BOOKS IN PRINT SUPPLEMENT
1980-1981

Senior staff of the Department of Bibliography includes:
Gertrude Jennings, Editor-in-Chief, Department of Bibliography,
Peter Simon and Brenda Sutton, Senior Database Production Managers,
Debra K. Brown, Manager, Product Development,
R. Dean Hollister, Ernest Lee, Scott D. MacFarland and Anne Wilson, Project Managers;
Beverly McDonough, Rebecca Olmo, and Jane Tiarsmith. Editorial Coordinators;
Jacqueline Artis, Joan Bethos, Ann Burns, Paul Deland, Tyrone Elliott, Brian Leonard,
Malcolm MacDermott, Hyacinth Myers, Michael Olenick, Beverly Palacio, Barbara Paone,
Vincent Parrillo, Brian Phair, Stuart Schwartzman, John Thompson, Rosemary Tobin,
Emilia Tomaszewski, Robert Tomlin and Frances Walsh, Assistant Editors.

Michael B. Howell, Business Systems Manager

Andrew H. Uszak, Vice President, Data Services/Systems

BOOKS IN PRINT SUPPLEMENT 1980-1981

Authors
Titles
Subjects

R. R. BOWKER COMPANY
New York & London

Published by R. R. Bowker Company (a Xerox Publishing Company)
1180 Avenue of the Americas, New York, N.Y. 10036

International Standard Book Number 0-8352-1328-5
International Standard Serial Number 0000-0310
Library of Congress Catalog Card Number 4-12648

Printed and Bound in the United States of America

CONTENTS

DATA BASES and PUBLICATIONS of the Department of Bibliography

BIPS DATA BASE

Books In Print Supplement 1980–1981 was produced from the BIPS Data Base of the R.R. Bowker Company. This data base is used to produce a complete, complementary line of bibliographic publications that give booksellers, librarians, publishers, and all other book users access to the latest bibliographic and ordering information. Following is a description of this data base and its publications.

The bibliographic data base was begun in 1948 primarily as a listing of titles included in Bowker's *Publishers' Trade List Annual (PTLA).* The computerization of this data base during the late nineteen-sixties using the Bibliographic Information Publication System (BIPS) made it possible for Bowker to expand the amount of information included in the bibliographic entries and to increase the number of essential tools of the trade we produced.

During the early nineteen-seventies the data base was greatly expanded to include information from additional publishers whose titles were not included in *PTLA.* Since that time the data base has been composed of and compiled from information received on an on-going basis directly from publishers. Prior to each publication from the data base, publishers review and correct their entries, providing current price, availability, and ordering information and update their list with recently published and forthcoming titles.

The data base includes scholarly, popular, adult, juvenile, reprint, and all other types of books covering all subjects provided they are published or exclusively distributed in the United States and are available to the trade or to the general public for single or multiple copy purchase. All editions and bindings are included: hardcover, paperbound, library binding, perfect binding, boards, spiral binding, text editions, teachers' editions, and workbooks.

Bibles as such are excluded, although commentaries, histories, and versions other than the standard English are extensively covered. Free books, books priced at less than 25 cents, unbound materials, pamphlets, periodicals, serials, government publications, puzzles, calendars, maps, microforms, audio-visual materials, and books available only to members of a particular organization, subscription-only titles or those sold only to schools are omitted. Spanish language books published outside of the United States are not included, but are covered in *Libros en venta.*

Bibliographic entries contain the following information when available: author, co-author, editor, co-editor, translator, co-translator, title, original title, number of volumes, volume number, edition, whether or not reprinted, Library of Congress number, subject information, series information, language if other than English, whether or not illustrated, grade range, date of publication, type of binding if other than cloth over boards, price, ISBN, imprint, publisher, and distributor, if other than the publisher.

Other data bases of the Data Services Division include: the Department of Bibliography's Textbook Data Base and Publishers' Authority Data Base; and the Serials Bibliography Department's Bowker Serial Bibliography Data Base.

Data Services Division's other computerized publications include: *American Book Publishing Record, Irregular Serials and Annuals, Ulrich's International Periodicals Directory,* and *Weekly Record.*

DESCRIPTION OF PUBLICATIONS

Books In Print

An annual publication listing all in-print and forthcoming titles from more than 8,400 publishers.

Indexes: • *Author/Title/Key to Publishers' & Distributors' Abbreviations/ Directory of U.S. Publishers & Distributors*

Subject Guide to Books In Print

A companion volume to *Books In Print,* this annual lists all in-print and forthcoming titles except fiction, literature, poetry, and drama by one author, under approximately 62,500 Library of

Congress (LC) subject headings.
Indexes: • *Subject/Key to Publishers' & Distributors' Abbreviations*

Publishers and Distributors of the United States

The main index of this publication contains the full name with editorial and ordering addresses for some 13,500 book publishers currently listed in Bowker's Publisher Authority Data Base and active in the United States. In addition, an ISBN Index supplies the ISBN prefixes, and a Key to Publishers' Abbreviations Index supplies the publishers' abbreviations from *Books In Print*. This directory is a useful companion tool to users of *Books In Print* as it increases the number of people who can use it simultaneously, and to librarians, booksellers, and others who need a comprehensive, up-to-date, and inexpensively-priced directory of U.S. publishing companies.
Indexes: • *Publisher Name/ISBN Prefix/ BIP Abbreviation*

Books In Print Supplement

An annual publication which updates *Books In Print* by listing all entries which have changes or additions to price, date of publication, ISBN, LC card number, or availability. Expands *Books In Print* by listing backlist titles new to the data base and titles published since January or forthcoming through July. Expands *Subject Guide To Books In Print* by listing all new and forthcoming titles under LC subject headings.
Indexes: • *Author/Title/Subject/Key to Publishers' & Distributors' Abbreviations*

Books In Series

A publication listing in-print *and* out-of-print titles in popular, scholarly, and professional series, arranged by the authoritative form for the series name as established in Library of Congress cataloging.
Indexes: • *Series/Author/Title/Subject Index to Series/Directory of Publishers & Distributors/Key to Publishers' & Distributors' Abbreviations*

Forthcoming Books

A bi-monthly cumulative publication listing forthcoming titles and titles published since July. Beginning with the November 1977 issue an asterisk indicates titles and publishers new to the data base since the last issue.
Indexes: • *Author/Title/Key to Publishers' & Distributors' Abbreviations*

Subject Guide To Forthcoming Books

A bi-monthly companion to *Forthcoming Books* covering the coming five-month season. Each issue overlaps and updates its predecessor. Adult and juvenile titles are listed under LC subject headings, as well as under additional headings created for literature, drama, and poetry by one author and for children's literature. In addition to their listing in the subject section, all titles for the juvenile market are listed by author in a separate section. Beginning with the July 1977 issue an asterisk indicates titles new to the data base since the last issue.
Indexes: • *Subject/Juvenile Books/Key to Publishers' & Distributors' Abbreviations*

Paperbound Books In Print

A semi-annual* publication listing all in-print and forthcoming paper trade and paper text editions. Entries are listed under approximately 470 subject headings.
Indexes: • *Author/Title/Subject/Key to Publishers' & Distributors' Abbreviations*
*semi-annual beginning 1978.

Children's Books In Print

An annual publication listing all books written for children or on the subject of children's literature. Grade or reading levels, where available, are indicated.
Indexes: • *Author/Title/Illustrator/Key to Publishers' & Distributors' Abbreviations*

Subject Guide To Children's Books In Print

A companion to *Children's Books In Print* this annual lists fiction and non-fiction titles under appropriate Sears or LC subject headings.
Indexes: • *Subject/Key to Publishers' & Distributors' Abbreviations*

Scientific And Technical Books And Serials In Print*

An annual subject selection of entries on science and technology *and* a selection of the same subject areas from the Bowker Serials Bibliography Data Base.
Indexes: • *Book Section: Subject/Author/ Title/Key to Publishers' & Distributors' Abbreviations*
• *Serial Section: Subject/Title*
*beginning with the 1978 edition. Prior editions (1972, 1973, 1974) were titled *Scientific And Technical Books In Print* and did not include serial publications.

Medical Books And Serials In Print*

An annual subject selection of entries on medicine, psychiatry, dentistry, nursing, and allied areas of the health field *and* a selection of the same subject areas from the Bowker Serials Bibli-

ography Data Base.

Indexes: • *Book Section: Subject/Author/ Title/Key to Publishers' & Distributors' Abbreviations*
• *Serial Section: Subject/Title*

*beginning with the 1978 edition. Prior editions (1972–1977) were titled *Bowker's Medical Books In Print* and did not include serial publications.

Business Books And Serials In Print* and Supplement

An annual subject selection of entries in the areas of economics, industry, finance, management, industrial psychology, vocational guidance, and other business-related topics *and* a selection of the same subject areas from the Bowker Serials Bibliography Data Base.

Indexes: • *Book Section: Subject/Author/ Title/Key to Publishers' & Distributors' Abbreviations*
• *Serial Section: Subject/Title*

*beginning with the 1977 edition. Prior editions (1973, 1974) were titled *Business Books In Print* and did not include serial publications.

Religious Books And Serials In Print

A subject selection of all entries on the world's religions and on allied religious and moral topics *and* a selection of the same subject areas from the Bowker Serials Bibliography Data Base. A Subject Area Directory provides access by broad areas to the subjects included. A Sacred Works Index provides a listing of the sacred books of the world's religions which are in-print and available in the U.S.

Indexes: • *Book Section: Subject/Author/ Title/Key to Publishers' & Distributors' Abbreviations/ Subject Area Directory/ Sacred Works Index*
• *Serial Section: Subject/Title*

Large Type Books In Print

A bi-annual* publication listing all books which are produced in 14 point or larger type and intended for the visually handicapped. This volume is printed in 18 point type.

Indexes: • *Subject/Textbook/Title/Author/ Key to Publishers' & Distributors' Abbreviations*

*Bi-annual beginning with the 1978 edition. Previous editions were issued in 1970 and 1976.

OTHER DATA BASES

TEXTBOOK DATA BASE

The Textbook Data Base was separated from the BIPS Data Base and expanded beyond the BIPS scope in 1973. Included are book and non-book materials for kindergarten through the first year of college as well as pedagogical material available and related to the educational world but not marketed to nor always available to the trade. The data base includes all editions and bindings (hardcover, paperbound, boards, spiral binding, reprints) as well as kits, maps, audio-visual materials and other teaching aids. Bibliographic entries contain the same elements as the BIPS Data Base.

PUBLICATIONS:

El-Hi Textbooks In Print

An annual publication listing in-print and forthcoming titles.

Indexes: • *Subject/Title/Author/Series/ Key to Publishers' & Distributors' Abbreviations*

PUBLISHERS' AUTHORITY DATA BASE

PUBLICATIONS:

Key to Publishers' and Distributors' Abbreviations

Provides the abbreviation, full name, ordering address, and ISBN prefix for all publishers and distributors whose bibliographic entries appear in the publication being indexed.

Directory of United States Publishers and Distributors

A listing of full name, editorial address, telephone number, and ISBN prefix for all active U.S. publishers and distributors currently on record in the files of the Department of Bibliography.

BOWKER SERIALS BIBLIOGRAPHY DATA BASE

This Data Base contains up-to-date information on 96,000 serial titles published by 60,000 serial publishers and corporate authors around the world. Maintained by the Bowker Serials Bibliography Department.

PUBLICATIONS:

Ulrich's International Periodicals Directory (annual); **Irregular Serials and Annuals** (biennial); **Ulrich's Quarterly**, a supplement to Ulrich's and Irregular Serials; **Sources of Serials**, an international directory of serial publishers and corporate authors and their titles by country.

ISBN
INTERNATIONAL STANDARD BOOK NUMBER

The 1980-1981 BOOKS IN PRINT SUPPLEMENT lists each title or edition of a title with an ISBN. All publishers were notified and requested to submit a valid ISBN for their titles.

During the past decade, the majority of the publishers complied with the requirements of the standard and implemented the ISBN. At present, approximately 95% of all new titles and all new editions are submitted for listing with a valid ISBN.

To fulfill the responsibility of accomplishing total book numbering, the ISBN Agency allocated the ISBN prefixes 0-685 and 0-686 to number the titles in the BOOKS IN PRINT database without an ISBN. Titles not having an ISBN at the closing date of this publication were assigned an ISBN with one of these prefixes by the International Standard Book Numbering Agency.

Titles numbered within the prefixes 0-685 and 0-686 are:

— Publishers who did not assign ISBN to their titles.
— Distributors with titles published and imported from countries not in the ISBN system, or not receiving the ISBN from the originating publisher.
— Errors from transposition and transcription which occurred in transmitting the ISBN to the BOOKS IN PRINT database.

All the ISBN listed in BOOKS IN PRINT SUPPLEMENT are validated by using the check digit control, and only valid ISBN are listed in the BIP database.

All publishers participating in the ISBN system having titles numbered within the prefixes 0-685 and 0-686 will receive a computer printout, requesting them to submit the correct ISBN.

Publishers not participating in the ISBN system may request from the ISBN Agency the assignment of an ISBN Publisher Prefix, and start numbering their titles.

By having an ISBN for each title and edition of a title, order fulfillment and inventory control systems will be able to operate more efficiently and economically. The ISBN Agency will produce and publish an ISBN Index on microfiche. Users encountering an ISBN in the range of 0-685 and 0-686 who are unable to identify the title in their file, will be able to refer to the ISBN microfiche Index. Each ISBN in the Index will have the information on title, author and publisher, or a cross reference to another ISBN. When publishing rights are sold and the title is published under the new imprint with a separate ISBN, the ISBN Index will carry a cross reference from the previous ISBN to the new one.

The Book Industry System Advisory Committee (BISAC) developed a standard format for data transmission, and many companies are already accepting orders transmitted on magnetic tape using the ISBN. Another standard format by BISAC for title updating is under development.

The ISBN Agency and the Data Services Division of the Bowker Company wish to express their appreciation to all publishers who collaborated in making the ISBN system the standard of the publishing industry.

For additional information related to the ISBN total numbering, please refer to Emery Koltay, Director of the ISBN Agency, R. R. Bowker Co.

How to Use BOOKS IN PRINT SUPPLEMENT 1980–1981

Books in Print Supplement 1980–1981, the ninth edition of an annual publication, is issued six months after the publication of *Books in Print 1980–1981* to update the information that appeared therein. It includes approximately 106,000 titles with price or other major changes, 15,000 titles which have gone out of print, and 21,700 titles received since *Books in Print 1980–1981* which have been published or announced from July, 1980 to July, 1981, plus an additional 9,200 titles published prior to July, 1980.

The *Supplement* includes author and title indexes. The subject index lists titles new to the data base since *Subject Guide to Books in Print 1980–1981.* A listing of the publishers represented plus any others which have indicated changes of name or address since *Books in Print* is also included.

Like *Books in Print,* the *Supplement* was produced from records stored on magnetic tape, edited by computer programs, and set in type by computer-controlled photocomposition.

AUTHOR AND TITLE INDEXES

Each of these indexes includes a single alphabetical listing of all corrected titles, those which have gone out of print or are out of stock indefinitely, those which were cancelled or postponed, and new titles. The notations "o.p." or "o.s.i." following the price information, indicate that the book is either out of print or out of stock indefinitely. All titles with price or other major changes and new titles which appear in the *March, 1981* issue of *Forthcoming Books* are also included.

ALPHABETICAL ARRANGEMENT OF AUTHOR AND TITLE INDEXES

Within each index entries are filed alphabetically by word, with the following exceptions:

Initial articles of titles in English, French, German, Italian, and Spanish are deleted from the title index.

M', Mc and *Mac* are filed as if they were *Mac* and are interfiled with other names beginning with *Mac;* for example, Macan, McAnally, Macardle, McAree, McArthur, Macarthur, M'Aulay, Macaulay, McAuley. Within a specific name grouping *Mc* and *Mac* are interfiled according to the given name of the author; for example, Macdonald, Agnes; McDonald, Annie L.; MacDonald, Austin F.; Macdonald, Betty. Compound names are listed under the first part of the name, and cross-references appear under the last part of the name.

Entries beginning with initial letters (whether authors' given names or titles) are filed first, e.g., Smith, H.C., comes before Smith, Harold A.; B E A M A Directory comes before Baal, Babylon.

Numerals, including year dates, are written out in most cases and filed alphabetically:

Seven years in Tibet
Seventeen
Seventeen famous operas
Seventeen-Fifteen to the present
Seventeen party book
Seventeen reader
Seventeenth century

U.S., UN, Dr., Mr., and St. are filed as though they were spelled out.

SPECIAL NOTE ON HOW TO FIND AN AUTHOR'S COMPLETE LISTING

In sorting author listings by computer it is not possible to group the entire listing for an author together unless a standard spelling and format for each name is used. If an author's name is given in various forms by the contributing publishers, his listings in the author index may be divided into several groups.

Variant forms of an author's first and middle names may not be adjacent in the filing sequence, as in Aiken, Conrad and Aiken, Conrad P. or Jung, C.G. and Jung, Carl G. For most surnames, variant forms of entry will fall close together, but for the most common surnames (Smith, Brown, etc.) it is suggested you check specifically for all variant forms of first and middle names.

Foreign names which may or may not be given with a prefix will not be adjacent in the filing sequence, such as: Balzac and de Balzac and Goethe or von Goethe. German names with umlauts may appear in two alphabets because of the varying treatment of the umlauted vowel: Müller, F. Max or Mueller, F. Max. Acronyms for names of corporate authors may appear in two or more groups of listings if one form is presented with no space between initials—UNESCO, and another with spaces, U N E S C O.

You will find cross-references to the variant forms of an author's name wherever we anticipated that his listings might not be filed together.

INFORMATION INCLUDED IN AUTHOR, TITLE, AND SUBJECT ENTRIES

Entries in all indexes include the following bibliographic information, when available: author, co-author, editor, co-editor, translator, co-translator, title, number of volumes, edition, Library of Congress number, series information, language if other than English, whether or not illustrated, grade range, year of publication, type of binding if other than cloth over boards, price, International Standard Book Number, publisher's order number, imprint and publisher. When an entry includes the prices for both the hardcover and paperback editions, the publication date within the entry refers to the hardcover binding; however, when the paperback binding is the only one included in the entry, the publication date is the paperback publication date. (Information on the International Standard Book Numbering System developing in the United States and other English-speaking countries is available from R.R. Bowker Company.)

GENERAL EDITORIAL POLICIES

In order to insure that the essential information in these listings is uniform, complete, and easy to find, the following editorial policies have been maintained:

When two authors or editors are responsible for a book, full bibliographic information is included in the author entry for the author or editor named first, and a cross-reference directs the user from the second author or editor to the primary entry; e.g., Wilson, Robert E., jt. auth. see Fensch, E.A. If more than two authors or editors are responsible for a certain publication, only the name of the first is given followed by *et al.*

Titles of single volumes as part of a set are given if the volumes are sold singly. Cross-references from single volume titles to set title are included whenever the former are distinctive. Some series are also listed in the title index.

Although the *Supplement* is designed to provide accurate, updated price and out-of-print information until the publication of *Books in Print 1981–1982,* a certain amount of additional price changes will occur and a certain number of titles will become unavailable in the interim.

A Bowker tool for keeping up with new titles is *Forthcoming Books,* a separate bimonthly publication which provides author-title indexes to all books due to appear in the coming 5 month period. In addition, it cumulates all books that have appeared since July 1980. Yearly subscriptions are available at $34.75 U.S.A., single copies for $8.00 U.S.A.

All prices are subject to change without notice. Most prices are list prices. Lack of uniformity by the participating publishers prohibits indicating trade discounts. A lowercase "a" follows some of the trade edition prices and indicates that a specially priced library edition is available; "t" indicates a tentative price; "g" a guaranteed binding on a juvenile title; and "x" a short discount—20% or less. PLB indicates a publishers' library binding. YA indicates that a title may be used for young adults.

On May 1, 1980 , Harper & Row introduced a new and innovative pricing policy for its college textbooks. Retail book stores and wholesalers purchase from Harper & Row at net prices and determine their own prices, without reference to any suggested retail price. Consumers who choose to buy single copies of Harper & Row college texts directly from the publisher will pay the "Single Copy, Direct To The Consumer Price." This price is identified in the *Supplement* by the abbreviation "scp". There is no relationship between this price and the price that may be charged by retail book stores and wholesalers.

Publishers' names, in most instances, are abbreviated. A key to the abbreviations together with the complete addresses of the various publishing firms will be found in the Key to Publishers' Abbreviations.

SUBJECT INDEX

The subject index supplements *Subject Guide to Books in Print 1980–1981* by listing titles published or announced for publication prior to July 1980 which did not appear in *Subject Guide to Books in Print 1980–1981.* It follows the headings assigned by the Library of Congress. Some books have been assigned a single heading, some two, three or more headings, and therefore some books appear two, three or more times in the subject index. Wherever official LC classification was unavailable, generally because the publication date was too recent or is in the future, provisional headings were assigned.

Headings and cross-references have been updated to conform with the latest supplement to the Ninth Edition of *Library of Congress Subject Headings* although many subheadings have been consolidated where they seem too cumbersome for the needs of the *Subject Guide to Books in Print* and this *Supplement,* and a few were changed when the needs of these books seemed to diverge from LC practice.

Where the Library of Congress does not assign subject headings to cataloged books, they are usually omitted from this subject listing. For example:

Fiction is omitted except where a work's background (biographical, historical, etc.) seemed extensive and authentic enough to warrant mention. However, collec-

tions of works of fiction may be included, and of course, criticism.

Poetry and drama are omitted, at least as regards works by a single author best sought in *Books in Print* or the Author Index of the *Supplement*. However, collections and criticism are included.

Juvenile fiction, like adult fiction, is usually omitted, though juvenile nonfiction (at least above the picture-book level) is represented. In some cases, juvenile titles have been set apart under a heading such as AERONAUTICS–JUVENILE LITERATURE. In other cases, juvenile titles are listed with adult books and are identified by grade range.

Bibles as such are omitted, though commentaries, histories, and versions other than the standard English are extensively covered.

Books priced at less than 25 cents are not listed.

Subject headings are arranged alphabetically:

ACCOUNTING
ACETYLENE
ACTING
ACTINOMYCETES
ADAMS, HENRY, 1838–1918
ADHESIVES

Many of the main entries are broken down still further:

ACCOUNTING
ACCOUNTING—DICTIONARIES
ACCOUNTING—EXAMINATIONS, QUESTIONS
ACCOUNTING—LAW
ACCOUNTING—PROBLEMS, EXERCISES

There are also many cross-references:

ACCOUNTING
see also Auditing; Bookkeeping; Business Losses; Business Mathematics; Cost Accounting; Depreciation; Financial Statements; Income Accounting; Inventories; Liquidation; Machine Accounting; Productivity Accounting; Tax Accounting

ACCOUNTING—FORMS, BLANKS, etc.
see Business—Forms, Blanks, etc.

ACCOUNTS, COLLECTING of
see Collecting of Accounts.

Headings, patterned after those used in the card catalog in the Library of Congress, are explicit rather than general. Thus books on cost accounting are under COST ACCOUNTING, not under ACCOUNTING. Books on actors are under ACTORS and ACTRESSES, not under THEATER.

Similarly, look first under PLASTICS rather than CHEMISTRY, or under ACRYLATES rather than PLASTICS.

In looking for books on painting, search past the main entry to the various subheadings:

PAINTING
PAINTING—DICTIONARIES
PAINTING—EARLY WORKS TO 1800
PAINTING—HISTORY
PAINTING—STUDY AND TEACHING
PAINTING—TECHNIQUE
PAINTING, AMERICAN
PAINTING, INDUSTRIAL
PAINTINGS

Note the sequence of the above cited headings and subheadings. The editors of the *Subject Guide* took as a guideline the *Filing Rules for the Dictionary Catalogs of the Library of Congress,* as prepared by the Processing Department of the Library of Congress.

Other typical examples of the sequences used are:

ART
ART—HISTORY
ART, AMERICAN
ART OBJECTS
ART OBJECTS—COLLECTORS AND COLLECTING
BIBLE—COMMENTARIES
BIBLE—COMMENTARIES—N.T.
BIBLE—COMMENTARIES—N.T. GOSPELS
GREAT BRITAIN
GREAT BRITAIN—HISTORY
GREAT BRITAIN—PARLIAMENT
GREAT BRITAIN—PARLIAMENT—HOUSE OF COMMONS

Although a constant effort is made to maintain consistency and to avoid splitting entries on a given subject among several headings, a certain amount is inevitable. The Library of Congress updates its subject headings constantly but cannot make such updating retroactive to cards and catalogs previously issued. For example, LC is now subdividing the heading EVOLUTION according to the subject matter of the material processed, e.g., HUMAN EVOLUTION; PLANTS—EVOLUTION. If old entries which belong in more precise subdivisions did not indicate by their titles where they should have been listed, a few were left under the main entry.

The editor's first principle is to list books where the user will be most likely to look for them with as many references as seem necessary. If an official heading is one under which the lay user might not think to look, additional popular cross-references have been added.

Each entry is filed alphabetically by author, or title when there is no author cited, under the appropriate subject. Filing rules are the same used in the author and title indexes.

KEY TO PUBLISHERS' AND DISTRIBUTORS' ABBREVIATIONS

Publishers' and distributors' names, in most instances, are abbreviated. A key to these abbreviations will be found in the *Key to Publishers' & Distributors' Abbreviations* at the end of this *Supplement*.

Entries in this "Key" are arranged alphabetically by the abbreviations used in the bibliographic entries. The full name, ISBN prefix, editorial address, telephone number, ordering address (if different from the editorial address), and imprints follow the abbreviation.

For example:

> **Bowker,** (Bowker, R.R., Co., 0-8352),
> A Xerox Publishing Co., 1180 Ave. of
> the Americas, New York, NY 10036
> Tel 212-764-5100; Orders To: P.O.
> Box 1807, Ann Arbor, MI 48106.

If an entry contains a "Pub. by" note after the price, the title should be ordered from the company whose abbreviation appears at the end of the entry. For example, an entry for a book published by Melbourne U Pr., but distributed by International Scholarly Book Services, Inc., will convey this information in the form "Pub. by Melbourne U Pr." after the price with "Intl Schol Bk Serv." at the end of the entry.

The R.R. Bowker Company has used its best efforts in collecting and preparing material for inclusion in *Books in Print Supplement 1980–1981* but does not assume, and hereby disclaims, any liability to any party for any loss or damage caused by errors or omissions in *Books in Print Supplement 1980–1981* whether such errors or omissions result from negligence, accident, or any other cause.

KEY TO ABBREVIATIONS

a	after price, specially priced library edition available
abr.	abridged
adpt.	adapted
Amer.	American
annot.	annotation(s), annotated
ans.	answer(s)
app.	appendix
approx.	approximately
assn.	association
auth.	author
bd.	bound
bdg.	binding
bds.	boards
bibl(s).	bibliography (ies)
bk(s).	book, books
bklet(s)	booklets
Bro.	Brother
coll.	college
comm.	commission, committee
co.	company
cond.	condensed
comp(s).	compiler(s)
corp.	corporation
dept.	department
diag(s).	diagram(s)
dir.	director
dist.	distributed
Div.	Division
doz.	dozen
ea.	each
ed.	editor, edited, edition
eds.	editions, editors
educ.	education
elem.	elementary
ency.	encyclopedia
Eng.	English
enl.	enlarged
exp.	expurgated
fac.	facsimile
fasc.	fascicule
fict.	fiction
fig(s).	figure(s)
for.	foreign
Fr.	French
frwd.	foreword
g	after price, guaranteed juvenile binding
gen.	general
Ger.	German
Gr.	Greek
gr.	grade, grades
hdbk.	handbook
Heb.	Hebrew
i.t.a.	initial teaching alphabet
Illus.	illustrated, illustration(s), illustrator(s)
in prep.	in preparation
incl.	includes, including
inst.	institute
intro.	introduction
It.	Italian
Jr.	Junior
jt. auth.	joint author
jt. ed.	joint editor
k	kindergarten audience level
l.p.	long playing
ltd. ed.	limited edition
lab.	laboratory
lang(s).	language(s)
Lat.	Latin
lea.	leather
lib.	library
lit.	literature, literary
math.	mathematics
mod.	modern
mor.	morocco
MS, MSS	manuscript, manuscripts
natl.	national
no., nos.	number, numbers
o.p.	out of print
orig.	original text, not a reprint
O.S.I.	out of stock indefinitely
pap.	paper
photos	photographs, photographer
PLB	publisher's library binding
Pol.	Polish
pop. ed.	popular edition
Port.	Portuguese
prep.	preparation
probs.	problems
prog. bk.	programmed book
ps	preschool audience level
pseud.	pseudonym
pt(s).	part, parts
pub.	published, publisher, publishing
pubn.	publication
ref(s).	reference(s)
repr.	reprint
reprod(s).	reproduction(s)
rev.	revised
rpm.	revolution per minute (phono records)
Rus.	Russian
s.p.	school price
scp	single copy, Direct to the Consumer Price
sec.	section
sel.	selected
ser.	series
Soc.	Society
sols.	solutions
Span.	Spanish
Sr. (after given name)	Senior
Sr. (before given name)	Sister
St.	Saint
subs.	subsidiary
subsc.	subscription
suppl.	supplement
t	after price, tentative price
tech.	technical
text ed.	text edition
tr.	translator, translated, translation
univ.	university
vol(s).	volume, volumes
wkbk.	workbook
x	after price, short discount (20% or less)
YA	young adult audience level
yrbk.	yearbook

AUTHOR INDEX

A

A., Herbie. Through Living Hell...from Alcohol & Back. 1981. 4.95 (ISBN 0-8062-1603-4). Carlton.

A. J. Wilson Mining Journal Books Ltd. The Pick & the Pen. 318p. 1980. 26.00x (ISBN 0-900117-16-8, Pub. by Mining Journal England). State Mutual Bk.

A P W A Research Foundation. Computer Assisted Mapping & Records Activity Manual. (CAMRAS: Pt. 1). 1979. 25.00 (ISBN 0-917084-31-4). Am Public Works.

Aaen, Bernhard. No Appointment Needed. Van Dolson, Bobbie J., ed. 128p. 1981. pap. write for info. (ISBN 0-8280-0025-5). Review & Herald.

AAG Consulting Panel, 1974. Self-Study Data Forms. pap. 1.00 (ISBN 0-89291-142-5). Assn Am Geographers.

Aaken, Ernst Van see Van Aaken, Ernst.

Aaker, David A. & Day, George S. Marketing Research: Private & Public Sector Decisions. LC 79-18532. (Wiley Series in Marketing). 1980. text ed. 21.95 (ISBN 0-471-00059-0); tchrs'. manual avail. (ISBN 0-471-07766-6). Wiley.

Aaker, David A. & Day, George S., eds. Consumerism: Search for the Consumer Interest. 3rd ed. LC 77-83163. (Illus.). 1978. 17.95 (ISBN 0-02-900050-5); pap. text ed. 9.95 (ISBN 0-02-900040-8). Free Pr.

Aalami, B., jt. auth. see Williams, D. G.

Aaltio, M. Finnish for Foreigners, 3 vols. Set. pap. 30.00 (ISBN 0-686-66991-6). Vol. 1 (ISBN 9-5110-0397-6). Vol. 2 (ISBN 9-5110-1483-8) (ISBN 9-5110-1919-8). Heinman.

Aaltio, M-H. Finnish for Foreigners: Pt 2, Lessons 27 to 40. 8th rev. ed. (Illus.). 192p. 1976. pap. text ed. 13.50x (ISBN 951-1-01483-8, F 562). Vanous.

Aaltio, M. J. Finnish for Foreigners, Pt. 1: Lessons 1-25. 9th ed. (Illus.). 254p. 1976. pap. text ed. 13.50x (ISBN 951-1-00397-6, F561); cassette a, 35.00x cassettes b-e, 100.00x open reel, 4.50x exercises 40.00x (ISBN 0-686-66923-1). Vanous.

Aalto, Alvar. Alvar Aalto-Sketches. Schildt, Goran, ed. Wrede, Stuart, tr. from Swed. & Finn. (Illus.). 1978. 27.50 (ISBN 0-262-01053-4). MIT Pr.

Aandahl, Andrew R. Soil Teaching Aid. LC 79-12843. (Illus.). 1979. pap. text ed. 100.00x with slide carousel (ISBN 0-8032-1012-4); tape cassette 5.00x (ISBN 0-686-65580-X). U of Nebr Pr.

Aardema, Verna. Bringing the Rain to Kapiti Plain. LC 80-25886. (Illus.). 32p. (ps). 1981. 9.95 (ISBN 0-8037-0809-2); PLB 9.43 (ISBN 0-8037-0807-6). Dial.

--Ji-Nongo-Nongo Means Riddles. LC 78-4038. (Illus.). 40p. (gr. 3 up). 1978. 7.95 (ISBN 0-590-07474-1, Four Winds). Schol Bk Serv.

Aardema, Verna, retold by. The Riddle of the Drum, A Tale from Tizapan, Mexico. LC 78-23791. (Illus.). 32p. (gr. k-3). 1979. 8.95 (ISBN 0-590-07489-X, Four Winds). Schol Bk Serv.

Aarle, Thomas Van. Don't Put Your Cart Before the Horse Race. (gr. k-3). 1980. reinforced bdg. 8.95 (ISBN 0-395-29095-3). HM.

Aarli, J. A. & Toender, O. Immunological Aspects of Neurological Diseases. (Monographs in Neural Sciences: Vol. 6). (Illus.). xiv, 190p. 1980. pap. 58.75 (ISBN 3-8055-0814-X). S Karger.

Aaron, Benjamin, ed. Labor Courts & Grievance Settlement in Western Europe. LC 72-123628. 1971. 28.50x (ISBN 0-520-01757-9). U of Cal Pr.

Aaron, Chester. Gideon. LC 80-12779. 192p. (gr. 7-11). 1981. cancelled (ISBN 0-525-30548-3). Dutton.

Aaron, Daniel. Writers on the Left. LC 61-13349. 1977. pap. 7.95 (ISBN 0-19-519970-7, GB512, GB). Oxford U Pr.

Aaron, Daniel, ed. American Men & Women of Letters, 31 vols. 1981. Set. pap. 160.00 (ISBN 0-87754-149-3). Chelsea Hse.

Aaron, Daniel, ed. see Aududon, Maria R.

Aaron, Daniel, ed. see George, Henry, Jr.

Aaron, Henry J. Politics & the Professors: The Great Society in Perspective. LC 77-91809. (Studies in Social Economics). 1978. 11.95 (ISBN 0-8157-0026-1); pap. 4.95 (ISBN 0-8157-0025-3). Brookings.

--Shelter & Subsidies: Who Benefits from Federal Housing Policies? (Studies in Social Economics). 200p. 1972. 11.95 (ISBN 0-8157-0018-0); pap. 4.95 (ISBN 0-8157-0017-2). Brookings.

--Who Pays the Property Tax? A New View. (Studies of Government Finance). 1975. 9.95 (ISBN 0-8157-0022-9); pap. 3.95 (ISBN 0-8157-0021-0). Brookings.

--Why Is Welfare So Hard to Reform? (Studies in Social Economics). 71p. 1973. 3.95 (ISBN 0-8157-0019-9). Brookings.

Aaron, Henry J., ed. Inflation & the Income Tax. LC 76-28669. (Studies of Government Finance). 1976. 15.95 (ISBN 0-8157-0024-5); pap. 6.95 (ISBN 0-8157-0023-7). Brookings.

Aaron, Howard. What the Worms Ignore the Birds Are Wild About. 1979. 2.50 (ISBN 0-918116-15-5). Jawbone Pr.

Aaron, Jan. The Art of Indoor Gardening: Green Magic for Blooming Miracles. LC 74-21357. 208p. 1981. 13.95 (ISBN 0-8303-0146-1). Fleet.

Aaron, Pietro. Trattato della natura, Vol. 129. 1980. 30.00x (ISBN 0-8450-2329-2). Broude.

Aaron, S. Jay. Guide to Vintage Wine Prices: Nineteen Seventy-Nine to Nineteen-Eighty Edition. 1979. pap. 7.95 (ISBN 0-446-97232-0). Warner Bks.

Aaron, Sam, jt. auth. see Fadiman, Clifton.

Aaron, Shirley L. A Study of Combined School-Public Libraries. LC 80-19785. 120p. 1980. pap. 7.00 (ISBN 0-8389-3247-9). ALA.

Aaron, Tossi, jt. auth. see Bisgaard, Erling.

Aaron, Tossi, ed. see Bisgaard, Erling & Stehouwer, Gulle.

Aarons, Edward S. Assignment--Afghan Dragon. (Assignment Ser.). 1978. pap. 1.95 (ISBN 0-449-14085-7, GM). Fawcett.

--Assignment--Amazon Queen. (Assignment Ser.). 1977. pap. 1.25 o.p. (ISBN 0-449-13544-6, GM). Fawcett.

--Assignment--Angelina. 1974. pap. 0.95 o.p. (ISBN 0-449-12989-6, M2989, GM). Fawcett.

--Assignment--Ankara. 176p. 1975. pap. 1.25 o.p. (ISBN 0-449-13377-X, P3377, Gm). Fawcett.

--Assignment--Bangkok. 192p. 1975. pap. 1.25 o.p. (ISBN 0-449-13343-5, P3343-125, GM). Fawcett.

--Assignment--Black Viking. (Assignment Ser.). 1978. pap. 1.75 o.p. (ISBN 0-449-14017-2, GM). Fawcett.

--Assignment--Budapest. 1977. pap. 1.25 o.p. (ISBN 0-449-13785-6, GM). Fawcett.

--Assignment--Ceylon. 208p. 1981. pap. 1.95 (ISBN 0-449-13583-7, 0-449-13583-7, GM). Fawcett.

--Assignment--Golden Girl. (Assignment Ser.). 1979. pap. 1.95 (ISBN 0-449-14140-3, GM). Fawcett.

--Assignment--Helene. (Sam Durrell Ser.). 1978. pap. 1.50 o.p. (ISBN 0-449-13955-7, GM). Fawcett.

--Assignment--Lili Lamaris. 1978. pap. 1.50 o.p. (ISBN 0-449-13934-4, GM). Fawcett.

--Assignment--Moon Girl. 1977. pap. 1.50 o.p. (ISBN 0-449-13856-9, GM). Fawcett.

--Assignment--Nuclear Nude. 192p. 1974. pap. 0.95 o.p. (ISBN 0-449-12815-6, M2815, GM). Fawcett.

--Assignment--Peking. 192p. 1975. pap. 1.25 o.p. (ISBN 0-449-13293-5, P3293, GM). Fawcett.

--Assignment--Quayle Question. 1979. pap. 1.75 o.p. (ISBN 0-449-14226-4, GM). Fawcett.

--Assignment--Silver Scorpion. 1976. pap. 1.95 o.p. (ISBN 0-449-14294-9, GM). Fawcett.

--Assignment--Star Stealers. 1978. pap. 1.50 o.p. (ISBN 0-449-13944-1, GM). Fawcett.

--Assignment--Sulu Sea. 160p. 1981. pap. 1.95 (ISBN 0-449-13875-5, GM). Fawcett.

--Assignment--Treason. 1977. pap. 1.50 o.p. (ISBN 0-449-13913-1, GM). Fawcett.

--Assignment--Unicorn. 1978. pap. 1.50 o.p. (ISBN 0-449-13998-0, GM). Fawcett.

--Assignment Ceylon. 208p. 1981. pap. 1.95 (ISBN 0-449-13583-7, GM). Fawcett.

Aarons, Will B. Assignment--Sheba. 192p. 1977. pap. 1.50 o.p. (ISBN 0-449-13696-5, GM). Fawcett.

--Assignment--Tiger Devil. 1978. pap. 1.75 o.p. (ISBN 0-449-14052-0, GM). Fawcett.

Aaronson, Joseph. The Encyclopedia of Furniture. 1970. 53.00 (ISBN 0-7134-0802-2, Pub. by Batsford England). David & Charles.

Aarseth, Sigmund, jt. auth. see Miller, Margaret M.

Aaseng, Nathan. Baseball's Finest Pitchers. LC 80-12275. (Sports Heroes Library). (Illus.). 72p. (gr. 4 up). 1980. PLB 5.95g (ISBN 0-8225-1061-8). Lerner Pubns.

--Eric Heiden: Winner in Gold. LC 80-16982. (The Achievers Ser.). (Illus.). (gr. 4-9). 1980. PLB 5.95g (ISBN 0-8225-0481-2). Lerner Pubns.

--Football's Breakaway Backs. LC 80-16691. (Sports Heroes Library). (Illus.). 72p. (gr. 4 up). 1980. PLB 5.95g (ISBN 0-8225-1063-4). Lerner Pubns.

--Football's Cunning Coaches. LC 80-29252. (The Sports Heroes Library). (Illus.). (gr. 4 up). 1981. PLB 5.95 (ISBN 0-8225-1065-0). Lerner Pubns.

--Football's Steadiest Kickers. LC 80-28868. (Sports Heroes Library). (Illus.). (gr. 4 up). 1981. PLB 5.95 (ISBN 0-8225-1069-3). Lerner Pubns.

--Football's Sure-Handed Receivers. LC 80-17762. (Sports Heroes Library). (Illus.). 72p. (gr. 4 up). 1980. PLB 5.95g (ISBN 0-8225-1064-2). Lerner Pubns.

--Football's Toughest Tight Ends. LC 80-27803. (Sports Heroes Ser.). (Illus.). (gr. 4 up). 1981. PLB 5.95 (ISBN 0-8225-1070-7). Lerner Pubns.

--Football's Winning Quarterbacks. LC 80-12074. (Sports Heroes Library). (Illus.). (gr. 4 up). 1980. PLB 5.95g (ISBN 0-8225-1062-6). Lerner Pubns.

--Pete Rose. LC 79-27377. (The Achievers Ser.). (Illus.). (gr. 4-9). 1981. PLB 5.95 (ISBN 0-8225-0480-4). Lerner Pubns.

--Track's Magnificent Milers. LC 80-27404. (The Sports Heroes Library). (Illus.). (gr. 4 up). 1981. PLB 5.95 (ISBN 0-8225-1066-9). Lerner Pubns.

--Walter Cronkite. (The Achievers Ser.). (Illus.). (gr. 4-9). 1981. PLB 5.95 (ISBN 0-8225-0486-3). Lerner Pubns.

--Winning Men of Tennis. LC 80-28598. (Sports Heroes Library). (Illus.). (gr. 4 up). 1981. PLB 5.95 (ISBN 0-8225-1068-5). Lerner Pubns.

--Winning Women of Tennis. (The Sports Heroes Library). (Illus.). (gr. 4 up). 1981. PLB 5.95 (ISBN 0-8225-1067-7). Lerner Pubns.

AASHTO Administrative Subcommittee on Computer Technology. Computer Systems Index. 1980. 10.00 (ISBN 0-686-20962-1, CSI). AASHTO.

AASHTO Annual Committee Meeting, 1974. Proceedings. 10.00 o.p. (ISBN 0-686-20946-X, P-74). AASHTO.
Aatec Publications, compiled by. Solar Census: The Directory for the Eighties. LC 80-68910. 484p. 1980. perfect-bound 45.00 (ISBN 0-937948-00-4). Aatec Pubns.
Aatre, V. K. Network Theory & Filter Design. 432p. 1981. 18.95 (ISBN 0-470-26934-0). Halsted Pr.
Aavani, Gholam R., tr. see Nasr, Seyyed H.
Abadinsky, Howard. Organized Crime. 400p. 1980. text ed. 13.95 (ISBN 0-205-07097-3, 827097X); instrs' manual (ISBN 0-205-07098-1, 827097-X). Allyn.
--Probation & Parole: Theory & Practice. (Illus.). 1977. text ed. 17.95 (ISBN 0-13-715953-6). P-H.
Abarbanel, Jay S. Co-Operative Farmer & Welfare State: Economic Change in an Israeli Moshav. (Illus.). 231p. 1974. text ed. 18.25x (ISBN 0-7190-0573-6). Humanities.
Abarbanel, Jerome. Redefining the Enviorment. (Key Issues Ser.: No. 9). 1972. pap. 2.00 (ISBN 0-87546-200-6). NY Sch Indus Rel.
Abarbanel, Karin & Siegel, Gonnie M. Woman's Work Book. 1977. pap. 2.50 (ISBN 0-446-81353-2). Warner Bks.
Abarbanel, Karin, jt. auth. see Hillman, Howard.
Abarbanol, Karin & Siegel, Gonnie M. The Woman's Work Book. 352p. 1981. pap. 3.50 (ISBN 0-446-91658-7). Warner Bks.
Abartis, Caesarea. The Tragicomic Construction of Cymberline & the Winter's Tale. (Salzburg Studies in English Literature: Jacobean Drama Studies: Vol. 73). (Orig.). 1977. pap. text ed. 25.00x (ISBN 0-391-01289-4). Humanities.
Abass, Alavi & Arger, Peter, eds. Abdomen. LC 80-24363. (Multiples Imaging Procedures Ser.). 1980. 44.50 (ISBN 0-8089-1306-9). Grune.
Abba, Giuseppe C. The Diary of One of Garibaldi's Thousand. Vincent, E. R., tr. from Ital. LC 80-24181. (Oxford Library of Italian Classics). (Illus.). xxi, 166p. 1981. Repr. of 1962 ed. lib. bdg. 18.75x (ISBN 0-313-22446-3, ABDO). Greenwood.
Abbagnano, Nicola. Critical Existentialism. Langiulli, Nino, ed. 6.75 (ISBN 0-8446-0450-X). Peter Smith.
Abbasi, Abdul S. Echocardiographic Interpretation. (Illus.). 448p. 1981. text ed. price not set (ISBN 0-398-04153-9). C C Thomas.
Abbe, Dorothy, compiled by. Stencilled Ornament & Illustration. pap. 15.00 (ISBN 0-89073-064-4). Boston Public Lib.
Abbe, George. Funeral. 4.95 (ISBN 0-912292-03-2). The Smith.
Abbe, Kathryn M., jt. auth. see Gill, Frances M.
Abbe Charles-Irenee, jt. auth. see Castel de Sainte-Pierre.
Abbett, R. W. Engineering Contracts & Specifications. 4th ed. LC 63-14072. 1963. 24.95 (ISBN 0-471-00035-3, Pub by Wiley-Interscience). Wiley.
Abbey, Edward. Black Sun. 160p. 1981. pap. 5.95 (ISBN 0-88496-192-3). Capra Pr.
--Cactus Country. (American Wilderness Ser.). (Illus.). 1973. 12.95 (ISBN 0-8094-1168-7). Time-Life.
--Cactus Country. LC 72-91599. (American Wilderness Ser). (Illus.). (gr. 6 up). 1973. PLB 11.97 (ISBN 0-8094-1169-5, Pub. by Time-Life). Silver.
--Desert Solitaire. rev. ed. (Literature of the American Wilderness). (Illus.). 296p. 1981. Repr. of 1968 ed. 12.50 (ISBN 0-87905-070-5). Peregrine Smith.
--Desert Solitaire: A Season in the Wilderness. 320p. 1977. pap. 2.50 (ISBN 0-345-27866-6). Ballantine.
--The Journey Home: Some Words in Defense of the American West. 1977. 10.95 (ISBN 0-525-13753-X); pap. 5.95 (ISBN 0-525-03700-4). Dutton.
--The Monkey Wrench Gang. LC 75-831. 352p. 1975. 8.95 o.s.i. (ISBN 0-397-01084-2). Lippincott.
Abbey, Edward, jt. auth. see Porter, Eliot.
Abbey, Edward, jt. auth. see Thollander, Earl.
Abbey, F., jt. auth. see Thomas, A. F.
Abbey, Harlan C. Horses & Horse Shows. LC 78-55449. (Illus.). 1980. 14.95 (ISBN 0-498-02247-1). A S Barnes.
--Horses & Horse Shows. LC 78-55449. (Illus.). 1979. pap. 7.95 cancelled (ISBN 0-498-02372-9). A S Barnes.
Abbey, Lester. A History of Music for Those Who Don't Want to Know Too Much About Music History. LC 80-124026. 1981. pap. 3.00. RWS Bks.
Abbey, Margaret. The Flight of the Kestrel. 1978. pap. 1.75 o.p. (ISBN 0-345-25424-4). Ballantine.
--Francesca. 1976. pap. 1.25 o.p. (ISBN 0-345-25423-6). Ballantine.
Abbey, Merrill R. & Edwards, O. C. Epiphany. LC 74-76935. (Proclamation 1: Aids for Interpreting the Lessons of the Church Year, Ser. A: Ser. A). 64p. (Orig.). 1974. pap. 1.95 (ISBN 0-8006-4062-4, 1-4062). Fortress.
Abbey, Staten. Book of the Rover. pap. 4.50x (ISBN 0-392-05798-0, SpS). Soccer.
--Book of the Triumph Two Thousand. pap. 4.50x (ISBN 0-392-05803-0, SpS). Soccer.
Abbiatico, Mario. Grandi Incisioni Su Armi D'Bagi. (Illus.). Repr. of 1976 ed. 30.00. Arma Pr.
Abbie, A. A. Studies in Physical Anthropology, Vols. 1 & 2. (AIAS Research & Regional Ser.: No. 5). (Illus., Orig.). 1975. pap. text ed. 10.00x (ISBN 0-391-01421-8); Vol. 1. pap. text ed. 6.25x (ISBN 0-391-01880-9); Vol. 2. pap. text ed. 7.25x (ISBN 0-391-01881-7). Humanities.
Abbing, Roscam H. International Organizations in Europe & the Right to Health Care. 1979. pap. 48.00 (ISBN 90-268-1077-6, Kluwer Law & Taxation). Kluwer Boston.
Abbondante, Paul J., jt. auth. see Moliver, Donald M.
Abbot, Alexander S. The Philosophical, Psychological & Moral Degeneration of the American Pragmatists. (Illus.). 114p. 1980. 41.75 (ISBN 0-89266-257-3). Am Classical Coll Pr.
Abbot, George. A Briefe Description of the Whole Worlde. LC 78-25701. (English Experience Ser.: No. 213). 68p. Repr. of 1599 ed. 9.50 (ISBN 90-221-0213-0). Walter J Johnson.
Abbot, John. The Iranians: How They Live & Work. 168p. 1978. text ed. 8.95 (ISBN 0-03-042496-8, HoltC). HR&W.
Abbot, Justin E. Life of Tukaram. 346p. 1980. text ed. 13.50 (ISBN 0-8426-1644-6); pap. text ed. 9.00 (ISBN 0-8426-1654-3). Verry.
Abbot, Morris W. Cog Railway to Pike's Peak. LC 73-9520. (Illus.). 48p. pap. 2.95 (ISBN 0-87095-052-5). Golden West.
Abbot, Rose Marie. Bride of Vengeance. (Candlelight Romance Ser.). (Orig.). 1981. pap. 1.50 (ISBN 0-440-10819-5). Dell.
Abbot, W. Practical Geometry & Engineering Graphics. 8th ed. (Illus.). 1971. pap. text ed. 16.50x (ISBN 0-216-89450-6). Intl Ideas.
Abbott & Anon. Railroads One Hundred Years Ago. (Sun Historical Ser.). (Illus.). 1980. 3.50 (ISBN 0-89540-048-0). Sun Pub.
Abbott, A. F. & Nelkon, M. Elementary Physics. Sayer, Michael, ed. 1971. pap. 5.50x ea. o.p.; Pt. 1. pap. (ISBN 0-435-67654-7); Pt. 2. pap. (ISBN 0-435-67655-5); pap. text ed. 9.50x combined ed. o.p. (ISBN 0-435-67656-3). Heinemann Ed.
Abbott, C. C., ed. see Hopkins, Gerard M.
Abbott, Carl. Boosters & Businessmen: Popular Economic Thought & Urban Growth in the Antebellum Middle West. LC 80-1795. (Contributions in American Studies: No. 53). (Illus.). 1981. lib. bdg. 27.50 (ISBN 0-313-22562-1, ABB/). Greenwood.
--The Great Extravaganza: Portland & the Lewis & Clark Expedition. LC 80-83179. (Illus.). 104p. 1981. pap. 5.95 (ISBN 0-87595-088-4). Oreg Hist Soc.
Abbott, Daniel J., jt. auth. see Clinard, Marshall B.
Abbott, David W. Getting Control of Your Weight. 144p. 1980. pap. cancelled (ISBN 0-89037-187-3). Anderson World.
Abbott, Derek & Pollit, Kimball. Hill Housing: A Guide to Design & Construction. 304p. 1981. 34.50 (ISBN 0-8230-7259-2, Whitney Lib). Watson-Guptill.
Abbott, Earl L. & Solomon, Erwin S., eds. Instructions for Virginia & West Virginia, 3 vols. 2nd ed. 1962. with 1980 suppl. 75.00 (ISBN 0-87215-077-1); 1980 suppl. 25.00 (ISBN 0-87215-343-6). Michie.
Abbott, Edwin A. Flatland: A Romance of Many Dimensions. 5th rev ed. 1963. pap. 2.95 (ISBN 0-06-463210-5, E*H 210, EH). Har-Row.
Abbott, Elisabeth, tr. see Artusi, Pellegrino.
Abbott, Frank F. The Common People of Ancient Rome: Studies of Roman Life & Literature. LC 65-23487. (gr. 7 up). 1911. 11.00x (ISBN 0-8196-0157-8). Biblo.
--A History & Description of Roman Political Institutions. 3rd ed. LC 63-10766. 451p. (gr. 7 up). 1910. 10.50x (ISBN 0-8196-0117-9). Biblo.
--Society & Politics in Ancient Rome: Essays & Sketches. LC 63-10767. 267p. (gr. 7 up). 1909. 10.50x (ISBN 0-8196-0118-7). Biblo.
Abbott, G. F. Israel in Europe. Aronsfeld, C. C., ed. & intro. by. 556p. 1972. text ed. 17.00x o.p. (ISBN 0-391-00182-5). Humanities.
Abbott, H. Porter. The Fiction of Samuel Beckett: Form & Affect. LC 79-186102. (Perspectives in Criticism Ser.: No. 22). 1973. 19.50x (ISBN 0-520-02202-5). U of Cal Pr.
Abbott, J. Student Life in a Class Society. 1971. 30.00 (ISBN 0-08-015654-1). Pergamon.
Abbott, Jacob. The Franconia Stories, 10 vols. in 2. LC 75-32164. (Classics of Children's Literature, 1621-1932: Vol. 28). (Illus.). 1976. Repr. of 1853 ed. Set. PLB 60.00 (ISBN 0-8240-2277-7); PLB 38.00 ea. Garland Pub.
--History of Elizabeth, Queen of England. 252p. 1980. Repr. lib. bdg. 20.00 (ISBN 0-8492-3226-0). R West.
--Makers of History, Charles I. 285p. 1980. Repr. of 1903 ed. lib. bdg. 20.00 (ISBN 0-89984-002-7). Century Bookbindery.
Abbott, James H., tr. see Zea, Leopoldo.
Abbott, Jean, et al. Protocols for Prehospital Emergency Care. (Illus.). 200p. 1980. softcover 11.95 (ISBN 0-683-01563-X). Williams & Wilkins.
Abbott, John R. Footwear Evidence: The Examination, Identification, & Comparison of Footwear Impressions. 100p. 1964. pap. 12.70 photocopy ed. spiral (ISBN 0-398-00003-4). C C Thomas.
Abbott, John S. Makers of History, Joseph Bonaparte. 391p. 1980. Repr. of 1903 ed. lib. bdg. 20.00 (ISBN 0-89984-049-3). Century Bookbindery.
Abbott, Katharine M. Old Paths & Legends of the New England Border: Connecticut, Deerfield, Berkshire. LC 72-75227. 1970. Repr. of 1907 ed. 18.00 (ISBN 0-8103-3562-X). Gale.
Abbott, Katherine M. Old Paths & Legends of New England: Saunterings Over Historic Roads with Glimpses of Picturesque Fields & Old Homesteads in Massachusetts, Rhode Island & New Hampshire. LC 76-75228. Repr. of 1903 ed. 18.00 (ISBN 0-8103-3564-6). Gale.
Abbott, Keith. Erase Words. LC 76-58861. (Illus.). 1977. pap. 2.95 (ISBN 0-912652-35-7, Dynamite Books); pap. 8.95 signed ed. (ISBN 0-912652-36-5). Blue Wind.
--Putty. (Illus.). 1971. signed lettered A-Z o.p. 7.50 (ISBN 0-912652-32-2); pap. 3.50 (ISBN 0-912652-31-4). Blue Wind.
--What You Know with No Name for It. 1976. signed ed. o.p. 7.00 (ISBN 0-912652-34-9); pap. 3.00 (ISBN 0-912652-33-0). Blue Wind.
Abbott, L. W. Law Reporting in England Fourteen Eighty Five-Fifteen Eighty Five. (University of London Legal Ser.: No. 10). (Illus.). 328p. 1973. text ed. 52.50x (ISBN 0-485-13410-1, Athlone Pr). Humanities.
Abbott, Lyman. Henry Ward Beecher. LC 80-19338. (American Men & Women of Letters Ser.). 475p. 1980. pap. 6.95 (ISBN 0-87754-163-9). Chelsea Hse.
Abbott, P. Calculus. (Teach Yourself Ser.). 1975. pap. 3.95 o.p. (ISBN 0-679-10391-0). McKay.
--Mechanics. (Teach Yourself Ser.). 1974. pap. 3.95 o.p. (ISBN 0-679-10403-8). McKay.
Abbott, R. T., ed. see McDonald, Gary R. & Nybakken, James W.
Abbott, R. Tucker, jt. auth. see Sandved, Kjell B.
Abbott, Richard H. Cobbler in Congress: The Life of Henry Wilson, 1812-1875. LC 70-147856. (Illus.). 308p. 1972. 17.00x (ISBN 0-8131-1249-4). U Pr of Ky.
Abbott, Susan & Van Willigen, John, eds. Predicting Sociocultural Change. LC 79-10193. (Southern Anthropological Society Proceedings Ser.: No. 13). 156p. 1980. 12.00x (ISBN 0-8203-0477-8); pap. 5.25 (ISBN 0-8203-0484-0). U of Ga Pr.
Abbott, T. K. Ephesians & Colossians. LC 40-15742. (International Critical Commentary Ser.). 392p. Repr. of 1979 ed. 21.00x (ISBN 0-567-05030-0). Attic Pr.
Abbott, Thomas K., tr. see Kant, Immanuel.
Abbott-Smith, G. A Manual Greek Lexicon of the New Testament. 3rd ed. 528p. 1977. text ed. 20.00 (ISBN 0-567-01001-5). Attic Pr.
Abbs, B., et al. Strategies. (Illus.). 1976. pap. text ed. 5.00x (ISBN 0-582-51872-5); tchr's ed. 9.00x (ISBN 0-582-51873-3). Longman.
Abbs, Peter. Approaches Ser., No. 2: Our World. 1974. pap. text ed. 2.95x (ISBN 0-435-10022-X). Heinemann Ed.
--Asking Questions. (Approaches Ser.: No. 3). 1974. pap. text ed. 2.95x o.p. (ISBN 0-435-10023-8). Heinemann Ed.
--Creating for Ourselves. (Approacher Ser.: No. 4). 1974. pap. text ed. 2.95x o.p. (ISBN 0-435-10024-6). Heinemann Ed.
--English Broadsheets. (Second Ser.). 1970. pap. text ed. 4.95x o.p. (ISBN 0-435-10005-X); tchrs's ed. 2.25x o.p. (ISBN 0-435-10007-6). Heinemann Ed.
--Stories for Today: First Series. Incl. Ron's Fight (ISBN 0-435-11140-X); Ginger & Sharon (ISBN 0-435-11141-8); Frank's Fire (ISBN 0-435-11142-6); Linda's Journey (ISBN 0-435-11143-4); Joe & Carol (ISBN 0-435-11144-2); Diane's Sister (ISBN 0-435-11145-0). 1972. pap. text ed. 9.75 mixed set-1 copy of ea. o.p. (ISBN 0-435-11150-7); Six-pack Of Single Titles. pap. text ed. 9.95x ea. o.p.; tchrs notes 0.75x o.p. (ISBN 0-435-11139-6). Heinemann Ed.
Abbs, Peter, ed. English Broadsheets. (Introductory Ser.). 1971. pap. text ed. 3.95x o.p. (ISBN 0-435-10008-4); tchr's ed. 2.95x o.p. (ISBN 0-435-10010-6). Heinemann Ed.
--English Broadsheets. (First Ser.). 1971. pap. text ed. 4.95x o.p. (ISBN 0-435-10002-5); tchrs' ed. 2.95x o.p. (ISBN 0-435-10003-3). Heinemann Ed.
--Into Action. (Approacher Ser.: No. 1). 1974. pap. text ed. 2.95x o.p. (ISBN 0-435-10021-1). Heinemann Ed.
Abcarius, J. John. An English-Arabic Reader's Dictionary. 1974. 16.00x (ISBN 0-685-72043-8). Intl Bk Ctr.
Abd Al-Kabir Al Munawarra, ed. see Sidi Ali Al-Jamal Of Fez.
Abdallah. Speaking Arabic. (Arabic.). pap. 3.50 (ISBN 0-685-82875-1). Intl Bk Ctr.
Abdeen, Adnan. English-Arabic Dictionary for Accounting & Finance. LC 79-41213. 1981. 22.95 (ISBN 0-471-27673-1, Pub. by Wiley-Interscience). Wiley.
Abdel-Fadil, M. Development, Income Distribution & Social Change in Rural Egypt 1952-1970. LC 75-17114. (Department of Applied Economics, Occasional Papers Ser.: No. 45). 1976. pap. 14.95x (ISBN 0-521-29019-8). Cambridge U Pr.
--The Political Economy of Nasserism. LC 80-49995. (Cambridge Department of Applied Economics, Occasional Papers: No. 52). (Illus.). 140p. 1980. 24.95 (ISBN 0-521-22313-X); pap. 13.95 (ISBN 0-521-29446-0). Cambridge U Pr.
Abdel-Fettah, Y. M., jt. ed. see Najim, M.
Abdel-Hady, M., jt. auth. see Tuma, J.
Abdel-Khalek, Goudal, jt. ed. see Tignor, Robert L.
Abdel-khalik, A. Rashad, ed. Government Regulation of Accounting & Information. LC 79-26555. (University of Florida Accounting Ser.: No. 11). (Illus.). vi, 320p. (Orig.). 1980. pap. 10.00 (ISBN 0-8130-0663-5). U Presses Fla.
Abdel-Malek, Zaki N. The Closed-List Classes of Colloquial Egyptian Arabic. (Janua Linguarum, Ser. Practica: No. 128). 240p. (Orig.). 1972. pap. text ed. 42.35x (ISBN 90-2792-322-1). Mouton.
Abdel-Massih, Ernest T. An Introduction to Egyptian Arabic. LC 75-24784. 1974. pap. text ed. 7.00 (ISBN 0-932098-09-6). Ctr for NE & North African Stud.
--Introduction to Moroccan Arabic. LC 72-154239. 1977. pap. text ed. 7.00 (ISBN 0-932098-80-0). Ctr for NE & North African Stud.
Abdel-Massih, Ernest T., et al. A Comprehensive Study of Egyptian Arabic: Lexicon, Vol. IV. Incl. Pt. I. Egyptian Arabic - English: 34 Cultural Categories; Pt. II. English - Arabic: 34 Cultural Categories. LC 76-24957. 1979. pap. text ed. 8.00 (ISBN 0-932098-14-2). Ctr for NE & North African Stud.
Abdel-Monem, Mahmoud M. & Henkel, James G. Essentials of Drug Product Quality: Concepts & Methodology. LC 77-27069. (Illus.). 1978. text ed. 19.95 (ISBN 0-8016-0031-6). Mosby.
Abdel Wahab, Farouk, ed. & tr. Modern Egyptian Drama: An Anthology. LC 72-94939. (Studies in Middle Eastern Literatures Ser: No. 3). 1974. 25.00x (ISBN 0-88297-005-4). Bibliotheca.
Abdi, Ali Issa. Commercial Banks & Economic Development: The Experience of Eastern Africa. LC 77-12813. (Praeger Special Studies). 1978. 20.95 (ISBN 0-03-023031-4). Praeger.
Abdill, George. Locomotive Engineer Album. (Encore Ed.). (Illus.). 9.95 (ISBN 0-87564-534-8). Superior Pub.
Abdo, D. Studies in Arabic Linguistics. (Arabic.). 1973. 14.00x (ISBN 0-685-72058-6). Intl Bk Ctr.
Abdul, Raoul. Blacks in Classical Music: A Personal History. LC 77-11645. 1978. 8.95 (ISBN 0-396-07394-8). Dodd.
Abdu'l-Baha. Christ's Promise Fulfilled. 1954. pap. 2.50 (ISBN 0-87743-049-7, 7-06-01). Baha'i.
--Memorials of the Faithful. Gail, Marzieh, tr. LC 77-157797. 1971. 9.00 (ISBN 0-87743-041-1, 7-06-12). Baha'i.
--Paris Talks. 11th ed. 1969. 8.00 (ISBN 0-900125-07-1, 7-06-15); pap. 4.50 (ISBN 0-900125-08-X, 7-06-16). Baha'i.
--Secret of Divine Civilization. 2nd ed. Gail, Marzieh, tr. LC 56-12427. 1970. 9.00 (ISBN 0-87743-008-X, 7-06-06). Baha'i.
--Selections from the Writings of Abdu'l-Baha. Effendi, Shoghi & Gail, Marzieh, trs. 1978. 10.00 (ISBN 0-85398-081-0, 7-06-25); pap. 5.00 (ISBN 0-85398-084-5, 7-06-26). Baha'i.
--Tablets of the Divine Plan. rev ed. 1980. pap. 4.00 (ISBN 0-87743-154-X, 7-06-11). Baha'i.
--Tablets of the Divine Plan. rev. ed. LC 76-10624. 1977. 10.00 (ISBN 0-87743-107-8, 7-06-09). Baha'i.

--A Traveler's Narrative: Written to Illustrate the Episode of the Bab. rev. ed. Browne, Edward G., tr. from Persian. LC 79-19025. 1980. 9.00 (ISBN 0-87743-134-5, 7-06-27); pap. 4.00 (ISBN 0-87743-134-5, 7-06-28). Baha'i.

Abdu'l-Baha, jt. auth. see Baha'u'llah.

Abdu'L-Baha, jt. auth. see Baha'u'llah.

Abdu'l-Baha, jt. auth. see Baha'u'llah.

Abdu'l-Baha, jt. auth. see Baha'U'Llah The Bab.

Abdu'L-Baha, jt. auth. see Baha'U'Llah The Bab.

Abdu'l-Baha, jt. auth. see Baha'U'Llah The Bab.

Abdulhadi, Hassan T. Energy--a Global Outlook: The Case for Effective International Co-operation. LC 80-41616. (Illus.). 300p. 1980. 40.00 (ISBN 0-08-027292-4); pap. 15.00 (ISBN 0-08-027293-2). Pergamon.

Abdullah, M., jt. auth. see Kuffel.

Abe, E. Hopf Algebras. LC 79-50912. (Cambridge Tracts in Mathematics Ser.: No. 74). 1980. 39.50 (ISBN 0-521-22240-0). Cambridge U Pr.

Abe, Kobo. Inter Ice Age Four. Saunders, E. Dale, tr. from Jap. (Perigee Japanese Library). 240p. 1981. pap. 4.95 (ISBN 0-399-50519-9, Perigee). Putnam.

Abe, M., et al, eds. Treatment of Radioresistant Cancers. 230p. 1979. 46.50 (ISBN 0-444-80179-0, North Holland). Elsevier.

Abe, Yuji, ed. Modern Japanese Prints: A Contemporary Selection. LC 70-120391. 1970. pap. 3.75 (ISBN 0-8048-0926-7). C E Tuttle.

A Beckett, Arthur W. A Becketts of Punch. LC 69-17341. 1969. Repr. of 1903 ed. 18.00 (ISBN 0-8103-3518-2). Gale.

Abegglen, James C. The Japanese Factory. rev. ed. LC 80-52878. 200p. 1981. pap. 6.25 (ISBN 0-8048-1372-8). C E Tuttle.

--Management & Worker: The Japanese Solution. LC 72-96130. 200p. 1973. 14.50x (ISBN 0-87011-199-X). Kodansha.

Abel, Alison M. Make Hay While the Sun Shines. (Illus.). 1977. 7.95 (ISBN 0-571-11006-1, Pub. by Faber & Faber). Merrimack Bk Serv.

Abel, Andrew B. Investment & the Value of Capital. LC 78-75063. (Outstanding Dissertations in Economics Ser.). 1979. lib. bdg. 22.00 (ISBN 0-8240-4139-9). Garland Pub.

Abel, Bob. The Book of Beer. LC 76-6254. (Illus.). 1976. pap. 6.95 o.p. (ISBN 0-8092-9126-6). Contemp Bks.

Abel, Doninick. Guide to the Wines of the United States. 1979. 2.95 (ISBN 0-346-12427-1). Cornerstone.

Abel, E. W., jt. auth. see Rochow, E. G.

Abel, Ernest L. Drugs & Behavior: A Primer in Neuropsychopharmacology. LC 80-11313. 240p. 1981. Repr. of 1974 ed. lib. bdg. write for info. (ISBN 0-89874-137-8). Krieger.

Abel, Ernest L., ed. The Scientific Study of Marihuana. LC 76-4508. 288p. 1976. 18.95 (ISBN 0-88229-144-0). Nelson-Hall.

Abel, H., ed. Advances in Cardiology, Vol. 28. (Illus.). 240p. 1980. 66.00 (ISBN 3-8055-1185-X). S Karger.

Abel, I. W. Collective Bargaining. 84p. 1976. 8.50x (ISBN 0-915604-05-1). Columbia U Pr.

Abel, Peter. Programming Assembler Language. (Illus.). 1979. text ed. 16.95 (ISBN 0-8359-5658-X); instrs'. manual avail. (ISBN 0-8359-5659-8). Reston.

--Structured PL-One & PL: A Problem Solving Approach. 1981. text ed. 18.95 (ISBN 0-8359-7120-1); pap. text ed. 12.95 (ISBN 0-8359-7119-8); instr's. manual avail. (ISBN 0-8359-7121-X). Reston.

Abel, Reuben. Man Is the Measure: A Cordial Invitation to the Central Problems of Philosophy. LC 75-16646. (Illus.). 1976. 12.95 (ISBN 0-02-900140-4); pap. text ed. 8.95 (ISBN 0-02-900110-2). Free Pr.

Abel, Reuben E., ed. Humanistic Pragmatism: The Philosophy of F. C. S. Schiller. (Orig.). 1966. pap. text ed. 4.95 (ISBN 0-02-900120-X). Free Pr.

Abel, Robert. Freedom Dues: Or, a Gentleman's Progress in the New World. 404p. 1980. 10.95 (ISBN 0-8037-2575-2). Dial.

Abel, Wilhelm. Agricultural Fluctuations in Europe: From the Thirteen to the Twentieth Centuries. Ordish, Olive, tr. LC 80-5072. 1980. 40.00 (ISBN 0-312-01465-1). St Martin.

Abelard, Felix. My Wife, the Condesa. 1978. 9.50 o.p. (ISBN 0-682-49054-7). Exposition.

Abeles, P. W.., et al. Prestressed Concrete Designers Handbook. 2nd ed. (C & CA Viewpoint Publication Ser.). (Illus.). 467p. 1976. pap. text ed. 42.50 (ISBN 0-7210-1028-8). Scholium Intl.

Abell, Aaron, ed. American Catholic Thought on Social Questions. LC 66-30548. 1968. pap. 10.95 (ISBN 0-672-60090-0, AHS58). Bobbs.

Abell, Corliss W., jt. auth. see Abell, Richard G.

Abell, Derek F. & Hammond, John. Strategic Market Planning: Problems & Analytical Approaches. 1979. text ed. 21.95 (ISBN 0-13-851089-X). P-H.

Abell, George D. & Singer, Barry. Science and the Paranormal. (Illus.). 320p. 1981. 12.95 (ISBN 0-684-16655-0, ScribT). Scribner.

Abell, Richard G. & Abell, Corliss W. Own Your Own Life. (Illus.). 288p. 1976. 9.95 o.p. (ISBN 0-679-50601-2). McKay.

Abella, Irving M. Nationalism, Communism & Canadian Labour: The CIO, the Communist Party, & the Canadian Congress of Labour, 1935-56. LC 72-80712. 304p. 1973. pap. 6.50 (ISBN 0-8020-6150-8). U of Toronto Pr.

Abeloe, William N. To the Top of the Mountain: The Life of Father Umberto Olivieri, "Padre of the Otomis". LC 76-7187. 1976. 8.00 o.p. (ISBN 0-682-48558-6). Exposition.

Abelow, Dan. Total Sex. 1977. pap. 2.75 (ISBN 0-441-81792-0). Ace Bks.

Abelow, Dan, jt. auth. see Barr, Samuel J.

Abels, Harriette S. Emmy, Beware! (Prime Time Adventures Ser.). (Illus.). 64p. (gr. 4 up). 1981. PLB 7.95 (ISBN 0-516-02105-2). Childrens.

--Future Business. Schroeder, Howard, ed. LC 80-14859. (Our Future World Ser.). (Illus.). 48p. (gr. 6-9). 1980. PLB 5.95 (ISBN 0-89686-081-7); pap. text ed. 2.95 (ISBN 0-89686-090-6). Crestwood Hse.

--Future Communication. Schroeder, Howard, ed. LC 80-16529. (Our Future World Ser.). (Illus.). 48p. (gr. 6-9). 1980. PLB 5.95 (ISBN 0-89686-084-1); pap. text ed. 2.95 (ISBN 0-89686-093-0). Crestwood Hse.

--Future Family. Schroeder, Howard, ed. LC 80-16400. (Our Future World Ser.). (Illus.). 48p. (gr. 6-9). 1980. PLB 5.95 (ISBN 0-89686-085-X); pap. text ed. 2.95 (ISBN 0-89686-094-9). Crestwood Hse.

--Future Food. Schroeder, Howard, ed. LC 80-14823. (Our Future World Ser.). (Illus.). 48p. (Orig.). (gr. 6-9). 1980. PLB 5.95 (ISBN 0-89686-083-3); pap. text ed. 2.95 (ISBN 0-89686-092-2). Crestwood Hse.

--Future Government. Schroeder, Howard, ed. LC 80-14940. (Our Future World Ser.). (Illus.). 48p. (gr. 4 up). PLB 5.95 (ISBN 0-89686-082-5); pap. 2.95 (ISBN 0-89686-091-4). Crestwood Hse.

--Future Government. Schroeder, Howard, ed. LC 80-14940. (Our Future World Ser.). (Illus.). (gr. 6-9). 1980. PLB 5.95 (ISBN 0-89686-082-5); pap. 2.95 (ISBN 0-89686-091-4). Crestwood Hse.

--Future Medicine. Schroeder, Howard, ed. LC 80-15523. (Our Future World Ser.). (Illus.). 48p. (Orig.). (gr. 6-9). 1980. PLB 5.95 (ISBN 0-89686-086-8); pap. 2.95 (ISBN 0-89686-095-7). Crestwood Hse.

--Future Science. Schroeder, Howard, ed. LC 80-19412. (Our Future World Ser.). (Illus.). 48p. (Orig.). (gr. 6-9). 1980. PLB 5.95 (ISBN 0-89686-080-9); pap. 2.95 (ISBN 0-89686-089-2). Crestwood Hse.

--Future Space. Schroeder, Howard, ed. LC 80-16457. (Our Future World Ser.). (Illus.). 48p. (Orig.). (gr. 4 up). PLB 5.95 (ISBN 0-89686-087-6); pap. 2.95 (ISBN 0-89686-096-5). Crestwood Hse.

--Future Travel. Schroeder, Howard, ed. (Our Future World Ser.). (Illus.). 48p. (gr. 6-9). 1980. PLB 5.95 (ISBN 0-89686-088-4); pap. 2.95 (ISBN 0-89686-097-3). Crestwood Hse.

--September Storm. (Prime Time Adventures Ser.). (Illus.). 64p. (gr. 4 up). PLB 7.95 (ISBN 0-516-02110-9). Childrens.

Abels, Linda F. Mosby's Manual of Critical Care: Practices & Procedures, Nineteen Seventy-Nine. LC 78-24358. (Illus.). 1979. pap. text ed. 16.95 (ISBN 0-8016-0055-3). Mosby.

Abels, Paul & Murphy, Michael J. Administration in the Human Sciences: A Normative Systems Approach. (P-H Ser. in Social Work). (Illus.). 256p. 1981. text ed. 16.95 (ISBN 0-686-68604-7). P-H.

Abel-Smith, Brian. British Doctors at Home & Abroad. 63p. 1964. pap. text ed. 3.75x (Pub. by Bedford England). Renouf.

--The Poor & the Poorest. 78p. 1965. pap. text ed. 5.00x (Pub. by Bedford England). Renouf.

Abel-Smith, Brian, et al. Legal Problems & the Citizen. 1973. text ed. 20.95x (ISBN 0-435-82865-7). Heinemann Ed.

Abelson, Harold & DiSessa, Andrea. Turtle Geometry: The Computer As a Medium for Exploring Mathematics. (Illus.). 576p. 1981. text ed. 35.00 (ISBN 0-262-01063-1). MIT Pr.

Abelson, Peter. Cost Benefit Analysis & Environmental Problems. 1979. 19.50 (ISBN 0-566-00267-1, 02837-1, Saxon Hse). Lexington Bks.

Aber. My Book of Memories & Miscellany-My Book of Autographs. (gr. 3-5). pap. 1.25 (ISBN 0-590-05390-6, Schol Pap). Schol Bk Serv.

Aberbach, Moses, jt. auth. see Grossfeld, Bernard.

Abercrombie, Lascelles. A Plea for the Liberty of Interpreting. 51p. 1980. Repr. of 1930 ed. lib. bdg. 5.50 (ISBN 0-89987-007-4). Darby Bks.

Abercrombie, D. The Elements of General Phonetics. 1967. 6.50x (ISBN 0-85224-028-7, Pub. by Edinburgh U Pr Scotland). Columbia U Pr.

Abercrombie, Lascelles. Theory of Poetry. LC 69-17712. 1969. Repr. of 1926 ed. 12.00x (ISBN 0-8196-0223-X). Biblo.

Abercrombie, M. L. The Anatomy of Judgement: An Investigation into the Processes of Perception & Reasoning. 1980. Repr. of 1960 ed. pap. text ed. write for info. o.p. (ISBN 0-391-01057-3). Humanities.

Abercrombie, Nicholas. Class, Structure & Knowledge: Problems in the Sociology of Knowing. LC 79-9650. 1980. 20.00x (ISBN 0-8147-0571-5). NYU Pr.

Abercrombie, Nicholas, et al. Dominant Ideology Thesis. 240p. 1980. text ed. 28.50x (ISBN 0-04-301117-9, 2531). Allen Unwin.

Abercrombie, V. T. & Gaylord, Louise. Catering Eleven Houston. Date not set. price not set. Brown Rabbit.

Abercrombie, V. T., jt. auth. see Gaylord, Elizabeth B.

Abercrombie, V. T. & Williams, Helen, eds. Christmas in Texas. LC 79-66212. (Illus., Orig.). 1979. pap. 4.50 (ISBN 0-933988-00-1). Brown Rabbit.

Aberle, D. F., jt. auth. see Dyen, D.

Abernathy, Charles F. Cases & Materials on Civil Rights. LC 79-24759. (American Casebook Ser.). 700p. 1980. text ed. 17.95 (ISBN 0-8299-2076-5). West Pub.

Abernathy, George L. & Langford, Thomas A. History of Philosophy. economy ed. 1975. pap. text ed. 13.95x (ISBN 0-8221-0223-4). Dickenson.

--Introduction to Western Philosophy: Pre-Socratics to Mill. student economy ed. 1976. pap. text ed. 11.95x (ISBN 0-8221-0179-3). Dickenson.

Abernathy, Glenn. The Right of Assembly & Association. 300p. 1981. pap. text ed. 7.95 (ISBN 0-87249-410-1). U of SC Pr.

Abernethy, Francis E., ed. Tales from the Big Thicket. (Illus.). 1966. 12.95 (ISBN 0-292-73636-3). U of Tex Pr.

Abernethy, Virginia. Population Pressure & Cultural Adjustment. LC 78-11676. 1979. 16.95 (ISBN 0-87705-329-4). Human Sci Pr.

Abers, Ernest S. & Kennel, Charles F. Matter in Motion: The Spirit & Evolution of Physics. 1977. pap. 15.95 o.p. (ISBN 0-205-05790-X, 7357907); tchr's. manual free o.p. (ISBN 0-205-05791-8, 7357915). Allyn.

Abersold, John & Howard, Wayne. Cases in Labor Relations: An Arbitration Experience. (Orig.). 1967. pap. text ed. 10.95 (ISBN 0-13-118794-5). P-H.

Abert, Hermann J. Grundprobleme der Operngeschichte. LC 80-2253. 1981. Repr. of 1926 ed. 14.00 (ISBN 0-404-18800-1). AMS Pr.

Abeson, Marion & Bailey, Charity. Playtime with Music. rev. ed. (Illus.). 1952. 4.95 o.p. (ISBN 0-87140-999-2). Liveright.

Abetti, Giorgio. The Sun. 2nd ed. (Illus.). 1963. 9.95 (ISBN 0-571-05389-0, Pub. by Faber & Faber). Merrimack Bk Serv.

Abhayadatta. Buddha's Lions. Robinson, James, tr. from Tibean. (Tibetan Translation Ser.). (Illus.). 1979. 16.95 (ISBN 0-913546-60-7). Dharma Pub.

Abhedananda, Swami. Bhagavad Gita: The Divine Message, 2 vols. 30.00 set o.s.i. (ISBN 0-87481-625-4). Vedanta Pr.

--How to Be a Yogi. 4.95 o.p. (ISBN 0-87481-609-2). Vedanta Pr.

--Reincarnation. 3.95 o.p. (ISBN 0-87481-604-1). Vedanta Pr.

Abian, Alexander. Linear Associative Algebras. 1971. text ed. 21.00 (ISBN 0-08-016564-8). Pergamon.

Abidin, Richard R. Parent Education & Intervention Handbook. (Illus.). 608p. 1980. 24.50 (ISBN 0-398-03937-2). C C Thomas.

Abiko, Yasushi, jt. ed. see Winbury, Martin.

Abikoff, W. The Real Analytic Theory of Teichmueller Space. (Lecture Notes in Mathematics Ser.: Vol. 820). (Illus.). 144p. 1981. pap. 11.80 (ISBN 0-387-10237-X). Springer-Verlag.

Abir, David, ed. Contributions to Mechanics. 1969. 67.00 (ISBN 0-08-012822-X). Pergamon.

Abir, Mordechai. Ethiopia & the Red Sea: The Rise & Decline of the Solomonic Dynasty & Muslim-European Rivalry in the Region. 272p. 1980. 25.00x (ISBN 0-7146-3164-7, F Cass Co). Biblio Dist.

--Oil, Power & Politics: Conflict in Arabia, the Red Sea & the Gulf. 210p. 1974. 25.00x (ISBN 0-7146-2990-1, F Cass Co). Biblio Dist.

Abi-Saab, Georges. The United Nations Operation in the Congo, 1960-1964. (International Crises & the Role of Law Ser.). 1979. pap. 7.95x (ISBN 0-19-825323-0). Oxford U Pr.

Abisch, Roz. Around the House That Jack Built: A Tale of Ecology. LC 70-174606. (Illus.). (gr. k-3). 1972. 5.95 o.s.i. (ISBN 0-8193-0553-7, Four Winds); PLB 5.41 o.s.i. (ISBN 0-8193-0554-5). Schol Bk Serv.

--Let's Find Out About Butterflies. LC 73-182899. (Let's Find Out Books). (Illus.). 48p. (gr. k-3). 1972. PLB 4.47 o.p. (ISBN 0-531-00077-X). Watts.

--The Make-It, Play-It Game Book. LC 74-78855. (Illus.). 96p. (gr. 1-5). 1974. 5.95 o.s.i. (ISBN 0-8027-6198-4). Walker & Co.

Abisch, Roz & Kaplan, Boche. Mixed Bag of Magic Tricks. LC 73-92656. (Illus.). 64p. (gr. 2-5). 1974. 5.95 o.s.i. (ISBN 0-8027-6189-5). Walker & Co.

--The Munchy, Crunchy, Healthy Kid's Snack Book. LC 75-16516. (Illus.). 64p. (gr. 2-5). 1976. 6.50 o.s.i. (ISBN 0-8027-6229-8); PLB 6.39 o.s.i. (ISBN 0-8027-6234-4). Walker & Co.

--Textiles. LC 74-13430. (Illus.). (gr. 5 up). 1974. PLB 4.47 o.p. (ISBN 0-531-00824-X). Watts.

Abish, Walter. How German Is It. LC 80-20838. 256p. 1980. 14.95 (ISBN 0-8112-0775-7); pap. 5.95 (ISBN 0-8112-0776-5, NDP508). New Directions.

Abler, Ronald, et al. Spatial Organization: The Geographer's View of the World. LC 71-123081. (Geography Ser). (Illus.). 1971. text ed. 22.95 (ISBN 0-13-824086-8). P-H.

Ablin, Richard J. Immunobiology of the Prostate. 320p. 1981. 27.50 (ISBN 0-87527-178-2). Green.

Ablon, Leon, et al. The Steps in Mathematics, 5 modules. 1981. softbound 3.95 ea. Module 1 (ISBN 0-8053-0131-3). Module 2 (ISBN 0-8053-0132-1). Module 3 (ISBN 0-8053-0133-X). Module 4. Module 5 (ISBN 0-8053-0135-6). Benjamin-Cummings.

Ablon, Leon J., et al. Series in Mathematics Modules: Six Modules. Incl. Module 1. Operations on Numbers. 2nd ed. 4.95 (ISBN 0-8465-0240-2); Module 1A. Arithmetic. 2nd ed. 3.95 (ISBN 0-8465-6713-X); Module 2. Operations on Numbers. 2nd ed. 4.95 (ISBN 0-8465-0241-0); Module 3. Linear Equations & Lines. 2nd ed. 4.95 (ISBN 0-8465-0242-9); Module 4. Factoring & Operations on Algebraic Functions. 2nd ed. 4.95 (ISBN 0-8465-0243-7); Module 5. Quadratic Equations & Curves. 2nd ed. 4.95 (ISBN 0-8465-0244-5); Module 6. Basic Trigonometry. 2nd ed. 3.75 (ISBN 0-8465-0260-7); Module M. Medical Dosage Calculations. 2nd ed. 6.95 (ISBN 0-8053-7570-8). LC 72-94408. 1973. instr's guide 3.95 (ISBN 0-8465-0245-3). Benjamin-Cummings.

ABM Service Corp. National Directory of CB Radio Channels. LC 78-12796. 1979. 15.00 (ISBN 0-88280-064-7); pap. 7.95 (ISBN 0-88280-065-5). ETC Pubns.

Abma, John S. Introductory Psychology, 7 vols. 2nd ed. Incl. Vol. 1-Introductory to Psychology (ISBN 0-86589-007-2); Vol. 2-Learning (ISBN 0-86589-008-0); Vol. 3-the Physiological Bases of Behavior (ISBN 0-86589-009-9); Vol. 4-Individual Differences & Group Processes (ISBN 0-86589-010-2); Vol. 5-Motivation & Stress (ISBN 0-86589-011-0); Vol. 6-Mental Health (ISBN 0-86589-012-9); Vol. 7-Measurements, Statistics & Analysis (ISBN 0-86589-013-7). 1973. Set. 16.75 (ISBN 0-86589-006-4). Individual Learn.

Abney, A. H. Life & Adventures of L. D. Lafferty: Being a True Biography of One of the Most Remarkable Men of the Great Southwest. LC 75-7116. (Indian Captivities Ser.: Vol. 89). 1976. Repr. of 1875 ed. lib. bdg. 44.00 (ISBN 0-8240-1713-7). Garland Pub.

Abney, Bonnie MacLean. Blueprint for MBO: Setting Goals, Objectives & Action Plans That Work. (Packaged books & materials). 1979. pap. 125.00 participant's material (ISBN 0-8224-7540-5); manager's material 195.00 (ISBN 0-8224-7558-8). Pitman Learning.

Abodaher, David J. Great Moments in Sports Car Racing. (Illus.). 96p. (gr. 4-6). 1981. PLB 7.29 (ISBN 0-686-69302-7). Messner.

--So You're Ready to Drive a Car. (Illus.). 128p. (gr. 7 up). 1981. PLB price not set. Messner.

Abolfathi, Farid, et al. The OPEC Market to Nineteen Eighty-Five. LC 76-44612. (Illus.). 1977. 24.95 (ISBN 0-669-01102-9). Lexington Bks.

Abouchar, Alan. Transportation Economics & Public Policy: With Urban Extensions. LC 76-51828. 1977. 29.95 (ISBN 0-471-02101-6, Pub. by Wiley-Interscience). Ronald Pr.

Aboucher, Alan. Economic Evaluation of Soviet Socialism. (Pergamon Policy Studies). 1979. text ed. 19.25 (ISBN 0-08-023870-X). Pergamon.

Aboud, Antone & Aboud, Grace S. Right to Strike in Public Employment. (Key Issues Ser.: No. 15). 1974. pap. 2.00 (ISBN 0-87546-201-4). NY Sch Indus Rel.

Aboud, Grace. Hiring & Training the Disadvantaged for Public Employment. (Key Issues Ser.: No. 11). 1973. pap. 2.00 (ISBN 0-87546-202-2). NY Sch Indus Rel.

Aboud, Grace S. & Doherty, Robert E. Practices & Procedures Under the Taylor Law: A Practical Guide in Narrative Form. 1974. pap. 2.00 (ISBN 0-87546-203-0). NY Sch Indus Rel.

Aboud, Grace S, jt. auth. see Aboud, Antone.

Aboul-Fetouh, Hilmi M. Morphological Study of Egyptian Colloquial Arabic. (Janua Linguarum, Ser. Practica: No. 33). 1969. pap. text ed. 36.50x (ISBN 90-2790-691-2). Mouton.

Abragam, A. Principles of Nuclear Magnetism. (International Series of Monographs on Physics). 1961. 89.00x (ISBN 0-19-851236-8). Oxford U Pr.

Abragam, A. & Bleaney, B. Electron Paramagnetic Resonance of Transition Ions. (International Series of Monographs on Physics). 1970. 84.00x (ISBN 0-19-851250-3). Oxford U Pr.

Abraham. The Judiciary: The Supreme Court in the Governmental Process. 5th ed. 264p. 1980. pap. text ed. 7.95 (ISBN 0-205-06848-0, 7668481). Allyn.

Abraham, A. Microscopic Innervation of the Heart & Blood Vessels in Vertebrates Including Man. 1969. 64.00 (ISBN 0-08-012342-2). Pergamon.

Abraham, Arthur. Mende Government & Politics Under Colonial Rule: A Historical Study of Political Change in Sierra Leone 1890-1937. (Illus.). 1979. 29.50x (ISBN 0-19-711638-8). Oxford U Pr.

Abraham, Claude. Jean Racine. (World Authors Ser.: No. 458). 1977. lib. bdg. 12.50 (ISBN 0-8057-6295-7). Twayne.

--Pierre Corneille. (World Authors Ser.: France: No. 214). lib. bdg. 10.95 (ISBN 0-8057-2244-0). Twayne.

Abraham, Claude K. Enfin Malherbe: The Influence of Malherbe on French Lyric Prosody, 1605-1674. LC 70-160042. 368p. 1971. 18.00x (ISBN 0-8131-1254-0). U Pr of Ky.

Abraham, David. The Collapse of the Weimar Republic: Political Economy & Crisis. LC 80-8533. 550p. 1981. 30.00x (ISBN 0-691-05322-7); pap. 12.50x (ISBN 0-691-10118-3). Princeton U Pr.

Abraham, E. P., jt. ed. see Baddiley, James.

Abraham, George. Green Thumb Book of Fruit & Vegetable Gardening. LC 78-85000. (Illus.). 1969. 11.95 (ISBN 0-13-365189-4). P-H.

Abraham, George & Abraham, Katy. Green Thumb Garden Handbook. rev & expanded ed. LC 77-22279. 1977. 14.95 (ISBN 0-13-365114-2). P-H.

Abraham, Gerald. Tradition of Western Music. (Ernest Bloch Lectures Ser). 1974. 14.50x (ISBN 0-520-02414-1); pap. 5.50x (ISBN 0-520-02615-2). U of Cal Pr.

Abraham, Gerald, ed. The History of Music in Sound, Vols. 1-3. Incl. Vol. 1. Ancient & Oriental Music. Wellesz, Egon, ed. (Illus.). 42p. 1957 (ISBN 0-19-323100-X); Vol. 2. Early Medieval Music up to 1300. Hughes, Dom A., ed. 70p. 1953 (ISBN 0-19-323101-8); Vol. 3. Ars Nova & the Renaissance, - C. 1300-1540. Westrup, J. A., ed. 70p. 1954 (ISBN 0-19-323102-6). 6.00 ea. Oxford U Pr.

--The History of Music in Sound, Vols. 4-10. Incl. Vol 4. The Age of Humanism, 1540-1630. Westrup, J. A., ed. 1954 (ISBN 0-19-323103-4); Vol 5. Opera & Church Music, 1630-1750. Westrup, J. A., ed. 1954 (ISBN 0-19-323104-2); Vol 6. The Growth of Instrumental Music 1630-1750. Westrup, J. A., ed. 1954 (ISBN 0-19-323105-0); Vol 7. Symphonic Outlook, 1750-90. Wellesz, Egon, ed. 1957 (ISBN 0-19-323106-9); Vol. 8. The Age of Beethoven, 1790-1830. Abraham, Gerald, ed. 1958 (ISBN 0-19-323107-7); Vol. 9. Romanticism, 1830-90. Abraham, Gerald, ed. 1958 (ISBN 0-19-323108-5); Vol. 10. Modern Music, 1890-1950. Abraham, Gerald, ed. 1959 (ISBN 0-19-323109-3). 6.00 ea. Oxford U Pr.

--The Music of Sibelius. LC 74-23413. (Music Ser.). 218p. 1975. Repr. of 1947 ed. lib. bdg. 21.50 (ISBN 0-306-70716-0). Da Capo.

Abraham, Gerald see Abraham, Gerald, et al.

Abraham, Gerald, et al, eds. New Oxford History of Music. Incl. Vol. 1. Ancient & Oriental Music. Wellesz, Egon, ed. (15 plates). 1957. 44.00 (ISBN 0-19-316301-2); Vol. 2. Early Medieval Music up to 1300. Hughes, Dom Anselm, ed. 1954. 49.95 (ISBN 0-19-316302-0); Vol 3. Ars Nova & the Renaissance, 1300-1540. Hughes, Dom Anselm & Abraham, Gerald, eds. 1960. 49.95 (ISBN 0-19-316303-9); Vol. 4. The Age of Humanism, 1540-1630. Abraham, Gerald, ed. (Illus.). 1968. 44.00x (ISBN 0-19-316304-7); Vol. 7. The Age of Enlightenment, 1745-1790. Wellesz, Egon & Sternfeld, Frederick, eds. (Illus.). 1973. 49.95 (ISBN 0-19-316307-1); Vol. 10. Modern Age, 1890-1960. Cooper, Martin, ed. 1974. 49.95x (ISBN 0-19-316310-1). Oxford U Pr.

Abraham, Henry & Pfeffer, Irwin. Enjoying World History. (gr. 10-12). 1977. text ed. 11.58 (ISBN 0-87720-620-1); pap. text ed. 7.50 (ISBN 0-87720-618-X). AMSCO Sch.

Abraham, Henry J. The Judiciary: The Supreme Court in the Governmental Process. 4th ed. 1977. pap. text ed. 5.95x o.p. (ISBN 0-205-05757-8). Allyn.

Abraham, Henry J. & Doherty, Grace. Freedom & the Court: Civil Rights & Liberties in the United States. 3rd ed. 1977. 22.50 (ISBN 0-19-502135-5); pap. 6.95x (ISBN 0-19-502134-7). Oxford U Pr.

Abraham, Katy, jt. auth. see Abraham, George.

Abraham, M. Francis. Perspectives on Modernization: Toward a General Theory of Third World Development. LC 79-6811. 262p. 1980. pap. text ed. 10.25 (ISBN 0-8191-0961-4). U Pr of Amer.

Abraham, Marc, jt. auth. see Jenner, Bruce.

Abraham, Michael R. & Pavelich, Michael J. Inquiries into Chemistry. (Illus.). 1979. 8.95x (ISBN 0-917974-32-8). Waveland Pr.

Abraham, Nicholas A. Doing Business in Egypt. Prinz, Karl E., ed. (Doing Business in the Middle East: Vol. 2). (Illus.). 280p. (Orig.). 1979. pap. text ed. 79.95x (ISBN 0-934592-00-4). Trade Ship Pub Co.

--Doing Business in Saudi Arabia. Hanna, Christine A., ed. (Doing Business in the Middle East: Vol. 1). (Illus.). 336p. (Orig.). 1980. pap. text ed. 79.95x (ISBN 0-934592-01-2). Trade Ship Pub Co.

Abraham, R. C. Tiv People. 2nd ed. (Illus.). 1968. text ed. 15.00x o.p. (ISBN 0-391-02060-9). Humanities.

Abraham, Roger D. & Troike, Rudolph D., eds. Language & Cultural Diversity in American Education. 384p. 1972. pap. text ed. 9.95 (ISBN 0-13-522888-3). P-H.

Abraham, Samuel & Kiefer, Ferenc. Theory of Structural Semantics. (Janua Linguarum, Ser. Minor: No. 49). 1966. 16.50x (ISBN 90-2790-581-9). Mouton.

Abraham, Stanley C. The Public Accounting Profession. LC 77-7804. (Illus.). 1978. 19.95 (ISBN 0-669-01606-3). Lexington Bks.

Abraham, Werner. Ut Videam: Contributions to an Understanding of Linguistics. 1975. pap. text ed. 33.00x (ISBN 90-316-0002-4). Humanities.

Abraham-Frois, Gilbert & Berrebi, E. Theory of Value, Prices & Accumulation: Two Mathematical Integration of Marx, Von Neumann & Straffa. Kregel-Javaux, M. P., tr. LC 78-16277. (Illus., Fr.). 1979. 29.50 (ISBN 0-521-22385-7). Cambridge U Pr.

Abrahams, Harold J. Heroic Efforts at Meteor Crater, Arizona: Selected Correspondence Between Daniel Moreau Barringer & Elihu Thomson. LC 78-75170. 480p. 1981. 20.00 (ISBN 0-8386-2399-9). Fairleigh Dickinson.

Abrahams, Olga. Seiko. Orig. Title: The Spiders Thread. 1973. pap. 1.25 (ISBN 0-85363-112-3). OMF Bks.

Abrahams, Peter. This Island, Now. 1971. pap. 1.95 o.s.i. (ISBN 0-02-048040-7, Collier). Macmillan.

Abrahams, R. G. The Nyamwezi Today: A Tenzanian People in the Seventies. LC 80-41012. (Changing Cultures Ser.). (Illus.). 176p. Date not set. price not set (ISBN 0-521-22694-5); pap. price not set (ISBN 0-521-29619-6). Cambridge U Pr.

Abrahams, Roger D. Deep Down in the Jungle: Negro Narrative Folklore from the Streets of Philadelphia. LC 78-124404. 1970. 16.95 (ISBN 0-202-00109-1); pap. 7.50 (ISBN 0-686-66359-4). Aldine Pub.

Abrahams, Roger D., jt. ed. see Bauman, Richard.

Abrahams, Roger D. & Rankin, Lois, trs. Counting Out Rhymes: A Dictionary. (Publications of the American Folklore Bibliographical & Special Ser.: Vol. 31). 288p. 1980. text ed. 17.50x (ISBN 0-292-71057-7). U of Tex Pr.

Abrahams, William. Prize Stories 1981: The O'henry Awards. 360p. 1981. text ed. 13.95 (ISBN 0-385-15977-3). Doubleday.

Abrahams, William, ed. Prize Stories of the Seventies from O'Henry Awards. LC 80-22790. 408p. 1981. 12.95 (ISBN 0-385-17158-7). Doubleday.

Abrahamsen, David. The Murdering Mind. LC 72-9742. 256p. 1973. 6.95 o.s.i. (ISBN 0-06-010022-2, HarpT). Har-Row.

--Psychology of Crime. LC 59-13606. 1960. 18.50x (ISBN 0-231-02274-3). Columbia U Pr.

Abrahamson, E. M. & Pezet, A. W. Body, Mind & Sugar. 1977. pap. 3.95 (ISBN 0-380-00903-X, 47415). Avon.

Abrahamson, Ira A., Jr. Know Your Eyes. LC 76-23195. 218p. (Orig.). 1977. 9.95 (ISBN 0-88275-928-0); pap. text ed. 6.95 (ISBN 0-88275-451-3). Krieger.

Abrahamson, James L. America Arms for a New Century: The Making of a Great Military Power. LC 80-69716. (Illus.). 1981. 17.95 (ISBN 0-02-900190-0). Free Pr.

Abrahamson, Julia. A Neighborhood Finds Itself. 370p. 1972. Repr. of 1959 ed. 16.00x (ISBN 0-8196-0268-X). Biblo.

Abrahamson, M. Functionalism. LC 77-6828. 1978. pap. 8.95 ref. (ISBN 0-13-331900-8). P-H.

Abrahamson, Mark. Urban Sociology. LC 75-25728. (Sociology Ser.). (Illus.). 320p. 1976. 17.95x (ISBN 0-13-939512-1). P-H.

--Urban Sociology. 2nd ed. (Ser. in Sociology). (Illus.). 1980. text ed. 17.95 (ISBN 0-13-939587-3). P-H.

Abrahamson, Royce L., jt. auth. see Pickle, Hal B.

Abrahamsson, Bengt & Brostrom, Anders. The Rights of Labor. LC 80-16233. 301p. 25.00 (ISBN 0-8039-1477-6). Sage.

Abrahamsson, Bernhard J., ed. Conservation & the Changing Direction of Economic Growth. LC 77-28753. (Westview Special Studies in Natural Resources & Energy Management Ser.). 1978. lib. bdg. 22.00x (ISBN 0-89158-413-7). Westview.

Abrahson, R. L., jt. auth. see Pickle, H. B.

Abram, Harry S. Psychological Aspects of Stress. 112p. 1970. pap. 11.75 photocopy ed. spiral (ISBN 0-398-00004-2). C C Thomas.

Abramo, Barbara A., et al. Teaching the Retarded Child. 1975. spiral bdg. 9.00 o.p. (ISBN 0-87488-967-7). Med Exam.

Abramoff, Peter & Thomson, Robert G. An Experimental Approach to Biology. 2nd ed. (Illus.). 1976. lab manual 10.95x (ISBN 0-7167-0578-8); individual experiments 0.50 (ISBN 0-685-55248-9); instr's hndbk. avail. (ISBN 0-685-55249-7). W H Freeman.

--Laboratory Outlines in Biology, II. (Illus.). 1972. lab. manual 10.95x (ISBN 0-7167-0694-6); individual experiments 0.50 (ISBN 0-686-66666-6); instr's handbk avail. W H Freeman.

--Laboratory Outlines in Zoology. (Illus.). 1978. lab manual 10.95x (ISBN 0-7167-0017-4); individual experiments 0.50 (ISBN 0-686-68019-7); instr's handbk avail. (ISBN 0-685-93659-7). W H Freeman.

Abramov, L. & Cafferty, B. Chess Move by Move. (Chess Player Ser.). 1977. pap. 4.95 o.p. (ISBN 0-900928-67-0, H-1188). Hippocrene Bks.

Abramov, S. Zalman. Perpetual Dilemma: Jewish Religion in the Jewish State. 1979. pap. 15.00 (ISBN 0-8074-0088-2, 382500, WUPJ). UAHC.

Abramovitch, R. A., ed. Reactive Intermediates, Vol. 1. (Illus.). 1980. 49.50 (ISBN 0-306-40220-3, Plenum Pr). Plenum Pub.

Abramowitz, Milton & Stegun, Irene A., eds. Handbook of Mathematical Functions. LC 65-12253. 1965. lib. bdg. 24.50x (ISBN 0-88307-589-X). Gannon.

Abramowitz, Molly. Elie Wiesel: A Bibliography. LC 74-17166. (Author Bibliographies Ser.: No. 22). 1974. 10.00 (ISBN 0-8108-0731-9). Scarecrow.

Abramowski, Luise & Goodman, Allan E., eds. Nestorian Collection of Christological Texts, 2 vols. Incl. Vol. 1. Syriac Text. 58.00 (ISBN 0-521-07578-5); Vol. 2. Introduction, Translation & Indexes. 49.50 (ISBN 0-521-08126-2). LC 77-130904. (Oriental Publications Ser.: No. 18, 19). 1972. Cambridge U Pr.

Abrams, A. J. & Albert, Sondra R. Sewing Hints for Men. 96p. 1980. 9.95 (ISBN 0-442-26782-7). Van Nos Reinhold.

Abrams, Alan E., ed. Journalist Biographies Master Index. 1st ed. LC 77-9144. (Gale Biographical Index Ser.: No. 4). 1979. 52.00 (ISBN 0-8103-1086-4). Gale.

--Media Personnel Directory. LC 79-12885. 1979. 40.00 (ISBN 0-8103-0421-X). Gale.

Abrams, Edwin D & Blackman, Edward B. Managing Low & Moderate Income Housing. LC 72-14209. (Special Studies in U.S. Economic, Social & Political Issues). 1973. 28.50x (ISBN 0-275-28816-1). Irvington.

Abrams, Jerome S. A Concise Handbook for the Care of Patients with Abdominal Stomas. (Illus.). 164p. 1981. 20.00 (ISBN 0-88416-292-3). PSG Pub.

Abrams, Joy, jt. auth. see Richards, Ruth.

Abrams, Kathleen & Abrams, Lawrence. Logging & Lumbering. LC 80-19473. (Illus.). 96p. (gr. 4 up). 1980. PLB 7.79 (ISBN 0-671-34007-7). Messner.

--Successful Landlording. Case, Virginia, ed. LC 80-36678. (Successful Ser.). (Illus.). 144p. 1980. 15.95 (ISBN 0-89999-006-1); pap. 6.95 (ISBN 0-89999-007-X). Structures Pub.

Abrams, Lawrence, jt. auth. see Abrams, Kathleen.

Abrams, M. H. Milk of Paradise: The Effects of Opium Visions on the Works of DeQuincey, Crabbe, Frances Thompson, & Coleridge. LC 79-120223. 1970. Repr. lib. bdg. 12.50 (ISBN 0-374-90028-0). Octagon.

--Natural Supernaturalism: Tradition & Revolution in Romantic Literature. 550p. 1973. pap. 6.95 (ISBN 0-393-00609-3). Norton.

Abrams, M. H., ed. English Romantic Poets: Modern Essays in Criticism. 2nd ed. 592p. 1975. pap. 7.95 (ISBN 0-19-501946-6, 35, GB). Oxford U Pr.

Abrams, M. H., et al, eds. The Norton Anthology of English Literature, 2 vols. 3rd ed. 5000p. 1974. text ed. 12.95x ea.; Vol. 1. (ISBN 0-393-09301-8). pap. text ed. 9.95x ea.; Vol. 1. pap. (ISBN 0-393-09304-2); Vol. 2. pap. (ISBN 0-393-09306-9). Norton.

--The Norton Anthology of English Literature, 2 vols. 4th ed. (Illus.). 1979. text ed. 16.95x (ISBN 0-393-95039-5); Vol. II. text ed. 16.95x (ISBN 0-393-95043-3); Vol. I. pap. text ed. 11.95x (ISBN 0-393-95048-4); Vol II. pap. text ed. 14.95x (ISBN 0-685-94872-2). Vol. II (ISBN 0-393-95051-4). Norton.

--Norton Anthology of English Literature: Third Major Authors Edition. 1975. text ed. 17.95x (ISBN 0-393-09298-4); pap. text ed. 14.95x (ISBN 0-393-09299-2). Norton.

Abrams, Marshall D. & Stein, Philip G. Computer Hardware & Software: An Interdisciplinary Introduction. LC 72-3455. 1973. text ed. 18.95 (ISBN 0-201-00019-9). A-W.

Abrams, Meyer H. Mirror & the Lamp: Romantic Theory & the Critical Tradition. pap. 6.95 (ISBN 0-19-501471-5, 360, GB). Oxford U Pr.

Abrams, Natalie & Buckner, Michael. Medical Ethics: A Clinical Textbook & Reference for the Health Care Professions. 1981. text ed. write for info. (ISBN 0-89706-012-1); pap. text ed. write for info. (ISBN 0-89706-013-X). Bradford Bks.

Abrams, P. & McCulloch, A. Communes, Sociology & Society. LC 75-40985. (Themes in the Social Sciences Ser.: No. 3). 200p. 1976. 29.50 (ISBN 0-521-21188-3); pap. 7.95x (ISBN 0-521-29067-8). Cambridge U Pr.

Abrams, P. & Wrigley, E. A., eds. Towns in Societies. LC 77-82481. (Past & Present Publications). 1978. 32.95 (ISBN 0-521-21826-8); pap. 10.50 (ISBN 0-521-29594-7). Cambridge U Pr.

Abrams, Philip, ed. see Locke, John.

Abrams, Richard M. The Burdens of Progress, 1900-1929. 1978. pap. text ed. 7.95x (ISBN 0-673-05778-X). Scott F.

Abrams, Robert, et al. FLEX Review. LC 80-83395. 1980. pap. 21.50 (ISBN 0-87488-158-7). Med Exam.

Abrams, Ruth D. Not Alone with Cancer: A Guide for Those Who Care; What to Expect; What to Do. 128p. 1976. pap. 8.75 (ISBN 0-398-02973-3). C C Thomas.

Abrams, Stanley. Polygraph Handbook for Attorneys. LC 77-6074. (Illus.). 1977. 19.95 (ISBN 0-669-01598-9). Lexington Bks.

Abrams, Stanley D. Guide to Maryland Zoning Decisions: With 1979 Supplement. LC 75-3716. 216p. 1975. 27.50 (ISBN 0-87215-166-2); 1979 suppl. 9.50 (ISBN 0-87215-241-3). Michie.

Abramson, David I. & Casey, M. Beth. Self-Assessment of Current Knowledge in Peripheral Vascular Disorders. 1980. pap. 18.00 (ISBN 0-87488-291-5). Med Exam.

Abramson, Harold J. & Sofios, Nicholas. Index to Sociology Readers, 1960-1965, 2 vols. LC 73-977. 1973. Set. 35.00 (ISBN 0-8108-0592-8). Scarecrow.

Abramson, J. H., ed. see Emanuel, N. M. & Evseenko, D. S.

Abramson, Joan. Old Boys-New Women: The Politics of Discrimination. LC 79-65933. (Praeger Special Studies). 270p. 1979. 24.95 (ISBN 0-03-049756-6); pap. 9.95 student edition (ISBN 0-03-049751-5). Praeger.

Abramson, Lillian & Robinson, Jessie. Alef Bet Fun. (Illus.). (gr. 2-4). 1957. pap. 2.75x (ISBN 0-8197-0028-2). Bloch.

Abramson, Paul R. The Political Socialization of Black Americans: A Critical Evaluation of Research on Efficacy & Trust. LC 76-25343. (Illus.). 1977. 16.95 (ISBN 0-02-900170-6). Free Pr.

Abrashkin, Raymond, jt. auth. see Williams, Jay.

Abravanel, Claude. Claude Debussy: A Bibliography. LC 72-90430. (Detroit Studies in Music Bibliography Ser.: No. 29). 1974. 9.50 (ISBN 0-685-26717-2); pap. 8.00 (ISBN 0-685-26717-2). Info Coord.

Abrecht, Paul, ed. Faith & Science in an Unjust World, Vol. 2: Reports & Recommendations. LC 80-81141. 224p. 1980. pap. 6.95 (ISBN 0-8006-1391-0, 1-1391). Fortress.

Abrera, Joseph B., jt. auth. see Davis, Jinnie Y.

Abreu, Beatriz. Physical Disabilities Manual. 362p. 1981. text ed. 26.50 (ISBN 0-89004-505-4). Raven.

Abreu, Maria I. & Rameh, Clea. Portugues Contemporaneo, 2 vols. Incl. Vol. 1. 256p. pap. 6.50 (ISBN 0-87840-025-7); 11 cassettes 55.00 (ISBN 0-87840-048-6); 22 reel-to-reel tapes 120.00 (ISBN 0-87840-075-3); Vol. 2. 346p. pap. 7.00 (ISBN 0-87840-026-5); 10 cassettes 65.00 (ISBN 0-87840-049-4); 20 tapes 120.00 (ISBN 0-87840-076-1). LC 66-25520. 1971. Georgetown U Pr.

Abreu, Rosendo, jt. auth. see Lanzano, Susan.

Abrey, Emilo. Canek: History & Legends of a Maya Hero. Davila, Mario L. & Wilson, Carter, trs. from Span. 1980. 11.50 (ISBN 0-520-03148-2, CAL. NO. 441); pap. 2.95 (ISBN 0-520-03982-3). U of Cal Pr.

Abriel, Vera. The Woman's Total Reshape Program: Have the Figure You Always Wanted. (Illus.). 256p. 1981. 12.95 (ISBN 0-525-93148-1). Dutton.

Abrikosov, A. A., et al. Quantum Field Theoretical Methods in Statistical Physics. (Vol. 4). 1965. text ed. 16.25 o.p. (ISBN 0-08-010406-1); pap. text ed. 8.75 o.p. (ISBN 0-08-013470-X). Pergamon.

Abroms, jt. auth. see Scheiner, Albert P.

Abruquah, Joseph. Torrent: A Novel. 1968. pap. text ed. 2.50x (ISBN 0-582-64009-1). Humanities.

Absalom, R. N. Passages for Translation from Italian. 1967. pap. 7.50x (ISBN 0-521-09431-3, 431). Cambridge U Pr.

Abse, D. Wilfred. Speech & Reason: Language Disorder in Mental Disease & a Translation of Philipp Wegener's The Life of Speech. LC 72-163981. 1971. 20.00x (ISBN 0-8139-0344-0). U Pr of Va.

Abse, Dannie. Collected Poems. LC 76-21049. (Pitt Poetry Ser.). 1977. pap. 4.95 (ISBN 0-685-75151-1). U of Pittsburgh Pr.

Abse, Dannie, ed. Best of the Poetry Year: Poetry Dimension Annual 7. 160p. 1980. 15.00x (ISBN 0-8476-3255-5). Rowman.

--The Best of the Poetry Year: Poetry Dimension Annual, 5. 171p. 1978. 11.50x (ISBN 0-8476-3139-7). Rowman.

--My Medical School. (Illus.). 211p. 1978. 14.50x (ISBN 0-8476-3124-9). Rowman.

Abse, Joan. The Art Galleries of Britain & Ireland: A Guide to Their Collections. LC 75-24944. (Illus.). 231p. 1975. 15.00 (ISBN 0-8386-1850-2). Fairleigh Dickinson.

Abse, Joan, ed. My LSE. (Illus.). 223p. 1977. 14.50x (ISBN 0-8476-3125-7). Rowman.

Abt, Clark C., ed. The Evaluation of Social Programs. (Illus.). 503p. 1979. pap. 12.95 (ISBN 0-8039-1412-1). Sage.

--The Evaluation of Social Programs. LC 76-40712. (Illus.). 503p. 1977. 29.95 (ISBN 0-8039-0735-4). Sage.

Abt, Lawrence, jt. auth. see Rosner, Stanley.

Abt, Lawrence E. & Weissman, Stuart L., eds. Acting Out. 2nd ed. LC 76-53942. 1976. Repr. 25.00x (ISBN 0-87668-287-5). Aronson.

Abt, Wendy P., et al. Reforming Schools: Problems in Program Implementation & Evaluation. LC 80-23339. (Contemporary Evaluation Research Ser.: Vol. 4). (Illus.). 200p. 1981. 20.00 (ISBN 0-8039-1459-8); pap. 9.95 (ISBN 0-8039-1460-1). Sage.

Abu-Jaber, Faiz S. American-Arab Relations from Wilson to Nixon. LC 78-65853. 1979. pap. 10.50 (ISBN 0-8191-0680-1). U Pr of Amer.

Abulafia, D. The Two Italies. LC 76-11069. (Cambridge Studies in Medieval Life & Thought Ser.: No. 9). (Illus.). 1977. 49.50 (ISBN 0-521-21211-1). Cambridge U Pr.

Abu-Lughod, Ibrahim, ed. The Transformation of Palestine: Essays on the Origin & Development of the Arab-Israeli Conflict. 1971. 15.75x o.s.i. (ISBN 0-8101-0345-1). Northwestern U Pr.

Abu-Lughod, Janet L. Rabat: Urban Apartheid in Morocco. LC 80-7508. (Princeton Studies on the Near East). (Illus.). 400p. 1981. 30.00 (ISBN 0-691-05315-4); pap. 12.50 (ISBN 0-691-10098-5). Princeton U Pr.

Abun-Nasr, J. M. A History of the Maghrib. 2nd ed. LC 74-25653. (Illus.). 432p. 1975. 49.50 (ISBN 0-521-20703-7); pap. 16.95x (ISBN 0-521-09927-7). Cambridge U Pr.

Abu-Saad, Huda. Nursing: A World View. LC 78-25860. (Illus.). 1979. text ed. 12.50 (ISBN 0-8016-0065-0). Mosby.

Abu-Samayah. Arabic for Beginners. 1976. pap. 8.00x (ISBN 0-685-88940-8). Intl Bk Ctr.

Abu-Sitta, S. H., jt. auth. see Gould, Phillip L.

Abzug, Robert H. Passionate Liberator: Theodore Dwight Weld & the Dilemma of Reform. LC 80-11819. (Illus.). 300p. 1980. 19.95 (ISBN 0-19-502771-X). Oxford U Pr.

Academy Forum. Coal As an Energy Resource: Conflict & Consensus. 1977. pap. 11.00 (ISBN 0-309-02728-4). Natl Acad Pr.

--Research with Recombinant DNA. 1977. pap. text ed. 8.50 (ISBN 0-309-02641-5). Natl Acad Pr.

Academy Forum, National Academy of Science. Experiments & Research with Humans: Values in Conflicts. LC 75-13985. (Illus.). 224p. 1975. pap. 7.00 (ISBN 0-309-02347-5). Natl Acad Pr.

Academy Forum, National Academy of Sciences. Sweeteners: Issues & Uncertainties. LC 75-29990. vi, 259p. 1975. pap. 8.00 (ISBN 0-309-02407-2). Natl Acad Pr.

Academy of Engineering. Technology, Trade & the U. S. Economy. 1978. pap. 8.25 (ISBN 0-309-02761-6). Natl Acad Pr.

Academy of Management, 40th Annual Meeting, 1980. Proceedings. Huseman, Richard C., ed. LC 40-2886. 436p. (Orig.). 1980. pap. text ed. 11.00 (ISBN 0-915350-19-X). Acad of Mgmt.

Academy of Motion Picture Arts & Sciences. Annual Index to Motion Picture Credits, 1979. Ramsay, Verna, ed. LC 79-644761. 430p. 1980. lib. bdg. 150.00 (ISBN 0-313-20951-0, AN79). Greenwood.

--Annual Index to Motion Picture Credits, 1978. Ramsey, Verna, ed. LC 79-644761. 1979. lib. bdg. 150.00 (ISBN 0-313-20950-2, AN78). Greenwood.

Academy of Motion Pictures Arts & Sciences. Annual Index to Motion Picture Credits, 1980: Nineteen Eighty. LC 79-644761. 450p. 1981. lib. bdg. 150.00 (ISBN 0-313-20952-9, AN80). Greenwood.

Acconci, Vito. Kay Price & Stella Pajunas: Work for a Poetry Context 1967-1969. LC 77-77011. 1981. pap. text ed. 10.95 (ISBN 0-915570-08-4). Oolp Pr.

Accurso, Frank. Machine Trades Projects & Procedures: Standard & Metric. LC 77-8691. 1978. pap. text ed. 9.50 (ISBN 0-672-97101-1); tchr's manual 3.33 (ISBN 0-672-97155-0). Bobbs.

ACEI Committee, et al. Selecting Educational Equipment & Materials for School & Home. rev. ed. Cohen, Monroe D., ed. LC 75-35900. (Illus.). 96p. (Orig.). 1976. 4.00x (ISBN 0-87173-010-3). ACEI.

Acerrano, Anthony J. The Practical Hunter's Handbook. (Illus.). 1978. 11.95 (ISBN 0-87691-276-5). Winchester Pr.

Aceves, J. B. & Douglass, W. A., eds. The Changing Faces of Rural Spain. LC 75-33744. 1976. text ed. 15.95 (ISBN 0-470-00236-0); pap. text ed. 8.95 (ISBN 0-470-00237-9). Halsted Pr.

Aceves, Joseph B. & King, H. Gill. Cultural Anthropology. 1978. pap. text ed. 11.95x (ISBN 0-673-15305-3); study guide 4.95x (ISBN 0-673-15292-8). Scott F.

--Introductory Anthropology. 1979. text ed. 15.95x (ISBN 0-673-15303-7). Scott F.

Achad, Frater. Ancient Mystical White Brotherhood. pap. 4.50 (ISBN 0-87516-212-6). De Vorss.

--Thirty-One Hymns to the Star Goddess. 5.00 o.p. (ISBN 0-685-54734-5). Weiser.

Achebe, Chinua. Chike & the River. 1966. text ed. 2.95x (ISBN 0-521-04003-5). Cambridge U Pr.

--A Man of the People. LC 66-22929. pap. 1.95 (ISBN 0-385-08616-4, A594, Anch). Doubleday.

--No Longer at Ease. 1977. pap. 2.25 (ISBN 0-449-30847-2, Prem). Fawcett.

--Things Fall Apart. LC 59-7114. 1959. 5.95 (ISBN 0-8392-1113-9); pap. 4.95 (ISBN 0-8392-5006-1). Astor-Honor.

Achelis, Elisabeth. World Calendar: Addresses & Occasional Papers Chronologically Arranged on the Progress of Calendar Reform Since 1930. LC 73-102214. Repr. of 1937 ed. 18.00 (ISBN 0-8103-3784-3). Gale.

Achenbach, Thomas M. Developmental Psychopathology. (Illus.). 726p. 1974. 24.95 (ISBN 0-8260-0210-2). Wiley.

Acherley, Roger. Free Parliaments. Berkowitz, David S. & Thorne, Samuel E., eds. LC 77-89218. (Classics of English Legal History in the Modern Era Ser.: Vol. 65). 334p. 1979. lib. bdg. 40.00 (ISBN 0-8240-3164-4). Garland Pub.

Acheson, David C., jt. ed. see McLellan, David S.

Acheson, Dean. Korean War. 1971. pap. text ed. 2.95x (ISBN 0-393-09978-4). Norton.

--Struggle for a Free Europe. 1971. pap. text ed. 3.95x (ISBN 0-393-09983-0). Norton.

Acheson, E. D., ed. Medicine: An Outline for the Intending Student. (Outlines Ser). 1970. cased 14.00 (ISBN 0-7100-6866-2); pap. 7.95x (ISBN 0-7100-6867-0). Routledge & Kegan.

Acheson, E. J., jt. auth. see Hutchinson, E. C.

Acheson, Keith & Gall, Meredith. Techniques in the Clinical Supervision of Teachers. 1980. pap. 9.95 (ISBN 0-582-28121-0). Longman.

Acheson, Sam & O'Connell, Julie, eds. George Washington Diamond's Account of the Great Hanging at Gainesville, 1862. 1963. 5.00 (ISBN 0-87611-000-6); pap. 3.50 (ISBN 0-87611-001-4). Tex St Hist Assn.

Achesone, James. The Military Garden: Instructions for All Young Souldiers. LC 74-80157. (English Experience Ser.: No. 637). 36p. 1974. Repr. of 1629 ed. 5.00 (ISBN 90-221-0637-3). Walter J Johnson.

Achtemeier, Elizabeth, et al, eds. see Borsch, Frederick H. & Napier, Davie.

Achtemeier, Elizabeth, et al, eds. see Burgess, Joseph A. & Winn, Albert C.

Achtemeier, Elizabeth, et al, eds. see Edwards, O. C., Jr. & Taylor, Gardner C.

Achtemeier, Elizabeth, et al, eds. see Fuller, Reginald H.

Achtemeier, Elizabeth, et al, eds. see Furnish, Victor P. & Thulin, Richard L.

Achtemeier, Elizabeth, et al, eds. see Jeske, Richard L. & Barr, Browne.

Achtemeier, Elizabeth, et al, eds. see Juel, Donald H. & Buttrick, David.

Achtemeier, Elizabeth, et al, eds. see Kee, Howard C. & Gomes, Peter J.

Achtemeier, Elizabeth, et al, eds. see Kingsbury, Jack D. & Pennington, Chester.

Achtemeier, Elizabeth, et al, eds. see Krentz, Edgar & Vogel, Arthur A.

Achtemeier, Elizabeth, et al, eds. see Micks, Marianne H. & Ridenhour, Thomas E.

Achtemeier, Elizabeth, et al, eds. see Minear, Paul S. & Adams, Harry B.

Achtemeier, Elizabeth, et al, eds. see Nieting, Lorenz.

Achtemeier, Elizabeth, et al, eds. see Pervo, Richard I. & Carl, William J., III.

Achtemeier, Elizabeth, et al, eds. see Reid, Richard & Crum, Milton, Jr.

Achtemeier, Elizabeth, et al, eds. see Thulin, Richard L.

Achtemeier, Elizabeth, et al, eds. see Tiede, David L. & Kavanagh, Aidan.

Achtemeier, Elizabeth, et al, eds. see Trotti, John B.

Achtemeier, Elizabeth R., jt. auth. see Achtemeier, Paul J.

Achtemeier, Paul J. Invitation to Mark: A Commentary on the Gospel of Mark with Complete Text from the Jerusalem Bible. LC 77-91555. 1978. pap. 2.95 (ISBN 0-385-12213-6, Im). Doubleday.

Achtemeier, Paul J. & Achtemeier, Elizabeth R. Epiphany. LC 73-79349. (Proclamation 1: Aids for Interpreting the Lessons of the Church Year, Ser. C). 64p. 1973. pap. 2.50 (ISBN 0-8006-4052-7, 1-4052). Fortress.

Achtemeier, Paul J., tr. see Marxsen, Willi.

Achtenberg, Gerhard, jt. auth. see Gatz, Konrad.

Achterberg, Jeanne & Lawlis, Frank. Bridges of the Bodymind. LC 80-16596. (Illus.). 1980. text ed. 19.50 (ISBN 0-918296-14-5). Inst Personality & Ability.

Achtert, Walter S., jt. auth. see Gibaldi, Joseph.

Achtmeier, Paul J., et al see Shelp, Earl E. & Sunderlan, Ronald.

ACI Committee 116. Cement & Concrete Terminology. 1967. pap. 11.25 (ISBN 0-685-85102-8, SP-19) (ISBN 0-685-85103-6). ACI.

ACI Committee 209. Shrinkage & Creep in Concrete. (Bibliography: No. 10). 1972. pap. 26.25 (ISBN 0-685-85150-8, B-10) (ISBN 0-685-85151-6). ACI.

ACI Committee 224. Causes, Mechanism, & Control of Cracking in Concrete. (Bibliography: No. 9). 1971. pap. 26.25 (ISBN 0-685-85148-6, B-9). ACI.

ACI Committee 311. ACI Manual of Concrete Inspection. 6th ed. 1975. 17.95 (ISBN 0-685-85096-X, SP-2) (ISBN 0-685-85097-8). ACI.

ACI Committee 315. Manual of Standard Practice for Detailing Reinforced Concrete Structures: ACI 315-74. 6th ed. 1974. loose-leaf 40.85 (ISBN 0-685-85073-0, 315-74) (ISBN 0-685-85074-9). ACI.

ACI Committee 318. Building Code Requirements for Reinforced Concrete: ACI 318-63 ANSI A89.1-1964. 1963. 12.00 (ISBN 0-685-85083-8, 318-63). ACI.

--Building Code Requirements for Reinforced Concrete: ACI 318-77 ANSI a89.1-1972. 1977. 20.75 (ISBN 0-685-03451-8, 318-77). ACI.

--Building Code Requirements for Reinforced Concrete: ACI 318-71 ANSI A89.1-1972. 1971. 19.00 (ISBN 0-685-85075-7, 318-71). ACI.

--Building Code Requirements for Reinforced Concrete SI Metric Edition: ACI 318-71. 1975. 20.00 (ISBN 0-685-85081-1, 318-7 SI). ACI.

--Commentary on Building Code Requirements for Reinforced Concrete: ACI 318-77. 1977. 20.75 (ISBN 0-685-03453-4, 318-77C) (ISBN 0-685-03454-2). ACI.

--Commentary on Building Code Requirements for Reinforced Concrete: ACI 318-71. 1971. 19.00 (ISBN 0-685-85077-3, 318-71C) (ISBN 0-685-85078-1). ACI.

--Supplement to ACI 318-71 & Commentary, 1975. 1975. 5.00 o.p. (ISBN 0-685-85079-X, 318-71 SUP); members 3.00 o.p. (ISBN 0-685-85080-3). ACI.

ACI Committee 340. Design Handbook in Accordance with the Strength Design Method of ACI 318-71, Vol. 1. 1973. 7-ring bnd. 43.75 (ISBN 0-685-85091-9, SP-17(73)) (ISBN 0-685-85092-7). ACI.

--Design Handbook in Accordance with the Strength Design Method of ACI 318-77: Columns, Vol. 2. 1978. binder 37.25 (ISBN 0-685-85093-5, SP-17A78). ACI.

ACI Committee 349. Code Requirements for Nuclear Safety Related Concrete Structures: ACI 349-76. 1976. 43.95 (ISBN 0-685-85087-0, 349-76) (ISBN 0-685-85088-9). ACI.

ACI Committee 515. Guide for the Protection of Concrete Against Chemical Attack by Means of Coatings & Other Corrosion-Resistant Materials. 1966. 20.65 (ISBN 0-685-85152-4, 515R-79). ACI.

Acker, D. Animal Science & Industry. 2nd ed. 1971. text ed. 21.95 (ISBN 0-13-037655-8). P-H.

Acker, Kathy. The Adult Life of Toulouse Lautrec by Henri Toulouse Lautrec. LC 78-58942. 1978. pap. text ed. 4.50 (ISBN 0-931106-21-4). Printed Matter.

Acker, Louis S., jt. auth. see Sakoian, Frances.

Ackerley, J. R. We Think the World of You. 180p. 1981. pap. 5.95 (ISBN 0-916870-36-7). Creative Arts Bk.

Ackerly, Salley M., jt. auth. see Riekes, Linda.

Ackerman. The Pathology of Malignant Melanoma, Vol. I. (Monographs in Dermatopathology, Vol. 1). 1981. price not set (ISBN 0-89352-132-9). Masson Pub.

Ackerman, A. Bernard, et al. Differential Diagnosis in Dermatopathology. (Illus.). 200p. 1981. text ed. 86.00 (ISBN 0-8121-0800-0). Lea & Febiger.

Ackerman, Allan. Craps by the Numbers. (System Check Ser.). 1978. pap. 2.95 (ISBN 0-89650-655-X). Gamblers.

--Roulette by the Dozens. (System Check Ser.). 1978. pap. 2.95 (ISBN 0-89650-885-4). Gamblers.

--Roulette Rouge et Noir. (System Check Ser.). 1978. pap. 2.95 (ISBN 0-89650-894-3). Gamblers.

Ackerman, Bruce A. Private Property & the Constitution. LC 76-47667. 1977. 15.00x (ISBN 0-300-02065-1); pap. 7.95x (ISBN 0-300-02237-9). Yale U Pr.

Ackerman, Bruce A. & Hassler, William T. Clean Coal - Dirty Air. (Illus.). 175p. 1981. 20.00x (ISBN 0-300-02628-5); pap. 5.95 (ISBN 0-300-02643-9). Yale U Pr.

Ackerman, Diane L. Getting Rich: The Smart Woman's Guide to Successful Money Management. 288p. 1981. 11.95 (ISBN 0-89479-063-3). A & W Pubs.

Ackerman, Diane L., jt. auth. see Ackerman, Martin S.

Ackerman, Eugene, et al. Biophysical Science. 2nd ed. (Illus.). 1979. ref. ed. 26.95 (ISBN 0-13-076901-0). P-H.

Ackerman, Gretchen P., jt. auth. see Ackerman, Robert W.

Ackerman, J. M., jt. auth. see Shelton, J. L.

Ackerman, John. Welsh Dylan: Dylan Thomas's Life, Writing & His Wales. 1981. pap. text ed. 5.25x (ISBN 0-586-08350-2). Humanities.

Ackerman, M. & Hermann, Robert. Sophus Lie's Eighteen Eighty Transformation Group Paper. LC 75-17416. (Lie Groups: History, Frontiers on Applications Ser.: No. 1). 1975. 45.00 (ISBN 0-915692-10-4). Math Sci Pr.

Ackerman, M., jt. auth. see Hermann, Robert.

Ackerman, Martin S. & Ackerman, Diane L. Living Rich. LC 80-80978. 224p. 1980. pap. 2.50 (ISBN 0-87216-697-X). Playboy Pbks.

Ackerman, Michael, tr. see Hermann, Robert.

Ackerman, Robert. Monarch Notes on Hardy's Tess of the D'Urbervilles. (Orig.). pap. 1.95 (ISBN 0-671-00619-3). Monarch Pr.

Ackerman, Robert W. Backgrounds to Medieval English Literature. (Orig.). 1966. 4.50x o.p. (ISBN 0-394-30627-9, RanC). Random.

Ackerman, Robert W. & Ackerman, Gretchen P. Sir Frederic Madden: A Bibliography & Biographical Sketch. LC 78-68237. 150p. 1979. lib. bdg. 18.00 (ISBN 0-8240-9819-6). Garland Pub.

Ackerman, Robert W. & Bauer, Raymond A. Corporate Social Responsiveness: The Modern Dilemma. (Illus.). 472p. 1976. text ed. 24.95x (ISBN 0-87909-137-1); pap. text ed. 11.95 (ISBN 0-87909-136-3). Reston.

Ackerman, Winona B. & Lohnes, Paul R. Research Methods for Nurses. (Illus.). 304p. 1981. text ed. 16.95x (ISBN 0-07-000182-0, HP). McGraw.

Ackermann, A. S. Popular Fallacies, a Book of Common Errors: Explained & Corrected with Copious References to Authorities. 4th ed. LC 79-121184. 1970. Repr. of 1950 ed. 38.00 (ISBN 0-8103-3295-7). Gale.

Ackermann, Gertrude see Nute, Grace L.

Ackermann, L. V., jt. auth. see Hamperl, H.

Ackermann, Paul K., ed. see Durrenmatt, Friedrich.

Ackermann, Paul K., ed. see Frisch, Max.

Ackermann, W., jt. auth. see Hilbert, David.

Ackland, Dojnald F. Broadman Comments, July-September, 1981. 1981. pap. 2.15 (ISBN 0-8054-1463-0). Broadman.

Ackland, Donald F. Broadman Comments: April-June, 1981. (Orig.). 1981. pap. 2.15 (ISBN 0-8054-1462-2). Broadman.

Ackland, Donald F., et al. Broadman Comments, Nineteen Eighty-One-Eighty-Two. 1981. pap. 4.75 (ISBN 0-8054-1465-7). Broadman.

--Broadman Comments, October-December, Nineteen Eighty. 1980. pap. 2.00 o.p. (ISBN 0-8054-1458-4). Broadman.

Ackley, Clifford S. Printed Portraits. LC 79-52929. (Illus.). 1979. pap. 3.95 (ISBN 0-87846-139-6). Mus Fine Arts Boston.
--Private Realities: Recent American Photography. (Illus.). 1974. 15.00 (ISBN 0-87846-077-2); pap. 6.95 (ISBN 0-87846-089-6). Mus Fine Arts Boston.
Ackley, Gardner, et al. Economic Freedom, Stability & Growth. 1972. 8.40 (ISBN 0-932826-05-9); pap. 3.95 (ISBN 0-685-85517-1). New Issues MI.
Ackley, P. O. Home Gun Care & Repair. LC 69-16147. 1974. pap. 6.95 (ISBN 0-8117-2028-4). Stackpole.
Ackoff, R. L. Concept of Corporate Planning. LC 74-100318. 1969. 14.95 (ISBN 0-471-00290-9, Pub. by Wiley-Interscience). Wiley.
--Progress in Operations Research. LC 61-10415. (Operations Research Ser.: Vol. 1). 1961. 35.95 (ISBN 0-471-00330-1, Pub by Wiley-Interscience). Wiley.
--Scientific Method: Optimizing Applied Research Decisions. LC 62-10914. 1962. 27.50 (ISBN 0-471-00297-6). Wiley.
Ackoff, R. L. & Rivett, Patrick. Manager's Guide to Operations Research. LC 63-14115. (Managers Guide Ser.). 1963. 15.95 (ISBN 0-471-00335-2, Pub by Wiley-Interscience). Wiley.
Ackoff, Russell. The Second Industrial Revolution. 1978. 0.75 (ISBN 0-686-28791-6). Forward Movement.
Ackoff, Russell L. The Art of Problem Solving: Accompanied by Ackoff's Fables. LC 78-5627. 1978. 15.50 (ISBN 0-471-04289-7, Pub. by Wiley-Interscience). Wiley.
--Redesigning the Future: A Systems Approach to Societal Problems. LC 74-10627. 320p. 1974. 17.95 (ISBN 0-471-00296-8, Pub. by. Wiley-Interscience). Wiley.
Ackoff, Russell L., ed. Designing a National Scientific & Technological Communication System. LC 76-20150. 1976. 19.50x (ISBN 0-8122-7716-3). U of Pa Pr.
Ackrill, J. L. Aristotle's Ethics. text ed. 15.00x (ISBN 0-391-00281-3). Humanities.
Ackrill, J. L., tr. see Aristotle.
Ackroyd, P. R., ed. Bible Bibliography, Nineteen Sixty-Seven to Nineteen Seventy-Three: Old Testament. 1975. 46.50x (ISBN 0-631-16070-1, Pub. by Basil Blackwell). Biblio Dist.
Ackroyd, Peter R. & Lindars, Barnabas, eds. Words & Meanings: Essays Presented to David Winton Thomas. LC 68-29649. 1968. 36.00 (ISBN 0-521-07270-0). Cambridge U Pr.
Ackroyd, Ted J., ed. Health & Medical Economics: A Guide to Information Sources. LC 73-17567. (Economics Information Guide Ser.: Vol. 7). 1977. 30.00 (ISBN 0-8103-1390-1). Gale.
Ackworth, Robert. The Takers. 1979. pap. 2.50 o.p. (ISBN 0-345-27632-9). Ballantine.
Acland, Robert D. Microsurgery Practice Manual. LC 79-17533. (Illus.). 1979. pap. text ed. 14.95 (ISBN 0-8016-0076-6). Mosby.
Acocella, Joan, jt. auth. see Calhoun, James F.
Acomb, Evelyn M., ed. see Von Closen, Ludwig.
Acosta, Antonio A. & Calvo, Joraida. Matematicas: Repaso Para el Examen De Equivalencia De la Escuela Superior En Espanol. rev. ed. LC 80-25182. 256p. (Orig.). 1981. pap. 5.00 (ISBN 0-668-04821-2, 4821-2). Arco.
Acosta, Virgilio, et al. Fisica Moderna. (Span.). 1975. pap. text ed. 10.50 (ISBN 0-06-310010-X, IntlDept). Har-Row.
Acosta-Belen, Edna & Christensen, Eli H. The Puerto Rican Women. LC 79-17638. (Praeger Special Studies Ser.). 186p. 1979. 20.95 (ISBN 0-03-052466-0). Praeger.
Acquaviva, Sabino & Santuccio, Mario. Social Structure in Italy: Crisis of a System. LC 76-13602. 272p. 1976. 35.00x (ISBN 0-89158-615-6). Westview.
Acree, James E. Rhythmic Thoughts. Date not set. 5.95 (ISBN 0-533-04855-9). Vantage.
Acri, Michael J., jt. auth. see Miller, Albert J.
ACS Committee on Chemistry & Public Affairs. Chemistry & the Food System. LC 80-11194. 1980. 15.00 (ISBN 0-8412-0557-4); pap. 9.00 (ISBN 0-8412-0563-9). Am Chemical.
Acton, C. R. Dog Sense. 12.50x (ISBN 0-392-06322-0, SpS). Soccer.
Acton, E. Alexander Herzen & the Role of the Intellectual Revolutionary. LC 78-56747. 1979. 22.95 (ISBN 0-521-22166-8). Cambridge U Pr.
Acton, H. B. The Illusion of the Epoch: Marxism-Leninism As a Philosophical Creed. 1955. cased 20.50 o.p. (ISBN 0-7100-1003-6). Routledge & Kegan.
--Illusion of the Epoch: Marxism-Leninism As a Philosophical Creed. 286p. 1973. pap. 8.95 (ISBN 0-7100-7657-6). Routledge & Kegan.
Acton, Harold. The Last Medici. rev. ed. (Illus.). 416p. 1980. Repr. of 1958 ed. 22.50 (ISBN 0-500-25074-X). Thames Hudson.
--Nancy Mitford: A Memoir. LC 75-34580. (Illus.). 288p. 1976. 10.00 o.p. (ISBN 0-06-010018-4, HarpT). Har-Row.
Acton, Susan, jt. auth. see Ross, Judith.
Acton, Thomas. Gypsy Politics & Social Change. 1974. 20.00x (ISBN 0-7100-7838-2). Routledge & Kegan.
Acus, Leah K. Quarreling Kids: Stop the Fighting & Develop Loving Relationship Within the Family. (Illus.). 192p. 1981. 10.95 (ISBN 0-13-748012-1, Spec); pap. 5.95 (ISBN 0-13-748004-0). P-H.
A.D. Little, Inc. Federal Funding of Civilian Research & Development: A Report to the Experimental Technology Incentives Program, U. S. Dept. of Commerce. new ed. Michaelis, Michael, ed. LC 76-43308. 1977. 35.50x (ISBN 0-89158-205-3). Westview.
Ada, Alma F., tr. see Simon, Norma.
Ada, Alma F., tr. see Vigna, Judith.
Adachi, Barbara. Living Treasures of Japan. LC 73-80959. (Illus.). 164p. 1973. 22.50 (ISBN 0-87011-204-X). Kodansha.
Adachi, Fumie, tr. see Fujimura, Kobon.
Adachi, Geraldine, ed. see Demura, Funio.
Adair, D., jt. auth. see Hamilton, W. H.
Adair, Douglass, jt. ed. see Schutz, John A.
Adair, Gilbert. Vietnam on Film. (Illus.). 208p. 1981. 12.95 (ISBN 0-906071-43-7). Proteus Pub NY.
Adair, Ian. The Complete Guide to Card Conjuring. LC 78-75281. (Illus.). 1979. 5.95 (ISBN 0-498-02099-1). A S Barnes.
Adair, Ian, jt. auth. see Amery, Heather.
Adair, J. & Blitt. Training for Series (Trilogy) 1978. text ed. 17.50x ea. (ISBN 0-685-96474-4, Pub. by Gower Pub Co England); No. 1. (ISBN 0-566-02110-2); No. 2. (ISBN 0-566-02111-0); No. 3. (ISBN 0-566-02112-9). Renouf.
Adair, John. Action Centered Leadership. 1979. text ed. 26.00x (ISBN 0-566-02143-9, Pub. by Gower Pub Co England). Renouf.
Adair, Robert. Concepts in Physics. 1969. 24.50 (ISBN 0-12-044050-4); tchrs' guide 4.95 (ISBN 0-12-044056-3). Acad Pr.
Adam, A. M., ed. see Plato.
Adam, Addie. Jenny Doone, Office Nurse. 192p. (YA) 1976. 4.95 o.p. (ISBN 0-685-62627-X, Avalon). Bouregy.
Adam, Alfred. Antike Berichte ueber die Essener. 2nd ed. Burchard, Christoph, ed. (Kleine Texte fuer Vorlesungen und Uebungen, 182). 80p. 1972. pap. text ed. 11.65x (ISBN 3-11-004183-9). De Gruyter.
Adam, Elaine P., jt. auth. see Stebbins, Richard P.
Adam, Elaine P., jt. ed. see Stebbins, Richard P.
Adam, Everett E., Jr. & Hershauer, James C. Productivity & Quality: Measurement As a Basis for Improvement. (Illus.). 192p. 1981. text ed. 18.95 (ISBN 0-13-725002-9). P-H.
Adam, G. Journalism, Communication & the Law. 1976. pap. 8.25 o.p. (ISBN 0-13-511170-6); 12.50 o.p. (ISBN 0-13-511188-9). P-H.
--Perception, Consciousness, Memory: Reflections of a Biologist. LC 73-20153. 215p. 1980. 22.50 (ISBN 0-306-30776-6, Plenum Pr). Plenum Pub.
Adam, H., ed. Transactions: International Vacuum Congress - 3rd - Stuttgart - 1965, Vol. 2, 3 Pts. text ed. 46.00 (ISBN 0-08-012127-6). Pergamon.
Adam, Helen. Gone Sailing. LC 80-10659. (Illus., Orig.). 1980. 20.00 (ISBN 0-915124-30-0, Bookslinger; Small Press Distribution); pap. 5.00 (ISBN 0-915124-29-7). Toothpaste.
Adam, Heribert. Modernizing Racial Domination: The Dynamics of South African Politics. LC 75-132422. (Perspectives on Southern Africa: No. 2). 1971. pap. 5.50x (ISBN 0-520-02251-3, CAMPUS229). U of Cal Pr.
Adam, J. & N. Divorce: How & When to Let Go. 9.95 (ISBN 0-13-216416-7); pap. 4.95 (ISBN 0-13-216408-6). P-H.
Adam, James, jt. auth. see Adam, Robert.
Adam, James, ed. see Plato.
Adam, Jan, ed. Wage Control & Inflation in the Soviet Bloc Countries. 266p. 1980. 22.95 (ISBN 0-03-057007-7). Praeger.
Adam, Jean-Michel. Linguistique et discours litteraire. new ed. (Collection L). (Orig., Fr.). 1976. pap. text ed. 19.95 (ISBN 0-685-66283-7). Larousse.
Adam, K. M., et al. Medical & Veterinary Protozoology. rev. ed. 1980. 50.00 (ISBN 0-443-00764-0). Churchill.
Adam, Michael. Wandering in Eden: Three Ways to the East Within Us. 1976. 10.00 o.p. (ISBN 0-394-49980-8); pap. 4.95 (ISBN 0-394-73141-7). Knopf.
--Womankind: A Celebration. LC 78-20623. (Illus.). 1979. 15.95 (ISBN 0-06-010032-X, HarpT). Har-Row.
Adam, Nabil R., jt. auth. see Dogramaci, Ali.
Adam, of Usk. Chronicon Adae de Usk, A.D. 1377 to 1421. Thompson, Edward M., ed. (Pilgrimages Ser.). 392p. 1980. Repr. of 1904 ed. 44.50 (ISBN 0-404-16367-X). AMS Pr.
Adam, Robert & Adam, James. The Works in Architecture of Robert & James Adam. LC 78-62405. (Illus.). 144p. 1980. 50.00 o.p. (ISBN 0-486-23810-5). Dover.
Adam, Ruth C. Living with Mysterious Epilepsy: My 48-Year Victory Over Fear. Alvarez, Walter C., ed. LC 73-92057. 1974. 6.00 o.p. (ISBN 0-682-47906-3, Banner). Exposition.
Adam, William S., et al. Microscopic Anatomy of the Dog: A Photographic Atlas. 304p. 1970. pap. 32.50 photocopy ed. spiral (ISBN 0-398-00006-9). C C Thomas.
Adamany, David. Financing Politics: Recent Wisconsin Elections. LC 79-84948. 1969. 24.50 (ISBN 0-299-05430-6). U of Wis Pr.
Adamec, Cannie S., ed. Sex Roles: Origins, Influences & Implications for Women. 1980. 17.95 (ISBN 0-920792-00-6). EPWP.
Adamec, Ludwig W. Afghanistan, Nineteen Hundred to Nineteen Twenty Three: A Diplomatic History. 1967. 20.00x (ISBN 0-520-00002-1). U of Cal Pr.
Adami, Marie. Fanny Keats. 1938. 34.50x (ISBN 0-686-51385-1). Elliots Bks.
Adamic, Louis. My America. LC 76-2050. (FDR & the Era of the New Deal). 1976. Repr. of 1938 ed. lib. bdg. 49.50 (ISBN 0-306-70801-9). Da Capo.
Adamic, Louis see Friedman, Leon.
Adams. Cosmic X-Ray Astronomy. 1980. 29.50 (ISBN 0-9960019-2-1, Pub. by a Hilger England). Heyden.
--Understanding Adolescence: Current Developments in Adolescent Psychology. 4th ed. 512p. 1980. text ed. 17.50 (ISBN 0-205-06931-2, 2469316). Allyn.
Adams, A., ed. see Hepworth, Barbara.
Adams, A., et al. Litterature francaise, 2 Vols. (Illus., Fr.). 76.50 ea. Larousse.
Adams, Adrian, tr. see Kourouma, Ahmadu.
Adams, Adrienne. The Easter Egg Artists. (Illus.). 32p. (gr. k-3). pap. 2.95 (ISBN 0-689-70479-8, A-106, Aladdin). Atheneum.
--The Great Valentine's Day Balloon Race. LC 80-19527. (Illus.). 32p. (gr. k-3). 1980. 9.95 (ISBN 0-684-16640-2). Scribner.
Adams, Alexander B. The Disputed Lands. 480p. 1981. 17.95 (ISBN 0-399-12530-2). Putnam.
Adams, Alice. Beautiful Girl. 1980. pap. write for info. (ISBN 0-671-83218-2). PB.
--Families & Survivors. 192p. 1976. pap. 1.50 o.s.i. (ISBN 0-446-78974-7). Warner Bks.
--Listening to Billie. 1977. 7.95 (ISBN 0-394-41069-6). Knopf.
Adams, Andrew. Ninja, the Invisible Assasins. Alston, Pat, ed. LC 75-130760. (Ser. 302s). (Illus.). 1970. 6.95 (ISBN 0-89750-030-X). Ohara Pubns.
Adams, Andy. Andy Adams' Campfire Tales. Hudson, Wilson M., ed. LC 75-29131. (Illus.). xxxii, 296p. 1976. 13.50x (ISBN 0-8032-0870-7); pap. 6.50 (ISBN 0-8032-5835-6, 615, Bison). U of Nebr Pr.
--The Log of a Cowboy. Orig. Title: Public Domain. 1976. pap. 1.25 o.p. (ISBN 0-685-64012-4, LB344ZK, Leisure Bks). Nordon Pubns.
Adams, Ansel. The Portfolios of Ansel Adams. 1981. 14.95 (ISBN 0-686-68992-5, 713953). NYGS.
Adams, Bill. Shrubs & Vines for Southern Landscapes. LC 76-15455. (Illus.). 1979. pap. 3.95 (ISBN 0-88415-804-7). Pacesetter Pr.
--Trees for Southern Landscapes. LC 76-15457. (Illus.). 1976. pap. 3.95 (ISBN 0-88415-881-0). Pacesetter Pr.
--Vegetable Growing for Southern Gardens. LC 75-18204. 1976. write for info. (ISBN 0-88415-888-8); pap. 3.95 (ISBN 0-685-54016-2). Pacesetter Pr.
Adams, Bob, tr. see Maston, T. B.
Adams, Brooks. The New Empire. (Social Science Classics Ser.). 1982. text ed. 19.95 (ISBN 0-87855-315-0); pap. text ed. 6.95 (ISBN 0-87855-691-5). Transaction Bks. Postponed.
Adams, Bruce & Kavanaugh-Baran, Kathryn. Promise & Performance: Carter Builds a New Administration. LC 78-24790. 224p. 1979. 21.00 (ISBN 0-669-02817-7). Lexington Bks.
Adams, C. J., jt. auth. see Downs, A. J.
Adams, C. K. A Beginner's Guide to Computers & Microprocessors--with Projects. (Illus.). (gr. 10 up). 1978. 10.95 (ISBN 0-8306-9890-6); pap. 7.95 (ISBN 0-8306-1015-4, 1015). TAB Bks.
--Build-It Book of Optoelectronic Projects. (Illus.). 1977. 8.95 (ISBN 0-8306-7935-9); pap. 5.95 (ISBN 0-8306-6935-3, 935). TAB Bks.
Adams, C. R., tr. see Falbe, J.
Adams, C. W. Research on Multiple Sclerosis. (Amer. Lec. Living Chemistry Ser.). (Illus.). 192p. 1972. 18.75 (ISBN 0-398-02214-3). C C Thomas.
Adams, Caren, jt. auth. see Fay, Jennifer.
Adams, Carl E., et al. Development of Design & Operational Criteria for Wastewater Treatment. LC 80-69077. (Illus.). 550p. 1980. text ed. 40.00 (ISBN 0-937976-00-8). Enviro Pr.
Adams, Carolyn & Winston, Kathryn. Mothers at Work. (Comparative Studies of Political Life). 1980. pap. text ed. 10.95 (ISBN 0-582-28064-8). Longman.
Adams, Charles F. Richard Henry Dana, 2 Vols. LC 67-23883. 1968. Repr. of 1890 ed. 20.00 (ISBN 0-8103-3038-5). Gale.
Adams, Charles F., Jr. Charles Francis Adams. LC 80-24115. (American Statesmen Ser.). 425p. 1980. pap. 6.95 (ISBN 0-87754-181-7). Chelsea Hse.
Adams, Charles J., ed. A Reader's Guide to the Great Religions. 2nd ed. LC 76-10496. 1977. 19.95 (ISBN 0-02-900240-0). Free Pr.
Adams, Charlotte. The Single's First Menu Cookbook. LC 72-23480. 192p. 1975. 6.95 (ISBN 0-396-07070-1). Dodd.
Adams, Chas F. The Antinomian Controversy. LC 74-164507. 1976. Repr. of 1892 ed. lib. bdg. 19.50 (ISBN 0-306-70290-8). Da Capo.
Adams, Chuck. The Lawless Ones. 1979. pap. 1.75 (ISBN 0-505-51399-4). Tower Bks.
Adams, Cindy. Lee Strasberg: The Imperfect Genius of the Actors Studio. LC 79-7191. 1980. 13.95 (ISBN 0-385-12496-1). Doubleday.
Adams, Clifton. Hard Times & Arnie Smith. 1976. pap. 1.75 (ISBN 0-441-31721-9). Ace Bks.
Adams, D., et al, eds. Electronic Equipment Wiring & Assembling: Part One. (Engineering Craftsmen: No. G5). 1968. spiral bdg. 15.50x (ISBN 0-85083-014-1). Intl Ideas.
--Electronic Inspection & Test, 2 vols. (Engineering Craftsmen: No. G26). (Illus.). 1969. Set. sprial bdg. 36.50x (ISBN 0-85083-035-4). Intl Ideas.
Adams, D. R., et al, eds. Static Electrical Equipment Testing. (Engineering Craftsmen: No. G21). (Illus.). 1969. spiral bdg. 23.50x (ISBN 0-685-90174-2). Intl Ideas.
Adams, David. Essentials of Oral Biology. (Dental Ser.). (Illus.). 152p. 1981. text ed. 12.50 (ISBN 0-443-02095-7). Churchill.
Adams, Don. Education & Modernization in Asia. LC 75-100852. 1970. pap. 6.95 (ISBN 0-201-00028-8). A-W.
Adams, Donald R., Jr. Finance & Enterprise in Early America: A Study of Stephen Girard's Bank, 1812-1831. LC 77-20301. 1978. 15.00x (ISBN 0-8122-7736-8). U of Pa Pr.
Adams, Dorothy & Kurtz, Margaret. Technical Secretary: Terminology & Transcription. (Diamond Jubilee Ser.). 1967. 15.30 (ISBN 0-07-000320-3, G); instructor's manual & key 5.20 (ISBN 0-07-000322-X); wkbk. 5.90 (ISBN 0-07-000321-1); tapes 195.00 (ISBN 0-07-088980-5). McGraw.
Adams, Doug. Humor in the American Pulpit from George Whitefield Through Henry Ward Beecher. rev. ed. 1981. 6.95 (ISBN 0-686-22745-X). Sharing Co.
Adams, Doug, ed. see Lyon, Barbara.
Adams, Elaine P., jt. ed. see Stebbins, Richard P.
Adams, Elizabeth. In Service Education & Teachers' Centers. 264p. 1975. text ed. 32.00 (ISBN 0-08-018291-7); pap. text ed. 21.00 (ISBN 0-08-018290-9). Pergamon.
Adams, Elizabeth, jt. auth. see Haggar, Reginald.
Adams, Elsie & Briscoe, Mary L. Up Against the Wall, Mother: On Women's Liberation. 1971. 8.95 (ISBN 0-02-470200-5, 47020). Macmillan.
Adams, Eric. Francis Danby: Varieties of Poetic Landscape. LC 72-75185. (Studies in British Art). (Illus.). 352p. 1973. 60.00x (ISBN 0-300-01538-0). Yale U Pr.
Adams, F. & Dams, R. Applied Gamma-Ray Spectrometry. 2nd rev. ed. LC 79-114847. 1970. text ed. 92.00 (ISBN 0-08-006888-X). Pergamon.
Adams, F. Gerard & Behrman, Jere R. Econometric Modeling of World Commodity Policy. LC 77-18596. (The Wharton Econometric Studies Ser.: No. 2). (Illus.). 1978. 21.00 (ISBN 0-669-02111-3). Lexington Bks.
--Econometric Models of World Agricultural Commodity Markets: Cocoa, Coffee, Tea, Wool, Cotton, Sugar, Wheat, Rice. LC 76-3624. 128p. 1976. text ed. 20.00 o.p. (ISBN 0-88410-290-4). Ballinger Pub.
Adams, F. Gerard & Glickman, Norman. Modeling the Multiregional Economic System: Perspectives for the Eighties. LC 79-48005. (Wharton Econometric Ser.). 1980. 24.95x (ISBN 0-669-03627-7). Lexington Bks.
Adams, F. Gerard & Klein, Sonia, eds. Stabilizing World Commodity Markets. LC 77-7805. (The Wharton Econometric Studies Ser.: No. 1). 1978. 24.95 (ISBN 0-669-01622-5). Lexington Bks.
Adams, Florence. Make Your Own Baby Furniture. LC 80-10495. (Illus.). 224p. 1980. pap. 9.95 (ISBN 0-87131-320-0). M Evans.
Adams, Forrest H., et al, eds. Pathophysiology of Congenital Heart Disease. LC 69-16626. (UCLA Forum in Medical Sciences: No. 10). (Illus.). 1970. 55.00x (ISBN 0-520-01630-0). U of Cal Pr.
Adams, Francis. A Child of the Age. Fletcher, Ian & Stokes, John, eds. LC 76-20045. (Decadent Consciousness Ser.: Vol. 1). 1977. Repr. of 1894 ed. lib. bdg. 38.00 (ISBN 0-8240-2750-7). Garland Pub.

Adams, Frederick B. Introduction to the Pierpont Morgan Library. Ryskamp, Charles, ed. LC 64-21147. 54p. 1974. pap. 4.00 (ISBN 0-87598-032-5). Pierpont Morgan.

Adams, George. Essentials of Geriatric Medicine. 1978. pap. text ed. 7.95x (ISBN 0-19-261216-6). Oxford U Pr.

--Nature Ever New: Essays on the Renewal of Agriculture. 1979. pap. 5.95 (ISBN 0-916786-40-4). St George Bk Serv.

Adams, George, tr. see Steiner, Rudolf.

Adams, Gerald. Neighborhood Guide. Leonard, Jan, ed. LC 80-66584. (Savvy San Francisco Ser.). (Illus.). 64p. (Orig.). 1980. pap. 2.50 (ISBN 0-89395-049-1). Cal Living Bks.

Adams, H. M. Catalogue of Books Printed on the Continent of Europe, 2 Vols. 1967. Set. 350.00 (ISBN 0-521-06951-3). Cambridge U Pr.

Adams, Harland B. Guide to Legal Gambling. LC 66-16484. (Funk & W Bk.). (Illus.). 1969. pap. 2.75 o.s.i. (ISBN 0-308-90102-9, F72, TYC-T). T Y Crowell.

Adams, Harry B., jt. auth. see Minear, Paul S.

Adams, Harry Baker. Priorities & People. 128p. 1975. pap. 0.65 (ISBN 0-8272-2924-0). Bethany Pr.

Adams, Henry. Albert Gallatin. LC 80-25555. (American Statesmen Ser.). 695p. 1981. pap. 8.95 (ISBN 0-87754-194-9). Chelsea Hse.

--Democracy, an American Novel. (Classics Ser). (YA) (gr. 9 up). pap. 1.50 (ISBN 0-8049-0164-3, CL-164). Airmont.

--Esther. Spiller, Robert, ed. LC 38-18393. 1976. Repr. lib. bdg. 34.00x (ISBN 0-8201-1187-2). Schol Facsimiles.

--John Randolph. LC 80-24498. (American Statesmen Ser.). 310p. 1981. pap. 4.95 (ISBN 0-87754-186-8). Chelsea Hse.

--The Life of George Cabot Lodge. LC 78-16619. 1978. Repr. of 1911 ed. 24.00x (ISBN 0-8201-1316-6). Schol Facsimiles.

Adams, Henry E. Abnormal Psychology. 750p. Date not set. text ed. price not set. Wm C Brown.

Adams, Herbert F., jt. auth. see Cooke, Nelson M.

Adams, Howard, ed. Jefferson & the Arts: An Extended View. LC 76-21951. 1976. 20.00x (ISBN 0-685-79644-2, National Gallery of Art). U Pr of Va.

Adams, J. Christian Counselor's Starter Packet. 12.50 o.p. (ISBN 0-87552-015-4). Presby & Reformed.

Adams, J. B., jt. auth. see O'Connell, K. J.

Adams, J. Frank. Infinite Loop Spaces. (Annals of Mathematics Studies Ser.: No. 90). 1978. 15.50x (ISBN 0-691-08207-3); pap. 5.50 (ISBN 0-691-08206-5). Princeton U Pr.

--Stable Homotopy & Generalized Homology. LC 74-5735. (Chicago Lectures in Mathematics Ser.). x, 374p. 1980. pap. text ed. 10.00x (ISBN 0-226-00524-0). U of Chicago Pr.

Adams, Jack. Learning & Memory: An Introduction. rev. ed. 1980. 18.95x (ISBN 0-256-02314-X). Dorsey.

Adams, Jack A. Learning & Memory: An Introduction. 1980. text ed. 17.50 o.p. (ISBN 0-256-01783-2). Dorsey.

Adams, James E. Electrical Principles & Practices. 2nd ed. 1973. text ed. 17.25 (ISBN 0-07-000281-9, G); ans. key 1.50 (ISBN 0-07-000282-7). McGraw.

--Liberacion: El Evangelo de Dios. 1980. pap. 2.45. Banner of Truth.

--Three to Win. (Radiant Life). pap. 1.50 (ISBN 0-88243-906-5, 02-0906); tchr's ed 2.50 (ISBN 0-88243-176-5, 32-0176). Gospel Pub.

Adams, James F. Understanding Adolescence: Current Developments in Adolescent Psychology. 3rd ed. 576p. 1976. text ed. 15.95x o.s.i. (ISBN 0-205-05410-2); tests free o.s.i. (ISBN 0-685-61042-X). Allyn.

Adams, James L. Conceptual Blockbusting: A Guide to Better Ideas. 2nd ed. (Illus.). 160p. 1980. 10.95 (ISBN 0-393-01223-9); pap. text ed. 3.95x (ISBN 0-393-95016-6). Norton.

Adams, James R. Media Planning. 2nd ed. 232p. 1977. pap. 12.25x (ISBN 0-220-66337-8, Pub. by Busn Bks England). Renouf.

Adams, James T. Album of American History, 3 vols. rev. ed. LC 74-91746. (gr. 5 up). 1969. Set. 165.00 (ISBN 0-684-16848-0, ScribR). Scribner.

Adams, Jan S. Citizen Inspectors in the Soviet Union: The Peoples Control Committee. LC 77-83460. (Praeger Special Studies). 1978. 27.95 (ISBN 0-03-023201-5). Praeger.

Adams, Jane. Jane Adams. LC 73-15838. 1974. PLB 5.95 (ISBN 0-87191-304-6). Creative Ed.

Adams, Jane L. An Education Curriculum for the Moderately, Severely & Profoundly Mentally Handicapped Pupil. 96p. 1980. pap. 11.75 (ISBN 0-398-03264-5). C C Thomas.

Adams, Jay. Communicating with Twentieth Century Man. 1979. pap. 1.95 (ISBN 0-87552-008-1). Presby & Reformed.

--Use of Scripture in Counseling. 1975. pap. 1.95 (ISBN 0-87552-063-4). Presby & Reformed.

Adams, Jay E. Marriage, Divorce & Remarriage. 120p. 1981. pap. 3.50 (ISBN 0-8010-0168-4). Baker Bk.

--Marriage, Divorce & Remarriage. 1980. pap. 3.50 (ISBN 0-87552-068-5). Presby & Reformed.

--Shepherding God's Flock. one vol. ed. 1979. pap. 8.95 (ISBN 0-87552-058-8). Presby & Reformed.

Adams, Jay E., ed. Journal of Practical Practice, Vol. 4, No. 2. 1980. pap. 5.00 (ISBN 0-87552-032-4). Presby & Reformed.

Adams, Jeannette T. Arco's Complete Woodworking Handbook. rev. ed. LC 80-18786. 768p. 1980. lib. bdg. 12.95 (ISBN 0-668-04829-8, 4829-8). Arco.

--Home Appliances: Selection, Use & Repair. LC 79-25773. (Illus.). 1132p. 1980. lib. bdg. 19.95 o.p. (ISBN 0-668-04530-2). Arco.

Adams, Joey. Strictly for Laughs. 224p. 1981. 8.95 (ISBN 0-89479-079-X). A & W Pubs.

Adams, John. Discourses on Davila. LC 70-87665. (American Constitutional & Legal History Ser.). 260p. 1973. Repr. of 1805 ed. lib. bdg. 25.00 (ISBN 0-306-71761-1). Da Capo.

--John Adams: A Biography in His Own Words. Peabody, James B., ed. LC 72-92141. (The Founding Fathers Ser.). (Illus.). 416p. (YA) 1973. 15.00 o.p. (ISBN 0-06-013308-2, HarpT). Har-Row.

--The Lenten Psalms. (Short Course Ser.). 124p. Repr. of 1912 ed. text ed. 2.95 (ISBN 0-567-08304-7). Attic Pr.

Adams, John, et al. Transition: Understanding & Managing Personal Change. LC 77-5833. 1977. text ed. 18.50x o.s.i. (ISBN 0-916672-98-0). Allanheld.

Adams, John A. A Defense of the Constitutions of Government of the United States of America, 3 Vols. LC 69-11328. (American Constitutional & Legal History Ser). 1971. Repr. of 1788 ed. lib. bdg. 125.00 (ISBN 0-306-71176-1). Da Capo.

Adams, John D. Understanding & Managing Stress: A Facilitator's Guide. LC 80-50474. 137p. 1980. pap. 39.50 with readings and workbook (ISBN 0-88390-157-9). Univ Assocs.

--Understanding & Managing Stress: A Workbook in Changing Life Styles, 5 vols. LC 80-50474. 101p. 1980. Set Of 5. pap. 44.50 (ISBN 0-88390-157-9). Set. Univ Assocs.

Adams, John D., ed. Understanding & Managing Stress: A Book of Readings. LC 80-50474. 217p. 1980. pap. 14.50; Set Of 5. pap. 62.50 (ISBN 0-88390-158-7). Univ Assocs.

Adams, John F. Algebraic Topology: A Student's Guide. LC 75-163178. (London Mathematical Lecture Note Ser.: No. 4). (Illus.). 1972. 23.95x (ISBN 0-521-08076-2). Cambridge U Pr.

--Two Plus Two Equals Minus Seven. LC 73-75392. (Cock Robin Mystery Ser). 1969. 4.50 o.s.i. (ISBN 0-02-500190-6). Macmillan.

Adams, John G. Pediatric Anesthesia Case Studies. 1976. spiral bdg. 14.00 (ISBN 0-87488-042-4). Med Exam.

Adams, John M. Newer Virus Diseases. (Illus.). 1960. 8.95 o.s.i. (ISBN 0-02-300490-8). Macmillan.

Adams, John P. At the Heart of the Whirlwind. LC 75-9343. 160p. 1976. 6.95 o.p. (ISBN 0-06-060080-2, HarpR). Har-Row.

--Bottle Collecting in America. LC 70-151175. (Illus.). 1971. pap. 5.95 o.p. (ISBN 0-912274-06-9). NH Pub Co.

--John P. Adams' Third Bottle Book. LC 72-80183. (Illus.). 128p. 1972. pap. 5.95 (ISBN 0-912274-19-0). NH Pub Co.

Adams, John P. & Marschall, Richard. Milton Caniff, Rembrandt of the Comic Strip. rev. ed. LC 80-70395. (Illus.). 64p. 1981. pap. 6.95x (ISBN 0-918348-04-8). Flying Buttress.

Adams, John Q. John Adams, 2 vols. LC 80-24028. (American Statesmen Ser.). 920p. 1981. Set. pap. 13.95 (ISBN 0-87754-177-9). Chelsea Hse.

Adams, John R. Edward Everett Hale. (U.S. Authors Ser.: No. 284). 1977. lib. bdg. 9.95 (ISBN 0-8057-7186-7). Twayne.

--Harriet Beecher Stowe. (U. S. Authors Ser.: No. 42). 1963. lib. bdg. 9.95 (ISBN 0-8057-0700-X). Twayne.

Adams, John S., ed. see Marshall, John.

Adams, Julian. The Student Journalist & Mass Communication. (Illus.). 190p. 1981. lib. bdg. 8.95 (ISBN 0-8239-0538-1); workbook 1.50 (ISBN 0-8239-0499-7). Rosen Pr.

Adams, June P. Minou: The Halfbreed. a Novel of Self-Discovery. LC 77-89859. 225p. 1980. 9.95 (ISBN 0-86533-006-9). Amber Crest.

Adams, Larry L. Walter Lippmann. (World Leaders Ser.: No. 58). 1977. lib. bdg. 10.95 (ISBN 0-8057-7709-1). Twayne.

Adams, Laura. Existential Battles: The Growth of Norman Mailer. LC 74-27710. 192p. 1976. 12.00x (ISBN 0-8214-0182-3); pap. 4.75 (ISBN 0-8214-0401-6). Ohio U Pr.

--Norman Mailer: A Comprehensive Bibliography. LC 74-14163. (Author Bibliographies Ser.: No. 20). 1974. 10.00 (ISBN 0-8108-0771-8). Scarecrow.

Adams, Laura, ed. Will the Real Norman Mailer Please Stand up. LC 73-83259. 288p. 1974. 16.00 (ISBN 0-8046-9066-9). Kennikat.

Adams, M. P. Rich Uncle from Fiji. (Gambler's Book Shelf). (Illus.). 1977. pap. 2.95 (ISBN 0-911996-82-6). Gamblers.

Adams, Mary. Natural Flower Arranging. (Illus.). 120p. 1981. 19.95 (ISBN 0-7134-2677-2, Pub. by Batsford England). David & Charles.

Adams, Mary, tr. see Steiner, Rudolf.

Adams, Maurianne. Autobiography. LC 67-23041. 1968. pap. 2.50 (ISBN 0-672-60898-7, CR12). Bobbs.

Adams, Maurice see Godwin, E. W.

Adams, Michael. Censorship: The Irish Experience. 265p. 1968. 15.00x (ISBN 0-686-28344-9, Pub. by Irish Academic Pr). Biblio Dist.

--Single-Minded: A Tract on Chastity, Mainly in the Context of Celibacy. 120p. 1979. pap. 10.00x (ISBN 0-7165-1819-8, Pub. by Irish Academic Pr). Biblio Dist.

--Voluntary Service Overseas. (Illus., Orig.). 1968. pap. 6.95 (ISBN 0-571-08337-4, Pub. by Faber & Faber). Merrimack Bk Serv.

Adams, Morley. Mudland. (Orig.). 1980. pap. 1.75 (ISBN 0-532-23146-5). Manor Bks.

Adams, Nancy M. Mountain Flowers in New Zealand. (Mobil New Zealand Nature Ser.). (Illus.). 80p. (Orig.). 1980. pap. 6.95 (ISBN 0-589-01328-9, Pub. by Reed Bks Australia). C E Tuttle.

--New Zealand Native Trees, Vol. 1. (Mobil New Zealand Nature Ser.). (Illus.). 84p. 1967. pap. 7.50 (ISBN 0-589-00052-7, Pub. by Reed Bks Australia). C E Tuttle.

Adams, Neal. Workover Well Control. 320p. 1981. 27.50 (ISBN 0-87814-142-1). Pennwell Pub.

Adams, Nicholson B., et al. Spanish Literature: A Brief Survey. 3rd ed. (Quality Paperback: No. 38). (Orig.). 1974. pap. 3.50 (ISBN 0-8226-0038-2). Littlefield.

Adams, Noland. The Complete Corvette Restoration & Technical Guide 1953 Through 1962, Vol. I. LC 80-65894. (Illus.). 424p. 1980. 59.95 (ISBN 0-915038-14-5); leather edition 69.95 (ISBN 0-915038-22-6). Princeton Pub.

Adams, Norman R., tr. see Raming, Ida.

Adams, Oscar F. Dictionary of American Authors. 5th ed. LC 68-2175. 1969. Repr. of 1904 ed. 26.00 (ISBN 0-8103-3148-9). Gale.

Adams, Paul. New Self-Hypnosis. pap. 4.00 (ISBN 0-87980-233-2). Wilshire.

Adams, Percy G. Travelers & Travel Liars, Sixteen Sixty-Eighteen Hundred. (Illus.). 1980. pap. 4.50 (ISBN 0-486-23942-X). Dover.

Adams, Peter. Fatal Necessity: British Intervention in New Zealand 1830-1847. 1978. 23.00x (ISBN 0-19-647950-9). Oxford U Pr.

--Successful Bonsai Growing. (Illus.). 102p. 1980. pap. 6.95 (ISBN 0-7063-5376-5, Pub. by Ward Lock England). Hippocrene Bks.

Adams, Priscilla, ed. Examining the Metric Issues. 85p. 1976. pap. 4.00 (ISBN 0-916148-08-4). Am Natl.

Adams, R., jt. auth. see Christ, F.

Adams, Ramon F. Come An' Get It: The Story of the Old Cowboy Cook. 171p. (Orig.). 1952. 7.95 (ISBN 0-8061-0254-3); pap. 3.95 (ISBN 0-8061-1013-9). U of Okla Pr.

--The Cowman Says It Salty. LC 73-174805. 1971. 5.95 o.p. (ISBN 0-8165-0311-7). U of Ariz Pr.

--A Fitting Death for Billy the Kid. LC 60-5112. (Illus.). 310p. 1981. 14.95 (ISBN 0-8061-0458-9). U of Okla Pr.

--Western Words: A Dictionary of the American West. LC 68-31369. 355p. 1981. pap. 9.95 (ISBN 0-8061-1173-9). U of Okla Pr.

Adams, Ramon F., ed. see Wolfenstine, Manfred R.

Adams, Ramon F., compiled by. The Adams One-Fifty. LC 76-8959. (Illus.). 100p. 1976. 30.00 (ISBN 0-8363-0143-9). Jenkins.

Adams, Raymond. The Thoreau Library of Raymond Adams. 80p. 1980. Repr. of 1936 ed. lib. bdg. 12.50 (ISBN 0-8495-0063-X). Arden Lib.

--The Thoreau Library of Raymond Adams. 24.50 (ISBN 0-686-28930-7). AMS Pr.

Adams, Raymond D., jt. auth. see Haymaker, Webb.

Adams, Rex. Doctor's Amazing Speed Reducing Diet. LC 79-11343. 1979. 10.95 (ISBN 0-13-216275-X, Parker). P-H.

--Miracle Medical Foods. 304p. (Orig.). 1981. pap. 2.50 (ISBN 0-446-91940-3). Warner Bks.

--Miracle Medicine Foods. LC 77-6245. 1977. pap. 3.95 (ISBN 0-13-585463-6, Reward). P-H.

Adams, Rhenna L, jt. auth. see Torrado, Ester.

Adams, Richard. The Girl in a Swing. 1980. pap. 3.50 (E9662, Signet Bks). NAL.

--The Girl in a Swing. LC 79-3480. 1980. 11.95 (ISBN 0-394-51049-6). Knopf.

--Nature Day & Night. (Illus.). 112p. 1980. pap. 7.95 (ISBN 0-14-005345-X). Penguin.

--Watership Down. deluxe ed. LC 73-6044. 448p. 1975. 12.95 (ISBN 0-02-700030-3, 70003). Macmillan.

--Watership Down. 1975. pap. 2.50 (ISBN 0-380-00293-0, 39586). Avon.

Adams, Richard E. The Ceramics of Altar De Sacrificios. LC 72-126638. (Peabody Museum Papers: Vol. 63, No. 1). 1971. pap. text ed. 25.00 (ISBN 0-87365-180-4). Peabody Harvard.

Adams, Robert. Castaways in Time. Freas, Polly & Freas, Kelly, eds. LC 79-11600. (Illus.). 1980. pap. 4.95 (ISBN 0-915442-96-5, Starblaze). Donning Co.

--The Coming of the Horseclans. 192p. (Orig.). 1980. pap. 1.95 o.p. (ISBN 0-523-40919-2). Pinnacle Bks.

--From the Missouri West. (Illus.). 1980. 20.00 (ISBN 0-89381-059-2); ltd. ed., 100 copies 400.00 (ISBN 0-89381-063-0). Aperture.

--Horseclans Odyssey. (Orig.). 1981. pap. 2.50 (ISBN 0-451-09744-0, E9744, Sig). NAL.

Adams, Robert E. A Companion to Shakespeare: The Non-Shakespearean Elizabethan Drama - An Introduction. LC 78-58821. 1978. pap. text ed. 9.50 (ISBN 0-8191-0540-6). U Pr of Amer.

--Encuentro Con Jesus. (Illus.). Date not set. pap. 1.20 (ISBN 0-311-04657-6). Casa Bautista.

Adams, Robert E., ed. How to Get Along in This World. pap. 5.95 (ISBN 0-911012-33-8). Nelson-Hall.

Adams, Robert L. Boston Job Bank. expanded ed. 168p. 1980. pap. 5.95 (ISBN 0-937860-01-8). Adams Inc MA.

Adams, Robert M. Bad Mouth: Fugitive Papers on the Dark Side. (Quantum Ser.). 1977. 11.50x (ISBN 0-520-03381-7); pap. 2.65 (ISBN 0-520-03530-5). U of Cal Pr.

--Heartland of Cities: Surveys of Ancient Settlement & Land Use on the Central Floodplain of the Euphrates. LC 80-13995. (Illus.). 384p. 1981. lib. bdg. 35.00x (ISBN 0-226-00544-5). U of Chicago Pr.

--Proteus: His Lies, His Truth. 192p. 1973. 7.95x o.p. (ISBN 0-393-04353-3). Norton.

--The Roman Stamp: Frame & Facade in Some Forms of Neo-Classicism. (Illus.). 1974. 20.00x (ISBN 0-520-02345-5); pap. 6.95 (ISBN 0-520-03715-4). U of Cal Pr.

Adams, Robert M., ed. see De Voltaire, Francois M.

Adams, Robert M., ed. & tr. see Machiavelli, Niccolo.

Adams, Robert M., ed. see Stendhal.

Adams, Robert M., et al. The Fitness of Man's Environment. LC 68-20988. (Smithsonian Annual, No. 2). 250p. 1968. 15.00x (ISBN 0-87474-058-4). Smithsonian.

Adams, Roger G. & Woods, T. F. Points to Watch in Elementary Russian. 1968. pap. text ed. 1.95x o.p. (ISBN 0-435-39301-4). Heinemann Ed.

Adams, Ronald C., et al, eds. Games, Sports & Exercises for the Physically Handicapped. 2nd ed. LC 75-1079. (Illus.). 308p. 1975. pap. 14.50 o.p. (ISBN 0-8121-0514-1). Lea & Febiger.

Adams, Russell B., Jr. The Boston Money Tree. LC 76-27388. 1977. 11.95 o.s.i. (ISBN 0-690-01209-8, TYC-T). T Y Crowell.

Adams, Russell E., jt. ed. see Lucas, Jay P.

Adams, Russell L. Great Negroes, Past & Present. 3rd rev. ed. Ross, David P., Jr., ed. LC 72-87924. (Orig.). 1976. 12.95 (ISBN 0-910030-07-3); pap. text ed. 7.95 (ISBN 0-910030-08-1); 9 portfolios of display prints 9.95 ea. Afro-Am.

Adams, Ruth. The Complete Home Guide to All the Vitamins. 432p. 1972. pap. 2.75 (ISBN 0-915962-05-5). Larchmont Bks.

--Eating in Eden. 196p. (Orig.). 1976. pap. 1.75 (ISBN 0-915962-16-0). Larchmont Bks.

Adams, Ruth & Murray, Frank. All You Should Know About Arthritis. 256p. (Orig.). 1979. pap. 2.25 (ISBN 0-915962-28-4). Larchmont Bks.

--All You Should Know About Beverages for Your Health & Well Being. 286p. 1976. pap. 1.75 (ISBN 0-915962-17-9). Larchmont Bks.

--All You Should Know About Health Foods. 352p. pap. 2.50 (ISBN 0-915962-01-2). Larchmont Bks.

--Body, Mind, & the B Vitamins. rev. ed. 317p. 1972. pap. 1.95x (ISBN 0-915962-02-0). Larchmont Bks.

--The Good Seeds, the Rich Grains, the Hardy Nuts for a Healthier, Happier Life. rev. ed. 303p. 1973. pap. 1.75 (ISBN 0-915962-07-1). Larchmont Bks.

--Improving Your Health with Vitamin A. (Larchmont Preventive Health Library). 125p. (Orig.). 1978. pap. 1.25 (ISBN 0-915962-24-1). Larchmont Bks.

--Is Blood Sugar Making You a Nutritional Cripple? rev. ed. 174p. (Orig.). 1975. pap. 1.75 (ISBN 0-915962-11-X). Larchmont Bks.

--Megavitamin Therapy. 277p. (Orig.). 1973. pap. 1.95. Larchmont Bks.

--Minerals: Kill or Cure. rev. ed. 366p. (Orig.). 1974. pap. 1.95 (ISBN 0-915962-16-0). Larchmont Bks.

--The New High Fiber Diet. 319p. (Orig.). 1977. pap. 2.25 (ISBN 0-915962-21-7). Larchmont Bks.

--The Vitamin B-Six Book. 176p. (Orig.). 1980. pap. 1.75 (ISBN 0-915962-30-6). Larchmont Bks.

Adams, Ruth B. Callaloo & Pastelles Too. LC 73-93096. 1973. 4.95 o.p. (ISBN 0-8163-0129-8, 03022-1). Pacific Pr Pub Assn.

Adams, Ruth S., jt. auth. see McNeill, William H.

Adams, Samuel H. Pony Express. (Landmark Ser.: No. 7). (Illus.). (gr. 4-6). 1950. PLB 5.99 (ISBN 0-394-90307-2, BYR). Random.

--Santa Fe Trail. (Landmark Ser.: No. 13). (Illus.). (gr. 4-6). 1951. PLB 5.99 (ISBN 0-394-90313-7, BYR). Random.

Adams, Scott. Medical Bibliography in an Age of Discontinuity. 256p. 1981. 21.50 (ISBN 0-912176-09-1). Med Lib Assn.

Adams, Sexton & Griffin, Adelaide. Modern Personnel Management. 330p. 1981. 14.95 (ISBN 0-87201-662-5). Gulf Pub.

Adams, Shirley J., jt. auth. see Jarvis, Gilbert A.

Adams, Susan, jt. auth. see Stove, Betty.

Adams, T. Police Patrol: Tactics & Techniques. LC 71-138484. (Essential of Law Enforcements Ser). 1971. ref. ed. 16.95x (ISBN 0-13-684662-9). P-H.

Adams, T. F. M. & Hoshii, Iwao. A Financial History of the New Japan. LC 75-185642. (Illus.). 547p. 1972. 22.50x (ISBN 0-87011-157-4). Kodansha.

Adams, T. F. M. & Kobayashi, N. World of Japanese Business. LC 71-82661. (Illus.). 326p. 1969. 14.95x (ISBN 0-87011-091-8). Kodansha.

Adams, Thomas F. Introduction to the Administration of Criminal Justice: An Overview of the Justice System & Its Components. 2nd ed. (Ser. in Criminal Justice). (Illus.). 1980. text ed. 15.95 (ISBN 0-13-477794-8). P-H.

--Training Officer's Handbook. 176p. 1964. pap. 14.50 photocopy ed. spiral (ISBN 0-398-00007-7). C C Thomas.

Adams, Thomas M. The Master Guide to Electronic Circuits. (Illus.). 616p. 1980. 19.95 o.p. (ISBN 0-8306-9971-6); pap. 15.95 (ISBN 0-8306-1184-3, 1184). TAB Bks.

Adams, Thomas R. The American Controversy: A Bibliographical Study of the British Pamphlets About the American Disputes, 1764-1783, 2 vols. LC 77-76348. 1980. Set. 60.00x (ISBN 0-87057-150-8, Pub. by Brown U Pr). Univ Pr of New England.

--The American Controversy: A Bibliographical Study of the British Pamphlets About the American Disputes, 1764-1783, 2 vols. LC 77-76348. 1140p. 1981. Set. text ed. 60.00 (ISBN 0-87057-150-8). U Pr of New Eng.

--The British Pamphlet Press & the American Controversy, 1764 to 1783. 1979. pap. 4.50 o.p. (ISBN 0-912296-37-2, Dist. by U Pr of Va). Am Antiquarian.

Adams, Virginia. Crime. (Human Behavior Ser.). 1976. 9.95 (ISBN 0-8094-1962-9). Time-Life.

Adams, W. Fundamentals of Mathematics for Business, Social, & Life Sciences. 1979. 21.95 (ISBN 0-13-341073-0). P-H.

Adams, W. J. Calculus for Business & Social Science. LC 74-5524. 1975. text ed. 18.50 (ISBN 0-471-00988-1). Wiley.

Adams, W. R. Nubia: Corridor to Africa. 1977. 45.00 o.p. (ISBN 0-691-09370-9). Princeton U Pr.

Adams, W. Royce. How to Read the Sciences. 1970. pap. 6.50x o.p. (ISBN 0-673-05864-6). Scott F.

Adams, Walter E. Crisis at the Twenty-Third Hour. 175p. 1981. pap. 4.50 (ISBN 0-937408-03-4). Gospel Pubns FL.

--The Devil Is a Mean Man. 140p. (Orig.). 1981. pap. 3.95 (ISBN 0-937408-01-8). Gospel Pubns Fl.

--Who Is God??? God Is Love!!! 115p. (Orig.). 1981. pap. 2.95 (ISBN 0-937408-02-6). Gospel Pubns Fl.

Adams, Willi P. The First American Constitutions: Republican Ideology & the Making of State Constitutions in the Revolutionary Era. Kimber, Rita & Kimber, Robert, trs. from Ger. LC 79-10887. xviii, 351p. 1980. 23.50x (ISBN 0-8078-1388-5). U of NC Pr.

Adams, William, ed. Afro-American Authors, American Indian Authors, Mexican-American Authors: Instructor's Guide. (Multo-Ethnic Literature Ser.). 1976. 5.32 (ISBN 0-395-24042-5). HM.

Adams, William, et al, eds. Afro-American Authors. LC 74-160035. (Multi-Ethnic Literature Ser.). (Illus.). 165p. (gr. 10-12). 1971. pap. text ed. 5.32 (ISBN 0-395-12700-9, 2-40591); inst guide 5.84 (ISBN 0-395-24042-5). HM.

--Afro-American Literature: Drama. (Afro-American Literature Ser.). (gr. 9-12). 1970. pap. 5.32 (ISBN 0-395-01973-7, 2-00200). HM.

--Afro-American Literature: Fiction. (Afro-American Literature Ser). (gr. 9-12). 1970. pap. 5.32 (ISBN 0-395-01977-X, 2-00204). HM.

--Afro-American Literature: Nonfiction. (Afro-American Literature Ser). (gr. 9-12). 1970. pap. 5.32 (ISBN 0-395-01979-6, 2-00206). HM.

--Afro-American Literature: Poetry. (Afro-American Literature Ser). (gr. 10-12). 1970. pap. 5.32 (ISBN 0-395-01975-3, 2-00202). HM.

--Asian-American Authors. (Multi-Ethnic Literature Ser.). pap. 5.32 (ISBN 0-395-24039-5); inst. guide 4.80 (ISBN 0-395-24042-5). HM.

Adams, William A. The Experience of Teaching & Learning: A Phenomenology of Education. LC 80-81902. 175p. (Orig.). 1980. pap. 6.95 (ISBN 0-937668-00-1). Psych Pr WA.

Adams, William B. Handbook of Motion Picture Production. LC 76-51818. (Wiley Ser. on Human Communication). 1977. 26.50 (ISBN 0-471-00459-6, Pub. by Wiley-Interscience). Wiley.

Adams, William D. Dictionary of English Literature. LC 66-25162. 1966. Repr. of 1880 ed. 34.00 (ISBN 0-8103-0150-4). Gale.

Adams, William D., ed. English Epigrams. LC 74-77039. 1974. Repr. of 1878 ed. 20.00 (ISBN 0-8103-3700-2). Gale.

Adams, William H. Atget's Gardens. LC 79-7037. (Illus.). 1979. 19.95 o.p. (ISBN 0-385-15319-8); pap. 9.95 o.p. (ISBN 0-385-15320-1). Doubleday.

--The French Garden, Fifteen-Hundred-Eighteen-Hundred. LC 78-24655. (Illus.). 1979. 19.95 (ISBN 0-8076-0918-8); pap. 9.95 (ISBN 0-8076-0919-6). Braziller.

Adams, William H. D. Curiosities of Superstition. LC 76-155434. 1971. 20.00 (ISBN 0-8103-3383-X). Gale.

--Witch, Warlock, & Magician. LC 73-5621. 1971. Repr. of 1889 ed. 30.00 (ISBN 0-8103-3619-7). Gale.

Adams, Williams D. Southern Flower Gardening. LC 79-29715. (Illus.). 1980. pap. 3.95 (ISBN 0-88415-291-X). Pacesetter Pr.

Adamson, Arthur. A Textbook of Physical Chemistry. 2nd ed. 953p. 1979. 26.50 (ISBN 0-12-044260-4); solutions manual 3.00 (ISBN 0-12-044265-5). Acad Pr.

Adamson, David. The Ruins of Time: Four & a Half Centuries of Conquest & Discovery Among the Maya. (Illus.). 1975. 12.50 o.p. (ISBN 0-04-972008-2, 2262). Allen Unwin.

Adamson, Donald, tr. see Balzac, Honore de.

Adamson, George. Finding One to Ten. (Illus.). (ps-5). 1968. 5.95 (ISBN 0-571-08330-7, Pub. by Faber & Faber). Merrimack Bk Serv.

--Widdecombe Fair. (Illus.). (ps-5). 1966. 6.50 (ISBN 0-571-06559-7, Pub. by Faber & Faber). Merrimack Bk Serv.

Adamson, Jane. Othello As Tragedy: Some Problems of Judgement & Feeling. LC 79-41437. 230p. 1980. 34.50 (ISBN 0-521-22368-7); pap. 11.50 (ISBN 0-521-29760-5). Cambridge U Pr.

Adamson, John W. Pioneers of Modern Education in the Seventeenth Century. LC 79-165366. 1971. text ed. 9.75 (ISBN 0-8077-1006-7); pap. text ed. 5.25x (ISBN 0-8077-1008-3). Tchrs Coll.

Adamson, Joy. Elsa. rev. ed. (Illus.). (gr. 1 up). 1963. PLB 4.99 o.s.i. (ISBN 0-394-91117-2). Pantheon.

--Queen of Shaba: The Story of an African Leopard. LC 80-7931. (Helen & Kurt Wolff Bk). (Illus.). 256p. 1980. 14.95 (ISBN 0-15-175651-1). HarBraceJ.

Adamson, Richard H. All for Nothing. Date not set. pap. price not set (ISBN 0-89126-075-7). Military Aff Aero.

Adamson, Simon. Seaside Piers. 1977. 16.95 o.p. (ISBN 0-7134-0242-3, Pub. by Batsford England). David & Charles.

Adamson, T. C., ed. see Project SQUID Workshop on Transonic Flow Problems in Turbomachinery, Feb. 1976.

Adamson, Walter L. Hegemony & Revolution: Antonio Gramsci's Political & Cultural Theory. 320p. 1980. 20.00x (ISBN 0-520-03924-6). U of Cal Pr.

Adamson, Wendy W. Saving Lake Superior. LC 74-17351. (Story of Environmental Action Ser.). (Illus.). (gr. 7 up). 1974. PLB 7.95 (ISBN 0-87518-083-3). Dillon.

--Who Owns a River? LC 76-53011. (Story of Environmental Action Ser.). (Illus.). (gr. 7 up). 1977. PLB 7.95 (ISBN 0-87518-140-6). Dillon.

Adarkar, Priya, tr. see Tendulkar, Vijay.

Adarkar, Vivek. We Could Be Happy Together. 105p. 1973. 4.00x (ISBN 0-210-22370-7). Asia.

Adas, Michael. The Burma Delta: Economic Development & Social Change on the Rice Frontier, 1852-1941. LC 73-15256. 288p. 1974. 21.50 (ISBN 0-299-06490-5). U of Wis Pr.

Adasko, Laura & Huberman, Alice. Batik in Many Forms. LC 74-16376. (Illus.). 176p. 1975. 12.95 o.p. (ISBN 0-688-00340-0). Morrow.

Adatto, I. J., jt. auth. see Snider, Arthur J.

Aday, LuAnn, et al. Health Care in the U. S. Equitable for Whom? LC 79-21841. 1980. 25.00x (ISBN 0-8039-1373-7). Sage.

Adby, P. R. Applied Circuit Theory: Matrix & Computer Methods. LC 79-41458. (Series in Electrical & Electronic Engineering). 1980. 94.95x (ISBN 0-470-26908-1). Halsted Pr.

Adby, P. R. & Dempster, M. A. Introduction to Optimization Methods. LC 74-4109. (Mathematics Ser.). 204p. 1974. pap. text ed. 11.95 (ISBN 0-412-11040-7, Pub. by Chapman & Hall). Methuen Inc.

--Introduction to Optimization Methods. LC 74-4109. (Mathematics Ser.). 204p. 1974. pap. text ed. 11.95 (ISBN 0-470-00830-X). Halsted Pr.

Adcock, C. V. Psychology & Theory. LC 78-321163. 1976. pap. 6.50x (ISBN 0-7055-0553-7). Intl Pubns Serv.

Adcock, Don & Segal, Marilyn. From One to Two Years. LC 80-13835. (Play & Learn Ser.). (Illus.). 1980. pap. 4.95 (ISBN 0-916392-51-1). Oak Tree Pubns.

--From Two to Three Years. LC 80-13834. (Play & Learn Ser.). (Illus.). 1980. pap. 5.95 (ISBN 0-916392-52-X). Oak Tree Pubns.

Adcock, Fleur. The Inner Harbour. 55p. 1981. pap. 8.95 (ISBN 0-19-211888-9). Oxford U Pr.

--The Scenic Route. 1974. pap. 4.95x (ISBN 0-19-211843-9). Oxford U Pr.

Adcock, Frank E. The Greek & Macedonian Art of War. (Sather Classical Lectures: No. 30). 1957. 12.75x (ISBN 0-520-02807-4); pap. 2.25 (ISBN 0-520-00005-6, CAL54). U of Cal Pr.

Adcock, Larry. How to Weigh Less for the Rest of Your Life. 1980. pap. 2.25 (ISBN 0-446-92084-3). Warner Bks.

Addams, Jane. Twenty Years at Hull-House. (Illus.). 1966. 6.95 o.s.i. (ISBN 0-02-500480-8). Macmillan.

Addams, Jane & Wells, Ida B. Lynching & Rape: An Exchange of Views. Aptheker, Bettina, ed. 1977. 1.25 (ISBN 0-89977-023-1). Am Inst Marxist.

Addams, Jane, et al. Women at the Hague: The International Congress of Women & Its Results. LC 73-147452. (Library of War & Peace; Peace Leaders: Biographies & Memoirs). lib. bdg. 38.00 (ISBN 0-8240-0246-6). Garland Pub.

Adde, Leo. Nine Cities: The Anatomy of Downtown Renewal. LC 73-85476. (Special Publications Ser.). 1969. pap. 4.25 o.p. (ISBN 0-87420-907-2). Urban Land.

Adderly, James G. Stephen Remarx: The Story of a Venture into Ethics, 1893. Wolff, Robert L., ed. Bd. with The Christian. Caine, Thomas H. Repr. of 1897 ed. LC 75-485. (Victorian Fiction Ser). 1975. lib. bdg. 66.00 (ISBN 0-8240-1562-2). Garland Pub.

Addi, Al-Sayyid. Dictionary of Persian Loan Words in the Arabic Language. 1980. 15.00x. Intl Bk Ctr.

Addie. Christopher for President. (Illus.). (gr. 2-5). 1973. PLB 10.69 o.p. (ISBN 0-307-65776-0, Golden Pr). Western Pub.

Addington, Whitney W., ed. see Gracey, Douglas R.

Addison, Daniel D. Lucy Larcom: Life, Letters & Diary. LC 75-99065. (Library of Lives & Letters). 1970. Repr. of 1894 ed. 18.00 (ISBN 0-8103-3611-1). Gale.

Addison, Jerome F. How Rules Eighteen & Eleven Can Succeed in Magnifying the Profit Potential of Commodity Futures Trading Operations. (Illus.). 129p. 1981. 39.85 (ISBN 0-918968-81-X). Inst Econ Fina.

Addison, John. Ancient Africa. LC 74-104309. (Young Historians Ser). (Illus.). (gr. 8-10). 1971. PLB 6.89 o.p. (ISBN 0-381-99998-X, A02900, JD-J). John Day.

--Apartheid. (Today's World Ser.). (Illus.). 72p. (gr. 7-9). 1981. 15.95 (ISBN 0-7134-2485-0, Pub. by Batsford England). David & Charles.

Addison, John, et al. Suleyman & the Ottoman Empire. Yapp, Malcolm & Killingray, Margaret, eds. (Illus.). (gr. 10). 1980. lib. bdg. 5.95 (ISBN 0-89908-038-3); pap. text ed. 1.95 (ISBN 0-89908-013-8). Greenhaven.

--Traditional Africa. Yapp, Malcolm, et al, eds. (World History Ser.). (Illus.). 32p. (gr. 10). 1980. lib. bdg. 5.95 (ISBN 0-89908-034-0); pap. text ed. 1.95 (ISBN 0-89908-009-X). Greenhaven.

Addison, Joseph. Critical Essays from The Spectator. Bond, Donald F., ed. (Orig.). 1970. pap. 4.95x (ISBN 0-19-501359-X). Oxford U Pr.

--Dialogues on the Usefulness of Ancient Medals. LC 75-27883. (Renaissance & the Gods Ser.: Vol. 38). (Illus.). 1976. Repr. of 1726 ed. lib. bdg. 73.00 (ISBN 0-8240-2087-1). Garland Pub.

Addison, Joseph & Steele, Richard. Selected Essays from the Tatler, the Spectator, & the Guardian. McDonald, Daniel, ed. LC 73-179472. (Library of Literature Ser: No. 15). 1973. pap. 5.95 (ISBN 0-672-60990-8). Bobbs.

Addison, Joseph, et al. Spectator, 4 Vols. 1958. Vol. 1. 6.00x (ISBN 0-460-00164-7, Evman); Vol. 2. 6.00x (ISBN 0-460-00165-5); Vol. 3. 17.95x (ISBN 0-460-00166-3); Vol. 4. 6.00x o.p. (ISBN 0-460-00167-1). Dutton.

Addison, William. Understanding English Place-Names. 1978. 17.95 (ISBN 0-7134-0295-4, Pub. by Batsford England). David & Charles.

--Understanding English Surnames. 1978. 19.95 (ISBN 0-7134-0295-4). David & Charles.

Addkison, Andrew R. Cooking on a Woodburning Stove: 150 Down-Home Recipes. LC 80-831192. 108p. (Orig.). 1980. pap. 7.95 (ISBN 0-915190-28-1). Jalmar Pr.

Addy, Sharon. We Didn't Mean to. LC 80-24976. (Life & Living from a Child's Point of View Ser.). (Illus.). 32p. (gr. k-5). 1981. PLB 9.65 (ISBN 0-8172-1370-8). Raintree Child.

Ade, George. The Old-Time Saloon: Not Wet--Not Dry, Just History. LC 77-181797. (Illus.). xii, 176p. 1975. Repr. of 1931 ed. 18.00 (ISBN 0-8103-4076-3). Gale.

Ade Ajayi, J. F., ed. see Davidson, Basil.

Adebayo, Augustus. Principles & Practice of Public Administration in Nigeria. 192p. 1981. 27.00 (ISBN 0-471-27897-1, Pub. by Wiley-Interscience); pap. 13.50 (ISBN 0-471-27898-X). Wiley.

Adeleye, R. A. Power & Diplomacy in Northern Nigeria, 1804-1906. (Ibadan History Ser). (Illus.). 1971. text ed. 11.50x (ISBN 0-391-00169-8). Humanities.

Adelman, Allen G. & Goldman, Bernard S., eds. Unstable Angina: Recognition & Management. LC 80-13211. 1980. 29.50 (ISBN 0-88416-271-0). PSG Pub.

Adelman, Benjamin & Adelman, Saul J. Bound for the Stars: An Enthusiastic Look at the Opportunities & Challenges Space Exploration Offers. (Illus.). 368p. 1980. text ed. 17.95 (ISBN 0-13-080390-1, Spec); pap. text ed. 8.95 (ISBN 0-13-080382-0). P-H.

Adelman, Bob. Gentleman of Leisure: A Year in the Life of a Pimp. (Illus.). 224p. 1973. pap. 1.95 (ISBN 0-451-05524-1, J5524, Sig). NAL.

Adelman, Irving & Dworkin, Rita. The Contemporary Novel: A Checklist of Critical Literature on the British & American Novel Since 1945. LC 72-4451. 1972. 20.50 (ISBN 0-8108-0517-0). Scarecrow.

Adelman, J. King Lear: Twentieth Century Interpretations. 1978. 8.95 (ISBN 0-13-516195-9, Spec); pap. 2.95 (ISBN 0-13-516187-8). P-H.

Adelman, Kenneth L. African Realities. LC 80-15828. 1980. 16.50x (ISBN 0-8448-1376-1). Crane-Russak Co.

Adelman, M. A. & Kaufman, G. M. Estimation of Resources & Reserves. 1981. price not set (ISBN 0-88410-644-6). Ballinger Pub.

Adelman, Richard, et al, eds. Neural Regulatory Mechanisms During Aging. (Modern Aging Ser.: Vol. 1). 230p. 1980. write for info. (ISBN 0-8451-2300-9). A R Liss.

Adelman, Saul J., jt. auth. see Adelman, Benjamin.

Adelphus, Johannes. Johannes Adelphus: Ausgewaehlte Schriften, 4 vols, Vol. 1, Barbarosssa. Gotzkowsky, Bodo, ed. (Ausgaben Deutscher Literatur des XV Bis XVIII Jahrhunderts). 1974. 123.50x (ISBN 3-11-003382-8). De Gruyter.

Adelson, Daniel, jt. ed. see Sarbin, Theodore R.

Adelson, Joseph, ed. Handbook of Adolescent Psychology. LC 79-21927. (Personality Processes Ser.). 1980. 35.95 (ISBN 0-471-03793-1, Pub. by Wiley-Interscience). Wiley.

Adelson, Lester. The Pathology of Homicide: A Vade Mecum for Pathologist, Prosecutor & Defense Counsel. (Illus.). 992p. 1974. text ed. 67.50 (ISBN 0-398-03000-6). C C Thomas.

Adelson, Sandra. Wrap Her in Light. 448p. 1981. 11.95 (ISBN 0-688-03753-4). Morrow.

Adelstein, Michael E. Contemporary Business Writing. 1971. text ed. 11.95 (ISBN 0-394-30373-3). Random.

Ademar, Guilhem. Poesies Du Troubadour Guilhem Ademar. LC 80-2180. 1981. Repr. of 1951 ed. 37.50 (ISBN 0-404-19006-5). AMS Pr.

Aden, John M. Pope's Once & Future Kings: Satire & Politics in the Early Career. LC 78-16618. 1978. 14.00x (ISBN 0-87049-252-7). U of Tenn Pr.

Adeney, Walter D. The Books of Ezra & Nehemiah. Date not set. 11.50 (ISBN 0-86524-050-7). Klock & Klock.

Ader, Robert, ed. Psychoneuroimmunology. LC 80-265. (Behavioral Medicine Ser.). 1981. price not set (ISBN 0-12-043780-5). Acad Pr.

Ader-Brin, Dianne, ed. see Ingebritsen, Karl J.

Aderman, Ralph M., ed. see Rebreau, Liviu.

Aderman, Ralph M., et al, eds. The Complete Works of Washington Irving: Letters, Eighteen Hundred Two to Eighteen Twenty-Three. (Twayne's Critical Editions Program: Vol. 1). 1978. lib. bdg. 30.00 (ISBN 0-8057-8522-1). G K Hall.

Ades, D. Dada & Surrealism. LC 77-76765. (Modern Movements in Art Ser.). 1978. pap. 1.95 (ISBN 0-8120-0877-4). Barron.

Adey, W. Ross. Brain Mechanisms & the Control of Behaviour. LC 75-311367. 1975. 19.50x (ISBN 0-8448-0611-0). Crane-Russak Co.

Adhikari, G. Documents of the History of the Communist Party of India, Vol. 1. LC 71-925316. 1971. 12.50x o.p. (ISBN 0-8364-0396-7). South Asia Bks.

--Documents of the History of the Communist Party of India, Vol. 2. 756p. 1974. 15.00x o.p. (ISBN 0-88386-560-2). South Asia Bks.

Adhikari, G., ed. Documents of the History of the Communist Party of India, Vol. 3 (1927) 1978. 11.50x o.p. (ISBN 0-8364-0213-8). South Asia Bks.

Adhikarya, R. Broadcasting in Peninsular Malaysia. (Case Studies on Broadcasting Systems). 1977. pap. 14.00 (ISBN 0-7100-8530-3). Routledge & Kegan.

Adi. Five Senses for One Death: Special Issue 18. pap. 1.00 o.p. (ISBN 0-685-78397-9). The Smith.

Adidevananda, Swami, tr. see Srinivasadasa.

Adie, Donald W. Marinas: A Working Guide to Their Development and Design. 2nd ed. LC 77-136. (Illus.). 1977. 52.50 (ISBN 0-8436-0151-5, Architectural Pr). CBI Pub.

Adie, Douglas K. An Evaluation of Postal Service Wage Rates. 1977. pap. 3.75 (ISBN 0-8447-3265-6). Am Enterprise.

Adie, R. & Poitras, G. Latin America: The Politics of Immobility. 1974. pap. 10.50 (ISBN 0-13-524272-X). P-H.

Adiga, M. G. The Song of the Earth & Other Poems. Ramanujan, A. K., tr. from Kannada. (Writers Workshop Redbird Ser.). 1975. 8.00 (ISBN 0-88253-640-0); pap. text ed. 4.00 (ISBN 0-88253-639-7). Ind-US Inc.

Adinarayan, S. P. Case for Colour. 1964. 10.00x (ISBN 0-210-26896-4). Asia.

Adinolfi, Matteo, ed. Developmental Immunology. (Clinics in Developmental Medicine Ser.: Vol. 34). 187p. 1969. 19.50 (ISBN 0-685-59041-0). Lippincott.

--Immunology & Development. (Illus.). 1970. 18.95x (ISBN 0-685-83591-X). Intl Ideas.

Adirondack Mountain Club, Map & Guidebook Committee. Guide to Adirondack Trails: High Peak Region. 10th ed. LC 80-15403. (Illus.). 324p. 1980. pap. 9.00 (ISBN 0-935272-11-9). ADK Mtn Club.

--Guide to the Northville-Placid Trail. LC 80-16626. (Illus.). 160p. (Orig.). 1980. pap. 5.00 (ISBN 0-935272-12-7). ADK Mtn Club.

Adivar, Halide E. The Turkish Ordeal. LC 79-3081. (Illus.). 407p. 1981. Repr. of 1928 ed. 32.50 (ISBN 0-8305-0057-X). Hyperion Conn.

Adizes, Ichak. How to Solve the Mismanagement Crisis: Diagnosis & Treatment of Management Problems. 300p. Repr. of 1979 ed. 16.00. Irvington.

Adizes, Ichak & Borgese, Elisabeth M. Self-Management: New Dimensions to Democracy. 162p. Repr. of 1975 ed. pap. text ed. 6.95x (ISBN 0-87436-202-4). Irvington.

Adizes, Ichak & Borgese, Elisabeth M., eds. Self-Management: New Dimensions to Democracy. LC 74-34220. (Studies in International & Comparative Politics: No. 7). 162p. 1975. text ed. 13.00 (ISBN 0-87436-202-4); pap. text ed. 4.60 (ISBN 0-87436-203-2). ABC-Clio.

Adkins, J. S., jt. auth. see Bodwell, C. E.

Adkins, Jan. Art & Industry of Sandcastles. LC 76-141615. (gr. k up). 1971. 7.95 (ISBN 0-8027-0336-4). Walker & Co.

--Heavy Equipment. LC 80-15213. (Illus.). 32p. (gr. 1-4). 1980. 7.95 (ISBN 0-686-62530-7). Scribner.

--Letterbox: The Art & History of Letters. (Illus.). (gr. 3 up). 1981. 10.95 (ISBN 0-8027-6385-5); PLB 11.85 (ISBN 0-8027-6386-3). Walker & Co.

--Moving Heavy Things. (gr. 5 up). 1980. reinforced bdg. 6.95 (ISBN 0-395-29206-9). HM.

--Toolchest: A Primer of Woodcraft. Cuyler, Margery, ed. LC 72-81374. (Illus.). 48p. 1973. 6.95 (ISBN 0-8027-6153-4); lib. bdg. 6.83 (ISBN 0-8027-6154-2). Walker & Co.

--The Wood Book: An Entertaining, Interesting, & Even Useful Compendium of Facts, Notions, Opinions, & Sentiments About Wood... & Its Growing, Cutting, Woodworking & Burning. 1980. pap. 9.95 (ISBN 0-316-01082-0). Little.

Adkins, Nelson F., ed. see Paine, Thomas.

Adkins, W. S. & Arick, M. B. Geology of Bell County, Texas. (Illus.). 92p. 1930. 1.00 (BULL 3016). Bur Econ Geology.

Adkins, W. S., jt. auth. see Winton, W. M.

Adkinson, A. Wyle & Fry, N., eds. The House of Horror: The Story of Hammer Films. LC 74-76299. 1974. 6.95 (ISBN 0-89388-163-5). Okpaku Communications.

Adlam, D. Code in Context. (Primary Socialization, Language & Education Ser.). 1977. 20.00x (ISBN 0-7100-8481-1). Routledge & Kegan.

Adlam, Diana, et al, eds. Ideology & Consciousness: Spring 1978, No. 3. 1978. pap. text ed. 3.25x (ISBN 0-391-01215-0). Humanities.

--Politics & Power: Problems in Labour Politics. (Politics & Power Ser.). 220p. (Orig.). 1981. pap. price not set (ISBN 0-7100-0716-7). Routledge & Kegan.

Adlard, John, ed. Fruit of That Forbidden Tree: Restoration Poems, Songs & Jests on the Subject of Sensual Love. (Fyfield Ser.). 1980. 6.95 (ISBN 0-85635-146-6, Pub. by Carcanet New Pr England); pap. 3.95 (ISBN 0-85635-147-4). Persea Bks.

Adleman, Robert. How to Write Anything. LC 80-81879. 1981. pap. 6.95 (ISBN 0-933350-37-6). Morse Pr.

Adler, Alfred. Cooperation Between the Sexes: Writings on Women, Love, Marriage & Its Disorders. LC 76-23804. 480p. 1980. Repr. of 1978 ed. 25.00 (ISBN 0-87668-443-6). Aronson.

--Individual Psychology of Alfred Adler: A Systematic Presentation in Selections from His Writings. Ansbacher, Heinz L. & Ansbacher, Rowena R., eds. pap. 6.95x (ISBN 0-06-131154-5, TB1154, Torch). Har-Row.

--Practice & Theory of Individual Psychology. Radin, P., tr. (International Library of Psychology Philosophy & Scientific Method Ser.). 1971. Repr. of 1929 ed. text ed. 27.50x (ISBN 0-7100-3015-0). Humanities.

--Science of Living. LC 69-12246. 1969. pap. 2.50 o.p. (ISBN 0-385-07139-6, A667, Anch). Doubleday.

--Understanding Human Nature. Wolfe, Walter B., tr. 1928. text ed. 19.50x (ISBN 0-04-150002-4). Allen Unwin.

--Understanding Human Nature. 1978. pap. 1.95 o.p. (ISBN 0-449-30833-2, Prem). Fawcett.

Adler, Alfred, ed. Co-Operation Between the Sexes: Writings on Women, Love & Marriage Sexuality, & Its Disorders. LC 76-23804. 1978. pap. 3.95 (ISBN 0-385-09562-7, Anch). Doubleday.

Adler, Bill. Still More Letters from Camp. 1973. pap. 0.95 (ISBN 0-451-07106-9, Q7106, Sig). NAL.

Adler, Bill & Feinman, Jeffrey. Woody Allen: Clown Prince of American Humor. (Illus.). 192p. (Orig.). 1975. pap. 1.75 o.p. (ISBN 0-523-00786-8). Pinnacle Bks.

Adler, Bill & Wagner, Gary. The Second Time Is Better. LC 78-70091. 1979. pap. 1.95 o.p. (ISBN 0-87216-515-9). Playboy Pbks.

--When I Fall in Love. LC 78-78051. 1979. pap. 1.95 o.p. (ISBN 0-87216-385-7). Playboy Pbks.

Adler, Bill, ed. Wit & Wisdom of Billy Graham. LC 80-65430. 256p. Date not set. 8.95 (ISBN 0-915684-61-6). Christian Herald. Postponed.

--Wit & Wisdom of Bishop Fulton J. Sheen. LC 78-82959. 1969. pap. 2.45 (ISBN 0-385-02691-9, D268, Im). Doubleday.

Adler, C. S. The Magic of the Glits. LC 78-12149. (Illus.). (gr. 5-8). 1979. 8.95 (ISBN 0-02-700120-2). Macmillan.

--Shelter on Blue Barns Road. LC 80-24715. (Illus.). 144p. (gr. 5-9). 1981. PLB 8.95 (ISBN 0-02-700280-2). Macmillan.

Adler, Charles S. We Are but a Moment's Sunlight: Understanding Death. 1976. pap. 1.95 (ISBN 0-671-48772-8). WSP.

Adler, Cyrus. I Have Considered the Days. (Illus.). 1969. 8.00x (ISBN 0-8381-3110-7). United Syn Bk.

Adler, David A. Base Five. LC 74-18325. (Young Math Ser.). (Illus.). (gr. k-3). 1975. 7.95 (ISBN 0-690-00668-3, TYC-J); PLB 7.89 (ISBN 0-690-00669-1). T Y Crowell.

--Cam Jansen & the Mystery of the U.F.O. (Cam Jansen Ser.). (Illus.). 64p. (gr. 7-10). 1980. 4.95 (ISBN 0-670-20041-7). Viking Pr.

--Finger Spelling Fun. (gr. 1-3). 1980. PLB 7.90 (ISBN 0-531-04140-9). Watts.

--Redwoods Are the Tallest Trees in the World. LC 77-4713. (A Let's-Read-and-Find-Out Science Bk). (Illus.). (gr. k-3). 1978. PLB 7.89 (ISBN 0-690-01368-X, TYC-J). T Y Crowell.

--Roman Numerals. LC 77-2270. (Young Math Ser.). (Illus.). (gr. 1-4). 1977. PLB 7.89 (ISBN 0-690-01302-7, TYC-J). T Y Crowell.

--Three-D, Two-D, One-D. LC 74-5156. (Young Math Ser.). (Illus.). 40p. (gr. k-3). 1974. 7.95 (ISBN 0-690-00456-7, TYC-J); 7.89 (ISBN 0-690-00543-1). T Y Crowell.

Adler, Denise. Five Women. 1980. pap. 1.95 (ISBN 0-8423-0874-1). Tyndale.

--Jonah. 1980. pap. 1.98 (ISBN 0-8423-1948-4). Tyndale.

--Philippines. 1980. pap. 1.95 (ISBN 0-8423-4844-1). Tyndale.

Adler, Denise R. Morning Star. 1977. pap. 1.50 (ISBN 0-89129-206-3). Jove Pubns.

Adler, Elkan N. About Hebrew Manuscripts. LC 78-136769. (Illus.). 1971. Repr. of 1905 ed. 12.50 (ISBN 0-87203-025-3). Hermon.

Adler, Freda & Simon, Rita J. The Criminology of Deviant Women. LC 78-69555. (Illus.). 1979. pap. text ed. 8.95 (ISBN 0-395-26719-6). HM.

Adler, G., et al, eds. see Jung, Carl G.

Adler, Gerald & Meyerson, Paul G. Confrontation in Psychotherapy. LC 72-93192. 1973. 25.00x (ISBN 0-87668-056-2). Aronson.

Adler, Gerhard, ed. see International Congress for Analytical Psychology, 5th.

Adler, H. I., jt. ed. see Lett, J. T.

Adler, Helmut E. Fish Behavior: Why Fish Do What They Do. (Illus.). 271p. 1975. 20.00 (ISBN 0-87666-162-2, PS-734). TFH Pubns.

Adler, Irving. Atomic Energy. LC 75-132946. (Illus.). (gr. 3-6). 1971. PLB 7.89 (ISBN 0-381-99613-1, AO6100, JD-J). John Day.

--Color in Your Life. LC 62-7784. (Illus.). (gr. 6 up). 1962. PLB 7.89 (ISBN 0-381-99995-5, A14860, JD-J). John Day.

--Energy. LC 71-10143. (Reason Why Ser). (Illus.). (gr. 3-6). 1970. PLB 7.89 (ISBN 0-381-99609-3, A23400, JD-J). John Day.

--The Environment. LC 75-35526. (Reason Why Ser.). (Illus.). 1976. lib. bdg. 7.89 (ISBN 0-381-99617-4, JD-J). John Day.

--Fire in Your Life. LC 55-9930. (Illus.). (YA) (gr. 5-9). 1955. PLB 7.89 (ISBN 0-381-99991-2, A27060, JD-J). John Day.

--Food. LC 76-54783. (The Reason Why Ser.). (Illus.). (gr. 2-5). 1977. PLB 6.89 (ISBN 0-381-90051-7, JD-J). John Day.

--Hot & Cold. rev. ed. LC 74-9357. (Illus.). 1975. PLB 7.89 (ISBN 0-381-99990-4, A34461, JD-J). John Day.

--Integers: Positive & Negative. LC 78-162589. (Reason Why Ser.). (Illus.). 48p. (gr. 3-6). 1972. PLB 7.89 (ISBN 0-381-99988-2, A39160, JD-J). John Day.

--Magic House of Numbers. LC 73-19471. (Illus.). 144p. (gr. 5-9). 1974. PLB 8.79 (ISBN 0-381-99986-6, JD-J). John Day.

--The New Mathematics. rev. & enl. ed. LC 72-2411. (Illus.). 224p. 1972. 9.95 (ISBN 0-381-98002-2, A55601, JD-J). John Day.

--Petroleum: Gas, Oil, & Asphalt. LC 78-2431. (Reason Why Ser.). (Illus.). (gr. 3-6). 1975. PLB 7.89 (ISBN 0-381-99624-7, JD-J). John Day.

--Seeing the Earth from Space. rev. ed. LC 61-18218. (Illus.). (gr. 6 up). 1961. 4.95 o.p. (ISBN 0-381-99985-8, A69000, JD-J). John Day.

--Stories of Hoaxes. 1962. pap. 0.95 o.s.i. (ISBN 0-02-016070-4, Collier). Macmillan.

--Story of Light. LC 79-93519. (Story of Science Ser). (Illus.). (gr. 5-8). 1971. PLB 7.29 (ISBN 0-8178-4752-9). Harvey.

--Sun & Its Family. rev. ed. LC 68-57377. (Illus.). (gr. 5-9). 1969. PLB 7.89 (ISBN 0-381-99983-1, A76000, JD-J). John Day.

--Thinking Machines: A Layman's Introduction to Logic, Boolean Algebra & Computers. rev ed. LC 73-19704. (Illus.). 1974. 5.95 o.p. (ISBN 0-381-98220-3, A78600, JD-J). John Day.

Adler, Irving & Adler, Joyce. Language & Man. LC 78-109148. (Reason Why Ser). (Illus.). (gr. 3-6). 1970. lib. bdg. 7.89 (ISBN 0-381-99978-5, A42100, JD-J). John Day.

Adler, Irving & Adler, Peggy. Adler Book of Puzzles & Riddles: Or, Sam Loyd Up-To-Date. LC 62-14898. (Illus.). (gr. 3-6). 1962. PLB 7.89 (ISBN 0-381-99977-7, A00800, JD-J). John Day.

Adler, Irving & Adler, Ruth. Calendar. LC 67-23865. (Reason Why Ser). (Illus.). (gr. 3-6). 1967. PLB 7.89 (ISBN 0-381-99975-0, A11200, JD-J). John Day.

--Directions & Angles. LC 69-10489. (Reason Why Ser). (Illus.). (gr. 3-6). 1969. PLB 6.89 o.p. (ISBN 0-381-99615-8, A18860, JD-J). John Day.

--The Earth's Crust. LC 63-10011. (Reason Why Ser.). (Illus.). (gr. 3-6). 1963. PLB 7.89 (ISBN 0-381-99971-8, JD-J). John Day.

--Houses. LC 64-20708. (Reason Why Ser). (Illus.). (gr. 3-6). 1965. PLB 7.89 (ISBN 0-381-99967-X, A35060, JD-J). John Day.

--Insects & Plants. LC 62-19714. (Reason Why Ser). (Illus.). (gr. 3-6). 1962. PLB 7.89 (ISBN 0-381-99966-1, A38660, JD-J). John Day.

--Numbers Old & New. LC 60-11126. (Reason Why Ser). (Illus.). (gr. 3-6). 1960. PLB 6.89 o.p. (ISBN 0-381-99961-0, A56400, JD-J). John Day.

--Taste, Touch & Smell. LC 66-11448. (Reason Why Ser). (Illus.). (gr. 3-6). 1966. PLB 7.89 (ISBN 0-381-99953-X, A76400, JD-J). John Day.

--Why: A Book of Reasons. LC 61-13113. (Reason Why Ser). (Illus.). (gr. 3-6). 1961. PLB 4.79 o.p. (ISBN 0-381-99950-5, A88600, JD-J). John Day.

--Your Eyes. LC 62-16223. (Reason Why Ser). (Illus.). (gr. 3-6). 1963. PLB 7.89 (ISBN 0-381-99947-5, A95000, JD-J). John Day.

Adler, Irving, jt. auth. see Adler, Peggy.

Adler, Jack. Fundamentals of Group Child Care: A Textbook & Instructional Guide for Child Care Workers. 1981. price not set reference (ISBN 0-88410-198-3). Ballinger Pub.

Adler, Jacob, ed. see Liholiho, Alexander.

Adler, Joseph. Guitar for a Singing Planet. 1976. pap. text ed. 9.95 (ISBN 0-8403-1428-0). Kendall-Hunt.

Adler, Joseph & Doherty, Robert E., eds. Employment Security in the Public Sector: A Symposium. 1974. pap. 2.00 (ISBN 0-87546-204-9). NY Sch Indus Rel.

Adler, Joyce, jt. auth. see Adler, Irving.

Adler, Joyce S. War in Melville's Imagination. (The Gotham Library). 208p. 1981. 17.50x (ISBN 0-8147-0574-X); pap. 7.95x (ISBN 0-8147-0575-8). NYU Pr.

Adler, K. The Art of Accompanying & Coaching. LC 79-147128. (Music Ser.). 260p. 1971. lib. bdg. 27.50 (ISBN 0-306-70360-2); pap. 7.95 (ISBN 0-306-80027-6). Da Capo.

Adler, L., jt. auth. see Wexler, M.

Adler, Larry. Man with a Mission: Pele. LC 76-11007. (Sports Profiles Ser.). (Illus.). 48p. (gr. 4-11). 1976. PLB 8.50 (ISBN 0-8172-0142-4). Raintree Pubs.

Adler, M. W., et al, eds. Factors Affecting the Action of Narcotics. LC 78-2999. (Monographs of the Mario Negri Institute for Pharmacological Research). 1978. 49.00 (ISBN 0-89004-272-1). Raven.

Adler, Manfred. A Parent's Manual: Answers to Questions on Child Development & Child Rearing. 124p. 1971. pap. 9.50 photocopy ed. spiral (ISBN 0-398-00010-7). C C Thomas.

Adler, Melvin J. A Pragmatic Logic for Commands. (Pragmatics & Beyond Ser.: No.3). 139p. 1980. pap. text ed. 17.25x (ISBN 90-272-2501-X). Humanities.

Adler, Morris. Voice Still Speaks. Chinitz, Jacob, ed. LC 68-57433. 1969. 10.00x (ISBN 0-8197-0052-5). Bloch.

Adler, Mortimer J. Aristotle for Everyone: Difficult Thought Made Easy. 1978. 10.95 (ISBN 0-02-503100-7). Macmillan.

--Philosopher at Large: An Intellectual Autobiography. LC 77-1383. 1977. 14.95 (ISBN 0-02-500490-5, 50049). Macmillan.

--Six Great Ideas. 256p. 1981. 12.95 (ISBN 0-02-500560-X). Macmillan.

Adler, Mortimer J., jt. auth. see Michael, Jerome.

Adler, Peggy. Geography Puzzles. (Illus.). (gr. 4-6). 1979. PLB 6.90 s&l (ISBN 0-531-02867-4). Watts.

--Second Adler Book of Puzzles & Riddles. LC 63-15912. (Illus.). (gr. 3-6). 1963. PLB 7.89 (ISBN 0-381-99946-7, A68801, JD-J). John Day.

Adler, Peggy & Adler, Irving. Math Puzzles. LC 78-2833. (Illus.). (gr. 4-6). 1978. PLB 6.90 s&l (ISBN 0-531-02216-1). Watts.

--Metric Puzzles. LC 77-1948. (gr. 4-6). 1977. PLB 6.90 s&l (ISBN 0-531-01295-6). Watts.

Adler, Peggy, jt. auth. see Adler, Irving.

Adler, Richard. All in the Family: A Critical Appraisal. LC 79-89505. (Illus.). 384p. 1979. 25.95 (ISBN 0-03-053996-X). Praeger.

Adler, Richard & Cater, Douglass, eds. Television As a Cultural Force. LC 76-10714. (Special Studies). 1976. text ed. 25.95 (ISBN 0-275-23180-1). Praeger.

Adler, Richard, jt. ed. see Cater, Douglass.

Adler, Richard B., et al. Introduction to Semiconductor Physics. (S. E. E. C. Ser.). (Illus.). pap. 14.95 (ISBN 0-471-00887-7). Wiley.

Adler, Robert J. The Geometry of Random Fields. 304p. 1981. 47.50 (ISBN 0-471-27844-0, Pub. by Wiley-Interscience). Wiley.

Adler, Roy D. Marketing & Society: Cases & Commentaries. (Illus.). 528p. 1981. text ed. 14.95 (ISBN 0-13-557074-3). P-H.

Adler, Roy D., jt. auth. see Robinson, Larry M.

Adler, Ruth, jt. auth. see Adler, Irving.

Adler, Sol, et al. An Interdisciplinary Language Intervention Program for the Moderately & Profoundly Language-Retarded Child. 1980. 19.50 (ISBN 0-8089-1301-8). Grune.

Adler, Stephen. International Migration & Dependence. 250p. 1980. text ed. 23.00x (ISBN 0-566-00202-7, Pub. by Gower Pub Co England). Renouf.

Adler, Thomas P. Robert Anderson. (United States Authors Ser: No. 300). 1978. lib. bdg. 12.50 (ISBN 0-8057-7204-9). Twayne.
Adler, Warren. Blood Ties. 1980. pap. write for info. (ISBN 0-671-83055-4). PB.
--The War of the Roses. (Orig.). 1981. 10.95 (ISBN 0-446-51220-6). Warner Bks.
Adler-Golden, Rachel & Gordon, Debbie. Beginning French with Preschoolers: A Montessori Handbook. LC 80-83136. (Illus.). 85p. 1980. pap. text ed. 6.00 (ISBN 0-915676-04-4). Montessori Wkshps.
Adler-Karlsson, Gunnar, jt. auth. see Wriggins, W. Howard.
Adlington, William, tr. see Apuleius, Lucius.
Adloff, Richard, jt. auth. see Thompson, Virginia.
Adlr, David A. Cam Jansen & the Mystery of the Dinosaur Bones. (Cam Jansen Adventure Ser.). (Illus.). 64p. (gr. 2-5). 1981. 5.95 (ISBN 0-670-20040-9). Viking Pr.
Admon, K., jt. auth. see Goldschmidt, Y.
Adnani, Muhammad. Dictionary of Common Language Errors & Their Corrections: Arabic-Arabic. 16.00x (ISBN 0-685-72039-X). Intl Bk Ctr.
Adoff, Arnold. Big Sister Tells Me That I'm Black. LC 75-32249. 32p. (gr. k-4). 1976. reinforced bdg. 5.95 (ISBN 0-03-014546-5). HR&W.
--Tornado! Poems. LC 76-47241. (Illus.). (gr. 1-3). 1977. 7.95 (ISBN 0-440-08964-6); PLB 7.45 (ISBN 0-440-08965-4). Delacorte.
Adoff, Arnold, ed. Black on Black: Commentaries by Negro Americans. LC 68-24101. (YA) (gr. 8 up). 1968. 5.95g o.s.i. (ISBN 0-02-700070-2). Macmillan.
--Black Out Loud: An Anthology of Modern Poems by Black Americans. LC 74-99117. (Illus.). (gr. 4 up). 1970. 5.95g o.s.i. (ISBN 0-02-700100-8). Macmillan.
--Brothers & Sisters. LC 76-102961. (Modern Stories by Black Americans Ser). (gr. 7 up). 1970. 6.95g o.s.i. (ISBN 0-02-700130-X). Macmillan.
--I Am the Darker Brother: An Anthology of Modern Poems by Negro Americans. LC 68-12077. (gr. 7 up). 1968. 8.95 (ISBN 0-02-700080-X); pap. text ed. 2.12 (ISBN 0-02-296520-3). Macmillan.
--My Black Me: A Beginning Book of Black Poetry. LC 73-16445. 96p. (gr. 3 up). 1974. PLB 8.95 (ISBN 0-525-35460-3). Dutton.
Adolph, L. & Lorenz, Rita. Diagnostico Enzimatico en las Enfermedades de Corazon, Higado y Pancreas. (Illus.). 126p. 1980. soft cover 13.25 (ISBN 3-8055-0506-X). S Karger.
Adomeit, Hannes, ed. Foreign Policy Making in Communist Countries. LC 78-70493. (Praeger Special Studies). 172p. 1979. 22.95 (ISBN 0-03-046201-0). Praeger.
Adomeit, Ruth. Three Centuries of Thumb Bibles. LC 78-68238. (Garland Reference Library of Humanities). (Illus.). 435p. 1980. 60.00 (ISBN 0-8240-9818-8). Garland Pub.
Adomian, G., ed. Applied Stochastic Processes. 1980. 21.00 (ISBN 0-12-044380-5). Acad Pr.
Adorjan, Carol. The Electric Man. LC 80-27107. (Prime Time Adventures Ser.). (Illus.). 64p. (gr. 4 up). 1981. PLB 7.95 (ISBN 0-516-02104-4). Childrens.
--The Pig Party. (Prime Time Adventures Ser.). (Illus.). 64p. (gr. 4 up). 1981. PLB 7.95 (ISBN 0-516-02108-7). Childrens.
Adorno, T. W., et al. Authoritarian Personality. 1969. pap. 9.95 o.p. (ISBN 0-393-00492-9, N492, Norton Lib). Norton.
Adorno, Theodor. In Search of Wagner. 160p. 1981. 14.50 (ISBN 0-8052-7087-6, Pub. by NLB England). Schocken.
Adorno, Theodor W. Minima Moralia: Reflexionen Aus Dem Beschaedigten Leben. (Gesammelte Schriften: Vol. 4). 350p. Date not set. text ed. 24.70 (ISBN 3-518-07496-2, Pub. by Insel Verlag Germany); pap. 16.90 quality paper (ISBN 3-518-07496-2). Suhrkamp.
--Negative Dialectics. LC 77-11720. 1973. 19.50 o.p. (ISBN 0-8164-9129-1). Continuum.
Adovasio, James M. Basketry Technology: A Guide to Identification & Analysis. (Manuals on Archeology Ser.: No. 1). (Illus.). x, 182p. 1977. 18.00x (ISBN 0-202-33035-4). Taraxacum.
Adriaansens, Hans P. Talcott Parsons & the Conceptual Dilemma. (International Library of Sociology). (Illus.). 224p. 1980. 27.50x (ISBN 0-7100-0519-9). Routledge & Kegan.
Adrian. CM: The Construction Management Process. (Illus.). 368p. 1981. text ed. 18.95 (ISBN 0-8359-0829-1). Reston.
Adrian, Edgar D. Mechanism of Nervous Action. rev ed. LC 33-4029. 1959. 12.50x (ISBN 0-8122-7118-1). U of Pa Pr.
Adrian, Mary. A Day & a Night in a Forest. (Illus.). Date not set. 4.95 (ISBN 0-8038-1513-1). Hastings.
--The Fireball Mystery. (Illus.). (gr. 2-6). 1977. 6.95 (ISBN 0-8038-2325-8). Hastings.
--Kite Mystery. LC 67-25609. (Illus.). (gr. 4-6). 1968. 5.95 (ISBN 0-8038-3937-5); PLB 3.33 (ISBN 0-8038-3938-3). Hastings.
--Secret Neighbors: Wildlife in a City Lot. (Illus.). (gr. 2-5). 1972. 5.95g (ISBN 0-8038-6708-5). Hastings.
--Skin Diving Mystery. Date not set. 5.95 (ISBN 0-8038-6719-0). Hastings.
Adrian, R. H. Reviews of Physiology, Biochemistry, & Pharmacology, Vol. 88. (Illus.). 280p. 1981. 52.00 (ISBN 0-387-10408-9). Springer-Verlag.
Adrian, R. H., ed. Reviews of Physiology, Biochemistry & Pharmacology, Vol. 89. (Illus.). 260p. 1981. 54.30 (ISBN 0-387-10495-X). Springer-Verlag.
Adrian, R. H., et al, eds. Reviews of Physiology, Biochemistry & Pharmacology, Vol. 77. LC 74-3674. (Illus.). 1977. 61.10 (ISBN 0-387-07963-7). Springer-Verlag.
Adrian, Werner. Freaks: Cinema of the Bizarre. (Illus.). 104p. 1976. pap. 3.95 o.s.i. (ISBN 0-446-87101-X). Warner Bks.
Adriani, John. The Chemistry & Physics of Anesthesia. 2nd ed. (Illus.). 862p. 1979. 39.75 (ISBN 0-398-00011-5). C C Thomas.
--Drugs, the Drug Industry & Prices. LC 70-176187. 192p. 1981. 10.50 (ISBN 0-87527-196-0). Green.
--Labat's Regional Anesthesia: Techniques & Clinical Applications. 4th ed. (Modern Concepts of Medicine). (Illus.). 600p. 1981. 48.75x (ISBN 0-87527-187-1). Green.
--Techniques & Procedures of Anesthesia. 3rd ed. 668p. 1972. pap. 48.75 photocopy ed. spiral (ISBN 0-398-00015-8). C C Thomas.
Adriani, John & Eaton, J. D. The Law & Health Professionals: Fundamentals of the Law & Malpractice. 144p. 1981. 10.50x (ISBN 0-87527-189-8). Green.
Adrichem, Christianus van. A Briefe Description of Hierusalem, Also a Mappe. Tymme, T., tr. LC 70-29008. (English Experience Ser.: No. 125). 1969. Repr. of 1595 ed. 21.00 (ISBN 90-221-0125-8). Walter J Johnson.
Adrienne. German in Thirty-Two Lessons. (Gimmick Ser.). 1979. 10.95 (ISBN 0-393-04527-7); pap. 5.95 (ISBN 0-393-04533-1). Norton.
Adrion. The Art of Magic. 1981. pap. 8.95 (ISBN 0-8120-2248-3). Barron.
Adult Education Association of the U. S. A., jt. auth. see ERIC.
Advanced Learning Inc. Auto Body Repair for the Do-It-Yourselfer. LC 76-1132. 1976. pap. 6.95 (ISBN 0-672-23238-3). Audel.
Advanced Learning, Inc. Can-Do Tune-up: Pinto & Vega Cars, 1971-74. 1975. pap. 4.95 (ISBN 0-672-23849-7); pap. 7.95, with cassette tape (ISBN 0-672-23831-4, 23831). Audel.
--Can-Do Tune-up: Toyota & Datsun Cars, 1964-74. 1975. pap. 4.95 (ISBN 0-672-23850-0); pap. 7.95, with cassette tape (ISBN 0-672-23835-7, 23835). Audel.
Advanced Study Institute on Toxicity of Pesticides Used on Livestock, Lethbridge, 13-21 July, 1970 & Khan, M. A. Toxicology, Biodegradation & Efficacy of Livestock Pesticides: Proceedings. 444p. 1972. text ed. 42.25 (ISBN 90-265-0158-7, Pub. by Swets Pub Serv Holland). Swets North Am.
Advances in Diagnosis & Therapy, Muenchen, November 1980. Congress on Microcirculation & Ischemic Vascular Diseases. Messmer, K. & Fagrell, B., eds. (Illus.). 240p. 1981. pap. 24.00 (ISBN 3-8055-2417-X). S Karger.
Advisory Board on Military Personnel Supplies. Cellular Plastics. 1967. 13.00 o.p. (ISBN 0-309-01462-X). Natl Acad Pr.
Advisory Committee For Assessment Of University Based Institutes For Research On Poverty. Policy & Program Research in a University Setting: A Case Study. LC 70-174752. 1971. pap. text ed. 3.00 (ISBN 0-309-01929-X). Natl Acad Pr.
Advisory Committee to the Dept of Housing & Urban Development. Revenue Sharing & the Planning Process: Shifting the Locus of Responsibility for Domestic Problem Solving. LC 74-6418. 108p. 1974. pap. 6.25 (ISBN 0-309-02214-2). Natl Acad Pr.
Advisory Group Meeting, Vienna, Jan. 27-31, 1975. Interpretation of Environmental Isotope and Hydrochemcal Data in Groundwater Hydrology: Proceedings. (Panel Proceedings Ser.). (Illus., Orig.). 1976. pap. 18.25 (ISBN 92-0-141076-X, IAEA). Unipub.
Ady, Cecilia M. Bentivoglio of Bologna: A Study in Despotism. 1937. 11.00x o.p. (ISBN 0-19-821481-2). Oxford U Pr.
Ady, Doris M. Curries from the Sultan's Kitchen. rev. ed. (Illus.). 126p. 1980. pap. 8.25 (ISBN 0-589-50188-7, Pub. by Reed Books Australia). C E Tuttle.
Adzema, Robert & Jones, Mablen. The Great Sundial Cutout Book. LC 78-52964. 1978. pap. 9.95 (ISBN 0-8015-3117-9, Hawthorn). Dutton.
Aebi, Harry, jt. auth. see Aebi, Ormond.
Aebi, Ormond & Aebi, Harry. The Art & Adventure of Beekeeping. LC 74-14661. (Illus.). 224p. 1975. 9.95 (ISBN 0-913300-39-X); pap. 5.95 (ISBN 0-913300-38-1). Unity Pr.
AElfric. AElfric's Catholic Homilies: The Second Series Text. Godden, Malcolm, ed. (Early English Text Soc., Supplementary Ser.: No. 5). (Illus.). 480p. 1979. text ed. 49.50x (ISBN 0-19-722405-9). Oxford U Pr.
Aelfric, Abbot. A Testimonie of Antique. LC 73-36208. (English Experience Ser.: No. 214). Repr. of 1567 ed. 13.00 (ISBN 90-221-0214-9). Walter J Johnson.
Aelianus, Tacitus. The Art of Embattailing an Army, or the Second Part of Aelian's Tacticks. Bingham, J., tr. LC 68-54605. (English Experience Ser.: No. 70). Repr. of 1629 ed. 21.00 (ISBN 90-221-0070-7). Walter J Johnson.
Aelinanus, Tacitus. The Tacticks of Aelign, or Art of Embattailing an Army. Bingham, J., tr. LC 68-54606. (English Experience Ser.: No. 14). (Illus.). Repr. of 1616 ed. 42.00 (ISBN 90-221-0014-6). Walter J Johnson.
Aelred Of Rievaulx. Dialogue on the Soul. (Cistercian Fathers Ser.: No. 22). Orig. Title: De Anima. 1981. price not set (ISBN 0-87907-222-9). Cistercian Pubns.
Aerial Photo. Aerial America: From Sea to Shining Sea. Date not set. 3.95 (ISBN 0-936672-11-0). Aerial Photo.
--The Blowing Rock: North Carolina. Date not set. 1.50 (ISBN 0-936672-08-0). Aerial Photo.
--Coastal North Carolina Picture Book. Date not set. 2.00 (ISBN 0-936672-10-2). Aerial Photo.
Aero Medical Center Staff, tr. see Surgeon General, USAF.
Aero, Rita. Things Chinese. LC 79-6852. (Illus.). 256p. 1980. 24.95 (ISBN 0-385-17258-3). Doubleday.
--Things Chinese. LC 79-6852. (Illus.). 320p. 1980. pap. 10.95 (ISBN 0-385-15673-1, Dolp). Doubleday.
Aero Staff. Airman's Information Manual, 1981. LC 70-186849. 256p. 1981. pap. write for info. (ISBN 0-8168-1360-4). Aero.
--Federal Aviation Regulations for Pilots. LC 60-10472. 112p. 1981. pap. write for info. (ISBN 0-8168-5737-7). Aero.
--Nineteen Eighty A. I. M. LC 70-186849. 192p. 1980. 4.50 (ISBN 0-8168-1359-0). Aero.
--Nineteen Eighty F. A. R. LC 60-10472. 112p. 1980. 3.50 (ISBN 0-8168-5736-9). Aero.
Aers, D., ed. see Milton, J.
Aerts, Jan. Pigeon Racing. 1973. 14.95 (ISBN 0-571-08287-4, Pub. by Faber & Faber). Merrimack Bk Serv.
--Pigeon Racing: Advanced Techniques. (Illus.). 192p. 1981. pap. 7.95 (ISBN 0-571-11572-1, Pub. by Faber & Faber). Merrimack Bk Serv.
Aeschylus. The Agamemnon. Murray, Gilbert, tr. 1920. pap. text ed. 3.95x (ISBN 0-04-882002-4). Allen Unwin.
--The Choephoroe. Murray, Gilbert, tr. 1923. pap. text ed. 3.95x (ISBN 0-04-882004-0). Allen Unwin.
--The Eumenides. Murray, Gilbert, tr. 1925. pap. text ed. 3.95x (ISBN 0-04-882007-5). Allen Unwin.
--Oresteian Trilogy. Vellacott, Philip, tr. Incl. Agamemnon; Choephori; Eumenides. (Classics Ser.). (Orig.). (YA) (gr. 9 up). 1956. pap. 2.50 (ISBN 0-14-044067-4). Penguin.
--Plays. Cookson, G. M., tr. 1956. 10.50x (ISBN 0-460-00062-4, Evman). Dutton.
--Prometheus Bound. Anderson, Warren D., tr. (Orig.). 1963. pap. 2.95 (ISBN 0-672-60357-8, LLA143). Bobbs.
--Prometheus Bound. Arrowsmith, William, ed. Scully, James & Herington, C. John, trs. from Greek. (The Greek Tragedy in New Translations Ser.). 112p. 1975. 10.95 (ISBN 0-19-501934-2). Oxford U Pr.
--Prometheus Bound & Other Plays. Vellacott, Philip, tr. Incl. Suppliants; Seven Against Thebes; Persians. (Classics Ser.). (Orig.). 1961. pap. 2.75 (ISBN 0-14-044112-3). Penguin.
--The Seven Against Thebes. Murray, Gilbert, tr. 1935. pap. text ed. 3.95x (ISBN 0-04-882015-6). Allen Unwin.
--Seven Against Thebes: Greek Tragedy Ser. Hecht, Anthony & Bacon, Helen, trs. (The Greek Tragedy in New Translations Ser.). 80p. 1973. 10.95 (ISBN 0-19-501732-3). Oxford U Pr.
--The Suppliant Women. Murray, Gilbert, tr. 1930. pap. text ed. 3.95x (ISBN 0-04-882017-2). Allen Unwin.
--The Suppliants. Arrowsmith, William, ed. Lembke, Janet, tr. from Greek. (The Greek Tragedy in New Translations Ser.). 110p. 1975. 10.95 (ISBN 0-19-501933-4). Oxford U Pr.
Aeschylus & Aeschylus. Agamemnon. Lloyd-Jones, Hugh, tr. from Greek. 1979. 20.00x (ISBN 0-7156-1365-0, Pub. by Duckworth England); pap. text ed. 6.75x (ISBN 0-7156-1367-7, Pub. by Duckworth England). Biblio Dist.
Aesop. The Book of the Subtyl Historyes & Fables of Esope. LC 76-177403. (English Experience Ser.: No. 439). 288p. Repr. of 1484 ed. 49.00 (ISBN 90-221-0439-7). Walter J Johnson.
--The Caldecott Aesop-Twenty Fables. LC 77-88424. (gr. 3-9). 1978. 12.95 (ISBN 0-385-12653-0); PLB (ISBN 0-385-12654-9). Doubleday.
--Fables of Aesop. Jacobs, Joseph, ed. (New Children's Classics). (gr. 3 up). 1964. 4.95g o.s.i. (ISBN 0-02-700160-1). Macmillan.
--The Morall Fabillis of Esope in Scottis Meter Be Maister Henrisone. LC 79-25964. (English Experience Ser.: No. 282). 104p. 1970. Repr. of 1570 ed. 14.00 (ISBN 90-221-0282-3). Walter J Johnson.
--Town Mouse & the Country Mouse. new ed. LC 78-18062. (Illus.). (gr. 1-4). 1979. PLB 5.21 (ISBN 0-89375-131-6); pap. 1.50 (ISBN 0-89375-109-X). Troll Assocs.
Aesopus. The Book of Subtyl Histories & Fables of Esope. Bd. with The Siege of Rhodes. Caoursin, Guillaume. LC 76-14086. 1975. Repr. of 1484 ed. 34.00x (ISBN 0-8201-1154-6). Schol Facsimilies.
Afanas'Ev, Aleksandr. Russian Fairy Tales. LC 44-37884. (gr. 6 up). 1976. pap. 6.95 (ISBN 0-394-73090-9). Pantheon.
Afanasev, Aleksandr N. Erotic Tales of Old Russia. Perkov, Yury, tr. (Orig., Eng. & Rus.). 1980. pap. 5.95 (ISBN 0-933884-07-9). Berkeley Slavic.
Afanasyev, Alexander, compiled By. Russian Folk Tales: Illustrated by Ivan Bilibin. Chandler, Robert, tr. from Russian. LC 80-50746. (Illus.). 80p. 1980. 14.95 (ISBN 0-394-51353-3). Shambhala Pubns.
Affleck, James Q., et al. Teaching the Mildly Handicapped in the Regular Classroom. 2nd ed. (Special Education Ser.). 192p. pap. text ed. 7.50 (ISBN 0-675-08132-7). Merrill.
Affonso, Dyanne D. Impact of Cesarean Childbirth. 1981. write for info. (ISBN 0-8036-0034-8). Davis Co.
Afgan, N., jt. ed. see Spalding, D. Brian.
Afgan, Naim H., jt. ed. see Spalding, D. Brian.
Afghan, B. K. & Mackay, D., eds. Hydrocarbons & Halogenated Hydrocarbons in the Aquatic Environment. LC 79-26462. (Environmental Science Research Ser.: Vol. 16). 602p. 1980. 59.50 (ISBN 0-306-40329-3, Plenum Pr). Plenum Pub.
AFIPS Taxonomy Committee & Ashenhurst, Robert L. Taxonomy of Computer Science & Engineering. LC 79-57474. ix, 462p. 1980. 35.00 (ISBN 0-88283-008-2). AFIPS Pr.
Aflalo, F. G., jt. ed. see Peek, Hedley.
Afriat, S. N. The Price Index. LC 77-2134. (Illus.). 1978. 29.50 (ISBN 0-521-21665-6). Cambridge U Pr.
Africa Information Service, ed. see Cabral, Amilcar.
Africa, Thomas W. Ancient World. (Illus., Orig.). 1969. pap. text ed. 12.50 (ISBN 0-395-04095-7, 3-00250). HM.
--The Immense Majesty: A History of Rome & the Roman Empire. LC 73-14536. 1974. 14.75x (ISBN 0-88295-700-7). AHM Pub.
African Literature Association. Artist & Audience. 1979. 22.00 (ISBN 0-89410-122-6); pap. 15.00 (ISBN 0-89410-123-4). Three Continents.
African Studies Association of the United Kingdom, 1972. The Population Factor in African Studies: Proceedings. Moss, R. P. & Rathbone, R. J., eds. 240p. 1975. text ed. 17.00 (ISBN 0-8419-6200-6). Holmes & Meier.
Africano, Lillian, jt. auth. see Stutman, Fred A.
Afrow, Mitchell L., jt. auth. see Alpers, Byron J.
Afshar, F., et al. Stereotaxic Atlas of the Human Brainstem & Cerebellar Nuclei: A Variability Study. LC 76-5676. 1978. 156.00 (ISBN 0-89004-132-6). Raven.
Afxentiou, Panayiotis C. Patterns of Government Revenue & Expenditure in Developing Countries & Their Relevance to Policy. LC 80-119979. (Center for Planning & Economic Research Ser.: No. 35). 70p. (Orig.). 1979. pap. 7.50x (ISBN 0-8002-2319-5). Intl Pubns Serv.
Afzelius, B., ed. The Functional Anatomy of the Spermatazoan. 1975. text ed. 79.00 (ISBN 0-08-018006-X). Pergamon.
Agajanian, A. H., ed. MOSFET Technology--a Comprehensive Bibliography. 305p. 1980. 95.00 (ISBN 0-306-65193-9). IFI Plenum.
Agapius, et al. The Rudder. Orthodox Christian Educational Society & Makrakis, Apostolos, eds. Cummings, Denver, tr. from Hellenic. Orig. Title: Pedalion. 1097p. 1957. 15.00x (ISBN 0-938366-00-9). Orthodox Chr.
Agar, Frederick A. The Deacon at Work. 1923. 3.25 (ISBN 0-8170-0783-0). Judson.
Agar, Herbert. The Perils of Democracy. LC 66-11684. (Background Ser.). 95p. 1965. 6.25 (ISBN 0-8023-1001-X). Dufour.
Agar, Michael H. The Professional Stranger: An Informal Introduction to Ethnography. LC 79-8870. (Studies in Anthropology). 1980. 12.50 (ISBN 0-12-043850-X). Acad Pr.

Agarbiceanu, I. I. & Popescu, I. M. Optical Methods of Radio-Frequency Spectroscopy. LC 74-22001. 310p. 1975. 62.95 (ISBN 0-470-00935-7). Halsted Pr.

Agard, A. The Reportorie of Records at Westminster. LC 72-225. (English Experience Ser.: No. 291). 1971. Repr. of 1631 ed. 22.00 (ISBN 90-221-0291-2). Walter J Johnson.

Agard, F. B., et al. English for Speakers of Spanish: El Ingles Hablado. 1980. text & cassettes 65.00 (ISBN 0-87950-312-2); cassettes, 5 dual tracts 60.00 (ISBN 0-87950-311-4). Spoken Lang Serv.

Agard, Frederick B., jt. auth. see Sola, Donald F.

Agard, Judith A., jt. auth. see Mopsik, Stanley I.

Agarwal, Bina. Monsoon-Poems. 1976. 8.00 (ISBN 0-89253-807-4); flexible cloth 4.00 (ISBN 0-89253-808-2). Ind-US Inc.

Agarwal, D. D., et al. Geometrical Drawing. 1980. text ed. 10.50x (ISBN 0-7069-0802-3, Pub. by Vikas India). Advent Bk.

Agarwala, Surendra, ed. see Heywood, John.

Agarwala-Rogers, Rekha, jt. auth. see Rogers, Everett M.

Agassi, Joseph, ed. see Gellner, Ernest.

Agassi, Judity B. Women on the Job: The Attitudes of Women to Their Work. LC 78-24789. (Illus.). 272p. 1979. 25.95 (ISBN 0-669-02815-0). Lexington Bks.

Agassiz, Louis. Lake Superior. 2nd ed. LC 73-89695. 476p. 1974. Repr. of 1850 ed. 24.50 o.p. (ISBN 0-88275-137-9). Krieger.

Agate, John. Geriatrics for Nurses & Social Workers. (Illus.). 1972. pap. 19.95x (ISBN 0-433-00204-2). Intl Ideas.

Agathias. Agathiae Myrinaei Historiarum Libri quinque. Keydell, Rudolfus, ed. (Corpus Fontium Historiae Byzantinae Ser. Berolinensis Vol. 2). 232p. (Lat). 1967. 48.25x (ISBN 3-11-001348-7). De Gruyter.

Agay, Denes. Best Loved Songs of the American People. LC 74-4502. 416p. 1975. 14.95 (ISBN 0-385-00004-9); pap. 7.95 (ISBN 0-385-14006-1). Doubleday.

--Teaching Piano. (Illus.). 1981. 29.95 (ISBN 0-8256-8039-5). Music Sales.

Agazarian, Yvonne & Peters, Richard. The Visible & Invisible Group: Two Perspectives on Group Psychotherapy & Group Process. (Illus.). 304p. 1981. 27.50 (ISBN 0-7100-0692-6). Routledge & Kegan.

Agee, Anne & Kline, Gary. The Basic Writer's Book. (Illus.). 384p. 1981. text ed. 11.95 (ISBN 0-13-069476-2). P-H.

Agee, James. Death in the Family. (Literature Ser). (gr. 10-12). 1970. pap. text ed. 4.25 (ISBN 0-87720-750-X). AMSCO Sch.

Agee, Joel. Twelve Years: An American Boyhood in East Germany. 1981. 10.95 (ISBN 0-374-27958-6). FS&G.

Agee, Vicki L. Treatment of the Violent Incorrigible Adolescent. LC 78-24653. (Illus.). 1979. 17.95 (ISBN 0-669-02811-8). Lexington Bks.

Agee, William C., jt. auth. see Hamilton, George H.

Agel, Jerome, ed. Rough Times. (Orig.). 1973. pap. 1.65 o.p. (ISBN 0-345-23059-0). Ballantine.

Ageloff, Roy & Mojena, Richard. Applied Basic Programming. 464p. 1980. pap. text ed. 14.95x (ISBN 0-534-00808-9). Wadsworth Pub.

Agenbroad, Larry D. The Hudson-Meng Site: An Alberta Bison Kill in the Nebraska High Plains. LC 78-57606. (Illus.). 1978. pap. text ed. 10.00 (ISBN 0-8191-0530-9). U Pr of Amer.

Ager, D. V. Introducing Geology. 2nd ed. (Illus.). 1975. 12.95 (ISBN 0-571-04857-9, Pub. by Faber & Faber); pap. 8.95 (ISBN 0-571-04858-7). Merrimack Bk Serv.

--Nature of the Stratigraphical Record. 2nd ed. 136p. 1981. 17.95 (ISBN 0-470-27052-7). Halsted Pr.

Ager, Derek V. The Geology of Europe. 576p. 1980. 44.95x (ISBN 0-470-26990-1). Halsted Pr.

Ager, Stanley & St. Auby, Fiona. Ager's Way to Easy Elegance: Ager the Butler's Guide to Clothes Care, Managing the Table, Running Your Home & Other Graces. LC 80-673. 176p. 1980. 14.95 (ISBN 0-672-52665-4). Bobbs.

Agerskov, Michael. Some Psychic Experiences & Their Results. LC 79-9596. Orig. Title: Nogle Psykiske Oplevelser. 84p. 1979. pap. 3.25 (ISBN 87-87871-54-8). Toward the Light.

Agerskov, Michael, ed. The Doctrine of Atonement & the Shorter Road. LC 79-9595. Orig. Title: Forsoningslaeren Og Genvejen. 1979. pap. 2.95 (ISBN 87-87871-56-4). Toward the Light.

--Questions & Answers: First & Second Supplement to "Toward the Light". LC 79-9594. Orig. Title: Sporgsmaal Og Svar. 244p. 1979. pap. 6.95 (ISBN 87-87871-52-1). Toward the Light.

--Toward the Light: A Message to Mankind from the Transcendental World. LC 79-9599. Orig. Title: Vandrer Mod Lyset. 348p. 1979. 11.95 (ISBN 87-87871-50-5); pap. 7.95 (ISBN 0-686-27618-3). Toward the Light.

Agerter, Sharlene & Glock, Waldo S. An Annotated Bibliography of Tree Growth & Growth Rings, 1950-62. LC 64-17274. 1965. 2.00 (ISBN 0-8165-0002-9). U of Ariz Pr.

Ageton, Arthur A. & Mack, William P. Naval Officer's Guide. 8th ed. LC 43-4401. (Illus.). 1970. 12.00x o.s.i. (ISBN 0-87021-432-2). Naval Inst Pr.

Agey, C. Buell, jt. auth. see Roberts, Leonard W.

Aggarwal, Raj. International Business Finance. 1981. 19.95 (ISBN 0-03-047191-5). Praeger.

Aggarwal, S. L., jt. auth. see Ambrose, R. J.

Aggarwala, S. N. Corrected Age Data of the 1931 Indian Census. 1967. 5.50x o.p. (ISBN 0-210-22722-2). Asia.

Agger, L. T. Introduction to Electricity. 1971. 29.95x (ISBN 0-19-859306-6). Oxford U Pr.

Agh, Attila. Labyrinth in the Mode of Production Controversy. (Studies on Developing Countries: No. 105). 79p. (Orig.). 1980. pap. 8.50x (ISBN 963-301-062-4). Intl Pubns Serv.

Agle, Nan H. Maple Street. LC 78-97034. (gr. 3-7). 1970. 6.95 (ISBN 0-395-28838-X, Clarion). HM.

--Princess Mary of Maryland. LC 70-12561. (Illus.). viii, 109p. 1967. Repr. 15.00 (ISBN 0-8103-5029-7). Gale.

--Susan's Magic. LC 73-7124. (Illus.). 140p. (gr. 3-6). 1973. 6.95 o.p. (ISBN 0-8164-3108-6, Clarion). HM.

Agle, Nan H. & Wilson, Ellen. Three Boys & H-Two-O. LC 68-12513. (Encore Ser.). (Illus.). (gr. 2-6). 1968. write for info. (ISBN 0-684-13950-2, ScribJ). Scribner.

Agnelli Foundation. Guide to European Foundations. 350p. 1972. 25.00x (ISBN 0-231-03701-5). Columbia U Pr.

Agnew, John A., ed. Innovation Research & Public Policy. LC 80-12054. (Syracuse Geographical Ser.: No. 5). (Illus.). 310p. (Orig.). 1980. pap. 19.75 (ISBN 0-8357-0510-2, IS-00109, Pub. by Syracuse U Dept Geog). Univ Microfilms.

Agnew, Joseph. Life's Christ Places. 206p. 1911. text ed. 2.95 (ISBN 0-567-02008-8). Attic Pr.

Agnew, Neil M. & Pike, S. W. The Science Game: An Introduction to Research in the Behavorial Sciences. 2nd ed. (P-H Ser. in Experimental Psychology). (Illus.). 1978. pap. 10.95 (ISBN 0-13-795336-4). P-H.

Agnew, Spiro. The Canfield Decision. 1977. pap. 1.95 o.p. (ISBN 0-425-03338-4, Medallion). Berkley Pub.

Agnihotri, O. P. & Gupta, B. K. Solar Selective Surfaces. LC 80-17392. (Alternative Energy Ser.). 250p. 1981. 25.00 (ISBN 0-471-06035-6, Pub. by Wiley Interscience). Wiley.

Agnihotri, V. K. India & Other Poems. (Writers Workshop Redbird Book Ser.). 39p. 1975. 8.00 (ISBN 0-88253-562-5); pap. text ed. 4.00 (ISBN 0-88253-561-7). Ind-US Inc.

Agnoli, A., ed. Sixth Meeting of the Italian League Against Parkinson's Disease & Extrapyramidal Disorders, 1981. (Journal: Pharmacology: Vol. 22, No. 1). (Illus.). 92p. 1981. pap. write for info. (ISBN 3-8055-2322-X). S Karger.

Agnos, T. J. & Schatt, S. The Practical Law Enforcement Guide to Writing Field Reports, Grant Proposals, Memos, & Resumes. 136p. 1980. pap. 11.75 (ISBN 0-398-04042-7). C C Thomas.

Agor, Weston H. Chilean Senate: Internal Distribution of Influence. (Latin American Monograph Ser.: No. 23). 1971. 11.95 (ISBN 0-292-70146-2). U of Tex Pr.

Agostini, Beatrice, tr. see McConkey, James H.

Agras, W. Stewart, et al. Behavior Therapy: Toward an Applied Clinical Science. LC 78-32069. (Psychology Ser.). (Illus.). 1979. text ed. 14.95x (ISBN 0-7167-1086-2); pap. text ed. 7.95x (ISBN 0-7167-1087-0). W H Freeman.

Agrawal, A. N. Indian Agriculture: Problems, Progress & Prospects. 1980. text ed. 25.00x (ISBN 0-7069-0683-7, Pub. by Vikas India). Advent Bk.

Agrawal, A. N. & Lal, Kundan. Economic Planning. 2nd rev. ed. 400p. 1980. text ed. 18.95 (ISBN 0-7069-1256-X, Pub. by Vikas India). Advent Bk.

Agrawal, Ashok K. & Guppy, James G., eds. Decay Heat Removal & Natural Convection in Fast Breeder Reactors. LC 81-329. 500p. 1981. text ed. 55.00 (ISBN 0-89116-196-1). Hemisphere Pub.

Agrawal, D. & Chakravarti, D., eds. Essays in Indian Protohistory. 1980. text ed. 42.00x (ISBN 0-391-01866-3). Humanities.

Agrawal, D. P. The Archaeology of India. (Scandinavian Institute of Asian Studies Monograph). (Illus.). 320p. 1981. pap. text ed. 23.50 (ISBN 0-7007-0140-0). Humanities.

Agrawal, H. N. A Portrait of Nationalised Banks. 334p. 1980. text ed. 18.00x (ISBN 0-391-02130-3). Humanities.

Agrawal, O. P. Paintings & MS of Southeast Asia. 1981. text ed. price not set. Butterworths.

Agree, Rose H. How to Eat a Poem & Other Morsels: A Collection of Food Poems for Children. (Illus.). (gr. 2-5). 1967. PLB 4.99 o.s.i. (ISBN 0-394-91622-0). Pantheon.

Agricola, Erhard. Semantische Relationen im Text und im System. (Janua Linguarum, Ser. Minor: No. 113). 1972. pap. text ed. 22.50x (ISBN 90-279-1977-1). Mouton.

Agricola, Johannes. Die Sprichwoertersammlungen, 2 vols. Gilman, Sander L., ed. (Ausgaben Deutscher Literatur des Xv. Bis Xviii Jahrhunders). 989p. 1971. 182.35x (ISBN 3-11-003710-6). De Gruyter.

Agricultural & Renewable Resources Board & Food & Nutrition Board, Natural Research Council. Fat Content & Composition of Animal Products. LC 76-6496. 1976. pap. 9.75 (ISBN 0-309-02440-4). Natl Acad Pr.

Agricultural Board. Aquatic Animal Health. LC 73-15707. 1973. pap. 3.00 (ISBN 0-309-02142-1). Natl Acad Pr.

--Body Composition in Animals & Man. 1968. pap. 14.25 (ISBN 0-309-01598-7). Natl Acad Pr.

--Communication for Change with the Rural Disadvantaged. LC 72-186371. 1972. pap. 4.25 (ISBN 0-309-01942-7). Natl Acad Pr.

--Nutrient Requirements of Laboratory Animals. rev. 3rd ed. LC 54-60841. (Illus.). 128p. 1978. pap. 6.75 (ISBN 0-309-02767-5). Natl Acad Pr.

--Nutrient Requirements of Trout, Salmon & Catfish. (Nutrient Requirements of Domestic Animals Ser). (Illus.). 64p. 1973. pap. 4.50 (ISBN 0-309-02141-3). Natl Acad Pr.

--Pest Control: Strategies for the Future. LC 79-188497. (Illus.). 1972. pap. 7.00 (ISBN 0-309-01945-1). Natl Acad Pr.

--Principles of Plant & Animal Pest Control, Vol. 1, Plant-Disease Development & Control. 1968. pap. 6.00 (ISBN 0-309-01596-0). Natl Acad Pr.

--Principles of Plant & Animal Pest Control, Vol. 2, Weed Control. 1968. pap. 9.25 (ISBN 0-309-01597-9). Natl Acad Pr.

--Quality of Rural Living. LC 78-184629. 160p. 1971. pap. 3.75 (ISBN 0-309-01940-0). Natl Acad Pr.

--Soils of the Humid Tropics. LC 78-189475. (Illus.). 224p. 1972. pap. 8.25 (ISBN 0-309-01948-6). Natl Acad Pr.

Agricultural Board, ed. see Animal Nutrition.

Agricultural Board - Division Of Biology And Agriculture. Guide to Environmental Research on Animals. LC 76-609948. (Illus., Orig.). 1971. pap. 11.25 (ISBN 0-309-01869-2). Natl Acad Pr.

Agricultural Board Division of Biology and Agriculture. Principles of Plant & Animal Pest Control, Vol. 3, Insect-Pest Management & Control. 1969. pap. 11.75 (ISBN 0-309-01695-9). Natl Acad Pr.

Agricultural Board-Division of Biology & Agriculture. Remote Sensing with Special Reference to Agriculture & Forestry. LC 77-600961. (Illus.). 1970. 13.75 o.p. (ISBN 0-309-01723-8). Natl Acad Pr.

Agricultural Board. National Research Council. Effect of Processing on the Nutritional Value of Feeds. (Illus.). 536p. 1973. pap. 14.50 (ISBN 0-309-02116-2). Natl Acad Pr.

Agriculture & Renewable Resources Board, National Research Council. Urea & Other Nonprotein Nitrogen Compounds in Animal Nutrition. LC 76-8240. 1976. pap. 5.50 (ISBN 0-309-02444-7). Natl Acad Pr.

Agriculture Board. Principles of Plant & Animal Pest Control, Vol. 6, Effects Of Pesticides On Fruit & Vegetable Physiology. 1968. pap. 4.50 (ISBN 0-309-01698-3). Natl Acad Pr.

Agriculture et Societes En Asie Du Sudest. Etudes Rurales, Vol. 14, Nos. 53-56. (Illus.). 1974. pap. 50.50x (ISBN 0-686-20910-9). Mouton.

Agricutural Economics Dept., U. of Nanking, Chengtu. Economic Facts, 4 vols. LC 78-74325. (The Modern Chinese Economy Ser.: Vol. 11). 1980. Set. lib. bdg. 165.00 (ISBN 0-8240-4260-3). Garland Pub.

Agrios, George N. Plant Pathology. 2nd ed. 1978. 23.95 (ISBN 0-12-044560-3). Acad Pr.

Agris, Paul F. The Modified Nucleosides of Transfer RNA: A Bibliography of Biochemical & Biophysical Studis from 1970 to 1979. LC 80-81197. 219p. 1980. 24.00 (ISBN 0-8451-0207-9). A R Liss.

Aguayo, A. G. & Karpati, G., eds. Current Topics in Nerve & Muscle Research. LC 79-13037. (International Congress Ser.: No. 455). 328p. 1979. 58.75 (ISBN 0-444-90057-8, North Holland). Elsevier.

Aguayo, Jorge, tr. see Dewey, Melvil.

Aguero, Kathleen & Goodman, Miriam. Thirsty Day & Permanent Wave. LC 76-55615. 88p. 1977. pap. 4.95 (ISBN 0-914086-17-0). Alicejamesbooks.

Aguiar, Walter R. Maya Land in Color. (Profiles of America Ser.). (Illus.). 1978. 6.95 (ISBN 0-8038-4703-3). Hastings.

Aguilar, Juan & Gonzalez, Armando E., eds. Basic Latin American Legal Materials 1970-1975. LC 77-78814. (American Association of Law Libraries Publication Ser: No. 13). 1977. pap. 12.50x (ISBN 0-8377-0111-2). Rothman.

Aguilar, Rodolfo J. Systems Analysis & Design in Engineering, Architecture, Construction, & Planning. (Civil Engineering & Engineering Mechanics Ser). (Illus.). 448p. 1973. ref. ed. 25.95 (ISBN 0-13-881458-9). P-H.

Aguilera, Donna, jt. auth. see Topalis, Mary.

Aguilera, Donna C. Review of Psychiatric Nursing. LC 76-40460. 1977. pap. text ed. 8.50 (ISBN 0-8016-0090-1). Mosby.

Aguilera-Malta, Demetrio. Don Goyo. Brushwood, John & Brushwood, Carolyn, trs. from Span. LC 80-81656. (Contemporary Literature Ser.). (Illus.). 228p. 1980. 9.95 (ISBN 0-89603-019-9). Humana.

Aguilera Malta, Demetrio. Manuela (La Caballeresa Del Sol) A Novel. Jones, Willis K., tr. from Span. LC 67-11700. (Contemporary Latin American Classic). 320p. 1967. 9.95x (ISBN 0-8093-0256-X). S Ill U Pr.

Agulhon, Maurice. Marianne into Battle: Republican Imagery & Symbolism in France, 1789-1880. Lloyd, Janet, tr. (Co-Publication with the Maison Des Sciences De L'homme). (Illus.). 224p. Date not set. price not set (ISBN 0-521-23577-4); pap. price not set (ISBN 0-521-28224-1). Cambridge U Pr.

--Une Ville Ouvriere au Temps du Socialisme Utopique: Toulon De 1815 a 1851. 2nd ed. (Civilisations et Societes: No. 18). 1977. pap. 24.70 (ISBN 90-2796-287-1). Mouton.

Aguolu, Christian C. Ghana in the Humanities & Social Sciences, 1900-71: A Bibliography. LC 73-9519. 1973. 16.50 (ISBN 0-8108-0635-5). Scarecrow.

Agusiobo, Obiora N., jt. auth. see Olaitan, Samson O.

Agustin, Ruiz V. Arpa Sagrada. 1979. pap. 1.95 (ISBN 0-311-08751-5). Casa Bautista.

Agwani, M. S. Communism in the Arab East. 1970. 8.50x (ISBN 0-210-98157-1). Asia.

Ahana, Doris N. & Kunishi, Marilyn M. Cancer Care Protocols for Hospital & Home Care Use. LC 80-20348. 1980. text ed. 21.50 (ISBN 0-8261-3290-1); pap. text ed. 21.50 (ISBN 0-8261-3291-X). Springer Pub.

Aharoni, Yair. The No-Risk Society. (Chatham House Series on Change in American Politics). 320p. (Orig.). 1981. pap. text ed. 9.95x (ISBN 0-934540-06-3). Chatham Hse Pubs.

Aharoni, Yohanon & Avi-Yonah, Michael. The Macmillan Bible Atlas. rev. ed. LC 77-4313. (Illus.). 1977. 24.95 (ISBN 0-02-500590-1). Macmillan.

Aharonson, E. F., et al, eds. Air Pollution & the Lung. LC 76-3488. 313p. 1976. 64.95 (ISBN 0-470-15049-1). Halsted Pr.

Ahearn, Daniel S. Federal Reserve Policy Reappraised, 1951-1959. LC 63-10522. 1963. 18.00x (ISBN 0-231-02575-0). Columbia U Pr.

Ahern, Dee Dee & Bliss, Betsy. The Economics of Being a Woman. 1976. 8.95 o.s.i. (ISBN 0-02-500610-X). Macmillan.

Ahern, Emily M., ed. The Anthropology of Taiwanese Society. Gates, Hill. LC 79-64212. 480p. 1981. 30.00x (ISBN 0-8047-1043-0). Stanford U Pr.

Ahern, James F. Police in Trouble: Our Frightening Crisis in Law Enforcement. 256p. 1971. 9.95 (ISBN 0-8015-5928-6, Hawthorn). Dutton.

Ahern, Jerry J. Textbook of Cosmetology. 330p. 1980. pap. text ed. 7.00 (ISBN 0-8299-0309-7); study guide 4.50 (ISBN 0-8299-0319-4); answers to study guide avail. (ISBN 0-8299-0354-2); state board review questions 0.75 (ISBN 0-8299-0375-5); answers to state board review questions avail. (ISBN 0-8299-0379-8). West Pub.

--West's Textbook of Cosmetology. (Illus.). 500p. 1980. text ed. 15.95 (ISBN 0-8299-0343-7). West Pub.

Ahern, John E. The Exergy Method of Energy Systems Analysis. LC 79-24500. 1980. 27.50 (ISBN 0-471-05494-1, Pub. by Wiley-Interscience). Wiley.

Ahern, Maureen, tr. see Asturias, Miguel.

Ahern, Mrs. Robert L., ed. The Fine Arts Cookbook. (Illus.). 1970. spiral bdg. 7.95 (ISBN 0-87846-163-9). Mus Fine Arts Boston.

Ahl, David H., ed. More Basic Computer Games. LC 80-57619. (Illus.). 188p. 1980. pap. 8.95 (ISBN 0-89480-137-6). Workman Pub.

Ahlberg, Allan. Burglar Bill. LC 76-40339. (Illus.). (gr. k-3). 1977. 8.25 (ISBN 0-688-80078-5); PLB 7.92 (ISBN 0-688-84078-7). Greenwillow.

--Cops & Robbers. LC 78-5354. (Illus.). (gr. k-3). 1979. 7.75 (ISBN 0-688-80178-1); PLB 7.44 (ISBN 0-688-84178-3). Greenwillow.

--Funnybones. LC 79-2472. (Illus.). 32p. (gr. k-3). 1981. 7.95 (ISBN 0-688-80238-9); PLB 7.63 (ISBN 0-688-84238-0). Greenwillow.

Ahlberg, Allan, jt. auth. see Ahlberg, Janet.

Ahlberg, Janet & Ahlberg, Allan. The Old Joke Book. (Illus.). (gr. 2-5). 1979. pap. 2.50 (ISBN 0-14-050333-1, Puffin). Penguin.

Ahlborn, Boye, et al, eds. Shock Tube & Shock Wave Research: Proceedings of the Eleventh International Symposium on Shock Tubes & Waves. LC 77-20168. (Illus.). 670p. 1978. 45.00 (ISBN 0-295-95582-1). U of Wash Pr.

Ahlborn, Lois A., jt. auth. see Strayer, Judy.

Ahlbrandt, Roger S. & Brophy, Paul C. Neighborhood Revitalization: Theory & Practice. LC 75-12483. 224p. 1975. 18.95 (ISBN 0-669-00026-4). Lexington Bks.

Ahlfeld, Helmut, ed. Licht's International Sugar Economic Yearbook & Directory 1979. LC 51-36145. (Illus.). 522p. (Eng. & Ger.). 1979. 85.00x (ISBN 0-8002-2348-9). Intl Pubns Serv.

Ahlstrand, Alan. Capri Service Repair Handbook All Models, 1970-1976. 2nd ed. Robinson, Jeff, ed. (Illus.). 1976. pap. text ed. 10.95 (ISBN 0-89287-110-5, A143). Clymer Pubns.

--Chevy Nova Nineteen Seventy-One to Nineteen Seventy-Nine: Shop Manual. Jorgensen, Eric, ed. (Illus.). 362p. (Orig.). 1980. pap. text ed. 10.95 (ISBN 0-89287-317-5, A133). Clymer Pubns.

--Datsun Five-Ten 1978-1979 Shop Manual. Jorgensen, Eric, ed. (Illus.). 313p. (Orig.). 1979. pap. text ed. 10.95 (ISBN 0-89287-244-6, A201). Clymer Pubns.

--Datsun Service-Repair Handbook L521, P1521, P1620 Pickups, 1968-1980. new ed. Robinson, Jeff, ed. (Illus.). 1977. pap. 10.95 (ISBN 0-89287-151-2, A-148). Clymer Pubns.

--Datsun Service Repair Handbook 510, 610, & 710, 1968-1977. 3rd ed. Robinson, Jeff, ed. (Illus.). 1979. pap. text ed. 10.95 (ISBN 0-89287-281-0, A149). Clymer Pubns.

--Datsun Twelve Hundred & B-Two Ten: 1971-78 Service-Repair Handbook. Robinson, Jeff, ed. (Illus.). 1978. pap. 10.95 (ISBN 0-89287-284-5, A151). Clymer Pubns.

--Datsun Two-Forty, Two-Sixty & Two-Eighty-Z & ZX: 1970-79 Service-Repair Handbook. 4th ed. Jorgensen, Eric, ed. (Illus.). 1978. pap. 10.95 (ISBN 0-89287-290-X, A152). Clymer Pubns.

--Datsun Two Hundred SX 1977-1979 Shop Manual. Jorgensen, Eric, ed. (Illus.). 184p. (Orig.). 1979. pap. text ed. 10.95 (ISBN 0-89287-294-2, A200). Clymer Pubns.

--Datsun Two Hundred Ten: Nineteen Seventy-Nine to Nineteen Eighty Shop Manual. Jorgensen, Eric, ed. (Illus.). 336p. (Orig.). 1980. pap. text ed. 11.95 (ISBN 0-89287-322-1, A 203). Clymer Pubns.

--Datsun 810: 1977-1980 Shop Manual. Jorgensen, Eric, ed. (Illus.). 296p. 1980. pap. 10.95 (ISBN 0-89287-334-5). Clymer Pubns.

--Mazda Service Repair Handbook. Jorgensen, Eric, ed. (RX-2 & RX-3, 1971-1977). (Illus.). 1978. pap. 10.95 (ISBN 0-89287-236-5, A164). Clymer Pubns.

--MGA-MGB All Models: 1956-1979 Service, Repair Handbook. 3rd ed. Robinson, Jeff, ed. (Illus.). 1978. pap. 10.95 (ISBN 0-89287-279-9, A165). Clymer Pubns.

--Pinto Service Repair Handbook: All Models 1971-1979. Jorgensen, Eric, ed. (Illus.). 1978. pap. 10.95 (ISBN 0-89287-211-X, A171). Clymer Pubns.

--Plymouth Arrow: 1976-1977 Shop Manual. Jorgensen, Eric, ed. (Illus.). 1979. pap. 10.95 (ISBN 0-89287-275-6, A178). Clymer Pubns.

--Sprite--MG Midget Service--Repair Handbook: All Models, 1958-1979. Robinson, Jeff, ed. (Illus.). 1977. pap. 10.95 (ISBN 0-89287-164-4, A205). Clymer Pubns.

--Toyota Service-Repair Handbook: Corona, Mark II & Celica, 1970-1978. Jorgensen, Eric, ed. (Illus.). 1978. pap. 10.95 (ISBN 0-89287-217-9, A192). Clymer Pubns.

--Toyota Service Repair Handbook: Pickups, 1968-1979. Jorgensen, Eric, ed. (Illus.). 1978. pap. 10.95 (ISBN 0-89287-205-5, A193). Clymer Pubns.

--Triumph Service-Repair Handbook: TR 7 Series, 1975-1978. Jorgensen, Eric, ed. (Illus.). 1978. pap. 10.95 (ISBN 0-89287-206-3, A211). Clymer Pubns.

Ahlstrand, Eric. Datsun F Ten & Three Hundred Ten: Nineteen Seventy-Six to Seventy-Nine Shop Manual. (Illus.). 186p. (Orig.). 1980. pap. text ed. 10.95 (ISBN 0-89287-318-3, A202). Clymer Pubns.

Ahlstrom, S. E. Religious History of the American People, 2 vols. LC 75-22362. (Illus.). 720p. 1975. pap. 3.50 ea. (Im); Vol. 1. pap. (ISBN 0-385-11164-9); Vol. 2. pap. (ISBN 0-385-11165-7). Doubleday.

Ahlstrom, Sydney E., ed. Theology in America: The Major Protestant Voices from Puritanism to Neo-Orthodoxy. LC 67-21401. 1967. pap. 13.50 (ISBN 0-672-60118-4, AHS73). Bobbs.

Ahluwalia, H. P. The Hermit Kingdom: Ladakh. (Illus.). 180p. 1981. text ed. 50.00x (ISBN 0-7069-1022-2, Pub. by Vikas India). Advent Bk.

Ahmad, Feroz. The Turkish Experiment in Democracy: 1950 to 1975. LC 76-25499. 1977. lib. bdg. 35.00x (ISBN 0-89158-629-6). Westview.

Ahmad, I. Letters from the Great Turke. LC 72-164. (English Experience Ser.: No. 292). 16p. Repr. of 1606 ed. 7.00 (ISBN 90-221-0292-0). Walter J Johnson.

Ahmad, Imtiaz. Muslim Political Behaviour: A Study of the Muslim Stratagem in Indian Electoral Politics. 1981. 14.00x (ISBN 0-88386-756-7). South Asia Bks.

Ahmad, Imtiaz, ed. Modernization & Social Change Among Muslims in India. 1981. 17.50x (ISBN 0-88386-892-X). South Asia Bks.

--Religion & Rituals Among Muslims in India. 1981. 14.00x (ISBN 0-685-74912-6). South Asia Bks.

Ahmad, Khurshid, ed. Islam: Its Meaning & Message. 279p. 1980. 17.50 (ISBN 0-86037-002-X, Pub. by Islamic Council of Europe England); pap. 8.95x (ISBN 0-86037-000-3). Intl Schol Bk Serv.

Ahmad, S. I. & Fung, Kwok. Introduction to Computer Design & Implementation. (Illus.). 1981. text ed. 19.95 (ISBN 0-914894-11-0). Computer Sci.

Ahmad, Sohrab, jt. auth. see Irons, Bruce.

Ahmad Abd al-Magid Haridi, ed. see Averroes.

Ahmann & Glock. Evaluating Student Progress: Principles of Tests & Measurements. 6th ed. 540p. 1980. text ed. 17.95 (ISBN 0-205-06561-9, 246561-2); test manual (ISBN 0-205-06562-7, 246562-0). Allyn.

Ahmann, J. Stanley & Glock, Marvin D. Evaluating Pupil Growth: Principles of Tests & Measurements. 5th ed. 492p. 1975. text ed. 17.95x o.p. (ISBN 0-205-04497-2, 2244969); tests free o.p. (ISBN 0-685-50740-8); workbook 3.95 o.p. (ISBN 0-685-50741-6). Allyn.

--Measuring & Evaluating Educational Achievement. 2nd ed. 324p. 1975. pap. text ed. 12.95 o.p. (ISBN 0-205-04776-9, 2247763). Allyn.

Ahmann, Mathew H. New Negro. LC 73-77031. 1969. Repr. of 1961 ed. 9.50x (ISBN 0-8196-0232-9). Biblo.

Ahmed & Coelho, eds. Toward a New Definition of Health: Psychosocial Dimensions. LC 79-9066. (Current Topics in Mental Health Ser.). (Illus.). 504p. 1979. 25.00 (ISBN 0-306-40248-3, Plenum Pr). Plenum Pub.

Ahmed, H. & Spreadbury, P. J. Electronics for Engineers. LC 72-93138. (Illus.). 280p. (Orig.). 1973. 34.95 (ISBN 0-521-20114-4); pap. 12.50x (ISBN 0-521-09789-4). Cambridge U Pr.

Ahmed, J. U., jt. auth. see Krishnamoorthy, P. N.

Ahmed, Manzoor, jt. auth. see Coombs, Philip H.

Ahmed, Nasir, jt. auth. see Unger, E. A.

Ahmed, S. Basheer. Nuclear Fuel & Energy Policy. LC 78-19673. 1979. 18.95 (ISBN 0-669-02714-6). Lexington Bks.

Ahmed Al Shahi & Moore, F. C., eds. Wisdom from the Nile: A Collection of Folk-Stories from Northern & Central Sudan. (Illus.). 270p. 1978. text ed. 37.50x (ISBN 0-19-815147-0). Oxford U Pr.

Ahmed-Ud-Din, Feroz. This Handful of Dust. (Redbird Bk.). 31p. 1975. 8.00 (ISBN 0-88253-835-7); pap. 4.80 (ISBN 0-88253-836-5). Ind-US Inc.

Ahn, Michael. Industrial Bibliography. LC 74-82273. (Research Report Ser.: No. 22). 1974. 6.00 (ISBN 0-87420-322-8). Urban Land.

Ahne, W., ed. Fish Diseases: Third COPRAQ-Session. (Proceedings in Life Sciences Ser.). (Illus.). 252p. 1981. 49.80 (ISBN 0-387-10406-2). Springer-Verlag.

Ahner, Walter. Laboratory Manual in Chemistry. (gr. 11-12). 1964. pap. 5.42 (ISBN 0-87720-123-4). AMSCO Sch.

Ahner, Walter L. Workbook & Laboratory Manual in Chemistry. rev. ed. (Illus.). (gr. 11-12). 1964. pap. 6.92 (ISBN 0-87720-125-0). AMSCO Sch.

Ahner, Walter L. & Diamond, Sheldon R. Laboratory Manual in Physics. 2nd ed. (Orig.). (gr. 10-12). 1967. 5.50 (ISBN 0-87720-174-9); tchrs' ed. 3.45 (ISBN 0-87720-175-7). AMSCO Sch.

--Workbook & Laboratory Manual in Physics. 2nd ed. (Illus., Orig.). (gr. 11-12). 1967. wkbk. 7.33 (ISBN 0-87720-176-5). AMSCO Sch.

Ahner, Walter L. & Kastan, Harold G. Review Text in Physics. (Illus., Orig.). (gr. 10-12). 1966. pap. text ed. 5.67 (ISBN 0-87720-171-4). AMSCO Sch.

Ahnne, Marlene & Burgess, Sara. SOS: A Communications Text with a Message. LC 72-81074. 446p. 1973. pap. text ed. 7.95x (ISBN 0-02-470850-X, 47085); tchr's manual free (ISBN 0-02-470860-7). Macmillan.

Aho, Alfred & Hopcroft, John. The Design & Analysis of Computer Algorithms. 480p. 1974. text ed. 21.95 (ISBN 0-201-00029-6). A-W.

Aho, Alfred V. & Ullman, Jeffrey D. Principles of Compiler Design. LC 77-73953. (Illus.). 1977. text ed. 21.95 (ISBN 0-201-00022-9). A-W.

--Theory of Parsing, Translation & Compiling: Vol. 1, Parsing. (Illus.). 592p. 1972. ref. ed. 24.95 (ISBN 0-13-914556-7). P-H.

Aho, Arnold J. Materials, Energies & Environmental Design. 1981. lib. bdg. 28.50 (ISBN 0-8240-7178-6). Garland Pub.

Ahrendts, Juergen, ed. Bibliographie zur alteuropaeischen Religionsgeschichte II, 1965-1969: Eine interdisziplinaere Auswahl von Literatur zu den Rand-und Nachfolgekulturen der Antike in Europa unter besonderer Beruecksichtigung der nichtchristlichen Religionen. LC 68-86477. (Arbeiten Zur Fruehmittelalterforschung: Vol. 5). xxvi, 591p. 1974. 87.05x (ISBN 3-11-003398-4). De Gruyter.

Ahrens, Christa, tr. see Kubler, Rolf.

Ahrens, Christa, tr. see Speicher, Klaus.

Ahrens, Christa, tr. see Thies, Dagmar.

Ahrens, Herman C., Jr. Keep in Touch. (Illus.). 96p. (Orig.). (gr. 7-12). 1978. pap. 4.95 (ISBN 0-8298-0351-3). Pilgrim NY.

Ahrens, L. H. Origin & Distribution of the Elements. 1979. text ed. 115.00 (ISBN 0-08-022947-6); pap. text ed. 50.00 (ISBN 0-08-022948-4). Pergamon.

Ahrens, Michael. Activities for Intellectually Handicapped Children. LC 76-357014. 1975. 6.10x (ISBN 0-7233-0423-8). Intl Pubns Serv.

Ahrens, Robert H., Jr. Monarch Notes on Aeschylus' Plays. (Orig.). pap. 2.50 (ISBN 0-671-00801-3). Monarch Pr.

Ahrens, Uwe, et al. Birth. LC 77-2603. (Illus.). 176p. 1981. pap. 9.95 (ISBN 0-06-090867-X, CN 867, CN). Har-Row.

Ahrland, S., et al. The Chemistry of the Actinides. (Pergamon Texts in Inorganic Chemistry: Vol. 10). 636p. 1975. text ed. 75.00 (ISBN 0-08-018794-3); pap. text ed. 35.00 (ISBN 0-08-018793-5). Pergamon.

Ahron, E. L. British Steam Railway Locomotive: Volume I, 1825-1925. 29.50x (ISBN 0-392-07695-0, SpS). Soccer.

Ahsan, M. M. Social Life Under the Abbasids. (Illus.). 1979. text ed. 33.00 (ISBN 0-582-78079-9). Longman.

Ahstrom, James P. Current Practice in Orthopaedic Surgery, Vol. 7. LC 63-18841. (Illus.). 1977. 34.50 o.p. (ISBN 0-8016-0095-2). Mosby.

Ahstrom, James P., Jr., ed. Current Practice in Orthopaedic Surgery, Vol. 6. LC 63-18841. (Illus.). 264p. 1975. text ed. 34.50 o.p. (ISBN 0-8016-0097-9). Mosby.

Ahuja, Elizabeth, jt. auth. see Roberts, Jean.

Ahuja, H. N. Construction Performance Control by Networks. LC 76-4774. (Construction Management & Engineering Ser.). 688p. 1976. 40.00 (ISBN 0-471-00960-1, Pub. by Wiley-Interscience). Wiley.

--Successful Construction Cost Control. LC 80-10156. (Construction Management & Engineering Ser.). 1980. 33.95 (ISBN 0-471-05378-3, Pub. by Wiley-Interscience). Wiley.

Ahuja, M. M. Epidemology of Diabetes in Developing Countries. 124p. 1980. pap. 5.95x (ISBN 0-89955-316-8, Pub. by Interprint India). Intl Schol Bk Serv.

Ahumada, Rodolfo. A History of Western Ontology from Thales to Heidegger. LC 78-60794. 1978. pap. text ed. 9.50 (ISBN 0-8191-0507-4). U Pr of Amer.

Ai, Fiore. Pasdale Welfare. 160p. 1981. 8.95 (ISBN 0-89962-207-0). Todd & Honeywell.

AIA Research Corporation. Passive Solar Design: A Short Bibliography for Practitioners. 1979. pap. 5.50 (ISBN 0-89934-040-7). Solar Energy Info.

--Passive Solar Design: A Survey of Monitored Buildings. 1979. pap. 19.50 (ISBN 0-930978-85-4). Solar Energy Info.

--Passive Solar Research & Development Project Summaries. 1979. pap. 11.95 (ISBN 0-89934-041-5). Solar Energy Info.

Aichele, George, Jr. Theology As Comedy: Critical & Theoretical Implications. LC 80-5384. 161p. 1980. lib. bdg. 15.75 (ISBN 0-8191-1082-5); pap. text ed. 8.75 (ISBN 0-8191-1083-3). U Pr of Amer.

Aichele, Jean & Olson, Nancy B. A Manual of AACR 2 Examples for Motion Pictures & Videorecordings. McClasky, Marilyn J. & Swanson, Edward, eds. 50p. 1980. pap. 6.00 (ISBN 0-936996-11-0). Soldier Creek.

Aichinger, Helga. The Shepherd. LC 67-18394. (Illus.). (gr. k-3). 1967. 8.95 (ISBN 0-690-73021-7, TYC-J). T Y Crowell.

Aichinger, Ilse see Otten, Anna.

Aickman, Robert. Cold Hand in Mine. LC 77-3042. (gr. 5 up). 1977. 8.95 o.p. (ISBN 0-684-15132-4, ScribT). Scribner.

Aidley, D. J. The Physiology of Excitable Cells. 2nd ed. LC 77-87375. (Illus.). 1979. 65.50 (ISBN 0-521-21913-2); pap. 17.95x (ISBN 0-521-29308-1). Cambridge U Pr.

Aidoo, Ama A. Anowa. (Sun-Lit Ser.). 64p. 1980. 9.00x (ISBN 0-89410-087-4); pap. 5.00x (ISBN 0-89410-088-2). Three Continents.

Aidoo, Ama A., illus. Dilemma of a Ghost. (African-American Lib). 1971. pap. 1.25 o.s.i. (ISBN 0-02-012020-6, Collier). Macmillan.

Aigner, Hal. Faint Trails: An Introduction to the Fundamentals of Adult Adoptee/Birth Parent Reunification Searches. 104p. (Orig.). 1980. pap. 4.95 (ISBN 0-937572-00-4). Paradigm Pr.

Aigner, Hal, et al. The Clear Creek Bike Book. Lawlor, Peter & Clear Creek Editors, eds. 192p. 1973. pap. 1.25 o.p. (ISBN 0-451-05459-8, Y5459, Sig). NAL.

Aihara, Cornellia. The Do of Cooking Ryorido: Winter. 1973. pap. 2.95 o.p. (ISBN 0-918860-15-6). G Ohsawa.

Aihara, Herman, et al. Smoking, Marijuana & Drugs. (Illus.). 1973. 1.50 o.p. (ISBN 0-918860-19-9). G Ohsawa.

Aijazuddin, F. S. Sikh Portraits by European Artists. (Illus.). 160p. 1979. 40.00x (ISBN 0-85667-059-6, Pub. by Sotheby Parke Bernet England). Biblio Dist.

Aijmer, Goran. Economic Man in Sha Tin: Vegetable Gardeners in a Hong Kong Valley. (Scandanavian Institute of Asian Studies Monograph: No. 43). (Orig.). 1980. pap. text ed. 9.25x (ISBN 0-7007-0135-4). Humanities.

Aikawa, Jerry K. Magnesium: Series in Cations of Biologic Significance. 144p. 1981. 49.95 (ISBN 0-8493-5871-X). CRC Pr.

--Relationship of Magnesium to Disease in Domestic Animals & in Humans. (Illus.). 160p. 1971. 16.75 (ISBN 0-398-02215-1). C C Thomas.

Aikawa, Jerry K. & Pinfield, Edward R. Computerizing a Clinical Laboratory. (Illus.). 112p. 1973. 12.75 (ISBN 0-398-02847-8). C C Thomas.

Aiken, Conrad. Gehenna. 1978. 14.50 o.p. (ISBN 0-685-86329-8). Porter.

Aiken, Conrad P. Collected Poems. 2nd ed. LC 79-120179. 1970. 25.00 (ISBN 0-19-501258-5). Oxford U Pr.

Aiken, George D., et al. Vermont for Every Season. (Illus.). 160p. 1980. 30.00 (ISBN 0-936896-00-0). VT Life Mag.

Aiken, Henry D., ed. see Hume, David.

Aiken, Joan. Arabel & Mortimer. LC 79-6577. (Illus.). 160p. (gr. 4 up). 1981. 9.95a (ISBN 0-385-15642-1); PLB (ISBN 0-385-15643-X). Doubleday.

--Died on a Rainy Sunday. LC 72-182777. 160p. (gr. 7 up). 1972. reinforced bdg. 4.95 o.p. (ISBN 0-03-089491-3). HR&W.

--The Faithless Lollybird. LC 77-72999. (gr. 6-9). 1978. PLB 6.95 (ISBN 0-385-13074-0). Doubleday.

--Go Saddle the Sea. LC 77-76958. (gr. 6-9). 1977. PLB 7.95 (ISBN 0-385-13226-3). Doubleday.

--Last Movement. LC 76-42055. 1977. 7.95 o.p. (ISBN 0-385-12620-4). Doubleday.

--Nightbirds on Nantucket. Date not set. pap. 1.75 (ISBN 0-440-96370-2, LE). Dell.

--Not What You Expected. LC 73-81121. 288p. 1974. 5.95 (ISBN 0-385-07518-9). Doubleday.

--The Shadow Guests. LC 80-65830. 160p. (gr. 5 up). 1980. 7.95 (ISBN 0-440-07746-X). Delacorte.

--A Touch of Chill. LC 79-3331. (YA) (gr. 8-12). 1980. 7.95 (ISBN 0-440-00007-6). Delacorte.

--The Wolves of Willoughby Chase. (gr. 7-12). 1981. pap. 1.75 (ISBN 0-440-99629-5, LE). Dell.

Aiken, Joan, tr. see De Segur, Comtesse.

Aiken, Joyce, jt. auth. see Laury, Jean R.

Aiken, Lewis R. Later Life. LC 77-11326. (Illus.). 1978. pap. text ed. 8.95 o.p. (ISBN 0-7216-1070-6). Saunders.

Aiken, Lewis R., Jr. Psychological Testing & Assessment. 3rd ed. 1978. text ed. 18.95 (ISBN 0-205-06613-5, 7966148). Allyn.

--Psychological Testing & Assessment. 2nd ed. 368p. 1976. text ed. 15.95x o.p. (ISBN 0-205-04861-7). Allyn.

Aiken, Linda, ed. Health Policy & Nursing Practice. (Illus.). 308p. 1980. pap. text ed. 6.95 (ISBN 0-07-000745-4, HP). McGraw.

Aiken, Michael, jt. auth. see Zey-Ferrell, Mary.

Aiken, William & LaFollette, Hugh, eds. Whose Child?: Children's Rights, Parental Authority, & State Power. 310p. 1980. 22.50x (ISBN 0-8476-6282-9). Rowman.

Aiken, Wm. A. Conduct of the Earl of Nottingham: 1689-1694. (Yale Historical Pubs., Manuscripts & Edited Texts: No. XVII). 1941. 47.50x (ISBN 0-685-69786-X). Elliots Bks.

Aikens, David A., et al. Integrated Experimental Chemistry, 2 vols. Incl. Vol. 1. Principles & Techniques. text ed. 11.95x (ISBN 0-205-05923-6); Vol. 2. Laboratory Experiments. lab manual 12.95x (ISBN 0-205-05924-4). 1978. pap. text ed. 14.95 ea. Allyn.

Aikins, Carrol, tr. see Grimm, George.

Aikman, Ann, jt. auth. see McQuade, Walter.

Aikman, Duncan. Calamity Jane & the Lady Wildcats. 1973. pap. 1.25 o.p. (ISBN 0-345-23507-X). Ballantine.

Aikman, Lonnelle. We, the People. LC 78-57740. 1978. text ed. 2.95 (ISBN 0-916200-13-2); pap. 2.00 (ISBN 0-916200-14-0). US Capitol Hist Soc.

Ai-Nai-Yim, Meir. Polychrome Historical Haggadah. (Illus.). 30.00 (ISBN 0-686-10317-3). J Freedman Liturgy.

Ainger, Alfred. Crabbe. LC 72-78107. (Library of Lives & Letters). 1970. Repr. of 1903 ed. 15.00 (ISBN 0-8103-3600-6). Gale.

Ainley, John, jt. auth. see Fordham, Adrian.

Ainsley, Tom. Ainsley's New Complete Guide to Harness Racing. rev. ed. 1981. Repr. of 1971 ed. 17.95 (ISBN 0-671-25257-7). S&S.

Ainslie, Douglas, tr. see Croce, Benedetto.

Ainsworth, Catherine H. American Calendar Customs, Vol. I. LC 79-52827. (Calendar Customs & Holidays Ser.). 104p. (Orig.). (gr. 5-12). 1979. pap. 5.00 (ISBN 0-933190-06-9). Clyde Pr.

--American Calendar Customs, Vol. II. LC 79-55784. (Calender Customs). 200p. (Orig.). 1980. pap. 10.00 (ISBN 0-933190-07-7). Clyde Pr.

--Black & White & Said All Over: Riddles. LC 78-54873. (Folklore Bks.). 36p. 1980. 2.00 (ISBN 0-933190-02-6). Clyde Pr.

--Folktales of America, Vol 1. LC 80-66300. (Folktales & Legends Ser.). 206p. 1980. pap. 10.00 (ISBN 0-933190-08-5). Clyde Pr.

--Italian-American Folktales. LC 76-52643. (Folklore Bks.). xii, 180p. 1980. 5.00 (ISBN 0-933190-03-4). Clyde Pr.

--Jump Rope Verses Around the United States. (Folklore Bks.). 24p. 1980. 2.00 (ISBN 0-933190-01-8). Clyde Pr.

--Legends of New York State. LC 78-54873. (Folklore Bks.). vi, 96p. 1980. 4.00 (ISBN 0-933190-05-0). Clyde Pr.

--Polish-American Folktales. LC 77-80771. (Folklore Bks.). x, 102p. 1980. 5.00 (ISBN 0-933190-04-2). Clyde Pr.

--Superstitions from Seven Towns of the United States. (Folklore Bks.). vi, 58p. 1980. 2.00 (ISBN 0-933190-00-X). Clyde Pr.

Ainsworth, G. C. Ainsworth & Bisby's Dictionary of the Fungi, Including the Lichens. 6th ed. LC 74-883641. (Illus.). 673p. 1971. 27.50x (ISBN 0-85198-075-9). Intl Pubns Serv.

--Introduction to the History of Mycology. LC 75-21036. (Illus.). 350p. 1976. 47.50 (ISBN 0-521-21013-5). Cambridge U Pr.

--Introduction to the History of Plant Pathology. LC 80-40476. 220p. Date not set. price not set (ISBN 0-521-23032-2). Cambridge U Pr.

Ainsworth, Henry. A True Confession of the Faith, Which Wee Falsley Called Brownists, Doo Hold. LC 78-26338. (English Experience Ser.: No. 158). 24p. 1969. Repr. of 1956 ed. 7.00 (ISBN 90-221-0158-4). Walter J Johnson.

Ainsworth, Henry & Johnson, Francis. An Apologie or Defence of Such True Christians As Are Commonly Called Brownists. LC 70-25742. (English Experience Ser.: No. 217). Repr. of 1604 ed. 16.00 (ISBN 90-221-0424-9). Walter J Johnson.

Ainsworth, Mary D., et al. Patterns of Attachment: A Psychological Study of the Strange Situation. LC 78-13303. 1979. 24.95 (ISBN 0-470-26534-5). Halsted Pr.

Ainsworth, Ralph M. Grain Trading As a Foundation for Total Futures Trading. (Illus.). 197p. 1980. 79.75 (ISBN 0-918968-74-7). Inst Econ Finan.

--Profitable Grain Trading. LC 80-53316. 256p. 1980. Repr. of 1933 ed. text ed. 25.00 (ISBN 0-934380-04-X). Traders Pr.

Ainsworth, Ruth. Mysterious Baba & Her Magic Caravan. (Illus.). (gr. k-5). 1980. 8.95 (ISBN 0-233-97200-5). Andre Deutsch.

--The Phantom Cyclist & Other Ghost Stories. (gr. 4-7). 1977. pap. 1.25 (ISBN 0-590-10311-3, Schol Pap). Schol Bk Serv.

--The Phantom Fisherboy. LC 79-92493. (Illus.). 168p. (gr. 1-5). 1980. 7.95 (ISBN 0-233-96569-6). Andre Deutsch.

--Talking Rock. (Illus.). (gr. k-4). 1979. PLB 8.95 (ISBN 0-233-97080-0). Andre Deutsch.

Ainsworth, Stanley. Positive Emotional Power: How to Manage Your Feelings. (Illus.). 256p. 1981. 12.95 (ISBN 0-13-687616-1); pap. 6.95 (ISBN 0-686-69330-2). P-H.

Ainsworth, Thomas H., Jr. Quality Assurance in Long Term Care. LC 77-70432. 1977. 27.50 (ISBN 0-912862-40-8). Aspen Systems.

Ainsworth, W. A. Mechanisms of Speech Recognitions. 1976. text ed. 30.00 (ISBN 0-08-020395-7); pap. text ed. 17.25 (ISBN 0-08-020394-9). Pergamon.

Ainsworth-Land, Vaune & Fletcher, Norma. Casting a Spell. (Illus., Orig.). 1980. pap. text ed. 7.95 (ISBN 0-914634-65-8, 7909). DOK Pubs.

--Making Waves with Creative Problem-Solving. (Illus.). 52p. (Orig.). 1979. pap. text ed. 3.95 (ISBN 0-914634-66-6, 7913). DOK Pubs.

Ainsztein, Reuben. Jewish Resistance in Nazi-Occupied Eastern Europe: With a Historical Survey of the Jew As Fighter & Soldier in Diaspora. LC 74-1759. 970p. 1974. 37.50x o.p. (ISBN 0-06-490030-4). B&N.

Aird, Catherine. His Burial Too. 208p. 1980. pap. 1.95 (ISBN 0-553-13949-5). Bantam.

--A Late Phoenix. 176p. 1981. pap. 2.25 (ISBN 0-553-14517-7). Bantam.

--Parting Breath. LC 77-12836. 1978. 7.95 o.p. (ISBN 0-385-13563-7). Doubleday.

--Passing Strange. LC 80-1120. (Crime Club Ser.). 192p. 1981. 9.95 (ISBN 0-385-17271-0). Doubleday.

--The Religious Body. 176p. 1980. pap. 1.95 (ISBN 0-553-13951-7). Bantam.

--Some Die Eloquent. 208p. 1981. pap. 2.25 (ISBN 0-553-14338-7). Bantam.

Aird, Edwin A. Introduction to Medical Physics. (Illus.). 1975. 22.50x (ISBN 0-433-00350-2). Intl Ideas.

Aird, Robert B. & Woodbury, Dixon M. The Management of Epilepsy. (American Lectures in Living Chemistry). (Illus.). 468p. 1974. 29.75 (ISBN 0-398-02881-8). C C Thomas.

Airey, T., et al, eds. Aircraft Erecting. (Engineering Craftsmen: No. H34). (Illus.). 1977. spiral bdg. 26.00x (ISBN 0-85083-413-9). Intl Ideas.

Airguide. Airguide Traveler: Bahamas, Florida, Florida Keys, & Sea Islands. (Illus.). 1980. pap. 11.00 (ISBN 0-911721-89-4). Aviation.

Airguide Publications. Flight Guide Airport & Frequency Manual, Vol. 1: Western States. Navarre, Monte, ed. 1980. small binder 16.00 (ISBN 0-911721-14-2, Pub. by Airguide). Aviation.

--Flight Guide Airport & Frequency Manual, Vol. 2: Eastern & Central States. Navarre, Monte, ed. 1980. small binder 22.00 (ISBN 0-911721-15-0, Pub. by Airguide). Aviation.

Airmart. Airmart Hardware Digest: AN, MS, & NAS. Date not set. pap. 4.95. Aviation.

Airola, Paavo. Are You Confused? 4.95 o.p. (ISBN 0-685-90564-0). Bi World Indus.

--Everywoman's Book. 1979. cloth 17.95 (ISBN 0-932090-00-1). Health Plus.

--Everywoman's Book. (Illus.). 640p. 1981. pap. 12.95 (ISBN 0-932090-10-9). Health Plus.

--Garlic. 2.00 o.s.i. (ISBN 0-89557-039-4). Bi World Indus.

--How to Get Well. 1974. cloth 12.95 (ISBN 0-932090-03-6). Health Plus.

--How to Get Well. 9.95 o.s.i. (ISBN 0-89557-036-X). Bi World Indus.

--How to Keep Slim, Healthy & Young with Juice Fasting. 3.25 o.p. (ISBN 0-685-90565-9). Bi World Indus.

--Hypoglycemia: A Better Approach. 4.95 o.s.i. (ISBN 0-89557-040-8). Bi World Indus.

Aisenberg, Nadya. The Justice-Worm. LC 80-53871. (Chapbook Ser.: No. 3). 64p. (Orig.). Date not set. pap. 4.95 (ISBN 0-937672-02-5). Rowan Tree.

Aisha Abd Ar-Rahman At-Tarjumana, tr. see Sidi Ali Al-Jamal Of Fez.

Aisner, Joseph, ed. Cancer Treatment Research. Chang, Paul. (Developments in Oncology Ser.: Vol. 2). (Illus.). xvi, 272p. 1980. lib. bdg. 44.75 (ISBN 90-247-2358-2, Martinus Nishoff Pubs). Kluwer Boston.

Aissen, Judith. The Syntax of Causative Constructions. Hankamer, Jorge, ed. LC 78-66533. (Outstanding Dissertations in Linguistics Ser.). 1979. lib. bdg. 27.50 (ISBN 0-8240-9690-8). Garland Pub.

Aistrop, Jack. Enjoying Nature's Marvels. LC 61-9014. (Illus.). (gr. 5-9). 1960. 6.95 (ISBN 0-8149-0250-2). Vanguard.

--Enjoying Pets. LC 55-7891. (gr. 5-10). 6.95 (ISBN 0-8149-0251-0). Vanguard.

Aita, John A. Neurologic Manifestations of General Diseases. 936p. 1975. 69.50 (ISBN 0-398-02675-0). C C Thomas.

Aitchinson, J. & Dunsmore, I. R. Statistical Prediction Analysis. LC 74-25649. (Illus.). 276p. 1975. 44.50 (ISBN 0-521-20692-8). Cambridge U Pr.

Aitchison, J. & Dunsmore, I. R. Statistical Prediction Analysis. (Illus.). 284p. 1980. pap. 14.95x (ISBN 0-521-29858-X). Cambridge U Pr.

Aitchison, John. Choice Against Chance: An Introduction to Statistical Decision Theory. LC 70-109505. (Business & Economics Ser). 1970. text ed. 17.95 (ISBN 0-201-00141-1). A-W.

Aitchison, John & Brown, J. A. Lognormal Distribution. (Cambridge Department of Applied Economic Monographs). 1957. 29.50 (ISBN 0-521-04011-6). Cambridge U Pr.

Aitchison, Stewart W. Oak Creek Canyon & the Red Rock Country of Arizona. LC 78-53385. (Illus., Orig.). 1978. pap. 5.95 (ISBN 0-933762-01-1). Stillwater Canyon Pr.

Aitken, A. J., et al, eds. A Dictionary of the Older Scottish Tongue: From the Twelfth Century to the End of the Seventeenth, Founded on the Collections of Sir Wm Craigie, Pt. 30. 1981. pap. price not set (ISBN 0-226-11721-9, Copub with Oxford). U of Chicago Pr.

Aitken, Amy. Kate & Mona in the Jungle. LC 80-15110. (Illus.). 32p. (gr. k-2). 1980. 8.95 (ISBN 0-87888-167-0). Bradbury Pr.

--Ruby! LC 78-21283. (Illus.). (gr. k-2). 1979. 8.95 (ISBN 0-87888-144-1). Bradbury Pr.

Aitken, C., ed. Psychosomatics & Pleasure: Proceedings of the Twenty-Third Annual Conference of the Society for Psychosomatic Research Held at the Royal College of Physicians, London, 19-20 November 1979. 88p. 1980. pap. 20.00 (ISBN 0-08-026797-1). Pergamon.

Aitken, D. J., ed. World List of Universities, Other Institutions of Higher Education & University Organizations 1979-1981. 693p. 1979. text ed. 57.64x (ISBN 3-11008-077-X). De Gruyter.

Aitken, Eleanor, ed. see Tolstoy, Leo.

Aitken, Hannah, ed. A Forgotten Heritage: Original Folk Tales of Lowland Scotland. (Illus.). 168p. 1973. 11.00x (ISBN 0-87471-430-3). Rowman.

Aitken, Hugh G. Syntony & Spark - the Origins of Radio Technology. LC 75-34247. (Science, Culture & Society Ser.). 1976. 25.50 (ISBN 0-471-01816-3, Pub. by Wiley-Interscience). Wiley.

Aitken, John J., jt. auth. see Hansell, Michael H.

Aitken, M. J. Physics & Archaeology. 2nd ed. (Illus.). 320p. 1975. 39.50x (ISBN 0-19-851922-2). Oxford U Pr.

Aitken, Thomas. The Multinational Man: The Role of the Manager Abroad. LC 73-10602. 176p. 1973. 14.95 (ISBN 0-470-01793-7). Halsted Pr.

Aitman, L., ed. see Electronics Magazine.

Aixala, Jerome, ed. see Arrupe, Pedro.

Aiyar, R. Krishnaswami, ed. see Sankaracharya, Srngeri.

Ajaegbu, H. I. Urban & Rural Development in Nigeria. 1976. text ed. 26.95 (ISBN 0-435-34030-1). Heinemann Ed.

Ajami, Fouad. The Arab Predicament: Arab Political Thought & Practice Since 1967. 250p. Date not set. price not set (ISBN 0-521-23914-1). Cambridge U Pr.

Ajami, Riad A. Arab Response to Multinationals. 1979. 20.95 (ISBN 0-03-048436-7). Praeger.

Ajay, Bose K., ed. see Manhas, Maghar S.

Ajayi, J. F. & Crowder, Michael, eds. The History of West Africa, Vol. 1. 2nd ed. 1976. 30.00x (ISBN 0-231-04102-0); pap. text ed. 17.50x (ISBN 0-231-04103-9). Columbia U Pr.

--History of West Africa, Vol. 2. 672p. 1974. 22.50x o.p. (ISBN 0-231-03737-6); pap. 12.50x o.p. (ISBN 0-231-03738-4). Columbia U Pr.

Ajayi, J. F. & Espie, Ian, eds. Thousand Years of West African History. 2nd ed. 1969. text ed. 12.00x (ISBN 0-391-00217-1). Humanities.

Ajdukiewicz, K. Problems & Theories of Philosophy. Quinton, A. & Skolimowski, H., trs. from Polish. LC 72-97878. 160p. 1973. 23.95 (ISBN 0-521-20219-1); pap. 6.95x (ISBN 0-521-09993-5). Cambridge U Pr.

Ajello, Libero E., et al. Histoplasmosis: Proceedings. (American Lecture in Clinical Microbiology Ser.). (Illus.). 540p. 1971. 49.50 (ISBN 0-398-02216-X). C C Thomas.

Ajmone-Marsan, C., jt. ed. see Pompeiano, O.

Ajmone-Marson, Cosimo, et al, eds. Neuropeptides & Neural Transmission. (International Brain Research Organization (IBRO) Monograph: Vol. 7). 412p. 1980. text ed. 40.00 (ISBN 0-89004-501-1). Raven.

Ajzen, Icek, jt. auth. see Fishbein, Martin.

Akagi, Roy. Japan's Foreign Relations, Fifteen Forty-Two to Nineteen Thirty-Six: A Short History. (Studies in Japanese History & Civilization). (Illus.). 560p. 1979. Repr. of 1936 ed. 36.50 (ISBN 0-89093-260-3). U Pubns Amer.

Akasofu, S. I. Polar & Magnetospheric Substorms. (Astrophysics & Space Science Library: Vol. 11). (Illus.). 1969. 18.00 o.p. (ISBN 0-387-91024-7). Springer-Verlag.

Akasofu, Syun-Ichi & Chapman, Sidney. Solar-Terrestrial Physics. (International Ser. of Monographs on Physics). (Illus.). 1000p. 1972. 112.00x (ISBN 0-19-851262-7). Oxford U Pr.

Ake, Claude. Revolutionary Pressures in Africa. 112p. 1978. 12.95 (Pub. by Zed Pr); pap. 6.95 (ISBN 0-905762-15-0). Lawrence Hill.

Akehurst, Michael. A Modern Introduction to International Law. 3rd ed. (Minerva Ser. of Students' Handbooks). 1977. text ed. 29.95x (ISBN 0-04-341013-8); pap. text ed. 13.75x (ISBN 0-04-341014-6). Allen Unwin.

Akel, jt. auth. see Dinaburg.

A'Kempis, Thomas. Of the Imitation of Christ. (Summit Bks). 1977. pap. 1.95 (ISBN 0-8010-0115-3). Baker Bk.

Akerman, M. Alfred. Demonstration of the First Visible Wave-Length Direct Nuclear Pumped Laser. LC 78-75011. (Outstanding Dissertations on Energy Ser.). 1979. lib. bdg. 11.00 (ISBN 0-8240-3984-X). Garland Pub.

Akeroyd, Richard H. He Is Nigh: Even at the Doors. (Illus.). 1981. 8.95 (ISBN 0-916620-53-0). Portals Pr.

Akeroyd, Richard H., tr. see Schlumberger, Jean.

Akers, Carl. Carl Akers' Colorado. Date not set. pap. 9.50 (ISBN 0-933472-53-6). Johnson Colo.

Akers, Glenn A. Phonological Variation in the Jamaican Continuum. 158p. 1981. pap. 8.50 (ISBN 0-89720-038-1). Karoma.

Akers, Ronald L. & Hawkins, Richard. Law & Control in Society. LC 74-22213. (Sociology Ser.). 384p. 1975. 17.95 (ISBN 0-13-526095-7). P-H.

Akerson, Charles B. Capitalization Theory & Techniques Study Guide. 1980. pap. 10.00 (ISBN 0-911780-48-3). Am Inst Real Estate Appraisers.

--An Introduction to Mortgage-Equity Capitalization. 1970. 3.00 (ISBN 0-911780-35-1). Am Inst Real Estate Appraisers.

Akert, Konrad, jt. auth. see Emmers, Raimond.

Akeson, A. & Ehrenburg, A. Structure & Function of Oxidation Reduction Enzymes. 788p. 1972. 130.00 (ISBN 0-08-016874-4). Pergamon.

Akhadov, Ya Y. Dielectric Properties of Binary Solutions: A Data Handbook. 400p. Date not set. 112.50 (ISBN 0-08-023600-6). Pergamon.

Akhiezer, A. I., et al. Collective Oscillations in a Plasma. 1967. 22.00 (ISBN 0-08-011894-1). Pergamon.

Akhilananda, Swami. Hindu Psychology: Its Meaning for the West. 1971. Repr. of 1948 ed. 20.00 (ISBN 0-7100-1006-0). Routledge & Kegan.

Akhmanova, O. Optimization of Natural Communication Systems. (Juana Linguarum, Ser. Minor: No. 92). 1977. 22.35 (ISBN 90-279-3146-1). Mouton.

Akhmanova, O. S., et al. Exact Methods in Linguistic Research. Haynes, David G. & Mohr, Dolores V., trs. 1963. 20.00x (ISBN 0-520-00542-2). U of Cal Pr.

Akhmanova, Olga. Linguostylistics: Theory & Method. (Janua Linguarum, Ser. Minor: No. 181). 1976. pap. text ed. 22.35x (ISBN 9-0279-3175-5). Mouton.

--Phonology, Morphonology, Morphology. LC 72-159459. (Janua Linguarum, Ser. Minor: No. 101). 135p. 1971. pap. text ed. 23.50x (ISBN 90-2791-748-5). Mouton.

Akhmanova, Olga & Mikael'An, Galina. Theory of Syntax in Modern Linguistics. LC 69-13300. (Janua Linguarum, Ser. Minor: No. 68). (Orig.). 1969. pap. text ed. 24.70x (ISBN 90-2790-683-1). Mouton.

Akhmatova, Anna. Chetki. 1972. pap. 3.00 (ISBN 0-88233-029-2). Ardis Pubs.

--Way of All the Earth. Thomas, D. M., tr. from Rus. LC 79-1953. 96p. 1980. 9.00 (ISBN 0-8214-0429-6); pap. 5.95 (ISBN 0-8214-0430-X). Ohio U Pr.

Aki, Keiiti & Richards, Paul G. Quantitative Seismology: Theory & Methods, Vol. I. LC 79-17434. (A Series of Books in Geology). (Illus.). 1980. text ed. 37.95x (ISBN 0-7167-1058-7). W H Freeman.

--Quantitative Seismology: Theory & Methods, Vol. II. LC 79-17434. (A Series of Books in Geology). (Illus.). 1980. text ed. 37.95x (ISBN 0-7167-1059-5). W H Freeman.

Akian, Gail G., jt. auth. see Breton, Raymond.

Akiba, K. Bond Switch at Hypervalent Sulfur in Thiathiophtene Analogous Systems. (Sulfur Reports Ser.). 29p. 1980. flexicover 7.50 (ISBN 3-7186-0037-4). Harwood Academic.

Akilov, G. P., jt. auth. see Kantorovich, L. V.

Akin, Johnnye, et al, eds. Language Behavior: A Book of Readings in Communication. LC 77-110948. (Janua Linguarum, Ser. Major: No. 41). 1970. text ed. 56.50x (ISBN 90-2791-244-0). Mouton.

Akin, Omar, ed. Representation & Architecture. 300p. 1981. pap. 19.50 o.p. (ISBN 0-8408-0506-3). Carrollton Pr.

Akin, Warren. Letters of Warren Akin, Confederate Congressman. Wiley, Bell I., ed. LC 59-15538. 151p. 1959. 10.00 (ISBN 0-8203-0116-7). U of Ga Pr.

Akin, William E. Technocracy & the American Dream: The Technocrat Movement, 1900-1941. 1977. 14.50x (ISBN 0-520-03110-5). U of Cal Pr.

Akins, Faren R., et al. Behavioral Development of Nonhuman Primates: An Abstracted Bibliography. LC 79-26700. 314p. 1980. 75.00 (ISBN 0-306-65189-0). IFI Plenum.

Akins, William R. ESP: Your Psychic Powers & How to Test Them. (gr. 4 up). 1980. PLB 6.45 (ISBN 0-531-02947-6). Watts.

Akintoye, S. A. Revolution & Power Politics in Yoruvaland 1840-1893: Ibadan Expansion & the Rise of Ekitparapo. (Ibadan History Ser). 1971. text ed. 11.00x o.p. (ISBN 0-391-00168-X). Humanities.

Akiyama, Terukazu & Matsubara, Saburo. Arts of China, Vol. 2: Buddhist Cave Temples. Soper, Alexander, tr. LC 68-17454. (Arts of China Ser: Vol. 2). (Illus.). 248p. 1969. 85.00 (ISBN 0-87011-089-6). Kodansha.

Akiyama, Terukazu, et al. Arts of China: Neolithic Cultures to the T'ang Dynasty, Vol. 1. LC 68-17454. (Arts of China Ser: Vol. 1). (Illus.). 1968. 85.00 (ISBN 0-87011-064-0). Kodansha.

Akkas, N. Process in Biomechanics. (NATO Advaned Study Institute Ser.). 395p. 1979. 37.50x (ISBN 90-286-0479-0). Sijthoff & Noordhoff.

Aklonis, John J., et al, eds. Introduction to Polymer Viscoelasticity. LC 72-473. 256p. 1972. 27.50 (ISBN 0-471-01860-0, Pub by Wiley-Interscience). Wiley.

Akmajian, Adrian. Aspects of the Grammar of Focus in English. Hankamer, Jorge, ed. LC 78-66534. (Outstanding Dissertations in Linguistics Ser.). 1979. lib. bdg. 37.50 (ISBN 0-8240-9691-6). Garland Pub.

Akmajian, Adrian & Heny, Frank. An Introduction to the Principles of Transformational Syntax. 448p. 1980. text ed. 20.00x (ISBN 0-262-01043-7); pap. text ed. 10.00x (ISBN 0-262-51022-7). MIT Pr.

Akmajian, Adrian & Heny, Frank W. An Introduction to the Principles of Transformational Syntax. LC 74-3054. 544p. 1975. 18.00x (ISBN 0-262-01043-7); pap. 10.00x (ISBN 0-262-51022-7). MIT Pr.

Akolkar, V. V. Social Psychology. 4th ed. 1972. pap. 4.75x o.p. (ISBN 0-210-33751-6). Asia.

Akpalu, Vinoko. When Sorrow-Song Descends on You. Awoonor, Kofi, tr. (Cross-Cultural Review Chapbook 14). 16p. (Ewe & Eng.). 1980. pap. 2.00 (ISBN 0-89304-813-5). Cross Cult.

Akpan, Ntieyong U. Wooden Gong: A Novel. (Orig.). 1965. pap. text ed. 2.00x (ISBN 0-582-64012-1). Humanities.

Aksenov, Arthur, tr. see Dubovik, Alexander.

Aksenov, Vasily P. Ozhog. (Rus.). 1980. 18.50 (ISBN 0-88233-600-2); pap. 10.50 (ISBN 0-88233-601-0). Ardis Pubs.

--Zolotaia Nasha Zhelezka. (Rus.). 1979. 15.00 (ISBN 0-88233-479-4); pap. 5.00 (ISBN 0-88233-480-8). Ardis Pubs.

Aksyonov, Andrei & Chernov, Alexander. Exploring the Deep. (gr. 7 up). 1980. PLB 6.90 (ISBN 0-531-02126-2, BO3). Watts.

Aksyonov, Vasiliy. It's Time, My Love, It's Time. LC 77-108294. 226p. 1974. 3.95 o.s.i. (ISBN 0-87695-026-8). Aurora Pubs.

Akutagawa, Ryunosuke. Hell Screen & Other Stories. Norman, W. H., tr. LC 78-98800. Repr. of 1948 ed. lib. bdg. 17.50x (ISBN 0-8371-3017-4, AKHS). Greenwood.

--Tu Tze-Chun. Britton, Dorothy, tr. LC 65-12283. (Illus.). 64p. 1965. 10.00x (ISBN 0-87011-013-6). Kodansha.

Al-Anon Family Group Headquarters. Al-Anon's Twelve Steps & Twelve Traditions. 140p. 5.00 (ISBN 0-910034-24-9). Al-Anon.

Alabaster, J. S., jt. ed. see Lloyd, Richard.

Alabiso, Frank P. & Hansen, James C. The Hyperactive Child in the Classroom. 336p. 1977. pap. 20.00 spiral (ISBN 0-398-03550-4). C C Thomas.

Aladjem, Silvio. Obstetrical Practice. LC 80-17356. (Illus.). 877p. 1980. text ed. 39.50 (ISBN 0-8016-0114-2). Mosby.

Aladjem, Silvio & Brown, Audrey K., eds. Clinical Perinatology. LC 74-8599. (Illus.). 1974. 45.00 o.p. (ISBN 0-8016-0100-2). Mosby.

Aladjem, Silvio, et al. Risks in the Practice of Modern Obstetrics, Vol. 2. LC 75-22148. (Illus.). 426p. 1975. 37.50 o.p. (ISBN 0-8016-0099-5). Mosby.

--Clinical Perinatology. 2nd ed. LC 79-24340. (Illus.). 1979. text ed. 52.50 (ISBN 0-8016-0103-7). Mosby.

Alagh, Y. K., jt. auth. see Bhalla, G. S.

Alagic, S. & Arbib, M. A. The Design of Well-Structured & Correct Programs. LC 77-27087. (Texts & Monographs in Computer Science). 1978. 14.80 (ISBN 0-387-90299-6). Springer-Verlag.

Alagille, Daniel & Odievre, Michel. Liver & Billiary Tract Disease in Children. LC 79-12254. 1979. 43.95 (ISBN 0-471-05256-6, Pub. by Wiley-Medical). Wiley.

Alagoa, Ebiegberi J. Small Brave City-State: A History of Nembe-Brass in the Niger Delta. (Illus.). 1964. 15.00x (ISBN 0-299-03110-1). U of Wis Pr.

Alaia, Cheri, jt. auth. see Rafter, Rosalie.

Alain. One, Two, Three, Going to Sea. (gr. k-3). 1969. pap. 1.25 (ISBN 0-590-02605-4, Schol Pap). Schol Bk Serv.

Alain, Hermano, jt. auth. see Leon, H.

Alain-Fournier. Wanderer. Bair, Lowell, tr. 1971. pap. 1.25 o.p. (ISBN 0-451-50538-7, CY538, Sig Classics). NAL.

Alain-Fournier, Henri. Lost Domain. Davison, Frank, tr. (World's Classics Ser.). 1959. 4.95 o.p. (ISBN 0-19-250569-6). Oxford U Pr.

Alan, Ray. Spanish Quest. (Illus.). 1969. 8.95 o.s.i. (ISBN 0-02-500650-9). Macmillan.

Aland, K., jt. ed. see Nestle, E.

Aland, Kurt, ed. Die Alten Uebersetzungen Des Neuen Testaments, Die Kirchenvaeterzitate und Lektionare: Der Gegenwaertige Stand Ihrer Erforschung und Ihre Bedeutung Fuer Die griechische Textgeschichte. (Arbeiten zur neutestamentlichen Textforschung 5). xxiv, 590p. 1972. 89.40x (ISBN 3-11-004121-9). De Gruyter.

--Repertorium der Griechischen Christlichen Papyri, Pt.1: Biblische Papyri, Altes Testament, Neues Testament, Varia, Apokryphen. (Patristische Texte und Studien, Vol. 18). 473p. 1976. 93.00x (ISBN 3-11-004674-1). De Gruyter.

--Synopsis of the Four Gospels: Greek - English Edition. 3rd ed. (Eng. & Gr.). 1979. 20.00 (ISBN 3-438-05405-1, 56691). United Bible.

--Synopsis Quattuor Evangeliorum. 10th ed. 1978. 20.00 (ISBN 3-438-05130-3, 56690). United Bible.

Aland, Kurt, et al, eds. The Greek New Testament. 3rd ed. 1975. leather 16.30 (ISBN 3-438-05111-7, 56491); vinyl 7.50 (ISBN 3-438-05110-9); With Dictionary. vinyl 9.75 (ISBN 3-438-05113-3, 56492). United Bible.

Al-Ani & Shammas. Arabic: Phonology & Script. 1980. 9.00x (ISBN 0-917062-04-3). Intl Bk Ctr.

Al-Ani, Salman H. Arabic Phonology: An Acoustical & Physiological Investigation. (Janua Linguarum, Ser. Practica: No. 61). 1970. pap. text ed. 31.75x (ISBN 90-2790-727-7). Mouton.

Alan Of Lille. The Art of Preaching. Evans, Gillian R., tr. (Cistercian Fathers Ser.: No. 23). (Orig., Lat.). 1981. pap. price not set (ISBN 0-87907-923-1). Cistercian Pubns.

Alarcon. Cuatro Comedias (in Spanish) 3.75x o.s.i. (ISBN 0-686-12052-3). Colton Bk.

Alarcon, Arthur L., jt. auth. see Fricke, Charles W.

Alarcon, Francisco X., ed. see Herrera, Juan F.

Alarcon, P. A. El Sombrero De Tres Picos. 2nd ed. 1965. 8.95 (ISBN 0-471-00004-3). Wiley.

Alas, Leopoldo. His Only Son. Jones, Julie, tr. from Span. LC 80-20837. 240p. 1981. 22.50x (ISBN 0-8071-0759-X). La State U Pr.

Alaska Geographic Staff. Southeast: Alaska's Panhandle. LC 72-92087. (Alaska Geographic: Vol. 5, No. 2). (Illus.). 1978. pap. 12.95 album style (ISBN 0-88240-107-6). Alaska Northwest.

Alaska Geographic Staff, ed. The Brooks Range: Environmental Watershed. LC 72-92087. (Alaska Geographic: Vol. 4, No. 2). (Illus.). 1977. pap. 9.95 o.p. (ISBN 0-88240-091-6). Alaska Northwest.

--Kodiak: Island of Change, Vol. 4, No. 3. LC 72-92087. (Alaska Geographic). (Illus.). 1977. pap. 7.95 o.p. (ISBN 0-88240-095-9). Alaska Northwest.

Alaska Magazine Editors, jt. auth. see Armstrong, Robert H.

Alaska Magazine Staff, et al. The Alaska Almanac: Facts About Alaska. 4th rev. ed. (Illus.). 1979. pap. 3.95 o.p. (ISBN 0-88240-135-1). Alaska Northwest.

Alasseur, Claude. La Comedie Francaise Au XVIIIe: Etude Economique. (Civilisation et Societes: No. 3). 1967. pap. 14.70x (ISBN 90-2796-074-7). Mouton.

Alaszewski, Andy, jt. auth. see Haywood, Stuart.

Alauzen, Andre & Ripert, Pierre. Monticelli. (Illus., Fr.). 1970. 60.00 (ISBN 0-685-02319-2). Newbury Bks Inc.

Alba. Alba's Medical Technology Board Examination Review, Vol. I. 9th ed. (Illus.). 1980. pap. text ed. 20.00 (ISBN 0-910224-05-6). Berkeley Sci.

--Alba's Medical Technology Board Examination Review, Vol. II. 4th ed. LC 72-172446. (Illus.). 1978. pap. text ed. 17.00 (ISBN 0-910224-02-1). Berkeley Sci.

Alba, Victor. The Mexicans: The Making of a Nation. LC 67-20469. 1970. pap. 5.95 (ISBN 0-672-63564-X). Pegasus.

--Peru. 1977. lib. bdg. 21.00x (ISBN 0-89158-111-1). Westview.

Albaiges, J., ed. see International Congress on Analytical Techniques in Environmental Chemistry, Barcelona, 27-30 November 1978.

Albanese, Anthony A., ed. Nutrition for the Elderly. LC 80-21565. (Current Topics in Nutrition & Disease: Vol. 3). 280p. 1980. 38.00 (ISBN 0-8451-1602-9). A R Liss.

Albanese, Jay S., et al. Is Probation Working: A Guide for Managers & Methodologists. LC 80-6311. 190p. 1981. lib. bdg. 17.75 (ISBN 0-8191-1507-X); pap. text ed. 8.75 (ISBN 0-8191-1508-8). U Pr of Amer.

Albanese, Robert. Management: Toward Accountability for Performance. rev. ed. 1978. text ed. 19.50x (ISBN 0-256-02039-6). Irwin.

Al-Banna, Hasan, jt. auth. see Wendell, Hasan.

Albano, Charles. TA on the Job. 1976. pap. 2.95 (ISBN 0-06-080385-1, P385, PL). Har-Row.

Albany County Sessions. Minutes of the Commissioners for Detecting & Defeating Conspiracies in the State of New York, 2 vols. Paltsits, Victor H., ed. LC 72-1835. (Era of the American Revolution Ser.). (Illus.). 1972. Repr. of 1909 ed. Set. lib. bdg. 95.00 (ISBN 0-306-70504-4). Da Capo.

Albarn, Keith, et al. The Language of Pattern: An Enquiry Inspired by Islamic Decoration. LC 73-20057. (Icon Editions). (Illus.). 112p. 1974. pap. 5.95x o.s.i. (ISBN 0-06-430050-1, IN-50, HarpT). Har-Row.

Al-Barrawi, Rashid. The Military Coup in Egypt. LC 79-2851. 269p. 1981. Repr. of 1952 ed. 21.00 (ISBN 0-8305-0027-8). Hyperion Conn.

Al-Bashir, Faisal S. A Structural Econometric Model of the Saudi Arabian Economy: 1960-1970. LC 77-441. 1977. 29.95 (ISBN 0-471-02177-6). Ronald Pr.

Albaugh, Dorothy P. The Kitchen Window. 1978. pap. 2.00x o.p. (ISBN 0-915020-15-7). Bardic.

Albeck, Chanoch. Einfuehrung in die Mischna. (Studia Judaica, 6). 493p. 1971. 41.75x (ISBN 3-11-006429-4). De Gruyter.

Albee, Edward. The Lady from Dubuque: A Play in Two Acts. pap. 2.50 (ISBN 0-686-69575-5). Dramatists Play.

Albee, George W. & Joffe, Justin M., eds. The Issues: An Overview of Primary Prevention. LC 76-53992. (Primary Prevention of Psychopathology Ser.: Vol. 1). (Illus.). 440p. 1977. text ed. 20.00x (ISBN 0-87451-135-6). U Pr of New Eng.

Albe-Fessard, Denise, ed. see World Congress on Pain, 1st, Florence, 1975.

Alber, Charles A., tr. see Semanov, V. I.

Alberger, Patricia L., ed. Building Your Alumni Program. 100p. (Orig.). 1980. pap. 14.50 (ISBN 0-89964-165-2). CASE.

Alberigo, Giuseppe & Weiler, Anton, eds. Election & Consensus in the Church. (Concilium Ser.: Religion in the Seventies: Church History, Vol. 77). 156p. 1972. pap. 4.95 (ISBN 0-8164-2533-7). Crossroad NY.

Alberione, James. Catechism for Adults. LC 75-160578. (Illus.). 1971. pap. 2.25 o.s.i. (ISBN 0-8198-0352-9). Dghtrs St Paul.

--Father Alberione's Prayerbook. 1974. plastic bdg. 4.00 o.s.i. (ISBN 0-8198-0291-3). Dghtrs St Paul.

--Mary, Hope of the World. 1958. 4.00 o.s.i. (ISBN 0-8198-0089-9); pap. 3.00 o.s.i. (ISBN 0-8198-0090-2). Dghtrs St Paul.

--Meditation Notes on Paul the Apostle. 1973. 2.00 o.s.i. (ISBN 0-8198-0252-2). Dghtrs St Paul.

Albers, Anni. On Designing. LC 62-12321. (Illus.). 1962. pap. 5.95 (ISBN 0-8195-6019-7, Pub. by Wesleyan U Pr). Columbia U Pr.

--On Weaving. LC 65-19855. (Illus.). 1965. 20.00x (ISBN 0-8195-3059-X, Pub. by Wesleyan U Pr); pap. 7.95 (ISBN 0-8195-6031-6). Columbia U Pr.

Albers, Henry H. Management: The Basic Concepts. 336p. 1981. Repr. of 1972 ed. lib. bdg. price not set (ISBN 0-89874-312-5). Krieger.

--Management: The Basic Concepts. LC 73-172949. 1979. text ed. 18.95 (ISBN 0-471-01925-9); text ed. 14.95 Arabic ed. (ISBN 0-471-06348-7); pap. 8.95 (ISBN 0-471-05142-X). Wiley.

Albers, Michael D. The Terror. (Orig.). 1980. pap. 2.25 (ISBN 0-532-23311-5). Manor Bks.

Albers, Vernon M. Amateur Cabinetmaking. LC 70-37801. (Illus.). 128p. 1972. 7.95 o.p. (ISBN 0-498-01012-0); large type 6.95 o.p. (ISBN 0-498-01855-5). A S Barnes.

Albert, A. Adrian. Fundamental Concepts of Higher Algebra. LC 56-5129. 1961. pap. 1.50 o.s.i. (ISBN 0-226-01177-1, P507, Phoen). U of Chicago Pr.

--Solid Analytic Geometry. 1966. pap. 1.95 o.s.i. (ISBN 0-226-01175-5, P530, Phoen). U of Chicago Pr.

Albert, Abraham A. Structure of Algebras. LC 41-9. (Colloquium Pbns. Ser.: Vol. 24). 1980. Repr. of 1939 ed. 25.20 (ISBN 0-8218-1024-3, COLL-24). Am Math.

Albert, Adrian A. Modern Higher Algebra. LC 63-11397. 1937. 9.00x o.s.i. (ISBN 0-226-01176-3). U of Chicago Pr.

Albert, Adrien. Selective Toxicity: The Physico-Chemical Basis of Theory. 6th ed. LC 78-15491. 662p. 1979. text ed. 39.95x (ISBN 0-412-15650-4, Pub. by Chapman & Hall). Methuen Inc.

--Selective Toxicity: The Physico-Chemical Basis of Theory. 6th ed. LC 78-15491. 1979. 42.50 (ISBN 0-470-26482-9). Halsted Pr.

Albert, Alain. The Crossing. LC 64-12397. 1964. 4.00 o.s.i. (ISBN 0-8076-0257-4). Braziller.

Albert, Burton. Codes for Kids. LC 76-25456. (Activity Bks). (Illus.). (gr. 4-6). 1976. 6.50g (ISBN 0-8075-1239-7). A Whitman.

--Mine, Yours, Ours. LC 77-9408. (Self-Starter Books). (Illus.). (ps). 1977. 6.50g (ISBN 0-8075-5148-1). A Whitman.

Albert, Burton, Jr. More Codes for Kids. Pacini, Kathy, ed. LC 79-245. (How-to Bks.). (Illus.). (gr. 3-6). 1979. 6.50g (ISBN 0-8075-5270-4). A Whitman.

Albert, Daniel M. & Puliafito, Carmen A., eds. Foundations of Ophthalmic Pathology. LC 78-9871. (Illus.). 1979. 49.75 (ISBN 0-8385-2690-X). ACC.

Albert, David H. Tell the American People: Perspectives on the Iranian Revolution. rev. ed. LC 80-83577. 1980. 14.95 (ISBN 0-86571-001-5); pap. 4.95 (ISBN 0-86571-003-1). Movement New Soc.

Albert, David H., ed. Tell the American People: Perspectives on the Iranian Revolution. LC 80-82242. 1980. pap. text ed. 3.80 (ISBN 0-86571-000-7). Movement New Soc.

Albert, Ethel M., jt. ed. see Vogt, Evon Z.

Albert, Helen M. Serving Successful Salads: A Merchandising Cookbook. LC 75-33339. 250p. 1975. 16.50 (ISBN 0-8436-2068-4). CBI Pub.

Albert, Kenneth J. Straight Talk About Small Business. (Illus.). 256p. 1980. 12.95 (ISBN 0-07-000949-X, P&RB). McGraw.

Albert, Kenneth S., ed. Statistical Considerations in Drug Absorption & Disposition. 256p. 1980. 18.00 (ISBN 0-917330-28-5). Am Pharm Assn.

Albert, Martin L., jt. auth. see Obler, Loraine K.

Albert, Marvin H. The Dark Goddess. LC 77-76219. 1978. 10.00 o.p. (ISBN 0-385-12182-2). Doubleday.

Albert, Marvin H., jt. auth. see Seidman, Theodore R.

Albert, Peter J., jt. ed. see Hoffman, Ronald.

Albert, Phyllis C. The Modernization of French Jewry: Consistory & Community in the Nineteenth Century. LC 76-50680. (Illus.). 472p. 1977. text ed. 27.50x (ISBN 0-87451-139-9). U Pr of New Eng.

Albert, Richard C. Trolleys from the Mines: Street Railways of Centre, Clearfield, Indiana & Jefferson Counties, Pennsylvania. (Illus.). 100p. (Orig.). 1980. pap. 9.00 (ISBN 0-911940-32-4). Cox.

Albert, Ronald & Hahnewald, Harry, eds. Eight Language Dictionary of Medical Technology. LC 78-40828. 1979. 75.00 (ISBN 0-08-023763-0). Pergamon.

Albert, Solomon N. Blood Volume & Extracellular Fluid Volume. 2nd ed. (Amer. Lec. Anesthesiology Ser.). (Illus.). 336p. 1971. 27.50 (ISBN 0-398-02193-7). C C Thomas.

Albert, Sondra R., jt. auth. see Abrams, A. J.

Albert, Stuart & Luck, Edward C., eds. On the Endings of Wars. (National University Publications, Political Science Ser.). 180p. 1980. 17.50 (ISBN 0-8046-9240-8). Kennikat.

Albert, William. Turnpike Road System, 1663-1840. LC 78-163062. (Illus.). 1972. 35.50 (ISBN 0-521-08221-8). Cambridge U Pr.

Alberti, Barbara. Delirium. Venuti, Lawrence, tr. from It. 1981. 15.00 (ISBN 0-374-13744-7). FS&G.

Alberti, Leon B. De re aedificatoria. (Documents of Art & Architectural History Series 2: Vol. 1). 420p. (Latin.). 1981. Repr. of 1485 ed. 45.00x (ISBN 0-89371-201-9). Broude Intl Edns.

Alberti, Rafael. The Lost Grove: Autobiography of a Spanish Poet in Exile. LC 74-79760. 1977. 12.95 (ISBN 0-520-02786-8); pap. 5.95 (ISBN 0-520-04265-4). U of Cal Pr.

--The Lost Grove: The Autobiography of a Spanish Poet in Exile. Berns, Gabriel, ed. (Illus.). 331p. 1981. pap. 5.95 (CAL 464). U of Cal Pr.

--The Other Shore: 100 Poems. Chantikian, Kosrof, ed. Elgorriaga, Jose A. & Paul, Martin, trs. from Span. LC 80-84602. (Modern Poets in Translation). 208p. (Orig.). 1981. 15.00 (ISBN 0-916426-05-X); pap. 7.95 (ISBN 0-916426-06-8). Kosmos.

Albertini Von, Rudolf see Von Albertini, Rudolf.

Alberts, Bruce & Fox, C. Fred, eds. Mechanistic Studies of DNA Replication & Genetic Recombination. (ICN-UCLA Symposia on Molecular & Cellular Biology Ser.: Vol. XIX). 1980. 48.00 (ISBN 0-12-048850-7). Acad Pr.

Alberts, Cecil D. Parent's Game Power for Phonics. (Illus.). 1979. pap. 25.00 (ISBN 0-915048-01-9). Spin-a-Test Pub.

--Parent's Power for Phonics. new ed. (Illus.). 1978. pap. text ed. 25.00 (ISBN 0-915048-01-9). Spin-A-Test Pub.

Alberts, David. Handbook of Mime & Pantomine. Date not set. 10.95 (ISBN 0-8238-0246-9). Plays. Postponed.

Alberts, Robert C. The Shaping of the Point: Pittsburgh's Renaissance Park. LC 79-26885. (Illus.). 264p. 1981. 12.95 (ISBN 0-8229-3422-1). U of Pittsburgh Pr.

Alberts, Ulvis. Poker Face. LC 80-70464. (Illus.). 144p. limited ed. 125.00 (ISBN 0-9605416-0-8); pap. 30.00 (ISBN 0-9605416-1-6). Angel City.

Albertson, Chris. Bessie. LC 79-163353. 253p. 1981. pap. 6.95. Stein & Day.

Albertson, Dean. Roosevelt's Farmer: Claude R. Wickard in the New Deal. LC 74-23430. (Fdr & the Era of the New Deal Ser.). 1975. Repr. of 1961 ed. lib. bdg. 39.50 (ISBN 0-306-70702-0). Da Capo.

Albertson, Dean, ed. Eisenhower As President. (Orig.). 1963. pap. 2.95 o.p. (ISBN 0-8090-0061-X, AmCen). Hill & Wang.

Albertson, Dorothy L. Business Machine Practice Set. (Illus.). 192p. (gr. 10-12). 1974. text ed. 7.36 o.p. (ISBN 0-07-000950-3, G); tchr's manual & key 3.95 o.p. (ISBN 0-07-000951-1). McGraw.

Albertson, Maurice L., et al. Fluid Mechanics for Engineers. 1960. text ed. 25.95 (ISBN 0-13-322578-X). P-H.

Albertson, Sandra H. Endings & Beginnings: A Harvesting. 1980. 8.95 (ISBN 0-394-50627-8). Random.

Albertus Magnus. The Boke of Secretes. LC 76-28227. (English Experience Ser: No. 116). 168p. 1969. Repr. of 1525 ed. 15.00 (ISBN 90-221-0116-9). Walter J Johnson.

Albery, John. Electrode Kinetics. (Oxford Chemistry Ser). (Illus.). 196p. 1975. 24.95x (ISBN 0-19-855433-8). Oxford U Pr.

Albery, W. J. & Hitchman, M. L. Ring-Disc Electrodes. (Oxford Science Research Papers Ser). (Illus.). 1971. pap. 29.00x (ISBN 0-19-855349-8). Oxford U Pr.

Albin, Edgar A., et al. Selections from the Permanent Collection of the Springfield Art Museum. Landwehr, William C., ed. LC 80-53333. 100p. (Orig.). 1980. pap. text ed. 9.95 (ISBN 0-934306-03-6). Springfield.

Albin, Mel & Cavallo, Dominick. Family Life in America. (Illus.). 350p. 1980. 8.95 (ISBN 0-686-64847-1). Revisionary.

Albin, Mel, et al, eds. New Directions in Psychohistory: The Adelphi Papers in Honor of Erik H. Erikson. LC 78-4410. 240p. 1980. 25.95x (ISBN 0-669-02350-7). Lexington Bks.

Albin, R. J. Handbook of Cryosurgery. (Science & Practice of Surgery: Vol. 1). 1980. 59.75 (ISBN 0-8247-6981-3). Dekker.

Albini, Joseph L. American Mafia: Genesis of a Legend. LC 70-147120. (Orig.). 1979. Repr. of 1971 ed. 22.50x (ISBN 0-89197-013-4). Irvington.

Albinoni, Tomaso. Zenobia Regina Di Palmireni. Brown, Howard M., ed. LC 76-21018. (Italian Opera 1640-1770 Ser.: Vol. 15). 1979. lib. bdg. 75.00 (ISBN 0-8240-2614-4). Garland Pub.

Albinski, Henry S. Canadian & Australian Politics in Comparative Perspective. 448p. 1973. text ed. 15.95x (ISBN 0-19-501682-3). Oxford U Pr.

Albion, Mark S. & Farris, Paul. Advertising Controversy: Evidence on the Economic Effects of Advertising. 224p. 1980. 19.95 (ISBN 0-86569-057-X). Auburn Hse.

Albion, Robert G. The Makers of Naval Policy Seventeen Ninety-Eight to Nineteen Forty-Seven. Reed, Rowena, ed. LC 79-90772. 752p. 1980. 22.95x (ISBN 0-87021-360-1). Naval Inst Pr.

Albion, Robert G., et al. New England & the Sea. LC 72-3694. (The American Maritime Library: Vol. 5). (Illus.). 303p. Date not set. 15.95 (ISBN 0-8195-4052-8); pap. 7.00 (ISBN 0-913372-23-4) (ISBN 0-8195-6046-4). Mystic Seaport.

Albrecht, Bob. My Computer Likes Me. LC 77-70966. 1972. pap. 4.95 (ISBN 0-918398-12-6). Dilithium Pr.

Albrecht, G., ed. Weyer's Warships of the World: 1979-81 Flottentaschenbuch. 55th ed. LC 46-43961. (Illus.). 680p. (Eng. & Ger.). 1979. 48.95x (ISBN 0-933852-20-7). Nautical & Aviation.

Albrecht, Julius, jt. ed. see Collatz, Lothar.

Albrecht, Karl. Executive Tune-Up: Personal Effectiveness Skills for Business & Professional People. (Illus.). 224p. 1981. text ed. 13.95 (ISBN 0-13-294215-1, Spec); pap. text ed. 6.95 (ISBN 0-13-294207-0, Spec). P-H.

--Stress & the Manager: Making It Work for You. (Illus.). 1978. 14.95 (ISBN 0-13-852681-8, Spec); pap. 5.95 (ISBN 0-13-852673-7). P-H.

--Successful Management by Objectives: An Action Manual. LC 77-14971. (Illus.). 1978. 14.95 (ISBN 0-13-863266-9, Spec); pap. 4.95 (ISBN 0-13-863258-8, Spec). P-H.

Albrecht, Karl G., jt. auth. see Boshear, Walton C.

Albrecht, Lillie V. Spinning Wheel Secret. (Illus.). (gr. 4-6). 1965. PLB 3.99 o.s.i. (ISBN 0-8038-6668-2). Hastings.

--Susanna's Candlestick. LC 77-126422. (Illus.). (gr. 4-6). 1970. PLB 4.44 o.s.i. (ISBN 0-8038-6691-7). Hastings.

Albrecht, P., jt. ed. see Birch, C.

Albrecht, Robert C., ed. World of Short Fiction. LC 69-11841. 1970. pap. text ed. 8.95 (ISBN 0-02-900350-4). Free Pr.

Albrecht, Robert L., et al. Basic. 2nd ed. LC 77-14998. (Self-Teaching Guide Ser.). 1978. pap. text ed. 8.95x (ISBN 0-471-03500-9). Wiley.

Albrecht, Val. Larger Than Life: Joe Namath. LC 75-42313. (Sports Profiles Ser.). (gr. 4-11). 1976. PLB 8.50 (ISBN 0-8172-0112-2). Raintree Pubs.

Albrecht, W., Jr. Macroeconomic Principles. 1979. pap. 10.95 (ISBN 0-13-542738-X); study guide & wkbk. 8.95 (ISBN 0-13-227553-8). P-H.

Albrecht, William P., Jr. Economics. 2nd ed. (Illus.). 1979. text ed. 18.95 o.p. (ISBN 0-13-227546-5); study guide & wkbk. 8.95 o.p. (ISBN 0-13-227553-8). P-H.

Albrecht, William P, Jr. Microeconomic Principles. (Illus.). 1979. pap. text ed. 10.95 (ISBN 0-13-581314-X); study guide & wkbk. 8.95 (ISBN 0-13-227553-8). P-H.

Albrecht-Carrie, Rene. Adolphe Thiers. (World Leaders Ser.: No. 67). 1977. lib. bdg. 12.50 (ISBN 0-8057-7717-2). Twayne.

--Italy from Napoleon to Mussolini. LC 49-50178. 1950. pap. 6.00x (ISBN 0-231-08508-7). Columbia U Pr.

Albrecht-Carrie, Rene, ed. Concert of Europe. LC 68-13327. (Documentary History of Western Civilization Ser.). 1968. 15.00x o.s.i. (ISBN 0-8027-2004-8). Walker & Co.

Albricus. Allegoriae Poeticae, Repr. Of 1520 Ed. Incl. Theologia Mythologica. Pictorius, Georg. Repr. of 1532 ed; Apotheoseos Tam Exterarum Gentium Quam Romanorum Deorum. Pictorius, Georg. Repr. of 1558 ed. LC 75-27845. (Renaissance & the Gods Ser.: Vol. 4). (Illus.). 1976. lib. bdg. 73.00 (ISBN 0-8240-2053-7). Garland Pub.

Albright, Arnita, jt. auth. see Albright, Hardie.

Albright, Bets P., jt. auth. see Albright, Peter.

Albright, Daniel. Representation & the Imagination: Beckett, Kafka, Nabokov, & Schoenberg. LC 80-26975. (Chicago Originals Ser.). 256p. 1981. lib. bdg. 20.00x (ISBN 0-226-01252-2). U of Chicago Pr.

Albright, David E. Communism & Political Systems in Western Europe. (Westview Special Studies in West European Politics & Society). 1979. lib. bdg. 27.50x (ISBN 0-89158-308-4). Westview.

Albright, Gretchen E. Survival Sanctuary: A Scouts Guide to Preparedness. LC 80-54281. (Illus.). 146p. (Orig.). 1980. pap. 4.95 (ISBN 0-938064-00-2). Secure Futures.

Albright, Hardie. Stage Direction in Transition. LC 70-163774. (Illus.). 352p. 1972. text ed. 15.95x (ISBN 0-8221-0013-4). Dickenson.

Albright, Hardie & Albright, Arnita. Acting: The Creative Process. 3rd ed. 432p. 1980. pap. text ed. 13.95x (ISBN 0-534-00744-9). Wadsworth Pub.

Albright, Horace M. & Taylor, Frank J. Oh, Ranger! rev. 14th ed. Jones, William R., ed. (Illus.). 176p. pap. 6.95 (ISBN 0-89646-068-1). Outbooks.

Albright, Peter & Albright, Bets P. Body, Mind & Spirit: The Journey Toward Wholeness. 2nd ed. (Illus.). 320p. 1981. pap. 9.95 (ISBN 0-8289-0386-7). Greene.

Albright, Priscilla, jt. auth. see Albright, Rod.

Albright, Rod & Albright, Priscilla. Walks in the Great Smokies. LC 79-4898. (Illus.). 192p. 1979. lib. bdg. 10.25 o.p. (ISBN 0-914788-14-0). East Woods.

Albright, Roger. Old Houses, New Homes. (Illus.). 256p. 1980. 14.95 (ISBN 0-8289-0395-6); pap. 9.95 (ISBN 0-8289-0396-4). Greene.

Albright, William F. Biblical Period from Abraham to Ezra: A Historical Survey. pap. 3.50x (ISBN 0-06-130102-7, TB102, Torch). Har-Row.

Albright, William Foxwell. From the Stone Age to Christianity. 2nd ed. 1957. pap. 2.50 (ISBN 0-385-09306-3, A100, Anch). Doubleday.

Alburger, Mary A. The Violin Makers: Portrait of a Living Craft. 1978. text ed. 26.25x (ISBN 0-575-02442-9). Humanities.

Albus, James S. Brains, Behavior, & Robotics. 400p. 1981. 16.95 (ISBN 0-07-000975-9, BYTE Bks). McGraw.

--Peoples' Capitalism: The Economics of the Robot Revolution. LC 75-44585. 157p. 1976. 10.50 (ISBN 0-685-66376-0); pap. 5.95 (ISBN 0-685-66377-9). New World Bks.

Al-Bustani, Butrus, jt. auth. see Al Muhit, Muhit.

Alcalay, Reuben. The Complete Hebrew-English, English-Hebrew Dictionary, 3 vols. 7180p. 1980. Repr. of 1965 ed. 62.00 set (ISBN 0-89961-017-X). Vol. 1 (ISBN 0-89961-003-X). Vol. 2 (ISBN 0-89961-007-2). Vol. 3 (ISBN 0-89961-008-0). SBS Pub.

Alcaly, Roger, jt. auth. see Mermelstein, David.

Alcantara, Shimon De see De Alcantara, Shimon.

Alcazar, Carol C. Medical Typist's Guide for Histories & Physicals. 2nd ed. 1974. spiral bdg. 7.00 (ISBN 0-87488-976-6). Med Exam.

Alchian, Armen A. & Allen, William R. Exchange & Production: Theory in Use. 2nd ed. 1977. pap. 14.95x (ISBN 0-534-00493-8). Wadsworth Pub.

--University Economics: Elements of Inquiry. 3rd ed. 1971. 21.95x (ISBN 0-534-00030-4); study guide 6.95x (ISBN 0-534-00184-X). Wadsworth Pub.

Alciati, Andrea. Emblematum Libellus Cum Commentariis. LC 75-27869. (Renaissance & the Gods Ser.: Vol. 25). (Illus.). 1977. Repr. of 1621 ed. lib. bdg. 73.00 (ISBN 0-8240-2074-X). Garland Pub.

Alcock, Anne. They're Off. (Illus.). 1979. 15.75 (ISBN 0-85131-299-3, Dist. by Sporting Book Center). J A Allen.

Alcock, C. B. Principles of Pyrometallurgy. 1977. 48.00 (ISBN 0-12-048950-3). Acad Pr.

Alcock, Gudrun. Run, Westy, Run. LC 66-14612. (Illus.). (gr. 4-7). 1966. PLB 7.44 o.p. (ISBN 0-688-51058-2). Lothrop.

Alcock, James E. Parapsychology-Science or Magic? A Psychological Perspective. (Foundations & Philosophy of Science & Technology Ser.). 300p. 1981. 45.00 (ISBN 0-08-025773-9); pap. 20.00 (ISBN 0-08-025772-0). Pergamon.

Alcock, John. Mons Perfectionis. LC 74-28823. (English Experience Ser.: No. 706). 1974. Repr. of 1497 ed. 6.00 (ISBN 90-221-0706-X). Walter J Johnson.

--Spousage of a Virgin to Christ. LC 74-80158. (English Experience Ser.: No. 638). (Illus.). 19p. 1974. Repr. of 1496 ed. 3.50 (ISBN 90-221-0638-1). Walter J Johnson.

Alcock, L. Arthur's Britain: History & Archaeology AD 367-634. 1972. 19.95 (ISBN 0-312-05530-7). St Martin.

Alcock, Randal H. Botanical Names for English Readers. LC 73-174935. xviii, 236p. 1971. Repr. of 1876 ed. 18.00 (ISBN 0-8103-3823-8). Gale.

Alcorn, Charles L., jt. auth. see Nicholson, Charles L.

Alcorn, George T., jt. ed. see Jordan, James M.

Alcorn, Pat. Success & Survival in the Family Owned Business. 256p. 1981. 17.95 (ISBN 0-07-000961-9). McGraw.

Alcosser, Edward, et al. How to Build a Working Digital Computer. (gr. 7 up). 1967. pap. 7.75 (ISBN 0-8104-0748-5). Hayden.

Alcott, Julia. Long Lost Love. Date not set. pap. 1.25 o.p. (ISBN 0-451-07190-5, Y7190, Sig). NAL.

Alcott, Louisa M. Good Wives. (gr. 4 up). 1979. pap. 2.25 (ISBN 0-14-031127-0, Puffin). Penguin.

--Jack & Jill. (gr. 5 up). 1879. 9.95 (ISBN 0-316-03092-9). Little.

--Little Men. (gr. 7 up). 1871. 9.95 (ISBN 0-316-03094-5). Little.

--Little Men. (gr. 6-8). 1963. 4.95g o.s.i. (ISBN 0-02-700150-4). Macmillan.

--Little Women. LC 68-21171. (gr. 7 up). 1868. 10.95 (ISBN 0-316-03095-3). Little.

--Little Women. (Illus.). (gr. 6-8). 1962. 6.95g o.s.i. (ISBN 0-02-700180-6). Macmillan.

--Little Women. 1963. 8.50 (ISBN 0-685-20188-0). Saphrograph.

--Little Women. LC 78-2919. (Raintree's Illustrated Classics). (Illus.). (gr. 5-8). 1978. PLB 9.65 (ISBN 0-8393-6210-2). Raintree Child.

--Rose in Bloom. (gr. 7 up). 1876. 9.95 (ISBN 0-316-03098-8). Little.

Alcott, Louisa May. Plots and Counterplots: More Unknown Thrillers of Louisa May Alcott. Stern, Madeleine, intro. by. (Illus.). 320p. 1976. 9.95 o.p. (ISBN 0-688-03046-7). Morrow.

Alcyone. At the Feet of the Master. 1970. pap. 1.95 (ISBN 0-8356-0196-X, Quest). Theos Pub Hse.

Alda, Arlene. Arlene Alda's ABC Book. LC 80-66261. (Illus.). 64p. (ps-2). 1981. 12.95 (ISBN 0-89742-043-8). Dawne-Leigh. Postponed.

Al-Daffa, A. A. ARA: A Brief Exposition of Arabic & Islamic Scientific Heritage. 1979. pap. text ed. 10.95 (ISBN 0-471-05348-1). Wiley.

Aldag, Ramon & Brief, Arthur. Managing Organizational Behavior. (Illus.). 500p. 1981. text ed. 15.95 (ISBN 0-8299-0306-2). West Pub.

Aldan, Daisy. The Art & Craft of Poetry. 96p. 1981. 7.95 (ISBN 0-88427-047-5, Dist. by Caroline Hse). North River.

--The Art & Craft of Poetry: A Guide for Students & Teachers. 7.95 (ISBN 0-88427-050-5). Green Hill.

--Breakthrough. 6.95 (ISBN 0-913152-02-1). Green Hill.

--A Golden Story. 6.95 (ISBN 0-913152-49-8). Green Hill.

--Or Learn to Walk on Water. 3.50 (ISBN 0-913152-20-X). Green Hill.

--Stones. 4.95 (ISBN 0-913152-14-5). Green Hill.

--Verses for the Zodiac. 7.95 (ISBN 0-913152-10-2). Green Hill.

Aldan, Daisy, tr. see Witzenman, Herbert.

Aldanov, Mark. Zagadka Tolstogo. LC 79-91652. (Slavic Reprint Ser.: No. 7). 127p. (Rus.). 1969. pap. 3.00 (ISBN 0-87057-114-1, Pub. by Brown U Pr). Univ Pr of New England.

Aldaraca, Bridget, et al, eds. Nicaragua in Revolution: The Poets Speak. LC 80-16304. (Studies in Marxism: Vol. 5). (Bilingual: spanish & english). 1980. 12.95 (ISBN 0-930656-10-5); pap. 6.95 (ISBN 0-930656-09-1). Marxist Educ.

Aldcroft, Derek & Fearon, Peter. Economic Growth in Twentieth Century Britain. 1970. 8.75x (ISBN 0-333-10041-7); pap. text ed. 4.75x (ISBN 0-333-10595-8). Humanities.

Aldcroft, Derek H. From Versailles to Wall Street: The International Economy in the 1920's. 1977. 20.00x (ISBN 0-520-03336-1). U of Cal Pr.

--Inter-War Economy: Britain 1919-1939. LC 70-20963. 1971. 21.50x (ISBN 0-231-03517-9). Columbia U Pr.

--Studies in British Transport History, 1870-1970. 1974. 17.50 o.p. (ISBN 0-7153-6505-3). David & Charles.

Aldcroft, Derek H. & Fearon, Peter, eds. British Economic Fluctuations: Seventeen-Ninety to Nineteen Thirty-Nine. LC 77-178900. 1972. text ed. 19.95 (ISBN 0-312-10045-0). St Martin.

Aldcroft, Derek H., jt. ed. see Buxton, Neil K.

Aldecoa, Ignacio. Cuentos. (Easy Readers). (Illus.). 1977. pap. text ed. 3.75 (ISBN 0-88436-283-3). EMC.

Alden, Betsey, jt. ed. see Castano, Francis A.

Alden, Daisy. Between High Tides. 6.95. Green Hill.

Alden, Dauril. Royal Government in Colonial Brazil: With Special Reference to the Administration of the Marquis of Lavradio, Viceroy, 1769-1779. (Illus.). 1968. 32.50x (ISBN 0-520-00008-0). U of Cal Pr.

Alden, Dauril, ed. Colonial Roots of Modern Brazil: Papers of the Newberry Library Conference. LC 78-174458. 1973. 21.50x (ISBN 0-520-02140-1). U of Cal Pr.

Alden, Douglas W., ed. French Twenty Bibliography: Critical & Bibliographical References for the Study of French Literature Since 1885, No. 32. LC 77-648803. (Orig.). 1981. pap. 42.00 (ISBN 0-933444-37-0). French Inst.

Alden, J. & Morgan, R. Regional Planning: A Comprehensive View. LC 74-12635. 1974. 24.95 (ISBN 0-470-02053-9). Halsted Pr.

Alden, John. European Americana: A Chronological Guide to Writings on the Americas Published in Europe 1493-1600, Vol. I. 467p. 1980. 50.00 (ISBN 0-918414-03-2). Readex Bks.

Alden, John R. American Revolution, Seventeen Seventy Five to Seventeen Eighty-Three. LC 53-11826. (New American Nation Ser). 1954. 19.95x (ISBN 0-06-010045-1, HarpT). Har-Row.

--Pioneer America. (The History of Human Society Ser.). (Illus.). 1966. 7.95 o.p. (ISBN 0-394-44089-7). Knopf.

Alden, Peter & Gooders, John. Finding Birds Around the World. (Illus.). 704p. 1980. 16.95 (ISBN 0-395-29114-3). HM.

Alden, Sue. The Magnificent Challenge. (YA) 1976. 4.95 o.p. (ISBN 0-685-69053-9, Avalon). Bouregy.

--Nurse of St. John. (YA) 1977. 4.95 o.p. (ISBN 0-685-75641-6, Avalon). Bouregy.

Alden, Thomas. Scientific Management: The Essential Knowledge Which Everyone, but Absolutely Everyone Ought to Possess of the Main Guiding Principles Which Intelligent Men Follow in the Management of Their Business & Personal Affairs. (The Essential Knowledge Ser.). 1978. plastic spiral bdg. 28.45 (ISBN 0-89266-120-8). Am Classical Coll Pr.

Alder, Henry L. & Roessler, Edward B. Introduction to Probability & Statistics. 6th ed. LC 76-13643. (Illus.). 1977. text ed. 19.95x (ISBN 0-7167-0467-6); answer book avail. W H Freeman.

Alder, Vera S. Finding of the Third Eye. 1980. pap. 3.95 (ISBN 0-87728-056-8). Weiser.

--From the Mundane to the Magnificent. 1980. pap. 5.95 (ISBN 0-87728-504-7). Weiser.

Alder, William H. & Nordin, Albert A. Immunology of Aging. 240p. 1981. 59.95 (ISBN 0-8493-5809-4). CRC Pr.

Alderfer, Clayton P. Existence, Relatedness & Growth: Human Needs in Organizational Settings. LC 78-156839. 1972. 15.95 (ISBN 0-02-900390-3). Free Pr.

Alderfer, Clayton P. & Brown, L. Dave. Learning from Changing: Organizational Diagnosis & Development. LC 75-34081. (Sage Library of Social Research: Vol. 19). 1975. 18.00x (ISBN 0-8039-0554-8); pap. 8.95x (ISBN 0-8039-0555-6). Sage.

Alderfer, Clayton P. & Cooper, Cary L. Advances in Experimental Social Processes, Vol. 2. 1980. 41.75 (ISBN 0-471-27623-5, Pub. by Wiley-Interscience). Wiley.

Alderfer, Harold F. Pennsylvania Local Government 1681-1974: Bicentennial Edition. LC 73-93891. 1975. pap. 2.95 o.p. (ISBN 0-931992-26-5). Penns Valley.

Alderman, Clifford. You Can Be a Writer: A Career & Leisure Guide. 160p. (gr. 9-12). 1981. PLB price not set (ISBN 0-671-34047-6). Messner.

Alderman, Clifford L. Colonists for Sale: The Story of Indentured Servants in America. 192p. (gr. 5-9). 1975. 8.95 (ISBN 0-02-700220-9, 70022). Macmillan.

--The Colony of Connecticut. LC 74-8893. (First Bks). (Illus.). 96p. (gr. 6 up). 1975. PLB 4.90 o.p. (ISBN 0-531-02773-2). Watts.

--The Dark Eagle: The Story of Benedict Arnold. LC 75-40087. 160p. (gr. 5-9). 1976. 8.95 (ISBN 0-02-700210-1, 70021). Macmillan.

--Rhode Island Colony. LC 69-10461. (Forge of Freedom Ser). (Illus.). (gr. 5 up). 1969. 8.95 o.s.i. (ISBN 0-02-700250-0, CCPr). Macmillan.

--Royal Opposition: The British Generals in the American Revolution. LC 73-119122. (Illus.). (gr. 7-12). 1970. 7.95 (ISBN 0-02-700240-3, CCPr). Macmillan.

--Rum, Slaves & Molasses: The Story of New England's Triangular Trade. LC 70-188772. (gr. 5-8). 1972. 4.95g o.s.i. (ISBN 0-02-700230-6, CCPr). Macmillan.

--Symbols of Magic: Amulets & Talismans. LC 76-51277. (Illus.). (gr. 7 up). 1977. PLB 7.79 o.p. (ISBN 0-671-32837-9). Messner.

Alderman, Geoffrey. British Elections. 1978. 30.00 (ISBN 0-7134-0195-8, Pub. by Batsford England); pap. 11.50 (ISBN 0-7134-0196-6). David & Charles.

Alderman, Harold G. Nietzsche's Gift. LC 76-25612. xvi, 184p. 1977. 15.00x (ISBN 0-8214-0231-5); pap. 5.50 (ISBN 0-8214-0385-0). Ohio U Pr.

Alderman, Karen C., jt. auth. see Levitan, Sar A.

Alderman, R. K. & Cross, J. A. Tactics of Resignation: A Study in British Cabinet Government. (Library of Political Studies). (Orig.). 1967. text ed. 5.25x (ISBN 0-7100-5130-1); pap. text ed. 2.75x (ISBN 0-7100-5119-0). Humanities.

Aldersey-Williams, Arthur, jt. auth. see Burberry, Peter.

Alderson, A. D. & Iz, Fahir, eds. Concise Oxford Turkish Dictionary. 1959. 17.95x (ISBN 0-19-864109-5). Oxford U Pr.

Alderson, Frederick. Bicycles. (Junior Reference Ser.). (Illus.). 64p. (gr. 7 up). 1974. 7.95 (ISBN 0-7136-1464-1). Dufour.

--Outdoor Games. (Junior Reference Ser.). (Illus.). 64p. (gr. 7 up). 1980. 7.95 (ISBN 0-7136-2031-5). Dufour.

Alderson, George & Sentman, Everett. How You Can Influence Congress: The Complete Handbook for the Citizen Lobbyist. 1979. 15.95 o.p.; pap. 9.95 (ISBN 0-87690-320-0). Dutton.

Alderson, John. Policing Freedom. 288p. 1979. 22.95x (ISBN 0-7121-1815-2, Pub. by Macdonald & Evans England). Intl Ideas.

Alderson, Michael. International Mortality Statistics. 380p. 1981. lib. bdg. 55.00 (ISBN 0-87196-514-3). Facts on File.

Alderson, Nannie T. & Smith, Helena H. A Bride Goes West. 5.00 o.p. (ISBN 0-8446-0452-6). Peter Smith.

Alderson, Philip O. Atlas of Pediatric Nuclear Medicine, Nineteen Seventy-Eight. LC 78-24369. (Illus.). 1978. text ed. 46.50 (ISBN 0-8016-0107-X). Mosby.

Alderson, William T. & Low, Shirley P. Interpretation of Historic Sites. LC 75-33292. (Illus.). 1976. pap. 6.95 (ISBN 0-910050-19-8). AASLH.

Alderton, David & Booker, John. The Batsford Guide to the Industrial Archaeology of East Anglia. LC 79-56490. (Illus.). 150p. 1980. 40.00 (ISBN 0-7134-2233-5, Pub. by Batsford England). David & Charles.

Aldgate, Anthony. Cinema & History: British Newsreels & the Spanish Civil War. (Illus.). 1979. text ed. 31.25x (ISBN 0-85967-485-1). Humanities.

Alding, Peter. A Man Condemned. 1981. 9.95 (ISBN 0-8027-5443-0). Walker & Co.

--Murder Is Suspected. 1978. 7.95 o.s.i. (ISBN 0-8027-5389-2). Walker & Co.

--Ransom Town. 1979. 7.95 o.s.i. (ISBN 0-8027-5409-0). Walker & Co.

Aldington, Richard. A Book of Characters from Theophrastus Joseph Hall, Sir Thomas Overbury, Nicolas Breton, John Earle, Thomas Fuller, & Other English Authors; Jean De la Bruyere, Vauvenargues, & Other French Authors. 559p. 1980. Repr. of 1924 ed. lib. bdg. 50.00 (ISBN 0-8482-0049-7). Norwood Edns.

Aldiss, Brian. Barefoot in the Head. 224p. 1981. pap. 2.25 (ISBN 0-380-53561-0, 53561). Avon.

--Brothers of the Head. (Illus.). 1977. pap. 7.95 (ISBN 0-8467-0386-6, Pub. by Two Continents). Hippocrene Bks.

--Earthworks. 1980. pap. 1.95 (ISBN 0-686-69267-5, 52159). Avon.

--Enemies of the System. 112p. 1981. pap. 1.95 (ISBN 0-380-53793-1, 53793). Avon.

--Enemies of the System: A Tale of Homo Uniformis. LC 77-11541. 1978. 7.95 o.s.i. (ISBN 0-06-010054-0, HarpT). Har-Row.

--Neanderthal Planet. 192p. 1981. pap. 2.25 (ISBN 0-380-54197-1, 54197). Avon.

--No Time Like Tomorrow. 160p. (RL 7). Date not set. pap. 1.25 (ISBN 0-451-06969-2, Y6969, Sig). NAL.

--Perilous Planets. 1979. pap. 2.50 (ISBN 0-380-47100-0, 47100). Avon.

--A Report on Probability. 144p. 1980. pap. 1.95 (ISBN 0-380-52498-8, 52498). Avon.

--The Saliva Tree. (Science Fiction Ser.). 1981. lib. bdg. 16.95 (ISBN 0-8398-2566-8). Gregg.

--Starswarm. 160p. (RL 9). Date not set. pap. 1.25 (ISBN 0-451-06883-1, Y6883, Sig). NAL.

Aldiss, Brian, ed. Galactic Empires, Vol. I. 1978. pap. 2.25 (ISBN 0-380-42341-3, 42341). Avon.

--Space Odysseys. 1978. pap. 1.95 o.p. (ISBN 0-425-03681-2, Medallion). Berkley Pub.

Aldiss, Brian W. An Island Called Moreau. 1981. 10.95 (ISBN 0-671-25453-7). S&S.

--The Shape of Further Things. 1970. 7.50 (ISBN 0-571-09472-4, Pub. by Faber & Faber). Merrimack Bk Serv.

Aldiss, Brian W. & Harrison, Harry, eds. Hell's Cartographers: Some Personal Histories of Science Fiction Writers. LC 75-25074. (Illus.). 256p. (YA) 1976. 8.95 o.p. (ISBN 0-06-010052-4, HarpT). Har-Row.

Aldiss, Brian W., jt. ed. see Harrison, Harry.

Al-Doory, Yousef. The Epidemiology of Human Mycotic Diseases. (Illus.). 364p. 1976. 36.50 (ISBN 0-398-03380-3). C C Thomas.

--Laboratory Medical Mycology. LC 79-22500. (Illus.). 410p. 1980. text ed. 24.50 (ISBN 0-8121-0695-4). Lea & Febiger.

Aldous, Joan, et al, eds. Politics & Programs of Family Policy: United States & European Perspectives. LC 80-50270. 224p. (Orig.). 1980. pap. text ed. 8.95 (ISBN 0-268-01539-2). U of Notre Dame Pr.

Aldous, Tony, ed. Trees and Buildings. 95p. 1980. pap. 9.50 (ISBN 0-900630-73-6, Pub. by RIBA). Intl Schol Bk Serv.

Aldred, Cyril. Egyptian Art. (World of Art Ser.). (Illus.). 300p. 1980. 17.95 (ISBN 0-19-520223-6); pap. 9.95 (ISBN 0-19-520224-4). Oxford U Pr.

Aldrich, Alexander. How to Write a Book: The Essential Knowledge Which Everyone, but Abolutely Everyone Should Possess on the Art of Writing for Fame & Profit. (The Essential Knowledge Ser. Books). (Illus.). 1978. plastic spiral bdg. 28.45 (ISBN 0-89266-123-2). Am Classical Coll Pr.

Aldrich, Arthur. Flowers & Flowering Plants. (Easy-Read Fact Book Ser.). (Illus.). 48p. (gr. 2-4). 1976. PLB 3.90 o.p. (ISBN 0-531-01214-X). Watts.

Aldrich, Dorothy, jt. ed. see Schwartz, Dorothy T.

Aldrich, Earl M., Jr. Modern Short Story in Peru. 1966. 17.50 (ISBN 0-299-03960-9). U of Wis Pr.

Aldrich, Frank T., jt. auth. see Lounsbury, John F.

Aldrich, Joseph C. Life-Style Evangelisim: Crossing Traditional Boundaries to Reach the Unbelieving World. (Critical Concern Bks.). 1981. 8.95 (ISBN 0-930014-46-4). Multnomah.

Aldrich, Pearl. The Impact of Mass Media. 192p. (gr. 10-12). 1975. pap. text ed. 6.95 (ISBN 0-8104-6000-9). Hayden.

Aldrich, Peggy. The Aldrich Report on Men. 1977. pap. text ed. 1.95 (ISBN 0-505-51158-4, BT51158). Tower Bks.

--My First. 1976. pap. 1.75 o.p. (ISBN 0-685-69148-9, LB355KK, Leisure Bks). Nordon Pubns.

--Nights in the Garden of Love. (Orig.). 1975. pap. 1.50 o.p. (ISBN 0-685-52939-8, LB256NK, Leisure Bks). Nordon Pubns.

Aldrich, Putnam. Ornamentation in J. S. Bach's Organ Works. LC 78-17258. (Music Reprint, 1978 Ser.). (Illus.). 1978. Repr. of 1950 ed. lib. bdg. 15.95 (ISBN 0-306-77590-5). Da Capo.

Aldrich, Ruth I. John Galt. (English Authors Ser.: No. 231). 1978. lib. bdg. 12.50 (ISBN 0-8057-6657-X). Twayne.

Aldrich, Ruth I., ed. see Holcroft, Thomas.

Aldrich, Thomas B. The Story of a Bad Boy. LC 75-32173. (Classics of Children's Literature, 1621-1932: Vol. 36). (Illus.). 1976. Repr. of 1870 ed. PLB 38.00 (ISBN 0-8240-2285-8). Garland Pub.

Aldrich, Virgil. Philosophy of Art. (Illus.). 1963. pap. 7.95x ref. ed. (ISBN 0-13-663765-5). P-H.

Aldrich, Winifred. Metric Pattern Cutting. (Illus.). 1977. pap. 18.95 (ISBN 0-263-06119-1). Transatlantic.

Aldridge. Quantitative Aspects of Science & Technology. LC 67-22016. 1967. pap. text ed. 11.95x (ISBN 0-675-09699-5). Merrill.

Aldridge, Adele. Notpoems. LC 72-23824. 1976. pap. 5.95 (ISBN 0-915600-01-3, 0753-5). Swallow.

Aldridge, Alan. Power, Authority & Restrictive Practices: A Sociological Essay on Industrial Relations. 1976. 25.00x (ISBN 0-631-17230-0, Pub. by Basil Blackwell). Biblio Dist.

Aldridge, Alan & Walker, Ted. The Lion's Cavalcade. (Illus.). (gr. 3 up). 1981. 10.95 (ISBN 0-224-01701-2, Pub. by Chatto-Bodley-Jonathan). Merrimack Bk Serv.

Aldridge, Alan, ed. Beatles Illustrated Lyrics. (Illus.). 1969. 5.95 o.s.i. (ISBN 0-440-00472-1, Sey Lawr). Delacorte.

Aldridge, Carter, tr. see Pasamanik, Luisa.

Aldridge, Fern. My Happy World. (Hello World Ser.). 1976. pap. 1.65 (ISBN 0-8163-0294-4). Pacific Pr Pub Assn.

Aldridge, G. J., ed. see International Association Of Gerontology - 5th Congress.

Aldridge, John W., ed. Critiques & Essays on Modern Fiction, 1920-1951: Representing the Achievement of Modern American & British Critics. LC 52-6180. 1952. 13.95 (ISBN 0-8260-0275-7). Wiley.

Aldridge, Robert C. Counterforce Syndrome: A Guide to U. S. Nuclear Weapons & Strategic Doctrine. rev. ed. (Illus.). 86p. 1979. pap. 4.95 (ISBN 0-89758-008-7). Inst Policy Stud.

Aldridge, Sarah. Cytherea's Breath. 1980. 6.50 (ISBN 0-930044-02-9). Naiad Pr.

--Tottie: The Tale of the Sixties. 181p. 1980. 5.95 (ISBN 0-930044-01-0). Naiad Pr.

Aldyne, Nathan. Vermilion. 1980. pap. 2.25 (ISBN 0-686-69261-6, 76596). Avon.

Aledort, L. M., et al. Outpatient Medicine. LC 78-51280. 1979. text ed. 10.50 (ISBN 0-89004-354-X). Raven.

Alee, John G., ed. Webster's Dictionary for Everyday Use. 445p. 1971. pap. 2.50 (ISBN 0-06-463330-6, E*H 330, EH). Har-Row.

Alefeld, G. & Crigorieff, R. D., eds. Fundamentals of Numerical Computation: International Conference. (Computing Supplementum: No. 2). (Illus.). 250p. 1980. pap. 57.90 (ISBN 0-387-81566-X). Springer-Verlag.

Alegria, Ciro. Broad & Alien Is the World. Onis, Harriet de, tr. from Span. 434p. 1973. 12.95 (ISBN 0-85036-176-1). Dufour.

--Mundo es Ancho y Ajeno. Wade, G. E. & Stiefel, W. E., eds. (Span.). 1945. text ed. 20.00x (ISBN 0-89197-309-5); pap. text ed. 9.50x (ISBN 0-89197-310-9). Irvington.

Alegria, Fernando. La Poesia Chilena: Origenes y desarrollo del siglo xvi al xix. 1954. 14.00x (ISBN 0-520-00009-9). U of Cal Pr.

--Retratos Contemporaneos. 247p. 1979. pap. text ed. 7.95 (ISBN 0-15-576680-5, HC). HarBraceJ.

Alegria, Ricardo E., ed. Three Wishes: A Collection of Puerto Rican Folktales. Culbert, Elizabeth, tr. LC 69-13770. (Illus.). (gr. 4-6). 1969. 6.75 o.p. (ISBN 0-15-286871-2, HJ). HarBraceJ.

Aleichem, Sholem. Hanukah Money. LC 77-26693. (Illus.). (gr. k-3). 1978. 7.95 (ISBN 0-688-80120-X); PLB 7.63 (ISBN 0-688-84120-1). Greenwillow.

Aleith, R. C. Bergsteigen: Basic Rock Climbing. LC 75-5853. (Illus.). 192p. 1975 (ISBN 0-684-15389-0, ScribT). pap. 6.95 (ISBN 0-684-14203-1, SL578, ScribT). Scribner.

Aleixandre, Vincente. The Cave of Night. 1980. 3.95. Solo Pr.

Alejandrino, Jose. The Testament of Paul Keller. 1981. 7.95 (ISBN 0-533-04819-2). Vantage.

Alekhine, Aleksandr. My Best Games of Chess, 1924-1937. 1960. text ed. 7.95 o.p. (ISBN 0-679-13026-8); pap. 5.95 (ISBN 0-679-14024-7, 19, Tartan). McKay.

Aleksander, Igor. Automata Theory: An Engineering Approach. LC 74-32509. (Computer Systems Engineering Ser.). 1975. 19.50x (ISBN 0-8448-0657-9). Crane-Russak Co.

Aleksin, Anatoli. Alik the Detective. Carey, Bonnie, tr. from Russ. (gr. 7-9). 1977. 8.25 (ISBN 0-688-22117-3); PLB 7.92 (ISBN 0-688-32117-8). Morrow.

Alent, Rose M. The Companion to Foreign Language Composition. LC 73-75127. (A German-English Guidebook to Literary Terms: Vol. 1). 143p. (Orig.). 1973. pap. text ed. 5.75x (ISBN 90-6203-337-7). Humanities.

Aler, Jan, ed. Proceedings of the Fifth International Congress of Aesthetics. 1968. pap. 205.90x (ISBN 90-2791-059-6). Mouton.

Aleramo, Sibilla. A Woman. Delmar, Rosalind, tr. from Italian. (Illus.). 200p. 1980. 10.95 (ISBN 0-520-04108-9). U of Cal Pr.

Alerich, W. N. Electricity-Four: Motors, Generators, Controls. 224p. 1975. pap. 6.20 o.p. (ISBN 0-8273-1155-9); instructor's guide 1.45 o.p. (ISBN 0-8273-1156-7). Delmar.

--Electricity-Three: Motors, Generators, Controls. 256p. 1974. pap. 6.00 o.p. (ISBN 0-8273-1153-2); instructor's guide 1.45 o.p. (ISBN 0-8273-1154-0). Delmar.

Alerich, Walter. Electric Motor Control. LC 73-13484. 236p. 1975. pap. 7.00 (ISBN 0-8273-1157-5); lab. manual 4.80 (ISBN 0-8273-1159-1); instructor's guide 1.60 (ISBN 0-8273-1158-3). Delmar.

Alerich, Walter N. Electricity Four: AC Motors & Generators, Controls, Alternators. LC 79-93325. (Electrical Trades Ser.). 224p. 1981. pap. 6.60 (ISBN 0-8273-1363-2); instructor's guide 1.10 (ISBN 0-8273-1364-0). Delmar.

--Electricity Three. LC 79-93324. (Electrical Trades Ser.). 232p. 1981. pap. 6.60 (ISBN 0-8273-1361-6); instructor's guide 1.50 (ISBN 0-8273-1362-4). Delmar.

Aleshkovsky, Yuz. Kangaroo. Glenny, Tamara, tr. from Rus. 1981. 12.95 (ISBN 0-374-18068-7). FS&G.

--Kenguru. 85p. (Rus.). 1980. 13.50 (ISBN 0-88233-566-9); pap. 5.00 (ISBN 0-88233-567-7). Ardis Pubs.

--Nikolai Nikolaevich. 80p. (Rus.). 1980. 12.50 (ISBN 0-88233-564-2); pap. 4.50 (ISBN 0-88233-565-0). Ardis Pubs.

--Ruka: (Roman O Palache) 400p. (Rus.). 1980. pap. 16.50 (ISBN 0-89830-015-0). Russica Pubs.

Alesi, Gladys & Pantell, Dora. Family Life in the U.S.A. (gr. 9-12). 1962. pap. text ed. 2.75 (ISBN 0-88345-055-0). Regents Pub.

Al-Esmani, Abed. Batal Al Abtal. pap. 5.95x. Intl Bk Ctr.

Alessandra, Anthony, jt. auth. see Hunsacker, Philip.

Alesse, Craig. Basic Thirty-Five mm Photo Guide. LC 79-54311. (Illus.). 110p. (Orig.). 1979. pap. 10.95 (ISBN 0-936262-00-1). Amherst Media.

Alessi, Vincie, ed. Programs for Advent & Christmas. 1978. pap. 3.75 (ISBN 0-8170-0808-X). Judson.

Alessio. The Secretes of Alexis of Piemount. Warde, W., tr. from Fr. LC 74-28825. (English Experience Ser.: No. 707). 1975. Repr. of 1558 ed. 21.00 (ISBN 90-221-0707-8). Walter J Johnson.

Aletti, Ann & Brinkley, Jeanne. Altering: Ready-to-Wear Fashions. (gr. 10-12). 1976. text ed. 13.28 (ISBN 0-87002-083-8); avail. tchr's guide 1.00 (ISBN 0-87002-110-9). Bennett IL.

Alex, Lynn M. Exploring Iowa's Past: A Guide to Prehistoric Archaeology. LC 80-21391. (Illus.). 180p. 1980. pap. 7.95 (ISBN 0-87745-108-7). U of Iowa Pr.

Alex, Nicholas. New York Cops Talk Back: A Study of a Beleaguered Minority. LC 76-1852. 1976. 18.95 (ISBN 0-471-02055-9, Pub. by Wiley-Interscience). Wiley.

Alex, William. Japanese Architecture. LC 63-7516. (Great Ages of World Architecture Ser). 1963. 7.95 o.s.i. (ISBN 0-8076-0211-6). Braziller.

Alexander, A. G., tr. see Makrakis, Apostolos.

Alexander, Albert G., tr. see Makrakis, Apostolos.

Alexander, Alex E. Bylina & Fairytale: The Origins of Russian Heroic Poetry. LC 72-94439. (Slavistic Printings & Reprintings: No. 281). 1973. 34.10x (ISBN 90-2792-512-7). Mouton.

Alexander, Alfred, ed. Stories of Sicily. 1979. 9.95 o.p. (ISBN 0-236-31079-8, Pub. by Paul Elek). Merrimack Bk Serv.

Alexander, Ann M., jt. auth. see Smith, Robert L.

Alexander, Archibald. The Log College. 1968. 9.95 (ISBN 0-686-12475-8). Banner of Truth.

--Thoughts on Religious Experience. 1978. 8.95 (ISBN 0-85151-080-9). Banner of Truth.

Alexander, Benjamin, tr. see Morgagni, John B.

Alexander, C. M. Alien Atlas. (Orig.). 1980. pap. 1.95 (ISBN 0-532-23189-9). Manor Bks.

Alexander, C. P. The Crane Flies of California. (Bulletin of the California Insect Survey: Vol. 8). 1967. pap. 10.00x (ISBN 0-520-09033-0). U of Cal Pr.

Alexander, Charles C. Here the Country Lies: Nationalism & the Arts in Twentieth-Century America. LC 80-7681. 384p. 1980. 32.50x (ISBN 0-253-15544-4). Ind U Pr.

Alexander, Christopher. The Linz Cafe. (Illus.). 96p. 1981. 19.95 (ISBN 0-19-520263-5). Oxford U Pr.

--The Oregon Experiment. (Illus.). 190p. 1975. 19.95 (ISBN 0-19-501824-9). Oxford U Pr.

Alexander, Christopher, jt. auth. see Chermayeff, Serge.

Alexander, Constance. Baghdad in Bygone Days: From the Journals and Correspondence of Claudius Rich, Traveler, Artist, Linguist, Antiquary, and British Resident of Baghdad, 1808-1821. LC 80-1939. 1981. Repr. of 1928 ed. 41.50 (ISBN 0-404-18951-2). AMS Pr.

Alexander, D. M. Some Avocado Varieties for Australia. 1980. 10.00x (ISBN 0-643-02276-7, Pub. by CSJRO Australia). State Mutual Bk.

Alexander, Daniel E. & Messer, Andrew C. FORTRAN Four Pocket Handbook. 96p. (Orig.). 1972. pap. 3.95 (ISBN 0-07-001015-3, SP). McGraw.

Alexander, David. Fotovision del Antiguo Testamento. Vega, Pedro, tr. from Eng. (Illus.). 157p. (Span.). 1976. 8.50 (ISBN 0-89922-062-2). Edit Caribe.

--Manual Biblico Llustrado. Vega, Pedro, et al, trs. from Eng. (Illus.). 680p. (Span.). 1976. 26.95 (ISBN 0-89922-077-0). Edit Caribe.

--Retailing in England During the Industrial Revolution. 1970. text ed. 28.75x (ISBN 0-485-11116-0, Athlone Pr). Humanities.

Alexander, David & Alexander, Patricia. Eerdmans' Handbook to the Bible. 1973. 19.95 (ISBN 0-8028-3436-1). Eerdmans.

Alexander, David & Alexander, Pat, eds. Eerdmans' Concise Bible Handbook. LC 80-20131. (Illus.). 384p. (Orig.). 1981. pap. 9.95 (ISBN 0-8028-1875-7). Eerdmans.

Alexander, David P. & Perlick, Walter W. Introduction to Business: Workbook. 3rd ed. 1979. pap. 6.50x (ISBN 0-256-01691-7). Business Pubns.

Alexander, David S. The Old Testament in Living Pictures. LC 73-85490. (Illus.). 1973. lib. bdg. 6.95 o.p. (ISBN 0-8307-0225-3, 51-062-06). Regal.

Alexander, Dennis C., jt. auth. see Faules, Don F.

Alexander, Diane, ed. see Capon, Jack.

Alexander, Diane, ed. see Hall, Tom.

Alexander, Don. To Any God Listening. 46p. 1974. 3.50 o.p. (ISBN 0-89015-069-9). Nortex Pr.

Alexander, Douglas G., jt. auth. see Alexander, Gordon.

Alexander, E. Curtis. Axioms & Quotations of Yosef Ben-Jochannan. LC 80-70287. (Illus.). 118p. (gr. 8-12). 1980. pap. 6.95 (ISBN 0-938818-01-5). ECA Pub.

--Axioms & Quotations of Yosef ben-Jochannan. LC 80-70287. (Illus.). 118p. (Orig.). 1980. pap. 6.95 (ISBN 0-938818-01-5). ECA Assoc.

Alexander, Edward. John Morley. (English Authors Ser.: No. 147). lib. bdg. 10.95 (ISBN 0-8057-1404-9). Twayne.

--Matthew Arnold & John Stuart Mill. LC 65-14321. 1965. 16.00x (ISBN 0-231-02786-9). Columbia U Pr.

Alexander, Edythe L. Nursing Administration in the Hospital Health Care System. 2nd ed. LC 77-18114. (Illus.). 1978. text ed. 16.95 (ISBN 0-8016-0110-X). Mosby.

Alexander, Frances. Orphans on the Guadalupe. 5.95 (ISBN 0-685-48788-1). Nortex Pr.

Alexander, Frank, ed. see Capon, Jack.

Alexander, Frank, ed. see Hall, Tom.

Alexander, Georgina. Fabric Printing & Dyeing at Home. (Illus.). 80p. 1976. 20.00 (ISBN 0-7135-1893-6). Transatlantic.

Alexander, Gerard L. Guide to Atlases - World, Regional, National, Thematic: An International Listing of Atlases Published Since 1950. LC 70-157728. 1971. 23.50 (ISBN 0-8108-0414-X). Scarecrow.

--Guide to Atlases Supplement, World, Regional, National, Thematic: An International Listing of Atlases Published 1971 Through 1975 with Comprehensive Indexes. LC 76-157728. 1977. 17.00 (ISBN 0-8108-1011-5). Scarecrow.

Alexander, Gerard L., jt. auth. see Kane, Joseph N.

Alexander, Gordon. General Zoology. 5th ed. (Illus., Orig.). 1964. pap. 4.50 (ISBN 0-06-460032-7, CO 32, COS). Har-Row.

Alexander, Gordon & Alexander, Douglas G. Biology. 9th ed. (Illus.). 1970. pap. 3.95 (ISBN 0-06-460004-1, CO 4, COS). Har-Row.

Alexander, Guy B. Chromatography: An Adventure in Graduate School. LC 77-8637. (Chemistry in Action Ser.). 1977. 7.50 o.p. (ISBN 0-8412-0277-X); pap. 4.50 (ISBN 0-8412-0616-3). Am Chemical.

Alexander, H. G. Religion in England, Fifteen Fifty-Eight to Sixteen Sixty-Two. 233p. 1968. 4.00x o.p. (ISBN 0-87471-292-0). Rowman.

Alexander, H. G., ed. The Leibniz Clarke Correspondence: Together with Extracts from Newton's "Principia" & "Opticks". (Philosophical Classics Ser.). 1976. pap. 15.00x (ISBN 0-06-490150-5). B&N.

Alexander, H. G., ed. see Leibniz.

Alexander Hamilton Institiue, Inc Moderne Budgetierungsverfahren. Jenks, James M., ed. (Illus.). 85p. (Orig., Ger.). 1978. pap. 49.50 (ISBN 0-86604-004-8, TX-150-972). Hamilton Inst.

Alexander Hamilton Institute, Inc Como los Ejecutivos Toman Decisiones. Jenks, James M., ed. (Illus.). 79p. (Orig., Span.). 1976. pap. 43.75 (ISBN 0-86604-006-4). Hamilton Inst.

--El Ejecutivo Bajo Stress. Jenks, James M., ed. (Illus.). 72p. (Orig., Span.). 1976. pap. 44.75x (ISBN 0-86604-008-0, A783158). Hamilton Inst.

--Executivo Sob Tensao. Jenks, James M., ed. (Illus.). 71p. (Orig., Portuguese.). 1978. pap. 50.75x (ISBN 0-86604-009-9). Hamilton Inst.

--How Executives Make Decisions. Jenks, James M., ed. (Illus.). 79p. (Orig.). 1976. pap. 48.25 (ISBN 0-86604-005-6, A783159). Hamilton Inst.

--Manual De Practicas Orcamentaries Modernas. Jenks, James M., ed. (Illus.). 84p. (Orig., Portuguese.). 1978. pap. 58.25x (ISBN 0-86604-002-1, TX-15-336). Hamilton Inst.

--Manual De Practicia Presupuestaria Moderna. Jenks, James M., ed. (Illus.). 90p. (Orig., Span.). 1976. pap. 52.75x (ISBN 0-86604-001-3, A783161). Hamilton Inst.

--The Manual of Modern Budgetary Practices. Jenks, James M., ed. (Illus.). 85p. (Orig.). 1976. pap. 57.25x (ISBN 0-86604-000-5, A783160). Hamilton Inst.

--Le Manuel De Pratiques Budgetaires Modernes. Jenks, Jjames M., ed. (Illus.). 87p. (Orig., Fr.). 1978. pap. 49.50 (ISBN 0-86604-003-X, TX-30-652). Hamilton Inst.

Alexander Hamilton Institute, Nc. La Medicion De la Moral: Clave Para Aumentar la Productividad. Jenks, James M., ed. (Illus.). 50p. (Orig., Span.). 1976. pap. 48.75x (ISBN 0-86604-011-0, A811102). Hamilton Inst.

Alexander Hamilton Unstitute, Inc. Measuring Morale: Key to Increased Productivity. (Illus.). 53p. (Orig.). 1976. pap. 53.25x (ISBN 0-86604-010-2, A806007). Hamilton Inst.

Alexander, Hartley B. World's Rim: Great Mysteries of the North American Indians. LC 53-7703. (Illus.). 1967. pap. 4.95 (ISBN 0-8032-5003-7, BB160, Bison). U of Nebr Pr.

Alexander, Herbert E. Campaign Money: Reform & Reality in the States. LC 76-21180. 1976. 12.95 (ISBN 0-02-900410-1); pap. text ed. 3.95 (ISBN 0-02-900420-9). Free Pr.

Alexander, Herbert E., ed. Political Finance. LC 78-24439. (Sage Electoral Studies Yearbook: Vol. 5). (Illus.). 1979. 20.00x (ISBN 0-8039-1175-0); pap. 9.95x (ISBN 0-8039-1176-9). Sage.

Alexander, Hiriam, et al. Creature Teachers. (Illus.). (gr. 1-3). 1974. student's book 3.99 (ISBN 0-87892-871-5); tchr's handbook 3.99 (ISBN 0-87892-875-8); tapes 167.25 (ISBN 0-87892-876-6). Economy Co.

Alexander, Horace. Gandhi Through Western Eyes. 9.00x (ISBN 0-210-22554-8). Asia.

Alexander, Hugh. The Penguin Book of Chess Positions. (Handbook Ser.). 1974. pap. 2.50 o.p. (ISBN 0-14-046199-X). Penguin.

Alexander Institute, Inc The Executive Under Stress. Jenks, Jamess M., ed. (Illus.). 71p. (Orig.). 1976. pap. 49.25x (ISBN 0-86604-007-2, A783157). Hamilton Inst.

Alexander, J. A. Acts of the Apostles, 2 vols. in 1. (Banner of Truth Geneva Series Commentaries). 1980. 19.95 (ISBN 0-85151-309-3). Banner of Truth.

Alexander, J. H. The Lay of the Last Minstrel: Vol. 1-2, Three Essays. (Salzburg Studies in English Literature, Romantic Reassessment: No. 77). 1978. pap. text ed. 25.00x (ISBN 0-391-01290-8). Humanities.

--The Reception of Scott's Poetry by His Correspondents, 2 vols. (SSEL Romantic Reassessment Ser.: No. 84). (Orig.). 1979. pap. text ed. 25.00x ea. Humanities.

--Two Studies in Romantic Reviewing: Edinburgh Reviewers & the English Tradition, Vol. 1. (Salzburg Studies in English Literature: No. 49). (Orig.). 1976. pap. text ed. 25.00x (ISBN 0-391-01293-2). Humanities.

--Two Studies in Romantic Reviewing: The Reviewing of Walter Scott's Poetry, 1805-1817, Vol. 2. (Salzburg Studies in English Literature Romantic Reassessment: No. 49). 1976. pap. text ed. 25,00x (ISBN 0-391-01294-0). Humanities.

Alexander, J. J., ed. The Decorated Letter. (Magnificent Paperback Ser.). 1978. 22.95 (ISBN 0-8076-0894-7); pap. 10.95 (ISBN 0-8076-0895-5). Braziller.

--Italian Renaissance Illuminations. LC 77-2841. (Magnificent Paperback Ser.). (Illus.). 1977. 19.95 (ISBN 0-8076-0863-7); pap. 9.95 (ISBN 0-8076-0864-5). Braziller.

Alexander, J. J. G. & Gibson, M. T., eds. Medieval Learning & Literature: Essays Presented to Richard William Hunt. (Illus.). 500p. 1976. 67.00x (ISBN 0-19-822402-8). Oxford U Pr.

Alexander, J. M. Strength of Materials: Fundamentals, Vol. 1. 190p. 1981. 47.95 (ISBN 0-470-27119-1). Halsted Pr.

Alexander, J. M., jt. auth. see Ford, High.

Alexander, J. W. Plan Para Memorizar las Escrituras. Orig. Title: Fire in My Bones. 1979. 1.45 (ISBN 0-311-03660-0). Casa Bautista.

--Thoughts on Preaching. 1975. 8.95 (ISBN 0-85151-210-0). Banner of Truth.

Alexander, Jason. In Praise of the Common Man. 86p. (Orig.). 1981. pap. price not set (ISBN 0-931826-02-0). Sitnalta Pr.

Alexander, Jean. Affidavits of Genius: Edgar Allan Poe & the French Critics, 1847-1924. LC 79-154033. 1971. 14.50 (ISBN 0-8046-9015-4, Natl U). Kennikat.

--Venture of Form in the Novels of Virginia Woolf. LC 73-83260. 1974. 13.50 (ISBN 0-8046-9052-9). Kennikat.

Alexander, Joan. One Sunny Day. 1978. pap. 1.95 o.p. (ISBN 0-425-03619-7, Medallion). Berkley Pub.

Alexander, John D., Jr. Make a Chair from a Tree: An Introduction to Working Green Wood. LC 78-58222. (Illus., Orig.). 1978. pap. 7.95 (ISBN 0-918804-01-9, Dist. by Van Nostrand Reinhold). Taunton.

Alexander, John L., et al. Handbook for Boys: Reproduction of the Nineteen Eleven Handbook. (Illus.). (gr. 7-12). Repr. of 1911 ed. pap. 6.80x (ISBN 0-8395-3100-1). BSA.

Alexander, John W. Economic Geography. 1963. text ed. 16.95 o.p. (ISBN 0-13-225144-2). P-H.

--Managing Our Work. rev. ed. LC 72-186572. (Illus.). 104p. 1975. pap. 3.50 (ISBN 0-87784-352-X). Inter-Varsity.

Alexander, John W. & Gibson, L. Economic Geography. 2nd ed. 1979. 20.95 (ISBN 0-13-225151-5). P-H.

Alexander, Joseph A. Commentaries on the Prophecies of Isaiah. 10th ed. 1980. 19.95 (ISBN 0-310-20000-8, 6526). Zondervan.

--Mark. (Thornapple Commentaries Ser.). 1980. pap. 8.95 (ISBN 0-8010-0150-1). Baker Bk.

--Matthew. (Thornapple Commentaries Ser.). 1980. pap. 8.95 (ISBN 0-8010-0146-3). Baker Bk.

Alexander, Josephine. America Through the Eye of My Needle: Common Sense for the 80's. 192p. 1981. 9.95 (ISBN 0-8037-0194-2). Dial.

Alexander, Joyce M., jt. auth. see Saaty, Thomas L.

Alexander, K. J., ed. The Political Economy of Change. 1975. 29.50x (ISBN 0-631-16540-1, Pub. by Basil Blackwell). Biblio Dist.

Alexander, Karen. Palaces of Desire. 1979. pap. 2.25 o.p. (ISBN 0-345-27997-2). Ballantine.

Alexander, Karl. A Private Investigation. 1980. 10.95 (ISBN 0-440-06834-7). Delacorte.

Alexander, Ken. How to Start Your Own Mail Order Business. rev. ed. (Illus.). 1960. 6.95 (ISBN 0-87396-000-9). Stravon.

Alexander, Kern. School Law. LC 79-24471. 939p. 1980. text ed. 18.95 (ISBN 0-8299-2078-1). West Pub.

Alexander, Kern & Solomon, Erwin. College & University Law. 1972. incl. 1976 suppl. 17.00 (ISBN 0-87215-146-8); 1976 suppl 6.50 (ISBN 0-87215-298-7). Michie.

Alexander, Kern, ed. see Seventeenth National Conference on School Finance.

Alexander, L. G. For & Against. 1975. pap. text ed. 3.00x (ISBN 0-582-52306-0). Longman.

--Situational English Language Picture Series. 14.50x (ISBN 0-582-52114-9). Longman.

--Sixty Steps to Precis. rev ed. 1975. pap. text ed. 2.50x (ISBN 0-582-52309-5). Longman.

Alexander, L. G. & Cornelius, E. T., Jr. COMP: Exercises in Comprehension & Composition. (Illus.). 1978. pap. text ed. 2.95x (ISBN 0-582-79703-9). Longman.

Alexander, L. G. & Wilson, C. In Other Words. 1974. pap. text ed. 3.00x (ISBN 0-582-55200-1). Longman.

Alexander, L. G., et al. Mainline: New Concept English. write for info. (ISBN 0-686-10913-9). Longman.

--English Grammatical Structure. 255p. 1975. text ed. 27.00x (ISBN 0-582-55325-3). Longman.

--Take a Stand: Discussion Topics for Intermediate Adult Students. (Illus.). 1978. pap. text ed. 2.50x (ISBN 0-582-79721-7); cassettes 7.95 (ISBN 0-582-79722-5). Longman.

Alexander, Leroy E., jt. auth. see Klug, Harold P.

Alexander, Lester, ed. Beyond Words. LC 76-29896. (Illus.). 1977. 8.95 o.p. (ISBN 0-03-020871-8); pap. 5.95 (ISBN 0-03-016911-9). HR&W.

Alexander, Lloyd. The Black Cauldron. (gr. 7-12). 1980. pap. 1.75 (ISBN 0-440-90649-0, LFL). Dell.

--Castle of Llyr. (gr. 4-8). 1969. pap. 1.50 (ISBN 0-440-41125-4, YB). Dell.

--Coll & His White Pig. LC 65-21540. (Illus.). 32p. (gr. k-3). 1965. reinforced bdg. 5.95 o.p. (ISBN 0-03-089751-3). HR&W.

--First Two Lives of Lukas-Kasha. LC 77-26699. (gr. 4-7). 1978. PLB 11.95 (ISBN 0-525-29748-0). Dutton.

--King's Fountain. (Illus.). (ps-3). 1971. PLB 7.95 o.p. (ISBN 0-525-33240-5). Dutton.

--Marvelous Misadventures of Sebastian. LC 70-166879. (gr. 4 up). 1970. PLB 10.95 (ISBN 0-525-34739-9); pap. 1.95 o.p. (ISBN 0-525-45009-2). Dutton.

--Taran Wanderer. (gr. 4-8). 1969. pap. 1.75 (ISBN 0-440-48483-9, YB). Dell.

--Time Cat. (Illus.). (gr. 2-4). 1975. pap. 1.25 o.s.i. (ISBN 0-380-00195-0, 39560, Camelot). Avon.

--The Town Cats & Other Tales. (gr. k-6). 1981. pap. 1.50 (ISBN 0-440-48989-X, YB). Dell.

--Westmark. LC 80-22242. (gr. 5 up). 1981. 9.95 (ISBN 0-525-42335-4). Dutton.

--The Wizard in the Tree. (gr. k-6). 1981. pap. 1.50 (ISBN 0-440-49556-3, YB). Dell.

Alexander, Lloyd, tr. see Sartre, Jean-Paul.

Alexander, M., ed. Advances in Microbial Ecology, Vol. 2. (Illus.). 311p. 1978. 24.50 (ISBN 0-306-38162-1, Plenum Pr). Plenum Pub.

Alexander, Martha. Four Bears in a Box. (Illus.). 32p. (ps-3). 1981. boxed set 6.95 (ISBN 0-8037-2756-9). Dial.

--I'll Protect You from the Jungle Beasts. LC 73-6015. (Illus.). 31p. (ps-2). 1980. Repr. of 1973 ed. pap. 1.95 (ISBN 0-8037-3900-1, Pied Piper Bk.). Dial.

--Move Over, Twerp. LC 80-21405. (Illus.). 32p. (ps-2). 1981. 6.95 (ISBN 0-8037-6139-2); PLB 6.46 (ISBN 0-8037-6140-6). Dial.

--Pigs Say Oink. (Illus.). 32p. (ps-3). 1981. PLB 4.99 (ISBN 0-394-93838-0); pap. 1.25 (ISBN 0-394-83838-6). Random.

Alexander, Martin. Introduction to Soil Microbiology. 2nd ed. LC 77-1319. 460p. 1977. text ed. 24.95 (ISBN 0-471-02179-2); arabic translation avail. Wiley.

--Microbial Ecology. LC 71-137105. (Illus.). 1971. 26.95 (ISBN 0-471-02054-0). Wiley.

Alexander, Mary J. Designing Your Own Room. (Career Concise Guides Ser.). (Illus.). (gr. 7 up). 1977. PLB 4.90 o.p. (ISBN 0-531-00091-5). Watts.

Alexander, Mary Jean. Decorating Made Simple. LC 64-13823. 1964. pap. 3.50 (ISBN 0-385-01695-6, Made). Doubleday.

Alexander, Meena. The Bird's Bright Ring. 1976. 8.00 (ISBN 0-89253-811-2); flexible cloth 4.80 (ISBN 0-89253-812-0). Ind-US Inc.

--The Poetic Self: Towards a Phenomenology of Romanticism. 280p. 1980. text ed. 14.00x (ISBN 0-391-01754-3). Humanities.

Alexander, Michael. The Poetic Achievement of Ezra Pound. 1979. 16.00 (ISBN 0-520-03739-1). U of Cal Pr.

Alexander, Michael Van Cleave see Van Cleave Alexander, Michael.

Alexander, Milton J. Information Systems Analysis: Theory & Application. LC 73-89599. (Illus.). 432p. 1974. text ed. 18.95 (ISBN 0-574-19100-3, 13-2100); instr's guide avail. (ISBN 0-574-19101-1, 13-2101). SRA.

Alexander, Morris. Israel & Me. LC 76-40091. 1977. 10.00 (ISBN 0-8467-0265-7, Pub. by Two Continents). Hippocrene Bks.

Alexander, Myrna. Behold Your God: A Woman's Workshop on the Attributes of God. pap. 2.50 (ISBN 0-310-37131-7). Zondervan.

Alexander, Olive. Developing Spiritually Sensitive Children. LC 80-23603. 132p. (Orig.). 1980. pap. 3.95 (ISBN 0-87123-111-5, 210111). Bethany Fell.

Alexander, P., jt. auth. see Bacq, Z. M.

Alexander, P. E., ed. Electrolytes & Neuropsychiatric Disorders. (Illus.). 351p. 1981. text ed. 45.00 (ISBN 0-89335-122-9). Spectrum Pub.

Alexander, Pat, ed. Eerdmans' Concise Bible Encyclopedia. LC 80-19885. (Illus.). 256p. (Orig.). 1981. pap. 8.95 (ISBN 0-8028-1876-5). Eerdmans.

Alexander, Pat, jt. ed. see Alexander, David.

Alexander, Patricia, jt. auth. see Alexander, David.

Alexander, Patrick. Death of a Thin-Skinned Animal. 1979. pap. 1.75 o.s.i. (ISBN 0-685-63661-5, 04679-5). Jove Pubns.

Alexander, Patsy R. Textile Products: Selection, Use & Care. LC 76-11955. (Illus.). 416p. 1977. text ed. 15.50 (ISBN 0-395-20358-9); inst. manual 1.50 (ISBN 0-395-20357-0). HM.

Alexander, Paul J. Religious & Political History & Thought in the Byzantine Empire. 360p. 1980. 60.00x (ISBN 0-86078-016-3, Pub. by Variorum England). State Mutual Bk.

Alexander, R. McNeill. The Chordates. LC 74-76580. (Illus.). 496p. 1975. 65.50 (ISBN 0-521-20472-0); pap. 18.95x (ISBN 0-521-09857-2). Cambridge U Pr.

--Functional Design in Fishes. 3rd ed. (Illus.). 1974. pap. text ed. 7.00 (ISBN 0-09-104751-X, Hutchinson U Lib). Humanities.

--The Invertebrates. LC 78-6275. (Illus.). 1979. 65.50 (ISBN 0-521-22120-X); pap. 17.95x (ISBN 0-521-29361-8). Cambridge U Pr.

Alexander, Rae P. & Lester, Julius, eds. Young & Black in America. (Sundial Paperbks.). 1972. pap. 1.95 (ISBN 0-394-70804-0, VS4, Vin). Random.

--Young & Black in America. (Illus.). 137p. Date not set. pap. 1.50 (ISBN 0-394-70804-0, Vin). Random.

Alexander, Ralph W. & Sparlin, Don M. Physics Laboratory Manual. 176p. 1981. pap. text ed. 11.95 (ISBN 0-8403-2289-5). Kendall-Hunt.

Alexander, Richard D., ed. Natural Selection & Social Behavior. Tinkle, Donald W. LC 80-65758. (Illus.). 550p. 1981. text ed. 49.95x (ISBN 0-913462-08-X). Chiron Pr.

Alexander, Robert J. Agrarian Reform in Latin American. LC 73-11733. (Latin American Ser.: Vol. 2). 120p. 1974. 5.95 o.s.i. (ISBN 0-02-500770-X). Macmillan.

--Communism in Latin America. 1957. 22.50 (ISBN 0-8135-0268-3). Rutgers U Pr.

--Juan Domingo Peron. 1979. lib. bdg. 20.00x (ISBN 0-89158-369-6). Westview.

--A New Development Strategy. LC 75-7783. 176p. 1976. 6.95x o.p. (ISBN 0-88344-328-7). Orbis Bks.

--The Right Opposition: The Lovestoneites & the International Communist Opposition of the 1930's. LC 80-1705. (Contributions in Political Science: No. 54). 312p. 1981. lib. bdg. 32.50 (ISBN 0-313-22070-0, AOP/). Greenwood.

--The Right Opposition: The Lovestoneites & the International Communist Opposition of the 1930's. LC 80-1711. (Contributions in Political Science Ser.: No. 54). 320p. 1981. lib. bdg. 32.50 (AOP/). Greenwood.

Alexander, Rodney & Sapery, Elizabeth, eds. The Shortchanged: Minorities & Women in Banking. LC 73-79033. 190p. 1973. 15.00 (ISBN 0-8046-7066-8); pap. 7.95 (ISBN 0-8046-7067-6). Kennikat.

Alexander, Roland, jt. auth. see Weber, Dick.

Alexander, Roy. Mehdi: Nothing Is Impossible. LC 77-95190. 1978. 8.95 (ISBN 0-87863-157-7). Farnswth Pub.

Alexander, Russel C. I Thought of It First. (Illus.). 102p. (Orig.). pap. 6.95 (ISBN 0-918146-21-6). Peninsula Pub WA.

Alexander, Sarane. Max Ernst. (Filipacchi Art Bks). (Illus.). 72p. 1980. cancelled (ISBN 2-85018-100-5); pap. cancelled (ISBN 2-85018-101-3). Hippocrene Bks.

Alexander, Scott. Rhinoceros Success. LC 80-51648. (Illus.). 123p. (Orig.). (gr. 7 up). 1980. pap. 4.95 (ISBN 0-937382-00-0). Rhinos Pr.

Alexander, Sidney. Running Healthy: A Guide to Cardiovascular Fitness. LC 80-12387. (Illus.). 1980. 12.95 (ISBN 0-8289-0387-5). Greene.

Alexander, Sidney, tr. see Guicciardini, Francesco.

Alexander, Sidney S., et al. Five Monographs on Business Income. LC 73-84377. 1973. Repr. of 1950 ed. text ed. 13.00 (ISBN 0-914348-00-0). Scholars Bk.

Alexander, Stella. Church & State in Yugoslavia Since Nineteen Forty-Five. LC 77-88668. (Soviet & East European Studies). 1979. 41.50 (ISBN 0-521-21942-6). Cambridge U Pr.

Alexander, Sue. Peacocks Are Very Special. 32p. (gr. 1-3). 1976. PLB 5.95 (ISBN 0-385-02169-0). Doubleday.

--Seymour the Prince. LC 78-31406. (I Am Reading Bks.). (Illus.). (gr. 2-4). 1979. 4.95 (ISBN 0-394-84141-7); PLB 5.99 (ISBN 0-394-94141-1). Pantheon.

--Small Plays for Special Days. LC 76-28424. (Illus.). (gr. 2-4). 1977. 7.95 (ISBN 0-395-28761-8, Clarion). HM.

--Small Plays for You & a Friend. LC 74-4019. (Illus.). 48p. (gr. 1-4). 1974. 6.95 (ISBN 0-395-28762-6, Clarion). HM.

--Witch, Goblin & Ghost in the Haunted Woods. LC 80-20863. (I Am Reading Ser.). (Illus.). 48p. (gr. 1-3). 1981. 4.95 (ISBN 0-394-84443-2); PLB 5.95 (ISBN 0-394-94443-7). Pantheon.

--Witch, Goblin & Ghost in the Haunted Woods. LC 80-20863. (I Am Reading Bk.). (Illus.). 72p. (gr. 1-4). 1981. 4.95 (ISBN 0-394-84443-2); PLB 5.99 (ISBN 0-394-94443-7). Pantheon.

Alexander, Taylor, et al. Botany. (Golden Guide Ser.). (Illus.). (gr. 7 up). 1970. PLB 9.15 (ISBN 0-307-63545-7, Golden Pr); pap. 1.95 o.p. (ISBN 0-307-24025-8). Western Pub.

Alexander, Taylor R. Ecology. (Golden Guide Ser). 160p. 1973. PLB 9.15 (ISBN 0-307-64359-X, Golden Pr); pap. 1.95 o.p. (ISBN 0-307-24359-1). Western Pub.

Alexander, Thea. A Macro Philosophy for the Aquarian Age. rev. 2nd ed. 160p. 1971. pap. 4.00 (ISBN 0-913080-01-2). Macro Bks.

--Twenty-One Fifty A.D. The Macro Love Story. 281p. (Orig.). 1971. pap. 4.00 (ISBN 0-913080-03-9). Macro Bks.

--Two Thousand One Hundred & Fifty A. D. 288p. (Orig.). 1976. pap. 2.50 (ISBN 0-446-91530-0). Warner Bks.

Alexander, Theron. Human Development in an Urban Age. (Illus.). 384p. 1973. ref. ed. 16.95 (ISBN 0-13-444786-7). P-H.

Alexander, Theron, et al. Developmental Psychology. (Illus.). 532p. 1980. text ed. 16.95 (ISBN 0-442-25212-9). Van Nos Reinhold.

Alexander, Thomas G., ed. Soul Butter & Hog Wash & Other Essays on the American West. LC 77-89974. (Charles Redd Monographs in Western History Ser.: No. 8). 1978. pap. 4.95 (ISBN 0-8425-1232-2). Brigham.

Alexander, Thomas G., ed. see Grant, Ulysses S.

Alexander, Tom. Project Apollo: Man to the Moon. LC 63-17719. (Illus.). 1964. 8.95 o.p. (ISBN 0-06-000120-8, HarpT). Har-Row.

Alexander, Wilbur. Beyond the Shadow of a Doubt. LC 74-181389. (Stories That Win Ser.). 1971. pap. 0.95 o.p. (ISBN 0-8163-0131-X, 02168-3). Pacific Pr Pub Assn.

Alexander, William. An Encouragement to Colonies. LC 68-54607. (English Experience Ser.: No. 63). (Illus.). 47p. 1968. Repr. of 1624 ed. 11.50 (ISBN 90-221-0063-4). Walter J Johnson.

--Film on the Left: American Documentary Film from 1931 to 1942. LC 80-8534. (Illus.). 364p. 1981. 27.50x (ISBN 0-691-04678-6); pap. 12.50x (ISBN 0-691-10111-6). Princeton U Pr.

--Image of China. (Oresko-Jupiter Art Bks). (Illus.). 96p. 1981. 17.95 (ISBN 0-933516-82-7, Pub. by Oresko-Jupiter England). Hippocrene Bks.

--The Tragedie of Darius. LC 72-6936. (English Experience Ser.: No. 293). 80p. Repr. of 1603 ed. 11.50 (ISBN 90-221-0293-9). Walter J Johnson.

Alexander, William J. An Introduction to the Poetry of Robert Browning. 210p. 1980. Repr. of 1889 ed. lib. bdg. 22.50 (ISBN 0-89987-006-6). Darby Bks.

Alexander, Yona & Chertoff, Mordecai, eds. Bibliography on Israel & Zionism. 1980. write for info. Herzl Pr.

Alexander, Yonah, ed. Behavioral & Quantitative Perspectives on Terrorism. Gleason, John M. LC 80-39752. (Pergamon Press Series on International Politics). 300p. 1981. 32.50 (ISBN 0-08-025989-8). Pergamon.

--International Terrorism: National, Regional, & Global Perspectives. rev. ed. LC 75-8396. 320p. 1981. text ed. 28.95 (ISBN 0-275-09480-4). Praeger.

Alexander, Yonah & Finger, Seymour M., eds. Terrorism: Interdisciplinary Perspectives. LC 77-7552. 1977. 15.00 (ISBN 0-89444-004-7). John Jay Pr.

Alexander, Yonah & Friedlander, Robert A., eds. Self-Determination: National, Regional, & Global Dimensions. (Special Studies in National & International Terrorism). 1980. lib. bdg. 27.50x (ISBN 0-89158-090-5). Westview.

Alexander, Yonah & Kilmarx, Robert A., eds. Political Terrorism & Business: The Threat & the Response. LC 79-16374. 360p. 1979. 26.95 (ISBN 0-03-046686-5). Praeger.

Alexander, Yonah & Nanes, Allan, eds. United States & Iran: A Documentary History. 450p. 1980. 24.00 (ISBN 0-89093-183-6); pap. 8.00 (ISBN 0-89093-184-4). U Pubns Amer.

Alexander, Yonah, et al, eds. Terrorism: Theory & Practice. (Westview Special Studies in National & International Terrorism). 200p. 1979. lib. bdg. 25.00x (ISBN 0-89158-089-1); pap. text ed. 12.00x (ISBN 0-86531-041-6). Westview.

Alexanderescu, Sorin, ed. Transformational Grammar & the Rumanian Language. (PDR Press Publications on Rumanian Ser.: No. 1). 1977. pap. text ed. 9.25x (ISBN 90-316-0144-6). Humanities.

Alexandersson, Gunnar. Geography of Manufacturing. 1967. pap. 6.95 ref. ed. (ISBN 0-13-351262-2). P-H.

Alexandersson, Gunnar & Kleverbring, Bjorn. World Resources: Energy & Minerals, Vol. 1. 1978. 21.25x (ISBN 3-11-006577-0). De Gruyter.

Alexandre, A., et al. Road Traffic Noise. LC 75-14297. 219p. 1975. 32.95 (ISBN 0-470-02160-8). Halsted Pr.

Alexandre, C., ed. see Swearer, Donald K.

Alexandre, Clement, ed. see Hubbard, David G.

Alexandre, Pierre, ed. French Perspectives in African Studies: A Collection of Translated Essays. (International African Institute Ser.). 348p. 1973. 24.95 o.p. (ISBN 0-19-724191-3). Oxford U Pr.

Alexandrian, Sarane. Surrealist Art. (World of Art Ser.). (Illus.). 256p. (Orig.). 1978. pap. 9.95 (ISBN 0-19-520009-8). Oxford U Pr.

Alexandroff, Paul S. & Hopf, H. Topologie. LC 65-21833. (Ger.). 18.50 (ISBN 0-8284-0197-7). Chelsea Pub.

Alexandrov, Eugene A., compiled by. Mineral & Energy Resources of the USSR: A Selected Bibliography of Sources in English. 160p. 1980. 10.00 (ISBN 0-913312-21-5). Am Geol.

Alexandrowicz, Charles H. Law of Global Communications. LC 79-163081. (International Legal Studies Ser). 1971. 14.50 (ISBN 0-231-03529-2). Columbia U Pr.

Alexandrowicz, Harry. Six Hundred Ninety-Nine Ways to Improve the Performance of Your Car. LC 79-93251. (Illus.). 192p. 1980. 14.95 (ISBN 0-8069-5550-3); lib. bdg. 13.29 (ISBN 0-8069-5551-1); pap. 6.95 (ISBN 0-8069-8900-9). Sterling.

Al-Exd, Kadhim A. Oil Revenues, Absorptive Capacity & Prospects for Accelerated Growth. 1979. 22.95 o.p. (ISBN 0-03-053306-6). Praeger.

Alexeev, Wassilij & Theofanis, Stavrou. The Great Revival: The Russian Church Under German Occupation. LC 76-83. text ed. 21.95 o.p. (ISBN 0-8087-0131-2). Burgess.

Alexenberg, Melvin L. Sound Science. LC 68-15760. (Illus.). (ps-3). 1968. pap. 0.95 o.p. (ISBN 0-13-823047-1). P-H.

Alexieva, Marguerite, tr. see Panayotova, Dora.

Alexiou, Margaret. The Ritual Lament in Greek Tradition. LC 72-97879. (Illus.). 216p. 1974. 34.00 (ISBN 0-521-20226-4). Cambridge U Pr.

Alexis, Marcus & Wilson, C. Organizational Decision Making. 1967. text ed. 17.95 (ISBN 0-13-641043-X). P-H.

Alexis, Marcus, et al. Black Consumer Profiles: Food Purchasing in the Inner City. (Illus.). 106p. 1980. pap. 4.00 (ISBN 0-87712-195-8). U Mich Busn Div Res.

Alexopoulos, Constantine J. & Mims, Charles W. Introductory Mycology. 3rd ed. LC 79-12514. 1979. text ed. 25.95 (ISBN 0-471-02214-4). Wiley.

Alexy, George, jt. auth. see Rector, Russell.

Al-Eyd, Kadhim A. Oil Revenues & Accelerated Growth: Absorptive Capacity in Iraq. LC 79-18596. 206p. 1979. 22.95 (ISBN 0-03-053306-6). Praeger.

Alfano, Genrose. All-RN Nursing Staff. LC 81-80201. (Nursing Dimensions Administration Ser.). 250p. 1981. pap. text ed. 11.95 (ISBN 0-913654-68-X). Nursing Res.

Alfaro, Julian H., jt. auth. see Bomse, Marguerite D.

Alfassa, Mira. Glimpses of the Mother's Life, Vol. 2. Das, Nilima, ed. 335p. 1980. 11.00 (ISBN 0-89071-291-3). Matagiri.

Alfassa, Mirra & Enginger, Bernard. Mother's Agenda, Vol. 2, 1961. Orig. Title: L'agenda De Mere. 500p. (Orig.). 1981. pap. 8.95 (ISBN 0-938710-01-X). Inst Evolutionary.

Alfers, Betty. Quilting. LC 78-55662. (Illus.). 1978. 14.95 o.p. (ISBN 0-672-52235-7). Bobbs.

Alfert, M., et al, eds. see Branton, D. & Deamer, D. W.

Alfert, M., et al, eds. see Satir, P.

Alfieri, et al. Laboratory for General Botany. 1977. pap. text ed. 4.50 (ISBN 0-917962-00-1). Peek Pubns.

Alfieri, Vittorio. An Ode to America's Independence: A Bilingual Edition. Caso, Adolph, tr. 60p. 1980. pap. text ed. 5.00 (ISBN 0-937832-01-4). Dante Univ Bkshlf.

Alfin-Slater, Roslyn & Kritchevsky, David, eds. Human Nutrition, a Comprehensive Treatise: Vol. 3B, Nutrition & the Adult-Micronutrients. (Illus.). 444p. 1980. 39.50 (ISBN 0-306-40288-2, Plenum Pr). Plenum Pub.

Alfoeldi, Andreas & Alfoeldi, Elisabeth. Die Kontorniat-Medaillons. (Antike Muenzen und Geschnittene Steine Ser., Vol. 6). 1976. 173.50x (ISBN 3-11-003484-0). De Gruyter.

Alfoeldi, Elisabeth, jt. auth. see Alfoeldi, Andreas.

Alfoeldy, Geza. Die Roemischen Inschriften von Tarraco. (Madrider Forschungen Ser.: Vol. 10). (Ger.). 1975. text & plate volume 188.25x (ISBN 3-11-004403-X). De Gruyter.

Alfonsi, Petrus. The Disciplina Clericalis of Petrus Alfonsi. Hermes, Eberhard, ed. Quarrie, P. R., tr. LC 73-94434. (Islamic World Ser.). 250p. 1977. 18.00x (ISBN 0-520-02704-3). U of Cal Pr.

Alfonso, Firth N. Instructional Supervision: A Behavior System. 2nd ed. 432p. 1980. text ed. 18.95 (ISBN 0-205-07142-2, 237142-1). Allyn.

Alford, Henry A. Alford's Greek Testament, 4 vols. 1980. Repr. 75.00 (ISBN 0-8010-0158-7). Baker Bk.

Alford, Jonathan, ed. The Impact of New Military Technolgy. LC 80-67839. (Adelphi Library: Vol. 4). 140p. 1981. text ed. 29.50 (ISBN 0-916672-74-3). Allanheld.

--Sea Power & Influence: Iold Issues & New Challenges. LC 80-67840. (Adelphi Library: Vol. 2). 224p. 1981. text ed. 31.50 (ISBN 0-916672-72-7). Allanheld.

Alford, M. H. & Alford, V. L. Russian-English Scientific & Technical Dictionary, 2 vols. LC 73-88348. 1970. Set. 87.00 (ISBN 0-08-012227-2). Pergamon.

Alford, V. L., jt. auth. see Alford, M. H.

Alford, Violet. Sword Dance & Drama. 1963. 8.95 o.p. (ISBN 0-85036-035-8). Dufour.

Alfred Benzon Symposium 5th. Transport Mechanisms in Epithelia. Ussing, H. H., et al, eds. 1973. 51.00 (ISBN 0-12-709550-0). Acad Pr.

Alfsen, E. M. Compact Convex Sets & Boundary Integrals. LC 72-136352. (Ergebnisse der Mathematik und Ihrer Grenzgebiete: Vol. 57). (Illus.). 1971. 27.60 (ISBN 0-387-05090-6). Springer-Verlag.

Alfven, Hannes. Atom, Man, & the Universe: The Long Chain of Complications. Hoberman, John, tr. LC 69-15872. 1969. text ed. 10.95x (ISBN 0-7167-0327-0). W H Freeman.

--Worlds-Antiworlds: Antimatter in Cosmology. Feichtner, Rudy, tr. LC 66-27947. 1966. 10.95x (ISBN 0-7167-0317-3). W H Freeman.

Alfven, Hannes & Alfven, Kerstin. Living on the Third Planet. Johnson, Eric, tr. from Swedish. LC 70-179799. 1972. text ed. 10.95x (ISBN 0-7167-0340-8). W H Freeman.

Alfven, Kerstin, jt. auth. see Alfven, Hannes.

Algar, Hamid. Mirza Malkum Khan: A Biographical Essay in 19th Century Iranian Modernism. LC 78-187750. 1973. 23.50x (ISBN 0-520-02217-3). U of Cal Pr.

--Religion & State in Iran, Seventeen Eighty-Five to Nineteen Six: The Role of the 'Ulama in the Qajar Period. LC 72-79959. (Near Eastern Center, UCLA). 1969. 18.50x (ISBN 0-520-01384-0). U of Cal Pr.

Algar, Hamid, jt. ed. see Khouri, Mounah A.

Algar, Hamid, tr. see Khouri, Mounah A. & Algar, Hamid.

Algarin, Miguel. On Call. LC 79-90764. (Illus., Orig.). 1980. pap. 5.00x (ISBN 0-934770-03-4). Arte Publico.

Algazi, Linda, jt. auth. see Sklansky, Gloria J.

Algee, Isabelle R. Moorings - Past & Present. (Illus.). 557p. 1980. lib. bdg. 35.00 (ISBN 0-918518-18-0); pap. 20.00 (ISBN 0-918518-17-2). St Luke TN.

Alger, Horatio. Digging for Gold: A Story of California. 1968. pap. 1.95 o.s.i. (ISBN 0-02-030230-4, Collier). Macmillan.

Al-Ghazzali. Worship in Islam. Calverley, Edwin E., ed. LC 79-2860. 242p. 1981. Repr. of 1925 ed. 21.50 (ISBN 0-8305-0032-4). Hyperion Conn.

Algie, Jimmy. Social Values, Objectives, & Action. LC 75-12902. 491p. 1975. 34.95 (ISBN 0-470-02250-7). Halsted Pr.

Algieri, Shirley. Events That Shook the World. Mooney, Thomas J., ed. (Pal Paperbacks Ser., Kit B). (Illus., Orig.). (gr. 7-12). 1974. pap. text ed. 1.25 (ISBN 0-8374-3513-7). Xerox Ed Pubns.

Algosaibi, Ghazi A. From the Orient & the Desert. (Illus.). 1978. pap. cancelled o.p. (ISBN 0-85362-176-4, Oriel). Routledge & Kegan.

Algozin, Keith, ed. see Rubel, Maximilien.

Algozzine, Bob, et al. Sourcebook of Research & Practice in Behavioral Disorders. 375p. 1981. text ed. price not set (ISBN 0-89443-345-8). Aspen Systems.

Algren, Nelson. The Man with the Golden Arm. LC 78-72524. 1979. Repr. of 1949 ed. lib. bdg. 12.50x (ISBN 0-8376-0425-7). Bentley.

Alhadeff, David A. Competition & Controls in Banking: A Study of the Regulation of Bank Competition in Italy, France & England. (Institute of Business & Economic Research & Institute of Industrial Relations, UC Berkeley). 1968. 25.50x (ISBN 0-520-00011-0). U of Cal Pr.

Al-Hakim, Tewfik. Fate of a Cockroach & Other Plays. Johnson-Davies, Denys, tr. from Arabic. 184p. 1980. 9.00 (ISBN 0-89410-196-X); pap. 5.00 (ISBN 0-89410-197-8). Three Continents.

Al-Hamdani & Al-Hasan Ibn Ahmad. The Antiquities of South Arabia. Faris, Nabih A., tr. from Arabic. LC 79-2864. (Illus.). 119p. 1981. Repr. of 1938 ed. 13.50 (ISBN 0-8305-0033-2). Hyperion Conn.

Alhara, Herman, ed. see Ohsawa, George.

Al-Hasan Ibn Ahmad, jt. auth. see Al-Hamdani.

Al Hashim, Dhia & Robertson, James W. Contemporary Issues in Accounting. LC 79-9840. (ITT Key Issue Lecture Ser.). 296p. 1979. text ed. 12.50 (ISBN 0-672-97331-6); pap. text ed. 6.95 (ISBN 0-672-97332-4). Bobbs.

Alhashim, Dhia D. & Robertson, James W. Accounting for Multinational Enterprises. LC 77-13732. (Key Issues Lecture Ser). 1978. 13.95 (ISBN 0-672-97209-3); pap. 7.95 (ISBN 0-672-97183-6). Bobbs.

Al-Hibri, Azizah. Deontic Logic: A Comprehensive Appraisal & a View Proposal. LC 78-66422. 1978. pap. text ed. 8.75 (ISBN 0-8191-0303-9). U Pr of Amer.

Al-Hibri, Azizah, jt. auth. see Hickman, Larry.

Al-Husaini, Ishak M. The Moslem Brethren: The Greatest of the Modern Islamic Movements. LC 79-2866. 186p. 1981. Repr. of 1956 ed. 18.00 (ISBN 0-8305-0039-1). Hyperion Conn.

Ali, A., jt. ed. see Mamak, A.

Ali, Agha S. Bone-Sculpture. (Writers Workshop Redbird Ser.). 32p. 1975. text ed. 8.00 (ISBN 0-89253-535-0); pap. text ed. 3.00 (ISBN 0-88253-727-X). Ind-US Inc.

Ali, Ahmed. Twilight in Dehli. 2nd ed. 290p. 1974. pap. 3.00 (ISBN 0-88253-281-2). Ind-US Inc.

Ali, Ahmed, ed. & tr. from Urdu. The Golden Tradition. (Studies in Oriental Culture). 350p. 1973. 20.00x (ISBN 0-231-03687-6); pap. 7.50x (ISBN 0-231-03688-4). Columbia U Pr.

Ali, Asghar & Kumar, Krishan. Bibliography. 2nd rev. ed. 1980. text ed. 12.50x (ISBN 0-7069-0738-8, Pub. by Vikas India). Advent Bk.

Ali, Chaudhri M. Emergence of Pakistan. LC 79-163081. 1967. 22.50x (ISBN 0-231-02933-0). Columbia U Pr.

Ali, Florence. Opposing Absolutes: Conviction & Convention in John Ford's Plays. (Salzburg Studies in English Literature, Jacobean Drama Studies: No.44). 1974. pap. text ed. 25.00x (ISBN 0-391-01295-9). Humanities.

Ali, Hamid. Outlines of Roman Law. 1964. 5.50x o.p. (ISBN 0-210-33703-6). Asia.

Ali, M. A., ed. Environmental Physiology of Fishes. (NATO Advanced Study Institutes Ser, A-Life Sciences: Vol. 35). 685p. 1981. 69.50 (ISBN 0-306-40574-1, Plenum Pr). Plenum Pub.

Ali, Majid, jt. ed. see Tracht, Myron E.

Ali, Majid, et al. Surgical Pathology Case Studies, Vol. 1. 1978. spiral bdg. 19.50 (ISBN 0-87488-068-8). Med Exam.

--Surgical Pathology Case Studies, Vol. 2. 1978. spiral bdg. 19.50 (ISBN 0-87488-089-0). Med Exam.

--Visa Qualifying Examination Review, Vol. 1: Basic Sciences. LC 78-61617. 1978. pap. 11.75 (ISBN 0-87488-124-2). Med Exam.

Ali, Maulana M. A Manual of Hadith: Arabic Text & English Translation. 2nd, 1944 ed. 1978. text ed. 13.00x (ISBN 0-391-00548-0). Humanities.

Ali, N., et al. Transactions of the Moscow Mathematical Society, 1975. LC 65-4713. 1977. 37.20 (ISBN 0-8218-1632-2, MOSCOW-32). Am Math.

Ali, Salim. Fieldguide to the Birds of the Eastern Himalayas. (Illus.). 1978. 15.95x (ISBN 0-19-560595-0). Oxford U Pr.

Ali, Salim & Ripley, Dillon. Compact Edition of the Handbook of the Birds of India & Pakistan, Together with Those of Bangladesh, Nepal, Bhutan & Sri Lanka. (Illus.). 816p. 1980. 96.95 (ISBN 0-19-561245-0). Oxford U Pr.

Ali, Salim & Ripley, S. D. Handbook of the Birds of India & Pakistan, Vol. II: Megapodes to Crab Plover. (Illus.). 345p. 1981. 34.00 (ISBN 0-19-561201-9). Oxford U Pr.

Ali, Salim & Ripley, S. Dillon. Handbook of the Birds of India & Pakistan: Together with Those of Nepal, Sikkim, Bhutan, & Ceylon, 7 vols. Incl. Vol. 2. Megapodes to Crab Plover. 362p. 1969. 20.00 o.p. (ISBN 0-19-635262-2); Vol. 3. Stone Curlews to Owls. 342p. 1969. 23.75x (ISBN 0-19-635264-9); Vol. 4. Frogmouths to Pittas. 282p. 1970. 23.75x (ISBN 0-19-635275-4); Vol. 5. Larks to the Grey Hypocolius. 292p. 1972. 29.50x (ISBN 0-19-560166-1); Vol. 6. Cuckoo-Shrikes to Babaxes. 262p. 1971. 23.50x (ISBN 0-19-560101-7); Vol. 7. Laughing Thrushes to the Mangrove Whistler. 252p. 1972. 23.50x (ISBN 0-19-560263-3); Vol. 8. Warblers to Redstarts. 294p. 1973. 29.50x (ISBN 0-19-560291-9); Vol. 9. Robins to Wagtails. 322p. 1973. 29.50x (ISBN 0-19-560349-4); Vol. 10. Flowerpeckers to Buntings. 1974. 29.50 (ISBN 0-19-560385-0). (Illus.). Oxford U Pr.

Ali, Syed A. The Spirit of Islam: A History of the Evolution & Ideals of Islam with a Life of the Prophet. rev ed. 515p. 1974. Repr. of 1922 ed. text ed. 17.00x (ISBN 0-391-00341-0). Humanities.

Aliano, Richard A. American Defense Policy from Eisenhower to Kennedy: The Politics of Changing Military Requirements, 1957-1961. LC 74-27709. xi, 309p. 1975. 16.00 (ISBN 0-8214-0181-5). Ohio U Pr.

--American Defense Policy from Eisenhower to Kennedy: The Politics of Changing Military Requirements, 1957-1961. LC 74-27709. xi, 309p. 1978. pap. 8.00x (ISBN 0-8214-0406-7). Ohio U Pr.

Aliber, Robert Z. Exchange Risk & Corporate International Finance. LC 78-4645. 1978. 24.95 (ISBN 0-470-26307-5). Halsted Pr.

Aliber, Robert Z., ed. The Political Economy of Monetary Reform. LC 76-26692. 320p. Date not set. 21.00 o.s.i. (ISBN 0-87663-810-8). Allanheld & Schram.

--The Political Economy of Monetary Reform. LC 76-26692. 320p. 1977. text ed. 21.00 (ISBN 0-86598-001-2). Allanheld.

Aliber, Robert Z., jt. ed. see Shultz, George P.

Aliboni, Roberto, ed. Arab Industrialization & Economic Integration. LC 78-10632. 1979. 23.95 (ISBN 0-312-04702-9). St Martin.

Al-Ibrahim, Mohamed S., jt. auth. see Novick, Lloyd F.

Alice. Dinky & Sam: And the Long Way Home. (Illus.). 1981. 4.95 (ISBN 0-533-04711-0). Vantage.

Aliesan, Jody. As If It Will Matter. LC 78-63399. 60p. (Orig.). 1978. 15.00 (ISBN 0-931188-04-0); pap. 4.00 (ISBN 0-931188-03-2). Seal Pr WA.

Aliev, A. I., et al. Handbook of Nuclear Data for Neutron Activation Analysis. 1972. 24.95 (ISBN 0-470-02260-4). Halsted Pr.

Aligarh Muslim University, ed. Messages of Freedom. 1964. 4.50x o.p. (ISBN 0-210-26962-6). Asia.

--Readings in Democracy. 4.75x o.p. (ISBN 0-210-26982-0). Asia.

Aliger, Margarita, et al. Three Russian Poets. Feinstein, Elaine, tr. from Rus. (Translation Ser.). 1979. pap. 4.95 o.s.i. (ISBN 0-85635-227-6, Pub. by Carcanet New Pr England). Persea Bks.

Alighar Muslim University. Significant Writings on Life & Man. 1963. 4.00x o.p. (ISBN 0-210-26967-7). Asia.

Alighiere, Dante. Paradiso. Ciardi, John, tr. 1970. pap. 2.75 (ISBN 0-451-61893-9, ME1893, Ment). NAL.

Alighieri, Dante see Dante Alighieri.

Ali-Khaklifa Al-Luwari. Oil Revenues in the Gulf Emirates. LC 78-7358. (Illus.). 1978. lib. bdg. 45.00x (ISBN 0-89158-831-0). Westview.

Aliki. At Mary Bloom's. LC 75-45482. (Illus.). 32p. (gr. k-3). 1976. PLB 7.92 (ISBN 0-688-84048-5). Greenwillow.

--Corn Is Maize: The Gift of the Indians. LC 75-6928. (A Let's-Read-&-Find-Out Science Bk). (Illus.). 40p. (gr. k-3). 1976. PLB 7.89 (ISBN 0-690-00975-5, TYC-J). T Y Crowell.

--Fossils Tell of Long Ago. LC 78-170999. (A Let's-Read-&-Find-Out Science Bk). (Illus.). 40p. (gr. k-3). 1972. PLB 7.89 (ISBN 0-690-31379-9, TYC-J). T Y Crowell.

--Hush Little Baby. (Illus.). (ps-1). 1968. PLB 7.95 (ISBN 0-13-448167-4); pap. 2.50 (ISBN 0-13-448175-5). P-H.

--June Seven. (gr. 1-5). 1972. 4.95g o.s.i. (ISBN 0-02-700400-7). Macmillan.

--The Long Lost Coelacanth & Other Living Fossils. LC 72-83773. (A Let's-Read-&-Find-Out Science Bk.). (Illus.). 40p. (gr. k-3). 1973. 7.95 (ISBN 0-690-50478-0, TYC-J); PLB 6.89 o.p. (ISBN 0-690-50479-9). T Y Crowell.

--My Five Senses. LC 62-7150. (A Let's-Read-&-Find-Out Science Bk). (Illus.). (gr. k-3). 1962. PLB 7.89 (ISBN 0-690-56763-4, TYC-J); filmstrip with record 11.95 (ISBN 0-690-56764-2); filmstrip with cassette 14.95 (ISBN 0-690-56766-9). T Y Crowell.

--My Five Senses. LC 62-7150. (Crocodile Paperbacks Ser.). (Illus.). 33p. (gr. k-3). 1972. pap. 2.95 (ISBN 0-690-56768-5, TYC-J). T Y Crowell.

--My Visit to the Dinosaurs. LC 70-78255. (A Let's-Read-&-Find-Out Science Bk). (Illus.). (gr. k-3). 1969. bds. 6.95 (ISBN 0-690-57401-0, TYC-J); PLB 7.89 (ISBN 0-690-57402-9); pap. 2.95 crocodile paperback ser. (ISBN 0-690-57403-7, TIYC-J). T Y Crowell.

--Story of William Penn. (gr. k-3). 1964. PLB 5.95 o.p. (ISBN 0-13-850446-6). P-H.

--The Twelve Months. LC 78-3554. (Illus.). (gr. k-3). 1978. 7.95 (ISBN 0-688-80164-1); PLB 7.63 (ISBN 0-688-84164-3). Greenwillow.

--The Two of Them. LC 79-10161. (Illus.). (gr. k-3). 1979. 7.95 (ISBN 0-688-80225-7); PLB 7.63 (ISBN 0-688-84225-9). Greenwillow.

--Wild & Woolly Mammoths. LC 76-18082. (A Let's-Read-&-Find-Out Science Bk). (Illus.). (gr. k-3). 1977. PLB 7.89 (ISBN 0-690-01276-4, TYC-J). T Y Crowell.

Alikonis, Justin J. Candy Technology. (Illus.). 1979. lib. bdg. 30.00 (ISBN 0-87055-280-5). AVI.

Ali Majid, et al. Pathology Review. 7th ed. (Medical Exam Review Ser.). 1980. pap. 8.50 spiral bdg. (ISBN 0-87488-204-4). Med Exam.

Alinder, James, ed. Discovery & Recognition. (Untitled Ser.: No. 25). 56p. (Orig.). 1981. pap. 9.95 (ISBN 0-933286-24-4). Friends Photography.

--New Landscapes. (Untitled Ser.: No. 24). (Illus.). 56p. 1981. pap. 8.95 (ISBN 0-933286-21-X). Friends Photography.

--Nine Critics - Nine Photographs. LC 80-68803. (Untitled Ser.: No. 23). (Illus.). 56p. (Orig.). 1980. pap. 8.95 (ISBN 0-933286-20-1). Friends Photography.

Alinder, James, ed. see Teske, Edmund.

Alinder, James, ed. see Watkins, Carleton E.

Alisjahbana, Takdir S. Language Planning for Modernization: The Case of Indonesian & Malaysian. (Contributions to the Sociology of Language Ser.: No. 14). 1976. pap. text ed. 20.00x (ISBN 90-279-7712-7). Mouton.

Alisky, Marvin. Historical Dictionary of Peru. LC 79-16488. (Latin American Historical Dictionaries Ser.: No. 20). 163p. 1979. 10.00 (ISBN 0-8108-1235-5). Scarecrow.

--Latin American Media: Guidance & Censorship. 1981. 16.50 (ISBN 0-8138-1525-8). Iowa St U Pr.

Alison, A. England in 1815 & 1845. 98p. 1971. Repr. of 1845 ed. 15.00x (ISBN 0-7165-1699-3, Pub. by Irish Academic Pr Ireland). Biblio Dist.

Alison, James. Poetry of Northeast Scotland. 1976. pap. text ed. 8.95x o.p. (ISBN 0-435-14021-3). Heinemann Ed.

Alitto, Guy S. The Last Confucian: Liang Shu-Ming & the Chinese Dilemma of Modernity. LC 75-27920. (Center for Chinese Studies). 1979. 19.00x (ISBN 0-520-03123-7). U of Cal Pr.

Alix, Ernest K. Ransom Kidnapping in America, 1874-1974: The Creation of a Capital Crime. LC 78-1985. (Perspectives in Sociology Ser.). 256p. 1978. 15.00 (ISBN 0-8093-0849-5). S Ill U Pr.

--Ransom Kidnapping in America, 1874-1974: The Creation of a Capital Crime. LC 78-1985. 256p. 1980. pap. 7.95 (ISBN 0-8093-0976-9). S Ill U Pr.

Alkazi, Roshan. Ancient Indian Costume, Six Hundred B.C - A.D. Seven Hundred & Fifty. (Illus.). 1978. text ed. 35.00x o.p. (ISBN 0-7069-0732-9). Humanities.

Alkazi, Roshen. Seventeen More Poems. (Writers Workshop Redbird Ser.). 1975. 8.00 (ISBN 0-88253-628-1); pap. text ed. 4.00 (ISBN 0-88253-627-3). Ind-US Inc.

--Seventeen Poems. 8.00 (ISBN 0-89253-549-0). Ind-US Inc.

Alkema, Chester J. Alkema's Complete Guide to Creative Art for Young People. LC 70-167654. (Illus.). 1971. 16.95 (ISBN 0-8069-5188-5); PLB 14.99 (ISBN 0-8069-5189-3). Sterling.

--Crafting with Nature's Materials. LC 72-81038. (Little Craft Book Ser.). (Illus.). 48p. (gr. 6 up). 1972. 5.95 (ISBN 0-8069-5214-8); PLB 6.69 (ISBN 0-8069-5215-6). Sterling.

--Mask-Making. LC 80-54343. (Illus.). 96p. 8.95 (ISBN 0-8069-7038-3); lib. bdg. 8.29 (ISBN 0-8069-7039-1). Sterling.

--Masks. (Little Craft Book Ser). (Illus.). (gr. 5 up). 1971. 4.95 o.p. (ISBN 0-8069-5166-4); PLB 5.89 o.p. (ISBN 0-8069-5167-2). Sterling.

--Monster Masks. (Little Craft Book Ser.). (Illus.). 48p. (gr. 7 up). 1973. 4.95 o.p. (ISBN 0-8069-5256-3); PLB 5.89 o.p. (ISBN 0-8069-5257-1). Sterling.

--Puppet-Making. LC 72-167668. (Little Craft Book Ser.). (Illus.). (gr. 4 up). 1971. 5.95 (ISBN 0-8069-5174-5); PLB 6.69 (ISBN 0-8069-5175-3). Sterling.

--Starting with Papier Mache. (Little Craft Book Ser). (Illus.). 48p. (gr. 2 up). 1974. 4.95 o.p. (ISBN 0-8069-5298-9); PLB 5.89 o.p. (ISBN 0-8069-5299-7). Sterling.

--Tissue Paper Creations. LC 73-83454. (Little Craft Book Ser.). (Illus.). 48p. (gr. 3-8). 1973. 5.95 (ISBN 0-8069-5288-1); PLB 6.69 (ISBN 0-8069-5289-X). Sterling.

Alkemade, Cornelis T. & Herrmann, Roland. Fundamentals of Analytical Flame Spectroscopy. LC 79-4376. 442p. 1979. 74.95 (ISBN 0-470-26710-0). Halsted Pr.

Al-Khalesi, Yasin M. The Court of the Palms: A Functional Interpretation of the Mari Palace. Buccellati, G., ed. LC 77-94987. (Bibliotheca Mesopotamica Ser.: Vol. 8). (Illus.). 85p. 1978. 18.00 (ISBN 0-89003-029-4); pap. 14.50 (ISBN 0-89003-030-8). Undena Pubns.

Alkin, Glyn. Sound Recording & Reproduction. LC 80-41481. (Illus.). 208p. 1981. 24.95 (ISBN 0-240-51070-4). Focal Pr.

--TV Sound Operation. (Media Manuals Ser.). pap. 7.95 (ISBN 0-8038-7148-1). Hastings.

Alkin, Marvin C., et al. Conducting Evaluations: Three Perspectives. LC 80-52791. 60p. (Orig.). 1980. pap. 2.95 (ISBN 0-87954-036-2). Foundation Ctr.

Al-Kindi. Medical Formulary or Agrabadhin. Levey, Martin, tr. (Medieval Science Pubns., No. 7). 1966. 32.50x (ISBN 0-299-03600-6). U of Wis Pr.

Alkire, Leland G., Jr., ed. Periodical Title Abbreviations. 2nd ed. LC 76-52617. 1977. 50.00 (ISBN 0-8103-0336-1). Gale.

--Periodical Title Abbreviations. 3rd ed. 500p. 1981. 50.00 (ISBN 0-8103-0337-X). Gale.

Alkire, William. Coral Islanders. Goldschmidt, Walter, ed. LC 77-90673. (World of Man Ser.). (Illus.). 1978. text ed. 11.50x (ISBN 0-88295-618-3); pap. text ed. 5.75x (ISBN 0-88295-619-1). AHM Pub.

Alkons, Nancy V. see Bottiglia, William F.

Alksne, Z. K. & Ikaunieks, Ya Y. Carbon Stars. rev. ed. Baumert, J. H., ed. (Astronomy & Astrophysics Ser.: Vol. 11). Orig. Title: Uglerodnye Zvevdy. (Illus.). 192p. pap. 24.00 (ISBN 0-912918-16-0). Pachart Pub Hse.

Allaback, Steven. Alexander Solzhenitsyn. 1979. pap. 2.50 (ISBN 0-446-71926-9). Warner Bks.

Allaby, M. World Food Resources: Actual & Potential. (Illus.). 1977. 52.90x (ISBN 0-85334-731-X, Pub. by Applied Science). Burgess-Intl Ideas.

Allaby, Michael. Making & Managing a Small Holding. LC 79-51103. (Making & Managing Ser.). (Illus.). 1980. 17.95 (ISBN 0-7153-7803-1). David & Charles.

--A Year in the Life of a Field. LC 80-68681. (Illus.). 192p. 1981. 22.50 (ISBN 0-7153-7889-9). David & Charles.

Allaby, Michael & Bunyard, Peter. The Politics of Self-Sufficiency. 208p. 1980. 21.00 (ISBN 0-19-217695-1). Oxford U Pr.

Allahan, Philip. Tuning in to Nature. (Illus.). 1980. 10.00 (ISBN 0-8159-6309-2). Devin.

Allahan, Philip S. Exploring the Spectrum. (Illus.). Date not set. 8.95 (ISBN 0-8159-5405-0). Devin. Postponed.

Allamong, Betty D. & Mertens, Thomas R. Energy for Life: Photosynthesis & Respiration. LC 76-10181. (Self-Teaching Guides Ser.). 1976. pap. text ed. 4.95 o.p. (ISBN 0-471-02263-2). Wiley.

Allan & Hartley. Hello, I'm Johnny Cash. 0.49 (ISBN 0-8007-8527-4). Revell.

Allan, D. G. William Shipley: Founder of the Royal Society of Arts--A Biography with Documents. (Illus.). 240p. 1979. 22.50x (ISBN 0-85967-483-5, Pub. by Scolar Pr England); pap. 9.95x (ISBN 0-85967-484-3). Biblio Dist.

Allan, D. G. & Schofield, R. E. Stephen Hales: Scientist & Philanthropist. (Illus.). 220p. 1980. 50.00x (ISBN 0-85967-482-7, Pub. by Scolar Pr England). Biblio Dist.

Allan, Grant. The Reluctant Hangman & Other Stories of Crime. Schantz, Tom & Schantz, Enid, eds. (Illus.). 56p. 1975. pap. 4.50 o.p. (ISBN 0-915230-00-3). Rue Morgue.

Allan, Henry C., Jr. College Credit by Examination: A Systematic Guide to CLEP. LC 74-6883. 144p. 1975. pap. 5.00 o.p. (ISBN 0-8092-8333-6). Contemp Bks.

Allan, James. The Life of James Allan, the Celebrated Northumberland Piper: Containing His Travels, Adventures, & Wonderful Escapes, Etc. LC 80-2469. 1981. Repr. of 1817 ed. 62.50 (ISBN 0-404-19101-0). AMS Pr.

Allan, Leslie, et al. Promised Lands 2: Subdivisions in Florida's Wetlands, Vol. 2. LC 76-46735. (Promised Lands). (Illus.). 1977. pap. 20.00x o.p. (ISBN 0-918780-05-5). Inform.

Allan, Mabel E. Bridge of Friendship. LC 76-53432. (gr. 5 up). 1977. 5.95 (ISBN 0-396-07431-6). Dodd.

--Catrin in Wales. LC 61-9009. (gr. 7-11). 1960. 5.95 (ISBN 0-8149-0258-8). Vanguard.

--The Mills Down Below. LC 80-2782. 192p. (gr. 7 up). 1981. PLB 7.95 (ISBN 0-396-07926-1). Dodd.

--Mystery in Arles. LC 64-23321. (gr. 7 up). 1964. 5.95 (ISBN 0-8149-0255-3). Vanguard.

--Mystery in Manhattan. LC 68-28342. (Illus.). (gr. 6 up). 1968. 5.95 (ISBN 0-8149-0252-9). Vanguard.

--Mystery in Rome. LC 72-90477. (gr. 7 up). 1975. 5.95 (ISBN 0-8149-0726-1). Vanguard.

--Mystery in Wales. LC 79-89664. (gr. 7 up). 1970. 5.95 (ISBN 0-8149-0664-8). Vanguard.

--New York for Nicola. LC 63-13791. (gr. 8-11). 5.95 (ISBN 0-8149-0256-1). Vanguard.

--The Rising Tide. LC 77-14653. (gr. 4-7). 1978. 6.95 o.s.i. (ISBN 0-8027-6317-0). Walker & Co.

--Romance in Italy. LC 62-11214. (gr. 8-11). 5.95 (ISBN 0-8149-0257-X). Vanguard.

--The View Beyond My Father. LC 78-7736. 1978. 5.95 (ISBN 0-396-07612-2). Dodd.

Allan, Margaret. The School Library Resource Centre. (Illus.). 192p. 1974. 18.00x o.p. (ISBN 0-8464-0815-5). Beekman Pubs.

Allan, Mea. Tom's Weeds. (Illus.). 1970. 5.95 o.p. (ISBN 0-571-08919-4, Pub. by Faber & Faber). Merrimack Bk Serv.

--Weeds. (Illus.). 1978. 14.95 o.p. (ISBN 0-670-75657-1). Viking Pr.

Allan Nairn & Associates. The Reign of Ets: The Corporation That Makes up Minds. LC 80-107761. (The Ralph Nader Report on the Educational Testing Service). 554p. (Orig.). 1980. pap. 30.00 (ISBN 0-936486-00-7). R Nader.

Allan, Peter & Rosenberg, Stephen. Public Personnel & Administrative Behavior: Text & Cases. 200p. 1981. pap. text ed. 8.95 (ISBN 0-87872-287-4). Duxbury Pr.

Allan, Stella. An Inside Job. 1980. pap. 2.25 (ISBN 0-380-50237-2, 50237). Avon.

Allan, Ted. Willie the Squowse. (Illus.). (gr. 2 up). 1978. 6.95 (ISBN 0-8038-8086-3). Hastings.

Allan, William. The African Husbandman. LC 75-17188. (Illus.). 1977. Repr. of 1965 ed. lib. bdg. 33.50x (ISBN 0-8371-8287-5, ALAH). Greenwood.

Alland, Alexander. Adaptation in Cultural Evolution: An Approach to Medical Anthropology. LC 78-100666. 1970. 17.50x (ISBN 0-231-03229-3); pap. 6.00x (ISBN 0-231-03997-2). Columbia U Pr.

--Human Diversity. LC 79-138293. 1971. 17.50x (ISBN 0-231-03227-7). Columbia U Pr.

--To Be Human: An Introduction to Cultural Anthropology. 401p. 1981. text ed. 13.95 (ISBN 0-471-06213-8). Wiley.

Alland, Alexander, Jr. The Human Imperative. LC 77-183227. 160p. 1972. 17.00x (ISBN 0-231-03228-5); pap. 6.00x (ISBN 0-231-08301-7, 132). Columbia U Pr.

--To Be Human: An Introduction to Anthropology. LC 79-19497. 1980. text ed. 19.95 (ISBN 0-471-01747-7); write for info tchr's ed (ISBN 0-471-06054-2). Wiley.

Allanson, George G. see Methvin, John J.

Allard, G. F., et al, eds. High Speed Can Manufacture, 2 vols. (Engineering Craftsmen: No. H301). (Illus.). 1972. Set. spiral bdg. 39.95x (ISBN 0-85083-159-8). Intl Ideas.

Allard, Harry. I Will Not Go to Market Today. LC 78-72474. (Illus.). 32p. (ps-2). 1981. pap. 2.75 (ISBN 0-8037-4178-2, Pied Piper Bk). Dial.

--The Stupids Die. (gr. k-3). 1981. 7.95 (ISBN 0-395-30347-8). HM.

--Tutti-Frutti Case. (Illus.). (ps-2). 1975. 5.95 (ISBN 0-13-933200-6, 933218); pap. 1.50 (ISBN 0-13-933218-9). P-H.

Allard, Harry, tr. see Waechter, Friedrich K.

Allard, R. J. An Approach to Econometrics. 227p. 1974. 18.75 (ISBN 0-470-02311-2). Krieger.

--An Approach to Econometrics. 240p. 1974. 27.00x (ISBN 0-86003-003-2, Pub. by Allan Pubs England); pap. 13.50x (ISBN 0-86003-102-0). State Mutual Bk.

Allard, Robert W. Principles of Plant Breeding. LC 60-14240. 1960. 22.95 (ISBN 0-471-02310-8). Wiley.

Allard, S. Metals: Thermal & Mechanical Data. 1969. text ed. 105.00 (ISBN 0-08-006588-0). Pergamon.

Allardyce, Alex & Genzel, Peter. Letters for the International Exchange of Publications, Vol. 13. (IFLA Publications Ser.). 148p. 1978. 17.25 (ISBN 0-89664-113-9, Pub. by K G Saur). Shoe String.

Allasio, John, et al. RCT Mathematics: A Workbook. 168p. (gr. 9-12). 1980. pap. 5.95 (ISBN 0-937820-00-8); ans. key 1.00 (ISBN 0-937820-01-6). Westsea Pub.

Allaud, Louis & Martin, Maurice H. Schlumberger, The History of a Technique. LC 77-23566. 1977. 34.95 (ISBN 0-471-01667-5, Pub. by Wiley-Interscience). Wiley.

Allbritton, Claude C., Jr. Abyss of Time: Changing Conceptions of the Earth's Antiquity After the 16th Century. LC 79-57131. (Illus.). 272p. 1980. text ed. write for info. (ISBN 0-87735-341-7). Freeman C.

Allbutt, Mary E., jt. ed. see Fraser, J. D.

Allchin, A. L., rev. by see Thunberg, Lars.

Allchin, F. R. Neolithic Cattle-Keepers of Southern India. (University of Cambridge Oriental Pubs). 1963. 38.50 (ISBN 0-521-04018-3). Cambridge U Pr.

Allcorn, Seth. Internal Auditing for Hospitals. LC 79-20072. 1979. text ed. 29.00 (ISBN 0-89443-163-3). Aspen Systems.

Alldridge, J. C. Ilse Aichinger. (Modern German Authors: Texts & Contexts Vol. 2). 8.95 (ISBN 0-8023-1235-7). Dufour.

Alldritt, Keith. The Good Pit Man. LC 76-5367. 1976. 8.95 o.p. (ISBN 0-312-33915-1). St Martin.

Alleger, Daniel E., ed. see Bard, Samuel A.

Allegro, J. M. Dead Sea Scrolls. 1956. pap. 3.50 (ISBN 0-14-020376-1, Pelican). Penguin.

Alleine, Joseph. Alarm. 1978. pap. 2.45 (ISBN 0-85151-081-7). Banner of Truth.

Alleman, Herbert C., ed. New Testament Commentary: A General Introduction to & a Commentary on the Books of the New Testament. rev. ed. LC 44-47049. 1944. 8.95 (ISBN 0-8006-0364-8). Fortress.

Allen, A. & Eberly, J. H. Optical Resonance & Two-Level Atoms. LC 74-18023. (Interscience Monographs & Texts in Physics & Astronomy: No. 28). 224p. 1975. 30.95 (ISBN 0-471-02327-2, Pub. by Wiley-Interscience). Wiley.

Allen, Agnes. The Story of Painting. 2nd ed. (Illus.). 1966. 5.95 o.p. (ISBN 0-571-06539-2, Pub. by Faber & Faber); pap. 2.95 (ISBN 0-571-09032-X). Merrimack Bk Serv.

--The Story of Sculpture. 2nd ed. (Illus.). 1967. 7.95 (ISBN 0-571-04601-0, Pub. by Faber & Faber). Merrimack Bk Serv.

Allen, Alex B. Basketball Toss up. LC 73-7317. (Springboard Ser.). (Illus.). 64p. (Remedial Reader). (gr. 3-8). 1972. 5.75g (ISBN 0-8075-0578-1). A Whitman.

--Danger on Broken Arrow Trail. LC 74-19499. (Springboard Sports Ser.). (Illus.). 64p. (gr. 3-6). 1974. 5.75g (ISBN 0-8075-1455-1). A Whitman.

--Fifth Down. LC 73-7317. (Springboard Sports Ser.). (Illus.). 64p. (gr. 3-5). 1974. 5.75g (ISBN 0-8075-2432-8). A Whitman.

--No Place for Baseball. LC 72-13346. (Springboard Ser.). (Illus.). 64p. (gr. 3-6). 1973. 5.75g (ISBN 0-8075-5697-1). A Whitman.

--The Tennis Menace. LC 72-83680. (Springboard Ser). (Illus.). 64p. (gr. 3-7). 1975. 5.75g (ISBN 0-8075-7773-1). A Whitman.

Allen, Anne S. Introduction to Health Professions. 3rd ed. LC 79-26136. (Illus.). 1980. pap. text ed. 11.50 (ISBN 0-8016-0113-4). Mosby.

Allen, Arnold O. Probability, Statistics & Queueing Theory: With Computer Science Application. (Computer Science & Applied Math Ser.). 1978. 29.50 (ISBN 0-12-051050-2). Acad Pr.

Allen, B. K., jt. auth. see Heywood, J. S.

Allen, B. L. Basic Anatomy: A Laboratory Manual: the Human Skeleton, the Cat. 2nd ed. (Illus.). 1980. 9.95x (ISBN 0-7167-1091-9). W H Freeman.

Allen, B. M. Soldering & Welding. LC 76-16388. (Drake Home Craftsman Ser.). (Illus.). 160p. 1975. pap. 4.95 o.p. (ISBN 0-8069-8676-X). Sterling.

Allen, Barbara A., jt. auth. see Allen, James.

Allen, Barbara A., jt. auth. see Allen, James R.

Allen, Barry, jt. auth. see Sports Illustrated Editors.

Allen, Bem P. Social Behavior: Fact & Falsehood. LC 77-28709. 1978. 15.95 (ISBN 0-88229-393-1); pap. 7.95 (ISBN 0-88229-611-6). Nelson-Hall.

Allen, C., jt. auth. see Harmon, T.

Allen, C. Curtis. The Saga of a Mud Road Doctor. (Illus.). 132p. 1975. 7.95 (ISBN 0-89015-099-0). Nortex Pr.

Allen, C. G. A Short Economic History of Modern Japan. 272p. 1980. 19.95 (ISBN 0-312-71771-7). St Martin.

Allen, C. W. Astrophysical Quantities. 3rd ed. (Illus.). 320p. 1973. text ed. 37.50x (ISBN 0-485-11150-0, Athlone Pr). Humanities.

Allen, Carleton K. Law in the Making. 7th ed. 1964. pap. 16.95x (ISBN 0-19-881029-6, OPB29). Oxford U Pr.

Allen, Carlos. Guia De Estudios Sobre Estudios En el Nuevo Testamento. (Illus.). 96p. Date not set. pap. price not set (ISBN 0-311-43502-5). Casa Bautista.

Allen, Carlton C. Space Station Eight. 1978. 7.95 o.p. (ISBN 0-533-03076-5). Vantage.

Allen, Catherine. The New Lottie Moon Story. LC 79-52336. 1980. 7.95 (ISBN 0-8054-6319-4). Broadman.

Allen, Cecil J. Great Eastern Railway. 14.95x (ISBN 0-392-07860-0, SpS). Soccer.

Allen, Charles. God's Psychiatry. 1963. pap. 1.75 (ISBN 0-515-05327-9). Jove Pubns.

Allen, Charles L. All Things Are Possible Through Prayer. (Orig.). pap. 1.95 (ISBN 0-515-05982-X). Jove Pubns.

--All Things Are Possible Through Prayer. 1975. pap. 1.25 (ISBN 0-89129-072-9, PV072). Jove Pubns.

--Life More Abundant. 1976. pap. 1.50 (ISBN 0-89129-212-8). Jove Pubns.

--The Miracle of Love. LC 72-5430. 128p. 1972. 6.95 (ISBN 0-8007-0543-2). Revell.

--Touch of the Master's Hand: Christ's Miracles for Today. 1956. pap. 1.25 (ISBN 0-8007-8093-0, Spire Bks). Revell.

Allen, Charlotte V. Hidden Meanings. 224p. (Orig.). 1976. pap. 1.50 o.s.i. (ISBN 0-446-88188-0). Warner Bks.

--Julia's Sister. (Orig.). 1978. pap. 1.95 o.s.i. (ISBN 0-446-89357-9). Warner Bks.

--The Marmalade Man. 1981. 13.95 (ISBN 0-525-15294-6). Dutton.

--Meet Me in Time. (Orig.). 1978. pap. 2.25 o.s.i. (ISBN 0-446-82530-1). Warner Bks.

--Promises. 1981. pap. 2.95 (ISBN 0-425-04843-8). Berkley Pub.

--Running Away. (Orig.). 1977. pap. 1.75 o.p. (ISBN 0-451-07740-7, E7740, Sig). NAL.

Allen, Clark L. Elementary Mathematics of Price Theory. 1966. pap. 9.95x (ISBN 0-534-00655-8). Wadsworth Pub.

Allen, Cleveland J. Brazilian Odyssey: Memoirs of a United Nations' Specialist. 160p. 1981. pap. 7.50 (ISBN 0-8059-2746-8). Dorrance.

Allen, Connie J., jt. auth. see Allen, Gerald R.

Allen, Daniel. Bibliography of Discographies: Jazz, Vol. II. 200p. 1981. 35.00 (ISBN 0-8352-1342-0). Bowker.

Allen, David. Infrared: The New Astronomy. LC 75-16584. 228p. 1976. 15.95 (ISBN 0-470-02334-1). Halsted Pr.

Allen, David G. In English Ways: The Movement of Societies & the Transferal of English Local Law & Custom to Massachusetts Bay in the Seventeenth Century. LC 80-13198. (Institute of Early American History & Culture Ser.). xxi, 312p. 1981. 27.00x (ISBN 0-8078-1448-2). U of NC Pr.

Allen, David G., ed. see Webster, Daniel.

Allen, David W. The Fear of Looking; or Scopophilic-Exhibitionistic Conflicts. LC 73-80875. 250p. 1974. 9.95x (ISBN 0-8139-0448-X). U Pr of Va.

Allen, Derek & Nash, Dephne. Coins of the Ancient Celts. (Illus.). 250p. 1980. 25.00x (ISBN 0-85224-371-5, Pub. by Edinburgh U Pr Scotland). Columbia U Pr.

Allen, Devere. Fight for Peace, 2 vols. LC 74-147439. (Library of War & Peace; Histories of the Organized Peace Movement). Set. lib. bdg. 76.00 (ISBN 0-8240-0228-8); lib. bdg. 38.00 ea. Garland Pub.

Allen, Diogenes. The Traces of God. LC 80-51570. 170p. (Orig.). 1981. pap. 5.00 (ISBN 0-936384-03-4). Cowley Pubns.

Allen, Don C., ed. Four Poets on Poetry. LC 80-20856. (Percy Graeme Turnbull Memorial Lectures on Poetry, 1958). 111p. 1980. Repr. of 1959 ed. lib. bdg. 19.50x (ISBN 0-313-22405-6, ALFP). Greenwood.

Allen, Donald & Guy, Rebecca. Conversation Analysis: The Sociology of Talk. (Janua Linguarum, Ser. Minor: No. 200). 284p. 1978. pap. text ed. 31.75x (ISBN 90-279-3002-3). Mouton.

Allen, Donald & Butterick, George F., eds. The Postmoderns: The New American Poetry Revised. rev. ed. LC 79-52054. 512p. 1981. pap. 9.95 postponed (ISBN 0-394-17458-5, Ever). Grove.

Allen, Donald, ed. see Creeley, Robert.

Allen, Donald, ed. see Dorn, Edward.

Allen, Donald, ed. see O'Hara, Frank.

Allen, Donald, ed. see Spicer, Jack.

Allen, Donald, ed. & intro. by see Welch, Lew.

Allen, Donald, ed. see Welch, Lew.

Allen, Donald, ed. see Whalen, Philip.

Allen, Donald M., ed. see Lorca, Federico Garcia.

Allen, Donald R. French Views of America in the 1930's. Freidel, Frank, ed. LC 78-62374. (Modern American History Ser.: Vol. 1). 1979. lib. bdg. 28.00 (ISBN 0-8240-3625-5). Garland Pub.

Allen, Dorothy S. Plaster Art: Step by Step. Cole, Tom, ed. LC 80-70317. (Illus.). 130p. (Orig.). (gr. 5). 1981. 15.95 (ISBN 0-686-28860-2); pap. 12.95 (ISBN 0-686-28861-0). Dots Pubns.

Allen, Douglas. Structure & Creativity in Religion. (Religion & Reason Ser.: No. 14). 1978. 28.80x (ISBN 90-279-7594-9). Mouton.

Allen, Durward L. Our Wildlife Legacy. rev. ed. LC 62-7980. (Funk & W Bk.). (Illus.). (YA) (gr. 9 up). 1962. 9.95 o.s.i. (ISBN 0-308-70309-X, 780100, TYC-T). T Y Crowell.

--Our Wildlife Legacy. LC 62-7980. (Funk & W Bk.). 432p. 1974. pap. 4.95 o.s.i. (ISBN 0-308-10096-4, F84, TYC-T). T Y Crowell.

Allen, E. L. From Plato to Nietzsche. Orig. Title: Guide Book to Western Thought. 192p. 1977. pap. 2.25 (ISBN 0-449-30768-9, Prem). Fawcett.

Allen, E. Waterhouse. How to Execute an Agency. LC 79-53977. (Illus., Orig.). 1980. pap. 4.95 (ISBN 0-9603338-1-9). Bark-Back.

Allen, Edith B. One Hundred Bible Games. (Paperback Program Ser). (YA) 1968. pap. 2.95 (ISBN 0-8010-0033-5). Baker Bk.

Allen, Edward B. Early American Wall Paintings, 1710-1850. LC 77-77694. (Library of American Art Ser.). 1971. Repr. of 1926 ed. lib. bdg. 27.50 (ISBN 0-306-71332-2). Da Capo.

Allen, Edward F. Complete Dream Book. 288p. 1973. pap. 2.75 (ISBN 0-446-95906-5). Warner Bks.

Allen, Edward L. Energy & Economic Growth in the United States. 1979. text ed. 22.50x (ISBN 0-262-01062-3). MIT Pr.

Allen, Edward S. Six-Place Tables. 256p. 1981. Repr. of 1922 ed. lib. bdg. price not set (ISBN 0-89874-287-0). Krieger.

Allen, Eleanor. Home Sweet Home: A History of Housework. (Junior Reference Ser.). (Illus.). 64p. (gr. 7 up). 7.95 (ISBN 0-7136-1927-9). Dufour.

--Victorian Children. (Junior Reference Ser.). (Illus.). 64p. (gr. 7 up). 7.95 (ISBN 0-7136-1324-6). Dufour.

--Wartime Children, 1939-1945. (Junior Reference Ser.). (Illus.). 64p. (gr. 7 up). 7.95 (ISBN 0-7136-1503-6). Dufour.

--Wash & Brush up. (Junior Reference Ser.). (Illus.). 64p. (gr. 7 up). 7.95 (ISBN 0-7136-1639-3). Dufour.

Allen, Ellen G. Japanese Flower Arrangement: A Complete Primer. rev. ed. LC 62-21731. (Illus.). 1963. Repr. 8.25 (ISBN 0-8048-0293-9). C E Tuttle.

--Japanese Flower Arrangement in a Nutshell. (Illus., Orig.). pap. 4.50 (ISBN 0-8048-0295-5). C E Tuttle.

Allen, Ethan. Baseball Play & Strategy. 2nd ed. LC 69-14668. (Illus.). 350p. 1969. 14.95 (ISBN 0-8260-0305-2). Wiley.

Allen, Ethel K. & Allen, O. N. The Leguminosae: A Source Book of Uses & Nodulation. 1152p. 1980. write for info. o.p. (ISBN 0-299-08400-0). U of Wis Pr.

Allen, Ethel K., jt. auth. see Allen, O. N.

Allen, Everett T., et al. Pension Planning: Pensions, Profit Sharing & Other Deferred Compensation Plans. 3rd ed. 1976. text ed. 17.50x (ISBN 0-256-01857-X). Irwin.

Allen, F. Sturges. Allen's Synonyms & Antonyms. rev. & enl. ed. Motter, T. H., ed. LC 38-12323. 1938. 12.50 o.p. (ISBN 0-06-010070-2, HarpT). Har-Row.

--Allen's Synonyms & Antonyms. pap. 3.50 (ISBN 0-06-463328-4, EH 328, EH). Har-Row.

Allen, F. W. Collected Poems. 1980. 5.95 (ISBN 0-533-04847-8). Vantage.

Allen, Francis A. The Decline of the Rehabilitative Ideal: Penal Policy & Social Purpose. LC 80-25098. (Storrs Lectures). 160p. 1981. 15.00x (ISBN 0-300-02565-3). Yale U Pr.

Allen, Frank C. A Critical Edition of Robert Browning's "Bishop Blougram's Apology". (Salzburg Studies in English Literature: Romantic Reassessment: No. 60). 243p. (Orig.). 1976. pap. 25.00x (ISBN 0-391-01296-7). Humanities.

Allen, Frank Kenyon, et al. Golfer's Bible. LC 68-11788. 1968. pap. 3.50 (ISBN 0-385-01402-3). Doubleday.

Allen, Fredrick W. Life's Way. 1981. 5.95 (ISBN 0-533-04847-8). Vantage.

Allen, G. & Pritchard, H. O. Statistical Mechanics & Spectroscopy. LC 74-7034. 1974. pap. 14.95 (ISBN 0-470-02331-7). Halsted Pr.

Allen, G. E. Life & Science in the Twentieth Century. LC 77-83985. (History of Science Ser.). (Illus.). 1978. 23.95 (ISBN 0-521-21864-0); pap. 8.50x (ISBN 0-521-29296-4). Cambridge U Pr.

Allen, Garland E., jt. auth. see Baker, Jeffrey J.

Allen, Garland E., jt. auth. see Baker, Jeffrey J. W.

Allen, Garland E., jt. auth. see Baker, Jeffrey W.

Allen, Gay W. American Prosody. 1966. Repr. lib. bdg. 20.00x (ISBN 0-374-90133-3). Octagon.

Allen, Gay W. & Clark, Harry H., eds. Literary Criticism: Pope to Croce. LC 61-12267. (Waynebooks Ser: No. 2). 1962. 9.95x (ISBN 0-8143-1157-1); pap. 6.50x (ISBN 0-8143-1158-X). Wayne St U Pr.

Allen, Gay Wilson. The Solitary Singer: A Critical Biography of Walt Whitman. LC 67-23414. 1967. 20.00x (ISBN 0-8147-0006-3). NYU Pr.

Allen, Gayle & Allen, Robert F. Three Worlds Cookbook. LC 75-19542. (Illus.). 239p. 1975. pap. 7.95 (ISBN 0-87983-096-4). Keats.

Allen, Gene P., jt. ed. see Wright, Nancy D.

Allen, George & Ritger, Dick. The Complete Guide to Bowling Strikes: The Encyclopedia of Strikes. LC 80-53200. (Illus.). 240p. 1981. 14.95 (ISBN 0-933554-02-8); pap. 9.95 (ISBN 0-933554-03-6). Ritger Sports.

Allen, George & Weiskopf, Don. Handbook of Winning Football. 1976. text ed. 16.95 (ISBN 0-205-05426-9); pap. text ed. 10.95 (ISBN 0-205-04880-3). Allyn.

Allen, George, jt. auth. see Ritger, Dick.

Allen, Gerald. Anemone Fishes. new ed. 20.00 (ISBN 0-87666-001-4, H-942). TFH Pubns.

--Charles Moore. (Illus.). 128p. 1980. 18.95 (ISBN 0-8230-7375-0). Watson-Guptill.

Allen, Gerald D., et al, eds. Dental Analgesia. LC 78-55278. (Postgraduate Dental Handbook Ser.: Vol. 6). (Illus.). 258p. 1979. casebound 25.00 (ISBN 0-685-47639-1). PSG Pub.

Allen, Gerald R. Butterfly & Angelfishes of the World, Vol. 2. LC 79-17351. 1980. 30.00 (ISBN 0-471-05618-9, Pub. by Wiley-Interscience). Wiley.

--Damselfishes. (Illus.). 240p. 1975. 9.95 (ISBN 0-87666-034-0, H-950). TFH Pubns.

Allen, Gerald R. & Allen, Connie J. All About Cockatiels. (Illus.). 1977. 4.95 (ISBN 0-87666-955-0, PS746). TFH Pubns.

Allen, Grant. An African Millionaire: Episodes in the Life of the Illustrious Colonel Clay. 1980. pap. 4.50 (ISBN 0-486-23992-6). Dover.

--The British Barbarians. Fletcher, Ian & Stokes, John, eds. LC 76-20062. (Decadent Consciousness Ser.). 1977. lib. bdg. 38.00 (ISBN 0-8240-2751-5). Garland Pub.

--Physiological Aesthetics. 283p. 1980. Repr. of 1877 ed. lib. bdg. 35.00 (ISBN 0-8495-0064-8). Arden Lib.

--Physiological Aesthetics. Fletcher, Ian & Stokes, John, eds. LC 76-20038. (Decadent Consciousness Ser.: Vol. 3). 1977. Repr. of 1877 ed. lib. bdg. 38.00 (ISBN 0-8240-2752-3). Garland Pub.

Allen, H. C. & Thompson, Roger, eds. Contrast and Connection: Bicentennial Essays in Anglo-American History. LC 76-7095. ix, 373p. 1976. 18.00x (ISBN 0-8214-0355-9). Ohio U Pr.

Allen, H. C., Jr. Molecular Vib-Rotors. 324p. 1963. text ed. 17.50 (ISBN 0-471-02325-6, Pub. by Wiley). Krieger.

Allen, H. G. Analysis & Design of Structural Sandwich Panels. 1969. text ed. 29.00 (ISBN 0-08-012870-X); pap. text ed. 17.00 (ISBN 0-08-012869-6). Pergamon.

Allen, H. G. & Bulson, P. S. Background to Buckling. (Illus.). 1980. text ed. 32.95x (ISBN 0-07-084100-4). McGraw.

Allen, H. Warner. A History of Wine. 2nd ed. (Illus.). 1962. 8.95 o.p. (ISBN 0-571-04409-3, Pub. by Faber & Faber). Merrimack Bk Serv.

Allen, Harold B. Linguistics & English Linguistics. 2nd ed. LC 75-42974. (Goldentree Bibliographies in Language & Literature Ser.). 1977. pap. text ed. 12.95x (ISBN 0-88295-558-6). AHM Pub.

Allen, Harry E. & Simonsen, Clifford E. Corrections in America. 2nd ed. 1978. text ed. 14.95 (ISBN 0-02-470830-5). Macmillan.

Allen, Harry E. & Beran, Nancy J., eds. Reform in Corrections: Problems & Issues. LC 76-12840. (Special Studies). 1977. text ed. 16.95 o.p. (ISBN 0-275-24270-6). Praeger.

Allen, Harry E., et al. Crime & Punishment: An Introduction to Criminology. LC 80-69715. (Illus.). 464p. 1981. text ed. 14.95 (ISBN 0-02-900460-8). Free Pr.

Allen, Herbert E. & Kramer, James R., eds. Nutrients in Natural Waters. LC 72-3786. (Environmental Science & Technology Ser.). 449p. 1972. 37.50 o.p. (ISBN 0-471-02328-0, Pub by Wiley-Interscience). Wiley.

Allen, Herman R. Open Door to Learning: The Land-Grant System Enters Its Second Century. LC 63-18672. 1963. 8.00 o.p. (ISBN 0-252-72590-5). U of Ill Pr.

Allen, Hervey. Anthony Adverse, Pt. 2: The Other Bronze Boy. 1978. pap. 2.50 o.s.i. (ISBN 0-446-81621-3). Warner Bks.

--Bedford Village: The City in the Dawn, Part 2. 1978. pap. 2.50 o.s.i. (ISBN 0-446-81436-9). Warner Bks.

--Toward the Morning: The City in the Dawn, Pt. 3. 1978. pap. 2.50 o.s.i. (ISBN 0-446-81438-5). Warner Bks.

Allen, Hilary. Norway & Europe in the Nineteen Seventies. 1979. 31.00x (ISBN 82-00-05230-3, Dist. by Columbia U Pr.). Universitet.

Allen, Horace T., Jr. A Handbook for the Lectionary. LC 80-19735. pap. 8.95. Geneva Pr.

--A Handbook for the Lectionary. 1980. softcover 9.95 (ISBN 0-664-24347-9). Westminster.

Allen, Howard W. Poindexter of Washington: A Study in Progressive Politics. LC 80-20123. 352p. 1981. price not set (ISBN 0-8093-0952-1). S Ill U Pr.

Allen, Hubert R. Air Warfare. LC 76-19593. (Pegasus Books: No. 18). 1968. 7.50x (ISBN 0-234-77156-9). Intl Pubns Serv.

Allen, Irving L., ed. New Towns & the Suburban Dream. (Interdisciplinary Urban Ser). 1976. 17.50 (ISBN 0-8046-9161-4, Natl U); pap. 8.95 (ISBN 0-8046-9165-7). Kennikat.

Allen, J., et al, eds. Grinding, Vol. 1. (Engineering Craftsmen: No. H5). 1968. spiral bdg. 21.00x (ISBN 0-85083-013-3). Intl Ideas.

Allen, J. P. & Widdowson, H. G. English in Physical Science. (English in Focus Ser). (Illus.). 1974. Student's Edition. pap. 6.95x (ISBN 0-19-437510-2); Tchr's Edition. 9.25x (ISBN 0-19-437504-8). Oxford U Pr.

Allen, J. P. & Corder, S. Pit, eds. The Edinburgh Course in Applied Linguistics, Vol. 2. (Language & Language Learning Ser). 388p. 1975. 24.00 o.p. (ISBN 0-19-437123-9); pap. text ed. 17.00x (ISBN 0-19-437058-5). Oxford U Pr.

--The Edinburgh Course in Applied Linguistics: Readings for Applied Linguistics, Vol. 1. (Language & Language Learning Ser.). 284p. 1973. 15.25 o.p. (ISBN 0-19-437122-0); pap. 9.00x (ISBN 0-19-437057-7). Oxford U Pr.

--The Edinburgh Course in Applied Linguistics: Techniques in Applied Linguistics, Vol. 3. (Language & Language Learning Ser.). 386p. 1974. 24.00 o.p. (ISBN 0-19-437124-7); pap. text ed. 13.95x (ISBN 0-19-437059-3). Oxford U Pr.

Allen, J. P. & Van Buren, Paul, eds. Chomsky: Selected Readings. 166p. 1981. pap. 6.95 (ISBN 0-19-437046-1). Oxford U Pr.

Allen, J. P., ed. see Chomsky, Noam.

Allen, J. S., jt. auth. see Rolt, L. T.

Allen, James. As a Man Thinketh. (Inspiration Classics Ser.). 4.95 (ISBN 0-8007-1076-2). Revell.

--From Poverty to Power. 184p. 1980. pap. 5.50 (ISBN 0-89540-061-8). Sun Pub.

Allen, James & Allen, Barbara A. Guide to Psychiatry: A Handbook on Psychiatry for Health Professionals. 1978. 17.50 (ISBN 0-87488-985-5); pap. 12.75 (ISBN 0-87488-716-X). Med Exam.

Allen, James C. Infectious Disease for the House Officer. (House Officer Ser.). (Illus.). 200p. 1981. price not set softcover (ISBN 0-683-00069-1). Williams & Wilkins.

Allen, James R. & Allen, Barbara A. Textbook Study Guide of Psychiatry. 2nd. ed. (Medical Examination Review Book: Vol. 7A). 1978. 8.50 (ISBN 0-87488-156-0). Med Exam.

Allen, James S. Popular French Romanticism: Authors, Readers, & Books in the 19th Century. (Illus.). 1980. 20.00 (ISBN 0-8156-2232-5). Syracuse U Pr.

--Popular French Romanticism: Authors, Readers, & Books in the Nineteenth Century. LC 80-27129. (Illus.). 304p. 1981. 20.00x (ISBN 0-8156-2232-5). Syracuse U Pr.

Allen, Jana & Gin, Margaret. Innards & Other Variety Meats. LC 73-91942. (Illus.). 144p. 1974. 7.95 (ISBN 0-912238-49-6); pap. 4.95 o.p. (ISBN 0-912238-48-8). One Hund One Prods.

Allen, Janet. Collage: The Art of Making Pictures from Odds & Ends. 80p. 1981. pap. 7.95 (ISBN 0-8120-2289-0). Barron.

Allen, Jeffrey. Mary Alice, Operator Number Nine. (Illus.). 32p. (gr. 1-3). 1976. 6.95 (ISBN 0-316-03425-8). Little.

Allen, Joan. The Happy Golden ABC. (Illus.). 24p. (gr. k-1). 1976. PLB 5.00 (ISBN 0-307-60344-X, Golden Pr). Western Pub.

Allen, Joan M. Candles & Carnival Lights: The Catholic Sensibility of F. Scott Fitzgerald. LC 77-82752. 1978. 15.00x (ISBN 0-8147-0563-4); pap. 5.00x (ISBN 0-8147-0564-2). NYU Pr.

Allen, John E. Early Aircraft. LC 78-64653. (Fact Finders Ser.). (Illus.). 1979. lib. bdg. 3.96 (ISBN 0-686-51127-1). Silver.

Allen, John R. Physical Geology. (Introducing Geology Ser.). 1975. pap. text ed. 9.95x (ISBN 0-04-550022-3). Allen Unwin.

Allen, John S. The Complete Book of Bicycle Commuting. (Illus.). 320p. 1980. 12.95 (ISBN 0-87857-342-9); pap. 9.95 (ISBN 0-87857-344-5). Rodale Pr Inc.

Allen, Jordan. Texas Fever. 224p. (Orig.). 1980. pap. 1.95 (ISBN 0-89083-664-7). Zebra.

Allen, Joseph, et al. Sandcastles. LC 80-1648. (Illus.). 164p. 1981. pap. 8.95 (ISBN 0-385-15931-5, Dolp). Doubleday.

Allen, Judson B. & Moritz, Theresa A. A Distinction of Stories: The Medieval Unity of Chaucer's Fair Chain of Narratives for Canterbury. 280p. 1981. write for info. (ISBN 0-8142-0310-8). Ohio St U Pr.

Allen, Judy L., jt. auth. see Sichel, Peter M.

Allen, K. Radway. Conservation & Management of Whales. LC 79-90505. (Washington Sea Grant). (Illus.). 120p. 1980. 12.50 (ISBN 0-295-95706-9). U of Wash Pr.

Allen, Kevin, ed. Balanced National Growth. LC 78-13820. 352p. 1979. 23.95 (ISBN 0-669-02668-9). Lexington Bks.

Allen, L. David. The Ballantine Teachers' Guide to Science Fiction. (Orig.). 1975. pap. 2.50 (ISBN 0-345-27989-1). Ballantine.

Allen, Linda. Mrs. Simkin's Bed. LC 80-12262. (Illus.). 32p. (gr. k-3). 1980. 6.95 (ISBN 0-688-22233-1); PLB 6.67 (ISBN 0-688-32233-6). Morrow.

Allen, Louis A. Time Before Morning: Art & Myth of the Australian Aborigines. LC 75-12812. 1976. 18.95 o.s.i. (ISBN 0-690-00411-7, TYC-T). T Y Crowell.

Allen, Loyd V., Jr. Drug Abuse: What Can We Do? LC 79-92950. 144p. (Orig.). 1981. pap. text ed. 2.50 (ISBN 0-8307-0744-1, 5016702). Regal.

Allen, M. W. & Noffsinger, Ella M. A Revision of the Marine Nematodes of the Superfamily Draconematoidea Filipjev. (Publications in Zoology Ser.: Vol. 109). 1978. 8.75x (ISBN 0-520-09583-9). U of Cal Pr.

Allen, Marcus. Tantra for the West: A Guide to Personal Freedom. LC 80-316. 220p. 1981. pap. 5.95 (ISBN 0-931432-06-5). Whatever Pub.

Allen, Marcus, et al. Reunion: Tools for Transformation. rev. ed. (Illus.). 1978. pap. 4.95 (ISBN 0-931432-01-4). Whatever Pub.

Allen, Margaret. Guides to Creative Motion Musicianship. 136p. 1979. 6.95 (ISBN 0-8059-2616-X). Dorrance.

Allen, Mark. Falconry in Arabia. (Illus.). 143p. Date not set. 40.00 (ISBN 0-89182-034-5). Charles River Bks.

Allen, Mary J. & Yen, Wendy M. Introduction to Measurement Theory. LC 78-25821. 1979. text ed. 16.95 (ISBN 0-8185-0283-5). Brooks-Cole.

Allen, Maury. Baseball's One Hundred: A Personal Ranking of the Best Players in Baseball History. (Illus.). 352p. 1981. 14.95 (ISBN 0-89104-208-3); pap. 6.95 (ISBN 0-89104-200-8). A & W Pubs.

--Jim Rice: Power Hitter. LC 79-91490. (Star People Ser.). (Illus.). 72p. (gr. 4-9). 1980. PLB 5.79 (ISBN 0-8178-6265-X). Harvey.

--Record Breakers. LC 68-31402. (Illus.). 1968. 5.95 o.p. (ISBN 0-13-767426-0). P-H.

--Where Have You Gone, Joe DiMaggio? The Story of America's Last Hero. (RL 9). 1976. pap. 1.50 o.p. (ISBN 0-451-06986-2, W6986, Sig). NAL.

Allen, Mearle L. Welcome to the Stork Club. LC 79-5424. 300p. Date not set. 14.95 (ISBN 0-498-02395-8). A S Barnes. Postponed.

Allen, Michael. Spence & the Holiday Murders. LC 78-51976. 1978. 7.95 o.s.i. (ISBN 0-8027-5390-6). Walker & Co.

--Spence & the Holiday Murders. 1981. pap. 2.25 (ISBN 0-440-18364-2). Dell.

Allen, Michael J., ed. Marsilio Ficino: The Philebus Commentary. 1981. 32.50x (ISBN 0-520-03977-7). U of Cal Pr.

Allen, N. S., ed. Developments in Polymer Photochemistry - One. (Illus.). x, 222p. 1980. 42.50x (ISBN 0-85334-911-8). Burgess-Intl Ideas.

Allen, N. S. & McKellar, J. F., eds. Photochemistry of Dyed & Pigmented Polymers. (Illus.). xii, 296p. 1980. 50.00x (ISBN 0-85334-898-7). Burgess-Intl Ideas.

Allen, Nancy. Homicide: Perspectives on Prevention. LC 79-11841. 192p. 1979. text ed. 15.95x (ISBN 0-87705-382-0); pap. text ed. 8.95x (ISBN 0-87705-412-6). Human Sci Pr.

Allen, O. Wildflower Gardening. LC 77-73630. (Encyclopedia of Gardening Ser.). (Illus.). (gr. 6 up). 1977. PLB 11.97 (ISBN 0-8094-2555-6, Pub. by Time-Life). Silver.

Allen, O. N. & Allen, Ethel K. The Leguminosae: A Source Book of Characteristics, Uses & Nodulation. LC 80-5104. (Illus.). 806p. 1981. 60.00 (ISBN 0-299-08400-0). U of Wis Pr.

Allen, O. N., jt. auth. see Allen, Ethel K.

Allen, Oliver. The Pacific Navigators. Time-Life Books Editors, ed. (The Seafarers Ser.). (Illus.). 176p. 1980. 13.95 (ISBN 0-8094-2685-4). Time-Life.

--Pruning & Grafting. Time-Life Books, ed. (Encyclopedia of Gardening). (Illus.). 1979. 11.95 (ISBN 0-8094-2633-1). Time-Life.

Allen, Oliver E. The Airline Builders. Time-Life Books, ed. (The Epic of Flight Ser.). (Illus.). 175p. 1981. 13.95 (ISBN 0-8094-3283-8). Time Life.

--The Windjammers. (The Seafarers Ser.). (Illus.). 1979. lib. bdg. 11.97 (ISBN 0-686-50989-7). Silver.

Allen, Oliver E., jt. auth. see Crockett, James U.

Allen, P. The Cambridge Apostles. LC 77-82482. (Illus.). 1979. 38.50 (ISBN 0-521-21803-9). Cambridge U Pr.

--Sales & Sales Management. 2nd ed. (Illus.). 288p. 1979. pap. 12.95x (ISBN 0-7121-1962-0, Pub. by Macdonald & Evans England). Intl Ideas.

Allen, P. E. & Patrick, C. R. Kinetics & Mechanisms of Polymerization Reactions: Applications of Physico-Chemical Principles. LC 74-3476. 596p. 1974. 64.95 (ISBN 0-470-02320-1). Halsted Pr.

Allen, P. W. Natural Rubber & the Synthetics. LC 72-5094. 255p. 1972. 22.95 (ISBN 0-470-02329-5). Halsted Pr.

Allen, Paul M. Vladimir Soloviev: Russian Mystic. (Illus.). 512p. 1978. pap. 9.95 (ISBN 0-8334-1750-9). Steinerbks.

Allen, Peter M., jt. ed. see Schieve, William C.

Allen, Philip M. & Segal, Aaron. The Traveler's Africa. 1975. 14.95 o.p. (ISBN 0-911974-07-5, ScribT). Scribner.

Allen, Phog, et al. Basketball. rev. ed. LC 65-20875. (Athletic Institute Ser). (Illus.). (gr. 5 up). 1968. 6.95 o.p. (ISBN 0-8069-4302-5); PLB 7.49 o.p. (ISBN 0-8069-4303-3). Sterling.

Allen, Polly R. & Kenen, Peter B. Asset Markets, Exchange Rates, & Economic Integration. LC 79-16874. (Illus.). 1980. 55.00 (ISBN 0-521-22982-0). Cambridge U Pr.

Allen, R. C. Professional Trading System. 1981. 20.00 (ISBN 0-910228-10-8). Best Bks.

Allen, R. E. Socrates & Legal Obligation. 176p. 1981. 17.50x (ISBN 0-8166-0962-4); pap. 8.95x (ISBN 0-8166-0965-9). U of Minn Pr.

Allen, R. E., jt. ed. see Furley, David J.

Allen, R. G. D. Index Numbers in Theory & Practice. LC 75-7612. 304p. 1975. 34.95x (ISBN 0-202-06071-3). Aldine Pub.

Allen, R. H., et al. Part-Time Farming in the Southeast. LC 74-165677. (FDR & the Era of the New Deal Ser). 1971. Repr. of 1937 ed. lib. bdg. 35.00 (ISBN 0-306-70341-6). Da Capo.

Allen, Ray & Thackery, Geral. The Last Survival Manual: A Citizen's Guide to Nuclear Survival. (Illus.). 288p. 1980. 24.95 (ISBN 0-937616-00-1). Am Res Pr.

Allen, Reginald. Gilbert & Sullivan in America. LC 79-54098. (Illus.). 26p. 1979. pap. 3.00. Pierpont Morgan.

--W. S. Gilbert: An Anniversary Survey & Exhibition Checklist. (Illus.). 1963. 5.50x o.p. (ISBN 0-8139-0002-6, Bibliographical Soc., U of Va). U Pr of Va.

Allen, Reginald E. Greek Philosophy: Thales to Aristotle. LC 66-10363. (Orig.). 1966. pap. text ed. 6.95 (ISBN 0-02-900500-0). Free Pr.

Allen, Reginald E., ed. Studies in Plato's Metaphysics. (International Library of Philosophy & Scientific Method). 1968. text ed. 25.50x (ISBN 0-7100-3626-4). Humanities.

Allen, Richard. A Short Introduction to the History & Politics of South-East Asia. (Illus.). 316p. 1968. 14.95 (ISBN 0-19-500815-4). Oxford U Pr.

--Social Passion: Religion & Social Reform in Canada, 1914-28. LC 71-151352. (Illus.). 1971. pap. 8.50 (ISBN 0-8020-6199-0). U of Toronto Pr.

Allen, Richard E., tr. see Heller, Agnes.

Allen, Richard E., tr. see Konrad, George & Szelenyi, Ivan.

Allen, Richard H. Star Names: Their Lore & Meaning. Orig. Title: Star-Names & Their Meanings. 11.00 (ISBN 0-8446-1527-7). Peter Smith.

Allen, Richard K. Organizational Management Through Communication. (Illus.). 1977. text ed. 15.50 scp (ISBN 0-06-040206-7, HarpC); inst. manual avail. (ISBN 0-685-79299-4). Har-Row.

Allen, Richard S. Covered Bridges of the Northeast. (Illus.). 128p. 1981. pap. 9.95 (ISBN 0-8289-0439-1). Greene.

Allen, Richard V., jt. auth. see Lee, Dorris M.

Allen, Roach V. Language Experience Activities. LC 75-31012. (Illus.). 384p. 1976. pap. text ed. 10.95 (ISBN 0-395-18626-9). HM.

--Language Experiences in Communication. LC 75-31011. (Illus.). 512p. 1976. text ed. 17.95 (ISBN 0-395-18624-2); inst. manual 1.25 (ISBN 0-395-18798-2). HM.

Allen, Robert. How to Save the World: Strategy for World Conservation. (Illus.). 144p. 1981. pap. 4.95 (ISBN 0-8226-0366-7). Littlefield.

--How to Save the World: Strategy for World Conservation. (Illus.). 150p. 1980. 12.95x (ISBN 0-389-20011-5). B&N.

--Nothing Down. Date not set. 10.95 (ISBN 0-671-24748-4). S&S.

Allen, Robert & Linde, Shirley. Lifegain: The Exciting New Program That Will Change Your Health - & Your Life. (Appleton Consumerhealth Guides). 288p. 1981. 12.95 (ISBN 0-8385-5671-X). ACC.

Allen, Robert & Maurer, H. Rainer, eds. Electrophoresis & Isoelectric Focusing in Polyacrylamide Gel: Advances of Methods & Theories, Biochemical & Clinical Applications. LC 73-94225. (Illus.). 1974. 61.75x (ISBN 3-11-004344-0). De Gruyter.

Allen, Robert D. & Wolfe, Thomas E. Real Estate Almanac. LC 80-12417. (Real Estate for Professional Practitioners Ser.). 456p. 1980. 16.95 (ISBN 0-471-05854-8). Wiley.

Allen, Robert F. & Kraft, Carlotte. Beat the System! A Way to Create More Human Environments. (Illus.). 1980. 15.95 (ISBN 0-07-001080-3). McGraw.

Allen, Robert F. & Kraft, Charlotte. Beat the System. (Illus.). 1980. 9.95 (ISBN 0-07-001080-3). McGraw.

Allen, Robert F., jt. auth. see Allen, Gayle.

Allen, Robert L. Black Awakening in Capitalist America: An Analytic History. LC 69-20059. pap. 3.50 (ISBN 0-385-07718-1, Anch). Doubleday.

Allen, Robert M. & Allen, Sue P. Intellectual Evaluation of the Mentally Retarded Child: A Handbook. rev ed. LC 66-29865. 1975. pap. 8.75x o.p. (ISBN 0-87424-086-7). Western Psych.

Allen, Robert M. & Cortazzo, Arnold D. Psychosocial & Educational Aspects & Problems of Mental Retardation. 1970. pap. 14.75 photocopy ed. spiral (ISBN 0-398-00031-X). C C Thomas.

Allen, Robert S., jt. auth. see Pearson, Drew.

Allen, Rodney F. Energy Education: Goals & Practices. LC 79-93115. (Fastback Ser.: No. 139). (Orig.). 1980. pap. 0.75 (ISBN 0-87367-139-2). Phi Delta Kappa.

Allen, Ron R., et al. Speech Communication in the Secondary School. 2nd ed. 461p. 1976. text ed. 15.95 (ISBN 0-205-05412-9, 4854128). Allyn.

Allen, Ronald R. & McKerrow, Ray. The Pragmatics of Public Communication. (Speech and Drama Ser.). 1977. pap. text ed. 8.95 (ISBN 0-675-08487-3); manual 3.95 (ISBN 0-686-67617-3). Merrill.

Allen, Roy. Introduction to National Accounts Statistics. 125p. 1980. text ed. 43.50x (ISBN 0-8419-5079-2). Holmes & Meier.

Allen, Roy F. German Expressionist Poetry. (World Authors Ser.: No. 421). 1979. lib. bdg. 13.50 (ISBN 0-8057-6386-4). Twayne.

Allen, S., jt. ed. see Barker, D. L.

Allen, Sally, jt. auth. see Foreman, Dale I.

Allen, Sandra Goose, ed. The Terrier Lovers Cookbook. 1977. 6.00 (ISBN 0-9600722-2-5). Skye Terrier.

Allen, Shirley S. Samuel Phelps & Sadler's Wells Theatre. LC 72-120259. (Illus.). 1971. 20.00x (ISBN 0-8195-4029-3, Pub. by Wesleyan U Pr). Columbia U Pr.

Allen, Stewart, et al. Chemical Analysis of Ecological Materials. LC 74-9819. 1975. 52.95 (ISBN 0-470-02318-X). Halsted Pr.

Allen, Sue P., jt. auth. see Allen, Robert M.

Allen, Susan W. & Talbot, Karen H. Preparing Preschoolers. 150p. (Orig.). 1981. pap. 9.95 (ISBN 0-88290-160-5, 2047). Horizon Utah.

--Projects for Preschoolers. 72p. (Orig.). 1981. pap. 5.95 (ISBN 0-88290-161-3, 2048). Horizon Utah.

Allen, T. D. Navahos Have Five Fingers. LC 63-17167. (The Civilization of the American Indian Ser.: Vol. 68). (Illus.). 249p. 1981. 13.95 (ISBN 0-8061-0575-5). U of Okla Pr.

Allen, T. D., jt. auth. see Mitchell, Emerson B.

Allen, T. Harrell. The Bottom Line: Communicating in the Organization. LC 78-24521. (Illus.). 1979. text ed. 16.95 (ISBN 0-88229-405-9). Nelson-Hall.

--New Methods in Social Science Research: Policy Sciences & Futures Research. LC 76-12840. (Praeger Special Studies). 1978. 21.95 (ISBN 0-275-23630-7). Praeger.

Allen, T. W., ed. see Homer.

Allen, Ted. The World of Cats in Color. rev. ed. (Illus.). 96p. 1974. 4.95 o.p. (ISBN 0-668-03416-5). Arco.

Allen, Thomas B. A Short Life. LC 77-11979. (YA) 1978. 9.95 o.p. (ISBN 0-399-11966-3). Berkley Pub.

Allen, Thomas J. Managing the Flow of Technology. 1977. text ed. 24.00x (ISBN 0-262-01048-8). MIT Pr.

Allen, Thomas T., tr. see Guyon, Madame.

Allen, Thomas W. The ASEAN Report, 2 vols. Wain, Barry, ed. Incl. Vol. 1. A Comparative Assessment of the ASEAN Countries; Vol. 2. The Evolution & Programs of ASEAN. (Illus.). 414p. 1980. Set. pap. 125.00 (ISBN 0-295-95740-9, 80-110683). U of Wash Pr.

Allen, W. C. St. Matthew. 3rd ed. (International Critical Commentary Ser.). 456p. Repr. of 1907 ed. text ed. 20.00x. Attic Pr.

Allen, W. S. Vox Latina. 2nd ed. LC 78-1153. (Illus.). 1978. 15.95 (ISBN 0-521-22049-1). Cambridge U Pr.

Allen, W. Sidney. Accent & Rhythm: Prosodic Features of Latin & Greek. LC 72-91361. (Studies in Linguistics). 432p. 1973. 57.50 (ISBN 0-521-20098-9). Cambridge U Pr.

--Sandhi: The Theoretical, Phonetic, & Historical Bases of Word-Junction in Sanskrit. (Janua Linguarum Ser. Minor: No. 17). 1972. pap. text ed. 18.80x (ISBN 90-2792-360-4). Mouton.

--Vox Graeca. 2nd ed. (Illus.). 1968. 15.95x (ISBN 0-521-20626-X). Cambridge U Pr.

Allen, W. Stannard. Living English Structure. rev. ed. 1974. pap. text ed. 5.50x (ISBN 0-582-52506-3); key 1.75 (ISBN 0-582-55204-4). Longman.

--Longman Structural Readers: Handbook. 1976. pap. text ed. 1.75x (ISBN 0-582-53699-5). Longman.

Allen, Walter. The British Isles in Colour. 1965. 27.00 (ISBN 0-7134-0002-1, Pub. by Batsford England). David & Charles.

--Reading a Novel. rev ed. 1975. pap. text ed. 3.00x (ISBN 0-391-00529-4). Humanities.

Allen, Warren D. Our Marching Civilization. LC 77-25408. (Music Reprint Ser., 1978). 1978. Repr. of 1943 ed. lib. bdg. 25.00 (ISBN 0-306-77568-9). Da Capo.

Allen, William. Halfmoons & Dwarf Parrots. pap. 4.95 (ISBN 0-87666-424-9, PS647). TFH Pubns.

--Starkweather. 1977. pap. 1.75 o.p. (ISBN 0-380-00973-0, 32508). Avon.

Allen, William A., jt. auth. see Hopper, C. Edmund.

Allen, William A., et al. Learning to Live Without Cigarettes. 1968. pap. 1.95 (ISBN 0-385-06511-6, Dolp). Doubleday.

Allen, William D., et al. Africa & South America. rev. ed. LC 77-87337. (World Cultures Ser.). (Illus.). (gr. 6 up). 1978. text ed. 12.43 ea. 1-4 copies, 5 or more 9.94 (ISBN 0-88296-166-7); tchrs'. guide 8.94 (ISBN 0-88296-369-4). Fideler.

Allen, William H., Jr. Budgerigars. (Orig.). pap. 2.00 (ISBN 0-87666-415-X, M502). TFH Pubns.

--How to Raise & Train Pigeons. enl. ed. LC 58-7602. (Illus.). 160p. (gr. 10 up). 1972. 9.95 (ISBN 0-8069-3706-8); PLB 9.29 (ISBN 0-8069-3707-6). Sterling.

Allen, William R. Midnight Economist I. 1980. pap. 1.45 (ISBN 0-89803-028-5). Caroline Hse.

Allen, William R., jt. auth. see Alchian, Armen A.

Allen, Woody. Annie Hall. 1978. 7.95 o.p. (ISBN 0-394-50071-7). Random.

--Bananas. 1978. 7.95 o.p. (ISBN 0-394-50049-0). Random.

--Getting Even. 128p. Date not set. pap. 1.95 (ISBN 0-394-72640-5, V-640, Vin). Random.

--Love & Death. 1978. 7.95 o.p. (ISBN 0-394-50070-9). Random.

--Non-Being & Somethingness. 96p. 1978. pap. 4.95 (ISBN 0-686-68485-0). Random.

--Sleeper. 1978. 7.95 o.p. (ISBN 0-394-50051-2). Random.

--Without Feathers. LC 74-29597. 1975. PLB 7.95 (ISBN 0-394-49743-0). Random.

Allenbright, J. P. The Ten-Dollar Wildcat. 1980. 14.95 (ISBN 0-87000-475-1). Arlington Hse.

Allendorf, Marlis. Women in Socialist Society. LC 75-17597. (Illus.). 223p. 1976. 12.95 o.p. (ISBN 0-7178-0442-9). Intl Pub Co.

Allensworth, Carl, et al. The Complete Play Production Handbook. LC 73-14814. (Illus.). 366p. 1973. 12.95 (ISBN 0-690-20752-2, TYC-T). T Y Crowell.

Allensworth, Don. Public Administration: The Execution of Public Policy. 250p. 1973. pap. text ed. 3.95 o.p. (ISBN 0-397-47272-2). Lippincott.

Allensworth, Don T., jt. auth. see Linowes, R. Robert.

Allentuck, Marcia, ed. Achievement of Isaac Bashevis Singer. LC 69-19747. (Crosscurrents-Modern Critique Ser.). 197p. 1969. 9.95 (ISBN 0-8093-0383-3). S Ill U Pr.

Allerhand, Melvin E., jt. auth. see Merry, Uri.

Allert, Kathy. Kate Greenaway Paper Dolls. (Illus.). 32p. (Orig.). 1981. pap. price not set (ISBN 0-486-24153-X). Dover.

Allerton, D. J., et al, eds. Function & Context in Linguistics Analysis. LC 78-11603. 1979. 26.95 (ISBN 0-521-22429-2). Cambridge U Pr.

Allerton, Frank W. Ring Culture. (Illus.). 1972. 9.95 (ISBN 0-571-04751-3, Pub. by Faber & Faber). Merrimack Bk Serv.

--Tomatoes for Everyone. (Illus., Orig.). 1971. pap. 3.95 (ISBN 0-571-09749-9, Pub. by Faber & Faber). Merrimack Bk Serv.

Alles, Alfred. Exhibitions: Universal Marketing Tools. LC 73-1796. 260p. 1973. 21.95 (ISBN 0-470-02332-5). Halsted Pr.

Alleton, V. Les Adverbes en Chinois Moderne. (Materiaux Pour L'etude De L'extreme-Orient Moderne et Comtemporain, Etudes Linguistiques: No. 4). 1972. pap. 24.10x (ISBN 90-2796-989-2). Mouton.

Alley, Brian, jt. auth. see Cargill, Jennifer S.

Alley, Robert. Honeysuckle Rose. 208p. 1980. pap. 2.25 (ISBN 0-553-14332-8). Bantam.

Alley, Robert, illus. Riddles. (Look Look Bks). (Illus.). 24p. (ps-3). 1981. pap. 1.25 (ISBN 0-307-11860-6, Golden Pr). Western Pub.

Alley, Ronald, ed. Catalogue of the Tate Gallery's Collection of Modern Art Other Than Works by British Artists. (Illus.). 800p. 1981. 120.00x (ISBN 0-85667-102-9, Pub. by Sotheby Parke Bernet England). Biblio Dist.

Alleyne, Mervyne C. Comparative Afro-American: An Historical-Comparative Study of English-Based Afro-American Dialects of the New World. (Linguistica Extranea: Studia: No. 11). 220p. pap. 8.50 (ISBN 0-89720-032-2). Karoma.

Allfrey, V. G., et al, eds. Organization & Expression of Chromosomes, LSRR 4. (Dahlem Workshop Reports Ser.). 1976. pap. 36.50 (ISBN 0-89573-088-X). Verlag Chemie.

Alliance of Perinatal Research & Services, Inc. The Father Book: Pregnancy & Beyond. 1981. 17.50 (ISBN 0-87491-618-6); pap. 8.95 (ISBN 0-87491-422-1). Acropolis.

Allibone, S. Austin. Critical Dictionary of English Literature & British & American Authors, 3 Vols. LC 67-295. 1965. Repr. of 1872 ed. Set. 130.00 (ISBN 0-8103-3017-2). Gale.

Allibone, Samuel A. Prose Quotations from Socrates to Macauley. LC 68-30642. 764p. 1973. Repr. of 1876 ed. 20.00 (ISBN 0-8103-3181-0). Gale.

Alliger, G. & Sjothun, I. J., eds. Vulcanization of Elastomers: Principles & Practice of Vulcanization of Commercial Rubbers. 1978. Repr. of 1964 ed. lib. bdg. 21.50 (ISBN 0-88275-686-9). Krieger.

Alliluyeva, Svetlana. Only One Year. Chavchavadze, Paul, tr. LC 79-81883. 1969. 12.50 o.p. (ISBN 0-06-010102-4, HarpT). Harper-Row.

Allin, Alfred, tr. see Keysser, Christian.

Allinger, Norman L. & Eliel, Ernest L. Topics in Stereochemistry, Vol. 9. 1976. 37.95 o.p. (ISBN 0-471-02472-4, Pub. by Wiley-Interscience). Wiley.

Allinger, Norman L., jt. auth. see Eliel, Ernest L.

Allinger, Norman L., et al. Organic Chemistry. 2nd ed. LC 75-18431. 1976. 26.95x (ISBN 0-87901-050-9). Worth.

Allingham, Michael G. Equilibrium & Disequilibrium: A Quantitative Analysis of Economic Interaction. LC 73-9639. 192p. 1973. text ed. 22.50 o.p. (ISBN 0-88410-252-1). Ballinger Pub.

Allingham, William. Lawrence Bloomfield in Ireland: A Modern Poem. Wolff, Robert L., ed. (Ireland Nineteenth Century Fiction - Ser. Two: Vol. 61). 304p. 1979. lib. bdg. 32.00 (ISBN 0-8240-3510-0). Garland Pub.

Allington, Richard & Strange, Michael. Learning Through Reading in the Content Areas. 1980. pap. text ed. 7.95 (ISBN 0-669-01375-7). Heath.

Allington, Richard L. Shapes. LC 79-19852. (Beginning to Learn About Ser.). (Illus.). (gr. k-2). 1979. PLB 9.65 (ISBN 0-8172-1277-9). Raintree Pubs.

Allington, Richard L. & Krull, Kathleen. Autumn. LC 80-25190. (Beginning to Learn About Ser.). (Illus.). 32p. (ps-2). 1981. PLB 9.65 (ISBN 0-8172-1343-0). Raintree Child.

--Reading. LC 80-16547. (Beginning to Learn About Ser.). (Illus.). 32p. (ps-2). 1980. PLB 9.65 (ISBN 0-8172-1322-8). Raintree Child.

--Spring. LC 80-25093. (Beginning to Learn About Ser.). (Illus.). 32p. (ps-2). 1981. PLB 9.65 (ISBN 0-8172-1342-2). Raintree Child.

--Summer. LC 80-25097. (Beginning to Learn About Ser.). (Illus.). 32p. (gr. k-2). 1981. PLB 9.65 (ISBN 0-8172-1341-4). Raintree Child.

--Talking. LC 80-17021. (Beginning to Learn About Ser.). (Illus.). 32p. (ps-2). 1980. PLB 9.65 (ISBN 0-8172-1320-1). Raintree Child.

--Thinking. LC 80-15390. (Beginning to Learn About Ser.). (Illus.). 32p. (ps-2). 1980. PLB 9.65 (ISBN 0-8172-1319-8). Raintree Child.

--Winter. LC 80-25115. (Beginning to Learn About Ser.). (Illus.). 32p. (ps-2). 1981. PLB 9.65 (ISBN 0-8172-1340-6). Raintree Child.

--Writing. LC 80-15334. (Beginning to Learn About Ser.). (Illus.). 32p. (ps-2). 1980. PLB 9.65 (ISBN 0-8172-1321-X). Raintree Child.

Allinson, Alec, et al. Language Stimulus Program. Incl. Level 1. Magic Seasons; Level 3. Multiworlds; Level 4. Mediamind; Level 5. Manspace. (gr. 3-6). 1973. pap. 1.60 o.p. (ISBN 0-685-33454-6, Satellite Books); classroom module 96.00 ea. o.p. Bowmar-Noble.

Allinson, Gary D. Japanese Urbanism: Industry & Politics in Kariya, 1872-1972. LC 74-84141. 296p. 1975. 24.00x (ISBN 0-520-02842-2). U of Cal Pr.

--Suburban Tokyo: A Comparative Study in Politics & Social Change. 1979. 20.00x (ISBN 0-520-03768-5). U of Cal Pr.

Allinson, J. R., ed. Criteria for Quality of Petroleum Products. LC 73-7958. 286p. 1973. 29.95 (ISBN 0-470-02500-X). Halsted Pr.

Allio, Robert J., jt. auth. see Pennington, Malcom W.

Allis, Jeannette B. West Indian Literature: An Index to Criticism, 1930-1975. (Reference Bks.). 1981. lib. bdg. 30.00 (ISBN 0-8161-8266-3). G K Hall.

Allis, John & Lehrman, Steve. The Bicycle Book for You. LC 78-2430. 1981. 8.95 (ISBN 0-689-10790-0). Atheneum.

Allis, Oswald T. The Five Books of Moses. 1977. Repr. of 1947 ed. pap. 4.95 (ISBN 0-8010-0108-0). Baker Bk.

Allis, Sarah. Nightwind. 1978. pap. 1.75 o.p. (ISBN 0-449-23693-5, Crest). Fawcett.

Allison, A. C., jt. auth. see Gregoriadis, G.

Allison, Alida. The Children's Manners Book. (Illus.). 32p. (Orig.). 1981. pap. 3.95 (ISBN 0-8431-0437-6). Price Stern.

Allison, C. FitzSimons. Fear, Love, & Worship. pap. 3.95 (ISBN 0-8164-2020-3, SP17). Crossroad NY.

--Guilt, Anger, & God. 1972. pap. 3.95 (ISBN 0-8164-2091-2). Crossroad NY.

Allison, C. Fitzsimons & Kelber, Werner H. Epiphany. LC 74-24900. (Proclamation 1: Aids for Interpreting the Lessons of the Church Year). 64p. 1974. pap. 1.95 (ISBN 0-8006-4072-1, 1-4072). Fortress.

Allison, Dorothy & Jacobson, Scott. Dorothy Allison: A Psychic Story. (Orig.). 1980. pap. 2.50 (ISBN 0-515-05304-X). Jove Pubns.

Allison, F. C., jt. auth. see Klaften, E. B.

Allison, Henry E. Benedict De Spinoza. LC 75-2059. (World Authors Ser.: No. 351). 1975. lib. bdg. 12.50 (ISBN 0-8057-2853-8). Twayne.

Allison, Ira S. & Palmer, Donald F. Geology: The Science of a Changing Earth. 7th, rev. ed. (Illus.). 1980. text ed. 17.95x (ISBN 0-07-001123-0); pap. text ed. 15.95x (ISBN 0-07-001121-4); instr's manual 4.95x (ISBN 0-07-001122-2). McGraw.

Allison, K. J., ed. Victoria History of the Counties of England: York East Riding, Vol. 3. (Illus.). 1976. text ed. 69.00x o.p. (ISBN 0-19-722744-9). Oxford U Pr.

Allison, R. Bruce, ed. Wisconsin's Champion Trees. (Illus.). 128p. (Orig.). 1980. lib. bdg. 15.00 (ISBN 0-913370-09-6); pap. 6.95 (ISBN 0-686-27407-5). Wisconsin Bks.

Allison, Sonia. Bisto Book of Meat Cookery. LC 80-66429. (Illus.). 128p. 1980. 14.95 (ISBN 0-7153-7893-7). David & Charles.

--Cooking in Style: Gourmet Recipes Without Meat or Fish. (Illus.). 176p. 1980. 19.95 (ISBN 0-241-10352-5, Pub. by Hamish Hamilton England). David & Charles.

Allison-Booth, William. Devils Island: Revelations of the French Penal Settlements in Guiana. LC 71-162504. (Illus.). 1971. Repr. of 1931 ed. 18.00 (ISBN 0-8103-3761-4). Gale.

Allman, Fred L., Jr., jt. auth. see Klein, Karl K.

Allman, James, ed. Women's Status & Fertility in the Muslim World. LC 78-5897. 1978. 29.95 (ISBN 0-03-042926-9). Praeger.

Allman, Lawrence R. & Jaffe, Dennis T., eds. Readings in Adult Psychology: Contemporary Perspectives. (Contemporary Perspectives Readers Ser.). 1977. pap. text ed. 10.50 scp (ISBN 0-06-047054-2, HarpC); inst. manual avail. (ISBN 0-685-77667-0). Har-Row.

Allman, Margaret see Chuan, Helen.

Allman, Marie Von see Nemiro, Beverly & Von Allman, Marie.

Allmond, Bayard W., et al. The Family Is the Patient: An Approach to Behavioral Pediatrics for the Clinician. LC 79-16622. 1979. pap. text ed. 19.95 (ISBN 0-8016-0131-2). Mosby.

Allnutt, Frank. After the Omen. 1978. pap. 1.95 (ISBN 0-89728-002-4, 704481). Omega Pubns OR.

--The Force of Star Wars. 1977. pap. 1.95 (ISBN 0-89728-030-X, 689135). Omega Pubns OR.

--The Peacemaker. 1977. pap. 1.95 (ISBN 0-89728-052-0, 693561). Omega Pubns OR.

Allon, Dafna, et al, trs. see Ringelblum, Emmanuel.

Allon, Yigal. The Making of Israel's Army. LC 73-133424. (Illus.). 1970. 10.00x o.s.i. (ISBN 0-87663-137-5). Universe.

Allosso, Michael. Your Career in Theater, Radio, Television or Filmmaking. LC 77-14145. (Career Guidance Ser.). (YA) 1978. lib. bdg. 6.97 (ISBN 0-668-04438-1); pap. 3.50 (ISBN 0-668-04445-4). Arco.

Allot, Robert. England's Parnassus: Or, the Choysest Flowers of Our Moderne Poets. LC 72-167. (English Experience Ser.: No. 216). 510p. Repr. of 1600 ed. 62.00 (ISBN 90-221-0216-5). Walter J Johnson.

--Wits Theatre of the World. LC 70-17131. (English Experience Ser.: No. 359). 560p. Repr. of 1599 ed. 51.00 (ISBN 90-221-0359-5). Walter J Johnson.

Allott, Miriam, ed. The Brontes: The Critical Heritage. (Critical Heritage Ser). 1974. 39.00x (ISBN 0-7100-7701-7). Routledge & Kegan.

--The Poems of John Keats. (Longman Annotated English Poets Ser.). (Illus.). 1972. pap. text ed. 15.95x (ISBN 0-582-48457-X). Longman.

Alloway, David N., jt. ed. see Cordasco, Francesco.

Allport, D. C. & Janes, W. H., eds. Block Copolymers. LC 72-10339. 620p. 1973. 57.95 (ISBN 0-470-02517-4). Halsted Pr.

Allport, Gordon W. Personality & Social Encounter: Selected Essays. LC 77-13911. x, 388p. 1981. pap. text ed. 17.00x (ISBN 0-226-01494-0). U of Chicago Pr.

Allport, J. A. & Stewart, C. M. Economics. LC 77-28479. 1978. 19.50 (ISBN 0-521-22013-0); pap. 15.50x. Cambridge U Pr.

Allred, Gordon. Lonesome Coyote. (gr. 6-11). 1969. 4.25 o.p. (ISBN 0-8313-0003-5); PLB 6.19 o.p. (ISBN 0-685-13775-9). Lantern.

Allred, Ruel A., et al. Continuous Progress in Spelling (Cps) Readiness. rev. ed. (Continuous Progress in Spelling Ser.). (gr. 1-3). 1977. pap. text ed. 2.85 (ISBN 0-87892-297-0); tchrs ed. 2.85 (ISBN 0-87892-298-9). Economy Co.

Allred, V. Dean, ed. Oil Shale Processing Technology. 208p. 1981. price not set (ISBN 0-86563-001-1). Ctr Prof Adv.

Allsburg, Chris Van see Van Allsburg, Chris.

Allsen, Philip E. & Witbeck, Alan R. Racquetball-Paddleball. 2nd ed. (Physical Education Activities & Dance Ser). 1977. pap. text ed. 3.25 o.p. (ISBN 0-697-07073-5). Wm C Brown.

Allshouse, Robert H., ed. Photographs for the Tsar: The Pioneering Color Photography of Sergei Mikhailovich Prokudin-Gorskii Commissioned by Tsar Nicholas II. (Illus.). 240p. 1980. 35.00 (ISBN 0-8037-6996-2). Dial.

Allsop, Bruce & Clark, Ursula. Architecture of England. (Illus.). 1964. 7.50 (ISBN 0-85362-006-7, Oriel); pap. 5.00. Routledge & Kegan.

Allsop, R. T. & Healey, J. A. Chemical Analysis, Chromatography, & Ion Exchange. 1974. pap. text ed. 4.95x (ISBN 0-435-65954-5); tchr's guide 3.25x (ISBN 0-435-65955-3). Heinemann Ed.

Allsopp, Bruce & Clark, Ursula. English Architecture. (Illus.). 1979. 18.00 (ISBN 0-85362-177-2, Oriel). Routledge & Kegan.

Allsopp, Michael. Management in the Professions: Guidelines to Improved Professional Performance. 201p. 1979. text ed. 29.50x (ISBN 0-220-67011-0, Pub. by Busn Bks England). Renouf.

--Survival in Business. 139p. 1977. text ed. 22.00x (ISBN 0-220-66320-3, Pub. by Busn Bks England). Renouf.

Allston, Washington. Lectures on Art - Poems. LC 75-171379. (Library of American Art Ser.). 1972. Repr. of 1892 ed. lib. bdg. 37.50 (ISBN 0-306-70414-5). Da Capo.

--Lectures on Art, & Poems, 1850, & Monaldi, 1841. LC 67-10124. 1967. 59.00x (ISBN 0-8201-1001-9). Schol Facsimiles.

Allswang, John M. A House for All Peoples: Ethnic Politics in Chicago, 1890-1936. LC 76-119810. (Illus.). 264p. 1971. 14.00x (ISBN 0-8131-1226-5). U Pr of Ky.

--The New Deal & American Politics: A Study in Political Change. LC 78-5733. (Critical Episodes in American Politics Ser.). 1978. text ed. 11.95 o.p. (ISBN 0-471-02515-1); pap. text ed. 8.95 (ISBN 0-471-02516-X). Wiley.

Allt, P., ed. see Yeats, William B.

Allt, Peter. Some Aspects of the Life & Works of James Augustine Joyce. 50p. 1980. Repr. of 1942 ed. lib. bdg. 7.50 (ISBN 0-89987-026-0). Darby Bks.

Alluisi, Earl A. & Fleishman, Edwin A., eds. Stress & Performance Effectiveness. (Human Performance & Productivity Ser.: Vol.3). 336p. 1981. professional ref. text 19.95 (ISBN 0-89859-091-4). L Erlbaum Assocs.

Allum, J. A. Photogeology & Regional Mapping. 1966. 21.00 (ISBN 0-08-012033-4); pap. 9.75 (ISBN 0-08-012032-6). Pergamon.

Allum, Nancy. Spina Bifida: The Treatment & Care of Spina Bifida Children. 1975. pap. text ed. 7.95x o.p. (ISBN 0-04-618014-1). Allen Unwin.

Allums, John F., jt. auth. see Saye, Albert B.

Alluntis, Felix & Wolter, Allan B., illus. John Duns Scotus: God & Creatures; the Quodlibetal Questions. Orig. Title: Quaestiones Quodlibetales. 548p. Repr. of 1975 ed. write for info. Cath U Pr.

Allwood, J., et al, eds. Logic in Linguistics. LC 76-46855. (Cambridge Textbooks in Linguistics Ser.). (Illus.). 1977. 29.95 (ISBN 0-521-21496-3); pap. 9.50 (ISBN 0-521-29174-7). Cambridge U Pr.

Allwood, John. The Great Exhibitions. 1978. 19.95 o.s.i. (ISBN 0-02-501710-1). Macmillan.

Allworth, Edward. Nationalities of the Soviet East: Publications & Writing Systems, a Bibliographical Directory & Transliteration Tables for Iranian & Turkic-Language Materials Located in U.S. Libraries. LC 73-110143. (Middle East Institute Ser). (Illus.). 1971. 25.00x (ISBN 0-231-03274-9). Columbia U Pr.

--Soviet Asia: Bibliographies. LC 73-9061. (Illus.). 756p. 1976. text ed. 54.95 (ISBN 0-275-07540-0). Praeger.

Allworth, Edward, ed. Central Asia. LC 66-16288. (Illus.). 1967. 27.00x (ISBN 0-231-02695-1). Columbia U Pr.

--Ethnic Russia in the U. S. S. R. The Dilemma of Dominance. LC 79-22959. (Pergamon Policy Studies Ser.). 270p. 37.50 (ISBN 0-08-023700-2). Pergamon.

--Nationality Group Survival in Multi-Ethnic States: Shifting Support Patterns in the Soviet Baltic Region. LC 77-4952. 1977. text ed. 30.95 (ISBN 0-275-24040-1). Praeger.

--The Nationality Question in Soviet Central Asia. LC 72-85986. (Special Studies in International Politics & Government Ser.). 1973. 34.50x (ISBN 0-275-28659-2). Irvington.

Allyn, Jane, jt. auth. see Cooper, Montgomery.

Allyn, Mildred V., compiled by. About Aging: A Catalog of Films. 4th ed. LC 79-64804. 1979. pap. 5.50 (ISBN 0-88474-091-9). USC Andrus Geron.

Allyn, Paul. The Picture Life of Herman Badillo. LC 79-185925. (Picture Life Bks). (Illus.). 48p. (gr. k-3). 1972. PLB 6.45 (ISBN 0-531-00985-8). Watts.

Allyne, Kerry. Across the Great Divide. (Harlequin Romances Ser.). (Orig.). 1980. pap. 1.25 o.p. (ISBN 0-373-02323-5, Pub. by Harlequin). PB.

--The Challenge. (Harlequin Romances). 192p. 1981. pap. 1.25 (ISBN 0-373-02389-8, Pub. by Harlequin). PB.

--Sweet Harvest. (Romances Ser.). 192p. (Orig.). 1980. pap. text ed. 1.25 (ISBN 0-373-02341-3, Pub. by Harlequin). PB.

Al Ma 'arri, Abu 'Ala, pseud. Luzumiyyat. Wormhoudt, Arthur, tr. from Arabic. (Arab Translation Ser.: No. 39). 1978. pap. 6.50 (ISBN 0-916358-89-5). Wormhoudt.

Almagor, Uri, jt. ed. see Baxter, P. T.

Al-Manar & Karmi, Hasan. English-Arabic Dictionary. 1971. lib. bdg. 25.00x (ISBN 0-685-77120-2). Intl Bk Ctr.

Almansi, Guido. Writer As Liar. 1975. 20.00x (ISBN 0-7100-8147-2). Routledge & Kegan.

Almanza, Francisco G., tr. see Baker, R. A.

Al-Mawrid & Ba'Albaki, Munir. English-Arabic Dictionary. 1980. 45.00 (ISBN 0-685-82805-0). Intl Bk Ctr.

--English-Arabic Dictionary. 1978. pocket dictionary 5.50x (ISBN 0-685-85419-1). Intl Bk Ctr.

Almeda, Frank, Jr. Systematics of the Genus Monochaetum (Melastomataceae) in Mexico & Central America. (Publications in Botany Ser.: Vol. 75). 1978. 11.00x (ISBN 0-520-09587-1). U of Cal Pr.

Almeder, Robert. The Philosophy of Charles S. Peirce: A Critical Introduction. Rescher, Nicholas, ed. (American Philosophical Quarterly Library of Philosophy). 224p. 1980. 27.50x (ISBN 0-8476-6854-1). Rowman.

Almedingen, E. M. Ladies of Saint Hedwig's. 1967. 7.95 o.s.i. (ISBN 0-8149-0015-1). Vanguard.

--Saint Francis of Assisi: A Great Life in Brief. (YA) 1967. 5.99 o.p. (ISBN 0-394-44429-9). Knopf.

--Too Early Lilac. LC 73-155661. 288p. 1974. 7.95 (ISBN 0-8149-0694-X). Vanguard.

Almeida, Hermione De see De Almeida, Hermione.

Almeida, Jose, et al. Descubrir y Crear. 2nd ed. (Illus.). 402p. (Span.). 1981. text ed. 18.95 scp (ISBN 0-06-040224-5, HarpC). Har-Row.

Almeida, Oscar. Metal Working. (Drake Home Craftsman Ser.). (Illus.). 1976. pap. 5.95 (ISBN 0-8069-8506-2). Sterling.

Almit, Zalman, jt. auth. see Sutherland, E. Ann.

Almon, Clopper. Matrix Methods in Economics. 1967. 14.95 (ISBN 0-201-00224-8). A-W.

Almon, Clopper, et al. Nineteen Eighty Five Interindustry Forecasts of the American Economy. LC 73-21608. (Illus.). 224p. 1974. 19.95 (ISBN 0-669-92494-6). Lexington Bks.

Almon, John, ed. A Collection of Papers Relative to the Dispute Between Great Britain & America, 1764-1775. LC 70-146272. (Era of the American Revolution Ser). 1971. Repr. of 1777 ed. lib. bdg. 32.50 (ISBN 0-306-70127-8). Da Capo.

Almond, Gabriel, jt. ed. see Smelser, Neil J.

Almond, Gabriel, et al. Freedom & Development. 4.75x (ISBN 0-210-22595-5). Asia.

Almond, Joseph P. Plumbers' Handbook. 5th ed. LC 79-64811. (Illus.). 1979. pap. 8.95 (ISBN 0-672-23339-8, 23339). Audel.

Almond, T., tr. see Bartknecht, W.

Almoznino, A. Hand Shadows. LC 70-105956. (Illus.). 1969. 7.95 (ISBN 0-87396-026-2); pap. 3.95 (ISBN 0-87396-027-0). Stravon.

Almquist, Elizabeth, et al. Sociology: Women, Men & Society. (Illus.). 1978. pap. text ed. 13.95 (ISBN 0-8299-0174-4); instrs.' manual avail. (ISBN 0-8299-0450-6). West Pub.

Almquist, Elizabeth M. Minorities, Gender & Work. LC 77-4537. 1979. 19.95 (ISBN 0-669-01488-5). Lexington Bks.

Almquist, John. The Sentence: How It Works. 1977. pap. text ed. 4.25x (ISBN 0-88334-100-X). Ind Sch Pr.

Al Muhit, Muhit & Al-Bustani, Butrus. Arabic-Arabic Dictionary. 50.00 (ISBN 0-686-53117-5). Intl Bk Ctr.

Almy, Millie & Genishi, Celia. Ways of Studying Children: An Observational Manual for Early Childhood Teachers. 2nd ed. LC 79-13881. 1979. pap. text ed. 8.50x (ISBN 0-8077-2551-X). Tchrs Coll.

Almy, Millie, et al. Young Children's Thinking: Studies of Some Aspects of Piaget's Theory. LC 66-16091. (Illus., Orig.). 1966. pap. text ed. 5.75 o.p. (ISBN 0-8077-1017-2). Tchrs Coll.

Alo, R. A. & Shapiro, H. L. Normal Topological Spaces. LC 73-79304. (Tracts in Mathematics Ser.: No. 65). (Illus.). 250p. 1974. 43.00 (ISBN 0-521-20271-X). Cambridge U Pr.

Aloi, G. Hotel-Motel (Architecture) (Illus.). 1970. 40.00 (ISBN 0-685-12023-6). Heinman.

--Restaurants (Architecture) (Illus.). 1972. 50.00 (ISBN 0-685-25486-0). Heinman.

Aloi, R. Fifty Villas of Our Time. (Illus.). 1970. 40.00 (ISBN 0-685-47307-4). Heinman.

--Museums: Architecture, Technics. (Illus.). 1962. 50.00 (ISBN 0-685-12032-5). Heinman.

--Theatres & Auditoriums. (Illus.). 1972. 50.00 (ISBN 0-685-30575-9). Heinman.

Aloi, R. & Bassi, C. Hospitals (Architecture) (Illus.). 1972. 50.00 (ISBN 0-685-30577-5). Heinman.

Aloisi, Ralph M. Principles of Immunodiagnostics. (Illus.). 1979. pap. text ed. 15.95 (ISBN 0-8016-0118-5). Mosby.

Alon, Azaria. The Natural History of the Land of the Bible. LC 77-91916. 1978. 12.95 o.p. (ISBN 0-385-14222-6). Doubleday.

Alonso, J. L. & Tarrach, R., eds. Quantum Chromodynamics: Proceedings. (Lecture Notes in Physics: Vol. 113). 306p. 1980. pap. 22.00 (ISBN 0-387-09731-7). Springer-Verlag.

Alonso, Marcelo & Valk, Henry. Quantum Mechanics: Principles & Applications. LC 73-6504. 1973. pap. text ed. 15.95 (ISBN 0-201-00244-2). A-W.

Alonso, Ricardo. Cimarron. LC 78-25876. (The Wesleyan Poetry Program: Vol. 94). 1979. 10.00x (ISBN 0-8195-2094-2, Pub. by Wesleyan U Pr); pap. 4.95 (ISBN 0-8195-1094-7). Columbia U Pr.

Alonso, William. Location & Land Use: Toward a General Theory of Land Rent. LC 63-17193. (Joint Center for Urban Studies Publications Ser). (Illus.). 1964. 10.00x (ISBN 0-674-53700-9). Harvard U Pr.

Alonzo, J., jt. auth. see Meservy, Jay A.

Al-Otaiba, Mana S. OPEC & the Petroleum Industry. LC 75-15447. 187p. 1975. 15.95 (ISBN 0-470-02252-3). Halsted Pr.

Alotta, Robert I. A Look at the Vice Presidency. 2ed ed. 1981. write for info. Messner.

--Number Two: A Look at the Vice Presidency. (Illus.). 256p. (gr. 8 up). 1981. PLB price not set. Messner.

Alpaugh, Patricia & Haney, Margaret. Counseling the Older Adult: A Training Manual. LC 77-99241. 1978. 7.50 (ISBN 0-88474-043-9). USC Andrus Geron.

Alper, Allan M., ed. Phase Diagrams: Materials Science & Technology Vol. 5: Crystal Chemistry, Stoichiometry, Spinodal Decomposition, Properties of Inorganic Phases. (Refractory Materials Ser.: Vol. 6-V). 1978. 43.50 (ISBN 0-12-053205-0). Acad Pr.

Alper, Allen, ed. Phase Diagrams: Materials Science & Technology. Incl. Part 1. Theory, Principles & Techniques of Phase Diagrams. 1970. 51.50 (ISBN 0-12-053201-8); Part 2. The Use of Phase Diagrams in Metals, Refractories, Ceramics, Glass & Electronic Materials. 1970. 51.50 (ISBN 0-12-053202-6); Part 3. The Use of Phase Diagrams in Electronic Materials & Glass Technology. 1970. 51.50 (ISBN 0-12-053203-4); Part 4. The Use of Phase Diagrams in Technical Materials. 1976. 49.00 (ISBN 0-12-053204-2). (Refractory Materials Ser: Vol. 6). Acad Pr.

Alper, Benedict S. & Nichols, Lawrence T. Beyond the Courtroom: Community Justice & Programs in Conflict Resolution. LC 78-20376. write for info. (ISBN 0-669-02724-3). Lexington Bks.

Alper, Philip R., ed. see Deaton, John G. & Pascoe, Elizabeth J.

Alper, T. Cell Survival After Low Doses of Radiation: Theoretical & Clinical Implications. LC 75-25578. (Sixth L. H. Gray Memorial Conference). 1975. 63.00 o.p. (ISBN 0-471-02513-5, Pub. by Wiley-Interscience). Wiley.

--Cellular Radiobiology. LC 78-68331. (Illus.). 1979. 47.50 (ISBN 0-521-22411-X); pap. 14.95x (ISBN 0-521-29479-7). Cambridge U Pr.

Alper, Victor M. America's Freedom Trail. LC 75-44414. (Illus.). 672p. 1976. pap. 7.95 o.s.i. (ISBN 0-02-097150-8, 09715, Collier). Macmillan.

--America's Heritage Trail. LC 75-45110. (Illus.). 351p. 1976. pap. 7.95 o.s.i. (ISBN 0-02-097160-5, 09716, Collier). Macmillan.

--America's Heritage Trail. (Illus.). 1976. 12.95 o.s.i. (ISBN 0-02-501690-3, 50169). Macmillan.

Alperin, Richard J. Rimmonim Bells: Ten Generations of the Behrman, Drucker, Hahn, Stockler & Sztynberg Families Plus Ten Related Lines. LC 80-65119. (Illus.). 249p. 1980. 39.95x (ISBN 0-9603932-0-X). Junius Inc.

Alpern, Andrew. Handbook of Specialty Elements in Architecture. (Illus.). 448p. 1981. 32.50 (ISBN 0-07-001360-8, P&RB). McGraw.

Alpers, Byron J. & Afrow, Mitchell L. Agriculture. (Shoptalk - Vocational Reading Skills). (gr. 9-12). 1978. pap. text ed. 5.12 (ISBN 0-205-05818-3, 4958187); 5.40 (ISBN 0-205-05824-8, 4958241). Allyn.

--The Automobile. (Shoptalk - Vocational Reading Skills). (gr. 9-12). 1978. pap. text ed. 5.12 (ISBN 0-205-05819-1, 4958195); 5.40 (ISBN 0-205-05824-8). Allyn.

--Carpentry. (Shoptalk - Vocational Reading Skills). (gr. 9-12). 1978. pap. text ed. 5.12 (ISBN 0-205-05820-5, 4958209); 5.40 (ISBN 0-205-05824-8). Allyn.

--Electricity. (Shoptalk - Vocational Reading Skills). (gr. 9-12). 1978. pap. text ed. 5.12 (ISBN 0-205-05821-3, 4958217); tchrs'. guide 5.40 (ISBN 0-205-05824-8). Allyn.

--Electronics. (Shoptalk - Vocational Reading Skills). (gr. 9-12). 1978. pap. text ed. 5.12 (ISBN 0-205-05822-1, 4958225); tchrs'. guide 5.40 (ISBN 0-205-05824-8). Allyn.

--Metal & Machines. (Shoptalk - Vocational Reading Skills). (gr. 9-12). 1978. pap. text ed. 5.12 (ISBN 0-205-05823-X, 4958233); tchr's guide 5.40 (ISBN 0-205-05824-8, 4958241). Allyn.

--You & Your Work. (Shoptalk - Vocational Reading Skills). (gr. 9-12). 1978. pap. text ed. 5.12 (ISBN 0-205-05825-6, 495825X). Allyn.

Alpers, Edward A. Ivory & Slaves in East Central Africa: Changing Patterns of International Trade to the Late Nineteenth Century. LC 73-93046. (Illus.). 1975. 20.00 (ISBN 0-520-02689-6). U of Cal Pr.

Alpers, Paul. The Singer of the Eclogues: A Study of Virgilian Pastoral. 1979. 17.50x (ISBN 0-520-03651-4). U of Cal Pr.

Alpert, Geoffrey P. Legal Rights of Prisoners: An Analysis of Legal Aid. LC 78-4343. (Illus.). 1978. 18.95 (ISBN 0-669-02347-7). Lexington Bks.

Alpert, Geoffrey P., ed. Legal Rights of Prisoners. LC 80-17241. (Sage Criminal Justice System Annuals: Vol. 14). (Illus.). 280p. 1980. 20.00 (ISBN 0-8039-1188-2). Sage.

--Legal Rights of Prisoners. LC 80-17241. (Sage Criminal Justice System Annuals: Vol. 14). (Illus.). 280p. 1980. pap. 9.95 (ISBN 0-8039-1189-0). Sage.

Alpert, Joseph E., jt. auth. see Dalen, James E.

Alpert, Joseph S. & Francis, Gary S. Manual of Coronary Care. 2nd ed. 1980. pap. 11.95 (ISBN 0-316-03503-3). Little.

--Manual of Coronary Care. 1977. spiral bdg. 10.95 o.p. (ISBN 0-316-03499-1). Little.

Alpert, Joseph S. & Rippe, James M. Manual of Cardiovascular Diagnosis & Therapy. 1980. 12.95 (ISBN 0-316-03502-5). Little.

Alpert, Nelson. Clinical Instrument Report. LC 75-25432. 1976. 24.50 (ISBN 0-912920-45-9). North Am Pub Co.

Alphonso-Karkala, John B. Comparative World Literature: Seven Essays. 98p. 1976. lib. bdg. 9.95 (ISBN 0-89253-048-0). Ind-US Inc.

--Jawaharlal Nehru. (World Authors Ser.: India: No. 345). 1975. lib. bdg. 10.95 (ISBN 0-8057-2649-7). Twayne.

Al Quareb, Al-Mawrid & Ba'Alabaki, Munir. English-Arabic Pocket Dictionary. 1980. pap. 5.50x. Intl Bk Ctr.

Alquie, Ferdinand, ed. Entretiens Sur le Surrealisme. (Decades Du Centre Culturel International De Cerisy-la-Salle, Nouvelle Ser.: No. 8). (Illus.). 1968. pap. 45.30x (ISBN 90-279-6018-6). Mouton.

Alquist, Tom. Getting Your Way with Parents. LC 80-68888. 128p. (Orig.). 1981. pap. 2.50 (ISBN 0-89636-065-2). Accent Bks.

Al-Rashid, Ibrahim, ed. Documents on the History of Saudi Arabia, 3 vols. Incl. Vol. I. Unification of Central Arabia Under Ibn Saud, 1909-1925 (ISBN 0-89712-053-1); Vol. 2. Consolidation of Power in Central Arabia Under Ibn Saud, 1925-1928 (ISBN 0-89712-054-X); Vol. 3. Establishment of the Kingdom of Saudi Arabia Under Ibn Saud, 1928-1935 (ISBN 0-89712-055-8). 1976. Set. lib. bdg. 60.00 (ISBN 0-89712-052-3). Documentary Pubns.

--The Unification of Central Arabia Under Ibn Saud 1909-1925. (Documents on the History of Saudi Arabia: Vol. 1). 1976. 60.00 (ISBN 0-89712-053-1). Documentary Pubns.

Al-Rashid, Rashid A. Pediatric Cancer Chemotherapy. (Medical Outline Ser.). 1979. 26.00 (ISBN 0-87488-685-6); pap. 17.00 (ISBN 0-87488-663-5). Med Exam.

--Pediatric Hematology Case Studies. 1972. spiral bdg. 14.00 (ISBN 0-87488-018-1). Med Exam.

--Pediatric Oncology Case Studies. 1975. spiral bdg. 15.00 o.p. (ISBN 0-87488-033-5). Med Exam.

Alred, Gerald J., et al. Business & Technical Writing: An Annotated Bibliography of Books, 1880-1980. LC 80-29211. 249p. 1981. 12.50 (ISBN 0-8108-1397-1). Scarecrow.

Al-Sabah, Y. S. F. The Oil Economy of Kuwait. 176p. 1981. write for info. (ISBN 0-7103-0003-4). Routledge & Kegan.

Al-Sayyid-Marsot, Afaf L. Egypt's Liberal Experiment, 1922-1936. 1977. 20.00x (ISBN 0-520-03109-1). U of Cal Pr.

Alsberg, P. In Quest of Man. 1970. text ed. 14.50 (ISBN 0-08-015680-0). Pergamon.

Alsen, Philip E. & Witbeck, Alan R. Racquetball. 3rd ed. 112p. 1980. write for info. (ISBN 0-697-07172-3). Wm C Brown.

Alsop, Joseph & Catledge, Turner. The One Hundred Sixty-Eight Days. LC 72-2362. (American Constitutional & Legal History Ser). 324p. 1973. Repr. of 1938 ed. lib. bdg. 32.50 (ISBN 0-306-70481-1). Da Capo.

Alsop, Stewart. Stay of Execution: A Sort of Memoir. LC 73-13691. 1973. 9.95 (ISBN 0-397-00897-X). Lippincott.

Alsop, Susan Mary. Lady Sackville: A Biography. 1978. 10.00 o.p. (ISBN 0-385-11379-X). Doubleday.

--To Marietta from Paris, Nineteen Forty-Five-Nineteen Sixty. LC 74-33628. 384p. 1975. 8.95 o.p. (ISBN 0-385-09774-3). Doubleday.

Alspach, R. K., ed. see Yeats, William B.

Alssid, Michael W. Dryden's Rhymed Heroic Tragedies: A Critical Study of the Plays & of Their Place in Dryden's Poetry, 2 vols. (Salzburg Studies in English Literature, Poetic Drama & Poetic Theory: No. 7). 429p. 1974. Set. pap. text ed. 50.25x (ISBN 0-391-01298-3). Humanities.

Alston, A. J. Devotional Poems of Mirabai. 144p. 1980. text ed. 13.50 (ISBN 0-8426-1643-8). Verry.

Alston, Eugenia. Growing up Chimpanzee. LC 74-12307. (Illus.). 32p. (gr. 1-4). 1975. 7.95 (ISBN 0-690-00015-4, TYC-J); PLB 7.89 (ISBN 0-690-00564-4). T Y Crowell.

Alston, Pat, ed. see Adams, Andrew.

Alston, Pat, ed. see Fong, Leo T.

Alston, Pat, ed. see Werner, E. T.

Alston, Pat, ed. see Yamaguchi, Gosei.

Alston, Walter & Weiskopf, Don. The Baseball Handbook: Strategies & Techniques for Winning. abr ed. 504p. 1974. pap. 17.95x (ISBN 0-205-04317-8). Allyn.

Alston, William P. Philosophy of Language. (Orig.). 1964. pap. 7.95x ref. ed. (ISBN 0-13-663799-X). P-H.

Alston, William P. & Brandt, Richard B. The Problems of Philosophy: Introductory Readings. 2nd ed. 804p. 1974. text ed. 18.50 o.p. (ISBN 0-205-03982-0, 6039820). Allyn.

--The Problems of Philosophy: Introductory Readings. 3rd ed. 1978. text ed. 18.50 (ISBN 0-205-06110-9, 6061109). Allyn.

Alstyne, Carol Van see Van Alstyne, Carol & Coldren, Sharon L.

Alstyne, Richard W. Van see Van Alstyne, Richard W.

Alsup, Fisher. The Lost Crucifix of Our Lady of Guadalupe. Koch, Polly, ed. 230p. 1977. 4.95 o.p. (ISBN 0-88319-028-1). Shoal Creek Pub.

Alsup, John E., tr. see Goppelt, Leonard.

Alszeghy, Zoltan & Flick, Maurizio. Introductory Theology. LC 79-88517. 1981. pap. text ed. cancelled (ISBN 0-87973-589-9). Our Sunday Visitor.

Alt, Arthur T. Theodor Storm. (World Authors Ser.: Germany: No. 252). 1971. lib. bdg. 10.95 (ISBN 0-8057-2865-1). Twayne.

Alta. The Shameless Hussy: Selected Prose & Poetry. LC 80-15551. (The Crossing Press Feminist Ser.). 1980. 10.95 (ISBN 0-89594-035-3); pap. 5.95 (ISBN 0-89594-036-1). Crossing Pr.

Altamirano, Ignacio M. El Zarco. Grismer, Raymond L. & Ruelas, Miguel, eds. 1933. 3.95x (ISBN 0-393-09442-1, NortonC). Norton.

Altbach, Philip G. Student Politics in Bombay. 7.50x (ISBN 0-210-22204-2). Asia.

Altbach, Philip G. & McVey, Sheila. Perspectives on Publishing. LC 75-3516. 272p. 1976. 24.95 (ISBN 0-669-99564-9). Lexington Bks.

Altbach, Philip G. & Rathgeber, Eva-Maria. Publishing in the Third World. LC 80-20146. 200p. 1980. 20.95 (ISBN 0-03-055931-6). Praeger.

Altbach, Philip G. & Uphoff, Norman T. The Student Internationals. LC 72-12980. 1973. 10.00 (ISBN 0-8108-0578-2). Scarecrow.

Altbach, Philip G., ed. Comparative Higher Education Abroad: Bibliography & Analysis. LC 75-33872. (Special Studies). 288p. 1976. text ed. 19.95 o.p. (ISBN 0-275-55500-3). Praeger.

--Comparative Perspectives on the Academic Profession. LC 77-83481. (Comparative Education Ser.: Vol. 1). 1978. 22.95 (ISBN 0-03-040781-8). Praeger.

Altbach, Philip G. & Kelly, Gail P., eds. Education & Colonialism. LC 77-22777. (Educational Policy, Planning, & Theory Ser.). 1978. pap. text ed. 10.95x (ISBN 0-582-28003-6). Longman.

Altekar, A. S. The Position of Women in Hindu Civilization. 1978. 12.50 (ISBN 0-8426-0713-7); pap. 9.00 (ISBN 0-686-67760-9). Orient Bk Dist.

Altemeier, William A, et al, eds. Manual on Control of Infection in Surgical Patients. LC 76-15400. 1976. 21.75 (ISBN 0-397-50355-5). Lippincott.

Altenstetter, Christa & Bjorkman, James W. Federal-State Health Policies & Impacts: The Politics of Implementation. LC 78-62173. (Illus.). 1978. pap. text ed. 7.75 (ISBN 0-8191-0503-1). U Pr of Amer.

Altenstetter, Christa, ed. Innovation in Health Policy & Service Delivery: A Cross-National Perspective, 3vols, Vol. 3. LC 80-39617. 256p. 1981. lib. bdg. 25.00 (ISBN 0-89946-078-X). Oelgeschlager.

Alter, Aaron A., et al. Medical Technology Examination Review Book, Vol. 1. 4th ed. 1977. spiral bdg. 9.50 (ISBN 0-87488-451-9). Med Exam.

--Medical Technology Examination Review Book, Vol. 2. 4th ed. 1978. spiral bdg. 9.50 (ISBN 0-87488-452-7). Med Exam.

Alter, Dinsmore, et al. Pictorial Astronomy. 4th, rev. ed. LC 73-15577. (Illus.). 352p. 1974. 14.95 (ISBN 0-690-00095-2, TYC-T). T Y Crowell.

Alter, G. & Ruprecht, J. System of Open Star Clusters & Galaxy Atlas of Open Star Clusters. 1963. 36.50 (ISBN 0-12-054250-1). Acad Pr.

Alter, J. Cecil. Jim Bridger. (Illus.). 1979. Repr. of 1962 ed. 14.95 (ISBN 0-8061-0546-1). U of Okla Pr.

Alter, Judy. After Pa Was Shot. (gr. 7-9). 1978. PLB 7.63 (ISBN 0-688-32136-4). Morrow.

Alter, Robert. The Art of Biblical Narrative. LC 80-68958. 208p. 1981. 13.95 (ISBN 0-465-04420-4). Basic.

--Partial Magic: The Novel As Self-Conscious Genre. 1975. 15.75x (ISBN 0-520-02755-8); pap. 3.95 (ISBN 0-520-03732-4). U of Cal Pr.

Alter, Robert M. The No-Nibbling Book: One Hundred Twenty-Eight Things to Do at the Refrigerator Door So You Won't Open It. 144p. 1981. 9.95 (ISBN 0-399-12581-7). Putnam.

Alter, Stephen. Silk & Steel. 327p. 1980. 11.95 (ISBN 0-374-26411-2). FS&G.

Alterman, Hyman. Counting People: The Census in History. LC 74-82635. (Illus.). (gr. 9-12). 1969. 7.50 o.p. (ISBN 0-15-220170-X, HJ). HarBraceJ.

--Introducing Statistics. (Illus.). 1968. 8.95 o.p. (ISBN 0-571-08429-X, Pub. by Faber & Faber). Merrimack Bk Serv.

Alterton, Margaret, ed. see Poe, Edgar A.

Altevogt, tr. see Rensch, Bernard.

Altfeld, E. Milton. The Jews Struggle for Religious & Civil Liberty in Maryland. LC 78-99859. (Civil Liberties in American History Ser). 1970. Repr. of 1924 ed. lib. bdg. 25.00 (ISBN 0-306-71859-6). Da Capo.

Altfest, Karen C. Robert Owen. (World Leaders Ser.: No. 60). 1977. lib. bdg. 12.50 (ISBN 0-8057-7711-3). Twayne.

Alth, Charlotte, jt. auth. see Alth, Max.

Alth, Max. All About Bikes & Bicycling. 1972. pap. 2.95 o.p. (ISBN 0-8015-0146-6). Dutton.

--All About Locks & Locksmithing. (Illus.). 1972. pap. 4.50 (ISBN 0-8015-0151-2, Hawthorn). Dutton.

--All About Mopeds. LC 78-2348. (Concise Guides Ser.). (Illus.). (gr. 7 up). 1978. PLB 6.45 (ISBN 0-531-01496-7). Watts.

--Do-It-Yourself Roofing & Siding. LC 76-56515. (Illus.). 1978. 9.95 o.p. (ISBN 0-8015-2150-5, Hawthorn); pap. 4.95 (ISBN 0-8015-2151-3, Hawthorn). Dutton.

--Homeowner's Quick-Repair & Emergency Guide. LC 77-6558. (Popular Science Skill Bk.). (Illus.). 1978. pap. 3.95 o.s.i. (ISBN 0-06-010142-3, TD-296, HarpT). Har-Row.

--Motorcycles & Motorcycling. (First Bks.). (Illus.). (gr. 4 up). 1979. PLB 6.45 s&l (ISBN 0-531-02945-X). Watts.

--The Stain Removal Handbook. 1977. 8.95 o.p. (ISBN 0-8015-7072-7); pap. 3.95 o.p. (ISBN 0-8015-7072-7). Dutton.

Alth, Max & Alth, Charlotte. The Furniture Buyer's Handbook: How to Buy, Arrange, Maintain & Repair Furniture. (Illus.). 1980. pap. 14.95 (ISBN 0-8027-0636-3); pap. 9.95 (ISBN 0-8027-7155-6). Walker & Co.

Al Tha'alibi. Dhikra al Babbaga, al Suri & al Nami. Wormhoudt, Arthur, tr. (Arab Translation Ser.: No. 24). 1976. pap. 6.50 (ISBN 0-916358-74-7). Wormhoudt.

Althaus, Catherine, jt. auth. see French-Hodges, Peter.

Althaus, Hans P. Die Cambridger Loewenfabel von 1382: Untersuchung und Edition eines defektiven Textes. (Quellen und Forschungen Zur Sprach-und Kulturgeschichte der Germanischen Voelker Ser.). (Illus.). 238p. 1971. 48.25x (ISBN 3-11-003939-7). De Gruyter.

Althea. About Bees & Honey. (ps-2). 1979. pap. 1.75 available in 5-pk (ISBN 0-85122-187-4, Pub. by Dinosaur Pubns). Merrimack Bk Serv.

--Herb for Presents. (ps-2). 1979. pap. 1.45 avail. in 5 pk. (ISBN 0-85122-179-3, Pub. by Dinosaur Pubns). Merrimack Bk Serv.

--Machines on a Farm. (Illus.). 24p. 1980. pap. 1.45 ea. (ISBN 0-85122-167-X, Pub. by Dinosaur Pubns); pap. in 5 pk. avail. Merrimack Bk Serv.

--A Visit to the Factory. (Illus.). 24p. 1980. pap. 1.45 ea.; pap. in 5 pk. avail. (ISBN 0-85122-192-0, Pub. by Dinosaur Pubns). Merrimack Bk Serv.

Altheide & Johnson. Bureaucratic Propaganda. 1980. text ed. 13.60 (ISBN 0-205-06716-6, 81617168). Allyn.

Altheide, David L. Creating Reality: How TV News Distorts Events. LC 76-22602. (Sage Library of Social Research: Vol. 33). 1976. 18.00x (ISBN 0-8039-0671-4); pap. 8.95x (ISBN 0-8039-0672-2). Sage.

Altheim, Franz & Stiehl, Ruth. Christentum am Roten Meer, Vol. 2. 1973. 170.55x (ISBN 3-11-003791-2). De Gruyter.

--Geschichte Mittelasiens im Altertum. (Illus., Ger.). 1970. 164.70x (ISBN 3-11-002677-5). De Gruyter.

Alther, Lisa. Kinflicks. 1976. 8.95 o.p. (ISBN 0-394-49836-4). Knopf.

--Original Sins. LC 80-22823. 608p. 1981. 13.95 (ISBN 0-394-51685-0). Knopf.

Althoen, Steven C. & Bumcrot, Robert J. Finite Mathematics. (Illus.). 1978. text ed. 16.95x (ISBN 0-393-09046-9). Norton.

Althoff, Philip, jt. ed. see Leachman, Robert B.

Althoff, Phillip & Rush, Michael. Introduction to Political Sociology. LC 77-180276. 1972. pap. 4.95 (ISBN 0-672-61311-5). Bobbs.

Altholz, Josef L. Churches in the Nineteenth Century. LC 66-30446. (Orig.). 1967. 7.15 o.p. (ISBN 0-672-51130-4); pap. 5.95 (ISBN 0-672-60682-8). Bobbs.

--Victorian England, Eighteen Thirty-Seven - Nineteen One. LC 71-108097. (Conference on British Studies Bibliographical Handbooks). 1970. 17.50 (ISBN 0-521-07880-6). Cambridge U Pr.

Althouse, Andrew, et al. Modern Refrigeration & Air Conditioning. LC 79-12403. (Illus.). 1979. text ed. 23.00 (ISBN 0-87006-275-1); lab manual 4.96 (ISBN 0-87006-265-4). Goodheart.

Altick, Richard D. Art of Literary Research. 2nd, rev. ed. 11.95x (ISBN 0-393-09227-5, NortonC); text ed. 5.95x (ISBN 0-393-09590-8). Norton.

--Robert Browning: The Ring & the Book. LC 80-53977. 707p. 1981. text ed. 30.00x (ISBN 0-300-02677-3); pap. 7.95. Yale U Pr.

--To Be in England. LC 68-20813. (Illus.). 1969. 6.95 o.p. (ISBN 0-393-04302-9). Norton.

--Victorian People & Ideas. (Illus.). 338p. 1974. pap. 6.95x (ISBN 0-393-09376-X). Norton.

Altizer, Thomas J. The Self Embodiment of God. LC 76-62952. 1977. 6.95 o.p. (ISBN 0-06-060160-4, HarpR). Har-Row.

--Total Presence: The Language of Jesus & the Language of Today. 128p. 1980. 9.95 (ISBN 0-8164-0461-5). Seabury.

Altland, Millard. The Pennsylvania Citizen. (gr. 8-12). 1964. 4.50 o.p. (ISBN 0-931992-22-2). Penns Valley.

Altland, Millard & Wildasin, John. A Workshop of Problems in Today's Pennsylvania. (gr. 8-12). 1968. pap. 1.85 o.p. (ISBN 0-931992-23-0). Penns Valley.

Altland, Millard, jt. auth. see Cornell, William A.

Altman. Readings: Organizational Behavior. 1979. pap. text ed. 11.95. Dryden Pr.

Altman, Alexander. Essays in Jewish Intellectual History. LC 80-54471. 336p. 1981. text ed. 20.00 (ISBN 0-87451-192-5). U Pr of New Eng.

Altman, Carole. Be Your Own Sex Therapist. (Illus.). 1976. pap. 7.95 o.p. (ISBN 0-399-11678-8). Berkley Pub.

Altman, Drew, et al. Health Planning & Regulation: Decision-Making Process. (Illus.). 350p. 1981. text ed. price not set (ISBN 0-914904-57-4). Health Admin Pr.

Altman, Edward I., ed. Bidding & Oil Leases, Vol. 25. Walter, Ingo I. LC 79-3169. (Contemporary Studies in Economic & Financial Analysis Monographs). 320p. (Orig.). 1980. lib. bdg. 28.50 (ISBN 0-89232-148-2). Jai Pr.

Altman, Howard B., ed. see PIE Seminar,Papers, Oxford, April 1979.

Altman, Ifrwin, et al, eds. Human Behavior & Environment - Advances in Theory & Research, Vol. 4: Environment & Culture. (Illus.). 368p. 1980. 25.00 (ISBN 0-306-40367-6, Plenum Pr). Plenum Pub.

Altman, Irwin & Wohlwill, J. F., eds. Human Behavior & Environment: Children & the Environment. (Advances in Theory & Environment Ser.: Vol. 3). (Illus.). 316p. 1978. 18.95 (ISBN 0-306-40090-1, Plenum Pr). Plenum Pub.

Altman, J. C. & Nieuwenhuysen, J. P. The Economic Status of Australian Aborigines. LC 78-14917. 1979. 34.50 (ISBN 0-521-22421-7). Cambridge U Pr.

Altman, Janet. Epistolarity: Approaches to a Form. 1981. write for info. (ISBN 0-8142-0313-2). Ohio St U Pr.

Altman, Joel B. The Tudor Play of Mind: Rhetorical Inquiry & the Development of Elizabethan Drama. LC 76-52022. 1978. 22.00x (ISBN 0-520-03427-9). U of Cal Pr.

Altman, Laurence, ed. see Electronics Magazine.

Altman, Liza & Gonella, Ronald R., eds. Great Events Two As Reported in the New York Times: Program Guide. 107p. (gr. 7-12). 1980. pap. text ed. 7.95 (ISBN 0-667-00600-1). Microfilming Corp.

Altman, Michael L. Standards Relating to Juvenile Records & Information Systems. (Juvenile Justice Standards Project Ser.). 1980. softcover 7.95 (ISBN 0-88410-819-8); casebound 16.50 (ISBN 0-88410-247-5). Ballinger Pub.

--Standards Relating to Juvenile Records & Information Systems. LC 77-3228. (Juvenile Justice Standards Project Ser.). 1977. softcover 7.95 o.p. (ISBN 0-88410-760-4); casebound 16.50 o.p. Ballinger Pub.

Altman, Nat. Ahimsa: Dynamic Compassion. LC 80-51548. 150p. (Orig.). 1981. pap. 4.95 (ISBN 0-8356-0537-X, Quest). Theos Pub Hse.

Altman, Nathaniel. The Chiropractic Alternative. LC 79-93020. 208p. 1981. 10.00 (ISBN 0-87477-132-3). J P Tarcher.

--Eating for Life. LC 73-1950. (Illus.). 1977. pap. 3.25 o.p. (ISBN 0-8356-0496-9, Quest). Theos Pub Hse.

--Nathaniel Altman's Vegetarian Book. LC 80-85343. 1981. pap. 2.95. Keats.

Altman, Norman H., jt. ed. see Melby, Edward C., Jr.

Altman, Richard. And the Envelopes Please. LC 77-26775. 1978. 7.95 o.p. (ISBN 0-397-01279-9); pap. 3.95 (ISBN 0-397-01270-5). Lippincott.

Altman, Stuart & Sapolsky, Harvey M., eds. Federal Health Programs: Improving the Health-Care System? LC 79-48059. (The University Health Policy Consortium Ser.). 1981. 24.95x (ISBN 0-669-03690-0). Lexington Bks.

Altmann, Alexander, tr. see Elaezer Of Worms.

Altmann, Horst. Poisonous Plants & Animals. (Illus.). 144p. 1981. pap. 5.95 (ISBN 0-7011-2526-8, Pub. by Chatto-Bodley-Jonathan). Merrimack Bk Serv.

Altmann, Jeanne. Baboon Mothers & Infants. LC 79-21568. (Illus.). 1980. text ed. 17.50x (ISBN 0-674-05856-9). Harvard U Pr.

Altmann, K. W., et al, eds. Current Topics in Pathology, Vol. 51-57. Incl. Vol. 51. 219p. 1970. 52.00 (ISBN 0-387-04788-3); Vol. 52. 244p. 1970. 52.00 (ISBN 0-387-04789-1); Vol. 53. 253p. 1970. 57.90 (ISBN 0-387-05070-1); Vol. 54. 191p. 1971. 62.60 (ISBN 0-387-05071-X); Vol. 55. 214p. 1971. 62.60 (ISBN 0-387-05428-6); Vol. 56. 236p. 1972. 62.60 (ISBN 0-387-05709-9); Vol. 57. 206p. 1973. 70.80 (ISBN 0-387-06000-6). (Illus.). Springer-Verlag.

Altmann, S. L. Band Theory of Metals. 1970. text ed. 32.00 (ISBN 0-08-015602-9); pap. text ed. 12.75 (ISBN 0-08-015601-0). Pergamon.

Altmeyer, Arthur J. Formative Years of Social Security. (Illus.). 1966. 22.50 (ISBN 0-299-03820-3); pap. 6.50 (ISBN 0-299-03824-6). U of Wis Pr.

Alton, W. G. Hats Galore. (Make & Play Ser.). (Illus.). 48p. (gr. k-6). 1976. pap. 1.50 (ISBN 0-263-05936-7). Transatlantic.

Altschul, M. Anglo-Norman England, Ten Sixty-Six to Eleven Fifty-Four. LC 78-80816. (Bibliographical Handbooks of the Conference on British Studies). 1969. 17.50 (ISBN 0-521-07582-3). Cambridge U Pr.

Altschule, Mark D., jt. auth. see Valeri, C. Robert.

Altschuler, Glenn C. Andrew M. White, Educator, Historian, Diplomat. LC 78-58065. (Illus.). 1978. 17.50x (ISBN 0-8014-1156-4). Cornell U Pr.

Altschuler, Thelma. Interactions: Themes for Thoughtful Writing. 1972. pap. text ed. 6.95x (ISBN 0-02-473300-8, 47330). Macmillan.

Altsheler, Joseph. Before the Dawn. 1976. lib. bdg. 16.70x (ISBN 0-89968-000-3). Lightyear.

--Border Watch. 1976. lib. bdg. 16.70x (ISBN 0-89968-001-1). Lightyear.

--Eyes of the Woods. 1976. lib. bdg. 12.95x (ISBN 0-89968-145-X). Lightyear.

--The Forest Runners. 1976. lib. bdg. 16.30x (ISBN 0-89968-002-X). Lightyear.

--In Hostile Red. 1976. lib. bdg. 15.80x (ISBN 0-89968-003-8). Lightyear.

--The Scouts of Stonewall. 1976. lib. bdg. 15.80x (ISBN 0-89968-004-6). Lightyear.

--The Young Trailers. 1976. lib. bdg. 15.30x (ISBN 0-89968-005-4). Lightyear.

Altsheler, Joseph A. Horsemen of the Plains. (Illus.). (gr. 7 up). 1967. 5.95x o.s.i. (ISBN 0-02-700650-6). Macmillan.

Altshul, Jack, jt. auth. see Lombardo, Guy.

Altshuler, Alan. Community Control: The Black Demand for Participation in Large American Cities. LC 72-110439. 1970. pap. 5.50 (ISBN 0-672-63517-8). Pegasus.

Altshuler, Alan, ed. Current Issues in Transportation Policies. LC 78-19631. (Policy Studies Organization Ser.). (Illus.). 224p. 1979. 19.95 (ISBN 0-669-02623-9). Lexington Bks.

Altshuler, Alan A. City Planning Process: A Political Analysis. LC 65-25498. 1966. 25.00x (ISBN 0-8014-0007-4); pap. 6.95 (ISBN 0-8014-9081-2, CP81). Cornell U Pr.

Altshuler, Alan A. & Thomas, Norman C., eds. Politics of the Federal Bureaucracy. 2nd ed. 1977. pap. text ed. 15.50 (ISBN 0-06-040246-6, HarpC). Har-Row.

Al'tshuler, S. A. & Kozyrev, B. M. Electron Paramagnetic Resonance in Compounds of Transition Elements. 2nd ed. Barouch, A., tr. from Rus. LC 74-8208. 589p. 1975. 82.95 (ISBN 0-470-02523-9). Halsted Pr.

Altstein, Howard, jt. auth. see Simon, Rita J.

Altura, B. M., jt. auth. see Kaley, G.

Altvater, Helen. From Eight to Eighty (Young Adult Poetry) 100p. (Orig.). 1981. pap. 5.95 (ISBN 0-933906-17-X). Gusto Pr.

Aluise, John J. The Physician As Manager. (Illus.). 357p. 1979. 29.95 (ISBN 0-89303-006-6). Charles.

Aluri, Rao, jt. auth. see Yannarella, Philip A.

Alvarenga, Beatriz. Fisica General, Vol. I. (Span.). 1980. pap. text ed. 5.00 (ISBN 0-06-310011-8, Pub. by HarLA Mexico). Har-Row.

Alvarenga, Beatriz & Alvarenga, Maximo. Curso De Fisica General. 1976. text ed. 8.50 (ISBN 0-06-310012-6, IntlDept). Har-Row.

Alvarenga, Maximo, jt. auth. see Alvarenga, Beatriz.

Alvares, Claude A. Homo Faber: Technology & Culture in India, China & the West from 1500 to the Present Day. xvi, 275p. 1980. lib. bdg. 47.50 (ISBN 90-247-2283-7, Martinus Nijhoff Pubs). Kluwer Boston.

Alvarez, A. Beyond All This Fiddle. LC 69-16460. 1969. 10.00 o.p. (ISBN 0-394-41674-0). Random.

--Hunt. 288p. 1981. pap. 2.75 (ISBN 0-553-13115-X). Bantam.

--The Savage God: A Study of Suicide. 1972. 7.95 o.p. (ISBN 0-394-47451-1). Random.

Alvarez, Joseph. Politics in America. Liberty, Gene, ed. LC 76-128850. (Understanding Bks.). (Illus.). (gr. 4-9). 1971. PLB 7.95 (ISBN 0-87191-068-3). Creative Ed.

Alvarez, Joseph, jt. auth. see Mattison, Charles W.
Alvarez, Paul, jt. ed. see Voros, Gerald J.
Alvarez, Roberto, tr. see Rhee, Jhoon.
Alvarez, Russell R De see De Alvarez, Russell R.
Alvarez, Walter C. Nerves in Collision. 1974. pap. 1.75 o.s.i. (ISBN 0-515-03414-2, M3414). Jove Pubns.
Alvarez, Walter C., ed. see Adam, Ruth C.
Alvarino, Angeles. Siphonophores of the Pacific, with a Review of the World Distribution. (Bulletin of the Scripps Institution of Oceanography: Vol. 16). pap. 8.00x (ISBN 0-520-09321-6). U of Cal Pr.
Alvera. The Tiny Little Tow Truck. (Illus.). 1980. 5.00 (ISBN 0-682-49542-5). Exposition.
Alverson, Dayton L., jt. ed. see Pruter, A. T.
Alves, A. Pereira. Triunfa En la Vida. (Illus.). 1977. pap. 1.90 (ISBN 0-311-46033-X). Casa Bautista.
Alves, Robert. Sketches of a History of Literature. LC 67-18714. 1967. Repr. of 1794 ed. 33.00x (ISBN 0-8201-1002-7). Schol Facsimiles.
Alves, Ron & Milligan, Charles. Living with Energy. (Illus.). 1978. 14.95 o.p. (ISBN 0-670-43584-8, Studio). Viking Pr.
Alves, Ronald & Milligan, C. Living with Energy: Alternative Sources in Your Home. (Large Format Ser). (Illus.). 1978. pap. 5.95 o.p. (ISBN 0-14-004681-X). Penguin.
Alvin, Juliette. Music Therapy for the Autistic Child. 1979. pap. 9.95x (ISBN 0-19-317414-6). Oxford U Pr.
Alvin, Kenneth. Observer's Book of Lichens. (Observer Bks.). (Illus.). 1977. 4.95 (ISBN 0-684-15202-9, ScribT). Scribner.
Alwin, Robert H. & Hackworth, R. Algebra Programmed, Pt. 4. LC 73-76042. (Illus.). 1971. pap. 9.50 (ISBN 0-13-022178-3). P-H.
Alwin, Robert H. & Hackworth, Robert D. Algebra Programmed, Pt. 2. 2nd ed. (Illus.). 1978. pap. text ed. 10.95 (ISBN 0-13-022020-5). P-H.
--Algebra Programmed, Pt. 1. 2nd ed. (Illus.). 1978. pap. text ed. 10.95 (ISBN 0-13-022038-8). P-H.
Alwin, Robert H., et al. Algebra Text: Intermediate. (Illus.). 1974. pap. 15.95 ref. ed. (ISBN 0-13-022400-6). P-H.
--Algebra Text: Elementary. (Illus.). 424p. 1974. pap. 15.95x ref. ed. (ISBN 0-13-022293-3). P-H.
Alworth, E. Paul. Will Rogers. (U. S. Authors Ser.: No. 236). 1974. lib. bdg. 10.95 (ISBN 0-8057-0634-8). Twayne.
Alyn, Irene B., jt. auth. see Gillies, Dee A.
AMA. AMA Drug Evaluations. 4th ed. LC 76-9254. 1470p. 1980. 58.00 (ISBN 0-471-08125-6, Pub. by Wiley Med). Wiley.
Amacher, et al, eds. Challenge to a Liberal International Economic Order. 1979. 16.25 (ISBN 0-8447-2151-4); pap. 9.25 (ISBN 0-8447-2152-2). Am Enterprise.
Amacher, P., jt. ed. see Gardner, L. I.
Amacher, Richard E. American Political Writers: 1588-1800. (United States Authors Ser.: No. 394). 1979. 13.50 (ISBN 0-8057-7217-0). Twayne.
--Edward Albee. LC 68-24299. (U. S. Authors Ser.: No. 141). 1968. lib. bdg. 10.95 (ISBN 0-8057-0011-0). Twayne.
Amada, Gerald. Mental Health on the Community College Campus. 157p. 1977. pap. text ed. 8.50 (ISBN 0-8191-0357-8). U Pr of Amer.
Amadi, Elechi. The Concubine. (African Writers Ser.). 1966. pap. text ed. 2.75 (ISBN 0-435-90025-0). Heinemann Ed.
Amado, Jorge. Dona Flor & Her Two Husbands. 1977. pap. 3.95 (ISBN 0-380-01796-2, 35402, Bard). Avon.
--Gabriela, Clove & Cinnamon. 1974. pap. 3.95 (ISBN 0-380-01205-7, 51839, Bard). Avon.
--Tieta. 688p. 1980. pap. 4.95 (ISBN 0-380-50815-X, 50815, Bard). Avon.
Amador, Antonio A., jt. auth. see Leo, Francisco D.
Amaducci, L., et al, eds. Aging of the Brain & Dementia. (Aging Ser.). 1980. text ed. 35.00 (ISBN 0-89004-457-0). Raven.
Amai, Robert L., jt. auth. see Clark, Ronald D.
Amalrik, Andrei. Involuntary Journey to Siberia, Russian Edition. LC 75-118829. (Rus). 1970. 10.00 (ISBN 0-15-145503-1). HarBraceJ.
Aman, Mohammed M., ed. Cataloging & Classification of Non-Western Materials: Concerns, Issues, & Practices. 1980. lib. bdg. 18.50x (ISBN 0-912700-06-8). Oryx Pr.
Aman, Reinhold, ed. Maledicta Yearbook, 1979. LC 77-649633. (Maledicta: International Journal of Verbal Aggression Ser.: Vol. 3, Nos. 1-2). (Illus.). 320p. (Orig.). 1980. pap. 20.00 (ISBN 0-916500-54-3). Maledicta.
Amann, Anton, ed. Open Care for the Elderly in Seven European Countries: A Pilot Study in the Possibilities & Limits of Care. LC 80-40816. 238p. 1980. 36.00 (ISBN 0-08-025215-X). Pergamon.
Amann, Charles A., jt. ed. see Mattavi, James N.
Amann, Dick. Airports: Today's Small Field, Tomorrow's Neighborhood Nightmare. 1981. 45.00 (ISBN 0-917194-05-5). Prog Studies.
Amann, R., et al, eds. The Technological Level of Soviet Industry. LC 77-76298. (Illus.). 1977. 45.00x (ISBN 0-300-02076-7). Yale U Pr.
Amaral, Anthony. How to Train Your Horse. (Illus.). 1977. 10.95 (ISBN 0-87691-193-9). Winchester Pr.
Amaral, Anthony A. Will James: The Last Cowboy Legend. rev. ed. LC 80-155. (Lancehead Ser.). (Illus.). xiv, 175p. 1980. 12.00 (ISBN 0-87417-058-3). U of Nev Pr.
Amarasinghe, Upali. Dryden & Pope in the Early 19th Century. 1962. 42.00 (ISBN 0-521-04026-4). Cambridge U Pr.
Amarchand, D. & Varadharajan, B. An Introduction to Marketing. 1980. text ed. 15.00x (ISBN 0-7069-0699-3, Pub. by Vikas India). Advent Bk.
Amarshu, Azeem, et al. Development & Dependency: The Political Economy of Papua New Guinea. (Illus.). 306p. 1979. text ed. 28.00x (ISBN 0-19-550582-4). Oxford U Pr.
Amary, A. B. Carpentry for Builders. (Drake Home Craftsman Ser.). (Illus.). 204p. (Orig.). 1976. pap. 5.95 (ISBN 0-8069-8198-9). Sterling.
Amary, Issam B. Creative Recreation for the Mentally Retarded. 128p. 1975. 14.75 (ISBN 0-398-03292-0). C C Thomas.
--Social Awareness, Hygiene, & Sex Education for the Mentally Retarded-Developmentally Disabled. (Illus.). 208p. 1980. text ed. 15.50 (ISBN 0-398-04096-6). C C Thomas.
Amateau, E. I., et al, eds. see Daudet, Alphonse.
Amato, Janet D' see D'Amato, Janet & D'Amato, Alex.
Amauri, Maurice & Decraon, Pierre. Les Chansons Attribuees Aux Seigneurs De Craon. Langfors, Arthur, ed. LC 80-2160. (Societe Neo-Philologique De Helsingfors, Memoires Ser.: Vol. 6). 1981. Repr. of 1917 ed. 17.50 (ISBN 0-404-19020-0). AMS Pr.
Amayo, R. K. & Stewart, I. Infinite-Dimensional Lie Algebras. 436p. 1974. 62.50x (ISBN 90-286-0144-9). Sijthoff & Noordhoff.
Ambekar, D. V., jt. ed. see Karve, D. G.
Amber Crest Bks. Staff, ed. see Howlett, Noel.
Amber, Lee. Chosen. 1978. pap. 2.98 o.s.i. (ISBN 0-88449-072-6). Vision Hse.
Amberger, Ronald, et al. Canal Boats, Interurbans & Trolleys: A History of the Rochester Subway. LC 80-82783. (Orig.). 1981. 12.95 (ISBN 0-9605296-1-6). Natl Rail Rochester.
Ambirajan, S. Classical Political Economy & British Policy in India. LC 76-21020. (South Asian Studies: No. 21). (Illus.). 1978. 44.50 (ISBN 0-521-21415-7). Cambridge U Pr.
Ambler, C. H., jt. auth. see Summers, Festus P.
Ambler, Charles H. Thomas Ritchie: A Study in Virginia Politics. (Law, Politics & History Ser). 1970. Repr. of 1913 ed. lib. bdg. 39.50 (ISBN 0-306-70092-1). Da Capo.
Ambler, Charles H., ed. Correspondence of Robert M. T. Hunter, 1826-1876. LC 76-75307. (American Scene Ser). 1971. Repr. of 1918 ed. lib. bdg. 39.50 (ISBN 0-306-71257-1). Da Capo.
Ambler, Eric. A Coffin for Dimitrios. 1977. pap. 1.75 o.p. (ISBN 0-345-25912-2). Ballantine.
--Journey into Fear. 1977. pap. 1.95 (ISBN 0-345-28256-6). Ballantine.
Ambler, Eric, intro. by. Great Cases of Scotland Yard. (Illus.). 1978. 12.95 (ISBN 0-89577-053-9, Pub. by Reader's Digest). Norton.
Ambrecht, Biliana C. Politicizing the Poor: The Legacy of the War on Poverty in a Mexican American Community. LC 74-31501. 1976. 29.95 (ISBN 0-275-05900-6). Praeger.
Ambron, Sueann R. & Brodzinsky, David M. Lifespan Human Development. 644p. 1979. text ed. 17.95 (ISBN 0-03-042406-2, HoltC); wkbk. 6.95 (ISBN 0-03-046046-8); instructor's manual avail. (ISBN 0-03-044991-X). HR&W.
Ambrose, Alice & Lazerowitz, Morris, eds. Ludwig Wittgenstein: Philosophy & Language. (Muirhead Library of Philosophy). 1972. text ed. 26.00x (ISBN 0-391-00190-6). Humanities.
Ambrose, David, jt. auth. see Willet, Shelagh M.
Ambrose, E. J. & Easty, Dorothy M. Cell Biology. LC 79-140833. (Biology Ser). 1970. text ed. 18.95 (ISBN 0-201-00233-7). A-W.
Ambrose, E. J. & Roe, F. J., eds. The Biology of Cancer. 2nd rev. ed. LC 74-26860. 315p. 1975. 57.95 (ISBN 0-470-02527-1). Halsted Pr.
Ambrose, E. R. Heat Pumps & Electric Heating: Residential, Commercial, Industrial Year-Round Air Conditioning. LC 65-27664. 1966. 25.00 (ISBN 0-471-02530-5, Pub by Wiley-Interscience). Wiley.
Ambrose, G. & Newbold, G. A Handbook of Medical Hypnosis. 4th ed. 1980. text ed. 25.95 (ISBN 0-02-857110-X). Macmillan.
Ambrose, James. Simplified Design of Building Foundations. 384p. 1981. 20.00 (ISBN 0-471-06267-7, Pub. by Wiley-Interscience). Wiley.
Ambrose, James & Vergun, Dimitry. Simplified Building Design for Wind & Earthquake Forces. LC 79-26660. 1980. 24.00 (ISBN 0-471-05013-X, Pub. by Wiley-Interscience). Wiley.
Ambrose, John W., jt. auth. see Buehner, William J.
Ambrose, K., jt. auth. see Gostling, E. P.
Ambrose, Mike & Walker, Nora S. Captain Mike's Complete Guide to Grunion Hunting. (Illus.). 93p. (Orig.). 1981. pap. 3.95 (ISBN 0-916392-70-8). Oak Tree Pubns.
Ambrose, R. J. & Aggarwal, S. L. Advances in Preparation & Characterization of Multiphase Polymer Systems. (Journal of Polymer Science Symposium: No. 60). 1977. 18.95 (ISBN 0-471-04714-7). Wiley.
Ambrose, Stephen E. Eisenhower & Berlin, Nineteen Forty Five: The Decision to Halt at the Elbe. (Essays in American History Ser). (Illus.). 1967. pap. 4.95 (ISBN 0-393-05342-3). Norton.
Ambrose, Stephen E. & Immerman, Richard H. Ike's Spies: Eisenhower & the Espionage Establishment. LC 80-1117. (Illus.). 384p. 1981. 14.95 (ISBN 0-385-14493-8). Doubleday.
Ambrose, Stephen E. & Barber, James A., Jr., eds. The Military & American Society. LC 77-163236. 1973. pap. text ed. 6.95 (ISBN 0-02-900550-7). Free Pr.
Ambrosek, Jim, et al. Third Season-Seven Poets: Poetry by Seven Eastern Oregon Poets. Gullikson, Sandra S., ed. 28p. (Orig.). 1980. pap. 3.50 (ISBN 0-9605512-0-4). Clearwater OR.
Ambrosius, Edgar E., et al. Mechanical Measurement & Instrumentation. (Illus.). 1966. 16.95 o.p. (ISBN 0-8260-0380-X). Wiley.
Ambrus, Victor G. The Valiant Little Tailor. (Illus.). 24p. (ps-3). 1980. 9.95 (ISBN 0-19-279727-1). Oxford U Pr.
Ambuter, Carolyn. Complete Book of Needlepoint. LC 70-178814. (Illus.). 1972. 9.95 (ISBN 0-690-00337-4, TYC-T). T Y Crowell.
Ambuter, Jeanne, jt. auth. see Crandall, Dorothy.
Amdursky, Robert S., ed. Basics for Municipal Bond Lawyers: Course Handbook. LC 80-82474. (Nineteen Seventy-Nine to Nineteen Eighty Corporate Law & Practice Course Handbook Ser.). 887p. 1980. pap. 25.00 (ISBN 0-686-69164-4, B4-6551). PLI.
Amedeo, Douglas & Golledge, Reginald G. Introduction to Scientific Reasoning in Geography. LC 75-1411. 437p. 1975. text ed. 29.95 (ISBN 0-471-02537-2). Wiley.
Ameican Psychological Association. Social Influences on Behavior: Teachers Handbook. (Human Behavior Curriculum Project Ser.). 48p. (Orig.). (gr. 9-12). 1981. pap. 9.95 (ISBN 0-8077-2620-6). Tchrs Coll.
Amelsvoort, Vincent van see Van Amelsvoort, Vincent.
Amen, Carol. Changing Problems into Challenges. (Uplook Ser.). 1972. pap. 0.75 (ISBN 0-8163-0068-2, 03109-6). Pacific Pr Pub Assn.
--For Rain As Well As Rainbow. (Uplook Ser.). 1975. pap. 0.65 o.p. (ISBN 0-8163-0173-5, 06433-7). Pacific Pr Pub Assn.
--Hyacinths to Feed the Soul. LC 74-33850. (Better Living Ser.). 64p. 1975. pap. text ed. 0.95 (ISBN 0-8127-0094-5). Southern Pub.
--Love Is the Motive. LC 77-12655. (Better Living Ser.). 1977. pap. 0.95 (ISBN 0-8127-0153-4). Southern Pub.
--Pass It on. (Uplook Ser.). 1977. pap. 0.75 (ISBN 0-8163-0310-X, 16027-5). Pacific Pr Pub Assn.
--Teetering on the Tightrope. LC 79-18718. (Orion Ser.). 1979. pap. 1.95 (ISBN 0-8127-0250-6). Southern Pub.
Amend, John R. Introductory Chemistry: Models & Basic Concepts. LC 76-41820. 1977. text ed. 16.95 o.p. (ISBN 0-471-02533-X); study guide 5.95 o.p. (ISBN 0-471-97715-2); experimental chemistry 7.95 o.p. (ISBN 0-471-02534-8). Wiley.
Amend, Karen, jt. auth. see Ruiz, Mary S.
Amend, Karen S., jt. auth. see Ruiz, Mary.
Amend, Victor E. & Hendrick, Leo T. Readings from Left to Right. LC 77-93111. 1970. pap. text ed. 6.95 o.s.i. (ISBN 0-02-900610-4). Free Pr.
Amend, Victor E. & Hendrick, Leo T., eds. Ten Contemporary Thinkers. LC 63-13536. (Orig.). 1964. pap. text ed. 6.95 o.s.i. (ISBN 0-02-900600-7). Free Pr.
Amendola, Giorgio. The Life I Chose. Packer, William, tr. from Ital. 1980. text ed. write for info. cancelled (ISBN 0-918294-06-1). Karz Pub.
Amendola, J. Ice Carving Made Easy. (Illus.). pap. 12.00x (ISBN 0-685-47434-8). Corner.
Amendola, Joseph. Baker's Manual for Quantity Baking & Pastry Making. rev., 3rd ed. (Illus.). 220p. 1972. 13.25x (ISBN 0-8104-9458-2). Hayden.
Amendola, Joseph, jt. auth. see Lundberg, Donald E.
Amendola, Joseph, jt. auth. see Wilkinson, Jule.
Amenta, Peter S., ed. Histology. 2nd ed. (Medical Outline Ser.). 1978. spiral bdg. 10.75 (ISBN 0-87488-662-7). Med Exam.
Amerian Society of Civil Engineers, compiled by. Legal, Institutional, & Social Aspects of Irrigation & Drainage & Water Resources Planning & Management. 912p. 1979. pap. text ed. 49.50 (ISBN 0-87262-140-5). Am Soc Civil Eng.
America Pulpwood Association. Chain Saw Manual. 118p. 1980. pap. text ed. 4.95 (ISBN 0-8134-2133-0). Interstate.
America, Richard F. Developing the Afro-American Economy: Building on Strength. LC 76-54557. (Illus.). 1977. 15.95 (ISBN 0-669-01304-8). Lexington Bks.
American Academy of Orthopaedic Surgeons. American Academy of Orthopaedic Surgeons: Instructional Course Lectures, Vols. 21-29. Incl. Vol. 21. 1972. 37.50 (ISBN 0-8016-0010-3); Vol. 22. 1973. 37.50 (ISBN 0-8016-0011-1); Vol. 23. 1974. 34.50 (ISBN 0-8016-0012-X); Vol. 24. 328p. 1975. 38.50 (ISBN 0-8016-0013-8); Vol. 25. 1976. 38.50 (ISBN 0-8016-0014-6); Vol. 26. 1977. 38.50 (ISBN 0-8016-0022-7); Vol. 27. 1978. 34.50 (ISBN 0-8016-0023-5); Vol. 28. 1979. 44.50 (ISBN 0-8016-0032-4); Vol. 29. 184p. 1980. 38.00 (ISBN 0-8016-0047-2). LC 43-17054. Mosby.
--Atlas of Limb Prosthetics: Surgical & Prosthetic Principles. (Illus.). 668p. 1980. 74.50 (ISBN 0-8016-0058-8). Mosby.
--Symposium on Anthroscopy & Arthrography of the Knee. LC 78-17015. (Illus.). 1978. text ed. 62.50 (ISBN 0-8016-0056-1). Mosby.
--Symposium on Microsurgery: Practical Use in Orthopaedics. Urbaniak, James R., ed. LC 79-14999. 1979. text ed. 52.50 (ISBN 0-8016-0066-9). Mosby.
--Symposium on Reconstructive Surgery of the Knee. LC 78-6486. (Illus.). 1978. 52.50 (ISBN 0-8016-0132-0). Mosby.
--Symposium on Tendon Surgery in the Hand. LC 75-37577. (Illus.). 314p. 1975. 37.50 o.p. (ISBN 0-8016-0046-4). Mosby.
--Symposium on the Athlete's Knee: Surgical Repair & Reconstruction. LC 80-19414. (Illus.). 218p. 1980. text ed. 39.50 (ISBN 0-8016-0077-4). Mosby.
American Academy of Podiatric Sports Medicine. Sports Medicine Eighty: A Publication by the Members of the American Academy of Podiatric Sports Medicine, Pt. II. Rinaldi, Robert R. & Sabia, Michael L., Jr., eds. LC 80-66360. (Sports Medicine, Supplement II to the Archives of Podiatric Medicine & Foot Surgery). 250p. 1980. pap. 19.50 monograph (ISBN 0-87993-143-4). Futura Pub.
American Academy of Political & Social Science. The Revolution, the Constitution & America's Third Century, 2 vols. 1980. 35.00x (ISBN 0-8122-7763-5). U of Pa Pr.
American Academy of Religion, 1972 & 1973. Women & Religion: Proceedings. rev. ed. Arnold, Joan & Romero, Joan A., eds. LC 74-83126. (American Academy of Religion. Aids for the Study of Religion). 1974. pap. 9.00 (ISBN 0-89130-224-7, 010301). Scholars Pr Ca.
American Academy of Religion, 1974. American Religion: Proceedings. Gaustad, Edwin S., ed. LC 74-14211. (American Academy of Religion. Section Papers). 1974. pap. 4.50 (ISBN 0-88420-116-3, 010910). Scholars Pr Ca.
--Asian Religions-History of Religion: Proceedings. Partin, Harry, ed. LC 74-14213. (American Academy of Religion. Section Papers). 1974. pap. 4.50 (ISBN 0-88420-114-7, 010912). Scholars Pr Ca.
--Biblical Literature: Proceedings. Francis, Fred O., ed. LC 74-14214. (American Academy of Religion. Section Papers). 1974. pap. 4.50 (ISBN 0-88420-112-0, 010914). Scholars Pr Ca.
American Adventures Association. International Adventure Travelguide, 1979. 1979. pap. 9.95 (ISBN 0-394-73723-7). Random.
--Worldwide Adventure Travelguide, 1980. (Illus.). 1980. pap. 9.95 (ISBN 0-394-73872-1). Random.
American Antiquarian Society. Catalogue of the Manuscript Collections of the American Antiquarian Society. 1979. lib. bdg. 375.00 (ISBN 0-8161-0258-9). G K Hall.
American Arbitration Association. Lawyers' Arbitration Letters, 1970 to 1979. 1981. 15.95 (ISBN 0-02-900570-1). Free Pr.
American Assoc. of Critical-Care Nurses. Critical Care Nursing of Children & Adolescents. Oakes, Annalee, ed. (Illus.). 750p. 1981. pap. write for info. (ISBN 0-7216-1003-X). Saunders.
American Association for Gifted Children. On Being Gifted. LC 78-58622. 1979. 8.95 (ISBN 0-8027-0616-9); pap. 5.95 (ISBN 0-8027-7138-6). Walker & Co.

--Reaching Out: Advocacy for the Gifted & Talented. Tannenbaum, Abraham J., ed. (Perspectives on Gifted & Talented Education Ser.). (Orig.). 1980. pap. text ed. 4.95x (ISBN 0-8077-2591-9). Tchrs Coll.

American Association for State & Local History. Directory of Historical Societies & Agencies in the United States & Canada. 11th ed. McDonald, Donna, ed. LC 56-4164. (Illus.). 1978. pap. 24.00x (ISBN 0-910050-36-8). AASLH.

American Association of College for Teacher Education. AACTE Directory 1980. 118p. (Orig.). 1980. pap. text ed. 6.00 (ISBN 0-89333-020-5). AACTE.

American Association of Critical Care Nurses. Critical Care Nursing of the Multi-Injured Patient. Mann, James K. & Oakes, Annalee R, eds. LC 79-67787. (Illus.). 168p. 1980. pap. 10.95 (ISBN 0-7216-1002-1). Saunders.

American Association of Genito-Urinary Surgeons. Transactions of the American Association of G-U Surgeons: Symposium, Vol. 69. 1978. pap. 19.00 o.p. (ISBN 0-683-00107-8). Williams & Wilkins.

American Automobile Association. Sportsmanlike Driving. rev. ed. Cranford, Carolyn E., ed. (Illus.). (gr. 10-12). 1979. text ed. 10.64 (ISBN 0-07-001330-6); pap. text ed. 6.92 (ISBN 0-07-001331-4); tchr's ed. 12.40 (ISBN 0-07-001332-2). Webster-McGraw.

American Bar Association. ABA Standards for Criminal Justice, 4 vols. 1980. Set. 195.00 (ISBN 0-316-03709-5); 50.00 ea. Little.

American Bar Association, Corporate, Banking & Business Law Committee of the Young Lawyers Div. Guidelines for a Corporate Law Office Manual. LC 79-88508. 75p. (Orig.). 1980. pap. text ed. 35.00 (ISBN 0-89707-023-2). Prof Educ IL.

American Bible Society. Good News for Modern Man: New Testament. 516p. 1980. pap. 2.95 (ISBN 0-553-14347-6). Bantam.

American Bible Society, ed. Scriptures of the World; a Compilation of 1,603 Languages in Which at Least One Book of the Bible Has Been Published. 6th ed. (Illus.). 1976. pap. 2.00 o.p. (ISBN 0-686-16537-3, 17602). United Bible.

American Bookseller's Association, ed. A Manual on Bookselling: How to Open & Run Your Own Bookstore. (Illus.). 146p. 1980. 11.95 (ISBN 0-517-53705-2, Harmony); pap. 6.95 (ISBN 0-517-53706-0, Harmony). Crown.

American Bureau of Metal Statistics Inc. ABMS Non-Ferrous Metal Data Publication. annual ed. 1978. 25.00 (ISBN 0-685-91837-8). Am Bur Metal.

American Bureau of Metal Statistics Staff, compiled by. ABMS Non-Ferrous Metal Data Publication: 1974 Yearbook. rev. ed. LC 21-15719. 1975. 25.00 (ISBN 0-910064-08-3). Am Bur Metal.

American Bureau of Metal Statistics Staff, ed. ABMS Non-Ferrous Metal Data Publication: 1975 Yearbook. rev. ed. LC 21-15719. 1976. 25.00 (ISBN 0-910064-09-1). Am Bur Metal.

--ABMS Non-Ferrous Metal Data Publication: 1976 Year Book. rev. ed. LC 21-15719. 1977. 25.00 (ISBN 0-910064-10-5). Am Bur Metal.

American Bureau of Metal Statistics Editorial Staff, ed. Fifty-Second Annual Yearbook. 1973. 25.00 (ISBN 0-685-39802-1). Am Bur Metal.

American Bureau of Metal Statistics Inc. Non-Ferrous Motal Data Yearbook, 1979. (Illus.). 1980. yrbk. 25.00 (ISBN 0-686-61434-8). Am Bur Metal.

American Bureau of Metal Statistics Staff, compiled by. Year Book of the American Bureau of Metal Statistics. annual 1972. 25.00 (ISBN 0-910064-05-9). Am Bur Metal.

--Year Book of the American Bureau of Metal Statistics. LC 21-15719. 1973. 25.00 (ISBN 0-910064-06-7). Am Bur Metal.

American Canal Society. The Best from American Canals. (Illus.). 84p. 1980. 6.00 (ISBN 0-933788-32-0). Am Canal & Transport.

American Civil Liberties Union. ACLU 1976 Policy Guide. LC 78-19573. (Orig.). 1978. pap. 13.95 (ISBN 0-669-01683-7); 1979 supplement 12.95 (ISBN 0-669-02624-7). Lexington Bks.

American College of Anesthesiology, jt. auth. see American Society of Anesthesiologists.

American College of Emergency Physicians. Emergency Department Organization & Management. 2nd ed. Jenkins, A. L. & Van De Leuv, John H., eds. LC 78-13594. (Illus.). 1978. text ed. 27.50 (ISBN 0-8016-0122-3). Mosby.

American College of Sports Medicine, ed. Guidelines for Graded Exercise Testing & Exercise Prescription. 2nd ed. LC 80-19484. (Illus.). 151p. 1980. pap. 6.50 (ISBN 0-8121-0769-1). Lea & Febiger.

American College of Surgeons. Early Care of the Injured Patient. 2nd ed. LC 76-8566. (Illus.). 1976. text ed. 17.00 (ISBN 0-7216-1161-3). Saunders.

--Surgical Nutrition. Ballinger, Walter F., ed. LC 75-19840. (Illus.). 527p. 1975. text ed. 26.00 (ISBN 0-7216-1525-2). Saunders.

American Consulting Engineers Council. ACEC International Engineering Directory: 1980-1981. 1980. 10.00 (ISBN 0-686-60619-1). Am Consul Eng.

--ACEC Membership Directory, 1980-1981. 1980. 25.00 (ISBN 0-686-60620-5). Am Consul Eng.

American Council Of Learned Societies. Dictionary of Scientific Biography. 1970. 55.00x ea. o.p.; Vol. 1. (ISBN 0-684-10112-2); Vol. 2. (ISBN 0-684-10113-0); Vol. 3. (ISBN 0-684-10114-9); Vol. 4. (ISBN 0-684-10115-7); Vol. 5. (ISBN 0-684-10116-5); Vol. 6. (ISBN 0-684-10117-3); lib. bdg. 36.00 o.p. (ISBN 0-685-20283-6). Scribner.

--Dictionary of Scientific Biography, Vol. 11. LC 69-18090. 1975. 44.00 o.p. (ISBN 0-684-10122-X); lib. bdg. 36.00 o.p. (ISBN 0-685-63862-6). Scribner.

--Dictionary of Scientific Biography, Vol. 12. LC 69-18090. 1975. 44.00 o.p. (ISBN 0-684-12924-8); lib. bdg. 36.00 o.p. (ISBN 0-685-63863-4). Scribner.

--Dictionary of Scientific Biography, Vol. 13. 1976. 44.00 o.p. (ISBN 0-685-63864-2); lib. bdg. 36.00 o.p. (ISBN 0-684-12925-6). Scribner.

--Dictionary of Scientific Biography, Vol. 14. LC 69-18090. 1976. 44.00 o.p. (ISBN 0-684-12926-4); lib. bdg. 36.00 o.p. (ISBN 0-685-63865-0). Scribner.

American Craft Council. Packing-Shipping Crafts. 1977. 2.70 (ISBN 0-88321-031-2). Am Craft.

--Photographing Crafts. 66p. 1974. 6.20 (ISBN 0-88321-006-1). Am Craft.

--Pricing & Promotion: A Guide for Craftspeople. McGuire, Patrick & Moran, Lois, eds. 93p. 1979. 7.20 (ISBN 0-88321-024-X). Am Craft.

American Dental Association - Bureau of Library & Indexing Service. Index to Dental Literature. 1980. annual cumulative 100.00 (ISBN 0-685-77438-4); quarterly cumulative 125.00. Am Dental.

American Dental Association-Bureau of Library Services. Index to Dental Literature, Nineteen Seventy-Nine. 1979. 100.00 (ISBN 0-685-96599-6). Am Dental.

American Diabetes Association & American Dietetic Association. The American Diabetes Association, American Dietetic Association Family Cookbook. LC 80-16722. 320p. 1980. 12.95 (ISBN 0-13-024901-7). P-H.

American Dietetic Association. Handbook of Clinical Dietetics. LC 80-11317. 480p. 1981. text ed. 20.00x (ISBN 0-300-02256-5). Yale U Pr.

American Dietetic Association, jt. auth. see American Diabetes Association.

American Dietetic Association Members. Your Future As a Dietician. LC 73-114126. (Career Guidance Ser). 1971. pap. 3.50 (ISBN 0-668-02240-X). Arco.

American Economic Association Committee, compiled by. Readings in Business Cycle Theory. LC 76-29403. (BCL Ser.). 736p. 1980. Repr. of 1951 ed. 33.50. AMS Pr.

--Readings in the Theory of Income Distribution. LC 76-29414. (BCL II Ser.). 736p. 1980. Repr. of 1946 ed. 45.00 (ISBN 0-404-15332-1). AMS Pr.

American Education Finance Association. Perspectives in State School Support Programs. Date not set. price not set prof. reference (ISBN 0-88410-197-5). Ballinger Pub.

American Ethnological Society, 1974. American Anthropology, the Early Years: Proceedings. Murra, John V., ed. (AES Ser). (Illus.). 235p. 1976. pap. text ed. 12.95 (ISBN 0-8299-0097-7). West Pub.

American-European Symposium, Vienna, Nov. 3-5, 1975, Sponsored by Physicians Associated for Continuing Education, Johns Hopkins University, & the University of Vienna & the Univ. of Innesbruck. Prostatic Disease: Proceedings. Marberger, H., et al, eds. LC 75-42905. (Progress in Clinical & Biological Research Ser.: Vol. 6). 1976. 32.00x (ISBN 0-8451-0006-8). A R Liss.

American Fabrics Magazine. Encyclopedia of Textiles. 55.00 (ISBN 0-87245-507-6). Textile Bk.

American Fabrics Magazine, ed. Encyclopedia of Textiles. 3rd ed. (Illus.). 1980. 49.95 (ISBN 0-13-276576-4, Busn). P-H.

American Federation of Arts, jt. auth. see Center for Inter-American Relations.

American Foreign Policy Association. Great Decisions Nineteen Eighty. (gr. 9-12). 1980. pap. text ed. 5.20 (ISBN 0-205-06889-8, 7668899); free tchrs' guide avail. (ISBN 0-205-06890-1). Allyn.

American Forestry Association. Trees Every Boy & Girl Should Know. Date not set. 3.50 (ISBN 0-686-26729-X, 31). Am Forestry.

American Foundation for Continuing Education at Syracuse University. Readings on Drug Education. Reagen, Michael V., ed. LC 72-7237. 1972. 10.00 (ISBN 0-8108-0548-0). Scarecrow.

American Foundation for the Blind. Directory of Agencies Serving the Visually Handicapped in the U. S. 21st ed. Mulholland, Mary E., ed. 450p. Date not set. pap. 16.00 (ISBN 0-89128-100-2). Am Foun Blind.

American Friends Service Committee. Anatomy of Anti-Communism: A Report Prepared for the Peace Education Division of the American Friends Service Committee. LC 68-30758. (Orig.). 1969. 2.25 o.p. (ISBN 0-8090-1346-0). Hill & Wang.

--Uncommon Controversy: Fishing Rights of the Muckleshoot, Puyallup, & Nisqually Indians. LC 73-103297. (Illus.). 264p. 1970. 7.50 o.p. (ISBN 0-295-95077-3). U of Wash Pr.

American Gas Association. Gas Engineers Handbook. Segeler, C. George, ed. (Illus.). 1965. 63.00 (ISBN 0-8311-3011-3). Indus Pr.

American Genealogical Research Institute Staff. How to Trace Your Family Tree. LC 73-88881. 200p. 1975. pap. 2.95 (ISBN 0-385-09885-5, Dolp). Doubleday.

American Geological Institute. Dictionary of Geological Terms. rev. ed. LC 73-9004. 600p. 1976. pap. 4.50 (ISBN 0-385-08452-8, Anch). Doubleday.

--Directory of Geoscience Departments: 1979-1980. 18th ed. 180p. (Orig.). 1979. pap. 12.00 (ISBN 0-913312-23-1). Am Geol.

--Directory of the Geologic Division, U. S. Geological Survey. (Illus.). 144p. 1980. pap. 6.00 (ISBN 0-913312-45-2). Am Geol.

--Geokhimiya Translations Nineteen Sixty-Nine: A Supplement to Geochemistry International, Vol. 6. LC 74-645947. 706p. (Orig., Rus.). 1980. pap. 35.00 (ISBN 0-913312-39-8). Am Geol.

American Girl Magazine Staff. American Girl Book of Horse Stories. (Illus.). (gr. 5-9). 1963. PLB 5.99 (ISBN 0-394-90899-6, BYR). Random.

--American Girl Book of Teen-Age Questions. (Illus.). (gr. 5-9). 1963. PLB 3.99 o.p. (ISBN 0-394-91807-X, BYR). Random.

--American Girl Cookbook. (Illus.). (gr. 5-9). 1966. PLB 5.99 (ISBN 0-394-91548-8). Random.

American Heart Association. The Heart Book. (Illus.). 1980. 25.00 (ISBN 0-525-93056-6). Dutton.

American Heart Association, Scientific Sessions, 52nd. Abstracts. (AHA Monograph: No. 65). 1979. pap. 8.00 (ISBN 0-686-58031-1). Am Heart.

American Heritage. Great Historic Places. 1980. pap. 4.95 (ISBN 0-686-60940-9, 24710). S&S.

--Historical Houses of America. pap. 4.95 (ISBN 0-686-60941-7, 24711). S&S.

--Natural Wonders of America. pap. 4.95 (ISBN 0-686-60942-5, 24712). S&S.

American Heritage & McCully, Helen, eds. The American Heritage Cookbook. LC 80-12470. (Illus.). 272p. 1980. 14.50 (ISBN 0-8281-0403-4, Dist. by Scribner). Am Heritage.

American Heritage Editors. The American Heritage Pictorial History of the Presidents of the United States, 2 vols. Leish, Kenneth W., ed. LC 68-15858. (Illus.). 1968. 9.98 o.p. (ISBN 0-8281-0320-8, B102R1-16). Am Heritage.

--Great Historic Places: An American Heritage Guide. Da Costa, Beverly, ed. LC 73-8836. (Illus.). 320p. 1973. 6.95 (ISBN 0-686-65705-5, 23074, Pub. by Am Heritage). S&S.

--Great Historic Places: An American Heritage Guide. Da Costa, Beverley, ed. LC 73-8836. (Illus.). 320p. 1973. pap. 6.95 (ISBN 0-8281-0295-3, B033G). Am Heritage.

--Historic Houses of America Open to the Public: An American Heritage Guide. Da Costa, Beverly, ed. LC 79-149725. (Illus.). 320p. 1971. 6.95 (ISBN 0-686-65707-1, 22991, Pub. by Am Heritage). S&S.

--Natural Wonders of America: An American Heritage Guide. Da Costa, Beverly, ed. LC 72-80700. (Illus.). 320p. 1972. 6.95 (ISBN 0-686-65711-X, 13065). S&S.

--Natural Wonders of America: An American Heritage Guide. Da Costa, Beverley, ed. LC 72-80700. (Illus.). 320p. 1972. pap. 6.95 (ISBN 0-8281-0296-1, B034G). Am Heritage.

American Hospital Assn. Digest of Hospital Cost Containment Projects. 3rd ed. LC 79-27674. (Orig.). 1980. pap. 6.25 (ISBN 0-87258-299-X, 1020). Am Hospital.

American Hospital Association. Alcoholism - Whose Responsibility? Coordinator's Guide. 1972. loose-leaf bdg 18.50 o.p. (ISBN 0-87258-082-2, 1225). Am Hospital.

--American Hospital Association Guide to the Health Care Field. 510p. 1980. pap. 50.00 (ISBN 0-87258-280-9, 2480). Am Hospital.

--Appropriateness Review of Health Services: Manual for Lawyers, Planners & Hospitals. LC 80-23209. 128p. 1980. pap. 18.75 (ISBN 0-87258-336-8, 1527). Am Hospital.

--Auxiliary Gift & Coffee Shop Management. LC 76-26604. (Orig.). 1976. pap. 18.25 (ISBN 0-87258-155-1, 1122). Am Hospital.

--Auxiliary: New Concepts, New Directions. LC 74-22174. 244p. (Orig.). 1974. pap. 16.25 (ISBN 0-87258-160-8, 1075). Am Hospital.

--Capital Financing for Hospitals. LC 73-87100. (Financial Management Ser.). 60p. (Orig.). 1974. pap. 8.75 (ISBN 0-87258-139-X, 1175). Am Hospital.

--Comparative Statistics on Health Facilities & Population: Metropolitan & Nonmetropolitan Areas. LC 78-7259. (Illus.). 1978. pap. 8.25 o.p. (ISBN 0-87258-222-1, 1802). Am Hospital.

--Cost Finding & Rate Setting for Hospitals. (Financial Management Ser.). (Illus.). 112p. 1968. pap. 15.00 (ISBN 0-87258-036-9, 1365). Am Hospital.

--CT Scanners: A Technical Report. LC 77-509. 1977. pap. 12.00 o.p. (ISBN 0-87258-188-8, 1100). Am Hospital.

--Cumulative Index of Hospital Literature: 1965-1969. 864p. 1970. 62.50 (ISBN 0-87258-055-5, 1384). Am Hospital.

--Cumulative Index of Hospital Literature. Incl. 1955-1959. 460p. 1960. casebound 31.25 (ISBN 0-87258-329-5, 1381); 1950-1954. 540p. 1955. 31.25 (ISBN 0-87258-328-7, 1380). Am Hospital.

--Diet & Menu Guide for Hospitals. (Illus.). 64p. 1969. pap. 10.25 o.p. (ISBN 0-87258-046-6, 1411). Am Hospital.

--Directory of Multihospital Systems. LC 80-363. 80p. 1980. pap. 30.00 (ISBN 0-87258-285-X, 1209). Am Hospital.

--Directory of Shared Services Organizations for Health Care Institutions. LC 79-18493. 444p. 1979. pap. 40.00 (ISBN 0-87258-286-8, 1202). Am Hospital.

--Educational Programs in the Health Field. LC 79-24621, 48p. 1979. pap. 7.50 (ISBN 0-87258-283-3, 3502). Am Hospital.

--Fire Safety Training in Health Care Institutions. LC 75-20295. (Illus.). 60p. 1975. pap. 10.00 (ISBN 0-87258-163-2, 1595). Am Hospital.

--A Guide for Hospital Participation in an Emergency Medical Communications System. LC 73-86669. 52p. 1973. pap. 8.75 (ISBN 0-87258-132-2, 1685). Am Hospital.

--The Hospital Admitting Department. LC 76-54284. (Illus.). 100p. (Orig.). 1977. pap. 13.75 (ISBN 0-87258-200-0, 1855). Am Hospital.

--Hospital Computer Systems Planning: Preparation of Request for Proposal. LC 80-18002. 124p. 1980. 25.00 (1445). Am Hospital.

--Hospital Cost Containment Through Operations Management, 2 pts. (Illus.). 1980. Instructor's Manual. loose-leaf 37.50 (ISBN 0-87258-304-X, 2435, 206 PAGES); Participant's Manual. loose-leaf 10.00 (ISBN 0-87258-305-8, 2436, 2434, 264 PAGES). Am Hospital.

--Hospital Design Checklist. 48p. 1965. 8.75 (ISBN 0-87258-016-4, 3310). Am Hospital.

--Hospital Housekeeping Handbook. 2nd ed. Orig. Title: Housekeeping Manual for Health Care. (Illus.). 1979. 18.75 (ISBN 0-87258-273-6, 2086). Am Hospital.

--Hospital Literature Index: 1978, Vol. 34. 350p. 75.00 (ISBN 0-87258-347-3, 1389). Am Hospital.

--Hospital Literature Index: 1979, Vol. 35. 736p. 1980. 75.00 (ISBN 0-87258-306-6, 1388). Am Hospital.

--Hospital Medical Records: Guidelines for Their Use & the Release of Medical Information. LC 70-188799. 70p. 1972. pap. 7.50 (ISBN 0-87258-087-3, 1250). Am Hospital.

--Hospital Statistics: Data from the American Hospital Association 1979 Annual Survey. 256p. 1980. pap. 18.75 (ISBN 0-87258-282-5, 2452). Am Hospital.

--The Hospital Trustee Reader: Selections from Trustee Magazine. LC 75-19443. 216p. 1975. pap. 13.75 (ISBN 0-87258-169-1, 1915). Am Hospital.

--Implementing Patient Education in the Hospital. LC 79-4292. (Illus.). 316p. 1979. pap. 34.25 (ISBN 0-87258-274-4, 1488). Am Hospital.

--Improving Work Methods in Small Hospitals. LC 75-32509. (Illus.). 88p. 1975. pap. 12.50 (ISBN 0-87258-165-9, 1910). Am Hospital.

--Interpreters' Services & the Role of Health Care Volunteers. LC 74-77268. (Illus.). 74p. (Orig.). 1974. pap. 6.25 (ISBN 0-87258-149-7, 2880). Am Hospital.

--Managerial Cost Accounting for Hospitals. LC 79-29708. (Financial Management Ser.). (Illus.). 144p. 1980. manual 20.00 (ISBN 0-87258-296-5, 1333). Am Hospital.

--Manual on Hospital Chaplaincy. 96p. 1970. pap. 8.75 (ISBN 0-87258-060-1, 1515). Am Hospital.
--Media Handbook: A Guide to Selecting, Producing & Using Media for Patient Education Programs. LC 78-13341. (Illus.). 136p. (Orig.). 1978. pap. 17.50 (ISBN 0-87258-230-2, 1258). Am Hospital.
--Medical Record Departments in Hospitals: Guide to Organization. 100p. 1972. pap. 10.00 (ISBN 0-87258-089-X, 2345). Am Hospital.
--Medical Staff Cost Containment: Digest of Hospital Projects & Selected Bibliography. 72p. 1980. pap. 8.75 (ISBN 0-87258-314-7, 1538). Am Hospital.
--Organizing a Cost Containment Committee in the Hospital. LC 76-26173. 104p. 1979. 15.00 (ISBN 0-87258-272-8, 1450). Am Hospital.
--Practical Approaches to Effective Functioning of the Department of Nursing Service: A Guide for Administrators of Nursing Service. (Illus.). 96p. 1972. loose-leaf bdg. 12.50 o.p. (ISBN 0-87258-076-8, 1375). Am Hospital.
--Readings in Hospital Risk Management. 64p. 1979. pap. 7.50 (ISBN 0-87258-284-1, 1360). Am Hospital.
--Readings in Materials Management. LC 73-87664. (Illus.). 100p. 1973. pap. 12.50 o.p. (ISBN 0-87258-136-5, 2510). Am Hospital.
--Reshaping Ambulatory Care Programs: Report & Recommendations of a Conference on Ambulatory Care. LC 73-86670. (Illus.). 68p. 1973. pap. 8.75 o.p. (ISBN 0-87258-133-0, 3615). Am Hospital.
--Selected Community Hospital Indicators: 1977 Data. LC 79-665. (Illus.). 1979. pap. 7.50 o.p. (ISBN 0-87258-275-2, 1893). Am Hospital.
--Selected Community Hospital Indicators: 1976 Data. LC 78-22110. (Illus.). 1978. pap. 6.25 o.p. (ISBN 0-87258-232-9, 1892). Am Hospital.
--Staff Manual for Teaching Patients About Chronic Obstructive Pulmonary Diseases. LC 78-27387. (Illus.). 424p. 1979. pap. 39.75 (ISBN 0-87258-249-3, 1317). Am Hospital.
--Technology Evaluation & Acquisition Methods (TEAM) for Hospitals. LC 79-21859. (Illus.). 212p. 1979. 200.00 (ISBN 0-87258-293-0, 1288). Am Hospital.
--Who Cares About an Alcoholism Program in the General Hospital? 56p. 1972. pap. 6.25 (ISBN 0-87258-088-1, 1245). Am Hospital.
--Winds of Change: Report of a Conference on Activity Programs in Long-Term Care Institutions. 48p. 1971. pap. 5.00 o.p. (ISBN 0-87258-081-4, 1890). Am Hospital.
American Hospital Association, et al. Sharing Responsibility for Patient Safety. 1979. 5.75 (ISBN 0-87258-248-5, 1152). Am Hospital.
American Hospital Association. American Society for Hospital Engineering. Medical Equipment Management in Hospitals. LC 78-1041. (Illus.). 528p. (Orig.). 1978. pap. 45.00 (ISBN 0-87258-241-8, 1272). Am Hospital.
American Hospital Association of the Hospital Management Systems Society. Selection & Employment of Management Consultants for Health Care. LC 78-4971. (Illus.). 64p. 1978. pap. 12.00 (ISBN 0-87258-233-7, 1062). Am Hospital.
American Hospital of Paris. Le Cookbook: Favorite Recipes of French & American Residents of Paris. 1976. pap. 7.50 o.p. (ISBN 0-8415-0412-1). Dutton.
American Indian Publishers, ed. Dictionary of Indian Tribes of the Americas, 4 vols. (Illus.). 1980. Set. lib. bdg. 225.00 (ISBN 0-937862-25-8). Am Hist Pubs.
American Institute of Architects. Glossary of Construction Industry Terms. pap. 1.50 (ISBN 0-913962-18-X). Am Inst Arch.
--New Towns in America: The Design & Development Process. LC 73-77292. 1973. 35.95 (ISBN 0-471-00975-X, Pub. by Wiley-Interscience). Wiley.
American Institute Of Certified Public Accountants. Management Services Technical Studies, 9 vols. Set. post binder 47.50 o.p. (ISBN 0-685-05615-5). Am Inst CPA.
American Institute of Graphic Arts. Symbol Signs. (Visual Communication Bks). (Illus.). 192p. (Orig.). 1981. pap. 12.95 (ISBN 0-8038-6777-8). Hastings.
American Institute of Physics. The Torque Wrench. (Physics of Technology Project Ser.). (Illus.). 40p. 1975. pap. text ed. 4.00 o.p. (ISBN 0-07-001725-5, G). McGraw.
American Institute of Real Estate Appraisers. The Appraisal of Real Estate. 7th ed. 1978. 22.50 (ISBN 0-911780-46-7). Am Inst Real Estate Appraisers.
American Institute of Real Estate Appraisers, ed. Condemnation Appraisal Practice, Vol. 2. 1973. 15.00 (ISBN 0-911780-32-7). Am Inst Real Estate Appraisers.
American Institute of Real Estate Appraisers. Study Guide Course 1-B: Capitalization Theory & Techniques. 1973. pap. 6.00 o.p. (ISBN 0-911780-34-3). Am Inst Real Estate Appraisers.
American Jewish Committee. The Jews in Nazi Germany. 1979. Repr. of 1935 ed. 11.50 (ISBN 0-86527-110-0). Fertig.
American Library Association Reference & Adult Services Division. Reference Books for Small & Medium-Sized Libraries. 3rd ed. LC 79-13004. 1979. pap. 9.00 (ISBN 0-8389-3227-4). ALA.
American Library Association - Young Adult Services Division. Doors to More Mature Reading: Detailed Notes on Adult Books for Use with Young People. LC 64-8298. 1964. pap. 5.00 o.p. (ISBN 0-8389-3029-8). ALA.
American Machines & Foundry Co. Silencers: Patterns & Principles, Vol. 2. (Illus.). 202p. 1972. pap. 9.95 (ISBN 0-87364-018-7). Paladin Ent.
American Map Co. Inc. Business Control Atlas of the United States & Canada: 1979 Edition. (Series 6500). 1979. plastic spiral bdg. 9.85 (ISBN 0-8416-9556-3). Am Map.
--General World Atlas, No. 9550. rev. ed. 1979. 0.95 (ISBN 0-8416-9550-4). Am Map.
American Map Company. Atlas Mundial, No. 9555. rev. ed. (Illus.). (gr. 7-12). 1979. pap. 1.10 (ISBN 0-8416-9555-5). Am Map.
--Executive Sales Control Atlas. rev. ed. 1979. 77.90 (ISBN 0-8416-9557-1). Am Map.
--Master Sales Control Atlas. rev. ed. 1979. 251.85 (ISBN 0-8416-9560-1). Am Map.
--Students Indexed World Atlas, No. 9551. (Illus.). (gr. 7-12). 1979. pap. 1.10 (ISBN 0-8416-9551-2). Am Map.
American Mathematical Society. Mathematical Reviews Cumulative Author Indexes. Incl. Twenty Volume Author Index of Mathematical Reviews, 1940-59, 2 pts. 1977. 140.00 set (ISBN 0-685-22496-1, MREVIN 40-59); Author Index of Mathematical Reviews, 1960-64, 2 pts. 1966. 90.00 set (ISBN 0-8218-0026-4, MREVIN 60-64); Author Index of Mathematical Reviews, 1965-72. 1974. 200.00 (ISBN 0-8218-0027-2, MREVIN 65-72). Repr. Am Math.
--Space Mathematics, 3 vols. Rosser, J. B., ed. Incl. Pt.1. (Vol. 5). 1979. 28.40 (ISBN 0-8218-1105-3, LAM-5); Pt. 2. (Vol. 6). 1974. Repr. of 1966 ed. 18.00 (ISBN 0-8218-1106-1, LAM-6); Pt. 3. (Vol. 7). 1966. 18.80 (ISBN 0-8218-1107-X, LAM-7). LC 66-20435. (Lectures in Applied Mathematics Ser). Am Math.
American Medical Association. The AMA Handbook of First Aid & Emergency Care. (Illus.). 256p. 1980. 5.95 (ISBN 0-394-73668-0). Random.
--American Medical Directory, 5 vols. LC 7-10295. (Vol. 5 is the Directory of Women Physicians). 1979. Set. 225.00 (ISBN 0-88416-274-5). Vol. 1 (ISBN 0-88416-275-3). Vol. 2 (ISBN 0-88416-276-1). Vol. 3 (ISBN 0-88416-277-X). Vol. 4 (ISBN 0-88416-278-8). Vol. 5 (ISBN 0-88416-279-6). PSG Pub.
American Medical Record Association. Glossary of Hospital Terms. 2nd rev. ed. 128p. 1974. 5.75 (ISBN 0-686-68577-6, 14911). Hospital Finan.
American Microscopical Society Symposium, 1980. Artificial Substrates: Proceedings. Cairns, John, Jr., ed. 1981. text ed. price not set. Ann Arbor Science.
American National Red Cross. Advanced First Aid & Emergency Care. 2nd ed. LC 79-53479. (American Red Cross Bks.). (Illus.). 1980. pap. 3.00 (ISBN 0-385-15737-1). Doubleday.
--Basic First Aid, 4 vols. (Illus.). Set. pap. 5.25 slipcased (ISBN 0-385-17211-7). Doubleday.
--Standard First Aid & Personal Safety. 2nd ed. LC 79-53478. (American Red Cross Bks.). 1979. pap. 2.50 (ISBN 0-385-15736-3). Doubleday.
American National Standards Institute, Standards Committee Z39 on Library Work, Documentation & Related Publishing Practices. American National Standard Compiling U. S. Microform Publishing Statistics. 1979. 3.50 (ISBN 0-686-28241-8, Z39.40). ANSI.
American Neurological Association. Transactions of the ANA, Vol. 105, 1980. 1981. text ed. price not set. Springer Pub.
American Peptide Symposium, Fifth see Goodman, Murray & Meienhofer, Johannes.
American Personnel & Guidance Assn. How to Visit Colleges. rev ed. 1972. pap. text ed. 3.75 pkg. of 5 o.p. (ISBN 0-686-04989-6). Am Personnel.
American Petroleum Institute. Manual of Petroleum Measurement Standards. LC 80-67080. (Chapter 11.1 -- Volume Correction Factors: Vol. VI). (Illus.). 563p. 1980. write for info. (ISBN 0-89364-027-1). Am Petroleum.
American Petroleum Institute. Manual of Petroleum Measurement Standards. LC 80-67080. (Chapter 11.1 -- Volume Correction Factors Ser.: Vol. I). (Illus.). 678p. 1980. write for info. (ISBN 0-89364-022-0). Am Petroleum.
--Manual of Petroleum Measurement Standards. LC 80-67080. (Chapter 11.1 -- Volume Correction Factors: Vol. II). (Illus.). 592p. 1980. write for info. (ISBN 0-89364-023-9). Am Petroleum.
--Manual of Petroleum Measurement Standards. LC 80-67080. (Chapter 11.1 -- Volume Correction Factors: Vol. III). (Illus.). 563p. 1980. write for info. (ISBN 0-89364-024-7). Am Petroleum.
--Manual of Petroleum Measurement Standards. LC 80-67080. (Chapter 11.1 -- Volume Correction Factors: Vol. IV). (Illus.). 878p. 1980. write for info. (ISBN 0-89364-025-5). Am Petroleum.
--Manual of Petroleum Measurement Standard. LC 80-67080. (Chapter 11.1 --Volume Corrections Factors: Vol. V). (Illus.). 812p. 1980. write for info. (ISBN 0-89364-026-3). Am Petroleum.
--Manual of Petroleum Measurement Standards. (Chapter 11.1 -- Volume Corrections Factors: Vol. VIII). (Illus.). 881p. 1980. write for info. (ISBN 0-89364-030-1). Am Petroleum.
--Manual of Petroleum Measurement Standards. LC 80-67080. (Chapter 11.1 -- Volume Correction Factors: Vol. IX). (Illus.). 587p. 1980. write for info. (ISBN 0-89364-032-8). Am Petroleum.
--Manual of Petroleum Measurement Standard. LC 80-67080. (Chapter 11.1 -- Volume Correction Factors: Vol. X). (Illus.). 420p. 1980. write for info. (ISBN 0-89364-033-6). Am Petroleum.
--Manual of Petroleum Measurement Standards. (Chapter 11.1 -- Vol. Correction Factors). (Illus.). 1980. write for info. (ISBN 0-89364-021-2). Am Petroleum.
--Manual of Petroleum Measurement Standards. LC 80-67080. (Chapter 11.1 -- Volume Correction Factors). 1980. write for info. (ISBN 0-89364-035-2). Am Petroleum.
--Manual of Petroleum Measurements Standards. LC 80-67080. (Chapter 11.1 -- Volume Correction Factors: Vol. VII). (Illus.). 958p. 1980. write for info. (ISBN 0-89364-029-8). Am Petroleum.
--Two Energy Futures: A National Choice for the 80's. LC 80-24004. (Illus.). 166p. (Orig.). 1980. pap. text ed. write for info. (ISBN 0-89364-037-9). Am Petroleum.
American Philosophical Society. Year Book. LC 39-2034. pap. 1.50 ea. 1937-1967 (ISBN 0-87169-991-5); pap. 3.00 ea. 1968-1970; pap. 5.00 ea. 1971-1978. Am Philos.
American Photographic Book Publishing Co. & Eastman Kodak Co. Encyclopedia of Practical Photography, 14 vols. 1978. Set. lib. bdg. 223.30 (ISBN 0-8174-3200-0); Set. 159.95 (ISBN 0-8174-3050-4). Amphoto.
American Physiological Society. Disturbances in Lipid & Lipoprotein Metabolism. Dietschy, John M., ed. (American Physiological Society Monograph Ser.). 1978. 25.00 (ISBN 0-683-02557-0). Williams & Wilkins.
--Handbook of Physiology, Section 3: Respiration, 2 Vols. Fenn, Wallace O. & Rahn, Hermann, eds. 1964-65. Vol. 1. 32.00 (ISBN 0-683-03148-1); Vol. 2. 32.00 (ISBN 0-683-03149-X). Williams & Wilkins.
--Handbook of Physiology, Section 5: Adipose Tissue. Renold, Albert E. & Cahill, George F., Jr., eds. 1965. 28.00 (ISBN 0-683-07232-3). Williams & Wilkins.
American Physiological Society, et al. Secretory Diarrhea. (American Physiological Society Clinical Physiology Ser.). (Illus.). 700p. 1980. lib. bdg. 30.00 (ISBN 0-683-03201-1). Williams & Wilkins.
--The Cardiovascular System, Vol. 2: Vascular Smooth Muscle. (APS Handbk. of Physiology: Section 2). (Illus.). 700p. 1980. lib. bdg. 95.00 (ISBN 0-683-00606-1). Williams & Wilkins.
American Phytopathological Society - Sourcebook Committee. Sourcebook of Laboratory Exercises in Plant Pathology. Kelman, Arthur, ed. (Illus.). 1967. 17.95x (ISBN 0-7167-0813-2). W H Freeman.
American Plant Studies Delegation, National Academy of Science. Plant Studies in the People's Republic of China: A Trip Report of the American Plant Studies Delegation. LC 75-13564. (Illus.). 1975. pap. 9.75 o.p. (ISBN 0-309-02348-3). Natl Acad Pr.
American Plywood Association. The Plywood Planbook. (Illus.). 1980. pap. 5.95 (ISBN 0-89586-034-1). H P Bks.
American Presbyterian Mission. The Isle of Palms: Sketches of Hainan. LC 78-74354. (The Modern Chinese Economy Ser.: Vol. 21). 141p. 1980. lib. bdg. 16.50 (ISBN 0-8240-4269-7). Garland Pub.
American Psychiatric Assn., ed. A Psychiatric Glossary. 5th ed. 1980. text ed. 9.95 (ISBN 0-316-03656-0). Little.
American Psychiatric Association. Behavior Therapy in Psychiatry. LC 74-3227. 182p. 1974. Repr. 17.50x (ISBN 0-87668-139-9). Aronson.
--Electroconvulsive Therapy. LC 78-69521. (Task Force Report: No. 14). 200p. 1978. pap. 10.00 (ISBN 0-685-94003-9, P228-0). Am Psychiatric.
American Psychiatric Association. Annual Meeting, 131st, Atlanta, Ga., May 1978. The Continuing Medical Education Syllabus & Scientific Proceedings in Summary Form. (Scientific Proceedings of the APA). 1978. pap. 10.00 o.p. (ISBN 0-685-94002-0, 153-8). Am Psychiatric.
American Psychiatric Association Annual Meeting, 132nd. Continuing Medical Education Syllabus & Scientific Proceedings in Summary Form. new ed. (Scientific Proceedings of the APA Ser.). 1979. pap. text ed. 10.00x o.p. (ISBN 0-685-96759-X, 153-9). Am Psychiatric.
American Psychiatric Association, Committee on Nomenclature & Statistics. Diagnostic & Statistical Manual of Mental Disorders. 2nd ed. 1968. pap. 3.50 o.p. (ISBN 0-685-24852-6, 145). Am Psychiatric.
American Psychiatric Association, Committee on the History of Psychiatry. New Directions in American Psychiatry, 1944-1968. lib. bdg. 5.00 o.p. (ISBN 0-685-24847-X, 230); pap. 3.00 o.p. (ISBN 0-685-24848-8). Am Psychiatric.
American Psychiatric Association Task Force. Professional Liability Insurance & Psychiatric Malpractice. LC 77-94900. (Task Force Report: No. 13). 1978. pap. 6.00 o.p. (ISBN 0-685-55998-X). Am Psychiatric.
American Psychiatric Association's Ad Hoc Committee on Professional Standards Review Organization, ed. Model Criteria Sets for Professional Standards Review Organization. 1974. 2.50 o.p. (ISBN 0-685-77443-0, 189). Am Psychiatric.
American Psychiatric Association's Task Force on Psychohistory, ed. The Psychiatrist As Psychohistorian. (Task Force Reports: No. 11). 33p. 1976. 5.00 (ISBN 0-685-76790-6, P221-0). Am Psychiatric.
American Psychiatric Association's Task Force on Religion & Psychiatry, ed. Psychiatrists' Viewpoints on & Their Services to Religious Institutions & the Ministry. (Task Force Reports: No. 10). 49p. 1975. 5.00 (ISBN 0-685-77445-7, P220-0). Am Psychiatric.
American Psychological Association. Changing Attitudes: Student Booklet. (Human Behavior Curriculum Project Ser.). 64p. (Orig.). (gr. 9-12). 1981. pap. text ed. 3.95 (ISBN 0-8077-2621-4). Tchrs Coll.
--Changing Attitudes: Teachers Handbook & Duplication Masters. (Human Behavior Curriculum Project Ser.). 48p. (Orig.). (gr. 9-12). 1981. 9.95 (ISBN 0-8077-2622-2). Tchrs Coll.
--Conditioning & Learning: Student Booklet. (Human Behavior Curriculum Project Ser.). 64p. (gr. 9-12). 1981. pap. text ed. 3.95 (ISBN 0-8077-2623-0). Tchrs Coll.
--Conditioning & Learning: Teachers Handbook & Duplication Masters. (Human Behavior Curriculum Project Ser.). 48p. (gr. 9-12). 1981. 9.95 (ISBN 0-8077-2624-9). Tchrs Coll.
--Ethical Principles in the Conduct of Research with Human Participants. 1973. pap. 4.50 (ISBN 0-685-56746-X). Am Psychol.
--Language & Communication: Student Booklet. (Human Behavior Curriculum Peoject Ser.). 64p. (Orig.). (gr. 9-12). 1981. pap. text ed. 3.95 (ISBN 0-8077-2625-7). Tchrs Coll.
--Language & Communication: Teachers Handbook & Duplication Masters. (Human Behavir Curriculum Project Ser.). 48p. (Orig.). (gr. 9-12). 1981. pap. 9.95 (ISBN 0-8077-2626-5). Tchrs Coll.
--Natural Behavior in Humans & Animals. (Human Behavior Curriculum Project Ser.). 64p. (Orig.). 1981. pap. text ed. 3.95x (ISBN 0-8077-2613-3); tchrs. manual & duplication masters 9.95 (ISBN 0-8077-2614-1). Tchrs Coll.
--School Life & Organizational Psychology. (Human Behavior Curriculum Project Ser.). 64p. (Orig.). 1981. pap. text ed. 3.95x (ISBN 0-8077-2617-6). Tchrs Coll.
--Social Influences on Behavior: Student Booklet. (Human Behavior Curriculum Project Ser.). 64p. (Orig.). (gr. 9-12). 1981. pap. text ed. 3.95x (ISBN 0-8077-2619-2). Tchrs Coll.
--Standards for Educational & Psychological Tests. LC 74-75734. 1974. pap. 4.00 (ISBN 0-685-56745-1). Am Psychol.
American Psychological Association, et al. States of Consciousness. (Human Behavior Curriculum Project Ser.). 64p. 1981. pap. text ed. 3.95x (ISBN 0-8077-2615-X); tchrs. manual & dup 9.95, ication masters (ISBN 0-8077-2616-8). Tchrs Coll.
American Psychological Association. Studying Personality: Student Booklet. (Human Behavior Curriculum Project Ser.). 64p. (Orig.). (gr. 9-12). 1981. pap. text ed. 3.95x (ISBN 0-8077-2627-3). Tchrs Coll.

--Studying Personality: Teachers Manual & Duplication Masters. (Human Behavior Curriculum Project Ser.). 48p. (Orig.). (gr. 9-12). 1981. pap. 9.95x (ISBN 0-8077-2628-1). Tchrs Coll.

American Psychological Association, Division 27. Issues in Community Psychology & Preventive Mental Health. LC 75-140047. 161p. (Orig.). 1971. 14.95 (ISBN 0-87705-022-8); pap. 7.95 (ISBN 0-87705-027-9). Human Sci Pr.

American Radio Relay League. Radio Amateur's Handbook: 1979 Edition. LC 41-3345. 1978. 9.75 o.p. (ISBN 0-87259-156-5); pap. write for info. o.p. (ISBN 0-87259-056-9). Am Radio.

--The Radio Amateur's V. H. F. Manual. LC 65-22343. 4.00 o.p. (ISBN 0-87259-553-6). Am Radio.

American Red Cross Seventh Annual Scientific Symposium, Washington, D.C., May 1975. Trace Components of Plasma: Isolation & Clinical Significance, Proceedings. Jamieson, G. A. & Greenwalt, Tibor J., eds. LC 75-38563. (Progress in Clinical & Biological Research: Vol. 5). 440p. 1976. 43.00 (ISBN 0-8451-0005-X). A R Liss.

American Scandinavian Foundation. Index Nordicus: A Cumulative Index to English-Language Periodicals on Scandinavian Studies. 1979. lib. bdg. 80.00 (ISBN 0-8161-0080-2). G K Hall.

American School of Classical Studies at Athens. Catalogue of the Gennadius Library: American School of Classical Studies at Athens. (Library Catalogs: Supplement 2). 1981. lib. bdg. 160.00 (ISBN 0-8161-0011-X). G K Hall.

American School of Needlework. The Great Afghan Book. Thomas, Mary, ed. (Illus.). 160p. 1981. 16.95 (ISBN 0-8069-5444-2, Columbia Hse). Sterling.

American Society for Hospital Engineering of the American Hospital Association. Controlling Waste Anesthetic Gases. (Illus.). 52p. 1980. 10.75 (ISBN 0-87258-308-2, 1222). Am Hospital.

American Society for Hospital Engineering. Hospital Engineering Handbook. 3rd ed. (Illus.). 348p. 1980. casebound 31.25 (ISBN 0-87258-311-2, 1820). Am Hospital.

--Mass Spectrometer Respiratory Monitoring Systems. LC 79-26957. (Illus., Orig.). 1980. pap. 9.75 (ISBN 0-87258-279-5, 1167). Am Hospital.

American Society for Hospital Engineering of the American Hospital Association. Multiphasic Health Testing. LC 79-11129. (Illus.). 1979. pap. 5.00 (ISBN 0-87258-269-8, 1103). Am Hospital.

American Society for Hospital Food Service Administrators. Hospital Food Service Management Review. LC 80-11834. 80p. (Orig.). 1980. 10.00 (ISBN 0-87258-323-6, 1410). Am Hospital.

American Society for Hospital Food Service Administrators of the American Hospital Association. Preparation of a Hospital Food Service Department Budget. LC 78-24399. 56p. 1978. pap. 9.50 (ISBN 0-87258-254-X, 1615). Am Hospital.

American Society for Training & Development. Training & Development Handbook. 1967. 25.00 o.p. (ISBN 0-07-001520-1, G). McGraw.

American Society of Anesthesiologists. ASA Refresher Courses in Anesthesiology. 170p. (Annual). 1975. Vol. 2 (1974) 8.00 (ISBN 0-685-59107-7); Vol. 3 (1975) 10.00 (ISBN 0-685-59108-5). Lippincott.

American Society of Anesthesiologists & American College of Anesthesiology. Regional Refresher Courses in Anesthesiology, Vol. 1. 1973. 10.00 (ISBN 0-685-34605-6). Lippincott.

American Society of Appraisers. Appraisal of Farmland: Use-Value Assessment Laws & Property Taxation, No. 8. new ed. LC 78-74140. (Monograph). 1979. pap. 5.00 (ISBN 0-937828-17-3). Am Soc Appraisers.

--The Bibliography of Appraisal Literature. LC 73-92529. 769p. 1974. 30.00 (ISBN 0-937828-18-1). Am Soc Appraisers.

American Society of Civil Engineers, jt. auth. see U. S. National Committee on Rock Mechanics, 15th, South Dakota School of Mines & Technology, Sept. 1973.

American Society of Civil Engineers, compiled By see ASCE Committee on Engineering Management, Aug. 1976.

American Society of Civil Engineers, compiled By see ASCE Conference, Alexandria, Mar. 1979.

American Society of Civil Engineers, compiled By see ASCE Conference, San Francisco, May 1978.

American Society of Civil Engineers, compiled By see ASCE Irrigation & Drainage Division, July 1976.

American Society of Civil Engineers, compiled By see ASCE Professional Activities Committee Conference, March 1977.

American Society of Civil Engineers, compiled By see ASCE Technical Council on Computer Practices, June 1978.

American Society of Civil Engineers, compiled By see ASCE Urban Transportation Division, May 1973.

American Society of Civil Engineers, compiled By see ASCE Urban Water Resources Research Council Conference, Nov. 1976.

American Society of Civil Engineers, compiled By see ASCE Waterway, Port Coastal & Ocean Division Conference, Charleston, Nov. 1977.

American Society of Civil Engineers, compiled By see Coastal Engineering International Conference, 11th, London, Sept. 1968.

American Society of Civil Engineers, compiled By see Coastal Engineering International Conference, 12th, September, 1970.

American Society of Civil Engineers, compiled By see Coastal Engineering International Conference, 16th, Hamburg, Germany, Aug. 1978.

American Society of Civil Engineers, compiled By see Engineering Foundation Conference, Aug. 1975.

American Society of Civil Engineers, compiled By see Engineering Foundation Conference, Jan. 1978.

American Society of Civil Engineers, compiled By see Engineering Foundation Conference, Mar. 1974.

American Society of Civil Engineers, compiled By see Engineering Foundation Conference, Nov. 1976.

American Society of Civil Engineers, ed. see Environmental Impact Analysis Research Council at the Chicago National Convention, Oct. 1978.

American Society of Civil Engineers, et al, eds. see Rock Mechanics International Society & the U. S. National Committee, 16th.

American Society of Civil Engineering, compiled by. Readings in Cost Engineering, Vol. 1. 732p. 1979. pap. text ed. 49.00 (ISBN 0-87262-147-2). Am Soc Civil Eng.

--Sedimentation Engineering. (Manual & Report on Engineering Practice Ser.: No. 54). 768p. 1975. text ed. 32.50 (ISBN 0-87262-001-8). Am Soc Civil Eng.

American Society of Civil Engineers, compiled By. Accommodation of Utility Plant Within the Rights of Way of Urban Streets & Highways. (ASCE Manual & Report on Engineering Practice Ser.: No. 14). 116p. 1974. pap. text ed. 18.00 (ISBN 0-87262-207-X). Am Soc Civil Eng.

American Society of Civil Engineers, et al, eds. Acid Rain. 76p. 1980. pap. text ed. 17.50 (ISBN 0-87262-202-9). Am Soc Civil Eng.

American Society of Civil Engineers, Conference, North Carolina State Univ., May 1977. Advances in Civil Engineering Through Engineering Mechanics: Proceedings. 640p. 1977. pap. text ed. 36.00 (ISBN 0-87262-087-5). Am Soc Civil Eng.

American Society of Civil Engineers, compiled By. Agricultural & Urban Considerations in Irrigation & Drainage. 808p. 1974. pap. text ed. 32.50 (ISBN 0-87262-067-0). Am Soc Civil Eng.

--Air Resource Management Primer. 280p. 1973. pap. text ed. 16.75 (ISBN 0-87262-055-7). Am Soc Civil Eng.

--Air Supported Structures. 104p. 1979. pap. text ed. 11.00 (ISBN 0-87262-196-0). Am Soc Civil Eng.

--American Wooden Bridges. 184p. 1976. pap. text ed. 24.75 (ISBN 0-87262-002-6). Am Soc Civil Eng.

--Analyses for Soil Structure Interaction: Effects for Nuclear Power Plants. 1979. pap. text ed. 13.50 (ISBN 0-87262-183-9). Am Soc Civil Eng.

--Analysis & Design in Geotechnical Engineering, 2 vols. 1975. Set. pap. text ed. 26.00 (ISBN 0-87262-121-9). Am Soc Civil Eng.

--Applied Techniques for Cold Environments, 2 vols. 1176p. 1978. pap. text ed. 64.00 (ISBN 0-87262-182-0). Am Soc Civil Eng.

--ASCE-ICE-CSCE: Joint Conference on Predicting & Designing for Natural & Man Made Hazards, 1978. 300p. 1979. pap. text ed. 30.00 (ISBN 0-87262-187-1). Am Soc Civil Eng.

--Assessment of Resources & Needs in Highway Technology Education. 232p. 1975. pap. text ed. 10.00 (ISBN 0-87262-117-0). Am Soc Civil Eng.

--Award Winning ASCE Papers in Geotechnical Engineering. 824p. 1977. pap. text ed. 32.00 (ISBN 0-87262-092-1). Am Soc Civil Eng.

--Bibliography of Bolted & Riveted Joints. (Manual & Report on Engineering Practice Ser.: No. 48). 200p. 1967. text ed. 14.75 (ISBN 0-87262-222-3). Am Soc Civil Eng.

--Bicycle-Pedestrian Planning & Design. 712p. 1974. pap. text ed. 22.50 (ISBN 0-87262-065-4). Am Soc Civil Eng.

--Bicycle Transportation: A Civil Engineer's Notebook. LC 80-70171. 189p. pap. text ed. 15.50 (ISBN 0-87262-260-6). Am Soc Civil Eng.

--A Biographical Dictionary of American Civil Engineers. 176p. 1972. pap. text ed. 13.75 (ISBN 0-87262-034-4). Am Soc Civil Eng.

American Society of Civil Engineers, et al, eds. City Planning Bibliography. 536p. 1972. pap. text ed. 16.75 (ISBN 0-87262-036-0). Am Soc Civil Eng.

American Society of Civil Engineers, compiled By. Civil Engineering Classics: Outstanding Papers of Thomas R. Camp. 418p. pap. text ed. 16.00 (ISBN 0-87262-053-0). Am Soc Civil Eng.

--Civil Engineering Education. 1024p. 1979. pap. text ed. 48.00 (ISBN 0-87262-195-2). Am Soc Civil Eng.

--Civil Engineering Education: Engineering Practice & Nations Needs, Vol. 3. 1975. pap. text ed. 48.00 (ISBN 0-87262-110-3). Am Soc Civil Eng.

--Civil Engineering in the Oceans III. 1560p. 1976. pap. text ed. 59.00 (ISBN 0-87262-162-6). Am Soc Civil Eng.

--Civil Engineering Software Center. 116p. 1973. pap. text ed. 16.50 (ISBN 0-87262-052-2). Am Soc Civil Eng.

--Clean Water for Our Future Environment. 384p. 1971. pap. text ed. 14.50 (ISBN 0-87262-030-1). Am Soc Civil Eng.

--Combined Sewer Seperation Using Pressure Sewers. 212p. 1969. pap. text ed. 12.00 (ISBN 0-87262-017-4). Am Soc Civil Eng.

--Composite or Mixed Steel: Concrete Construction for Buildings. 160p. 1977. pap. text ed. 11.50 (ISBN 0-87262-079-4). Am Soc Civil Eng.

--Conservation & Utilization of Water & Energy Resources. 544p. 1979. pap. text ed. 34.75 (ISBN 0-87262-189-8). Am Soc Civil Eng.

--Construction Cost Control. 108p. 1979. pap. text ed. 10.00 (ISBN 0-87262-003-4). Am Soc Civil Eng.

--Consulting Engineering: A Guide to the Engagement of Engineering Services. (Manual & Report on Engineering Practice Ser.: No. 45). 96p. 1972. pap. text ed. 3.00 (ISBN 0-87262-220-7). Am Soc Civil Eng.

--Consumptive Use of Water. 232p. 1974. pap. text ed. 10.75 (ISBN 0-87262-068-9). Am Soc Civil Eng.

--Contribution of Irrigation & Drainage to World Food Supply. 432p. 1975. pap. text ed. 22.00 (ISBN 0-87262-114-6). Am Soc Civil Eng.

--Current Geotechnical Practice in Mine Waste Disposal. 272p. 1979. pap. text ed. 19.25 (ISBN 0-87262-141-3). Am Soc Civil Eng.

--Current Research on Tall Buildings. 144p. 1972. pap. text ed. 5.50 (ISBN 0-87262-039-5). Am Soc Civil Eng.

--Design & Construction of Sanitary & Storm Sewers. 352p. 1969. text ed. 17.00 (ISBN 0-87262-214-2). Am Soc Civil Eng.

--Design & Construction of Steel Chimney Liners. 232p. pap. text ed. 9.00 (ISBN 0-87262-111-1). Am Soc Civil Eng.

--A Design Guide & Commentary on Wood Structures. 432p. 1975. pap. text ed. 16.00 (ISBN 0-87262-109-X). Am Soc Civil Eng.

--Design of Cylindrical Concrete Shell Roofs. (Manual & Report on Engineering Practice Ser.: No. 31). 192p. 1953. pap. 6.75 (ISBN 0-87262-209-6). Am Soc Civil Eng.

--Design of Foundations to Control Settlements. 602p. 1966. pap. text ed. 29.50 (ISBN 0-87262-007-7). Am Soc Civil Eng.

--Dredging & Its Environmental Effects. 1048p. 1976. pap. text ed. 30.00 (ISBN 0-87262-165-0). Am Soc Civil Eng.

--Dynamic Planning for Environmental Quality in the Eighties. 288p. 1978. pap. text ed. 19.75 (ISBN 0-87262-098-0). Am Soc Civil Eng.

--Economical Construction of Concrete Dams. 568p. 1973. pap. text ed. 19.75 (ISBN 0-87262-043-3). Am Soc Civil Eng.

American Society of Civil Engineers & Steyert, Richard D., eds. The Economics of High-Rise Apartment Buildings of Alternate Design Configuration. 192p. 1972. pap. text ed. 6.00 (ISBN 0-87262-038-7). Am Soc Civil Eng.

American Society of Civil Engineers, compiled By. Effective Project Management Techniques. 84p. 1973. pap. 5.00 (ISBN 0-87262-058-1). Am Soc Civil Eng.

--Electric Power & the Civil Engineer: Proceedings. 688p. 1974. pap. text ed. 39.50 (ISBN 0-87262-070-0). Am Soc Civil Eng.

--Electric Power Today. 80p. 1979. pap. text ed. 6.75 (ISBN 0-87262-180-4). Am Soc Civil Eng.

--Engineering & Contracting Procedure for Foundations. (Manual & Report on Engineering Practice Ser.: No. 8). 1953. pap. text ed. 3.00 (ISBN 0-87262-204-5). Am Soc Civil Eng.

--Engineering Ethics: Proceedings. 120p. 1977. pap. text ed. 7.00 (ISBN 0-87262-173-1). Am Soc Civil Eng.

--Engineering Mechanics Specialty Conference, 3rd. 952p. 1979. pap. text ed. 55.00 (ISBN 0-87262-192-8). Am Soc Civil Eng.

--Environmental Impacts of International Civil Engineering Projects & Practices: Proceedings. 272p. pap. text ed. 18.00 (ISBN 0-87262-129-4). Am Soc Civil Eng.

--Fatigue Life of Prestressed Concrete Beams: Reinforced Concrete Research Council, No. 19. 96p. 1977. pap. text ed. 7.00 (ISBN 0-87262-094-8). Am Soc Civil Eng.

--Field Test Sections Save Cost in Tunnel Support. 64p. 1975. pap. text ed. 9.75 o.p. (ISBN 0-87262-161-8). Am Soc Civil Eng.

--Financing & Charges for Wastewater Systems. 72p. 1973. pap. text ed. 4.00 (ISBN 0-87262-057-3). Am Soc Civil Eng.

--Ground Water Management. (Manual & Report on Engineering Practice: No. 40). 1972. pap. text ed. 13.75 (ISBN 0-87262-216-9). Am Soc Civil Eng.

--Guide for Field Testing of Bridges. LC 80-69154. 72p. 1980. pap. text ed. 12.00 (ISBN 0-87262-255-X). Am Soc Civil Eng.

--Guide for the Design of Steel Transmission Towers. (Manual & Report on Engineering Practice Ser.: No. 52). 1971. pap. text ed. 5.00 (ISBN 0-87262-226-6). Am Soc Civil Eng.

--Guide to Investigation of Structural Failures. 88p. 1979. pap. text ed. 6.50 (ISBN 0-87262-184-7). Am Soc Civil Eng.

--Hydraulic Engineering & the Environment. 480p. 1973. pap. text ed. 12.50 (ISBN 0-87262-054-9). Am Soc Civil Eng.

--Hydraulics in the Coastal Zone. 376p. 1977. pap. text ed. 19.75 (ISBN 0-87262-085-9). Am Soc Civil Eng.

--Implementing Highway Safety Improvements. LC 79-93190. 320p. 1980. pap. text ed. 22.50 (ISBN 0-87262-009-3). Am Soc Civil Eng.

--In Situ Measurement of Soil Properties. 1975. pap. text ed. 28.00 (ISBN 0-87262-156-1). Am Soc Civil Eng.

--Inspection, Maintenance & Rehabilitation of Old Dams. 960p. 1974. pap. text ed. 34.00 (ISBN 0-87262-061-1). Am Soc Civil Eng.

--Interdisciplinary Analysis of Water Resource Systems. 416p. 1975. pap. text ed. 21.00 (ISBN 0-87262-115-4). Am Soc Civil Eng.

--International Air Transport Conference. 424p. 1977. pap. text ed. 28.00 (ISBN 0-87262-093-X). Am Soc Civil Eng.

--International Seminar on Probabilistic & Extreme Load Design of Nuclear Plant Facilities. 464p. 1979. pap. text ed. 27.00 (ISBN 0-87262-146-4). Am Soc Civil Eng.

--International Symposium on Stratified Flow. 760p. 1973. pap. text ed. 32.50 (ISBN 0-87262-059-X). Am Soc Civil Eng.

--Irrigation & Drainage in an Age of Competition for Resources. 560p. 1975. pap. text ed. 19.00 (ISBN 0-87262-123-5). Am Soc Civil Eng.

--Irrigation & Drainage in the Nineteen Eighties. 448p. 1979. pap. text ed. 27.00 (ISBN 0-87262-181-2). Am Soc Civil Eng.

--Is Water Quality Enhancement Feasible. 144p. 1970. pap. text ed. 11.75 (ISBN 0-87262-025-5). Am Soc Civil Eng.

--Land Application of Residual Materials. 192p. 1977. pap. text ed. 10.00 (ISBN 0-87262-081-6). Am Soc Civil Eng.

--Lateral Stresses in the Ground & Design of Earth Retaining Structures. 336p. 1970. pap. text ed. 8.50 (ISBN 0-87262-023-9). Am Soc Civil Eng.

--Lessons from Dam Incidents. 392p. 1975. pap. text ed. 18.00 (ISBN 0-87262-104-9). Am Soc Civil Eng.

--Lifeline Earthquake Engineering. 496p. 1977. pap. text ed. 23.00 (ISBN 0-87262-086-7). Am Soc Civil Eng.

--A List of Translations of Foreign Literature on Hydraulics. (ASCE Manual & Report on Energy Practice Ser.: No. 35). 144p. 1968. pap. text ed. 6.00 (ISBN 0-87262-212-6). Am Soc Civil Eng.

--Man-Transportation Interface. 384p. 1972. pap. text ed. 12.50 (ISBN 0-87262-041-7). Am Soc Civil Eng.

--Management of Engineering of Control Systems for Water Pipelines. 208p. 1978. pap. text ed. 16.25 (ISBN 0-87262-132-4). Am Soc Civil Eng.

--Mathematical Model of Aggregate Plant Production. 120p. 1974. pap. text ed. 6.50 (ISBN 0-87262-071-9). Am Soc Civil Eng.

--Metal Bridges. 448p. 1974. pap. text ed. 49.00 (ISBN 0-87262-101-4). Am Soc Civil Eng.

--Methods of Structural Analysis. 1120p. 1976. pap. text ed. 39.50 (ISBN 0-87262-163-4). Am Soc Civil Eng.

--Modeling Seventy-Five. 1712p. 1975. pap. text ed. 67.00 (ISBN 0-87262-124-3). Am Soc Civil Eng.

--Modes of Transportation. 160p. 1970. pap. text ed. 8.75 (ISBN 0-87262-021-2). Am Soc Civil Eng.

--National Conference on Construction Contracts. 84p. 1968. pap. text ed. 11.75 o.p. (ISBN 0-87262-010-7). Am Soc Civil Eng.

--National Conference on Environmental Engineering. 480p. 1978. pap. text ed. 29.00 (ISBN 0-87262-128-6). Am Soc Civil Eng.

--National Specialty Conference on Disinfection. 712p. 1971. text ed. 22.50 (ISBN 0-87262-027-1). Am Soc Civil Eng.

--Need for National Policy for the Use of Underground Space. 240p. 1975. pap. text ed. 14.50 (ISBN 0-87262-102-2). Am Soc Civil Eng.

--New Approaches to Urban Transportation Needs. 218p. pap. text ed. 11.00 (ISBN 0-87262-032-8). Am Soc Civil Eng.

--New Horizons in Rock Mechanics. 800p. 1973. text ed. 25.00 (ISBN 0-87262-050-6). Am Soc Civil Eng.

--Nineteen Seventy-Nine Conference on Environmental Engineering. 840p. 1979. pap. text ed. 48.00 (ISBN 0-87262-185-5). Am Soc Civil Eng.

--Nineteen Seventy-Nine International Air Transportation Conference. 836p. 1980. pap. text ed. 59.00 (ISBN 0-87262-201-0). Am Soc Civil Eng.

American Society of Civil Engineers & Desai, C. S., eds. Numerical Methods in Geomechanics. 1568p. 1976. pap. text ed. 52.00 (ISBN 0-87262-168-5). Am Soc Civil Eng.

American Society of Civil Engineers, compiled by. Ocean Wave Measure & Analysis. 1240p. 1974. pap. text ed. 62.00 (ISBN 0-87262-116-2). Am Soc Civil Eng.

--Operation & Maintenance of Irrigation & Drainage Systems. LC 79-55951. (Manuel & Report on Engineering Practice Ser: No. 57). 280p. 1980. pap. text ed. 28.00 (ISBN 0-87262-231-2). Am Soc Civil Eng.

--An Overview of the Alaska Highway Gas Pipeline. 136p. 1978. pap. text ed. 11.00 (ISBN 0-87262-130-8). Am Soc Civil Eng.

--Passenger Psychological Dynamics. 192p. 1969. pap. text ed. 8.75 (ISBN 0-87262-020-4). Am Soc Civil Eng.

--Performance of Earth & Earth-Supported Structures. 1972. pap. text ed. 75.00 (ISBN 0-87262-046-8). Am Soc Civil Eng.

--Pipeline Design for Hydrocarbon Gases & Liquids. 88p. 1975. pap. text ed. 6.00 (ISBN 0-87262-118-9). Am Soc Civil Eng.

--Pipeline Design for Water & Wastewater. 136p. 1975. pap. text ed. 7.50 (ISBN 0-87262-106-5). Am Soc Civil Eng.

--Pipelines in Adverse Environments. 564p. 1979. pap. text ed. 39.50 (ISBN 0-87262-176-6). Am Soc Civil Eng.

--Pipelines in the Oceans. 120p. 1974. pap. text ed. 6.00 (ISBN 0-87262-062-X). Am Soc Civil Eng.

--Placement & Improvement of Soils. 448p. 1971. text ed. 19.75 (ISBN 0-87262-031-X). Am Soc Civil Eng.

--Planning, Design & Implementation of Bicycle & Pedestrian Facilities. 616p. 1976. pap. text ed. 20.00 (ISBN 0-87262-170-7). Am Soc Civil Eng.

--Planning, Engineering, & Constructing the Super Projects. 536p. 1979. pap. text ed. 27.00 (ISBN 0-87262-178-2). Am Soc Civil Eng.

--Plastic Design in Steel-A Guide & Commentary. (ASCE Manual & Report of Energy Practice Ser.: No. 41). 352p. 1971. pap. text ed. 15.00 (ISBN 0-87262-217-7). Am Soc Civil Eng.

--Port Structure Costs. 188p. 1974. pap. text ed. 39.50 o.p. (ISBN 0-87262-072-7). Am Soc Civil Eng.

--Ports Seventy-Seven. 1024p. 1977. pap. text ed. 36.00 (ISBN 0-87262-084-0). Am Soc Civil Eng.

--Practical Highway Esthetics. 80p. 1977. pap. text ed. 17.50 (ISBN 0-87262-096-4). Am Soc Civil Eng.

--Probabalistic Mechanics & Structural Reliability. 436p. 1979. pap. text ed. 32.50 (ISBN 0-87262-138-3). Am Soc Civil Eng.

--Prospects for Metropolitan Water Management. 256p. 1971. pap. text ed. 5.25 (ISBN 0-87262-026-3). Am Soc Civil Eng.

--Public Works & Society. 256p. 1974. pap. text ed. 17.00 (ISBN 0-87262-064-6). Am Soc Civil Eng.

--Pumped Storage. 608p. 1975. pap. text ed. 19.00 (ISBN 0-87262-120-0). Am Soc Civil Eng.

--Quality System in Construction. 224p. 1974. pap. text ed. 11.00 (ISBN 0-87262-073-5). Am Soc Civil Eng.

--Recreation Planning & Development. 784p. 1980. pap. text ed. 56.50 (ISBN 0-87262-200-2). Am Soc Civil Eng.

--Reevaluating Spillway Adequacy of Existing Dams. 64p. 1975. pap. text ed. 9.50 (ISBN 0-87262-119-7). Am Soc Civil Eng.

--Reinforced Concrete Floor Slabs-Research & Design. 224p. 1978. pap. text ed. 15.00 (ISBN 0-87262-136-7). Am Soc Civil Eng.

--Repair & Strengthening of Old Steel Truss Bridges. 144p. 1979. pap. text ed. 14.00 (ISBN 0-87262-194-4). Am Soc Civil Eng.

--Report on Highway & Bridge Surveys. (Manual & Report on Engineering Practice Ser.: No. 44). 160p. 1962. pap. text ed. 7.50 (ISBN 0-87262-219-3). Am Soc Civil Eng.

--Report on Pipeline Location. (Manual & Report on Engineering Practice Ser.: No. 46). 88p. 1965. pap. text ed. 8.50 (ISBN 0-87262-040-9). Am Soc Civil Eng.

--Report on Small Craft Harbors. (Manual & Report on Engineering Practice Ser.: No. 50). 148p. 1969. pap. 10.00 (ISBN 0-87262-224-X). Am Soc Civil Eng.

--Research Conference on Shear Strength of Cohesive Soils. 1174p. 1966. pap. text ed. 37.50 (ISBN 0-87262-004-2). Am Soc Civil Eng.

--Research Directions in Computer Control of Urban Traffic Systems. 400p. 1979. pap. text ed. 20.00 (ISBN 0-87262-179-0). Am Soc Civil Eng.

--Residential Erosion & Sediment Control. 64p. 1978. pap. text ed. 10.00 (ISBN 0-87262-133-2). Am Soc Civil Eng.

--Residential Storm Water Management. 64p. 1976. pap. text ed. 7.50 (ISBN 0-87262-160-X). Am Soc Civil Eng.

--Residential Streets. 48p. 1974. pap. text ed. 7.50 (ISBN 0-87262-159-6). Am Soc Civil Eng.

--Responsibility & Liability of Public & Private Interests on Dams. 216p. 1976. pap. text ed. 12.00 (ISBN 0-87262-167-7). Am Soc Civil Eng.

--Rivers Seventy-Six. 1824p. 1976. pap. text ed. 72.50 (ISBN 0-87262-164-2). Am Soc Civil Eng.

--Rock Engineering for Foundations & Slopes. 728p. 1976. pap. text ed. 27.50 (ISBN 0-87262-082-4). Am Soc Civil Eng.

--Safety & Reliability of Metal Structures. 464p. 1972. pap. text ed. 12.75 (ISBN 0-87262-042-5). Am Soc Civil Eng.

--Safety of Small Dams. 472p. 1975. pap. text ed. 23.00 (ISBN 0-87262-112-X). Am Soc Civil Eng.

--Sanitary Landfill, Manual 39. (ASCE Manual & Report on Engineering Practice Ser.: No. 39). 92p. looseleaf binder 27.50 (ISBN 0-87262-215-0). Am Soc Civil Eng.

--Second International Waterbone Transportation Conference. 780p. 1978. pap. text ed. 42.00 (ISBN 0-87262-099-9). Am Soc Civil Eng.

--Selected Abstracts on Structural Applications of Plastics. (Manual & Report on Engineering Practices Ser.: No. 47). 80p. 1967. pap. text ed. 4.00 (ISBN 0-87262-221-5). Am Soc Civil Eng.

--Selected Papers by Alfred M. Freudenthal. 816p. 1981. pap. text ed. 54.00 (ISBN 0-87262-263-0). Am Soc Civil Eng.

--Site Characterization & Exploration. 408p. 1979. pap. text ed. 15.00 (ISBN 0-87262-186-3). Am Soc Civil Eng.

--Soil Improvement: History, Capability & Outlook. 192p. 1978. pap. text ed. 8.75 (ISBN 0-87262-126-X). Am Soc Civil Eng.

--Solid Waste Research & Development Needs for Emerging Coal Technologies. 272p. 1980. pap. text ed. 21.50 (ISBN 0-87262-199-5). Am Soc Civil Eng.

--Source Book on Environmental & Safety Considerations for Planning & Design of LNG Marine Terminals. 48p. 1976. pap. text ed. 7.00 (ISBN 0-87262-158-8). Am Soc Civil Eng.

--Stability & Performance of Slopes & Embankments. 704p. 1969. text ed. 33.00 (ISBN 0-87262-016-6). Am Soc Civil Eng.

American Society of Civil Engineers & Cording, Edward J., eds. Stability of Rock Slopes. 1008p. 1972. text ed. 34.50 (ISBN 0-87262-047-6). Am Soc Civil Eng.

American Society of Civil Engineers, compiled by. Stability of Structures Under Static & Dynamic Loads. 836p. 1978. pap. text ed. 30.00 (ISBN 0-87262-095-6). Am Soc Civil Eng.

--Structural Analysis & Design of Nuclear Plant Facilities. LC 80-65828. (ASCE Manual & Report on Engineering Practice Ser.: No. 58). 576p. 1980. text ed. 140.00 (ISBN 0-87262-238-X). Am Soc Civil Eng.

--Structural Design of Nuclear Plant Facilities. 1975. pap. text ed. 73.00 (ISBN 0-87262-172-3). Am Soc Civil Eng.

--Structural Design of Nuclear Plant Facilities. 1973. pap. text ed. 52.00 (ISBN 0-87262-155-3). Am Soc Civil Eng.

--Structural Failures-Modes, Causes, Responsibilities. 112p. 1973. pap. text ed. 5.00 (ISBN 0-87262-051-4). Am Soc Civil Eng.

American Society of Civil Engineers & Medearis, Kenneth G., eds. Structural-Induced Response to Explosion-Induced Motions. 148p. 1975. pap. text ed. 8.00 (ISBN 0-87262-150-2). Am Soc Civil Eng.

American Society of Civil Engineers, compiled by. Structural Plastics-Properties & Possibilities. 248p. 1969. pap. text ed. 6.50 (ISBN 0-87262-015-8). Am Soc Civil Eng.

--A Study of Damage to Residential Structures from Blast Vibrations. 80p. 1974. pap. text ed. 4.50 (ISBN 0-87262-074-3). Am Soc Civil Eng.

--Subsurface Exploration for Underground Excavation & Heavy Construction. 414p. 1974. pap. text ed. 13.50 (ISBN 0-87262-105-7). Am Soc Civil Eng.

--Subsurface Investigation for Design & Construction for Foundations of Buildings. (Manuel & Report on Engineering Practice Ser.: No. 56). 68p. 1976. pap. text ed. 6.00 (ISBN 0-87262-230-4). Am Soc Civil Eng.

--Survey of Current Structural Research. (Manual & Report on Engineering Practice Ser.: No. 51). 336p. 1970. pap. text ed. 29.75 (ISBN 0-87262-225-8). Am Soc Civil Eng.

--Symposium on Earth Reinforcement. 912p. 1979. pap. text ed. 40.00 (ISBN 0-87262-144-8). Am Soc Civil Eng.

--Symposium on Rearation Research. 376p. 1979. pap. text ed. 26.00 (ISBN 0-87262-142-1). Am Soc Civil Eng.

--Technical Procedure for City Surveys. (Manual & Report on Engineering Practice Ser.: No. 10). 128p. 1963. pap. text ed. 4.00 (ISBN 0-87262-205-3). Am Soc Civil Eng.

--Technology & Decisions in Airport Access. 168p. 1970. pap. text ed. 19.75 o.p. (ISBN 0-87262-022-0). Am Soc Civil Eng.

--Terzaghi Lectures. 432p. 1974. pap. text ed. 25.00 (ISBN 0-87262-060-3). Am Soc Civil Eng.

--Timber Piles & Construction Timbers. (Manual & Report on Engineering Practice Ser.: No. 17). 48p. 1953. pap. text ed. 3.00 (ISBN 0-87262-208-8). Am Soc Civil Eng.

--Transportation & Energy. 456p. 1978. pap. text ed. 15.00 (ISBN 0-87262-135-9). Am Soc Civil Eng.

--Transportation Facilities Workshop. 576p. 1975. pap. text ed. 24.75 (ISBN 0-87262-107-3). Am Soc Civil Eng.

--Underground Rock Chambers. 608p. 1972. text ed. 29.50 (ISBN 0-87262-033-6). Am Soc Civil Eng.

--Urban Planning Guide. (Manual & Report on Engineering Practice Ser.: No. 49). 308p. 1969. pap. text ed. 8.00 (ISBN 0-87262-223-1). Am Soc Civil Eng.

--Urban Runoff-Quantity & Quality. 280p. 1975. pap. text ed. 14.00 (ISBN 0-87262-103-0). Am Soc Civil Eng.

--Urban Transportation Efficiency. 448p. 1977. pap. text ed. 19.75 (ISBN 0-87262-174-X). Am Soc Civil Eng.

--Urban Transportation Innovation. 432p. 1971. pap. text ed. 18.75 (ISBN 0-87262-044-1). Am Soc Civil Eng.

--Use of Shotcrete for Underground Structural Support. 480p. 1974. pap. text ed. 24.00 (ISBN 0-87262-066-2). Am Soc Civil Eng.

--The Use of Underground Space to Achieve National Goals. 360p. 1973. pap. text ed. 22.00 (ISBN 0-87262-045-X). Am Soc Civil Eng.

--Verification of Mathematical & Physical Models in Hydraulic Engineering. 904p. 1978. pap. text ed. 40.00 (ISBN 0-87262-131-6). Am Soc Civil Eng.

--Wastewater Treatment Plant Design. (Manual & Report on Engineering Practice Ser.: No. 36). 550p. 1977. text ed. 20.00 (ISBN 0-87262-213-4). Am Soc Civil Eng.

--Water & Metropolitan Man. 96p. 1969. pap. text ed. 7.75 (ISBN 0-87262-011-5). Am Soc Civil Eng.

--Water & Wastewater Control Engineering: Glossary. 400p. 1969. text ed. 15.00 o.p. (ISBN 0-87262-014-X). Am Soc Civil Eng.

--Water Conservation-Needs & Implementing Strategies. 280p. 1979. pap. text ed. 19.50 (ISBN 0-87262-198-7). Am Soc Civil Eng.

--Water for the Southwest: Historical Survey & Guide to Historic Sites. 224p. 1973. pap. text ed. 13.00 (ISBN 0-87262-056-5). Am Soc Civil Eng.

--Water Management for Irrigation & Drainage. 640p. 1977. pap. text ed. 46.00 (ISBN 0-87262-097-2). Am Soc Civil Eng.

--Water Problems of Urbanizing Areas. 360p. 1979. pap. text ed. 20.00 (ISBN 0-87262-145-6). Am Soc Civil Eng.

--Water Systems Nineteen Seventy-Nine. 240p. 1979. pap. text ed. 17.75 (ISBN 0-87262-143-X). Am Soc Civil Eng.

--Water Treatment Plant Design. 364p. 1969. text ed. 15.00 (ISBN 0-87262-012-3). Am Soc Civil Eng.

--Watershed Management. 792p. 1975. pap. text ed. 29.50 (ISBN 0-87262-122-7). Am Soc Civil Eng.

American Society of Composers, Authors & Publishers. Copyright Law Symposium, No. 24. 1980. 16.00x (ISBN 0-231-04864-5). Columbia U Pr.

American Society of Hospital Attorneys. Federal Regulation: Hospital Attorney's Desk Reference. 244p. (Orig.). 1980. pap. 35.00 (ISBN 0-87258-321-X, 1430). Am Hospital.

American Society of Hospital Pharmacists Institute on Oncology Pharmacy Practice. Proceedings. Caro, J. P., ed. 128p. 1979. 23.00 (ISBN 0-444-00369-X); pap. 15.00 (ISBN 0-444-00373-8). Elsevier.

American Society of Hospital Pharmacists. Sourcebook on Clinical Pharmacy. 2nd ed. LC 79-24069. (Illus.). 404p. 1980. pap. text ed. 20.00 (ISBN 0-88416-303-2). PSG Pub.

American Society Of International Law. International Law in the Twentieth Century. Gross, Leo, ed. LC 69-16894. (Orig.). 1969. pap. text ed. 18.95x (ISBN 0-89197-234-X). Irvington.

American Society of Planning Officials. Planned Unit Development Ordinances. 1973. 8.00 o.s.i. (ISBN 0-685-71649-X). Urban Land.

American Society of Plastic & Reconstructive Surgeons & McDowell, Frank. The McDowell Series of Plastic Surgery Indexes: Nineteen Forty-Six to Nineteen Seventy-One the Great Index, Vol. Iv. (Illus.). 1168p. 1981. 225.00 (ISBN 0-686-69564-X, 5767-7). Williams & Wilkins.

American Sunbeam Staff. Weather Made to Whose Order? (Illus.). 56p. Date not set. self cover 2.00 (ISBN 0-918700-04-3). Duverus Pub. Postponed.

American Theatre Planning Board. Theatre Check List: A Guide to the Planning & Construction of Proscenium & Open Stage Theatres. LC 69-19619. (Illus.). 1969. pap. 10.00x (ISBN 0-8195-6005-7, Pub. by Wesleyan U Pr). Columbia U Pr.

American Water Works Association. Annual Conference: Proceedings, 1979. (AWWA Handbooks). (Illus.). 1200p. 1979. pap. text ed. 48.00 (ISBN 0-89867-229-5). Am Water Wks Assoc.

--Annual Conference Proceedings, 1980. (AWWA Handbooks Ser.). (Illus.). 1452p. 1980. pap. text ed. 48.00 (ISBN 0-89867-238-4). Am Water Wks Assn.

--AWWA Distribution System Symposium Nineteen Eighty: Proceedings: 1980. (AWWA Handbooks Proceedings Ser.). (Illus.). 179p. 1980. pap. text ed. 9.50 (ISBN 0-89867-235-X). Am Water Wks Assn.

--Computer-Based Automation in Water Systems. (AWWA Handbooks-General Ser.). (Illus.). 104p. 1980. pap. text ed. 10.00 (ISBN 0-89867-230-9). Am Water Wks Assn.

--Concrete Pressure Pipe-M9: AWWA Manuals. (Illus.). 1979. pap. text ed. 11.00 (ISBN 0-89867-067-5). Am Water Wks Assn.

--Distribution Systems: Actions & Innovations. (General Handbooks). (Illus.). 256p. 1980. pap. text ed. 20.00 (ISBN 0-89867-246-5). Am Water Wks Assn.

--Energy & Water Use Forecasting. (AWWA Handbooks-General Ser.). (Illus.). 104p. 1980. pap. text ed. 10.00 (ISBN 0-89867-236-8). Am Water Wks Assn.

--Journal AWWA, Vol. 70, 1978. (Journal Bound Volumes). (Illus.). 788p. 1979. text ed. 36.50 (ISBN 0-89867-205-8). Am Water Wks Assn.

--Journal AWWA, Vol. 71, 1979. (Journal Bound Volumes). (Illus.). 788p. 1980. lib. bdg. 28.80 (ISBN 0-89867-232-5); text ed. 36.50 (ISBN 0-686-68527-X). Am Water Wks Assn.

--Managing Water Rates & Finances Handbook. (AWWA Handbooks-General Ser.). (Illus.). 208p. 1980. pap. text ed. 17.00 (ISBN 0-89867-228-7). Am Water Wks Assn.

--Officers & Committee Directory Nineteen Seventy-Nine to Nineteen Eighty. (Rosters & Directories). (Illus.). 121p. 1979. pap. text ed. 4.00 o.p. (ISBN 0-89867-226-0). Am Water Wks Assn.

--Operator Certification Study Guide. (AWWA Handbooks Ser.: General). (Illus.). 104p. 1979. pap. 12.00 (ISBN 0-89867-227-9). Am Water Wks Assn.

--Opflow, Vol. 4, 1978. (OpFlow Bound Volumes). (Illus.). 104p. 1979. text ed. 14.00 (ISBN 0-89867-221-X). Am Water Wks Assn.

--Reference Handbook: Basic Science Concepts & Applications. (General References Ser.). (Illus.). 756p. 1980. text ed. 18.50 (ISBN 0-89867-202-3). Am Water Wks Assn.

--Safe Water: A Factbook on the SDWA for Noncommunity Water Systems. (Illus.). 52p. 1980. pap. 1.50 (ISBN 0-89867-224-4). Am Water Wks Assn.

--Upgrading Water Treatment Plants to Improve Water Quality. (Handbooks-Proceedings). (Illus.). 132p. 1980. pap. text ed. 10.50 (ISBN 0-89867-245-7). Am Water Wks Assn.

--Water Customer Information: Proceedings. (AWWA Handbooks Proceedings Ser.). (Illus.). 56p. 1979. pap. text ed. 6.00 (ISBN 0-89867-222-8). Am Water Wks Assn.

--Water Disinfection with Ozone, Chloramines, or Chlorine Dioxide. (Handbooks-Proceedings Ser.). (Illus.). 224p. 1980. pap. text ed. 10.00 (ISBN 0-89867-244-9). Am Water Wks Assn.

--Water Quality Technology Conference - Nineteen Seventy-Nine. (AWWA Handbooks Proceedings Ser.). (Illus.). 350p. 1980. pap. text ed. 10.00 (ISBN 0-89867-231-7). Am Water Wks Assn.
--Water Utility Accounting. 2nd ed. (General References Ser.). (Illus.). 288p. 1980. text ed. 28.00 (ISBN 0-89867-237-6). Am Water Wks Assn.
American Youth Hostels. The American Bicycle Atlas. 1981. pap. 5.95 (ISBN 0-525-93172-4). Dutton.
American Youth Hostels Inc. Hosteling U. S. A. The Official American Youth Hostels Handbook. LC 79-936. (Illus.). 224p. 1979. pap. 9.25 o.p. (ISBN 0-686-27149-1); pap. 5.95 o.p. (ISBN 0-914788-26-4). East Woods.
Amerine, M. A., et al. Technology of Wine Making. 4th ed. (Illus.). 1980. text ed. 39.50 (ISBN 0-87055-333-X). AVI.
Amerine, Maynard, jt. auth. see Stewart, George.
Amerine, Maynard A. & Berg, H. W. Technology of Wine Making. 3rd. ed. (Illus.). 500p. 1972. text ed. 38.50 o.p. (ISBN 0-87055-116-7). AVI.
Amerine, Maynard A. & Roessler, Edward B. Wines: Their Sensory Evaluation. LC 76-13441. (Illus.). 1976. text ed. 13.95x (ISBN 0-7167-0553-2). W H Freeman.
Amerine, Maynard A., ed. Wine Production Technology in the United States. LC 80-28041. (Symposium Ser.: No. 145). 1981. price not set (ISBN 0-8412-0596-5); pap. price not set (ISBN 0-8412-0602-3). Am Chemical.
Amerongon, Charles Van see Gunter, Altner.
Amery, Colin, ed. Three Centuries of Architectural Craftsmanship. (Illus.). 1977. pap. 14.50 (ISBN 0-85139-662-3, Pub. by Architectural Pr). Nichols Pub.
Amery, Heather. The Know How Book of Experiments. LC 78-17788. (Know How Books). (gr. 4-5). 1978. text ed. 6.95 (ISBN 0-88436-531-X). EMC.
Amery, Heather & Adair, Ian. The Know How Book of Jokes & Tricks. LC 78-14807. (Know How Books). (gr. 4-5). 1978. text ed. 6.95 (ISBN 0-88436-530-1). EMC.
Amery, Jean. At the Mind's Limits: Contemplations by a Survivor on Auschwitz & Its Realities. Rosenfeld, Sidney & Rosenfeld, Stella P., trs. LC 80-7682. 160p. 1980. 12.50 (ISBN 0-253-17724-3). Ind U Pr.
Ames. Private Lives of Our Natural Neighbors. Date not set. 15.00 (ISBN 0-8076-0960-9). Braziller.
Ames & Ilg. Your Three-Year Old. 1980. pap. 4.95 (ISBN 0-440-59478-2, Delta). Dell.
--Your Two Year Old. 1980. pap. 4.95 (ISBN 0-440-59477-4, Delta). Dell.
Ames, Adelbert, Jr. The Morning Notes of Adelbert Ames, Jr. Including a Correspondence with John Dewey. Cantril, Hadley, ed. 1960. 17.00 (ISBN 0-8135-0354-X). Rutgers U Pr.
Ames, Blanche A. Adelbert Ames, 1835-1933. (Illus.). 1964. 15.00 (ISBN 0-87266-000-1). Argosy.
Ames, Evelyn. Dust on a Precipice. LC 80-26142. 1981. 8.95 (ISBN 0-87233-055-9); pap. 4.95 (ISBN 0-686-69211-X). Bauhan.
Ames, Felicia. The Bird You Care for. Date not set. pap. 1.75 (ISBN 0-451-07527-7, E7527, Sig). NAL.
--The Cat You Care for. Date not set. pap. 1.75 o.p. (ISBN 0-451-07862-4, E7862, Sig). NAL.
Ames, Gerald & Wyler, Rose. Earth's Story. LC 66-30640. (Creative Science Ser). (gr. 4-9). 1967. PLB 7.95 (ISBN 0-87191-012-8). Creative Ed.
Ames, Gerald, jt. auth. see Wyler, Rose.
Ames, H. B. City Below the Hill. LC 78-163831. (Social History of Canada Ser.). 112p. 1972. pap. 3.50 (ISBN 0-8020-6142-7). U of Toronto Pr.
Ames, Herman V., ed. State Documents on Federal Relations. LC 78-77697. (American Constitutional & Legal History Ser). 1970. Repr. of 1900 ed. lib. bdg. 35.00 (ISBN 0-306-71335-7). Da Capo.
Ames, Kenneth L. Beyond Necessity: Art in the Folk Tradition. (Illus.). 1978. 14.95x (ISBN 0-393-04499-8). Norton.
Ames, Lee. Graff-a-Doodle Do. (Illus.). 96p. 1981. pap. 3.95 (ISBN 0-686-69181-4). G&D.
Ames, Lee J. Draw Fifty Dogs. LC 79-6853. (Illus.). 64p. (gr. 4-6). 1981. 6.95a (ISBN 0-385-15686-3); PLB (ISBN 0-385-15687-1). Doubleday.
--Draw Fifty Vehicles. LC 77-94862. (gr. 1 up). 1978. pap. 2.95 (ISBN 0-385-14154-8). Doubleday.
Ames, Louise B. Your Three Year Old. 1976. 7.95 (ISBN 0-440-09883-1). Delacorte.
--Your Two Year Old. 1976. 7.95 (ISBN 0-440-09882-3). Delacorte.
Ames, Louise B. & Ilg, Frances L. Your Five Year Old. 1981. pap. 4.95 (ISBN 0-440-59494-4, Delta). Dell.
Ames, Louise B., et al. Stop School Failure. LC 79-181603. (Illus.). 256p. 1972. 8.95 o.p. (ISBN 0-06-010114-8, HarpT). Har-Row.
Ames, Marjorie. Miniature Macrame for Dollhouses. Date not set. pap. price not set (ISBN 0-486-23960-8). Dover. Postponed.
Ames, Mary E. Outcome Uncertain: Science & the Political Process. LC 77-81692. 1978. PLB 13.95x (ISBN 0-89461-028-7); pap. 7.95x (ISBN 0-89461-029-5). Comm Pr Inc.
Ames, Maurice U., jt. auth. see Schneider, Leo.
Ames, Mildred. Anna to the Infinite Power. 204p. (gr. 7 up). 1981. 9.95 (ISBN 0-684-16855-3). Scribner.
--Is There Life on a Plastic Planet? 144p. (gr. 4-6). 1975. PLB 9.95 (ISBN 0-525-32594-8). Dutton.
--Nicky & the Joyous Noise. LC 80-384. (gr. 4-6). 1980. 8.95 (ISBN 0-684-16524-4). Scribner.
Ames, Oakes. Orchidaceae: Illustrations & Studies of the Family Orchidaceae Volume IV: the Genus Habenaria in North America. (Orchid Ser.). (Illus.). 1980. Repr. of 1910 ed. text ed. 25.00 (ISBN 0-930576-23-3). E M Coleman Ent.
Ames, R., jt. auth. see Archer, Robert M.
Ames, Robert. Off Road Drivers Handbook. LC 77-92562. (Illus.). 176p. 1981. pap. 6.95 (ISBN 0-89632-002-2). Del Oeste. Postponed.
Ames, Ruth M. Fulfillment of the Scriptures: Abraham, Moses & Piers. 1970. 9.95x o.s.i. (ISBN 0-8101-0301-X). Northwestern U Pr.
Ames, Seth, ed. Works of Fisher Ames, 2 Vols. LC 69-14409. (American Scene Ser). 1969. Repr. of 1854 ed. Set. lib. bdg. 69.50 (ISBN 0-306-71122-2). Da Capo.
Ames, Sue Ann, jt. auth. see Kneisl, Carol R.
Ames, Walter L. Police & Community in Japan. (Illus.). 300p. 1981. 16.50 (ISBN 0-520-04070-8). U of Cal Pr.
Ames, William. Anti-Theatrical Tracts Seventeen Two-Seventeen Four: Stage Plays Arraigned & Condemned. Bd. with A Scourge for the Play-Houses. Burridge, Richard; An Humble Application to the Queen...to Suppress Playhouses. Feild, John; A Letter from Several Members of the Society for Reformation of Manners. LC 77-170480. (The English Stage Ser.: Vol. 44). lib. bdg. 50.00 (ISBN 0-8240-0627-5). Garland Pub.
--Technometry. Gibbs, Lee W., tr. from Lat. LC 78-65117. (Haney Foundation Ser.). (Illus.). 1979. 17.95x (ISBN 0-8122-7756-2). U of Pa Pr.
Amesbury, James E. A Sporting Chance. 242p. 1980. 9.95 (ISBN 0-8037-7865-1). Dial.
Amey, J., jt. auth. see Coveney, James.
Amey, Peter. Imperialism. Yapp, Malcolm, et al, eds. (World History Ser.). (Illus.). (gr. 10). 1980. Repr. of 1977 ed. lib. bdg. 5.95 (ISBN 0-89908-226-2); pap. text ed. 1.95 (ISBN 0-89908-201-7). Greenhaven.
--Pax Romana. Yapp, Malcolm, et al, eds. (World History Ser.). (Illus.). 32p. (gr. 10). 1980. Repr. of 1977 ed. lib. bdg. 5.95 (ISBN 0-89908-027-8); pap. text ed. 1.95 (ISBN 0-89908-002-2). Greenhaven.
--The Scientific Revolution. Yapp, Malcolm, et al, eds. (World History Ser.). (Illus.). (gr. 10). 1980. lib. bdg. 5.95 (ISBN 0-89908-132-0); pap. text ed. 1.95 (ISBN 0-89908-107-X). Greenhaven.
Amey, Peter, et al. Leonardo Da Vinci. Yapp, Malcolm, et al, eds. (World History Ser.). (Illus.). (gr. 10). 1980. lib. bdg. 5.95 (ISBN 0-89908-041-3); pap. text ed. 1.95 (ISBN 0-89908-016-2). Greenhaven.
--Luther, Erasmus & Loyola. Yapp, Malcolm, et al, eds. (World History Ser.). (Illus.). (gr. 10). 1980. lib. bdg. 5.95 (ISBN 0-89908-043-X); pap. text ed. 1.95 (ISBN 0-89908-018-9). Greenhaven.
Amey, Vera E., jt. auth. see Eaton, Margaret H.
Amfitheatrof, Erik. The Enchanted Ground: Americans in Italy, 1760-1980. 256p. 1980. 14.95 (ISBN 0-316-03700-1). Little.
Amherst Student. The Student Guide to Fellowships & Internships. 356p. 1980. 15.95 (ISBN 0-525-93155-4); pap. 7.95 (ISBN 0-525-93147-3). Dutton.
Amichai, Yehuda. Amen. LC 76-50164. 1977. 7.95 o.s.i. (ISBN 0-06-010090-7, HarpT); pap. 4.95 o.s.i. (ISBN 0-06-010089-3, TD-278, HarpT). Har-Row.
--Not of This Time, Not of This Place. Katz, Shlomo, tr. from Hebrew. 345p. 1973. 12.50x (ISBN 0-85303-180-0, Pub. by Vallentine Mitchell England). Biblio Dist.
--Poems. Gutman, Assia, tr. LC 69-15293. 1969. 6.95 o.s.i. (ISBN 0-06-010111-3, HarpT). Har-Row.
--Songs of Jerusalem & Myself. LC 72-181604. 96p. 1973. 6.95 o.s.i. (ISBN 0-06-010097-4, HarpT); pap. 2.95 o.s.i. (ISBN 0-06-010101-6, TD-124, HarpT). Har-Row.
Amichai, Yehuda, ed. see Yeshurun, Avoth.
Amick, Daniel J. & Walberg, Herbert, eds. Introductory Multivariate Analysis (for Educational Psychological and Social Research) LC 74-30754. (Illus.). 275p. 1975. 17.90 (ISBN 0-8211-0013-0); text ed. 16.20 in ten or more copies (ISBN 0-685-52138-9). McCutchan.
Amick, Robert G., jt. auth. see Brennecke, John H.
Amidei, Rosemary E., compiled by. Environment, The Human Impact. 1973. pap. 5.00 (ISBN 0-87355-001-3). Natl Sci Tchrs.
Amidon, Edmund J. & Hough, John B. Interaction Analysis: Theory, Research & Application. LC 67-23976. (Education Ser). (Illus., Orig.). 1967. pap. 9.95 (ISBN 0-201-00234-5). A-W.
Amidon, Eva V. Easy Quillery: Projects with Paper Coils & Scrolls. (Illus.). (gr. 3-8). 1977. 7.25 (ISBN 0-688-22130-0); PLB 6.96 (ISBN 0-688-32130-5). Morrow.
Amiel, Barbara, jt. auth. see Jonas, George.
Amiet, Pierre. Art of the Ancient Near East. (Illus.). 604p. 1980. 95.00 (ISBN 0-686-62712-1, 0638-4). Abrams.
Amigo, Eleanor & Neuffer, Mark. Beyond the Adirondacks: The Story of St. Regis Paper Company. LC 80-1798. (Contributions in Economics & Economic History: No. 35). (Illus.). xi, 219p. 1980. lib. bdg. 22.95 (ISBN 0-313-22735-7, AFN/). Greenwood.
Amin & Mayor. Seeing the Real New York. 1981. pap. 7.95 (ISBN 0-8120-2242-4). Barron.
Amin, Karima, jt. auth. see Stanford, Barnara D.
Amin, Samir. The Arab Nation: Nationalism & Class Struggle. 116p. 1978. 12.95 (Pub. by Zed Pr); pap. 4.95 (ISBN 0-905762-23-1). Lawrence Hill.
--The Law of Value & Historical Materialism. 1978. 6.50 o.p. (ISBN 0-85345-470-1, CL-4701). Monthly Rev.
Amin, Samir, ed. Modern Migrations in Western Africa: Studies Presented & Discussed at the 11th Int'l African Seminar, Dakar, 4/1972. (International African Institute Ser.). 428p. 1974. 37.50x (ISBN 0-19-724193-X). Oxford U Pr.
Amiri, Imanu see Harrison, Paul C.
Amis, Kingsley. Collected Poems, 1944-1979. 162p. 1980. 10.00 (ISBN 0-670-22910-5). Viking Pr.
--Green Man. LC 76-95862. 1970. 5.95 o.p. (ISBN 0-15-137040-0). HarBraceJ.
--Jake's Thing. 1980. pap. 3.50 (ISBN 0-14-005096-5). Penguin.
--Lucky Jim. 256p. 1976. Repr. of 1954 ed. lib. bdg. 12.95x (ISBN 0-89244-069-4). Queens Hse.
Amis, Kingsley, ed. see Chesterton, G. K.
Amis, Martin. Other People: A Mystery Story. 1981. 11.95 (ISBN 0-670-52948-6). Viking Pr.
Ami Sha'Ked. Human Sexuality & Rehabilitation Medicine: Sexual Functioning Following Spinal Cord Injury. (Illus.). 228p. 1981. write for info. (7749-X). Williams & Wilkins.
Amiss, John M. & Jones, Franklin D. The Use of Handbook Tables & Formulas. 21st ed. Ryffel, Henry H., ed. LC 75-10949. (Illus.). 224p. 8.00 (ISBN 0-8311-1131-3). Indus Pr.
Amiss, John M., jt. auth. see Jones, Franklin D.
Amitai, P., jt. auth. see Levy, G.
Amitay, Noach, et al. Theory & Analysis of Phased Array Antennas. LC 70-174768. 1972. 38.00 o.p. (ISBN 0-471-02553-4, Pub. by Wiley-Interscience). Wiley.
Amkreutz, Carl. Dictionary of Data Processing: Hardware-Software. 905p. (Ger, Eng, Fr.). 1972. 32.50x (ISBN 0-8002-1258-4). Intl Pubns Serv.
Amlaner, C. & Macdonald, D., eds. A Handbook on Biotelemetry & Radio Tracking: International Conference: Biotelemetry & Radio Tracking in Biology & Medicine, Oxford, 20-22 March 1979. LC 79-41234. (Illus.). 826p. 1980. 105.00 (ISBN 0-08-024928-0). Pergamon.
Amlick, B. Get Started in Dried Flower Craft. 1974. pap. 2.95 o.s.i. (ISBN 0-02-011110-X, Collier). Macmillan.
Amling, Fred. Plaid for Principles of Investments. 1977. pap. 5.50 (ISBN 0-256-02003-5, 06-0815-02). Learning Syst.
Amlung, Susan, ed. see League of Women Voters of New York State.
Amman, L. A. Self Liberation. 1981. pap. 6.95 (ISBN 0-87728-511-X). Weiser.
Ammer, Christine & Ammer, Dean S. Dictionary of Business and Economics. LC 76-41625. 1977. 22.50 (ISBN 0-02-900590-6). Free Pr.
Ammer, Dean S. Manufacturing Management & Control. (Illus.). 1968. pap. 8.95 (ISBN 0-13-555839-5). P-H.
--Materials Management. 3rd ed. 1974. text ed. 17.95x o.p. (ISBN 0-256-01556-2). Irwin.
--Materials Management & Purchasing. 4th ed. 1980. 20.95x (ISBN 0-256-02146-5). Irwin.
--Purchasing & Materials Management for Health Care Institutions. LC 74-11416. (Illus.). 1975. 16.95 (ISBN 0-669-95604-X). Lexington Bks.
Ammer, Dean S., jt. auth. see Ammer, Christine.
Ammerman, C. R., jt. auth. see Edmond, Joseph B.
Ammerman, David. In the Common Cause: American Response to the Coercive Acts of 1774. LC 74-2417. 1974. 10.95x (ISBN 0-8139-0525-7). U Pr of Va.
--In the Common Cause: American Response to the Coercive Acts of 1775. 184p. pap. 2.95 (ISBN 0-393-00787-1, Norton Lib). Norton.
Ammerman, Gale. Your Future in Food Technology. rev. ed. (Careers in Depth Ser.). 1980. lib. bdg. 5.97 (ISBN 0-8239-0314-1). Rosen Pr.
Ammerman, Thomas J. God, If You Exist, Prove It to Me. 1981. 6.95 (ISBN 0-8062-1595-X). Carlton.
Ammon, Harry. The Genet Mission. (Essays in American History Ser.). 208p. 1973. 6.95x (ISBN 0-393-05475-6); pap. text ed. 3.95x (ISBN 0-393-09420-0). Norton.
Ammons, A. R. The Coast of Trees. 1981. 12.95 (ISBN 0-393-01447-9); pap. 4.95 (ISBN 0-393-00051-6). Norton.
Ammons, Elizabeth. Edith Wharton's Argument with America. LC 79-48000. 232p. 1980. 15.00x (ISBN 0-8203-0513-8). U of Ga Pr.
Amoia, Alba. Edmond Rostand. (World Authors Ser.: No. 420). 1978. lib. bdg. 12.50 (ISBN 0-8057-6260-4). Twayne.
Amon, Aline. The Earth Is Sore: Native Americans on Nature. LC 80-36854. (Illus.). 96p. 1981. PLB 9.95 (ISBN 0-689-30798-5). Atheneum.
Amon Carter Museum. Future Directions for Museums of American Art. LC 80-80501. 68p. 1980. pap. 7.95 (ISBN 0-88360-033-1). Amon Carter.
Amon, Frank. Othello, Macbeth, & King Lear: A Formal Approach. LC 78-58445. 1978. pap. text ed. 9.00 (ISBN 0-8191-0533-3). U Pr of Amer.
Amon-Ra, Juba. Flights into Time. LC 80-81579. (Illus.). 52p. (Orig.). 1980. 7.50 (ISBN 0-936874-01-5, JNP-01); pap. 4.50 (ISBN 0-936874-00-7, JNP-00); special ed. 15.00 (ISBN 0-936874-02-3, JNP-02). Joyful Noise.
Amoore, John E. Molecular Basis of Odor. (American Lecture in Living Chemistry Ser). (Illus.). 216p. 1970. 21.00 (ISBN 0-398-00039-5). C C Thomas.
Amore, Roy C. & Shinn, Larry D. Lustful Maidens & Ascetic Kings: Buddhist & Hindu Stories of Life. (Illus.). 150p. 1981. 14.95 (ISBN 0-19-502838-4); pap. 5.95 (ISBN 0-19-502839-2). Oxford U Pr.
Amoros, J. L. & Amoros, M. Molecular Crystals: Their Transforms & Diffuse Scattering. 479p. 1968. text ed. 26.00 (ISBN 0-471-02555-0, Pub. by Wiley). Krieger.
Amoros, M., jt. auth. see Amoros, J. L.
Amory, Cleveland. The Trouble with Nowadays: A Curmudgeon Strikes Back. 272p. 1981. pap. 6.95 (ISBN 0-345-29720-2). Ballantine.
Amory, Mark, ed. see Waugh, Evelyn.
Amory, Martha B. The Domestic & Artistic Life of John Singleton Cop. LC 71-77698. (Library of American Art Ser). 1882. Repr. of 1969 ed. lib. bdg. 39.50 (ISBN 0-306-71336-5). Da Capo.
Amory, Thomas. The Life of John Buncle, Esq., 1756-1766, 2 vols. in 1. LC 74-31048. (Novel in England, 1700-1775 Ser). 1974. lib. bdg. 50.00 (ISBN 0-8240-1144-9). Garland Pub.
Amos, Eileen, tr. see Vestly, Anne-Catherine.
Amos, H. D. & Lang, A. G. These Were the Greeks. (Illus.). 224p. 1980. 12.95 (ISBN 0-7175-0789-0). Dufour.
Amos, John M. & Sarchet, Bernard R. Management for Engineers. (P-H Ser. in Industrial Systems Engineering). (Illus.). 384p. 1981. text ed. 18.95 (ISBN 0-686-68606-3). P-H.
Amos, John W. Arab-Israeli Military Political Relations: Arab Perceptions & the Politics of Escalation. 1979. text ed. 39.50 (ISBN 0-08-023865-3). Pergamon.
--The Palestinian Liberation Organization (P.L.O.) Organization of a Nationalise Movement. (Pergamon Policy Studies). 1981. 45.00 (ISBN 0-08-025094-7). Pergamon.
Amos, John W., II. Palestinian Resistance: Organization of a Nationalist Movement. LC 80-16134. (Pergamon Policy Studies on International Politics). 496p. 1981. 45.00 (ISBN 0-08-025094-7). Pergamon.
Amos, Martha T. Fanny Runs in Honolulu. (Illus.). 64p. 1981. 5.00 (ISBN 0-682-49718-5). Exposition.
Amos, S. W. Dictionary of Electronics. 1981. text ed. price not set (ISBN 0-408-00331-6, Newnes-Butterworth). Butterworth.
Amos, William E. & Grambs, Jean D. Counseling the Disadvantaged Youth. 1968. text ed. 18.95x (ISBN 0-13-183129-1). P-H.
Amos, William E. & Manella, Raymond L. Readings in the Administration of Institutions for Delinquent Youth. 228p. 1965. pap. 18.75 photovopy ed. spiral (ISBN 0-398-00041-7). C C Thomas.

Amos, William E. & Manella, Raymond L., eds. Delinquent Children in Juvenile Correctional Institutions: State Administered Reception & Diagnostic Centers. (Illus.). 176p. 1973. pap. 14.75 (ISBN 0-398-00040-9). C C Thomas.

Amoss, Berthe. The Chalk Cross. LC 75-4778. 192p. (gr. 5-12). 1976. 6.95 (ISBN 0-395-28887-8, Clarion). HM.

--The Great Sea Monster or a Book by You. LC 74-30422. (Illus.). 36p. (gr. k-3). 1975. 5.95 o.s.i. (ISBN 0-685-53908-3, Four Winds); PLB 5.41 o.s.i. (ISBN 0-8193-0798-X). Schol Bk Serv.

--Old Hasdrubal & the Pirates. LC 76-153787. (Illus.). (gr. k-3). 1971. 5.95 o.s.i. (ISBN 0-8193-0519-7, Four Winds); PLB 5.41 o.s.i. (ISBN 0-8193-0520-0). Schol Bk Serv.

--The Very Worst Thing. LC 77-174605. (Illus.). 48p. (gr. k-3). 1972. 5.95 o.s.i. (ISBN 0-8193-0559-6, Four Winds); PLB 5.41 o.s.i. (ISBN 0-8193-0560-X). Schol Bk Serv.

Amoss, Pamela T. & Harrell, Stevan, eds. Other Ways of Growing Old: Anthropological Perspectives. LC 79-66056. 1981. 18.50x (ISBN 0-8047-1072-4). Stanford U Pr.

Amr, et al. Energy Systems in the United States. Date not set. price not set (ISBN 0-8247-1275-7). Dekker.

Amrine, Bill, ed. see Amrine, Lowell.

Amrine, Lowell. Sierra Railroad: A Portfolio. Amrine, Bill, ed. (Illus.). 32p. 1980. pap. 6.95 (ISBN 0-936616-01-6). Galliard Pr.

Amsbury. Bridge: Bidding Naturally. 1979. 17.95 (ISBN 0-7134-1619-X, Pub. by Batsford England). David & Charles.

Amsden, Alice H., ed. The Economics of Women & Work. LC 80-15970. 1980. write for info. (ISBN 0-312-23670-0). St Martin.

Amse-De Jong, Tine H. The Meaning of the Finite Verb Forms in the Old Church Slavonic Codex Suprasliensis: A Synchronic Study. (Slavistic Printings & Reprintings Ser.: No. 319). 228p. (Orig.). 1974. pap. text ed. 52.95x (ISBN 90-2793-012-0). Mouton.

Amstead, B. H., et al. Manufacturing Processes. 7th ed. LC 76-26542. 1977. 26.95x (ISBN 0-471-06245-6). Wiley.

--Manufacturing Processes. 7th ed. LC 78-16185. 1979. text ed. 27.95 (ISBN 0-471-03575-0); solutions manual avail. (ISBN 0-471-03679-X). Wiley.

Amstutz, Beverly. Benjamin & the Bible Donkies. (Illus.). 1981. pap. 2.50 (ISBN 0-937836-03-6). Precious Res.

--The Fly Has Lots of Eyes. (Illus.). 1981. pap. 2.50 (ISBN 0-937836-04-4). Precious Res.

--I Love My Foster Grandparents. (Illus.). 204p. (gr. k-7). 1981. pap. 2.50 (ISBN 0-937836-06-0). Precious Res.

--Moccasins & Sneakers. (Illus.). 1980. pap. 2.50 (ISBN 0-937836-02-8). Precious Res.

--Sharing Is Fun. 22p. (ps-6). 1979. pap. 2.25 (ISBN 0-937836-00-1). Precious Res.

--That Boy, That Girl. LC 80-80372. 24p. (ps-6). 1979. pap. 2.25 (ISBN 0-937836-01-X). Precious Res.

--Too Big for the Bag. (Illus.). 1981. pap. 2.50 (ISBN 0-937836-05-2). Precious Res.

Amstutz, Mark R. Economics & Foreign Policy: A Guide to Information Sources. LC 74-11566. (Vol. 7). 1977. 30.00 (ISBN 0-8103-1321-9). Gale.

Amundsen, Kirsten. Norway, NATO & the Forgotten Soviet Challenge. (Policy Papers in International Affairs: No. 14). (Illus.). iv, 60p. 1981. pap. 2.95x (ISBN 0-87725-514-8). U of Cal Pr.

Amundsen, Lou. Cardiac Rehabilitation. (Clinics in Physical Therapy Ser.). (Illus.). 224p. 1981. lib. bdg. 18.00 (ISBN 0-443-08147-6). Churchill.

Amundson, Neal R. Mathematical Methods in Chemical Engineering: Matrices & Their Application. 1966. ref. ed. 25.95 (ISBN 0-13-561084-2). P-H.

Amur, G. S. Images & Impressions. 1980. text ed. 11.00x (ISBN 0-391-01917-1). Humanities.

--Manohar Malgonkar. (Indian Writers Ser.). 1976. 8.50 (ISBN 0-89253-506-7). Ind-US Inc.

Ana, Julio De Santa see De Santa Ana, Julio.

Anagnostakos, Nicholos, jt. auth. see Tortora, Gerald.

Anagnostopoulos, Athan, tr. see Odysseus Elytis.

Anagnostou, C. Demetrius "On Style". A New Edition with Commentary. (London Studies in Classical Philology). 1980. pap. text ed. write for info. (ISBN 0-391-01158-8). Humanities.

Anak, Gde Agung. Twenty Years Indonesian Foreign Policy 1945-1965. LC 72-93180. 1973. text ed. 67.65x (ISBN 0-686-22635-6). Mouton.

Analytical Chemical Conference, 3rd, Budapest, 1970. Proceedings, 2 vols. Buzas, I., ed. Incl. Vol. 1. Separation Methods; Vol. 2. Organic Analysis. LC 72-184389. 777p. 1970. Set. 25.00x (ISBN 0-8002-1840-X). Intl Pubns Serv.

Ananchenko, S. N. & Ananchenko, S. N., eds. Proceedings of the International Symposium on Frontiers of Bioorganic Chemistry & Molcular Biology, Moscow & Tashkent, USSR, 1978: Proceedings of the International Symposium on Frontiers of Biorganic Chemistry & Molecular Biology, Moscow & Tashkent, USSR 1978. (IUPAC Symposium Ser.). (Illus.). 435p. Date not set. 92.00 (ISBN 0-08-023967-6). Pergamon. Postponed.

Anand, D. K. Introduction to Control Systems. LC 72-12834. 1974. text ed. 31.00 (ISBN 0-08-017104-4); pap. text ed. 17.60 (ISBN 0-08-019005-7). Pergamon.

Anand, Mulk R. Apology for Heroism: A Brief Autobiography of Ideas. 143p. 1974. 3.60 (ISBN 0-88253-478-5). Ind-US Inc.

--Between Tears & Laughter. 171p. 1974. pap. 2.75 (ISBN 0-88253-311-8). Ind-US Inc.

--Indian Fairy Tales. 2nd. ed. (Illus.). 166p. 1966. 4.00 (ISBN 0-88253-333-9). Ind-US Inc.

--More Indian Fairy Tales. 80p. (gr. 5-7). 1975. 4.00 (ISBN 0-88253-684-2). Ind-US Inc.

--Untouchable. 181p. 1974. pap. 2.75 (ISBN 0-88253-280-4). Ind-US Inc.

Anand, Mulk Raj & Hutheesing, Krishina N. The Book of Indian Beauty. LC 80-52066. (Illus.). 1981. 12.95 (ISBN 0-8048-1180-6). C E Tuttle.

Anand, Narender K., jt. auth. see Srivastava, Girish.

Anand, R. P. Compulsory Jurisdiction of the International Court of Justice. 10.00x (ISBN 0-210-33826-1). Asia.

Anand, Shahla. Of Costliest Emblem: Paradise Lost & the Emblem Tradition. LC 78-59853. (Illus.). 1978. pap. text ed. 11.25 (ISBN 0-8191-0556-2). U Pr of Amer.

Anand, Uma. The Tale of Lumbdoom, the Long-Tailed Langoor. (Illus.). 1968. 1.00 (ISBN 0-88253-325-8). Ind-US Inc.

Anand, Valerie. Gildenford. 1979. pap. 2.50 o.p. (ISBN 0-445-04336-9). Popular Lib.

Anania, Michael. Color of Dust. LC 71-116681. (New Poetry Ser.: No. 40). 70p. 1970. 6.50 (ISBN 0-8040-0048-4); pap. 4.50 (ISBN 0-8040-0049-2). Swallow.

Anania, Michael, ed. New Poetry Anthology One. LC 69-20470. (New Poetry Ser). 111p. (Orig.). 1969. 7.95x (ISBN 0-8040-0224-X); pap. 4.95x (ISBN 0-8040-0225-8). Swallow.

Ananikian, Mardiros H. Armenian Mythology & African Mythology. (Mythology of All Races Ser.: Vol. VII). Repr. of 1932 ed. 23.50 (ISBN 0-8154-0011-X). Cooper Sq.

Anan Isho, compiled by. The Wit & Wisdom of the Christian Fathers of Egypt: The Syrian Version of the Apophthegmata Patrum. Wallis Budge, Ernest A., tr. LC 80-2354. 1981. Repr. of 1934 ed. 53.50 (ISBN 0-404-18900-8). AMS Pr.

Anantanarayanan, M. The Silver Pilgrimage. (Indian Novels Ser.). 160p. 1976. pap. 2.75 (ISBN 0-89253-022-7). Ind-US Inc.

Anantendra-Yati. Vedanta-Sara-Sangraha. Mahadevan, T. M., tr. 1974. pap. 2.00 (ISBN 0-89744-124-9, Pub. by Ganesh & Co. India). Auromere.

Ananthanarayan, R. & Paniker, C. K. Textbook of Microbiology. 608p. 1979. 25.00x (ISBN 0-86131-032-2, Pub. by Orient Longman India). State Mutual Bk.

Anapol'Skaya, L. E. & Gandin, L. S. Environmental Factors in the Heating of Buildings. Greenberg, P., ed. Olaru, H., tr. from Rus. LC 75-6609. 238p. 1975. 32.50 (ISBN 0-470-02557-3). Halsted Pr.

Anastaplo, George. Human Being & Citizen: Essays on Virtue, Freedom & the Common Good. new ed. LC 75-21909. xiv, 332p. 1975. 16.95 (ISBN 0-8040-0677-6). Swallow.

--Human Being & Citizen: Essays on Virtue, Freedom & the Common Good. LC 75-21909. 1978. pap. 7.95 (ISBN 0-8040-0678-4). Swallow.

Anastasi, Thomas E., Jr. Communicating for Results. LC 72-82619. 200p. 1972. pap. text ed. 9.95 (ISBN 0-8465-0292-5). Benjamin-Cummings.

--How to Manage.., 4 vols. Incl. How to Manage Your Writing. 123p (ISBN 0-932078-46-X); How to Manage Your Speaking. 128p (ISBN 0-932078-45-1); How to Manage Your Reading. 129p (ISBN 0-932078-44-3); Face to Face Communication. 198p (ISBN 0-932078-47-8). 1974. pap. 6.50 ea.; pap. 24.50 set of four (ISBN 0-932078-43-5). GE Tech Prom & Train.

--The Manager's Desk Guide to Communication. 300p. 1981. 15.95 (ISBN 0-8436-0855-2). CBI Pub.

Anastasio, Dina. Careful Melinda, That Footstep Belongs to... !! (Write-It-Yourself Bks.). (Illus.). 48p. 1981. pap. 1.75 (ISBN 0-8431-0282-9). Price Stern.

--Crazy Freddy's in Trouble Again & His Parents Are Going to... !! (Write-It-Yourself Bks.). (Illus.). 48p. 1981. pap. 1.75 (ISBN 0-8431-0280-2). Price Stern.

--My Own Book, No. 6. 48p. (Orig.). 1981. pap. 1.75 (ISBN 0-8431-0698-0). Price Stern.

--Something Weird Is Happening to Matthew, & He's a Little... !! (Write-It-Yourself Bks.). (Illus.). 48p. 1981. pap. 1.75 (ISBN 0-8431-0281-0). Price Stern.

Anastos, Milton V. Studies in Byzantine Intellectual History. 432p. 1980. 78.00x (ISBN 0-86078-031-7, Pub. by Variorum England). State Mutual Bk.

Anaya, Rudolfo, tr. see Griego, Jose & Maestas.

Ancelet, Danielle. Cuisine of France. (Illus.). 184p. 1981. 15.95 (ISBN 0-312-17834-4). St Martin.

Anchin, Jack C. & Kiesler, Donald J., eds. Handbook of Interpersonal Psychotherapy. (Pergamon General Psychology Ser.). 400p. Date not set. price not set (ISBN 0-08-025959-6). Pergamon.

Anchor, R. D. Design of Liquid-Retaining Concrete Structures. 176p. 1981. 49.95 (ISBN 0-470-27123-X). Halsted Pr.

Anchor, Robert. The Enlightenment Tradition. LC 78-62855. (Cal Ser.: No. 411). 1979. 12.50x (ISBN 0-520-03805-3); pap. 3.95 (ISBN 0-520-03784-7). U of Cal Pr.

--Germany Confronts Modernization: German Culture & Society, 1790-1890. (Civilization & Society Ser). 224p. 1972. pap. 5.95x o.p. (ISBN 0-669-81026-6). Heath.

--Modern Western Experience. (Illus.). 1978. pap. text ed. 12.95 (ISBN 0-13-599357-1). P-H.

Anchor, Robert, tr. see Lukacs, Georg.

Anckarsvard, Karin. Aunt Vinnie's Invasion. LC 62-17039. (Illus.). 128p. (gr. 5-9). 1962. 4.50 o.p. (ISBN 0-15-204621-6, HJ). HarBraceJ.

Ancona, George. It's a Baby! LC 79-10453. (Illus.). (gr. k-3). 1979. PLB 8.95 (ISBN 0-525-32598-0). Dutton.

--Monster on Wheels. (Illus.). 48p. (gr. 3 up). 1974. PLB 8.95 (ISBN 0-525-35155-8). Dutton.

Ancowitz, Arthur M. Strokes & Their Prevention. (Orig.). pap. 2.75 (ISBN 0-515-05723-1). Jove Pubns.

Ancsel, Eva. The Dilemmas of Freedom. 1978. 9.00x (ISBN 9-6305-1694-2). Intl Pubns Serv.

Andacht, Sandra. Satsuma: An Illustrated Guide. 1978. softbound 7.95 o.p. (ISBN 0-87069-227-5). Wallace-Homestead.

Andancht, Sandra, et al. Wallace-Homestead Price Guide to Oriental Antiques. (Illus.). 308p. 1980. pap. 17.95 (ISBN 0-87069-295-X). Wallace-Homestead.

Anday, Melih C. Rain One Step Away. Halman, Talat & Swann, Brian, trs. LC 80-68880. 1980. 7.50 (ISBN 0-686-62254-5). Charioteer.

Andelin, Helen. Fascinating Womanhood. 320p. 1980. pap. 2.75 (ISBN 0-553-13988-6). Bantam.

Andelin, Helen B. La Mujer Encantadora. (Span.). 5.95 (ISBN 0-911094-02-4). Pacific Santa Barbara.

Andelson, G. W., jt. ed. see Bentzen, Aage.

Andenaes, Johannes. General Part of the Criminal Law of Norway. Ogle, T. P., tr. (New York University Comparative Criminal Law Project, Pubns: No. 3). 1965. 22.50x (ISBN 0-8377-0202-X). Rothman.

Anderegg, G., ed. see International Union of Pure & Applied Chemistry.

Anderegg, Michael. William Wyler. (Theatrical Arts Ser.). 1979. lib. bdg. 10.95 (ISBN 0-8057-9268-6). Twayne.

Anderman, Nancy. United States Supreme Court Decisions: An Index to Their Locations. LC 76-8479. 323p. 1976. 14.50 (ISBN 0-8108-0932-X). Scarecrow.

Anders, Edward, ed. see Heide, Fritz.

Anders, Gerhard, et al, eds. The Economics of Mineral Extraction. Gramm, W. Phillip. LC 79-22949. 334p. 1980. 29.95 (ISBN 0-03-053171-3). Praeger.

Anders, Mary E. Libraries & Library Services in the Southeast: A Report of the Southeastern States Cooperative Library Survey, 1972-1974. LC 75-44140. (Illus.). 272p. 1976. 18.50 (ISBN 0-8173-9705-1). U of Ala Pr.

Anders, Nedda C. Chafing Dish Specialties. LC 54-11633. 2.50 o.p. (ISBN 0-685-56521-1, 8208-0205). Hearthside.

Anders, Robert L. & Bermosk, Loretta S. Group Therapy: A Source of New Meaning. 1981. cancelled (ISBN 0-8036-0142-5). Davis Co.

Andersch, Alfred. Winterspelt. LC 76-56262. 1978. 10.00 o.p. (ISBN 0-385-01368-X). Doubleday.

Andersen, Ann H., jt. ed. see Huck, Virginia.

Andersen, Arlow W. The Norwegian-Americans. (The Immigrant Heritage of American Ser). 1975. lib. bdg. 9.95 (ISBN 0-8057-3249-7). Twayne.

Andersen, Christian A., ed. Microprobe Analysis. LC 72-8837. 656p. 1973. 43.00 (ISBN 0-471-02835-5, Pub. by Wiley-Interscience). Wiley.

Andersen, Christopher P. The Book of People. (Illus.). 500p. 1981. 19.95 (ISBN 0-399-12617-1, Perigee); pap. 9.95 (ISBN 0-399-50530-X). Putnam.

--A Star, Is a Star, Is a Star: The Life & Loves of Susan Hayward. LC 80-908. (Illus.). 288p. 1980. 12.95 (ISBN 0-385-15598-0). Doubleday.

Andersen, Francis I. The Sentence in Biblical Hebrew. (Janua Linguarum, Ser. Practica: No. 231). 209p. 1974. pap. text ed. 34.10x (ISBN 90-2792-673-5). Mouton.

Andersen, Gretchen. Creative Exploration in Crafts. (Illus.). 368p. 1976. 14.95 (ISBN 0-87909-169-X); pap. 9.95 (ISBN 0-87909-168-1). Reston.

Andersen, Hans C. Andersen's Fairy Tales. (gr. 1-5). 1963. 4.95g o.s.i. (ISBN 0-02-700920-3). Macmillan.

--Emperor & the Nightingale. LC 78-18065. (Illus.). (gr. 1-4). 1979. PLB 5.21 (ISBN 0-89375-134-0); pap. 1.50 (ISBN 0-89375-112-X). Troll Assocs.

--Emperor's New Clothes. Delano, Jack & Delano, Irene, eds. (Illus.). 1971. 4.95 o.p. (ISBN 0-394-82105-X, BYR); PLB 5.99 (ISBN 0-394-92105-4). Random.

--First Three Tales. 3rd ed. pap. 5.00x (ISBN 87-14-27297-0, D715). Vanous.

--Little Match Girl. LC 68-28050. (Illus.). (gr. k-3). 1968. reinforced bdg 7.95 (ISBN 0-395-21625-7); pap. 1.95 (ISBN 0-395-13712-8). HM.

--Little Mermaid. 3rd ed. pap. 5.00x (ISBN 8-7142-7783-2, D714). Vanous.

--The Princess & the Pea. LC 77-12707. (Illus.). (ps-2). 1978. 8.95 (ISBN 0-395-28807-X, Clarion). HM.

--Snow Queen. Magito, Suria & Weil, Rudolf, eds. LC 59-15639. 1960. pap. 2.95x (ISBN 0-87830-538-6). Theatre Arts.

--Tales & Stories by Hans Christian Andersen. Conroy, Patricia & Rossel, Sven H., trs. LC 80-50867. (Illus.). 316p. 1980. 17.50 (ISBN 0-295-95769-7). U of Wash Pr.

--Thumbeline. Winston, Richard & Winston, Clara, trs. from Danish. LC 80-13012. Orig. Title: Tommelise. (Illus.). 40p. (gr. k-3). 1980. 8.95 (ISBN 0-688-22235-8); PLB 8.59 (ISBN 0-688-32235-2). Morrow.

Andersen, Hans C., jt. auth. see Brown, Marcia.

Andersen, Hans Christian. The Complete Fairy Tales & Stories. LC 73-83583. 1152p. (gr. 1 up). 1974. 17.95a (ISBN 0-385-01901-7); PLB (ISBN 0-385-05867-5). Doubleday.

Andersen, Hans H., ed. Bibliography & Index of Experimental Range & Stopping Power Data. LC 77-22415. 1978. text ed. 48.00 (ISBN 0-08-021604-8). Pergamon.

Andersen, Hans H. & Ziegler, James F., eds. Hydrogen Stopping Powers & Ranges in All Elements. LC 77-3068. 1977. text ed. 40.00 (ISBN 0-08-021605-6). Pergamon.

Andersen, Ian. Making Money. LC 77-93232. 1978. 10.00 (ISBN 0-8149-0797-0). Vanguard.

Andersen, Jeul. The Tofu Primer: A Beginner's Book of Bean Cake Cookery. (Illus.). 50p. (Orig.). 1981. pap. 2.95 (ISBN 0-916870-33-2). Creative Arts Bk.

Andersen, Karen B. What's the Matter, Sylvie, Can't You Ride? LC 80-12514. (Illus.). 32p. (ps-3). 1981. 8.95 (ISBN 0-8037-9607-2); PLB 8.44 (ISBN 0-8037-9621-8). Dial.

Andersen, Kurt. The Real Thing. LC 78-22787. 192p. 1980. 8.95 (ISBN 0-385-14636-1). Doubleday.

Andersen, P. Vikings of the West-Expansion of Norway in Middle Ages. (Tanum of Norway Tokens Ser). (Illus.). pap. 11.00x (ISBN 82-518-0026-9, N508). Vanous.

Andersen, Paul. Obsolete Fractional Coinage of the United States. LC 79-55915. (Illus.). 67p. (Orig.). (gr. 9 up). 1980. pap. 2.95 (ISBN 0-9604720-0-2). P Andersen.

--Statically Indeterminate Structures: Their Analysis & Design. (Illus.). 1953. 14.95 o.p. (ISBN 0-8260-0395-8). Wiley.

Andersen, Poul-Gerhard. Organ Building & Design. Curnutt, Joanne, tr. (Illus.). 359p. 1969. 28.50 (ISBN 0-04-786003-0). Allen Unwin.

Andersen, R. & Barlag, R. They Were There. 1977. pap. 4.50 (ISBN 0-570-03769-7, 12-2704). Concordia.

Andersen, Richard. The Bread of Christmas. 32p. 1981. pap. 1.50 (ISBN 0-570-06983-1, 12-2605). Concordia.

--William Goldman. (United States Authors Ser.: No. 326). 1979. lib. bdg. 10.95 (ISBN 0-8057-7259-6). Twayne.

Andersen, Roger W., ed. New Dimensions in Second Language Acquisition Research. (Illus.). 280p. (Orig.). 1981. pap. text ed. 14.95 (ISBN 0-88377-180-2). Newbury Hse.

Andersen, Uell S. Three Magic Words. pap. 5.00 (ISBN 0-87980-165-4). Wilshire.

Anderson. Analysis of Teaching Physical Education. LC 79-20074. 1979. pap. 8.95 (ISBN 0-8016-0179-7). Mosby.

--Searching for Shona. (gr. 3-5). Date not set. pap. cancelled (ISBN 0-590-30313-9, Schol Pap). Schol Bk Serv.

Anderson & Becker. Pathology of Congenital Heart Disease. 1981. text ed. price not set. Butterworth.

Anderson & Sobieski. Introduction to Microbiology. 2nd ed. LC 79-20560. 1980. pap. 17.95 (ISBN 0-8016-0206-8). Mosby.

Anderson, jt. auth. see Farmer.

Anderson, et al. Canyon De Chelly: The Story Behind the Scenery. LC 79-157461. (Illus.). 1971. 7.95 (ISBN 0-916122-34-4); pap. 2.50 (ISBN 0-916122-09-3). K C Pubns.

--An Introduction to Management Science: Quantitative Approaches to Decision Making. 2nd ed. 1979. text ed. 19.95 (ISBN 0-8299-0193-0); study guide 7.50 (ISBN 0-8299-0283-X); instrs.' manual avail. (ISBN 0-8299-0451-4); transparency masters avail. (ISBN 0-8299-0452-2). West Pub.

Anderson, A. J. E. B. White: A Bibliography. LC 78-2783. (Author Bibliographies Ser.: No. 37). 1978. 10.00 (ISBN 0-8108-1121-9). Scarecrow.

Anderson, A. L. The Way. 1978. pap. 1.75 (ISBN 0-8100-0006-7, 12N1715). Northwest Pub.

Anderson, Alan, Jr., ed. see Smith, Dwight.

Anderson, Alan R., ed. Minds & Machines. (Orig.). 1964. pap. 7.95 ref. ed. (ISBN 0-13-583393-0). P-H.

Anderson, Alexandra, jt. auth. see Cohen, Randy.

Anderson, Anders H. Bibliography of Arizona Ornithology. LC 76-163008. 272p. (Orig.). 1972. pap. 2.00 (ISBN 0-8165-0313-3). U of Ariz Pr.

Anderson, Andrew R. Alexander's Gate, Gog & Magog & the Inclosed Nations. 1932. 7.50 o.p. (ISBN 0-910956-07-3). Medieval.

Anderson, Anita L., ed. Hidden Places, Secret Words. LC 80-81307. 1980. 9.95 (ISBN 0-89002-158-9); pap. 2.95 (ISBN 0-89002-149-X). Northwoods Pr.

Anderson, Annelise G. The Business of Organized Crime: A Cosa Nostra Family. (Publications 201 Ser.). (Illus.). 200p. 1979. 10.95 (ISBN 0-8179-7011-8). Hoover Inst Pr.

Anderson, Arthur J., tr. see De Sahagun, Bernardino.

Anderson, Arthur J., et al. Beyond the Codices: The Nahua View of Colonial Mexico. LC 74-29801. 225p. 1976. 21.50x (ISBN 0-520-02974-7). U of Cal Pr.

Anderson, B. Ray. How You Can Use Inflation to Beat IRS: All the Legal Ways to Keep Your Money for Yourself & Your Family... Without Getting in Trouble with the IRS. LC 80-8429. (Illus.). 416p. 1981. 12.95 (ISBN 0-06-014825-X, HarpT). Har-Row.

Anderson, B. Robert. Professional Selling. (Illus.). 400p. 1981. text ed. 16.50 (ISBN 0-13-725960-3). P-H.

--Professional Selling. (Illus.). 1977. text ed. 15.95 (ISBN 0-13-725937-9). P-H.

Anderson, B. Wylie, et al. Guide to Economic Analysis. 1978. pap. text ed. 8.95 (ISBN 0-8403-1827-8). Kendall-Hunt.

Anderson, Barbara & Shapiro, Pamela. Emergency Childbirth Handbook. 1979. pap. 7.40 (ISBN 0-8273-1761-1). Delmar.

--Obstetrics for the Nurse. LC 77-83424. 1979. pap. text ed. 7.40 (ISBN 0-8273-1330-6); instructor's guide 1.60 (ISBN 0-8273-1331-4). Delmar.

--Obstetrics for the Nurse. 272p. 1981. text ed. 13.95 (ISBN 0-442-21840-0). Van Nos Reinhold.

Anderson, Barbara A. Internal Migration During Modernization in Late Nineteenth-Century Russia. LC 80-7509. (Illus.). 248p. 1980. 18.00 (ISBN 0-691-09386-5). Princeton U Pr.

Anderson, Barbara G. The Aging Game: Success, Sanity, & Sex After 60. 252p. 1981. pap. 4.95 (ISBN 0-07-001761-1). McGraw.

Anderson, Barry F. Cognitive Psychology: The Study of Knowing, Learning & Thinking. 1975. 16.95 (ISBN 0-12-057850-6). Acad Pr.

Anderson, Bernhard W. Understanding the Old Testament. 3rd ed. 608p. 1975. 18.95 (ISBN 0-13-936153-7). P-H.

Anderson, Bert M. Write True to Yourself So You Sell: 19 Lessons in Folios. write for info. (ISBN 0-917628-02-0). Coraco.

Anderson, Beverly M. & Hamilton, Donna M. The New High Altitude Cookbook. LC 80-5287. (Illus.). 320p. 1980. 13.95 (ISBN 0-394-51308-8). Random.

Anderson, Bob, ed. Best of on the Run. pap. cancelled o.s.i. (ISBN 0-89037-208-X). Anderson World.

Anderson, Brian & Moore, John B. Optimal Filtering. 1979. 27.95 (ISBN 0-13-638122-7). P-H.

Anderson, Bruce & Riordan, Michael. The Solar Home Book: Heating, Cooling, & Designing with the Sun. LC 76-29494. (Illus.). 1976. o.p. (ISBN 0-917352-02-5); pap. 9.50 (ISBN 0-917352-01-7). Brick Hse Pub.

Anderson, Bruce & Wells, Malcolm. Passive Solar Energy: A Complete Guide to Heating & Cooling with Solar Power. LC 80-70147. (Illus.). 208p. 1980. 17.95 (ISBN 0-931790-51-4); pap. 8.95 (ISBN 0-931790-09-3). Brick Hse Pub.

--Passive Solar Energy: The Homeowners Guide to Natural Heating & Cooling. (Illus., Orig.). 1981. 17.95 (ISBN 0-931790-51-4); pap. 8.95 (ISBN 0-931790-09-3). Brick Hse Pub.

Anderson, Burton. Vino: The Wine & Winemakers of Italy. (Illus.). 416p. 1980. 19.95 (ISBN 0-316-03948-9). Little.

Anderson, Byron. A Bibliography of Master's Theses & Doctoral Dissertations on Milwaukee Topics, 1911-1977. LC 80-27261. 136p. (Orig.). 1981. pap. 3.95x (ISBN 0-87020-202-2). State Hist Soc Wis.

Anderson, C. Arnold, jt. auth. see Carnegie Commission on Higher Education.

Anderson, C. Dixon. Spanish in Context: A Basic Course. (Illus.). 1978. text ed. 16.95 (ISBN 0-13-824235-6); pap. 7.95 student wkbk (ISBN 0-13-824243-7). P-H.

Anderson, C. L. Health Principles & Practice. rev. ed. 6th ed. LC 74-106045. (Illus.). 1970. text ed. 12.50 o.p. (ISBN 0-8016-0239-4). Mosby.

Anderson, C. L. & Creswell, William H., Jr. School Health Practice. 6th ed. LC 75-37562. (Illus.). 480p. 1976. 13.95 o.p. (ISBN 0-8016-0215-7). Mosby.

Anderson, C. L. & Morton, Richard R. Community Health. 3rd ed. LC 77-23864. (Illus.). 1978. text ed. 15.95 (ISBN 0-8016-0182-7). Mosby.

Anderson, C. N., ed. see Kohner, Frederick.

Anderson, C. Richard. OSHA & Accident Control Through Training. LC 74-16444. (Illus.). 225p. 1975. 20.00 (ISBN 0-8311-1094-5). Indus Pr.

Anderson, C. W. Blaze & the Gray Spotted Pony. LC 68-10997. (Illus.). 48p. (gr. k-3). 1974. pap. 2.95 (ISBN 0-02-041480-3, 04148, Collier). Macmillan.

Anderson, Carl L. & Creswell, William H., Jr. School Health Practice. 7th ed. LC 79-27664. (Illus.). 1980. text ed. 16.95 (ISBN 0-8016-0216-5). Mosby.

Anderson, Chaney & Pierce, R. C., Jr. Elementary Calculus for Business, Economics & Social Sciences. 1975. text ed. 17.50 (ISBN 0-395-18960-8); instructors manual 1.90 (ISBN 0-395-18959-4). HM.

Anderson, Charles. Political Economy of Social Class. 384p. 1974. text ed. 17.95 (ISBN 0-13-685149-5). P-H.

Anderson, Charles H. & Gibson, Jeffry R. Toward a New Sociology. 3rd ed. 1978. pap. text ed. 10.95x (ISBN 0-256-02062-0). Dorsey.

Anderson, Charles J., ed. Fact Book for Academic Administrators 1980. 1980. 25.00 (ISBN 0-8268-1197-3). ACE.

Anderson, Charles W. Political Economy of Modern Spain: Policy-Making in an Authoritarian System. LC 72-106036. (Illus.). 1970. 25.00 (ISBN 0-299-05611-2); pap. 7.95 (ISBN 0-299-05614-7). U of Wis Pr.

--Statecraft: An Introduction to Political Choice & Judgment. LC 76-22740. 1977. text ed. 16.95 (ISBN 0-471-02896-7); tchrs. manual 2.00 (ISBN 0-471-02429-5). Wiley.

Anderson, Chester. Fox & Hare. LC 80-66869. (Illus.). 192p. 1980. 20.00 (ISBN 0-9601428-0-0); pap. 9.95 (ISBN 0-9601428-9-4). Entwhistle Bks.

Anderson, Chris. The Name Game. 1979. pap. 2.50 (ISBN 0-515-04857-7). Jove Pubns.

Anderson, Christian & Hawes, J. L. Basic Experimental Chemistry: A Laboratory Manual for Beginning Students. rev. ed. 1971. pap. 9.95 (ISBN 0-8053-0222-0). Benjamin-Cummings.

Anderson, Clarence W. Afraid to Ride. (Illus.). (gr. 3-7). 1962. 4.95g o.s.i. (ISBN 0-02-701440-1). Macmillan.

--Another Man O' War. (Illus.). (gr. 4-6). 1966. 4.95g o.s.i. (ISBN 0-02-701610-2). Macmillan.

--Billy & Blaze. (Illus.). (gr. k-3). 1962. 6.95 (ISBN 0-02-701880-6). Macmillan.

--Blaze & the Forest Fire. (Illus.). (gr. k-3). 1962. 8.95 (ISBN 0-02-702080-0). Macmillan.

--Blaze & the Gray Spotted Pony. LC 68-10997. (Illus.). (ps-2). 1968. 6.95 (ISBN 0-02-701150-X). Macmillan.

--Blaze & the Lost Quarry. (Illus.). (gr. 1-3). 1966. 4.95g o.s.i. (ISBN 0-02-702490-3). Macmillan.

--Blaze & the Mountain Lion. (gr. 1-3). 1959. 8.95 (ISBN 0-02-702630-2). Macmillan.

--Blaze & Thunderbolt. (Illus.). (gr. 1-3). 1962. 8.95 (ISBN 0-02-702870-4). Macmillan.

--Blaze Finds Forgotten Roads. LC 76-117970. (Illus.). (gr. k-3). 1970. 6.95 (ISBN 0-02-701340-5). Macmillan.

--Blaze Finds the Trail. (Illus.). (gr. 1-3). 1962. 4.50g o.s.i. (ISBN 0-02-703130-6). Macmillan.

--Blaze Shows the Way. LC 74-78090. (Illus.). (gr. 1-3). 1969. 6.95 (ISBN 0-02-701990-X). Macmillan.

--Blind Connemara. (Illus.). (gr. 4-6). 1971. 4.95g o.s.i. (ISBN 0-02-705000-9). Macmillan.

--Crooked Colt. (Illus.). (gr. k-3). 1966. 7.95 (ISBN 0-02-703410-0). Macmillan.

--Filly for Joan. (Illus.). (gr. 3-7). 1962. 4.95g o.s.i. (ISBN 0-02-703620-0). Macmillan.

--Heads Up, Heels Down. (Illus.). (gr. 8 up). 1944. 5.95g o.s.i. (ISBN 0-02-704160-3). Macmillan.

--High Courage. (Illus.). (gr. 7 up). 1968. 6.95 (ISBN 0-02-704280-4). Macmillan.

--Horse of Hurricane Hill. (Illus.). (gr. 3-7). 1962. 4.95g o.s.i. (ISBN 0-02-704520-X). Macmillan.

--Lonesome Little Colt. (gr. k-3). 1961. 4.95g o.s.i. (ISBN 0-02-704840-3). Macmillan.

--Outlaw. (gr. 3-6). 1967. 5.95g o.s.i. (ISBN 0-02-700940-8). Macmillan.

--Phantom, Son of the Gray Ghost. LC 69-18233. (Illus.). (gr. 4-6). 1969. 6.95g (ISBN 0-02-701350-2). Macmillan.

--Pony for Linda. (Illus.). (gr. k-3). 1951. 7.95 (ISBN 0-02-705050-5). Macmillan.

--Pony for Three. (Illus.). (gr. 1-3). 1958. 7.95 (ISBN 0-02-705160-9). Macmillan.

--Rumble Seat Pony. LC 71-127466. (Illus.). (gr. k-3). 1971. 7.95 (ISBN 0-02-705490-X). Macmillan.

--Salute. (Illus.). (gr. 2-4). 1967. 3.95g o.s.i. (ISBN 0-02-705270-2). Macmillan.

--Twenty Gallant Horses. (gr. 5 up). 1965. 8.95 (ISBN 0-02-705530-2). Macmillan.

Anderson, Courtney. To the Golden Shore: The Life of Adoniram Judson. 1977. pap. 6.95 (ISBN 0-310-36131-1). Zondervan.

Anderson, D. Blood Brothers. LC 67-17800. (Illus.). 1969. 5.95 o.p. (ISBN 0-312-08400-5). St Martin.

Anderson, D., et al, eds. Pipe & Tube Fabrication. 2nd ed. (Engineering Craftsmen: No. D3). (Illus.). 1978. spiral bdg. 16.50x (ISBN 0-85083-415-5). Intl Ideas.

Anderson, D. A. All the Trees & Woody Plants of the Bible. 1979. cloth 10.95 (ISBN 0-8499-0138-3). Word Bks.

Anderson, D. Carl. Trial by Death & Fire. LC 80-14446. (Orion Ser.). 160p. 1980. pap. 2.95 (ISBN 0-8127-0292-1). Southern Pub.

Anderson, D. Chris & Borkowski, John G. Experimental Psychology: Research Tactics & Their Applications. 1978. 16.95x (ISBN 0-673-07866-3). Scott F.

Anderson, D. Chris, jt. auth. see Borkowski, John G.

Anderson, D. J., ed. Physiology: Past, Present, & Future: A Symposium in Honour of Yngve Zotterman, University of Bristol, July 11 & 12, 1979. LC 80-40957. (Illus.). 168p. 1980. 27.00 (ISBN 0-08-025480-2). Pergamon.

Anderson, D. L. Embryology & Phylogeny in Annelids & Arthropods. LC 73-1019. 492p. 1974. 50.00 (ISBN 0-08-017069-2). Pergamon.

Anderson, D. R., et al. Instructional Programming for the Handicapped Student. (Illus.). 1024p. 1976. 49.75 (ISBN 0-398-03339-0); pap. 37.50 (ISBN 0-398-03340-4). C C Thomas.

Anderson, Dave. Great Pass Receivers of the NFL. (NFL Punt, Pass & Kick Library). (gr. 5-9). 1966. PLB 3.69 (ISBN 0-394-90196-7, BYR). Random.

Anderson, David & Smith, William A. Forest & Forestry. 2nd ed. LC 75-23932. (gr. 10-12). 1976. 15.35 o.p. (ISBN 0-8134-1764-3); text ed. 11.50x o.p. (ISBN 0-685-71178-1, 1764). Interstate.

Anderson, David & Smith William, A., eds. Forest & Forestry. 3rd ed. (gr. 10-12). 1981. 14.00 (ISBN 0-8134-2169-1); text ed. 10.50x. Interstate.

Anderson, David, tr. from Greek. On the Divine Images: St. John of Damascus. LC 80-13409. 106p. 1980. pap. 3.95 (ISBN 0-913836-62-1). St Vladimirs.

Anderson, David, tr. see St. Basil The Great.

Anderson, David, et al. Essentials of Management Science: Applications to Decision Making. (Illus.). 1978. text ed. 19.95 (ISBN 0-8299-0147-7); study guide 7.95 (ISBN 0-8299-0202-3); test bank avail. (ISBN 0-8299-0455-7); instrs.' manual avail. (ISBN 0-8299-0453-0); transparency masters avail. (ISBN 0-8299-0454-9). West Pub.

Anderson, David D. Abraham Lincoln. (U. S. Authors Ser.: No. 153). 1970. lib. bdg. 9.95 (ISBN 0-8057-0452-3). Twayne.

--Ignatius Donnelly. (United States Author Ser.: No. 362). 1980. lib. bdg. 14.50 (ISBN 0-8057-7303-7). Twayne.

Anderson, David D., ed. Dimensions of His Literary Art: A Collection of Critical Essays. 141p. 1976. 9.50x (ISBN 0-87013-204-0). Mich St U Pr.

Anderson, David R., et al. Practical Controllership. 3rd ed. 1973. text ed. 18.50x o.p. (ISBN 0-256-00008-5). Irwin.

Anderson, Dean A. Laboratory Instructions in Microbiology. 2nd ed. LC 73-18202. 1974. text ed. 7.95 o.p. (ISBN 0-8016-0171-1). Mosby.

Anderson, Decima M. Computer Programming: Fortran Four. (Illus., Orig.). 1966. pap. 13.95 (ISBN 0-13-164822-5). P-H.

Anderson, Dennis R. American Flower Painting. (Illus.). 84p. 1980. text ed. 25.00 (ISBN 0-8230-0211-X). Watson-Guptill.

Anderson, Diann, jt. auth. see Cosgriff, James H., Jr.

Anderson, Digby C., ed. The Ignorance of Social Intervention. 163p. 1980. 27.50x (ISBN 0-7099-0270-0, Pub. by Croom Helm Ltd England). Biblio Dist.

Anderson, Donald K., Jr. John Ford. (English Authors Ser.: No. 129). lib. bdg. 10.95 (ISBN 0-8057-1204-6). Twayne.

Anderson, Donald K., Jr., ed. see Ford, John.

Anderson, Donald L. & Raun, Donald L. Information Analysis in Management Accounting. LC 77-14938. (Accounting & Information Systems Ser.). 1978. pap. text ed. 24.50 (ISBN 0-471-02815-0); tchrs. manual 6.00 (ISBN 0-471-05664-2). Wiley.

Anderson, Dorothy M. Women, Design, & the Cambridge School. LC 80-81341. (Illus.). 246p. 1980. 15.95 (ISBN 0-914886-10-X). PDA Pubs.

Anderson, Doug. Eye Spy: A Collection of Tricky, Sneaky, Puzzling Pictures to Test Your Eyes & Memory. LC 80-52329. (Illus.). 128p. (gr. 4 up). 1980. 6.95 (ISBN 0-8069-4628-8); PLB 6.69 (ISBN 0-8069-4629-6). Sterling.

Anderson, Douglas. All About Cribbage. 1978. pap. 3.95 (ISBN 0-87691-262-5). Winchester Pr.

--The One Real Poem Is Life. LC 72-93478. 1973. 5.95 o.s.i. (ISBN 0-8076-0669-3). Braziller.

Anderson, Douglas A. New Approaches to Family Pastoral Care. LC 79-8898. (Creative Pastoral Care & Counseling Ser.). 96p. (Orig.). 1980. pap. 3.25 (ISBN 0-8006-0564-0, 1-564). Fortress.

--Washington Merry-Go-Round of Libel Actions. LC 79-18126. 1980. 19.95x; pap. 9.95 (ISBN 0-88229-746-5). Nelson-Hall.

Anderson, Douglas D. Regulatory Politics & Electric Utilities. 200p. 1981. 19.95 (ISBN 0-86569-058-8). Auburn Hse.

Anderson, Duane C. & Semken, Holmes, eds. The Cherokee Excavations: Holocene Ecology & Human Adaptations in Northwestern Iowa. (Studies in Archaeology). 1980. 23.00 (ISBN 0-12-058260-0). Acad Pr.

Anderson, E. B., et al. The Oxford Book of Garden Flowers. (Illus.). 1963. 27.50 (ISBN 0-19-910002-0). Oxford U Pr.

Anderson, Edna M. Tamsen: The Donner Party. 1973. pap. 1.50 (ISBN 0-87508-761-2). Chr Lit.

Anderson, Edwin P., jt. auth. see Miller, Rex.

Anderson, Elaine. With God's Help Flowers Bloom. 1978. pap. 3.75 (ISBN 0-89137-411-6); study guide 2.45 (ISBN 0-89137-412-4). Quality Pubns.

Anderson, Eleanor. How to Raise & Train a Puli. (Orig.). pap. 1.79 o.p. (ISBN 0-87666-367-6, DS1108). TFH Pubns.

Anderson, Elijah. A Place on the Corner. LC 78-1879. (Studies of Urban Society). 248p. 1981. pap. 5.50 (ISBN 0-226-01954-3). U of Chicago Pr.

Anderson, Elisabeth, et al. Cabin Comments: A Journal of Life in Jackson Hole. LC 80-53090. (Illus.). 286p. (gr. 7-12). 1980. 14.95 (ISBN 0-933160-08-9); pap. 7.75 (ISBN 0-933160-07-0). Teton Bkshop.

Anderson, Elizabeth, ed. Directory of Newspaper Libraries in the U. S. & Canada. 2nd ed. LC 76-9751. 1980. write for info. (ISBN 0-87111-265-5). SLA.

Anderson, Ella. Jo-Jo. 1975. pap. 1.25 (ISBN 0-87508-693-4). Chr Lit.

Anderson, Ellen M. & Vervoren, Thora M. Workbook of Solutions & Dosage of Drugs, Including Arithmetic. 10th ed. (Illus.). 168p. 1976. pap. 7.95 o.p. (ISBN 0-8016-0235-1). Mosby.

Anderson, Elliott, jt. ed. see Hayman, David.

Anderson, Eloise. Carlos Goes to School. LC 72-89478. (Illus.). 32p. (gr. 1-3). 1973. PLB 4.95 (ISBN 0-7232-6095-8). Warne.

Anderson, Eric, jt. auth. see Ingraham, F.

Anderson, Erica, ed. see Schweitzer, Albert.

Anderson, Erland. Harmonious Madness: A Study of Musical Metaphors in the Poetry of Coleridge, Shelley & Keats. (Salzburg Studies in English Literature, Romantic Reassessment Ser.: No. 12). 321p. 1975. pap. text ed. 25.00x (ISBN 0-391-01299-1). Humanities.

Anderson, Eugene N. & Anderson, Pauline R. Political Institutions & Social Change in Continental Europe in the Nineteenth Century. 1967. 23.50x (ISBN 0-520-00022-6). U of Cal Pr.

Anderson, Evelyn M. Only a Woman. (Ultra Bks Ser). 1969. 3.50 (ISBN 0-8010-0062-9). Baker Bk.

Anderson, Evelyn M., jt. ed. see Carney, Andrew L.

Anderson, F. Douglas, jt. auth. see Tait, James A.

Anderson, Frances E. Christopher Smart. (English Authors Ser.: No. 161). 1974. lib. bdg. 10.95 (ISBN 0-8057-1502-9). Twayne.

Anderson, Frank. Orchids. (Abbeville Library of Art Ser.). (Illus.). 112p. 1981. pap. 4.95 (ISBN 0-89659-122-0). Abbeville Pr.
--Redoute Roses. (Abbeville Library of Art Ser.). (Illus.). 112p. 1981. pap. 4.95 (ISBN 0-89659-096-8). Abbeville Pr.
Anderson, Frank J. Cultivated Flowers. (Abbeville Library of Art Ser.). (Illus.). 112p. (Orig.). 1981. pap. 4.95 (ISBN 0-89659-182-4). Abbeville Pr.
--An Illustrated History of the Herbals. LC 77-8821. (Illus.). 1977. 20.00x (ISBN 0-231-04002-4). Columbia U Pr.
--An Illustrated Treasury of Cultivated Flowers. LC 79-64989. (Illus.). 160p. 1980. 17.95 (ISBN 0-89659-066-6). Abbeville Pr.
--An Illustrated Treasury of Orchids. LC 79-88367. (Illus.). 160p. 1980. 17.95 (ISBN 0-89659-067-4). Abbeville Pr.
Anderson, Frank R. Quality Controlled Investing: Or How to Avoid the Pick & Pray Method. LC 78-7607. 1978. 19.95 (ISBN 0-471-04382-6, Pub. by Wiley-Interscience). Wiley.
Anderson, Frederick, et al, eds. see Twain, Mark.
Anderson, Frederick, et al, eds. see Twain, Mark & Howells, William D.
Anderson, Fredrick, ed. Mark Twain: The Critical Heritage. (The Critical Heritage Ser.). 1971. 30.00 (ISBN 0-7100-7084-5). Routledge & Kegan.
Anderson, Fulton H., ed. see Bacon, Francis.
Anderson, G. Douglas. All About Cribbage. 1971. 8.95 (ISBN 0-87691-041-X). Winchester Pr.
Anderson, G. L., ed. Asian Literature in English: A Guide to Information Sources. (American, English Literature & World Literatures in English Information Guide Ser.: Vol. 31). 300p. 1981. 30.00 (ISBN 0-8103-1362-6). Gale.
Anderson, G. L, ed. Masterpieces of the Orient. pap. 8.95x (ISBN 0-393-09542-8, NortonC); expanded pap. 1976 15.95x (ISBN 0-393-09196-1). Norton.
Anderson, G. W. The History and Religion of Israel. (New Clarendon Bible Ser.). (Illus.). 222p. 1966. pap. 6.95x (ISBN 0-19-836915-8). Oxford U Pr.
Anderson, Gene. Coring & Core Analysis Handbook. LC 74-33713. 1975. 23.00 (ISBN 0-87814-058-1). Pennwell Pub.
Anderson, Gene C. & Raff, Beverly, eds. Newborn Behavioral Organization: Nursing Research &Implications. LC 79-2597. (Alan R. Liss Ser.: Vol. 15, No. 7). 1979. 24.00 (ISBN 0-8451-1032-2). March of Dimes.
Anderson, George B. One Hundred Booming Years. Row, H. J. & Stupek, D., eds. (Illus.). 305p. 1980. 32.50 (ISBN 0-9604136-0-X). Bucyrus-Erie Co.
Anderson, George K. Legend of the Wandering Jew. LC 65-14290. 489p. 1970. Repr. of 1965 ed. 20.00 (ISBN 0-87057-094-3, Pub. by Brown U Pr). Univ Pr of New England.
Anderson, George K. & Buckler, William E. The Literature of England: Single Volume Edition. rev. ed. 1967. 17.95x (ISBN 0-673-05656-2). Scott F.
Anderson, George K., tr. The Saga of the Volsungs. LC 80-65685. 200p. 1981. 18.00 (ISBN 0-87413-172-3). U Delaware Pr.
Anderson, George M. The Work of Adalbert Johann Volck, 1828-1912: Who Chose for His Name the Anagram, V. Blada, 1861-1865. (Illus.). 1970. 35.00 (ISBN 0-938420-19-4). Md Hist.
Anderson, Gerald H. & Stransky, Thomas F. Christ's Lordship & Religious Pluralism. LC 80-25406. 256p. (Orig.). 1981. pap. 8.95 (ISBN 0-88344-088-1). Orbis Bks.
Anderson, Gerald H. & Stransky, Thomas F., eds. Mission Trends No. Five: Faith Meets Faith. (Mission Trends Ser.). 320p. (Orig.). 1981. pap. 3.95 (ISBN 0-8028-1821-8). Eerdmans.
--Mission Trends No.5: Faith Meets Faith, No. 5. (Orig.). 1981. pap. 3.95 (ISBN 0-8091-2356-8). Paulist Pr.
Anderson, Gerald H., jt. ed. see Stransky, Thomas.
Anderson, Glen E. Water Skiing Skill. (Quick & Easy Ser). (gr. 7-12). 1968. pap. 1.95 o.s.i. (ISBN 0-02-079080-5, Collier). Macmillan.
Anderson, H. G. & Trigg, C. F. Case-Histories in Engineering Geology. (Illus.). 1977. 35.00 (ISBN 0-236-40049-5, Pub. by Paul Elek). Merrimack Bk Serv.
Anderson, H. George, tr. see Thielicke, Helmut.
Anderson, Henry R. & Raiborn, Mitchell H. Basic Cost Accounting Concepts. LC 76-12017. (Illus.). 720p. 1977. text ed. 19.95 (ISBN 0-395-20646-4); instructor's manual with solutions 7.25 (ISBN 0-395-20648-0); test bank 3.25 (ISBN 0-395-20649-9). HM.
Anderson, Howard J. Primer on Labor Relations. 160p. pap. 7.50. BNA.
Anderson, Howard R., ed. see Kublin, Hyman.
Anderson, Hoyt. The Disabled Homemaker. (Illus.). 328p. 1980. 19.50 (ISBN 0-398-04077-X); pap. 12.75 (ISBN 0-398-04078-8). C C Thomas.
Anderson, I. G., ed. Councils, Committees & Boards: A Handbook of Advisory, Cunsultative, Executive & Similar Bodies in British Public Life. 4th ed. 409p. 1980. 100.00x (ISBN 0-900246-32-4). Intl Pubns Serv.
--Current Asian & Australian Directories. 264p. 1978. 85.00x (ISBN 0-900246-25-1). Intl Pubns Serv.
--Current British Directories. 9th ed. LC 53-26894. 1979. 105.00x (ISBN 0-900246-31-6). Intl Pubns Serv.
--Current British Directories: A Guide to the Directories Published in Great Britain, Ireland, British Commonwealth & South Africa. 9th ed. 369p. 1979. 120.00 (ISBN 0-900246-31-6). Gale.
--Directory of European Associations: National Industrial, Trade & Professional Associations, Pt. One. 3rd ed. 500p. 1981. 125.00. Gale.
--Directory of European Associations: Part 1 - National Industrial, Trade & Professional Associations. 2nd ed. LC 76-11697. 1976. 125.00 (ISBN 0-685-67342-1, Pub. by CBD Research). Gale.
--Directory of European Associations: Part 2-National Learned, Scientific & Technical Societies. 2nd ed. LC 76-11697. 1979. 130.00 (ISBN 0-900246-29-4, Pub. by CBD Research). Gale.
Anderson, Irvine H. Aramco, the United States, & Saudi Arabia: A Study of the Dynamics of Foreign Oil Policy, 1933-1950. LC 80-8535. 288p. 1981. 15.00x (ISBN 0-691-04679-4). Princeton U Pr.
Anderson, J. A., jt. auth. see Grahame, R.
Anderson, J. C., et al. Data & Formulae for Engineering Students. 2nd ed. 1969. text ed. 8.50 (ISBN 0-08-013989-2); pap. text ed. 3.50 (ISBN 0-08-013988-4). Pergamon.
--Materials Science. 2nd ed. LC 74-9620. 1975. 21.95 (ISBN 0-470-02830-0). Halsted Pr.
Anderson, J. D., et al, eds. Nuclear Isospin. 1969. 52.50 (ISBN 0-12-058150-7). Acad Pr.
Anderson, J. E., tr. see Lefebvre, Georges.
Anderson, J. Edward. Transit Systems Theory. LC 77-11856. (Illus.). 1978. 24.95 (ISBN 0-669-01902-X). Lexington Bks.
Anderson, J. G. The Structure of Western Europe. 1978. text ed. 30.00 (ISBN 0-08-022045-2); pap. text ed. 14.00 (ISBN 0-08-022046-0). Pergamon.
Anderson, J. G. & Owen, T. R. The Structure of the British Isles. 1968. 18.00 (ISBN 0-08-012423-2); pap. 11.25 (ISBN 0-08-012422-4). Pergamon.
--The Structure of the British Isles. 2nd ed. LC 80-41075. (Illus.). 242p. 1980. 28.00 (ISBN 0-08-023998-6); pap. 13.50 (ISBN 0-08-023997-8). Pergamon.
Anderson, J. G. C. & Owen, T. R. Field Geology in Britain. Date not set. 36.01 (ISBN 0-08-022054-1); pap. 12.01 (ISBN 0-08-022055-X). Pergamon.
Anderson, J. K. Ancient Greek Horsemanship. (Illus.). 1961. 28.50x (ISBN 0-520-00023-4). U of Cal Pr.
--Military Theory & Practice in the Age of Xenophon. LC 74-104010. 1970. 25.75x (ISBN 0-520-01564-9). U of Cal Pr.
Anderson, J. M., jt. auth. see Lass, R.
Anderson, J. M. & MacFadden, A., eds. The Role of Terrestrial & Aquatic Organisms in Decomposition Processes. LC 76-9830. (British Ecological Society Symposia Ser.). 474p. 1977. 38.95 (ISBN 0-470-15105-6). Halsted Pr.
Anderson, J. R. High Mountains & Cold Seas: A Biography of H. W. Tilman. LC 80-81520. (Illus.). 364p. 1980. 20.00 (ISBN 0-89886-008-3). Mountaineers.
--Sprig of Sea Lavender. 1980. pap. 2.25 (ISBN 0-440-18321-9). Dell.
Anderson, Jack & Boyd, James. Confessions of a Muckraker. 416p. 1980. pap. 2.95 (ISBN 0-345-26025-2). Ballantine.
Anderson, Jack & Pronzini, Bill. The Cambodia File. LC 80-5447. 456p. 1981. 13.95 (ISBN 0-385-14984-0). Doubleday.
Anderson, Jacqulyn. Dewey Decimal & Sears Update: Supplement to How to Classify, Catalog, & Maintain Media. 1981. Repr. saddle wire 2.25 (ISBN 0-8054-3705-3). Broadman.
Anderson, James E., ed. Economic Regulatory Policies. LC 76-44023. 232p. 1977. pap. 6.95 (ISBN 0-8093-0818-5). S Ill U Pr.
Anderson, James L. & Cohen, Martin. The Competitive Edge: The West Point Guide for the Weekend Athlete. (Illus.). 1981. 14.95. Morrow.
--The Competitive Edge: The West Point Guide for the Weekend Athlete. LC 80-23535. (Illus.). 352p. 1981. 14.95 (ISBN 0-688-00352-4). Morrow.
--The West Point Fitness & Diet Book. 1978. pap. 3.95 (ISBN 0-380-01894-2, 37342). Avon.
--The West Point Fitness & Diet Book. 256p. 1981. pap. 2.95 (ISBN 0-380-54205-6, 54205). Avon.
Anderson, James L., jt. auth. see Kennett, Lee.
Anderson, James M. Structural Aspects of Language Change. (Linguistics Library Ser.: No. 13). (Illus.). 1973. 14.95x (ISBN 0-582-55032-7); pap. 10.95x (ISBN 0-582-55033-5). Longman.
Anderson, James M. & Creore, JoAnn. Readings in Romance Linguistics. (Illus.). 472p. (Orig.). 1972. pap. text ed. 38.25x (ISBN 90-2792-303-5). Mouton.
Anderson, Jane. Inn Perspective: A Guide to New England Country Inns. LC 74-1785. (Illus.). 288p. 1976. 12.50 o.p. (ISBN 0-06-010138-5, HarpT); pap. 4.95 (ISBN 0-06-010137-7, TD-223, HarpT). Har-Row.
Anderson, Jean & Hanna, Elaine. The Doubleday Cookbook: Complete Contemporary Cooking. LC 75-1000. 1344p. 1975. 15.95 (ISBN 0-385-09088-9). Doubleday.
Anderson, Jennifer. Cave Exploring. (Illus.). 128p. 1974. pap. 4.95 o.p. (ISBN 0-8096-1889-3, Assn Pr). Follett.
Anderson, Jennifer, ed. see Woodman, Bill.
Anderson, Jim. How to Live Rent Free in the 1980's: It's Not Too Late! 1980. write for info. (ISBN 0-932574-04-1). Brun Pr.
--Jim Anderson's How to Live Rent in the 1980's, Vol. 2. (Illus.). 324p. 1980. 25.00 (ISBN 0-932574-02-5); pap. 15.00 (ISBN 0-932574-03-3). Brun Pr.
Anderson, Joanne. For the People: A Consumer Action Handbook. LC 77-73065. 1977. pap. 5.95 o.p. (ISBN 0-201-00200-0). A-W.
Anderson, Johannes E. Myths & Legends of the Polynesians. LC 69-13509. (Illus.). (gr. 9 up). 1969. Repr. of 1928 ed. 15.00 (ISBN 0-8048-0414-1). C E Tuttle.
Anderson, John. Education & Inquiry. Phillips, D. Z., ed. 228p. 1980. 27.00x (ISBN 0-389-20075-1). B&N.
--An Essay Concerning Aspect: Some Considerations of a General Character Arising from the Abbe Darrigol's Analysis of the Basque Verb. (Janua Linguarum Ser. Minor: No. 167). 1973. pap. text ed. 20.00x (ISBN 90-2792-408-2). Mouton.
--Reptilia & Batrachia. (Zoology of Egypt: No. 1). (Illus.). 1965. Repr. of 1898 ed. 150.00 (ISBN 3-7682-0240-2). Lubrecht & Cramer.
Anderson, John, ed. Language Form & Linguistic Variation. (Current Issue in Linguistic Theory: No. 15). 370p. 1980. text ed. 45.75x (ISBN 0-686-65680-6). Humanities.
Anderson, John B., et al, eds. Congress & Conscience. LC 77-120331. 1970. 4.95 o.p. (ISBN 0-397-10099-X). Lippincott.
Anderson, John D. Gasdynamic Lasers: An Introduction. (Quantum Electronic Ser.). 1976. 29.50 (ISBN 0-12-056950-7). Acad Pr.
Anderson, John F., jt. auth. see Berdie, Douglas R.
Anderson, John G. Technical Shop Mathematics. 510p. 1974. 17.50 (ISBN 0-8311-1085-6); wkd.-out solutions 6.00 (ISBN 0-8311-1106-2). Indus Pr.
Anderson, John M. Grammar of Case: Towards a Localistic Theory. LC 71-145602. (Studies in Linguistics Ser: No. 4). (Illus.). 1971. 35.00 (ISBN 0-521-08035-5); pap. 11.95 (ISBN 0-521-29057-0). Cambridge U Pr.
Anderson, John R. Cognitive Psychology & Its Implications. LC 80-14354. (Psychology Ser.). (Illus.). 1980. text ed. 15.00x (ISBN 0-7167-1197-4). W H Freeman.
Anderson, John R., ed. Cognitive Skills & Their Acquisition. (Carnegie Symposia on Cognition). 384p. 1981. ref. 24.95 (ISBN 0-89859-093-0). L Erlbaum Assocs.
Anderson, Justo C. Historia De los Bautistas Tomo I: Sus Bases y Principios. 1978. pap. 4.25 (ISBN 0-311-15036-5). Casa Bautista.
Anderson, Karen. Wartime Women: Sex Roles, Family Relations, & the Status of Women During World War II. LC 80-1703. (Contributions in Women's Studies Ser.: No. 20). 224p. 1981. lib. bdg. 22.95 (ISBN 0-313-20884-0, AWW/). Greenwood.
Anderson, Ken. The Sterno Guide to the Outdoors. 5.95 (ISBN 0-916752-16-X). Green Hill.
Anderson, Ken & Carlson, Morry. Games for All Occasions. pap. 2.50 (ISBN 0-310-20152-7). Zondervan.
Anderson, Kenneth, ed. Expense Analysis: Condominiums, Cooperatives, & Planned Unit Developments. 1980. lib. bdg. 30.00 (ISBN 0-912104-41-4). Inst Real Estate.
--Income, Expense Analysis: Apartments. 1979. lib. bdg. 45.00 o.p. (ISBN 0-912104-39-2). Inst Real Estate.
--Income, Expense Analysis: Suburban Office Buildings. 1979. lib. bdg. 30.00 o.p. (ISBN 0-912104-40-6). Inst Real Estate.
Anderson, Kenneth, ed. see Inst. of Real Estate Management.
Anderson, Kenneth A., ed. see Institute of Real Estate Management.
Anderson, Kenneth E. & Haugh, Oscar M. A Handbook for the Preparation of Research Reports & Theses. LC 78-61395. 1978. pap. text ed. 4.75 (ISBN 0-8191-0597-X). U Pr of Amer.
Anderson, Kenneth N. Eagle Claw Fish Cookbook. LC 77-89549. (Illus.). 1978. 6.95 (ISBN 0-916752-17-8). Dorison Hse.
Anderson, Kent, ed. Career Education & the Art Teaching Profession. 48p. 1980. 4.50 (ISBN 0-686-27491-1). Natl Art Ed.
--Television Fraud: The History & Implications of the Quiz Show Scandals. LC 77-94755. (Contributions in American Studies: No. 39). lib. bdg. 22.50x (ISBN 0-313-20321-0, ATF/). Greenwood.
Anderson, Kim E. & Scott, Ronald M. Fundamentals of Industrial Toxicology. (Illus.). 1981. 14.95 (ISBN 0-250-40378-1). Ann Arbor Science.
Anderson, L. O. Wood Houses for Country Living. LC 77-6213. (Illus.). 1977. pap. 5.95 o.p. (ISBN 0-8069-8800-2). Sterling.
Anderson, L. W. Light & Color. LC 77-27460. (Read About Science Ser.). (Illus.). (gr. k-3). 1978. PLB 9.95 (ISBN 0-8393-0077-8). Raintree Child.
Anderson, Larry L. & Tillman, David A. Synthetic Fuels from Coal: Overview & Assessment. LC 79-17786. 1979. 19.50 (ISBN 0-471-01784-1, Pub. by Wiley-Interscience). Wiley.
Anderson, Laurie. Package. 3.95 o.p. (ISBN 0-672-51604-7). Bobbs.
Anderson, Lavere. Allan Pinkerton. (gr. k-6). Date not set. pap. price not set (ISBN 0-440-40210-7, YB). Dell.
Anderson, Lee. Economic Analysis of Fisheries Management Plans. 300p. 1981. text ed. 49.95 (ISBN 0-250-40389-7). Ann Arbor Science.
Anderson, Lee G. & Settle, Russell F. Benefit-Cost Analysis. LC 77-3108. (Illus.). 1977. 16.95 (ISBN 0-669-01465-6). Lexington Bks.
Anderson, Leonard. Electric Machines & Transformers. (Illus.). 336p. 1980. text ed. 18.95 (ISBN 0-8359-1615-4); instr's. manual free. Reston.
Anderson, Leroy. Leroy Anderson: Twenty-Five Melodies for Piano Solo. Orig. Title: Leroy Anderson (Almost Complete) (Illus.). 1980. pap. 6.95. Dover.
Anderson, Lewis E., jt. auth. see Crum, Howard A.
Anderson, Linda. Person You Are. 1978. text ed. 11.15 (ISBN 0-913310-42-5). PAR Inc.
Anderson, Luther A. Hunting the Uplands with Rifle & Shotgun. (Illus.). 1977. 12.95 (ISBN 0-87691-191-2). Winchester Pr.
Anderson, Lydia. Death. (gr. 4 up). 1980. PLB 6.45 (ISBN 0-531-04107-7). Watts.
Anderson, M. Government in France: An Introduction to the Executive Power. 1970. 23.00 (ISBN 0-08-015562-6); pap. 11.25 (ISBN 0-08-015561-8). Pergamon.
Anderson, Mrs. M. D. Book Indexing. (Authors' & Printers' Guides Ser.: No. 8). 1971. 4.50 (ISBN 0-521-08202-1). Cambridge U Pr.
Anderson, M. S. The Ascendancy of Europe: Aspects of European History 1815-1914. 1972. pap. text ed. 11.50 (ISBN 0-582-48348-4). Longman.
--Europe in the Eighteenth Century 1713-1783. 2nd ed. (A General History of Europe Ser.). 1977. text ed. 24.00x (ISBN 0-582-48671-8); pap. text ed. 11.50x (ISBN 0-582-48672-6). Longman.
--Historians & Eighteenth-Century Europe 1715-1789. 1979. 37.50x (ISBN 0-19-822548-2). Oxford U Pr.
Anderson, Madelyn K. The Census. LC 79-67813. (Illus.). (gr. 4-7). 1980. 7.95 (ISBN 0-8149-0824-1). Vanguard.
--Counting on You: The U. S. Census. 7.95 (ISBN 0-686-63972-3). Vanguard.
--Oil on the Waters: Cleaning up Oil Spills. LC 80-21139. (Illus.). 128p. 1981. 8.95 (ISBN 0-8149-0842-X). Vanguard.
Anderson, Margaret. Arabic Materials in English Translation: A Bibliography of Works from the Pre-Islamic Period to 1977 Arabic. 1980. lib. bdg. 22.50 (ISBN 0-8161-7954-9). G K Hall.
--Let's Talk About God. LC 75-6055. (Illus.). 192p. (Orig.). (YA) 1975. 3.50 (ISBN 0-87123-340-1, 210340). Bethany Fell.
Anderson, Margaret J. Happy Moments with God. (Illus.). 192p. 1969. pap. 3.50 (ISBN 0-87123-212-X, 210212). Bethany Fell.
Anderson, Margaret M. Insect Friends & Enemies. (Illus.). 64p. 1981. 7.50 (ISBN 0-682-49689-8). Exposition.
Anderson, Marie. A First Course in Modern Mathematics, Vol. 1. 1973. text ed. 5.95x o.p. (ISBN 0-435-50018-X); pap. text ed. 5.95x with answers o.p. (ISBN 0-435-50019-8). Heinemann Ed.
--A First Course in Modern Mathematics, Vol. 2. 1972. text ed. 3.95x o.p. (ISBN 0-435-50020-1); pap. text ed. 5.95x with answers o.p. (ISBN 0-435-50021-X). Heinemann Ed.

--A First Course in Modern Mathematics, Vol. 3. 1973. text ed. 3.95x o.p. (ISBN 0-435-50022-8); pap. text ed. 5.95x with answers o.p. (ISBN 0-435-50023-6). Heinemann Ed.

--A First Course in Modern Mathematics, Vol. 4. 1971. text ed. 3.95x o.p. (ISBN 0-435-50016-3); pap. text ed. 5.95x with answers o.p. (ISBN 0-435-50017-1). Heinemann Ed.

Anderson, Marjorie C. Kings & Kingship in Early Scotland. 304p. 1981. 20.00x (ISBN 0-7073-0179-3, Pub. by Scottish Academic Pr Scotland). Columbia U Pr.

Anderson, Marlene, jt. auth. see Brearley, Joan McD.

Anderson, Martin. Welfare: The Political Economy of Welfare Reform in the United States. LC 77-20644. (Publications 181). 276p. 1978. 12.95 (ISBN 0-8179-6811-3). Hoover Inst Pr.

Anderson, Martin P., jt. auth. see Potter, David.

Anderson, Mary. The Rise & Fall of a Teen-Age Wacko. LC 80-12396. 180p. (gr. 5-9). 1980. 8.95 (ISBN 0-689-30767-5). Atheneum.

Anderson, Mary, ed. see Burnett, C. W.

Anderson, Maxwell. Off Broadway: Essays About the Theatre. LC 75-77699. (Theater, Film, & the Performing Arts Ser.). 92p. 1971. Repr. of 1947 ed. lib. bdg. 17.50 (ISBN 0-306-71337-3). Da Capo.

Anderson, Michael. Family Structure in Nineteenth Century Lancashire. LC 79-164448. (Cambridge Studies in Sociology: No. 5). (Illus.). 1971. 29.50 (ISBN 0-521-08237-4). Cambridge U Pr.

Anderson, Mildred. Beyond All This. 1979. pap. 4.95 o.p. (ISBN 0-8010-0128-5). Baker Bk.

--Papier Mache Crafts. LC 75-14520. (Illus.). 132p. 1975. 9.95 (ISBN 0-8069-5338-1); lib. bdg. 9.29 (ISBN 0-8069-5339-X). Sterling.

Anderson, Mildred, jt. ed. see Wright, Rita.

Anderson, Mildred C., jt. auth. see Plaut, Thomas R.

Anderson, Miles H. Upper Extremities Orthotics. (Illus.). 476p. 1979. 34.50 (ISBN 0-398-00044-1). C C Thomas.

Anderson, Miles H., ed. A Manual of Lower Extremities Orthotics. (Illus.). 552p. 1978. 40.50 (ISBN 0-398-02217-8). C C Thomas.

Anderson, Miles H., et al. Manual of Above Knee Wood Socket Prosthetics. rev. ed. (Illus.). 296p. 1980. pap. 21.50 spiral bdg. (ISBN 0-398-04071-0). C C Thomas.

Anderson, Neil V., ed. Veterinary Gastroenterology. LC 79-20234. (Illus.). 720p. 1980. text ed. 65.00 (ISBN 0-8121-0632-6). Lea & Febiger.

Anderson, Nels. The Hobo: The Sociology of the Homeless Man. LC 23-10481. (Midway Reprint Ser). (Illus.). xxxii, 296p. 1975. pap. 11.50x o.s.i. (ISBN 0-226-01965-9). U of Chicago Pr.

--Men on the Move. LC 74-7427. (FDR & the Era of the New Deal Ser.). xii, 357p. 1974. Repr. of 1940 ed. lib. bdg. 37.50 (ISBN 0-306-70588-5). Da Capo.

Anderson, Nels, ed. Studies in Multilingualism. (International Studies in Sociology & Social Anthropology: No. 8). 1969. text ed. 10.50x o.p. (ISBN 90-0403-036-0). Humanities.

Anderson, Norma J. Pediatric Nursing: A Self Study Guide. 3rd ed. LC 77-26632. (Illus.). 1978. pap. text ed. 10.50 (ISBN 0-8016-0195-9). Mosby.

Anderson, Norman. Law Reform in the Muslim World. (Univ. of London Logical Ser.: No. 11). 1976. text ed. 27.25x (ISBN 0-485-13411-X, Athlone Pr). Humanities.

Anderson, Norman, jt. auth. see Brown, Walter.

Anderson, Norman D., jt. auth. see Simpson, Ronald D.

Anderson, Norman E. & Macdermot, C. G. PA-Four Locomotive. (Illus.). 1978. 19.95 (ISBN 0-89685-035-8). Chatham Pub CA.

Anderson, O. D. Time Series Analysis & Forecasting: The Box Jenkins Approach. 168p. 1975. pap. 15.95 (ISBN 0-686-15234-4). Butterworths.

Anderson, O. Roger. Structure in Teaching. LC 76-150210. (Illus.). 1969. text ed. 7.50x (ISBN 0-8077-1030-X). Tchrs Coll.

Anderson, Odin W. Health Care: Can There Be Equity? the United States, Sweden, & England. LC 72-7449. 1972. 22.95 (ISBN 0-471-02760-X, Pub by Wiley-Interscience). Wiley.

Anderson, Olov B. Bushu: A Key to the 'Radicals' of the Japanese Language. (Scandinavian Institute of Asian Studies). 1980. pap. text ed. 6.50x (ISBN 0-7007-0127-3). Humanities.

Anderson, P. C. The Dental Assistant. 3rd ed. 372p. 1974. pap. 11.00 (ISBN 0-8273-1339-X); instructor's guide 1.60 (ISBN 0-8273-1340-3). Delmar.

Anderson, P. Howard. Forgotten Railways: The East Midlands. (Forgotten Railways Ser.). (Illus.). 208p. 1973. 17.95 (ISBN 0-7153-6094-9). David & Charles.

Anderson, P. M. & Fouad, A. A. Power System Control & Stability. 1977. 45.95 (ISBN 0-8138-1245-3). Iowa St U Pr.

Anderson, Patricia A. Promoted to Glory: The Apotheosis of George Washington. (Illus.). 68p. (Orig.). 1980. pap. 8.75 (ISBN 0-87391-017-6). Smith Coll Mus Art.

Anderson, Patrick. High in America. LC 80-51772. 360p. 1981. 13.95 (ISBN 0-670-11990-3). Viking Pr.

Anderson, Paul. Building Christian Character. (Trinity Teen Curriculum Ser.). 96p. (Orig.). 1980. wkbk. 2.95 (ISBN 0-87123-019-4, 240019). Bethany Fell.

--Day of Their Return. pap. 1.50 (ISBN 0-451-07941-8, W7941, Sig). NAL.

--The Devil's Game. 1980. pap. write for info. (ISBN 0-671-83689-7). PB.

--Mirkheim. 1979. pap. 1.75 (ISBN 0-425-04309-6). Berkley Pub.

--Regional Landscape Analysis. LC 80-6837. 1980. pap. 19.50 (ISBN 0-918436-11-7). Environ Des VA.

--Vault of the Ages. 1978. pap. 1.95 (ISBN 0-425-04336-3, Medallion). Berkley Pub.

Anderson, Paul, et al. Addison Wesley General Mathematics: Level One. 1980. text ed. 13.40 (ISBN 0-201-03825-0, Sch Div); tchr's. manual 15.28 (ISBN 0-201-03826-9, Sch Div); tests & d.m. avail. A-W.

Anderson, Paul F. Financial Aspects of Industrial Leasing Decisions: Implications for Marketing. LC 77-75139. (MSU Business Studies Ser.). 1977. pap. 6.50 (ISBN 0-87744-145-6). Mich St U Busn.

Anderson, Paul G. Brass Solo & Study Guide. 15.00 (ISBN 0-686-15889-X). Instrumentalist Co.

Anderson, Paul L. With the Eagles. LC 57-9447. (Illus.). (gr. 7-11). 1929. 8.50x (ISBN 0-8196-0100-4). Biblo.

Anderson, Pauline. Dental Radiology. 96p. 1974. pap. 5.80 (ISBN 0-8273-0341-6); instructor's guide 1.60 (ISBN 0-8273-0342-4). Delmar.

Anderson, Pauline C. The Dental Assistant. 3rd ed. 372p. 1981. text ed. 14.95 (ISBN 0-442-21873-7). Nos Van Reinhold.

Anderson, Pauline H. The Library in the Independent School. 42p. 1980. pap. 6.50 (ISBN 0-934338-43-4). NAIS.

Anderson, Pauline R., jt. auth. see Anderson, Eugene N.

Anderson, Peggy. Nurse. 1980. pap. 2.75 (ISBN 0-425-04685-0). Berkley Pub.

Anderson, Perry & Blackburn, Robin, eds. Towards Socialism. 397p. 1966. 25.00x o.p. (ISBN 0-8014-0012-0). Cornell U Pr.

Anderson, Phil. General-Class Amateur Study Guide. LC 79-63865. 1979. pap. 6.50 (ISBN 0-672-21617-5). Sams.

Anderson, Poul. The Avatar. 1979. pap. 2.50 (ISBN 0-425-04861-6). Berkley Pub.

--Conan the Rebel, No. 5. 224p. (Orig.). 1980. pap. 2.25 (ISBN 0-553-13831-6). Bantam.

--Fire Time. 256p. 1975. pap. 2.25 (ISBN 0-345-28692-8). Ballantine.

--The Golden Slave. 256p. (Orig.). 1980. pap. 2.25 (ISBN 0-89083-651-5). Zebra.

--The High Crusade. 1978. pap. 1.75 (ISBN 0-425-04307-X, Medallion). Berkley Pub.

--Homeward & Beyond. 1979. pap. 1.75 (ISBN 0-425-03162-4). Berkley Pub.

--The Merman's Children. 1980. pap. 2.50 (ISBN 0-425-04643-5). Berkley Pub.

--The Psychotechnic Leagues. Stine, Hank, ed. 450p. 1981. 20.00 (ISBN 0-89865-084-4, Starblaze); pap. 5.95 (ISBN 0-89865-083-6). Donning Co.

--The Road of the Sea Horse. (The Last Viking Ser.: No. 2). 400p. (Orig.). 1980. pap. 2.50 (ISBN 0-89083-610-8). Zebra.

--Time & Stars. 1978. pap. 1.50 o.p. (ISBN 0-425-03621-9, Medallion). Berkley Pub.

--The Trouble Twisters. pap. 1.25 o.p. (ISBN 0-425-03245-0). Berkley Pub.

--Virgin Planet. 1973. pap. 1.50 o.s.i. (ISBN 0-446-88334-4). Warner Bks.

Anderson, Poul & Dickson, Gordon R. Earthman's Burden. 1979. pap. 1.75 (ISBN 0-380-47993-1, 47993, Camelot). Avon.

--Star Prince Charlie. 1976. pap. 1.75 o.p. (ISBN 0-425-03078-4, Medallion). Berkley Pub.

Anderson, Poul, jt. auth. see Eklund, Gordon.

Anderson, Poul, tr. The Method of Holding the Three Ones. (Studies on Asian Topics: No. 1). (Orig.). 1980. pap. text ed. 6.50x (ISBN 0-7007-0113-3). Humanities.

Anderson, Poul, et al. The Day the Sun Stood Still - Three Original Novellas of Science Fiction. LC 77-38748. 1972. 7.95 o.p. (ISBN 0-525-66206-5). Elsevier-Nelson.

Anderson, R. Anglo-Scandinavian Law Dictionary. 1977. pap. 15.00x (ISBN 82-00-02365-6, Dist. by Columbia U Pr). Universitet.

Anderson, R., et al. Developing Children's Thinking Through Science. 1970. ref. ed. 17.95 (ISBN 0-13-204214-2). P-H.

Anderson, R. A. You Can Be Free. LC 76-5074. (Harvest Ser.). 1977. pap. 3.95 (ISBN 0-8163-0292-8). Pacific Pr Pub Assn.

Anderson, R. C. & Frankis, G. A History of the Western National. LC 79-51082. (Illus.). 1979. 19.95 (ISBN 0-7153-7771-X). David & Charles.

Anderson, R. D. Education in France 1848-1870. 300p. 1975. 29.95x (ISBN 0-19-827311-8). Oxford U Pr.

--France, 1870-1914: Politics & Society. 1977. 22.50x (ISBN 0-7100-8575-3). Routledge & Kegan.

Anderson, R. E. Unfolding the Prophecies of Daniel. LC 75-16526. (Dimension Ser.). 1975. pap. 4.50 o.p. (ISBN 0-8163-0180-8, 21390-0). Pacific Pr Pub Assn.

Anderson, R. G. Business Systems. (Illus.). 240p. (Orig.). 1977. pap. 9.95x (ISBN 0-7121-0254-X, Pub. by Macdonald & Evans England). Intl Ideas.

--Case Studies in Systems Design. (Illus.). 208p. (Orig.). 1980. pap. text ed. 10.00x (ISBN 0-7121-0387-2). Intl Ideas.

--Data Processing & Management Information Systems. 3rd ed. (Illus.). 480p. 1980. pap. text ed. 15.95x (ISBN 0-7121-0417-8). Intl Ideas.

Anderson, R. M., et al, eds. Population Dynamics: (the Twentieth Symposium of the British Ecological Society) 1980. 76.95x (ISBN 0-470-26816-6). Halsted Pr.

Anderson, R. R., jt. ed. see Whitby, W. M.

Anderson, R. S., ed. Nutrition of the Dog & Cat: Proceedings of an International Symposium 26 June 1978, Hanover. LC 80-40449. (Illus.). 212p. 1980. 32.00 (ISBN 0-08-025526-4). Pergamon.

Anderson, R. S. & De Hoog, F. R., eds. Application & Numberical Solution of Intergral Equations. (Mechanics Analysis Ser.: No. 6). 265p. 1980. 27.50x (ISBN 90-286-0450-2). Sijthoff & Noordhoff.

Anderson, R. T., et al, eds. Electrical Fitting, Vol. 1. (Engineering Craftsmen: No. G3). (Illus.). 1968. spiral bdg. 18.50x (ISBN 0-85083-015-X). Intl Ideas.

--Rotating Electrical Equipment Winding & Building, 2 vols. (Engineering Craftsmen: No. G2). (Illus.). 1969. Set. spiral bdg. 46.95x (ISBN 0-85083-030-3). Intl Ideas.

Anderson, Ralph E. & Carter, Irl. Human Behavior in the Social Environment. 2nd ed. LC 77-95322. 1978. text ed. 15.95x (ISBN 0-202-36021-0); pap. text ed. 7.50x (ISBN 0-202-36022-9). Aldine Pub.

Anderson, Ralph R., jt. ed. see Johnson, J. Alan.

Anderson, Raymond L., jt. auth. see Maass, Arthur.

Anderson, Richard. Inspirational Meditations for Sunday Church School Teachers. 1980. pap. 2.25 (ISBN 0-570-03810-3, 12-2919). Concordia.

--Representation in the Juvenile Court. (Direct Editions Ser). (Orig.). 1978. pap. 10.00 (ISBN 0-7100-8578-8). Routledge & Kegan.

--Roads to Recovery. 1974. pap. 1.50 (ISBN 0-570-03175-3, 12-2578). Concordia.

--Robert Coover. (United States Authors Ser.: No. 300). 1981. lib. bdg. 11.95 (ISBN 0-8057-7330-4). Twayne.

--Your Keys to the Executive Suite. 32p. 1973. pap. 1.50 (ISBN 0-570-06981-5, 12-2558). Concordia.

Anderson, Richard L. Art in Primitive Societies. (Illus.). 1979. pap. 10.95 ref. ed. (ISBN 0-13-048108-4). P-H.

Anderson, Robert. The Cultural Context: An Introduction to Cultural Anthropology. LC 75-16796. 1976. pap. text ed. 12.95 (ISBN 0-8087-0126-6). Burgess.

--Forgotten Truths. LC 80-17526. (Sir Robert Anderson Library). 1980. pap. 3.50 (ISBN 0-8254-2130-6). Kregel.

--Redemption Truths. LC 80-16161. (Sir Robert Anderson Library). Orig. Title: For Us Men. 192p. 1980. pap. 3.50 (ISBN 0-8254-2131-4). Kregel.

--Semasia: Beitrage Zue Germanischromanischen Sorachforschung, Band IV. 1977. pap. text ed. 23.00x (ISBN 0-391-02045-5). Humanities.

Anderson, Robert, jt. auth. see Williams, Alan.

Anderson, Robert, jt. auth. see Wolf, James M.

Anderson, Robert, ed. Semasia: Beitrage zur Germanisch-Romanischen Sprachforschung, Band 5. (Orig.). 1980. pap. text ed. 19.50x (ISBN 0-391-02047-1). Humanities.

Anderson, Robert, et al, eds. Semasia: Beitrage Zur Germanisch-Romanischen Sprachforschung, Band 2. (Orig., Ger.). 1975. pap. text ed. 40.00x (ISBN 0-391-02045-5). Humanities.

--Semasia: Beitrage Zur Germanisch-Romanischen Sprachforschung, Band 1. (Orig., Ger.). 1974. pap. text ed. 15.00x (ISBN 0-391-02046-3). Humanities.

Anderson, Robert A. Stress Power: How to Turn Tension into Energy. LC 78-8308. 225p. 1978. 14.95 (ISBN 0-87705-328-6). Human Sci Pr.

Anderson, Robert H. & Shane, Harold G., eds. As the Twig Is Bent: Readings in Early Childhood Education. LC 71-135675. 1971. pap. text ed. 11.50 (ISBN 0-395-11218-4, 3-01135). HM.

Anderson, Robert L. & Barry, Thomas E. Advertising Management: Test & Cases. (Marketing & Management Ser.). 1979. text ed. 18.95 (ISBN 0-675-08302-8); instructor's manual 3.95 (ISBN 0-685-60799-2). Merrill.

Anderson, Robert M. American Law of Zoning, 5 vols. LC 68-28408. 1976. 212.50 (ISBN 0-686-14539-9, 024A). Lawyers Co-Op.

--Vision of the Disinherited: The Making of American Pentecostalism. 1979. 16.95 (ISBN 0-19-502502-4). Oxford U Pr.

Anderson, Robert M. & Romfh, Richard F. Technique in the Use of Surgical Tools. 208p. 1980. 16.50 (ISBN 0-8385-8843-3). ACC.

Anderson, Robert M., et al. Instructional Resources for Teachers of the Culturally Disadvantaged & Exceptional. (Illus.). 320p. 1971. text ed. 24.50 (ISBN 0-398-00045-X). C C Thomas.

Anderson, Robert P. & Halcomb, Charles G. Learning Disability-Minimal Brain Dysfunction Syndrome: Research Perspectives & Applications. (Illus.). 296p. 1976. 24.50 (ISBN 0-398-03395-1). C C Thomas.

Anderson, Robert R. Spanish American Modernism: A Selected Bibliography. LC 73-82616. 1970. 2.00 (ISBN 0-8165-0193-9). U of Ariz Pr.

Anderson, Robert S., ed. Reloading for Shotgunners. LC 81-65119. (Illus.). 224p. 1981. pap. 7.95 (ISBN 0-910676-25-9, 2606). DBI.

Anderson, Rodney U., jt. auth. see Kessler, Robert.

Anderson, Roger F. Forest & Shade Tree Entomology. LC 60-11714. 1960. 25.50 (ISBN 0-471-02739-1). Wiley.

Anderson, Ronald A. Couch on Insurance, 24 vols. 2nd ed. LC 59-1915. 1971. 876.00 set (ISBN 0-686-14510-0). Lawyers Co-Op.

--Uniform Commercial Code, 5 vols. 2nd ed. LC 77-138263. 1970. 200.00 (ISBN 0-686-14491-0); legal forms vol. 65.00 (ISBN 0-686-14492-9); pleading & practice forms 2 vols. 65.00 (ISBN 0-686-14493-7). Lawyers Co-Op.

Anderson, Ronald T. Agent's Legal Responsibility. LC 80-83690. 168p. 1980. text ed. 12.75 (ISBN 0-87218-307-6). Natl Underwriter.

Anderson, Rosemarie. Crochet for the Connoisseur. (Illus.). 120p. 1980. 22.50 (ISBN 0-7134-1144-9, Pub. by Batsford England). David & Charles.

Anderson, Roy A. Unfolding the Revelation. LC 61-10884. (Dimension Ser.). 223p. 1961. pap. 5.95 (ISBN 0-8163-0027-5, 21400-7). Pacific Pr Pub Assn.

Anderson, Rubin. Adsorption of Inorganics at Solid Liquid Interfaces. 1981. text ed. 39.95 (ISBN 0-250-40226-2, Dist. by Butterworths). Ann Arbor Science.

Anderson, Ruth, jt. auth. see Woolsey, Raymond H.

Anderson, Ruth L. Lost Hill. (Illus.). (gr. 4-6). 1976. pap. 2.25x (ISBN 0-933892-06-3). Child Focus Co.

Anderson, S. D. & Woodhead, R. W. Project Manpower Management: Management Process in Construction Practice. LC 80-22090. 350p. 1981. 32.95 (ISBN 0-471-95979-0, Pub. by Wiley-Interscience). Wiley.

Anderson, Sharon, et al. Statistical Methods for Comparative Studies: Techniques for Bias Reduction. LC 79-27220. (Wiley Series in Probability & Mathematical Statistics: Applied Probability & Statistics). 1980. 24.95 (ISBN 0-471-04838-0, Pub. by Wiley-Interscience). Wiley.

Anderson, Shauna C. Introductory Laboratory Exercises for Medical Technologists. LC 77-8819. (Illus.). 1978. pap. text ed. 8.50 (ISBN 0-8016-0173-8). Mosby.

Anderson, Stanley F. & Hull, Raymond. Art of Making Beer. 1971. pap. 3.50 (ISBN 0-8015-0380-9, Hawthorn). Dutton.

--Art of Making Wine. 1971. pap. 2.95 (ISBN 0-8015-0390-6, Hawthorn). Dutton.

Anderson, Sydney. Lives of Animals. LC 65-28581. (Lives of Animals Ser). (Illus.). (gr. 6 up). 1966. PLB 7.95 (ISBN 0-87191-007-1). Creative Ed.

Anderson, Sydney & Jones, J. Knox, Jr., eds. Recent Mammals of the World: A Synopsis of Families. (Illus.). 1967. 24.95 (ISBN 0-8260-0440-7, Pub. by Wiley-Interscience). Wiley.

Anderson, T. & Randell, B., eds. Computing Systems Reliability. LC 78-75253. (Illus.). 1979. 41.95 (ISBN 0-521-22767-4). Cambridge U Pr.

Anderson, T. W. & Sclove, Stanley L. An Introduction to the Statistical Analysis of Data. LC 77-78890. (Illus.). 1978. text ed. 18.50 (ISBN 0-395-15045-0); sol. manual 0.75 (ISBN 0-395-15046-9). HM.

Anderson, Teresa, tr. see Neruda, Pablo.

Anderson, Terry H. The United States, Great Britain, & the Cold War: 1944-1947. LC 80-25838. 256p. 1981. text ed. 23.00x (ISBN 0-8262-0328-0). U of Mo Pr.

Anderson, Terry L. & Hill, Peter J. The Birth of a Transfer Society. 130p. (Orig.). 1980. pap. 6.95 (ISBN 0-8179-7292-7). Hoover Inst Pr.

Anderson, Theodore W. Statistical Analysis of Time Series. LC 70-126222. (Probability & Mathematical Statistics Ser.). 1971. 31.95 (ISBN 0-471-02900-9). Wiley.

Anderson, Thomas J. & Trotter, William R. Word Processing Users' Manual. LC 73-94097. 1976. pap. 10.95 (ISBN 0-8144-5424-0). Am Mgmt.

Anderson, Thomas P., et al, eds. see Gas Dynamics Symposium - 5th Biennial - 1964.

Anderson, Tim. Modern Algebra: An Introduction. LC 73-82414. 1974. text ed. 16.95x (ISBN 0-675-08904-2). Merrill.

Anderson, Tom. Silence Is Not Golden - It's Yellow. LC 73-176510. 1973. 7.00 (ISBN 0-88279-227-X). Western Islands.

Anderson, Valborg, ed. & tr. see Strindberg, August.

Anderson, Vernon E. & Gruhn, William T. Principles & Practices of Secondary Education. 2nd ed. LC 62-11648. 1962. 13.50x o.p. (ISBN 0-8260-0470-9). Wiley.

Anderson, Virgil A. Training the Speaking Voice. 3rd ed. (Illus.). 1977. text ed. 14.95x (ISBN 0-19-502150-9). Oxford U Pr.

Anderson, W. A. & Scotti, W. A. Synopsis of Pathology. 10th ed. LC 80-13985. (Illus.). 786p. 1980. pap. text ed. 26.00 (ISBN 0-8016-0231-9). Mosby.

Anderson, W. A. D. & Kissane, John M. Pathology. 7th ed. LC 77-1052. (Illus.). 1977. 54.50 (ISBN 0-8016-0186-X). Mosby.

Anderson, W. A. D. & Scotti, Thomas M. Synopsis of Pathology. 9th ed. LC 75-31874. (Illus.). 1152p. 1976. 19.95 o.p. (ISBN 0-8016-0230-0). Mosby.

Anderson, W. Steve & Cox, Don R. The Technical Reader: Readings in Technical Business & Scientific Communication. LC 79-29677. 378p. (Orig.). 1980. pap. text ed. 7.95 (ISBN 0-03-048771-4, HoltC). HR&W.

Anderson, Walter E. The German Enigma: The Elitist Tradition in German Literature. LC 79-66491. 225p. 1981. 9.95 (ISBN 0-533-04398-0). Vantage.

Anderson, Warren D., tr. see Aeschylus.

Anderson, Wayne & Logue, Christopher. The Magic Circus. (Illus.). 1979. 7.95 o.p. (ISBN 0-670-44809-5, Studio). Viking Pr.

--Ratsmagic. (Illus.). 1979. 7.95 o.p. (ISBN 0-670-58977-2, Studio). Viking Pr.

Anderson, Wayne F., et al, eds. Managing Human Services. LC 77-2464. (Municipal Management Ser.). (Illus.). 1977. text ed. 22.00 (ISBN 0-87326-017-1). Intl City Mgt.

Anderson, Wayne I. Geology of Iowa. (Illus.). 1981. write for info. (ISBN 0-8138-1505-3). Iowa St U Pr.

Anderson, William. In His Light: A Path into Catholic Belief. 216p. 1979. pap. 4.95 (ISBN 0-697-01716-8). Wm C Brown.

--The Strawberry: A World Bibliography Nineteen Twenty to Nineteen Sixty Six. LC 72-3866. 1969. 20.50 (ISBN 0-8108-0262-7). Scarecrow.

Anderson, William C. BAT-Twenty-One: Based on the True Story of Lt. Col. Iceal E. Hambleton, USAF. LC 80-20648. 1980. 9.95 (ISBN 0-13-069500-9). P-H.

Anderson, William G. In-Car Instruction: Methods & Content. 2nd ed. (Illus.). 1977. pap. text ed. 13.95 (ISBN 0-201-00217-5). A-W.

Anderson, William S., ed. Ballantine's Law Dictionary with Pronunciations. 3rd ed. LC 68-30931. 1969. 17.00x o.p. (ISBN 0-686-14540-2). Lawyers Co-Op.

Anderson, William S. & Puhvel, Jaan, eds. California Studies in Classical Antiquity, Vol. 12. LC 68-26906. (Illus.). 400p. 1981. 15.00x (ISBN 0-520-04055-4). U of Cal Pr.

Anderson, Williams. Jobs. (gr. 10-12). 1972. pap. text ed. 8.50 incl. suppl. & tchrs' manual (ISBN 0-8449-3050-4). Learning Line.

Anderson-Evangelista, Anita. Hypnosis: A Journey into the Mind. LC 79-27817. (Illus.). 256p. 1980. 10.95 (ISBN 0-668-04908-1, 4908-1). Arco.

Anderson Imbert, Enrique. Other Side of the Mirror (el Rimonio) Reade, Isabel, tr. LC 66-11155. (Contemporary Latin American Classic). 239p. 1966. 7.95x (ISBN 0-8093-0227-6). S Ill U Pr.

Anderson-Imbert, Enrique & Kiddle, Lawrence B., eds. Veinte Cuentos Espanoles Del Siglo Veinte. (Orig., Span.). (gr. 10-12). 1961. pap. text ed. 9.50 (ISBN 0-13-941567-X). P-H.

Anderson-Sannes, Barbara. Alma on the Mississippi, 1848-1932. Doyle, Michael, et al, eds. LC 80-68241. (Illus.). 198p. (Orig.). 1980. pap. 11.95 (ISBN 0-9604684-0-4). Alma Hist Soc.

Anderson Sweeney, David R. & Williams, Thomas A. Introduction to Statistics: An Applications Approach. (Illus.). 750p. text ed. 14.36 (ISBN 0-8299-0361-5). West Pub.

Andersson, Theodore see Kellenberger, Hunter.

Andersson, Theodore, ed. see Chaucer, Geoffrey.

Anderton, Craig. Electronic Projects for Musicians. LC 75-27789. 136p. (Orig.). 1975. pap. 7.95 (ISBN 0-8256-9502-3). Guitar Player.

--Home Recording for Musicians. LC 77-87208. (Illus.). 184p. 1978. pap. 9.95 (ISBN 0-89122-011-9). Guitar Player.

Anderton, R., et al. A Dynamic Stratigraphy of the British Isles. (Illus.). 1979. text ed. 35.00x (ISBN 0-04-551027-X); pap. text ed. 19.95x (ISBN 0-04-551028-8). Allen Unwin.

Andino, Alrto. Frutos De Mi Trasplante. LC 79-52356. (Coleccion Caniqui). 102p. (Span.). 1980. pap. 5.95 (ISBN 0-89729-230-8). Ediciones.

Andler, Kenneth. Mission to Fort No. Four. (N. H.-Vermont Historiettes). (Illus.). 64p. (gr. 6-7). 1975. 4.95 (ISBN 0-915892-04-9); pap. 1.95 (ISBN 0-915892-15-4). Regional Ctr Educ.

Andoh, Elizabeth. At Home with Japanese Cooking. LC 79-3501. (Illus.). 228p. 1980. 15.00 (ISBN 0-394-41219-2). Knopf.

Andolfi, Maurizio, ed. Dimensions of Family Therapy. Zwerling, Israel. 280p. 1980. text ed. 20.00 (ISBN 0-89862-602-1). Guilford Pr.

Andorka, Rudolf. Determinants of Fertility in Advanced Societies. LC 78-62993. 431p. 1978. Repr. 25.00 (ISBN 0-02-900780-1). Free Pr.

Andrade, Carlos D. The Minus Sign. De Araujo, Virginia, ed. 160p. 1980. 15.00x (ISBN 0-933806-03-5). Black Swan CT.

Andrade, Edward N. Sir Isaac Newton. LC 79-15162. 140p. 1979. Repr. of 1958 ed. lib. bdg. 14.50x (ISBN 0-313-22022-0). Greenwood.

Andrade, Mario I. From Deep Within Me. 48p. 1978. 2.95 (ISBN 0-8059-2620-8). Dorrance.

Andrae, Tor. Mohammed: The Man & His Faith. LC 60-5489. 1977. pap. text ed. 4.95x (ISBN 0-06-130062-4, TB 62, Torch). Har-Row.

Andraeson, Tjalve & Schmidt. Engineering Graphic Modelling. (Illus.). 1979. 11.95 (ISBN 0-408-00305-7). Butterworths.

Andrasko, Kenneth, ed. see Setnicka, Timothy J.

Andrassy, Juraj. International Law & the Resources of the Sea. LC 76-130960. (International Legal Studies). (Illus.). 1970. 16.00x (ISBN 0-231-03409-1). Columbia U Pr.

Andrassy, Stella. The Solar Cookbook. LC 79-88818. 1981. pap. 4.95 (ISBN 0-87100-142-X, 2142). Morgan.

--The Solar Still Connection: History, Purpose, & Application. 128p. 1981. pap. 4.95 (ISBN 0-87100-173-X). Morgan.

Andre, Nevin, jt. auth. see Palmore, Phyllis.

Andre, Rae. Homemakers: The Forgotten Workers. LC 80-21258. 1981. 15.00 (ISBN 0-226-01993-4). U of Chicago Pr.

Andrea, Bob. Akron-Canton Epicure. (Epicure Ser.). 1981. pap. 4.95 (ISBN 0-89716-080-0). Peanut Butter.

Andrea, Johann V. Johann Valentin Andreae's Christianopolis: An Ideal State of the Seventeenth Century. Held, Felix E., tr. from Lat. (Illus.). x, 287p. 1981. Repr. of 1916 ed. lib. bdg. 20.00x (ISBN 0-87991-958-2). Porcupine Pr.

Andreadis, Harriette, ed. see Lyly, John.

Andreano, Ralph & Siegfried, John J., eds. The Economics of Crime: An Anthology of Recent Work. 1980. 16.25x (ISBN 0-470-26836-0); pap. text ed. 10.50 (ISBN 0-470-26837-9). Halsted Pr.

Andreas, Burton G. Experimental Psychology. 2nd ed. LC 78-171910. 1972. text ed. 23.95x (ISBN 0-471-02905-X). Wiley.

Andreas Capellanus. Art of Courtly Love. Perry, John J., tr. 1969. pap. text ed. 4.95x (ISBN 0-393-09848-6, NortonC). Norton.

Andreasen, Alan R. The Disadvantaged Consumer. LC 75-2805. (Illus.). 1975. 16.95 (ISBN 0-02-900960-X). Free Pr.

Andreasen, Alan R. & Sturdivant, Frederick D., eds. Minorities & Marketing: Research Challenges. LC 77-6819. (Illus.). 1977. pap. text ed. 7.00 o.p. (ISBN 0-87757-095-7). Am Mktg.

Andreasen, Niels-Erik A. The Old Testament Sabbath: A Tradition-Historical Investigation. LC 72-88671. (Society of Biblical Literature. Dissertation Ser.). 1974. pap. 9.00 (ISBN 0-89130-163-1, 060107). Scholars Pr Ca.

Andreas-Salome, Lou. Selected Essays of Lou Andreas-Salome. Binion, Rudolph, ed. 500p. (Orig.). 1981. price not set (ISBN 0-937406-15-5); pap. price not set (ISBN 0-937406-14-7); price not set limited ed. (ISBN 0-937406-16-3). Logbridge-Rhodes.

Andree, R., et al. Computer Programming: Techniques, Analyses & Mathematics. 1973. ref. ed. 21.95 (ISBN 0-13-166082-9). P-H.

Andree, Robert G. Collective Negotiations: A Guide to School Board-Teacher Relations. LC 74-121401. 1970. 29.50x (ISBN 0-89197-704-X). Irvington.

Andreev, K. The Patriarchs of Constantinople Between the Council of Chalcedon & Photius. LC 80-2353. 1981. Repr. of 1895 ed. 38.50 (ISBN 0-404-18901-6). AMS Pr.

Andren, Nils & Birnbaum, Karl E. Belgrade & Beyond: The CSCE Process in Perspective. (East West Perspectives: No. 5). 27.50x (ISBN 90-286-0250-X). Sijthoff & Noordhoff.

Andreoli, Kathleen, et al. Comprehensive Cardiac Care: A Text for Nurses, Physicians & Other Health Practitioners. 4th ed. LC 78-9905. (Illus.). 1979. text ed. 14.95 (ISBN 0-8016-0256-4). Mosby.

Andreoli, M., jt. ed. see Cassano, C.

Andreoli, Thomas E., et al, eds. Physiology of Membrane Disorders. LC 78-4071. (Illus.). 1148p. 1978. 75.00 (ISBN 0-306-31054-6, Plenum Pr). Plenum Pub.

Andreopoulos, Spyros, ed. National Health Insurance: Can We Learn from Canada? LC 75-2348. (Sun Valley Forum on National Health Ser.). 304p. 1975. 20.95 (ISBN 0-471-02925-4, Pub. by Wiley Medical). Wiley.

Andres, Ann A. & Coil, Ann P. Buying & Selling: You & Your Legal Rights. (Orig.). 1981. pap. 2.95 (ISBN 0-671-42131-X). Monarch Pr.

Andres, Glenn M. The Villa Medici in Rome, 2 vols. LC 75-23778. (Outstanding Dissertations in the Fine Arts - Sixteenth Century). (Illus.). 1976. Set. lib. bdg. 121.00 (ISBN 0-8240-1975-X). Garland Pub.

Andres, P. G., et al. Basic Mathematics for Science & Engineering. LC 55-8369. 1955. text ed. 27.95 (ISBN 0-471-02970-X). Wiley.

Andres, U. Magnetohydrodynamic & Magnetohydrostatic Methods of Mineral Separation. 1976. 39.95 (ISBN 0-470-15014-9). Halsted Pr.

Andresen, A. F. & Maeland, A., eds. Hydrides for Energy Storage: Proceedings of an International Symposium Held in Norway, Aug. 1977. 1978. text ed. 90.00 (ISBN 0-08-022715-5). Pergamon.

Andresen, Gail & Weinhold, Barry. Connective Bargaining: Communicating About Sex. (Illus.). 224p. 1980. 13.95 (ISBN 0-13-167791-8, Spec); pap. 5.95 (ISBN 0-13-167783-7). P-H.

Andreski, Stanislav. Military Organization & Society. 1968. pap. 5.85x (ISBN 0-520-00026-9, CAMPUS 7). U of Cal Pr.

--The Uses of Comparative Sociology. 1964. 19.00x (ISBN 0-520-00024-2); pap. 2.65 (ISBN 0-520-01413-8, CAL180). U of Cal Pr.

Andress, Michael. PSL Model Railroad Guide Five: Operating Your Layout. (Illus.). 64p. 1981. pap. 9.95 (ISBN 0-85059-436-7). Aztex.

--PSL Model Railroad Guide Six: Branchline Modelling. (Illus.). 64p. 1981. pap. 9.95 (ISBN 0-85059-437-5). Aztex.

--Scenery: Model Railway Guide 4. 64p. 1980. pap. 9.95 (ISBN 0-85059-401-4). Aztex.

--Structures. (Model Railway Guide Ser.: No. 3). (Illus.). 1980. pap. 9.95 (ISBN 0-85059-400-6). Aztex.

--Structures: Model Railway Guide 3. 64p. 1980. pap. 9.95 (ISBN 0-85059-400-6). Aztex.

Andrew, Bryan H., ed. Interstellar Molecules. (International Astronomical Union Symposia: No. 87). 500p. 1980. PLB 76.50 (ISBN 90-277-1160-7, Pub. by D. Reidel); pap. 34.00 (ISBN 90-277-1161-5). Kluwer Boston.

Andrew, Christopher M. & Kanya-Forstner, A. S. The Climax of French Imperial Expansion, 1914-1924. (Illus.). 304p. 1981. 29.50x (ISBN 0-8047-1101-1). Stanford U Pr.

Andrew, Edwin R. Nuclear Magnetic Resonance. (Cambridge Monographs on Physics Ser). 1956. 49.95 (ISBN 0-521-04030-2). Cambridge U Pr.

Andrew, H. E. Creative Rubbings. 1972. 16.95 (ISBN 0-7134-2257-2, Pub. by Batsford England). David & Charles.

Andrew, J. Dudley. The Major Film Theories: An Introduction. (Illus.). 275p. (Orig.). 1976. pap. 5.95 (ISBN 0-19-501991-1, 450, GB). Oxford U Pr.

Andrew, Jan. Divorce & the American Family. (gr. 7 up). 1978. PLB 7.45 (ISBN 0-531-01470-3). Watts.

Andrew, John A., III. Rebuilding the Christian Commonwealth: New England Congregationalists & Foreign Missions, 1800-1830. LC 75-38214. 1976. 17.00x (ISBN 0-8131-1333-4). U Pr of Ky.

Andrew, Larry D. & Andrew, Patricia. Math Exercises (in Addition) 1980. pap. 1.95 (ISBN 0-931992-36-2). Penns Valley.

--Math Exercises (in Division) 1980. pap. 1.95 (ISBN 0-931992-39-7). Penns Valley.

--Math Exercises (in Multiplication) 1980. pap. 1.95 (ISBN 0-931992-38-9). Penns Valley.

--Math Exercises (in Subtraction) 1980. pap. 1.95 (ISBN 0-931992-37-0). Penns Valley.

Andrew, Malcolm & Waldron, Ronald, eds. The Poems of the Pearl Manuscript. LC 78-64464. (York Medieval Texts). 1979. 35.00x (ISBN 0-520-03794-4). U of Cal Pr.

Andrew, Nancy, tr. see Murakami, Ryu.

Andrew, Patricia, jt. auth. see Andrew, Larry D.

Andrew, Robert. The Lucky Dream & Number Book. 1966. pap. 1.95 (ISBN 0-446-84939-1). Warner Bks.

Andrew, S. O., tr. see Homer.

Andrew, Warren. Six Anatomists Worth Knowing. LC 73-707. 280p. 1981. 13.50 (ISBN 0-87527-174-X). Green.

Andrew, Warren & Hickman, Cleveland P., Sr. Histology of the Vertebrates: A Comparative Text. LC 73-17378. 1974. text ed. 17.95 o.p. (ISBN 0-8016-0247-5). Mosby.

Andrew, William G. & Williams, H. B. Applied Instrumentation in the Process Industries: A Survey, Vol. 1. 2nd ed. 1979. 37.95 (ISBN 0-87201-382-0). Gulf Pub.

Andrewes, A. The Greek Tyrants. 1956. pap. 7.00x (ISBN 0-09-029564-1, Hutchinson U Lib). Humanities.

Andrewes, Antony. Greeks. LC 66-19367. (The History of Human Society Ser.). (Illus.). (YA) 1967. 7.95 o.p. (ISBN 0-394-42722-X). Knopf.

Andrewes, Lancelot. Sermons. Story, G. M., ed. 1967. 22.00x o.p. (ISBN 0-19-811467-2). Oxford U Pr.

Andrews. Mountain Witch. pap. 2.75 o.s.i. (ISBN 0-515-04780-5). Jove Pubns.

Andrews, Albert H., ed. Microscopic & Endoscopic Surgery with the Carbon Dioxide Laser. 1981. write for info. (ISBN 0-88416-211-7). PSG Pub.

Andrews, Barry. Price Warung (William Astley) (World Authors Ser.: Australia: No. 383). 1976. lib. bdg. 12.50 (ISBN 0-8057-6225-6). Twayne.

Andrews, Barry G. & Wilde, William H., eds. Australian Literature to Nineteen Hundred: A Guide to Information Sources. LC 74-11521. (American Literature, English Literature & World Literatures in English Information Guide Ser.: Vol. 22). 472p. 1980. 30.00 (ISBN 0-8103-1215-8). Gale.

Andrews, Bart. Lucy & Ricky & Fred & Ethel: The Story of "I Love Lucy". 1977. pap. 2.50 (ISBN 0-445-04028-9). Popular Lib.

--Worst TV Shows--Ever. (Illus.). 1980. pap. 6.95 (ISBN 0-525-47592-3). Dutton.

Andrews, Bart & Ervin, Judy. TV or Not TV: An Irreverent Look at Television. (Orig.). 1977. pap. 1.25 o.p. (ISBN 0-451-07660-5, Y7660, Sig). NAL.

Andrews, Bart & Watson, Thomas. Loving Lucy. (Illus.). 224p. 1980. 10.95 (ISBN 0-312-49974-4). St Martin.

Andrews, Benny. Between the Lines. LC 78-60633. (Illus.). 111p. 1978. 19.95 (ISBN 0-918618-13-4); lib. bdg. 9.95 (ISBN 0-918618-12-6). Pella Pub.

Andrews, Charles. Fell's International Coin Book. 6th rev. ed. LC 53-11213. 320p. 1976. 7.95 (ISBN 0-8119-0367-2); pap. 4.95 (ISBN 0-88391-052-7). Fell.

--Fell's U.S Coin Book. 8th rev. ed. LC 73-11213. (Illus.). 1975. pap. 4.95 (ISBN 0-8119-0371-0). Fell.

Andrews, Charles J. Fell's United States Coin Book. 9th rev. ed. LC 73-11213. (Illus.). 156p. 1981. 9.95 (ISBN 0-8119-0349-4); pap. 5.95 (ISBN 0-8119-0421-0). Fell.

Andrews, Charles M. Colonial Background of the American Revolution: Four Essays in American Colonial History. rev. ed. LC 31-2404. 1961. 16.00x (ISBN 0-300-00268-8); pap. 5.95x (ISBN 0-300-00004-9, Y44). Yale U Pr.

Andrews, Clarence. Growing up in the Midwest. 168p. 1981. 11.25 (ISBN 0-8138-0250-4). Iowa St U Pr.

Andrews, Clarence A. Writing: Growth Through Structure. (gr. 10 up). 1972. pap. text ed. 5.95x (ISBN 0-02-470900-X, 47090). Macmillan.

Andrews, Clarence A., tr. see Gravel, Fern.

Andrews, E. H., ed. Developments in Polymer Fracture, Vol. 1. (Illus.). 1979. 59.60x (ISBN 0-85334-819-7, Pub. by Applied Science). Burgess-Intl Ideas.

Andrews, Edward D. People Called Shakers. new & enl. ed. 8.75 (ISBN 0-8446-1535-8). Peter Smith.

Andrews, Edward D. & Andrews, F. Shaker Furniture: The Craftmanship of an American Communal Sect. (Illus.). 9.00 (ISBN 0-8446-1537-4). Peter Smith.

Andrews, Edward D. & Andrews, Faith. Religion In Wood: A Book of Shaker Furniture. LC 66-12722. (Illus.). 128p. 1966. 7.95x (ISBN 0-253-17360-4). Ind U Pr.

Andrews, Emma. The Films of Michael Caine. Castell, David, ed. (The Films of...Ser.). (Illus.). (gr. 7-12). 1978. Repr. of 1974 ed. PLB 5.95 (ISBN 0-912616-90-3). Greenhaven.

--The Films of Sean Connery. Castell, David, ed. (The Films of...Ser.). (Illus.). (gr. 7-12). 1978. Repr. of 1974 ed. PLB 5.95 (ISBN 0-912616-85-7). Greenhaven.

Andrews, F., jt. auth. see Andrews, Edward D.

Andrews, F., ed. Scientific Productivity. LC 78-21978. (Illus.). 1979. 29.95 (ISBN 0-521-22586-8). Cambridge U Pr.

Andrews, F. Emerson. Nobody Comes to Dinner. (Illus.). (gr. 1-3). 1977. 6.95 (ISBN 0-316-04221-8). Little.

--Numbers, Please. 2nd enlarged ed. LC 77-20492. 1977. pap. 5.25x (ISBN 0-8077-2545-5). Tchrs Coll.
Andrews, Faith, jt. auth. see Andrews, Edward D.
Andrews, Felicia. Moonwitch. (Historical Romance Ser.). 1980. pap. 2.50 (ISBN 0-515-04781-3). Jove Pubns.
--Mountainwitch. 352p. (Orig.). 1980. pap. 2.75 (ISBN 0-515-05846-7). Jove Pubns.
--Riverrun. (Orig.). 1979. pap. 2.50 (ISBN 0-515-04545-4). Jove Pubns.
--Riverwitch. (Orig.). 1979. pap. 2.75 (ISBN 0-515-05861-0). Jove Pubns.
Andrews, Frances. Helpers with Hammers. (Home Mission Graded Ser.). (Illus.). (gr. 1-3). 1977. pap. 0.75 o.p. (ISBN 0-686-19020-3). Home Mission.
Andrews, Frank C. Equilibrium Statistical Mechanics. 2nd ed. LC 74-17197. 288p. 1975. 20.95 (ISBN 0-471-03123-2, Pub by Wiley-Interscience). Wiley.
--Thermodynamics: Principles & Applications. LC 77-150607. 1971. 19.50 (ISBN 0-471-03183-6, Pub. by Wiley-Interscience). Wiley.
Andrews, Frank M. & Messenger, Robert C. Multivariate Nominal Scale Analysis: A Report on a New Analysis Technique & a Computer Program. LC 72-629721. 114p. 1973. cloth 8.00 (ISBN 0-87944-135-6); pap. 5.00 (ISBN 0-87944-134-8). U of Mich Soc Res.
Andrews, Frank M., et al. Multiple Classification Analysis: A Report on a Computer Program for Multiple Regression Using Categorical Predictors. rev. ed. LC 73-620206. 105p. 1973. cloth 9.00 (ISBN 0-87944-148-8); pap. 5.50 (ISBN 0-87944-055-4). U of Mich Soc Res.
Andrews, Freida. The Night the Sky Lit Up. Verdick, Mary, ed. (Pal Paperbacks - Pal Skills Ser.). (Illus., Orig.). (gr. 7-12). 1978. pap. text ed. 1.25 (ISBN 0-8374-6704-7). Xerox Ed Pubns.
Andrews, G. Reid. The Afro-Argentines of Buenos Aires, 1800-1900. LC 80-5105. 336p. 1980. 21.50 (ISBN 0-299-08290-3). U of Wis Pr.
Andrews, George E. Number Theory: The Theory of Partitions. LC 76-41770. (Encyclopedia of Mathematics & Its Applications: Vol. 2). (Illus.). 1976. text ed. 21.50 (ISBN 0-201-13501-9). A-W.
--Partitions: Yesterday & Today. 56p. (Orig.). 1980. pap. text ed. 7.95 (ISBN 0-9597579-0-2). Bks Australia.
Andrews, Gini. Esther: The Star & the Sceptre. 272p. 1980. 9.95 (ISBN 0-310-20180-2). Zondervan.
Andrews, Glenn. How to Be Food Self-Sufficient: Organically, of Course! Andrews, Viola, ed. 1978. 8.95 o.p. (ISBN 0-533-02913-9). Vantage.
Andrews, Hank. How to Fish for Smallmouth Bass. 1979. 12.95 o.p. (ISBN 0-8092-7645-3); pap. 5.95 (ISBN 0-8092-7644-5). Contemp Bks.
Andrews, Harry C. & Hunt, B. R. Digital Image Restoration. (Signal Processing Ser.). (Illus.). 1977. 28.95 (ISBN 0-13-214213-9). P-H.
Andrews, Henry N. Ancient Plants & the World They Lived In. (Illus.). 288p. 1947. 19.50x o.p. (ISBN 0-8014-0015-5). Comstock.
--The Fossil Hunters: In Search of Ancient Plants. LC 79-24101. (Illus.). 664p. 1980. 28.50 (ISBN 0-8014-1248-X). Cornell U Pr.
Andrews, Henry N., Jr. Studies in Paleobotany. LC 61-6768. (Illus.). 1961. 24.95 (ISBN 0-471-03168-2). Wiley.
Andrews, Hilda, tr. see Cortot, Alfred.
Andrews, Hilda, tr. see Walicki, Andrzei.
Andrews, Howard, jt. auth. see Lapp, Ralph.
Andrews, I. Pompeii. (Introduction to the History of Mankind Ser.). 1978. 3.95 (ISBN 0-521-20973-0). Cambridge U Pr.
Andrews, Ian. Boudicca's Revolt. (Introduction to the History of Mankind Ser.). 1972. 3.95 (ISBN 0-521-08031-2). Cambridge U Pr.
Andrews, J. & Von Hahn, H. P., eds. Rational Geraitrics. (Illus.). vi, 194p. 1981. pap. 23.50 (ISBN 3-8055-1803-X). S Karger.
Andrews, J. Austin & Wardian, Jeanne. Introduction to Music Fundamentals. 4th ed. 1978. pap. text ed. 13.95 (ISBN 0-13-489575-4). P-H.
Andrews, J. David. Choosing the Best Form for Your Poem: An Illustrated Guide to Fifteen Noteworthy Verse Forms. 92p. (gr. 6-12). 1979. pap. 6.50; pap. text ed. 5.50. Planetary Pr.
--The Magic Bullet: A Novel of Presidential Assassination. 185p. (Orig.). 1980. pap. 7.50 (ISBN 0-938330-00-4). Planetary Pr.
--New Sonnets from Shakespeare: Thirty Famous Passages & Thirty New Sonnets from Shakespeare's Best-Loved Plays. 71p. (gr. 8-12). 1979. pap. 5.00. Planetary Pr.
--Oh, My Comet, Shine! Found Haiku and Senryu, Based on "Thought Forms" by Mirtala Bentov. 60p. (Orig.). 1979. pap. 5.00; pap. text ed. 5.00. Planetary Pr.
Andrews, J. David, ed. see Andrews, Melvin B.
Andrews, J. H. A Paper Landscape: The Ordnance Survey in Nineteenth-Century Ireland. (Illus.). 366p. 1975. 75.00x (ISBN 0-19-823209-8). Oxford U Pr.
Andrews, James R. Essentials of Public Communicaton. LC 78-18182. 1979. text ed. 11.95 (ISBN 0-471-02357-4); tchrs. manual avail. (ISBN 0-471-04278-1). Wiley.
Andrews, Jim. Catamarans for Cruising. (Illus.). 224p. 1976. 14.00 (ISBN 0-370-10339-4); pap. 8.95 (ISBN 0-370-10294-0). Transatlantic.
Andrews, John. Birds. (Hamlyn Nature Guide Ser.). (Illus.). 1978. 8.95 (ISBN 0-600-31413-8). Transatlantic.
Andrews, John & Taylor, Jennifer. Architecture: A Performing Art. (Illus.). 208p. 1981. cancelled (ISBN 0-19-550557-3). Oxford U Pr.
Andrews, John T. & Milne, Marvis J. Nuclear Medicine: Clinical & Technological Bases. LC 77-5040. 1977. 39.50 (ISBN 0-471-01594-6, Pub. by Wiley Medical). Wiley.
Andrews, Julian, ed. & tr. see Tassi, Roberto.
Andrews, K. R. The Spanish Caribbean: Trade & Plunder, 1530-1630. LC 77-90944. 1978. 25.00x (ISBN 0-300-02197-6). Yale U Pr.
Andrews, K. W. Physical Metallurgy: Techniques & Applications, 2 vols. LC 72-11309. 1973. Vol. 1. 34.95 (ISBN 0-470-03150-6); Vol. 2. 30.95 (ISBN 0-470-03151-4). Halsted Pr.
Andrews, Kenneth R. The Concept of Corporate Strategy. rev. ed. 1980. pap. 8.95x (ISBN 0-256-02371-9). Irwin.
--Elizabethan Privateering Fifteen Eighty-Three - Sixteen Three. 1964. 35.50 (ISBN 0-521-04032-9). Cambridge U Pr.
Andrews, Lawrence. Education Act, Nineteen Eighteen. (Students Library of Education Ser.). 1976. 9.95x (ISBN 0-7100-8409-9). Routledge & Kegan.
Andrews, Leila. Family, No. Three: Commitments. LC 76-56770. 1977. pap. 1.50 o.p. (ISBN 0-345-25706-5). Ballantine.
--Family, No. Two: Transitions. 1977. pap. 1.50 o.p. (ISBN 0-345-25705-7). Ballantine.
Andrews, Lewis M., jt. auth. see Karlins, Marvin.
Andrews, Linda, jt. auth. see Leggett, Linda.
Andrews, Linda. Philosophy of Economics. (Foundations of Philosophy Ser.). (Illus.). 200p. 1981. pap. text ed. 7.95 (ISBN 0-13-663336-6). P-H.
Andrews, Lorrin. A Dictionary of the Hawaiian Language. LC 72-89745. 1973. 17.50 (ISBN 0-8048-1087-7). C E Tuttle.
Andrews, Lyman. Kaleidoscope. LC 74-160170. 1979. 9.95 (ISBN 0-7145-1024-6, Pub. by M Boyars); pap. 5.95 (ISBN 0-7145-1025-4). Merrimack Bk Serv.
Andrews, M. C., ed. Port Dues, Charges & Accommodation Throughout the World. 37th ed. 1978-79. 80.00 (ISBN 0-540-07386-5). Heinman.
Andrews, Mark. Body Rub. 1976. pap. 1.50 o.p. (ISBN 0-685-74567-8, LB419DK, Leisure Bks). Nordon Pubns.
Andrews, Marta, et al. Platicas: Conversational Spanish. LC 80-84024. 304p. 1981. pap. text ed. 11.95 (ISBN 0-8403-2328-X). Kendall-Hunt.
Andrews, Melvin B. Carolina Adventures: Brief Sketches of Growing up in Eastern North Carolina at the Turn of the Century (1889-1915) Andrews, J. David, ed. (Illus.). 92p. (Orig.). 1979. pap. 5.00. Planetary Pr.
Andrews, Oliver, Jr; see Bird, Thomas E.
Andrews, Patrick. The Kiowa Flats Raiders. (Orig.). 1980. pap. 1.75 (ISBN 0-532-23145-7). Manor Bks.
Andrews, Peter, ed. Classic Country Inns of America, 3 vols. LC 77-71352. (Illus.). 1978. Set. slip-cased 49.95x o.s.i. (ISBN 0-03-045556-1). Knapp Pr.
Andrews, R. V. Wilkie Collins, a Critical Survey of His Prose Fiction with a Bibliography. Bleiler, E. F., ed. LC 78-60801. (The Fiction of Popular Culture Ser.: Vol. 1). 367p. 1979. lib. bdg. 35.00 (ISBN 0-8240-9667-3). Garland Pub.
Andrews, R. W. Curtis' Western Indians: Life & Worksof Edw. C. Curtis. encore ed. LC 62-14491. (Illus.). 1962. encore ed. 9.95 (ISBN 0-87564-336-1). Superior Pub.
Andrews, Ralph W. This Was Logging. 1954. 19.95 (ISBN 0-87564-901-7). Superior Pub.
Andrews, Raymond. Rosibelle Lee Wildcat Tennessee. (Illus.). 1980. 9.95 (ISBN 0-8037-8336-1). Dial.
Andrews, Richard B. Urban Land Economics & Public Policy. LC 77-122281. 1971. 12.95 (ISBN 0-02-900710-0). Free Pr.
Andrews, Richard B., ed. Urban Land Use Policy. LC 70-169230. 1972. 15.95 (ISBN 0-02-900700-3). Free Pr.
Andrews, Richard N. Environmental Policy & Administrative Change: Implementation of the National Environmental Policy Act. LC 76-7265. (Illus.). 1976. 21.50 (ISBN 0-669-00682-3). Lexington Bks.
Andrews, Richard N., ed. Land in America. LC 77-14735. (Illus.). 1979. 21.00 (ISBN 0-669-01989-5). Lexington Bks.
Andrews, Robert & Ericson, E. E. Teaching Industrial Education: Principles & Practices. 1976. pap. text ed. 7.12 (ISBN 0-87002-079-X). Bennett IL.
Andrews, Robert C., jt. auth. see Bush, Clifford L.
Andrews, Roy C. All About Dinosaurs. (Allabout Ser.: No. 1). (Illus.). (gr. 4-6). 1953. 3.95 (ISBN 0-394-80201-2, BYR); PLB 5.39 (ISBN 0-394-90201-7). Random.
--All About Strange Beasts of the Past. (Allabout Ser.: No. 17). (Illus.). (gr. 4-6). 1956. PLB 5.39 (ISBN 0-394-90217-3, BYR). Random.
--Ends of the Earth. LC 78-164078. (Towers Bks). (Illus.). x, 355p. 1972. Repr. of 1929 ed. 18.00 (ISBN 0-8103-3923-4). Gale.
--In the Days of the Dinosaurs. (Gateway Ser.: No. 11). (Illus.). (gr. 3-5). 1959. 3.50 (ISBN 0-394-80111-3, BYR); PLB 5.99 (ISBN 0-394-90111-8). Random.
Andrews, Siri, ed. Hewins Lectures, 1947-1962. LC 63-21644. 1963. 11.00 (ISBN 0-87675-054-4); pap. 6.00 (ISBN 0-87675-056-0). Horn Bk.
Andrews, Theodora. A Bibliography of Drug Abuse: A Supplement, 1977 to 1980. 200p. 1981. lib. bdg. price not set (ISBN 0-87287-252-1). Libs Unl.
--Bibliography of the Socioeconomic Aspects of Medicine. LC 74-34054. 1975. lib. bdg. 13.50x o.p. (ISBN 0-87287-104-5). Libs Unl.
Andrews, V. C. Flowers in the Attic. pap. 2.95 (ISBN 0-686-68323-4). PB.
--If There Be Thorns. Date not set. pap. price not set. PB.
--Petals in the Wind. 1980. Repr. 14.95 (ISBN 0-671-41125-X). S&S.
--Petals on the Wind. 1980. pap. 2.95 (ISBN 0-671-82977-7). PB.
Andrews, Victor L. & Hunt, Pearson. Financial Management: Cases & Readings. rev. ed. 1976. text ed. 19.95x (ISBN 0-256-01746-8). Irwin.
Andrews, Viola, ed. see Andrews, Glenn.
Andrews, W. Guide to the Study of Freshwater Ecology. 1971. 11.36 (ISBN 0-13-370866-7); pap. text ed. 7.36 (ISBN 0-13-370759-8). P-H.
Andrews, W. T., ed. Critics on Shakespeare. (Readings in Literary Criticism). 1973. pap. text ed. 6.75x (ISBN 0-04-821034-X). Allen Unwin.
Andrews, Wayne. Architecture, Ambition, & Americans: A Social History of American Architecture. rev. ed. LC 78-50786. (Illus.). 1978. 17.95 (ISBN 0-02-900770-4). Free Pr.
--Architecture, Ambition, & Americans: A Social History of American Architecture. rev. ed. LC 78-50786. (Illus.). 1979. pap. text ed. 7.95 (ISBN 0-02-900750-X). Free Pr.
--Voltaire. LC 80-29565. (Illus.). 1981. 13.95 (ISBN 0-8112-0800-1); pap. 5.95 (ISBN 0-8112-0802-8, NDP519). New Directions.
--Voltaire. (Illus.). 13.95 (ISBN 0-8112-0800-1); pap. 5.95 (ISBN 0-8112-0802-8, NDP519). New Directions.
Andrews, William. At the Sign of the Barber's Pole. LC 74-77164. 1969. Repr. of 1904 ed. 15.00 (ISBN 0-8103-3846-7). Gale.
--Bygone England: Social Studies in Its Historic Byways & Highways. LC 67-23910. (Social History Reference Ser). (Illus.). 1968. Repr. of 1892 ed. 15.00 (ISBN 0-8103-3246-9). Gale.
--Doctor in History, Literature, Folklore. LC 74-99779. 1970. Repr. of 1896 ed. 18.00 (ISBN 0-8103-3595-6). Gale.
--England in the Days of Old. LC 68-21752. 1968. Repr. of 1897 ed. 18.00 (ISBN 0-8103-3545-X). Gale.
--Old Time Punishments. LC 78-124585. 1970. Repr. of 1890 ed. 15.00 (ISBN 0-8103-3841-6). Gale.
Andrews, William G. & Williams, H. B. Applied Instrumentation in the Process Industries, Vol. 2. 2nd ed. (Practical Guidelines Ser.). (Illus.). 330p. 1980. 37.95 (ISBN 0-87201-383-9). Gulf Pub.
Andrews, William L. Literary Romanticism in America. LC 80-24365. 168p. 1981. 14.95x (ISBN 0-8071-0760-3). La State U Pr.
Andrian, Gustave W. & Davies, Jane. Pret a Lire. 1980. pap. write for info. (ISBN 0-02-303440-8). Macmillan.
Andrianov, A. N., et al, eds. Algebra, Number Theory, & Their Applications. (Trudy Steklov: No. 148). Date not set. 88.00 (ISBN 0-8218-3046-5). Am Math.
Andrisani, Paul J., et al. Work Attitudes & Labor Market Experience: Evidence from the National Longitudinal Surveys. LC 78-2520. 1978. 24.95 (ISBN 0-03-041586-1). Praeger.
Andrist, Friedrich. Mares, Foals & Foaling. Dent, A., tr. pap. 3.35 (ISBN 0-85131-053-2, Dist. by Sporting Book Center). J A Allen.
Andrist, Ralph, ed. see Washington, George.
Andrist, Ralph K. Steamboats on the Mississippi. LC 62-10384. (Illus.). 153p. (gr. 6 up). 1962. 9.95 (ISBN 0-8281-0387-9, J009-1); lib. bdg. 12.89 (ISBN 0-06-020136-3, Distr. by Harrow). Am Heritage.
Andrist, Ralph K. & Dufek, George J. Heroes of Polar Exploration. LC 62-16256. (Horizon Caravel Bks). (Illus.). 153p. (gr. 6-12). 1962. 9.95 (ISBN 0-8281-0352-6, J023-0). Am Heritage.
Andrist, Ralph K. & Hanna, Archibald. California Gold Rush. LC 61-10677. (American Heritage Junior Library). (Illus.). 153p. (gr. 5 up). 1961. 9.95 (ISBN 0-8281-0388-7, JOO6-0). Am Heritage.
Andronescu, Serban. Bye Cadmos: A Journal of Aesthetic Analogies. 5.00 (ISBN 0-686-65394-7). Am Inst Writing Res.
--English-Rumanian Dictionary. 15.00 (ISBN 0-685-20187-2, 064-X). Saphrograph.
--Rumanian-English Dictionary. 15.00 (ISBN 0-685-20189-9); thumb indexed o.p. 11.50 (ISBN 0-685-20190-2). Saphrograph.
Andronicos, Manolis, et al. Philip of Macedon. Hatzopoulos, Miltiades B. & Loukopoulos, Louisa D., eds. (Illus.). 254p. 1980. 45.00 (ISBN 0-89241-330-1). Caratzas Bros.
Andronis, Constantine. Apostolos Makrakis--An Evaluation of Half A Century. 369p. (Orig.). 1966. pap. 4.00x (ISBN 0-938366-33-5). Orthodox Chr.
Andronov, A. A., et al. Qualitative Theory of Second-Order Dynamic Systems. LC 43-4704. 524p. 1973. 64.95 (ISBN 0-470-03195-6). Halsted Pr.
Andronov, Alexander, et al. Theory of Oscillators. (Illus.). 1966. text ed. 41.25 o.p. (ISBN 0-08-009981-5). Pergamon.
Andrus, Lisa F. Measure & Design in American Painting, 1760-1860. LC 76-23601. (Outstanding Dissertations in the Fine Arts - American). (Illus.). 1977. Repr. lib. bdg. 56.00 (ISBN 0-8240-2675-6). Garland Pub.
Andrusyshen, C. H. & Kirkconnell, Watson, trs. The Ukrainian Poets, Eleven Hundred & Eight-Nine to Nineteen Sixty-Two. (Scholarly Reprint Ser.). 1980. Repr. of 1963 ed. 15.00 (ISBN 0-8020-3100-5). U of Toronto Pr.
And Thomas, T. R., jt. auth. see Leaver, R. H.
Andujar, Claudia & Reit, Seymour. Week in Bico's World: Brazil. (Face to Face Bks). (Illus.). (gr. k-3). 1970. 6.95 (ISBN 0-02-705550-7, CCPr). Macmillan.
Andujar, Julio I. Mastering Spanish Verbs. (Orig.). (gr. 9 up). 1968. pap. text ed. 3.95 (ISBN 0-88345-100-X, 17452). Regents Pub.
Andujar, Julio I., ed. see Clarey, M. Elizabeth & Dixson, Robert J.
Andujar, Maria D. & Iglesias, Jose L. Mecanografia Al Dia. rev. ed. (gr. 10 up). 1977. pap. text ed. 2.45 (ISBN 0-88345-306-1). Regents Pub.
Anell, Lars & Nygren, Birgitta. The Developing Countries & the World Economic Order. 208p. 1980. pap. 8.95 (ISBN 0-416-74630-6, 2002). Methuen Inc.
Anema, Durlynn. Get Hired: Thirteen Ways to Get a Job. (Illus.). 64p. (gr. 7-12). 1979. pap. text ed. 2.95 (ISBN 0-915510-35-9). Janus Bks.
Anene, A. International Boundaries of Nigeria: The Framework of an Emergent African Nation. (Ibadan History Ser). 1970. text ed. 10.50x (ISBN 0-391-00080-2). Humanities.
Anfinsen, C. B., et al, eds. Advances in Protein Chemistry, Vol. 34. (Serial Publication). 1981. price not set (ISBN 0-12-034234-0); price not set lib. ed. (ISBN 0-12-034284-7); price not set microfiche. Acad Pr.
Ang, A. H. & Tang, W. H. Probability & Concepts in Engineering Planning & Design: Basic Principles, Vol. 1. LC 75-5892. 409p. 1975. text ed. 24.95x (ISBN 0-471-03200-X); solutions manaul avail. (ISBN 0-471-03198-4). Wiley.
--Probability & Design: Concepts in Engineering Planning & Design, Vol. 2. 1982. 15.95 (ISBN 0-471-03201-8). Wiley.
Angebert, Jean & Angebert, Michel. The Occult & the Third Reich. LC 73-2748. (Illus.). 288p. 1974. 8.95 o.p. (ISBN 0-02-502150-8). Macmillan.
Angebert, Michel, jt. auth. see Angebert, Jean.
Angehrn, Emil. Freiheit und System Bei Hegel. 1977. 73.00x (ISBN 3-11-006969-5). De Gruyter.
Angel, Allen R. & Porter, Stuart R. Survey of Mathematics: With Applications. LC 80-19471. (Mathematics Ser.). (Illus.). 576p. 1981. text ed. write for info. (ISBN 0-201-00045-8). A-W.
Angel, H. Flowers. 1975. pap. 5.00 o.p. (ISBN 0-85242-424-8, Pub. by Fountain). Morgan.
--Fungi. 1975. pap. 5.00 (ISBN 0-85242-425-6, Pub. by Fountain). Morgan.
--Insects. 1975. pap. 5.00 o.p. (ISBN 0-85242-402-7, Pub. by Fountain). Morgan.
--Seashore. 1975. pap. 5.00 o.p. (ISBN 0-85242-403-5, Pub. by Fountain). Morgan.
--Trees. 1975. pap. 5.00 o.p. (ISBN 0-85242-401-9, Pub. by Fountain). Morgan.
Angel, Heather. Life on the Seashore. LC 78-64656. (Fact Finders Ser.). (Illus.). 1979. lib. bdg. 3.96 (ISBN 0-686-51128-X). Silver.

--Nature Photography: Its Art & Techniques. 14.95 o.p. (ISBN 0-85242-105-2, Pub. by Fountain). Morgan.
--The World of an Estuary. (Illus.). 1974. 7.95 (ISBN 0-571-10378-2, Pub. by Faber & Faber). Merrimack Bk Serv.
Angel, Judie. Tina Gogo. (gr. 7-12). 1980. pap. 1.50 (ISBN 0-440-98738-5, LFL). Dell.
Angel, Juvenal L. & Dixson, Robert J. Metodo Directo De Conversacion En Espanol, 2 Bks. (gr. 9 up). 1969. Bk. 1. pap. text ed. 2.75 (ISBN 0-88345-102-6, 17761); Bk. 2. pap. text ed. 2.75 (ISBN 0-88345-103-4, 17762). Regents Pub.
--Tests & Drills in Spanish Grammar, 2 bks. (Orig., Span. & Eng., Lessons correlated to Conversacion en Espanol). (gr. 9 up). 1973. Bk. 1. pap. text ed. 2.75 (ISBN 0-88345-161-1, 18100); Bk. 2. pap. text ed. 2.75 (ISBN 0-88345-162-X, 18101). Regents Pub.
Angel, Marie. The Art of Calligraphy: A Practical Guide. (Illus.). 1978. pap. 7.95 (ISBN 0-684-15518-4, ScribT). Scribner.
Angel, Martin V. & Harris, Tegwyn. Animals of the Oceans: The Ecology of Marine Life. LC 77-2490. (Illus.). 1977. 10.95 o.p. (ISBN 0-8467-0344-0, Pub. by Two Continents). Hippocrene Bks.
Angel, Martin V., ed. A Voyage of Discovery: George Deacon 70th Anniversary Volume. new ed. LC 76-57958. 1977. 120.00 (ISBN 0-08-021380-4). Pergamon.
Angel, Myron. History of San Luis Obispo County, California, with Illustrations & Biographical Sketches of Its Prominent Men & Pioneers, 1883. (Illus.). 1979. Repr. of 1883 ed. 25.00 o.p. (ISBN 0-913548-66-9, Pub. by Thompson & West). Western Tanager.
Angel, Nicholas. Capsize in a Trimaran: A Story of Survival in the North Atlantic. (Illus.). 1981. 15.95 (ISBN 0-393-03264-7). Norton.
Angel, Roger B. Relativity: The Theory & Its Philosophy. (Foundations & Philosophy of Science & Technology Ser.). (Illus.). 320p. 1980. 48.00 (ISBN 0-08-025197-8); pap. 21.00 (ISBN 0-08-025196-X). Pergamon.
Angela. Daffy Definitions of Medical Terms. Date not set. 5.95 (ISBN 0-533-04834-6). Vantage.
Angele, H. Four-Language Technical Dictionary of Chromatography: English, German, French, Russian. LC 76-103000. 1971. text ed. 42.00 (ISBN 0-08-015865-X). Pergamon.
Angelella, Michael. Trail of Blood. 1981. pap. 1.95 (ISBN 0-451-09673-8, J9673, Sig). NAL.
Angeles, Peter, ed. Critiques of God. LC 76-43520. (Skeptic's Bookshelf Ser.). 371p. 1976. 13.95 (ISBN 0-87975-077-4); pap. 8.95 (ISBN 0-87975-078-2). Prometheus Bks.
--Critiques of God. pap. 7.00 (ISBN 0-87980-349-5). Wilshire.
Angeli, Daniel & Dousset, Jean-Paul, photos by. Private Pictures. 96p. 1980. pap. 9.95 (ISBN 0-670-57849-5, Studio). Viking Pr.
Angeli, Marguerite De see De Angeli, Marguerite.
Angelini, Anthony, et al. International Lending, Risk & the Euromarkets. LC 79-10712. 213p. 1979. 21.95x (ISBN 0-470-26653-8). Halsted Pr.
Angell, C. Roy. God's Gold Mines. LC 62-9194. 1962. 3.95 (ISBN 0-8054-5113-7). Broadman.
--Price Tags of Life. LC 59-9692. 1959. 3.95 (ISBN 0-8054-5108-0). Broadman.
Angell, Ellen. The Layman's Handbook of Interior Design. 1972. 5.00 o.p. (ISBN 0-682-47363-4, Banner). Exposition.
Angell, George. Computer Proven Commodity Spreads. 1981. write for info. Windsor.
--Winning in the Commodities Market: A Money-Making Guide to Commodity Futures Trading. LC 78-18129. 1979. 12.95 (ISBN 0-385-14208-0). Doubleday.
Angell, George W., ed. Faculty & Teacher Bargaining: The Impact of Unions on Education. LC 80-8769. 1981. write for info. (ISBN 0-669-04360-5). Lexington Bks.
Angell, J. R., et al. Darwinism. Bd. with Natural Inheritance. Galton, Francis. (Contributions to the History of Psychology Ser., Vol. IV, Pt. D: Comparative Psychology). 1978. 30.00 (ISBN 0-89093-173-9). U Pubns Amer.
Angell, J. William & Helm, Robert M. Meaning & Value in Western Thought: A History of Ideas in Western Culture. LC 80-67174. (The Ancient Foundations Ser.: Vol. I). 434p. 1981. lib. bdg. 22.75 (ISBN 0-8191-1368-9); pap. text ed. 13.95 (ISBN 0-8191-1369-7). U Pr of Amer.
Angell, James W. Learning to Manage Our Fears. 128p. 1981. 6.95 (ISBN 0-687-21329-0). Abingdon.
Angell, Judie. Dear Lola: Or How to Build Your Own Family: a Tale. LC 80-15111. 160p. (gr. 4-6). 8.95 (ISBN 0-87888-170-0). Bradbury Pr.
--In Summertime It's Tuffy. LC 76-57810. (gr. 5-7). 1977. 8.95 (ISBN 0-87888-117-4). Bradbury Pr.
--Ronnie & Rosey. (YA) 1979. pap. 1.50 (ISBN 0-440-97491-7, LFL). Dell.
--Ronnie & Rosey. LC 77-75362. (gr. 6-9). 1977. 8.95 (ISBN 0-87888-124-7). Bradbury Pr.
--Secret Selves. LC 79-12710. (gr. 5-7). 1979. 8.95 (ISBN 0-87888-158-1). Bradbury Pr.
--Tina Gogo. LC 77-16439. (gr. 5 up). 1978. 8.95 (ISBN 0-87888-132-8). Bradbury Pr.
--What's Best for You. 192p. (gr. 6 up). 1981. 8.95 (ISBN 0-87888-181-6). Bradbury Pr.
--A Word from Our Sponsor. (gr. 7 up). 1981. pap. 1.75 (ISBN 0-440-99525-6, LE). Dell.
--Word from Our Sponsor: Or My Friend Alfred. LC 78-25716. (gr. 5-7). 1979. 8.95 (ISBN 0-87888-142-5). Bradbury Pr.
Angell, Madeline. One Hundred Twenty Questions & Answers About Birds. 6.95 o.p. (ISBN 0-672-51771-X). Bobbs.
Angell, Norman. War & the Workers. LC 74-147518. (Library of War & Peace; Labor, Socialism & War). lib. bdg. 38.00 (ISBN 0-8240-0455-8). Garland Pub.
Angell, Tony. Owls. 80p. text ed. 12.95 (ISBN 0-919654-25-8). Hancock Hse.
Angell, Tony & Balcomb, Kenneth. Mammals & Waterbirds of Puget Sound. 1981. write for info. U of Wash Pr.
Angelo, Frank, ed. see Walker, Morton.
Angelopoulos, Angelos. The Third World & the Rich Countries: Prospects for the Year 2000. LC 72-75694. (Special Studies in International Economics & Development). 1972. text ed. 28.50x (ISBN 0-275-28608-8); pap. text ed. 9.50x (ISBN 0-89197-963-8). Irvington.
Angelopoulos, Angelos T. For a New Policy of International Development. LC 77-24420. (Praeger Special Studies). 1977. text ed. 17.95 o.p. (ISBN 0-03-022816-6); pap. 7.95 o.p. (ISBN 0-03-022821-2). Praeger.
Angelucci, Enzo & Matricardi, Paolo. World Aircraft: Military, 1945-1960. (Illus.). 1980. pap. 7.95 (ISBN 0-528-88205-8). Rand.
Anger, Kathryn. Breakout. LC 79-55871. (Feminist Novels Ser.). 128p. (Orig.). 1980. pap. 4.95 (ISBN 0-935772-01-4). Diotima Bks.
Angerman, David, jt. auth. see Norwood, James E.
Angeville, A. d' Essai Sur la Statistique De la Population Francaise: Consideree Sous Quelque-Uns De Ses Rapports Physiques et Moraux. (Reeditions: No. 6). 1970. 65.30 (ISBN 0-686-20911-7). Mouton.
Angevine, Jay B. & Cotman, Carl W. Principles of Neuroanatomy. (Illus.). 300p. 1981. text ed. 18.95x (ISBN 0-19-502885-6); pap. text ed. 11.95x (ISBN 0-19-502886-4). Oxford U Pr.
Angevine, Jay B., Jr., ed. see Womack, Lester.
Angier, Bradford. Feasting Free on Wild Edibles. LC 72-6088. (Illus.). 320p. 1972. pap. 6.95 (ISBN 0-8117-2006-3). Stackpole.
--Field Guide to Edible Wild Plants. LC 73-23042. (Illus.). 256p. 1974. write for info. (ISBN 0-8117-0616-8); pap. 8.95 (ISBN 0-8117-2018-7). Stackpole.
--Field Guide to Medicinal Wild Plants. LC 78-19112. (Illus.). 320p. 1978. pap. 9.95 (ISBN 0-8117-2076-4). Stackpole.
--Field Guide to Medicinal Wild Plants. LC 78-19112. (Illus.). 320p. 1978. 14.95 (ISBN 0-8117-0552-8). Stackpole.
--How to Live in the Woods on Pennies a Day. LC 70-140741. (Illus.). 192p. 1971. pap. 7.95 (ISBN 0-8117-2009-8). Stackpole.
--Looking for Gold. (Illus.). 224p. 1981. pap. 8.95 (ISBN 0-8117-2034-9). Stackpole.
--Wilderness Neighbors. LC 76-26303. 228p. 1981. pap. 5.95 (ISBN 0-8128-6100-0). Stein & Day.
Angier, Bradford & Taylor, Zack. Introduction to Canoeing. (Illus.). 192p. (Orig.). 1981. pap. 8.95 (ISBN 0-8117-2010-1). Stackpole.
Angier, R. H. Firearms Blueing & Browning. 160p. 1936. 9.95 (ISBN 0-685-20387-5). Stackpole.
Angione, Genevieve. All Bisque & Half Bisque Dolls. LC 76-77265. (Illus.). 357p. 1981. Repr. 25.00 (ISBN 0-916838-39-0). Schiffer.
Angira, Jared. Cascades. 143p. (Orig.). (gr. 10 up). 1979. pap. 5.00 (ISBN 0-582-64225-6, Drum Beat). Three Continents.
--Silent Voices. (African Writers Ser.). 1972. pap. text ed. 1.95x (ISBN 0-435-90111-7). Heinemann Ed.
Angle, Burr, ed. Hints & Tips for Plastic Modelers. (Illus.). 1980. pap. 3.95 (ISBN 0-89024-546-0). Kalmbach.
Angle, Burr, ed. see Marks, Fred M.
Angle, Burr, ed. see Pratt, Douglas R.
Angle, Burr, ed. see Siposs, George G.
Angle, Burr, ed. see Wilkins, Lester.
Angle, Carol R., jt. ed. see McIntire, Matilda S.
Angle, Harold L., jt. auth. see Perry, James L.
Angle, Paul M., ed. The Lincoln Reader. LC 80-25663. (Illus.). xii, 564p. 1981. Repr. of 1947 ed. lib. bdg. 49.50x (ISBN 0-313-22757-8, ANLR). Greenwood.
Anglemyer, Mary, ed. see International Institute for Environment & Development (I.I.E.D.).
Anglemyer, Mary, et al, eds. A Search for Environmental Ethics: An Initial Bibliography. LC 80-15026. 119p. (Orig.). 1980. text ed. 8.95x (ISBN 0-87474-212-9). Smithsonian.
Anglin, Donald L., jt. auth. see Crouse, William H.
Anglin, Douglas G. & Shaw, Timothy M. Zambia's Foreign Policy: Studies in Diplomacy & Dependence. 1979. 29.50 (ISBN 0-89158-191-X). Westview.
Anglin, Douglas G., jt. auth. see Shaw, Timothy M.
Anglin, Douglas G., et al, eds. Conflict & Change in Southern Africa: Papers from a Scandinavian-Canadian Conference. LC 78-70693. 1978. pap. text ed. 10.00 (ISBN 0-8191-0647-X). U Pr of Amer.
Anglo, Sydney, ed. The Damned Art: Essays in the Literature of Witchcraft. 1977. 25.00 (ISBN 0-7100-8589-3). Routledge & Kegan.
Anglund, Joan W. Almost a Rainbow: A Book of Poems. (Illus.). 64p. 1980. 4.95 (ISBN 0-394-50072-5). Random.
--A Gift of Love, 5 vols. (Illus.). 32p. 1980. Set. pap. 8.95 (ISBN 0-15-230790-7, VoyB). HarBraceJ.
--The Joan Walsh Anglund Storybook. LC 78-55913. (Illus.). (ps-2). 1978. 4.95 (ISBN 0-394-83803-3, BYR); PLB 5.99 (ISBN 0-394-93803-8). Random.
Anglund, Joan W. & Walsh, Joan. Slice of Snow: A Book of Poems. LC 70-11830. (gr. 1-5). 1970. 3.95 o.p. (ISBN 0-15-183015-0, HJ). HarBraceJ.
Angnostopoulos, Athan, tr. see Seferis, George.
Angoff, Allan, ed. Public Relations for Libraries: Essays in Communications Techniques. LC 72-776. (Contributions in Librarianship & Information Science: No. 5). 1973. lib. bdg. 17.50x (ISBN 0-8371-6060-X, ANP/). Greenwood.
Angoff, Allan, ed. see International Conference, Amsterdam, 1972.
Angoff, Allan, ed. see International Conference, France, 1971.
Angoff, Allan, ed. see International Conference London, 1973.
Angoff, Allan, ed. see Proceedings of an International Conference, France, 1969.
Angoff, Charles, ed. & frwd. by. Twenty Years of the Literary Review: Essays, Stories, Poems, Plays, Epigrams. LC 77-92563. 500p. 1981. 18.00 (ISBN 0-8386-2221-6). Fairleigh Dickinson.
Angold, M. J. A Byzantine Government in Exile: Government & Society Under the Laskairds of Nicaea 1204-1261. 260p. 1975. 29.50x (ISBN 0-19-821854-0). Oxford U Pr.
Angrave, Bruce. Magnificat. 1978. pap. 2.25 o.p. (ISBN 0-425-03823-8, Medallion). Berkley Pub.
Angress, R. K. The Early German Epigram: A Study in Baroque Poetry. LC 70-111501. (Studies in Germanic Languages & Literatures: No. 2). 136p. 1971. 9.00x (ISBN 0-8131-1231-1). U Pr of Ky.
Angrist, B., et al, eds. Recent Advances in Neuropsychopharmacology: Selected Papers from the 12th Congress of the Collegium Internationale Neuro-Psychopharmacologicum Goteborg, Sweden, 22-26 June, 1980. (Illus.). 422p. 1981. 110.00 (ISBN 0-08-026382-8). Pergamon.
Angrist, Stanley W. Direct Energy Conversion. 3rd ed. 1976. text ed. 26.95x (ISBN 0-205-05581-8). Allyn.
Angsburger, David. The Freedom of Forgiveness. 128p. 1973. pap. 1.50 (ISBN 0-8024-2875-4). Moody.
Angus, Douglas & Angus, Sylvia, eds. Contemporary American Short Stories. 1978. pap. 2.50 (ISBN 0-449-30832-4, Prem). Fawcett.
--Great Modern European Short Stories. 1977. pap. 2.50 (ISBN 0-449-30781-6, Prem). Fawcett.
Angus, Fay. Between Your Status & Your Quo. LC 74-15512. (Orig.). 1975. pap. 1.65 o.p. (ISBN 0-8307-0321-7, 50-131-00). Regal.
--Catalyst. 1979. pap. 3.95 (ISBN 0-8423-0210-7). Tyndale.
Angus, H. T. Cast Iron: Physical & Engineering Properties. 542p. 1976. 89.00 (ISBN 0-408-70933-2). Butterworths.
Angus, Ian. Fell's Guide to Coins & Money Tokens of the World. LC 74-75383. Orig. Title: Coins & Money Tokens. (Illus.). 128p. 1974. 8.95 (ISBN 0-8119-0237-4). Fell.
Angus, Ian, ed. see Orwell, George.
Angus, M., ed. see Haydon, Dorothy & Gordon, Elayne.
Angus, M., ed. see Reid, G. A. & Thompson, Evelina.
Angus, Robert B., Jr. Electrical Engineering Fundamentals. 2nd ed. (Illus.). 1968. 18.95 (ISBN 0-201-00250-7). A-W.
Angus, S., ed. International Thermodynamic Tables of the Fluid State-5. 1978. text ed. 60.00 (ISBN 0-08-021981-0). Pergamon.
--International Thermodynamic Tables of the Fluid State-6. 1979. text ed. 82.00 (ISBN 0-08-022372-9). Pergamon.
--International Thermodynamic Tables of the Fluid State-7. 1980. text ed. 100.00 (ISBN 0-08-022373-7). Pergamon.
Angus, Samuel. Religious Quest of the Graeco-Roman World: A Study in the Historical Background of Early Christianity. LC 66-30791. 1929. 15.00x (ISBN 0-8196-0196-9). Biblo.
Angus, Sylvia, jt. ed. see Angus, Douglas.
Anhalt, John P., jt. auth. see Gerson, Benjamin.
Anholt, Uni V. In Search of Heffalumps. (Illus.). 88p. (Orig.). pap. 5.95 (ISBN 0-9601996-0-8). Beeberry Bks.
Anikouchine, W. & Sternberg, R. World Ocean: An Introduction to Oceanography. 1973. 18.95 (ISBN 0-13-967752-6). P-H.
Anikouchine, William & Sternberg, Richard. The World Ocean. 2nd ed. (Illus.). 512p. 1981. 19.95 (ISBN 0-13-967778-X). P-H.
Animal Behavior Society Symposium, 1977. Behavioral Significance of Color: Proceedings. new ed. Burtt, Edward H., Jr., ed. LC 77-14618. 1979. lib. bdg. 42.00x (ISBN 0-8240-7016-X, Garland STPM Pr). Garland Pub.
Animal Nutrition. Nutrient Requirements of Poultry. 7th rev ed. Agricultural Board, ed. LC 54-60841. (Nutrient Requirements of Domestic Animals Ser). 1978. pap. 4.50 (ISBN 0-309-02725-X). Natl Acad Pr.
Animal Welfare Institute. Animal Expressions. rev. ed. (Illus.). 54p. 1974. pap. text ed. 2.00 (ISBN 0-938414-06-2). Animal Welfare.
--Comfortable Quarters for Laboratory Animals. 7th ed. (Illus.). 108p. 1979. pap. text ed. 3.00 (ISBN 0-938414-01-1). Animal Welfare.
--Humane Biology Projects. 3rd ed. (Illus.). 57p. 1977. pap. text ed. 2.00 (ISBN 0-938414-05-4). Animal Welfare.
Animal Welfare Institute, ed. see Diner, Jeff.
Animal Welfare Institute, jt. ed. see Walker, Ernest P.
Animal Welfare Institute, tr. see Nilsson, Great, et al.
Animalu, Alex O. E. Intermediate Quantum Theory of Crystalline Solids. LC 76-16858. (Illus.). 1977. 27.95 (ISBN 0-13-470799-0). P-H.
Anjaneyulu, M. S. Elements of Modern Pure Geometry. 6.50x (ISBN 0-210-26948-0). Asia.
Ank, John A., jt. auth. see Breyer, Donald E.
Ankeny, Nesmith. Poker Strategy. LC 80-68177. 272p. 1981. 11.95 (ISBN 0-465-05839-6). Basic.
Ankrum, Paul. Semiconductor Electronics. LC 76-135025. (Illus.). 1971. 26.95 (ISBN 0-13-806257-9). P-H.
Ann, Fay, ed. see Corey, Dorothy.
Ann, Fay, ed. see Nixon, Joan L.
Ann, Ruth. Miracle of the Tulips. (Orig.). 1980. pap. 5.50 (ISBN 0-8309-0296-1). Herald Hse.
Annand, William S. & Wise, Sheldon. The ALA TOEFL Course. 2nd ed. (Orig.). 1980. Set Includes Tchrs.' Handbk, Classwork Bk, Homework Bk. pap. text ed. write for info. (ISBN 0-934270-00-7). Antiquary Pr.
Annarino, A. Bowling: Individualized Instructional Program. 1973. pap. 4.25 (ISBN 0-13-080440-1). P-H.
--Individualized Instructional Programs in Archery, Badminton, Bowling, Golf & Tennis, 5 bklts. 1973. pap. 12.95 o.p. (ISBN 0-13-457093-6); instructor's guide 1.95 o.p. (ISBN 0-13-457127-4). P-H.
Annarino, Anthony A. Developmental Conditioning for Women & Men. 2nd ed. LC 75-9879. (Illus.). 262p. 1976. pap. text ed. 8.95 o.p. (ISBN 0-8016-0249-1). Mosby.
Annarino, Anthony A., et al. Curriculum Theory & Design in Physical Education. LC 80-282. (Illus.). 1980. text ed. 15.95 (ISBN 0-8016-0297-1). Mosby.
Annas, Julia, ed. see Aristotle.
Anne, Fay, ed. see Heide, Florence P. & Heide, Roxanne.
Annegan, Charles, ed. see Baird, Samuel E.
Annenberg, Maurice. Advertising: Three Thousand B. C. to Nineteen Hundred A.D. LC 77-75421. 1969. 20.00 o.p. (ISBN 0-916526-02-X). Maran Pub.
--Type Foundries of America & Their Catalogs. LC 73-94198. 1978. Repr. of 1975 ed. 30.00 o.p. (ISBN 0-916526-03-8). Maran Pub.
Annenberg, Maurice, compiled by. A Typographical Journey Through the Inland Printer. LC 77-89269. 1977. write for info. Maran Pub.
Annenberg, Maurice, intro. by. A Typographical Journey Through the Inland Printer 1880-1900. LC 77-89269. casebound 45.00 (ISBN 0-916526-04-6). Maran Pub.
Annenkov, Yury. Portraits. Lowe, David, tr. from Rus. (Illus.). 1981. 60.00 (ISBN 0-931554-18-7). Strathcona.
Annensky, Innokenty. Cypress Chest-Kiparisovy Larets. Morrison, R., tr. (Rus & Eng.). 1981. pap. 7.50 (ISBN 0-88233-474-3). Ardis Pubs.
Annese, Lucius. Pope John Paul II in America. LC 79-56497. (Orig.). 1980. 10.00 (ISBN 0-933402-10-4); pap. 4.95 (ISBN 0-933402-09-0). Charisma Pr.

--The Purpose of Authority? LC 78-72295. 1980. text ed. 10.00 (ISBN 0-933402-12-0); pap. text ed. 4.95 (ISBN 0-933402-00-7). Charisma Pr.
--The Purpose of Authority: A Drama. LC 79-57037. (Orig.). 1980. pap. write for info. (ISBN 0-933402-02-3). Charisma Pr.
--Write & Publish. LC 79-57036. 100p. 1980. write for info. (ISBN 0-933402-13-9); pap. 4.95 (ISBN 0-933402-14-7). Charisma Pr.
Annesley, James. Memoirs of an Unfortunate Young Nobleman, Returned from a Thirteen Years' Slavery in America, 1743. LC 75-16366. (Novel in England, 1700-1775 Ser). 1974. lib. bdg. 50.00 (ISBN 0-8240-1107-4). Garland Pub.
Annett, Cora. Dog Who Thought He Was a Boy. (Illus.). (gr. k-3). 1965. reinforced bdg. 8.95 (ISBN 0-395-18471-1). HM.
--How the Witch Got Alf. LC 74-8808. (Illus.). 64p. (gr. 1-4). 1975. PLB 4.90 o.p. (ISBN 0-531-02791-0). Watts.
Annexton, May & Schillinger, Brent. Coping with Skin Care. (Coping with Ser.). 1981. lib. bdg. 7.97 (ISBN 0-8239-0525-X). Rosen Pr.
Annis. Techniques of Critical Reasoning. LC 73-81554. 1974. pap. text ed. 8.95 (ISBN 0-675-08906-9). Merrill.
Annis, L., et al, eds. Turning, Vol. 1. 2nd ed. (Engineering Craftsmen: No. H2). (Illus.). 1977. spiral bdg. 14.95x (ISBN 0-85083-403-1). Intl Ideas.
Annixter, Jane & Annixter, Paul. Monkeys & Apes. LC 76-9834. (First Bks.). (Illus.). 72p. (gr. 4-6). 1976. PLB 4.90 o.p. (ISBN 0-531-00322-1). Watts.
Annixter, Paul, jt. auth. see Annixter, Jane.
Annual Asse Professional Development Conference, 1968, 70, 72, 78 & 79. Proceedings. 1980. 20.00 (ISBN 0-686-21675-X). ASSE.
Annual Attitude Research Conference, 7th, Hilton Head, S.C., Feb. 1976. Moving a Head with Attitude Research: Proceedings. Wind, Yoram & Greenberg, Marshall, eds. LC 77-5548. 1977. pap. text ed. 12.00 o.p. (ISBN 0-87757-088-4). Am Mktg.
Annual Clinical Conference on Cancer, 22nd. Immunotherapy of Human Cancer: Proceedings. M. D. Anderson Hospital & Tumor Institute, ed. LC 77-17701. (Illus.). 1978. 41.00 (ISBN 0-89004-263-2). Raven.
Annual Conference for Psychosomatic Research, 20th, London, Nov. 15-16, 1976. The Psychosomatic Approach to Prevention of Disease: Proceedings. Carruthers, M. & Priest, R., eds. 1978. pap. text ed. 22.00 (ISBN 0-08-022253-6). Pergamon.
Annual Conference of Microbeam Analysis Society, 9th, 1974. Microbeam Analysis: Proceedings. 20.00 (ISBN 0-686-50179-9); 1975 (10th conf.) 20.00 (ISBN 0-686-50180-2); 1976 (11th conf.) 20.00 (ISBN 0-686-50181-0); 1978 (13th conf.) o. 20.00 (ISBN 0-686-50183-7); 1979 (14th conf.) 25.00 (ISBN 0-686-67766-8); 1980 (15th conf.) 25.00 (ISBN 0-686-67767-6). San Francisco Pr.
Annual Conference of the Society of Psychosomatic Research, 21st, Royal College of Physicians, London, November 21-22 1977 & Mellett, P. The Coming Age of Psychosomatics: Proceedings of the 21st Annual Conference of the Society of Psychosomatic Research, November 21-22 1977, Royal College of Physicians. (Illus.). 163p. 1979. 29.50 (ISBN 0-08-023736-3). Pergamon.
Annual Educators Conference Chicago, Illinois, August, 1980. Marketing in the Eighties, Changes & Challenges: Proceedings. Bagozzi, Richard P., et al, eds. LC 80-15934. (No. 46). (Illus., Orig.). 1980. pap. text ed. 30.00 (ISBN 0-87757-141-4). Am Mktg.
Annual Legal Conference on the Representation of Aliens 1978. In Defense of the Alien: Proceedings, Vol. 1. Fragomen, Austin L. & Tomasi, Lydio F., eds. (In Defense of the Alien Ser.). 144p. 1979. lib. bdg. 25.00x (ISBN 0-913256-41-2). Ctr Migration.
Annual Meeting of the Ohio Valley Philosophy of Educ. Society, August 1979. Philosophical Studies in Education: Proceedings. Carter, John E., ed. 1980. write for info. (ISBN 0-686-22976-2). Ind St Univ.
Annual of Trade Mark Design. Trademarks, No. 7. Carter, David E., ed. LC 72-76493. (The Book of American Trade Marks). (Illus.). Date not set. price not set (ISBN 0-910158-61-4). Art Dir.
Annual Symposium of Basic Medical Sciences, 10th & Piper, Priscilla J. SRS-A & Leukotrienes: Proceedings. (Prostaglandis Research Studies Press Ser.). 304p. 1981. 63.00 (ISBN 0-471-27959-5, Pub. by Wiley-Interscience). Wiley.
Annual Symposium on Fundamental Cancer Research, No. 31. Carcinogens: Identification & Mechanisms of Action. Griffin, A. Clark & Shaw, Charles R., eds. LC 78-23366. 1979. text ed. 45.00 (ISBN 0-89004-286-1). Raven.
Annual Uranium Seminar, 3rd. Proceedings. LC 79-48044. (Illus.). 177p. 1980. pap. 15.00x (ISBN 0-89520-260-3). Soc Mining Eng.
Anobile, Richard, ed. Why a Duck. (Illus.). 288p. 1974. pap. 5.95 large-format (ISBN 0-380-00452-6, 40774). Avon.
Anobile, Richard J. Outland: The Movie. (Orig.). 1981. pap. 9.95 (ISBN 0-686-69396-5). Warner Bks.
--The Wiz Scrapbook. 1978. pap. 7.95 o.p. (ISBN 0-425-03963-3, Medallion). Berkley Pub.
Anobile, Richard J., ed. A Flask of Fields. 1975. pap. 3.95 (ISBN 0-380-01189-1, 17533). Avon.
Anokhin, Peter K. Biology & Neurophysiology of the Conditioned Reflex & Its Role in Adaptive Behavior. Corson, Samuel A., tr. LC 73-744. 592p. 1974. 94.00 (ISBN 0-08-017160-5); pap. text ed. 21.00 (ISBN 0-08-021516-5). Pergamon.
Anon. Joseph Conrad, a Pen Portrait. 24p. 1980. Repr. of 1913 ed. lib. bdg. 10.00 (ISBN 0-8482-1309-2). Norwood Edns.
Anon, jt. auth. see Abbott.
Anonym, Kenneth. Understanding the Recovering Alcoholic. 1980. pap. 3.95 (ISBN 0-89486-103-4). Hazelden.
Anonymous. Frank & I. LC 68-56363. 272p. 1980. pap. 3.50 (ISBN 0-394-17751-7, B444, BC). Grove.
--Man with a Maid. LC 8-27284. 1968. pap. 2.95 (ISBN 0-394-17479-8, B181, BC). Grove.
--A Man with a Maid, Bk. 2. LC 79-15758. 1979. pap. 2.95 (ISBN 0-394-17091-1, B434, BC). Grove.
Anosike, Benji O. Draw up Your Own Will Without a Lawyer, or Else... Why You Can't Afford to Live--or Die--Without One! LC 80-966444. 84p. (Orig.). 1980. pap. text ed. 5.95x (ISBN 0-932704-05-0). Do-It-Yourself Pubns.
Anouilh, Jean. Alouette. Thomas, Merlin & Lee, Simon, eds. (Orig., Fr.,). 1975. pap. text ed. 8.95x incl. exercises (ISBN 0-89197-005-3). Irvington.
--Anouilh: Five Plays, Vol. 1. Incl. Romeo & Jeannette; Rehearsal; Ermine; Antigone; Eurydice. 340p. (Orig.). 1958. pap. 4.95 (ISBN 0-8090-0710-X, Mermaid). Hill & Wang.
--Jean Anouilh: Five Plays, Vol. 2. Incl. Ardele; Time Remembered; Mademoiselle Colombe; Restless Heart; Lark. 302p. (Orig.). 1959. pap. 6.95 (ISBN 0-8090-0713-4, Mermaid). Hill & Wang.
--Jean Anouilh: Seven Plays, Vol. 3. Incl. Thieves Carnival; Medea; Cecile (or the School for Fathers; Traveller Without Luggage; Orchestra; Episode in the Life of an Author; Catch As Catch Can. 379p. (Orig.). 1967. pap. 4.25 (ISBN 0-8090-0739-8, Mermaid). Hill & Wang.
Anozie, Sunday O. Structural Models & African Poetics: Towards a Pragmatic View of Literature. 220p. 1981. 37.50 (ISBN 0-7100-0467-2). Routledge & Kegan.
Anozie, Sunday O., et al. Phenomenology in Modern African Studies, No. 5. (Studies in African Semiotics). 1981. 25.00 (ISBN 0-914970-69-0); pap. text ed. 12.95 (ISBN 0-914970-70-4). Conch Mag.
Anpilogova, B. B., et al. A Foundation Dictionary of Russian. Korotky, V., tr. Date not set. 4.50 (ISBN 0-8446-1538-2). Peter Smith.
Anrais, David. Man & the Zodiac. pap. 5.95 (ISBN 0-87728-014-2). Weiser.
Anrep, G. V., ed. see Pavlov, Ivan P.
Ansara, Michael. Games for Two. (Illus.). 224p. 1981. pap. 8.95 (ISBN 0-906071-26-7). Proteus Pub NY.
Ansari, M. A. Muslims & the Congress: Correspondence of Dr. M. A. Ansari. Hasan, M., ed. 1979. 18.50 (ISBN 0-8364-0381-9). South Asia Bks.
Ansari, N. Economics of Irrigation Rates - a Study of Punjab & Uttar Phadesh. 1968. 9.00x o.p. (ISBN 0-210-22536-X). Asia.
Ansbacher, Heinz L., ed. see Adler, Alfred.
Ansbacher, Rowena R., ed. see Adler, Alfred.
Ansberger, Carolyn & Green, Mary J. Here's How to Handle "L". 1980. 50.00 (ISBN 0-88450-709-2, 30598-B). Communication Bks.
Anschel, Eugene, ed. American Appraisals of Soviet Russia: 1917-1977. LC 78-5920. 1978. 18.00 (ISBN 0-8108-1135-9). Scarecrow.
Anscombe, Elizabeth, ed. see Descartes, Rene.
Anscombe, Elizabeth, tr. see Descartes, Rene.
Anscombe, G. E. Introduction to Wittgenstein's Tractatus. 1971. pap. 5.95x (ISBN 0-8122-1019-0, Pa Paperbks). U of Pa Pr.
--Introduction to Wittgenstein's Tractatus. 3rd ed. 1967. pap. text ed. 4.00 (ISBN 0-09-051131-X, Hutchinson U Lib). Humanities.
Anscombe, G. E., ed. see Wittgenstein, Ludwig.
Anscombe, G. E., tr. see Wittgenstein, Ludwig.
Anscombe, G. E. M., ed. see Wittgenstein, Ludwig.
Anscombe, G. E. M, tr. see Wittgenstein, Ludwig.
Ansdale, R. F. Wankel RC Engine. LC 69-18692. (Illus.). 1969. 15.00 o.p. (ISBN 0-498-07410-2). A S Barnes.
Ansel, Howard C. Introduction to Pharmaceutical Dosage Forms. 3rd ed. LC 80-16842. (Illus.). 408p. 1981. text ed. write for info. (ISBN 0-8121-0771-3). Lea & Febiger.
Ansel, Howard C., jt. auth. see Stoklosa, Mitchell J.
Ansel, Willits D. Restoration of the Smack Emma C. Berry. LC 72-95937. (Illus.). 94p. 1973. pap. 7.00 (ISBN 0-913372-08-0). Mystic Seaport.
Ansel, Willits D., jt. auth. see Blair, Carvel H.
Ansell, Barbara M. Rheumatic Disorders in Childhood. LC 80-40275. (Postgraduate Paediatrics Ser.). (Illus.). 344p. 1980. text ed. 66.95 (ISBN 0-407-00186-7). Butterworths.
Ansell, Jack. Giants. 1976. pap. 1.95 o.p. (ISBN 0-685-72627-4, T3271). Berkley Pub.
Ansell, Thomas. The Many-Coloured Mantle. 10.00 (ISBN 0-89253-452-4); flexible cloth 4.80 (ISBN 0-89253-453-2). Ind-US Inc.
Anselmo, Kathy. Things Once Secret. 33p. 1980. 3.95 (ISBN 0-8059-2750-6). Dorrance.
Anselm Of Canterbury. Anselm of Canterbury: Why God Became Man. Hopkins, Jasper & Richardson, Herbert, eds. 105p. 1980. cover 4.95 0soft (ISBN 0-88946-009-4). E Mellen.
Ansen, Alan. Disorderly Houses. LC 61-14240. (Wesleyan Poetry Program: Vol. 11). (Orig.). 1962. 10.00x (ISBN 0-8195-2011-X, Pub. by Wesleyan U Pr); pap. 5.00 (ISBN 0-8195-1011-4). Columbia U Pr.
Ansheim, Lester, jt. auth. see Berelson, Bernard.
Anshen, Melvin. Corporate Strategies for Social Performance. LC 79-7888. (Studies of the Modern Corporation). 1980. 15.95 (ISBN 0-02-900730-5). Macmillan.
Anshen, Melvin, ed. Managing the Socially Responsible Corporation. LC 73-13364. (Studies of the Modern Corporation). (Illus.). 288p. 1974. 15.95 (ISBN 0-02-900680-5). Macmillan.
Anshen, Ruth N., ed. see Delgado, Jose M.
Anshen, Ruth N., ed. see Illich, Ivan.
Anshen, Ruth N., ed. see Mead, Margaret.
Ansite, Pat. No Longer Lonely. 1977. pap. 2.95 (ISBN 0-89728-048-2, 670689). Omega Pubns OR.
Ansoff, H. Igor, ed. Business Strategy. (Education Ser). (Orig.). 1977. pap. 2.95 o.p. (ISBN 0-14-080072-7). Penguin.
Anson, Barbara. God Made Them Superstars. 1976. pap. 1.50 o.p. (ISBN 0-685-73454-4, LB405, Leisure Bks). Nordon Pubns.
Anson, Barry & Donaldson, James A. Surgical Anatomy of the Temporal Bone. 3rd ed. (Illus.). 500p. 1980. write for info. (ISBN 0-7216-1292-X). Saunders.
Anson, Edward, et al. Perceptions of Reality: A Sourcebook for the Social History of Western Civilization. LC 80-81665. 240p. 1980. pap. text ed. 10.95 (ISBN 0-8403-2224-0). Kendall-Hunt.
Anson, Jay. Six Sixty-Six. 13.95 (ISBN 0-671-25144-9). S&S.
Anson, Robert S. Gone Crazy & Back Again: The Rise & Fall of the Rolling Stone Generation. LC 80-5448. 384p. 1981. 14.95 (ISBN 0-385-13114-3). Doubleday.
Anson, Ronald J., jt. auth. see Rist, Ray C.
Anson, W. S. Mottoes & Badges of Families, Regiments, Schools, Colleges, States, Towns, Livery Companies, Societies, Etc. LC 74-14502. 192p. 1975. Repr. of 1904 ed. 20.00 (ISBN 0-8103-4055-0). Gale.
Ansorge, Peter. Disrupting the Spectacle: Five Years of Experience & Fringe Theatre in Britain. 1975. pap. 10.00x (ISBN 0-273-00351-8, Pub. by Wesleyan U Pr); pap. 5.00x (ISBN 0-273-00255-4). Columbia U Pr.
Ansorge, Rainer, et al. Numerical Mathematics-Numerische Mathematik. (International Series of Numerical Mathematics: No. 49). 210p. (Eng. Ger.). 1979. 28.00 (ISBN 3-7643-1099-5). Birkhauser.
Ansteinsson, J., ed. Norwegian Technical Dictionary: Norwegian-English, Vol. 2. rev. ed. 1954. 25.00x (ISBN 8-2702-8006-2, N432). Vanous.
Anstey, Edgar. Committees: How They Work & How to Work Them. 1962. pap. 3.95 o.p. (ISBN 0-04-380001-7). Allen Unwin.
Anstey, Thomas, et al. The Lawes Resolutions of Women's Rights. Thorne, Samuel E., ed. LC 77-89253. (Classics of English Legal History in the Modern Era Ser.: Vol. 82). 529p. 1979. lib. bdg. 40.00 (ISBN 0-8240-3181-4). Garland Pub.
Anstie, J. Observations on the Importance & Necessity of Introducing Improved Machinery into the Woollen Manufactory. 104p. 1971. Repr. of 1803 ed. 17.00x (ISBN 0-7165-1575-X, Pub. by Irish Academic Pr Ireland). Biblio Dist.
Anstis, R. D., et al. Practical Business Education, 2 vols. (Illus.). 576p. 1978. pap. text ed. 21.00x (ISBN 0-7121-2336-9, Pub. by Macdonald & Evans England). Intl Ideas.
Anstruther, Sir William. Essays, Moral & Divine. LC 74-170474. (The English Stage Ser.: Vol. 40). lib. bdg. 50.00 (ISBN 0-8240-0623-2). Garland Pub.
Antal, Evelyn, ed. see Klingender, Francis D.
Antal, Frederick. Florentine Painting & Its Social Background. (Icon Editions). (Illus.). 576p. 1975. pap. 8.95x o.s.i. (ISBN 0-06-430067-6, IN-67, HarpT). Har-Row.
Antalffy, Gyula. A Thousand Years of Travel in Old Hungary. Hoch, Elisabeth, tr. Orig. Title: Igy Utaztunk Hajdanaban. (Illus.). 337p. (Orig.). 1980. pap. 8.50x (ISBN 963-13-0909-6). Intl Pubns Serv.
Antcliff, A. J. Major Wine Grape Varieties of Australia. 1980. 15.00x (ISBN 0-643-02517-0, Pub. by CSJRO Australia). State Mutual Bk.
Antek, Samuel & Hupka, Robert. This Was Toscanini. LC 63-15196. (Illus.). 1963. 19.50 (ISBN 0-8149-0018-6). Vanguard.
Antell, Gerson. Economics: Institutions & Analysis. (gr. 10-12). 1970. 5.83 (ISBN 0-87720-609-0). AMSCO Sch.
Antell, Gerson & Harris, Walter. Current Issues in American Democracy. (Orig.). (gr. 10-12). 1975. pap. text ed. 6.75 (ISBN 0-87720-605-8). AMSCO Sch.
--Economics for Everybody. (Orig.). (gr. 11-12). 1973. text ed. 12.50 (ISBN 0-87720-621-X); pap. text ed. 5.83 (ISBN 0-87720-610-4). AMSCO Sch.
Antes, Richard L., jt. auth. see Hopkins, Charles D.
Anthes, Richard, et al. The Atmosphere. 3rd ed. (Illus.). 384p. 1981. text ed. 17.95 (ISBN 0-675-08043-6); instr's. manual 3.95 (ISBN 0-686-69485-6). Merrill.
Anthes, Richard A., et al. The Atmosphere. 2nd ed. (Physical Science Ser.). 1978. text ed. 18.95 (ISBN 0-675-08423-7). Merrill.
Anthimos. The Reply of the Orthodox Church to Roman Catholic Overtures on Reunion. 1977. pap. 1.00 (ISBN 0-913026-15-8). St Nectarios.
Anthony, Anne. Orienteering Handbook: Physical Education Ser. (Illus.). 64p. 1980. pap. text ed. 5.95 (ISBN 0-88839-047-5). Hancock Hse.
Anthony, Carol K. A Guide to the I Ching. LC 79-93376. 184p. (Orig.). 1980. pap. 4.95 (ISBN 0-9603832-0-4). Anthony Pub Co.
Anthony, Catherine P. & Thibodeau, Gary A. Anatomy & Physiology Laboratory Manual. 10th ed. LC 78-11927. (Illus.). 1979. pap. text ed. 9.95 (ISBN 0-8016-0270-X). Mosby.
--Basic Concepts in Anatomy & Physiology: A Programmed Presentation. 4th ed. LC 79-19392. (Illus.). 1979. pap. text ed. 10.50 (ISBN 0-8016-0260-2). Mosby.
--Structure & Function of the Body. 6th ed. LC 75-30936. 1980. text ed. 12.95 (ISBN 0-8016-0273-4); pap. text ed. 9.95 (ISBN 0-8016-0287-4). Mosby.
--Textbook of Anatomy & Physiology. 10th ed. LC 79-11405. (Illus.). 1978. text ed. 21.95 (ISBN 0-8016-0255-6). Mosby.
Anthony, Courtney L., et al. Pediatric Cardiology. (Medical Outline Ser.). 1979. pap. 18.00 (ISBN 0-87488-607-4). Med Exam.
Anthony, D. W., tr. see Morishima, M.
Anthony, Don. Success in Volleyball. (Illus.). 80p. 1974. 10.95 (ISBN 0-7195-2584-5). Transatlantic.
Anthony, E. James, et al. The Child in His Family. Incl. Vol. 2. The Impact of Disease & Death. 1973. 30.50 o.p. (ISBN 0-471-03226-3); Vol. 3. Children at Psychiatric Risk. LC 74-6169. 1974. 28.50 (ISBN 0-471-03228-X); Vol. 4. Vulnerable Children. LC 78-120701. 1978. 31.50 (ISBN 0-471-04433-4); Vol. 5. Children & Their Parents in a Changing World. LC 78-120701. 1978. 29.95 (ISBN 0-471-04432-6); Vol. 6. Preventative Child Psychiatry in an Age of Transition. 1980. 32.50 (ISBN 0-471-08403-4). LC 72-11702. (International Association for Child Psychiatry & Allied Professions Yearbook, Pub. by Wiley-Interscience). Wiley.
Anthony, Earl & Taylor, Dawson. Winning Bowling. LC 77-75718. (Winning Ser.). (Illus.). 1977. 8.95 o.p. (ISBN 0-8092-7792-1); pap. 5.95 (ISBN 0-8092-7791-3). Contemp Bks.
Anthony, Earl, jt. ed. see King, Woodie.
Anthony, Evelyn. The Assassin. 1978. pap. 1.50 o.p. (ISBN 0-425-03678-2, Medallion). Berkley Pub.
--The Cardinal & the Queen. 1977. pap. 1.50 o.p. (ISBN 0-425-03591-3, Medallion). Berkley Pub.
--Charles the King. 427p. 1976. Repr. of 1961 ed. lib. bdg. 15.95x (ISBN 0-89244-067-8). Queens Hse.
--The Janus Imperative. 1981. pap. 2.95 (ISBN 0-451-09890-0, E9890, Sig). NAL.
--The Legend. 1976. pap. 1.50 o.p. (ISBN 0-345-25473-2). Ballantine.
--Mission to Malaspiga. 1975. pap. 1.75 o.p. (ISBN 0-451-06706-1, E6706, Sig). NAL.
--The Rendezvous. 1977. pap. 1.95 o.p. (ISBN 0-425-03573-5, Medallion). Berkley Pub.
Anthony, Gene, jt. auth. see Anthony, Jill.

Anthony, Geraldine. John Coulter. (World Authors Ser.: Canada: No. 400). 1976. lib. bdg. 10.95 (ISBN 0-8057-6240-X). Twayne.
--Stage Voices: Twelve Canadian Playwrights Talk About Their Lives & Work. LC 77-76223. 1978. pap. 7.95 o.p. (ISBN 0-385-13540-8). Doubleday.

Anthony, Irvin. Paddle Wheels & Pistols. 329p. 1980. Repr. of 1929 ed. lib. bdg. 30.00 (ISBN 0-8495-0075-3). Arden Lib.

Anthony, James E. & Gilpin, Doris C., eds. Three Further Clinical Faces of Childhood. (Illus.). 340p. 1981. text ed. 25.00 (ISBN 0-89335-110-5). Spectrum Pub.

Anthony, James R., ed. see Delalande, Michel-Richard.

Anthony, Jill & Anthony, Gene. The Great Cable Car Adventure Book. (Illus.). 192p. (Orig.). 1981. pap. 6.95 (ISBN 0-89141-120-8). Presidio Pr.

Anthony, John. The Gardens of Britain, Six: Derbyshire, Leicestershire, Lincolnshire, Northamptonshire & Nottinghamshire. 1979. 24.00 (ISBN 0-7134-1745-5, Pub. by Batsford England). David & Charles.

Anthony, John D. Historical & Cultural Dictionary of the Sultanate of Oman & the Emirates of Eastern Arabia. LC 76-42216. (Historical & Cultural Dictionaries of Asia Ser.: No. 9). 1976. 10.00 (ISBN 0-8108-0975-3). Scarecrow.

Anthony, Julie & Bollitieri, Nick. A Winning Combination. (Illus.). 224p. 1980. 12.50 (ISBN 0-684-16710-7, ScribT). Scribner.

Anthony, Julie, jt. auth. see Bollitier, Nick.

Anthony, Michael. Handbook of Small Business Advertising. 192p. 1981. text ed. price not set (ISBN 0-201-00086-5). A-W.
--Sandra Street & Other Stories. (Heinemann Secondary Readers Ser.). 1973. pap. text ed. 2.95x (ISBN 0-435-92512-1). Heinemann Ed.

Anthony, Ole. Cross Fire. LC 75-38198. 1976. pap. 2.95 o.p. (ISBN 0-88270-157-6). Logos.

Anthony, P. P., jt. auth. see Woolf, Neville.

Anthony, Piers. Castle Roogna. 1979. pap. 2.50 (ISBN 0-345-29421-1, Del Rey Bks). Ballantine.
--God of Tarot. (Orig.). 1979. pap. 1.75 (ISBN 0-515-05134-9). Jove Pubns.
--God of Tarot. (Orig.). 1981. pap. 2.25 (ISBN 0-425-05031-9). Berkley Pub.
--Hasan. LC 77-24589. (Illus.). 1977. lib. bdg. 10.95x (ISBN 0-89370-115-7); pap. 4.95 (ISBN 0-89370-215-3). Borgo Pr.
--Mutes. 448p. 1981. pap. 2.95 (ISBN 0-380-77578-6). Avon.
--Orn, No. 2. 1975. pap. 1.75 (ISBN 0-380-00266-3, 40964). Avon.
--Ox, No. 3. 1976. pap. 1.75 (ISBN 0-380-00461-5, 41392). Avon.

Anthony, R. N. Essentials of Accounting. 2nd ed. LC 76-10413. 1977. pap. 10.95 (ISBN 0-201-00252-3); instr's guide 0.50 (ISBN 0-201-00258-2). A-W.

Anthony, Raymond G., jt. auth. see Holland, Charles D.

Anthony, Robert & Herzlinger, Regina E. Management Control in Nonprofit Organizations. rev. ed. 1980. 20.50x (ISBN 0-256-02326-3). Irwin.

Anthony, Robert N. Accounting for the Cost of Interest. LC 75-12484. 128p. 1975. 15.95 (ISBN 0-669-00027-2). Lexington Bks.
--Plaid for Management Accounting. 1974. pap. 5.50 (ISBN 0-256-01277-6, 01-0814-00). Learning Syst.

Anthony, Robert N. & Dearden, John. Management Control Systems. 4th ed. 1980. 20.95x (ISBN 0-256-02325-5). Irwin.
--Management Control Systems. 3rd ed. 1976. 18.50x o.p. (ISBN 0-256-01816-2). Irwin.

Anthony, Robert N. & Herzlinger, Regina E. Management Control in Nonprofit Organizations. 1975. text ed. 16.95x o.p. (ISBN 0-256-01748-4). Irwin.

Anthony, Robert N. & Reece, James S. Accounting Principles. 4th ed. 1979. text ed. 17.95x (ISBN 0-256-02147-3). Irwin.
--Accounting: Text & Cases. 6th ed. 1979. text ed. 19.95x (ISBN 0-256-02148-1). Irwin.

Anthony, Robert N. & Welsch, Glenn A. Fundamentals of Management Accounting. rev. ed. 1977. text ed. 18.95x (ISBN 0-256-01896-0); practice set 5.95x (ISBN 0-256-01957-6); study guide 6.50x (ISBN 0-256-01603-8). Irwin.

Anthony, Robert N., jt. auth. see Reece, James S.

Anthony, Robert N., jt. auth. see Welsch, Glenn A.

Anthony, Travis D., ed. Sunshine & Shadows. (Illus.). 190p. 1981. price not set (ISBN 0-9604686-1-7). T D Anthony.

Anthony, Vivian. Objective Tests in Introductory Economics with Answers. 1975. pap. text ed. 3.95x o.p. (ISBN 0-435-33150-7). Heinemann Ed.

Anthony, William A. The Art of Health Care. LC 75-40867. 104p. 1976. pap. text ed. 8.95x (ISBN 0-914234-25-0). Human Res Dev Pr.

Anthony, William E., jt. auth. see Hill, Richard T.

Anthony, William P. Management: Competencies & Incompetencies. LC 79-25171. 604p. 1981. text ed. price not set (ISBN 0-201-00085-7). A-W.
--Participative Management. LC 77-83035. 1978. pap. text ed. 8.95 (ISBN 0-201-00253-1); instr's guide 1.25 (ISBN 0-201-00219-1). A-W.

Anthraquinone Symposium, Buergenstock-Luzern, September, 1978. Natural Anthraquinone Drugs. Fairbairn, J. W., ed. (Pharmacology Journal: Vol. 20, Suppl. 1). (Illus.). 140p. 1980. pap. 24.00 (ISBN 3-8055-0683-X). S Karger.

Anticaglia, Elizabeth. Heroines of Seventy-Six. LC 74-24583. (Illus.). (gr. 3-6). 1975. 5.95 o.s.i. (ISBN 0-8027-6210-7); PLB 6.83 o.s.i. (ISBN 0-8027-6209-3). Walker & Co.
--A Housewife's Guide to Women's Liberation. LC 72-85889. 1972. 12.95 (ISBN 0-911012-69-9). Nelson-Hall.
--Twelve American Women. LC 74-23229. (Illus.). 272p. 1975. 17.95 (ISBN 0-88229-102-5). Nelson-Hall.

Antico, John & Hazelrigg, Meredith K. Insight Through Fiction: Dealing Effectively with the Short Story. LC 71-127360. (English Ser). (Orig.). 1970. pap. 4.95 o.p. (ISBN 0-8465-0253-4, 50253). Benjamin-Cummings.

Antieau, C. J., et al. Current Constitutional Issues: A Symposium. LC 77-153885. (Symposia on Law & Society Ser.). 1971. Repr. of 1967 ed. lib. bdg. 19.50 (ISBN 0-306-70154-5). Da Capo.

Antieau, Chester J. Modern Constitutional Law, 2 vols. LC 69-19951. 1969. 100.00 (ISBN 0-686-14506-2). Lawyers Co-Op.

Antilla, Raimo & Brewer, Warren. Analogy: A Basic Bibliography. (Library & Information Sources in Linguistics: No. 1). 1977. text ed. 17.25x (ISBN 0-391-01677-6). Humanities.

Antin, David, tr. see Gunther, Werner A.

Antique Airplane Association. Classic Airplanes of the Thirties - Aircraft of the Roaring Twenties. Gilbert, James, ed. LC 79-7238. (Flight: Its First Seventy-Five Years Ser.). (Illus.). 1979. Repr. of 1965 ed. lib. bdg. 15.00x (ISBN 0-405-12153-9). Arno.

Antler. Factory. LC 80-25727. (Pocket Poets Ser.: No. 38). (Orig.). 1980. 8.50 (ISBN 0-87286-123-6); pap. 3.00 (ISBN 0-87286-122-8). City Lights.

Antoine, George H., jt. auth. see Owen, Wyn F.

Antoine, Jaen-Pierre & Tirapegui, Enrique, eds. Functional Integration--Theory & Applications. 355p. 1980. 42.50 (ISBN 0-306-40573-3, Plenum Pr). Plenum Pub.

Antoine, Robert. Rama & the Bards: Epic Memory in the Ramayana. (Greybird Book). 114p. 1975. 12.00 (ISBN 0-88253-821-7); pap. 6.75 (ISBN 0-88253-822-5). Ind-US Inc.

Antoine, Robert, tr. see Kalidasa.

Anton, Ferdinand, et al. Primitive Art: Pre-Columbian, American Indian, African, Oceanic. (Illus.). 1979. 35.00 (ISBN 0-8109-1459-X). Abrams.

Anton, Hans H. Studien Zu Den Klosterprivilegien der Paepste Im Fruehen Mittelalter Unter Besonderer Beruecksichti der Privilegierung Von St. Maurice D'agaune. (Beitraege Zur Geschichte und Quellenkunde Des Mittelalters Ser.: Vol. 4). 1975. pap. 47.00x (ISBN 3-11-004686-5). De Gruyter.

Anton, Hector R., et al. Contemporary Issues in Cost & Managerial Accounting: A Discipline in Transition. 3rd ed. LC 77-74383. (Illus.). 1977. text ed. 18.95 (ISBN 0-395-25435-3). HM.

Anton, Howard. Calculus with Analytic Geometry. LC 79-11469. 1980. 27.95 (ISBN 0-471-03248-4); tchrs' manual avail. (ISBN 0-471-06360-6); solution manual avail. Wiley.
--Elementary Linear Alebra. 3rd ed. 384p. 1981. text ed. 19.95 (ISBN 0-471-05338-4). Wiley.

Anton, Howard & Kalman, Bernard. Applied Finite Mathematics. 1974. 13.95 o.p. (ISBN 0-12-059550-8). Acad Pr.

Anton, Howard & Kolman, Bernard. Applied Finite Mathematics. 2nd ed. 558p. 1978. 16.95 (ISBN 0-12-059565-6); instrs'. manual avail. (ISBN 0-12-059564-8). Acad Pr.
--Applied Finite Mathematics with Calculus. 760p. 1978. 17.95 (ISBN 0-12-059560-5); instrs'. manual 3.00 (ISBN 0-12-059567-2). Acad Pr.

Anton, Howard & Rorres, Chris. Applications of Linear Algebra. 2nd ed. 1979. pap. text ed. 8.95 (ISBN 0-471-05337-6). Wiley.

Anton, Thomas J. Governing Greater Stockholm: A Study of Policy Development & System Change. LC 79-94447. 1975. 20.00x (ISBN 0-520-02718-3). U of Cal Pr.

Anton, Thomas J., et al. Moving Money: An Empirical Analysis of Federal Expenditure Patterns. LC 80-21700. 272p. 1980. text ed. 20.00 (ISBN 0-89946-066-6). Oelgeschlager.

Antonaccio, Michael J., ed. Cardiovascular Pharmacology. LC 74-14469. 1977. 31.00 (ISBN 0-89004-063-X). Raven.

Antoniades, Anthony C. Architecture & Allied Design: An Environmental Design Perspective. (Illus.). 384p. (Orig.). 1980. pap. text ed. 17.95 (ISBN 0-8403-2154-6). Kendall-Hunt.

Antonio, Robert J. & Ritzer, George. Social Problems: Values & Interests in Conflict. 350p. 1975. text ed. 10.95x o.p. (ISBN 0-205-04713-0, 8147132). Allyn.

Antoniou, Jim. Greece. LC 75-44871. (Macdonald Countries). (Illus.). (gr. 6 up). 1976. PLB 7.95 (ISBN 0-382-06104-7, Pub. by Macdonald Ed.). Silver.

Antonius, George. The Arab Awakening. 16.00x (ISBN 0-685-77089-3). Intl Bk Ctr.

Antonovskii, et al. Topological Semifields & Their Applications to General Topology. LC 77-11046. (Translation Ser. No 2: Vol. 106). 1979. Repr. of 1977 ed. 16.40 (ISBN 0-8218-3056-2, TRAN 2/106). Am Math.

Antonovsky, Helen F., et al. Adolescent Sexuality: A Study of Attitudes & Behavior. LC 80-8337. 176p. 1980. 18.95 (ISBN 0-669-04030-4). Lexington Bks.

Antony, Arthur. Guide to Basic Information Sources in Chemistry. LC 79-330. (Information Resources Ser.). 1979. 15.95 (ISBN 0-470-26587-6). Halsted Pr.

Antosiewicz, H. A., ed. International Conference on Differential Equation: Procedings. 1975. 48.50 (ISBN 0-12-059650-4). Acad Pr.

Antoun, Richard T. Arab Village: A Social Structural Study of a Transjordanian Peasant Community. LC 70-633555. (Social Science Ser.: No. 29). (Illus.). 210p. 1972. pap. 15.00x (ISBN 0-253-38450-8). Ind U Pr.

Anttila. Analogy. (Trends in Lingusitics: No. 10). 1977. 25.30 (ISBN 9-0279-7975-8). Mouton.

Anttila, Elizabeth K. English Oral Production. 1980. pap. write for info. (ISBN 0-8477-3333-5). U of PR Pr.
--English Structure Exercises. pap. 1.85 (ISBN 0-8477-3300-9). U of PR Pr.

Anttila, Raimo, jt. auth. see Slagle, Uhlan.

Antwerp, Emily S. Van see Van Antwerp, Emily S.

Antwi, Anthony K. Public Expenditures: The Impact of Distribution on Income - the Ghana Case. LC 78-63269. 1978. pap. text ed. 9.50 (ISBN 0-8191-0620-8). U Pr of Amer.

Anuil, Christopher. Warlord's World. (Science Fiction Ser). pap. 1.25 o.p. (ISBN 0-87997-201-7, UY1201). DAW Bks.

Anwar, M. H. Memories of Afghanistan. 1981. 8.95 (ISBN 0-8062-1696-4). Carlton.

Anyan, Walter R. Adolescent Medicine in Primary Care. LC 78-16772. 1978. 19.50 (ISBN 0-471-03976-4, Pub. by Wiley Medical). Wiley.

Anyanwu, Chukwulozie K. Nature of Black Cultural Reality. 1976. pap. text ed. 16.75x o.p. (ISBN 0-8191-0013-7). U Pr of Amer.

Anzaldua, Gloria, jt. ed. see Lawrence, Cherrie M.

Anzalone, Joseph T., jt. auth. see Phillips, Celeste R.

Anzia, Joan M., jt. auth. see Durkin, Mary G.

Aoki, Harro. Nez Perce Grammar. (California Library Reprint). 1974. 20.00x (ISBN 0-520-02524-5). U of Cal Pr.

Aoki, Haruo. Nez Perce Texts. LC 77-91776. (Publications in Linguistics: Vol. 90). 1979. 12.75x (ISBN 0-520-09593-6). U of Cal Pr.

Aoutomobile Association. Nine Hundred Ninety-Nine Places to Eat for Around Five Pounds. rev. ed. (Illus.). 288p. 1981. pap. price not set (ISBN 0-86145-055-8, Pub. by Auto Assn-British Tourist Authority England). Merrimack Bk Serv.

Aoyagi, Akiko, jt. auth. see Shurtgleff, William.

Aoyagi, Akiko, jt. auth. see Shurtleff, William.

APA Library. Psychiatry & Confidentiality: An Annotated Bibliography. Jones, Jean C., ed. 51p. 1974. pap. 5.00 (ISBN 0-685-65578-4, P215-0). Am Psychiatric.

APA Task Force on Standards for Psychiatric Facilities for Children. Standards for Psychiatric Facilities Serving Children and Adolescents. 136p. 1971. 5.00 (ISBN 0-685-37536-6, P160-0). Am Psychiatric.

Apadeva. Mimansa Nyaya Prakasa. Edgerton, Franklin, tr. 1929. 65.00x (ISBN 0-685-69815-7). Elliots Bks.

Apczynski, John V. Doers of the Word. LC 76-51640. (American Academy of Religion. Dissertation Ser.). 1977. pap. 7.50 (ISBN 0-89130-128-3, 010118). Scholars Pr Ca.

Apel, Karl-Otto. Charles Sanders Peirce: From Pragmatism to Pragmaticism. Krois, John M., tr. from Ger. Orig. Title: Der Denkweg Von Charles Sanders Peirce. 336p. 1981. lib. bdg. 20.00x (ISBN 0-87023-177-4). U of Mass Pr.
--Towards a Transformation of Philosophy. (International Library of Phenomenology & Moral Sciences). 1980. 30.00x (ISBN 0-7100-0403-6). Routledge & Kegan.

Apel, Max & Luds, Peter. Philosophiches Woerterbuch. 6th ed. (Sammlung Goeschen: 2202). (Ger). 1976. pap. 5.80x (ISBN 3-11-006729-3). De Gruyter.

Apelt, Otto. Platonis Sophista: Recentsuit, Prolegomenis et Commentariis Instruxit. Taran, Leonardo, ed. LC 78-66612. (Ancent Philosophy Ser.: Vol. 1). 225p. lib. bdg. 20.00 (ISBN 0-8240-9611-8). Garland Pub.

Apfel, Necia H. It's All Relative: Einstein's Theory of Relativity. LC 80-28188. (Illus.). 144p. (gr. 5 up). 1981. 8.95 (ISBN 0-688-41981-X); PLB 8.59 (ISBN 0-688-51981-4). Morrow.

Apfelbaum, H. Jack & Ottesen, Walter O. Basic Engineering Sciences & Structural Engineering for Engineer-in-Training Examinations. Hollander, Lawrence J., ed. (Professional Engineering Examinations Ser.). (Illus.). 1970. 23.95 (ISBN 0-8104-5712-1). Hayden.

Apilado, Vincent P., et al. Cases in Financial Management. 1977. pap. text ed. 9.50 (ISBN 0-8299-0120-5); instrs.' manual avail. (ISBN 0-8299-0456-5). West Pub.

Apley, Alan, jt. auth. see Smith, Roger.

Apley, J. Modern Trends in Pediatrics-4. 1974. 28.95 (ISBN 0-407-30803-2). Butterworths.

Apley, J., ed. see O'Donohue, Niall F.

Apley, John, jt. auth. see Craig, Oman.

Apley, John, ed. see Stone, Fred H.

Apley, M. J., ed. see Nixon.

Apollinaire, Guillaume. Alcools. Greet, Anne Hyde, tr. & annotations by. 1966. 16.00x (ISBN 0-520-00028-5); pap. 3.75 (ISBN 0-520-00029-3, CAL121). U of Cal Pr.
--Alcools. Rees, Garnet, ed. (French Poets Ser.). 192p. 1975. text ed. 19.75x (ISBN 0-485-14708-4, Athlone Pr); pap. text ed. 10.00x (ISBN 0-485-12708-3, Athlone Pr). Humanities.
--Le Bestaire ou Cortege d'Orphee. Shakely, Lauren, tr. from Fr. LC 77-23500. (Illus.). 1977. 20.00 (ISBN 0-87099-165-5). Metro Mus Art.
--Bestiary, or the Parade of Orpheus. Karmel, Pepe, tr. from Fr. LC 80-66191. (Illus.). 80p. 1980. 10.00 (ISBN 0-87923-319-2); pap. 5.95 (ISBN 0-87923-359-1). Godine.
--Calligrammes. Greet, Anne H., tr. 600p. (Fr. & Eng.). 1980. 19.95 (ISBN 0-520-01968-7). U of Cal Pr.

Apostle, H. G. Aristotle's Categories & Propositions (De Interpretatione) LC 80-80777. 157p. (Orig.). 1980. lib. bdg. 12.00 (ISBN 0-9602870-4-3); pap. text ed. 6.00 (ISBN 0-9602870-5-1). Peripatetic.
--Aristotle's Posterior Analytics. LC 81-80233. (Apostle Translations of Aristotle's Works Ser.: Vol. 4). 350p. (Orig.). 1981. text ed. 19.20x (ISBN 0-9602870-6-X); pap. text ed. 9.60x (ISBN 0-9602870-7-8). Peripatetic.

Apostle, Hippocrates G. Aristotle's Physics. LC 80-80037. 386p. 1980. lib. bdg. 17.50 (ISBN 0-9602870-2-7); pap. text ed. 8.50 (ISBN 0-9602870-3-5). Peripatetic.

Apostol, Robert Z., ed. Human Values in a Secular World. 1970. text ed. 7.50x (ISBN 0-391-00120-5). Humanities.

Apostol, T. M. Calculus: One-Variable Calculus with an Introduction to Linear Algebra, Vol. 1. 2nd ed. LC 73-20899. 1967. text ed. 25.50 (ISBN 0-471-00005-1). Wiley.

Apostol, Tom M. Mathematical Analysis: A Modern Approach to Advanced Calculus. 2nd ed. LC 72-11473. 1974. text ed. 21.95 (ISBN 0-201-00288-4). A-W.

Apostolakis, G., et al, eds. Synthesis & Analysis Methods for Safety & Reliability Studies. 470p. 1980. 49.50 (ISBN 0-306-40316-1, Plenum Pr). Plenum Pub.

Apostolon, Billy. Fifty Two Special Day Invitation Illustrations. (Preaching Helps Ser.). pap. 1.95 o.p. (ISBN 0-8010-0082-3). Baker Bk.
--Preach the Word. (Sermon Outline Ser). 1978. pap. 1.95 (ISBN 0-8010-0039-4). Baker Bk.

App, Austin J. The Sudeten-German Tragedy. (Illus.). 84p. (Orig.). 1979. pap. 3.00x (ISBN 0-911038-66-3, Inst Hist Rev). Noontide.

Appadorai, A. Essays in Politics & International Relations. 15.00x (ISBN 0-210-98160-1). Asia.

Appadurai, Arjun. Worship & Conflict Under Colonial Rule: A South India Case. (Cambridge South Asian Studies: No. 27). (Illus.). 282p. Date not set. price not set (ISBN 0-521-23122-1). Cambridge U Pr.

Appel, Alfred, Jr. & Newman, Charles, eds. Nabokov. LC 76-96906. (Triquarterly Book). 1970. 16.95x o.p. (ISBN 0-8101-0292-7). Northwestern U Pr.

Appel, Alfred, Jr., ed. see Nabokov, Vladimir.

Appel, Allan. Judah. 1976. pap. 1.75 o.p. (ISBN 0-685-74570-8, LB418KK, Leisure Bks). Nordon Pubns.

Appel, Benjamin. The Devil & W. Kaspar. 1977. pap. 1.50 o.p. (ISBN 0-445-03190-5). Popular Lib.
--Heart of Ice. LC 76-4815. (Illus.). (gr. 1 up). 1977. 5.95 (ISBN 0-394-83245-0); PLB 6.99 (ISBN 0-394-93245-5). Pantheon.

Appel, Carl L. Provenzalische Lautlehre: Mit Einer Karte. LC 80-2165. (Provenzalische Chrestomathie Ser.). 1981. Repr. of 1918 ed. 30.00 (ISBN 0-404-19027-8). AMS Pr.

--Die Singweisen Bernarts Von Ventadorn Nach Den Handschriften Mitgeteilt. LC 80-2171. 1981. Repr. of 1934 ed. 17.50 (ISBN 0-404-19002-2). AMS Pr.

--Der Trobador Uc Brunec Oder Brunenc: Abhandlungen Herrn Prof. Adolf Tobler. LC 80-2177. 1981. Repr. of 1895 ed. 15.00 (ISBN 0-404-19003-0). AMS Pr.

Appel, Gerald. Double Your Money Every Three Years. 1974. 25.00 o.p. (ISBN 0-87000-896-X). Arlington Hse.

Appel, Martin, jt. auth. see Stolle, Fred.

Appel, Odette M., jt. auth. see Sobieszek, Robert A.

Appel, Stanley H., ed. Current Neurology, Vol. 3. LC 78-68042. (Current Ser.). (Illus.). 545p. 1981. text ed. price not set (ISBN 0-89289-112-2). HM Prof Med Div.

Appelbaum, Judith & Evans, Nancy. How to Get Happily Published: A Complete & Candid Guide. LC 77-3737. 1978. 10.95 (ISBN 0-06-010141-5, HarpT). Har-Row.

Appelbaum, Richard P. Size, Growth, & U. S. Cities. LC 78-61885. (Praeger Special Studies). 1978. 20.95 (ISBN 0-03-045336-4). Praeger.

Appelbaum, Richard P., et al. The Effects of Urban Growth: A Population Impact Analysis. LC 75-23952. (Illus.). 1976. 32.50 (ISBN 0-275-55980-7). Praeger.

Appelbaum, Stanley. The Chicago World's Fair of Eighteen Ninety-Three: A Photographic Record. (Illus.). 144p. (Orig.). 1980. pap. 6.00 (ISBN 0-486-23990-X). Dover.

Appelbaum, Stanley, ed. Scenes from the Nineteenth-Century Stage in Advertising Woodcuts. (Pictorial Archive Ser.). (Illus.). 176p. 1977. pap. 6.00 (ISBN 0-486-23434-7). Dover.

Appelbaum, Stanley & Kelly, Richard, eds. Great Drawings & Illustrations from Punch Eighteen Forty-One to Nineteen Hundred-One: One Hundred Ninety-Two Works by Leech, Keene, du Maurier, May & 21 Others. (Illus.). 144p. (Orig.). 1981. pap. price not set (ISBN 0-486-24110-6). Dover.

Appelbaum, Stanley, ed. see Posada, Jose G.

Appelbaum, Steven. Stress Management for Health Care Professionals. 350p. 1980. text ed. 24.95 (ISBN 0-89443-332-6). Aspen Systems.

Appell, Madeleine. One-Stitch Stitchery. LC 78-51063. (Little Craft Book). (Illus.). 1978. 5.95 (ISBN 0-8069-5384-5); lib. bdg. 6.69 (ISBN 0-8069-5385-3). Sterling.

Appelman, D. Ralph. Science of Vocal Pedagogy: Theory & Application. LC 67-10107. (Illus.). 448p. 1967. 19.50x (ISBN 0-253-35110-3); of 3 tapes 15.00 set (ISBN 0-253-35115-4); Tape 1. tapes 15.00 (ISBN 0-253-35112-X); Tape 2. tapes 15.00 (ISBN 0-253-35113-8); Tape 3. tapes 5.95 (ISBN 0-253-35114-6). Ind U Pr.

Appelman, Hyman. Appelman's Outlines & Illustrations. (Pocket Pulpit Library). 128p. 1981. pap. 2.95 (ISBN 0-8010-0072-6). Baker Bk.

Appelo, C. A. J., jt. auth. see DeVries, J. J.

Appels, A. & Falger, P., eds. The Role of Psychosocial Factors in the Pathogenesis of Coronary Heart Disease, 1980. (Journal: Psychotherapy & Psychosomatics: Vol. 34, No. 2-3). (Illus.). iv, 160p. 1981. pap. price not set (ISBN 3-8055-2286-X). S Karger.

Appels, J. T. & Geels, B. H. Handbook of Relay Switching Technique. (Illus.). 1966. 14.90 o.p. (ISBN 0-387-91005-0). Springer-Verlag.

Appenzeller, Herb & Appenzeller, Thomas. Sports & the Courts. 423p. 1980. 15.00 (ISBN 0-87215-243-X). Michie.

Appenzeller, Otto, jt. auth. see Raskin, Neil H.

Appenzeller, Thomas, jt. auth. see Appenzeller, Herb.

Apperlman, Hyman. Sermons on Evangelism. (Pocket Pulpit Library). 96p. 1981. pap. 1.95 (ISBN 0-8010-0068-8). Baker Bk.

Apperson, George L. English Proverbs & Proverbial Phrases: A Historical Dictionary. LC 70-76017. 1969. Repr. of 1929 ed. 24.00 (ISBN 0-8103-3881-5). Gale.

Appiah, Peggy. The Pineapple Child & Other Tales from Ashanti. (Illus.). 176p. (gr. 2-7). 1981. 7.95 (ISBN 0-233-95875-4). Andre Deutsch.

--A Smell of Onions. 84p. (Orig.). 1979. pap. 4.00 (ISBN 0-686-27212-9, Dist. by Three Continents Pr). Longman.

--A Smell of Onions. 84p. (Orig.). 1979. pap. 5.00 (ISBN 0-686-64550-2). Three Continents.

--Tales of an Ashanti Father. LC 80-2697. (Illus.). 160p. (gr. 2-7). 1981. 8.95 (ISBN 0-233-95927-0). Andre Deutsch.

Appiah-Kubi, Kofi. Healing & Religion in Rural Ghana. (Orig.). 1981. pap. 10.95 (ISBN 0-377-00114-7). Friend Pr.

--Healing & Religion in Rural Ghana: A Sociological Study of Health Care Among the Akans. (Illus.). 224p. 1981. text ed. 25.00 (ISBN 0-86598-011-X). Allanheld.

Appian. Civil Wars, Bk. 1. Strachan-Davidson, J. L., ed. 1902. 2.50x o.p. (ISBN 0-19-814104-1). Oxford U Pr.

Appisson, Barbara, jt. auth. see McQueen-Williams, Morvyth.

Applbaum, Ronald & Hart, Roderick, eds. MODCOM Modules in Speech Communication, 22 modules. 1976. Individual Modules. pap. text ed. 2.25 (ISBN 0-686-68014-6); Set. pap. 49.50 (ISBN 0-574-22529-3, 13-5529). SRA.

Applbaum, Ronald, ed. see Campbell, John A.

Applbaum, Ronald, ed. see Colburn, William & Weinberg, Sanford.

Applbaum, Ronald, ed. see Felsenthal, Norman.

Applbaum, Ronald, ed. see Leathers.

Applbaum, Ronald, et al. The Process of Group Communication. 2nd ed. LC 78-18501. 1979. text ed. 13.95 (ISBN 0-574-22710-5, 13-5710); instr's guide avail. (ISBN 0-574-22711-3, 13-5711). SRA.

Apple, David J. & Rabb, Maurice F. Clinicopathologic Correlation of Ocular Disease: A Stereoscopic Atlas. 2nd ed. LC 78-15635. 1978. text ed. 115.00 (ISBN 0-8016-0272-6). Mosby.

Apple, James M. Material Handling Systems Design. (Illus.). 600p. 1972. 33.00 (ISBN 0-8260-0485-7, Pub. by Wiley-Interscience). Wiley.

Apple, Max. Zip. 1978. 8.95 o.p. (ISBN 0-670-79692-1). Viking Pr.

Apple, Max, ed. Southwest Fiction Anthology. 368p. (Orig.). 1981. pap. 2.95 (ISBN 0-553-14256-9). Bantam.

Apple, Michael W. Ideology & Curriculum. (Education Bks.). 1979. 18.00x (ISBN 0-7100-0136-3). Routledge & Kegan.

Apple, Michael W., jt. ed. see Haubrich, Vernon F.

Apple, Michael W., et al. Educational Evaluation: Analysis & Responsibility. LC 73-17611. 1974. 17.90 (ISBN 0-8211-0011-4); text ed. 16.20 in ten or more copies (ISBN 0-685-42624-6). McCutchan.

Applebaum, Edward L. & Bruce, David L. Tracheal Intubation. LC 75-19837. (Illus.). 130p. 1976. text ed. 13.95 (ISBN 0-7216-1311-X). Saunders.

Applebaum, Louis, et al. Glossary of United States Patent Practice. LC 70-103702. (Eng, Fr & Ger.). 1969. 25.00 (ISBN 0-87632-037-X). Boardman.

Applebaum, Sada, jt. auth. see Applebaum, Samuel.

Applebaum, Samuel & Applebaum, Sada. The Way They Play, Bk. 2. (Illus.). 384p. 1973. 9.95 (ISBN 0-87666-438-9, Z-4). Paganiniana Pubns.

Applebaum, Samuel & Roth, Henry. The Way They Play, Bk. 7. (Illus.). 288p. 1980. 9.95 (ISBN 0-87666-619-5, Z-33). Paganiniana Pubns.

--The Way They Play, Bk. 8. (Illus.). 288p. 1980. 9.95 (ISBN 0-87666-622-5, Z-34). Paganiniana Pubns.

Applebaum, Shimon. Jews & Greeks in Ancient Cyrene. (Illus.). 367p. 1980. text ed. 64.00x (ISBN 90-04-05970-9). Humanities.

Applebaum, William. Guide to Store Location Research: With Emphasis on Super Markets. 1968. text ed. 23.95 (ISBN 0-201-00285-X). A-W.

--Store Location Strategy Cases. (Retailing Ser.). 1968. text ed. 19.95 (ISBN 0-201-00290-6); instructor's manual 2.50 (ISBN 0-201-00291-4). A-W.

Appleberg, Marilyn, compiled by. The I Love New York Guide, 1981. (Illus.). 208p. 1981. pap. 3.95 (ISBN 0-02-097220-2, Collier). Macmillan.

Appleby, Joyce O. Economic Thought & Ideology in Seventeenth-Century England. LC 77-85527. 304p. 1980. pap. 4.95 (ISBN 0-691-00779-9). Princeton U Pr.

Appleby, Paul H. Citizens As Sovereigns. LC 62-10727. 1962. 10.00x (ISBN 0-8156-0024-0). Syracuse U Pr.

Applegate, Dorothy. Mission A-Go-Go. LC 78-73043. (Illus.). 1979. 9.95 (ISBN 0-9602122-2-1). Apple-Gems.

Applegate, Rex. Riot Control: Materiel & Techniques. 4th rev. ed. (Illus.). 320p. 1981. 15.95 (ISBN 0-8117-1489-6). Paladin Ent.

--Scouting & Patrolling. (Illus.). 135p. 1980. 15.95 (ISBN 0-87364-184-1). Paladin Ent.

Appleman, Philip, ed. Darwin. 2nd ed. (Norton Critical Edition). 1979. 24.95 (ISBN 0-393-01192-5); pap. 6.95x (ISBN 0-393-95009-3). Norton.

Appleman, Philip, ed. see Darwin, Charles.

Appleman, Phillip. Shame the Devil. Michaelman, Herbert, ed. 160p. 1981. 10.00 (ISBN 0-517-54286-2, Michaelman Books). Crown.

Applequist, Harry A., jt. auth. see Means, Louis E.

Appleton, J. D. Labour Economics. 2nd ed. (Illus.). 240p. 1979. pap. text ed. 9.95 (ISBN 0-7121-1246-4, Pub. by Macdonald & Evans England). Intl Ideas.

Appleton, Jane & Appleton, William, M.D. How Not to Split up. LC 77-89874. 1978. 7.95 (ISBN 0-385-13201-8). Doubleday.

Appleton, Victor. The City in the Stars. Barish, Wendy, ed. (Tom Swift Ser.). 192p. (Orig.). (gr. 2-7). 1981. 7.95 (ISBN 0-671-41120-9); pap. 1.95 (ISBN 0-671-41115-2). Wanderer Bks.

--Tom Swift: The Alien Probe. Barish, Wendy, ed. (Tom Swift Ser.). 192p. (Orig.). (gr. 3-7). 1981. 7.95 (ISBN 0-671-42538-2); pap. 1.95 (ISBN 0-671-42578-1). Wanderer Bks.

--Tom Swift: The War in Outer Space. Barish, Wendy, ed. (Tom Swift Ser.). 192p. (Orig.). (gr. 3-7). 1981. 7.95 (ISBN 0-671-42539-0); pap. 1.95 (ISBN 0-671-42579-X). Wanderer Bks.

Appleton, William, M.D., jt. auth. see Appleton, Jane.

Appleton, William W. Madame Vestris & the London Stage. LC 73-10106. (Illus.). 240p. 1974. text ed. 17.50x (ISBN 0-231-03794-5). Columbia U Pr.

Appleton, William W., ed. see Cibber, Colley.

Appleton, William W., ed. see Fielding, Henry.

Applewhite, Cynthia. Sundays. 1978. pap. 1.95 (ISBN 0-380-42358-8, 42358). Avon.

Applewhite, Edgar J. The Cosmic Fishing. 1977. 10.95 (ISBN 0-02-502710-7, 50271). Macmillan.

Applewhite, Karen M. On the Road to Nowhere: A History of Greer, Arizona, 1879-1979. LC 79-54966. (Illus., Orig.). 1979. pap. text ed. 6.95 (ISBN 0-9603472-0-8). Applewhite.

Applewhite, Philip B. Molecular Gods: How Molecules Determine Our Behavior. (Illus.). 288p. 1981. 10.95 (ISBN 0-13-599530-2). P-H.

Applewwhite, James. Following Gravity. LC 80-21578. 1981. 7.95x (ISBN 0-8139-0885-X). U Pr of Va.

Appley, Dee G. & Winder, Alvin E. T-Groups & Therapy Groups in a Changing Society. LC 73-10934. (Social & Behavioral Science Ser.). 224p. 1973. 14.95x o.p. (ISBN 0-87589-201-9). Jossey-Bass.

Appley, Lawrence A. Formula for Success: A Core Concept of Management. LC 73-87546. 1974. 11.95 (ISBN 0-8144-5339-2). Am Mgmt.

Appley, M. H., jt. auth. see Cofer, Charles N.

Appleyard, Donald. Liveable Streets. 336p. 1981. 27.50 (ISBN 0-520-03689-1). U of Cal Pr.

Applied Geochemistry Research Group. The Wolfson Geochemical Atlas of England & Wales. (Illus.). 1978. 98.00x (ISBN 0-19-891113-0). Oxford U Pr.

Applied Science Publishers Ltd., ed. see World Petroleum Congress, 9th, Japan, 1975.

Applied Science Publishers Ltd. London, ed. Biodegradation of Polymers & Synthetic Polymers: Sessions of the 3rd International Biodegradation Symposium. (Illus.). 1976. 26.00x (ISBN 0-85334-708-5, Pub. by Applied Science). Burgess-Intl Ideas.

Applied Science Publishers Ltd London, ed. Materials Deterioration & Mechanisms of Deterioration. (Illus.). 1976. 50.40x (ISBN 0-85334-705-0). Intl Ideas.

--Metabolism of Hydrocarbons, Oils, Fuels & Lubricants. (Illus.). 1976. 50.40x (ISBN 0-85334-703-4). Intl Ideas.

Apps, Jerry. Mills of Wisconsin. LC 80-24684. (Illus., Orig.). 1980. pap. 12.50 (ISBN 0-915024-22-5). Tamarack Pr.

Apps, Jerry W. The Adult Learner on Campus: A Guide for Instructors & Administrators. 288p. 1981. 17.95 (ISBN 0-695-81577-6, Assn Pr). Follett.

Apps, R. L., jt. auth. see Milner, D. R.

Aprahamian, Felix, tr. see Martin, Frank.

Apresjan, Ju. D. Principles & Methods of Contemporary Structural Linguistics. Crockett, Dina B., tr. from Dutch. LC 72-94441. (Janua Linguarum, Ser. Minor: No. 144). (Illus.). 349p. (Orig.). 1973. pap. text ed. 38.25x (ISBN 90-2792-386-8). Mouton.

Apresjan, Yuri D. Lexical Semantics. Lehrman, Alexander, tr. from Rus. (Linguistica Extranea: Studia: No. 13). 450p. 1981. 35.00 (ISBN 0-89720-039-X); pap. 22.50 (ISBN 0-89720-040-3). Karoma.

April, Ernest W., ed. Anatomy. 2nd ed. LC 79-83717. (Basic Sciences PreTest Self-Assessment & Review Ser.). (Illus.). 1980. 9.95 (ISBN 0-07-050961-1). McGraw-Pretest.

April, Koral. Headlines & Deadlines. 64p. (gr. 4-7). 1981. write for info. Messner.

ApRoberts, Ruth. The Moral Trollope. LC 75-141383. 203p. 1971. 12.00x (ISBN 0-8214-0089-4). Ohio U Pr.

Apsimon, John. The Total Synthesis of Natural Products, Vol. 4. LC 72-4075. (The Total Synthesis of Natural Products Ser.). 450p. 1981. 37.00 (ISBN 0-471-05460-7, Pub. by Wiley-Interscience). Wiley.

Apsler, Alfred. An Introduction to Social Science. 3rd ed. 541p. 1981. text ed. 16.95 (ISBN 0-394-32534-6). Random.

--An Introduction to Social Science. 2nd ed. 1976. text ed. 13.95 o.p. (ISBN 0-394-31974-5). Random.

Apt, Charles. Flavor: Its Chemical, Behavioral & Commercial Aspects. LC 77-13274. 1978. lib. bdg. 36.50x (ISBN 0-89158-233-9). Westview.

Apte, Robert Z. Halfway Houses. 125p. 1968. pap. text ed. 5.00x (ISBN 0-7135-1522-8, Pub. by Bedford England). Renouf.

Apte, Robert Z., jt. auth. see Friedlander, Walter A.

Apte, V. S. Practical Sanskrit-English Dictionary. rev. ed. 1978. Repr. 24.00 (ISBN 0-89684-294-0). Orient Bk Dist.

--Student's English-Sanskrit Dictionary. 501p. 1973. text ed. 7.50x (ISBN 0-8426-0507-X). Verry.

Apte, Vaman S. Practical Sanskrit-English Dictionary. new ed. 1975. 30.00x (ISBN 0-8426-0996-2). Verry.

Aptekar, Herbert. Anjea; Infanticide, Abortion & Contraception in Savage Society. LC 79-2929. 192p. 1981. Repr. of 1931 ed. 17.50 (ISBN 0-8305-0097-9). Hyperion Conn.

Aptekar, Jane. Icons of Justice: Iconography & Thematic Imagery in Book Five of the Faerie Queen. LC 79-79189. (Illus.). 1969. 17.50x (ISBN 0-231-03246-3). Columbia U Pr.

Apter, David E., ed. Ideology & Discontent. LC 64-20305. 1964. 17.95 (ISBN 0-02-900760-7). Free Pr.

Apter, T. E. Virginia Woolf: A Study of Her Novels. LC 78-78175. (The Gotham Library). 1979. Cusa. 17.50x (ISBN 0-8147-0568-5); Cusa. pap. 9.00x (ISBN 0-8147-0569-3). NYU Pr.

Aptheker, Bettina. Women's Legacy: Interpretive Essays in U. S. History. (Orig.). Date not set. 10.00 (ISBN 0-7178-0572-7); pap. 3.50 (ISBN 0-7178-0566-2). Intl Pub Co. Postponed.

Aptheker, Bettina, ed. see Addams, Jane & Wells, Ida B.

Aptheker, Bettina, et al. Kent State Ten Years After. Bills, Scott, ed. (Illus.). 88p. (Orig.). 1980. pap. 3.95 (ISBN 0-933522-04-5). Kent Popular.

Aptheker, Herbert. Nature of Democracy, Freedom & Revolution. LC 67-29076. (Orig.). (YA) (gr. 9-12). 1967. pap. 1.50 o.p. (ISBN 0-7178-0137-3). Intl Pub Co.

Aptheker, Herbert, ed. Contributions by Du Bois in Government Publications & Proceedings. LC 80-13063. (The Complete Published Works of W. E. Du Bois). 1981. lib. bdg. 70.00 (ISBN 0-527-25292-1). Kraus Intl.

--One Continual Cry: Walker's Appeal to the Colored Citizens of the World, 1829. (Historical Ser.: No. 1). 7.50 (ISBN 0-686-19223-0). Am Inst Marxist.

--Writings by Du Bois in Periodicals Edited by Others, 4 vols. (The Completed Published Works of W. E. B. Du Bois). 1981. Set. lib. bdg. 240.00 (ISBN 0-527-25358-8). Kraus Intl.

--Writings in Periodicals Edited by Du Bois: Selections from Phylon. LC 80-13721. (The Complete Published Works of W. E. B. Du Bois Ser.). 1980. lib. bdg. 65.00 (ISBN 0-527-25353-7). Kraus Intl.

Aptheker, Herbert, ed. see Du Bois, W. E.

Aptheker, Herbert, ed. see Du Bois, William E.

Apuleius, Lucius. Golden Ass. Schnur, Harry C., ed. Adlington, William, tr. 1962. pap. 0.95 o.s.i. (ISBN 0-02-048240-X, Collier). Macmillan.

Aquadro, Charles, et al. Canoeing the Brandywine: A Naturalist's Guide. 1980. 2.25x. Brandywine Conserv.

Aquila, Mirella. Selected Poems. 64p. (Orig.). 1981. pap. 5.00 (ISBN 0-682-49666-9). Exposition.

Aquilano, Nicholas J., jt. auth. see Chase, Richard B.

Aquilina, Joseph. Teach Yourself Maltese. (Teach Yourself Ser). pap. 2.95 o.p. (ISBN 0-679-10188-8). McKay.

Aquilina, Alfred P. The Mackenzie Today. Campbell, Margaret, ed. (Illus.). 50p. (Orig.). 1981. pap. 4.00 (ISBN 0-88839-082-3). Hancock Hse.

--The Mackenzie: Yesterday & Beyond. (Illus.). pap. 6.95 (ISBN 0-88839-083-1). Hancock Hse.

Aquinas, Thomas. Commentary on the Gospel of St. John, 2 pts. Weisheipl, James A., ed. Larcher, Fabian R., tr. from Lat. LC 66-19306. (Aquinas Scripture Ser.: Vol. 4, Pt. 1). (Illus.). 512p. 1980. 35.00x (ISBN 0-87343-031-X). Magi Bks.

Aquinas, Thomas see Thomas Aquinas, Saint.

Arabi, Ibn. Journey to the Lord of Power. Harris, Rabia, tr. from Arab. (Illus.). 1981. 9.95 (ISBN 0-89281-024-6); pap. 7.95 (ISBN 0-89281-018-1). Inner Tradit.

Arabinda, Ray. The Manager Beyond the Organization. 1980. 9.50x (ISBN 0-8364-0636-2, Pub. by Macmillan India). South Asia Bks.

Arac, Jonathan. Commissioned Spirits: The Shaping of Social Motion in Dickens, Carlyle, Melville, & Hawthorne. 1979. 15.00 (ISBN 0-8135-0874-6). Rutgers U Pr.

Arad, Miriam, tr. see Megged, Aharon.

Aradoon, Zarifa. Belly Dance Costume Book. rev. ed. Bain, David, ed. LC 77-88919. (Illus.). 1981. pap. 15.00 (ISBN 0-930486-04-8). Dream Place.

--The Oldest Dance: Origins & Philosophy of Danse Orientale. LC 78-67210. (Illus.). 1979. 14.95 o.p. (ISBN 0-930486-02-1); pap. 15.00 (ISBN 0-930486-03-X). Dream Place.

Aragno, Anna. The Story of Felicity. (Illus.). 64p. 1980. 5.00 (ISBN 0-682-49633-2). Exposition.

Aragon, George, jt. auth. see Viscione, Jerry.

Aragones, Sergio. Mad About Mad. (Mad Ser.). (Illus.). 1977. pap. 1.75 (ISBN 0-446-94394-0). Warner Bks.

--Mad As a Hatter. (Mad Ser.). (Illus., Orig.). 1981. pap. 1.75 (ISBN 0-446-94116-6). Warner Bks.

--Mad As the Devil. (Mad Ser.). (Illus.). 1975. pap. 1.75 (ISBN 0-446-94395-9). Warner Bks.

--Mad-ly Yours. (Mad Ser.). (Illus.). 192p. 1972. pap. 1.75 (ISBN 0-446-94396-7). Warner Bks.

--Mad Marginals. (Mad Ser.). (Illus.). 1974. pap. 1.75 (ISBN 0-446-94284-7). Warner Bks.

--Shootin' Mad. (Mad Ser.). (Illus., Orig.). 1979. pap. 1.75 (ISBN 0-446-94397-5). Warner Bks.

Arai, Hisao, ed. Biology of the Tapeworm Hymenolepis Diminuta. 1980. 45.00 (ISBN 0-12-058980-X). Acad Pr.

Arakawa, Kohman Y. Shells on Stamps of the World. (Illus.). 234p. (Jap.). 1979. 15.95 (ISBN 0-915826-07-0). Am Malacologists.

Araki, Chiyo. Origami in the Classroom, 2 vols. LC 65-13412. (Illus.). (gr. 1 up). 1965-68. bds. 8.95 ea. Vol. 1 (ISBN 0-8048-0452-4). Vol. 2 (ISBN 0-8048-0453-2). C E Tuttle.

Aram, John D. Dilemmas of Administrative Behavior. 144p. 1976. Ref. Ed. 9.95 (ISBN 0-13-214247-3). P-H.

Arambulo, Primo & Steele, James H., eds. Handbook Series in Zoonoses, CRC, Section C: Parasitic Zoonoses. Date not set. 64.95 (ISBN 0-8493-2916-7). CRC Pr. Postponed.

Arana, Alice see Knorre, Marty, et al.

Arana, Oswaldo see Knorre, Marty, et al.

Arana Q., Pedro. Providencia y Revolucion. 1.40 o.p. (ISBN 0-686-12563-0). Banner of Truth.

Arand, Louis A., tr. see Wuasten, J. & Plumpe, J.

Aranda, Francisco. Luis Bunuel: A Critical Biography. Robinson, David, ed. LC 76-7621. 1976. lib. bdg. 22.50 (ISBN 0-306-70754-3); pap. 4.95 (ISBN 0-306-80028-4). Da Capo.

Arango, E. Ramon. The Spanish Political System: Franco's Legacy. LC 78-8979. (Westview Special Studies in West European Politics & Society). 1978. lib. bdg. 26.50x (ISBN 0-89158-177-4). Westview.

Arango, Tony, tr. Armonias Corales, Vol. 1. 144p. (Orig., Span.). 1977. pap. 4.75 (ISBN 0-89922-082-7). Edit Caribe.

Aranibar, A., jt. ed. see Lechner, H.

Aranson, Peter H. American Government: Strategy & Choice 1980. (Political Science Ser.). (Illus.). 600p. 1981. text ed. 18.95 (ISBN 0-87626-023-7). Winthrop.

Aranya, Hariharananda. Samkhya-Sutras of Pancasikha & the Samkhyatattvalcka. 1977. 9.50 (ISBN 0-89684-313-0, Pub. by Motilal Banarsidass India); pap. 6.50 (ISBN 0-89684-346-7). Orient Bk Dist.

Arapura, J. G. Radhakrishnan & Integral Experience. 6.25x o.p. (ISBN 0-210-33813-X). Asia.

--Religion As Anxiety & Tranquillity: An Essay in Comparative Phenomenology of the Spirit. (Religion & Reason Ser.: No. 5). 1973. 21.20x (ISBN 90-2797-180-3). Mouton.

Arasaratnam, Sinnappah. Indians in Malaysia & Singapore. 1980. pap. 8.95x (ISBN 0-19-580427-9). Oxford U Pr.

A-Rashid, Ibrahim. The Consolidation of Power in Central Arabia Under Ibn Saud, 1925-1928. (Documents on the History of Saudi Arabia: Vol. 2). 60.00 (ISBN 0-89712-054-X). Documentary Pubns.

Arasteh, A. R. Teaching Through Research. 1966. 22.50 (ISBN 0-685-12048-1). Heinman.

Arasteh, A. R. & Arasteh, J. D. Creativity in Human Development: An Interpretive & Annotated Bibliography. 1976. 12.95 (ISBN 0-470-98933-5). Halsted Pr.

Arasteh, A. Reza. Growth to Selfhood: The Sufi Contribution. (Orig.). 1980. pap. 8.50 (ISBN 0-7100-0355-2). Routledge & Kegan.

Arasteh, J. D., jt. auth. see Arasteh, A. R.

Arata, Esther S. More Black American Playwrights: A Bibliography. LC 78-15231. 1978. lib. bdg. 16.50 (ISBN 0-8108-1158-8). Scarecrow.

Arata, Esther S. & Rotoli, Nicholas J. Black American Playwrights, Eighteen Hundred to the Present: A Bibliography. LC 76-2376. 302p. 1976. 14.50 (ISBN 0-8108-0912-5). Scarecrow.

Arato, Andrew. Frankfurt School Reader, Vol. II: The Post-War Years. Date not set. 17.50 (ISBN 0-89396-035-7); pap. 7.95 (ISBN 0-89396-036-5). Urizen Bks.

Arato, Andrew, tr. see Konrad, George & Szelenyi, Ivan.

Arato, Andrew, et al. The Essential Frankfurt School Reader. 1978. 17.50 (ISBN 0-916354-30-X); pap. 7.95 (ISBN 0-916354-31-8). Urizen Bks.

Araujo, Aloisio & Gine, Evarist. The Central Limit Theorem for Real & Banach Valued Random Variables. (Ser. in Probability & Mathematical Statistics). 1980. 26.95 (ISBN 0-471-05304-X, Pub. by Wiley-Interscience). Wiley.

Araujo, Virginia De see Andrade, Carlos D.

A Raujo-Haugse, Vera L. De, jt. auth. see Lauerhass, Ludwig.

Arb, Sondra Von see Von Arb, Sondra.

Arbeiter, Jean S., jt. auth. see Weiser, Marjorie P.

Arbeitman & Bomhard, eds. Bono Homini Donum: Essays in Historical Linguistics, in Memory of J. Alexander Kerns. (Current Issues in Linguistic Theory: No. 16). 700p. 1980. text ed. 80.00x (ISBN 90-272-3507-4). Humanities.

Arbel, A. F. Analog Signal Processing & Instrumentation. LC 79-13461. (Illus.). 1980. 77.50 (ISBN 0-521-22469-1). Cambridge U Pr.

Arber, Edward, ed. English Garner, 12 Vols. Repr. of 1890 ed. write for info. Cooper Sq.

Arber, Edward, ed. see Selden, John.

Arber, W., et al, eds. Current Topics in Microbiology & Immunology, Vols. 40-55. Incl. Vol. 40. Chronic Infections Neuropathic Agents & Other Slow Virsus Infections. Brody, J. A., et al, eds. (Illus.). vii, 74p. 1967. 22.90 (ISBN 0-387-03754-3); Vol. 41. (Illus.). iv, 183p. 1967. 49.00 (ISBN 0-387-03755-1); Vol. 42. Insect Viruses. Maramorosch, K., ed. (Illus.). viii, 192p. 1968. 25.40 (ISBN 0-387-04071-7); Vol. 43. (Illus.). iii, 233p. (Incl. 32 pp. in German). 1968. 52.00 (ISBN 0-387-04072-2); Vol. 44. (Illus.). iii, 175p. 1968. 52.00 (ISBN 0-387-04073-0); Vol. 45. (Illus.). iii, 237p. (Incl. 61 pp. in German). 1968. 52.00 (ISBN 0-387-04074-9); Vol. 46. (Illus.). iii, 203p. (Incl. 90 pp. in German). 1968. 57.90 (ISBN 0-387-04075-7); Vol. 47. (Illus.). iii, 222p. (Incl. 29 pp. in German). 1969. 55.50 (ISBN 0-387-04445-0); Vol. 48. (Illus.). iii, 206p. 1969. 55.50 (ISBN 0-387-04446-9); Vol. 49. (Illus.). iii, 250p. 1969. 555.50 (ISBN 0-387-04447-7); Vol. 50. (Illus.). iii, 238p. 1969. 55.50 **(ISBN 0-387-04448-5); Vol. 52. (Illus.). iv, 197p. 1970. 55.50 (ISBN 0-387-04787-5); Vol. 53. (Illus.). 236p. 1970. 58.50 (ISBN 0-387-05069-8); Vol. 54. (Illus.). 230p. 1971. 58.50 (ISBN 0-387-05289-5); Vol. 55. Arthropod Cell Cultures & Their Application to the Study of Viruses. Weiss, E., ed. (Illus.). 340p. 1971. 49.10 (ISBN 0-387-05451-0). (Illus., Eng. & Ger.). Springer-Verlag.**

--Current Topics in Microbiology & Immunology, Vol. 77. LC 15-12910. (Illus.). 1977. 41.50 (ISBN 0-387-08401-0). Springer-Verlag.

--Current Topics in Microbiology & Immunology, Vols. 86-87. (Illus.). 1980. Vol. 86. 37.40 (ISBN 0-387-09432-6); Vol. 87. 37.40 (ISBN 0-387-09433-4). Springer-Verlag.

--Current Topics in Microbiology & Immunology, Vol. 90. (Illus.). 147p. 1980. 51.90 (ISBN 0-387-10181-0). Springer-Verlag.

Arberry, A. J. The Doctrine of the Sufis. LC 76-58075. 1977. 32.50 (ISBN 0-521-21647-8); pap. 8.95x (ISBN 0-521-29218-2). Cambridge U Pr.

--Shiraz: Persian City of Saints & Poets. (Centers of Civilization Ser.: No. 2). 1960. 5.95 o.p. (ISBN 0-8061-0461-9). U of Okla Pr.

Arberry, A. J., ed. see Hafiz.

Arberry, A. J., tr. see Attar, Farid.

Arberry, A. J., tr. see Rumi, Jalal A.

Arberry, A. J., tr. see Rumi, Jalal Al-Din.

Arberry, Arthur J. Arabic Poetry: A Primer for Students. (Orig.). 1965. 36.00 (ISBN 0-521-04037-X); pap. 13.50x (ISBN 0-521-09257-4). Cambridge U Pr.

--Fitzgerald's Salaman & Absal. (Cambridge Oriental Ser.: No. 2). 1956. 36.00 (ISBN 0-521-05011-1). Cambridge U Pr.

--Koran Interpreted. 1964. pap. 11.95 (ISBN 0-02-083260-5). Macmillan.

--Religion in the Middle East, 2 Vols. LC 68-21187. (Illus.). 1969. Set. 88.00 (ISBN 0-521-07400-2); 54.00 ea.; Vol. 1. (ISBN 0-521-20543-3); Vol. 2. (ISBN 0-521-20544-1). Cambridge U Pr.

--Revelation and Reason in Islam. LC 80-1936. 1981. Repr. of 1957 ed. 20.00 (ISBN 0-404-18952-0). AMS Pr.

Arbetman, Lee, et al. Street Law: A Course in Practical Law. 2nd ed. 383p. 1980. pap. text ed. write for info. (ISBN 0-8299-1031-X). West Pub.

Arbib, M. A., jt. auth. see Alagic, S.

Arbib, Michael. Computers & the Cybernetic Society. 494p. 1977. 16.95 (ISBN 0-12-059040-9); instrs'. manual 3.00 (ISBN 0-12-059042-5); avail. transparency masters (ISBN 0-12-059045-X). Acad Pr.

--The Metaphorical Brain: An Introduction to Cybernetics As Artificial Intelligence & Brains Theory. LC 72-2490. (Illus.). 243p. 1972. 24.95 (ISBN 0-471-03249-2, Pub by Wiley-Interscience). Wiley.

Arbib, Michael A., jt. auth. see Bobrow, Leonard S.

Arbib, Michael A., jt. auth. see Padulo, Louis.

Arbital, Samuel L. Cities & Metropolitan Areas. Ress, Etta S., ed. LC 67-25673. (Illus.). (gr. 4-9). 1968. PLB 7.50 o.p. (ISBN 0-87191-004-7). Creative Ed.

Arbiter, N., jt. ed. see Somasundaran, P.

Arbitman, Dena C., jt. auth. see Safford, Philip L.

Arblay, Frances B. Fanny Burney & Her Friends: Select Passages from Her Diary & Other Writings. LC 75-76135. 1969. Repr. of 1890 ed. 15.00 (ISBN 0-8103-3896-3). Gale.

Arboleda, Amadio, jt. auth. see Petit, Gaston.

Arbor, Jane. Where the Wolf Leads. (Harlequin Romances). 192p. 1981. pap. 1.25 (ISBN 0-373-02396-0, Pub. by Harlequin). PB.

Arbuckle, Dugald S. Counseling & Psychotherapy: An Existential-Humanistic View. 3rd ed. 500p. 1975. text ed. 17.95x o.p. (ISBN 0-205-04634-7, 2246341). Allyn.

Arbuckle, J. Gordon, et al. Environmental Law Handbook. 6th rev. ed. LC 76-41637. 349p. 1979. 39.50 (ISBN 0-86587-076-4). Gov Insts.

Arbuckle, W. S. Ice Cream Service Handbook. (Illus.). 1976. pap. text ed. 7.50 (ISBN 0-87055-211-2). AVI.

Arbuckle, Wendell S. Ice Cream. 3rd ed. (Illus.). 1977. lib. bdg. 26.50 (ISBN 0-87055-256-2). AVI.

Arbuthnot, Archibald. Memoirs of the Remarkable Life & Surprizing Adventures of Miss Jenny Cameron: Philamours & Philamena; or, Genuine Memoirs of a Late Affecting Transaction, 1746. LC 74-26901. (Novel in England, 1700-1775 Ser). 1974. lib. bdg. 50.00 (ISBN 0-8240-1117-1). Garland Pub.

Arbuthnot, F. F., tr. see Burton, Richard.

Arbuthnot, Jack & Faust, David. Teaching Moral Reasoning: Theory & Practice. (Illus.). 304p. 1980. text ed. 18.50 scp (ISBN 0-06-040321-7, HarpC). Har-Row.

Arbuthnot, May H. & Taylor, Mark. Time for Old Magic. 1970. 11.95x o.p. (ISBN 0-673-05844-1). Scott F.

Arbuthnot, May H., jt. auth. see Sutherland, Zena.

Arbuthnot, May H., et al. Childrens Books Too Good to Miss: Revised Edition 1979. 7th ed. LC 79-53812. (Illus.). 125p. 1980. 7.95 (ISBN 0-8295-0287-4). UPBS.

Arbuthnott, J. P. & Beeley, J. A., eds. Isoelectric Focusing. 400p. 1976. 59.95 (ISBN 0-408-70659-7). Butterworths.

Arcalli, Franco, jt. auth. see Bertolucci, Bernardo.

Arcamone, Federico. Doxorubicin. LC 80-1106. (Medicinal Chemistry Ser.). 1981. price not set (ISBN 0-12-059280-0). Acad Pr.

Arce, Hector. Gary Cooper: An Intimate Biography. 272p. 1980. pap. 2.75 (ISBN 0-553-14130-9). Bantam.

Arce de Vazquez, Margot, ed. see Pales Matos, Luis.

Arch, E. L. First Immortals. (YA) 5.95 (ISBN 0-685-07433-1, Avalon). Bouregy.

--Man with Three Eyes. (YA) 5.95 (ISBN 0-685-07446-3, Avalon). Bouregy.

Archambault, Reginald D., ed. Philosophical Analysis & Education. 1972. text ed. 9.50x (ISBN 0-7100-1021-4); pap. text ed. 3.75x (ISBN 0-391-00239-2). Humanities.

Archdiocese of Newark. Growing in Faith with Your Child. Ivory, Thomas P., ed. 48p. (Orig.). pap. 2.50 (ISBN 0-697-01693-5). Wm C Brown.

Archenhold, W. F., jt. auth. see Treloar, L. R.

Archenhold, W. F., et al. School Science Laboratories: A Handbook of Design, Management & Organisation. 303p. 1980. 35.00x (ISBN 0-7195-3436-4, Pub. by Murray Pubs England). State Mutual Bk.

--Social Science Laboratories: A Handbook of Design, Management & Organisation. 303p. 1980. 35.00x (ISBN 0-7195-3436-4, Pub. by Murray Pubs England). State Mutual Bk.

Archer. Infantry Weapons Nineteen Eighty to Nineteen Eighty-One. 1980. 135.00 (ISBN 0-531-03936-6). Watts.

--Infantry Weapons Nineteen Seventy-Nine to Nineteen Eighty. 1980. 89.50 (ISBN 0-531-03905-6). Watts.

Archer, Carol R. Computed Tomography of the Larynx. (Illus.). 200p. 1981. 19.75 (ISBN 0-87527-240-1). Green.

Archer, Clive & Maxwell, Stephen. The Nordic Model. 1980. text ed. 28.00x (ISBN 0-566-00341-4, Pub. by Gower Pub Co England). Renouf.

Archer, Clive & Main, John, eds. Scotland's Voice in International Affairs. 160p. 1980. 19.95x (ISBN 0-7735-0512-1). McGill-Queens U Pr.

Archer, Denis, ed. Jane's Infantry Weapons 1977. 1977. 72.50 o.p. (ISBN 0-531-03905-6). Watts.

Archer, E. C. & Pemberton, LeRoy A. Typing Skill Drills. 1973. pap. text ed. 3.85 (ISBN 0-89420-103-4, 143000). Natl Book.

Archer, J. E. & Dalton, T. H. Fieldwork in Geography. 1970. 25.00 (ISBN 0-7134-2101-0, Pub. by Batsford England). David & Charles.

Archer, Jeffrey. Kane & Abel. 480p. 1981. pap. 3.75 (ISBN 0-449-24376-1, Crest). Fawcett.

Archer, John. The Archer Method of Winning at 21. LC 73-6449. 240p. 1973. 7.95 o.p. (ISBN 0-8092-9021-9). Contemp Bks.

Archer, John B; see Bottiglia, William F.

Archer, Jules. China in the Twentieth Century. LC 73-6050. (Illus.). 240p. (gr. 7 up). 1974. 9.95 (ISBN 0-02-705620-1, 70562). Macmillan.

--Ho Chi Minh: Legend of Hanoi. LC 79-151161. (gr. 7-12). 1971. 7.95 (ISBN 0-02-705630-9, CCPr). Macmillan.

--Indian Foe, Indian Friend. LC 72-93280. (Illus.). (gr. 7-12). 1970. 6.95 (ISBN 0-02-705650-3, CCPr). Macmillan.

--Superspies: The Secret Side of Government. LC 77-72640. (gr. 7up). 1977. 7.95 o.p. (ISBN 0-440-08136-X). Delacorte.

--Who's Running Your Life: A Look at Young People's Rights. (Illus.). (gr. 7 up). 1979. PLB 7.95 (ISBN 0-15-296058-9, HJ). HarBraceJ.

Archer, Kathy & Feeley, Pat. Perfect Needlepoint Projects from Start to Finish. LC 75-40786. (Illus.). 1977. 12.95 o.p. (ISBN 0-312-60070-4). St Martin.

Archer, M. S., ed. Current Research in Sociology: Published on the Occasion of the 8th World Congress of Sociology. (Current Sociology, Supplementary Ser: Vol. 1). 430p. 1974. pap. text ed. 37.05x (ISBN 90-2797-325-3). Mouton.

Archer, Margaret S. Social Origins of Educational Systems. LC 77-84072. (Illus.). 815p. 1979. 40.00 (ISBN 0-8039-9876-7). Sage.

Archer, Margaret S., jt. ed. see Giner, Salvador.

Archer, Maurice, jt. auth. see Rashid, S. Anwar.

Archer, Michael, jt. auth. see Garner, F. H.

Archer, Mildred. Early Views of India: The Picturesque Journeys of Thomas & William Daniell 1788-1793. (Illus.). 240p. 1980. 37.50 (ISBN 0-500-01238-5). Thames Hudson.

--India & British Portraiture Seventeen Seventy to Eighteen Twenty-Five. (Illus.). 536p. 1979. 105.00x (ISBN 0-85667-054-5, Pub by Sotheby Parke Bernet England). Biblio Dist.

--Natural History Drawings in the India Office Library. (Illus.). 116p. 1962. 22.50x (ISBN 0-85667-082-0, Pub. by Sotheby Parke Bernet England). Biblio Dist.

Archer, Myrtle. The Young Boys Gone. LC 77-78983. (gr. 7 up). 1978. 7.95 o.s.i. (ISBN 0-8027-6304-9). Walker & Co.

Archer, Peter. Christian Calendar & the Gregorian Reform. 1941. 20.00 o.p. (ISBN 0-8232-0001-9). Fordham.

Archer, Peter & Lord Reay. Freedom at Stake. LC 67-15647. (Background Ser.). 1967. 6.25 (ISBN 0-8023-1118-0). Dufour.

Archer, R. K. & Jeffcott, L. B., eds. Comparative Clinical Haematology. 1977. 64.00x o.p. (ISBN 0-397-60454-8, Blackwell Scientific). Mosby.

Archer, R. L., tr. from Fr. & see Rousseau, Jean-Jacques.

Archer, R. W. Land Pooling by Local Government for Planned Urban Development in Perth. (Lincoln Institute Monograph: No. 80-4). (Illus.). 69p. 1980. pap. 5.00 (Australian Institute of Urban Studies). Lincoln Inst Land.

--Site Value Taxation in Central Business District Redevelopment (Sydney, Aus.) LC 72-93820. (Research Report Ser.: No. 19). (Illus.). 44p. 1972. pap. 4.75 (ISBN 0-87420-319-8). Urban Land.

Archer, Richard P., ed. Concept Spelling Teacher's Manual. 132p. 1979. 50.00 (ISBN 0-935276-03-3). Am Spelling.

Archer, Robert M. & Ames, R. Basic Business Communications. 1971. text ed. 16.95 (ISBN 0-13-057299-3). P-H.

Archer, Ruth. Dayspring. 1981. pap. 2.95 (ISBN 0-935236-18-X). Nurseco.

Archer, S. H., jt. auth. see Meier, R. C.

Archer, S. H., et al. Financial Management: An Introduction. 724p. 1979. 23.50 (ISBN 0-471-02987-4); study guide 9.50 (ISBN 0-471-02988-2). Wiley.

Archer, Stephen H., jt. auth. see Francis, Clark.

Archer, Victor E., jt. ed. see Rom, William N.

Archibald, Katherine. Wartime Shipyard: A Study in Social Disunity. LC 76-7621. (FDR & the Era of the New Deal Ser.). 1976. Repr. of 1947 ed. 22.50 (ISBN 0-306-70802-7). Da Capo.

Archibald, Ralph. Introduction to the Theory of Numbers. LC 76-118978. 1970. text ed. 17.95 (ISBN 0-675-09351-1). Merrill.

Archibald, Russell D. Managing High-Technology Programs & Projects. LC 76-3789. 288p. 1976. 29.95 (ISBN 0-471-03308-1, Pub. by Wiley-Interscience). Wiley.
Archibald, Russell D. & Villoria, R. Network-Based Management Systems. LC 66-25216. (Information Science Ser.). 1967. 27.95 o.p. (ISBN 0-471-03250-6, Pub. by Wiley-Interscience). Wiley.
Architects' Emergency Committee. Great Georgian Houses of America, 2 Vols. (Illus.). 1970. pap. 8.95 ea. Vol. 1 (ISBN 0-486-22491-0). Vol. 2 (ISBN 0-486-22492-9). Dover.
Architectural Digest Editors, ed. American Interiors. (Illus.). 1978. 35.00 o.p. (ISBN 0-670-11972-5, Studio). Viking Pr.
--Celebrity Homes. (Studio Bk). (Illus.). 1977. 35.00 o.p. (ISBN 0-670-20964-3). Viking Pr.
Architectural Record, ed. see Architectural Record Magazine.
Architectural Record Magazine. Architecture 1970-1980: A Decade of Change. Davern, Jeanne & Architectural Record, eds. (Architectural Record Book). (Illus.). 320p. 1980. 29.50 (ISBN 0-07-002352-2). McGraw.
--Contextual Architecture: Responding to Existing Styles. Ray, Keith, ed. (Architecture Ser.). (Illus.). 1980. 27.50 (ISBN 0-07-002332-8). McGraw.
--Energy-Efficient Buildings. Wagner, Walter F., Jr. & Architectural Record, eds. (Architectural Record Book). (Illus.). 256p. 1980. 22.95 (ISBN 0-07-002344-1). McGraw.
--Interior Spaces Designed by Architects. 2nd ed. (Architectural Record Ser.). (Illus.). 224p. 1981. 32.50 (ISBN 0-07-002354-9, P&RB). McGraw.
--Record Houses of 1980. (Architectural Record Bks.). 128p. 1980. pap. 5.95 (ISBN 0-07-002333-6). McGraw.
Arcipreste de Hita. Libro de Buen Amor. (Span.). 7.95 (ISBN 84-241-5640-4). E Torres & Sons.
Arco Editorial Board. Aviation Weather. LC 78-23251. (Illus.). 1979. pap. text ed. 8.00 o.p. (ISBN 0-668-04413-6, 4413). Arco.
--California High School Proficiency Examination. LC 78-4628. 1978. pap. text ed. 6.00 (ISBN 0-668-04412-8, 4412). Arco.
--Case Worker. 5th ed. LC 75-21849. 1975. pap. 8.00 o.p. (ISBN 0-668-01528-4). Arco.
--Construction Foreman - Supervisor - Inspector. 2nd ed. (Orig.). 1970. pap. 8.00 o.p. (ISBN 0-668-01085-1). Arco.
--English Language & Literature: Teaching Area Exam for the National Teacher Examination. LC 65-23055. (Orig.). 1967. pap. 3.95 o.s.i. (ISBN 0-668-01319-2). Arco.
--Food Service Supervisor, School Lunch Manager. LC 65-27819. (Orig.). 1968. lib. bdg. 8.50 o.p. (ISBN 0-668-02022-9). Arco.
--Gardener--Assistant Gardener. 2nd ed. LC 75-27588. (Orig.). 1975. pap. 8.00 (ISBN 0-668-01340-0, 1340). Arco.
--Graduate Management Admission Test. 3rd ed. LC 79-1214. (Arco Professional Career Examination Ser.). (Illus.). 408p. (Orig.). 1980. pap. 6.95 (ISBN 0-668-04914-6, 4914); lib. bdg. 10.00 o. p. (ISBN 0-668-04917-0). Arco.
--Graduate Record Examination Aptitude Test. 5th ed. LC 78-15173. (Arco Professional Career Examination Ser.). (Illus.). 428p. (Orig.). 1980. pap. 6.95 (ISBN 0-668-04910-3, 4910-3); lib. bdg. 10.00 (ISBN 0-668-04915-4). Arco.
--Investigator-Inspector. 3rd ed. LC 67-22816. (Orig.). 1967. lib. bdg. 7.50 (ISBN 0-668-01711-2); pap. 5.00 o. p. (ISBN 0-668-01670-1). Arco.
--Laboratory Aide. 2nd ed. LC 73-100662. 224p. 1972. pap. 8.00 o.p. (ISBN 0-668-01121-1). Arco.
--Laborer: Federal, State & City Jobs. 2nd ed. LC 62-18801. (Orig.). 1969. lib. bdg. 6.50 o. p. o.p. (ISBN 0-668-02147-0); pap. 4.00 o.p. (ISBN 0-668-00566-1). Arco.
--Librarian. 4th ed. LC 75-37087. (Orig.). 1975. lib. bdg. 14.00 o. p. (ISBN 0-668-01403-2); pap. 10.00 (ISBN 0-668-00060-0). Arco.
--Machinist--Machinist's Helper. 3rd ed. LC 79-28693. 256p. 1980. pap. 8.00 (ISBN 0-668-04933-2). Arco.
--Mathematics, Simplified & Self Taught. 5th ed. LC 65-21203. (Orig.). 1968. pap. 5.00 (ISBN 0-668-00567-X); lib. bdg. 10.00 (ISBN 0-668-01399-0). Arco.
--National Teacher Examination. 5th ed. LC 79-148866. 1974. pap. 6.75 (ISBN 0-668-00823-7). Arco.
--Post Office Clerk-Carrier. 13th ed. LC 76-23985. 1980. pap. 6.00 (ISBN 0-668-04846-8, 4846-8). Arco.
--Postal Service Officer. LC 67-22817. (Orig.). 1967. pap. 5.00 o.p. (ISBN 0-668-01658-2). Arco.
Arctic Institute of North America (Montreal, Canada) Catalogue of the Library of the Arctic Institute of North America, Third Supplement. 1980. lib. bdg. 395.00 (ISBN 0-8161-1162-6). G K Hall.
Ard, Ben N., Jr. Rational Sex Ethics. LC 78-62739. 1978. pap. text ed. 7.75 (ISBN 0-8191-0592-9). U Pr of Amer.
Arden. Mystery of the Laughing Shadow. (gr. 5-6). Date not set. pap. cancelled (ISBN 0-590-30053-9, Schol Pap). Schol Bk Serv.
Arden, Bruce W. & Astill, Kenneth N. Numerical Algorithms: Origins & Applications. LC 76-100853. 1970. 17.95 (ISBN 0-201-00336-8). A-W.
Arden, Bruce W., ed. What Can Be Automated? The Computer Science & Engineering Research Study (COSERS) 920p. 1980. text ed. 29.95x (ISBN 0-262-01060-7). MIT Pr.
Arden, Kelvin J. & Whalen, William J. Effective Publications for Colleges & Universities. rev. ed. 1978. pap. 16.50 (ISBN 0-89964-034-6). CASE.
Arden, Leon. One Fine Day: A Novel. 1981. 10.95 (ISBN 0-393-01423-1). Norton.
Arden, Linda. The Fine Art of Being Clever...for Fun & Profit. LC 78-55993. (Illus.). 1978. softcover 12.95 o.p. (ISBN 0-930490-11-8). Future Shop.
--Health & Beauty Secrets from Hollywood. LC 78-5591. (Illus.). 1978. softcover 12.95 o.p. (ISBN 0-686-66477-9). Future Shop.
--Keeping Healthy in an Unhealthy World. (Illus.). 1980. pap. 12.95 o.p. (ISBN 0-930490-25-8). Future Shop.
Arden, William. Alfred Hitchcock & the Three Investigators in the Mystery of the Moaning Cave. Hitchcock, Alfred, ed. LC 68-23677. (Three Investigators Ser.: No. 10). (Illus.). (gr. 4-7). 1968. 2.95 (ISBN 0-394-81423-1, BYR); PLB 5.39 (ISBN 0-394-91423-6); pap. 1.95 (ISBN 0-394-83773-8). Random.
--Alfred Hitchcock & the Three Investigators in the Mystery of the Shrinking House. Hitchcock, Alfred, ed. (Three Investigators Ser.: No. 18). (Illus.). (gr. 4-7). 1972. 2.95 (ISBN 0-394-82482-2, BYR); PLB 5.39 (ISBN 0-394-92482-7); pap. 1.95 (ISBN 0-394-83777-0). Random.
--Alfred Hitchcock & the Three Investigators in the Mystery of the Deadly Double. LC 78-55960. (Illus.). (gr. 4-7). 1978. 2.95 (ISBN 0-394-83902-1, BYR); PLB 5.39 (ISBN 0-394-93902-6); pap. 1.95 (ISBN 0-394-84491-2). Random.
--Alfred Hitchcock & the Three Investigators in the Mystery of the Dead Man's Riddle. LC 74-4934. (Three Investigators Ser.). (Illus.). 160p. (gr. 4-7). 1974. 2.95 (ISBN 0-394-82927-1, BYR); PLB 5.39 (ISBN 0-394-92927-6); pap. 1.95 (ISBN 0-394-84451-3). Random.
--Alfred Hitchcock & the Three Investigators in the Mystery of the Dancing Devil. LC 76-8134. (Illus.). (gr. 4-7). 1976. 2.95 (ISBN 0-394-83289-2, BYR); PLB 5.39 (ISBN 0-394-93289-7). Random.
--Alfred Hitchcock & the Three Investigators in the Secret of Phantom Lake. Hitchcock, Alfred, ed. (Three Investigators Ser.: No. 19). (Illus.). (gr. 4-7). 1973. 2.95 (ISBN 0-394-82651-5, BYR); PLB 5.39 (ISBN 0-394-92651-X); pap. 1.95 (ISBN 0-394-84257-X). Random.
--The Mystery of the Deadly Double. LC 79-29638. (Alfred Hitchcock & the Three Investigators Ser.). 160p. (gr. 4-7). 1981. pap. 1.95 (ISBN 0-394-84491-2). Random.
Ardener, Shirley, ed. Perceiving Women. LC 75-12662. 1975. 22.95 (ISBN 0-470-03309-6); pap. 10.95 (ISBN 0-470-99264-6). Halsted Pr.
Ardery, Mrs. Wm. B., ed. see Clift, G. Glenn, et al.
Ardiff, Martha B. & Seaward, Eileen. Great Ideas. (Readers Ser.: Stage 4-Intermediate). (Orig.). 1980. pap. text ed. 2.80 (ISBN 0-88377-159-4). Newbury Hse.
Arditi, Luigi. My Reminiscences. LC 77-5500. (Music Reprint Ser.). (Illus.). 1977. Repr. of 1896 ed. lib. bdg. 25.00 (ISBN 0-306-77417-6). Da Capo.
Arditti, Joseph, ed. Orchid Biology: Reviews & Perspectives, I. LC 76-25648. (Illus.). 328p. 1977. 35.00x (ISBN 0-8014-1040-1). Comstock.
Ardizzone, Edward. Ardizzone's Hans Anderson. 1979. 10.95 (ISBN 0-689-50128-5, Mcelderry Bk). Atheneum.
--Johnny the Clockmaker. (Illus.). 48p. (ps-3). 1981. pap. 4.95 (ISBN 0-19-272120-8). Oxford U Pr.
--Ship's Cook Ginger. LC 78-7518. (Illus.). (gr. 1-4). 1978. 8.95 (ISBN 0-02-705680-5, 70568). Macmillan.
--Tim & Charlotte. (Illus.). 48p. (ps-3). 1981. pap. 4.95 (ISBN 0-19-272118-6). Oxford U Pr.
--Tim & Ginger. (Illus.). 48p. (ps-3). 1981. pap. 4.95 (ISBN 0-19-272113-5). Oxford U Pr.
--Tim to the Lighthouse. (Illus.). (gr. 1-4). 1980. pap. 3.95 (ISBN 0-19-272107-0). Oxford U Pr.
--Tim's Friend Towser. (Illus.). 48p. (ps-3). 1981. pap. 4.95 (ISBN 0-19-272112-7). Oxford U Pr.
--Young Ardizzone: An Autobiographical Fragment. (Illus.). 1971. 7.95 o.s.i. (ISBN 0-02-503000-0). Macmillan.
Ardizzone, Edward, illus. Ardizzone's Kilvert: Selections from the Diary of the Rev. Francis Kilvert 1870-79. abr. ed. (Illus.). 176p. (gr. 5-7). 1980. 7.95 (ISBN 0-224-01276-2, Pub. by Chatto Bodley Jonathan). Merrimack Bk Serv.
Ardizzone, Tony, ed. Intro Twelve. (Intro Ser.). 244p. 1981. pap. 6.95 (ISBN 0-936266-02-3). Assoc Writing Progs.
Ardsdell, P. M. Van see Van Arsdell, P. M.
Ardura, Ernesto. America En el Horizonte: Una Perspectiva Cultural. LC 79-54965. (Coleccion De Estudios Hispanicos: Hispanic Studies Collection). (Illus.). 161p. (Orig., Span.). Date not set. pap. 9.95 (ISBN 0-89729-240-5). Ediciones.
Are, Ennio T., tr. see Gumina, Deanna P.
A.R.E. New York Members. Economic Healing. rev. ed. 29p. 1974. pap. 1.25 (ISBN 0-87604-074-1). ARE Pr.
ARE Study Group No. 1. Suche Nach Gott, Bk I. Kronberger, Helge F., tr. from Eng. 135p. (Ger.). 1978. pap. 10.00 (ISBN 0-87604-131-4). ARE Pr.
Arechiga, H., jt. ed. see Valverde-Rodriguez, C.
Areeda, Phillip E. & Turner, Donald F. Antitrust Law. lawyers ed. 1980. Vol, I-V. text ed. 235.00 set (ISBN 0-316-05052-0). Little.
Areen, Judith. Standards Relating to Youth Service Agencies. (Juvenile Justice Standards Project Ser.). 1980. softcover 7.95 (ISBN 0-88410-804-X); casebound 16.50 (ISBN 0-88410-756-6). Ballinger Pub.
--Standards Relating to Youth Service Agencies. LC 77-14496. (Juvenile Justice Standards Project Ser.). 1977. softcover 7.95 o.p. (ISBN 0-88410-782-5); casebound 16.50 o.p. Ballinger Pub.
Arehart-Treichel, Joan. Poisons & Toxins. LC 76-15034. (Illus.). 160p. (gr. 5 up). 1976. 8.95 (ISBN 0-8234-0288-6). Holiday.
Arellano, Michael. Teach Yourself to Swim...Despite Your Fear of Water. LC 77-90092. (Illus.). 1978. 7.95 (ISBN 0-8015-7462-5, Hawthorn); pap. 4.95 (ISBN 0-8015-7463-3). Dutton.
Aremu, Odaleye, jt. auth. see Stevick, E. W.
Aremu, Odaleye, jt. auth. see Stevick, Earl.
Arena, John I., ed. Building Number Skills in Dyslexic Children. LC 72-83250. 1972. pap. 4.00x o.p. (ISBN 0-686-57621-7). Acad Therapy.
--Building Spelling Skills in Dyslexic Children. LC 72-97517. 1968. pap. 4.00x o.p. (ISBN 0-87879-001-2). Acad Therapy.
Arenas, Rosa Maria. She Said Yes. 26p. 1980. pap. 3.00 (ISBN 0-931598-09-5). Fallen Angel.
Arendt, Hannah. Eichmann in Jerusalem: A Report of the Banality of Evil. rev ed. 1977. pap. 3.50 (ISBN 0-14-004450-7). Penguin.
--Imperialism. LC 66-22273. Orig. Title: Origins of Totalitarianism Pt. 2. (2). 1968. pap. 4.95 (ISBN 0-15-644200-0, HB132, Harv). HarBraceJ.
--On Violence. LC 74-95867. 1970. pap. 2.95 (ISBN 0-15-669500-6, HB177, Harv). HarBraceJ.
Arendt, Jermaine D., et al, eds. Foreign Language Learning, Today & Tomorrow: Essays in Honor of Emma M. Birkmaier. 1979. 19.25 (ISBN 0-08-024628-1). Pergamon.
Arens, A. & Loebbecke, J. Auditing: An Integrated Approach. (Illus.). 1976. 19.95 o.p. (ISBN 0-13-051698-8). P-H.
--Auditing: An Integrated Approach. 2nd ed. 1980. 21.00 (ISBN 0-13-051656-2). P-H.
Arens, Alvin A., jt. auth. see Loebbecke, James K.
Arens, Richard & Lasswell, Harold D. In Defense of Public Order: The Emerging Field of Sanction Law. LC 61-7946. 1961. 22.00x (ISBN 0-231-02430-4). Columbia U Pr.
Arens, W. The Man-Eating Myth: Anthropology & Anthropophagy. (Illus.). 220p. 1980. pap. 4.95 (ISBN 0-19-502793-0, GB 615). Oxford U Pr.
Arens, W. & Montague, Susan. The American Dimension: Cultural Myths & Social Realities. 2nd ed. LC 80-26355. 250p. 1976. pap. text ed. 8.95x (ISBN 0-88284-030-4). Alfred Pub.
Arensberg, Conrad M. & Niehoff, Arthur H. Introducing Social Change: A Manual for Community Development. 2nd ed. LC 78-14936. 1971. 16.95x (ISBN 0-202-01072-4). Aldine Pub.
Arensberg, Susan M. Javanese Batiks. LC 78-54015. (Illus.). 64p. 1978. pap. 7.00 (Pub. by Mus Fine Arts Boston). C E Tuttle.
--Javanese Batiks. LC 78-54015. (Illus.). 1978. pap. text ed. 5.50 (ISBN 0-87846-128-0). Mus Fine Arts Boston.
Arenstein, Misha, jt. auth. see Hopkins, Lee Bennett.
Arents, J. S., jt. auth. see Labowitz, L. C.
Aresvik, Oddvar. The Agricultural Development of Jordan. LC 75-8399. 1976. 41.95 (ISBN 0-275-00450-3). Praeger.
--The Agricultural Development of Turkey. LC 74-3575. (Illus.). 244p. 1975. text ed. 19.95 o.p. (ISBN 0-275-28851-X). Praeger.
Arewa, E. O., jt. auth. see Shreve, G. M.
Arey, Leslie B. Human Histology: A Textbook in Outline Form. 4th ed. LC 73-88256. (Illus.). 338p. 1974. text ed. 19.00 (ISBN 0-7216-1392-6). Saunders.
Arfken, George. Mathematical Methods for Physicists. 2nd ed. 1970. text ed. 25.95 (ISBN 0-12-059851-5). Acad Pr.
Argall, George O., Jr., ed. see International Symposium on the Transportation & Handling of Minerals, 3rd British Columbia, Canada, Oct. 1979.
Argandona, Mario & Kiev, Ari. Mental Health in the Developing World: A Case Study in Latin America. LC 72-78606. 1972. 9.95 o.s.i. (ISBN 0-02-900850-6). Free Pr.
Argens, Jean Baptiste De Boyer see Baptiste De Boyer Argens, Jean.
Argenti, J. Corporate Collapse: The Causes & Symptoms. LC 76-982. 1976. 19.95 (ISBN 0-470-15111-0). Halsted Pr.
Argenti, John. A Management System for the Seventies. 1972. text ed. 16.50x (ISBN 0-04-658044-1). Allen Unwin.
Arger, Peter, jt. ed. see Abass, Alavi.
Argersinger, Peter H. Populism & Politics: William Alfred Peffer & the People's Party. LC 73-86400. (Illus.). 352p. 1974. 20.00x (ISBN 0-8131-1306-7). U Pr of Ky.
Argon, A. S., jt. auth. see McClintock, F. A.
Argy, Victor. The Post War International Money Crisis: An Analysis. 472p. (Orig.). 1981. text ed. 38.95x (ISBN 0-04-332075-9, 2576); pap. text ed. 17.50x (ISBN 0-04-332076-7, 2577). Allen Unwin.
Argyle, M. & Cook, M. Gaze & Mutual Gaze. LC 75-12134. (Illus.). 160p. 1976. 27.50 (ISBN 0-521-20865-3). Cambridge U Pr.
Argyle, M., jt. ed. see Furnham, A.
Argyle, M., et al. Social Situations. (Illus.). 450p. Date not set. price not set (ISBN 0-521-23260-0); pap. price not set (ISBN 0-521-29881-4). Cambridge U Pr.
Argyle, Michael. The Psychology of Interpersonal Behaviour. lib. bdg. 9.50x o.p. (ISBN 0-88307-297-1). Gannon.
Argyle, Michael & Beit-Hallahmi, Benjamin. Social Psychology of Religion. 1975. 20.00x (ISBN 0-7100-8043-3); pap. 10.00 (ISBN 0-7100-7997-4). Routledge & Kegan.
Argyle, Michael & Trower, Peter. Person to Person: Ways of Communicating. (Life Cycle Ser.). 1979. pap. text ed. 4.95 scp (ISBN 0-06-384746-9, HarpC). Har-Row.
Argyris, C. The Applicability of Organizational Sociology. (Illus.). 138p. 1974. 24.50 (ISBN 0-521-08448-2); pap. 7.95x (ISBN 0-521-09894-7). Cambridge U Pr.
Argyris, Chris. Inner Contradictions of Rigorous Research. LC 79-6792. (Organizational & Occupational Psychology Ser.). 1980. 16.00 (ISBN 0-12-060150-8). Acad Pr.
--Integrating the Individual & the Organization. LC 64-13209. 1964. 26.95 (ISBN 0-471-03315-4). Wiley.
--Intervention Theory & Method: A Behavioral Science View. LC 79-114331. (Business Ser). 1970. text ed. 18.95 (ISBN 0-201-00342-2). A-W.
Argyris, Chris & Cyert, Richard M. Leadership in the Eighties: Essays on Higher Education. LC 80-80425. 100p. 1980. pap. text ed. 4.50 (ISBN 0-934222-01-0). Inst Ed Manage.
Argyris, Chris & Schon, Donald A. Organizational Learning: A Theory of Action Perspective. LC 77-81195. 1978. text ed. 10.95 (ISBN 0-201-00174-8). A-W.
Arhipov, G. I., et al. Multiple Trigonometric Sums. (Trudy Steklov: No. 151). Date not set. cancelled (ISBN 0-8218-3067-8). Am Math.
Arian, Asher, ed. Israel: A Developing Society. 456p. 1980. pap. text ed. 14.25x (ISBN 90-232-1710-1). Humanities.
Arias, Esther & Arias, Mortimer. Cry of My People. (Orig.). 1980. pap. 2.95 (ISBN 0-377-00095-7). Friend Pr.
Arias, Mortimer, jt. auth. see Arias, Esther.
Aricha, Amos. The Hour of the Clown. (Orig.). 1981. pap. 2.95 (ISBN 0-451-09717-3, E9717, Sig). NAL.
Arichea, D. C. & Nida, E. A. Translators Handbook on the First Letter from Peter. (Helps for Translators Ser.). 1980. softcover 2.35 (ISBN 0-8267-0152-3, 08624). United Bible.
Arichea, D. C., Jr. & Nida, E. A. Translators Handbook on Paul's Letter to the Galatians. (Helps for Translators Ser.). 1979. Repr. of 1976 ed. soft cover 2.95 (ISBN 0-8267-0142-6, 08527). United Bible.
Arick, M. B., jt. auth. see Adkins, W. S.
Ariel, Irving M. Malignant Melanoma. 544p. 1981. 42.50 (ISBN 0-8385-6114-4). ACC.
Ariel, Robert. Freud: The Psychoanalytic Adventure. LC 77-29220. 1978. pap. 10.00 o.p. (ISBN 0-03-021696-6). HR&W.
Ariens, C. U., et al. The Comparative Anatomy of the Nervous System of Vertebrates Including Man, 3 vols. 2nd ed. (Illus.). 1845p. 1936. 97.50 (ISBN 0-02-840400-9). Hafner.

Ariens, E. J. Drug Design. (Medicinal Chemistry Ser.: Vol. 11). Vol. 1 1971: 56.00 (ISBN 0-12-060301-2); Vol. 2 1972. 56.00, by subscription 48.00 (ISBN 0-12-060302-0); Vol.3 1972. 53.00 (ISBN 0-12-060303-9); Vol 4. 1973. 54.00 (ISBN 0-12-060304-7); Vol. 5 1975. 52.50, by subscription 43.00 (ISBN 0-12-060305-5); Vol. 6 1975. 52.50, by subscription 45.00 (ISBN 0-12-060306-3); Vol. 7 1976. 50.50, by subscription 43.50 (ISBN 0-686-66291-1); Vol. 8, 1978. 51.50, by subscription 44.00 (ISBN 0-12-060308-X). Acad Pr.

Aries. Dictionary of Telecommunication. 1981. text ed. price not set (ISBN 0-408-00328-6). Butterworth.

Aries, Philippe. The Hour of Our Death. LC 79-2227. (Illus.). 800p. 1981. 20.00 (ISBN 0-394-41074-2). Knopf.

Arieti, Silvano. Abraham & the Contemporary Mind. LC 80-68187. 187p. 1981. 11.95 (ISBN 0-465-00005-3). Basic.

--Understanding & Helping the Schizophrenic: A Guide for Family & Friends. 1981. pap. 4.95 (ISBN 0-671-41252-3, Touchstone Bks). S&S.

Arieti, Silvano & Brodie, Keith H. American Handbook of Psychiatry: Advances & New Directions, Vol. VII. LC 80-68960. (American Handbook of Psychiatry Ser.). 784p. 1981. 45.50x (ISBN 0-465-00157-2). Basic.

Ariman, T., jt. ed. see Shibata, H.

Arinc Research Corporation. Reliability Engineering. 1964. ref. ed. 29.95 (ISBN 0-13-773127-2). P-H.

Ariosto, Ludovico. Orlando Furioso: A New Prose Translation. Waldman, Guido, tr. from It. 700p. 1974. text ed. 19.25x (ISBN 0-19-212576-1); pap. text ed. 6.95 o.p. (ISBN 0-19-281161-4). Oxford U Pr.

--Orlando Furioso in English Heroical Vers. LC 77-25638. (English Experience Ser.: No. 259). (Illus.). 424p. Repr. of 1591 ed. 51.00 (ISBN 90-221-0259-9). Walter J Johnson.

Aris, Reinhold. History of Political Thought in Germany, 1789-1815. 414p. 1965. Repr. 28.00x (ISBN 0-7156-1646-3, F Cass Co). Biblio Dist.

Aris, Rutherford. The Mathematical Theory of Diffusion & Reaction in Permeable Catalysts, 2 vols. Incl. Vol. 1. Theory of the Steady State. 470p. 55.00x (ISBN 0-19-851931-1); Vol. 2. Questions of Uniqueness, Stability, & Transient Behaviour. 232p. 34.95x (ISBN 0-19-851942-7). (Illus.). 1975. 75.00x set (ISBN 0-19-519829-8). Oxford U Pr.

Aris, Rutherford & Varma, Arvind, eds. The Mathematical Understanding of Chemical Engineering Systems: Selected Papers of Neal R. Amundson. LC 79-40686. (Illus.). 1980. 130.00 (ISBN 0-08-023836-X). Pergamon.

Aristophanes. Acharnians. Graves, Charles E., ed. (Gr.). 1905. text ed. 6.50x (ISBN 0-521-04045-0). Cambridge U Pr.

--The Birds. pap. 1.50 (ISBN 0-451-61671-5, M*W1671, Ment). NAL.

--The Birds. Arnott, Peter D., ed. & tr. Bd. with The Brothers Menaechmus. Plautus. LC 58-12716. (Crofts Classics Ser.). 1958. pap. text ed. 2.95x (ISBN 0-88295-004-5). AHM Pub.

--The Birds. Murray, Gilbert, tr. 1950. pap. text ed. 3.95x (ISBN 0-04-882019-9). Allen Unwin.

--The Clouds. Arnott, Peter D., ed. & tr. Bd. with The Pot of Gold. Plautus. LC 67-17194. (Crofts Classics Ser.). 1967. pap. text ed. 2.95x (ISBN 0-88295-005-3). AHM Pub.

--Comodiae, 2 Vols. Hall, F. W. & Geldart, W. M., eds. (Oxford Classical Texts Ser). Vol. 1. 18.95x (ISBN 0-19-814504-7); Vol. 2. 16.95x (ISBN 0-19-814505-5). Oxford U Pr.

--Ecclesiazusae. Ussher, Roland G., ed. 300p. 1973. 14.50x o.p. (ISBN 0-19-814191-2). Oxford U Pr.

--Four Comedies: Lysistrata, the Congresswomen, the Acharnians, the Frogs. Arrowsmith, William, ed. (Illus.). 432p. 1969. pap. 5.95 (ISBN 0-472-06152-6, 152, AA). U of Mich Pr.

--Four Major Plays. new ed. Incl. The Acharnians; The Birds; The Clouds; Lysistrata. (Classics Ser). (gr. 11 up). 1968. pap. 1.50 (ISBN 0-8049-0189-9, CL-189). Airmont.

--The Frogs. Murray, Gilbert, tr. 1908. pap. text ed. 3.95x (ISBN 0-04-882021-0). Allen Unwin.

--Frogs & Other Plays. Barrett, David, tr. Incl. Wasps; Poet & the Women. (Classics Ser.). (Orig.). 1964. pap. 2.50 (ISBN 0-14-044152-2). Penguin.

--Lysistrata. Webb, Robert H., tr. 106p. 1963. 4.95 (ISBN 0-8139-0010-7). U Pr of Va.

--Peace. Webb, Robert H., tr. LC 64-22630. 1964. pap. 2.95 (ISBN 0-8139-0013-1). U Pr of Va.

--Plays. Dickinson, Patric, tr. (Oxford Paperbacks Ser.). 1971. pap. 4.95x; Vol. 1. pap. (ISBN 0-19-281054-5); Vol. 2. pap. o.p. (ISBN 0-19-281093-6). Oxford U Pr.

--Scenes from the Birds. Oldaker, Wilfred H., ed. (Gr). 1926. text ed. 6.50x (ISBN 0-521-04047-7). Cambridge U Pr.

--Three Comedies: The Birds, the Clouds, the Wasps. Arrowsmith, William, ed. (Illus.). 400p. 1969. pap. 5.95 (ISBN 0-472-06153-4, 153, AA). U of Mich Pr.

--Wasps. MacDowell, Douglas M., ed. 1971. text ed. 22.50x (ISBN 0-19-814182-3). Oxford U Pr.

Aristotle. Aristotle: Selections from Seven Books. enl. ed. Wheelwright, Philip, ed. 1951. pap. 7.50 (ISBN 0-672-63010-9). Odyssey Pr.

--Aristotle's Physics. Hope, Richard, tr. LC 61-5498. 1961. pap. 4.50x (ISBN 0-8032-5093-2, BB122, Bison). U of Nebr Pr.

--Art of Poetry: A Greek View of Poetry & Drama. Fyfe, W. Hamilton, ed. 1940. 6.95x (ISBN 0-19-814106-8). Oxford U Pr.

--Categories & De Interpretatione. Ackrill, J. L., tr. (Clarendon Aristotle Ser.). 1963. pap. 12.50x (ISBN 0-19-872086-6). Oxford U Pr.

--Categories Et Liber De Interpretatione. Minio-Paluello, L., ed. (Oxford Classical Texts Ser). 1949. 14.95 (ISBN 0-19-814507-1). Oxford U Pr.

--Constitution of Athens & Related Texts. (Library of Classics Ser.: No. 13). pap. text ed. 4.25 (ISBN 0-02-840420-3). Hafner.

--De Anima. Ross, W. David, ed. (Oxford Classical Texts Ser). 1956. 14.95x (ISBN 0-19-814508-X). Oxford U Pr.

--De Anima, Bks. 2 & 3. Hamlyn, D. W., tr. & intro. by. (Clarendon Aristotle Ser). 184p. (With certain passages from bk. 1). 1975. pap. 13.50x (ISBN 0-19-872076-9). Oxford U Pr.

--De Arte Poetica. Kassel, Rudolf V., ed. (Oxford Classical Texts Ser.). 1965. 10.50x (ISBN 0-19-814564-0). Oxford U Pr.

--Ethics. Warrington, John, tr. 1963. 12.95x (ISBN 0-460-00547-2, Evman). Dutton.

--Metaphysica. Jaeger, Werner, ed. (Oxford Classical Texts Ser). 1957. 24.00x (ISBN 0-19-814513-6). Oxford U Pr.

--Metaphysics, Bks. 4-6. Kirwan, Christopher, tr. (Clarendon Aristotle Ser.). 214p. 1971. 16.95x (ISBN 0-19-872027-0). Oxford U Pr.

--Metaphysics: Books M & N. Annas, Julia, ed. (Clarendon Aristotle Ser.). 1976. 24.95x (ISBN 0-19-872085-8). Oxford U Pr.

--Nicomachean Ethics. Ostwald, Martin, tr. LC 62-15690. (Orig.). 1962. pap. 4.50 (ISBN 0-672-60256-3, LLA75). Bobbs.

--On Poetry & Style. Grube, G. M., tr. LC 58-13827. 1958. pap. 3.95 (ISBN 0-672-60244-X, LLA68). Bobbs.

--On the Art of Poetry with a Supplement on Music. 2nd ed. Nahm, Milton C., ed. Butcher, S. H., tr. 1976. pap. 2.50 (ISBN 0-672-60168-0, LLA 6). Bobbs.

--Physica. Ross, W. David, ed. (Oxford Classical Texts Ser). 1950. 17.50x (ISBN 0-19-814514-4). Oxford U Pr.

--Poetics. 1970. pap. 3.95 (ISBN 0-472-06166-6, 166, AA). U of Mich Pr.

--Politica. Ross, W. David, ed. (Oxford Classical Texts). 1957. 18.95x (ISBN 0-19-814515-2). Oxford U Pr.

--Politics. Barker, Ernest, tr. (YA) (gr. 9 up). 1946. pap. 6.95x (ISBN 0-19-500306-3). Oxford U Pr.

--Posterior Analytics. Barnes, Jonathan, ed. (Clarendon Aristotle Ser). 1975. 19.95x (ISBN 0-19-872066-1); pap. 17.95x (ISBN 0-19-872067-X). Oxford U Pr.

--Prior & Posterior Analytics. Warrington, John, tr. 1964. 5.00x o.p. (ISBN 0-460-00450-6, Evman). Dutton.

--Secreta Secretorum. Copland, Robert, tr. LC 71-26095. (English Experience Ser.: No. 220). 72p. Repr. of 1528 ed. 11.50 (ISBN 90-221-0220-3). Walter J Johnson.

Ariza, A. K. & Ariza, I. F., eds. Lauro Olmo: La Camisa. 1968. 7.50 (ISBN 0-08-012616-2); pap. 3.50 (ISBN 0-08-012615-4). Pergamon.

Ariza, I. F., jt. ed. see Ariza, A. K.

Arizona State University Library. Solar Energy Index. 1980. 150.00 (ISBN 0-08-023888-2). Pergamon.

Arjas, A., et al. The Performance of Paper Made with Thermomechanical Pulp: A Workshop on Thermomechanical Pulp. (TAPPI PRESS Reports). (Illus.). 1978. pap. 14.95 (ISBN 0-89852-374-5). TAPPI.

Arje, Frances B., et al. Psychiatric-Mental Health Nursing. 3rd ed. (Nursing Examination Review Book: Vol. 2). 1972. spiral bdg. 6.00 (ISBN 0-87488-502-7). Med Exam.

Arjona, Carlos V., jt. auth. see Arjona, Doris K.

Arjona, Doris K. & Arjona, Carlos V. Quince Cuentos De Las Espanas. LC 71-135971. 1971. pap. text ed. 5.95x (ISBN 0-684-41153-9, ScribC). Scribner.

Arjona, Doris K. & Helman, Edith F., eds. Cuentos Contemporaneos. (Orig., Span.). 1935. pap. 6.95x (ISBN 0-393-09432-4, NortonC). Norton.

Arjona, Doris K., jt. ed. see Helman, Edith F.

Arkell, Claudia, jt. auth. see Van Etten, Glen.

Arkes, Hadley. The Philosopher in the City: The Moral Dimensions of Urban Politics. LC 80-8536. 496p. 1981. 27.50x (ISBN 0-691-09356-3); pap. 6.95x (ISBN 0-691-02822-2). Princeton U Pr.

Arkhurst, Frederick S., ed. U. S. Policy Toward Africa. LC 74-33028. (Illus.). 272p. 1975. text ed. 27.95 (ISBN 0-275-05330-X); pap. 9.95 o.p. (ISBN 0-275-64250-X). Praeger.

Arkhurst, Joyce C. The Adventures of Spider. (Illus.). (gr. 2-6). 1964. 7.95 (ISBN 0-316-05106-3). Little.

Arkin, Alan. Halfway Through the Door. 128p. 1981. pap. 2.50 (ISBN 0-553-13816-2). Bantam.

Arkin, Arthur M. Sleep-Talking: Psychology & Psychophysiology. (Illus.). 576p. 1981. text ed. 29.95 (ISBN 0-89859-031-0). L Erlbaum Assocs.

Arkin, Arthur M., et al, eds. The Mind in Sleep: Psychology & Psychophysiology. LC 78-6025. 1978. 29.95 (ISBN 0-470-26369-5). Halsted Pr.

Arkin, Herbert & Colton, Raymond R. Statistical Methods. 5th ed. 344p. (Orig.). 1970. pap. 4.95 (ISBN 0-06-460027-0, CO 27, COS). Har-Row.

--Tables for Statisticians. 2nd ed. (Illus.). 168p. 1963. pap. 2.95 (ISBN 0-06-460075-0, CO 75, COS). Har-Row.

Arkin, William. IPS Research Guide to Current Military & Strategic Affairs. 160p. 1981. pap. 5.95 (ISBN 0-89758-025-7). Inst Policy Stud.

Arkoff. Psychology & Personal Growth. 2nd ed. 1980. text ed. 13.95 (ISBN 0-205-06822-7, 7968221). Allyn.

Arkoff, Abe. Psychology & Personal Growth. 480p. 1975. pap. text ed. 9.95x o.s.i. (ISBN 0-205-04682-7, 7946821); test items avail. o.s.i. (ISBN 0-205-04683-5). Allyn.

Arland, Marcel & Mouton, Jean, eds. Entretiens Sur Andre Gide: Decades Du Centre Culturel International De Cerisy-la-Salle. (Nouvelle Ser.: No. 3). 1967. pap. 20.50x (ISBN 90-2796-014-3). Mouton.

Arlen, Leslie. Love & Honor. 384p. 1980. pap. 2.95 (ISBN 0-515-05868-8, Jove). Jove Pubns.

--War & Passion. (The Borodins Ser.: No. 2). 368p. (Orig.). 1981. pap. 2.75 (ISBN 0-515-05481-X). Jove Pubns.

Arlen, Michael. London Venture. Van Thal, Herbert, ed. 1920-1968. pap. 2.50 (ISBN 0-304-92614-0). Dufour.

Arlen, Michael J. The Camera Age: Essays on Television. 1981. 12.95 (ISBN 0-374-11822-1). FS&G.

--Exiles. 160p. 1976. pap. 1.75 o.p. (ISBN 0-345-25196-2). Ballantine.

--Exiles - Passage to Ararat. 1978. pap. 5.95 (ISBN 0-374-51460-7). FS&G.

--Thirty Seconds. 224p. 1981. pap. 2.95 (ISBN 0-14-005810-9). Penguin.

--Thirty Seconds. 211p. 1980. 9.95 (ISBN 0-374-27576-9). FS&G.

Arlen, Richard T., jt. auth. see Woltz, Phebe M.

Arlin, M., et al. Music Sources: A Collection of Excerpts & Complete Movements. 1979. pap. 16.95 (ISBN 0-13-607168-6). P-H.

Arlotto, Anthony. Introduction to Historical Linguistics. LC 80-6309. 284p. 1981. lib. bdg. 19.75 (ISBN 0-8191-1459-6); pap. text ed. 10.25 (ISBN 0-8191-1460-X). U Pr of Amer.

Arlt, Gustave O., ed. see Werfel, Franz.

Armacost, Michael H. Politics of Weapons Innovation: The Thor-Jupiter Controversy. LC 70-90213. 1969. 22.00x (ISBN 0-231-03206-4). Columbia U Pr.

Armah, Ayi. Two Thousand Seasons. 1980. 10.00 (ISBN 0-88378-084-4); pap. 6.95 (ISBN 0-88378-046-1). Third World.

Armand, Frances U. De see De Armand, Frances U.

Armand, Octavio, ed. Contemporary Latin American Poetry. 300p. (Orig.). 1981. price not set (ISBN 0-937406-09-0); pap. price not set (ISBN 0-937406-08-2); price not set limited ed. (ISBN 0-937406-10-4). Logbridge-Rhodes.

Armanino, Dominic C. Dominoes: Popular Games, Rules & Strategy. LC 77-93308. (Illus.). 1978. 7.95 (ISBN 0-8069-4948-1); lib. bdg. 7.49 (ISBN 0-8069-4949-X). Sterling.

Armbrister, Trevor. Act of Vengeance. 1980. pap. 2.75 (ISBN 0-446-85767-6). Warner Bks.

Armbruster, C. H. Dongolese Nubian: A Grammar. 1965. text ed. 170.00 (ISBN 0-521-04050-7). Cambridge U Pr.

--Dongolese Nubian, a Lexicon. 1965. text ed. 145.00 (ISBN 0-521-04051-5). Cambridge U Pr.

Armbruster, David A., et al. Sports & Recreational Activities for Men & Women. 7th ed. LC 78-31629. (Illus.). 1979. pap. text ed. 10.95 (ISBN 0-8016-0286-6). Mosby.

Armbruster, David A., Sr. & Musker, Frank F. Basic Skills in Sports for Men & Women. 6th ed. LC 74-14684. 1975. pap. text ed. 8.50 o.p. (ISBN 0-8016-0285-8). Mosby.

Armbruster, Gisela & Brinker, Helmut, eds. Brush & Ink. (Illus.). 1979. pap. 17.50 (ISBN 0-87773-714-2). Great Eastern.

Armbruster, Maxim. The Presidents of the United States & Their Administrations from Washington to the Present. (Illus.). 400p. 1981. 14.95 (ISBN 0-8180-0812-1). Horizon.

Armbruster, Maxim E. The Presidents of the United States & Their Administrations from Washington to Ford. 6th ed. (Illus.). 1975. 10.00 o.p. (ISBN 0-8180-0815-6). Horizon.

Armbruster, Wally. A Bag of Noodles. (Illus.). (YA) 1973. pap. 2.50 (ISBN 0-570-03158-3, 12-2543). Concordia.

--Noodles du Jour. LC 75-42818. (Illus.). 192p. 1976. pap. 4.50 (ISBN 0-570-03729-8, 12-2631). Concordia.

Armed Forces - NRC Committee On Vision. Recent Developments in Vision Research. 1965. pap. 5.00 (ISBN 0-309-01272-4). Natl Acad Pr.

Armen, H. & Stiansen, S. Computational Methods for Offshore Structures. (AMD: Vol. 37). 154p. 1980. 24.00 (G00170). ASME.

Armengaud, Andre. Les Populations De L'est-Aquitain Au Debut De L'epoque Contempoaine: Recherche Sur une Region Moins Developpee, 1845-1871. (Societe, Mouvements Sociaux et Ideologis, Etudes: No. 3). 1961. pap. 51.20x (ISBN 90-2796-236-7). Mouton.

Armengol, Joseph, et al, eds. English-Spanish Guide for Medical Personnel. 1966. pap. 3.50 (ISBN 0-87488-721-6). Med Exam.

Armentano, D. T. The Myths of Antitrust: Economic Theory & Legal Cases. 1972. 11.95 o.p. (ISBN 0-87000-159-0). Arlington Hse.

Armento, Richard. Automotive Cooling System Training & Reference Manual. (Illus.). 1979. text ed. 16.95 (ISBN 0-8359-0265-X); pap. text ed. 10.95 (ISBN 0-8359-0264-1). Reston.

Armentrout, J. Michael, jt. auth. see Doman, Glenn.

Armentrout, John M., ed. Pacific Northwest Cenozoic Biostratigraphy. LC 80-82937. (Special Paper Ser.: No. 184). (Illus., Orig.). 1980. pap. write for info. (ISBN 0-8137-2184-9). Geol Soc.

Armer, G. S. & Garas, F. K., eds. Offshore Structures: The Use of Physical Models in Their Design. (Illus.). 420p. 1981. 55.00 (ISBN 0-86095-874-4). Longman.

Armer, G. S. T., jt. ed. see Garas, F. K.

Armerding, George D. & Landrum, Phil. The Dollars & Sense of Honesty: Stories from the Business World. LC 77-7854. 1979. 6.95 o.p. (ISBN 0-06-060301-1, HarpR). Har-Row.

Armerding, Hudson T. A Word to the Wise. 1980. pap. 3.95 (ISBN 0-8423-0099-6). Tyndale.

Armes, Jay J. Jay J. Armes, Investigator: The World's Most Successful Private Eye. Nolan, Frederick, ed. (Illus.). 1976. 8.95 o.s.i. (ISBN 0-02-503200-3). Macmillan.

Armes, Roy. Ambiguous Image: Narrative Style in Modern European Cinema. LC 75-37266. (Illus.). 256p. 1976. 15.00x (ISBN 0-253-30560-8). Ind U Pr.

Armey, Richard K. Price-Theory: A Policy-Welfare Approach. (Illus.). 1977. 17.95 (ISBN 0-13-699694-9). P-H.

Armiger, William B., ed. Computer Applications in Fermentation Technology, No. 9. (Biotechnology & Bioengineering Symposium). 398p. 1980. pap. 28.00 (ISBN 0-471-05746-0, Pub. by Wiley-Interscience). Wiley.

Armin, Robert. The History of the Two Maids of More-Clacke. Liddie, Alexander S. & Orgel, Stephen, eds. LC 78-66849. (Renaissance Drama Ser.). 1979. lib. bdg. 35.00 (ISBN 0-8240-9742-4). Garland Pub.

Armistead, J. M. Nathaniel Lee. (English Authors Ser.: No. 270). 1979. 14.50 (ISBN 0-8057-6748-7). Twayne.

Armistead, Samuel G. & Silverman, Joseph H. Folk-Literature of the Sephardic Jews, Vol. 1. The Judeo-Spanish Ballad Chapbooks of Yacob Abraham Yona. LC 71-78565. 1971. 38.50x (ISBN 0-520-01648-3). U of Cal Pr.

Armit, A. P. Advanced Level Vectors. 1973. pap. text ed. 5.95x o.p. (ISBN 0-435-51036-3). Heinemann Ed.

Armitage. Principles of Modern Biology. (gr. 9-12). 1972. pap. text ed. 9.00 each incl. 9 texts & tchrs' manual (ISBN 0-8449-0450-3). Learning Line.

Armitage, Andrew, jt. auth. see Tudor, Dean.

Armitage, Andrew D. & Tudor, Dean. Annual Index to Popular Music Record Reviews 1972. LC 73-8909. 1973. 16.50 (ISBN 0-8108-0636-3). Scarecrow.

--Annual Index to Popular Music Record Reviews 1973. LC 73-8909. 1974. 24.00 (ISBN 0-8108-0774-2). Scarecrow.

--Annual Index to Popular Music Record Reviews 1974. LC 73-8909. 1976. 24.00 (ISBN 0-8108-0865-X). Scarecrow.

--Annual Index to Popular Music Record Reviews 1975. LC 73-8909. 1976. 24.00 (ISBN 0-8108-0934-6). Scarecrow.

Armitage, Andrew D., jt. ed. see Tudor, Dean.

Armitage, Angus. The World of Copernicus. 1972. pap. 5.95x (ISBN 0-8464-0979-8). Beekman Pubs.

Armitage, Kenneth B. Investigations in General Biology. 1970. text ed. 9.50 (ISBN 0-12-062460-5). Acad Pr.

Armitage, P. Sequential Medical Trials. 2nd ed. LC 75-2211. 194p. 1975. 25.95 (ISBN 0-470-03323-1). Halsted Pr.

--Statistical Methods in Medical Research. 509p. 1971. 32.95 (ISBN 0-471-03320-0). Halsted Pr.

Armitage, Paul. The Common Market. LC 78-61095. (Countries Ser.). (Illus.). 1978. lib. bdg. 7.95 (ISBN 0-686-51150-6). Silver.

Armitage, Richard, et al. Beginning Spanish: A Cultural Approach. 4th ed. (Illus.). 1979. text ed. 15.00 (ISBN 0-395-27507-5); wkbk. 6.25 (ISBN 0-395-27508-3). HM.

--Fundamentals of Spanish Grammar. 1975. pap. text ed. 6.60 (ISBN 0-395-19865-8). HM.

Armitage, Ronda. Don't Forget, Matilda. (Illus.). (ps-2). 1979. PLB 8.95 (ISBN 0-233-97075-4). Andre Deutsch.

--Lighthouse Keeper's Lunch. (Illus.). (ps-2). 1979. PLB 8.95 (ISBN 0-233-96868-7). Andre Deutsch.

Armor, D. J. & Couch, A. S. Data-Text Primer. LC 78-165564. 1972. pap. text ed. 10.95 (ISBN 0-02-901020-9). Free Pr.

Armor, David J., jt. auth. see Polich, J. Michael.

Armor, David J., et al. Alcoholism & Treatment. LC 77-17421. (Personality Processes Ser.). 1978. 23.50 (ISBN 0-471-02558-5, Pub. by Wiley-Interscience). Wiley.

Armor, Reginald. Ernest Holmes: The Man. 1977. pap. 4.95 (ISBN 0-911336-66-4). Sci of Mind.

Armore, Sidney J. Statistics: A Conceptual Approach. new ed. LC 74-22892. (Mathematics Ser). 288p. 1975. text ed. 17.95 (ISBN 0-675-08730-9). Merrill.

Armour & Company Kitchens. The Quick-Easy Armour Cookbook. (Orig.). 5.95 (ISBN 0-87502-082-8). Benjamin Co.

Armour, David, ed. Treason at Michilimackinac. LC 67-81179. (Illus.). 103p. 1967. pap. 2.50 (ISBN 0-911872-32-9). Mackinac Island.

Armour, David A. & Widder, Keith R. Michilimackinac: A Handbook to the Site. 1st ed. (Illus.). 48p. (Orig.). 1980. pap. 1.50 (ISBN 0-911872-39-6). Mackinac Island.

Armour, David A., ed. Attack at Michilimackinac, 1763: Alexander Henry's Travels & Adventures in Canada & the Indian Territories Between the Years 1760 & 1764. (Illus.). 1971. pap. 2.50 (ISBN 0-911872-37-X). Mackinac Island.

Armour, Leslie. The Concept of Truth. 1979. text ed. 29.50 (ISBN 90-232-0728-9). Humanities.

Armour, Leslie & Bartlett, Edward T., 3rd. The Conceptualization of the Inner Life: A Philosophical Exploration. 1981. text ed. 17.50 (ISBN 0-391-01759-4). Humanities.

Armour, Richard. Adventures of Egbert the Easter Egg. (Illus.). (gr. k-3). 1965. PLB 7.95 o.p. (ISBN 0-07-002236-4, GB). McGraw.

--Armour's Almanac: Around the Year in 365 Days. (Illus.). 1962. 4.95 o.p. (ISBN 0-07-002253-4, GB). McGraw.

--Writing Light Verse & Prose Humor. 7.95 (ISBN 0-87116-064-1). Writer.

Armour, Robert. Fritz Lang. (Theatrical Art Ser.). 1978. 12.50 (ISBN 0-8057-9259-7). Twayne.

Armour, Robert A. Film: A Reference Guide. LC 79-6566. (American Popular Culture). xxiv, 251p. 1980. lib. bdg. 29.95 (ISBN 0-313-22241-X, AFR/). Greenwood.

Armour, Tommy. How to Play Your Best Golf All the Time. 1978. pap. 1.50 o.p. (ISBN 0-449-23516-5, Crest). Fawcett.

Arms, George, et al, eds. see Howells, W. D.

Arms, John, jt. auth. see Arms, Suzanne.

Arms, Suzanne & Arms, John. Season to Be Born. 1973. pap. 4.50 o.p. (ISBN 0-06-090323-6, CN323, CN). Har-Row.

Arms, W. Y., et al. A Practical Approach to Computing. LC 75-15787. 376p. 1976. 38.50 (ISBN 0-471-03324-3); pap. 21.95 (ISBN 0-471-99736-6). Wiley.

Armstrong. ORACLS: A Design System for Linear Multivariable Control. 256p. 1980. 35.00 (ISBN 0-8247-1239-0). Dekker.

--Renaissance Miniature Painters & Classical Imagery. 1980. write for info. (ISBN 0-905203-24-0, Pub. by H Miller England). Heyden.

Armstrong, A. Stability & Change in an English County Town. LC 73-92785. (Illus.). 272p. 1974. 23.95 (ISBN 0-521-20423-2). Cambridge U Pr.

Armstrong, A. H. Cambridge History of Later Greek & Early Medieval Philosophy. 1967. 59.50 (ISBN 0-521-04054-X). Cambridge U Pr.

Armstrong, Allen. Belief, Truth & Knowledge. LC 72-83586. 240p. 1973. 35.50 (ISBN 0-521-08706-6); pap. 10.50x (ISBN 0-521-09737-1). Cambridge U Pr.

Armstrong, Anne, tr. Viendo Lo Invisible. (Spanish Bks.). (Span.). 1979. 1.90 (ISBN 0-8297-0670-4). Vida Pub.

Armstrong, B. H. & Nicholls, R. W. Emission, Absorption & Transfer of Radiation in Heated Atmospheres. 319p. 1972. text ed. 50.00 (ISBN 0-08-016774-8). Pergamon.

Armstrong, Barry L. & Murphy, James B. The Natural History of Mexican Rattlesnakes. Wiley, E. O. & Collins, Joseph T., eds. (U of KS Museum of Nat. Hist. Special Publication: No. 5). (Illus.). 88p. (Orig.). Date not set. pap. 6.00 (ISBN 0-89338-010-5). U of KS Mus Nat Hist.

Armstrong, Ben. The Electric Church. LC 78-27699. 1979. pap. 4.95 (ISBN 0-8407-5685-2). Nelson.

Armstrong, Brian G. Calvinism & the Amyraut Heresy: Protestant Scholasticism & Humanism in Seventeenth-Century France. LC 72-84949. (Illus.). 1969. 27.50 (ISBN 0-299-05490-X). U of Wis Pr.

Armstrong, Bruce. Sable Island. LC 80-2745. (Illus.). 256p. 1981. 19.95 (ISBN 0-385-13113-5). Doubleday.

Armstrong, Charlotte. A Little Less Than Kind. large type ed. pap. 1.25 o.p. (ISBN 0-425-03018-0). Berkley Pub.

--The Trouble in Thor. 1977. pap. 1.50 o.p. (ISBN 0-425-03631-6, Medallion). Berkley Pub.

--The Unsuspected. large type ed. pap. 0.95 o.p. (ISBN 0-425-03070-9). Berkley Pub.

--The Witch's House. 1975. pap. 0.95 o.p. (ISBN 0-425-02797-X, Medallion). Berkley Pub.

Armstrong, Christopher. Evelyn Underhill. LC 75-33401. 1976. 8.95 o.p. (ISBN 0-8028-3474-4). Eerdmans.

--The Politics of Federalism: Ontario's Relations with the Federal Government 1867-1942. (Ontario Historical Studies). 316p. 1981. 20.00 (ISBN 0-8020-3374-1). U of Toronto Pr.

Armstrong, D., et al. The Old Church Slavonic Translation of the Andron Hagion Biblos in the Edition of Nikolas Van Wijk. Van Schooneveld, C. H., ed. (Slavistic Printings & Reprintings Ser: No. 1). 310p. 1975. text ed. 98.80x (ISBN 90-2793-196-8). Mouton.

--Opportunistic Infections in Cancer Patients. LC 77-94828. (Illus.). 207p. 1978. 29.75 (ISBN 0-89352-014-4). Masson Pub.

Armstrong, D. M. Universals & Scientific Realism: A Theory of Universals, Vol. 2. LC 77-80824. 1978. 26.95 (ISBN 0-521-21950-7). Cambridge U Pr.

--Universals & Scientific Realism: Nominalism & Realism, Vol. 1. LC 77-80824. 1978. 23.95 (ISBN 0-521-21741-5). Cambridge U Pr.

--Universals & Scientific Realism: Vol. 1, Nominalism. LC 77-80824. 165p. 1980. pap. 8.95 (ISBN 0-521-28033-8). Cambridge U Pr.

--Universals & Scientific Realism: Vol. 2, A Theory of Universals. LC 77-80824. 200p. 1980. pap. 8.95 (ISBN 0-521-28032-X). Cambridge U Pr.

Armstrong, Daniel & Schooneveld, C. H., eds. Roman Jakobson: Echoes of His Scholarship. 1977. pap. text ed. 68.50x (ISBN 90-316-0147-0). Humanities.

Armstrong, David. A Trumpet to Arms: Alternative Media in America. 384p. 1981. 12.95 (ISBN 0-87477-158-7). J P Tarcher.

Armstrong, David M. Perception & the Physical World. (International Library of Philosophy & Scientific Method). 1961. text ed. 14.50x (ISBN 0-7100-3603-5). Humanities.

Armstrong, Diana. Bicycle Camping. (Illus., Orig.). 1981. pap. 8.95. Dial.

Armstrong, Edward A. St. Francis, Nature Mystic: The Derivation & Significance of the Nature Stories in the Franciscan Legend. 1963. 20.00x (ISBN 0-520-01966-0); pap. 5.95 (ISBN 0-520-03040-0). U of Cal Pr.

--A Study of Bird Song. 2nd, enl. ed. (Illus.). 1980. 7.50 (ISBN 0-8446-4704-7). Peter Smith.

Armstrong, Elizabeth. Or Give Me Death. 1977. 7.95 o.p. (ISBN 0-533-02951-1). Vantage.

Armstrong, Frederick H., et al. Bibliography of Canadian Urban History: Part V: Western Canada. (Public Adminstration Ser.: Bibliography P-541). 72p. 1980. pap. 7.50. Vance Biblios.

Armstrong, Garner T. The Real Jesus. 1978. pap. 2.25 (ISBN 0-380-40055-3, 40055). Avon.

Armstrong, George P., jt. auth. see Darst, Paul W.

Armstrong, Gregory. Wanderers All: An American Pilgrimage. LC 76-26210. 1977. 6.95 o.p. (ISBN 0-06-010139-3, HarpT). Har-Row.

Armstrong, H. C. & Lewis, C. V. Practical Boiler Firing. 4th ed. 387p. 1954. 10.95x (ISBN 0-85264-065-X, Pub. by Griffin England). State Mutual Bk.

Armstrong, Harvey & Taylor, Jim. Regional Economic Policy & Its Analysis. 352p. 1978. 43.50x (ISBN 0-86003-015-6, Pub. by Allan Pubs England); pap. 21.75x (ISBN 0-86003-116-0). State Mutual Bk.

Armstrong, Isobel, ed. Victorian Scrutinies: Reviews of Poetry, 1830-1870. 1972. text ed. 28.75x (ISBN 0-485-11131-4, Athlone Pr). Humanities.

--Writers & Their Background: Robert Browning. LC 72-96846. (Writers & Their Background Ser). xxvi, 365p. 1974. 15.00x (ISBN 0-8214-0131-9); pap. 6.00x (ISBN 0-8214-0132-7). Ohio U Pr.

Armstrong, J. D. Revolutionary Diplomacy: Chinese Foreign Policy & the United Front Doctrine. 259p. 1981. 21.00x (ISBN 0-520-03251-9, CAMPUS 268); pap. 5.95x (ISBN 0-520-04273-5). U of Cal Pr.

Armstrong, J. L., jt. auth. see Leecing, W.

Armstrong, J. Scott. Long-Range Forecasting: From Crystal Ball to Computer. LC 77-25176. 1978. 33.50 (ISBN 0-471-03002-3, Pub by Wiley-Interscience). Wiley.

Armstrong, Joe E. & Harman, Willis W. Strategies for Conducting Technology Assessments. (Westview Special Studies in Science, Technology, & Public Policy). 130p. 1980. lib. bdg. 17.50x (ISBN 0-89158-672-5). Westview.

Armstrong, John A. Ukranian Nationalism. 2nd ed. LC 79-25529. 361p. 1980. Repr. of 1963 ed. 30.00x (ISBN 0-87287-193-2). Libs Unl.

Armstrong, John A., ed. Soviet Partisans in World War Two. (Illus.). 1964. 45.00x (ISBN 0-299-03060-1). U of Wis Pr.

Armstrong, John W. The Water of Life. 136p. 1971. pap. 4.75x (ISBN 0-8464-1060-5). Beekman Pubs.

Armstrong, Judith. The Novel of Adultery. LC 76-15793. 1976. text ed. 18.50x o.p. (ISBN 0-06-490203-X). B&N.

Armstrong, Kathleen. Joys & Teardrops. 1976. pap. 2.95 (ISBN 0-917578-02-3). Eternal Ent.

Armstrong, L. & Guy, P. K. Metalcraft Today. 1975. pap. text ed. 3.95x (ISBN 0-435-75700-8). Heinemann Ed.

Armstrong, Larry. Disaster & Deliverance. LC 79-88400. 1979. pap. 4.25 (ISBN 0-933350-22-8). Morse Pr.

Armstrong, Lee H., jt. auth. see Pettofrezzo, Anthony J.

Armstrong, Lilian. The Paintings & Drawings of Marco Zoppo. LC 75-23779. (Outstanding Dissertations in the Fine Arts - 15th Century). (Illus.). 1976. lib. bdg. 60.50 (ISBN 0-8240-1976-8). Garland Pub.

Armstrong, Louise. Arthur Gets What He Spills. LC 78-32029. (Let Me Read Ser.). (Illus.). (gr. 6-10). 1979. 4.95 (ISBN 0-685-94651-7, HJ); pap. 1.95 o.p. (ISBN 0-15-607945-3). HarBraceJ.

--Saving the Big-Deal Baby. LC 79-22838. (Illus.). (gr. 7 up). 1980. PLB 7.95 (ISBN 0-525-38805-2, Skinny Book); pap. 2.50 (ISBN 0-525-45050-5, Skinny Book). Dutton.

--The Thump, Blam, Bump Mystery. LC 74-24582. (Illus.). (gr. k-3). 1975. 5.95 o.s.i. (ISBN 0-8027-6208-5); PLB 5.83 o.s.i. (ISBN 0-8027-6207-7). Walker & Co.

Armstrong, Louise V. We Too Are the People. LC 74-168679. (FDR & the Era of the New Deal Ser.). Repr. of 1938 ed. lib. bdg. 42.50 (ISBN 0-306-70367-X). Da Capo.

Armstrong, Lyn. Woodcolliers & Charcoal Burning. 96p. 1980. pap. 6.95x (ISBN 0-905259-05-X, Pub. by Coach Pub Hse England). Intl Schol Bk Serv.

Armstrong, Michael. Case Studies in Personnel Management. 1979. 30.00x (ISBN 0-85038-243-2). Nichols Pub.

--Personnel & Training Management Yearbook & Directory: United Kingdom 1980. 1979. 35.00x (ISBN 0-686-60659-0, Pub by Kogan Pg). Nichols Pub.

Armstrong, Michael, frwd. by. The Knapp Commission Report on Police Corruption. LC 73-76969. 1973. 10.00 o.s.i.; pap. 5.95 (ISBN 0-8076-0689-8). Braziller.

Armstrong, Nancy. Victorian Jewelry. (Illus.). 1976. 19.95 o.s.i. (ISBN 0-02-503220-8). Macmillan.

Armstrong, O. K., jt. auth. see Parkinson, C. Northcote.

Armstrong, Paul W. & Baigrie, Ronald S. Hemodynamic Monitoring in the Critically Ill. (Illus.). 250p. 1980. text ed. 14.95 (ISBN 0-06-140268-0, Harper Medical). Har-Row.

Armstrong, R. D., ed. Solid Ionic & Ionic-Electronic Conductors. LC 77-747. 1977. text ed. 34.00 (ISBN 0-08-021592-0). Pergamon.

Armstrong, R. D., ed. see International Meeting on Solid Electrolytes, 2nd, University of St. Andrews, Sep. 20-22, 1978.

Armstrong, Ray L. The Poems of James Shirley. 108p. 1980. Repr. of 1941 ed. lib. bdg. 27.50 (ISBN 0-8495-0062-1). Arden Lib.

Armstrong, Regina B. Regional Accounts. LC 79-3659. 256p. 1980. 18.50x (ISBN 0-253-17965-3). Ind U Pr.

Armstrong, Robert. The Centers. (Stars of the NBA Ser.). (Illus.). (gr. 4-12). 1977. PLB 7.50 o.p. (ISBN 0-87191-565-0). Creative Ed.

--The Coaches. (Stars of the NBA Ser.). (Illus.). (gr. 4-12). 1977. PLB 7.95 (ISBN 0-87191-566-9). Creative Ed.

--Dave Cowens. (Sports Superstars Ser.). (Illus.). (gr. 3-9). 1978. PLB 5.95 (ISBN 0-87191-668-1); pap. 2.95 (ISBN 0-89812-182-5). Creative Ed.

--The Forwards. (Stars of the NBA Ser.). (Illus.). (gr. 3-7). 1977. PLB 7.95 (ISBN 0-87191-563-4). Creative Ed.

--The Guards. (Stars of the NBA Ser.). (Illus.). (gr. 4-12). 1977. PLB 7.95 (ISBN 0-87191-564-2). Creative Ed.

--Pete Maravich. (Sports Superstars Ser.). (Illus.). (gr. 3-9). 1978. PLB 5.95 (ISBN 0-87191-669-X); pap. 2.95 (ISBN 0-89812-183-3). Creative Ed.

--Rick Barry. (Sports Superstars Ser.). (Illus.). (gr. 3-9). 1977. PLB 5.95 (ISBN 0-87191-539-1); pap. 2.95 (ISBN 0-89812-185-X). Creative Ed.

Armstrong, Robert D. Nevada Printing History: A Bibliography of Imprints & Publications, 1858-1880. (Illus.). 540p. 1981. price not set (ISBN 0-87417-063-X). U of Nev Pr.

Armstrong, Robert H. & Alaska Magazine Editors. Guide to the Birds of Alaska. 320p. 1980. pap. 15.95 (ISBN 0-88240-143-2). Alaska Northwest.

Armstrong, Robert P. Wellspring: On the Myth & Source of Culture. LC 73-85781. (Illus.). 100p. 1975. 15.50x (ISBN 0-520-02571-7). U of Cal Pr.

Armstrong, Roger. Wax & Casting: A Notebook of Process & Technique. (Illus.). 160p. 1981. pap. write for info. (ISBN 0-89863-038-X). Star Pub CA.

Armstrong, Roger W. Laboratory Manual for Chemistry: A Lige Science Approach. 1980. pap. write for info. (ISBN 0-02-303920-5). Macmillan.

Armstrong, Ronald M., jt. auth. see Steele, Marion A.

Armstrong, Russ, jt. auth. see Hemingway, Muffet.

Armstrong, Russell M. Modular Programming in COBOL. LC 73-4030. (Business Data Processing Ser.). 224p. 1973. 23.95 (ISBN 0-471-03325-1, Pub. by Wiley-Interscience). Wiley.

Armstrong, Scott, jt. auth. see Woodward, Bob.

Armstrong, Terry, et al, eds. A Reader's Hebrew-English Lexicon of the Old Testament: (Genesis-Deuteronomy, Vol. 1. 1978. 9.95 (ISBN 0-310-37020-5). Zondervan.

Armstrong, Tom. Love in Being. (Illus.). 64p. 1981. 5.95 (ISBN 0-9604246-1-X). Jemta Pr.

Armstrong, Virginia I., ed. I Have Spoken: American History Through the Voices of the Indians. LC 74-150755. xxii, 260p. 1971. 10.00 o.p. (ISBN 0-8040-0529-X, SB); pap. 5.95 (ISBN 0-8040-0530-3, Sb). Swallow.

Armstrong, W., jt. auth. see Etherington, J. R.

Armstrong, Walter. Art in Great Britain & Ireland. 332p. 1980. Repr. of 1913 ed. lib. bdg. 65.00 (ISBN 0-8492-3206-6). R West.

Armstrong, William, ed. see Bacon, Francis.

Armstrong, William, ed. see King, Cecil.

Armstrong, William E. Purser's Handbook. LC 65-21748. (Illus.). 1966. 10.00x (ISBN 0-87033-086-1). Cornell Maritime.

Armstrong, William H. Barefoot in the Grass: The Story of Grandma Moses. LC 74-122338. (gr. 5 up). 1970. PLB 4.95 (ISBN 0-385-00454-0). Doubleday.

--Organs for America: The Life & Work of David Tannenberg. LC 67-26221. 1968. 9.95x o.p. (ISBN 0-8122-7000-2). U of Pa Pr.

--Sounder. 1969. pap. 1.95 (ISBN 0-06-080379-7, P379, PL). Har-Row.

Armytage, W. H. American Influence on English Education. (Students Library of Education). (Orig.). 1967. text ed. 5.50x (ISBN 0-7100-4201-9); pap. text ed. 3.25x (ISBN 0-7100-4206-X). Humanities.

--French Influence on English Education. (Students Library of Education). 1968. pap. text ed. 2.50x (ISBN 0-7100-4216-7). Humanities.

--Russian Influence on English Education. (Students Library of Education). 1969. text ed. 7.25x (ISBN 0-7100-6492-6). Humanities.

Arn, Winfield C., jt. auth. see McGavran, Donald A.

Arnakis, George & Vucinish. History of the Near East in Modern Times, 3 vols. Incl. Vol. 1. The Ottoman Empire & the Balkan States to 1900. (Illus.). 452p (ISBN 0-8363-0046-7); Vol. 2. Forty Crucial Years: 1900-1940 (ISBN 0-8363-0047-5). 15.00 ea. Jenkins.

Arnason, H. H. Robert Motherwell. 2nd, rev. ed. (Illus.). 252p. 1980. 65.00 (ISBN 0-686-62702-4, 0289-3). Abrams.

Arnason, H. Horvard. History of Modern Art. 2nd ed. (Illus.). 1976. 21.95 (ISBN 0-13-390351-6). P-H.

Arnason, K. Quantity in Historical Phonology. LC 79-41363. (Cambridge Studies in Linguistics: No. 30). (Illus.). 256p. 1980. 44.50 (ISBN 0-521-23040-3). Cambridge U Pr.

Arnaud, Pierre, jt. ed. see Berredo Carneiro, Paulo E.

Arnaudet, Martin L. & Barrett, Mary E. Paragraph Development: A Guide for Students of English As a Second Language. (ESL Ser.). (Illus.). 160p. 1981. pap. text ed. 7.95 (ISBN 0-13-648618-5). P-H.

Arnauld, Antoine. The Arraignment of the Whole Societie of Jesuites in Fraunce: Holden-the Twelfth & Thirteenth of July, 1594. LC 79-84084. (English Experience Ser.: No. 904). 68p. 1979. Repr. of 1594 ed. lib. bdg. 8.00. Walter J Johnson.

--Art of Thinking: Port-Royal Logic. Dickoff, James & James, Patricia, trs. LC 63-16933. (Orig.). 1964. pap. 10.95 (ISBN 0-672-60358-6, LLA144). Bobbs.

Arnauld, Antoine & Lancelot, Claude. General & Rational Grammar: The Port-Royal Grammar. Rieux, Jacques & Rollin, Bernard E., eds. LC 74-84245. (Janua Linguarum, Series Minor: No. 208). 197p. 1975. pap. text ed. 34.10x (ISBN 90-2793-004-X). Mouton.

Arndt, Clara & Huckabee, Loucine. Nursing Administration: Theory for Practice with a Systems Approach. 2nd ed. LC 80-14034. (Illus.). 1980. pap. 15.95 (ISBN 0-8016-0305-6). Mosby.

Arndt, Clara & Huckabay, Loucine M. Nursing Administration: Theory for Practice with a Systems Approach. LC 75-4893. (Illus.). 336p. 1975. text ed. 14.95 o.p. (ISBN 0-8016-0312-9). Mosby.

Arndt, H. W. The Rise & Fall of Economic Growth. 1978. text ed. 16.00 (ISBN 0-582-71214-9); pap. text ed. 10.95 (ISBN 0-582-71213-0). Longman.

Arndt, Hans W. Methodo Scientifica pertractatum: Mos geometricus und Kalkuelbegriff in der Philosophischen Theorienbildung des 17. und 18. (Quellen und Studien Zur Philosophie Ser.: Vol. 4). 1971. 42.35x (ISBN 3-11-003942-7). De Gruyter.

Arndt, Karl J. George Rapp's Separatists: 1700-1803. LC 80-82896. (Illus.). 512p. (Ger. & Eng.). 1980. bilingual ed. 32.50 (ISBN 0-937640-00-X). Harmony Soc.

--Harmony on the Connoquenessing: George Rapp's First American Harmony: 1803-1815. LC 80-828. (Documentary History of Rapp's Harmony Society, 1700-1916 Ser.). (Illus.). 1072p. (Eng. & Ger.). 1981. 38.00 (ISBN 0-937640-01-8). Harmony Soc.

Arndt, Karl J. & Olson, May. German Language Press of the Americas, 3 vols. 1980. Set. text ed. 321.00 (Pub. by K G Saur). Gale.

Arndt, Rolf D., et al. Peripheral & Joint Arthrography. (Illus.). 188p. 1981. write for info. (0253-8). Williams & Wilkins.

Arndt, Walter, tr. see Goethe, Johann W. Von.

Arndt, Walter, tr. see Pushkin, Alexander.

Arndt, William F. Bible Difficulties. 1981. 3.75 (ISBN 0-570-03120-6, 12-2357). Concordia.

Arndt, William F., et al, eds. see Gingrich, F. Wilbur.

Arneil, Steve & Dowler, Bryan. Better Karate: The Key to Better Technique. (Better Bks.). (Illus.). 98p. 1980. text ed. 14.50 (ISBN 0-7182-1444-7, SpS). Soccer.

Arneson, Donald. Doing Something Nice, Inc. & Other Short Plays for Kids. (Illus.). 72p. (Orig.). (gr. 3-6). 1978. write for info. (ISBN 0-934778-00-0); pap. write for info. Bookmaker.

Arnett, Caroline. Christina. (Coventry Romance Ser.: No. 65). 224p. 1980. pap. 1.75 (ISBN 0-449-50096-9, Coventry). Fawcett.

--Claudia. 1978. pap. 1.75 o.p. (ISBN 0-449-23647-1, Crest). Fawcett.

--Stephanie. (A Regency Romance Ser.). 1979. pap. 1.75 o.p. (ISBN 0-449-24081-9, Crest). Fawcett.

--Theodora. 1977. pap. 1.50 o.p. (ISBN 0-449-23347-2, Crest). Fawcett.

Arnett, Harold & Danos, Paul. CPA Firm Viability: A Study of Major Environmental Factors Affecting Firms of Various Sizes & Characteristics. LC 79-18672. (Illus., Orig.). 1979. pap. 6.50 (ISBN 0-87712-199-0). U Mich Busn Div Res.

Arnett, John A. Bibliopegia; or, the Art of Bookbinding in All Its Branches. Bidwell, John, ed. LC 78-74390. (Nineteenth-Century Book Arts & Printing History Ser.: Vol. 5). (Illus.). 1980. lib. bdg. 27.50 (ISBN 0-8240-3879-7). Garland Pub.

Arnett, Ross H. The Beetles of the United States. 2nd ed. 1980. write for info. o.p. (ISBN 0-916846-08-3). World Natural Hist.

Arnett, Ross H. & Bazinet, George F. Plant Biology: A Concise Introduction. 4th ed. LC 76-26531. (Illus.). 1977. text ed. 15.95 (ISBN 0-8016-0316-1). Mosby.

Arnett, Ross H., Jr., jt. auth. see Blackwelder, Richard E.

Arnett, Ross H., Jr., et al. How to Know the Beetles. 2nd ed. (Pictured Key Nature Ser.). 1980. text ed. 10.95x (ISBN 0-697-04777-6); wire coil 7.95x (ISBN 0-697-04776-8). Wm C Brown.

Arnett, Willard E. George Santayana. (World Leaders Ser). lib. bdg. 9.95 (ISBN 0-8057-3718-9). Twayne.

Arnett, Willard E., ed. Modern Reader in the Philosophy of Religion. LC 66-20470. (Century Philosophy Ser.). 1966. 29.50x (ISBN 0-89197-482-2); pap. text ed. 16.95x (ISBN 0-89197-483-0). Irvington.

Arnez, John A. A Slovenian Community in Bridgeport, Conn. LC 73-170467. (Studia Slovenica, Special Series). 96p. 1971. 4.00 (ISBN 0-686-28388-0). Studia Slovenica.

Arnheim, Daniel B. & Pestolesi, Robert A. Elementary Physical Education: A Developmental Approach. 2nd ed. LC 77-26214. 1978. text ed. 15.95 (ISBN 0-8016-0326-9). Mosby.

Arnheim, Daniel D. Dance Injuries: Their Prevention & Care. 2nd ed. LC 79-24524. (Illus.). 1980. pap. text ed. 12.00 (ISBN 0-8016-0311-0). Mosby.

Arnheim, Daniel D. & Klafs, Carl E. Athletic Training: A Study & Laboratory Guide. LC 78-145. 1978. pap. text ed. 9.95 (ISBN 0-8016-0329-3). Mosby.

Arnheim, Daniel D. & Schlaich, Joan. Dance Injuries: Their Prevention & Care. LC 74-22491. 1975. pap. text ed. 10.50 o.p. (ISBN 0-8016-0313-7). Mosby.

Arnheim, Daniel D. & Sinclair, William A. The Clumsy Child: A Program of Motor Therapy. 2nd ed. LC 78-2. (Illus.). 1979. pap. 12.00 (ISBN 0-8016-0310-2). Mosby.

Arnheim, Daniel D., jt. auth. see Klafs, Carl E.

Arnheim, Rudolf. The Genesis of a Painting: Picasso's Guernica. (Illus.). 148p. 1981. 30.00x (ISBN 0-520-00037-4, CAL 485); pap. text ed. 10.95 (ISBN 0-520-04266-2, 485). U of Cal Pr.

--Kunst und Sehen: Eine Psychologie Des Schopferischen Auges. 2nd ed. (Illus.). 1978. 24.70x (ISBN 3-11-006682-3). De Gruyter.

--Radio: The Psychology of an Art of Sound. LC 73-164504. (Cinema Ser). 1972. Repr. of 1936 ed. lib. bdg. 29.50 (ISBN 0-306-70291-6). Da Capo.

--Toward a Psychology of Art. 1966. 18.50x (ISBN 0-520-00038-2); pap. 5.95 (ISBN 0-520-02161-4, CAL242). U of Cal Pr.

--Visual Thinking. (Illus.). 1980. 13.95x (ISBN 0-686-64912-5, CAL229); pap. 6.95 (ISBN 0-520-01871-0). U of Cal Pr.

Arnim, J. Von. Stoicorum Veterum Fragmenta, 4 vols. (Classical Studies Ser.). (Lat. & Gr.). Repr. of 1903 ed. Set. lib. bdg. 96.50x (ISBN 0-89197-950-6); Vol. 1. lib. bdg. 26.00x (ISBN 0-697-00024-9); Vol. 2. lib. bdg. 28.50x (ISBN 0-697-00025-7); Vol. 3. lib. bdg. 28.50x (ISBN 0-697-00026-5); Vol. 4. lib. bdg. 24.00x (ISBN 0-697-00027-3). Irvington.

Arno, Ed, illus. The Gingerbread Man. (Illus.). (gr. k-3). 1970. pap. 1.25 (ISBN 0-590-01554-0, Schol Pap); pap. 3.95 gingerbread man & three billy goats gruff (2 bks.) & 1 record (ISBN 0-590-04405-2). Schol Bk Serv.

Arno, Peter. Peter Arno. LC 79-19540. (Illus.). 1979. 10.95 (ISBN 0-396-07772-2). Dodd.

Arno, Stephen F. Northwest Trees. LC 77-82369. (Illus.). 1977. 30.00 (ISBN 0-916890-55-4); pap. 6.95 (ISBN 0-916890-50-3). Mountaineers.

Arnoff, Mark & Kean, Mary-Louise, eds. Juncture. (Studia Linguistica et Philologica: Ovol. 7). 144p. 1980. pap. 25.00 (ISBN 0-915838-46-X). Anma Libri.

Arnold. World Book of Children's Games. 1977. pap. 1.75 o.p. (ISBN 0-449-23044-9, Crest). Fawcett.

Arnold, Adele. Red Son Rising. LC 74-17283. (Illus.). (gr. 5 up). 1974. 6.95 (ISBN 0-87518-077-9). Dillon.

Arnold, Alan. Once Upon a Galaxy: A Journal of the Making of the Empire Strikes Back. 1980. pap. 2.75 (ISBN 0-345-29075-5, Del Rey Bks). Ballantine.

Arnold, Armin. Friedrich Durrenmatt. LC 78-178169. (Modern Literature Ser.). 128p. 1972. 10.95 (ISBN 0-8044-2000-9). Ungar.

--James Joyce. LC 68-31445. (Modern Literature Ser.). 1969. 10.95 (ISBN 0-8044-2007-6); pap. 3.45 (ISBN 0-8044-6008-6). Ungar.

Arnold, Arnold. Career Choices for the Seventies. LC 79-132860. (gr. 7 up). 1971. 7.95 (ISBN 0-02-705670-8, CCPr). Macmillan.

--Pictures & Stories from Forgotten Children's Books. (Illus., Orig.). (gr. k-6). 1970. pap. 5.00 (ISBN 0-486-22041-9). Dover.

--World Book of Children's Games. LC 77-142134. (Illus.). 1972. 9.95 o.s.i. (ISBN 0-690-00372-2, TYC-T). T Y Crowell.

Arnold, Arnold, ed. Antique Paper Dolls: Nineteen Fifteen to Nineteen Twenty. LC 75-3822. 1975. pap. 5.00 (ISBN 0-486-23176-3). Dover.

Arnold, Bob. Habitat. (Orig.). 1980. pap. 5.00x sewn (ISBN 0-915316-75-7). Pentagram.

--Thread. 1981. pap. 4.00 (ISBN 0-915316-87-0); pap. 10.00 lmtd. signed ed. (ISBN 0-915316-90-0). Pentagram.

Arnold, Bruce. A Concise History of Irish Art. LC 77-76835. (World of Art Ser.). (Illus.). 1977. 17.95 (ISBN 0-19-519962-6); pap. 9.95 (ISBN 0-19-519966-9). Oxford U Pr.

--A Singer at the Wedding. 285p. 1980. 17.95 (ISBN 0-241-89825-0, Pub. by Hamish Hamilton England). David & Charles.

--The Song of the Nightingale. 256p. 1980. 19.95 (ISBN 0-241-10497-1, Pub. by Hamish Hamilton England). David & Charles.

Arnold, Caroline. Electric Fish. LC 80-12479. (Illus.). 64p. (gr. 4-6). 1980. 6.95 (ISBN 0-688-22237-4); PLB 6.67 (ISBN 0-688-32237-9). Morrow.

--My Friend from Outer Space. (Easy-Read Story Bks). (Illus.). 32p. (gr. k-3). 1981. 3.95 (ISBN 0-531-02473-3). Watts.

Arnold, Carroll, jt. auth. see Wilson, John.

Arnold, Corliss R. Organ Literature: A Comprehensive Survey. LC 72-8824. 1973. 18.50 (ISBN 0-8108-0559-6). Scarecrow.

Arnold, Darlene B. & Doyle, Kenneth O., Jr. Education-Psychology Journals: A Scholar's Guide. LC 74-23507. 1975. 10.00 (ISBN 0-8108-0779-3). Scarecrow.

Arnold, Denis. Baroque Operatic Arias, Bk.1. Ford, Anthony, ed. 1971. 13.10x o.p. (ISBN 0-19-713412-2). Oxford U Pr.

Arnold, Denis, ed. see Marenzio, Luca.

Arnold, Denis V. Management of the Information Department. LC 76-43375. 1978. lib. bdg. 18.50x (ISBN 0-89158-716-0). Westview.

Arnold, Eddie & Stocks, Broan. Men's Gymanastics. (EP Sport Ser.). (Illus.). 1979. 12.95 (ISBN 0-8069-9128-3, Pub. by EP Publishing England); pap. 6.95 (ISBN 0-8069-9130-5). Sterling.

Arnold, Edwin, tr. The Light of Asia & the Indian Song of Songs: Gita Govinda. 1949. pap. 2.00 (ISBN 0-88253-115-8). Ind-US Inc.

--The Song Celestial or Bhaggvad-Gita: From the Mahabharata, Being a Discourse Between Arjuna, Prince of India, & the Supreme Being Under the Form of Krishna. 1967. pap. 4.00 (ISBN 0-7100-6268-0). Routledge & Kegan.

Arnold, Edwin L. The Wonderful Adventures of Phra the Phoenician. Reginald, R. & Menville, Douglas, eds. LC 80-19173. (Newcastle Forgotten Fantasy Library Ser.: Vol. 11). 329p. 1980. Repr. of 1977 ed. lib. bdg. 10.95x (ISBN 0-89370-510-1). Borgo Pr.

Arnold, Edwin P. Gulliver of Mars. 1976. lib. bdg. 12.95x (ISBN 0-89968-173-5). Lightyear.

--Phra the Phoenician. 1976. lib. bdg. 12.95x (ISBN 0-89968-174-3). Lightyear.

Arnold, Edwin T., ed. see Perry, Benjamin F.

Arnold, Elliot. The Commandos. 1979. pap. 1.75 (ISBN 0-505-51332-3). Tower Bks.

Arnold, Eric A. Fouche, Napoleon, & the General Police. LC 79-62894. 1979. pap. text ed. 9.50 (ISBN 0-8191-0716-6). U Pr of Amer.

Arnold, Francena H. Brother Beloved. 1967. pap. 2.25 (ISBN 0-8024-0050-7). Moody.

--Deepening Stream. pap. 2.50 (ISBN 0-310-20212-4). Zondervan.

--Fruit for Tomorrow. pap. 2.50 (ISBN 0-310-20222-1). Zondervan.

--Straight Down a Crooked Lane. (gr. 9-12). 1959. pap. 2.25 (ISBN 0-8024-0041-8). Moody.

--Then Am I Strong. 1969. pap. 2.50 (ISBN 0-8024-0060-4). Moody.

--Three Shall Be One. (Orig.). (gr. 9-12). 1966. pap. 2.50 (ISBN 0-8024-0085-X). Moody.

Arnold, G. Economic Co-operation in the Commonwealth. 1967. 22.00 (ISBN 0-08-012449-6); pap. 10.75 (ISBN 0-08-012448-8). Pergamon.

Arnold, Godfrey E., jt. auth. see Luchsinger, Richard.

Arnold, Guy. Britain's Oil. (Illus.). 1979. 27.00 (ISBN 0-241-89995-8, Pub. by Hamish Hamilton England). David & Charles.

--Held Fast for England: G. A. Henty, Imperialist Boys' Writer. 224p. 1980. 27.00 (ISBN 0-241-10373-8, Pub. by Hamish Hamilton England). David & Charles.

--Modern Nigeria. 1977. pap. text ed. 8.95x (ISBN 0-582-64643-X). Longman.

Arnold, Hans. Foriegn Cultural Policy: A Survey from a German Point of View. 1979. pap. 18.50 (ISBN 0-85496-210-7). Dufour.

Arnold, Harry L., Jr. & Fasal, Paul. Leprosy: Diagnosis & Management. 2nd ed. (American Lecture Dermatology Ser.). (Illus.). 108p. 1973. 18.75 (ISBN 0-398-02681-5). C C Thomas.

Arnold, Henri. Jumble: That Scrambled Word Game, No. 16. 128p. (Orig.). 1980. pap. 1.50 (ISBN 0-451-09311-9, W9311, Sig). NAL.

Arnold, Henri & Lee, Bob. Jumble: No. 19. (Orig.). 1981. pap. price not set (ISBN 0-451-09907-9, Sig). NAL.

--Jumble: That Scrambled Word Game, No. 17. (Orig.). 1980. pap. 1.50 (ISBN 0-451-09492-1, W9492, Sig). NAL.

--Jumble: That Scrambled Word Game, No. 18. (Orig.). 1981. pap. 1.50 (ISBN 0-451-09740-8, W9240, Sig). NAL.

Arnold, Herbert, tr. see Scheurig, Bodo.

Arnold, J. M. Loligo Pealei. LC 74-77352. 1974. 7.00 (ISBN 0-685-52859-6). Marine Bio.

Arnold, James. All Drawn by Horses. LC 79-51087. (Illus.). 1979. 24.00 (ISBN 0-7153-7682-9). David & Charles.

--Farm Waggons & Carts. LC 76-57081. 1977. 22.50 (ISBN 0-7153-7330-7). David & Charles.

Arnold, Janet. Patterns of Fashion: 1660-1860, Vol. 1. 3rd rev. ed. LC 76-189820. (Illus.). 1977. text ed. 12.50x (ISBN 0-89676-026-X). Drama Bk.

--Patterns of Fashion: 1860-1940, Vol. 2. 3rd rev. ed. LC 76-189820. (Illus.). 1977. text ed. 12.50x (ISBN 0-89676-027-8). Drama Bk.

Arnold, Joan, ed. see American Academy of Religion, 1972 & 1973.

Arnold, Joanne M. Man-Killer. McCarthy, Patricia, ed. (Pal Paperbacks Ser., Kit A). (Illus., Orig.). 1974. pap. text ed. 1.25 (ISBN 0-8374-3474-2). Xerox Ed Pubns.

Arnold, John. Shooting the Executive Rapids: The First Year in a New Assignment. Newton, William R., ed. (Illus.). 288p. 1981. price not set (ISBN 0-07-002312-3, P&RB). McGraw.

Arnold, John, et al. Topics in Management Accounting. 256p. 1980. 33.00x (ISBN 0-86003-508-5, Pub. by Allan Pubs England); pap. 16.50x (ISBN 0-86003-609-X). State Mutual Bk.

Arnold, Joseph & Schank, Kenneth, eds. Exploratory Electricity. (gr. 9-12). 1960. text ed. 5.00 (ISBN 0-87345-276-3). McKnight.

Arnold, Julean & Myers, Ramon H. Commerical Handbook of China, 2 vols. LC 78-24800. (Modern Chinese Economy Ser.: Vol. 16). (Illus.). 1979. Set. lib. bdg. 110.00 (ISBN 0-8240-4264-6). Garland Pub.

Arnold, Julius. Student's Guide to Basic French. 2nd ed. 184p. (gr. 9-11). 1980. pap. text ed. 5.50 (ISBN 0-88334-021-6). Ind Sch Pr.

Arnold, Lois B. Preparing Young Children for Science: A Book of Activities. LC 79-26119. (Illus.). 128p. (Orig.). 1980. text ed. 11.95x (ISBN 0-8052-3740-2); pap. 6.95 (ISBN 0-8052-0641-8). Schocken.

Arnold, Lorna, jt. auth. see Gowing, Margaret.

Arnold, Ludwig. Stochastic Differential Equations: Theory & Applications. LC 73-22256. 1974. 30.95 (ISBN 0-471-03359-6, Pub. by Wiley-Interscience). Wiley.

Arnold, M. H. Agricultural Research for Development. 368p. 1976. 57.50 (ISBN 0-521-21051-8). Cambridge U Pr.

Arnold, Margot. The Villa on the Palatine. 1978. pap. 1.75 o.p. (ISBN 0-425-03656-1, Medallion). Berkley Pub.

Arnold, Mary E. & Reed, Mabel. In the Land of the Grasshopper Song: Two Women in the Klamath River Indian Country in 1908-09. LC 80-12556. (Illus.). iv, 330p. 1980. 17.95x (ISBN 0-8032-1804-4); pap. 5.95 (ISBN 0-8032-6703-7, BB 740, Bison). U of Nebr Pr.

Arnold, Matthew. Culture & Anarchy. 1932. 36.50 (ISBN 0-521-04061-2); pap. 7.95 (ISBN 0-521-09103-9, 103). Cambridge U Pr.

--Culture & Anarchy: An Essay in Political & Social Criticism. Gregor, Ian, ed. LC 79-95714. (Library of Literature Ser). 1971. pap. 6.95 (ISBN 0-672-60994-0, LL17). Bobbs.

--Poetical Works. Tinker, C. B. & Lowry, H. F., eds. (Standard Authors Ser). 1950. 24.95 (ISBN 0-19-254110-2). Oxford U Pr.

Arnold, Millard, ed. Steve Biko: Black Consciousness in South Africa. 1978. 12.95 o.p. (ISBN 0-394-50282-5). Random.

Arnold, Millard, ed. see Biko, Steve.

Arnold, Morris S., et al, eds. On the Laws & Customs of England: Essays in Honor of Samuel E. Thorne. LC 80-11909. (Studies in Legal History). xx, 426p. 1981. 25.00x (ISBN 0-8078-1434-2). U of NC Pr.

Arnold, Nellie D. The Interrelated Arts in Leisure: Perceiving & Creating. LC 75-30965. (Illus.). 224p. 1976. 10.50 o.p. (ISBN 0-8016-0328-5). Mosby.

Arnold, Oren. Story of Cattle Ranching. LC 68-22983. (Story of Science Ser.). (Illus.). (gr. 5-8). 1968. PLB 7.29 (ISBN 0-8178-4292-6). Harvey.

--What's in a Name: Famous Brand Names. LC 79-15555. 128p. (gr. 7 up). 1979. PLB 7.79 (ISBN 0-671-32932-4). Messner.

--Wit of the West. 1975. 2.95 (ISBN 0-685-59275-8). Nortex Pr.

Arnold, Oren & Hale, John P. Hot Irons. LC 71-188637. 1972. Repr. of 1940 ed. lib. bdg. 11.00x (ISBN 0-8154-0416-6). Cooper Sq.

Arnold, Rhodes. The Republic F-Eighty-Four: From Lead Sled to Super Hawg. (Illus.). 128p. 1981. pap. 9.95 (ISBN 0-89404-054-5). Aztex.

--Shooting Star, T-Bird & Starfire: A Famous Lockheed Family. (Illus.). 128p. 1981. pap. 12.95 (ISBN 0-89404-035-9). Aztex.

Arnold, Richard. Better Roller Skating: The Key to Improved Performance. (Illus.). (gr. 7 up). 1977. 8.95 (ISBN 0-8069-4106-5); PLB 8.29 (ISBN 0-8069-4107-3). Sterling.

--Come Sea Fishing with Me. 9.95x (ISBN 0-392-06448-0, SpS). Soccer.

Arnold, Richard, jt. auth. see Lamb, Pose.

Arnold, Richard D., jt. auth. see Lamb, Pose M.
Arnold, Robert E. Poisonous Plants. LC 77-84881. (Orig.). 1979. pap. 5.95 (ISBN 0-8467-0585-0, Pub. by Two Continents). Hippocrene Bks.
--What to Do About Bites & Stings of Venomous Animals. 128p. 1973. 9.95 (ISBN 0-02-503250-X). Macmillan.
Arnold, Robert F. Abacus in Modern Math. Date not set. price not set (ISBN 0-685-46523-3). Pacific Bks.
Arnold, Robert R., et al. Modern Data Processing. 3rd ed. LC 77-14941. 1978. 21.95 (ISBN 0-471-03361-8); instructors' manual (ISBN 0-471-03405-3); wkbk. 8.50x (ISBN 0-471-03362-6). Wiley.
Arnold, Steven F. The Theory of Linear Models & Multivariate Analysis. LC 80-23017. (Wiley Ser. in Probability & Math Statistics). 500p. 1981. 30.00 (ISBN 0-471-05065-2). Wiley.
Arnold, Thomas. Letters of Thomas Arnold the Younger: Eighteen Fifty to Nineteen Hundred. Bertram, James, ed. 336p. 1980. 38.00x (ISBN 0-19-647980-0). Oxford U Pr.
Arnold, Thurman W. The Bottlenecks of Business. LC 72-2363. (FDR & the Era of the New Deal Ser.). 352p. 1973. Repr. of 1940 ed. lib. bdg. 35.00 (ISBN 0-306-70470-6). Da Capo.
--Folklore of Capitalism. 1937. 29.50x o.p. (ISBN 0-686-51386-X). Elliots Bks.
Arnold, Tom & Vaden, Frank S. Invention Protection for Practicing Engineers. LC 73-133266. 1971. 10.95 (ISBN 0-8436-0312-7); pap. 8.95 (ISBN 0-8436-0313-5). CBI Pub.
Arnold, W. D. Oakfield, or Fellowship in the East. (The Victorian Library Ser.). 298p. 1973. Repr. of 1854 ed. text ed. 14.50x (ISBN 0-391-00275-9, Leicester). Humanities.
Arnold, William. Shadowland. 1979. pap. 2.25 (ISBN 0-515-05124-1). Jove Pubns.
Arnold, William D. Oakfield; or, Fellowship in the East, 1854. 2nd ed. Wolff, Robert L., ed. LC 75-1522. (Victorian Fiction Ser.). 1975. lib. bdg. 66.00 (ISBN 0-8240-1594-0). Garland Pub.
Arnold, William J. & Cole, James K., eds. Nebraska Symposium on Motivation, 1975: Conceptual Foundations of Psychology. LC 53-11655. (Nebraska Symposium on Motivation Ser.: Vol. 23). 1976. 22.50x (ISBN 0-8032-0618-6); pap. 11.95x (ISBN 0-8032-5624-8). U of Nebr Pr.
Arnold, William J., jt. ed. see Page, Monte M.
Arnold, Zach M. Observations on the Biology of Protozoan Gromia Oviformis Dujardin. (U. C. Publ. in Zoology: Vol. 100). 1973. pap. 9.50x (ISBN 0-520-09455-7). U of Cal Pr.
Arnold-Foster, Mark. World at War. (RL 8). 1974. pap. 1.95 (ISBN 0-451-05775-9, J5775, Sig). NAL.
Arnon, Isaac. Organisation & Administration of Agricultural Research. 1968. 44.60x (ISBN 0-444-20028-2). Intl Ideas.
Arnon-Ohanna, Yuval, jt. auth. see Yodfat, Aryeh.
Arnot, R. Page. The Miners: One Union, One Industry: A History of the National Union of Mineworkers 1939-46. (Illus.). 1979. text ed. 30.00x (ISBN 0-04-331074-5). Allen Unwin.
Arnot, William. The Lesser Parables of Our Lord. LC 80-8066. 464p. 1981. Repr. of 1884 ed. 10.95 (ISBN 0-8254-2121-7). Kregel.
--The Parables of Our Lord. LC 80-8065. 532p. 1981. Repr. of 1865 ed. 10.95 o.p. (ISBN 0-8254-2119-5). Kregel.
Arnott, Anne. The Secret Country of C. S. Lewis. (YA) 1975. 4.95 o.p. (ISBN 0-8028-3468-X). Eerdmans.
Arnott, James F. & Robinson, J. W. English Theatrical Literature Fifteen Fifty-Nine to Nineteen Hundred: A Bibliography Incorporating Lowe's Bibliographical Account. 1971. Repr. 45.00 (ISBN 0-8277-0415-1). British Bk Ctr.
Arnott, Peter. The Theater in Its Time: An Introduction. 1981. text ed. 15.95 (ISBN 0-316-05194-2). Little.
Arnott, Peter D., ed. & tr. see Aristophanes.
Arnoudt, Peter J. The Imitation of the Sacred Heart of Jesus. LC 79-112463. 1974. pap. 7.50 (ISBN 0-89555-012-1, 149). TAN Bks Pubs.
Arnould, E. J., ed. see Beaumarchais, Pierre.
Arnov, Boris. Water: Experiments to Understand It. (gr. 5 up). 1980. 6.95 (ISBN 0-688-41927-5); lib. bdg. 6.67 (ISBN 0-688-51927-X). Morrow.
Arnow, E. Earle. Food Power: A Doctor's Guide to Commonsense Nutrition. LC 75-185419. (Illus.). 320p. 1972. 14.95 (ISBN 0-911012-37-0). Nelson-Hall.
Arnow, H. S. The Dollmaker. 1962. pap. 1.50 o.s.i. (ISBN 0-02-016310-X, Collier). Macmillan.
Arnow, Harriet. The Dollmaker. (YA) 1972. pap. 2.95 (ISBN 0-380-00947-1, 53926, Bard). Avon.
Arnow, Harriette S. Dollmaker. 1967. 9.95 o.s.i. (ISBN 0-02-503360-3); large print ed 8.95 o.s.i. (ISBN 0-02-489370-6). Macmillan.
Arnow, L. Earle. Introduction to Laboratory Chemistry. 9th ed. (Illus.). 102p. 1976. pap. text ed. 8.50 (ISBN 0-8016-0325-0). Mosby.
Arnson, Cynthia & Klare, Michael T. Supplying Repression: U. S. Support for Authoritarian Regimes Abroad. rev. ed. 100p. 1981. pap. 4.95 (ISBN 0-89758-024-9). Inst Policy Stud.
Arnstein, Helene S. The Roots of Love: Helping Your Child Learn to Love in the First Three Years of Life. LC 74-17674. 240p. 1975. 8.95 o.p. (ISBN 0-672-51845-7). Bobbs.
--When a Parent Is Mentally Ill: What to Say to Your Child. 36p. 1974. pap. 1.25 (ISBN 0-686-12282-8). Jewish Bd Family.
Arnstein, Walter, ed. The Past Speaks: Sources & Problems in British History Since 1688. 448p. 1981. pap. text ed. 7.95 (ISBN 0-669-02919-X). Heath.
Arnstein, Walter L. see Smith, Lacey B.
Arntzen, Helmnt, et al, eds. Literatur Wissenschaft und Geschichtsphilosophie: Festschrift Fuer Wilhelm Emrich. 602p. 1975. 115.00x (ISBN 3-11-005726-3). De Gruyter.
Aron, Jean P., et al. Anthropologie Du Conscrit Francais D'apres les Comptes Numeriques et Sommaires Du Recrutement De L'armee, 1819-1826: Presentation Cartographique. (Civilisation et Societes: No. 28). 1972. 41.75 (ISBN 90-2797-167-6). Mouton.
Aron, Joan B. The Quest for Regional Cooperation: A Study of the New York Metropolitan Regional Council. LC 69-16738. (California Studies in Urbanization & Environmental Design). 1969. 19.50x (ISBN 0-520-01505-3). U of Cal Pr.
Aron, Joel D. Program Development Process, Pt. 1: The Individual Programmer. (IBM Systems Programming Ser.). (Illus.). 280p. 1974. text ed. 16.95 (ISBN 0-201-14451-4). A-W.
Aron, R. The Imperial Republic: The United States & the World 1945-1973. 1975. 9.95 (ISBN 0-13-451781-4). P-H.
Aron, Raymond. Main Currents in Sociological Thought: Durkhelm, Pareto & Weber, Vol. 2. LC 68-14142. 1970. pap. 3.95 (ISBN 0-385-01976-9, A600B, Anch). Doubleday.
--Main Currents in Sociological Thought: Montesquieu, Comte, Marx, Tocqueville, the Sociologists, & the Revolution of 1848, Vol. 1. LC 68-14142. 1968. pap. 3.95 (ISBN 0-385-08804-3, A600A, Anch). Doubleday.
--On War. Kilmartin, Terence, tr. 1968. pap. 3.45 (ISBN 0-393-00107-5, Norton Lib). Norton.
--Opium of the Intellectuals. 1962. pap. 3.45 o.p. (ISBN 0-393-00106-7, Norton Lib). Norton.
--Politics & History: Selected Essays. Conant, Miriam B., ed. LC 78-54122. 1978. 19.95 (ISBN 0-02-901000-4). Free Pr.
Aronoff, Craig, et al. Getting Your Message Across: A Practical Guide to Business Communication. (Illus.). 500p. 1981. text ed. 13.95 (ISBN 0-8299-0362-3). West Pub.
Aronoff, Myron J. Frontiertown: The Politics of Community Building in Israel. 306p. 1974. text ed. 17.00x (ISBN 0-7190-0574-4). Humanities.
Aronoff, Myron J., ed. Freedom & Constraint: A Memorial Tribute to Max Gluckman. (Illus.). 1976. pap. text ed. 22.25x (ISBN 90-232-1392-0). Humanities.
Aronoff, S. Techniques of Radiobiochemistry. (Illus.). 1967. Repr. of 1956 ed. 13.75 o.s.i. (ISBN 0-02-840460-2). Hafner.
Aronofsky, Julius S., et al. Managerial Planning with Linear Programming: In Process Industry Operations. LC 78-2848. 1978. 41.95 (ISBN 0-471-03360-X). Ronald Pr.
Aronowicz, Annette, et al, trs. see Dumezil, Georges.
Aronowitz, Stanley. Class, Politics, & Culture. 256p. 1981. 25.95 (ISBN 0-03-059031-0). Praeger.
Arons, Arnold. The Various Language: An Inquiry Approach to the Physical Sciences. (Illus.). 1977. 14.95x (ISBN 0-19-502147-9). Oxford U Pr.
Aronsfeld, C. C., ed. & intro. by see Abbott, G. F.
Aronson. The Scorecard. 1979. Set Of 5. pap. 6.95 (ISBN 0-7216-1409-4). Dryden Pr.
Aronson, Arnold E. Clincal Voice Disorders. 1980. 19.50. Thieme Stratton.
Aronson, Elliot. Readings About the Social Animal. 2nd ed. LC 76-22435. (Psychology Ser.). (Illus.). 1977. text ed. 18.75x o.p. (ISBN 0-7167-0380-7); pap. text ed. 7.75x o.p. (ISBN 0-7167-0379-3). W H Freeman.
--The Social Animal. 3rd ed. LC 79-27721. (Psychology Ser.). (Illus.). 1980. text ed. 15.95x (ISBN 0-7167-1229-6); pap. text ed. 7.95x (ISBN 0-7167-1230-X); test & study questions avail. W H Freeman.
Aronson, Elliot, ed. Readings About the Social Animal. 3rd ed. LC 80-18208. (Psychology Ser.). (Illus.). 1981. text ed. 19.95x (ISBN 0-7167-1267-9); pap. text ed. 9.95x (ISBN 0-7167-1268-7). W H Freeman.
Aronson, Harvey & McGrady, Mike. Establishment of Innocence. 1977. pap. 1.95 o.p. (ISBN 0-425-03288-4). Berkley Pub.
Aronson, Harvey B. Love & Sympathy in Theravada Buddhism. 1980. 11.00x (ISBN 0-8364-0627-3, Pub. by Motilal Banarsidass). South Asia Bks.
Aronson, J. Richard, jt. auth. see Maxwell, James A.
Aronson, J. Richard & Schwartz, Eli, eds. Management Policies in Local Government Finance. LC 75-9500. (Municipal Management Ser.). 1975. 20.00 o.p. (ISBN 0-87326-000-7). Intl City Mgt.
Aronson, James, jt. auth. see Belfrage, Cedric.
Aronson, Jonathan D., ed. Debt & the Less Developed Countries. (Special Studies in National Security & Defense Policy). 1979. lib. bdg. 28.50x (ISBN 0-89158-370-X). Westview.
Aronson, Lester R., et al, eds. Development & Evolution of Behavior, Essays in Memory of T. C. Schneirla. LC 76-84600. (Illus.). 1970. text ed. 31.95x (ISBN 0-7167-0921-X). W H Freeman.
Aronson, Marvin L., jt. ed. see Wolberg, Lewis R.
Aronson, Nicole. Mademoiselle De Scudery. (World Authors Ser.: No. 441 France). 1978. 12.50 (ISBN 0-8057-6278-7). Twayne.
Aronson, Robert H. & Weckstein, Donald T. Professional Responsibility in a Nutshell. LC 80-15007. (Nutshell Ser.). 448p. 1980. pap. text ed. 6.95 (ISBN 0-8299-2095-1). West Pub.
Aronson, S. M. & Volk, B. W., eds. Inborn Disorders of Sphingolipid Metabolism. 1967. 64.00 (ISBN 0-08-012038-5). Pergamon.
Aronson, Sam. Everyone's Guide to Opening Doors by Telephone. 2nd ed. (Illus.). 338p. 1981. 17.95 (ISBN 0-686-27230-7). S Aronson.
Aronson, Theo. Victoria & Disraeli: The Making of a Romantic Partnership. 1978. 12.95 (ISBN 0-02-503490-1). Macmillan.
Aronson, Virginia & Fitzgerald, Barbara. Guidebook for Nutrition Counselors. 448p. 1980. 19.50 (ISBN 0-8158-0387-7). Chris Mass.
Aronstein, Michael, jt. auth. see Rankin, Judy.
Arora, David. Mushrooms Demystified. LC 79-8513. (Illus.). 1979. 18.95 (ISBN 0-89815-010-8); pap. 11.95 (ISBN 0-89815-009-4). Ten Speed Pr.
Arora, Jasbir S., jt. auth. see Haug, Edward J.
Arora, S. P. Office Organisation & Management. 1980. text ed. 18.95x (ISBN 0-7069-0795-7, Pub. by Vikas India). Advent Bk.
Arora, Shirley L. Proverbial Comparisons & Related Expressions in Spanish. (Publications in Folklore & Mythology Ser.: Vol.29). 1977. 20.00x (ISBN 0-520-09552-9). U of Cal Pr.
--Proverbial Comparisons in Ricardo Palma's Tradiciones Peruanas. (U. C. Publ. in Folklore Studies: Vol. 16). 1966. pap. 11.00x (ISBN 0-520-09138-8). U of Cal Pr.
Aros, Andrew A. Actor's Guide to the Talkies, Nineteen Sixty-Five to Nineteen Seventy-Four. LC 77-21589. 1977. 32.50 (ISBN 0-8108-1052-2). Scarecrow.
--A Title Guide to the Talkies, Nineteen Sixty-Four to Nineteen Seventy-Four. LC 76-40451. 1977. 15.00 (ISBN 0-8108-0976-1). Scarecrow.
Arp, Claudia, jt. auth. see Dillow, Linda.
Arp, Gerald. Tropical Gardening Along the Gulf Coast. LC 78-53815. (Illus.). 1978. pap. 3.95 (ISBN 0-88415-883-7). Pacesetter Pr.
Arpaci, Vedat S. Conduction Heat Transfer. 1966. 23.95 (ISBN 0-201-00359-7). A-W.
Arpan, Jeffrey S., et al. The U. S. Apparel Industry: International Challenge - Domestic Response. (Research Monograph: No. 88). 1981. pap. 14.95 (ISBN 0-88406-141-8). Ga St U Busn Pub.
Arpel, Adrien. How to Look Ten Years Younger. 1981. pap. 8.95 (ISBN 0-446-97823-X). Warner Bks.
Arpin, Gary Q. The Poetry of John Berryman. (National University Publications Literary Criticism Ser.). 1977. 8.95 o.p. (ISBN 0-8046-9205-X). Kennikat.
Arrabal, Fernando. Guernica & Other Plays. Wright, Barbara, tr. from Fr. Incl. Labyrinth; Tricycle; Picnic on the Battlefield. 1969. pap. 4.95 (ISBN 0-394-17318-X, E521, Ever). Grove.
Arrabel, Fernando. Burial of the Sardine. 1980. pap. 4.95 (ISBN 0-7145-0146-8). Riverrun NY.
Arrastia, Cecelio. Itinerario De la Pasion: Meditacion De la Semana Santa. 1978. pap. 2.50 (ISBN 0-311-43036-8). Casa Bautista.
Arratia, Alejandro & Hamilton, Carlos D. Diez Cuentos Hispanoamericanos. (Span). 1958. pap. 5.95x (ISBN 0-19-500818-9). Oxford U Pr.
Arredondo, Larry A. Getting Started in Telecommunications Management. 1980. softcover 30.00 (ISBN 0-936648-04-X). Telecom Lib.
Arreola, Allysia J. Elephant Eater. Kamei, Marlene, ed. 12p. (Orig.). 1977. pap. 2.00 (ISBN 0-935684-00-X). Plumbers Ink.
Arreola, Juan J. Confabulario & Other Inventions. Schade, George D., tr. LC 64-13315. (Pan American Paperbacks Ser.). 264p. 1964. 9.95x (ISBN 0-292-73196-5); pap. 5.00x (ISBN 0-292-71030-5). U of Tex Pr.
Arrick, Fran. Steffie Can't Come Out to Play. LC 78-4423. (gr. 8 up). 1978. 8.95 (ISBN 0-87888-135-2). Bradbury Pr.
--Tunnel Vision. LC 79-25939. (YA) (gr. 8 up). 1980. 9.95 (ISBN 0-87888-163-8). Bradbury Pr.
Arridge, R. G. Mechanics of Polymers. (Illus.). 276p. 1975. 28.00x (ISBN 0-19-859136-5). Oxford U Pr.
Arrighi, Frances E., et al, eds. see M. D. Anderson Symposia on Fundamental Cancer Research, 33rd.
Arrighi, Mel. Turkish White. LC 76-54620. 1977. 7.95 o.p. (ISBN 0-15-191390-0). HarBraceJ.
--Turkish White. 1978. pap. 1.95 o.s.i. (ISBN 0-515-04549-7). Jove Pubns.
Arrigoni, Patricia. Making the Most of Marin. (Illus., Orig.). 1981. pap. 7.95 (ISBN 0-89141-108-9). Presidio Pr.
Arrington, Fred. History of Dickens County: Ranches & Rolling Plains. 17.95 (ISBN 0-685-48795-4). Nortex Pr.
Arrington, French L. New Testament Exegesis: Examples. 1977. 7.25 (ISBN 0-8191-0108-7). U Pr of Amer.
--Paul's Aeon Theology in First Corinthians. 1977. pap. text ed. 9.00x (ISBN 0-8191-0119-2). U Pr of Amer.
Arrington, George E., Jr. History of Ophthalmology. LC 58-13433. 1959. 4.00 o.p. (ISBN 0-910922-10-1). MD Pubns.
Arrington, Leonard J. Great Basin Kingdom: An Economic History of the Latter-Day Saints, 1830-1900. LC 58-12961. (Illus.). 1966. pap. 6.95 (ISBN 0-8032-5006-1, BB342, Bison). U of Nebr Pr.
Arrington, Leonard J., jt. auth. see Cornwall, Rebecca.
Arriola, Lewis. Vengenance of God. 240p. 1981. 9.50 (ISBN 0-682-49687-1). Exposition.
Arrow, K. J. & Hurwicz, L., eds. Studies in Resource Allocation Process. LC 76-9171. (Illus.). 1977. 47.50 (ISBN 0-521-21522-6). Cambridge U Pr.
Arrow, Kenneth J. & Kalt, Joseph P. Petroleum Price Regulation: Should We Decontrol? 1979. pap. 4.25. Am Enterprise.
Arrow, William. Return to the Planet of the Apes, No.2. (Orig.). 1976. pap. 1.50 o.p. (ISBN 0-345-25167-9). Ballantine.
--Return to the Planet of the Apes: Man, the Hunted Animal, No.3. (YA) 1976. pap. 1.50 o.p. (ISBN 0-345-25211-X). Ballantine.
Arrowood, Clinton, jt. auth. see Elliott, Donald.
Arrowsmith, John P. Art of Instructing the Infant Deaf & Dumb: Including De L'Epee's Method of Educating Mutes. (Contributions to the History of Psychology B, Psychometrics & Educational Psychology Ser.). 1980. Repr. of 1819 ed. 30.00 (ISBN 0-89093-319-7). U Pubns Amer.
Arrowsmith, William, ed. see Aeschylus.
Arrowsmith, William, ed. see Aristophanes.
Arrowsmith, William see Euripides.
Arrowsmith, William, tr. see Euripides.
Arrowsmith, William, tr. see Petronius.
Arroyo, Anita. America En Su Literatura. 2nd ed. LC 77-3041. (Illus.). 1978. 15.00 (ISBN 0-8477-3175-8); pap. text ed. 12.00 (ISBN 0-8477-3182-0). U of PR Pr.
--Narrativa Hispanoamericana Actual: America y Sus Problemas. LC 79-19468. (Mente y Palabra Ser.). v, 517p. 1980. 20.00 (ISBN 0-8477-0563-3); pap. 15.00 (ISBN 0-8477-0563-3). U of PR Pr.
Arroyo, Stephen. Astrology, Karma & Transformation: The Inner Dimensions of the Birthchart. LC 76-21588. (Illus.). 1978. 10.95 (ISBN 0-916360-04-0); pap. 7.95 (ISBN 0-916360-03-2). CRCS Pubns NV.
--Astrology, Psychology & the Four Elements. LC 75-27828. 208p. (Orig.). 1975. 9.95 (ISBN 0-916360-02-4); pap. 6.95 (ISBN 0-916360-01-6). CRCS Pubns NV.
--Relationships & Life Cycles: Modern Dimensions of Astrology. LC 79-53979. 1979. pap. 6.95 (ISBN 0-916360-12-1). CRCS Pubns NV.
Arrupe, Pedro. Justice with Faith Today: Selected Letters & Addresses--II. Aixala, Jerome, ed. LC 80-81055. 336p. 1980. 8.00 (ISBN 0-912422-51-3); pap. 7.00 (ISBN 0-912422-50-5). Inst Jesuit.
Arsan, Emmanuelle. Emmanuelle One. Bair, Lowell, tr. LC 78-139255. 1980. pap. 2.95 (ISBN 0-394-17657-X, B439, BC). Grove.
--Emmanuelle Two. Hollo, Anselm, tr. from Fr. LC 74-24995. 1974. 3.25 (ISBN 0-394-17891-2, B453, BC). Grove.
--Illustrated Emmanuelle. LC 80-999. 144p. 1980. 25.00 (ISBN 0-8021-0206-9, GP837); pap. 9.95 (ISBN 0-8021-4316-4, E765 EVER). Grove.

Arsanes. Orations of Arsanes Agaynst Philip: Of the Embassadors of Venice. LC 70-26068. (English Experience Ser.: No. 233). 164p. Repr. of 1560 ed. 14.00 (ISBN 90-221-0233-5). Walter J Johnson.

Arsanjani, Mahnoush H. International Regulation of Internal Resources: A Study of Law & Policy. LC 80-21169. 1981. write for info. (ISBN 0-8139-0879-5). U Pr of Va.

Arsdel, Wallace B. Van see Van Arsdel, Wallace B., et al.

Arsdell, Paul M. Van see Van Arsdell, Paul M.

Arsenyev, Vladimir. With Dersu the Hunter. LC 65-25971. (gr. 6-9). 3.95 o.p. (ISBN 0-8076-0325-2). Braziller.

Arsove, Maynard & Leutwiler, Heinz. Algebraic Potential Theory. LC 79-24384. (Memoirs of the American Mathematical Society Ser.). 1980. 7.60 (ISBN 0-8218-2226-8). Am Math.

Arstila, A. U., jt. ed. see Trump, Benjamin F.

Arsuaga De Vila, Maria. Manual De Espanol. rev. ed. LC 80-36752. 253p. 1980. Set. write for info. (ISBN 0-8477-3177-4). Vol. 1,pt. 1 (ISBN 0-8477-3195-2). Vol. 1,pt. 2 (ISBN 0-8477-3196-0). U of PR Pr.

--Manual De Espanol, 2 pts, Vol. 1. new ed. 1980. Pt. 1. pap. 5.60 (ISBN 0-8477-3178-2); Pt. 2. pap. 5.60. U of PR Pr.

Art Directors Club of N. Y. & Copy Club of N. Y. The Fifty-Second Annual of Advertising, Editorial & Television Art & Design with the 13th Annual Copy Awards. (Illus.). 576p. 1973. slipcased 29.95 o.p. (ISBN 0-8230-1905-5, Pub. by Art Directors Club). Watson-Guptill.

Art Directors Club of New York. The Fifty-Fifth Annual of Advertising, Editorial & Television Art & Design. (Illus., Orig.). 1976. 29.95 o.p. (ISBN 0-8230-1908-X, Pub. by Art Directors Club). Watson-Guptill.

--The Fifty-Ninth Art Directors Annual. Solomon, Miriam L., ed. (Illus.). 672p. 1980. 34.95 (ISBN 0-937414-00-X). ADC NY.

Art Gallery of Ontario. Exposure. 1976. 29.95 o.p. (ISBN 0-688-03052-1). Morrow.

Art Institute of Chicago & Joachim, Harold. French Drawings & Sketchbooks of the Eighteenth Century. LC 77-20132. 1978. write for info. (ISBN 0-226-68795-3, Chicago Visual Lib) (ISBN 0-685-84958-9). U of Chicago Pr.

--Italian Drawings of the Fifteenth, Sixteenth, & Seventeenth Centuries. LC 79-14276. (Chicago Visual Library: No. 31). (Illus.). 1979. text ed. 80.00 incl. microfiche (ISBN 0-226-68801-1). U of Chicago Pr.

Art Institute of Chicago & Speyer, A. James. Twentieth Century European Paintings. (Illus.). 112p. 1981. incl fiche 60.00x (ISBN 0-226-68804-6). U of Chicago Pr.

Art, Robert J. & Waltz, Kenneth N., eds. The Use of Force: International Politics & Foreign Policy. 2nd ed. 575p. 1981. write for info. U Pr of Amer.

Artandi, Susan B. An Introduction to Computers in Information Science. 2nd ed. LC 68-12643. (Illus.). 1972. 10.00 (ISBN 0-8108-0485-9). Scarecrow.

Artaud, Antonin. Artaud: Four Texts. Eshleman, Clayton, tr. from Fr. (Illus.). 80p. 1981. 9.95 (ISBN 0-915572-57-5); pap. 4.50 (ISBN 0-915572-56-7). Panjandrum.

--Collected Works. Corti, V. & Hamilton, A., trs. Incl. Vol. 1. Correspondence with J. Riviere-Umbilical Limbo-Nerve Scales- Art & Death-Cup & Ball-Seven Letters-Unpublished Prose & Poetry. 247p. 1968. 17.50x (ISBN 0-7145-0169-7); Vol. 2. The Alfred Jarry Theatre-Two Stage Scenarios & Two Production Plans-Reviews-On Literature & the Plastic Arts. (Illus.). 240p. 1971. 13.50x (ISBN 0-7145-0171-9); Vol. 3. Scenarios-On the Cinema-Interviews-Letters. (Illus.). 255p. 1972. 15.00x (ISBN 0-7145-0778-4); Vol. 4. The Theatre & Its Double-The Cenci-Documents. 1974. 15.00x (ISBN 0-7145-0622-2). LC 76-369595. (French Surrealism Ser.). Intl Pubns Serv.

--Death of Satan. 1980. pap. 3.95 (ISBN 0-7145-1085-8). Riverrun NY.

--The Death of Satan. Hamilton, Alastair, tr. 1980. pap. 3.95 (ISBN 0-7145-1085-8). Riverrun NY.

--The Peyote Dance. Weaver, Helen, tr. from Fr. LC 75-26919. 105p. 1976. 7.95 o.p. (ISBN 0-374-23090-0); pap. 2.45 (ISBN 0-374-51100-4). FS&G.

Arth, Marvin & Ashmore, Helen. Newsletter Editor's Desk Book. 2nd rev. ed. LC 80-83042. (Illus.). 168p. (gr. 11-12). 1980. pap. 9.95 (ISBN 0-938270-00-1). Kindinger.

--The Newsletter Editor's Desk Book. 2nd, rev. ed. 168p. (Orig.). 14.95 (ISBN 0-938270-00-1); pap. 8.95 (ISBN 0-686-28910-2). Kindinger.

--The Newsletter Editor's Deskbook. 1981. 14.95 (ISBN 0-938270-01-X). Kindinger.

Arthanari, Subramanvam & Dodge, Yadolah. Mathematical Programming in Statistics. LC 80-21637. (Probability & Math Statistics Ser.: Applied Probability & Statistics). 375p. 1981. 25.00 (ISBN 0-471-08073-X, Pub. by Wiley-Interscience). Wiley.

Arther, Richard O. The Scientific Investigator. (Illus.). 248p. 1976. pap. 18.75 photocopy edition, spiral (ISBN 0-398-00055-7). C C Thomas.

Arthey, V. D. Quality of Horticultural Products. 1975. 21.95 (ISBN 0-470-03425-4). Halsted Pr.

Arthos, John. The Status of the Humanities. LC 80-84732. 1981. 12.50 (ISBN 0-686-68870-8). Philos Lib.

Arthur. The Mystery Ofthe Screaming Clock. (gr. 5-6). Date not set. pap. cancelled (ISBN 0-590-30330-9, Schol Pap). Schol Bk Serv.

Arthur, Budd, jt. auth. see Arthur, Burt.

Arthur, Burt. The Black Rider. 1978. pap. 1.25 (ISBN 0-505-51258-0). Tower Bks.

--Gunsmoke in Paradise. 1978. pap. 1.25 (ISBN 0-505-51246-7). Tower Bks.

--Lead Hungry Lobos. 1978. pap. 1.25 (ISBN 0-505-51255-6). Tower Bks.

--Outlaw Fury. 1976. pap. 0.95 o.p. (ISBN 0-685-72359-3, LB385NK, Leisure Bks). Nordon Pubns.

--Return of the Texan. 1975. pap. 0.95 o.p. (ISBN 0-685-61048-9, LB321, Leisure Bks). Nordon Pubns.

Arthur, Burt & Arthur, Budd. Ride a Crooked Trail. 1979. pap. 1.25 (ISBN 0-505-51389-7). Tower Bks.

--The Saga of Denny McCune. 1979. pap. 1.25 (ISBN 0-505-51397-8). Tower Bks.

Arthur, Chris. The Dialectic of Revolution. (Philosophy Now Ser.). 1980. text ed. write for info. (ISBN 0-391-00841-2); pap. text ed. write for info. (ISBN 0-391-00842-0). Humanities.

Arthur D. Little, Inc., et al. Civil Aviation Development: A Policy & Operation Analysis. LC 70-185656. (Special Studies in U.S. Economic, Social & Political Issues). 1980. Repr. of 1972 ed. 39.50x (ISBN 0-89197-697-3). Irvington.

Arthur D. Little Inc., et al. Corporate Director. LC 75-4838. 1975. 19.95 (ISBN 0-8436-0739-4). CBI Pub.

Arthur, Elizabeth. Island Sojourn. LC 79-2611. (Illus.). 1980. 9.95 (ISBN 0-06-010156-3, HarpT). Har-Row.

Arthur, J. Morality & Moral Controversies. 1981. pap. 10.95 (ISBN 0-13-601278-7). P-H.

Arthur, Joe, jt. auth. see Arthur, Pat.

Arthur, John. Realism Photo-Realism. LC 80-83113. (Illus.). 123p. 1980. 25.00 (ISBN 0-86659-002-1); pap. 16.50 (ISBN 0-86659-003-X). Philbrook.

Arthur, Michael, jt. auth. see Leiner, Katherine.

Arthur, Pat & Arthur, Joe. The Bananas B-Guide to School Survival. 96p. (Orig.). (gr. 7 up). 1980. pap. 1.25 (ISBN 0-590-30028-8, Schol Pap). Schol Bk Serv.

Arthur, Phyllis. Goddess in the Home. (YA) 1971. 5.95 (ISBN 0-685-03334-1, Avalon). Bouregy.

Arthur, Robert. Alfred Hitchcock & the Three Investigators in the Mystery of the Fiery Eye. LC 77-28860. (Three Investigators Ser.: No. 7). (Illus.). (gr. 4-8). 1967. 2.95 (ISBN 0-394-81661-7, BYR); PLB 5.39 (ISBN 0-394-91661-1); pap. 1.95 (ISBN 0-394-83770-3). Random.

--Alfred Hitchcock & the Three Investigators in the Mystery of the Green Ghost. Hitchcock, Alfred, ed. (Three Investigators Ser.: No. 4). (Illus.). (gr. 4-8). 1965. 2.95 (ISBN 0-394-81228-X, BYR); PLB 5.39 (ISBN 0-394-91228-4); pap. 1.95 (ISBN 0-394-84258-8). Random.

--Alfred Hitchcock & the Three Investigators in the Mystery of the Silver Spider. (Three Investigators Ser.: No. 8). (Illus.). (gr. 4-8). 1967. 2.95 (ISBN 0-394-81663-3, BYR); PLB 5.39 (ISBN 0-394-91663-8); pap. 1.95 (ISBN 0-394-83771-1). Random.

--Alfred Hitchcock & the Three Investigators in the Mystery of the Screaming Clock. Hitchcock, Alfred, ed. LC 68-23676. (Three Investigators Ser.: No. 9). (Illus.). (gr. 4-7). 1968. 2.95 (ISBN 0-394-81288-3, BYR); PLB 5.39 (ISBN 0-394-91288-8); pap. 1.95 (ISBN 0-394-83772-X). Random.

--Alfred Hitchcock & the Three Investigators in the Mystery of the Stuttering Parrot. Hitchcock, Alfred, ed. (Three Investigators Ser.: No. 1). (Illus.). (gr. 4-8). 1964. 2.95 (ISBN 0-394-81243-3, BYR); PLB 5.39 (ISBN 0-394-91243-8); pap. 1.95 (ISBN 0-394-83767-3). Random.

--Alfred Hitchcock & the Three Investigators in the Mystery of the Talking Skull. Hitchcock, Alfred, ed. LC 69-20274. (Three Investigators Ser.: No. 11). (Illus.). (gr. 4-7). 1969. 2.95 (ISBN 0-394-81380-4, BYR); PLB 5.39 (ISBN 0-394-91380-9); pap. 1.95 (ISBN 0-394-83774-6). Random.

--Alfred Hitchcock & the Three Investigators in the Mystery of the Vanishing Treasure. Hitchcock, Alfred, ed. (Three Investigators Ser.: No. 5). (Illus.). (gr. 4-8). 1966. 2.95 (ISBN 0-394-81550-5, BYR); PLB 5.39 (ISBN 0-394-91550-X); pap. 1.95 (ISBN 0-394-84452-1). Random.

--Alfred Hitchcock & the Three Investigators in the Mystery of the Whispering Mummy. Hitchcock, Alfred, ed. (Three Investigators Ser.: No. 3). (Illus.). (gr. 4-8). 1965. 2.95 (ISBN 0-394-81220-4, BYR); PLB 5.39 (ISBN 0-394-91220-9); pap. 1.95 (ISBN 0-394-83768-1). Random.

--Alfred Hitchcock & the Three Investigators in the Secret of Skeleton Island. Hitchcock, Alfred, ed. (Three Investigators Ser.: No. 6). (Illus.). (gr. 4-9). 1966. 2.95 (ISBN 0-394-81552-1, BYR); PLB 5.39 (ISBN 0-394-91552-6); pap. 1.95 (ISBN 0-394-83769-X). Random.

--Alfred Hitchcock & the Three Investigators in the Secret of Terror Castle. Hitchcock, Alfred, ed. (Three Investigators Ser.: No. 2). (Illus.). (gr. 4-8). 1964. 2.95 (ISBN 0-394-81241-7, BYR); PLB 5.39 (ISBN 0-394-91241-1); pap. 1.95 (ISBN 0-394-83766-5). Random.

Arthur, Robert P., jt. auth. see Weinstock, E. B.

Arthur, Ruth M. Miss Ghost. LC 79-63117. (gr. 5-9). 1979. 7.95 (ISBN 0-689-30702-0). Atheneum.

Arthur, William. Etymological Dictionary of Family & Christian Names. LC 68-17911. 1969. Repr. of 1857 ed. 24.00 (ISBN 0-8103-3107-1). Gale.

--Italy in Transition. 469p. 1980. Repr. of 1860 ed. lib. bdg. 50.00 (ISBN 0-89760-005-3). Telegraph Bks.

Arthurs, A. M. Complementary Variational Principles. 2nd ed. (Mathematical Monographs). 160p. 1980. 49.00 (ISBN 0-19-853532-5). Oxford U Pr.

--Probability Theory. (Library of Mathematics). 1965. pap. 4.50 (ISBN 0-7100-4359-7). Routledge & Kegan.

Arthurs, A. M. & Bhagavan, M. R., eds. Functional Integration & Its Applications. 300p. 1975. 45.00x (ISBN 0-19-853346-2). Oxford U Pr.

Arthus, Gothard. Dialogues in the English & Malaiane Languages. Spalding, A., tr. LC 74-80160. (English Experience Ser.: No. 640). 1974. Repr. of 1614 ed. 8.00 (ISBN 90-221-0640-3). Walter J Johnson.

Artin, E. Geometric Algebra: Pure & Applied Mathematics. (A Wiley-Interscience Ser. of Texts, Monographs & Tracts). 214p. 1957. 26.50 (ISBN 0-470-03432-7, Pub. by Wiley-Interscience). Wiley.

Artis, M. J., ed. Essays in Economic Analysis. Nobay, A. R. LC 75-46207. (Illus.). 422p. 1976. 49.50 (ISBN 0-521-21154-9). Cambridge U Pr.

Artis, M. J., ed. see Association of University Teachers of Economics, Edinburgh, 1976.

Artis, Vicki K. Pajama Walking. (gr. k-3). 1981. 6.95 (ISBN 0-395-30343-5). HM.

Artley, Sterl. F Book of Readings for Teaching Reading in Elementary School. 1974. pap. text ed. 6.95x (ISBN 0-87543-114-3). Lucas.

--Inventory of Teacher Knowledge of Reading. (Lucas Text Ser). text ed. 1.35x saddle stitched (ISBN 0-87543-102-X). Lucas.

--Study Guide for Teaching Reading in the Elementary Schools. rev. ed. 1976. pap. text ed. 4.25x (ISBN 0-87543-130-5). Lucas.

--Word Perception for Teachers. 3rd ed. (Lucas Text Ser). 1978. text ed. 2.75x saddle stitched (ISBN 0-87543-141-0). Lucas.

Artusi, Pellegrino. Italianissimo: Italian Cooking at Its Best. Abbott, Elisabeth, tr. from It. 552p. 1975. 12.50 o.p. (ISBN 0-87140-596-2). Liveright.

Artwick, B. Microcomputer Interfacing. 1980. 21.95 (ISBN 0-13-580902-9). P-H.

Artz, Curtis P., et al. Brief Textbook of Surgery. LC 75-19839. (Illus.). 1976. text ed. 19.95 o.p. (ISBN 0-7216-1415-9). Saunders.

Artz, Frederick B. The Mind of the Middle Ages: An Historical Survey: A. D. 200-1500. 3rd rev. ed. LC 79-16259. 1980. lib. bdg. 20.00x (ISBN 0-226-02839-9); pap. 7.50 (ISBN 0-226-02840-2, P859, Phoen). U of Chicago Pr.

Artz, Robert J. Experimental Chemistry: An Introduction. (Illus.). 311p. 1980. instructor's manual free (ISBN 0-316-05279-5); lab manual 7.95 (ISBN 0-316-05278-7). Little.

Artz, Thomas & Haley, Ruth M. Helping Your Child Appreciate the Mass & the Sacraments. 144p. (Orig.). 1980. pap. 2.95 (ISBN 0-89243-132-6). Liguori Pubns.

Artzner, James H. The Black Minute. 170p. (Orig.). 1980. 10.95 (ISBN 0-938936-00-X); pap. 4.95 (ISBN 0-938936-01-8). Daring Pr.

Aruego, Ariane, jt. auth. see Aruego, Jose.

Aruego, Jose & Aruego, Ariane. Cuento De un Cocodrilo. Palacios, Agentina, tr. from Span. (gr. k-3). 1979. pap. 1.95 (ISBN 0-590-10310-5, Schol Pap). Schol Bk Serv.

Aruego, Jose & Dewey, Ariane. We Hide, You Seek. LC 78-13638. (Illus.). (gr. k-3). 1979. 7.95 (ISBN 0-688-80201-X); PLB 7.63 (ISBN 0-688-84201-1). Greenwillow.

Aruego, Jose, jt. auth. see Kraus, Robert.

Arundale, George S. Kundalini. 1972. 3.50 (ISBN 0-8356-7102-X). Theos Pub Hse.

Arundel, Honor. A Family Failing. LC 72-3231. 160p. (gr. 6 up). 1972. 7.95 o.p. (ISBN 0-525-66256-1). Elsevier-Nelson.

Arundel, Jocelyn. Little Stripe. (gr. 2-4). 1967. 4.95g o.s.i. (ISBN 0-8038-4245-7). Hastings.

Arup, H. & Parkins, R. N. Stress Corrosion Research. (NATO Advanced Study Institute Ser.). 279p. 1979. 30.00x (ISBN 90-286-0647-5). Sijthoff & Noordhoff.

Arup, Jens see Ibsen, Henrik.

Arvey, Richard D. Fairness in Selecting Employees. LC 78-74678. 1979. pap. text ed. 6.95 (ISBN 0-201-00070-9). A-W.

Arvidson, Lucy. Alaawich. 1978. 2.00 (ISBN 0-686-25512-7). Malki Mus Pr.

Arvidson, Paul W. A New Look at Earthquakes. 1979. 9.55 o.p. (ISBN 0-914330-18-7). Pioneer Pub Co.

Arvin, Jack. The Footsteps of Jesus. (Ser. Outlines). 4.95 (ISBN 0-89315-053-3). Lambert Bk.

Arvine, Kazlitt. Cyclopedia of Anecdotes of Literature. LC 67-14020. 1967. Repr. of 1851 ed. 22.00 (ISBN 0-8103-3296-5). Gale.

Arvy, L. Histoenzymology of the Endocrine Gland. 1971. 64.00 (ISBN 0-08-015649-5). Pergamon.

Arwas, Victor. Art Deco. (Illus.). 304p. 1980. 45.00 (ISBN 0-686-62692-3, 0691-0). Abrams.

Arwikar, J. S. & Mishra, C. B. Heat Engines Through Theory & Examples. pap. 15.00x (ISBN 0-210-31219-X). Asia.

Arx, J. A. Von. Genera of Fungi Sporulating in Pure Culture. 2nd ed. (Illus.). 1974. 50.00 o.p. (ISBN 3-7682-0693-9). Lubrecht & Cramer.

Arx, William S. Von see Von Arx, William S.

Ary, Sheila & Gregory, Mary. Oxford Book of Wild Flowers. (Illus.). 1970. 27.50 (ISBN 0-19-910001-2). Oxford U Pr.

Arya, Atam P. Elementary Modern Physics. new ed. LC 73-1466. 1974. text ed. 18.95 (ISBN 0-201-00304-X). A-W.

Arya, J. C. & Lardner, R. W. Mathematics for the Biological Sciences. (Illus.). 1979. 22.95 (ISBN 0-13-562439-8). P-H.

Arya, Jagdish C. & Lardner, Robin W. Applied Calculus for Business & Economics. (Illus.). 528p. 1981. text ed. 18.95 (ISBN 0-13-039255-3). P-H.

--Mathematical Analysis for Business & Economics. (Illus.). 768p. 1981. text ed. 19.95 (ISBN 0-13-561019-2). P-H.

Arzans de Orsua y Vela, Bartolome. Historia de la Villa Imperial de Potosi, 3 =vols. Mendoza, Gunnar & Hanke, Lewis, eds. LC 63-13533. (Illus.). 1464p. 1965. Set. 60.00x (ISBN 0-87057-097-8, Pub. by Brown U Pr). Univ. Pr of New England.

--Tales of Potosi. Padden, R. C., ed. Lopez-Morillas, Frances M., tr. from Span. LC 74-6574. 209p. 1975. 12.50 (ISBN 0-87057-144-3, Pub. by Brown U Pr). Univ Pr of New England.

Arzelies, H. Relativistic Point Dynamics. LC 72-142173. 416p. 1972. text ed. 60.00 (ISBN 0-08-015842-0). Pergamon.

Asad, Muhammad. The Road to Mecca. LC 80-1937. 1981. Repr. of 1954 ed. 42.00 (ISBN 0-404-18953-9). AMS Pr.

Asai, Kazuhiko. Miracle Cure: Organic Germanium. LC 79-91512. (Illus.). 256p. 1980. 12.95 (ISBN 0-87040-474-1). Japan Pubns.

Asakawa, K. The Russo-Japanese Conflict: It Causes & Issues. (Illus.). 399p. 1972. Repr. of 1904 ed. 31.00x (ISBN 0-7165-2048-6, Pub. by Irish Academic Pr Ireland). Biblio Dist.

Asalache, Khadambi. Calabash of Life. (Orig.). 1967. pap. text ed. 2.25x (ISBN 0-582-64001-6). Humanities.

Asals, A. Heather. Equivocal Predication: George Herbert's Way to God. 152p. 1981. 25.00x (ISBN 0-8020-5536-2). U of Toronto Pr.

Asano, Osamu & Ishiwata, Mutsuko, eds. The Japanese Press, 1980. 32nd ed. Henshu-sha, Century E. & Higashi, Shinbu, trs. from Japanese. LC 49-25552. (Illus.). 172p. (Orig.). 1980. pap. 25.00x (ISBN 0-8002-2699-2). Intl Pubns Serv.

Asano, Shuzo, ed. Structure of the Transition Zone. (Advances in Earth & Planetary Sciences Ser.: No. 8). 184p. 1980. lib. bdg. 26.50 (ISBN 90-277-1149-6, Pub. by D. Reidel). Kluwer Boston.

Asante, Molefi K. & Vandi, Abdulai S., eds. Contemporary Black Thought: Alternative Analyses in Social & Behavioral Science. LC 80-15186. (Sage Focus Editions Ser.: Vol. 26). (Illus.). 302p. 1980. 18.95 (ISBN 0-8039-1500-4). Sage.

--Contemporary Black Thought: Alternative Analyses in Social & Behavioral Science. LC 80-15186. (Sage Focus Editions: Vol. 26). (Illus.). 302p. 1980. pap. 9.95 (ISBN 0-8039-1501-2). Sage.

Asante, S. K. Pan African Protest: West Africa & the Italo-Ethiopian Crisis, 1934-41. (Legon History). (Illus.). 1977. text ed. 22.00x (ISBN 0-582-64194-2). Longman.

Asanuma, Tsuyoshi, ed. see International Symposium on Flow Visualization, Tokyo, Oct. 12-14, 1977.

Asaria, Gerald & Quemere, Erwan, eds. The World of Sail & Power, No. 3. (Illus.). 1980. 28.95 (ISBN 0-914814-25-7). Sail Bks.

Asbell, Bernard. The Senate Nobody Knows. LC 80-8928. 480p. 1981. pap. text ed. 6.95x (ISBN 0-8018-2620-9). Johns Hopkins.

Asbjornsen, P. C. & Moe, Jorgen E. East of the Sun & West of the Moon & Other Tales. (Illus.). (gr. k-3). 1953. 3.95g o.s.i. (ISBN 0-02-705740-2). Macmillan.

Asbjornsen, P. Chr. & Moe, Jorgen. Norwegian Folk Tales. (Illus.). 188p. 1961. 20.00x (ISBN 82-09-01603-2, N449). Vanous.

ASCAP, ed. American Society of Composers, Authors, & Publishers Copyright Symposium, No. 25. 1980. 17.50x (ISBN 0-231-04866-1). Columbia U Pr.

ASCE Committee on Engineering Management, Aug. 1976. Civil Engineer's Role in Productivity in the Construction Industry: Proceedings, 2 vols. American Society of Civil Engineers, compiled By. 408p. 1976. Set. pap. text ed. 17.75 (ISBN 0-87262-075-1). Am Soc Civil Eng.

ASCE Conference, Alexandria, Mar. 1979. Coastal Structures, 2 vols. American Society of Civil Engineers, compiled By. 1232p. 1979. pap. text ed. 75.00 (ISBN 0-87262-149-9). Am Soc Civil Eng.

ASCE Conference, San Francisco, May 1978. Coastal Zone: Proceedings. American Society of Civil Engineers, compiled By. 3180p. 1978. pap. text ed. 118.00 (ISBN 0-87262-134-0). Am Soc Civil Eng.

ASCE Conference, Urban Transportation Division, 1979. Urban Transportation Financing: Proceedings. LC 80-66290. 320p. 1980. pap. text ed. 25.50 (ISBN 0-87262-241-X). Am Soc Civil Eng.

ASCE Irrigation & Drainage Division, July 1976. Environmental Aspects of Irrigation & Drainage: Proceedings. American Society of Civil Engineers, compiled By. 752p. 1976. pap. text ed. 37.50 (ISBN 0-87262-171-5). Am Soc Civil Eng.

ASCE Professional Activities Committee Conference, March 1977. Ethics, Professionalism, & Maintaining Competence: Proceedings. American Society of Civil Engineers, compiled By. 360p. 1977. pap. text ed. 18.50 (ISBN 0-87262-076-X). Am Soc Civil Eng.

ASCE Technical Council on Computer Practices, June 1978. Computing in Civil Engineering: Proceedings. American Society of Civil Engineers, compiled By. 864p. 1978. pap. text ed. 42.00 (ISBN 0-87262-127-8). Am Soc Civil Eng.

ASCE Urban Transportation Division, May 1973. Environmental Impact: Proceedings. American Society of Civil Engineers, compiled By. 400p. 1974. pap. text ed. 16.00 (ISBN 0-87262-063-8). Am Soc Civil Eng.

ASCE Urban Water Resources Research Council Conference, Nov. 1976. Guide for Collection, Analysis, & Use of Urban Stormwater Data: Proceedings. American Society of Civil Engineers, compiled By. 128p. 1977. pap. text ed. 5.75 (ISBN 0-87262-077-8). Am Soc Civil Eng.

ASCE Waterway, Port Coastal & Ocean Division Conference, Charleston, Nov. 1977. Coastal Sediments: Proceedings. American Society of Civil Engineers, compiled By. 1100p. 1977. pap. text ed. 47.00 (ISBN 0-87262-090-5). Am Soc Civil Eng.

Asch. Turtle Tale. (Illus.). (gr. 3). Date not set. pap. cancelled (ISBN 0-590-30386-4, Schol Pap). Schol Bk Serv.

Asch, Berta & Mangus, A. R. Farmers on Relief & Rehabilitation. LC 78-165678. (FDR & the Era of the New Deal Ser.). 1971. Repr. of 1937 ed. lib. bdg. 22.50 (ISBN 0-306-70340-8). Da Capo.

Asch, Frank. City Sandwich. LC 77-18902. (Illus.). (gr. 1-4). 1978. 6.95 (ISBN 0-688-80156-0); PLB 6.67 (ISBN 0-688-84156-2). Greenwillow.

--Country Pie. LC 78-14837. (Illus.). (gr. 1-3). 1979. 7.50 (ISBN 0-688-80188-9); PLB 7.20 (ISBN 0-688-84188-0). Greenwillow.

--The Last Puppy. (Illus.). (gr. 3-7). 8.95 (ISBN 0-13-524058-1). P-H.

--Monkey Face. LC 76-18101. (Illus.). 40p. (ps-2). 1977. 5.95 o.s.i. (ISBN 0-8193-0862-5, Four Winds); PLB 5.41 o.s.i. (ISBN 0-8193-0863-3). Schol Bk Serv.

Asch, Peter. Economic Theory & the Antitrust Dilemma. LC 78-127658. (Illus.). 1970. 24.95 (ISBN 0-471-03443-6, Pub. by Wiley-Interscience). Wiley.

Ascham, R. English Works. Wright, W. A., ed. 1970. Repr. of 1904 ed. 49.50 (ISBN 0-521-07768-0). Cambridge U Pr.

Ascham, Roger. The Scholemaster: Or, Plaine & Perfite Way of Teachyng Children the Latin Tong. LC 68-54609. (English Experience Ser.: No. 15). 134p. 1968. Repr. of 1570 ed. 14.00 (ISBN 90-221-0015-4). Walter J Johnson.

--Taxophilus, the Schole of Shootinge, 2 bks. LC 75-76431. (English Experience Ser.: No. 79). 184p. 1969. Repr. of 1545 ed. 25.00 (ISBN 90-221-0079-0). Walter J Johnson.

Aschbacher, Michael. The Finite Simple Groups & Their Classifications. LC 79-20927. (Yale Mathematical Monograph: No. 7). (Orig.). 1980. pap. text ed. 6.95 (ISBN 0-300-02449-5). Yale U Pr.

Aschburner, Steve. Ted Kennedy: The Politician & the Man. LC 79-27299. (Illus.). 48p. (gr. 4-8). 1980. PLB 7.95 (ISBN 0-8172-0430-X). Raintree Pubs.

Asche, Frank. Good Lemonade. LC 72-1361. 32p. (gr. k-3). 1976. 5.90 (ISBN 0-531-01093-7). Watts.

Ascher, Carol. Simone De Beauvoir: A Life of Freedom. LC 80-70361. 256p. 1981. 13.95 (ISBN 0-8070-3240-9). Beacon Pr.

Ascher, Scott & Shadburne, William. Scuba Handbook for Humans. 2nd ed. LC 75-3832. (Illus.). 1977. pap. text ed. 6.95 (ISBN 0-8403-1126-5). Kendall-Hunt.

Ascoli, David. The Queen's Peace. (The Origins & Development of the Metropolitan Police 1829-1979). (Illus.). 364p. 1980. 30.00 (ISBN 0-241-10296-0, Pub. by Hamish Hamilton England). David & Charles.

Asdell, S. A. Patterns of Mammalian Reproduction. 2nd ed. (Illus.). 1964. 35.00x (ISBN 0-8014-0021-X). Comstock.

Asfaw, Girma-Selassie, et al, eds. The Ampharic Letters of Emperor Theodore of Ethiopia. (Oriental Documents-British Academy Ser.). 1979. pap. 24.00x (ISBN 0-19-725988-X). Oxford U Pr.

Asgar Ali Engineer. Islamic State. 192p. 1980. text ed. 17.95x (ISBN 0-89891-002-1). Advent Bk.

Ash, Anthony L. Acts of the Apostles, Pt. I. LC 79-63269. (Living Word Commentary Ser.: Vol. 6). 1979. 7.95 (ISBN 0-8344-0069-3). Sweet.

--Decide to Love. LC 80-80294. (Journey Books). 140p. (Orig.). 1980. pap. 2.35 (ISBN 0-8344-0116-9). Sweet.

--The Gospel According to Luke, 2 parts. Ferguson, Everett, ed. LC 72-77838. (The Living Word Commentary Ser., Vol. 4). 1972. 7.95 ea.; Pt 1. (ISBN 0-8344-0067-7); Pt 2. (ISBN 0-8344-0077-4). Sweet.

Ash, Brian. Who's Who in H. G. Wells. 1979. 22.50 (ISBN 0-241-89597-9, Pub. by Hamish Hamilton). David & Charles.

--Who's Who in Science Fiction. LC 76-11667. (YA) (gr. 9 up). 1976. 10.95 (ISBN 0-8008-8274-1). Taplinger.

Ash Deposit & Corrosion from Impurities in Combustion Gases Symposium, June 26-July 1, 1977, New England College, Henniker, New Hampshire. Ash Deposits & Corrosion Due to Impurities in Combustion Gases: Proceedings. new ed. Bryers, R. W., ed. LC 78-7001. 1978. text ed. 57.50 (ISBN 0-89116-074-4, Co-Pub by McGraw Intl). Hemisphere Pub.

Ash, Douglas. How to Identify English Silver Drinking Vessels. 15.00x (ISBN 0-392-07924-0, SpS). Soccer.

Ash, I., jt. auth. see Ash, M.

Ash, J. & Hyde, E., eds. Chemical Information Systems. LC 74-14904. 309p. 1975. 49.95 (ISBN 0-470-03444-0). Halsted Pr.

Ash, Lawrence R. & Orihel, Thomas C. Atlas of Human Parasitology. LC 80-25291. (Illus.). 176p. 1980. text ed. 45.00 (ISBN 0-89189-081-5, 16-7-001-00). Am Soc Clinical.

Ash, Lawrence R., jt. auth. see Garcia, Lynne S.

Ash, Lee. Serial Publications Containing Medical Classics. 2nd ed. 1979. 22.50 (ISBN 0-9603990-0-3). Antiquarium.

Ash, M. & Ash, I. Encyclopedia of Surfactants, Vol. 2. 1981. 75.00 (ISBN 0-8206-0287-6). Chem Pub.

--Formulary of Detergents & Other Cleaning Agents. 1980. 22.50 (ISBN 0-8206-0247-7). Chem Pub.

Ash, McKinley, Jr., jt. auth. see Ramfjord, Sigurd.

Ash, Maurice. Regions of Tommorrow: Towards the Open City. LC 70-85676. (Illus.). 1969. 5.95x (ISBN 0-8052-3221-4). Schocken.

Ash, R. B. Information Theory. LC 65-24284. (Pure & Applied Mathematics Ser.). 1965. 33.50 (ISBN 0-470-03445-9, Pub by Wiley-Interscience). Wiley.

Ash, Rene L. The Motion Picture Film Editor. LC 74-4072. 1974. 10.00 (ISBN 0-8108-0718-1). Scarecrow.

Ash, Robert. Measure, Integration, & Functional Analysis. 284p. 1971. 22.95 (ISBN 0-12-065260-9). Acad Pr.

Ash, Robert B. Basic Probability Theory. LC 76-109394. 1970. 25.95 (ISBN 0-471-03450-9). Wiley.

--Complex Variables. 1971. text ed. 22.95 (ISBN 0-12-065250-1). Acad Pr.

--Real Analysis & Probability. (Probability & Mathematical Statistics Ser.). 476p. 1972. 22.50 (ISBN 0-12-065201-3); solutions to problems 3.00 (ISBN 0-12-065240-4). Acad Pr.

Ash, William. Morals & Politics: The Ethics of Revolution. (Direct Editions Ser.). 1977. pap. 9.00 (ISBN 0-7100-8558-3). Routledge & Kegan.

Ashabranner, B., jt. auth. see Davis, Russell G.

Ashbee, C. R. Craftsmanship in Competitive Industry. Stansky, Peter & Shewan, Rodney, eds. LC 76-17772. (Aesthetic Movement & the Arts & Crafts Movement Ser.). 1978. Repr. of 1908 ed. lib. bdg. 44.00x (ISBN 0-8240-2477-X). Garland Pub.

--A Few Chapters in Workshop Reconstruction & Citizenship, Repr. Of 1894. Stansky, Peter & Shewan, Rodney, eds. Bd. with An Endeavor Towards the Teaching of John Ruskin & William Morris (1901. LC 76-18324. (Aesthetic Movement & the Arts & Crafts Movement Ser.: Vol. 27). 1978. lib. bdg. 44.00 (ISBN 0-8240-2476-1). Garland Pub.

--Manual of the Guild of Handicraft. Stansky, Peter & Shewan, Rodney, eds. LC 76-17776. (Aesthetic Movement & the Arts & Crafts Movement Ser.: Vol. 32). 1978. Repr. of 1892 ed. lib. bdg. 44.00 (ISBN 0-8240-2481-8). Garland Pub.

--Should We Stop Teaching Art? Stansky, Peter & Shewan, Rodney, eds. LC 76-17774. (Aesthetic Movement & the Arts & Crafts Movement Ser.). 1978. Repr. of 1911 ed. lib. bdg. 44.00x (ISBN 0-8240-2478-8). Garland Pub.

Ashbee, C. R., tr. see Cellini, Benvenuto.

Ashbee, K. H., jt. auth. see Smallman, R. E.

Ashberry, Anne. Miniature Gardens. 1977. 9.95 o.p. (ISBN 0-7153-7289-0). David & Charles.

Ashbery, John. Paradoxes & Oxymorons. 64p. 1981. 8.95 (ISBN 0-670-63786-6). Viking Pr.

--Paradoxes & Oxymorons: Fifty Lyrics. 1981. pap. 4.95 (ISBN 0-14-042288-9). Penguin.

Ashbery, John, et al. Apparitions. 60p. ltd. signed ed. 50.00 (ISBN 0-935716-10-6). Lord John.

Ashbery, John, et al, trs. see Jacob, Max.

Ashbrook, Stanley. The United States One Cent Stamp of 1851-1857. Date not set. 100.00x (ISBN 0-88000-082-1). Quarterman. Postponed.

Ashburn, Shirley, jt. auth. see Schuster, Clara.

Ashburner, Jenni, jt. auth. see Green, David.

Ashby, Cliff. The Dogs of Dewsbury. (Poetry Ser.). 1979. 5.95 o.s.i. (ISBN 0-685-96487-6, Pub. by Carcanet New Pr England). Persea Bks.

Ashby, E., ed. see Carnegie Commission On Higher Education.

Ashby, Gordon P. & Heilman, Robert L. Introduction to I-O Concepts & Job Control Language for the IBM Operating System 360. 1971. pap. 13.95x (ISBN 0-8221-0004-5). Dickenson.

Ashby, M. F. & Jones, D. R. Engineering Materials: An Introduction to Their Properties & Applications. (International Ser. on Materials Science & Technology: Vol. 34). (Illus.). 120p. 1980. 36.00 (ISBN 0-08-026139-6); pap. 11.50 (ISBN 0-08-026138-8). Pergamon.

Ashby, Philip H. Modern Trends in Hinduism. (Lectures in the History of Religions Ser.: No. 10). 176p. 1974. 16.00x (ISBN 0-231-03768-6). Columbia U Pr.

Ashcraft, Laura, jt. auth. see Nickles, Elizabeth.

Ashcraft, Morris. The Will of God. LC 80-65714. 1980. pap. 4.25 (ISBN 0-8054-1620-X). Broadman.

Ashcraft, Norman. Colonialism & Underdevelopment: Processes of Political Economic Change in British Honduras. LC 72-92055. 1973. pap. text ed. 7.00x (ISBN 0-8077-2407-6). Tchrs Coll.

Ashcraft, Norman & Scheflen, Albert E. People Space: The Making & Breaking of Human Boundaries. LC 76-2844. 1976. pap. 2.50 o.p. (ISBN 0-385-11229-7, Anch). Doubleday.

Ashdown, Peter. Caribbean History in Maps. (Illus.). 84p. 1979. pap. text ed. 9.95 (ISBN 0-582-76541-2). Longman.

Ashdown-Sharp, Patricia. A Guide to Pregnancy & Parenthood for Women on Their Own. 1977. pap. 3.95 (ISBN 0-394-72272-8, V-272, Vin). Random.

Ashe, Amy E., jt. auth. see Bossone, Richard M.

Ashe, Arthur. Arthur Ashe's Tennis Clinic. LC 80-84951. (Illus.). 144p. 1981. 12.95 (ISBN 0-914178-44-X, 42904-3). Golf Digest Bks.

--Off the Court. 1981. price not set (ISBN 0-453-00400-8, H400). NAL.

Ashe, Arthur, et al. Mastering Your Tennis Strokes. Sheehan, Larry, ed. LC 75-41854. 1976. 12.95 (ISBN 0-689-10718-8); pap. 8.95 (ISBN 0-689-70562-X). Atheneum.

Ashe, Dora J., ed. see Beaumont, Francis & Fletcher, John.

Ashe, Jim. Handbook of IC Circuit Projects. LC 72-94804. (Illus.). 224p. 1973. pap. 5.95 o.p. (ISBN 0-8306-2629-8, 629). TAB Bks.

Ashe, Penelope. Viva la Difference. 304p. 1976. pap. 1.95 o.p. (ISBN 0-345-24126-6). Ballantine.

Ashe, Rosalind. The Hurricane Wake. 1978. pap. 1.95 o.s.i. (ISBN 0-446-89448-6). Warner Bks.

--The Hurricane Wake. LC 77-71366. 1977. 7.95 o.p. (ISBN 0-03-021366-5). HR&W.

--Moths. 1977. pap. 1.95 o.s.i. (ISBN 0-446-89447-8). Warner Bks.

Asheim, Lester & Fenwick, Sara I., eds. Differentiating the Media. (Studies in Library Science). vi, 74p. 1975. 10.00x (ISBN 0-226-02964-6). U of Chicago Pr.

Ashem, Beatrice A. & Poser, Ernest G., eds. Adaptive Learning: Behavior Modification with Children. LC 72-156903. 460p. 1975. pap. 15.00 (ISBN 0-08-017683-6). Pergamon.

Ashenfelter, Orley, jt. ed. see Bowen, William G.

Ashenfelter, Orley C. & Oates, Wallace, eds. Essays in Labor Market Analysis. LC 77-9421. 1978. 41.95 (ISBN 0-470-99222-0). Halsted Pr.

Ashenhurst, Robert L., jt. auth. see AFIPS Taxonomy Committee.

Asher, A. Bibliographical Essay on the Collection of Voyages & Travels: Nuremburg, 1598-1660. Hulsius, Levinus, ed. 1962. pap. text ed. 11.50x (ISBN 90-6041-001-7). Humanities.

Asher, C. Postural Variations in Childhood. (Postgraduate Pediatric Ser.). 1975. 14.95 (ISBN 0-407-00032-1). Butterworths.

Asher, Don. Blood Summer. 1979. pap. 1.95 o.p. (ISBN 0-425-03949-8). Berkley Pub.

--Honeycomb. LC 78-75155. (Illus.). 1979. 3.95 (ISBN 0-89395-021-1). Cal Living Bks.

Asher, Don, jt. auth. see Hawes, Hampton.

Asher, Herbert. Presidential Elections & American Politics: Voters, Candidates, & Campaigns Since 1952. 1980. pap. 10.95x (ISBN 0-256-02322-0). Dorsey.

Asher, Maxine K. Ancient Energy: Key to the Universe. LC 78-19497. (Illus.). 1979. 8.95 (ISBN 0-06-060308-9, HarpR). Har-Row.

Asher, Mukul G. Revenue Systems of Asean Countries. 76p. 1980. pap. 5.00 (ISBN 0-8214-0546-2). Swallow.

Asher, R., jt. auth. see Henderson, E. J.

Asher, R. E. & Radharkrishnan, R. Tamil Prose Reader. LC 73-93705. 1971. text ed. 38.50 (ISBN 0-521-07214-X). Cambridge U Pr.

Asher, R. E., tr. see Pillai, Thakazhi S.

Asher, R. E., tr. see Varkom Muhammed Basheer.

Asher, Robert E., jt. auth. see Mason, Edward S.

Asher, Robert E., et al. Development Assistance in the Seventies: Alternatives for the United States. 1970. 11.95 (ISBN 0-8157-0542-5). Brookings.

--Development of the Emerging Countries: An Agenda for Research. 239p. 1962. pap. 3.95 (ISBN 0-8157-0539-5). Brookings.

Asher, Sandy. Daughters of the Law. LC 80-20400. 160p. (gr. 7 up). 1980. 7.95 (ISBN 0-8253-0006-1). Beaufort Bks NY.

--Just Like Jenny. LC 80-27653. 160p. (gr. 7 up). 1981. 7.95 (ISBN 0-8253-0040-1). Beaufort Bks NY.

Asher, Steven & Gottman, John, eds. The Development of Children's Friendships. LC 80-25920. (Illus.). 336p. Date not set. price not set (ISBN 0-521-23103-5); pap. price not set (ISBN 0-521-29806-7). Cambridge U Pr.

Ashfield, Helen. Beau Barron's Lady. 192p. 1981. 9.95 (ISBN 0-312-07057-8). St Martin.

Ashford, Douglas E. Policy & Politics in Britain: The Limits of Consensus. (Policy & Politics in Industrial States Ser.). 400p. 1980. 19.50 (ISBN 0-87722-194-4); pap. text ed. 9.95 (ISBN 0-87722-195-2). Temple U Pr.

Ashford, Douglas E., ed. Comparing Public Policies: New Concepts & Methods. LC 77-79492. (Sage Yearbooks in Politics & Public Policy: Vol. 4). 1978. 20.00x (ISBN 0-8039-0904-7); pap. 9.95x (ISBN 0-8039-0905-5). Sage.

Ashford, Gerald. Spanish Texas: Yesterday & Today. LC 72-157044. (Illus.). 1971. 12.50 (ISBN 0-8363-0090-4). Jenkins.

Ashford, Jane. Gwendeline. 1981. pap. 1.75 (ISBN 0-446-94247-2). Warner Bks.

--Man of Honour. 2400p. (Orig.). 1981. pap. 1.75 (ISBN 0-446-94797-0). Warner Bks.

Ashin, Deborah. Inside L. A. Art: A Guide to Museums & Galleries from Santa Barbara to San Diego. LC 80-22527. (Illus.). 112p. (Orig.). 1980. pap. 6.95 (ISBN 0-87701-153-2). Chronicle Bks.

Ashkar, F. S., ed. Thyroid & Endocrine System Investigations with Radionuclides & Radioassays. (Illus.). 544p. 1979. 40.50 (ISBN 0-89352-070-5). Masson Pub.

Ashley, Alma. Love's Raging Torment. 1978. pap. 2.25 (ISBN 0-505-51250-5). Tower Bks.

Ashley, Bernard. All My Men. LC 78-12683. (gr. 6 up). 1978. 9.95 (ISBN 0-87599-228-5). S G Phillips.

--A Break in the Sun. (Illus.). 186p. (gr. 6 up). 1980. 9.95 (ISBN 0-87599-230-7). S G Phillips.

--A Kind of Wild Justice. LC 78-10899. (Illus.). (gr. 7 up). 1979. 9.95 (ISBN 0-87599-229-3). S G Phillips.

--Terry on the Fence. LC 76-39898. (Illus.). (gr. 5-9). 1977. 9.95 (ISBN 0-87599-222-6). S G Phillips.

Ashley, Brian. Law & Order. (Past into Present Ser.). (Illus.). 15.00x o.p. (ISBN 0-392-03663-0, LTB). Soccer.

Ashley, Clifford W. Ashley Book of Knots. 1944. 19.95 (ISBN 0-385-04025-3). Doubleday.

Ashley, J. P. & Harvey, E. R. Modern Trigonometry. 1974. text ed. 10.95 kivar bdg. (ISBN 0-02-473480-2, 47348); dupl. masters 9.95x (ISBN 0-02-473390-3, 47339). Macmillan.

Ashley, John. Principles of Intermediate Algebra. 1977. text ed. 13.95x (ISBN 0-02-473170-6). Macmillan.

Ashley, John P. & Harvey, E. R. Modern Geometry: Complete Course. Maier, Eugene, ed. (Mathematics for Individualized Instruction Ser). (Orig., Prog. Bk.). 1970. pap. text ed. 10.95x (ISBN 0-02-473490-X, 47349); dupl. masters 10.95x (ISBN 0-02-473400-4, 47340). Macmillan.

Ashley, Mark. Ring Twice to Enter. 320p. (Orig.). 1980. pap. 2.50 (ISBN 0-441-72703-4). Charter Bks.

Ashley, Maurice. England in the Seventeenth Century. new ed. 273p. 1980. 20.00x; pap. 9.95. B&N.

--A History of Europe: 1648-1815. (Illus.). 304p. 1973. pap. text ed. 12.95 (ISBN 0-13-390062-2). P-H.

--Life in Stuart England. 1967. 19.95 (ISBN 0-7134-1457-X, Pub. by Batsford England). David & Charles.

--Louis the Fourteenth & the Greatness of France. 1965. pap. 5.95 (ISBN 0-02-901080-2). Free Pr.

--Magna Carta in the Seventeenth Century. LC 65-23456. (Illus., Orig.). 1965. pap. 1.95x (ISBN 0-8139-0014-X). U Pr of Va.

Ashley, Michael. Fantasy Readers Guide, No. 1: The John Spencer Fantasy Publications. 54p. 1980. Repr. of 1979 ed. lib. bdg. 8.95 cancelled (ISBN 0-89370-099-1). Borgo Pr.

--Fantasy Readers Guide to Ramsey Campbell. 64p. 1980. Repr. lib. bdg. 8.95x (ISBN 0-89370-098-3). Borgo Pr.

Ashley, Mike. Souls in Metal: An Anthology of Robot Futures. 1978. pap. 1.75 o.s.i. (ISBN 0-515-04546-2). Jove Pubns.

Ashley, Percy. Modern Tariff History: Germany, United States, France. LC 68-9645. 1970. Repr. of 1926 ed. 17.50 (ISBN 0-86527-131-3). Fertig.

Ashley, Rebecca. An Intriguing Innocent. (Orig.). 1980. pap. 1.50 o.p. (ISBN 0-440-10258-8). Dell.

--A Season of Surprises. (Orig.). 1981. pap. 1.50 (ISBN 0-440-18281-6). Dell.

Ashley, Richard. Cocaine: Its History, Uses & Effects. 240p. 1976. pap. 2.75 (ISBN 0-446-95978-2). Warner Bks.

Ashley, Richard K. Political Economy of War & Peace. 320p. 1980. 30.00 (ISBN 0-89397-087-5). Nichols Pub.

Ashley, Roy. Matchstick Modelling. (Illus.). 80p. 1980. 10.95 (ISBN 0-7207-1150-9, Pub. by Michael Joseph). Merrimack Bk Ser V.

Ashley, Ruth. Human Anatomy. LC 76-65. (Self-Teaching Guides Ser.). 1976. pap. text ed. 6.95 (ISBN 0-471-03508-4). Wiley.

--Structured Cobol: A Self Teaching Guide. LC 79-27340. (Wiley Self-Teaching Guides). 320p. 1980. pap. text ed. 8.95 (ISBN 0-471-05362-7). Wiley.

Ashley, Ruth, jt. auth. see Fernandez, Judi.

Ashley, Ruth, ed. see Fernandez, Judi N.

Ashley Montagu. Man, His First Two Million Years: A Brief Introduction to Anthropology. LC 80-15749. (Illus.). vi, 262p. 1980. Repr. of 1969 ed. lib. bdg. 23.50x (ISBN 0-313-22600-8, MOMH). Greenwood.

Ashley Montagu & Darling, Edward. Ignorance of Certainty. LC 78-123955. 1970. 8.95 o.s.i. (ISBN 0-06-012997-2, HarpT). Har-Row.

Ashley Montagu, jt. auth. see Steen, Edwin B.

Ashley Montagu, ed. Culture & Human Development: Insights into Growing Human. LC 74-18338. 192p. 1974. 8.95 (ISBN 0-13-195578-0, Spec); pap. 2.95 o.p. (ISBN 0-13-195560-8, Spec). P-H.

Ashline, Nelson F., et al, eds. Education, Inequality & National Policy. LC 75-21833. 224p. 1976. 18.95 (ISBN 0-669-00053-1). Lexington Bks.

Ashlock, P. D. A Generic Classification of the Orsillinae of the World (Hemiptera-Heteroptera: Lygaeidae) (U. C. Publ. in Entomology: Vol. 48). 1967. pap. 6.00x (ISBN 0-520-09120-5). U of Cal Pr.

Ashlock, Patrick. Teaching Reading to Individuals with Learning Difficulties. 216p. 1974. pap. 14.75 (ISBN 0-398-03050-2). C C Thomas.

Ashlock, Patrick & Grant, Sister Marie. Educational Therapy Materials from the Ashlock Learning Center. (Illus.). 440p. 1976. pap. 34.50 (ISBN 0-398-02218-6). C C Thomas.

Ashlock, Patrick & Stephen, Alberta. Educational Therapy in the Elementary School: An Educational Approach to the Learning Problems of Children. 120p. 1970. pap. 14.75 photocopy ed. spiral (ISBN 0-398-00060-3). C C Thomas.

Ashlock, Robert B. Error Patterns in Computation. 2nd ed. (Elementary Education Ser.). 128p. 1976. pap. text ed. 7.95x (ISBN 0-675-08654-X). Merrill.

Ashmole, Bernard. Architect & Sculptor in Classical Greece. LC 72-76019. (The Wrightsman Lectures Ser.). (Illus.). 218p. 1972. 22.50 (ISBN 0-8147-0553-7). NYU Pr.

Ashmole, Bernard, jt. auth. see Groenewegen Frankfort, Mrs. H.

Ashmore, Harry S. Arkansas. (States & the Nation Ser.). (Illus.). 1978. 12.95 (ISBN 0-393-05669-4, Co-Pub by AASLH). Norton.

Ashmore, Harry W., ed. The William O. Douglas Inquiry into the State of Individual Freedom. 1979. lib. bdg. 23.50x (ISBN 0-89158-371-8). Westview.

Ashmore, Helen, jt. auth. see Arth, Marvin.

Ashmore, Wendy, ed. Lowland Maya Settlement Patterns. (School of American Research Advanced Seminar Ser.). 464p. 1980. 30.00x (ISBN 0-8263-0556-3). U of NM Pr.

Ashmore, Wendy A., jt. auth. see Sharer, Robert J.

Ashmun, Richard, jt. auth. see Ernest, John.

Ashner, Sonie S., jt. auth. see Christensen, Jo I.

Ashpaugh, Bill & Miller, Holly. Powerlift. LC 80-81758. 150p. 1981. pap. 4.95 (ISBN 0-914850-67-9). Impact Tenn.

Ashtar. In Days to Come. (Illus.). 1975. pap. 3.95 o.p. (ISBN 0-685-59370-3). Saucerian.

Ashton, Ann. Concession. LC 79-7484. (Romantic Suspense Ser.). 192p. 1981. 9.95 (ISBN 0-385-13210-7). Doubleday.

Ashton, Dore. The New York School: A Cultural Reckoning. (Illus.). 1979. pap. 6.95 (ISBN 0-14-005263-1). Penguin.

--Picasso on Art. 1977. pap. 5.95 (ISBN 0-14-004528-7). Penguin.

--Pol Bury. (The Maeght Gallery Ser.). (Illus.). 1977. Repr. 39.95 (ISBN 0-8120-5178-5). Barron.

Ashton, Dore & Hare, Denise B. Rosa Bonheur: A Life & a Legend. LC 80-36749. (Illus.). 192p. 1981. 20.00 (ISBN 0-670-60813-0). Viking Pr.

Ashton, Dudley. Administration of Physical Education for Women. (Illus.). 1968. 10.50 o.p. (ISBN 0-8260-0545-4). Wiley.

Ashton, E. B., tr. see Kant, Immanuel.

Ashton, E. O. Swahili Grammar. 2nd ed. 1976. pap. text ed. 6.50x (ISBN 0-582-62701-X). Longman.

Ashton, Eliyahu. Studies on the Levantine Trade in the Middle Ages. 372p. 1980. 60.00x (ISBN 0-86078-020-1, Pub. by Variorum England). State Mutual Bk.

Ashton, Elizabeth. Borrowed Plumes. (Harlequin Romances). 192p. 1981. pap. 1.25 (ISBN 0-373-02395-2, Pub. by Harlequin). PB.

--The Rekindled Flame. (Harlequin Romances Ser.). 192p. 1980. pap. 1.25 (ISBN 0-373-02347-2, Pub. by Harlequin). PB.

--Reluctant Partnership. (Harlequin Romance Ser.). (Orig.). 1980. pap. 1.25 o.p. (ISBN 0-373-02324-3, Pub. by Harlequin). PB.

--Sicilian Summer. (Harlequin Romances Ser.). 192p. 1981. pap. 1.25 (ISBN 0-373-02401-0, Pub. by Harlequin). PB.

Ashton, Floyd M. & Crafts, Alden S. Mode of Action of Herbicides. 2nd ed. 464p. 1981. 42.50 (ISBN 0-471-04847-X, Pub. by Wiley-Interscience). Wiley.

Ashton, Floyd M., jt. auth. see Klingman, Glenn C.

Ashton, Gordon C. & McMillan, Ian. A Medley of Statistical Techniques for Researchers. 64p. 1981. pap. 6.25 (ISBN 0-686-69139-3). Kendall-Hunt.

Ashton, John. Adventures & Discourses of Captain John Smith. LC 76-78108. (Illus.). 1969. Repr. of 1883 ed. 15.00 (ISBN 0-8103-3565-4). Gale.

--Century of Ballads. LC 67-23925. 1968. Repr. of 1887 ed. 18.00 (ISBN 0-8103-3406-2). Gale.

--Curious Creatures in Zoology. LC 68-57297. 1968. Repr. of 1890 ed. 20.00 (ISBN 0-8103-3525-5). Gale.

--Dawn of the Nineteenth Century in England. LC 67-23941. (Social History Reference Ser). 1968. Repr. of 1886 ed. 18.000 (ISBN 0-8103-3247-7). Gale.

--Devil in Britain & America. LC 73-18391. Repr. of 1896 ed. 26.00 (ISBN 0-8103-3626-X). Gale.

--The Devil in Britain & America. LC 80-19692. 363p. 1980. Repr. of 1972 ed. lib. bdg. 10.95x (ISBN 0-89370-608-6). Borgo Pr.

--Eighteenth Century Waifs. LC 68-58971. 1968. Repr. of 1887 ed. 18.00 (ISBN 0-8103-3517-4). Gale.

--Fleet: Its River, Prison, & Marriages. LC 68-21753. 1969. Repr. of 1888 ed. 20.00 (ISBN 0-8103-3414-3). Gale.

--Gossip in the First Decade of Victoria's Reign. LC 67-23942. 1968. Repr. of 1903 ed. 15.00 (ISBN 0-8103-3249-3). Gale.

--History of English Lotteries. LC 67-23945. (Illus.). 1969. Repr. of 1893 ed. 18.00 (ISBN 0-8103-3250-7). Gale.

--History of Gambling in England. LC 68-21520. 1968. Repr. of 1899 ed. 15.00 (ISBN 0-8103-3501-8). Gale.

--Humour, Wit & Satire of the Seventeenth Century. LC 67-24350. (Social History Reference). 1968. Repr. of 1883 ed. 15.00 (ISBN 0-8103-3251-5). Gale.

--Modern Street Ballads. LC 67-23926. (Illus.). 1968. Repr. of 1888 ed. 18.00 (ISBN 0-8103-3407-0). Gale.

--Old Times. LC 67-23944. (Illus.). 1969. Repr. of 1885 ed. 15.00 (ISBN 0-8103-3252-3). Gale.

--Social England Under the Regency. LC 67-23940. 1968. Repr. of 1899 ed. 15.00 (ISBN 0-8103-3253-1). Gale.

--Social Life in the Reign of Queen Anne: Taken from Original Sources. LC 67-23939. (Illus.). 474p. 1968. Repr. of 1883 ed. 18.00 (ISBN 0-8103-3254-X). Gale.

--Varia. LC 68-9573. (Illus.). 1968. Repr. of 1894 ed. 15.00 (ISBN 0-8103-3502-6). Gale.

--When William Fourth Was King. LC 67-23943. (Social History Reference Ser). 1968. Repr. of 1896 ed. 15.00 (ISBN 0-8103-3255-8). Gale.

Ashton, John, jt. auth. see Mew, James.

Ashton, Leila. Checks from God. (My Church Teaches Ser.). 32p. (ps-1). 1981. pap. 1.50 (ISBN 0-8127-0314-6). Southern Pub.

Ashton, M. L. Mind at Ease. 1961. pap. 2.25 (ISBN 0-87508-902-X). Chr Lit.

Ashton, R. The City & the Court: Sixteen Hundred & Three to Sixteen Forty-Three. LC 78-67296. 1979. 29.50 (ISBN 0-521-22419-5). Cambridge U Pr.

Ashton, Sylvia, ed. see Bassett, Steve.

Ashton, Sylvia, ed. see Carter, Frank B., Jr.

Ashton, Sylvia, ed. see Farrar, Kenneth.

Ashton, Sylvia, ed. see Peskin, Dean B.

Ashton, Sylvia, ed. see Terrell, Elizabeth.

Ashton, Violet. Love's Rebellious Pleasure. 1978. pap. 1.95 o.p. (ISBN 0-449-13979-4, GM). Fawcett.

--Love's Triumphant Heart. 1977. pap. 1.75 o.p. (ISBN 0-449-13771-6, 0-449-13771-6, GM). Fawcett.

--Swan Song. 1979. pap. 2.25 o.p. (ISBN 0-449-14263-9, GM). Fawcett.

Ashtor, E. Social & Economic History of the Near East in the Middle Ages. LC 74-29800. 1976. 25.00x (ISBN 0-520-02962-3). U of Cal Pr.

Ashurst, Henry F. A Many-Colored Toga: The Diary of Henry Fountain Ashurst. Sparks, George, ed. LC 62-10625. (Illus.). 1962. 2.00 (ISBN 0-8165-0056-8). U of Ariz Pr.

Ashwal, Stephen, jt. auth. see Swaiman, Kenneth.

Ashworth, jt. auth. see Bourbousson.

Ashworth, J. H. Catalogue of the Chaetopoda in the British Museum (Natural History) A. Polychaeta. (Illus.). xii, 175p. 1912. 15.00x (ISBN 0-565-00102-7, Pub. by British Mus Nat Hist England). Sabbot-Natural Hist Bks.

Ashworth, J. M. & Smith, J. E., eds. Microbial Differentiation. (Society for General Microbiology Ser.: No. 23). (Illus.). 500p. 1973. 49.50 (ISBN 0-521-20104-7). Cambridge U Pr.

Ashworth, Lou S., et al. The Dell Encyclopedia of Dogs. (Illus.). 240p. 1974. 8.95 o.s.i. (ISBN 0-440-01784-X). Delacorte.

Ashworth, M. F. Analytical Methods for Organic Cyano Groups. 1971. text ed. 27.00 (ISBN 0-08-016191-X). Pergamon.

Ashworth, M. R., tr. see Fischer, Helmut A. & Werner, Gottfried.

Ashworth, Pat M. Care to Communicate. (RCN Research Monographs). 184p. (Orig.). 1980. pap. 10.00 (ISBN 0-443-02412-X). Churchill.

Ashworth, Philip A., tr. see Gneist, Rudolph.

Ashworth, Robert. Highway Engineering. 1966. pap. text ed. 18.50x o.p. (ISBN 0-435-72302-2). Heinemann Ed.

Ashworth, Tony. Trench Warfare. LC 80-13696. 258p. 1980. text ed. 43.50x (ISBN 0-8419-0615-7). Holmes & Meier.

Ashworth, William. A Short History of the International Economy Since 1850. 3rd ed. 1976. text ed. 20.00x (ISBN 0-582-44060-2); pap. text ed. 12.95x (ISBN 0-582-44061-0). Longman.

--Under the Infulence: Congress, Lobbies, & the American Park Barreling System. 1981. pap. 7.95 (ISBN 0-8015-5929-4, Hawthorn). Dutton.

Asian Cultural Centre for Unesco, compiled by. Festivals in Asia. LC 75-30415. (Illus.). 68p. (gr. 9-12). 1975. 7.95 (ISBN 0-87011-265-1). Kodansha.

--More Festivals in Asia. LC 75-34740. (Illus.). 68p. (gr. 9-12). 1975. 7.95 (ISBN 0-87011-273-2). Kodansha.

Asian Development Bank. Rural Asia: Challenge & Opportunity. LC 77-25907. (Praeger Special Studies Ser.). 1978. 34.95 (ISBN 0-03-042601-4). Praeger.

Asiatic Research Center, Korea University CSIS. Northeast Asia: Prosperity & Vulnerability, Vol. I. LC 79-65209. (Significant Issues Ser.: No. 2). 79p. 1979. 5.95 (ISBN 0-89206-008-5). CSI Studies.

Asihene, E. V. Introduction to Traditional Art of Western Africa: Representative Examples from Various Regions. (Illus.). 96p. 1972. 14.50x o.p. (ISBN 0-8448-0077-5). Crane-Russak Co.

Asimov, Isaac. Adding a Dimension. 1975. pap. 1.50 (ISBN 0-380-00278-7, 36871). Avon.

--Animals of the Bible. LC 77-16893. (gr. 2-5). 1978. 7.95a (ISBN 0-385-07195-7); PLB (ISBN 0-385-07215-5). Doubleday.

--Asimov on Astronomy. LC 73-80946. 288p. 1975. pap. 4.50 (ISBN 0-385-06881-6, Anch). Doubleday.

--Asimov on Physics. 1978. pap. 2.50 (ISBN 0-380-41848-7, 41848). Avon.

--Asimov on Science Fiction. LC 80-2246. 288p. 1981. 13.95 (ISBN 0-385-17443-8). Doubleday.

--Asimov's Guide to the Bible, Vol. 1. LC 68-23566. 12.50 (ISBN 0-385-07399-2). Doubleday.

--Asimov's Guide to the Bible: The New Testament. 1971. pap. 5.95 (ISBN 0-380-01031-3, 46862). Avon.

--Asimov's Mysteries. 1979. pap. 1.95 (ISBN 0-449-24011-8, Crest). Fawcett.

--Before the Golden Age, Bk. 2. 320p. 1975. pap. 1.50 o.p. (ISBN 0-449-22715-4, Q2452, Crest). Fawcett.

--Before the Golden Age: Book 3. 1978. pap. 1.95 o.p. (ISBN 0-449-23593-9, Crest). Fawcett.

--Buy Jupiter & Other Stories. 1978. pap. 1.95 (ISBN 0-449-23828-8, Crest). Fawcett.

--Casebook of the Black Widowers. 256p. 1981. pap. 2.25 (ISBN 0-449-24384-2, Crest). Fawcett.

--A Choice of Catastrophes. 384p. 1981. pap. 6.95 (ISBN 0-449-90048-7, Columbine). Fawcett.

--Comets & Meteors. LC 72-2499. (Beginning Science Ser.). (Illus.). 32p. (gr. 2-5). 1972. 2.50 o.p. (ISBN 0-695-80047-7); PLB 2.97 titan ed. o.p. (ISBN 0-695-40047-9). Follett.

--The Currents of Space. 1978. pap. 1.95 (ISBN 0-449-23829-6, Crest). Fawcett.

--Eight Stories from the Rest of the Robots. 1978. pap. 1.50 (ISBN 0-515-04551-9). Jove Pubns.

--Foundation & Empire. 1976. pap. 1.95 (ISBN 0-380-00774-6, 42689). Avon.

--Foundation Trilogy. 1974. pap. 7.95 (ISBN 0-380-00101-2, 54403). Avon.

--Galaxies. LC 68-13034. (Beginning Science Ser). (Illus.). (gr. 2-4). 1968. 2.50 o.p. (ISBN 0-695-83315-4); PLB 2.97 o.p. (ISBN 0-695-43315-6). Follett.

--How Did We Find Out About Black Holes? LC 73-4320. (How Did We Find Out Ser.). (Illus.). (gr. 5 up). 1978. 0.p. 6.95 (ISBN 0-8027-6336-7); PLB 6.85 (ISBN 0-8027-6337-5). Walker & Co.

--How Did We Find Out About Coal? LC 80-50448. (History of Science (How Did We Find Out About...?) Ser.). (Illus.). 64p. (gr. 5-8). 1980. 6.95 (ISBN 0-8027-6400-2); PLB 7.85 (ISBN 0-8027-6401-0). Walker & Co.

--How Did We Find Out About Earthquakes. LC 77-78984. (gr. 6 up). 1978. 5.95 o.p. (ISBN 0-8027-6305-7); PLB 7.85 (ISBN 0-8027-6306-5). Walker & Co.

--How Did We Find Out About Nuclear Power? LC 76-12067. (How Did We Find Out Ser.). (Illus.). (gr. 4 up). 1976. 6.95 o.s.i. (ISBN 0-8027-6265-4); PLB 6.85 (ISBN 0-8027-6266-2). Walker & Co.

--How Did We Find Out About Outer Space? 1977. 6.85 o.p. (ISBN 0-8027-6283-2); PLB 6.85 (ISBN 0-8027-6284-0). Walker & Co.

--How Did We Find Out About Solar Power? (History of Science Ser.). (Illus.). 64p. (gr. 4-7). 1981. 6.95 (ISBN 0-8027-6422-3); PLB 7.85 (ISBN 0-8027-6423-1). Walker & Co.

--How Did We Find Out About Volcanoes? (History of Science Ser.). (Illus.). 64p. (gr. 4-7). 1981. 6.95 (ISBN 0-8027-6411-8); PLB 7.85 (ISBN 0-8027-6412-6). Walker & Co.

--How Did We Find Out the Earth Is Round? Selsam, Millicent, ed. LC 72-81378. (How Did We Find Out Ser.). (Illus.). 64p. (gr. 5-8). 1972. 4.95 o.p. (ISBN 0-8027-6121-6); PLB 5.85 (ISBN 0-8027-6122-4). Walker & Co.

--The Hugo Winners, Vol. 1. 320p. 1977. pap. 2.25 (ISBN 0-449-23917-9, Crest). Fawcett.

--Human Brain: Its Capacities & Functions. pap. 2.25 (ISBN 0-451-61901-3, ME1901, Ment). NAL.

--I, Robot. LC 63-6943. 6.95 o.p. (ISBN 0-385-05048-8). Doubleday.

--Lecherous Limericks. LC 75-7922. (Illus.). 96p. 1975. 6.95 o.p. (ISBN 0-8027-0515-4); pap. 3.95 (ISBN 0-8027-7096-7). Walker & Co.

--Lucky Starr & the Big Sun of Mercury. pap. 0.95 (ISBN 0-451-06772-X, Q6772, Sig). NAL.

--Lucky Starr & the Moons of Jupiter. 144p. (RL 5). 1972. pap. 0.95 (ISBN 0-451-07048-8, Q7048, Sig). NAL.

Asimov, Isaac, pseud. Lucky Starr & the Moons of Jupiter. (Lucky Star Ser.). 1978. pap. 1.50 o.p. (ISBN 0-449-23422-3, Crest). Fawcett.

Asimov, Isaac. Lucky Starr & the Pirates of the Asteroids. (David Starr Ser). (RL 5). 1971. pap. 0.95 o.p. (ISBN 0-451-07047-X, Q7047, Sig). NAL.

--Lucky Starr & the Pirates of the Asteroids. (Lucky Star Ser.). 1979. pap. 1.50 o.p. (ISBN 0-449-23421-5, Crest). Fawcett.

--The Martian Way & Other Stories. 1978. pap. 1.95 (ISBN 0-449-23783-4, Crest). Fawcett.

--Moon. (Beginning Science Ser.). (Illus.). (gr. 2-4). 1966. 2.50 o.p. (ISBN 0-695-45875-2); lib. bdg. 3.59 o.p. (ISBN 0-685-10943-7). Follett.

--Murder at the ABA. LC 75-21206. 240p. 1976. 7.95 o.p. (ISBN 0-385-11305-6). Doubleday.

--Nightfall & Other Stories. 1978. pap. 2.25 (ISBN 0-449-23672-2, Crest). Fawcett.

--Nine Tomorrows. LC 59-6347. 1970. 4.95 o.p. (ISBN 0-385-05314-2). Doubleday.

--Of Matters Great & Small. (Isaac Asimov Collection Ser). 320p. 1976. pap. 2.25 (ISBN 0-441-61072-2). Ace Bks.

--Of Time, Space, & Other Things. 1975. pap. 1.75 (ISBN 0-380-00325-2, 35584, Discus). Avon.

--Only a Trillion. (Isaac Asimov Collection Ser.). 224p. 1976. pap. 2.25 (ISBN 0-441-63121-5). Ace Bks.

--Realm of Algebra. 1977. pap. 1.50 o.p. (ISBN 0-449-30804-9, Prem). Fawcett.

--Realm of Numbers. 1977. pap. 1.50 o.p. (ISBN 0-449-30805-7, Prem). Fawcett.

--The Road to Infinity. 256p. 1981. pap. 2.75 (ISBN 0-380-54155-6, 54155). Avon.

--Science, Numbers, & I. LC 68-14207. 1968. 5.50 o.p. (ISBN 0-385-01908-4). Doubleday.

--Second Foundation. 1976. pap. 1.95 (ISBN 0-380-00823-8, 45351). Avon.

--A Short History of Biology. LC 80-15464. (American Museum Science Bks.). (Illus.). ix, 189p. 1980. Repr. of 1964 ed. lib. bdg. 17.25x (ISBN 0-313-22583-4, ASSB). Greenwood.

--The Solar System & Back. LC 78-89121. 5.95 o.p. (ISBN 0-385-02345-6). Doubleday.

--Stars, Like Dust. 1978. pap. 1.95 (ISBN 0-449-23595-5, Crest). Fawcett.

--The Sun. LC 70-184458. (Beginning Science Ser.). (Illus.). 32p. (gr. 2-5). 1972. 2.50 o.p. (ISBN 0-695-80320-4); PLB 2.97 o.p. (ISBN 0-695-40320-6). Follett.

--To the Ends of the Universe. new ed. LC 75-10524. 144p. 1976. 6.50 (ISBN 0-8027-6236-0); PLB 7.85 (ISBN 0-8027-6235-2). Walker & Co.

--Twentieth Century Discovery. 1976. pap. 1.95 (ISBN 0-441-83227-X). Ace Bks.

--Understanding Physics, 3 Vols. LC 66-17227. 8.95 ea. Vol.1 O.s.i (ISBN 0-8027-0294-5). Vol. 2 (ISBN 0-8027-0295-3). Vol.3 (ISBN 0-8027-0296-1). Walker & Co.

--The Universe: From Flat Earth to Quasar. 1976. pap. 2.95 (ISBN 0-380-01596-X, 42192, Discus). Avon.

--Venus, Near Neighbor of the Sun. (Illus.). 224p. (gr. 5 up). 1981. 8.95 (ISBN 0-688-41976-3); PLB 8.59 (ISBN 0-688-51976-8). Morrow.

--A Whiff of Death. 1979. pap. 1.95 (ISBN 0-449-23660-9, Crest). Fawcett.

Asimov, Isaac & Baron, Carole. In the Beginning. 1981. 10.95 (ISBN 0-517-54336-2). Crown.

Asimov, Isaac see Dr. A., pseud.

Asimov, Isaac, ed. The Annotated Gulliver's Travels. (Illus.). 1980. 19.95 (ISBN 0-517-53949-7). Potter.

Asimov, Isaac & Conklin, Groff, eds. Fifty Short Science Fiction Tales. 1963. pap. 2.95 (ISBN 0-02-016390-8, Collier). Macmillan.

Asimov, Isaac & Greenberg, Martin H., eds. Isaac Asimov Presents the Great SF Stories, No. 5. 1981. pap. 2.50 (ISBN 0-87997-604-7, UE1604). Daw Bks.

Asimov, Isaac, ed. & intro. by see Swift, Jonathan.

Asimov, Isaac, et al. Miniature Mysteries: One Hundred Malicious Little Mystery Stories. 256p. 1981. 12.95 (ISBN 0-8008-5251-6). Taplinger.

Asimov, Isaac, et al, eds. One Hundred Great Science Fiction Short Short Stories. 1980. pap. 2.50 (ISBN 0-686-69237-3, 50773). Avon.

--Isaac Asimov Presents the Best Science Fiction of the 19th Century. LC 80-27721. 192p. 1981. 9.95 (ISBN 0-8253-0038-X). Beaufort Bks NY.

--The Seven Deadly Sins of Science Fiction. 1980. pap. 2.50 (ISBN 0-449-24349-4, Crest). Fawcett.

Asimov, Issac. The Solar System. LC 73-93548. (Beginning Science Ser.). 32p. (gr. 2-4). 1974. PLB 3.39 o.p. (ISBN 0-695-40473-3). Follett.

Asimov, Issac & Ciardi, John. Limericks: Too Gross. 1978. 8.95 (ISBN 0-393-04522-6); pap. write for info. (ISBN 0-393-04530-7). Norton.

Asinger, H. Mono-Olefins: Chemistry & Technology. 1969. text ed. 150.00 (ISBN 0-08-011547-0). Pergamon.

ASIS Annual Meeting, 43rd, 1980. Communicating Information: Proceedings, Vol. 17. Benenfeld, Alan R., ed. LC 64-8303. (Illus.). 417p. 1980. pap. text ed. 19.50 (ISBN 0-914236-73-3, American Society for Information Science). Knowledge Indus.

Asiwaju, A. I., ed. see Tarikh.

Asiwaju, A. I., et al, eds. Tarikh: Pan-Africanism, Vol. 6. (Illus.). 69p. 1980. pap. text ed. 3.25x (ISBN 0-582-60374-9). Humanities.

Ask, Gunvor & Ask, Harriet. Simple Paper Craft. 1971. 16.95 (ISBN 0-7134-2293-9, Pub. by Batsford England). David & Charles.

Ask, Harriet, jt. auth. see Ask, Gunvor.

Askari, Hossein & Cummings, John T. Agricultural Supply Response: A Survey of the Econometric Evidence. LC 76-23376. 1976. 49.95 (ISBN 0-275-23260-3). Praeger.

--Middle East Economies in the 1970's: A Comparative Approach. (Illus.). 1976. text ed. 46.95 (ISBN 0-275-23130-5). Praeger.

Askeland, J. Norwegian Painting: A Survey. (Tanum of Norway Tokens Ser). (Illus.). pap. 10.00x (ISBN 82-518-1122-8, N505). Vanous.

Askeland, Jan. Norwegian Printmakers: A Hundred Years of Graphic Arts. Shaw, Pat, tr. from Norwegian. LC 79-305965. (Tokens of Norway Ser.). (Illus.). 55p. (Orig.). 1978. pap. 10.50x (ISBN 82-518-0688-7). Intl Pubns Serv.

Askenasy, Alexander. Attitudes Towards Mental Patients. (New Babylon, Studies in the Social Sciences). 1974. text ed. 34.10x (ISBN 90-2797-891-3). Mouton.

Asker, jt. auth. see Hauglid.

Askh, Upendranath. Sorrow of the Snows. Ratan, Jai, tr. (Translated from Hindi). 9.00 (ISBN 0-89253-639-X); flexible cloth 6.75 (ISBN 0-89253-640-3). Ind-US Inc.

Askham, Janet. Fertility & Deprivation. LC 75-2718. (Papers in Sociology Ser.: No. 5). (Illus.). 192p. 1975. 24.95 (ISBN 0-521-20795-9). Cambridge U Pr.

Askin, A. Bradley, ed. How Energy Affects the Economy. LC 77-70084. 1978. 17.95 (ISBN 0-669-01365-X). Lexington Bks.

Askins, Bill, ed. see Askins, Charles.

Askins, Charles. Askins on Pistols & Revolvers. Bryant, Ted & Askins, Bill, eds. 144p. 1980. text ed. 25.00 (ISBN 0-935998-22-5); pap. 8.95 (ISBN 0-935998-21-7). Natl Rifle Assn.

Askwith, Herbert. Your Retirement. 157p. 1976. pap. 1.95 o.s.i. (ISBN 0-346-12224-4). Cornerstone.

Aslam, Abukamil Shuja Ibn see Shuja Ibn Aslam, Abukamil.

Aslanapa, Oktay. Turkish Art & Architecture. 1971. 68.00 (ISBN 0-571-08781-7, Pub. by Faber & Faber). Merrimack Bk Serv.

Aslanian, Carol B., jt. ed. see Schmelter, Harvey B.

Aslett, Don. Is There Life After Housework. (Illus.). 109p. (Orig.). 1980. pap. 4.50. Article One.

Aslin, Elizabeth. Nineteenth Century English Furniture. 1962. 22.50 o.p. (ISBN 0-571-05046-8, Pub. by Faber & Faber). Merrimack Bk Serv.

Asmal, Louise, tr. see Hadjinicolaou, Nicos.

Asmussen, Patricia D. Simplified Recipes for Day Care Centers. LC 74-222. 224p. 1976. spiral bdg. 12.95 (ISBN 0-8436-0590-1). CBI Pub.

Asp, Carolyn. A Study of Thomas Middleton's Tragicomedies. (Salzburg Studies in English Literature, Jacobean Drama Studies: No. 28). 282p. 1974. pap. text ed. 25.00x (ISBN 0-391-01303-3). Humanities.

Aspaklaria, Shelley & Geltner, Gerson. What You Should Know About Your Husband's Money... Before the Divorce. LC 80-52403. Orig. Title: Everything You Want to Know About Your Husband's Money... & Need to Know Before the Divorce. 256p. 1981. pap. 5.95 (ISBN 0-87223-646-3). Wideview Bks.

Aspaturian, Vernon V., et al, eds. Eurocommunism between East & West. LC 80-7489. 384p. 1980. 32.50x (ISBN 0-253-32346-0); pap. 9.95x (ISBN 0-253-20248-5). Ind U Pr.

Aspden, George. One Piece of Card. 1973. 13.50 (ISBN 0-7134-2866-X, Pub. by Batsford England). David & Charles.

Aspenstrom, Werner. You & I & the World. Barkan, Stanley H., ed. Cedering, Siv, tr. from Swedish & Eng. (Cross-Cultural Review Chapbook 5). 40p. pap. 3.50 (ISBN 0-89304-803-8). Cross Cult.

Asperheim, Mary K. Pharmacology: An Introduction Text. 5th ed. (Illus.). 272p. 1981. text ed. 10.50 (ISBN 0-7216-1446-9). Saunders.

Asperheim, Mary K. & Eisenhauer, Laurel A. The Pharmacologic Basis of Patient Care. 4th ed. (Illus.). 624p. 1981. text ed. write for info. (ISBN 0-7216-1438-8). Saunders.

--Pharmacological Basis of Patient Care. 3rd ed. LC 76-28937. (Illus.). 1977. text ed. 15.00 (ISBN 0-7216-1437-X). Saunders.

Aspinall, A., ed. see George, Prince of Wales.

Aspinall, A., ed. see George Third.

Aspinall, D., ed. The Microprocessor & Its Application. LC 78-54572. (Illus.). 1978. 47.50 (ISBN 0-521-22241-9). Cambridge U Pr.

Aspinall, John. The Best of Friends. LC 76-26211. (Illus.). 1977. 15.00 o.s.i. (ISBN 0-06-010153-9, HarpT). Har-Row.

Aspinall, Mary Jo. Aortic Arch Surgery. (Surgical Aspects of Cardiovasculardisease: Nursing Intervention Series). 100p. 1980. pap. 6.95 (ISBN 0-686-69603-4). ACC.

Aspinall, Mary Jo & Tanner, Christine. Experiences in Medical Surgical Nursing. 480p. 1981. pap. 14.95 (ISBN 0-8385-2481-8). ACC.

Aspinwall, Dorothy. Modern Verse Translations from French. 220p. 1980. 9.95 (ISBN 0-89962-020-5). Todd & Honeywell.

Aspinwall, Dorothy B. French Poems in English Verse, Eighteen Fifty to Nineteen Seventy. LC 73-1782. 113p. 1973. lib. bdg. 10.00 (ISBN 0-8108-0599-5). Scarecrow.

Aspinwall, Margaret, jt. auth. see Lipman, Jean.

Aspinwall, Margaret, ed. The Painterly Print: Monotypes from the Seventeenth to the Twentieth Century. (Illus.). 262p. 1980. 29.95 (ISBN 0-87099-223-6); pap. 14.95 (ISBN 0-87099-224-4). Metro Mus Art.

ASPIRA of New York, tr. see Fernandez, Happy.

ASPIRA of New York, tr. see Fernandez, Happy & NCCE.

Aspitall, A., ed. see Latham, Robert.

Aspiz, Harold. Walt Whitman & the Body Beautiful. LC 79-28280. 288p. 1980. 19.95 (ISBN 0-252-00799-9). U of Ill Pr.

Aspland, C. W. Syntactical Study of Epic Formulas. 1970. text ed. 13.25x (ISBN 0-391-00422-0). Humanities.

Aspler, Tony, jt. auth. see Pape, Gordon.

Asprey, Robert B. War in the Shadows: The Guerrilla in History, 2 vols. LC 72-92400. 1632p. 1975. Set. Two-volumes, slipcased 35.00 o.p. (ISBN 0-385-03470-9). Doubleday.

Aspril, Elizabeth. As Battles Raged. (Illus., Orig.). 12.95 (ISBN 0-9604750-1-X); pap. 7.95 (ISBN 0-9604750-0-1). E Keys.

--WW II Historical Romance. Date not set. price not set. E Keys.

Asprin, Robert. The Cold Cash War. 1978. pap. 1.75 o.p. (ISBN 0-440-11364-4). Dell.

--Myth Conceptions. Freas, Polly & Freas, Kelly, eds. LC 79-9216. (Illus.). 1980. pap. 4.95 (ISBN 0-915442-94-9, Starblaze). Donning Co.

Asquith, Glenn H. Church Officers at Work. pap. 2.50 (ISBN 0-8170-0048-8). Judson.

Asquith, Peter D. & Giere, Ronald, eds. PSA 1980, Vol. 1. 315p. 1980. 9.50 (ISBN 0-917586-14-X); pap. 7.50 (ISBN 0-917586-13-1). Philos Sci Assn.

Asquith, Peter D., ed. see Philosophy of Science Biennial Meeting, 1976.

Asqwith, Peter D., ed. see Philosophy of Science Association, Biennial Meeting, 1978.

Asratian, E. A. Compensatory Adaptations, Reflex Activity & the Brain. 1965. text ed. 37.00 (ISBN 0-08-010591-2). Pergamon.

Assad, Mike, jt. auth. see Duffy, Neil.

Assagioli, Roberto. Act of Will. 1974. pap. 4.50 (ISBN 0-14-003866-3). Penguin.

Assaiante, Paul, ed. Championship Tennis by the Experts. LC 80-83978. (West Point Sports Fitness Ser.: Vol. 13). (Illus.). 208p. (Orig.). 1981. pap. text ed. 6.95 (ISBN 0-918438-23-3). Leisure Pr.

Asscher, A. W. The Challenge of Urinary Tract Infections. 1980. 34.50 (ISBN 0-8089-1268-2). Grune.

Asscher, A. W., jt. ed. see Brumfitt, William.

Assefi, Touraj. Stochastic Processes & Estimation Theory with Applications. LC 79-17872. 1979. 26.00 (ISBN 0-471-06454-8, Pub. by Wiley-Interscience). Wiley.

Asselineau, Roger. The Transcendentalist Constant in American Literature. (The Gotham Library). 1981. 17.50x (ISBN 0-686-64289-9); pap. 7.00 (ISBN 0-8147-0573-1). NYU Pr.

Assembly of Behavioral & Social Sciences. Deterrence & Incapacitation: Estimating the Effects of Criminal Sanctions on Crime Rates. 1977. pap. 15.25 (ISBN 0-309-02649-0). Natl Acad Pr.

Assembly of Behavioral & Social Sciences, National Research Council. Knowledge & Policy in Manpower: A Study of the Manpower, Research & Development Program in the Department of Labor. LC 75-37384. xi, 171p. 1975. pap. 6.25 (ISBN 0-309-02439-0). Natl Acad Pr.

Assembly of Behavioral & Social Sciences. Knowledge & Policy: The Uncertain Connection. 1978. pap. 8.25 (ISBN 0-309-02732-2). Natl Acad Pr.

--Noise Abatement: Policy Alternatives for Transportation. 1977. pap. 8.00 (ISBN 0-309-02648-2). Natl Acad Pr.

Assembly of Behavioral and Social Sciences, National Research Council. Toward a National Policy for Children & Families. LC 76-56640. 1976. pap. 6.25 (ISBN 0-309-02533-8). Natl Acad Pr.

Assembly of Engineering, Institute of Medicine, National Research Council. Medical Technology & the Health Care System: A Study of the Diffusion of Equipment-Embodied Technology. 1979. pap. text ed. 10.75 (ISBN 0-309-02865-5). Natl Acad Pr.

Assembly of Life Sciences, National Research Council. Seriously Handicapping Orthodontic Conditions. LC 76-16344. 1976. pap. 5.25 (ISBN 0-309-02501-X). Natl Acad Pr.

Assembly of Mathematical & Physical Sciences, National Research Council. Long-Term Worldwide Effects of Multiple Nuclear - Weapons Detonations. LC 75-29733. xvi, 213p. 1975. pap. 8.50 (ISBN 0-309-02418-8). Natl Acad Pr.

Assis, Joaquim M. The Attendant's Confession, the Fortune Teller, & Life. Goldberg, Isaac, ed. & tr. (International Pocket Library). pap. 2.00 (ISBN 0-8283-1426-8). Branden.

--Hand & the Glove. Bagby, Albert I., Jr., tr. LC 74-111502. (Studies in Romance Languages: No. 2). 144p. 1970. 8.00x (ISBN 0-8131-1211-7). U Pr of Ky.

--Iaia Garcia. Bagby, Albert I., Jr., tr. LC 76-24338. (Studies in Romance Languages: No. 17). 192p. 1977. 15.50x (ISBN 0-8131-1353-9). U Pr of Ky.

Assis, Joaquim M. Machado De see Machado de Assis, Joaquim M.

Assis, Machado De see De Assis, Machado.

Assmann, E. Principles of Forest Yield Study. 1971. text ed. 79.00 (ISBN 0-08-006658-5). Pergamon.

Assn Ed Comm Tech, ed. see Frederick, Franz J.

Associated Press. The World in Nineteen Seventy-Five: History As We Lived It. (Illus.). 300p. (gr. 7 up). 1976. PLB 9.85 o.p. (ISBN 0-531-00331-0). Watts.

--The World in Nineteen-Seventy Seven. (Illus.). 1978. lib. bdg. 11.90 s&l o.p. (ISBN 0-531-01414-2). Watts.

Associated Women's Organization, Mars Hill Bible School. Something Special. Simpson, Peggy & Stanley, Linda, eds. 1977. pap. 3.75 (ISBN 0-89137-408-6). Quality Pubns.

--What Are We Doing Here? 1972. pap. 3.75 (ISBN 0-89137-404-3). Quality Pubns.

Association for Biology Laboratory Education, 1st Workshop. Tested Studies for Laboratory Teaching: Proceedings. Glase, Jon C., ed. LC 80-82832. 288p. 1980. text ed. 19.95 (ISBN 0-8403-2271-2). Kendall-Hunt.

Association for Childhood Education International. And Everywhere, Children! LC 78-25932. (gr. 4-7). 1979. 9.50 (ISBN 0-688-80215-X). Greenwillow.

--Sung Under the Silver Umbrella. (Illus.). (gr. k-3). 1972. 4.95g o.s.i. (ISBN 0-02-706180-9). Macmillan.

--Told Under the Blue Umbrella. (Illus.). (gr. k-3). 1962. 4.95g o.s.i. (ISBN 0-02-706390-9). Macmillan.

--Told Under the Christmas Tree. (Illus.). (gr. 4-6). 1962. 6.95g o.s.i. (ISBN 0-02-706500-6). Macmillan.

Association for Childhood Education, ed. Told Under the City Umbrella. LC 72-165107. (Illus.). (gr. 4-6). 1972. 8.95 (ISBN 0-02-707600-8). Macmillan.

Association For Childhood Education International. Told Under the Green Umbrella. (gr. 4-6). 1935. 4.95g o.s.i. (ISBN 0-02-706830-7). Macmillan.

--Told Under the Magic Umbrella. (Illus.). (gr. k-3). 1967. 5.95g o.s.i. (ISBN 0-02-707050-6). Macmillan.

--Told Under the Stars & Stripes. (Illus.). (gr. 4-6). 1967. 4.25g o.s.i. (ISBN 0-02-707490-0). Macmillan.

--Toward Self-Discipline: Guide for Parents & Teachers. 1980. write for info. (ISBN 0-87173-089-8). ACEI.

Association for Educational & Training Technology. Aspects of Educational Technology: Educational Technology to the Year 2000, Vol. 14. Evans, Leo & Winterburn, Roy, eds. 450p. 1980. 37.50x (ISBN 0-85038-383-8). Nichols Pub.

--International Yearbook of Educational & Instructional Technology 1980-81. 500p. 1980. 36.00x (ISBN 0-89397-082-4). Nichols Pub.

Association for Programmed Learning & Educational Technology. Aspects of Educational Technology XII: Educational Technology in a Changing World. 1978. 32.50x (ISBN 0-85038-137-1, Pub by Kogan Pg). Nichols Pub.

Association for Programmed Learning & Educational Technology Conference, 1979. Aspects of Educational Technology XIII: Educational Technology 20 Years on. Page, G. Terry & Whitlock, Quentin, eds. 1979. 35.00x (ISBN 0-85038-247-5). Nichols Pub.

Association for Research in Nervous & Mental Disease. Biology of the Major Psychoses: A Comparative Analysis. Freedman, D. X., ed. LC 75-14571. (Research Publications: Vol. 54). 384p. 1975. 31.50 (ISBN 0-89004-034-6). Raven.

Association for Research in Nervous Mental Disease. The Brain & Human Behavior. 1966. 30.25 o.s.i. (ISBN 0-02-846390-0). Hafner.

Association for Research in Nervous & Mental Disease. Brain Dysfunction in Metabolic Disorders, Vol. 53. Plum, Fred, ed. LC 74-79190. 1974. 34.50 (ISBN 0-911216-81-2). Raven.

Association for Research in Nervous Mental Disease. The Circulation of the Brain & Spinal Cord, Vol. 18. 1966. 27.50 (ISBN 0-02-842900-1). Hafner.

Association For Research In Nervous And Mental Disease. Disorders of Communication: Proceedings, Vol. 42. 1969. Repr. 30.25 o.s.i. (ISBN 0-02-846430-3). Hafner.

--Hypothalamus & Central Levels of Autonomic Function: Proceedings, Vol. 20. (Illus.). 1966. Repr. of 1940 ed. 32.75 o.s.i. (ISBN 0-02-846330-7). Hafner.

Association for Research in Nervous Mental Disease. Patterns of Organization in the Central Nervous System. 1968. 30.25 (ISBN 0-02-846370-6). Hafner.

Association For Science Education. Teaching Science at the Secondary Stage. text ed. 8.50x (ISBN 0-7195-1707-9). Transatlantic.

Association for the Library Service to Children. The Arbuthnot Lectures Nineteen-Seventy to Nineteen Seventy-Nine. LC 79-26095. 214p. 1980. 12.50 (ISBN 0-8389-3240-1). ALA.

Association for University Business & Economic Research-AUBER. AUBER Membership Directory 1980. (Orig.). 1980. pap. 10.00. Bureau Busn Res U Wis.

--Readings in Business & Economic Research Management: Execution & Enterprise, Vol. 1. 1980. pap. 7.50 (ISBN 0-86603-000-X). Bureau Busn Res U Wis.

Association of American Colleges. Reflections on the Role of Liberal Education. 1964. 3.00 o.p. (ISBN 0-685-26072-0). ACE.

Association Of American Law School. Law Books Recommended for Libraries. (Compilation of 46 subject lists complete in six binders). 1967-70. loose leaf 475.00x, with 1974-1976 suppl. (ISBN 0-8377-0201-1). Rothman.

Association of American University Presses, ed. One Book-Five Ways: The Publishing Procedures of Five University Presses. LC 78-9505. (Illus.). 350p. 1978. 18.75 (ISBN 0-913232-53-X); pap. 10.95 (ISBN 0-913232-54-8). W Kaufmann.

Association of Bone & Join Surgeons. Newest Views on Scoliosis, Vol. 93. Urist, Marshall, ed. (Clinical Orthopaedics & Related Research Ser.). 1973. 12.00 o.p. (ISBN 0-685-34614-5). Lippincott.

Association of Bone & Joint Surgeons. A. R. Shands, Jr. Birthday Celebration Issue. Urist, Marshall R., ed. (Clinical Orthopaedics Ser., Vol. 76). 1971. 15.00 (ISBN 0-685-22854-1). Lippincott.

--Ankylosing Spondylitis & Its Variants. Urist, Marshall R., ed. (Clinical Orthopaedics Ser., Vol. 74). 1971. 12.00 o.p. (ISBN 0-685-22852-5). Lippincott.

--Articular Cartilage in Health & Disease. Urist, Marshall R., ed. (Clinical Orthopaedics Ser., Vol. 64). 1969. 15.00 (ISBN 0-685-22845-2). Lippincott.

--Bone Grafts & Inplants, Vol. 87. Urist, Marshall, ed. (Clinical Orthopaedics & Related Research Ser.). 1972. 12.00 o.p. (ISBN 0-685-34608-0). Lippincott.

--Bone Mass. Urist, Marshall R., ed. (Clinical Orthopaedics Ser., Vol. 65). 1969. 15.00 (ISBN 0-685-22846-0). Lippincott.

--Calcium Transfer Mechanisms. Urist, Marshall R. & Depalma, Anthony F., eds. (Clinical Orthopaedics & Related Research Ser. No. 78). (Illus.). 1971. 15.00 (ISBN 0-685-24733-3). Lippincott.

--Chemonucleolysis. Urist, M. R., ed. (Clinical Orthopaedics Ser, Vol. 67). 1969. 12.00 o.p. (ISBN 0-685-14224-8). Lippincott.

--Clavicle. Urist, Marshall R., ed. (Clinical Orthopaedics Series, Vol. 58). 1968. 12.00 o.p. (ISBN 0-685-14225-6). Lippincott.

--Clinical Orthopaedics & Related Research: Vol. 85, AOFS Surgery of the Foot. Urist, Marshall R., ed. 1972. 15.00 (ISBN 0-685-27031-9). Lippincott.

--Clinical Orthopaedics & Related Research: Vol. 86, Progress in Hip Joint Surgery. Urist, Marshall R., ed. 1972. 15.00 (ISBN 0-685-27032-7). Lippincott.

--Clinical Orthopaedics & Related Research: Vol. 80, Problems of Unusual Interest. Urist, Marshall R., ed. 1971. 15.00 (ISBN 0-685-27028-9). Lippincott.

--Clinical Orthopaedics & Related Research: Vol. 81, Spinal Column. Urist, Marshall R., ed. 1971. 12.00 o.p. (ISBN 0-685-27029-7). Lippincott.

--Clinical Orthopaedics & Related Research: Vol. 82, Subjects of Current Interest. Urist, Marshall R., ed. 1972. 12.00 o.p. (ISBN 0-685-27030-0). Lippincott.

--Club Foot. Urist, Marshall R. & De Palma, Anthony F., eds. (Clinical Orthopaedics & Related Research Ser. No. 84). (Illus.). 1972. 12.00 o.p. (ISBN 0-685-24745-7); new subseribers 8.00 o.p. (ISBN 0-685-24746-5). Lippincott.

--Contemporary Views, Vol. 88. Urist, Marshall, ed. (Clinical Orthopaedics & Related Research Ser.). 1972. 12.00 o.p. (ISBN 0-685-34609-9). Lippincott.

--Creativity in Orthopaedics: Marius N. Smith-Peterson Commemoration. Urist, Marshall R., ed. (Clinical Orthopaedics Ser., Vol. 66). 1969. 15.00 (ISBN 0-685-22847-9). Lippincott.

--The Education of Orthopaedic Surgeons. Urist, Marshall R., ed. (Clinical Orthopaedics Ser., Vol. 75). 1971. 15.00 (ISBN 0-685-22853-3). Lippincott.

--Exigent Subjects. Urist, Marshall R., ed. (Clinical Orthopaedics Ser., Vol. 68). 1970. 12.00 o.p. (ISBN 0-685-22848-7). Lippincott.

--Fluorides for Better Bones & Teeth. Urist, Marshall R., ed. (Clinical Orthopaedics Ser, Vol. 55). 1967. 15.00 (ISBN 0-685-14231-0). Lippincott.

--Fractures of the Hip, Vol. 92. Urist, Marshall, ed. (Clinical Orthopaedics & Related Research Ser.). 1973. 15.00 (ISBN 0-685-34613-7). Lippincott.

--Gout. Urist, Marshall R., ed. (Clinical Orthopaedics Ser., Vol. 71). 1970. 15.00 (ISBN 0-685-22851-7). Lippincott.

--Hand, Pt. 2. Urist, Marshall, ed. (Clinical Orthopaedics Ser.). (Illus.). 1959. 15.00. Lippincott.

--Hip Manifestations of Systemic Disease, Vol. 90. Urist, Marshall, ed. (Clinical Orthopaedics & Related Research Ser.). 1973. 15.00 (ISBN 0-685-34611-0). Lippincott.

--Metastatic Bone Disease. Urist, Marshall R., ed. (Clinical Orthopaedics Ser., Vol. 73). 1970. 15.00 (ISBN 0-685-22889-4). Lippincott.

--Muscle Structure, Chemistry & Function. Urist, Marshall R. & De Palma, Anthony F., eds. (Clinical Orthopaedics & Related Research Ser. No. 85). (Illus.). 12.00 o.p. (ISBN 0-685-24747-3). Lippincott.

--New Surgical Approaches, Vol. 91. Urist, Marshall, ed. (Clinical Orthopaedics & Related Research Ser.). 1973. 15.00 (ISBN 0-685-34612-9). Lippincott.

--Orthopaedics & the Arts & Letters, Vol. 89. Urist, Marshall, ed. (Clinical Orthopaedics & Related Research Ser.). 1972. 15.00 (ISBN 0-685-34610-2). Lippincott.

--The Present Status of Calciphylaxis. Urist, Marshall R., ed. (Clinical Orthopaedics Ser., Vol. 69). 1970. 15.00 (ISBN 0-685-22849-5); new subscribers 8.00 (ISBN 0-685-22850-9). Lippincott.

--Recent Advances in Orthopaedic Surgery in Infancy & Childhood. Urist, Marshall R., ed. (Clinical Orthopaedics Ser, Vol. 14). 1959. 15.00 (ISBN 0-685-14257-4). Lippincott.

--Robert W. Johnson Jr., 77th Birthday Celebration. Urist, Marshall R. & De Palma, Anthony F., eds. (Clinical Orthopaedics & Related Research Ser. No. 56). (Illus.). 15.00 (ISBN 0-685-24742-2). Lippincott.

--Soft-Tissue Tumors. Depalma, Anthony F., ed. (Clinical Orthopaedics Ser, Vol. 19). (Illus.). 1961. 15.00 (ISBN 0-685-14259-0). Lippincott.

--Solutions to Pediatric Problems. (Clinical Orthopaedics & Related Research Ser No. 79). 15.00 (ISBN 0-685-24743-0). Lippincott.

--Three Endeavors or Walter Blount: A Trubute to Dr. Walter P. Blount on His Seventieth Birthday. Urist, Marshall R., ed. (Clinical Orthopaedics Ser., Vol. 77). 1971. 15.00 (ISBN 0-685-22855-X). Lippincott.

--Total Hip Replacement: Clinical Orthopaedics Ser., Vol. 72. Urist, Marshall R., ed. 1970. 12.00 o.p. (ISBN 0-685-22888-6). Lippincott.

--Wrist & Hand: Clinical Orthopaedics & Related Research Ser. No. 83. Urist, Marshall R. & De Palma, Anthony F., eds. (Illus.). 1971. 15.00 (ISBN 0-685-24744-9). Lippincott.

Association of Commonwealth Universities. The Compendium of University Entrance Requirements: For First Degree Courses in the United Kingdom 1981-82. 18th ed. LC 74-648109. 1980. pap. 12.50x (ISBN 0-85143-065-1). Intl Pubns Serv.

Association of Commonwealth Universities. Compendium of University Entrance Requirements for First Degree Courses in the United Kingdom, 1981-82. 18th ed. LC 74-648109. 347p. (Orig.). 1980. pap. 12.50x (ISBN 0-85143-065-1). Intl Pubns Serv.

--Schedule of Postgraduate Courses in United Kingdom Universities, 1979-1980. 16th ed. LC 75-644246. 109p. 1979. pap. 7.50x (ISBN 0-85143-061-9). Intl Pubns Serv.

--Scholarships Guide for Commonwealth Postgraduate Students, 1980-82. 4th ed. 326p. (Orig.). 1979. pap. 13.50x (ISBN 0-85143-062-7). Intl Pubns Serv.

Association of Desk & Derrick Clubs of America. D & D Standard Oil Abbreviator. 2nd ed. LC 72-96172. 256p. 9.50 (ISBN 0-87814-017-4). Pennwell Pub.

Association of Pacific Coast Geographers. Yearbooks of the Association of Pacific Coast Geographers, Vol. 1-35. Incl. Vols. 1-19. 1935 - 1957. pap. 3.00 ea.; Vol. 20-27. 1958 - 1965. pap. 3.00 ea; Vols. 28, 29, 31. 1966 - 1967, 1969. pap. 3.00 ea; Vol. 30, 1968. 6.00 (ISBN 0-686-66693-3); Vols. 32-40. 1970 - 1978. pap. 5.00 ea. LC 37-13376. Oreg St U Pr.

Association of Specialized & Cooperative Library Agencies. Standards of Service for the Library of Congress Network of Libraries for the Blind & Physically Handicapped. LC 79-22963. 76p. 1980. pap. 4.50 (ISBN 0-8389-0298-7). ALA.

Association of Teachers of Management. Breaking Down Barriers. Garratt, Bob & Stopford, John, eds. 333p. text ed. 41.00x (ISBN 0-566-02122-6, Pub. by Gower Pub Co England). Renouf.

Association of Teachers of Social Studies in the City of New York. A Handbook for the Teaching of Social Studies. new ed. 1977. text ed. 18.95 (ISBN 0-205-05769-1). Allyn.

Association of the Bar of the City of New York, jt. auth. see Medina, H. R.

Association of the Bar of the City of New York. Report of the Special Committee on the Federal Loyalty Security Program. LC 74-6494. (Civil Liberties in American History Ser.). 301p. 1974. Repr. of 1956 ed. lib. bdg. 32.50 (ISBN 0-306-70596-6). Da Capo.

Association of University Teachers of Economics, Edinburgh, 1976. Studies in Modern Economic Analysis: Proceedings. Artis, M. J. & Nobay, A. R., eds. 1977. 36.50x (ISBN 0-631-17970-4, Pub. by Basil Blackwell). Biblio Dist.

Association of Voluntary Agency for Rural Development, India. Block-Level Planning. 128p. 1980. text ed. 18.95x (ISBN 0-7069-1063-X, Pub by Vikas India). Advent Bk.

Assosciated Press & Grolier, eds. The Olympic Story Nineteen Eighty. (Illus.). 256p. 1981. 14.95 (ISBN 0-531-09942-3). Watts.

Astaire, Fred. Steps in Time. (Quality Paperbacks Ser.). (Illus.). 327p. 1981. pap. 7.95 (ISBN 0-306-80141-8). Da Capo.

Asthana, Rama K. Henry James: A Study in the Aesthetics of the Novel. 130p. 1980. Repr. of 1936 ed. text ed. 11.25 (ISBN 0-391-02180-X). Humanities.

Asthma & Allergy Foundation of America & Norback, Craig T., eds. The Allergy Encyclopedia. (Orig.). 1981. pap. price not set (ISBN 0-452-25270-9, Z5270, Plume Bks). NAL.

Astill, Kenneth N., jt. auth. see Arden, Bruce W.

Astin, A. Predicting Academic Performance in College. LC 78-128470. 1971. 19.95 (ISBN 0-02-901100-0). Free Pr.

Astin, A., ed. see Carnegie Commission on Higher Education.

Astin, Alexander W. Academic Gamesmanship: Student-Oriented Change in Higher Education. LC 76-12520. (Illus.). 1976. text ed. 22.95 (ISBN 0-275-56720-6). Praeger.

Astin, Alexander W., et al. The Power of Protest: A National Study of Student & Faculty Disruptions with Implications for the Future. LC 75-24007. (Higher Education Ser.). (Illus.). 224p. 1975. 14.95x o.p. (ISBN 0-87589-266-3). Jossey-Bass.

Astin, Helen S., jt. auth. see Harway, Michele.

Astin, Helen S., ed. Some Action of Her Own. LC 75-43476. 208p. 1976. 18.95 (ISBN 0-669-00567-3). Lexington Bks.

Astley, John. The Art of Riding: Set Forthe in a Breefe Treatise. LC 68-54610. (English Experience Ser.: No. 10). 80p. 1968. Repr. of 1584 ed. 13.00 (ISBN 90-221-0010-3). Walter J Johnson.

Aston, Graham & Tiffney, John. Guide to Improving Food Hygiene. (Illus.). 1977. pap. 11.95x (ISBN 0-7198-2644-6). Intl Ideas.

Aston, S. C., jt. auth. see Peirol D'Auvergne.

Astone, N. A., jt. auth. see Martin, J. A.

Astor, Michael & Rowley, Trevor. Landscape Archaeology: An Introduction to Fieldwork Techniques on Post Roman Landscapes. 1975. 16.95 (ISBN 0-7153-6670-X). David & Charles.

Astor, Saul D. Loss Prevention: Controls & Concepts. LC 77-28164. 1978. 15.95 (ISBN 0-913708-29-1). Butterworths.

Astro Publishers. Military Competency Exam, with Explanations. Date not set. pap. 7.95 (Pub. by Astro). Aviation.

Astro, Richard, jt. ed. see Nagel, James.

Astrov, Nicholas J., jt. auth. see Gronsky, Paul P.

Astrup, Christian. The Chronic Schizophrenias. (Orig.). 1979. pap. 18.00x (ISBN 82-00-01810-5, Dist. by Columbia U. Pr.). Universitet.

Asturias, Miguel. Guatemalan Sociology. Ahern, Maureen, tr. LC 77-8270. 1977. 12.95x o.p. (ISBN 0-87918-035-8); pap. 7.95x (ISBN 0-87918-037-4). ASU Lat Am St.

--El Senor Presidente. Partridge, Frances, tr. from Span. LC 64-10908. 1975. pap. text ed. 4.95x (ISBN 0-689-70521-2, 211). Atheneum.

Asturias, Miguel A. Leyendas De Guatemala. (Easy Readers, C). 1978. pap. text ed. 3.75 (ISBN 0-88436-290-6). EMC.

Asturius, Miguel A. The Eyes of the Interred. 1973. 15.00 o.p. (ISBN 0-440-02378-5, Sey Lawr). Delacorte.

--Men of Maize. 400p. 1975. 10.00 o.p. (ISBN 0-440-05583-0, Sey Lawr). Delacorte.

Astwood, E. B. see Laurentian Hormone Conferences.

Astwood, William, jt. auth. see Neuhaus, Edmund C.

Asua, L. Jimenez de see Jimenez de Asua, L.

Aswad, Betsy. Winds of the Old Days. 288p. 1980. 9.95 (ISBN 0-8037-9638-2). Dial.

Aszalos, Adorjan, ed. Antitumor Compounds of Natural Origin. 1981. Vol. 1. 64.95 (ISBN 0-8493-5520-6); Vol. 2. 67.95 (ISBN 0-8493-5521-4). CRC Pr.

Atanasijevic, I. Selected Exercises in Galactic Astronomy. LC 73-159652. (Astrophysics & Space Science Library: Vol. 26). (Illus.). 156p. 1972. 12.80 o.p. (ISBN 0-387-91087-5). Springer-Verlag.

Atassi, M. Z., ed. Immunochemistry of Proteins, 3 vols. LC 76-2596. (Illus.). 1979. Vol. 1, 485p, 1977. 44.50 (ISBN 0-306-36221-X, Plenum Pr); Vol. 2, 438p, 1977. 44.50 (ISBN 0-306-36222-8); Vol. 3, 339p, 1979. 35.00 (ISBN 0-306-40131-2). Plenum Pub.

Atcheson, Marguerite. The Mouse Who Didn't Believe in Santa Claus. LC 80-69472. (Illus.). 64p. (Orig.). 1980. pap. 4.50x (ISBN 0-9603118-6-6). Davenport.

Atchinson, Joseph E., et al. Nonwood Pulp Fiber Pulping: Progress Report, No. 9. (TAPPI PRESS Reports). (Illus.). 1978. pap. 38.95 (ISBN 0-89852-375-3, 01 01 R075). TAPPI.

Atchison, Evelyn, jt. auth. see Glass, Marion.

Atchison, Joseph E. Nonwood Plant Fiber Pulping, Progress Report, No. 10. (TAPPI PRESS Reports). (Illus.). 1979. pap. 38.95 (ISBN 0-89852-381-8, 01-01-R081). TAPPI.

Atchley, Robert C. Social Forces in Later Life. 3rd ed. 480p. 1980. text ed. 16.95x (ISBN 0-534-00828-3). Wadsworth Pub.

--Social Forces in Later Life: An Introduction to Social Gerontology. 2nd ed. 1977. 15.95x o.p. (ISBN 0-534-00463-6). Wadsworth Pub.

Atchley, W. R. & Bryant, E. H. Multivariate Statistical Methods: Among-Groups Covariation. LC 75-9893. (Benchmark Papers in Systematic & Evolutionary Biology: Vol. 1). 480p. 1975. 43.50 (ISBN 0-12-786085-1). Acad Pr.

Atchley, W. R. & Woodruff, David S. Evolution & Speciation: Essays in Honor of M.J.D. White. (Illus.). 496p. Date not set. price not set (ISBN 0-521-23823-4). Cambridge U Pr.

Atchley, William R., jt. auth. see Wirth, Willis W.

Aten, James. The Denver Auditory Phoneme Sequencing Test. LC 79-651. (Illus.). 310p. 1979. clinical test 59.95 (ISBN 0-933014-51-1). College-Hill.

Aten, Marilyn J. & McAnarney, Elizabeth R. A Behavioral Approach to the Care of Adolescents. 200p. 1981. pap. text ed. 10.50 (ISBN 0-8016-3201-3). Mosby.

Athanassakis, Apostolos N. The Life of Pachomius. LC 75-37766. (Society of Biblical Literature. Texts & Translation-Early Christian Literature Ser.). 1976. pap. 9.00 (ISBN 0-89130-065-1, 060207). Scholars Pr Ca.

Athanassakis, Apostolos N., ed. The Orphic Hymns. LC 76-54179. (Society of Biblical Literature. Texts & Translation - Graeco-Roman Religion Ser.). (Illus.). 1977. pap. text ed. 7.50 (ISBN 0-89130-119-4, 060212). Scholars Pr Ca.

Athanassova, Theodora, tr. see Panayotova, Dora.

Athans, George, Jr. & Ward, Clint. Waterskiing. LC 75-7706. (Illus.). 120p. 1975. pap. 4.95 o.p. (ISBN 0-312-85715-2). St Martin.

Athans, Greg. Ski Free. 1978. 12.95 o.p. (ISBN 0-87690-321-9); pap. 7.95 o.p. (ISBN 0-87690-322-7). Dutton.

Athas, Daphne. Cora. 1978. 10.95 o.p. (ISBN 0-670-24116-4). Viking Pr.

Athayde, Roberto. Miss Margarida's Way. 1979. pap. 1.95 (ISBN 0-380-40568-7, 40568, Bard). Avon.

Athearn, James L. Risk & Insurance. 4th ed. (Illus.). 550p. 1981. text ed. 15.96 (ISBN 0-8299-0298-8). West Pub.

Athearn, Robert G. The Denver & Rio Grande Western Railroad: Rebel of the Rockies. LC 76-30296. (Illus.). 1977. 18.50x (ISBN 0-8032-0920-7); pap. 8.95 (ISBN 0-8032-5861-5, 641, Bison). U of Nebr Pr.

--Forts of the Upper Missouri. LC 67-24466. (Illus.). xii, 340p. 1972. pap. 7.50 (ISBN 0-8032-5762-7, 555, Bison). U of Nebr Pr.

Athens, Lonnie. Violent Criminal Acts & Actors: A Symbolic Interactionist Study. (International Library of Sociology). 1980. 14.00x (ISBN 0-7100-0342-0). Routledge & Kegan.

Atherly, Gordon. Occupational Health & Safety Concepts. 1978. 22.50x. Intl Ideas.

Atherton, Alexine L., ed. International Organizations: A Guide to Information Sources. LC 73-17502. (International Relations Guide Ser.: Vol. 1). 1976. 30.00 (ISBN 0-8103-1324-3). Gale.

Atherton, D. P., ed. Multivariable Technological Systems. 1978. text ed. 115.00 (ISBN 0-08-022010-X). Pergamon.

Atherton, Henry V. & Newlander, John A. Chemistry & Testing of Dairy Products. 4th ed. (Illus.). 1977. text ed. 17.00 (ISBN 0-87055-253-8). AVI.

Atherton, James S. The Books at the Wake: A Study of Literary Allusions in James Joyce's "Finnegans.Wake". LC 74-5407. (Arcturus Books Paperbacks). 308p. 1974. pap. 7.95 (ISBN 0-8093-0687-5). S Ill U Pr.

Atherton, Lewis E. The Pioneer Merchant in Mid-America. LC 75-77700. (American Scene Ser). 1969. Repr. of 1939 ed. 19.50 (ISBN 0-306-71338-1). Da Capo.

Atherton, N. M. Electron Spin Resonance. LC 73-14031. (Illus.). 435p. 1973. 66.95 (ISBN 0-470-03600-1). Halsted Pr.

Atherton, Pauline, jt. auth. see Meadow, Charles T.

Athey, Patricia A. & Hadlock, Frank P. Ultrasound in Obstetrics & Gynecology. (Illus.). 400p. 1981. text ed. 45.00 (ISBN 0-8016-0374-9). Mosby.

Athey, Robert D., Jr., et al. Water Resistance in Paper Coatings: A Panel Discussion. (TAPPI PRESS Reports). 1979. pap. 33.95 (ISBN 0-89852-382-6, 01-01-R082). TAPPI.

Athos, A. & Gabarro, J. Interpersonal Behavior. 1978. 21.95 (ISBN 0-13-475004-7). P-H.

Atie, Van Der Meer see Van Der Meer, Ron & Van Der Meer, Atie.

Atil, Esin. Ceramics from the World of Islam. LC 73-92017. (Illus.). 225p. 1973. pap. 12.50x (ISBN 0-87474-217-X). Smithsonian.

--Kalila Wa Dimna: Fables from a Fourteenth Century Arabic Manuscript. (Illus.). 96p. (Orig.). 1981. 17.50 (ISBN 0-87474-216-1); pap. 9.95 (ISBN 0-87474-215-3). Smithsonian.

--Renaissance of Islam: Art of the Mamluks. LC 80-607866. (Illus.). 256p. (Orig.). 1981. 47.50 (ISBN 0-87474-214-5); pap. 19.95 (ISBN 0-87474-213-7). Smithsonian.

Atil, Esin, ed. Turkish Art. LC 79-22171. (Illus.). 386p. 1981. 65.00 (ISBN 0-87474-218-8). Smithsonian.

--Turkish Art. (Illus.). 400p. 1980. 65.00 (ISBN 0-686-62717-2, 1659-2). Abrams.

Atimono, Emiko. Law & Diplomacy in Commodity Economics. 200p. 1981. text ed. 57.95x (ISBN 0-8419-5080-6). Holmes & Meier.

Atiya, Aziz S. History of Eastern Christianity. LC 80-232. 1980. Repr. lib. bdg. 52.00 (ISBN 0-527-03703-6). Kraus Repr.

Atiyah, Edward. The Arabs. (Arab Background Ser.). 1968. pap. 6.95x (ISBN 0-685-77090-7). Intl Bk Ctr.

Atiyah, Edward S. An Arab Tells His Story; a Study in Loyalties. LC 79-3071. (Illus.). 229p. 1981. Repr. of 1946 ed. 19.75 (ISBN 0-8305-0023-5). Hyperion Conn.

Atiyah, M. F., et al. Representation Theory of Lie Groups. LC 78-73820. (London Mathematical Society Lecture Note: No. 34). 1980. pap. 29.50x (ISBN 0-521-22636-8). Cambridge U Pr.

Atiyah, Michael F. & Macdonald, I. G. Introduction to Commutative Algebra. 1969. text ed. 17.95 (ISBN 0-201-00361-9). A-W.

Atiyah, P. S. Accidents, Compensation & the Law. 3rd ed. (Law in Context Ser.). xxiv, 695p. 1980. 47.00x (ISBN 0-297-77754-8, Pub. by Weidenfeld & Nicolson England). Rothman.

Atiyah, Patrick S. The Rise & Fall of Freedom of Contract. 804p. 1979. 59.00 (ISBN 0-19-825342-7). Oxford U Pr.

Atkeson, Ray. Western Impressions. Shangle, Robert D., ed. LC 78-102327. 1976. 27.50 (ISBN 0-915796-11-2). Beautiful Am.

Atkeson, Ray & Atkeson, Ray, photos by. Portrait of Oregon. LC 79-91507. (Portrait of America Ser.). (Illus., Orig., Photos by ray atkeson). 1980. pap. 5.95 (ISBN 0-912856-52-1). Graphic Arts Ctr.

Atkin, Edith & Rubin, Estelle. Part-Time Father. LC 75-25146. 1976. 8.95 (ISBN 0-8149-0766-0). Vanguard.

Atkin, J. K. Computer Science. 2nd ed. (Illus.). 224p. (Orig.). 1980. pap. 12.95x (ISBN 0-7121-0396-1). Intl Ideas.

Atkin, John, jt. auth. see Atkin, William.

Atkin, William & Atkin, John. The Book of Boats. LC 76-25311. (Illus.). 1976. Repr. of 1948 ed. 9.95 (ISBN 0-87742-081-5). Intl Marine.

Atkins. Highway Materials, Soils & Concretes. (Illus.). 1980. text ed. 24.95 (ISBN 0-8359-2828-4). Reston.

Atkins, jt. auth. see Spence.

Atkins, A. G. & Beard, W. A History of GWR Goods Wagons: Vol. 2, Detail. LC 76-45508. 1977. 15.95 o.p. (ISBN 0-7153-7290-4). David & Charles.

Atkins, A. G., et al. A History of GWR & Goods Wagons: Vol. 1, General. LC 75-11. (Illus.). 96p. 1975. 15.95 o.p. (ISBN 0-7153-6532-0). David & Charles.

Atkins, Chet & Knowles, John. Chet Atkins Note-for-Note. LC 75-14957. 72p. (Orig.). 1978. pap. 5.95 (ISBN 0-8256-9510-4). Guitar Player.

Atkins, Dorothy. George Eliot & Spinoza. (Salzburg Studies in English Literature: Romantic Reassessment Ser.: No. 78). 1979. pap. text ed. 25.00x (ISBN 0-391-01302-5). Humanities.

Atkins, Fred C. Guide to Mushroom Growing. (Illus.). 1974. 12.95 o.p. (ISBN 0-571-10190-9, Pub. by Faber & Faber). Merrimack Bk Serv.

--Mushroom Growing Today. 6th ed. (Illus.). 1973. 9.95 o.p. (ISBN 0-571-04793-9, Pub. by Faber & Faber). Merrimack Bk Serv.

Atkins, Frederick C. Mushroom Growing To-Day. 5th ed. (Illus.). 1967. 5.95 o.s.i. (ISBN 0-02-504150-9). Macmillan.

Atkins, G. Douglas. The Faith of John Dryden: Change & Continuity. LC 80-12890. 208p. 1980. 14.00x (ISBN 0-8131-1401-2). U Pr of Ky.

Atkins, G. Pope. Arms & Politics in the Dominican Republic. (Special Studies on Latin America & the Caribbean). 158p. 1981. lib. bdg. 20.00x (ISBN 0-86531-112-9). Westview.

--Latin America in the International Political System. LC 76-20882. (Illus.). 1977. text ed. 16.95 (ISBN 0-02-901060-8). Free Pr.

Atkins, Guy. Jorn, Vol III. (Asger Jorn Complete Work Ser.). 250p. 1980. write for info. (ISBN 0-8150-0927-5). Wittenborn.

Atkins, Jeannette see Levy, Harold L.

Atkins, John. Sex in Literature, Vol. 2. 1980. 15.95 (ISBN 0-7145-0919-1); pap. 6.95 (ISBN 0-7145-1138-2). Riverrun NY.

--Sex in Literature, Vol. 3. 1981. 25.00 (ISBN 0-7145-3668-7). Riverrun NY.

--Six Novelists Look at Society. 1980. 11.95 (ISBN 0-7145-3535-4). Riverrun NY.

Atkins, John W. Literary Criticism in Antiquity, 2 vols. Incl. Vol. 1. Greek. 6.00; Vol. 2. Graeco-Roman. 6.75 (ISBN 0-8446-1033-X). Peter Smith.

Atkins, Kenneth R. Physics. 3rd ed. LC 75-11677. 818p. 1976. text ed. 24.95 (ISBN 0-471-03629-3); instr's manual 2.75 (ISBN 0-471-01824-4). Wiley.

Atkins, M. H. & Lowe, J. F. Case Studies in Pollution Control in the Textile Dyeing & Finishing Industries: A Study in Non-Technical Language of Essential Information on the Economics of Control, the Problems & Their Solutions. 1979. 45.00 (ISBN 0-08-022457-1). Pergamon.

--Economics of Pollution Control in the Non-Ferrous Metals Industry. (Illus.). 1979. 35.00 (ISBN 0-08-022458-X). Pergamon.

--Pollution Control Costs in Industry: An Economic Study. text ed. 23.00 (ISBN 0-08-021851-2); pap. text ed. 13.75 (ISBN 0-08-021841-5). Pergamon.

Atkins, Meg E. Samain. pap. 1.50 o.p. (ISBN 0-345-26006-6). Ballantine.

--Secret Loving Shadows. 1977. pap. 1.75 o.p. (ISBN 0-685-75034-5, 345-25301-9-175). Ballantine.

Atkins, Michael D., jt. auth. see Cox, George W.

Atkins, P. W. Molecular Quantum Mechanics: An Introduction to Quantum Chemistry, 2 vols. Vol. 1, Pts. 1-2. pap. 14.95x (ISBN 0-19-855129-0); Vol. 2. pap. 19.95x (ISBN 0-19-855130-4). Oxford U Pr.

--Physical Chemistry. LC 77-21208. (Illus.). 1978. text ed. 26.95x (ISBN 0-7167-0187-1); solutions manual 6.95x (ISBN 0-7167-1071-4). W H Freeman.

Atkins, Robert. Dr. Atkins Diet Revolution. 336p. 1981. pap. 2.95 (ISBN 0-553-14736-6). Bantam.

Atkins, Thomas. The Blue Man. LC 77-77116. 1978. 7.95 o.p. (ISBN 0-385-12844-4). Doubleday.

Atkinson, A. B. The Economics of Inequality. (Illus.). 308p. 1975. 16.50x (ISBN 0-19-877024-3); pap. 9.95x (ISBN 0-19-877076-6). Oxford U Pr.

--Poverty in Britain & the Reform of Social Security. LC 76-85711. (Department of Applied Economic, Occasional Papers Ser). 1969. 15.95 (ISBN 0-521-07522-X); pap. 8.50 (ISBN 0-521-09607-3, 607). Cambridge U Pr.

Atkinson, A. B. & Harrison, A. J. Distribution of Personal Wealth in Britain. LC 77-2715. 1978. 41.50 (ISBN 0-521-21735-0). Cambridge U Pr.

Atkinson, A. B., ed. Personal Distribution of Incomes. (Illus.). 1977. pap. text ed. 25.00x (ISBN 0-04-332065-1). Allen Unwin.

--Wealth, Income, & Inequality. 2nd ed. (Illus.). 450p. 1981. 42.00x (ISBN 0-19-877143-6); pap. 21.00x (ISBN 0-19-877144-4). Oxford U Pr.

Atkinson, A. B., et al. Wealth & Personal Incomes. LC 77-30556. 1978. text ed. 37.00 (ISBN 0-08-022450-4). Pergamon.

Atkinson, Alta. Volume Feeding Menu Selector. Blair, Eulalia, ed. LC 78-145861. 1971. 16.95 (ISBN 0-8436-0528-6). CBI Pub.

Atkinson, Anthony B., ed. The Personal Distribution of Incomes. LC 75-34050. 1976. 35.00x (ISBN 0-89158-526-5). Westview.

Atkinson, Betty J. The Medical Assistant: Clinical Practice. LC 76-5301. 1976. pap. 8.00 (ISBN 0-8273-0351-3); instructor's guide 1.60 (ISBN 0-8273-0352-1). Delmar.

Atkinson, Brooks. Broadway. rev. ed. LC 74-12077. (Illus.). 640p. 1974. 12.95 o.s.i. (ISBN 0-02-504180-0). Macmillan.

--Sean O'Casey: From Times Past by Brooks Atkinson. Lowery, Robert G., ed. 1980. 26.50x (ISBN 0-389-20180-4). B&N.

Atkinson, Brooks & Olson, W. Kent. New England's White Mountains: At Home in the Wild. LC 78-55506. 1978. 35.00 (ISBN 0-913890-18-9, 936065). NYGS.

Atkinson, Brooks J. Henry Thoreau the Cosmic Yankee. LC 80-2678. 1981. Repr. of 1927 ed. 22.50 (ISBN 0-404-19075-8). AMS Pr.

Atkinson, Chuck. Inventory Management for Small Computers. 140p. 1981. pap. 16.95 (ISBN 0-918398-48-7). Dilithium Pr.

Atkinson, D., et al, eds. Mineral Nutrition of Fruit Trees. LC 79-41647. (Studies in the Agricultural & Food Sciences). 1980. text ed. 79.95 (ISBN 0-408-10662-X). Butterworths.

Atkinson, David. Hotel & Catering French: A New Approach for Advanced Students & Practitioners. (Illus.). 1980. text ed. 26.00 (ISBN 0-08-023731-2); pap. text ed. 11.50 (ISBN 0-08-023730-4). Pergamon.

--Menu French. (International Ser. in Hospitality Management). (Illus.). 96p. 1980. 15.00 (ISBN 0-08-024309-6); pap. 6.75 (ISBN 0-08-024308-8). Pergamon.

Atkinson, Frank. Industrial Archaeology of North-East England, 2 vols. LC 74-81052. (Industrial Archaeology of British Isles Ser). (Illus.). 342p. 1974. Vol. 1. 5.95 (ISBN 0-7153-5911-8); Vol. 2, The Sites. 5.95 (ISBN 0-7153-6740-4). David & Charles.

Atkinson, G. Origin & Chemistry of Petroleum: Oriceedings of the Third Annual Karcher Symposium, Oklahoma, May 4, 1979. Zuckerman, J. J., ed. (Illus.). 120p. 1981. 24.00 (ISBN 0-08-026179-5). Pergamon.

Atkinson, Geoffroy. The Sentimental Revolution: French Writers of 1690-1740. Keller, Abraham C., ed. LC 64-18424. 200p. 1966. 10.50 (ISBN 0-295-74024-8). U of Wash Pr.

Atkinson, H. J., jt. auth. see Lee, Donald Lewis.

Atkinson, I. The Viking Ships. LC 77-17510. (Introduction to the History of Mankind Ser.). 1979. 3.95 (ISBN 0-521-21951-5). Cambridge U Pr.

Atkinson, J. E. A Commentary on Q. Curtius' Historiae Alexandri Magni. (London Studies in Classical Philology: No. 3). 1980. text ed. 68.50x (ISBN 90-70265-61-3). Humanities.

Atkinson, James, ed. Luther: Early Theological Works. (Library of Christian Classics Ichthus Edition). 1980. pap. 9.95 (ISBN 0-664-24166-2). Westminster.

Atkinson, James, jt. ed. see Lehmann, Helmut T.

Atkinson, James, ed. see Machiavelli, Niccolo.

Atkinson, James C. The Two Forms of Subject Inversion in Modern French. (Janua Linguarum Ser. Practica: No. 168). 1973 pap. text ed. 18.25x (ISBN 90-2792-481-3). Mouton.

Atkinson, John W. & Raynor, Joel O. Personality, Motivation & Achievement. abr. ed. LC 77-24985. 1978. Repr. of 1974 ed. text ed. 10.95 (ISBN 0-470-99336-7). Halsted Pr.

Atkinson, Jon, jt. auth. see Sandwell, Beryl.

Atkinson, Julia. Eleven Out of Twelve: A Bibliography. 95p. (Orig.). 1980. pap. 4.00x (ISBN 0-931040-03-5). Independence Unltd.

--Emergence. 360p. 1974. pap. 9.00 ltd. ed. (ISBN 0-931040-02-7). Independence Unltd.

--Seeing Is Perceiving. 312p. 1978. pap. 5.00 (ISBN 0-931040-02-7). Independence Unltd.

Atkinson, K. B., ed. Developments in Close Range Photogrammetry - One. (Illus.). xii, 220p. 1980. 45.00x (ISBN 0-85334-882-0). Burgess-Intl Ideas.

Atkinson, Kendall E. An Introduction to Numerical Analysis. LC 78-6706. 1978. text ed. 26.95 (ISBN 0-471-02985-8); solutions manual 5.00 (ISBN 0-471-03749-4). Wiley.

Atkinson, Kenneth, jt. auth. see Smith, Richard T.

Atkinson, Laurence. Pascal Programming. LC 80-40126. 300p. 1980. 49.50 (ISBN 0-471-27773-8); pap. 21.00 (ISBN 0-471-27774-6). Wiley.

Atkinson, Linda. Alternatives to College. LC 78-5957. (Career Concise Guides Ser.). (Illus.). 1978. lib. bdg. 6.95 s&l (ISBN 0-531-01495-9). Watts.

--Incredible Crimes. (Triumph Bks.). (gr. 5 up). 1980. PLB 6.90 (ISBN 0-531-04170-0, F21). Watts.

Atkinson, Margaret E., ed. see Tiek, Ludwig & Brentano.

Atkinson, Mary. Maria Teresa. LC 79-90393. (Illus.). 40p. (gr. k-3). 1979. pap. 3.00 (ISBN 0-914996-21-5). Lollipop Power.

Atkinson, Michael M., jt. auth. see Jackson, Robert J.

Atkinson, Richard C., intro. by. Psychology in Progress: Readings from Scientific American. LC 74-23602. (Illus.). 1975. text ed. 19.95x (ISBN 0-7167-0517-6); pap. text ed. 9.95x (ISBN 0-7167-0516-8); test questions avail. (ISBN 0-685-99783-9). W H Freeman.

Atkinson, Rita L., intro. by. Mind & Behavior: Readings from Scientific American. LC 80-15307. (Illus.). 1980. text ed. 19.95x (ISBN 0-7167-1215-6); pap. text ed. 9.95x (ISBN 0-7167-1216-4). W H Freeman.

Atkinsson, C. Clifford, Jr., et al, eds. Evaluation in the Management of Human Services. 1978. 33.00 (ISBN 0-12-066350-3). Acad Pr.

Atlantic Council Committee on East-West Trade. East-West Trade: Managing Encounter & Accomodation. LC 76-39928. 1977. pap. text ed. 8.25 o.p. (ISBN 0-89158-216-9). Westview.

Atlantic Council of the United States. GATT Plus-A Proposal for Trade Reform: With the Text of the General Agreement. LC 76-126. (Special Studies). 208p. 1976. text ed. 24.95 (ISBN 0-275-23010-4). Praeger.

Atlantic Council Working Group on Nuclear Fuels Policy. Nuclear Power & Nuclear Weapons Proliferation, 2 vols. Gray, John E. & Harned, Joseph W., eds. (Atlantic Council Policy Papers). (Illus.). 1978. pap. text ed. 8.25x ea. Vol. 1 (ISBN 0-917258-13-4). Vol. 2. Westview.

Atlantic Council Working Group on the U.S. & the Developing Countries & Martin, Edwin M. The United States & the Developing Countries. LC 77-9102. (Atlantic Council Policy Ser.). (Illus.). 1977. text ed. 19.50x (ISBN 0-89158-400-5); pap. 9.25x (ISBN 0-89158-401-3). Westview.

Atlantic Council's Working Group on Security Affairs, et al. After Afghanistan: The Long Haul Safeguarding Security & Independence in the Third World. (Atlantic Council Policy Paper Ser.). 71p. 1980. pap. text ed. 6.50x (Pub. by Atlantic Council of the U.S.). Westview.

Atlas, Allan, ed. see Morton, Robert.

Atlas Corporation, ed. Proceedings of the Workshop on Economic & Operational Requirements & Status of Large Scale Wind Systems. 447p. 1979. pap. 22.95 (ISBN 0-89934-022-9). Solar Energy Info.

Atlas, Stephen L. Single Parenting: A Practical Resource Guide. 256p. 1981. 12.95 (ISBN 0-13-810622-3, Spec); pap. 5.95 (ISBN 0-13-810614-2). P-H.

Atmore, A., jt. auth. see Oliver, R.

Atmore, Anthony, jt. ed. see Marks, Shula.

Atre, Shakuntala. Data Base Structured Techniques to Designing Performance & Management: A Case Study Approach. LC 80-14808. (Business Data Processing Wiley Ser.). 500p. 1980. 27.95 (ISBN 0-471-05267-1, Pub. by Wiley-Interscience). Wiley.

Atreya, B. L. Deification of Man: Its Methods & Stages According to the Yoga Vasistha Including a Translation of the Essence of Vasistha's Teachings. 116p. 1980. pap. 4.50 (ISBN 0-935548-02-5). Santarasa Pubns.

Atta, Dale Van see Bradlee, Ben, Jr. & Van Atta, Dale.

Atta, Frieda Van see Van Atta, Frieda.

Atta, Jacob K. A Macroeconometric Model of a Developing Economy: Ghana (Simulations & Policy Analysis) LC 80-67178. 346p. (Orig.). 1981. pap. text ed. 12.50 (ISBN 0-8191-1504-5). U Pr of Amer.

Atta, Winfred Van see Van Atta, Winfred.

Attanasio, A. A. Sugarat. 544p. 1981. 14.95 (ISBN 0-688-00135-1); pap. 7.95 (ISBN 0-688-00508-X). Morrow.

Attanasio, Salvator, tr. see Rustow, Alexander.

Attar, Farid. Muslim Saints & Mystics: Episodes from the Tadhkirat Al-Auliya (Memorial of the Saints) Arberry, A. J., tr. from Persian. (Persian Heritage Ser.). 1979. pap. 7.95 (ISBN 0-7100-0169-X). Routledge & Kegan.

Attaway, John, jt. ed. see Nagy, Steven.

Atteberry, Pat H. Power Mechanics. LC 77-16075. (Illus.). 1978. text ed. 4.80 (ISBN 0-87006-243-3). Goodheart.

--Power Mechanics. LC 80-20581. (Illus.). 112p. 1980. text ed. 4.40 (ISBN 0-87006-307-3). Goodheart.

Atteberry, William. Modern Real Estate Finance. 3rd ed. LC 79-24627. (Grid Ser. in Finance & Real Estate). 1980. text ed. 20.95 (ISBN 0-88244-212-0). Grid Pub.

Atteberry, William L., et al. Real Estate Law. 2nd ed. LC 77-85043. (Real Estate-Business Law Ser.). 1978. text ed. 20.95 (ISBN 0-88244-161-2). Grid Pub.

Attebery, Brian. Fantasy Tradition in American Literature: From Irving to le Guin. LC 80-7670. 256p. 1980. 17.50x (ISBN 0-253-35665-2). Ind U Pr.

Attenberger, Walburga. Who Knows the Little Man? (Illus.). (ps-1). 1972. PLB 3.39 o.p. (ISBN 0-394-92427-4). Random.

Attenborough, Bessie M. Craft of Tatting. (Illus.). 1973. 5.25 o.p. (ISBN 0-8231-5039-9). Branford.

Atteraas, L., et al, eds. Underwater Technology-Offshore Petroleum: Proceedings of the International Conference, Bergen, Norway, April 14-16 1980. LC 80-40414. 450p. 1980. 66.00 (ISBN 0-08-026141-8). Pergamon.

Atterbury, P., jt. auth. see Philip, P.

Atterbury, Paul. Berthold Wolpe. (Illus.). 96p. 1981. 22.00 (ISBN 0-571-11655-8, Pub. by Faber & Faber). Merrimack Bk Serv.

Atterbury, Rowley S. The Contributors. (Illus.). 14.50 (ISBN 0-913720-03-8). Sandstone.

Atterbury, Stella. The Smallest Freezers. 1977. 11.95 o.p. (ISBN 0-571-10888-1, Pub. by Faber & Faber); pap. 5.95 (ISBN 0-571-11176-9). Merrimack Bk Serv.

Atthill, Robin. Mendip: A New Study. LC 76-45509. (Illus.). 1977. 28.00 (ISBN 0-7153-7297-1). David & Charles.

--The Somerset & Dorset Railway. LC 80-69344. (Illus.). 224p. 1981. 12.95 (ISBN 0-7153-4164-2). David & Charles.

Attinger, E. O. Global Systems Dynamics. 1970. 29.95 (ISBN 0-471-03640-4). Halsted Pr.

Attitude Research Conference, October, 1974, San Francisco. Attitude Research at Bay: Proceedings. Johnson, Deborah K. & Wells, William D., eds. LC 76-24880. 1976. pap. 12.00 o.p. (ISBN 0-87757-078-7). Am Mktg.

Attiyeh & Lumsden. The American Economics Ser. (gr. 10-12). 1972. pap. text ed. 9.00 each incl. 7 texts, tchrs' manuals, test plus 1 suppl. (ISBN 0-8449-0700-6). Learning Line.

Attiyeh, Richard E., et al. Macroeconomics: A Programmed Book. 3rd ed. (Illus.). 272p. (Prog. Bk.). 1974. pap. 9.95 ref. ed. (ISBN 0-13-542662-6). P-H.

--Microeconomics: A Programmed Book. 3rd ed. (Illus.). 256p. pap. 9.95 ref. ed. (ISBN 0-13-581421-9). P-H.

Attkisson, Frank. How to Cut Your Energy Bill Thirty to Fifty Percent. (Illus., Orig.). 1979. pap. 5.95 o.p. (ISBN 0-9602440-1-8). Jesus-First.

Attridge, D. Well-Weighed Syllables. LC 74-80362. (Illus.). 280p. 1975. 42.50 (ISBN 0-521-20530-1); pap. 12.95 (ISBN 0-521-29722-2). Cambridge U Pr.

Attridge, Harold W. First-Century Cynicism in the Epistles of Heraclitus. LC 76-20736. (Harvard Theological Review. Harvard Theological Studies: No. 29). 1976. pap. 6.00 (ISBN 0-89130-111-9, 020029). Scholars Pr Ca.

--The Interpretation of Biblical History in the Antiquitates Judaicae of Flavius Josephus. LC 76-26597. (Harvard Theological Review, Dissertations in Religion). 1976. pap. 7.50 (ISBN 0-89130-081-3, 020107). Scholars Pr Ca.

Attwater, Donald. Names & Name-Days: A Dictionary of Catholic Christian Names in Alphabetical Order with Origins & Meanings. LC 68-30595. 1968. Repr. of 1939 ed. 20.00 (ISBN 0-8103-3108-X). Gale.

Attwell, Arthur A. & Clabby, D. A. The Retarded Child: Answers to Questions Parents Ask. LC 72-182924. 139p. 1975. pap. 7.95x (ISBN 0-87424-120-0). Western Psych.

Attwood, C., ed. Practical Tables, Vol. 1: Six-Figure Trigonometrical Functions of Angles in Degrees & Minutes. 5th ed. 1965. 8.50 (ISBN 0-08-009894-0); pap. 4.20 (ISBN 0-08-009893-2). Pergamon.

Attwood, Stephen S. Electric & Magnetic Fields. 3rd ed. (Illus.). 1966. pap. 4.50 o.p. (ISBN 0-486-61753-X). Dover.

Atwater, Harry A. Introduction to Microwave Theory. rev. ed. Repr. of 1962 ed. lib. bdg. write for info. (ISBN 0-89874-192-0). Krieger.

Atwater, Mary M. Byways in Handweaving. 1968. 12.95 (ISBN 0-02-504320-X). Macmillan.

--Shuttle-Craft Book of American Hand-Weaving. rev. ed. (Illus.). 1951. 16.95 (ISBN 0-02-504380-3). Macmillan.

Atwater, Maxine H. Rollin' on: A Wheelchair Guide to U. S. Cities. LC 78-15289. (Illus.). 1978. 9.95 (ISBN 0-396-07548-7). Dodd.

Atwater, Montgomery M. Avalanche Patrol. (gr. 7-9). 1963. PLB 5.69 o.p. (ISBN 0-394-90923-2, BYR). Random.

Atwater, Warren E. Psychology of Adjustment: Personal Growth in a Changing World. (Illus.). 1979. pap. 14.95 (ISBN 0-13-734830-4). P-H.

Atwell, Lee. G. W. Pabst. (Theatrical Arts Ser.). 1977. lib. bdg. 12.50 (ISBN 0-8057-9251-1). Twayne.

Atwell, Sterling. The Philosophy of History in Schematic Representations. (Illus.). 1980. deluxe ed. 39.55 (ISBN 0-89266-230-1). Am Classical Coll Pr.

Atwood, A. C., jt. auth. see Blake, Sidney F.

Atwood, Ann. Fly with the Wind, Flow with the Water. (Illus.). 32p. (gr. 1-5). 1979. 9.95 (ISBN 0-684-16103-6). Scribner.

--Wild Young Desert. LC 73-106536. (Illus.). (gr. 6 up). 1970. 5.95 o.p. (ISBN 0-684-12625-7, ScribJ). Scribner.

Atwood, Beth, et al. Reading About Science, Skills & Concepts, 3 bks. Kane, Joanne E., ed. (Reading About Science, Skills & Concepts Ser.). (Illus.). (gr. 5-7). 1980. Bk. E, 144 Pgs. pap. text ed. 5.04x (ISBN 0-07-002425-1, W); Bk. F, 160 Pgs. pap. text ed. 5.28x (ISBN 0-07-002426-X); Bk. G, 160 Pgs. pap. text ed. 5.28x (ISBN 0-07-002427-8); tchrs. ed. 3.24 (ISBN 0-686-68698-5). McGraw.

Atwood, Beth S. Building Independent Learning Skills. LC 74-16807. (Learning Handbooks Ser.). 1974. pap. 3.95 (ISBN 0-8224-1973-4). Pitman Learning.

Atwood, E. Bagby. The Regional Vocabulary of Texas. 2nd ed. LC 62-9784. (Illus.). 1969. pap. 6.95 (ISBN 0-292-77008-1). U of Tex Pr.

Atwood, Jerry W. The Systems Analyst: How to Design Computer-Based Systems. 1977. text ed. 13.25x (ISBN 0-8104-5102-6). Hayden.

Atwood, June, jt. auth. see Cronan, Marion.

Atwood, June, jt. auth. see Cronan, Marion L.

Atwood, Margaret. The Circle Game. (House of Anansi Poetry Ser.: No. 3). 80p. 1967. 8.95 (ISBN 0-88784-103-1, Pub. by Hse Anansi Pr Canada). U of Toronto Pr.

--Edible Woman. 1976. pap. 2.25 (ISBN 0-445-08466-9). Popular Lib.

--Lady Oracle. 1977. pap. 1.95 (ISBN 0-380-01799-7, 35444). Avon.

--Life Before Man. 304p. 1981. pap. 2.95 (ISBN 0-445-04636-8). Popular Lib.

--Power Politics. LC 73-146455. (House of Anansi Poetry Ser.: No. 20). 56p. 1971. 8.95 (ISBN 0-88784-120-1, Pub. by Hse Anansi Pr Canada); pap. 3.95 (ISBN 0-88784-020-5). U of Toronto Pr.

--Surfacing. 224p. 1981. pap. 2.50 (ISBN 0-445-08465-0). Popular Lib.

--Two-Headed Poems. 1981. 9.95 (ISBN 0-686-68755-8, Touchstone Bks); pap. 5.95 (ISBN 0-686-68756-6). S&S.

Atwood, Mary A. Hermetic Philosophy & Alchemy. LC 79-8592. Repr. of 1960 ed. 49.50 (ISBN 0-404-18446-4). AMS Pr.

Atwood, Rodney. The Hessians: Mercenaries from Hessen Kassel in the American Revolution. LC 79-20150. 1980. 28.50 (ISBN 0-521-22884-0). Cambridge U Pr.

Au, Tung. Elementary Structural Mechanics. 1963. text ed. 26.95 (ISBN 0-13-260455-8). P-H.

Au, Tung & Stelson, Thomas E. Introduction to Systems Engineering: Deterministic Models. (Civil Engineering Ser). (Illus.). 1969. text ed. 22.95 (ISBN 0-201-00363-5); instructor's manual 3.00 (ISBN 0-201-00364-3). A-W.

Auber, Daniel F. Gustave ou le Bal Masque, 2 vols. LC 76-49212. (Early Romantic Opera Ser.: Vol. 31). 1980. lib. bdg. 82.00 (ISBN 0-8240-2930-5). Garland Pub.

--La Muette De Portici, 2 vols. Grossett, Philip & Rosen, Charles, eds. LC 76-49211. (Early Romantic Opera Ser.: Vol. 30). 1980. lib. bdg. 82.00 (ISBN 0-8240-2929-1). Garland Pub.

Aubert, J. J., jt. ed. see Preparata, G.

Aubert, Marcel. French Sculpture at the Beginning of the Gothic Period, 1140-1225. LC 75-143337. (Illus.). 1972. Repr. of 1929 ed. 40.00 o.p. (ISBN 0-87817-057-X). Hacker.

Aubert, Roger, ed. Church History in Future Perspective. (Concilium Ser.: Religion in the Seventies: Vol. 57). 1970. pap. 4.95 (ISBN 0-8164-2513-2). Crossroad NY.

--History, Self-Understanding of the Church: Concilium, Vol.67. LC 75-168655. (Religion in the Seventies). 1971. pap. 4.95 (ISBN 0-8164-2523-X). Crossroad NY.

Aubert, Vilhelm. The Hidden Society. (Social Science Classics Ser.). 351p. 1982. 19.95 (ISBN 0-87855-327-4); pap. 6.95 (ISBN 0-87855-730-X). Transaction Bks. Postponed.

Aubin, Jean-Pierre. Applied Abstract Analysis. LC 77-2382. (Pure & Applied Mathematics, a W-I Ser. of Texts, Monographs & Tracts). 1977. 33.95 (ISBN 0-471-02146-6, Pub. by Wiley-Interscience). Wiley.

--Applied Functional Analysis. LC 78-20896. (Pure & Applied Mathematics: Texts, Monographs & Tracts). 1979. 28.95 (ISBN 0-471-02149-0, Pub. by Wiley-Interscience). Wiley.

--Approximation of Elliptic Boundary-Value Problems. new ed. LC 79-26276. 386p. 1980. Repr. of 1972 ed. lib. bdg. 26.00 (ISBN 0-89874-077-0). Krieger.

Aubin, Penelope. The Life of Madam De Beaumont, a French Lady. Bd. with The Strange Adventures of the Count De Vinevil & His Family. LC 75-170548. (Foundations of the Novel 1700-1739). lib. bdg. 50.00 (ISBN 0-8240-0548-1). Garland Pub.

Aubin, Penelope see Haywood, Eliza.

Auboyer, J. Daily Life in Ancient India. 1965. 6.95 o.s.i. (ISBN 0-02-504420-6). Macmillan.

Auboyer, Jeannine, intro. by. Rarities of the Musee Guimet. LC 74-81967. (Illus.). 124p. 1975. 19.50 (ISBN 0-87848-043-9). Asia Soc.

Aubrey, Edmund. Sherlock Holmes in Dallas. LC 80-15980. 240p. 1980. 9.95 (ISBN 0-396-07904-0). Dodd.

Aubrey, John, jt. auth. see Washburn, W-Ilcomb E.

Aubrey, Ruth H. Selected Free Materials for Classroom Teachers. 6th ed. LC 77-90627. 1978. pap. 5.50 (ISBN 0-8224-6560-4). Pitman Learning.

Aubrey, Vickey. Chinese Brush Painting for Children. (Illus.). 32p. (gr. 2 up). 1981. 9.95 (ISBN 0-8149-0851-9). Vanguard.

Aubrey, Wilson, jt. auth. see Stacey, Nicholas A.

Aubry, Arthur S., Jr. & Caputo, Rudolph R. Criminal Interrogation. 3rd ed. 464p. 1980. 18.75 (ISBN 0-398-03978-X). C C Thomas.

Aubuchon, jt. auth. see Moran.

Auburn, Mark & Burkman, Katherine. Drama Through Performance. LC 76-19458. (Illus.). 1977. pap. text ed. 12.95 (ISBN 0-395-24548-6); inst. manual 1.25 (ISBN 0-395-24550-8). HM.

Auby, J. M., et al. Traite De Science Administrative: Anatomie et Physiologie De L'administration Publique. 1966. 61.75x (ISBN 90-2796-376-2). Mouton.

Aubyn, F. C. St. see St. Aubyn, F. C.

Auchincloss, Louis. The Cat & the King. 192p. 1981. 9.95 (ISBN 0-395-30225-0). HM.

--The House of the Prophet. (Large Print Bks.). 1980. lib. bdg. 14.95 (ISBN 0-8161-3133-3). G K Hall.

--The Partners. 256p. 1975. pap. 1.75 o.s.i. (ISBN 0-446-59714-7). Warner Bks.

--Pursuit of the Prodigal. 1971. pap. 0.95 o.p. (ISBN 0-380-01380-0, 06965). Avon.

--The Winthrop Covenant. 1977. pap. 1.95 o.p. (ISBN 0-345-25668-9). Ballantine.

Audefroi Le Bastard. Die Lieder und Romanzen Des Audefroi le Bastard. LC 80-2159. 1981. Repr. of 1914 ed. 26.50 (ISBN 0-404-19021-9). AMS Pr.

Audemars, Pierre. And One for the Dead. Date not set. 9.95 (ISBN 0-8027-5440-6). Walker & Co.

Auden, ed. see MacNeice, Louis.

Auden, W. H. Collected Longer Poems. LC 69-16429. 1969. 7.95 o.p. (ISBN 0-394-40321-5). Random.

--Collected Longer Poems (Giant) 1975. pap. 3.95 (ISBN 0-394-72014-8, V-2014, Vin). Random.

--Collected Shorter Poems: 1927 to 1957. 352p. Date not set. pap. 3.95 (ISBN 0-394-72015-6, V-2015, Vin). Random.

--Collected Shorter Poems 1927-1957. 1967. 15.95 (ISBN 0-394-40333-9). Random.

--Dyer's Hand & Other Essays. 1968. pap. 3.95 (ISBN 0-394-70418-5, V-418, Vin). Random.

--Selected Poems. Mendelson, Edward, ed. LC 78-55719. 1979. pap. 5.95 (ISBN 0-394-72506-9, V-506, Vin). Random.

--Selected Poems of W. H. Auden. 2nd ed. Date not set. pap. 2.45 (ISBN 0-394-71102-5, Vin). Random.

--Shield of Achilles. 1955. 6.95 o.p. (ISBN 0-394-40446-7). Random.

Auden, W. H. & Kallman, Chester. An Elizabethan Song Book. Greenberg, Noah, ed. 1968. pap. 6.50 (ISBN 0-686-16377-X, Pub. by Faber & Faber). Merrimack Bk Serv.

Auden, W. H., ed. Portable Greek Reader. (Viking Portable Library: No. 39). 1955. pap. 5.95 (ISBN 0-14-015039-0, P39). Penguin.

Auden, W. H., ed. see Dryden, John.

Auden, W. H., jt. ed. see Taylor, Paul B.

Auden, W. H., tr. Collected Poems of St. John Perse. LC 70-100357. (Bollingen Ser., No. 87). 1972. 27.50x o.p. (ISBN 0-691-09858-1). Princeton U Pr.

Auden, W. H., tr. see Perse, St. John.

Audet, Thelma, jt. auth. see Dreizen, LaVerne.

Audette, Vicki. Dress for Less: One Thousand & One for Saving Money on Clothes. Grooms, Kathe, ed. (A Consumer-Aid Bk.). (Illus.). 160p. 1981. pap. 3.95 (ISBN 0-915658-33-X). Meadowbrook Pr.

Audley, Noel F. Cornucopia: Homespun Philosophy. 1981. 6.95 (ISBN 0-533-04631-9). Vantage.

Audsley, G., jt. auth. see Audsley, W.

Audsley, W. & Audsley, G. Designs & Patterns from Historic Ornaments. Orig. Title: Outlines of Ornament in the Leading Styles. (Illus.). 9.00 (ISBN 0-8446-1565-X). Peter Smith.

Audubon, John J. Birds of America, 7 vols. (Illus.). Repr. of 1840 ed. Set. 56.00 (ISBN 0-8446-1567-6); 8.00 ea. Peter Smith.

--Birds of America. (Illus.). (gr. 5 up). 1947. 24.95 (ISBN 0-02-504440-0). Macmillan.

Aududon, Maria R. Audubon & His Journal, 2 vols. Aaron, Daniel, ed. (American Men & Women of Letters Audubon & His Journals Ser.). (Illus.). 1100p. 1981. pap. 14.95 (ISBN 0-87754-174-4). Chelsea Hse.

Aue, A. E., tr. see Wittgenstein, Ludwig.

Aue, Hartmann Von see Hartmann, Von Aue.

Aue, Hartmann Von see Hartmann Von Aue.

Auer, J. Jeffery, ed. Brigance's Speech Communication. 3rd ed. Orig. Title: Speech Communication. 1967. pap. 11.95 (ISBN 0-13-082933-1). P-H.

Auer, J. Jeffery & Jenkinson, Edward B., eds. On Teaching Speech in Elementary & Junior High Schools. LC 73-138412. (English Curriculum Study Ser). 1971. 7.50x o.p. (ISBN 0-253-34240-6); pap. 3.25x o.p. (ISBN 0-253-34241-4). Ind U Pr.

Auer, Marilyn M., ed. see Russell, James E.

Auer, Peter, ed. Energy & the Developing Nations. (Pergamon Policy Studies on Energy). (Illus.). 400p. 1981. 50.00 (ISBN 0-08-027527-3). Pergamon.

Auerbach & Harper. Immigration Laws of the United States. 3rd ed. 756p. 1975. 44.00, with 1979 suppl (ISBN 0-672-83703-X, Bobbs-Merrill Law); 1978 suppl. 9.00 (ISBN 0-672-83691-2). Michie.

Auerbach, Aline B. Parents Learn Through Discussion: Principles & Practices of Parent Group Education. 372p. 1980. Repr. of 1968 ed. lib. bdg. 18.75 (ISBN 0-89874-183-1). Krieger.

Auerbach, Aline B., jt. auth. see Wolf, Katherine M.

Auerbach, Carl & Zinnes, Joseph L. Psychological Statistics: A Case Approach. text ed. 16.95 scp (ISBN 0-397-47376-1, HarpC); inst. manual free (ISBN 0-06-379301-6); scp student wkbk. 6.50 (ISBN 0-397-47398-2). Har-Row.

Auerbach, Erich. Dante, Poet of the Secular World. Silverstein, Theodore, ed. Manheim, Ralph, tr. 1961. 6.00x (ISBN 0-226-03207-8). U of Chicago Pr.

--Literary Language & Its Public in Late Latin Antiquity & in the Middle Ages. Manheim, R., tr. (Bollingen Ser.: No. 74). 1965. 21.00 o.p. (ISBN 0-691-09782-8). Princeton U Pr.

Auerbach, Jerold S. Unequal Justice. 1976. 19.95 (ISBN 0-19-501939-3). Oxford U Pr.

Auerbach, Jerold S., ed. American Labor: The Twentieth Century. LC 69-14822. (American Heritage Ser). 1969. pap. 9.50 (ISBN 0-672-60128-1, 78). Bobbs.

Auerbach, Stevanne. The Whole Child: A Sourcebook. (Illus.). 320p. 1981. 17.95 (ISBN 0-399-12364-4). Putnam.

Auerbach, Stevanne, ed. Child Care: A Comprehensive Guide, 2 vols. Incl. Vol. 1. Rationale for Child Care: Programs Vs. Politics. LC 74-11877. 215p. 1975. text ed. 16.95 (ISBN 0-87705-218-2); Vol. 2. Model Programs & Their Components. LC 76-10121. 297p. 1976. 19.95 (ISBN 0-87705-256-5). Human Sci Pr.

Auerbach, Sylvia. A Woman's Book of Money-a Guide to Financial Independence. LC 75-44952. 220p. 1976. pap. 4.95 (ISBN 0-385-09883-9, Dolp). Doubleday.

Auf Der Heide, Ralph. The Illustrated Wine Making Book. LC 72-90968. pap. 1.50 o.p. (ISBN 0-385-06939-1, Dolp). Doubleday.
Auffret, Pierre. The Literary Structure of Psalm Two. (JSOT Supplement Ser.: No. 3). 43p. 1977. pap. text ed. 3.00x o.p. (ISBN 0-905774-02-7, Pub by JSOT Pr England). Eisenbrauns.
Aufmann, Richard N. & Barker, Vernon C. Arithmetic: An Applied Approach. LC 77-77005. (Illus.). 1978. pap. text ed. 15.25 (ISBN 0-395-25791-3); inst. manual 0.50 (ISBN 0-395-25790-5). HM.
Augarde, Steve. Barnaby Shrew, Black Dan & the Mighty Wedgwood. (Illus.). (ps-3). 1980. 7.95 (ISBN 0-233-97104-1). Andre Deutsch.
--Barnaby Shrew Goes to Sea. (Illus.). (ps-3). 1979. PLB 8.95 (ISBN 0-233-96957-8). Andre Deutsch.
--Mr. Mick. LC 80-65660. (Illus.). 32p. (ps-3). 1980. 9.95 (ISBN 0-233-97254-4). Andre Deutsch.
Augelli, John P. Caribbean Lands. rev. ed. LC 77-84154. (American Neighbors Ser.). (Illus.). (gr. 5 up). 1978. text ed. 9.95 ea. 1-4 copies (ISBN 0-88296-112-8); text ed. 7.96 ea. 5 or more; tchrs'. guide 6.96 (ISBN 0-88296-353-8). Fideler.
Augelli, John P. & West, Robert C. Middle America: Its Lands & Peoples. 2nd ed. (Anthropology Ser.). (Illus.). 576p. 1976. text ed. 22.95 (ISBN 0-13-581546-0). P-H.
Augenstein, Moshe & Tenenbaum, Aaron. Data Structures & PL-1 Programming. (Illus.). 1979. text ed. 25.95 (ISBN 0-13-197731-8); exercise manual 6.95 (ISBN 0-13-197756-3). P-H.
Augenstein, Moshe & Tenenbaum, Aaron M. Data Structures Using PASCAL. (Illus.). 528p. 1981. text ed. 23.95 (ISBN 0-13-196501-8). P-H.
Auger, C. P., ed. Engineering Eponyms. 2nd rev. ed. 1975. 15.50x (ISBN 0-85365-437-9, Pub. by Lib Assn England). Oryx Pr.
Augerbauer, George J. Electronics for Modern Communication. (Illus.). 672p. 1974. ref. ed. 21.95 (ISBN 0-13-252338-8). P-H.
Augier see Stanton, Stephen S.
Augier, F. R. & Gordon, Shirley C., eds. Sources of West Indian History: A Compilation of Writings of Historical Events in the West Indies. (Orig.). (YA) 1962. pap. text ed. 3.75x (ISBN 0-582-76303-7). Humanities.
Augsberger, tr. Livre Para Perdoar. (Portuguese Bks.). 1979. 1.30 (ISBN 0-8297-0735-2). Life Pubs Intl.
Augsburger, David. Caring Enough to Forgive. LC 80-50545. 1981. pap. 4.95 (ISBN 0-8307-0749-2). Regal.
--Cherishable: Love & Marriage. 1975. pap. 1.25 (ISBN 0-89129-065-6, PV065). Jove Pubns.
Augsburger, David W. Anger & Assertiveness in Pastoral Care. Clinebell, Howard J. & Stone, Howard W., eds. LC 78-14660. (Creative Pastoral Care & Counseling Ser.). 96p. 1979. pap. 2.95 (ISBN 0-8006-0562-4, 1-562). Fortress.
Augspurg, Casey, jt. auth. see Augspurg, Gus.
Augspurg, Gus & Augspurg, Casey. Monkey Business. (Illus.). 1957. pap. 1.79 o.p. (ISBN 0-87666-211-4, AP8052). TFH Pubns.
Auguet, Roland. Festivals & Celebrations. (International Library). 128p. (gr. 7 up). 1975. PLB 6.90 o.p. (ISBN 0-531-02117-3). Watts.
Augur, Helen. The Book of Fairs. LC 75-159875. (Tower Bks). (Illus.). xviii, 308p. 1972. Repr. of 1939 ed. 20.00 (ISBN 0-8103-3927-7). Gale.
Augusiobo, Obiora N., jt. auth. see Olaitan, Samson O.
August, Bonnie & Count, Ellen. Dress Thin, Look Thin. LC 80-51245. (Illus.). 304p. 1981. 13.95 (ISBN 0-89256-137-8). Rawson Wade.
August, Eugene R., ed. see Carlyle, Thomas.
Augusteyn, R. C. & Collin, H. B. The Eye, Vol. 2. Horrobin, David F., ed. (Annual Research Reviews). 344p. 1980. 36.00 (ISBN 0-88831-083-8). Eden Med Res.
Augustin, Ann S. Help! I Want to Remodel My Home: The New Woman's Guide to Home Improvement. LC 74-28307. (Illus.). 230p. 1975. 12.95 (ISBN 0-88229-214-5). Nelson-Hall.
Augustine, Don & Fass, Peter M. Private Real Estate Limited Partnerships 1980: A Course Handbook. LC 80-81320. (Real Estate Law & Practice Course Handbook Ser.). 950p. 1980. pap. text ed. 25.00 (ISBN 0-686-68828-7, N4-4353). PLI.
Augustine, St. Against Julian. (Fathers of the Church Ser.: Vol. 35). 21.00 (ISBN 0-8132-0035-0). Cath U Pr.
Augustine, Saint Against the Academicians. Garvey, Sr. M. Patricia, tr. 1957. pap. 5.95 (ISBN 0-87462-202-6). Marquette.
--City of God, 2 Vols. Tasker, R. V., ed. Healey, John, tr. 1957. 10.50x ea. (ISBN 0-686-66408-6, Evman). Vol. 1 (ISBN 0-460-00982-6). Vol. 2 (ISBN 0-460-00983-4). Dutton.
Augustine, St. City of God, Bks. 1-7. (Fathers of the Church Ser.: Vol. 8). 24.00 (ISBN 0-8132-0008-3). Cath U Pr.
--Immortality of the Soul. (Fathers of the Church Ser.: Vol. 4). 24.00 (ISBN 0-8132-0004-0). Cath U Pr.
--Letters: 165-203. (Fathers of the Church Ser.: Vol. 30). 21.00 (ISBN 0-8132-0030-X). Cath U Pr.
--Letters: 204-272. (Fathers of the Church Ser.: Vol. 32). 16.00 (ISBN 0-8132-0032-6). Cath U Pr.
Augustine, Saint On Christian Doctrine. Robertson, D. W., tr. LC 58-9956. 1958. pap. 4.95 (ISBN 0-672-60262-8). Bobbs.
--On Free Choice of the Will. Benjamin, A. S. & Hackstaff, L. H., trs. LC 63-16932. (Orig.). 1964. pap. 4.95 (ISBN 0-672-60368-3, LLAS150). Bobbs.
--Presdestinacion of Saintes. Bd. with Perserveraunce Unto Thende. LC 68-54611. (English Experience Ser.: No. 32). Repr. of 1556 ed. 20.00 (ISBN 90-221-0032-4). Walter J Johnson.
Augustine, St. St. Augustine, Sermons for Christmas & Epiphany. Quasten, J. & Plumpe, J., eds. Lawler, Thomas, tr. (Ancient Christian Writers Ser.: No. 15). 250p. 1952. 10.95 (ISBN 0-8091-0137-8). Paulist Pr.
--St. Augustine: The Greatness of the Soul, Vol. 9. Quasten, J. & Plumpe, J., eds. Colleran, Joseph M., tr. (Ancient Christian Writers Ser.: No. 9). 255p. 1950. 11.95 (ISBN 0-8091-0060-6). Paulist Pr.
--Sermons of the Liturgical Seasons. (Fathers of the Church Ser.: Vol. 38). 23.00 (ISBN 0-8132-0038-5). Cath U Pr.
Augustithis, S. S. Atlas of the Textural Patterns of Basic & Ultrabasic Rocks & Their Genetic Significance. 1979. 150.00x (ISBN 3-11-006571-1). De Gruyter.
Augustus. Res Gestae Divi Augusti. Brunt, P. A. & Moore, J. M., eds. 1967. pap. 6.95x (ISBN 0-19-831772-7). Oxford U Pr.
Aukema, Susan & Kostick, Marilyn. The Curity Baby Book. 7.95 (ISBN 0-916752-06-2). Green Hill.
Auker, Jim & Cey, Ron. How to Play Third Base. 1977. pap. 2.50 o.p. (ISBN 0-695-80867-2). Follett.
Aukerman, Louise R., jt. auth. see Aukerman, Robert C.
Aukerman, Robert C. Approaches to Beginning Reading. LC 70-144330. (Illus.). 1971. pap. text ed. 14.95 (ISBN 0-471-03691-9). Wiley.
--The Basal Reader Approach to Reading. 400p. 1981. text ed. 14.95 (ISBN 0-471-03082-1); pap. text ed. 8.95 (ISBN 0-471-09066-2). Wiley.
Aukerman, Robert C. & Aukerman, Louise R. How Do I Teach Reading. LC 80-23380. 550p. 1981. text ed. 14.95 (ISBN 0-471-03687-0). Wiley.
Aulard, Alphonse. Christianity & the French Revolution. 1966. 15.00 (ISBN 0-86527-025-2). Fertig.
Auld, James. Real Personality. 1981. 7.75 (ISBN 0-8062-1597-6). Carlton.
Auld, Margaret E. & Birum, Linda H. The Challenge of Nursing: A Book of Readings. LC 72-87648. 224p. 1973. pap. text ed. 8.95 o.p. (ISBN 0-8016-0410-9). Mosby.
Auld, Rhoda L. Molas: What They Are; How to Make Them; Ideas They Suggest for Creative Applique. 136p. 1980. pap. 9.95 (ISBN 0-442-20050-1). Van Nos Reinhold.
Aulen, Gustaf. The Faith of the Christian Church. rev. ed. Wahlstrom, Eric H., tr. from Swedish. LC 61-5302. 416p. 1973. pap. 5.75 (ISBN 0-8006-1655-3, 1-1655). Fortress.
Auletta, Ken. The Streets Were Paved with Gold: The Decline of New York--An American Tragedy. LC 79-22305. 1980. pap. 4.95 (ISBN 0-394-74355-5, V-355, Vin). Random.
Aulls, Mark W. Developmental & Remedial Reading in the Middle Grades. new ed. 1978. text ed. 19.95 (ISBN 0-205-06092-7). Allyn.
--Developmental & Remedial Reading in the Middle Grades. abr. ed. 1978. pap. text ed. 10.95 (ISBN 0-205-06081-1). Allyn.
Aulnoy, Marie C. Hypolitus Earl of Douglas... with the Secret History of Mack-Beth King of Scotland. Bd. with The Island of Content: A New Paradise Discovered. LC 70-170517. LC 76-170516. (Foundations of the Novel Ser.: Vol. 12). lib. bdg. 50.00 (ISBN 0-8240-0524-4). Garland Pub.
--The Prince of Carency. LC 70-170541. (Novel in England, 1700-1775 Ser). lib. bdg. 50.00 (ISBN 0-8240-0542-2). Garland Pub.
Ault, Addison. Techniques: Experiments for Organic Chemistry. 3rd ed. 1979. text ed. 18.95x (ISBN 0-205-06528-7, 6865283); instr's man. o.p. avail. (ISBN 0-205-06545-7). Allyn.
Ault, Addison & Ault, Margaret R. A Handy & Systematic Catalog of NMR Spectra: Instruction Through Examples. LC 79-57227. 425p. 1980. 15.00 (ISBN 0-935702-00-8). Univ Sci Bks.
Ault, Hugh J. & Radler, Albert J., trs. from Ger. German Corporation Tax Reform Law 1977. 1977. pap. text ed. 15.00x (ISBN 3-7875-5261-8). Rothman.
Ault, Margaret R., jt. auth. see Ault, Addison.
Ault, Phil. By the Seat of Their Pants. LC 78-7738. (Illus.). (gr. 5 up). 1978. 6.95 (ISBN 0-396-07613-0). Dodd.
Ault, Ruth L. Children's Cognitive Development: Piaget's Theory & the Process Approach. (Illus.). 1977. text ed. 11.95x (ISBN 0-19-502092-8); pap. text ed. 4.95x (ISBN 0-19-502093-6). Oxford U Pr.
Ault, Warren O. Private Jurisdiction in England. LC 80-1998. 1981. Repr. of 1923 ed. 37.00 (ISBN 0-404-18550-9). AMS Pr.
Aultman, Dick & Golf Digest Editors. One Hundred & One Ways to Win at Golf. LC 80-66689. 248p. (Orig.). 1980. pap. 5.95 (ISBN 0-914178-40-7, 41417-8). Golf Digest.
Aultman, Dick, jt. auth. see Runyan, Paul.
Aultman, Dick, jt. auth. see Toski, Bob.
Aultman, Dick, jt. auth. see Trevino, Lee.
Aultman, Donald S. Guiding Youth. 1977. pap. 3.50 (ISBN 0-87148-358-0). Pathway Pr.
Auluck, Sunita V. Intracity Residential Mobility in an Industrial City: A Case Study of Ludhiana. 180p. 1980. text ed. 10.25x (ISBN 0-391-02134-6). Humanities.
Aumann, Francis R. Changing American Legal System: Some Selected Phases. LC 79-92625. (Law, Politics, & History Ser). 1969. Repr. of 1940 ed. 29.50 (ISBN 0-306-71762-X). Da Capo.
Aumann, Jordan, tr. see John Paul, Pope, II.
Aumiaux, M. The Use of Microprocessors. LC 79-42904. (Wiley Ser. in Computing). 198p. 1980. 36.00 (ISBN 0-471-27689-8, Pub. by Wiley Interscience). Wiley.
Aumiller, Dr. Jochen. You Don't Have to Be Next. 1980. pap. 5.95 (ISBN 0-8065-0683-0). Lyle Stuart.
Aumra. As of a Trumphet. 1968. 4.95 (ISBN 0-686-27649-3). Cole-Outreach.
Aune, B. A. Knowledge, Mind & Nature. 1979. lib. bdg. 22.00 (ISBN 0-917930-27-4); pap. text ed. 7.50x (ISBN 0-917930-07-X). Ridgeview.
Aung, M. Htin see Htin Aung, M.
Aung, Maung Htin & Trager, Helen G. Kingdom Lost for a Drop of Honey. LC 68-11653. (Illus.). 96p. (gr. 3-7). 1968. 5.95 o.s.i. (ISBN 0-8193-0219-8, Four Winds); PLB 5.41 o.s.i. (ISBN 0-8193-0220-1). Schol Bk Serv.
Aunger, Edmund A. In Search of Political Stability: A Comparative Study of New Brunswick & Northern Ireland. 238p. 1981. 21.95x (ISBN 0-7735-0366-8). McGill-Queens U Pr.
AUPHA Task Force on Financial Management. Financial Management of Health Care Organizations: A Referenced Outline & Annotated Bibliography. 237p. 1978. 8.00 (ISBN 0-686-68588-1, 14921). Hospital Finan.
Auran, John H. Skiing Is a Family Sport. LC 68-31329. 4.95 (ISBN 0-910294-33-X). Brown Bk.
Aurand, L. W., jt. auth. see Woods, A. E.
Aurand, Leonard W. & Woods, A. E. Food Chemistry. (Illus.). 1973. text ed. 19.50 o.p. (ISBN 0-87055-142-6). AVI.
Aurandt, Paul. More of Paul Harvey's the Best of the Story. 208p. 1981. pap. 2.50 (ISBN 0-553-14594-0). Bantam.
--Paul Harvey's the Rest of the Story. LC 77-75381. 1977. 8.95 (ISBN 0-385-12768-5). Doubleday.
Aurelia, Joseph C. Aphasia Therapy Manual. 2nd ed. 1980. pap. text ed. 3.95x (ISBN 0-8134-2112-8, 2112). Interstate.
--Aphasia Therapy Manual. LC 73-90607. 1974. pap. text ed. 2.95x o.p. (ISBN 0-8134-1627-2, 1627). Interstate.
Aurelius, Marcus. The Meditations. Grube, G. M., tr. LC 63-12205. (Orig.). 1963. pap. 3.95 (ISBN 0-672-60402-7). Bobbs.
--Meditations. Staniforth, Maxwell, tr. (Classics Ser.). (Orig.). (YA) (gr. 9 up). 1964. pap. 2.75 (ISBN 0-14-044140-9). Penguin.
Aurigemma, Luigi. Le Signe Zodiacal Du Scorpion Dans les Traditions Occidentales De L'antiquite Grego-Latine a la Renaissance. (Civilisations et Societes.: No. 54). (Illus.). 1976. text ed. 47.05x (ISBN 90-2797-573-6). Mouton.
Aurobindo. Glossary of Terms in Sri Aurobindo's Writings. 1979. 9.50 (ISBN 0-89744-980-0, Pub. by Sri Aurobindo Ashram Trust India); pap. 7.50 (ISBN 0-89744-981-9, Pub. by Sri Aurobindo Ashram Trust India). Auromere.
Aurobindo, Sri. Dictionary of Sri Aurobindo's Yoga. Pandit, Sri M., ed. 1979. Repr. of 1966 ed. 7.50 (ISBN 0-89744-905-3). Auromere.
--Essays on the Gita. 1979. 7.50 (ISBN 0-89744-907-X); lib. bdg. 14.00 (ISBN 0-89744-906-1); pap. 6.00 (ISBN 0-89744-908-8). Auromere.
--Foundations of Indian Culture. 1979. pap. 10.00 (ISBN 0-89744-909-6). Auromere.
--The Life Divine, 2 vols. 1977. 12.50 o.p. (ISBN 0-89071-269-7); pap. 10.00 o.p. (ISBN 0-89071-270-0). Matagiri.
--More Lights on Yoga. 1979. pap. 2.00 (ISBN 0-89744-950-9). Auromere.
--Practical Guide to Integral Yoga. 7th ed. Manibhai, ed. 1979. 6.00 o.p. (ISBN 0-89744-941-X); pap. 4.50 (ISBN 0-89744-942-8). Auromere.
--The Synthesis of Yoga. 1976. pap. 8.00 (ISBN 0-89071-268-9). Matagiri.
Aurobindo, Sri, tr. see Sri Aurobindo.
Aurobindo, Sri, tr. see The Mother.
Aurora, V. K., jt. auth. see Kumar, Girja.
Ausband, John R., ed. Ear, Nose and Throat Disorders: A Practitioners Guide. 1974. spiral bdg. 12.00 o.p. (ISBN 0-87488-705-4). Med Exam.
Ausberger, Carloyn & Green, Mary J. Here's How to Handle "S". 1979. 50.00 (ISBN 0-88450-708-4, 3057-B). Communications Skill.
Ausberger, Carolyn & Green, Mary J. Here's How to Handle "R". 1975. 50.00 (ISBN 0-88450-707-6, 2023-B). Communication Skill.
Auslander, David & Sagues, Paul. Microprocessors for Measurement & Control. 300p. (Orig.). 1981. pap. 15.99 (ISBN 0-931988-57-8). Osborne-McGraw.
Ausloos, P. Fundamental Processes in Radiation Chemistry. 753p. 1968. text ed. 32.50 (ISBN 0-470-03834-9, Pub. by Wiley). Krieger.
Austen, D. E. & Rhymes, I. L. A Laboratory Manual of Blood Coagulation. (Illus.). 160p. 1976. 17.00 (ISBN 0-8016-0376-5, Blackwell). Mosby.
Austen, Jane. The Complete Novels of Jane Austen. Incl. Vol. 1. Sense & Sensibility, Pride & Prejudice, Mansfield Park (ISBN 0-394-71891-7, V-891); Vol. 2. Emma, Northanger Abbey, Persuasion (ISBN 0-394-71892-5, V-892). 1976. pap. 4.95 ea. (Vin). Random.
--Emma. pap. 1.75. Bantam.
--Emma. 1964. pap. 1.75 (ISBN 0-451-51357-6, CE1357, Sig Classics). NAL.
--Emma. Blythe, Ronald, ed. (English Library Ser). 1966. pap. 2.50 (ISBN 0-14-043010-5). Penguin.
--Emma. new ed. Parrish, Stephen, ed. (Norton Critical Editions). 430p. 1972. pap. 4.95x (ISBN 0-393-09667-X). Norton.
--Emma. lib. bdg. 15.95x (ISBN 0-89966-242-0). Buccaneer Bks.
--Jane Austen's Letters to Her Sister Cassandra & Others. 2nd ed. Chapman, R. W., ed. 716p. 1979. 45.00x (ISBN 0-19-212102-2). Oxford U Pr.
--Love & Friendship & Other Early Works. Bell, Harriet, ed. (Illus.). 128p. 1981. 8.95 (ISBN 0-517-54459-8, Harmony); pap. 3.95 (ISBN 0-517-54372-9). Crown.
--Mansfield Park. Lucas, John, ed. (Oxford English Novels Ser.). 1970. 11.95x o.p. (ISBN 0-19-255336-4). Oxford U Pr.
--Mansfield Park. (Illus.). 1955. 10.50x (ISBN 0-460-00023-3, Evman); pap. 2.95 (ISBN 0-460-01023-9, EP1023). Dutton.
--Mansfield Park. (The Zodiac Press Ser.). 1978. 9.95 (ISBN 0-7011-1233-6, Pub. by Chatto Bodley Jonathan). Merrimack Bk Serv.
--Mansfield Park. Kinsley, James & Lucas, John, eds. (The World's Classics Ser.). 256p. 1981. pap. 2.95 (ISBN 0-19-281526-1). Oxford U Pr.
--Mansfield Park. lib. bdg. 15.95x (ISBN 0-89966-244-7). Buccaneer Bks.
--Northanger Abbey. (World's Classics Ser.). 8.95 o.p. (ISBN 0-19-250355-3). Oxford U Pr.
--Northanger Abbey. 1977. pap. 2.25 o.p. (ISBN 0-460-01893-0, Evman). Dutton.
--Northanger Abbey. (Macdonald Classics Ser.). 266p. 1974. 9.95x (ISBN 0-8464-0676-4). Beekman Pubs.
--Northanger Abbey. (The Zodiac Press Ser.). 1978. 9.95 (ISBN 0-7011-1234-4, Pub. by Chatto Bodley Jonathan). Merrimack Bk Serv.
--Northanger Abbey. Kinsley, James & Davie, John, eds. Bd. with Lady Susan; The Watsons; Sandition. (The World's Classics Ser.). 350p. 1981. pap. 2.95 (ISBN 0-19-281525-3). Oxford U Pr.
--The Oxford Illustrated Jane Austen, 6 vols. 3rd ed. Chapman, R. W., ed. Incl. Sense & Sensibility. 1933. Vol. 1. 15.95x (ISBN 0-19-254701-1); Pride & Prejudice. 1932. Vol. 2. 16.95x (ISBN 0-19-254702-X); Mansfield Park. 1934. Vol. 3. 15.95x (ISBN 0-19-254703-8); Emma. 1933. Vol. 4. 17.95x (ISBN 0-19-254704-6); Northanger Abbey & Persuasion. 1933. Vol. 5. 17.95x (ISBN 0-19-254705-4); Minor Works. (1st ed.). 1954. Vol. 6. 17.95x (ISBN 0-19-254706-2). Oxford U Pr.
--Persuasion. (World's Classics Ser.). 5.95 o.p. (ISBN 0-19-250356-1). Oxford U Pr.
--Persuasion. (The Zodiac Press Ser.). 1978. 9.95 (ISBN 0-7011-1235-2, Pub. by Chatto Bodley Jonathan). Merrimack Bk Serv.
--Persuasion. Kinsley, James & Davie, John, eds. (The World's Classics Ser.). 256p. 1981. pap. 2.95 (ISBN 0-19-281546-6). Oxford U Pr.
--Pride & Prejudice. pap. 1.50. Bantam.

--Pride & Prejudice. (Literature Ser). (gr. 7-12). 1969. pap. text ed. 3.50 (ISBN 0-87720-711-9). AMSCO Sch.

--Pride & Prejudice. (Illus.). (gr. 9 up). 1962. PLB 5.25 o.s.i. (ISBN 0-02-707710-1). Macmillan.

--Pride & Prejudice. 1980. lib. bdg. 13.95 (ISBN 0-8161-3076-0, Large Print Bks). G K Hall.

--Pride & Prejudice. 1976. pap. 2.95 (ISBN 0-460-01022-0, Evman). Dutton.

--Pride & Prejudice. Tanner, Tony, ed. Date not set. pap. 1.95 (ISBN 0-14-005774-9). Penguin.

--Pride & Prejudice. lib. bdg. 15.95x (ISBN 0-89966-243-9). Buccaneer Bks.

--Sense & Sensibility. (Literature Ser). (gr. 10-12). 1970. pap. text ed. 3.58 (ISBN 0-87720-738-0). AMSCO Sch.

--Sense & Sensibility. (The Zodiac Press Ser). 1978. 10.95 (ISBN 0-7011-1237-9, Pub. by Chatto Bodley Jonathan). Merrimack Bk Serv.

--Sense & Sensibility. 544p. 1981. Repr. lib. bdg. 19.95x (ISBN 0-89966-287-0). Buccaneer Bks.

--The Watsons. LC 72-9808. 318p. 1973. Repr. of 1958 ed. lib. bdg. 24.75x (ISBN 0-8371-6598-9, AUTW). Greenwood.

--The Works of Jane Austen. (Spring Books Ser. of Classics). 1979. 14.00 (ISBN 0-600-00603-4). Transatlantic.

Austen, K. F., jt. ed. see Lichtenstein, L. M.

Austen, K. Frank, jt. ed. see Mahmoud, Adel A.

Austen, W. Gerald, jt. auth. see Behrendt, Douglas M.

Auster, Paul, tr. see Clastres, Pierre.

Austerlitz, Roberg, ed. The Scope of American Linguistics. 1977. text ed. 10.25x (ISBN 90-316-0003-2). Humanities.

Austerlitz, Robert, tr. see Kruszewski, Mikolaj.

Austern, David T., ed. see O'Brien, Edward L. & Fisher, Margaret E.

Austin, Aleine. Matthew Lyon: "New Man" of the Democratic Revolution, 1749-1822. LC 80-281. (Illus.). 208p. 1980. 16.50x (ISBN 0-271-00262-X). Pa St U Pr.

Austin, Alicia. The Illustrated Night Before Christmas. (Illus.). 96p. (gr. k-5). 1980. pap. 1.95 (ISBN 0-448-14151-5, Tempo). G&D.

Austin, Allan E. Roy Fuller. (English Authors Ser.: No. 253). 1979. lib. bdg. 12.95 (ISBN 0-8057-6743-6). Twayne.

Austin, Bill. The Back Side of God. 1980. pap. 3.95 (ISBN 0-8423-0115-1). Tyndale.

Austin, C. K. Site Carpentry. (Illus.). 1979. 19.95x; wire bdg. 14.95x (ISBN 0-7198-2730-2). Intl Ideas.

Austin, C. R. & Short, R. V., eds. Human Sexuality. LC 78-18959. (Reproduction in Mammals Ser.: Bk. 8). (Illus.). 110p. 1980. 24.95 (ISBN 0-521-22361-X); pap. 7.95 (ISBN 0-521-29461-4). Cambridge U Pr.

Austin, Colinus, ed. Comicorum Graecorum Fragmenta in papyris reperta (1838-1971) 1973. 197.00x (ISBN 3-11-004046-8). De Gruyter.

Austin, D. & Crosfield, T. English for Nurses. (Illus.). 144p. 1976. pap. text ed. 4.50x (ISBN 0-582-55019-X); tchrs' notes 2.25x (ISBN 0-582-55244-3). Longman.

Austin, D. G. Chemical Engineering Drawing Symbols. 1979. 22.95 (ISBN 0-470-26601-5). Halsted Pr.

Austin, David. Year of the Capricorn. 1981. 9.95 (ISBN 0-533-04467-7). Vantage.

Austin, Dennis. Ghana Observed: Essays on the Politics of a West African Republic. LC 76-15398. 1976. text ed. 28.50x (ISBN 0-8419-0278-X, Africana). Holmes & Meier.

--Politics in Africa. LC 77-95397. 212p. 1978. text ed. 12.50x (ISBN 0-87451-150-X); pap. text ed. 7.50x (ISBN 0-87451-152-6). U Pr of New Eng.

Austin, Donald F. & Werner, S. Benson. Epidemiology for the Health Sciences: A Primer on Epidemiologic Concepts & Their Uses. (Illus.). 88p. 1979. pap. 5.25 (ISBN 0-398-02949-0). C C Thomas.

Austin, Eileen K. Guidelines for the Development of Continuing Education Offerings for Nurses. 176p. 1981. pap. 11.00 (ISBN 0-8385-3524-0). ACC.

Austin, Elizabeth S. Penguins: The Birds with Flippers. (gr. 3-6). 1968. PLB 5.99 (ISBN 0-394-90148-7); pap. 1.95. Random.

Austin, Erik W., ed. see Geda, Carolyn L., et al.

Austin, H. Russell. The Wisconsin Story. rev. ed. (Illus.). 650p. (gr. 6 up). 1948. pap. 6.00 (ISBN 0-686-27878-X). Milwaukee Journal.

Austin, James, jt. ed. see Krisberg, Barry.

Austin, James E., ed. Nutrition Programs in the Third World: Cases & Concepts. LC 80-21083. 464p. 1981. lib. bdg. 27.50 (ISBN 0-89946-024-0). Oelgeschlager.

Austin, James E. & Zeitlin, Marian F., eds. Nutrition Intervention in Developing Countries: An Overview. LC 80-29223. (Nutrition Intervention in Developing Countries Ser.). 256p. 1981. lib. bdg. 20.00 (ISBN 0-89946-077-1). Oelgeschlager.

Austin, James H. Chase, Chance, & Creativity. LC 77-23011. 1978. 15.00x (ISBN 0-231-04294-9). Columbia U Pr.

Austin, James T. The Life of Elbridge Gerry, 2 Vols. LC 77-99470. (American Public Figures Ser). 1970. Repr. of 1828 ed. lib. bdg. 69.50 (ISBN 0-306-71841-3). Da Capo.

Austin, Karen O., tr. see Galdos, Benito P.

Austin, L. & Lindberg, Roy. Zero-Base Planning & Budgeting: A Key to Raising Productivity. (Illus.). 1980. 25.00 o.p. (ISBN 0-89433-107-8). Petrocelli.

Austin, L. Allan & Cheek, Logan M. Zero-Base Budgeting: A Decision Package Manual. (Illus.). 1979. 16.95 (ISBN 0-8144-5513-1). Am Mgmt.

Austin, M. M. & Vidal-Naquet, P. Economic & Social History of Ancient Greece: An Introduction. 1978. 27.50x (ISBN 0-520-02658-6); pap. 6.95 (ISBN 0-520-04267-0). U of Cal Pr.

Austin, Marilyn. Holly Hathaway, Physical Therapist. 192p. (YA) 1976. 4.95 o.p. (ISBN 0-685-64241-0, Avalon). Bouregy.

Austin, Mary. The Flock. LC 73-83228. (Illus.). 266p. 1973. Repr. of 1906 ed. 15.00 (ISBN 0-88307-509-1). Gannon.

--The Textbook of Acupuncture Therapy. rev. 2nd ed. LC 72-78147. (Illus.). 280p. 1975. text ed. 20.00 (ISBN 0-88231-003-8). ASI Pubs Inc.

Austin, Mary S. Philip Freneau, the Poet of the Revolution. Vreeland, Helen K., ed. LC 67-23885. 1968. Repr. of 1901 ed. 15.00 (ISBN 0-8103-3040-7). Gale.

Austin, Michael J. Professionals & Paraprofessionals. LC 77-26273. 295p. 1978. text ed. 22.95 (ISBN 0-87705-305-7). Human Sci Pr.

--Supervisory Management for the Human Services. (P-H Ser. in Social Work Practices). 352p. 1981. text ed. 16.95 (ISBN 0-13-877068-9). P-H.

Austin, Norman. Archery at the Dark of the Moon: Poetic Problems in Homer's Odyssey. LC 73-94442. 300p. 1975. 20.00x (ISBN 0-520-02713-2). U of Cal Pr.

Austin, P. A Grammar of Diyari, South Australia. (Cambridge Studies in Linguistics Monographs: No. 32). (Illus.). 230p. Date not set. price not set (ISBN 0-521-22849-2). Cambridge U Pr.

Austin, Paul, jt. auth. see Lindfors, Viveca.

Austin, Paul B., tr. see Gripe, Maria.

Austin, R. G., ed. see Cicero.

Austin, R. G., ed. see Virgil.

Austin, R. W. Sufis of Andalusia: The Ruh Al-Quds & Al-Durrat Al-Fakhirah of Ibn 'arabi. (Library Reprint Ser.: Vol. 91). 1978. 16.00x (ISBN 0-520-03553-4). U of Cal Pr.

Austin, Reid, jt. auth. see Vargas, Alberto.

Austin, Stephen F. Establishing Austin's Colony: The First Book Printed in Texas, with the Laws, Orders, & Contracts of Colonization. Gracy, David B., 2nd, ed. (Illus.). 9.50 (ISBN 0-8363-0031-9). Jenkins.

Austin, William. Music in the Twentieth Century. (Illus.). 1966. 19.95x (ISBN 0-393-09704-8, NortonC). Norton.

Austin, William M., ed. Papers in Linguistics in Honor of Leon Dostert. (Janua Linguarum, Ser. Major: No. 25). 1967. text ed. 34.10x (ISBN 90-2790-616-5). Mouton.

Austin, William W. Susanna, Jeanie & the Old Folks at Home: The Songs of Stephen C. Foster from His Time to Ours. LC 75-17635. 448p. 1975. 17.95 o.s.i. (ISBN 0-02-504500-8, 50450). Macmillan.

Austin-Lett, Genelle & Sprague, Janet. Talk to Yourself: Experiencing Intrapersonal Communication. LC 75-31037. (Illus.). 160p. 1976. pap. text ed. 7.25 (ISBN 0-395-18576-9). HM.

Austrin, Miriam G., et al. Workbook for Medical Assistants. (Illus.). 198p. 1980. pap. text ed. 10.95 (ISBN 0-8016-0409-5). Mosby.

Austwick, Brian, jt. auth. see Austwick, Jill.

Austwick, Jill & Austwick, Brian. The Decorative Tile: An Illustrated History of English Tile-Making & Design. (Illus.). 1981. 30.00 (ISBN 0-684-16761-1). Scribner.

Austwick, K., et al. Objective Questions in "A" Level Modern Mathematics. 1973. pap. text ed. 3.95x o.p. (ISBN 0-435-51040-1). Heinemann Ed.

Austwick, Kenneth. Sistemas De Ecuaciones. (Span). 1970. pap. 1.40 (ISBN 0-06-310040-1, IntlDept). Har-Row.

Ausubel, Nathan, ed. A Treasury of Jewish Folklore. 544p. 1980. pap. 3.95 (ISBN 0-553-13807-3). Bantam.

Auten, James H. Training in the Small Department. 144p. 1973. 12.75 (ISBN 0-398-02719-6). C C Thomas.

Autenrieth, Georg. Homeric Dictionary for Schools & Colleges. Flagg, Isaac, ed. Keep, Robert P., tr. (Illus.). (YA) (gr. 9 up). 1979. Repr. of 1958 ed. 7.95x (ISBN 0-8061-0394-9). U of Okla Pr.

Autgaerden, S., jt. auth. see Thomas, Andre.

Auto Racing Magazine Staff, jt. auth. see Engel, Lyle K.

Autocar Editors. MG Sports Cars. LC 78-65889. 1979. 14.95 (ISBN 0-312-50156-0). St Martin.

Automation Industries. Solar Energy Reports Available from the National Solar Data Program. 50p. 1981. pap. 11.95 (ISBN 0-89934-104-7). Solar Energy Info.

Automobile Assication. AA Camping & Caravanning in Europe. rev. ed. (Illus.). 416p. 1981. pap. write for info. (Pub. by Auto Assn-British Tourist Authority England). Merrimack Bk Serv.

Automobile Association. AA Camping & Caravanning in Britain. rev. ed. (Illus.). 256p. 1981. pap. write for info. (ISBN 0-86145-041-8, Pub. by Auto Assn-British Tourist Authority England). Merrimack Bk Serv.

--AA Guesthouses & Inns in Britain. rev. ed. (Illus.). 264p. 1981. pap. write for info. (ISBN 0-86145-042-6, Pub. by Auto Assn-British Tourist Authority England). Merrimack Bk Serv.

--AA Guesthouses, Farmhouses & Inns in Europe. rev. ed. (Illus.). 256p. 1981. pap. write for info. (Pub. by Auto Assn-British Tourist Authority England). Merrimack Bk Serv.

--AA Hotels & Restaurants in Britain. rev. ed. (Illus.). 600p. 1981. pap. write for info. (ISBN 0-86145-040-X, Pub. by Auto Assn-British Tourist Authority England). Merrimack Bk Serv.

--AA Ireland: Where to Go, What to Do. (Illus.). 204p. 1981. pap. write for info. (ISBN 0-86145-035-3, Pub. by Auto Assn-British Tourist Authority England). Merrimack Bk Serv.

--AA Motoring in Europe. rev. ed. (Illus.). 416p. 1981. pap. write for info. (Pub. by Auto Assn-British Tourist Authority England). Merrimack Bk Serv.

--AA Self Catering in Britain. rev. ed. (Illus.). 272p. 1981. pap. write for info. (ISBN 0-86145-043-4, Pub. by Auto Assn-British Tourist Authority England). Merrimack Bk Serv.

--AA Stately Homes, Museums, Castles & Gardens. rev. ed. (Illus.). 272p. 1981. pap. price not set (ISBN 0-86145-044-2, Pub. by Auto Assn-British Tourist Authority England). Merrimack Bk Serv.

--AA The Motorists' Atlas of Western Europe. (Illus.). Date not set. pap. price not set (ISBN 0-86145-029-9, Pub. by Auto Assn-British Tourist Authority England). Merrimack Bk Serv.

--AA Touring Map of Western Europe. (Illus.). Date not set. pap. price not set (ISBN 0-86145-001-9). Merrimack Bk Serv.

Automobile Association & British Tourist Authority. A-Z Visitors' London Atlas & Guide. (Illus.). 96p. 1981. pap. write for info. (ISBN 0-85039-107-5, Pub. by Auto Assn-British Tourist Authority England). Merrimack Bk Serv.

--AA -BTA Where to Go in Britain. (Illus.). 224p. 1981. write for info. (ISBN 0-86145-028-0, Pub. by Auto Assn-British Tourist Authority England). Merrimack Bk Serv.

--Britain: Four Countries, One Kingdom. (Illus.). 64p. Date not set. pap. price not set (ISBN 0-85122-188-2, Pub. by Auto Assn-British Tourist Authority England). Merrimack Bk Serv.

--Guide to Outdoor Britain: North of England. (Illus.). 160p. 1981. pap. write for info. (ISBN 0-7099-0385-5, Pub. by Auto Assn-British Tourist Authority England). Merrimack Bk Serv.

--London: Hotels & Restaurants Incl. Budget Accom. rev. ed. (Illus.). 146p. 1981. pap. write for info. (ISBN 0-7095-0576-0, Pub. by Auto Assn-British Tourist Authority England). Merrimack Bk Serv.

Automobile Association British Tourist Authority. A-Z London Map. (Illus.). 1981. pap. write for info. (ISBN 0-85039-021-4, Pub. by Auto Assn-British Tourist Authority England). Merrimack Bk Serv.

Automobile Association - British Tourist Authority. Castles & Historic Places in Wales. (Illus.). 1979. pap. 3.95 o.p. (ISBN 0-900784-63-6, Pub. by B T a). Merrimack Bk Serv.

--Hotels in England. 1979. pap. 8.95 (ISBN 0-686-24020-0, Pub. by B T a). Merrimack Bk Serv.

--Mid-Wales. (Regional Guide Ser.). (Illus.). 1979. pap. 2.95 o.p. (ISBN 0-900784-51-2, Pub. by B T a). Merrimack Bk Serv.

--North Wales. (Regional Guide Ser.). (Illus.). 1979. pap. 2.95 o.p. (ISBN 0-900784-50-4, Pub. by B T a). Merrimack Bk Serv.

--Royal Britain. (Illus.). 1979. pap. 9.95 (ISBN 0-09-128200-4, Pub. by B T a). Merrimack Bk Serv.

--Scotland for the Motorist. 1979. pap. 2.50 o.p. (ISBN 0-686-24008-1, Pub. by B T a). Merrimack Bk Serv.

--Touring Guide to Britain. (Illus.). 1979. pap. 13.95 (ISBN 0-85630-854-4, Pub. by B T a). Merrimack Bk Serv.

--Where to Stay: East Anglia. 1979. pap. 2.95 o.p. (ISBN 0-86143-005-0, Pub. by B T a). Merrimack Bk Serv.

--Where to Stay: East Midlands. 1979. pap. 2.95 o.p. (ISBN 0-86143-003-4, Pub. by B T a). Merrimack Bk Serv.

Automobile Association -British Tourist Authority. Where to Stay: English Lakeland. 1979. pap. 2.95 o.p. (ISBN 0-903265-98-2, Pub. by B T a). Merrimack Bk Serv.

Automobile Association - British Tourist Authority. Where to Stay: Heart of England. 1979. pap. 2.95 o.p. (ISBN 0-86143-002-6, Pub. by B T a). Merrimack Bk Serv.

--Where to Stay in Wales. (Illus.). 1979. pap. 4.50 o.p. (ISBN 0-900784-70-9, Pub. by B T a). Merrimack Bk Serv.

--Where to Stay: North West England. 1979. pap. 2.95 o.p. (ISBN 0-86143-000-X, Pub. by B T a). Merrimack Bk Serv.

--Where to Stay: Northumbria. 1979. pap. 2.95 o.p. (ISBN 0-903265-99-0, Pub. by B T a). Merrimack Bk Serv.

--Where to Stay: South East England. 1979. pap. 2.95 o.p. (ISBN 0-86143-009-3, Pub. by B T a). Merrimack Bk Serv.

--Where to Stay: South of England. 1979. pap. 2.95 o.p. (ISBN 0-86143-008-5, Pub. by B T a). Merrimack Bk Serv.

--Where to Stay: Thames & Chilterns. 1979. pap. 2.95 o.p. (ISBN 0-86143-004-2, Pub. by B T a). Merrimack Bk Serv.

--Where to Stay: West Country. 1979. pap. 2.95 o.p. (ISBN 0-86143-007-7, Pub. by B T a). Merrimack Bk Serv.

--Where to Stay: Yorkshire & Humberside. 1979. pap. 2.95 o.p. (ISBN 0-86143-001-8, Pub. by B T a). Merrimack Bk Serv.

Automobile Association of England, ed. Treasures of Britain. 3rd ed. (Illus.). 1976. 24.95 (ISBN 0-393-08743-3). Norton.

Automobile Associations of New Zealand. AA Road Atlas of New Zealand. LC 77-372880. (Illus.). 1975. 15.00x (ISBN 0-600-07347-5). Intl Pubns Serv.

Automobile Club of Italy, ed. World Cars 1977. LC 7-643381. (Illus.). 1977. 33.95 (ISBN 0-910714-09-6). Herald Bks.

--World Cars 1979. LC 7-643381. (Illus.). 1979. 33.95 (ISBN 0-910714-11-8). Herald Bks.

Automobile Quarterly Editors. American Car Since Seventeen Seventy-Five: An Encyclopedic Survey. (Illus.). 1971. 17.95 o.p. (ISBN 0-525-05300-X). Dutton.

--Great Cars & Grand Marques: Automobile Quarterly's Great Cars & Grand Marques. (Automobile Quarterly Marques History Ser.). 1976. 29.50 o.p. (ISBN 0-525-11612-5). Dutton.

Autor, Anne P. Active Oxygen in Medicine. Date not set. text ed. cancelled (ISBN 0-89004-410-4). Raven.

Autret, Jean, ed. see Proust, Marcel.

Autret, Jean, tr. see Proust, Marcel.

Autrum, H., ed. Comparative Physiology & Evolution of Vision in Invertebrates B: Invertebrate Visual Centers & Behavior I. (Handbook of Sensory Physiology: Vol. VII, Pt. 6B). (Illus.). 650p. 1980. 159.30 (ISBN 0-387-08703-6). Springer-Verlag.

Autry, Ewart A. & Autry, Lola M. Bible Puppet Plays. (Paperback Program Ser.). pap. 3.95 (ISBN 0-8010-0032-7). Baker Bk.

Autry, Lola M., jt. auth. see Autry, Ewart A.

Autton, Norman. In Times of Sickness. 1978. 1.40 (ISBN 0-686-28781-9). Forward Movement.

Autumn, Violeta. Flavors of Northern Italy. LC 80-83215. (Illus.). 168p. (Orig.). 1980. pap. 5.95 (ISBN 0-89286-164-9). One Hund One Prods.

Auty, R. & Obolensky, D., eds. Cambridge Companion to Russian Studies, Vol. 1. LC 75-10691. 1976. 44.50 (ISBN 0-521-20893-9); pap. 16.95 (ISBN 0-521-28038-9). Cambridge U Pr.

Auty, Robert. Handbook of Old Church Slavonic, Text & Glossary. (London East European Ser.). 1977. pap. text ed. 17.50x (ISBN 0-485-17518-5, Athlone Pr). Humanities.

Auty, Susan G. The Comic Spirit of Eighteenth Century Novels. (National University Publications Literary Criticism Ser.). 200p. 1975. 15.00 (ISBN 0-8046-9120-7, Natl U.). Kennikat.

Auvil, Daniel L. & Poluga, Charles. Elementary Algebra. LC 77-76194. (Illus.). 1978. text ed. 14.95 (ISBN 0-201-00137-3); student supplement 3.25 (ISBN 0-201-00138-1). A-W.

Auvil, Kenneth W. Serigraphy: Silk Screen Techniques for the Artist. (Illus., Orig.). 1965. 9.95 (ISBN 0-13-807164-0). P-H.

Auvray, J. & Fourrier, M. Problems in Electronics. LC 73-7617. 444p. 1974. text ed. 46.00 (ISBN 0-08-016982-1); pap. text ed. 17.50 (ISBN 0-08-017871-5). Pergamon.

Auvray, Louis, jt. auth. see De La Chavignerie, Emile B.

Au-Yang, M. K., ed. Flow-Induced Vibration of Power Plant Components. (PVP: No. 41). 176p. 1980. 24.00 (H00168). ASME.

Avallone, Michael. Where Monsters Walk. (gr. 7 up). 1978. pap. 1.25 (ISBN 0-590-11914-1, Schol Pap). Schol Bk Serv.

Avalov, Zurab D. The Independence of Georgia in International Politics, 1918-1920. LC 79-2890. 286p. 1981. Repr. of 1940 ed. 23.50 (ISBN 0-8305-0059-6). Hyperion Conn.

Avanesov, R. I. Modern Russian Stress. (Pergamon Oxford Russian Ser.). 1963. pap. 4.00 o.p. (ISBN 0-08-010300-6). Pergamon.

Avary, Myrta L. Dixie After the War: An Exposition of Social Conditions Existing in the South, During the 12 Years Succeeding the Fall of Richmond. LC 79-77701. (American Scene Ser). (Illus.). 1970. Repr. of 1937 ed. 35.00 (ISBN 0-306-71339-X). Da Capo.

Avary, Myrta L., ed. Recollections of Alexander H. Stephens: His Diary Kept When a Prisoner at Fort Warren, Boston Harbor, 1865. LC 76-124914. (American Public Figures Ser). 1971. Repr. of 1910 ed. lib. bdg. 55.00 (ISBN 0-306-71984-3). Da Capo.

Avebury. The Dread & the Love of Nature. (Illus.). 1980. Repr. of 1909 ed. deluxe ed. 29.75 deluxe binding (ISBN 0-89901-012-1). Found Class Reprints.

Avedon, Elliott M. Therapeutic Recreation Service: An Applied Behavioral Science Approach. 256p. 1974. ref. ed. 15.95 (ISBN 0-13-914879-5). P-H.

Avedon, John F. An Interview with the Dalai Lama. LC 80-83015. (Illus.). 83p. (Orig.). 1980. pap. 6.95 (ISBN 0-937896-00-4). Littlebird.

Avedon, Luciana & Molli, Jeanne. Luciana Avedon's Body Book. LC 76-15189. (Illus.). 208p. 1976. 12.95 (ISBN 0-87131-211-5). M Evans.

Aveline, Claude see Otten, Anna.

Aveling, Eleanor M., tr. see Plekhanov, Georgii V.

Aveling, Harry, tr. Arjuna in Meditation. 1976. 14.00 (ISBN 0-89253-799-X); flexible cloth 8.00 (ISBN 0-89253-800-7). Ind-US Inc.

Aveni, Anthony F. Skywatchers of Ancient Mexico. (Texas Pan American Ser.). (Illus.). 360p. 1980. text ed. 20.00x (ISBN 0-686-60148-3); pap. 6.95 (ISBN 0-292-77557-1). U of Tex Pr.

Avens, Robert. Imagination Is Reality. rev. ed. Severson, Bedford A., ed. 128p. 1979. pap. 7.00 (ISBN 0-88214-311-5). Spring Pubns.

Avens, Roberts. Imagination: A Way Toward Western Nirvana. LC 78-68693. 1979. pap. text ed. 8.25 (ISBN 0-8191-0697-6). U Pr of Amer.

Avent, Sue. Spells, Chants, & Potions. LC 77-22779. (Myth, Magic & Superstition Ser.). (Illus.). (gr. 4-5). 1977. PLB 9.65 (ISBN 0-8172-1035-0). Raintree Pubs.

Averbach, Albert. Handling Accident Cases: 1963-73, 7 vols. in 8 bks. LC 58-4149. 1973. Set. 320.00 (ISBN 0-686-14528-3); Vols. 1-2. 85.00; Vols. 3a-3b. 42.50 ea.; Vols. 4-5. 85.00; Vols. 6-7. 85.00. Lawyers Co-Op.

Averbach, Bonnie & Chein, Orin. Mathematics: Problem Solving Through Recreational Mathematics. LC 80-11989. (Mathematical Sciences Ser.). (Illus.). 1980. text ed. 16.95x (ISBN 0-7167-1124-9); instrs'. guide avail. W H Freeman.

Averbakh, Y. Chess Endings - Essential Knowledge. text ed. 11.50 (ISBN 0-08-011823-2); pap. text ed. 5.75 (ISBN 0-08-011822-4). Pergamon.

--Chess Endings: Essential Knowledge. (Pergamon Chess Ser.). (Illus.). 1966. 11.50 (ISBN 0-08-011823-2); pap. 5.75 (ISBN 0-08-011822-4). Pergamon.

Averbakh, Yuri. Bishop Endings. 1977. 18.95 (ISBN 0-7134-0096-X). David & Charles.

--Bishop V. Knight Endings. 1977. 18.95 (ISBN 0-7134-3179-2). David & Charles.

--Queen & Pawn Endings. 1976. 15.95 (ISBN 0-7134-3041-9). David & Charles.

--Queen V. Rook Minor Piece Endings. 1978. 22.50 (ISBN 0-7134-0866-9, Pub. by Batsford England). David & Charles.

--Rock v. Minor Piece Endings. 1978. 18.95 (ISBN 0-7134-0868-5, Pub. by Batsford England). David & Charles.

Averbakh, Yuri & Chekhover, V. Knight Endings. 1977. 18.95 (ISBN 0-7134-0552-X). David & Charles.

Averbakh, Yuri & Maizelis, I. Pawn Endings. 1974. 22.50 (ISBN 0-7134-2797-3). David & Charles.

Averill, Gerald. Ridge Runner. LC 79-14339. (Illus.). 1979. lib. bdg. 10.50 o.p. (ISBN 0-89621-031-6); pap. 4.95 (ISBN 0-89621-030-8). Thorndike Pr.

Averkamp, Marcella. Preserving Paper & Photographic Materials: A Handbook for Curators & Librarians. LC 80-26028. (Illus.). 88p. (Orig.). 1981. pap. 7.95x (ISBN 0-87020-203-0). State Hist Soc Wis.

Averroes. Middle Commentary on Aristotle Topics. Butterworth, Charles E. & Ahmad Abd al-Magid Haridi, eds. (Corpvs Commentariorvm Averrois in Aristotelem). 317p. (Orig., Arabic.). 1979. pap. 10.00 (ISBN 0-936770-03-1). Am Res Ctr Egypt.

Averrois. Averrois Cordubensis Commentarium Medium in Porphyrii Isagogen et Aristoelis Categorias, Eng. Ed. Davidson, Herbert A., ed. 1969. 7.50 (ISBN 0-910956-53-7). Medieval Acad.

Avers, Charlotte J. Cell Biology. 2nd ed. 1981. text ed. price not set (ISBN 0-442-25770-8). D Van Nostrand.

Avery, Arthur C. A Modern Guide to Foodservice Equipment. LC 79-20831. (Illus.). 1980. text ed. 26.95 (ISBN 0-8436-2179-6). CBI Pub.

Avery, Benedict R., tr. see Gregorius I.

Avery, Charles. Florentine Renaissance Sculpture. LC 78-148429. (Icon Editions). (Illus.). 282p. 1971. pap. 5.95x o.s.i. (ISBN 0-06-430038-2, IN-38, HarpT). Har-Row.

Avery, Connie, jt. ed. see Brown, Alan R.

Avery, Craig, ed. see Portland Cement Association.

Avery, David D., jt. auth. see Singh, Devendra.

Avery, David R., jt. auth. see McDonald, Ralph E.

Avery, Emmett L. London Stage, Seventeen Hundred to Seventeen Twenty-Nine: A Critical Introduction, Pt. 2. LC 60-6539. (Arcturus Books Paperbacks). (Illus.). 199p. 1968. pap. 5.95 (ISBN 0-8093-0337-X). S Ill U Pr.

Avery, Emmett L. & Scouten, Arthur H. London Stage, Sixteen Sixty to Seventeen-Hundred: A Critical Introduction, Pt. 1. LC 60-6539. (Arcturus Books Paperbacks Ser.). (Illus.). 203p. 1968. pap. 5.95 (ISBN 0-8093-0336-1). S Ill U Pr.

Avery, Emmett L., ed. see Congreve, William.

Avery, Ernest. Jungle Oil: Hazardous Times. 1981. 8.95 (ISBN 0-533-04889-3). Vantage.

Avery, Evelyn. Rebels & Victims: The Fiction of Richard Wright & Bernard Malamud. (National Univ. Pubns. Literary Criticism Ser.). 1979. 10.00 (ISBN 0-8046-9234-3). Kennikat.

Avery, Gillian. Ellen & the Queen. LC 74-10287. (Illus.). 128p. (gr. 3-5). 1975. 5.95 o.p. (ISBN 0-525-66415-7). Elsevier-Nelson.

Avery, Gillian, et al. Authors' Choice. LC 76-126978. (Illus.). (gr. 7 up). 1971. 8.95 o.p. (ISBN 0-690-11141-X, TYC-J). T Y Crowell.

Avery, J. H. & Ingram, A. W. Objective Tests in Advanced Level Physics. 1970. pap. text ed. 1.50x o.p. (ISBN 0-435-68042-0); pap. text ed. 2.95x with answers o.p. (ISBN 0-435-68043-9). Heinemann Ed.

--Objective Tests in Ordinary Level Physics, Bk. 1. 1969. pap. text ed. 2.95x with ans. o.p. (ISBN 0-435-67043-3). Heinemann Ed.

--Objective Tests in Ordinary Level Physics, Bk. 2. 1975. pap. text ed. 2.25x with ans. o.p. (ISBN 0-435-67044-1). Heinemann Ed.

Avery, Kevin Quinn. The Numbers of Life. LC 76-45969. 354p. 1977. pap. 4.50 (ISBN 0-385-12629-8, Dolp). Doubleday.

Avery, Lois, jt. auth. see Debnam, Betty.

Avery, Mary E., et al. The Lung & Its Disorders in the Newborn Infant. 4th ed. (Major Problems in Clinical Pediatrics: Vol. 1). (Illus.). 560p. 1981. text ed. price not set (ISBN 0-7216-1462-0). Saunders.

Avery, Robert K. & Pepper, Robert. The Politics of Interconnection: A History of Public Television at the National Level. 66p. 1979. pap. 3.00 (Pub Telecom). NAEB.

Avery, Robert K., et al. Research Index of NAEB Journals, 1957 to 1979. 169p. 1980. pap. 13.50. NAEB.

Avery, Robert S. Experiment in Management: Personnel Decentralization in the Tennessee Valley Authority. LC 54-11202. 1954. 12.50x (ISBN 0-87049-010-9). U of Tenn Pr.

Avery, William P., et al, eds. Rural Change & Public Policy: Eastern Europe, Latin America & Australia. (Pergamon Policy Studies). 1980. 39.00 (ISBN 0-08-023109-8). Pergamon.

Avery Jones, J. F., ed. Tax Havens & Measures Against Tax Evasion & Avoidance in the EEC. 144p. 1974. text ed. 25.00x (ISBN 0-85227-027-5). Rothman.

Averyt, William F., Jr. Agropolitics in the European Community: Interest Groups & the Common Agricultural Policy. LC 77-10619. 1977. 21.95 (ISBN 0-03-039666-2). Praeger.

Avesta, English. Zend-Avesta, 3 Vols. LC 68-30997. 1880-87. Repr. lib. bdg. 49.00x (ISBN 0-8371-3070-0, AVZE). Greenwood.

Aveyard, R. & Haydon, D. A. An Introduction to the Principles of Surface Chemistry. LC 72-89802. (Illus.). 200p. 1973. 42.50 (ISBN 0-521-20110-1); pap. 15.95x (ISBN 0-521-09794-0). Cambridge U Pr.

Avi. Emily Upham's Revenge. LC 77-13739. (gr. 5-8). 1978. 6.95 (ISBN 0-394-83506-9); PLB 6.99 (ISBN 0-394-93506-3). Pantheon.

--The History of Helpless Harry: To Which Is Added a Variety of Amusing & Entertaining Adventures. (Illus.). 1980. 8.95 (ISBN 0-394-84505-6). Pantheon.

--A Place Called Ugly. LC 80-23326. (Illus.). 224p. (YA) (gr. 7-9). 1981. 8.95 (ISBN 0-394-84755-5); PLB 8.99 (ISBN 0-394-94755-X). Pantheon.

Aviado, D. M., jt. auth. see Salem, H.

Aviation Book Company, ed. see Federal Aviation Administration.

Aviation Book Company Editors, jt. auth. see Federal Aviation Administration.

Aviation Consumer. The Aviation Consumer Used Aircraft Guide. Weeghman, Richard, ed. (McGraw-Hill Series in Aviation). (Illus.). 224p. 1981. 18.95 (ISBN 0-07-002543-6). McGraw.

Aviation Maintenance Publishers. Airframe Logbook. 77p. 1975. pap. 4.95 (ISBN 0-89100-190-5, E*A-A*F*L-1). Aviation Maintenance.

--Engine Logbook. 77p. 1975. pap. 4.95 (ISBN 0-89100-187-5, E*A-E*F*L-1). Aviation Maintenance.

--Pilot Logbook. 72p. 1979. text ed. 3.95 (ISBN 0-89100-112-3, E*A-P*L*O-2). Aviation Maintenance.

--Radio Logbook. 70p. 1974. pap. 3.95 (ISBN 0-89100-186-7, EA-ARL-1). Aviation Maintenance.

--Radio Logbook. 70p. 1974. text ed. 4.95 (ISBN 0-89100-195-6, EA-ARL-2). Aviation Maintenance.

Aviation Mechanincs Journal. Nineteen Eighty Aircraft & Helicopter Digest. (Illus.). 204p. 1980. text ed. 13.25 (ISBN 0-89100-184-0, E*A-184-0). Aviation Maintenance.

Avicenna. Avicenna'a Psychology. Rahman, F., ed. LC 79-2848. 127p. 1981. Repr. of 1952 ed. 14.50 (ISBN 0-8305-0024-3). Hyperion Conn.

Avi-Itzhak, Benjamin, jt. auth. see Vardi, Joseph.

Avila, Donald L., et al. The Helping Relationship Source Book. 2nd ed. 1977. pap. text ed. 10.50 (ISBN 0-205-05843-4). Allyn.

Avineri, Shlomo. Hegel's Theory of the Modern State. LC 70-186254. (Cambridge Studies in the History & Theory of Politics Ser.). 266p. 1973. 32.50 (ISBN 0-521-08513-6); pap. 8.95x (ISBN 0-521-09832-7). Cambridge U Pr.

--Social & Political Thought of Karl Marx. LC 68-12055. (Studies in the History & Theory of Politics). 1971. 32.50 (ISBN 0-521-04071-X); pap. 8.95x (ISBN 0-521-09619-7). Cambridge U Pr.

Aviram, Uri, jt. auth. see Segal, Steven P.

Avis, Paul D. The Church in the Theology of the Reformers. Toon, Peter & Martin, Ralph, eds. LC 80-16186. (New Foundations Theological Library). 256p. 1981. 18.50 (ISBN 0-8042-3708-5); pap. 11.95 (ISBN 0-8042-3728-X). John Knox.

Avital, Samuel. Mime Workbook. 2nd, rev. ed. Reed, Ken, ed. LC 77-84487. (Illus.). 176p. 1977. pap. 8.95 (ISBN 0-914794-30-2). Wisdom Garden.

Avi-Yonah, Michael, jt. auth. see Aharoni, Yohanon.

Avi Yonah, Michael & Shatzman, Israel, eds. Illustrated Encyclopedia of the Classical World. LC 73-14245. (Illus.). 510p. 1976. 20.00 o.p. (ISBN 0-06-010178-4, HarpT). Har-Row.

Avogaro, P., jt. ed. see Galli, C.

Avon, Dennis & Tilford, Tony. Birds of Britain & Europe. (Illus.). 1975. 11.95 (ISBN 0-7137-0762-3, Pub by Blandford Pr England). Sterling.

Avon Products. Looking Good, Feeling Beautiful. 14.95 (ISBN 0-671-25224-0). S&S.

Avrich, Paul. The Russian Anarchists. LC 80-21590. (Studies of the Russian Institute, Columbia University). (Illus.). vii, 303p. 1980. Repr. of 1967 ed. lib. bdg. 28.50x (ISBN 0-313-22571-0, AVRA). Greenwood.

Avriel, Mordecai, ed. Advances in Geometric Programming. (Mathematical Concepts & Methods in Science & Engineering Ser.: Vol. 21). 470p. 1980. 39.50 (ISBN 0-306-40381-1, Plenum Pr). Plenum Pub.

Avrin, Cookie, jt. auth. see Sassen, Georgia.

Awad, A. G., et al. Evaluation of Quality of Care in Psychiatry: Proceedings of a Symposium Held at the Queen St. Mental Health Centre, Toronto, Canada, June 22, 1979. LC 80-94280. 140p. 1980. 21.00 (ISBN 0-08-025364-4). Pergamon.

Awad, Elias M. Business Data Processing. 5th ed. (Illus.). 1980. text ed. 19.95 (ISBN 0-13-093807-6); student wkbk. 7.95 (ISBN 0-13-093757-6). P-H.

--Introduction to Computers in Business. (Illus.). 512p. 1977. text ed. 19.95 (ISBN 0-13-479378-1); student guide 7.95 (ISBN 0-13-479360-9). P-H.

--Systems Analysis & Design. 1979. 17.95x (ISBN 0-256-02091-4). Irwin.

Awad, Elias M., jt. auth. see Cascio, Wayne F.

Awad, Joseph. The Neon Distances. 1980. 5.50 (ISBN 0-8233-0320-9). Golden Quill.

Awad, Sheikh M., jt. auth. see Hiskett, M.

Awbery, Gwen. The Syntax of Welsh. LC 76-11489. (Cambridge Studies in Linguistics: No. 18). 1977. 35.00 (ISBN 0-521-21341-X). Cambridge U Pr.

Awh, Robert Y. Microeconomics: Theory & Applications. LC 75-38643. 1976. text ed. 22.95 (ISBN 0-471-03849-0); instructors manual (ISBN 0-471-03854-7); wkbk 6.50 (ISBN 0-471-03853-9). Wiley.

Awolalu, Joseph O. Yoruba Beliefs & Sacrificial Rites. (Illus.). 1979. text ed. 28.00x (ISBN 0-582-64203-5); pap. text ed. 13.50 (ISBN 0-582-64244-2). Longman.

Awoonor, Kofi, tr. see Akpalu, Vinoko.

Awwad, Tawfiq Y. Death in Beirut. McLoughlin, Leslie, tr. from Arabic. 1978. 9.00 (ISBN 0-914478-86-9); pap. 5.00 (ISBN 0-914478-87-7). Three Continents.

Axelbank, Albert. Black Star Over Japan: Rising Forces of Militarism. 1972. 7.95 o.p. (ISBN 0-8090-3045-4). Hill & Wang.

--The China Challenge. (Illus.). (gr. 7 up). 1978. PLB 5.90 s&l o.p. (ISBN 0-531-01478-9). Watts.

--Japan Destiny. LC 73-1810. (Illus.). 160p. (gr. 7-12). 1973. PLB 5.88 o.p. (ISBN 0-531-02615-9). Watts.

--Soviet Dissent: Intellectuals, Jews & Detente. LC 74-13635. (Illus.). 112p. (gr. 7 up). 1975. PLB 5.95 o.p. (ISBN 0-531-02800-3). Watts.

Axelrod, Daniel. The Eocene Copper Basin Flora of Northeastern Nevada. (U. C. Publ. in Geological Sciences: Vol. 59). 1966. pap. 7.50x (ISBN 0-520-09160-4). U of Cal Pr.

--The Pleistocene Soboba Flora of Southern California. (U. C. Publ. in Geological Sciences: Vol. 60). 1966. pap. 6.00x (ISBN 0-520-09161-2). U of Cal Pr.

Axelrod, Daniel I. History of the Amritime Closed-Cone Pines, Alta & Baja California. (U. C. Publications in Geological Sciences: Vol. 120). 1980. pap. 8.00 (ISBN 0-520-09620-7). U of Cal Pr.

Axelrod, Daniel I., jt. auth. see Raven, Peter H.

Axelrod, David B. A Dream of Feet. LC 76-21123. (Poetry Ser.). (Illus.). 1976. o. p. 8.95x (ISBN 0-89304-004-5, CCC105); signed ltd. ed. 15.00 (ISBN 0-89304-042-8); pap. 3.95x (ISBN 0-89304-007-X); pap. 3.95x signed ltd. ed. o.p. (ISBN 0-89304-043-6). Cross Cult.

--The Man Who Fell in Love with a Chicken. Barkan, Stanley H., ed. (Cross-Cultural Review Chapbook 2). 16p. 1980. pap. 2.00 (ISBN 0-89304-801-1). Cross Cult.

--A Meeting with Dacid B. Axelrod & Gnazino Russo. Scammacca, Nat, ed. & tr. LC 79-90012. (Sicilian Antigruppo Ser.: No. 3). (Illus.). 1979. signed ltd. o. s. i. 10.00 (ISBN 0-89304-505-5); pap. 3.00x (ISBN 0-89304-507-1); signed ltd. ed. 6.00x (ISBN 0-89304-506-3). Cross Cult.

Axelrod, H., et al. Exotic Tropical Fishes. rev. ed. (Illus.). 1302p. 1980. 25.00 (ISBN 0-87666-543-1, H-1028); looseleaf 30.00. TFH Pubns.

Axelrod, Herbert & Vorderwinkler, W. Tropical Fish in Your Home. LC 56-7698. (gr. 10 up). 8.95 (ISBN 0-8069-3710-6); PLB 8.29 (ISBN 0-8069-3711-4). Sterling.

Axelrod, Herbert, jt. auth. see Emmens, C. W.

Axelrod, Herbert R. African Cichlids of Lakes Malawi & Tanganyika. (Illus.). 224p. 1973. 14.95 (ISBN 0-87666-515-6, PS-703). TFH Pubns.

--Breeding Aquarium Fishes, Bk.6. (Illus.). 288p. 1980. 12.95 (ISBN 0-87666-536-9, H-995). TFH Pubns.

--Freshwater Fishes, Bk. 1. (Illus.). 320p. 1974. 20.00 (ISBN 0-87666-076-6, PS-713). TFH Pubns.

--Photography for Aquarists. (Illus.). 1970. pap. 2.95 o.p. (ISBN 0-87666-132-0, PS664). TFH Pubns.

--Sand Painting for Aquariums & Terrariums. (Illus.). 128p. 1975. pap. 1.00 (ISBN 0-87666-626-8, P-902). TFH Pubns.

--Tropical Fish for Beginners. (Illus.). 1972. 4.95 (ISBN 0-87666-752-3, PS-304). TFH Pubns.

Axelrod, Herbert R. & Vorderwinkler, William. Tropical Fish in Your Home. (Illus.). 144p. 1973. pap. 2.25 (ISBN 0-06-463356-X, E*H 356, EH). Har-Row.

Axelrod, Herbert R. & Welty, Edwin C., Jr. Pigeon Racing. LC 72-81050. 160p. (gr. 10 up). 1973. 11.95 (ISBN 0-8069-3720-3); PLB 10.79 (ISBN 0-8069-3721-1). Sterling.

Axelrod, Herbert R. & Whitern, Wilfred H. Guppies. (Orig.). pap. 2.00 (ISBN 0-87666-082-0, M505). TFH Pubns.

Axelrod, Herbert R., jt. auth. see Burgess, Warren E.

Axelrod, Herbert R., jt. auth. see Gordon, Myron.

Axelrod, Herbert R., ed. Heifetz. 2nd ed. (Illus.). 507p. 1980. 20.00 (ISBN 0-87666-600-4, Z-24). Paganiniana Pubns.

Axelrod, Herbert R., et al. Exotic Tropical Fishes. 9.95 (ISBN 0-87666-051-0, H-907); looseleaf 20.00 (ISBN 0-87666-052-9, H-907L). TFH Pubns.

--Exotic Marine Fishes. (Illus.). 608p. 1973. 15.00 (ISBN 0-87666-102-9, H938); looseleaf bdg. o.p. 20.00 (ISBN 0-87666-103-7). Tfh Pubns.

Axelrod, Nathan. Executive Leadership. 1969. pap. text ed. 9.10 (ISBN 0-672-96054-0); tchr's manual 5.00 (ISBN 0-672-96055-9). Bobbs.

--Selected Cases in Fashion Marketing, 2 vols. 3rd ed. 1968. pap. 11.00 ea.; Vol. 1. pap. (ISBN 0-672-96037-0); Vol. 2. pap. (ISBN 0-672-96038-9). Bobbs.

Axelrod, Nathan, jt. auth. see Packard, Sidney.

Axelrod, R. Herbert, jt. auth. see Sheppard, Leslie.

Axelrod, Regina S., ed. Energy & the Urban Environment. LC 79-3523. (Conflict & Resolution). (Illus.). 1981. write for info. (ISBN 0-669-03460-6). Lexington Bks.

Axelsen, J., jt. ed. see Vinterberg, H.

Axelsson, R. A., jt. auth. see Oehman, R. L.

Axenrod, Theodore & Webb, Graham. Nuclear Magnetic Resonance Spectroscopy of Nuclei Other Than Protons. 424p. Repr. of 1974 ed. lib. bdg. write for info. (ISBN 0-89874-290-0). Krieger.

Axford, H. William. Gilpin County Gold: Peter McFarlane, Mining Entrepreneur in Central City, Colorado. LC 76-115034. (Illus.). xii, 210p. 1976. 12.95 (ISBN 0-8040-0550-8, SB). Swallow.

Axford, Lavonne. Weaving, Spinning, and Dyeing. LC 75-16436. (Spare Time Guides Ser.: No. 7). 148p. 1975. lib. bdg. 11.50x o.p. (ISBN 0-87287-080-4). Libs Unl.

Axford, Lavonne, ed. English Language Cookbooks, Sixteen Hundred to Nineteen Seventy-Three. LC 76-23533. 1976. 62.00 (ISBN 0-8103-0534-8). Gale.

Axford, Lavonne B. An Index to the Poems of Ogden Nash. LC 72-7266. 1972. 10.00 (ISBN 0-8108-0547-2). Scarecrow.

Axinn, Donald E. Sliding Down the Wind. LC 77-90082. 1977. 5.95 o.p. (ISBN 0-8040-0793-4); pap. 3.50 o.s.i. (ISBN 0-8040-0794-2). Swallow.

Axler, Bruce H. Adding Eye Appeal to Foods. 1974. pap. 3.70 o.p. (ISBN 0-672-96115-6). Bobbs.

--Breakfast Cookery. 1974. pap. 3.55 (ISBN 0-672-96120-2). Bobbs.

--Building Care for Hospitality Operations. 1974. pap. 3.95 (ISBN 0-672-96124-5). Bobbs.

--Buying & Using Convenience Foods. 1974. pap. 3.55 (ISBN 0-672-96122-9). Bobbs.

--Increasing Lodging Revenues & Restaurant Checks. 1974. pap. 3.95 (ISBN 0-672-96121-0). Bobbs.

--Practical Wine Knowledge. 1974. pap. 3.95 (ISBN 0-672-26119-7). Bobbs.

--Profitable Catering. 1974. pap. 3.95 (ISBN 0-672-26118-9). Bobbs.

--Room Care for Hotels & Motels. 1974. pap. 3.95 (ISBN 0-672-96125-3). Bobbs.

--Sanitation, Safety, & Maintenance Management. 1974. 13.25 o.p. (ISBN 0-672-96106-7); tchrs' manual 5.00 o.p. (ISBN 0-672-96108-3); wkbk 6.45 o.p. (ISBN 0-672-96107-5). Bobbs.

--Security for Hotels, Motels, & Restaurants. 1974. pap. 3.95 (ISBN 0-672-96123-7). Bobbs.

--Showmanship in the Dining Room. 1974. pap. 3.95 (ISBN 0-672-96117-2). Bobbs.

--Tableservice Techniques. 1974. pap. 3.95 (ISBN 0-672-96116-4). Bobbs.

Axline, Virginia M. Dibs: In Search of Self. 224p. 1976. pap. 2.50 (ISBN 0-345-29536-6). Ballantine.

Axsom, Richard H. Parade: Cubism As Theater. LC 78-74361. (Outstanding Dissertations in the Fine Arts, Fourth Ser.). (Illus.). 1979. lib. bdg. 38.00 (ISBN 0-8240-3950-5). Garland Pub.

Axtell, James, ed. The Indian Peoples of Eastern America: A Documentary History of the Sexes. (Illus.). 232p. 1981. text ed. 11.95x (ISBN 0-19-502740-X); pap. text ed. 6.95 (ISBN 0-19-502741-8). Oxford U Pr.

Axtell, James L., ed. see Locke, John.

Axthelm, Pete. The Kid. (Illus.). 1978. 10.00 o.p. (ISBN 0-670-41296-1). Viking Pr.

Axton, David. Prison of Ice. 1977. pap. 1.75 o.p. (ISBN 0-449-23345-6, Crest). Fawcett.

Axton, Marie & Williams, R., eds. English Drama. LC 76-57099. 1977. 32.00 (ISBN 0-521-21588-9). Cambridge U Pr.

Aya, R. & Miller, N. New American Revolution. LC 74-142353. 1971. 10.95 o.s.i. (ISBN 0-02-901110-8); pap. text ed. 4.50 o.s.i. (ISBN 0-02-901090-X). Free Pr.

Aya, R., jt. auth. see Miller, N.

Ayal, Eliezer B., ed. Micro Aspects of Development. LC 72-89641. (Special Studies in International Economics & Development). 1973. 28.75x (ISBN 0-275-28685-1); pap. text ed. 10.95x (ISBN 0-89197-846-1). Irvington.

Ayala, Felipe, jt. ed. see Sanchez-Camara, Florencio.

Ayala, Francisco & Kiger, John. Solutions Manual for Modern Genetics. 1980. pap. 2.95 (ISBN 0-8053-0313-8, 800F00). Benjamin Cummings.

Ayala, Francisco & Dobzhansky, Theodosius, eds. Studies in the Philosophy of Biology: Reduction & Related Problems. LC 73-90656. 1975. 30.00x (ISBN 0-520-02649-7). U of Cal Pr.

Ayala, Francisco J. & Valentine, James W. Evolving: The Theory & Processes of Organic Evolution. 1979. text ed. 18.95 (ISBN 0-8053-0310-3). Benjamin-Cummings.

Ayala, Mitzi. The Farmers' Cookbook: A Collection of Favorite Recipes, Economical Meal Planning Methods & Other Tips & Pointers for America's Farm Kitchens. (Illus.). 240p. 1981. 12.50 (ISBN 0-686-69457-0). Harbor Pub CA.

Ayala, Ramon Perez De see Perez de Ayala, Ramon.

Ayalon, David. The Mamluk Military Society. 364p. 1980. 69.00x (Pub. by Variorum England). State Mutual Bk.

--Studies on the Mamluks of Egypt. 360p. 1980. 60.00x (ISBN 0-86078-006-6, Pub. by Variorum England). State Mutual Bk.

Ayandele, E. A., et al. Making of Modern Africa, Vol. 2: The Late 19th Century to the Present Day. (Growth of African Civilization Ser). (Orig.). 1971. pap. text ed. 7.75x (ISBN 0-391-00149-3). Humanities.

Ayandele, Emmanuel A. Missionary Impact on Modern Nigeria, 1842-1914. (Ibadan History Ser.). 1967. pap. text ed. 13.75x (ISBN 0-582-64512-3). Humanities.

Ayatey, Siegfried B. Essentials of Economic Analysis: Vol. 1, Microeconomics. LC 79-66234. 1979. pap. text ed. 10.50 (ISBN 0-8191-0803-0). U Pr of Amer.

--Essentials of Economic Analysis: Vol. 2, Macroeconomics. LC 79-66234. 1979. pap. text ed. 9.00 (ISBN 0-8191-0804-9). U Pr of Amer.

Aycoberry, Pierre. The Nazi Question. 1981. price not set. Pantheon.

Aycock, Dale. Stardrifter. 1981. pap. 1.95 (ISBN 0-8439-0855-6, Leisure Bks). Nordon Pubns.

Aycock, Don M. The E. Y. Mullins Lectures on Preaching with Reference to the Aristotelian Triad. LC 79-6080. 113p. 1980. text ed. 15.75 (ISBN 0-8191-0981-9); pap. text ed. 7.50 (ISBN 0-8191-0982-7). U Pr of Amer.

Aycock, Wendell M. see Zyla, Wolodymyr T.

Aycock, Wendell M. & Klein, Theodore M., eds. Classical Mythology in Twentieth-Century Thought & Literature. (Proceedings of the Comparative Literature Symposium). (Illus.). 221p. (Orig.). 1980. pap. 12.00 (ISBN 0-89672-079-9). Tex Tech Pr.

Aycock, Wendell M., ed. see Comparative Literature Symposium, No. 12.

Aydelotte, William O. Quantification in History. LC 76-150517. (History Ser). 1971. pap. 5.95 (ISBN 0-201-00350-3). A-W.

Aydelotte, William O., et al, eds. Dimensions of Quantitative Research in History. LC 72-736. (Quantitative Studies in History Ser). 420p. 1972. 19.50x (ISBN 0-691-07544-1); pap. 7.50 (ISBN 0-691-10045-4, 45). Princeton U Pr.

Aydon, Cyril. How to Finance Your Company. 206p. 1976. text ed. 19.50x (ISBN 0-220-66309-2, Pub. by Busn Bks England). Renouf.

Ayensu, E. S. see Metcalfe, C. R.

Ayensu, Edward S. Medicinal Plants of the West Indies. Irvine, Keith, ed. LC 79-48009. (Medicinal Plants of the World Ser.). (Illus.). 1981. 29.95 (ISBN 0-917256-12-3). Ref Pubns.

Ayensu, Edward S. & DeFilipps, Robert A. Endangered & Threatened Plants of the United States. LC 77-25138. (Illus.). 403p. 1978. 25.00x (ISBN 0-87474-222-6). Smithsonian.

Ayer, jt. auth. see Barbato.

Ayer, A. J. Hume. 108p. 1980. 7.95 (ISBN 0-8090-5615-1); pap. 2.95 (ISBN 0-8090-1409-2). Hill & Wang.

--Probability & Evidence: The John Dewey Lectures in Philosophy, No. 2. 1979. pap. 6.00x (ISBN 0-231-04767-3). Columbia U Pr.

Ayer, Alfred J. Language, Truth & Logic. 2nd ed. 1936. pap. 2.00 (ISBN 0-486-20010-8). Dover.

--Probability & Evidence. LC 71-185572. (John Dewey Lecture Ser). 1972. 12.50x (ISBN 0-231-03650-7). Columbia U Pr.

Ayer, Alfred J., ed. Logical Positivism. LC 58-6467. 1966. pap. text ed. 9.95 (ISBN 0-02-900130-7). Free Pr.

Ayer, Jacqueline, ed. & illus. Rumpelstiltskin. LC 67-20165. (gr. k-3). 7.50 (ISBN 0-15-269525-7, HJ). HarBraceJ.

Ayers, Gwendoline M. England's First State Hospitals & the Metropolitan Asylums Board 1867-1930. LC 75-126766. (Wellcome Institute of the History of Medicine). (Illus.). 1971. 30.00x (ISBN 0-520-01792-7). U of Cal Pr.

Ayers, Peter K., ed. see Ogali, Ogali.

Aylen, R., et al, eds. Vehicle Fitting. (Engineering Craftsmen: No. H8). (Illus.). 1978. spiral bdg. 21.00x (ISBN 0-685-90188-2). Intl Ideas.

Aylesworth, Jim. Tonight's the Night. Fay, Ann, ed. (Self-Starter Bks.). (Illus.). 32p. (ps-1). 1981. 6.50 (ISBN 0-8075-8020-1). A Whitman.

Aylesworth, Thomas. Astrology & Foretelling the Future: A Concise Guide. LC 72-8797. (Illus.). 96p. (gr. 5 up). 1973. PLB 4.90 o.p. (ISBN 0-531-02606-X). Watts.

--Spoon Bending & Other Feats. LC 80-20901. (gr. 4-10). 1980. pap. 1.95 (ISBN 0-88436-767-3). EMC.

Aylesworth, Thomas C. & Klein, Stanley, eds. Science Update: 1977 Issue. pap. 29.95 o.p. (ISBN 0-685-42982-2, 9365/77). Gaylord Prof Pubns.

Aylesworth, Thomas G. Cars, Boats, Trains & Planes of Today & Tomorrow. LC 74-31906. (Illus.). 128p. (gr. 3-7). 1975. 6.95 o.s.i. (ISBN 0-8027-6236-0). Walker & Co.

--Geological Disasters: Earthquakes & Volcanoes. (Impact Bks.). (Illus.). 1979. PLB 6.90 s&l (ISBN 0-531-02288-9). Watts.

--Monsters from the Movies. 160p. (gr. 4-6). pap. 1.95 (ISBN 0-553-15091-X, Skylark). Bantam.

--Palmistry. LC 75-38964. (Career Concise Guides Ser.). (Illus.). 96p. (gr. 7 up). 1976. PLB 4.90 o.p. (ISBN 0-531-01129-1). Watts.

--Science at the Ballgame. (gr. 4). 1977. 5.95 o.s.i. (ISBN 0-8027-6279-4); PLB 5.85 o.s.i. (ISBN 0-8027-6280-8). Walker & Co.

--Storm Alert: Understanding Weather Disasters. LC 80-19580. (Illus.). 160p. (gr. 7 up). 1980. PLB 8.29 (ISBN 0-671-34052-2). Messner.

--Understanding Body Talk. LC 78-12446. (Impact Bks.). (Illus.). (gr. 7 up). 1979. PLB 6.90 s&l (ISBN 0-531-02200-5). Watts.

Aylesworth, Tom. ESP. LC 74-26797. (Impact Bks.). (Illus.). 72p. (gr. 4-8). 1975. PLB 6.90 (ISBN 0-531-00826-6). Watts.

--Graphology. LC 76-7048. (Career Concise Guides Ser.). (Illus.). 72p. (gr. 6 up). 1976. PLB 4.90 o.p. (ISBN 0-531-00323-X). Watts.

Ayliffe, G. A., jt. auth. see Lowbury, E. J.

Ayling, Alan, et al, trs. Folding Screen Chinese Lyrics. (Writing in Asia Ser.). 1976. pap. text ed. 5.95 (ISBN 0-686-60433-4, 00204). Heinemann Ed.

Ayling, Ronald. Continuity & Innovation in Sean O'Casey's Drama. (Salzburg Studies in English Literature Poetic Drama & Poetic Theory: No. 23). 1976. pap. 25.00x (ISBN 0-391-01304-1). Humanities.

Ayling, Stanley. John Wesley. 1980. Repr. 10.95 (ISBN 0-687-20376-7). Abingdon.

--John Wesley. 1979. 12.95 (ISBN 0-529-05688-7, RB5688, Pub. by Collins Pubs). Abingdon.

Ayllon, Teodoro & Azrin, Nathan H. Token Economy: A Motivational System for Therapy & Rehabilitation. (Orig.). 1968. pap. 12.95 (ISBN 0-13-919357-X). P-H.

Aylmer, G. E. The King's Servants: The Civil Service of Charles I, 1625-1645. 2nd rev ed. 1974. 45.00x (ISBN 0-7100-1037-0). Routledge & Kegan.

--Struggle for the Constitution, 1603-1689: England in the Seventeenth Century. (History of England Ser.). 1968. text ed. 6.25x o.p. (ISBN 0-7137-0309-1). Humanities.

Aylsworth, Jim. Hush Up! LC 79-2137. (Illus.). 32p. (gr. k-2). 1980. 6.95 (ISBN 0-03-054841-1). HR&W.

Aylward, Jim. Things No One Ever Tells You. 144p. (Orig.). 1981. pap. 1.95 (ISBN 0-446-90707-3). Warner Bks.

Aymar, Brandt, ed. see Blum, Daniel.

Aymar, Brandt, ed. see Fromme, Babbette B.

Aymar, Brandt, ed. see Meilach, Dona Z.

Aymar, Brandt, ed. see Trachtman, Paula.

Aymar, Brandt, ed. see Willis, John.

Aymar, Brant, ed. see Brandt, Babette.

Aymar, Brant, ed. see Meilach, Dona Z.

Aymar, Brant, ed. see Merrill, Virginia & Richardson, Susan M.

Aynsley, R. M., et al. Architectural Aerodynamics. (Illus.). 1977. text ed. 49.70x (ISBN 0-85334-698-4, Pub. by Applied Science). Burgess-Intl Ideas.

Ayoub, Aktoine. Energy: International Cooperation or Crisis. 272p. 1980. pap. 20.00x (ISBN 0-686-63152-8, Pub. by Laval). Intl Schol Bk Serv.

Ayres. Care of the Critically Ill. 2nd ed. 1974. 17.50 o.p. (ISBN 0-8385-1053-1). ACC.

Ayres, A. Jean. Sensory Integration & Learning Disorders. LC 72-91446. 294p. 1973. 15.50x (ISBN 0-87424-303-3). Western Psych.

--Sensory Integration & the Child. LC 79-66987. 191p. 1979. pap. text ed. 8.95 (ISBN 0-87424-158-8). Western Psych.

Ayres, C. E. The Theory of Economic Progress. 3rd ed. 1978. pap. 6.95 (ISBN 0-932826-03-2). New Issues MI.

Ayres, J. A., ed. Decontamination of Nuclear Reactors & Equipment. (Illus.). 815p. 1970. 50.00 (ISBN 0-471-06687-7, Pub. by Wiley-Interscience). Wiley.

Ayres, James. English Naive Painting. (Illus.). 168p. 1980. 29.95 (ISBN 0-500-23308-X). Thames Hudson.

--The Shell Book of the Home in Britain: Decoration, Design & Construction of Vernacula Interiors, 1500-1850. (Shell Book Ser.). (Illus.). 240p. 1981. 25.00 (ISBN 0-571-11625-6, Pub. by Faber & Faber). Merrimack Bk Serv.

Ayres, John C. & Kirschman, John C., eds. Impact of Toxiology on Food Processing. (Institute of Food Technologists Basic Symposia Ser.). (Illus.). 1981. lib. bdg. price not set (ISBN 0-87055-388-7). AVI.

Ayres, John C., et al. Microbiology of Foods. LC 79-16335. (Food & Nutrition Ser.). (Illus.). 1980. text ed. 21.95x (ISBN 0-7167-1049-8). W H Freeman.

Ayres, N., jt. auth. see Taylor, George.

Ayres, Phillip J., ed. see Munday, Anthony.

Ayres, R. L., jt. ed. see Mann, W. B.

Ayres, Robert. Banking on the Poor: The World Bank's Antipoverty Work in Developing Countries. 384p. 1981. write for info. Overseas Dev Council.

Ayres, Robert U. Resources, Environment & Economics: Applications of the Materials-Energy Balance Principle. LC 77-20049. 1978. 34.00 (ISBN 0-471-02627-1, Pub. by Wiley-Interscience). Wiley.

Ayres, Stanleigh. College Business Mathematics: An Audio Tutorial Approach. 1977. pap. text ed. 13.95 (ISBN 0-675-08500-4); cassettes 95.00 (ISBN 0-675-08499-7). Merrill.

Ayres, William. The Warner Collectors' Guide to American Toys. (Orig.). 1981. pap. 9.95 (ISBN 0-446-97632-6). Warner Bks.

Ayrout, Henry H. The Fellaheen. Wayment, Hilary, tr. LC 79-2849. 179p. 1981. Repr. of 1945 ed. 17.00 (ISBN 0-8305-0025-1). Hyperion Conn.

Ayscough, Florence. Chinese Women: Yesterday & Today. LC 74-32095. (China in the 20th Century Ser). (Illus.). xiv, 324p. 1975. Repr. of 1937 ed. lib. bdg. 29.50 (ISBN 0-306-70700-4). Da Capo.

Azad, Abul K. Tarjuman Al-Qur'an, 2 Vols. Vol. 1. o.p. (ISBN 0-210-33966-7); Vol. 2. 13.95x (ISBN 0-210-31193-2). Asia.

Azar, Ines. Discurso Retorico y Mundo Pastoral en la "Egloga Segunda" de Garcilaso. (Purdue Univ. Monographs in Romance Languages: No. 5). 160p. (Span.). 1980. text ed. 23.00x (ISBN 90-272-1715-7). Humanities.

Azar, J. J. Matrix Structural Analysis. 1972. text ed. 28.00 (ISBN 0-08-016781-0). Pergamon.

Azar, Miguel M., jt. ed. see Schwartz, Lagar M.

Azariah, Isaiah. Lord Bentinck & Indian Education, Crime, & Status of Women. LC 78-64822. 1978. pap. text ed. 9.00 (ISBN 0-8191-0641-0). U Pr of Amer.

Azarian, Mary. A Farmer's Alphabet. (gr. 1-4). 1981. 10.95 (ISBN 0-87923-394-X); pap. 6.95 (ISBN 0-87923-397-4). Godine.

Azarnoff, Pat & Flegal, Sharon. A Pediatric Play Program: Developing a Therapeutic Play Program for Children in Medical Settings. (Illus.). 112p. 1980. pap. 9.75 (ISBN 0-398-03272-6). C C Thomas.

Azarnoff, Pat & Hardgrove, Carol. The Family in Child Health Care. 240p. 1981. pap. 14.95 (ISBN 0-471-08663-0, Pub. by Wiley-Med). Wiley.

Azarpay, Guitty. Sogdian Painting: The Pictorial Epic in Oriental Art. 300p. 1981. 50.00x (ISBN 0-520-03765-0). U of Cal Pr.

Azbel, David. Two Phase Flows in Chemical Engineering. LC 80-20936. (Illus.). 400p. Date not set. price not set (ISBN 0-521-23772-6). Cambridge U Pr.

Azbel, Mark Y. Refusenik: Trapped in the Soviet Union. Forbes, Grace P., ed. (Illus.). 528p. 1981. 17.95 (ISBN 0-395-30226-9). HM.

Azel, Jan & McCready, Karen. Porcelain: Traditions & New Visions. 200p. 1981. 30.00 (ISBN 0-8230-4091-7). Watson-Guptill.

Azevedo, Aluisio. A Brazilian Tenement. Brown, Harry W., tr. 320p. 1977. Repr. of 1926 ed. 15.75 (ISBN 0-86527-222-0). Fertig.

Azevedo, Milton M. & McMahon, Kathryn K. Lecturas Periodisticas. 2nd ed. 272p. 1981. pap. text ed. 8.95 (ISBN 0-669-04026-6). Heath.

--Lecturas Periodisticas. 1978. pap. text ed. 7.95x o.p. (ISBN 0-669-00576-2). Heath.

Azevedo, Ross. Labor Economics: A Guide to Information Sources. LC 73-17568. (Economics Information Guide Ser.: Vol. 8). 1978. 30.00 (ISBN 0-8103-1297-2). Gale.

Azif, Herbert B. China Trade: A Guide to Doing Business with the People's Republic of China. LC 80-84105. (Illus.). 200p. (Orig.). Date not set. pap. price not set (ISBN 0-9605190-0-9). Intraworld Trade.

Azikiwe, Nnamdi. My Odyssey: An Autobiography. 1970. 15.00 (ISBN 0-685-71645-7). Univ Place.

--Renascent Africa. (Africana Modern Library: No. 6). 1968. Repr. of 1937 ed. text ed. 11.75x (ISBN 0-7146-1744-X). Humanities.

Aziz, Abdul. Organizing Agricultural Labourers in India. 1980. 7.50x (ISBN 0-8364-0651-6, Pub. by Minerva India). South Asia Bks.

Aziz, Harry. Police Procedures & Defense Tactics Training Manual. Halet, Sydney S., ed. (Illus.). 1979. 19.95 (ISBN 0-87040-451-2). Japan Pubns.

Aziz, Khalid. Step by Step Guide to Indian Cooking. 1976. 11.95 (ISBN 0-600-38093-9). Transatlantic.

Aziz, Madbool, ed. see James, Henry.

Aziz, Maqbool, ed. see James, Henry.

Aziz, Nasima. No Metaphor, Remember. 10.00 (ISBN 0-89253-646-2); flexible cloth 5.00 (ISBN 0-89253-647-0). Ind-US Inc.

--One More: Poems. (Redbird Bk). 43p. 1975. 8.00 (ISBN 0-88253-837-3); pap. 4.80 (ISBN 0-88253-838-1). Ind-US Inc.

Aziz, Sartaj, ed. Hunger, Politics & Markets: The Real Issues in the Food Crisis. LC 75-34674. 130p. 1975. 10.00x (ISBN 0-8147-0559-6); pap. 5.00x (ISBN 0-8147-0560-X). NYU Pr.

Azmeh, A. Ibn Khaldun: A Re-Interpretation. 1981. 25.00x (ISBN 0-7146-3140-X, F Cass Co). Biblio Dist.

Aznar, Marina. Home Book of Spanish Cookery. LC 67-94477. (Home Cookery Book Ser). 1967. 10.50x (ISBN 0-571-10655-2). Intl Pubns Serv.

Azrael, Jeremy R., ed. Soviet Nationality Policies & Practices. LC 77-83478. 1978. 35.95 (ISBN 0-03-041476-8). Praeger.

Azrin, Nathan H. & Besalel, V. A. How to Use Overcorrection. 1980. 3.25 (ISBN 0-89079-047-7). H & H Ent.

Azrin, Nathan H. & Besalel, Victoria A. A Parent's Guide to Bedwetting Control: A Step by Step Method. 1981. pap. price not set (ISBN 0-671-82774-X). PB.

Azrin, Nathan H., jt. auth. see Ayllon, Teodoro.

Azuela, M., et al, eds. Los De Abajo: Novela De la Revolucion Mexicana. rev. ed. 1971. pap. write for info. (ISBN 0-13-540690-0). P-H.

Azumi, Koya. Higher Education & Business Recruitment in Japan. LC 71-81593. 1969. pap. 5.75x (ISBN 0-8077-1042-3). Tchrs Coll.

Azur, Betty S. Understanding & Using English Grammar. (Illus.). 416p. 1981. pap. text ed. 10.95 (ISBN 0-13-936492-7, Spec). P-H.

Azzam, Salem, frwd. by. The Muslim World & the Future Economic Order. 383p. 1980. 29.95x (ISBN 0-906041-10-4, Pub. by Islamic Council of Europe England); pap. 14.95x (ISBN 0-906041-09-0). Intl Schol Bk Serv.

B

B., Bill. Compulsive Overeater. 1981. 10.95 (ISBN 0-89638-046-7). CompCare.

B., Mel. Is There Life After Sobriety. 1980. pap. 4.95. Hazelden.

Baal, J. Van see Van Baal, J.

Ba'Alabaki, Munir, jt. auth. see Al Quareb, Al-Mawrid.

Ba'Albaki. English-Arabic Student Dictionary. 12.00 (ISBN 0-686-53115-9). Intl Bk Ctr.

Ba'Albaki, Munir. English-Arabic Dictionary: Al-Mawrid. 1981. 45.00 (ISBN 0-686-69401-5). Intl Bk Ctr.

Ba'Albaki, Munir, jt. auth. see Al-Mawrid.

Baalen, Jan K. Van see Van Baalen, Jan K.

Baar, Carl, jt. auth. see Millar, Perry S.

Baar, H. S. & Stransky, E. Disorders of Blood & Blood-Forming Organs in Childhood. (Illus.). 1963. 71.50 o.s.i. (ISBN 0-02-840710-5). Hafner.

Baark, Erik. Catalogue of Chinese Manuscripts in the Danish Archives: Chinese Diplomatic Correspondence from the Ch'ing Dynasty (1644-1911) (Studies on Asian Topics: No. 2). (Orig.). 1979. pap. text ed. 11.00x (ISBN 0-7007-0120-6). Humanities.

Baark, Erik & Sigurdson, Jon, eds. India-China Comparative Research: Technology & Science for Development. (Studies on Asian Topics: No. 3). 180p. 1980. pap. text ed. 10.50x (ISBN 0-7007-0138-9). Humanities.

Baase, Sara. Computer Algorithms: Introduction to Design & Analysis. LC 77-81197. 1978. text ed. 19.95 (ISBN 0-201-00327-9). A-W.

Baatz, Charles A., ed. Philosophy of Education: A Guide to Information Sources. (Education Information Guide Ser.: Vol. 6). 1980. 30.00 (ISBN 0-8103-1452-5). Gale.

Baatz, Charles A. & Baatz, Olga K., eds. The Psychological Foundations of Education: A Guide to Information Sources. (Education Information Guide Ser.: Vol. 10). 350p. 1981. 30.00 (ISBN 0-8103-1467-3). Gale.

Baatz, Olga K., jt. ed. see Baatz, Charles A.

Baba, Bangali. The Yogasutra of Patanjali. 2nd rev. ed. 1979. pap. 6.50 (ISBN 0-8426-0916-4, Pub. by Motilal Banarsidass India). Orient Bk Dist.

Baba, Meher. Life at Its Best. 1976. pap. 2.50 o.p. (ISBN 0-525-47434-X). Dutton.

Baba, Noburo. Eleven Hungry Cats. Tresselt, Alvin, tr. LC 79-93858. Orig. Title: Eleven Pikino Neko. (Illus.). (gr. k-3). 1970. 5.95 o.s.i. (ISBN 0-8193-0384-4, Four Winds); PLB 5.41 o.s.i. (ISBN 0-8193-0385-2). Schol Bk Serv.

Baba, S., et al, eds. The Biology of the Fluids of the Female Genital Tract. 456p. 1979. 80.50 (ISBN 0-444-90069-1, Excerpta Medica). Elsevier.

Bababunmi, E. A. & Smith, R. L. Toxicology in the Tropics. 280p. 1980. 37.50 (ISBN 0-85066-194-3, Pub. by Taylor & Francis England). J K Burgess.

Babaevsky, P. G., et al. English-Russian Dictionary of Chemistry & Technology of Polymers. Yashinskaya, F. I. & Trostyanskaya, E. B., eds. 1978. text ed. 75.00 o.p. (ISBN 0-08-022944-1). Pergamon.

Baba Hari Dass. Harikhan Baba--Known, Unknown. LC 75-3838. (Illus.). 93p. (Orig.). 1975. pap. 1.95 (ISBN 0-918100-00-3). Sri Rama.

Babb, Charles. Pontius Pilate, Vol. 2. 1981. 9.75 (ISBN 0-8062-1564-X). Carlton.

Babb, Hugh W. & Martin, Charles. Business Law. 3rd ed. 400p. (Orig.). 1981. pap. 4.95 (ISBN 0-06-460198-6, COS 198, COS). Har-Row.

--Business Law: Uniform Commercial Code Edition. 2nd ed. LC 74-77984. 1969. pap. 3.95 (ISBN 0-06-460040-8, CO 40, COS). Har-Row.

Babb, Janice B. & Dordick, B. F., eds. Real Estate Information Sources. LC 63-16246. (Management Information Guide Ser.: No. 1). 1963. 30.00 (ISBN 0-8103-0801-0). Gale.

Babb, Jewel. Border Healing Woman: The Story of Jewel Babb. 152p. 1981. text ed. 14.95 (ISBN 0-292-70729-0); pap. 5.95 (ISBN 0-292-70730-4). U of Tex Pr.

Babb, Lawrence A. The Divine Hierarchy: Popular Hinduism in Central India. (Illus.). 272p. 1975. 17.50x (ISBN 0-231-03882-8). Columbia U Pr.

Babbage, C. Reflections on the Decline of Science in England & on Some of Its Causes. 256p. 1971. Repr. of 1830 ed. 25.00x (ISBN 0-7165-1578-4, Pub. by Irish Academic Pr Ireland). Biblio Dist.

Babbage, Ross. Rethinking Australia's Defence. (Illus.). 312p. 1981. text ed. 30.25x (ISBN 0-7022-1486-8). U of Queensland Pr.

Babbidge, I. Beginning in Bookselling: Grafton Books on Library Science. 1977. PLB 9.00x (ISBN 0-233-96019-8). Westview.

Babbie, Earl R. Practice of Social Research. 2nd ed. 1979. text ed. 19.95x (ISBN 0-534-00630-2); wkbk. 7.95x (ISBN 0-534-00702-3). Wadsworth Pub.

--Science & Morality in Medicine: A Survey of Medical Educators. LC 71-92674. 1970. 19.50x (ISBN 0-520-01559-2). U of Cal Pr.

--Sociology: An Introduction. 2nd ed. 640p. 1980. text ed. 18.95x (ISBN 0-534-00797-X); 6.95 (ISBN 0-534-00798-8). Wadsworth Pub.

--Survey Research Methods: A Cookbook & Other Fables. 320p. 1973. 13.95x (ISBN 0-534-00224-2). Wadsworth Pub.

Babbit, Irving. The New Laokoon. 259p. 1980. Repr. of 1910 ed. lib. bdg. 40.00 (ISBN 0-89760-049-5). Telegraph Bks.

Babbit, Natalie. Goldyhall. 1976. pap. 1.25 (30163, Camelot). Avon.

Babbitt, Bruce. Grand Canyon: An Anthology. LC 78-58470. (Illus.). 1978. 15.95 (ISBN 0-87358-180-6). Northland.

--Grand Canyon: An Anthology. LC 78-58470. (Illus.). 276p. 1980. pap. 8.95 (ISBN 0-87358-275-6). Northland.

Babbitt, Diane H. & Haas, Werner. Gymnastic Apparatus Exercises for Girls. (Illus.). 1964. 10.95 (ISBN 0-8260-0590-X). Wiley.

Babbitt, Edwin D. Principles of Light & Color. (Illus.). 578p. Date not set. 20.00 (ISBN 0-89540-060-X). Sun Pub. Postponed.

Babbitt, Edwin S. The Principles of Light and Color. 1980. pap. text ed. 7.95 (ISBN 0-8065-0748-9). Lyle Stuart.

Babbitt, Ellen C. Jataka Tales. (Illus.). (gr. 7-12). 1912. text ed. 6.50 (ISBN 0-13-509729-0). P-H.

Babbitt, Harold E. & Baumann, E. R. Sewerage & Sewage Treatment. 8th ed. LC 58-13453. (Illus.). 1958. 33.95 o.p. (ISBN 0-471-03927-6). Wiley.

Babbitt, Natalie. Knee-Knock Rise. (gr. 3-6). 1974. pap. 1.50 o.s.i. (ISBN 0-380-00849-1, 44875, Camelot). Avon.

--The Search for Delicious. (gr. 3-7). 1974. pap. 1.50 o.s.i. (ISBN 0-380-01541-2, 42085, Camelot). Avon.

Babbush, Charles A. Surgical Atlas of Dental Implant Techniques. LC 78-65373. (Illus.). 280p. 1980. text ed. 49.00 (ISBN 0-7216-1474-4). Saunders.

Babby, Leonard H. Existential Sentences & Negation in Russian. (Linguistica Extranea: Studia: No. 8). 199p. 1980. 12.50 (ISBN 0-89720-013-6); pap. 7.50 (ISBN 0-89720-014-4). Karoma.

--A Transformational Grammar of Russian Adjectives. LC 73-83929. (Janua Linguarum, Ser. Practica: No. 235). 242p. 1975. pap. text ed. 52.65x (ISBN 90-2793-022-8). Mouton.

Babcock, C. L. Silicate Glass Technology Methods. LC 76-30716. (Pure & Applied Optics Ser). 1977. 38.95 (ISBN 0-471-03965-9, Pub. by Wiley-Interscience). Wiley.

Babcock, David, jt. auth. see Gruenberger, Fred.

Babcock, Henry. Appraisal Principles & Procedures. 289p. 1980. pap. text ed. 20.00 (ISBN 0-937828-19-X). Am Soc Appraisers.

Babcock, J. C., et al, eds. Zalacain el Aventurero. LC 49-8551. (Graded Spanish Readers, Bk. 4). (Span). 1954. pap. text ed. 4.15 (ISBN 0-395-04127-9). HM.

Babcock, J. G., Jr., et al. Cuentos De Ambos Mundos. (Graded Spanish Readers: Bk. 2). 1950. pap. text ed. 3.90 (ISBN 0-395-04125-2). HM.

Babcock, James C., et al, eds. Amalia. LC 49-8551. (Graded Spanish Readers, Bk. 1). (Span). (gr. 10-11). 1949. pap. text ed. 3.65 (ISBN 0-395-04124-4, 3-02245). HM.

--Contigo Pan y Cebolla. LC 49-8551. (Graded Spanish Readers, Bk. 3). (Span). (gr. 10-11). 1953. pap. text ed. 4.15 (ISBN 0-395-04126-0, 3-02255). HM.

Babcock, Molly, jt. auth. see Tiger, Peggy.

Babcock, Richard F. Zoning Game: Municipal Practices & Policies. (Illus.). 1966. 17.50 (ISBN 0-299-04091-7); pap. 6.95 (ISBN 0-299-04094-1). U of Wis Pr.

Babcock, Richard F., jt. auth. see Weaver, Clifford L.

Babcock, Robert H. Gompers in Canada: A Study in American Continentalism Before the First World War. LC 74-78507. 1974. pap. 6.50 (ISBN 0-8020-6242-3). U of Toronto Pr.

Babcock, Winifred. Jung, Harold, Hesse: Contributions of C. G. Jung, Preston Harold & Hermann Hesse Toward a Spiritual Psychology. 275p. 1981. 12.95 (ISBN 0-686-68720-5). World Authors.

Babe, Thomas. Fathers & Sons. pap. 2.50 (ISBN 0-686-69574-7). Dramatists Play.

Babel, Isaak. Zabytye Proizvedelniia. Stroud, N., ed. (Rus.). 1979. 15.00 (ISBN 0-88233-118-3); pap. 7.50 o.p. (ISBN 0-88233-119-1). Ardis Pubs.

Babeuf, F. N. Journal de la Confederation. (Fr.). 1977. lib. bdg. 17.50x o.p. (ISBN 0-8287-0048-6); pap. text ed. 7.50x o.p. (ISBN 0-685-75752-8). Clearwater Pub.

--Journal de la Liberte de la Presse, No. 1-22: Prospectus du Tribun du Peuple, le Tribun de Peuple ou le Defenseur des DrOits de l'Homme, No. 23-43, 2 vols. (Fr.). 1977. lib. bdg. 70.00x o.p. (ISBN 0-8287-0049-4); pap. text ed. 50.00x o.p. (ISBN 0-685-75754-4). Clearwater Pub.

Babin, Claude. Elements of Palaeontology. LC 79-13223. 446p. 1980. 57.00 (ISBN 0-471-27577-8, Pub. by Wiley-Interscience); pap. 22.50 (ISBN 0-471-27576-X). Wiley.

Babin, David E. Week in-Week Out: A New Look at Liturgical Preaching. 1976. 7.95 (ISBN 0-8164-0287-6). Crossroad NY.

Babin, Lawrence J. The School Library. 1981. pap. 1.95 (ISBN 0-912492-17-1). Pyquag.

--Singles Are Suckers. 1981. pap. 6.95 (ISBN 0-912492-16-3). Pyquag.

Babin, Lawrence J., jt. auth. see Potz, Veronica.

Babin, Maria T. & Steiner, Stan, eds. Borinquen: An Anthology of Puerto Rican Literature. 1974. 10.00 o.p. (ISBN 0-394-47462-7). Knopf.

Babin, Pierre. Faith & the Adolescent. 1967. 3.95 (ISBN 0-8164-1030-5). Crossroad NY.

Babington, John. A Short Treatise of Geometrie. LC 76-25837. (English Experience Ser.: No. 296). 200p. Repr. of 1635 ed. 35.00 (ISBN 90-221-0296-3). Walter J Johnson.

Babister, A. W. Aircraft Dynamic Stability & Response. (Illus.). 230p. 1980. 41.00 (ISBN 0-08-024769-5); pap. 17.00 (ISBN 0-08-024768-7). Pergamon.

Babits, Mihaly. The Nightmare. Racz, Eva, tr. 6.50x (ISBN 0-89918-348-4, H348). Vanous.

Babitz, Eve. Sex & Rage. 208p. 1981. pap. 2.50 (ISBN 0-380-53009-0, 53009). Avon.

Bablet, Denis. Edward Gordon Craig. Woodward, D., tr. LC 66-23134. (Illus.). 1966. 7.75 (ISBN 0-87830-042-2). Theatre Arts.

Babson, Marian. Dangerous to Know. 1981. 9.95 (ISBN 0-8027-5442-2). Walker & Co.

--Twelve Deaths of Christmas. 180p. 1980. 9.95 (ISBN 0-8027-5426-0). Walker & Co.

Babson, S. Gorham, et al. Diagnosis & Management of the Fetus & Neonate at Risk: A Guide for Team Care. 4th ed. LC 79-16957. (Illus.). 1979. text ed. 21.95 (ISBN 0-8016-0415-X). Mosby.

Babson, Walt. All Kinds of Codes. LC 76-17529. (Illus.). 144p. (gr. 4 up). 1976. 8.95 (ISBN 0-590-07427-X, Four Winds). Schol Bk Serv.

Babula, William. Wishes Fall Out As They're Willed: Shakespeare & the Tragicomic Archetype. (Salzburg Studies in English Literature, Elizabethan & Renaissance Studies Ser.: No. 48). 133p. 1975. pap. text ed. 25.00x (ISBN 0-391-01305-X). Humanities.

Baca Fabiola, Cabeza De see Cabeza De Baca, Fabiola.

Bacal, Azril, tr. see Jackins, Harvey.

Bacall, Lauren. Lauren Bacall by Myself. 1980. pap. 2.95 (ISBN 0-345-29216-2). Ballantine.

Bacciocco, Edward J., Jr. The New Left in America: Reform to Revolution 1956-1970. LC 73-75887. (Publications Ser.: No. 130). 300p. 1974. 8.95 (ISBN 0-8179-6301-4). Hoover Inst Pr.

Bach, Alice. Millicent the Magnificent. (gr. k-6). Date not set. pap. 1.25 (ISBN 0-440-45456-5, YB). Dell.

--Waiting for Johnny Miracle. LC 79-2813. 256p. (YA) (gr. 7-12). 1980. 8.95 (ISBN 0-06-020348-X, HarpJ); PLB 8.79 (ISBN 0-06-020349-8). Har-Row.

Bach, Alice, tr. see Belves, Pierre & Mathey, Francois.

Bach, Carl P. Essay on the True Art of Playing Keyboard Instruments. Mitchell, William J., ed. (Illus.). 1948. 16.95x (ISBN 0-393-09716-1, NortonC). Norton.

Bach, Fritz H., et al, eds. see ICN-UCLA Symposia on Molecular & Cellular Biology, 1979.

Bach, G. Microeconomics: Analysis & Applications. 1977. pap. 10.95 (ISBN 0-13-581306-9). P-H.

Bach, G. L. The New Inflation: Causes, Effects, Cures. LC 72-2451. (Illus.). 103p. 1974. Repr. of 1972 ed. 7.50 (ISBN 0-87057-136-2, Pub. by Brown U Pr). Univ Pr of New England.

Bach, George L. Economics: An Introduction to Analysis & Policy. 10th ed. (Illus.). 1980. text ed. 19.95 (ISBN 0-13-227231-8); student wkbk. 8.95 (ISBN 0-13-227199-0). P-H.

Bach, George R. & Deutsch, Ronald M. Pairing. 1971. pap. 2.50 (ISBN 0-380-00394-5, 40675). Avon.

--Stop! You're Driving Me Crazy. 1981. pap. 2.95 (ISBN 0-425-04738-5). Berkley Pub.

Bach, George R. & Wyden, Peter. The Intimate Enemy: How to Fight Fair in Love & Marriage. 384p. 1981. pap. 2.95 (ISBN 0-380-00392-9, 54452). Avon.

Bach, J. S. Organ Music. 357p. 1970. pap. 7.95 (ISBN 0-486-22359-0). Dover.

Bach, Jean F., ed. Immunology. 2nd ed. 950p. 1981. 62.50 (ISBN 0-471-08044-6, Pub. by Wiley Med). Wiley.

Bach, Jean-Francois, ed. Immunology. LC 77-12139. 1978. 55.00 (ISBN 0-471-01760-4, Pub. by Wiley Medical). Wiley.

Bach, Johann S. Clavier-Buchlein Vor Wilhelm Friedmann Bach. (Music Reprint Ser.). 1979. Repr. of 1959 ed. 19.50 (ISBN 0-306-79558-2). Da Capo.

--Eleven Great Cantatas in Full Vocal & Instrumental Score. 352p. 1976. pap. 8.50 (ISBN 0-486-23268-9). Dover.

--The Six Brandenburg Concertos & the Four Orchestral Suites in Full Score. 273p. 1976. pap. 6.95 (ISBN 0-486-23376-6). Dover.

--Six Great Secular Cantatas in Full Score. 288p. (Orig.). 1980. pap. 7.95 (ISBN 0-486-23934-9). Dover.

Bach, Marcus. Power of Perception. 1973. pap. 2.95 (ISBN 0-8015-5976-6, Hawthorn). Dutton.

--The Power of Total Living. LC 77-13279. (Illus.). 1977. 7.95 (ISBN 0-396-07510-X). Dodd.

--Will to Believe. 1973. pap. 6.50 (ISBN 0-911336-46-X). Sci of Mind.

Bach, Orville E., Jr. Hiking the Yellowstone Backcountry. LC 72-96121. (Totebook Ser.). (Illus.). 240p. 1973. pap. 7.95 (ISBN 0-87156-078-X). Sierra.

Bach, R. Jonathan Livingston Seagull. (Keith Jennison Large Type Ser). 8.95 o.p. (ISBN 0-531-00320-5). Watts.

Bach, Richard. Illusions. 1978. gift ed. 12.95 o.s.i. (ISBN 0-440-04105-8, E Friede). Delacorte.

--Jonathan Livingston Seagull. LC 75-119617. (Illus.). 1970. 8.95 (ISBN 0-02-504540-7). Macmillan.

--Stranger to the Ground. LC 63-14370. (Illus.). 192p. (YA) 1972. 10.00 o.p. (ISBN 0-06-010180-6, HarpT). Har-Row.

Bach, Shirley J., jt. auth. see Binkin, Martin.

Bach, W., et al, eds. see Conference on Non-Fossil Fuel & Non-Nuclear Fuel Energy Strategies, Honolulu, USS, January 1979.

Bach, Wilfrid, et al, eds. Interactions of Energy & Climate. 568p. 1980. lib. bdg. 58.00 (ISBN 90-277-1179-8, Pub. by D. Reidel); pap. 26.50 (ISBN 90-277-1177-1). Kluwer Boston.

Bachand, Shirley, jt. auth. see Catlin, Alberta P.

Bacharach, A. L., jt. ed. see Laurence, D. R.

Bacharach, Alfred L., jt. ed. see Gray, Charles H.

Bacharach, Bert. How to Do Almost Everything. 304p. 1975. pap. 1.50 o.p. (ISBN 0-445-03054-2). Popular Lib.

Bacharach, M. Biproportional Matrices & Input Output Change. LC 77-75823. (Department of Applied Economics Monographs: No. 16). (Illus.). 1970. 29.50 (ISBN 0-521-07594-7). Cambridge U Pr.

Bacharach, Michael. Economics & the Theory of Games. LC 76-27665. 1977. lib. bdg. 23.50x (ISBN 0-89158-704-7). Westview.

Bachelard, Gaston. On Poetic Imagination & Reverie: Selections from the Works of Gaston Bachelard. Gaudin, C., ed. LC 73-148015. (Library of Liberal Arts Ser). 1971. pap. 3.95 (ISBN 0-672-61187-2). Bobbs.

Bacheller, Martin A., ed. The Hammond Almanac of a Million Facts, Records & Forecasts 1979. (Illus.). 1978. 6.95 o.p. (ISBN 0-8437-4014-0). Hammond Inc.

--Hammond Almanac of a Million Facts, Records, Forecasts 1981. (Illus.). 1980. 7.95 (ISBN 0-8437-4021-3). Hammond Inc.

Bachem, Michael. Heimito Von Doderer. (World Authors Ser.: No. 595). 1981. lib. bdg. 14.95 (ISBN 0-8057-6437-2). Twayne.

Bacher, Max, jt. auth. see Heinle, Erwin.

Bacher, Wilhelm. Die Anfange der Hebraischen Grammaik (1895) Together with Die Hebraische Sprachwissenschaft Vom 10, Bus Zum 16. Jahrhundert (1892) (Studies in the History of Linguistics: No. 4). 1974. text ed. 42.75x (ISBN 0-391-01676-8). Humanities.

Bachhuber, Andrew H. Introduction to Logic. (Illus.). 1957. text ed. 11.95 (ISBN 0-13-487280-0). P-H.

Bachhuber, Thomas D. & Harwood, Richard K. Directions: A Guide to Career Planning. LC 77-78015. (Illus.). 1978. pap. text ed. 9.50 (ISBN 0-395-25385-3). HM.

Bachman, George & Narici, Lawrence. Functional Analysis. 1966. text ed. 22.95 (ISBN 0-12-070250-9). Acad Pr.

Bachman, Richard. Roadwork: A Novel of the First Energy Crisis. (Orig.). 1981. pap. 2.25 (ISBN 0-451-09668-1, Sig). NAL.

Bachman, V. John. The Rebellious Thought of Albert Camus. LC 77-73998. 1979. 7.00 o.p. (ISBN 0-89430-008-3). Morgan-Pacific.

Bachmann, Alberto. An Encyclopedia of the Violin. Weir, Albert E., ed. Martens, Frederick H., tr. from Ger. LC 65-23406. (Music Ser). 1966. Repr. of 1925 ed. lib. bdg. 29.50 (ISBN 0-306-70912-0). Da Capo.

Bachmann, Donna G. & Piland, Sherry. Women Artists: An Historical, Contemporary & Feminist Bibliography. LC 78-19182. 1978. 16.50 (ISBN 0-8108-1149-9). Scarecrow.

Bachmann, E. Theodore, tr. see Froer, Hans.

Bachmann, Jul & Von Moos, Stanislaus. New Directions in Swiss Architecture. LC 72-78052. (New Directions in Architecture Ser). (Illus., Orig.). 1969. 7.95 o.s.i. (ISBN 0-8076-0525-5); pap. 3.95 o.s.i. (ISBN 0-8076-0529-8). Braziller.

Bachmann, Paul. Niedere Zahlentheorie, 2 Vols. in 1. LC 66-20395. (Ger). 1968. Repr. of 1902 ed. text ed. 19.50 o.p. (ISBN 0-8284-0217-5). Chelsea Pub.

--Zahlentheorie, 5 vols. (Nos. 15-20). (Ger). Repr. Set. 131.00 (ISBN 0-384-02990-6). Johnson Repr.

Bachmann, Theodore & Lehmann, Helmut T., eds. Luther's Works, Vol. 35: Word & Sacrament I. LC 55-9893. 426p. 1960. 14.50 (ISBN 0-8006-0335-4, 1-335). Fortress.

Bachmeyer, jt. auth. see Hauenstein.

Bachmeyer, Steven A., jt. auth. see Hauenstein, A. Dean.

Bachmeyer, T. J., jt. auth. see Everett, William W.

Bachner, John P. Public Relations for Nursing Homes. (Illus.). 184p. 1974. text ed. 13.75 o.p. (ISBN 0-398-03111-8). C C Thomas.

Bachofen, J. J. Myth, Religion, & Mother Right: Selected Writings of Johann Jakob Bachofen. Manheim, Ralph, tr. LC 67-22343. (Bollingen Series, No. 84). 368p. 1967. 19.00x (ISBN 0-691-09799-2); pap. 5.95 (ISBN 0-691-01797-2, 303). Princeton U Pr.

Bachrach, Arthur J. Psychological Research: An Introduction. 4th ed. 205p. 1981. pap. text ed. 6.95 (ISBN 0-394-32288-6). Random.

Bachrack, Stanley D. The Committee of One Million: China Lobby Politics, 1953-1971. LC 76-18117. 1976. 18.00x (ISBN 0-231-03933-6). Columbia U Pr.

Bachrich, Jack L. Dry Kiln Handbook. (Illus.). 400p. 1980. 50.00 (ISBN 0-87930-087-6, Pub. by H a Simons Intl Canada). Miller Freeman.

Bachtold, Louise M. Gifted Women in Politics & the Arts & Sciences. LC 80-69361. 135p. 1981. perfect bdg. 10.95 (ISBN 0-86548-022-2). Century Twenty One.

Bach-Y-Rita, P., jt. ed. see Lennerstrand, G.

Bacigalupo, Leonard F. The American Franciscan Missions in Central America. LC 80-68205. 480p. 1980. 14.50 (ISBN 0-933402-20-1); pap. 8.95 (ISBN 0-933402-21-X). Charisma Pr.

Back, Kurt W. Social Psychology. LC 76-30835. 1977. text ed. 21.50 (ISBN 0-471-03983-7); instructor's manual avail. (ISBN 0-471-02656-5). Wiley.

Back, Kurt W., ed. In Search for Community. LC 77-90415. (AAAS Selected Symposium Ser.: No. 4). 1978. lib. bdg. 20.00x (ISBN 0-89158-431-5). Westview.

--Life Course: Integrative Theories & Exemplary Populations. (AAAS Selected Symposium: No. 41). 160p. 1980. lib. bdg. 18.50x (ISBN 0-89158-777-2). Westview.

Back, M. & Laidler, K. J., eds. Selected Readings in Chemical Kinetics. 1967. text ed. 19.50 (ISBN 0-08-012344-9); pap. text ed. 12.75 (ISBN 0-08-012343-0). Pergamon.

Backer, Theodore B. A Compact Anthology of Bartlett's Quotations. LC 74-1964. 1974. 8.95 o.p. (ISBN 0-685-50518-9). Jonathan David.

Background GmbH. Without a Trace. Partisan Press Staff, ed. (Illus.). 128p. (Orig.). 1980. pap. 4.95 (ISBN 0-935150-00-5). Partisan Pr.

Backhaut, Bernard, jt. ed. see Spiegel, Allen D.

Backhouse, John K. Pass or Fail? A Study of Pass Rates in the G. C. E. at the "O" Level. (General Ser.). (Illus.). 44p. 1974. pap. text ed. 5.75x (ISBN 0-85633-036-1, NFER). Humanities.

Backhurst, J. R., et al. Problems in Heat & Mass Transfer. (Illus.). 1974. pap. text ed. 14.95x (ISBN 0-7131-3327-9). Intl Ideas.

Backman, Beth, ed. see Gupta, Pranati Sen.

Backman, Beth, ed. see Virion, Charles.

Backman, Jules. Advertising & Competition. LC 67-17108. (Illus.). 1967. 12.00x (ISBN 0-8147-0020-9). NYU Pr.

--Business Problems of the Eighties. (ITT Key Issues Lecture Ser.). 1980. pap. 6.95 (ISBN 0-672-97499-1). Bobbs.

Backman, Jules, jt. auth. see Czepiel, John.

Backman, Jules, ed. Economic Growth or Stagnation. LC 78-10874. (ITT Key Issue Lecture Ser.). 168p. text ed. 9.95 (ISBN 0-672-97323-5); pap. text ed. 4.95 (ISBN 0-672-97322-7). Bobbs.

Backofen, Walter A. Deformation Processing. LC 71-132054. (Engineering Science Ser). 1972. text ed. 21.95 (ISBN 0-201-00388-0). A-W.

Backpacker Magazine, ed. see Bunnelle, Hasse R.

Backris, J. O'M & Khan, S. U. Quantum Electrochemistry. 480p. 1979. 49.50 (ISBN 0-306-31143-7, Plenum Pr). Plenum Pub.

Backscheider, Paula R., ed. The Plays of Arthur Murphy, 4 vols. LC 78-66610. (Eighteenth-Century English Drama Ser.: Vol. 30). 1980. Set. lib. bdg. 200.00 (ISBN 0-8240-3604-2); lib. bdg. 50.00 ea. Garland Pub.

--The Plays of Charles Gildon. LC 78-66609. (Eighteenth-Century English Drama Ser.: Vol. 17). 1979. lib. bdg. 50.00 (ISBN 0-8240-3591-7). Garland Pub.

--The Plays of James Thomson. LC 78-66637. (Eighteenth-Century English Drama Ser.: Vol. 35). 1980. lib. bdg. 50.00 (ISBN 0-8240-3609-3). Garland Pub.

--The Plays of John Dennis. LC 78-66657. (Eighteenth-Century English Drama Ser.: Vol. 14). 1980. lib. bdg. 50.00 (ISBN 0-8240-3588-7). Garland Pub.

Backscheider, Paula R., jt. ed. see Drucker, Trudy.

Backscheider, Paula R., jt. ed. see Link, Frederick M.

Backscheider, Paula R., jt. ed. see Malek, James S.

Backscheider, Paula R., jt. ed. see Maynard, Temple.

Backscheider, Paula R., jt. ed. see Nussbaum, Felicity.

Backscheider, Paula R., jt. ed. see Siebert, Donald T.

Backstrom, Charles H. & Hursch-Cesar, Gerald. Survey Research. 2nd ed. 400p. 1981. text ed. 8.95 (ISBN 0-471-02543-7). Wiley.

Backus, Charles E. Solar Cells. LC 75-46381. (IEEE Press Selected Reprint Ser.). 1976. 29.95 (ISBN 0-471-01981-X); pap. 19.50 o.p. (ISBN 0-471-01980-1, Pub. by Wiley-Interscience). Wiley.

Backus, Isaac. The Diary of Isaac Backus, 3 vols. McLoughlin, William G., ed. LC 76-12018. (Illus.). 1780p. 1980. Set. 120.00x (ISBN 0-87057-148-6, Pub. by Brown U Pr). Univ Pr of New England.

Backus, Richard H., jt. auth. see Lineaweaver, Thomas H., 3rd.

Backus, Sharron. Inside Softball for Women. 1979. 9.95 o.p. (ISBN 0-8092-7491-4); pap. 5.95 (ISBN 0-8092-7490-6). Contemp Bks.

Backus, William & Chapian, Marie. Telling Yourself the Truth. LC 80-10136. 192p. (Orig.). 1980. pap. 4.95 (ISBN 0-87123-562-5, 210562); study guide 1.25 (ISBN 0-87123-567-6). Bethany Fell.

Backus, William & Malte, Paul. Perspective. pap. 4.85 (ISBN 0-933350-06-6). Morse Pr.

--Really Living. pap. 4.85 (ISBN 0-933350-04-X). Morse Pr.

Backus, William, et al. Adventuring in the Church. pap. 4.85 (ISBN 0-933350-08-2); tchrs' ed. 1.95 (ISBN 0-933350-58-9). Morse Pr.

Bacon & Boyce. Towns & Cities. rev. ed. (People: Cultures, Times, Places). (gr. 2-4). 1976. text ed. 11.00 (ISBN 0-201-42474-6, Sch Div); tchr's. ed. 15.48 (ISBN 0-201-42475-4). A-W.

Bacon & Stephens. Mechanical Science for Higher Technicians, Nos. 4-5. 1981. text ed. price not set (ISBN 0-408-00570-X). Butterworth.

Bacon, jt. auth. see Johnston.

Bacon, A. W. Public Accountability & School System. 1979. text ed. 15.70 (ISBN 0-06-318082-0, Pub. by Har-Row Ltd England). Har-Row.

Bacon, Edmund N. Design of Cities. rev ed. (Illus.). 336p. 1976. pap. 18.95 (ISBN 0-14-004236-9). Penguin.

Bacon, Elizabeth. Central Asians Under Russian Rule: A Study in Cultural Change. LC 66-16739. (Cornell Paperback Ser.). (Illus.). 291p. 1980. pap. 5.95 (ISBN 0-8014-9211-4). Cornell U Pr.

Bacon, Eve. Orlando, a Centennial History, 2 vols. Incl. Vol. 1. (Illus.). 1975. 17.76 (ISBN 0-913122-08-4); Vol. 2. (Illus.). 1977. 19.95 (ISBN 0-913122-10-6). LC 75-21374. 35.00 set (ISBN 0-913122-13-0). Mickler Hse.

Bacon, Frances. Wisedome of the Ancients. Gorges, A., tr. LC 68-54614. (English Experince Ser.: No. 1). 176p. 1968. Repr. of 1619 ed. 13.00 (ISBN 90-221-0001-4). Walter J Johnson.

Bacon, Francis. The Advancement of Learning. Kitchin, G. W., ed. (Rowman & Littlefield University Library). 246p. 1973. 11.50x (ISBN 0-87471-664-0); pap. 6.50x (ISBN 0-87471-665-9). Rowman.

--The Advancement of Learning, Bk. 1. Armstrong, William, ed. 154p. 1975. text ed. 10.75x (ISBN 0-485-13605-8, Athlone Pr). Humanities.

--Certaine Miscellany Works. LC 79-25440. (English Experience Ser.: No. 222). 166p. Repr. of 1629 ed. 21.00 (ISBN 90-221-0222-X). Walter J Johnson.

--The Charge of Sir F. Bacon Touching Duells. LC 68-27475. (English Experience Ser.: No. 7). 62p. Repr. of 1614 ed. 8.00 (ISBN 90-221-0007-3). Walter J Johnson.

--De Sapientia Veterum, Repr. Of 1609 Ed. Bd. with The Wisedome of the Ancients. Gorges, Arthur, tr. Repr. of 1619 ed. LC 75-27863. (Renaissance & the Gods Ser.: Vol. 20). (Illus.). 1976. lib. bdg. 73.00 (ISBN 0-8240-2068-5). Garland Pub.

--The Elements of the Common Lawes of England. LC 77-26477. (English Experience Ser.: No. 164). 104p. 1969. Repr. of 1630 ed. 25.00 (ISBN 90-221-0164-9). Walter J Johnson.

--Essayes or Counsels, Civill & Morall. 1974. text ed. 16.95x o.p. (ISBN 0-8277-2150-1); pap. text ed. 12.00x o.p. (ISBN 0-8277-3730-0). British Bk Ctr.

--Essays: Religious Meditations; Places of Perswasion & Disswasion. LC 68-54612. (English Experience Ser.: No. 17). Repr. of 1597 ed. 9.50 (ISBN 90-221-0017-0). Walter J Johnson.

--Francis Bacon - Essays. (Rowman & Littlefield University Library). 200p. 1972. 10.95x (ISBN 0-87471-666-7); pap. 4.50x (ISBN 0-87471-667-5). Rowman.

--Francis Bacon: A Selection of His Works. Warhaft, Sidney, ed. LC 65-20259. (College Classics in English Ser). 1965. pap. 8.55 (ISBN 0-672-63011-7). Odyssey Pr.

--Great Insaturation & New Atlantis. Weinberger, J., ed. (Croft Classics Ser.). 1980. text ed. 9.95 (ISBN 0-88295-115-7); pap. text ed. 2.95 (ISBN 0-88295-113-0). AHM Pub.

--The Historie of Life & Death: With Observations Naturall & Experimentall. LC 68-54613. (English Experience Ser.: No.20). 324p. Repr. of 1638 ed. 21.00 (ISBN 90-221-0020-0). Walter J Johnson.

--History of the Reign of King Henry the Seventh. Levy, Fritz J., ed. LC 70-177471. (European Historiography Ser). 1972. 6.95 (ISBN 0-672-61420-0). Bobbs.

--New Organon & Related Writings. Anderson, Fulton H., ed. LC 60-11682. 1960. pap. 6.95 (ISBN 0-672-60289-X, LLA97). Bobbs.

--Two Books...of the Proficience & Advancement of Learning. LC 70-25525. (English Experience Ser.: No. 218). 236p. Repr. of 1605 ed. 39.00 (ISBN 90-221-0218-1). Walter J Johnson.

--Works, 1857-74, 15 Vols. Spedding, James, et al, eds. 1951. Set. 595.00 (ISBN 0-403-00003-3). Scholarly.

Bacon, Francis & Francis, Richard. Examples of a Treatise on Universal Justice or the Fountains of Equity, by Aphorisms. Berkowitz, David S. & Thorne, Samuel E., eds. LC 77-86639. (Classics of English Legal History in the Modern Era Ser.: Vol. 33). 125p. 1979. lib. bdg. 40.00 (ISBN 0-8240-3082-6). Garland Pub.

Bacon, Sir Francis. The Elements of the Common Lawes of England, 2 pts, Repr. Of 1630. Bd. with John Cowell: The Institutes of the Lawes of England, Digested into the Method of the Civilll or Imperiall Institutions. Repr. of 1651 ed. LC 77-86558. (Classics of English Legal History in the Modern Era: Vol. 67). 1978. lib. bdg. 55.00 (ISBN 0-8240-3054-0). Garland Pub.

--Reading on the Statute of Uses. Berkowitz, David S. & Thorne, Samuel E., eds. LC 77-89249. (Classics of English Legal History in the Modern Era Ser.: Vol. 140). 1979. lib. bdg. 55.00 (ISBN 0-8240-3177-6). Garland Pub.

Bacon, G. E. Neutron Diffraction. 3rd ed. (Monographs on the Physics & Chemistry of Materials). (Illus.). 652p. 1975. 109.00x (ISBN 0-19-851353-4). Oxford U Pr.

--X-Ray & Neutron Diffraction. 1966. text ed. 44.00 (ISBN 0-08-011999-9); pap. text ed. 19.50 (ISBN 0-08-011998-0). Pergamon.

Bacon, G. E. & Noakes, G. R. Neutron Physics. (Wykeham Science Ser.: Vol. 2). (Illus.). 1969. pap. 4.40 o.p. (ISBN 0-387-91046-8). Springer-Verlag.

--Neutron Physics. (Wykeham Science Ser.: No. 2). 1969. 9.95x (ISBN 0-8448-1104-1). Crane-Russak Co.

Bacon, Helen, tr. see Aeschylus.

Bacon, Helen H. Barbarians in Greek Tragedy. 1961. 22.50x o.p. (ISBN 0-685-69787-8). Elliots Bks.

Bacon, Jack, ed. Eros in Art. (Illus.). 1969. 10.00 (ISBN 0-910550-03-4). Elysium.

Bacon, James. Hollywood Is a Four Letter Town. 1977. pap. 1.95 (ISBN 0-380-01671-0, 33399). Avon.

Bacon, Jo A. Don't Die Baby. McCarthy, Patricia, ed. (Pal Paperbacks Ser., Kit A). (Illus., Orig.). (gr. 7-12). 1974. pap. text ed. 1.25 (ISBN 0-8374-3468-8). Xerox Ed Pubns.

Bacon, Joan. Pussycat Tiger. (Illus.). 24p. (ps-4). 1972. PLB 5.00 (ISBN 0-307-60362-8, Golden Pr). Western Pub.

Bacon, Joan C. Boo & the Flying Flews. (Eager Readers Ser). (gr. k-3). 1975. PLB 5.00 (ISBN 0-307-60803-4, Golden Pr). Western Pub.

--A Hat for the Queen. (Eager Readers Ser.). (Illus.). (gr. k-3). 1975. PLB 5.00 (ISBN 0-307-60802-6, Golden Pr). Western Pub.

Bacon, R. L. Boy & the Taniwha. 1976. 4.55x o.p. (ISBN 0-8002-0767-X). Intl Pubns Serv.

Bacon, Richard M. The Art & Craft of Wall Stenciling. LC 76-41361. (Funk & W Bk.). 1977. 9.95 (ISBN 0-308-10274-6, TYC-T). T Y Crowell.

Bacon, Roy. The Motorcycle Manual. 1977. pap. 12.50 (ISBN 0-408-00260-3). Transatlantic.

Bacon, Theo. D. Leonard Bacon: A Statesman in the Church. 1931. 47.50x (ISBN 0-685-69788-6). Elliots Bks.

Bacon, Thomas I. Martin Luther & the Drama. (Amsterdamer Pulkationen Zur Sprache und Literature: No. 25). 1976. text ed. 14.25x (ISBN 90-6203-359-8). Humanities.

Bacon, Walter M., Jr., ed. Behind Closed Doors: Secret Papers on the Failure of Romanian-Soviet Negotiations 1931-1932. LC 77-78050. (Archival Documentation Publications Ser.: No. 180). (Illus.). 228p. 1979. 17.50 (ISBN 0-8179-6801-6). Hoover Inst Pr.

Bacou, Roseline. The German, Flemish, & Dutch Drawings. (Great Drawings of the Louvre Museum Ser: Vol. 3). (Illus.). 1968. 20.00 o.s.i. (ISBN 0-8076-0474-7). Braziller.

--The Italian Drawings. LC 68-23040. (Great Drawings of the Louvre Museum Ser: Vol. 2). (Illus.). 1968. 20.00 o.s.i. (ISBN 0-8076-0475-5). Braziller.

Bacou, Roseline, et al. French Landscape Drawings, & Sketches of the Eighteenth Century. Date not set. 16.50 (ISBN 0-374-85311-8); pap. 7.50 (ISBN 0-374-86233-8). FS&G. Postponed.

Bacovcin, Helen, tr. The Way of a Pilgrim-& the Pilgrim Continues His Way. LC 76-52000. 1978. pap. 2.45 (ISBN 0-385-12400-7, Im). Doubleday.

Bacq, Z. M. Sulfur Containing Radio-Protective Agents. 344p. 1976. text ed. 94.00 (ISBN 0-08-016298-3). Pergamon.

Bacq, Z. M. & Alexander, P. Fundamentals of Radiobiology. 2nd ed. 1971. 32.00 (ISBN 0-08-009406-6); pap. text ed. 4.15 (ISBN 0-08-012166-7). Pergamon.

Bacq, Z. M., et al, eds. Fundamentals of Biochemical Pharmacology. LC 75-135101. 1971. text ed. 52.00 (ISBN 0-08-016453-6); pap. text ed. 24.00 (ISBN 0-08-017775-1). Pergamon.

Baczko, Bronislaw. Rousseau: Solitude et Communaute. Brendhel-Lamhout, Claire, tr. (Civilisation et Societes: No. 30). 1974. pap. 35.90x (ISBN 90-2797-505-1). Mouton.

Baczynsky, Mark. Photocrafts Book of Guides, Vol. 2. LC 78-70581. (Illus.). 104p. 1980. pap. 19.95 (ISBN 0-89816-002-2). Embee Pr.

Badaczewski, Dennis, jt. auth. see Rodrigues, Raymond J.

Badash, Lawrence & Broida, H. P., eds. Reminiscences of Los Alamos: 1943-1945. (Studies in the History of Modern Science: No. 5). 180p. 1980. lib. bdg. 26.50 (ISBN 90-277-1097-X); pap. 9.95 (ISBN 90-277-1098-8). Kluwer Boston.

Badawi, A. Dictionary of Social Sciences: English-French-Arabic. 25.00x (ISBN 0-686-63544-2). Intl Bk Ctr.

Badawi, M. M. Coleridge: Critic of Shakespeare. LC 72-86417. 240p. 1973. 38.00 (ISBN 0-521-20040-7). Cambridge U Pr.

--A Critical Introduction to Modern Arabic Poetry. LC 75-9279. 275p. 1976. 48.00 (ISBN 0-521-20699-5); pap. 16.95x (ISBN 0-521-29023-6). Cambridge U Pr.

Badawi, M. Zaki, jt. ed. see Sardar, Ziauddin.

Badawy, Alexander. History of Egyptian Architecture -The Empire (the New Kingdom) From the 18th Dynasty to the End of the 20th Dynasty, 1580-1085 B. C. 1968. 40.00x (ISBN 0-520-00057-9). U of Cal Pr.

--The Tomb of Nyhetep-Ptah at Giza & the Tomb of 'Ankhm' Ahor at Saqqara. (Occasional Papers Archaeology Ser.: Vol. II). 1978. pap. 18.50x (ISBN 0-520-09575-8). U of Cal Pr.

--The Tombs of Iteti, Sekhem'ankh-Ptah, & Kaemnofert at Giza. LC 75-620057. (Publications, Occasional Papers, Archaeology: Vol. 9). 1976. pap. 14.50x (ISBN 0-520-09544-8). U of Cal Pr.

Badayev, A. The Bolsheviks in the Tsarist Duma. 1973. 16.50 (ISBN 0-86527-013-9). Fertig.

Badcock, jt. auth. see Tingay.

Badcock, C. R. The Psychoanalysis of Culture. 264p. 1980. 36.50x (ISBN 0-631-11701-6, Pub. by Basil Blackwell). Biblio Dist.

Badcock, W. & Reynolds, J. A New Touch-Stone for Gold & Silver Wares. 390p. Repr. of 1679 ed. 10.00x (ISBN 0-686-28346-5, Pub. by Irish Academic Pr). Biblio Dist.

Baddeley, Clinton. My Foe Outstretch'd Beneath the Tree. 1981. pap. 2.25 (ISBN 0-440-15685-8). Dell.

Baddiley, James & Abraham, E. P., eds. Penicillin Fifty Years After Fleming. 2nd ed. (Royal Society Ser.). 378p. 1980. lib. bdg. 62.00x (ISBN 0-85403-140-5, Pub. by Royal Soc London). Scholium Intl.

Baddour, Raymond F. & Timmins, Robert S., eds. Application of Plasmas to Chemical Processing. 1967. 23.00x (ISBN 0-262-02027-0). MIT Pr.

Baden, John. Earth Day Reconsidered. LC 80-81670. 1980. 4.00 (ISBN 0-89195-028-1). Heritage Found.

Baden, John & Stroup, Richard. Myths & Management of Natural Resources. (Pacific Institute for Public Policy Research Ser.). 1981. price not set professional reference (ISBN 0-88410-380-3). Ballinger Pub.

Baden, John, jt. ed. see Hardin, Garrett.

Baden, Marian. Being in God's Family. (Concordia Weekday Ser. - Gr. 3-4. Bk. 4, 2-V). 1967. pap. text ed. 2.15 (ISBN 0-570-06658-1, 22-2028); manual 4.85 (ISBN 0-685-08548-1, 22-2029). Concordia.

Baden, Wayne F., et al. The Obstetrician-Gynecologist & Primary Care. (Illus.). 197p. 1980. lib. bdg. 22.00 (ISBN 0-683-00301-1). Williams & Wilkins.

Baden-Fuller, A. J. Engineering Field Theory. 272p. 1973. text ed. 32.00 (ISBN 0-08-017033-1); pap. text ed. 16.25 (ISBN 0-08-017034-X). Pergamon.

--Microwaves: An Introduction to Microwave Theory & Techniques. 1979. 41.00 (ISBN 0-08-024228-6); pap. 16.25 (ISBN 0-08-024227-8). Pergamon.

Baden-Fuller, A. J., ed. Worked Examples in Engineering Field Theory. 1977. text ed. 42.00 (ISBN 0-08-018143-0); pap. text ed. 15.00 (ISBN 0-08-018142-2). Pergamon.

Badenhuizen, N. P. Chemistry & Biology of the Starch Granule. (Protoplasmatologia Ser.: Vol. 2B, Pt. 2bs). (Illus.). 1959. pap. 26.00 o.p. (ISBN 0-387-80522-2). Springer-Verlag.

Bader, Barbara. Trademark Scandinavia. LC 76-8502. (Illus.). (gr. 4-7). 1976. 8.25 (ISBN 0-688-80015-7); PLB 7.92 (ISBN 0-688-84015-9). Greenwillow.

Bader, Julia. Crystal Land: Patterns of Artifice in Vladimir Nabokov's English Novels. 1973. 18.50x (ISBN 0-520-02167-3). U of Cal Pr.

Badger, Geoffrey M. Aromatic Character & Aromaticity. LC 68-29650. (Chemistry Texts Ser). (Illus., Orig.). 1969. 26.95 (ISBN 0-521-07339-1). Cambridge U Pr.

Badgley, Anne V. The Rembrandt Decisions. LC 79-13159. 1979. 8.95 (ISBN 0-396-07622-X). Dodd.

Badgley, John. Asian Development: Problems & Prognosis. LC 78-142354. 1971. pap. text ed. 4.50 o.s.i. (ISBN 0-02-901140-X). Free Pr.

Badi, Joseph, ed. Fundamental Laws of the State of Israel. LC 61-8605. 451p. 1961. text ed. 34.00x (ISBN 0-8290-0174-3). Irvington.

Badia, Leonard F. & Sarno, Ronald. Morality: How to Live It Today. LC 79-20498. 1980. pap. 7.95 (ISBN 0-8189-0391-0). Alba.

Badian, E. Roman Imperialism in the Late Republic. 2nd ed. 1969. 8.50x (ISBN 0-8014-0024-4); pap. 2.45 (ISBN 0-8014-9109-6, CP109). Cornell U Pr.

--Studies in Greek & Roman History. 1964. 30.50x (ISBN 0-631-08140-2, Pub. by Basil Blackwell). Biblio Dist.

Badian, E., ed. see Polybius.

Badian, E., ed. see Syme, Ronald.

Badnow, William R., ed. Edmund's Nineteen Eighty-One Foreign Car Prices. (Edmund's Car Price Guides Ser.). (Orig.). 1981. pap. 2.50 (ISBN 0-440-02207-X, Pub. by Edmund). Dell.

--Edmund's Nineteen Eighty-One New Car Prices. (Orig.). 1981. pap. 2.50 (ISBN 0-440-02236-3, Pub. by Edmund). Dell.

--Edmund's Nineteen Eighty-One Used Car Prices. (Edmund's Car Price Guides Ser.). (Orig.). 1981. pap. 2.50 (ISBN 0-440-02209-6, Pub. by Edmund). Dell.

--Edmund's United States Coin Prices. (Orig.). 1981. pap. 2.50 (ISBN 0-440-01794-7, Pub. by Edmund). Dell.

--Edmund's Used Car Prices. (Orig.). Date not set. pap. price not set (ISBN 0-440-02952-X, Pub by Edmund). Dell.

Badr, Albirt Y. & Siksek, Simon G. Manpower & Oil in Arab Countries. LC 79-2850. (Illus.). 270p. 1981. Repr. of 1959 ed. 22.50 (ISBN 0-8305-0026-X). Hyperion Conn.

Badzinski, S. Carpentry in Commercial Construction. 2nd ed. 1980. 14.95 (ISBN 0-13-115220-3). P-H.

Badzinski, S., Jr. Carpentry in Residential Construction. 1981. 16.95 (ISBN 0-13-115238-6). P-H.

Bae, Yoong. Alien Starships. (Illus.). 32p. 1980. pap. 3.50 (ISBN 0-89844-014-9). Troubador Pr.

--Paper Robots. (Illus.). 32p. (Orig.). 1981. pap. 3.50 (ISBN 0-686-69425-2). Troubador Pr.

--Paper Rockets. (Illus.). 32p. 1980. pap. 3.50 (ISBN 0-89844-022-X). Troubador Pr.

Baeckler, Virginia. Sparkle: PR for Library Staff. LC 80-50566. (Illus.). 80p. (Orig.). 1980. pap. 5.00x (ISBN 0-9603232-1-X). Sources.

Baeckler, Virginia & Larson, Linda. Go, Pep, & Pop: Two Hundred Fifty Tested Ideas for Lively Libraries. LC 75-20328. 1976. pap. 4.50 (ISBN 0-916444-01-5). UNABASHED Lib.

Baedeker, Karl. Baedeker's Great Britain, Vol. 3. (Illus.). 1971. 7.95 o.s.i. (ISBN 0-02-504970-4). Macmillan.

--Berlin. 1966. 6.95 o.s.i. (ISBN 0-02-504750-7). Macmillan.

Baedeker, Karl, ed. Baedeker's United States. LC 76-77703. (American Scene Ser.). Orig. Title: The United States with an Excursion into Mexico. (Illus.). 520p. 1971. Repr. of 1893 ed. lib. bdg. 17.50 (ISBN 0-306-71341-1). Da Capo.

Baegert, Johann J. Observations in Lower California. Brandenburg, M. M. & Baumann, Carl L., trs. from Ger. (Library Reprint Ser.: No. 100). 1979. Repr. of 1952 ed. 17.50x (ISBN 0-520-03873-8). U of Cal Pr.

Baeher, Helen, ed. Women & Media. LC 80-41424. (Illus.). 150p. 1980. 14.25 (ISBN 0-08-026061-6). Pergamon.

Baehler, James R. The New Manager's Guide to Success. 160p. 1980. 19.95 (ISBN 0-03-058014-5). Praeger.

Baehr, Consuelo. Best Friends. 1980. 11.95 (ISBN 0-440-00841-7). Delacorte.

Bae Hrens, Aemilius. Poetae Latini Minores, Leipzig, 1879-1883, 5 vols. Commager, Steele, ed. LC 77-70775. (Latin Poetry Ser.). 1979. Set. lib. bdg. 170.00 (ISBN 0-8240-2950-X). Garland Pub.

Baelz, Peter. Ethics & Belief. LC 76-15425. 1977. pap. 3.95 (ISBN 0-8164-1229-4). Crossroad NY.

Baen, James P., ed. see Dickson, Gordon R.

Baen, James P., ed. see Leiber, Fritz.

Baen, Jim, ed. see Heinlein, Robert A.

Baer, Daniel M. & Dito, William R., eds. Interpretation of Therapeutic Drug Levels. (Illus.). 400p. 1981. text ed. 35.00 (ISBN 0-89189-080-7, 45-9-009-00). Am Soc Clinical.

Baer, Donald M., jt. auth. see Bijou, Sidney W.

Baer, Edith. A Frost in the Night: A Childhood on the Eve of the Third Reich. LC 79-27774. 224p. 1980. 8.95 (ISBN 0-394-84364-9); lib. bdg. 8.99 (ISBN 0-394-94364-3). Pantheon.

--Wonder of Hands. LC 77-93852. (gr. k-3). 1970. 5.95 o.s.i. (ISBN 0-8193-0420-4, Four Winds); PLB 5.41 o.s.i. (ISBN 0-8193-0421-2). Schol Bk Serv.

Baer, Eleanora A. Titles in Series: A Handbook for Librarians & Students, 4 vols. 3rd ed. LC 78-14452. 1978. Set. 99.50 (ISBN 0-8108-1043-3). Scarecrow.

Baer, Gabriel. Fellah & Townsman in the Middle East: Studies in Social History. 1981. 30.00x (ISBN 0-7146-3126-4, F Cass Co). Biblio Dist.

--Population & Society in the Arab East. Szoke, Hanna, tr. LC 76-16835. (Illus.). 1976. Repr. of 1964 ed. lib. bdg. 21.25x (ISBN 0-8371-8963-2, BAPSA). Greenwood.

Baer, Hans P. & Drummond, George I. Physiological & Regulatory Functions of Adenosine & Adenine Nucleotides. LC 78-55809. 1979. text ed. 44.50 (ISBN 0-89004-305-1). Raven.

Baer, Helene G. Heart Is Like Heaven: The Life of Lydia Maria Child. LC 64-10895. 1964. 10.00x o.p. (ISBN 0-8122-7442-3). U of Pa Pr.

Baer, Herbert R. Admiralty Law of the Supreme Court. 3rd ed. 1978. 50.00 (ISBN 0-87215-216-2); 1980 supplement 12.50 (ISBN 0-87215-339-8). Michie.

Baer, Howard F. St. Louis to Me. 1978. 10.95 (ISBN 0-86629-005-2). Sunrise MO.

Baer, Jean. Single Girl Goes to Town. 1968. 5.95 o.s.i. (ISBN 0-02-505190-3). Macmillan.

Baer, Judith A. The Chains of Protection: The Judicial Response to Women's Labor Legislation. LC 77-82695. (Contributions in Women's Studies: No. 1). 1978. lib. bdg. 18.95x (ISBN 0-8371-9785-6, BCP/). Greenwood.

Baer, Larry L. The Parker Gun. rev. ed. LC 77-75333. 196p. 1980. 24.95 (ISBN 0-917714-18-0). Beinfeld Pub.

Baer, Morley, et al. Adobes in the Sun. LC 72-85173. (Illus.). 144p. 1980. pap. 8.95 (ISBN 0-87701-168-0). Chronicle Bks.

Baer, Steve. Sunspots. write for info. (ISBN 0-88930-062-3); pap. write for info. (ISBN 0-88930-061-5). Zomeworks Corp.

--Sunspots. LC 75-20779. 1977. pap. 4.00 o.p. (ISBN 0-686-21779-9). Zomeworks Corp.

Baer, Werner & Samuelson, Larry. Latin America in the Post-Import Substitution Era. 1977. pap. text ed. 21.00 (ISBN 0-08-021822-9). Pergamon.

Baerends, Gerard, et al, eds. Essays on Function & Evolution in Behaviour. (Illus.). 350p. 1975. 55.00x (ISBN 0-19-857382-0). Oxford U Pr.

Baernreither, Joseph M. English Associations of Working Men. Taylor, A., tr. LC 66-28040. 1966. Repr. of 1889 ed. 22.000 (ISBN 0-8103-3078-4). Gale.

Baert, A. L. Atlas of Computer Tomography: Volume Two, Abdominal Computer Tomography. (Illus.). 210p. 1980. 116.90 (ISBN 0-387-10093-8). Springer-Verlag.

Baert, Andre E., jt. ed. see Mednick, Sarnoff A.

Baerthlein, Karl. Transzendentalienlehre der alten Ontologie, Pt. 1: Transzendentalienlehre im Corpus Aristotelicum. 415p. 1972. 52.00x (ISBN 3-11-004021-2). De Gruyter.

Baerwald, H. H. Japan's Parliament: An Introduction. LC 73-90810. 200p. 1974. 19.95x (ISBN 0-521-20387-2). Cambridge U Pr.

Baerwald, Sara, jt. auth. see Handelsman, Judith.

Baetz, Ruth. Lesbian Crossroads: Personal Stories of Lesbian Struggles & Triumphs. LC 80-12440. 288p. 1980. 10.95 (ISBN 0-688-03712-7). Morrow.

Baez, Joan. And Then I Wrote... (Illus.). 352p. 1980. 14.95 (ISBN 0-671-44849-8). Summit Bks.

Baez, Tony, et al. Desegregation & Hispanic Students: A Community Perspective. LC 80-80311. 84p. (Orig.). 1980. pap. 3.50 (ISBN 0-89763-023-8). Natl Clearinghse Bilingual Ed.

Baez-Camargo, Gonzalo. Comentario Arqueologica de la Biblia. 339p. (Orig., Span.). 1979. pap. 7.25 (ISBN 0-89922-148-3). Edit Caribe.

Bagaturov, S. A. Multicomponent Distillation & Rectification. 10.00x (ISBN 0-210-98104-0). Asia.

Bagby, Albert I., Jr., tr. see Assis, Joaquim M.

Bagby, English. The Psychology of Personality. 236p. 1980. Repr. of 1928 ed. lib. bdg. 35.00 (ISBN 0-8492-3590-1). R West.

Bagby, Wesley M. Contemporary American Economic & Political Problems. LC 80-22510. 296p. 1981. text ed. 19.95 (ISBN 0-88229-328-1); pap. text ed. 9.95 (ISBN 0-88229-765-1). Nelson-Hall.

Bagchi, Amiya K. Private Investment in India & Pakistan, 1900-1939. LC 79-152631. (South Asian Studies: No. 10). (Illus.). 1971. 53.50 (ISBN 0-521-07641-2). Cambridge U Pr.

Bagchi, Asoke K. An Introduction to Head Injuries. (Illus.). 1981. text ed. 12.95x (ISBN 0-19-561151-9). Oxford U Pr.

Bagder, George P. An English-Arabic Lexicon. 75.00x (ISBN 0-685-72042-X). Intl Bk Ctr.

Bagdikian, Ben H. Caged: Eight Prisoners & Their Keepers. LC 74-20398. 438p. (YA) 1976. 12.95 o.s.i. (ISBN 0-06-010174-1, HarpT). Har-Row.

Bage, Robert. Barham Downs, 2 vols. Paulson, Ronald, ed. LC 78-60850. (Novel 1720-1805 Ser.: Vol. 9). 1979. Set. lib. bdg. 62.00 (ISBN 0-8240-3659-X). Garland Pub.

--The Fair Syrian, 2 vols. LC 78-60845. (Novel 1720-1805 Ser.: Vol. 10). 1980. Set. lib. bdg. 62.00 (ISBN 0-8240-3659-X). Garland Pub.

--Hermsprong; or, Man As He Is Not, 3 vols. LC 78-60853. (Novel 1720-1805 Ser.: Vol. 13). 1980. Set. lib. bdg. 93.00 (ISBN 0-8240-3662-X). Garland Pub.

--James Wallace, 3 vols. Paulson, Ronald, ed. LC 78-60847. (Novel 1720-1805 Ser.: Vol. 11). 1979. 31.00 ea. (ISBN 0-8240-3660-3). Garland Pub.

--Mount Henneth, 2 vols. Paulson, Ronald, ed. LC 78-60846. (Novel 1720-1805 Ser.: Vol. 8). 1980. Set. lib. bdg. 62.00 (ISBN 0-8240-3657-3); lib. bdg. 31.00 ea. Garland Pub.

Bage, Robert & Paulson, Ronald. Man As He Is, 4 vols. LC 78-60853. (Novel 1720-1805 Ser.: Vol. 12). 1979. Set. 124.00 (ISBN 0-8240-3661-1); lib. bdg. 31.00 ea. Garland Pub.

Bageant, Robert A., jt. auth. see Heironimus, Terring W., 3rd.

Bagehot, Walter. English Constitution. (World's Classics Ser.). 1933. 10.95 (ISBN 0-19-250330-8). Oxford U Pr.

--The English Constitution. LC 77-86594. (Classics of English Legal History in the Modern Era Ser.: Vol. 84). 1978. Repr. of 1867 ed. lib. bdg. 55.00 (ISBN 0-8240-3071-0). Garland Pub.

--Estimates of Some Englishmen & Scotchmen. 453p. 1980. Repr. of 1858 ed. lib. bdg. 40.00 (ISBN 0-89987-060-0). Darby Bks.

Bagemihl, Frederick, tr. see Knopp, Konrad.

Bagenal, T. B. The Observer's Book of Sea Fishes. (The Observer Bks). (Illus.). 1979. 3.95 (ISBN 0-684-16032-3, ScribT). Scribner.

Bagg, Elma W. Cooking Without a Grain of Salt. LC 64-13870. 1964. 9.95 (ISBN 0-385-05432-7). Doubleday.

Bagg, Robert. Madonna of the Cello. LC 61-6972. (Wesleyan Poetry Program: Vol. 9). (Orig.). 1961. 7.50x (ISBN 0-8195-2009-8); pap. 4.00 (ISBN 0-8195-1009-2). Columbia U Pr.

Bagg, Robert, tr. see Euripides.

Baggaley, Andrew R. Mathematics for Introductory Statistics: A Programmed Review. 1969. pap. 11.95 (ISBN 0-471-04008-8). Wiley.

Baggaley, J. P. & Duck, Steve. The Dynamics of Television. 1977. 21.95 (ISBN 0-347-01124-1, 00255-0, Pub. by Saxon Hse). Lexington Bks.

Baggaley, J. P., et al. Aspects of Educational Technology VIII: Findings of the 1974 Conference for Programmed Learning & Educational Technology. 384p. 1975. 21.00x o.p. (ISBN 0-8464-0156-8). Beekman Pubs.

--Psychology of the TV Image. LC 79-92118. 1980. 21.95 (ISBN 0-03-046206-1). Praeger.

Baggelaar, Kristin & Milton, Donald. Folk Music: More Than a Song. LC 76-3547. (Illus.). 1976. 14.95 o.p. (ISBN 0-690-01159-8, TYC-T). T Y Crowell.

Baggett, Lee. Utilice Su Casa Para Evangelizar. 1980. Repr. of 1979 ed. 1.10 (ISBN 0-311-13832-2). Casa Bautista.

Baggett, Richard C. A Programmed Approach to Good Spelling! 160p. 1981. pap. text ed. 6.95 (ISBN 0-13-729764-5). P-H.

Baggiolini, M., jt. ed. see Brune, K.

Baginski, Frank & Dodson, Reynolds. Splitsville. (Illus.). 96p. 1980. pap. 4.95 (ISBN 0-8015-7042-5, Hawthorn). Dutton.

Bagley, Christopher & Verma, Gajendra K. Racial Prejudice, the Individual & Society. 1979. 19.95 (ISBN 0-566-00294-9, 03085-6, Pub. by Saxon Hse England). Lexington Bks.

Bagley, Christopher, et al. Personality, Self-Esteem & Prejudice. 1979. 18.50 (ISBN 0-566-00265-5, 02836-3, Pub. by Saxon Hse England). Lexington Bks.

Bagley, Desmond. The Enemy. LC 76-42058. 1978. 7.95 o.p. (ISBN 0-385-04873-4). Doubleday.

--Running Blind. LC 71-135711. 1971. 5.95 o.p. (ISBN 0-385-06551-5). Doubleday.

--The Snow Tiger. 272p. 1977. pap. 1.75 o.p. (ISBN 0-449-23107-0, Crest). Fawcett.

--The Tightrope Men. 256p. 1977. pap. 1.75 o.p. (ISBN 0-449-23159-3, Crest). Fawcett.

Bagley, F. R., tr. see Ghazali.

Bagley, J. J. Medieval People. (People in Period Ser.). 1978. 16.95 (ISBN 0-7134-1046-9, Pub. by Batsford England). David & Charles.

Bagley, James R. The Alchemist & the Other Poems. 1980. 5.50 (ISBN 0-8233-0318-7). Golden Quill.

Bagley, John J. History of Lancashire. rev. ed. (County History Ser.). (Illus.). 1961. 10.95 (ISBN 0-85208-047-6). Dufour.

Bagley, Richard, et al. Identifying the Talented & Gifted. (Ser. on Talented & Gifted Education). (Illus., Orig.). 1979. 2.95 (ISBN 0-89354-125-7). Northwest Regional.

Bagley, Val C. Puppy Love. (Illus.). 96p. 1981. pap. 3.95 (ISBN 0-88290-158-3, 2043). Horizon Utah.

--Very Anxiously Engaged. (Illus.). 96p. (Orig.). 1981. pap. 3.95 (ISBN 0-88290-157-5, 2042). Horizon Utah.

Bagnall, Nicholas, ed. New Movements in the Study & Teaching of English. 1977. 12.00 (ISBN 0-85117-044-7). Transatlantic.

Bagnall, Roger S. & Worp, K. A. Regnal Formulas in Byzantine Egypt. LC 79-1316. (Supplements to the Bulletin of American Society of Papyrologists). 1979. pap. 9.00 (ISBN 0-89130-280-8, 311102). Scholars Pr Ca.

Bagnasco, Erminio. Submarines of World War Two. LC 77-81973. Orig. Title: I Sommergibili. 1978. 24.95 (ISBN 0-87021-962-6). Naval Inst Pr.

Bagni, Gwen & Dubov, Paul. With Six You Get Eggroll. (Willow Bks). (gr. 7-8). 1971. pap. 0.75 o.s.i. (ISBN 0-515-00055-8, JT55). Jove Pubns.

Bagnold, Enid. National Velvet. (gr. 7-9). 1971. pap. 1.95 (ISBN 0-671-42893-4). Archway.

--National Velvet. (Illus.). (gr. 7 up). 1949. Repr. of 1935 ed. 9.50 (ISBN 0-688-21422-3); PLB 9.12 (ISBN 0-688-31422-8). Morrow.

Bagnole, John W. Cultures of the Islamic Middle East. (America-Mideast Educational & Training Servies, Inc. - Occasional Paper: No. 4). 86p. (Orig.). 1978. pap. text ed. 4.00 (ISBN 0-89192-296-2). Interbk Inc.

Bagozzi, Richard P. Casual Models in Marketing. LC 79-11622. (Theories in Marketing Ser.). 1980. text ed. 21.95 (ISBN 0-471-01516-4). Wiley.

Bagozzi, Richard P., et al, eds. see Annual Educators Conference Chicago, Illinois, August, 1980.

Bagwell, Elizabeth, jt. auth. see Meeks, Esther.

Bagwell, P. S. Industrial Relations in Nineteenth Century Britain. 106p. 1974. 15.00x (ISBN 0-7165-2215-2, Pub. by Irish Academic Pr Ireland). Biblio Dist.

Bagwell, Philip S. The Transport Revolution, from Seventeen Seventy. 1974. 16.95 (ISBN 0-7134-1386-7, Pub. by Batsford England). David & Charles.

Bahadur, Dinesh. Come Fight a Kite. (Illus.). (gr. 5 up). 1978. PLB 6.79 (ISBN 0-8178-5928-4); pap. 3.95 (ISBN 0-8178-5927-6). Harvey.

Bahadur, K. P., tr. The Parrot & the Starling. (UNESCO Collection of Representative Works: Indian Ser). 1977. text ed. 21.00x (ISBN 0-8426-1034-0). Verry.

Baha'i Committee on Music. Dawn Song: Choral Music. 1969. pap. 5.00 (ISBN 0-87743-061-6, 7-58-03). Baha'i.

Baha'i Committee on Music, compiled by. A New Wind Blowing. (Illus., Orig.). 1970. pap. 3.00 (ISBN 0-87743-040-3, 7-58-04). Baha'i.

Baha'i Publishing Committee, tr. see Walcott, Cynthia.

Bahan, Bill, et al. Spirit of Sunrise. 1925. 1980. 16.00x (ISBN 0-7051-0270-X, Pub. by Skilton & Shaw England); pap. 6.00x (ISBN 0-7051-0271-8). State Mutual Bk.

Baha'u'llah. Blessed Is the Spot. LC 58-8815. (Illus.). (gr. k-2). 1958. 4.50 (ISBN 0-87743-014-4, 7-52-40). Baha'i.

--Epistle to the Son of the Wolf. rev. ed. Effendi, Shoghi, tr. LC 53-18798. 1976. 10.00 (ISBN 0-87743-048-9, 7-03-01). Baha'i.

Baha'u 'llah. Gleanings from the Writings of Baha'u'llah. 2nd rev. ed. Shoghi Effendi, tr. LC 76-45364. 1976. 10.00 (ISBN 0-87743-111-6, 7-03-03); pap. 6.35 o.s.i. (ISBN 0-87743-112-4, 7-03-04). Baha'i.

Baha'u'llah. The Hidden Words of Baha'u'llah. rev. ed. Effendi, Shoghi, tr. LC 54-7328. 1954. 4.00 (ISBN 0-87743-007-1, 7-03-05); pap. 2.50 (ISBN 0-87743-002-0, 7-03-06). Baha'i.

--The Kitab-i-Iqan: The Book of Certitude. 2nd ed. Shoghi Efferdi, tr. from Persian. LC 51-22838. 9.00 (ISBN 0-87743-022-5, 7-03-08). Baha'i.

--Prayers & Meditations. Effendi, Shoghi, tr. LC 53-10767. 1938. 10.00 (ISBN 0-87743-024-1, 7-03-10). Baha'i.

--The Proclamation of Baha'u'llah. LC 72-237435. 1967. 7.50 (ISBN 0-87743-064-0, 7-03-12); pap. 2.00 (ISBN 0-87743-065-9, 7-03-13). Baha'i.

--Selected Writings of Baha'u'llah. rev. ed. 1975. pap. 1.50 (ISBN 0-87743-077-2, 7-03-23). Baha'i.

--Selected Writings of Baha'u'llah. LC 79-15136. 1979. Repr. of 1975 ed. 9.00 (ISBN 0-87743-133-7, 7-03-24). Baha'i.

--The Seven Valleys & the Four Valleys. 3rd rev. ed. Gail, Marzieh, tr. LC 77-23326. 1978. 4.00 (ISBN 0-87743-113-2, 7-03-15); pap. 2.50 (ISBN 0-87743-114-0, 7-03-16). Baha'i.

--Tablets of Baha'u'llah Revealed After the Kitab-i-Aqdas. Effendi, Shoghi & Taherzadeh, Habib, trs. LC 79-670079. 1978. 9.00 (ISBN 0-85398-077-2, 7-03-21, Pub. by Universal Hse. of Justice). Baha'i.

Baha'u'llah & Abdu'L-Baha. Baha'i Prayers & Tablets for the Young. LC 77-2228. (Illus.). 1978. 4.00 (ISBN 0-87743-115-9, 7-15-54). Baha'i.

--Baha'i World Faith. 2nd ed. LC 56-8259. 1956. 10.00 (ISBN 0-87743-013-6, 7-15-23). Baha'i.

--The Divine Art of Living: Selections from Writings of Baha'u'llah & Abdu'l-Baha. 4th rev. ed. LC 77-27001. 1979. pap. 3.00 (ISBN 0-87743-123-X, 7-15-23). Baha'i.

Baha'u'llah, et al. The Pattern of Baha'i Life. 3rd ed. 1963. pap. 1.00 (ISBN 0-900125-15-2, 7-15-30). Baha'i.

Baha'u'llah, the Bab & Abdu'l-Baha. Baha'i Prayers. LC 54-10901. 4.00 (ISBN 0-87743-012-8, 7-15-05). Baha'i.

Baha'U'Llah The Bab & Abdu'l-Baha. Communion with God. large-type ed. 1976. pap. 1.50 (ISBN 0-87743-110-8, 7-15-11). Baha'i.

--The Glad Tidings of Baha'u'llah: Being Extracts from the Sacred Writings of the Baha'is. rev. ed. 1975. 4.95 (ISBN 0-85398-046-2, 7-15-51, Pub. by G Ronald England); pap. 2.00 (ISBN 0-85398-045-4, 7-15-52, Pub. by G Ronald England). Baha'i.

--O God, Guide Me! A Selection of Prayers Revealed. LC 66-22165. (Illus.). (gr. 2-6). 1974. 4.00 (ISBN 0-87743-080-2, 7-52-47). Baha'i.

Bahiri, S., jt. auth. see Norman, R. G.

Bahl, Roy W. Metropolitan City Expenditures: A Comparative Analysis. LC 68-12965. (Illus.). 152p. 1969. 10.00x (ISBN 0-8131-1173-0). U Pr of Ky.

--The Taxation of Urban Property in Less Developed Countries. LC 78-65018. 1979. 19.50 (ISBN 0-299-07860-4). U of Wis Pr.

Bahl, Roy W., jt. ed. see Campbell, Alan K.

Bahlke, George W. The Later Auden: From "New Year Letter" to About the House. LC 74-98179. 1970. 14.50 (ISBN 0-8135-0626-3). Rutgers U Pr.

Bahlman, Dudley W., ed. see Hamilton, Edward W.

Bahlmann, J. & Brod, J., eds. Disturbances of Water & Electrolyte Metabolism. (Contributions to Nephrology Ser.: Vol. 21). (Illus.). 1980. soft cover 45.00 (ISBN 3-8055-0215-X). S Karger.

Bahm, Archie J. The Heart of Confucius: Interpretations of "Genuine Living" & "Great Wisdom". LC 76-83638. (Arcturus Books Paperbacks). (Illus.). 159p. 1977. pap. 4.95 (ISBN 0-8093-0828-2). S Ill U Pr.

--World's Living Religions. (Arcturus Books Paperbacks). 384p. 1971. pap. 6.95 (ISBN 0-8093-0529-1). S Ill U Pr.

--Yoga: Union with the Ultimate. LC 60-53365. 1961. 6.50 (ISBN 0-8044-5056-0); pap. 3.95 (ISBN 0-8044-6015-9). Ungar.

Bahniuk, Margaret H., jt. auth. see Mansfield, Carmella E.

Bahr, Alice. Video in Libraries: A Status Report, 1979-80. 2nd ed. LC 79-25951. (Professional Librarian Ser.). (Illus.). 1979. softcover professional 24.50x (ISBN 0-914236-49-0). Knowledge Indus.

Bahr, Alice H. Automated Library Circulation Systems, 1979-1980. LC 79-16189. (Professional Librarian Ser.). (Illus.). 1979. softcover 24.50x (ISBN 0-914236-34-2). Knowledge Indus.

--Book Theft & Library Security Systems: 1981-82. 2nd ed. LC 77-25284. (Illus.). 120p. 1980. pap. 24.50 (ISBN 0-914236-71-7). Knowledge Indus.

--Microforms: The Librarians' View, 1980-1981. 3rd ed. (Professional Librarian Ser.). (Illus.). 135p. 1981. pap. text ed. 24.50 (ISBN 0-914236-70-9). Knowledge Indus.

Bahr, Donald M., et al. Piman Shamanism & Staying Sickness: Ka: cim Mumkidag. LC 72-92103. 400p. 1974. pap. 9.95x (ISBN 0-8165-0303-6). U of Ariz Pr.

Bahr, Ehrhard & Kunzer, Ruth G. Georg Lukacs. LC 70-190350. (Modern Literature Ser.). 1972. 10.95 (ISBN 0-8044-2014-9). Ungar.

Bahr, Howard M. & Caplow, Theodore. Old Men Drunk & Sober. LC 72-96370. (Illus.). 407p. 1974. 20.00x (ISBN 0-8147-0965-6). NYU Pr.

Bahr, Howard M., et al. American Ethnicity. 1979. text ed. 17.95x (ISBN 0-669-90399-X). Heath.

Bahr, Jerome. The Lonely Scoundrel: A Supplement to the Perishing Republic. LC 73-80240. 89p. 1974. 7.00 o.p. (ISBN 0-686-63592-2). Trempealeau.

--The Perishing Republic. LC 79-129182. 148p. 1971. 8.00 o.p. (ISBN 0-686-63593-0). Trempealeau.

Bahr, Robert. The Blizzard. LC 80-14956. 1980. 9.95 (ISBN 0-13-077842-7). P-H.

Bahr, Robert, jt. auth. see Hess, Lucille.

Bahre, Conrad J. Destruction of the Natural Vegetation of North-Central Chile. LC 78-50836. (Publications in Geography Ser.: Vol. 23). 1979. 10.50x (ISBN 0-520-09594-4). U of Cal Pr.

Bahro, Rudolph. The Alternative in Eastern Europe. 464p. 1981. 19.50 (ISBN 0-8052-7056-6, Pub. by NLB England); pap. 9.50 (ISBN 0-8052-7098-1). Schocken.

Bahti, Mark. Collecting Southwestern Native American Jewelry. (Illus.). 1980. pap. 8.95 (ISBN 0-679-50960-7). McKay.

Bahti, Tom. Southwestern Indian Arts & Crafts. LC 65-499. (Illus.). 1966. 7.95 (ISBN 0-916122-25-5); pap. 2.00 (ISBN 0-916122-00-X). K C Pubns.

--Southwestern Indian Ceremonials. LC 79-136004. (Illus.). 1970. 7.95 (ISBN 0-916122-27-1); pap. 3.00 (ISBN 0-916122-02-6). K C Pubns.

--Southwestern Indian Tribes. LC 68-31188. (Illus.). 1968. 7.95 (ISBN 0-916122-26-3); pap. 3.75 (ISBN 0-916122-01-8). K C Pubns.

Baier, Kurt & Rescher, Nicholas. Values & the Future. LC 68-14109. 1971. pap. text ed. 7.95 (ISBN 0-02-901190-6). Free Pr.

Baierlein, Ralph. Atoms & Information Theory: An Introduction to Statistical Mechanics. LC 71-116369. (Illus.). 1971. text ed. 24.95x (ISBN 0-7167-0332-7). W H Freeman.

Baig, Tara A. Moon in Rahu: A Novel. 10.00x (ISBN 0-210-33812-1). Asia.

Baigell, Matthew. The Western Art of Frederic Remington. Date not set. pap. 9.95 (ISBN 0-345-29026-7). Ballantine.

Baigrie, Ronald S., jt. auth. see Armstrong, Paul W.

Bailar, John C., et al. Chemistry. 940p. 1978. 21.95 (ISBN 0-12-072850-8); instr's. manual 3.00 (ISBN 0-12-072852-4); study guide 6.95 (ISBN 0-12-072854-0). Acad Pr.

Bailard, Thomas E., et al. Personal Money Management. 3rd ed. 1979. text ed. 16.95 (ISBN 0-574-19395-2, 13-2395); instr's guide avail. (ISBN 0-574-19396-0, 13-2396); study guide 6.50 (ISBN 0-574-19397-9, 13-2397). SRA.

Bailes, Frederick W. Hidden Power for Human Problems. new rev. deluxe ed. 1957. deluxe ed. 7.95 o.p. (ISBN 0-13-386953-9). P-H.

Bailes, Kendall E. Technical Elites & Soviet Society Under Lenin & Stalin. LC 77-85558. (Studies of the Russian Institute, Columbia University). 1978. 33.00x (ISBN 0-691-05260-3); pap. 12.50 (ISBN 0-691-10063-2). Princeton U Pr.

Bailes, Mary A. Ryme & Thought. 48p. (Orig.). 1981. pap. 2.95 (ISBN 0-938468-00-6). Marcella.

Bailey. America: Framing of a Nation, 2 vols. LC 74-15253. 1975. Vol. 1. pap. text ed. 11.95 (ISBN 0-675-08756-2); Vol. 2. pap. text ed. 11.95 (ISBN 0-675-08749-X). Merrill.

--Organic Chemistry: A Brief Survey of Concepts & Applications. 2nd ed. 500p. 1981. text ed. 19.95 (ISBN 0-205-07233-X, 6872336); free tchr's ed. (ISBN 0-205-07234-8); free student's guide (ISBN 0-205-07235-6). Allyn.

Bailey, jt. auth. see Draper.

Bailey, A. E., et al, eds. see Kaye, G. W. & Laby, T. H.

Bailey, Adrian. Cooking of the British Isles. LC 69-19833. (Foods of the World Ser). (Illus.). (gr. 6 up). 1969. PLB 14.94 (ISBN 0-8094-0065-0, Pub. by Time-Life). Silver.

--Cooking of the British Isles. (Foods of the World Ser). (Illus.). 1969. 14.95 (ISBN 0-8094-0038-3). Time-Life.

Bailey, Afred M. & Niedrach, Robert J. Stepping Stones Across the Pacific. (Museum Pictorial: No. 3). 1951. pap. 1.10 o.p. (ISBN 0-916278-32-8). Denver Mus Natl Hist.

Bailey, Afred M., et al. The Red Crossbills of Colorado. (Museum Pictorial: No. 9). 1953. pap. 1.10 o.p. (ISBN 0-916278-38-7). Denver Mus Natl Hist.

Bailey, Alfred G. The Conflict of European & Eastern Algonkian Cultures, 1504-1700: A Study in Canadian Civilization. 2nd ed. LC 78-434310. 1969. pap. 6.50 (ISBN 0-8020-6310-1). U of Toronto Pr.

Bailey, Alfred M. Dusky & Swallow-Tailed Gulls of the Galapagos Islands. (Museum Pictorial: No. 15). 1961. pap. 1.10 o.p. (ISBN 0-916278-42-5). Denver Mus Natl Hist.

--Field Work of a Museum Naturalist: Alaska Southeast, 1919-1921; Alaska Far North, 1921-1922. (Museum Pictorial: No. 22). 1971. pap. 2.25 o.p. (ISBN 0-916278-49-2). Denver Mus Natl Hist.

--Galapagos Islands. (Museum Pictorial: No. 9). 1970. pap. 1.10 o.p. (ISBN 0-916278-46-8). Denver Mus Natl Hist.

--The Hawaiian Monk Seal. (Museum Pictorial: No. 7). 1949. pap. 1.10 o.p. (ISBN 0-916278-36-0). Denver Mus Natl Hist.

--Laysan & Black Footed Albatrosses. (Museum Pictorial: No. 6). 1952. pap. 1.10 o.p. (ISBN 0-916278-35-2). Denver Mus Natl Hist.

--Nature Photography with Miniature Cameras. (Museum Pictorial: No. 1). 1951. pap. 1.10 o.p. (ISBN 0-916278-30-1). Denver Mus Natl Hist.

Bailey, Alfred M. & Sorenson, J. H. Subantarctic Campbell Island. (Proceedings: No. 10). 1962. 5.50 o.p. (ISBN 0-916278-62-X); pap. 4.00 o.p. (ISBN 0-916278-63-8). Denver Mus Natl Hist.

Bailey, Alice A. Initiation, Human & Solar. 1977. 11.25 (ISBN 0-85330-010-0); pap. 4.75 (ISBN 0-85330-110-7). Lucis.

--Labours of Hercules. 1977. pap. 3.25 (ISBN 0-85330-130-1). Lucis.

--A Treatise on the Seven Rays, 5 vols. Incl. Vol. 1. Esoteric Psychology. 1979. 17.00 (ISBN 0-85330-018-6); pap. 5.75 (ISBN 0-85330-118-2); Vol. 2. Esoteric Psychology. 1970. 12.00 (ISBN 0-85330-019-4); pap. 7.25 (ISBN 0-85330-119-0); Vol. 3. Esoteric Astrology. 1975. 15.00 (ISBN 0-85330-020-8); pap. 7.75 (ISBN 0-85330-120-4); Vol. 4. Esoteric Healing. 1978. 22.00 (ISBN 0-85330-021-6); pap. 8.00 (ISBN 0-85330-121-2); Vol. 5. The Rays & the Initiations. 1970. 11.50 (ISBN 0-85330-022-4); pap. 7.25 (ISBN 0-85330-122-0). Lucis.

Bailey, Alice A. & Khul, Djwhal. A Compilation on Sex. 160p. (Orig.). pap. 5.00 (ISBN 0-85330-136-0). Lucis.

Bailey, Anne & Reit, Seymour. The West in the Middle Ages. Shapiro, Irwin, ed. (Universal History Ser.). (Illus.). (gr. 7-10). 1966. PLB 6.08 o.p. (ISBN 0-307-60986-3, Golden Pr). Western Pub.

Bailey, Anne M., ed. The Asiatic Mode of Production: Science & Politics. (Illus.). 352p. 1981. price not set (ISBN 0-7100-0737-X) (ISBN 0-7100-0738-8). Routledge & Kegan.

Bailey, Anthony. America, Lost & Found. 1981. 9.95 (ISBN 0-394-51088-7). Random.

Bailey, Bernadine. American Shrines in England. LC 75-20586. 1977. 15.00 o.p. (ISBN 0-498-01727-3). A S Barnes.

--Bells, Bells, Bells. LC 77-16859. (Illus.). (gr. 4 up). 1978. 5.95 (ISBN 0-396-07551-7). Dodd.

--Our Nation's Capital, Washington, D. C. rev. ed. LC 62-19727. (Illus.). (gr. 3-5). 1967. 5.50g (ISBN 0-8075-9558-6). A Whitman.

--Picture Book of Alabama. rev. ed. LC 59-9658. (Illus.). (gr. 3-5). 1975. 5.50g (ISBN 0-8075-9501-2). A Whitman.

--Picture Book of Alaska. rev. ed. LC 57-7143. (Illus.). (gr. 3-5). 1968. 5.50g (ISBN 0-8075-9502-0). A Whitman.

--Picture Book of Arizona. rev. ed. LC 57-7146. (Illus.). (gr. 3-5). 1967. 5.15g (ISBN 0-8075-9503-9). A Whitman.

--Picture Book of Arkansas. rev. ed. LC 66-2711. (Illus.). (gr. 3-5). 1967. 5.50g (ISBN 0-8075-9504-7). A Whitman.

--Picture Book of California. rev ed. (gr. 3-5). 1981. 5.50g. A Whitman.

--Picture Book of California. rev. ed. LC 66-687. (Illus.). (gr. 3-5). 1968. 5.00g o.p. (ISBN 0-8075-9505-5). A Whitman.

--Picture Book of Colorado. rev. ed. LC 55-8827. (Illus.). (gr. 3-5). 1971. 5.50g (ISBN 0-8075-9506-3). A Whitman.

--Picture Book of Connecticut. rev. ed. LC 60-11567. (Illus.). (gr. 3-5). 1974. 5.50g (ISBN 0-8075-9507-1). A Whitman.

--Picture Book of Delaware. rev. ed. LC 68-4252. (Illus.). (gr. 3-5). 1977. 5.50g (ISBN 0-8075-9509-8). A Whitman.

--Picture Book of Florida. rev. ed. LC 68-4252. (Illus.). (gr. 3-5). 1980. 5.50g (ISBN 0-8075-9510-1). A Whitman.

--Picture Book of Georgia. rev. ed. LC 60-11566. (Illus.). (gr. 3-5). 1966. 5.00g o.p. (ISBN 0-8075-9512-8). A Whitman.

--Picture Book of Hawaii. rev. ed. LC 62-10660. (Illus.). (gr. 3-5). 1978. 5.50g (ISBN 0-8075-9513-6). A Whitman.

--Picture Book of Idaho. rev. ed. LC 62-10660. (Illus.). (gr. 3-5). 1967. 5.50g (ISBN 0-8075-9514-4). A Whitman.

--Picture Book of Illinois. rev. ed. LC 66-5264. (Illus.). (gr. 3-5). 1967. 5.50g (ISBN 0-8075-9515-2). A Whitman.

--Picture Book of Indiana. rev. ed. LC 66-705. (Illus.). (gr. 3-5). 1974. 5.50g (ISBN 0-8075-9516-0). A Whitman.

--Picture Book of Iowa. rev. ed. LC 62-19727. (Illus.). 32p. (gr. 3-5). 1969. 5.50g (ISBN 0-8075-9517-9). A Whitman.

--Picture Book of Kansas. rev. ed. LC 65-29625. (Illus.). (gr. 3-5). 1969. 5.50g (ISBN 0-8075-9518-7). A Whitman.

--Picture Book of Kentucky. rev. ed. LC 55-8828. (Illus.). (gr. 3-5). 1967. 5.50g (ISBN 0-8075-9519-5). A Whitman.

--Picture Book of Louisiana. rev. ed. LC 54-9944. (Illus.). (gr. 3-5). 1967. 5.50g (ISBN 0-8075-9520-9). A Whitman.

--Picture Book of Maine. rev. ed. LC 57-7144. (Illus.). (gr. 3-5). 1967. 5.50g (ISBN 0-8075-9521-7). A Whitman.

--Picture Book of Maryland. rev. ed. LC 55-8829. (Illus.). (gr. 3-5). 1970. 5.50g (ISBN 0-8075-9522-5). A Whitman.

--Picture Book of Massachusetts. rev. ed. LC 65-5509. (Illus.). (gr. 3-5). 1969. 5.50g (ISBN 0-8075-9523-3). A Whitman.

--Picture Book of Michigan. rev. ed. (Illus.). (gr. 3-5). 1967. 5.50g (ISBN 0-8075-9524-1). A Whitman.

--Picture Book of Minnesota. rev. ed. (Illus.). (gr. 3-5). 1967. 5.50g (ISBN 0-8075-9526-8). A Whitman.

--Picture Book of Mississippi. rev. ed. LC 68-4457. (Illus.). (gr. 3-5). 1972. 5.00g o.p. (ISBN 0-8075-9527-6). A Whitman.

--Picture Book of Missouri. rev. ed. LC 66-31256. (Illus.). (gr. 3-5). 1974. 5.50g (ISBN 0-8075-9528-4). A Whitman.

--Picture Book of Montana. rev. ed. LC 65-8994. (Illus.). (gr. 3-5). 1969. 5.50g (ISBN 0-8075-9529-2). A Whitman.

--Picture Book of Nebraska. rev. ed. LC 56-7756. (Illus.). (gr. 3-5). 1966. 5.50g (ISBN 0-8075-9530-6). A Whitman.

--Picture Book of Nevada. rev. ed. LC 73-89402. (Illus.). (gr. 3-5). 1974. 5.50g (ISBN 0-8075-9531-4). A Whitman.

--Picture Book of New Hampshire. rev. ed. LC 61-9971. (Illus.). (gr. 3-5). 1971. 5.50g (ISBN 0-8075-9532-2). A Whitman.

--Picture Book of New Jersey. rev. ed. LC 65-9016. (Illus.). (gr. 3-5). 1968. 5.00g o.p. (ISBN 0-8075-9533-0). A Whitman.

--Picture Book of New Mexico. rev. ed. LC 60-11568. (Illus.). (gr. 3-5). 1966. 5.50g (ISBN 0-8075-9534-9). A Whitman.

--Picture Book of New York. rev. ed. LC 66-1262. (Illus.). (gr. 3-5). 1968. 5.50g (ISBN 0-8075-9535-7). A Whitman.

--Picture Book of North Carolina. rev. ed. LC 74-134956. (Illus.). (gr. 3-5). 1970. 5.50g (ISBN 0-8075-9536-5). A Whitman.

--Picture Book of North Dakota. rev. ed. LC 58-12319. (Illus.). (gr. 3-5). 1971. 5.50g (ISBN 0-8075-9537-3). A Whitman.

--Picture Book of Ohio. rev. ed. (Illus.). (gr. 3-5). 1967. 5.50g (ISBN 0-8075-9538-1). A Whitman.

--Picture Book of Oklahoma. rev. ed. (Illus.). (gr. 3-5). 1967. 5.50g (ISBN 0-8075-9540-3). A Whitman.

--Picture Book of Oregon. rev. ed. LC 54-9942. (Illus.). (gr. 3-6). 1967. 5.50g (ISBN 0-8075-9541-1). A Whitman.

--Picture Book of Pennsylvania. rev. ed. LC 66-2707. (Illus.). (gr. 3-5). 1972. 5.00g o.p. (ISBN 0-8075-9543-8). A Whitman.

--Picture Book of Rhode Island. rev. ed. LC 58-12320. (Illus.). (gr. 3-5). 1971. 5.50g (ISBN 0-8075-9545-4). A Whitman.

--Picture Book of South Carolina. rev. ed. LC 56-7757. (Illus.). (gr. 3-5). 1975. 5.50g (ISBN 0-8075-9546-2). A Whitman.

--Picture Book of South Dakota. rev. ed. LC 60-11569. (Illus.). (gr. 3-5). 1966. 5.00g o.p. (ISBN 0-8075-9547-0). A Whitman.

--Picture Book of Tennessee. rev. ed. LC 66-5266. (Illus.). (gr. 3-5). 1974. 5.50g (ISBN 0-8075-9548-9). A Whitman.

--Picture Book of Texas. rev. ed. (Illus.). (gr. 3-5). 1967. 5.50g (ISBN 0-8075-9549-7). A Whitman.

--Picture Book of Utah. rev. ed. LC 57-7145. (Illus.). (gr. 3-5). 1967. 5.50g (ISBN 0-8075-9550-0). A Whitman.

--Picture Book of Vermont. rev. ed. LC 65-9015. (Illus.). (gr. 3-5). 1968. 5.50g (ISBN 0-8075-9551-9). A Whitman.

--Picture Book of Virginia. rev. ed. LC 66-4792. (Illus.). (gr. 3-5). 1970. 5.50g (ISBN 0-8075-9552-7). A Whitman.

--Picture Book of Washington. rev. ed. LC 62-10660. (Illus.). (gr. 3-5). 1966. 5.50g (ISBN 0-8075-9553-5). A Whitman.

--Picture Book of West Virginia. rev. ed. LC 56-7755. (Illus.). (gr. 3-6). 1970. 5.00g o.p. (ISBN 0-8075-9554-3). A Whitman.

--Picture Book of Wisconsin. rev. ed. (Illus.). (gr. 3-5). 1975. 5.50g (ISBN 0-8075-9555-1). A Whitman.

--Picture Book of Wyoming. rev. ed. LC 58-12321. (Illus.). (gr. 3-5). 1972. 5.50g (ISBN 0-8075-9557-8). A Whitman.

Bailey, C. J. Effect of Surface on Behavior of Metals. 6.00 o.p. (ISBN 0-685-28357-7). Philos Lib.

Bailey, Carolyn S. For the Story Teller, Story Telling & Stories to Tell. LC 74-23576. 1975. Repr. of 1913 ed. 24.00 (ISBN 0-8103-3802-5). Gale.

--Stories for Every Holiday. LC 73-20149. 277p. 1974. Repr. of 1918 ed. 26.00 (ISBN 0-8103-3957-9). Gale.

Bailey, Carolyn S. & Lewis, Clara M. For the Children's Hour. LC 73-20186. (Illus.). 336p. 1974. Repr. of 1920 ed. 30.00 (ISBN 0-8103-3958-7). Gale.

Bailey, Charity, jt. auth. see Abeson, Marion.

Bailey, Christina A., jt. auth. see Bailey, Philip S.

Bailey, Conner. Broker, Mediator, Patron, & Kinsman: An Historical Analysis of Key Leadership Roles in a Rural Malaysian District. LC 75-620140. (Papers in International Studies, Southeast Asia Ser.). 89p. 1980. pap. 9.00 (ISBN 0-89680-024-5). Ohio U Ctr Intl.

Bailey, Cyril, ed. Legacy of Rome. (Illus.). 524p. 1923. 22.50x (ISBN 0-19-821906-7). Oxford U Pr.

Bailey, D. K., et al, eds. see Mineralogical Society Geochemistry Group, November 1 & 2, 1978.

Bailey, D. R. Two Studies in Roman Nomenclature. (American Philological Association, American Classical Studies). 1976. pap. 6.00 (ISBN 0-89130-243-3, 400403). Scholars Pr Ca.

Bailey, D. R., ed. Cicero: Epistulae Ad Quintum Fratrem et M. Brutum. (Cambridge Classical Texts & Commentaries Ser.: No. 22). 300p. Date not set. 49.50 (ISBN 0-521-23053-5). Cambridge U Pr.

Bailey, D. R., ed. see Cicero.

Bailey, D. Shackleton, ed. Harvard Studies in Classical Philology, Vol. 84. LC 44-32100. 1980. text ed. 30.00x (ISBN 0-674-37931-4). Harvard U Pr.

Bailey, David C. Viva Cristo Rey: The Cristero Rebellion & the Church-State Conflict in Mexico. (Illus.). 358p. 1974. 17.50x (ISBN 0-292-78700-6). U of Tex Pr.

Bailey, E. B. Tectonic Essays, Mainly Alpine. 1935. 19.50x (ISBN 0-19-854368-9). Oxford U Pr.

Bailey, F. G. Stratagems & Spoils: A Social Anthropology of Politics. (Pavilion Ser.). 240p. 1980. pap. 12.95x (ISBN 0-631-11760-1, Pub. by Basil Blackwell). Biblio Dist.

Bailey, F. Lee. The Defense Never Rests. pap. 2.50 (ISBN 0-451-08236-2, E9236, Sig). NAL.

Bailey, F. Lee & Rothblatt, Henry. Cross-Examination in Criminal Trials, Vol. 1. LC 78-18628. 1978. 47.50. Lawyers Co-Op.

Bailey, F. Lee & Rothblatt, Henry B. Complete Manual of Criminal Forms, 2 vols. 2nd ed. LC 74-17692. (Criminal Law Library). 1974. 85.00 (ISBN 0-686-14486-4). Lawyers Co-Op.

--Crimes of Violence: Homicide & Assault. LC 72-97625. (Criminal Law Library). 543p. 1973. 47.50 (ISBN 0-686-05455-5). Lawyers Co-Op.

--Crimes of Violence: Rape & Other Sex Crimes. LC 72-97625. (Criminal Law Library). 1973. 47.50 (ISBN 0-686-14500-3). Lawyers Co-Op.

--Defending Business & White Collar Crimes. LC 77-83168. (Criminal Law Library). 1969. 47.50 (ISBN 0-686-14487-2). Lawyers Co-Op.

--Fundamentals of Criminal Advocacy. LC 73-90861. 1974. 18.00x o.p. (ISBN 0-686-14542-9). Lawyers Co-Op.

--Handling Misdemeanor Cases. new ed. LC 76-12668. (Criminal Law Library). 1976. 47.50 (ISBN 0-686-20648-7). Lawyers Co-Op.

--Handling Narcotic & Drug Cases. LC 72-84855. (Criminal Law Library). 652p. 1972. 47.50 (ISBN 0-686-05452-0). Lawyers Co-Op.

--Successful Techniques for Criminal Trials. LC 72-161700. (Criminal Law Library). 1971. 47.50 (ISBN 0-686-14485-6). Lawyers Co-Op.

Bailey, Faith. George Mueller: Young Rebel in Bristol. 1958. pap. 1.95 o.p. (ISBN 0-8024-0031-0). Moody.

Bailey, Faith C. D. L. Moody. 1959. pap. 2.50 (ISBN 0-8024-0039-6). Moody.

--D. L. Moody. 160p. 1980. pap. 2.50 o.p. (ISBN 0-686-62771-7). Moody.

--George Mueller. 160p. 1980. pap. 2.50 (ISBN 0-8024-0031-0). Moody.

Bailey, Flora L. Sex Beliefs & Practices in a Navaho Community with Comparative Material from Other Navaho Areas. LC 52-8354. (Papers: Vol. 40, No. 2). 1950. pap. 10.00 (ISBN 0-87365-118-9). Peabody Harvard.

Bailey, Frank. Small Boat Design for Beginners. (Illus.). 88p. (Orig.). 1980. pap. 8.25 (ISBN 0-589-50203-4, Pub. by Reed Bks Australia). C E Tuttle.

Bailey, Frank A. Basic Mathematics. 1977. pap. 10.95x (ISBN 0-673-15064-X). Scott F.

Bailey, Frank E. British Policy & the Turkish Reform Movement: A Study in Anglo-Turkish Relations, 1826-1853. LC 74-80519. 1970. Repr. of 1942 ed. 17.50 (ISBN 0-86527-019-8). Fertig.

Bailey, Frederick G. Caste & the Economic Frontier. 1957. text ed. 10.50x (ISBN 0-7190-0249-4). Humanities.

--Tribe, Caste & Nation. 1971. Repr. of 1960 ed. text ed. 19.50x (ISBN 0-7190-0250-8). Humanities.

Bailey, Geoffrey, jt. auth. see Landau, Susanne.

Bailey, Geoffrey, jt. auth. see Landau, Suzanne.

Bailey, George. Germans: The Biography of an Obsession. 1974. pap. 3.50 (ISBN 0-380-00140-3, 53918, Discus). Avon.

Bailey, George, jt. auth. see Time-Life Books Editors.

Bailey, George W. Privacy & the Mental. (Elementa Ser.: No. 6). 1979. pap. text ed. 23.00x (ISBN 90-6203-862-X). Humanities.

Bailey, Gerald E. Sword of Poyana. 1979. pap. 1.75 o.p. (ISBN 0-425-04055-0). Berkley Pub.

--Sword of the Nurlingas. 1979. pap. 1.75 o.p. (ISBN 0-425-03954-4). Berkley Pub.

Bailey, H. W. Dictionary of Khotan Saka. LC 77-80825. 1979. 210.00 (ISBN 0-521-21737-7). Cambridge U Pr.

Bailey, Harold W. Khotanese Texts, 4 bks. 1961-1967. Vols. 1-3. 156.00 (ISBN 0-521-06961-0); Vol. 4. 75.00 (ISBN 0-521-04080-9); Vol. 5. 136.00 (ISBN 0-521-04081-7); Vol. 6. 150.00 (ISBN 0-521-07113-5). Cambridge U Pr.

Bailey, Helen M. & Grijalva, Maria C. Fifteen Famous Latin Americans. (gr. 1-6). 1971. text ed. 6.64 o.p. (ISBN 0-13-314609-X). P-H.

Bailey, Helen M. & Nasatir, Abraham P. Latin America: The Development of Its Civilization. 3rd ed. (Illus.). 896p. 1973. ref. ed. 20.95x (ISBN 0-13-524264-9). P-H.

Bailey, Henry J., jt. auth. see Hursh, Robert D.

Bailey, Henry T. & Pool, Ethel. Symbolism for Artists. LC 68-18018. (Illus.). 239p. 1973. Repr. of 1925 ed. 15.00 (ISBN 0-8103-3870-X). Gale.

Bailey, Herbert. Vitamin Pioneers. 1970. pap. 0.95 (ISBN 0-515-02239-X). Jove Pubns.

Bailey, Herbert S., Jr. Art & Science of Book Publishing. LC 73-95935. (Illus.). 1970. 10.00 o.p. (ISBN 0-06-010192-X, HarpT). Har-Row.

Bailey, J. O., jt. ed. see Brown, Edward K.

Bailey, James A., et al, eds. Readings in Wildlife Conservation. LC 74-28405. (Illus.). 722p. (Orig.). 1974. pap. 9.00 (ISBN 0-933564-02-3). Wildlife Soc.

Bailey, James O. Pilgrims Through Space & Time: Trends & Patterns in Scientific & Utopian Fiction. LC 76-38126. 341p. 1972. lib. bdg. 25.75x (ISBN 0-8371-6323-4, BAPS); pap. 4.95 (ISBN 0-8371-7351-5). Greenwood.

Bailey, Joan H., jt. auth. see Jung, John.

Bailey, John C. Milton. 256p. 1980. Repr. of 1945 ed. lib. bdg. 20.00 (ISBN 0-8495-0463-5). Arden Lib.

Bailey, John K. San Francisco Insider's Guide: A Unique Guide to Bay Area Restaurants, Bars, Best Bets, Bargains, Sex & Sensuality, & More... 224p. 1980. pap. 4.95 (ISBN 0-936816-00-7). Non Stop Bks.

Bailey, John M. Liberal Arts Physics: Invariance & Change. LC 73-21531. (Illus.). 1974. text ed. 22.95x (ISBN 0-7167-0343-2); tchr's manual avail. W H Freeman.

Bailey, June T. & Claus, Karen E. Decision Making in Nursing: Tools for Change. LC 74-28268. 168p. 1975. pap. text ed. 10.50 (ISBN 0-8016-0422-2). Mosby.

Bailey, June T., jt. auth. see Claus, Karen E.

Bailey, Keith M. Leader's Guide for Opening the Old Testament. 50p. (Orig.). 1980. pap. 1.25 (ISBN 0-87509-283-7). Chr Pubns.

Bailey, Kenneth. Through Peasant Eyes: More Lucan Parables. LC 80-14297. 208p. 1980. 16.95 (ISBN 0-8028-3528-7). Eerdmans.

Bailey, Kenneth D. Methods of Social Research. LC 77-6938. (Illus.). 1978. text ed. 16.95 (ISBN 0-02-901250-3). Free Pr.

Bailey, L. H. The Cultivated Conifers in North America: Comprising the Pine Family & the Taxads. (Landmark Reprints in Plant Science). 1933. text ed. 27.00 (ISBN 0-86598-007-1). Allanheld.

Bailey, Larry J. & Stadt, Ronald W. Career Education: New Approaches to Human Development. 403p. 1974. pap. 16.09 (ISBN 0-87345-601-7). McKnight.

Bailey, Liberty H. The Holy Earth. LC 80-27854. (Illus.). 124p. 1980. pap. 4.95 (ISBN 0-9605314-6-7). NY St Coll Ag.

--How Plants Get Their Names. LC 73-30611. 1975. Repr. of 1933 ed. 15.00 (ISBN 0-8103-3763-0). Gale.

--Manual of Cultivated Plants. rev. ed. 1949. 29.95 (ISBN 0-02-505520-8). Macmillan.

Bailey, Lynn R. The Long Walk. 1979. 8.95 (ISBN 0-87026-047-2). Westernlore.

Bailey, M. Thomas. Reconstruction in Indian Territory. LC 77-189551. 1972. 13.50 (ISBN 0-8046-9022-7). Kennikat.

Bailey, Mark W. Electricity. LC 77-27324. (Read About Science Ser.). (Illus.). (gr. k-3). 1978. PLB 9.95 (ISBN 0-8393-0085-9). Raintree Child.

Bailey, Martha J. Supervisory & Middle Managers in Libraries. LC 80-23049. 218p. 1981. 12.00 (ISBN 0-8108-1400-5). Scarecrow.

Bailey, Martin J., jt. ed. see Harberger, Arnold C.

Bailey, N. Louise & Cooper, Elizabeth I., eds. Biographical Directory of the South Carolina House of Representatives: Seventeen-Seventy-Five to Seventeen-Ninty, Vol. 3. 780p. 1981. text ed. 14.95 (ISBN 0-87249-406-3). U of SC Pr.

Bailey, Norman T. Elements of Stochastic Processes with Applications to the Natural Sciences. LC 63-23220. (Probability & Mathematical Statistics Ser.: Applied Probability & Statistics Section). 1964. 29.50 (ISBN 0-471-04165-3, Pub by Wiley-Interscience). Wiley.

Bailey, Norman T., ed. Statistical Methods in Biology. 2nd ed. LC 80-15774. 1981. pap. 12.95 (ISBN 0-470-27006-3). Halsted Pr.

Bailey, Patrick. Orkney. (Island Ser.). (Illus.). 245p. 1974. 16.95 (ISBN 0-7153-5000-5). David & Charles.

--Teaching Geography. (Teaching Ser.). (Illus.). 261p. 1975. 17.95 (ISBN 0-7153-6860-5). David & Charles.

Bailey, Paul C. & Wagner, K. A. Introduction to Modern Biology. 2nd ed. LC 72-183720. 1972. pap. text ed. 18.50 scp (ISBN 0-7002-2361-4, HarpC). Har-Row.

Bailey, Philip S. & Bailey, Christina A. Organic Chemistry: A Brief Survey of Concepts & Applications. 1978. text ed. 19.95 (ISBN 0-205-05925-2, 6859259); study guide o.p. 5.95 (ISBN 0-205-05926-0); lab manual 8.95 (ISBN 0-205-05927-9, 6859275). Allyn.

Bailey, R., jt. auth. see Foren, R.

Bailey, Raymond. Thomas Merton on Mysticism. LC 74-32570. 280p. 1976. pap. 1.95 (ISBN 0-385-12071-0, Im). Doubleday.

Bailey, Richard. Africa's Industrial Future. LC 76-30919. 1977. text ed. 25.00x (ISBN 0-89158-726-8). Westview.

Bailey, Richard M. Clinical Laboratories & the Practice of Medicine: An Economic Perspective. LC 78-70545. (Health Care Ser.). 1979. 20.50 (ISBN 0-8211-0132-3); text ed. 18.50 in ten or more copies (ISBN 0-685-63680-1). McCutchan.

Bailey, Robert L. & Hafner, Anne L. Minority Admissions. LC 77-18360. (Illus.). 1978. 21.00 (ISBN 0-669-02095-8). Lexington Bks.

Bailey, Robert Q. The Servant Story (Mark) Study Guide. (New Horizons Bible Study Ser.). 64p. 1980. pap. 2.25 (ISBN 0-89367-049-9). Light & Life.

Bailey, Robert W. God's Questions & Answers: Contemporary Studies in Malachi. LC 76-56513. 1977. pap. 3.95 (ISBN 0-8164-1228-6). Crossroad NY.

--New Ways in Christian Worship. 1981. pap. 5.95. Broadman.

Bailey, Roger C., jt. auth. see Hankins, Norman E.

Bailey, Ronald. Air War in Europe. (World War II Ser.). 1979. 12.95 (ISBN 0-8094-2494-0). Time-Life.

--The Air War in Europe. (World War II Ser.). (Illus.). 1979. lib. bdg. 14.94 (ISBN 0-686-51053-4). Silver.

--The Home Front: U. S. A. LC 77-87556. (World War II Ser.). (Illus.). 1977. lib. bdg. 14.94 (ISBN 0-686-51046-1). Silver.

--The Home Front: USA. Time Life Books, ed. (World War II Ser.). (Illus.). 1978. 12.95 (ISBN 0-8094-2478-9). Time-Life.

--Partisans & Guerrillas. (World War II Ser.). (Illus.). 1978. lib. bdg. 14.94 (ISBN 0-686-51049-6). Silver.

--The Role of the Brain. (Human Behavior Ser.). (Illus.). 176p. 1975. 9.95 (ISBN 0-8094-1920-3); lib. bdg. avail. (ISBN 0-685-53584-3). Time-Life.

--The Role of the Brain. LC 75-939. (Human Behavior). (Illus.). (gr. 6 up). 1975. PLB 9.99 o.p. (ISBN 0-8094-1921-1, Pub. by Time-Life). Silver.

--Violence & Aggression. LC 76-1293. (Human Behavior). (Illus.). (gr. 5 up). 1976. PLB 9.99 o.p. (ISBN 0-8094-1951-3, Pub. by Time-Life). Silver.

--Violence & Aggression. (Human Behavior Ser.). 9.95 (ISBN 0-8094-1950-5). Time-Life.

Bailey, Ronald H. The Partisans & Guerrillas. Time-Life Books, ed. (World War II Ser.). 1978. 12.95 (ISBN 0-8094-2490-8). Time-Life.

Bailey, S. F., jt. auth. see Gentile, A. G.

Bailey, Sydney D. The General Assembly of the United Nations: A Study of Procedure & Practice. rev. ed. LC 78-2810. (Carnegie Endowment for International Peace, United Nations Studies: No. 9). (Illus.). 1978. Repr. of 1964 ed. lib. bdg. 28.50x (ISBN 0-313-20336-9, BAGA). Greenwood.

--The Procedure of the UN Security Council. (Illus.). 438p. 1975. 34.50x (ISBN 0-19-827199-9). Oxford U Pr.

--The Secretariat of the United Nations. LC 78-2880. (Carnegie Endowment for International Studies: No. 11). 1978. Repr. of 1964 ed. lib. bdg. 15.17x (ISBN 0-313-20338-5, BASU). Greenwood.

Bailey, T. Grahame. Teach Yourself Urdu. (Teach Yourself Ser). pap. 3.95 o.p. (ISBN 0-679-10201-9). McKay.

Bailey, Thomas A. America Faces Russia. 1964. 8.75 (ISBN 0-8446-1037-2). Peter Smith.

--Art of Diplomacy: The American Experience. LC 68-11680. 1968. 18.95x (ISBN 0-89197-032-0); pap. text ed. 6.95x (ISBN 0-89197-033-9). Irvington.

--The Pugnacious Presidents: White House Warriors on Parade. LC 80-1646. (Illus.). 1980. 17.95 (ISBN 0-02-901220-1). Free Pr.

--Voices of America: The Nation's Story in Slogans, Sayings, & Songs. LC 76-8143. 1976. 17.95 (ISBN 0-02-901260-0). Free Pr.

Bailey, Thomas A. & Kennedy, David M. The American Pageant: A History of the Republic, 2 vols. 6th ed. 1979. complete ed. 19.95 (ISBN 0-669-00355-7); 12.95x ea. Vol. I (ISBN 0-669-00353-0). Vol. II (ISBN 0-669-00354-9). guidebk. 6.95x (ISBN 0-669-01697-7); quizbk. free (ISBN 0-669-01698-5). Heath.

Bailey, Thomas A. & Ryan, Paul B. The Lusitania Disaster: An Episode in Modern Warfare & Diplomacy. LC 75-2806. (Illus.). 1975. 12.95 (ISBN 0-02-901240-6). Free Pr.

Bailey, Vernon. Mammals of the Southwestern United States: With Special Reference to New Mexico. (Illus.). 8.00 (ISBN 0-8446-0016-4). Peter Smith.

Bailey, Walter. A Short Discourse of the Three Kindes of Peppers in Common Use. LC 77-38145. (English Experience Ser.: No 425). 48p. Repr. of 1588 ed. 7.00 (ISBN 90-221-0425-7). Walter J Johnson.

--Two Treatises Concerning the Preservation of Eye-Sight. LC 74-28827. (English Experience Ser.: No. 709). 1975. Repr. of 1616 ed. 5.00 (ISBN 90-221-0709-4). Walter J Johnson.

Bailey, William. Man, Religion, & Science: A Functional View. LC 80-65860. (Illus.). 242p. (Orig.). 1981. pap. 9.95 (ISBN 0-9604196-0-8). W Bailey Pub.

Bailie, J. M., ed. The British Crossword Dictionary. LC 77-84889. 1978. 8.95 o.p. (ISBN 0-385-13625-0). Doubleday.

Bailie, Richard C. Energy Conversion Engineering. LC 78-11969. (Ser. of Graduate Textbooks, Monographs & Research Papers). (Illus.). 1978. text ed. 21.50 (ISBN 0-201-00840-8). A-W.

Bailin, George. Collapsing Spaces, Tilting Times. (Poetry Ser.: No. 11). 48p. (Orig.). 1981. pap. 4.50 (ISBN 0-930020-10-3). Stone Country.

Bailkey, Nels, ed. Readings in Ancient History: From Gilgamesh to Diocletian. 2nd ed. 1977. pap. text ed. 8.95x (ISBN 0-669-00249-6). Heath.

Baillie, D. M. God Was in Christ. 1977. pap. 6.50 (ISBN 0-571-05685-7, Pub. by Faber & Faber). Merrimack Bk Serv.

Baillie, G. H. & Loomes, Brian. Watchmakers & Clockmakers of the World, 2 vols. 3rd ed. (Illus.). 1976. 29.95x set (ISBN 0-686-65563-X). Vol. 1 (ISBN 0-7198-0040-4). Vol. 2 (ISBN 0-7198-0080-3). Intl Ideas.

Baillie, J. B., tr. see Hegel, G. W.

Baillie, Joanna. The Family Legend, Repr. Of 1810 Ed. Bd. with Metrical Legends of Exalted Characters. Repr. of 1821 ed. LC 75-31147. (Romantic Context: Poetry 1789-1830 Ser.: Vol. 4). 1977. lib. bdg. 47.00 (ISBN 0-8240-2103-7). Garland Pub.

--Miscellaneous Plays. LC 75-31146. (Romantic Context: Poetry 1789-1830 Ser.: Vol. 3). 1977. Repr. of 1804 ed. lib. bdg. 47.00 (ISBN 0-8240-2102-9). Garland Pub.

--A Series of Plays: In Which It Is Attempted to Delineate the Strongest Passions of the Mind, 3 vols. LC 75-31145. (Romantic Context: Poetry 1789-1830 Ser.: Vol. 2). 1977. Repr. of 1812 ed. Set. lib. bdg. 47.00 ea. (ISBN 0-8240-2101-0). Garland Pub.

Baillie, John. Diary of Private Prayer. 1949. pap. 5.95 (ISBN 0-684-30997-1, ScribT). Scribner.

--The Idea of Revelation in Recent Thought. LC 56-8158. 1956. 12.00x (ISBN 0-231-02142-9); pap. 5.00x (ISBN 0-231-08554-0, 54). Columbia U Pr.

Baillie, Thomas W., jt. ed. see De Boer, Jan.

Bailly, R. Dictionnaire des synonymes. (Fr). 23.50 (ISBN 0-685-13870-4, 3621) Larousse.

Baily, F. E. The Perfect Age. 187p. 1981. Repr. of 1946 ed. lib. bdg. 30.00 (ISBN 0-89987-064-3). Darby Bks.

Baily, Keith M. Care of Converts. 95p. (Orig.). 1979. pap. 1.75 (ISBN 0-87509-157-1); leader's guide 0.75 (ISBN 0-686-65443-9). Chr Pubns.

Baily, Leslie. Gilbert & Sullivan: Their Lives & Times. (Large Format Ser.). (Illus.). 1979. pap. 5.95 o.p. (ISBN 0-14-005106-6). Penguin.

Baily, Martin. Union of Tanganyika & Zanzibar-a Study in Political Intergration. (Foreign & Comparative Studies-Eastern African Ser.: No.9). 114p. 1973. pap. 4.50x (ISBN 0-915984-05-9). Syracuse U Foreign Comp.

Baily, Samuel L. Labor, Nationalism, & Politics in Argentina. 1967. 16.00 (ISBN 0-8135-0556-9). Rutgers U Pr.

Baily, Samuel L. & Hyman, Ronald T., eds. Perspectives on Latin America, Vol. 1. LC 73-10689. (Latin America Series). (Illus.). 128p. 1974. 5.95 o.p. (ISBN 0-02-505830-4). Macmillan.

Bailyn, Bernard. The Apologia of Robert Keane: The Self-Portrait of a Puritan Merchant. 6.50 (ISBN 0-8446-0470-4). Peter Smith.

--Origins of American Politics. LC 68-12665. 1968. 5.95 o.p. (ISBN 0-394-43941-4). Knopf.

Bailyn, Bernard, et al. The Great Republic: A History of the American People. 1977. text ed. 18.95x o.p. (ISBN 0-669-86629-6); Vol. 1. pap. text ed. 11.95x o.p. (ISBN 0-669-86637-7); Vol. 2. pap. text ed. 10.95x o.p. (ISBN 0-669-86645-8); instructor's manual free o.p. (ISBN 0-669-97881-7); study guide 5.95x o.p. (ISBN 0-669-97865-5); test item file to adopters free o.p. (ISBN 0-669-00962-8). Heath.

--The Great Republic: A History of the American People. 2nd ed. 1008p. 1981. text ed. 19.95 (ISBN 0-669-02753-7); pap. text ed. 12.95 vol. 1 (ISBN 0-669-02754-5); pap. text ed. 12.95 vol. 2 (ISBN 0-669-02755-3); instr's guide avail. (ISBN 0-669-02757-X); student guide 5.95 (ISBN 0-669-02756-1). Heath.

Bailyn, Lotte. Living with Technology: Issues at Mid-Career. 160p. 1980. text ed. 15.00x (ISBN 0-262-02153-6). MIT Pr.

Bain, A. D., et al. Company Financing in the U.K. A Flow of Funds Model. 1975. 28.00x (ISBN 0-85520-094-4, Pub by Martin Robertson England). Biblio Dist.

Bain, A. G. & Bonnington, S. T. Hydraulic Transport of Solids by Pipelines. 1971. text ed. 31.00 o.p. (ISBN 0-08-015778-5). Pergamon.

Bain, Alexander. Emotions & the Will. (Contributions to the History of Psychology Ser.: No. 5, Pt. a: Orientations). 1978. Repr. of 1859 ed. 30.00 (ISBN 0-89093-154-2). U Pubns Amer.

--On the Study of Character, Including an Estimate of Phrenology. (Contributions to the History of Psychology Ser.: Orientations). 1980. Repr. of 1861 ed. 30.00 (ISBN 0-89093-316-2). U Pubns Amer.

--Senses & the Intellect. (Contributions to the History of Psychology Ser.: No. 4, Pt. A Orientations). 1978. Repr. of 1855 ed. 30.00 (ISBN 0-89093-153-4). U Pubns Amer.

Bain, Carl E., et al, eds. The Norton Introduction to Literature. 3rd ed. 1536p. 1981. pap. text ed. 11.95x (ISBN 0-393-95146-4); classroom guide avail. (ISBN 0-393-95158-8). Norton.

--The Norton Introduction to Literature. 2nd ed. 1977. pap. 9.95 (ISBN 0-393-09119-8); tchr's manual 2.95x (ISBN 0-393-09127-9). Norton.

Bain, Carolyn. It's Easy to Become a Citizen. LC 68-28131. 1968. pap. 3.50 (ISBN 0-8015-4134-4, Hawthorn). Dutton.

Bain, David, ed. see Aradoon, Zarifa.

Bain, David H. Aftershocks: A Tale of Two Victims. 320p. 1980. 10.95 (ISBN 0-416-00681-7). Methuen Inc.

Bain, Donald. Long John Nebel: Biography of Charlatan. (Illus.). 1974. 8.95 o.s.i. (ISBN 0-02-505950-5). Macmillan.

Bain, G. S. & Elsheikh, Farouk. Union Growth & the Business Cycle: An Econometric Analysis. 1976. 35.50x (ISBN 0-631-16650-5, Pub. by Basil Blackwell). Biblio Dist.

Bain, G. S., et al. Social Stratification & Trade Unionism. 184p. 1974. 12.50x o.p. (ISBN 0-8448-0896-2). Crane-Russak Co.

Bain, George. Celtic Art: The Methods of Construction. (Illus.). 160p. 1973. pap. 5.00 (ISBN 0-486-22923-8). Dover.

--The Methods of Construction of Celtic Art. (Illus.). 9.50 (ISBN 0-8446-4706-3). Peter Smith.

Bain, George, ed. see Mellish, Michael.

Bain, George, ed. see Rimmer, M.

Bain, Georgia, ed. Understanding the Sunday Readings: July, August, September 1980. (Understanding the Sunday Readings Ser.). 173p. 1980. 8.95 (ISBN 0-8434-0741-7, Consortium). McGrath.

Bain, Iain, ed. see Bewick, Thomas.

Bain, J. S. & Jain, R. B., eds. Contemporary Political Theory. 300p. 1980. text ed. 13.25x (ISBN 0-391-01901-5). Humanities.

--Perspectives in Political Theory. 275p. 1980. text ed. 13.25 (ISBN 0-391-01900-7). Humanities.

Bain, John A. The Foundations of Christian Faith. 112p. Repr. of 1936 ed. 2.95 (ISBN 0-567-02015-0). Attic Pr.

Bain, Kenneth R. & Gormly, James L. The Restless Centuries: Student Study Guide. (Orig.). 1979. pap. 4.25 (ISBN 0-8087-4029-6). Burgess.

Bain, R. Nisbet. Turkish Fairy Tales & Folk Tales. (Illus.). (gr. k-8). 1969. pap. 2.50 o.p. (ISBN 0-486-22344-2). Dover.

Bain, Richard C. & Parris, Judith H. Convention Decisions & Voting Records. rev. 2nd ed. (Studies in Presidential Selection). 500p. 1973. 15.95 (ISBN 0-8157-0768-1). Brookings.

Bainbridge, A., jt. ed. see Scott, P. R.

Bainbridge, Beryl. Another Part of the Wood. 8.95 (ISBN 0-8076-0965-X). Braziller.

--Harriet Said. pap. 1.50 (ISBN 0-451-06058-X, W6058, Sig). NAL.

--Winter Garden. 1981. 8.95 (ISBN 0-8076-1011-9). Braziller.

Bainbridge, Brian W. The Genetics of Microbes. (Tertiary Level Biology Ser.). 204p. 1980. pap. 30.95x (ISBN 0-470-26995-2). Halsted Pr.

Bainbridge, C. Welding. (Teach Yourself Ser.). 1974. pap. 3.95 o.p. (ISBN 0-679-10495-X). McKay.

Bainbridge, David A. The Second Passive Solar Catalog. (Illus.). 110p. (Orig.). 1980. pap. 11.95 (ISBN 0-933490-02-X). Passive Solar.

Bainbridge, John. Astronomical Description of the Late Comet from the 18. of Novemb. 1618 to the 16. of December Following. LC 74-28828. (English Experience Ser.: No. 710). 1975. Repr. of 1619 ed. 6.00 (ISBN 90-221-0710-8). Walter J Johnson.

Bainbridge, William S. Satan's Power: A Deviant Psychotherapy Cult. LC 77-80466. 1978. 18.50x (ISBN 0-520-03546-1). U of Cal Pr.

--The Spacefight Revolution: A Sociological Study. LC 76-21349. (Science, Culture, & Society Ser.). 1976. 27.50 (ISBN 0-471-04306-0, Pub. by Wiley-Interscience). Wiley.

Baine, David, jt. auth. see Das, J. P.

Baine, Sean. Community Action & Local Government. 96p. 1975. pap. text ed. 8.75x (ISBN 0-7135-1842-1, Pub. by Bedford England). Renouf.

Bainer, Roy, jt. auth. see Kepner, R. A.

Baines, A., et al. Research in the Chemical Industry: The Environment, Objectives & Strategy. (Illus.). 1969. 33.60x (ISBN 0-444-20035-5, Pub. by Applied Science). Burgess-Intl Ideas.

Baines, Anthony, ed. Musical Instruments Through the Ages. LC 66-22505. (Illus.). 352p. 1975. 15.00 (ISBN 0-8027-0469-7). Walker & Co.

Baines, Barbara J. The Lust Motif in the Plays of Thomas Middleton. (Salzburg Studies in English Literature, Jacobean Drama Studies: No. 29). 160p. 1973. pap. text ed. 25.00x (ISBN 0-391-01306-8). Humanities.

Baines, Harry. Science of Photography. 3rd ed. LC 73-19208. 1967. 17.95 (ISBN 0-471-04340-0). Halsted Pr.

Baines, Jennifer. Mandelstam: The Later Poetry. LC 76-8515. 1977. 36.00 (ISBN 0-521-21273-1). Cambridge U Pr.

Baines, John & Malek, Jaromir. Atlas of Ancient Egypt. (Illus.). 240p. 1980. 29.95 (ISBN 0-87196-334-5). Facts on File.

Baines, Keith, tr. see Malory, Thomas.

Baines, Patricia. Spinning Wheels & Spinning. LC 77-78709. (Illus.). 1978. 14.95 o.p. (ISBN 0-684-15307-6, ScribT). Scribner.

--Spinning Wheels, Spinners & Spinning. 1980. 14.95 (ISBN 0-686-27277-3). Robin & Russ.

Bains, J. S., ed. Studies in Political Science. 7.50x o.p. (ISBN 0-210-33962-4). Asia.

Bainton, Roland. Here I Stand. (Festival Bks.). 1978. pap. 2.25 (ISBN 0-687-16894-5). Abingdon.

Bainton, Roland H. Christendom: A Short History of Christianity & Its Impact on Western Civilization, Vol. 1. rev. ed. (Illus.). pap. 5.50x (ISBN 0-06-130131-0, TB131, Torch). Har-Row.

Bainton, Roland H., tr. Martin Luther Christmas Book with Celebrated Woodcuts by His Contemporaries. LC 59-2930. 80p. 1948. pap. 3.25 (ISBN 0-8006-1843-2, 1-1843). Fortress.

Bair, Frank, jt. ed. see Ruffner, James.

Bair, Frieda. Twilight Tapestry. 1977. 3.95 (ISBN 0-8059-2470-1). Dorrance.

Bair, Lowell, tr. see Alain-Fournier.

Bair, Lowell, tr. see Arsan, Emmanuelle.

Bair, Lowell, tr. see Desmarest, Marie A.

Baird. Using Media in the Music Program. write for info. (ISBN 0-87628-211-7). Ctr Appl Res.

Baird, C. Direlle, jt. auth. see Fluck, Richard C.

Baird, Charles. Rent Control: The Perennial Folly. LC 80-16317. (Cato Public Policy Research Cato Monograph: No. 2). 110p. (Orig.). 1980. pap. 5.00 (ISBN 0-932790-22-4). Cato Inst.

Baird, Charles W. John Bunyan: A Study in Narrative Technique. LC 76-53813. (National University Publications in Literary Criticism Ser.). 1977. 12.00 (ISBN 0-8046-9162-2). Kennikat.

Baird, Charles W. & Cassuto, Alexander E. Macroeconomics. 2nd ed. 336p. 1980. text ed. 16.95 (ISBN 0-574-19400-2, 13-2400); instr's. guide avail. (ISBN 0-574-19401-0, 13-2401). SRA.

Baird, D. H., jt. ed. see Dodge, D.

Baird, D. T., jt. auth. see Short, R. V.

Baird, Eric. Horse Care. (Illus.). 1979. 11.95 (ISBN 0-87691-296-X). Winchester Pr.

Baird, Eva-Lee & Wyler, Rose. Going Metric the Fun Way. LC 77-16895. (Illus.). (gr. 8-9). 1980. 7.95a (ISBN 0-385-13641-2); PLB (ISBN 0-385-13642-0). Doubleday.

Baird, Eva-Lee, jt. auth. see Wyler, Rose.

Baird, Forrest, jt. auth. see Rogers, Jack B.

Baird, Frank L., ed. Mexican Americans: Political Power, Influence, or Resource. (Graduate Studies: No. 14). (Illus., Orig.). 1977. pap. 7.00 (ISBN 0-89672-024-1). Tex Tech Pr.

Baird, Irwin L., jt. auth. see Munger, Bryce L.

Baird, J. C. Psychophysical Analysis of Visual Space. 1970. text ed. 72.00 (ISBN 0-08-013876-4). Pergamon.

Baird, J. G., ed. Private Letters of the Marquess of Dalhousie. (Illus.). 448p. 1972. Repr. of 1910 ed. 30.00x (ISBN 0-686-28317-1, Pub. by Irish Academic Pr). Biblio Dist.

Baird, Jack. Irish Setters. rev. ed. (Illus.). 128p. 1974. pap. 2.95 o.p. (ISBN 0-87666-321-8, HS 1055). TFH Pubns.

Baird, Jack, jt. auth. see Sopher, Charles.

Baird, Jack V., jt. auth. see Sopher, Charles D.

Baird, James, et al see Kurtz, David L. & Boone, Louis E.

Baird, John C. & Noma, Elliot. Fundamentals of Scaling & Psychophysics. LC 78-6011. (Wiley Ser. in Behavior). 1978. 25.95 (ISBN 0-471-04169-6, Pub. by Wiley-Interscience). Wiley.

Baird, John D. Fifteen Years in Hawken Lode. 15.00 (ISBN 0-88227-011-7). Gun Room.

--Hawken Rifles: The Mountain Man's Choice. 15.00 (ISBN 0-88227-010-9). Gun Room.

Baird, John D., ed. Editing Texts of the Romantic Period. (Conference on Editorial Problems Ser.). 1976. lib. bdg. 16.50 (ISBN 0-8240-2406-0). Garland Pub.

Baird, John D., ed. see Cooper, William.

Baird, John E., Jr. Speaking for Results: Communication by Objectives. (Illus.). 301p. 1981. text ed. 10.95 scp (ISBN 0-06-040457-4, HarpC); avail. Har-Row. Postponed.

Baird, John E., Jr. & Weinberg, Sanford B. Group Communication: Essence of Synergy. 270p. 1981. pap. text ed. write for info. (ISBN 0-697-04181-6); resourse manual avail. (ISBN 0-697-04187-5). Wm C Brown.

Baird, Joseph A., Jr. The Churches of Mexico, 1530-1810. (Illus.). 1962. 35.00x (ISBN 0-520-00066-8). U of Cal Pr.

Baird, Leonard. The Elite Schools: A Profile of Prestigious Independent College Preparatory Schools. LC 76-48376. 1977. 17.95 (ISBN 0-669-01146-0). Lexington Bks.

Baird, Marie T. A Lesson in Love. 1975. pap. 1.25 o.p. (ISBN 0-445-00246-8). Popular Lib.

Baird, Robert. Religion in America: A Critical Abridgment. 7.50 (ISBN 0-8446-0471-2). Peter Smith.

Baird, Robert D. Category Formation & the History of Religions. (Religion & Reason Ser: No. 1). 178p. 1971. text ed. 22.95x (ISBN 90-2796-889-6). Mouton.

Baird, Robert D., ed. Methodological Issues in Religious Studies. LC 75-44170. (Orig.). 1976. lib. bdg. 14.95x (ISBN 0-914914-08-1); pap. text ed. 5.95x (ISBN 0-914914-07-3). New Horizons.

Baird, Ronald J. Contemporary Industrial Teaching. LC 78-185957. (Illus.). 200p. 1972. text ed. 9.28 (ISBN 0-87006-130-5). Goodheart.

--Industrial Plastics. LC 75-139249. (Illus.). 1976. text ed. 10.86 (ISBN 0-87006-213-1). Goodheart.

--Oxyacetylene Welding. LC 79-6555. (Illus.). 1980. pap. text ed. 4.96 (ISBN 0-87006-290-5). Goodheart.

Baird, Ronald J., jt. auth. see Kicklighter, Clois E.

Baird, Samuel E. With Merrill's Cavalry. Annegan, Charles, ed. LC 80-69601. (Illus.). 64p. 1981. 15.95 (ISBN 0-9605200-0-7). Bk Habit.

Baird, Thomas. People Who Pull You Down. 1978. pap. 1.75 (ISBN 0-380-39339-5, 39339). Avon.

--The Way to the Old Sailors Home. LC 76-26260. 1977. 8.95 o.s.i. (ISBN 0-06-010173-3, HarpT). Har-Row.

Baird, W. David. Medical Education in Arkansas, Eighteen Seventy Nine-Nineteen Seventy Eight. LC 79-126280. (Illus.). 1979. 21.95x (ISBN 0-87870-052-8). Memphis St Univ.

Baird, Wesley. Guyana Gold: The Story of Wesley Baird, Guyana's Greatest Miner. 210p. (Orig.). 1981. 18.00x (ISBN 0-89410-192-7); pap. 7.00x (ISBN 0-89410-193-5). Three Continents.

Baird, William. Corinthians I & II. Hayes, John, ed. LC 79-92064. (Knox Preaching Guides Ser.). 112p. (Orig.). 1980. pap. 4.50 (ISBN 0-8042-3239-3). John Knox.

Bairoch, Paul. The Economic Development of the Third World Since 1900. Postan, Cynthia, tr. LC 74-16706. (Illus.). 1975. pap. 7.50x (ISBN 0-520-03554-2). U of Cal Pr.

Bairstow, Jeffrey, jt. auth. see Lott, George.

Bairstow, Jeffrey, et al. IT: Interval Training for Lifetime Fitness. (Illus.). 194p. 1980. 8.95 (ISBN 0-8037-4087-5). Dial.

Baitsell, George A., ed. The Centennial of the Sheffield Scientific School (Yale University) 1950. 32.50x (ISBN 0-686-51350-9). Elliots Bks.

Baity, W. A., ed. see Committee on Space Research.

Baiulescu, G. E. & Cosofret, V. V. Applications of Ion Selective Membrane Electrodes in Organic Analysis. (Series in Analytical Chemistry). 1977. 59.95 (ISBN 0-470-99192-5). Halsted Pr.

Baiulescu, G. E. & Ilie, A. V. Stationary Phases in Gas Chromatography. 1975. text ed. 55.00 (ISBN 0-08-018075-2). Pergamon.

Bajandas, F. J., jt. ed. see Brooks, B. A.

Bajema, Carl, jt. auth. see Hardin, Garrett.

Bajema, Carl J., ed. Eugenics: Then & Now. LC 75-43761. (Benchmark Papers in Genetics Ser: Vol. 5). 400p. 1976. 40.50 (ISBN 0-12-786110-6). Acad Pr.

Bajpai, A. C., et al. Fortran & Agol: A Programmed Course for Students of Science & Technology. LC 73-5712. (Applied Mathematics for Scientists & Technologists Ser). 276p. 1972. 20.95 o.p. (ISBN 0-471-04371-0, Pub by Wiley-Interscience). Wiley.

--Specialist Techniques in Engineering Mathematics. 416p. 1980. 57.25 (ISBN 0-471-27907-2, Pub. by Wiley-Interscience); pap. 26.00 (ISBN 0-471-27908-0). Wiley.

Bajura, R. A., ed. Polyphase Flow & Transport Technology. 270p. 1980. 40.00 (H00158). ASME.

Bajusz, E., ed. Physiology & Pathology of Adaptation Mechanisms: Neural-Neuroendocrine-Hormonal. 598p. 1968. text ed. 90.00 (ISBN 0-08-012023-7). Pergamon.

Bajwa, Fauja S. Military System of the Sikhs (During the Period 1799-1899) (Illus.). 1964. 4.95 (ISBN 0-89684-280-0). Orient Bk Dist.

Bakacs, Anna. Beautiful Film Stories. 1978. 7.95 o.p. (ISBN 0-533-03297-0). Vantage.

Bakaitis, Helmut. The Incredible Mind-Blowing Trial of Jack Smith. (Australian Theatre Workshop Ser.). 1973. pap. text ed. 4.25x (ISBN 0-686-65320-3, 00524). Heinemann Ed.

Bakal, Yitzhak & Polsky, Howard W. Reforming Corrections for Juvenile Offenders. LC 73-11680. 1979. 17.95 (ISBN 0-669-90209-8). Lexington Bks.

Bakal, Yitzhak, jt. auth. see Vachss, Andrew H.

Bakal, Yitzhak, ed. Closing Correctional Institutions. LC 73-998. 275p. 1973. 16.95 (ISBN 0-669-86140-5). Lexington Bks.

Bakalar, James B., jt. auth. see Grinspoon, Lester.

Bakalla, M. The Morphological & Phonological Components of the Arabic Verb. (Meccan Arabic.). 1979. 20.00x. Intl Bk Ctr.

Bakan, David. Sigmund Freud & the Jewish Mystical Tradition. 1975. pap. 4.95 o.p. (ISBN 0-8070-2963-7, BP510). Beacon Pr.

Bakay, Louis & Glasauer, Franz E. Head Injury. 1980. text ed. 28.95 (ISBN 0-316-07774-7). Little.

Bake, William A. & Kilpatrick, James J. The American South: Four Seasons of the Land. LC 80-80754. (Illus.). 224p. 1980. 29.95 (ISBN 0-8487-0495-9). Oxmoor Hse.

Bakeless, Katherine L. Story-Lives of Great Composers. rev. ed. (Illus.). (gr. 7-9). 1962. 10.00 o.p. (ISBN 0-397-30253-3). Lippincott.

Baker & Breach. Medical Microbiological Techniques. LC 80-40010. 1980. 49.00 (ISBN 0-407-00099-2). Butterworths.

Baker, jt. auth. see Goldstein.

Baker, A. A. Border War. 192p. (YA) 1976. 5.95 (ISBN 0-685-61051-9, Avalon). Bouregy.

--Rebel Guns. 192p. (YA) 1975. 5.95 (ISBN 0-685-52653-4, Avalon). Bouregy.

--Vengeance Rides West. 192p. (YA) 1976. 4.95 o.p. (ISBN 0-685-67083-X, Avalon). Bouregy.

Baker, A. D. & Betteridge, D. Photoelectron Spectroscopy: Chemical & Analytical Aspects. 190p. 1972. text ed. 27.00 (ISBN 0-08-016910-4). Pergamon.

Baker, A. Ernest. Tennyson Concordance. 1965. 75.00x (ISBN 0-7100-6557-4). Routledge & Kegan.

Baker, A. R. & Butlin, R. A., eds. Studies of Field Systems in the British Isles. LC 72-91359. (Illus.). 744p. 1973. 77.50 (ISBN 0-521-20121-7). Cambridge U Pr.

Baker, Abe B., et al, eds. see Loose Leaf Reference Services.

Baker, Adelaide N. Return to Arcady. LC 73-80849. (Illus.). 192p. 1973. 8.95 o.p. (ISBN 0-88208-018-0). Lawrence Hill.

Baker, Alan H. & Butlin, R. A., eds. Studies of Field Systems in the British Isles. (Illus.). 728p. 1980. pap. 28.95 (ISBN 0-521-29790-7). Cambridge U Pr.

Baker, Alan J. Investment, Valuation & the Managerial Theory of the Firm. 336p. 1978. text ed. 25.25x (ISBN 0-566-00192-6, Pub. by Gower Pub Co England). Renouf.

Baker, Alan R., ed. Progress in Historical Geography. LC 72-75031. (Studies in Historical Geography). 1972. 15.95 (ISBN 0-471-04550-0). Halsted Pr.

Baker, Archibald G., ed. Short History of Christianity. LC 40-34185. 1940. 10.00x (ISBN 0-226-03529-8); pap. 7.50x (ISBN 0-226-03530-1). U of Chicago Pr.

Baker, Arthur. Arthur Baker's Historic Calligraphic Alphabets. (Pictorial Archive Ser.). (Illus.). 96p. (Orig.). 1980. pap. 3.50 (ISBN 0-486-24054-1). Dover.

--Calligraphic Alphabets. LC 79-8223. (Pictorial Archive Ser.). (Illus.). 160p. (Orig.). 1974. pap. 4.50 (ISBN 0-486-21045-6). Dover.

--Calligraphy. (Illus.). 10.00 (ISBN 0-8446-4619-9). Peter Smith.

--New Calligraphic Ornaments & Flourishes. (Pictorial Archive Ser.). (Orig.). 1981. pap. price not set (ISBN 0-486-24095-9). Dover.

Baker, Arthur D. & Engel, Robert. Organic Chemistry: Problems & Solutions. 1978. pap. text ed. 10.95 (ISBN 0-205-06118-4). Allyn.

Baker, B. N., jt. ed. see Williams, Theodore P.

Baker, Betty. All-by-Herself. (Illus.). (gr. 1-3). 1980. 5.95 (ISBN 0-688-80242-7); lib. bdg. 5.71 (ISBN 0-688-84242-9). Morrow.

--And One Was a Wooden Indian. LC 77-117957. (gr. 5-9). 1970. 4.95g o.s.i. (ISBN 0-02-708310-1). Macmillan.

--At the Center of the World. LC 72-88820. (Illus.). 64p. (gr. 3-6). 1973. PLB 4.95g o.s.i. (ISBN 0-02-708290-3). Macmillan.

--Danby & George. LC 80-15707. (Illus.). 64p. (gr. 3-5). 1981. 7.95 (ISBN 0-688-80289-3); PLB 7.63 (ISBN 0-688-84289-5). Greenwillow.

--Do Not Annoy the Indians. (Illus.). (gr. 4-6). 1968. 4.95g o.s.i. (ISBN 0-02-708300-4). Macmillan.

--The Great Desert Race. LC 80-16483. (Illus.). 144p. (gr. 5-9). 1980. PLB 8.95 (ISBN 0-02-708200-8). Macmillan.

--Latki & the Lightning Lizard. LC 79-11197. (Illus.). (gr. 1-3). 1979. 8.95 (ISBN 0-02-708210-5). Macmillan.

--Rat Is Dead & Ant Is Sad. LC 78-1943. (I Can Read Bks.). (Illus.). 64p. (gr. k-3). 1981. 6.95 (ISBN 0-06-020346-3, HarpJ); PLB 7.89g (ISBN 0-06-020347-1). Har-Row.

--Santa Rat. LC 79-24904. (Illus.). 64p. (gr. 3-5). 1980. 7.95 (ISBN 0-688-80262-1); PLB 7.63 (ISBN 0-688-84262-3). Greenwillow.

--Save Sirrushany! (Also Agotha, Princess Gwyn & All the Fearsome Beasts) LC 77-20137. (gr. 5-9). 1978. 8.95 (ISBN 0-02-708230-X, 70823). Macmillan.

--Settlers & Strangers: Native Americans of the Desert Southwest & History As They Saw It. LC 77-4925. (Illus.). (gr. 3-6). 1977. 8.95 (ISBN 0-02-708220-2, 70822). Macmillan.

--Spirit Is Willing. LC 73-8576. 128p. (gr. 5-9). 1974. 8.95 (ISBN 0-02-708270-9, 70827). Macmillan.

--Three Fools & a Horse. LC 75-14272. (Illus.). 64p. (gr. 1-4). 1975. 8.95 (ISBN 0-02-708250-4, 70825). Macmillan.

--Worthington Botts & the Steam Machine. LC 80-24627. (Ready-to-Read Ser.). (Illus.). 56p. (gr. 1-4). 1981. PLB 7.95 (ISBN 0-02-708190-7). Macmillan.

Baker, Bill. House of Ideas. LC 73-11734. (Illus.). 288p. 1974. 19.95 (ISBN 0-02-506280-8, 50628). Macmillan.

Baker, Brian H. Fundamental Skills in Hematology. 508p. 1980. pap. 28.50 photocopy ed. spiral (ISBN 0-398-04101-6). C C Thomas.

Baker, Bruce L., et al. As Close As Possible. LC 77-81502. 1977. text ed. 13.95 (ISBN 0-316-07827-1); pap. text ed. 9.95 (ISBN 0-316-07829-8). Little.

--Steps to Independence: A Skills Training Series for Children with Special Needs. Incl. Early Self-Help Skills. pap. text ed. 7.95 spiral bd. (ISBN 0-87822-167-0); Intermediate Self-Help Skills. pap. text ed. 7.95 spiral bdg. (ISBN 0-87822-168-9); Advanced Self-Help Skills. pap. text ed. 7.95 spiral bdg. (ISBN 0-87822-169-7); Behavior Problems. pap. text ed. 7.95 spiral bdg. (ISBN 0-87822-170-0); Training Guide. 1976. pap. 2.95 (ISBN 0-87822-171-9); Toilet Training. LC 77-81303. 1977. pap. text ed. 7.95 spiral bdg. (ISBN 0-87822-144-1); Speech & Language, 2 levels. LC 78-51500. 1978. pap. text ed. 7.95 ea. spiral bdg.; Level 1. (ISBN 0-87822-181-6); Level 2. (ISBN 0-87822-182-4). (Illus., Orig.). Set. 59.95 (ISBN 0-87822-166-2). Res Press.

--Toward Independent Living: A Skills Training Series for Children with Special Needs. LC 80-51922. (Steps to Independence Ser.). (Illus.). 118p. 1980. pap. text ed. 7.95 spiral bdg. (ISBN 0-87822-221-9, 2219). Res Press.

Baker, C. C., jt. auth. see Oram, R. B.

Baker, C. J. & Washbrook, D. A. South India: Political Institutions & Political Change 1880-1940. 1975. text ed. 27.50x (ISBN 0-8419-5016-4). Holmes & Meier.

Baker, C. R. & Hayes, R. S. Lease Financing: A Practical Guide. 256p. 1981. 17.95 (ISBN 0-471-06040-2, Pub. by Wiley Interscience). Wiley.

Baker, C. Richard & Hayes, Rick S. Accounting, Finance, & Taxation: A Basic Guide for Small Business. LC 79-16481. 1980. 22.50 (ISBN 0-8436-0784-X). CBI Pub.

Baker, Caleb. Two Roads & Two Destinies. 59p. pap. 0.25; chart 0.50. Walterick Pubs.

Baker, Carlos. Ernest Hemingway: A Life Story. 1980. pap. 4.95 (ISBN 0-380-50039-6, 50039, Discus). Avon.

Baker, Carlos, ed. Ernest Hemingway: Selected Letters. 960p. 1981. 25.00 (ISBN 0-684-16765-4, ScribT). Scribner.

Baker, Charlotte & Battison, Robbin. Sign Language & the Deaf Community: Essays in Honor of William Stokoe. (Illus.). 267p. 1981. text ed. 12.00 (ISBN 0-913072-37-0); pap. text ed. 8.00 (ISBN 0-913072-36-2). Natl Assn Deaf.

Baker, Charlotte A. True Stories of New England Captives Carried to Canada During the Old French & Indian Wars. LC 75-7128. (Indian Captivities Ser.: Vol. 101). 1976. Repr. of 1897 ed. lib. bdg. 44.00 (ISBN 0-8240-1725-0). Garland Pub.

Baker, Clara B. Sing & Be Happy: Songs for the Young Child. LC 80-13421. (Illus.). 96p. 1980. pap. 6.95 (ISBN 0-687-38547-4). Abingdon.

Baker, D., ed. Heresy, Schism & Religious Protest. LC 75-184899. (Studies in Church History: Vol. 9). 1972. 52.00 (ISBN 0-521-08486-5). Cambridge U Pr.

Baker, D. & Wadstrom, T., eds. Natural Toxins: Proceedings of the 6th International Symposium on Animal, Plant & Microbial Toxins, Uppsala, August, 1979. LC 80-40898. (Illus.). 704p. 1980. 110.00 (ISBN 0-08-024952-3). Pergamon.

Baker, D., jt. ed. see Cuming, G. J.

Baker, D. A., jt. auth. see Hall, J. L.

Baker, D. K., jt. auth. see Goble, Alfred T.

Baker, D. Phillip & Bender, David R. Library Media Programs & the Special Learner. 400p. 1981. 18.50 (ISBN 0-208-01852-2, Lib Prof Pubns); pap. text ed. 14.50x (ISBN 0-208-01846-8, Lib Prof Pubns). Shoe String.

Baker, Dan & Weisgerber, Bill. Television Production. Duane, James E., ed. LC 80-23479. (The Instructional Media Library: Vol. 15). (Illus.). 112p. 1981. 13.95 (ISBN 0-87778-175-3). Educ Tech Pubns.

Baker, David. The Larousse Guide to Astronomy. LC 78-54635. (Illus.). 1980. o.p. (ISBN 0-88332-095-9); pap. 8.95 (ISBN 0-88332-094-0). Larousse.

Baker, David N., et al. The Black Composer Speaks. LC 77-24146. 1978. 24.00 (ISBN 0-8108-1045-X). Scarecrow.

Baker, Derek. Medieval Women. (Illus.). 412p. 1981. pap. 16.95x (ISBN 0-631-12539-6, Pub. by Basil Blackwell England). Biblio Dist.

--Religious Motivation: Biographical & Sociological Problems for the Church Historian. (Studies in Church History: Vol. 15). 1978. 36.00x (ISBN 0-631-19250-6, Pub. by Basil Blackwell England). Biblio Dist.

--Renaissance & Renewal in Christian History. (Studies in Church History: Vol. 14). 1977. 36.00x (ISBN 0-631-17780-9, Pub. by Basil Blackwell). Biblio Dist.

Baker, Derek, ed. Bibliography of the Reform, Fourteen Fifty to Sixteen Forty-Eight: Relating to the United Kingdom & Ireland for the Years 1955-70. 1975. 25.00x (ISBN 0-631-15960-6, Pub. by Basil Blackwell). Biblio Dist.

--The Church in Town & Countryside: Papers Read at the Seventeenth Summer Meeting & the Eighteenth Winter Meeting of the Ecclesiastical History Society. (Studies in Church History: Vol. 16). 1980. 36.00x (ISBN 0-631-11421-1, Pub. by Basil Blackwell). Biblio Dist.

--Church Society & Politics. (Studies in Church History Ser.: Vol. 12). 1975. 36.00x (ISBN 0-631-16970-9, Pub. by Basil Blackwell). Biblio Dist.

--Medieval Women. (Illus.). 1978. 35.50x (ISBN 0-631-19260-3, Pub. by Basil Blackwell England). Biblio Dist.

--The Orthodox Churches & the West. (Studies in Church History Ser.: Vol. 13). 1976. 36.00x (ISBN 0-631-17180-0, Pub. by Basil Blackwell). Biblio Dist.

--Reform & Reformation: England & the Continent c.1380-c.1750. (Studies in Church History: Subsidia 2). (Illus.). 1979. 36.00x (ISBN 0-631-19270-0, Pub. by Basil Blackwell England). Biblio Dist.

--Religion & Humanism. (Studies in Church History: Vol. 17). 500p. 1981. 36.00x (ISBN 0-631-18050-8, Pub. by Basil Blackwell). Biblio Dist.

Baker, Derek, jt. ed. see Cuming, G. J.

Baker, Donald G. & Sheldon, Charles H. Postwar America: The Search for Identity. (Insight Series: Studies in Contemporary Issues). 1969. pap. 4.95x (ISBN 0-02-473840-9, 47384). Macmillan.

Baker, Donald G., ed. Politics of Race: Comparative Studies. 324p. 1975. 24.95 (ISBN 0-347-01076-8, 97311-4, Pub. by Saxon Hse). Lexington Bks.

Baker, Dorothy, ed. see Masters, Roy.

Baker, Doug. River Place. 176p. 1980. pap. 7.95 (ISBN 0-917304-57-8, Pub. by Timber Pr). Intl Schol Bk Serv.

Baker, E. C., jt. auth. see Hess, T. B.

Baker, E. H., et al. Structural Analysis of Shells. 2nd ed. LC 79-27250. 364p. 1981. Repr. lib. bdg. write for info. (ISBN 0-89874-118-1). Krieger.

Baker, Elizabeth. Love Around the House. 1979. pap. 2.50 (ISBN 0-88207-603-5). Victor Bks.

Baker, Elizabeth & Baker, Elton. Uncook Book: Raw Food Adventures to a New Health High. 210p. 1981. pap. 5.95 (ISBN 0-937766-05-4). Comm Creat.

--The Uncook Book: Raw Food Adventures to a New Health High. (Illus.). 198p. 1981. pap. 5.95 (ISBN 0-937766-05-4). Drelwood Pubns.

Baker, Elizabeth F. Henry Wheaton: 1785-1848. LC 70-154698. (American Constitutional & Legal History Ser.). 1971. Repr. of 1937 ed. lib. bdg. 42.50 (ISBN 0-306-70152-9). Da Capo.

Baker, Elliott. Klynt's Law. 1977. pap. 1.95 o.p. (ISBN 0-345-25720-0). Ballantine.

Baker, Elsworth F. Foreword by see Eden, Jerome.

Baker, Elton, jt. auth. see Baker, Elizabeth.

Baker, Eugene. I Want to Be a Postal Clerk. LC 75-38520. (I Want to Be Bks.). (Illus.). 32p. (gr. k-4). 1976. PLB 7.95 o.p. (ISBN 0-516-01738-1). Childrens.

--I Want to Be a Service Station Attendant. LC 70-178495. (I Want to Be Books). (Illus.). 32p. (gr. k-4). 1972. PLB 7.95 o.p. (ISBN 0-516-01797-7). Childrens.

--Secret Writing-Codes & Messages. (Junior Detective Bks.). (Illus.). 1980. 7.35g (ISBN 0-516-06473-8). Childrens.

--What's Right. Buerger, Jane, ed. (Illus.). 1980. 5.95 (ISBN 0-89565-175-0, 4932). Standard Pub.

Baker, Eva, jt. auth. see Popham, James.

Baker, Eva, jt. auth. see Popham, W.

Baker, F. J. & Silverton, R. E. Introduction to Medical Laboratory Technology. 5th ed. 1976. 29.95 (ISBN 0-407-73251-9). Butterworths.

Baker, F. Robert. Warhead. 304p. (Orig.). 1981. pap. 2.50 (ISBN 0-553-14790-0). Bantam.

Baker, Frank & Northman, John E. Helping: Human Services for the 80's. 221p. 1981. pap. text ed. 8.75 (ISBN 0-8016-0424-9). Mosby.

Baker, Frank, ed. Organizational Systems: General Systems Approaches to Complex Organizations. 1973. text ed. 16.50x (ISBN 0-256-00236-3). Irwin.

Baker, Frank, jt. ed. see Schulberg, Herbert C.

Baker, Fred, et al. Galactic Adventures. LC 80-80321. (Illus.). 192p. (gr. 3-7). 1980. 7.95 (ISBN 0-528-82374-4). Rand.

Baker, G. Communism in America: Liberty & Security in Conflict. Brown, Richard H. & Halsey, Van R., eds. (Amherst Ser.). (gr. 9-12). 1970. pap. text ed. 4.52 o.p. (ISBN 0-201-00455-0, Sch Div); tchr's manual 1.72 o.p. (ISBN 0-201-00457-7). A-W.

Baker, George, jt. ed. see Needleman, Jacob.

Baker, George P. Dramatic Technique. LC 77-77706. (Theatre, Film & the Performing Arts Ser). 532p. 1971. Repr. of 1919 ed. lib. bdg. 35.00 (ISBN 0-306-71344-6). Da Capo.

Baker, Glenn E. & Crow, Leonard R. Electricity Fundamentals. LC 73-131131. 1971. 13.95 (ISBN 0-672-20795-8). Bobbs.

Baker, Glenn E. & Miller, Rex. Carpentry Fundamentals. (Contemporary Construction Ser.). (Illus.). 512p. (gr. 10-12). 1981. 16.95 (ISBN 0-07-003361-7, G); tchrs. manual & key 1.50 (ISBN 0-07-003363-3); write for info wkbk. (ISBN 0-07-003362-5). McGraw.

Baker, Glenn E. & Yeager, L. Dayle. Wood Technology. LC 72-83817. 1974. 20.95 (ISBN 0-672-20917-9); student's manual 6.95 (ISBN 0-672-97107-0). Bobbs.

Baker, Glenn E., jt. auth. see Yeager, L. Dayle.

Baker, H. F. Introduction to Plane Geometry. LC 70-141879. 1971. text ed. 14.95 (ISBN 0-8284-0247-7). Chelsea Pub.

Baker, Harry. The Step-by-Step Guide to Fruits. (Illus.). 1980. 7.95 (ISBN 0-686-60919-0, 24834). S&S.

Baker, Hendrik. Stage Management & Theatrecraft. new & rev. ed. LC 68-16449. (Illus.). pap. 14.85 (ISBN 0-87830-559-9). Theatre Arts.

Baker, Herbert G. Plants & Civilization. 3rd ed. (Fundamentals of Botany Ser.). 1978. pap. text ed. 7.95x (ISBN 0-534-00575-6). Wadsworth Pub.

Baker, Herschel, ed. Later Renaissance in England: Nondramatic Verse & Prose, 1600-1660. 1975. text ed. 21.50 (ISBN 0-395-16038-3). HM.

Baker, Houston A., Jr. Long Black Song: Essays in Black American Literature & Culture. LC 72-77261. 1972. 10.95x (ISBN 0-8139-0403-X). U Pr of Va.

Baker, Howard. Ode to the Sea & Other Poems. LC 66-20097. 77p. 1966. 4.95 (ISBN 0-8040-0228-2). Swallow.

Baker, Hugh. Chinese Family & Kinship. LC 78-26724. 1979. 20.00x (ISBN 0-231-04768-1). Columbia U Pr.

Baker, Hugh R. Chinese Family & Kinship. 1980. pap. 7.50x (ISBN 0-231-04769-X). Columbia U Pr.

Baker, Ivon. Death & Variations. LC 77-157. Date not set. cancelled (ISBN 0-312-18880-3). St Martin.

Baker, J. & Nicholson, E. W., eds. The Commentary of Rabbi David Kimhi on Psalms 120-150. (Cambridge Oriental Publications Ser.: No. 22). 34.50 (ISBN 0-521-08670-1). Cambridge U Pr.

Baker, J. A., tr. see Von Campenhausen, Hans.

Baker, J. E. The Right to Participate: Inmate Involvement in Prison Administration. LC 74-7071. 1974. 10.00 (ISBN 0-8108-0727-0). Scarecrow.

Baker, J. F. Steel Skeleton, 2 vols. Incl. Vol. 1. Elastic Behaviour & Design. 1954. 35.50 (ISBN 0-521-04086-8); Vol. 2. Plastic Behaviour & Design. 1956. 57.50 (ISBN 0-521-04088-4). Cambridge U Pr.

Baker, J. K. & Juergenson, E. M. Approved Practices in Swine Production. 5th ed. LC 79-142330. 1979. 14.00 (ISBN 0-8134-2038-5, 2038); text ed. 10.50x (ISBN 0-685-41955-X). Interstate.

Baker, J. R. Parasitic Protozoa. (Biological Sciences Ser). 1969. pap. text ed. 6.50x (ISBN 0-09-099161-3, Hutchinson U Lib). Humanities.

Baker, J. Wayne. Heinrich Bullinger & the Covenant: The Other Reformed Tradition. LC 80-11667. xxvi, 300p. 1980. 18.95 (ISBN 0-8214-0554-3). Ohio U Pr.

Baker, J. Wayne, jt. auth. see Riede, David C.

Baker, James. International Bank Regulation. LC 76-19545. (Praeger Special Studies). 1978. 23.95 (ISBN 0-275-23570-X). Praeger.

Baker, James C. & Bradford, M. Gerald. American Banks Abroad: Edge Act Companies & Multinational Banking. LC 73-18135. (Special Studies). 202p. 1974. text ed. 21.95 o.p. (ISBN 0-275-28819-6). Praeger.

Baker, James C., jt. auth. see Scrivner, C. L.

Baker, James H., ed. Poems of Bishop Henry King. LC 60-8067. 138p. 1960. 5.95 (ISBN 0-8040-0249-5); pap. 3.95 o.p. (ISBN 0-8040-0249-5). Swallow.

Baker, James K. & Greer, William J. Animal Health. LC 78-62054. 1980. 24.65 (ISBN 0-8134-2053-9, 2053); text ed. 18.50x (ISBN 0-686-67467-7). Interstate.

Baker, James R. & Staley, Thomas F. James Joyce's Dubliners. 1969. pap. 4.95x o.p. (ISBN 0-534-00682-5). Wadsworth Pub.

Baker, James W. Elements of Stagecraft. LC 77-25899. 1978. pap. text ed. 11.50x (ISBN 0-88284-053-3). Alfred Pub.

Baker, Jan. The Church of England. 1978. pap. 2.90 (ISBN 0-08-021408-8). Pergamon.

Baker, Jeannie. Grandfather. LC 78-74759. (Illus.). (gr. k-2). 1980. 8.95 (ISBN 0-233-96864-4). Andre Deutsch.

--Grandmother. (Illus.). (ps-2). 1979. PLB 8.95 (ISBN 0-233-96975-6). Andre Deutsch.

--Millicent. (Illus.). (ps-2). 1980. 8.95 (ISBN 0-233-97201-3). Andre Deutsch.

Baker, Jeffrey. Time & Mind in Wordsworth's Poetry. 216p. 1980. 14.95 (ISBN 0-8143-1655-7). Wayne St U Pr.

Baker, Jeffrey A., jt. auth. see Cline, Gloria S.

Baker, Jeffrey J. & Allen, Garland E. Course in Biology. 3rd ed. LC 78-67451. (Life Sciences Ser.). 1979. text ed. 18.95 (ISBN 0-201-00308-2). A-W.

--Hypothesis, Prediction, & Implication in Biology. LC 68-30687. (Biology Ser). (Illus., Orig.). 1968. pap. 6.95 (ISBN 0-201-00482-8). A-W.

--The Process of Biology. LC 73-93981. (Biology Ser). 1970. pap. 7.95 (ISBN 0-201-00372-4). A-W.

--Study of Biology. 3rd ed. LC 76-15460. (Illus.). 1977. text ed. 21.95 (ISBN 0-201-00349-X); instr's manual 3.00 (ISBN 0-201-00413-5). A-W.

Baker, Jeffrey J. W. & Allen, Garland E. Matter, Energy, & Life: An Introduction to Chemical Concepts, 4-E. LC 80-17946. (Life Sciences Ser.). 256p. 1981. 8.95 (ISBN 0-201-00169-1). A-W.

Baker, Jeffrey W. & Allen, Garland E. Matter, Energy & Life: An Introduction for Biology Students. 3rd ed. 1975. pap. text ed. 8.50 o.p. (ISBN 0-201-00389-9). A-W.

Baker, Jennifer. The Horse Show. (Illus.). 1977. 7.95 o.p. (ISBN 0-04-798001-X). Allen Unwin.

Baker, Jerry & Kibbie, Dan. Farm Fever: Finding & Buying Country Land. LC 76-30861. (Funk & W Bk.). 1977. 11.95 o.s.i. (ISBN 0-308-10299-1, TYC-T). T Y Crowell.

Baker, Jim, tr. Tranportez-Vous Montagnes. (French Bks.). (Fr.). 1979. 1.80 (ISBN 0-8297-0817-0). Life Pubs Intl.

Baker, John & Heyman, J. Plastic Design of Frames, 2 vols. Incl. Vol. 1. Fundamentals. 32.95 (ISBN 0-521-07517-3); pap. 15.95 (ISBN 0-521-29778-8); Vol. 2. Applications. 33.95 (ISBN 0-521-07984-5). LC 69-19370. (Illus.). 1969-1971. Cambridge U Pr.

Baker, John M. How to Build a House with an Architect. LC 79-203. 1979. pap. 6.95 (ISBN 0-397-01325-6). Lippincott.

--How to Build a House with an Architect. LC 76-49974. (Illus.). 1977. 14.95 o.p. (ISBN 0-397-01124-5). Lippincott.

Baker, Joseph T. & Murphy, Vreni. Compounds from Marine Organisms, Vol. 2. (Section B, Handbook of Marine Science). 192p. 1981. 39.95 (ISBN 0-8493-0214-5). CRC Pr.

Baker, Josephine & Bouillon, Jo. Josephine. LC 76-26212. (Illus.). 1977. 12.95 o.s.i. (ISBN 0-06-010212-8, HarpT). Har-Row.

Baker, K. & Fane, X. Understanding & Guiding Young Children. 3rd ed. 1975. 13.32 (ISBN 0-13-935825-0). P-H.

Baker, Keith & Rubel, Tobert J. Violence & Crime in the Schools. LC 79-5325. 320p. 1980. 16.95 (ISBN 0-669-03389-8). Lexington Bks.

Baker, Keith, et al. Comprehensive Services to Rural Poor Families: An Evaluation of the Arizona Job College Program. LC 75-36414. (Special Studies). (Illus.). 1976. text ed. 22.95 (ISBN 0-275-56310-3). Praeger.

Baker, Keith M., ed. Condorcet: Selected Writings. LC 75-38680. (Library of Liberal Arts No. 159). 1976. pap. 9.50 (ISBN 0-672-60381-0). Bobbs.

Baker, Ken F., et al, eds. Annual Review of Phytopathology, Vol. 13. LC 63-8847. (Illus.). 1975. text ed. 17.00 (ISBN 0-8243-1313-5). Annual Reviews.

Baker, Krystyna. Masks. Date not set. price not set (ISBN 0-89672-086-1); price not set ltd. signed ed. (ISBN 0-89672-092-6); pap. price not set (ISBN 0-89672-085-3). Tex Tech Pr.

Baker, L. E., jt. auth. see Geddes, L. A.

Baker, Leonard. Days of Sorrow & Pain: Leo Baeck & the Berlin Jews. (Illus.). 412p. 1980. pap. 7.95 (ISBN 0-19-502800-7, GB 611). Oxford U Pr.

--John Marshall: A Life in Law. LC 73-2751. (Illus.). 1974. 19.75 o.s.i. (ISBN 0-02-506360-X). Macmillan.

Baker, Leslie A. The Art Teacher's Resource Book. (Illus.). 1978. ref. 16.95 (ISBN 0-87909-022-7). Reston.

Baker, Lillian. One Hundred Years of Collectible Jewelry. (Illus.). 1980. pap. 8.95 (ISBN 0-89145-066-1). Collector Bks.

Baker, Liva. I'm Radcliff Fly Me! 1976. 12.95 (ISBN 0-02-506310-3). Macmillan.

Baker, Lynn S. The Fertility Fallacy: Sexuality in the Post-Pill Age. LC 80-50715. 224p. 1981. 11.95 (ISBN 0-7216-1492-2). Saunders.

--The Fertility Fallacy: Sexuality in the Post Pill Age. LC 80-50715. 224p. 1981. 11.95 (ISBN 0-03-057656-3). HR&W.

Baker, Margaret. Food & Cooking. (Junior Reference Ser.). (Illus.). 64p. (gr. 7 up). 7.95 (ISBN 0-7136-1465-X). Dufour.

--Gardener's Magic & Folklore. LC 77-73799. (Illus.). 1978. 12.50x (ISBN 0-87663-299-1). Universe.

Baker, Margret. Folklore of the Sea. (Illus.). 1979. 14.50 (ISBN 0-7153-7568-7). David & Charles.

Baker, Mark. Nam. 288p. 1981. 10.95 (ISBN 0-688-00086-X). Morrow.

Baker, Mary F. Florida Wild Flowers. 1977. Repr. 5.95 (ISBN 0-9600046-1-0). Horticultural.

Baker, Marybob. Smiley Lion Book. (Illus.). (ps-1). 1964. PLB 5.38 (ISBN 0-307-68907-7, Golden Pr). Western Pub.

Baker, Michael A. Visa Qualifying Examination Review, Vol. 2: Clinical Sciences. LC 78-61618. 1978. pap. 11.75 (ISBN 0-87488-125-0). Med Exam.

Baker, Michael A., ed. Medicine. 7th ed. (Medical Examination Review Ser.: Vol. 2). 1980. pap. 8.50 (ISBN 0-87488-102-1). Med Exam.

Baker, Muriel L. Stumpwork: The Art of Raised Embroidery. LC 77-13204. (Illus.). 1978. 14.95 o.p. (ISBN 0-684-15360-2, ScribT). Scribner.

Baker, Nancy C. Act Two: Mid-Career Job Changes. LC 79-56027. 256p. 1980. 10.00 (ISBN 0-8149-0833-0). Vanguard.

--Babyselling: The Scandal of Black-Market Adoption. LC 77-93231. 1978. 8.95 (ISBN 0-8149-0798-9). Vanguard.

Baker, Nina B. Nickels & Dimes: The Story of F. W. Woolworth. LC 54-9621. (gr. 4-7). 1966. pap. 0.50 o.p. (ISBN 0-15-665590-X, AVB17, VoyB). HarBraceJ.

Baker, Olaf. Where the Buffaloes Begin. LC 80-23319. (Illus.). 48p. (gr. 1-4). 1981. 9.95g (ISBN 0-7232-6195-4). Warne.

Baker, Oleda. Reluctant Goddess. 480p. (Orig.). 1981. pap. 2.75 (ISBN 0-515-05869-6). Jove Pubns.

Baker, Oleda & Gale, Bill. The Model's Way to Beauty, Slenderness & Glowing Health. 256p. 1976. pap. 1.75 o.p. (ISBN 0-345-24444-3). Ballantine.

Baker, Oleda & Petty, Francey. How to Create the Illusion of a More Perfect Figure. LC 77-22825. (Illus.). 1978. 8.95 o.p. (ISBN 0-13-404475-4). P-H.

Baker, P. F. & Reute, H. Calcium Movement in Excitable Cells. 1976. pap. text ed. 18.25 (ISBN 0-08-018298-4). Pergamon.

Baker, P. J. & Jacobs, B. E. Guide to Slurry Pipeline Systems. (Illus.). 58p. (Orig.). 1980. PLB 32.00 (ISBN 0-906085-38-1, Dist. by Air Science Co.). BHRA Fluid.

Baker, P. T., ed. The Biology of High-Altitude Peoples. LC 76-50311. (International Biological Programme Ser.: No. 14). (Illus.). 1978. 68.00 (ISBN 0-521-21523-4). Cambridge U Pr.

Baker, P. T. & Little, Michael A., eds. Man in the Andes: A Multidisciplinary Approach of High Altitude Quechua. LC 76-17025. 1976. 37.50 (ISBN 0-12-786115-7). Acad Pr.

Baker, Pat. Giving God What You Are. 1981. pap. 3.95 (ISBN 0-8054-5333-4). Broadman.

--Help! I've Just Given Birth to a Teenager. 128p. (Orig.). 1981. pap. 4.95 (ISBN 0-8010-0799-2). Baker Bk.

Baker, Paul. Why Should the Devil Have All the Good Music: Jesus Music, Where It Began, Where It Is, & Where It Is Going. 1979. 7.95 (ISBN 0-8499-2858-3). Word Bks.

Baker, Pauline H. Urbanization & Political Change: The Politics of Lagos, 1917-1967. 1975. 28.50x (ISBN 0-520-02066-9). U of Cal Pr.

Baker, R. A. Compendio De la Historia Cristiana. Almanza, Francisco G., tr. Orig. Title: A Summary of Christian History. 372p. (Span.). Date not set. pap. price not set (ISBN 0-311-15032-2). Casa Bautista.

Baker, R. Robin. The Evolutionary Ecology of Animal Migration. LC 78-34. (Illus.). 1978. text ed. 117.50x (ISBN 0-8419-0368-9). Holmes & Meier.

Baker, Ralph & Meyer, Fred, Jr. The Criminal Justice Game. 1980. pap. text ed. 8.95 (ISBN 0-87872-240-8). Duxbury Pr.

Baker, Ralph & Meyer, Fred, eds. Evaluating Alternative Law-Enforcement Policies. LC 79-1541. (Policy Studies Organization Bk.). (Illus.). 240p. 1979. 19.95 (ISBN 0-669-02898-3). Lexington Bks.

Baker, Ralph, jt. ed. see Meyer, Fred.

Baker, Ray P., ed. see Haliburton, Thomas C.

Baker, Richard. Richard Baker's Music Guide. LC 79-52366. (Illus.). 144p. 1980. 11.95 (ISBN 0-7153-7782-5). David & Charles.

Baker, Richard, ed. Controlled Release of Bioactive Materials. 1980. 34.50 (ISBN 0-12-074450-3). Acad Pr.

Baker, Richard D. Judicial Review in Mexico: A Study of the Amparo Suit. (Latin American Monographs, No. 22). 304p. 1971. 13.50 (ISBN 0-292-70105-5). U of Tex Pr.

Baker, Robert, jt. auth. see Fredrick, Laurence.

Baker, Robert & Elliston, Frederick, eds. Philosophy & Sex. LC 75-21670. 397p. 1975. 11.95 (ISBN 0-87975-055-3); pap. 6.95 (ISBN 0-87975-050-2). Prometheus Bks.

Baker, Robert J. I'm Listening Lord, Keep Talking. 200p. 1981. pap. 6.95 (ISBN 0-8361-1953-3). Herald Pr.

Baker, Robert J., et al, eds. Biology of Bats of the New World Family Phyllostomatidae, Pt. I. (Special Publications: No. 10). (Illus., Orig.). 1976. pap. 8.00 (ISBN 0-89672-036-5). Tex Tech Pr.

Baker, Robert K. Doing Library Research: An Introduction for Community College Students. (Westview Guides to Library Research Ser.). 260p. 27.50x (ISBN 0-89158-778-0). Westview.

--Introduction to Library Research in French Literature. LC 77-18074. (A Westview Special Study Ser.). 1978. lib. bdg. 22.50x (ISBN 0-89158-060-3); pap. text ed. 9.00 (ISBN 0-89158-082-4). Westview.

Baker, Robin, ed. The Mystery of Migration. LC 80-16839. (Illus.). 256p. 1981. 29.95 (ISBN 0-670-50286-3). Viking Pr.

Baker, Ronald L. & Carmony, Marvin. Indiana Place Names. LC 74-17915. 224p. 1976. 7.95x o.p. (ISBN 0-253-14167-2); pap. 3.95x (ISBN 0-253-28340-X). Ind U Pr.

Baker, Russell. So This Is Depravity. 256p. 1980. 10.95 (ISBN 0-312-92782-7). St Martin.

--So This Is Depravity & Other Observations. 1980. 10.95 (ISBN 0-312-92782-7); deluxe signed, limited ed. 40.00 (ISBN 0-312-92783-5). Congdon & Lattes.

Baker, Ruth. Getting Rich in Real Estate Partnerships. (Orig.). 1981. 11.95 (ISBN 0-446-51222-2). Warner Bks.

Baker, S. The Crowell College Reader. 1974. pap. text ed. 10.50 scp (ISBN 0-690-00170-3, HarpC); instructor's manual avail. (ISBN 0-685-99798-7). Har-Row.

--The Practical Stylist. 4th ed. 1977. pap. text ed. 7.50 scp (ISBN 0-690-00873-2, HarpC). Har-Row.

Baker, Samm S. & Stillman, Irwin M. The Doctor's Quick Teenage Diet. 256p. 1972. pap. 1.25 o.s.i. (ISBN 0-446-76808-1). Warner Bks.

Baker, Samm S., jt. auth. see Bella, Leopold.

Baker, Samm S., jt. auth. see Tarnower, Herman.

Baker, Scott. Symbiote's Crown. 1978. pap. 1.75 o.p. (ISBN 0-425-03839-4, Medallion). Berkley Pub.

Baker, Sheridan. The Complete Stylist & Handbook. 2nd ed. 1980. text ed. 11.50 scp (ISBN 0-06-040452-3, HarpC); instructor's manual avail. (ISBN 0-685-95565-6). Har-Row.

--The Practical Stylist. 5th ed. 224p. 1980. pap. text ed. 7.50 scp (ISBN 0-06-040454-X, HarpC); avail. Har-Row.

--Practice in Exposition: Supplementary Exercises for the Practical Stylist. 2nd ed. 160p. 1980. pap. text ed. 6.50 scp (ISBN 0-690-00875-9, HarpC). Har-Row.

Baker, Stanley L. The Railroadiana Collector's Price Guide. (Illus.). 1977. pap. 4.95 o.p. (ISBN 0-8015-6219-8). Dutton.

Baker, Susan R. Collaboration et Originalite Chez la Rochefoucauld. LC 79-21085. (U. of Fla. Humanities Monographs: No. 48). 135p. (Orig.). 1980. pap. 9.00 (ISBN 0-8130-0657-0). U Presses Fla.

Baker, T. F., ed. Victoria History of the Counties of England: Middlesex, Vol. 5. (Illus.). 1976. text ed. 85.00x o.p. (ISBN 0-19-722742-2). Oxford U Pr.

Baker, T. Lindsay. The Early History of Panna Maria, Texas. (Graduate Studies: No. 9). (Illus., Orig.). 1975. pap. 4.00 (ISBN 0-89672-016-0). Tex Tech Pr.

--The First Polish Americans: Silesian Settlements in Texas. LC 78-6373. 1979. 14.95 (ISBN 0-89096-060-7). Tex A&M Univ Pr.

Baker, Theodore. Dictionary of Musical Terms. 1923. 7.95 (ISBN 0-02-870200-X). Schirmer Bks.

--On the Music of the North American Indians. Buckley, Ann, tr. from Ger. (Music Reprint Ser., 1977). 1977. lib. bdg. 17.50 (ISBN 0-306-70888-4). Da Capo.

--Schirmer Pronouncing Pocket Manual of Musical Terms. 4th ed. LC 77-5236. 1978. pap. 3.50 (ISBN 0-02-870250-6). Schirmer Bks.

Baker, Thomas H. Memphis Commercial Appeal: The History of a Southern Newspaper. LC 74-165066. 1971. 20.00 (ISBN 0-8071-0944-4). La State U Pr.

Baker, V., jt. auth. see Costa, J.

Baker, Victor R., jt. auth. see Costa, John E.

Baker, W. M. Bell's Acrostic Dictionary. LC 77-141772. 1971. Repr. of 1927 ed. 15.00 (ISBN 0-8103-3379-1). Gale.

Baker, Wilfred, et al. Similarity Methods in Engineering Dynamics: Theory & Practice of Scale Modeling. (Illus.). 1973. 22.95x (ISBN 0-8104-9214-8). Hayden.

Baker, William. George Eliot and Judaism: A Study of George Eliot's Interest & Knowledge of Judaism. (Salzburg Studies in English Literature, Romantic Reassessment Ser.: No. 45). 272p. 1975. pap. text ed. 25.00x (ISBN 0-391-01312-2). Humanities.

--Some George Eliot Notebooks: An Edition of the Carl H. Pforzheimer Library's George Eliot Holography Notebooks, Mss. 707, 5 vols. (Salzburg Studies in English Literature, Romantic Reassessment: No. 46). 332p. 1977. pap. text ed. 25.00x set (ISBN 0-391-01307-6). Humanities.

--Some George Eliot Notebooks: An Edition of the Carl H. Pforzheimer Library's George Eliot Ecolgrph Notebooks Mss 707, 708, 709, 710, Vol.iII-711. (Romantic Reassessment Ser.: No.46). 267p. 1980. pap. text ed. 25.00 (ISBN 0-391-01309-2). Humanities.

Baker, William, jt. auth. see Smith, Harold.

Baker, William E. Syntax in English Poetry, 1870-1930. (Perspectives in Criticism: No. 18). 1968. 14.00x (ISBN 0-520-00069-2). U of Cal Pr.

Baker, William H., jt. auth. see Lewis, Phillip V.

Baker, William O. Miles Conrad Memorial Lecture, 1977. 10.00. NFAIS.

Baker, William S. Bibliotheca Washingtoniana. LC 67-14022. 1967. Repr. of 1889 ed. 15.00 (ISBN 0-8103-3318-X). Gale.

Bakere, Jane A. The Cornish Ordinalia: A Critical Study. 191p. 1980. text ed. 50.00x (ISBN 0-7083-0745-0). Verry.

Baker of Windrush, Lord. Enterprise Versus Bureaucracy: The Development of Structural Air-Raid Precautions During the 2nd World War. 1978. text ed. 12.75 (ISBN 0-08-022149-1). Pergamon.

Bakewell, K. G. A Manual of Cataloguing Practice. LC 73-171838. 312p. 1972. text ed. 50.00 (ISBN 0-08-016697-0). Pergamon.

Bakewell, K. G., ed. Management Principles & Practice: A Guide to Information Sources. LC 76-16127. (Management Information Guide Series: No. 32). 1977. 30.00 (ISBN 0-8103-0832-0). Gale.

Bakhtin, M. M. The Dialogic Imagination: Four Essays. Holquist, Michael, ed. Emerson, Caryl, tr. from Rus. LC 80-15450. (No. 1). 480p. 1981. text ed. 25.00x (ISBN 0-292-71527-7). U of Tex Pr.

--Problems of Dostoevsky's Poetics. Rotsel, R. W., tr. from Rus. (Illus.). 340p. (Orig.). 1973. 10.00 o.p. (ISBN 0-88233-040-3); pap. 3.95 o.p. (ISBN 0-88233-041-1). Ardis Pubs.

Bakish, David. Richard Wright. LC 71-190353. (Modern Literature Ser.). 121p. 1973. 10.95 (ISBN 0-8044-2015-7). Ungar.
Bakish, David, jt. ed. see Margolies, Edward.
Bakken, Lavolla J. Land of the North Umpquas: Peaceful Indians of the West. LC 73-84954. (Illus.). 1973. pap. 1.00 (ISBN 0-913508-03-9). Te Cum Tom.
Bakken, Terry, jt. auth. see Monahan, Evelyn.
Bakker, Dirk J., ed. Temporal Order in Disturbed Reading: Developmental & Neuropsychological Aspects in Normal & Reading-Retarded Children. (Modern Approaches to the Diagnosis & Instruction of Multi-Handicapped Children: Vol. 7). 100p. 1972. text ed. 21.50 (ISBN 90-237-4108-0, Pub. by Swets Pub Serv Holland). Swets North Am.
Bakker, Dirk J. & Satz, Paul, eds. Specific Reading Disability: Advances in Theory & Method. (Modern Approaches to the Diagnosis & Instruction of Multi-Handicapped Children: Vol. 3). 166p. 1970. text ed. 21.50 (ISBN 90-237-4103-X, Pub. by Swets Pub Serv Holland). Swets North Am.
Bakker, F. Facets of Prayer. Pronk, Cornelis & Pronk, Fredericka, trs. from Dutch. (Summit Bks.). 96p. 1981. pap. 2.45 (ISBN 0-8010-0796-8). Baker Bk.
Bakker, J. W. & Leeuwen, J. Van, eds. Automata, Languages & Programming: Seventh Colloquim. (Lecture Notes in Computer Sciences: Vol. 85). 671p. 1980. pap. 31.90 (ISBN 0-387-10003-2). Springer-Verlag.
Bakker, Jan, jt. auth. see Butler, Francelia.
Bakker, Jan & Wilkinson, D. R., eds. From Cooper to Philip Roth: Essays on American Literature Presented to J. G. Riewald on the Occasion of His Seventieth Birthday. (Costerus New Ser.). 130p. 1980. pap. text ed. 14.25x (ISBN 90-6203-851-4). Humanities.
Bakker, Jim. Survival: Unity to Live. Boneck, John & Dudley, Cliff, eds. LC 80-84504. 150p. 1980. 7.95 (ISBN 0-89221-081-8). New Leaf.
Bakker, Jim, tr. Tres Factores Para Mover Montanas. (Spanish Bks.). (Span.). 1978. 1.60 (ISBN 0-8297-0488-4). Life Pubs Intl.
Bakker, Jim, et al. PTL Devotional Guide. Marco, Anton, ed. LC 80-81170. 370p. 1980. pap. 3.95 (ISBN 0-89221-077-X). New Leaf.
Baklanoff, Eric N. The Economic Transformation of Spain & Portugal. LC 76-12842. (Praeger Special Studies). 1978. 24.95 (ISBN 0-275-23380-4). Praeger.
Baklanov, Grigory, tr. from Rus. South of the Main Offensive. LC 64-25464. 1963. 6.25 (ISBN 0-8023-1006-0). Dufour.
Bakr, A. Studies in Arabic Philology. (Arabic.). 1969. 14.00x (ISBN 0-685-72059-4). Intl Bk Ctr.
Baks, C. see Pillai, S. Devadas.
Bakshi, Trilochan S. & Naveh, Zev, eds. Environmental Education: Principles, Methods & Applications. (Environmental Science Research Ser.: Vol. 18). 300p. 1980. 32.50 (ISBN 0-306-40433-8, Plenum Pr). Plenum Pub.
Bakst, Leon. The Decorative Art of Leon Bakst. Melvill, Harry, tr. LC 73-187844. (Illus.). 144p. 1973. pap. 6.00 (ISBN 0-486-22871-1). Dover.
Bakunin, Mikhail A. Political Philosophy of Bakunin. Maximoff, G. P., ed. 1964. 10.95 o.s.i. (ISBN 0-02-901200-7); pap. text ed. 8.95 (ISBN 0-02-901210-4). Free Pr.
Bakutis, Alice R. Nurse Anesthetists Continuing Education Review. 1975. spiral bdg. 10.75 (ISBN 0-87488-356-3). Med Exam.
--Self-Assessment of Current Knowledge for the Nurse Anesthetist. 2nd ed. 1976. spiral bdg. 9.50 (ISBN 0-87488-715-1). Med Exam.
Bakvis, Herman. Catholic Power in the Netherlands. (Illus.). 550p. 1981. 35.95x (ISBN 0-7735-0367-6); pap. 18.95x (ISBN 0-7735-0368-4). McGill-Queens U Pr.
Bakwin, Harry & Bakwin, Ruth M. Behavior Disorders in Children. 4th ed. LC 75-173330. (Illus.). 690p. 1972. 29.00 (ISBN 0-7216-1502-3). Saunders.
Bakwin, Ruth M., jt. auth. see Bakwin, Harry.
Baky, John S., ed. Humans & Animals. (Reference Shelf Ser.). 1980. 6.25 (ISBN 0-8242-0647-9). Wilson.
Bal, Sant S. George Orwell: The Ethical Imagination. 144p. 1981. text ed. 9.25 (ISBN 0-391-02202-4). Humanities.
Balaam, David N. & Carey, Michael J., eds. Food Policies: The Regional Conflict. LC 79-48097. 280p. 1981. text ed. 24.50 (ISBN 0-916672-52-2). Allanheld.
Balaam, L. N. Fundamentals of Biometry. 1972. 16.95 (ISBN 0-470-04571-X). Halsted Pr.
Balaban, A. T., et al, eds. Steric Fit in Quantitative Structure-Activity Relations. (Lecture Notes in Chemistry: Vol. 15). (Illus.). 178p. 1980. pap. 17.50 (ISBN 0-387-09755-4). Springer-Verlag.
Balaban, M., ed. Molecular Mechanisms of Biological Recognition. 516p. 1979. 68.50 (ISBN 0-444-80130-8). Elsevier.
Balabanian, Norman & Bickert, Theodore. Linear Network Theory: Analysis, Properties, Design & Synthesis. 450p. 1981. text ed. 32.95 (ISBN 0-916460-10-X). Matrix Pubns.
Balabanian, Norman & LePage, Wilbur. Electrical Science, Bk. 1. 1970. 14.95 o.p. (ISBN 0-07-003543-1, C). McGraw.
Balabanoff, Angelica. Impressions of Lenin. Cesari, Isotta, tr. pap. 1.75 o.p. (ISBN 0-472-06133-X, 133, AA). U of Mich Pr.
Balabkins, Nicholas. Germany Under Direct Controls: Economic Aspects of Industrial Disarmament, 1945-1948. 1964. 16.00 (ISBN 0-8135-0449-X). Rutgers U Pr.
--West German Reparations to Israel. LC 70-152724. 1971. 25.00 (ISBN 0-8135-0691-3). Rutgers U Pr.
Balachandran, M., ed. Regional Statistics: A Guide to Information Sources. LC 80-14260. (Economics Information Guide Ser.: Vol. 13). 230p. 1980. 30.00 (ISBN 0-8103-1463-0). Gale.
Balachandran, M., jt. ed. see Balachandran, S.
Balachandran, S. & Balachandran, M., eds. Reference Sources Nineteen Eighty. 1981. 65.00 (ISBN 0-87650-127-7). Pierian.
Balachandran, Sarojini, ed. Energy Statistics: A Guide to Information Sources. LC 80-13338. (Natural World Information Guide Ser.: Vol. 1). 272p. 1980. 30.00 (ISBN 0-8103-1419-3). Gale.
--New Product Planning. LC 79-24046. (Management Information Guide Ser.: No. 38). 1980. 30.00 (ISBN 0-8103-0838-X). Gale.
Balachdran, M., jt. ed. see Balachdran, S.
Balachdran, S. & Balachdran, M., eds. Reference Sources, 1980. 1981. 65.00 (ISBN 0-87650-127-7). Pierian.
Balaguer, Josemaria E. de. The Way. 228p. 1979. pap. 2.95 (ISBN 0-933932-35-9). Scepter Pubs.
Balaguer, Josemaria E. de see De Balaguer, Josemaria E.
Balakian, Anna. Literary Origins of Surrealism: A New Mysticism in French Poetry. 1966. 10.00x (ISBN 0-8147-0024-1); pap. 4.00x (ISBN 0-8147-0025-X). NYU Pr.
--Surrealism: The Road to the Absolute. rev. ed. 1970. 7.95 o.p. (ISBN 0-525-21270-1). Dutton.
--The Symbolist Movement: A Critical Appraisal. LC 77-76044. 320p. 1977. 15.00x (ISBN 0-8147-0993-1); pap. 6.00x (ISBN 0-8147-0994-X). NYU Pr.
Balakrishnan, A. V., ed. Control Theory & the Calculus of Variations. LC 74-91431. 1969. 37.50 (ISBN 0-12-076953-0). Acad Pr.
Balakrishnan, A. V., ed. see International Conference on Computing Methods in Optimization Problems - 2nd San Remo, Italy - 1968.
Balakrishnan, A. V., tr. see Kolchin, Valentin F., et al.
Balakrishnan, B. & Ramabhadran, N. A Textbook of Modern Algebra. 1978. 12.95 (ISBN 0-7069-0636-5, Pub. by Vikas India). Advent Bk.
Balalaev, G. A. Corrosion Prevention Practice. Sapronova, I., tr. from Rus. 343p. 1972. text ed. 15.00x o.p. (ISBN 0-8464-0293-9). Beekman Pubs.
Balan, Jorge, et al. Men in a Developing Society: Geographic & Social Mobility in Monterrey, Mexico. LC 72-6282. (Latin American Monographs Ser.: No. 30). 432p. 1973. 15.00x (ISBN 0-292-75004-8). U of Tex Pr.
Balanchine, George & Mason, Francis. Balanchine's Complete Stories of the Great Ballets. LC 76-55684. 1977. 19.95 (ISBN 0-385-11381-1). Doubleday.
--One Hundred One Stories of the Great Ballets. LC 73-9140. 560p. 1975. pap. 5.95 (ISBN 0-385-03398-2, Dolp). Doubleday.
Balanger, Terry & La Casce, Steward. The Art of Persuasion: How to Write Effectively About Almost Anything. LC 78-38278. 1972. pap. 3.95x (ISBN 0-684-15053-0, ScribT). Scribner.
Balassa, Bela. The Newly Industrialized Countries in the World Economy. LC 80-20787. 450p. 1981. 42.50 (ISBN 0-08-026336-4); pap. 15.00 (ISBN 0-08-026335-6). Pergamon.
--Policy Reform in Developing Countries. 1977. text ed. 27.00 (ISBN 0-08-021477-0); pap. text ed. 16.25 (ISBN 0-08-021478-9). Pergamon.
Balassa, Bela, ed. World Trade: Constraints & Opportunities in the 80's. (Atlantic Papers: No.36). 70p. 1979. write for info. (ISBN 0-916672-76-X). Allanheld.
Balasubrahmanyam, V. Verse with Prose. 8.00 (ISBN 0-89253-559-8); flexible cloth 4.00 (ISBN 0-89253-560-1). Ind-US Inc.
--Verses. 8.00 (ISBN 0-89253-561-X); flexible cloth 4.00 (ISBN 0-89253-562-8). InterCulture.
Balawyder, Aloysius. The Maple Leaf & the White Eagle: Canadian-Polish Relations, 1918-1978. (East European Monographs: No. 66). 1980. 20.00x (ISBN 0-914710-59-1, Dist. by Columbia U Pr). East Eur Quarterly.
Balawyder, Aloysius, ed. Cooperative Movements in Eastern Europe. LC 79-55001. (Illus.). 200p. 1980. text ed. 18.00 (ISBN 0-916672-45-X). Allanheld.
Balazs, R. & Cremer, J. E., eds. Metabolic Compartmentation in the Brain. LC 72-11227. 383p. 1973. 37.95 (ISBN 0-470-04582-5). Halsted Pr.
Balbani, Niccolo. Newes from Italy of a Second Moses or, the Life of Galeacius Carracciolus the Noble Marquese of Vico. Crashaw, W., tr. LC 79-84085. (English Experience Ser.: No. 905). 92p. 1979. Repr. of 1608 ed. lib. bdg. 10.00 (ISBN 90-221-0905-4). Walter J Johnson.
Balbert, Peter. D. H. Lawrence & the Psychology of Rhythm: The Meaning of Form in the Rainbow. (Studies in English Literature: No. 99). 1974. pap. 20.00x (ISBN 0-686-22634-8). Mouton.
Balbin, Julius. Strangled Cries. Barkan, Stanley H., ed. Rizzuto, Charlz, tr. (Cross-Cultural Review Chapbook 8). 24p. (Esperanto & Eng.). 1980. pap. 2.50 (ISBN 0-89304-807-0). Cross Cult.
Balch, Edwin S. Glacieres or Freezing Caverns. Repr. of 1900 ed. 11.50 (ISBN 0-914264-32-X, Dist. by Caroline Hse). Zephyrus Pr.
Balch, Glenn. Book of Horses. (Illus.). 96p. (gr. 3-7). 1967. 8.95 (ISBN 0-590-07048-7, Four Winds). Schol Bk Serv.
--Horse of Two Colors. LC 69-11079. (Illus.). (gr. 3-9). 1969. 7.95 o.p. (ISBN 0-690-40360-7, TYC-J). T Y Crowell.
Balch, Marston S. Thomas Middleton's No Wit, No Help Like a Woman's & the Counterfeit Bridegroom (1677) & Further Adaptations. (Jacobean Drama Studies: No. 94). 1980. pap. text ed. 25.00x (ISBN 0-391-01921-X). Humanities.
Balchin, N. C., ed. Manual Metal-Arc Welding. (Engineering Craftsmen: No. F24). (Illus.). 1977. spiral bdg. 16.50x (ISBN 0-85083-395-7). Intl Ideas.
Balchin, N. C., et al, eds. Metal-Arc Gas Shielded Welding. (Engineering Craftsmen: No. F23). (Illus.). 1977. spiral bdg. 17.50x (ISBN 0-85083-385-X). Intl Ideas.
--Oxy-Acetylene Welding. (Engineering Craftsmen: No. F25). (Illus.). 1977. spiral bdg. 14.95x (ISBN 0-85083-396-5). Intl Ideas.
--Tungsten-Arc Gas Shielded Welding. (Engineering Craftsmen: No. F22). (Illus.). 1977. spiral bdg. 15.95x (ISBN 0-85083-394-9). Intl Ideas.
Balchin, Paul N. Housing Improvement & Social Inequality. 1979. text ed. 31.25x (ISBN 0-566-00274-4, Pub. by Gower Pub Co England). Renouf.
Balchum, Oscar J. & Jung, Ralph C., eds. Chest Disease Case Studies. 1973. spiral bdg. 12.00 o.s.i. (ISBN 0-87488-012-2). Med Exam.
Balcomb, Kenneth, jt. auth. see Angell, Tony.
Balcomb, Kenneth C. A Boy's Albuquerque, 1898-1912. LC 79-2774. (Illus.). 1980. 8.95 (ISBN 0-8263-0525-3). U of NM Pr.
Bald, R. C., ed. see Shakespeare, William.
Bald, Robert C., ed. see Shakespeare, William.
Baldanza, Frank. Iris Murdoch. (English Authors Ser.: No. 169). 169p. 1974. lib. bdg. 10.95 (ISBN 0-8057-1410-3). Twayne.
Baldassare, Mark. Residential Crowding in Urban America. LC 77-83102. 1979. 13.95x (ISBN 0-520-03563-1). U of Cal Pr.
Baldauf, Richard B. A Handy Guide to Grammar & Punctuation. (Programmed Instruction - Communications Skills Ser.). 160p. (Prog. Bk.). 1973. pap. text ed. 8.95 (ISBN 0-201-00382-1). A-W.
Baldausky, Karen, jt. auth. see Gos, Francois.
Balder, A. P. Complete Manual of Skin Diving. LC 68-23060. (YA) 1968. 10.95 (ISBN 0-02-506410-X). Macmillan.
Balderige, Letitia, rev. by see Vanderbilt, Amy.
Balderston, Katherine G., ed. see Goldsmith, Oliver.
Baldi, Sergio see Muir, Kenneth.
Baldini, Baccio. Discorso Sopra la Mascherata Della Genealogia Delg'Iddei, Repr. Of 1565 Ed. Bd. with Discorso Sopra Li Dei De'Gentili. Zucchi, Jacopo. Repr. of 1602 ed. LC 75-27852. (Renaissance & the Gods Ser.: Vol. 10). (Illus.). 1976. lib. bdg. 73.00 (ISBN 0-8240-2059-6). Garland Pub.
Baldini, Gabriele. The Story of Giuseppe Verdi. Parker, Roger, tr. from Ital. LC 79-41376. 330p. 1980. 34.50 (ISBN 0-521-22911-1); pap. 9.95 (ISBN 0-521-29712-5). Cambridge U Pr.
Baldisan, James R. A Manual of Ancient Sex & Sun Worship Rituals. 1979. Repr. of 1857 ed. deluxe ed. 51.75 (ISBN 0-930582-26-8). Gloucester Art.
Baldock, Peter. Community Work & Social Work. (Library of Social Work Ser.). 1974. 12.50x (ISBN 0-7100-8026-3); pap. 7.95 (ISBN 0-7100-8027-1). Routledge & Kegan.
Baldonado, Ardelina A. & Stahl, Dulcelina A. Cancer Nursing. (Nursing Outline Ser.). 1977. spiral bdg. 8.00 o.p. (ISBN 0-87488-374-1). Med Exam.
Baldridge, H. David. Shark Attack. (Orig.). 1975. pap. 1.95 (ISBN 0-425-03988-9, Medallion). Berkley Pub.
Baldridge, J. Victor, et al, eds. Managing Change in Educational Organizations: Sociological Perspectives Stragegies & Case Studies. LC 74-24479. 500p. 1975. 20.50 (ISBN 0-8211-0128-5); text ed. 18.50 (ISBN 0-685-51463-3). McCutchan.
Baldridge, Letitia. Amy Vanderbilt Complete Book of Etiquette. rev. ed. LC 77-16896. 1978. 11.95 (ISBN 0-385-13375-8); thumb-indexed 12.95 (ISBN 0-385-14238-2). Doubleday.
Baldridge, Victor J., jt. ed. see Riley, Gary L.
Baldry, H. C. Unity of Mankind in Greek Thought. 1965. 36.00 (ISBN 0-521-04091-4). Cambridge U Pr.
Baldry, J. C. General Equilibrium Analysis: An Introduction to the Two Sector Model. LC 80-82652. 256p. 1980. 29.95 (ISBN 0-470-27024-1, Pub. by Halsted Pr). Wiley.
Baldry, P. E. The Battle Against Bacteria: A Fresh Look. LC 76-639. (Illus.). 140p. 1976. 18.95 (ISBN 0-521-21268-5). Cambridge U Pr.
Baldwin & Richardson. International Trade & Finance. 2nd ed. 1981. pap. text ed. 8.95 (ISBN 0-316-07922-7). Little.
Baldwin, jt. auth. see Richardson.
Baldwin, A. The Coinages of Lapsakos. (Illus.). 111p. 1980. 30.00 (ISBN 0-916710-70-X). Obol Intl.
Baldwin, Alfred L. Theories of Child Development. 2nd ed. LC 80-24517. 675p. 1981. text ed. 22.95 (ISBN 0-471-04583-7). Wiley.
Baldwin, Bob, jt. auth. see Golden, Jim.
Baldwin, Bruce, jt. auth. see Burgess, Ann W.
Baldwin, C. S. Medieval Rhetoric & Poetic to 1400. 1959. 7.50 (ISBN 0-8446-1043-7). Peter Smith.
Baldwin, Carl R. Echoes of Their Voices. 400p. 1978. 10.95 (ISBN 0-86629-003-6). Sunrise MO.
Baldwin, Charles. Colorado Gem & Mineral Collecting Localities. pap. 4.95 (ISBN 0-933472-08-0). Johnson Colo.
Baldwin, Charles C. Stanford White. LC 78-150512. (Architecture & Decorative Art Ser.: Vol. 39). 1971. Repr. of 1931 ed. lib. bdg. 39.50 (ISBN 0-306-70138-3). Da Capo.
Baldwin, Christopher. The Major Problems of the World at the End of the 20th Century & Possible Solutions to Avoid an Epochal Catastrophe. (Illus.). 106p. 1980. 49.75 (ISBN 0-930008-65-0). Inst Econ Pol.
Baldwin, Dane L. & Broughton, L. N. Concordance to the Poems of John Keats. 1963. 35.00 (ISBN 0-8446-1044-5). Peter Smith.
Baldwin, David A., ed. America in an Interdependent World: Problems of United States Foreign Policy. LC 75-41909. (Illus.). 372p. 1976. pap. text ed. 8.50x (ISBN 0-87451-127-5). U Pr of New Eng.
Baldwin, Deidra. An Occasional Suite. (Jazz Press Chapbook Ser.). 20p. (Orig.). 1981. pap. 1.50 (ISBN 0-937310-08-5). Jazz Pr.
Baldwin, E. Differentiation & Co-Operation in an Israeli Veteran Moshav. 1972. text ed. 14.00x (ISBN 0-7190-0438-1). Humanities.
Baldwin, Edward. The Cross-Country Skiing Handbook. rev. ed. 1973. pap. 4.95 o.p. (ISBN 0-684-13420-9, SL397, ScribT). Scribner.
Baldwin, Ernest. Nature of Biochemistry. 2nd ed. (Orig.). 1962. 19.50 (ISBN 0-521-04097-3); pap. 6.95x (ISBN 0-521-09177-2, 177). Cambridge U Pr.
Baldwin, Ewart M. Geology of Oregon. 3rd ed. LC 76-4346. (Illus.). 1981. perfect bdg. 11.95 (ISBN 0-8403-2321-2). Kendall-Hunt.
Baldwin, Faith. Adam's Eden. LC 76-29898. 1977. 7.95 o.p. (ISBN 0-03-018896-2). HR&W.
--Change of Heart. 1980. pap. write for info. (ISBN 0-671-83091-0). PB.
--Give Love the Air. 1980. pap. write for info. (ISBN 0-671-83092-9). PB.
--Gove Love the Air. 1980. pap. write for info. (ISBN 0-671-83092-9). PB.
--The Heart Has Wings. 1981. pap. price not set (ISBN 0-671-83094-5). PB.
--The Lonely Man. 1980. pap. write for info. (ISBN 0-671-83095-3). PB.
--No Bed of Roses. 1980. pap. write for info. (ISBN 0-671-83096-1). PB.
--Take What You Want. 1980. pap. write for info. (ISBN 0-671-83097-X). PB.
--Three Women. 1980. pap. write for info. (ISBN 0-671-83098-8). PB.
--Thursday's Child. LC 75-18668. 1976. 7.95 o.p. (ISBN 0-03-014916-9). HR&W.
Baldwin, Gordon C. The Apache Indians: Raiders of the Southwest. LC 77-21439. (Illus.). 240p. (gr. 7 up). 1978. 9.95 (ISBN 0-590-07321-4, Four Winds). Schol Bk Serv.
--How the Indians Really Lived. (Science Survey Ser.). (Illus.). (gr. 5-9). 1967. 5.49 o.p. (ISBN 0-399-60268-2). Berkley Pub.

--Inventors & Inventions of the Ancient World. LC 73-76461. (Illus.). 256p. (gr. 7-11). 1973. 7.95 (ISBN 0-590-07164-5, Four Winds). Schol Bk Serv.

Baldwin, Hanson W. The Crucial Years: Nineteen Thirty-Nine to Nineteen Forty-One. LC 74-15808. (Illus.). 516p. 1976. 20.00 o.s.i. (ISBN 0-06-010186-5, HarpT). Har-Row.

Baldwin, Helen G., tr. see Binet, Alfred.

Baldwin, Henry. A General View of the Origin & Nature of the Constitution & Government of the United States. LC 72-118027. (American Constitutional & Legal History Ser). 1970. Repr. of 1837 ed. lib. bdg. 22.50 (ISBN 0-306-71944-4). Da Capo.

Baldwin, Horace S. Our Host the World. LC 78-66223. 1980. 6.95 (ISBN 0-533-04152-X). Vantage.

Baldwin, J. Story of Roland. (Illustrated Classic). (Illus.). (gr. 7 up). 1930. 12.50 o.p. (ISBN 0-684-20731-1, ScribT). Scribner.

--Story of Siegfried. (Illustrated Classic). (Illus.). (gr. 9 up). 1931. 12.50 o.p. (ISBN 0-684-20732-X, ScribT). Scribner.

Baldwin, James. Just Above My Head. 1980. pap. 3.50 (ISBN 0-440-14777-8). Dell.

Baldwin, James F. King's Council in England During the Middle Ages. 1913. 19.95x (ISBN 0-19-821394-8). Oxford U Pr.

Baldwin, Janice I., jt. auth. see Baldwin, John D.

Baldwin, John & McConville, Michael J. Negotiated Justice: Pressure to Plead Guilty. (Law in Society Ser.). 128p. 1977. 19.00x (ISBN 0-85520-171-1, Pub. by Martin Robertson England). Biblio Dist.

Baldwin, John & Bottomley, A. Keith, eds. Criminal Justice: Selected Readings. 311p. 1978. 36.00x (ISBN 0-85520-234-3, Pub by Martin Robertson England); pap. 12.50x (ISBN 0-85520-233-5). Biblio Dist.

Baldwin, John D. & Baldwin, Janice I. Behavior Principles in Everyday Life. (Illus.). 336p. 1981. text ed. 14.95 (ISBN 0-13-072751-2). P-H.

Baldwin, John W. The Scholastic Culture of the Middle Ages: 1000-1300. LC 70-120060. (Civilization & Society Ser). 192p. 1971. pap. 5.95x (ISBN 0-669-62059-9). Heath.

Baldwin, Joseph. Flush Times of Alabama & Mississippi. 1959. 7.50 (ISBN 0-8446-1589-7). Peter Smith.

Baldwin, Leland D. The Keelboat Age on Western Waters. LC 41-10342. (Illus.). x, 264p. 1980. pap. 5.95 (ISBN 0-8229-5319-6). U of Pittsburgh Pr.

--Reframing the Constitution: An Imperative for Modern America. LC 78-187927. (Illus.). 145p. 1972. text ed. 16.50 (ISBN 0-87436-082-X); pap. text ed. 2.50 (ISBN 0-87436-083-8). ABC-Clio.

Baldwin Library of Childrens Literature, Universityof Florida, Gainesville. Index to Children's Literature in English Before 1900: Catalog of the Baldwin Library of the University of Florida at Gainesville. (Library Catalogs Supplements). 1981. lib. bdg. 325.00 (ISBN 0-686-69555-0). G K Hall.

Baldwin, Linda & Pierce, Ruth. Mobile Intensive Care: A Problem Oriented Approach. LC 78-18240. (Illus.). 1978. pap. 12.95 (ISBN 0-8016-0428-1). Mosby.

Baldwin, Lindley. March of Faith: Samuel Morris. 1969. pap. 1.95 (ISBN 0-87123-360-6, 200360). Bethany Fell.

Baldwin, Marshall W., ed. Christianity Through the Thirteenth Century. 15.00x o.s.i (ISBN 0-8027-2003-X). Walker & Co.

Baldwin, Marshall W. see Setton, Kenneth M.

Baldwin, Nick. Trucks of the Sixties & Seventies. (Warne's Transport Library). (Illus.). 1980. 10.95 (ISBN 0-7232-2364-5). Warne.

Baldwin, Nick, ed. Vintage Lorry Annual. (Illus.). 96p. 1979. 16.50x (ISBN 0-906116-07-4). Intl Pubns Serv.

Baldwin, Norman F., jt. ed. see Seligman, Milton.

Baldwin, Orrel. Makers of American History. rev. ed. (Illus.). 480p. (gr. 4-6). 1979. text ed. 8.19 (ISBN 0-8372-3692-4); tchrs' guide 2.40 (ISBN 0-686-60060-6). Bowmar-Noble.

Baldwin, R. L., ed. Animals, Feed, Food & People: An Analysis of the Role of Animals in Food Production. (AAAS Selected Symposium: No. 42). 150p. 1980. lib. bdg. 16.00x (ISBN 0-89158-779-9). Westview.

Baldwin, R. W., ed. Secondary Spread of Cancer. 1978. 35.00 (ISBN 0-12-076850-X). Acad Pr.

Baldwin, Rebecca. A Gentleman from Philadelphia. 1978. pap. 1.50 o.p. (ISBN 0-449-23559-9, Crest). Fawcett.

Baldwin, Robert E. Multilateral Trade Negotiations: Toward Greater Liberalization? 1979. pap. 3.75 (ISBN 0-8447-1082-2). Am Enterprise.

--Nontariff Distortions of International Trade. 1970. 12.95 (ISBN 0-8157-0786-X). Brookings.

Baldwin, Sally, jt. ed. see Brown, Muriel.

Baldwin, Stanley C. What Did Jesus Say About That? 156p. 1975. pap. 3.50 (ISBN 0-88207-718-X). Victor Bks.

Baldwin, Stanley C., jt. auth. see Cook, Jerry.

Baldwin, Stanley C., jt. auth. see MacGregor, Malcolm.

Baldwin, Stanley C., jt. auth. see Mallory, James D.

Baldwin, T. W. On Act & Scene Division in the Shakespere First Folio. LC 64-20255. 190p. 1965. 6.50x (ISBN 0-8093-0153-9). S Ill U Pr.

--Shakespeare's "Love's Labor's Won". LC 56-9515. 54p. 1957. 5.00x (ISBN 0-8093-0010-9). S Ill U Pr.

Baldwin, Victor, jt. auth. see Fredericks, H. D.

Baldwin, Victor L., et al. Isn't It Time He Outgrew This? or A Training Program for Parents of Retarded Children. (Illus.). 230p. 1980. 13.50 (ISBN 0-398-02636-X). C C Thomas.

Baldwin, William. Treatise of Morall Philosophie. rev. ed. LC 67-10126. 1967. Repr. of 1620 ed. 41.00 (ISBN 0-8201-1003-5). Schol Facsimiles.

Baldwin, Woodrow W. & O'Neill, John T., eds. Readings in Business. LC 74-12552. (Illus.). 99p. 1973. pap. text ed. 6.20 (ISBN 0-913310-17-4). PAR Inc.

Baldwinson, John. Plonk & Super-Plonk. 1975. 7.95 o.p. (ISBN 0-7181-1407-8, Pub. by Michael Joseph). Merrimack Bk Serv.

Bale, Don, Jr. Fabulous Investment Potential of Singles. 4th, rev. ed. 1980. pap. 5.00. Bale Bks.

--The Fabulous Investment Potential of Liberty Walking Half Dollars. rev. 3rd ed. 1975. pap. 5.00 o.p. (ISBN 0-912070-05-6). Bale Bks.

--The Fabulous Investment Potential of Singles. rev. 3rd ed. 1975. pap. 5.00 o.p. (ISBN 0-912070-13-7). Bale Bks.

--Fabulous Investment Potential of Uncirculated Singles. 4th, rev. ed. 1980. pap. 5.00. Bale Bks.

--The Fabulous Investment Potential of Uncirculated Singles. rev. 3rd ed. 1975. pap. 5.00 o.p. (ISBN 0-912070-11-0). Bale Bks.

--Gold Mine in Gold. 4th, rev. ed. 1980. pap. 5.00. Bale Bks.

--A Gold Mine in Gold. rev. 3rd ed. 1975. pap. 5.00 o.p. (ISBN 0-912070-12-9). Bale Bks.

--Gold Mine in Your Pocket. 4th, rev. ed. 1980. pap. 5.00. Bale Bks.

--A Gold Mine in Your Pocket. rev. 3rd ed. 1975. pap. 5.00 o.p. (ISBN 0-912070-07-2). Bale Bks.

--How to Find Valuable Old & Scarce Coins. 4th, rev. ed. 1980. pap. 5.00. Bale Bks.

--How to Find Valuable Old & Scarce Coins. 3rd ed. 1973. pap. 5.00 o.p. (ISBN 0-912070-15-3). Bale Bks.

--How to Invest in Singles. 4th, rev. ed. 1980. pap. 5.00. Bale Bks.

--How to Invest in Singles. rev. 3rd ed. 1975. pap. 5.00 o.p. (ISBN 0-912070-09-9). Bale Bks.

--How to Invest in Uncirculated Singles. 4th, rev. ed. 1980. pap. 5.00. Bale Bks.

--How to Invest in Uncirculated Singles. rev. 3rd ed. 1975. pap. 5.00 o.p. (ISBN 0-912070-10-2). Bale Bks.

--Out of Little Coins, Big Fortunes Grow. 4th, rev. ed. 1980. pap. 5.00. Bale Bks.

--Out of Little Coins, Big Fortunes Grow. rev. 3rd ed. 1975. pap. 5.00 o.p. (ISBN 0-912070-08-0). Bale Bks.

Bale, Don, Jr., ed. Fabulous Investment Potential of Liberty Walking Half Dollars. 4th, rev. ed. 1980. pap. 5.00. Bale Bks.

Bale, John. The First Two Partes of the Acts or Unchaste Examples of the Englyshe Votaryes. LC 79-84086. (English Experience Ser.: No. 906). 540p. 1979. Repr. of 1560 ed. lib. bdg. 40.00 (ISBN 90-221-0906-2). Walter J Johnson.

--The Image of Bothe Curhces, After the Moste Wonderfull & Heavenly Revelation of Sainct John the Evangelist. LC 72-5965. (English Experience Ser.: No. 498). 872p. 1973. Repr. of 1548 ed. 51.00 (ISBN 90-221-0498-2). Walter J Johnson.

Bales. Christ: The Fulfillment of the Law & Prophets. pap. 3.95 (ISBN 0-89315-009-6). Lambert Bk.

Bales, James. Communism Killed Kennedy but Did America Learn? 3.95 (ISBN 0-89315-015-0). Lambert Bk.

Bales, James D. The Cross & the Church. pap. 1.95 (ISBN 0-89315-011-8). Lambert Bk.

--The Deacon & His Work. pap. 1.95 (ISBN 0-89315-025-8). Lambert Bk.

--The Finality of Faith. pap. 2.50 (ISBN 0-89315-051-7). Lambert Bk.

--The Holy Spirit & the Christian. 3.75 o.p. (ISBN 0-89315-102-5); pap. 3.50 (ISBN 0-89315-103-3). Lambert Bk.

--Soils & Seeds of Sectarianism. 1977. pap. 4.50 (ISBN 0-89315-264-1). Lambert Bk.

--The Sower Goes Forth. 4.50 (ISBN 0-89315-259-5). Lambert Bk.

--Studies in Hebrews. pap. 3.50 (ISBN 0-89315-260-9). Lambert Bk.

--What Think Ye of Christ's Church? pap. 0.50 o.p. (ISBN 0-89315-353-2). Lambert Bk.

Bales, Peter. The Art of Brachygraphie: That Is, to Write As Fast As a Man Speaketh Treatably, Writing but One Letter for a Word. LC 70-38146. (English Experience Ser.: No. 426). 120p. 1972. Repr. of 1597 ed. 11.50 (ISBN 90-221-0426-5). Walter J Johnson.

--The Writing Schoolemaster: Brachygraphie, Orthographie, Calygraphie. LC 70-26226. (English Experience Ser.: No. 194). 122p. 1969. Repr. of 1590 ed. 16.00 (ISBN 90-221-0194-0). Walter J Johnson.

Bales, Robert F., et al, eds. Small Groups: Studies in Social Interaction. rev ed. 1965. 14.95 o.p. (ISBN 0-394-30227-3). Knopf.

Balestra, Pietro. Demand for Natural Gas in the United States. (Contributions to Economic Analysis Ser.: No. 46). 1967. text ed. 16.50x (ISBN 0-7204-3142-5, Pub. by North Holland). Humanities.

Balestrino, Philip. Hot As an Ice Cube. LC 70-139092. (A Let's-Read-&-Find-Out Science Bk). (Illus.). (gr. k-3). 1971. PLB 7.89 (ISBN 0-690-40415-8, TYC-J). T Y Crowell.

--Skeleton Inside You. LC 72-132290. (A Let's-Read-and-Find-Out Science Bk). (Illus.). (gr. k-3). 1971. PLB 7.89 (ISBN 0-690-74123-5, TYC-J); filmstrip with cassette 14.95 (ISBN 0-690-74126-X); filmstrip with record 11.95 (ISBN 0-690-74124-3). T Y Crowell.

Balet, Jan. Joanjo, a Portuguese Tale. LC 67-10705. (Illus.). (ps-2). 1967. 4.95 (ISBN 0-440-04236-4, Sey Lawr); PLB 4.58 o.s.i. (ISBN 0-440-04233-X, Sey Lawr). Delacorte.

Baley, James A. & Field, David A. Physical Education & the Physical Educator. 2nd ed. 400p. 1976. text ed. 17.95x (ISBN 0-205-05052-2, 6250521). Allyn.

Baley, John, et al. Algebra: A First Course. 432p. 1979. pap. text ed. 15.95x (ISBN 0-534-00727-9). Wadsworth Pub.

Baley, John D., et al. Basic Mathematics: A Program for Semi-Independent Study. 1978. pap. text ed. 13.95x (ISBN 0-669-01019-7); inst. resource bk. free (ISBN 0-669-01020-0); Set. cassette 125.00 (ISBN 0-669-01165-7); free tapescript (ISBN 0-669-01022-7). Heath.

Balfour, A. & Beveridge, W. T. Basic Numerical Analysis with FORTRAN. 1977. text ed. 12.25 o.p. (ISBN 0-686-67891-5); pap. text ed. 9.95x (ISBN 0-435-77484-0). Heinemann Ed.

Balfour, Campbell. Incomes Policy & the Public Sector. 1972. 22.00x (ISBN 0-7100-7306-2). Routledge & Kegan.

Balfour, Edward G. Cyclopaedia of India & of Eastern & Southern Asia: Commercial, Industrial & Scientific; Products of Mineral, Vegetable & Animal Kingdoms, Useful Arts & Manufactures, 3 vols. 3rd ed. LC 5-12913. 3632p. 1968. Repr. of 1885 ed. Set. 387.50x (ISBN 3-201-00028-0). Intl Pubns Serv.

Balfour, John. The Armoured Train. (Illus.). 168p. 1981. 25.50 (ISBN 0-7134-2547-4, Pub. by Batsford England). David & Charles.

Balfour, Michael. The Adversaries: America, Russia and the Open World 1941-1962. 224p. 1981. price not set (ISBN 0-7100-0687-X). Routledge & Kegan.

Balfour, Neil & Mackay, Sally. Paul of Yugoslavia. (Illus.). 364p. 1980. 45.00 (ISBN 0-241-10392-4, Pub. by Hamish Hamilton England). David & Charles.

Balian, Lorna. Humbug Witch. (Illus.). (gr. k-2). 1965. 7.95 (ISBN 0-687-18023-6). Abingdon.

--Leprechauns Never Lie. LC 79-25950. (Illus.). 32p. (gr. k-3). 1980. PLB 7.95g (ISBN 0-687-21371-1). Abingdon.

Balin, Peter. Xultun Tarot. 2nd ed. (Illus., Orig.). 1981. 12.00 (ISBN 0-914794-33-7). Wisdom Garden.

Balinsky, Benjamin. Improving Personnel Selection Through Effective Interviewing: Essentials for Management. LC 77-94944. (Orig.). 1979. true bindery 8.13 (ISBN 0-935198-04-0); pap. 7.74 saddle stitch (ISBN 0-935198-05-9). M M Bruce.

Balint, Michael, ed. see Ferenczi, Sandor.

Balio, Tino. United Artists: The Company Built by the Stars. LC 75-12208. (Illus.). 304p. 1976. 22.50x (ISBN 0-299-06940-0); pap. 7.95 (ISBN 0-299-06944-3). U of Wis Pr.

Balio, Tino, ed. The American Film Industry. LC 75-32070. (Illus.). 1976. 25.00 (ISBN 0-299-07000-X); pap. 8.95 (ISBN 0-299-07004-2). U of Wis Pr.

--The Jazz Singer. LC 78-53295. (Screenplay Ser.). (Illus.). 1979. 15.00 (ISBN 0-299-07660-1); pap. 5.95 (ISBN 0-299-07664-4). U of Wis Pr.

--Mystery of the Wax Museum. LC 78-53296. (Wisconsin-Warner Bros. Screenplay Ser.). (Illus.). 1979. 15.00 (ISBN 0-299-07670-9); pap. 5.95 (ISBN 0-299-07674-1). U of Wis Pr.

--Treasure of Sierra Madre. LC 78-53298. (Screenplay Ser.). (Illus.). 1979. 15.00 (ISBN 0-299-07680-6); pap. 5.95 (ISBN 0-299-07684-9). U of Wis Pr.

Baliozian, Ara, tr. see Zarian, Gostan.

Balis, George, et al, eds. Psychiatric Foundations of Medicine, 6 vols. (Illus.). 1978. text ed. 200.00x set (ISBN 0-409-95160-9). Butterworths.

Balizet, Carol. The Seven Last Years. 368p. 1980. pap. 2.75 (ISBN 0-553-14136-8). Bantam.

Balje, O. E. Turbomechanics: A Guide to Design, Selection & Theory. LC 80-21524. 525p. 1981. 35.00 (ISBN 0-471-06036-4, Pub. by Wiley-Interscience). Wiley.

Baljeu, Joost. Theodore Van Doesburg. LC 74-7400. (Illus.). 208p. 1975. 15.95 o.s.i. (ISBN 0-02-506440-1, 50644). Macmillan.

Baljian-Gara, N. R. Sonic Scotia. 53p. 1980. 3.50 (ISBN 0-8059-2751-4). Dorrance.

Balkan, Sheila & Berger, Ronald. Crime & Deviance in America. 416p. 1980. pap. text ed. 12.95x (ISBN 0-534-00803-8). Wadsworth Pub.

Balkanski, M., jt. auth. see International Conference on Light Scattering in Solids, 3rd.

Balkin, Richard. Writer's Guide to Book Publishing. rev. ed. 288p. 1981. 15.95 (ISBN 0-8015-8925-8, Hawthorn); pap. 8.95 (ISBN 0-8015-8926-6, Hawthorn). Dutton.

--A Writer's Guide to Book Publishing. 1977. 9.95 o.p. (ISBN 0-8015-8935-5); pap. 4.95 o.p. (ISBN 0-8015-8936-3). Dutton.

Ball. Light Construction Techniques: From Foundation to Finish. (Illus.). 416p. 1980. ref. ed. 24.95; text ed. 17.95 (ISBN 0-8359-4035-7). Reston.

Ball, jt. auth. see McDonnell.

Ball, Adrian. SS Great Britain. LC 80-68903. (Illus.). 96p. 1981. 22.50 o.p. (ISBN 0-7153-8096-6); pap. 14.50 o.p. (ISBN 0-7153-8089-3). David & Charles.

Ball, Allan P. Seneca's Apocolocyntosis, New York, Nineteen Hundred & Two. Commager, Steele, ed. LC 77-70769. (Latin Poetry Ser.). 1979. lib. bdg. 27.50 (ISBN 0-8240-2951-8). Garland Pub.

Ball, Barbara. Coffee Talk: Sharing Christ Through Friendly Gatherings. 80p. 1980. pap. 3.50 (ISBN 0-934396-08-6). Churches Alive.

Ball, Baron V. Alpha Backgammon. LC 80-19226. (Illus.). 1980. pap. 5.95 (ISBN 0-688-08714-0, Quill). Morrow.

Ball, Brian. Death of a Low Handicap Man. 1978. 8.95 o.s.i. (ISBN 0-8027-5403-1). Walker & Co.

--Montenegrin Gold. 1978. 7.95 o.s.i. (ISBN 0-8027-5384-1). Walker & Co.

Ball, C. J. Introduction to the Theory of Diffraction. 1971. text ed. 25.00 (ISBN 0-08-015787-4); pap. text ed. 12.75 (ISBN 0-08-015786-6). Pergamon.

Ball, Derek S. An Introduction to Real Analysis. LC 72-84200. (Mathematical Topics). (Illus.). 324p. 1973. text ed. 23.00 o.p. (ISBN 0-08-016936-8); pap. text ed. 9.90 o.p. (ISBN 0-08-016937-6). Pergamon.

Ball, Desmond J. Politics & Force Levels: The Strategic Missile Program of the Kennedy Administration. 400p. 1981. 27.50x (ISBN 0-520-03698-0). U of Cal Pr.

Ball, Don, Jr. & Whitaker, Rogers E. M. Decade of the Trains: The 1940s. LC 75-37282. (Illus.). 1977. 24.95 (ISBN 0-8212-0706-7, 178853); pap. 12.95 (ISBN 0-8212-0759-8, 178861). NYGS.

Ball, Donald W. Microecology: Social Situations & Intimate Space. LC 72-10541. (Studies in Sociology Ser). 40p. 1973. pap. text ed. 2.50 (ISBN 0-672-61209-7). Bobbs.

Ball, Donald W. & Loy, John W. Sport & the Social Order: Contributions to the Sociology of Sport. LC 74-30694. 592p. 1975. text ed. 19.95 (ISBN 0-201-00408-9). A-W.

Ball, Dorothy W. Dream for Sale. (YA) 1969. 4.95 o.p. (ISBN 0-685-07430-7, Avalon). Bouregy.

Ball, Douglas & Turner, Dan S. This Fascinating Oil Business. LC 64-15660. 1965. 15.95 (ISBN 0-672-50829-X). Bobbs.

Ball, Edith L. & Cipriano, Robert E. Leisure Services Preparation: A Competency Based Approach. (Illus.). 1978. ref. ed. 16.95 (ISBN 0-13-528273-X). P-H.

Ball, Eve. Ma'am Jones of the Pecos. LC 68-9336. (Illus.). 1969. pap. 7.50 (ISBN 0-8165-0404-0). U of Ariz Pr.

Ball, Eve, jt. auth. see Crosby, Thelma.

Ball, F. Carlton. Decorating Pottery. 3.95 (ISBN 0-934706-05-0). Prof Pubns Ohio.

Ball, Frances. The Development of Reading Skills: A Book of Resources for Teachers. 1977. 18.00x (ISBN 0-631-17660-8, Pub. by Basil Blackwell); pap. 9.50x (ISBN 0-631-18290-X, Pub. by Basil Blackwell). Biblio Dist.

Ball, Geraldine. Having Good Feelings in the Magic Circle at School: A Human Development Program Book. (Illus.). 1972. pap. 0.40 (ISBN 0-86584-015-6); pap. 3.95 set of 10 (ISBN 0-86584-015-6). Human Dev Train.

--Innerchange Career Education Resource Set for Senior High. 1977. 95.00 (ISBN 0-86584-022-9). Human Dev Train.

--Innerchange Career Educational Resource Set for Junior High. 1977. 95.00 (ISBN 0-86584-027-X). Human Dev Train.

--Innerchange Conflict Mgt. Resources Set for Sr. High. 95.00 (ISBN 0-86584-023-7). Human Dev Train.

--Innerchange Drug Abuse Prevention Resource Set for Jr. High. 95.00 (ISBN 0-86584-029-6). Human Dev Train.

--Innerchange Experiences: Reproducible Masters for Senior High. 1977. 24.95 (ISBN 0-86584-018-0). Human Dev Train.

--Innerchange for Junior High. 1977. 175.00 (ISBN 0-86584-021-0). Human Dev Train.

--Innerchange for Senior High. 1977. 175.00 (ISBN 0-86584-020-2). Human Dev Train.

--Innerchange Language Arts Resource Ser for Junior High. 1977. 95.00 (ISBN 0-86584-031-8). Human Dev Train.

--Innerchange Language Arts Resource Set for Senior High. 1977. 95.00 (ISBN 0-86584-026-1). Human Dev Train.

--Innerchange Leader's Manual. 1977. 12.95 (ISBN 0-86584-017-2). Human Dev Train.

--Magic Circle: An Overview of the Human Development Program. 1974. 4.95 (ISBN 0-86584-007-5). Human Dev Train.

Ball, Geraldine, jt. auth. see Bessell, Harold.

Ball, Gerry. Circle of Warmth: Family Program. 1980. 34.95 (ISBN 0-86584-040-7). Human Dev Train.

--Grounds for Growth: Comprehensive Theory Manual. 1980. 14.95 (ISBN 0-86584-009-1). Human Dev Train.

Ball, Gerry, jt. auth. see Palomares, Uvaldo.

Ball, Howard. Constitutional Powers: Cases on the Separation of Powers & Federalism. LC 80-12820. 371p. 1980. pap. text ed. 11.95 (ISBN 0-8299-2090-0). West Pub.

--No Pledge of Privacy: The Watergate Tapes Litigation, 1973-1974. (National University Pubns. Multi-Disciplinary Studies in the Law). 1977. 15.00 (ISBN 0-8046-9181-9). Kennikat.

Ball, J. Dyer. Things Chinese: Or Notes Connected with China. rev. 5th ed. Werner, Chalmers, ed. LC 74-164085. (Tower Bks). 1971. Repr. of 1926 ed. 32.00 (ISBN 0-8103-3917-X). Gale.

Ball, J. N., jt. auth. see Holmes, R. L.

Ball, John. Miss One Thousand Spring Blossoms. 1979. pap. 1.95 (ISBN 0-380-42325-1, 42325). Avon.

--Rescue Mission. LC 66-13854. 1966. 8.95 o.s.i. (ISBN 0-06-010196-2, HarpT). Har-Row.

--Trouble for Tallon. LC 80-1983. (Crime Club Ser.). 192p. 1981. 9.95 (ISBN 0-385-17329-6). Doubleday.

Ball, John, jt. auth. see McDonnell, Leo.

Ball, John, ed. Cop Cade. LC 78-7750. 1978. 7.95 o.p. (ISBN 0-385-14374-5). Doubleday.

--From Beowulf to Modern British Writers. 3rd ed. 1959. 18.95 (ISBN 0-672-63168-7). Odyssey Pr.

Ball, John E. Architectural Drafting Fundamentals. (Illus.). 336p. 1980. text ed. 13.95 (ISBN 0-8359-0254-4). Reston.

--Carpenters & Builders Library. LC 76-24079. 1977. 35.95 set (ISBN 0-672-23244-8); 9.95 ea. Vol. 1 (ISBN 0-672-23240-5). Vol. 2 (ISBN 0-672-23241-3). Vol. 3 (ISBN 0-672-23242-1). Vol. 4 (ISBN 0-672-23243-X). Audel.

--Exterior & Interior Trim. LC 75-6060. 264p. 1975. pap. 8.60 (ISBN 0-8273-1120-6); instructor's guide 1.60 (ISBN 0-8273-1121-4). Delmar.

--Practical Problems in Mathematics for Masons. LC 78-74431. (Mathematics - Construction Ser.). 112p. 1980. 5.00 (ISBN 0-8273-1283-0); instructor's guide 2.00 (ISBN 0-8273-1284-9). Delmar.

Ball, John N., jt. auth. see Pearson, Ronald.

Ball, Kenneth R., jt. auth. see Willcutt, J. Robert.

Ball, Max W., et al. This Fascinating Oil Business. LC 64-15660. (Illus.). 1979. pap. 10.95 (ISBN 0-672-52584-4). Bobbs.

Ball, Nicole. World Hunger: A Guide to the Economic & Political Dimensions. Burns, Richard D., ed. (War-Peace Bibliography Ser.: No. 15). (Illus.). 1981. lib. bdg. price not set (ISBN 0-87436-308-X). ABC-Clio.

Ball, Patricia M. The Central Self: A Study in Romantic & Victorian Imagination. 1968. text ed. 23.50x (ISBN 0-485-11102-0, Athlone Pr). Humanities.

--The Heart's Events: The Victorian Poetry of Relationships. 240p. 1976. text ed. 21.50x (ISBN 0-485-11163-2, Athlone Pr). Humanities.

Ball, Robert H. Shakespeare on Silent Film. LC 68-14014. (Illus.). 1968. 3.10 (ISBN 0-87830-116-X). Theatre Arts.

Ball, Robert H., jt. auth. see Bowman, Walter P.

Ball, Robert M. Social Security: Today & Tomorrow. LC 77-13713. 1978. 19.00 (ISBN 0-231-04254-X). Columbia U Pr.

Ball, Robert W. & Radford, K. W. Laboratory Studies in General Biology. rev. ed. 1981. pap. 8.95 (ISBN 0-917962-66-4). Peek Pubns.

Ball, Samuel. An Account of the Cultivation & Manufacture of Tea in China. LC 78-74309. (The Modern Chinese Economy Ser.). 382p. 1980. lib. bdg. 38.00 (ISBN 0-8240-4250-6). Garland Pub.

Ball, Thomas. My Threescore Years & Ten. 2nd ed. LC 75-28884. (Art Experience in Late 19th Century America Ser.: Vol. 18). (Illus.). 1976. Repr. of 1892 ed. lib. bdg. 37.00 (ISBN 0-8240-2242-4). Garland Pub.

Ball, Thomas S. Itard, Sequin & Kephart: Sensory Education, a Learning Interpretation. LC 70-154658. 1971. text ed. 7.95x (ISBN 0-675-09191-8). Merrill.

Ball, V. K. Architecture & Interior Design: A Basic History of the Eighteenth Through Twentieth Centuries, 2 vol. set. 1980. Set. 80.00 (ISBN 0-471-08721-1, Pub. by Wiley-Interscience); Set. pap. 50.00 (ISBN 0-471-08720-3); pap. 27.50 (ISBN 0-471-08722-X). Wiley.

--Architecture & Interior Design: A Basic History of the Eighteenth Through Twentieth Centuries. 464p. 1980. pap. 27.50 (ISBN 0-471-08722-X, Pub. by Wiley-Interscience). Wiley.

Ball, Victoria K. Architecture & Interior Design: A Basic History Through the Seventeenth Century. LC 79-21371. 1980. 45.00 (ISBN 0-471-05162-4, Pub. by Wiley-Interscience); pap. 27.50 (ISBN 0-471-08719-X). Wiley.

--Architecture & Interior Design: Europe & America from the Colonial Era to Today. LC 79-24851. 1980. 45.00 (ISBN 0-471-05161-6, Pub. by Wiley-Interscience); pap. 27.50 (ISBN 0-471-08722-X). Wiley.

Ball, W. R; see Ball, W. Rouse, et al.

Ball, W. Rouse. Mathematical Recreations & Essays. rev. ed. 1960. 12.95 (ISBN 0-02-506430-4); pap. 1.95 (ISBN 0-02-091480-6). Macmillan.

Ball, W. Rouse, et al, eds. String Figures & Other Monographs, 4 vols. in 1. Incl. String Figures. Ball, W. R; History of the Slide Rule. Cajori, F; Non Euclidean Geometry. Carslaw, Horatio S; Methods Geometrical Construction. Petersen, Julius. LC 59-11780. 12.95 (ISBN 0-8284-0130-6). Chelsea Pub.

Ball, W. W. A Short Account of the History of Mathematics. LC 60-3187. 1960. lib. bdg. 13.50x (ISBN 0-88307-009-X). Gannon.

Ball, Walter W. & Coxeter, H. S. Mathematical Recreations & Essays. 12th ed. LC 72-186276. 446p. 1974. pap. 6.00 (ISBN 0-8020-6138-9). U of Toronto Pr.

Ball, Zachary. Bristle Face. (Illus.). 206p. (gr. 5 up). 1962. 8.95 (ISBN 0-8234-0013-1). Holiday.

--Kep. 208p. (gr. 7-9). 1961. 4.95 o.p. (ISBN 0-8234-0064-6). Holiday.

Ballabh, R. Hydrodynamic Superposability. pap. 3.75x o.p. (ISBN 0-210-26873-5). Asia.

Ballabon, M. B., ed. Economic Perspectives: An Annual Survey of Economics, Vol. 2. 300p. 1980. lib. bdg. 45.00 (ISBN 0-470-26662-7). Harwood Academic.

Ballagh, James C., ed. The Letters of Richard Henry Lee, 2 Vols. LC 79-107678. (Era of the American Revolution Ser). 1970. Repr. of 1914 ed. 85.00 (ISBN 0-306-71894-4). Da Capo.

Ballan, Lorna. Where in the World Is Henry? LC 79-10391. (Illus.). (gr. k-11). 1980. Repr. 5.95g (ISBN 0-687-45092-6). Abingdon.

Ballance, P. F. & Reading, H. G., eds. Sedimentation of Oblique-Slip Mobile Zones. (International Association of Sedimentologists & the Societ As Internationalis Limnological Symposium). 265p. 1980. pap. 37.50x (ISBN 0-470-26927-8). Halsted Pr.

Ballantine, Betty. Frazetta Four. 96p. 1980. pap. 8.95 (ISBN 0-553-01267-3). Bantam.

Ballantine, Jeanne H., jt. auth. see Cargan, Leonard.

Ballantine, William. Piano: An Introduction to the Instrument. LC 79-114926. (Keynote Bks). (Illus.). (gr. 7 up). 1971. PLB 4.90 o.p. (ISBN 0-531-01843-1). Watts.

--Violin: An Introduction to the Instrument. LC 75-115772. (Keynote Bks). (Illus.). (gr. 7 up). 1971. PLB 4.90 o.p. (ISBN 0-531-01845-8). Watts.

Ballantyne, J. Ear. Rob & Smith, eds. (Operative Surgery Ser). 1976. text ed. 45.00 (ISBN 0-407-00097-6). Butterworths.

Ballantyne, John & Groves, John, eds. Scott Brown's Diseases of the Ear, Nose, & Throat. 4th ed. Incl. Vol. 1. Ear, Nose & Throat Diseases. 115.00 (ISBN 0-407-00147-6); Vol. 2. The Ear. 145.00 (ISBN 0-407-00148-4); Vol. 3. The Nose. 69.95 (ISBN 0-407-00149-2); Vol. 4. The Throat. 99.95 (ISBN 0-407-00150-6). LC 79-41008. (Illus.). 1979. Set. text ed. 400.00 (ISBN 0-407-00143-3). Butterworths.

Ballantyne, R. M. The Dog Crusoe. (Childrens Illustrated Classics Ser). (Illus.). 1972. Repr. of 1966 ed. 9.00x o.p. (ISBN 0-460-05070-2, Pub. by J. M. Dent England). Biblio Dist.

Ballantyne, Robert. The Coral Island. Lurie, Alison & Schiller, Justin G., eds. LC 75-32167. (Classics of Children's Literature Ser.: 1621-1932). PLB 38.00 (ISBN 0-8240-2280-7). Garland Pub.

Ballard. Gold Tried in the Fire. pap. 3.00 (ISBN 0-686-12401-4). Church History.

Ballard, Adolphus, ed. British Borough Charters,1042-1216. LC 80-2236. 1981. Repr. of 1913 ed. 49.50 (ISBN 0-404-18750-1). AMS Pr.

Ballard, Dorothy. Horseback Honeymoon. LC 75-15042. 1975. 8.95 (ISBN 0-89430-021-0). Morgan-Pacific.

Ballard, Edward B., et al, eds. A Technical Glossary of Horticultural & Landscape Terminology. LC 78-165521. 1971. 9.95 (ISBN 0-686-26652-8); text ed. 9.95 (ISBN 0-686-26653-6); tchrs' ed. 6.00 (ISBN 0-686-26654-4). Horticult Research.

Ballard, F., et al, eds. Press Toolmaking. 2nd ed. (Engineering Craftsmen: No. H21). (Illus.). 1972. spiral bdg. 16.50x (ISBN 0-85083-168-7). Intl Ideas.

Ballard, G. A. The Black Battlefleet. 264p. 1980. 66.00x (ISBN 0-245-53030-4, Pub. by Nautical England). State Mutual Bk.

--The Black Battlefleet: Early Ironclads of the Royal Navy. LC 79-49435. (Illus.). 245p. 1980. 38.95 (ISBN 0-87021-924-3). Naval Inst Pr.

--The Influence of the Sea on the Political History of Japan. 312p. 1972. Repr. of 1921 ed. 25.00x (ISBN 0-7165-2048-6, Pub. by Irish Academic Pr Ireland). Biblio Dist.

Ballard, J. G. Chronopolis. 1979. pap. 2.25 (ISBN 0-425-04191-3). Berkley Pub.

--Crash. 1973. 6.95 o.p. (ISBN 0-374-13072-8). FS&G.

--High Rise. 1978. pap. 1.95 o.p. (ISBN 0-445-04181-1). Popular Lib.

--High-Rise. LC 76-29899. 1977. 6.95 o.p. (ISBN 0-03-020651-0). HR&W.

Ballard, Jan. If Young Adult Is the Answer, What Is the Question? (Neal-Schuman Professional Bk.). Date not set. cancelled (ISBN 0-912700-14-9). Oryx Pr.

Ballard, Jim. Dibble & the Great Blob: A Parable for Children Over & Under 21. LC 75-25393. (Mandala Ser. in Education). 1975. pap. text ed. 2.50 (ISBN 0-916250-06-7). Irvington.

--Seeing Circle: A Parable for Children Over & Under 21. LC 75-25393. (Mandala Ser. in Education). 1975. pap. 2.50 (ISBN 0-916250-07-5). Irvington.

--Warm Snuggles & Cold Ouchies: A Parable for Children Over & Under 21. LC 75-25393. (Mandala Ser. in Education). 1975. pap. 2.50 (ISBN 0-916250-05-9). Irvington.

Ballard, Jim & Quinn, Brennan. Connection: Golf's Master Fundamental. LC 80-66691. (Illus.). 176p. (Orig.). 1981. 12.95 (ISBN 0-914178-38-5). Golf Digest.

Ballard, Jim, jt. auth. see Timmermann, Tim.

Ballard, Juliet B. The Hidden Laws of Earth. 241p. (Orig.). 1979. pap. 5.95 (ISBN 0-87604-117-9). ARE Pr.

--Treasures from Earth's Storehouse. 311p. (Orig.). 1980. pap. 7.95 (ISBN 0-87604-128-4). ARE Pr.

Ballard, L. S., jt. auth. see Warren, Thomas B.

Ballard, Lou E., jt. auth. see Levie, Robert C.

Ballard, Mignon F. Aunt Matilda's Ghost. (gr. 11 up). 1978. 5.95 o.s.i. (ISBN 0-87695-210-4); pap. 3.95 (ISBN 0-87695-211-2). Aurora Pubs.

Ballard, R. E. Photoelectron Spectroscopy & Molecular Orbital Theory. LC 78-40817. 1979. 57.95 (ISBN 0-470-26542-6). Halsted Pr.

Ballard, Todhunter. Fight or Die. Orig. Title: Westward the Monitors Roar. 1977. pap. 1.50 (ISBN 0-505-51184-3). Tower Bks.

Ballas, George C. & Hollas, Dave. The Making of an Entrepreneur: Keys to Your Success. (Illus.). 1980. 12.95 (ISBN 0-13-546788-8, Spec); pap. 6.95 (ISBN 0-13-546770-5). P-H.

Ballas, Samir K. Self-Assessment of Current Knowledge in Hematology, Part One: Textbook Review. 2nd ed. 1977. 15.00 (ISBN 0-87488-248-6). Med Exam.

Ballast, Daniel L. & Shoemaker, Ronald L. Coactive Guidance: A Blueprint for the Future. 200p. 1980. 19.95 (ISBN 0-398-04089-3). C C Thomas.

Ballbon, M. B., ed. Economic Perspectives: An Annual Survey of Economics, Vol. 1. 280p. 1979. 35.00 (ISBN 3-7186-0001-3). Harwood Academic.

Ballem, John. Sacrifice Play. 256p. 1981. pap. 2.25 (ISBN 0-449-14381-3, GM). Fawcett.

Ballenger, Dean W. Terror at Sea. (Orig.). 1981. pap. 2.50 (ISBN 0-451-09670-3, E9670, Sig). NAL.

Baller, Warren B. Bed-Wetting: Origins & Treatment. rev. ed. 300p. 1976. 21.00 (ISBN 0-08-017859-6). Pergamon.

Ballerini, Luigi. Che Figurato Muore. Milazzo, Richard, tr. from It. LC 78-58982. 1981. 7.95 (ISBN 0-915570-11-4). Oolp Pr.

Ballesteros, Antonio M. Tres Farsas Contemporaneas y un Secuestro. Maroto, Angel R. & Whitehead, Charles E., eds. (Orig.). (gr. 10-12). 1980. pap. text ed. 3.25x (ISBN 0-88334-125-5). Ind Sch Pr.

Ballesteros, Octavio A. Preparing Teachers for Bilingual Education: Basic Readings. LC 78-68567. 1979. pap. text ed. 9.50 (ISBN 0-8191-0695-X). U Pr of Amer.

Ballet, Arthur H., ed. Playwrights for Tomorrow: A Collection of Plays. Incl. Vol. 3. 1967. 7.95x (ISBN 0-8166-0430-4); Vol. 4. (Orig.). 1967. 7.95x (ISBN 0-8166-0432-0); Vol. 5. (Orig.). 1969. 5.50x (ISBN 0-8166-0534-3); Vol. 6. (Orig.). 1969. o.p. (ISBN 0-8166-0537-8); Vol. 7. 10.00x (ISBN 0-8166-0579-3); Vol. 8. 10.00x (ISBN 0-8166-0650-1); Vol. 9. 10.00x (ISBN 0-8166-0653-6); Vol. 10. 1973. 10.00x (ISBN 0-8166-0693-5); Vol. 11. 1973. 10.00x (ISBN 0-8166-0695-1). LC 66-19124. U of Minn Pr.

Balley, F. J. Introduction to Semiconductor Devices. 1972. pap. text ed. 9.50x o.p. (ISBN 0-04-621017-2). Allen Unwin.

Ballhatchet, K. & Harrison, J., eds. The City in South Asia. 1980. text ed. 15.75x (ISBN 0-391-01129-4). Humanities.

Balliett, G. Getting Started in Private Practice. 1978. 21.50 (ISBN 0-87489-134-5). Med Economics.

--How to Close a Medical Practice. 1978. 21.50 (ISBN 0-87489-142-6). Med Economics.

Balliett, Whitney. Night Creature: A Journal of Jazz, 1975-1980. (Illus.). 275p. 1981. 15.95 (ISBN 0-19-502908-9). Oxford U Pr.

--The Sound of Surprise. LC 77-17852. (Roots of Jazz Ser.). 1978. Repr. of 1961 ed. lib. bdg. 19.50 (ISBN 0-306-77543-3). Da Capo.

Ballin, Karen, tr. see Marosi, Esteban & Whidden, Angela.

Ballinger, R., ed. see Visigli, R.

Ballinger, Raymond A. Layout & Graphic Design. 96p. 1980. pap. 8.95 (ISBN 0-442-20178-8). Van Nos Reinhold.

Ballinger, Rex E., ed. see Usigli, Rodolfo.

Ballinger, Ronald G. The Anisotropic Mechanical Behavior of Zircalor-2. LC 78-74995. (Outstanding Dissertations on Energy Ser.). 1979. lib. bdg. 27.50 (ISBN 0-8240-3986-6). Garland Pub.

Ballinger, Walter F., ed. see American College of Surgeons.

Ballmer, T. & Brennenstuhl, W. Speech Art Classification. (Springer Series in Language & Communication: Vol. 8). (Illus.). 304p. 1981. 29.50 (ISBN 0-387-10294-9). Springer-Verlag.

Ballon, R. J., et al. Financial Reporting in Japan. LC 75-30179. (Illus.). 305p. 1976. 15.00x (ISBN 0-87011-269-4). Kodansha.

Ballon, Robert J., ed. Marketing in Japan. LC 73-79771. (Illus.). 200p. 1973. 14.50x (ISBN 0-87011-200-7). Kodansha.

Ballon, Robert J. & Lee, Eugene H., eds. Foreign Investment & Japan. LC 72-85427. 340p. 1972. 12.50x (ISBN 0-87011-186-8). Kodansha.

Ballonoff, Paul A., ed. Genetics & Social Structure: Mathematical Structuralism in Population Genetics & Social Theory. LC 73-20412. (Benchmark Papers in Genetics Ser). 520p. 1974. 40.50 (ISBN 0-12-786125-4). Acad Pr.

Ballou, Adin. Christian Non-Resistance. LC 70-121104. (Civil Liberties in American History Ser). 1970. Repr. of 1910 ed. lib. bdg. 29.50 (ISBN 0-306-71980-0). Da Capo.

Ballou, D. H., jt. auth. see Steen, Frederick H.

Ballou, Judith. The Psychology of Pregnancy. LC 78-57242. 1978. 16.95 (ISBN 0-669-02377-9). Lexington Bks.

Ballou, Maturin M. Notable Thoughts About Women: A Literary Mosaic. LC 78-141602. 1971. Repr. of 1882 ed. 20.00 (ISBN 0-8103-3771-1). Gale.

Ballou, Ronald H. Basic Business Logistics. (Illus.). 1978. ref. ed. 19.95 (ISBN 0-13-057364-7). P-H.

Ballou, Stephen V. Model for Theses & Research Papers. LC 72-125125. (Illus., Orig.). 1970. pap. text ed. 6.85 (ISBN 0-395-10806-3, 3-02700). HM.

Ballou, Stephen V., jt. auth. see Campbell, William G.

Ballow, Henry, et al, eds. see Fonblanque, John.

Ball-Rokeach, Sandra, jt. auth. see De Fleur, Melvin L.

Balls, M. & Billett, F. S., eds. The Cell Cycle in Development & Differentiation. (British Society for Developmental Biological Symposia Ser.). (Illus.). 450p. 1973. 71.50 (ISBN 0-521-20136-5). Cambridge U Pr.

Balls, M. & Monnickendam, Marjorie, eds. Organ Culture in Biomedical Research. LC 75-21034. (British Society for Cell Biology Symposium Ser.: No. 1). (Illus.). 600p. 1976. 99.00 (ISBN 0-521-21001-1). Cambridge U Pr.

Balls, M. & Wild, A. E., eds. The Early Development of Mammals. (British Society for Developmental Biology Symposium Ser). (Illus.). 500p. 1975. 92.00 (ISBN 0-521-20771-1). Cambridge U Pr.

Balls, M., jt. ed. see Newth, D. R.

Balmain, K. G., jt. auth. see Jordan, Edward C.

Balmer, Edwin, jt. auth. see Wylie, Philip.

Balmer, Philip & Wylie, Edwin. When Worlds Collide. 192p. 1975. pap. 2.25 (ISBN 0-446-92812-7). Warner Bks.

Balmuth, Daniel. Censorship in Russia, Eighteen Sixty-Five to Nineteen Five. LC 79-52510. 1979. pap. text ed. 10.50 (ISBN 0-8191-0773-5). U Pr of Amer.

Balogh, Thomas. Fact & Fancy in International Economic Relations: An Essay on International Monetary Reform. LC 73-7993. 132p. 1973. text ed. 19.50 (ISBN 0-08-017740-9). Pergamon.

Balon, Eugene K. African Fishes of Lake Kariba. (Illus.). 144p. 1974. 4.95 (ISBN 0-87666-073-1, PS-706). TFH Pubns.

Balon, Joseph. Etudes Franques, I: Aux Origines De la Noblesse. LC 80-2202. 1981. Repr. of 1963 ed. 16.50 (ISBN 0-404-18551-7). AMS Pr.

Balows, Albert & Isenberg, Henry. Biotyping in the Clinical Microbiology Laboratory. (Amer. Lec. Clinical Microbiology). (Illus.). 128p. 1978. 12.00 (ISBN 0-398-03806-6). C C Thomas.

Balsam, M. S. & Sagarin, Edward, eds. Cosmetics: Science & Technology, 3 vols. 2nd ed. LC 75-177888. Set. 145.75 (ISBN 0-471-04650-7); Vol. 1. 1972. 52.75 (ISBN 0-471-04646-9); Vol. 2. 1972. 52.75 (ISBN 0-471-04647-7); Vol. 3 1974. 58.25 (ISBN 0-471-04649-3, Pub. by Wiley-Interscience). Wiley.

Balsama, George D. The Politics of National Despair: French Royalism in the Post-Reformation Era. 1977. pap. text ed. 7.75x (ISBN 0-8191-0142-7). U Pr of Amer.

Balse, Mayah. Mystics & Men of Miracles in India. (Illus.). 1976. 4.50 (ISBN 0-913244-10-4). Hapi Pr.

Balseiro, Jose, ed. see Casona, Alejandro.

Balshofer, Fred J. & Miller, Arthur C. One Reel a Week. (Illus.). 1968. 17.50 (ISBN 0-520-00073-0). U of Cal Pr.

Balshone, Bruce L., et al. Bicycle Transit: Its Planning & Design. LC 75-55. (Special Studies). (Illus.). 186p. 1975. text ed. 21.95 (ISBN 0-275-05410-1). Praeger.

Balsiger, Dave, jt. auth. see Musgraves, Don.

Balsiger, David W., jt. auth. see Johnson, James E.

Balsley, Howard L. Basic Statistics for Business & Economics. LC 76-24237. 1978. text ed. 19.95 o.p. (ISBN 0-88244-086-1); student problem manual 8.25 o.p. (ISBN 0-88244-154-X). Grid Pub.

Balsley, Howard L., jt. auth. see Clover, Vernon T.

Balson, Diane. Yo-Yo. LC 75-25723. 288p. 1976. 7.95 o.p. (ISBN 0-688-02979-5). Morrow.

Balston, Thomas. James Whatman, Father & Son. Bidwell, John, ed. LC 78-74386. (Nineteenth-Century Book Arts & Printing History Ser.: Vol. 1). (Illus.). 1979. lib. bdg. 22.00 (ISBN 0-8240-3875-4). Garland Pub.

--William Balston, Paper Maker, 1759-1849. Bidwell, John, ed. LC 78-74387. (Nineteenth-Century Book Arts & Printing History Ser.: Vol. 2). (Illus.). 1979. lib. bdg. 22.00 (ISBN 0-8240-3876-2). Garland Pub.

Balstrino, Philip. Fat & Skinny. LC 74-12306. (A Let's-Read-&-Find-Out Science Bk). (Illus.). (gr. k-3). 1975. 7.95 (ISBN 0-690-00454-0, TYC-J); PLB 7.89 (ISBN 0-690-00565-9). T Y Crowell.

Baltay, Charles & Rosenfeld, Arthur H., eds. Experimental Meson Spectroscopy. LC 78-137009. (Illus.). 1970. 32.50x (ISBN 0-231-03477-6). Columbia U Pr.

Baltazzi, Evan S. Self-Protection at Close Quarters & Beyond. (Illus.). 50.00 (ISBN 0-918948-03-7). Evanel.

Balter, Deborah J. Air Traffic Control Communications Manual. Date not set. pap. 14.95. Aviation.

--Intermediate Aeronautical Language Manual. Date not set. pap. 14.95. Aviation.

--Primary Aeronautical Language Manual. Date not set. pap. 30.95. Aviation.

Baltes, H. P., ed. Inverse Scattering Problems in Optics. (Topics in Current Physics: Vol. 20). (Illus.). 313p. 1980. 42.00 (ISBN 0-387-10104-7). Springer-Verlag.

Baltes, P. B. & Brim, O. C., Jr., eds. Life-Span Development & Behavior, Vol. 3. 1980. 35.00 (ISBN 0-12-431803-7). Acad Pr.

Balthasar, Hans Urs Von. A First Glance at Adrienne Von Speyr. Lawry, Antje & Englund, Sr. Sergia, trs. from Ger. LC 79-91933. Orig. Title: Erster Blick Auf Adrienne Von Speyr. 220p. (Orig.). 1981. pap. 6.95 (ISBN 0-89870-003-5). Ignatius Pr.

Balthasar, Hans Urs von see Von Balthasar, Hans Urs.

Balthazar, Vera, ed. see Nee, T. S.

Balthazar, Vera, tr. see Leenhouts, Keith.

Baltz, Howard B. Fundamentals of Inferential Statistics for Business Analysis. 2nd ed. 416p. 1980. pap. text ed. 18.95 (ISBN 0-8403-2217-8). Kendall-Hunt.

Baltz, Lewis & Blaisdell, Gus. Park City. (Illus.). 252p. 1980. 75.00 (ISBN 0-9604140-0-2). Castelli-Artspace.

Baltzer, Dieter. Ezechiel und Deuterojesaja: Beruehrungen in der Heilserwartung der beiden grossen Exilspropheten. (Beiheft 121 Zur Zeitschrift fuer die alttestamentliche Wissenschaft Ser.). 1971. 34.00x (ISBN 3-11-001756-3). De Gruyter.

Baltzer, Fritz. Theodor Boveri: The Life & Work of a Great Biologist, 1862-1915. Rudnick, Dorothea, tr. (Illus.). 1967. 19.00x (ISBN 0-520-00074-9). U of Cal Pr.

Baltzer, Klaus, ed. see Zimmerli, Walther.

Baly, Dennis. God & History in the Old Testament. LC 76-9984. 256p. 1976. pap. 6.95x (ISBN 0-06-060369-0, RD 186, HarpR). Har-Row.

Baly, Monica E. Nursing & Social Change. (Illus.). 1973. pap. text ed. 13.95x (ISBN 0-433-01160-2). Intl Ideas.

Balyuzi, H. M. Abdu'l-Baha: The Centre of the Covenant of Baha'u'llah. (Illus.). 1971. 11.95 (ISBN 0-85398-029-2, 7-31-36, Pub. by George Ronald England); pap. 5.95 (ISBN 0-85398-043-8, 7-31-37, Pub. by G Ronald England). Baha'i.

--The Bab: The Herald of the Day of Days. (Illus.). 1973. 9.95 (ISBN 0-85398-048-9, 7-31-50, Pub. by G Ronald England); pap. 3.65 (ISBN 0-85398-054-3, 7-31-51, Pub. by G Ronald England). Baha'i.

--Baha'u'llah: The King of Glory. (Illus.). 1980. 22.50 (ISBN 0-85398-090-X, 7-32-47, Pub. by G Ronald England). Baha'i.

--Edward Granville Browne & the Baha'i Faith. (Illus.). 1970. 10.95 o.s.i. (ISBN 0-85398-023-3, 7-31-14, Pub. by G Ronald England). Baha'i.

--Muhammad & the Course of Islam. (Illus.). 1976. 18.50 (ISBN 0-85398-060-8, 7-39-01, Pub. by G Ronald England). Baha'i.

Balzac. Le Pere Goriot. (Easy Reader, D). pap. 3.75 (ISBN 0-88436-043-1, FRA301051). EMC.

Balzac, Honore de. The Black Sheep. Adamson, Donald, tr. (Classics Ser.). 352p. 1976. pap. 2.95 (ISBN 0-14-044237-5). Penguin.

--Eugenie Grandet. Marriage, Ellen, tr. 1955. 7.95x (ISBN 0-460-00169-8, Evman); pap. 1.95 o.p. (ISBN 0-460-01169-3, EP1169). Dutton.

--History of the Thirteen. Hunt, Herbert J., tr. from Fr. (Classics Ser). 1978. pap. 3.95 (ISBN 0-14-044301-0). Penguin.

--Le Medecin de campagne. new ed. (Documentation thematique). (Illus.). 167p. (Orig., Fr.). 1975. pap. 2.95 (ISBN 0-685-54485-0, 116). Larousse.

--Seraphita. LC 76-12203. 188p. 1976. pap. 2.50 (ISBN 0-8336-1757-5). Steinerbks.

Balzac, Honore De see De Balzac, Honore.

Balzhiser, R. E. & Samuels, M. R. Engineering Thermodynamics. (Illus.). 1977. text ed. 26.95 (ISBN 0-13-279570-1). P-H.

Balzhiser, R. E., et al. Chemical Engineering Thermodynamics. (International Physical & Chemical Engineering Sciences Ser). (Illus.). 1972. ref. ed. 27.95 (ISBN 0-13-128603-X). P-H.

Bambas, Rudolph C. The English Language: Its Origin & History. LC 80-5237. (Illus.). 333p. 1980. 12.95x (ISBN 0-8061-1661-7). U of Okla Pr.

Bambeck, Manfred. Goettliche Komoedie und Exegese. viii, 253p. 1975. pap. 47.10x (ISBN 3-11-004874-4). De Gruyter.

Bamberg, Robert D., ed. see James, Henry.

Bamberger, Bernard J. Commentary on Leviticus. Plaut, W. Gunther, ed. (The Torah: a Modern Commentary Ser.). 1979. 17.50 (ISBN 0-8074-0011-4, 381608). UAHC.

--Story of Judaism. rev. ed. 1970. 6.50 (ISBN 0-8074-0193-5, 959291). UAHC.

Bamberger, Jeanne S. & Brofsky, Howard. The Art of Listening: Developing Musical Perception. 4th ed. LC 78-20837. 1979. pap. text ed. 15.50 scp (ISBN 0-06-040943-6, HarpC); inst. manual free (ISBN 0-06-360966-5); Set Of 5 Records. scp 26.50 (ISBN 0-06-040981-9). Har-Row.

Bamborough, J. B. Ben Jonson. (English Literature Ser.). 1970. pap. text ed. 4.75x (ISBN 0-09-101691-6, Hutchinson U Lib). Humanities.

Bamborough, J. B; see Henderson, Philip.

Bambrough, Renford, ed. New Essays on Plato & Aristotle. (International Library of Philosophy & Scientific Method). 1965. text ed. 14.50x (ISBN 0-391-00979-6). Humanities.

Bame, E. Allen & Cummings, Paul. Exploring Technology. (Technology Series). (Illus.). 288p. 1980. text ed. 12.95 (ISBN 0-87192-112-X, 000-3); tchr's. guide 13.25 (ISBN 0-87192-114-6); activity manual 6.95 (ISBN 0-87192-113-8). Davis Pubns.

Bamert, Arnold. Africa: Tribal Art of Forest & Savanna. (Illus.). 332p. 1980. 60.00 (ISBN 0-500-23318-7). Thames Hudson.

Bamford, C. H., et al. Synthetic Polypeptides: Preparation, Structure, & Properties. (Physical Chemistry Ser.: Vol. 5). 1956. 49.00 o.p. (ISBN 0-12-077650-2). Acad Pr.

Bamford, Francis & Bankes, Viola. Vicious Circle: The Case of the Missing Irish Crown Jewels. (Illus.). 5.95 o.p. (ISBN 0-8180-0807-5). Horizon.

Bamford, G. S., jt. auth. see Bennion, Edmond.

Bamford, Joan. Collecting Antiques for the Future. (Illus.). 1976. 16.95x (ISBN 0-7188-7008-5). Intl Ideas.

Bamford, Samuel. The Autobiography of Samuel Bamford, 2 vols. Chaloner, W. H., ed. & intro. by. Incl. Vol. 1. Early Days. Repr. of 1849 ed; Vol. 2. Passages in the Life of a Radical. Repr. of 1844 ed. LC 67-23461. 30.00x (ISBN 0-678-05025-2). Kelley.

Bamford, T. W. Thomas Arnold on Education. LC 79-108099. (Texts & Studies in the History of Education: No. 8). 1970. 22.95 (ISBN 0-521-07785-0). Cambridge U Pr.

Bamman, et al. Target Spelling Skills Program, 2 pts. (gr. 3-12). 1977. 291.21 ea. (Sch Div); Pt. 1. (ISBN 0-201-21050-9); Pt. 2. (ISBN 0-201-21100-9); tchr's man. incl. A-W.

Bamman, H. & Whitehead, R. Checkered Flag Ser. (gr. 6-12). 1968. pap. text ed. 7.52 ea. (Sch Div); tchr's. manual o.p. 2.72 (ISBN 0-685-83973-7); o.p. Vol. 2 (ISBN 0-201-40102-9). Vol. 3 (ISBN 0-201-40103-7). Vol. 4 (ISBN 0-201-40104-5). Vol. 5 (ISBN 0-201-40105-3). Vol. 6 (ISBN 0-201-40106-1). Vol. 7. o.p. (ISBN 0-201-40107-X). A-W.

Bamman, H. A., et al. Free to Read: A Guide to Effective Reading. rev. ed. LC 74-84819. 1975. 9.95 (ISBN 0-8465-5835-1, 55835); 0.75 (ISBN 0-8465-5836-X, 55836). Benjamin-Cummings.

--World of Ideas: A Guide to Effective Reading. LC 74-84819. 1970. text ed. 8.95 (ISBN 0-8464-3003-7). Benjamin-Cummings.

--World of Ideas: A Guide to Effective Reading. 1970. 8.95 (ISBN 0-201-43003-7); tchr's guide 4.50 (ISBN 0-201-43004-5). A-W.

Bamman, Henry A. & Whitehead, R. J. Top Flight Readers Series, 7 bks. Incl. Chopper (ISBN 0-201-21501-2); Test Pilot (ISBN 0-201-21502-0); Hang Glider (ISBN 0-201-21503-9); Bush Pilot. o.p.; Barnstormers. o.p. (ISBN 0-201-21505-5); Balloon. o.p. (ISBN 0-201-21506-3). (gr. 5-12). 1977. pap. text ed. 6.92 ea. (Sch Div); tchr's. ed. 4.08 (ISBN 0-201-21500-4). A-W.

Bamman, Henry A., ed. see Dawson, Mildred A., et al.

Ban, John & Ciminillo, Lewis. Violence & Vandalism. LC 77-87607. text ed. 6.95x (ISBN 0-8134-1981-6, 1981). Interstate.

Ban, T. A. & Hollender, M. H. Psychopharmacology for Everyday Practice. vi, 190p. 1981. pap. 19.75 (ISBN 3-8055-2241-X). S Karger.

Ban, T. A. & Freyhan, F. A., eds. Drug Treatment of Sexual Dysfunction. (Modern Problems of Pharmacopsychiatry: Vol. 15). (Illus.). viii, 196p. 1980. 58.75 (ISBN 3-8055-2906-6). S Karger.

Ban, T. H., ed. Psychopharmacologh for the Aged. xii, 216p. 1980. softcover 23.50 (ISBN 3-8055-1204-X). S Karger.

Ban, Thomas A. Psychopharmacology of Depression. (Illus.). 104p. 1980. pap. 14.00 (ISBN 3-8055-1154-X). S Karger.

--Psychopharmacology of Thiothixene. LC 75-43191. 1978. 20.50 (ISBN 0-89004-108-3). Raven.

Banach, William J., et al. Releasing Test Scores. 1976. pap. text ed. 5.75 o.p. (ISBN 0-87545-006-7). Natl Sch Pr.

Banas & Goebel. Measures of Noncompactness in Banach Spaces. 112p. 1980. 59.75 (ISBN 0-8247-6981-3). Dekker.

Banasinski, A., jt. auth. see Lange, Oskar.

Banasinski, Antoni, ed. see Lange, Oskar.

Banathy, Bela H. Instructional Systems. LC 68-31771. 1968. pap. text ed. 3.32 o.p. (ISBN 0-8224-3930-1). Pitman Learning.

Bance, S. Handbook of Practical Organic Micro-Analysis: Recommended Methods for Determining Elements & Groups. LC 80-40145. (Ellis Horwood Ser. in Analytical Chemistry). 200p. 1980. 58.95x (ISBN 0-470-26972-3). Halsted Pr.

Banchek, Linda. Snake In, Snake Out. LC 78-51935. (Illus.). (ps-1). 1978. 6.95 (ISBN 0-690-03852-6, TYC-J); PLB 6.89 (ISBN 0-690-03853-4). T Y Crowell.

Bancroft, Caroline. Augusta Tabor: Her Side of the Scandal. 1955. pap. 1.50 (ISBN 0-933472-14-5). Johnson Colo.

--Brown Palace in Denver. 1955. pap. 1.50 (ISBN 0-933472-15-3). Johnson Colo.

--Silver Queen: The Fabulous Story of Baby Doe Tabor. pap. 2.75 (ISBN 0-933472-21-8). Johnson Colo.

--Six Racy Madams of Colorado. 1965. pap. 2.50 (ISBN 0-933472-22-6). Johnson Colo.

Bancroft, Edward. The History of Charles Wentworth, Esq., 1770, 3 vols. (The Flowering of the Novel, 1740-1775 Ser: Vol. 93). 1974. lib. bdg. 50.00 ea (ISBN 0-8240-1192-9). Garland Pub.

Bancroft, Emery. Christian Theology. Mayers, Ronald B., pref. by. 1976. 12.95 (ISBN 0-310-20440-2). Zondervan.

Bancroft, G. M. Mossbauer Spectroscopy: An Introduction for Chemists & Geochemists. LC 73-3326. 252p. 1974. text ed. 29.95 (ISBN 0-470-04665-1). Halsted Pr.

Bancroft, George. The Life & Letters of George Bancroft, 2 Vols. in 1. Howe, Mark D., ed. LC 78-106990. (American Public Figures Ser). 1970. Repr. of 1908 ed. lib. bdg. 65.00 (ISBN 0-306-71877-4). Da Capo.

Bancroft, Griffing. Vanishing Wings: A Tale of Three Birds of Prey. LC 77-182289. (Illus.). 160p. (gr. 9 up). 1972. PLB 5.88 o.p. (ISBN 0-531-02041-X). Watts.

Bancroft, Henrietta & Van Gelder, Richard G. Animals in Winter. LC 63-17543. (A Let's-Read-&-Find-Out Science Bk). (Illus.). (gr. k-3). 1963. 7.89 (ISBN 0-690-09261-X, TYC-J). T Y Crowell.

Bancroft, Hubert H. California Inter Pocula. LC 67-29422. (Works of Hubert Howe Bancroft Ser.). 1967. Repr. of 1888 ed. 25.00x (ISBN 0-914888-28-5). Bancroft Pr.

--Essays & Miscellany. LC 67-29422. (Works of Hubert Howe Bancroft Ser.). 1967. Repr. of 1888 ed. 25.00x (ISBN 0-914888-42-0). Bancroft Pr.

--History of California, 7 vols. LC 67-29422. Repr. of 1888 ed. Set. 100.00x (ISBN 0-914888-20-X). Bancroft Pr.

--History of Central America, 3 vols. LC 67-29422. (Works of Hubert Howe Bancroft Ser.). 1967. Repr. of 1888 ed. Set. 75.00x (ISBN 0-914888-06-4). Bancroft Pr.

--History of Mexico, 6 vols. LC 67-29422. (Works of Hubert Howe Bancroft Ser.). 1967. Repr. of 1888 ed. Set. 150.00x (ISBN 0-914888-10-2). Bancroft Pr.

--Literary Industries. LC 67-29422. (Works of Hubert Howe Bancroft Ser.). 1967. Repr. of 1888 ed. 25.00x (ISBN 0-914888-43-9). Bancroft Pr.

--The Native Races, 5 vols. LC 67-29422. (Works of Hubert Howe Bancroft Ser.). 1967. Repr. of 1888 ed. Set. 125.00x (ISBN 0-914888-00-5). Bancroft Pr.

--Popular Tribunals, 2 vols. LC 67-29422. (Works of Hubert Howe Bancroft Ser.). 1967. Repr. of 1888 ed. 50.00x (ISBN 0-914888-39-0). Bancroft Pr.

Bancroft, Iris. Love's Burning Flame. 1980. pap. cancelled (ISBN 0-686-68083-9). Bantam.

Bancroft, J. D. Histochemical Technique. 2nd ed. 336p. 1975. 39.95 (ISBN 0-407-00033-X). Butterworths.

Bancroft, John D. & Stevens, Alan, eds. Theory and Practice of Histological Techniques. LC 76-20829. 1977. text ed. 37.50 o.s.i. (ISBN 0-443-01534-1). Churchill.

Bancroft, Richard. Dangerous Positions & Proceedings. LC 74-38147. (English Experience Ser.: No. 427). 192p. 1972. Repr. of 1593 ed. 28.50 (ISBN 90-221-0427-3). Walter J Johnson.

--A Survey of the Pretended Holy Dicipline. LC 78-38148. (English Experience Ser.: No. 428). 472p. 1972. Repr. of 1593 ed. 67.00 (ISBN 90-221-0428-1). Walter J Johnson.

Band, Arnold J. Nostalgia and Nightmare: A Study in the Fiction of S. Y. Agnon. (Near Eastern Center, UCLA). 1968. 30.00x (ISBN 0-520-00076-5). U of Cal Pr.

Bandel, Betty. Sing the Lord's Song in a Strange Land: The Life of Justin Morgan. LC 78-73309. 280p. 1981. 17.50 (ISBN 0-8386-2411-1). Fairleigh Dickinson.

--Sing the Lord's Song in a Strange Land: The Life of Justin Morgan. LC 78-73309. 264p. 1981. 24.50 (ISBN 0-8386-2411-1). Fairleigh Dickinson.

Bandelier, Adolph F. The Discovery of New Mexico by the Franciscan Monk Friar Marcos de Niza in 1539. Rodack, Madeleine T., tr. from Fr. LC 80-25083. 1981. 10.95x (ISBN 0-8165-0717-1). U of Ariz Pr.

Bandelier, Adolph F. & Hewett, Edgar L. Indians of the Rio Grande Valley. LC 72-95268. (Illus.). 274p. 1973. Repr. of 1939 ed. lib. bdg. 16.50x (ISBN 0-8154-0462-X). Cooper Sq.

Bander, E. Mr. Dooley & Mr. Dunne. 150p. 1981. text ed. 12.50 (ISBN 0-87215-329-0). Michie.

Bander, Edward J. Dictionary of Legal Terms & Maxims, Vol. 58. 2nd ed. 1979. 5.95 (ISBN 0-379-11119-5). Oceana.

Bander, Edward J., jt. auth. see Marke, Julius J.

Bander, Edward J., ed. Corporations in a Democratic Society. (Reference Shelf Ser: Vol. 46, No. 6). 1974. 6.25 (ISBN 0-8242-0526-X). Wilson.
--Turmoil on the Campus. (Reference Shelf Ser: Vol. 42, No. 3). 1970. 6.25 (ISBN 0-8242-0411-5). Wilson.
Bander, Joseph J., et al. Cardiac Arrest & CPR: Assessment, Planning & Intervention. 232p. 1980. text ed. cancelled (ISBN 0-89443-328-8). Aspen Systems.
Bander, Peter. The Prophecies of St. Malachy & St. Columbkille. 3rd ed. 1979. pap. text ed. 6.00x (ISBN 0-901072-10-9). Humanities.
Bandhopadyaya, Vibhuti Bhushan. Pather Panchali, 3 vols. Varma, Monika, tr. from Bengali. 1974. Set. 25.00 (ISBN 0-89253-783-3); Set. pap. text ed. 12.00 (ISBN 0-88253-390-8); Vol. 1. 8.00 (ISBN 0-89253-780-9). Vol. 2. 14.00 (ISBN 0-89253-781-7); pap. text ed. 8.00 (ISBN 0-88253-808-X); Vol.3. 8.00 (ISBN 0-89253-782-5); pap. text ed. 4.00 (ISBN 0-88253-809-8). InterCulture.
Bandlow, Richard F., jt. auth. see Yehl, Joan K.
Bandura, A. Social Learning Theory. 1977. text ed. 15.95 (ISBN 0-13-816751-6); pap. text ed. 9.95 (ISBN 0-13-816744-3). P-H.
Bandura, Albert. Aggression: A Social Learning Analysis. (P-H Social Learning Ser). (Illus.). 368p. 1973. ref. ed. 17.95 (ISBN 0-13-020743-8). P-H.
Bandy, Dale & Swad, Randy. Federal Income Taxation. 1981. 250p. 1981. pap. text ed. 12.95 (ISBN 0-13-308502-3). P-H.
Bandyopadhyay, R. & Padwal, S. M. Introduction to Operational Research & Data Management. 400p. 1981. text ed. 25.00x (ISBN 0-7069-1234-9, Pub. by Vikas India). Advent Bk.
Bane, Donald & Kutscher, Austin H. Death & Ministry: Pastoral Care of the Dying & Bereaved. 196p. 1975. 10.95 (ISBN 0-8164-0260-4). Crossroad NY.
Bane, Mary Jo, jt. auth. see Masnick, George.
Bane, Suda L. & Lutz, Ralph, eds. The Blockade of Germany After the Armistice, 1918-1919: Selected Documents of the Supreme Economic Council, Superior Blockade Council, American Relief Administration, & Other Wartime Organizations. LC 79-80520. 874p. 1973. Repr. of 1942 ed. 28.00 o.p. (ISBN 0-86527-012-0). Fertig.
Banerjea, D. Coordination Chemistry: Twentieth International Conference on Coordination Chemistry, Calcutta, India, 10-14 Dec. 1979. LC 80-41163. 286p. 1980. 75.00 (ISBN 0-08-023942-0). Pergamon.
Banerjea, Pramathanath. Indian Finance in the Days of the Company. (Perspectives in Asian History: No. 5). Repr. of 1928 ed. lib. bdg. 25.00x (ISBN 0-87991-820-9). Porcupine Pr.
Banerjee, A. C. Constitutional History of India: 1858-1919, 2 vols. 1978. Vol. 1. 20.00x o.p. (ISBN 0-8364-0286-3); Vol. 2. 22.50 o.p. (ISBN 0-685-81684-2). South Asia Bks.
Banerjee, Anukul C. Studies in Chinese Buddhism. 1977. 6.00x o.p. (ISBN 0-8364-0047-X). South Asia Bks.
Banerjee, P. K. & Butterfield, R., eds. Developments in Boundary Element Methods, Vol. 1. (Illus.). 1979. 69.90 (ISBN 0-85334-845-6, Pub. by Applied Science). Burgess-Intl Ideas.
Banerjee, Pradeep, tr. Some Post-Independence Bengali Poems. (Translated from Bengali). 8.00 (ISBN 0-89253-606-3). Ind-US Inc.
Banerjee, Sumanta. Family Planning Communication: A Critique of the Indian Programme. (Illus.). 218p. 1980. text ed. 10.50x (ISBN 0-391-02169-9). Humanities.
--In the Wake of Naxalbari: A History of the Naxalite Movement in India. 436p. 1980. text ed. 22.50 (ISBN 0-8426-1656-X). Verry.
Banerjee, Utpal K. Operational Analysis & Indian Defence. 1980. text ed. 40.50x (ISBN 0-391-01839-6). Humanities.
Banerji, Barenya K. Towards Quiescence & Immortality. LC 80-81693. 1981. 10.00 (ISBN 0-8022-2366-4). Philos Lib.
Banerji, Dilip & Raymond, Jacque. Elements of Microprogramming. (Illus.). 416p. 1981. text ed. 24.50 (ISBN 0-13-267146-8). P-H.
Banerji, R. B., ed. see Systems Symposium - 4th - Case Western Reserve University, Institute of Technology.
Banerji, Ranjit. Energy Economy in Design. LC 77-13289. 1979. lib. bdg. 16.00 (ISBN 0-88275-621-4). Krieger.
Banff Centre. Banff Purchase: An Exhibition of Photography in Canada. 112p. 1980. 19.95 (ISBN 0-471-99829-X). Wiley.
Banfield, Edward C. Government Project. 1951. 7.25 o.s.i. (ISBN 0-02-901440-9). Free Pr.
--Political Influence. LC 60-12182. 1965. pap. text ed. 7.95 (ISBN 0-02-901590-1). Free Pr.
Banfield, Edward C. & Banfield, L. F. Moral Basis of a Backward Society. LC 58-9398. 1958. 12.95 (ISBN 0-02-901520-0); pap. text ed. 5.95 (ISBN 0-02-901510-3). Free Pr.
Banfield, Edward C., jt. auth. see Meyerson, Martin.
Banfield, Edward C., ed. Urban Government: Reader in Administration & Politics. 2nd ed. LC 69-11169. 1969. text ed. 15.95 (ISBN 0-02-901690-8). Free Pr.
Banfield, L. F., jt. auth. see Banfield, Edward C.
Bang, Betsy. The Demons of Rajpur. LC 80-10467. (Illus.). 96p. (gr. 3-6). 1980. 7.95 (ISBN 0-688-80263-X); PLB 7.63 (ISBN 0-688-84263-1). Greenwillow.
--The Old Woman & the Rice Thief. LC 76-30671. (Illus.). (gr. k-3). 1978. 7.95 (ISBN 0-688-80098-X); PLB 7.63 (ISBN 0-688-84098-1). Greenwillow.
Bang, Betsy, adapted by. The Old Woman & the Red Pumpkin. LC 74-13057. (Illus.). 32p. (gr. k-3). 1975. 8.95g (ISBN 0-02-708360-8). Macmillan.
Bang, Garrett, tr. from Japanese. & illus. Men from the Village Deep in the Mountains, & Other Japanese Folk Tales. LC 72-92431. (Illus.). 96p. (gr. 3-6). 1973. 7.95 (ISBN 0-02-708350-0). Macmillan.
Bang, Molly. The Goblins Giggle & Other Stories. LC 72-9033. (Illus.). 57p. (gr. 4-7). 1973. reinforced bdg. 5.95 o.p. (ISBN 0-684-13226-5, ScribJ). Scribner.
--The Grey Lady & the Strawberry Snatcher. LC 79-21243. (Illus.). 48p. (gr. 1 up). 1980. 10.95 (ISBN 0-590-07547-0, Four Winds). Schol Bk Serv.
Bang, Molly G. Tye May & the Magic Brush. LC 80-16488. (Read-Along Books). (Illus.). 56p. (gr. 1-3). 1981. 5.95 (ISBN 0-688-80290-7); PLB 5.71 (ISBN 0-688-84290-9). Greenwillow.
--Wiley & the Hairy Man: Adapted from an American Folk Tale. LC 75-38581. (Ready-to-Read Ser). (Illus.). 64p. (gr. 1-4). 1976. 8.95 (ISBN 0-02-708370-5, 70837). Macmillan.
Bangert, Jeff, jt. auth. see Diedrich, William M.
Bangert, William V. A History of the Society of Jesus. LC 78-188687. (Original Studies Composed in English Ser.: No. 3). (Illus.). 570p. 1972. 14.75 o.s.i. (ISBN 0-912422-05-X); pap. 7.00; Smyth sewn 9.00 (ISBN 0-912422-23-8). Inst Jesuit.
Bangerter, Lowell A. Hugo Von Hofmannsthal. LC 76-20408. (Modern Literature Ser.). 1977. 10.95 (ISBN 0-8044-2028-9). Ungar.
Bangs, Edward. Yankee Doodle. LC 80-17024. (Illus.). 40p. (ps-3). 1980. Repr. of 1976 ed. 9.95 (ISBN 0-590-07782-1, Four Winds). Schol Bk Serv.
Bangs, John K. Ghosts I Have Met, & Some Others. LC 80-19172. 191p. 1980. Repr. of 1971 ed. lib. bdg. 9.95x (ISBN 0-89370-605-1). Borgo Pr.
Bangs, Tina E. Language & Learning Disorders of the Pre-Academic Child. (Illus.). 1968. 18.95 (ISBN 0-13-522797-6). P-H.
Banham, Martin. African Theatre Today. (Theatre Today Ser). 1976. pap. 4.95 (ISBN 0-685-50819-6, Pitman Pub); pap. 4.95 o.p. Columbia U Pr.
Banham, Reyner. Los Angeles: The Architecture of Four Ecologies. LC 72-148430. (Icon Editions). (Illus.). 1971. 8.95x o.s.i. (ISBN 0-06-430370-5, HarpT). Har-Row.
--Megastructure: Urban Futures of the Recent Past. LC 76-12061. (Icon Editions Ser.). (Illus.). 240p. 1977. 25.00 o.s.i. (ISBN 0-06-430371-3, HarpT). Har-Row.
Banhidi, Zoltan, et al. Learn Hungarian. 1965. text ed. 22.00x (ISBN 963-17-0971-X). Intl Learn Syst.
Banier, Antoine. The Mythology & Fables of the Ancients, Explain'd from History, 4 vols. LC 75-27885. (Renaissance & the Gods Ser.: Vol. 40). (Illus.). 1976. Repr. of 1740 ed. Set. lib. bdg. 292.00 (ISBN 0-8240-2089-8); lib. bdg. 73.00 ea. Garland Pub.
Banim, John & Banim, Michael. The Anglo-Irish of the Nineteenth Century, 3 vols. Wolff, Robert L., ed. (Ireland Nineteenth Century Fiction Ser. Two: Vol. 20). 934p. 1979. Set. lib. bdg. 96.00 (ISBN 0-8240-3469-4). Garland Pub.
--The Bit O'writin' & Other Tales. Wolff, Robert L., ed. (Ireland Nineteenth Century Fiction Ser. Two: Vol. 24). 928p. 1979. lib. bdg. 32.00 (ISBN 0-8240-3473-2). Garland Pub.
--The Boyne Water: A Tale of the O'Hara Family, 3 vols. Wolff, Robert L., ed. (Ireland Nineteenth Century Fiction Ser. Two: Vol. 17). 1329p. 1979. Set. lib. bdg. 96.00 (ISBN 0-8240-3466-X). Garland Pub.
--The Croppy: A Tale of 1798, 3 vols. Wolff, Robert L., ed. (Ireland Nineteenth Century Fiction Ser. Two: Vol. 19). 948p. 1979. Set. lib. bdg. 96.00 (ISBN 0-8240-3468-6). Garland Pub.
--The Denounced, 3 vols. Wolff, Robert L., ed. (Ireland Nineteenth Century Fiction Ser. Two: Vol. 21). 1979. Set. lib. bdg. 138.00 (ISBN 0-8240-3470-8). Garland Pub.
--The Ghost-Hunter & His Family. Wolff, Robert L., ed. (Ireland Nineteenth Century Fiction - Ser. Two: Vol. 22). 348p. 1979. lib. bdg. 32.00 (ISBN 0-8240-3471-6). Garland Pub.
--The Life of John Banim, the Irish Novelist. Wolff, Robert L., ed. (Ireland, Nineteenth Century Fiction - Ser. Two: Vol. 25). 350p. 1979. lib. bdg. 32.00 (ISBN 0-8240-3474-0). Garland Pub.
--The Mayor of Wind-Gap & Canvassing, 3 vols. Wolff, Robert L., ed. (Ireland Nineteenth Century Fiction - Ser. Two). 1066p. 1979. lib. bdg. 96.00 (ISBN 0-8240-3472-4). Garland Pub.
--Tales by the O'Hara Family, Eighteen Twenty-Five, 3 vols. Wolff, Robert L., ed. (Ireland Nineteenth Century Fiction - Ser. Two: Vol. 16). 1278p. 1979. lib. bdg. 96.00 (ISBN 0-8240-3465-1). Garland Pub.
--Tales of the O'Hara Family, 3 vols. Wolff, Robert L., ed. (Ireland Nineteenth Century Fiction - Ser. Two: Vol. 18). 1080p. 1979. lib. bdg. 96.00 (ISBN 0-8240-3467-8). Garland Pub.
Banim, Michael, jt. auth. see Banim, John.
Banin, A., ed. see Soil Chemistry, Soil Fertility & Soil Clay Mineralogy Commissions of the International Society of Soil Science, 13-18 July 1976, Jerusalem.
Banis, Carolyn S., jt. auth. see Shipley, Kenneth G.
Banister, John. The Historie of Man. LC 74-26164. (English Experience Ser.: No. 122). (Illus.). 250p. 1969. Repr. of 1578 ed. 42.00 (ISBN 90-221-0122-3). Walter J Johnson.
--A Needfull, New & Necessarie Treatise of Chyrugerie. LC 73-171732. (English Experience Ser.: No. 300). 276p. Repr. of 1575 ed. 22.00 (ISBN 90-221-0300-5). Walter J Johnson.
Banister, Keith. A Closer Look at Fish. (gr. 5 up). 1980. PLB 6.90 (ISBN 0-531-03413-5). Watts.
Banister, Manly. Woodblock Cutting & Printing. LC 76-19813. (Illus.). (YA) 1976. 7.95 o.p. (ISBN 0-8069-5374-8); PLB 7.49 o.p. (ISBN 0-8069-5375-6). Sterling.
Banister, Manly, tr. see Pfluger, A.
Banister, Richard. A Treatise of One Hundred & Thirteene Diseases of the Eyes. LC 79-37135. (English Experience Ser.: No. 297). 480p. Repr. of 1622 ed. 35.00 (ISBN 90-221-0297-1). Walter J Johnson.
Bank, Adrianne, et al. A Practical Guide to Program Planning: A Teaching Models Approach. (Orig.). 1981. pap. 14.95 (ISBN 0-8077-2641-9). Tchrs Coll.
Bank, Arthur, et al, eds. see Cooley's Anemia Symposium, 4th, et al.
Bank, Dena C. How Things Get Done: The Nitty-Gritty of Parliamentary Procedure. LC 79-1287. 1979. 3.95 (ISBN 0-87249-343-1). U of SC Pr.
Bankes, Viola, jt. auth. see Bamford, Francis.
Bank-Jensen, Thea. Play with Paper. (gr. 1-4). 1962. 4.95g o.s.i. (ISBN 0-02-708240-7). Macmillan.
Banko, Winston E. The Trumpeter Swan: Its History, Habits, & Population in the United States. LC 80-12533. (Illus.). x, 214p. 1980. pap. 5.95 (ISBN 0-8032-6057-1, BB 731, Bison). U of Nebr Pr.
Bankoff, S. George, et al, eds. Heat Transfer in Nuclear Reactor Safety: Proceedings of the International Centre for Heat & Mass Transfer. (International Centre for Heat & Mass Transfer). (Illus.). 1981. text ed. 95.00 (ISBN 0-89116-223-2). Hemisphere Pub.
Bankowski, Zenon, jt. ed. see Mungham, Geoff.
Banks. Multiethnic Eduction: Theory & Practice. 300p. 1981. text ed. 17.50 (ISBN 0-205-07300-X, 2373009); pap. text ed. 10.50 (ISBN 0-205-07293-3, 2372932). Allyn.
Banks, Ann. First-Person America. LC 80-7660. (Illus.). 320p. 1980. 13.95 (ISBN 0-394-41397-0). Knopf.
Banks, Arthur S. Cross-Polity Time-Series Data. 328p. 1971. 50.00 (ISBN 0-262-02071-8). MIT Pr.
Banks, Arthur S, ed. Political Handbook of the World: Nineteen Eighty. 6th ed. (Political Handbook of the World Ser.). 1980. 34.95 (ISBN 0-07-003626-8). McGraw.
Banks, Bruce & Kenny, Dick. Looking at Sails. (Illus.). 1980. 12.95 (ISBN 0-393-03251-5). Norton.
Banks, Carolyn. Mr. Right. 1980. pap. 2.50 (ISBN 0-446-91191-7). Warner Bks.
Banks, Ferdinand E. Bauxite & Aluminum: An Introduction to the Economics of Non-Fuel Minerals. LC 78-24632. 208p. 1979. 21.00 (ISBN 0-669-02771-5). Lexington Bks.
--The International Economy: A Modern Approach. LC 77-26560. (Illus.). 1979. 17.95 (ISBN 0-669-01504-0). Lexington Bks.
--The Political Economy of Oil. LC 79-3340. 1980. 25.95 (ISBN 0-669-03402-9). Lexington Bks.
--Scarcity, Energy and Economic Progress. LC 77-4630. 1977. 21.00 (ISBN 0-669-01781-7). Lexington Bks.
Banks, James A. Teaching Strategies for Ethnic Studies. 2nd ed. 1979. pap. text ed. 10.95 (ISBN 0-205-06585-6, 2365855). Allyn.
Banks, James A. & Clegg, Ambrose A., Jr. Teaching Strategies for the Social Studies: Inquiry, Valuing & Decision-Making. 2nd ed. LC 76-5081. (Illus.). 1977. text ed. 16.50 (ISBN 0-201-00412-7). A-W.
Banks, James A. & Joyce, William W., eds. Teaching Social Studies to Culturally Different Children. LC 72-132057. (Education Ser). 1971. pap. 8.95 (ISBN 0-201-00391-0). A-W.
Banks, James A., jt. ed. see Joyce, William W.
Banks, Jane, jt. auth. see Dong, Collin H.
Banks, Jerry & Hohenstein, Charles L., Jr. Procurement & Inventory Ordering Tables. LC 77-8663. 1978. pap. text ed. 14.50 (ISBN 0-08-021945-4). Pergamon.
Banks, Jimmy. Money, Marbles & Chalk. LC 70-180195. 1971. 2.95 o.p. (ISBN 0-685-48119-0). Shoal Creek Pub.
Banks, Lynne R. The Adventures of King Midas. (Illus.). 1976. 9.00x o.p. (ISBN 0-460-06752-4, Pub. by J. M. Dent England). Biblio Dist.
--Path to the Silent Country. 1978. 8.95 o.s.i. (ISBN 0-440-06985-8). Delacorte.
Banks, Lynne Reid. The Farthest-Away Mountain. LC 77-72412. (gr. 4-7). 1977. 5.95 (ISBN 0-385-12876-2). Doubleday.
Banks, Noel. Six Inner Hebrides. 1977. 16.95 (ISBN 0-7153-7368-4). David & Charles.
Banks, Oliver. The Rembrandt Panel. large print ed. LC 80-27955. 1981. Repr. of 1980 ed. 11.95 (ISBN 0-89621-264-5). Thorndike Pr.
--Watteau & the North Studies in the Dutch & Flemish Baroque Influence on French Rocco Painting. LC 76-23602. (Outstanding Dissertations in the Fine Arts Ser.). 1977. lib. bdg. 63.00x (ISBN 0-8240-2676-4). Garland Pub.
Banks, P. M. & Kockarts, G. Aeronomy. Incl. Pt. A. 1973. 47.00 (ISBN 0-12-077801-7); Set. 38.50 (ISBN 0-12-077801-7); Pt. B. 1973. 48.00 (ISBN 0-12-077802-5). Set. 39.50 (ISBN 0-12-077802-5). Acad Pr.
Banks, Peter M. & Doupnik, Joseph. Introduction to Computer Science. LC 75-20407. 384p. 1976. text ed. 21.95 (ISBN 0-471-04710-4); instructors manual avail. (ISBN 0-471-01552-0). Wiley.
Banks, R. C., et al. Introductory Problems in Spectroscopy. 1980. pap. 12.95 (ISBN 0-8053-0572-6). A-W.
Banks, R. E. Organofluorine Chemicals & Their Industrial Applications. LC 79-40251. (Industrial Chemistry Ser.). 255p. 1979. 54.95x (ISBN 0-470-26720-8). Halsted Pr.
Banks, Robert. Paul's Idea of Community: The Early House Churches in the Historical Setting. 1980. pap. 5.95 (ISBN 0-8028-1830-7). Eerdmans.
Banks, Ronald F. A History of Maine: A Collection of Readings on the History of Maine 1600-1976. 4th ed. (History Series). 1976. pap. text ed. 12.95 o.p. (ISBN 0-8403-0020-4). Kendall-Hunt.
Banks, Sam W. & Laufman, Harold. Atlas of Surgical Exposures of the Extremities. LC 52-12872. (Illus.). 1973. 32.00 (ISBN 0-7216-1530-9). Saunders.
Banks, Stuart. The Complete Handbook of Poultry Keeping. LC 79-14305. (Illus.). 216p. 1979. 14.95 (ISBN 0-442-23382-5); pap. 8.95 (ISBN 0-442-23383-3). Van Nos Reinhold.
Banks, William J. Applied Veterinary Histology. (Illus.). 540p. 1981. write for info. (0410-7). Williams & Wilkins.
Banks, William K., ed. see Lanzano, Susan & Abreu, Rosendo.
Bankson, N. Bankson Language Screening Test. 1977. 18.95 (ISBN 0-8391-1126-6). Univ Park.
Banna, M., jt. auth. see Hankinson, John.
Banner, Angela. Ant & Bee. LC 63-20113. (Ant & Bee Bks). (Illus.). (gr. k-3). 1958. 2.95 o.p. (ISBN 0-531-01155-0). Watts.
--Ant & Bee & the ABC. LC 66-16692. (Ant & Bee Bks). (Illus.). (gr. k-3). 1967. 2.95 o.p. (ISBN 0-531-01156-9). Watts.
--Ant & Bee & the Doctor. LC 77-152853. (Ant & Bee Ser). (Illus.). (gr. k-3). 1971. PLB 2.95 o.p. (ISBN 0-531-01167-4). Watts.
--Ant & Bee & the Rainbow. (Ant & Bee Bks). (Illus.). (gr. k-3). 1963. 2.95 o.p. (ISBN 0-531-01157-7). Watts.
--Ant & Bee Go Shopping. LC 74-185921. (Ant & Bee Bks.). (Illus.). 80p. (gr. k-3). 1972. 2.95 o.p. (ISBN 0-531-01168-2). Watts.
--Ant & Bee Time. LC 69-12354. (Ant & Bee Bks). (Illus.). (gr. k-3). 1969. 2.95 o.p. (ISBN 0-531-01163-1). Watts.
--More & More Ant & Bee. (Ant & Bee Bks). (gr. k-3). 1970. 2.95 o.p. (ISBN 0-531-01164-X). Watts.
--More Ant & Bee. (Ant & Bee Bks). (gr. k-3). 1958. 2.50 o.p. (ISBN 0-531-01161-5). Watts.
--One, Two, Three with Ant & Bee. (Ant & Bee Bks). (Illus.). (gr. k-3). 1959. 2.95 o.p. (ISBN 0-531-01162-3). Watts.
Banner, Hubert S. Calamities of the World. LC 74-159880. (Tower Bks). (Illus.). 1971. Repr. of 1932 ed. 18.000 (ISBN 0-8103-3918-8). Gale.

Banner, Lois W. Elizabeth Cady Stanton: A Radical for Women's Rights. (Library of American Biography). 189p. 1980. pap. text ed. 4.95 (ISBN 0-316-08030-6). Little.
Banner, William A. Moral Norms & Moral Order. LC 80-24206. x, 111p. 1981. 10.00 (ISBN 0-8130-0661-9). U Presses Fla.
Bannerjee, M. Invitation to Hinduism. 1979. pap. 5.95 (ISBN 0-89684-081-6, Pub. by Arnold Heinemann India). Orient Bk Dist.
Bannerman, Glenn & Fakkema, Robert. Guide for Recreation Leaders. LC 74-28523. 120p. (Orig.). 1975. pap. 3.95 (ISBN 0-8042-2154-5). John Knox.
Bannerman, Helen, jt. auth. see Hay, Elizabeth.
Bannerman, James. The Church of Christ, 2 vols. Set. 15.95 o.p. (ISBN 0-686-12499-5). Banner of Truth.
Banning, Evelyn I. Mary Lyons of Putnam Hill. LC 66-10683. (gr. 4 up). 1965. 6.95 (ISBN 0-8149-0269-3). Vanguard.
Banning, Lance. The Jeffersonian Persuasion: Evolution of a Party Ideology. LC 77-14666. (Cornell Paperbacks Ser.). 328p. 1980. pap. 5.95 (ISBN 0-8014-9203-3). Cornell U Pr.
Banning, Margaret C. Country Club People. 1976. lib. bdg. 14.85x (ISBN 0-89968-006-2). Lightyear.
--Spellbinders. 1976. lib. bdg. 14.35x (ISBN 0-89968-008-9). Lightyear.
Bannister, D., jt. auth. see Fransella, F.
Bannister, Don. Long Day at Shiloh. LC 80-24112. 288p. 1981. 11.95 (ISBN 0-394-50680-4). Knopf.
Bannister, Peter. Introduction to Physiological Plant Ecology. LC 76-16743. 1978. pap. text ed. 18.95 (ISBN 0-470-99389-8). Halsted Pr.
Bannister, Robert C., Jr. Ray Stannard Baker: The Mind of a Progressive. Freidel, Frank, ed. LC 78-66516. (The History of the United States Ser.: Vol. 1). 372p. 1979. lib. bdg. 28.00 (ISBN 0-8240-9711-4). Garland Pub.
Bannock, Graham. The Economics of Small Firms: Return from the Wilderness. 120p. 1981. 14.50x (ISBN 0-631-11391-6, Pub. by Basil Blackwell). Biblio Dist.
Bannon, George. Fisherman's Handbook. 12.50x (ISBN 0-392-06420-0, SpS). Soccer.
Bannon, John F. Spanish Borderlands Frontier, 1513-1821. LC 74-110887. (Histories of the American Frontier Series). (Illus.). 308p. 1974. pap. 6.50x (ISBN 0-8263-0309-9). U of NM Pr.
Bannon, John F. & Miller, Robert R. Latin America. 4th ed. 1977. text ed. 14.95 (ISBN 0-02-474350-X). Macmillan.
Bannon, John F., ed. see Bolton, Herbert E.
Bannon, Joseph J. Problem Solving in Recreation & Parks. LC 70-38797. (Illus.). 336p. 1972. pap. text ed. 16.50 (ISBN 0-13-711648-9). P-H.
Bannon, Laura. Who Walks the Attic. LC 62-20174. (Pilot Book Ser). (Illus.). (gr. 3-5). 1967. 6.95g (ISBN 0-8075-9064-9). A Whitman.
Banov, Abel & Lytle, Marie-Jeanne. Successful Wallcoverings & Decoration. 2nd ed. Case, Virginia A., ed. (Successful Ser.). (Illus.). 136p. 1981. 17.95 (ISBN 0-89999-021-5); pap. 7.95 (ISBN 0-89999-022-3). Structures Pub.
--Wall Coverings & Decoration. LC 76-28710. (Illus.). 1976. 13.95 (ISBN 0-912336-24-2); pap. 6.95 (ISBN 0-912336-25-0). Structures Pub.
Banovetz, James M., ed. Managing the Modern City. LC 58-9090. (Muncipal Management Ser.). 1971. text ed. 22.00 (ISBN 0-87326-004-X). Intl City Mgt.
Bansil, P. C. Agricultural Problems in India. 1977. 18.95 (ISBN 0-7069-0363-3, Pub. by Vikas India). Advent Bk.
--Agricultural Problems of India. 2nd ed. LC 75-903617. 608p. 1975. 11.50x (ISBN 0-7069-0363-3). Intl Pubns Serv.
Banta, David. Toward Rational Technology in Medicine: Considerations for Health Policy. (Health Care & Society Ser.: No. 5) 1981. text ed. 28.50 (ISBN 0-8261-3200-6); pap. text ed. cacelled (ISBN 0-8261-3201-4). Springer Pub.
Banta, R. E. Ohio Valley. LC 66-19221. (gr. 7 up). 1967. pap. 2.95x (ISBN 0-8077-1044-X). Tchrs Coll.
Banta, R. E., ed. Hoosier Caravan: A Treasury of Indiana Life & Lore. new ed. LC 75-16521. 640p. 1975. limited ed. 10.95 (ISBN 0-253-13863-9); deluxe ed. 10.95 o.p. (ISBN 0-253-13862-0). Ind U Pr.
Banthin, Joanna, jt. auth. see Stelzer, Leigh.
Bantick, G. H. Freedom & Authority in Education. 1970. 5.95 (ISBN 0-571-09328-0, Pub. by Faber & Faber). Merrimack Bk Serv.
Bantleman, Lawrence. The Award. 9.00 (ISBN 0-89253-648-9); flexible cloth 4.80 (ISBN 0-89253-649-7). Ind-US Inc.
--Graffiti: Poems. 3rd ed. (Redbird Bk.). 1976. lib. bdg. 8.00 (ISBN 0-89253-095-2); pap. text ed. 4.00 (ISBN 0-89253-132-0). Ind-US Inc.
--Kanchanjanga. 8.00 (ISBN 0-89253-493-1); flexible cloth 4.00 (ISBN 0-89253-494-X). Ind-US Inc.
--New Poems. 8.00 (ISBN 0-89253-491-5); flexible cloth 4.00 (ISBN 0-89253-492-3). Ind-US Inc.
Bantock, G. H. Dilemmas of the Curriculum. LC 80-11764. 146p. 1980. 15.95x (ISBN 0-470-26920-0). Halsted Pr.
--Education in an Industrial Society. 1973. 8.50 (ISBN 0-571-04791-2, Pub. by Faber & Faber). Merrimack Bk Serv.
Bantock, Geoffrey H. Culture, Industrialization & Education. (Students Library of Education). 1968. text ed. 5.50x (ISBN 0-7100-6132-3); pap. text ed. 2.00x (ISBN 0-7100-6133-1). Humanities.
Banton, Michael. The Idea of Race. 1979. lib. bdg. 22.00x (ISBN 0-89158-719-5). Westview.
Banville, John. Doctor Copernicus. 1977. 8.95 o.p. (ISBN 0-393-08757-3). Norton.
Banville, Thomas G. How to Listen-How to Be Heard. LC 77-17961. 1978. 12.95 (ISBN 0-88229-332-X); pap. 7.95 (ISBN 0-686-68003-0). Nelson-Hall.
Banwart, George J. Basic Food Microbiology. (Illus.). 1979. pap. text ed. 31.50 (ISBN 0-87055-322-4). AVI.
Banwart, L., jt. ed. see Stucki, J. W.
Banzhaf, Jane C., jt. auth. see Greendyke, Robert M.
Bapat, Meera. Shelter for the Poor: The Case of Poona. (Progress in Planning Ser.: Vol. 15, Pt. 3). 85p. 1981. pap. 13.50 (ISBN 0-08-026811-0). Pergamon.
Baptiste, H. Prentice, Jr. & Baptiste, Mira L. Developing the Multicultural Process in Classroom Instruction: Competencies for Teachers. LC 79-89993. 1979. pap. text ed. 11.75 (ISBN 0-8191-0855-3). U Pr of Amer.
Baptiste, Mira L., jt. auth. see Baptiste, H. Prentice, Jr.
Baptiste De Boyer Argens, Jean. Chinese Letters, Seventeen Forty-One. (The Flowering of the Novel, 1740-1775 Ser: Vol. 4). 1974. lib. bdg. 50.00 (ISBN 0-8240-1103-1). Garland Pub.
Bapton, Douglas. Modern Oscilloscope Handbook. (Illus.). 1979. ref. 18.95 (ISBN 0-8359-4582-0). Reston.
Bar, Antonio. Syndicalism & Revolution in Spain. (History of Anarchism Ser.). 1981. lib. bdg. 69.95 (ISBN 0-8490-3208-3). Gordon Pr.
Bar Association of the City of New York. The Law of Presidential Impeachment. 57p. 1974. pap. 1.00 o.p. (ISBN 0-06-087074-5, HW). Har-Row.
Bar, Lois E. Le see Le Bar, Lois E.
Bar, Ulrich. Encyclopedia of Business Letters in Four Languages, 3 vols. LC 72-3331. 1972. Set. 59.00 o.p. (ISBN 0-668-02670-7). Arco.
Barach, Jeffrey. The Individual, Business & Society. (Illus.). 1977. 16.95 (ISBN 0-13-458075-3); pap. text ed. 13.95x (ISBN 0-13-458067-2). P-H.
Barack, Nathan A. The Jewish Way to Life. LC 74-19272. 216p. 1975. 7.95 o.p. (ISBN 0-685-53375-1). Jonathan David.
Barad, Dianne S. K-Speech News. (gr. 7-12). 1981. manual 15.00. Communication Skill.
Bar-Adon, Aaron. The Rise & Decline of a Dialect: A Study in the Revival of Modern Hebrew. LC 74-80121. (Janua Linguarum, Ser. Practica: No. 197). 116p. (Orig.). 1975. pap. text ed. 28.25x (ISBN 90-2793-206-9). Mouton.
Baragan, Joseph, et al. Dynamic Auscultation & Phonocardiography. Tavel, Morton E. & Tavel, Morton E., eds. (Illus.). 314p. 1979. 31.95 (ISBN 0-87619-458-7). Charles.
Baragwanath, Albert K. Currier & Ives. LC 79-57412. (Abbeville Library of Art: No. 6). (Illus.). 112p. (Orig.). 1980. pap. 4.95 (ISBN 0-89659-092-5). Abbeville Pr.
Baraheni, Reza. The Crowned Cannibals: Writings on Repression in Iran. 1977. pap. 3.95 (ISBN 0-394-72357-0, V-357, Vin). Random.
Barak, Michael. The Phantom Conspiracy. LC 80-13591. 324p. 1980. 11.95 (ISBN 0-688-03689-9). Morrow.
Baraka, Imamu A. Blues People: Negro Music in White America. LC 80-15648. 244p. 1980. Repr. of 1963 ed. lib. bdg. 19.75x (ISBN 0-313-22519-2, BABP). Greenwood.
Baraka, Imamu A., pseud. Raise Race Rays Raze: Essays Since 1965. 1971. 10.00 (ISBN 0-685-77057-5). Univ Place.
Baram, Michael S. Environmental Law & the Siting of Facilities: Issues in Land Use & Coastal Zone Management. LC 76-2664. 200p. 1976. text ed. 17.50 o.p. (ISBN 0-88410-417-6). Ballinger Pub.
Baram, R., et al, eds. see Meeting of the Midwest Autumn Immunology Conference, 7th, Michigan, Nov. 1978.
Baran, Kathryn Kavanaugh see Adams, Bruce & Kavanaugh-Baran, Kathryn.
Baran, Stanley J. The Viewer's Television Book: A Personal Guide to Understanding Television & Its Influence. LC 80-81369. 109p. (Orig.). 1980. pap. 6.95 (ISBN 0-936522-00-3). Penrith.
Baran, Stanley J., jt. auth. see Davis, Dennis K.
Baranowski, Zdzislaw. The International Horseman's Dictionary. (Illus.). 9.10 (ISBN 0-85131-262-4, Dist. by Sporting Book Center). J A Allen.
Baranski, Matthew. Mask Making. rev ed. LC 54-12542. (Illus.). (gr. 3-9). 1966. 7.75 o.p. (ISBN 0-87192-016-6). Davis Mass.
Baranson, Jack. Technology & the Multinationals. LC 77-14699. 1978. 18.95 (ISBN 0-669-02021-4). Lexington Bks.
Barany, F. R., et al, eds. Gastrointestinal Emergencies Two: Proceedings of the 2nd International Symposium on Gastrointestinal Emergencies, Rome, 7-8 June 1979. (Advances in the Biosciences: Vol. 27). (Illus.). 186p. 1980. 30.00 (ISBN 0-08-024927-2). Pergamon.
Baranyay, E. P. Mentally Handicapped Adolescent: The Slough Project of the National Society for Mentally Handicapped Children. 1971. text ed. 22.00 (ISBN 0-08-016271-1). Pergamon.
Baras, Victor, jt. ed. see Himmelfarb, Milton.
Barasch, Clarence S., jt. ed. see Biskind, Elliott L.
Barasch, Frances. Monarch Notes on Shakespeare's Henry Fourth, Part 2. (Orig.). pap. 1.95 (ISBN 0-671-00634-7). Monarch Pr.
Barasch, Marc, jt. auth. see Powers, Bob.
Barasch, Moshe. Gestures of Despair in Medieval & Early Renaissance Art. LC 76-4601. 1976. 28.50x (ISBN 0-8147-1006-9). NYU Pr.
Barash, David. The Whisperings Within. 288p. 1981. pap. 4.95 (ISBN 0-14-005699-8). Penguin.
Barath, Betty. Little Lion That Couldn't Roar. 1980. 4.00 (ISBN 0-8062-1299-3). Carlton.
Baratta & Lorton, Mary B. Workjobs for Parents. new ed. (gr. k-3). 1975. 5.50 (ISBN 0-201-04303-3). A-W.
Baratta-Lorton, Mary. Mathematics: A Way of Thinking. new ed. (gr. 1-8). 1977. tchr's. ed. 19.75 (ISBN 0-201-04322-X, Sch Div). A-W.
Baratta-Lorton, Mary B. Workjobs: Activity-Centered Learning for Early Childhood Education. 1972. text ed. 11.95 (ISBN 0-201-04311-4, Sch Div). A-W.
Barba, Harry. One of a Kind (the Many Faces & Voices of America) LC 75-41743. 1976. 6.95 o.s.i. (ISBN 0-911906-11-8); pap. 5.95 (ISBN 0-911906-12-6). Harian Creative.
Barba, Harry, ed. Harian Creative Awards No. One: Featuring the Gospel According to Everyman by Baron Mikan. 220p. 1981. lib. bdg. 8.95 (ISBN 0-911906-09-6); pap. 2.95 (ISBN 0-911906-16-9). Harian Creative.
Barba, Sharon, jt. ed. see Chester, Laura.
Barbach, Lonnie & Levine, Linda. Shared Intimacies: Women's Sexual Experiences. LC 80-917. 384p. 1980. 12.95 (ISBN 0-385-17177-3, Anchor Pr). Doubleday.
Barbach, Lonnie Garfield. For Yourself - the Fulfillment of Female Sexuality. LC 74-4873. 240p. 1975. 7.95 o.p. (ISBN 0-385-05825-X); pap. 3.95 (ISBN 0-385-11245-9). Doubleday.
Barban, jt. auth. see Green, P.
Barbara, Dominick A. How to Make People Listen to You. 188p. 1971. pap. 9.75 photocopy ed. spiral (ISBN 0-398-02223-2). C C Thomas.
--Questions & Answers on Stuttering. 112p. 1965. pap. 7.25 photocopy ed., spiral (ISBN 0-398-00088-3). C C Thomas.
--Your Speech Reveals Your Personality. 192p. 1970. pap. 8.75 photocopy, spiral (ISBN 0-398-00089-1). C C Thomas.
Barbaresi, Nina, illus. The Three Little Pigs. (Golden Storytime Bk.). (Illus.). 24p. 1981. 1.95 (ISBN 0-307-11955-6, Golden Pr). Western Pub.
Barbaresi, Sara M. How to Raise & Train a Boxer. pap. 2.00 (ISBN 0-87666-253-X, DS1006). TFH Pubns.
--How to Raise & Train a Collie. pap. 2.00 (ISBN 0-87666-272-6, DS1010). TFH Pubns.
--How to Raise & Train a German Shepherd. pap. 2.00 (ISBN 0-87666-296-3, DS1017). TFH Pubns.
Barbaresi, Sara M., jt. auth. see Ferguson, Estelle.
Barbaresi, Sara M., jt. auth. see Martin, Leda B.
Barbaresi, Sara M., jt. auth. see Meistrell, Lois.
Barbaresi, Sara M., jt. auth. see Shay, Sunny.
Barbaresi, Sara M., jt. auth. see Stebbins, Natalie.
Barbaresi, Sara M., jt. auth. see Ward, Mary A.
Barbash, Heather, jt. auth. see Marshall, John L.
Barbato & Ayer. Atmospheres. 250p. Date not set. text ed. price not set (ISBN 0-08-025583-3); pap. text ed. price not set (ISBN 0-08-025582-5). Pergamon.
Barbauld, Anna L. Hymns in Prose for Children, Repr. Of 1781 Ed. Bd. with Cheap Repository Tracts: The Shepherd of Salisbury Plain, the Two Wealthy Farmers, History of Tom White the Postilion, Black Giles the Poacher, & the History of Tawny Rachel the Fortune Teller, Black Giles' Wife. More, Hannah. Repr. of 1797 ed. LC 75-32144. (Classics of Children's Literature, 1621-1932: Vol. 10). 1976. PLB 38.00 (ISBN 0-8240-2259-9). Garland Pub.
Barbe, Louis A. Viscount Dundee. 159p. 1980. Repr. lib. bdg. 20.00 (ISBN 0-89987-053-8). Darby Bks.
Barbe, W. B. & Renzulli, J. S., eds. Psychology & Education of the Gifted. 2nd ed. LC 75-14330. 1975. 15.95 o.p. (ISBN 0-470-04775-5). Halsted Pr.
Barbe, Walter B. Resource Book for the Kindergarten Teacher. (Illus.). 1980. 34.95 (ISBN 0-88309-103-8). Zaner-Bloser.
--Teaching Reading: Selected Materials. 1965. pap. 6.95x (ISBN 0-19-500823-5). Oxford U Pr.
--Zaner-Bloser Handwriting Workbook: Cursive. (Illus.). 1977. 3.95 (ISBN 0-88309-098-8). Zaner-Bloser.
--Zaner-Bloser Handwriting Workbook: Manuscript. (Illus.). 1977. 3.95 (ISBN 0-88309-097-X). Zaner-Bloser.
Barbe, Walter B. & Swassing, Raymond H. Teaching Through Modality Strengths: Concepts & Practices. LC 79-66953. 1979. 10.00 (ISBN 0-88309-100-3). Zaner-Bloser.
Barbe, Walter B. & Renzulli, Joseph S., eds. Psychology & Education of the Gifted. 3rd ed. 544p. 1981. text ed. 16.95x (ISBN 0-8290-0234-0). Irvington.
Barbe, Walter B., et al. Charting Compass Points. (Design for Reading Ser). (Illus.). (gr. 8). 1972. text ed. 13.28 (ISBN 0-06-516011-8, SchDept); tchr's. manual 13.80 (ISBN 0-06-516209-9). Har-Row.
--Shining Searchlights. (Design for Reading Ser). (Illus.). (gr. 7). 1972. text ed. 13.28 (ISBN 0-06-516010-X, SchDept); tchrs' manual 13.80 (ISBN 0-06-516208-0). Har-Row.
--Creative Growth with Handwriting. Incl. Readiness (ISBN 0-88309-233-6); Grade One. tchrs.' manual 9.95 (ISBN 0-88309-245-X); consumable (ISBN 0-88309-234-4); non-consumable (ISBN 0-88309-256-5); Grade Two. tchrs.' manual 9.95 (ISBN 0-88309-246-8); consumable (ISBN 0-88309-235-2); non-consumable; Book 2T. tchrs.' manual 9.95 (ISBN 0-88309-247-6); consumable (ISBN 0-88309-236-0); non-consumable (ISBN 0-88309-236-0); Grade 3T. tchrs.' manual 9.95 (ISBN 0-88309-248-4); consumable (ISBN 0-88309-259-X); non-consumable (ISBN 0-88309-237-9); Grade 4. tchrs.' manual 9.95 (ISBN 0-88309-250-6); consumable (ISBN 0-88309-239-5); non-consumable; Grade 5. tchrs.' manual 9.95 (ISBN 0-88309-251-4); consumable (ISBN 0-88309-262-X); non-consumable (ISBN 0-88309-240-9); Grade 6. tchrs.' manual 9.95 (ISBN 0-88309-252-2); consumable (ISBN 0-88309-263-8); non-consumable (ISBN 0-88309-241-7); Grade 7. tchrs.' manual 6.96 (ISBN 0-88309-253-0); consumable (ISBN 0-88309-264-6); non-consumable (ISBN 0-88309-242-5); Grade 8. tchrs.' manual 6.96 (ISBN 0-88309-254-9); consumable; non-consumable. (Illus.). 1979. pupil bk., consumable or non-consumable 1.97 ea. Zaner-Bloser.
--Basic Skills in Kindergarten: Foundations for Formal Learning. 1980. 10.00 (ISBN 0-88309-104-6). Zaner-Bloser.
Barbeau, A., ed. see Canadian-American Conference on Parkinson's Disease, 2nd.
Barbeau, A., et al, eds. Huntington's Chorea: Advances in Neurology, Vol. 1. LC 72-93317. 1973. 73.50 (ISBN 0-911216-40-5). Raven.
Barbeau, Andre & Huxtable, Ryan, eds. Taurine & Neurological Disorders. LC 77-85076. 1978. 45.00 (ISBN 0-89004-202-0). Raven.
Barbeau, Andre, jt. ed. see Huxtable, Ryan.
Barbeau, Andre, et al, eds. Choline & Lecithin in Brain Disorders. LC 78-68608. (Nutrition & the Brain Ser.: Vol. 5). 1979. text ed. 47.50 (ISBN 0-89004-366-3). Raven.
Barbeau, Anne T. Intellectual Design of John Dryden's Heroic Plays. LC 71-81412. 1970. 18.50x o.p. (ISBN 0-300-01111-3). Yale U Pr.
Barbeau, Clayton D. Creative Marriage: The Middle Years. 160p. 1976. 6.95 (ISBN 0-8164-0284-1). Crossroad NY.
Barber, Albert A., jt. auth. see Grinnell, Alan.
Barber, Aldyth & Barber, Cyril. Your Marriage Has Possibilities. 200p. (Orig.). 1981. pap. 4.95 (ISBN 0-89840-012-0). Heres Life.
Barber, Antonia. The Ghosts. (gr. 5-7). 1975. pap. 1.95 (ISBN 0-671-42454-8). Archway.
--The Ghosts. (gr. 5-7). 1975. pap. 1.75 (ISBN 0-671-56001-8). PB.
Barber, Benjamin. Marriage Voices: A Novel. LC 80-18831. 256p. 1981. 10.95 (ISBN 0-671-44808-0). Summit Bks.

Barber, Benjamin & McGrath, Michael J., eds. The Artist & Political Vision. 300p. 1981. 19.95 (ISBN 0-87855-380-0). Transaction Bks.
Barber, Bernard. Science & the Social Order. LC 78-1569. 228p. 1978. Repr. of 1952 ed. lib. bdg. 22.25x (ISBN 0-313-20356-3, BASSO). Greenwood.
Barber, C. L. Shakespeare's Festive Comedy. 1972. 16.50x (ISBN 0-691-06043-6); pap. 4.95 (ISBN 0-691-01304-7, 271). Princeton U Pr.
Barber, Cyril, jt. auth. see Barber, Aldyth.
Barber, Cyril J. Periodic Supplement Three to Minister's Library. 1980. pap. 4.95 (ISBN 0-8010-0787-9). Baker Bk.
--Study Guide for Nehemiah & the Dynamics of Effective Leadership. (Illus.). 96p. 1980. pap. text ed. 3.25 (ISBN 0-87213-022-3). Loizeaux.
Barber, Daniel M. Citizen Participation in American Communities: Strategies for Success. LC 80-83336. 144p. 1980. pap. 8.95 (ISBN 0-8403-2299-2). Kendall-Hunt.
Barber, DeNonie. Their Last Lap at Indy: A Book of Tributes. (Illus.). 1980. 8.95 (ISBN 0-916620-49-2). Portals Pr.
Barber, Derek, ed. Data Networks: Development & Uses. 690p. 1980. pap. text ed. 160.00x (ISBN 0-903796-59-7, Pub. by Online Conferences England). Renouf.
Barber, E. A., jt. ed. see Powell, J. U.
Barber, E. A., et al, eds. see Liddell, Henry G. & Scott, Robert.
Barber, Edwin A. The Ceramic Furniture & Silver Collectors' Glossary. LC 76-8172. (Architecture & Decorative Art Ser). 1967. Repr. of 1914 ed. 14.50 (ISBN 0-306-70967-8). Da Capo.
Barber, Elsie M. Trembling Years. (gr. 7 up). 1949. 5.95 o.s.i. (ISBN 0-02-506850-4). Macmillan.
Barber, Florence H. Fellow of Infinite Jest: Recollections & Anecdotes of William Lyon Phelps. 1949. 19.50x (ISBN 0-685-89752-4). Elliots Bks.
Barber, H. R. Immunobiology for the Clinician. LC 76-23386. 1977. 38.95 (ISBN 0-471-04785-6). Wiley.
Barber, Henry. British Family Names. 2nd ed. LC 68-17914. 1968. Repr. of 1903 ed. 18.00 (ISBN 0-8103-3109-8). Gale.
Barber, Hugh. Ovarian Carcinoma: Etiology, Diagnosis & Treatment. LC 77-846077. (Illus.). 1978. 41.25 (ISBN 0-89352-009-8). Masson Pub.
Barber, Hugh O. Manual of Electronystagmography. LC 80-17349. (Illus.). 232p. 1980. text ed. 32.50 (ISBN 0-8016-0449-4). Mosby.
Barber, Hugh R. Manual of Gynecologic Oncology. 356p. 1980. pap. text ed. 17.75 (ISBN 0-397-50474-8). Lippincott.
Barber, Hugh R., jt. ed. see Van Nagell, John R., Jr.
Barber, J. H. & Kratz, Charlotte R., eds. Towards Team Care. (Illus.). 176p. 1980. pap. text ed. 10.00x (ISBN 0-443-02031-0). Churchill.
Barber, James. Imperial Frontier. LC 70-14208. (Illus.). 1968. 9.00x (ISBN 0-8002-1279-7). Intl Pubns Serv.
Barber, James A., Jr., jt. ed. see Ambrose, Stephen E.
Barber, James D. The Presidential Character: Predicting Performance in the White House. 2nd ed. LC 77-4094. 1977. 11.95 o.p. (ISBN 0-13-697466-X); pap. 10.95 (ISBN 0-13-697847-9). P-H.
Barber, Janet & Dillman, Peter. Emergency Patient Care for the EMT: A Workbook for the EMT. 1981. 15.95 (ISBN 0-8359-1671-5). Reston.
Barber, Janet, jt. auth. see Budassi, Susan A.
Barber, Janet M. & Budassi, Susan A. Mosby's Manual of Emergency Care: Practices & Procedures. LC 79-31708. (Illus.). 1979. pap. text ed. 19.95 (ISBN 0-8016-0447-8). Mosby.
Barber, Janet M., et al. Adult & Child Care: A Client Approach to Nursing. 2nd ed. LC 76-26637. (Illus.). 1977. 26.95 (ISBN 0-8016-0444-3). Mosby.
Barber, John. Soviet Historians in Crisis Nineteen Twenty-Eight to Nineteen Thirty-Two. LC 80-13798. 250p. 1981. text ed. 33.00x (ISBN 0-8419-0614-9). Holmes & Meier.
Barber, Laird H., ed. see Heywood, Thomas.
Barber, Lester E., ed. see Rudd, Anthony.
Barber, Lucie W. The Religious Education of Preschool Children. LC 80-27623. 190p. (Orig.). 1981. pap. price not set (ISBN 0-89135-026-8). Religious Educ.
--The Religious Education of Preschool Children. 190p. (Orig.). 1981. pap. write for info. (ISBN 0-89135-026-8). Religious Educ.
Barber, Lynn. The Heyday of Natural History. LC 79-6533. (Illus.). 324p. 1981. 17.95 (ISBN 0-385-12574-7). Doubleday.
Barber, M. C. The Trial of the Templars. LC 77-85716. 320p. 1978. 41.50 (ISBN 0-521-21896-9); pap. 11.95x (ISBN 0-521-21896-9). Cambridge U Pr.
Barber, Marie-Claire, tr. see Ferraris, Luigi V.
Barber, Noel. Tanamera. 416p. 1981. 13.95 (ISBN 0-02-506840-7). Macmillan.
Barber, Phyllis. Smiley Snake's Adventure. Jordan, Alton, ed. (Buppet Series). (Illus.). (gr. k-3). 1981. PLB 4.50 (ISBN 0-89868-098-0, Read Res); pap. text ed. 1.95 (ISBN 0-89868-109-X). ARO Pub.
Barber, Richard. Edward Prince of Wales & Aquitaine: A Biography of the Black Prince. (Illus.). 1978. 17.50 o.p. (ISBN 0-684-15864-7, ScribT). Scribner.
--The Knight & Chivalry. 2nd ed. (Illus.). 400p. 1975. 17.50x (ISBN 0-87471-653-5). Rowman.
--Samuel Pepys Esq. LC 70-123622. (Illus.). 1970. 11.95 (ISBN 0-520-01763-3). U of Cal Pr.
--A Strong Land & a Sturdy: Life in Medieval England. LC 75-43895. (Illus.). (gr. 6 up). 1976. 8.95 (ISBN 0-395-28888-6, Clarion). HM.
Barber, Theodore, ed. see Sherwood, Sylvia, et al.
Barber, Theodore X. LSD, Marijuana, Yoga, & Hypnosis. LC 73-115935. 1970. 18.95x (ISBN 0-202-25004-0). Aldine Pub.
Barber, Theodore X., et al. Hypnosis, Imagination & Human Potentialities. LC 73-19539. 1974. 23.00 (ISBN 0-08-017932-0). Pergamon.
Barber, Theodore X., et al, eds. Biofeedback & Self-Control: An Aldine Reader on the Regulation of Bodily Processes & Consciousness. LC 71-167858. 1971. 34.95x (ISBN 0-202-25048-2). Aldine Pub.
--Biofeedback & Self-Control 1975-76: An Aldine Annual on the Regulation of Bodily Processes & Consciousness. LC 74-151109. 225p. 1976. 34.95x (ISBN 0-202-25110-1). Aldine Pub.
Barber, William J. British Economic Thought & India Sixteen Hundred to Eighteen Fifty-Eight: A Study in the History of Development Economics. 264p. 1975. 29.95x (ISBN 0-19-828265-6). Oxford U Pr.
Barberis, P. Pere Goriot de Balzac: Ecriture, structures, significations. new ed. (Collection themes et textes). 296p. (Orig., Fr.). 1972. pap. 6.75 (ISBN 2-03-035010-9, 2681). Larousse.
Barberis, Pierre, ed. see Goupil, Armand.
Barbet, Pierre. Cosmic Crusaders. (Science Fiction Ser.). 1980. pap. 2.25 (ISBN 0-87997-583-0, UE1583). DAW Bks.
Barbet, Pierre, M.D. Doctor at Calvary. pap. 2.95 (ISBN 0-385-06687-2, D155, Im). Doubleday.
Barbezieux, Rigaut De. Le Canzoni: Testi E Commento a Cura Di Mauro Braccini. LC 80-2188. 1981. Repr. of 1960 ed. 26.00 (ISBN 0-404-19017-0). AMS Pr.
--Liriche Di Rigaut De Berbezilh, a Cura Di Alberto Varvaro. LC 80-2187. 1981. Repr. of 1960 ed. 39.50 (ISBN 0-404-19018-9). AMS Pr.
Barbier, E., ed. The Application of Nuclear Techniques to Geothermal Studies: Proceedings. 1978. pap. text ed. 77.00 (ISBN 0-08-021670-6). Pergamon.
--Cerro Prieto Geothermal Field: Prodeedings of the First Symposium Held at San Diego, California, Sept. 1978. (Illus.). 300p. 1981. 77.00 (ISBN 0-08-026241-4). Pergamon.
Barbier, Jean, jt. auth. see Gorree, Georges.
Barborka, Geoffrey. Divine Plan: Commentary on the Secret Doctrine. 3rd ed. 1972. 11.95 (ISBN 0-8356-7167-4). Theos Pub Hse.
Barborka, Geoffrey A. Glossary of Sanskrit Terms & Key to Their Correct Pronunciation. 76p. (Orig.). 1972. pap. 1.75 (ISBN 0-685-29054-9, 913004-04). Point Loma Pub.
--H. P. Blavatsky, Tibet & Tulku. (Illus.). 1974. 12.95 (ISBN 0-8356-7159-3). Theos Pub Hse.
Barbour, Arthur. Painting the Seasons in Watercolor. (Illus.). 160p. 1975. 18.95 o.p. (ISBN 0-8230-3858-0). Watson-Guptill.
Barbour, Beverly. The Complete Food Preservation Book: How to Can, Freeze, Preserve, Pickle, & Cure Edibles. 1978. 12.95 o.p. (ISBN 0-679-50806-6); pap. 6.95 o.p. (ISBN 0-679-50825-2). McKay.
--Easy, Elegant Luncheon Menus. (Illus.). 1980. 14.95 (ISBN 0-8019-6831-3). Chilton.
Barbour, George M. Florida for Tourists, Invalids & Settlers. Peter, Emmett B., Jr., ed. LC 64-19152. (Floridiana Facsimile & Reprint Ser). (Illus.). 1964. Repr. of 1882 ed. 10.75 (ISBN 0-8130-0012-2). U Presses Fla.
Barbour, Ian. Earth Might Be Fair: Reflections on Ethics, Religion & Ecology. LC 73-167916. 1972. pap. text ed. 7.95 (ISBN 0-13-222679-0). P-H.
Barbour, Ian G. Issues in Science & Religion. 1971. pap. 8.50x (ISBN 0-06-131566-4, TB1566, Torch). Har-Row.
Barbour, Ian G., ed. Western Man & Environmental Ethics. LC 72-1936. 1973. pap. text ed. 6.50 (ISBN 0-201-00387-2). A-W.
Barbour, James Murray. Tuning & Temperament: A Historical Survey. LC 74-37288. (Illus.). 228p. 1972. Repr. of 1951 ed. lib. bdg. 21.50 (ISBN 0-306-70422-6). Da Capo.
Barbour, John A. In the Wake of the Whale. LC 69-11397. (Surveyor Books Ser). (Illus.). (gr. 7-10). 1969. 3.95g o.s.i. (ISBN 0-02-708330-6, CCPr). Macmillan.
Barbour, Michael, et al. Botany: A Laboratory Manual for Weier. 5th ed. 1975. 10.95 (ISBN 0-471-04800-3). Wiley.
Barbour, Michael G., et al. Coastal Ecology: Bodega Head. (Illus.). 1974. 15.00x (ISBN 0-520-02147-9); pap. 6.95x (ISBN 0-520-03276-4). U of Cal Pr.
Barbour, Murray. The Church Music of William Billings. LC 72-39000. 168p. 1972. Repr. of 1960 ed. lib. bdg. 15.00 (ISBN 0-306-70434-X). Da Capo.
Barbour, R. Glassblowing for Laboratory Technicians. 2nd ed. 1978. text ed. 45.00 (ISBN 0-08-022155-6); pap. text ed. 14.00 (ISBN 0-08-022156-4). Pergamon.
Barbour, Roger W., et al. Kentucky Birds: A Finding Guide. LC 72-91662. (Illus.). 328p. 1973. 13.50 (ISBN 0-8131-1281-8). U Pr of Ky.
Barbree, Jay. Six Million Dollar Man, No. 4: Pilot Error. 1975. pap. 1.25 o.s.i. (ISBN 0-446-76835-9). Warner Bks.
Barbrook, Alec & Bolt, Christine. Power & Protest in American Life. 1980. write for info. (ISBN 0-312-63369-6). St Martin.
Barca, Pedro Calderon de la see Calderon de la Barca, Pedro.
Barca Pedro Calderon, De La see Calderon De La Barca, Pedro.
Barcelo, J. R. Spanish-English - English-Spanish Chemical Vocabulary. vii, 111p. (Orig.). 1980. pap. 7.50 (ISBN 84-205-0696-6). Heinman.
Barcelona, Biblioteca Central, Seccion De Musica. La Musica De la Cantigas De Santa Maria del Rey Alfonso el Sabio, 4 pts. in 3 vols. LC 80-2193. 1981. Set. 375.00 (ISBN 0-404-19046-4). Vol. 1 (ISBN 0-404-19047-2). Vol. 2 (ISBN 0-404-19048-0). Vol. 3 (ISBN 0-404-19049-9). AMS Pr.
Barcham, William L. The Imaginary View Scenes of Antonio Canaletto. LC 76-23603. (Outstanding Dissertations in the Fine Arts - 18th Century). (Illus.). 1977. Repr. of 1974 ed. lib. bdg. 63.00 (ISBN 0-8240-2677-2). Garland Pub.
Barcia, Jose R. Americo Castro & the Meaning of Spanish Civilization. 1977. 20.00x (ISBN 0-520-02920-8). U of Cal Pr.
Barcia, Jose R., tr. see Vallejo, Cesar.
Barclay, G. W. Techniques of Population Analysis. LC 58-59899. 1958. 21.95 (ISBN 0-471-04818-6). Wiley.
Barclay, Ian. He Is Everything to Me. LC 75-29735. 96p. 1976. 1.95 o.p. (ISBN 0-684-14543-X, SL628, ScribT). Scribner.
Barclay, Pamela. Charley Pride. LC 74-14659. (Rock'n Pop Stars Ser.). (Illus.). 32p. (gr. 4-12). 1974. PLB 5.95 (ISBN 0-87191-397-6); pap. 2.95 (ISBN 0-89812-108-6). Creative Ed.
--Duke Ellington. LC 74-8211. (Illus.). 40p. (gr. 4-8). 1975. PLB 5.75 o.p. (ISBN 0-87191-367-4). Creative Ed.
--Secretariat. LC 74-11378. (Sports Superstars Ser.). (Illus.). 32p. (gr. 3-6). 1974. PLB 5.95 (ISBN 0-87191-377-1); pap. 2.95 (ISBN 0-89812-189-2). Creative Ed.
Barclay, Scotty. Poker: The Small-Limit Game. 64p. (Orig.). 1980. pap. 2.95 (ISBN 0-89650-835-8). Gamblers.
Barclay, William. The Beatitudes & the Lord's Prayer for Everyman. LC 75-9309. 256p. 1975. pap. 4.95 (ISBN 0-06-060393-3, RD112, HarpR). Har-Row.
--The Daily Study Bible, 18 vols. rev. ed. Incl. Vol. 1. The Gospel of Matthew. (ISBN 0-664-21300-6); softcover (ISBN 0-664-24100-X); Vol. 2. The Gospel of Matthew. (ISBN 0-664-21301-4); softcover (ISBN 0-664-24101-8); The Gospel of Mark. (ISBN 0-664-21302-2); softcover (ISBN 0-664-24102-6); The Gospel of Luke. (ISBN 0-664-21303-0); softcover (ISBN 0-664-24103-4); Vol. 1. The Gospel of John. (ISBN 0-664-21304-9); softcover (ISBN 0-664-24104-2); Vol. 2. The Gospel of John. (ISBN 0-664-21305-7); softcover (ISBN 0-664-24105-0); The Acts of the Apostles. (ISBN 0-664-21306-5); softcover (ISBN 0-664-24106-9); The Letter to the Romans. (ISBN 0-664-21307-3); softcover (ISBN 0-664-24107-7); The Letters to the Corinthians. (ISBN 0-664-21308-1); softcover (ISBN 0-664-24108-5); The Letters to the Galatians & Ephesians. (ISBN 0-664-21309-X); softcover (ISBN 0-664-24109-3); The Letters to the Philippians, Colossians & Thessalonians. (ISBN 0-664-21310-3); softcover (ISBN 0-664-24110-7); The Letters to Timothy, Titus & Philemon. (ISBN 0-664-21311-1); softcover (ISBN 0-664-24111-5); The Letter to the Hebrews. (ISBN 0-664-21312-X); softcover (ISBN 0-664-24112-3); The Letters of James & Peter. (ISBN 0-664-21313-8); softcover (ISBN 0-664-24113-1); The Letters of John & Jude. (ISBN 0-664-21314-6); softcover (ISBN 0-664-24114-X); Vol. 1. The Revelation of John. (ISBN 0-664-21315-4); softcover (ISBN 0-664-24115-8); Vol. 2. The Revelation of John. (ISBN 0-664-21316-2); softcover (ISBN 0-664-24116-6). 1977. Set. deluxe ed. 150.00 (ISBN 0-664-21318-9); Set. softcover 76.00 (ISBN 0-664-24098-4); deluxe ed. 8.95 ea.; softcover 4.50 ea.; index vol. (ISBN 0-664-21370-7); softcover (ISBN 0-664-24215-4). Westminster.
--Ethics in a Permissive Society. LC 70-175157. 1972. 9.95 (ISBN 0-06-060415-8, Harpr). Har-Row.
--Everyday Prayers. LC 60-5326. (Harper Jubilee Bk.). 1976. pap. 1.95 o.p. (ISBN 0-06-060394-1, HJ-27, HarpR). Har-Row.
--Guide to Daily Prayer. LC 62-11473. 1974. pap. 3.95 (ISBN 0-06-060401-8, RD75, HarpR). Har-Row.
--In the Hands of God. LC 80-25261. 1981. pap. price not set (ISBN 0-664-24362-2). Westminster.
--Jesus of Nazareth. 288p. 1981. pap. 10.95 (ISBN 0-8407-5759-X). Nelson.
--Jesus of Nazareth. 1977. pap. 1.95 (ISBN 0-345-27253-6). Ballantine.
--A Life of Christ. LC 76-9989. (Harper Jubilee Giant). (Illus.). 96p. 1977. pap. 3.95 o.p. (ISBN 0-06-060403-4, HJG O1, HarpR). Har-Row.
--The Life of Jesus for Everyman. LC 75-12282. 96p. 1975. pap. 3.95 (ISBN 0-06-060404-2, RD 319, HarpR). Har-Row.
--The Master's Men. (Festival Books). 1976. pap. 1.75 (ISBN 0-687-23732-7). Abingdon.
--The Master's Men. (Orig.). pap. 1.50 (ISBN 0-89129-132-6). Jove Pubns.
--The Mind of St. Paul. LC 75-9310. 256p. 1975. pap. 5.95 (ISBN 0-06-060471-9, RD110, HarpR). Har-Row.
--The New Testament: A New Translation. 576p. (Orig.). 1980. pap. 2.95x (ISBN 0-664-24358-4). Westminster.
--Palabras Griegas Del Nuevo Testamento. Marin, Javier J., tr. 1979. pap. 3.60 (ISBN 0-311-42052-4). Casa Bautista.
--Prayers for Help & Healing. LC 74-25682. 128p. 1975. pap. 2.95 (ISBN 0-06-060481-6, RD-89, HarpR). Har-Row.
--Ten Commandments for Today. 1977. pap. 1.95 (ISBN 0-89129-228-4). Jove Pubns.
--Turning to God: A Study of Conversion in the Book of Acts & Today. pap. 2.95 (ISBN 0-8010-0564-7). Baker Bk.
Barcley, Alexander, tr. see Brant, Sebastian.
Barcus, F. Earle & Wolkin, Rachel. Children's Television: An Analysis of Programming & Advertising. LC 76-12843. (Special Studies). 1977. text ed. 25.95 (ISBN 0-275-23210-7). Praeger.
Barcus, James E., ed. Shelley: The Critical Heritage. (The Critical Heritage Ser.). 1975. 38.00x (ISBN 0-7100-8148-0). Routledge & Kegan.
Bard, Allen J. & Faulkner, Larry R. Electrochemical Methods: Fundamentals & Applications. LC 79-24712. 718p. 1980. text ed. 29.95 (ISBN 0-471-05542-5); tchrs' manual avail. (ISBN 0-471-07788-7). Wiley.
Bard, James A. Rational Emotive Therapy in Practice. LC 80-51923. 192p. 1980. pap. text ed. 8.95 (ISBN 0-87822-213-8, 2138). Res Press.
Bard, Patti, jt. auth. see Culbertson, Judi.
Bard, Rachel. Successful Wood Book: Selection & Use, Fastening & Finishing. LC 78-15547. 1978. 13.95 (ISBN 0-912336-73-0); pap. 6.95 (ISBN 0-912336-74-9). Structures Pub.

Bard, Ray & Davis, Larry. Winning Ways. LC 79-20395. 1979. write for info 3 ring notebk. (ISBN 0-89384-043-2). Learning Concepts.

Bard, Samuel A., pseud. Waikna, or, Adventures on the Mosquito Shore. Alleger, Daniel E., ed. LC 65-28697. (Latin American Gateway Ser.). (Illus.). 1965. Repr. of 1855 ed. 9.00 (ISBN 0-8130-0217-6). U Presses Fla.

Bard, William E. As a Wild Bird Returning. 4.50 o.p. (ISBN 0-685-48826-8). Nortex Pr.

Bardach, Eugene. The Skill Factor in Politics: Repealing the Mental Commitment Laws in California. LC 79-157820. 300p. 1972. 20.00x (ISBN 0-520-02042-1). U of Cal Pr.

Bardeen, Charles W., ed. see Comenius, John A.

Barden, L. W. The Ruy Lopez: Winning Chess with IP-K4. 11.25 (ISBN 0-08-013006-2); pap. 5.75 (ISBN 0-08-009997-1). Pergamon.

Barden, Leonard. An Introduction to Chess. 112p. 1968. pap. 4.95 (ISBN 0-7100-5221-9). Routledge & Kegan.

--Introduction to Chess Moves & Tactics Simply Explained. (Illus., Orig.). 1959. pap. 2.00 (ISBN 0-486-21210-6). Dover.

Barden, Leonard, et al. King's Indian Defence. 1973. 22.50 (ISBN 0-7134-0367-5). David & Charles.

Barder, Richard. Dry Fly Trouting for Beginners. 1976. 5.95 (ISBN 0-7153-7055-3). David & Charles.

Bardeschi, Marco D. & Segoloni, Giulio. Italian Villas Today. (Eng, Fr, It. & Ger.). 25.00 (ISBN 0-685-20599-1). Transatlantic.

Bardet, Jean-Pierre, et al, eds. Le Batiment: Enquete D'histoire Economidue XIVe-XIXe Siecles, Tome 1. (Maisons Rurales et Urbaines Dans la France Traditionnello Industrite et Artisanat: No. 6). 1971. pap. 51.20x (ISBN 90-2796-880-2). Mouton.

Bardi. Saint Gemma, the Passion Flower. 3.50 o.s.i. (ISBN 0-8198-0136-4). Dghtrs St Paul.

Bardi, Edward, jt. auth. see Coyle, John J.

Bardi, P. M. Architecture: The World We Build. LC 77-153826. (International Library). (Illus.). 128p. (gr. 7-12). 1972. PLB 6.90 o.p. (ISBN 0-531-02104-1). Watts.

Bardin, Pierre. La Vie D'un Dovar: Essai Sur la Vie Rurale Dans les Grades Plaines De la Haute Medjerda, Tunisio. (Recherches Mediterraneennes, Documents: No. 2). 1965. pap. 20.50x (ISBN 90-2796-225-1). Mouton.

Bardoff, O., jt. auth. see Downing, Frank.

Bardon, Edward J. The Sexual Arena & Women's Liberation. LC 77-23937. 1978. 15.95 (ISBN 0-88229-219-6); pap. 7.95 (ISBN 0-88229-558-6). Nelson-Hall.

Bardon, Jack I. & Bennett, Virginia C. School Psychology. LC 73-11419. (Foundations of Modern Psychology Ser). (Illus.). 224p. 1973. pap. text ed. 7.95 (ISBN 0-13-79442-8). P-H.

Bardsley, Charles W. Romance of the London Directory. LC 72-78115. 1971. Repr. of 1879 ed. 18.00 (ISBN 0-8103-3782-7). Gale.

Bardwell, Denver. Calamity at Devil's Crossing. (YA) 1973. 5.95 (ISBN 0-685-28397-6, Avalon). Bouregy.

Bardwick, Judith M., et al. Feminine Personality & Conflict. LC 80-24191. (Contemporary Psychology Ser.). vii, 102p. 1981. Repr. of 1970 ed. lib. bdg. 19.75 (ISBN 0-313-22504-4, BAFP). Greenwood.

Bare, Colleen S. The Durable Desert Tortoise. LC 79-12806. (A Skylight Bk.). (Illus.). (gr. 2-5). 1979. 4.95 (ISBN 0-396-07706-4). Dodd.

--Ground Squirrels. LC 80-13649. (A Skylight Bk.). (Illus.). 64p. (gr. 2-5). 1980. PLB 5.95 (ISBN 0-396-07852-4). Dodd.

Barefoot, A. C. & Hankins, Frank W. Identification of Modern Tertiary Woods. (Illus.). 220p. 1981. 54.00x (ISBN 0-19-854378-6). Oxford U Pr.

Barefoot, Patience. Community Services. 1977. pap. 7.95 (ISBN 0-571-11052-5, Pub. by Faber & Faber). Merrimack Bk Serv.

Bareham, Terence. George Crabbe. (Critical Studies Ser.). 245p. 1977. 19.50x (ISBN 0-06-490305-2). B&N.

Bareham, Tony, ed. Anthony Trollope. (Barnes & Noble Critical Studies). 207p. 1980. 26.00x (ISBN 0-389-20027-1). B&N.

Barell, John. Playgrounds of Our Minds. LC 79-27084. 1980. pap. text ed. 9.95x (ISBN 0-8077-2580-3). Tchrs Coll.

Baren, Martin, et al. Overcoming Learning Disabilities: A Team Approach (Parent-Teacher-Physician-Child) 1978. text ed. 16.95 (ISBN 0-8359-5365-3). Reston.

Barenblatt, ed. Similarity, Self-Similarity & Intermediate Asymptotics. (Illus.). 1979. 35.00 (ISBN 0-306-10956-5, Consultants). Plenum Pub.

Barendse, Michael A. Social Expectations & Perception: The Case of the Slavic Anthracite Workers. LC 80-8610. (Penn State Studies: No. 47). (Illus.). 90p. (Orig.). 1981. pap. text ed. 3.50x (ISBN 0-271-00277-8). Pa St U Pr.

Barenholtz, Bernard & McClintock, Inez. American Antique Toys, Eighteen-Thirty to Nineteen-Hundred. (Illus.). 264p. 1980. 45.00 (ISBN 0-686-62681-8, 0668-6). Abrams.

Bares, Jiri, et al. Collection of Problems in Physical Chemistry. 1962. text ed. 27.00 (ISBN 0-08-009577-1). Pergamon.

Barfield, Janice. You Can Fly: But That Cocoon Has Got to Go. (Orig.). 1981. 7.95 (ISBN 0-310-43920-5). Zondervan.

Barfield, Owen. History, Guilt, & Habit. LC 79-65333. 1979. 12.50x (ISBN 0-8195-5038-8, Pub. by Wesleyan U Pr). Columbia U Pr.

--History in English Words. (Orig.). 1962. pap. 2.95 o.p. (ISBN 0-571-06283-0, Pub. by Faber & Faber). Merrimack Bk Serv.

--Poetic Diction: A Study in Meaning. 3rd ed. LC 72-10631. 232p. 1973. pap. 7.50 (ISBN 0-8195-6026-X, Pub. by Wesleyan U Pr). Columbia U Pr.

--What Coleridge Thought. LC 73-153100. 1971. 17.50 (ISBN 0-8195-4040-4, Pub. by Wesleyan U Pr). Columbia U Pr.

--Worlds Apart. LC 63-17798. 1964. pap. 7.45 (ISBN 0-8195-6017-0, Pub. by Wesleyan U Pr). Columbia U Pr.

Barfoot, Audrey. Everyday Costume in Britain. 1972. 14.95 (ISBN 0-7134-1901-6, Pub. by Batsford England). David & Charles.

Barfoot, Edith. The Witness of Edith Barfoot: The Joyful Vocation to Suffering. 1977. 4.25x (ISBN 0-631-17910-0, Pub by Basil Blackwell England). Biblio Dist.

Barford, Carol. Let Me Hear the Music. LC 78-23966. (gr. 6 up). 1979. 7.95 (ISBN 0-395-28959-9, Clarion). HM.

Barge, Lura La see La Barge, Lura.

Bargebuhr, Fredrick P. The Alhambra: A Cycle of Studies on the Eleventh Century in Moorish Spain. 1968. 100.00x (ISBN 3-11-000524-7). De Gruyter.

Barger, Bill, ed. see Boyle, Robert.

Barger, Gerald L., jt. ed. see Wang Jen-Yu.

Barger, M. Susan. Bibliography of Photographic Processes in Use Before 1880: Their Materials, Processing, & Conservation. LC 80-84390. 160p. 1980. pap. 37.50 (ISBN 0-89938-003-4). Graph Arts Res RIT.

Barghoorn, Frederick C. Detente & the Democratic Movement in the USSR. LC 76-4425. 1976. 15.95 (ISBN 0-02-901850-1). Free Pr.

Bargmann, V., ed. Group Representations in Mathematics & Physics: Battelle Seattle 1969 Rencontres. LC 75-146233. (Lecture Notes in Physics: Vol. 6). 1971. pap. 18.30 (ISBN 0-387-05310-7). Springer-Verlag.

Bargo, Michael, Jr. Choices & Decisions: A Guidebook for Constructing Values. LC 79-67019. 164p. 1980. pap. 12.00 (ISBN 0-88390-153-6); facilitator's manual with guidebook 25.00 (ISBN 0-88390-152-8). Univ Assocs.

Bargyla, ed. see Corley, Hugh.

Bargyla, ed. see Hainsworth, P. H.

Bargyla, ed. see Leatherbarrow, Margaret.

Bargyla, ed. see Stephenson, W. A.

Barham, Jerry N. Mechanical Kinesiology. LC 77-23969. (Illus.). 1978. 18.95 (ISBN 0-8016-0476-1). Mosby.

Barham, Jerry N., jt. auth. see Krause, J. V.

Barham, Patte, jt. auth. see Rasputin, Maria.

Barhes, Harold, ed. Proceedings of the Ninth European Marine Biology Symposium, Oban 1974. 1976. 55.00x (ISBN 0-900015-34-9). Taylor-Carlisle.

Barhydt, Hap. Voyage of a Lifetime: A Journal. (Illus.). 75p. (Orig.). 1980. pap. 4.95 (ISBN 0-9605346-0-1). Remarkable Pubns.

Barica, J. & Mur, L., eds. Hypertrophic Ecosystems. (Developments in Hydrobiology Ser.: No. 2). 330p. 1981. PLB 87.00 (ISBN 90-6193-752-3, Pub. by Dr. W. Junk). Kluwer Boston.

Barich, Bill. Laughing in the Hills. 240p. 1981. pap. 3.95 (ISBN 0-14-005832-X). Penguin.

Barigozzi, Claudio, ed. Origin & Natural History of Cell Lines: Proceedings of a Conference Held at Accademia Nazionale Dei Lincei, Rome, Italy, October 1977. LC 78-12805. (Progress in Clinical & Biological Research: Vol. 26). 1979. 22.00 (ISBN 0-8451-0026-2). A R Liss.

Baring, Maurice. A Year in Russia. LC 79-2891. 296p. 1981. Repr. of 1917 ed. 23.50 (ISBN 0-8305-0060-X). Hyperion Conn.

Baring-Gould, Sabine. Book of Folklore. LC 69-16807. Repr. of 1913 ed. 18.00 (ISBN 0-8103-3603-0). Gale.

--Book of Werewolves: Being an Account of Terrible Superstition. Repr. of 1865 ed. 15.00 (ISBN 0-685-32595-4). Gale.

--Cliff Castles & Cave Dwellings of Europe. LC 68-17983. (Illus.). 1968. Repr. of 1911 ed. 15.000 (ISBN 0-8103-3423-2). Gale.

--Early Reminiscences, 1834-1864. LC 67-23868. 1967. Repr. of 1923 ed. 15.00 (ISBN 0-8103-3049-0). Gale.

--Family Names & Their Story. LC 68-23136. 1969. Repr. of 1910 ed. 15.00 (ISBN 0-8103-0151-2). Gale.

--Freaks of Fanaticism & Other Strange Events. LC 68-21754. 1968. Repr. of 1891 ed. 18.00 (ISBN 0-8103-3503-4). Gale.

--Further Reminiscences, 1864-1894. LC 67-23869. 1967. Repr. of 1925 ed. 15.00 (ISBN 0-8103-3050-4). Gale.

--Old Country Life. LC 78-77086. 1969. Repr. of 1890 ed. 18.00 (ISBN 0-8103-3848-3). Gale.

--Old English Home & Its Dependencies. LC 74-77085. 1969. Repr. of 1898 ed. 18.00 (ISBN 0-8103-3847-5). Gale.

--Strange Survivals, Some Chapters in the History of Man. LC 67-23909. (Illus.). 1968. Repr. of 1892 ed. 15.00 (ISBN 0-8103-3422-4). Gale.

Barish & Schla. Seeing the Real London. Date not set. pap. 7.95 (ISBN 0-8120-2241-6). Barron. Postponed.

Barish, Jonas. The Antitheatrical Prejudice. 1981. 20.00 (ISBN 0-520-03735-9). U of Cal Pr.

Barish, Louis & Barish, Rebecca. Varieties of Jewish Belief. 1979. Repr. 9.95 (ISBN 0-8246-0242-0). Jonathan David.

Barish, Rebecca, jt. auth. see Barish, Louis.

Barish, Wendy, ed. The Anything Goes, Bk. I. 1981. 2.95 (ISBN 0-671-43051-3). Wanderer Bks.

--The Anything Goes, Bk. II. 192p. 1981. price not set. Wanderer Bks.

Barish, Wendy, ed. see Appleton, Victor.

Barish, Wendy, ed. see Dixon, Franklin W.

Barish, Wendy, ed. see Hope, Laura Lee.

Barish, Wendy, ed. see Keene, Carolyn.

Barish, Wendy, ed. see Sheldon, Ann.

Baritz, Loren. The Servants of Power. LC 73-17924. 273p. 1974. Repr. of 1960 ed. lib. bdg. 19.75x (ISBN 0-8371-7275-6, BASP). Greenwood.

Baritz, Loren, ed. The Culture of the Twenties. LC 69-14821. (American Heritage Ser). (Illus.). 1970. 9.50 (ISBN 0-672-60138-9, AHS83). Bobbs.

Barjon, J. Radio-Diagnosis of Pleuro-Pulmonary Affections. 1918. 47.50x (ISBN 0-685-89775-3). Elliots Bks.

Bark, Dennis L. Berlin-Frage Nineteen Forty-Nine to Nineteen Fifty-Five: Verhandlungsgrundlagen und Eindaemmungspolitik. (Veroeffentlichungen der Historischen Kommission Zu Berlin Ser.: Vol. 36). xiv, 544p. 1972. 72.80x (ISBN 3-11-003639-8). De Gruyter.

Bark, L. S. & Bark, S. M. Thermometric Titrimetry. 1969. 22.00 (ISBN 0-08-013047-X). Pergamon.

Bark, S. M., jt. auth. see Bark, L. S.

Barkai, Meyer, tr. The Ghetto Fighters. 1977. pap. text ed. 1.75 (ISBN 0-505-51159-2). Tower Bks.

Barkan, Joel D. & Okumu, John J. Politics & Public Policy in Kenya & Tanzania. LC 78-19470. (Praeger Special Studies). 1979. 27.95 (ISBN 0-03-023206-6); pap. 10.95 student edition (ISBN 0-03-052336-2). Praeger.

Barkan, Stanley H. The Blacklines Scrawl. (Poetry Ser.). 1976. 8.95 o.p. (ISBN 0-89304-017-7, CCC108); signed ltd. ed. 10.00 (ISBN 0-89304-017-7); pap. 3.00x (ISBN 0-89304-010-X); pap. 3.00 signed ltd. ed. (ISBN 0-89304-018-5). Cross Cult.

Barkan, Stanley H., ed. Five Contemporary Turkish Poets. Sait, Talat, tr. (Cross-Cultural Review No. 6). 48p. (Turkish & Eng.). 1980. 10.00 (ISBN 0-89304-610-8); pap. 4.00 (ISBN 0-89304-611-6). Cross Cult.

--Four Contemporary Swedish Poets. Fulton, Robin & Hollo, Anselm, trs. (Cross-Cultural Review No.5). 48p. Date not set. 10.00 (ISBN 0-89304-608-6); pap. 4.00 (ISBN 0-89304-609-4). Cross Cult.

--To Struga with Love. LC 78-67775. (Illus., Orig.). 1978. in-folio 10.00 (ISBN 0-89304-028-2, CCC115); in-folio boxed 15.00 (ISBN 0-89304-050-9). Cross Cult.

Barkan, Stanley H. & Feiler, Eva, eds. International Poetry Festival. (International Poetry Festival Ser.: No. 1). (Illus.). 1972. pap. 5.00 o.p. (ISBN 0-89304-001-0, CCC100). Cross Cult.

Barkan, Stanley H. & Scammacca, Saverio A., eds. Sicilian Antigruppo. (Illus.). 30p. Date not set. 5.00 (ISBN 0-89304-008-8). Cross Cult.

Barkan, Stanley H., ed. see Aspenstrom, Werner.

Barkan, Stanley H., ed. see Axelrod, David B.

Barkan, Stanley H., ed. see Balbin, Julius.

Barkan, Stanley H., ed. see Bruchac, Joseph.

Barkan, Stanley H., ed. see Butscher, Edward.

Barkan, Stanley H., ed. see Daglarca, Fazil Husnu.

Barkan, Stanley H., ed. see Dame, Enid.

Barkan, Stanley H., jt. ed. see De Wit, Joost.

Barkan, Stanley H., ed. see Dobrin, Arthur.

Barkan, Stanley H., jt. ed. see Halman, Talat S.

Barkan, Stanley H., jt. ed. see Harding, Gunnar.

Barkan, Stanley H., ed. see Hartman, Susan.

Barkan, Stanley H., ed. see Lev, Donald.

Barkan, Stanley H., ed. see Mulisch, Harry.

Barkan, Stanley H., ed. see Scammacca, Nat.

Barkan, Stanley H., ed. see Van de Warsenburg, Hans.

Barkas, J. L. The Celebrity Vegetarian Cookbook. LC 78-3837. (Illus.). 1978. pap. 2.50 o.p. (ISBN 0-668-04616-3, 4616). Arc Bks.

--Victims. 1978. 10.95 o.p. (ISBN 0-684-15191-X, ScribT). Scribner.

Barke, Harvey E., jt. auth. see Pyenson, Louis L.

Barkely, William D., jt. auth. see Martin, Alexander C.

Barkenbus, Jack N. Deep Seabed Resources: Politics & Technology. LC 78-73024. 1979. 17.95 (ISBN 0-02-901830-7). Free Pr.

Barker, A. J. Afrika Korps. LC 78-70063. (Illus.). 192p. 1979. 17.95 o.p. (ISBN 0-89196-017-1, Domus Bks). Quality Bks IL.

Barker, A. J., tr. see Piekalkiewicz, Janusz.

Barker, A. Trevor, compiled by. The Mahatma Letters to A. P. Sinnett. 2nd, facsimile of 1926 ed. LC 75-10574. 1975. 10.00 (ISBN 0-911500-20-0); pap. 5.95 softcover (ISBN 0-911500-21-9). Theos U Pr.

Barker, Alan. Civil War in America. LC 61-11594. pap. 1.95 (ISBN 0-385-09871-5, A274, Anch). Doubleday.

Barker, Albert. The Spice Adventure. LC 80-18754. (Illus.). 96p. (gr. 4-6). 1980. PLB 7.79 (ISBN 0-671-33097-7). Messner.

Barker, Andrew. A Report of Captaine Ward & Danseker, Pirates. LC 68-54615. (English Experience Ser.: No. 21). 56p. 1968. Repr. of 1609 ed. 8.00 (ISBN 90-221-0021-9). Walter J Johnson.

Barker, Anthony. Public Participation in Britain. 192p. 1979. pap. text ed. 17.40x (ISBN 0-7199-1029-3, Pub. by Bedford England). Renouf.

Barker, Berta LaVan. A Thousand Happiness. (YA) 1978. 5.95 (ISBN 0-685-87351-X, Avalon). Bouregy.

Barker, Cicely M. Fairy's Gift. (Cicely Mary Barker Storybks). (Illus.). (gr. k-4). 1977. 3.95 (ISBN 0-685-78524-6, Pub. by Two Continents). Hippocrene Bks.

--The Flower Fairies Alphabet Book. (Illus.). 1978. 3.95 (ISBN 0-8467-0512-5, Pub. by Two Continents). Hippocrene Bks.

--Flower Fairies of Autumn. (Flower Fairies Ser.). (Illus.). (gr. 2-5). 1976. 3.95 (ISBN 0-8467-0191-X, Pub. by Two Continents). Hippocrene Bks.

--Flower Fairies of Spring. (Flower Fairies Ser.). (Illus.). (gr. 2-5). 1976. 3.95 (ISBN 0-8467-0193-6, Pub. by Two Continents). Hippocrene Bks.

--Flower Fairies of Summer. (Flower Fairies Ser.). (Illus.). (gr. 2-5). 1976. 3.95 (ISBN 0-8467-0194-4, Pub. by Two Continents). Hippocrene Bks.

--Flower Fairies of the Garden. (Flower Fairies Ser.). (Illus.). (gr. 2-5). 1976. 3.95 (ISBN 0-8467-0192-8, Pub. by Two Continents). Hippocrene Bks.

--Flower Fairies of the Trees. (Flower Fairies Ser.). (Illus.). (gr. 2-5). 1976. 3.95 (ISBN 0-8467-0195-2, Pub. by Two Continents). Hippocrene Bks.

--Flower Fairies of the Wayside. (Flower Fairies Ser.). (Illus.). (gr. 2-5). 1976. 3.95 (ISBN 0-8467-0196-0, Pub. by Two Continents). Hippocrene Bks.

--Flower Fairy - a Little Book of Old Rhymes. (Cicely Mary Barker Storybks.). (Illus.). (gr. k-4). 1977. 3.95 (ISBN 0-8467-0257-6, Pub. by Two Continents). Hippocrene Bks.

--The Lord of Rushie River. (Cicely Mary Barker Storybooks). (Illus.). (gr. k-4). 1977. 2.95 (ISBN 0-8467-0258-4, Pub. by Two Continents). Hippocrene Bks.

--The Rhyming Rainbow. (Cicely Mary Barker Storybks). (Illus.). (gr. k-4). 1977. 3.95 (ISBN 0-8467-0259-2, Pub. by Two Continents). Hippocrene Bks.

Barker, Cicely M., illus. Flower Fairies Birthday Book. (Illus.). 157p. 1980. 5.95 (ISBN 0-216-90814-0, Pub. by Blackie England). Hippocrene Bks.

Barker, Craig. Starting a Marine Aquarium. 1972. pap. 2.95 (ISBN 0-87666-751-5, PS-305). TFH Pubns.

Barker, D. L. & Allen, S., eds. Dependence & Exploitation in Work & Marriage. LC 75-43517. 1976. text ed. 20.00x (ISBN 0-582-48673-4); pap. text ed. 10.95x (ISBN 0-582-48674-2). Longman.

Barker, Danny, jt. auth. see Buerkle, Jack V.

Barker, Dave. TA & Training: The Theory & Use of Transactional Analysis. 226p. 1980. text ed. 29.50x (ISBN 0-566-02118-8, Pub. by Gower Pub Co England). Renouf.

Barker, David. Inside the Big O. 1980. 1.50 (ISBN 0-917554-03-5). Maelstrom.

--Scenes from a Marriage. 40p. 1979. pap. 2.00 (ISBN 0-935390-04-9). Wormwood Rev.

Barker, Elliott S. Beatty's Cabin: Adventures in Pecos High Country. LC 77-88836. 1977. Repr. of 1953 ed. 17.50 (ISBN 0-88307-537-7); pap. 6.95 o.p. (ISBN 0-88307-536-9). Gannon.

Barker, Eric J. & Millard, W. F. Science Projects & Experiments, 4 bks. Incl. Materials & Elements (ISBN 0-668-01498-9); Nature & Engergy (ISBN 0-668-01500-4); Five Senses (ISBN 0-668-01497-0); Machines & Energy (ISBN 0-668-01499-7). (YA) 1964. 4.50 ea. o.p. Arco.

Barker, Ernest. Political Thought in England, Eighteen Forty-Eight to Nineteen Fourteen. 2nd ed. LC 80-19766. (Home University Library of Modern Knowledge: 104). 256p. 1980. Repr. of 1928 ed. lib. bdg. 22.50x (ISBN 0-313-22216-9, BAPL). Greenwood.

--Political Thought of Plato & Aristotle. 11.50 (ISBN 0-8446-1594-3). Peter Smith.

Barker, Ernest, ed. Social Contract: Essays by Locke, Hume & Rousseau. (YA) (gr. 9 up). 1962. pap. 4.95x (ISBN 0-19-500309-8, 68). Oxford U Pr.

--Social Contract: Essays by Locke, Hume, & Rousseau. LC 80-22006. xliv, 307p. 1980. Repr. of 1947 ed. lib. bdg. 27.50x (ISBN 0-313-22409-9, BACT). Greenwood.

Barker, Ernest, tr. see Aristotle.

Barker, Eugene C. Life of Stephen F. Austin, Founder of Texas, 1793-1836. LC 68-27723. (American Scene Ser). (Illus.). 1968. Repr. of 1925 ed. 49.50 (ISBN 0-306-71153-2). Da Capo.

Barker, Eugene C., jt. ed. see Williams, Amelia W.

Barker, Evelyn M. Everyday Reasoning. (Illus.). 304p. 1981. pap. text ed. 8.95 (ISBN 0-13-293407-8). P-H.

Barker, Forrest. Problems in Technical Mathematics for Electricity-Electronics. LC 76-12728. 1976. pap. 8.95 (ISBN 0-8465-0403-0). Benjamin-Cummings.

Barker, George. In Memory of David Archer. 1973. 6.50 (ISBN 0-571-10398-7, Pub. by Faber & Faber). Merrimack Bk Serv.

Barker, George E. Death & After Death. LC 78-65349. 1978. pap. text ed. 7.25 (ISBN 0-8191-0653-4). U Pr of Amer.

Barker, George F; see Draper, John W.

Barker, Gerard A. Henry Mackenzie. (English Authors Ser.: No. 184). 1975. lib. bdg. 10.95 (ISBN 0-8057-6651-0). Twayne.

--Twice-Told Tales: An Anthology of Short Fiction. LC 78-69561. 1978. pap. text ed. 8.75 (ISBN 0-395-26635-1); inst. manual 0.65 (ISBN 0-395-26636-X). HM.

Barker, Gray. Silver Bridge. 1970. 9.95 o.p. (ISBN 0-685-20203-8). Saucerian.

Barker, Gray, ed. The Strange Case of Dr. M. K. Jessup. 4th ed. (Illus.). 82p. 1975. pap. 7.95 (ISBN 0-685-51759-4). Saucerian.

Barker, H. A., tr. see Piekalkiewicz, Janusz.

Barker, Harriett. The One-Burner Gourmet. rev. ed. (Illus.). 1981. pap. 7.95 (ISBN 0-8092-5883-8). Contemp Bks.

Barker, Howard. Fair Slaughter. 1980. pap. 3.95 (ISBN 0-7145-3654-7). Riverrun NY.

--The Hang of the Gaol. 1981. pap. 4.50 (ISBN 0-7145-3769-1). Riverrun NY.

--The Love of a Good Man. 1981. pap. 9.95 (ISBN 0-7145-3767-5). Riverrun NY.

--Stripwell & Claw. 1980. pap. 4.95 (ISBN 0-7145-3572-9). Riverrun NY.

--That Good Between Us. 1981. pap. 9.95 (ISBN 0-7145-3765-9). Riverrun NY.

Barker, J. & Smith, T., eds. The Role of Peptides in Neuronal Function. 1980. 95.00 (ISBN 0-8247-6926-0). Dekker.

Barker, Jane. Exilius; or The Banish'd Roman. LC 70-170536. (Foundations of the Novel Ser.: Vol. 25). lib. bdg. 50.00 (ISBN 0-8240-0537-6). Garland Pub.

--Love's Intrigues. Bd. with The Lovers Week. Hearne, Mary; The Female Deserters. Hearne, Mary. LC 70-170528. (Foundations of the Novel 1700-1739). lib. bdg. 50.00 (ISBN 0-8240-0531-7). Garland Pub.

--A Patchwork Screen for the Ladies. Bd. with The Prude: A Novel by a Young Lady. LC 74-170553. (Novel in England, 1700-1775 Ser). lib. bdg. 50.00 (ISBN 0-8240-0551-1). Garland Pub.

Barker, Jane V. & Downing, Sybil. Wagons & Rails. (Colorado Heritage Ser.: Bk. 9). (Illus.). 44p. (gr. 3-4). 1980. pap. 3.00x (ISBN 0-87108-225-X). Pruett.

Barker, Jane V., jt. auth. see Downing, Sybil.

Barker, John N. & Bray, John. The Indian Princess, 2 vols in 1. LC 77-169587. (Earlier American Music Ser.: No. 11). Repr. of 1808 ed. 19.50 (ISBN 0-306-77311-2). Da Capo.

Barker, John W. Justinian & the Later Roman Empire. LC 66-11804. 336p. 1976. pap. text ed. 7.95 (ISBN 0-299-03944-7). U of Wis Pr.

--Manuel Ii Palaeologus, 1391-1425: A Study in Late Byzantine Statesmanship. 1969. 40.00 (ISBN 0-8135-0582-8). Rutgers U Pr.

Barker, June. Decorative Braiding & Weaving. (Illus.). 112p. 1973. 9.95 (ISBN 0-8231-7031-4). Branford.

Barker, L. & Barker, T. Civil Liberties & the Constitution. 3rd ed. 1978. pap. 12.95 (ISBN 0-13-134957-0). P-H.

Barker, Larry L. Communication. 2nd ed. (Illus.). 448p. 1981. text ed. 13.95 (ISBN 0-13-153346-0); pap. 5.95 study guide (ISBN 0-13-153445-9). P-H.

--Communication Vibrations. (Speech Communication Ser.). (Illus.). 160p. 1974. pap. text ed. 111.95 (ISBN 0-13-153007-0). P-H.

Barker, Larry L. & Kibler, Robert J., eds. Speech Communication Behavior: Perspectives & Principles. LC 74-143585. 1971. pap. text ed. 14.95 (ISBN 0-13-827337-5). P-H.

Barker, Lewis M., et al, eds. Learning Mechanisms in Food Selection. 632p. 1977. 19.00 (ISBN 0-918954-19-3). Baylor Univ Pr.

Barker, M. A. Spoken Baluchi, 2 bks. Incl. Bk. I. 526p. cancelled (ISBN 0-87950-425-0); cancelled (ISBN 0-87950-427-7); cancelled (ISBN 0-87950-428-5); Bk. II. 667p. 1980. cancelled (ISBN 0-87950-426-9); cancelled Bks. I & II (ISBN 0-87950-429-3). (Spoken Language Ser.). 1980. Spoken Lang Serv.

Barker, Michael, ed. Studies in Renewable Resource Policy, 10 vols, Vol. 1. 1981. pap. write for info. (ISBN 0-934842-74-4). Coun State Plan.

--Studies in State Development Policy, 9 vols, Vol. 1. 1979. pap. 66.00x (ISBN 0-934842-24-8). Coun State Plan.

Barker, Muhammad Abd-al-Rahman. Reader of Classical Urdu Poetry, 3 vols. Incl. Vol. 1. pap. 10.00x (ISBN 0-87950-430-7); Vol. 2. pap. 10.00x (ISBN 0-87950-431-5); Vol. 3. pap. 10.00x (ISBN 0-87950-432-3). LC 77-73779. (Spoken Language Ser.). (Prog. Bk.). 1977. Set. pap. 24.00x (ISBN 0-87950-433-1); 6 dual track cassetes 75.00 (ISBN 0-87950-434-X); Set. incl. cassettes 95.00x (ISBN 0-87950-435-8). Spoken Lang Serv.

Barker, Muhammad Abd-al-Rahman, et al. Urdu Newspaper Reader. LC 74-21940. (Spoken Language Ser.). (Illus.). 1974. Repr. of 1968 ed. 10.00x (ISBN 0-87950-337-8); cassettes 4 dual track 50.00x (ISBN 0-87950-338-6); cassettes with course-bk. 55.00x (ISBN 0-87950-339-4). Spoken Lang Serv.

--Spoken Urdu, a Course in Urdu. Incl. Vol. 1. pap. 10.00x (ISBN 0-87950-340-8); Vol. 2. pap. 10.00x (ISBN 0-87950-341-6); Vol. 3. pap. 8.00x (ISBN 0-87950-342-4); Vols 1-3. Set. pap. 25.00x (ISBN 0-87950-343-2); Vol. 1-Cassettes, Six Dual Track. 90.00x (ISBN 0-87950-344-0); Vol. 1-Cassette Course-Bk. & Cassettes. pap. 95.00x (ISBN 0-87950-347-5); Vol. 2-Cassettes Six Dual Track. 75.00x (ISBN 0-87950-345-9); Vol. 2-Cassette Course & Cassettes. pap. 80.00x (ISBN 0-87950-348-3); Combined Cassette Course & Cassettes for Vols. 1 & 2. pap. 165.00x (ISBN 0-87950-349-1). LC 75-15183. (Spoken Language Ser). Orig. Title: A Course in Urdu. (Illus.). 520p. (Prog. Bk.). 1976. Set. pap. 25.00 (ISBN 0-87950-343-2). Spoken Lang Serv.

Barker, Nancy N. Distaff Diplomacy: The Empress Eugenie & the Foreign Policy of the Second Empire. 1967. 12.50x (ISBN 0-292-73694-0). U of Tex Pr.

Barker, Nancy N., ed. French Legation in Texas, 2 vols. (Illus.). 1971-73. 12.00 ea. Vol. 1 (ISBN 0-87611-026-X). Vol. 2 (ISBN 0-87611-030-8). Tex St Hist Assn.

Barker, Peter, ed. see Einstein Centennial Celebration, Memphis State University, March 14-16, 1979.

Barker, Philip, ed. The Residential Psychiatric Treatment of Children. LC 74-7208. 354p. 1974. 33.50 (ISBN 0-470-04910-3). Halsted Pr.

Barker, Ralph. Not Here, but in Another Place. (Illus.). 352p. 1980. 13.95 (ISBN 0-312-57961-6). St Martin.

Barker, Raymond C., jt. auth. see Holmes, Ernest.

Barker, Raymond C., jt. auth. see Maltz, Maxwell.

Barker, Robert. Love Forty. LC 75-2241. 216p. 1975. 7.95 o.p. (ISBN 0-397-01069-9). Lippincott.

--Organic Chemistry of Biological Compounds. (Modern Biochemistry Ser). (Illus.). 1971. pap. 13.95x ref. ed. (ISBN 0-13-640623-8). P-H.

Barker, Robert L. & Briggs, Thomas L. Differential Use of Social Work Manpower. LC 68-27158. 1968. 5.00x o.p. (ISBN 0-87101-049-6, CHO-049-C). Natl Assn Soc Wkrs.

Barker, Stephen. Elements of Logic. 2nd ed. (Illus.). 336p. 1974. text ed. 12.95 o.p. (ISBN 0-07-003718-3, C); instructor's manual 3.95 o.p. (ISBN 0-07-003719-1); study guide by A, Levinson 6.95 o.p. (ISBN 0-07-037382-5). McGraw.

Barker, T., jt. auth. see Barker, L.

Barker, Thomas. Greenberg's Operating & Repair Manual for American Flyer Trains. Greenberg, Linda, ed. LC 79-54103. (Illus.). 1979. pap. 6.95 (ISBN 0-89778-218-6). Greenberg Pub Co.

Barker, Thomas M. & Moritsch, Andreas. The Slovenes of Carinthia. 2nd ed. LC 79-15399. (Eastern European Studies of Columbia University). 1981. 22.50x (ISBN 0-231-04862-9). Columbia U Pr.

Barker, Vernon C., jt. auth. see Aufmann, Richard N.

Barker, Wayne G. Cryptanalysis of an Enciphered Code Problem: Where an "Additive" Method of Encipherement Has Been Used. (Cryptographic Ser.). (Orig.). 1979. pap. 22.40 (ISBN 0-89412-037-9). Aegean Park Pr.

Barker, Wayne G., ed. The History of Codes & Ciphers in the United States During World War I. (Cryptographic Ser.). (Illus.). 1979. 19.60 (ISBN 0-89412-031-X). Aegean Park Pr.

Barker, Will. Familiar Reptiles & Amphibians of America. LC 62-14599. (Familiar Nature Ser.). (Illus.). 1964. PLB 9.87 o.p. (ISBN 0-06-070421-7, HarpT). Har-Row.

Barker, William F. & Doeff, Annick M. Preschool Behavior Rating Scale. LC 80-11444. (Orig.). 1980. pap. text ed. 3.95 instructions & scoring sample (ISBN 0-87868-148-5); blank scale 0.50 (ISBN 0-87868-185-X); Methodology 2.25 (ISBN 0-87868-187-6). Child Welfare.

Bar-Khama, Amos, et al. The Israeli Fitness Strategy: Based on the Physical Training Program of the Israel Defense Forces. LC 80-15443. (Illus.). 192p. 1980. 10.95 (ISBN 0-688-03628-7). Morrow.

--Israeli Fitness Strategy: Based on the Physical Training Program of the Israel Defense Forces. LC 80-17222. (Illus.). 192p. 1980. pap. 5.95 (ISBN 0-688-08628-4, Quill). Morrow.

Barkhouse, Bob. Engine Repair: Head Assembly & Valve Gear. LC 74-21562. 500p. (gr. 10-12). 1974. text ed. 18.48 (ISBN 0-87345-101-5). McKnight.

Barkin, Carol & James, Elizabeth. Are We Still Best Friends? LC 75-19482. (Moods & Emotions Ser.). (Illus.). 32p. (gr. k-3). 1975. PLB 8.95 (ISBN 0-8172-0032-0). Raintree Pubs.

--Doing Things Together. LC 75-20083. (Moods & Emotions Ser.). (Illus.). 32p. (gr. k-2). 1975. PLB 8.95 (ISBN 0-8172-0036-3). Raintree Pubs.

--I'd Rather Stay Home. LC 75-19481. (Moods & Emotions Ser.). (Illus.). 32p. (gr. k-2). 1975. PLB 8.95 (ISBN 0-8172-0030-4). Raintree Pubs.

--Sometimes I Hate School. LC 75-20143. (Moods & Emotions Ser.). (Illus.). 32p. (gr. k-2). 1975. PLB 8.95 (ISBN 0-8172-0034-7). Raintree Pubs.

Barkin, Carol, jt. auth. see James, Elizabeth.

Barkin, Solomon, ed. Worker Militancy & Its Consequences, 1965-75: New Directions in Western Industrial Relations. LC 75-3745. (Special Studies). (Illus.). 448p. 1975. text ed. 31.95 (ISBN 0-275-07410-2); pap. 11.95 (ISBN 0-275-89440-1). Praeger.

Barkins, Evelyn. From an Understanding Heart. LC 76-43626. (Illus.). 34p. 1977. pap. 2.95 (ISBN 0-8119-0373-7). Fell.

--A Grandparent's Garden of Verses. LC 72-96892. 1973. pap. 2.95 (ISBN 0-8119-0374-5). Fell.

--Hospital Happy. 1976. pap. 3.95 (ISBN 0-8119-0376-1). Fell.

--Love Poems of a Marriage. LC 74-20656. 1970. pap. 2.95 (ISBN 0-8119-0387-7). Fell.

--My Ocean, My Love. LC 77-28151. 1977. pap. 2.95 (ISBN 0-8119-0391-5). Fell.

Barkman, Alma. Times to Treasure. 96p. 1980. text ed. 9.95 (ISBN 0-686-66054-4). Moody.

Bar-Kochva, B. The Seleucid Army. (Cambridge Classical Studies Ser.). 1976. 26.50 (ISBN 0-521-20667-7). Cambridge U Pr.

Barkow, Al, jt. auth. see Venturi, Ken.

Barkowski, Renee. My Home. (Illus.). (ps-4). 1971. PLB 5.00 (ISBN 0-307-60115-3, Golden Pr). Western Pub.

Barks, Carl, illus. Donald Duck. LC 78-14844. (Walt Disney Best Comics Ser.). (Illus.). 1978. 17.95 (ISBN 0-89659-006-2). Abbeville Pr.

--Donald Duck & the Golden Helmet. (Illus.). 36p. 1981. 3.95 (ISBN 0-89659-178-6). Abbeville Pr.

--Donald Duck & the Magic Hourglass. (Illus.). 36p. 1981. 3.95 (ISBN 0-89659-177-8). Abbeville Pr.

--Uncle Scrooge & the Secret of Old Castle. (Illus.). 36p. 1981. 3.95 (ISBN 0-89659-180-8). Abbeville Pr.

Barks, Herb. Prime Time. 144p. 1981. pap. 3.95 (ISBN 0-8407-5768-9). Nelson.

Barksdale, E. C. Cosmologies of Consciousness. 148p. 1980. text ed. 16.50x (ISBN 0-87073-969-7); pap. text ed. 11.25x (ISBN 0-87073-970-0). Schenkman.

Barksdale, Jelks. Titanium, Its Occurrence, Chemistry & Technology. 2nd ed. 1966. 43.50 (ISBN 0-8260-0725-2, Pub. by Wiley-Interscience). Wiley.

Barksdale, William C., jt. auth. see Wood, Oliver G., Jr.

Barkuizen, B. The Succulents of Southern Africa. 1980. 60.00x (Pub. by Bailey & Swinton South Africa). State Mutual Bk.

Barlag, R., jt. auth. see Andersen, R.

Barlay, Stephen. The Search for Air Safety. (Illus.). 1970. 7.95 o.p. (ISBN 0-688-02441-6). Morrow.

--Sex Slavery. 1977. pap. 1.75 o.p. (ISBN 0-685-79746-5). Ballantine.

Barlett, Peggy F., ed. Agricultural Decision Making: Anthropological Contributions to Rural Development. LC 80-513. (Studies in Anthropology Ser.). 1980. 28.00 (ISBN 0-12-078880-2). Acad Pr.

Barletta, N. A., et al, eds. Conference on the Western Hemisphere. LC 76-175023. 1971. pap. 1.25 o.p. (ISBN 0-913456-80-2). Interbk Inc.

Barley, M. W. Guide to British Topographical Collections. 160p. 1980. pap. 17.95x (ISBN 0-900312-24-6, Pub. by Coun Brit Arch England). Intl Schol Bk Serv.

Barley, Margaret, jt. auth. see Jeffers, Janet.

Barling, John. Solar Fun Book. 1980. 7.95 (ISBN 0-931790-04-2). Brick Hse Pub.

Barlingay & Kulkarni. A Critical Survey of Western Philosophy. 1980. write for info (ISBN 0-391-01767-5). Humanities.

Barlough, J. Ernest. The Archaicon: A Collection of Unusual Archaic English. LC 73-14926. 1974. 11.00 (ISBN 0-8108-0683-5). Scarecrow.

--Minor British Poetry 1680-1800: An Anthology. LC 73-4878. 1973. 13.00 (ISBN 0-8108-0619-3). Scarecrow.

Barlow. Introduction to Criminology. 2nd ed. 1981. text ed. 16.95 (ISBN 0-316-08115-9); tchrs'. manual free (ISBN 0-316-08116-7). Little.

Barlow, A. R. English-Kikuyu Dictionary. Benson, T. G., tr. 340p. 1975. 24.95x (ISBN 0-19-864407-8). Oxford U Pr.

Barlow, Anna M; see Corrigan, Robert W.

Barlow, B. V. & Everest, A. S. The Astronomical Telescope. (Wykeham Science Ser.: No. 31). 1975. 9.95x (ISBN 0-8448-1158-0). Crane Russak Co.

Barlow, Christopher. The Third World. 1979. 14.95 (ISBN 0-7134-1878-8, Pub. by Batsford England). David & Charles.

Barlow, D. W., et al, eds. Grinding, Vol. 2. (Engineering Craftsmen: No. H.31). 1972. spiral bdg. 28.50x (ISBN 0-85083-380-9). Intl Ideas.

Barlow, David. Sexually Transmitted Diseases: The Facts. (Illus.). 1979. text ed. 11.95x (ISBN 0-19-261157-7). Oxford U Pr.

Barlow, David H., jt. auth. see Hersen, Michel.

Barlow, David H., ed. Behavioral Assessment of Adult Disorders. (The Guilford Behavioral Assessment Ser.). 500p. 1981. 25.00 (ISBN 0-89862-140-2). Guilford Pr.

Barlow, David H., jt. ed. see Mavissakalian, Matig.

Barlow, Derrick, ed. see Fontane, Theodor.

Barlow, Frank. Edward the Confessor. LC 70-104107. (English Monarchs Series). (Illus.). 1970. 19.50x (ISBN 0-520-01671-8). U of Cal Pr.

--The English Church, Ten Hundred to Ten Sixty-Six. 1979. pap. text ed. 13.95 (ISBN 0-582-49049-9). Longman.

--The Feudal Kingdom of England: 1042-1216. (Illus.). 1972. pap. text ed. 10.95 (ISBN 0-582-48237-2). Longman.

--Winchester in the Early Middle Ages: An Edition & Discussion of the Winton Domesday. (Winchester Studios). (Illus.). 1977. 98.00x (ISBN 0-19-813169-0). Oxford U Pr.

Barlow, Frank, ed. The Life of King Edward Who Rests at Westminster: Attributed to a Monk of St. Bertin. Barlow, Frank, tr. LC 80-2170. 1981. Repr. of 1962 ed. 34.50 (ISBN 0-404-18751-X). AMS Pr.

Barlow, Fred M. Timeless Truth for Twentieth Century Times. 123p. 1970. 3.25 (ISBN 0-87398-838-8, Pub. by Bibl Evang Pr). Sword of Lord.

Barlow, George. Gumbo. LC 80-2557. 96p. 1981. 8.95 (ISBN 0-385-17529-9); pap. 4.95 (ISBN 0-385-17530-2). Doubleday.

Barlow, George W. & Silverberg, James, eds. Sociobiology: Beyond Nature-Nurture. (AAAS Selected Symposium: No. 35). 625p. 1980. lib. bdg. 35.00x (ISBN 0-89158-372-6); pap. text ed. 15.00x (ISBN 0-89158-960-0). Westview.

Barlow, I. M. Spatial Dimensions of Urban Government. (Geographical Research Studies Press Ser.). 900p. 1981. 49.00 (ISBN 0-471-27978-1, Pub by Wiley Interscience). Wiley.

Barlow, Iola. Dolls in National Costume. (gr. 6 up). 6.50 (ISBN 0-8231-3023-1). Branford.

Barlow, Joel. Works 2 Vols: Vol. 1. Prose, Vol. 2. Poetry. LC 68-17012. 1970. Set. 120.00x (ISBN 0-8201-1062-0). Schol Facsimiles.

Barlow, John see Holland, Henry.

Barlow, Joseph W. Basic Oral Spanish. (Illus.). 1947. text ed. 16.95x (ISBN 0-89197-042-8); pap. text ed. 9.95x o.p. (ISBN 0-89197-043-6). Irvington.

Barlow, Judith, ed. Plays by American Women: The Early Years. 368p. 1981. pap. 3.95 (ISBN 0-380-76620-5, 76620, Bard). Avon.
Barlow, Max G. Medicinal Botany II: From the Shepard's Purse. 1981. 25.95x (ISBN 0-9602812-1-5). Spice West.
Barlow, Melvin L. History of Industrial Education in the United States. 1967. pap. text ed. 23.44 (ISBN 0-87002-241-5). Bennett IL.
Barlow, N., jt. auth. see Jones, A. J.
Barlow, Nora, ed. Darwin & Henslow: The Growth of an Idea, Letters 1831-1860. 1967. 20.00x (ISBN 0-520-00080-3). U of Cal Pr.
Barlow, Richard B. Citizenship & Conscience: A Study in the Theory & Practice of Religious Toleration in England During the Eighteenth Century. LC 62-7197. 1963. 12.00x o.p. (ISBN 0-8122-7395-8). U of Pa Pr.
Barlow, Roger. The Diesel Car Book. LC 80-8913. (Illus.). 288p. (Orig.). 1981. pap. 7.95 (ISBN 0-394-17895-5, Ever). Grove.
Barlow, Ronald S. How to Be Successful in the Antique Business. rev. ed. (Illus.). 185p. 1981. 10.95 (ISBN 0-686-69481-3, ScribT). Scribner.
Barlow, T. Ed. Small Group Ministry in the Contemporary Church. LC 72-90357. 1972. pap. 4.50 o.p. (ISBN 0-8309-0080-2). Herald Hse.
Barlow, Wayne. Foundations of Music. LC 53-8987. (Illus.). 1953. 28.50x (ISBN 0-89197-176-9); pap. 16.50x. Irvington.
Barlow, Wilfred. Alexander Technique. 1980. pap. 4.95 (ISBN 0-446-97280-0). Warner Bks.
Barlow, William. A Briefe Discovery of the Idle Animadversions of Mark Ridley, Doctor of Phisicke. LC 71-38149. (English Experience Ser.: No. 429). 16p. 1972. Repr. of 1618 ed. 7.00 (ISBN 90-221-0429-X). Walter J Johnson.
--A Dyaloge Descrybyng the Orygynall Ground of These Lutheran Saccyons, That Is, Faccyons. LC 74-80161. (English Experience Ser.: No. 641). 200p. 1974. Repr. of 1531 ed. 13.00 (ISBN 90-221-0641-1). Walter J Johnson.
--Magneticall Advertisements. LC 68-54616. (English Experience Ser.: No. 47). Repr. of 1616 ed. 14.00 (ISBN 90-221-0047-2). Walter J Johnson.
--The Navigators Supply. LC 76-38150. (English Experience Ser.: No. 430). 100p. Repr. of 1597 ed. 16.00 (ISBN 90-221-0430-3). Walter J Johnson.
--The Summe & Substance of the Conference at Hampton Court, January 14, 1603. LC 74-28829. (English Experience Ser.: No. 711). 1975. Repr. of 1604 ed. 9.50 (ISBN 90-221-0711-6). Walter J Johnson.
--Summe & Substance of the Conference. LC 65-10395. 1965. Repr. of 1604 ed. 20.00x (ISBN 0-8201-1004-3). Schol Facsimiles.
Barlowe, Raleigh. Land Resource Economics: The Economics of Real Estate. 3rd ed. (Illus.). 1978. ref. ed. 21.95 (ISBN 0-13-522532-9). P-H.
Barloy, J. J. Man & Animals: One Hundred Centuries of Man's Relationship with Animals. LC 77-30501. (Illus.). 1978. 9.95 o.p. (ISBN 0-86033-012-5). Gordon-Cremonesi.
Barman, Alicerose S. Mental Health in Classroom & Corridor. LC 68-25763. 1968. 9.20 o.p. (ISBN 0-672-75107-0). Bobbs.
Barman, Charles R., et al. Science & Societal Issues: A Guide for Science Teachers. (Illus.). 152p. 1981. pap. text ed. 9.00 (ISBN 0-8138-0485-X). Iowa St U Pr.
Barman, Christian. The Man Who Built London Transport: A Biography of Frank Pick. 1979. 24.00 (ISBN 0-7153-7753-1). David & Charles.
Barman, T. E. Enzyme Handbook, 2 Vols. LC 69-19293. 1969. Set. 51.70 (ISBN 0-387-04423-X). Springer-Verlag.
Barmann, Lawrence F. Baron Friedrich Von Hugel & the Modernist Crisis in England. LC 77-153014. 1972. 39.00 (ISBN 0-521-08178-5). Cambridge U Pr.
Barmark, Jan, ed. Perspectives in Metascience. (Regiae Societatis-Interdisciplinaria: No. 2). 199p. 1980. text ed. 19.75x (ISBN 91-85252-21-2). Humanities.
Barmash, Isadore. The Chief Executives. 10.95 o.s.i. (ISBN 0-397-01285-3). Lippincott.
--Net Net. LC 77-180292. 320p. 1972. 5.95 o.s.i. (ISBN 0-02-507200-5). Macmillan.
Barme, Geremie, jt. auth. see Lee, Bennett.
Barna, Arpad & Porat, Dan I. Introduction to Microcomputers & Microprocessors. LC 75-31675. 1976. 15.00 (ISBN 0-471-05051-2, Pub. by Wiley-Interscience). Wiley.
Barna, Arpad, jt. auth. see Porat, Dan I.
Barna, Luba, tr. see Bulgakov, Sergei.
Barna, Victor. Your Book of Table Tennis. (gr. 7 up). 1971. 6.50 (ISBN 0-571-09345-0). Transatlantic.
--Your Book of Table Tennis. 1977. 6.95 (ISBN 0-571-09345-0, Pub. by Faber & Faber). Merrimack Bk Serv.
Barnaby, Frank. Prospects for Peace. (Illus.). 105p. 1980. 21.50 (ISBN 0-08-027399-8); pap. 11.50 (ISBN 0-08-027398-X). Pergamon.
Barnaby, Jack. Winning Squash Racquets. new ed. 1979. 17.95 (ISBN 0-205-06175-3). Allyn.
Barnaby, Jack M. Advantage Tennis: Racket Work, Tactics & Logic. (Illus.). 300p. 1975. text ed. 17.95 (ISBN 0-205-04686-X, 6246869). Allyn.
Barnard, A. D., rev. by see Gill, N. T. & Vear, K. C.
Barnard, C. In the Night Season. 1978. 8.95 o.p. (ISBN 0-13-453654-1). P-H.
--One Life. 1970. 7.95 o.s.i. (ISBN 0-02-507230-7). Macmillan.
Barnard, C. S. & Nix, J. S. Farm Planning & Control. LC 72-85436. (Illus.). 522p. 1973. 52.50 (ISBN 0-521-08738-4); pap. 19.95x (ISBN 0-521-29079-1). Cambridge U Pr.
--Farm Planning & Control. 2nd ed. LC 79-10572. 1980. 72.50 (ISBN 0-521-22658-9); pap. 23.95x (ISBN 0-521-29604-8). Cambridge U Pr.
Barnard, Charles N. It Was a Wonderful Summer for Running Away. LC 78-17282. 1978. 8.95 (ISBN 0-396-07574-6). Dodd.
Barnard, Charles N., jt. auth. see Hamilton, Richard.
Barnard, Charles P. Families, Alcoholism & Therapy. (Illus.). 184p. 1981. text ed. 16.50 (ISBN 0-398-04157-1); pap. text ed. 12.75 (ISBN 0-398-04173-3). C C Thomas.
Barnard, Christiaan. Good Life Good Death: A Doctor's Case for Euthanasia & Suicide. LC 80-18839. 120p. 1980. 7.95 (ISBN 0-13-360370-9). P-H.
--Heart Attack: You Don't Have to Die. 1972. 6.95 o.s.i. (ISBN 0-440-03536-8). Delacorte.
--South Africa: Sharp Dissection. LC 77-99151. 1977. 9.95 (ISBN 0-916728-02-1). Bks in Focus.
Barnard, D. P. Figure It Out. 1976. pap. 1.25 o.p. (ISBN 0-449-13532-2, P3532, GM). Fawcett.
Barnard, Ellsworth. English for Everybody. LC 79-18238. (Orig.). 1979. pap. 5.00 (ISBN 0-686-26670-6). Dinosaur.
Barnard, Ellsworth, ed. Edwin Arlington Robinson: Centenary Essays. LC 77-111377. 192p. 1969. 12.00x (ISBN 0-8203-0252-X). U of Ga Pr.
Barnard, F. M., ed. J. G. Herder on Social & Political Culture. LC 69-11022. (Cambridge Studies in the History & Theory of Politics). (Illus.). 1969. 39.95 (ISBN 0-521-07336-7). Cambridge U Pr.
Barnard, H. C. Education & the French Revolution. (Cambridge Texts & Studies in the History of Education: No. 5). 1969. 32.50 (ISBN 0-521-07256-5). Cambridge U Pr.
--Fenelon on Education. (Cambridge Texts & Studies in the History of Education: No. 1). 1966. 24.50 (ISBN 0-521-04107-4). Cambridge U Pr.
--Were Those the Days? 1969. 16.00 (ISBN 0-08-007107-4). Pergamon.
Barnard, Henry. Reformatory Education. 361p. 1980. Repr. of 1857 ed. lib. bdg. 20.00 (ISBN 0-8492-3589-8). R West.
Barnard, Henry & Butler, J. D. Armsmear. (Illus.). 399p. 1976. 16.95 (ISBN 0-686-68856-2). Beinfeld Pub.
Barnard, Henry, ed. Slavery: A Bibliography & Union List of the Microfilm Collection, Part I. 1980. pap. write for info. (ISBN 0-667-00613-3). Microfilming Corp.
Barnard, Jerry. Something Worse Than Hell & Better Than Heaven. 1979. pap. 1.95 (ISBN 0-917726-31-6). Hunter Bks.
Barnard, John, ed. Pope: The Critical Heritage. (Critical Heritage Ser). 550p. 1973. 42.00x (ISBN 0-7100-7390-9). Routledge & Kegan.
Barnard, Julian. Collecting Victorian Ceramic Tiles. (The Christies International Collectors Ser.). (Illus.). 128p. 1980. 14.95 (ISBN 0-8317-9168-3). Mayflower Bks.
Barnard, Kathryn E. & Erickson, Marcene L. Teaching Children with Developmental Problems, a Family Care Approach. 2nd ed. LC 75-31520. (Illus.). 184p. 1976. pap. 10.50 (ISBN 0-8016-0496-5). Mosby.
Barnard, Martha U., et al. Human Sexuality for Health Professionals. LC 77-84663. (Illus.). 1978. pap. text ed. 10.95 (ISBN 0-7216-1544-9). Saunders.
Barnard, Max, jt. auth. see Herbert, Frank.
Barnard, Philip. The Tackle Box Fishing Guide. LC 78-69685. (Illus.). 128p. 1981. 7.95 (ISBN 0-498-02254-4). A S Barnes.
Barnard, R. D. Thermoelectricity in Metals & Alloys. LC 72-10919. 259p. 1973. 29.95 (ISBN 0-470-05053-5). Halsted Pr.
Barnard, Robert. Death in a Cold Climate. 196p. 1981. 8.95 (ISBN 0-684-16795-6, ScribT). Scribner.
--Death of an Old Goat. 1977. 6.95 o.s.i. (ISBN 0-8027-5365-5). Walker & Co.
--Death on the High C's. 1978. 7.95 o.s.i. (ISBN 0-8027-5398-1). Walker & Co.
--Death on the High C's. 1981. pap. 2.25 (ISBN 0-440-11900-6). Dell.
--A Talent to Deceive: An Appreciation of Agatha Christie. LC 79-27435. 208p. 1980. 10.00 (ISBN 0-396-07827-3). Dodd.
Barnard, Robert L. Intrusion Detection Systems. 300p. 1981. text ed. 21.95 (ISBN 0-409-95026-2). Butterworths.
Barnard, T. C. Cromwellian Ireland: English Government & Reform in Ireland 1649-1660. (Oxford Historical Monographs). 352p. 1975. text ed. 45.00x (ISBN 0-19-821858-3). Oxford U Pr.
Barnard, William D. Dixiecrats & Democrats: Alabama Politics 1942-1950. LC 73-22711. 1974. 13.95 (ISBN 0-8173-4820-4). U of Ala Pr.
Barnds, William J., ed. Japan & the United States: Challenges & Opportunities. LC 79-1551. 1979. 15.00x (ISBN 0-8147-1020-4); pap. 7.00x (ISBN 0-8147-1021-2). NYU Pr.
Barndt, Deborah. Education & Social Change: A Photographic Study of Peru. 1980. pap. text ed. 19.95 (ISBN 0-8403-2283-6). Kendall-Hunt.
Barndt, Joseph R., jt. auth. see Smith, Louis A.
Barner, Herbert E. & Scheuerman, Richard V. Handbook of Thermochemical Data for Compounds & Aqueous Species. LC 77-20244. 1978. 26.95 (ISBN 0-471-03238-7, Pub. by Wiley-Interscience). Wiley.
Barnes. Plaid for Business Law. 3rd ed. 1978. 5.50 (ISBN 0-256-02123-6, 02-0816-03). Learning Syst.
Barnes & Todd. Communication & Learning in Small Groups. (Direct Editions Ser.). (Orig.). 1977. pap. 9.75 (ISBN 0-7100-8512-5). Routledge & Kegan.
Barnes, A. D., jt. ed. see Clarke, D. B.
Barnes, B. J., jt. auth. see Ellner, Carolyn L.
Barnes, Barnabe. The Devil's Charter (1607) Pogue, Jim C. & Orgel, Stephen, eds. LC 79-54358. (Renaissance Drama Second Ser.). 225p. 1980. lib. bdg. 25.00 (ISBN 0-8240-4474-6). Garland Pub.
Barnes, Barry. Interests & the Growth of Knowledge. (Direct Editions Ser). (Orig.). 1977. pap. 11.00 (ISBN 0-7100-8669-5). Routledge & Kegan.
--Scientific Knowledge & Sociological Theory. (Monographs in Social Theory). 1974. 16.50 (ISBN 0-7100-7961-3); pap. 8.95 (ISBN 0-7100-7962-1). Routledge & Kegan.
Barnes, Barry & Shapin, Steven, eds. Natural Order: Historical Studies of Scientific Culture. LC 78-19650. (Sage Focus Editions: Vol. 6). 1979. 18.95x (ISBN 0-8039-0958-6); pap. 9.95x (ISBN 0-8039-0959-4). Sage.
Barnes, Ben, jt. auth. see Gay, Kathlyn.
Barnes, Broda & Galton, Lawrence. Hypothyroidism: The Unsuspected Illness. LC 75-29251. 224p. 1976. 10.95 (ISBN 0-690-01029-X, TYC-T). T Y Crowell.
Barnes, Broda O. & Barnes, Charlotte W. Heart Attack Rareness in Thyroid-Treated Patients. 104p. 1972. pap. 11.75 photocopy ed. spiral (ISBN 0-398-02519-3). C C Thomas.
Barnes, Burton V. & Wagner, Warren H., Jr. Michigan Trees: A Guide to the Trees of Michigan & the Great Lakes. (Biological Science). (Illus.). 360p. 1981. text ed. 10.95 (ISBN 0-472-08017-2); pap. text ed. 5.95 (ISBN 0-472-08018-0). U of Mich Pr.
Barnes, Burton V., jt. auth. see Spurr, Stephen H.
Barnes, C. D. & Eltherington, L. G. Drug Dosage in Laboratory Animals: A Handbook. 2nd rev. & enl. ed. 1973. 26.75x (ISBN 0-520-02273-4). U of Cal Pr.
Barnes, C. D., jt. ed. see Orem, J.
Barnes, Charles D., jt. ed. see Hughes, Maysie J.
Barnes, Charlotte W., jt. auth. see Barnes, Broda O.
Barnes, Christopher J., ed. Studies in Twentieth-Century Russian Literature. LC 75-40543. 91p. 1976. text ed. 11.50x (ISBN 0-06-490316-8). B&N.
Barnes, Clive. Inside the American Ballet Theatre. 1977. pap. 9.95 (Hawthorn). Dutton.
Barnes, Cyril G. Medical Disorders in Obstetric Practice. 4th ed. (Illus.). 1974. text ed. 42.50 (ISBN 0-632-09810-4, Blackwell). Mosby.
Barnes, D. & Wilson, F. Chemistry & Unit Operations in Sewage Treatment. (Illus.). 1978. text ed. 51.30x (ISBN 0-85334-783-2, Pub. by Applied Science). Burgess-Intl Ideas.
--The Design & Operation of Small Sewage Works. LC 76-48093. 1977. 19.95 o.p. (ISBN 0-470-99015-5). Halsted Pr.
Barnes, Dallas. See the Woman. 1974. pap. 1.50 o.p. (ISBN 0-451-07768-7, W7768, Sig). NAL.
Barnes, David, photos by. Seattle. LC 80-60. (Illus.). 80p. 1980. 22.50 (ISBN 0-914718-51-7); pap. 12.95 (ISBN 0-914718-50-9). Pacific Search.
Barnes, Djuna. Ryder. 1979. 10.95 (ISBN 0-312-69640-X). St Martin.
--The Selected Works of Djuna Barnes. 1980. 12.95 (ISBN 0-374-25936-4). FS&G.
Barnes, Donald L. & Burgdorf, Arlene. Study Skills for Information Retrieval, Bk. 1. (gr. 4-8). 1979. pap. text ed. 4.40 (ISBN 0-205-06436-1, 4964365); tchrs'. ed. 4.80 (ISBN 0-205-06440-X, 4964403). Allyn.
--Study Skills for Information Retrieval, Bk. 2. (gr. 4-8). 1979. pap. text ed. 4.40 (ISBN 0-205-06437-X, 4964373); tchrs'. ed. 4.80 (ISBN 0-205-06441-8, 4964411). Allyn.
--Study Skills for Information Retrieval, Bk. 3. (gr. 4-8). 1979. pap. text ed. 4.40 (ISBN 0-205-06438-8, 496438-1); tchrs'. ed. 4.80 (ISBN 0-205-06442-6, 496442-X). Allyn.
--Study Skills for Information Retrieval, Bk. 4. (gr. 4-8). 1974. pap. text ed. 4.40 (ISBN 0-205-03994-4, 4939948); tchrs. ed. 4.80 (ISBN 0-205-03995-2, 4939956). Allyn.
Barnes, Dorothy L., jt. ed. see Stephens, Irving E.
Barnes, Duncan. History of Winchester Firearms, Eighteen Sixty-Six to Nineteen Eighty. rev. ed. (Illus.). 272p. 1980. 21.95 (ISBN 0-87691-324-9). Winchester Pr.
Barnes, F. S. Laser Theory. (IEEE Press Selected Reprint Ser.). 469p. 1972. 14.95 o.p. (ISBN 0-471-05190-X); pap. 11.45 o.p. (ISBN 0-471-05191-8, Pub. by Wiley-Interscience). Wiley.
Barnes, Frances Johnson, ed. Love-from Black Men to Black Women. 1976. 5.00 o.p. (ISBN 0-682-48569-1). Exposition.
Barnes, George W. How to Make Bamboo Fly Rods. 1977. 11.95 (ISBN 0-87691-237-4). Winchester Pr.
Barnes, Gilbert H. & Dumond, Dwight L., eds. Letters of Theodore Dwight Weld, Angelina Grimke Weld, & Sarah Grimke. LC 77-121103. (American Public Figures Ser). 1970. Repr. of 1934 ed. lib. bdg. 75.00 (ISBN 0-306-71981-9). Da Capo.
Barnes, Grace M., et al. Alcohol & the Elderly: A Comprehensive Bibliography. LC 80-1786. xvii, 138p. 1980. lib. bdg. 25.00 (ISBN 0-313-22132-4, BAE/). Greenwood.
Barnes, Gregory. Crisscross: Structured Writing in Context. (Illus.). 208p. 1981. pap. text ed. 8.95 (ISBN 0-13-193920-3). P-H.
Barnes, H., ed. Oceanography & Marine Biology. Incl. Vol. 8. 1970. 40.50 (ISBN 0-02-840940-X); Vol. 10. 1972. 40.50 (ISBN 0-02-840960-4); Vol. 11. 1973. 40.50 (ISBN 0-02-840970-1); Vol. 12. 1974. 40.50 (ISBN 0-02-841010-6); Vol. 13. 1975. 57.75 (ISBN 0-02-841020-3). Hafner.
Barnes, H. L., ed. Geochemistry of Hydrothermal Ore Deposits. 2nd ed. LC 79-354. 1979. 33.00 (ISBN 0-471-05056-3, Pub by Wiley-Interscience). Wiley.
Barnes, Harold, ed. Oceanography & Marine Biology: An Annual Review, Vol. 15. 1977. 70.00 (ISBN 0-900015-39-X). Taylor-Carlisle.
--Oceanography & Marine Biology: An Annual Review, Vol. 16. 1978. 75.00 (ISBN 0-900015-44-6). Taylor-Carlisle.
--Oceanography & Marine Biology: Annual Review, Vol. 14. 1976. 70.00 (ISBN 0-900015-37-3). Taylor-Carlisle.
Barnes, Harold, jt. ed. see Barnes, Margaret.
Barnes, Harry E. Revisionism: A Key to Peace & Other Essays, 3 essays. LC 80-15902. (Cato Paper Ser.: No. 12). Orig. Title: Revisionism: a Key to Peace & the Historical Blackout & How 1984 Trends Threaten American Peace, Freedom, & Prosperity. 200p. 1980. pap. 4.00 (ISBN 0-932790-18-6). Cato Inst.
Barnes, Hazel. Sartre. LC 72-13764. 1973. 6.95 o.s.i. (ISBN 0-397-00750-7). Lippincott.
Barnes, Hazel E. Humanistic Existentialism: The Literature of Possibility. LC 59-11732. 1962. pap. 3.95 (ISBN 0-8032-5229-3, BB 145, Bison). U of Nebr Pr.
Barnes, Hazel E., tr. see Sartre, Jean-Paul.
Barnes, Irston R. Public Utility Control in Massachusetts. 1930. 47.50x (ISBN 0-685-89774-5). Elliots Bks.
Barnes, Isabel J., et al. Microbes & Man: A Laboratory Manual for Students in the Health Sciences. (Illus.). 1974. lab. man 10.95x (ISBN 0-7167-0585-0); tchr's manual avail. W H Freeman.
Barnes, J., jt. auth. see Murdoch, J.
Barnes, J. A. Three Styles in the Study of Kinship. LC 74-142057. 1972. 17.50x (ISBN 0-520-01879-6); pap. 5.85x (ISBN 0-520-02481-8). U of Cal Pr.
Barnes, Jack. Social Care Research. 163p. 1978. pap. text ed. 8.75x (ISBN 0-7199-0947-3, Pub. by Bedford England). Renouf.
Barnes, James J. & Barnes, Patience P. Hitler's Mein Kampf in Britain & America: A Publishing History, 1930-39. LC 79-54014. 1980. pap. 18.95 (ISBN 0-521-22691-0). Cambridge U Pr.
Barnes, Jane. Double Lives. LC 79-7795. 264p. 1981. 11.95 (ISBN 0-385-15647-2). Doubleday.
Barnes, Jim, tr. see Nick, Dagmar.
Barnes, Joanna. Pastora. LC 77-79533. 1980. 13.95 (ISBN 0-87795-170-5). Arbor Hse.
Barnes, John. Evita--First Lady: A Biography of Eva Peron. LC 78-3185. 1979. pap. 2.95 (ISBN 0-394-17087-3, B425, BC). Grove.
--More Money for Your Retirement. 320p. 1980. pap. 4.95 (ISBN 0-686-61976-5, EH 514, EH). Har-Row.
Barnes, John, jt. auth. see Middlemas, Keith.

Barnes, John G. Titmice of the British Isles. LC 74-33156. (Illus.). 224p. 1975. 15.95 (ISBN 0-7153-6955-5). David & Charles.
Barnes, Jonathan, ed. see Aristotle.
Barnes, Jonathan, et al, eds. Articles on Aristotle: Ethics & Politics, Vol. 2. LC 77-2064. 1979. 25.00 (ISBN 0-312-05478-5). St Martin.
--Articles on Aristotle: Vol. I: Metaphysics. LC 77-20604. 1979. 25.00 (ISBN 0-312-05479-3). St Martin.
--Articles on Aristotle: Vol. IV: Psychology & Aesthetics. LC 77-20604. 25.00 (ISBN 0-312-05480-7). St Martin.
Barnes, Kathleen & Pearce, Virginia. You & Yours. (Illus.). 41p. (Orig.). (gr. 3-6). 1980. pap. 2.95 (ISBN 0-87747-823-6). Deseret Bk.
Barnes, Lawrence G. Miocene Desmatophocinae (Mammalia: Carnivora) from California. (U. C. Publ. in Geological Sciences: Vol. 89). 1972. pap. 7.00x (ISBN 0-520-09384-4). U of Cal Pr.
Barnes, Leslie W. Canada's Guns: An Illustrated History of Artillery. (Illus.). 1979. pap. 9.95 (ISBN 0-660-00137-3, 56297-2, Pub. by Natl Mus Canada). U of Chicago Pr.
Barnes, Louis B., jt. auth. see Lorsch, Jay W.
Barnes, M. C., et al. Company Organization: Theory & Practice. (Unwin Professional Management Library). 1970. text ed. 10.95x o.p. (ISBN 0-04-658031-X). Allen Unwin.
Barnes, Margaret & Barnes, Harold, eds. Oceanography & Marine Biology: An Annual Review, Vol. 18. (Illus.). 528p. 1980. 84.00 (ISBN 0-08-025732-1). Pergamon.
Barnes, Mark & May, Ron. Mexican Majolica in Northern New Spain. 1980. Repr. 4.95 (ISBN 0-686-62076-3). Acoma Bks.
Barnes, Marvin P. Computer-Assisted Mineral Appraisal & Feasibility. LC 79-52270. (Illus.). 167p. 1980. text ed. 30.00x (ISBN 0-89520-262-X). Soc Mining Eng.
Barnes, Mary. Is There a Chef in the Kitchen. (Illus., Orig.). 1969. pap. 7.50x (ISBN 0-392-06983-0, AUS68-2523, LTB). Soccer.
Barnes, Mary & Berke, Joe. Mary Barnes: Two Accounts of a Journey Through Madness. 1978. pap. 2.50 o.p. (ISBN 0-345-27527-6). Ballantine.
Barnes, Mary & Berke, Joseph. Mary Barnes: Two Accounts of Journey Through Madness. 1973. pap. 1.95 o.p. (ISBN 0-345-23221-6). Ballantine.
Barnes, Melvyn P. Best Detective Fiction: A Guide from Godwin to the Present. (Guides to Subject Literature Ser.). 121p. (Orig.). 1975. 10.00 (ISBN 0-208-01376-8, Linnet). Shoe String.
Barnes, Michael J., ed. Politics & Personality Seventeen Sixty-Eighteen Twenty-Seven. LC 68-97214. (Selections from History Today Ser.: No. 6). (Illus.). 1967. 5.00 (ISBN 0-05-001533-8); pap. 3.95 (ISBN 0-685-09195-3). Dufour.
Barnes, Mildred, jt. ed. see Barnes, Virgil.
Barnes, Mildred J. Women's Basketball. 2nd ed. (Illus.). 1980. text ed. 18.95x (ISBN 0-205-06604-6, 6266045). Allyn.
--Women's Basketball. (Illus.). 250p. 1972. text ed. 13.95x o.s.i. (ISBN 0-686-66634-8, 623450X). Allyn.
Barnes, Mildred J. & Kentwell, Richard G. Field Hockey: The Coach & the Player. 2nd ed. 1978. text ed. 18.95 (ISBN 0-205-06512-0). Allyn.
Barnes, N. Sue, jt. auth. see Curtis, Helena.
Barnes, Patience P., jt. auth. see Barnes, James J.
Barnes, Patricia, jt. auth. see Mack, Earle.
Barnes, R. H. Kedang: A Study of the Collective Thought of an Eastern Indonesian People. (Oxford Monographs in Social Anthropology). (Illus.). 359p. 1974. 29.50x (ISBN 0-19-823185-7). Oxford U Pr.
Barnes, R. J. Economic Analysis: An Introduction. 412p. 1971. 12.95 (ISBN 0-408-70220-6); pap. 7.95 (ISBN 0-408-70233-8). Butterworths.
Barnes, R. S. Coastal Lagoons. LC 80-40041. (Cambridge Studies in Modern Biology: No. 1). (Illus.). 130p. 1980. 29.50 (ISBN 0-521-23422-0); pap. 11.95 (ISBN 0-521-29945-4). Cambridge U Pr.
Barnes, R. S., ed. Estuarine Environment. Green, J. (Illus.). 1972. 26.00x (ISBN 0-85334-539-2, Pub. by Applied Science). Burgess-Intl Ideas.
Barnes, Ralph M. Motion & Time Study: Design & Measurement of Work. 6th ed. LC 68-20097. 1968. 26.50 o.p. (ISBN 0-471-05350-3). Wiley.
--Motion & Time Study: Design & Measurement of Work. 7th ed. LC 80-173. 689p. 1980. text ed. 23.95 (ISBN 0-471-05905-6). Wiley.
Barnes, Ramon M., ed. Applications of Inductively Coupled Plasmas to Emission Spectroscopy. LC 78-70143. (Eastern Analytical Symposium Ser). (Illus., Orig.). 1978. pap. 21.75 (ISBN 0-89168-020-9). Franklin Inst Pr.
--Emission Spectroscopy. LC 75-30672. 1976. 49.00 (ISBN 0-12-786137-8). Acad Pr.
Barnes, Richard, jt. auth. see Giffin, Kim.
Barnes, Richard E., jt. auth. see Mabry, Edward A.
Barnes, Robert. A Supplicatyon... Unto Henry the Eighth. LC 73-6098. (English Experience Ser.: No. 567). 1973. Repr. of 1534 ed. 18.50 (ISBN 90-221-0567-9). Walter J Johnson.
Barnes, Robert M. Technical Commodity Yearbook, 1981. 128p. 1980. text ed. 37.50 (ISBN 0-686-69348-5). Van Nos Reinhold.
Barnes, Roger W., et al. Urology. 3rd. ed. (Medical Outline Ser.). 1980. pap. 20.00 (ISBN 0-87488-611-2). Med Exam.
Barnes, Sandra T. Ogun: An Old God for a New Age. LC 79-26577. (ISHI Occasional Papers in Social Change: No. 3). 1980. pap. text ed. 4.95x (ISBN 0-89727-011-8). Inst Study Human.
Barnes, T. R. English Verse. 1967. 49.50 (ISBN 0-521-04109-0); pap. 10.95x (ISBN 0-521-09433-X, 433). Cambridge U Pr.
Barnes, Thomas A. & Israel, Jacob S. Brady's Programmed Introduction to Respiratory Therapy. 2nd ed. LC 79-27753. (Illus.). 365p. 1980. pap. text ed. 14.95 (ISBN 0-87619-624-5). R J Brady.
Barnes, Thomas C., et al. Northern New Spain: A Research Guide. LC 80-24860. 1981. pap. text ed. 9.95x (ISBN 0-8165-0709-0). U of Ariz Pr.
Barnes, Thomas G. & Feldman, Gerald D., eds. Rationalism & Revolution Sixteen Sixty to Eighteen Fifteen, Vol. II. LC 79-66686. 1979. pap. text ed. 9.25 (ISBN 0-8191-0850-2). U Pr of Amer.
--Renaissance, Reformation, & Absolutism Fourteen Hundred to Sixteen Sixty, Vol. I. LC 79-66685. 1979. pap. text ed. 9.25 (ISBN 0-8191-0847-2). U Pr of Amer.
Barnes, V. E. & Schofield, D. A. Potential Low-Grade Iron Ore & Hydraulic-Fracturing Sand in Cambrian Sandstones, Northwestern Llano Region, Texas. (Illus.). 58p. 1964. 2.00 (RI 53). Bur Econ Geology.
Barnes, V. E., et al. Geology of the Llano Region & Austin Area. rev. ed. 154p. 1976. Repr. of 1972 ed. 1.50 (GB 13). Bur Econ Geology.
--Utilization of Texas Serpentine. (Illus.). 52p. 1950. 0.60 (PUB 5020). Bur Econ Geology.
Barnes, Valerie, jt. auth. see Murray, Thomas C.
Barnes, Virgil & Barnes, Mildred, eds. Tektites. LC 72-95942. (Benchmark Papers in Geology Ser). 400p. 1973. 42.50 (ISBN 0-12-786138-6). Acad Pr.
Barnes, W. Emery. Gospel Criticism & Form Criticism. 83p. 1936. pap. text ed. 3.50 (ISBN 0-567-02020-7). Attic Pr.
Barnes, Wesley. Existentialism. LC 67-28536. (Orig.). (gr. 10 up). 1968. pap. text ed. 3.25 (ISBN 0-8120-0275-X). Barron.
Barnes-Ostrander, Marilyn. Music: Reflections in Sound. 1976. tchr's ed avail. (ISBN 0-06-371056-0, HarpC). Har-Row.
Barness, Lewis A., et al, eds. Nutrition & Medical Practice. (Illus.). 1981. text ed. 17.00 (ISBN 0-87055-365-8). AVI.
Barnet, et al. An Introduction to Literature. 7th ed. 1981. pap. text ed. 9.95 (ISBN 0-316-08211-2); tchrs'. manual free (ISBN 0-316-08212-0). Little.
--Types of Drama. 3rd ed. Date not set. pap. text ed. 11.95 (ISBN 0-316-08208-2). Little.
Barnet, G., et al, eds. Mechanical Fitting, Vol. 2. 2nd ed. (Engineering Craftsmen: No. H25). (Illus.). 1973. spiral bdg. 17.95x (ISBN 0-85083-186-5). Intl Ideas.
Barnet, Richard J. Intervention & Revolution. rev. ed. 336p. 1972. pap. 1.75 o.p. (ISBN 0-451-61156-X, ME 1156, Ment). NAL.
Barnet, Sylvan & Stubbs, Marcia. Barnet & Stubbs's Practical Guide to Writing. 3rd ed. 424p. 1980. pap. text ed. 7.95 (ISBN 0-316-08155-8); instructor's manual free (ISBN 0-316-08156-6). Little.
Barnet, Sylvan, jt. auth. see Stubbs, Marcia.
Barnet, Sylvan, et al, eds. Genius of the Early English Theater: Abraham & Isaac, Second Shepherd's Play, Everyman, Doctor Faustus, Macbeth, Volpone, Samson Agonistes. 1962. pap. 2.50 (ISBN 0-451-61889-0, ME1889, Ment). NAL.
Barnetson, John. Critter Chronicles: Tales for Next Tuesday. LC 80-66262. (Illus.). 96p. 1981. 12.95 (ISBN 0-89742-037-3). Dawne-Leigh. Postponed.
Barnett, A. Doak. China & the Major Powers in East Asia. 1977. 15.95 (ISBN 0-8157-0824-6); pap. 6.95 (ISBN 0-8157-0823-8). Brookings.
--China & the World Food System. LC 79-87912. (Monographs: No. 12). 128p. 1979. 5.00 (ISBN 0-686-28683-9). Overseas Dev Council.
--China Policy: Old Problems & New Challenges. LC 76-51538. 1977. 9.95 (ISBN 0-8157-0822-X); pap. 3.95 (ISBN 0-8157-0821-1). Brookings.
--A New U.S. Policy Toward China. LC 70-166508. 1971. 9.95 (ISBN 0-8157-0818-1); pap. 3.95 (ISBN 0-8157-0817-3). Brookings.
--Uncertain Passage: China's Transition to the Post-Mao Era. LC 73-22482. 378p. 1974. 14.95 (ISBN 0-8157-0820-3); pap. 5.95 (ISBN 0-8157-0819-X). Brookings.
Barnett, Canon. The Ideal City. Meller, Helen, ed. (The Victorian Library). 1979. text ed. 16.25 (ISBN 0-7185-5061-7, Leicester). Humanities.
Barnett, Doak A. Cadres, Bureaucracy, & Political Power in Communist China. LC 67-15895. 1967. 22.50x (ISBN 0-231-03035-5). Columbia U Pr.
Barnett, G. J., tr. see Moreau, J. J., et al.
Barnett, Gene A. Denis Johnston. (English Author Ser.: No. 230). 1978. 12.50 (ISBN 0-8057-6701-0). Twayne.
Barnett, George L. Charles Lamb. (English Author Ser.). 1976. lib. bdg. 12.50 (ISBN 0-8057-6668-5). Twayne.
Barnett, H. J., et al, eds. Acetylsalicylic Acid: New Uses for an Old Drug. 1981. text ed. price not set (ISBN 0-89004-647-6). Raven.
Barnett, Henry L. see Walcher, Dwain N., et al.
Barnett, Herbert E. & Fraser, Hugh, eds. Who's Who in Canada 1980-81. 70th ed. (Illus.). 1496p. 1980. 75.00x (ISBN 0-8002-2744-1). Intl Pubns Serv.
Barnett, Homer. Indian Shakers: A Messianic Cult of the Pacific Northwest. LC 72-5482. (Arcturus Books Paperbacks). (Illus.). 383p. 1972. pap. 7.95 (ISBN 0-8093-0595-X). S Ill U Pr.
Barnett, J. A., et al. A Guide to Identifying & Classifying Yeasts. LC 79-11136. (Illus.). 1979. 82.50 (ISBN 0-521-22762-3). Cambridge U Pr.
Barnett, James. Head of the Force. LC 78-19614. 1979. 8.95 o.p. (ISBN 0-312-36499-7). St Martin.
Barnett, Laurie, jt. ed. see Kaylin, Arleen.
Barnett, Lincoln. The Ancient Adirondacks. (The American Wilderness Ser.). (Illus.). 184p. 1974. 12.95 (ISBN 0-8094-1233-0). Time-Life.
--The Ancient Adirondacks. LC 74-75617. (American Wilderness). (Illus.). (gr. 6 up). 1974. PLB 11.97 (ISBN 0-8094-1234-9, Pub. by Time-Life). Silver.
Barnett, M. E., jt. auth. see Klemperer, O. E.
Barnett, M. T. & Smith, J. L. Effective Communication for Public Safety Personnel. LC 76-46125. 1978. pap. text ed. 9.20 (ISBN 0-8273-1658-5); instructor's guide 1.60 (ISBN 0-8273-1659-3). Delmar.
Barnett, M. Y. Elements of Technical Writing. LC 73-13487. 1974. 10.00 (ISBN 0-8273-0356-4); instructor's guide 1.60 (ISBN 0-8273-0357-2). Delmar.
Barnett, Marguerite R. & Hefner, James, eds. Public Policy for the Black Community: Strategies & Perspectives. LC 76-24466. (Illus.). 225p. 1976. pap. text ed. 7.95x (ISBN 0-88284-038-X). Alfred Pub.
Barnett, Peter H. Can You Tell Me How What You Are Doing Now Is to Do Something Philosophical? pap. 5.00 (ISBN 0-686-62107-7). Assembling Pr.
Barnett, R. D. Illustrations of Old Testament History. (British Museum Publications). 1978. 9.95 o.p. (ISBN 0-374-83335-4); pap. 4.95 o.p. (ISBN 0-374-84336-8). FS&G.
Barnett, Raymond. Analytic Trigonometry with Applications. 2nd ed. 1980. text ed. 17.95x (ISBN 0-534-00728-7). Wadsworth Pub.
Barnett, Raymond A. College Algebra. 2nd ed. (Illus.). 1979. text ed. 14.95 (ISBN 0-07-003778-7, C); ans. manual 2.95 (ISBN 0-07-003779-5); tests 5.95 (ISBN 0-07-003784-1). McGraw.
Barnett, Regina R. Create, One. 31p. (Orig.). (ps). 1978. pap. text ed. 4.95 student work pad (ISBN 0-697-01678-1); tchr's manual 10.75 (ISBN 0-697-01677-3). Wm C Brown.
--Create, Two. 31p. (Orig.). (ps). 1979. pap. text ed. 4.95 student work pad (ISBN 0-697-01705-2); tchr's manual 10.75 (ISBN 0-697-01706-0). Wm C Brown.
--Let Out the Sunshine. 144p. (Orig.). 1981. pap. text ed. 12.00 (ISBN 0-697-01762-1). Wm C Brown.
Barnett, Richard B. North India Between Empires: Awadh, the Mughals, & the British, 1720-1801. (Center for South & Southeast Asian Studies). 400p. 1981. 25.00x (ISBN 0-520-03787-1). U of Cal Pr.
Barnett, Robert M. Analysis, Computation, Presentation of Engineering Information. 8.50 (ISBN 0-89741-000-9); pap. 5.00 (ISBN 0-89741-000-9). Roadrunner Tech.
Barnett, Rosalind C. & Baruch, Grace K. Competent Woman. LC 78-8380. (Irvington Social Relations Ser.). 1980. pap. text ed. 6.95x (ISBN 0-8290-0092-5). Irvington.
Barnett, Roy N. Clinical Laboratory Statistics. 2nd ed. (Series in Laboratory Medicine). 224p. 1978. 17.95 (ISBN 0-316-08196-5). Little.
Barnett, S. A. Modern Ethology. (Illus.). 720p. 1981. text ed. 19.95x (ISBN 0-19-502780-9). Oxford U Pr.
Barnett, Stephen. Introduction to Mathematical Control Theory. (Oxford Applied Mathematics & Engineering Sciences Ser). (Illus.). 280p. 1975. 21.00x (ISBN 0-19-859618-9). Oxford U Pr.
Barnett, Ted. Golf Is Madness. LC 77-80365. (Illus.). 128p. 1977. 5.95 (ISBN 0-671-22974-5). Golf Digest.
Barnett, Ursula A. Ezekiel Mphahlele. LC 76-18881. (World Authors Ser: No. 417). 1976. lib. bdg. 12.50 (ISBN 0-8057-6257-4). Twayne.
Barnett, Vic. Elements of Sampling Theory. 1975. pap. text ed. 12.50x (ISBN 0-8448-0614-5). Crane-Russak Co.
Barnett, Vivian E. The Guggenheim Museum: Justin K. Thannhauser Collection. new ed. LC 78-66357. (Illus.). 1978. 24.50 (ISBN 0-89207-016-1); pap. 15.50 (ISBN 0-685-91431-3). S R Guggenheim.
--Handbook: The Guggenheim Museum Collection, 1900-1980. (Illus.). 1980. 14.85 (ISBN 0-89207-021-8). S R Guggenheim.
Barnett, Walter. Jesus: the Story of His Life: A Modern Retelling Based on the Gospels. LC 75-28260. 1976. 13.95 (ISBN 0-88229-308-7). Nelson Hall.
Barnett, Winston & Winskell, Cyril. A Study in Conservation. 1978. 11.95 (ISBN 0-85362-168-3, Oriel); pap. 8.95 (ISBN 0-85362-172-1). Routledge & Kegan.
Barnette, Henlee H. Introducing Christian Ethics. LC 61-5629. 1961. 6.50 (ISBN 0-8054-6102-7). Broadman.
Barnewall, Gordon G. Succeed as a Job Applicant. LC 75-18877. (Career Guidance Ser.). 160p. (YA) 1976. pap. 3.50 (ISBN 0-668-03861-6). Arco.
Barney, C. W., jt. auth. see Goor, A. Y.
Barney, Frances. Lantern in the Night. 192p. (YA) 1976. 4.95 o.p. (ISBN 0-685-64247-X, Avalon). Bouregy.
Barney, Gerald O., ed. The Global Two Thousand Report to the President of the U. S.--Entering the 21st Century: The Summary Report--Special Edition with Environment Projections & the Government's Global Model, Vol. 1. (Pergamon Policy Studies Ser.). 200p. 1980. 30.00 (ISBN 0-08-024617-6); pap. 9.50 (ISBN 0-08-024616-8). Pergamon.
--The Unfinished Agenda. LC 76-30486. 1977. 8.95 o.s.i. (ISBN 0-690-01481-3, TYC-T). T Y Crowell.
Barney, Joseph see Brown, O. Z.
Barney, Kenneth D. A Faith to Live by. LC 76-27929. (Radiant Life). 128p. 1977. pap. 1.95 (ISBN 0-88243-899-9, 02-0899); teacher's ed. 2.50 (ISBN 0-88243-171-4, 32-0171). Gospel Pub.
--Freedom: A Guarantee for Everybody. (Radiant Life Ser). 128p. 1976. pap. 1.25 (ISBN 0-88243-891-3, 02-0891, Radiant Books); teacher's ed 2.50 (ISBN 0-88243-165-X, 32-0165). Gospel Pub.
--If You Love Me... LC 75-22611. (Radiant Life Ser). 1977. pap. 1.50 (ISBN 0-88243-889-1, 02-0889); teacher's ed 2.50 (ISBN 0-88243-163-3, 32-0163). Gospel Pub.
--You'd Better Believe It! LC 75-22608. (Radiant Bk). 1976. pap. 1.95 (ISBN 0-88243-887-5, 02-0887); teacher's ed 2.50 (ISBN 0-88243-161-7, 32-0161). Gospel Pub.
Barney, Richard W., et al. How to Make Knives. Beinfeld, Wallace, ed. 182p. 1977. 13.95 (ISBN 0-917714-13-X). Beinfeld Pub.
Barney, Stephen, ed. Chaucer's "Troilus": Essays in Criticism. 323p. 1980. 22.50 (ISBN 0-208-01822-0, Archon). Shoe String.
Barney, William L. Flawed Victory: A New Perspective on the Civil War. LC 80-68972. 225p. 1980. lib. bdg. 19.00 (ISBN 0-8191-1273-9); pap. text ed. 8.75 (ISBN 0-8191-1274-7). U Pr of Amer.
Barnfield, Richard. The Encomion of Lady Pecunia: Or, the Praise of Money. LC 74-80162. (English Experience Ser.: No. 642). 24p. 1974. Repr. of 1598 ed. 3.50 (ISBN 90-221-0642-X). Walter J Johnson.
Barngrover, Charles L., et al. Personal Finance. 2nd ed. LC 80-18010. (Finance Ser.). 520p. 1981. text ed. 19.95 (ISBN 0-88244-216-3). Grid Pub.
Barnhart, Clarence L., ed. Scott, Foresman Advanced Dictionary. 1978. 15.95 (ISBN 0-385-14852-6). Doubleday.
--Scott, Foresman Beginning Dictionary. 12.95 (ISBN 0-385-13330-8). Doubleday.
--Scott, Foresman Intermediate Dictionary. 1978. 15.95 (ISBN 0-385-14853-4). Doubleday.
--The World Book Dictionary, 2 vols. rev. ed. Barnhart, Robert K. LC 79-53618. (Illus.). (gr. 4-12). 1980. Set. PLB write for info. (ISBN 0-7166-0280-6). World Bk-Childcraft.
Barnhart, Clarence L. & Halsey, William D., eds. New Century Handbook of English Literature. rev. ed. (gr. 9-12). 1956. 23.95 (ISBN 0-13-611962-X). P-H.

Barnhart, Clarence L., et al. Second Barnhart Dictionary of New English. LC 79-6815. 1980. 19.95 (ISBN 0-06-010154-7, HarpT). Har-Row.

Barnhart, Clarence L., et al, eds. The Barnhart Dictionary of New English Since 1963. LC 73-712. 512p. (YA) 1973. 14.95 o.s.i. (ISBN 0-06-010223-3, HarpT). Har-Row.

Barnhart, J. The Study of Religion & Its Meaning. 1977. 27.05x (ISBN 90-279-7762-3). Mouton.

Barnhart, John D. & Riker, Dorothy L. Indiana to Eighteen Sixteen: The Colonial Period. 536p. 1971. 15.00x (ISBN 0-253-37018-3). Ind U Pr.

Barnhart, Phillip H. Seasonings for Sermons. 88p. (Orig.). 1980. pap. text ed. 5.50 (ISBN 0-89536-451-4). CSS Pub.

Barnhart, Robert K. see Barnhart, Clarence L.

Barnhart, Russell T., tr. see Villiod, Eugene.

Barnhart, Sarah A. Introduction to Interpersonal Communication. 1967. pap. text ed. 6.50 scp (ISBN 0-690-00855-4, HarpC). Har-Row.

Barnhouse, Donald G. Genesis: A Devotional Commentary in One Volume. 564p. 1973. 12.95 (ISBN 0-310-20470-4). Zondervan.

--The Invisible War. 288p. 1980. pap. 6.95 (ISBN 0-310-20481-X). Zondervan.

--The Love Life. LC 72-94754. 1977. pap. 2.95 (ISBN 0-8307-0451-5, S270-1-29). Regal.

--Revelation: An Expositional Commentary. 1971. 12.95 (ISBN 0-310-20490-9). Zondervan.

--Thessalonians: An Expositional Commentary. 116p. 1980. pap. 3.95 (ISBN 0-310-20501-8). Zondervan.

Barnhouse, Ruth T. Homosexuality: A Symbolic Confusion. 1976. 8.95 (ISBN 0-8164-0303-1). Crossroad NY.

--Homosexuality: A Symbolic Confusion. 2nd ed. 1979. pap. 4.95 (ISBN 0-8164-2235-4). Crossroad NY.

Barnhouse, Ruth T. & Holmes, Urban T. Male & Female: Christian Approaches to Sexuality. (Orig.). 1976. pap. 4.95 (ISBN 0-8164-2118-8). Crossroad NY.

Barnick, Bernard C. Penn's Woods: A Love Story. 64p. 1980. 10.00x (ISBN 0-682-49660-X, Banner). Exposition.

Barnicoat, John. A Concise History of Posters. LC 78-22019. (World of Art Ser.). (Illus.). 1979. pap. 9.95 (ISBN 0-19-520131-0). Oxford U Pr.

Barnidge, Thomas & Grow, Douglas. The Jim Hart Story. (Illus.). 1977. 6.95 (ISBN 0-8272-1705-6); pap. 4.95 (ISBN 0-8272-1704-8). Bethany Pr.

Barnitz, Jacqueline. Abstract Currents in Ecuadorian Art. annual (Illus.). 48p. 1977. pap. text ed. 3.00 (ISBN 0-89192-235-0). Interbk Inc.

Barnouw. Plaid for Cultural Anthropology. rev. ed. 1978. 4.95 (ISBN 0-256-02100-7, 01-0356-02). Learning Syst.

--Plaid for Physical Anthropology & Archaeology. rev. ed. 1978. 4.95 (ISBN 0-256-02117-1, 01-0355-02). Learning Syst.

Barnouw, Erik. Documentary: A History of the Non-Fiction Film. LC 74-79618. (Illus.). 336p. 1976. pap. 5.95 (ISBN 0-19-502005-7, 451, GB). Oxford U Pr.

--The Magician & the Cinema. (Illus.). 112p. 1981. 12.95 (ISBN 0-19-502918-6). Oxford U Pr.

--The Sponsor: Notes on a Modern Potentate. (Illus.). 1979. pap. 4.95 (ISBN 0-19-502614-4, GB 580, GB). Oxford U Pr.

Barnouw, Erik & Krishnaswamy, S. Indian Film. 2nd ed. (Illus.). 1980. 15.95 (ISBN 0-19-502682-9, 592); pap. 5.95 (ISBN 0-19-502683-7). Oxford U Pr.

Barnouw, Victor. Anthropology: A General Introduction. 1979. 18.50 (ISBN 0-256-02113-9); pap. text ed. 2.50 study guide (ISBN 0-256-02113-9). Dorsey.

--Culture & Personality. 3rd ed. 1979. text ed. 19.50x (ISBN 0-256-02193-7). Dorsey.

--Dream of the Blue Heron. LC 66-20995. (Illus.). (gr. 4-6). 1966. 4.50 o.s.i. (ISBN 0-440-02150-2, Sey Lawr). Delacorte.

--Introduction to Anthropology, 2 vols. 3rd ed. Incl. Vol. 1. Physical Anthropology & Archaeology (ISBN 0-256-02000-0); Vol. 2. Ethnology (ISBN 0-256-02001-9). 1978. pap. text ed. 12.95x ea. Dorsey.

Barns, Cass G. Sod House. LC 73-100812. (Illus.). 1970. 13.95x (ISBN 0-8032-1153-8); pap. 3.95 (ISBN 0-8032-5700-7, BB 511, Bison). U of Nebr Pr.

Barns, J. W., jt. ed. see Reymond, E. A.

Barnsley, Alan. Introducing Expanded Polystyrene. 1973. 14.95 (ISBN 0-7134-2442-7, Pub. by Batsford England). David & Charles.

Barnsley, John H. The Social Reality of Ethics: The Comparative Analysis of Moral Codes. (International Library of Sociology). 464p. 1972. 35.00x (ISBN 0-7100-7286-4). Routledge & Kegan.

Barnstone, Aliki. Real Tin Flower: Poems About the World at Nine. LC 68-22122. (Illus.). 1968. 7.95 (ISBN 0-02-708430-2, CCPr). Macmillan.

Barnstone, Willis. A Snow Salmon Reached the Andes Lake. LC 80-65064. 1980. 6.95 (ISBN 0-931604-02-8); pap. 3.95 (ISBN 0-931604-03-6). Curbstone Pub NY TX.

Barnstone, Willis, tr. from Span. The Dream Below the Sun: Selected Poems of Antonio Machado. rev., enl ed. (Illus.). 176p. (Span., Eng.). 1981. 12.95 (ISBN 0-89594-048-5); pap. 6.95 (ISBN 0-89594-047-7). Crossing Pr.

Barnum, Marvin R., et al. Audio-Tutorial Introductory Biology: Principles. rev. ed. (Illus., Orig.). 1969. text ed. 6.95x (ISBN 0-02-473600-7, 47360); tapes 375.00 (ISBN 0-02-473580-9, 47358); tape script 6.95 (ISBN 0-02-473610-4, 47361). Macmillan.

Barnum, Phineas T. Humbugs of the World. LC 68-21755. 1970. Repr. of 1865 ed. 15.00 (ISBN 0-8103-3580-8). Gale.

Barnum, Priscilla H., ed. Dives & Pauper, Vol. I, Pt. 2. (Early English Text Society Original Ser.). (Illus.). 400p. 1980. 29.50 (ISBN 0-19-722282-X). Oxford U Pr.

Barnwell, H. T., ed. see Corneille, Pierre.

Barnwell, William. Imram: Vol. II of the Blessing Trilogy. (Orig.). 1981. pap. 2.95 (ISBN 0-671-41272-8). PB.

Baro, Gene. Robert Gordy: Paintings & Drawings. (Illus.). 1981. pap. price not set (ISBN 0-89494-011-2). New Orleans Mus Art.

Baro, Gene, intro. By. Claes Oldenburg: Drawings & Prints. LC 68-8894. (Illus.). 274p. 1981. pap. 19.95 (ISBN 0-87754-202-3). Chelsea Hse.

Barocas, David N., tr. see Magriso, Yitzchak.

Barocci, Thomas A. Non-Profit Hospitals: Their Structure, Human Resources, & Economic Importance. LC 80-22075. (Illus.). 224p. 1980. 19.95 (ISBN 0-86569-054-5). Auburn Hse.

Barocci, Thomas A., jt. auth. see Jerrett, Robert.

Baroja, Pio. Caesar or Nothing. How, Louis, tr. from Span. 337p. 1976. Repr. of 1919 ed. 17.50 (ISBN 0-86527-224-7). Fertig.

Baron, Carol, ed. see Burton, Ian J.

Baron, Carole, jt. auth. see Asimov, Isaac.

Baron, Carole, ed. see Comings, Pamela.

Baron, Carole, ed. see Warner, Jack, Jr.

Baron, Dona, ed. The National Purpose Reconsidered. 1978. 15.00x (ISBN 0-231-04472-0). Columbia U Pr.

Baron, G. Society, Schools & Progress in England. 1966. 22.00 (ISBN 0-08-011594-2); pap. text ed. 10.75 (ISBN 0-08-011593-4). Pergamon.

Baron, G., ed. The Politics of School Government. (International Studies in Education & Social Change). 260p. Date not set. 36.01 (ISBN 0-08-025213-3). Pergamon.

Baron, George & Howell, D. A. The Government & Management of Schools. 270p. 1974. text ed. 20.75x (ISBN 0-485-11142-X, Athlone Pr). Humanities.

Baron, Hans. Crisis of the Early Italian Renaissance: Civic Humanism & Republican Liberty in an Age of Classicism & Tyranny. rev. ed. 1966. 25.00 (ISBN 0-691-05114-3); pap. 5.95 (ISBN 0-691-00752-7). Princeton U Pr.

Baron, Herman. Author Index to Esquire 1933-1973. LC 76-10625. 299p. 1976. 13.50 (ISBN 0-8108-0935-4). Scarecrow.

Baron, J. H. & Moody, F., eds. Gastroenterology: Foregut, Vol. 1. (Butterworth International Medical Reviews). 1981. text ed. price not set (ISBN 0-407-02287-2). Butterworth.

Baron, Michael. Water & Plant Life. 1967. pap. text ed. 5.95x (ISBN 0-435-61054-6). Heinemann Ed.

Baron, Richard, et al. Raid: The Untold Story of Patton's Secret Mission. 288p. 1981. 12.95 (ISBN 0-399-12597-3). Putnam.

Baron, Robert A. & Byrne, Donn. Exploring Social Psychology. 1978. text ed. 13.95x (ISBN 0-205-06529-5); instr's man. avail. (ISBN 0-205-06546-5). Allyn.

Baron, Salo W. The Russian Jew Under Tsars & Soviets. rev. ed. 480p. 1976. 14.95 o.s.i. (ISBN 0-02-507300-1). Macmillan.

--Social & Religious History of the Jews: Byzantines, Mamelukes, & Maghribians, Vol. 17. 1980. 25.00 (ISBN 0-231-08854-X). Columbia U Pr.

--A Social & Religious History of the Jews, 16 vols. 2nd, rev. & enl. ed. Incl. Vol. 1. Ancient Times: To the Beginning of the Christian Era. 1952 (ISBN 0-231-08838-8); Vol. 2. Ancient Times: Christian Era: the First Five Centuries. 1952 (ISBN 0-231-08839-6); Vol. 3. High Middle Ages: Heirs of Rome & Persia. 1957 (ISBN 0-231-08840-X); Vol. 4. High Middle Ages: Meeting of the East & West. 1957 (ISBN 0-231-08841-8); Vol. 5. High Middle Ages: Religious Controls & Dissensions. 1957 (ISBN 0-231-08842-6); Vol. 6. High Middle Ages: Laws, Homilies & the Bible. 1958 (ISBN 0-231-08843-4); Vol. 7. High Middle Ages: Hebrew Language & Letters. 1958 (ISBN 0-231-08844-2); Vol. 8. High Middle Ages: Philosophy & Science. 1958 (ISBN 0-231-08845-0); Vol. 9. Late Middle Ages & Era of European Expansion, 1200-1650: Under Church & Empire. 1965 (ISBN 0-231-08846-9); Vol. 10. Late Middle Ages & Era of European Expansion, 1200-1650: On the Empire's Periphery. 1965 (ISBN 0-231-08847-7); Vol. 11. Late Middle Ages & Era of European Expansion, 1200-1650: Citizen or Alien Conjurer. 1967 (ISBN 0-231-08848-5); Vol. 12. Late Middle Ages & Era of European Expansion, 1200-1650: Economic Catalyst. 1967 (ISBN 0-231-08849-3); Vol. 13. Late Middle Ages & Era of European Expansion, 1200-1650: Inquisition, Renaissance & Reformation. 1969 (ISBN 0-231-08850-7); Vol. 14. Late Middle Ages & Era of European Expansion, 1200-1650: Catholic Restoration & Wars of Religion. 1969 (ISBN 0-231-08851-5); Vol. 15. Late Middle Ages & Era of European Expansion, 1200-1650: Resettlement Era. 1973 (ISBN 0-231-08852-3); Index (ISBN 0-231-08877-9). LC 52-404. 27.00x ea. Columbia U Pr.

--A Social & Religious History of the Jews: Late Middle Ages and Era of European Expansion (1200-1650) Poland-Lithuania 1500-1650, Vol 16. 400p. 1976. 27.00x (ISBN 0-231-08853-1). Columbia U Pr.

Baron, Salo W. & Blau, Joseph L., eds. Judaism: Post Biblical & Talmudic Period. LC 55-1342. 1954. 5.25 o.p. (ISBN 0-672-60344-6, LLA135). Bobbs.

Baron, Samuel H. Muscovite Russia. 362p. 1980. 75.00x (ISBN 0-86078-063-5, Pub. by Variorum England). State Mutual Bk.

Baron, W. M. Organization in Plants. 3rd ed. LC 78-12085. 1979. pap. 19.95 (ISBN 0-470-26558-2). Halsted Pr.

Barone, Antonio & Paterno, Gianfranco. The Physics & Applications of the Josephson Effect. 450p. 1981. 40.00 (ISBN 0-471-01469-9, Pub. by Wiley-Interscience). Wiley.

Barone, Jory H., jt. auth. see Sandhu, Harpreet K.

Barone, Michael, et al. Almanac of American Politics - 1972. LC 70-160417. (Illus.). 1972. 15.00 (ISBN 0-87645-053-2); pap. 6.95 (ISBN 0-87645-056-7). Gambit.

Baroni, T. J. A Revision of the Genus Rhodocybe Maire: Agaricales. (Nova Hedwigia Beiheft). (Illus.). 300p. 1981. lib. bdg. 60.00x (ISBN 3-7682-5467-4). Lubrecht & Cramer.

Baronio, Joyce. Forty-Second Street Studio. LC 80-80678. (Illus.). 96p. 1980. 40.00 (ISBN 0-936568-00-3). Pyxidium Pr.

Barons, Keith C. Are Pesticides Really Necessary? 280p. 1981. pap. 6.95 (ISBN 0-89526-888-4). Regnery-Gateway.

Barons, Richard I., ed. The American Hearth. (Illus.). 1976. pap. 6.00 (ISBN 0-89062-085-7, Pub. by Roberson Ctr). Pub Ctr Cult Res.

--Franck Taylor Bowers, Eighteen Seventy-Five-Nineteen Thirty-Two. LC 77-72387. 1977. pap. 5.00 (ISBN 0-937318-02-7, Pub. by Roberson Ctr.). Pub Ctr Cult Res.

Baron Von Mullenheim-Rechberg, Burkhard. Battleship Bismark: A Survivor's Story. LC 80-81093. 284p. 1980. 15.95 (ISBN 0-87021-096-3). Naval Inst Pr.

Barooshian, Stephen M. My Story. 1978. 5.95 o.p. (ISBN 0-533-03000-5). Vantage.

Barouch, A., tr. see Al'tshuler, S. A. & Kozyrev, B. M.

Barouch, A., tr. see Strazhesko, D. N.

Barquero, J. A. Estampas Espanolas. (Span.). 7.50 (ISBN 84-241-5632-3). E Torres & Sons.

Barr, Allan. A Diagram of Synoptic Relationships. Repr. of 1938 ed. text ed. 9.50x (ISBN 0-567-02021-5). Attic Pr.

Barr, Alwyn. Black Texans: A History of Negroes in Texas 1528-1971. LC 72-97935. (Negro Heritage Ser., No. 12). (Illus.). 259p. 1973. 12.50 (ISBN 0-8363-0016-5). Jenkins.

Barr, Amelia. Remember the Alamo. 329p. 1980. Repr. of 1880 ed. lib. bdg. 11.95x (ISBN 0-89968-215-4). Lightyear.

Barr, Avron & Feigenbaum, Edward, eds. The Handbook of Artificial Intelligence, 3 vols. 1981. 90.00 set (ISBN 0-86576-004-7); 30.00 ea. Vol. 1 (ISBN 0-86576-005-5). Vol. 2 (ISBN 0-86576-006-3). Vol. 3 (ISBN 0-86576-007-1). W Kaufmann.

Barr, Ben & Grinaker, Robert L. Short Audit Case: The Valley Publishing Company. 3rd ed. 1976. text ed. 11.95x o.p. (ISBN 0-256-01629-1). Irwin.

--Short Audit Case: The Valley Publishing Company. 4th ed. 1980. pap. 13.95x (ISBN 0-256-02327-1). Irwin.

Barr, Ben B., jt. auth. see Grinaker, Robert L.

Barr, Browne. The Well Church Book. 1976. 7.95 (ISBN 0-8164-0304-X). Crossroad NY.

Barr, Browne, jt. auth. see Jeske, Richard L.

Barr, Charles W. Waterfront Development: A Bibliography. (Public Administration Ser.: Bibliography P-462). 51p. 1980. pap. 5.50. Vance Biblios.

Barr, David & Gordon, Andrew. Water Polo. (Illus.). 112p. (YA) 1981. 12.95 (Pub. by EP Publishing England). Sterling.

Barr, Donald. A Planet in Arms. 288p. 1981. pap. 2.25 (ISBN 0-449-24407-5, Crest). Fawcett.

Barr, Doris W. Communication for Business, Professional & Technical Students. 2nd ed. 512p. 1980. pap. text ed. 18.95x (ISBN 0-534-00777-5). Wadsworth Pub.

Barr, Elisabeth. Castle Heritage. 1979. pap. 1.75 (ISBN 0-87216-669-4). Playboy Pbks.

--The Sea Treasure. LC 80-82847. 208p. (Orig.). 1981. pap. 1.95 (ISBN 0-87216-780-1). Playboy Pbks.

Barr, George. Who's Who in the Bible. LC 74-6570. 1974. 8.95 o.p. (ISBN 0-685-50512-X). Jonathan David.

Barr, Guy, tr. see Nernst, W.

Barr, Howard N. Fifty Best of Baltimore & Ohio Railroad, Bk. 1. (Illus.). 1977. 12.00 (ISBN 0-934118-16-7). Barnard Robert.

Barr, Howard N. & Barringer, W. A. Q-Baltimore & Ohio Railroad Q-Class Mikado Locomotives. LC 78-52708. (Illus.). 1978. 30.00 (ISBN 0-934118-15-9). Barnard Robert.

Barr, J., et al, eds. Instrument Fitting. (Engineering Craftsmen: No. H24). (Illus.). 1969. spiral bdg. 15.95x (ISBN 0-85083-069-9). Intl Ideas.

Barr, James. The Scope & Authority of the Bible. LC 80-21394. 1981. pap. 7.95 (ISBN 0-664-24361-4). Westminster.

--Semantics of Biblical Language. 1961. 27.50x (ISBN 0-19-826607-3). Oxford U Pr.

Barr, James R, jt. auth. see Schleicher, Robert.

Barr, Jene. Mister Zip & U. S. Mail. LC 64-16364. (Career Awareness-Community Helpers Ser.). (Illus.). (gr. k-2). 1964. 4.75g o.p. (ISBN 0-8075-5180-5). A Whitman.

--This Is My Country. rev. ed. LC 59-14393. (Community Helpers Ser). (Illus.). (gr. k-2). 1966. 4.75g o.p. (ISBN 0-8075-7879-7). A Whitman.

Barr, John R; see O'Neal, William B.

Barr, Justin, et al. Hellinger's Law. (Orig.). pap. 2.25 (ISBN 0-515-05809-2). Jove Pubns.

Barr, M. Autonomous Categories. (Lecture Notes in Mathematics: Vol. 752). 1979. pap. 9.00 (ISBN 0-387-09563-2). Springer-Verlag.

Barr, Pat. Japan. (Illus.). 160p. 1980. 24.00 (ISBN 0-7134-0578-3, Pub. by Batsford England). David & Charles.

Barr, R. S., et al. The Alternating Basis Algorithm for Assignment Problems. 1977. 2.50 (ISBN 0-686-64191-4). U CO Busn Res Div.

Barr, Robert D., et al. The Nature of the Social Studies. LC 77-2014. 1978. pap. 6.95 (ISBN 0-88280-049-3). ETC Pubns.

Barr, Robert M. Basic Skills in Technical Mathematics, Vols. 1-4. 1977. Vol. 1. pap. 5.50 o.p. (ISBN 0-205-05831-0); Vol. 2. 5.00x o.p. (ISBN 0-205-05833-7); Vol. 3. 6.00x o.p. (ISBN 0-205-05834-5); Vol. 4. 6.25x o.p. (ISBN 0-205-05835-3). Allyn.

Barr, Robert R. Main Currents in Early Christian Thought. (Guide to the Fathers of the Church Ser). (Orig.). 1966. pap. 3.95 (ISBN 0-8091-1625-1). Paulist Pr.

Barr, Robert S., jt. auth. see Blecher, Melvin.

Barr, Samuel J. & Abelow, Dan. A Woman's Choice: The Best Modern Guide to Unplanned Pregnancy. pap. 4.95 (ISBN 0-934954-11-9). Public Info Pr.

Barr, Stringfellow & Standard, Stella. Kitchen Garden Book: Vegetables from Seed to Table. (Handbooks Ser). 1977. pap. 2.95 o.p. (ISBN 0-14-046257-0). Penguin.

Barr, William D. Counseling with Confidence. (Orig.). 1981. pap. 4.95 (ISBN 0-88270-492-3). Logos.

Barra, Jean-Rene & Herbach, L. Mathematical Basis of Statistics. LC 80-519. (Probability & Mathematical Statistical Ser.). 1981. write for info. (ISBN 0-12-079240-0). Acad Pr.

Barraclaugh, Geoffrey, ed. see Chesneaux, Jean.

Barraclough, E. M. Flags of the World. rev. ed. LC 68-22445. (Illus.). (gr. 7 up). 1979. 30.00 (ISBN 0-7232-2015-8). Warne.

Barraclough, Geoffrey. The Crucible of Europe: The Ninth & Tenth Centuries in European History. LC 75-21934. (Illus.). 180p. 1976. 22.50x (ISBN 0-520-03105-9); pap. 6.95 (ISBN 0-520-03118-0, CAL 362). U of Cal Pr.

Barraclough, Geoffrey, ed. see Historical Association, London.

Barraclough, Norman. Preology: The Scientific Study of the Planning of Human Development. LC 80-40600. 265p. 1980. pap. 13.25 (ISBN 0-08-026083-7). Pergamon.

Barraclough, Robin I., jt. auth. see Jarman, Lytton P.

Barraclough, Solon & Collarte, Juan. Agrarian Structure in Latin America. LC 72-7020. 272p. 1973. 21.95 o.p. (ISBN 0-669-83006-2). Lexington Bks.

Barrager, Diane & Perkins, Rodney. The Hearing Book. Orig. Title: Come Again, Please... (Illus.). 128p. 1980. pap. 8.95 (ISBN 0-89106-016-2, 7274). Consulting Psychol.

Barranger, Milly S. Theatre: A Way of Seeing. 320p. 1980. pap. text ed. 13.95x (ISBN 0-534-00763-5). Wadsworth Pub.

Barrante, James R. Applied Mathematics for Physical Chemistry. (Illus.). 160p. 1974. pap. text ed. 10.95 (ISBN 0-13-041384-4). P-H.

Barrante, Paul. Physical Chemistry for the Life Sciences. (Illus.). 1977. text ed. 18.95 (ISBN 0-13-665984-5). P-H.

Barrass, Robert. Biology: Food & People. LC 74-21791. 224p. 1975. 18.95 (ISBN 0-312-08050-6). St Martin.

--The Locust. (Illus.). 73p. (gr. 10 up). 1975. 8.95x (ISBN 0-903330-11-3). Transatlantic.

--Scientists Must Write: A Guide to Better Writing for Scientists, Engineers & Students. LC 77-18561. 176p. 1978. text ed. 9.95x o.p. (ISBN 0-412-15440-4, Pub. by Chapman & Hall); pap. 8.50x o.p. (ISBN 0-412-15430-7). Methuen Inc.

--Scientists Must Write: A Guide to Better Writing for Scientists, Engineers & Students. LC 77-18561. 1978. 9.95 o.p. (ISBN 0-470-99388-X). Halsted Pr.

Barratt, Glen. The Russians at Port Jackson. 1980. text ed. write for info. (ISBN 0-391-02165-6); pap. text ed. write for info. (ISBN 0-391-02166-4). Humanities.

Barratt, John, jt. ed. see Rotberg, Robert I.

Barratt, S., jt. auth. see Haszonics, J. J.

Barre, Weston La see La Barre, Weston.

Barrell, John. Idea of Landscape & the Sense of Place, 1730-1840: An Approach to the Poetry of John Clare. LC 77-160092. (Illus.). 1972. 39.50 (ISBN 0-521-08254-4). Cambridge U Pr.

Barrer, Harry G., ed. Orthodontics: The State of the Art. LC 79-5043. (Illus.). 448p. 1981. 60.00x (ISBN 0-8122-7767-8). U of Pa Pr.

Barrera, Mario. Race & Class in the Southwest: A Theory of Racial Inequality. LC 78-62970. 261p. 1980. pap. text ed. 5.95 (ISBN 0-268-01601-1). U of Notre Dame Pr.

Barrere, Albert. Dictionary of Slang, Jargon & Cant, 2 Vols. Leland, Charles G., ed. LC 66-27828. 1967. Repr. of 1889 ed. Set. 52.00 (ISBN 0-8103-3242-6). Gale.

Barrese, Pauline N. Italian Cookery-Home Style. rev. ed. LC 74-82514. 1977. pap. 5.95 (ISBN 0-912656-69-7). H P Bks.

Barret, Robert. The Theorike & Practike of Moderne Warres. LC 74-26523. (English Experience Ser.: No. 155). (Illus.). 247p. 1969. Repr. of 1598 ed. 42.00 (ISBN 90-221-0155-X). Walter J Johnson.

Barrett & Hanson, Marvin L. Oral Myofunctional Disorders. 2nd ed. LC 78-7029. 1978. text ed. 36.50 (ISBN 0-8016-0497-4). Mosby.

Barrett, jt. auth. see Bass.

Barrett, C. Strategy & Society. 161p. 1976. 7.00x (ISBN 0-7190-0627-9, Pub. by Manchester U Pr England). State Mutual Bk.

Barrett, C., et al. The Principles of Engineering Materials. 1973. 26.95 (ISBN 0-13-709394-2). P-H.

Barrett, C. S. & Massalski, T. B. Structure of Metals: Crystallographic Methods, Principles & Data. 3rd rev. ed. LC 80-49878. (International Ser. on Materials Science & Technology: Vol. 14). (Illus.). 675p. 1980. 65.00 (ISBN 0-08-026171-X); pap. 20.00 (ISBN 0-08-026172-8). Pergamon.

Barrett, Charles D. Understanding the Christian Faith. (Illus.). 1980. text ed. 15.00 (ISBN 0-13-935882-X). P-H.

Barrett, Charles K., ed. New Testament Background: Selected Documents. pap. 4.95x (ISBN 0-06-130086-1, TB86, Torch). Har-Row.

Barrett, Charls R. Short Story Writing. 257p. 1981. Repr. lib. bdg. 30.00 (ISBN 0-8495-0465-1). Arden Lib.

Barrett, David, tr. see Aristophanes.

Barrett, David, et al. Financing the Solar Home. LC 77-3858. 1977. 22.95 (ISBN 0-669-01684-5). Lexington Bks.

Barrett, Douglas. Early Cola Architecture & Sculpture, 866-1014 A.D. 1974. 52.00 o.p. (ISBN 0-571-10507-6, Pub. by Faber & Faber). Merrimack Bk Serv.

Barrett, Eaton S. All the Talents; a Satirical Poem, in Four Dialogues. to Which Is Added, a Pastoral Epilogue, Repr. Of 1807. Reiman, Donald H., ed. Bd. with The Second Titan War Against Heaven; or, the Talents Buried Under Portland-Isle. Repr. of 1807 ed; The Talents Run Mad; or, Eighteen Hundred & Sixteen. a Satirical Poem. Repr. of 1816 ed. LC 75-31150. (Romantic Context Ser.: Poetry 1789-1830). 1979. lib. bdg. 47.00 (ISBN 0-8240-2104-5). Garland Pub.

Barrett, Ethel. Don't Look Now. LC 68-25807. (Illus., Orig.). 1968. pap. 2.25 o.p. (ISBN 0-8307-0019-6, 5000602). Regal.

--God & a Boy Named Joe. LC 74-16957. (Venture Stories Ser.). (Illus.). 160p. (Orig.). (gr. 4-8). 1975. pap. 1.95 (ISBN 0-8307-0324-1, 57-006-04). Regal.

--God, Have You Got It All Together. LC 76-29888. (Venture Stories Ser.). 1977. pap. 1.95 (ISBN 0-8307-0434-5, S064-1-54). Regal.

--Gregory the Grub. (ps-1). 1978. pap. 6.95 o.p. (ISBN 0-8307-0421-3, 56-028-07). Regal.

--Historias Biblicas Favoritas. Mercado, Benjamin, ed. De Lobo, Virginia P., tr. from Eng. 103p. (Span.). (gr. 3). 1979. pap. 1.80 (ISBN 0-8297-0871-5). Vida Pubs.

--Historias Biblicas Para Ninos, Vol. 1. Mercado, Benjamin, ed. De Lobo, Virginia P., tr. from Eng. 117p. (Span.). (gr. 3). 1979. pap. text ed. 2.10 (ISBN 0-8297-0872-3). Vida Pubs.

--John Welch. 128p. (gr. 5-9). 1980. pap. 2.95 (ISBN 0-310-43151-4). Zondervan.

--People Who Couldn't Be Stopped. LC 79-96703. (Orig.). (gr. 4-8). 1970. pap. 1.95 (ISBN 0-8307-0007-2, S063107). Regal.

--Quacky & Wacky. (ps-1). 1978. pap. 6.95 book & cassette pac (ISBN 0-8307-0418-3, 5602505). Regal.

--Rules - Who Needs Them? LC 73-90623. (Orig.). (gr. 4-8). 1974. pap. 1.95 (ISBN 0-8307-0282-2, 54-070-01). Regal.

--Ruth. LC 80-52961. (Great Heroes of the Bible Ser.). 128p. (gr. 3-9). 1980. pap. 1.95 (ISBN 0-8307-0764-6, 5810418). Regal.

--Sometimes I Feel Like a Blob. LC 79-92649. 1977. pap. 2.75 (ISBN 0-8307-0482-5, 50-003-27). Regal.

--The Strangest Thing Happened... LC 76-84599. (gr. 4-8). 1971. pap. 1.95 (ISBN 0-8307-0005-6, S061104). Regal.

--There I Stood in All My Splendor. pap. 2.25 o.p. (ISBN 0-8307-0016-1, 5000408). Regal.

--Which Way to Nineveh. LC 79-96703. (Venture Bks.). (gr. 4-8). 1970. pap. 1.95 (ISBN 0-8307-0006-4, S062100). Regal.

Barrett, Ethell, tr. Que Se Ponga De Pie el Verdadero Farsante! (Spanish Bks.). (Span.). 1978. 1.75 (ISBN 0-8297-0850-2). Life Pubs Intl.

Barrett, Florence E. A Pocket in a Petticoat: Memoirs. 1974. 4.00 o.p. (ISBN 0-682-48075-4, Lochinvar). Exposition.

Barrett, Franklin A. Worcester Porcelain & Lund's Bristol. 2nd ed. 1966. 25.00 (ISBN 0-571-06739-5, Pub. by Faber & Faber). Merrimack Bk Serv.

Barrett, Franklin A. & Thorpe, Arthur L. Derby Porcelain, 1750-1848. 1971. 43.00 (ISBN 0-571-09577-1, Pub. by Faber & Faber). Merrimack Bk Serv.

Barrett, H. J., jt. auth. see Rohl, J. S.

Barrett, Harold, ed. Rhetoric of the People: Is There Any Better or Equal Hope in the World? 335p. (Orig.). 1974. pap. text ed. 16.75x (ISBN 90-6203-001-7). Humanities.

Barrett, Hugh. Early to Rise: A Suffolk Morning. 1967. 6.95 (ISBN 0-571-08140-1, Pub. by Faber & Faber). Merrimack Bk Serv.

Barrett, James & Williams, Geoffrey. Test Your Own Job Aptitude: Exploring Your Career Potential. 128p. 1981. pap. 2.95 (ISBN 0-14-005809-5). Penguin.

Barrett, James E., ed. Stress & Mental Disorder. LC 79-2202. (American Psychopathological Association Ser.). 1979. text ed. 28.00 (ISBN 0-89004-384-1). Raven.

Barrett, James E., jt. ed. see Cole, Jonathan O.

Barrett, James T. Basic Immunology & Its Medical Application. 2nd ed. LC 80-14328. (Illus.). 304p. 1980. pap. text ed. 14.95 (ISBN 0-8016-0495-8). Mosby.

--Textbook of Immunology: An Introduction to Immunochemistry & Immunobiology. 3rd ed. LC 77-16208. (Illus.). 1978. text ed. 19.95 (ISBN 0-8016-0500-8). Mosby.

Barrett, John. The Bear Who Slept Through Christmas. 32p. (gr. k-6). 2.95 (ISBN 0-89542-943-8); pap. 2.25 o.p. (ISBN 0-89542-942-X). Ideals.

Barrett, John G., jt. ed. see Yearns, W. Buck.

Barrett, Judi. Animals Should Definitely Not Act Like People. LC 80-13364. (Illus.). 32p. (ps-2). 1980. 9.95 (ISBN 0-689-30768-3). Atheneum.

--I Hate to Go to Bed. LC 77-1583. (Illus.). 32p. (gr. k-3). 1977. 5.50 (ISBN 0-590-07472-5, Four Winds). Schol Bk Serv.

--I Hate to Take a Bath. LC 75-6955. (Illus.). 32p. (gr. k-3). 1975. 5.95 (ISBN 0-590-07429-6, Four Winds). Schol Bk Serv.

Barrett, Judi, ed. I'm Too Small: You're Too Big. LC 80-23883. (Illus.). 32p. (ps-1). 1981. PLB 9.95 (ISBN 0-689-30800-0). Atheneum.

Barrett, Martha B. Maggie's Way. (Orig.). 1981. pap. 2.75 (ISBN 0-451-09601-0, E9601, Sig). NAL.

Barrett, Mary E. American Beauty. 288p. 1980. 12.95 (ISBN 0-525-05285-2). Dutton.

Barrett, Mary E., jt. auth. see Arnaudet, Martin L.

Barrett, Maye. The Crystal Palace. 1978. pap. 1.95 o.p. (ISBN 0-425-03677-4, Medallion). Berkley Pub.

--The Thorn in the Rose. 192p. (Orig.). 1980. pap. 1.75 (ISBN 0-515-05631-6). Jove Pubns.

--The Threat of Love. (Orig.). pap. 1.75 (ISBN 0-515-05727-4). Jove Pubns.

Barrett, Michael. Last Flowers. 256p. 1957. 3.50 o.p. (ISBN 0-374-18344-9). FS&G.

Barrett, Michele. Women's Oppression Today: Problems in Marxist Feminst Analysis. 280p. 1981. 19.50x (ISBN 0-8052-7091-4, Pub. by NLB England); pap. 8.50 (ISBN 0-8052-7090-6). Schocken.

Barrett, Nancy S. The Theory of Macroeconomic Policy. 2nd ed. (Illus.). 480p. 1975. 17.95 o.p. (ISBN 0-13-913830-7). P-H.

Barrett, Paul, tr. see Dumery, Henry.

Barrett, Paul, et al, eds. Concordance to Darwin's "Origin of Species". 864p. 1981. 38.50x (ISBN 0-8014-1319-2). Cornell U Pr.

Barrett, Paul H., ed. see Darwin, Charles.

Barrett, Roger C. & Jackson, Daphne F. Nuclear Sizes & Structure. (International Series of Monographs on Physics). 1977. 69.00x (ISBN 0-19-851272-4). Oxford U Pr.

Barrett, Roger K. Depression--What It Is & What to Do About It. 1979. pap. 3.95 (ISBN 0-89191-179-0). Cook.

Barrett, S. L. Parties with a Purpose. 128p. 1980. pap. 10.50 spiral (ISBN 0-398-03986-0). C C Thomas.

Barrett, Stephen, jt. auth. see Cornacchia, Harold J.

Barrett, Stephen & Knight, Gilda, eds. The Health Robbers: How to Protect Your Money & Your Life. new ed. LC 76-22281. (Illus.). 352p. 1976. 10.50 o.p. (ISBN 0-89313-001-X). G F Stickley Co.

Barrett, Susan E. Inbetween Yesterday. 2nd ed. LC 77-74036. (Illus.). 1976. pap. 4.00 (ISBN 0-89430-001-6). Morgan-Pacific.

--Ms Noah Touches Earth. (Illus.). 1979. pap. 5.95 (ISBN 0-9603916-0-6). Artichoke.

Barrett, Thomas C., jt. auth. see Smith, Richard J.

Barrett, William. Irrational Man. LC 58-8081. 1958. pap. 4.50 (ISBN 0-385-03138-6, A371, Anch). Doubleday.

Barrett, William A. English Folk Songs Collected, Arranged & Provided with Symphonies & Accompaniments for the Pianoforte. 95p. 1980. Repr. of 1891 ed. lib. bdg. 15.00 (ISBN 0-8492-3758-0). R West.

Barrett, William A. & Couch, John D. Compiler Construction: Theory & Practice. LC 78-26183. 512p. 1979. text ed. 24.95 (ISBN 0-574-21160-8, 13-4335); inst. guide o.p. 2.00 (ISBN 0-574-18508-9, 13-4161). SRA.

Barrett, William T., II, ed. The Overland Journal of Amos Piatt Josselyn. 129p. 1978. octavo 10.00. Holmes.

Barrett-Connor, Elizabeth, et al, eds. Epidemiology for the Infection Control Nurse. LC 77-13128. (Illus.). 1978. text ed. 18.95 (ISBN 0-8016-0744-2). Mosby.

Barrette, Paul. Robert de Blois' Floris et Lyriope. (U. C. Publications in Modern Philology, Vol. 92). 1968. pap. 9.50x (ISBN 0-520-09287-2). U of Cal Pr.

Barrette, Pierre P. The Microcomputer & the School Library Media Specialist. 200p. 1981. lib. bdg. 13.50x (ISBN 0-87287-226-2). Libs Unl.

Barrham, Patte, jt. auth. see Rasputin, Maria.

Barricelli, Gian P. Alessandro Manzoni. LC 76-16481. (World Authors Ser.: No. 411). 1976. lib. bdg. 11.95 (ISBN 0-8057-6251-5). Twayne.

Barrick, Mac E., ed. see Gomez De Toledo, Gaspar.

Barrie. Peter Pan. Josette, Frank, ed. (gr. 3). Date not set. pap. cancelled (ISBN 0-590-30054-7, Schol Pap). Schol Bk Serv.

--Plays & Stories. 1975. pap. 2.25 o.p. (ISBN 0-460-01184-7, Evman). Dutton.

Barrie, D. S. A Regional History of the Railways of Great Britain: South Wales, Vol. 12, Vol. 12. LC 80-67609. (Illus.). 1980. 30.00 (ISBN 0-7153-7970-4). David & Charles.

Barrie, Donald S. Directions in Managing Construction: A Critical Look at Present & Future Industry Practices, Problems & Policies. (Construction Management & Engineering Ser.). 500p. 1981. 34.95 (ISBN 0-471-04642-6, Pub. by Wiley-Interscience). Wiley.

Barrie, James M. Peter Pan. abridged ed. Frank, Josette, adapted by. (Illus.). (gr. 1-4). 1957. 3.95 (ISBN 0-394-80749-9, BYR); PLB 4.79 (ISBN 0-394-90749-3). Random.

--Peter Pan. Unwin, Noras, ed. (Illus.). (gr. 4-6). 1950. 8.95 (ISBN 0-684-13214-1, ScribJ). Scribner.

Barrie, James M; see Salerno, Henry F.

Barrier, Gerald, jt. ed. see Juergensmeyer, Mark.

Barrier, N. Gerald. Banned: Controversial Literature & Political Control in British India, 1907-1947. LC 73-92241. 1974. 17.50x o.p. (ISBN 0-8262-0159-8). U of Mo Pr.

Barriere, Steven L., jt. auth. see Conte, John E., Jr.

Barringer, Bugs, et al. Rocky Mount: A Pictorial History. LC 77-8620. (Illus.). 1977. 14.95 (ISBN 0-915442-31-0). Donning Co.

Barringer, Leslie. Gerfalcon. Reginald, R. & Menville, Douglas, eds. LC 80-19243. (Newcastle Forgotten Fantasy Library: Vol. 7). 310p. 1980. Repr. of 1976 ed. lib. bdg. 10.95x (ISBN 0-89370-506-3). Borgo Pr.

--Joris of the Rock: The Neustrian Cycle, Bk. 2. Reginald, R. & Menville, Douglas, eds. LC 80-19241. (Newcastle Forgotten Fantasy Library: Vol. 9). 318p. 1980. Repr. of 1976 ed. lib. bdg. 10.95x (ISBN 0-89370-508-X). Borgo Pr.

--Shy Leopardess: The Neustrian Cycle, Bk. 3. Reginald, R. & Menville, Douglas, eds. LC 80-19240. (Newcastle Forgotten Fantasy Library Ser.: Vol. 13). 392p. 1980. Repr. of 1977 ed. lib. bdg. 11.95x (ISBN 0-89370-512-8). Borgo Pr.

Barringer, Robert, tr. see Staniloae, Dumitru.

Barringer, W. A., jt. auth. see Barr, Howard N.

Barringhaus, Sr. Francita, ed. see Catholic Hospital Association.

Barrington, E. J. Environmental Biology. LC 80-12090. (Resource & Environmental Science). 244p. 1980. pap. 17.95x (ISBN 0-470-26967-7). Halsted Pr.

--Intervertebrate Structure & Function. 2nd ed. 1979. 32.95 o.p. (ISBN 0-470-26502-7); pap. 18.95x (ISBN 0-470-26503-5). Halsted Pr.

Barrington, E. J., jt. ed. see Hamburgh, Max.

Barrington, George. The Life, Times, & Adventures of George Barrington, the Celebrated Thief & Pickpocket. Bd. with The Memoirs of George Barrington, Containing Every Emarkable Circumstance, from His Birth to the Present Time. LC 80-2470. 1981. 29.50 (ISBN 0-404-19102-9). AMS Pr.

Barrio, Raymond. The Devil's Apple Corps. (Illus.). 50p. 1976. pap. 1.50 (ISBN 0-917438-06-X). Ventura Pr.

--Plum Plum Pickers. (Orig.). 1970. 8.50 (ISBN 0-917438-04-3); pap. 3.75 (ISBN 0-917438-04-3). Ventura Pr.

Barrios, Alfred A. Towards Greater Freedom & Happiness. new ed. LC 78-63152. 1978. 12.95 (ISBN 0-9601926-1-1); pap. 8.95 (ISBN 0-9601926-0-3). Self-Prog Control.

Barris, Alex. Hollywood's Other Women. LC 74-6933. (Illus.). 300p. 1975. 17.50 o.p. (ISBN 0-498-01488-6). A S Barnes.

--Stop the Presses! LC 74-30718. 300p. 1976. 17.50 o.p. (ISBN 0-498-01603-X). A S Barnes.

Barris, Chuck. You & Me Babe. 1980. pap. write for info. (ISBN 0-671-81654-3). PB.

Barris, George & Scagnetti, Jack. Famous Custom & Show Cars. (Illus.). 160p. (YA) 1973. PLB 12.95 (ISBN 0-525-29610-7). Dutton.

Barro, R. J. & Grossman, H. I. Money, Employment & Inflation. LC 75-13449. (Illus.). 304p. 1976. 24.50x (ISBN 0-521-20906-4). Cambridge U Pr.

Barro, Robert J. Money, Expectations & Business Cycles: Essays in Macroeconomics. (Economic Theory, Econometrics & Mathematical Economic Ser.). 1981. write for info. (ISBN 0-12-079550-7). Acad Pr.

Barrois, George. Jesus Christ & the Temple. LC 80-19700. 164p. 1980. pap. 5.95. St Vladimirs.

Barrois, Georges A. Jesus Christ & the Temple. LC 80-19700. 163p. (Orig.). 1980. pap. 5.95 (ISBN 0-913836-73-7, BS680 T4837). St Martin.

Barrois, Maurice, ed. Journal de l'annee: 1974-1975. new ed. (Illus.). 415p. (Fr.). 1975. 25.00x (ISBN 0-686-67325-5). Larousse.

Barroll, Clare. Season of the Heart. 1978. pap. 1.95 o.p. (ISBN 0-345-25902-5). Ballantine.

Barron, Ann F. Banner Bold & Beautiful. 1978. pap. 1.95 o.p. (ISBN 0-449-13877-1, GM). Fawcett.

--Firebrand. 1977. pap. 1.95 o.p. (ISBN 0-449-13863-1, GM). Fawcett.

Barron, Cheryl C. & Scherzer, Cathy C. Great Parties for Young Children. (Illus.). 160p. 1981. 9.95 (ISBN 0-8027-0684-3); pap. 5.95 (ISBN 0-8027-7175-0). Walker & Co.

Barron, D. W. Computer Operating Systems. 135p. 1971. text ed. 10.95x o.p. (ISBN 0-412-09010-4, Pub. by Chapman & Hall). Methuen Inc.

--Computer Operating Systems. 135p. 1971. 9.95 o.p. (ISBN 0-470-05426-3). Halsted Pr.

--An Introduction to the Study of Programming Languages. LC 76-11070. (Cambridge Computer Science Texts Ser.: No. 7). (Illus.). 1977. 22.50 (ISBN 0-521-21317-7); pap. 8.95x (ISBN 0-521-29101-1). Cambridge U Pr.

--Pascal: The Language & Its Implementation. 1981. price not set (ISBN 0-471-27835-1, Pub. by Wiley-Interscience). Wiley.

Barron, Frank. The Shaping of Personality: Conflict, Choice & Growth. 1979. text ed. 19.50 scp (ISBN 0-06-040504-X, HarpC). Harper-Row.

Barron, Gloria J. Leadership in Crisis: FDR & the Path to Intervention. LC 73-75576. 1973. 9.95 (ISBN 0-8046-9038-3, Natl U). Kennikat.

Barron, J. B. & Saad, M. N., eds. Operative Plastic & Reconstructive Surgery, Vol. 3. (Illus.). 352p. 1980. text ed. 59.00 (ISBN 0-443-02212-7). Churchill.

Barron, J. N. & Saad, M. N. Operative Plastic & Reconstructive Surgery, 3 vols. 1981. text ed. 220.00 (ISBN 0-443-01600-3). Churchill.

Barron, Jerome A. & Dienes, C. Thomas. Constitutional Law: Principles & Policy, Cases & Materials. LC 74-2945. (Contemporary Legal Education Ser.). 1975. text ed. 24.00 (ISBN 0-672-81774-8, Bobbs-Merrill Law); 1980 cum. suppl. 8.00 (ISBN 0-672-83549-5). Michie.

Barron, Jerome A., jt. auth. see Gillmor, Donald M.

Barron, John. The KGB. 1979. pap. 2.50 (ISBN 0-88264-085-2). Diane Bks.

--MIG Pilot: The Final Escape of Lieutenant Belenko. 232p. 1981. pap. 2.95 (ISBN 0-380-53868-7). Avon.

--MIG Pilot: The Story of Viktor Belenko. 1980. 10.95 (ISBN 0-07-003850-3). McGraw.

Barron, Jonathan C. Computer-Assisted Mathematics of Finance. LC 78-53421. 1978. pap. text ed. 11.25 (ISBN 0-8191-0496-5). U Pr of Amer.

Barron, Sr. Mary C. Unveiled Faces: Men & Women of the Bible. (Illus.). 120p. 1981. pap. 4.50 (ISBN 0-8146-1212-1). Liturgical Pr.

Barron, Neil. Anatomy of Wonder. 2nd ed. 450p. 1981. 22.50 (ISBN 0-8352-1339-0). Bowker.

Barron, Neil & Reginald, R. Science Fiction & Fantasy Annual, Vol. 1. LC 80-392. (Borgo Reference Library). 1980. lib. bdg. 11.95x cancelled (ISBN 0-89370-141-6); pap. 5.95 cancelled (ISBN 0-89370-241-2). Borgo Pr.

Barron, Stephanie & Tuchman, Maurice, eds. The Avant-Garde in Russia: New Perspectives. (Illus.). 250p. 1980. 27.50 (ISBN 0-262-20040-6). MIT Pr.

Barron, Stephanie, et al. The Avant-Garde in Russia, 1910-1930: New Perspectives. Hirshman, Jack & Wojciechowski, Andrzej, trs. (Illus.). 288p. (Orig., Rus. Ger. Fr. Pol.). 1980. pap. 11.95 o.p. (ISBN 0-87587-095-3). La Co Art Mus.

Barron, W. R. Trawthe & Treason: The Sin of Gawain Reconsidered; A Thematic Study of "Sir Gawain & the Green Knight". 150p. 1980. 23.00x (ISBN 0-389-20028-X). B&N.

Barrons Educational College Division Staff. Profiles of American Colleges, Vol. 1. 12th ed. LC 80-21243. 1980. text ed. 23.95 (ISBN 0-8120-5407-5); pap. 9.95 (ISBN 0-8120-2201-7). Barron.

Barron's Educational Series Staff, College Division. Profiles of American Colleges: Regional Editions-the Midwest. LC 79-50110. (gr. 10-12). 1978. pap. 5.75 (ISBN 0-8120-2078-2). Barron.

--Profiles of American Colleges: Regional Editions-the Northeast. rev. ed. LC 79-50110. (gr. 10-12). 1979. pap. text ed. 5.75 (ISBN 0-8120-2075-8). Barron.

Barros, James. Office Without Power: Secretary-General Sir Eric Drummond 1919-1933. 1979. 48.00x (ISBN 0-19-822551-2). Oxford U Pr.

Barros, James & Johnston, Douglas M. International Law of Pollution. LC 73-6491. 1974. text ed. 19.95 (ISBN 0-02-901910-9). Free Pr.

Barros, Leda Watson de see Sutton, Joan L. & Watson de Barros, Leda.

Barros-Neto, Jose. An Introduction to the Theory of Distributions. LC 80-11323. 234p. 1980. Repr. of 1973 ed. lib. bdg. write for info. (ISBN 0-89874-128-9). Krieger.

Barrow, Andrew. The Flesh Is Weak: An Intimate History of the Church of England. (Illus.). 254p. 1981. 29.95 (ISBN 0-241-10234-0, Pub. by Hamish Hamilton England). David & Charles.

Barrow, Charles G. French Art at the End of the Nineteenth Century: An Illustrated Survey. (Illus.). 123p. 1981. 39.45 (ISBN 0-930582-88-8). Gloucester Art.

Barrow, Clayton R., Jr., ed. America Spreads Her Sails: U. S. Seapower in the 19th Century. LC 73-76271. 1973. 11.00 o.s.i. (ISBN 0-87021-071-8). Naval Inst Pr.

Barrow, G. W. The Anglo-Norman Era in Scottish History. 220p. 1980. 49.50x (ISBN 0-19-822473-7). Oxford U Pr.

Barrow, G. W. S. Robert Bruce & the Community of the Realm of Scotland. 1965. 23.50x (ISBN 0-520-00083-8). U of Cal Pr.

Barrow, Georgia & Smith, Patricia. Aging, Ageism, & Society. (Illus.). 1979. pap. text ed. 13.95 (ISBN 0-8299-0237-6); instrs.' manual avail. (ISBN 0-8299-0458-1). West Pub.

Barrow, Gordon M. Introduction to Chemistry. 1976. text ed. 21.95x (ISBN 0-534-00326-5). Wadsworth Pub.

Barrow, Loyd M., jt. auth. see Dintiman, George B.

Barrow, M. H., jt. auth. see Rase, H. F.

Barrow, Robin. Plato, Utilitarianism & Education. (International Library of the Philosophy of Education Ser.). 1975. 20.00x (ISBN 0-7100-8044-1). Routledge & Kegan.

--Radical Education: A Critique of Freeschooling & Deschooling. LC 78-1972. 1978. 21.95 (ISBN 0-470-26329-6); pap. 11.95 (ISBN 0-470-26845-X). Halsted Pr.

Barrow, W. J. Manuscripts & Documents: Their Deterioration & Restoration. rev. ed. LC 72-89855. (Illus.). 86p. 1972. 8.95x (ISBN 0-8139-0408-0). U Pr of Va.

Barrowman, J. A. Physiology of the Gastro-Intestinal Lymphatic System. LC 77-22823. (Physiological Society Monographs: No. 33). (Illus.). 1978. 59.50 (ISBN 0-521-21710-5). Cambridge U Pr.

Barrows, A. B. Everyday Production of Baked Goods. 2nd ed. (Illus.). 1975. text ed. 17.95 (ISBN 0-8436-2062-5). CBI Pub.

Barrows, Anita, tr. see Cixous, Helen.

Barrows, Anita, tr. see Duras, Marguerite.

Barrows, Edith. Faith, Hope, & Charity: Mother's Poems. 4.00 o.p. (ISBN 0-8062-1183-0). Carlton.

Barrows, Howard S. Guide to Neurological Assessment. (Illus.). 144p. 1980. text ed. 9.95 (ISBN 0-397-52093-X). Lippincott.

--Simulated Patients (Programmed Patients) The Development & Use of a New Technique in Medical Education. (Illus.). 80p. 1971. pap. 9.75 (ISBN 0-398-02227-5). C C Thomas.

Barrows, Marjorie. One Thousand Beautiful Things. (Library of Beautiful Things: Vol. 1). (gr. 7 up). 1955. 9.95 (ISBN 0-8015-5562-0, Hawthorn). Dutton.

Barry, Sr. Anna. Aortic Andtricuspid Valvular Disease. (Surgical Aspects of Cardiovascular Disease: Nursing Intervention Series). 100p. 1980. pap. 6.95 (ISBN 0-8385-0189-3). ACC.

Barry, Austin, jt. auth. see Brinker, Russell C.

Barry, Brian. The Liberal Theory of Justice: A Critical Examination of the Principal Doctrines in - A Theory of Justice by John Rawls. (Illus.). 180p. 1973. text ed. 15.95 o.p. (ISBN 0-19-824509-2); pap. text ed. 4.95x (ISBN 0-19-875032-3). Oxford U Pr.

Barry, Canon W. The New Antigone. LC 75-462. (Victorian Fiction Ser.). 1975. Repr. of 1887 ed. lib. bdg. 66.00 (ISBN 0-8240-1540-1). Garland Pub.

Barry, Carol B., jt. auth. see Barry, Donald D.

Barry, Donald D. & Barry, Carol B. Contemporary Soviet Politics: An Introduction. LC 77-10871. (Illus.). 1978. pap. 11.50x ref. ed. (ISBN 0-13-170225-4). P-H.

Barry, Donald D. & Whitcomb, Howard R. The Legal Foundations of Public Administration. 407p. 1980. text ed. 17.95 (ISBN 0-8299-2120-6). West Pub.

Barry, Elaine. Robert Frost. LC 72-79942. (Modern Literature Ser.). 1973. 10.95 (ISBN 0-8044-2016-5). Ungar.

--Robert Frost on Writing. 1974. 14.00 (ISBN 0-8135-0692-1); pap. 3.95 (ISBN 0-8135-0789-8). Rutgers U Pr.

Barry, F. V., intro. by. Jane Taylor: Prose & Poetry. 177p. 1980. Repr. of 1925 ed. lib. bdg. 30.00 (ISBN 0-89760-075-4). Telegraph Bks.

Barry, Florence V. A Century of Children's Books. LC 68-23467. 18.000 (ISBN 0-8103-3472-0). Gale.

Barry, Jackson G. Dramatic Structure: The Shaping of Experience. LC 78-100607. 1970. 20.00x (ISBN 0-520-01624-6). U of Cal Pr.

Barry, James, ed. Ethics on a Catholic University Campus: Symposium. 1980. pap. 5.95 (ISBN 0-8294-0369-8). Loyola.

Barry, James C., ed. see McElrath, William N.

Barry, James P. Berlin Olympics, Nineteen Thirty-Six: Black American Athletes Counter Nazi Propaganda. LC 74-20173. (World Focus Bks). (Illus.). 88p. (gr. 7 up). 1975. PLB 4.90 o.p. (ISBN 0-531-01090-2). Watts.

--The Great Lakes. LC 76-15641. (First Bks.). (Illus.). 72p. (gr. 4-6). 1976. PLB 4.90 o.p. (ISBN 0-531-00337-X). Watts.

--The Louisiana Purchase, April 1803: Thomas Jefferson Doubles the Area of the United States. LC 72-6836. (Focus Bks.). (Illus.). 96p. (gr. 7-12). 1973. PLB 4.90 o.p. (ISBN 0-531-02460-1). Watts.

--The Noble Experiment, 1920-1933: The Eighteenth Amendment Prohibits Liquor in America. LC 72-180165. (Focus Books). (Illus.). 72p. (gr. 7 up). 1972. PLB 4.47 o.p. (ISBN 0-531-02454-7). Watts.

Barry, Jan, ed. Peace Is Our Profession: Poems & Passages of War Protest. LC 80-70115. 1981. pap. 5.95 (ISBN 0-917238-03-6). East River Anthol.

Barry, Jane T., jt. auth. see Miller, Dulcy B.

Barry, John R. & Wingrove, C. Ray, eds. Let's Learn About Aging: A Book of Readings. LC 76-45168. 1977. text ed. 8.50 (ISBN 0-470-98965-3); pap. text ed. 12.95 (ISBN 0-470-98967-X). Halsted Pr.

Barry, John W. & Henry, Porter J. Effective Sales Incentive Compensation. (Illus.). 192p. 1980. write for info. (ISBN 0-07-003860-0, P&RB). McGraw.

Barry, Joseph. France. (Illus.). (gr. 7 up). 1965. 4.95 o.s.i. (ISBN 0-02-708460-4). Macmillan.

--The Infamous Woman: The Life of George Sand. LC 76-5335. 1978. pap. 5.95 o.p. (ISBN 0-385-13366-9, Anchor Pr). Doubleday.

Barry, Kathleen. Female Sexual Slavery. 336p. 1981. pap. 3.95 (ISBN 0-380-54213-7, 54213, Discus). Avon.

Barry, Louise. The Beginning of the West: Annals of the Kansas Gateway to the American West 1540-1854. LC 78-172225. (Illus.). 1972. 14.75 (ISBN 0-87726-001-X). Kansas St Hist.

Barry, Norman P. Hayek's Social & Economic Philosophy. 1979. text ed. 31.25x (ISBN 0-333-25618-2). Humanities.

--An Introduction to Modern Political Theory. 1980. write for info. (ISBN 0-312-43098-1). St Martin.

Barry, Patricia S. The King n Tudor Drama. (Salzburg Studies in English Literature: Elizabethan & Renaissance Studies: No. 58). (Orig.). 1977. pap. text ed. 25.00x (ISBN 0-391-01313-0). Humanities.

Barry, Patrick. The Theory & Practice of the International Trade of the United States & England, & of the Trade of the United States & Canada. (The Neglected American Economists Ser.). 1974. lib. bdg. 50.00 (ISBN 0-8240-1014-0). Garland Pub.

Barry, R. Construction of Buildings, 5 vols. (Illus.). 508p. 1971. Set. spiral bdg. 40.00x (ISBN 0-8464-0276-9). Beekman Pubs.

Barry, R. D., jt. ed. see Mahy, B. W.

Barry, Richard, tr. see Hoffmann, Peter.

Barry, Robert. Snowman's Secret. LC 75-15801. (Illus.). 32p. (ps-2). 1975. 8.95 (ISBN 0-02-708390-X, 70839). Macmillan.

Barry, Robert, tr. see Staniloae, Dumitru.

Barry, Robert E. Business English for the Eighties. (Illus.). 1980. pap. text ed. 12.95 (ISBN 0-13-095372-5). P-H.

Barry, Roger D. Basic Chemistry. LC 74-79831. (Allied Health Ser). 1975. pap. text ed. 9.65 (ISBN 0-672-61376-X); lab manual 6.35 (ISBN 0-672-61377-8); answer key 3.33 (ISBN 0-672-61432-4). Bobbs.

--Organic Chemistry. LC 74-79834. (Allied Health Ser). 1975. pap. text ed. 8.35 (ISBN 0-672-61378-6); lab manual 4.80 (ISBN 0-672-61379-4). Bobbs.

Barry, Ruth & Wolf, Beverly. Epitaph for Vocational Guidance: Myths, Actualities, Implications. LC 62-13471. 1962. text ed. 10.25x (ISBN 0-8077-1047-4). Tchrs Coll.

--Modern Issues in Guidance-Personnel Work. rev. ed. LC 57-11977. 1963. pap. 4.25x (ISBN 0-8077-1050-4). Tchrs Coll.

Barry, S. M. Engineering Craft Studies: Monitoring a New Syllabus. (General Ser.). (Illus.). 28p. 1974. pap. text ed. 3.75x (ISBN 0-85633-048-5, NFER). Humanities.

Barry, S. M. see Van Der Eyken, W.

Barry, Sheila A. Super-Colossal Book of Puzzles, Tricks & Games. LC 77-93325. (Illus.). (gr. 4 up). 1978. 17.95 (ISBN 0-8069-4580-X); PLB 15.99 (ISBN 0-8069-4581-8). Sterling.

Barry, Thomas E., jt. auth. see Anderson, Robert L.

Barry, Vincent. Looking at Ourselves. 1977. 15.95x o.p. (ISBN 0-534-00464-4). Wadsworth Pub.

--Moral Issues in Business. 1979. text ed. 17.95x (ISBN 0-534-00709-0). Wadsworth Pub.

--Philosophy: A Text with Readings. 544p. 1980. text ed. 17.95x (ISBN 0-534-00767-8). Wadsworth Pub.

Barry, Wallace. Structural Functions in Music. (Illus.). 512p. 1976. 20.95 (ISBN 0-13-853903-0). P-H.

Barry, William. Heralds of Revolt. LC 78-11333. 1971. Repr. of 1904 ed. 13.25 o.p. (ISBN 0-8046-1182-3). Kennikat.

Barry, William F. The Two Standards. Wolff, Robert L., ed. LC 75-466. (Victorian Fiction Ser). 1975. Repr. of 1898 ed. lib. bdg. 66.00 (ISBN 0-8240-1544-4). Garland Pub.

Barrymore, John. The Life & Times of John Barrymore. 1978. Repr. of 1943 ed. 15.85x (ISBN 0-89966-250-1). Buccaneer Bks.

Barsam, Richard M. Non-Fiction Film - A Critical History. 1973. pap. 4.95 o.p. (ISBN 0-525-47331-9). Dutton.

Barsch, Jeffrey & Creson, Betty. Spelling Plus. 96p. 1980. pap. text ed. 6.00 (ISBN 0-87879-246-5). Acad Therapy.

Barsch, Ray H. Parent of the Handicapped Child: The Study of Child-rearing Practices. (American Lecture in Special Education Ser.). (Illus.). 452p. 1976. pap. 14.75 (ISBN 0-398-03559-8). C C Thomas.

Barschall, Henry H., ed. see Symposium - 3rd - Madison - 1970.

Barsh, Laurence I. Dental Planning for the Adult Patient. (Illus.). 376p. 1981. text ed. price not set (ISBN 0-7216-1533-3). Saunders.

Barshay, Robert H. Philip Wylie: The Man & His Work. LC 79-63682. 1979. pap. text ed. 7.50 (ISBN 0-8191-0733-6). U Pr of Amer.

Bar-Siman-Tov, Yaacov. The Israeli-Egyptian War of Attrition, Nineteen Sixty-Nine to Nineteen Seventy: A Case-Study of Limited Local War. LC 80-11124. 256p. 1980. 19.50x (ISBN 0-231-04982-X). Columbia U Pr.

Barskaya, Anna & Izerghina, Antonina. French Painting from the Hermitage Museum. (Illus.). 1977. 60.00 (ISBN 0-8109-0908-1). Abrams.

Barskaya, Anna, compiled By. Claude Monet. (Illus.). 50p. 1980. pap. 4.95 (ISBN 0-686-62716-4, 2219-3). Abrams.

Barslow, Melvin L. Burkett: Latest Word from Washington. 169p. 1977. pap. 3.00 (ISBN 0-89514-001-2, 10177). Am Voc Assn.

Barsocchini, Peter, jt. auth. see Griffin, Merv.

Barson, Alan. Motivational Games for Mathematics. (Illus.). 40p. (gr. 3-7). 1981. pap. 6.00 (ISBN 0-937138-02-9). Fabmath.

Barson, John, jt. auth. see Rolfe, Stan.

Barstow, D. R. Knowledge-Based Program Construction. (Programming Language Ser.: Vol. 6). 1979. 16.95 (ISBN 0-444-00340-1, North Holland); pap. 9.95 (ISBN 0-444-00341-X). Elsevier.

Barstow, Stan. An Enemy of the People. 1980. pap. 3.95 (ISBN 0-7145-3651-2). Riverrun NY.

Bart, Benjamin F. Flaubert. LC 67-27410. (Illus.). 1967. 16.00 o.p. (ISBN 0-8156-0057-7); pap. 6.95 (ISBN 0-8156-0087-9). Syracuse U Pr.

Bart, Sheldon. Ruby Sweetwater & the Ringo Kid. LC 80-14683. 384p. 1980. 11.95 (ISBN 0-07-003872-4, GB). McGraw.

Bartal, Lee & Ne'eman, Nira. Movement Awareness & Creativity. LC 75-36735. 1976. 7.95 o.p. (ISBN 0-685-82483-7, HarpR). Harper-Row.

Bartalini, Gualtiero. Opera Therapy. 176p. 1981. 8.50 (ISBN 0-682-49703-7). Exposition.

Bartas, Sieur Du see De Saluste, Guillaume & Du Bartas, Sieur.

Bartchy, S. Scott. First-Century Slavery & the Interpretation of I Corinthians 7: 21. LC 73-83723. (Society of Biblical Literature. Dissertation Ser.). 1973. pap. 9.00 (ISBN 0-89130-220-4, 060111). Scholars Pr Ca.

Barteau, F. Les Romans de Tristan et Iseut: Introduction a une lecture plurielle. new ed. (Collection L). 288p. (Orig., Fr.). 1972. pap. 19.95 (ISBN 2-03-036007-4). Larousse.

Bartee, Thomas. Digital Computer Fundamentals. 5th ed. (Illus.). 576p. 1981. text ed. 22.95 (ISBN 0-07-003894-5, C); instr's manual 4.95 (ISBN 0-07-003895-3). McGraw.

Bartel, Nettie R., jt. auth. see Hammil, Donald D.

Bartel, Pauline. Biorhythm: Discovering Your Natural Ups & Downs. (Impact Books Ser.). (Illus.). 1978. lib. bdg. 6.90 (ISBN 0-531-01355-3). Watts.

Bartels, H. Methods in Pulmonary Physiology. Workman, M., tr. (Illus.). 1963. 45.75 o.s.i. (ISBN 0-02-840980-9). Hafner.

Bartels, Robert. Global Development & Marketing. LC 80-11542. (Marketing Ser.). 90p. 1981. pap. text ed. 7.95 (ISBN 0-88244-223-6). Grid Pub.

--The History of Marketing Thought. 2nd ed. LC 76-6015. (Marketing Ser.). 1976. text ed. 19.95 o.p. (ISBN 0-88244-085-3). Grid Pub.

Bartenev, G. M. & Zuyev, Yu. S. Strength & Failure of Visco-Elastic Materials. 1968. 60.00 (ISBN 0-08-012183-7). Pergamon.

Bartenev, G. M. & Zelenev, Y. V., eds. Relaxation Phenomena in Polymers. LC 74-13015. 349p. 1974. 49.95 (ISBN 0-470-05429-8). Halsted Pr.

Bartenieff, I., jt. auth. see Lewis, D.

Barth, ed. see Symposium on Theory of Argumentation, Groningen, October 11-13, 1978.

Barth, Alan. The Price of Liberty. LC 74-176486. (Civil Liberties in American History Ser.). 1972. Repr. of 1961 ed. lib. bdg. 25.00 (ISBN 0-306-70416-1). Da Capo.

--Prophets with Honor. 1974. 8.95 o.p. (ISBN 0-394-48557-2). Knopf.

--Prophets with Honor: Great Dissenters in the Supreme Court. 254p. Date not set. pap. 2.95 (ISBN 0-394-71571-3, Vin). Random.

Barth, Diana, ed. see International Conference London, 1973.

Barth, Edna. Balder & the Mistletoe: A Story for the Winter Holidays. LC 78-4523. (Illus.). (gr. 2-5). 1979. 7.95 (ISBN 0-395-28956-4, Clarion). HM.

--Cupid & Psyche: A Love Story. LC 76-8821. (Illus.). (gr. 3-6). 1976. 7.95 (ISBN 0-395-28840-1, Clarion). HM.
--Hearts, Cupids & Red Roses. LC 73-7128. (Illus.). (gr. 2-6). 8.95 (ISBN 0-395-28841-X, Clarion). HM.
--Holly, Reindeer, & Colored Lights: The Story of the Christmas Symbols. LC 71-157731. (Illus.). (gr. 2-5). 1971. 8.95 (ISBN 0-395-28842-8, Clarion). HM.
--I'm Nobody, Who Are You: The Story of Emily Dickinson. LC 72-129211. (Illus.). (gr. 3-7). 1971. 6.95 (ISBN 0-395-28843-6, Clarion). HM.
--Jack O'Lantern. LC 73-20194. (Illus.). 48p. (gr. 1-4). 1974. 6.95 (ISBN 0-395-28763-4, Clarion). HM.
--Lilies, Rabbits, & Painted Eggs: The Story of the Easter Symbols. LC 74-79033. (Illus.). (gr. 2-5). 1970. 8.95 (ISBN 0-395-28844-4, Clarion). HM.
--Lilies, Rabbits, & Painted Eggs: The Story of the Easter Symbols. (Illus.). 64p. (gr. 3-6). 1981. pap. 3.95 (ISBN 0-686-69042-7, Clarion). HM.
--Shamrocks, Harps, and Shillelaghs: The Story of the St. Patrick's Day Symbols. LC 77-369. (gr. 3-6). 1977. 8.95 (ISBN 0-395-28845-2, Clarion). HM.
--Turkeys, Pilgrims, & Indian Corn: The Story of the Thanksgiving Symbols. LC 75-4703. (Illus.). 96p. (gr. 2-6). 1975. 8.95 (ISBN 0-395-28846-0, Clarion). HM.
--Witches, Pumpkins & Grinning Ghosts: The Story of the Halloween Symbols. LC 72-75705. (Illus.). 96p. (gr. 2-6). 1972. 8.95 (ISBN 0-395-28847-9, Clarion). HM.
Barth, Fredrik. Features of Person & Society in Swat-Collected Essays on Pathans: Selected Essays of Frederik Barth, Vol. II. (International Library of Anthropology Ser.). 208p. 1981. 32.00 (ISBN 0-7100-0620-9). Routledge & Kegan.
--Political Leadership Among Swat Pathans. (Monographs on Social Anthropology: No. 19). 1970. pap. text ed. 7.50x (ISBN 0-485-19619-0, Athlone Pr). Humanities.
--Selected Essays of Fredrik Barth: Process & Form in Social Life. (International Library of Anthropology). 1981. 35.00 (ISBN 0-7100-0720-5). Routledge & Kegan.
Barth, Hans. Truth & Ideology. LC 74-81430. Orig. Title: Wahrheit und Ideologie. 1977. 19.50x (ISBN 0-520-02820-1). U of Cal Pr.
Barth, Heinrich, ed. Travels & Discoveries in North & Central Africa, 3 vols. 1965. 150.00x set (ISBN 0-7146-1790-3, F Cass Co). Biblio Dist.
Barth, Henrik. Internationale Wagner-Bibliographie, International Wagner Bibliography, 4 vols. Incl. Vol. 2. 1956-1960. Vol. 1. 7.50x (ISBN 3-921733-05-7); Vol. 2. 1956-1960. Vol. 2. 7.50x (ISBN 3-921733-05-7); 1961-1966. Vol. 3. 7.50 (ISBN 3-921733-06-5). LC 79-455691. Intl Pubns Serv.
Barth, Herbert, ed. Internationale Wagner - Bibliographie: 1967-1978. LC 80-483676. 175p. (Orig.). 1979. pap. 12.50 (ISBN 3-921733-08-1). Intl Pubns Serv.
Barth, James L. Elementary & Middle School Social Studies Curriculum Program, Activities, Materials. LC 78-71367. 1979. pap. text ed. 11.00 (ISBN 0-8191-0667-4). U Pr of Amer.
--Methods of Instruction in Social Studies Education. LC 79-66224. 1979. pap. text ed. 11.25 (ISBN 0-8191-0817-0). U Pr of Amer.
Barth, Karl. Anselm: Fides Quaerens Intellectum. Robertson, Ian W., tr. from Ger. LC 76-10795. (Pittsburgh Reprint Ser.: No. 2). 1976. text ed. 3.75 (ISBN 0-915138-09-3). Pickwick.
--The Christian Life. Bromiley, Geoffrey W., ed. LC 80-39942. 328p. 1981. 14.95 (ISBN 0-8028-3523-6). Eerdmans.
--Church Dogmatics. Incl. Vol. 4. Doctrine of Reconciliation, 2 pts. Pt. 3, Repr. Of 1962 Ed., 492p. 23.00x (ISBN 0-567-09044-2); Pt. 4, Repr. Of 1969 Ed., 240p. 12.95x (ISBN 0-567-09045-0); Vol. 5. Index: with Aids to the Preacher. Bromiley, G. W. & Torrance, G. F. 584p. Repr. of 1977 ed. 32.00x (ISBN 0-567-09046-9). Attic Pr.
--Church Dogmatics: The Doctrine of Creation, Vol. III, Pt. I. 440p. 1958. text ed. 23.00x (ISBN 0-567-09031-0). Attic Pr.
--Church Dogmatics: The Doctrine of God, Vol. II, Pt. I. Parker, T. H., et al, trs. from Ger. 710p. 1957. text ed. 23.00x (ISBN 0-567-09021-3). Attic Pr.
--Church Dogmatics: The Doctrine of God, Vol. II, Pt. II. Bromiley, G. W., tr. from Ger. 820p. 1957. text ed. 23.00x (ISBN 0-567-09022-1). Attic Pr.
--Church Dogmatics: The Doctrine of the Word of God (Prolegomena to Church Dogmatics, Vol. 1, Pt. 2. Thomson, G. T. & Knight, Harold, eds. 924p. 1956. text ed. 23.00x (ISBN 0-567-09012-4). Attic Pr.
--Church Dogmatics, Vol. III: The Doctrine of Creation, Pt. 3. 560p. Repr. of 1961 ed. text ed. 23.00x (ISBN 0-567-09033-7). Attic Pr.
--Church Dogmatics Vol. III: The Doctrine of Creation Pt. 4. 720p. Repr. of 1961 ed. text ed. 23.00 (ISBN 0-567-09034-5). Attic Pr.
--Church Dogmatics, Vol IV: The Doctrine of Reconciliation-Part 1. 814p. Repr. of 1956 ed. text ed. 23.00x (ISBN 0-567-09041-8). Attic Pr.
--Church Dogmatics, Vol. IV: The Doctrine of Reconciliation-Part 2. 882p. Repr. of 1958 ed. text ed. 23.00x (ISBN 0-567-09042-6). Attic Pr.
--Church Dogmatics, Vol. IV: The Doctrine of Reconciliation-Part 3, (I) 496p. Repr. of 1961 ed. text ed. 23.00 (ISBN 0-567-09043-4). Attic Pr.
--Church Dogmatics, Vol. 1: The Doctrine of the Word of God (Prolegomena to Church Dogmatics), Pt. 1. 2nd ed. Bromiley, G. W., tr. from Ger. 592p. Repr. of 1975 ed. text ed. 23.00x (ISBN 0-567-09013-2). Attic Pr.
--Epistle to the Romans. 6th ed. Hoskyns, Edwyn C., tr. 1968. pap. 8.95 (ISBN 0-19-500294-6, GB). Oxford U Pr.
--Final Testimonies. LC 77-8088. 1977. 3.95 o.p. (ISBN 0-8028-3497-3). Eerdmans.
--Humanity of God. Weiser, Thomas & Thomas, John N., trs. LC 60-3479. 1960. pap. 3.95 (ISBN 0-8042-0612-0). John Knox.
--Karl Barth Letters: 1961 to 1968. Bromiley, Geoffrey W., tr. LC 80-29140. 288p. 1981. 14.95 (ISBN 0-8028-3536-8). Eerdmans.
Barth, Richard. The Rag Bag Clan. 1979. pap. 1.95 (ISBN 0-380-46078-5, 46078). Avon.
--A Ragged Plot. 224p. 1981. 9.95 (ISBN 0-686-69089-3). Dial.
Barthel, Bruce, photos by. Skiing the Rockies. LC 80-65133. (Belding Imprint Ser.). (Illus.). 128p. (Text by Charlie Meyers). 1980. 27.50 (ISBN 0-912856-60-2). Graphic Arts Ctr.
Barthel, J. Thermometric Titrations. (Chemical Analysis Ser: Vol. 45). 209p. 1975. 29.95 (ISBN 0-471-05448-8, Pub. by Wiley-Interscience). Wiley.
Barthelme, Donald. Great Days. 1980. pap. write for info. (ISBN 0-671-83185-2). PB.
--Sadness. 183p. 1972. 7.95 o.p. (ISBN 0-374-25333-1). FS&G.
Barthes, Roland. Barthes Reader. Sontag, Susan, ed. 1981. 17.95 (ISBN 0-8090-2815-8); pap. 8.95 (ISBN 0-8090-1394-0). Hill & Wang.
--Critical Essays. Howard, Richard, tr. xxi, 279p. 1972. 15.95x (ISBN 0-8101-0370-2); pap. 6.95x (ISBN 0-8101-0589-6). Northwestern U Pr.
--The Eiffel Tower & Other Mythologies. Howard, Richard, tr. 152p. 1979. 9.95 (ISBN 0-8090-4115-4); pap. 4.95 (ISBN 0-8090-1391-6). Hill & Wang.
--Mythologies. Lavers, Annette, tr. LC 75-185427. 160p. 1972. 5.95 (ISBN 0-8090-7193-2); pap. 3.95 (ISBN 0-8090-1369-X). Hill & Wang.
--New Critical Essays. Howard, Richard, tr. from Fr. 121p. 1980. 10.95 (ISBN 0-8090-7257-2). Hill & Wang.
--S-Z. Miller, Richard, tr. 271p. 1974. 8.95 (ISBN 0-8090-8375-2); pap. 5.95 (ISBN 0-8090-1377-0). Hill & Wang.
--Writing Degree Zero. Laver & Smith, trs. 94p. 1977. 8.95 (ISBN 0-8090-9865-2); pap. 4.50 (ISBN 0-8090-1384-3). Hill & Wang.
Barthleme, Donald. Sadness. 1980. pap. write for info. (ISBN 0-671-83204-2). PB.
Barthlet, John. The Pedegrewe of Heretiques. LC 79-76432. (English Experience Ser.: No. 76). 180p. 1969. Repr. of 1566 ed. 21.00 (ISBN 90-221-0076-6). Walter J Johnson.
Barthold, Bonnie J. Black Time: Fiction of Africa, the Caribbean, & the United States. LC 80-24336. (Illus.). 224p. 1981. 17.50x (ISBN 0-300-02573-4). Yale U Pr.
Barthold, Helga, tr. see Morgenstern, Christian.
Bartholomaeo, Paulinus S. Dissertation on the Sanskrit Language. Rocher, L., ed. (Studies in the History of Linguistics: No. 12). 1979. text ed. 37.00x (ISBN 0-391-01675-X). Humanities.
Bartholomaeus, Anglicus. Medieval Lore. Steele, R., ed. LC 66-23970. (Medieval Library). Repr. of 1926 ed. 8.50x (ISBN 0-8154-0016-0). Cooper Sq.
Bartholomeusz, Dennis. Macbeth & the Players. LC 69-10270. (Illus.). 1969. 48.00 (ISBN 0-521-06925-4, 4); pap. 10.95 (ISBN 0-521-29322-7). Cambridge U Pr.
Bartholomew, A., ed. see Hamilton, Alistair.
Bartholomew, Alick, ed. see Ellis, Christopher.
Bartholomew, Alick, ed. see Langley, Noel.
Bartholomew, Alick, ed. see Nicholson, T. R.
Bartholomew, Cecilia. Outrun the Dark. pap. 2.25 (ISBN 0-515-04648-5). Jove Pubns.
--Second Sight. 1981. pap. 2.75 (ISBN 0-425-04798-9). Berkley Pub.
Bartholomew, David. Guidebook for Social Scientists. 148p. 1981. 34.50 (ISBN 0-471-27932-3, Pub. by Wiley-Interscience); pap. 19.95 (ISBN 0-471-27933-1). Wiley.
Bartholomew, Mel. Square Foot Gardening: A New Way to Garden in Less Space with Less Work. Halpin, Anne, ed. (Illus.). 288p. 1981. 13.95 (ISBN 0-87857-340-2); pap. 9.95 (ISBN 0-87857-341-0). Rodale Pr Inc.
Bartholomew, Paul C. Public Administration. 3rd ed. (Quality Paperback: No. 29). (Orig.). 1977. 3.95 (ISBN 0-8226-0029-3). Littlefield.
Bartholomew, Paul C. & Menez, Joseph F. Summaries of the Leading Cases on the Constitution. 10th ed. LC 68-7178. (Quality Paperback: No. 50). 1979. pap. 5.95 (ISBN 0-8226-0050-1). Littlefield.
Bartholomew, Richard. Poems. (Writers Workshop Redbird Ser.). 1975. 8.00 (ISBN 0-88253-610-9); pap. text ed. 4.00 (ISBN 0-88253-609-5). Ind-US Inc.
--The Story of Siddhartha's Release. (Writers Workshop Redbird Ser.). 1975. 8.00 (ISBN 0-88253-648-6); pap. text ed. 4.00 (ISBN 0-88253-647-8). Ind-US Inc.
Bartholomew, Rolland & Crawley, Frank. A Sourcebook of Laboratory Techniques for Science Teachers. (gr. 9-12). 1980. pap. text ed. 12.50 (ISBN 0-201-00354-6, Sch Div). A-W.
Bartholomew, Roy A. & Orr, Francis S. Learning to Read Mechanical Drawings. rev. ed. (gr. 9-12). 1970. pap. text ed. 5.20 (ISBN 0-87002-040-4); tchr. guide avail. (ISBN 0-685-03308-2). Bennett IL.
Barthwell, Akosua. Trade Unionism in North Carolina: The Strike in Reynolds Tobacco, 1947. 1977. 1.25 (ISBN 0-89977-029-0). Am Inst Marxist.
Bartilucci, A. & Durgin, J. Giving Medications Correctly & Safely. 1978. pap. 9.95 (ISBN 0-87489-216-3). Med Economics.
Bartke, Wolfgang. Who's Who in the People's Republic of China. (Illus.). 750p. 1981. 100.00 (ISBN 0-87332-183-9). M E Sharpe.
Bartknecht, W. Explosions: Course, Prevention, Protection. Burg, H. & Almond, T., trs. from Ger. (Illus.). 251p. 1981. 74.40 (ISBN 0-387-10216-7). Springer-Verlag.
Bartkowiak, Robert A. Electric Circuits. LC 72-14366. 478p. 1973. text ed. 21.50 scp (ISBN 0-7002-2421-1, HarpC); sol. manual scp 4.50 (ISBN 0-8102-0040-6). Har-Row.
Bartle, Jim. Trails of the Cordillaras Blanca & Huayhuash of Peru. (Illus.). 160p. (Orig.). 1980. pap. 7.95 (ISBN 0-933982-10-0). Bradt Ent.
Bartle, Nicole, tr. see Decarpentry.
Bartle, Robert G. The Elements of Real Analysis. 2nd ed. LC 75-15979. 480p. 1975. text ed. 24.95 (ISBN 0-471-05464-X); arabic translation avail. Wiley.
Bartleman, Frank. Azusa Street. 1980. pap. 4.95 (ISBN 0-88270-439-7). Logos.
Bartlett, A., jt. auth. see Cooper, B.
Bartlett, A. J., jt. auth. see Garbutt, J. W.
Bartlett, Bruce R. A Walk on the Supply Side: Economic Policies for the Eighties & Beyond. 256p. 1981. 14.95 (ISBN 0-87000-505-7). Arlington Hse.
Bartlett, C. J. A History of Postwar Britain, 1945-74. LC 77-3000. 1977. pap. text ed. 12.95 (ISBN 0-582-48320-4). Longman.
Bartlett, C. J., ed. Britain Pre-Eminent: Studies in British World Influence in the Nineteenth Century. LC 75-93447. (Problems in Focus Ser). 1969. 18.95 (ISBN 0-312-09835-9). St Martin.
Bartlett, Carol, jt. auth. see Bartlett, David.
Bartlett, David & Bartlett, Carol. Adam's New Friend & Other Stories from the Bible. 96p. 1980. pap. 4.95 (ISBN 0-8170-0882-9). Judson.
Bartlett, E. G. Basic Fitness. LC 76-1402. (Illus.). 128p. 1976. 10.50 (ISBN 0-7153-7172-X). David & Charles.
--Basic Judo. LC 75-2707. (Illus.). 1975. pap. 2.95 o.p. (ISBN 0-668-03790-3). Arco.
--Summer Day at Ajaccio. 168p. 1980. 15.00x (ISBN 0-7050-0075-3, Pub. by Skilton & Shaw England). State Mutual Bk.
Bartlett, Edward T., 3rd, jt. auth. see Armour, Leslie.
Bartlett, Fred S., frwd. by. Walt Kuhn: An Imaginary History of the West. LC 64-+012. (Illus.). 52p. 1964. pap. 2.50 (ISBN 0-88360-008-0). Amon Carter.
Bartlett, Frederic C. Remembering: A Study in Experimental & Social Psychology. 1932. 35.00 (ISBN 0-521-04114-7); pap. 9.95x (ISBN 0-521-09441-0). Cambridge U Pr.
Bartlett, Gene E. Postscript to Preaching: After Forty Years, How Will I Preach Today? 88p. 1981. pap. 3.95 (ISBN 0-8170-0909-4). Judson.
Bartlett, Harriett M. Common Base of Social Work Practice. LC 72-116893. (Orig.). 1970. pap. 6.00x (ISBN 0-87101-054-2, CBO-054-C). Natl Assn Soc Wkrs.
Bartlett, Hazel & Gregory, Julia. Catalogue of Early Books on Music (Before 1800) LC 69-12684. (Music Ser). 1969. Repr. of 1913 ed. lib. bdg. 32.50 (ISBN 0-306-71223-7). Da Capo.
Bartlett, Irving H. Windell & Ann Phillips: The Community of Reform 1840-1880. (Illus.). 1981. 17.95 (ISBN 0-393-01426-6): Norton.
Bartlett, J. L., jt. auth. see Helmrath, M. O.
Bartlett, J. V. Handy Farm & Home Devices. (Illus.). 320p. (Orig.). 1981. pap. price not set. MIT Pr.
Bartlett, Jean A. Eliza. (Torment of Aaron Burr Ser.: No. 3). 1977. pap. 1.75 o.p. (ISBN 0-445-04012-2). Popular Lib.
Bartlett, Jerry F. Getting Started in Alabama Real Estate. (Real Estate Ser.). 1978. pap. text ed. 12.50 (ISBN 0-8403-1879-0). Kendall-Hunt.
Bartlett, John. Bartlett's Familiar Quotations: Fifteenth & 125th Anniversary Edition. rev. & enl. ed. LC 68-15664. 1980. 24.95 (ISBN 0-316-08275-9). Little.
Bartlett, John, ed. Familiar Quotations. 1958. 4.75 o.p. (ISBN 0-8022-0077-X). Philos Lib.
Bartlett, Jonathan, ed. The First Amendment in a Free Society. (Reference Shelf Ser.: Vol. 50, No. 6). 1979. 6.25 (ISBN 0-8242-0627-4). Wilson.
--The Ocean Environment. (Reference Shelf Ser.). 1977. 6.25 (ISBN 0-8242-0600-2). Wilson.
Bartlett, Laile. PSI Trek. 300p. 1981. 12.95 (ISBN 0-07-003915-1, GB). McGraw.
Bartlett, Lee. The Beats: Essays in Criticism. LC 80-28179. 250p. 1981. lib. bdg. write for info (ISBN 0-89950-026-9). McFarland & Co.
Bartlett, Lee & Campo, Allan. William Everson: A Descriptive Bibliography, 1934-1976. LC 77-5397. (Author Bibliographies Ser.: No. 33). 1977. 10.00 (ISBN 0-8108-1037-9). Scarecrow.
Bartlett, Lee, ed. Benchmark & Blaze: The Emergence of William Everson. LC 78-2137. 1979. lib. bdg. 13.50 (ISBN 0-8108-1198-7). Scarecrow.
Bartlett, Lee, ed. see Spender, Stephen.
Bartlett, M. S. Introduction to Stochastic Processes. 3rd ed. LC 76-57094. (Illus.). 404p. Date not set. pap. 17.95 (ISBN 0-521-28085-0). Cambridge U Pr.
--An Introduction to Stochastic Processes with Special Reference to Methods & Applications. 3rd ed. LC 76-57094. (Illus.). 1978. 57.50 (ISBN 0-521-21585-4). Cambridge U Pr.
--Probability, Statistics & Time: A Collection of Essays. LC 75-24171. 148p. 1976. text ed. 15.95x o.p. (ISBN 0-412-14150-7, Pub. by Chapman & Hall); pap. 12.95x o.p. (ISBN 0-412-22260-4). Methuen Inc.
--Probability, Statistics & Time: A Collection of Essays. LC 75-24171. (Monographs on Applied Probability & Statistics). 1975. text ed. 15.95 o.p. (ISBN 0-470-05466-2). Halsted Pr.
--The Statistical Analysis of Spatial Pattern. LC 75-31673. (Monographs on Applied Probability & Statistics). 1976. 11.95 o.p. (ISBN 0-470-05467-0). Halsted Pr.
--The Statistical Analysis of Spatial Patterns. LC 75-31673. 90p. 1978. text ed. 12.95x o.p. (ISBN 0-412-14290-2, Pub. by Chapman & Hall). Methuen Inc.
Bartlett, Margaret F. Clean Brook. LC 60-8257. (A Let's-Read-&-Find-Out Science Bk). (Illus.). (gr. k-3). 1960. PLB 7.89 (ISBN 0-690-19556-7, TYC-J). T Y Crowell.
--Where the Brook Begins. LC 60-9773. (A Let's-Read-&-Find-Out Science Bk). (Illus.). (gr. k-3). 1961. 7.95 (ISBN 0-690-88428-1, TYC-J). T Y Crowell.
Bartlett, Margaret F., jt. auth. see Bassett, Preston R.
Bartlett, Michael. The Golf Book. (Illus.). 1980. 22.95 (ISBN 0-87795-297-3) (ISBN 0-686-64654-1). Arbor Hse.
Bartlett, R., jt. auth. see Clendenning, P. H.
Bartlett, R. E. Surface Water Sewerage. LC 75-46624. 1976. 29.95 (ISBN 0-470-15020-3). Halsted Pr.
Bartlett, R. E., ed. Developments in Sewerage, Vol. 1. (Illus.). 1979. 31.00x (ISBN 0-85334-831-6, Pub. by Applied Science). Burgess-Intl Ideas.
Bartlett, R. P. Human Capital: The Settlement of Foreigners in Russia, 1762-1804. LC 78-68337. 1980. 53.00 (ISBN 0-521-22205-2). Cambridge U Pr.
Bartlett, Randall. Economic Foundations of Political Power. LC 73-3899. 1973. 12.95 (ISBN 0-02-901870-6). Free Pr.
Bartlett, Raymond C. Medical Microbiology: Quality Cost & Clinical Relevance. LC 73-18482. (Quality Control Methods in the Clinical Laboratory Ser.). 272p. 1974. 32.50 (ISBN 0-471-05475-5, Pub. by Wiley-Medical). Wiley.
Bartlett, Richard A. Great Surveys of the American West. LC 62-16475. (The American Exploration & Travel Ser.: Vol. 38). (Illus.). 464p. 1980. pap. 9.95 (ISBN 0-8061-1653-6). U of Okla Pr.
--The New Country: A Social History of the American Frontier 1776-1890. LC 74-79619. (Illus.). 495p. 1976. pap. 8.95 (ISBN 0-19-502021-9, 452, GB). Oxford U Pr.

Bartlett, Robert M. Thanksgiving Day. LC 65-16178. (Holiday Ser.). (Illus.). (gr. 1-3). 1965. PLB 7.89 (ISBN 0-690-81045-8, TYC-J). T Y Crowell.

Bartlett, Ronald E. Public Health Engineering: Sewerage. 2nd ed. (Illus.). 1979. 31.00x (ISBN 0-85334-796-4). Intl Ideas.

--Pumping Stations for Water & Sewage. LC 73-22472. 150p. 1974. 24.95 (ISBN 0-470-05477-8). Halsted Pr.

Bartlett, Ruhl J. John C. Fremont & the Republican Party. LC 73-87663. (American Scene Ser). 1970. Repr. of 1930 ed. lib. bdg. 19.50 (ISBN 0-306-71763-8). Da Capo.

Bartlett, Sy, jt. auth. see Lay, Beirne, Jr.

Bartlett, Truman H. The Art Life of William Rimmer: Sculptor, Painter, & Physician. LC 68-27718. (Library of American Art Ser.). (Illus.). 1970. Repr. of 1890 ed. lib. bdg. 27.50 (ISBN 0-306-71166-4). Da Capo.

Bartley, Douglas. Job Evaluation-Wage & Salary Administration. LC 80-21099. 272p. 1981. text ed. 14.95 (ISBN 0-201-00095-4). A-W.

Bartley, Numan V. & Graham, Hugh D. Southern Elections: County & Precinct Data, 1950-1972. LC 78-5525. 1977. 24.95x (ISBN 0-8071-0278-4). La State U Pr.

Bartley, S. Howard. Introduction to Perception. (Illus.). 1980. pap. 18.95 scp (ISBN 0-06-040514-7, HarpC). Har-Row.

Bartling, V., jt. auth. see Moellering, H. A.

Bartmess, Carolyn. For You. 1981. 4.95 (ISBN 0-8062-1701-4). Carlton.

Bartok, John W. Heating with Coal. (Illus.). 160p. 1980. pap. 6.95 (ISBN 0-88266-243-0). Garden Way Pub.

Bartol, Curt R. Criminal Behavior: A Psychosocial Approach. (Criminal Justice Ser.). (Illus.). 1980. text ed. 17.95 (ISBN 0-13-193169-5). P-H.

Bartolke-Bergmann. Integrated Cooperatives in the Industrial Society. 1980. text ed. 22.50x (ISBN 90-232-1772-1). Humanities.

Bartollas, Clemens. Introduction to Corrections. (Illus.). 496p. 1981. text ed. 18.50 scp (ISBN 0-06-040516-3, HarpC); avail. instrs manual. Har-Row.

Bartollas, Clemens & Miller, Stuart J. The Juvenile Offender: Control, Correction & Treatment. 1978. text ed. 17.95 (ISBN 0-205-06069-2, 826069-9). Allyn.

Bartolo, Baldassare De, ed. Spectroscopy of the Excited State. LC 75-38526. (NATO Advanced Study Institutes Ser., Series B: Physics: Vol. 12). 416p. 1976. 37.50 (ISBN 0-306-35712-7, Plenum Pr). Plenum Pub.

Bartolo, Dick De see De Bartolo, Dick & North, Henry.

Bartolome, Fernando, jt. auth. see Evans, Paul.

Bartolozzi, Bruno. New Sounds for Woodwind. Brindle, Reginald S., ed. 80p. 1981. 22.50x (ISBN 0-19-318611-X). Oxford U Pr.

Barton, A. F. Resource Recovery & Recycling. LC 78-13601. (Environmental Science & Technology Ser.). 1979. 32.00 (ISBN 0-471-02773-1, Pub. by Wiley-Interscience). Wiley.

Barton, Allen, et al. Decentralizing City Government. (Illus.). 1977. 22.95 (ISBN 0-669-01098-7). Lexington Bks.

Barton, Allen H., jt. ed. see Weiss, Carol H.

Barton, Anne. Shakespeare & the Idea of the Play. LC 76-58419. 1977. Repr. of 1962 ed. lib. bdg. 17.00x (ISBN 0-8371-9446-6, BASI). Greenwood.

Barton, Bernard. A Day in Autumn: A Poem, Repr. Of 1820 Ed. Bd. with Napoleon, & Other Poems. Repr. of 1822 ed; Verses on the Death of Percy Bysshe Shelley. Repr. of 1822 ed. LC 75-31153. (Romantic Context: Poetry 1789-1830 Ser.: Vol. 9). 1977. lib. bdg. 47.00 (ISBN 0-8240-2108-8). Garland Pub.

--Poems, by an Amateur, Repr. Of 1818 Ed. Bd. with Poems. Repr. of 1820 ed. LC 75-31152. (Romantic Context: Poetry 1789-1830 Ser.: Vol. 8). 1977. lib. bdg. 47.00 (ISBN 0-8240-2107-X). Garland Pub.

Barton, Bruce. Man Nobody Knows. 1925. pap. 4.85 (ISBN 0-672-50743-9). Bobbs.

Barton, Byron. Building a House. LC 80-22674. (Illus.). 32p. (ps-1). 1981. 7.95 (ISBN 0-688-80291-5); PLB 7.63 (ISBN 0-688-84291-7). Greenwillow.

--Buzz, Buzz, Buzz. LC 73-1965. (Illus.). 32p. (gr. k-2). 1973. 7.95 (ISBN 0-02-708450-7). Macmillan.

--Elephant. LC 74-154301. (Illus.). (ps-2). 1971. 4.95 (ISBN 0-395-28764-2, Clarion). HM.

--Harry Is a Scaredy-Cat. LC 73-6039. (Illus.). 32p. (ps-2). 1974. 5.95g o.s.i. (ISBN 0-02-708440-X, 70844). Macmillan.

--Hester. LC 75-9668. (Illus.). 32p. (ps-3). 1975. 8.25 (ISBN 0-688-80009-2); PLB 7.92 (ISBN 0-688-84009-4). Greenwillow.

--Jack & Fred. (Illus.). 32p. (gr. k-2). 1974. 8.95 (ISBN 0-02-708400-0, 70840). Macmillan.

--Wheels. LC 78-20541. (Illus.). (ps-3). 1979. 7.95 (ISBN 0-690-03951-4, TYC-J); PLB 6.89 (ISBN 0-690-03952-2). T Y Crowell.

--Where's Al. LC 78-171866. (Illus.). 32p. (ps-2). 1972. 7.95 (ISBN 0-395-28765-0, Clarion). HM.

Barton, D. H., jt. auth. see Simonsen, J. L.

Barton, David. Dying & Death. 1977. pap. text ed. 15.95 (ISBN 0-683-00440-9). Williams & Wilkins.

Barton, Del. A Good Day to Die. 320p. 1981. pap. 2.75 (ISBN 0-445-04646-5). Popular Lib.

Barton, Donald K., et al. Beginning Spanish Course. 3rd ed. 1976. text ed. 16.95x (ISBN 0-669-96776-9); wkbk. 5.95x (ISBN 0-669-96784-X); tape set 8 reels 40.00 (ISBN 0-669-96792-0); 8 cassettes 40.00 (ISBN 0-669-00082-5). Heath.

Barton, Donald W. Journey into the Word. 130p. (Orig.). 1981. pap. 3.50 (ISBN 0-938736-00-0). Life Enrich.

--Training of the Twelve: How to Teach Yourself & Others to Pray. 165p. (Orig.). 1981. pap. 3.95 (ISBN 0-938736-01-9). Life Enrich.

Barton, Felix. The Most Beautiful Women in British History. (Illus.). 1978. deluxe ed. 47.75 (ISBN 0-930582-07-1). Gloucester Art.

Barton, G. A. Ecclesiastes. LC 8-15777. (International Critical Commentary Ser.). 236p. Repr. of 1908 ed. 17.50x (ISBN 0-567-05014-9). Attic Pr.

Barton, Gretchen, jt. auth. see Greenlaw, Jean.

Barton, Henry M. Eversonian Plateau. 1981. 4.95 (ISBN 0-8062-1567-4). Carlton.

Barton, J. Amos' Oracles Against the Nations. LC 78-67630. (Society for Old Testament Study Ser.). 1980. 17.50 (ISBN 0-521-22501-9). Cambridge U Pr.

Barton, J. J. Small-Bore Heating & Hot Water Supply for Small Dwellings. 2nd ed. 1971. 9.75 (ISBN 0-408-00351-0). Transatlantic.

Barton, Jack S., et al. Future Technical Needs & Trends in the Paper Industry - II. (TAPPI PRESS Reports). (Illus.). 1976. pap. 33.95 (ISBN 0-89852-364-8, 01-01-R064). TAPPI.

Barton, John & Barton, Margaret. Allergies: How to Find & Conquer. (Illus.). 280p. 1980. pap. 15.00 (ISBN 0-937216-01-1). J&M Barton.

--Biokinesiology: Vol II Neurovasculars. 3rd ed. (Encyclopedia of Mind & Body). (Illus.). 110p. (Orig.). 1980. pap. 10.00 (ISBN 0-937216-05-4). J&M Barton.

--Emotions Can Heal, Emotions Can Harm. rev. 2nd ed. Orig. Title: Loving Affirmations. (Illus.). 157p. 1978. pap. 5.00 (ISBN 0-937216-02-X). J&M Barton.

--Flow Lines to Health. 4th ed. (Illus.). 158p. 1980. pap. 8.00 (ISBN 0-937216-04-6). J&M Barton.

--How to Take Care of Yourselves Naturally. 4th ed. LC 77-80393. Orig. Title: Flow Lines to Health. (Illus.). 158p. 1980. pap. 8.00 (ISBN 0-937216-04-6). J & M Barton.

--Now to Take Care of Yourselves Naturally. 2nd ed. LC 77-80393. (Illus.). 158p. (Orig.). 1980. pap. 8.00 o.p. (ISBN 0-937216-00-3). J&M Barton.

Barton, John, jt. ed. see Imai, Ryukichi.

Barton, John E. & Barton, Margaret. Be Your Own Chiropractor: Through Biokinetic Exercises. rev. 2nd ed. Orig. Title: Biokinetic Exercises. (Illus.). 210p. 1979. pap. 8.00 (ISBN 0-937216-03-8). J&M Barton.

Barton, John H. The Politics of Peace: An Evaluation of Arms Control. LC 79-67776. 296p. 1981. text ed. 18.50x (ISBN 0-8047-1081-3). Stanford U Pr.

Barton, John J. Electric Floor Warming with Notes on Ceiling Heating. 1967. 23.50x o.p. (ISBN 0-685-20576-2). Transatlantic.

--Estimating for Heating & Ventilating. 3rd ed. (Illus.). 29.50x (ISBN 0-408-00072-4). Transatlantic.

Barton, Lucy. Appreciating Costume. 1969. pap. 4.50 (ISBN 0-685-06786-6). Baker's Plays.

Barton, Lucy & Edson, Doris. Period Patterns. (Illus.). 1942. 5.95 (ISBN 0-685-06788-2). Baker's Plays.

Barton, Margaret, jt. auth. see Barton, John.

Barton, Margaret, jt. auth. see Barton, John E.

Barton, Michael, jt. ed. see Blain, Daniel.

Barton, Paule. The Woe Shirt. Norman, Howard, tr. from Creole. LC 80-81728. (Illus.). 64p. 12.50 (ISBN 0-915778-37-8); deluxe ed. 40.00x (ISBN 0-915778-36-X). Penmaen Pr.

Barton, Robert. The Oceans. 336p. 1980. 19.95x (ISBN 0-87196-414-7). Facts on File.

Barton, S. R., jt. auth. see O'Rourke, Karen.

Barton, Thomas F. John Smith: Jamestown Boy. (Childhood of Famous Americans Ser). (Illus.). (gr. 3-7). 1966. 3.95 (ISBN 0-672-50110-4). Bobbs.

Barton, Walter E. In the Twilight of My Memory: Windows to the Past. 100p. 1981. 5.00 (ISBN 0-8059-2762-X). Dorrance.

Barton, Walter E. & Sanborn, Charlotte J., eds. An Assessment of the Community Mental Health Movement. LC 76-54610. (Illus.). 1977. 22.95 (ISBN 0-669-01309-9). Lexington Bks.

Barton, Wilfrid C. Shelley & the New Criticism: The Anatomy of a Critical Misvaluation. (Salzburg Studies in English Literature, Romantic Reassessment: No. 5). 228p. 1973. pap. text ed. 25.00x (ISBN 0-391-01314-9). Humanities.

Barton, William E. Safed & Keturah. LC 69-19473. 1969. pap. 2.45 (ISBN 0-8042-3425-6). John Knox.

--Safed the Sage: Selections from Wit & Wisdom of Safed the Sage. LC 65-13377. 1965. pap. 2.45 (ISBN 0-8042-3424-8). John Knox.

Bartos, Bob. All About Puppies-- Your Dog's First Year. (Illus.). 1980. pap. 1.95 (ISBN 0-451-09177-9, J9177, Sig). NAL.

Bartosek, I., et al, eds. Isolated Liver Perfusion & Its Applications. LC 72-95635. (Mario Negri Institute for Pharmacological Research Monographs). (Illus.). 1973. 25.00 (ISBN 0-911216-43-X). Raven.

Bartow, Donald W. The Adventures of Healing: How to Use New Testament Practices & Receive New Testament Results. rev. ed. 371p. 1981. pap. 5.95 (ISBN 0-938736-02-7). Life Enrich.

Bartram, George, pseud. Fair Game. LC 73-7356. 250p. 1973. 6.95 o.s.i. (ISBN 0-02-507580-2). Macmillan.

Bartram, George. A Job Abroad. 224p. 1975. 7.95 o.s.i. (ISBN 0-02-521030-0). Macmillan.

--A Job Abroad. 1976. pap. 1.75 o.p. (ISBN 0-445-08482-0). Popular Lib.

Bartram, Graham & Waine, Anthony, eds. Brecht in Perspective. (German Literature & Society: Vol. 2). 1980. text ed. write for info. (ISBN 0-85496-076-7). Humanities.

Bartram, William. Travels. Van Doren, Mark, ed. (Illus.). 9.00 (ISBN 0-8446-1600-1). Peter Smith.

--The Travels of William Bartram. Peck, Robert M., ed. & intro. by. (Literature of the American Wilderness). 388p. 1980. pap. 3.95 (ISBN 0-87905-079-9). Peregrine Smith.

--Travels Through North & South Carolina, Georgia, & East & West Florida. LC 73-84685. (Illus.). 520p. 1980. Repr. of 1973 ed. 14.95 (ISBN 0-8139-0871-X). U Pr of Va.

Bartruff, Bryce, compiled by. Insight Proverbs NASV. LC 73-10830. 128p. 1973. pap. 1.25 (ISBN 0-87123-248-0, 200248). Bethany Fell.

Bartruff, Bryce D. Sayings of Jesus: A Pocket Guide. 1976. pap. 1.95 (ISBN 0-87123-461-0, 200461). Bethany Fell.

Bartrum, Douglas. Water in the Garden. 1968. 5.95 o.p. (ISBN 0-8231-6025-4). Branford.

Bartrum, Royal J., Jr. & Crow, Harte C. Gray-Scale Ultrasound: A Manual for Physician & Technical Personnel. LC 77-72802. (Illus.). 1977. text ed. 16.50 (ISBN 0-7216-1548-1). Saunders.

Bartsch, K. Chrestomathie de l'Ancien Francais (VIII-XV Siecles) 12th rev. ed. 1969. 14.25 (ISBN 0-02-841100-5). Hafner.

Bartsch, Karl & Sandmeyer, Louise. Skills in Life-Career Planning. LC 78-24615. (Psychology Ser.). (Illus.). 1979. pap. text ed. 8.95 (ISBN 0-8185-0322-X). Brooks-Cole.

Bartsch, William H. Employment & Technology Choice in Asian Agriculture. LC 76-58540. (Special Studies). 1977. text ed. 20.95 (ISBN 0-275-24280-3). Praeger.

Bartscht, Waltraud. Goethe's "Das Marchen". Translation and Analysis. LC 72-132826. (Studies in Germanic Langauges & Literatures: No. 3). 112p. 1972. 9.00x (ISBN 0-8131-1237-0). U Pr of Ky.

Bartsh, Thomas C., et al. A Class-Action Suit That Worked. new ed. LC 78-58814. 1978. 19.95 (ISBN 0-669-02409-0). Lexington Bks.

Bartsocas, Christos S. & Papadatos, Constantine J., eds. The Management of Genetic Disorders: Proceedings. LC 79-5298. (Progress in Clinical & Biological Research Ser.: Vol. 34). 1979. 32.00x (ISBN 0-8451-0034-3). A R Liss.

Bartz, Albert E. Basic Statistical Concepts. 2nd ed. 438p. 1981. 15.95 (ISBN 0-8087-4041-5); write for info. wkbk by george g. seifert (ISBN 0-8087-4201-9). Burgess.

Bartz, Patricia M. South Korea. (Illus.). 248p. 1972. 24.95x (ISBN 0-19-874008-5). Oxford U Pr.

Bartz, Walter H. Testing Oral Communication in the Foreign Language Classroom. (Language in Education Ser.: No. 17). 1979. pap. 2.95 (ISBN 0-87281-103-4). Ctr Appl Ling.

Baruch, Bernard M. The Making of the Reparation & Economic Sections of the Treaty. LC 68-9615. 1970. Repr. 17.50 (ISBN 0-86527-120-8). Fertig.

Baruch, Geoffrey & Treacher, Andrew. Psychiatry Observed: The Conflict Between Theory & Practice in a General Hospital Psychiatric Unit. 1978. pap. 14.95 (ISBN 0-7100-8876-0). Routledge & Kegan.

Baruch, Grace K., jt. auth. see Barnett, Rosalind C.

Barut, A. O. Electrodynamics & Classical Theory of Fields & Particles. (Illus.). 256p. 1980. pap. text ed. 4.50 (ISBN 0-486-64038-8). Dover.

Barwell, F. T. Automation & Control in Transport. 1972. 42.00 (ISBN 0-08-016962-7). Pergamon.

Barwick, Humphrey. Concerning the Force & Effect of Manuall Weapons of Fire. LC 74-80163. (English Experience Ser.: No. 643). 86p. 1974. Repr. of 1594 ed. 8.00 (ISBN 90-221-0643-8). Walter J Johnson.

Barwick, James. The Hangman's Crusade. 320p. 1981. 11.95 (ISBN 0-698-11037-4). Coward.

Barwin, B. Norman, et al. Self-Assessment of Current Knowledge in Infertility & Gynecologic Endocrinology. 1979. spiral bdg. 14.50 (ISBN 0-87488-231-1). Med Exam.

Bary, Constantine W. Operational Economics of Electric Utilities. LC 63-9807. 1963. 22.50x (ISBN 0-231-02614-5). Columbia U Pr.

Bary, William T. De see De Bary, William T.

Baryshnikov, Mikhail. Baryshnikov. France, Charles E., ed. (Illus.). 64p. 1980. 12.95 (ISBN 0-686-62682-6, 2225-8). Abrams.

Barzel, Yoram & Hall, Christopher D. The Political Economy of the Oil Import Quota. LC 76-41087. (Publications Ser.: No. 172). 1977. 8.95 (ISBN 0-8179-6721-4). Hoover Inst Pr.

Barzini, Luigi. O America: When You & I Were Young. LC 76-5110. 1977. 10.00 o.p. (ISBN 0-06-010226-8, HarpT). Har-Row.

Barzman, Sol. Credit in Early America. 1975. pap. 2.95 (ISBN 0-934914-11-7). NACM.

--Everyday Credit Checking. new ed. 256p. Date not set. (ISBN 0-690-01875-4). Lippincott & Crowell. Postponed.

--Everyday Credit Checking: A Practical Guide. 256p. 1973. 9.95 (ISBN 0-690-27107-7, TYC-T). T Y Crowell.

--Everyday Credit Checking: A Practical Guide. rev. ed. LC 80-82080. 289p. 1980. 13.95 (ISBN 0-934914-36-2). NACM.

Bar Zohar, Michael. The Deadly Document. 1981. pap. 2.50 (ISBN 0-440-12165-5). Dell.

Barzun, Isabel, tr. see Brandys, Kazimierz.

Barzun, Jacques. Berlioz & the Romantic Century, 2 vols. 3rd ed. LC 77-97504. (Illus.). 1969. Set. 50.00x (ISBN 0-231-03135-1). Columbia U Pr.

--Classic, Romantic & Modern. xvi, 256p. 1975. pap. 5.50 (ISBN 0-226-03852-1, P643, Phoen). U of Chicago Pr.

--Darwin, Marx, & Wagner: Critique of a Heritage. rev. ed. LC 58-2647. 1958. pap. 2.95 (ISBN 0-385-09341-1, A127, Anch). Doubleday.

--Science: The Glorious Entertainment. LC 62-14520. 1964. 8.95 o.s.i. (ISBN 0-06-010240-3, HarpT). Har-Row.

--Teacher in America. LC 80-82370. 496p. 1981. 9.00 (ISBN 0-913966-78-9, Liberty Pr); pap. 4.00 (ISBN 0-913966-79-7). Liberty Fund.

Barzun, Jacques & Graff, Henry F. The Modern Researcher. 3rd ed. 378p. 1977. pap. text ed. 9.95 (ISBN 0-15-562511-X, HC). HarBraceJ.

Barzun, Jacques & Taylor, Wendell H. A Catalog of Crime. LC 73-20705. (Illus.). 864p. 1974. 25.00 o.p. (ISBN 0-06-010266-7, HarpT). Har-Row.

Barzun, Jacques, ed. see Follett, Wilson.

Barzun, Jacques, tr. see Diderot, Denis.

Basa, Eniko M. Sandor Petofi. (World Author Ser.: No. 587). 1980. lib. bdg. 13.50 (ISBN 0-8057-6429-1). Twayne.

Basagni, Fabio & Uri, Pierre, eds. Monetary Relations & World Development. LC 77-15650. (Praeger Special Studies). 1977. 19.85 (ISBN 0-03-041591-8). Praeger.

Basagni, Fabio, jt. ed. see Cohen, Benjamin.

Basak, R. Asokan Inscriptions. (Illus.). 1959. 5.50x o.p. (ISBN 0-8426-1147-9). Verry.

Basansky, Bill & Manuel, David. Escape from Terror. Orig. Title: Babunia. 1977. pap. 1.95 pocketsize o.p. (ISBN 0-88270-254-8). Logos.

Basart, Ann. Serial Music: A Classified Bibliography of Writings on 12 Tone & Electronic Music. LC 75-45460. 151p. 1976. Repr. of 1961 ed. lib. bdg. 16.50x (ISBN 0-8371-8753-2, BASM). Greenwood.

Bascio, Patrick. Building a Just Society. LC 80-27238. 176p. (Orig.). 1981. pap. text ed. 5.95 (ISBN 0-88344-205-1). Orbis Bks.

Bascom, Willard. Waves & Beaches: The Dynamics of the Ocean Surface. rev. updated ed. LC 79-7038. (Illus.). 1980. 12.00 (ISBN 0-385-14845-3, Anchor Pr); pap. 6.95 (ISBN 0-385-14844-5, Anchor Pr). Doubleday.

Bascom, William. African Art in Cultural Perspective: An Introduction. new ed. (Illus.). 192p. 1973. 7.95x (ISBN 0-393-04368-1); pap. 4.95x (ISBN 0-393-09375-1). Norton.

--If a Divination: Communication Between Gods & Men in West Africa. LC 69-10349. (Illus.). 604p. 1969. 35.00x (ISBN 0-253-32890-X). Ind U Pr.

Bascom, William R., ed. Frontiers of Folklore. LC 77-12784. (AAAS Selected Symposium Ser.: No. 5). (Illus.). 1978. lib. bdg. 17.00x (ISBN 0-89158-432-3). Westview.

Bascombe, George. The Preacher & the Strumpet: And Other Short Stories. 1978. 4.50 o.p. (ISBN 0-533-03499-X). Vantage.

Basdekis, Demetrios. Miguel De Unamuno. LC 74-92029. (Columbia Essays on Modern Writers Ser.: No. 44). (Orig.). 1969. pap. 2.00 (ISBN 0-231-03259-5). Columbia U Pr.

Basehart, Harry W. Apache Indians XII. Horr, David A., ed. (American Indian Ethnohistory Ser.). 1978. lib. bdg. 42.00 (ISBN 0-8240-0713-1). Garland Pub.

Basehore, C. J. & Marantette, Carter H. Securing an Executive Position in the Sunbelt. 57p. (Orig.). 1980. pap. 5.95 (ISBN 0-939148-00-5). Exec West.

Baserga, Renato, et al, eds. Introduction of Macromolecules into Viable Mammalian Cells. LC 79-91743. (Wistar Symposium Ser.: Vol. 1). 354p. 1980. 26.00x (ISBN 0-8451-2000-X). A R Liss.

Basevi, Abramo. Studio Sulle Opere Di Giuseppe Verdi. LC 80-2255. 1981. Repr. of 1859 ed. 35.50 (ISBN 0-404-18802-8). AMS Pr.

Basgoz, Ihlan & Tietze, Andreas. Bilmece: A Corpus of Turkish Riddles. (Publications in Folklore Studies Vol. 22). 1974. pap. 34.50x (ISBN 0-520-09145-0). U of Cal Pr.

Bash, Deborah M. & Gold, Winifred A. The Nurse & the Childbearing Family. LC 80-22945. 800p. 1981. 17.95 (ISBN 0-471-05520-4). Wiley.

Bash, Ewald. Legends from the Future. (Orig.). 1972. pap. 1.75 o.p. (ISBN 0-377-02101-6). Friend Pr.

Bash, Frank N. Astronomy. (Illus.). 1977. pap. 16.95 (ISBN 0-06-043853-3, HarpC). Har-Row.

Basham, A. L., ed. A Cultural History of India. (Illus.). 642p. 1975. 34.00x (ISBN 0-19-821914-8). Oxford U Pr.

Basham, Don. Deliver Us from Evil. 1972. 4.95 (ISBN 0-912376-06-6); pap. 2.95 o.p. (ISBN 0-685-56346-4). Chosen Bks Pub.

--Handbook on Tongues, Interpretation & Prophecy. (Handbk. Ser.: No. 2). 1971. pap. 2.95 (ISBN 0-88368-004-1). Whitaker Hse.

--Spiritual Power. rev ed. 92p. 1976. pap. 2.95 (ISBN 0-88368-005-X). Whitaker Hse.

Bashaw, W. L. Mathematics for Statistics. LC 69-16123. 1969. pap. 13.95 (ISBN 0-471-05531-X). Wiley.

Bashford, James W., jt. auth. see Ellwood, Robert S., Jr.

Bashinski, Marian C. Improving Sentences: A Diagnostic Approach. 200p. 1980. tchrs. ed. 7.95 (ISBN 0-89892-034-5). Contemp Pub Co Raleigh.

Bashir, Iskandar. Civil Service Reform in Lebanon. 1977. 15.00x (ISBN 0-8156-6050-2, Am U Beirut). Syracuse U Pr.

Basho, Matsuo. A Haiku Journey: Basho's Narrow Road to a Far Province. Britton, Dorothy G., tr. from Jap. LC 74-24903. 124p. 1980. pap. 3.95 (ISBN 0-87011-423-9). Kodansha.

Bashshur, Rashid L., et al. Telemedicine: Explorations in the Use of Telecommunications in Health Care. (Illus.). 376p. 1975. 36.50 (ISBN 0-398-03276-9); pap. 26.75 (ISBN 0-398-03311-0). C C Thomas.

Basicevic, Dimitrije. Primitive Paintings. (Alpine Fine Arts Collection). (Illus.). 300p. 1981. 85.00 (ISBN 0-933516-12-6, Pub by Alpine Fine Arts). Hippocrene Bks.

Basil, Cynthia. Breakfast in the Afternoon. LC 78-10366. (Illus.). (gr. k-3). 1979. 7.50 (ISBN 0-688-22175-0); PLB 7.20 (ISBN 0-688-32175-5). Morrow.

--Nailheads & Potato Eyes. LC 75-23180. (Illus.). 32p. (gr. k-3). 1976. PLB 7.63 (ISBN 0-688-32056-2). Morrow.

Basil, Douglas C., et al, eds. Purchasing Information Sources. LC 76-7037. (Management Information Guide Ser.: No. 30). 380p. 1977. 30.00 (ISBN 0-8103-0830-4). Gale.

Basile, Frank M. Back to Basics with Basile. Glick, Marianne, ed. 305p. (Orig.). 1979. pap. 13.00 (ISBN 0-937008-01-X). Charisma Pubns.

Basile, Ralph J., et al. Downtown Development Handbook. LC 80-50928. (Community Builder Handbook Ser.). (Illus.). 278p. 1980. 34.00 (ISBN 0-87420-591-3, D12). Urban Land.

Basilius. The Ascetic Works of Saint Basil. Clarke, W. K., tr. & intro. by. LC 80-2352. 1981. Repr. of 1925 ed. 47.50 (ISBN 0-404-18902-4). AMS Pr.

Basilius, Harold A., tr. see Feuchtwanger, Lion.

Basily, Lascelle De see De Basily, Lascelle.

Basinger, Jeanine. Anthony Mann. (Theatrical Arts Ser.). 1979. lib. bdg. 12.50 (ISBN 0-8057-9263-5). Twayne.

Basinger, Jeanine, ed. Working with Kazan. (Illus.). 1973. pap. 4.00 (ISBN 0-8195-8016-3, Pub. by Wesleyan U Pr). Columbia U Pr.

Basinger, Louis F. The Techniques of Observation & Learning Retention: A Handbook for the Policeman & the Lawyer. (Illus.). 88p. 1973. pap. 8.75 (ISBN 0-398-02935-0). C C Thomas.

Basiuk, Victor. Technology, World Politics, & American Policy. LC 76-51841. (Institute of War & Peace Studies). 1977. 22.50x (ISBN 0-685-74998-3). Columbia U Pr.

Baskerville, David. Music Business Handbook & Career Guide. 2nd ed. LC 78-57949. (Illus.). 1979. 18.95 (ISBN 0-933056-00-1). Sherwood Co.

Baskett, Mary. Footprints of the Buddha. LC 80-80133. (Illus.). 125p. (Orig.). 1980. pap. 8.95 (ISBN 0-87633-034-0). Phila Mus Art.

Baskin, Leonard, et al. Hosie's Alphabet. (Illus.). 64p. (gr. k-3). 1972. PLB 10.00 (ISBN 0-670-37958-1). Viking Pr.

Baskin, Wade & Runes, Richard N. Dictionary of Black Culture. LC 72-78162. 400p. 1973. 15.00 o.p. (ISBN 0-8022-2090-8). Philos Lib.

Baskin, Wade see Brehier, Emile.

Baskin, Wade, tr. see De Saussure, Ferdinand.

Baskiyar, Dharni D. The Inextinguishable Flame: Shelley Poetic & Creative Practice. (Salzburg Studies in English Literature: Romantic Reassessment Ser.: No. 68). 1977. pap. text ed. 25.00x (ISBN 0-391-01315-7). Humanities.

Basler, Beatrice K. & Basler, Thomas G., eds. Health Sciences Librarianship: A Guide to Information Sources. LC 74-11552. (Books, Publishing, & Libraries Information Guide Ser.: Vol. 1). 180p. 1977. 30.000 (ISBN 0-8103-1284-0). Gale.

Basler, Roy P., ed. see Lincoln, Abraham.

Basler, Thomas G., jt. ed. see Basler, Beatrice K.

Basmajian, John V. Grant's Method of Anatomy. 10th ed. (Illus.). 644p. 1980. 26.95 (ISBN 0-683-00373-9). Williams & Wilkins.

Basmajian, John V. & Blumenstein, R. Electrode Placement for EMG Biofeedback. (Illus.). 96p. 1980. softcover 8.95 (ISBN 0-683-00376-3). Williams & Wilkins.

Basolo, F. Inorganic Synthesis, Vol. 16. 1976. 27.50 o.p. (ISBN 0-07-004015-X, P&RB). McGraw.

Basolo, F. & Johnson, R. C. Coordination Chemistry: The Chemistry of Metal Complexes. 1964. pap. text ed. 8.95 (ISBN 0-8053-0651-X, 30651). Benjamin-Cummings.

Basolo, F., jt. auth. see Eliel, E. L.

Basow, Susan. Sex Role Stereotypes: Traditions & Alternatives. LC 80-19086. 320p. (Orig.). 1980. pap. text ed. 10.95 (ISBN 0-8185-0394-7). Brooks-Cole.

Basquette, Lina. How to Raise & Train a Great Dane. (Illus.). pap. 2.00 (ISBN 0-87666-308-0, DS1019). TFH Pubns.

Bass & Barrett. People, Work & Organizations: An Introduction to Industrial & Organizational Psychology. 2nd ed. 1980. text ed. 18.95 (ISBN 0-205-06809-X, 7968094). Allyn.

Bass, Alan, tr. see Derrida, Jacques.

Bass, Bernard M. & Ryterband, Edward C. Organizational Psychology. 2nd ed. 1979. text ed. 20.95 (ISBN 0-205-06010-2, 7960107). Allyn.

Bass, Bernard M., et al. Assessment of Managers: An International Comparison. LC 78-24670. (Illus.). 1979. 17.95 (ISBN 0-02-901960-5). Free Pr.

Bass, Eben E. Aldous Huxley: An Annotated Bibliography. LC 79-7907. (Garland Reference Library of Humanities). 275p. 1981. 30.00 (ISBN 0-8240-9525-1). Garland Pub.

Bass, Ellen. I'm Not Your Laughing Daughter. LC 73-79503. 96p. 1973. 8.00x (ISBN 0-87023-128-6); pap. 3.95 (ISBN 0-87023-129-4). U of Mass Pr.

Bass, Ellen, jt. ed. see Howe, Florence.

Bass, F. G. & Fuchs, M. Wave Scattering from Statistically Rough Surfaces. 1978. text ed. 105.00 (ISBN 0-08-019896-1). Pergamon.

Bass, Feris A., Jr., jt. auth. see Brunson, R. R.

Bass, George F., ed. A History of Seafaring Based on Underwater Archaeology. LC 72-81455. (Illus.). 320p. 1972. 22.50 o.s.i. (ISBN 0-8027-0390-9). Walker & Co.

Bass, George M., jt. auth. see Kemper, Frederick.

Bass, Howard L. & Rein, M. L. Divorce or Marriage: A Legal Guide. 1976. 9.95 o.p. (ISBN 0-685-67125-9, Spec). P-H.

Bass, Lee W. & Wolfson, Jerome H. The Style & Management of a Pediatric Practice. LC 76-50882. (Contemporary Community Health Ser.). 1977. pap. 7.95 (ISBN 0-8229-3341-1). U of Pittsburgh Pr.

Bass, R. M. Credit Management: How to Manage Credit Effectively. 352p. 1979. pap. 14.75x (ISBN 0-220-67029-3, Pub. by Busn Bks England). Renouf.

Bass, Robert D. Green Dragon: The Lives of Banastre Tarleton & Mary Robinson. LC 57-6183. 1973. Repr. 6.95 o.p. (ISBN 0-87844-019-4). Sandlapper Store.

--Ninety-Six: The Struggle for the South Carolina Back Country. LC 77-20551. (Illus.). 1978. 12.50 (ISBN 0-87844-039-9); ltd. signed 25.00 (ISBN 0-87844-017-8). Sandlapper Store.

Bass, Robert E. Some Features of Organization in Nature: A Contribution to Philosophy. 1980. 6.00. Print Mail Serv.

Bass, Ronald J. The Perfect Thief. (Orig.). 1978. pap. 1.75 o.s.i. (ISBN 0-515-04622-1). Jove Pubns.

Bass, T. J. Half Past Human. 288p. 1975. pap. 1.50 o.p. (ISBN 0-345-24635-7). Ballantine.

Bass, Tom. Power Plays. (Illus.). 40p. (Orig.). Date not set. pap. 3.00 (ISBN 0-934996-07-5). Am Stud Pr. Postponed.

Bassani, F. & Parravicini, Pastori. Electron States & Optical Transitions in Solids. 312p. 1976. text ed. 44.00 (ISBN 0-08-016846-9). Pergamon.

Basset, Bernard, S.J. And Would You Believe It! Thoughts About the Creed. 1978. pap. 2.45 (ISBN 0-385-13367-7, Im). Doubleday.

--Guilty, O Lord: Yes, I Still Go to Confession. LC 74-9475. 120p. 1976. pap. 1.45 o.p. (ISBN 0-385-11372-2, Im). Doubleday.

--How to Be Really with It: Guide to the Good Life. LC 70-89099. 1971. pap. 1.45 o.p. (ISBN 0-385-04227-2, Im). Doubleday.

--Let's Start Praying Again. 120p. 1973. pap. 1.95 o.p. (ISBN 0-385-05091-7, Im). Doubleday.

--We Agnostics: On the Tight Rope to Eternity. 1968. pap. 0.95 (ISBN 0-385-08106-5, Im). Doubleday.

Basset, William W. & Huizing, Peter J., eds. Future of Christian Marriage. (Concilium Ser.: Religion in the Seventies: Vol. 87). 1976. pap. 4.95 (ISBN 0-8164-2571-X). Crossroad NY.

Basset, Williams, jt. ed. see Huizing, Peter.

Bassett, Allen M. & O'Dunn, Shannon. General Geology of the Western United States: A Laboratory Manual. rev. ed. (Illus.). 176p. 1980. pap. text ed. 9.95x (ISBN 0-917962-67-2). Peek Pubns.

Bassett, D. C. Principles of Polymer Morphology. (Cambrige Solid State Science Ser.). (Illus.). 220p. Date not set. price not set (ISBN 0-521-23270-8); pap. price not set (ISBN 0-521-29886-5). Cambridge U Pr.

Bassett, Edward, ed. see Miles International Symposium, 12th.

Bassett, Edward G., jt. ed. see Beers, Roland F.

Bassett, Edward G., jt. ed. see Beers, Roland F., Jr.

Bassett, Fletcher S. Legends & Superstitions of the Sea & of Sailors, in All Lands & at All Times. LC 70-119444. (Illus.). 1974. Repr. of 1885 ed. 28.00 (ISBN 0-8103-3375-9). Gale.

Bassett, J. Inorganic Chemistry. 1965. text ed. 23.00 (ISBN 0-08-011207-2); pap. text ed. 9.75 o.p. (ISBN 0-08-011206-4). Pergamon.

Bassett, J., et al, eds. see Vogel, A. I.

Bassett, John, ed. William Faulkner: The Critical Heritage. (The Critical Heritage Ser.). 1975. 36.00 (ISBN 0-7100-8124-3). Routledge & Kegan.

Bassett, John S see Gabriel, Ralph H.

Bassett, Margaret. Profiles & Portraits of American Presidents. 1980. cancelled (ISBN 0-686-65651-2). McKay.

Bassett, Michael G. & Cocks, Leonard R. A Review of Silvrian Brachiopods from Gotland. (Fossils & Strata Ser: No. 3). 1974. 10.50x (ISBN 8-200-09349-2, Dist. by Columbia U Pr). Universitet.

Bassett, Preston R. & Bartlett, Margaret F. Raindrop Stories. LC 80-19036. (Illus.). 40p. (gr. k-3). 1981. 9.95 (ISBN 0-590-07628-0, Four Winds). Schol Bk Serv.

Bassett, R. G. Road Transport Management. 1975. 19.95x (ISBN 0-434-90097-4). Intl Ideas.

Bassett, Ronald. The Tinfish Run. LC 76-50167. 1977. 8.95 o.s.i. (ISBN 0-06-010233-0, HarpT). Har-Row.

Bassett, S. Denton. Public Religious Services in the Hospital. (Illus.). 80p. 1976. 12.675 (ISBN 0-398-03563-6). C C Thomas.

Bassett, Steve. The Battered Rich. Ashton, Sylvia, ed. 1980. 11.95 (ISBN 0-87949-159-0). Ashley Bks.

Bassett, William & Huizing, Peter, eds. The Financial Administration of the Church. (Concilium Ser.: Vol. 117). (Orig.). 1978. pap. 4.95 (ISBN 0-8164-2197-8). Crossroad NY.

--Judgement in the Church. (Concilium Ser.: Vol. 107). 1978. pap. 4.95 (ISBN 0-8164-2166-8). Crossroad NY.

Bassett, William, jt. ed. see Huizing, Peter.

Bassett, William W. & Huizing, Peter J., eds. Celibacy in the Church. LC 72-3943. (Concilium Ser.: Religion in the Seventies: Vol. 78). 156p. 1972. pap. 4.95 (ISBN 0-8164-2534-5). Crossroad NY.

Bassey, Linus A., ed. African Wise Sayings. 1980. pap. write for info. African Policy.

Bassey, M. School Science for Tomorrow's Citizens. 1963. pap. 4.20 (ISBN 0-08-009797-9). Pergamon.

Bassey, Michael. Nine Hundred Primary School Teachers. (General Ser.). (Illus.). 1978. pap. text ed. 12.50x (ISBN 0-85633-157-0, NFER). Humanities.

Bassham, Ben L., ed. see Warshawsky, Abel G.

Bassi, C., jt. auth. see Aloi, R.

Bassiouni, M. Cherif. International Criminal Law: A Draft International Criminal Code. LC 80-50452. 286p. 1980. 50.00x (ISBN 90-286-0130-9). Sijthoff & Noordhoff.

--International Terrorism & Political Crimes. 624p. 1975. pap. 29.75 (ISBN 0-398-03296-3). C C Thomas.

Bassiouni, M. Cherif & Nanda, Ved P. A Treatise on International Criminal Law, Vol.2: Jurisdiction & Cooperation. 448p. 1973. 59.50 (ISBN 0-398-02573-8); pap. 49.50 (ISBN 0-398-02628-9). C C Thomas.

Bassiouni, M. Cherif & Savitski, V. M. The Criminal Justice System of the USSR. 296p. 1979. text ed. 27.50 (ISBN 0-398-03868-6). C C Thomas.

Bassiouni, M. Cherif & Nanda, Ved P., eds. A Treatise on International Criminal Law, Vol. 1: Crimes & Punishment. 778p. 1973. pap. text ed. 54.75 (ISBN 0-398-02557-6). C C Thomas.

Bassler, G. Clayton, jt. auth. see Silverstein, Robert M.

Basso, Aldo P. Coins, Medals & Tokens of the Philippines. (Illus.). 144p. 1968. 5.95 (ISBN 0-912496-10-X). Shirjieh Pubs.

Basso, Bill. The Top of the Pizzas. LC 77-6085. (gr. 2-5). 1977. 6.50 (ISBN 0-396-07463-4). Dodd.

Basso, Keith H. Portraits of the Whiteman. LC 78-31535. 1979. 17.95 (ISBN 0-521-22640-6); pap. 4.95 (ISBN 0-521-29593-9). Cambridge U Pr.

Basson, Marc D., ed. Rights & Responisbilities in Modern Medicine: The Second Volume in a Series on Ethics, Humanism, & Medicine. (Progress in Clinical & Biological Research: Vol. 50). 250p. 1980. write for info. A R Liss.

Bassow, H. Construction & Use of Atomic & Molecular Models. 1968. 19.50 (ISBN 0-08-012925-0); pap. 9.75 (ISBN 0-08-012924-2). Pergamon.

Basten, Fred E. Bruin Country: A Pictorial Grand Tour of the Famed UCLA Campus. LC 80-83610. (Illus.). 128p. (Orig.). 1980. pap. 9.95 (ISBN 0-937536-02-4). Graphics Calif.

--An Illustrated Guide to the Legendary Trees of Santa Monica Bay. LC 80-83609. (Illus.). 128p. (Orig.). 1980. pap. 10.95 (ISBN 0-937536-01-6). Graphics Calif.

--Main St. to Malibu: Yesterday & Today. LC 80-83608. (Illus.). 128p. (Orig.). 1980. pap. 9.95 (ISBN 0-937536-00-8). Graphics Calif.

Bastenie, Paul A. & Ermans, A. M. Thyroiditis & Thyroid Function: Clinical, Morphological, & Physiopathological Studies. 360p. 1972. text ed. 82.00 (ISBN 0-08-016628-8). Pergamon.

Bastian, F. Defoe's Early Life. (Illus.). 456p. 1981. 36.00x (ISBN 0-389-20094-8). B&N.

Bastide, Marianne. Aspects De la Reforme De L'enseignement En Chine Au Debut Du XXe Siecle D'apres Des Ecrits De Zhang Jian. (Recherches: No. 64). (Illus.). 1971. pap. 28.80 (ISBN 0-686-22139-7). Mouton.

Bastien. I Want to Be Me. (gr. 7-12). pap. 0.95 o.p. (ISBN 0-686-68467-2, Schol Pap). Schol Bk Serv.

Bastille, Anne La see LaBastille, Anne.

Bastin, Bruce. Crying for the Carolines. (The Paul Oliver Blues Ser.). pap. 2.95 (ISBN 0-913714-31-3). Legacy Bks.

Bastin, E. W., ed. Quantum Theory & Beyond: Essays & Discussions Arising from a Colloquium. LC 77-127237. (Illus.). 1971. 43.00 (ISBN 0-521-07956-X). Cambridge U Pr.

Basu, Arindam. Picaro or Me. (Writers Workshop Greenbird Ser.). 90p. 1975. 12.00 (ISBN 0-88253-608-7); pap. text ed. 4.80 (ISBN 0-88253-607-9). Ind-US Inc.

Basu, Asoke, jt. auth. see Segalman, Ralph.

Basu, Keith. Revealed Preference of Government. LC 78-67300. 1980. 24.95 (ISBN 0-521-22489-6). Cambridge U Pr.

Basu, Manoje. The Beauty. Ghosh, Sachindra L., tr. 103p. 1969. pap. 1.80 (ISBN 0-88253-011-9). Ind-US Inc.

--Trappings of Gold. Ghosh, S. L., tr. 176p. 1969. pap. 2.00 (ISBN 0-88253-013-5). Ind-US Inc.

Basu, Rabindranath. Critical Study of the Malindapanha: Critique of Buddhist Philosophy. 1978. 7.50x o.p. (ISBN 0-8364-0141-7). South Asia Bks.

Basu, Romen. A Gift of Love. (Greenbird Bk.). 176p. 1975. 12.00 (ISBN 0-88253-823-3); pap. 5.00 (ISBN 0-88253-824-1). Ind-US Inc.

--The Tamarind Tree. (Greenbird Bk.). 1976. lib. bdg. 14.00 (ISBN 0-89253-119-3); flexible bdg. 8.00 (ISBN 0-89253-144-4). Ind-US Inc.

Basu, S. K. Economics of Hire Purchase Credit. 1971. 10.00x (ISBN 0-210-98135-0). Asia.

Basu, S. N. Jagadis Chandra Bose. (National Biography Ser.). (Orig.). 1979. pap. 2.50 (ISBN 0-89744-205-9). Auromere.

Basu, Sajal. The Politics of Violence: A Case Study of West Bengal. 1981. 11.00x (ISBN 0-685-59390-8). South Asia Bks.

Basu, T. K. Clinical Implications of Drug Use, 2 vols. 1981. Vol. 1, 160p. 49.95 (ISBN 0-8493-5391-2); Vol. 2, 144p. 49.95 (ISBN 0-8493-5392-0). CRC Pr.

Bata, L., ed. Advances in Liquid Crystal Research & Applications: Proceedings of the Third Liquid Crystal Conference of the Socialist Countries, Budapest, 27-31 August 1979. 1000p. 1981. 170.00 (ISBN 0-08-026191-4). Pergamon.

Bataille, George. Abbe C. Georges Bataille. Date not set. 10.00 (ISBN 0-89396-017-9). Urizen Bks.

Bataille, Georges. Literature & Evil. Hamilton, Alastair, tr. 1981. 12.95 (ISBN 0-89396-013-6); pap. 6.95 (ISBN 0-89396-014-4). Urizen Bks.

Bataille, Leon, ed. A Turning Point for Literacy-Adult Education for Development-Spirit & Declaration of Persepolis: Proceedings of the International Symposium for Literacy, Iran, 1975. LC 76-46206. 1976. text ed. 29.00 (ISBN 0-08-021385-5); pap. text ed. 16.00 (ISBN 0-08-021386-3). Pergamon.

Batalden, Paul B. & O'Conner, J. Paul. Quality Assurance in Ambulatory Care. LC 79-24700. 1980. text ed. 55.00 loose-leaf 3-ring binder (ISBN 0-89443-165-X). Aspen Systems.

Batch, Donald L., jt. auth. see Branson, Branley A.

Batchelder, Alan & Haitani, Kanji. International Economics: Theory & Practice. LC 70-21770. (Economics Ser.). 420p. 1981. text ed. 20.95 (ISBN 0-88244-231-7). Grid Pub.

Batchelder, J. W. Metric Madness: One Hundred Fifty Reasons for Not Converting to the Metric System. (Illus.). 250p. 1981. 12.95 (ISBN 0-8159-6220-7); pap. 5.95 (ISBN 0-8159-6219-3). Devin.

Batcheller. Music in Early Childhood. write for info. (ISBN 0-87628-212-5). Ctr Appl Res.

Batchelor, Edward, ed. Homosexuality & Ethics. LC 80-10533. 1980. 10.95 (ISBN 0-8298-0392-0). Pilgrim NY.

Batchelor, G. K., ed. see Taylor, Geoffrey I.

Batchelor, George K. Introduction to Fluid Dynamics. (Illus.). 634p. 1967. 71.50 (ISBN 0-521-04118-X); pap. 19.95x (ISBN 0-521-09817-3). Cambridge U Pr.

Batchelor, Ivor R., ed. see Henderson, David & Gillespie, R. D.

Batchelor, John. Existence & Imagination: The Theatre of Henry De Montherlant. 1967. text ed. 11.50x (ISBN 0-391-00421-2). Humanities.

Batchelor, John C. The Further Adventures of Halley's Comet. 640p. 1981. 17.95 (ISBN 0-312-92231-0); pap. 8.95 (ISBN 0-312-92232-9). Congdon & Lattes.

Batchelor, Kay & Brent, Kurt. You: The Complete Book of Self-Knowledge. LC 77-93326. (Illus.). 1978. 10.95 (ISBN 0-8069-4592-3); lib. bdg. 9.89 (ISBN 0-8069-4593-1). Sterling.

Batchelor, Mary. Bible Stories to Grow by. LC 80-65436. (Illus.). 96p. 1980. 8.95 (ISBN 0-915684-68-3). Christian Herald.

Batchelor, R. A., et al. Industrialisation & the Basis for Trade. LC 79-41582. (Economic & Social Studies: No. 32). 350p. 1980. 39.50 (ISBN 0-521-23302-X). Cambridge U Pr.

Bate, Lucy. Little Rabbit's Loose Tooth. (gr. k-3). 1978. pap. 1.95 (ISBN 0-590-11870-6, Schol Pap); pap. 3.50 bk. & record (ISBN 0-590-20621-4). Schol Bk Serv.

Bate, Marjorie D. & Casey, Mary C. Legal Office Procedures. 2nd ed. (Illus.). 544p. 1980. pap. text ed. 15.25 (ISBN 0-07-004058-3, G); instructor's manual & key avail. (ISBN 0-07-004059-1). McGraw.

Bate, Norman. Who Built the Bridge. (Encore Edition). (Illus.). (gr. k-5). 1954. 1.49 o.p. (ISBN 0-684-15828-0, ScribT). Scribner.

Bate, Paul, jt. auth. see Mangham, Ian.

Bate, Philip. The Flute. rev. ed. (Instruments of the Orchestra Ser.). 1980. 17.95 (ISBN 0-393-01292-1). Norton.

--The Oboe. 3rd ed. (Instruments of the Orchestra Ser). (Illus.). 1975. 13.95x o.p. (ISBN 0-393-02166-1). Norton.

Bate, R. T., jt. auth. see Carter, D. L.

Bate, Walter J., ed. Keats: A Collection of Critical Essays. (Orig.). 1964. pap. 2.95 (ISBN 0-13-514745-X, STC43, Spec). P-H.

Bately, Janet, ed. The Old English Orosius. (Early English Text Society Ser.). (Illus.). 558p. 1981. 65.00 (ISBN 0-19-722406-7). Oxford U Pr.

Bateman & Trott. The Foot & Ankle. 1980. 32.00. Thieme Stratton.

Bateman, A. M., jt. auth. see Jensen, M. L.

Bateman, Barbara, jt. auth. see Haring, Norris.

Bateman, David N., jt. auth. see Sigband, Norman B.

Bateman, Fred & Weiss, Thomas. A Deplorable Scarcity: The Failure of Industrialization in the Slave Economy. LC 80-13238. xii, 237p. 1981. 19.00x (ISBN 0-8078-1447-4). U of NC Pr.

Bateman, Harry. Differential Equations. LC 66-23754. 1967. 11.95 (ISBN 0-8284-0190-X). Chelsea Pub.

Bateman, J. E. Trapping: A Practical Guide. (Illus.). 190p. 1979. 14.95 (ISBN 0-8117-1743-7). Stackpole.

Bateman, James A. Animal Traps & Trapping. LC 70-144110. (Illus.). 228p. 1971. 10.95 (ISBN 0-8117-0103-4). Stackpole.

Bateman Manuscript Project, Calif. Inst. Technology. Higher Transcendental Functions, 3 vols. Incl. Vol. 1. 316p. Repr. of 1953 ed (ISBN 0-89874-206-4); Vol. 2. 414p. Repr. of 1953 ed; Vol. 3. 310p. Repr. of 1955 ed (ISBN 0-89874-207-2). LC 79-26544. 1980. lib. bdg. write for info. Krieger.

Bateman, Peter. Household Pests: A Guide to the Identification & Control of Insect, Rodent Damp & Fungoid Problems in the Home. (Illus.). 1979. 14.95 (ISBN 0-7137-0915-4, Pub by Blandford Pr England). Sterling.

Bateman, Py. Fear into Anger: A Manual of Self-Defense for Women. LC 77-19122. (Illus.). 1978. 15.95 (ISBN 0-88229-441-5); pap. 8.95 (ISBN 0-88229-603-5). Nelson-Hall.

Bateman, Wayne. Introduction to Computer Music. LC 79-26361. 314p. 1980. 24.95 (ISBN 0-471-05266-3, Pub. by Wiley-Interscience). Wiley.

Bater, James H. The Soviet City: Ideal & Reality. LC 80-51193. (Explorations in Urban Analysis: Vol. 2). 196p. 1980. 18.95x (ISBN 0-8039-1466-0); pap. 8.95x (ISBN 0-8039-1467-9). Sage.

Bates. Better Eyesight Without Glasses. 1970. pap. 2.95 (ISBN 0-515-05897-1, A2332). Jove Pubns.

Bates, Alan P. & Julian, Joseph. Sociology: Understanding Social Behavior. 1975. 19.50 (ISBN 0-395-18652-8); instructor's guide & resource manual by patricia a. harvey 1.75 (ISBN 0-395-18794-X). HM.

Bates, Albert C. The Work of Hartford's First Printer. 1925. pap. 0.50 (ISBN 0-686-26791-5). Conn Hist Soc.

Bates, Betty. Love Is Like Peanuts. 1981. pap. 1.75 (ISBN 0-671-56109-X). PB.

--Picking up the Pieces. LC 80-8811. 160p. 1981. 8.95 (ISBN 0-8234-0390-4). Holiday.

--The Ups & Downs of Jone Jenkins. 1981. pap. 1.75 (ISBN 0-671-29950-6). Archway.

Bates, Billy P. I. S. Q. D. (Identification System for Questioned Documents) (Illus.). 112p. 1970. text ed. 9.75 (ISBN 0-398-00108-1). C C Thomas.

Bates, D. R., ed. Quantum Theory. Incl. Pt. 1. Elements. 1961. 51.50 o.p. (ISBN 0-12-081401-3); Pt. 2. Aggregates of Particles. 1961. 51.50 o.p. (ISBN 0-12-081402-1); Pt. 3. Radiation & High Energy Physics. 1961. 51.50 o.p. (ISBN 0-12-081403-X). Acad Pr.

Bates, D. R., et al, eds. Advances in Atomic & Molecular Physics, Vols. 1-14. Incl. Vol. 1. 1965. 50.00 (ISBN 0-12-003801-3); Vol. 2. 1966. 50.00 (ISBN 0-12-003802-1); Vol. 3. 1968. 50.00 (ISBN 0-12-003803-X); Vol. 4. 1968. 50.00 (ISBN 0-12-003804-8); Vol. 5. 1969. 50.00 (ISBN 0-12-003805-6); Vol. 6. 1970. 50.00 (ISBN 0-12-003806-4); Vol. 7. 1971. 50.00 (ISBN 0-12-003807-2); Vol. 8. 1972. 50.00 (ISBN 0-12-003808-0); Vol. 9. 1974. 50.00 (ISBN 0-12-003809-9); Vol. 10. 1974. 50.00 (ISBN 0-12-003810-2); Vol. 11. 1976. 67.00 (ISBN 0-686-66770-0); lib ed. 86.25 (ISBN 0-12-003874-9); microfiche 47.75 (ISBN 0-12-003875-7); Vol. 12. 1976. 59.00 (ISBN 0-12-003812-9); lib ed. 76.00 (ISBN 0-12-003876-5); microfiche 42.25 (ISBN 0-12-003877-3); Vol. 13. 1978. 58.00 (ISBN 0-12-003813-7); lib ed. 74.50 (ISBN 0-12-003878-1); microfiche 36.00 (ISBN 0-12-003879-X); Vol. 14. 1979. 48.50 (ISBN 0-12-003814-5); lib ed. 62.50 (ISBN 0-12-003880-3); microfiche 35.00 (ISBN 0-12-003881-1). Acad Pr.

Bates, Daniel & Plog, Fred. Cultural Anthropology. 1979. pap. text ed. 12.95 (ISBN 0-394-32094-8). Knopf.

Bates, Daniel G. & Lees, Susan H. Contemporary Anthropology: An Anthology. 332p. 1981. pap. 8.95 (ISBN 0-394-32043-3). Knopf.

Bates, Darrell. The Abyssinian Difficulty: The Emperor Theodorus & the Magdala Campaign, 1867-68. (Illus.). 256p. 27.50x (ISBN 0-19-211747-5). Oxford U Pr.

Bates, David R., ed. Atomic & Molecular Processes. (Pure & Applied Physics Ser.: Vol. 13). 1962. 52.50 (ISBN 0-12-081450-1). Acad Pr.

Bates, Sir David R. & Bederson, Benjamin, eds. Advances in Atomic & Molecular Physics, Vol. 16. LC 65-18423. 1980. write for info. (ISBN 0-12-003816-1); lib. bdg. 61.50 (ISBN 0-12-003884-6); microfiche ed. 33.50 (ISBN 0-12-003885-4). Acad Pr.

Bates, Ernest. This Land of Liberty. LC 73-19817. (Civil Liberties in American History Ser.). 383p. 1974. Repr. of 1930 ed. lib. bdg. 35.00 (ISBN 0-306-70597-4). Da Capo.

Bates, G. L., jt. auth. see Gill, F. W.

Bates, Henry & Busenbark, Robert. Parrots. (Orig.). pap. 2.00 (ISBN 0-87666-427-3, M506). TFH Pubns.

Bates, Henry W. Naturalist on the Amazons. 1969. 5.00x o.p. (ISBN 0-460-00446-8, Evman). Dutton.

Bates, Herbert E. Oh to Be in England. 167p. 1963. 4.50 o.p. (ISBN 0-374-22492-7). FS&G.

Bates, Jefferson D. Dictating Effectively: A Time Saving Manual. (Illus.). 1980. 12.50 (ISBN 0-87491-411-6); pap. 5.95 (ISBN 0-87491-414-0). Acropolis.

Bates, Joseph D., Jr. Fishing: An Encyclopedic Guide to Tackle & Tactics for Fresh & Salt Water. 1974. 16.95 (ISBN 0-87690-110-0). Dutton.

Bates, Kenneth F. Basic Design: Principles & Practice. LC 74-25356. (Funk & W Bk.). (Illus.). 176p. 1975. pap. 3.95 o.p. (ISBN 0-308-10151-0, F-110, TYC-T). T Y Crowell.

Bates, M., et al. Nucleus. write for info. (ISBN 0-686-19151-X). Longman.

Bates, M. Searle. Religious Liberty: An Inquiry. LC 77-166096. (Civil Liberties in American History Ser.). 1972. Repr. of 1945 ed. lib. bdg. 39.50 (ISBN 0-306-70235-5). Da Capo.

Bates, Margaret. The Belfast Cookery Book. 222p. 1975. pap. 10.00 (ISBN 0-08-018952-0). Pergamon.

--Talking About Cakes with an Irish & Scottish Accent. 1964. text ed. 15.00 (ISBN 0-08-010004-X). Pergamon.

Bates, Marilyn, jt. auth. see Keirsey, David.

Bates, Marston. Animal Worlds. (Illus.). (YA) 1963. 20.00 o.p. (ISBN 0-394-41533-7). Random.

--Forest & the Sea. 1965. pap. 2.45 (ISBN 0-394-70292-1, V-292, Vin). Random.

--Gluttons & Libertines: Human Problems of Being Natural. LC 66-11978. 1971. pap. 2.45 (ISBN 0-394-71267-6, V-267, Vin). Random.

--Land & Wildlife of South America. LC 64-19009. (Life Nature Library). (Illus.). (gr. 5 up). 1964. PLB 8.97 o.p. (ISBN 0-8094-0630-6, Pub. by Time-Life). Silver.

--The Natural History of Mosquitos. (Illus.). 8.25 (ISBN 0-8446-0480-1). Peter Smith.

Bates, Matthew. Worked Examples in Engineering in Si Units: Vol. 1 Engineering Science. 1974. pap. text ed. 7.95x o.p. (ISBN 0-04-620003-7). Allen Unwin.

--Worked Examples in Engineering in Si Units: Vol. 2 Electrical Science. 1974. pap. text ed. 7.95x o.p. (ISBN 0-04-620005-3). Allen Unwin.

--Worked Examples in Engineering in Si Units: Vol. 3 Electrical Engineering. 1974. pap. text ed. 7.95x o.p. (ISBN 0-04-620007-X). Allen Unwin.

Bates, R. C. The Fine Art of Understanding Patients. 1968. pap. 5.95 (ISBN 0-87489-019-5). Med Economics.

Bates, R. W. & Fraser, N. M. Investment Decisions in the Nationalized Fuel Industries. LC 74-76575. (Illus.). 208p. 1974. 29.50 (ISBN 0-521-20455-0). Cambridge U Pr.

Bates, Robert B. & Beavers, William A. Carbon-Thirteen NMR Spectral Problems. LC 79-92216. (Organic Chemistry Ser.). 288p. 1981. text ed. 24.50x (ISBN 0-89603-010-5); pap. text ed. 12.50x (ISBN 0-89603-016-4). Humana.

Bates, Robert H. Ethnicity in Contemporary Africa. LC 73-86994. (Foreign & Comparative Studies-Eastern African Ser.: No. 14). 59p. 1973. pap. 3.50x (ISBN 0-915984-11-3). Syracuse U Foreign Comp.

Bates, Robert H. & Lofchie, Michael F. Agricultural Development in Africa: Issues of Public Policy. LC 79-24914. 464p. 1980. 36.95 (ISBN 0-03-056173-6). Praeger.

Bates, Robert L. Geology of the Industrial Rocks & Minerals. (Illus.). 10.00 (ISBN 0-8446-0481-X). Peter Smith.

Bates, Scott. Guillaume Apollinaire. (World Authors Ser.: France: No. 14). lib. bdg. 10.95 (ISBN 0-8057-2052-9). Twayne.

Bates, Susannah. The Pendex: An Index of Pen Names & House Names in Fantastic, Thriller & Series Literature. LC 80-8486. 200p. 1981. lib. bdg. 22.50 (ISBN 0-8240-9501-4). Garland Pub.

Bates, T. D. & Berry, R. J., eds. High Dose-Rate Afterloading in the Treatment of Cancer of the Uterus. 1980. 90.00x (Pub. by Brit Inst Radiology). State Mutual Bk.

Bates, Timothy & Bradford, William. Financing Black Economic Development. (Institute for Research on Poverty Policy Analysis Ser.). 1979. 17.50 (ISBN 0-12-081650-4); pap. 8.50 (ISBN 0-12-081652-0). Acad Pr.

Bates, Timothy M. Black Capitalism: A Quantitative Analysis. LC 73-9060. (Special Studies in U.S. Economic,Social & Political Issues). 1973. 27.50x (ISBN 0-89197-680-9). Irvington.

Bates, W. H. Better Eyesight Without Glasses. 208p. (Orig.). 1981. pap. 2.95 (ISBN 0-03-058012-9). HR&W.

Bateson. Introduction to Control Systems Technology. 2nd ed. (Technology Ser.). 560p. 1980. text ed. 23.95 (ISBN 0-675-08255-2); instructor's manual 3.95 (ISBN 0-686-63341-5). Merrill.

Bateson, F. W. A Guide to English & American Literature. 3rd ed. 352p. 1977. pap. text ed. 13.95 (ISBN 0-582-48417-0). Longman.

Bateson, Gregory. Naven. 2nd ed. (Illus.). 1958. 17.50x (ISBN 0-8047-0519-4); pap. 6.95 (ISBN 0-8047-0520-8). Stanford U Pr.

Bateson, P. P. & Hinde, R. A., eds. Growing Points in Ethology. LC 76-8291. (Illus.). 500p. 1976. 57.50 (ISBN 0-521-21287-1); pap. 16.95x (ISBN 0-521-29086-4). Cambridge U Pr.

Bateson, P. P. & Klopfer, Peter H., eds. Perspectives in Ethology: Advantages of Diversity, Vol. 4. 230p. 1980. 25.00 (ISBN 0-306-40511-3, Plenum Pr). Plenum Pub.

Bates-Yakobson, Helen, jt. auth. see Von Gronicka, Andre.

Batey, Richard. Letter of Paul to the Romans. Ferguson, Everett, et al, eds. LC 68-58865. (Living Word New Testament Commentary Ser.: Vol. 7). 1969. 7.95 (ISBN 0-8344-0002-2). Sweet.

Batey, Richard A. Thank God, I'M O.K. The Gospel According to T.A. LC 76-14358. 1976. pap. 2.95 o.p. (ISBN 0-687-41389-3). Abingdon.

Bath, Geoffrey, ed. The State of the Universe. (Illus.). 200p. 1980. 24.95x (ISBN 0-19-857549-1). Oxford U Pr.

Bath, Tony. Hannibal's Campaigns. (Illus.). 160p. 1981. 31.95 (ISBN 0-85059-492-8). Aztex.

Batham, M. J. Guide to Travel Agency Accounting. LC 78-60276. 1979. 12.00 o.p. (ISBN 0-916032-05-1). Merton Hse.

Bathe, Klaus, et al, eds. Formulations & Computational Algorithms in Finite-Element Analysis: U. S. German Symposium. 1977. text ed. 47.50x (ISBN 0-262-02127-7). MIT Pr.

Bathe, Klaus-Jurgen & Wilson, Edward L. Numerical Methods in Finite Element Analysis. (Illus.). 544p. 1976. 33.95 (ISBN 0-13-627190-1). P-H.

Batherman, Muriel. Before Columbus. (gr. k-3). 1981. 8.95 (ISBN 0-395-30088-6). HM.

Bathes, Roland. Camera Lucida: Reflections on Photography. Howard, Richard, tr. (Illus.). 1981. 11.95 (ISBN 0-8090-3340-2). Hill & Wang.

Batho, Edith C., ed. Wordsworth Selection. 1962. pap. text ed. 1.75x (ISBN 0-485-61004-3, Athlone Pr). Humanities.

Bathory, Peter D. Political Theory As Public Confession. 307p. 1981. 24.95 (ISBN 0-87855-405-X); text ed. 24.95 (ISBN 0-686-68058-8). Transaction Bks.

Bathrick, David D. Agricultural Credit for Small Farm Development: Policies & Practices. (Westview Special Studies in Social, Political, & Economic Development). (Illus.). 1981. lib. bdg. 17.50x (ISBN 0-86531-037-8). Westview.

Bathurst, P. E. & Butler, D. A. Building Cost Control Techniques & Economics. 1973. pap. 14.95x (ISBN 0-434-90101-6). Intl Ideas.

Batist, Bessie, ed. A Treasure for My Daughter. pap. 3.95 (ISBN 0-8015-7939-2, Hawthorn). Dutton.

Batlelier, Pieter Dom, ed. Saint Benedict. (Illus.). 450p. 125.00 (ISBN 0-933516-19-3). Alpine Fine Arts.

Batman, Stephen. The Golden Booke of the Leaden Gods, Repr. Of 1577 Ed. Bd. with The Third Part of the Countess of Pembroke's Yvychurch. Fraunce, Abraham. Repr. of 1592 ed; The Fountaine of Ancient Fiction. Lynche, Richard. Repr. of 1599 ed. LC 75-27856. (Renaissance & the Gods Ser.: Vol. 13). (Illus.). 1976. lib. bdg. 73.00 (ISBN 0-8240-2062-6). Garland Pub.

Batog, Tadeusz. Axiomatic Method in Phonology. 1968. text ed. 8.50x (ISBN 0-7100-2980-2). Humanities.

Batra, Gretchen, jt. ed. see Markson, Elizabeth.

Batra, Lekh R., ed. Insect Fungus Symbiosis: Nutrition, Mutualism & Commensalism. LC 78-20640. 288p. 1979. text ed. 27.50 (ISBN 0-470-26671-6). Allanheld.

Batra, Neelam. Clinical Pathology for Medical Students. 240p. 1981. text ed. 18.95x (ISBN 0-7069-1117-2, Pub. by Vikas India). Advent Bk.

Batra, R. N. The Pure Theory of International Trade Under Uncertainty. LC 74-4820. 1975. text ed. 24.95 (ISBN 0-470-05687-8). Halsted Pr.

Batra, Ravi. Prout: The Alternative to Capitalism & Marxism. LC 80-67184. 221p. 1980. lib. bdg. 16.75 (ISBN 0-8191-1187-2); pap. text ed. 8.50 (ISBN 0-8191-1188-0). U Pr of Amer.

Batsakis, John G., et al. Pathology of the Salivary Glands. LC 77-3537. (Head & Neck Atlas Ser.). (Illus.). 1977. slide atlas 95.00 (ISBN 0-89189-031-9, 15-1-0019-00). Am Soc Clinical.

Batschelet, E. Introduction to Mathematics for Life Scientists. 2nd ed. LC 75-11755. (Biomathematics Ser.: Vol. 2). (Illus.). 643p. 1975. 29.00 o.p. (ISBN 0-387-07293-4); pap. text ed. 13.20 o.p. (ISBN 0-387-07350-7). Springer-Verlag.
Batschelet, Ralph J. The Flick & I. 176p. 1981. 9.00 (ISBN 0-682-49717-7). Exposition.
Batshaw, Mark L. & Perret, Yvonne M. Children with Handicaps: A Medical Primer. (Illus.). 300p. 1981. price not set (ISBN 0-933716-16-8). P H Brookes.
Batson, H. E., tr. see Von Mises, Ludwig.
Batson, Larry. Bill Walton. LC 74-16498. (Sports Superstars Ser.). (Illus.). 32p. (gr. 3-9). 1974. PLB 5.50 o.p. (ISBN 0-87191-379-8). Creative Ed.
--Evel Knievel. LC 74-18302. (Sports Superstars Ser). (Illus.). 32p. (gr. 3-6). 1974. PLB 5.95 (ISBN 0-87191-385-2); pap. 2.75 o. p. (ISBN 0-89812-191-4). Creative Ed.
--An Interview with Alan Page. (Interviews Ser.). (Illus.). (gr. 3-8). 1977. PLB 6.75 (ISBN 0-87191-569-3). Creative Ed.
--An Interview with Bobby Knight. (Interviews Ser.). (Illus.). (gr. 3-8). 1977. PLB 6.75 (ISBN 0-87191-574-X). Creative Ed.
--An Interview with Jim Plunkett. (Interviews Ser.). (Illus.). (gr. 3-8). 1977. PLB 6.75 (ISBN 0-87191-570-7). Creative Ed.
--An Interview with Rod Carew. (Interviews Ser.). (Illus.). (gr. 3-8). 1977. PLB 5.95 o.p. (ISBN 0-87191-568-5). Creative Ed.
--Walt Frazier. LC 74-2013. (Creative Superstars Ser.). 32p. 1974. PLB 5.95 (ISBN 0-87191-348-8); pap. 2.95 (ISBN 0-89812-179-5). Creative Ed.
Batson, Wade T. Wild Flowers in South Carolina. LC 64-23760. (Illus.). 146p. 1980. pap. 5.95 (ISBN 0-87249-257-5). U of SC Pr.
Batstone, Eric, et al. The Social Organization of Strikes. (Warwick Studies in Industrial Relations). 1978. 14.50x (ISBN 0-631-18320-5, Pub. by Basil Blackwell England). Biblio Dist.
--Shop Stewards in Action: The Organization of Workplace Conflict & Accomodation. 1977. 20.00x o.p. (ISBN 0-631-17260-2, Pub. by Basil Blackwell); pap. 11.50x (ISBN 0-631-16690-4). Biblio Dist.
Battagila, Frederick C. & Hagerman, Dwain D. Perinatal Medicine: Review & Comments. 2nd ed. Meschia, Giacomo & Quilligan, E. J., eds. (Illus.). 1978. text ed. 25.00 o.p. (ISBN 0-8016-0513-X). Mosby.
Battaglia, Aurelius, illus. Animals Sounds. (Golden Sturdy Bk.). (Illus.). 22p. 1981. 3.50 (ISBN 0-307-12122-4, Golden Pr). Western Pub.
Battaglia, R. A. & Mayrose, V. Handbook of Animal Management Techniques. 608p. 1981. write for info. (ISBN 0-8087-2957-8). Burgess.
Battan, Louis J. Fundamentals of Meteorology. 1979. 17.95 (ISBN 0-13-341131-1). P-H.
--The Nature of Violent Storms. LC 80-24986. (Science Study Ser.: No. S19). (Illus.). 158p. 1981. Repr. of 1961 ed. lib. bdg. 19.50x (ISBN 0-313-22582-6, BANV). Greenwood.
--The Unclean Sky: A Meteorologist Looks at Air Pollution. LC 80-23434. (Selected Topics in the Atmospheric Sciences, Science Study Ser.). (Illus.). xii, 141p. 1980. Repr. of 1966 ed. lib. bdg. 19.50x (ISBN 0-313-22710-1, BAUS). Greenwood.
Battcher, Joyce, jt. auth. see Dlugosch, Sharon.
Battcock, Gregory. Breaking the Sound Barrier: A Critical Anthology of the New Music. (Thomas Congdon Bk.). (Illus.). 1981. pap. 9.95 (ISBN 0-525-47640-7). Dutton.
Battcock, Gregory, ed. & intro. by. Minimal Art: A Critical Anthology. 1968. pap. 7.50 (ISBN 0-525-47211-8). Dutton.
--New Ideas in Art Education: A Critical Anthology. 1973. pap. 2.95 o.p. (ISBN 0-525-47345-9). Dutton.
--Super Realism: A Critical Anthology. 352p. 1975. pap. 10.95 (ISBN 0-525-47377-7). Dutton.
Battelle Columbus Laboratories. Preliminary Environmental Assessment of Biomass Conversion to Synthetic Fuels. 346p. 1980. pap. 24.95 (ISBN 0-89934-049-0, B049-PP). Solar Energy Info.
Battelle Columbus Labs. Solar Energy Employment & Requirements: 1978-1983. 200p. 1981. pap. 24.50 (ISBN 0-89934-102-0). Solar Energy Info.
Batten, A. H. Binary & Multiple Systems of Stars. LC 72-88026. 288p. 1973. 32.00 (ISBN 0-08-016986-4). Pergamon.
Batten, Charles L., Jr. Pleasurable Instruction: Form & Convention in Eighteenth-Century Travel Literature. LC 76-14316. 1978. 16.50x (ISBN 0-520-03260-8). U of Cal Pr.
Batten, H. Mortimer. Singing Forest. (Illus.). 214p. (gr. 6 up). 1964. 3.95 (ISBN 0-374-26468-6). FS&G.
Batten, J. D. Developing a Tough-Minded Climate for Results. LC 65-16483. 1965. 14.95 (ISBN 0-8144-5101-2). Am Mgmt.
--Tough-Minded Management. 3rd rev. ed. 1978. 14.95 (ISBN 0-8144-5477-1). Am Mgmt.
Batten, Jack. The Complete Jogger. (Illus.). 1978. pap. 1.95 (ISBN 0-515-04858-5). Jove Pubns.
Batten, Jack, jt. auth. see McKay, Heather.
Batten, Joseph D. Expectations & Possiblities. LC 80-17102. 368p. 1981. text ed. write for info. (ISBN 0-201-00093-8). A-W.
Batten, L. W. Ezra & Nehemiah. LC 13-12806. (International Critical Commentary Ser.). 400p. Repr. of 1913 ed. 20.00x (ISBN 0-567-05008-4). Attic Pr.
Batten, Peter & Stancil, Deborah. Living Trophies: A Shocking Look at the Conditions in America's Zoos. LC 75-40211. (Illus.). 272p. 1976. 9.95 o.s.i. (ISBN 0-690-01096-6, TYC-T). T y Crowell.
Batten, Robert W. Mortality Table Construction. LC 77-12349. (Risk, Insurance & Security Ser.). (Illus.). 1978. 17.95 (ISBN 0-13-601302-3). P-H.
Batten, Roger L., jt. auth. see Dott, Robert H.
Batten, Thomas R. Communities & Their Development: An Introductory Study with Special Reference to the Tropics. LC 80-14699. (Illus.). vi, 248p. 1980. Repr. of 1957 ed. lib. bdg. 22.50x (ISBN 0-313-22447-1, BACD). Greenwood.
Batten, William T. Understanding the IBM Three-Sixty & Three-Seventy Computer with Machine Language Programming. (Illus.). 480p. 1974. 17.95 (ISBN 0-13-936096-4). P-H.
Batterberry, Michael, jt. auth. see Ruskin, Ariane.
Batterham, R. G. Slipform Concrete. (Illus.). 96p. 1980. text ed. 19.95 cased (ISBN 0-86095-855-8). Longman.
Battersby, W. J. De la Salle: A Pioneer of Modern Education. 236p. 1981. Repr. of 1949 ed. lib. bdg. 40.00 (ISBN 0-89987-065-1). Darby Bks.
Battersfy, Martin. Decorative Thirties. 208p. 1975. pap. 7.95 o.s.i. (ISBN 0-02-000210-6, Collier). Macmillan.
--The Decorative Twenties. 216p. 1975. pap. 7.95 o.s.i. (ISBN 0-02-000200-9, Collier). Macmillan.
Battershaw, Brian, tr. see Gorlitz, Walter.
Battershill, Norman. Painting & Drawing Skies. 156p. 1981. 19.95 (ISBN 0-8230-3558-1). Watson-Guptill.
--Painting Landscapes in Oils. (Leisure Arts Painting Ser.). (Illus.). 32p. 1980. pap. 2.50 (ISBN 0-8008-6202-3, Pentalic). Taplinger.
--Working with Oils. (Leisure Arts Painting Ser.). (Illus.). 32p. 1980. pap. 2.50 (ISBN 0-8008-8542-2, Pentalic). Taplinger.
Battestin, Martin, ed. see Fielding, Henry.
Battestin, Martin C. Moral Basis of Fielding's Art: A Study of Joseph Andrews. LC 59-10177. 1959. 15.00x (ISBN 0-8195-3007-7, Pub. by Wesleyan U Pr); pap. 6.00 (ISBN 0-8195-6038-3). Columbia U Pr.
Battey, M. H. Mineralogy for Students. (Illus.). 1975. pap. text ed. 17.95 (ISBN 0-582-44159-5). Longman.
Battey, M. H., ed. see Vlasov, K. A., et al.
Battezzati, M. & Donini, I. The Lymphatic System. Cameron-Curry, U., tr. from It. LC 73-9924. 496p. 1974. 52.95 (ISBN 0-470-05706-8). Halsted Pr.
Battino, R. Oxygen & Ozone: Gas Solubilities. (Solubility Data Ser.: Vol. 5). 1981. 100.00 (ISBN 0-08-023915-3). Pergamon.
Battison, Edward A. & Kane, Patricia E. The American Clock, 1725-1865: From the Mabel Brady Garvan & Other Collections at Yale University. LC 72-93856. (Illus.). 208p. 1973. 19.95 (ISBN 0-8212-0493-9, 036706). NYGS.
Battison, Robbin, jt. auth. see Baker, Charlotte.
Battista, O. A. Quotoons: A Speakers Dictionary. 472p. 1981. 13.95 (ISBN 0-399-12573-6, Perigee); 5.95 (ISBN 0-399-50514-8). Putnam.
--World Olympiad of Knowledge - 1984, a Novel. 1981. 9.95. Research Servs.
Battiste see Jackson, et al.
Battistella, Roger M. & Rundall, Thomas G., eds. Health Care Policy in a Changing Environment. LC 78-57148. 1979. 23.50 (ISBN 0-8211-0131-5); text ed. 21.00 in ten or more copies (ISBN 0-686-67039-6). McCutchan.
Battistin, Leontino, et al, eds. Neurochemistry & Clinical Neurology. LC 80-7475. (Progress in Clinical & Biological Research Ser.: Vol. 39). 512p. 1980. 38.00 (ISBN 0-8451-0039-4). A R Liss.
Battle, Dennis M. America's Future in Symbolic Prophecy. (Illus.). 52p. 1981. pap. 2.50 (ISBN 0-933464-10-X). D M Battle Pubns.
--Armageddon: Heaven's Holy War on Earth. LC 80-65197. 56p. 1980. pap. 2.50 (ISBN 0-933464-07-X). D M Battle Pubns.
--The Beast's Mark & Number: 666. (Illus.). 52p. 1981. pap. 2.50 (ISBN 0-933464-11-8). D M Battle Pubns.
--The Gospel Religion of Jesus Christ. 52p. 1980. pap. 2.25 (ISBN 0-933464-08-8). D M Battle Pubns.
--Life After Death? (Illus.). 52p. 1981. pap. 2.00 (ISBN 0-933464-13-4). D M Battle Pubns.
--UFO Invaders Deceive Every Nation. LC 80-65199. 52p. 1980. pap. 2.50 (ISBN 0-933464-06-1). D M Battle Pubns.
Battle, Edith K. Our Children Ask About God. 1944. pap. 0.25 (ISBN 0-687-29515-7). Abingdon.
Battle, Gerald N. Simon Peter: The Boy Who Became a Fisherman. LC 75-135353. (Illus.). (gr. 3-7). 1970. 3.95 o.p. (ISBN 0-87680-179-3). Word Bks.
Battle, James. Canadian Self-Esteem Inventories for Children & Adults. 1981. pap. 45.50 for complete battery (ISBN 0-686-69429-5). Spec Child.
Battles, Edith. Eddie Couldn't Find the Elephants. LC 74-13997. (Self Starter Bks.). (Illus.). 32p. (gr. k-2). 1974. 6.50g (ISBN 0-8075-1877-8). A Whitman.
--One to Teeter-Totter. LC 72-13348. (Self Starter Bks.). (Illus.). 32p. (ps-1). 1973. 6.50g (ISBN 0-8075-6103-7). A Whitman.
--What Does the Rooster Say, Yoshio? Pacini, Kathy, ed. LC 78-12824. (Self-Starter Bks). (Illus.). (ps-2). 1978. 6.50g (ISBN 0-8075-8833-4). A Whitman.
Battles, Ford L. & Walchenbach, John. An Analysis of "The Institute of the Christian Religion" of John Calvin. 1980. pap. 10.95 (ISBN 0-8010-0766-6). Baker Bk.
Battles, Ford L., jt. auth. see Rosenstock-Huessy, Eugen.
Battley, Harry. Single Finger Prints: A New & Practical Method of Classifying & Filing Single Finger Prints & Fragmentary Impressions. (Illus.). 1931. 42.50x (ISBN 0-686-51311-8). Elliots Bks.
Battocletti, Joseph H. see Rose, J. & Weidener, E. W.
Batts, Michael S. Gottfried von Strassburg. (World Authors Ser.: Germany: No. 167). lib. bdg. 10.95 (ISBN 0-8057-2866-X). Twayne.
Battuta, Ibn. Ibn Battuta in Black Africa. Hamdun, Said & King, Noel, trs. from Arabic. 99p. (Orig.). 1978. pap. 5.00x (ISBN 0-901720-57-7, Dist. for Rex Collings, London). Three Continents.
Batty, Eric. Coaching Modern Soccer: Attack. (Illus.). 128p. 1980. 15.95 (ISBN 0-571-09840-1, Pub. by Faber & Faber); pap. 6.95 (ISBN 0-571-11605-1, Pub. by Faber & Faber). Merrimack Bk Serv.
--Soccer Coaching the Modern Way. 2nd ed. (Illus., Orig.). 1975. pap. 5.95 o.p. (ISBN 0-571-10648-X, Pub. by Faber & Faber). Merrimack Bk Serv.
Batty, Eric G., et al, eds. International Football Book, No. 22. (Illus.). 142p. (YA) 1980. text ed. 17.50x (ISBN 0-285-62445-8, SpS). Soccer.
Batty, I., jt. auth. see Sterne, M.
Batty, J. Accounting for Research & Development. 237p. 1976. text ed. 23.50x (Pub. by Busn Bks England). Renouf.
--The Board & the Presentation of Financial Information to Management. 340p. 1978. text ed. 36.75x (ISBN 0-220-66352-1, Pub. by Busn Bks England). Renouf.
Batty, J., ed. Cost & Management Accountancy for Students. 2nd ed. 1970. pap. text ed. 15.95x (ISBN 0-434-90112-1). Intl Ideas.
Batty, J., et al. Industrial Administration & Management. 4th ed. (Illus.). 592p. 1979. pap. 16.95x (ISBN 0-7121-0954-4, Pub. by Macdonald & Evans England). Intl Ideas.
Batty, J. W. Textile Auxiliaries. 1967. pap. 5.75 (ISBN 0-08-012381-3). Pergamon.
Batty, M. Urban Modelling. (Cambridge Urban & Architectural Studies). (Illus.). 384p. 1976. 60.00 (ISBN 0-521-20881-5). Cambridge U Pr.
Battye, Marguerite, jt. auth. see White, Edwin.
Baty, jt. auth. see Himstreet.
Baty, Gordon. Entrepreneurship in the Eighties. 1981. text ed. 17.95 (ISBN 0-8359-1745-2); pap. text ed. 12.95 (ISBN 0-8359-1744-4). Reston.
Baty, Wayne M., jt. auth. see Himstreet, William C.
Batya, Judith, jt. auth. see Penn, Gerald M.
Batzler, L. Richard, jt. auth. see Tauraso, Nicola M.
Bau, Mingchien J. Modern Democracy in China: Studies in Chinese Government & Law. 467p. 1977. Repr. of 1923 ed. 25.00 (ISBN 0-89093-060-0). U Pubns Amer.
Bauby, Cathrina. Between Consenting Adults. 252p. 1973. 7.95 o.s.i. (ISBN 0-02-507700-7). Macmillan.
Baucom, Marta E. & Causby, Ralph E. Total Communication Used in Experience Based Speechreading & Auditory Training Lesson Plans: For Hard of Hearing & Deaf Individuals. (Illus.). 96p. 1981. 12.50 (ISBN 0-398-04124-5); pap. 7.75 (ISBN 0-398-04125-3). C C Thomas.
Baud, Charles A. Harmonie der Gesichtszuege. (Illus.). 1981. pap. 29.50 (ISBN 3-8055-0067-X). S Karger.
Baudeau, Nicolas. Explication Du Tableau Economique. (Fr.). 1977. lib. bdg. 24.00x o.p. (ISBN 0-8287-0063-X); pap. text ed. 14.00x o.p. (ISBN 0-685-74925-8). Clearwater Pub.
Baudelaire, Charles. Eugene Delacroix: His Life & Works. Freedberg, Sydney J., ed. LC 77-18676. (Connoisseurship Criticism & Art History Ser.: Vol. 2). (Illus.). 1979. lib. bdg. 24.00 (ISBN 0-8240-3258-6). Garland Pub.
--Fatal Destinies: The Edgar Poe Essays. Mele, Joan F., tr. from Fr. 1981. 10.95 (ISBN 0-916696-16-2); pap. 4.95 (ISBN 0-916696-17-0). Cross Country.
--Les Fleurs du Mal. Starkie, Enid, ed. (French Texts Ser.). 1970. pap. text ed. 10.50x (ISBN 0-631-00410-6, Pub. by Basil Blackwell). Biblio Dist.
--Intimate Journals. Isherwood, Christopher, tr. from Fr. LC 75-1454. 1977. Repr. of 1930 ed. 13.25 (ISBN 0-86527-262-X). Fertig.
--Oeuvres critiques: Petits Poemes en prose. (Nouveaux Classiques Larousse). (Fr). pap. 2.95 (ISBN 0-685-14010-5, 20). Larousse.
--The Painter of Modern Life & Other Essays. Freedberg, Sydney J., ed. LC 77-18671. (Connoisseurship Criticism & Art History Ser.: Vol. 1). 224p. 1979. lib. bdg. 27.00 (ISBN 0-8240-3257-8). Garland Pub.
--Paris Spleen. Varese, Louise, tr. LC 48-5012. 1970. pap. 3.95 (ISBN 0-8112-0007-8, NDP294). New Directions.
--Selected Flowers of Evil. rev. ed. Mathews, Marthiel & Mathews, Jackson, eds. LC 58-9276. (Eng & Fr). 1946. pap. 2.95 (ISBN 0-8112-0006-X, NDP71). New Directions.
Baudelaire, Charles P. Baudelaire: A Self-Portrait. Hyslop, Lois B. & Hyslop, Francis E., eds. LC 78-20447. 1981. Repr. of 1957 ed. 22.00 (ISBN 0-88355-827-0). Hyperion Conn.
Baudendistel, Robert F. Horticulture: A Basic Awareness. (Illus.). 1978. pap. 15.95 ref. ed. (ISBN 0-8359-2891-8); instrs'. manual avail. Reston.
Baudin, Louis. Daily Life in Peru Under the Last Incas. Bradford, Winifred, tr. (Illus.). 1962. 10.95 (ISBN 0-02-507870-4). Macmillan.
Baudin, Robert. Confessions of a Promiscuous Counterfeiter. LC 78-22243. 1979. 9.95 (ISBN 0-15-121853-6). HarBraceJ.
Baudoin, E. Margaret, et al. Reader's Choice: A Reading Skills Textbook for Students of English As a Second Language. 1977. pap. 7.50x (ISBN 0-472-08100-4). U of Mich Pr.
Baudot, Marcel, et al. Historical Encyclopedia of World War II. Dilson, Jesse, tr. 500p. 1980. 24.95 (ISBN 0-87196-401-5). Facts on File.
Baudouin, Frans. Rubens. LC 77-82339. (Illus.). 1977. 60.00 o.p. (ISBN 0-8109-1586-3). Abrams.
Baudouin, Jean. Mythologie, 2 vols. LC 75-27871. (Renaissance & the Gods Ser.: Vol. 26). (Illus.). 1976. Repr. of 1627 ed. Set. lib. bdg. 146.00 (ISBN 0-8240-2075-8); lib. bdg. 73.00 ea. Garland Pub.
Baudouin, Jean, tr. see Ripa, Cesare.
Baudouin de Courtenay, Jan. Baudouin de Courtenay Anthology: The Beginnings of Structural Linguistics. Stankiewicz, Edward, tr. LC 78-135012. (History & Theory of Linguistics Ser.). 412p. 1972. 21.95x (ISBN 0-253-31120-9). Ind U Pr.
Baudrillard, Jean. For a Critique of the Political Economy of the Sign. Levin, Charles, tr. from Fr. lib. bdg. 14.00 (ISBN 0-914386-23-9); pap. 4.50 (ISBN 0-914386-24-7). Telos Pr.
--The Mirror of Production. Poster, Mark, tr. LC 74-82994. 1975. pap. 3.95 (ISBN 0-914386-06-9). Telos Pr.
Bauer, A. J. Chilean Rural Society from the Spanish Conquest to 1930. LC 75-2724. (Cambridge Latin American Studies: No. 21). (Illus.). 311p. 1975. 32.95 (ISBN 0-521-20727-4). Cambridge U Pr.
Bauer, Arnold. Carl Zuckmayer. LC 75-29600. (Modern Literature Ser.). 1976. 10.95 (ISBN 0-8044-2026-2). Ungar.
--Rainer Maria Rilke. Lamm, Ursula, tr. LC 75-163151. (Modern Literature Ser.). 128p. 1972. 10.95 (ISBN 0-8044-2025-4). Ungar.
--Thomas Mann. Henderson, Alexander & Henderson, Elizabeth, trs. from Ger. LC 71-139221. (Modern Literature Ser.). 1971. 10.95 (ISBN 0-8044-2023-8); pap. 3.45 (ISBN 0-8044-6018-3). Ungar.
Bauer, Barbara & Moss, Robert. Judge Horton & the Scottsboro Boys. 1977. pap. 1.75 o.p. (ISBN 0-345-25268-3). Ballantine.
Bauer, C. R. & Peluso, A. P. Basic FORTRAN IV with WATFOR & WATFIV. 1974. 13.95 (ISBN 0-201-00411-9) (ISBN 0-686-67380-8). A-W.
Bauer, Camille. France Actuelle. rev. ed. (Illus.). 1971. text ed. 10.50 (ISBN 0-395-04150-3, 3-03207). HM.
Bauer, Camille & Bond, Otto, eds. Graded French Reader: Premiere Etape. 3rd ed. 1978. pap. text ed. 6.95x (ISBN 0-669-00876-1). Heath.

Bauer, Carol & Ritt, Lawrence, eds. Free & Ennobled: Source Readings in the Development of Victorian Feminism. (Illus.). 1979. 46.00 (ISBN 0-08-022272-2); pap. 18.50 (ISBN 0-08-022271-4). Pergamon.
Bauer, Ernest. Mysterious World of Caves. (International Library). (Illus.). 1978. pap. 4.95 o.p. (ISBN 0-531-02378-8). Watts.
Bauer, Ernst W. Mysterious World of Caves. (International Library). (Illus.). (gr. 7 up). 1971. PLB 6.90 o.p. (ISBN 0-531-02102-5). Watts.
Bauer, Erwin & Bauer, Peggy. Photographing the West a State-by-State Guide. LC 80-81770. (Illus.). 192p. 1980. 27.50 (ISBN 0-87358-269-1); pap. 14.95 (ISBN 0-87358-268-3). Northland.
Bauer, Erwin, jt. auth. see Laycock, George.
Bauer, Erwin A. Cross-Country Skiing & Snowshoeing. (Illus.). 256p. 1975. 11.95 (ISBN 0-87691-200-5). Winchester Pr.
--Salt-Water Fisherman's Bible. LC 62-14182. pap. 3.50 (ISBN 0-385-02337-5). Doubleday.
Bauer, F. L., et al. Introduction to ALGOL. 1964. ref. ed. 13.95 (ISBN 0-13-477828-6). P-H.
Bauer, Fred. The Faith of America. (Illus.). 1980. 19.95 (ISBN 0-8499-0280-0). Word Bks.
Bauer, Frederic M., jt. auth. see Forgione, Albert G.
Bauer, Frederick, jt. auth. see Bollinger, Edward T.
Bauer, G., jt. auth. see Breitmaier, E.
Bauer, G. C., jt. auth. see Breitmaier, E.
Bauer, H. J., ed. Progress in Multiple Sclerosis Research. (Illus.). 630p. 1980. 46.60 (ISBN 0-387-09867-4). Springer-Verlag.
Bauer, Hank. Championship Baseball. LC 67-15347. 1968. 6.95 o.p. (ISBN 0-385-08573-7). Doubleday.
Bauer, Hanskurt. Color Atlas of Colposcopy. LC 78-62047. (Illus.). 1979. 45.00 (ISBN 0-89640-031-X). Igaku-Shoin.
Bauer, Harry. The Flying Mystique. (Illus.). 1980. 9.95 (ISBN 0-440-02722-5, E Friede). Delacorte.
Bauer, Henry H., et al. Instrumental Analysis. 1978. text ed. 26.95 (ISBN 0-205-05922-8). Allyn.
Bauer, J. B. Encyclopedia of Biblical Theology: The Concise Sacramentum Verbi. 1172p. 1981. 29.50 (ISBN 0-8245-0042-3). Crossroad NY.
Bauer, John D., et al. Clinical Laboratory Methods. 8th ed. LC 73-6928. 1974. pap. 36.50 (ISBN 0-8016-0507-5). Mosby.
Bauer, K. Jack. The Mexican War (1846-1848) LC 74-3489. (Illus.). 480p. 1974. 14.95 o.s.i. (ISBN 0-02-507890-9). Macmillan.
Bauer, K. Jack, ed. The New American State Papers: Naval Affairs, 1949 to 1979, 10 vols. LC 80-53884. 3000p. 1981. Set. lib. bdg. 595.00 (ISBN 0-686-69283-7). Scholarly Res Inc.
Bauer, Marianne & Wertheimer, Micheal. Study Guide to Accompany Psychology: A Brief Introduction. 1972. pap. 3.95x o.p. (ISBN 0-673-07786-1). Scott F.
Bauer, Marion. Twentieth Century Music: How It Developed, How to Listen to It. (Music Ser.). 1978. Repr. of 1933 ed. lib. bdg. 24.50 (ISBN 0-306-79503-5). Da Capo.
Bauer, Marion D. Shelter from the Wind. LC 75-28184. 128p. (gr. 5-12). 1976. 6.95 (ISBN 0-395-28890-8, Clarion). HM.
Bauer, Marion Dane. Foster Child. LC 76-54291. (gr. 5 up). 1977. 6.95 (ISBN 0-395-28889-4, Clarion). HM.
Bauer, Otto F. Fundamentals of Debate: Theory & Practice. 1966. pap. 6.95x o.p. (ISBN 0-673-05715-1). Scott F.
Bauer, Peggy, jt. auth. see Bauer, Erwin.
Bauer, R. & Loeschen, R. Chemistry for the Allied Health Sciences. 1980. 19.95 (ISBN 0-13-129205-6); lab manual 7.95 (ISBN 0-13-129213-7); student guide 6.95 (ISBN 0-13-129197-1). P-H.
Bauer, R. A. & Gergen, K. J. Study of Policy Formation. 1971. pap. text ed. 7.95 (ISBN 0-02-901930-3). Free Pr.
Bauer, Raymond A., jt. auth. see Ackerman, Robert W.
Bauer, Raymond A., et al. American Business & Public Policy: The Politics of Foreign Trade. 2nd ed. LC 63-8171. (Illus.). 1972. 24.95x (ISBN 0-202-24128-9); pap. 13.95x (ISBN 0-202-24129-7). Aldine Pub.
Bauer, Royal D. & Darby, Paul H. Elementary Accounting. rev. 4th ed. (Orig.). 1973. pap. 3.95 (ISBN 0-06-460150-1, CO 50, COS). Har-Row.
Bauer, Wolfgang. Change & Other Plays. 249p. 1973. 10.00 (ISBN 0-8090-3403-4, Mermaid); pap. 3.95 o.p. (ISBN 0-8090-0750-9). Hill & Wang.
Bauer, Yehuda. American Jewry & the Holocaust: The American Jewish Joint Distribution Committee, 1939-1945. 550p. 1981. 25.00 (ISBN 0-8143-1672-7). Wayne St U Pr.
Bauer, Yehuda & Rotenstreich, Nathan, eds. Holocaust As Historical Experience. 300p. 1981. text ed. 24.50x (ISBN 0-8419-0635-1); pap. text ed. 12.50x (ISBN 0-8419-0636-X). Holmes & Meier.
Bauerfeind, Jack C., ed. Carotenoid As Colorants & Vitamin A Precursors: Technological & Nutritional Applications. LC 79-8850. (Food Science & Technology Ser.). 1981. write for info. (ISBN 0-12-082850-2). Acad Pr.
Bauerle, Richard E. & Kemper, Frederick W. Up to Jerusalem. 1979. pap. 5.50 (ISBN 0-570-03795-6, 12-2777). Concordia.
Bauerle, Ruth. A Word List to James Joyce's "Exiles". LC 80-8487. 240p. 1981. lib. bdg. 40.00 (ISBN 0-8240-9500-6). Garland Pub.
Bauer-Lechner, Natalie. Recollections of Gustav Mahler. Franklin, P., ed. Newlin, D., tr. from Ger. LC 80-834. (Illus.). 241p. 1980. 22.50 (ISBN 0-521-23572-3). Cambridge U Pr.
Bauernfeind, R. H. Building a School Testing Program: Uses & Misuses of Standardized Tests. 226p. 1978. 8.75 (ISBN 0-936224-00-2). Schol Test.
Baues, Hans J. Geometry of Loop Spaces & the Cobar Construction. LC 80-12430. (Memoirs of the American Mathematical Society Ser.). 1980. 6.40 (ISBN 0-8218-2230-6, MEMO-230). Am Math.
Baugh, A., ed. Chaucers Major Poetry. 1963. 18.95 (ISBN 0-13-128223-9). P-H.
Baugh, A., et al, eds. Literary History of England. 2nd student ed. 1967. 34.95 (ISBN 0-13-537605-X). P-H.
--Mechanical Maintenance: Part One. (Engineering Craftsmen: No. J1). (Illus.). 1978. spiral bdg. 21.00x (ISBN 0-85083-016-8). Intl Ideas.
Baugh, Jack W. & Morgan, Jefferson. Why Have They Taken Our Children? 1978. 8.95 o.s.i. (ISBN 0-440-09463-1). Delacorte.
Baughan, Peter E. Chester & Holyhead Railway: The Main Line up 1880, Vol. 1. (Railway History Ser.). (Illus.). 17.95 (ISBN 0-7153-5617-8). David & Charles.
--A Regional History of the Railways of Great Britain: Vol. Eleven-North & Mid Wales. LC 79-56255. (Illus.). 208p. 1980. 24.00 (ISBN 0-7153-7850-3). David & Charles.
Baughman, Ernest W. Type & Motif-Index of the Folktales of England & North America. 1966. pap. text ed. 65.90x (ISBN 90-2790-046-9). Mouton.
Baughman, James P., et al. Environmental Analysis for Management. 1974. text ed. 19.50x (ISBN 0-256-01561-9). Irwin.
Baughman, Kenneth L. & Greene, Bruce L. Clinical Diagnostic Manual for the House Officer. (House Officer Ser.). (Illus.). 110p. 1981. write for info. (ISBN 0-683-03553-3). Williams & Wilkins.
Baughman, Kenneth L. & Greene, Bruce M. Clinical Diagnostic Manual for the House Officer. 110p. 1981. write for info. soft cover (3553-3). Williams & Wilkins.
Baughman, Martin L., et al. Electric Power in the United States: Models & Policy Analysis. 1979. text ed. 32.50x (ISBN 0-262-02130-7). MIT Pr.
Baulch, D. L., et al. Evaluated Kinetic Data for High Temperature Reactions, Vol. 3. 1977. 99.95 (ISBN 0-408-70787-9). Butterworths.
Bauldree, John, et al. Biophysical Lab Manual. 1976. spiral bdg. 16.95 (ISBN 0-88252-057-1). Paladin Hse.
Baum. Basic Nuclear Medicine. 1975. 17.50 o.p. (ISBN 0-8385-0613-5). ACC.
Baum, Alan. Montesquieu & Social Theory. 1979. 27.50 (ISBN 0-08-024317-7). Pergamon.
Baum, Allyn Z. Antarctica: The Worst Place in the World. (gr. 5-8). 1967. 4.95g o.s.i. (ISBN 0-02-708490-6). Macmillan.
Baum, Andrew & Mackmin, David. The Income Approach to Property Valuation. rev. ed. 216p. (Orig.). 1981. pap. 14.95 (ISBN 0-7100-0833-3). Routledge & Kegan.
--The Income Approach to Property Valuation. 1979. pap. 12.00 (ISBN 0-7100-0018-9). Routledge & Kegan.
Baum, Andrew & Epstein, Yakov M., eds. Human Response to Crowding. LC 78-6875. (Environmental Psychology Ser.). 1978. 24.95 (ISBN 0-470-26374-1). Halsted Pr.
Baum, Andrew & Singer, Jerome E., eds. Applications of Personal Control. LC 79-25025. (Advances in Environmental Psychology Ser.: Vol. 2). (Illus.). 208p. 1980. text ed. 19.95 (ISBN 0-89859-018-3). L Erlbaum Assocs.
--Energy Conservation: Psychological Perspectives. (Advances in Environmental Psychology Ser.: Vol. 3). 224p. 1981. text ed. 19.95 (ISBN 0-89859-063-9). L Erlbaum Assocs.
Baum, Arline & Baum, Joseph. One Bright Monday Morning. (Illus.). (ps). 1962. pap. 0.95 (ISBN 0-394-82650-7). Random.
Baum, Daniel J. Teenage Pregnancy. 192p. 1980. pap. 6.95 (ISBN 0-8253-0024-X). Beaufort Bks NY.
Baum, David, jt. ed. see Buckley, Mary.
Baum, Frank L. Glinda of Oz. 224p. 1981. pap. 2.25 (ISBN 0-345-28236-1, Del Rey). Ballantine.
Baum, G., et al, eds. see Calvin, Jean.
Baum, Gregory. Man Becoming: God in Secular Experience. (Library of Contemporary Theology). 1979. pap. 8.95 (ISBN 0-8164-2203-6). Crossroad NY.
Baum, Gregory & Greeley, Andrew. The Church As Institution. LC 73-6430. (Concilium Ser.: Religion in the Seventies: Vol. 91). 156p. 1974. pap. 4.95 (ISBN 0-8164-2575-2). Crossroad NY.
Baum, Gregory, ed. Sociology & Human Destiny: Studies in Sociology, Religion & Society. 224p. 1980. 12.95 (ISBN 0-8164-0110-1). Crossroad NY.
--Work & Religion, Concilium 131. (New Concilium 1980). 128p. 1980. pap. 5.95 (ISBN 0-8164-4764-0). Crossroad NY.
Baum, Gregory & Greeley, Andrew, eds. Communication in the Church Concilium, Vol. III. 1978. pap. 4.95 (ISBN 0-8164-2170-6). Crossroad NY.
Baum, Gregory, jt. ed. see Greeley, Andrew.
Baum, H. & Gergely, J., eds. Molecular Aspects of Medicine, Vol. 2. LC 80-40473. (Illus.). 453p. 1980. 70.00 (ISBN 0-08-026355-0). Pergamon.
Baum, Hank, ed. California Art Review Books. Incl. California Art Review. 272p. pap. 12.95 (ISBN 0-89087-310-0); San Francisco Art Review. 160p. pap. 9.95 (ISBN 0-89087-308-9); Los Angeles Art Review. 160p. pap. 9.95 (ISBN 0-89087-319-4). (Illus., Orig.). 1980. Celestial Arts.
--California Art Review Books, 3 bks. Incl. Bk. 1. California. LC 80-70751. 272p. pap. 12.95 (ISBN 0-89087-310-0); Bk. 2. Los Angeles. LC 80-70752. 160p. pap. 9.95 (ISBN 0-89087-319-4); Bk. 3. San Francisco. LC 80-70753. 160p. pap. 9.95 (ISBN 0-89087-308-9). (Illus.). Date not set. Celestial Arts.
Baum, Harold, jt. auth. see Green, David E.
Baum, Joan M. The Theatrical, Composition of the Major English Romantic Poets. (Salzburg Studies in Poetic Drama: No. 57). 1980. pap. text ed. 25.00x (ISBN 0-391-02187-7). Humanities.
Baum, Joseph, jt. auth. see Baum, Arline.
Baum, L. Frank. Land of Oz. (Classics Ser). (Illus.). (gr. 4 up). 1968. pap. 1.25 (ISBN 0-8049-0181-3, CL-181). Airmont.
--The Magic of Oz. 256p. 1981. pap. 2.25 (ISBN 0-345-28235-3, Del Rey). Ballantine.
--The Purple Dragon & Other Fantasies. LC 76-44600. (Illus.). 1976. 8.50 (ISBN 0-934882-01-0). Fictioneer Bks.
--Queen Zix of Ix: The Story of the Magic Cloak. (Illus.). 7.50 (ISBN 0-8446-0026-1). Peter Smith.
--The Tin Woodman of Oz. 272p. 1981. pap. 2.25 (ISBN 0-345-28234-5, Del Rey). Ballantine.
--The Wiz Book. 1978. pap. 1.95 o.p. (ISBN 0-425-03959-5, Medallion). Berkley Pub.
--Wizard of Oz. (Illus.). (gr. 3-6). 1970. 5.95g o.s.i. (ISBN 0-02-708520-1). Macmillan.
--Wizard of Oz. Chaffee, Allen, ed. (Illus.). (gr. k-3). 1950. 4.95 (ISBN 0-394-80689-1, BYR); PLB 5.99 (ISBN 0-394-90689-6). Random.
--The Wizard of Oz. (gr. 4-6). 1967. pap. 1.50 (ISBN 0-590-08604-9, Schol Pap). Schol Bk Serv.
--The Wizard of Oz. (Tempo Classic Ser.). 1980. pap. 1.50 (ISBN 0-448-17134-1, Tempo). G&D.
--The Wonderful Wizard of Oz. (gr. 3 up). 1979. pap. 1.25 (ISBN 0-307-21620-9, Golden Pr). Western Pub.
Baum, Lloyd, ed. Restorative Techniques for Individual Teeth. LC 80-81989. (Masson Monographs in Dentistry: Vol. 2). (Illus.). 224p. 1980. 29.50 (ISBN 0-89352-113-2). Masson Pub.
Baum, Lloyd, et al. Textbook of Operative Dentistry. (Illus.). 450p. 1981. text ed. price not set (ISBN 0-7216-1601-1). Saunders.
Baum, Lyman F. By the Candelabra's Glare. Repr. of 1898 ed. write for info. (ISBN 0-8201-1361-1). Schol Facsimil.
Baum, Martha, jt. auth. see Baum, Rainer.
Baum, Rainer & Baum, Martha. Growing Old: A Social Perspective. (Ser. in Sociology). (Illus.). 1980. pap. text ed. 10.95 (ISBN 0-13-367797-4). P-H.
Baum, Rainer C. Genocide & National Suicide. 1981. 25.00x (ISBN 0-8476-6970-X). Rowman.
Baum, Richard. Prelude to Revolution: Mao, the Party, & the Peasant Question, 1962-66. LC 74-23894. 240p. 1975. 17.50x (ISBN 0-231-03900-X). Columbia U Pr.
Baum, Richard, ed. China's Four Modernizations: The New Technological Revolution. (Westview Special Studies on China & East Asia). 276p. 1980. lib. bdg. 22.00x (ISBN 0-89158-673-3); pap. 9.50x (ISBN 0-89158-755-1). Westview.
Baum, Robert J. Ethics & Engineering Curricula. LC 80-10099. (The Teaching of Ethics Ser.). 79p. 1980. pap. 4.00 (ISBN 0-916558-12-6). Hastings Ctr Inst Soc.
Baum, S. J., et al, eds. Experimental Hematology Today: 1980. (Illus.). xii, 290p. 1980. 84.50 (ISBN 3-8055-1705-X). S Karger.
--Experimental Hematology Today 1981. (Illus.). xiv, 240p. 1981. 84.50 (ISBN 3-8055-2255-X). S Karger.
Baum, Sheldon, et al. Atlas of Nuclear Medicine Imaging. 432p. 1980. 78.00x (ISBN 0-8385-0447-7). ACC.
Baum, Stuart J. Introduction to Organic & Biological Chemistry. 3rd ed. Date not set. 19.50 (ISBN 0-686-65087-5); pap. 2.95 answer bk. (ISBN 0-02-306580-X). Macmillan. Postponed.
Baum, Thomas. Carny. 224p. (Orig.). 1980. pap. 2.50 (ISBN 0-515-05431-3). Jove Pubns.
Bauman, Carl E. Predicting Adolescent Drug Use: Utility Structure & Marijuana. 192p. 1980. 22.95 (ISBN 0-03-050636-0). Praeger.
Bauman, James J. Guide to Issues in Indian Language Retention. 1980. pap. text ed. 5.50 (ISBN 0-87281-132-8). Ctr Appl Ling.
Bauman, John A., jt. auth. see York, Kenneth H.
Bauman, John F., jt. auth. see Coode, Thomas H.
Bauman, Karl E. Research Methods for Community Health & Welfare: An Introduction. 160p. 1980. 13.95x (ISBN 0-19-502698-5); pap. 7.95x (ISBN 0-19-502699-3). Oxford U Pr.
Bauman, Kathleen. On Stage with Elvis Presley. (gr. 4-8). 1975. PLB 5.95 o.p. (ISBN 0-87191-488-3); pap. 2.95 o.p. (ISBN 0-685-61189-2). Creative Ed.
Bauman, Kurt. Joseph, the Border Guard. LC 70-178743. (gr. k-3). 1972. 5.95 o.s.i. (ISBN 0-8193-0548-0, Four Winds); PLB 5.41 o.s.i. (ISBN 0-8193-0549-9). Schol Bk Serv.
Bauman, Louis. The Faith. pap. 2.50 (ISBN 0-88469-026-1). BMH Bks.
Bauman, Mark K. Warren Akin Candler: The Conservative As Idealist. LC 80-22230. 290p. 1981. 16.00 (ISBN 0-8108-1368-8). Scarecrow.
Bauman, R. S., jt. auth. see Shugar, G. J.
Bauman, Richard & Abrahams, Roger D., eds. And Other Neighborly Names: Social Process & Cultural Image in Texas Folklore. (Illus.). 333p. 1981. text ed. 25.00x (ISBN 0-292-70352-X). U of Tex Pr.
Bauman, Toni & Zinkgraf, June. Winter Wonders. (gr. k-6). 1978. 12.95 (ISBN 0-916456-29-3, GA89). Good Apple.
Bauman, W. Scott, jt. auth. see Hayes, Douglas A.
Bauman, Wes. Country Kitchen Cookbook. 8.95 (ISBN 0-8423-0448-7). Tyndale.
Bauman, Zygmunt. Culture As Praxis. (Monographs in Social Theory). 204p. 1973. 15.95x (ISBN 0-7100-7606-1). Routledge & Kegan.
--Hermeneutics & Social Science. 1978. 17.50x (ISBN 0-231-04546-8). Columbia U Pr.
Baumann, Carl L., tr. see Baegert, Johann J.
Baumann, Cecilia C. Wilhelm Muller: The Poet of the Schubert Song Cycles. LC 80-12806. (Studies in German Literature). (Illus.). 208p. 1981. 17.50x (ISBN 0-271-00266-2). Pa St U Pr.
Baumann, Charles H. The Influence of Angus Snead MacDonald & the Snead Bookstack on Library Architecture. LC 74-171928. (Illus.). 1972. 11.50 (ISBN 0-8108-0390-9). Scarecrow.
Baumann, Dan. Which Way to Happiness. 160p. 1981. pap. price not set (ISBN 0-8307-0773-5). Regal.
Baumann, Duane & Dworkin, Daniel. Water Resources for Our Cities. Natoli, Salvatore J., ed. LC 78-59100. (Resource Papers for College Geography Ser.). (Illus.). 1978. pap. text ed. 4.00 (ISBN 0-89291-130-1). Assn Am Geographers.
Baumann, E. R., jt. auth. see Babbitt, Harold E.
Baumann, Elwood. Bigfoot: America's Abominable Snowman. LC 74-11407. (Illus.). 128p. (gr. 5 up). 1975. PLB 7.90 (ISBN 0-531-02793-7). Watts.
--The Loch Ness Monster. LC 72-182896. (Illus.). 160p. (gr. 6 up). 1972. PLB 7.45 (ISBN 0-531-02031-2). Watts.
Baumann, Elwood D. The Devil's Triangle. LC 75-22020. (Illus.). 160p. (gr. 7 up). 1976. PLB 7.45 (ISBN 0-531-01094-5). Watts.
--Monsters of North America. (Illus.). (gr. 5 up). 1978. PLB 7.90 s&l (ISBN 0-531-02246-3). Watts.
--They Came from Space. LC 76-44435. (Illus.). (gr. 6 up). 1977. PLB 6.90 s&l (ISBN 0-531-00388-4). Watts.
--Vampires. PLB 5.90 o.p. (ISBN 0-531-00128-8). Watts.
Baumann, Hans. Caves of the Great Hunters. rev. ed. (Illus.). (gr. 5 up). 1962. PLB 6.99 o.s.i. (ISBN 0-394-91006-0). Pantheon.
Baumann, Ludwig. Introduction to Ore Deposits. LC 74-26527. 163p. 1976. 19.95 (ISBN 0-470-05937-0). Halsted Pr.

Baumann, Roland & Wallace, Diane S. Guide to the Microfilm Collections in the Pennsylvania State Archives. 117p. 1980. pap. 5.00 (ISBN 0-89271-013-6). Pa Hist & Mus.
Baumann, Roland M., ed. Dissertations on Pennsylvania History, 1886-1976: A Bibliography. 1978. pap. 3.00 (ISBN 0-911124-93-4). Pa Hist & Mus.
--Guide to the Microfilm of the Records of Pennsylvania's Revolutionary Governments, 1775-1790. 10.00 (ISBN 0-911124-96-9); pap. 8.00 (ISBN 0-911124-95-0). Pa Hist & Mus.
--A Manual of Archival Techniques. (Illus.). 127p. 1979. pap. 4.00 (ISBN 0-89271-000-4). Pa Hist & Mus.
Baumbach, Jonathan. The Landscape of Nightmare: Studies in the Contemporary American Novel. LC 65-11761. (The Gotham Library). (Orig.). 1965. 12.00x (ISBN 0-8147-0031-4); pap. 4.00x (ISBN 0-8147-0032-2). NYU Pr.
Baumbach, Richard O., Jr. & Borah, William E. The Second Battle of New Orleans: A History of the Vieux Carre Riverfront Expressway Controversy. (Illus.). 1980. 27.50 (ISBN 0-8173-4840-9); pap. 12.95 (ISBN 0-8173-4841-7). U of Ala Pr.
Baumback, C. Baumback's Guide to Entrepreneurship. 1981. 13.95 (ISBN 0-13-066761-7). P-H.
Baumback, Clifford M. & Lawyer, Kenneth. How to Organize & Operate a Small Business. 6th ed. (Illus.). 1979. ref. ed. 18.95 (ISBN 0-13-425694-8); study guide & wkbk. 7.95 (ISBN 0-13-425686-7). P-H.
Baumback, Clifford M. & Mancuso, Joseph R. Entrepreneurship & Venture Management: Text & Readings. (Illus.). 368p. 1975. pap. text ed. 12.95 (ISBN 0-13-283119-8). P-H.
Baume, Louis. Sivalaya: Explorations of the Eight-Thousand Metre Peaks of the Himalaya. LC 79-20964. 336p. 1979. 12.95 (ISBN 0-916890-97-X); pap. 9.95 (ISBN 0-916890-71-6). Mountaineers.
Baumel, Howard B. & Berger, J. Joel. Biology-Its People & Its Papers. 1973. pap. 3.50 (ISBN 0-87355-002-1, 471-14652). Natl Sci Tchrs.
Baumer, Franz. Franz Kafka. Farbstein, Abraham, tr. from Ger. LC 68-3144. (Modern Literature Ser.). 1971. 10.95 (ISBN 0-8044-2024-6); pap. 3.45 (ISBN 0-8044-6014-0). Ungar.
--Hermann Hesse. Conway, John, tr. LC 68-31446. (Modern Literature Ser.). 1969. 10.95 (ISBN 0-8044-2027-0). Ungar.
Baumer, Mary P. Seasonal Kindergarten Units. 1972. pap. 5.95 o.p. (ISBN 0-8224-6330-X). Pitman Learning.
Baumer, Rachel & Brandon, James R. Sanskrit Drama in Performance. (Illus.). 352p. 1981. text ed. 27.50x (ISBN 0-8248-0688-3). U Pr of Hawaii.
--Sanskrit Drama in Performance. 1981. 27.50 (ISBN 0-8248-0688-3). U Pr of Hawaii.
Baumer, William H., jt. auth. see Darby, William O.
Baumert, J. H., ed. see Alksne, Z. K. & Ikaunieks, Ya Y.
Baumert, John H., jt. auth. see Jackson, Joseph H.
Baumgart, Winfried, jt. ed. see Saab, Ann P.
Baumgartel, Elise J. The Cultures of Prehistoric Egypt. LC 80-24186. (Illus.). 268p. 1981. Repr. of 1955 ed. lib. bdg. 60.00x (ISBN 0-313-22524-9, BACU). Greenwood.
--The Cultures of Prehistoric Egypt, 2 vols. in one. LC 80-24186. (Illus.). xxiii, 286p. 1981. Repr. of 1960 ed. lib. bdg. 63.33 (ISBN 0-313-22524-9, BAUC). Greenwoodd.
Baumgarten, Alexander & Richards, Frank F. Handbook Series in Clinical Laboratory Science, CRC: Section F, Immunology, 2 pts, Vol. 1. 1978-79. Pt. 1. 63.95 (ISBN 0-8493-7021-3); Pt. 2, 480p. 62.95 (ISBN 0-8493-7022-1). CRC Pr.
Baumgarten, Henry E., jt. auth. see Linstromberg, Walter W.
Baumgarten, Henry F., jt. auth. see Linstromberg, Walter W.
Baumgarten, Murray, tr. see Perez de Ayala, Ramon.
Baumgarten, Paul, jt. auth. see Farber, Donald C.
Baumgartner, Diane. Melissa. (Orig.). 1980. pap. 4.95 (ISBN 0-89191-233-9). Cook.
Baumgartner, Richard A., ed. see Nagel, Fritz.
Baumgartner, Ted A. & Jackson, Andrew S. Measurement for Evaluation in Physical Education. 2nd ed. (Illus.). 576p. 1981. text ed. write for info. (ISBN 0-395-29623-4); write for info. instr's manual (ISBN 0-395-29637-4). HM.
Baumhammers, Andrejs. Temporary & Semipermanent Splinting: An Atlas of Clinical Procedures. 128p. 1971. pap. 14.75 photovopy ed. spiral (ISBN 0-398-00117-0). C C Thomas.
Baumhoff, Martin A., jt. auth. see Heizer, Robert F.
Bauml, Betty J. & Bauml, Franz H. A Dictionary of Gestures. LC 75-3144. 1975. 12.00 (ISBN 0-8108-0863-3). Scarecrow.
Bauml, Franz H., jt. auth. see Bauml, Betty J.
Bauml, Franz H., ed. Kudrun: Die Handschrift. (Ger). 1969. 58.00x (ISBN 3-11-000376-7). De Gruyter.
Baumol, W. Economic Theory & Operations Analysis. 4th ed. 1977. 20.95 (ISBN 0-13-227132-X). P-H.
Baumol, William J. & Oates, Wallace E. The Theory of Environmental Policy: The Externalities, Public Outlays, & the Quality of Life. LC 74-11205. (Illus.). 304p. 1975. ref. ed. 19.95 (ISBN 0-13-913673-8). P-H.
Baumol, William J., et al. Economics, Environmental Policy & the Quality of Life. 1979. 15.95 (ISBN 0-13-231365-0); pap. 9.95 (ISBN 0-13-231357-X). P-H.
Baumstark, Reinhold. Masterpieces from the Collection of the Princes of Liechtenstein. Wolf, Robert E., tr. from Ger. LC 80-18070. (Illus.). 298p. 1981. 100.00 (ISBN 0-933920-09-1). Hudson Hills. Postponed.
Baun, Elizabeth. T. S. Eliot Als Kritiker. (Salzburg Studies in Elizabethan Literature: Poetic Drama Ser.: No. 58). 1980. pap. text ed. 25.00x (ISBN 0-391-01906-6). Humanities.
Baunach, Phyllis J., jt. ed. see Price, Barbara R.
Baur, G. R. & George, L. O. Helping Children Learn Mathematics: A Competency Based Laboratory Approach. LC 75-16772. 1976. 17.95 (ISBN 0-8465-0408-1); instr's guide 3.95 (ISBN 0-8465-0409-X). Benjamin-Cummings.
Baur, John I. American Painting, Nineteen Hundred to Nineteen Seventy-Six. LC 75-27361. (Illus.). 102p. 1975. pap. 6.00 (ISBN 0-89062-022-9, Pub. by Katonah). Pub Ctr Cult Res.
Baur, K., jt. auth. see Crooks, R.
Baur, Karla, jt. auth. see Crooks, Robert.
Baus, Herbert M. The Experts Crossword Puzzle Dictionary. LC 72-84960. pap. 4.50 (ISBN 0-385-04788-6, Dolp). Doubleday.
--The Master Crossword Puzzle Dictionary. (Thumb Indexed). 1981. 27.50 (ISBN 0-385-15118-7). Doubleday.
Bausch, Michael & Duck, Ruth. Everflowing Streams. 96p. (Orig.). 1981. pap. 3.95 (ISBN 0-8298-0428-5). Pilgrim NY.
Bausch, Richard. Real Presence. 1980. 9.95 (ISBN 0-8037-7779-5). Dial.
--Take Me Back. 372p. 1981. 11.95 (ISBN 0-686-69093-1). Dial.
Bausell, Baker, jt. auth. see Waltz, Carolyn.
Bausell, R. Barker, jt. auth. see Waltz, Carolyn F.
Bautista, Sara, tr. see Thomas, Terry C.
Bauwens, Eleanor E., ed. The Anthropology of Health. LC 78-6776. 1978. pap. text ed. 11.95 (ISBN 0-8016-0516-4). Mosby.
Bauzen, Peter & Bauzen, Susanne. Flower Pressing. Kuttner, Paul, tr. from Ger. LC 77-167661. (Little Craft Book Ser.). (gr. 7 up). 1971. 5.95 (ISBN 0-8069-5186-9); PLB 6.69 (ISBN 0-8069-5187-7). Sterling.
Bauzen, Susanne, jt. auth. see Bauzen, Peter.
Bava, Domenick. Favorite Stories for Boys & Girls. 160p. (gr. k-6). 1980. PLB 6.95 (ISBN 0-89962-023-X). Todd & Honeywell.
Baver, Leonard D., et al. Soil Physics. 4th ed. LC 72-5318. 496p. 1972. 29.95 (ISBN 0-471-05974-9). Wiley.
Bavier, Richard. Study of Judaism: Bibliographic Essays. 1972. 17.50 (ISBN 0-685-38395-4, 87068-180-4, Pub. by Anti-Defamation League). Ktav.
Bavinck, Herman. The Doctrine of God. Hendricksen, W., tr. (Student's Reformed Theological Library Ser.). 1977. 14.95 (ISBN 0-85151-255-0). Banner of Truth.
--Doctrine of God. (Twin Brooks Ser.). 1977. pap. 7.95 (ISBN 0-8010-0723-2). Baker Bk.
Baviskar, B. S. The Politics of Development: Sugar Cooperatives in Rural Maharashtra. (Illus.). 240p. 1981. 18.95 (ISBN 0-19-561206-X). Oxford U Pr.
Bawa Muhaivadeeen, M. R. The Truth & Unity of Man: Letters in Response to a Crisis. LC 80-18050. 144p. 1980. 10.00 (ISBN 0-914390-15-5); pap. 3.95 (ISBN 0-914390-14-7). Fellowship Pr PA.
Bawa Muhaiyaddeen, M. R. The Asma'ul-Husna: The 99 Beautiful Names of Allah. (Illus.). 211p. 1979. pap. 4.95 (ISBN 0-914390-13-9). Fellowship Pr PA.
--A Book of God's Love. Marcus, Sharon & Marcus, Karin, eds. Macan-Markar, Ajwad, et al, trs. from Tamil. (Illus.). 126p. 1981. 7.95 (ISBN 0-914390-19-8). Fellowship Pr.
--The Divine Luminous Wisdom That Dispels the Darkness God-Man Man-God. rev. ed. (Illus.). 288p. 1977. pap. 5.95 (ISBN 0-914390-12-0). Fellowship Pr PA.
--God, His Prophets & His Children. (Illus.). 1978. pap. 4.95 (ISBN 0-914390-09-0). Fellowship Pr PA.
--The Guidebook to the True Secret of the Heart, 2 vols. (Illus.). 1976. pap. 4.95 ea. Vol. 1, 224p (ISBN 0-914390-07-4). Vol. 3, 223p (ISBN 0-914390-08-2). Fellowship Pr PA.
Bawa Muhaiy Addeen, M. R. Songs of God's Grace. LC 73-91016. (Illus.). 154p. 1974. pap. 3.50 (ISBN 0-914390-02-3). Fellowship Pr PA.
Bawa Muhaiyaddeen, M. R. Truth & Light: Brief Explanations. LC 74-76219. (Illus.). 144p. 1974. pap. 2.95 (ISBN 0-914390-04-X). Fellowship Pr PA.
--Wisdom of Man: Selected Discourses. LC 80-20541. (Illus.). 168p. 1980. 10.00 (ISBN 0-914390-16-3). Fellowship Pr PA.
Bawcutt, N. W., ed. see Ford, John.
Bawcutt, Paul. Captive Insurance Companies. 160p. 1980. 54.00x (ISBN 0-85941-077-3, Pub. by Woodhead-Faulkner England). State Mutual Bk.
Bawden, D. Lee, jt. auth. see Bendick, Marc, Jr.
Bawden, Nina. Carrie's War: T.V. Ed. (Illus.). 1980. pap. 2.95 (ISBN 0-14-005581-9). Penguin.
--Rebel on a Rock. (gr. 7-12). 1980. pap. 1.50 (ISBN 0-440-97423-2, LFL). Dell.
--Three on the Run. (Illus.). (gr. 4-6). 1968. pap. 1.25 (ISBN 0-686-68481-8). PB.
--The Witchs Daughter. (gr. 4-6). 1974. pap. 0.95 o.s.i. (ISBN 0-671-29720-1). Archway.
--Witch's Daughter. (gr. 4-6). 1973. pap. 0.95 (ISBN 0-671-29720-1). PB.
Bax, Clifford. Leonardo Da Vinci. 160p. 1980. Repr. of 1932 ed. lib. bdg. 27.50 (ISBN 0-8495-0464-3). Arden Lib.
Bax, Mart. Harpstrings & Confessions: Machine-Style Politics in the Irish Republic. 1977. pap. text ed. 23.25x (ISBN 90-232-1481-1). Humanities.
Baxandall, Lee & Morawski, Stefan, eds. Marx & Engels on Literature & Art: A Selection of Writings. LC 73-93501. 150p. 1973. 9.50 (ISBN 0-914386-01-8); pap. 3.95 (ISBN 0-914386-02-6). Telos Pr.
Baxandall, Lee, ed. see Marx, Karl & Engels, Frederick.
Baxandall, Lee, ed. see Reich, Wilhelm.
Baxandall, Michael. Painting & Experience in Fifteenth Century Italy: A Primer in the Social History of Pictorial Style. (Illus.). 180p. 1972. 12.95 o.p. (ISBN 0-19-817321-0). Oxford U Pr.
--Painting & Experience in Fifteenth Century Italy: A Primer in the Social History of Pictorial Style. 172p. 1974. pap. 7.95 (ISBN 0-19-881329-5, GB411, GB). Oxford U Pr.
Baxendale, Jean. First Bible Lessons. (Illus., Orig.). (ps). 1955. pap. 6.95 (ISBN 0-87239-328-3, 2861). Standard Pub.
Baxter, Anne. Intermission. 1978. pap. 2.50 (ISBN 0-345-29267-7). Ballantine.
Baxter, Annette K., ed. see Brown, Harriet C.
Baxter, Annette K., ed. see Carson, Ann.
Baxter, Annette K., ed. see Dorr, Rheta C.
Baxter, Annette K., ed. see Jones, Amanda T.
Baxter, Annette K., ed. see Terhune, Mary V.
Baxter, Annette K., ed. see Van Hoosen, Bertha.
Baxter, B. Naval Architecture: Examples & Theory. 450p. 1978. 39.95x (ISBN 0-85264-179-6, Pub. by Griffin England). State Mutual Bk.
Baxter, B., ed. see Walton, T.
Baxter, Batsell B. I Believe Because. 1971. pap. 5.95 (ISBN 0-8010-0548-5). Baker Bk.
--Speaking for the Master. pap. 3.95 (ISBN 0-8010-0588-4). Baker Bk.
--When Life Tumbles in. (Direction Books). 136p. 1976. pap. 2.25 (ISBN 0-8010-0668-6). Baker Bk.
Baxter, Batsell Barrett & Harless, Dan. The Search for Happiness, Futility or Fulfillment. (Direction Bks). 1977. pap. 1.95 o.p. (ISBN 0-8010-0707-0). Baker Bk.
Baxter, Brian. The Films of Judy Garland. Castell, David, ed. (The Films of...Ser.). (Illus.). (gr. 7-12). 1978. Repr. of 1974 ed. PLB 5.95 (ISBN 0-912616-81-4). Greenhaven.
Baxter, Caroline. The Stolen Telesm. LC 76-17307. (gr. 5-12). 1976. 7.95 o.p. (ISBN 0-397-31686-0). Lippincott.
Baxter, Cheryl A. The Cocoon. 90p. 1980. 4.95 (ISBN 0-87747-830-9). Deseret Bk.
Baxter, Claude & Melnechuk, Theodore, eds. Perspectives in Schizophrenia Research. 463p. 1980. text ed. 42.00 (ISBN 0-89004-517-8). Raven.
Baxter, D. Victorian Locomotives. 129p. 1980. 25.00x (ISBN 0-903485-62-1, Pub. by Moorland England). State Mutual Bk.
Baxter, Davis R. Big Dallas Kill. 1980. 4.95 o.p. (ISBN 0-8062-1539-9). Carlton.
Baxter, Gerald D., jt. auth. see Dye, O. David.
Baxter, Gordon. How to Fly. 288p. 1981. 12.95 (ISBN 0-671-44801-3). Summit Bks.
Baxter, Ian F. Marital Property. LC 72-97627. (American Family Law Library). 640p. 1973. 47.50 (ISBN 0-686-05456-3). Lawyers Co-Op.
Baxter, J. Sidlow. Explore the Book, 6 vols. in 1. 24.85 (ISBN 0-310-20620-0). Zondervan.
--A New Call to Holiness. 256p. 1973. pap. 5.95 (ISBN 0-310-20581-6). Zondervan.
Baxter, James K. The Labyrinth: Some Uncollected Poems 1944-1972. 76p. 1974. 8.00x o.p. (ISBN 0-19-640018-X). Oxford U Pr.
--New Zealand in Colour, Vol. 1. (Illus.). 1961. 13.50 o.s.i. (ISBN 0-589-00259-7, Dist. by C E Tuttle). Reed.
Baxter, James P. The Picneers of New France in New England. 450p. 1980. Repr. of 1894 ed. 20.00 (ISBN 0-917890-20-5). Heritage Bk.
Baxter, John. The Kid. LC 80-25042. 312p. 1981. 13.95 (ISBN 0-670-41297-X). Viking Pr.
Baxter, Kathleen M. Come & Get It: A Natural Foods Cookbook for Children. 2nd ed. LC 78-73448. (Illus.). 128p. 1978. pap. 8.50 (ISBN 0-9603696-1-9). Children First.
Baxter, Lorna. The White Rose & the Black. 147p. (gr. 3-7). 1981. 10.95 (ISBN 0-571-11413-X, Pub. by Faber & Faber). Merrimack Bk Serv.
Baxter, Norman. A Line on Texas. LC 80-15870. (Illus.). 1980. pap. 6.95 (ISBN 0-88415-429-7). Pacesetter Pr.
--Selections from "A Line on Texas". abr. ed. (Illus.). 128p. 1980. pap. 6.95 (ISBN 0-88415-429-7). Gulf Pub.
Baxter, P. T. & Almagor, Uri, eds. Age, Generation & Time: Some Features of East African Age Organizations. LC 78-18952. (Illus.). 1978. 25.00 (ISBN 0-312-01172-5). St Martin.
Baxter, R., jt. auth. see Perraton, J.
Baxter, R. E. & Phillips, C. Ports, Inland Waterways & Civil Aviation. Maunder, W. F., ed. 1979. text ed. 55.00 (ISBN 0-08-022460-1). Pergamon.
Baxter, Raymond. Raymond Baxter's Farnborough Commentary. (Illus.). 120p. 1980. 27.95 (ISBN 0-85059-434-0). Aztex.
Baxter, Richard. The Reformed Pastor. 1979. pap. 3.95 (ISBN 0-85151-191-0). Banner of Truth.
Baxter, Robert. Baxter's Alaska. 1981. 9.95 (ISBN 0-913384-47-X). Rail Europe-Baxter.
--Baxter's Britrail Guide. LC 72-83184. 1979. 8.95 (ISBN 0-913384-28-3). Rail-Europe-Baxter.
--Baxter's Eurailpass Travel Guide. LC 74-169913. 1980-81. 9.95 (ISBN 0-913384-33-X). Rail-Europe-Baxter.
--Baxter's Florida. 1981. 9.95 (ISBN 0-913384-34-8). Rail-Europe-Baxter.
--Baxter's Mexico. 1981. 9.95 (ISBN 0-913384-42-9). Rail-Europe-Baxter.
--Baxter's U. S. A. (the U. S. A. by Car, Bus, Train & Plane) LC 77-92700. 1980-81. perfect bdg. 12.95 (ISBN 0-913384-44-5). Rail-Europe-Baxter.
--Baxter's Western Canada. 1981. 9.95 (ISBN 0-913384-41-0). Rail-Europe-Baxter.
--Bicentennial Images. 1976. perfect bdg. 14.95 (ISBN 0-913384-19-4). Rail-Europe-Baxter.
Baxter, Willard E. & Sloyer, Clifford W. Calculus with Probability. LC 72-1937. 1973. text ed. 19.95 (ISBN 0-201-00401-1); instructor's manual 2.00 (ISBN 0-201-00404-6). A-W.
Baxter, William. Life of Walter Scott. 8.00 (ISBN 0-89225-114-X). Gospel Advocate.
Baxter, William F., et al. Retail Banking in the Electronic Age: The Law & Economics of Electronic Funds Transfer. LC 76-28594. (Illus.). 208p. 1977. text ed. 18.50 (ISBN 0-916672-06-9). Allanheld.
Bay, Adela. Method & Techniques for Understanding Music Notation. LC 80-10292. (Illus.). 143p. 1980. pap. 11.95 (ISBN 0-89116-190-2). Hemisphere Pub.
Bay, Christian. Strategies of Political Emancipation. LC 80-53117. 240p. 1981. text ed. 18.95 (ISBN 0-268-01702-6). U of Notre Dame Pr.
Bay, Howard. Stage Design. LC 73-15948. (Illus.). 1978. pap. text ed. 12.95x (ISBN 0-910482-98-5). Drama Bk.
Bay, Kenneth, jt. auth. see Kessler, Herman.
Bay, Kenneth E. & Vinciguerra, Matthew M. How to Tie Freshwater Flies. 1974. 10.00 o.p. (ISBN 0-87691-148-3). Winchester Pr.
Bay, Kenneth E., ed. The American Fly Tyer's Handbook. (Illus.). 1979. 14.95 (ISBN 0-87691-287-0). Winchester Pr.
Bay, Timothy. Fake Giants & Other Great Hoaxes. LC 80-21132. (gr. 4-10). 1980. pap. 1.95 (ISBN 0-88436-766-5). EMC.
Bayard, Tania. Bourges Cathedral: the West Portals. LC 75-23780. (Outstanding Dissertations in the Fine Arts - Medieval). (Illus.). 1976. lib. bdg. 45.00 (ISBN 0-8240-1977-6). Garland Pub.
Baydot. Historical Encyclopedia of World War II. Date not set. 25.00 (ISBN 0-87196-401-5). Facts on File.
Baydun, M. Quran. (Arabic.). 25.00x (ISBN 0-686-63558-2). Intl Bk Ctr.
--Quran. (Arabic.). medium sized. 19.00x (ISBN 0-686-63559-0). Intl Bk Ctr.
--Quran. (Arabic.). with jacket. 10.95x (ISBN 0-686-63560-4). Intl Bk Ctr.
--Quran. (Arabic.). pocket sized. 4.95x (ISBN 0-686-63561-2). Intl Bk Ctr.
--Quran. (Arabic.). pap. 2.95x small pocket sized. (ISBN 0-686-63562-0). Intl Bk Ctr.

Bayer, Herbert, et al, eds. Bauhaus Nineteen Nineteen to Nineteen Twenty-Eight. LC 77-169299. (Illus.). 1976. pap. 8.95 (ISBN 0-87070-240-3). Museum Mod Art.

Bayer, R. & Graham, R. M., eds. Operating Systems: An Advanced Course. (Lecture Notes in Computer Science: Vol. 60). 1978. pap. 22.50 o.p. (ISBN 0-387-08755-9). Springer-Verlag.

Bayer, Ronald. Homosexuality & American Psychiatry: The Politics of Diagnosis. LC 80-68182. (Illus.). 224p. 1980. 12.95 (ISBN 0-465-03048-3). Basic.

Bayer, William. Punish Me with Kisses. 1980. 10.95 (ISBN 0-312-92664-2). Congdon & Lattes.

--Visions of Isabelle. 1976. 7.95 o.s.i. (ISBN 0-440-09315-5). Delacorte.

Bayerl, Elizabeth. Interdisciplinary Studies in the Humanities: A Directory. LC 77-22960. 1977. 40.00 (ISBN 0-8108-1076-X). Scarecrow.

Bayes, Ronald H., ed. see Sibley, Susan K.

Bayes, Thomas. Facsimiles of Two Papers by Bayes, 2 vols. in 1. Deming, W. Edwards, ed. 1963. 7.50 o.s.i. (ISBN 0-02-841120-X). Hafner.

Bayes De Luna, A. J., ed. see International Symposium on Diagnosis & Treatment of Cardiac Arrhythmias, Barcelona, Spain, 5-8 October 1977.

Baygan, Lee. Makeup for Theatre, Film & Television: A Step by Step Photographic Guide. (Illus.). 206p. 1981. 22.50x (ISBN 0-89676-023-5). Drama Bk.

Bayha, Franklin H., jt. auth. see Karger, Delmar W.

Bayle, Pierre. Historical & Critical Dictionary: Selections. Popkin, Richard H., tr. LC 64-16703. (Orig.). 1965. pap. 11.50 (ISBN 0-672-60406-X, LLA175). Bobbs.

--Oeuvres diverses, 5 Vols. Labrousse, E., ed. Orig. Title: Oeuvres completes. 1969. Repr. of 1727 ed. 780.00 set (ISBN 0-685-05263-X). Adler.

Baylen, J. O. & Grossman, N. J. The Biographical Dictionary of Modern British Radicals Since 1770: 1833-1914, Vol.2. 1980. text ed. write for info. (ISBN 0-391-01058-1). Humanities.

Baylen, J. O. & Gossman, N. J., eds. The Biographical Dictionary of Modern British Radicals Since 1770: 1915-1970, Vol. 3. 1980. text ed. write for info. (ISBN 0-391-01059-X). Humanities.

Bayler, Byrd. Yes Is Better Than No. 1980. pap. 1.95 (ISBN 0-686-69248-9, 50625). Avon.

Bayless, Gordon E. How to (Easily) Eliminate the Smoking Habit. rev. ed. Ide, Arthur F., ed. (Studies in Health). (Illus.). 50p. 1981. pap. 16.95 (ISBN 0-86663-653-6). Ide Hse.

Bayless, Kathleen, jt. auth. see Ramsey, Marjorie E.

Bayley, Ada E. Donovan, a Novel, 1882. Wolff, Robert L., ed. LC 75-1529. (Victorian Fiction Series). 1975. lib. bdg. 66.00 (ISBN 0-8240-1601-7). Garland Pub.

Bayley, Barrington J. Annihilation Factor. 144p. 1980. 11.95 (ISBN 0-85031-311-2, Pub. by Allison & Busby England); pap. 4.95 (ISBN 0-85031-320-1, Pub. by Allison & Busby England). Schocken.

Bayley, C. C. War & Society in Renaissance Florence: The De Militia of Leonardo Bruni. LC 62-3048. 1961. 30.00x o.p. (ISBN 0-8020-7047-7). U of Toronto Pr.

Bayley, D. H. & Mendelsohn, H. Minorities & the Police. LC 69-12119. 1969. 9.95 o.s.i. (ISBN 0-02-901980-X); pap. text ed. 3.50 o.s.i. (ISBN 0-02-901970-2). Free Pr.

Bayley, David H. Forces of Order: Police Behavior in Japan & the United States. LC 75-17304. 1976. 16.50x (ISBN 0-520-03069-9); pap. 3.95 (ISBN 0-520-03641-7). U of Cal Pr.

Bayley, Gordon. Local Government: Is Is Manageable? 1979. 15.00 (ISBN 0-08-024279-0). Pergamon.

Bayley, J. An Essay on Hardy. LC 77-80826. 1978. 23.95 (ISBN 0-521-21814-4). Cambridge U Pr.

Bayley, John. Shakespeare & Tragedy. 224p. 1981. price not set (ISBN 0-7100-0632-2); pap. price not set (ISBN 0-7100-0607-1). Routledge & Kegan.

Bayley, John B., ed. see Letarouilly, Paul.

Bayley, Michael. Mental Handicap & Community Care: A Study of Mentally Handicapped People in Sheffield. (Int'l. Library of Social Policy). (Illus.). 420p. 1973. 32.50x (ISBN 0-7100-7662-2). Routledge & Kegan.

Bayley, Stephen. In Good Shape: Style in Industrial Products Nineteen Hundred to Nineteen Sixty. 225p. 1979. pap. text ed. 12.95 (ISBN 0-442-26333-3). Van Nos Reinhold.

Baylis, Fred S. Rhyme & Reason. 1978. 4.00 o.p. (ISBN 0-682-49040-7). Exposition.

Baylis, Maggie. House Plants for the Purple Thumb. LC 72-94894. (Illus.). 192p. (Orig.). 1973. 4.95 (ISBN 0-912238-33-X); pap. 4.95 (ISBN 0-912238-32-1). One Hund One Prods.

--Practicing Plant Parenthood. LC 75-22361. (Illus.). 192p. (Orig.). 1975. 4.95 (ISBN 0-912238-62-3); pap. 4.95 (ISBN 0-912238-61-5). One Hund One Prods.

Baylis, Maggie & Castle, Coralie. Real Bread. LC 80-21929. (Illus.). 240p. (Orig.). 1980. pap. 6.95 (ISBN 0-89286-179-7). One Hund One Prods.

Baylis, Robert. Ephesians: Living in God's Household. LC 76-43523. (Fisherman Bible Study Guide). 45p. 1976. pap. 1.95 (ISBN 0-87788-223-1). Shaw Pubs.

Baylis, Thomas A. The Technical Intelligentsia & the East German Elite: Legitimacy & Social Change in Mature Communism. (Illus.). 1974. 21.50x (ISBN 0-520-02395-1). U of Cal Pr.

Bayliss, B. T. & Philip, A. Butt. Capital Markets & Industrial Investment in Germany & France: Lessons for the U. K. 1979. text ed. 29.50x (ISBN 0-566-00335-X, Pub. by Gower Pub Co England). Renouf.

Bayliss, Leonard E. Living Control Systems. (Illus.). 1966. 13.95x (ISBN 0-7167-0651-2). W H Freeman.

Baylor, Byrd. The Desert Is Theirs. (Illus.). 32p. (gr. 1-5). pap. 2.95 (ISBN 0-689-70481-X, A-108, Aladdin). Atheneum.

--Desert Voices. (Illus.). 32p. (gr. 1-5). 1981. 9.95 (ISBN 0-684-16712-3). Scribner.

--A God on Every Mountain Top. (Illus.). 64p. (gr. 3-7). 1981. 8.95 (ISBN 0-684-16758-1). Scribner.

--When Clay Sings. (Illus.). 32p. (gr. 1-5). pap. 2.95 (ISBN 0-689-70482-8, A-109, Aladdin). Atheneum.

--Your Own Best Secret Place. LC 78-21243. (Illus.). (gr. 1-4). 1979. 9.95 (ISBN 0-684-16111-7). Scribner.

Baylor County Historical Society. History of Baylor County: Salt Pork to Sirloin. 19.95 (ISBN 0-685-48790-3). Nortex Pr.

Bayly, Brian. Introduction to Petrology. 1968. text ed. 23.95 (ISBN 0-13-491621-2). P-H.

Bayly, Joseph. I Love to Tell the Story. 1978. pap. 1.50 o.p. (ISBN 0-89191-162-6). Cook.

Bayly, Thomas H. Epistles from Bath, or, Q's Letters to His Yorkshire Relations, Repr. Of 1817. Bd. with Rough Sketches of Bath, Imitations of Horace & Other Poems. Repr. of 1817 ed; Parliamentary Letters, & Other Poems. Repr. of 1818 ed; The Dandies of the Present & the Macaronies of the Past: A Rough Sketch. Repr. of 1819 ed; The Tribute of a Friend. Repr. of 1819 ed; Mournful Recollections. Repr. of 1820 ed; Small Talk. Repr. of 1820 ed; Erin, & Other Poems. Repr. of 1822 ed; Outlines of Edinburgh, & Other Poems. Repr. of 1822 ed. LC 75-31154. (Romantic Context Ser.: Poetry 1789-1830: Vol. 10). 1979. lib. bdg. 47.00 (ISBN 0-8240-2109-6). Garland Pub.

Baym, Nina. Woman's Fiction: A Guide to Novels by & About Women in America, 1820-1870. 1980. 17.50 (ISBN 0-8014-1128-9); pap. 4.95. Cornell U Pr.

Bayne, B. L., ed. Marine Mussels. LC 75-25426. (International Biological Programme Ser.: No. 10). (Illus.). 400p. 1976. 99.00 (ISBN 0-521-21058-5). Cambridge U Pr.

Bayne, Keith G., jt. auth. see Nystrom, Dennis C.

Bayne, Stephen F., Jr. Christian Living. (Orig.). 1956. pap. 4.95 (ISBN 0-8164-2007-6, SP5). Crossroad NY.

Baynes, Cary F., tr. see Jung, Emma.

Baynes, Kate, jt. ed. see Baynes, Ken.

Baynes, Ken. Art in Society. LC 74-21587. (Illus.). 288p. 1975. 45.00 (ISBN 0-87951-027-7). Overlook Pr.

Baynes, Ken & Pugh, Francis. The Art of the Engineer. LC 80-29190. (Illus.). 240p. 1981. 60.00 (ISBN 0-87951-128-1). Overlook Pr.

Baynes, Ken & Baynes, Kate, eds. The Shoe Show: British Shoes Since Seventeen Ninety. 96p. 1979. 20.00x (ISBN 0-903798-37-9, Pub. by Jolly & Barber England). State Mutual Bk.

Baynes, Norman H. Byzantine Studies & Other Essays. LC 74-11586. (Illus.). 392p. 1974. Repr. of 1955 ed. lib. bdg. 29.75x (ISBN 0-8371-7673-5, BABYS). Greenwood.

Baynes, Pauline, jt. auth. see Squire, Geoffrey.

Baynes, Richard W. God's OK -- You're OK? Perspective on Christian Worship. LC 79-67440. 96p. (Orig.). 1981. pap. 1.95 (ISBN 0-87239-382-8, 40088). Standard Pub.

Baynton, Barbara. The Portable Barbara Baynton. Krimmer, Sally & Lawson, Alan, eds. (Portable Australian Authors Ser.). 340p. 1981. text ed. 30.25 (ISBN 0-7022-1377-2); pap. 12.00 (ISBN 0-7022-1469-8). U of Queensland Pr.

Bayraktar, B. A., et al, eds. Education in Systems Science: Report & Procedings, Germany, 21-25 Feb., 1978. LC 79-83871. 1979. 44.95 (ISBN 0-470-26704-6). Halsted Pr.

Bayramian, Mary. Chicken & Fish. (Illus.). 1978. 3.95 (ISBN 0-912300-85-X, 85-X). Troubador Pr.

Bayrd, Edwin, jt. auth. see National Press Photographers Association & the University of Missouri School of Journalism.

Bayrd, Edwin, ed. see Grunfeld, Frederic V.

Bayrd, Edwin, ed. see Hemming, John.

Bayrd, Edwin A., jt. auth. see Kyle, Robert A.

Baysinger, Barry D., et al. Barriers to Corporate Growth. LC 80-8603. 1981. price not set (ISBN 0-669-04323-0). Lexington Bks.

Baysinger, Patricia R. see Dewey, John.

Bayt, Phyllis T. Administering Medications. (Health Occupations Ser.). 1981. pap. write for info. (ISBN 0-672-61522-3). Bobbs.

Bazak Guidebook Publishers, Ltd. Bazak Guide to Israel 1980-1981. (Illus.). 1980. pap. 7.95 o.p. (ISBN 0-06-090758-4, CN 758, CN). Har-Row.

Bazak, Jacob. Jewish Law & Jewish Life, 8 bks. in 4 vols. Passamaneck, Stephen M., ed. Incl. Bk. 1. Selected Rabbinical Response (ISBN 0-8074-0034-3, 180210); Bks. 2-4. Contracts, Real Estate, Sales & Usury (180211); Bks. 5-6. Credit, Law Enforcement & Taxation (180212); Bks. 7-8. Criminal & Domestic Relations (ISBN 0-8074-0037-8, 180213). 1978. pap. 12.50 complete vol. (ISBN 0-8074-0038-6, 180218); pap. 5.00 ea. UAHC.

--Judaism & Psychical Phenomena. LC 71-184295. 6.50 o.p. (ISBN 0-912326-27-1). Garrett-Helix.

Bazalgette, Leon. Henry Thoreau Bachelor of Nature. Brooks, Wyck Van, tr. LC 80-2679. 1981. Repr. of 1924 ed. 37.50 (ISBN 0-404-19076-6). AMS Pr.

Bazan, Emilia Pardo see Pardo Bazan, Emilia.

Bazan, N. G. & Lolley, R. N., eds. Neurochemistry of the Retina: Proceedings of the International Symposium on the Neurochemistry of the Retina, 28 August - 1 September 1979, Athens, Greece. (Illus.). 584p. 1980. 70.00 (ISBN 0-08-025485-3). Pergamon.

Bazant, J. A Concise History of Mexico from Hidalgo to Cardenas 1805-1940. (Illus.). 1977. 26.95 (ISBN 0-521-21495-5); pap. 7.95x (ISBN 0-521-29173-9). Cambridge U Pr.

Bazaraa, M. S. & Shetty, C. M. Foundations of Optimization. (Lecture Notes in Economics & Mathematical Systems Ser.: Vol. 122). 1976. pap. 9.00 (ISBN 0-387-07680-8). Springer-Verlag.

Bazaraa, Mokhtar S. & Jarvis, John J. Linear Programming & Network Flows. LC 76-42241. 1977. text ed. 29.95 (ISBN 0-471-06015-1). Wiley.

Bazaraa, Mokhtar S. & Shetty, C. M. Nonlinear Programming: Theory & Algorithms. LC 78-986. 1979. text ed. 30.95 (ISBN 0-471-78610-1). Wiley.

Bazelon, Irwin. Knowing the Score: Notes on Film Music. LC 80-24925. (Illus.). 352p. 1981. pap. 6.95 (ISBN 0-668-05132-9, 5132). Arco.

Bazerman, Charles. The Informed Writer. LC 80-68140. 320p. 1981. pap. text ed. 9.50 (ISBN 0-395-29715-X); instr's manual 0.50 (ISBN 0-395-29716-8). HM.

Bazerman, Charles, jt. auth. see Wiener, Harvey.

Bazerman, Charles, jt. auth. see Wiener, Harvey S.

Bazin, Andre. Orson Welles: A Critical View. Rosenbaum, Jonathan, tr. from Fr. LC 74-15810. (Illus.). 1978. 12.50 o.s.i. (ISBN 0-06-010274-8, HarpT). Har-Row.

--What Is Cinema? Gray, Hugh, tr. LC 67-18899. 1967. 12.95x (ISBN 0-520-00091-9); pap. 3.45 (ISBN 0-520-00092-7, CAL151). U of Cal Pr.

--What Is Cinema, Vol. 2. Gray, Hugh, tr. & compiled by. 1971. 12.95x (ISBN 0-520-02034-0); pap. 4.50 (ISBN 0-520-02255-6, CAL250). U of Cal Pr.

Bazin, Germain. Baroque & Rococo Art. (World of Art Ser.). (Illus.). 1964. pap. 9.95 (ISBN 0-19-519927-8). Oxford U Pr.

Bazinet, George F., jt. auth. see Arnett, Ross H.

BCC Staff. Big Potential for Rigid Oriented Containers: P-037. (Illus.). 1976. 625.00 o.p. (ISBN 0-89336-051-1). BCC.

--Blow Molding Markets, P-029. rev. ed. 1976. 500.00 o.p. (ISBN 0-89336-042-2). BCC.

--Data-Telecommunications Progress Report. 1981. 850.00 (ISBN 0-89336-241-7, G-009R). BCC.

--Fluorocarbons: Alternatives, Markets, Problems. (Illus.). 1976. 500.00 o.p. (ISBN 0-89336-092-9). BCC.

--Fuel & Lubricant Additives. 1981. 800.00 (ISBN 0-89336-239-5, C-027). BCC.

--Future Utility Requirements. rev. ed. 1977. 650.00 (ISBN 0-89336-003-1, E-028). BCC.

--G-046 Growing Markets for Security Monitoring & Alarm Systems: G-046. 1980. 750.00 (ISBN 0-89336-111-9). BCC.

--Healthy Foods: Markets, Trends. 1981. 750.00 (ISBN 0-89336-245-X, GA-047). BCC.

--New Burgeoning Video Industries. 1980. cancelled (ISBN 0-89336-264-6, G-058). BCC.

--Nutritional Food Additives, GA-040. 1979. 675.00 (ISBN 0-89336-119-4). BCC.

--Office of the Future. 1980. cancelled (ISBN 0-89336-242-5, G-056). BCC.

--The Pet Industry: Outlook. 1981. 750.00 (ISBN 0-89336-164-X, GA-034). BCC.

--Plastics in Food Packaging P-034. 1980. 975.00 (ISBN 0-89336-163-1). BCC.

--The Resurging Plastics Pipe Industry P-043. (Illus.). 1980. 750.00 (ISBN 0-89336-165-8). BCC.

--The Telephone Instrument: Access, Business. 1980. cancelled (ISBN 0-89336-243-3, G-057). BCC.

--Transparent Plastics: Developments Trends, P-053. 1981. 950.00 (ISBN 0-89336-201-8). BCC.

--Vitamins & Food Supplements, GA-036. 1980. 975.00 (ISBN 0-89336-090-2). BCC.

--Wind Power: Who's Doing What, Why & Where. 1981. 750.00 (ISBN 0-89336-240-9, E-040). BCC.

BCC Staff, ed. Fermentation Products & Processes, C-018: Developments. 1978. 750.00 o.p. (ISBN 0-89336-145-3). BCC.

--The Superconductivity Industry. 1980. 750.00 (ISBN 0-89336-144-5, E-032R). BCC.

Beable, William H. Epitaphs: Graveyard Humour & Eulogy. LC 79-154494. 246p. Repr. of 1925 ed. 15.000 (ISBN 0-8103-3374-0). Gale.

Beach, Beatrice, jt. auth. see Hu, C. T.

Beach, Charles M., et al. Distribution of Income & Wealth: Theory & Evidence for Ontario. (Ontario Economic Council Research Studies). 1981. pap. 17.50 (ISBN 0-8020-3369-5). U of Toronto Pr.

Beach, D. N. The Shona & Zimbabwe Nine Hundred to Eighteen Fifty: An Outline of Shona History. LC 80-14116. 424p. 1980. text ed. 45.00x (ISBN 0-8419-0624-6, Africana). Holmes & Meier.

Beach, E. F. Economic Models: An Exposition. 227p. 1957. text ed. 11.25 (ISBN 0-471-06072-0, Pub. by Wiley). Krieger.

Beach, Mark. Editing Your Own Newsletter. 76p. 1980. pap. 6.95x (ISBN 0-9602664-2-9, Pub. by Coast to Coast Bks). Intl Schol Bk Serv.

Beach, Sunny. Stan Goes on Safari. 1981. 4.95 (ISBN 0-533-04641-6). Vantage.

Beach, Vincent. Charles X. LC 69-14471. (Illus.). 1970. 25.00x (ISBN 0-87108-103-2). Pruett.

Beach, Waldo & Niebuhr, H. Richard, eds. Christian Ethics-Sources of the Living Tradition. 2nd ed. 550p. 1973. text ed. 16.95 (ISBN 0-8260-0786-4). Wiley.

Beacham, Daniel W. & Beacham, Woodard D. Synopsis of Gynecology. 9th ed. LC 77-3544. (Illus.). 1977. pap. 19.95 (ISBN 0-8016-0525-3). Mosby.

Beacham, Hans. Architecture of Mexico: Yesterday & Today. 1969. 15.00 (ISBN 0-8038-0013-4). Architectural.

--Architecture of Mexico: Yesterday & Today. Date not set. 15.00 o.p. (ISBN 0-8038-0013-4). Hastings.

Beacham, Woodard D., jt. auth. see Beacham, Daniel W.

Beachley, Michael C., jt. ed. see Hazra, Tapan A.

Beaconsfield, P. Placenta-a Neglected Experimental Animal. 1979. 68.00 (ISBN 0-08-024430-0); pap. 28.00 (ISBN 0-08-024435-1). Pergamon.

Beadle, Leigh. The New Brew It Yourself. 150p. 1981. 5.95 (ISBN 0-374-51529-8). FS&G.

Beadle, Muriel. Child's Mind. LC 75-89079. 1971. pap. 3.50 (ISBN 0-385-08228-2, Anch). Doubleday.

Beadles, William T., jt. auth. see Greider, Janice E.

Beadnell, Charles M. Encyclopaedic Dictionary of Science & War. LC 74-164093. 1971. Repr. of 1943 ed. 20.00 (ISBN 0-8103-3753-3). Gale.

Beagle, Legal. The Legal Beagle. LC 79-56874. 1980. 8.95 (ISBN 0-533-04538-X). Vantage.

Beagle, Peter. Last Unicorn. 1976. pap. 2.25 (ISBN 0-345-27505-5). Ballantine.

Beagle, Peter S. A Fine & Private Place. 256p. 1976. pap. 2.25 (ISBN 0-345-29001-1). Ballantine.

Beagle, Peter S., jt. auth. see Derby, Pat.

Beahm, George. Kirk's Works. (Fantasy Artists Ser.: No. 2). (Illus., Orig.). 1980. pap. 10.00 (ISBN 0-9603276-1-4). Heresy Pr.

Beahrs, Oliver H., jt. auth. see Jackman, Raymond J.

Beahrs, Oliver H., ed. General Surgery Therapy Update Service. (Illus.). 1979. 80.00 (ISBN 0-89289-300-1). HM Prof Med Div.

Beak, Linda. Wire Fox Terriers. Foyle, Christina, ed. (Foyle's Handbks). 1973. 3.95 (ISBN 0-685-55789-8). Palmetto Pub.

Beal, tr. see Mueller, F. Max.

Beal, Doone. A Pleasure of Cities. 1975. 10.95 o.p. (ISBN 0-7181-1430-2, Pub. by Michael Joseph). Merrimack Bk Serv.

Beal, Edwin F., et al. Practice of Collective Bargaining. 5th ed. 1976. text ed. 19.50x (ISBN 0-256-01821-9). Irwin.

Beal, Fred E. Proletarian Journey. LC 70-146158. (Civil Liberties in American History Ser). 1971. Repr. of 1937 ed. lib. bdg. 39.50 (ISBN 0-306-70096-4). Da Capo.

Beal, H. How to Run a Restaurant. 1978. 16.50 o.p. (ISBN 0-685-04998-1, 0-911156-27-6). Porter.

Beal, Kathleen. Bob Dylan. LC 74-13936. (Rock'n Pop Stars Ser.). (Illus.). 32p. (gr. 4-12). 1974. PLB 5.95 (ISBN 0-87191-399-2); pap. 2.95 (ISBN 0-89812-107-8). Creative Ed.

Beal, Merrill D. Grand Canyon: The Story Behind the Scenery. rev. ed. DenDooven, Gweneth R., ed. LC 75-14775. (Illus.). 1978. 7.95 (ISBN 0-916122-31-X); pap. 3.00 (ISBN 0-916122-06-9). K C Pubns.

--I Will Fight No More Forever. 1975. pap. 2.50 (ISBN 0-345-28461-5). Ballantine.

--I Will Fight No More Forever: Chief Joseph & the Nez Perce War. LC 62-13278. (Illus.). 384p. 1963. pap. 6.95 (ISBN 0-295-74009-4). U of Wash Pr.

Beal, Peter W; see O'Neal, William B.

Beal, Richard S. Systems Analysis of International Crises. LC 79-66860. 1979. text ed. 19.75 (ISBN 0-8191-0858-8); pap. text ed. 13.75 (ISBN 0-8191-0859-6). U Pr of Amer.

Beal, Richard S., jt. ed. see Misra, K. P.

Beal, Virginia A. Nutrition in the Life Span. LC 79-24610. 1980. text ed. 19.95 (ISBN 0-471-03664-1). Wiley.

Beale, Calvin L., jt. auth. see Bogue, Donald J.

Beale, Helen P. Bibliography of Plant Viruses. 1700p. 1976. 80.00x (ISBN 0-231-03763-5). Columbia U Pr.

Beale, Howard K. Theodore Roosevelt & the Rise of America to World Power. 1962. pap. 1.50 o.s.i. (ISBN 0-02-030380-7, Collier). Macmillan.

Beale, I. L., jt. auth. see Corballis, M. C.

Beale, Jack G. The Manager & the Environment: General Theory & Practice of Environmental Management. LC 79-40712. (Illus.). 192p. 1980. 33.00 (ISBN 0-08-024043-7); pap. 16.75 (ISBN 0-08-024044-5). Pergamon.

Beale, Walter H. Old & Middle English Poetry: A Guide to Information Sources. LC 74-11538. (American Literature, English Literature & World Literatures in English Information Guide Ser.: Vol. 7). 1976. 30.00 (ISBN 0-8103-1247-6). Gale.

Bealer, Alex W. Old Ways of Working Wood. rev. ed. (Illus.). 1980. 12.50 (ISBN 0-517-54047-9, 540479). Potter.

--Old Ways of Working Wood. rev ed. (Illus.). 256p. 1980. 12.50 (ISBN 0-517-54047-9). Barre.

Bealer, Alex W., 3rd. The Art of Blacksmithing. LC 76-4546. (Funk & W Bk.). (Illus.). 448p. 1976. 16.95 (ISBN 0-308-10254-1, TYC-T). T Y Crowell.

Bealey, Frank. Constituency Politics. LC 65-27451. 1966. 9.95 o.s.i. (ISBN 0-02-902010-7). Free Pr.

Beall, Gretchen H. Music As Experience: Structure & Sequence for the Elementary School. 352p. 1981. pap. text ed. write for info. (ISBN 0-697-03444-5). Wm C Brown.

Beall, James R. & Downing, Robert E. Helicopter Utilization in Municipal Law Enforcement: Administrative Considerations. (Illus.). 96p. 1973. text ed. 14.75 (ISBN 0-398-02780-3). C C Thomas.

Beall, Pamela & Nipp, Susan. Wee Sing & Play. (Illus.). 64p. (Orig.). 1981. pap. 2.25 (ISBN 0-8431-0391-4). Price Stern.

Beals, Alan R. Village Life in South India: Cultural Design & Environmental Variation. LC 74-76547. (Worlds of Man Ser). 1974. 11.00x (ISBN 0-88295-600-0); pap. 5.75x (ISBN 0-88295-601-9). AHM Pub.

Beals, Carleton. Colonial Rhode Island. LC 73-99437. (Colonial History Ser). (Illus.). (gr. 5 up). 1970. PLB 6.75 o.p. (ISBN 0-8407-7107-X). Elsevier-Nelson.

Beals, Ralph L. California Indians Six. Horr, David A., ed. (American Indian Ethnohistory Ser.). 1978. lib. bdg. 42.00 (ISBN 0-8240-0776-X). Garland Pub.

--The Peasant Marketing System of Oaxaca, Mexico. 1975. 30.00x (ISBN 0-520-02435-4). U of Cal Pr.

Beals, Ralph L., ed. see Driver, Harold, et al.

Beals, Richard. National Real Estate Examination Study Guide. 1980. pap. text ed. 10.00 (ISBN 0-89764-002-0). Lincoln's Leadership.

Beam, F. N., ed. Ideas That Become Big Business. 1981. 28.50 o.p. (ISBN 0-686-68304-8). Porter.

Beam, George, jt. auth. see Simpson, Dick.

Beam, R. M., et al. Computational Fluid Dynamics. Keller, Herbert B., ed. LC 78-9700. 1978. 17.60 (ISBN 0-8218-1331-5, SIAM-11). Am Math.

Beaman, Arthur. The Chesapeake Bay Retriever. 1980. 19.95 (ISBN 0-87714-075-8). Caroline Hse.

Beaman, Donald R., et al, eds. Eighth International Congress on X-Ray Optics & Microanalysis. LC 77-18656. 665p. 90.00 (ISBN 0-87812-180-3). Pendell Pub.

Beame, Rona. Emergency! LC 76-5778. (Illus.). 64p. (gr. 3-5). 1977. PLB 6.97 (ISBN 0-671-32824-7). Messner.

Beamer, Charles. Lightning in the Bottle. 320p. 1981. pap. 8.95 (ISBN 0-8407-5233-4). Nelson.

Beames, John, tr. see Glanville, Ranulph de.

Beamish, F. E. & Van Loon, J. C. Recent Advances in the Analytical Chemistry of the Noble Metals. LC 77-166010. 527p. 1972. text ed. 105.00 (ISBN 0-08-016751-9). Pergamon.

Beams, Floyd A. Advanced Accounting. 1979. text ed. 21.95 (ISBN 0-13-010124-9). P-H.

Bean, A. R. & Simons, R. H. Lighting Fittings, Performance & Design. (International Series in Electrical Engineering: Vol. 1). 1968. 23.10 o.p. (ISBN 0-08-012594-8). Pergamon.

Bean, Barbara, jt. auth. see Erdstein, Erich.

Bean, George E. Aegean Turkey. (Illus.). 1980. 17.50 o.p. (ISBN 0-393-01328-6). Norton.

Bean, Geraldine. Charles Boettcher: A Study in Pioneer Western Enterprise. LC 76-6472. 1976. 19.00x (ISBN 0-89158-049-2). Westview.

Bean, Joseph J., Jr. & Laliberty, Rene. Understanding Hospital Labor Relations: An Orientation for Supervisors. LC 76-20014. 110p. 1977. pap. text ed. 8.95 (ISBN 0-201-00496-8). A-W.

Bean, Joseph, Jr. & Laliberty, Rene. Decentralizing Hospital Management: A Manual for Supervisors. 1980. pap. text ed. 8.95 (ISBN 0-201-00556-5). A-W.

Bean, Lowell J. Mukat's People: The Cahuilla Indians of Southern California. LC 78-145782. (Illus.). 300p. 1972. 14.00x (ISBN 0-520-01912-1); pap. 4.50x (ISBN 0-520-02627-6). U of Cal Pr.

Bean, Philip. Compulsory Admissions to Mental Hospitals. LC 79-41786. 1980. 46.00 (ISBN 0-471-27758-4, Pub. by Wiley-Interscience). Wiley.

--The Social Control of Drugs. LC 74-1342. 176p. 1974. 15.95 o.p. (ISBN 0-470-06090-5). Halsted Pr.

Bean, Reynold & Clemes, Harris. How to Discipline Children Without Feeling Guilty. rev. ed. (The Whole Child Ser.). (Illus.). 80p. 1980. pap. 3.95 (ISBN 0-933358-77-6). Enrich.

--How to Raise Children's Self-Esteem. rev. ed. (The Whole Child Ser.). (Illus.). 80p. 1980. pap. 3.95 (ISBN 0-933358-75-X). Enrich.

--How to Teach Children Responsibility. rev. ed. (The Whole Child Ser.). (Illus.). 80p. 1980. pap. 3.95 (ISBN 0-933358-78-4). Enrich.

Bean, Reynold, et al. How to Raise Teenagers' Self-Esteem. rev. ed. (The Whole Child Ser.). (Illus.). 96p. 1980. pap. 3.95 (ISBN 0-933358-76-8). Enrich.

Bean, W. J., compiled by. Trees & Shrubs: Hardy in the British Isles, 4 vols. 8th ed. Clarke, D. L. & Taylor, George, eds. (Illus.). 850p. 1981. 280.00x set (ISBN 0-312-81742-8). St Martin.

Beanblossom, Ronald E., ed. see Reid, Thomas.

Beane, Wendell C., ed. see Eliade, Mircea.

Beaney, Jan. Fun with Collage. (Learning with Fun Ser.). (Illus.). 64p. (gr. 5 up). 1980. text ed. 11.50x (ISBN 0-7182-1320-3, LTB). Soccer.

Beaney, William M., jt. auth. see Mason, A. T.

Beany, Jan. Adventures with Collage. LC 79-128406. (Illus.). (gr. 5-9). 1970. 6.95 (ISBN 0-7232-6033-8). Warne.

Bear, Fred. Fred Bear's Field Notes. LC 76-2752. 1976. 11.95 (ISBN 0-385-11690-X). Doubleday.

--Fred Bear's World of Archery. (Illus.). 1979. 15.95 (ISBN 0-385-11275-0). Doubleday.

Bear, H. S. Intermediate Algebra for College Students. LC 72-104058. 1970. text ed. 12.95 o.p. (ISBN 0-8465-0420-0). Benjamin-Cummings.

--Introduction to Differential Equations. (Illus.). 490p. 1981. pap. text ed. 19.50 (ISBN 0-9605502-0-8). Manoa Pr.

Bear, H. S. & Mouck, N. G. Elementary Algebra for College Students. 1968. text ed. 12.95 o.p. (ISBN 0-201-00432-1, 00433). A-W.

Bear, Jacob. Hydraulics of Ground Water. (Water Resources & Environmental Engineering Ser.). (Illus.). 1980. text ed. 48.95 (ISBN 0-07-004170-9). McGraw.

Bear, James A., Jr., jt. auth. see Nichols, Frederick D.

Bear, John. United States of America. LC 75-44862. (Macdonald Countries). (Illus.). (gr. 6 up). 1976. PLB 7.95 (ISBN 0-382-06109-8, Pub. by Macdonald Ed). Silver.

Beard, Charles. The Reformation of the Sixteenth Century in Its Relation to Modern Thought & Knowledge. LC 80-12915. xxviii, 450p. 1980. Repr. of 1962 ed. lib. bdg. 33.50x (ISBN 0-313-22410-2, BERF). Greenwood.

Beard, Charles A. & Beard, Mary R. America in Mid Passage. (Rise of American Civilization Ser. Vol. 3). 1966. 15.00 (ISBN 0-8446-1062-3). Peter Smith.

Beard, Charles A. & Schultz, Birl E. Documents on the State-Wide Initiative, Referendum & Recall. LC 70-120853. (Law, Politics & History Ser). 1970. Repr. of 1912 ed. lib. bdg. 39.50 (ISBN 0-306-71958-4). Da Capo.

Beard, Charles R. Lucks & Talismans: A Chapter of Popular Superstition. LC 74-174903. xxii, 258p. Repr. of 1934 ed. 22.00 (ISBN 0-8103-3871-8). Gale.

Beard, Crowell. Ptosis. 3rd ed. LC 80-21576. (Illus.). 276p. 1980. text ed. 44.50 (ISBN 0-8016-0532-6). Mosby.

Beard, Edmund. Developing the ICBM: A Study in Bureaucratic Politics. (Institute of War & Peace Studies). 288p. 1976. 17.50x (ISBN 0-231-04012-1). Columbia U Pr.

Beard, Edmund & Horn, Stephen. Congressional Ethics: The View from the House. LC 74-1434. 60p. 1975. pap. 3.95 (ISBN 0-8157-0855-6). Brookings.

Beard, Henry & McKie, Roy. Sailing. LC 80-54621. (Illus.). 96p. 1981. 8.95 (ISBN 0-89480-158-9); pap. 4.95 (ISBN 0-89480-144-9). Workman Pub.

Beard, Isobel R. Draw with Dots. (Activity Fun Books). (Illus., Orig.). (ps-3). 0.99 o.p. (ISBN 0-695-90180-X). Follett.

--Join the Dots. (Activity Fun Books). (Illus.). (ps-3). 1969. 0.99 o.p. (ISBN 0-695-90390-X). Follett.

--Link the Dots. 2nd ed. (Activity Fun Books). (Illus.). (ps-3). 1969. 0.99 o.p. (ISBN 0-695-90456-6). Follett.

--Play with Dots. 2nd ed. (Activity Fun Books). (Illus.). (ps-3). 1969. 0.99 o.p. (ISBN 0-695-90625-9). Follett.

Beard, J. Turfgrass: Science & Culture. (Illus.). 1972. ref. ed. 23.95 (ISBN 0-13-933002-X). P-H.

Beard, James. Barbecue with Beard. 1976. pap. 2.25 o.s.i. (ISBN 0-446-82975-7). Warner Bks.

--Delights & Prejudices. (Illus.). 1964. 6.95 (ISBN 0-689-00007-3); pap. 7.95 (ISBN 0-689-70605-7). Atheneum.

--James Beard Cookbook. rev. ed. 1970. 14.95 (ISBN 0-525-13621-5, Hawthorn). Dutton.

--James Beard's American Cookery. 1980. pap. 9.95 (ISBN 0-686-63303-2). Little.

--James Beard's Casserole Cookbook. 1977. pap. 1.50 o.p. (ISBN 0-449-13871-2, GM). Fawcett.

--James Beard's Fish Cookery. 1967. pap. 2.75 (ISBN 0-446-95680-5). Warner Bks.

Beard, James & Jerome, Carl. New Recipes for the Cuisinart Food Processor. 4th ed. 96p. 1978. pap. 5.00 (ISBN 0-936662-00-X, FP-250). Cuisinart Cooking.

Beard, James B. Turfgrass Management: The Golf Course. (Orig.). 1981. write for info. (ISBN 0-8087-2872-5). Burgess.

Beard, Mary R., jt. auth. see Beard, Charles A.

Beard, Miriam. History of Business, Vol. 2: From the Monopolists to the Organization Man. 298p. 1963. pap. 2.25 o.p. (ISBN 0-472-06076-7, 76, AA). U of Mich Pr.

Beard, Paul. Living on: How Consciousness Continues & Evolves After Death. 212p. 1981. 12.95 (ISBN 0-8264-0036-1); pap. 5.95 (ISBN 0-8264-0037-X). Continuum.

Beard, Peter, ed. Longing for Darkness: Kamante's Tales from Out of Africa. LC 74-19092. (Illus.). 242p. 1975. 19.95 o.p. (ISBN 0-15-153080-7). HarBraceJ.

Beard, R. E., et al. Risk Theory: The Stochastic Basis of Insurance. 2nd ed. LC 77-1637. 195p. 1977. text ed. 17.95x o.p. (ISBN 0-412-15100-6, Pub. by Chapman & Hall). Methuen Inc.

--Risk Theory: The Stochastic Basis of Insurance. 2nd ed. LC 77-1637. 1977. 13.95 o.p. (ISBN 0-470-99119-4). Halsted Pr.

Beard, R. W. & Nathanielsz, P. W. Fetal Physiology & Medicine. LC 76-20126. (Illus.). 1976. text ed. 32.00 (ISBN 0-7216-1600-3). Saunders.

Beard, Ray, jt. auth. see Matthews, Velda.

Beard, Ross E., Jr. Carbine: The Story of David Marshall Williams. LC 76-20847. 1977. 12.50 (ISBN 0-87844-036-4); ltd ed, signed 25.00 (ISBN 0-87844-047-X). Sandlapper Store.

Beard, W., jt. auth. see Atkins, A. G.

Bearden, H. Joe, jt. auth. see Fuquay, John W.

Bearden, Romare & Henderson, Harry. Six Black Masters of American Art. LC 70-175358. 4.95 o.p. (ISBN 0-385-01211-X). Doubleday.

Bearden, Romare & Holty, Carl. The Painter's Mind: A Study of the Relations of Srtructure & Space in Painting a New Printing. LC 80-8527. 240p. 1981. lib. bdg. 25.00 (ISBN 0-8240-9457-3). Garland Pub.

Bearden, Thomas E. The Excalibur Briefing: Understanding Paranormal Phenomena. LC 78-12936. (A Walnut Hill Bk.). (Illus., Orig.). 1980. pap. 8.95 (ISBN 0-89407-015-0). Strawberry Hill.

Beardmore, Nellie. Come Walk with Me. 1981. 5.95 (ISBN 0-533-04850-8). Vantage.

Beardow, Keith. The Volvo Penta Aquamatic Boat Engine. (Illus.). 224p. 1980. 27.00 (ISBN 0-7153-8000-1). David & Charles.

Beards, Peter. Electronics: Level II. (Illus.). 192p. 1980. pap. text ed. 12.95x (ISBN 0-7121-0581-6). Intl Ideas.

Beardsell, P. R., ed. Ricardo Guiraldes: Don Segundo Sombra. 252p. 1973. text ed. 8.65 (ISBN 0-08-017009-9); pap. text ed. 8.30 (ISBN 0-08-017010-2). Pergamon.

Beardslee, Edward C., jt. auth. see Jerman, Max E.

Beardslee, John W., III, ed. see Turretin, Francis.

Beardslee, William A. Literary Criticism of the New Testament. Via, Dan O., Jr., ed. LC 77-94817. (Guides to Biblical Scholarship: New Testament Ser.). 96p. (Orig.). 1970. pap. 2.50 (ISBN 0-8006-0185-8, 1-185). Fortress.

Beardslee, William A., ed. see Calloud, Jean.

Beardslee, William A., ed. see Detweiler, Robert.

Beardslee, William A., ed. see Tannehill, Robert C.

Beardsley, Aubrey V. Last Letters of Aubrey Beardsley. 158p. 1980. Repr. of 1904 ed. lib. bdg. 20.00 (ISBN 0-8482-4200-9). Norwood Edns.

Beardsley, Charles. Fourth Blow. 1980. pap. 2.50 (ISBN 0-445-04623-6). Popular Lib.

Beardsley, Edward H. Harry L. Russell & Agricultural Science in Wisconsin. (Illus.). 1969. 20.00x (ISBN 0-299-05470-5). U of Wis Pr.

Beardsley, John. Probing the Earth: Contemporary Land Projects. LC 77-12419. (Illus.). 112p. 1978. 17.50 (ISBN 0-87474-232-3). Smithsonian.

Beardsley, Lou. How to Be a Better Mother-in-Law. 176p. (Orig.). 1981. pap. 4.95 (ISBN 0-89081-281-0). Harvest Hse.

--Mother-in-Laws Can Be Fun. LC 80-84763. 1981. pap. 4.95 (ISBN 0-89081-281-0). Harvest Hse.

Beardsley, M. C. Writing with Reason: Logic for Composition. (Illus.). 176p. 1976. pap. text ed. 6.95 (ISBN 0-13-970301-2). P-H.

Beardsley, Monroe. Practical Logic. 1950. text ed. 14.95 (ISBN 0-13-692111-6). P-H.

Beardsley, Monroe C. Aesthetics: Problems in the Philosophy of Criticism. 2nd ed. (Illus.). 688p. 1981. 25.00 (ISBN 0-915145-09-X); pap. text ed. 14.50 (ISBN 0-915145-08-1). Hackett Pub.

--Literature & Aesthetics. LC 68-57656. 1968. pap. 2.50 (ISBN 0-672-60903-7). Bobbs.

--Modes of Argument. LC 67-18663. 1967. pap. 2.50 (ISBN 0-672-60893-6). Bobbs.

Beardsley, Monroe C., et al, eds. Theme & Form: An Introduction to Literature. 4th ed. 704p. 1975. text ed. 17.95 (ISBN 0-13-912972-3). P-H.

Beardsley, Philip L. Redefining Rigor: Ideology & Statistics in Political Inquiry. (Sage Library of Social Research: Vol. 104). (Illus.). 199p. 1980. 18.00x (ISBN 0-8039-1472-5); pap. 8.95x (ISBN 0-8039-1473-3). Sage.

Beardsley, Rick, ed. The Videolog: General Interest & Education. 1980-81 ed. (Videolog Ser.). 500p. 1981. pap. 34.50 (ISBN 0-88432-071-5). J Norton Pubs.

--The Videolog in Business. 1980-81 ed. (Videolog Ser.). 300p. 1981. pap. 39.50 (ISBN 0-88432-070-7). J Norton Pubs.

--The Videolog in the Health Sciences. 1980-81 ed. (Videolog Ser.). 1981. pap. 49.50 (ISBN 0-88432-069-3). J Norton Pubs.

Beardsley, Theodore S., Jr. Hispano-Classical Translations. 188p. 1970. 7.95 (ISBN 0-89192-064-1). Interbk Inc.

Beardsley, William R. The Way Out Must Lead in: Life Histories of the Civil Rights Movement. rev. ed. 187p. 1981. pap. 4.95 (ISBN 0-88208-120-9). Lawrence Hill.

Beardwell, C. Clinical Endocrinology: Pituitary, Vol. 1. (Butterworths International Medical Reviews Ser.). 1981. text ed. price not set (ISBN 0-407-02272-4). Butterworth.

Beardwood, Lynette, et al. A First Course in Technical English, Bk. 2. (Illus.). 1979. pap. text ed. 5.95x (ISBN 0-435-28758-3); tchr's ed. 7.50x (ISBN 0-435-28759-1); 24.00tape (ISBN 0-435-28760-5); cassette 22.00 (ISBN 0-435-28031-7). Heinemann Ed.

Bearman, Graham, jt. auth. see Lee, Peter.

Bearman, Jane. The Eight Nights: A Chanukah Counting Book. Syme, Daniel B., ed. LC 78-60781. (Illus.). 1979. pap. 4.50 (ISBN 0-8074-0025-4, 102562). UAHC.

Bear Nicol, W. B. De see Jones, Thora B. & De Bear, Nicol.

Bearns, Robert J. The Awakening Electromagnetic Spectrum. new ed. LC 74-76050. (Illus.). 128p. (Orig.). 1974. pap. 7.98 (ISBN 0-914706-00-4). Awakening Prods.

Bearse, Ray. The Canoe Camper's Handbook. 1974. 9.95 (ISBN 0-87691-094-0). Winchester Pr.

--The Canoe Camper's Handbook. (Illus.). 1979. pap. 7.95 (ISBN 0-87691-281-1). Winchester Pr.

Beasch, Anthony, tr. see Milnes, John, et al.

Beasley. Hand Injuries. (Illus.). 320p. 1981. text ed. write for info. (ISBN 0-7216-1607-0). Saunders.

Beasley, Barbara. No Place to Run. (YA) (gr. 7-9). 1978. pap. 1.95 (ISBN 0-671-43291-5). PB.

Beasley, Conger. Hidalgo's Beard: A California Fantasy. 1979. 9.95 o.p. (ISBN 0-8362-6103-8); pap. 5.95 o.p. (ISBN 0-8362-6100-3). Andrews & McMeel.

Beasley, Daniel S. & Davis, G. A., eds. Aging: Communication Processes & Disorders. 1980. 29.50 (ISBN 0-8089-1281-X). Grune.

Beasley, Jerry, ed. English Fiction, Sixteen Sixty to Eighteen Hundred: A Guide to Information Sources. LC 74-11526. (American Literature, English Literature & World Literatures in English Information Guide Ser.: Vol. 14). 1978. 30.00 (ISBN 0-8103-1226-3). Gale.

Beasley, M. Robert. Fell's Guide to Buying, Building & Financing a Home. LC 63-21657. 1963. 9.95 (ISBN 0-8119-0039-8). Fell.

Beasley, Manley & Robinson, Ras. Laws for Liberated Living. 212p. 1980. pap. 4.95 (ISBN 0-937778-01-X); 3.00 (ISBN 0-937778-02-8). Fulness Hse.

Beasley, Maurine, jt. ed. see Lowitt, Richard.

Beasley, Maurine H. & Harlow, Richard R. Voices of Change: Southern Pulitzer Winners. LC 79-52511. 1979. pap. text ed. 8.50 (ISBN 0-8191-0771-9). U Pr of Amer.

Beasley, N., jt. auth. see Smith, R.

Beasley, Sonia. The Spirulina Cookbook: Recipes for Rejuvenating the Body. (Illus.). 160p. (Orig.). 1981. pap. 6.95 (ISBN 0-916438-39-2). Univ of Trees.

Beasley, Victor. Your Electro-Vibratory Body: A Study of Life Force in the Human Chakras. Hills, Christopher, ed. LC 79-5085. (Illus.). 1979. pap. 9.95 (ISBN 0-916438-27-9). Univ of Trees.

Beasley, W. G., ed. Modern Japan: Aspects of History, Literature & Society. (Campus Ser.: No. 195). 1977. pap. 6.95x (ISBN 0-520-03495-3). U of Cal Pr.

Beasley, W. G., tr. Select Documents on Japanese Foreign Policy, 1853-1868. 1955. 27.50x (ISBN 0-19-713508-0). Oxford U Pr.

Beasley-Murray, G. R. Revelation. Black, Matthew, ed. (New Century Bible Commentary Ser.). 352p. (Orig.). 1981. pap. 7.95 (ISBN 0-8028-1885-4). Eerdmans.

Beasley-Murray, G. R., ed. Revelation. (New Century Bible Ser.). 1974. 13.95 o.p. (ISBN 0-551-00533-5). Attic Pr.

Beater, Jack. Electric Motor Test & Repair. 2nd ed. LC 66-24043. 1966. vinyl 6.95 o.p. (ISBN 0-8306-6097-6, 97). TAB Bks.

Beath, Paul R., compiled by. Febold Feboldson: Tall Tales from the Great Plains. LC 62-8725. (Illus.). 1962. pap. 4.95 (ISBN 0-8032-5012-6, BB 161, Bison). U of Nebr Pr.

Beatie, Russel H. Saddles. LC 79-6708. (Illus.). 375p. 1980. 35.00 (ISBN 0-8061-1584-X). U of Okla Pr.

Beatley, R., jt. auth. see Birkhoff, George D.

Beaton, G. H. & McHenry, E. W., eds. Nutrition: A Comprehensive Treatise, 3 vols. Incl. Vol. 1. Macronutrients & Nutrient Elements. 1964. 62.00 (ISBN 0-12-084101-0); Vol. 2. Vitamins, Nutrient Requirements & Food Selections. 1964. 62.00 (ISBN 0-12-084102-9); Vol. 3. Nutritional Status: Assessment & Application. 1966. 53.00 (ISBN 0-12-084103-7). 143.00 (ISBN 0-685-23127-5). Acad Pr.

Beaton, J. R., et al, eds. Horizontal Boring. 2nd ed. (Engineering Craftsmen: No. H28/2). (Illus.). 1976. spiral bdg. 16.50x (ISBN 0-85083-307-8). Intl Ideas.

Beaton, Roderick. Folk Poetry of Modern Greece. LC 79-7644. (Illus.). 272p. 1980. 29.50 (ISBN 0-521-22853-0). Cambridge U Pr.

Beaton, W. R. & Robinson, T. Real Estate Investment. 2nd ed. 1977. text ed. 18.95 (ISBN 0-13-762971-0). P-H.

Beaton, William R. Real Estate Finance. (Illus.). 288p. 1975. 18.95 (ISBN 0-13-762708-4). P-H.

Beatson, Elizabeth H. see Meiss, Millard.

Beattie, Ann. Chilly Scenes of Winter. 1978. pap. 2.75 (ISBN 0-445-04261-3). Popular Lib.

--Falling in Place. 352p. 1981. pap. 2.95 (ISBN 0-445-04650-3). Popular Lib.

Beattie, Arthur H., tr. see Montaigne, Michel De.

Beattie, Eleanor. A Handbook of Canadian Film. 2nd ed. (Take One-PMA Film Ser). (Illus.). 1977. 16.95 o.p. (ISBN 0-88778-130-6); pap. 8.00 (ISBN 0-88778-131-4). NY Zoetrope.

Beattie, Hilary J. Land & Lineage in China. LC 77-91080. (Cambridge Studies in Chinese History, Literature & Institutions). 1979. 34.95 (ISBN 0-521-21974-4). Cambridge U Pr.

Beattie, J. Anatomy of the Common Marmoset. LC 78-72711. 1980. Repr. of 1927 ed. 27.50 (ISBN 0-404-18281-X). AMS Pr.

Beattie, J. H. & Lienhardt, R. G., eds. Studies in Social Anthropology: Essays in Memory of E. E. Evans-Pritchard by His Former Oxford Colleagues. (Illus.). 408p. 1975. 29.95x (ISBN 0-19-823183-0). Oxford U Pr.

Beattie, James. Elements of Moral Science, 2 vols. Wellek, Rene, ed. LC 75-11195. (British Philosophers & Theologians of the 17th & 18th Centuries: Vol. 2). 1976. Repr. of 1793 ed. Set. lib. bdg. 84.00 (ISBN 0-8240-1751-X); lib. bdg. 42.00 ea. Garland Pub.

--Elements of Moral Science. LC 75-45348. 1168p. 1976. Repr. of 1790 ed. lib. bdg. 85.00 (ISBN 0-8201-1167-8). Schol Facsimilies.

Beattie, John. Lifeboats to the Rescue. LC 80-70704. (Illus.). 160p. 1981. 17.95 (ISBN 0-7153-8103-2). David & Charles.

--The Nyoro State. 294p. 1971. 29.95x (ISBN 0-19-823171-7). Oxford U Pr.

--Other Cultures. LC 64-16952. 1968. 9.95 o.s.i. (ISBN 0-02-902040-9); pap. text ed. 7.95 (ISBN 0-02-902050-6). Free Pr.

Beatts, Anne, jt. auth. see Stillman, Deanne.

Beatts, Anne & Head, John, eds. Saturday Night Live. (Illus.). 1977. pap. 7.95 (ISBN 0-380-01801-2, 51342). Avon.

Beatty, Grace J., jt. auth. see Gardner, David C.

Beatty, J. Kelly, jt. ed. see O'Leary, Brian.

Beatty, Jackson. Introduction to Physiological Psychology: Information Processing in the Nervous System. LC 74-17631. (Illus.). 1975. text ed. 15.95x o.p. (ISBN 0-8185-0123-5). Brooks-Cole.

Beatty, James W. & Scamehorn, Richard G. Reaction Kinetics. 1978. pap. text ed. 9.25x (ISBN 0-8191-0376-4). U Pr of Amer.

Beatty, Jerome, Jr. Maria Looney & the Cosmic Circus. 1978. pap. 1.95 (ISBN 0-380-40311-0, 40311, Camelot). Avon.

--Matthew Looney, 4 vols. Incl. Matthew Looney & the Space Pirates. 1975. Vol. 1. pap. 1.25 (ISBN 0-380-00848-3, 24315); Matthew Looney in the Outback. 1973. Vol. 2. pap. 1.50 (ISBN 0-380-00847-5, 31575); Matthew Looney's Invasion of the Earth. 1973. Vol. 3. pap. 1.25 (ISBN 0-380-01493-9, 23069); Matthew Looney's Voyage to the Earth. Vol. 4. pap. 1.50 (ISBN 0-380-01494-7, 47423). (gr. 8 up). 1978. pap. 5.25 boxed set (ISBN 0-380-39693-9, 39693, Camelot). Avon.

--Matthew Looney & the Space Pirates. (gr. 4-8). 1974. pap. 1.50 (ISBN 0-380-00848-3, 50484, Camelot). Avon.

--Matthew Looney's Voyage to the Earth. (Illus.). 176p. (gr. 3-7). 1972. pap. 1.50 (ISBN 0-380-01494-7, 53660, Camelot). Avon.

Beatty, Jim, et al. We Own It: Starting & Managing Co-Ops, Collectives & Employee Owned Ventures. 1981. 14.00 (ISBN 0-917510-02-X); pap. 9.00 (ISBN 0-917510-03-8). Bell Springs Pub.

Beatty, John & Beatty, Patricia. At the Seven Stars. (Illus.). (gr. 7-10). 1967. 4.95g o.s.i. (ISBN 0-02-708550-3). Macmillan.

--Campion Towers. (gr. 7 up). 1965. 4.95g o.s.i. (ISBN 0-02-708670-4). Macmillan.

--Holdfast. LC 75-187902. 224p. (gr. 7-9). 1972. PLB 7.44 o.p. (ISBN 0-688-31434-1). Morrow.

--Master Rosalind. LC 74-5050. 224p. (gr. 7 up). 1974. 8.25 (ISBN 0-688-21819-9); PLB 7.92 (ISBN 0-688-31819-3). Morrow.

--Pirate Royal. (gr. 5-8). 1969. 4.95g o.s.i. (ISBN 0-02-708600-3). Macmillan.

--The Royal Dirk. (gr. 7 up). 1966. 8.75 o.p. (ISBN 0-688-21431-2). Morrow.

--Witch Dog. LC 68-11213. (gr. 7 up). 1968. 7.75 o.p. (ISBN 0-688-21433-9). Morrow.

Beatty, LaMond F. Filmstrips. Duane, James E., ed. LC 80-21338. (The Instructional Media Library: Vol. 4). (Illus.). 104p. 1981. 13.95 (ISBN 0-87778-164-8). Educ Tech Pubns.

--Instructional Materials Centers. Duane, James E., ed. LC 80-21451. (The Instructional Media Library: Vol. 5). (Illus.). 104p. 1981. 13.95 (ISBN 0-87778-165-6). Educ Tech Pubns.

--Motion Pictures. Duane, James E., ed. LC 80-21340. (The Instructional Media Library: Vol. 8). (Illus.). 112p. 1981. 13.95 (ISBN 0-87778-168-0). Educ Tech Pubns.

--Still Pictures. Duane, James E., ed. LC 80-21448. (The Instructional Media Library: Vol. 14). (Illus.). 112p. 1981. 13.95 (ISBN 0-87778-174-5). Educ Tech Pubns.

Beatty, Patricia. The Bad Bell of San Salvador. (Illus.). 256p. (gr. 5-9). 1973. PLB 7.25 o.p. (ISBN 0-688-20081-8); PLB 7.92 (ISBN 0-688-30081-2). Morrow.

--Billy Bedamned, Long Gone by. (gr. 5-9). 1977. 8.25 (ISBN 0-688-22101-7); PLB 7.92 (ISBN 0-688-32101-1). Morrow.

--By Crumbs, It's Mine. LC 75-31574. 256p. (gr. 5-9). 1976. PLB 7.92 (ISBN 0-688-32062-7). Morrow.

--Hail Columbia. (gr. 5-9). 1970. PLB 8.40 (ISBN 0-688-31371-X). Morrow.

--How Many Miles to Sundown. LC 73-10770. (Illus.). (gr. 5-9). 1974. PLB 7.92 (ISBN 0-688-30102-9). Morrow.

--I Want My Sunday, Stranger. (gr. 7 up). 1977. 9.25 (ISBN 0-688-22118-1); PLB 8.88 (ISBN 0-688-32118-6). Morrow.

--Just Some Weeds from the Wilderness. (gr. 7-9). 1978. 8.95 (ISBN 0-688-22137-8); PLB 8.59 (ISBN 0-688-32137-2). Morrow.

--Lacy Makes a Match. LC 79-9813. (gr. 7-9). 1979. 8.50 (ISBN 0-688-22200-5); PLB 8.16 (ISBN 0-688-32200-X). Morrow.

--A Long Way to Whiskey Creek. LC 75-134486. (Illus.). (gr. 5-9). 1971. pap. 7.20 o.p. (ISBN 0-688-31427-9). Morrow.

--Lupita Manana. LC 81-505. 192p. (gr. 7-9). 1981. 8.95 (ISBN 0-688-00358-3); 8.59 (ISBN 0-688-00359-1). Morrow.

--Red Rock Over the River. LC 72-5883. 256p. (gr. 7-9). 1973. PLB 8.40 (ISBN 0-688-30065-0). Morrow.

--Rufus, Red Rufus. LC 74-26981. (Illus.). 192p. (gr. 7 up). 1975. 8.25 (ISBN 0-688-22021-5); PLB 7.92 (ISBN 0-688-32021-X). Morrow.

--Something to Shout About. LC 76-22185. (gr. 5-9). 1976. PLB 7.92 (ISBN 0-688-32078-3). Morrow.

--Wait for Me, Watch for Me, Eula Bee. (gr. 7-9). 1978. 8.95 (ISBN 0-688-22151-3); PLB 8.59 (ISBN 0-688-32151-8). Morrow.

Beatty, Patricia, jt. auth. see Beatty, John.

Beatty, R. W., jt. auth. see Kerns, D. M.

Beatty, Richard W. & Schneier, Craig E. Personnel Administration: An Experiential Skill-Building Approach. 576p. 1981. pap. text ed. 14.95 (ISBN 0-201-00172-1). A-W.

Beatty, Richard W., jt. auth. see Schneier, Craig E.

Beatty, Richmond C., ed. see Clemens, Samuel L.

Beatty, William K., jt. auth. see Marks, Geoffrey.

Beaty, David. The Water Jump: The Story of Transatlantic Flight. LC 76-5116. (Illus.). 288p. (YA) 1977. 10.00 o.p. (ISBN 0-06-010296-9, HarpT). Har-Row.

Beaty, Janice J. Classroom Skills for Preschool Teachers: A Self-Taught Modular Training Program. (Early Childhood Education Ser.). 1979. pap. 8.95 (ISBN 0-675-08283-8). media 195.00 (ISBN 0-675-08282-X); 2-4 sets 155.00 (ISBN 0-686-67284-4); 6 or more 125.00 (ISBN 0-686-67285-2); manual 3.95 (ISBN 0-686-67286-0). Merrill.

Beaty, Jerome, ed. The Norton Introduction to Fiction. 2nd ed. 640p. 1981. pap. text ed. 8.95x (ISBN 0-393-95156-1); classroom guide avail. (ISBN 0-393-95159-6). Norton.

Beau, Francis N. Quantity Food Purchasing Guide. rev. ed. 1974. pap. 9.95 spiral bdg. (ISBN 0-8436-2046-3). CBI Pub.

Beaucamp, Ernest & Hansen, Dorothea. Take Thirty Dictionary. (gr. 12). 1971. pap. 5.25 (ISBN 0-89420-099-2, 219905). Natl Book.

Beaucamp, Ernest & Hansen, Dorthea. Take Thirty Shorthand: Student Syllabus, 2 vols. (gr. 11-12). 1970. Vol. 1. pap. text ed. 5.95 (ISBN 0-89420-097-6, 218999); cassette recordings 244.75 (ISBN 0-89420-211-1, 219105); Vol. 2. pap. text ed. 5.80 (ISBN 0-89420-098-4, 219105). Natl Book.

Beauchamp, Dan E. Beyond Alcoholism: Alcohol & Public Health Policy. 250p. 1980. 17.50 (ISBN 0-87722-189-8). Temple U Pr.

Beauchamp, George A. Curriculum Theory. 3rd ed. 1975. cancelled 5.75 (ISBN 0-912200-05-7). Kagg Pr.

--Curriculum Theory. 4th ed. LC 80-84104. 225p. 1981. pap. text ed. 8.50 (ISBN 0-87581-270-8). Peacock Pubs.

Beauchamp, K. G. & Yuen, C. K. Data Acquisitions for Signal Analysis. (Illus.). 288p. 1980. text ed. 50.00x (ISBN 0-04-621028-8, 2530). Allen Unwin.

Beauchamp, Thom & Perlin, Seymour. Ethical Issues in Death & Dying. 1978. pap. 11.50 (ISBN 0-13-290114-5). P-H.

Beauchamp, Tom L. & Rosenberg, Alexander. Hume & the Problem of Causation. 352p. 1981. 22.50. Oxford U Pr.

Beauchamp, Tom L. & Walters, LeRoy. Contemporary Issues in Bioethics. 1978. 19.95x (ISBN 0-8221-0200-5). Dickenson.

Beauchamp, Tom L. & Bowie, Norman E., eds. Ethical Theory & Business. (Illus.). 1979. text ed. 17.50 (ISBN 0-13-290460-8). P-H.

Beauchamp, Tom L., et al. Philosophy & the Human Condition. (Illus.). 640p. 1980. text ed. 15.95 (ISBN 0-13-662528-2). P-H.

Beauchamp, Virgil. The Life of Christ in the Paintings by Tissot. 1979. deluxe ed. 29.75 (ISBN 0-930582-29-2). Gloucester Art.

Beauchamp, William M. Aboriginal Place Names of New York. LC 68-17915. 333p. 1972. Repr. of 1907 ed. 21.00 (ISBN 0-8103-3231-0). Gale.

Beaudreau, George S., ed. see Biology Colloquium, 34th, Oregon State University, 1973.

Beaudry, Antoinette. Strands of Desire. 288p. (Orig.). 1981. pap. 2.50 (ISBN 0-523-40925-7). Pinnacle Bks.

Beaudry, Harry R. The English Theatre & John Keats. (Salzburg Studies in English Literature, Poetic Drama & Poetic Theory: No. 13). 240p. 1973. pap. 25.00x (ISBN 0-391-01321-1). Humanities.

Beaufait, F. Basic Concepts of Structural Analysis. 1977. text ed. 27.95 (ISBN 0-13-058347-2). P-H.

Beaujeu-Garnier, J. France. LC 75-28288. (World's Landscapes). (Illus.). 160p. 1976. pap. text ed. 9.50x (ISBN 0-582-48178-3). Longman.

--Geography of Population. 2nd ed. Beaver, S. H., tr. from Fr. (Geographies for Advanced Study Ser). (Illus.). 1978. text ed. 25.00x (ISBN 0-582-48569-X); pap. text ed. 13.50x (ISBN 0-582-48570-3). Longman.

--Methods & Perspectives in Geography. Bray, Jennifer, tr. from French. LC 75-23484. (Illus.). 144p. 1976. text ed. 11.95x (ISBN 0-582-48069-8). Longman.

Beaujeu-Garnier, J. & Chabot, G. Urban Geography. (Geography for Advanced Study Ser.). 1967. 14.95 (ISBN 0-471-06115-8). Halsted Pr.

Beaujeu-Garnier, J. & Delobez, A. Geography of Marketing. (Geographies for Advanced Study). (Illus.). 1979. pap. text ed. 19.95 (ISBN 0-582-48991-1). Longman.

Beaujour, Elizabeth K. Invisible Land: A Study of the Artistic Imagination of Iurii Olesha. LC 71-130959. 1970. 20.00x (ISBN 0-231-03428-8). Columbia U Pr.

Beaulac, Willard L. The Fractured Continent: Latin America in Close-Up. LC 78-70885. (Publication Ser.: No. 225). (Illus.). 252p. 1980. 11.95 (ISBN 0-8179-7251-X). Hoover Inst Pr.

Beaulieu, Harry J. & Buchan, Roy M. Quantitative Industrial Hygiene. 1981. lib. bdg. 17.50 (ISBN 0-8240-7180-8). Garland Pub.

Beaulieu, John E. Stretching for All Sports. (Illus.). 214p. 7.95 (ISBN 0-87095-079-7). Athletic.

Beaulieu, Mirabelle. Cooking for Myself. (Illus.). 1978. pap. 5.95 o.s.i. (ISBN 0-7715-9435-6, Pub. by Gage). Vanguard.

--The Cooking of Provincial Quebec. (Illus.). 158p. 1976. 9.95 o.s.i. (ISBN 0-7715-9942-0). Vanguard.

Beaumarchais, Pierre. Le Barbier de Seville. Arnould, E. J., ed. (French Texts Ser.). 1977. pap. text ed. 10.00x (ISBN 0-631-00620-6, Pub. by Basil Blackwell). Biblio Dist.

--Le Mariage De Figaro. Arnould, E. J., ed. (French Texts Ser.). 1976. pap. text ed. 10.00x (ISBN 0-631-00540-4, Pub. by Basil Blackwell). Biblio Dist.

Beaumier, John P. & Camp, Lewis. The Pipesmoker. LC 79-1770. (Illus.). 144p. 1980. 9.95 (ISBN 0-06-250376-6, HarpR). Har-Row.

Beaumont, Anthony. Traction Engines Past & Present. 1974. 11.95 o.p. (ISBN 0-7153-6379-4). David & Charles.

Beaumont, Cyril W. Michel Fokine & His Ballets. LC 80-69956. (Illus.). 1981. pap. 8.95 (ISBN 0-87127-120-6). Dance Horiz.

Beaumont, Ernest V. The Intellectual Cowardice of the American Philosophers. (Illus.). 1980. deluxe ed. 49.75 (ISBN 0-89266-262-X). Am Classical Coll Pr.

Beaumont, Francis. Knight of the Burning Pestle. Doebler, John, ed. LC 67-11462. (Regents Renaissance Drama Ser). 1967. 9.50x (ISBN 0-8032-0250-4); pap. text ed. 2.45x (ISBN 0-8032-5250-1, BB 223, Bison). U of Nebr Pr.

Beaumont, Francis & Fletcher, John. A King & No King. LC 77-171733. (English Experience Ser.: No. 290). 88p. Repr. of 1619 ed. 15.00 (ISBN 90-221-0290-4). Walter J Johnson.

--The Knight of the Burning Pestle. LC 70-25848. (English Experience Ser.: No. 152). 76p. 1969. Repr. of 1613 ed. 8.00 (ISBN 90-221-0152-5). Walter J Johnson.

--The Maides Tragedy. LC 70-38151. (English Experience Ser.: No. 431). 82p. 1972. Repr. of 1619 ed. 13.00 (ISBN 90-221-0431-1). Walter J Johnson.

--Maid's Tragedy. Norland, Howard B., ed. LC 67-21895. (Regents Renaissance Drama Ser). 1968. pap. 1.85x (ISBN 0-8032-5253-6, BB 224, Bison). U of Nebr Pr.

--Philaster. Ashe, Dora J., ed. LC 75-127980. (Regents Renaissance Drama Ser). xxxii, 152p. 1974. 9.95x (ISBN 0-8032-0291-1); pap. 2.75x (ISBN 0-8032-5290-0, BB 236, Bison). U of Nebr Pr.

--Phylaster: Or, Love Lyes a Bleeding. LC 68-54617. (English Experience Ser.: No. 18). 66p. 1968. Repr. of 1620 ed. 8.00 (ISBN 90-221-0018-9). Walter J Johnson.

--The Scornfyl Lady. LC 73-38152. (English Experience Ser.: No. 432). 70p. 1972. Repr. of 1616 ed. 9.50 (ISBN 90-221-0432-X). Walter J Johnson.

--Selected Plays. 1953. 6.00x o.p. (ISBN 0-460-00506-5, Evman). Dutton.

--Wit Without Money: A Comedy. LC 73-25968. (English Experience Ser.: No. 264). 66p. Repr. of 1639 ed. 11.50 (ISBN 90-221-0264-5). Walter J Johnson.

Beaumont, George. Warrior's Looking Glass: Wherein Is Shewn from Many High Authorities the Trivial Causes, Cruel Nature, Direful Effects & Anti-Christian Spirit & Practice of War. LC 76-147426. (Library of War & Peace; Proposals for Peace: a History). lib. bdg. 38.00 (ISBN 0-8240-0218-0). Garland Pub.

Beaumont, Gustave De see De Beaumont, Gustave & De Tocqueville, Alexis.

Beaumont, John. The Metamorphasis of Tobacco. LC 70-171734. (English Experience Ser.: No. 360). 44p. Repr. of 1602 ed. 7.00 (ISBN 90-221-0360-9). Walter J Johnson.

Beaumont, P. B., jt. auth. see Thomson, A. W. J.

Beaumont, Roger A. & Edmonds, Martin, eds. War in the Next Decade. LC 73-77251. 1974. 14.00x (ISBN 0-8131-1291-5). U Pr of Ky.
Beaumont, William. The Career of William Beaumont & the Reception of His Discovery: An Original Anthology. Cohen, I. Bernard, ed. LC 79-7949. (Three Centuries of Science in America Ser.). (Illus.). 1980. lib. bdg. 20.00x (ISBN 0-405-12530-5). Arno.
Beauregard, J. Histoire de France illustree. 1968. 15.00 (ISBN 0-08-013198-0); pap. 7.00 (ISBN 0-08-013197-2). Pergamon.
Beauregard, Raymond A. & Fraleigh, John B. A First Course in Linear Algebra. LC 72-5648. 1973. text ed. 20.50 (ISBN 0-395-14017-X, 3-03230); solutions manual. pap. 2.15 (ISBN 0-395-14018-8, 3-03231). HM.
Beaurline, L., ed. see Jonson, Ben.
Beaurline, Lester A., ed. Mirror for Modern Scholars: Essays in Methods of Research in Literature. LC 65-26779. (Orig.). 1966. pap. 9.50 o.p. (ISBN 0-672-63064-8). Odyssey Pr.
Beauvoir, Simone De see De Beauvoir, Simone.
Beaven, Betsey, et al, eds. The Political Palate: A Feminist Vegetarian Cookbook. (Illus.). 352p. (Orig.). 1980. pap. 8.95 (ISBN 0-9605210-0-3, Dist. by Crossing Press). Sanguinaria.
Beaven, D. W., et al. Self Teaching Guide to Physical Examination. 1976. pap. 9.95x (ISBN 0-433-01770-8). Intl Ideas.
Beaver & Beaver. SG Understanding Statistics. 1980. pap. text ed. write for info. (ISBN 0-87872-241-6). Duxbury Pr.
Beaver, Bonnie. Comparative Anatomy of Domestic Animals: A Guide. (Illus.). 180p. 1980. pap. 9.95 (ISBN 0-8138-1545-2). Iowa St U Pr.
--Veterinary Aspect of Feline Behavior. LC 80-12085. (Illus.). 1980. text ed. 28.50 (ISBN 0-8016-0542-3). Mosby.
Beaver, Bonnie V. Comparative Anatomy of Domestic Animals: A Guide. (Illus.). 209p. pap. 9.95 (ISBN 0-8138-1545-2). Iowa St U Pr.
Beaver, Harold, ed. see Melville, Herman.
Beaver, James N., Jr. John Garfield: His Life & Films. LC 75-38450. (Illus.). 1977. 17.50 o.p. (ISBN 0-498-01890-3). A S Barnes.
Beaver, Ninette, et al. Caril. LC 74-9843. 1974. 10.00 o.p. (ISBN 0-397-00997-6). Lippincott.
Beaver, Patrick. A History of Lighthouses. (Illus.). 158p. 1976. pap. 4.95 (ISBN 0-8065-0256-8). Citadel Pr.
--A History of Tunnels. (Illus.). 155p. 1976. pap. 4.95 (ISBN 0-8065-0527-3). Citadel Pr.
--The Spice of Life: Pleasures of the Victorian Age. (Illus.). 1979. 24.00 (ISBN 0-241-89366-6, Pub. by Hamish Hamilton England). David & Charles.
Beaver, Paul. Ark Royal: A Pictorial History of the Royal Navy's Last Conventional Aircraft Carrier. (Illus.). 96p. 1980. 19.95 (ISBN 0-85059-381-6). Aztex.
--E-Boats & Coastal Craft. (Worldwar Two Photo Album: No. 17). (Illus.). 96p. 1981. pap. 5.95 (ISBN 0-89404-045-6). Aztex.
--German Capital Ships. (World War Two Photo Album Ser.: No. 14). (Illus.). 1980. 17.95 o.p. (ISBN 0-85059-395-6); pap. 11.95 o.p. (ISBN 0-85059-396-4). Aztex.
--German Capital Ships: World War Two Photo Album. (Illus.). 96p. 1981. pap. 5.95 (ISBN 0-89404-038-3). Aztex.
--German Destroyers & Escorts: World War Two Photo Album. (Illus.). 96p. 1981. pap. 5.95 (ISBN 0-89404-060-X). Aztex.
--U-Boats in the Atlantic. (WW 2 Photo Album Ser.: No. 11). 1980. 17.95 o.p. (ISBN 0-85059-386-7); pap. 11.50 o.p. (ISBN 0-85059-388-3). Aztex.
--U-Boats in the Atlantic: World War Two Photo Album. (Illus.). 96p. 1981. pap. 5.95 (ISBN 0-89404-057-X). Aztex.
--World War Two Photo Album: German Destroyers & Escorts. (Illus.). 96p. 1981. pap. 5.95 (ISBN 0-89404-060-X). Aztex.
--World War 2 Photo Album 14: German Capital Ships. 96p. 1980. 17.95 o.p. (ISBN 0-85059-395-6); pap. 11.95 o.p. (ISBN 0-85059-396-4). Aztex.
Beaver, R. Pierce. American Protestant Women in World Mission. rev. ed. LC 80-14366. Orig. Title: All Loves Excelling. 224p. 1980. pap. 7.95 (ISBN 0-8028-1846-3). Eerdmans.
Beaver, R. Pierce, ed. American Missions in Bicentennial Perspective. LC 77-7569. 1977. pap. 10.95 (ISBN 0-87808-153-4). William Carey Lib.
--The Native American Christian Community: A Directory of Indian, Aleut, & Eskimo Churches. 1979. text ed. 10.95 (ISBN 0-912552-25-5). MARC.
Beaver, Rachel, jt. auth. see Beaver, Richard.
Beaver, Richard & Beaver, Rachel. All About the St. Bernard. (All About Ser.). 1980. 16.95 (ISBN 0-7207-1197-5, Pub. by Michael Joseph). Merrimack Bk Serv.
Beaver, Roy C. Bessemer & Lake Erie Railroad, 1869-1969. LC 73-97230. 1969. 17.95 (ISBN 0-87095-033-9). Golden West.
Beaver, S. H., jt. auth. see Stamp, L. Dudley.
Beaver, S. H., tr. see Beaujeu-Garnier, J.
Beaver, S. H., tr. see Gourou, Pierre.
Beaver, William C., jt. auth. see Noland, George B.
Beaver, William H. Financial Reporting: An Accounting Revolution. (Contemporary Topics in Accounting Ser.). (Illus.). 240p. 1981. text ed. 12.95 (ISBN 0-13-316141-2); pap. text ed. 9.95 (ISBN 0-13-316133-1). P-H.
Beavers, Dorothy J. Autism: Nightmare Without End. Hammond, Debbie, ed. 1980. 14.95 (ISBN 0-87949-167-1). Ashley Bks.
Beavers, William A., jt. auth. see Bates, Robert B.
Beavis, Bill, jt. auth. see Jarman, Colin.
Beavon, K. S. Central Place Theory: A Reinterpretation. LC 76-42282. (Illus.). 1977. text ed. 16.95x (ISBN 0-582-48678-5); pap. text ed. 12.95x (ISBN 0-582-48683-1). Longman.
Beazer, William F. The Commercial Future of Hong Kong. LC 76-24343. (Praeger Special Studies). 1978. 22.95 (ISBN 0-275-23670-6). Praeger.
Beazley, Elizabeth. Maddocks & the Wonder of Wales. (Illus.). 1967. 9.50 (ISBN 0-571-08023-5, Pub. by Faber & Faber). Merrimack Bk Serv.
Beazley, Elizabeth & Brett, Lionel. North Wales: A Shell Guide. (Shell Guide Ser.). (Illus.). 1971. 14.95 (ISBN 0-571-09756-1, Pub. by Faber & Faber). Merrimack Bk Serv.
Beazley, John D. Attic Red-Figure Vase-Painters, 3 Vols. 2nd ed. 1963. Set. 175.00x (ISBN 0-19-813146-1). Oxford U Pr.
Beazley, Mitchell. The Atlas of World Wildlife. LC 73-3724. (Illus.). 208p. 1973. 16.95 (ISBN 0-528-83039-2). Rand.
Bebbington, D. W. Patterns in History. LC 79-3062. 1980. pap. 7.25 (ISBN 0-87784-737-1). Inter-Varsity.
Bebbington, Jim. The Young Player's Guide to Soccer. LC 78-66970. 1979. 11.95 (ISBN 0-7153-7536-9). David & Charles.
Bebek, Borna. Santhana: One Man's Road to the East. 224p. 1981. 11.95 (ISBN 0-370-30260-5, Pub. by Chatto-Bodley-Jonathan). Merrimack Bk Serv.
Bebe Patten. Give Me Back My Soul. 1973. pap. 1.25 o.p. (ISBN 0-8007-0645-5). Revell.
Beccaria, Cesare. On Crimes & Punishments. Paolucci, Henry, tr. LC 61-18589. 1963. pap. 3.95 (ISBN 0-672-60302-0, LLA107). Bobbs.
Beccar-Varela, Adele, jt. auth. see Lappe, Frances M.
Becher, Rolf. Schooling by the Natural Method. (Illus.). 8.75 (ISBN 0-85131-105-9, Dist. by Sporting Book Center). J A Allen.
Becher, Tony & Maclure, Stuart, eds. Accountability in Education. (General Ser.). (Illus.). 1978. pap. text ed. 20.00x (ISBN 0-85633-167-8, NFER). Humanities.
Becher, Udo. Early Tin Plate Model Railways. (Illus.). 180p. 1980. 33.95 (ISBN 0-8038-1964-1). Hastings.
Becher, William D. Logical Design Using Integrated Circuits. 1977. text ed. 21.50x (ISBN 0-8104-5859-4). Hayden.
Bechet, Sidney. Treat It Gentle: An Autobiography. LC 74-23412. (Roots of Jazz Ser). (Illus.). vi, 245p. 1975. lib. bdg. 22.50 (ISBN 0-306-70657-1); pap. 5.95 (ISBN 0-306-80086-1). Da Capo.
Becht, J. Edwin & Belzung, L. D. World Resource Management: Key to Civilizations & Social Achievement. (Illus.). 336p. 1975. text ed. 19.95 (ISBN 0-13-968107-8). P-H.
Bechtel, Helmut. Cactus Identifier. LC 76-51168. (Illus.). 256p. 1981. pap. 6.95 (ISBN 0-8069-8960-2). Sterling.
--Cactus Identifier. (Identifier Ser.). (Illus.). (gr. 6 up). 1977. 6.95 o.p. (ISBN 0-8069-3080-2); PLB 6.69 o.p. (ISBN 0-8069-3081-0). Sterling.
--House Plant Identifier. LC 72-95203. (Identifier Bks.). (Illus.). 256p. (gr. 6 up). 1973. 6.95 (ISBN 0-8069-3056-X); PLB 6.69 (ISBN 0-8069-3057-8). Sterling.
Bechtel, John H. Slips of Speech. LC 77-159889. Repr. of 1901 ed. 18.00 (ISBN 0-8103-4041-0). Gale.
Bechtel, Louise S. Books in Search of Children: Essays & Speeches. Haviland, Virginia, ed. LC 79-78078. 1969. 6.95 o.s.i. (ISBN 0-02-508290-6). Macmillan.
Bechtereva, N. P., ed. Psychophysiology Today & Tomorrow: Proceedings of International Union of Physiological Sciences Conference on Psychophysiology, 1979. (Illus.). 270p. 1980. 60.00 (ISBN 0-08-025930-8). Pergamon.
Bechtold, Peter K. Politics in the Sudan: Parliamentary & Military Rule in an Emerging African Nation. LC 76-6466. (Special Studies). (Illus.). 375p. 1976. text ed. 33.95 (ISBN 0-275-22730-8). Praeger.
Beck, A. E. Physical Principles of Exploration Methods: An Introduction Text for Geology & Geophysics Students. 256p. 1981. 39.95 (ISBN 0-470-27124-8); pap. 18.95 (ISBN 0-470-27128-0). Halsted Pr.
Beck, A. H. Handbook of Vacuum Physics. Vol. 2, Pt. 1 1965. pap. 19.50 (ISBN 0-08-010888-1); Vol. 3, Pts. 1-3. 1965. pap. 22.00 (ISBN 0-08-011051-7). Pergamon.
Beck, Aaron T. Depression: Causes & Treatment. LC 67-23826. 1972. 15.00x (ISBN 0-8122-7652-3); pap. 8.50x (ISBN 0-8122-1032-8, Pa Paperbks). U of Pa Pr.
--Diagnosis & Management of Depression. LC 73-83290. 160p. 1973. 11.95x (ISBN 0-8122-7674-4, Pa Paperbks). U of Pa Pr.
Beck, Anatole, et al. Excursions into Mathematics. LC 68-57963. (Illus.). 1969. text ed. 16.95x (ISBN 0-87901-004-5). Worth.
Beck, Arthur C. & Hillmar, Ellis D. Making MBO-R Work. LC 75-18151. 239p. 1975. text ed. 8.95 (ISBN 0-201-00469-0). A-W.
Beck, Arthur C., Jr. & Hillmar, Ellis D. A Practical Approach to Organization Development Through MBO: Selected Readings. LC 71-183665. (Illus.). 280p. 1972. pap. text ed. 8.95 (ISBN 0-201-00447-X). A-W.
Beck, Barbara. First Book of the Ancient Maya. LC 65-11746. (First Bks). (Illus.). (gr. 4-6). 1965. PLB 6.45 (ISBN 0-531-00464-3). Watts.
--First Book of the Aztecs. LC 66-18671. (First Bks). (Illus.). (gr. 4-6). 1966. PLB 6.45 (ISBN 0-531-00476-7). Watts.
--First Book of the Incas. LC 66-16579. (First Bks). (Illus.). (gr. 4-6). 1966. PLB 4.90 o.p. (ISBN 0-531-00558-5). Watts.
Beck, Barbara L. First Book of Vegetables. (First Bks). (gr. 4-6). 1970. PLB 4.90 o.p. (ISBN 0-531-00717-0). Watts.
--The Pilgrims of Plymouth. LC 79-187970. (First Bks). (Illus.). 96p. (gr. 4-6). 1972. PLB 4.47 o.p. (ISBN 0-531-00776-6). Watts.
Beck, Brenda E. Perspectives on a Regional Culture: Essays About the Coimbatore Area of South India. 1979. text ed. 17.95x (ISBN 0-7069-0723-X, Pub. by Vikas India). Advent Bk.
Beck, Brenda E., ed. Perspectives on a Regional Culture: Essays About the Coimbatore Area of South India. 211p. 1980. 18.00x (ISBN 0-7069-0723-X, Pub. by Croom Helm Ltd England). Biblio Dist.
Beck, Brian E. Reading the New Testament Today: An Introduction to the Study of the New Testament. LC 78-14420. (Biblical Foundations Ser.). 1978. pap. 4.95 (ISBN 0-8042-0391-1). John Knox.
Beck, Carl. Contempt of Congress: A Study of the Prosecutions Initiated by the Committee on un-American Activities, 1945-1957. LC 75-166090. (Studies in American History & Government Ser.). 264p. 1974. Repr. of 1959 ed. lib. bdg. 25.00 (ISBN 0-306-70229-0). Da Capo.
Beck, Carleton E. Philosophical Foundations of Guidance. 1963. pap. text ed. 9.95 (ISBN 0-13-662262-3). P-H.
Beck, Charles B., ed. Origin & Early Evolution of Angiosperms. (Illus.). 416p. 1976. 25.00x (ISBN 0-231-03857-7). Columbia U Pr.
Beck, David. Ski Touring in California. 2nd ed. LC 79-90502. (Illus.). 1979. pap. 7.95 (ISBN 0-686-59506-8). Pika Pr.
Beck, Donald R. Basic Hospital Financial Management. 350p. 1980. text ed. 24.00 (ISBN 0-89443-329-6). Aspen Systems.
Beck, Doris M. Custom Tailoring for Homemakers. (Illus.). (gr. 10-12). 1972. text ed. 8.80 (ISBN 0-87002-122-2). Bennett IL.
Beck, Earl R. A Time of Triumph & of Sorrow: Spanish Politics During the Reign of Alfonso Xii, Eighteen Seventy-Four to Eighteen Eighty-Five. LC 78-23282. 320p. 1979. 18.95x (ISBN 0-8093-0902-5). S Ill U Pr.
Beck, Evelyn T. Kafka & the Yiddish Theater: Its Impact on His Work. LC 75-143763. 1971. 19.50 (ISBN 0-299-05881-6). U of Wis Pr.
Beck, F., jt. ed. see Lierse, W.
Beck, Harry S. & Gerrard, James W. God Is Speaking to You. 6.95 (ISBN 0-686-05779-1). Prod Hse.
Beck, Henry J. & Parrish, Roy J., Jr. Computerized Accounting. (Business Ser.). 1977. pap. text ed. 8.95 (ISBN 0-675-08449-0); card deck 3.95 (ISBN 0-685-79549-7); manual 3.95 (ISBN 0-686-67826-5); source dick 3.95 (ISBN 0-686-67827-3). Merrill.
Beck, Horace. Classification & Nomenclature of Beads & Pendants. (Illus.). 80p. 1973. pap. 10.00 (ISBN 0-87387-083-2). Shumway.
--Folklore & the Sea. 1st ed. LC 73-6011. (The American Maritime Library: Vol. 6). (Illus.). 1973. pap. 9.95 (ISBN 0-8195-6052-9). Columbia U Pr.
Beck, Hubert S. Stay in the Son-Shine. (Orig.). 1980. pap. text ed. 3.95 (ISBN 0-89536-460-3). CSS Pub.
Beck, J. Walter & Davies, John E. Medical Parasitology. 3rd ed. LC 80-25201. (Illus.). 300p. 1981. text ed. 21.95 (ISBN 0-8016-0552-0). Mosby.
Beck, James. Raphael. LC 73-12198. (Library of Great Painters). 1976. 35.00 (ISBN 0-8109-0432-2). Abrams.
Beck, Jane. The General Store in Vermont: An Oral History. 1980. pap. 3.50x (ISBN 0-934720-23-1). VT Hist Soc.
Beck, John & Cox, Charles. Advances in Management Education. LC 80-40117. 1980. 47.50 (ISBN 0-471-27775-4, Pub. by Wiley-Interscience). Wiley.
Beck, Julian. Blaise Cendrars: Pathe Baby. (Pocket Poets Ser.). 112p. 1980. pap. 3.50 o.p. (ISBN 0-87286-108-2). City Lights.
Beck, Kirsten. How to Run a Small Box Office. 1980. pap. 4.95 (ISBN 0-933750-01-3). Off off Broadw.
Beck, L. & Holms, R. Philosophic Inquiry: An Introduction to Philosophy. 2nd ed. 1968. 16.50 (ISBN 0-13-662494-4). P-H.
Beck, L. W., et al, trs. see Kant, Immanuel.
Beck, Lewis W. Eighteenth Century Philosophy. LC 66-10364. (Orig.). 1966. pap. text ed. 6.95 (ISBN 0-02-902100-6). Free Pr.
Beck, Lewis W., ed. see De Vleeschauwer, H. J.
Beck, Lewis W., ed. see Fischer, Kuno.
Beck, Lewis W., ed. see Kant, Immanuel.
Beck, Lewis W., ed. see Macmillan, R. A.
Beck, Lewis W., ed. see Prichard, H. A.
Beck, Lewis W., ed. see Schilpp, Paul A.
Beck, Lewis W., ed. see Seth, Andrew.
Beck, Lewis W., ed. see Vaihinger, Hans.
Beck, Lewis W., ed. see Ward, James.
Beck, Lewis W., ed. see Watson, John.
Beck, Lewis W., tr. see Kant, Immanuel.
Beck, Madeline H. & Williamson, Lamar, Jr. Mastering Old Testament Facts, 3 bks. Incl. Bk. 1. Introduction on-Deut. 1979 (ISBN 0-8042-0134-X); Bk. 2. Joshua-Esther. 1979 (ISBN 0-8042-0135-8); Bk. 3. Job, Psalms, Proverbs, Ecclesiastes, Song of Solomon. 106p. (gr. 9-12). 1980 (ISBN 0-8042-0136-6). (Illus., Orig.). pap. text ed. 4.95 ea. John Knox.
Beck, Mary E. Nutrition & Dietectics for Nurses. 6th ed. (Churchill Livingstone Nursing Texts Ser.). (Illus.). 288p. 1980. pap. text ed. 9.75 (ISBN 0-443-02009-4). Churchill.
--Nutrition and Dietetics for Nurses. 5th ed. LC 76-51312. (Illus.). 1977. pap. text ed. 8.25 o.p. (ISBN 0-443-01557-0). Churchill.
Beck, P. G. & Forster, M. C. Six Rural Problem Areas: Relief-Resources-Rehabilitation. LC 71-165679. (Franklin D. Roosevelt & the Era of the New Deal Ser). 1971. Repr. of 1935 ed. lib. bdg. 17.50 (ISBN 0-306-70333-5). Da Capo.
Beck, Phillip. Oratour: Village of the Dead. 124p. 1979. 15.00. Shoe String.
Beck, R., et al. Table of Laser Lines in Gases & Vapors. (Springer Series in Optical Sciences: Vol. 2). 1976. 21.70 o.p. (ISBN 3-540-07808-8). Springer-Verlag.
Beck, R. N. & Orr, J. B. Ethical Choice. LC 70-122282. 1970. pap. text ed. 7.95 (ISBN 0-02-902060-3). Free Pr.
Beck, Robert. Experiencing Biography. (Literature Ser.). (gr. 10 up). 1978. pap. text ed. 6.20x (ISBN 0-8104-6034-3); 1.75 (6125). Hayden.
Beck, Robert, jt. auth. see Kolman, Bernard.
Beck, Robert C. Motivation: Theories & Principles. 1978. ref. ed. 18.95 (ISBN 0-13-603902-2). P-H.
Beck, Robert N. & Steinkraus, Warren E., eds. Studies in Personalism: Selected Writings of Edgar Sheffield Brightman. LC 75-4133. (Philosophy Ser.: No. 603). 15.00 o.s.i. (ISBN 0-89007-603-0). C Stark.
Beck, S. William. Gloves: Their Annals & Associations. LC 75-75801. 1969. Repr. of 1883 ed. 15.00 (ISBN 0-8103-3825-4). Gale.
Beck, Stanley. Insect Photoperiodism. 1968. 40.50 o.p. (ISBN 0-12-084350-1). Acad Pr.
Beck, Thomas. French Legislators 1800-1834: A Study in Quantitative History. 1975. 22.75x (ISBN 0-520-02535-0). U of Cal Pr.
Beck, Warren. Rest Is Silence & Other Stories. LC 63-12585. 132p. (Orig.). 1963. pap. 3.95 (ISBN 0-8040-0261-4, 46). Swallow.
Beck, Warren A. New Mexico: A History of Four Centuries. (Illus.). 1979. Repr. of 1962 ed. 11.95 (ISBN 0-8061-0533-X). U of Okla Pr.
Beck, Warren A. & Haase, Ynez D. Historical Atlas of New Mexico. LC 68-31366. (Illus.). 1969. 9.95 o.p. (ISBN 0-8061-0819-3); pap. 6.95 (ISBN 0-8061-0817-7). U of Okla Pr.
Beck, Warren A. & Haase, Ynez P. Historical Atlas of California. LC 74-5952. (Illus.). 240p. 1975. 12.50 (ISBN 0-8061-1211-5); pap. 7.95 (ISBN 0-8061-1212-3). U of Okla Pr.
Beck, William C. & Trier, James R. Programmed Course in Basic Algebra. (Mathematics Ser). 1971. 13.95 (ISBN 0-201-00445-3); 3.95 (ISBN 0-201-00446-1). A-W.
Becke, Donna, jt. ed. see Wilson, Paul T.
Beckenbach, Edwin, et al. College Algebra. 4th ed. 1978. text ed. 18.95x (ISBN 0-534-00536-5); study guide 5.95x (ISBN 0-534-00537-3). Wadsworth Pub.
Beckenbach, Edwin F. & Drooyan, Irving. Modern College Algebra & Trigonometry. 3rd ed. 1977. 18.95x (ISBN 0-534-00468-7). Wadsworth Pub.

Beckenbach, Edwin F., ed. Applied Combinatorial Mathematics. 630p. 1981. lib. bdg. write for info. (ISBN 0-89874-172-6). Krieger.

Beckenstein, Alan, et al. Performance Measurement of the Petroleum Industry: Functional Profitability & Alternatives. LC 79-1951. (Illus.). 1979. 19.95 (ISBN 0-669-03017-1). Lexington Bks.

Becker. Seven Little Rabbits. (gr. k-3). 1977. pap. 1.50 (ISBN 0-590-04429-X); pap. 3.50 bk. & record (ISBN 0-590-20620-6). Schol Bk Serv.

--Timothy & Titus. pap. 1.75 (ISBN 0-8024-2646-8). Moody.

Becker, jt. auth. see Anderson.

Becker, A. C., Jr. The Complete Book of Fishing. LC 76-18477. (Illus.). 217p. 1981. Repr. of 1977 ed. 20.00 (ISBN 0-498-01973-X). A S Barnes.

--Waterfowl in the Marshes. LC 69-13030. (Illus.). 1969. 9.95 o.p. (ISBN 0-498-06948-6). A S Barnes.

Becker, Abraham S. Soviet National Income, 1958-1964: National Accounts of the USSR in the Seven Year Plan Period. (Illus.). 1969. 35.00x (ISBN 0-520-01437-5). U of Cal Pr.

Becker, Arthur P., ed. see Committee on Taxation Resources and Economic Development Symposium, 4th.

Becker, Betty G. & Fendler, Dolores T. Vocational & Personal Adjustments in Practical Nursing. 3rd ed. LC 77-10153. (Illus.). 1978. pap. text ed. 9.50 (ISBN 0-8016-0565-2). Mosby.

Becker, Bob. It's Easy to Raise & Train a Puppy. 1950. pap. 1.95 (ISBN 0-385-00102-9, Dolp). Doubleday.

Becker, Bruce. Backgammon for Blood. 1974. 8.95 (ISBN 0-87690-123-2). Dutton.

Becker, Calvin W. First & Second Timothy & Titus: Letters to Two Young Men. (Teach Yourself the Bible Ser). 1961. pap. 1.75 (ISBN 0-8024-2646-8). Moody.

Becker, Carl L. Declaration of Independence: A Study in the History of Political Ideas. 1958. pap. 2.45 (ISBN 0-394-70060-0, V-60, Vin). Random.

--History of Political Parties in the Province of New York, 1760-1776. 1960. pap. 7.95x (ISBN 0-299-02024-X). U of Wis Pr.

Becker, Carl M. The Village: A History of Germantown, Ohio, 1804-1976. LC 80-16683. (Historical Society of Germantown, Ohio Ser.). (Illus.). 209p. 1980. 15.00 (ISBN 0-8214-0550-0). Ohio U Pr.

Becker, D. E., ed. Recommendations for the Presentation of Infrared Absorption Spectra in Data Collections-A: Condensed Phases. 1978. pap. text ed. 10.00 (ISBN 0-08-022376-1). Pergamon.

Becker, Dennis & Becker, Nancy. How to Succeed with Your Money: Leader's Guide. (Leader's Guide Ser.). (Illus.). 1978. text ed. 3.25 (ISBN 0-8024-3661-7). Moody.

Becker, Donald. Reverse Dictionary of Urdu. 1980. 38.00x (ISBN 0-8364-0656-7, Pub. by Manohaar India). South Asia Bks.

Becker, E. Lovell, ed. Seminars in Nephrology. LC 76-28438. (Perspectives in Nephrology & Hypertension Ser.). 1976. 25.00 o.p. (ISBN 0-471-01804-X, Pub. by Wiley Medical). Wiley.

Becker, Edna. Nine Hundred Buckets of Paint. (Illus.). (gr. k-2). 1949. 3.95 o.p. (ISBN 0-687-28013-3). Abingdon.

Becker, Eric B., et al. Finite Elements: An Introduction, Vol. I. (Illus.). 256p. 1981. 24.95 (ISBN 0-13-317057-8). P-H.

Becker, Eric V. de see De Becker, Eric V.

Becker, Ernest. Angel in Armor. LC 69-12803. 1969. 5.95 o.s.i. (ISBN 0-8076-0488-7). Braziller.

--Angel in Armor: A Post-Freudian Perspective on the Nature of Man. LC 69-12803. 1975. pap. 3.95 (ISBN 0-02-902280-0). Free Pr.

--Birth & Death of Meaning. 2nd ed. LC 62-15359. 1971. 9.95 (ISBN 0-02-902170-7); pap. 5.95 (ISBN 0-02-902190-1). Free Pr.

--The Denial of Death. LC 73-1860. 1973. 12.95 (ISBN 0-02-902150-2); pap. 3.95 (ISBN 0-02-902310-6). Free Pr.

--Escape from Evil. LC 75-12059. 1976. pap. 3.95 (ISBN 0-02-902340-8). Free Pr.

--The Lost Science of Man. LC 75-142076. 1971. 6.95 o.s.i.; pap. 2.95 (ISBN 0-8076-0599-9). Braziller.

--The Revolution in Psychiatry: The New Understanding of Man. LC 64-11213. 1974. pap. 3.95 (ISBN 0-02-902130-8). Free Pr.

--The Structure of Evil. LC 68-12890. (Illus.). 1968. 8.50 o.s.i. (ISBN 0-8076-0446-1). Braziller.

Becker, Frederick F., ed. Cancer: A Comprehensive Treatise. Incl. Vol. 1. Etiology: Chemical & Physical Carcinogenesis. LC 74-31195. 524p. 1975. 42.50 (ISBN 0-306-35201-X); Vol. 2. Etiology: Viral Carcinogenesis. LC 75-11770. 439p. 1975. 42.50 (ISBN 0-306-35202-8); Vol. 3. Biology of Tumors: Cellular Biology & Growth. LC 74-31196. 473p. 1975. 42.50 (ISBN 0-306-35203-6); Vol. 4, Biology of Tumors: Surfaces,Immunology & Comparative Pathology. 440p. 1975. 42.50 (ISBN 0-306-35204-4); Vol. 5, Chemotherapy. LC 77-1142. 666p. 1977. 42.50 (ISBN 0-306-35205-2); Vol. 6. Radiotherapy, Surgery, & Immunotherapy. LC 74-31196. 544p. 42.50 (ISBN 0-306-35206-0). (Illus., Plenum Pr). Plenum Pub.

Becker, Gaylene. Growing Old in Silence. 160p. 1980. 10.00 (ISBN 0-520-03900-9). U of Cal Pr.

Becker, George J. D. H. Lawrence. LC 79-48075. (Modern Literature Ser.). 160p. 1980. 10.95 (ISBN 0-8044-2029-7); pap. 4.95 (ISBN 0-8044-6033-7). Ungar.

--John Dos Passos. LC 74-78437. (Modern Literature Ser.). 142p. 1974. 10.95 (ISBN 0-8044-2034-3). Ungar.

Becker, H. A. Dimensionless Parameters: Theory & Methodology. LC 76-1570. 128p. 1976. 24.95 (ISBN 0-470-15048-3). Halsted Pr.

Becker, Hal B. Functional Analysis of Information Networks. 296p. 1981. Repr. of 1973 ed. lib. bdg. write for info. (ISBN 0-89874-028-2). Krieger.

Becker, Harold K. Issues in Police Administration. LC 72-9389. 1970. 10.00 (ISBN 0-8108-0281-3). Scarecrow.

--Police Systems of Europe: A Survey of Selected Police Organizations. 2nd ed. (Illus.). 256p. 1980. pap. 13.75 (ISBN 0-398-04023-0). C C Thomas.

Becker, Harold K. & Whitehouse, Jack E. Police of America: A Personal View, Introduction & Commentary. (Illus.). 108p. 1979. 11.75 (ISBN 0-398-03895-3). C C Thomas.

Becker, Harold K., jt. auth. see Felkenes, George T.

Becker, Helmut, jt. ed. see Thorelli, Hans.

Becker, Howard S. Outsiders: Studies in the Sociology of Deviance. LC 63-8413. 1963. 12.95 (ISBN 0-02-902200-2); pap. 3.95 (ISBN 0-02-902140-5). Free Pr.

Becker, Howard S., ed. Other Side: Perspectives on Deviance. LC 64-16953. 1967. pap. 5.95 (ISBN 0-02-902210-X). Free Pr.

Becker, J. Marxian Political Economy. LC 76-9172. (Illus.). 1977. 26.50x (ISBN 0-521-21349-5). Cambridge U Pr.

Becker, Jillian. Hitler's Children: The Story of the Baader - Meinhof Terrorist Gang. LC 76-55730. (Illus.). 1977. 10.00 o.p. (ISBN 0-397-01153-9). Lippincott.

Becker, Joachim. Messianic Expectation in the Old Testament. Green, David E., tr. from Ger. LC 79-8891. 96p. 1980. 7.95 (ISBN 0-8006-0545-4, 1-545). Fortress.

Becker, John. Jaimie. LC 80-65424. 176p. 1980. 10.00 (ISBN 0-87923-340-0). Godine.

--Seven Little Rabbits. LC 72-86974. (Illus.). 4.95 o.p. (ISBN 0-8027-6129-1); PLB 5.85 (ISBN 0-8027-6130-5). Walker & Co.

Becker, John, jt. auth. see Faulkner, Georgene.

Becker, Joseph & Hayes, Robert M. Information Storage & Retrieval: Tools, Elements & Theories. LC 62-12279. (Information Science Ser.). 1963. 28.95 (ISBN 0-471-06129-8, Pub by Wiley-Interscience). Wiley.

Becker, Joseph, jt. auth. see Hayes, Robert M.

Becker, Joseph E. de see De Becker, Joseph E.

Becker, Joseph M. Unemployment Benefits: Should There Be a Compulsory Federal Standard? 1980. pap. 4.25 (ISBN 0-8447-3389-X). Am Enterprise.

Becker, Judith. Traditional Music in Modern Java. LC 80-19180. (Illus.). 1980. text ed. 30.00x (ISBN 0-8248-0563-1). U Pr of Hawaii.

Becker, Judith, et al. Fine-Tuning: An NCCB Report on Noncommercial Radio. 1980. pap. 3.00 (ISBN 0-9603466-4-3). NCCB.

Becker, Julie. Animals of the Fields & Meadows. LC 77-8496. (Animals Around Us Ser.). (Illus.). (gr. 2-6). 1977. PLB 6.95 (ISBN 0-88436-394-5). EMC.

--Animals of the Ponds & Streams. LC 77-8497. (Animals Around Us Ser.). (Illus.). (gr. 2-6). 1977. PLB 6.95 (ISBN 0-88436-398-8). EMC.

--Animals of the Seashore. LC 77-8106. (Animals Around Us Ser.). (Illus.). (gr. 2-6). 1977. PLB 6.95 (ISBN 0-88436-392-9). EMC.

--Animals of the Woods & Forests. LC 77-8253. (Animals Around Us Ser.). (Illus.). (gr. 2-6). 1977. PLB 6.95 (ISBN 0-88436-396-1). EMC.

Becker, Kenneth M. A Monograph of the Genus Lasianthaea (Asteraceae) (Memoirs Ser.: Vol. 31, No. 2). 1979. pap. 6.50 (ISBN 0-89327-211-6). NY Botanical.

Becker, Lawrence C. Property Rights: Philosophic Foundations. 148p. 1980. pap. 5.95 (ISBN 0-7100-0606-3). Routledge & Kegan.

--Property Rights: Philosophic Foundations. 1977. 17.00x (ISBN 0-7100-8679-2). Routledge & Kegan.

Becker, Lawrence W., jt. auth. see Stone, George N.

Becker, Leonard, Jr. & Gustafson, Clair. Encounter with Sociology: The Term Paper. 2nd ed. 1976. pap. 4.95x (ISBN 0-87835-056-X). Boyd & Fraser.

Becker, Lois. How to Make & Sell Your Arts & Crafts. LC 75-29939. (Illus.). 1975. 8.95 (ISBN 0-8119-0250-1); pap. 4.95 (ISBN 0-88391-056-X). Fell.

Becker, Lucille F. Georges Simenon. (World Authors Ser.: No. 456). 1977. lib. bdg. 12.50 (ISBN 0-8057-6293-0). Twayne.

Becker, Marion R. & Rombauer, Irma. The Joy of Cooking, Vol. 1. pap. 2.50 (ISBN 0-451-08625-2, E8625, Sig). NAL.

--The Joy of Cooking, Vol. 2. pap. 2.50 (ISBN 0-451-08072-6, E8691, Sig). NAL.

Becker, Marion R., jt. auth. see Rombauer, Irma S.

Becker, Mark, ed. see Elwood, Ann & Raht, John.

Becker, Martin, et al, eds. Advances in Nuclear Science & Technology, Vol. 12. 350p. 1980. 39.50 (ISBN 0-306-40315-3, Plenum Pr). Plenum Pub.

Becker, Mary K. & Coburn, Patricia. Superspill: An Account of the 1978 Grounding at Bird Rocks. LC 74-76954. 1974. pap. 3.95 (ISBN 0-914842-02-1). Madrona Pubs.

Becker, Nancy, jt. auth. see Becker, Dennis.

Becker, Norman. The Complete Book of Home Inspection. (McGraw Hill Paperbacks). (Illus., Orig.). 1980. 16.95 (ISBN 0-07-004181-4); pap. 8.95 (ISBN 0-07-004180-6). McGraw.

Becker, Paul & Wood, Elizabeth C. Beard's Massage. 1981. pap. price not set (ISBN 0-7216-9592-2). Saunders.

Becker, Peter. Inland Tribes of South Africa. 1980. text ed. 39.00x (ISBN 0-246-10926-2). Humanities.

--Inland Tribes of Southern Africa. 1979. 44.95x (ISBN 0-8464-0058-8). Beekman Pubs.

Becker, R. P. & Johari, O. Scanning Electron Microscopy 1980, No. II. LC 72-626068. (Illus.). xiv, 658p. 50.00 (ISBN 0-931288-12-6). Scanning Electron.

Becker, R. P., jt. ed. see Johari, Om.

Becker, R. S. The Data Processing Security Game: Fundamentals of Data Processing Security. 1977. text ed. 8.25 (ISBN 0-08-021790-7). Pergamon.

Becker, Ralph & Wentworth, Wayne. General Chemistry. LC 72-5642. 1973. text ed. 19.50 o.p. (ISBN 0-395-16002-2, 3-03295); instructor's manual. pap. 1.50 o.p. (ISBN 0-395-16003-0, 3-03296); study guide 7.75 o.p. (ISBN 0-395-14516-3, 3-03297). HM.

Becker, Ralph S. & Wentworth, Wayne E. General Chemistry. LC 79-87864. 1980. text ed. 21.95 (ISBN 0-395-25316-0); instrs'. manual 1.10 (ISBN 0-395-25317-9); study guide 8.50 (ISBN 0-395-25318-7). HM.

Becker, Robert A., jt. ed. see Jensen, Merrill.

Becker, Robert D. Pathways to the Present: The United States Since the Civil War. LC 78-68694. 1979. pap. text ed. 10.25 (ISBN 0-8191-0696-8). U Pr of Amer.

Becker, Robert O. Mechanisms of Growth Control. (Illus.). 377p. write for info. (ISBN 0-398-04469-4). C C Thomas.

Becker, Robert P. & Johari, Om. Cell Surface Labeling. (Illus.). 100p. 1979. pap. text ed. 10.00 (ISBN 0-931288-07-X). Scanning Electron.

Becker, Robin, et al. Personal Effects. LC 75-46406. 88p. 1976. pap. 4.95 (ISBN 0-914086-15-4). Alicejamesbooks.

Becker, Russell J. When Marriage Ends. Julme, Willam E., ed. LC 74-152366. (Pocket Counsel Bks). 64p. (Orig.). 1971. pap. 1.75 (ISBN 0-8006-1102-0, 1-1102). Fortress.

Becker, Siegbert. Wizards That Peep. Kujath, Mentor, ed. 1978. pap. 5.95 (ISBN 0-8100-0054-7, 15N0366). Northwest Pub.

Becker, Stephen. The Chinese Bandit. 1977. pap. 1.95 o.p. (ISBN 0-425-03403-8, Medallion). Berkley Pub.

--Dog Tags. 1978. pap. 1.95 o.p. (ISBN 0-425-03664-2, Medallion). Berkley Pub.

Becker, Stephen, tr. see Philippe, Louis.

Becker, Stephen, tr. see Schwarz-Bart, Andre.

Becker, Teresa M. Cancer Chemotherapy: A Manual for Nurses. (Little, Brown Spiral Training Manual Ser.). 1981. pap. text ed. price not set. Little.

Becker, Theodore L. American Government: Past, Present, Future. 560p. 1976. pap. text ed. 12.95x o.p. (ISBN 0-205-04726-2); instr's manual free o.p. (ISBN 0-685-62607-5). Allyn.

Becker, Theodore L., ed. Political Trials. LC 78-126303. 1971. 9.50 (ISBN 0-672-60744-1). Bobbs.

Becker, Theodore L., et al. Unvote for a New America. 1976. pap. 8.50x o.p. (ISBN 0-205-05720-9). Allyn.

Becker, Warren, jt. auth. see Gleason, Harold.

Becker, Wesley. An Empirical Basis for Change in Education. LC 73-156886. (Illus.). 1971. pap. text ed. 10.95 (ISBN 0-574-18426-0, 13-1426); instr's guide avail. (ISBN 0-574-18427-9, 13-1427). SRA.

Becker, Wesley C. Parents Are Teachers: A Child Management Program. LC 72-75091. (Illus.). 200p. (Orig.). 1971. pap. 6.95 (ISBN 0-87822-019-4); leader's guide 3.95 (ISBN 0-87822-020-8); Set Of 5 Review Tests. 6.95 (ISBN 0-87822-022-4). Res Press.

Becker, Wesley C., et al. Teaching 2: Cognitive Learning & Instruction. LC 75-5563. (Illus.). 306p. 1975. pap. text ed. 10.95 (ISBN 0-574-18030-3, 13-6030); instr's guide avail. (ISBN 0-574-18026-5, 13-6026). SRA.

--Teaching 1: Classroom Management. LC 74-31012. (Illus.). 1975. pap. text ed. 10.95 (ISBN 0-574-18025-7, 13-6025); instr's guide avail. (ISBN 0-574-18026-5, 13-6026). SRA.

Becker, Willi. Barriers to Higher Education in the Federal Republic of Germany. (Access to Higher Education). 1977. pap. 2.50 (ISBN 0-89192-216-4). Interbk Inc.

Becker, William E., jt. ed. see Lewis, Darrell R.

Becker-Cantarino, Baerbel. Daniel Heinsius. (World Author Ser.: No. 477). 1978. lib. bdg. 12.50 (ISBN 0-8057-6318-X). Twayne.

Beckerman, Bernard. Dynamics of Drama. LC 79-65301. 1979. pap. text ed. 7.95x (ISBN 0-89676-019-7). Drama Bk.

Beckerman, Emma. Not So Long Ago. LC 79-57538. 6.95 (ISBN 0-8197-0477-6). Bloch.

Beckerman, Jay, jt. auth. see Rosner, Bernard.

Beckerman, Stephen, jt. ed. see Cordell, Linda S.

Beckett, A. H. & Stenlake, J. B. Practical Pharmaceutical Chemistry, 2 pts. 1975-76. Pt. 1 3rd Ed. text ed. 35.00x (ISBN 0-485-11156-X, Athlone Pr); Pt.2 3rd Ed. text ed. 43.75x (ISBN 0-485-11159-4). Humanities.

Beckett, Arthur W. A see A Beckett, Arthur W.

Beckett, Derrick. Brunels Britain. LC 80-66092. (Illus.). 256p. 1980. 25.00 (ISBN 0-7153-7973-9). David & Charles.

--Concrete Bridges: An Introduction to Structural Design. (Illus.). 1973. 24.00x (ISBN 0-903384-01-9). Intl Ideas.

--An Introduction to Structural Design: Concrete Bridges, No. 1. (Illus.). 240p. 1975. 18.00x (ISBN 0-903384-01-9). Transatlantic.

--Limit State Design of Reinforced Concrete Structures. LC 74-20975. 134p. 1975. 19.95 (ISBN 0-470-06128-6). Halsted Pr.

Beckett, Derrick & Marsh, Paul. Introduction to Structural Design: Timber. (Illus.). 1974. 22.50x (ISBN 0-903384-02-7). Intl Ideas.

--An Introduction to Structural Design: Timber, No. 2. (Illus.). 216p. 1975. 18.00x (ISBN 0-903384-02-7). Transatlantic.

Beckett, Derrick, jt. auth. see Marsh, Paul.

Beckett, J. V. Coal & Tobacco. (Illus.). 280p. 1981. 47.50 (ISBN 0-521-23486-7). Cambridge U Pr.

Beckett Jackson Raeder, Inc. Soil Erosion & Sedimentation Control. (Illus.). 150p. 1980. pap. text ed. 20.00 (ISBN 0-918436-15-X). Environ Design.

Beckett, James C. Short History of Ireland. 6th ed. 1975. 17.50x (ISBN 0-391-02079-X, Hutchinson U Lib); pap. text ed. 8.25x (ISBN 0-391-02080-3). Humanities.

Beckett, Kenneth A. Amateur Greenhouse Gardening. 1980. 14.95 (ISBN 0-8464-0991-7). Beekman Pubs.

Beckett, Lucy. Richard Wagner: Parsifal. (Cambridge Opera Handbooks Ser.). (Illus.). 220p. Date not set. price not set (ISBN 0-521-22825-5); pap. price not set (ISBN 0-521-29662-5). Cambridge U Pr.

Beckett, R. B., ed. see Constable, John.

Beckett, Richard, jt. auth. see Boddy, Michael.

Beckett, Samuel. The Collected Works of Samuel Beckett, 23 vols. LC 74-28586. 1981. Set. 125.00 (ISBN 0-394-49789-9). Grove.

--Company. LC 80-995. 64p. 1980. 8.95 (ISBN 0-394-51394-0, GP 833). Grove.

--Endgame. Beckett, Samuel, tr. from Fr. 1958. pap. 2.45 (ISBN 0-394-17208-6, E96, Ever). Grove.

--Rockaby & Other Works. LC 80-8916. 128p. 1981. 12.50 (ISBN 0-394-51953-1, Ever); pap. 4.95 (ISBN 0-394-17924-2). Grove.

--Stories & Texts for Nothing. 1967. pap. 4.95 (ISBN 0-394-17268-X, E466, Ever). Grove.

--Waiting for Godot. Beckett, Samuel, tr. from Fr. 1954. pap. 2.95 (ISBN 0-394-17204-3, E33, Ever). Grove.

Beckett, Samuel, tr. see Pinget, Robert.

Beckett, Samuel, et al. New Writing & Writers Thirteen. 1980. pap. 6.00 (ISBN 0-7145-3541-9). Riverrun NY.

Beckett, Samuel, et al, trs. see Bosquet, Alain.

Beckett, Sarah. Herbs for Feminine Ailments. LC 80-53449. (Everybody's Home Herbal Ser.). (Illus.). 63p. (Orig.). 1981. pap. 1.95 (ISBN 0-394-74836-0). Shambhala Pubn.

--Herbs to Soothe Your Nerves. LC 80-53448. (Everybody's Home Herbal Ser.). (Illus.). 64p. (Orig.). 1981. pap. 1.95 (ISBN 0-394-74835-2). Shambhala Pubn.

Beckey, Fred. Cascade Alpine Guide: Climbing & High Routes-Rainy Pass to Fraser River, Vol. III. Ferber, Peggy, ed. (Illus.). 356p. (Orig.). 1981. pap. 12.95 (ISBN 0-89886-002-4). Mountaineers.

--Darrington & Index Rock Climbing Guide. LC 76-8296. (Illus.). 64p. (Orig.). 1976. pap. 2.95 (ISBN 0-916890-41-4). Mountaineers.

Beckey, Fred & Bjorstad, Eric. Guide to Leavenworth Rock Climbing Areas. (Illus.). 88p. (Orig.). 1973. pap. 3.50 o.p. (ISBN 0-916890-05-8). Mountaineers.

Beckey, H. D. Field Ionization & Field Desorption Mass Spectroscopy. 1978. text ed. 46.00 (ISBN 0-08-020612-3). Pergamon.

--Field Ionization Mass Spectrometry. LC 79-146601. 1971. 52.00 (ISBN 0-08-017557-0). Pergamon.

--Principles of Field Ionization & Field Desorption Mass Spectrometry. LC 77-33014. 1978. text ed. 52.00 (ISBN 0-686-67953-9). Pergamon.

Beckford, Grania. Virtues & Vices. 304p. 1981. 13.95 (ISBN 0-312-84954-0); pap. 5.95 (ISBN 0-312-84955-9). St Martin.

Beckford, James A. The Trumpet of Prophecy: A Sociological Study of Jehovah's Witnesses. LC 75-14432. 246p. 1975. 24.95 (ISBN 0-470-06138-3). Halsted Pr.

Beckford, William. Azemia: A Descriptive & Sentimental Novel, Interspersed with Pieces of Poetry, by Jaquetta Agneta Mariana Jenks, 2 vols. Luria, Gina, ed. LC 74-8006. (The Feminist Controversy in England, 1788-1810 Ser.). 1974. Set. lib. bdg. 76.00 (ISBN 0-8240-0850-2); lib. bdg. 50.00 ea. Garland Pub.

--Modern Novel Writing, 4 vols. in 1. Incl. Azemia. Repr. of 1797 ed. LC 74-81366. 264p. 1970. Repr. of 1796 ed. 35.00x (ISBN 0-8201-1063-9). Schol Facsimiles.

--Modern Novel Writing, or the Elegant Enthusiast: And Interesting Emotions of Arabella Bloomville, a Rhapsodical Romance, Interspersed with Poetry, by the Right Hon. Lady Harriet Marlow, 2 vols. (The Feminist Controversy in England, 1788-1810 Ser.). 1974. Set. lib. bdg. 100.00 (ISBN 0-8240-0851-0); lib. bdg. 50.00 ea. Garland Pub.

Beckham, Joseph. Legal Implications of Minimum Competency Testing. LC 79-93114. (Fastback Ser.: No. 138). (Orig.). 1980. pap. 0.75 (ISBN 0-87367-138-4). Phi Delta Kappa.

Beckham, Stephen D. Requiem for a People: The Rogue Indians & the Frontiersmen. LC 79-145497. (Civilization of the American Indian Ser.: Vol. 108). (Illus.). 1971. 9.95 (ISBN 0-8061-0942-4); pap. 4.95 (ISBN 0-8061-1036-8). U of Okla Pr.

Beckhard, R. & Harris, R. T. Organizational Transitions: Managing Complex Change. 1977. 6.50 (ISBN 0-201-00335-X). A-W.

Beckhard, Richard. Organization Development: Strategies & Models. Schein, Edgar, et al, eds. (Ser. in Organization Development). 1969. pap. text ed. 6.50 (ISBN 0-201-00448-8). A-W.

Beckhard, Richard, jt. ed. see Burke, W. Warner.

Beckhardt, Benjamin H. Federal Reserve System. LC 70-184746. 1971. 25.00x o.p. (ISBN 0-231-03536-5). Columbia U Pr.

Beckinsale, Monica, jt. auth. see Beckinsale, Robert.

Beckinsale, Robert & Beckinsale, Monica. The English Heartland. (Illus.). 434p. 1980. 39.50x (ISBN 0-7156-1389-8, Pub. by Duckworth England). Biblio Dist.

Beckley, Helen, jt. auth. see White, Paul B.

Beckley, Tim, jt. auth. see Machlin, Milt.

Beckley, Timothy G. Subterranean World. 1971. pap. 6.95 o.p. (ISBN 0-685-04796-2). Saucerian.

Beckley, Timothy G., ed. Book of Space Brothers. (Illus., Orig.). 1968. pap. 6.95 o.p. (ISBN 0-685-20194-5). Saucerian.

Beckman, Bjorn. Organising the Farmers: Cocoa Politics & National Development in Ghana. 1976. pap. text ed. 14.00x (ISBN 0-8419-9722-5). Holmes & Meier.

Beckman, Delores. My Own Private Sky. LC 79-23341. 160p. (gr. 4-6). 1980. 8.95 (ISBN 0-525-35510-3). Dutton.

Beckman, Frank S. Mathematical Foundations of Programming. LC 79-1453. 1980. text ed. 20.95 (ISBN 0-201-14462-X). A-W.

Beckman, Gunnel. Girl Without a Name. Parker, Anne, tr. from Swedish. LC 75-124840. (Illus.). (gr. 4-6). 1970. 5.50 o.p. (ISBN 0-15-230980-2, HJ). HarBraceJ.

Beckman, Patti. The Beachcomber. 192p. (Orig.). 1980. pap. 1.50 (ISBN 0-671-57037-4). S&S.

--Captive Heart. 192p. (Orig.). 1980. pap. 1.50 (ISBN 0-671-57008-0). S&S.

--Shrimpers Woman. 192p. 1981. pap. 1.50 (ISBN 0-671-57054-4). S&S.

Beckman, Theodore N., et al. Wholesaling. 3rd ed. (Illus.). (gr. 9-12). 1959. text ed. 22.50 (ISBN 0-471-06585-4, Pub. by Ronald Pr). Wiley.

--Marketing. 9th ed. 642p. 1973. 19.95 o.p. (ISBN 0-8260-0831-3); instructors' manual avail. o.p. (ISBN 0-471-07435-7). Wiley.

Beckman, Tom. Cincinnati Companion. (Illus.). 1979. pap. text ed. 4.95 o.p. (ISBN 0-930556-00-3). T Beckman & Assoc.

Beckman, W. A., jt. auth. see Duffie, J. A.

Beckman, William A., et al. Solar Heating Design: By the F-Chart Method. LC 77-22168. 1977. 20.95 (ISBN 0-471-03406-1, Pub. by Wiley-Interscience). Wiley.

Beckmann, Martin, et al. Studies in the Economics of Transportation. 1956. 42.50x (ISBN 0-685-89787-7). Elliots Bks.

Beckmann, Neal W. Negotiations, Understanding the Bargaining Process. 1981. write for info. (ISBN 0-87527-242-8). Green.

--Student Guide for Negotiations: Understanding the Bargaining Process. 1981. write for info. (ISBN 0-87527-241-X). Green.

Beckner, Morton. Money Plays. 1980. 10.95 (ISBN 0-686-68751-5, 25122). S&S.

Beckson, Karl, ed. Oscar Wilde: The Critical Heritage. 1970. 40.00x (ISBN 0-7100-6929-4). Routledge & Kegan.

Beckwith, B. K. The Longden Legend. LC 72-5185. (Illus.). 256p. 1973. 9.95 o.p. (ISBN 0-498-01242-5); pap. 2.95 o.p. (ISBN 0-498-01950-0). A S Barnes.

Beckwith, B. P. Radical Essays. 1981. 6.00 (ISBN 0-686-69571-2). Beckwith.

Beckwith, Elizabeth. If I Take the Wings of the Morning. 1979. 2.00 (ISBN 0-686-28780-0). Forward Movement.

Beckwith, John. Early Medieval Art. (World of Art Ser.). (Illus.). 1964. pap. 9.95 (ISBN 0-19-519922-7). Oxford U Pr.

Beckwith, Osmond. Vernon: An Anecdotal Novel. LC 81-65121. (Illus.). 204p. 1981. 10.00. Breaking Point.

Beckwith, Paul, et al, eds. Hymns II. LC 76-47503. 1976. text ed. 9.50 (ISBN 0-87784-898-X); pap. text ed. 5.95 (ISBN 0-87784-783-5); pap. text ed. 5.95 spiral text (ISBN 0-87784-750-9). Inter-Varsity.

Beckwith, Roger T. & Stott, Wilfrid. The Christian Sunday: A Biblical & Historical Study. (Canterbury Ser.). 192p. 1980. pap. 4.95 (ISBN 0-8010-0784-4). Baker Bk.

Beckwith, Thomas G. & Buck, N. Lewis. Mechanical Measurements. 2nd ed. (Mechanical Engineering Ser). 1969. text ed. 24.95 (ISBN 0-201-00454-2). A-W.

Becky, Steven K. The Hard Money Book: An Insider's Guide to Successful Investment in Currency, Gold, Silver, & Precious Stones. (Illus.). 160p. 1980. 14.95 (ISBN 0-8015-3281-7, Hawthorn); pap. 7.95 (ISBN 0-8015-3282-5). Dutton.

Becon, Thomas. The Demaundes of Holy Scripture, with Answeres to the Same. LC 79-84087. (English Experience Ser.: No.907). 116p. 1979. Repr. of 1577 ed. lib. bdg. 9.00 (ISBN 90-221-0907-0). Walter J Johnson.

--The Physyke of the Soule. LC 74-28831. (English Experience Ser.: No. 713). 1975. Repr. of 1549 ed. 3.50 (ISBN 90-221-0713-2). Walter J Johnson.

Becque see Bentley, Eric.

Becquer, G. Rimas, Leyendas & Narraciones. (Span). 4.50x o.s.i. (ISBN 0-686-00884-7). Colton Bk.

Becton, Randy. The Beauty of God's Whisper. 1980. pap. 3.95 (ISBN 0-89137-310-1). Quality Pubns.

--The Gift of Life: A Message of Hope for the Seriously Ill. (Illus.). 1978. pap. 3.95 (ISBN 0-89137-309-8). Quality Pubns.

Becvar, J., ed. Mathematical Foundations of Computer Science 1979: Proceedings, 8th Symposium, Olomouc, Czechoslovakia, September 3-7, 1979. (Lecture Notes in Computer Science: Vol. 74). 1979. pap. 26.40 (ISBN 0-387-09526-8). Springer-Verlag.

Becvar, Raphael J. Skills for Effective Communication: A Guide to Building Relationships. LC 73-19914. (Self-Teaching Guides Ser). 1974. pap. text ed. 7.95x (ISBN 0-471-06143-3). Wiley.

Beda. The History of the Church of Englande. (English Experience Ser.: No. 234). 382p. Repr. of 1565 ed. 55.00 (ISBN 90-221-0234-3). Walter J Johnson.

Bedard, Roger L. Dramatic Literature for Children: A Century in Review. Date not set. text ed. price not set (ISBN 0-87602-019-8); pap. text ed. price not set (ISBN 0-87602-020-1). Anchorage.

Bedarida, Francois, jt. ed. see Johnson, Douglas.

Bedau, Hugo. Justice & Equality. (Central Issues of Philosophy Ser). (Illus.). 1971. pap. 9.00 ref. ed. (ISBN 0-13-514125-7). P-H.

Bedau, Hugo A. The Courts, the Constitution, & Capital Punishment. LC 76-53666. 1977. 18.95 (ISBN 0-669-01290-4). Lexington Bks.

Bedau, Hugo A., ed. Civil Disobedience: Theory & Practice. LC 69-27984. (Orig.). 1969. pap. 6.95 (ISBN 0-672-63514-3). Pegasus.

--Death Penalty in America: An Anthology. 2nd ed. LC 68-19886. 1967. 29.95x (ISBN 0-202-24000-2). Aldine Pub.

Bedbrook, G., ed. The Care & Management of Spinal Cord Injuries. (Illus.). 351p. 1981. 39.80 (ISBN 0-387-90494-8). Springer-Verlag.

Bedbrook, Gerald S. Keyboard Music from the Middle Ages to the Beginnings of the Baroque. 2nd ed. LC 69-15605. (Music Ser). (Illus.). 1973. Repr. of 1949 ed. 19.50 (ISBN 0-306-71056-0). Da Capo.

Beddall, Barbara G., ed. Wallace & Bates in the Tropics: An Introduction to the Theory of Natural Selection. LC 69-12174. (Illus.). (gr. 7 up). 1969. 5.95g o.s.i. (ISBN 0-02-708680-1). Macmillan.

Bedde, Derk, ed. see Fung, Yu-Lan.

Beddome, R. H. The Flora Sylvatica for Southern India, 3 vols. 800p. 1980. 240.00 (ISBN 0-89955-313-3, Intl Bk). Intl Schol Bk Serv.

Bede. Ecclesiastical History of England. Repr. 45.00 o.p. (ISBN 0-686-12351-4). Church History.

--Ecclesiastical History of the English Nation. Stevens, John, tr. 1973. 12.95x (ISBN 0-460-00479-4, Evman). Dutton.

--Emile Zola. (Columbia Essays on Modern Writers Ser.: No. 69). 1974. pap. 2.00 (ISBN 0-231-02977-2). Columbia U Pr.

Bedeian, Arthur G. Organizations: Theory & Analysis. 350p. 1980. text ed. 19.95 (ISBN 0-03-052956-5). Dryden Pr.

Bedekar, V. M., tr. see Deussen, Paul.

Bedell, Beverly. The Magic Little Ones. LC 75-2964. (Beginning-to-Read Bks). (Illus.). 32p. (gr. 1-3). 1975. PLB 3.39 o.s.i. (ISBN 0-695-80588-6); pap. 1.50 o.s.i. (ISBN 0-695-30588-3). Follett.

Bedell, Estle H. When Life Calls. 1979. 6.95 o.p. (ISBN 0-8062-1191-1). Carlton.

Bedell, Harry. Brooklyn: Where Else. 1981. 8.50 (ISBN 0-8062-1621-2). Carlton.

Bedenbaugh, John H. & Howell, J. Emory. Introductory Chemistry. 1978. lib. bdg. 17.95 (ISBN 0-205-05943-0); instr's man. avail. (ISBN 0-205-05945-7); programmed supplement 5.95 (ISBN 0-205-05944-9). Allyn.

Beder, Harold & Smith, Franceska. Developing an Adult Education Program Through Community Linkages. 1977. 5.75 (ISBN 0-685-82348-2). Adult Ed.

Beder, O. E. Fundamentals for Maxillofacial Prosthetics. (American Lectures in Dentistry Ser.). (Illus.). 246p. 1974. 29.50 (ISBN 0-398-02916-4). C C Thomas.

Bederson, B. see Marton, L.

Bederson, Benjamin, jt. ed. see Bates, Sir David R.

Bedeschi, Guilio. The Science of Medicine. LC 74-12752. (International Library). 128p. (gr. 7 up). 1975. PLB 6.90 o.p. (ISBN 0-531-02122-X). Watts.

Bedeski, Robert E. State Building in Modern China. (China Research Monographs: No. 18). 200p. 1981. pap. 8.00 (ISBN 0-912966-28-9). IEAS Ctr Chinese Stud.

Bedford. Income Determination Theory: An Accounting Framework. 1976. 17.95 (ISBN 0-201-00460-7). A-W.

Bedford, A. D. The Defence of Truth. 271p. 1979. 51.00x (ISBN 0-7190-0740-2, Pub. by Manchester U Pr England). State Mutual Bk.

Bedford, Anne, ed. Walt Disney's Mary Poppins. (Illus.). (ps-3). 1976. PLB 7.62 (ISBN 0-307-60850-6, Golden Pr). Western Pub.

Bedford, Annie N. The Jolly Barnyard. (Illus.). (ps-1). 1950. PLB 5.00 (ISBN 0-307-60067-X, Golden Pr). Western Pub.

--Walt Disney's Peter Pan & Wendy. (Illus.). 24p. (gr. k-3). 1976. PLB 5.00 (ISBN 0-307-60110-2, Golden Pr). Western Pub.

Bedford, Arthur. The Evil & Danger of Stage Plays. LC 72-170479. (The English Stage Ser.: Vol. 43). lib. bdg. 50.00 (ISBN 0-8240-0626-7). Garland Pub.

--Serious Reflections on the Scandalous Abuse & Effects of the Stage. Bd. with A Second Advertisement Concerning the Profaneness of the Play-House; A Sermon Preached in the Parish-Church of St. Butolph's Algate, in the City of London: Occasioned by the Erecting of a Play-House in the Neighborhood. (The English Stage Ser.: Vol. 41). lib. bdg. 50.00 (ISBN 0-8240-0624-0). Garland Pub.

Bedford, Emmett G. & Dilligan, Robert J., eds. Concordance to the Poems of Alexander Pope, 2 vols. LC 74-852. 1656p. 1974. Set. 125.00 (ISBN 0-8103-1008-2). Gale.

Bedford, Jessie. English Children in the Olden Time. 336p. 1980. Repr. of 1907 ed. lib. bdg. 30.00 (ISBN 0-8492-3777-7). R West.

Bedford, John R. Basic Course of Practical Metalwork. (gr. 9-12). pap. text ed. 8.95 (ISBN 0-7195-0079-6). Transatlantic.

Bedford, Norton M., et al. Advanced Accounting: An Organizational Approach. 4th ed. LC 78-6961. (Accounting & Information Systems Ser.). 1979. text ed. 26.95 (ISBN 0-471-02927-0); solutions manual avail. (ISBN 0-471-04275-7). Wiley.

Bedford, Stewart. Stress & Tiger Juice: How to Manage Your Stress & Improve Your Life & Your Health. LC 79-92277. 128p. 1980. 9.95x (ISBN 0-935930-00-0); pap. 4.95x (ISBN 0-935930-01-9). Scott Pubns CA.

Bedfrod, Arthur. A Serious Remonstrance in Behalf of the Christian Religion Against English Play-Houses. LC 79-170478. (The English Stage Ser.: Vol. 42). lib. bdg. 50.00 (ISBN 0-8240-0625-9). Garland Pub.

Bedi, Ajit S. Freedom of Expression & Security: A Comparative Study of the Function of the Supreme Courts of the United States of American & India. 1966. 13.95x (ISBN 0-210-31224-6). Asia.

Bedi, Rajinder S. I Take This Woman. Singh, Khushwant, tr. 103p. 1967. pap. 2.25 (ISBN 0-88253-014-3). Ind-US Inc.

Bedichek, Roy. Adventures with a Texas Naturalist. (Illus.). 1961. pap. 7.95 (ISBN 0-292-70311-2). U of Tex Pr.

Bedier, Joseph. The Romance of Tristan & Iseult. 1965. pap. 1.65 (ISBN 0-394-70271-9, Vin, V271). Random.

Bedinger, Margery. Indian Silver: Navajo & Pueblo Jewelers. LC 72-94659. 1976. pap. 8.95 o.p. (ISBN 0-8263-0416-8). U of NM Pr.

Bedini, Silvio. The Spotted Stones: A Story About the Game of Dominoes. LC 78-3283. (Illus.). (gr. 3-6). 1978. 5.95 (ISBN 0-394-83573-5); PLB 5.99 (ISBN 0-394-93573-X). Pantheon.

Bednar, Michael J., ed. Proceedings of the Sixty-Seventh A.C.S.A. Annual Meeting. 288p. 1980. 25.00 (ISBN 0-686-64816-1); pap. 17.50 (ISBN 0-686-64817-X). Carrollton Pr.

Bednarski, Betty, tr. see Ferron, Jacques.

Bednarski, Gloriana, jt. auth. see Hitchcock, James.

Bednarski, Mary W. & Florczyk, Sandra E. Nursing Home Care As a Public Policy Issue. (Learning Packages in Policy Issues: No. 4). 62p. (Orig.). 1978. pap. text ed. 3.50 (ISBN 0-936826-13-4). Pol Stud Assocs.

Bednarski, Mary W., jt. auth. see Lubliner, Jerry.

Bedore, James, jt. auth. see Turner, Louis.

Bedrick, Christina, jt. auth. see Bedrick, Ed.

Bedrick, Ed & Bedrick, Christina. One Hundred Seventy Seven Free Oregon Campgrounds. new ed. LC 79-66696. (Illus., Orig.). 1980. pap. 6.95 (ISBN 0-913140-33-3). Signpost Bk Pub.

Bedrossian, E. Howard. Surgical & Nonsurgical Management of Strabismus. (Illus.). 240p. 1969. 24.50 (ISBN 0-398-00123-5). C C Thomas.

Bedrossian, Mathias. Armenian-English Dictionary. 30.00x (ISBN 0-685-85420-5). Intl Bk Ctr.

Bedts, Ralph F. De see De Bedts, Ralph F.

Bedwell, C., ed. Developments in Electronics for Offshore Fields, Vol. 1. (Illus.). 1978. text ed. 42.60x (ISBN 0-85334-753-0, Pub. by Applied Science). Burgess-Intl Ideas.

Bedwell, William. Mesolabium Architectonicum That Is a Most Rare Instrument of Measuring. LC 72-172. (English Experience Ser.: No. 224). 24p. Repr. of 1631 ed. 7.00 (ISBN 90-221-0224-6). Walter J Johnson.

Bedworth, David D. Industrial Systems: Planning, Analysis, Control. 510p. 1973. 25.95 (ISBN 0-8260-0867-4). Wiley.

Bee, Clair, ed. Winning Basketball Plays: By America's Foremost Coaches. 2nd ed. (Illus.). 1963. 18.50 o.p. (ISBN 0-8260-0875-5). Ronald Pr.

Bee, Helen. Desarollo Del Nino. (Span.). 1977. pap. text ed. 8.00 (ISBN 0-06-310061-4, IntlDept). Har-Row.

--The Developing Child. 2nd ed. (Illus.). 1978. text ed. 19.50 scp (ISBN 0-06-040583-X, HarpC); inst. manual free (ISBN 0-06-360560-0); study guide scp 6.50 (ISBN 0-06-040864-2). Har-Row.

Bee, Helen & Mitchell, Sandra. The Developing Person. 3rd ed. 1980. text ed. 19.50 scp (ISBN 0-06-040579-1, HarpC); scp study guide 6.50 (ISBN 0-06-040586-4); instr's. manual free (ISBN 0-06-360561-9). Har-Row.

Bee, Martha. The Adventures of Barney Bean. (Illus.). 1977. 6.95 o.p. (ISBN 0-533-02890-6). Vantage.

Bee, Robert L. Crosscurrents Along the Colorado: The Impact of Government Policy on the Quechan Indians. 1981. text ed. 20.00x (ISBN 0-8165-0558-6); pap. 9.50x (ISBN 0-686-69385-X). U of Ariz Pr.

--Patterns & Processes: An Introduction to Anthropological Strategies for the Study of Sociocultural Change. LC 73-10791. 1974. pap. text ed. 6.95 (ISBN 0-02-902090-5). Free Pr.

Beebe, Ann. Easy Cooking, Simple Recipes for Beginning Cooks. (Illus.). 48p. (gr. 4-6). 1972. PLB 6.96 (ISBN 0-688-30039-1). Morrow.

Beebe, Brooke. Best Bets for Babies. (Orig.). pap. 4.95 (ISBN 0-440-50453-8, Dell Trade Pbks). Dell.

Beebe, Brooke, et al. Nutrition & Good Health. LC 78-731300. (Illus.). 1978. pap. text ed. 99.00 (ISBN 0-89290-099-7, A576-SATC). Soc for Visual.

Beebe, Brooke M. & Rosenblatt, Ruth Y. The Dictionary. LC 77-730283. (Illus.). (gr. 3-5). 1977. pap. text ed. 64.00 (ISBN 0-89290-121-7, A151-SAR). Soc for Visual.

Beebe, Hugh G. Complications in Vascular Surgery. LC 73-7978. (Illus.). 402p. 1973. 37.50 (ISBN 0-397-50269-9). Lippincott.

Beebe, Lucius & Clegg, Charles. Virginia & Truckee. LC 63-14279. (Illus.). 64p. 1980. pap. 2.95 (ISBN 0-8310-6007-7). Howell-North.

Beebe, Ralph A., jt. auth. see Langford, Cooper H.

Beebe, William. The Arcturus Adventure. (Nature Library Ser.). 450p. 1981. pap. 5.95 (ISBN 0-06-090846-7, CN 846, CN). Har-Row.

Beebe, William, intro. by. Autofact West Proceedings, Vol. 1. LC 80-53423. (Illus.). 939p. 1980. pap. 55.00 (ISBN 0-87263-065-X). SME.

Beech, H. R. & Fransella, F. Research & Experiment in Stuttering. 1968. 34.00 (ISBN 0-08-012539-5). Pergamon.

Beech, Thomas R., jt. auth. see Chaney, Warren H.

Beecham, Thomas. A Mingled Chime: An Autobiography. LC 76-40182. (The Lyric Stage Ser.). Repr. of 1943 ed. 22.50 (ISBN 0-306-70791-8). Da Capo.

Beecham, Tom, illus. The Lone Ranger. LC 80-52867. (Rocking Bks.). (Illus.). 24p. (ps-3). 1981. pap. 2.95 saddle stitched (ISBN 0-394-84690-7). Random.

Beechcroft, William. Position of Ultimate Trust. LC 80-26561. 256p. 1981. 8.95 (ISBN 0-396-07933-4). Dodd.

Beecher, Gary R., ed. Human Nutrition Research. LC 79-91006. (Beltsville Symposia in Agricultural Research Ser.: No. 4). (Illus.). 400p. 1980. text ed. 32.50 (ISBN 0-916672-48-4). Allanheld.

Beecher, John. Collected Poems, Nineteen Twenty-Four to Nineteen Seventy-Four. LC 73-10560. 352p. 1974. 12.95 (ISBN 0-02-508310-4). Macmillan.

Beechick, Allen. The Pre-Tribulation Rapture. LC 79-53291. 256p. (Orig.). 1980. pap. 4.95 (ISBN 0-89636-040-7). Accent Bks.

Beechick, Ruth. Teaching Juniors. LC 80-68886. (Teacher Training Ser.). 192p. (Orig.). 1981. pap. 3.95 (ISBN 0-89636-062-8). Accent Bks.

--Teaching Primaries. LC 80-66723. (Accent Teacher Training Ser.). 128p. (Orig.). 1980. pap. 3.95 (ISBN 0-89636-054-7). Accent Bks.

--While Waiting for the Bell to Ring. LC 79-53445. (Orig.). 1981. pap. 3.25 (ISBN 0-89636-032-6). Accent Bks.

Beeching, Brian. Interpreting Dental Radiographs. (Illus.). 142p. 1981. PLB 33.55 (ISBN 0-906141-20-6, Pub. by Update Books Ltd). Kluwer Boston.

Beeching, Jack. The Chinese Opium Wars. LC 75-16414. (Illus.). 368p. 1976. 14.95 o.p. (ISBN 0-15-117650-7). HarBraceJ.

--Open Path: Christian Missionaries, 1515-1914. LC 80-21270. 350p. 1981. 14.95 (ISBN 0-915520-37-0). Ross-Erikson.

Beecroft, Glynis. Casting Techniques for Sculpture. 1979. 24.00 (ISBN 0-7134-3314-0, Pub. by Batsford England). David & Charles.

Beede, J. W. & Kniker, H. T. Species of the Genus Schwagerina & Their Stratigraphic Significance. (Illus.). 96p. 1924. 1.00 (BULL 2433). Bur Econ Geology.

Beedell, Suzanne. Country Living by Sea & Estuary. LC 79-91479. (Illus.). 1980. 22.50 (ISBN 0-7153-7796-5). David & Charles.

Beeding, Francis. Death Walks in Eastrepps. 272p. 1980. pap. 4.00 (ISBN 0-486-24014-2). Dover.

Beedle, Lynn S. Plastic Design of Steel Frames. LC 58-13454. 1958. 34.50 (ISBN 0-471-06171-9, Pub by Wiley-Interscience). Wiley.

Beefr, Lucius. Virginia & Truckee. (Illus.). 68p. 1980. 2.95 o.p. (ISBN 0-89685-102-8). Chatham Pub CA.

Beeftink, Wim G., ed. Vegetation Dynamics. 135p. 1980. pap. 31.60 (ISBN 90-6193-606-3). Kluwer Boston.

Beegle, Shirley. Bible Game Ideas. (Ideas Ser.). (Illus.). 1977. pap. text ed. 1.75 (ISBN 0-87239-118-3, 7958). Standard Pub.

--Christmas Games & Crafts for Children. (Standard Ideas Ser.). 1978. pap. 1.75 (ISBN 0-87239-215-5, 2816). Standard Pub.

Beegle, Shirley, ed. Creative Craft Ideas for All Ages. (Illus., Orig.). (gr. k up). 1966. pap. 5.50 (ISBN 0-87239-321-6, 2795). Standard Pub.

Beehler, Paul J. Contemporary Cash Management: Principles, Practices, Perspectives. LC 77-18998. (Systems & Controls for Financial Management Ser.). 1978. 27.95 (ISBN 0-471-06172-7). Ronald Pr.

Beekes, R. S. Development of the Proto-Indo-European Laryngeals in Greek. (Janua Linguarum, Ser. Practica: No. 42). 1969. pap. text ed. 68.25x (ISBN 90-2790-693-9). Mouton.

Beekett, Lucy. Wallace Stevens. 208p. 1974. 36.00 (ISBN 0-521-20278-7); pap. 10.50x (ISBN 0-521-29194-1). Cambridge U Pr.

Beekman, Betty, jt. auth. see Sutton, Valerie J.

Beekman, E. M., ed. & tr. from Dutch. The Oyster & the Eagle: Selected Aphorisms of Multatuli. LC 73-93171. 124p. 1974. lib. bdg. 8.00x (ISBN 0-87023-123-5). U of Mass Pr.

Beekman, John A. Two Stochastic Processes. LC 73-21380. 176p. 1974. text ed. 25.95 o.p. (ISBN 0-470-06175-8). Halsted Pr.

Beelen, Geertruida C., jt. auth. see Sadee, Wolfgang.

Beeler, John. Warfare in Feudal Europe, 730-1200. LC 74-148018. (Illus.). 288p. 1971. 19.50x (ISBN 0-8014-0638-2); pap. 4.95 (ISBN 0-8014-9120-7, CP120). Cornell U Pr.

Beeler, M. Fancher, et al. Measuring the Quality of Library Service: A Handbook. LC 74-12107. (Illus.). 1974. 10.00 (ISBN 0-8108-0732-7). Scarecrow.

Beeler, M. S., ed. The Ventureno Confesionario of Jose Senan, O.F.M. (U. C. Publ. in Linguistics: Vol. 47). 1967. pap. 7.00x (ISBN 0-520-09242-2). U of Cal Pr.

Beeler, Myrton F. Interpretations in Clinical Chemistry. LC 77-95109. (Illus.). 1978. text ed. 35.00 binder (ISBN 0-89189-045-9, 45-2-036-00). Am Soc Clinical.

Beeler, Nelson F. & Branley, Franklyn M. Experiments in Optical Illusion. LC 51-5642. (Illus.). (gr. 5-9). 1951. 7.95 (ISBN 0-690-27507-2, TYC-J). T Y Crowell.

--Experiments with a Microscope. LC 56-9796. (Illus.). (gr. 5-11). 1957. 7.95 (ISBN 0-690-28004-1, TYC-J). T Y Crowell.

--Experiments with Light. LC 58-5591. (Illus.). (gr. 5-11). 1957. 7.95 (ISBN 0-690-28217-6, TYC-J). T Y Crowell.

Beeler, Valerie. Dining in-Cincinnati. (Dining in Ser.). 1981. pap. 7.95 (ISBN 0-89716-079-7). Peanut Butter.

Beeley, J. A., jt. ed. see Arbuthnott, J. P.

Beeley, Ray. Amos. pap. 1.45 o.p. (ISBN 0-686-12507-X). Banner of Truth.

Beem. The Lorentzian Distance Function & Global Lorentzian Geometry. Date not set. price not set (ISBN 0-8247-1369-9). Dekker.

Beeman, Richard R. The Old Dominion & the New Nation, 1788-1801. LC 76-190531. 296p. 1972. 15.00x (ISBN 0-8131-1269-9). U Pr of Ky.

Beemer, Eleanor. My Luiseno Neighbors. (Illus.). 91p. (Orig.). 1980. pap. 9.95 (ISBN 0-916552-20-9). Acoma Bks.

Beemer, Halsey, jt. ed. see Plucknett, Donald L.

Been, Margaret L. Wilderness & Gardens: An American Lady's Prospect. (Illus.). 1974. pap. 5.00 (ISBN 0-87423-011-X). Westburg.

Beene, Wayne, jt. ed. see Woodhead, Daniel.

Beenstock, M. A Neoclassical Analysis of Macroeconomic Policy. LC 79-8961. 1981. 32.50 (ISBN 0-521-23077-2). Cambridge U Pr.

Beenstock, Michael. Health, Migration & Development. 192p. 1980. text ed. 27.75x (ISBN 0-566-00369-4, Pub. by Gower Pub Co England). Renouf.

Beer, A., jt. auth. see Beer, P.

Beer, A. C., jt. ed. see Willardson, R. K.

Beer, A. C., jt. ed. see Willardson, Robert.

Beer, Alan E. & Billingham, Rupert E. The Immunobiology of Mammalian Reproduction. (Illus.). 275p. 1976. 22.95x (ISBN 0-13-451666-4). P-H.

Beer, Alice S. & Graham, Richard. Teaching Music to the Exceptional Child: A Handbook for Mainstreaming. (Illus.). 1980. text ed. 14.95 (ISBN 0-13-893982-9); pap. text ed. 9.95 (ISBN 0-13-893974-8). P-H.

Beer, Arthur, ed. see Jordan, Pascual.

Beer, Ferdinand P. & Johnston, E. Russell, Jr. Mechanics of Materials. (Illus.). 672p. 1981. text ed. 26.95x (ISBN 0-07-004284-5, C); write for info solutions manual (ISBN 0-07-004291-8). McGraw.

Beer, Francis A. Peace Against War: The Ecology of International Violence. LC 80-27214. (International Relations Ser.). (Illus.). 1981. text ed. 18.95x (ISBN 0-7167-1250-4); pap. text ed. 9.95x (ISBN 0-7167-1251-2). W H Freeman.

Beer, Gavin De see Darwin, Charles & Huxley, Thomas H.

Beer, Gillian. Meredith: A Change of Masks, a Study of the Novels. 1970. text ed. 23.25x (ISBN 0-485-11122-5, Athlone Pr). Humanities.

Beer, J. E., jt. auth. see King, B. J.

Beer, John. Wadsworth & the Human Heart. 1979. 20.00x (ISBN 0-231-04646-4). Columbia U Pr.

Beer, Lawrence W., ed. Constitutionalism in Asia: Asian Views of the American Influence. 1979. 20.00x (ISBN 0-520-03701-4). U of Cal Pr.

Beer, P. & Beer, A. Vistas in Astronomy, Vol. 23 Complete. 1980. 112.50 (ISBN 0-08-026046-2). Pergamon.

Beer, Patricia. An Introduction to the Metaphysical Poets. 1972. 7.50x o.p. (ISBN 0-87471-134-7). Rowman.

Beer, Samuel, et al. Patterns of Government: The Major Political Systems of Europe. 3rd ed. 1972. 16.95 (ISBN 0-394-31387-9). Random.

Beer, Stafford. Brain of the Firm. 2nd ed. LC 80-49979. 448p. 1981. 29.50 (ISBN 0-471-27687-1, Pub. by Wiley-Interscience). Wiley.

Beer, Tom. Atmospheric Waves. LC 74-13429. 300p. 1974. 59.95 (ISBN 0-470-06185-5). Halsted Pr.

Beer, William R. The Unexpected Rebellion: Ethnic Activism in Contemporary France. LC 79-3515. 1980. 18.50x (ISBN 0-8147-1029-8). NYU Pr.

Beer, William R., tr. see Bloch, Mark.

Beerbower, J. R. Field Guide to Fossils. (Earth Science Curriculum Project Pamphlet Ser). 1971. pap. 3.20 (ISBN 0-395-02618-0, 2-14604). HM.

Beerbower, James R. Search for the Past: An Introduction to Paleontology. 2nd ed. LC 68-18060. (Illus.). 1968. ref. ed. 22.95 (ISBN 0-13-797316-0). P-H.

Beermann, W., ed. Biochemical Differentiation in Insect Glands. LC 77-23423. (Results & Problems in Cell Differentiation: Vol. 8). (Illus.). 1977. 41.50 (ISBN 0-387-08286-7). Springer-Verlag.

Beers, Burton F. China in Old Photographs, Eighteen Sixty-Five to Nineteen Ten. (Illus.). 1978. 5.95 (ISBN 0-684-16532-5, ScribT). Scribner.

Beers, Burton F., jt. auth. see Clyde, Paul H.

Beers, Clifford W. A Mind That Found Itself. 5th ed. LC 80-5256. (Contemporary Communities Health Ser). 232p. 1981. 14.95 (ISBN 0-8229-3442-6); pap. 6.95 (ISBN 0-8229-5324-2). U of Pittsburgh Pr.

Beers, Gil. Cats & Bats & Things Like That. 32p. (gr. 1-3). 1972. 4.95 (ISBN 0-8024-1211-4). Moody.

Beers, Gilbert. The Children's Illustrated Bible Dictionary. Mairani, Alvaro, tr. LC 77-12650. (Illus.). 1977. 8.95 o.p. (ISBN 0-8407-4987-2). Nelson.

Beers, Gilbert V. Around the World with My Red Balloon. (ps-3). 1973. 4.95 (ISBN 0-8024-0303-4). Moody.

Beers, Henry A. Initial Studies in American Letters. 291p. 1980. Repr. of 1395 ed. lib. bdg. 30.00 (ISBN 0-89987-063-5). Darby Bks.

Beers, Howard W. An American Experience in Indonesia: The University of Kentucky Affiliation with the Agricultural University at Bogor. LC 75-132824. (Illus.). 288p. 1971. 16.00x (ISBN 0-8131-1235-4). U Pr of Ky.

Beers, John C., jt. auth. see Gafney, Leo.

Beers, Paul B. Pennsylvania Politics Today & Yesterday: The Tolerable Accomodation. LC 79-65826. (Keystone Bks.). (Illus.). 416p. 1980. 16.75 (ISBN 0-271-00233-7). Pa St U Pr.

Beers, Roland F. & Bassett, Edward G., eds. Mechanisms of Pain & Analgesic Compounds. LC 78-52524. (Miles Symposium Ser.: No. 11). 1979. text ed. 52.50 (ISBN 0-89004-304-3). Raven.

--Nutritional Factors: Modulating Effects on Metabolic Processes. (Miles International Symposium Ser.: Vol. 13). 1981. text ed. price not set (ISBN 0-89004-592-5). Raven.

Beers, Roland F., ed. see Miles International Symposium, 12th.

Beers, Roland F., Jr. & Bassett, Edward G., eds. Cell Membrane Receptors for Viruses, Anticens & Antibodies, Polypeptide Hormones, & Small Molecules. LC 75-25108. (Miles International Symposium Ser.: No.9). 1976. 49.50 (ISBN 0-89004-091-5). Raven.

--Recombinant Molecules: Impact on Science & Society. LC 77-5276. (Miles International Symposium Ser: 10th). 1977. 49.00 (ISBN 0-89004-131-8). Raven.

--The Role of Immunological Factors in Infectious, Allergic, & Autoimmune Processes. LC 75-25109. (Miles International Symposium Ser: No. 8). 1976. 45.00 (ISBN 0-89004-073-7). Raven.

Beers, V. G. Out of the Treasure Chest. (Muffin Family Ser.). (Illus.). 96p. (ps-6). 1981. 8.95 (ISBN 0-8024-6099-2). Moody.

Beers, V. Gilbert. The Children's Illustrated Bible Dictionary. 1981. pap. 6.95 (ISBN 0-8407-5755-7). Nelson.

--Coco's Candy Shop. 32p. (gr. 3-6). 1973. 4.95 (ISBN 0-8024-1586-5). Moody.

--A Gaggle of Green Geese. (Christian Home Library). (Illus.). 32p. (ps-3). 1974. 5.50 (ISBN 0-8024-2911-4). Moody.

--Honeyphants & Elebees. (Christian Home Library). 32p. (ps-3). 1974. 4.95 (ISBN 0-8024-3612-9). Moody.

--Learning to Read from the Bible, 4 vols. Incl. Vol. 1. God Is My Helper (ISBN 0-310-20780-0). kivar (ISBN 0-310-20781-9); Vol. 2. God Is My Friend (ISBN 0-310-20790-8). kivar (ISBN 0-310-20791-6); Vol. 3. Jesus Is My Teacher (ISBN 0-310-20800-9). kivar (ISBN 0-310-20801-7); Vol. 4. Jesus Is My Guide (ISBN 0-310-20810-6). kivar (ISBN 0-310-20811-4). (Illus.). 96p. (Readers). (ps up). 1973. 6.95 ea.; kivar 3.95. Zondervan.

--Learning to Read from the Bible Primers: Primers, 4bks. Incl. May I Help You. pap. (ISBN 0-310-20821-1); Do You Know My Friend (ISBN 0-310-20830-0). pap. (ISBN 0-310-20831-9); Do You Love Me (ISBN 0-310-20840-8). pap. (ISBN 0-310-20841-6); Will You Come with Me (ISBN 0-310-20850-5). pap. (ISBN 0-310-20851-3). (ps-1). 1976. 6.95 ea.; pap. 3.95 ea. kivar. Zondervan.

--The Magic Merry-Go-Round. 32p. (gr. 2-4). 1973. 4.95 (ISBN 0-8024-5138-1). Moody.

--With Mini & Maxi in Muffkinland. (Muffin Family Adventure Ser.). 79p. (gr. k-4). 1981. text ed. 8.95 (ISBN 0-8024-4063-0). Moody.

Beers, Yardley. Theory of Error. 2nd ed. LC 53-8616. (Physics Ser). (Orig.). 1957. pap. 4.95 (ISBN 0-201-00470-4). A-W.

Beery, Lydia A. Mennonite Maid Cookbook. 1971. pap. 5.00 (ISBN 0-87813-205-8). Park View.

Beery, W. T., ed. see International Clean Air Congress, 2nd.

Beesley, Alan, ed. see Murray, Sheila.

Beesley, M. J. Lasers & Their Applications. 2nd ed. 1976. 27.95 (ISBN 0-470-15166-8). Halsted Pr.

Beesly, Patrick. Very Special Admiral. (Illus.). 256p. 1981. 30.00 (ISBN 0-241-10383-5, Pub. by Hamish Hamilton England). David & Charles.

--Very Special Intelligence. LC 77-82615. 1978. 10.00 o.p. (ISBN 0-385-13206-9). Doubleday.

Beeson, Paul B., et al. Cecil Textbook of Medicine, 2 vols. 15th ed. (Illus.). 2478p. 1979. Single Vol. Ed. 49.00 (ISBN 0-7216-1663-1); Two Vol. Set. 60.00 (ISBN 0-7216-1667-4); Vol. 1. 30.00 (ISBN 0-7216-1664-X); Vol. 2. 30.00 (ISBN 0-7216-1666-6). Saunders.

Beeston, A. F., ed. Selections from the Poetry of Bassar. LC 77-928. 1977. 28.50 (ISBN 0-521-21664-8); pap. 7.95x (ISBN 0-521-29223-9). Cambridge U Pr.

Beeston, Alfred F. Historical Phraseology: Supplement to Written Arabic. 1969. 12.50x (ISBN 0-521-09578-6). Cambridge U Pr.

--Written Arabic: An Approach to the Basic Structures. (Orig.). 1968. 10.95 (ISBN 0-521-09559-X, 559). Cambridge U Pr.

Beetham, David. Max Weber & the Theory of Modern Politics. 1974. text ed. 17.95x o.p. (ISBN 0-04-329018-3). Allen Unwin.

Beetham, William P., Jr., jt. auth. see Pieroni, Robert E.

Beethoven, Ludwig Van. Complete Piano Sonatas, 2 vols. Schenker, Heinrich, ed. LC 74-83473. 1975. pap. 7.50 ea. Vol. 1 (ISBN 0-486-23134-8). Vol. 2 (ISBN 0-486-23135-6). Dover.

Beeton, Beverly, jt. ed. see Canning, Ray R.

Beets, M. G., ed. Structure-Activity Relationships in Human Chemoreception. (Illus.). 1978. text ed. 71.30x (ISBN 0-85334-746-8, Pub. by Applied Science). Burgess-Intl Ideas.

Beetz, Kirk H. John Ruskin: A Bibliography, 1900-1974. LC 76-13611. (Author Bibliographies Ser.: No. 28). 1976. 10.00 (ISBN 0-8108-0938-9). Scarecrow.

--Wilkie Collins: An Annotated Bibliography 1889-1976. LC 77-26609. (Author Bibliographies Ser.: No. 35). 1978. 10.00 (ISBN 0-8108-1103-0). Scarecrow.

Beevers, John. Storm of Glory. 1977. pap. 2.45 (ISBN 0-385-12617-4, Im). Doubleday.

Befu, Ben. Ihara Saikaku: Worldy Mental Calculations. (Publications in Occasional Papers: No. 5). 1976. pap. 13.50x (ISBN 0-520-09406-9). U of Cal Pr.

Begemann, H. & Rastetter, J. Atlas of Clinical Haematology. 2nd ed. Heilmeyer, L., ed. Hirsch, H. J., tr. from Ger. LC 72-86892. (Illus.). xv, 324p. 1972. 118.50 (ISBN 0-387-05949-0). Springer-Verlag.

Begg, Paul. Into Thin Air: People Who Disappear. (Illus.). 1979. 17.95 (ISBN 0-7153-7724-8). David & Charles.

Beggs, Donald L. & Lewis, Ernest L. Measurement & Evaluation in the Schools. 1975. 15.75 (ISBN 0-395-18609-9); insturctor's manual 1.50 (ISBN 0-395-18795-8). HM.

Begin, Menachem. The Revolt. (Illus.). 1977. Repr. 12.95 o.p. (ISBN 0-8402-1370-0). Nash Pub.

--White Nights: The Story of a Prisoner in Russia. LC 78-69610. 1979. 8.95 o.s.i. (ISBN 0-06-010289-6, HarpT). Har-Row.

Begner, Edith. Just off Fifth. 352p. 1981. pap. 2.95 (ISBN 0-380-77321-X, 77321). Avon.

Begue, A., jt. auth. see Wylie, L.

Begun, James W. Professionalism & Public Interest. (Health & Public Policy Ser.). 176p. 1981. text ed. 17.50x (ISBN 0-262-02156-0). MIT Pr.

Behague, Gerard. Music in Latin America: an Introduction. (History of Music Ser.). (Illus.). 1979. text ed. 16.95 (ISBN 0-13-608919-4); pap. text ed. 14.95 (ISBN 0-13-608901-1). P-H.

Beharrel, Peter, ed. Trade Unions & the Media. Greg, Philo. (Critical Social Studies). 1977. pap. text ed. 6.50x (ISBN 0-333-22055-2). Humanities.

Behavior of Offshore Structures, 2nd International Conference. Boss Seventy-Nine: Proceedings, 3 vols. 1500p. Set. pap. 169.00 (ISBN 0-906085-34-9, Dist. by Air Science Co). BHRA Fluid.

Behbehani, Abbas M. Human Viral, Bedsonial & Rickettsial Diseases: A Diagnostic Handbook for Physicians. (Illus.). 370p. 1972. text ed. 37.50 (ISBN 0-398-02228-3). C C Thomas.

--Laboratory Diagnosis of Viral, Bedsonial & Rickettsial Diseases: A Handbook for Laboratory Workers. (Illus.). 244p. 1972. 27.50 (ISBN 0-398-02229-1). C C Thomas.

Behenna, John. West Country Shipwrecks (England) A Pictorial Record, 1866-1973. LC 74-76205. 1975. 10.50 (ISBN 0-7153-6569-X). David & Charles.

Behler, Ernst, et al, eds. Nietzsche-Studien. (Internationales Jahrbuch Fur Die Nietzsche-Forschung: Vol. 9). 400p. 1980. text ed. 92.50x (ISBN 3-11-008241-1). De Gruyter.

Behling, John H. Research Methods: Statistical Concepts & Research Practicum. 1977. pap. text ed. 6.00x (ISBN 0-8191-0084-6). U Pr of Amer.

Behling, Orlando & Schriesheim, Chester A. Organizational Behavior: Theory, Research & Application. 400p. 1976. text ed. 16.95 o.p. (ISBN 0-205-04690-8, 0846902). Allyn.

Behn, Aphra. Rover. Link, Frederick M., ed. LC 66-20828. (Regents Restoration Drama Ser). 1967. 8.95x (ISBN 0-8032-0350-0); pap. 3.95x (ISBN 0-8032-5350-8, BB 260, Bison). U of Nebr Pr.

Behn, Harry. The Faraway Lurs. (Children's Literature Ser.). 1981. PLB 8.95 (ISBN 0-8398-2722-9). Gregg.

Behn, Henry. The Faraway Lurs. (YA) (gr. 7 up). 1975. pap. 1.25 (ISBN 0-380-00696-0, 22053). Avon.

Behn, Judith, ed. see Public Interest Economics Foundation.

Behn, Noel. The Brinks Job. (Illus.). 1978. pap. 2.50 o.s.i. (ISBN 0-446-91108-9). Warner Bks.

Behnke, Albert R., Jr. & Wilmore, Jack H. Evaluation & Regulation of Body Build & Composition. (International Research Monograph Series in Physical Education). (Illus.). 224p. 1974. ref. ed. 11.95 (ISBN 0-13-292284-3). P-H.

Behnke, John A. & Bok, Sissela, eds. The Dilemmas of Euthanasia. LC 75-5267. 200p. 1975. pap. 2.95 (ISBN 0-385-09730-1, Anch). Doubleday.

Behnke, Leo. Impromptu Magic from the Castle. LC 79-57654. (Wizards of the Magic Castle Ser.: Vol. 1). (Illus.). 235p. 1980. 11.95 (ISBN 0-87477-135-8). J P Tarcher.

Behr, jt. auth. see Bowen.

Behr, Marlyn J. & Jungst, Dale. Fundamentals of Elementary Mathematics Geometry. 326p. 1972. 17.95 (ISBN 0-12-084740-X); answer suppl. 3.00 (ISBN 0-12-084746-9). Acad Pr.

Behr, Robert V. The Search for Black Identity. (gr. 10-12). 1970. pap. text ed. 3.50x o.p. (ISBN 0-88334-023-2); tchrs' manual avail. o.p. (ISBN 0-685-39241-4). Ind Sch Pr.

Behrendt, Douglas M. & Austen, W. Gerald. Patient Care in Cardiac Surgery. 3rd ed. (Little, Brown Spiral Manual Series). 1980. pap. write for info. (ISBN 0-316-08756-4). Little.

Behrendt, Hans & Green, Marvin. Patterns of Skin ph from Birth Through Adolescene: With a Synopsis on Skin Growth. (Illus.). 116p. 1971. 14.75 (ISBN 0-398-00125-1). C C Thomas.

Behrendt, Harry M., jt. auth. see Unthank, L. L.

Behrendt, Walter C. Modern Building: Its Nature, Problems & Forms. LC 78-59005. (Illus.). 1981. Repr. of 1937 ed. 25.00 (ISBN 0-88355-681-2). Hyperion Conn.

Behrens, D., ed. see Gmehling, J., et al.

Behrens, David W. Pacific Coast Nudibranchs. (Illus.). 112p. 1980. pap. 14.95 (ISBN 0-930118-05-7). Western Marine.

--Pacific Coast Nudibranchs: A Guide to the Opisthobranchs of the Northeastern Pacific. LC 80-51439. (Illus.). 112p. 1980. 24.95 (ISBN 0-930118-04-9, Dist. by Western Marine Enterprises); pap. 14.95 (ISBN 0-930118-05-7). Sea Chall.

Behrens, John C. The Typewriter Guerillas: Closeups of Twenty Top Investigative Reporters. LC 77-3439. 1977. 13.95 (ISBN 0-88229-266-8); pap. 7.95 (ISBN 0-88229-506-3). Nelson-Hall.

Behrens, Richard. Ceramic Glazemaking. 3.95 (ISBN 0-934706-07-7). Prof Pubns Ohio.

--Glaze Projects. 3.95 (ISBN 0-934706-06-9). Prof Pubns Ohio.

Behrens, Robert. The Conservative Party from Heath to Thatcher: Policy & Politics 1974 to 1979. 152p. 15.95x (ISBN 0-566-00268-X, 03778-8, Pub. by Gower Pub Co England). Lexington Bks.

Behringer, Marjorie P. Techniques & Materials in Biology. LC 80-12458. 608p. 1981. Repr. of 1973 ed. lib. bdg. write for info. (ISBN 0-89874-175-0). Krieger.

Behrman, Carol H. The Remarkable Writing Machine. (Illus.). 64p. (gr. 3-5). 1981. PLB 6.97 (ISBN 0-686-69297-7). Messner.

Behrman, Cynthia F. Victorian Myths of the Sea. LC 76-51694. 188p. 1977. 12.95 (ISBN 0-8214-0351-6). Ohio U Pr.

Behrman, Jack & Mikesell, Raymond. The Impact of U. S. Foreign Direct Investment on U. S. Export Competitiveness in Third World Markets, Vol. II. LC 80-65189. (Significant Issues Ser.: No. 1). 34p. 1980. 5.95 (ISBN 0-89206-014-X). CSI Studies.

Behrman, Jack H. & Wallender, Harvey W. Transfer of Manufacturing Technology Within Multinational Enterprises. LC 76-5866. 272p. 1976. text ed. 20.00 o.p. (ISBN 0-88410-048-0). Ballinger Pub.

Behrman, Jack N. Discourses on Ethics & Business. LC 80-23626. 192p. 1981. lib. bdg. 20.00 (ISBN 0-89946-064-X). Oelgeschlager.

--Tropical Diseases: Responses of Pharmaceutical Companies. 1980. pap. 4.25 (ISBN 0-8447-3393-8). Am Enterprise.

Behrman, Jere R. International Commodity Agreements: An Evaluation of the UNCTAD Integrated Commodity Programme. LC 77-90146. (Monographs: No. 9). 112p. 1977. 5.00 (ISBN 0-686-28686-3). Overseas Dev Council.

Behrman, Jere R., jt. auth. see Adams, F. Gerard.

Behrman, Marion, ed. see Bernstein, Richard K.

Behrman, Marion, ed. see Callen, Anna T.

Behrmann, Polly, jt. auth. see Millman, Joan.

Behrstock, Barry & Trubo, Richard. The Parent's When-Not-to Worry Book: Straight Talk About All Those Myths You've Learned from Your Parents, Friends-- & Even Doctors. LC 80-7894. 256p. 1981. 10.95 (ISBN 0-690-01972-6, HarpT). Har-Row.

Beidelman, William. Story of the Pennsylvania Germans: Embracing an Account of Their Origin, Their History, Their Dialect. LC 70-81759. 1969. Repr. of 1898 ed. 20.00 (ISBN 0-8103-3571-9). Gale.

Beidler, John X. X. Beidler: Vigilante. Sanders, Helen F. & Bertsche, William H., Jr., eds. (Western Frontier Library Ser.: Vol. 8). (Illus.). 1969. Repr. of 1957 ed. 4.95 o.p. (ISBN 0-8061-0373-6). U of Okla Pr.

Beidler, Peter G. & Egge, Marion F. The American Indian in Short Fiction: An Annotated Bibliography. LC 79-20158. 1979. 11.00 (ISBN 0-8108-1256-8). Scarecrow.

Beier, Ernst G. & Valens, Evans G. People-Reading: How We Control Others, How They Control Us. 320p. 1976. pap. 2.95 (ISBN 0-446-93642-1). Warner Bks.

Beier, H. U. African Poetry. (Illus., Orig.). 1966. 10.95 (ISBN 0-521-04140-6); pap. 5.50x (ISBN 0-521-04141-4). Cambridge U Pr.

Beier, Helen & Hanfmann, Eugenia. Six Russian Men - - Lives in Turmoil. LC 75-32060. 220p. 1976. pap. 5.95 o.p. (ISBN 0-8158-0333-8). Chris Mass.

Beier, Ulli. Introduction to African Literature. 2nd ed. 1979. pap. text ed. 9.95 (ISBN 0-582-64228-0). Longman.

--The Stolen Images. 64p. 1976. pap. 2.25x (ISBN 0-521-20901-3). Cambridge U Pr.

--Yoruba Myths. LC 79-7645. (Illus.). 88p. 1980. 13.95 (ISBN 0-521-22995-2); pap. 4.50 (ISBN 0-521-22865-4). Cambridge U Pr.

Beierle, Herbert L. Making Energy Work. 1980. 5.00 (ISBN 0-686-23895-8). God Unltd U of Healing.

--Quiet Healing Zone. 1980. 10.00 (ISBN 0-686-23897-4). God Unltd U of Healing.

--Why I Can Say I Am God. 1978. 1.00 (ISBN 0-686-23898-2). God Unltd U of Healing.

Beightler, C., jt. auth. see Wilde, Douglass.

Beightler, Charles S. & Phillips, Donald T. Applied Geometric Programming. LC 75-44391. 1976. 34.95 (ISBN 0-471-06390-8). Wiley.

Beightler, Charles S., et al. Foundations of Optimization. 2nd ed. (International Ser. in Industrial & Systems Engineering). (Illus.). 1979. text ed. 24.95 (ISBN 0-13-330332-2). P-H.

Beigie, Carl E. & Hero, Alfred O., Jr., eds. Natural Resources in U. S. - Canadian Relations: Patterns & Trends in Resource Supplies & Policies, Vol. 2. 1980. lib. bdg. 27.50x (ISBN 0-89158-555-9); pap. text ed. 12.00x (ISBN 0-89158-878-7). Westview.

--Natural Resources in U. S. - Canadian Relations: Perspectives, Prospects, & Policy Options, Vol. 3. 240p. 1981. lib. bdg. 18.50x (ISBN 0-89158-556-7); pap. text ed. 8.50x (ISBN 0-89158-879-5). Westview.

Beijbom, Ulf. Swedes in Chicago: A Demographic & Social Study of the 1846-1880 Immigration. LC 71-182869. (Illus.). 381p. 1971. pap. 20.00 o.p. (ISBN 91-24-68690-5). Chicago Hist.

Beik, Paul H. French Revolution. LC 71-142852. (Documentary History of Western Civilization Ser). 1971. 15.00x o.s.i. (ISBN 0-8027-2036-6). Walker & Co.

--The French Revolution Seen from the Right. p ed. LC 70-80523. 1971. Repr. of 1956 ed. 13.75 (ISBN 0-86527-074-0). Fertig.

Beil, Donald. File Processing with Cobol. (Illus.). 1981. text ed. 19.95 (ISBN 0-8359-1985-4); pap. text ed. 13.95 (ISBN 0-8359-1984-6). Reston.

Beil, Norman, et al, eds. see Beverly Hills Bar Association. Barristers Committee for the Arts.

Beilenson, Laurence W. Survival & Peace in the Nuclear Age. LC 80-51729. 169p. 1980. 10.95 (ISBN 0-89526-672-5). Regnery-Gateway.

Beilharz, Edwin A., jt. auth. see DeMers, Donald O., Jr.

Beilke, Marlan. Family, Friends, & Poetry. 12p. 1980. pap. 5.00 (ISBN 0-918466-09-1). Quintessence.

--Shining Clarity: God & Man in the Works of Robinson Jeffers. LC 77-70786. 1978. separate ed. 100.00x (ISBN 0-918466-01-6); separate ed. 100.00x (ISBN 0-918466-01-6). Quintessence.

--Shining Clarity: God & Man in the Works of Robinson Jeffers. rev. ed. (Illus., Orig.). 1980. pap. write for info o.p (ISBN 0-918466-05-9). Quintessence.

Beim, George. Principles of Modern Soccer. LC 76-11986. (Illus.). 1977. pap. text ed. 15.75 (ISBN 0-395-24415-3). HM.

Beim, Jerrold. Andy & the School Bus. (Illus.). (gr. k-3). 1947. PLB 7.44 (ISBN 0-688-31022-2). Morrow.

--The Smallest Boy in the Class. (Illus.). (gr. k-3). 1949. PLB 7.44 (ISBN 0-688-31442-2). Morrow.

--Swimming Hole. (Illus.). (gr. k-3). 1951. PLB 7.44 (ISBN 0-688-31442-2). Morrow.

Beinfeld, Wallace, ed. see Barney, Richard W., et al.

Beinhorn, George, tr. see Van Aaken, Ernst.

Beintema, David. A Neurological Study of Newborn Infants. (Clinics in Developmental Medicine Ser. No. 28). 170p. 1968. 13.00 (ISBN 0-685-24725-2). Lippincott.

Beintema, David, jt. auth. see Prechtl, Heinz.

Beirne, Francis F. The Amiable Baltimoreans. LC 68-9401. xiv, 400p. 1968. Repr. 22.00 (ISBN 0-8103-5031-9). Gale.

Beiser, Arthur. Basic Concepts of Physics. 2nd ed. LC 70-168762. 1972. text ed. 18.95 (ISBN 0-201-00491-7). A-W.

--Concepts of Modern Physics. 3rd ed. (Illus.). 512p. 1981. text ed. 22.50 (ISBN 0-07-004382-5, C). McGraw.

--The Earth. (Young Readers Library). (Illus.). 1977. lib. bdg. 7.95 (ISBN 0-686-51088-7). Silver.

--The Earth. LC 62-16141. (Life Nature Library). 1970. lib. bdg. 8.97 o.p. (ISBN 0-8094-0618-7). Silver.

--The Mainstream of Physics. 1962. 15.95 (ISBN 0-201-00495-X). A-W.

--Modern Physics: An Introductory Survey. LC 68-12695. (Physics Ser). (Illus., Orig.). 1968. pap. 7.95 (ISBN 0-201-00515-8). A-W.

--Modern Technical Physics. 3rd ed. LC 78-31596. 1979. 22.95 (ISBN 0-8053-0680-3); instr's guide 3.95 (ISBN 0-8053-0681-1). Benjamin-Cummings.

--Physics. 2nd ed. LC 77-87340. 1978. 22.95 (ISBN 0-8053-0379-0); instr's guide 7.95 (ISBN 0-8053-0380-4). Benjamin-Cummings.

--Proper Yacht. 1966. 10.95 o.s.i. (ISBN 0-685-15800-4). Macmillan.

--The Proper Yacht. LC 77-85406. (Illus.). 1978. 27.50 (ISBN 0-87742-096-3). Intl Marine.

--The Sailor's World. 1972. 19.95 o.p. (ISBN 0-394-46852-X, Co-Pub. by Ridge Pr). Random.

--Schaum's Outline of Mathematics for Electricity & Electronics. (Schaum's Outline Ser.). (Illus.). 208p. 1980. pap. 4.95 (ISBN 0-07-004378-7, SP). McGraw.

Beiser, Arthur, jt. auth. see Beiser, Germaine.

Beiser, Germaine & Beiser, Arthur. Story of Cosmic Rays. (Illus.). (gr. 7 up). 1962. PLB 5.95 o.p. (ISBN 0-525-40121-0). Dutton.

Beisner, Monika. An Address Book with Riddles, Rhymes, Tales & Tongue Twisters. (Illus.). 1979. 6.95 (ISBN 0-374-30053-4). FS&G.

--The Birthday Box of Dreams. LC 74-18130. (Picture Bk). (Illus.). 32p. (ps-1). 1975. 4.95 o.s.i. (ISBN 0-695-80532-0); PLB 4.98 o.s.i. (ISBN 0-695-40532-2). Follett.

--Fantastic Toys. LC 74-79249. (Picture Bk). (Illus.). 24p. (gr. k-2). 1974. 5.95 o.s.i. (ISBN 0-695-80504-5); PLB 6.99 o.s.i. (ISBN 0-695-40504-7). Follett.

Beit-Hallahmi, Benjamin, jt. auth. see Argyle, Michael.

Beith-Halahmi, Esther Y. Angell Fayre or Strumpet Lewd: Jane Shaw As an Example of Erring Beauty in 16th Century Literature, 2 vols. (Salzburg Studies in English Literature, Elizabethan & Renaissance Studies: Nos. 26-27). 361p. 1974. Set. pap. text ed. 50.25x (ISBN 0-391-01322-X). Humanities.

Beitler, Arline. Adventures of a Cheap Antiquer. 1979. pap. 1.95 (ISBN 0-380-42804-0, 43804). Avon.

Beitler, Ethel J. Creating from Remnants: Stitchery with Imperfect Fabrics. LC 74-82325. (Little Craft Bk.). (Illus.). 48p. (gr. 6 up). 1974. 5.95 (ISBN 0-8069-5306-3); PLB 6.69 (ISBN 0-8069-5307-1). Sterling.

Beitman, Hartford. Directory of Antique Radio Collectors & Suppliers. 5th ed. (Orig.). 1980. pap. 3.00x (ISBN 0-938630-00-8); notebook 4.00x (ISBN 0-938630-01-6). Antique Radio.

Beitman, Lawrence. Beginner's Guide to Weather Forecasting. (Beginners Guide Ser.). 1975. 10.95 o.p. (ISBN 0-7207-0819-2, Pub. by Michael Joseph). Merrimack Bk Serv.

Beitz, Les. Treasury of Frontier Relics. 2nd,rev. ed. 12.00 o.p. (ISBN 0-498-01688-9). A S Barnes.

Beitzel, Wallace, jt. auth. see Harter, James.

Beitzell, Robert, ed. Tehran-Yalta-Potsdam: The Soviet Protocols. 16.00 (ISBN 0-87569-013-0). Academic Intl.

Beja, Morris. Film & Literature. 1979. pap. text ed. 10.95 (ISBN 0-582-28094-X). Longman.

Bejerot, Nils. Addiction: An Artificially Induced Drive. (Illus.). 96p. 1972. 12.50 (ISBN 0-398-02527-4). C C Thomas.

--Addiction & Society. (Illus.). 272p. 1970. text ed. 27.50 (ISBN 0-398-00126-X). C C Thomas.

Beker, J. C., jt. auth. see Hageman, Howard G.

Beker, J. Christiaan. Paul the Apostle: The Triumph of God in Life & Thought. LC 79-8904. 468p. 1980. 22.95 (ISBN 0-8006-0633-7, 1-633). Fortress.

Beker, Jerome, jt. auth. see Willie, Charles V.

Beker G., Simon, jt. auth. see Grases, Pedro J.

Bekker, Cajus. The Luftwaffe War Diaries. Ziegler, Frank, tr. 608p. 1975. pap. 3.95 (ISBN 0-345-28799-1). Ballantine.

Bekker, Leander J. De see Vizetelly, Frank H. & De Bekker, Leander J.

Bekker, M. G. Off-The-Road Locomotion: Research & Development in Terramechanics. LC 61-5020. (Illus.). 1960. 10.00 o.p. (ISBN 0-472-04142-8). U of Mich Pr.

Bekker, Paul. The Changing Opera. Mendel, Arthur, tr. LC 80-2256. 1981. Repr. of 1935 ed. 35.50 (ISBN 0-404-18803-6). AMS Pr.

Bekkum, D. W. Van see VanBekkum, D. W.

Belaief, Gail. Spinoza's Philosophy of Law. LC 78-118275. (Studies in Philosophy: No. 24). (Illus.). 151p. (Orig.). 1971. pap. text ed. 17.65x (ISBN 90-2791-851-1). Mouton.

Belanger, Maurice, jt. auth. see Purpel, David.

Belasco, Bernard. The Entrepreneur As Culture Hero: Preadaptations for Nigerian Economic Development. LC 79-10475. (Praeger Special Studies). (Illus.). 256p. 1980. 23.95 (ISBN 0-03-052096-7). Praeger.

Belasco, James A. & Hampton, David R. Managemant Today. 2nd ed. 550p. 1981. text ed. 18.95 (ISBN 0-471-08579-0); write for info. tchr's. ed. (ISBN 0-471-08934-6). Wiley.

Belasco, James A., et al. Management Today. LC 74-28245. 528p. 1975. text ed. 19.95 (ISBN 0-471-06365-7); instructor's manual avail. (ISBN 0-471-06366-5). Wiley.

Belasco, Simon see Bottiglia, William F.

Belch, Jean, ed. Contemporary Games: a Directory & Bibliography Describing Play Situations or Simulations, Vol. 2. LC 72-6353. 1974. 65.00 (ISBN 0-8103-0969-6). Gale.

Belch, Stanislaus F. Paulus Vladimiri & His Doctrine Concerning International Law & Politics, 2 Vols. 1965. Set. text ed. 247.00x (ISBN 90-2790-977-6). Mouton.

Belchamber, David, tr. see Wein, Horst.

Belcher, C. Francis. Logging Railroads of the White Mountains. (Illus.). 250p. (Orig.). 1980. pap. 6.95 (ISBN 0-910146-32-2). Appalach Mtn.

Belcher, David W. Compensation Administration. (Industrial Relations & Personnel Ser). (Illus.). 576p. 1974. ref. ed. 19.95 (ISBN 0-13-154161-7). P-H.

Belcher, Harold H. Subnuclear Resonance Science Unification Key: Old Data-New Concepts. 1977. 14.50 o.p. (ISBN 0-682-48884-4, University). Exposition.

Belcher, R., ed. see Jeffery, P. G.

Belcher, Richard. Layman's Guide to the Inerrancy Debate. 1980. pap. 2.50 (ISBN 0-8024-2379-5). Moody.

Belcher, Supply. The Harmony of Maine. Hitchcock, H. Wiley, ed. LC 77-169607. (Earlier American Music Ser: Vol. 6). 104p. 1972. Repr. of 1794 ed. lib. bdg. 18.50 (ISBN 0-306-77306-6). Da Capo.

Belden, Bernard R. The Eighth Day of the Week. 3rd ed. Henry, Bamman A., ed. (Kaleidoscope Ser.). 1978. pap. text ed. 6.08 (ISBN 0-201-40881-3, Sch Div); tchr's. ed. 6.64 (ISBN 0-201-40882-1). A-W.

Belden, Henry M., ed. Ballads & Songs Collected by the Missouri Folk-Lore Society. 2nd ed. LC 55-7519. 1955. 15.00x (ISBN 0-8262-0142-3). U of Mo Pr.

Belden, Jack. Retreat with Stillwell. (China in the 20th Century Ser). (Illus.). 368p. 1975. Repr. of 1943 ed. lib. bdg. 22.50 (ISBN 0-306-70734-9). Da Capo.

--Still Time to Die. (China in the 20th Century Ser). xi, 322p. 1975. Repr. of 1944 ed. lib. bdg. 25.00 (ISBN 0-306-70735-7). Da Capo.

Belden, L. Burr. Mines of Death Valley. (Illus.). 1966. wrappers 2.95 (ISBN 0-910856-16-8). La Siesta.

Belden, Wilanne S. Mind-Call. LC 80-18488. 252p. (gr. 5-9). 1981. PLB 10.95 (ISBN 0-689-30796-9, Argo). Atheneum.

Belenitsky, Alexandr. Central Asia. Hogarth, James, tr. from Rus. (Archaeologia Mundi Ser.). 256p. 1968. 29.50 (ISBN 0-88254-147-1). Hippocrene Bks.

Belew, Wendell. The Leaven & the Salt. (Home Mission Graded Ser.). 1977. pap. 1.50 (ISBN 0-937170-14-3). Home Mission.

Belfield, Eversley. Defy & Endure: Great Sieges of Modern History. LC 68-21302. Orig. Title: Great Sieges. (Illus.). (gr. 7-10). 1968. 4.50g o.s.i. (ISBN 0-02-709030-2, CCPr). Macmillan.

Belfield, Robert, jt. auth. see Sagafi-nejad, Tagi.

Belfiglio, Valentine J. American Foreign Policy. LC 78-66047. (Illus.). 1979. pap. text ed. 8.00 (ISBN 0-8191-0681-X). U Pr of Amer.

Belfiore, F. Enzyme Regulation & Metabolic Diseases. (Illus.). xxiv, 880p. 1980. 149.25 (ISBN 3-8055-0005-X). S Karger.

Belford, Barbara, ed. Redbook's the Young Mothers. (Orig.). 1977. pap. 1.95 o.s.i. (ISBN 0-446-89381-1). Warner Bks.

Belfrage, Cedric & Aronson, James. Something to Guard. 1978. 25.00x (ISBN 0-231-04510-7). Columbia U Pr.

Belfrage, Sally. Flowers of Emptiness: Reflections on an Ashram. 256p. 1981. 10.95 (ISBN 0-8037-2523-X). Dial.

Belgardt, Raimund. Romantische Poesie. (Ger). 1970. text ed. 40.00x (ISBN 90-2791-248-3). Mouton.

Bel Geddes, Joan. How to Parent Alone: A Guide for Single Parents. LC 74-8241. 192p. 1974. 8.95 o.p. (ISBN 0-8164-9243-3). Continuum.

Belgrave, Charles. Personal Column. (Arab Background Ser.). (Illus.). 13.00x (ISBN 0-685-72054-3). Intl Bk Ctr.

--The Pirate Coast. (Arab Background Ser.). 13.00x (ISBN 0-685-72055-1). Intl Bk Ctr.

Belgum, David. Religion & Personality in the Spiral of Life. LC 79-66478. 1979. pap. text ed. 11.50 (ISBN 0-8191-0832-4). U Pr of Amer.

Belgum, David R. Alone, Alone, All, All Alone. (The Crossroads Ser.). 80p. (Orig.). 1972. pap. 1.95 (ISBN 0-570-06764-2, 12-2391). Concordia.

Beliaev, Alexander. Professor Dowell's Head. Bouis, Antonina W., tr. (Best of Soviet Science Fiction Ser.). 156p. 1981. pap. 2.95 (ISBN 0-02-016580-3, Collier). Macmillan.

Belina, Virginia S. Planning for Your Own Apartment. (gr. 7 up). 1975. pap. 3.96 (ISBN 0-8224-5420-3); tchrs manual free (ISBN 0-8224-5421-1). Pitman Learning.

Belinfante, F. J. Measurements of Time Reversal in Objective Quantum Theory. 1975. text ed. 18.75 (ISBN 0-08-018152-X). Pergamon.

--Survey of Hidden Variables Theories. 376p. 1973. text ed. 50.00 (ISBN 0-08-017032-3). Pergamon.

Beling, Carl, ed. The LH - Releasing Hormone. (Illus.). 368p. 1979. text ed. 39.50 (ISBN 0-89352-045-4). Masson Pub.

Beling, Willard A., ed. Role of Labor in African Nation-Building. 15.00 (ISBN 0-685-37307-X). Univ Place.

Belinkoff, Stanton. Introduction to Respiratory Care. 2d ed. LC 76-1045. 1976. text ed. 10.95 o.p. (ISBN 0-316-08802-1). Little.

Belinskii, Vissarion G. Selected Philisophical Works. LC 79-2893. li, 552p. 1981. Repr. of 1948 ed. 37.50 (ISBN 0-8305-0061-8). Hyperion Conn.

Belitt, Ben. The Double Witness: Poems. LC 77-2534. (Princeton Series of Contemporary Poets). 1977. 9.00 (ISBN 0-691-06346-X); pap. 3.75 (ISBN 0-691-01341-1). Princeton U Pr.

Belitt, Ben, tr. see Machado, Antonio.

Beliveau, Andre, jt. auth. see French, Richard.

Belk, J. A., ed. Electron Microscopy & Microanalysis of Crystalline Materials. (Illus.). 1979. 36.30x (ISBN 0-85334-816-2, Pub. by Applied Science). Burgess-Intl Ideas.

Belk, Russell W., jt. auth. see Gardner, David M.

Belkaoui, Ahmed. Conceptual Foundations of Management Accounting. LC 80-16086. (A-W Paperback Series in Accounting). 125p. 1980. pap. 6.50 (ISBN 0-201-00097-0). A-W.

Belkin, Gary S. Practical Counseling in the Schools. 480p. 1975. text ed. 12.95x o.p. (ISBN 0-697-06006-3). Wm C Brown.

Belkin, Gary S. & Skydell, Ruth H. Foundations of Psychology. LC 78-69566. (Illus.). 1979. text ed. 17.50 (ISBN 0-395-25363-2); annot. inst. ed. 18.95 (ISBN 0-395-25364-0); study guide 6.95 (ISBN 0-395-25365-9); test items 0.65 (ISBN 0-395-25366-7); test items manual il 0.60 (ISBN 0-395-28483-X). HM.

Belknap, Jeremy. Foresters, an American Tale, 1792. LC 71-100127. 1969. Repr. of 1792 ed. 23.00x (ISBN 0-8201-1071-X). Schol Facsimiles.

Belknap, Jodi P. Felisa & the Magic Tikling Bird. LC 73-79571. (gr. 1-7). 1973. 5.95g (ISBN 0-89610-014-6). Island Her.

Belknap, Michael R. Cold War Political Justice: The Smith Act, the Communist Party, & American Civil Liberties. LC 77-4566. (Contributions in American History: No. 66). 1977. lib. bdg. 18.95x (ISBN 0-8371-9692-2, BCW/). Greenwood.

Bell. I Learn to Write: 1978 Ed, 9 bks. Incl. Bk. A. (gr. k). pap. text ed. 2.92 (ISBN 0-8009-0255-6); tchr's. ed. 4.40 (ISBN 0-8009-0257-2); Bks. B-I. (gr. 1-8). pap. text ed. 2.44 ea. Bk. B (ISBN 0-8009-0259-9). Bk. C (ISBN 0-8009-0263-7). Bk. D (ISBN 0-8009-0269-6). Bk. E (ISBN 0-8009-0274-2). Bk. F (ISBN 0-8009-0278-5). Bk. G (ISBN 0-8009-0282-3). Bk. H (ISBN 0-8009-0288-2). Bk. I (ISBN 0-8009-0292-0); Bks. B-I, Tchr's. Eds. pap. 3.88 ea. Bk. B (ISBN 0-8009-0261-0). Bk. C (ISBN 0-8009-0265-3). Bk. D (ISBN 0-8009-0272-6). Bk. E (ISBN 0-8009-0276-9). Bk. F (ISBN 0-8009-0280-7). Bk. G (ISBN 0-8009-0286-6). Bk. H (ISBN 0-8009-0290-4). Bk. I (ISBN 0-8009-0294-7); Bks. C-G, Texas Edition. (gr. 2-6). Bk. C, Transition. pap. text ed. 2.00 (ISBN 0-8009-0250-5); Bks. D-G. pap. text ed. 2.20 ea. Bk. D (ISBN 0-8009-0240-8). Bk. E (ISBN 0-8009-0242-4). Bk. F (ISBN 0-8009-0244-0). Bk. G (ISBN 0-8009-0246-7). tchr's. ed. for Bk. C 3.88 (ISBN 0-8009-0252-1); Helping the Left-Handed Child. **pap. 0.44 (ISBN 0-8009-0305-6); How Parents Help Pre-School Children Write. pap. 0.64 (ISBN 0-8009-0302-1); Learn Manuscript Writing - Student Bk. pap. 2.32 (ISBN 0-8009-0300-5); Transition - When? pap. 0.044 (ISBN 0-8009-0307-2). (gr. k-8). ABC reference & desk cards, charts, practice paper, pencils & pens avail.; 1968 & 1973 eds. of texts & tchr's. bks. also avail. Write for further info. McCormick-Mathers.**

--Petroleum Regulations: Handbook. 1980. pap. 75.00 (ISBN 0-917386-37-X). Exec Ent.

Bell, A. A., jt. ed. see Mace, M. E.

Bell, A. W. Waterpape: The Conspiracy That Succeeded. 1977. 5.95 o.p. (ISBN 0-533-02982-1). Vantage.

Bell, Alan. Sydney Smith. (Illus.). 240p. 1980. 29.95 (ISBN 0-19-812050-8). Oxford U Pr.

Bell, Alexis T. & Hair, Michael L., eds. Vibrational Spectroscopies for Absorbed Species. LC 80-21181. (ACS Symposium Ser.: No. 137). 1980. 31.00 (ISBN 0-8412-0585-X). Am Chemical.

Bell, Alexis T., jt. ed. see Hollahan, John R.

Bell, Ann O., ed. see Woolf, Virginia.

Bell, Anthea. The Great Menagerie: An Adaptation of the Antique Pop-up Book. LC 79-67762. (Illus.). (gr. k-3). 1980. 7.95 (ISBN 0-670-34979-8, Co-Pub. by Kestrel Books). Viking Pr.

Bell, Anthea, tr. see Goscinny & Uderzo.

Bell, Anthea, tr. see Nostlinger, Christine.

Bell, Anthea, tr. see Preussler, Otfried.

Bell, Anthea, tr. see Sonnleitner, A. T.

Bell, Aubrey F. Portuguese Literature. (Reprints Ser). 1922. 24.00x (ISBN 0-19-815396-1). Oxford U Pr.

Bell, Belden, ed. Nicaragua: An Ally Under Seige. 1978. pap. 10.00 (ISBN 0-685-59450-5). Coun Am Affair.

Bell, Bob. The Digest Book of Upland Game Shooting. (The Sports & Leisure Library). (Illus.). 96p. 1979. pap. 2.95 (ISBN 0-686-66063-3). Follett.

Bell, Bruce W. A Little Dab of Color. (gr. 5 up). 1980. 7.95 (ISBN 0-688-51956-3); lib. bdg. 7.63 (ISBN 0-688-51956-3). Morrow.

Bell, C., tr. see Meyer, Conrad F.

Bell, C., tr. see Perez Galdos, Benito.

Bell, C. A. English-Tibetan Colloquial Dictionary. 1977. Repr. of 1920 ed. 18.50x (ISBN 0-8364-0401-7). South Asia Bks.

Bell, C. F. Syntheses & Physical Studies of Inorganic Compounds. LC 79-178772. 253p. 1972. text ed. 46.00 (ISBN 0-08-016651-2). Pergamon.

Bell, C. Gordon, et al. Computer Engineering: A DEC View of Hardware Systems Design. LC 77-91677. (Illus.). 1978. 25.00 (ISBN 0-932376-00-2). Digital Pr.

Bell, C. R. Men at Work. (Advances in Psychology). (Illus.). 1974. pap. text ed. 5.95x (ISBN 0-04-150046-6). Allen Unwin.

--Nature of Sociology. LC 78-57600. (Studies in Society). 1980. text ed. cancelled o.p. (ISBN 0-86861-328-2); pap. text ed. 9.95x o.p. (ISBN 0-86861-336-3). Allen Unwin.

Bell, Carolyn. Delivery. (Outlaws Ser.: Vol. 3). 1980. pap. 4.50x (ISBN 0-917624-19-X). Lame Johnny.

Bell, Cecil H., Jr., jt. auth. see French, Wendell L.

Bell, Charles Frederic M. Khedives and Pashas: Sketches of Contemporary Egyptian Rulers and Statesmen. by One Who Knows Them Well. LC 80-2196. 1981. Repr. of 1884 ed. 30.00 (ISBN 0-404-18954-7). AMS Pr.

Bell, Charles G. & Price, Charles M. California Government Today: Politics of Reform. 1980. pap. 9.95x (ISBN 0-256-02185-6). Dorsey.

Bell, Sir Charles. Grammar of Colloquial Tibetan. 1977. pap. 4.00 o.p. (ISBN 0-486-23466-5). Dover.

Bell, Clinton C. Maintenance Mechanics Qualification Program. (Illus.). 56p. 1981. pap. write for info. (ISBN 0-89852-389-3). TAPPI.

--Preventive Maintenance in a Corrugated Container Plant. (TAPPI Press Reports Ser.). (Illus.). 56p. 1981. pap. write for info. (ISBN 0-89852-388-5, 01-01-R088). Tappi.

Bell, Colin & Encel, Sol, eds. Inside the Whale: Ten Personal Accounts of Social Research. 1978. text ed. 29.00 (ISBN 0-08-022244-7); pap. text ed. 15.25 (ISBN 0-08-022243-9). Pergamon.

Bell, Colin & Newby, Howard, eds. Doing Sociological Research. LC 77-84959. 1978. 16.95 (ISBN 0-02-902350-5). Free Pr.

Bell, Colin E. Quantitative Methods for Administration. 1977. 19.25x (ISBN 0-256-01875-8). Irwin.

Bell, Colin F. Principles & Applications of Metal Chelation. (Oxford Chemistry Ser.). (Illus.). 1977. 21.00x (ISBN 0-19-855485-0). Oxford U Pr.

Bell, Coral, ed. Agenda for the Eighties. LC 80-65340. 256p. 1980. pap. text ed. 18.95 (ISBN 0-7081-1086-X, 0469, Pub. by ANUP Australia). Bks Australia.

Bell, D. J. & Freemon, B. M., eds. Physiology & Biochemistry of the Domestic Fowl, 3 vols. 1972. Vol. 1. 96.00 (ISBN 0-12-085001-X); Vol. 2. 94.50 (ISBN 0-12-085002-8); Vol. 3. 67.50 (ISBN 0-12-085003-6). Acad Pr.

Bell, D. Rayford. The Philosophy of Christ. LC 80-67408. 104p. 1980. 6.95 (ISBN 0-9604820-0-8); pap. 4.95 (ISBN 0-9604820-1-6). D R Bell.

Bell, D. S., jt. ed. see Kolinsky, Martin.

Bell, Daniel. Teletext: The New Networks of Information & Knowledge in Computer Society. LC 78-19820. Date not set. cancelled (ISBN 0-465-08402-8). Basic.

--The Winding Passage: Essays & Sociological Journeys, 1960-1980. LC 79-57350. (Illus.). 446p. 1980. 25.00 (ISBN 0-89011-545-1). Abt Assoc.

Bell, Daniel & Kristol, Irving, eds. The Crisis in Economic Theory. LC 80-70392. 242p. 1981. 13.95 (ISBN 0-465-01476-3); pap. 4.95. Basic.

Bell, David. Frege's Theory of Judgement. 178p. 1979. text ed. 24.95x (ISBN 0-19-827423-8). Oxford U Pr.

--Fundamentals of Electric Circuits. 2nd ed. 688p. 1981. text ed. 18.95 (ISBN 0-8359-2128-X); instrs. manual avail. Reston.

--Fundamentals of Electric Circuits. (Illus.). 1978. ref. ed. 19.95 (ISBN 0-87909-318-8); students manual avail. Reston.

Bell, David & Tepperman, Lorne. The Roots of Disunity: A Look at Canadian Political Culture. 262p. 1980. pap. 10.00x (ISBN 0-7710-1196-2). NYU Pr.

Bell, David A. Fundamentals of Electronic Devices. (Illus.). 480p. 1974. 19.95 (ISBN 0-87909-276-9); students manual avail. Reston.

Bell, David S., ed. Labour into the Eighties. 168p. 1980. 25.00x (ISBN 0-7099-0443-6, Pub. by Croom Helm Ltd England). Biblio Dist.

Bell, Derrick, ed. Shades of Brown: New Perspectives on School Desegregation. LC 80-21877. 1980. text ed. 12.95x (ISBN 0-8077-2595-1). Tchrs Coll.

Bell, Diane & Ditton, Pam. Law. (Illus.). 147p. 1980. pap. text ed. 9.95 (ISBN 0-908160-77-1). Bks Australia.

Bell, Enid H. Storming the Citadel: The Rise of the Woman Doctor. LC 79-2931. 200p. 1981. Repr. of 1953 ed. 17.50 (ISBN 0-8305-0098-7). Hyperion Conn.

Bell, F. G. Engineering Properties of Soils & Rocks. (Illus.). 144p. 1981. pap. text ed. 12.50 (ISBN 0-408-00537-8). Butterworths.

--Foundation Engineering in Difficult Ground. 1978. 79.95 (ISBN 0-408-00311-1). Butterworths.

Bell, Frederic. Jenny's Corner. LC 73-18741. (Illus.). 72p. 1974. 3.95 (ISBN 0-394-82741-4); PLB 5.99 (ISBN 0-394-92741-9). Random.

Bell, Frederick W. Food from the Sea: The Economics & Politics of Ocean Fisheries. LC 77-28756. (Special Studies in Natural Resources & Energy Management Ser.). (Illus.). 1978. lib. bdg. 30.00x (ISBN 0-89158-403-X); pap. text ed. 12.50x (ISBN 0-89158-353-X). Westview.

Bell, Garrett De see DeBell, Garrett.

Bell, Gary & Seay, David R. The Gary Bell Story. 176p. (Orig.). 1981. pap. 4.95 (ISBN 0-89081-253-5). Harvest Hse.

Bell, Gary & Seay, Davin R. Lost but Not Forever. LC 80-81472. 1981. pap. 4.95 (ISBN 0-89081-253-5). Harvest Hse.

Bell, Geoffrey. Euro-Dollar Market & the International Finance System. 112p. 1973. 18.95 o.p. (ISBN 0-470-06405-6). Halsted Pr.

Bell, George. Day & Night in the Wynds of Edinburgh. Incl. Blackfriars' Wynd Analysed. 1973. Repr. of 1850 ed. text ed. 12.50 (ISBN 0-8277-1536-6). British Bk Ctr.

Bell, George H., et al, eds. Textbook of Physiology. 10th ed. (Illus.). 600p. 1980. text ed. 33.00x (ISBN 0-443-02152-X). Churchill.

Bell, Gerald D. Achievers. LC 73-79581. 200p. 1973. pap. 8.95 (ISBN 0-914616-00-5). Preston-Hill.

Bell, Gertrude. First Crop. LC 72-89608. (Illus.). (gr. 5-8). 1973. 6.50 o.p. (ISBN 0-8309-0082-9). Independence Pr.

Bell, Gertrude L., jt. auth. see Ramsay, W. M.

Bell, Gwen, ed. Strategies for Human Settlements: Habitat & Environment. LC 76-5416. (Illus.). 200p. (Orig.). 1976. 9.95 o.p. (ISBN 0-8248-0414-7, Eastwest Ctr); pap. 3.95 (ISBN 0-8248-0469-4). U Pr of Hawaii.

Bell, Harriet, ed. see Austen, Jane.

Bell, Harriet, ed. see Haubrick, Judd.

Bell, Harriet, ed. see Tunnard, Christopher & Pushkarev, Boris.

Bell, I., et al. Art As You See It: Wiley Self Teaching Guide. 326p. 1979. write for info. (ISBN 0-471-03826-1). Wiley.

Bell, Ian. The Dominican Republic. LC 80-13968. (Nations of the Modern World Ser.). (Illus.). 360p. 1981. lib. bdg. 26.50x (ISBN 0-89158-780-2). Westview.

Bell, Irene W. & Wieckert, Jeanne E. Basic Classroom Skills Through Games. LC 80-351. 1980. 17.50 (ISBN 0-87287-207-6). Libs Unl.

--Basic Media Skills Through Games. LC 79-941. 1979. 17.50 (ISBN 0-87287-194-0). Libs Unl.

Bell, Irene W., jt. auth. see Wieckert, Jeanne E.

Bell, Irving. Christmas in Old New England. 54p. (gr. 3-8). 1981. 8.95 (ISBN 0-917780-02-7). April Hill.

Bell, J., tr. see Nicod, Jean.

Bell, J., et al, eds. General Welding & Cutting. (Engineering Craftsmen: No. F10). (Illus.). 1976. spiral bdg. 26.00x (ISBN 0-85083-330-2). Intl Ideas.

--Welding Practices, 6 vols. Incl. Vol. 1. General Welding & Cutting; Vol. 2. Advanced Pipe & Tube Welding; Vol. 3. Tungsten Arc Gas Shielded Welding; Vol. 4. Metal Arc Gas Shielded Welding; Vol. 5. Manual Metal Arc Welding; Vol. 6. Oxy-Acetlene Welding. 1977. Set. 115.00x (ISBN 0-685-91105-5). Intl Ideas.

Bell, J. Ellis, ed. Spectroscopy in Biochemistry, 2 vols. 288p. 1981. 69.95 ea. Vol. 1 (ISBN 0-8493-5551-6). Vol. 2 (ISBN 0-8493-5552-4). CRC Pr.

Bell, James B., jt. auth. see Doane, Gilbert H.

Bell, James K. & Cohn, Adrian. Bell & Cohn's Handbook of Grammar, Style & Usage. 2nd ed. 1976. pap. text ed. 3.95x (ISBN 0-02-470630-2, 470630). Macmillan.

--Rhetoric in a Modern Mode, with Selected Readings. 3rd ed. 1976. pap. text ed. 9.95 (ISBN 0-02-470600-0). Macmillan.

--Rhetoric Three: The Rhetoric Section from Rhetoric in a Modern Mode. 3rd ed. 1976. pap. text ed. 4.95 (ISBN 0-02-470620-5). Macmillan.

Bell, James W. Little Rock Handbook. (Illus.). iv, 88p. (Orig.). 1980. pap. 7.95 (ISBN 0-939130-00-9). J W Bell.

Bell, Jimmy, jt. ed. see Owens, Charles E.

Bell, Joan K., jt. auth. see Bell, Richard O.

Bell, John. Bell's British Theatre, Consisting of the Most Esteemed English Plays, 41 vols. 1776-1802. Set. 1127.50 (ISBN 0-404-00800-3); 27.50 ea.; write for info. listing (ISBN 0-685-05697-X). AMS Pr.

--Bell's New Pantheon, 2 vols. Feldman, Burton & Richardson, Robert D., eds. LC 78-60919. (Myth & Romanticism Ser.: Vol. 4). 809p. 1979. Set. lib. bdg. 120.00 (ISBN 0-8240-3553-4). Garland Pub.

Bell, John, ed. see Owen, Wilfred.

Bell, John L. Boolean-Valued Models & Independence Proofs in Set Theory. (Oxford Logic Guides Ser.). 1978. 23.50x (ISBN 0-19-853168-0). Oxford U Pr.

Bell, John M., ed. see Purdue University Industrial Waste Conference, 35th.

Bell, John P. Crisis in Costa Rica: The Nineteen Forty-Eight Revolution. LC 77-165920. (Latin American Monographs Ser.: No. 24). 192p. 1971. 9.95x (ISBN 0-292-70147-0). U of Tex Pr.

Bell, Josephine. A Question of Inheritance. 1981. 9.95 (ISBN 0-8027-5438-4). Walker & Co.

--Stroke of Death. LC 77-79963. 1977. 6.95 o.s.i. (ISBN 0-8027-5378-7). Walker & Co.

--Treachery in Type. (Walker Mystery Ser.). 1980. 8.95 o.s.i. (ISBN 0-8027-5402-3). Walker & Co.

Bell, Kathleen. Tribunals in the Social Services, an Introductory Study. (Library of Social Policy & Administration). 1969. text ed. 6.00x (ISBN 0-7100-6339-3); pap. text ed. 3.00x (ISBN 0-7100-6345-8). Humanities.

Bell, Ken & Major, Henriette. A Man & His Mission: Cardinal Leger in Africa. Springer, Jane, tr. 1976. 35.00 o.p. (ISBN 0-13-548115-5). P-H.

Bell, L. J., ed. The Large Print Book & Its User. 1980. pap. 33.00x (ISBN 0-85365-632-0, Pub. by Lib Assn England). Oryx Pr.

Bell, Louis. The Telescope. 287p. 1981. pap. price not set (ISBN 0-486-24151-3). Dover.

Bell, M. Robert, jt. auth. see Steinaker, Norman.

Bell, Malcolm. Morgantina Studies: Vol. 1, the Terracottas. LC 80-8537. (Illus.). 416p. 1981. 55.00x (ISBN 0-691-03946-1). Princeton U Pr.

Bell, Margaret E. Love Is Forever. (gr. 7 up). 1954. PLB 8.40 (ISBN 0-688-31449-X). Morrow.

Bell, Maria A. Guess Who's Cooking Dinner: One Hundred & Fifty Recipes from the Famous, the Near Famous & the Super Famous. (Illus.). 1979. 12.95 (ISBN 0-8027-0614-2); pap. 6.95 (ISBN 0-8027-7141-6). Walker & Co.

Bell, Martin. Nenshu & the Tiger: Parables of Life & Death. 128p. 1975. 5.95 (ISBN 0-8164-0261-2). Crossroad NY.

--Way of the Wolf: The Gospel in New Images. LC 77-120366. (Illus.). 1970. 6.95 (ISBN 0-8164-0202-7); 2 records 7.95 ea. Crossroad NY.

Bell, Martin L. Marketing: Concepts & Strategy. 3rd ed. LC 78-69572. (Illus.). 1979. text ed. 19.95 (ISBN 0-395-26503-7); inst. manual 1.50 (ISBN 0-395-26504-5). HM.

Bell, Max S., et al. Algebraic & Arithmetic Structures: A Concrete Approach for Elementary School Teachers. LC 75-2807. (Illus.). 1976. text ed. 16.95 (ISBN 0-02-902270-3). Free Pr.

Bell, Mervyn, ed. Britain's National Parks. LC 74-20450. (Illus.). 160p. 1975. 17.95 (ISBN 0-7153-6792-7). David & Charles.

Bell, Michael. The Salesman in the Field: Conditions of Work & Employment of Commercial Travellers & Representatives. International Labour Office, Geneva, ed. viii, 108p. (Orig.). 1980. pap. 8.55 (ISBN 92-2-102308-7). Intl Labour Office.

Bell, Michael, ed. The Context of English Literature, Nineteen Hundred to Nineteen-Thirty. LC 80-7792. (The Context of English Literature Ser.). 250p. 1980. text ed. 29.50x (ISBN 0-8419-0423-5); pap. text ed. 16.95x (ISBN 0-8419-0424-3). Holmes & Meier.

Bell, Michael D. Development of American Romance: The Sacrifice of Relation. LC 80-12241. 272p. 1981. lib. bdg. 22.50x (ISBN 0-226-04211-1). U of Chicago Pr.

Bell, Millicent. Edith Wharton & Henry James: The Story of Their Friendship. LC 65-10196. 1965. 6.50 o.p. (ISBN 0-8076-0295-7). Braziller.

Bell, Norman T., et al. Self-Instructional Program in Educational Psychology. 1970. pap. 4.95x o.p. (ISBN 0-673-05859-X). Scott F.

Bell, Norman W. & Vogel, Ezra F., eds. Modern Introduction to the Family. rev. ed. LC 68-12830. 1968. text ed. 15.95 (ISBN 0-02-902330-0). Free Pr.

Bell, O. O. Goaling up. LC 77-91672. (Illus.). 1978. 13.95 (ISBN 0-931034-01-9). Everest Pub.

Bell, Oliver, ed. America's Changing Population. (Reference Shelf Ser.). 1974. 6.25 (ISBN 0-8242-0522-7). Wilson.

Bell, P., tr. see Von Denffer, Dietrich, et al.

Bell, R. L. Negative Electron Affinity Devices. (Monographs in Electrical & Electronic Engineering). (Illus.). 148p. 1973. 29.95x (ISBN 0-19-859313-9). Oxford U Pr.

Bell, Richard O. & Bell, Joan K. Auditions & Scenes: American & British Theatre. LC 80-80119. 200p. Date not set. pap. 9.95 (ISBN 0-9603626-1-4). Armado & Moth.

--Auditions & Scenes from Shakespeare. LC 79-54914. 161p. (Orig.). 1979. pap. 7.95 (ISBN 0-9603626-0-6). Armado & Moth.

Bell, Robert & Grant, Nigel. Patterns of Education in the British Isles. (Unwin Education Books). 1977. text ed. 21.00x (ISBN 0-04-370082-9); pap. text ed. 9.95x (ISBN 0-04-370083-7). Allen Unwin.

Bell, Robert, ed. Early Ballads, Illustrative of History, Traditions, & Customs. LC 67-23928. 1968. Repr. of 1877 ed. 20.00 (ISBN 0-8103-3408-9). Gale.

Bell, Robert C. Monographs on Plastic Surgery, Vol. 1. (Illus.). 200p. 1973. text ed. 18.50x o.p. (ISBN 0-19-265106-4). Oxford U Pr.

Bell, Robert E. Dictionary of Classical Mythology: Symbols, Attributes, & Associations. Schlachter, Gail, ed. (No. 1). 1981. write for info. (ISBN 0-87436-305-5). ABC Clio.

--Wichita Indians: Wichita Indian Archaeology & Ethnology: a Pilot Study. Horr, David A., ed. (Plains Indians - American Indian Ethnohistory Ser.). 1974. lib. bdg. 42.00 (ISBN 0-8240-0770-0). Garland Pub.

Bell, Robert R. Marriage & Family Interaction. 5th ed. 1979. text ed. 18.50x (ISBN 0-256-02110-4); pap. study guide 5.95 (ISBN 0-256-02243-7). Dorsey.

--Social Deviance: A Substantive Analysis. rev. ed. 1976. pap. text ed. 10.50 o.p. (ISBN 0-256-01663-1). Dorsey.

Bell, Robert W. & Smotherman, William F., eds. Maternal Influences & Early Behavior. new ed. LC 78-17074. (Illus.). 465p. 1980. text ed. 45.00 (ISBN 0-89335-059-1). Spectrum Pub.

Bell, Roseann P., et al. Sturdy Black Bridges: Visions of Black Women in Literature. LC 77-16898. 1979. pap. 6.95 (ISBN 0-385-13347-2, Anch). Doubleday.

Bell, Ruth, et al. Changing Bodies, Changing Lives: A Book for Teens on Sex & Relationships. (Illus.). 1981. 14.95 (ISBN 0-394-50304-X); pap. 7.95 (ISBN 0-394-73632-X). Random.

Bell, S. Peter. Dissertations on British History, 1815-1914: An Index to British & American Theses. LC 75-15489. 1974. 8.50 o.p. (ISBN 0-8108-0733-5). Scarecrow.

Bell, Sallie L. The Bond Slave. 1978. pap. 2.50 (ISBN 0-310-21092-5). Zondervan.

--By Strange Paths. 192p. 1974. pap. 2.25 (ISBN 0-310-20992-7). Zondervan.

--The Last Surrender. new ed. 192p. (Orig.). 1974. pap. 2.25 (ISBN 0-310-21002-X). Zondervan.

--Romance Along the Bayou. new ed. 192p. (Orig.). 1974. pap. 2.25 (ISBN 0-310-21022-4). Zondervan.

--The Substitute. 1976. pap. 2.25 (ISBN 0-310-21042-9). Zondervan.

--Through Golden Meadows. LC 72-146582. 1971. pap. 1.95 (ISBN 0-310-21052-6). Zondervan.

Bell, Sam, jt. auth. see Steben, Ralph E.

Bell, Stephen, jt. auth. see Williams, Michael.

Bell, Susan. Women: From the Greeks to the French Revolution. 1972. pap. 6.95 o.p. (ISBN 0-534-00284-6). Wadsworth Pub.

Bell, Susan G., ed. Women: From the Greeks to the French Revolution. LC 80-51750. xiv, 313p. 1980. 17.50x (ISBN 0-8047-1094-5); pap. 5.95x (ISBN 0-8047-1082-1). Stanford U Pr.

Bell, T. H. & Thorum, Arden R. Your Child's Intellect: A Guide to Home-Based Preschool Education. LC 73-159374. (Illus.). 192p. 1972. 8.95 (ISBN 0-913420-02-6); pap. 6.95 o.p. (ISBN 0-913420-03-4). Olympus Pub Co.

Bell, Terrel H. Performance Accountability System for School Administrators. 1974. 11.95 o.p. (ISBN 0-13-657189-1). P-H.

Bell, Thomas. The Anatomie of Popish Tyrannie. LC 74-28833. (English Experience Ser.: No. 714). 1975. Repr. of 1603 ed. 16.00 (ISBN 90-221-0714-0). Walter J Johnson.

Bell, Vereen. Swamp Water. LC 80-24570. (Brown Thrasher Ser.). 272p. 1981. pap. 6.95 (ISBN 0-8203-0546-4). U of Ga Pr.

Bell, W. Bruce. A Little Dab of Color. LC 80-11986. 192p. (gr. 5 up). 1980. 7.95 (ISBN 0-688-41956-9); PLB 7.63 (ISBN 0-688-51956-3). Lothrop.

Bell, Wendell. Jamaican Leaders: Political Attitudes in a New Nation. 1964. 19.00x (ISBN 0-520-00103-6). U of Cal Pr.

Bell, Whitfield J., jt. auth. see Donovan, Frank R.

Bell, Whitfield J., Jr. Towards a National Spirit. 1979. pap. 3.00 (ISBN 0-89073-057-1). Boston Public Lib.

Bell, William E. & McCormick, William. Neurologic Infections in Children. 2nd ed. (Major Problems in Clinical Pediatrics Ser.: Vol. 12). (Illus.). 600p. 1981. text ed. price not set (ISBN 0-7216-1676-3). Saunders.

Bell, William H., et al. Surgical Correction of Dentofacial Deformities. LC 76-27050. 1979. text ed. 150.00 (ISBN 0-7216-1671-2); Vol. 1. 70.00 (ISBN 0-7216-1675-5); Vol. 2. 80.00 (ISBN 0-7216-1707-7). Saunders.

Bell, Winthrop P. Foreign Protestants & the Settlement of Nova Scotia: The History of a Piece of Arrested British Policy in the Eighteenth Century. LC 61-4799. xiv, 673p. 1961. 45.00x o.p. (ISBN 0-8020-7000-0). U of Toronto Pr.

Bella, Geoffrey A. Di see Di Bella, Geoffrey A., et al.

Bella, Leopold & Baker, Samm S. Reading Faces. LC 80-19235. (Illus.). 160p. 1981. 9.95 (ISBN 0-03-057869-8). HR&W.

Bellack, Alan, jt. ed. see Hersen, Michel.

Bellack, Alan S., jt. ed. see Hersen, Michel.

Bellack, Arno A. & Kliebard, Herbert E., eds. Curriculum & Evaluation. LC 76-18040. (Readings in Educational Research Ser.). 1977. 25.00 (ISBN 0-8211-0129-3); text ed. 22.50 10 or more copies (ISBN 0-686-67488-X). McCutchan.

Bellack, Arno A., ed. see Fey, James T.

Bellack, Arno A., jt. ed. see Westbury, Ian.

Bellafiore, Joseph. Adventures with Words, 2 bks. (gr. 9-12). 1971. Bk. 1. wkbk. 5.25 (ISBN 0-87720-353-9); Bk. 2. wkbk 5.25 (ISBN 0-87720-355-5). AMSCO Sch.

--College English Workshop. 1976. 8.17 (ISBN 0-87720-951-0). AMSCO Sch.

--English Language Arts, Intermediate Level. (Illus.). (gr. 7-9). 1969. text ed. 10.00 (ISBN 0-87720-308-3); pap. text ed. 5.83 (ISBN 0-87720-307-5); wkbk. ed. 6.83 (ISBN 0-87720-347-4). AMSCO Sch.

--English Made Easier. (Orig.). (gr. 7-12). 1974. wkbk. 7.33 (ISBN 0-87720-344-X); pap. text ed. 5.92 (ISBN 0-87720-342-3). AMSCO Sch.

--Essentials of English. (gr. 7-9). 1970. pap. text ed. 4.42 (ISBN 0-87720-341-5); wkbk. 5.67 (ISBN 0-87720-349-0). AMSCO Sch.

--Reviewing English Preliminary. (gr. 7-12). 1958. pap. text ed. 4.33 (ISBN 0-87720-305-9). AMSCO Sch.

--Words at Work. 2nd ed. (gr. 10-12). 1968. pap. text ed. 4.42 (ISBN 0-87720-320-2). AMSCO Sch.

Bellah, Melanie. Bow Wow! Meow! A First Book of Sounds. (Illus.). (ps-3). 1963. PLB 5.00 (ISBN 0-307-60523-X, Golden Pr). Western Pub.

Bellah, Robert N. Beyond Belief: Essays on Religion in a Post-Traditional World. LC 77-109058. 1970. 8.95 o.p. (ISBN 0-06-060774-2, RD-129, HarpR). Har-Row.

--The Broken Covenenant: American Civil Religion in Time of Trail. 1976. pap. 4.95 (ISBN 0-8164-2123-4). Crossroad NY.

--Tokugawa Religion. 1959. 8.95 o.s.i. (ISBN 0-02-902400-5). Free Pr.

Bellah, Robert N. & Hammond, Phillip E. Varieties of Civil Religion. LC 80-7742. 256p. 1981. 14.95 (ISBN 0-06-060776-9, HarpR). Har-Row.

Bellah, Robert N., jt. ed. see Glock, Charles Y.

Bellaire, Marc. Brush Decoration for Ceramics. 3.95 (ISBN 0-934706-02-6). Prof Pubns Ohio.

--Underglaze Decoration. 3.95 (ISBN 0-934706-01-8). Prof Pubns Ohio.

Bellairs, Angus. Life of Reptiles, 2 Vols. LC 70-99976. (Natural History Ser.). (Illus.). 1970. Set. 27.50x o.s.i. (ISBN 0-87663-113-8). Universe.

Bellairs, George. Fear Round About. 1981. 9.95 (ISBN 0-8027-5441-4). Walker & Co.

Bellairs, Herbert J., et al. Modern Real Estate Practice in Pennsylvania. 2nd ed. 576p. 1978. pap. 25.00 (ISBN 0-88462-280-0). Real Estate Ed Co.

Bellairs, John. The Treasure of Alpheus Winterborn. 192p. (gr. 3-8). 1980. pap. 1.95 (ISBN 0-553-15095-2). Bantam.

Bellak, Leopold & Faithorn, Peri E. Crises & Special Problems in Psychoanalysis & Psychotherapy. 264p. 1981. 17.50 (ISBN 0-87630-257-6). Brunner-Mazel.

Bellak, Leopold, et al. Ego Functions in Schizophrenics, Neurotics, & Normals: A Systematic Study of Conceptual, Diagnostic, & Therapeutic Aspects. LC 73-3199. (Personality Processes Ser.). 688p. 1973. 39.95 (ISBN 0-471-06413-0, Pub. by Wiley-Interscience). Wiley.

Bellak, Rhoda & Voehl, Dick. Five Pennies Make a Nickel: A Piggybank Book. (Piggybank Bks.). 12p. (gr. k-2). 1981. text ed. 4.95 (ISBN 0-671-42562-5). Wanderer Bks.

Bellamy, A. J. Introduction to Conservation of Orbital Symmetry: A Programmed Text. 160p. (Orig.). 1974. pap. text ed. 8.95x (ISBN 0-582-44089-0). Longman.

Bellamy, B. E. Private Presses & Publishing in England Since 1945. 1980. text ed. 30.00 (ISBN 0-89664-180-5, Pub. by K G Saur). Shoe String.

Bellamy, Edward. Looking Backward. (Literature Ser). (gr. 9-12). 1970. pap. text ed. 3.50 (ISBN 0-87720-733-X). AMSCO Sch.

Bellamy, Frank. Mexico & Central America. LC 76-55108. 1977. 10.00 (ISBN 0-8467-0272-X, Pub. by Two Continents); pap. 6.95 (ISBN 0-8467-0336-X). Hippocrene Bks.

Bellamy, Joyce M. & Saville, John, eds. Dictionary of Labour Biography, 5 vols. LC 78-185417. 414p. 1972. Vol. 1. lib. bdg. 37.50x (ISBN 0-678-07008-3); Vol. 2. lib. bdg. 47.50x (ISBN 0-678-07018-0); Vols. 3. lib. bdg. 37.50x (ISBN 0-333-14415-5); Vol. 4. lib. bdg. 37.50x (ISBN 0-333-19704-6); Vol. 5. lib. bdg. 37.50x (ISBN 0-333-22015-3). Kelley.

Bellamy, Margot A., ed. African Agriculture & Rural Development, 5 vols. Incl. Vol. 1. General. 33p (ISBN 0-85198-359-6); Vol. 2. North & Northeast Africa. 33p (ISBN 0-85198-360-X); Vol. 3. East Africa. 60p (ISBN 0-85198-361-8); Vol. 4. South & Central Africa. 37p (ISBN 0-85198-363-4); Vol. 5. West Africa. 70p (ISBN 0-85198-362-6). (Annotated Bibliography Ser.: B., 1970 to 1974). 1975. Set. pap. 67.50x (ISBN 0-8002-2412-4). Intl Pubns Serv.

Bellamy, Rex. The Peak District Companion: A Walker's Guide. LC 80-70294. (Illus.). 208p. 1981. 24.00. David & Charles.

Belland, F. W. Fleshwound. 224p. (Orig.). 1981. pap. 2.25 (ISBN 0-515-05652-9). Jove Pubns.

Bellanti, J. A. & Dayton, D. H., eds. The Phagocytic Cell in Host Resistance. LC 74-14147. 365p. 1975. 31.50 (ISBN 0-911216-90-1). Raven.

Bellas, Ralph A. Christina Rossetti. (English Authors Ser.: No. 201). 1977. lib. bdg. 9.95 (ISBN 0-8057-6671-5). Twayne.

Bellaschi, Jules. To Lead & Manage. LC 80-83869. 70p. (Orig.). 1980. pap. 4.95 (ISBN 0-9605144-0-6). MJ Pubns.

Bellasis, Edward. Cherubini: Memorials Illustrative of His Life & Work. LC 70-138497. (Music Ser). 1971. Repr. of 1912 ed. lib. bdg. 29.50 (ISBN 0-306-70071-9). Da Capo.

Bellavance, Diane. Advertising & Public Relations for a Small Business. (Illus.). 80p. 1980. pap. 5.95 (ISBN 0-9605276-0-5). DBA Bks.

Bellavance, Russell C., ed. see Institute for Paralegal Training.

Belleggia, Sr. Concetta. God & the Problem of Evil. 1980. 3.75 (ISBN 0-8198-3007-0); pap. 2.50 (ISBN 0-8198-3008-9). Dghtrs St Paul.

Bellenger, Danny N. & Berl, Robert L. Sales Management: A Review of the Current Literature. (Research Monograph: No. 89). 1981. spiral bdg. 10.00 (ISBN 0-88406-147-7). GA St U Busn Pub.

Bellenger, Danny N. & Greenberg, Barnett A. Marketing Research: A Management Information Approach. 1978. text ed. 18.95x (ISBN 0-256-01990-8). Irwin.

Beller, A., et al. Coding the Universe. (London Mathematical Society Lecture Notes: No. 47). 300p. Date not set. price not set (ISBN 0-521-28040-0). Cambridge U Pr.

Beller, Anne S. Bed & Board: The Economics of Love, Marriage, & Dependency. 1981. 10.95 (ISBN 0-686-68238-6). FS&G.

Bellestri, Joseph. Sins of the Father. 1981. 7.75 (ISBN 0-8062-1612-3). Carlton.

Bellette, Emile. La Succession Aux Fiefs Dans les Coutumes Flamandes. LC 80-1997. 1981. Repr. of 1926 ed. 23.50 (ISBN 0-404-18553-3). AMS Pr.

Bellevue Art Museum. Glen Alps Retrospective: The Collagraph Idea, Nineteen Fifty Six to Nineteen Eighty. LC 79-54958. (Illus.). pap. 4.95 (ISBN 0-295-95703-4). U of Wash Pr.

Belli, Giuseppe G. The Roman Sonnets of Giuseppe Gioacchino Belli. Norse, Harold, tr. from It. & intro. by. LC 73-79284. (Perivale Translation Ser.: No. 1). 54p. 1974. pap. 3.75 (ISBN 0-912288-06-X). Perivale Pr.

--Some of the Sonnets. Williams, Miller, tr. from Ital. LC 80-24331. 177p. 1981. 9.95x (ISBN 0-8071-0762-X); pap. 4.95x (ISBN 0-8071-0763-8). La State U Pr.

Bellimin-Noel, J. Le Texte et l'avant-texte: Les Brouillons d'un poeme de Milosz. new ed. (Collection L). 144p. (Orig., Fr.). 1972. pap. 8.95 (ISBN 2-03-036003-1). Larousse.

Bellin. Classical Dutch. 19.95 (ISBN 0-7134-3211-X, Pub. by Batsford England). David & Charles.

Bellin, Lowell E. The Challenge of Administering Health Services. Weeks, Lewis E., ed. (Illus.). 400p. 1981. write for info. (ISBN 0-914904-64-7). Health Admin Pr.

Bellin, Mildred G. The Jewish Cookbook. 1980. write for info. (ISBN 0-8197-0058-4). Bloch.

Bellin, Robert. Chess Olympiad Skopje Nineteen Seventy-Two. 1977. 12.75 o.p. (ISBN 0-7134-3211-X). David & Charles.

--The Classical Dutch. (Batsford Chess Ser.). (Illus.). 1977. 12.95 o.s.i. (ISBN 0-7134-3211-X). Hippocrene Bks.

Bellini, Vincenzio. Beatrice Di Tenda, 2 vols. Rosen, Charles & Gosset, Philip, eds. LC 76-49178. (Early Romantic Opera Ser.: Vol. 5). 567p. 1980. lib. bdg. 82.00 (ISBN 0-8240-2904-6). Garland Pub.

Bellini, Vincenzo. Epistolario, a Cura Di Luisa Cambi. LC 80-2262. (Illus.). 1981. Repr. of 1943 ed. 56.00 (ISBN 0-404-18815-X). AMS Pr.

--Norma, 2 vols. Rosen, Charles & Gossett, Philip, eds. LC 76-49177. (Early Romantic Opera Ser.: Vol. 4). Date not set. lib. bdg. 82.00 (ISBN 0-8240-2903-8). Garland Pub. Postponed.

Bellisimo, Lou. The Bowler's Manual. 3rd ed. (Illus.). 128p. 1975. pap. text ed. 6.50 (ISBN 0-13-080432-0). P-H.

Belliston, Larry, jt. auth. see Hanks, Kurt.

Bellman, Beryl L. Village of Curers & Assassins: On the Production of Fala Kpelle Cosmological Categories. LC 73-76893. (Approaches to Semiotics: No. 39). 196p. 1975. text ed. 44.10x (ISBN 90-2793-042-2). Mouton.

Bellman, Guenter. Slavoteutonica: Lexikalische Untersuchungen Zum Slawisch-deutschen Sprachkontakt Im Ostmitteldeutschen. (Studia Linguistica Germanica Ser.: Vol. 4). (Illus.). 356p. 1971. 51.75x (ISBN 3-11-003344-5). De Gruyter.

Bellman, R. Analytic Number Theory: An Introduction. 1980. 19.50 (ISBN 0-8053-0360-X). A-W.

Bellman, R., ed. see Symposia in Applied Mathematics-New York-1958.

Bellman, R., ed. see Symposia in Applied Mathematics-New York-1963.

Bellman, Richard & Cooke, Kenneth. Modern Elementary Differential Equations. 2nd ed. (Mathematics Ser). 1971. text ed. 19.95 (ISBN 0-201-00511-5). A-W.

Bellman, Richard & Wing, Milton G. An Introduction to Invariant Imbedding. LC 74-18455. (Pure & Applied Mathematics Ser.). 288p. 1975. 30.50 o.p. (ISBN 0-471-06416-5, Pub. by Wiley-Interscience). Wiley.

Bellman, Richard E. & Dreyfus, S. Applied Dynamic Programming. (Rand Corporation Research Studies). 1962. 20.00 (ISBN 0-691-07913-7). Princeton U Pr.

Bellman, Samuel I. Marjorie Kinnan Rawlings. (U. S. Authors Ser.: No. 241). 1974. lib. bdg. 10.95 (ISBN 0-8057-0610-0). Twayne.

Bellman, W. F. Lighting the Stage: Art & Practices. 2nd ed. 1974. text ed. 24.50 scp (ISBN 0-7002-2421-1, HarpC). Har-Row.

Belloc, Hilaire. Bad Child's Book of Beasts. (Illus.). 6.50 (ISBN 0-8446-1627-3). Peter Smith.

--Cautionary Tales. (Children's Literature Ser.). 1980. PLB 5.95 (ISBN 0-8398-2602-8). Gregg.

--Cautionary Verses. (Illus.). 1959. 10.00 (ISBN 0-394-40314-2). Knopf.

--The Crisis of Civilization. LC 73-114465. 245p. 1973. Repr. of 1937 ed. lib. bdg. 19.75x (ISBN 0-8371-4761-1, BECC). Greenwood.

--The Path to Rome. 1902. text ed. 13.95x (ISBN 0-04-914017-5). Allen Unwin.

--The Yak, the Python, the Frog: Three Beast Poems. LC 74-12441. (Illus.). (ps-3). 1975. 5.95 o.s.i. (ISBN 0-8193-0785-8, Four Winds); PLB 5.41 o.s.i. (ISBN 0-8193-0786-6). Schol Bk Serv.

Belloc, Hillare. The Path to Rome. 1981. pap. text ed. 5.95 (ISBN 0-89526-884-1). Regnery-Gateway.

Bellon, Jerry J., et al. Instructional Improvement: Principles & Processes. 1978. pap. text ed. 5.95 (ISBN 0-8403-1838-3). Kendall-Hunt.

Bellone, Carl J. Organization Theory & the New Public Administration. 336p. 1980. text ed. 18.85 (ISBN 0-205-06997-5, 766997-6). Allyn.

Bellos, David. Balzac Criticism in France, 1850-1900: The Making of a Reputation. 1976. 37.50x (ISBN 0-19-815530-1). Oxford U Pr.

Bellow, Saul. Henderson: The Rain King. 1976. pap. 2.50 (ISBN 0-380-00832-7, 54320). Avon.

--Seize the Day. 1977. pap. 1.75 (ISBN 0-380-01649-4, 33076). Avon.

--Victim. LC 47-12088. 9.95 (ISBN 0-8149-0050-X). Vanguard.

--The Victim. 1975. pap. 1.95 (ISBN 0-380-00334-1, 36780). Avon.

Bellow, Saul, et al. Frontiers of Knowledge: The Frank Nelson Doubleday Lectures at the National Museum of History & Technology at the Smithsonian Institution, Washington, D. C. 416p. 1975. Limited Edition. 20.00 (ISBN 0-385-04826-2). Doubleday.

Bellow, Saul, et al, trs. see Singer, Isaac B.

Bellows, John G., ed. Glaucoma: Contemporary International Concepts. LC 79-88728. (Illus.). 448p. 1980. 54.50 (ISBN 0-89352-058-6). Masson Pub.

Bellows, Thomas J. The People's Action Party of Singapore: Emergence of a Dominant Party System. (Mongraph: No. 14). (Illus.). xii, 195p. 1970. 5.75 o.p. (ISBN 0-686-63728-3). Yale U Pr.

Bellows, Thomas J., jt. auth. see Winter, Herbert R.

Bellringer, A. W. & Jones, C. B., eds. The Romantic Age in Prose. (Costerus Ser.: Vol. XXXIX). 159p. 1981. pap. text ed. 28.50x (Pub. by Radopi, Holland). Humanities.

Bellrose, Frank C., rev. by see Kortright, E. H.

Bellugi, U. & Studdert-Kennedy, M., eds. Signed & Spoken Language: Biological Constraints on Linguistic Form. (Dahlem Workshop Reports, Life Science Research Report Ser.: No. 19). (Illus.). 379p. (Orig.). 1980. pap. 35.70 (ISBN 0-89573-034-0). Verlag Chemie.

Bellush, Bernard. The Failure of the NRA. (Norton Essays in American History Ser). 197p. 1976. 8.95x (ISBN 0-393-05548-5); pap. 4.95x (ISBN 0-393-09223-2). Norton.

Bell-Villada, Gene H. Borges & His Fiction: A Guide to His Mind & Art. LC 80-17426. 352p. 1981. 19.00x (ISBN 0-8078-1458-X); pap. 10.00x (ISBN 0-8078-4075-0). U of NC Pr.

Bellwood, Peter. Man's Conquest of the Pacific: The Prehistory of Southeast Asia & Oceania. 1979. 35.00x (ISBN 0-19-520103-5). Oxford U Pr.

Belman, A. Barry & Kaplan, George W. Urologic Problems in Pediatrics. (Major Problems in Clinical Pediatrics Ser.: Vol. 22). (Illus.). 200p. 1981. text ed. price not set (ISBN 0-7216-1678-X). Saunders.

Belmar, Terri. Brezhia. 128p. 1981. 7.00 (ISBN 0-682-49721-5). Exposition.

Belmonte, Thomas. The Broken Fountain. LC 78-32167. 1979. 12.50 (ISBN 0-231-04542-5). Columbia U Pr.

Belo, Fernando. A Materialist Reading of the Gospel of Mark. O'Connell, Matthew, tr. LC 80-24756. 384p. (Orig.). 1981. pap. 12.95 (ISBN 0-88344-323-6). Orbis Bks.

Beloff, John, ed. New Directions in Parapsychology: With a Postscript by Arthur Koestler. LC 75-15489. 1975. 10.00 (ISBN 0-8108-0866-8). Scarecrow.

Beloff, Max. Age of Absolutism, Sixteen Sixty to Eighteen Fifteen. 1971. Repr. of 1954 ed. text ed. 11.50x (ISBN 0-09-020271-6, Hutchinson U Lib). Humanities.

--The Foreign Policy of Soviet Russia: 1929-1941, 2 vols. Incl. Vol. 1. 1929-1936. 1947. (ISBN 0-19-214505-3); Vol. 2. 1936-1941. 1949 (ISBN 0-19-214506-1). (Royal Institute of International Affairs Ser.). 14.95x ea. o.p. Oxford U Pr.

Beloff, Max & Peele, Gillian. The Government of the United Kingdom: Political Authority in a Changing Society. (Comparitive Modern Goverment Ser.). (Orig.). 1980. 17.95x (ISBN 0-393-01344-8); pap. text ed. 6.95x (ISBN 0-393-95135-9). Norton.

Belokhovstikova, V. I., jt. auth. see Kornilovich, Yu. E.

Belote, James H. & Belote, William M. Corregidor. LC 80-80981. (World War Two Ser.). (Illus.). 272p. 1980. pap. 2.25 (ISBN 0-87216-696-1). Playboy Pbks.

Belote, William M., jt. auth. see Belote, James H.

Belousov, V. V. Geotectonics. (Illus.). 330p. 1981. 29.80 (ISBN 0-387-09173-4). Springer-Verlag.

Belov, jt. ed. see Williams.

Belov, N. V., jt. auth. see Shubnikov, A. V.

Belozerskaya-Bulgakova, L. E. My Life with Mikhail Bulgakov. Thompson, M., tr. from Rus. 105p. 1981. 13.50 (ISBN 0-88233-433-6). Ardis Pubs.

Belpre, Pura. Perez & Martina. rev. ed. (Illus.). (gr. 2-5). 1961. 7.95 (ISBN 0-7232-6017-6). Warne.

Bels, Albert. The Inspector. Cedrins, Inara, tr. from Latvian. 125p. Date not set. 13.50 (ISBN 0-931556-08-2); pap. 4.50 (ISBN 0-931556-09-0). Translation Pr. Postponed.

Belsey, Catherine. Critical Practice. 176p. 1980. 17.00 (ISBN 0-416-72940-1, 2022); pap. 7.95 (ISBN 0-416-72950-9, 2021). Methuen Inc.

Belshaw, Cyril S. The Sorcerer's Apprentice: An Anthropology of Public Policy. 360p. 1976. text ed. 26.00 (ISBN 0-08-018313-1); pap. text ed. 16.75 (ISBN 0-08-018312-3). Pergamon.

--Under the Ivi Tree: Society & Economic Growth in Rural Fiji. 1964. 18.50x (ISBN 0-520-00106-0). U of Cal Pr.

Belshaw, Michael H. Village Economy: Land & People of Huecorio. LC 66-28489. (Illus.). 1967. 22.50x (ISBN 0-231-02928-4). Columbia U Pr.

Belsley, David A., et al. Regression Diagnostics: Identifying Influential Data & Sources of Collinearity. LC 79-19876. (Ser. in Probability & Mathematical Statistics: Applied Probability & Statistics). 1980. 21.95 (ISBN 0-471-05856-4, Pub. by Wiley-Interscience). Wiley.

Belson, W. A. & Thompson, B. A. Bibliography on Methods of Social & Business Research. LC 72-11488. 300p. 1973. 24.95 (ISBN 0-470-06420-X). Halsted Pr.

Belson, William A. Public & the Police. 1975. 4.80 o.p. (ISBN 0-06-318025-1, IntlDept). Har-Row.

--Television Violence & the Adolescent Boy. (Illus.). 1978. 21.00 (ISBN 0-566-00211-6, 02081-8, Pub. by Saxon Hse England). Lexington Bks.

Belsterling, C. A. Fluidic Systems Design. LC 80-12189. 248p. 1981. Repr. of 1971 ed. lib. bdg. write for info. (ISBN 0-89874-169-6). Krieger.

Belt, Forest H. Pictorial Guide to CB Radio Installation & Repair. LC 73-85407. 1973. 8.95 o.p. (ISBN 0-8306-3683-8); pap. 5.95 (ISBN 0-8306-2683-2, 683). TAB Bks.

Belt, Guy Chester. Love's Answer from Eternity. 1973. 4.00 o.p. (ISBN 0-682-47696-X). Exposition.

Belt, T. Edwin. Wines from Jams & Preserved Fruits. 1973. pap. 2.50 (ISBN 0-263-51655-5). Transatlantic.

Belting, Natalia. Our Fathers Had Powerful Songs. LC 73-13968. (Illus.). 32p. (gr. 2-6). 1974. PLB 7.95 o.p. (ISBN 0-525-36485-4). Dutton.

Belton, John & Cramblit, Joella. Card Games. LC 75-42319. (Games & Activities Ser.). (Illus.). 48p. (gr. 3 up). 1976. PLB 9.30 (ISBN 0-8172-0021-5). Raintree Pubs.

--Dice Games. LC 75-43625. (Games & Activities Ser.). (Illus.). 48p. (gr. k-3). 1976. 9.30 (ISBN 0-8172-0024-X); PLB 6.60 (ISBN 0-8172-0023-1). Raintree Pubs.

--Domino Games. LC 76-8864. (Games & Activities Ser.). (Illus.). 48p. (gr. 4-9). 1976. PLB 8.95 (ISBN 0-8172-0625-6). Raintree Pubs.

--Let's Play Cards. LC 75-9606. (Games & Activities Ser.). (Illus.). 48p. (gr. k-3). 1975. PLB 9.30 (ISBN 0-8172-0025-8). Raintree Pubs.

--Solitaire Games. LC 75-25956. (Games & Activities Ser.). (Illus.). 48p. (gr. 3 up). 1975. PLB 9.30 (ISBN 0-8172-0027-4). Raintree Pubs.

Beltroy, Manuel, tr. see Hume, Roberto E.

Beltsville Symposia in Agricultural Research. Biosystematics in Agriculture. Romberger, John A., ed. LC 77-84408. 1978. 29.95x (ISBN 0-470-26416-0). Halsted Pr.

Belves, Pierre & Mathey, Francois. Enjoying the World of Art. (Illus.). (gr. 6 up). 1966. PLB 12.00 (ISBN 0-87460-100-2). Lion.

--How Artists Work. Bach, Alice, tr. (gr. 6 up). 1968. PLB 12.00 (ISBN 0-87460-101-0). Lion.

Belvianes, Marcel. The Madonna in the Paintings of the Great Masters. (Illus.). 1980. Repr. 37.50 (ISBN 0-89901-010-5). Found Class Reprints.

Belvins, James L., tr. see Herrmann, Siegfried.

Bely, V. A., et al. Friction & Wear in Polymer-Based Materials. LC 80-41825. (Illus.). 400p. 1981. 85.00 (ISBN 0-08-025444-6). Pergamon.

Belyayev, N. M. Problems in the Strength of Materials. 1966. text ed. 34.00 (ISBN 0-08-010306-5); pap. 21.00 (ISBN 0-08-013664-8). Pergamon.

Belyi, Andrei. Serebriannyi Golub' (Rus.). 1980. pap. 6.50 (ISBN 0-88233-398-4). Ardis Pubs.

Belz, Herman. Emancipation & Equal Rights: Politics & Constitutionalism in the Civil War Era. 1978. 10.95 (ISBN 0-393-05692-9); pap. 4.95x (ISBN 0-393-09016-7). Norton.

Belzung, L. D., jt. auth. see Becht, J. Edwin.

Bemelmans, Ludwig. Madeline. LC 39-21791. (gr. k-3). 1977. pap. 2.75 (ISBN 0-14-050198-3, Puffin). Penguin.

Bement, Peter. George Chapman: Action & Contemplation in His Novels. (Salzburg Studies in English Literature, Jacobean Drama Studies: No. 8). 292p. 1974. pap. text ed. 25.00x (ISBN 0-391-01323-8). Humanities.

Bemis, E. W; see Haynes, J.

Bemis, Pat. Astrology: An Illustrated Manual for Teachers & Students. 1978. pap. 6.00 (ISBN 0-686-68269-6). Macoy Pub.

--Pluto. 1978. pap. 3.50 (ISBN 0-686-68270-X). Macoy Pub.

Bemis, Samuel F. Diplomacy of the American Revolution. LC 57-7878. (Midland Bks.: No. 6). 1957. pap. 2.95x o.p. (ISBN 0-253-20006-7). Ind U Pr.

--John Quincy Adams & the Foundations of American Foreign Policy. LC 80-23039. (Illus.). xix, 588p. 1981. Repr. of 1949 ed. lib. bdg. 49.75x (ISBN 0-313-22636-9, BEAD). Greenwood.

--Latin American Policy of the U. S. (Illus.). 1967. pap. 3.45 o.p. (ISBN 0-393-00412-0, Norton Lib). Norton.

Bemis, Samuel Flagg. John Quincy Adams & the Union. LC 80-20402. (Illus.). xv, 546p. 1980. Repr. of 1965 ed. lib. bdg. 45.00x (ISBN 0-313-22637-7, BEJQ). Greenwood.

Benabo, Brian. Moonlight Kingdom. LC 75-29608. (Illus.). 92p. (YA) 1976. 6.95 o.p. (ISBN 0-312-54705-6). St Martin.

Benacerraf, Baruj & Unanue, Emil. Textbook of Immunology. 2nd ed. 300p. 1981. write for info. softcover (0528-6). Williams & Wilkins.

Benack, Raymond T. What Is Allergy? A Guide for the Allergic Person. (Illus.). 172p. 1967. 17.50 (ISBN 0-398-00128-6). C C Thomas.

Benade, Arthur H. Horns, Strings & Harmony. LC 60-10663. pap. 2.50 (ISBN 0-385-09471-X, S11). Doubleday.

Benagh, Jim. Making It to Number One. LC 75-42497. 1976. 10.00 (ISBN 0-396-07210-0). Dodd.

Ben-Ami, Shlomo. The Origins of the Second Republic in Spain. (Historical Monographs). 1978. 36.00x (ISBN 0-19-821871-0). Oxford U Pr.

Ben-Amos, D. & Goldstein, K., eds. Folklore: Performance & Communication. LC 74-80122. (Approaches to Semiotics Ser.: No. 40). (Illus.). 308p. 1975. pap. text ed. 70.50x (ISBN 90-2793-143-7). Mouton.

Ben-Amos, Dan & Mintz, Jerome R., eds. In Praise of the Baal Shem Tov (Shivhei ha-Besht) The Earliest Collection of Legends About the Founder of Hasidism. Ben-Amos, Dan & Mintz, Jerome R., trs. LC 76-98986. (Illus.). 384p. 1970. 15.00x (ISBN 0-253-14050-1); pap. 5.95x (ISBN 0-253-14051-X). Ind U Pr.

Ben-Amos, Dan, tr. see Ben-Amos, Dan & Mintz, Jerome R.

Ben-Amos, Paula. The Art of Benin. (Tribal Art Ser.). (Illus.). 96p. 1980. pap. 9.95 (ISBN 0-500-06009-6). Thames Hudson.

Benamou, Michel & Carduner, Jean. Le Moulin a paroles. 2nd ed. LC 71-126958. (Illus., Fr.). 1971. pap. text ed. 10.95 (ISBN 0-471-06450-5); tapes avail. (ISBN 0-471-00024-8). Wiley.

Benaquist, Lawrence M. Tripartite Structure of Christopher Marlowe's Tamburlaine Plays & Edward II. (Salzburg Studies in English Literature; Elizabethan & Renaissance Studies: No. 43). 223p. (Orig.). 1975. pap. text ed. 25.00x (ISBN 0-391-01324-6). Humanities.

Benarde, Anita. Games from Many Lands. LC 71-86975. (Illus.). 64p. (gr. 3-7). 1971. PLB 7.95 (ISBN 0-87460-147-9). Lion.

--The Pumpkin Smasher. LC 76-189792. (Illus.). 32p. (gr. k-3). 1972. 4.95 o.s.i. (ISBN 0-8027-6109-7); PLB 4.85 o.s.i. (ISBN 0-8027-6110-0). Walker & Co.

Benardete, Jane & Moe, Phyllis, eds. Companions of Our Youth: Stories by Women for Young People's Magazines, 1865-1900. LC 80-5339. (Illus.). 1980. 12.95 (ISBN 0-8044-2043-2); pap. 5.95 (ISBN 0-8044-6047-7). Ungar.

Benarie, Michael M. Urban Air Pollution Modeling. (Illus.). 1980. text ed. 45.00x (ISBN 0-262-02140-4). MIT Pr.

Benario, Herbert W. A Commentary on the Vita Hadriana in the Historia Augusta. LC 80-11953. (American Classical Studies: No. 7). 1980. 13.50x (ISBN 0-89130-391-X, 400407); pap. 9.00x. Scholars Pr CA.

--An Introduction to Tacitus. LC 73-85025. 184p. 1975. text ed. 7.50x o.p. (ISBN 0-8203-0328-3); pap. text ed. 5.00x (ISBN 0-8203-0361-5). U of Ga Pr.

Benary-Isbert, Margot. Long Way Home. LC 59-7519. (gr. 7-9). 1959. 5.95 o.p. (ISBN 0-15-248830-8, HJ). HarBraceJ.

--Under a Changing Moon. LC 64-17084. (gr. 10 up). 1964. 5.95 o.p. (ISBN 0-15-292800-6, HJ). HarBraceJ.

Ben-Asher, Naomi & Leaf, Hayim, eds. Junior Jewish Encyclopedia. 9rev. ed. LC 79-66184. (Illus.). (gr. 9-12). 1979. 14.95 (ISBN 0-88400-066-4). Shengold.

Benassi, Victor, jt. auth. see Houston, John P.

Benasutti, Marion. No Steady Job for Papa. 1966. 7.95 o.s.i. (ISBN 0-8149-0051-8). Vanguard.

Benavides, Rodolfo. Then We Shall Be Gods. (The Living Path Ser: No. 3). 1975. pap. 6.50 (ISBN 0-914732-03-X). Bro Life Bks.

Benbow, Audrey M. How to Raise & Train a Scottish Deerhound. (Orig.). pap. 1.79 o.p. (ISBN 0-87666-382-X, DS1115). TFH Pubns.

Benbow, R. Mark, ed. see Wager, W.

Bence, Richard. Handbook of Clinical Endodontics. 2nd ed. LC 80-15722. (Illus.). 262p. 1980. pap. text ed. 16.95 (ISBN 0-8016-0587-3). Mosby.

Ben-Chieh Liu, et al. Earthquake Risk & Damage Functions: Applications to New Madrid. (Special Studies in Earth Sciences). 300p. 1981. lib. bdg. 24.50x (ISBN 0-86531-144-7). Westview.

Benchley, Nathaniel. All Over Again. LC 80-1800. (Illus.). 240p. 1981. 11.95 (ISBN 0-385-15859-9). Doubleday.

--Red Fox & His Canoe. (gr. k-3). 1969. pap. 0.95 o.p. (ISBN 0-590-08089-X, Schol Pap); pap. 2.95 bk. & record o.p. (ISBN 0-590-20794-6). Schol Bk Serv.

--Snip. LC 80-696. (Illus.). 64p. (gr. 4). 1981. 8.95a (ISBN 0-385-15997-8); PLB (ISBN 0-385-15998-6). Doubleday.

--Sweet Anarchy. (Large Print Bks.). 1980. lib. bdg. 15.50 (ISBN 0-8161-3134-1). G K Hall.

--Sweet Anarchy. 304p. 1981. pap. 2.50 (ISBN 0-380-53777-X, 53777). Avon.

--Walter, the Homing Pigeon. LC 79-2696. (Illus.). 32p. (gr. 1-4). 1981. 7.95 (ISBN 0-06-020507-5, HarpJ); PLB 7.89g (ISBN 0-06-020508-3). Har-Row.

Benchley, Robert. Benchley Lost & Found: Thirty-Nine. (Illus.). 6.75 o.p. (ISBN 0-8446-0484-4). Peter Smith.

Benczer-Koller, Noemie & Koller, Earl L. Power & Energy. LC 59-13619. (Illus.). (gr. 4-6). 1960. PLB 6.95 (ISBN 0-87396-009-2). Stravon.

Bendall, Cecil. A Journey in Nepal & Northern India. (Illus.). 1975. 5.95x (ISBN 0-685-89508-4). Himalaya Hse.

Bendall, J. R. Muscles, Molecules & Movement. 1969. text ed. 6.50x o.p. (ISBN 0-435-62054-1). Heinemann Ed.

Bendann, Effie. Death Customs: An Analytical Study of Burial Rites. 1971. 20.00 (ISBN 0-8103-3733-9). Gale.

Bendat, Julius S. & Piersol, Allan G. Engineering Applications of Correction & Spectral Analysis. LC 79-25926. 1980. 29.95 (ISBN 0-471-05887-4, Pub. by Wiley-Interscience). Wiley.

--Random Data: Analysis & Measurement Procedures. LC 71-160211. (Illus.). 1971. 36.95 (ISBN 0-471-06470-X, Pub. by Wiley-Interscience). Wiley.

Bendavid, Avrom. Regional Economic Analysis for Practitioners: An Introduction to Common Descriptive Methods. rev. ed. LC 73-22260. (Special Studies). (Illus.). 1974. text ed. 17.95 o.p. (ISBN 0-275-08450-7); pap. text ed. 11.95 (ISBN 0-275-88820-7). Praeger.

Ben-David, Joseph, jt. auth. see Carnegie Commission on Higher Education.

Bendavid-Val, Leah, et al. Discover Wildlife in Your Backyard. Stone, John C., ed. (Illus.). 1977. 24.95 (ISBN 0-912186-25-9). Natl Wildlife.

Bender, jt. auth. see McCabe.

Bender, Averam B. Apache Indians IX. Horr, David A., ed. (American Indian Ethnohistory Ser.). 1978. lib. bdg. 42.00 (ISBN 0-8240-0711-5). Garland Pub.

Bender, Averam B., et al. Apache Indians V. Horr, David A., ed. (American Indian Ethnohistory Ser.). 1978. lib. bdg. 42.00 (ISBN 0-8240-0720-4). Garland Pub.

Bender, David, jt. auth. see Glock, Marvin D.

Bender, David L. America's Prisons: Opposing Viewpoints. (Opposing Viewpoints Ser.). 140p. (gr. 12). 1980. lib. bdg. 8.95 (ISBN 0-89908-330-7); pap. text ed. 3.95 (ISBN 0-89908-305-6). Greenhaven.

--Constructing a Life Philosophy: Opposing Viewpoints. (Opposing Viewpoints Ser.). 144p. (gr. 12). 1980. lib. bdg. 8.95 (ISBN 0-89908-329-3); pap. text ed. 3.95 (ISBN 0-89908-304-8). Greenhaven.

--The Political Spectrum: Opposing Viewpoints. (Opposing Viewpoints Ser.). (gr. 12). 1981. lib. bdg. 8.95 (ISBN 0-89908-325-0); pap. text ed. 3.95 (ISBN 0-89908-300-5). Greenhaven.

Bender, David L., ed. American Values. (Opposing Viewpoints Ser.: Vol. 10). (Illus.). 1975. lib. bdg. 10.95 (ISBN 0-912616-35-0); pap. text ed. 4.95 (ISBN 0-912616-16-4). Greenhaven.

--Constructing a Life Philosophy: An Examination of Alternatives. rev.,3rd ed. (Opposing Viewpoints Ser.: Vol. 4). (Illus.). (gr. 9 up). 1976. lib. bdg. 10.60 o.p. (ISBN 0-912616-28-8); pap. text ed. 4.60 o.p. (ISBN 0-912616-18-0). Greenhaven.

--Criminal Justice: Opposing Viewpoints. (Opposing Viewpoints Ser.). (gr. 12). 1981. lib. bdg. 8.95 (ISBN 0-89908-332-3); pap. text ed. 3.95 (ISBN 0-89908-307-2). Greenhaven.

--Death & Dying: Opposing Viewpoints. (Opposing Viewpoints Ser.). (gr. 12). 1980. lib. bdg. 8.95 (ISBN 0-89908-331-5); pap. text ed. 3.95 (ISBN 0-89908-306-4). Greenhaven.

--Liberals & Conservatives: A Debate on the Welfare State. rev. ed. (Opposing Viewpoints Ser.: Vol. 2). (Illus.). (gr. 9 up). 1973. lib. bdg. 8.95 (ISBN 0-912616-26-1); pap. 3.95 (ISBN 0-912616-08-3). Greenhaven.

--Problems of Death: Opposing Viewpoints. (Opposing Viewpoints Ser.: Vol. 8). (Illus.). 1974. lib. bdg. 8.95 (ISBN 0-912616-32-6); pap. text ed. 3.95 (ISBN 0-912616-13-X). Greenhaven.

Bender, David L. & McCuen, Gary E., eds. American Foreign Policy: Opposing Viewpoints. (Opposing Viewpoints Ser.: Vol. 6). (Illus.). 88p. (gr. 9-12). 1972. lib. bdg. 8.95 (ISBN 0-912616-30-X); pap. 3.95 (ISBN 0-912616-05-9). Greenhaven.

--Crime & Criminals: Opposing Viewpoints. (Opposing Viewpoints Ser: Vol. 13). (Illus.). 1977. lib. bdg. 8.95 (ISBN 0-912616-39-3); pap. text ed. 3.95 (ISBN 0-912616-20-2). Greenhaven.

--Economics in America: Opposing Viewpoints. (Opposing Viewpoints Ser.: Vol. 13). (Illus.). (gr. 9-12). 1976. lib. bdg. 10.95 (ISBN 0-912616-38-5); pap. text ed. 4.95 (ISBN 0-912616-19-9). Greenhaven.

--The Indochina War: Why Our Policy Failed. (Opposing Viewpoints Ser.: Vol. 11). (Illus.). 1975. lib. bdg. 8.95 (ISBN 0-912616-36-9); pap. text ed. 3.95 (ISBN 0-912616-17-2). Greenhaven.

--The Sexual Revolution: Traditional Mores Versus New Values. (Opposing Viewpoints Ser.: Vol. 7). (Illus.). (gr. 9 up). 1972. lib. bdg. 8.95 (ISBN 0-912616-31-8); pap. 3.95 (ISBN 0-912616-12-1). Greenhaven.

Bender, David L., ed. see Church, Carol B.

Bender, David L., ed. see Leone, Bruno.

Bender, David L., jt. ed. see McCuen, Gary.

Bender, David L., jt. ed. see McCuen, Gary E.

Bender, David R., jt. auth. see Baker, D. Phillip.

Bender, Edward A. An Introduction to Mathematical Modeling. LC 77-23840. 1978. 22.95 (ISBN 0-471-02951-3, Pub by Wiley-Interscience); solutions manual 4.50 (ISBN 0-471-03407-X). Wiley.

Bender, Ernest & Riccardi, Theodore, Jr. Introductory Hindi Readings. LC 75-133202. 1971. text ed. 12.00x (ISBN 0-8122-7626-4). U of Pa Pr.

Bender, Filmore, et al. Systems Analysis for the Food Industry. (Illus.). 1976. pap. text ed. 24.50 (ISBN 0-87055-306-2). AVI.

Bender, Gerald J. Angola Under the Portuguese: The Myth & the Reality. (Illus.). 315p. 1981. pap. 6.95x (ISBN 0-520-04274-3, CAMPUS 269). U of Cal Pr.

--Angola Under the Portuguese: The Myth & the Reality. (Perspectives on Southern Africa Ser.: No. 23). 1978. 19.50x (ISBN 0-520-03221-7); pap. 7.95x (ISBN 0-520-04274-3). U of Cal Pr.

Bender, Harold S. & Erb, Paul. Later History & Poetry. rev. ed. (Bible Survey Course No. 2). 1956. pap. 1.00 o.p. (ISBN 0-8361-1317-9). Herald Pr.

Bender, I. B., jt. auth. see Seltzer, Samuel.

Bender, James F. N. B. C. Handbook of Pronunciation. 3rd, rev. ed. Crowell, Thomas, Jr., ed. 1964. 11.95 (ISBN 0-690-57472-X, TYC-T). T Y Crowell.

Bender, Jan. Organ Improvisation for Beginners. LC 75-2934. (Illus.). 71p. 1975. bds. 7.50 (ISBN 0-570-01312-7, 99-1229). Concordia.

Bender, Leonard F. Prostheses & Rehabilitation After Arm Amputation. (Illus.). 196p. 1974. text ed. 19.75 (ISBN 0-398-03094-4). C C Thomas.

Bender, Louis W. The States, Communities, & Control of the Community Colleges. 60p. 1975. pap. 1.50 (ISBN 0-87117-083-3). Am Assn Comm Jr Coll.

Bender, Lynn D. Perspectivas Politicas, Vol. 1. 2nd, rev. ed. (Illus.). 116p. pap. text ed. 4.55 (ISBN 0-913480-50-9). Inter Am U Pr.

Bender, Mark. EFTS: Electronic Funds Transfer Systems - Elements & Impact. 112p. 1975. 12.95 (ISBN 0-8046-9119-3, Natl U). Kennikat.

Bender, Michael & Bender, Rosmary K. Disadvantaged Preschool Children: A Source Book for Teachers. LC 79-12001. (Illus.). 308p. (Orig.). 1979. pap. text ed. 14.95 (ISBN 0-933716-00-1). P H Brookes.

Bender, Michael & Valletuhi, Peter J. Teaching the Moderately & Severely Handicapped: Curriculum, Objectives, Strategies & Activites, 3 vols. (Illus.). 1000p. 1976. Set. ed. 3 vol. set 39.50 (ISBN 0-685-64022-1); vol. 1 & 2 28.50 (ISBN 0-685-64023-X); Vol. 1. 14.95 (ISBN 0-8391-0869-9); Vol. 2. 19.95 (ISBN 0-8391-0868-0); Vol. 3. 13.95 (ISBN 0-8391-0963-6). Univ Park.

Bender, P. L., ed. see I.A.U Symposium No. 78, Kiev, USSR, May 23-28, 1977, et al.

Bender, Roger J. & Odegard, Warren W. Uniforms, Organization & History of the Panzertruppe. (Illus.). 336p. 1980. 24.95 (ISBN 0-912138-18-1). Bender Pub CA.

Bender, Rosmary K., jt. auth. see Bender, Michael.

Bender, Stephen J., jt. auth. see Sorochan, Walter D.

Bender, Thomas. Community & Social Change in America. (Sanford-Erpf Lecture Ser.). 1978. 10.50 (ISBN 0-8135-0858-4). Rutgers U Pr.

--Toward an Urban Vision: Ideas & Institutions in 19th-Century America. LC 74-18930. (Illus.). 296p. 1975. 17.00x (ISBN 0-8131-1326-1). U Pr of Ky.

Bender, Todd K. Concordances to Conrad's Victory. LC 79-8416. 150p. 1980. lib. bdg. 35.00 (ISBN 0-8240-9520-0). Garland Pub.

Bender, Todd K. & Parins, James W. A Concordance to Conrad's Nigger of the Narcissus. LC 79-8417. 150p. 1981. lib. bdg. 35.00 (ISBN 0-8240-9519-7). Garland Pub.

Benderly, Beryl L. Dancing Without Music: Deafness in America. LC 79-6092. 312p. 1980. 11.95 (ISBN 0-385-14703-1, Anchor Pr). Doubleday.

Bendick. The Big Strawberry Book of the Earth: Our Ever-Changing Planet. 110p. Date not set. 6.95 (ISBN 0-07-004514-3). McGraw.

Bendick, J. Ecology. LC 75-8904. (Science Experiences Ser). (gr. 3-5). 1975. 4.90 o.p. (ISBN 0-531-01442-8). Watts.

Bendick, James. Automobiles. rev. ed. LC 78-6252. (First Bks.). (Illus.). (gr. 4-6). 1978. PLB 6.45 s&l (ISBN 0-531-02227-7). Watts.

Bendick, Jeanne. The First Book of Airplanes. rev. ed. LC 75-31880. (First Bks. Ser). (Illus.). 72p. (gr. 4). 1976. PLB 6.45 (ISBN 0-531-00455-4). Watts.

--First Book of Automobiles. 2nd rev. ed. LC 66-10586. (First Bks). (Illus.). (gr. 4-6). 1971. PLB 6.45 (ISBN 0-531-00475-9). Watts.

--First Book of Space Travel. rev. ed. (First Bks). (Illus.). (gr. 4-6). 1969. PLB 4.90 o.p. (ISBN 0-531-00639-5). Watts.

--Heat & Temperature. LC 73-19885. (Science Experiences Ser.). (Illus.). 72p. (gr. 3-6). 1974. PLB 4.90 o.p. (ISBN 0-531-01438-X). Watts.

--How to Make a Cloud. LC 74-134834. (Finding-Out Book). (Illus.). 64p. (gr. 2-3). PLB 6.95 (ISBN 0-8193-0441-7). Enslow Pubs.

--Human Senses. (Science Experiences Ser). (Illus.). (gr. 4-6). PLB 4.90 o.p. (ISBN 0-531-01431-2); pap. 1.25 o.p. (ISBN 0-531-01884-9). Watts.

--Living Things. LC 69-12869. (Science Experiences Ser). (Illus.). (gr. 4-6). 1969. PLB 4.90 o.p. (ISBN 0-531-01432-0); pap. 1.25 o.p. (ISBN 0-531-02324-9). Watts.

--Measuring. LC 76-150734. (Science Experiences Ser). (Illus.). (gr. 3-5). 1971. PLB 4.90 o.p. (ISBN 0-531-01435-5). Watts.

--Motion & Gravity. LC 72-4085. (Science Experiences Ser.). (Illus.). 72p. (gr. 3-5). 1972. PLB 4.90 o.p. (ISBN 0-531-01439-8). Watts.

--The Mystery of Super People: Will They Replace Us? LC 79-14486. (Illus.). (gr. 7 up). 1980. 7.95 (ISBN 0-07-004503-8). McGraw.

--Names, Sets & Numbers. LC 73-137151. (Science Experiences Ser.). (Illus.). (gr. 4-6). 1971. PLB 5.90 (ISBN 0-531-01436-3); pap. 1.25 o.p. (ISBN 0-531-02321-4). Watts.

--Observation. LC 72-6053. (Science Experiences Ser). (Illus.). 72p. (gr. 3-5). 1972. PLB 4.90 o.p. (ISBN 0-531-01440-1). Watts.

--A Place to Live: A Study of Ecology. LC 74-99133. (Finding-Out Book). (Illus.). 64p. (gr. 1-4). 1970. PLB 6.95 (ISBN 0-686-64141-8). Enslow Pubs.

--Shapes. LC 68-11889. (Science Experiences Ser.). (Illus.). (gr. 4-6). 1968. PLB 4.90 o.p. (ISBN 0-531-01433-9); pap. 1.25 o.p. (ISBN 0-531-02322-2). Watts.

--Solids, Liquids & Gases. LC 73-13976. (Illus.). 72p. (gr. 4-6). 1974. PLB 4.90 o.p. (ISBN 0-531-01441-X). Watts.

Bendick, Jeanne & Levin, Marcia. Take Shapes, Lines & Letters: New Horizons in Math. (Illus.). (gr. 4-6). 1962. PLB 6.95 o.p. (ISBN 0-07-004487-2, GB). McGraw.

Bendick, Marc, Jr. & Bawden, D. Lee. Income Conditioned Programs & Their Clients: A Research Agenda. (An Institute Paper). 96p. 1977. pap. 4.00 o.p. (ISBN 0-685-99486-4, 19600). Urban Inst.

Bendick, Marc, Jr., jt. auth. see Campbell, Toby H.

Bendick, Marc, Jr., et al. The Anatomy of AFDC Errors. (An Institute Paper). 158p. 1978. pap. 4.00 (ISBN 0-87766-217-7, 20500). Urban Inst.

Bendick, Mark, Jr., jt. ed. see Stryk, Raymond J.

Bendiner, Elmer. A Time for Angels: The Tragicomic History of the League of Nations. 1975. 12.95 o.p. (ISBN 0-394-48183-6). Knopf.

--The Virgin Diplomats. 1976. 10.00 o.p. (ISBN 0-394-48977-2). Knopf.

Bendiner, Robert. The Fall of the Wild, the Rise of the Zoo. (Illus.). 256p. 1981. 13.95 (ISBN 0-525-10270-1). Dutton.

--Politics of Schools: A Crisis in Self-Government. LC 73-83585. 1969. 10.00 o.p. (ISBN 0-06-010301-9, HarpT). Har-Row.

Bending, C. W. Communication & the Schools. LC 71-103930. 1970. 22.00 (ISBN 0-08-015663-0); pap. 10.75 (ISBN 0-08-015662-2). Pergamon.

Bendix, Reinhard. Kings or People: Power & the Mandate to Rule. 1978. 25.00 (ISBN 0-520-02302-1); pap. 9.95 (ISBN 0-520-04090-2). U of Cal Pr.

--Max Weber: An Intellectual Portrait. 1978. 25.00x (ISBN 0-520-03503-8, CAMPUS 187); pap. 6.95x (ISBN 0-520-03194-6). U of Cal Pr.

--Nation-Building & Citizenship: Studies of Our Changing Social Order. 400p. 1977. 25.75x (ISBN 0-520-02676-4); pap. 6.95x (ISBN 0-520-02761-2, CAMPUS 138). U of Cal Pr.

--Work & Authority in Industry: Ideologies of Management in the Course of Industrialization. 1974. pap. 6.95x (ISBN 0-520-02628-4). U of Cal Pr.

Bendix, Reinhard & Lipset, S. M., eds. Class, Status & Power: A Reader in Social Stratification. rev. ed. LC 65-23025. 1966. text ed. 17.95 (ISBN 0-02-902630-X). Free Pr.

Bendixen, H. H., et al. Respiratory Care. LC 65-27642. (Illus.). 1965. 22.50 o.p. (ISBN 0-8016-0605-5). Mosby.

Ben-Dor, Gabriel. The Druzes in Israel: A Political Study: Political Innovation & Integration in a Middle Eastern Minority. 287p. 1980. lib. bdg. 30.00x (ISBN 0-686-64555-3, Pub. by Magnes Pr). Westview.

Benecerraf, Paul, tr. see Mehlberg, Henry.

Benecke, G. F., et al, eds. see Hartmann Von Aue.

Benecke, G. F., et al, eds. see Hartmann von Ave.

Benecke, Gerhard, jt. auth. see Scribner, Bob.

Benedek, G., jt. ed. see Obal, F.

Benedek, George, jt. auth. see Miller, David.

Benedetti, Robert. The Actor at Work. 3rd ed. (Illus.). 1981. text ed. 14.95 (ISBN 0-13-003673-0). P-H.

Benedetti, Robert L. Actor at Work. rev. & enl ed. (Illus.). 272p. 1976. 14.95 (ISBN 0-13-003665-X). P-H.

Benedict, Burton, ed. Problems of Smaller Territories. 1967. text ed. 8.75x (ISBN 0-485-17610-6, Athlone Pr). Humanities.

Benedict, Manson, et al. Nuclear Chemical Engineering. 2nd ed. (Illus.). 1008p. 1981. text ed. 44.50 (ISBN 0-07-004531-3). McGraw.

Benedict, Michael L. The Impeachment & Trial of Andrew Johnson. (Norton Essays in American History Ser). 224p. 1973. 6.95x (ISBN 0-393-05473-X); pap. text ed. 3.95x (ISBN 0-393-09418-9). Norton.

Benedict, Paul K. Sino-Tibetan: A Conspectus. LC 78-154511. (Princeton-Cambridge Studies in Chinese Linguistics: No. 2). 1972. 75.00 (ISBN 0-521-08175-0). Cambridge U Pr.

Benedict, R. Ralph. Electronics for Scientists & Engineers. 2nd ed. (Illus.). 1975. 25.95x (ISBN 0-13-252353-1). P-H.

Benedict, Robert P. Fundamentals of Temperature, Pressure, & Flow Measurements. 2nd ed. LC 76-54341. 1977. 37.50 (ISBN 0-471-06561-7, Pub. by Wiley-Interscience). Wiley.

Benedict, Ruth. Tales of the Cochiti Indians. 256p. 1981. pap. price not set (ISBN 0-8263-0569-5). U of NM Pr.

Benedict, Saint Rule of Saint Benedict. Gasquet, Cardinal, tr. LC 66-30730. (Medieval Library). Repr. of 1926 ed. 15.00x (ISBN 0-8154-0022-5). Cooper Sq.

Benedict, Stephen, compiled by. Arts Management: An Annotated Bibliography. rev. ed. LC 80-25918. 48p. 1980. pap. 5.00 (ISBN 0-89062-046-6, Pub. by Ctr for Arts Info). Pub Ctr Cult Res.

Benedict, Stephen, ed. see Thurston, Ellen.

Benedict, Verne. Where Do Bastards Go to Die. 1981. 9.95 (ISBN 0-533-04879-6). Vantage.

Benedictine Sisters Of Peking Editors. Art of Chinese Cooking. LC 56-11125. (Illus., Orig.). 1956. pap. 5.95 (ISBN 0-8048-0035-9). C E Tuttle.

Benedictus, David. The Antique Collector's Guide. LC 80-69368. 1981. 14.95 (ISBN 0-689-11146-0). Atheneum.

--The Rabbi's Wife. 1977. pap. 1.75 o.p. (ISBN 0-449-23394-4, Crest). Fawcett.

Benedictus, Edouard. Benedictus' Art Deco Designs in Color. (Illus.). 1980. pap. 6.00 (ISBN 0-486-23971-3). Dover.

Benedikt, Michael. The Badminton at Great Barrington; or, Gustave Mahler & the Chattanooga Choo-Choo. LC 80-5258. (Pitt Poetry Ser.). xii, 81p. 1980. 9.95 (ISBN 0-8229-3423-X); pap. 4.50 (ISBN 0-8229-5322-6). U of Pittsburgh Pr.

--The Body. LC 68-27539. (Wesleyan Poetry Program: Vol. 40). 1968. pap. 10.00x (ISBN 0-8195-2040-3, Pub. by Wesleyan U Pr); pap. 4.95 (ISBN 0-8195-1040-8). Columbia U Pr.

--Mole Notes. LC 78-161695. (Illus.). 1971. 12.00x (ISBN 0-8195-4038-2, Pub. by Wesleyan U Pr). Columbia U Pr.

--Night Cries. LC 75-32526. (Wesleyan Poetry Program: Vol. 80). 1976. 10.00x (ISBN 0-8195-2080-2, Pub. by Wesleyan U Pr); pap. 4.95 (ISBN 0-8195-1080-7). Columbia U Pr.

--Sky. LC 75-120257. (Wesleyan Poetry Program: Vol. 52). 1970. 10.00x (ISBN 0-8195-2052-7, Pub. by Wesleyan U Pr); pap. 4.95x (ISBN 0-8195-1052-1). Columbia U Pr.

Benedikt, Moriz. Anatomical Studies Upon Brains of Criminals. Fowler, E. P., tr. from Ger. (Historical Foundations of Forensic Psychiatry & Psychology Ser.). (Illus.). 185p. 1980. Repr. of 1881 ed. lib. bdg. 22.50 (ISBN 0-306-76071-1). Da Capo.

Benedikz, S., tr. see Blondal, S.

Benefield, Larry D., jt. auth. see Randall, Clifford W.

Beneke, E. S. & Rogers, A. L. Medical Mycology Manual with Human Mycoses Monograph. 4th ed. 76p. 1980. pap. 19.95 (ISBN 0-8087-4042-3). Burgess.

Beneke, Raymond R. & Winterboer, Ronald D. Linear Programming Applications to Agriculture. LC 72-2298. (Illus.). 251p. 1973. text ed. 12.95 (ISBN 0-8138-1035-3). Iowa St U Pr.

Benenfeld, Alan R., ed. see ASIS Annual Meeting, 43rd, 1980.

Benenson, Walter, jt. ed. see Nolen, Jerry A.

Ben-Ephraim, Gavriel. The Moon's Dominion: Narrative Dichotomy & Female Dominance in the First Five Novels of D. H. Lawrence. LC 78-75172. 300p. 1981. 18.50 (ISBN 0-8386-2266-6). Fairleigh Dickinson.

Benes, Josef. Prehistoric Animals & Plants. (Illus.). 311p. 1979. 13.95 (ISBN 0-600-30341-1). Transatlantic.

Benes, Vaclav & Porends, Norman J. Poland. (Nations of the Modern World Ser.). 1976. 19.00x (ISBN 0-510-38911-2). Westview.

Benet. Economic Studies on Hungary's Agriculture. 1977. 14.00 (ISBN 0-9960000-4-6, Pub. by Kaido Hungary). Heyden.

Benet, Mary K. The Politics of Adoption. LC 76-14287. 1976. 12.95 (ISBN 0-02-902500-1). Free Pr.

--Writers in Love. LC 76-25560. 1977. 9.95 o.s.i. (ISBN 0-02-508900-5, 50890). Macmillan.

Benet, Stephen V. The Devil & Daniel Webster & Other Stories. (gr. 7-9). 1972. pap. 1.75 (ISBN 0-671-42889-6). Archway.

--Devil & Daniel Webster & Other Stories. (Illus.). (YA) (gr. 7-9). 1967. pap. 1.50 (ISBN 0-671-29943-3). PB.

Benet, William R. The Great White Wall. 1916. 24.50x o.p. (ISBN 0-686-51397-5). Elliots Bks.

Benet, William R., jt. ed. see Briggs, Wallace A.

Benevolo, Leonard. Architecture of the Renaissance. Landry, Judith, tr. LC 76-54186. 1978. Repr. lib. bdg. 75.00 o.p. (ISBN 0-89158-720-9). Westview.

Benevot, Maurice, ed. see Cyprian.

Benfey, Otto T. Names & Structures of Organic Compounds: A Programmed Text. LC 66-16550. 1966. pap. 10.95 (ISBN 0-471-06575-7). Wiley.

Benford, Gregory. The Jupiter Project. 1980. pap. 2.25 (ISBN 0-425-04569-2). Berkley Pub.

Benford, Gregory & Eklund, Gordon. Find the Changeling. 1980. pap. 2.50 (ISBN 0-440-12604-5). Dell.

--If the Stars Are Gods. 1978. pap. 1.75 o.p. (ISBN 0-425-03761-4, Medallion). Berkley Pub.

--If the Stars Are Gods. LC 76-28692. (YA) 1977. 7.95 o.p. (ISBN 0-686-57865-1). Berkley Pub.

Benford, Gregory & Rotsler, William. Shiva Descending. 400p. 1979. pap. 2.50 (ISBN 0-380-75168-2, 75168). Avon.

Benge, Eugene J. How to Lick Inflation Before It Licks You. LC 80-70954. 204p. 1981. 9.95 (ISBN 0-8119-0342-7). Fell.

Bengtson, Athene, ed. see Newhouse, Flower A.

Bengtson, Melodie N., ed. see Newhouse, Flower A.

Bengtson, Vern L. The Social Psychology of Aging. LC 73-4918. 1973. pap. 2.95 (ISBN 0-672-61339-5). Bobbs.

Ben-Gurion, David. Israel: Years of Challenge. 1963. 5.00 o.p. (ISBN 0-03-030985-9). HR&W.

--Rebirth & Destiny of Israel. (Return to Zion Ser.). 539p. 1980. Repr. of 1954 ed. lib. bdg. 35.00x (ISBN 0-87991-139-5). Porcupine Pr.

Benham, Amy & Ensminger, Doris. Science Fun Every Day in Every Way, a Total Environment Calendar. (Illus.). 1977. pap. 9.50 (ISBN 0-87355-017-X). Natl Sci Tchrs.

Benham, Hugh. Latin Church Music in England, Fourteen Sixty to Fifteen Seventy-Five. (Music Reprint Ser.: 1980). (Illus.). 1980. Repr. of 1977 ed. lib. bdg. 22.50 (ISBN 0-306-76025-8). Da Capo.

Benham, P. P. Elementary Mechanics of Solids. (Illus.). 1965. 19.50 (ISBN 0-08-011216-1); pap. text ed. 8.25 o.p. (ISBN 0-08-011215-3). Pergamon.

Benham, William G. Laws of Scientific Hand Reading. rev. ed. (Illus.). 1946. 16.95 (ISBN 0-8015-4446-7, Hawthorn). Dutton.

Ben-Horim, Moshe & Levy, Haim. Statistics: Decisions & Applications in Business & Economics. Incl. Mastering Business Statistics: A Student Guide to Problem Solving. Coccari, Ronald L. 320p. wkbk. 7.95 (ISBN 0-394-32484-6). 592p. 1981. text ed. 21.95 (ISBN 0-394-32297-5). Random.

Benice, Daniel D. Arithmetic & Algebra. 2nd ed. (Illus.). 1979. pap. text ed. 14.95 (ISBN 0-13-046094-X). P-H.

--Introduction to Computers & Data Processing. (Applied Mathematics Ser). 1970. ref. ed. 16.95 (ISBN 0-13-479543-1). P-H.

--Mathematics: Ideas & Applications. 1978. 14.95 (ISBN 0-12-088250-7); instrs'. ed. 3.00 (ISBN 0-12-088252-3). Acad Pr.

--Modern Business Data Processing. (Illus.). 416p. 1973. ref. ed. 18.95 (ISBN 0-13-589648-7). P-H.

--Precalculus Algebra & Trigonometry. (Illus.). 348p. 1976. text ed. 17.95 (ISBN 0-13-695072-8); study guide 3.95 (ISBN 0-13-695171-6). P-H.

Beniner, Winifred, jt. auth. see Schoenfeld, Susan.

Beningfield, Gordon. Beningfield's Countryside. LC 80-5366. 144p. 1980. 19.95 (ISBN 0-670-15815-1, Studio). Viking Pr.

Benington, John, jt. auth. see Newell, Pete.

Benis, Leslie M., jt. auth. see Beregi, Oscar.

Ben-Israel, Adi, et al. Optimality in Nonlinear Programming: A Feasible Directions Approach. LC 80-36746. (Wiley Pure & Applied Mathematics Ser.). 250p. 1981. 19.95 (ISBN 0-471-08057-8, Pub. by Wiley-Interscience). Wiley.

Benitez, Fernando. In the Magic Land of Peyote. 1976. pap. 1.95 o.s.i. (ISBN 0-446-89306-4). Warner Bks.

Benitez, Frank & Benitez, Sharon. Practical Spanish for the Health Professions. 1973. 9.95 o.p. (ISBN 0-914330-01-2). Pioneer Pub Co.

Benitez, Sharon, jt. auth. see Benitez, Frank.

Benitez, Zuleyka. Trouble in Paradise. Wright, C. D., intro. by. (Lost Roads Ser.: No. 19). (Illus.). 56p. (Orig.). 1980. pap. 9.00 (ISBN 0-918786-20-7). Lost Roads.

Benjamin, A. Cooking with Conscience. 1977. pap. 2.95 (ISBN 0-8164-0902-1). Crossroad NY.

Benjamin, A. S., tr. see Augustine, Saint.

Benjamin, Alan. One Thousand Inventions. LC 80-80659. (Illus.). 10p. (ps up). 1980. spiral bdg. 4.95 (ISBN 0-590-07749-X, Four Winds). Schol Bk Serv.

--One Thousand Monsters. LC 79-10682. (Illus.). 10p. (ps up). 1979. spiral 4.95 (ISBN 0-590-07636-1, Four Winds). Schol Bk Serv.

--One Thousand Space Monsters--"Have Landed". LC 79-55339. (Illus.). 10p. (ps up). 1980. spiral 3.95 (ISBN 0-590-07667-1, Four Winds). Schol Bk Serv.

Benjamin, Alexander & Helal, Basil. Surgical Repair & Reconstruction in Rheumatoid Disease. 256p. 1980. 45.00 (ISBN 0-471-08291-0, Pub. by Wiley Med). Wiley.

Benjamin, Alfred. Behavior in Small Groups. LC 77-73213. 1977. pap. text ed. 6.25 (ISBN 0-395-25447-7). HM.

Benjamin, Alfred D. The Helping Interview. 3rd ed. LC 80-81650. 208p. 1981. pap. text ed. 7.95 (ISBN 0-395-29648-X). HM.

Benjamin, Asher. The Works of Asher Benjamin: Boston, 1806-1843, 7 vols. Incl. The Country Builder's Assistant: 1797. 84p. (ISBN 0-306-71027-7); The American Builder's Companion: 1806. 158p. (ISBN 0-306-71026-9); The Rudiments of Architecture: 1814. 162p. (ISBN 0-306-71031-5); The Practical House Carpenter: 1830. 248p. (ISBN 0-306-71029-3); The Practice of Architecture: 1833. 236p. (ISBN 0-306-71030-7); The Builder's Guide: 1839. 174p. 40.00 (ISBN 0-306-70971-6); Elements of Architecture: 1843. 290p. 35.00 (ISBN 0-306-71028-5). (Architecture & Decorative Art Ser.). 1974. 37.50 ea.; Set. 225.00 (ISBN 0-306-71032-3). Da Capo.

Benjamin, Ben A. Let's Talk Hebrew. 1961. 4.00 (ISBN 0-914080-01-6). Shulsinger Sales.

Benjamin, Ben E. Are You Tense? The Benjamin System of Muscular Therapy. LC 77-88778. 1978. 15.95 (ISBN 0-394-49511-X); pap. 7.95 (ISBN 0-394-73499-8). Pantheon.

Benjamin, Bernard. Demographic Analysis. (Studies in Sociology Ser.). 1969. text ed. 14.95x (ISBN 0-04-519002-X); pap. text ed. 6.50x o.p. (ISBN 0-04-519003-8). Allen Unwin.

--Medical Records. 1977. 24.60x (ISBN 0-433-02450-X). Intl Ideas.

Benjamin, Bruce. Atlas of Paediatric Endoscopy: Upper Respiratory Tract & Oesophagus. (Illus.). 1981. text ed. 37.50x (ISBN 0-19-261179-8). Oxford U Pr.

Benjamin, Carol. The Rib Section. (Orig.). 1981. pap. 4.95 (ISBN 0-88270-498-2). Logos.

Benjamin, Carol Lea. Dog Problems. LC 80-1082. 192p. 1981. 10.95 (ISBN 0-385-15710-X). Doubleday.

Benjamin, Claude. Medical Itch. (Illus.). 1964. 7.95 (ISBN 0-8392-1067-1). Astor-Honor.

Benjamin, Francis S., Jr. & Toomer, G. J., eds. Campanus of Novara & Medieval Planetary Theory: Theorica Planetarum. (Medieval Science Ser: No. 16). (Illus.). 1971. 37.50x (ISBN 0-299-05960-X). U of Wis Pr.

Benjamin, Harry. Everyone's Guide to Theosophy. 1969. 10.95 (ISBN 0-7229-0130-5). Theos Pub Hse.

--The Transsexual Phenomenon. (Illus.). 1977. pap. 2.25 o.s.i. (ISBN 0-446-82426-7). Warner Bks.

Benjamin, Helena. Marion Bentley. LC 79-66926. 93p. 1980. 6.95 (ISBN 0-533-04428-6). Vantage.

Benjamin, Jacob. Sing Me a Love Song. (Orig.). 1980. pap. 1.75 (ISBN 0-532-23173-2). Manor Bks.

Benjamin, James J., et al. Financial Accounting. 3rd ed. LC 80-67311. (Illus.). 737p. 1980. pap. text ed. 18.95 (ISBN 0-931920-21-3); practice problems 4.95x; study guide 5.95x; work papers 6.95x. Dame Pubns.

--Principles of Accounting. LC 80-67313. 1100p. 1981. text ed. 18.95x (ISBN 0-931920-24-8); study guide 5.95 (ISBN 0-686-68562-8); working papers 6.95 (ISBN 0-686-68563-6); practice problem 4.95 (ISBN 0-686-68564-4). Dame Pubns.

Benjamin, Libby, jt. auth. see Walz, Garry R.

Benjamin, Libby, ed. see Jones, Brian, et al.

Benjamin, Libby, ed. see Lamb, Jackie & Lamb, Wesley.

Benjamin, Libby, ed. see Sinick, Daniel.

Benjamin, Martin & Curtis, Joy. Ethics in Nursing. 250p. 1981. text ed. 13.95x (ISBN 0-19-502836-8); pap. text ed. 7.95x (ISBN 0-19-502837-6). Oxford U Pr.

Benjamin, Robert. Making Schools Work: A Reporter's Journey Through Some of America's Most Remarkable Schools. 208p. 1981. 12.95 (ISBN 0-8264-0040-X). Continuum.

Benjamin, Robert L. Semantics & Language Analysis. LC 77-75141. (Speech Communication Ser). 1970. pap. 3.35 o.p. (ISBN 0-672-61085-X, SC15). Bobbs.

Benjamin, S. G. Art in America: A Critical & Historical Sketch. Weinberg, H. Barbara, ed. LC 75-28872. (Art Experience in Late 19th Century America Ser.: Vol. 8). (Illus.). 1976. Repr. of 1880 ed. lib. bdg. 58.00x (ISBN 0-8240-2232-7). Garland Pub.

--Contemporary Art in Europe. Weinberg, H. Barbara, ed. LC 75-28868. (Art Experiences in Late 19th Century America Ser.: Vol. 4). (Illus.). 1976. Repr. of 1877 ed. lib. bdg. 60.00 (ISBN 0-8240-2228-9). Garland Pub.

--Our American Artists: With Portraits, Studios & Engravings of Paintings, Repr. Of 1879 Ed. Bd. with Second Series. Painters, Sculptors, Illustrators, Engravers & Architects. Repr. of 1881 ed. LC 75-28870. (Art Experience in Late 19th Century America Ser.: Vol. 6). (Illus.). 1976. lib. bdg. 58.00 (ISBN 0-8240-2230-0). Garland Pub.

Benjamin, Susan. English Enamel Boxes. (Illus.). 1978. 15.95 o.p. (ISBN 0-670-29679-1, Studio). Viking Pr.

Benjamin, Thomas. The Craft of Modal Counterpoint: A Practice Approach. LC 77-90012. 1979. pap. text ed. 10.95 (ISBN 0-02-870480-0). Schirmer Bks.

Benjamin, Thomas, et al. Music for Analysis: Examples from the Common Practice Period & the Twentieth Century. LC 77-78237. 1978. pap. text ed. 12.95 (ISBN 0-395-25507-4). HM.

Benjamin, Thomas E., et al. Techniques & Materials of Tonal Music: With an Introduction to Twentieth Century Techniques. 2nd ed. LC 78-69578. (Illus.). 1979. text ed. 16.25 (ISBN 0-395-27066-9). HM.

Benjamin, Walter. Moskauer Tagebuch. (Edtion Suhrkamp: Neue Folge). 200p. (Orig.). 1980. pap. text ed. 6.50 (ISBN 3-518-11020-9, Pub. by Insel Verlag Germany). Suhrkamp.

Benjamin, William A., jt. ed. see Kingston, Irene.

Benjamine, Elbert. How to Use the Modern Ephemeris. 1940. pap. 1.00 (ISBN 0-933646-08-9). Aries Pr.

--The Influence of the Planet Pluto, Including an Ephemeris of Pluto 1840-1960. 1968. pap. 1.00 (ISBN 0-933646-09-7). Aries Pr.

Benko, Lorand & Imre, Samu, eds. The Hungarian Language. (Janua Linguarum, Ser. Practica: No. 134). (Illus.). 377p. (Orig.). 1972. pap. text ed. 64.70x (ISBN 90-2792-075-3). Mouton.

Benko, Stephen. Los Evangelicos, los Catolicos y la Virgen Maria. Olmedo, Alfonso, tr. from Eng. Orig. Title: Protestants, Catholics & Mary. Date not set. pap. price not set (ISBN 0-311-05041-7). Casa Bautista.

Benlliure, Felix, tr. see Hester, H. I.

Benmaman, Virginia & Moore, Suzanne. Individualized Learning Program for En Camino! 1981. pap. text ed. 4.95x (ISBN 0-673-15392-4). Scott F.

Ben-Meir, Alon. Israel: The Challenge of the Fourth Decade. 224p. 1978. text ed. 12.95x (ISBN 0-8290-0392-4). Irvington.

Ben-Menachem, Yoram. Angiography in Trauma: A Work Atlas. (Illus.). 350p. Date not set. text ed. 75.00 (ISBN 0-7216-1733-6). Saunders.

Benmussa, Simone, jt. auth. see Cixous, Helene.

Benn, J. Solomon. Preaching from the Bible. (Resources for Black Ministries Ser.). 80p. (Orig.). 1981. pap. 2.95 (ISBN 0-8010-0801-8). Baker Bk.

--Preaching in Ebony. (Resources for Black Ministries Ser.). 128p. (Orig.). 1981. pap. 3.45 (ISBN 0-8010-0803-4). Baker Bk.

Benn, M. B. The Drama of Revolt: A Critical Study of Georg Buchner. LC 75-3974. (Anglica Germanica Ser.: No. 2). (Illus.). 300p. 1976. 49.50 (ISBN 0-521-20828-9); pap. 13.95x (ISBN 0-521-29415-0). Cambridge U Pr.

Benn, S. I. & Peters, R. S. The Principles of Political Thought. 1965. pap. text ed. 5.95 o.s.i. (ISBN 0-02-902670-9). Free Pr.

--Social Principles & the Democratic State. 1959. pap. text ed. 15.95x (ISBN 0-04-300028-2). Allen Unwin.

Benn, Solomon J., III. God's Soul Medicine. (Resources for Black Ministries Ser.). 64p. (Orig.). 1981. pap. 2.45 (ISBN 0-8010-0802-6). Baker Bk.

Ben-Naim, Arieh. Hydrophobic Interactions. LC 79-510. (Illus.). 325p. 1980. 32.50 (ISBN 0-306-40222-X, Plenum Pr). Plenum Pub.

Bennani, B., tr. from Arabic. Bread, Hashish & Moon: Four Modern Arab Poets. (Keepsake Ser.: Vol. 10). (Illus.). 1981. 10.00 (ISBN 0-87775-134-X); pap. 5.00 (ISBN 0-87775-135-8). Unicorn Pr.

Bennathan, Esra & Walters, Alan A. Port Pricing & Investment Policy for Developing Countries. 1979. 16.95x (ISBN 0-19-520092-6); pap. 7.95x (ISBN 0-19-520093-4). Oxford U Pr.

Benne, Kenneth D. Education for Tragedy: Essays in Disenchanted Hope for Modern Man. LC 67-17847. 216p. 1967. pap. 3.75x (ISBN 0-8131-0124-7). U Pr of Ky.

Bennemann, Karl H. & Ketterson, J. B., eds. Physics of Liquid & Solid Helium, 2 pts. LC 75-20235. (Interscience Monographs & Texts in Physics & Astronomy). Pt. 1, 1976, 608p. 43.50 (ISBN 0-471-06600-1, Pub. by Wiley-Interscience); Pt. 2, 1978. 80.95 (ISBN 0-471-06601-X). Wiley.

Benner, Allen R., ed. see Homer.

Benner, Samuel. Commodity Prophecy & the Mastery of Commodity Futures Trading. (Illus.). 1979. Repr. of 1879 ed. deluxe ed. 69.75 (ISBN 0-918968-40-2). Inst Econ Finan.

Bennet, Arthur. Valley of Vision. pap. 4.95 o.p. (ISBN 0-686-12544-4). Banner of Truth.

Bennet, D. J. The Elements of Nuclear Power. LC 72-13693. 207p. 1972. pap. 17.95x (ISBN 0-470-01354-0). Halsted Pr.

Bennet, Donald. Scottish Mountain Climbs. (Illus.). 192p. 1980. 30.00 (ISBN 0-7134-1048-5, Pub. by Batsford England). David & Charles.

Bennet, G. A. Electricity & Modern Physics. 2nd ed. 1974. pap. text ed. 17.95x (ISBN 0-7131-2459-8). Intl Ideas.

Bennet, John & Masia, Seth. Walks in the Catskills. LC 74-81304. (Illus.). 204p. 1974. lib. bdg. 10.25 o.p. (ISBN 0-914788-00-0); pap. 6.95 (ISBN 0-914788-00-0). East Woods.

Bennett. Spaces for People: Human Factors in Design. LC 76-30847. 1977. pap. 4.95 (ISBN 0-13-823955-X, Spec). P-H.

--Successful Communication & Effective Speaking. pap. 3.95 (ISBN 0-13-860437-1, Parker). P-H.

Bennett & Siy. Blueprint Reading for Welders. LC 76-29579. (Illus.). 180p. 1978. pap. 8.40 (ISBN 0-8273-1059-5); instructor's guide 1.60 (ISBN 0-8273-1060-9); wall charts 4.00 (ISBN 0-8273-1063-3); transparencies 85.00 (ISBN 0-8273-1889-8). Delmar.

Bennett, et al. Introduction to Statistics. LC 77-21394. write for info. o.p. (ISBN 0-87618-920-6). R J Brady.

Bennett, A., et al, eds. Workshops in Cognitive Processes. (Illus.). 120p. 1980. write for info. (ISBN 0-7100-0579-2); pap. 9.75 (ISBN 0-7100-0580-6). Routledge & Kegan.

Bennett, A. Wayne. Introduction to Computer Simulation. LC 74-4509. 480p. 1974. text ed. 20.95 (ISBN 0-8299-0017-9); solutions manual avail. (ISBN 0-8299-0459-X). West Pub.

Bennett, Addison C. Improving Management Performance in Health Care Institutions: A Total Systems Approach. LC 78-8010. (Illus., Orig.). 1978. casebound 26.00 (ISBN 0-87258-246-9, 1066); pap. 25.00 (ISBN 0-87258-229-9, 1056). Am Hospital.

--Managing Hospital Costs Effectively As a System: A Primer for Hospital Administration. (Illus.). 72p. (Orig.). 1980. pap. 18.75 (ISBN 0-87258-327-9, 1404). Am Hospital.

Bennett, Alan. Enjoy. 80p. 1981. pap. 8.95 (ISBN 0-571-11734-1, Pub. by Faber & Faber). Merrimack Bk Serv.

--Office Suite. 60p. 1981. pap. 8.50 (ISBN 0-571-11744-9, Pub. by Faber & Faber). Merrimack Bk Serv.

--Prostaglandins & the Gut, Vol. 1. 14.40 (ISBN 0-904406-49-0). Eden Med Res.

Bennett, Alan D. Unlocking the Beauty of the Bible: A Study Guide. 5.00. UAHC.

Bennett, Albert B. & Nelson, Leonard T. Mathematics: An Activity Approach. 1979. text ed. 11.50 (ISBN 0-205-06518-X, 5665183); avail. instr's man. 3.95 (ISBN 0-205-06540-6, 566540X). Allyn.

--Mathematics: An Informal Approach. 1979. text ed. 17.80 (ISBN 0-205-06519-8, 5665191); avail. instr's man. 4.50 (ISBN 0-205-06541-4, 5665418). Allyn.

Bennett, Alice S., jt. auth. see Mertens, Thomas.

Bennett, Anna E. Little Witch. (Illus., Orig.). (gr. 3-5). pap. 1.25 o.p. (ISBN 0-590-08066-0, Schol Pap). Schol Bk Serv.

--Little Witch. (Illus.). 128p. (gr. 2-5). 1981. pap. 1.95 (ISBN 0-06-440119-7, Trophy). Har-Row.

Bennett, Arnold. Author's Craft & Other Critical Writings of Arnold Bennett. Hynes, Samuel, ed. LC 68-12706. (Regents Critics Ser). 1968. 11.95x (ISBN 0-8032-0451-5); pap. 3.95x (ISBN 0-8032-5451-2, BB 410, Bison). U of Nebr Pr.
Bennett, Barbara C. Berryhill. (Orig.). 1979. pap. 1.95 (ISBN 0-686-68907-0). Manor Bks.
Bennett, Ben. Death, Too, for The-Heavy-Runner. (Illus.). 192p. 1981. 15.95 (ISBN 0-87842-131-9); pap. 7.95 (ISBN 0-87842-132-7). Mountain Pr.
Bennett, Betty T., ed. British War Poetry in the Age of Romanticism: 1793-1815. LC 75-31144. (Romantic Context: Poetry 1789-1830 Ser.: Vol. 1). 1977. lib. bdg. 47.00 (ISBN 0-8240-2100-2). Garland Pub.
Bennett, Bill, jt. auth. see Martin, Ken.
Bennett, Boyce M., Jr., ed. see Miller, Madeleine S. & Miller, J. Lane.
Bennett, Bruce, jt. auth. see Van Dalen, Deobold B.
Bennett, Bruce, ed. The Literature of Western Australia. 1980. 17.95x (ISBN 0-85564-152-5, Pub by U of W Austral Pr). Intl Schol Bk Serv.
Bennett, C. Richard. Conscious Sedation in Dental Practice. 2nd ed. LC 78-4565. 1978. text ed. 26.50 (ISBN 0-8016-0612-8). Mosby.
--Monheim's General Anesthesia in Dental Practice. 4th ed. LC 73-4653. (Illus.). 446p. 1974. text ed. 21.00 o.p. (ISBN 0-8016-0608-X). Mosby.
Bennett, Charles A. History of Manual & Industrial Education, 2 Vols, Vol. 1. to 1870, Vol. 2. 1870-1917. Vol. 1. text ed. 18.00 (ISBN 0-87002-005-6); Vol. 2. text ed. 20.68 (ISBN 0-87002-006-4). Bennett IL.
Bennett, Charles E. Syntax of Early Latin, 2 Vols. Repr. of 1910 ed. Set. 100.60 (ISBN 0-685-05294-X). Adler.
Bennett, Clarence E. College Physics. 6th ed. LC 67-16622. (Illus.). 1967. pap. 3.95 (ISBN 0-06-460021-1, CO 21, COS). Har-Row.
--Physics Problems & How to Solve Them. 2nd ed. (Orig.). 1973. pap. 3.95 (ISBN 0-06-460149-8, CO 149, COS). Har-Row.
--Physics Without Mathematics. rev. ed. LC 76-124362. 1970. pap. 3.95 (ISBN 0-06-460067-X, CO 67, COS). Har-Row.
Bennett, Clifford. Nursing Home Life: What It Is & What It Could Be. LC 80-52650. (Illus.). 192p. 1980. pap. text ed. 6.95 (ISBN 0-913292-19-2). Tiresias Pr.
Bennett, Clois W. Clinical Serology. (Illus.). 304p. 1980. text ed. 13.50 (ISBN 0-398-00130-8). C C Thomas.
Bennett, D. Machine Embroidery with Style. LC 80-13914. (Connecting Threads Ser.). (Illus.). 100p. 1980. pap. 8.95 (ISBN 0-914842-45-5). Madrona Pubs.
Bennett, D. R., et al, eds. Atlas of Electroencephalography in Coma & Cerebral Death: EEG at the Bedside or in the Intensive Care Unit. LC 74-14470. 254p. 1976. 92.00 (ISBN 0-911216-91-X). Raven.
Bennett, D. W. Secrets of Baitfishing. Campbell, M., ed. (North East Fishing Ser.). (Illus.). 128p. 1981. pap. 4.95 (ISBN 0-88839-087-4). Hancock Hse.
--Secrets of Blue Fishing. Campbell, M., ed. (North East Fishing Ser.). (Illus.). 50p. (Orig.). 1981. pap. 3.95 (ISBN 0-88839-086-6). Hancock Hse.
--Secrets of Striped Bass Fishing. (N. E. Fishing Ser.). (Illus.). 70p. (Orig.). 1981. pap. 6.95 (ISBN 0-88839-103-X). Hancock Hse.
Bennett, Daphne. King Without a Crown: Albert, Prince Consort of England 1819-1861. LC 77-22108. (Illus.). 1977. 12.95 o.p. (ISBN 0-397-01143-1). Lippincott.
Bennett, David. Spatial & Temporal Uses of English Prepositions: An Essay in Stratificational Semantics. (Longman Linguistics Library). 256p. 1975. text ed. 17.50x (ISBN 0-582-52453-9). Longman.
Bennett, De Robigne M. Anthony Comstock: His Career of Cruelty & Crime. LC 73-121102. (Civil Liberties in American History Ser). 1971. Repr. of 1878 ed. lib. bdg. 17.50 (ISBN 0-306-71968-1). Da Capo.
Bennett, Dean B. & Young, Barbara E., eds. Maine Dirigo: I Lead. LC 80-68242. (Maine Studies Curriculum Project). (Illus.). 300p. 1980. text ed. 13.50 (ISBN 0-89272-103-0). Down East.
Bennett, Dennis & Bennett, Rita, trs. El Espiritu Santo y Tu. (Spanish Bks.). (Span.). 1978. 1.95 (ISBN 0-8297-0439-6). Life Pubs Intl.
Bennett, Donald P. & Humphries, David A. Introduction to Field Biology. 2nd ed. 1974. pap. text ed. 13.50x (ISBN 0-7131-2458-X). Intl Ideas.
Bennett, Dorothea. Between Friends. 1980. pap. 2.25 (ISBN 0-446-92604-3). Warner Bks.
--The Jigsaw Man. 1977. pap. 1.95 o.s.i. (ISBN 0-446-89414-1). Warner Bks.
Bennett, Dudley. TA & the Manager. (AMACOM Executive Bks). 1978. pap. 5.95 (ISBN 0-8144-7511-6). Am Mgmt.
--TA & the Manager. (Illus.). 1976. 13.95 (ISBN 0-8144-5422-4). Am Mgmt.
Bennett, Dwight. Disaster Creek. LC 80-1061. (Double D Western Ser.). 192p. 1981. 9.95 (ISBN 0-385-15629-4). Doubleday.
Bennett, E. J. Fluids for Anesthesia & Surgery in the Newborn & Infant. (Illus.). 248p. 1975. 25.50 (ISBN 0-398-03279-3). C C Thomas.
Bennett, E. K. History of the German Novelle. rev. ed. Waidson, H. M., rev. by. (Orig.). 1961. 47.50 (ISBN 0-521-04152-X); pap. 11.50 (ISBN 0-521-09152-7). Cambridge U Pr.
Bennett, Earl, et al. Business Policy: Case Problems of the General Manager. 3rd ed. (Marketing & Management Ser.). 1978. text ed. 19.95x (ISBN 0-675-08401-6); manual 3.95 (ISBN 0-686-67971-7). Merrill.
Bennett, Edward H., jt. auth. see Burnham, Daniel H.
Bennett, Edward M., jt. ed. see Burns, Richard D.
Bennett, Ernest N. Apparitions & Haunted Houses: A Survey of Evidence. LC 76-164100. Repr. of 1939 ed. 22.00 (ISBN 0-8103-3752-5). Gale.
Bennett, Frances C. & Chang, Sung-wen. Page a Day SAT Study Guide. 320p. (Orig.). 1981. pap. 3.95 (ISBN 0-668-05196-5, 5196). Arco.
Bennett, G. V. The Tory Crisis in Church & State 1688-1730: The Career of Francis Atterbury, Bishop of Rochester. (Illus.). 260p. 1975. 42.00x (ISBN 0-19-822444-3). Oxford U Pr.
Bennett, Geoffry. The Battle for Trafalgar. 1977. 27.00 (ISBN 0-7134-3269-1, Pub. by Batsford England). David & Charles.
Bennett, Georgaan. What the Bible Says About Goodness. LC 80-69626. (What the Bible Says Ser.). 350p. 1981. 13.50 (ISBN 0-89900-080-0). College Pr Pub.
Bennett, George & Hamill, Pete. Fighters. LC 77-12839. (Illus.). 1978. pap. 7.95 o.p. (ISBN 0-385-13524-6, Dolp). Doubleday.
Bennett, Gordon. Huadong: The Story of a Chinese People's Commune. (Westview Special Studies on China & East Asia Ser.). 1978. lib. bdg. 21.50x (ISBN 0-89158-094-8); pap. text ed. 8.75 (ISBN 0-89158-095-6). Westview.
Bennett, Gordon C. Readers Theatre Comes to Church. LC 72-1763. (Illus.). 128p. (Orig.). 1972. pap. 4.95 (ISBN 0-8042-1963-X). John Knox.
Bennett, H. Encyclopedia of Chemical Trademarks & Synonyms, Vol. 1 A-E. 1981. 55.00 (ISBN 0-8206-0286-8). Chem Pub.
--Industrial Waxes, 2 vols. Incl. Vol. 1. Natural Waxes; Synthetic Waxes (ISBN 0-8206-0224-8); Vol. 2. Compounded Waxes; Technology (ISBN 0-8206-0225-6). 1975. 30.00 ea. (ISBN 0-686-67154-6). Chem Pub.
--New Cosmetic Formulary. 1970. 25.00 o.p. (ISBN 0-8206-0088-1). Chem Pub.
Bennett, H., ed. Chemical Formulary, 22 vols. Incl. Vol. 1, 1933 (ISBN 0-8206-0259-0). Vol. 2, 1935 (ISBN 0-8206-0260-4). Vol. 3, 1936 (ISBN 0-8206-0261-2). Vol. 4, 1939 (ISBN 0-8206-0262-0). Vol. 5, 1941 (ISBN 0-8206-0263-9). Vol. 6, 1943 (ISBN 0-8206-0264-7). Vol. 7, 1945 (ISBN 0-8206-0265-5); Vol. 8, 1948 (ISBN 0-8206-0266-3). Vol. 9, 1950 (ISBN 0-8206-0267-1). Vol. 10, 1957 (ISBN 0-8206-0268-X). Vol. 11, 1961 (ISBN 0-8206-0269-8). Vol. 12, 1965 (ISBN 0-8206-0270-1). Vol. 13, 1967 (ISBN 0-8206-0271-X). Vol. 14, 1968 (ISBN 0-8206-0272-8); Vol. 15, 1970 (ISBN 0-8206-0273-6). Vol. 16, 1971 (ISBN 0-8206-0274-4). Vol. 17, 1973 (ISBN 0-8206-0275-2). Vol. 18, 1975 (ISBN 0-8206-0276-0). Vol. 19, 1976 (ISBN 0-8206-0277-9). Vol. 20, 1977 (ISBN 0-8206-0278-7). Vol. 21, 1979 (ISBN 0-8206-0279-5). Vol. 22, 1979 (ISBN 0-8206-0280-9). 22.50 ea. Chem Pub.
--Chemical Formulary, Vol. 23. 1981. 22.50 (ISBN 0-8206-0282-5). Chem Pub.
Bennett, H. Stith. On Becoming a Rock Musician. LC 80-5378. 272p. 1981. lib. bdg. 15.00x (ISBN 0-87023-311-4). U of Mass Pr.
Bennett, Hal & Samuels, Michael. The Well-Body Book. (YA) 1973. pap. 7.95 (ISBN 0-394-70969-1). Random.
Bennett, Hal Z. The Doctor Within. (Illus.). 160p. 1981. 11.95 (ISBN 0-517-54178-5); pap. 5.95 (ISBN 0-517-54299-4). Potter.
Bennett, Hank & Helms, Harry L. The Complete Shortwave Listener's Handbook. 2nd ed. (Illus.). 308p. 1980. 14.95 (ISBN 0-8306-9941-4); pap. 9.95 (ISBN 0-8306-1255-6, 1255). Tab Bks.
Bennett, Harold & Bennett, Judy. Cambridge Glass Book. 1970. pap. 7.95 o.p. (ISBN 0-87069-012-4). Wallace-Homestead.
Bennett, Heather, ed. see Davis, Joyce E.
Bennett, Heather, ed. see Flack, Dora B.
Bennett, Henry S. Chaucer & the Fifteenth Century. (Oxford History of English Literature Ser.). 1947. 37.50x (ISBN 0-19-812201-2). Oxford U Pr.
--English Books & Readers, 3 vols. 1970. Vol 1. 65.00 (ISBN 0-521-07609-9); Vol 2. 54.00 (ISBN 0-521-04153-8); Vol 3. 47.00 (ISBN 0-521-07701-X); 140.00 set (ISBN 0-521-08857-7). Cambridge U Pr.
--Life on the English Manor. (Cambridge Studies in Medieval Life & Thought). 1960. 32.95 (ISBN 0-521-04154-6); pap. 8.95x (ISBN 0-521-09105-5). Cambridge U Pr.
--Pastons & Their England. 2nd ed. LC 68-23175. (Cambridge Studies in Medieval Life & Thought). 1968. 32.95 (ISBN 0-521-07173-9); pap. 8.95x (ISBN 0-521-09513-1). Cambridge U Pr.
Bennett, J. Linguistic Behavior. LC 75-44575. 260p. 1976. 31.95 (ISBN 0-521-21168-9). Cambridge U Pr.
--Linguistic Behaviour. LC 75-44575. 1979. pap. 11.50x (ISBN 0-521-29751-6). Cambridge U Pr.
Bennett, J. A. & Smithers, G. V., eds. Early Middle English Verse & Prose. 2nd ed. 1968. text ed. 22.50x (ISBN 0-19-811493-1). Oxford U Pr.
Bennett, J. F. The Way to Be Free. 1980. pap. 6.95 (ISBN 0-87728-491-1). Weiser.
Bennett, J. G. The Masters of Wisdom. 1980. pap. 5.95 (ISBN 0-87728-466-0). Weiser.
--Sex. 128p. 1981. pap. 5.95 (ISBN 0-87728-533-0). Weiser.
Bennett, James C. & Demos, George D. Drug Abuse & What We Can Do About It. 148p. 1972. 14.75 (ISBN 0-398-00132-4). C C Thomas.
Bennett, James D. Frederick Jackson Turner. LC 74-32112. (U. S. Authors Ser.: No. 254). 1975. lib. bdg. 10.95 (ISBN 0-8057-7150-6). Twayne.
Bennett, James O. Much Loved Books. (Black & Gold Lib). 7.95 o.p. (ISBN 0-87140-979-8). Liveright.
Bennett, Jay. The Birthday Murderer. (YA) 1980. pap. 1.50 (ISBN 0-440-90576-1, LFL). Dell.
--The Birthday Murderer. LC 76-47239. (YA) 1977. 7.95 (ISBN 0-440-00584-1). Delacorte.
--The Dangling Witness: A Mystery. LC 74-5502. 160p. (gr. 7 up). 1974. 5.95 o.s.i. (ISBN 0-440-03483-3). Delacorte.
--Deathman, Do Not Follow Me. (gr. 7 up). 1968. 6.95 o.p. (ISBN 0-8015-1998-5). Dutton.
--The Killing Tree. LC 76-189567. 128p. (gr. 7-12). 1972. PLB 4.90 o.p. (ISBN 0-531-02559-4). Watts.
Bennett, Jean, ed. Japanese Love Poems. LC 76-2753. 1976. 6.95 o.p. (ISBN 0-385-03085-1). Doubleday.
Bennett, Jeffrey, jt. auth. see Bennett, Meryl.
Bennett, Jill, compiled by. Roger Was a Razor Fish & Other Poems. LC 80-17166. (Illus.). 48p. (gr. 2-6). 1981. 7.95 (ISBN 0-688-41986-0). Morrow.
Bennett, Joan. Five Metaphysical Poets: Donne, Herbert, Vaughan, Crashaw, Marvell. 1964. 27.50 (ISBN 0-521-04156-2); pap. 8.95x (ISBN 0-521-09238-8). Cambridge U Pr.
--George Eliot: Her Mind & Her Art. (Orig.). 1948. 27.50 (ISBN 0-521-04158-9); pap. 8.95x (ISBN 0-521-09174-8, 174). Cambridge U Pr.
--Sir Thomas Browne. 1962. 42.00 (ISBN 0-521-04159-7). Cambridge U Pr.
--Virginia Woolf. 2nd ed. 1945. 19.95 (ISBN 0-521-04160-0); pap. 7.95x (ISBN 0-521-09951-X). Cambridge U Pr.
Bennett, John E., ed. Building Voluntary Support for the Two-Year College. 1979. pap. 16.50 (ISBN 0-89964-017-6). CASE.
Bennett, John M. Nips Poem. (Illus.). 40p. (Orig.). 1980. pap. 3.00 (ISBN 0-935350-00-4); signed & lettered 6.00. Luna Bisonte.
Bennett, John P. Chemical Contraception. LC 73-7910. 272p. 1973. 25.00x (ISBN 0-231-03434-2). Columbia U Pr.
Bennett, John W. The Ecological Transition. 1976. text ed. 27.00 (ISBN 0-08-017867-7); pap. text ed. 16.00 (ISBN 0-08-017868-5). Pergamon.
--Northern Plainsmen: Adaptive Strategy & Agrarian Life. LC 76-75043. (Worlds of Man Ser.). (Illus.). 1970. text ed. 13.95x (ISBN 0-88295-602-7); pap. text ed. 8.75x (ISBN 0-88295-603-5). AHM Pub.
Bennett, Jonathan. Kant's Analytic. (Orig.). 1966. 35.50 (ISBN 0-521-04157-0); pap. 9.95x (ISBN 0-521-09389-9, 389). Cambridge U Pr.
--Kant's Dialectic. LC 73-89762. 290p. 1974. 38.50 (ISBN 0-521-20420-8); pap. 9.95x (ISBN 0-521-09849-1). Cambridge U Pr.
--Rationality: An Essay Towards an Analysis. (Studies in Philosophical Psychology). 1971. text ed. 4.50x (ISBN 0-7100-3841-0); pap. text ed. 3.50x (ISBN 0-391-00198-1). Humanities.
Bennett, Jonathan, ed. see Leibniz, G. W.
Bennett, Joseph. Luxury Cruise. LC 62-11667. 1962. 4.50 o.s.i. (ISBN 0-8076-0170-5). Braziller.
Bennett, Josephine W. Measure for Measure As Royal Entertainment. LC 66-15764. 1966. 20.00x (ISBN 0-231-02921-7). Columbia U Pr.
Bennett, Judith. Sex Signs. 384p. 1981. pap. 7.95 (ISBN 0-312-71339-8). St Martin.
Bennett, Judy, jt. auth. see Bennett, Harold.
Bennett, Linda A. Personal Choice in Ethnic Identity Maintenance: Serbs, Croats & Slovenes in Washington, D. C. LC 77-93261. 230p. 1978. soft cover 10.00 (ISBN 0-918660-06-8). Ragusan Pr.
Bennett, M. R. Automatic Neuromuscular Transmission. LC 76-182026. (Physiological Society Monographs: No. 30). (Illus.). 400p. 1973. 54.00 (ISBN 0-521-08463-6). Cambridge U Pr.
Bennett, M. V., ed. Synaptic Transmission & Neuronal Interaction. LC 73-83886. (Society of General Physiologists Ser: Vol. 28). 401p. 1974. 34.50 (ISBN 0-911216-56-1). Raven.
Bennett, Margaret. Peripatetic Diabetic. LC 69-16019. (Illus.). 1969. pap. 5.95 (ISBN 0-8015-5840-9, Hawthorn). Dutton.
Bennett, Marian. My Book of Special Days. (Illus.). (gr. 4-8). 1977. 4.95 (ISBN 0-87239-156-6, 3049). Standard Pub.
Bennett, Marian, ed. Songs for Preschool Children. LC 80-25091. 96p. 1981. pap. 5.95 (ISBN 0-87239-429-8, 5754). Standard Pub.
Bennett, Meryl & Bennett, Jeffrey. The Renovator's Primer. LC 77-87470. (Illus.). 1978. pap. 6.95 o.p. (ISBN 0-8069-8618-2, 034700). Sterling.
Bennett, Michael, et al. Papers in Cognitive-Stratificational Linguistics. Copeland, James E. & Davis, Philip W., eds. (Rice University Studies: Vol. 66, No. 2). 208p. 1980. pap. 5.50x (ISBN 0-89263-245-3). Rice Univ.
Bennett, Mildred R. World of Willa Cather. LC 61-7235. (Illus.). 1961. 13.95x (ISBN 0-8032-1151-1); pap. 3.95 (ISBN 0-8032-5013-4, BB 112, Bison). U of Nebr Pr.
Bennett, Norman R. Studies in East African History. LC 63-11193. (Pub. by Boston U Pr). 1963. 5.50x (ISBN 0-8419-8701-7, Africana). Holmes & Meier.
Bennett, Norman R., ed. Leadership in Eastern Africa: Six Political Biographies. LC 68-21921. (Pub. by Boston U Pr). 1968. 15.00x (ISBN 0-8419-8705-X, Africana). Holmes & Meier.
--Stanley's Despatches to the New York Herald, 1871-1872, 1874-1877. LC 72-96999. (Pub. by Boston U Pr). 1970. 24.50x (ISBN 0-8419-8702-5, Africana). Holmes & Meier.
Bennett, Norman R., jt. ed. see Gabel, Creighton.
Bennett, P. What Happened on Lexington Green: An Inquiry into the Nature & Methods of History. Brown, Richard H. & Halsey, Van R., eds. (Amherst Ser.). (gr. 9-12). 1970. pap. text ed. 4.52 (ISBN 0-201-00461-5, Sch Div); tchr's. manual 1.92 (ISBN 0-201-00463-1). A-W.
Bennett, Paul. Up Your Accountability: How to up Your Serviceability & Funding Credibility by Upping Your Accounting Ability. LC 73-89364. (Nonprofit-Ability Ser.). (Illus.). 1973. pap. 9.95 (ISBN 0-914756-02-8). Taft Corp.
Bennett, Paul J. Conference Under the Tamarind Tree: Three Essays in Burmese History. (Monograph: No. 15). (Illus.). viii, 153p. 1971. 5.75 o.p. (ISBN 0-686-63727-5). Yale U Pr.
Bennett, Philip M., jt. auth. see Rosen, Harold J.
Bennett, Ralph. Ultra in the West. (Illus.). 306p. 1980. 17.50 (ISBN 0-684-16704-2, ScribT). Scribner.
Bennett, Rita. I'm Glad You Asked That. 207p. 4.95 (ISBN 0-930756-56-8, 4290-BE6, Pub. by Logos). Women's Aglow.
Bennett, Rita, jt. tr. see Bennett, Dennis.
Bennett, Robert A. & Edwards, O. C. The Bible for Today's Church. (The Church's Teaching Ser.: Vol. 2). 1979. 9.50 (ISBN 0-8164-0419-4); pap. 3.95 (ISBN 0-8164-2215-X). Crossroad NY.
Bennett, Robert J., jt. ed. see Wrigley, Neil.
Bennett, Robert L. Careers Through Cooperative Work Experience. 1977. 11.95 (ISBN 0-471-06634-6); tchrs'. manual (ISBN 0-471-02416-3). Wiley.
--Earning & Learning. LC 80-65003. (Illus.). 256p. (Orig.). 1980. pap. 7.95 (ISBN 0-936148-01-2). Action Link.
Bennett, Roger, ed. see Donne, John.
Bennett, S. A History of Control Engineering, Eighteen Hundred to Nineteen Thirty. (IEE Control Engineering Ser.: No. 8). (Illus.). 224p. 1979. 39.50 (ISBN 0-906048-07-9). Inst Elect Eng.
Bennett, Virginia C., jt. auth. see Bardon, Jack I.
Bennett, W. A. Aspects of Language & Language Teaching. (Illus., Orig.). 1968. 24.95 (ISBN 0-521-04164-3); pap. 6.95x (ISBN 0-521-09512-3, 512). Cambridge U Pr.
Bennett, Wayne W. & Hess, Karen M. Criminal Investigation. (Criminal Justice Ser.). 450p. 1980. text ed. 15.95 (ISBN 0-8299-0342-9). West Pub.
Bennett, William H. An Introduction to the Gothic Language. 4th, rev. ed. Lehmann, Winfred P., ed. LC 79-87574. (Introductions to the Older Languages of Europe Ser.: No. 2). xvii, 190p. 1981. 18.50x (ISBN 0-87352-290-7). Modern Lang.

Bennett, William P. First Baby in Camp. 68p. pap. 3.50 (ISBN 0-8466-0161-3, SJS161). Shorey.

Bennett, Wilma. Occupations Filing Plan & Bibliography. LC 68-56288. 138p. 1968. pap. text ed. 3.95x (ISBN 0-8134-1055-X, 1055). Interstate.

Bennett, Wilma E. Checklist-Guide to Selecting a Small Computer. LC 80-13996. 1980. pap. 5.00 (ISBN 0-87576-091-0). Pilot Bks.

Bennetts, R. G. Introduction to Digital Board Testing. (Computer Systems Engineering Ser.). 1981. text ed. price not set (ISBN 0-8448-1385-0). Crane-Russak Co.

Bennett-Sandler, Georgette, et al. Law Enforcement & Criminal Justice: An Introduction. LC 78-69537. (Illus.). 1979. text ed. 15.75 (ISBN 0-395-27467-2); inst. manual 0.25 (ISBN 0-395-27466-4). HM.

Benning, Lee Edwards. How to Bring up a Child Without Spending a Fortune. LC 75-25436. 320p. 1976. pap. 2.95 (ISBN 0-385-11513-X, Dolp). Doubleday.

Benningfield, L. M., jt. auth. see Lago, G.

Bennion, Edmond & Bamford, G. S. Technology of Cake Making. 5th ed. (Illus.). 1973. 45.00x (ISBN 0-249-44121-7). Intl Ideas.

Bennion, Junius, jt. auth. see Schneider, Edward W.

Bennion, Lowell. Jesus, The Master Teacher. 63p. 1980. 4.95 (ISBN 0-87747-833-3). Deseret Bk.

Bennis, Warren. The Unconscious Conspiracy: Why Leaders Can't Lead. (AMACOM Executive Bks). 1978. pap. 5.95 (ISBN 0-8144-7507-8). Am Mgmt.

Bennis, Warren, et al. Essays in Interpersonal Dynamics. 1979. pap. text ed. 7.95x (ISBN 0-256-02231-3). Dorsey.

Bennis, Warren G. Organization Development: Its Nature, Origins & Prospects. Schein, Edgar, et al, eds. (Ser. in Organization Development). 1969. pap. text ed. 6.50 (ISBN 0-201-00523-9). A-W.

Bennison, D. J. & Davies, R. L. The Impact of Town Centre Shopping Schemes in Britain: Their Impact on Traditional Retail Environments. (Progress in Planning Ser.: Vol. 14, Part 1). (Illus.). 104p. 1980. pap. 13.50 (ISBN 0-08-026789-0). Pergamon.

Bennison, G. M. Introduction to Geological Structures & Maps: Metric. 3rd ed. (Illus.). 1975. pap. text ed. 9.95x (ISBN 0-7131-2513-6). Intl Ideas.

Benois, George, jt. auth. see Cox, Beverly.

Benoist, Elizabeth. The Dish Ran Away with the Spoon. 212p. 1980. pap. 5.95 (ISBN 0-86629-007-9). Sunrise MO.

--Swift As a Shadow. 256p. 1980. 9.95 (ISBN 0-86629-002-8). Sunrise MO.

Benoist-Mechin, Jacques. History of the German Army Since the Armistice. 345p. 1979. Repr. of 1939 ed. 22.50 (ISBN 0-86527-094-5). Fertig.

Benoit. Le Dejeuner De Sousceyrac. (Easy Readers Ser.). 1978. pap. text ed. 3.75 (ISBN 0-88436-293-0). EMC.

Benoit, Emile. Progress & Survival: An Essay on the the Future of Mankind. Gohn, Jack B., ed. 144p. 1980. 17.95 (ISBN 0-03-056911-7). Praeger.

Benoit, Jehane. Madame Benoit's World of Food. (Illus.). 304p. 1980. 16.95 (ISBN 0-07-082974-8, GB). McGraw.

Benoit, P. Jesus & the Gospel, Vol. 1. 264p. 1973. 9.75 (ISBN 0-8164-1055-0). Crossroad NY.

Benoit, Pierre & Murphy, Roland, eds. Immortality & Resurrection. LC 71-129759. (Concilium Ser.: Religion in the Seventies: Vol. 60). 1970. pap. 4.95 (ISBN 0-8164-2516-7). Crossroad NY.

Benoit, Raymond. Single Nature's Double Name: The Collectedness of the Conflicting in British & American Romanticism. (De Proprietatibus Litterarum Ser.: No. 26). 1973. text ed. 23.50x (ISBN 90-2792-599-2). Mouton.

Benouis, Mustapha K. Le Dialoque Philosophique Dans la Litterature Francaise Du Seizieme Siecle. (De Proprietatibus Litterarum, Series Maior: No. 31). 1976. text ed. 48.25x (ISBN 90-2793-201-8). Mouton.

Benrey, Ronald. How to Get the Most Out of Your Low-Cost Electronic Calculator. 1976. pap. 5.95 (ISBN 0-8104-5942-6). Hayden.

Benrey, Ronald M. Fifty IC Projects You Can Build. (Illus.). 1970. pap. 7.15 (ISBN 0-8104-0723-X). Hayden.

Ben-Sasson, H. H. Trial & Achievement: Currents in Jewish History. (Illus.). 327p. 1975. 10.95 (ISBN 0-7065-1420-3). Bloch.

Benseler, David P. & Schultz, Renate A. Intensive Foreign Language Courses. (Language in Education Ser.: No. 18). 55p. 1979. pap. 4.95 (ISBN 0-87281-104-2). Ctr Appl Ling.

Bensen, D. R. Sherlock Holmes in New York. (Orig.). 1976. pap. 1.50 o.p. (ISBN 0-345-25571-2). Ballantine.

Bensen, Donald R., ed. The Unknown. 1978. pap. 1.75 o.s.i. (ISBN 0-515-04820-8). Jove Pubns.

Bensen, Robert, ed. see Gillespie, Netta.

Bensen, Robert, ed. see Klein, Elizabeth.

Bensimon-Donath, Doris. L'integration Des Juifs Nord-Africains En France. (Publications De L'institut D'etudes et De Recherches Interethniques et Interculturelles: No. 1). 1971. pap. 20.50x (ISBN 90-2796-930-2). Mouton.

Bensinger, Charles. The Home Video Handbook. 2nd, rev. ed. 1980. pap. 8.95 (ISBN 0-931294-02-9). Video-Info.

--The Video Guide. 2nd, rev. ed. LC 78-66194. (Illus.). 1980. pap. 14.95 (ISBN 0-931294-03-7). Video-Info.

Bension, Shmuel. New York Production Manual 1979-80: The "Producer's Masterguide" for Motion Picture, Television, Commercials & Videotape Industries. 1979. pap. 35.00 (ISBN 0-935744-00-2). NY Prod Manual.

--New York Production Manual 1981: The "Producer's MasterGuide" for: Motion Picture, Television, Commercials & Videotape Industries. 1000p. (Orig.). 1981. pap. 49.50 (ISBN 0-935744-01-0). NY Prod Manual.

Benskina, Princess Orelia. I Have Loved You Already. 1975. 3.50 o.p. (ISBN 0-682-47871-7). Exposition.

Bensko, John. Green Soldiers. LC 80-26052. (Younger Poet Ser.: No. 76). 80p. 1981. 9.95 (ISBN 0-300-02637-4); pap. 4.95 (ISBN 0-300-02644-7). Yale U Pr.

Bensman, Joseph. Dollars & Sense. 1967. 9.95 (ISBN 0-02-509000-3). Macmillan.

Benson, A. C. The Memoirs of Arthur Hamilton B.A. LC 76-20043. (The Decadent Consciousness Ser.: Vol. 4). 1977. Repr. of 1886 ed. lib. bdg. 38.00 (ISBN 0-8240-2753-1). Garland Pub.

Benson, Arthur C. Walter Pater. LC 67-23876. (Library of Lives & Letters: British Writers Ser.). 1968. Repr. of 1906 ed. 15.00 (ISBN 0-8103-3054-7). Gale.

Benson, Bob. In Quest of the Shared Life. 168p. 1981. pap. 4.95 (ISBN 0-914850-55-5). Impact Tenn.

Benson, C. H. El Arte De Ensenar. Villalobos, Fernando P., tr. from Eng. (Curso Para Maestros Cristianos: No. 5). Orig. Title: Teaching Techniques. 128p. (Span.). 1971. pap. 2.50 (ISBN 0-89922-016-9); instructor's manual 1.50 (ISBN 0-89922-017-7). Edit Caribe.

--Conozcamos Al Alumno. Villalobos, Fernando P., tr. from Eng. (Curso para Maestros Cristianos: No. 4). Orig. Title: Understanding Children & Youth. 128p. (Span.). 1972. pap. 2.50 (ISBN 0-89922-014-2); instr's manual 1.50 (ISBN 0-89922-015-0). Edit Caribe.

--Escuela Dominical En Accion. Villalobos, Fernando P., tr. from Eng. (Curso Para Maestros Cristianos: No. 6). Orig. Title: Sunday School Success. 122p. (Span.). 1972. pap. 2.50 (ISBN 0-89922-018-5); instructor's manual 1.50 (ISBN 0-89922-019-3). Edit Caribe.

--Poesia y Profecia del Antiquo Testamento. Villalobos, Fernando P., tr. from Eng. (Curso Para Maestros Cristianos: No. 2). Orig. Title: Old Testament Survey - Poetry & Prophecy. 122p. (Span.). 1972. pap. 2.50 (ISBN 0-89922-010-X); instructor's manual 1.50 (ISBN 0-89922-011-8). Edit Caribe.

Benson, Carmen. This Earth's End: New Testament Prophecy of the End Times. 152p. 1972. pap. 1.95 o.p. (ISBN 0-912106-89-1). Logos.

Benson, Carmen, jt. auth. see Jarman, Ray C.

Benson, Charles S. The Economics of Public Education. 3rd ed. LC 77-77670. (Illus.). 1978. text ed. 20.50 (ISBN 0-395-18619-6). HM.

Benson, Clarence H. Sunday School Success. rev. ed. LC 64-13765. 1964. pap. text ed. 3.75 o.p. (ISBN 0-910566-06-2); instructor's guide by bill bynum 3.75 o.p. (ISBN 0-910566-22-4). Evang Tchr.

--Teaching Techniques. rev. ed. 1974. pap. text ed. 3.75 (ISBN 0-910566-05-4); instr's guide by janet m. loth 3.75 (ISBN 0-686-66315-2). Evang Tchr.

Benson, Donald R., ed. Unknown Five. 1978. pap. 1.75 o.s.i. (ISBN 0-515-04833-X). Jove Pubns.

Benson, E. F. Dodo. LC 78-19214. 1978. 14.95 o.s.i. (ISBN 0-690-01782-0, TYC-T). T Y Crowell.

--Make Way for Lucia: The Complete Lucia, Including Queen Lucia, Miss Mapp, Mapp & Lucia, Lucia in London, Trouble for Lucia & the Worshipful Lucia & the Male Impersonator. LC 76-783. 576p. 1977. 14.95 o.p. (ISBN 0-690-01105-9, TYC-T). T Y Crowell.

Benson, Elizabeth & Conklin, William. Museums of the Andes. Lafarge, Henry, ed. LC 80-8912. 1981. 16.95 (ISBN 0-88225-306-9). Newsweek.

Benson, Elizabeth P. The Maya World. rev. ed. LC 77-4955. (Illus.). 1977. 11.95 (ISBN 0-690-01673-5, TYC-T). T Y Crowell.

Benson, Elizabeth P., jt. auth. see Coe, Michael D.

Benson, Elizabeth P., ed. Dumbarton Oaks Conference on the Olmec: October 28 & 29, 1967. LC 68-58523. (Illus.). 186p. 1968. 7.50 (ISBN 0-88402-027-4, Ctr Pre-Columbian). Dumbarton Oaks.

Benson, Elizabeth P., ed. see Conference at Dumbarton Oaks, October 18 & 19, 1975.

Benson, Ellis, jt. ed. see Stefanini, Mario.

Benson, Evelyn P. & DeVitt, Joan Q. Community Health & Nursing Practices. 2nd ed. (Illus.). 1980. text ed. 16.95 (ISBN 0-13-153171-9). P-H.

Benson, George C. The Politics of Urbanism: The New Federalism. new ed. Dillon, Mary E., ed. LC 70-189864. (Politics of Government Ser.). 142p. (Orig.). 1972. pap. 2.50 o.p. (ISBN 0-8120-0445-0). Barron.

Benson, George C., et al. Political Corruption in America. LC 77-88815. 1978. write for info. (ISBN 0-669-02008-7). Lexington Bks.

Benson, Ginny. Mark Twain. LC 74-2105. (People to Remember Ser.). 40p. 1974. 5.95 (ISBN 0-87191-325-9). Creative Ed.

Benson, Herbert. The Mind-Body Effect. 1980. pap. 2.50 (ISBN 0-425-04699-0). Berkley Pub.

--The Relaxation Response. LC 75-14309. (Illus.). 128p. 1975. 5.95 o.p. (ISBN 0-688-02955-8). Morrow.

Benson, Howard. The Business Brokers' Manual. 136p. (Orig.). 1977. 15.00 (ISBN 0-686-27499-7). Business Brokers.

Benson, J. L. Bamboula at Kourion: The Necropolis & the Finds, Excavated by J. F. Daniel. LC 72-133204. (Haney Foundation Ser). (Illus.). 192p. 1973. 60.00x (ISBN 0-8122-7635-3). U of Pa Pr.

Benson, J. L., jt. auth. see Stillwell, Agnes N.

Benson, Jackson J., ed. The Short Stories of Ernest Hemingway: Critical Essays. LC 74-75815. xv, 375p. 1975. 14.75 (ISBN 0-8223-0320-5); pap. 7.75 (ISBN 0-8223-0386-8). Duke.

Benson, Jeffrey & MacKenzie, Alastair. Sauternes: A Study of the Great Sweet Wines of Bordeaux. (Illus.). 172p. 1979. 26.00 (ISBN 0-85667-062-6, Pub. by Sotheby Parke Bernet England). Biblio Dist.

Benson, Jim, jt. auth. see Okagaki, Alan.

Benson, Jim, jt. auth. see Schaefer, Elizabeth.

Benson, L. Images, Heroes & Self Perceptions: The Struggle for Identity from Maskwearing to Authenticity. 1974. 17.95 (ISBN 0-13-451187-5). P-H.

Benson, Larry. King Arthur's Death: The Middle English 'stanzaic Morte Arthur' & 'alliterative Morte Arthur' LC 73-13545. (Library of Literature Ser). 1974. pap. text ed. 8.35 o.p. (ISBN 0-672-61010-8). Bobbs.

Benson, Larry, ed. see Chaucer, Geoffrey.

Benson, Larry D & Leyerle, John, eds. Chivalric Literature: Essays on Relations Between Literature and Life in the Later Middle Ages. LC 80-17514. (Studies in Medieval Culture: XIV). (Illus.). 176p. (Orig.). 1980. pap. 10.80 (ISBN 0-918720-09-5). Medieval Inst.

Benson, Lee. Turner & Beard, American Historical Writing Reconsidered. 1965. pap. 1.95 o.s.i. (ISBN 0-02-902710-1). Free Pr.

Benson, Lyman & Darrow, Robert A. Trees & Shrubs of the Southwestern Deserts. rev. ed. 1981. text ed. 49.50x (ISBN 0-8165-0591-8). U of Ariz Pr.

Benson, Morton, ed. Dictionary of Russian Personal Names. LC 64-19386. 1964. 12.00x (ISBN 0-8122-7452-0). U of Pa Pr.

--Serbocroatian-English Dictionary. LC 79-146959. 1971. text ed. 35.00x (ISBN 0-8122-7636-1). U of Pa Pr.

Benson, Nettie L., ed. Mexico & the Spanish Cortes, 1810-1822: Eight Essays. (Latin American Monograph Ser.: No. 5). 1966. 10.95x (ISBN 0-292-73606-1). U of Tex Pr.

Benson, Oliver E. Political Science Laboratory. LC 69-10596. 1969. 11.95 o.p. (ISBN 0-675-09593-X). Merrill.

Benson, Oscar H., jt. auth. see Tod, Osma G.

Benson, Philip F. The Biochemistry of Development. (Clinics in Developmental Medicine Ser. No. 37). 273p. 1971. 19.50 (ISBN 0-685-24729-5). Lippincott.

Benson, Rita, ed. see Debussy, Claude.

Benson, Robert. Great Winemakers of California. (Illus.). 1977. 15.00 o.p. (ISBN 0-88496-107-9). Capra Pr.

Benson, Rowland S. & Whitehouse, N. D. Internal Combustion Engines, 2 vols. LC 79-40359. (Thermodynamics & Fluid Mechanics for Mechanical Engineers). (Illus.). 1979. Set. 68.00 (ISBN 0-08-022717-1); Vol. 1. pap. 15.75 (ISBN 0-08-022718-X); Vol. 2. pap. 15.75 (ISBN 0-08-022720-1). Pergamon.

Benson, S. Vere. Observer's Book of Birds. (Observer Bks.). (Illus.). 1977. 4.95 (ISBN 0-684-15204-5, ScribT). Scribner.

Benson, Sally. Jiunior Miss. (YA) (gr. 7-9). 1969. pap. 1.50 (ISBN 0-671-29981-6). PB.

--Junior Miss. (gr. 7-9). 1969. pap. 1.75 (ISBN 0-671-42066-6). Archway.

--Stories of the Gods & Heroes. (gr. 4-6). 1979. pap. 1.75 (ISBN 0-440-98291-X, LFL). Dell.

Benson, Sidney W. Foundations of Chemical Kinetics. 722p. 1981. Repr. of 1960 ed. lib. bdg. write for info. (ISBN 0-89874-194-7). Krieger.

Benson, Susan, ed. see El Shazly, Saad.

Benson, T. G., ed. Kikuyu-English Dictionary. 1964. 24.95x (ISBN 0-19-864405-1). Oxford U Pr.

Benson, T. G., tr. see Barlow, A. R.

Benson, Tedd & Gruber, James. Building the Timber Frame House. (Illus.). 1980. 17.95 (ISBN 0-684-16446-9, ScribT). Scribner.

Benson, Warren E., Jr., ed. The Car Buyer's Illustrated Fact & Figure Guidebook 1981. LC 80-319. (Illus.). 160p. (Orig.). 1981. pap. 5.00 (ISBN 0-394-17881-5, E 761, Ever). Grove.

--Car Buyer's Illustrated Fact & Figure Book 1980. (Illus.). 1981. pap. 5.00 (ISBN 0-394-17881-5, E761, Ever). Grove.

Benson, William E. Retinal Detachment Diagnosis & Treatment. (Illus.). 208p. 1980. text ed. 27.50 (ISBN 0-06-140410-1, Harper Medical). Har-Row.

Bensoussan, A. & Lions, J. L., eds. Analysis & Optimization of Systems: Proceedings. (Lecture Notes in Control & Information Sciences Ser.: Vol. 28). 999p. 1981. pap. 57.90 (ISBN 0-387-10472-0). Springer-Verlag.

Benstead, C. R. Portrait of Cambridge. LC 68-99210. (Portrait Bks.). (Illus.). 1968. 10.50x (ISBN 0-7091-0112-0). Intl Pubns Serv.

Benston, George J. Contemporary Cost Accounting & Control. 2nd ed. LC 76-27552. 1977. pap. 9.95 (ISBN 0-8221-0186-6). CBI Pub.

--Corporate Financial Disclosure in the UK & the USA. 1976. 21.95 (ISBN 0-347-01133-0, 00409-X, Pub. by Saxon Hse.). Lexington Bks.

Bent, Arthur C. Life Histories of North American Birds of Prey, 2 vols. (Illus.). Set. 22.00 (ISBN 0-8446-1630-3). Peter Smith.

--Life Histories of North American Flycatchers, Larks, Swallows & Their Allies. (Illus.). 12.00 (ISBN 0-8446-1634-6). Peter Smith.

--Life Histories of North American Jays, Crows & Titmice, 2 vols. (Illus.). Set. 18.00 (ISBN 0-8446-1638-9). Peter Smith.

--Life Histories of North American Marsh Birds. (Illus.). 1927. pap. 6.50 (ISBN 0-486-21082-0). Dover.

--Life Histories of North American Nuthatches, Wrens, Thrashers & Their Allies. (Illus.). 111.50 (ISBN 0-8446-1640-0). Peter Smith.

Bent, Margaret. Dunstaple. (Studies of Composers: No. 17). 96p. 1981. pap. 14.95 (ISBN 0-19-315225-8). Oxford U Pr.

Bent, Ralph D. & McKinley, James L. Aircraft Electricity & Electronics. rev. ed. (Aviation Technology Ser.). (Illus.). 432p. 1981. pap. text ed. 16.95x (ISBN 0-07-004793-6, G). McGraw.

Bent, Robert J. & Sethares, George C. Business Basic. LC 79-18502. 1980. pap. text ed. 11.95 (ISBN 0-8185-0359-9). Brooks-Cole.

--Fortran. LC 80-28581. 448p. (Orig.). 1981. pap. text ed. 16.95 (ISBN 0-8185-0436-6). Brooks-Cole.

Bent, Samuel A., ed. Familiar Short Sayings of Great Men. LC 68-30643. 1968. Repr. of 1887 ed. 22.00 (ISBN 0-8103-3182-9). Gale.

Bent, Susan, ed. Back in Town. LC 80-23860. (Illus.). 1980. pap. text ed. 7.95 (ISBN 0-918606-02-0). Heidelberg Graph.

Bente, Elizabeth H. The Farm Plan. 64p. 1981. 6.00 (ISBN 0-682-49671-5). Exposition.

Benteen, John. Bandolero. (Fargo). 1977. pap. 1.25 (ISBN 0-505-51144-4). Tower Bks.

--Bounty Killer. (Sundance: No. 15). 1979. pap. 1.25 (ISBN 0-8439-0704-5, Leisure Bks). Nordon Pubns.

--Dakota Badlands. (Fargo Ser.). 1977. pap. 1.50 (ISBN 0-505-51173-8). Tower Bks.

--Dakota Territory. (Sundance: No. 3). 1979. pap. 1.75 (ISBN 0-8439-0708-8, Leisure Bks). Nordon Pubns.

--Dead Man's Canyon. (Sundance: No. 2). 1979. pap. 1.75 (ISBN 0-8439-0709-6, Leisure Bks). Nordon Pubns.

--Death in the Lava. (Sundance: No. 4). 1979. pap. 1.75 (ISBN 0-8439-0707-X, Leisure Bks). Nordon Pubns.

--Fargo, No. 1. 1980. pap. 1.75 (ISBN 0-505-51481-8). Tower Bks.

--Fargo & the Texas Rangers. 1977. pap. 1.25 (ISBN 0-505-51126-6, BT51126). Tower Bks.

--Fargo No. 3: Alaska Steel. (Orig.). 1980. pap. 1.50 (ISBN 0-505-51502-4). Tower Bks.

--Fargo No. 4: Massacre River. (Orig.). 1980. pap. 1.50 (ISBN 0-505-51521-0). Tower Bks.

--Fargo: Panama Gold, No. 2. 1980. pap. 1.75 (ISBN 0-505-51482-6). Tower Bks.

--Overkill. (Sundance Ser.: No. 1). 1976. pap. 1.50 (Leisure Bks). Nordon Pubns.

--The Pistoleros. (Sundance: No. 5). 1979. pap. 1.75 (ISBN 0-8439-0706-1, Leisure Bks). Nordon Pubns.

--War Party. (Sundance Ser.: No. 14). 1974. pap. 1.50 (Leisure Bks). Nordon Pubns.

--War Trail. (Sundance Ser. No. 19: No. 19). 1976. pap. 1.50 (ISBN 0-8439-0373-2, Leisure Bks). Nordon Pubns.
--The Wild Stallions. (Sundance: No. 7). 1979. pap. 1.75 (ISBN 0-8439-0705-3, Leisure Bks). Nordon Pubns.
Benthall, Jonathan. The Limits of Human Nature: Essays Based on a Course of Lectures Given at the Institute of Contemporary Arts, London. 1974. pap. 3.95 o.p. (ISBN 0-525-47359-9). Dutton.
Bentham see Bentham, Jeremy & Mill, John S.
Bentham, C. G., jt. auth. see Haynes, R. M.
Bentham, Frederick. Art of Stage Lighting. rev. ed. (Illus.). 1976. 16.95 (ISBN 0-87830-009-0). Theatre Arts.
Bentham, G. The Botany of the Voyage of H. M. S. Sulphur: Under the Command of Captain Sir Edward Belcher 1836-42. (Illus.). 1968. 100.00 (ISBN 3-7682-0542-8). Lubrecht & Cramer.
Bentham, Jeremy. A Comment on the Commentaries & a Fragment on Government. Burns, J. H. & Hart, H. L., eds. (Collected Works of Jeremy Bentham Ser.). 1977. text ed. 69.00x (ISBN 0-485-13212-5, Athlone Pr). Humanities.
--The Correspondence of Jeremy Bentham, 3 vols. Sprigge, T. L., ed. Incl. Vols. 1-2. 1752-1780. 1968 (ISBN 0-485-13201-X); Vol. 3. January 1781-October 1788. 1971 (ISBN 0-485-13203-6). text ed. 74.00x ea. (Athlone Pr). Humanities.
--Elements of the Art of Packing As Applied to Special Juries Particularly in Cases of Libel Law. Berkowitz, David & Thorne, Samuel, eds. LC 77-86672. (Classics of English Legal History in the Modern Era Ser.: Vol. 116). 1979. Repr. of 1821 ed. lib. bdg. 55.00 (ISBN 0-8240-3153-9). Garland Pub.
--An Introduction to the Principles of Morals & Legislation. Burns, J. H. & Hart, H. L., eds. (Collected Works of Jeremy Bentham Ser.). 1970. text ed. 47.00x (ISBN 0-485-13211-7, Athlone Pr). Humanities.
--Of Laws in General. Hart, H. L., ed. (Collected Works of Jeremy Bentham Ser.). 1970. text ed. 27.00x (ISBN 0-485-13210-9, Athlone Pr). Humanities.
--Rationale of Judicial Evidence, Specially Applied to English Practice, 5 vols. Berkowitz, David & Thorne, Samuel, eds. LC 77-86645. (Classics of English Legal History in the Modern Era Ser.: Vol. 98). 1979. Set. lib. bdg. 225.00 (ISBN 0-8240-3085-0); lib. bdg. 55.00 ea. Garland Pub.
--A Treatise on Judicial Evidence, Extracted from the Manuscripts of Jeremy Bentham. Dumont, M., ed. xvi, 366p. 1981. Repr. of 1825 ed. lib. bdg. 35.00x (ISBN 0-8377-0318-2). Rothman.
Bentham, Jeremy & Mill, John S. The Utilitarians. Incl. Principles of Morals & Legislation. Bentham; Utilitarianism & on Liberty. Mill, John S. LC 62-2159. pap. 3.50 (ISBN 0-385-08256-8, C265, Anch). Doubleday.
Bentinck, William A. The Correspondence of Lord William Bentinck, Governor General of India 1828-1835, 2 vols. Philips, Cyril H., ed. 1977. 169.00x set (ISBN 0-19-713571-4). Oxford U Pr.
Bentkover, Judith D., jt. auth. see Sloan, Frank A.
Bentley, jt. auth. see Bryson.
Bentley, Anne. The Groggs Day Out. LC 80-2689. 32p. (gr. k-3). 1981. 9.95 (ISBN 0-233-97348-6). Andre Deutsch.
--Groggs Have a Wonderful Summer. (Illus.). (ps-2). 1980. 8.95 (ISBN 0-233-97199-8). Andre Deutsch.
Bentley, Arnold. Music in Education: A Point View. (General Ser.). 125p. 1975. pap. text ed. 10.00x (ISBN 0-85633-066-3, NFER). Humanities.
Bentley, Arthur F., jt. auth. see Dewey, John.
Bentley, Barbara. Mistress Nancy. LC 80-14264. 384p. 1980. 12.95 (ISBN 0-07-016722-2). McGraw.
Bentley, Beth. Country of Resemblances. LC 75-14549. 78p. 1976. 8.95 (ISBN 0-8214-0196-3); pap. 5.95 (ISBN 0-8214-0210-2). Ohio U Pr.
--Phone Calls from the Dead. LC 76-122096. 78p. 1970. 7.00 (ISBN 0-8214-0076-2). Ohio U Pr.
Bentley, D. J., ed. see Keir, David L. & Lawson, Frederick H.
Bentley, E. C. Trent Intervenes. 259p. 1981. pap. price not set (ISBN 0-486-24098-3). Dover.
--Trent's Last Case. LC 75-44955. (Crime Fiction Ser). 1976. Repr. of 1912 ed. lib. bdg. 17.50 (ISBN 0-8240-2353-6). Garland Pub.
--Trent's Last Case. 1976. lib. bdg. 13.95x (ISBN 0-89968-165-4). Lightyear.
--Trent's Own Case. LC 80-7836. 1980. pap. 1.95 (ISBN 0-06-080516-1, P 516, PL). Har-Row.
--Woman in Black. 1976. lib. bdg. 13.95x (ISBN 0-89968-166-2). Lightyear.
Bentley, Eric. Brecht Commentaries. LC 80-998. 320p. (Orig.). 1981. 17.50 (ISBN 0-394-51994-9, GP838, Ever); pap. text ed. 9.50 (ISBN 0-394-17734-7, E743, Ever). Grove.
--Rallying Cries: Three Plays. LC 77-1973. 1977. o.s.i 10.00 o.p. (ISBN 0-915220-23-7); pap. 4.50 o.p. (ISBN 0-915220-24-5, 23034). New Republic.
--A Time to Die & a Time to Live: Two Plays. 1970. pap. 11.40 (ISBN 0-686-66227-X, ST00047). Grove.
Bentley, Eric, ed. From the Modern Repertoire: Series One. Incl. La Parisienne. Becque; The Threepenny Opera. Brecht; Danton's Death. Buchner; The Infernal Machine. Cocteau; Fantasio. De Musset; Sweeney Agonistes. Eliot; The Love of Don Perlimplin. Lorca; Belisa in the Garden. Lorca; Round Dance. Schnitzler; The Snob. Sternheim; A Full Moon in March. Yeats. 424p. 1949. 12.50x (ISBN 0-253-12900-1). Ind U Pr.
--From the Modern Repertoire: Series Two. Incl. Galileo. Brecht; Him. Cummings; The King & The Duke. Fergusson; Electra. Giraudoux; Jest; Satire; Irony. Grabbe; The Dark Tower. MacNeice; The Epidemic. Mirabeau; Venus & Adonis. Obey; Easy Money. Ostrovsky; The Marquis of Keith. Wedekind. (Illus.). 528p. 1952. 15.00x (ISBN 0-253-12901-X). Ind U Pr.
Bentley, Eric, ed. see Pirandello, Luigi.
Bentley, Eric, tr. from German see Brecht, Bertolt.
Bentley, G. Orthopedics, Vol. 1. (Operative Surgery Ser.). 1979. 125.00 (ISBN 0-407-00630-3). Butterworths.
Bentley, G., ed. Orthopedics, Vol. 2. (Operative Surgery Ser.). 1979. 125.00 (ISBN 0-407-00631-1). Butterworths.
Bentley, G. E., ed. see Blake, William.
Bentley, Gerald E. Shakespeare & His Theater. LC 64-11350. (Landmark Eds.). viii, 128p. 1964. 11.50x (ISBN 0-8032-0220-2). U of Nebr Pr.
Bentley, Gerald E., jt. auth. see Millett, Fred B.
Bentley, Howard B., ed. Building Construction Information Sources. LC 64-16502. (Management Information Guide Ser.: No. 2). 1964. 30.00 (ISBN 0-8103-0802-9). Gale.
Bentley, John. A Historical View of the Hindu Astronomy from the Earliest Dawn of That Science in India to the Present Time. LC 5-29507. 1970. Repr. of 1825 ed. 35.00x (ISBN 3-7648-0107-7). Intl Pubns Serv.
--Oldtime Steam Cars. LC 53-4010. (Illus.). 1969. lib. bdg. 3.50 o.p. (ISBN 0-668-02073-3). Arco.
Bentley, Judith. State Government. (American Government Ser.). (Illus.). (gr. 7 up). 1978. PLB 6.90 s&l (ISBN 0-531-01343-X). Watts.
Bentley, K. W. & Kirby, G. W. Techniques of Chemistry: Vol. 4, 2 Pts. Elucidation of Organic Structures by Physical & Chemical Methods. 2nd ed. 1250p. 1972. Pt. 1. 57.00 (ISBN 0-471-92896-8); Pt. 2. 58.00 (ISBN 0-471-92897-6). Wiley.
Bentley, K. W. see Weissberger, A.
Bentley, M. The Liberal Mind 1914-1929. LC 76-11072. (Cambridge Studies in the History & Theory of Politics). 1977. 36.00 (ISBN 0-521-21243-X). Cambridge U Pr.
Bentley, P. J. Comparative Vertebrate Endocrinology. LC 75-10235. (Illus.). 480p. 1976. 52.50 (ISBN 0-521-20726-6); pap. 17.50x (ISBN 0-521-09935-8). Cambridge U Pr.
--Endocrine Pharmacology: Physiological Basis & Theraputic Applications. LC 79-19487. (Illus.). 700p. 1981. 75.00 (ISBN 0-521-22673-2). Cambridge U Pr.
Bentley, Richard. Eight Boyle Lectures on Atheism. Wellek, Rene, ed. LC 75-11196. (British Philosophers & Theologians of the 17th & 18th Centuries: Vol. 3). 1976. Repr. of 1692 ed. lib. bdg. 42.00 (ISBN 0-8240-1752-8). Garland Pub.
--Q. Horatius Flaccus, 2 vols. 3rd ed. Commager, Steele, ed. LC 77-24817. (Latin Poetry Ser.: Vol. 3). 1979. Repr. of 1869 ed. Set. lib. bdg. 73.00 (ISBN 0-8240-2952-6). Garland Pub.
Bentley, Robert H. & Crawford, Samuel D. Black Language Reader. 200p. 1973. pap. 5.95x o.p. (ISBN 0-673-07683-0). Scott F.
Bentley, Sean. Into the Bright Oasis: The Great Knight Reason. 1976. 2.50 (ISBN 0-918116-01-5). Jawbone Pr.
Bentley, Stacy. Weight Training. (Burns Sports Ser.). 156p. Date not set. pap. 4.95 (ISBN 0-695-81572-5). Follett. Postponed.
Bentley, W. A. & Humphreys, W. J. Snow Crystals. (Illus.). 1931. pap. 8.95 (ISBN 0-486-20287-9). Dover.
Bentley, William H., ed. see McCray, Walter A.
Bently, G. E., Jr., ed. Editing Eighteenth Century Novels. (Conference on Editorial Problems Ser.). 1976. lib. bdg. 16.50 (ISBN 0-8240-2408-7). Garland Pub.
Benton, Angelo Ames. The Church Cyclopaedia: A Dictionary of Church Doctrine, History, Organization & Ritual, & Containing Original Articles on Special Topics, Written Expressly for This Work by Bishops, Presbyters, & Laymen. LC 74-31499. 810p. 1975. Repr. of 1883 ed. 32.00 (ISBN 0-8103-4204-9). Gale.
Benton, Arthur L., ed. Dyslexia: An Appraisal of Current Knowledge. (Illus.). 1978. 19.50x o.p. (ISBN 0-19-502384-6). Oxford U Pr.
Benton, Bill, et al. Social Services: Federal Legislation vs. State Implemention. (An Institute Paper). 157p. 1978. pap. 4.50 (ISBN 0-87766-237-1, 23700). Urban Inst.
Benton, Curtis D., Jr. & Welsh, Robert C. Spectacles for Aphakia. (Illus.). 176p. 1977. 17.50 (ISBN 0-398-00135-9). C C Thomas.
Benton, Elbert J. The Movement for Peace Without a Victory During the Civil War. LC 70-176339. (The American Scene Ser.). 1972. Repr. of 1918 ed. lib. bdg. 12.50 (ISBN 0-306-70420-X). Da Capo.
Benton, Gregor, tr. see Wang Fan-Hsi.
Benton, John. Cindy. 1978. pap. 2.50 (ISBN 0-8007-8319-0, Spire). Revell.
--Lori. (Spire Bks.). 160p. 1980. pap. 2.50 (ISBN 0-8007-8385-9). Revell.
Benton, John B. Managing the Organizational Decision Process. LC 72-12933. (Illus.). 288p. 1973. 19.95 (ISBN 0-669-85589-8). Lexington Bks.
Benton, Mrs. L. G. see Methvin, John J.
Benton, Minnie M. Boomtown: A Portrait of Burkburnett. 7.95 (ISBN 0-685-48792-X). Nortex Pr.
Benton, Peggie & Lyon, Ninette. Eggs, Milk & Cheese. 1971. 10.95 (ISBN 0-571-08302-1, Pub. by Faber & Faber). Merrimack Bk Serv.
Benton, Peggie, jt. auth. see Lyon, Ninette.
Benton, Richard. Bedlam Patterns: Love & the Idea of Madness in Poe's Fiction. 1979. pap. 2.75 (ISBN 0-910556-13-X). Enoch Pratt.
Benton, Ted. Philosophical Foundations of the Three Sociologies. (International Library of Sociology). 1978. pap. 8.95 (ISBN 0-7100-0045-6). Routledge & Kegan.
--Philosophical Foundations of the Three Sociologies. (International Library of Sociology Ser). 1977. 21.00x (ISBN 0-7100-8593-1). Routledge & Kegan.
Benton, Thomas H. An Artist in America. 3rd rev. ed. LC 68-20096. (Illus.). 1968. 15.00 o.p. (ISBN 0-8262-0071-0). U of Mo Pr.
Bentov, Itzhak. Stalking the Wild Pendulum: On the Mechanics of Consciousness. LC 76-46349. 1977. pap. 6.95 (ISBN 0-525-47458-7). Dutton.
Bentsi-Enchill, Kwamina, jt. auth. see Smock, David R.
Bentwich, Norman. For Zion's Sake: A Biography of Judah L. Magnes. (Return to Zion Ser.). (Illus.). 329p. 1980. Repr. of 1954 ed. lib. bdg. 25.00x (ISBN 0-87991-144-1). Porcupine Pr.
Bentz, Edward J., Jr. & Salmon, Eliahi J. Synthetic Fuels Technology Overviews with Health & Environmental Impacts. 136p. 1981. text ed. 19.95 (ISBN 0-250-40423-0). Ann Arbor Science.
Bentz, William F., jt. ed. see Sterling, Robert R.
Bentzen, Aage & Andelson, G. W., eds. King & Messiah. 2nd ed. 1970. 12.50x o.p. (ISBN 0-631-12850-6, Pub. by Basil Blackwell). Biblio Dist.
Benveniste, Guy. Bureaucracy. LC 77-75390. 1977. lib. bdg. 14.00x (ISBN 0-87835-063-2); pap. text ed. 7.95x (ISBN 0-87835-059-4). Boyd & Fraser.
--Politics of Expertise. 2nd ed. 1977. text ed. 14.00x (ISBN 0-87835-067-5); pap. text ed. 7.95x (ISBN 0-87835-060-8). Boyd & Fraser.
Benvenuti, Judi & Cataldo, Mary Ann. Morristown: The War Years, Seventeen Seventy-Five to Seventeen Eighty-Three. (Illus.). 124p. 1979. 15.95 (ISBN 0-686-27870-4, Pub. by Eastern Natl Park). Eastern Acorn.
Benward, Bruce. Music in Theory & Practice. 2nd ed. 1980. 13.95 (ISBN 0-697-03423-2). Wm C Brown.
Ben-Yami, M. Tuna Fishing with Pole & Line. 1980. 21.50x (ISBN 0-686-64740-8, Pub. by Fishing News England); pap. 19.50x. State Mutual Bk.
Ben-Yehuda, Eliezer, ed. Dictionary & Thesaurus of the Hebrew Language, 8 Vols. Set. 150.00 (ISBN 0-498-07038-7, Yoseloff); lea. bd. set o.p. 250.00 (ISBN 0-498-08915-0). A S Barnes.
Benz, A. Facts About Finland. 1976. pap. 4.50x (ISBN 9-5110-4105-3, F525). Vanous.
Benz, C. William. Passion: Program for Algebraic Sequences Specifically of Input-Output Nature. LC 72-126524. (Illus.). 1971. pap. text ed. 7.95x (ISBN 0-7167-0441-2). W H Freeman.
Benz, Morris. Flowers: Free Form-Interpretive Design. LC 59-15356. (Illus.). 1960. 15.00 (ISBN 0-89096-103-4). San Jacinto.
--Flowers: Geometric Form. LC 66-25443. (Illus.). 1973. 35.00 o.p. (ISBN 0-911982-07-8). San Jacinto.
--Flowers: Geometric Form. rev., 5th ed. LC 80-50568. (Illus.). 336p. 1980. 42.50 (ISBN 0-911982-12-4). San Jacinto.
Benziger, Barbara. Controlling Your Weight. (gr. 7-9). 1975. pap. 1.25 o.s.i. (ISBN 0-671-29735-X). Archway.
--Controlling Your Weight. (Illus.). (YA) (gr. 7-9). 1975. pap. 1.25 (ISBN 0-671-29735-X). PB.
--Controlling Your Weight: A Concise Guide. LC 73-5888. (Career Concise Guides Ser.). (gr. 5 up). 1973. PLB 4.90 o.p. (ISBN 0-531-02639-6). Watts.
Benziger, Barbara F. The Prison of My Mind. LC 80-54811. 184p. 1981. pap. 5.95 (ISBN 0-8027-7172-6). Walker & Co.
Benzing, David H. Biology of the Bromeliads. 300p. (Orig.). 1980. pap. write for info (ISBN 0-916422-21-6). Mad River.
Benzoni, Juliette. Belle Catherine. 1973. pap. 1.95 (ISBN 0-380-01855-1, 36525). Avon.
--Catherine's Time for Love. 1973. pap. 1.95 (ISBN 0-380-40949-6, 40949). Avon.
--A Snare for Catherine. 1976. pap. 1.95 o.p. (ISBN 0-380-00651-0, 41343). Avon.
Beowulf. Beowulf, the Oldest English Epic. Kennedy, Charles W., tr. 1940. 11.95x (ISBN 0-19-500929-0). Oxford U Pr.
Bequai, August. The Cashless Society: EFTS at the Crossroads. LC 80-21517. 350p. 1981. 19.95 (ISBN 0-471-05654-5, Pub. by Wiley-Interscience). Wiley.
--Computer Crime. LC 77-3857. 1978. 17.95 (ISBN 0-669-01728-0). Lexington Bks.
--Organized Crime. LC 77-18574. 1979. 17.95 (ISBN 0-669-02104-0). Lexington Bks.
--White-Collar Crime. LC 77-11242. (Illus.). 1978. 16.95 (ISBN 0-669-01900-3). Lexington Bks.
Beraha, E. & Shipigler, B. Color Metallography. (TN 690.b47). 1977. 68.00 (ISBN 0-87170-045-X). ASM.
Beran, George. Viral Zoonoses. (CRC Handbook in Zoonoses Sect B: Vol. 1). 480p. 1981. 64.95 (ISBN 0-8493-2911-6). CRC Pr.
Beran, George, ed. Viral Zoonoses. (Handbook Series in Zoonoses Sect. B: Vol. 2). 464p. 1981. 64.95 (ISBN 0-8493-2912-4). CRC Pr.
Beran, George & Steele, James H., eds. Handbook Series in Zoonoses: Viral Zoonoses. (CRC Handbook Ser. in Zoonoses). 1980. 64.95 (ISBN 0-8493-2911-6). CRC Pr.
Beran, J. A. & Brady, J. E. Laboratory Manual for General Chemistry. 1978. pap. text ed. 10.95 (ISBN 0-471-03290-5). Wiley.
Beran, Nancy J. & Toomey, Beverly G., eds. Mentally Ill Offenders & the Criminal Justice System: Issues in Forensic Services. LC 78-19782. (Praeger Special Studies). 1979. 24.95 (ISBN 0-03-046426-9). Praeger.
Beran, Nancy J., jt. ed. see Allen, Harry E.
Beranek, William & Ranis, Gustav, eds. Science, Technology & Economic Development: A Historical & Comparative Study. LC 78-5660. 1978. 32.95 (ISBN 0-03-041801-1). Praeger.
Berard, Victor. British Imperialism & Commercial Supremacy. LC 70-80613. 298p. 1973. Repr. of 1906 ed. 16.50 (ISBN 0-86527-018-X). Fertig.
Berardo, Felix M., jt. ed. see Nye, F. Ivan.
Berberi, Dilaver. Arabic in a Nutshell. (Funk & W Bk.). 256p. 1975. pap. 2.95 o.s.i. (ISBN 0-308-10145-6, F106, TYC-T). T Y Crowell.
Berberian, Sterling K. An Introduction to Hilbert Space. 2nd ed. LC 75-29231. 206p. 1976. text ed. 9.95 (ISBN 0-8284-0287-6). Chelsea Pub.
--Measure & Integration. LC 74-128871. 1970. Repr. of 1965 ed. text ed. 11.95 (ISBN 0-8284-0241-8). Chelsea Pub.
Berbrich, Joan D. One Hundred One Ways to Learn Vocabulary. (Orig.). (gr. 10-12). 1971. wkbk. 6.25 (ISBN 0-87720-343-1). AMSCO Sch.
--Wide World of Words. (Orig.). (gr. 7-10). 1975. 7.17 (ISBN 0-87720-340-7). AMSCO Sch.
--Writing About Curious Things. (Orig.). (gr. 8). 1981. pap. text ed. 5.67 (ISBN 0-87720-394-6). AMSCO Sch.
--Writing About Fascinating Things. (Orig.). (gr. 8-10). 1980. wkbk. 5.83 (ISBN 0-87720-391-1). AMSCO Sch.
--Writing About People & Yourself. (gr. 10-12). 1979. wkbk. 7.33 (ISBN 0-87720-382-2). AMSCO Sch.
--Writing Creatively. (gr. 10-12). 1977. wkbk 9.08 (ISBN 0-87720-375-X). AMSCO Sch.
--Writing Logically. (gr. 11-12). 1978. wkbk 8.00 (ISBN 0-87720-332-6). AMSCO Sch.
--Writing Practically. (Orig.). (gr. 10-12). 1976. wkbk. 7.17 (ISBN 0-87720-338-5). AMSCO Sch.
Berchman, Evelyn. Victims of Piracy: The Admirality Court 1575-1678. 1978. 22.50 (ISBN 0-241-10105-0, Pub by Hamish Hamilton). David & Charles.
Berci. Endoscopy. (Illus.). 1976. 84.50 o.p. (ISBN 0-8385-2216-5). ACC.

Berci, George & Hamlin, J. A. Operative Biliary Radiology. (Illus.). 290p. 1980. lib. bdg. 37.50 (ISBN 0-683-00602-9). Williams & Wilkins.

Bercovici, Alfred. House of Bondage. 1978. pap. 1.75 o.p. (ISBN 0-445-04170-6). Popular Lib.

Bercovici, Konrad. The Story of the Gypsies. LC 78-164051. (Illus.). xii, 294p. 1975. Repr. of 1928 ed. 20.00 (ISBN 0-8103-4042-9). Gale.

Bercovitch, S. The American Puritan Imagination. LC 73-94136. 256p. 1974. 36.00 (ISBN 0-521-20392-9); pap. 10.50x (ISBN 0-521-09841-6). Cambridge U Pr.

Bercuson. Opening the Canadian West. (gr. 6-10). 1980. PLB 6.90 (ISBN 0-531-00448-1). Watts.

Bercuson, David J. Confrontation at Winnipeg: Labour, Industrial Relations & the General Strike. 224p. 1974. 10.00x o.p. (ISBN 0-7735-0215-7); pap. 9.95 (ISBN 0-7735-0226-2). McGill-Queens U Pr.

Berczynski, Thomas, tr. see Olesha, Yury.

Berdanier, Carolyn D., ed. Carbohydrate Metabolism: Regulation & Physiological Role, Vol. 1. LC 76-27944. (Advances in Modern Nutrition Ser.). 1976. 24.50 o.p. (ISBN 0-470-15047-5). Halsted Pr.

Berdecio, Robert, ed. see Posada, Jose G.

Berdichewsky, Bernardo, ed. Anthropology & Change in Rural Areas. (World Anthropology Ser.). (Illus.). 564p. text ed. 52.65x (ISBN 90-279-7810-7). Mouton.

Berdie, Douglas R. & Anderson, John F. Questionnaires: Design & Use. LC 74-4174. 1974. 10.00 (ISBN 0-8108-0719-X). Scarecrow.

Berdie, Mitchell, jt. auth. see Muldoon, Joseph A.

Berdine, jt. auth. see Blackhurst.

Berdine, William H. & Cegelka, Patricia T. Teaching the Trainable Retarded. (Special Education Ser.). 312p. 1980. text ed. 16.95 (ISBN 0-675-08200-5). Merrill.

Berdy, Janos. Heterocyclic Antibiotics. (CRC Handbook of Antibiotic Compounds: Vol. 5). 640p. 1981. 62.95 (ISBN 0-8493-3456-X). CRC Pr.

Berdy, Janos, ed. Handbook of Antibiotic Compounds, 4 vols. Incl. Vol. 1. Carbohydrate Antibiotics. 59.95 (ISBN 0-8493-3451-9); Vol. 2. Macrocyclic Lactone (Lactam) Antibiotics. 64.95 (ISBN 0-8493-3452-7); Vol. 3. 59.95 (ISBN 0-8493-3453-5); Vol. 4, 2 pts. Pt. 1. 64.95 (ISBN 0-8493-3454-3); Pt. 2, 576p. 59.95 (ISBN 0-8493-3455-1). 1980. CRC Pr.

Berdyaev, Nicholas. Dostoevsky. pap. 2.95 o.p. (ISBN 0-452-00415-2, F415, Mer). NAL.

Berdyaev, Nicolas. Origin of Russian Communism. 1960. pap. 3.95 (ISBN 0-472-06034-1, 34, AA). U of Mich Pr.

--The Origin of Russian Communism. 239p. 1980. Repr. of 1937 ed. lib. bdg. 30.00 (ISBN 0-89760-047-9). Telegraph Bks.

--Russian Revolution. 1961. pap. 1.75 o.p. (ISBN 0-472-06055-4, 55, AA). U of Mich Pr.

Bereano, Philip L. Technology As a Social & Political Phenomenon. LC 76-18723. 1976. text ed. 22.95 (ISBN 0-471-06875-6). Wiley.

Beregi, Oscar & Benis, Leslie M. How to Raise & Train a Komondor. (Orig.). 1966. pap. 1.79 o.p. (ISBN 0-87666-328-5, DS1093). TFH Pubns.

Bereiter, Carl & Englemann, S. Teaching Disadvantaged Children in the Preschool. (Illus.). 1966. text ed. 18.95 (ISBN 0-13-892455-4). P-H.

Berelson, Bernard. Content Analysis in Communications Research. 1971. 20.00 (ISBN 0-02-841210-9). Hafner.

Berelson, Bernard & Ansheim, Lester. The Library's Public: A Report of the Public Library Inquiry. LC 75-31430. 174p. 1976. Repr. of 1949 ed. lib. bdg. 21.50x (ISBN 0-8371-8499-1, BELP). Greenwood.

Berenbaum, Esai. Municipal Public Safety: A Guide for the Implementation of Consolidated Police-Fire Services. (Illus.). 104p. 1977. 15.75 (ISBN 0-398-03612-8). C C Thomas.

Berenbaum, Michael. The Vision of the Void: Theological Reflections on the Works of Elie Wiesel. LC 78-27321. 1979. 15.00 (ISBN 0-8195-5030-2, Pub. by Wesleyan U Pr). Columbia U Pr.

Berenblum, I. Cancer Research Today. 1967. 16.50 (ISBN 0-08-012451-8); pap. 8.50 (ISBN 0-08-012452-6). Pergamon.

Berend, Ivan T. & Ranki, Gyorgy, trs. Economic Development in East Central Europe. LC 73-6542. (Institute on East Central Europe Ser.). 1976. pap. 10.00x (ISBN 0-231-08349-1). Columbia U Pr.

Berendes, H. W., jt. ed. see Garattini, S.

Berenson, Bernard. Studies in Medieval Painting. LC 73-153884. (Graphic Art Ser.). (Illus.). 148p. 1971. Repr. of 1930 ed. lib. bdg. 35.00 (ISBN 0-306-70292-4). Da Capo.

Berenson, Bernard G. & Mitchel, Kevin M. Confrontation for Better or Worse. LC 74-75370. (Perspectives Ser.). (Illus.). 106p. 1974. pap. text ed. 10.95 (ISBN 0-914234-81-1). Human Res Dev Pr.

Berenson, F. M. Understanding Persons: Personal & Impersonal Relations. 19.95 (ISBN 0-312-83154-4). St Martin.

Berenson, M. & Levine, D. Basic Business Statistics: Concepts & Applications. 1979. 21.00 (ISBN 0-13-057596-8); studyguide & wkbk. 7.50 (ISBN 0-13-057588-7). P-H.

Berenstain, Jan, jt. auth. see Berenstain, Stan.

Berenstain, Janice, jt. auth. see Berenstain, Stan.

Berenstain, Janice, jt. auth. see Berenstain, Stanley.

Berenstain, Stan & Berenstain, Jan. How to Teach Your Children About Sex. 1980. pap. 2.95. Ballantine.

Berenstain, Stan & Berenstain, Janice. The Berenstain Bears Go to School. LC 77-79853. (Picturebacks Ser.). (Illus.). (ps-2). 1978. PLB 4.99 (ISBN 0-394-93736-8, BYR); pap. 1.25 (ISBN 0-394-83736-3). Random.

--Papa's Pizza: A Berenstain Bear Sniffy Book. LC 78-55907. (Illus.). (ps-2). 1978. 0.95 (ISBN 0-394-83922-6, BYR). Random.

Berenstain, Stanley & Berenstain, Janice. The Bears Almanac. (gr. 1-4). 1973. 3.95 (ISBN 0-394-82693-0, BYR); PLB 5.99 (ISBN 0-394-92693-5). Random.

--The New Baby. LC 74-2535. (Picturebacks Ser). (Illus.). 32p. (Orig.). (ps-1). 1974. pap. 1.25 (ISBN 0-394-82908-5, BYR). Random.

Bereny, et al. Baseline Study of U.S. Industry Solar Exports for Nineteen Seventy-Nine. 73p. 1981. Repr. of 1980 ed. 35.00 (ISBN 0-89934-080-6). Solar Energy Info.

Bereny, J. A., ed. see Central Intelligence Agency.

Bereny, J. A., ed. see Energy Information Administration.

Bereny, J. A., ed. see Rockwell International, et al.

Bereny, Justin, ed. Alcohol Fuels Information Series, Vol. 5: Gasohol. Date not set. price not set (ISBN 0-89934-033-4, B942-SS); pap. price not set (ISBN 0-89934-034-2, B042-SS). Solar Energy Info.

--Alcohol Fuels Information Series, Vol. 6: Ethanol. Date not set. price not set (ISBN 0-89934-035-0, B943-SS); pap. price not set (ISBN 0-89934-036-9, B043-SS). Solar Energy Info.

--Alcohol Fuels Information Series, Vol. 7: Methanol. Date not set. price not set (ISBN 0-89934-037-7, B944-SS); pap. price not set (ISBN 0-89934-038-5, B044-SS). Solar Energy Info.

Bereny, Justin & Kittle, Linda, eds. Alcohol Fuels Information Series, Vol. 1: U. S. Government Overviews, Gasohol: the Alcohol Fuel Issue Brief; Gasohol: a Technical Memorandum; Will Gasohol Help Power America's Future? the Report of the Alcohol Fuels Policy Review; LC 80-51918. 1980. 49.95 (ISBN 0-89934-031-8, B941-SS); pap. 34.95 (ISBN 0-89934-032-6, B041-SS). Solar Energy Info.

Bereny, Justin A. Survey of the Emerging Solar Energy Industry. De Winter, Francis, ed. LC 77-71664. (Illus.). 1977. 69.50 (ISBN 0-930978-00-5); pap. cancelled (ISBN 0-930978-01-3). Solar Energy Info.

Bereny, Justin A., ed. State Government Overviews. (Alcohol Fuels Information Ser.: Vol. 4). 1981. 49.95 (ISBN 0-89934-115-2); pap. 34.95 (ISBN 0-89934-114-4). Solar Energy Info.

Beres, Louis R. Apocalypse: Nuclear Catastrophe in World Politics. LC 80-13541. (Illus.). 1980. 20.00 (ISBN 0-226-04360-6). U of Chicago Pr.

--People, States, & World Order. LC 80-83099. 300p. 1981. pap. text ed. 7.95 (ISBN 0-87581-267-8). Peacock Pubs.

Beres, Louis R. & Targ, Harry R., eds. Planning Alternative World Futures: Values, Methods, & Models. LC 74-33030. (Illus.). 342p. 1975. text ed. 25.95 o.p. (ISBN 0-275-05340-7); pap. text ed. 8.95 o.p. (ISBN 0-275-89420-7). Praeger.

Beresfod, Elisabeth. The Treasure Hunters. (Illus.). (gr. 3-7). 1980. 7.95 (ISBN 0-525-66702-4). Elsevier-Nelson.

Beresford, Anne. Songs a Thracian Taught Me. 64p. 1981. 8.95 (ISBN 0-7145-2724-6, Pub. by M. Boyars); pap. 4.50 (ISBN 0-7145-2725-4). Merrimack Bk Serv.

Beresford, Elisabeth. Teasure Hunters. (gr. 3-7). 1980. 7.95 o.p. (ISBN 0-525-66702-4). Elsevier-Nelson.

Beresford, Elizabeth. Curious Magic. (gr. 4-8). 1980. 7.95 (ISBN 0-525-66682-6). Elsevier-Nelson.

Beresford, M. W. & St. Joseph, J. K. Medieval England: An Aerial Survey. 2nd ed. LC 77-90200. (Cambridge Air Surveys). 1979. 29.95 (ISBN 0-521-21961-2). Cambridge U Pr.

Beresford, Michael. Complete Russian Course for Beginners. 1965. 14.50x (ISBN 0-19-815642-1). Oxford U Pr.

Beresford, W. A. Chonroid Bone, Secondary Cartilage & Metaplasia. LC 80-13411. (Illus.). 360p. (Orig.). 1980. text ed. 42.50 (ISBN 0-8067-0261-3). Urban & S.

Beresin, Victor E. & Schiesser, Frank J. The Neutral Zone in Complete & Partial Dentures. 2nd ed. LC 78-59658. (Illus.). 1978. text ed. 39.50 (ISBN 0-8016-0617-9). Mosby.

Bereswell, Joe, jt. auth. see Moriarty, Tim.

Berey, David. Earth Science. LC 57-58736. (High School Regents Exams & Answer Ser.). (gr. 9-12). 1976. pap. 3.95 (ISBN 0-8120-0194-X). Barron.

Berezin, B. D. Coordination Compounds of Porphyrins & Phthalocyanine. 256p. 1981. 52.00 (ISBN 0-471-27857-2, Pub. by Wiley-Interscience). Wiley.

Berezin, Nancy. The Gentle Birth Book: A Practical Guide to Leboyer Family-Centered Delivery. 1981. pap. 2.95 (ISBN 0-671-41990-0). PB.

Berg, Alan. The Nutrition Factor: Its Role in National Development. 1973. 14.95 (ISBN 0-8157-0914-5); pap. 5.95 (ISBN 0-8157-0913-7). Brookings.

Berg, Barbara. The Remembered Gate: Origins of American Feminism - the Woman & the City 1800-1860. (Urban Life in America Ser.). 1978. 16.95x (ISBN 0-19-502280-7). Oxford U Pr.

Berg, C. Circumpolar Problems: Habitat, Economy & Social Relations in the Arctic. 1973. text ed. 46.00 (ISBN 0-08-017038-2). Pergamon.

Berg, Dave. Dave Berg Looks Around. (Mad Ser.). (Illus.). 192p. 1975. pap. 1.75 (ISBN 0-446-94399-1). Warner Bks.

--Dave Berg Looks at Living. (Mad Ser.). (Illus.). 192p. (Orig.). 1973. pap. 1.50 (ISBN 0-446-88735-8). Warner Bks.

--Dave Berg Looks at Modern Thinking. (Mad Ser.). (Illus.). 192p. 1976. pap. 1.75 (ISBN 0-446-94401-7). Warner Bks.

--Dave Berg Looks at Things. (Mad Ser.). (Illus.). 192p. 1974. pap. 1.75 (ISBN 0-446-94403-3). Warner Bks.

--Dave Berg: Our Sick World. (Mad Ser.). (Illus.). 1978. pap. 1.75 (ISBN 0-446-94404-1). Warner Bks.

--Mad's Dave Berg Looks, Listens & Laughs. (Mad Ser.). (Illus.). 1979. pap. 1.50 (ISBN 0-446-88667-X). Warner Bks.

Berg, David N., jt. auth. see Mirvis, Philip H.

Berg, Francie M. How to Lose Weight the Action Way: Young Adult-Teen Edition. (Illus.). 176p. (gr. 9 up). 1980. 12.95 (ISBN 0-918532-03-5); pap. 8.95 (ISBN 0-918532-04-3); leaders guide for action groups, 48p. 4.95 (ISBN 0-918532-05-1). Flying Diamond Bks.

Berg, Gary. Using Calculators for Business Problems. LC 78-10173. 1979. pap. text ed. 10.75 (ISBN 0-574-20565-9, 13-3565); instr's guide avail. (ISBN 0-574-20566-7, 13-3566). SRA.

Berg, Gertrude & Waldo, Myra. Molly Goldberg Jewish Cookbook. 1972. pap. 1.75 o.s.i. (ISBN 0-515-04777-5, V2398). Jove Pubns.

Berg, H. K. & Giloi, W. K., eds. The Use of Formal Specification of Software & Firmware. (Informatik-Fachberichte Ser.: Vol. 36). 388p. 1981. pap. 27.50 (ISBN 0-387-10442-9). Springer-Verlag.

Berg, H. W., jt. auth. see Amerine, Maynard A.

Berg, Ian, jt. ed. see Hersov, Lionel.

Berg, Ivar, ed. Sociological Perspectives on Labor Markets. (Quantitative Studies in Social Relations). 1981. price not set. Acad Pr.

Berg, Ivar, et al. Managers & Work Reform: A Limited Engagement. LC 77-83165. (Illus.). 1978. 15.95 (ISBN 0-02-902900-7). Free Pr.

Berg, Ivar E., Jr., ed. Human Resources & Economic Welfare. LC 72-8331. 200p. 1972. 17.00x (ISBN 0-231-03710-4). Columbia U Pr.

Berg, J. M. Genetic Counseling in Relation to Mental Retardation. 1971. pap. 6.25 (ISBN 0-08-016315-7). Pergamon.

Berg, J. M., et al. The DeLange Syndrome. LC 72-124065. 1970. 22.00 (ISBN 0-08-016125-1). Pergamon.

Berg, Jean. Wee Little Man. (Beginning-to-Read Ser.). (ps-3). 1963. 3.95 o.p. (ISBN 0-695-89220-7); lib. ed. 2.97 o.p. (ISBN 0-695-49220-9); pap. 1.50 o.p. (ISBN 0-695-39220-4). Follett.

Berg, Larry, jt. auth. see Schmidhauser, John.

Berg, Leila. Reading & Loving. 1976. 13.50 (ISBN 0-7100-8475-7); pap. 4.95 (ISBN 0-7100-8476-5). Routledge & Kegan.

Berg, Leo Van Den see Van Den Berg, Leo, et al.

Berg, Mark R., et al. Jobs & Energy in Michigan: The Next Twenty Years. LC 80-24884. (Illus.). 262p. 1981. 17.95 (ISBN 0-87944-264-6); pap. 11.95 (ISBN 0-87944-263-8). U of Mich Soc Res.

Berg, Mary G., tr. see Moreno, Cesar F. & Schulman, Ivan A.

Berg, Maxine. The Machinery Question & the Making of Political Economy: 1815-1848. LC 79-51223. (Illus.). 1980. 39.50 (ISBN 0-521-22782-8). Cambridge U Pr.

--Technology & Toil: In 19th Century Britain. (Illus.). 1979. text ed. 26.00x (ISBN 0-906336-02-3); pap. text ed. 10.50x (ISBN 0-906336-03-1). Humanities.

Berg, Miguel. El Placer De Estudiar la Biblia. 127p. (Orig., Span.). 1973. pap. 2.50 o.s.i. (ISBN 0-89922-026-6). Edit Caribe.

Berg, Miguel, jt. auth. see Lebar, Lois.

Berg, Patty & Schiewe, March. Inside Golf for Women. LC 77-75715. (Inside Ser.). (Illus.). 1977. 7.95 o.p. (ISBN 0-8092-8041-8); pap. 4.95 (ISBN 0-8092-7738-7). Contemp Bks.

Berg, R. T. & Butterfield, R. M. New Concepts of Cattle Growth. LC 75-32561. 1976. 18.95 (ISBN 0-470-06888-4). Halsted Pr.

Berg, Rick. The Art & Adventure of Traveling Cheaply. 1981. pap. 2.95 (ISBN 0-451-09729-7, E9729, Sig). NAL.

Berg, Robert C., jt. auth. see Landreth, Garry L.

Berg, Sandra B. The Book of Esther: Motifs, Themes & Structure. LC 78-32035. (SBL Dissertation Ser.). 1979. 12.00 (ISBN 0-89130-306-5); pap. 7.50 (ISBN 0-89130-279-4, 060144). Scholars Pr Ca.

Berg, Sheila R., ed. Microbiology for Medical Technologists: PreTest Self-Assessment & Review. LC 78-51703. (PreTest Self-Assessment & Review Ser.). (Illus.). 1979. pap. 9.95 (ISBN 0-07-051572-7). McGraw-Pretest.

Berg, Stephen. With Akhmatova at the Black Gates. LC 80-14469. 1981. 10.00 (ISBN 0-252-00833-2); pap. 3.95 (ISBN 0-252-00834-0). U of Ill Pr.

Berg, Stephen & Mezey, Robert, eds. Naked Poetry: Recent American Poetry in Open Forms. LC 69-16527. 1969. pap. 7.95 (ISBN 0-672-60669-0). Bobbs.

--The New Naked Poetry: Recent American Poetry in Open Forms. LC 75-12999. 1976. pap. 9.50 (ISBN 0-672-61354-9). Bobbs.

Berg, Stephen, tr. see Sophocles.

Berg, Stuart F., et al, eds. The Oxford American Dictionary. 832p. 1980. pap. 4.95 (ISBN 0-380-51052-9, 51052). Avon.

Berg, William. Early Virgil. 198p. 1974. text ed. 20.75x (ISBN 0-485-11145-4, Athlone Pr). Humanities.

Bergaigne, Abel. Vedic Religion. Paranjpe, V. G., tr. 1978. 25.00 (ISBN 0-89684-006-9, Pub. by Motilal Banarsidass India). Orient Bk Dist.

Bergamini, David. Land & Wildlife of Australia. rev. ed. LC 64-16421. (Life Nature Library). (Illus.). (gr. 5 up). 1968. PLB 8.97 o.p. (ISBN 0-8094-0629-2, Pub. by Time-Life). Silver.

--Universe. LC 62-18337. (Life Nature Library). (Illus.). (gr. 5 up). 1969. PLB 8.97 o.p. (ISBN 0-8094-0619-5, Pub. by Time-Life). Silver.

--The Universe. (Young Readers Library). (Illus.). 1977. lib. bdg. 7.95 (ISBN 0-686-51095-X). Silver.

Bergamini, David, jt. auth. see Margenau, Henry.

Bergan, John J. & Yao, James S., eds. Operative Techniques in Vascular Surgery. 1980. write for info. (ISBN 0-8089-1334-4). Grune.

Bergan, John R. & Dunn, James A. Psychology & Education: A Science for Instruction. LC 75-14321. 542p. 1976. text ed. 23.95 (ISBN 0-471-06910-8). Wiley.

Bergan, John R., jt. auth. see Henderson, Ronald W.

Berge, Andre, et al, eds. Entretiens Sur L'art et la Psychanalyse: Decades Du Centre International De Cerisy-la-Salle. (Nouvelle Serie: No. 6). 1968. pap. 27.05x (ISBN 90-2796-017-8). Mouton.

Berge, Yvonne. Body Alive! Toward an Education in Movement. LC 76-62748. (Illus.). 160p. 1977. 7.95 o.p. (ISBN 0-312-08723-3). St Martin.

Bergelson, David. When All Is Said & Done. Martin, Bernard, tr. from Yiddish. LC 76-25614. xxi, 310p. 1978. 15.00 (ISBN 0-8214-0360-5); pap. 7.25 (ISBN 0-8214-0392-3). Ohio U Pr.

Bergen, Henry, ed. see Lydgate, John.

Bergen, John. All About Upholstering. LC 77-85359. (Illus.). 1978. pap. 7.50 (ISBN 0-8015-0169-5, Hawthorn). Dutton.

Bergen, Stephen F., jt. auth. see Preston, Jack D.

Bergen, T., jt. ed. see Norris, J. R.

Bergen, Werner Von see Von Bergen, Werner.

Bergendoff, Conrad & Lehman, Helmut H., eds. Luther's Works: Church & Ministry II, Vol. 40. LC 55-9893. 1958. 10.95 (ISBN 0-8006-0340-0, 1-340). Fortress.

Bergens, A. & Noakes, D., eds. Prevert Vous Parle. (Fr.). 1968. pap. 8.50 (ISBN 0-13-699231-5). P-H.

Berger. Nineteen Eighty Berger Building Cost File, 4 vols. Incl. Eastern Edition (ISBN 0-442-12214-4); Western Edition; Central Edition (ISBN 0-442-12220-9); Southern Edition (ISBN 0-442-12215-2). 1980. 27.95 ea. Van Nos Reinhold.

--Nineteen Eighty-One Building Cost File, 4 vols, Vol. 1. Incl. Eastern Edition. 34.95 (ISBN 0-442-21240-2); Western Edition. 34.95 (ISBN 0-442-21238-0); Central Edition. 34.95 (ISBN 0-442-21237-2); Southern Edition. 34.95. 1981. Van Nos Reinhold.
--Nineteen Eighty-One Building Cost File, 4 vols, Vol. 2. Incl. Eastern Edition. 24.95 (ISBN 0-442-21235-6); Western Edition. 24.95 (ISBN 0-442-21234-8); Central Editin. 24.95 (ISBN 0-442-21232-1); Southern Edition. 24.95 (ISBN 0-442-21231-3). 1981. Van Nos Reinhold.
Berger, jt. auth. see McCoy.
Berger, et al. Management for Nurses: A Multidisciplinary Approach. 2nd ed. LC 79-19965. 1980. pap. 11.50 (ISBN 0-8016-4815-7). Mosby.
Berger, A., jt. auth. see Pitcher, W.
Berger, Adolf. Encyclopedic Dictionary of Roman Law. LC 53-7641. (Transactions Ser.: Vol. 43, Pt. 2). 1980. Repr. of 1953 ed. 10.00 (ISBN 0-87169-435-2). Am Philos.
Berger & Associated Cost Consultants, Inc. Design Cost File, Nineteen Seventy-Eight. 299p. 1980. pap. text ed. 29.95 (ISBN 0-442-12217-9). Van Nos Reinhold.
Berger, Andrew J., jt. auth. see George, J. C.
Berger, Arthur. Aaron Copland. LC 79-136055. (Illus.). 1971. Repr. of 1953 ed. lib. bdg. 16.50x (ISBN 0-8371-5205-4, BEAC). Greenwood.
Berger, Brian. Beautiful Chicago. Shangle, Robert D., ed. LC 80-13116. (Illus.). 72p. 1980. 14.95 (ISBN 0-89802-117-0); pap. 7.95 (ISBN 0-89802-116-2). Beautiful Am.
--Beautiful Iowa. Shangle, Robert D., ed. LC 79-28596. (Illus.). 72p. 1980. 14.95 (ISBN 0-89802-107-3); pap. 7.95 (ISBN 0-89802-106-5). Beautiful Am.
--Beautiful Louisiana. Shangle, Robert D., ed. (Illus.). 72p. 1981. 14.95 (ISBN 0-89802-111-1); pap. 7.95 (ISBN 0-89802-110-3). Beautiful Am.
--Beautiful New Orleans. Shangle, Robert D., ed. (Illus.). 72p. 1981. 14.95 (ISBN 0-89802-123-5); pap. 7.95 (ISBN 0-89802-122-7). Beautiful Am.
--Beautiful Oklahoma. LC 80-10968. (Illus.). 72p. 1980. 14.95 (ISBN 0-89802-008-5); pap. 7.95 (ISBN 0-89802-007-7). Beautiful Am.
--Beautiful Oregon Country. Shangle, Robert D., ed. LC 79-1107. (Illus.). 72p. 1979. 14.95 (ISBN 0-89802-092-1); pap. 7.95 (ISBN 0-89802-091-3). Beautiful Am.
--Beautiful Vancouver U. S. A. Shangle, Robert D., ed. LC 79-19900. (Illus.). 72p. 1980. 14.95 (ISBN 0-89802-090-5); pap. 7.95 (ISBN 0-89802-089-1). Beautiful Am.
--Beautiful Wyoming. Shangle, Robert D., ed. LC 79-25372. (Illus.). 72p. 1980. 14.95 (ISBN 0-89802-094-8); pap. 7.95 (ISBN 0-89802-093-X). Beautiful Am.
--Beauty of Oregon. Shangle, Robert D., ed. (Illus.). 160p. 1980. 27.50 (ISBN 0-89802-128-6). Beautiful Am.
--Los Angeles: Commemorating Two Hundred Years. Shangle, Robert D., ed. LC 80-16824. 1980. 27.50 (ISBN 0-89802-176-6). Beautiful Am.
Berger, Brigitte & Callahan, Sidney, eds. Child Care & Mediating Structures. 1979. 9.25 (ISBN 0-8447-2162-X); pap. 4.25. Am Enterprise.
Berger, Bruce. Gordon Snidow Portrays the Cowboy Heritage Hangin'on. LC 80-83021. (Illus.). 128p. 1980. 40.00 (ISBN 0-87358-266-7); pap. 18.50 (ISBN 0-87358-265-9); ltd. ed. avail. (ISBN 0-87358-267-5). Northland.
Berger, Carl. Korea Knot. rev. ed. LC 57-7459. 1964. 9.00x o.p. (ISBN 0-8122-7471-7). U of Pa Pr.
Berger, Charles J. How to Raise & Train an Alaskan Malamute. (Orig.). pap. 2.00 (ISBN 0-87666-235-1, DS1042). TFH Pubns.
Berger, Curtis J. Land Ownership & Use: Cases, Statutes & Other Materials. 2nd ed. 1975. 24.50 (ISBN 0-316-09152-9). Little.
Berger, Dorothea. Jean Paul Friedrich Richter. (World Authors Ser.: Germany: No. 192). lib. bdg. 10.95 (ISBN 0-8057-2762-0). Twayne.
Berger, Edward G. The Physiology of Adequate Perfusion. LC 78-15591. (Illus.). 1979. 21.95 (ISBN 0-8016-0618-7). Mosby.
Berger, Elena L. Labour, Race & Colonial Rule: The Copperbelt from 1924 to Independence. (Oxford Studies in African Affairs). 272p. 1974. 29.50x (ISBN 0-19-821690-4). Oxford U Pr.
Berger, Elmer. Memoirs of an Anti-Zionist Jew. 159p. (Orig.). 1978. pap. 5.00x (ISBN 0-911038-87-6, Inst Hist Rev). Noontide.
Berger, Eugenia H. Parents As Partners in the Educational Process. (Illus.). 360p. 1981. pap. text ed. 11.95 (ISBN 0-8016-0637-3). Mosby.
Berger, Evelyn & Winters, Bonnie. Social Studies in the Open Classroom: A Practical Guide. LC 72-97667. 108p. 1973. pap. text ed. 5.00x (ISBN 0-8077-2398-3). Tchrs Coll.
Berger, Evelyn M. Triangle: The Betrayed Wife. LC 70-170883. 1971. 13.95 (ISBN 0-911012-13-3). Nelson-Hall.
Berger, F. Studying Deductive Logic. 1977. pap. 8.95 (ISBN 0-13-858811-2). P-H.
Berger, Fred R. Freedom of Expression. 224p. 1979. pap. text ed. 7.95x (ISBN 0-534-00749-X). Wadsworth Pub.
Berger, Gary S., et al, eds. Second Trimester Abortion. 456p. 1981. text ed. 29.50 (ISBN 0-88416-256-7). PSG Pub.
Berger, Gaston. Recherches Sur les Conditions De la Connaissance Essai D'une Theoretique Pure. Natanson, Maurice, ed. LC 78-66755. (Phenomenology Ser.: Vol. 1). 194p. 1979. lib. bdg. 20.00 (ISBN 0-8240-9569-3). Garland Pub.
Berger, Gene. Bowling for Everyone. (Illus.). 1974. 5.50 o.p. (ISBN 0-312-09380-2). St Martin.
Berger, Gerold. Grand Prix Culinaire. 528p. Date not set. 29.95 (ISBN 0-8436-2196-6). CBI Pub.
Berger, Gilda. All in the Family: Animal Species Around the World. (Science Is What & Why Bk.). (Illus.). 48p. (gr. 7-10). 1981. PLB 5.99 (ISBN 0-698-30730-5). Coward.
--Apes in Fact & Fiction. (gr. 5 up). 1980. PLB 7.90 (ISBN 0-531-04152-2). Watts.
--Home Economics Careers. LC 77-837. (Career Concise Guides Ser.). (gr. 7 up). 1977. PLB 6.45 s&l (ISBN 0-531-01280-8). Watts.
--Kuwait & the Rim of Arabia: Kuwait, Bahrain, Quatar, United Arab Emirates, Yemen, Oman, People's Democratic Republic of Yemen. (First Bks). (Illus.). (gr. 4-6). 1978. PLB 6.45 s&l (ISBN 0-531-02235-8). Watts.
--Learning Disabilities & Handicaps. (Impact Bks.). (Illus.). (gr. 7 up). 1978. PLB 6.90 s&l (ISBN 0-531-01457-6). Watts.
--Physical Disabilities. LC 78-10106. (Illus.). 1979. s&l 7.45 (ISBN 0-531-02927-1). Watts.
Berger, Gilda, jt. auth. see Berger, Melvin.
Berger, H., jt. auth. see Nelson, Richard.
Berger, J. Joel, jt. auth. see Baumel, Howard B.
Berger, Jason. A New Deal for the World: Eleanor Roosevelt & American Foreign Policy, 1920-1962. 240p. 1981. 20.00x (ISBN 0-930888-07-3). Brooklyn Coll Pr.
Berger, Joel S., ed. Making Your News Service More Effective. 1978. looseleaf bdg. 16.50 (ISBN 0-89964-029-X). CASE.
Berger, John. Art in Revolution. LC 68-26045. 1969. pap. 4.95 (ISBN 0-394-41562-0). Pantheon.
Berger, Josef & Wroth, Lawrence C. Discoverers of the New World. LC 60-10300. (American Heritage Junior Library). (Illus.). 153p. (gr. 5 up). 1960. 9.95 (ISBN 0-8281-0353-4, J002-0). Am Heritage.
Berger, Joseph, et al, trs. see Heinle, Erwin & Bacher, Max.
Berger, Karen & Fields, Willa. Pocket Guide to Health Assessment. (Illus.). 1980. pap. text ed. 11.95 (ISBN 0-8359-5582-6). Reston.
Berger, Karle F. Cat in a Monastery. 63p. 1981. 5.95 (ISBN 0-533-04717-X). Vantage.
Berger, Kathleen S. The Developing Person. (Illus.). 1980. 17.95x (ISBN 0-87901-117-3); study guide 5.95x (ISBN 0-87901-118-1). Worth.
Berger, Kermit C. Sun, Soil, & Survival: An Introduction to Soils. LC 72-3608. (Illus.). 371p. pap. 8.95 (ISBN 0-8061-1388-X). U of Okla Pr.
Berger, Klaus. Die Amen-Worte Jesu: Eine Untersuchung zum Problem der Legitimation in apokalyptischer Rede. (Beiheft 39 Zur Zeitschrift fuer Die neutestamentliche Wissenschaft Ser.). (Ger). 1970. 26.00x (ISBN 3-11-006445-6). De Gruyter.
Berger, Louis S. Introductory Statistics: A New Approach for Behavioral Science Students. LC 79-2484. 350p. 1981. text ed. 24.95 (ISBN 0-8236-2775-6). Intl Univs Pr.
Berger, M. L. & Berger, P. J., eds. Group Training Techniques: Cases, Applications & Research. LC 72-9008. 191p. 1973. 24.95 (ISBN 0-470-06960-0). Halsted Pr.
Berger, Margaret A., ed. see Ford Foundation.
Berger, Mark L. The Revolution in the New York Party System: 1840-1860. LC 72-89990. 1973. 11.00 (ISBN 0-8046-9030-8, Natl U). Kennikat.
Berger, Maxine, jt. auth. see Mays, Willie.
Berger, Melvin. Bionics. (Impact Books Ser.). (Illus.). (gr. 7 up). 1978. PLB 6.90 s&l (ISBN 0-531-01354-5). Watts.
--Building Construction. LC 78-6258. (Industry at Work Ser.). (Illus.). (gr. 4-6). 1978. PLB 5.90 s&l (ISBN 0-531-02206-4). Watts.
--Cancer Lab. LC 74-9369. (gr. 8-11). 1975. PLB 8.79 o.p. (ISBN 0-381-99626-3, JD-J). John Day.
--Comets, Meteors & Asteroids. (Illus.). 64p. (gr. 10 up). 1981. PLB 6.99 (ISBN 0-399-61148-7). Putnam.
--Disease Detectives. LC 77-26589. (Scientists at Work Ser.). (Illus.). (gr. 4 up). 1978. 8.95 (ISBN 0-690-03907-7, TYC-J); PLB 8.79 (ISBN 0-690-03908-5). T Y Crowell.
--Energy from the Sun. LC 75-33310. (A Let's-Read-&-Find-Out Bk). (Illus.). 40p. (gr. k-3). 1976. PLB 7.89 (ISBN 0-690-01056-7, TYC-J). T Y Crowell.
--FBI. LC 77-1395. (First Books Ser.). (gr. 4-6). 1977. PLB 6.45 (ISBN 0-531-01285-9). Watts.
--Food Processing Plant. (Industry at Work Ser.). (gr. 4-6). 1977. 5.90 (ISBN 0-531-01336-7). Watts.
--Mad Scientists in Fact & Fiction. (gr. 5 up). 1980. PLB 7.90 (ISBN 0-531-04153-0). Watts.
--Medical Center Lab. LC 76-12964. (Scientists at Work Seires). (Illus.). (gr. 3 up). 1976. PLB 9.89 (ISBN 0-381-99602-6, JD-J). John Day.
--The New Earth Book: Our Changing Planet. LC 79-7828. (Illus.). 128p. (gr. 5 up). 1980. 7.95 (ISBN 0-690-00735-3, TYC-J); PLB 7.89 (ISBN 0-690-04074-1). T Y Crowell.
--The New Water Book. LC 73-3395. (Illus.). 128p. (gr. 3-6). 1973. 7.95 (ISBN 0-690-58146-7, TYC-J). T Y Crowell.
--Oceanography Lab. LC 72-2417. (Scientists at Work Ser.). (Illus.). 128p. (gr. 2-4). 1973. PLB 9.89 (ISBN 0-381-99940-8, A56700, JD-J). John Day.
--Police Lab. LC 75-33198. (Illus.). 1976. PLB 9.89 (ISBN 0-381-99620-4, JD-J). John Day.
--Pollution Lab. LC 73-18542. (Illus.). 128p. (gr. 3-5). 1974. lib. bdg. 9.89 (ISBN 0-381-99629-8, JD-J). John Day.
--Printing Plant. LC 78-2529. (Industry at Work Ser.). (Illus.). (gr. 4-6). 1978. PLB 5.90 s&l (ISBN 0-531-02207-2). Watts.
--South Pole Station. LC 79-132947. (Scientists at Work Ser). (Illus.). (gr. 2-4). 1971. PLB 8.79 (ISBN 0-381-99942-4, A73420, JD-J). John Day.
--The Story of Folk Music. LC 76-18159. (Illus.). (gr. 6 up). 1976. PLB 9.95 (ISBN 0-87599-215-3). S G Phillips.
--The Supernatural: From ESP to UFO's. LC 77-2829. (gr. 6 up). 1977. 8.95 (ISBN 0-381-90054-1, JD-J). John Day.
--Tools of Modern Biology. LC 73-94788. (Illus.). (gr. 5-8). 1970. 7.95 o.p. (ISBN 0-690-83032-7, TYC-J). T Y Crowell.
--The World of Dance. LC 78-14498. (Illus.). (gr. 5 up). 1978. 9.95 (ISBN 0-87599-221-8). S G Phillips.
Berger, Melvin & Berger, Gilda. The New Food Book: Nutrition, Diet, Consumer Tips & Foods of the Future. LC 77-7976. (gr. 4-6). 1978. 7.95 (ISBN 0-690-01295-0, TYC-J); PLB 7.89 (ISBN 0-690-03841-0). T Y Crowell.
Berger, Michael. Firearms in American History. LC 78-11652. (First Bks.). (Illus.). (gr. 5 up). 1979. PLB 6.45 (ISBN 0-531-02255-2). Watts.
Berger, Michael L. The Public Education System. (American Government Ser). (Illus.). (gr. 7 up). 1977. lib. bdg. 6.90 s&l (ISBN 0-531-00399-X). Watts.
Berger, Morroe. Islam in Egypt Today: Social & Political Aspects of Popular Religion. LC 70-113597. 1970. 23.95 (ISBN 0-521-07834-2). Cambridge U Pr.
Berger, Nomi. Echoes of Yesterday. LC 80-82848. 384p. (Orig.). 1981. pap. 2.95 (ISBN 0-87216-777-1). Playboy Pbks.
Berger, P. J., jt. ed. see Berger, M. L.
Berger, Pam, jt. ed. see Dyer, Esther.
Berger, Peter. Protocol of a Damnation: A Novel. 250p. 1975. 7.95 (ISBN 0-8164-0280-9). Crossroad NY.
Berger, Peter & Neuhaus, Richard J. Against the World for the World: The Hartford Appeal & the Future of American Religion. 180p. 1976. pap. 3.95 (ISBN 0-8164-2121-8). Crossroad NY.
Berger, Peter L. Invitation to Sociology: A Humanistic Perspective. LC 63-8758. 1963. pap. 2.95 (ISBN 0-385-06529-9, A346, Anch). Doubleday.
Berger, Phil. Championship Teams of the N. F. L. LC 68-23667. (NFL Punt, Pass & Kick Library: No. 10). (Illus.). (gr. 5-9). 1968. 2.50 o.p. (ISBN 0-394-80640-9, BYR). Random.
--Heroes of Pro Basketball. (Pro Basketball Library: No. 1). (Illus.). (gr. 5-9). 1968. PLB 3.69 (ISBN 0-394-90871-6, BYR). Random.
Berger, Phil & Bortstein, Larry. The Boys of Indy. 1978. pap. 1.95 o.p. (ISBN 0-523-40327-5). Pinnacle Bks.
Berger, Philip A., jt. ed. see Davis, Kenneth L.
Berger, Rainer, ed. Scientific Methods in Medieval Archaeology. LC 75-99771. (UCLA Center for Medieval & Renaissance Studies). (Illus.). 1971. 36.50x (ISBN 0-520-01626-2). U of Cal Pr.
Berger, Rainer & Suess, Hans E., eds. Radiocarbon Dating. 1980. 60.00x (ISBN 0-520-03680-8). U of Cal Pr.
Berger, Ralph. Psyclosis: The Circularity of Experience. LC 77-24398. (Biology Ser.). (Illus.). 1977. text ed. 17.95x (ISBN 0-7167-0018-2). W H Freeman.
Berger, Raoul. Impeachment: The Constitutional Problems. LC 72-75428. (Studies in Legal History). 360p. 1973. 16.00 (ISBN 0-674-44475-2); pap. 5.95x (ISBN 0-674-44476-0). Harvard U Pr.
Berger, Raymond M. Computer Programmer Job Analysis Reference Text. (Illus.). 195p. 1974. pap. 10.00 (ISBN 0-88283-021-X). AFIPS Pr.
Berger, Robert O. Practical Accounting for Lawyers. (Modern Accounting Perspectives & Practice Ser.). 450p. 1981. 25.00 (ISBN 0-471-08486-7, Pub. by Wiley-Interscience). Wiley.
Berger, Ronald, jt. auth. see Balkan, Sheila.
Berger, Seymour & Godel, Jules B. Estimating & Project Management for Small Construction Firms. 1977. pap. text ed. 8.80 o.p. (ISBN 0-8273-1763-8). Delmar.
Berger, Sidney E., ed. see Clemens, Samuel L.
Berger, Suzanne. French Political System. (Patterns of Government Ser.). 1974. pap. text ed. 4.95 (ISBN 0-394-31818-8). Random.
Berger, Suzanne & Piore, Michael. Dualism & Discontinuity in Industrial Societies. LC 79-25172. (Illus.). 176p. 1980. 17.95 (ISBN 0-521-23134-5). Cambridge U Pr.
Berger, Suzanne, ed. Organizing Interests in Western Europe: Pluralism, Corporatism & the Transformation of Politics. LC 80-16378. (Cambridge Studies in Modern Political Economies). (Illus.). 464p. Date not set. price not set (ISBN 0-521-23174-4). Cambridge U Pr.
Berger, Terry. Being Alone, Being Together. LC 75-20302. (Moods & Emotions Ser.). (Illus.). 32p. (gr. k-3). 1976. Repr. of 1974 ed. PLB 8.95 (ISBN 0-8172-0047-9). Raintree Pubs.
--Big Sister Little Brother. LC 75-19467. (Identity II Ser.). (Illus.). 32p. (gr. k-3). 1975. Repr. of 1974 ed. PLB 7.95 o.p. (ISBN 0-8172-0049-5). Raintree Pubs.
--A Friend Can Help. LC 75-19325. (Moods & Emotions Ser.). (Illus.). 32p. (gr. k-3). 1975. Repr. of 1974 ed. PLB 8.95 (ISBN 0-8172-0051-7). Raintree Pubs.
--Friends. (Illus.). 64p. (gr. 3-5). 1981. PLB 6.97 (ISBN 0-686-69300-0). Messner.
--A New Baby. LC 75-19415. (Moods & Emotions Ser.). (Illus.). 32p. (gr. k-3). 1975. Repr. of 1974 ed. PLB 8.95 (ISBN 0-8172-0053-3). Raintree Pubs.
Berger, Thomas. Arthur Rex. 1980. pap. 3.25 (ISBN 0-440-10362-2). Dell.
--Little Big Man. 448p. 1978. pap. 2.95 (ISBN 0-449-23854-7, Crest). Fawcett.
Bergeret, et al. Nourrir En Harmonie Avec L'environment. 1977. 21.75x (ISBN 90-279-7684-8). Mouton.
Bergeron, J. Self Instructional Workbook for Emergency Care. 2nd ed. (Illus.). 1978. pap. 7.95 (ISBN 0-87618-996-6). R J Brady.
Bergersen, Betty, et al, eds. Current Concepts in Clinical Nursing, Vol. 2. LC 67-30797. (Illus.). 1969. 15.50 o.p. (ISBN 0-8016-0636-5). Mosby.
Bergersen, Betty S. Pharmacology in Nursing. 14th ed. LC 66-10935. (Illus.). 1979. text ed. 22.95 (ISBN 0-8016-0632-2). Mosby.
Bergersen, Betty S. & Sakalys, Jurate A. Review of Pharmacology in Nursing. 2nd ed. LC 78-5717. 1978. pap. text ed. 11.00 (ISBN 0-8016-0624-1). Mosby.
Bergersen, F. J., ed. Methods for Evaluating Biological Nitrogen Fixation. LC 79-41785. 640p. 1980. 114.00 (ISBN 0-471-27759-2, Pub. by Wiley-Interscience). Wiley.
Bergert, Fritz. Die Von Den Trobadors Genannten Oder Gefeierten Damen. LC 80-2164. 1981. Repr. of 1913 ed. 26.50 (ISBN 0-404-19028-6). AMS Pr.
Bergerud, Marly & Gonzalez, Jean. Word Information Processing Concepts: Careers Technology, & Applications. 512p. 1981. text ed. 16.95 (ISBN 0-471-08499-9). Wiley.
--Word Processing: Concepts & Careers. 2nd ed. (Wiley Word Processing Ser.). 256p. 1981. text ed. 14.95 (ISBN 0-471-06010-0); write for info. tchrs'. ed. (ISBN 0-471-09093-X); write for info. resource manual (ISBN 0-471-09093-X). Wiley.
--Word Processing: Concepts & Careers. LC 77-15794. (Word Processing Ser.). 1978. pap. text ed. 13.95 (ISBN 0-471-02748-0); tchrs. manual 2.95 (ISBN 0-471-03778-8). Wiley.
Berges, Ruth. The Collector's Cabinet. LC 77-84560. (Illus.). 1980. 20.00 (ISBN 0-498-02117-3). A S Barnes.
Bergethon, Bjorner, jt. auth. see Nye, Robert E.
Bergethon, K. Roald & Finger, Ellis. Grammar for Reading German, Form C. rev. ed. 1979. pap. text ed. 9.40 (ISBN 0-395-26085-X); instrs'. answer key 6.60 (ISBN 0-395-26084-1). HM.
Bergevin, Paul. A Philosophy of Adult Education. 1970. pap. 4.95 (ISBN 0-8164-2056-4, SP62). Crossroad NY.
Bergevin, Paul, et al. Adult Education Procedures: A Handbook of Tested Patterns for Effective Participation. 1963. pap. 3.95 (ISBN 0-8164-2000-9, SP29). Crossroad NY.

Bergey, Alyce. El Mundo que Dios Creo. Ross, Ronald, tr. from Eng. (Libros Arco). (Illus.). 32p. (Orig., Span.). (gr. 1-3). 1972. pap. 0.95 o.s.i. (ISBN 0-89922-041-X). Edit Caribe.

--El Nino que Salvo a su Familia. Villalobos, Fernando, tr. from Eng. (Libros Arco). (Illus.). 32p. (Orig., Span.). (gr. 1-3). 1970. pap. 0.95 o.s.i. (ISBN 0-89922-043-6). Edit Caribe.

--La Sopresa de los Pescadores. Villalobos, Fernando, tr. from Eng. (Libros Arco Ser.). (Illus.). 32p. (Orig., Span.). (gr. 1-3). 1978. pap. 0.95 (ISBN 0-89922-122-X). Edit Caribe.

--El Sueno de un Pordiosero. Villalobos, Fernando, tr. from Eng. (Libros Arco Ser.). (Illus.). 32p. (Orig., Span.). (gr. 1-3). 1978. pap. 0.95 (ISBN 0-89922-126-2). Edit Caribe.

Bergfield, Philip B. California Real Estate Law. 1974. text ed. 16.50x o.p. (ISBN 0-256-01571-6). Irwin.

Bergh, Arpad A. & Dean, Paul J. Light-Emitting Diodes. (Monographs in Electrical & Electronic Engineering). (Illus.). 1976. text ed. 89.00x (ISBN 0-19-859317-1). Oxford U Pr.

Bergh, Kit. Northern Pike Fishing: The Angler's Complete Handbook. LC 75-6532. (Illus.). 1975. 8.95 (ISBN 0-87518-096-5). Dillon.

Bergh, T. Van Den see Van Den Bergh, T.

Berghahn, Volker & Kitchen, Martin. Germany in the Age of Total War. 272p. 1981. 25.00x (ISBN 0-389-20186-3). B&N.

Berghe, Christian van den. Dictionnaire Des Idees Dans L'oeuvre De Simone de Beauvoir. (Collection Dictionnaires Des Idees, Litterature Francaise: No. 1). 1966. 20.50x (ISBN 0-686-20917-6). Mouton.

Berghe, Pierre L. Van Den. Caneville: The Social Structure of a South African Town. LC 63-17796. (Illus.). 1964. 17.50x (ISBN 0-8195-3042-5, Pub. by Wesleyan U Pr). Columbia U Pr.

Berghe, Pierre Van den see Van den Berghe, Pierre.

Berghe, Pierre van Den see Van den Berghe, Pierre.

Berghorn, Forrest J., et al. Dynamics of Aging: Original Essays on the Process & Experience of Growing Old. 542p. 1980. lib. bdg. 32.50x (ISBN 0-89158-781-0); pap. text ed. 13.50x (ISBN 0-89158-782-9). Westview.

--The Urban Elderly: A Study of Life Satisfaction. LC 77-84407. 1978. text ed. 18.50x (ISBN 0-916672-98-0). Allanheld.

Bergin, Allen E., jt. auth. see Garfield, Sol L.

Bergin, James J. & Holmes, Geraldine C. Continuing Medical Education in the Community Hospital. LC 79-55326. (Illus.). 1979. text ed. 22.00x (ISBN 0-935466-00-2); pap. text ed. 16.00x (ISBN 0-935466-01-0). Pierson Pubs.

Bergin, Thomas G. Petrarch. (World Authors Ser.: Italy: No. 81). lib. bdg. 10.95 (ISBN 0-8057-2694-2). Twayne.

Bergin, Victoria. Special Education Needs in Bilingual Programs. 64p. (Orig.). 1980. pap. 3.00 (ISBN 0-89763-026-2). Natl Clearinghse Bilingual Ed.

Bergler, Edmund. Divorce Won't Help. 1978. 12.95 (ISBN 0-87140-635-7); pap. 3.95 (ISBN 0-87140-124-X). Liveright.

--Tensions Can Be Reduced to Nuisances. 12.95 (ISBN 0-87140-976-3); pap. 3.95 (ISBN 0-87140-976-3). Liveright.

Bergles, Arthur E. & Ishigai, Seiken, eds. Two-Phase Flow Dynamics & Reactur Safety: The Japan-U. S. Seminar 1979. (Illus.). 1981. text ed. 75.00 (ISBN 0-89116-198-8). Hemisphere Pub.

Bergles, Arthur E., et al, eds. Two-Phase Flow & Heat Transfer in the Power & Process Industries. LC 80-22025. (Illus.). 450p. 1980. text ed. 55.00 (ISBN 0-89116-197-X). Hemisphere Pub.

Berglund, Berndt & Bolsby, Clare. Wilderness Cookbook. LC 72-12158. 192p. 1973. 4.95 (ISBN 0-684-14661-4, ScribT); pap. 3.95 (ISBN 0-684-14715-7, ScribT). Scribner.

Berglund, Berndt & Bolsby, Clare E. Complete Outdoorsman's Guide to Edible Wild Plants. LC 78-162948. (Illus.). 1971. pap. 4.95 (ISBN 0-684-15481-1, SL278, ScribT). Scribner.

Berglund, Bjorn. Noah's Ark Is Stranded. 1976. 12.95 o.p. (ISBN 0-440-06434-1, Sey Lawr). Delacorte.

Bergman, Abby, jt. auth. see Jacobson, Willard.

Bergman, Andrew. Hollywood & le Vine. 192p. 1976. pap. 1.75 o.p. (ISBN 0-345-25006-0). Ballantine.

--We're in the Money. 1975. pap. 3.95 (ISBN 0-06-131948-1, TB1948, Torch). Har-Row.

--We're in the Money: Depression America & Its Films. LC 74-159533. (Illus.). 1971. 12.00x, cusa (ISBN 0-8147-0964-8). NYU Pr.

Bergman, Carol. Stories for Today, 6 pk. single titles. Incl. Paul (ISBN 0-435-11133-7); Donnovan (ISBN 0-435-11134-5); Naomi (ISBN 0-435-11135-3); Junes Work (ISBN 0-435-11136-1); Rescue at Night (ISBN 0-435-11137-X); The Big Game (ISBN 0-435-11138-8). (Second Series). 1972. pap. text ed. 9.95 ea. mixed set 1 copy o.p. (ISBN 0-435-11149-3). Heinemann Ed.

Bergman, Drew, jt. auth. see Willig, George.

Bergman, Elihu, et al, eds. American Energy Choices Before the Year Two Thousand. LC 78-7122. (Illus.). 1978. 16.95 (ISBN 0-669-02398-1). Lexington Bks.

Bergman, G. Merle. Realtheism: A Religion & Bible for the Humanist Age. 160p. 1981. 10.95 (ISBN 0-938986-03-1); pap. 6.95 (ISBN 0-938986-04-X). Fellowship Pr.

Bergman, Hannah E. Luis Quinones de Benavente. (World Authors Ser.: Spain: No. 216). lib. bdg. 10.95 (ISBN 0-8057-2140-1). Twayne.

Bergman, Ingmar. From the Life of the Marionettes. Blair, Alan, tr. 1980. 8.95 (ISBN 0-394-51317-7); pap. 2.95 (ISBN 0-394-73970-1). Pantheon.

Bergman, Ingrid & Burgess, Alan. Ingrid Bergman: My Story. 1980. 14.95 (ISBN 0-440-03299-7). Delacorte.

Bergman, Jules. Anyone Can Fly. rev. ed. LC 73-9141. 1977. 12.95 (ISBN 0-385-02830-X). Doubleday.

Bergman, M., ed. Subsurface Space--Environment Protection, Low Cost Storage, Energy Savings: Proceedings of the International Symposium, Stockholm, Sweden, June 23-27, 1980, 3 vols. (Illus.). 1500p. 1980. 250.00 (ISBN 0-08-026136-1). Pergamon.

Bergman, Madeleine. Hieronymus Bosch & Alchemy: A Study on the St. Anthony Triptych. (Stockholm Studies in History of Art Ser.: No. 31). (Illus.). 139p. 1979. pap. text ed. 17.50x (ISBN 91-22-00292-8). Humanities.

Bergman, Magnus, ed. Rockstore Seventy-Seven: Proceedings of the First International Symposium on Storage in Excavated Rock Caverns, Stockholm, Sweden, Sept. 5-8 1977, 3 vols. LC 77-30591. 1978. Set. text ed. 375.00 (ISBN 0-08-022407-5). Pergamon.

Bergman Publ. Co, ed. Chronological History of the Negro in America. (RL 7). pap. 1.50 o.p. (ISBN 0-451-60937-9, MW937, Ment). NAL.

Bergman, R. N., jt. auth. see Cobelli, E.

Bergman, Ray & Janes, Edward C. Trout. 1976. 15.00 (ISBN 0-394-49957-3); pap. 9.95 (ISBN 0-394-73144-1). Knopf.

Bergman, Robert P. The Salerno Ivories: Ars Sacra from Medieval Amalfi. LC 79-22616. 1980. 37.50x (ISBN 0-674-78528-2). Harvard U Pr.

Bergman, Samuel & Bruckner, Steven. Introduction to Computers & Computer Programming. LC 72-140834. 1972. text ed. 17.95 (ISBN 0-201-00552-2); instructor's guide & soultions manuals 2.50 (ISBN 0-201-00553-0). A-W.

Bergmann, Frederick L., jt. ed. see Pedicord, Harry W.

Bergmann, Fredrick L., jt. ed. see Pedicord, Harry W.

Bergmann, Gustav. Meaning & Existence. (Orig.). 1960. pap. 7.95x (ISBN 0-299-01984-5). U of Wis Pr.

--Realism: A Critique of Brentano & Meinong. (Orig.). 1967. 25.00x (ISBN 0-299-04330-4); pap. 9.95x (ISBN 0-299-04334-7). U of Wis Pr.

Bergmann, John F. Tips for You: Thirty-One Ways to Please Customers & Increase Your Earning Power. LC 79-14759. 1979. pap. 4.95 (ISBN 0-8436-2155-9); tips for your poster set 19.95 (ISBN 0-686-66175-3). CBI Pub.

Bergmann, Josef. The Peafowl of the World. 142p. 1980. 29.95x (ISBN 0-904558-52-5, Pub. by Saiga England). State Mutual Bk.

Bergmann, Leola N. Music Master of the Middle West: The Story of F. Melius Christiansen & the St. Olaf Choir. 2nd ed. LC 68-16222. (Music Ser). 1968. Repr. of 1944 ed. 22.50 (ISBN 0-306-71057-9). Da Capo.

Bergmann, Merrie, et al. The Logic Book. 608p. 1980. text ed. 17.95 (ISBN 0-394-32323-8). Knopf.

Bergner, H., ed. English Short Stories of the Nineteenth Century. 1969. bound 31.20 (ISBN 0-685-05222-2); pap. 12.90 (ISBN 0-685-05223-0). Adler.

Bergner, Jeffrey T. The Origin of Formalism in Social Science. LC 80-17484. 160p. 1981. lib. bdg. 16.00 (ISBN 0-226-04362-2). U of Chicago Pr.

Bergon, Frank. Stephen Crane's Artistry. 224p. 1975. 17.50x (ISBN 0-231-03905-0). Columbia U Pr.

--The Wilderness Reader. (Orig.). 1980. pap. 3.50 (ISBN 0-451-61902-1, ME1902, Ment). NAL.

Bergon, Frank, ed. see Burroughs, John.

Bergone, Frank, ed. see Burroughs, John.

Bergonzi, Bernard. Heroes Twilight. 1980. text ed. write for info. (ISBN 0-391-01137-5). Humanities.

--T. S. Eliot. (Masters of World Literature). 1972. 6.95 o.s.i. (ISBN 0-02-509960-4). Macmillan.

--T. S. Eliot. Roberts, Ray, ed. 1972. pap. 2.95 o.s.i. (ISBN 0-02-048580-8, Collier). Macmillan.

Bergonzi, Bernard, ed. see Eliot, T. S.

Bergquist, Gordon N. The Pen & the Sword: War & Peace in the Prose & Plays of Bernard Shaw. (Salzburg Studies in English Literature, Poetic Drama & Poetic Theory: No. 28). 1977. pap. text ed. 25.00x (ISBN 0-391-01325-4). Humanities.

Bergquist, Patricia R. Sponges. LC 77-93644. 1978. 30.00x (ISBN 0-520-03658-1). U of Cal Pr.

Bergquist, William H. & Phillips, Steven R. Handbook for Faculty Development, Vol. 3. Quehl, Gary H. & Bernard, Jean B., eds. LC 80-69254. 1981. pap. 15.00 (ISBN 0-937012-11-4). Coun Advance Small Colleges.

Bergreen, Laurence. Look Now, Pay Later: The Rise of Network Broadcasting. 1981. pap. 3.95 (ISBN 0-451-61966-8, ME1966, Ment). NAL.

Bergren, Ann L. The Etymology & Usage of Peirar in Early Greek Poetry. (American Philological Association, American Classical Studies). 1975. pap. 6.00 (ISBN 0-89130-242-5, 400402). Scholars Pr Ca.

Bergsma, Daniel, ed. Birth Defects Compendium. 2nd ed. LC 78-20651. 1222p. 1979. 50.00x (ISBN 0-8451-0203-6). A R Liss.

--Human Gene Mapping 4, Vol. 4. LC 78-61294. (S. Karger Ser.: Vol. 14, No. 4). 1978. 50.00. March of Dimes.

--An International System for Human Cytogenetic Namenclature. LC 78-61295. (S. Karger Ser.: Vol. 14, No. 8). 1978. 10.00. March of Dimes.

Bergsma, Daniel & Goldstein, Allan L., eds. Neurochemical & Immunologic Components in Schizophrenia: Proceedings of a Conference Held at the University of Texas Medical Branch, Oct. 1976. LC 78-8534. (Birth Defects Original Article Ser.: Vol. 14, No. 5). 447p. 1978. 46.00 (ISBN 0-8451-1019-5). A R Liss.

Bergsma, Daniel & Pulver, Ann E., eds. Developmental Disabilities: Psychologic & Social Implications; Proceedings of a Symposium Sponsored by the National Foundation March of Dimes & the Johns Hopkins University School of Hygiene & Public Health, Baltimore, Md., LC 76-44446. (Birth Defects - Original Article Ser.: Vol. 12, No. 4.). 204p. 1976. 21.00 (ISBN 0-8451-1007-1). A R Liss.

Bergsma, Daniel, ed. see Birth Defects Annual Conference, 10th Memphis, Tenn., June, 1977.

Bergsma, Daniel, ed. see Birth Defects Conference, Kansas City, Mo., May 1975.

Bergsma, Daniel, ed. see Birth Defects Conference-1975, Kansas City, Missouri.

Bergsma, Daniel, ed. see Birth Defects Conference, 1975, Kansas City, Missouri.

Bergsma, Daniel, ed. see Conference Held at Jackson Laboratory, Bar Harbor, Maine, Sept. 1976.

Bergsma, Daniel, ed. see International Workshop on Morphogenesis & Malformation, 4th, Grand Canyon, Ariz., 1977.

Bergsma, Daniel, jt. ed. see Myrianthopoulos, Ntinos C.

Bergsma, Daniel, jt. ed. see Rosenquist, Glenn C.

Bergsma, Daniel, et al, eds. see Conference Sponsored by National Foundation-March of Dimes, Key Biscayne, Florida, Nov. 1975.

Bergsma, Daniel, et al, eds. see Symposium Held at the Radcliffe Infirmary, Oxford, England, April, 1975 Sponsod by the National Foundation - March of Dimes.

Bergson, Abram. The Economics of Soviet Planning. LC 80-13737. (Studies in Comparative Economics: No. 5). (Illus.). xxii, 394p. 1980. Repr. of 1964 ed. lib. bdg. 30.00x (ISBN 0-313-22413-7, BEES). Greenwood.

--Planning & Productivity Under Soviet Socialism. LC 68-24703. 1968. 15.00x (ISBN 0-231-03116-5). Columbia U Pr.

Bergson, Henri. An Introduction to Metaphysics. 2nd ed. Hulme, T. E., tr. LC 49-3135. 1955. pap. 1.95 (ISBN 0-672-60171-0, LLA10). Bobbs.

--An Introduction to Metaphysics: The Creative Mind. (Quality Paperback: No. 164). 1975. pap. 3.95 (ISBN 0-8226-0164-8). Littlefield.

--Time & Free Will. (Muirhead Library of Philosophy). 1971. text ed. 20.00x (ISBN 0-04-194002-4). Humanities.

Bergstein, Eleanor. Advancing Paul Newman. 320p. 1976. pap. 1.75 o.p. (ISBN 0-445-08438-3). Popular Lib.

Bergsten, A. C. Fred & Krause, Lawrence B., eds. World Politics & International Economics. 1975. 18.95 (ISBN 0-8157-0916-1); pap. 6.95 (ISBN 0-8157-0915-3). Brookings.

Bergsten, C. Fred. American Multinationals & American Interests. LC 77-91786. 1978. 21.95 (ISBN 0-8157-0920-X); pap. 13.95 (ISBN 0-8157-0919-6). Brookings.

--Managing International Economic Interdependence: Selected Papers of C. Fred Bergsten. LC 77-2517. 1977. 23.95 (ISBN 0-669-01516-4). Lexington Bks.

Bergsten, C. Fred, ed. Toward a New World: Trade Policy. LC 74-22304. 1975. 24.95 (ISBN 0-669-96743-2). Lexington Bks.

Bergsten, Fred C. Toward a New International Economic Order. LC 74-16635. 1975. 23.95 (ISBN 0-669-96677-0). Lexington Bks.

Bergsten, Staffan. Osten Sjostrand. (World Authors Ser.: Spain: No. 309). 174p. 1974. lib. bdg. 12.50 (ISBN 0-8057-2844-9). Twayne.

Bergstrom, Corinne. Losing Your Best Friend. LC 79-20622. 32p. 1980. 8.95 (ISBN 0-87705-471-1). Human Sci Pr.

Bergstrom, Jan. Organization, Life & Systematics of Trilobites. (Fossils & Strata Ser: No. 2). 1973. 12.00x (ISBN 8-200-09330-1, Dist. by Columbia U Pr). Universitet.

Bergstrom, Len V. see Rosenberg, Marie E.

Bergstrom, Louise. Claudia's Secret. (YA) 1969. 5.95 (ISBN 0-685-07426-9, Avalon). Bouregy.

--Dangerous Paradise. 192p. (YA) 1975. 5.95 (ISBN 0-685-52655-0, Avalon). Bouregy.

--The House of the Evening Star. 192p. (YA) 1976. 5.95 (ISBN 0-685-66574-7, Avalon). Bouregy.

--Pink Camellia. (YA) 1968. 5.95 (ISBN 0-685-07453-6, Avalon). Bouregy.

--Strange Legacy. (YA) 4.95 o.p. (ISBN 0-685-07459-5, Avalon). Bouregy.

Bergstrom, Sune, jt. ed. see Vane, John R.

Bergstrom, Theo. Hadrian's Wall. (Illus.). 1978. pap. 4.95 (ISBN 0-8467-0502-8, Pub. by Two Continents). Hippocrene Bks.

--Stonehenge. (Illus.). 1977. pap. 4.95 (ISBN 0-8467-0323-8, Pub. by Two Continents). Hippocrene Bks.

--The Thames. (Illus.). 1978. 8.95 (ISBN 0-8467-0501-X, Pub. by Two Continents). Hippocrene Bks.

Bergveld, P. Electromedical Instrumentation: A Guide for Medical Personnel. LC 77-85711. (Techniques of Measurement in Medicine Ser.: No. 2). (Illus.). 1980. 29.50 (ISBN 0-521-21892-6); pap. 9.95 (ISBN 0-521-29305-7). Cambridge U Pr.

Beri, G. C. Measurements of Production & Productivity in Indian Industry. 5.25x o.p. (ISBN 0-210-33666-8). Asia.

Beringer, Johann B. The Lying Stones of Johann Bartholomew Adam Beringer Being His Lithographiae Wirceburgensis. Jahn, Melvin E. & Woolf, Daniel J., trs. 1963. 26.75x (ISBN 0-520-00110-9). U of Cal Pr.

Beringer, Richard E. Historical Analysis: Contemporary Approaches to Clio's Craft. LC 77-10589. 1978. pap. text ed. 15.95 (ISBN 0-471-06996-5); pap. text ed. 12.95 o.p. (ISBN 0-686-67925-3). Wiley.

Berington, Simon. The Memoirs of Signior Guadentio Di Lucca. LC 74-170596. (Novel in England, 1700-1775 Ser.). lib. bdg. 50.00 (ISBN 0-8240-0578-3). Garland Pub.

Berio, Paquita. Ahora Brillan las Estrellas. 134p. (Orig., Span.). 1981. pap. 2.50 (ISBN 0-89922-201-3). Edit Caribe.

Berk, Fred. Chasidic Dance. (gr. 9 up). 1975. pap. 5.00 (ISBN 0-8074-0083-1, 582050). UAHC.

Berk, Fred, ed. Ha-Rikud: The Jewish Dance. (Illus.). 112p. (Orig.). 1972. pap. 5.00 o.p. (ISBN 0-685-24136-X, 582040). UAHC.

Berk, J. Edward, ed. Developments in Digestive Diseases, Vol. 3. (Illus.). 258p. 1980. text ed. 24.00 (ISBN 0-8121-0754-3). Lea & Febiger.

Berk, Paul D. & Chalmers, Thomas C., eds. Frontiers in Liver Disease. (Illus.). 300p. 1981. text ed. 35.00 (ISBN 0-86577-017-4). Thieme-Stratton.

Berk, Phyllis L. Duke's Command. (Illus.). (gr. 2-5). 4.25 o.p. (ISBN 0-8313-0005-1); PLB 6.19 (ISBN 0-685-13772-4). Lantern.

Berk, Robert N. & Lasser, Elliot C. Radiology of the Ileocecal Area. LC 74-11684. (Monographs in Clinical Radiology: Vol. 5). (Illus.). 327p. 1975. text ed. 23.50 o.p. (ISBN 0-7216-1689-5). Saunders.

Berk, Sarah F., ed. Women & Household Labor. LC 79-23003. (Sage Yearbooks in Women's Policy Studies: Vol. 5). (Illus.). 295p. 1980. 20.00 (ISBN 0-8039-1211-0); pap. 9.95 (ISBN 0-8039-1212-9). Sage.

Berk, Susan. California: A Programmed History. (gr. 10-12). 1976. pap. text ed. 5.67 (ISBN 0-87720-617-1). AMSCO Sch.

Berke, Art. Unsung Heroes of the Major Leagues. LC 75-34909. (Illus.). 160p. (gr. 5 up). 1976. PLB 3.69 (ISBN 0-394-93096-7, BYR). Random.

Berke, Joe, jt. auth. see Barnes, Mary.

Berke, Joel S. Answers to Inequity. LC 73-7237. 1974. 17.90 (ISBN 0-685-42625-4); text ed. 16.20 (ISBN 0-685-42626-2). McCutchan.

Berke, Joel S., et al. Financing Equal Educational Opportunity: Alternatives for State Finance. LC 79-190059. 300p. 1972. 16.60x (ISBN 0-8211-0120-X); text ed. 15.00x (ISBN 0-685-24959-X). McCutchan.

Berke, Joseph & Hernton, Calvin C. The Cannabis Experience: An Interpretative Study of the Effects of Marijuana & Hashish. 288p. 1974. text ed. 17.00x (ISBN 0-7206-0073-1). Humanities.

Berke, Joseph, jt. auth. see Barnes, Mary.

Berke, Joseph, ed. Counter Culture: The Creation of an Alternative Society. (Illus.). 19.95x (ISBN 0-8464-0295-5). Beekman Pubs.

Berke, Roberta. Bounds Out of Bounds: A Compass for Recent American & British Poetry. 192p. 1981. 14.95 (ISBN 0-19-502872-4). Oxford U Pr.

Berke, Sally. Monster at Loch Ness. LC 77-24715. (Great Unsolved Mysteries Ser.). (Illus.). (gr. 4-5). 1977. PLB 9.65 (ISBN 0-8172-1054-7). Raintree Pubs.

--When T V Began: The First TV Shows. LC 78-15168. (Famous Firsts Ser.). (Illus.). 1978. lib. bdg. 7.35 (ISBN 0-686-50003-2). Silver.

Berkeley, Anthony. Trial & Error. 1981. pap. 2.25 (ISBN 0-440-18766-4). Dell.

Berkeley, C. F. Ialy in the Making, 3 vols. Incl. Vol. 1. Eighteen Fifteen to Eighteen Forty-Six. Repr. of 1932 ed. 38.50 (ISBN 0-521-07427-4); Vol. 2. Eighteen Forty-Six to Eighteen Forty-Eight. Repr. of 1936 ed. 44.50 (ISBN 0-521-07428-2); Vol. 3. January 1, Eighteen Forty-Eight to November 16, Eighteen Forty-Eight. Repr. of 1940 ed. 53.50 (ISBN 0-521-07429-0). (Illus.). 1969. Cambridge U Pr.

Berkeley, David S. Inwrought with Figures Dim: A Reading of Milton's Lycidas. (De Proprietatibus Litterarum Ser. Didactica: No. 2). 1974. pap. text ed. 22.35x (ISBN 90-2792-605-0). Mouton.

Berkeley, George. Berkeley-Philosophical Works: Including the Works on Vision. (Rowman & Littlefield University Library). 1980. pap. 8.75x (ISBN 0-8476-6231-4). Rowman.

--New Theory of Vision. 1954. 5.00x o.p. (ISBN 0-460-00483-2, Evman). Dutton.

--Philosophical Works: Including the Works on Vision. 1981. 18.50; pap. 8.75. Rowman.

--Principles, Dialogues & Philosophical Correspondence. Turbayne, Colin M., tr. LC 64-66065. 1965. pap. 5.95 (ISBN 0-672-60453-1, LLA208). Bobbs.

--Three Dialogues Between Hylas & Philonous. Turbayne, Colin M., ed. 1954. pap. 3.95 (ISBN 0-672-60206-7, LLA39). Bobbs.

--Three Dialogues Between Hylas & Philonous. McCormack, Thomas J., ed. vi, 136p. 1969. 9.95 (ISBN 0-87548-068-3); pap. 3.50 (ISBN 0-87548-069-1). Open Court.

--Treatise Concerning the Principles of Human Knowledge. Turbayne, Colin M., ed. LC 57-1290. 1957. pap. 3.95 (ISBN 0-672-60225-3, LLA53). Bobbs.

--A Treatise Concerning the Principles of Human Knowledge: Text & Critical Essays. Turbayne, Colin M., ed. LC 69-16531. (Text & Critical Essays Ser). 1970. pap. 6.55 (ISBN 0-672-61115-5, TC2). Bobbs.

Berkeley Holistic Health Center. The Holistic Health Lifebook. (Illus.). 384p. 1980. soft cover 9.95 (ISBN 0-915904-53-5). And-Or Pr.

Berkeley, Humphry. The Life & Death of Rochester Sneath. (Illus.). 96p. 1981. 11.95 (ISBN 0-241-10416-5, Pub. by Hamish Hamilton England). David & Charles.

--The Odyssey of Enoch: A Political Memoir. (Illus.). 1978. 17.95 (ISBN 0-241-89623-1, Pub. by Hamish Hamilton England). David & Charles.

Berkeley, James P. Paul & Philippians. (Orig.). 1969. pap. 1.50 o.p. (ISBN 0-8170-0434-3). Judson.

Berkeley Poets Cooperative, ed. Berkeley Poets Cooperative Anthology, 1970-1980. 300p. 1980. pap. 6.95 (ISBN 0-917658-12-4). Berkeley Poets.

Berkeley, R. C., et al. Microbial Adhesion to Surfaces. LC 80-41358. 600p. 1981. 110.00 (ISBN 0-470-27083-7). Halsted Pr.

Berkeley, S. G. & Jackson, B. E. Your Career As a Medical Secretary-Transcriber. LC 74-34233. 1975. 12.95 (ISBN 0-471-07020-3, Pub. by Wiley Medical). Wiley.

Berkeley Solar Group. Solar for Your Present Home. 1978. pap. 12.00 (ISBN 0-930978-83-8). Solar Energy Info.

Berker, Paul de see De Berker, Paul.

Berkey, Barry R. Save Your Marriage. LC 75-45338. 224p. 1976. 15.95 (ISBN 0-88229-235-8). Nelson-Hall.

Berkey, Gordon, jt. auth. see Holloway, Gordon F.

Berkhof, Hendrikus. Doctrine of the Holy Spirit. LC 64-16279. 1976. pap. 3.95 (ISBN 0-8042-0551-5). John Knox.

Berkhof, Louis. History of Christian Doctrines. (Twin Brooks Ser). 288p. 1975. pap. 5.95 (ISBN 0-8010-0636-8). Baker Bk.

--The History of Christian Doctrines. 1978. 11.95 (ISBN 0-85151-005-1). Banner of Truth.

Berkhofer, Robert, ed. see Hansen, Stephen L.

Berkhofer, Robert, ed. see Harlan, David.

Berkhofer, Robert, ed. see Holmes, Richard.

Berkhofer, Robert, ed. see Rosenberg, Ann E.

Berkhofer, Robert, ed. see Young, Christine A.

Berkhofer, Robert F., Jr. Behavioral Approach to Historical Analysis. LC 69-11485. (Illus.). 1971. pap. text ed. 6.95 (ISBN 0-02-902960-0). Free Pr.

--The White Man's Indian: Images of the American Indian from Columbus to the Present. LC 78-11047. (Illus.). 1979. pap. 4.95 (ISBN 0-394-72794-0, V-794, Vin). Random.

Berkin, Carol & Norton, Mary B. Women of America: A History. LC 78-69589. (Illus.). 1979. pap. text ed. 10.95 (ISBN 0-395-27067-7). HM.

Berkin, Carol R. & Lovett, Clara M., eds. Women, War & Revolution. LC 79-26450. 1980. text ed. 27.50x (ISBN 0-8419-0502-9); pap. text ed. 9.75x (ISBN 0-8419-0545-2). Holmes & Meier.

Berkley & Gould, Saundra. The Short Story Reader. 3rd ed. pap. 5.95 (ISBN 0-672-73292-0). Bobbs.

Berkley, George. Cancer: How to Prevent It, & How to Help Your Doctor Fight It. LC 77-26954. 1978. 10.95 (ISBN 0-13-113399-3, Spec); pap. 5.95 (ISBN 0-13-113381-0, Spec). P-H.

Berkley, George & Fox, William J. Eighty Thousand Governments: The Politics of Subnational America. 1978. text ed. 17.95 (ISBN 0-205-06007-2). Allyn.

Berkley, George E. The Craft of Public Administration. 3rd ed. 550p. 1980. text ed. 19.90 (ISBN 0-205-07211-9, 767211-X); tchrs'. ed. avail. (ISBN 0-205-07212-7). Allyn.

--The Craft of Public Administration. 2nd ed. 1978. text ed. 16.95x o.p. (ISBN 0-205-06060-9). Allyn.

Berkley, George E., et al. Introduction to Criminal Justice: Police, Courts, Corrections. 1976. text ed. 16.95 (ISBN 0-205-05448-X, 825448-6); instr's manual free (ISBN 0-205-04993-1, 825449-4). Allyn.

Berkley Holistic Health Center, compiled by. Holistic Health Lifebook. 384p. 1981. pap. 9.95 (ISBN 0-915904-53-5). And-or Pr.

Berkman, Al. It's How You Say It. 1977. 12.50 (ISBN 0-934972-04-4). Melrose Pub Co.

--The Psychology of Singing. 1977. 10.00 (ISBN 0-934972-08-7). Melrose Pub Co.

--The Science of Popular Voice: Voice Production for the Pop Singer. 1979. 12.95 (ISBN 0-934972-09-5). Melrose Pub Co.

--Sex & the Singing Girl. 1975. 12.50 (ISBN 0-934972-03-6). Melrose Pub Co.

--Sight Reading for the Pop Singer. 1969. 4.50 (ISBN 0-934972-05-2). Melrose Pub Co.

--Singers Glossary of Show Business Jargon. 1961. 3.00 (ISBN 0-934972-06-0). Melrose Pub Co.

--Singing Takes More Than a Voice. 1961. 3.00 (ISBN 0-934972-00-1). Melrose Pub Co.

--Song Presentation for Polular Singers: Book II. 1977. 8.50 (ISBN 0-934972-02-8). Melrose Pub Co.

--Song Presentation for Popular Singers: Book I. 1976. 10.00 (ISBN 0-934972-01-X). Melrose Pub Co.

--Vocal Gymnastics for the Pop Singer. 1976. 8.00 (ISBN 0-934972-07-9). Melrose Pub Co.

Berkman, Joyce. Olive Schreiner: Feminism on the Frontier. LC 78-74842. 1979. 11.95 (ISBN 0-88831-031-5). EPWP.

Berkman, Ronald. Opening the Gates: The Rise of the Prisoners Movement. 224p. 1979. 21.95 (ISBN 0-669-02828-2). Lexington Bks.

Berkman, Sue, et al. A Doctor Discusses Care of the Feet. (Illus.). 110p. 1979. pap. 2.50 (ISBN 0-685-46330-3). Budlong.

Berko, Frances G., et al. Management of Brain Damaged Children: A Parents' & Teachers' Guide. 84p. 1970. 12.75 (ISBN 0-398-00141-3). C C Thomas.

Berko, Roy M. & Wolvin, Andrew D. Communicating: A Social & Career Focus. 2nd ed. (Illus.). 432p. 1981. pap. text ed. 10.50 (ISBN 0-395-29170-4). HM.

Berko, Roy M., et al. Communicating: A Social & Career Focus. LC 76-12008. (Illus.). 336p. 1977. pap. text ed. 12.95 (ISBN 0-395-24073-5); instructor's manual 2.10 (ISBN 0-395-24074-3). HM.

Berkoben, L. D. Coleridge's Decline As a Poet. (Studies in English Literature: No. 98). 171p. (Orig.). 1975. pap. text ed. 28.25x (ISBN 90-2793-226-3). Mouton.

Berkoff, Steven. East & Other Plays. 1980. pap. 4.95 (ISBN 0-7145-3637-7). Riverrun NY.

--Gross Intrusion & Other Stories. 1980. 9.95 (ISBN 0-7145-3685-7); pap. 4.95 (ISBN 0-7145-3685-7). Riverrun NY.

Berkofsky, Louis, et al, eds. Settling the Desert. 272p. 1981. write for info. (ISBN 0-677-16280-4). Gordon.

Berkove, Laurence I. Ambrose Bierce: A Braver Man Than Anybody Knew. (Illus.). 1981. 16.00 (ISBN 0-88233-349-6). Ardis Pubs.

Berkovitch, Israel. Coal on the Switchback: The Coal Industry Since Nationalisation. 1977. text ed. 25.00x (ISBN 0-04-622002-X). Allen Unwin.

Berkovsky, Boris, ed. see International Advanced Course & Workshop on Thermomechanics of Magnetic Fluids, Udine, Italy, Oct. 3-7, 1977.

Berkow, Ira. The Man Who Robbed the Pierre. 288p. 1981. 11.95 (ISBN 0-87460-381-1). Lion.

Berkow, Ira, jt. auth. see Frazier, Walt.

Berkow, Robert, ed. The Merck Manual of Diagnosis and Therapy. 13th ed. LC 1-31760. (Illus.). 1980p. 1977. 14.50 (ISBN 0-911910-02-6). Merck.

Berkowits, David S., ed. see Nelson, William.

Berkowitz, A. E. & Kneller, E., eds. Magnetism & Metallurgy, 2 Vols. Vol. 1 1970. 61.00 (ISBN 0-12-091701-7); Vol. 2 1969. 52.50 (ISBN 0-12-091702-5); 92.50 set (ISBN 0-685-05134-X). Acad Pr.

Berkowitz, Alan. A Guide to the Bright Angel Trail. 1979. pap. 1.00 (ISBN 0-938216-09-0). GCNHA.

--A Guide to the North Kaibab Trail. 1980. pap. 1.00 (ISBN 0-938216-10-4). GCNHA.

Berkowitz, Alan D., jt. auth. see Dereshinsky, Ralph M.

Berkowitz, Bernard, jt. auth. see Newman, Mildred.

Berkowitz, David & Thorne, Samuel, eds. The Law of Commons & Commoners; or a Treatise Shewing the Original & Nature of Common, & the Several Kinds Thereof. LC 77-89244. (Classics of English Legal History in the Modern Era Ser.: Vol. 138). 1979. Repr. of 1698 ed. lib. bdg. 55.00 (ISBN 0-8240-3175-X). Garland Pub.

--Treatise of Feme Converts; or, Lady's Law. Containing All the Laws & Statutes Relating to Women. LC 77-86663. (Classics of English Legal History in the Modern Era Ser.: Vol. 44). 1979. Repr. of 1732 ed. lib. bdg. 60.50 (ISBN 0-8240-3093-1). Garland Pub.

Berkowitz, David, ed. see Bentham, Jeremy.

Berkowitz, David, ed. see Best, William M.

Berkowitz, David, ed. see Brydall, John.

Berkowitz, David, ed. see Chitty, Joseph.

Berkowitz, David, ed. see De Lolme, Jean L.

Berkowitz, David, ed. see Finch, Sir Henry.

Berkowitz, David, ed. see Hale, Sir Matthew.

Berkowitz, David, ed. see Hallam, Henry.

Berkowitz, David, ed. see Holt, Francis L.

Berkowitz, David, ed. see Kyd, Stewart.

Berkowitz, David, ed. see Lodowick, Lloyd.

Berkowitz, David, ed. see Manwood, John.

Berkowitz, David, ed. see Nolan, Michael.

Berkowitz, David, ed. see Palmer, Sir Francis B.

Berkowitz, David, ed. see Petyt, George.

Berkowitz, David, ed. see Powell, John J.

Berkowitz, David, ed. see Sheppard, William.

Berkowitz, David S. In Remembrance of Creation: Evolution of Art & Scholarship in the Medieval & Renaissance Bible. LC 68-28658. (Illus.). 324p. 1968. 20.00 (ISBN 0-87451-059-7). U Pr of New Eng.

Berkowitz, David S. & Thorne, Samuel E., eds. Baron & Feme. LC 77-86664. (Classics of English Legal History in the Modern Era Ser.: Vol. 43). 445p. 1979. lib. bdg. 40.00 (ISBN 0-8240-3092-3). Garland Pub.

--British Liberties. LC 77-89201. (Classics of English Legal History in the Modern Era Ser.: Vol. 57). 486p. 1979. lib. bdg. 40.00 (ISBN 0-8240-3156-3). Garland Pub.

--An Enquiry into the Doctrine Concerning Libels, Warrants, & the Seizure of Papers. LC 77-86678. (Classics of English Legal History in the Modern Era Ser.: Vol. 52). 99p. 1979. lib. bdg. 40.00 (ISBN 0-8240-3151-2). Garland Pub.

--George Meriton. Sir Henry Spelman. Anon. Charles Fearne. (English Legal History Ser.: Vol. 137). 370p. 1979. lib. bdg. 55.00 (ISBN 0-8240-3174-1). Garland Pub.

--Sir Edward Coke, 4 vols. (English Legal History Ser.). 1468p. 1979. lib. bdg. 55.00 (ISBN 0-8240-3053-2). Garland Pub.

--Sir Henry Finch. Edmund Wingate. William Phillips. (English Legal History Ser.: Vol. 68). 462p. 1979. lib. bdg. 55.00 (ISBN 0-8240-3055-9). Garland Pub.

--Sir William Staunford. William Dickinson. Roger Maynwaring. Robert Sibthorpe. Sir Walter Raleigh. (English Legal History Ser.: Vol. 131). 426p. 1979. lib. bdg. 55.00 (ISBN 0-8240-3168-7). Garland Pub.

Berkowitz, David S., ed. see Acherley, Roger.

Berkowitz, David S., ed. see Bacon, Francis & Francis, Richard.

Berkowitz, David S., ed. see Bacon, Sir Francis.

Berkowitz, David S., ed. see Best, William M. & Stephen, James F.

Berkowitz, David S., ed. see Blackstone, Sir William.

Berkowitz, David S., ed. see Blount, Charles, et al.

Berkowitz, David S., ed. see Bott, Edmund.

Berkowitz, David S., ed. see Brydall, John & Highmore, Anthony.

Berkowitz, David S., ed. see Buller, Francis.

Berkowitz, David S., ed. see Chitty, Joseph.

Berkowitz, David S., ed. see Chitty, Joseph, Jr.

Berkowitz, David S., ed. see Coke, Edward & Highmore, Anthony, Jr.

Berkowitz, David S., ed. see Davenport, Humphrey.

Berkowitz, David S., ed. see De Lolme, Jea L.

Berkowitz, David S., ed. see Filmer, Sir Robert.

Berkowitz, David S., ed. see Gilbert, Sir Gefrey & Peake, Thomas.

Berkowitz, David S., ed. see Hale, Matthew & Giles, Jacob.

Berkowitz, David S., ed. see Hammond, Henry.

Berkowitz, David S., ed. see Haslam, John.

Berkowitz, David S., ed. see Hawkins, William.

Berkowitz, David S., ed. see Heale, William & Swinburne, Henry.

Berkowitz, David. S., ed. see Jacob, Giles, et al.

Berkowitz, David S., ed. see Jenkins, David, et al.

Berkowitz, David S., ed. see Jones, Sir William.

Berkowitz, David S., ed. see Littlton, Thomas.

Berkowitz, David S., ed. see Mantell, Walter, et al.

Berkowitz, David S., ed. see Perkins, John.

Berkowitz, David S., ed. see Pettus, Sir John.

Berkowitz, David S., ed. see Pratt, John T.

Berkowitz, David S., ed. see Prynne, Wiliam, et al.

Berkowitz, David S., ed. see Pulton, Ferdinand.

Berkowitz, David S., ed. see Raleigh, Sir Walter, et al.

Berkowitz, David S., ed. see Robinson, Henry, et al.

Berkowitz, David S., ed. see Russell, Sir William O.

Berkowitz, David S., ed. see Somers, John & Jacob, Giles.

Berkowitz, David S., ed. see Staunford, William & Romilly, Samuel.

Berkowitz, David S., ed. see Stephen, Henry J.

Berkowitz, David S., ed. see Swinburne, Henry.

Berkowitz, David S., ed. see Theloall, Simon.

Berkowitz, David S., ed. see Toland, John, et al.

Berkowitz, David S., ed. see Towers, Joseph & Maseres, Francis.

Berkowitz, David S., ed. see Tyrrell, Sir James.

Berkowitz, David S., ed. see Webb, Philip C. & Grove, Joseph.

Berkowitz, David S., ed. see West, Richard, et al.

Berkowitz, David S., ed. see West, William.

Berkowitz, David S., ed. see White, George.

Berkowitz, David S., ed. see Williams, Thomas & Somers, John.

Berkowitz, David S., ed. see Wood, Thomas.

Berkowitz, Edward & McQuaid, Kim. Creating the Welfare State: The Political Economy of Twentieth Century Reform. LC 79-22524. 1980. 22.95 (ISBN 0-03-056243-0). Praeger.

Berkowitz, Freda P. Popular Titles & Subtitles of Musical Compositions. 2nd ed. LC 75-4751. 217p. 1975. 10.00 (ISBN 0-8108-0806-4). Scarecrow.

Berkowitz, Gerald, jt. auth. see Neimark, Paul.

Berkowitz, Joan B., et al, eds. Unit Operations for Treatment of Hazardous Industrial Wastes. LC 78-62520. (Pollution Technology Review: No. 47). (Illus.). 1979. 42.00 (ISBN 0-8155-0717-8). Noyes.

Berkowitz, Joseph. Photoabsorption, Photoionization & Photoelectron Spectroscopy. (Pure & Applied Physics Ser.). 1979. 42.50 (ISBN 0-12-091650-9). Acad Pr.

Berkowitz, Leonard, ed. Advances in Experimental Social Psychology. Incl. Vol. 2. 1966. 31.00 (ISBN 0-12-015202-9); Vol. 3. 1967. 31.00 (ISBN 0-12-015203-7); Vol. 4. 1969. 31.00 (ISBN 0-12-015204-5); Vol. 5. 1971. 31.00 (ISBN 0-12-015205-3); Vol. 6. 1972. 31.00 (ISBN 0-12-015206-1); Vol. 7. 1974. 31.00 (ISBN 0-12-015207-X); Vol. 8. 1975. 31.00 (ISBN 0-12-015208-8); microfiche 22.50 (ISBN 0-12-015275-4); Vol. 10. 1977. 31.00 (ISBN 0-12-015210-X); lib ed. 40.50 (ISBN 0-12-015278-9); microfiche 22.50 (ISBN 0-12-015279-7); Vol. 11. 1978. 26.50 (ISBN 0-12-015211-8). LC 64-23452. Acad Pr.

--Advances in Experimental Social Psychology, Vol. 13. (Serial Publication Ser.). 1980. 22.50 (ISBN 0-12-015213-4); lib. ed. 29.50 (ISBN 0-12-015284-3); microfiche 16.00 (ISBN 0-12-015285-1). Acad Pr.

Berkowitz, M., et al. The Politics of American Foreign Policy: The Social Contexts of Decisions. (Illus.). 1977. pap. text ed. 10.50 (ISBN 0-13-685073-1). P-H.

Berkowitz, Mona. How to Raise & Train an Old English Sheepdog. pap. 2.00 (ISBN 0-87666-344-7, DS1103). TFH Pubns.

Berkowitz, Monroe, et al. An Evaluation of Policy-Related Rehabilitation Research. LC 75-23957. (Illus.). 244p. 1975. text ed. 23.95 (ISBN 0-275-01260-3). Praeger.

--Public Policy Toward Disability. LC 76-25081. (Illus.). 1976. 23.95 (ISBN 0-275-23290-5). Praeger.

Berkowitz, Pearl H. & Rothman, Esther P. The Disturbed Child: Recognition & Psychoeducational Therapy in the Classroom. LC 60-6418. 1960. 12.00x (ISBN 0-8147-0040-3). NYU Pr.

Berkowitz, Richard L., et al. A Guide to the Use of Medications During Pregnancy. 1980. pap. write for info. (ISBN 0-316-09173-1). Little.

--Handbook for Prescribing Medications During Pregnancy. 1981. pap. text ed. write for info (ISBN 0-316-09173-1). Little.

Berkowitz, Sol. Improvisation Through Keyboard Harmony. (Illus.). 288p. 1975. pap. 14.50 (ISBN 0-13-453472-7). P-H.

Berkshire Traveller. Treasured Recipes of Country Inns. new ed. LC 73-91008. (Illus.). 128p. 1973. pap. 3.95x (ISBN 0-912944-08-0). Berkshire Traveller.

Berkshire Traveller, ed. Country Inn Cookbook. rev. ed. LC 75-2520. (Illus.). 1975. pap. 3.95 (ISBN 0-912944-18-8). Berkshire Traveller.

Berkson, Bill & LeSeuer, Joe, eds. Homage to Frank O'Hara. (Illus.). 250p. 1980. pap. 8.95 (ISBN 0-916870-29-4). Creative Arts Bk.

Berkson, Larry, jt. auth. see Chian, Nancy.

Berkson, Larry C. The Concept of Cruel & Unusual Punishment. LC 75-16331. 272p. 1975. 22.95 (ISBN 0-669-00063-9). Lexington Bks.

--The Supreme Court & Its Publics. LC 77-14793. (Illus.). 1978. 16.95 (ISBN 0-669-01994-1). Lexington Bks.

Berkson, Larry C., jt. auth. see Carbon, Susan B.

Berkson, Larry C. & Vandenberg, Donna, eds. National Roster of Women Judges, 1980. 120p. (Orig.). 1980. pap. 2.95 (8563). Am Judicature.

Berkson, Lee. Away from Home. 36p. 1980. pap. 2.50 (ISBN 0-933180-19-5). Spoon Riv Poetry.

Berkson, William. Fields of Force: The Development of a World View from Faraday to Einstein. 1974. 30.00 (ISBN 0-7100-7626-6). Routledge & Kegan.

Berl, Robert L, jt. auth. see Bellenger, Danny N.

Berl, W. G. & Powell, W. R. Efficient Comfort Conditioning. 1979. lib. bdg. 23.00x (ISBN 0-89158-290-8). Westview.

Berl, Walter G., ed. Physical Methods in Chemical Analysis, 4 vols. Incl. Vol. 1. 2nd rev. ed. 1960. 62.00 (ISBN 0-12-092061-1); Vol. 2. 1951. 51.00 (ISBN 0-12-092002-6); Vol. 3. 1956. 51.00 (ISBN 0-12-092003-4); Vol. 4. 1961. 51.00 (ISBN 0-12-092004-2). Acad Pr.

Berland, A. Culture & Conduct in the Novels of Henry James. 225p. Date not set. 39.95 (ISBN 0-521-23343-7). Cambridge U Pr.

Berland, Theodore. The Fitness Fact Book: A Guide to Diet, Exercise & Sport. 1981. pap. 1.95 (ISBN 0-686-69109-1, J9730, Sig). NAL.

Berland, Theodore & Perritt, Richard A. Living with Your Eye Operation. 1974. 5.95 o.p. (ISBN 0-312-49175-1). St Martin.

Berland, Theodore, jt. auth. see Jordan, Henry A.

Berlandier, Jean L., et al. Journey to Mexico During the Years Eighteen Twenty-Six to Eighteen Thirty-Four, 2 vols. Ohlendorf, Sheila M. & Bigelow, Josette, eds. LC 80-52705. (Illus.). 1980. boxed 75.00 (ISBN 0-87611-044-8); special limited ed. 150.00 (ISBN 0-87611-051-0). Tex St Hist Assn.

Berlant, Jeffrey L. Profession & Monopoly: A Study of Medicine in the United States & Great Britain. 1975. 20.00x (ISBN 0-520-02734-5). U of Cal Pr.

Berley, Lawrence F. Holographic Mind, Holographic Vision: A New Theory of Vision in Art & Physics. LC 79-92384. (Illus.). 1980. 14.95x (ISBN 0-9603706-0-9); pap. 9.95x (ISBN 0-9603706-1-7). Lakstun Pr.

Berlin, Brent. Tzeltal Numerical Classifiers: A Study in Ethnographic Semantics. (Janua Linguarum, Ser. Practica: No. 70). (Orig.). 1968. pap. text ed. 52.50x (ISBN 0-686-22422-1). Mouton.

Berlin, Brent & Kay, Paul. Basic Color Terms: Their Universality & Evolution. LC 70-76541. (Illus.). 1969. 15.75x (ISBN 0-520-01442-1). U of Cal Pr.

Berlin, Ellin. The Best of Families. 1978. pap. 1.95 o.p. (ISBN 0-449-23541-6, Crest). Fawcett.

Berlin, G. Lennis. Earthquakes & the Urban Environment, 3 vols. 1980. Vol. 1. 59.95 (ISBN 0-8493-5173-1); Vol. 2. 69.95 (ISBN 0-8493-5174-X); Vol. 3. 78.95 (ISBN 0-8493-5175-8). CRC Pr.

Berlin, Helene, ed. see Harrison, Henry S. & Leonard, Margery B.

Berlin, Howard M. Design of Op-Amp Circuits, with Experiments. LC 78-56606. 1978. pap. 8.95 (ISBN 0-672-21537-3). Sams.

--Design of Phase-Locked Loop Circuits, with Experiments. LC 78-57203. 1978. pap. 9.95 (ISBN 0-672-21545-4). Sams.

--Five Hundred & Fifty-Five Timer Applications Sourcebook. LC 78-56584. 1976. pap. 6.95 (ISBN 0-672-21538-1). Sams.

Berlin, Howard M., jt. auth. see Stone, Robert T.

Berlin, Ira. Slaves Without Masters: The Free Negro in the Antebellum South. 446p. 1981. pap. 6.95 (ISBN 0-19-502905-4, GB 629, OPB). Oxford U Pr.

Berlin, Irving, jt. auth. see French, Alfred.

Berlin, Irving N., ed. Bibliography of Child Psychiatry with a Selected List of Films. LC 74-11813. 528p. 1976. 29.95 (ISBN 0-87705-244-1); pap. text ed. 14.95 (ISBN 0-87705-277-8). Human Sci Pr.

Berlin, Isaiah. Four Essays on Liberty. 1970. 14.95 (ISBN 0-19-501242-9). Oxford U Pr.

--Personal Impressions. Hardy, Henry, ed. LC 79-56278. (Illus.). 240p. 1981. 13.95 (ISBN 0-670-54833-2). Viking Pr.

Berlin, Louis, jt. auth. see Smith, Alexander B.

Berlin, Lucia, ed. Angel's Laundromat. (New World Writing Ser). (Illus.). 96p. (Orig.). 1981. pap. 4.95 (ISBN 0-686-69426-0). Turtle Isl Foun.

Berlin, Normand. Thomas Sackville. (English Authors Ser.: No. 165). 1974. lib. bdg. 10.95 (ISBN 0-8057-1471-5). Twayne.

Berlin, Saretta, jt. auth. see Haft, Jacob I.

Berliner, Burt. Fifty Famous Faces in Transition. 1980. pap. write for info. (ISBN 0-671-41127-6, Fireside). S&S.

Berliner, Don. Aerobatics. LC 80-10914. (Superwheels & Thrill Sports Bks.). (Illus.). 48p. (gr. 4 up). 1980. PLB 6.95 (ISBN 0-8225-0436-7). Lerner Pubns.

Berliner, Paul F. The Soul of Mbira: Music & Tradition of the Shona People of Zimbabwe. (Perspectives on Southern Africa Ser.: No. 26). 1978. 20.00x (ISBN 0-520-03315-9); pap. 4.95 (ISBN 0-520-04268-9). U of Cal Pr.

Berliner, William M. Managerial & Supervisory Practice. 7th ed. 1979. 17.95x (ISBN 0-256-02040-X). Irwin.

Berlinghoff, William P., et al. A Mathematical Panorama: Topics for the Liberal Arts. 1980. text ed. 15.95 (ISBN 0-669-02423-6). Heath.

Berlioz, Hector. Berlioz Symphonie Fantastique. Cone, Edward T., ed. (Critical Scores Ser). 1971. pap. 5.95x (ISBN 0-393-09926-1). Norton.

Berlitz, Charles. Doomsday Nineteen Ninety-Nine A.D. LC 80-1084. (Illus.). 240p. 1981. 11.95 (ISBN 0-385-15982-X). Doubleday.

--Passport to German. 1974. pap. 1.75 (ISBN 0-451-09444-1, E9444, Sig). NAL.

--Without a Trace: New Information from the Triangle. LC 76-41438. 1977. 7.95 o.p. (ISBN 0-385-11139-8). Doubleday.

Berlitz, Charles & Moore, William L. The Roswell Incident. 1980. 10.00 (ISBN 0-686-69014-1). G&D.

Berlitz, Charles, jt. auth. see Moore, William.

Berlitz, Charles, ed. see Carrier, Rick & Carrier, Barbara.

Berlitz, Charles, ed. see Mawson, C. O.

Berlyand, M. E., ed. Air Pollution & Athmospheric Diffusion. LC 73-1982. 221p. 1974. Vol. 1. 27.95 (ISBN 0-470-07034-X); Vol. 2. 36.95 (ISBN 0-470-07038-2). Halsted Pr.

Berlye, Milton. Your Career in the World of Work. LC 75-12236. 1975. pap. 13.00 (ISBN 0-672-21050-9). Bobbs.

Berlyn. Your Future in Television Careers. (Careers in Depth Ser.). 1980. lib. bdg. 5.97 (ISBN 0-8239-0404-0). Rosen Pr.

Berlyn, David. Your Future in a Television Career. (Careers in Depth). 1978. lib. bdg. 5.97 o.p. (ISBN 0-8239-0404-0). Rosen Pr.

Berlyne, D. E. Structure & Direction in Thinking. (Illus.). 378p. 1965. text ed. 14.50 (ISBN 0-471-07035-1, Pub. by Wiley). Krieger.

Berlyne, D. E., ed. Studies in the New Experimental Aesthetics. LC 74-13600. 1974. 14.95 o.p. (ISBN 0-470-07039-0). Halsted Pr.

Berman. Relationships. 1978. pap. 8.95 (ISBN 0-8015-6269-4, Hawthorn). Dutton.

Berman & Shevitz. The Basics & Beyond. 1981. pap. text ed. write for info. (ISBN 0-8302-0992-1). Goodyear.

Berman, Alvin & Jones, Edward G. The Thalamus & Basal Telencephalon of the Cat. (Illus.). 180p. 1980. write for info. (ISBN 0-299-08440-X). U of Wis Pr.

Berman, Alvin L. Brain Stem of the Cat: A Cytoarchitectonic Atlas with Stereotaxic Coordinates. (Illus.). 1968. 175.00 (ISBN 0-299-04860-8). U of Wis Pr.

Berman, Avis, intro. by. Lamar Briggs: Paintings & Works on Paper. LC 80-69965. (Illus.). 108p. 1980. text ed. 260.00 (ISBN 0-938454-01-3); pap. text ed. 25.00 (ISBN 0-938454-00-5). Ai.

Berman, Bernard A. & MacDonnell, Kenneth F. Differential Diagnosis & Treatment of Pediatric Allergy. 1981. text ed. write for info (ISBN 0-316-09182-0). Little.

Berman, Connie. Diana Ross - Supreme Lady. 1978. pap. 1.75 o.p. (ISBN 0-445-04283-4). Popular Lib.

Berman, Danieal S. & Mason, Dean T. Clinical Nuclear Cardiology. (Clinical Cardiology Monographs Ser.). 1981. write for info. (ISBN 0-8089-1356-5). Grune.

Berman, Daniel M. Death on the Job. LC 78-13914. 1979. 12.95 o.p. (ISBN 0-85345-462-0, CL-4620). Monthly Rev.

Berman, David R. State & Local Politics. 3rd ed. 336p. 1980. text ed. 17.95 (ISBN 0-205-07219-4, 767219-5). Allyn.

--State & Local Politics. 2nd ed. 1978. text ed. 16.95 o.p. (ISBN 0-205-05974-0, 765974-1). Allyn.

Berman, David R. & Bollens, John C. American Government: Ideas & Issues. LC 80-83670. 1981. pap. 6.95 (ISBN 0-913530-22-0). Palisades Pubs.

Berman, Edgar. The Politician Primeval: From the Amoeba to the White House. LC 73-22527. 256p. 1974. 6.95 o.s.i. (ISBN 0-02-510060-2). Macmillan.

--The Solid Gold Stethescope. 252p. 1976. 7.95 o.s.i. (ISBN 0-02-510050-5). Macmillan.

Berman, Edward H. African Reaction to Missionary Education. LC 74-22497. (Orig.). 1975. pap. text ed. 9.95x (ISBN 0-8077-2445-9). Tchrs Coll.

Berman, Elaine R., jt. ed. see Michaelson, I. C.

Berman, Eleanor. Re-Entering: Successful Back-to-Work Strategies for Women Seeking a Fresh Start. 192p. 1980. 8.95 (ISBN 0-517-53943-8). Crown.

Berman, Elizabeth. Mathematics Revealed. 546p. 1979. 12.95 (ISBN 0-12-092450-1); instrs'. manual 3.00 (ISBN 0-12-092452-8). Acad Pr.

Berman, Gerald & Fryer, K. D. Introduction to Combinatorics. 1972. text ed. 19.95 (ISBN 0-12-092750-0). Acad Pr.

Berman, H., jt. auth. see Ginzberg, Eli.

Berman, Howard J. & Weeks, Lewis E. The Financial Management of Hospitals. 4th ed. LC 79-16947. (Illus.). 1979. text ed. 29.50 (ISBN 0-914904-33-7). Health Admin Pr.

Berman, Howard J., jt. ed. see Weeks, Lewis E.

Berman, Howard W. & Weeks, Lewis E. The Financial Management of Hospitals. 3rd ed. (Illus.). 585p. 1976. 17.50 (ISBN 0-686-68573-3, 1496). Hospital Finan.

Berman, I. & Schroeder, J. W., eds. Explosive Welding, Forming, Plugging, & Compaction. (PVP: No. 44). 119p. 1980. 20.00 (H00171). ASME.

Berman, Kathleen & Landesman, Bill. How to Care for Your Older Dog. LC 78-19063. 1979. 9.95 (ISBN 0-8119-0280-3). Fell.

--How to Train Your Dog in Six Weeks. LC 75-45459. 224p. 1976. 9.95 (ISBN 0-8119-0266-8). Fell.

Berman, Louise M. From Thinking to Behaving. LC 67-19025. (Orig.). 1967. pap. text ed. 4.00x (ISBN 0-8077-1071-7). Tchrs Coll.

--New Priorities in the Curriculum. LC 68-28703. (International Education Ser). 1968. text ed. 16.95 (ISBN 0-675-09612-X). Merrill.

Berman, Louise M. & Roderick, Jessie A. Curriculum: Teaching the What, How, and Why of Living. (Elementary Education Ser.). 1977. text ed. 15.95 (ISBN 0-675-08480-6). Merrill.

Berman, Martin M., jt. auth. see Foster, James H.

Berman, Michael. Materials for Listening Comprehension & Note Taking in English. pap. 3.95 (ISBN 0-08-025316-4). Pergamon.

--Read & Recall: Passages for Advanced Reading Comprehension in English. 1980. pap. 3.95 (ISBN 0-08-024531-5). Pergamon.

Berman, Neil D. Playful Fictions & Fictional Players: Game, Sport & Survival in Contemporary American Fiction. (National University Publications, Literary Criticism Ser.). 125p. 1981. 13.50 (ISBN 0-8046-9265-3). Kennikat.

Berman, P., jt. auth. see Miller, F.

Berman, Peter I. Inflation & the Money Supply in the United States, 1956-1977. LC 78-4344. 1978. 14.95 (ISBN 0-669-02346-9). Lexington Bks.

Berman, R. Thermal Conduction in Solids. (Oxford Studies in Physics). 1980. 12.95x (ISBN 0-19-851430-1). Oxford U Pr.

Berman, Robert P. Soviet Air Power in Transition. (Studies in Defense Policy). 1978. pap. 3.95 (ISBN 0-8157-0923-4). Brookings.

Berman, Ronald. America in the Sixties. LC 68-10365. 1968. 9.95 o.s.i. (ISBN 0-02-902980-5). Free Pr.

--The Signet Classic Book of Restoration Drama. 1980. pap. 3.95 (ISBN 0-451-51402-5, CE1402, Sig Cl). NAL.

Berman, Ronald, ed. Solzhenitsyn at Harvard: The Address, Twelve Early Responses, & Six Later Reflections. 160p. 1980. 9.50 (ISBN 0-89633-034-6); pap. 5.00 (ISBN 0-89633-023-0). Ethics & Public Policy.

Berman, Sanford. Joy of Cataloging. 1981. lib. bdg. 22.50 (ISBN 0-912700-51-3); pap. 16.50 (ISBN 0-912700-94-7). Oryx Pr.

Berman, Sharon L. With a Face Like Mine. 160p. 1981. 8.95 (ISBN 0-87777-062-X, Pub. by R W Baron). Dutton.

Berman, Steve. How to Create Your Own Publicity for Names, Products or Services & Get It for Free. LC 77-2736. 128p. 1977. pap. 4.95 (ISBN 0-8119-0378-8). Fell.

Berman, Susan. Driver, Give a Soldier a Lift. 1977. pap. 1.50 o.p. (ISBN 0-425-03500-X, Medallion). Berkley Pub.

Bermann, Richard A. The Mahdi of Alah: The Story of the Dervish, Mohammed Ahmed. John, Robin, tr. LC 80-1935. 1981. Repr. of 1932 ed. 36.00 (ISBN 0-404-18955-5). AMS Pr.

Bermant, C. The Cousinhood. 1972. 10.95 o.s.i. (ISBN 0-02-510080-7). Macmillan.

Bermant, Chaim. Now Newman Was Old. LC 78-3993. 1978. 8.95 o.p. (ISBN 0-312-57971-3). St Martin.

--The Patriarch. 448p. 1981. 14.95 (ISBN 0-312-59804-1). St Martin.

--The Walled Garden: The Saga of Jewish Family Life & Tradition. (Illus.). 272p. 1975. 12.95 o.s.i. (ISBN 0-02-510100-5). Macmillan.

Bermant, Gordon, et al. Psychology & the Law. LC 75-40628. 1976. 21.95 (ISBN 0-669-00452-9). Lexington Bks.

Bermel, Albert. Artaud's Theatre of Cruelty. LC 77-76510. 1977. 3.95 (ISBN 0-8008-0395-7). Taplinger.

Bermingham, Alan, et al. The Small TV Studio: The Equipment & Facilities. (Media Manuals Ser.). Date not set. pap. 7.95 (ISBN 0-8038-6725-5). Hastings.

Bermont, Hubert, jt. auth. see Garvin, Andrew.

Bermont, Hubert, jt. auth. see Thomas, David S.

Bermosk, Loretta S., jt. auth. see Anders, Robert L.

Bermudez, Antonio J. The Mexican National Petroleum Industry. 268p. 1963. pap. 4.00 o.p. (ISBN 0-912098-00-7). Cal Inst Intl St.

Bernace, Salvatore & Walters, Janet L. Living with Your Digestive System: This Book Can Save Your Life. (Illus.). 224p. 1981. 10.95 (ISBN 0-525-93133-3). Dutton.

Bernal, jt. auth. see Diaz Del Castillo.

Bernal, jt. auth. see Ludwig.

Bernal, Ivan, et al. Symmetry: A Stereoscopic Guide for Chemists. LC 75-178258. (Illus.). 1972. text ed. 25.95x (ISBN 0-7167-0168-5). W H Freeman.

Bernanos, Georges. The Diary of a Country Priest. 240p. 1974. pap. 2.95 (ISBN 0-385-09600-3, Im). Doubleday.

Bernard, Bruce. Photodiscovery: Masterworks of Photography 1840-1940. (Illus.). 256p. 1980. 35.00 (ISBN 0-8109-1453-0, 1453-0). Abrams.

Bernard, C. H. & Epp, C. D. Laboratory Experiments in College Physics. 5th ed. 1981. 13.50 (ISBN 0-471-05441-0). Wiley.

Bernard, C. Henry. Laboratory Experiments in College Physics. 4th ed. 1972. pap. text ed. 14.95 o.p. (ISBN 0-471-00029-9). Wiley.

Bernard, Carl & Norquay, Karen. Practical Effects in Photography. LC 80-40794. (Practical Photography Ser.). (Illus.). 168p. 1981. 19.95 (ISBN 0-240-51082-8). Focal Pr.

Bernard, Claude. Lectures on the Phenomena of Life Common to Animals & Plants, Vol. 1. Hoff, Hebbel E., et al, trs. (American Lectures in History of Medicine & Science Ser.). (Illus.). 336p. 1974. 34.75 (ISBN 0-398-02857-5). C C Thomas.

Bernard, Dan, et al, eds. Charging for Computer Services: Principles & Guidelines. Emery, James C. & Nolan, Richard. LC 77-23811. (Computer & Data Processing Professionals Ser). 1977. text ed. 14.00 (ISBN 0-89433-055-1); pap. text ed. 12.00 (ISBN 0-89433-051-9). Petrocelli.

Bernard, G., jt. auth. see Katz, W. L.

Bernard, Guy. Ville Africaine, Famille Urbaine: Les Enseignants De Kinshasa. (Recherches Africaines: No. 6). 1968. pap. 23.50x (ISBN 90-2797-543-4). Mouton.

Bernard, H. A., et al. Recent Sediments of Southeast Texas-A Field Guide to the Brazos Alluvial & Deltaic Plains & the Galveston Barrier Island Complex. 132p. 1970. Repr. 5.00 (GB 11). Bur Econ Geology.

Bernard, H. Y. Law of Death & Disposal of the Dead. 2nd ed. 1979. 5.95 (ISBN 0-379-11000-8). Oceana.

Bernard, Harold. The Greenhouse Effect. 1980. 12.95 (ISBN 0-88410-633-0). Ballinger Pub.

--The Greenhouse Effect. LC 80-8710. 256p. 1981. pap. 4.95 (ISBN 0-06-090855-6, C*N 855, CN). Har-Row.

Bernard, Harold W. Human Development in Western Culture. 5th ed. 1978. text ed. 17.95x o.p. (ISBN 0-205-05911-2); instr's man. avail. o.p. (ISBN 0-205-05933-3). Allyn.

Bernard, Harold W. & Huckins, Wesley C. Dynamics of Personal Adjustment. 3rd ed. 476p. 1978. text ed. 16.95 (ISBN 0-205-06032-3, 7960328); instr's manual o.p. (ISBN 0-205-06033-1). Allyn.
--The Dynamics of Personal Adjustment. 3rd ed. 1978. text ed. 18.95 (ISBN 0-205-06032-3, 7960328). Allyn.
Bernard, J. H. Saint John, 2 vols. LC 29-17737. (International Critical Commentary Ser.). Repr. of 1928 ed. Vol. 1, 480p. 22.00x (ISBN 0-567-05024-6); Vol. 2, 456p. 22.00x (ISBN 0-567-05025-4). Attic Pr.
Bernard, Jack, ed. see Hartmann, Sven & Hartner, Thoman.
Bernard, Jacqueline. The Children You Gave Us. LC 72-87122. (Illus.). 1972. 6.95 (ISBN 0-8197-0356-7). Bloch.
Bernard, Jean. Vital Signs: A Doctor Diagnoses the Medical Profession. LC 75-8715. 322p. 1975. 9.95 o.s.i. (ISBN 0-02-510150-1). Macmillan.
Bernard, Jean B., ed. see Bergquist, William H. & Phillips, Steven R.
Bernard, Jessie. The Female World. LC 80-69880. (Illus.). 1981. 17.95 (ISBN 0-02-903000-5). Free Pr.
Bernard, Jessie, jt. ed. see Lipman-Blumen, Jean.
Bernard, John. The Tranquillitie of the Minde. LC 73-6099. (English Experience Ser.: No. 568). 1973. Repr. of 1570 ed. 15.00 (ISBN 90-221-0568-7). Walter J Johnson.
Bernard, Joseph, et al. HALO: A Data Base Management System. 1981. pap. 12.95 (ISBN 0-8359-2720-2). Reston.
Bernard, L. L. Instinct: A Study in Social Psychology. 550p. 1980. Repr. of 1924 ed. lib. bdg. 40.00 (ISBN 0-89760-046-0). Telegraph Bks.
Bernard, Luther L. War & Its Causes. LC 71-147465. (Library of War & Peace; the Character & Causes of War). lib. bdg. 38.00 (ISBN 0-8240-0256-3). Garland Pub.
Bernard, Mary. How to Find Real Love & Keep It. Date not set. 8.50 (ISBN 0-533-04684-X). Vantage.
Bernard, Michael M., ed. Annotated Bibliography on Taxation As an Instrument of Land Planning Policy. (Lincoln Institute Monograph: No. 80-8). 90p. 1980. pap. text ed. 4.00. Lincoln Inst Land.
Bernard, Nora. Hollywood's Irish Rose. 1978. pap. 1.95 (ISBN 0-380-41061-3, 41061). Avon.
Bernard, Paul P. Rush to the Alps. (Eastern European Monographs: No. 37). 1978. 15.00x (ISBN 0-914710-30-3, Dist. by Columbia U Pr). East Eur Quarterly.
Bernard, Philippe J. Le Travailleurs Estrangers En Europe Occidentale: Actes Du Colloque Organise Par la Commission Nationale Pour les Etudes et les Recherches Inter-Ethniques, Paris-Sorbonne, Du 5 Au 7 Juin 1974. (Publications De l'Institut d'Etudes et De Recherches Interethniques et Inter Culturelles: No. 6). (Fr.). 1976. pap. text ed. 39.40x (ISBN 0-686-22611-9). Mouton.
Bernard, Richard M. The Poles in Oklahoma. LC 79-6714. (Newcomers to a New Land Ser.). (Illus.). 96p. (Orig.). 1980. pap. 2.95 (ISBN 0-8061-1630-7). U of Okla Pr.
Bernard, Sidney. This Way to the Apocalypse: The Politics of the 1960's. LC 77-92709. 1969. 5.95 (ISBN 0-912292-09-1). The Smith.
Bernard, Thomas. Of the Education of the Poor. (Social History of Education Ser.: Second Series, No. 1). 380p. 1981. Repr. of 1809 ed. 22.50x (ISBN 0-7130-0010-4, Woburn Pr England). Biblio Dist.
--The Progress of Doctrine in the New Testament. 1978. 9.00 (ISBN 0-686-12959-8). Klock & Klock.
Bernard De Clairvaux, Saint. On Loving God, & Selections from Sermons by St. Bernard of Clairvaux. Martin, Hugh, ed. LC 79-8706. (A Treasury of Christian Books). 125p. 1981. Repr. of 1959 ed. lib. bdg. 17.50x (ISBN 0-313-20787-9, BEOL). Greenwood.
Bernard de Clairvaux, St. On Loving God: Selections from Sermons by St. Bernard of Clairvaux. Martin, Hugh, ed. LC 79-8706. (A Treasury of Christian Books). 125p. 1981. Repr. of 1959 ed. lib. bdg. 17.50x (ISBN 0-313-20787-9, BEOL). Greenwood.
Bernardin, Joseph B. Introduction to the Episcopal Church. rev ed. (Orig.). 1978. pap. 3.75 (ISBN 0-8192-1231-8). Morehouse.
Bernardin De Saint-Pierre, Jacques H. Paul et Virginie. (Documentation thematique). (Illus., Fr.). pap. 2.95 (ISBN 0-685-14023-7, 29). Larousse.
Bernardo, F. P., Jr. Design & Implementation of Low Cost Automation. LC 72-86487. 116p. 1972. 7.75 (ISBN 92-833-1020-9, APO17, APO). Unipub.
Bernardo, Roberto M. Popular Management & Pay in China. 1977. pap. text ed. 8.00x (ISBN 0-8248-0741-3). U Pr of Hawaii.
Bernardo, Sorj, jt. ed. see Henfrey, Colin.
Bernardo, Stephanie. The Ethnic Almanac. LC 78-14694. (Illus.). 576p. 1981. 19.95 (ISBN 0-385-14143-2). Doubleday.
--The Ethnic Almanac. LC 80-14694. (Illus.). 576p. 1981. pap. 10.95 (ISBN 0-385-14144-0, Dolp). Doubleday.
Bernard Of Clairvaux. Bernard of Clairvaux: Sermons I on Conversations; Lenten Sermons on the Psalm "He Who Dwells". Said, Marie-Bernard, tr. (Cistercian Fathers Ser.: No. 25). (Lat.). 1981. price not set (ISBN 0-87907-125-7); pap. price not set (ISBN 0-87907-925-8). Cistercian Pubns.
Bernardus Silvestris. Commentary on the First Six Books of Virgil's "Aeneid". Schreiber, E. G. & Maresca, Thomas E., trs. LC 79-9138. xxxvi, 129p. 1980. 11.50x (ISBN 0-8032-4108-9). U of Nebr Pr.
Bernart De Ventadorn. Bernart Von Ventadorn. LC 80-2176. 1981. Repr. of 1915 ed. 49.50 (ISBN 0-404-19004-9). AMS Pr.
Bernath, Stuart L. Squall Across the Atlantic: American Civil War Prize Cases & Diplomacy. LC 76-79042. 1970. 18.50x (ISBN 0-520-01562-2). U of Cal Pr.
Bernays, Anne. The First to Know. 1975. pap. 1.25 o.p. (ISBN 0-445-00247-6). Popular Lib.
Bernays, Edward L. Public Relations. 1977. 9.95 o.p. (ISBN 0-8061-0243-8); pap. 6.95 (ISBN 0-8061-1457-6). U of Okla Pr.
Bernbaum, Gerald. Knowledge & Ideology in the Sociology of Education. (Studies in Sociology Ser.). 1977. pap. text ed. 4.00x (ISBN 0-333-15762-1). Humanities.
Bernd, Clifford A. German Poetic Realism. (World Authors Ser.: No. 605). 1981. lib. bdg. 12.95 (ISBN 0-8057-6447-X). Twayne.
Bernd, Joseph L., ed. Mathematical Applications in Political Science, Vol. 4. LC 67-28023. (Illus.). 122p. 1969. 7.50x (ISBN 0-8139-0262-2). U Pr of Va.
Bernd, Joseph L. & Herndon, James F., eds. Mathematical Applications in Political Science, Vol. 5. LC 67-28023. (Illus.). 100p. 1971. 7.50x (ISBN 0-8139-0313-0). U Pr of Va.
--Mathematical Applications in Political Science, Vol. 6. LC 67-28023. (Illus.). 1972. 10.00x (ISBN 0-8139-0386-6). U Pr of Va.
--Mathematical Applications in Political Science, Vol. 7. LC 67-28023. (Illus.). 90p. 1974. 10.00x (ISBN 0-8139-0506-0). U Pr of Va.
Bernd, Joseph L. & Jones, Archer, eds. Mathematical Applications in Political Science, Vol. 3. LC 67-28023. 1967. 7.50x (ISBN 0-8139-0027-1). U Pr of Va.
Berndt, Alan F. & Stearns, Robert I. Dental Fluoride Chemistry. (Illus.). 144p. 1978. 14.75 (ISBN 0-398-03753-1). C C Thomas.
Berne, Bruce J. & Pecora, Robert. Dynamic Light Scattering: With Applications to Chemistry, Biology & Physics. LC 75-19140. 376p. 1976. 40.95 (ISBN 0-471-07100-5, Pub. by Wiley-Interscience). Wiley.
Berne, Eric. Games People Play. 1978. pap. 2.75 (ISBN 0-345-29477-7). Ballantine.
--Intuition & Ego States: The Origins of Transactional Analysis. LC 76-57549. 1977. 8.95 o.p. (ISBN 0-06-060784-X, HarpR). Har-Row.
--Layman's Guide to Psychiatry & Psychoanalysis. 1976. pap. 2.50 (ISBN 0-345-28472-0). Ballantine.
--The Structure & Dynamics of Organizations & Groups. 1973. pap. 2.50 o.p. (ISBN 0-345-28473-9). Ballantine.
Berne, Eric & Steiner, C. Beyond Games & Scripts. 1978. pap. 2.50 (ISBN 0-345-28471-2). Ballantine.
Berne, Robert M. & Levy, Matthew N. Cardiovascular Physiology. 4th ed. (Illus.). 304p. 1981. pap. text ed. 16.50 (ISBN 0-8016-0655-1). Mosby.
Berne, Stanley & Zekowski, Arlene. A First Book of the Neo-Narrative. 1954. 75.00 (ISBN 0-913844-09-8). Am Canadian.
Berne, Stanley, jt. auth. see Zekowski, Arlene.
Berner, Jeff. The Holography Book. Date not set. 12.95x o.s.i. (ISBN 0-440-03680-1). Delacorte. Postponed.
Berner, P., et al, eds. Aktuelle Perspektiven der Lithiumprophylaxe: Current Perspectives in Lithium Prophilaxis. (Bibliotheca Psychiatrica: No. 161). (Illus.). vi, 294p. 1981. pap. 90.00 (ISBN 3-8055-1753-X). S Karger.
Berner, R. Thomas. Language Skills for Journalists. LC 78-69584. 1978. pap. text ed. 10.50 (ISBN 0-395-26789-7); inst. manual 0.65 (ISBN 0-395-26790-0). HM.
Berner, Robert A. Early Diagenesis: A Theoretical Approach. LC 80-7510. (Princeton Series in Geochemistry: No. 1). (Illus.). 256p. 1980. 25.00x (ISBN 0-691-08258-8); pap. 9.50 (ISBN 0-691-08260-X). Princeton U Pr.
Bernero, Jacqueline R., jt. ed. see Wasserman, Paul.
Berners, Juliana. The Book of Hawking, Hunting & Blasing of Arms. LC 74-25849. (English Experience Ser.: No. 151). 180p. 1969. Repr. of 1486 ed. 42.00 (ISBN 90-221-0151-7). Walter J Johnson.
--A Treatise on Fishing with a Hook. 9.95. Green Hill.
--A Treatise on Fishing with a Hook. LC 79-20603. (Angling Classics Ser.). 1979. Repr. 9.95 (ISBN 0-88427-038-6, Dist. by Caroline Hse). North River.
Bernet, Eleanor H., jt. ed. see Wirth, Louis.
Berney, Donald W. American Government for Law Enforcement Training. LC 75-8915. (Nelson Hall Law Enforcement Ser.). 1976. 20.95x (ISBN 0-88229-152-1). Nelson-Hall.
Berney, William, jt. auth. see Richardson, Howard.
Bernfeld, Siegfried. Sisyphus; or, the Limits of Education. Lilge, Frederic, tr. from Ger. 1973. 14.50x (ISBN 0-520-01407-3). U of Cal Pr.
Bernfeld, Stephen R. & Lakshmikantham, V. An Introduction to Boundary Value Problems. (Mathematics in Science & Engineering: A Series of Monographs & Textbooks, Vol. 109). 1974. 33.00 (ISBN 0-12-093150-8). Acad Pr.
Bernhard, Thomas. The Force of Habit, a Comedy. Plaice, Neville & Plaice, Stephen, trs. (National Theatre Plays Ser.). 1976. pap. text ed. 4.25x (ISBN 0-435-23120-0). Heinemann Ed.
Bernhard, Winfred E., jt. ed. see McGiffert, Michael.
Bernhardi, Robert. Building of Oakland with a Section on Piedmont. 116p. 1979. 14.95 (ISBN 0-9605472-0-7). Forest Hill.
Bernhardsen, Christian. Fight in the Mountains. Sinding, Franey, tr. LC 68-28800. (gr. 7 up). 1968. 4.50 o.p. (ISBN 0-15-227523-1, HJ). HarBraceJ.
Bernhardt, David K., ed. see Bernhardt, Karl S.
Bernhardt, Frances S. Introduction to Library Technical Services. 1979. 15.00 (ISBN 0-8242-0637-1). Wilson.
Bernhardt, Karl S. Being a Parent: Unchanging Values in a Changing World. Bernhardt, David K., ed. LC 74-484635. 1970. pap. 4.00 (ISBN 0-8020-6106-0). U of Toronto Pr.
Bernhardt, Kenneth L. & Kinnear, Thomas C. Cases in Marketing Management. 1978. 19.95x (ISBN 0-256-02081-7). Business Pubns.
Bernhardt-Kabisch, Ernest. Robert Southey. (English Authors Ser.: No. 223). 1977. lib. bdg. 10.95 (ISBN 0-8057-6692-8). Twayne.
Bernheim, Evelyne, jt. auth. see Bernheim, Marc.
Bernheim, Kayla F. & Lewine, Richard R. J. Schizophrenia: Symptoms, Causes, Treatments. 1979. 14.95 (ISBN 0-393-01174-7); pap. 6.95 (ISBN 0-393-09017-5). Norton.
Bernheim, Marc & Bernheim, Evelyne. Growing Up in Old New England. LC 75-151160. (Illus.). (gr. 5-9). 1971. 9.95 (ISBN 0-02-709060-4, CCPr). Macmillan.
--Week in Aya's World: The Ivory Coast. LC 70-75391. (Face to Face Books Ser). (Illus.). (gr. k-3). 1969. 4.50g (ISBN 0-02-709050-7, CCPr); text ed. 1.36 o.p. (ISBN 0-02-709070-1, CCPr). Macmillan.
Bernheimer, Alan W. Mechanisms in Bacterial Toxinology. LC 76-8274. (Developments in Medical Microbiology & Infectious Disease Ser). 288p. 1976. 40.50 o.p. (ISBN 0-471-07105-6, Pub by Wiley Medical). Wiley.
Bernheimer, Alan W., ed. Perspectives in Toxicology. LC 80-11261. 218p. 1981. Repr. of 1977 ed. lib. bdg. write for info. (ISBN 0-89874-131-9). Krieger.
Berni, Rosemarian & Fordyce, Wilbert E. Behavior Modification & the Nursing Process. 2nd ed. LC 76-57775. (Illus.). 1977. pap. text ed. 9.00 (ISBN 0-8016-0656-X). Mosby.
Berni, Rosemarian & Readey, Helen. Problem-Oriented Medical Record Implementation: Allied Health Peer Review. 2nd ed. LC 77-18278. (Illus.). 1978. pap. text ed. 10.00 (ISBN 0-8016-0648-9). Mosby.
Bernick, Deborah, jt. auth. see Bershad, Carol.
Bernier, Donald R., et al. Nuclear Medicine: Technology & Techniques. LC 80-17455. (Illus.). 450p. 1981. pap. text ed. 34.50 (ISBN 0-8016-0662-4). Mosby.
Bernier, Olivier. Pleasure & Privilege: Life in France, Naples & America. LC 79-6174. (Illus.). 304p. 1981. 14.95 (ISBN 0-385-15780-0). Doubleday.
Berninger, Louis M. Profitable Garden Center Management. (Illus.). 1978. 14.95 (ISBN 0-8359-5632-6); instrs's manual avail. Reston.
Bernot, Lucien. Les Paysans Arakanais Du Pakistan Oriental: L'histoire le Monde Vegetal et L'organisation Sociale Des Refugies Marma (Mog, 2 vols. (Le Monde D'outre-Mer Passe et Present, Etudes: No. 16). (Illus.). 1967. pap. text ed. 95.30x (ISBN 90-2796-172-7). Mouton.
Berns, Barrie, jt. auth. see Lewis, Alfred A.
Berns, Gabriel, ed. see Alberti, Rafael.
Berns, Gabriel, tr. see Perez de Ayala, Ramon.
Berns, Joel M. The Story of Impacted Wisdom Teeth Kit. 1980. pap. 24.00 (ISBN 0-931386-14-4). Quint Pub Co.
Berns, Michael W. Cells. LC 77-2815. 163p. 1977. pap. text ed. 5.50 (ISBN 0-03-013456-0, HoltC). HR&W.
Bernstein. Digital Image Processing for Remote Sensing. LC 77-94520. (IEEE Reprint Ser.). 1978. 35.95 (ISBN 0-471-04939-5); pap. 23.50 (ISBN 0-471-04938-7, Pub. by Wiley-Interscience). Wiley.
Bernstein, et al, eds. The Presidential Transcripts. 736p. 1974. 10.00 o.s.i. (ISBN 0-440-06056-7). Delacorte.
Bernstein, Anne E. & Warner, Gloria. An Introduction to Contemporary Psychoanalysis. LC 80-70246. 300p. 1981. 25.00 (ISBN 0-87668-442-8). Aronson.
Bernstein, Basil. Class, Codes & Control Vol. 1: Theoretical Studies Towards a Sociology of Language. (Primary Socialization, Language & Education Ser.). 1971. 30.00 (ISBN 0-7100-7060-8). Routledge & Kegan.
--Class, Codes & Control, Vol. 3: Towards a Theory of Educational Transmissions. (Primary Socialization, Language & Education Ser.). 1977. pap. 6.95 (ISBN 0-7100-8666-0). Routledge & Kegan.
Bernstein, Basil, ed. Class, Codes & Control, Vol. 2: Applied Studies Towards a Sociology of Language. (Primary Socialization, Language & Education Ser). 1973. 30.00 (ISBN 0-7100-7396-8). Routledge & Kegan.
Bernstein, Bernard, jt. auth. see Nassi, Robert.
Bernstein, Bernard, jt. auth. see Nassi, Robert J.
Bernstein, Bonnie, ed. Day by Day: Three Hundred Calendar-Related Activities, Crafts, & Bulletin Board Ideas for the Elementary Grades. LC 80-81680. (Learning Ideabooks Ser.). 1980. pap. 12.95 (ISBN 0-8224-4252-3). Pitman Learning.
Bernstein, Carl & Woodward, Bob. All the President's Men. (Illus.). 1976. pap. 3.50 (ISBN 0-446-96983-4). Warner Bks.
Bernstein, Carl, jt. auth. see Woodward.
Bernstein, Eduard. Cromwell & Communism. LC 63-18392. 1930. 21.00x (ISBN 0-678-05153-4). Kelley.
Bernstein, Eugene F., et al, eds. Noninvasive Diagnostic Techniques in Vascular Disease. new ed. LC 78-892. (Illus.). 1978. text ed. 45.50 (ISBN 0-8016-0670-5). Mosby.
Bernstein, George see Cordasco, Francesco.
Bernstein, Harry. The Smile. LC 80-53806. (Illus.). 192p. (Orig.). 1980. pap. 5.00 (ISBN 0-931122-21-X). West End.
Bernstein, Ilene N., ed. Validity Issues in Evaluative Research. LC 75-32373. (Sage Contemporary Social Science Issues: Vol. 23). 1976. 4.95x (ISBN 0-8039-0581-5). Sage.
Bernstein, Irving. The New Deal Collective Bargaining Policy. LC 75-8997. (FDR & the Era of the New Deal Ser.). xi, 178p. 1975. Repr. of 1950 ed. lib. bdg. 20.00 (ISBN 0-306-70703-9). Da Capo.
Bernstein, J. S., tr. see Garcia-Marquez, Gabriel.
Bernstein, Jacob. The Investor's Quotient: The Psychology of Successful Investing in Commodities & Stock. LC 80-17127. 296p. 1980. 16.95 (ISBN 0-471-07849-2). Wiley.
Bernstein, Jane. Departures. 304p. 1981. pap. 2.50 (ISBN 0-380-53736-2). Avon.
Bernstein, Jeremy. The Analytical Engine: Computers-Past, Present, & Future. rev. ed. 128p. 1981. 8.95; pap. 4.95. Morrow.
--Elementary Particles & Their Currents. LC 68-21404. (Physics Ser.). (Illus.). 1968. text ed. 26.95x (ISBN 0-7167-0324-6). W H Freeman.
--Experiencing Science: Profiles in Discovery. 1980. pap. 5.95 (ISBN 0-525-47636-9). Dutton.
--Hans Bethe: Prophet of Energy. LC 80-50555. (Illus.). 224p. 1980. pap. 12.95 (ISBN 0-465-02903-5). Basic.
Bernstein, Jerold G. Handbook of Drug Therapy in Psychiatry. 1981. write for info. (ISBN 0-88416-323-7). PSG Pub.
Bernstein, Joanna. Loss & How to Cope with It. 160p. (gr. 6 up). 1981. pap. 3.95 (ISBN 0-395-30012-6, Clarion). HM.
BerNstein, Joanne. Loss & How to Cope with It. LC 76-50027. (gr. 5 up). 7.95 (ISBN 0-395-28891-6, Clarion). HM.
Bernstein, Joel. For the Going. LC 74-24492. (Illus.). 1974. 3.95 (ISBN 0-915298-00-7). Sagarin Pr.
Bernstein, John A. Shaftsbury, Rousseau & Kant: An Introduction to the Conflict Between Aesthetic & Moral Values in Modern Thought. LC 78-75190. 192p. 1980. write for info. (ISBN 0-8386-2351-4). Fairleigh Dickinson.
Bernstein, Ken. Intercept. 1978. pap. 1.50 o.p. (ISBN 0-523-40366-6, Dist. by Independent News Co.). Pinnacle Bks.
Bernstein, Lawrence F., ed. see Gero, Ihan.
Bernstein, Leopold A. The Analysis of Financial Statements. LC 78-55533. 1978. 13.95 (ISBN 0-87094-164-X). Dow Jones-Irwin.
--Financial Statement Analysis: Theory, Application & Interpretation. rev. ed. 1978. 20.95x (ISBN 0-256-02004-3). Irwin.
Bernstein, Lewis & Bernstein, Rosalyn S. Interviewing: A Guide for Health Professionals. 3rd ed. 1974. pap. 11.95 (ISBN 0-8385-4307-3). ACC.

Bernstein, Margery & Kobrin, Janet. The Summer Maker: An Ojibway Indian Myth. LC 76-14875. (Myths You Can Read by Yourself). 48p. (gr. 1-3). 1977. binding 5.95reinforced (ISBN 0-684-14716-5, ScribJ). Scribner.

Bernstein, Marver H. The Job of the Federal Executive. 1958. 10.95 (ISBN 0-8157-0918-8). Brookings.

Bernstein, Marvin D. Foreign Investment in Latin America: Cases & Attitudes. (Borzoi Books on Latin America Ser). 1966. pap. 3.50 o.p. (ISBN 0-394-30054-8). Knopf.

Bernstein, Merton C. Private Dispute Settlement. LC 68-17521. (Illus.). 1969. 20.95 o.s.i. (ISBN 0-02-903030-7). Free Pr.

Bernstein, Michael A. The Tale of the Tribe: Ezra Pound & the Modern Verse Epic. LC 80-129. 1980. 22.50 (ISBN 0-691-06434-2); pap. 9.95 (ISBN 0-691-10105-1). Princeton U Pr.

Bernstein, Morey. Search for Bridey Murphy. rev. ed. LC 65-17244. 1965. 7.95 o.p. (ISBN 0-385-06621-X). Doubleday.

Bernstein, Richard J. Praxis & Action: Contemporary Philosophies of Human Activity. LC 77-157048. 1971. 15.00x (ISBN 0-8122-7640-X); pap. 7.95x (ISBN 0-8122-1016-6, Pa Paperbks). U of Pa Pr.

--The Restructuring of Social & Political Theory. LC 76-12544. 1978. pap. 7.95x (ISBN 0-8122-7742-2). U of Pa Pr.

Bernstein, Richard J., ed. Perspectives on Peirce: Critical Essays on Charles Sanders Peirce. LC 80-13703. 157p. 1980. Repr. of 1965 ed. lib. bdg. 15.75x (ISBN 0-313-22414-5, BEPP). Greenwood.

Bernstein, Richard K. Diabetes: The Glucograph Method for Normalizing Blood Sugar. Behrman, Marion, ed. (Illus.). 320p. 1981. 14.95 (ISBN 0-517-54155-6). Crown.

Bernstein, Robert A. & Dyer, James A. An Introduction to Political Science Methods. (Illus.). 1979. pap. 10.95 ref. ed. (ISBN 0-13-493304-4). P-H.

Bernstein, Rosalyn S., jt. auth. see Bernstein, Lewis.

Bernstein, Rosella. English at Your Fingertips: Teacher's Manual. 1979. pap. text ed. 3.95x o.p. (ISBN 0-87789-141-9). English Lang.

Bernstein, Samuel J. The Strands Entwined. LC 80-12740. 171p. 1980. 17.95x (ISBN 0-930350-07-3). NE U Pr.

Bernstein, Samuel J. & Mellon, W. Giles. Selected Readings in Quantitative Urban Analysis. LC 77-30458. 1978. text ed. 34.00 (ISBN 0-08-019593-8); pap. text ed. 22.00 (ISBN 0-08-019592-X). Pergamon.

Bernstein, Samuel J., ed. Computers in Public Administration: An International Perspective. 450p. 1976. text ed. 46.00 (ISBN 0-08-017869-3). Pergamon.

Bernstein, Saul, ed. Explorations in Group Work: Essays in Theory & Practice. LC 76-50518. 1976. text ed. 12.00x (ISBN 0-89182-000-0); pap. text ed. 6.75x (ISBN 0-89182-001-9). Charles River Bks.

--Further Explorations in Group Work. 1976. text ed. 12.00 (ISBN 0-89182-002-7); pap. 5.75 (ISBN 0-89182-003-5). Charles River Bks.

Bernstein, Serge & Poussin, Charles D. Approximation, 2 Vols. in 1. LC 69-16996. (Fr). 13.95 (ISBN 0-8284-0198-5). Chelsea Pub.

Bernstein-Tarrow, Norma, jt. auth. see Lundsteen, Sara.

Bernstine, R. L., jt. auth. see Thompson, H. E.

Bernthal, Patricia J. & Spiller, James D. Understanding the Language of Medicine: A Programmed Learning Text. (Illus.). 300p. 1981. pap. text ed. 11.95x (ISBN 0-19-502879-1). Oxford U Pr.

Berntzen, Allen K., jt. auth. see Macy, Ralph W.

Bernus, Alexander Von see Von Bernus, Alexander.

Bernus, Edmond. Les Illabakan (Niger) Une Tribu Touaregue Sahelienne et Son Aire De Nomadisation. (Atlas Des Structures Agraires Au Sud Du Sahara: No. 10). 1974. 44.10x (ISBN 90-2797-535-3). Mouton.

Bernzweig, Eli. The Nurse's Liability for Malpractice: A Programed Course. 3rd ed. 368p. 1980. pap. text ed. 11.95 (ISBN 0-07-005058-9, HP); prepub. 2.95 test bank (ISBN 0-07-005059-7). McGraw.

Bernzweig, Eli P. By Accident, Not Design: The Case for Comprehensive Injury Reparations. 238p. 1980. 23.95 (ISBN 0-03-056961-3). Praeger.

Berofsky, Bernard. Determinism. LC 70-112994. 1971. 16.50 (ISBN 0-691-07169-1). Princeton U Pr.

Berolzheimer, Ruth, ed. The American Woman's Cook Book. rev ed. 960p. 1973. 10.95 (ISBN 0-385-00732-9). Doubleday.

--Culinary Arts Institute Encyclopedic Cookbook. 1980. 8.95 (ISBN 0-671-41408-9, Fireside). S&S.

Beroul. The Romance of Tristan: A Poem of the Twelfth Century, Vol. 1 & 2. Ewert, Alfred, ed. 1977. Vol. 1. pap. 8.00x o.p. (ISBN 0-631-02510-3, Pub. by Basil Blackwell); Vol. 2. pap. 9.00x o.p. (ISBN 0-631-12770-4, Pub. by Basil Blackwell). Biblio Dist.

Berque, Jacques. Egypt. (Illus.). 1972. 37.50 o.p. (ISBN 0-686-24608-X, Pub. by Faber & Faber). Merrimack Bk Serv.

Berrall, Julia S. The Garden: An Illustrated History. (Illus.). 1978. 22.50 o.p. (ISBN 0-670-33433-2). Viking Pr.

Berrebi, E., jt. auth. see Abraham-Frois, Gilbert.

Berredo Carneiro, Paulo E. & Arnaud, Pierre, eds. Auguste Comte: Correspondance Generale et Confessions, Tome 1, 1814-1840. (Archives Positivistes). 1973. pap. 40.00x (ISBN 90-2797-192-7). Mouton.

--Auguste Comte: Ecrits De Jeunesse 1816-1828. (Archives Positivistes). 1971. pap. 52.35x (ISBN 90-2796-767-9). Mouton.

Berreman, Gerald D. Hindus of the Himalayas: Ethnography & Change. 2nd ed. LC 73-156468. (Center for South & Southeast Asia Studies, UC Berkeley). 1972. 24.50x (ISBN 0-520-01423-5); pap. 6.95x (ISBN 0-520-02035-9, CAMPUS66). U of Cal Pr.

--Social Inequality: Comparative & Developmental Approaches. (Studies in Anthroplogy). 1981. price not set (ISBN 0-12-093160-5). Acad Pr.

Berrett, Arnold, et al, eds. Modern Thin-Section Tomography. (Illus.). 352p. 1973. 39.50 (ISBN 0-398-02468-5). C C Thomas.

Berrian, Howard. How to Manage the Sales Territory for Maximum Growth. (Illus.). 49.95 o.p. (ISBN 0-89846-031-X). Sales & Mktg.

Berrichon, Paterne. La Vie De Jean-Arthur Rimbaud. LC 77-10252. (Symbolists Ser.). 264p. (Fr.). 1980. Repr. of 1897 ed. 27.50 (ISBN 0-404-16307-6). AMS Pr.

Berridge, A. E. Product Innovation & Development. 236p. 1977. text ed. 24.50x (ISBN 0-220-66325-4, Pub. by Busn Bks England). Renouf.

Berrien, F. Kenneth. General & Social Systems. LC 68-29552. (Illus.). 1968. 15.00x (ISBN 0-8135-0585-2). Rutgers U Pr.

Berrien, Polly, adapted by. Doctor Dolittle & His Friends. (Illus.). (gr. k-4). 1967. PLB 3.99 o.p. (ISBN 0-394-90739-6, BYR). Random.

Berrien, Polly, ed. Games to Play with the Very Young. (Illus.). (ps-2). 1967. 1.95 o.p. (ISBN 0-394-80654-9, BYR). Random.

Berrigan, D. Love, Love at the End. 1971. pap. 1.45 o.s.i. (ISBN 0-02-083750-X, Collier). Macmillan.

Berrigan, Daniel. Beside the Sea of Glass: The Song of the Lamb. (Classic Prayer Ser.). (Illus.). 1978. pap. 4.95 (ISBN 0-8164-2174-9). Crossroad NY.

--A Book of Parables. 1977. 7.95 (ISBN 0-8164-0328-7). Crossroad NY.

--Consequences, Truth and. LC 67-12794. 1967. 3.95 o.p. (ISBN 0-02-510220-6); pap. 1.45 (ISBN 0-02-083780-1). Macmillan.

--Prison Poems. LC 73-76683. 124p. 1973. 10.00 (ISBN 0-87775-049-1). Unicorn Pr.

--Ten Commandments for the Long Jaul. (Journeys in Faith Ser.). 128p. 1981. 7.95 (ISBN 0-687-41240-4). Abingdon.

--Uncommon Prayer: A Book of Psalms. (Illus.). 1978. 7.95 (ISBN 0-8164-0382-1). Crossroad NY.

--We Die Before We Live: Talking with the Very Ill. 160p. 1980. 9.95 (ISBN 0-8164-0462-3). Seabury.

Berrigan, Daniel & Lockwood, Lee. Absurd Convictions, Modest Hopes: Conversation After Prison. 256p. 1973. pap. 1.95 o.p. (ISBN 0-394-71912-3, Vin). Random.

Berrill, Deborah, jt. auth. see Berrill, Michael.

Berrill, Michael & Berrill, Deborah. A Sierra Club Naturalist's Guide to the North Atlantic Coast. (Sierra Club Naturalist's Guides). (Illus.). 512p. (Orig.). 1981. 24.95 (ISBN 0-87156-242-1); pap. 10.95 (ISBN 0-87156-243-X). Sierra.

Berrill, N. J. You & the Universe. 224p. 1973. pap. 4.95 (ISBN 0-911336-47-8). Sci of Mind.

Berrill, N. J., jt. auth. see Karp, Gerald.

Berrill, Norman J. Growth, Development, & Pattern. LC 61-8356. (Illus.). 1961. 26.95x (ISBN 0-7167-0607-5). W H Freeman.

Berriman, D. Master Hi-Fi Loudspeakers & Enclosures. 1979. pap. 5.95 (ISBN 0-8104-0845-7, Co-Pub. by Newnes Butterworth England). Hayden.

Berriman, W. Thomas, et al. Capital Projects for Health Care Facilities. LC 76-15771. 1976. 27.50 (ISBN 0-912862-24-6). Aspen Systems.

Berrington, Hugh B. Backbench Opinion in the House of Commons, 1945-1955. 1974. text ed. 32.00 (ISBN 0-08-016748-9). Pergamon.

Berrisford, Judith. Backyards & Tiny Gardens. 1977. 8.95 o.p. (ISBN 0-571-11034-7, Pub. by Faber & Faber); pap. 5.95 (ISBN 0-571-10837-7). Merrimack Bk Serv.

--Gardening on Chalk, Lime & Clay. 1979. 14.95 (ISBN 0-571-10952-7, Pub. by Faber & Faber); pap. 6.95 (ISBN 0-571-11129-7). Merrimack Bk Serv.

--Rhododencrons & Azaleas. (Illus.). 1973. 17.95 (ISBN 0-571-04798-X, Pub. by Faber & Faber). Merrimack Bk Serv.

--Wild Garden. 1973. 8.95 (ISBN 0-571-04821-8, Pub. by Faber & Faber). Merrimack Bk Serv.

Berrurier, Diane O. le see Le Berrurier, Diane O.

Berry, A. J., ed. see European Symposium on Marine Biology, 12th.

Berry, Ana M. Animals in Art. LC 79-162506. (Tower Bks). (Illus.). 1971. Repr. of 1929 ed. 18.00 (ISBN 0-8103-3900-5). Gale.

Berry, B. J. City Classification Handbook: Methods & Applications. LC 71-171911. (Urban Research Ser.). 394p. 1972. 38.00 (ISBN 0-471-07115-3, Pub. by Wiley-Interscience). Wiley.

Berry, Brewton. You & Your Superstitions. LC 78-174904. (Illus.). 249p. 1974. Repr. of 1940 ed. 20.00 (ISBN 0-8103-3985-4). Gale.

Berry, Brewton & Tischler, Henry L. Race & Ethnic Relations. 4th ed. LC 77-78901. (Illus.). 1978. text ed. 19.50 (ISBN 0-395-25508-2); inst. manual 0.60 (ISBN 0-395-04188-0). HM.

Berry, Brian. Geography of Market Centers & Retail Distribution. 1967. pap. 6.95 ref. ed. (ISBN 0-13-351304-1). P-H.

Berry, Brian J. Theories of Urban Location. LC 68-8949. (CCG Resource Papers Ser.: No. 1). (Illus.). 1968. pap. text ed. 4.00 (ISBN 0-89291-048-8). Assn Am Geographers.

Berry, Brian J. & Horton, Frank E. Geographic Perspectives on Urban Systems with Integrated Readings. 1970. ref. ed. 22.95 (ISBN 0-13-351312-2). P-H.

--Urban Environmental Management: Planning for Pollution Control. (Illus.). 448p. 1974. 20.95 (ISBN 0-13-939611-X). P-H.

Berry, Brian J. L., ed. Urbanization & Counterurbanization. (Urban Affairs Annual Reviews: Vol. 11). (Illus.). 1976. 20.00x (ISBN 0-8039-0499-1); pap. 9.95x (ISBN 0-8039-0682-X). Sage.

Berry, Charles R. The Reform in Oaxaca, 1856-76: A Microhistory of the Liberal Revolution. LC 80-15378. (Illus.). xx, 282p. 1981. 20.00x (ISBN 0-8032-1158-9). U of Nebr Pr.

Berry, Cicely. Voice & the Actor. (Illus.). 144p. 1974. 11.95 (ISBN 0-02-510370-9). Macmillan.

Berry, Claude. Portrait of Cornwall. LC 64-2200. (Portrait Bks.). (Illus.). 1964. 10.50x (ISBN 0-7091-1872-4). Intl Pubns Serv.

Berry, David. Central Ideas in Sociology: An Introduction. 185p. 1975. pap. text ed. 5.95 o.p. (ISBN 0-87581-181-7). Peacock Pubs.

Berry, David, jt. ed. see Smith, John E.

Berry, Dorothea M. A Bibliographic Guide to Educational Research. LC 75-20134. 1975. 8.00 o.p. (ISBN 0-8108-0825-0). Scarecrow.

--A Bibliographic Guide to Educational Research. 2nd ed. LC 80-20191. 224p. 1980. 11.00 (ISBN 0-8108-1351-3). Scarecrow.

Berry, Duane. Psychic Manual. 1978. pap. 1.95 (ISBN 0-686-01317-4). Cathedral of Knowledge.

Berry, Edmund G. Emerson's Plutarch. LC 80-2525. 1981. Repr. of 1961 ed. 37.00 (ISBN 0-404-19250-5). AMS Pr.

Berry, Elizabeth, jt. auth. see Berry, William D.

Berry, G. C. & Sroog, C. E. Rigid Chain Polymers: Synthesis & Properties. (Journal of Polymer Science Symposium Ser.: No. 65). 226p. 1979. 20.50 (ISBN 0-471-05802-5). Wiley.

Berry, George R. A Dictionary of New Testament Greek Synonyms. 1979. 5.95 (ISBN 0-310-21160-3). Zondervan.

Berry, Gerald L. Religions of the World. (Orig.). 1956. pap. 2.50 (ISBN 0-06-463224-5, EH 224, EH). Har-Row.

Berry, Henry & Cook, Bob. A Baseball Century: The First 100 Years of the National League. (Illus.). 256p. 1976. 19.95 o.s.i. (ISBN 0-02-510380-6). Macmillan.

Berry, I. William. The Skier's Almanac. LC 78-15441. 1978. 12.95 o.p. (ISBN 0-684-15791-8, ScribT); pap. 5.95 o.p. (ISBN 0-684-15792-6, ScribT). Scribner.

Berry, J. W., ed. see International Conference of Selected Papers, 2nd, Kingston. Ont. August, 6-10, 1974.

Berry, James. Heroin Was My Best Friend. LC 70-153761. (gr. 6-12). 1971. 4.95 o.s.i. (ISBN 0-02-709700-5, CCPr). Macmillan.

--Heroin Was My Best Friend. LC 70-153761. 160p. (gr. 7 up). 1974. pap. 0.95 o.s.i. (ISBN 0-02-041560-5, 04156, Collier). Macmillan.

--My Experiences As an Executioner. Ward, H. Snowden, ed. LC 70-170299. (Illus.). iv, 148p. Repr. of 1892 ed. 15.00 (ISBN 0-8103-3898-X). Gale.

--Tales of the West of Ireland. 3rd ed. Horgan, Gertrude M., ed. (Yeats Cent. Papers Ser.: Vol. 8). 186p. 1975. text ed. 13.25x (ISBN 0-85105-285-1, Dolmen Pr); pap. text ed. 4.50x (ISBN 0-85105-286-X). Humanities.

Berry, James R. Kids on the Run: The Stories of Seven Teen-Age Runaways. LC 77-15845. 112p. (gr. 7 up). 1978. 6.95 (ISBN 0-590-07507-1, Four Winds). Schol Bk Serv.

Berry, Jo. Proverbs for Easier Living. LC 80-50540. 160p. 1980. pap. 4.95 (ISBN 0-8307-0748-4, 5413605). Regal.

Berry, Juliet. Daily Experience in Residential Life. (Library of Social Work). 1975. 16.95x (ISBN 0-7100-8115-4); pap. 7.95 (ISBN 0-7100-8116-2). Routledge & Kegan.

--Social Work with Children. (Library of Social Work). 1972. pap. 7.95 (ISBN 0-7100-7268-6). Routledge & Kegan.

Berry, L. G., jt. auth. see Mason, Brian.

Berry, L. H. Gastrointestinal Pan-Endoscopy. (Illus.). 688p. 1974. 49.75- (ISBN 0-398-02912-1). C C Thomas.

Berry, Lemuel, Jr. Biographical Dictionary of Black Musicians & Music Educators, Vol. II. (Illus.). 389p. (gr. 5-12). 1981. 20.00 (ISBN 0-932188-02-8). Ed Bk Pubs OK.

--Biographical Dictionary of Black Musicians & Music Educators, Vol. I. LC 78-62404. (gr. 5-12). 1978. 16.95 (ISBN 0-932188-00-1); pap. 12.95 (ISBN 0-932188-01-X). Ed Bk Pubs OK.

Berry, Leonard & Kates, Robert W., eds. Making the Most of the Least: Alternative Development for Poor Nations. LC 79-11619. 1980. text ed. 35.00x (ISBN 0-8419-0434-0). Holmes & Meier.

Berry, Leonard G. & Mason, Brian. Mineralogy: Concepts, Descriptions, Determinations. LC 59-7841. (Geology Ser.). (Illus.). 1959. 26.95x (ISBN 0-7167-0203-7). W H Freeman.

Berry, Linda. Christmas Plays for Older Children. (gr. 5-7). 1981. saddle wire 1.65 (ISBN 0-8054-9733-1). Broadman.

Berry, Lloyd E., ed. Bibliography of Studies in Metaphysical Poetry, Nineteen Thirty-Nine to Nineteen Sixty. 1964. 12.50x (ISBN 0-299-03120-9). U of Wis Pr.

Berry, Lloyd E. & Crummey, Robert O., eds. Rude & Barbarous Kingdom: Russia in the Accounts of Sixteenth-Century English Voyagers. LC 68-16059. (Illus.). 416p. 1972. 25.00 (ISBN 0-299-04760-1, 476); pap. 9.95x (ISBN 0-299-04764-4). U of Wis Pr.

Berry, Lloyd E., ed. see Fletcher, Giles.

Berry, M. Black Resistance - White Law: A History of Institutional Racism in America. 1971. pap. text ed. 11.95 (ISBN 0-13-077735-8). P-H.

--Principles of Cosmology and Gravitation. LC 75-22559. (Illus.). 200p. 1976. 34.95 (ISBN 0-521-21061-5); pap. 11.95x (ISBN 0-521-29028-7). Cambridge U Pr.

Berry, M., jt. auth. see Majer, J. R.

Berry, M., jt. auth. see Mott, Nevill.

Berry, M., jt. auth. see Nonhebel, G.

Berry, M. F. & Floyd, C. M., eds. A History of the Eton College Hunt, 1857-1968. (Illus.). 12.25 (ISBN 0-85131-029-X, Dist. by Sporting Book Center). J A Allen.

Berry, Margaret C. U. T. Austin Traditions & Nostalgia. new ed. LC 75-8061. 126p. 1980. 6.75 (ISBN 0-88319-021-4); pap. 3.95. Shoal Creek Pub.

Berry, Mary. Cooking with Cheese. (Illus.). 144p. 1980. 17.95 (ISBN 0-7134-1925-3, Pub. by Batsford England). David & Charles.

Berry, Mary, ed. Cantors. LC 78-56178. (Resources of Music Ser.). 1979. pap. 4.95 (ISBN 0-521-22149-8). Cambridge U Pr.

Berry, Mary F. Military Necessity & Civil Rights Policy: Black Citizenship & the Constitution, 1861-1868. LC 76-53822. (National University Publications Ser. in American Studies). 1977. 10.00 (ISBN 0-8046-9166-5). Kennikat.

Berry, Mildred F. Language Disorders of Children: The Bases & Diagnoses. (Illus.). 1969. 18.95 (ISBN 0-13-522854-9). P-H.

Berry, Mildred F. & Eisenson, Jon. Speech Disorders: Principles & Practices of Therapy. (Illus.). 1956. 19.95 (ISBN 0-13-827352-9). P-H.

Berry, R. How to Write a Research Paper. 1969. pap. 6.50 (ISBN 0-08-006392-6). Pergamon.

Berry, R. Albert, ed. Economic Policy & Income Distribution in Columbia. Soligo, Ronald. (Westview Replica Edition Ser.). 1979. lib. bdg. 25.50x (ISBN 0-89158-558-3). Westview.

Berry, R. J., ed. Computerized Tomographic Scanners on Radiotheraopy in Europe. 1980. 20.00x (Pub. by Brit Inst Radiology England). State Mutual Bk.

Berry, R. J., jt. ed. see Bates, T. D.

Berry, R. L. Adventures in the Land of Canaan. 128p. pap. 1.00. Faith Pub Hse.

--Around Old Bethany. 83p. pap. 0.75. Faith Pub Hse.

--Steps Heavenward. 123p. pap. 1.00. Faith Pub Hse.

Berry, R. Stephen, et al. Physical Chemistry. LC 79-790. 1980. comb. text ed. 34.95 (ISBN 0-471-04829-1); solutions manual 10.95 (ISBN 0-471-04844-5). Wiley.

Berry, Richard C. Industrial Marketing for Results. LC 80-18222. (Illus.). 144p. 1981. text ed. 19.95 (ISBN 0-201-00075-X). A-W.

Berry, Roger L. God's World: His Story. 1981. pap. 11.45 tchrs'. guide (ISBN 0-87813-914-1). Christian Light.

Berry, Roland. Berry's Book of How It Works. 1976. 5.95 (ISBN 0-7136-1585-0). Transatlantic.

Berry, Sara S. Cocoa, Custom, & Socio-Economic Change in Rural Western Nigeria. (Oxford Studies in African Affairs Ser). (Illus.). 256p. 1975. 37.50x (ISBN 0-19-821697-1). Oxford U Pr.

Berry, Stewart, jt. auth. see Sheldrake, Peter.

Berry, Thomas. Buddhism. 1967. pap. 5.95 (ISBN 0-89012-017-X). Anima Pubns.

--Management: The Managerial Ethos & the Future of Planet Earth. 1980. pap. 2.00 (ISBN 0-89012-016-1). Anima Pubns.

--The New Story. 1978. 2.00 (ISBN 0-89012-012-9). Anima Pubns.

Berry, Thomas E. The Craft of Writing. 1974. pap. text ed. 3.95 (ISBN 0-07-005051-1, SP). McGraw.

Berry, Turner W. & Johnson, A. F. Catalogue of Specimens of Printing Types by English & Scottish Printers & Founders 1665-1830. LC 78-74404. (Nineteenth-Century Book Arts & Printing History Ser.: Vol. 12). 1980. lib. bdg. 38.00 (ISBN 0-8240-3886-X). Garland Pub.

Berry, Virginia G., ed. & tr. see Odo of Deuil.

Berry, W. B. & Murphy, M. A. Silurian & Devonian Graptolites of Central Nevada. (Publications in Geological Sciences: Vol. 110). 1975. pap. 12.50x (ISBN 0-520-09515-4). U of Cal Pr.

Berry, W. T., Jr., et al. Basic Animal Science. (Illus.). 187p. Repr. wire coil lab. manual 6.95 (ISBN 0-89641-052-8). American Pr.

Berry, Wallace. Form in Music: An Examination of Traditional Techniques of Musical Structure & Their Application in Historical & Contemporary Styles. 1966. text ed. 20.95 (ISBN 0-13-329201-0). P-H.

Berry, Wallace & Chudacoff, Edward. Eighteenth Century Imitative Counterpoint: Music for Analysis. (Orig.). 1969. pap. 20.95 (ISBN 0-13-246843-3). P-H.

Berry, Wendell. The Memory of Old Jack. LC 73-15432. 1974. 6.95 o.p. (ISBN 0-15-158865-1). HarBraceJ.

--The Memory of Old Jack. LC 75-6530. 223p. 1975. pap. 3.50 (ISBN 0-15-658670-3, HPL64, HPL). HarBraceJ.

Berry, William B. Growth of a Prehistoric Time Scale, Based on Organic Evolution. LC 68-14224. (Illus.). 1968. pap. 6.95x (ISBN 0-7167-0237-1). W H Freeman.

Berry, William D. Deneki: An Alaskan Moose. (gr. 4-6). 1965. 4.50g o.s.i. (ISBN 0-02-709510-X). Macmillan.

Berry, William D. & Berry, Elizabeth. Mammals of the San Francisco Bay Region. (California Natural History Guides: No. 2). 1959. 12.95x (ISBN 0-520-03088-5); pap. 3.95 (ISBN 0-520-00116-8). U of Cal Pr.

Berry, William L., et al. Management Decision Sciences: Cases & Readings. 1980. 19.95x (ISBN 0-256-02219-4). Irwin.

Berryman, John. Homage to Mistress Bradstreet & Other Poems. LC 68-24596. 1968. pap. 3.50 (ISBN 0-374-50660-4, N337). FS&G.

Bers, Lipman see Knopp, Konrad.

Bersani, Leo. Baudelaire & Freud. (Quantum Ser.). 1978. 11.95x (ISBN 0-520-03402-3); pap. 2.65 (ISBN 0-520-03535-6). U of Cal Pr.

Berscheid, Ellen & Walster, Elaine H. Interpersonal Attraction. 2nd ed. LC 77-77726. (Topics in Social Psychology). (Illus.). 1978. pap. text ed. 8.95 (ISBN 0-201-00569-7). A-W.

Berse, P. A., ed. see Fraser, G. M. & Blockley, J.

Bershad, Carol & Bernick, Deborah. Bodyworks: The Kids' Guide to Food & Physical Fitness. (Illus.). 240p. (gr. 5-9). 1981. PLB 8.99 (ISBN 0-394-94752-5); pap. 5.95 (ISBN 0-394-84752-0). Random.

Bershady, H. Ideology & Social Knowledge. LC 73-5337. 178p. 1973. 13.95 (ISBN 0-470-07155-9). Halsted Pr.

Berson, Harold. Larbi & Leila: A Tale of Two Mice. LC 73-12378. (Illus.). (ps-3). 1974. 5.50 (ISBN 0-395-28766-9, Clarion). HM.

--The Thief Who Hugged a Moonbeam. LC 70-190382. (Illus.). 40p. (gr. k-3). 1972. 4.50 (ISBN 0-395-28767-7, Clarion). HM.

--Truffles for Lunch. LC 80-13367. (Illus.). (gr. k-3). 1980. PLB 8.95 (ISBN 0-02-709800-1). Macmillan.

--Why the Jackal Won't Speak to the Hedgehog. LC 69-13439. (Illus.). (ps-2). 1969. 6.95 (ISBN 0-395-28768-5, Clarion). HM.

Berssen, William. Pacific Boating Almanac: Pacific Northwest & Alaska Edition 1981. annual ed. 416p. 1981. pap. 6.95 (ISBN 0-686-66131-1). Western Marine Ent.

--Pacific Boating Almanac 1981: Northern California & Nevada Edition. annual ed. 416p. 1981. pap. 6.95 (ISBN 0-686-66130-3). Western Marine Ent.

--Pacific Boating Almanac 1981: Southern California, Arizona, Baja Edition. annual ed. 416p. 1981. pap. 6.95 (ISBN 0-686-66129-X). Western Marine Ent.

Berssenbrugge, Mei-mei. Random Possession. LC 78-66087. 1979. pap. 5.95 (ISBN 0-918408-13-X). Reed & Cannon.

Berston, Hyman M. California Real Estate Practice. 3rd. ed. 1977. text ed. 17.95x (ISBN 0-256-01929-0). Irwin.

--California Real Estate Principles. 3rd. ed. 1979. text ed. 17.95x (ISBN 0-256-02149-X). Irwin.

Berston, Hyman M. & Fisher, Paul. Collegiate Business Mathematics. rev. ed. 1978. Repr. text ed. 12.95x (ISBN 0-256-01395-0). Irwin.

Bert, C. W., ed. Mechanics of Bimodulus Materials, Bk. No. G00150. LC 90-75422. (Applied Mechanics Division Ser.: Vol. 33). 96p. 1979. 18.00 (ISBN 0-686-62957-4). ASME.

Bertalanffy, Ludwig Van see Von Bertalanffy, Ludwig.

Bertalanffy, Ludwig Von see Von Bertalanffy, Ludwig.

Bertalanffy, Ludwig von see Von Bertalanffy, Ludwig.

Bertalanffy, Maria von see Von Bertalanffy, Ludwig.

Bertcher, Harvey J. Group Participation: Techniques for Leaders & Members. LC 79-175. (Sage Human Services Guides: Vol. 10). 1979. pap. 8.00x (ISBN 0-8039-1204-8). Sage.

Bertcher, Harvey J. & Maple, Frank F. Creating Groups. LC 77-22401. (Sage Human Services Guides: Vol. 2). 1977. pap. 6.00x (ISBN 0-8039-0881-4). Sage.

Berteaux, H. O. Buoy Engineering. LC 75-20046. (Ocean Engineering Ser). 336p. 1976. 35.00 (ISBN 0-471-07156-0, Pub. by Wiley-Interscience). Wiley.

Bertela, G. Gaeta. Donatello. (Scala Art Book). (Illus., Orig.). 1978. pap. 5.95 (ISBN 0-8467-0471-4, Pub. by Two Continents). Hippocrene Bks.

Bertels, Frank. The First Book on Male Liberation & Sex Equality. (Illus.). 352p. 1981. lib. bdg. 25.00 (ISBN 0-932574-05-X); pap. 15.00 (ISBN 0-932574-06-8). Brun Pr.

Bertelsen, Judy S., ed. Non-State Nations in International Politics: Comparative System Analyses. LC 75-36404. 1978. text ed. 29.95 (ISBN 0-275-56320-0). Praeger.

Bertelson, David. The Lazy South. LC 80-24033. ix, 284p. 1980. Repr. of 1967 ed. lib. bdg. 25.00x (ISBN 0-313-22696-2, BELS). Greenwood.

Bertens, Hans. The Fiction of Paul Bowles: The Soul Is the Weariest Part of the Body. (Costerus Ser.: No. XXI). (Orig.). 1979. pap. text ed. 28.50x (ISBN 90-6203-992-8). Humanities.

Bertensson, Sergei & Leyda, Jay. Sergei Rachmaninoff: A Lifetime in Music. LC 55-10065. (Illus.). 1956. 17.50x (ISBN 0-8147-0044-6). NYU Pr.

Bertensson, Sergei, jt. ed. see Leyda, Jay.

Berthoff, Ann E. Forming-Thinking-Writing: The Composing Imagination. (gr. 10-12). 1978. pap. text ed. 7.50x (ISBN 0-8104-6033-5). Hayden.

Berthoff, Warner. Example of Melville. 1972. pap. 2.25 o.p. (ISBN 0-393-00595-X, Norton Lib). Norton.

Berthoff, Werner. A Literature Without Qualities: American Writing Since 1945. (Quantum Bks.). 1980. 11.95 (ISBN 0-520-03696-4). U of Cal Pr.

Berthollet, Claude-Louis. Researches into the Laws of Chemical Affinity. 2nd ed. LC 65-23404. 1966. Repr. of 1809 ed. 22.50 (ISBN 0-306-70914-7). Da Capo.

Berthoud, Jacques. Joseph Conrad: The Major Phase. LC 77-8242. (British Authors Ser.). 1978. 22.50 (ISBN 0-521-21742-3); pap. 8.95x (ISBN 0-521-29273-5). Cambridge U Pr.

Berti, Luciano. The Uffizi. (Illus.). 1978. pap. 9.95 (ISBN 0-8467-0453-6, Pub. by Two Continents). Hippocrene Bks.

Berti, Luciano, intro. by. The Official Catalogue of the Uffizi. (Illus.). 1980. 350.00 (ISBN 88-7038-017-3, Centro Di). Gale.

Bertin, John J. & Smith, Michael L. Aerodynamics for Engineers. (Illus.). 1979. text ed. 29.95 (ISBN 0-13-018234-6). P-H.

Berting, Jan, et al. Problems in International Comparative Research in the Social Sciences. 186p. 1979. 28.00 (ISBN 0-08-025247-8). Pergamon.

Berting, Jan, et al, eds. The Socio-Economic Impact of Microelectronics: International Conference on Socio-Economic Problems & Potentialities of Microelectronics, Sept. 1979, Zandvoort, Netherlands. LC 80-49810. (Vienna Centre Ser.). (Illus.). 263p. 1980. 50.00 (ISBN 0-08-026776-9). Pergamon.

Bertisch, Jan, ed. see Harvey, Bill.

Bertke, Eldridge M., jt. auth. see Brown, Walter V.

Bertocci, Peter A., ed. Mid-Twentieth Century American Philosophy: Personal Statements. LC 73-18467. 251p. 1974. text ed. 12.50x (ISBN 0-391-00340-2). Humanities.

Bertol, Roland. Charles Drew. LC 77-94789. (Biography Ser.). (Illus.). (gr. 2-5). 1970. PLB 7.89 o.p. (ISBN 0-690-18598-7, TYC-J). T Y Crowell.

Bertolucci, Bernardo & Arcalli, Franco. Bernardo Bertolucci's Last Tango in Paris. (Illus.). 256p. 1974. 7.95 o.p. (ISBN 0-440-02041-7). Delacorte.

Berton, Alberta D., compiled by. Asbestosis: A Comprehensive Bibliography. (Biomedical Information Guides Ser.: Vol. 1). 395p. 1980. 85.00 (ISBN 0-306-65176-9, IFI). Plenum Pub.

--Nuclear Medicine: A Comprehensive Bibliography. (Biomedical Information Guides Ser.: Vol. 2). 355p. 1980. 85.00 (ISBN 0-306-65178-5, IFI). Plenum Pub.

--Smoking & Health: A Comprehensive Bibliography. (Biomedical Information Guides Ser.: Vol. 3). 535p. 1980. 95.00 (ISBN 0-306-65184-X, IFI). Plenum Pub.

Berton, Pierre. The Invasion of Canada: 1812-1813. 320p. 1980. 17.50 (ISBN 0-686-62570-6, An Atlantic Monthly Press Book). Little.

Bertonasco, Marc F., jt. auth. see Miles, Robert.

Bertone, Pamela S., jt. auth. see Dickens, E. Larry.

Bertotti-Scamozzi, Ottavio. The Buildings & Designs of Andrea Palladio, 2 vols. 1976. boxed 400.00x (ISBN 0-685-73875-2); Plates. boxed 200.00x (ISBN 0-686-67583-5); 30 plates 30.00x (ISBN 0-686-67584-3); 10 plates 20.00x (ISBN 0-686-67585-1); eng. trans. only 50.00x (ISBN 0-686-67586-X). U Pr of Va.

Bertozzi, W., et al, eds. Electron & Pion Interactions with Nuclei at Intermediate Energies. (Studies in High Energy Physics: Vol. 2). 716p. 1981. 55.00 (ISBN 3-7186-0015-3). Harwood Academic.

Bertram, Christoph. New Conventional Weapons & East-West Security. LC 78-78216. (Praeger Special Studies Ser.). 102p. 1979. 20.95 (ISBN 0-03-052091-6). Praeger.

Bertram, Christoph, ed. Arms Control & Military Force. LC 80-67836. (Adelphi Library: Vol. 3). 272p. 1981. text ed. 32.50 (ISBN 0-916672-70-0). Allanheld.

--Prospects of the Soviet Power in the Nineteen Eighties. 126p. 1980. 19.50 (ISBN 0-208-01885-9, Archon). Shoe String.

--Strategic Deterrence in a Changing Environment. LC 80-67841. (Adelphi Library: Vol. 6). 200p. 1981. text ed. 29.50 (ISBN 0-916672-75-1). Allanheld.

Bertram, James, ed. see Arnold, Thomas.

Bertram, James M. First Act in China: The Story of the Sian Mutiny. LC 74-31223. (China in the 20th Century Ser). Orig. Title: Crisis in China. (Illus.). xxii, 284p. 1975. Repr. of 1938 ed. lib. bdg. 27.50 (ISBN 0-306-70687-3). Da Capo.

--Unconquered: Journal of a Year's Adventure Among the Fighting Peasants of North China. (China in the 20th Century Ser). (Illus.). ix, 340p. 1975. Repr. of 1939 ed. lib. bdg. 29.50 (ISBN 0-306-70688-1). Da Capo.

Bertram, Paul. White Spaces in Shakespeare. 112p. 1981. 12.50x (ISBN 0-934958-01-7); pap. 8.00x (ISBN 0-934958-02-5). Arete Pr.

Bertram, Paul D. Shakespeare & the "Two Noble Kinsmen". 1965. 21.00 (ISBN 0-8135-0499-6). Rutgers U Pr.

Bertrand, A. & Cebula, J. Test & Measurement: A Developmental Approach. 1980. 14.50 (ISBN 0-201-00778-9). A-W.

Bertrand, Arthur & Cebula, Joseph P. Tests, Measurement & Evaluation: A Developmental Approach. LC 79-21032. (Education Ser.). (Illus.). 1980. 14.50 (ISBN 0-201-00778-9). A-W.

Bertrand, F. E., ed. Giant Multipole Resonances Oak Ridge, Tennessee, October 15-17, 1979. (Nuclear Science Research Conference Ser.: Vol. 1). 481p. 1980. 42.50 (ISBN 0-686-61662-6). Harwood Academic.

Bertrand, Joseph. Calcul Des Probabilites. 2nd ed. LC 78-113114. 389p. (Fr.). 1972. text ed. 11.95 (ISBN 0-8284-0262-0). Chelsea Pub.

Bertrand, Marc. L'Oeuvre de Jean Prevost. (U. C. Publ. in Modern Philology: Vol. 90). 1968. pap. 8.00x (ISBN 0-520-09285-6). U of Cal Pr.

Bertsch, Gary K. & Ganschow, Thomas W., eds. Comparative Communism: The Soviet, Chinese, & Yugoslav Models. LC 75-20464. (Illus.). 1976. text ed. 21.95x (ISBN 0-7167-0733-0); pap. text ed. 10.95x (ISBN 0-7167-0732-2). W H Freeman.

Bertsch, Gary K., et al. Comparing Political Systems: Power & Policy in Three Worlds. LC 77-27575. 1978. text ed. 16.95 (ISBN 0-471-02674-3); tchrs. manual avail. (ISBN 0-471-04047-9). Wiley.

Bertsche, William H., Jr., ed. see Beidler, John X.

Berube, Maurice R. The Urban University in America. LC 77-87917. 1978. lib. bdg. 15.00 (ISBN 0-313-20031-9, BUU/). Greenwood.

Berulfsen, B. English-Norsk Dictionary: Gyldendals. new ed. 1978. 18.50x (ISBN 8-2573-0007-1, N481); Norsk-English. 18.50x (ISBN 8-2573-0006-3, N-482). Vanous.

Berulfsen, B. & Berulfsen, T. Norwegian Dictionary: Engelsk-Norwegina. rev. ed. 433p. 1978. 18.50x (ISBN 82-573-0007-1, N481). Vanous.

Berulfsen, B. & Svenkerud, A. Norwegian Deluxe Dictionary: English-Norse. 1968. 90.00x (ISBN 82-02-06627-1, N461). Vanous.

Berulfsen, T., jt. auth. see Berulfsen, B.

Berwick, Donald M., et al. Cholesterol, Children, & Heart Disease: An Analysis of Alternatives. (Illus.). 416p. 1980. 32.95x (ISBN 0-19-502669-1). Oxford U Pr.

Berwick, Thurso, jt. ed. see Law, T. S.

Berwick, W. E. Integral Bases. (Cambridge Tracts in Mathematics & Mathematical Physics Ser.: No. 22). 1964. Repr. of 1927 ed. 9.75 o.s.i. (ISBN 0-02-841310-5). Hafner.

Berwitz, Clement J. The Job Analysis Approach to Affirmative Action. LC 75-11660. 327p. 1975. 34.50 (ISBN 0-471-07157-9, Pub. by Wiley-Interscience). Wiley.

Beryl & Newman, Michael. A Guide to Prayer for Busy People. (Jubilee Ser.). (Illus.). 48p. (Orig.). 1980. pap. 1.95 (ISBN 0-89570-196-0). Claretian Pubns.

Berzon, Judith R. Neither White nor Black: The Mulatto Character in American Fiction. LC 77-94392. 1978. 15.00x (ISBN 0-8147-0996-6); pap. 7.00x (ISBN 0-8147-0997-4). NYU Pr.

Berztiss, A. T. Data Structures: Theory & Practice. 2nd ed. (Computer Science & Applied Mathematics Ser.). 586p. 1975. 21.95 (ISBN 0-12-093552-X). Acad Pr.

Besalel, V. A., jt. auth. see Azrin, Nathan H.

Besalel, Victoria A., jt. auth. see Azrin, Nathan H.

Besancon, Alain. Education et Societe En Russie Dans le Second Tiers Du XIXe Siecle. (Civilisations et Societes: No. 40). 1974. pap. 18.80x (ISBN 90-2797-545-0). Mouton.

--The Rise of the Gulag: Intellectual Origins of Leninism. 272p. 1980. 19.50 (ISBN 0-8264-0014-0). Continuum.

Besancon, Alain, ed. L' Histoire Psychanalytique: Une Anthologie. (Le Savoir Historique: No. 7). 1974. pap. 23.00x (ISBN 90-2797-326-1). Mouton.

Besant, Annie. Ancient Wisdom. 9th ed. 1972. 5.95 (ISBN 0-8356-7038-4). Theos Pub Hse.

--Introduction to Yoga. 1972. 3.25 (ISBN 0-8356-7120-8). Theos Pub Hse.

--Karma. 10th ed. 1975. 3.25 (ISBN 0-8356-7035-X). Theos Pub Hse.

--Reincarnation. 11th ed. 1975. 2.50 (ISBN 0-8356-7019-8). Theos Pub Hse.

--Study in Consciousness. 6th ed. 1972. 6.25 (ISBN 0-8356-7287-5). Theos Pub Hse.

Besant, Annie & Leadbeater, Charles W. Thought Forms. abr. ed. (Illus.). 1969. pap. 4.95 (ISBN 0-8356-0008-4, Quest). Theos Pub Hse.

Besant, Annie, tr. Bhagavad Gita, 8th prts. 1974. 1.75 (ISBN 0-8356-7001-5). Theos Pub Hse.

Besant, C. B. Computer-Aided Design & Manufacture. LC 79-40971. 1980. 42.95 (ISBN 0-470-26868-9). Halsted Pr.

Besant, Walter. East London: London, Nineteen One. LC 79-56945. (The English Working Class Ser.). 1980. lib. bdg. 32.00 (ISBN 0-8240-0100-1). Garland Pub.

--In Deacon's Orders, 1895. Wolff, Robert L., ed. Bd. with Red Pottage, 1899. Cholmondely, Mary. LC 75-1541. (Victorian Fiction Ser). 1975. lib. bdg. 66.00 (ISBN 0-8240-1612-2). Garland Pub.

Besaw, Victor. The Alien. 1979. pap. 1.75 o.p. (ISBN 0-449-14197-7, GM). Fawcett.

Besch, Anthony, tr. see Milnes, John, et al.

Bescherelle. Art De Conjuguer: Huit Milles Verses. (Fr). 7.00 (ISBN 0-685-20225-9). Schoenhof.

Beshers, James M. Urban Social Structure. LC 80-27972. vii, 207p. 1981. Repr. of 1962 ed. lib. bdg. 19.75x (ISBN 0-313-22714-4, BEUR). Greenwood.

Besov, Oleg V., et al. Integral Representations of Functions & Imbedding Theorems, 2 vols. (Scripta Ser. in Mathematics). 1979. 19.95 ea. Vol. 1 (ISBN 0-470-26540-X). Vol. 2 (ISBN 0-470-26593-0). Halsted Pr.

Bess, Barbara, et al. A Sexual Profile of Men in Power. 1978. pap. 2.50 (ISBN 0-446-81484-9). Warner Bks.
Bess, Fred H. & McConnell, Freeman E. Audiology, Education & the Hearing Impaired Child. (Illus.). 325p. 1981. pap. text ed. 15.95 (ISBN 0-8016-0671-3). Mosby.
Bess, Nancy, jt. auth. see Gilman, Rachel.
Bessant, J. R., et al. The Impact of Microelectronics: A Review of the Literature. LC 80-54414. (Illus.). 174p. 1981. text ed. 25.00 (ISBN 0-87663-729-2, Pica Special Studies). Universe.
Besse, A. L. Manifolds All of Whose Geodesics Are Closed. (Ergebnisse der Mathmatik und Ihrer Grenzbebiete: Vol. 93). (Illus.). 1978. 41.00 (ISBN 0-387-08158-5). Springer-Verlag.
Bessel, Richard & Feuchtwanger, E. J., eds. Social Change & Political Development in Weimar Germany. 297p. 1981. 27.00x (ISBN 0-389-20176-6). B&N.
Bessell, Harold. Methods in Human Development: Theory Manual. rev. ed. 1973. 7.95 o.p. (ISBN 0-686-05865-8). Human Dev Train.
Bessell, Harold & Ball, Geraldine. Methods in Human Development: Activity Guide for Pre-School & Kindergarten. rev. ed. 1972. 9.95 (ISBN 0-86584-000-8). Human Dev Train.
Bessell, Robert. Interviewing & Counselling. 1976. 22.50 (ISBN 0-7134-0965-7, Pub. by Batsford England). David & Charles.
Besser, Gretchen R. Nathalie Sarraute. (World Authors Ser.: No. 534). 1979. lib. bdg. 13.50 (ISBN 0-8057-6376-7). Twayne.
Besset, Maurice. Le Corbusier. LC 76-11507. (Illus.). 1976. 50.00 o.p. (ISBN 0-8478-0048-2). Rizzoli Intl.
Bessiere, Irene. Recit fantastique: La Poetique de l'incertain. new ed. (Collection Themes et Textes). 256p. (Orig., Fr.). 1974. pap. 6.75 (ISBN 2-03-035023-0, 2674). Larousse.
Bessiere, J. Fitzgerald: La Vocation de l'echec. (Collection themes et textes). 256p. (Orig., Fr.). 1972. pap. 6.75 (ISBN 2-03-035002-8, 2682). Larousse.
Bessler, Helen. Beresheet: A Kindergarten Guide. LC 68-30816. (Orig.). 1969. pap. text ed. 4.50 (ISBN 0-8074-0130-7, 244310). UAHC.
Besson, Pablo, tr. from Greek. Nuevo Testamento De Nuestro Senor Jesucristo. 576p. (Span.). 1980. pap. write for info. (ISBN 0-311-48710-6, Edit Mundo). Casa Bautista.
Bessonov, L. Applied Electricity for Engineers. 2nd ed. Kuznetsov, Boris, tr. from Rus. (Illus.). 792p. 1973. 20.00x o.p. (ISBN 0-8464-0142-8). Beekman Pubs.
Best, Alan C. & Blij, Harm J. An African Survey. LC 76-44520. 1977. text ed. 23.95 (ISBN 0-471-20063-8). Wiley.
Best, Alan D. & Wolfshutz, Hans, eds. Modern Austrian Writing: Literature & Society After 1945. 307p. 1980. 24.50x (ISBN 0-389-20038-7). B&N.
Best, Arthur. When Consumers Complain. LC 80-21789. 256p. 1981. 16.95 (ISBN 0-231-05124-7). Columbia U Pr.
Best, David. Philosophy & Human Movement. (Unwin Education Bks.). 1979. text ed. 21.95x (ISBN 0-04-370088-8); pap. text ed. 7.95x (ISBN 0-04-370089-6). Allen Unwin.
Best, E. & Wilson, R. McL., eds. Text & Interpretation. LC 78-2962. 1979. 39.00 (ISBN 0-521-22021-1). Cambridge U Pr.
Best, Elsdon. Maori Storehouses & Kindred Structures: Houses, Platforms, Racks & Pits Used for Storing Food, Etc. (New Zealand Dominion Museum Bulletin: No. 5). (Illus.). 1977. text ed. 9.50x o.p. (ISBN 0-8426-1041-3). Verry.
Best, Fred. Flexible Life Scheduling: Breaking the Education-Work-Retirement Lockstep. 1979. 23.95 (ISBN 0-03-050586-0); pap. 8.95 (ISBN 0-03-050591-7). Praeger.
Best, Gary A. Individuals with Physical Disabilities: An Introduction for Educators. LC 78-1206. (Illus.). 1978. text ed. 16.50 (ISBN 0-8016-0665-9). Mosby.
Best, Geoffrey & Wheatcroft, Andrew, eds. War, Economy & the Military Mind. 136p. 1976. 12.50x (ISBN 0-87471-757-4). Rowman.
Best, Gerald M. Iron Horses to Promontory Railroad: Central Pacific Union Pacific. LC 69-20447. (Illus.). 1969. 18.95 (ISBN 0-87095-001-0). Golden West.
--Ships & Narrow Gauge Rails: The Story of the Pacific Coast Company. (Illus.). 155p. Date not set. Repr. of 1964 ed. 15.00 (ISBN 0-8310-7042-0). Howell-North.
Best, John. Research in Education. 4th ed. (Illus.). 400p. 1981. text ed. 18.95 (ISBN 0-13-774026-3). P-H.
Best, John H., ed. Benjamin Franklin on Education. LC 62-20697. (Orig.). 1962. text ed. 8.75 (ISBN 0-8077-1080-6); pap. text ed. 4.00x (ISBN 0-8077-1077-6). Tchrs Coll.
Best, John W. Research in Education. 3rd ed. (Illus.). 1977. text ed. 18.95 (ISBN 0-13-774018-2). P-H.
Best, Judith. The Mainstream of Western Political Thought. 144p. 1980. text ed. 17.95x (ISBN 0-87705-271-9); pap. text ed. 8.95x (ISBN 0-87705-243-3). Human Sci Pr.
Best, Leo, jt. auth. see Hein, Morris.
Best, Michael H. & Connolly, William E. The Politicized Economy. 1976. pap. text ed. 5.95x (ISBN 0-669-97162-6). Heath.
Best, Otto F. Peter Weiss. Molinaro, Ursule, tr. from Ger. LC 75-10104. (Modern Literature Ser.). 170p. 1976. 10.95 (ISBN 0-8044-2038-6). Ungar.
Best, Robin H., jt. auth. see Coppock, J. T.
Best, Simon & Lollerstrom, Nick. Planting by the Moon - Nineteen Eighty-One. rev. ed. (Illus.). 128p. 1981. pap. 2.95 (ISBN 0-917086-25-2). Astro Comp Serv.
Best, Thomas W. Jacob Bidermann. (World Authors Ser.: Germany: No. 314). 1974. lib. bdg. 12.50 (ISBN 0-8057-2154-1). Twayne.
--Macropedius. (World Authors Ser.: Netherlands: No. 218). lib. bdg. 10.95 (ISBN 0-8057-2560-1). Twayne.
Best, William M. William Mawdesley Best: Treatise on the Principles of Evidence & Practice As to Proofs in Courts of Common Law, Repr. Of 1849 Ed. Berkowitz, David & Thorne, Samuel, eds. Bd. with Sir James Fitzjames Stephen: Digest of the Law of Evidence. Stephen, Sir James F. Repr. of 1876 ed. LC 77-86653. (Classics of English Legal History in the Modern Era Ser.). 1979. lib. bdg. 55.00 (ISBN 0-8240-3086-9). Garland Pub.
Best, William M. & Stephen, James F. A Treatise on the Principles of Evidence & Practice As to Proofs in the Court of Common Law. Berkowitz, David S. & Thorne, Samuel E., eds. LC 77-86653. (Classics of English Legal History in the Modern Era Ser.: Vol.37). 594p. 1979. lib. bdg. 40.00 (ISBN 0-8240-3086-9). Garland Pub.
Bester, Alfred. Computer Connection. LC 74-30544. (YA) 1975. 6.95 o.p. (ISBN 0-399-11481-5). Berkley Pub.
--The Computer Connection. 1976. pap. 1.75 o.p. (ISBN 0-425-03039-3, Medallion). Berkley Pub.
--Golem. 1981. pap. 2.50 (ISBN 0-671-82047-8). PB.
--Star Light, Star Bright: The Great Short Fiction of Alfred Bester, Vol. 2. LC 76-17377. (YA) 1976. 7.95 o.p. (ISBN 0-399-11816-0). Berkley Pub.
--Starlight: The Best of Bester. 1977. pap. 1.95 o.p. (ISBN 0-425-03451-8, Medallion). Berkley Pub.
--The Stars My Destination. 1975. pap. 2.25 (ISBN 0-425-04365-7, Medallion). Berkley Pub.
--The Stars My Destination. (Science Fiction Ser). 244p. 1975. Repr. of 1957 ed. lib. bdg. 12.50 (ISBN 0-8398-2300-2). Gregg.
Bester, John, tr. see Enchi, Fumiko.
Bester, John, tr. see Ibuse, Masuji.
Bester, John, tr. see Mishima, Yukio.
Bester, John, tr. see Nakagawa, Sensaka.
Bester, John, tr. see Oe, Kenzaburo.
Bester, John, tr. see Yoshiyuki, Junnosuke.
Besterman, T. Bibliography of Sir James George Frazer, O. M. (Illus.). 1968. 11.00 o.p. (ISBN 0-7129-0245-7, Dist. by Shoe String). Dawson Pub.
Besterman, Theodore. Collected Papers on the Paranormal. LC 66-28500. (Illus.). 1968. 12.50 o.p. (ISBN 0-912326-21-2). Garrett-Helix.
--Early Printed Books to the End of the Sixteenth Century: A Bibliography of Bibliographies. 2nd rev. & enl. ed. 344p. 1969. 21.50x (ISBN 0-87471-008-1). Rowman.
Besterman, Theodore, ed. see Crawley, Ernest.
Beston & Coatsworth. Chimney Farm Bedtime Stories. 1977. pap. 3.50 (ISBN 0-89272-040-9). Down East.
Bestor, Arthur. Backwoods Utopias: The Sectarian Origins & the Owenite Phase of Communitarian Socialism in America: 1663-1829. 2nd ed. LC 76-92852. 1971. 15.00x (ISBN 0-8122-7193-9); pap. 8.50x (ISBN 0-8122-1004-2, Pa Paperbks). U of Pa Pr.
Bestor, William S., jt. ed. see Leakey, L. S.
Betancourt, Philip P. The Aeolic Style in Architecture: A Survey of Its Development in Palestine, the Halikarnassos Peninsula, & Greece, 1000-500 B.C. LC 76-45890. (Illus.). 1977. text ed. 30.00 (ISBN 0-691-03922-4). Princeton U Pr.
Betancourt, Roger & Clague, Christopher. Capacity Utilization: A Theoretical & Empirical Analysis. LC 80-22410. (Illus.). 320p. Date not set. price not set (ISBN 0-521-23583-9). Cambridge U Pr.
Betcherman, Barbara. Suspicions. 1981. pap. 2.75 (ISBN 0-425-04839-X). Berkley Pub.
Beteille, Andre. Caste, Class & Power: Changing Patterns of Stratification in a Tanjore Village. 1965. pap. 7.50x (ISBN 0-520-02053-7). U of Cal Pr.
--Inequality Among Men. (Pavilion Ser.). 1977. 36.00x (ISBN 0-631-17410-9, Pub. by Basil Blackwell); pap. 12.00x (ISBN 0-631-17420-6, Pub. by Basil Blackwell). Biblio Dist.
Betensky, Mala. Self-Discovery Through Self-Expression: Use of Art in Psychotherapy with Children & Adolescents. (Illus.). 384p. 1973. 34.75 (ISBN 0-398-02574-6). C C Thomas.
Beter, Thais R. & Cragin, Wesley E. The Mentally Retarded Child & His Motor Behavior: Practical Diagnosis & Movement Experiences. (Illus.). 208p. 1972. 19.75 (ISBN 0-398-02230-5). C C Thomas.
Beth Israel Hospital, Boston. Respiratory Intensive Care Nursing. 2nd ed. 1979. spiral bdg. 12.95 (ISBN 0-316-09237-1). Little.
Bethancourt, Ernesto T. Dr. Doom Superstar. 128p. (gr. 6-9). 1980. pap. 1.75 (ISBN 0-553-13929-0). Bantam.
Bethancourt, T. Ernesto. Dr. Doom: Superstar. LC 78-6315. (YA) 1978. 8.95 (ISBN 0-8234-0333-5). Holiday.
--The Dog Days of Arthur Cane. LC 76-15033. (gr. 7 up). 1976. 8.95 (ISBN 0-8234-0286-X). Holiday.
--The Dog Days of Arthur Cane. 160p. 1981. pap. 1.75 (ISBN 0-553-14835-4). Bantam.
--Doris Fein: Phantom of the Casino. LC 80-8814. 160p. (YA) 1981. 8.95 (ISBN 0-8234-0391-2). Holiday.
--Doris Fein: Quartz Boyar. LC 80-15920. 160p. (YA) (gr. 9 up). 1980. 8.95 (ISBN 0-8234-0378-5). Holiday.
--Doris Fein: Superspy. LC 79-23339. 160p. (YA) (gr. 9 up). 1980. 8.95 (ISBN 0-8234-0407-2). Holiday.
--Tune in Yesterday. 144p. 1981. pap. 1.75 (ISBN 0-553-13324-1). Bantam.
--Tune in Yesterday. LC 77-15640. (YA) 1978. 8.95 (ISBN 0-8234-0316-5). Holiday.
--Where the Deer & the Cantaloupe Play. 90p. 1980. write for info. (ISBN 0-916392-69-4). Oak Tree Pubns.
Bethe, Hans A. & Jackiw, Roman W. Intermediate Quantum Mechanics. 2nd ed. LC 68-24363. (Lecture Notes & Supplements in Physics Ser.: No. 9). 1968. pap. 17.50 (ISBN 0-8053-0755-9, Adv Bk Prog). Benjamin-Cummings.
Bethe, Monica, tr. see Ito, Toshiko.
Bethe, Monica, tr. see Nishikawa, Kyotaro.
Bethel, Dell. Coaching Winning Baseball. 1979. 14.95 o.p. (ISBN 0-8092-7460-4); pap. 7.95 (ISBN 0-8092-7459-0). Contemp Bks.
--Inside Baseball: Tips & Techniques for Coaches & Players. LC 69-17434. (Illus.). 1969. 7.95 (ISBN 0-8092-8871-0); pap. 4.95 o.p. (ISBN 0-8092-8870-2). Contemp Bks.
Bethel, James S. & Massengale, Martin A., eds. Renewable Resource Management for Forestry & Agriculture. LC 78-25994. (Geo. S. Long Publication Ser.). 136p. 1979. 10.00 (ISBN 0-295-95624-0). U of Wash Pr.
Bethell, E., et al, eds. Electrical Assembly & Wiring. (Engineering Craftsmen: No. G4). (Illus.). 1969. spiral bdg. 21.00x (ISBN 0-85083-031-1). Intl Ideas.
Bethell, Jean. How to Care for Your Dog. LC 67-23535. (Illus.). 64p. (gr. 2-5). 1967. 5.95 (ISBN 0-590-07076-2, Four Winds). Schol Bk Serv.
--Playmates. LC 80-20542. 32p. (gr. k-2). 1981. 7.95 (ISBN 0-03-053821-1). HR&W.
Bethell, Nicholas. Russia Besieged. LC 77-77799. (World War II Ser.). (Illus.). (gr. 6 up). 1977. PLB 14.94 (ISBN 0-8094-2471-1, Pub. by Time-Life). Silver.
--Russia Besieged. Time-Life Books, ed. (World War II Ser.). 1977. 12.95 (ISBN 0-8094-2470-3). Time-Life.
Bethell, Tom. George Lewis: A Jazzman from New Orleans. 1977. 14.50 (ISBN 0-520-03212-8). U of Cal Pr.
--Television Evening News Covers Inflation: Nineteen Seventy-Eight to Seventy-Nine. Media Institute, ed. (Illus.). 52p. (Orig.). 1980. pap. 5.00 (ISBN 0-937790-00-1). Media Inst.
Bethge, Eberhard. Bonhoeffer: Exile & Martyr. 192p. 1976. 7.95 (ISBN 0-8164-1211-1). Crossroad NY.
Bethke, Emil G. Basic Drawing for Biology Students. (Illus.). 100p. 1969. 10.75 (ISBN 0-398-00148-0). C C Thomas.
Bethke, Robert D. Adirondack Voices: Woodsmen & Woods Lore. LC 80-24054. (Music in American Life Ser.). (Illus.). 180p. 1981. 12.50 (ISBN 0-252-00829-4). U of Ill Pr.
Bethune, James D. Basic Electronic & Electrical Drafting. (Illus.). 1980. text ed. 17.95 (ISBN 0-13-060301-5). P-H.
Bethurum, Dorothy, ed. Critical Approaches to Medieval Literature: Selected English Institute Papers 1958-1959. LC 60-13104. 1960. 15.00x (ISBN 0-231-02417-7). Columbia U Pr.
Bethurum, Truman. People of the Planet Clarion. 1975. 6.95 o.p. (ISBN 0-685-20199-6). Saucerian.
Beti, Mongo. King Lazarus. 1971. pap. 1.50 o.s.i. (ISBN 0-02-048600-6, Collier). Macmillan.
Beti, Mongo, pseud. Remember Ruben. 350p. (Orig.). 1981. 14.00x (ISBN 0-89410-240-0); pap. 7.00x (ISBN 0-89410-241-9). Three Continents.
Betjeman, John. Cornwall: A Shell Guide. (Shell Guide Ser.). (Illus.). 1969. 8.95 o.p. (ISBN 0-571-05862-0, Pub. by Faber & Faber). Merrimack Bk Serv.
--London's Historic Railway Stations. (Illus.). 1978. pap. 10.95 (ISBN 0-7195-3426-7). Transatlantic.
--Victorian & Edwardian London. 1969. pap. 13.50 (ISBN 0-7134-2185-1, Pub. by Batsford England). David & Charles.
Betjeman, John & Rowse, A. L. Victorian & Edwardian Cornwall. 1977. pap. 11.95 (ISBN 0-7134-3167-9, Pub. by Batsford England). David & Charles.
Betjeman, John & Vaisey, David. Victorian & Edwardian Oxford. 1972. 19.95 o.p. (ISBN 0-7134-0118-4, Pub. by Batsford England). David & Charles.
Betjeman, John & Taylor, Geoffrey, eds. English Love Poems. 1964. pap. 6.95 (ISBN 0-571-07065-5, Pub. by Faber & Faber). Merrimack Bk Serv.
Betnun, Nathan S. Housing Finance Agencies: A Comparison Between State Agencies & Hud. LC 76-2899. 1976. text ed. 32.95 (ISBN 0-275-56660-9). Praeger.
Betsky, Sarah Z, ed. Onions & Cucumbers & Plums: Fourty-Six Yiddish Poems in English. Betsky, Sarah Z., tr. from Yiddish. 280p. 1981. 12.50 (ISBN 0-8143-1080-X); pap. 6.95 (ISBN 0-8143-1674-3). Wayne St U Pr.
Betsky, Sarah Z., tr. see Betsky, Sarah Z.
Bett, Henry. English Myths & Traditions. (Illus.). 144p. 1980. Repr. of 1952 ed. lib. bdg. 17.50 (ISBN 0-8414-2921-9). Folcroft.
--Games of Children, Their Origin & History. LC 68-31218. 1968. Repr. of 1929 ed. 15.00 (ISBN 0-8103-3473-9). Gale.
--Nursery Rhymes & Tales, Their Origin & History. LC 68-21756. 1968. Repr. of 1924 ed. 18.00 (ISBN 0-8103-3474-7). Gale.
Bettelheim, Bruno. Children of the Dream. 1970. pap. 2.50 (ISBN 0-380-01097-6, 49130, Discus). Avon.
--Dialogues with Mothers. LC 62-10583. 1962. text ed. 14.95 (ISBN 0-02-903120-6). Free Pr.
--The Empty Fortress: Infantile Autism & the Birth of the Self. LC 67-10886. 1967. 16.95 (ISBN 0-02-903130-3); pap. text ed. 8.95 (ISBN 0-02-903140-0). Free Pr.
--Informed Heart: Autonomy in a Mass Age. 1960. 12.95 (ISBN 0-02-903200-8). Free Pr.
--Love Is Not Enough. 1950. 17.95 (ISBN 0-02-903280-6). Free Pr.
--Love Is Not Enough. 1971. pap. 2.95 (ISBN 0-380-01405-X, 47498, Discus). Avon.
--Truants from Life: The Rehabilitation of Emotionally Disturbed Children. LC 55-7331. 1955. 15.95 (ISBN 0-02-903440-X); pap. 4.95 (ISBN 0-02-903450-7). Free Pr.
Bettelheim, Bruno & Janowitz, M. B. Social Change & Prejudice. LC 64-11214. 1964. 15.95 (ISBN 0-02-903480-9). Free Pr.
Bettelheim, Charles. The Transition to Socialist Economy. Mepham, John, ed. Pearce, Brian, tr. from Fr. (Marxist Theory & Contemporary Capitalism Ser). 248p. 1975. text ed. 18.50x (ISBN 0-391-00396-8); pap. text ed. 10.00x (ISBN 0-391-00884-6). Humanities.
Bettembourg, Georges & Brame, Michael. Himalayan Confessions. 12.95 (ISBN 0-932998-05-4). Noit Amrofer.
Bettenson, Henry, ed. Documents of the Christian Church. 2nd ed. 1970. pap. 5.95 (ISBN 0-19-501293-3, GB). Oxford U Pr.
Bettenson, Henry, tr. Early Christian Fathers: A Selection from the Writings of the Fathers from St. Clement of Rome to St. Athanasius. (Oxford Paperbacks Ser). 1969. pap. 5.95x (ISBN 0-19-283009-0, 174). Oxford U Pr.
Better Business Bureau. The Better Business Bureau Guide to Wise Buying. (Illus.). 1980. pap. 6.95 (ISBN 0-448-22075-X). Paddington.
--Better Business Bureau Wise Buying Guide. 1980. lib. bdg. 17.50 (ISBN 0-87196-419-8). Facts on File.
Better Homes & Gardens. Better Homes & Gardens New Cookbook. 832p. 1981. pap. 3.95 (ISBN 0-553-14866-4). Bantam.
--Woodworking Projects You Can Build. 1980. 4.95 (ISBN 0-696-00325-2). BH&G.
Better Homes & Gardens, ed. Better Homes & Gardens New Baby Book. 416p. 1980. pap. 2.75 (ISBN 0-553-13941-X). Bantam.
Better Homes & Gardens Book Editors. Better Homes & Gardens Gourmet Recipes Made Easy. (Illus.). 96p. 1980. 4.95 (ISBN 0-696-00525-5). Meredith Corp.
Better Homes & Gardens Books, ed. Better Homes & Gardens All-Time Favorite Hamburger & Ground Meats Recipes. (All-Time Favorite Ser.). (Illus.). 1980. 4.95 (ISBN 0-696-00505-0). Meredith Corp.

--Better Homes & Gardens Complete Guide to Home Repair, Maintenance & Improvement. (Illus.). 1980. 19.95 (ISBN 0-696-00545-X). Meredith Corp.
--Better Homes & Gardens Low-Cost Cooking. (Illus.). 1980. 4.95 (ISBN 0-696-00541-7). Meredith Corp.
Better Homes & Gardens Books Editors. Better Homes & Gardens After-40 Health & Medical Guide. (Illus.). 480p. 1980. 24.95 (ISBN 0-696-00810-6). Meredith Corp.
--Better Homes & Gardens All-Time Favorite Cake & Cookie Recipes. (All-Time Favorite Recipes Ser.). (Illus.). 96p. 1980. 4.95 (ISBN 0-696-00620-0). Meredith Corp.
--Better Homes & Gardens All-Time Favorite Fish & Seafood Recipes. (All-Time Favorite Recipes Ser.). (Illus.). 96p. 1980. 4.95 (ISBN 0-696-00495-X). Meredith Corp.
Better Homes & Gardens Books Editors, ed. Better Homes & Gardens All-Time Favorite Pies. (Illus.). 1978. 4.95 (ISBN 0-696-00455-0). Meredith Corp.
Better Homes & Gardens Books Editors. Better Homes & Gardens Calorie-Trimmed Recipes. (Illus.). 96p. 1980. 4.95 (ISBN 0-696-00605-7). Meredith Corp.
Better Homes & Gardens Books Editors, ed. Better Homes & Gardens Complete Step-by-Step Cook Book. (Illus.). 1978. 19.95 (ISBN 0-696-00125-X). Meredith Corp.
Better Homes & Gardens Books Editors. Better Homes & Gardens More from Your Microwave. (Illus.). 96p. 1980. 4.95 (ISBN 0-696-00615-4). Meredith Corp.
--Better Homes & Gardens Step-by-Step Basic Wiring. (Illus.). 96p. 1980. 4.95 (ISBN 0-696-00555-7). Meredith Corp.
--Better Homes & Gardens Treasury of Christmas Crafts & Foods. (Illus.). 384p. 1980. 18.95 (ISBN 0-696-00025-3). Meredith Corp.
Better Homes & Gardens Books Editors, ed. Easy Bazaar Crafts. (Illus.). 96p. 1981. 4.95 (ISBN 0-696-00665-0). Meredith Corp.
--Good Food & Fitness. (Illus.). 96p. 1981. 4.95 (ISBN 0-696-00635-9). Meredith Corp.
--Meatless Main Dishes. (Illus.). 96p. 1981. 4.95 (ISBN 0-696-00645-6). Meredith Corp.
--Short-Cut Recipes. (Illus.). 96p. 1981. 4.95 (ISBN 0-696-00655-3). Meredith Corp.
--Woman's Health & Medical Guide. (Illus.). 96p. 1981. 24.95 (ISBN 0-696-00275-2). Meredith Corp.
Better Homes & Gardens Editors. Better Homes & Gardens All-Time Favorite Barbecue Recipes. 176p. 1980. pap. 2.25 (ISBN 0-553-13659-3). Bantam.
--Better Homes & Gardens All-Time Favorite Fruit Recipes. (All Time Favorite Ser.). (Illus.). 1980. 4.95 (ISBN 0-696-00515-8). Meredith Corp.
--Better Homes & Gardens Calorie Counter's Cookbook. 176p. 1981. pap. 2.50 (ISBN 0-553-14267-4). Bantam.
--Better Homes & Gardens Woodworking Projects You Can Build. (You Can Build Ser.). (Illus.). 1980. 4.95 (ISBN 0-696-00325-2). Meredith Corp.
Better Homes & Gardens Editors, ed. Better Homes & Gardens Decorating Book. LC 74-25586. (Illus.). 400p. 1975. 15.95 o.p. (ISBN 0-696-00091-1). Meredith Corp.
--Better Homes & Gardens Family Medical Guide. rev. ed. (Illus.). 1084p. 1973. 22.95 (ISBN 0-696-00342-2); prepub. 26.95 deluxe (ISBN 0-696-00343-0). Meredith Corp.
--Casual Entertaining Cook Book. (Illus.). 96p. 1981. 4.95 (ISBN 0-696-00490-9). Meredith Corp.
Betteridge, Clair B. Primer for Change. 1981. 8.95 (ISBN 0-8062-1717-0). Carlton.
Betteridge, D., jt. auth. see Baker, A. D.
Betteridge, W. Nickel & Its Alloys. (Illus.). 160p. 1977. pap. 12.95x (ISBN 0-7121-0947-1, Pub. by Macdonald & Evans England). Intl Ideas.
Bettetini, Gianfranco. The Language & Technique of the Film. (Approaches to Semiotics Ser: No. 28). 1973. text ed. 33.00x (ISBN 90-2792-412-0). Mouton.
Bettex, M. & Koch, A., eds. Kinderchirurgische Probleme in der paediatrische Praxis. (Paediatrische Fortbildungskurse fuer die Praxis: Vol. 49). (Illus.). 1980. soft cover 29.50 (ISBN 3-8055-0232-X). S Karger.
Bettinghaus, Erwin P. The Nature of Proof. 2nd ed. LC 76-173979. (Orig.). 1972. pap. 3.50 (ISBN 0-672-61295-X, SC1). Bobbs.
Bettman, James R. Information Processing Theory of Consumer Choice. LC 78-52496. (Advances in Marketing). 1979. text ed. 16.95 (ISBN 0-201-00834-3). A-W.
Bettman, Otto L., jt. auth. see Brooks, Van Wyck.
Bettmann, Otto L. Good Old Days - They Were Terrible! LC 74-6050. (Illus.). 1974. 10.00 o.p. (ISBN 0-394-48689-7); pap. 4.95 (ISBN 0-394-70941-1). Random.
Betts, D. S. Refrigeration & Thermometry Below One Kelvin. LC 75-34695. (Illus.). 304p. 1976. 29.50x (ISBN 0-8448-0853-9). Crane-Russak Co.
Betts, Doris. Beasts of the Southern Wild & Other Stories. LC 73-4138. 202p. 1973. 7.95 o.s.i. (ISBN 0-06-010321-3, HarpT). Har-Row.
Betts, Edward. Creative Seascape Painting. 160p. 1981. 19.15 (ISBN 0-8230-1113-5). Watson-Guptill.
Betts, Glynne R. Writers in Residence: American Authors at Home. 1981. 16.95 (ISBN 0-670-79108-3, Studio). Viking Pr.
Betts, Jim, jt. auth. see Brewer, Edward S.
Betts, John E. Physics for Technology. 2nd ed. (Illus.). 675p. 1981. text ed. 22.95 (ISBN 0-8359-5544-3); solutions manual free (ISBN 0-8359-5545-1). Reston.
Betts, John R. America's Sporting Heritage: 1850-1950. LC 73-10590. 1974. text ed. 16.95 (ISBN 0-201-00557-3). A-W.
Betts, Leonard C. Garden Pools. (Illus.). 1952. pap. 2.50 (ISBN 0-87666-077-4, M513). TFH Pubns.
Betts, Peter W. The Board & Administrative Management: Management for the Board. 192p. 1977. text ed. 23.50x (ISBN 0-220-66338-6, Pub. by Busn Bks England). Renouf.
Betts, R. R. Essays in Czech History. 1969. text ed. 25.75x (ISBN 0-485-11095-4, Athlone Pr). Humanities.
Betts, Raymond F. Europe in Retrospect: A Brief History of the Past Two Hundred Years. (Orig.). 1979. pap. 6.95 (ISBN 0-669-01366-8). Heath.
Betts, Richard K., jt. auth. see Gelb, Leslie H.
Betts, Richard M., jt. auth. see McKenzie, Dennis J.
Betz, Don. Cultivating Leadership: An Approach. LC 80-69039. 120p. (Orig.). 1981. pap. text ed. 4.95 (ISBN 0-8191-1441-3). U Pr of Amer.
Betz, Hans D. Christology & a Modern Pilgrimage: A Discussion with Norman Perrin. LC 75-31605. (Scholars Press Homage Ser.: No. 1). 1974. pap. 7.50 (ISBN 0-89130-185-2, 001601). Scholars Pr Ca.
--Galatians. LC 77-78625. (Hermenia: a Critical & Historical Commentary on the Bible). 1979. 27.95 (ISBN 0-8006-6009-9, 20-6009). Fortress.
Betz, Margaret. Faith & Justice. LC 80-50259. 176p. (gr. 11-12). 1980. pap. text ed. 4.20x (ISBN 0-88489-114-3); tchr's guide 5.00x (ISBN 0-88489-121-6). St Mary's.
Betz, Norm. A A C C Technical Guide to Key Cereal & Making Ingredients. LC 80-68710. 138p. 1980. write for info. (ISBN 0-913250-18-X). Am Assn Cereal Chem.
Betz, Paul, ed. see Wordsworth, William.
Beuchame, L., tr. see Melanchthon, Philip.
Beuchat, L. R. Food & Beverage Mycology. (Illus.). 1978. lib. bdg. 35.50 o.p. (ISBN 0-87055-247-3); pap. text ed. 22.50 (ISBN 0-87055-293-7). AVI.
Beudell, Martin, ed. Offshore Oil & Gas Yearbook 1980-81. 500p. 1980. 115.00x (ISBN 0-85038-336-6). Nichols Pub.
Beuf, Ann H. Biting off the Bracelet: A Study of Children in Hospitals. LC 79-5047. 1979. 10.95 (ISBN 0-8122-7766-X). U of Pa Pr.
--Red Children in White America. LC 76-49737. 168p. 1977. 10.95x (ISBN 0-8122-7719-8). U of Pa Pr.
Beukenkamp, Cornelius, Jr. Fortunate Strangers. LC 80-19260. 269p. 1980. Repr. of 1971 ed. lib. bdg. 9.95x (ISBN 0-89370-600-0). Borgo Pr.
Beum, R., jt. auth. see Shapiro, Karl J.
Beurdeley, Cecile & Beurdeley, Michel. A Connoisseur's Guide to Chinese Ceramics. Watson, Katherine, tr. from Fr. LC 74-1792. (Illus.). 320p. 1974. 75.00 o.s.i. (ISBN 0-06-010322-1, HarpT). Har-Row.
Beurdeley, Michel, jt. auth. see Beurdeley, Cecile.
Beutel, Frederick K. Experimental Jurisprudence & the Scienstate. (Illus.). 404p. (Orig.). 1975. text ed. 55.00x o.p. (ISBN 3-7694-0400-9); pap. text ed. 34.00 o.p. (ISBN 3-7694-0404-1). Rothman.
Beutlich, Tadek. Technique of Woven Tapestry. 1979. 22.50 o.p. (ISBN 0-7134-2513-X, Pub. by Batsford England). David & Charles.
Beutner, E. H., et al. Immunopathology of the Skin. 2nd ed. LC 78-24139. 1979. 47.50 (ISBN 0-471-03514-9, Pub. by Wiley Medical). Wiley.
Bevan, Bernard, tr. see Gomez-Moreno, Manuel.
Bevan, D. & Hagenmuller, P. Non-Stoichiometric Compounds: Tungsten Bronzes; Vanadium Bronzes; & Related Compounds. (Pergamon Texts in Inorganic Chemistry: Vol. 1). 154p. 1975. text ed. 27.00 (ISBN 0-08-018776-5); pap. text ed. 14.00 (ISBN 0-08-018775-7). Pergamon.
Bevan, David. Charles-Ferdinand Ramuz. (World Authors Ser.: No. 512). 1979. lib. bdg. 14.95 (ISBN 0-8057-6353-8). Twayne.
Bevan, Elizabeth, jt. auth. see Weckselmann, David.
Bevan, Gloria. Half a World Away. (Harlequin Romances Ser.). 192p. (Orig.). 1981. pap. 1.25 (ISBN 0-373-02377-4, Pub. by Harlequin). PB.
Bevan, John A., et al, eds. Vascular Neuroeffector Mechanisms. 1979. 42.50 (ISBN 0-89004-302-7). Raven.
Bevans, Michael H. Book of Reptiles & Amphibians. LC 55-9715. (gr. 4-9). 5.95 (ISBN 0-385-02196-8). Doubleday.
Bevelander, Gerrit. Outline of Histology. rev. ed. 7th ed. (Illus., Orig.). 1971. text ed. 12.95 (ISBN 0-8016-0680-2). Mosby.
Bevelander, Gerrit & Ramaley, Judith A. Essentials of Histology. 8th ed. LC 78-4847. 1979. text ed. 19.95 (ISBN 0-8016-0669-1). Mosby.
Bever, M. B., jt. ed. see Henstock, M.
Bever, Thomas G., ed. Dips in Learning. 300p. 1981. prof. - refer. 19.95 (ISBN 0-89859-096-5). L Erlbaum Assocs.
Beveridge, Albert J. John Marshall, 4 vols. LC 80-24550. (American Statesmen Ser.). 2400p. 1981. Set. pap. 30.00 (ISBN 0-87754-178-7). Chelsea Hse.
Beveridge, Andrew A. & Oberschall, Anthony R. African Businessmen & Social Change in Zambia. LC 79-83978. 1979. 22.50x (ISBN 0-691-03121-5). Princeton U Pr.
Beveridge, Charles E. & McLaughlin, Charles C., eds. The Papers of Frederick Law Olmsted: Vol. II: Slavery & the South, 1852-1857. LC 80-8881. (The Papers of Frederick Law Olmsted). (Illus.). 528p. 1981. text ed. 27.50x (ISBN 0-8018-2242-4). Johns Hopkins.
Beveridge, James. John Grierson: Film Master. LC 77-17799. 1978. 22.95 (ISBN 0-02-510530-2). Macmillan.
Beveridge, W. E. The Interview in Staff Appraisal. 1975. text ed. 16.50x (ISBN 0-04-658212-6). Allen Unwin.
Beveridge, W. E. B. Seeds of Discovery. (Illus.). 1981. 12.95 (ISBN 0-393-01444-4). Norton.
Beveridge, W. H. Unemployment: A Problem of Industry, London 1912. LC 79-59646. (The English Workinh Class Ser.). 1980. lib. bdg. 35.00 (ISBN 0-8240-0101-X). Garland Pub.
Beveridge, W. T., jt. auth. see Balfour, A.
Beveridge, William H. Causes & Cures of Unemployment. LC 75-41030. 1976. Repr. of 1931 ed. 9.00 (ISBN 0-685-70886-1). Ams Pr.
--Prices & Wages in England: From the Twelfth to the Nineteenth Century, Vol. 1 Price Tables-mercantile Era. LC 66-6277. 1939. 45.00x (ISBN 0-678-05154-2). Kelley.
Beveridge, William H. & Bew, P. London School of Economics & Its Problems, 1919-1937. 1960. text ed. 6.50x (ISBN 0-391-02007-2). Humanities.
Beveridge-Wavering, Agnes & Seibert-Shook, Mavis. Reinforcing Home Activities: Program for Articulation Improvement. 1981. pap. 7.50 (ISBN 0-8134-2158-6, 2158). Interstate.
Beverley, John. Aspects of Gongora's Soledades. (Purdue University Monograhs in Romance Languages: No. 1). 1981. text ed. 23.00x (ISBN 90-272-1711-4). Humanities.
Beverley, Robert. History & Present State of Virginia. Wright, Louis B., ed. LC 68-58999. (Illus.). 366p. 1968. pap. 3.95 (ISBN 0-8139-0028-X). U Pr of Va.
Beverly Hills Bar Association. Barristers Committee for the Arts. The Actor's Manual: A Practical Legal Guide. Beil, Norman, et al, eds. 288p. 1981. 13.95 (ISBN 0-8015-0040-0); pap. 9.95 (ISBN 0-8015-0041-9). Dutton.
Beverly Hills Bar Association Barristers Committee for the Arts. The Musician's Manual: A Practical Career Guide. Halloran, Mark, ed. 288p. 1981. 17.95 o.p. (ISBN 0-8015-5203-6); pap. 9.95 (ISBN 0-8015-5204-4). Dutton.
Bevin, A. Griswold, jt. auth. see Salisbury, Roger E.
Bevington, David. The Complete Works of Shakespeare. 3rd ed. 1980. text ed. 21.95x (ISBN 0-673-15193-X). Scott F.
--Medieval Drama. 1975. text ed. 21.95 (ISBN 0-395-13915-5). HM.
Bevington, David, compiled by. Shakespeare. LC 76-5220. (Goldentree Bibliographies in Language & Literature). 1978. text ed. 17.95x (ISBN 0-88295-556-X); pap. text ed. 12.95x (ISBN 0-88295-555-1). AHM Pub.
Bevington, G. C. Remarkable Miracles. LC 73-85242. 209p. 1974. pap. text ed. 2.50 o.p. (ISBN 0-88270-063-4). Logos.
Bevington, Helen. Along Came the Witch: A Journal of the 1960's. LC 75-31653. 216p. 1976. 8.95 o.p. (ISBN 0-15-105080-5). HarBraceJ.
Bevington, S., ed. Twentieth Century Interpretations of Hamlet. (Orig.). (YA) (gr. 9-12). 1968. 8.95 (ISBN 0-13-372375-5, Spec); pap. 2.95 (ISBN 0-13-372367-4, Spec). P-H.
Bevington, S., et al, eds. see Shakespeare, William.
Bevis, Em O., jt. auth. see Bower, Fay L.
Bevis, Em O., jt. auth. see Douglass, Laura M.
Bevis, Em Olivia. Curriculum Building in Nursing: A Process. 2nd ed. LC 77-13045. (Illus.). 1978. pap. text ed. 12.95 (ISBN 0-8016-0668-3). Mosby.
Bew, P., jt. auth. see Beveridge, William H.
Bew, Paul. C. S. Parnell. (Gill's Irish Lives Ser.). 152p. 1980. 20.00 (ISBN 0-7171-1079-6, Pub. by Gill & Macmillan); pap. 6.50 (ISBN 0-7171-0963-1). Irish Bk Ctr.
Bewell, D. A., jt. ed. see Repacholi, M. H.
Bewer, Julius A. Literature of the Old Testament. 3rd ed. Kraeling, Emil G., ed. LC 62-17061. 1962. 27.50x (ISBN 0-231-02478-9). Columbia U Pr.
Bewes, Richard. Talking About Prayer. LC 80-7781. 128p. (Orig.). 1980. pap. 2.95 (ISBN 0-87784-465-8). Inter-Varsity.
Bewick, Thomas. Thomas Bewick: Vignettes. Bain, Iain, ed. (Illus.). 1977. 15.95 (ISBN 0-85967-410-X, Pub. by Scolar Pr England). Biblio Dist.
Bewley, Marius. The Eccentric Design: Form in the Classic American Novel. LC 59-13769. 1959. pap. 10.00x (ISBN 0-231-08542-7, 42). Columbia U Pr.
Bewtra, J. K. Water Pollution Control Technology. (Theoretical & Applied Environmental Reviews: Vol. 1). 200p. 1981. 25.00 (ISBN 3-7186-0027-7). Harwood Academic.
Beyea, Basil. Notorious Eliza. 1979. pap. 1.95 o.p. (ISBN 0-449-23998-5, Crest). Fawcett.
Beyer, Andrew. My Fifty Thousand Year at the Races. LC 78-53918. 1978. 8.95 o.p. (ISBN 0-15-163693-1). HarBraceJ.
Beyer, Carlos, ed. Endocrine Control of Sexual Behavior. LC 78-24620. (Comprehensive Endocrinology Ser.). 1979. text ed. 39.00 (ISBN 0-89004-207-1). Raven.
Beyer, Douglas. Basic Beliefs of Christmas. 64p. 1981. pap. 3.50 (ISBN 0-8170-0896-9). Judson.
Beyer, Harald. A History of Norwegian Literature. Haugen, Einar, tr. LC 56-6801. 1956. pap. 7.00x (ISBN 0-8147-1023-9). NYU Pr.
Beyer, Jan Erik. Aquatic Ecosystems: An Operational Research Approach. LC 79-57217. (Illus.). 316p. 1981. 20.00 (ISBN 0-295-95719-0). U of Wash Pr.
Beyer, Janice M. & Trice, Harrison M. Implementing Change: Alcoholism Policies in Work Organizations. LC 78-54127. 1978. 17.95 (ISBN 0-02-903460-4). Free Pr.
Beyer, R. & Trawicki, D. J. Profitability Accounting: For Planning & Control. 2nd ed. 403p. 1972. 29.95 (ISBN 0-471-06523-4). Wiley.
Beyer, Robert & Trawicki, Donald J. Profitability Accounting: For Planning & Control. 2nd ed. (Illus.). 400p. 1972. 29.95 (ISBN 0-8260-1055-5, 06961). Ronald Pr.
Beyer, Stephen. The Buddhist Experience: Sources & Interpretations. 1974. pap. text ed. 7.95x (ISBN 0-8221-0127-0). Dickenson.
Beyer, William, et al, eds. see Ulam, Stanislaw M.
Beyerhaus, Peter. Missions - Which Way? (Contemporary Evangelical Perspectives Ser). 128p. 1971. kivar 2.45 o.p. (ISBN 0-310-21191-3). Zondervan.
Beyerly, Elizabeth. The Europe Centric Historiography of Russia: An Analysis of the Contribution by Russian Emigre Historians in the USA, 1925-55, Concerning 19th Century Russian History. LC 72-94444. (Studies in European History: No. 11). 385p. 1973. text ed. 88.25x (ISBN 90-2792-515-1). Mouton.
Beyersdorff, Gerald & Sanders, Peter. Inside Track. LC 75-1204. (The Venture Ser, a Reading Incentive Program). (Illus.). 80p. (gr. 7-12,RL 4.5-6.5). 1975. In Packs Of 5. text ed. 23.25 ea. pack (ISBN 0-8172-0214-5). Follett.
Beyl, Judith. Sunshine, Rainbows & Friends. LC 80-50828. (Illus.). 1980. pap. 5.95 (ISBN 0-933308-01-9). West Village.
Beyle, Henri see Stendhal, pseud.
Beyle, Marie H. Armance. Sale, Gilbert & Sale, Suzanne, trs. 7.25 o.p. (ISBN 0-85036-090-0). Dufour.
Beyme, K. Von see Von Beyme, Klaus.
Beyme, Klaus Von see Kaase, Max & Von Beyme, Klaus.
Beyme, Klaus Von see Von Beyme, Klaus.
Beynon, Huw, jt. auth. see Nichols, Theo.
Beynon, J. H., ed. Recommendations for Symbolism & Nomenclature for Mass Spectroscopy. new ed. 1978. pap. text ed. 6.60 o.p. (ISBN 0-08-022368-0). Pergamon.
Beynon, John. Conduction of Electricity Through Gases. 1972. pap. text ed. 12.50x (ISBN 0-245-50580-6). Intl Ideas.
Beynon, L. R. & Cowell, E. B., eds. Ecological Aspects of Toxicity Testing of Oils & Dispersants. 1974. 22.95 (ISBN 0-470-07190-7). Halsted Pr.
Bezanson, Walter E., ed. Clarel. 772p. 1959. 12.50 (ISBN 0-87532-011-2). Hendricks House.

Bezboruah, Monoranjan. U. S. Strategy in the Indian Ocean: The International Response. LC 77-2786. (Praeger Special Studies). 1977. 29.95 (ISBN 0-03-021811-X). Praeger.

Bezdanov, Stevan. A Community School in Yugoslavia. (Experiments & Innovations in Education Ser., No. 6). 40p. (Orig.). 1974. pap. 2.50 (ISBN 92-3-101130-8, U92, UNESCO). Unipub.

Bezdekova, Zdenka. They Called Me Leni. LC 77-175227. 1973. 4.50 o.p. (ISBN 0-672-51331-5). Bobbs.

Beze, Theodore de. Abraham Sacrifiant: Tragedie Francoise (Geneve, 1550) (Classiques De la Renaissance En France: No. 2). 1970. 15.30 (ISBN 90-2796-344-4). Mouton.

Bezirgan, Basima Q., jt. ed. see Fernea, Elizabeth W.

Bezkorovainy, Anatoly. Biochemistry of Nonheme Iron. (Biochemistry of the Elments Ser.: Vol. 1). 430p. 1981. 45.00 (ISBN 0-306-40501-6, Plenum Pr). Plenum Pub.

Bezold, C. The Future of Pharmaceuticals. 144p. 1980. 12.00 (ISBN 0-471-08343-7, Pub. by Wiley Med). Wiley.

Bezruchka, Stephen. A Guide to Trekking in Nepal. 4th ed. (Illus.). 240p. 1981. pap. 8.95 (ISBN 0-89886-003-2). Mountaineers.

Bezy, John. Bryce Canyon: The Story Behind the Scenery. Dendooven, Gweneth R., ed. LC 79-93079. (Illus.). 1980. 7.95 (ISBN 0-916122-70-0); pap. 3.00 (ISBN 0-916122-69-7). K C Pubns.

Bezymenski, Lev. The Death of Adolph Hitler. 1978. pap. 1.75 o.s.i. (ISBN 0-515-04594-2). Jove Pubns.

Bhaduri, R. K., jt. auth. see Preston, M. A.

Bhaduri, S. Vigil (a Novel) 6.50x o.p. (ISBN 0-210-22621-8). Asia.

Bhagavan, M. R. Poems. 2nd ed. (Redbird Bk.). 1976. lib. bdg. 8.00 (ISBN 0-89253-125-8); flexible bdg. 4.80 (ISBN 0-89253-139-8). Ind-US Inc.

Bhagavan, M. R., jt. ed. see Arthurs, A. M.

Bhagowalia, Urmila. Vaisnavism & Society in Northern India. 1980. 22.00x (ISBN 0-8364-0664-8, Pub. by Intellectual India). South Asia Bks.

Bhagwati, Jagdish, ed. International Trade: Selected Readings. 456p. 1981. text ed. 25.00x (ISBN 0-262-02160-9); pap. text ed. 9.95x (ISBN 0-262-52060-5). MIT Pr.

Bhagwati, Jagdish N. Amount & Sharing of Aid. LC 73-123777. (Monographs: No. 2). 208p. 1970. 1.50 (ISBN 0-686-28693-6). Overseas Dev Council.

--Indian Economic Policy & Performance: A Framework for a Progressive Society. (Working Papers on Development Ser.: No. 1). 1975. pap. 1.25x (ISBN 0-87725-401-X). U of Cal Intl St.

Bhagwati, Jagdish N., ed. Economics & World Order: From the 1970's to the 1990's. LC 73-179966. 1972. 16.95 (ISBN 0-02-895600-1); pap. text ed. 5.95 (ISBN 0-02-903470-1). Free Pr.

Bhajan, Yogi. The Golden Temple Cookbook. LC 78-52267. (Orig.). 1979. pap. 5.95 (ISBN 0-8015-3067-9, Hawthorn). Dutton.

--The Teachings of Yogi Bhajan. 1977. pap. 5.95 (ISBN 0-8015-7461-7, Hawthorn). Dutton.

Bhaktivedanta, A. C. Easy Journey to Other Planets. 96p. 1972. pap. 1.25 o.s.i. (ISBN 0-02-083590-6, Collier). Macmillan.

--Krishna Consciousness: The Topmost Yoga System. 96p. 1972. pap. 1.25 o.s.i. (ISBN 0-02-083570-1, Collier). Macmillan.

--The Perfection of Yoga. (Illus.). 123p. 1973. pap. 1.50 o.s.i. (ISBN 0-02-083610-4, Collier). Macmillan.

Bhaktivedanta, Swami. The Science of Self Realization. (Illus.). 1977. 9.95 (ISBN 0-89213-101-2). Bhaktivedanta.

Bhaktivedanta, Swami A. C. Beyond Birth & Death. LC 72-84844. (Illus.). 1972. pap. 1.50 (ISBN 0-912776-41-2). Bhaktivedanta.

--The Bhagavad-Gita As It Is. abr. ed. LC 75-34536. (Illus.). 330p. 1976. 6.95 (ISBN 0-912776-80-3); text ed. 3.95 (ISBN 0-685-65672-1); pap. write for info. (ISBN 0-685-65673-X); pap. text ed. 2.95 (ISBN 0-685-65674-8). Bhaktivedanta.

--Easy Journey to Other Planets. LC 70-118080. (Illus.). 1970. pap. 1.50 (ISBN 0-912776-10-2). Bhaktivedanta.

--Krsna: The Supreme Personality of Godhead, 3 vols. LC 74-118081. (Illus.). 1970. Set. pap. 6.95 (ISBN 0-912776-30-7); pap. 2.95 ea.; Vol. 1. pap. (ISBN 0-912776-31-5); Vol. 2. pap. (ISBN 0-912776-32-3); Vol. 3. pap. (ISBN 0-912776-33-1). Bhaktivedanta.

--Life Comes from Life. LC 75-39756. (Illus.). 1979. 5.95 (ISBN 0-912776-84-6); text ed. 5.95 (ISBN 0-685-70923-X). Bhaktivedanta.

--Perfection of Yoga. LC 72-76302. (Illus.). 1972. pap. 1.50 (ISBN 0-912776-36-6). Bhaktivedanta.

--Teachings of Lord Caitanya. LC 75-2060. (Illus.). 1974. 7.95 (ISBN 0-912776-08-0); pap. 2.95 (ISBN 0-912776-07-2). Bhaktivedanta.

Bhaktivedanta, Swami Prabhupada A. C. Srimad-Bhagavatam: Tenth Canto, Part 3. (Illus.). 112p. 1980. 6.95 (ISBN 0-89213-107-1). Bhaktivedanta.

Bhaktivedanta Swami Prabhupada, A. C. The Path of Perfection: Yoga for the Modern Age. 1979. 5.95 (ISBN 0-89213-103-9). Bhaktivedanta.

Bhalla, A. S., ed. Towards Global Action for Appropriate Technology: Expert Meeting on International Action for Appropriate Technology, December 5-9 1977, Geneva. LC 78-41191. (Illus.). 240p. 1979. 30.00 (ISBN 0-686-60416-4); pap. 13.00 (ISBN 0-686-60417-2). Pergamon.

Bhalla, B. M. Major Indian Novels: The Pattern of Meaning. 204p. 1980. text ed. price not set o.p. (ISBN 0-391-02075-7). Humanities.

Bhalla, G. S. & Alagh, Y. K. Performance of Indian Agriculture: A Districtwise Study. (Illus.). 239p. 1979. 15.00x (ISBN 0-8002-0994-X). Intl Pubns Serv.

Bham, Thamsanqa E. The Will to Live. LC 79-66395. 115p. 1980. 6.95 (ISBN 0-533-04383-2). Vantage.

Bhandakhar, R. G. Vaisnavism, Saivism & Minor Religious Systems: Strassburg, 1913. LC 78-74263. (Oriental Religions Ser.: Vol. 1). 167p. 1980. lib. bdg. 22.00 (ISBN 0-8240-3900-9). Garland Pub.

Bhandarkar, R. Early History of the Dekkan. 1975. Repr. 8.50x o.p. (ISBN 0-88386-670-6). South Asia Bks.

Bhanoji Rae, V. V. Malaysia: Development Patterns & Policy, 1947 to 1971. 270p. 1981. 17.50 (ISBN 0-8214-0512-8). Swallow.

Bhappu, R. B., jt. ed. see Mular, A. L.

Bharadwaj, K. Production Conditions in Indian Agriculture. (Department of Applied Economics, Occasional Papers: No. 33). 175p. 1974. 25.50 (ISBN 0-521-08494-6); pap. 10.95 (ISBN 0-521-09862-9). Cambridge U Pr.

Bharath, A. V. The Black Princess & Other Stories. (Illus.). 96p. 1967. 1.00 (ISBN 0-88253-413-0). Ind-US Inc.

Bharatha, S., jt. auth. see Truesdell, C.

Bharati, Agahananda. The Ochre Robe: An Autobiography. 2nd ed. 300p. 1980. 14.95 (ISBN 0-915520-40-0); pap. 7.95. Ross-Erikson.

Bharati, Agehananda. Asians in East Africa: Jayhind & Uhuru. LC 72-85882. 416p. 1972. 19.95x (ISBN 0-911012-49-4). Nelson-Hall.

--The Light at the Center: Context & Pretext of Modern Mysticism. 1976. lib. bdg. 11.95 (ISBN 0-915520-03-6); pap. 6.95 (ISBN 0-915520-04-4). Ross-Erikson.

--Ochre Robe: An Autobiography. rev. ed. LC 80-24101. 300p. 1980. 14.95 o.p. (ISBN 0-915520-40-0); pap. 7.95 o.p. (ISBN 0-915520-28-1). Ross-Erikson.

Bharati, Subramania. Songs to Krishna. Bunce, David, tr. from Tamil. (Writers Workshop Saffronbird Ser.). 1975. 14.00 (ISBN 0-88253-642-7); pap. text ed. 4.80 (ISBN 0-88253-641-9). Ind-US Inc.

Bhardwaj, Surinder M. Hindu Places of Pilgrimage in India: A Study in Cultural Geography. LC 73-174454. (Illus.). 1973. 24.50x (ISBN 0-520-02135-5). U of Cal Pr.

Bhargava, Ashok. The Poetry of W. B. Yeats: Myth As Metaphor. 1979. text ed. 11.50x (ISBN 0-391-01006-9). Humanities.

Bharti, Ma S., ed. see Rajneesh, Bhagwan S.

Bharti, Ma Satya. Death Comes Dancing: Celebrating Life with Bhagwan Shree Rajneesh. 200p. 1981. pap. 9.95 (ISBN 0-7100-0705-1). Routledge & Kegan.

Bharucha-Reid, Albert T. Elements of the Theory of Markov Processes & Their Applications. (Probability & Statistics Ser). 1960. 38.00 o.p. (ISBN 0-07-005156-9, P&RB). McGraw.

Bhaskar, Krish. Future of the U. K. Motor Industry. 1979. 37.50x (ISBN 0-85038-259-9). Nichols Pub.

--Future of the World Motor Industry. 300p. 1980. 42.50x (ISBN 0-89397-083-2). Nichols Pub.

Bhaskar, Roy. Possibility of Naturalism: Social Science & Social Ideologies. (Philosophy Now Ser.). 1978. text ed. 28.75x (ISBN 0-391-00843-9); pap. text ed. 11.75x (ISBN 0-391-00844-7). Humanities.

Bhaskar, S. N. Orban's Oral Histology & Embryology. 9th ed. LC 80-11972, (Illus.). 1980. pap. text ed. 29.95 (ISBN 0-8016-4609-X). Mosby.

--Radiographic Interpretation for the Dentist. 3rd ed. LC 74-14785. 1979. 34.50 (ISBN 0-8016-0690-X). Mosby.

--Synopsis of Oral Pathology. 6th ed. (Illus.). 676p. 1981. text ed. 27.50 (ISBN 0-8016-0685-3). Mosby.

Bhaskaran, M. K., tr. see Pillai, Thakazhi S.

Bhaskaran, M. P. The Dancer & the Ring. 8.00 (ISBN 0-89253-459-1); flexible cloth 4.00 (ISBN 0-89253-460-5). Ind-US Inc.

Bhaskaran, R. Sociology of Politics. 1967. 6.50x o.p. (ISBN 0-210-27169-8). Asia.

Bhasker, S. N. & Sicher, Harry, eds. Orban's Oral Histology & Embryology. 8th ed. LC 75-31628. (Illus.). 1976. text ed. 22.50 o.p. (ISBN 0-8016-4608-1). Mosby.

Bhat, U. Narayan. Elements of Applied Stochastic Processes. LC 70-178140. (Probability & Mathematical Statistics Ser.). 368p. 1972. 35.95 (ISBN 0-471-07199-4, Pub. by Wiley-Interscience). Wiley.

Bhate, Vaijayanti, jt. auth. see Dandekar, Kumudini.

Bhatia, B., et al, eds. Selected Topics in Environmental Biology. 530p. 1980. 47.50x (ISBN 0-89955-317-6, Pub. by Interprint India). Intl Schol Bk Serv.

Bhatia, B. M. Famines in India, 1850-1965. 2nd ed. 10.50x (ISBN 0-210-33854-7). Asia.

Bhatia, H. L. History of Economic Thought. rev. 2nd ed. 1980. text ed. 25.00x (ISBN 0-7069-0585-7, Pub. by Vikas India). Advent Bk.

Bhatia, K. S., jt. auth. see Varute, A. T.

Bhatia, Prem. All My Yesterdays. (Illus.). 179p. 1972. 6.75x (ISBN 0-685-30444-2). Intl Pubns Serv.

Bhatia, Shyam. India's Nuclear Bomb. 1980. text ed. 13.95x (ISBN 0-7069-0972-0, Pub. by Vikas India). Advent Bk.

Bhatnagar, S. K. History of M. A. O. College, Aligarh. 8.50 o.p. (ISBN 0-210-22303-0). Asia.

Bhatnagar, S. P., jt. auth. see Bhojwani, S. S.

Bhatnagar, U. S. Electrical Engineering Experiments. 5.50x o.p. (ISBN 0-210-33848-2). Asia.

Bhatnagar, ViJay M. Nonwovens & Disposables: New Technical-Marketing Developments. 86p. 1978. pap. 25.00 (ISBN 0-87762-256-6). Technomic.

Bhatnagar, ViJay M., ed. Fire Retardants: Proceeding of the First European Conference on Flammability & Fire Retardants. LC 78-66105. 1979. pap. 35.00 (ISBN 0-87762-264-7). Technomic.

--Nonwovens & Disposables: Proceedings of the First Canadian Symposium of Nonwovens & Disposables. LC 78-68591. (Illus.). 1978. pap. 25.00 (ISBN 0-87762-268-X). Technomic.

Bhatnager, V. M. Building Materials. 300p. 1981. 40.00x (ISBN 0-86095-866-3). Longman.

Bhatt, Anil, jt. auth. see Rao, T. V.

Bhatt, Kiran U., jt. auth. see Kirby, Ronald F.

Bhatt, Kiran U., et al. An Analysis of Road Expenditures & Payments by Vehicle Class (1956-1975) (An Institute Paper). 282p. 1977. pap. 7.00 (ISBN 0-87766-188-X, 18400). Urban Inst.

--Implementation Procedures for Pricing Urban Roads. (An Institute Paper). 49p. 1976. pap. 2.00 (ISBN 0-87766-178-2, 16400). Urban Inst.

--Congressional Intent & Road User Payments. (An Institute Paper). 97p. 1977. pap. 4.00 (ISBN 0-87766-189-8, 18500). Urban Inst.

Bhatt, Kjmarila. Anthology of Kumarila Bhatt's Works. Sharma, P. S., ed. 96p. 1980. text ed. 9.00x (ISBN 0-8426-1647-0). Verry.

Bhatt, S. Aviation, Environment & World Order. 196p. 1980. text ed. 15.00x (ISBN 0-391-01809-4). Humanities.

Bhatt, V. V. Development Perspectives: Problems, Strategies & Policies. (Illus.). 352p. 1980. 50.00 (ISBN 0-08-025774-7). Pergamon.

Bhattacarya, Jagadishvhra. Hasyarnava-the Ocean of Laughter. Nelson, David & Munda, Ramdayal, trs. (Translated from Sanskrit). 1976. 8.00 (ISBN 0-89253-805-8); flexible cloth 4.80 (ISBN 0-89253-806-6). Ind-US Inc.

Bhattacharji, Sukumari. The Indian Theogony: Comparative Study of Indian Mythology from the Vedas to the Puranas. rev. ed. 1978. Repr. of 1970 ed. 18.50x (ISBN 0-8364-0160-3). South Asia Bks.

Bhattacharya, A. N. & Vyas, R. N. Habitat, Economy & Society: A Study of the Dangis. 1979. text ed. 12.50x (ISBN 0-391-01818-3). Humanities.

Bhattacharya, Anindya K. The Asian Dollar Market: International Offshore Financing. LC 76-2900. (Praeger Special Studies). 1977. 17.95 o.p. (ISBN 0-275-56610-2). Praeger.

--Foreign Trade & International Development. LC 75-27807. (Illus.). 1976. 15.95 (ISBN 0-669-00252-6). Lexington Bks.

Bhattacharya, Bhabani. Goddess Named Gold. 306p. 1969. pap. 3.40 (ISBN 0-88253-016-X). Ind-US Inc.

--Music for Mohini. 2nd ed. 1976. pap. 2.75 (ISBN 0-89253-071-5). Ind-US Inc.

--Shadow from Ladakh. 359p. 1969. pap. 3.00 (ISBN 0-88253-018-6). Ind-US Inc.

--Steel Hawk & Other Stories. 143p. 1968. pap. 1.95 (ISBN 0-88253-020-8). Ind-US Inc.

Bhattacharya, Bhabani, ed. Contemporary Indian Short Stories, 2 vols. 1967. Vol. 1. 2.50 (ISBN 0-88253-409-2); Vol. 2. 2.50 (ISBN 0-88253-327-4). Ind-US Inc.

Bhattacharya, Lokenath. Fifteen Prose Poems. Guha, Nikhiles, tr. from Bengali. (Saffronbird Book Ser). 25p. 1975. flexible cloth 4.80 (ISBN 0-88253-709-1). Ind-US Inc.

--The Virgin Fish of Babughat. Mukherjee, Meenakshi, tr. from Bengali. (Indian Novels Ser.). 160p. 1975. 8.00 (ISBN 0-89253-016-2). Ind-US Inc.

Bhattacharya, Mohit. Rural Self-Government in Metropolitan Calcutta. 1965. 4.50x o.p. (ISBN 0-210-22662-5). Asia.

Bhattacharya, P. B. & Jain, S. K. First Course in Rings, Fields & Vector Spaces. 1977. 10.95 (ISBN 0-470-99047-3, 76-55303). Halsted Pr.

Bhattacharya, P. K. Marxism & Buddhism. 1976. 3.50x o.p. (ISBN 0-686-59641-2). South Asia Bks.

Bhattacharya, Rameswar. Dynamics of Marine Vehicles. LC 78-950. (Ocean Engineering Ser.). 1978. text ed. 50.00 (ISBN 0-471-07206-0, Pub. by Wiley-Interscience). Wiley.

Bhattacharya, Srinibas. Long Road to Peace. 1977. 5.00 o.p. (ISBN 0-533-02008-5). Vantage.

--Our Sweetest Songs. LC 77-74557. 1978. 4.95 o.p. (ISBN 0-533-02900-7). Vantage.

Bhattacharyya, et al, eds. The Cultural Heritage of India, 4 vols. Incl. Vol. 1. Early Phases. Radhakrishnan, S., intro. by. (ISBN 0-87481-560-6); Vol. 2. Itihasas, Puranas, Dharma & Other Shastras (ISBN 0-87481-561-4); Vol. 3. The Philosophies (ISBN 0-87481-562-2); Vol. 4. The Religions (ISBN 0-87481-563-0). (Illus.). 30.00x ea.; Set. 150.00x (ISBN 0-87481-558-4). Vedanta Pr.

Bhattacharyya, Amitabha, jt. auth. see Ham, Inyong.

Bhattacharyya, Benoytosh. An Introduction to Buddhist Esoterism. 1980. Repr. of 1931 ed. 19.00x (ISBN 0-686-69019-2, Pub. by Motilal Banarsidas). South Asia Bks.

Bhattacharyya, Bhaskar. To Catch the Uncatchable. (Illus.). 1981. 9.95 (ISBN 0-89281-019-X, Destiny Bks). Inner Tradit.

Bhattacharyya, D. K. Demand for Financial Assets. 200p. 1978. text ed. 25.25x (ISBN 0-566-00228-0, Pub. by Gower Pub Co England). Renouf.

--Demand for Financial Assets. 1978. text ed. 25.25x (ISBN 0-566-00228-0, Pub. by Gower Pub Co England). Renouf.

Bhattacharyya, M. N. Comparison of Box-Jenkins & Bonn Monetary Prediction Performance. (Lecture Notes in Economics & Mathematical Systems: Vol. 178). (Illus.). 146p. 1980. pap. 15.00 (ISBN 0-387-10011-3). Springer-Verlag.

Bhattacharyya, S. C. Some Aspects of Indian Society. 1977. 10.00x o.p. (ISBN 0-685-74588-0). South Asia Bks.

Bhattasali, B. N. Transfer of Technology Among the Developing Countries. LC 70-186286. 94p. 1972. 10.50 o.p. (ISBN 92-833-1013-6, APO5, APO). Unipub.

Bhattatiri, M. N. Narayaneeyam. Tapasyananda, Swami, tr. from Sanskrit. 1976. 8.50 o.p. (ISBN 0-87481-474-X). Vedanta Pr.

Bhavnani, Enakshi. Dance in India. 3rd ed. 261p. 1979. 45.00x (ISBN 0-8002-0696-7). Intl Pubns Serv.

Bhebe, A. H. Lobengula of Zimbabwe. (Illus.). 48p. 1977. pap. text ed. 2.75x (ISBN 0-435-94476-2). Heinemann Ed.

Bhely-Quenum, Olympe. Snares Without Ending. Blair, Dorothy, tr. from Fr. (Sun-Lit Ser.). Orig. Title: Un Piege Sans Fin. 220p. (Orig.). 1981. 10.00x (ISBN 0-89410-184-6); pap. 6.00x (ISBN 0-686-64485-9). Three Continents.

Bhikkhu, Suratano. In the Conquest of True Freedom. LC 78-63079. 100p. 1980. 5.95 (ISBN 0-533-03965-7). Vantage.

Bhikshu Heng Yo, et al, trs. see Ch'An Master Yung Chia.

Bhikshuni Heng Hsien, et al, trs. see Ch'An Master Hua.

Bhiksuni Heng Hsien, tr. see Master Hua, Ch'An.

Bhojwani, S. S. & Bhatnagar, S. P. The Embryology of Angiosperms. 1978. 14.00 (ISBN 0-7069-0335-8, Pub. by Vikas India). Advent Bk.

Bhooshan, B. S., ed. Towards Alternative Settlement Strategies: The Role of Small & Intermediate Centers in Development Process. x, 404p. 1980. text ed. 25.00x (ISBN 0-86590-005-1). Apt Bks.

Bhutani, Surendra, ed. Contemporary Gulf. 1980. 12.00x (ISBN 0-8364-0667-2, Pub. by Academic India). South Asia Bks.

Bhutto, Z. My Execution. 1980. 10.00x (ISBN 0-8364-0650-8, Pub. by Muswati India). South Asia Bks.

Biagi, Adele, jt. ed. see Ragazzini, Giuseppe.

Bial, Morrison D. Liberal Judaism at Home: The Practices of Modern Reform Judaism. rev. ed. 1971. pap. 5.00 (ISBN 0-8074-0075-0, 383110); tchrs'. guide 1.50 (ISBN 0-8074-0225-7, 203110). UAHC.

--Your Jewish Child. Syme, Daniel B., ed. 1978. pap. 5.00 (ISBN 0-8074-0012-2, 101200). UAHC.

Bialer & Sluzar, eds. Strategies & Impact of Contemporary Radicalism: Radicalism in the Contemporary Age. LC 76-39890. (Studies of the Research Institute on International Change, Columbia University: Vol. 3). 1977. lib. bdg. 24.00x (ISBN 0-89158-129-4); lib. bdg. 60.00 3 vol. set. Westview.

Bialer, S. & Sluzar, S., eds. Sources of Contemporary Radicalism, Vol. 1. LC 76-39890. (Studies of the Research Institute of International Change, Columbia University). 1977. lib. bdg. 24.00x (ISBN 0-89158-130-8); lib. bdg. 60.00 3 vol. set. Westview.

Bialer, Seweryn, ed. The Domestic Context of Soviet Foreign Policy. 500p. 1980. lib. bdg. 35.00x (ISBN 0-89158-783-7); pap. text ed. 15.00x (ISBN 0-89158-891-4). Westview.

Bialer, Seweryn & Sluzar, Sophia, eds. Radical Visions of the Future. LC 76-39890. (Studies of the Research Institute on International Change, Columbia, University: Vol. 2). 1977. lib. bdg. 21.50x (ISBN 0-89158-131-6); lib. bdg. 60.00 3 vol. set. Westview.

Biallas, Franz X. Konfuzius und Sein Kult: Peking & Leipzig, 1928. LC 78-74282. (Oriental Religions Ser.: Vol. 13). 187p. 1981. lib. bdg. 22.00 (ISBN 0-8240-3915-7). Garland Pub.

Bialoszewski, Miron. A Memoir of the Warsaw Uprising. Levine, Madeline, tr. from Polish. 1977. 15.00 (ISBN 0-88233-275-9). Ardis Pubs.

--The Revolution of Things. Czaykowski, Bogdan & Busza, Andrzej, trs. LC 74-81212. 1974. 7.50 (ISBN 0-685-41660-7). Charioteer.

Bialyniccy-Birula, J. Quantum Electrodynamics. LC 74-4473. 541p. 1975. text ed. 44.00 (ISBN 0-08-017188-5). Pergamon.

Biancani, Laurent. Nude Photography: The French Way. Orig. Title: Te Nu. (Illus.). 1980. 25.00 (ISBN 0-8174-5095-5); pap. 9.95 (ISBN 0-8174-5096-3). Amphoto.

Bianchi, C. Paul & Hilf, Russell, eds. Protein Metabolism & Biological Functions. 1970. 18.50x o.p. (ISBN 0-8135-0617-4). Rutgers U. Pr.

Bianchi, C. Paul, jt. ed. see Narahashi, Toshio.

Bianchi, John. Blue Steel & Gunleather. Mason, James D., ed. (Illus.). 213p. 1978. 9.95 (ISBN 0-917714-15-6). Beinfeld Pub.

Bianchi, Martha D. The Life & Letters of Emily Dickinson. LC 70-162296. 386p. 1972. Repr. of 1924 ed. 15.00x (ISBN 0-8196-0276-0). Biblo.

Bianchi, Raymond, jt. auth. see Lyle, Carl.

Bianchi, Robert S., jt. auth. see El Mallakh, Kamal.

Bianchin, Helen. Devil in Command. (Harlequin Presents Ser.). 192p. (Orig.). 1981. pap. 1.50 (ISBN 0-373-10409-X, Pub. by Harlequin). PB.

--Edge of Spring. (Harlequin Presents Ser.). 192p. 1981. pap. 1.50 (ISBN 0-373-10415-4, Pub. by Harlequin). PB.

--Master of Urulu. (Harlequin Romances Ser.). 192p. (Orig.). 1981. pap. 1.25 (ISBN 0-373-02378-2, Pub. by Harlequin). PB.

Bianco, David, compiled by. Who's New Wave in Music, 1976 to 1980: A Catalog & Directory. LC 80-21534. 300p. (Orig.). 1981. pap. 5.50 (ISBN 0-938136-00-3). Lunchroom Pr.

Bianco, Margery. Little Wooden Doll. (Illus.). (gr. 3-4). 1967. 6.95 (ISBN 0-02-710110-X). Macmillan.

Biardeau, Madeleine. Theorie De la Connaissance et Philosophie De la Parole Dans le Brahmanisme Classique. (Le Monde D'outre-Mer Passe et Present, Etudes: No. 23). 1963. pap. 51.20x (ISBN 90-2796-178-6). Mouton.

Bias, Clifford, compiled by. Ritual Book of Magic. 160p. 1981. pap. 6.95 (ISBN 0-87728-532-2). Weiser.

Biasini, Americole, et al. Manhattanville Music Curriculum Project Interaction: Early Childhood Music Curriculum. 2nd ed. 119p. (Orig.). 1972. pap. text ed. 5.50 o.p. (ISBN 0-686-63974-X). Media Materials.

Bibaud, M. Histoire Du Canada et Des Canadiens Sous la Domination Anglaise. (Canadiana Avant 1867: No. 2). 1968. 38.25x (ISBN 90-2796-323-1). Mouton.

--Histoire Du Canada Sous la Domination Francaise. (Canadiana Avant 1867: No. 3). 1968. 38.25x (ISBN 0-686-20918-4). Mouton.

Bibb, Porter, et al. The CB Bible. 1976. pap. 4.95 (ISBN 0-385-12323-X). Doubleday.

Bibby, John F., et al. Vital Statistics on Congress Nineteen Eighty. 1980. 12.25 (ISBN 0-8447-3408-X); pap. 5.25 (ISBN 0-8447-3401-2). Am Enterprise.

Bibby, Violet. Many Waters Cannot Quench Love. LC 75-14446. 160p. (gr. 7 up). 1975. 7.25 (ISBN 0-688-22042-8); PLB 6.96 (ISBN 0-688-32042-2). Morrow.

--Tinner's Quest. (gr. 6-8). 1978. 10.95 (ISBN 0-571-11029-0, Pub. by Faber & Faber). Merrimack Bk Serv.

Bibeau, R. W. Math Skills for Science. (gr. 10-12). 1973. 4.00 o.p. (ISBN 0-201-00437-2, Sch Div); tchr's guide 2.22 o.p. (ISBN 0-201-05753-0); dupl. masters 36.12 o.p. (ISBN 0-685-64744-7, 0438). A-W.

Bibeault, Donald. Corporate Turnaround: How Managers Turn Losers into Winners. 416p. 1981. 22.95 (ISBN 0-07-005190-9). McGraw.

Bibel, W. & Kowalski, R., eds. Fifth Conference on Automated Deduction, les Arcs Proceedings. (Lecture Notes in Computer Science: Vol. 87). (Illus.). 385p. 1980. pap. 22.00 (ISBN 0-387-10009-1). Springer-Verlag.

Bibliographic Society of Northern Illinois. Index to Reviews of Bibliographical Publications, Nineteen Seventy-Seven, Vol. 2. Oggel, Terry, ed. (Reference Bks.). 1979. lib. bdg. 20.50 (ISBN 0-8161-8477-1). G K Hall.

Bibliotheek der Rijksuniversiteit Utrecht, Department of Classification, ed. Dutch Theses Nineteen Seventy-Seven. 132p. 1980. text ed. 30.95 (ISBN 90-265-0330-X, Pub. by Swets Pub Serv Holland). Swets North Am.

Bibo, Istvan. The Paralysis of International Institutions & the Remedies: A Study of Self-Determination, Concord Among the Major Powers & Political Arbitration. LC 75-17182. 152p. 1976. 24.95 (ISBN 0-470-07208-3). Halsted Pr.

Bicanic, R. Economic Policy in Socialist Yugoslavia. LC 72-80588. (Soviet & East European Studies). (Illus.). 270p. 1973. 38.50 (ISBN 0-521-08631-0). Cambridge U Pr.

Bicanic, Rudolf. Problems of Planning, East & West. (Publications of the Institute of Social Studies: No. 15). 1967. text ed. 17.05x (ISBN 90-2790-112-0). Mouton.

--Turning Points in Economic Development. 1972. text ed. 48.25x (ISBN 90-2792-101-6). Mouton.

Bice, David A. The Legend of John Henry - the Steel Drivin' Man. (The Pringle Tree Ser.). (Illus.). 32p. (gr. 3-6). 1980. PLB 5.95 (ISBN 0-934750-05-X). Jalamap.

--Mad Anne Bailey. (The Pringle Tree Ser.). (Illus.). 36p. (gr. 3-6). 1980. 5.95 (ISBN 0-934750-06-8). Jalamap.

--A Panorama of West Virginia. LC 79-89608. 319p. (gr. 8). 1979. text ed. 12.95 (ISBN 0-934750-00-9); tchr's guide 4.00 (ISBN 0-934750-01-7); wkbk. 3.50 (ISBN 0-934750-03-3). Jalamap.

Bice, Thomas, jt. auth. see Salkever, David.

Bichat, Xavier. Physiological Researches on Life & Death. Gold, F., tr. from Fr. Bd. with Outlines of Phrenology; Phrenology Examined. (Contributions to the History of Psychology, Vol. II, Pt. E: Physiological Psychology). 1978. Repr. of 1827 ed. 30.00 (ISBN 0-89093-175-5). U Pubns Amer.

Bick, T. A. Introduction to Abstract Mathematics. 1971. text ed. 18.50 o.p. (ISBN 0-12-095850-3). Acad Pr.

Bickel, Alexander M. The Least Dangerous Branch: The Supreme Court at the Bar of Politics. LC 62-20685. (Orig.). 1962. pap. 6.95 (ISBN 0-672-60757-3). Bobbs.

--The Morality of Consent. LC 75-10988. 176p. 1975. 12.50x (ISBN 0-300-01911-4); pap. 4.95x (ISBN 0-300-02119-4). Yale U Pr.

--Politics & the Warren Court. LC 73-398. (American Constitutional & Legal History Ser.). 314p. 1973. Repr. of 1955 ed. lib. bdg. 27.50 (ISBN 0-306-70573-7). Da Capo.

--The Supreme Court & the Idea of Progress. LC 77-18365. 1978. 17.50x (ISBN 0-300-02238-7); pap. 4.95x (ISBN 0-300-02239-5). Yale U Pr.

Bickel, H., et al, eds. Neonatal Screening for Inborn Errors of Metabolism. (Illus.). 300p. 1980. 50.70 (ISBN 0-387-09779-1). Springer-Verlag.

Bickel, Hans, ed. Palatability & Flavor Use in Animal Feeds. (Advances in Animal Physiology & Animal Nutrition: Vol. 11). (Illus.). 148p. (Orig.). 1980. pap. text ed. 34.10 (ISBN 3-490-41115-3). Parey Sci Pubs.

Bickel, Lennard. The Deadly Element: The Story of Uranium. LC 78-66243. (Illus.). 320p. 1980. pap. 7.95 (ISBN 0-8128-6089-6). Stein & Day.

--Mawson's Will. 1978. pap. 2.95 (ISBN 0-380-39131-7, 52076, Discus). Avon.

Bickel, P. J. & Doksum, K. A. Mathematical Statistics: Basic Ideas & Selected Topics. LC 76-8724. 1977. 28.95x (ISBN 0-8162-0784-4). Holden-Day.

Bickel, Walter, ed. Hering's Dictionary of Classical & Modern Cookery. 5th ed. 1974. 27.95 (ISBN 3-8057-0232-9, Pub. by Virtuea Col Ltd. England). CBI Pub.

Bickel, Walter, tr. see Hering, Richard.

Bickelhaupt, David L. General Insurance. 10th ed. 1979. text ed. 19.50x (ISBN 0-256-02150-3). Irwin.

Bickerman, Elias J., ed. see Rostovtzeff, Mikhail I.

Bickers, Richard L. Marketing in Europe. 1971. 21.50 (ISBN 0-7161-0058-4). CBI Pub.

Bickersteth, Geoffrey, tr. see Dante Alighieri.

Bickersteth, J. Burgon. The Land of Open Doors: Being Letters from Western Canada, 1911-1913. LC 76-41611. 1976. pap. 5.50 (ISBN 0-8020-6266-0); pap. 5.50 (ISBN 0-8020-6266-0). U of Toronto Pr.

Bickert, Theodore, jt. auth. see Balabanian, Norman.

Bickerton, Derek. King of the Sea. 1981. pap. 2.50 (ISBN 0-425-04846-2). Berkley Pub.

Bickerton, Derek, et al. The Genesis of Language: The First Michigan Colloquium, 1979. Hill, Kenneth C., ed. 159p. 1979. 15.50 (ISBN 0-89720-024-1); pap. 12.50 (ISBN 0-89720-025-X). Karoma.

Bickford, John. New Media in Printmaking. (Illus., Orig.). 1976. 17.95 o.p. (ISBN 0-8230-3165-9). Watson-Guptill.

Bickham, Jack. All the Days Were Summer. LC 80-2895. 240p. 1981. 10.95 (ISBN 0-385-17597-3). Doubleday.

Bickham, Jack M. Baker's Hawk. LC 73-79644. 240p. 1974. 6.95 o.p. (ISBN 0-385-01852-5). Doubleday.

--The War on Charity Ross. 1976. pap. 1.75 (ISBN 0-441-87262-X). Ace Bks.

Bickhard, Mark H. Cognition, Convention, & Communication. 210p. 1980. 24.95 (ISBN 0-03-056098-5). Praeger.

Bickley, A. C. see Gomme, George L., et al.

Bickley, Harmon C. Practical Concepts in Human Disease. 2nd ed. (Illus.). 335p. 1980. softcover 18.95 (ISBN 0-683-00914-1). Williams & Wilkins.

Bickley, John S., jt. ed. see Osler, Robert W.

Bickley, R. Bruce, Jr. Joel Chandler Harris. (United States Authors Ser.: No. 308). 1978. lib. bdg. 12.50 (ISBN 0-8057-7215-4). Twayne.

Bicknell, A. J. Wooden & Brick Buildings with Details. (Architecture & Decorative Art Ser.). 1977. Repr. of 1875 ed. 75.00 (ISBN 0-306-70832-9). Da Capo.

Bicknell, Alexander. The Benevolent Man; or, the History of Mr. Belville, 1775, 2 vols. in 1. Shugrue, Michael F., ed. (The Flowering of the Novel, 1740-1775 Ser: Vol. 108). 1974. lib. bdg. 50.00 (ISBN 0-8240-1207-0). Garland Pub.

Bicknell, J. & McQuiston, L., eds. Design for Need. 1977. pap. 19.25 o.p. (ISBN 0-08-021500-9). Pergamon.

Bicks, Alexander. Contracts for the Sale of Realty. Glassner, Herman M. & Kufeld, William M., eds. 1973. text ed. 10.00 o.p. (ISBN 0-685-85373-X, N1-0333). PLI.

Bicksler, James L., ed. Capital Market Equilibrium & Efficiency: Implications for Accounting, Finance, & Portfolio Decision Making. 1977. 38.50 (ISBN 0-669-86660-1). Lexington Bks.

Bicksler, James L. & Samuelson, Paul A., eds. Investment Portfolio Decision-Making. LC 73-1561. 1974. 19.95 (ISBN 0-669-86215-0). Lexington Bks.

Bicycling Magazine, ed. Bicycle Commuting. 1980. pap. 2.95 (ISBN 0-87857-301-1). Rodale Pr Inc.

--The Most Frequently Asked Questions About Bicycling. 1980. pap. 2.95 (ISBN 0-87857-300-3). Rodale Pr Inc.

Bidde, K. H. & Rivinus, M. W. Lights Along the Delaware. 1965. 4.95 (ISBN 0-8059-0245-7). Dorrance.

Biddle, Arthur. A Treatise on the Law of Warranties in the Sale of Chattels. xx, 308p. 1981. Repr. of 1884 ed. lib. bdg. 30.00x (ISBN 0-8377-0316-6). Rothman.

Biddle, Arthur W. & Eschholz, Paul A., eds. The Literature of Vermont: A Sampler. LC 73-76017. (Illus.). 390p. 1973. 17.50 (ISBN 0-87451-074-0); pap. 6.50 o.p. (ISBN 0-87451-078-3). U Pr of New Eng.

Biddle, B. J. & Thomas, E. J. Role Theory: Concepts & Research. 468p. 1979. Repr. of 1966 ed. lib. bdg. 21.00 (ISBN 0-88275-817-9). Krieger.

Biddle, Francis. Fear of Freedom. LC 76-138496. (Civil Liberties in American History Ser). 1971. Repr. of 1951 ed. lib. bdg. 37.50 (ISBN 0-306-70073-5). Da Capo.

--In Brief Authority. LC 76-5432. (Illus.). 494p. 1976. Repr. of 1962 ed. lib. bdg. 19.75x (ISBN 0-8371-8807-5, BIIB). Greenwood.

Biddle, Gordon. Victorian Stations: Railway Stations in England & Wales, 1836-1923. LC 74-154891. 224p. 1973. 16.95 (ISBN 0-7153-5949-5). David & Charles.

Biddle, Gordon & Spence, Geoffrey. British Railway Station. LC 77-89382. 1977. 13.50 (ISBN 0-7153-7467-2). David & Charles.

Biddle, Gordon, jt. auth. see Hadfield, Charles.

Biddle, Marcia. Tony Dorsett. LC 80-18302. (Illus.). 192p. (gr. 7 up). 1980. PLB 8.79 (ISBN 0-671-34040-9). Messner.

Biddle, Marcia M. Contributions of Women: Labor. LC 78-23303. (Contributions of Women Ser.). (Illus.). (gr. 6 up). 1979. PLB 8.95 (ISBN 0-87518-167-8). Dillon.

Biddle, Maureen. Fifty Craft Projects with Bible Verses & Patterns. LC 80-53872. (Illus.). 64p. (Orig.). 1981. pap. 3.50 (ISBN 0-87239-428-X, 2148). Standard Pub.

Biddle, Sheila. Bolingbroke & Harley. LC 73-20749. 1974. 10.00 o.p. (ISBN 0-394-46974-7). Knopf.

Biddle, W. Earl. Hypnosis in the Psychoses. 152p. 1967. pap. 12.75 photocopy ed. spiral (ISBN 0-398-00152-9). C C Thomas.

Biddle, Wayne. Coming to Terms: A Lexicon for Science-Watchers. 1981. 8.95 (ISBN 0-670-33092-2). Viking Pr.

--Coming to Terms: Lexicon for the Science Watcher. LC 80-54198. (Illus.). 128p. 1981. 8.95 (ISBN 0-670-33092-2). Viking Pr.

Biderman, A. D. & Drury, T. F., eds. Measuring Work Quality for Social Reporting. 1976. 22.95 (ISBN 0-470-15218-4). Halsted Pr.

Bidermann, Jacob. Cenodoxus. Dyer, D. G. & Longrigg, Cecily, trs. from Latin. LC 74-15527. (Edinburgh Bilingual Library: No. 9). 203p. 1976. 9.50x (ISBN 0-292-71027-5); pap. 4.95x (ISBN 0-292-71028-3). U of Tex Pr.

Bidgood, Reginald. Consulting Overseas: A Guide for Professionals in Construction. (Illus.). 1976. 18.95x (ISBN 0-7198-2640-3). Intl Ideas.

--Future Markets for Consultancy: Professional Business Development Abroad. (Illus.). 160p. 1980. 21.00x (ISBN 0-7198-2830-9). Intl Ideas.

Bidlack, Russell E. The ALA Accreditation Process, 1973-1976: A Survey of Library Schools Whose Programs Were Evaluated Under the 1972 Standards for Accreditation. LC 77-21153. 1977. pap. 5.00 o.p. (ISBN 0-8389-3205-3). ALA.

Bidwell, John, ed. see Arnett, John A.

Bidwell, John, ed. see Balston, Thomas.

Bidwell, John, ed. see De Vinne, Theodore L.

Bidwell, John, ed. see Legros, Lucien & Grant, John C.

Bidwell, John, ed. see Munsell, Joel.

Bidwell, John, ed. see Nicholson, James B.

Bidwell, John, ed. see R. Hoe & Co.

Bidwell, John, jt. ed. see Ringwalt, J. Luther.

Bidwell, John, ed. see Thompson, John S.

Bidwell, Percy W. History of Agriculture in the Northern United States: 1620-1860. 12.50 (ISBN 0-8446-1075-5). Peter Smith.

Bidwell, R. G., ed. Rusi & Brassey's Defense Yearbook 1976-77, Vol. 87. LC 76-29923. (Defense Publications Ser.). 1977. lib. bdg. 36.00x (ISBN 0-89158-630-X). Westview.

Bidwell, R. L., jt. ed. see Serjeant, R. B.

Bie, John De see De Bie, John.

Bie, Oscar. History of the Pianoforte & Pianoforte Players. 2nd ed. LC 66-28445. 1966. Repr. of 1899 ed. lib. bdg. 18.50 (ISBN 0-306-70938-4). Da Capo.

Biebel, David. Jonathan: You Left Too Soon. 192p. 1981. 8.95 (ISBN 0-8407-5235-0). Nelson.

Biebel, P., ed. Second International Symposium on Desmid Research Lake Itasca, Minnesota 1976: Proceedings. (Beiheft Zur Nova Hedwigia 56 Ser.). 1981. lib. bdg. 60.00 (ISBN 3-7682-5456-9). Lubrecht & Cramer.

Bieber, Doris M. Dictionary of Legal Abbreviations Used in American Law Books. LC 78-60173. 1979. lib. bdg. 19.50 (ISBN 0-930342-61-5); pap. text ed. 7.50 (ISBN 0-930342-96-8). W S Hein.

Bieber, Irving. Cognitive Psychoanalysis. LC 80-66921. 300p. 1980. 30.00 (ISBN 0-87668-419-3). Aronson.

Bieber, Konrad. Simone de Beauvoir. (World Authors Ser.: No. 532). 1979. lib. bdg. 13.50 (ISBN 0-8057-6374-0). Twayne.

Bieber, Margaret. History of the Greek & Roman Theater. rev. ed. (Illus.). 360p. 1980. 40.00x (ISBN 0-691-03521-0); pap. 15.00 (ISBN 0-691-00212-6). Princeton U Pr.

Bieberbach, Ludwig. Conformal Mapping. LC 53-7209. 6.95 (ISBN 0-8284-0090-3); pap. 2.95 (ISBN 0-8284-0176-4). Chelsea Pub.

Biebuyck, Daniel. Hero & Chief: Epic Literature from the Banyanga(Zaire Republic) LC 76-50242. 1978. 25.00x (ISBN 0-520-03386-8). U of Cal Pr.

--Lega Culture: Art, Initiation, & Moral Philosophy Among a Central African People. LC 71-165226. 1973. 33.50x (ISBN 0-520-02085-5). U of Cal Pr.

--Tradition & Creativity in Tribal Art. LC 69-12457. 1969. 30.00x (ISBN 0-520-01509-6); pap. 4.95 (ISBN 0-520-02487-7). U of Cal Pr.

Biebuyck, Daniel & Mateene, Kahombo C., eds. The Mwindo Epic from the Banyanga (Congo Republic) 1969. 20.00x (ISBN 0-520-01502-9); pap. 2.45 (ISBN 0-520-02049-9, CAL233). U of Cal Pr.

Biechler, James E. The Religious Language of Nicholas of Cusa. LC 75-23096. (American Academy of Religion. Dissertation Ser.). 1975. pap. 7.50 (ISBN 0-89130-021-X, 010108). Scholars Pr Ca.

Bieda, K. Structure & the Operation of the Japanese Economy. LC 76-127033. 1970. pap. 14.50 o.p. (ISBN 0-471-07225-7, Pub. by Wiley-Interscience). Wiley.

Biedenharn, Norma W. Basic Language: Messages & Meanings 1978, Level 4. (gr. 10). 1978. 11.96 (ISBN 0-06-530109-9, SchDept); tchr's guide 11.16 (ISBN 0-06-530209-5). Har-Row.

Biedenharn, Norma W. & Davis, Pauline C. Basic Language: Messages & Meanings 1973, Level 2. (gr. 8). 11.32 (ISBN 0-06-530101-3, SchDept); tchr's manual 10.00 (ISBN 0-06-530201-X); wkbk. 5.16 (ISBN 0-06-530301-6); tchr's. wkbk. 10.24 (ISBN 0-06-530401-2). Har-Row.

Biedenharn, Norma W., et al. Basic Language: Messages & Meanings, Level 3. (gr. 9). 1978. 11.96 (ISBN 0-06-530108-0, SchDept); tchr's guide 11.16 (ISBN 0-06-530208-7). Har-Row.

Biedenharn, Norma W, et al. Basic Language: Messages & Meanings Level 5. (gr. 11). 1973. 11.96 (ISBN 0-06-530104-8, SchDept); tchrs manual 10.00 (ISBN 0-06-530204-4); wkbk. 5.88 (ISBN 0-06-530304-0); tchr's. wkbk. 11.16 (ISBN 0-06-530404-7). Har-Row.

Biedenharn, Norma W., et al. Basic Language: Messages & Meanings 1973, Level 1. (gr. 7). 11.32 (ISBN 0-06-530100-5, SchDept); tchrs. manual 10.00 (ISBN 0-06-530200-1); wkbk. 5.16 (ISBN 0-06-530300-8); tchr's wkbk. 10.24 (ISBN 0-06-530400-4). Har-Row.

--Basic Language: Messages & Meanings 1973, Level 3. (gr. 9). 11.96 (ISBN 0-06-530102-1, SchDept); tchrs manual 10.00 (ISBN 0-06-530202-8); wkbk. 5.64 (ISBN 0-06-530302-4); tchr's. wkbk. 11.16 (ISBN 0-06-530402-0). Har-Row.

--Basic Language: Messages & Meanings 1973, Level 4. (gr. 10). 11.96 (ISBN 0-06-530103-X, SchDept); tchr's. manual 10.00 (ISBN 0-06-530203-6); wkbk. 5.64 (ISBN 0-06-530303-2); tchr's. wkbk. 11.16 (ISBN 0-06-530403-9). Har-Row.

--Basic Language: Messages & Meanings 1973, Level 6. (gr. 12). 11.96 (ISBN 0-06-530105-6, SchDept); tchr's manual 10.00 (ISBN 0-06-530205-2); wkbk. 5.88 (ISBN 0-06-530305-9); tchr's. wkbk. 11.16 (ISBN 0-06-530405-5). Har-Row.

--Basic Languages: Messages & Meanings 1978, Level 5. (gr. 11). 1978. 11.96 (ISBN 0-06-530110-2, SchDept); tchr's guide 11.16 (ISBN 0-06-530210-9). Har-Row.

--Basic Languages: Messages & Meanings 1978, Level 6. (gr. 12). 1978. 11.96 (ISBN 0-06-530111-0, SchDept); tchr's guide 11.16 (ISBN 0-06-530211-7). Har-Row.

Biederman, Charles. Search for New Arts. LC 79-90835. 1979. 20.00 (ISBN 0-935476-01-6); pap. 15.00 (ISBN 0-686-64371-2). Art History.

Biederman, Donald E. Legal & Business Aspects of the Music Industry: Music, Videocassettes & Records, Course Handbook. LC 80-81531. (Patents, Copyrights, Trademarks & Literary Property 1979-80 Course Handbook Ser.). 736p. 1980. pap. text ed. 25.00 (ISBN 0-686-68825-2, G4-3676). PLI.

Biederman-Thorson, M. A., tr. see Larcher, W.

Biederstadt, Lynn. The Eye of the Mind. 256p. 1981. 12.95 (ISBN 0-399-90108-6). Marek.

Biegert, E., ed. A Topical Guide to "Folia Primatologica", Volumes 1-30 (1963-1978) 160p. 1980. pap. 23.50 (ISBN 3-8055-0781-X). S Karger.

Biehl, Bobb & Hagelganz, James W. Praying: How to Start & Keep Going. 144p. 1981. pap. text ed. 2.50 (ISBN 0-8307-0781-6). Regal.

Biehler, Robert F. Child Development - an Introduction. LC 75-31014. 1976. text ed. 17.95 (ISBN 0-395-20650-2); inst. manual 3.50 (ISBN 0-395-20651-0); inst. suppl. 1.25 (ISBN 0-395-25079-X); study guide 6.60 (ISBN 0-395-20652-9). HM.

--Child Development: An Introduetion. 2nd ed. LC 80-82347. (Illus.). 704p. 1981. text ed. write for info. (ISBN 0-395-29833-4); price not set study guide (ISBN 0-395-29835-0); price not set instr's. manual (ISBN 0-395-29834-2). HM.

--Psychology Applied to Teaching. 3rd ed. LC 77-77665. (Illus.). 1978. pap. text ed. 16.95 (ISBN 0-395-25489-2); study guide & tching. handbook 7.30 (ISBN 0-395-25491-4); inst. manual 1.65 (ISBN 0-395-25490-6). HM.

Biel, Raymond. Bacterium. 320p. 1980. pap. 9.95 (ISBN 0-934444-07-2). Aazunna.

Bielefeld, Carole, jt. auth. see Young, Lorelle.

Bielennstein, Hans. The Bureaucracy of Han Times. LC 78-72080. (Cambridge Studies in Chinese History, Literature & Institutions). (Illus.). 1980. 37.50 (ISBN 0-521-22510-8). Cambridge U Pr.

Bielenstein, Hans. The Restoration of the Han Dynasty, 2 vols. in 1. (Perspectives in Asian History Ser.: No. 8). 161p. Repr. of 1954 ed. lib. bdg. 37.50x (ISBN 0-87991-479-3). Porcupine Pr.

Bieler, Arthur, jt. auth. see Haac, Oscar A.

Bieler, Arthur, et al. Perspectives De France. abr. rev. ed. (Illus.). 1972. text ed. 16.95 (ISBN 0-13-660571-0); wkbk. 7.95 (ISBN 0-13-660803-5); tapes 175.00 (ISBN 0-13-660779-9). P-H.

Bieler, Henry G. Food Is Your Best Medicine. 256p. 1973. pap. 2.45 (ISBN 0-394-71837-2, V-837, Vin). Random.

Bieler, L., ed. see O'Meara, John J.

Bieliauskas, Linas A. The Influence of Indiviual Differences in Health & Illness. (Behavioral Sciences for Health Care Professionals). 128p. (Orig.). 1981. lib. bdg. 15.00x (ISBN 0-86531-004-1); pap. text ed. 6.00x (ISBN 0-86531-005-X). Westview.

--Stress & Its Relationship to Health & Illness. (Behavioral Sciences for Health Care Professionals Ser.). 128p. (Orig.). 1981. lib. bdg. 15.00x (ISBN 0-86531-002-5); pap. text ed. 6.00x (ISBN 0-86531-003-3). Westview.

Bielski, Benon H., jt. auth. see Capellos, Christos.

Biemiller, Carl L. Escape from the Crater: More Adventures of the Hydronauts. LC 74-2714. 216p. (gr. 6-9). 1974. 4.95 o.p. (ISBN 0-385-07133-7). Doubleday.

Bien, Joseph, ed. see Ricoeur, Paul.

Bien, Peter. Constantine Cavafy. LC 64-22641. (Columbia Essays on Modern Writers Ser.: No. 5). (Orig.). 1964. pap. 1.50 o.p. (ISBN 0-231-02661-7, MW5). Columbia U Pr.

Bien, Peter, tr. see Myrivilis, Stratis.

Bienayme, Alain. Systems of Higher Education: France. 144p. 1978. pap. 7.00 (ISBN 0-89192-205-9). Interbk Inc.

Bienecker, Fritz. A Linguistic Key to the Greek New Testament, 2 vols. Vol. 1. 14.95 (ISBN 0-310-32020-8); Vol. 2. 17.95; Set. 31.90 (ISBN 0-310-32048-8). Zondervan.

Bienek, Horst. The Cell. Mahlendorf, tr. from Ger. LC 74-134739. 1973. 7.50 (ISBN 0-87775-024-6); pap. 2.95 (ISBN 0-87775-070-X). Unicorn Pr.

Bienen, Henry. Center for International Affairs, Harvard University: The Politics of Participation & Control. LC 73-2461. 192p. 1974. 14.00x (ISBN 0-691-03096-0); pap. 4.95 o.p. (ISBN 0-691-00022-0). Princeton U Pr.

Bienen, Henry & Diejomaoh, V. P., eds. The Political Economy of Income Distribution in Nigeria. LC 80-16860. (The Political Economy of Income Distribution in Developing Countries Ser.: No. 2). 500p. 1981. text ed. 45.00x (ISBN 0-8419-0618-1). Holmes & Meier.

Bienen, Leigh B., jt. auth. see Feild, Hubert S.

Bienenfeld, Arthur. Beachview Tower: A High-Rise Saga. LC 78-61219. 1978. 10.00 (ISBN 0-89430-029-6). Morgan-Pacific.

Bienert, Wolfgang. Dionysius Von Alexandrien Zur Frage Des Originismus. (Patristische Texte und Studien, 21). 1978. 51.75x (ISBN 3-11-007442-7). De Gruyter.

Bienkowski, W. Theory & Reality: The Development of Social Systems. (Allison & Busby Motive Ser.). 272p. 1981. 17.95x (ISBN 0-8052-8093-6, Pub. by Allison & Busby England); pap. 8.95 (ISBN 0-8052-8092-8). Schocken.

Bienz, D. R. The Why & How of Home Horticulture. LC 79-19915. (Illus.). 1980. text ed. 17.95x (ISBN 0-7167-1078-1). W H Freeman.

Bierce, Ambrose. Can Such Things Be? 314p. 1976. Repr. of 1910 ed. lib. bdg. 13.25 (ISBN 0-89190-195-7). Am Repr-Rivercity Pr.

--The Devil's Dictionary. 6.75 (ISBN 0-8446-0492-5). Peter Smith.

--The Devil's Dictionary. LC 78-13294. (Illus.). 1978. 14.95 (ISBN 0-916144-34-8); pap. 7.95 (ISBN 0-916144-35-6). Stemmer Hse.

--Fantastic Fables. 160p. 1976. Repr. of 1911 ed. lib. bdg. 8.75 (ISBN 0-89190-184-1). Am Repr-Rivercity Pr.

--Ghost & Horror Stories. 7.00 (ISBN 0-8446-0493-3). Peter Smith.

--The Monk & the Hangman's Daughter. 143p. 1976. Repr. of 1911 ed. lib. bdg. 8.35 (ISBN 0-89190-183-3). Am Repr-Rivercity Pr.

--An Occurrence at Owl Creek Bridge. (Creative's Classics Ser.). (Illus.). 40p. (gr. 4-9). 1980. PLB 6.95 (ISBN 0-87191-770-X). Creative Ed.

--Stories & Fables of Ambrose Bierce. Wagenknecht, Edward, ed. LC 77-20146. (Illus.). 1977. 14.95 (ISBN 0-916144-19-4); pap. 7.95 (ISBN 0-916144-20-8). Stemmer Hse.

Bierhorst, John. A Cry from the Earth: Music of the North American Indians. LC 78-21538. (Illus.). 128p. (gr. 5 up). 1979. 9.95 (ISBN 0-590-07533-0, Four Winds). Schol Bk Serv.

Bierhorst, John, ed. The Girl Who Married a Ghost & Other Tales from the North American Indian. LC 77-21515. (Illus.). (gr. 5 up). 1978. 10.95 (ISBN 0-590-07505-5, Four Winds). Schol Bk Serv.

Bierhorst, John, tr. from Fr. The Glass Slipper: Charles Perrault's Tales of Times Past. LC 80-66243. (Illus.). 128p. 1981. 9.95t (ISBN 0-590-07603-5, Four Winds). Schol Bk Serv. Postponed.

Bierlein, Lawrence W. Red Book on Transportation of Hazardous Materials. LC 76-44394. 1977. 80.00 (ISBN 0-8436-1407-2). CBI Pub.

Bierley, Paul E. Office Fun! LC 76-39578. (Cartoon Ser.). (Illus., Orig.). pap. 2.00 autographed ed. (ISBN 0-918048-01-X). Integrity.

Bierman. Financial Accounting. 3rd ed. 1978. 20.95 (ISBN 0-7216-1704-2). Dryden Pr.

Bierman, A. K. The Philosophy of Urban Existence: A Prolegomenon. LC 72-96393. x, 194p. 1973. 12.00x (ISBN 0-8214-0123-8). Ohio U Pr.

Bierman, H. Decision Making & Planning for the Corporate Treasurer. 195p. 1977. 27.95 (ISBN 0-471-07238-9). Wiley.

Bierman, Harold, Jr. Decision Making & Planning for the Corporate Treasurer. LC 76-58435. (Systems & Controls for Financial Management Ser.). 1977. 27.95 (ISBN 0-471-07238-9). Ronald Pr.

--Strategic Financial Planning: A Manager's Guide to Improving Profit Performance. LC 80-1058. (Illus.). 1980. 15.95 (ISBN 0-02-903560-0). Free Pr.

Bierman, Harold, Jr. & Haas, Jerome. An Introduction to Managerial Finance. 1973. text ed. 12.95x (ISBN 0-393-09353-0). Norton.

Bierman, Harold, Jr., et al. Quantitative Analysis for Business Decisions. 5th ed. 1977. text ed. 19.95x (ISBN 0-256-01918-5). Irwin.

Bierman, Howard. How to Plan & Install Electronic Burglar Alarms. (gr. 10 up). 1977. pap. 5.95 (ISBN 0-8104-5734-2). Hayden.

Bierman, Howard & Bierman, Marvin. Color TV: Principles & Servicing. (Illus.). 1973. pap. 8.30 (ISBN 0-8104-5929-9). Hayden.

Bierman, Judah, jt. ed. see Laszlo, Ervin.

Bierman, June & Toohey, Barbara. The Diabetic's Sports & Exercise Book. 1978. pap. 2.25 (ISBN 0-515-04513-6). Jove Pubns.

Bierman, Marvin, jt. auth. see Bierman, Howard.

Bierman, Richard B. Aviation Quarterly. (Illus.). Date not set. 12.00 (Pub. by Avn Quarterly). Aviation.

Bierman, Sheldon L., et al. Geothermal Energy in the Western United States: Innovation Versus Monopoly. LC 77-16078. (Praeger Special Studies). 1978. 34.50 (ISBN 0-03-041470-9). Praeger.

Bierman, Stanley M. The World's Greatest Stamp Collectors. LC 80-70957. (Illus.). 400p. 1981. 17.95 (ISBN 0-8119-0347-8). Fell.

Biermann, June & Toohey, Barbara. The Diabetic's Sports & Exercise Book: How to Play Your Way to Better Health. LC 76-17894. (Illus.). 1977. 10.95 o.s.i. (ISBN 0-397-01115-6); pap. 5.95 (ISBN 0-397-01202-0). Lippincott.

Biermann, Ludwig, jt. auth. see Schatzman, Evry.

Biernat, Russ, illus. The Great Piggy Bank Robbery. (Illus.). 32p. (Orig.). (ps). 1980. pap. 1.95 o.p. (ISBN 0-89542-934-9). Ideals.

Bierre, John, ed. see Coleridge, Samuel T.

Bierschwale, Margaret. Fort McKavett, Texas. (Illus.). 1966. 15.00 (ISBN 0-685-05001-7). A Jones.

Biersdorf, John E. Hunger for Experience: Vital Religious Communities in America Today. 160p. 1975. 7.95 (ISBN 0-8164-1198-0). Crossroad NY.

Biersteker, Thomas J. Distortion or Development? Contending Perspectives on the Multinational Corporation. 1979. text ed. 20.00x (ISBN 0-262-02133-1), MIT Pr.

Bierfliet, Alan Van see Van Bieryliet, Alan & Sheldon-Wildgen, Jan.

Bierwisch, Manfred. Modern Linguistics, Its Development Methods & Problems. (Janua Linguarum, Ser. Minor: No. 110). 103p. 1971. pap. text ed. 15.30x (ISBN 90-2791-657-8). Mouton.

Bierwisch, Manfred & Heidolph, Karl E., eds. Progress in Linguistics: A Collection of Papers. LC 78-123127. (Janua Linguarum Ser.: No. 43). 1970. text ed. 48.25x (ISBN 90-2790-723-4). Mouton.

Biesanz, John & Biesanz, Mavis. Modern Society with Revisions. 3rd ed. 1971. text ed. 17.95 (ISBN 0-13-597732-0). P-H.

Biesanz, John, jt. auth. see Biesanz, Mavis.

Biesanz, Mavis & Biesanz, John. Introduction to Sociology. 3rd ed. (Illus.). 1978. text ed. 17.95 (ISBN 0-13-497412-3); study guide 4.95 (ISBN 0-13-497404-2). P-H.

Biesanz, Mavis, jt. auth. see Biesanz, John.

Biesele, Igildo. Graphic Design Education. (Illus.). 190p. 1981. 67.50 (ISBN 0-8038-2712-1, Visual Communication). Hastings.

Biesenthal, Linda, jt. auth. see Tudor, Dean.

Bietz, Reinhold R. Happiness Under One Roof. LC 76-62562. (Harvest Ser.). 1977. pap. 3.95 (ISBN 0-8163-0315-0, 08104-2). Pacific Pr Pub Assn.

Biffle, Kent. Fire & Ice: The Arkansas Diamonds. (Illus.). 220p. Date not set. pap. 5.95 (ISBN 0-87870-108-7). Memphis St Univ.

Bigazzi, Pierluigi E., jt. auth. see Rose, Noel.

Bigelow, Bo, jt. auth. see Hansen, William.

Bigelow, Donald, ed. Schoolworlds 1976. LC 76-15293. 1976. 17.50x (ISBN 0-8211-0130-7); text ed. 15.65x ea. 10 or more copies. McCutchan.

Bigelow, Elfreda M. Hairdresser's Memoirs. 1981. 6.75 (ISBN 0-8062-1643-3). Carlton.

Bigelow, Erastus B. The Tariff Policy of England & of the United States Contrasted. (The Neglected American Economists Ser.). 1974. lib. bdg. 50.00 (ISBN 0-8240-1015-9). Garland Pub.

Bigelow, John. William Cullen Bryant. LC 79-78114. (Library of Lives & Letters). 1970. Repr. of 1890 ed. 18.00 (ISBN 0-8103-3369-4). Gale.

--William Cullen Bryant. LC 80-19850. (American Men & Women of Letters Ser.). 360p. 1980. pap. 5.95 (ISBN 0-87754-160-4). Chelsea Hse.

Bigelow, Josette, ed. see Berlandier, Jean L., et al.

Bigelow, Melville M. History of Procedure in England from the Norman Conquest: The Norman Period (1066-1204) LC 80-2235. 1981. Repr. of 1880 ed. 44.50 (ISBN 0-404-18752-8). AMS Pr.

--The Law of Fraud & the Procedure Pertaining to the Redress Thereof. lix, 696p. 1981. Repr. of 1877 ed. lib. bdg. 45.00x (ISBN 0-8377-0317-4). Rothman.

--Placita Anglo - Normannica: Law Cases from William First to Richard First. 328p. 1970. Repr. of 1881 ed. text ed. 15.00x (ISBN 0-8377-1928-3). Rothman.

Bigg, Charles. Saint Peter & Saint Jude, 2 vols. LC 2-12311. (International Critical Commentary Ser.). 376p. Repr. of 1978 ed. Vol. 1, 534p. 20.00x (ISBN 0-567-05036-X); Vol. 2, 580p. 22.00x (ISBN 0-567-05012-2). Attic Pr.

Bigge, June L. & O'Donnell, Patrick A. Teaching the Physically & Multiply Disabled. (Special Education Ser.). 1977. text ed. 18.95 (ISBN 0-675-08527-6). Merrill.

Biggers, Earl D. Seven Keys to Baldpate. (Charlie Chan Mysteries Ser.). 1976. Repr. of 1917 ed. lib. bdg. 17.15x (ISBN 0-89966-076-2). Buccaneer Bks.

Biggers, J. V., jt. auth. see Hamer, D. W.

Biggers, W. Watts, jt. auth. see Goodman, Joseph I.

Biggle, Lloyd, Jr. All the Colors of Darkness. 1975. pap. 1.25 o.p. (ISBN 0-685-54123-1, LB2956K, Leisure Bks). Nordon Pubns.

--The Fury Out of Time. 1975. pap. 1.25 o.p. (ISBN 0-685-61045-4, LB318, Leisure Bks). Nordon Pubns.

--Watchers of the Dark. 1975. pap. 0.95 o.p. (ISBN 0-685-53128-7, LB275NK, Leisure Bks). Nordon Pubns.

Biggs, Barbara E., jt. auth. see Felton, Gary S.

Biggs, Bradley. Gavin. (Illus.). 1980. 17.50 (ISBN 0-208-01748-6, Archon). Shoe String.

Biggs, Bruce, ed. The Complete English-Maori Dictionary. 250p. 1981. 34.00 (ISBN 0-19-647989-4). Oxford U Pr.

Biggs, Don. Survival Afloat. (Illus.). 1976. 9.95 o.p. (ISBN 0-679-50579-2); pap. 4.95 o.p. (ISBN 0-679-50629-2). McKay.

Biggs, Donald A., jt. auth. see Williamson, Edmund G.

Biggs, E. & MacLean, J. Freedom to Learn: An Active Learning Approach to Mathematics. 1969. text ed. 14.00 (ISBN 0-201-00572-7). A-W.

Biggs, J., jt. auth. see Fajana, A.

Biggs, J. B. Mathematics & the Conditions of Learning: A Study of Arithmetic in the Primary School. (General Ser.). 1970. Repr. of 1967 ed. text ed. 22.50x (ISBN 0-901225-24-X, NFER). Humanities.

Biggs, J. B., jt. ed. see Kirby, John R.

Biggs, N. L. Algebraic Graph Theory. LC 73-86042. (Tracts in Mathematics Ser.: No. 67). (Illus.). 180p. 1974. 28.95x (ISBN 0-521-20335-X). Cambridge U Pr.

--Interaction Models. LC 77-80827. (London Mathematical Society Lecture Ser.: No. 30). (Illus.). 1977. 14.50x (ISBN 0-521-21770-9). Cambridge U Pr.

Biggs, N. L. & White, A. T. Permutation Groups & Combinatorial Structures. LC 78-21485. (London Mathematical Society Lecture Note: No. 33). (Illus.). 1979. pap. 17.95x (ISBN 0-521-22287-7). Cambridge U Pr.

Biggs, Norman, et al. Graph Theory: Seventeen Thirty-Six to Nineteen Thirty-Six. (Illus.). 1976. 45.00x (ISBN 0-19-853901-0). Oxford U Pr.

Biggs, P. & Dalwood, C. Les Orleanais ont la Parole. (Illus.). 1977. pap. text ed. 4.00x (ISBN 0-582-33121-8); tchr's ed. 4.50x (ISBN 0-582-33122-6); tapes 17.50x (ISBN 0-582-37746-3). Longman.

Bigl, Joseph H., et al. Blade Coating Technology. Clark, C. Wells, ed. (TAPPI Press Reports). (Illus., Orig.). 1978. pap. 33.95 (ISBN 0-89852-373-7, 01 01 R073). TAPPI.

Bigland, Eileen. Helen Keller. LC 67-22810. (Illus.). (gr. 7-10). 1967. 9.95 (ISBN 0-87599-134-3). S G Phillips.

--Madame Curie. LC 57-5540. (Illus.). (gr. 7-9). 1957. 9.95 (ISBN 0-87599-013-4). S G Phillips.

Bigler, Carole L. & Lloyd-Watts, Valery. Studying Suzuki Piano: More Than Music: A Handbook for Teachers, Parents & Students. LC 78-73088. (Illus., Orig.). 1979. pap. 19.95 (ISBN 0-918194-06-7). Accura.

Bigler, James C., jt. auth. see Pantaleoni, C. A.

Bigler, Robert M. The Politics of German Protestantism: The Rise of the Protestant Church Elite in Prussia, 1815-1848. 1972. 24.50x (ISBN 0-520-01881-8). U of Cal Pr.

Bigliani, Raymond E., jt. auth. see Nolan, Peter J.

Bigman, David. Coping with Hunger: Toward a System of Food Security & Price Stabilization. 1981. write for info. (ISBN 0-88410-371-4). Ballinger Pub.

Bigman, David & Taya, Teizo, eds. The Functioning of Floating Exchange Rates: Theory, Evidence & Policy Implications. LC 79-21589. 1980. ref. ed. 37.50 (ISBN 0-88410-492-3). Ballinger Pub.

Bignon, Jean P. see Shugrue, Michael F.

Bigongiari, Dino, ed. see Thomas Aquinas, Saint.

Bigsby, C. W. Superculture: American Popular Culture & Europe. LC 74-84638. 1975. 13.95 (ISBN 0-87972-070-0); pap. 7.95 (ISBN 0-87972-163-4). Bowling Green Univ.

Bigsten, Arne. Regional Inequality & Development: A Case Study of Kenya. 200p. 1980. text ed. 44.00x (ISBN 0-566-00382-1, Pub. by Gower Pub Co England). Renouf.

Biguenet, John, ed. Foreign Fictions: An Anthology of Contemporary International Short Fiction. 1978. pap. 4.95 (ISBN 0-394-72493-3, V-493, Vin). Random.

Bigwood, E. J., ed. Protein & Amino Acid Functions. 536p. 1972. text ed. 130.00 (ISBN 0-08-016464-1). Pergamon.

Bigwood, Jeremy, jt. ed. see Ott, Jonathan.

Bihalji-Merin, Oto. The Art of the Primitives. (Pocket Art Ser.). (Illus.). 1981. pap. 5.50 (ISBN 0-8120-2185-1). Barron.

Bijalwan, C. D. Hindu Omens. 176p. 1980. 8.95x (ISBN 0-89955-321-4, Pub. by Interprint India). Intl Schol Bk Serv.

Bijlani, L. Eating Scientifically. 188p. 1979. 10.00x (ISBN 0-86125-049-4, Pub. by Orient Longman India). State Mutual Bk.

Bijou, Sidney W. & Baer, Donald M. Behavior Analysis of Child Development. (Child Psychology Ser.). 1978. pap. 9.50 ref. ed. (ISBN 0-13-066712-9). P-H.

Bijou, Sidney W. & Ruiz, Roberto. Contribution of Behavior Modification to Education. 352p. 1980. text ed. 24.95 (ISBN 0-89859-024-8). L Erlbaum Assocs.

Bijou, Sidney W. & Ruiz, Roberto, eds. Contribution of Behavior Modification to Education. 224p. 1981. 24.95 (ISBN 0-89859-051-5). L Erlbaum Assocs.

Bijur, Hilda & Smith, Nancy. Jason the Lobsterman. LC 78-58577. 1978. write for info. o.p. (ISBN 0-932384-00-5). Tashmoo.

Bikales, N. M. & Segal, L. Cellulose & Cellulose Derivatives, Vol. 5, Pts. 4 & 5. 1411p. 1971. Set. 130.00 (ISBN 0-471-39038-0). Wiley.

Biklen, Douglas, jt. auth. see Taylor, Steven J.

Biklen, Sari K. & Branningan, Marilyn. Women & Educational Leadership. LC 79-7748. 288p. 1980. 23.95 (ISBN 0-669-03216-6). Lexington Bks.

Biko, Steve. Black Consciousness in South Africa. Arnold, Millard, ed. LC 78-65570. 1979. pap. 5.95 (ISBN 0-394-72739-8, V-739, Vin). Random.

Bila, Dennis, et al. Arithmetic. LC 76-19446. 1976. 5.95x (ISBN 0-87901-058-4). Worth.

--Geometry & Measurement. LC 76-19445. 1976. 5.95x (ISBN 0-87901-059-2). Worth.

--Core Mathematics. LC 74-82696. (Illus.). ix, 603p. (Prog. Bk.). 1975. text ed. 13.95x (ISBN 0-87901-035-5). Worth.

--Intermediate Algebra. LC 74-84642. (Illus.). xvii, 625p. (Prog. Bk.). 1975. text ed. 13.95x (ISBN 0-87901-038-X). Worth.

--Introductory Algebra. LC 74-84641. (Illus.). xviii, 610p. (Prog. Bk.). 1975. text ed. 13.95x (ISBN 0-87901-037-1). Worth.

Bilan, R. P. The Literary Criticism of F. R. Leavis. LC 78-18089. 1979. 32.50 (ISBN 0-521-22324-5). Cambridge U Pr.

Bilancia, Phillip R. Dictionary of Chinese Law & Government: Chinese-English. LC 73-80618. 832p. 1981. 45.00x (ISBN 0-8047-0864-9). Stanford U Pr.

Bilboul, Roger R., ed. Retrospective Index to Theses of Great Britain & Ireland: Vol 1, Social Sciences & Humanities. new ed. 1975. text ed. 168.75 o.p. (ISBN 0-903450-03-8). ABC-Clio.

Bilciu, C., jt. ed. see Rose, J.

Bilderberg Conference - Arnhem - Holland - 1968. Structure of the Quiet Photosphere & the Low Chromosphere: Proceedings. De Jager, C., ed. 1968. 9.90 o.p. (ISBN 0-387-91015-8). Springer-Verlag.

Bilenky, S. M. Introduction to Feynman Diagrams. LC 73-21657. 1974. text ed. 37.00 (ISBN 0-08-017799-9). Pergamon.

Biles, Jack I. & Evans, Robert O., eds. William Golding: Some Critical Considerations. LC 77-73705. 296p. 1978. 18.00x (ISBN 0-8131-1362-8). U Pr of Ky.

Biles, William E. & Swain, James J. Optimization & Industrial Experimentation. LC 79-9516. 1980. 35.00 (ISBN 0-471-04244-7, Pub. by Wiley-Interscience). Wiley.

Biles, William E., jt. auth. see Gajda, Walter J., Jr.

Bilgrami, K. S. & Dube, H. C. A Textbook of Modern Plant Pathology. 1976. text ed. 16.95 (ISBN 0-7069-0421-4, Pub. by Vikas India). Advent Bk.

Bilgrami, S. J. International Organization. (Illus.). 1979. text ed. 17.50x (ISBN 0-7069-0548-2, Pub. by Vikas India). Advent Bk.

Bilibin. Das Maerchen Vom Herrlichen Falken. (Insel Taschenbucher Fur Kinder: It 487). 64p. (Ger.). 1980. pap. text ed. 4.55 (ISBN 3-458-32187-X, Pub. by Insel Verlag Germany). Suhrkamp.

Bilik, Dorothy S. Immigrant-Survivors: Post-Holocaust Consciousness in Recent Jewish-American Literature. 295p. 1981. 19.95x (ISBN 0-8195-5046-9). Wesleyan U Pr.

Bill, Alfred H. The Beleaguered City: Richmond, 1861-1865. LC 80-16702. (Illus.). xiv, 313p. 1980. Repr. of 1946 ed. lib. bdg. 29.75x (ISBN 0-313-22568-0, BIBE). Greenwood.

Billcliffe, Roger. Mackintosh Watercolours. LC 78-53795. (Illus.). 144p. 1979. pap. 12.50 (ISBN 0-8008-5043-2). Taplinger.

Bille, Donald A. Practical Approaches to Patient Teaching. 1981. pap. text ed. write for info (ISBN 0-316-09498-6). Little.

Biller, Henry B. Father, Child & Sex Role: Paternal Determinants in Personality Development. 1971. pap. 9.95 (ISBN 0-669-02517-8). Lexington Bks.

--Paternal Deprivation: Family, School, Sexuality & Society. LC 74-928. 1974. pap. 9.95 (ISBN 0-669-02517-8). Lexington Bks.

Biller, Henry B., jt. auth. see Gershon, Michael.

Biller, Henry, Ph.D. & Meredith, Dennis. Father Power. 400p. 1975. pap. 3.50 (ISBN 0-385-11125-8, Anch). Doubleday.

Biller, Martie, jt. auth. see Biller, Tom A.

Biller, Tom A. & Biller, Martie. Simple Object Lessons for Children. (Object Lesson Ser.). 160p. 1980. pap. 4.95 (ISBN 0-8010-0793-3). Baker Bk.

Billeskov-Jansen, F. J. & Mitchell, P. M., eds. Anthology of Danish Literature. new bilingual ed. LC 72-132475. 1971. Repr. of 1964 ed. 25.00x o.p. (ISBN 0-8093-0487-2). S Ill U Pr.

--Anthology of Danish Literature: Middle Ages to Romanticism. bilingual ed. LC 72-5610. (Arcturus Books Paperbacks). 272p. 1972. pap. 6.95 (ISBN 0-8093-0596-8). S Ill U Pr.

--Anthology of Danish Literature: Realism to the Present. bilingual ed. LC 72-5610. (Arcturus Books Paperbacks). 352p. 1972. pap. 7.95 (ISBN 0-8093-0597-6). S Ill U Pr.

Billetdoux, Francois. Billetdoux: Two Plays. Rudkin, Mark, tr. Incl. Tchin-Tchin; Chez Torpe. 1964. 3.50 o.p. (ISBN 0-8090-3010-1, Mermaid). Hill & Wang.

Billett, F. S., jt. ed. see Balls, M.

Billett, M. G. A Handbook of Industrial Lubrication. 1979. 28.00 (ISBN 0-08-024232-4). Pergamon.

Billias, G. A. & Grob, G. N. American History: Retrospect & Prospect. LC 71-128471. 1971. 14.95 (ISBN 0-02-903490-6); pap. text ed. 7.95 (ISBN 0-02-903510-4). Free Pr.

Billias, George, ed. see Great Britain Historical Manuscripts Commission.

Billias, George, ed. see Great Britain Historical Manuscripts Commission. Report on Manuscripts in Various Collections.

Billias, George A., jt. auth. see Grob, Gerald N.

Billig, O. & Burton-Bradley, B. G. The Painted Message. 1978. 19.50 (ISBN 0-470-99126-7). Wiley.

Billig, Otto. Flying Saucers: Magic in the Skies. 256p. 1981. text ed. 14.95x (ISBN 0-87073-833-X). Schenkman.

Billigmeier, Jon C. Kadmos & the Possibility of a Semitic Presence in Halladic Greece. (Publications of the Henri Frankfort Foundation Ser.: No. 6). 1980. pap. text ed. write for info. (ISBN 90-6032-110-3). Humanities.

Billingham, J. & Pesek, R., eds. Communication with Extraterrestial Intelligence. (Astronautica: Vol. 6, Nos. 1-2). 1979. 47.00 (ISBN 0-08-024727-X). Pergamon.

Billingham, John, et al, eds. Life in the Universe. 400p. 1981. text ed. 20.00x (ISBN 0-262-02155-2); pap. text ed. 12.50x (ISBN 0-262-52062-1). MIT Pr.

Billingham, Katherine A. Developmental Psychology for the Health Care Professions: Prenatal Through Adolescent Development, Pt. 1. (Behavioral Sciences for Health Care Professionals Ser.). 128p. (Orig.). 1981. lib. bdg. 15.00x (ISBN 0-86531-000-9); pap. text ed. 6.00x (ISBN 0-86531-001-7). Westview.

Billingham, N. C. Molar Mass Measurements in Polymer Science. LC 77-2823. 1977. 41.95 (ISBN 0-470-99125-9). Halsted Pr.

Billingham, Richard & Goodkin, Marie. First Steps to Musicianship. 256p. 1980. pap. text ed. 9.95x (ISBN 0-917974-38-7). Waveland Pr.

Billingham, Rupert E., jt. auth. see Beer, Alan E.

Billings, Charlene W. Salamanders. LC 80-21838. (A Skylight Bk.). (Illus.). 48p. (gr. 2-5). 1981. PLB 5.95 (ISBN 0-396-07913-X). Dodd.

--Spring Peepers Are Calling. LC 78-7735. (Illus.). (gr. 3-5). 1979. 5.95 (ISBN 0-396-07584-3). Dodd.

Billings, Diane, jt. auth. see Ellis, Diane.

Billings, Dwight B., Jr. Planters & the Making of a "New South". Class, Politics, & Development in North Carolina, 1865-1900. LC 78-25952. xiii, 284p. 1979. 15.00x (ISBN 0-8078-1315-X). U of NC Pr.

Billings, Grace H. The Art of Transition in Plato. Taran, Leonardo, ed. LC 78-66578. (Ancient Philosophy Ser.: Vol. 2). 110p. 1979. lib. bdg. 13.00 (ISBN 0-8240-9609-6). Garland Pub.

Billings, John S. History & Literature of Surgery. 1970. Repr. of 1895 ed. 15.00 (ISBN 0-87266-038-9). Argosy.

Billings, Karen & Moursund, David. Are You a Computer Literate? LC 79-56396. 150p. 1979. pap. 8.95 (ISBN 0-686-61254-X). Dilithium Pr.

--Problem Solving with Calculators. 150p. 1979. pap. 7.95 (ISBN 0-918398-30-4). Dilithium Pr.

Billings, Richard N., jt. auth. see Blakey, G. Robert.

Billings, Thomas H. The Platonism of Philo Judaeus. Taran, Leonardo, ed. LC 78-66560. (Ancient Philosophy Ser.: Vol. 3). 117p. 1979. lib. bdg. 13.00 (ISBN 0-8240-9608-8). Garland Pub.

Billings, W. D. Plants, & the Ecosystem. 3rd ed. 1978. pap. 7.95x (ISBN 0-534-00571-3). Wadsworth Pub.

Billings, William. The Psalm Singer's Amusement. LC 73-5100. (Earlier American Music Ser.: Vol. 20). 104p. 1974. Repr. of 1781 ed. lib. bdg. 22.50 (ISBN 0-306-70587-7). Da Capo.

Billings, William R. Some Details of Water-Works Construction. LC 72-80387. (History of Technology Ser., Vol. 2). (Illus.). 96p. 1972. Repr. of 1898 ed. 10.00x o.p. (ISBN 0-8155-5006-5, NP). Noyes.

Billingsley, jt. auth. see Huntsberger.

Billingsley, P. Convergence of Probability Measures. (Probability & Mathematical Statistics Tracts: Probability & Statistics Section). 1968. 27.50 (ISBN 0-471-07242-7, Pub by Wiley-Interscience). Wiley.

Billingsley, Patrick. Probability & Measure. LC 78-25632. (Probability & Mathematical Statistics Ser.). 1979. 28.95 (ISBN 0-471-03173-9, Pub. by Wiley-Interscience). Wiley.

Billingsley, Patrick, jt. auth. see Huntsberger, David V.

Billington, David P. Thin-Shell Concrete Structures. 2nd ed. (Illus.). 432p. 1981. 24.50. McGraw.

Billington, Dora & Colbeck, John. The Technique of Pottery. 1979. 27.00 (ISBN 0-7134-2836-8, Pub. by Batsford England). David & Charles.

Billington, E. W. & Tate, A. The Physics of Deformation & Flow. (Illus.). 720p. 1981. text ed. 59.00 (ISBN 0-07-005285-9, C). McGraw.

Billington, Elizabeth T. Adventure with Flowers. LC 66-15814. (Illus.). (gr. 5-9). 1966. 6.95 (ISBN 0-7232-6021-4). Warne.

Billington, James H. Fire in the Minds of Men. LC 79-2750. 677p. 1980. 25.00 (ISBN 0-465-02405-X). Basic.

Billington, Mary F. Woman in India. (Illus.). 269p. 1973. 17.50x (ISBN 0-8002-0978-8). Intl Pubns Serv.

Billington, Michael. How Tickled I Am: A Celebration of Ken Dodd. (Illus.). 11.95 (ISBN 0-241-89345-3, Pub. by Hamish Hamilton England). David & Charles.

Billington, Monroe & Leach, Duane, eds. American Democracy on Trial. 1968. pap. text ed. 5.95x o.p. (ISBN 0-8211-0102-1). McCutchan.

Billington, Monroe L. The Political South in the Twentieth Century. LC 73-1312. 1975. pap. text ed. 8.95x o.p. (ISBN 0-684-13986-3, ScribT). Scribner.

Billington, N. S. & Roberts, B. M. Building Services Engineering: A Review of Its Development. (International Series on Building Environmental Engineering: Vol. 1). 500p. 1981. 80.00 (ISBN 0-08-026741-6); pap. 24.00 (ISBN 0-08-026742-4). Pergamon.

Billington, Rachel. A Woman's Age. LC 79-23723. 469p. 1980. 12.95 (ISBN 0-671-40115-7). Summit Bks.

--A Woman's Age. 528p. 1981. pap. 2.95 (ISBN 0-553-14142-2). Bantam.

Billington, Ray A. Far Side of Despair: Eighteen Thirty to Eighteen Sixty. (New American Nation Ser.). (Illus.). pap. 4.95x (ISBN 0-06-133012-4, TB 3012, Torch). Har-Row.

--Limericks Historical & Hysterical: Plagiarized, Arranged, Annotated & Some Written by Ray Allen Billington. 1981. 9.95 (ISBN 0-393-01453-3). Norton.

Billington, Ray A., ed. see Forten, Charlotte L.

Billink, Alan, jt. auth. see Kaplan, Donald.

Billip, K., jt. auth. see Stanislawski, J.

Billmeyer, Fred W. & Kelley, Richard N. Entering Industry: A Guide for Young Professionals. LC 75-22283. 281p. 1975. 25.50 (ISBN 0-471-07285-0, Pub. by Wiley-Interscience). Wiley.

Billmeyer, Fred W., Jr. Textbook of Polymer Science. 2nd ed. LC 78-142713. 1971. 28.95 (ISBN 0-471-07296-6, Pub. by Wiley-Interscience). Wiley.

Billmeyer, Fred W., Jr. & Saltzman, Max. Principles of Color Technology. LC 80-21561. 272p. 1980. 19.95 (ISBN 0-471-03052-X, Pub. by Wiley-Interscience). Wiley.

Billnitzer, Harold. It's Your Death, Make the Most of It. LC 79-88402. 1979. pap. 6.95 (ISBN 0-933350-27-9). wkbk. 0.90 (ISBN 0-933350-28-7). Morse Pr.

Billon, Francois De see De Billon, Francois.

Billot, Marcel & Wells, F. V. Perfumery Technology: Art, Science, Industry. LC 75-5768. (Illus.). 353p. 1975. 54.95 (ISBN 0-470-07298-9). Halsted Pr.

Billows, F. L. The Techniques of Language Teaching. 1961. pap. text ed. 9.75x (ISBN 0-582-52505-5). Longman.

Bills, Scott, ed. see Aptheker, Bettina, et al.

Billups, Ann. Discussion Starters for Youth Groups: Series 1. (Orig.). 1966. pap. 7.95 (ISBN 0-8170-0351-7). Judson.

--Discussion Starters for Youth Groups: Series 2. LC 70-75185. 1969. pap. 7.95 (ISBN 0-8170-0443-2). Judson.

--Discussion Starters for Youth Groups, Series 3. LC 70-75185. 224p. 1976. pap. 7.95 (ISBN 0-8170-0687-7). Judson.

--Perspectives: Discussion Starters on Attitudes & Values for Church Groups. 224p. 1981. pap. 11.95 (ISBN 0-8170-0905-1). Judson.

Bilnitzer. Check Your Chances of Success in a Mixed Marriage. pap. 1.00 o.p. (ISBN 0-686-12318-2). Christs Mission.

Bilokur, Borys. A Concordance to the Russian Poetry of Fedor I. Tiutchev. LC 75-9419. 343p. 1975. 20.00x (ISBN 0-87057-145-1, Pub. by Brown U Pr). Univ Pr of New England.

Biloon, F. Medical Equipment Service Manual: Theory & Maintenance Procedures. LC 77-513. 1978. 23.95 (ISBN 0-13-572644-1). P-H.

Bilsen, F. A., ed. see International Symposium on Hearing, Fifth, Noordwijkerhout, the Netherlands, April 8-12, 1980.

Bimba, Anthony. History of the American Working Class. 3rd ed. LC 68-30818. (Illus.). 1968. Repr. of 1936 ed. lib. bdg. 25.00x (ISBN 0-8371-0020-8, BIWC). Greenwood.

Bimler, Rich. Pray, Praise & Hooray. LC 77-175306. (Illus.). 150p. (Orig.). (YA) 1972. pap. 3.95 (ISBN 0-570-03130-3, 12-2380). Concordia.

Bimler, Richard. Seventy-Seven Ways of Involving Youth in the Church. (Illus.). 1976. pap. 4.50 (ISBN 0-570-03737-9, 12-2641). Concordia.

Bimson, John J. Redating the Exodus & Conquest. (JSOT Supplement Ser.: No. 5). 351p. 1978. text ed. o.p. (ISBN 0-905774-10-8, Pub. by JSOT Pr England); pap. text ed. 23.95x (ISBN 0-905774-03-5, Pub. by JSOT Pr England). Eisenbrauns.

Binchy, D. A. Church & State in Fascist Italy. (Royal Institute of International Affairs Ser.). 1941. 39.50x (ISBN 0-19-821486-3). Oxford U Pr.

Bindeman, Steven L. Heidegger & Wittgenstein: The Poetics of Silence. LC 80-6066. 159p. 1980. lib. bdg. 15.75 (ISBN 0-8191-1350-6); pap. text ed. 7.50 (ISBN 0-8191-1351-4). U Pr of Amer.

Binder, Eando. Enslaved Brains. (YA) 1971. 4.95 o.p. (ISBN 0-685-23397-9, Avalon). Bouregy.

Binder, Frederick M. Coal Age Empire: Pennsylvania Coal & Its Utilization to 1860. LC 75-621822. 184p. 1974. 8.50 (ISBN 0-911124-75-6). Pa Hist & Mus.

Binder, Leonard. The Study of the Middle East: Research & Scholarship in the Humanities & Social Sciences. LC 76-7408. 648p. 1976. 39.95 (ISBN 0-471-07304-0, Pub. by Wiley-Interscience). Wiley.
Binder, Otto O. Flying Saucers Are Watching Us. 1978. pap. 1.50 (ISBN 0-505-51304-8). Tower Bks.
Binder, Raymond C. Fluid Mechanics. 5th ed. (Illus.). 448p. 1973. ref. ed. 25.95x (ISBN 0-13-322594-1). P-H.
Binder, Raymond C., et al see Heat Transfer & Fluid Mechanics Institute.
Binder, V., et al. Modern Therapies. 1976. 11.95 (ISBN 0-13-599001-7, Spec); pap. 5.95 (ISBN 0-13-598995-7). P-H.
Binding, G. J. Vegetables & Herbs with a Difference. 1980. 19.50x (ISBN 0-85032-178-6, Pub. by Daniel Co England). State Mutual Bk.
--Vegetables & Herbs with a Difference. 64p. 1972. pap. 3.00x (ISBN 0-8464-1059-1). Beekman Pubs.
Bindingarmynstur, Foroysk. Faroese Knitting Patterns. 60p. 1980. pap. 10.95 (ISBN 0-906191-17-3, Pub. by Thule Pr England). Intl Schol Bk Serv.
Bindley, T. Herbert, ed. The Ecumenical Documents of the Faith: The Creed of Nicea; Three Epistles of Cyril; the Tome of Leo; the Chalcedonian Definition. 4th ed. LC 79-8708. viii, 246p. 1980. Repr. of 1950 ed. lib. bdg. 22.25x (ISBN 0-313-22197-9, BIOD). Greenwood.
Bindman, David. Hogarth. (World of Art Ser.). (Illus.). 288p. 1981. 17.95 (ISBN 0-19-520239-2); pap. 9.95 (ISBN 0-19-520240-6). Oxford U Pr.
Bindoff, S. T. The Pelican History of England: Tudor England, Vol. 5. 1950. pap. 3.50 (ISBN 0-14-020212-9, Pelican). Penguin.
--Tudor England. lib. bdg. 10.50x (ISBN 0-88307-022-7). Gannon.
Bindra, Dalbir. A Theory of Intelligent Behavior. LC 75-46519. 1976. 27.50 (ISBN 0-471-07320-2, Pub by Wiley-Interscience). Wiley.
Bindschedler-Robert, Denise. The Law of Armed Conflicts. 1971. pap. 2.25 (ISBN 0-87003-021-3). Carnegie Endow.
Bindseil, Kenneth R. & Dickey, Imogene B. Effective Writing: Methods & Examples. LC 77-72907. (Illus.). 1977. pap. text ed. 10.95 (ISBN 0-395-24950-3); inst. manual & suppl. tests 0.25 (ISBN 0-395-24949-X). HM.
Binet, Alfred. Alterations of Personality. Baldwin, Helen G., tr. from Fr. Bd. with On Double-Consciousness. Repr. of 1890 ed. (Contributions to the History of Psychology Ser., Vol. V, Pt. C: Medical Psychology). 1978. Repr. of 1896 ed. 30.00 (ISBN 0-89093-169-0). U Pubns Amer.
Binet, Alfred see Magendie, Francois.
Binet, Alfred, et al see Stern, William L.
Binford, Lewis R. Bones: Ancient Men & Modern Myths. LC 80-2327. (Studies in Archaeology Ser.). 1981. price not set (ISBN 0-12-100035-4). Acad Pr.
Binford, Lewis R. & Binford, Sally R., eds. New Perspectives in Archeology. LC 67-27386. 1968. 28.95x (ISBN 0-202-33022-2). Aldine Pub.
Binford, Sally R., jt. ed. see Binford, Lewis R.
Bing, David H., ed. see Sponsored by the Center for Blood Research.
Bing, Jon & Harvold, Trygve. Legal Decisions & Information Systems. 1977. 25.00x (ISBN 82-00-05031-9, Dist. by Columbia U Pr). Universitet.
Bing, Jon & Selmer, Knut S. A Decade of Computers & Law. 480p. 1980. pap. 35.00x (ISBN 82-0005-376-8). Universitet.
Bing, Samuel. Artistic America, Tiffany Glass & Art Nouveau. (Illus.). 288p. (Orig.). 1980. pap. 9.95 (ISBN 0-262-52025-7). MIT Pr.
Bing, Stephen & Brown, Larry. Standards Relating to Monitoring. (Juvenile Justice Standards Project Ser.). 1980. softcover 7.95 (ISBN 0-88410-805-8); casebound 16.50 (ISBN 0-88410-753-1). Ballinger Pub.
--Standards Relating to Monitoring. LC 77-3939. (Juvenile Justice Standards Project Ser.). 1977. softcover 5.95 o.p. (ISBN 0-88410-761-2); casebound 12.50 o.p. Ballinger Pub.
Bingaman, Ronald, jt. auth. see Shook, Robert.
Binger, Jane, jt. auth. see Huntsman, Ann.
Binger, Norman H., tr. see Busch, Moritz.
Bingham, C. D. Rural Biology. 1965. pap. text ed. 5.50x o.p. (ISBN 0-435-59090-1). Heinemann Ed.
Bingham, Caleb. Young Lady's Accidence. 1980. Repr. of 1785 ed. 30.00 (ISBN 0-8201-1360-3). Schol Facsimiles.
Bingham, Doris. Lovers & Liars. 1981. pap. 2.25 (ISBN 0-8439-0905-6, Leisure Bks). Nordon Pubns.
Bingham, Earl G. Pocketbook for Writers: A Guide to Writing & Revision. 416p. 1980. pap. text ed. 8.95x (ISBN 0-534-00773-2). Wadsworth Pub.
Bingham, Edwin R. & Love, Glen A., eds. Northwest Perspectives: Essays on the Culture of the Pacific Northwest. LC 77-15189. 264p. 1981. pap. 7.95 (ISBN 0-295-95805-7). U of Wash Pr.
Bingham, Hiram. Across South America. (Latin America in the 20th Century Ser.). 1976. Repr. of 1911 ed. lib. bdg. 32.50 (ISBN 0-306-70834-5). Da Capo.
--The Monroe Doctrine. (Latin America in the 20th Century Ser.). 1976. Repr. of 1913 ed. lib. bdg. 15.00 (ISBN 0-306-70833-7). Da Capo.
--A Residence of Twenty-One Years in the Sandwich Islands: A Civil, Religious, & Political History. rev. 3rd ed. LC 77-83041. 1981. 27.50 (ISBN 0-8048-1252-7). C E Tuttle.
Bingham, J., tr. see Aelianus, Tacitus.
Bingham, J., tr. see Aelinanus, Tacitus.
Bingham, Jane & Scholt, Grayce, eds. Fifteen Centuries of Children's Literature: An Annotated Chronology of British & American Works in Historical Context. LC 79-8584. (Illus.). l, 540p. 1980. lib. bdg. 35.00 (ISBN 0-313-22164-2, BCL/). Greenwood.
Bingham, Joan, jt. auth. see Riccio, Dolores.
Bingham, John. The Handbook for Apartment Living. LC 80-70350. 288p. (gr. 11-12). 1981. 13.95 (ISBN 0-686-69519-4); pap. 8.95 (ISBN 0-686-69520-8). Chilton.
Bingham, John E. & Davies, Garth W. A Handbook of Systems Analysis. 2nd ed. LC 77-28954. 229p. 1980. pap. text ed. 17.95x (ISBN 0-470-26997-9). Halsted Pr.
--A Handbook of Systems Analysis. 2nd ed. LC 77-28954. 1978. 18.95 o.p. (ISBN 0-470-99129-1). Halsted Pr.
--Planning for Data Communications. 218p. 1979. pap. 17.95x (ISBN 0-470-26843-3). Halsted Pr.
Bingham, John E & Davies, Garth W. Planning for Data Communications. LC 77-7193. 1978. 29.95 (ISBN 0-470-99187-9). Halsted Pr.
Bingham, Madeline. Earls & Girls. (Illus.). 150p. 1980. 27.00 (ISBN 0-241-10270-7, Pub. by Hamish Hamilton England). David & Charles.
--Sheridan: The Track of a Comet. 1972. text ed. 17.95x o.p. (ISBN 0-04-928024-4); pap. 7.50 o.p. (ISBN 0-04-928036-8). Allen Unwin.
Bingham, Millicent T., ed. see Dickinson, Emily.
Bingham, Peregrine. The Law of Infancy & Coverture. 2nd ed. viii, 396p. 1980. Repr. of 1849 ed. lib. bdg. 35.00x (ISBN 0-8377-0311-5). Rothman.
Bingham, Richard D. The Adoption of Innovation by Local Government. LC 75-41922. 1976. 22.95 (ISBN 0-669-00484-7). Lexington Bks.
--Public Housing & Urban Renewal: An Analysis of Federal-Local Relations. LC 74-19822. (Special Series). (Illus.). 282p. 1975. text ed. 27.95 (ISBN 0-275-05810-7). Praeger.
Bingham, Richard D., et al. The Politics of Raising State & Local Revenue. LC 78-8392. (Praeger Special Studies). 1978. 23.95 (ISBN 0-03-022306-7); pap. 9.95 (ISBN 0-03-041471-7). Praeger.
Bingham, Robert C. Economic Concepts: A Programmed Approach. 6th ed. (Illus.). 384p. 1981. pap. text ed. 7.95 (ISBN 0-07-044936-8, C). McGraw.
Bingley, William. Musical Biography, Two Vols. LC 70-127286. (Music Ser). 1971. Repr. of 1834 ed. Set. lib. bdg. 65.00 (ISBN 0-306-70032-8). Da Capo.
Binh, Duong T. Tagmemic Comparison of the Structure of English & Vietnamese Sentences. LC 74-123126. (Janua Linguarum, Ser. Practica: No. 110). (Orig.). 1971. pap. text ed. 51.75x (ISBN 90-2791-598-9). Mouton.
Binhammer, R. T., jt. auth. see Crafts, R. C.
Bining, Arthur C. Pennsylvania Iron Manufacture in the Eighteenth Century. rev. ed. (Illus.). 214p. 1973. 8.50 (ISBN 0-911124-72-1); pap. 4.50 (ISBN 0-911124-71-3). Pa Hist & Mus.
Binion, Alice. Antonio & Francesco Guardi: Their Life & Milieu: With a Catalogue of Their Figure Drawings. LC 75-23782. (Outstanding Dissertations in the Fine Arts - 17th & 18th Century). (Illus.). 1976. lib. bdg. 48.00 (ISBN 0-8240-1979-2). Garland Pub.
Binion, Rudolph. Frau Lou: Nietzsche's Wayward Disciple. LC 68-10389. 602p. 1968. 25.00x (ISBN 0-691-06142-4, 313); pap. 7.95 o.p. (ISBN 0-691-01312-8). Princeton U Pr.
--Soundings. 275p. 1981. 18.95 (ISBN 0-914434-16-0); pap. 8.95 (ISBN 0-914434-17-9). Psychohistory Pr.
Binion, Rudolph, ed. see Andreas-Salome, Lou.
Binkin, Martin. The Military Pay Muddle. (Studies in Defense Policy). 60p. 1975. pap. 3.95 (ISBN 0-8157-0961-7). Brookings.
--Shaping the Defense Civilian Work Force: Economics, Politics, & National Security. LC 78-14897. (Studies in Defense Policy). 1978. pap. 3.95 (ISBN 0-8157-0967-6). Brookings.
--Support Costs in the Defense Budget: The Submerged One-Third. (Studies in Defense Policy). 49p. 1972. pap. 3.95 (ISBN 0-8157-0957-9). Brookings.
--U. S. Reserve Forces: The Problem of the Weekend Warrior. (Studies in Defense Policy). 63p. 1974. pap. 3.95 (ISBN 0-8157-0959-5). Brookings.
Binkin, Martin & Bach, Shirley J. Women & the Military. (Studies in Defense Policy). 1980. 9.95 (ISBN 0-8157-0966-8); pap. 3.95 (ISBN 0-8157-0965-X). Brookings.
Binkin, Martin & Kyriakopoulos, Irene. Paying the Modern Military. LC 80-70080. (Studies in Defense Policy). 100p. 1981. pap. 3.95 (ISBN 0-8157-0971-4). Brookings.
--Youth or Experience? Manning the Modern Military. (Studies in Defense Policy). 1979. pap. 3.95 (ISBN 0-8157-0969-2). Brookings.
Binkin, Martin & Record, Jeffrey. Where Does the Marine Corps Go from Here? (Studies in Defense Policy). 1976. pap. 3.95 (ISBN 0-8157-0963-3). Brookings.
Binkley, Harold R. & Tulloch, Rodney W. Teaching Vocational Agriculture-Agribusiness. (Illus.). 250p. 1981. pap. write for info. (ISBN 0-8134-2153-5). Interstate.
Binkley, Thomas, tr. see Winckel, Fritz.
Binkley, William C. The Texas Revolution. LC 79-63065. 1979. 10.95 (ISBN 0-87611-041-3); pap. 4.50 (ISBN 0-87611-042-1). Tex St Hist Assn.
Binks, Gerald S. Best in Show: Breeding & Exhibiting Budgerigans. 1976. 11.95 (ISBN 0-85223-064-8, Pub. by Michael Joseph). Merrimack Bk Serv.
Binmore, K. G. Foundations of Analysis: Bk. 1, a Straightforward Introduction: Logic, Sets & Numbers. LC 79-41790. (Illus.). 200p. Date not set. 24.95 (ISBN 0-521-23322-4); pap. 12.95 (ISBN 0-521-29915-2). Cambridge U Pr.
--Foundations of Analysis: Bk. 2, a Straightforward Introduction: Topological Ideas. LC 79-41790. (Illus.). 350p. Date not set. price not set (ISBN 0-521-23350-X); pap. price not set (ISBN 0-521-29930-6). Cambridge U Pr.
--Mathematical Analysis. LC 76-28006. (Illus.). 1977. 47.00 (ISBN 0-521-21480-7); pap. 13.95x (ISBN 0-521-29167-4). Cambridge U Pr.
Binney, Horace. An Enquiry into the Formation of Washington's Farewell Address. LC 74-98692. 1969. Repr. of 1859 ed. lib. bdg. 32.50 (ISBN 0-306-71840-5). Da Capo.
Binnie, C. D. Data Processing in Electroencephalography: Medical Computing, Vol. 2. 1979. 14.95 o.p. (ISBN 0-89355-003-5). Res Stud Pr.
Binning, Emily. Gordon Takes a Wife. 138p. 1977. 3.75 (ISBN 0-930756-26-6, 4230-EB1). Women's Aglow.
Binns, J. W., ed. The Latin Poetry of English Poets. 1974. 18.00x (ISBN 0-7100-7845-5). Routledge & Kegan.
--Ovid. (Greek & Latin Studies). 1973. 20.00x (ISBN 0-7100-7639-8). Routledge & Kegan.
Binny, J., jt. auth. see Mayhew, Henry.
Binstead, Herbert E. The Book of Decorative Details for Artists, Upholsterers, Architects, Builders, Cabinet & Furniture Makers. (Illus.). 1979. deluxe ed. 49.75x (ISBN 0-930582-40-3). Gloucester Art.
Binstock, Robert H., jt. auth. see Morris, Robert.
Binyon, J. Physiology of Echinoderms. 212p. 1972. text ed. 36.00 (ISBN 0-08-016991-0). Pergamon.
Binyon, Lawrence. Engraved Designs of William Blake. LC 67-25542. (Graphic Art Ser). 1967. Repr. of 1926 ed. lib. bdg. 65.00 (ISBN 0-306-70956-2). Da Capo.
Binzen, Bill. Alfred Goes House Hunting. LC 73-81425. 32p. (gr. 1-4). 1974. 5.95a o.p. (ISBN 0-385-04820-3); PLB (ISBN 0-385-08223-1). Doubleday.
--Alfred, the Little Bear. LC 78-99465. (gr. 1-3). 1970. PLB 5.95 (ISBN 0-385-08967-8). Doubleday.
--El Primer Dia de Clases. LC 76-23788. (ps-k). 1977. PLB 4.95 (ISBN 0-385-12007-9). Doubleday.
--The Rory Story. LC 73-9011. 32p. (gr. 1-3). 1974. 4.95 o.p. (ISBN 0-385-09332-2). Doubleday.
Binzen, Peter. White Town, U.S.A. LC 70-85565. 1971. pap. 2.45 (ISBN 0-394-71077-0, V-77, Vin). Random.
Bioavailability of Drug Products Project. The Bioavailability of Drug Products. LC 77-94131. 1978. 18.00 (ISBN 0-917330-18-8). Am Pharm Assn.
Biobaku, S. O., ed. Sources of Yoruba History. (Oxford Studies in African Affairs). (Illus.). 250p. 1973. 27.00x (ISBN 0-19-821669-6). Oxford U Pr.
Biochemical Societies of France, Great Britain, Italy, & the Netherlands. Joint Meeting, Venice, 1976. Phosphorylated Proteins & Related Enzymes: Proceedings. 121p. 8.00. Info Retrieval.
Biogas & Other Rural Energy Resources Workshop, Suva. Proceedings. Bd. with Proceedings: Rural Energy Development Roving Seminar; Bangkok, Manila, Tehran & Jakarta. (Energy Resources Development Ser.: No. 19). 152p. 1979. pap. text ed. 10.00 (79/2F10, UN). Unipub.
Biological Science Curriculum Study. Investigating Your Environment Ser. Incl. Bk. 1. The Environment: Some Viewpoints. pap. text ed. 3.92 (ISBN 0-201-00933-1); Bk. 2. The Price of Progress. pap. text ed. 4.52 (ISBN 0-201-00934-X); Bk. 3. Food for Humanity. pap. text ed. 4.52 (ISBN 0-201-00935-8); Bk. 4. Human Population. pap. text ed. 4.52 (ISBN 0-201-00936-6); Bk. 5. Solid Waste. pap. text ed. 4.52 (ISBN 0-201-00937-4); Bk. 6. Pesticides. pap. text ed. 4.52 (ISBN 0-201-00938-2); Bk. 7. Land Use. pap. text ed. 4.52 (ISBN 0-201-00939-0); Bk. 8. Water Quality. pap. text ed. 4.52 (ISBN 0-201-00940-4). (gr. 10-12). 1975. pap. text ed. 8.80 student hndbk. (ISBN 0-201-00931-5, Sch Div); tchr's hndbk. 8.00 (ISBN 0-201-00932-3). A-W.
Biology & Agriculture Division. Biochronometry. LC 79-610527. (Illus.). 1971. text ed. 16.75 (ISBN 0-309-01866-8). Natl Acad Pr.
Biology Colloquium, 34th, Oregon State University, 1973. The Biology of Tumor Viruses: Proceedings. Beaudreau, George S., ed. LC 52-19235. (Illus.). 144p. 1976. pap. text ed. 7.00 (ISBN 0-87071-173-3). Oreg St U Pr.
Biology Colloquium, 35th,Oregon State University,1974. Chromosomes - from Simple to Complex: Proceedings. Roberts, Paul, ed. LC 76-5880. (Illus.). 96p. 1977. pap. text ed. 6.00 (ISBN 0-87071-174-1). Oreg St U Pr.
Biology Colloquium, 37th, Oregon State University, 1976. Historical Biogeography, Plate Tectonics, & the Changing Environment: Proceedings. Gray, Jane & Boucot, Arthur J., eds. LC 78-31376. (Illus.). 512p. 1979. 59.75 (ISBN 0-87071-176-8). Oreg St U Pr.
Biology Coloquium, 29th, Oregon State Univ. Biochemical Coevolution: Proceedings. Chambers, Kenton L., ed. LC 52-19235. 128p. 1970. text ed. 6.00 (ISBN 0-87071-168-7). Oreg St U Pr.
Bion, W. R. Experiences in Groups. LC 61-7884. 1981. text ed. 12.95x (ISBN 0-465-02174-3). Basic.
Biophy, Mary A. see Bottiglia, William F.
Biraben, Jean N. Les Hommes et la Peste En France et Dans les Pays Europeens et Mediterraneens: Le Peste Dans L'mistoire, Tome 1. (Civilisations et Societies: No. 35). (Illus.). 451p. 1975. pap. text ed. 63.50 (ISBN 90-2797-555-8). Mouton.
Biram, John, tr. see Wegener, Alfred.
Birau, N. & Schlott, W., eds. Melatonin - Current Status & Perspectives: Proceedings of an International Symposium on Melatonin, Held in Bremen, F. R. Germany, September 18-30, 1980. (Advances in the Biosciences Ser.: Vol. 29). (Illus.). 420p. 1981. 65.00 (ISBN 0-08-026400-X). Pergamon.
Birch, A. H. The British System of Government. 3rd ed. (Minerva Ser. of Students' Handbooks). 1973. text ed. 16.50x o.p. (ISBN 0-04-320091-5); pap. text ed. 8.95x o.p. (ISBN 0-04-320092-3). Allen Unwin.
Birch, A. H., et al. Britain: Progress & Decline, Vol. 17. 154p. 1980. lib. bdg. 17.50 (ISBN 0-930598-18-0). Tulane Stud Pol.
Birch, Alison Wyrley. Poetry for Peace of Mind. LC 77-76959. 1978. 6.95 o.p. (ISBN 0-385-13253-0). Doubleday.
Birch, Anthony H. British System of Government. 4th ed. (Minerva Series of Students Handbooks). (Illus.). 320p. 1980. text ed. 19.95x (ISBN 0-04-320142-3, 2485); pap. text ed. 7.95x (ISBN 0-04-320143-1, 2486). Allen Unwin.
Birch, Austin. The Boy's Brigade. 7.50 (ISBN 0-392-07678-0, SpS). Soccer.
Birch, Bruce C. The Rise of the Israelite Monarchy: The Growth & Development of I Samuel 7-15. LC 76-20680. (Society of Biblical Literature. Dissertation Ser.). 1976. pap. 7.50 (ISBN 0-89130-112-7, 060127). Scholars Pr Ca.
Birch, C. & Albrecht, P., eds. Genetics & the Quality of Life. 1976. text ed. 32.00 (ISBN 0-08-018210-0); pap. text ed. 14.30 (ISBN 0-08-019861-9). Pergamon.
Birch, Cyril, ed. & intro. by. Studies in Chinese Literary Genres. LC 77-157825. 1975. 18.50x (ISBN 0-520-02037-5). U of Cal Pr.
Birch, Cyril & Keene, Donald, eds. Anthology of Chinese Literature, Vol. 2. From the Fourteenth Century to the Present. Birch, Cyril, tr. from Chinese. (Illus.). 1972. pap. 4.95 (ISBN 0-394-17766-5, E584, Ever). Grove.
Birch, Cyril, tr. see Birch, Cyril & Keene, Donald.
Birch, Cyril, tr. see Tang, Xianzu.
Birch, D., jt. auth. see Rissover, F.

Birch, G. G., jt. auth. see Shallenberger, R. S.
Birch, G. G., ed. Sweetness & Sweeteners. (Illus.). 1971. 26.00x (ISBN 0-85334-503-1, Pub. by Applied Science). Burgess-Intl Ideas.
Birch, G. G. & Green, L. F., eds. Molecular Structure & Function of Food Carbohydrate. LC 73-16299. 308p. 1974. 44.95 (ISBN 0-470-07323-3). Halsted Pr.
Birch, G. G. & Parker, K. J., eds. Sugar: Science & Technology. (Illus.). 1979. 82.80x (ISBN 0-85334-805-7, Pub. by Applied Science). Burgess-Intl Ideas.
--Vitamin C: Recent Aspects of Its Physiological & Technological Importance. LC 74-16050. 259p. 1974. 44.95 (ISBN 0-470-07325-X). Halsted Pr.
Birch, G. G. & Shallenberger, R. S., eds. Developments in Food Carbohydrate, Vol. 1. (Illus.). 1977. text ed. 43.50x (ISBN 0-85334-733-6, Pub. by Applied Science). Burgess-Intl Ideas.
Birch, G. G., et al, eds. Food from Waste. (Illus.). 1976. 67.20x (ISBN 0-85334-659-3, Pub. by Applied Science). Burgess-Intl Ideas.
--Sensory Properties of Food. (Illus.). 1977. 49.70x (ISBN 0-85334-744-1). Burgess-Intl Ideas.
Birch, I., et al. Intergovernmental Relations & Australian Education. LC 79-55415. (Centre for Research on Federal Financial Relations - Research Monograph: No. 29). 107p. (Orig.). 1980. pap. text ed. 11.95 (ISBN 0-908160-46-1, 0566). Bks Australia.
Birch, Jack, jt. auth. see Sellin, Don.
Birch, Jack W. & Johnstone, B. Kenneth. Designing Schools & Schooling for the Handicapped. (Illus.). 244p. 1975. 22.50 (ISBN 0-398-03362-5). C C Thomas.
Birch, Jack W. & Reynolds, Maynard C., eds. Teaching Exceptional Children in All America's Schools: A First Course for Teachers & Principals. 1977. text ed. 10.00 (ISBN 0-86586-084-X). Coun Exc Child.
Birch, Jillian, ed. see International Cancer Congress, 12th, Buenos Aires, 5-11 October.
Birch, N. H. & Bramson, A. E. Associated Ground Subjects, Vol. 4. (Flight Briefing for Pilots Ser.). (Illus.). 1978. 6.95 o.p. (ISBN 0-685-59598-6, Flying-Zd). Ziff-Davis Pub.
--An Introductory Manual of Flying Training, Vol. 1. (Flight Briefing for Pilots Ser.). (Illus.). 1978. 6.95 o.p. (ISBN 0-685-59601-X, Flying-Zd). Ziff-Davis Pub.
Birch, Robert L., jt. auth. see Fauver, William.
Birch, William D., tr. see Birch, Williiam D.
Birch, William G. & Meilach, Dona Z. Doctor Discusses Pregnancy. (Illus.). 1980. pap. 2.50 (ISBN 0-910304-00-9). Budlong.
Birch, Williiam D., ed. Vita Haroldi: The Romance of the Life of Harold, King of England. Birch, William D., tr. LC 80-2232. 1981. Repr. of 1885 ed. 32.50 (ISBN 0-404-18753-6). AMS Pr.
Birchall, M. Joyce. King Charles Spaniels. Foyle, Christina, ed. (Foyle's Handbks). (Illus.). 1973. 3.95 (ISBN 0-685-55788-X). Palmetto Pub.
Birchenall, Joan M. & Streight, Mary E. Introduction to Health Careers. LC 77-26305. 1978. text ed. cancelled (ISBN 0-397-54215-1); pap. text ed. 6.95x (ISBN 0-397-54210-0). Lippincott.
Bircher, Ruth. Eating Your Way to Health. 1961. 10.95 (ISBN 0-571-06984-3, Pub. by Faber & Faber). Merrimack Bk Serv.
Birchfield, Jane. The Taste of Goodness: Great Aunt Jane's Cook & Garden Book. LC 76-22729. (Illus.). 1976. 8.95 o.p. (ISBN 0-397-01176-8). Lippincott.
Birchfield, John C. Foodservice Operations Manual. LC 79-15622. 1979. spiral bd. 39.95 (ISBN 0-8436-2145-1). CBI Pub.
Birchfield, John C., et al. Contemporary Quantity Recipe File. LC 75-12917. 346p. 1975. 21.50 (ISBN 0-8436-2065-X). CBI Pub.
Bird & May. Mathematics Two: Checkbook. 1981. text ed. price not set (ISBN 0-408-00610-2). Butterworths.
Bird, Alan. The Plays of Oscar Wilde. (Critical Studies Ser.). 220p. 1977. 18.50x (ISBN 0-06-490415-6). B&N.
Bird, Byron R., et al. Dynamics of Polymeric Liquids, 2 vols. Incl. Vol. 1. Fluid Mechanics. 43.95 (ISBN 0-471-07375-X); Vol. 2. Kinetic Theory. 41.95 (ISBN 0-471-01596-2). LC 76-15408. 1977. Wiley.
Bird, Caroline. Invisible Scar: The Great Depression, & What It Did to American Life, from Then Until Now. LC 65-24266. (gr. 10 up). 1978. pap. 9.95x (ISBN 0-582-28016-8). Longman.
Bird, Charles S., jt. ed. see Karp, Ivan.
Bird, Christopher, jt. auth. see Tompkins, Peter.
Bird, E. A. Electronic Data Processing & Computers for Commercial Students. (Illus.). 1972. text ed. 19.95x (ISBN 0-434-90140-7); pap. text ed. 11.95x (ISBN 0-434-90141-5). Intl Ideas.
Bird, G. A. Molecular Gas Dynamics. (Oxford Engineering & Science Ser.). 1976. text ed. 49.50x (ISBN 0-19-856120-2). Oxford U Pr.
Bird, G. J. Radar Precision & Resolution. LC 74-8158. 151p. 1974. 24.95 (ISBN 0-470-07380-2). Halsted Pr.
Bird, Graham. The International Monetary System & the Less Developed Countries. LC 78-65139. (Praeger Special Studies Ser.). 1979. 28.95 (ISBN 0-03-051211-5). Praeger.
--Kant's Theory of Knowledge: An Outline of One Central Argument in the Critique of Pure Reason. (International Library of Philoaophy & Scientific Method Ser.). 1973. Repr. of 1962 ed. text ed. 10.00x (ISBN 0-391-00316-X). Humanities.
--Philosophical Tasks. 1972. text ed. 7.00x (ISBN 0-09-113250-9, Hutchinson U Lib). Humanities.
Bird, Harold L., Jr. Laboratory Studies in General, Organic, & Biological Chemistry. (Illus.). 1972. lab manual 9.00x o.p. (ISBN 0-7167-0162-6). W H Freeman.
Bird, Isabella L. Englishwoman in America. 1966. pap. 9.50x (ISBN 0-299-03524-7). U of Wis Pr.
Bird, J., jt. auth. see Totterdell, B.
Bird, Jean D. Factory Outlet Shopping Guide for New Jersey & Rockland County-1980. 1979. pap. 2.95 o.p. (ISBN 0-913464-43-0). FOSG Pubns.
--Factory Outlet Shopping Guide for New York City-Westchester-Long Island-1980. 1979. pap. text ed. 2.95 o.p. (ISBN 0-913464-44-9). FOSG Pubns.
--Factory Outlet Shopping Guide for North & South Carolina-1980. 1979. pap. 2.95 o.p. (ISBN 0-913464-46-5). FOSG Pubns.
--Factory Outlet Shopping Guide for Washington D. C.-Maryland-Virginia-Delaware-1980. 1979. pap. 2.95 o.p. (ISBN 0-913464-45-7). FOSG Pubns.
Bird, John. Science from Water Play. LC 77-82984. (Teaching Primary Science Ser.). (Illus.). 1977. pap. text ed. 6.95 (ISBN 0-356-05071-8). Raintree Child.
Bird, John & Catherall, Ed. Fibres & Fabrics. LC 77-82983. (Teaching Primary Science Ser.). (Illus.). 1977. pap. text ed. 6.95 (ISBN 0-356-05076-9). Raintree Child.
Bird, John & Diamond, Dorothy. Candles. LC 77-82987. (Teaching Primary Science Ser.). 1977. pap. text ed. 6.95 (ISBN 0-356-05070-X). Raintree Child.
Bird, Joseph W. & Bird, Lois F. Freedom of Sexual Love. LC 67-10377. 1970. pap. 2.75 (ISBN 0-385-04341-4, Im). Doubleday.
--Marriage Is for Grownups. LC 79-78725. 1971. pap. 2.95 (ISBN 0-385-04256-6, Im). Doubleday.
--Power to the Parents. LC 77-176346. 240p. 1974. pap. 1.95 (ISBN 0-385-08423-4, Im). Doubleday.
Bird, Junius B., intro. by. Peruvian Painting by Unknown Artists: 800 B. C. to 1700 A. D. (Illus.). 1973. pap. 3.00 (ISBN 0-913456-20-9). Interbk Inc.
Bird, Keith W. Weimar, the German Naval Officer Corps & the Rise of National Socialism. 1977. pap. text ed. 34.25x (ISBN 90-6032-094-8). Humanities.
Bird, Lois F., jt. auth. see Bird, Joseph W.
Bird, May. Electrical Principles Three Checkbook. text ed. write for info. (ISBN 0-408-00636-6); pap. text ed. write for info. (ISBN 0-408-00601-3). Butterworth.
--Electrical Principles Two Checkbook. 1981. text ed. price not set (ISBN 0-408-00635-8); pap. text ed. price not set (ISBN 0-408-00600-5). Butterworth.
--Mathematics Two Checkbook. 1981. text ed. price not set (ISBN 0-408-00633-1); pap. text ed. price not set (ISBN 0-408-00609-9). Butterworths.
Bird, Patricia. Once Upon a Dream. (YA) 1977. 4.95 o.p. (ISBN 0-685-73812-4, Avalon). Bouregy.
--Staged for Death. 192p. (YA) 1976. 5.95 (ISBN 0-685-64250-X, Avalon). Bouregy.
Bird, Peter, jt. auth. see King, Derek.
Bird, Richard M. Bibliography on Taxation in Underdeveloped Countries. LC 62-17751. 85p. (Orig.). 1962. pap. 2.00x o.p. (ISBN 0-915506-03-3). Harvard Law Intl Tax.
--The Growth of Public Employment in Canada. 190p. 1979. pap. text ed. 12.95x (ISBN 0-920380-17-4, Pub. by Inst Res Pub Canada). Renouf.
Bird, Roy. Topeka: A Pictorial History. Friedman, Donna R., ed. (Illus.). 208p. 1981. pap. price not set (ISBN 0-89865-114-X). Donning Co.
Bird, Thomas E., ed. Foreign Language Learning: Research & Development. Incl. The Classroom Revisited. Simches, Seymour O; Innovative Foreign Language Programs. Andrews, Oliver, Jr; Liberated Expression. Edgerton, F. Mills. 118p. 1968. pap. 7.95x (ISBN 0-915432-68-4). NE Conf Teach Foreign.
--Foreign Languages: Reading, Literature, Requirements. Incl. The Teaching of Reading. Moulton, William G; The Times & Places for Literature. Paquette, F. Andre; Trends in Foreign Language Requirements & Placement. Gummere, John F. 124p. 1967. pap. 7.95x (ISBN 0-915432-67-6). NE Conf Teach Foreign.
Bird, V. Portrait of Birmingham. LC 70-546349. (Portrait Bks.). 1970. 10.50x (ISBN 0-7091-4582-9). Intl Pubns Serv.
Bird, Viola, et al. Order Procedures. (AALL Publications Ser.: No. 2). 62p. (Orig.). 1960. pap. 8.50x (ISBN 0-8377-0102-3). Rothman.
Birdsall, Stephen S. & Florin, John W. Regional Landscapes of the United States & Canada. LC 77-28103. 1978. text ed. 20.95 (ISBN 0-471-07397-0). Wiley.
Birdsall, Steve. The B-Seventeen Flying Fortress. LC 65-16862. (Famous Aircraft Ser.). (Illus.). 1979. pap. 4.95 (ISBN 0-8168-5646-X). Aero.
--Flying Buccaneers: The Illustrated Story of Kenney's Fifth Air Force. LC 77-74293. 1977. 15.00 o.p. (ISBN 0-385-03218-8). Doubleday.
Birdsall, Steven. Saga of the Superfortress: The Dramatic Story of the B-29 & the Twentieth Air Force. LC 78-22303. (Illus.). 352p. 1980. 19.95 (ISBN 0-385-13668-4). Doubleday.
Birdsong, Craig W., jt. auth. see Stinnett, Nick.
Birdsong, Robert E. Introspection-Panacea or Pitfall? (Aquarian Academy Supplementary Lecture No. 1: No. 1). 1975. pap. 0.75 (ISBN 0-917108-16-7). Sirius Bks.
--Soul Mates: The Facts & the Fallacies. (Aquarian Academy Supplementary Lecture Ser.: No. 9). 22p. (Orig.). 1980. pap. 1.25 (ISBN 0-917108-32-9). Sirius Bks.
--Way of the Immortal Threefold Self: The Straight Path. (Aquarian Academy Monograph: Ser. E, No. 4). 1980. pap. 1.45 (ISBN 0-917108-29-9). Sirius Bks.
Birdsong, Sam. Weather or Not: A Study of Weather Control. pap. 1.75 (ISBN 0-918700-09-4). Duverus Pub.
Birdwell, Cleo. Amazons. LC 80-80241. 400p. 1980. 12.95 (ISBN 0-03-055426-8). HR&W.
Birdwhistell, Ralph K. & O'Connor, Rod, eds. Freeman Library of Laboratory Separates in Chemistry, 1083-1122, 40 studies. 1971. loose-leaf 0.50 ea. o.p.; tchr's manual avail. o.p. W H Freeman.
Birdwhistell, Ray L. Kinesics & Context: Essays on Body Motion Communication. LC 77-122379. (Conduct & Communication Ser.: No. 2). 1970. 12.00x o.p. (ISBN 0-8122-7605-1); pap. 7.95x (ISBN 0-8122-1012-3, Pa Paperbks). U of Pa Pr.
Biren, Helen A., jt. auth. see Savage, E. Lynn.
Birenbaum, Arnold. Health Care & Society: Patients, Professions, Programs & Policies. LC 80-67092. 350p. 1981. text ed. 28.50 (ISBN 0-916672-57-3). Allanheld.
Birenbaum, Arnold & Seiffer, Samuel. Resettling Retarded Adults in a Managed Community. LC 75-19765. (Special Studies). 150p. 1976. text ed. 24.95 (ISBN 0-275-55520-8). Praeger.
Birk, Genevieve B., jt. auth. see Birk, Newman P.
Birk, Newman P. & Birk, Genevieve B. A Handbook of Grammar, Rhetoric, Mechanics & Usage. LC 71-179751. 148p. 1972. pap. text ed. 5.95 (ISBN 0-672-63275-6). Odyssey Pr.
--The Odyssey Reader: Ideas & Style. LC 68-13057. 1968. 12.95 (ISBN 0-672-63187-3); pap. 7.95 (ISBN 0-672-63075-3). Odyssey Pr.
--Practice for Understanding & Using English: Eighty Exercises. 2nd ed. LC 71-189751. 1972. pap. 4.95 (ISBN 0-672-63291-8). Odyssey Pr.
--Understanding & Using English. 5th ed. LC 71-179751. 1972. 12.50 (ISBN 0-672-63214-4). Odyssey Pr.
Birkbeck, Morris. Letters from Illinois. LC 68-8685. (American Scene Ser). 1970. Repr. of 1818 ed. lib. bdg. 19.50 (ISBN 0-306-71170-2). Da Capo.
Birke, G., et al, eds. Physiology & Pathophysiology of Plasma Protein Metabolism. 1968. 40.00 (ISBN 0-08-012965-X). Pergamon.
Birkeland, Peter W. Pedology, Weathering & Geomorphological Research. (Illus.). 304p. 1974. text ed. 15.95x (ISBN 0-19-501730-7). Oxford U Pr.
Birkeland, Torger. Echoes of Puget Sound: Fifty Years of Logging & Steamboating. (Illus.). 252p. pap. 10.00 (ISBN 0-8466-0315-2). Shorey.
Birkenhead, Lord. Rudyard Kipling. 1978. 15.00 (ISBN 0-394-50315-5). Random.
Birker, D., tr. see Kaiser, Artur.
Birket-Smith, Kaj. Paths of Culture: A General Ethnology. Fennow, Karin, tr. LC 64-8488. (Illus.). 1970. 15.00 (ISBN 0-299-03381-3); pap. 7.50x (ISBN 0-299-03384-8). U of Wis Pr.
Birkhoff, Garrett & Gian-Carlo Rota. Ordinary Differential Equations. 3rd ed. LC 78-8304. 1978. text ed. 21.95 (ISBN 0-471-07411-X). Wiley.
Birkhoff, Garrett, ed. see Society for Industrial & Applied Mathematics - American Mathematical Society Symposia - New York - March, 1971.
Birkhoff, George D. & Beatley, R. Basic Geometry. 3rd ed. LC 59-7308. (gr. 9-12). 1959. text ed. 12.00 (ISBN 0-8284-0120-9); tchr's manual 2.50 (ISBN 0-8284-0034-2); answer bk. 1.50 (ISBN 0-8284-0162-4). Chelsea Pub.
Birkholz, Heinz, ed. War Album Five. (Illus.). 96p. (Orig.). 1979. pap. 10.00x (ISBN 0-85242-667-4). Intl Pubns Serv.
Birkin, Stanley J., jt. auth. see Richardson, Gary L.
Birkinshaw, Elsye. Turn off Your Age. LC 79-27693. 1980. pap. 4.95 (ISBN 0-912800-77-1). Woodbridge Pr.
Birkos, Alexander S. & Tambs, Lewis A. African & Black American Studies. LC 74-31262. (Academic Writer's Guide to Periodicals Ser.: Vol. 3). 205p. 1975. lib. bdg. 13.50x o.p. (ISBN 0-87287-109-6). Libs Unl.
--East European and Soviet Economic Affairs: A Bibliography (1965-1973) LC 74-28495. 170p. 1975. lib. bdg. 13.50x o.p. (ISBN 0-87287-097-9). Libs Unl.
Birks, H. J. The Past & Present Vegetation of the Isle of Skye. LC 76-189591. (Illus.). 300p. 1973. 99.00 (ISBN 0-521-08533-0). Cambridge U Pr.
Birks, H. J., ed. Quaternary Plant Ecology: Fourteenth Symposium of the British Ecological Society, University of Cambridge 28-30 March 1972. LC 73-10215. (British Ecological Society Symposia Ser.). 1974. 61.95 (ISBN 0-470-07534-1). Halsted Pr.
Birks, L. S. X-Ray Spectrochemical Analysis, Vol. 2. 2nd ed. (Illus.). 143p. 1969. text ed. 11.25 (ISBN 0-471-07525-6, Pub. by Wiley). Krieger.
Birks, Tony. Potter's Companion: The Complete Guide to Pottery Making. (Illus.). 1977. pap. 4.95 (ISBN 0-87690-246-8). Dutton.
Birla Institute of Scientific Research. Structural Transformation & Economic Development. 126p. 1980. text ed. 9.50 (ISBN 0-391-01790-X). Humanities.
Birla, L. N. Folk Tales from Rajasthan. 1964. 4.75x o.p. (ISBN 0-210-34031-2). Asia.
Birley, Anthony. Life in Roman Britain. 1976. pap. 13.50 (ISBN 0-7134-3161-X, Pub. by Batsford England). David & Charles.
--The People of Roman Britain. 240p. 1980. 22.50x (ISBN 0-520-04119-4). U of Cal Pr.
Birley, Anthony, ed. Universal Rome. LC 68-78675. (Selections from History Today Ser.: No. 4). (Illus.). 1969. pap. 3.95 (ISBN 0-05-000020-9). Dufour.
Birley, Derek. The Education Officer & His World. 1970. 10.50 (ISBN 0-7100-6811-5); pap. 4.95 (ISBN 0-7100-7704-1). Routledge & Kegan.
Birman, et al, eds. Light Scattering in Solids. 535p. 1979. 55.00 (ISBN 0-306-40313-7, Plenum Pr). Plenum Pub.
Birmingham, Frederic A., jt. auth. see Turgeon, Charlotte.
Birmingham, Jacqueline J. Medical Terminology: A Self-Learning Module. (Illus.). 448p. 1981. pap. text ed. 11.95 (ISBN 0-07-005386-3, HP). McGraw.
Birmingham, Stephen. California Rich. 1980. 13.95 (ISBN 0-671-24127-3). S&S.
--The Golden Dream: Surburbia in the 1970's. LC 76-57891. 1978. 10.00 o.s.i. (ISBN 0-06-010334-5, HarpT). Har-Row.
--Life at the Dakota: New York's Most Unusual Address. LC 79-4800. (Illus.). 1979. 12.95 (ISBN 0-394-41079-3). Random.
Birn, Randi. Johan Borgen. (World Authors Ser.: Norway: No. 311). 1974. lib. bdg. 10.95 (ISBN 0-8057-2167-3). Twayne.
Birn, Randi & Gould, Karen, eds. Orion Blinded: Essays on Claude Simon. LC 79-17687. 320p. 1981. 18.50 (ISBN 0-8387-2420-5). Bucknell U Pr.
Birnbaum, George see Marton, L.
Birnbaum, Henrik. On Medieval & Renaissance Slavic Writings. LC 73-85243. (Slavistic Printings & Reprintings Ser.: No. 266). 381p. 1974. text ed. 76.50x (ISBN 90-2792-680-8). Mouton.
Birnbaum, Henrik & Eekman, Thomas. Fiction & Drama in Eastern & Southeastern Europe: Evolution & Experiment in the Postwar Period. (UCLA Slavic Studies: Vol. 1). ix, 463p. 1980. 24.95 (ISBN 0-89357-064-8). Slavica.
Birnbaum, Henrik, et al, eds. Studia Linguistica Alexandro Vasilii Filio Issatschenko a Collegis Amicisque Oblata. 1978. pap. text ed. 70.50x (ISBN 0-685-59424-6). Humanities.
Birnbaum, Howard. The Cost of Catastrophic Illness. LC 77-9192. 1978. 14.95 (ISBN 0-669-01773-6). Lexington Bks.
Birnbaum, Karl E., jt. auth. see Andren, Nils.
Birnbaum, Max, jt. auth. see Cass, James.
Birnbaum, Michael, jt. auth. see Sonnenberg, David E.

Birnbaum, Norman. Crisis of Industrial Society. 1969. pap. 4.95 (ISBN 0-19-500794-8, 295, GB). Oxford U Pr.
--Toward a Critical Sociology. 468p. 1973. pap. 5.95 (ISBN 0-19-501664-5, GB). Oxford U Pr.

Birnbaum, Philip, ed. Karaite Studies. LC 76-136771. 1971. Repr. 12.50 o.p. (ISBN 0-87203-027-X). Hermon.

Birnbaum, Robert. Creative Academic Bargaining: Managing Conflict in the Unionized College & University. 288p. 1981. text ed. 19.95x (ISBN 0-8077-2631-1). Tchrs Coll.

Birnbaum, Stephen. South America, Nineteen Eighty-One. (Get 'em & Go Travel Guides). 1980. 15.00 (ISBN 0-395-29756-7); pap. 9.95 (ISBN 0-395-29757-5). HM.

Birnbaumer, L., jt. ed. see O'Malley, B. W.

Birney, A. A. Noon Sight Navigation: Simplified Celestial. LC 72-88042. (Illus.). 1972. pap. 5.00 (ISBN 0-87033-171-X). Cornell Maritime.

Birney, Alice L. Satiric Catharsis in Shakespeare: A Theory of Dramatic Structure. 1973. 18.50x (ISBN 0-520-02214-9). U of Cal Pr.

Birney, Earle. The Mammoth Corridors. 1980. pap. 5.00 (ISBN 0-936892-07-2). Stone Pr MI.

Birnholz, Jason C. Clinical Diagnostic Pearls. 1971. spiral bdg. 7.50 (ISBN 0-87488-730-5). Med Exam.

Birnie, G. D. Subnuclear Components: Preparation & Fractionation. 160p. 1976. 31.50 (ISBN 0-408-70729-1). Butterworths.

Birnie, G. D. & Rickwood, D. Centrifugal Seperations in Molecular & Cell Biology. (Illus.). 1978. 29.95 (ISBN 0-408-70803-4). Butterworths.

Biro, Val. Gumdrop Posts a Letter. (Illus.). 24p. (gr. k-3). 1977. PLB 6.00 (ISBN 0-516-03596-7). Childrens.

Biro, Z., et al, eds. Homeostasis in Injury & Shock: Proceedings of a Satellite Symposium of the 28th International Congress of Physiological Sciences, Budapest, Hungary, 1980. LC 80-42104. (Advances in Physiological Sciences: Vol. 26). (Illus.). 360p. 1981. 40.00 (ISBN 0-08-027347-5). Pergamon.

Biros, Francis J., jt. ed. see Haque, Rizwanel.

Birot, Pierre. The Cycle of Erosion in Different Climates. 1968. 16.50x (ISBN 0-520-00121-4). U of Cal Pr.

Birr, Shirley, jt. auth. see Rouch, Roger L.

Birrell, Derek & Murie, Alan. Policy & Government in Northern Ireland: Lessons of Devolution. 353p. 1980. 32.50x (ISBN 0-389-20019-0). B&N.

Birrell, Susan, jt. auth. see Hart, Marie.

Birrell, Vivian T. The Psychological Theory of the Sexual Temptations. 1979. deluxe ed. 43.15 (ISBN 0-930582-28-4). Gloucester Art.

Birren, Faber. The Textile Colorist. 64p. 1980. pap. 12.95 (ISBN 0-442-23854-1). Van Nos Reinhold.

Birren, James E. Psychology of Aging. 1964. text ed. 17.95 (ISBN 0-13-733428-1). P-H.

Birren, James E. see Davis, Richard H.

Birren, James E., jt. auth. see Welford, A. T.

Birren, James E. & Sloane, R. Bruce, eds. Handbook of Mental Health & Aging. (Illus.). 1980. text ed. 72.00 (ISBN 0-13-380261-2). P-H.

Birren, James E., et al. Developmental Psychology: A Life-Span Approach. LC 80-82839. (Illus.). 736p. 1981. write for info. (ISBN 0-395-29717-6); price not set instr's manual (ISBN 0-395-29718-4); price not set test-bank (ISBN 0-395-29720-6). HM.
--Life-Span Developmental Psychology. (Illus.). 640p. 1981. text ed. 18.95 o.p. (ISBN 0-395-29717-6); price not set instr's. manual o.p. (ISBN 0-395-29718-4). HM.

Birrer, Cynthia. Multiple Sclerosis: A Personal View. (Illus.). 304p. 1979. text ed. 24.75 (ISBN 0-398-03864-3); pap. text ed. 18.75 (ISBN 0-398-03886-4). C C Thomas.

Birth Defects Annual Conference, 10th Memphis, Tenn., June, 1977. Annual Review of Birth Defects, 1977: Proceedings, 3 vols. Summitt, Robert L. & Bergsma, Daniel, eds. Incl. No. 6A. Cell Surface Factors,Immune Deficiencies, Twin Studies. LC 78-17058. 240p. 28.00 (ISBN 0-8451-1020-9); No. 6B. Recent Advances & New Syndromes. LC 78-17056. 400p. 46.00 (ISBN 0-8451-1021-7); No. 6C. Sex Differentiation & Chromosomal Abnormalities. LC 78-17057. 51.00 (ISBN 0-8451-1022-5). (Birth Defects: Original Article Ser.: Vol. 14, No. 6). (Illus.). 1978. Set. 125.00 (ISBN 0-8451-0951-0). A R Liss.

Birth Defects Conference, Kansas City, Mo., May 1975. Growth Problems & Clinical Advances: Proceedings. Bergsma, Daniel & Schimke, R. Neil, eds. LC 76-21714. (Birth Defects - Original Article Ser.: Vol. 12, No. 6). 340p. 1976. 35.00x (ISBN 0-8451-1005-5). A R Liss.

Birth Defects Conference-1975, Kansas City, Missouri. Cancer & Genetics: Proceedings. Bergsma, Daniel, ed. LC 75-43622. (Birth Defects-Original Article Ser.: Vol. 12, No. 1). 1976. 23.00x (ISBN 0-8451-1002-0). A R Liss.

Birth Defects Conference, 1975, Kansas City, Missouri. Cytogenetics, Environment, & Malformation Syndromes: Proceedings. Bergsma, Daniel & Schimke, R. Neil, eds. LC 76-20510. (Birth Defects Original Article Ser.: Vol. 12, No. 5). 364p. 1976. 35.00x (ISBN 0-8451-1004-7). A R Liss.

Birth Defects Converence, 1978, San Francisco. Risk, Communication, & Decision Making in Genetic Counseling: Proceedings, Annual Review of Birth Defects, 1978, Pt. C. Epstein, Charles J., et al, eds. LC 79-5120. (Birth Defects: Original Article Ser.: Vol. XV, No. 5C). 1979. 36.00x (ISBN 0-8451-1030-6). A R Liss.

Birum, Linda H., jt. auth. see Auld, Margaret E.

Biryukov, I. P. & Voroknov, M. G. Tables of Nuclear Quadruple Resonance Frequencies. LC 70-15351. 1972. 17.50 o.p. (ISBN 0-470-07549-X). Halsted Pr.

Birzle, Hermann, et al. Radiology of Trauma. Kaufmann, Herbert, tr. LC 76-20070. 1978. text ed. 69.00 (ISBN 0-7216-1703-4). Saunders.

Birzon, Paul I., jt. ed. see Gershenson, Milton G.

Bisagno, John. Power of Positive Praying. 1965. pap. 1.95 (ISBN 0-310-21212-X). Zondervan.

Bisagno, Juan. El Poder De la Oracion Tenaz. De Lerin, Olivia S. D., tr. from Eng. Orig. Title: The Power of Positive Praying. 96p. (Span.). 1980. pap. 1.70 (ISBN 0-311-40029-9). Casa Bautista.

Bisbee, Gerald E., Jr. & Vraciu, Robert A., eds. Managing the Finances of Health Care Organizations. (Illus.). 1980. text ed. 28.95 (ISBN 0-914904-50-7); pap. text ed. 15.95 (ISBN 0-914904-51-5). Health Admin Pr.

Bisbee Press Collective, ed. The Bisbee Anthology Nineteen Eighty: Poetry. 62p. (Orig.). 1980. pap. 5.00 (ISBN 0-938196-00-6). Bisbee Pr.

Bisby, J. R., et al, eds. Electrical Fitting, Vol. 2. (Engineering Craftsmen: No. G23). (Illus.). 1969. spiral bdg. 23.50x (ISBN 0-685-90132-7). Intl Ideas.

Bisch, Louis E., ed. Cure Your Nerves Yourself. rev. ed. 1977. pap. 1.75 o.p. (ISBN 0-449-23433-9, Crest). Fawcett.

Bischel, Leonard. A Merry-Go-Round. (Illus.). 72p. (Orig.). (gr. 1-5). 1980. pap. 4.95 (ISBN 0-935110-01-1, 28711-TXU). Blackjack Ent.

Bischof, Eunice S., jt. auth. see Bischof, George P.

Bischof, George P. Atoms at Work. LC 51-100007. (Illus.). (gr. 5-8). 1951. 4.50 o.p. (ISBN 0-15-204617-8, HJ). HarBraceJ.

Bischof, George P. & Bischof, Eunice S. Sun, Earth, & Man. LC 56-8352. (Illus.). (gr. 5 up). 1957. 4.50 o.p. (ISBN 0-15-282643-2, HJ). HarBraceJ.

Bischoff, Dave, jt. auth. see White, Ted.

Bischoff, David. The Phantom of the Opera. (gr. 7 up). 1977. pap. 1.25 (ISBN 0-590-10312-1, Schol Pap). Schol Bk Serv.
--Star Fall. (Orig.). 1980. pap. 1.95 o.p. (ISBN 0-686-62032-1). Berkley Pub.
--The Vampires of the Nightworld. (Orig.). 1981. pap. 2.25 (ISBN 0-345-28763-0, Del Rey). Ballantine.

Bischoff, David, ed. Quest. LC 76-44815. (Science Fiction Ser.). (Illus.). (gr. 3-6). 1977. PLB 7.75 (ISBN 0-8172-0527-6). Raintree Pubs.
--Strange Encounters. LC 76-45662. (Science Fiction Ser.). (Illus.). (gr. 3-6). 1977. 7.75 (ISBN 0-8172-0525-X). Raintree Pubs.

Bischoff, Ernst P. Microscopic Analysis of the Anastomoses between the Cranial Nerves. Sachs, Ernest, Jr. & Valtin, Eva W., trs. from Ger. LC 77-72520. (Illus.). 148p. 1977. text ed. 13.50x (ISBN 0-87451-143-7). U Pr of New Eng.

Bischoff, J. Comprehensive History of the Woollen & the Worsted Manufacturers, 2 vols. (Illus.). 1968. Repr. of 1842 ed. 75.00x (ISBN 0-7146-1387-8, F Cass). Biblio Dist.

Bischoff, James. Comprehensive History of the Woollen & Worsted Manufactures, 2 Vols. LC 68-108156. (Illus.). 1842. 47.50x (ISBN 0-678-05155-0). Kelley.

Bischoff, Kenneth B., jt. auth. see Froment, Gilbert F.

Bisconti, Ann S. & Kessler, Jean G. Other Stepping Stones: A Study of Learning Experiences That Contribute to Effective Performance in Early & Long-Run Jobs. pap. 8.95 (ISBN 0-913936-15-4). Coll Placement.

Bisconti, Ann S., et al. Labor Market for Humanities. (Praeger Special Studies Ser.). (Illus.). 1979. 16.50 o.p. (ISBN 0-03-021981-7). Praeger.

Bisgaard, Erling & Aaron, Tossi. In Canon. 1978. pap. 5.00 (ISBN 0-918812-03-8). Magnamusic.

Bisgaard, Erling & Stehouwer, Gulle. Musicbook 0: Pulse, Pitch, Rhythm, Form, Dynamics. Aaron, Tossi, ed. 1976. pap. 6.00 (ISBN 0-918812-04-6). Magnamusic.

Bisgrove, Richard. The Gardens of Britain, Three: Berkshire, Oxfordshire, Buckinghamshire, Bedfordshire, Hertfordshire. 1978. 24.00 (ISBN 0-7134-1178-3, Pub. by Batsford England). David & Charles.
--Your Problem Garden. 1980. 19.95 (ISBN 0-7134-1184-8, Pub. by Batsford England). David & Charles.

Bishay, A. & McGinnies, W. B. Advances in Desert & Arid Land Technology & Development, Vol. 2. 350p. 1981. price not set (ISBN 3-7186-0002-1). Harwood Academic.

Bishay, A., ed. see Cairo International Workshop on Applications of Science & Technology for Desert Development September 9-15, 1978.

Bisher, Furman. Strange But True Baseball Stories. (Major League Baseball Library). (Illus.). (gr. 5-9). 1966. 2.95 (ISBN 0-394-80184-9, BYR); PLB 4.39 (ISBN 0-394-90184-3); pap. 1.95 (ISBN 0-394-82191-2). Random.

Bishko, Charles J. Studies in Medieval Spanish Frontier History. 336p. 1980. 75.00x (ISBN 0-86078-069-4, Pub. by Variorum England). State Mutual Bk.

Bishop, A. S. Rise of a Central Authority for English Education. LC 70-128634. (Cambridge Texts & Studies in the History of Education). (Illus.). 1971. 34.50 (ISBN 0-521-08023-1). Cambridge U Pr.

Bishop, Ada L. All About the Collie. (All About Ser.). (Illus.). 1980. 16.95 (ISBN 0-7207-1215-7, Pub. by Michael Joseph). Merrimack Bk Serv.
--All About the Collie. 1971. 8.95 o.p. (ISBN 0-7207-0450-2, Pub. by Michael Joseph). Merrimack Bk Serv.

Bishop, Ann. Annie O'Kay's Riddle Roundup. (Illus.). 40p. (gr. 2-5). 1981. 7.95 (ISBN 0-525-66727-X). Elsevier-Nelson.
--Chicken Riddle. LC 72-83681. (Riddle Bk.). (Illus.). 40p. (gr. 1-3). 1972. 5.75g (ISBN 0-8075-1140-4). A Whitman.
--Cleo Catra's Riddle Book. (Illus.). (gr. 2-5). 1981. 6.95 (ISBN 0-525-66706-7). Elsevier-Nelson.
--The Ella Fannie Elephant Riddle Book. LC 74-14931. (Riddle Bk.). (Illus.). 40p. (gr. 1-3). 1974. 5.75g (ISBN 0-8075-1966-9). A Whitman.
--Hey, Riddle Riddle. LC 66-16074. (Riddle Bk.). (Illus.). (gr. 2-4). 1968. 5.75g (ISBN 0-8075-3257-6). A Whitman.
--Merry-Go-Riddle. LC 73-7321. (Riddle Bk.). (Illus.). 40p. (gr. 1-3). 1973. 5.75g (ISBN 0-8075-5072-8). A Whitman.
--Noah Riddle? LC 71-115893. (Riddle Bk.). (gr. 1-3). 1970. 5.75g (ISBN 0-8075-5702-1). A Whitman.
--Oh, Riddlesticks! Rubin, Caroline, ed. LC 76-41418. (Riddle Bk.). (Illus.). (gr. 2-6). 1976. 5.75g (ISBN 0-8075-5916-4). A Whitman.
--Riddle Ages. Rubin, Caroline, ed. LC 77-12828. (Riddle Bk.). (Illus.). (gr. 1-4). 1977. 5.75g (ISBN 0-8075-6965-8). A Whitman.
--Riddle-Iculous Rid-Alphabet Book. LC 78-150799. (Riddle Bk.). (Illus.). (gr. 2-4). 1971. 5.75g (ISBN 0-8075-6970-4). A Whitman.
--Riddle Raddle, Fiddle Faddle. LC 68-22189. (Riddle Bk.). (Illus.). (gr. 2-4). 1966. 5.75g (ISBN 0-8075-6974-7). A Whitman.
--Riddle Red Riddle Book. LC 72-79549. (Riddle Bk.). (Illus.). (gr. 2-5). 1969. 5.75g (ISBN 0-8075-6979-8). A Whitman.
--Wild Bill Hiccup's Riddle Book. Rubin, Caroline, ed. LC 75-33161. (Riddle Bk.). (Illus.). 1975. 5.75g (ISBN 0-8075-9097-5). A Whitman.

Bishop, Arthur C. Outline of Crystal Morphology. 1970. pap. text ed. 5.50x (ISBN 0-09-079423-0). Humanities.

Bishop, Beverly. Neurophysiology Study Guide. 2nd ed. (Illus.). 1973. spiral bdg. 8.50 (ISBN 0-87488-600-7). Med Exam.

Bishop, Calvin C. Slide Rule: How to Use It. 3rd ed. (Orig.). 1955. pap. 1.75 o.p. (ISBN 0-06-463254-7, 254, EH). Har-Row.

Bishop, Carol. Massinger & Field's "the Fatal Dowry". A Critical Edition. (Salzburg Studies in English Literature, Jacobean Drama Studies: No. 63). 267p. 1976. pap. text ed. 25.00x (ISBN 0-391-01326-2). Humanities.

Bishop, Charles E. Farm Labor in the United States. LC 66-28037. 1967. 27.50x (ISBN 0-231-02985-3). Columbia U Pr.

Bishop, Charles E. & Toussaint, W. D. Introduction to Agricultural Economic Analysis. LC 58-12715. (Illus.). 1958. 20.50 (ISBN 0-471-07557-4). Wiley.

Bishop, Claire H. Twenty & Ten. (Illus.). (gr. 4-6). 1952. 6.50 o.p. (ISBN 0-670-73407-1); pap. 1.95 o. p. o.p. (ISBN 0-685-59582-X). Viking Pr.

Bishop, Curtis. Little League Little Brother. LC 68-10778. (gr. 4-6). 1968. PLB 4.69 o.p. (ISBN 0-397-31030-7). Lippincott.
--Little League Stepson. LC 65-13432. (gr. 4-6). 1965. PLB 4.69 o.p. (ISBN 0-397-30814-0). Lippincott.
--Little League Victory. LC 67-10343. (gr. 4-6). 1967. 5.50 o.p. (ISBN 0-397-30962-7). Lippincott.
--Lonesome End. LC 63-18501. (gr. 7-9). 1963. PLB 4.69 o.p. (ISBN 0-397-30695-4). Lippincott.

Bishop, D. H., ed. & pref. by. Indian Thought: An Introduction. LC 73-13206. 1975. 10.95 (ISBN 0-470-07580-5). Halsted Pr.

Bishop, David M. Group Theory & Chemistry. (Illus.). 310p. 1973. 39.00x (ISBN 0-19-855140-1). Oxford U Pr.

Bishop, Denis, jt. auth. see Ingram, Arthur.

Bishop, Dennis & Ellis, Christopher. Vehicles at War. LC 75-20588. 1979. 25.00 (ISBN 0-498-01699-4). A S Barnes.

Bishop, Duane S. Behavioral Problems & the Disabled: Assessment & Management. (Rehabilitation Medicine Library Ser.). (Illus.). 480p. 1980. lib. bdg. 39.00 (ISBN 0-683-00751-3). Williams & Wilkins.

Bishop, E. Indicators. 756p. 1973. text ed. 105.00 (ISBN 0-08-016617-2). Pergamon.

Bishop, E., tr. see Ivanov, E. K.

Bishop, Elizabeth. The Complete Poems. LC 69-15407. 216p. 1969. 10.00 (ISBN 0-374-12744-1); pap. 6.95 (ISBN 0-374-51516-6). FS&G.

Bishop, Elizabeth & Brasil, Emanuel, eds. An Anthology of Twentieth-Century Brazilian Poetry. Blackburn, Paul, et al, trs. from Port. LC 75-184359. 224p. (Orig.). 1972. pap. 7.50x (ISBN 0-8195-6023-5, Pub. by Wesleyan U Pr). Columbia U Pr.

Bishop, Ferman. Henry Adams. (United States Authors Ser.: No. 293). 1979. lib. bdg. 10.95 (ISBN 0-8057-7257-X). Twayne.

Bishop, G. Reginald, Jr., ed. Culture in Language & Learning. Incl. An Anthropological Concept of Culture. Friedl, Ernestine; Language As Culture. Welmers, William E; Teaching of Classical Cultures. Kibbe, Doris E; Teaching of Western European Cultures. Wade, Ira; Teaching of Slavic Cultures. Twarog, Leon I. 1960. pap. 7.95x (ISBN 0-915432-60-9). NE Conf Teach Foreign.
--Foreign Language Teaching: Challenges to the Profession. Incl. The Case for Latin. Parker, William R; The Challenge of Bilingualism. Gaarder, A. Bruce; From School to College: The Problem of Continuity. Dufau, Micheline; Study Abroad. Freeman, Stephen A. 158p. 1965. pap. 7.95x (ISBN 0-915432-65-X). NE Conf Teach Foreign.

Bishop, Gale B. & Hill, Winfred, eds. Dimensions of Psychology: Introductory Readings. LC 79-155877. 400p. 1972. pap. text ed. 5.95 o.p. (ISBN 0-397-47210-2). Lippincott.

Bishop, George. Capital Formation Through Life Insurance. 1976. text ed. 9.25x o.p. (ISBN 0-256-01850-2). Irwin.
--The Encyclopedia of Motorcycling. (Illus.). 1980. 16.95 (ISBN 0-686-68350-1). Putnam.

Bishop, George F., et al, eds. The Presidential Debates: Media Electeral & Policy Perspective. Meadow, Robert G. & Jackson-Beeck, Marilyn. LC 78-70323. (Praeger Special Studies). 1978. 32.95 (ISBN 0-03-044271-0); pap. 11.95 (ISBN 0-03-057707-1). Praeger.

Bishop, Gerald. New British Science Fiction & Fantasy Books Published During 1970 & 1971. LC 80-20579. 1980. Repr. of 1972 ed. lib. bdg. 9.95x (ISBN 0-89370-057-6). Borgo Pr.
--Science Fiction Books Published in Britain, 1972 & 1973. LC 80-20590. 64p. 1980. Repr. of 1975 ed. lib. bdg. 9.95 (ISBN 0-89370-086-X). Borgo Pr.
--Science Fiction Books Publishing in Britain: 1974 to 1978. LC 80-20576. 82p. 1980. Repr. of 1979 ed. lib. bdg. 15.95x (ISBN 0-89370-087-8). Borgo Pr.

Bishop, Harriet E. Dakota War Whoop; or Indian Massacres & War in Minnesota. Washburn, Wilcomb E., ed. LC 75-7103. (Narratives of North American Indian Captivities Ser.: Vol. 78). 1978. Repr. of 1863 ed. lib. bdg. 44.00x (ISBN 0-8240-1702-1). Garland Pub.

Bishop, Hillman, jt. auth. see Hendel, Samuel.

Bishop, Ian. Pearl in Its Setting: A Critical Study of the Structure & Meaning of the Middle English Poem. 24.00x (ISBN 0-631-11410-6, Pub. by Basil Blackwell). Biblio Dist.

Bishop, Jim. A Bishop's Confession. 448p. 1981. 14.95 (ISBN 0-316-09669-5). Little.
--The Day Christ Died. LC 57-6125. 1978. pap. 2.95 (ISBN 0-06-060786-6, HJ 38, HarpR). Har-Row.
--Day Kennedy Was Shot. 2nd ed. LC 68-31633. (Funk & W Bk.). (Illus.). 1972. 9.95 o.s.i. (ISBN 0-308-70271-9, 770530, TYC-T). T Y Crowell.
--Day Lincoln Was Shot. 1964. pap. 2.25 (ISBN 0-06-080005-4, P5, PL). Har-Row.

Bishop, John Peale. The Collected Essays of John Peale Bishop. Wilson, Edmund, ed. 508p. 1975. Repr. of 1948 ed. lib. bdg. 25.00 (ISBN 0-374-90643-2). Octagon.

Bishop, Jonathan. Emerson on the Soul. LC 80-2527. 1981. Repr. of 1964 ed. 29.50 (ISBN 0-404-19251-3). AMS Pr.
Bishop, Joseph. The Eye of the Storm. 1976. pap. 4.95 (ISBN 0-912376-16-3). Chosen Bks Pub.
Bishop, Marcus W., ed. Advances in Reproductive Physiology, Vol. 6. 1973. 39.95x o.p. (ISBN 0-236-17670-6, Pub. by Paul Elek). Merrimack Bk Serv.
Bishop, Michael. A Little Knowledge. (YA) 1977. 8.95 o.p. (ISBN 0-399-11943-4). Berkley Pub.
--A Little Knowledge. 1978. pap. 1.75 o.p. (ISBN 0-425-04305-3, Medallion). Berkley Pub.
--Stolen Faces. LC 76-26262. 1977. 7.95 o.s.i. (ISBN 0-06-010362-0, HarpT). Har-Row.
Bishop, Mike. Arctic Cat: Snowmobile Service-Repair, 1974-1979. Jorgensen, Eric, ed. (Illus.). 1977. pap. 8.95 (ISBN 0-89287-172-5, X951). Clymer Pubns.
--BMW Five Hundred & Six Hundred cc Twins, Nineteen Fifty-Five to Nineteen Sixty-Nine: Service-Repair-Performance. Jorgensen, Eric, ed. (Illus.). 1978. pap. 9.95 (ISBN 0-89287-224-1, M308). Clymer Pubns.
--BMW Service, Repair, Performance: 500-1000cc Twins, 1970-79. Jorgensen, Eric, ed. (Illus.). 1978. pap. 9.95 (ISBN 0-89287-225-X, M309). Clymer Pubns.
--Chevrolet & GMC--4-Wheel Drive Maintenance: Blazer, Jimmy, Pickups & Suburbans, 1967-1979. Robinson, Jeff, ed. (Illus.). 1978. pap. 7.95 (ISBN 0-89287-159-8, A230). Clymer Pubns.
--Chevrolet & GMC Tune-up-Maintenance: Vans, Pickups, & Suburban, 1967-1980. 2nd ed. Robinson, Jeff, ed. (Illus.). 1977. pap. text ed. 10.95 o.p. (ISBN 0-89287-207-1, A238). Clymer Pubns.
--Chevy & GMC Vans Nineteen Sixty-Seven to Nineteen Eighty Shop Manual. Jorgensen, Eric, ed. (Illus.). 1979. pap. text ed. 10.95 (ISBN 0-89287-300-0, A239). Clymer Pubns.
--Chevy GMC Pickups Nineteen Sixty-Seven to Nineteen Eighty: Includes Suburbans Shop Manual. Jorgensen, Eric, ed. (Illus.). 1979. pap. text ed. 9.95 (ISBN 0-89287-207-1, A238). Clymer Pubns.
--CZ Service-Repair Handbook: Single Exhaust Models-Through 1978. Robinson, Jeff, ed. (Illus.). 1976. pap. text ed. 9.95 (ISBN 0-89287-102-4, M425). Clymer Pubns.
--Dodge Plymouth Ramcharger, Trail Duster & Pickups: 4-Wheel Drive Maintenance, 1965-1978. Jorgensen, Eric, ed. (Illus.). 1978. pap. 7.95 (ISBN 0-89287-289-6, A231). Clymer Pubns.
--Dodge Plymouth Tune-up Maintenance: Vans & Pickups, 1965-1978. Jorgensen, Eric, ed. (Illus.). 1978. pap. 7.00 o.p. (ISBN 0-89287-239-X, A241). Clymer Pubns.
--Fiat Service--Repair Handbook: 124 Series, 1967-1980. Robinson, Jeff, ed. (Illus.). 1978. pap. 10.95 (ISBN 0-89287-156-3, A156). Clymer Pubns.
--Fiat: 128 & X1-9, 1971-1979--Service, Repair Handbook. 3rd ed. Jorgensen, Eric, ed. (Illus.). 1978. pap. 10.95 (ISBN 0-89287-282-9, A157). Clymer Pubns.
--Ford Tune-up & Maintenance: Vans & Pickups, 1969-1978. Jorgensen, Eric, ed. (Illus.). 1978. pap. 7.00 o.p. (ISBN 0-89287-231-4, A242). Clymer Pubns.
--Honda Service-Repair Handbook: Civic, 1973-1979. Jorgensen, Eric, ed. (Illus.). 1978. pap. 10.95 (ISBN 0-89287-216-0, A227). Clymer Pubns.
--Honda 125-250 Elsinores 1973-1978: Service, Repair, Performance. Jorgensen, Eric, ed. (Illus.). 1977. pap. 9.95 (ISBN 0-89287-176-8, M317). Clymer Pubns.
--International Tune-up-Maintenance, Scouts, Wagons, Pickups, Through 1980. new ed. Robinson, Jeff, ed. (Illus.). 1977. pap. 7.95 (ISBN 0-89287-137-7, A233). Clymer Pubns.
--Jeep All Models: 1969-1978, 4-Wheel Drive Maintenance. Jorgensen, Eric, ed. (Illus.). 1978. pap. 7.95 (ISBN 0-89287-291-8, A234). Clymer Pubns.
--Kawasaki Snowmobiles Nineteen Seventy-Six to Nineteen Eighty: Service, Repair, Maintenance. Jorgensen, Eric, ed. (Illus.). 152p. (Orig.). 1980. pap. text ed. 8.95 (ISBN 0-89287-320-5, X995). Clymer Pubns.
--Maico Service-Repair Handbook: 250-501cc Singles, 1968-1975. Robinson, Jeff, ed. (Illus.). 120p. 1975. pap. text ed. 9.95 (ISBN 0-89287-019-2, M357). Clymer Pubns.
--Mercedes-Benz Tune-up Maintenance: Gas & Diesel, 1958-1978. Jorgensen, Eric, ed. (Illus.). 1977. pap. 10.95 (ISBN 0-89287-175-X, A180). Clymer Pubns.
--Norton Service Repair Handbook: 750 & 850 Commandos, All Years. Robinson, Jeff, ed. (Illus.). 1977. pap. 9.95 (ISBN 0-89287-158-X, M361). Clymer Pubns.
--Polaris Snowmobile Service-Repair: 1973-1977. Jorgensen, Eric, ed. (Illus.). 1977. pap. 8.95 (ISBN 0-89287-177-6, X952). Clymer Pubns.
--Sachs Engine Service-Repair Handbook: 100 & 125cc, All Years. Robinson, Jeff, ed. (Illus.). 144p. 1974. pap. text ed. 9.95 (ISBN 0-89287-025-7, M427). Clymer Pubns.
--Suzuki GS750 Fours, 1977-1979: Service, Repair, Performance. Jorgensen, Eric, ed. (Illus.). 1979. pap. 9.95 (ISBN 0-89287-189-X, M370). Clymer Pubns.
--Yamaha Snowmobiles: Nineteen Seventy-Five to Nineteen Eighty Service, Repair & Maintenance. Jorgensen, Eric, ed. (Illus.). 180p. (Orig.). 1980. pap. text ed. 8.95 (ISBN 0-89287-323-X, X954). Clymer Pubns.
--Yamaha SR500 Singles: 1977-1979 Service-Repair-Performance. Jorgensen, Eric, ed. (Illus.). 191p. (Orig.). 1979. pap. 9.95 (ISBN 0-89287-212-8, M407). Clymer Pubns.
Bishop, Milo E. Mainstreaming: Practical Ideas for Educating Hearing-Impaired Students. 1979. 10.00 (ISBN 0-88200-126-4). Bell Assn Deaf.
Bishop, Morris. The Best of Bishop: Light Verse from the New Yorker & Elsewhere. Reppert, Charlotte P., ed. LC 80-66902. (Illus.). 224p. 1980. 12.95 (ISBN 0-8014-1310-9). Cornell U Pr.
Bishop, Nathaniel Holmes. Four Months in a Sneak Box: A Boat Voyage of Twenty Six Hundred Miles Down the Ohio & Mississippi Rivers. LC 71-142572. (Illus.). xii, 322p. 1976. Repr. of 1879 ed. 26.00 (ISBN 0-8103-4170-0). Gale.
Bishop, Olga B. Bibliography of Ontario History, 1867-1976: Cultural, Economic, Political, Social, 2 vols. 1980. 75.00 (ISBN 0-8020-2359-2). U of Toronto Pr.
--Canadian Official Publications. (Guides to Official Publications Ser.: Vol. 9). 308p. 1981. 40.00 (ISBN 0-08-024697-4). Pergamon.
Bishop, R. E. Vibration. 2nd ed. LC 79-11172. (Illus.). 1979. 29.50 (ISBN 0-521-22779-8); pap. 10.50 (ISBN 0-521-29639-0). Cambridge U Pr.
Bishop, R. E. & Johnson, D. C. The Mechanics of Vibration. (Illus.). 1979. 97.50 (ISBN 0-521-04258-5). Cambridge U Pr.
Bishop, R. E. & Price, W. G. Hydroelasticity of Ships. LC 78-67297. 1980. 90.00 (ISBN 0-521-22328-8). Cambridge U Pr.
Bishop, R. E., et al. The Matrix Analysis of Vibration. (Illus.). 1979. 83.50 (ISBN 0-521-04257-7). Cambridge U Pr.
Bishop, Richard & Goldberg, Samuel. Tensor Analysis on Manifolds. (Illus.). 1980. pap. 6.00 (ISBN 0-486-64039-6). Dover.
Bishop, Richard L. & Crittenden, R. J. Geometry of Manifolds. (Pure and Applied Mathematics Ser.: Vol. 15). 1964. text ed. 19.50 o.p. (ISBN 0-12-102450-4). Acad Pr.
Bishop, Robert. A Gallery of American Weathervanes & Whirligigs. (Illus.). 128p. 1981. 27.50 (ISBN 0-525-93151-1); pap. 16.95 (ISBN 0-525-47652-0). Dutton.
--Treasures of American Folk Art. 12.50 (ISBN 0-8109-2218-5). Abrams.
Bishop, Ron. Basic Microprocessors & Sixty-Eight Hundred. 1979. pap. 13.95 (ISBN 0-8104-0758-2). Hayden.
Bishop, Sharon & Weinzweig, Marjorie. Philosophy & Women. 1979. pap. text ed. 12.95x (ISBN 0-534-00609-4). Wadsworth Pub.
Bishop, Sheila. Lucasta. 1978. pap. 1.50 o.p. (ISBN 0-449-23458-4, Crest). Fawcett.
--The Rules of Marriage. (Regency Romance Ser.). 1978. pap. 1.75 o.p. (ISBN 0-449-23819-9, Crest). Fawcett.
Bishop, Tom, ed. L' Avant-Garde Theatrale: French Theatre Since 1950. LC 74-29373. 1975. 15.00x (ISBN 0-8147-0985-0); pap. 7.00x (ISBN 0-8147-0986-9). NYU Pr.
Bishop, Virginia E. Teaching the Visually Limited Child. (Illus.). 224p. 1978. 16.50 (ISBN 0-398-00158-8). C C Thomas.
Bishop, Wiley L., jt. auth. see Weaver, Barbara N.
Bishop, William A. Winged Warfare. (Air Combat Classics Ser.). (Illus.). 288p. 1981. 11.95 (ISBN 0-668-05162-0); pap. 5.95 (ISBN 0-668-05164-7). Arco.
Bishop, William H. Saint Louis in 1884. Jones, William R., ed. (Illus.). 24p. 1977. Repr. of 1884 ed. pap. 2.50 (ISBN 0-89646-024-X). Outbooks.
Bishop, Yvonne, et al. Discrete Multivariate Analysis: Theory & Practice. 1977. text ed. 40.00x (ISBN 0-262-02113-7); pap. 15.00 (ISBN 0-262-52040-0). MIT Pr.
Biskind, Elliot L., ed. see Harvey, David C.
Biskind, Elliott L., ed. Boardman's Estate Management & Accounting, 2 Vols. rev. ed. LC 64-8482. 1969. looseleaf with 1980 suppl. 80.00 (ISBN 0-87632-056-6). Boardman.
--Boardman's New York Family Law. rev. ed. LC 64-17549. 1972. looseleaf with 1980 suppl. 60.00 (ISBN 0-87632-058-2). Boardman.
Biskind, Elliott L. & Barasch, Clarence S., eds. Law of Real Estate Brokers, N.Y. LC 70-83769. 1969. with 1979 suppl. 45.00 (ISBN 0-87632-050-7). Boardman.
Bisko, W. Mowimy Po Polski: A Beginners Course. 1977. pap. 7.00x (ISBN 0-89918-519-3, P519); 3-12" l.p. records 20.00x (ISBN 0-89918-520-7). Vanous.
Bisley, Geoffrey G. A Handbook of Ophthalmology for Developing Countries. 2nd ed. (Illus.). 1981. 160p. 1981. pap. text ed. 13.95x (ISBN 0-19-261244-1). Oxford U Pr.
Bisman, Ron. Cardigan Bay: The Horse That Won a Million Dollars. (Illus.). 154p. 1972. 6.95 o.p. (ISBN 0-668-02840-8). Arco.
Bison, Mountie. Mountie Bison's 1st Flying Smirk Book. (gr. 3-5). pap. 1.25 o.p. (ISBN 0-590-11926-5, Schol Pap). Schol Bk Serv.
Bisplinghoff, R. L., et al. Aeroelasticity. 1955. 34.95 (ISBN 0-201-00595-6). A-W.
Bisquier, Arthur & Soltis, Andy. American Chess Masters from Morphy to Fischer. LC 73-18510. (Illus.). 260p. 1974. 9.95 o.s.i. (ISBN 0-02-511050-0). Macmillan.
Bissainthe, Max. Dictionnaire De Bibliographie Haitienne: Premier Supplement. LC 51-12164. 1973. 10.00 (ISBN 0-8108-0667-3). Scarecrow.
Bisschop, W. R. Rise of the London Money Market 1640-1826. LC 67-31557. Repr. of 1910 ed. 25.00x (ISBN 0-678-05027-9). Kelley.
Bissel, Richard E. & Crocker, Chester A., eds. South Africa into the Nineteen Eighties. (Special Studies on Africa). 1979. lib. bdg. 25.00x (ISBN 0-89158-373-4). Westview.
Bissell, Richard E. South Africa & the United States: The Erosion of an Influence Relationship. 1981. 19.95 (ISBN 0-03-047026-9); pap. 9.95 (ISBN 0-03-047021-8). Praeger.
Bisseret, Noelle. Education, Class Language & Ideology. 1979. 16.00x (ISBN 0-7100-0118-5). Routledge & Kegan.
Bisset, George, tr. see Skogsberg, Bertil.
Bisset, James & Stephensen, P. R. Sail Ho. LC 58-5447. (Illus.). 1958. 14.95 (ISBN 0-87599-015-0). S G Phillips.
--Tramps & Ladies. LC 59-12193. (Illus.). 1959. 14.95 (ISBN 0-87599-014-2). S G Phillips.
Bissex, Glenda. Gnys at Wrk: A Child Learns to Write & Read. LC 80-14558. 1980. text ed. 17.50x (ISBN 0-674-35485-0). Harvard U Pr.
Bisson, L., ed. see Hugo, Victor.
Bisson, Roy, jt. auth. see Wright, Chris.
Bisson, Thomas N. Conservation of Coinage: Monetary Exploitation & Its Restraint in France, Catalonia, & Aragon C.1000-1225 A.D. (Illus.). 1979. 45.00 (ISBN 0-19-828275-3). Oxford U Pr.
Bissoondayal, Basdeo. The Essence of the Vedas & Allied Scriptures. 1966. pap. 1.80 (ISBN 0-88253-126-3). Ind-US Inc.
Bisswanger, Hans & Schmincke-Ott, Eva, eds. Multifunctional Proteins. LC 79-16055. 1980. 37.50 (ISBN 0-471-04270-6, Pub. by Wiley-Interscience). Wiley.
Bistner, Stephen I., jt. auth. see Kirk, Robert W.
Biswas, A. K., jt. ed. see Golubev, G. N.
Biswas, Anita, jt. auth. see Biswas, S. B.
Biswas, Asit K. Models for Water Quality Management. (M-H Series in Water Resources & Environmental Engineering). (Illus.). 392p. 1980. text ed. 44.50 (ISBN 0-07-005481-9). McGraw.
Biswas, Asit K., jt. auth. see Biswas, Margaret R.
Biswas, Asit K., ed. The Ozone Layer: Synthesis of Papers Based on the UNEP Meeting on the Ozone Layer, Washington DC, March 1977. LC 79-42879. (Environmental Sciences & Applications Ser.: Vol. 4). 1980. 58.00 (ISBN 0-08-022429-6). Pergamon.
--United Nations Water Conference: Summary & Main Documents. new ed. LC 77-30461. 1978. text ed. 42.00 (ISBN 0-08-022392-3). Pergamon.
Biswas, Margaret R. & Biswas, Asit K. Desertification: Associated Case Studies Prepared for the United Nations Conference on Desertification. LC 80-40024. (Environmental Sciences & Applications: Vol. 12). (Illus.). 532p. 1980. 87.00 (ISBN 0-08-023581-6). Pergamon.
Biswas, N. N. Principles of Telegraphy. 1968. Repr. pap. 5.00x (ISBN 0-210-98177-6). Asia.
Biswas, S. B. & Biswas, Anita. An Introduction to Viruses. 1976. 12.50 (ISBN 0-7069-0411-7, Pub. by Vikas India). Advent Bk.
Bisztray, George. Marxist Models of Literary Realism. LC 77-23833. 1978. 14.00x (ISBN 0-231-04310-4). Columbia U Pr.
Bitel, Jane. Jane Butel's Tex-Mex Cookbook. 224p. 1980. 10.95 (ISBN 0-517-53986-1, Harmony). Crown.
Bitensky, M., et al, eds. see ICN-UCLA Symposium on Transmembrane Signaling, Keystone, Colorado, February, 1978.
Bithell, Jethro, ed. see Carossa, Hans.
Bithell, Jethro, tr. Contemporary French Poetry. 227p. 1980. Repr. lib. bdg. 20.00 (ISBN 0-89760-041-X). Telegraph Bks.
Bitker, Marjorie M. A Different Flame. 1976. pap. 1.50 o.p. (ISBN 0-445-03126-3). Popular Lib.
--Gold of the Evening. Orig. Title: The Forest Path. 240p. 1975. pap. 1.25 o.p. (ISBN 0-445-00268-9). Popular Lib.
Bitsilli, P. M., et al. O Dostoevskom: Stat'i. LC 66-23779. (Slavic Reprint Ser.: No. 4). 229p. (Rus). 1966. pap. 4.00 (ISBN 0-87057-098-6, Pub. by Brown U Pr). Univ Pr of New England.
Bitsilli, Peter. Chekhov's Art: A Stylistic Analysis. Clyman, Toby & Cruise, Edwina, trs. from Rus. 1981. 15.00 (ISBN 0-88233-100-0). Ardis Pubs.
Bittar, E. Edward. Membrane Structure & Function, 3 vols. LC 79-14969. (Membrane Structure & Function Ser.). 1980. Vol. 1. 24.00 (ISBN 0-471-03816-4, Pub. by Wiley-Interscience); Vol. 2. 42.50 (ISBN 0-471-03817-2); Vol. 3. 22.50 (ISBN 0-471-03818-0). Wiley.
--Membrane Structure & Function, Vol. 4. (Membrane Structure & Function Ser.). 200p. 1980. 24.50 (ISBN 0-471-08774-2, Pub. by Wiley-Interscience). Wiley.
Bittel, Lester R. Essentials of Supervisory Management. LC 80-13784. (Illus.). 288p. 1980. softcover 12.95 (ISBN 0-07-005571-8, G); instrs'. manual & key 4.50 (ISBN 0-07-005572-6). McGraw.
--Management by Exception: Systematizing & Simplifying the Manager's Job. 1964. 18.50 o.p. (ISBN 0-07-005484-3, P&RB). McGraw.
--Skills Development Portfolio for What Every Supervisor Should Know, The Basics of Supervisory Management. 4th ed. 1979. 5.30 (ISBN 0-07-005562-9). McGraw.
--What Every Supervisor Should Know, the Basics of Supervisory Management. 4th ed. LC 79-16387. 1980. 18.95x (ISBN 0-07-005573-4); text ed. 16.75x (ISBN 0-07-005561-0); Skills Development portfolio 5.95 (ISBN 0-07-005562-9); Course & Management key 4.50 (ISBN 0-07-005563-7). McGraw.
Bitter & Mikesell. Activities Handbook for Teaching with the Hand Held Calculator. 1979. text ed. 14.65 (ISBN 0-205-06713-1, 2367130). Allyn.
Bitter, Gary. Exploring with Computers. (Illus.). (gr. 4-7). 1981. PLB price not set (ISBN 0-671-34034-4). Messner.
Bitter, James A. Introduction to Vocational Rehabilitation. LC 78-24530. (Illus.). 1979. text ed. 16.95 (ISBN 0-8016-0693-4). Mosby.
Bitter, John. Practical Public Relations for the Public Schools. LC 77-71467. 1977. text ed. 9.95 (ISBN 0-916624-08-0). TSU Pr.
Bittermann, Henry J. The Refunding of International Debt. LC 72-93542. 234p. 1973. 14.75 (ISBN 0-8223-0280-2). Duke.
Bitting, Katherine G. Gastronomic Bibliography. LC 71-168559. (Illus.). 1971. Repr. of 1939 ed. 34.00 (ISBN 0-8103-3758-4). Gale.
Bittinger, M. S. Logic & Proof. 1970. pap. 5.95 (ISBN 0-201-00597-2). A-W.
Bittinger, Marvin L. Calculus: A Modeling Approach. 2nd ed. LC 79-18272. (Illus.). 1980. text ed. 19.95 (ISBN 0-201-01247-2). A-W.
Bittinger, Marvin L. & Crown, J. Conrad. Finite Mathematics: A Modeling Approach. LC 76-14656. (Illus.). 1977. text ed. 16.95 o.p. (ISBN 0-201-00832-7); instr's manual 2.50 o.p. (ISBN 0-201-00833-5). A-W.
--Mathematics: A Modeling Approach. 1981. write for info. (ISBN 0-201-03116-7). A-W.
Bittinger, Marvin L., jt. auth. see Crown, J. Conrad.
Bittinger, Marvin L., jt. auth. see Keedy, Mervin L.
Bittinger, Marvin L., ed. Living with Our Hyperactive Children: Parents' Own Stories. (Illus.). 1977. 8.95 (ISBN 0-8467-0275-4, Pub. by Two Continents). Hippocrene Bks.
Bittinger, Marvin L., et al. Mathematics for Consumer Survival. (Illus.). 640p. text ed. 10.00 (ISBN 0-87150-501-0); tchr's manual 5.00 (ISBN 0-686-64028-4); wkbk 4.00 (ISBN 0-686-64029-2). Prindle.
Bittinger, Morton N. & Green, Elizabeth B. You Never Miss the Water till... The Ogallala Story. 1981. 12.00 (ISBN 0-918334-33-0). WRP.
Bittleston, Adam. Our Spiritual Companions. 1980. pap. 13.50 (ISBN 0-903540-39-8, Pub. by Floris Books). St George Bk Serv.
--The Spirit of the Circling Stars: Human Problems in a Cosmic Setting. 1975. 8.95 (ISBN 0-900285-25-7, Pub. by Floris Books). St George Bk Serv.
Bittleston, Gisela. The Healing Art of Glove Puppetry. 1978. 7.95 (ISBN 0-903540-15-0, Pub. by Floris Bks). St George Bk Serv.
Bittlinger, Arnold. Gifts & Ministries. LC 72-96403. 104p. 1973. pap. 1.95 o.p. (ISBN 0-8028-1497-2). Eerdmans.
--Letter of Joy. Wiesmann, Susan, tr. from Ger. LC 75-2265. 128p. 1975. pap. 3.50 (ISBN 0-87123-338-X, 210338). Bethany Fell.
Bittlingmayer, George, jt. auth. see Gould, John.

Bittman, Sam & Zalk, Sue. Expectant Fathers. LC 78-54666. 1979. 12.95 (ISBN 0-8015-2444-X, Hawthorn). Dutton.

Bittner, Denise A. & Bittner, John R. Radio Journalism. LC 76-29048. (Speech Communication Ser.). (Illus.). 1977. pap. text ed. 12.95 (ISBN 0-13-750455-1). P-H.

Bittner, Egon & Krantz, Sheldon. Standards Relating to Police Handling of Juvenile Problems. (Juvenile Justice Standards Project Ser.). 1980. softcover 7.95 (ISBN 0-88410-806-6); final casebound 16.50 (ISBN 0-88410-755-8). Ballinger Pub.

--Standards Relating to Police Handling of Juvenile Problems. LC 77-3376. (Juvenile Justice Standards Project Ser.). 1977. final casebound 16.50 o.p.; softcover 7.95 o.p. (ISBN 0-88410-762-0). Ballinger Pub.

Bittner, Egon & Messinger, Sheldon L., eds. Criminology Review Yearbook, Vol. 2. (Illus.). 733p. 1980. 35.00 (ISBN 0-8039-1309-5). Sage.

Bittner, J. Mass Communication: An Introduction Theory & Practice of Mass Media in Society. (Speech Communication Ser.). 1977. text ed. 14.95 o.p. (ISBN 0-13-559310-7); pap. text ed. 11.95 o.p. (ISBN 0-13-559302-6); teaching mass communication o.p. avail. o.p. (ISBN 0-685-78781-8). P-H.

--Professional Broadcasting: A Brief Introduction. 1981. pap. 12.95 (ISBN 0-13-725465-2). P-H.

Bittner, John R. Mass Communication. 2nd ed. (Ser. in Speech Communication). (Illus.). 1980. pap. text ed. 14.95 (ISBN 0-13-559278-X). P-H.

Bittner, John R., jt. auth. see Bittner, Denise A.

Bitzer, G. W. Billy Bitzer, His Story. (Illus.). 1973. 10.00 o.p. (ISBN 0-374-11294-0). FS&G.

Bitzer, Lloyd F., ed. see Campbell, George.

Bivand, Ewa S., jt. auth. see Bivand, Roger.

Bivand, Roger & Bivand, Ewa S. Britain: Continuity & Change. LC 80-40778. (Illus.). 196p. 1981. 7.95 (ISBN 0-08-025312-1). Pergamon.

Biviano, Ronald S. Medical Conditions & Terms Made Simple. LC 80-68397. 100p. (Orig.). 1981. pap. 10.00 (ISBN 0-9605476-0-6). Biviano.

Bix, Cynthia & Dillon, Ann. Contributions of Women: Theater. LC 77-13094. (Contributions of Women Ser.). (Illus.). (gr. 6 up). 1978. PLB 8.95 (ISBN 0-87518-152-X). Dillon.

Bixler, David, jt. ed. see Melnick, Michael.

Biyidi, Alexandre see Beti, Mongo, pseud.

Bizet, Georges. Carmen. Bleiler, Ellen, ed. & tr. LC 68-10868. (Opera Guide & Libretto Ser). (Illus., Orig.). 1970. pap. 4.00 (ISBN 0-486-22111-3). Dover.

Bizien, Yves. Population & Economic Development. LC 78-19768. 202p. 1979. 22.95 (ISBN 0-03-048896-6). Praeger.

Bizzarro, Salvatore. Historical Dictionary of Chile. LC 72-3161. (Latin American Historical Dictionaries Ser.: No. 7). 1972. 10.00 (ISBN 0-8108-0497-2). Scarecrow.

--Pablo Neruda: All Poets the Poet. LC 78-24437. 1979. lib. bdg. 10.00 (ISBN 0-8108-1189-8). Scarecrow.

Bizzell, jt. auth. see Deitrick.

Bjaerevoll, Olav, jt. auth. see Ronning, Olaf.

Bjaerke, Tor & Manum, Svein B. Mesozoic Palynology of Svalbard. (Norsk Polarinstitutt Skrifter: No. 165). (Illus.). 1978. pap. 8.00x (ISBN 82-00-29719-5, Dist. by Columbia U Pr). Universitet.

Bjelica, Mihalo, jt. auth. see Lekovic, Zdravko.

Bjelland, Harley. How to Sell Your Own House: Without a Broker! 1979. pap. 4.95 (ISBN 0-346-12381-X). Cornerstone.

Bjerke, L. & Soraas, H., eds. Norwegian Dictionary: English-Norwegian. 1963. 26.00x (N434). Vanous.

Bjerre, Andreas. The Psychology of Murder: A Study in Criminal Psychology. Classen, E., tr. from Swedish. (Historical Foundations of Forensic Psychiatry & Psychology Ser.). 164p. 1980. Repr. lib. bdg. 19.50 (ISBN 0-306-76067-3). Da Capo.

Bjerreskov, Merete. Llandoverian & Wenlockian Graptolites from Bornholm. (Fossils & Strata: No.8). 1975. pap. text ed. 25.00x (ISBN 8-200-09392-1, Dist. by Columbia U Pr). Universitet.

Bjorge, James R. And Heaven & Nature Sings. (Illus.). 1977. pap. 4.95 (ISBN 0-570-03047-1, 6-1172). Concordia.

Bjorgum, Kenneth L. Bloodstone. 256p. (Orig.). 1980. pap. 2.25 (ISBN 0-515-05475-5). Jove Pubns.

Bjork, Daniel W. The Victorian Flight: Russell Conwell & the Crisis of American Individualism. LC 78-50767. 1978. pap. text ed. 7.75x (ISBN 0-8191-0464-7). U Pr of Amer.

Bjork, Gordon C. Life, Liberty, & Property: The Economics & Politics of Land-Use Planning & Environmental Controls. LC 80-8038. 160p. 1980. 16.50x (ISBN 0-669-03952-7). Lexington Bks.

Bjork, Robert M. & Fraser, Stewart E. Population, Education, & Children's Futures. LC 80-82683. (Fastback Ser.: No. 150). (Orig.). 1980. pap. 0.75 (ISBN 0-87367-150-3). Phi Delta Kappa.

Bjorkhagen, I. Modern Swedish Grammar. 9th, rev. ed. 1966. 12.50 o.p. (ISBN 0-685-47300-7). Heinman.

Bjorkhagen, Immanuel. Modern Swedish Grammar. 9th ed. 1962. 12.50x o.s.i. (ISBN 0-686-00876-6). Colton Bk.

Bjorklund, Gail. Planning for Play: A Developmental Approach. 1978. pap. text ed. 5.95 (ISBN 0-675-08434-2); filmstrips or cassettes avail. 60.00, 2-4 sets (ISBN 0-686-52447-0). manual 3.95 (ISBN 0-686-67983-0). Merrill.

Bjorklund, Oddvar, et al. Historical Atlas of the World. LC 64-26. (Illus.). 1972. pap. 10.00x (ISBN 0-06-490435-0). B&N.

Bjorkman, James W., jt. auth. see Altenstetter, Christa.

Bjorkman, Nancy R. Wilma & the Water Pistol That Wouldn't Shoot Straight. (Illus.). (gr. k-4). 1976. PLB 7.62 o.p. (ISBN 0-307-65695-0, Golden Pr). Western Pub.

Bjorn, L. O. Light & Life. LC 76-27618. 1976. pap. 7.95x (ISBN 0-8448-1006-1). Crane-Russak Co.

Bjorn, Thyra F. The Home Has a Heart. (Spire Bks). 1975. pap. 1.75 o.p. (ISBN 0-8007-8222-4). Revell.

--The Home Has a Heart. (Orig.). pap. 1.75 (ISBN 0-89129-033-8). Jove Pubns.

--This Is My Life. (A Spire Bk). 1976. pap. 1.50 o.p. (ISBN 0-8007-8234-8). Revell.

--This Is My Life. 1976. pap. 1.50 (ISBN 0-89129-137-7). Jove Pubns.

Bjorn, Thyre F. Dear Papa. 1976. pap. 1.75 (ISBN 0-89129-138-5). Jove Pubns.

Bjorner, D., ed. Abstract Software Specifications. (Lecture Notes in Computer Sciences: Vol. 86). 567p. 1980. pap. 31.00 (ISBN 0-387-10007-5). Springer-Verlag.

Bjornson, Richard. The Picaresque Hero in European Fiction. LC 76-11312. 1977. 25.00x (ISBN 0-299-07100-6); pap. 8.95 (ISBN 0-299-07104-9). U of Wis Pr.

Bjornstad, James. The Moon Is Not the Son: A Close Look at the Religion of Rev. Son Myung Moon. LC 76-46208. 1977. pap. 2.50 (ISBN 0-87123-380-0, 200380). Bethany Fell.

--The Transcendental Mirage. LC 76-6614. 1976. pap. 1.50 (ISBN 0-87123-556-0, 200556). Bethany Fell.

--Twentieth Century Prophecy. 1976. pap. 1.25 (ISBN 0-89129-150-4). Jove Pubns.

--Twentieth Century Prophecy: Jean Dixon-Edgar Cayce. 1969. pap. 1.95 (ISBN 0-87123-546-3, 200546). Bethany Fell.

Bjornstad, James & Johnson, Shildes. Stars, Signs, & Salvation in the Age of Aquarius. (Orig.). 1971. pap. 1.50 o.p. (ISBN 0-87123-524-2). Bethany Fell.

Bjorstad, Eric, jt. auth. see Beckey, Fred.

Bjurstedt, H. A., tr. see Gazenko, O. G.

Blaauw, Gerritt A. Digital System Implementation. (Illus.). 1976. 25.95 (ISBN 0-13-212241-3). P-H.

Blache, M. T., ed. Vicus, Arquelogia, Antropologia, Cultural, Etnologia, Vol.1. 1979. text ed. 34.25x (ISBN 0-391-01246-0). Humanities.

--Vicus, Arquelogia, Antropologia, Cultural, Etnologia, Vol. 2. 1980. text ed. 34.25x (ISBN 0-391-01245-2). Humanities.

Blachly, Paul H., jt. auth. see Western Institute of Drug Problems Summer School, 3rd Annual.

Blachly, Paul H., ed. Drug Abuse: Data & Debate. (Illus.). 340p. 1973. 21.50 (ISBN 0-398-00159-6). C C Thomas.

Black. Little Old Man Who Could Not Read. (gr. 2-3). 1980. pap. 3.50 incl. record (ISBN 0-590-24004-8, Schol Pap). Schol Bk Serv.

--Materials in the Biological Environment. 320p. 1981. 32.50 (ISBN 0-8247-1267-6). Dekker.

Black, A. J. Monarchy & Community. LC 72-108101. (Studies in Medieval Life & Thought). 1970. 32.95 (ISBN 0-521-07739-7). Cambridge U Pr.

Black, A. N., jt. auth. see Coles, K. Adlard.

Black, Algernon D. First Book of Ethics. LC 65-13677. (First Bks). (Illus.). (gr. 4-6). 1965. PLB 4.90 o.p. (ISBN 0-531-00526-7). Watts.

Black, Betty, jt. auth. see Green, Karen.

Black, Bruce J. Workshop Processes, Practices & Materials. (Illus.). 282p. 1979. pap. 13.95x (ISBN 0-7131-3409-7). Intl Ideas.

Black, C. A. Soil-Plant Relationships. 2nd ed. LC 67-28946. (Orig.). 1968. 41.50 (ISBN 0-471-07723-2). Wiley.

Black, C. E. & Helmreich, E. C. Twentieth Century Europe: A History. 4th ed. (Illus.). 1972. 18.95 o.p. (ISBN 0-394-47274-8); text ed. 18.95 (ISBN 0-394-31638-X). Knopf.

Black, C. E. & Falk, Richard A., eds. Future of International Legal Order, 4 vols. Incl. Vol. 1. Trends & Patterns. 1969. 25.00x (ISBN 0-691-09215-X); Vol. 2. Wealth & Resources. 1970. 20.00x (ISBN 0-691-09217-6); Vol. 3. Conflict Management. 416p. 1971. 22.00x (ISBN 0-691-09220-6); Vol. 4. The Structure of the International Environment. 600p. 1972. 22.50x (ISBN 0-691-09221-4); pap. o.p. (ISBN 0-691-10005-5). (Center of International Studies, Princeton Univ.). Princeton U Pr.

Black, C., Jr. Perspectives in Constitutional Law with Revisions. 1970. pap. 5.95 o.p. (ISBN 0-13-660746-2). P-H.

Black, Campbell. Brainfire. 1980. pap. 2.50 (ISBN 0-451-09481-6, E9481, Sig). NAL.

Black, Charles. Owls Bay in Babylon. (The American Dust Ser.: No. 13). 90p. 1980. 7.95 (ISBN 0-913218-92-8); pap. 2.95 (ISBN 0-913218-91-X). Dustbooks.

Black, Charles, jt. auth. see Eckhardt, Bob.

Black, Charles L., Jr. Decision According to Law: Nineteen Seventy-Nine Holmes Lectures. 1981. 12.95 (ISBN 0-393-01452-5). Norton.

--Structure & Relationship in Constitutional Law. LC 69-17621. (Edward Douglass White Lectures). 1969. 7.95 (ISBN 0-8071-0305-5). La State U Pr.

Black, Clementina. Married Women's Work: Being the Report of an Inquiry Undertaken by the Women's Industrial Council, London Nineteen Fifteen. LC 79-56947. (The Englishworking Class Ser.). 1980. lib. bdg. 25.00 (ISBN 0-8240-0102-8). Garland Pub.

Black, Colette. Art of Parisian Cooking. (Orig.). 1962. pap. 0.95 o.s.i. (ISBN 0-02-009160-5, Collier). Macmillan.

--French Provincial Cookbook. (Orig.). 1967. pap. 0.95 o.s.i. (ISBN 0-02-009230-X, Collier). Macmillan.

Black, Colin. A Handbook of Free Conversation. 48p. 1970. pap. text ed. 2.50x (ISBN 0-19-432773-6). Oxford U Pr.

Black, Cyril E. The Dynamics of Modernization: A Study in Comparative History. 1967. pap. 4.95x (ISBN 0-06-131321-1, TB1321, Torch). Har-Row.

Black, Cyril E., jt. auth. see Halliday, E. M.

Black, Cyril E., ed. Comparative Modernization: A Reader. LC 75-16647. (Perspectives on Modernization Ser). 1976. 16.95 (ISBN 0-02-903530-9). Free Pr.

Black, Cyril E., et al. The Modernization of Japan & Russia. LC 75-8429. (Perspectives on Modernization Ser.). 1975. 19.95 (ISBN 0-02-906850-9). Free Pr.

Black, David. Like Father. LC 78-6841. 1978. 8.95 (ISBN 0-396-07587-8, Dist. by W.W. Noryon). Dembner Bks.

Black, David, ed. see Fabre, Jean H.

Black, David, ed. see Linnaeus, Carl von.

Black, Donald. The Manners & Customs of the Police. 1980. 28.00 (ISBN 0-12-102880-1); pap. 9.50 (ISBN 0-12-102885-2). Acad Pr.

Black, Duncan. Incidence of Income Taxes. LC 66-76596. Repr. of 1939 ed. 21.00x (ISBN 0-678-05156-9). Kelley.

--Theory of Committees & Elections. 1958. 29.95 (ISBN 0-521-04262-3). Cambridge U Pr.

Black, Edwin. Rhetorical Criticism: A Study in Method. LC 77-91050. 1978. 15.00 (ISBN 0-299-07550-8); pap. text ed. 6.95 (ISBN 0-299-07554-0). U of Wis Pr.

Black, Esther B. Rancho Cucamonga & Dona Merced. new ed. LC 75-21294. (Illus.). 340p. 1975. 9.50 o.p. (ISBN 0-915158-09-4); pap. 7.50 o.p. (ISBN 0-915158-08-6). San Bernardino.

Black, F. William, jt. auth. see Strub, Richard L.

Black, Floyd. Alphabet Cat. LC 79-1911. (Illus.). (ps-3). 1979. 1.95 (ISBN 0-525-69008-5, Gingerbread Bks); PLB 5.95 (ISBN 0-525-69009-3, Gingerbread Bks). Dutton.

Black, Frank G. & Black, Renee M., eds. Harney Papers. (Publications on Social History Ser: No. 5). 1969. text ed. 25.25x (ISBN 90-232-0270-8). Humanities.

Black, George F. Gypsy Bibliography. LC 74-149780. 1971. Repr. of 1914 ed. 18.00 (ISBN 0-8103-3708-8). Gale.

Black, Gilbert J. Trends in Managemment Development Educations: An Economic Study. LC 79-4435. (Communications Library). 1979. 24.95x (ISBN 0-914236-24-5). Knowledge Indus.

Black, Hallie. Animal Cooperation: A Look at Sociobiology. (Illus.). 64p. (gr. 7-9). 1981. 7.95 (ISBN 0-688-00360-5); PLB 7.63 (ISBN 0-688-00361-3). Morrow.

--Dirt Cheap: Evolution of Renewable Resource Management. LC 79-11353. (Illus.). (gr. 4-6). 1979. 8.50 (ISBN 0-688-22184-X); PLB 8.16 (ISBN 0-688-32184-4). Morrow.

Black, Harry G. Trails to Hoosier Heritage. LC 80-81608. (Illus.). 114p. (Orig.). 1981. pap. 3.95 (ISBN 0-937086-00-2). HMB Pubns.

Black, Helen, ed. The Berkeley Co-Op Food Book. (Orig.). 1980. pap. 7.95 (ISBN 0-915950-43-X). Bull Pub.

Black, Henry C. Black's Law Dictionary. 5th ed. Nolan, Joseph R. & Connolly, Michael J., eds. LC 79-12547. 1511p. 1979. text ed. 17.95 (ISBN 0-8299-2041-2); deluxe ed. 35.00 (ISBN 0-8299-2045-5). West Pub.

--An Essay on the Constitutional Prohibitions Against Legislation Impairing the Obligation of Contracts, & Against Retroactive & Ex Post Facto Laws. xxvi, 355p. 1980. Repr. of 1887 ed. lib. bdg. 32.50x (ISBN 0-8377-0312-3). Rothman.

Black, Hermina. Dangerous Masquerade-a World of Love. 1977. pap. 1.75 o.p. (ISBN 0-451-07703-2, E7703, Sig). NAL.

Black, Homer A., et al. Accounting in Business Decisions: Theory, Method, & Use. 3rd ed. (Illus.). 752p. 1973. 19.95x (ISBN 0-13-001545-8); accounting forms 4.95x (ISBN 0-13-001644-6); practice case 2.95x (ISBN 0-13-001230-0). P-H.

Black, Hugh C., et al. The Great Educators: Readings for Leaders in Education. LC 72-88717. 1972. 19.95 (ISBN 0-911012-48-6). Nelson-Hall.

Black, Hugo L. Constitutional Faith. 1968. 4.95 o.p. (ISBN 0-394-42020-9). Knopf.

Black, Ian S. The Man on the Bridge. 1977. pap. 1.95 o.s.i. (ISBN 0-515-04416-4). Jove Pubns.

Black, Irma S. Doctor Proctor & Mrs. Merriweather. LC 78-150800. (Concept Bks). (Illus.). (gr. k-2). 1971. 5.75g o.p. (ISBN 0-8075-1654-6). A Whitman.

--Is This My Dinner? LC 72-83682. (Self Starter Bks.). (Illus.). 32p. (ps-2). 1972. 6.50g (ISBN 0-8075-3665-2). A Whitman.

Black, J. Neonatal Emergencies & Other Problems. 288p. 1972. 27.50 (ISBN 0-407-32780-0). Butterworths.

Black, J. & Bradley, J. F. Essential Mathematics for Economists. 2nd ed. LC 79-40826. 1980. 48.50 (ISBN 0-471-27659-6, Pub. by Wiley-Interscience); pap. cancelled (ISBN 0-471-27660-X). Wiley.

Black, J. B. Reign of Elizabeth, Fifteen Fifty-Eight to Sixteen Three. 2nd ed. (Oxford History of England Ser.). 1959. 33.00x (ISBN 0-19-821701-3). Oxford U Pr.

Black, J. L., ed. Essays on Karamzin: Russian Man of Letters, Political Thinker, Historian, 1766-1826. (Slavistic Printings & Reprints: No.309). 232p. 1975. pap. text ed. 43.50x (ISBN 90-2793-251-4). Mouton.

Black, J. Thomas. The Changing Economic Role of Central Cities. LC 78-66446. (Issue Paper Ser.). 30p. 1978. pap. text ed. 4.75 (ISBN 0-87420-577-8). Urban Land.

--Prospects for Rental Housing Production Under Rent: A Case Study of Washington, D.C. (Research Report Ser.: No. 24). 1976. pap. 3.75 (ISBN 0-87420-561-1). Urban Land.

Black, J. Thomas & Hoben, James E., eds. Urban Land Markets: Price Indices, Supply Measures, & Public Policy Effects. LC 80-53134. (ULI Research Report: No. 30). (Illus.). 238p. 1980. pap. 14.75 (ISBN 0-87420-593-X). Urban Land.

Black, J. Thomas, et al. Private Market Housing Renovation in Older Urban Areas. LC 77-80214. (ULI Research Report: No. 26). (Illus.). 40p. 1977. pap. text ed. 9.75 (ISBN 0-87420-326-0). Urban Land.

--UDAG Partnerships: Nine Case Studies. (Illus.). 108p. 1980. pap. 10.00 (ISBN 0-87420-594-8, U12). Urban Land.

Black, James. The Mystery of Preaching. 1978. pap. 4.95 (ISBN 0-310-36991-6). Zondervan.

Black, James, ed. see Tate, Nahum.

Black, James A. & Champion, Dean J. Methods & Issues in Social Research. LC 75-26659. 445p. 1976. 18.95 (ISBN 0-471-07705-4). Wiley.

Black, James M. Positive Discipline. LC 70-121834. 1970. 12.95 o.p. (ISBN 0-8144-5227-2). Am Mgmt.

Black, Jan K. United States Penetration of Brazil. LC 76-53192. 1977. 17.00x (ISBN 0-8122-7720-1). U of Pa Pr.

Black, Jeannette D. The Blathwayt Atlas: Vol. 2, Commentary. LC 78-654217. 235p. 1975. 25.00x (ISBN 0-87057-139-7, Pub. by Brown U Pr). Univ Pr of New England.

Black, Jeannette D., ed. Blathwayt Atlas, Vol. 1, The Maps. LC 78-654217. (Illus.). 1970. Set. unbound boxed 500.00x (ISBN 0-87057-125-7, Pub. by Brown U Pr). Univ Pr of New England.

Black, Joan, jt. auth. see Holloway, John.

Black, John. The Economics of Modern Britain: An Introduction to Macroeconomics. 2nd ed. 256p. 1981. 24.50x (ISBN 0-686-28828-9, Pub. by Martin Robertson England); pap. 9.95x (ISBN 0-686-28829-7). Biblio Dist.

--The Economics of Modern Britain: An Introduction to Macroeconomics. 272p. 1979. 24.50x (ISBN 0-85520-274-2, Pub by Martin Robertson England); pap. 9.95x (ISBN 0-85520-273-4). Biblio Dist.

Black, John, jt. auth. see Stanley, Del.
Black, John A. Water Pollution Technology. (Illus.). 1977. ref. ed. 16.95 o.p. (ISBN 0-87909-875-9). Reston.
Black, John D. Parity, Parity, Parity. LC 72-2364. (FDR & the Era of the New Deal Ser.). 367p. 1972. Repr. of 1942 ed. 37.50 (ISBN 0-306-70482-X). Da Capo.
Black, John W. American Speech for Foreign Students. 272p. 1970. pap. 22.75 photocopy ed. spiral (ISBN 0-398-00161-8). C C Thomas.
Black, Jonathan. The House on the Hill. 1977. pap. 1.95 o.p. (ISBN 0-425-03648-0, Medallion). Berkley Pub.
--Megacorp. (Orig.). 1981. pap. 3.95 (ISBN 0-451-09889-7, E9889, Sig). NAL.
--Ride the Golden Tiger. new ed. LC 75-30828. 312p. 1976. 8.95 o.p. (ISBN 0-688-03001-7). Morrow.
--Streisand. 1975. pap. 1.50 o.p. (ISBN 0-685-57553-5, LB298DK, Leisure Bks). Nordon Pubns.
Black, Jonathan & Dumbleton, John. Clinical Biomechanics: A Case History Approach. (Illus.). 416p. 1980. text ed. 40.00x (ISBN 0-443-08022-4). Churchill.
Black, K., jt. auth. see Huebner, A.
Black, K., jt. auth. see Huebner, S. S.
Black, Kenneth, jt. auth. see Russell, George H.
Black, Kenneth, jt. auth. see Russell, Hugh.
Black, Laura. Glendraco. LC 77-5017. 1977. 10.00 o.p. (ISBN 0-312-32917-2). St Martin.
--Ravenburn. (Large Print Bks.). 1980. lib. bdg. 16.95 (ISBN 0-8161-3129-5). G K Hall.
--Wild Cat. 416p. 1981. pap. 2.75 (ISBN 0-446-95754-2). Warner Bks.
Black, Lionel. The Penny Murders. 1979. pap. 1.95 (ISBN 0-380-48090-5, 48090). Avon.
Black, M. & Smalley, W. A., eds. On Language, Culture & Religion: In Honor of Eugene A. Nida. (Approaches to Semiotics Ser: No. 56). (Illus.). 386p. 1974. text ed. 45.90x (ISBN 90-2793-236-0). Mouton.
Black, Maggie & Howard, Pat. Eating Naturally: Recipes for Food with Fibre. 148p. 1981. 21.00 (ISBN 0-571-11602-7, Pub. by Faber & Faber); pap. 9.50 (ISBN 0-571-11603-5). Merrimack Bk Serv.
Black, Martha E. Speech Therapy in the Public Schools. LC 72-81498. (Studies in Communicative Disorders Ser). 1972. pap. 1.95 (ISBN 0-672-61287-9). Bobbs.
Black, Mary E. The Key to Weaving. rev. ed. (Illus.). 1980. 24.95 (ISBN 0-02-511170-1). Macmillan.
Black, Matthew. Aramaic Approach to the Gospels & Acts. 3rd ed. 1967. 32.00x (ISBN 0-19-826157-8). Oxford U Pr.
Black, Matthew, ed. see Beasley-Murray, G. R.
Black, Matthew, ed. see Bruce, F. F.
Black, Matthew, ed. see Martin, Ralph P.
Black, Matthew W., ed. see Shakespeare, William.
Black, Max. Critical Thinking. 2nd ed. 1952. text ed. 16.50 (ISBN 0-13-194092-9). P-H.
Black, Max, ed. Importance of Language. 1968. pap. 4.95 (ISBN 0-8014-9077-4, CP77). Cornell U Pr.
--The Social Theories of Talcott Parsons: A Critical Examination. LC 75-40325. (Arcturus Books Paperbacks). 384p. 1976. pap. 8.95 (ISBN 0-8093-0759-6). S Ill U Pr.
Black, Max, jt. ed. see Bloomfield, Morton W.
Black, Max, ed. see Frege, Gottlob.
Black, Max, ed. see Frye, Northrop, et al.
Black, Merle. Social Science Perspectives of the South, Vol. 1. Reed, John S., ed. 1981. price not set (ISBN 0-677-16260-X). Gordon.
Black, Nancy B. & Weidman, Bette S., eds. White on Red: Images of the American Indian. 1976. 17.50 (ISBN 0-8046-9084-7, Natl U). Kennikat.
Black, Nelson W., ed. see Huttman, Elizabeth D.
Black, P. Strength of Materials. 1966. 22.00 (ISBN 0-08-011555-1). Pergamon.
Black, Perry. Brain Dysfunction in Children: Etiology, Diagnosis & Management. 200p. 1980. text ed. 19.00 (ISBN 0-89004-022-2). Raven.
Black, Perry O. Diesel Engine Manual. 3rd ed. LC 64-23154. (Illus.). 480p. 1964. 10.95 (ISBN 0-672-23199-9, 23199). Audel.
Black, Peter M. The Complete Handbook of Orchid Growing. 160p. 1981. 19.95 (ISBN 0-8129-0951-8). Times Bks.
Black, Renee M., jt. ed. see Black, Frank G.
Black, Rhona M. Elements of Palaeontology. (Illus.). 1970. 54.50 (ISBN 0-521-07445-2); pap. 16.95x (ISBN 0-521-09615-4). Cambridge U Pr.
--Observer's Book of Fossils. (Observer Bks.). (Illus.). 1977. 4.95 (ISBN 0-684-15209-6, ScribT). Scribner.
Black, William C. Fly-Fishing the Rockies. (Illus.). 160p. 1976. 9.95 o.p. (ISBN 0-87108-507-0). Pruett.
Black, William T. Mormon Athletes. (Illus.). 6.95 (ISBN 0-87747-842-2). Deseret Bk.
Blackaby, F. T. British Economic Policy: Nineteen Sixty to Nineteen Seventy-Four. LC 77-28282. (NIESR Economic & Social Policy Studies: No. 31). (Illus.). 1979. 67.50 (ISBN 0-521-22042-4); pap. 19.95x (ISBN 0-521-29597-1). Cambridge U Pr.
Blackaby, Linda, et al. In Focus: A Guide to Using Films. (Cine Information Ser.). 1980. 20.00 o.p. (ISBN 0-918432-23-5); pap. 9.95 (ISBN 0-918432-22-7). NY Zoetrope.
Blackall, Eric A. Goethe & the Novel. LC 75-38426. 344p. 1976. 22.50x (ISBN 0-8014-0978-0). Cornell U Pr.
Blackall, W. E., jt. ed. see Grieve, B. J.
Blackbeard, Bill & Williams, Martin, eds. The Smithsonian Collection of Newspaper Comics. LC 77-608090. (Illus.). 336p. 1978. 29.95; pap. 14.95 (ISBN 0-87474-167-X). Smithsonian.
Blackbourn, David. Class, Religion, & Local Politics: The Centre Party in Wurttemberg Before 1914. LC 80-11878. 288p. 1980. text ed. 25.00x (ISBN 0-300-02464-9). Yale U Pr.
Blackburn, Alexander. The Cold War of Kitty Pentecost: A Novel. LC 78-58533. (A Writers West Book). 232p. 1979. 8.95 o.p. (ISBN 0-8040-9015-7); pap. 4.50 (ISBN 0-8040-9011-4). Swallow.
Blackburn, Charles. Needlepoint Designs for Traditional Furniture. LC 79-67255. (Illus.). 160p. 1980. 17.50 (ISBN 0-8149-0815-2); pap. 12.95 (ISBN 0-8149-0835-7). Vanguard.
--The Pillow Book. LC 77-93302. (Illus.). 1979. 12.95 (ISBN 0-8149-0799-7); pap. 7.95 (ISBN 0-8149-0801-2). Vanguard.
Blackburn, Emily, jt. auth. see Thomas, Art.
Blackburn, Graham. The Illustrated Encyclopedia of Ships, Boats, Vessels & Other Water-Borne Craft. LC 78-16565. (Illus.). 1978. 17.95 (ISBN 0-87951-082-X). Overlook Pr.
--The Overlook Illustrated Dictionary of Nautical Terms. LC 80-39640. (Illus.). 416p. 1981. 19.95 (ISBN 0-87951-124-9). Overlook Pr.
Blackburn, Henry. Randolph Caldecott. LC 68-21757. 1969. Repr. of 1886 ed. 15.00 (ISBN 0-8103-3490-9). Gale.
Blackburn, Joyce. A Book of Praises. 128p. (Orig.). (YA) 1980. pap. 3.95 (ISBN 0-310-42061-X). Zondervan.
Blackburn, Laurence H. God Wants You to Be Well. 160p. 1974. pap. 3.75 (ISBN 0-8192-1189-3). Morehouse.
Blackburn, Lois H. A Handbook for Planning & Conducting Tennis Tournaments. (Illus.). 1979. pap. 4.50 (ISBN 0-938822-04-7). USTA.
Blackburn, Lois J. Florida Food Fare: & Food for Thought. (Illus.). 120p. (Orig.). 1980. pap. 5.00 (ISBN 0-938910-00-0). Pecalhen.
Blackburn, Lorraine A., jt. ed. see Brewton, John E.
Blackburn, Paul, tr. Proensa: An Anthology of Troubador Poetry. LC 75-7466. 1978. 15.95x (ISBN 0-520-02985-2). U of Cal Pr.
Blackburn, Paul, tr. see Cortazar, Julio.
Blackburn, Paul, et al, trs. see Bishop, Elizabeth & Brasil, Emanuel.
Blackburn, R. M., ed. see Stewart, Alexander, et al.
Blackburn, Robin, ed. Revolution & Class Struggle: A Reader in Marxist Politics. LC 77-1640. 1978. text ed. 24.75x (ISBN 0-391-00712-2). Humanities.
Blackburn, Robin, jt. ed. see Anderson, Perry.
Blackburn, Robin, ed. see Debray, Regis.
Blackburn, Roderic H. Cherry Hill: The History & Collections of a Van Rensselaer Family. LC 75-44844. (Illus.). 186p. 1976. 16.00x (ISBN 0-89062-098-9, Pub. by Historic Cherry); pap. 11.95x (ISBN 0-89062-099-7). Pub Ctr Cult Res.
Blackburn, Roderic H., jt. auth. see Piwonka, Ruth.
Blackburn, S., ed. Meaning & Reference. 192p. 1975. 29.50x (ISBN 0-521-20720-7). Cambridge U Pr.
Blacker, Carmen. Japanese Enlightenment. (University of Cambridge Oriental Pubns). 1964. 32.50 (ISBN 0-521-04267-4). Cambridge U Pr.
Blacker, Charles P. Eugenics: Galton & After. LC 78-20452. 1981. Repr. of 1952 ed. 25.00 (ISBN 0-88355-832-7). Hyperion Conn.
Blacker, Ken, ed. Vintage Bus Annual, No. 1. (Illus.). 96p. 1979. 16.50x (ISBN 0-906116-09-0). Intl Pubns Serv.
Blackey, Robert. Modern Revolutions & Revolutionists: A Bibliography. LC 75-45301. (War-Peace Bibliography Ser.: No. 5). 257p. 1976. text ed. 17.00 (ISBN 0-87436-223-7). ABC-Clio.
Blackham, Garth J. & Silberman, Adolph. Modification of Child & Adolescent Behavior. 3rd ed. 1979. pap. text ed. 10.95x (ISBN 0-534-00725-2). Wadsworth Pub.
Blackham, H. J. Education for Personal Autonomy. 211p. 1978. pap. text ed. 7.40x (ISBN 0-7199-0936-8, Pub. by Bedford England). Renouf.
Blackham, H. J., ed. Moral & Religious Education in County Primary Schools. (General Ser.). (Orig.). 1976. pap. text ed. 5.75x (ISBN 0-85633-115-5, NFER). Humanities.
Blackhurst & Berdine. An Introduction to Special Education. 1981. text ed. 15.95 (ISBN 0-316-09060-3); tchrs'. manual free (ISBN 0-316-09061-1). Little.
Blackie, C. Geographical Etymology: A Dictionary of Place-Names Giving Their Derivations. LC 68-17916. 1968. Repr. of 1887 ed. 15.00 (ISBN 0-8103-3882-3). Gale.
Blackie, M. J., jt. auth. see Dent, J. B.
Blackie, M. J. & Dent, J. B., eds. Information Systems for Agriculture. (Illus.). 1979. 28.50x (ISBN 0-85334-829-4). Intl Ideas.
Blacking, John. How Musical Is Man? LC 72-6710. (John Danz Lecture Ser). (Illus.). 132p. 1973. 9.50 (ISBN 0-295-95218-0, WP72); pap. 5.95 (ISBN 0-295-95338-1); tapes 17.50 (ISBN 0-295-75510-5); c-60 cassette 17.50 (ISBN 0-295-75517-2). U of Wash Pr.
Blacking, John & Kealiinohomoku, Joann W., eds. The Performing Arts: Music & Dance. (World Anthropology Ser.). 1979. text ed. 44.00x (ISBN 90-279-7870-0). Mouton.
Blackistone, Mick & McLendon, Charles. Signage Communication Standards. (Illus.). 192p. 1982. 24.95 (ISBN 0-07-005740-0, P&RB). McGraw.
Blackith, R. E., tr. see Gabe, M.
Blackler, F. H. & Brown, C. A. Job Redesign & Management Control. LC 78-60430. 1978. 22.95 (ISBN 0-03-046210-X). Praeger.
--Whatever Happened to Shell's New Philosophy of Management? 184p. 1980. text ed. 29.00x (ISBN 0-566-00306-6, Pub. by Gower Pub Co England). Renouf.
Blackman, Clifford L. Our Foolish Ways. 1981. 5.75 (ISBN 0-8062-1718-9). Carlton.
Blackman, Edward B, jt. auth. see Abrams, Edwin D.
Blackman, James R. The Big Book of Tricks & Magic. (gr. 2 up). 1966. 3.95 (ISBN 0-394-80632-8, BYR). Random.
Blackman, Laura. Marina. 1981. pap. 2.95 (ISBN 0-451-09721-1, E9721, Sig). NAL.
Blackman, Martin E. Representing the Professional Athlete, Nineteen Seventy-Eight. LC 78-58673. (Patents, Copyrights, Trademarks, & Literary Property Course Handbook Ser.: 1978-1979). 1978. pap. text ed. 20.00 o.p. (ISBN 0-686-59560-2, G4-3641). PLI.
Blackman, Martin E. & Hochberg, Phillip R. Representing Professional Athletes & Teams 1980. LC 80-81911. (Real Estate Law & Practice Course Handbook Ser.). 699p. 1980. pap. text ed. 25.00 (ISBN 0-686-68830-9, G4-3678). PLI.
Blackman, Murray. A Guide to Jewish Themes in American Fiction, 1940-1980. LC 80-24953. 271p. 1981. lib. bdg. 15.00 (ISBN 0-8108-1380-7). Scarecrow.
Blackman, Philip. Ethics of the Fathers. 166p. 1980. pap. 3.95 (ISBN 0-910818-15-0). Judaica Pr.
Blackman, R. L., et al. Insect Cytogenetics. (Royal Entomological Society of London Symposium Ser.). 272p. 1981. 69.95 (ISBN 0-470-27126-4). Halsted Pr.
Blackman, Rodger. Aphids. (Invertebrate Types Ser.). (Illus.). 176p. 1981. pap. 12.00 (ISBN 0-08-025943-X). Pergamon.
Blackman, Sheldon, jt. auth. see Goldstein, Kenneth M.
Blackmore, D. R. & Thomas, A. Fuel Economy of the Gasoline Engine. LC 77-3916. 1977. 27.95 (ISBN 0-470-99132-1). Halsted Pr.
Blackmore, Jane. Hawkridge. 1976. pap. 1.95 (ISBN 0-441-31930-0). Ace Bks.
--Perilous Waters. 1981. pap. 1.50 (ISBN 0-440-17309-4). Dell.
Blackmur, R. P. Language As Gesture. LC 80-28610. (Morningside Book Ser.). 448p. 1981. pap. 8.50 (ISBN 0-231-05295-2). Columbia U Pr.
Blackmur, R. P., ed. Henry Adams. LC 79-1812. 1980. 19.95 (ISBN 0-15-139997-2). HarBraceJ.
Blacksell, Mark. Post-War Europe: A Political Geography. LC 77-82814. (Illus.). 1978. lib. bdg. 22.00x (ISBN 0-89158-822-1). Westview.
Blacksell, Mark & Gilg, Andrew. The Countryside: Planning & Change. (Resource Management Ser.: No. 2). (Illus.). 288p. (Orig.). 1981. text ed. 35.00x (ISBN 0-04-711008-2, 2599); pap. text ed. 17.50x (ISBN 0-04-711009-0, 2560). Allen Unwin.
Blackshear, P. J. Key References in Internal Medicine. 1981. pap. text ed. write for info. (ISBN 0-443-08079-8). Churchill.
Blackstock, Charity. A House Possessed. 222p. 1976. Repr. of 1962 ed. lib. bdg. 12.95x (ISBN 0-89244-077-5). Queens Hse.
Blackstock, L. S. Ruy Lopez: Breyer System. 1976. 15.95 (ISBN 0-7134-3124-5, Pub. by Batsford England); pap. 12.50 (ISBN 0-7134-3142-3). David & Charles.
Blackstock, Mary L. The Beachcomber. 3.95 o.p. (ISBN 0-685-48829-2). Nortex Pr.
Blackstock, Paul W. & Schaf, Frank, Jr. Intelligence, Espionage, Counterespionage & Covert Operations: A Guide to Information Sources. LC 74-11567. (International Relations Information Guide Ser.: Vol. 2). 1978. 30.00 (ISBN 0-8103-1323-5). Gale.
Blackstock, Paul W., tr. see Solzhenitsyn, Aleksandr.
Blackstone, Bernard. Byron: A Survey. 320p. 1975. text ed. 22.00x (ISBN 0-582-48354-9); pap. text ed. 13.95 (ISBN 0-582-48355-7). Longman.
--Virginia Woolf. Dobree, Bonamy, et al, eds. Bd. with E. M. Forster. Warner, Rex; Katherine Mansfield. Gordon, Ian A. LC 63-63095. (British Writers & Their Work Ser: Vol. 3). 1964. pap. 2.35x (ISBN 0-8032-5652-3, BB 452, Bison). U of Nebr Pr.
Blackstone, Harry. Blackstone's Modern Card Tricks. rev. ed. LC 58-5566. 1958. 5.95 o.p. (ISBN 0-385-00305-6). Doubleday.
Blackstone, Harry, Jr. There's One Born Every Minute. 1978. pap. 1.50 o.s.i. (ISBN 0-515-04465-2). Jove Pubns.
Blackstone, Tessa. Education & Day Care for Young Children in Need: The American Experience. 72p. 1973. pap. text ed. 1.90x (ISBN 0-7199-0875-2, Pub. by Bedford England). Renouf.
Blackstone, Sir William. Commentaries on the Law of England, 4 vols. Berkowitz, David S. & Thorne, Samuel E., eds. LC 77-86570. (Classics of English Legal History in the Modern Era Ser.: Vol. 10). 2025p. 1979. Set. lib. bdg. 160.00 (ISBN 0-8240-3059-1). Garland Pub.
--Tracts Chiefly Relating to the Antiquities & Laws of England. 3rd ed. 1979. Repr. of 1771 ed. lib. bdg. 30.00x (ISBN 0-87991-750-4). Porcupine Pr.
Blackstone, William T. & Heslep, Robert D., eds. Social Justice & Preferential Treatment: Women & Racial Minorities in Education & Business. LC 76-28921. 216p. 1977. pap. 5.95x (ISBN 0-8203-0434-4). U of Ga Pr.
Blackwelder, Richard E. Taxonomy: A Text & Reference Book. LC 67-13520. 1967. 33.50 (ISBN 0-471-07800-X). Wiley.
Blackwelder, Richard E. & Arnett, Ross H., Jr. The Tiger Beetles, Ground Beetles, & Water Beetles: Families 1-9, Part 1, 10 parts. (Checklist of Beetles, Yellow Version). 1977. 20.00 o.p. (ISBN 0-89140-016-8); 200.00 set o.p. (ISBN 0-686-16918-2). World Natural Hist.
Blackwelder, Sheila K. Science for All Seasons. (Human Science Ser.). (Illus.). 272p. 1980. 11.95 (ISBN 0-13-795286-4, Spec); pap. 5.95 (ISBN 0-13-795278-3). P-H.
Blackwell, et al. Contemporary Cases Consumer Behavior. 1977. 10.95. Dryden Pr.
Blackwell, Alice S. Lucy Stone: Pioneer of Woman's Rights. LC 77-164111. (Illus.). viii, 301p. 1971. Repr. of 1930 ed. 18.00 (ISBN 0-8103-3824-6). Gale.
Blackwell, Alice S., tr. Some Spanish-American Poets. LC 68-22694. (Eng. & Span.). 1968. Repr. of 1937 ed. 15.00x (ISBN 0-8196-0217-5). Biblo.
Blackwell, David. Basic Statistics. LC 69-16250. 1969. text ed. 12.95 o.p. (ISBN 0-07-005531-9, C); instructors' commentary 1.50 o.p. (ISBN 0-07-005544-0). McGraw.
Blackwell, David A. & Girshick, M. A. Theory of Games & Statistical Decisions. 368p. 1980. pap. 5.00 (ISBN 0-486-63831-6). Dover.
Blackwell, Gene. The Private Investigator. LC 79-4560. (Illus.). 1979. 16.95 (ISBN 0-913708-34-8). Butterworths.
Blackwell, Jim, jt. auth. see Firestone, Eve.
Blackwell, Liz. The Craft of Crocheted Afghans. LC 73-5169. (Illus.). 96p. 1973. pap. 3.95 o.p. (ISBN 0-684-13574-4, SL472, ScribT). Scribner.
Blackwell, Marian. Care of the Mentally Retarded. 1979. 15.95 (ISBN 0-316-09890-6). Little.
Blackwell, Muriel F. The Secret Dream. (gr. 6-8). 1981. 7.95 (ISBN 0-8054-4804-7). Broadman.
Blackwell, Peter M., et al. Sentences & Other Systems: A Language & Learning Curriculum for Hearing-Impaired Children. 1978. 11.75 (ISBN 0-88200-118-3). Bell Assn Deaf.
Blackwell, Richard, tr. see Wolff, Christian.
Blackwell, Robert B. & Joynt, Robert R. Mainstreaming: What to Expect...What to Do. 1980. 15.95 (ISBN 0-87804-416-7). Mafex.
Blackwell, Robert B. & Joynt, Robert R., eds. Learning Disabilities Handbook for Teachers. 208p. 1976. text ed. 16.50 (ISBN 0-398-02234-8). C C Thomas.
Blackwell, Roger D. & Talarzyk, W. Wayne. Consumer Attitudes Toward Health Care & Medical Malpractice. LC 77-78191. 1977. pap. 9.95 o.p. (ISBN 0-88244-155-8). Grid Pub.

Blackwell, Thomas. Letters Concerning Mythology. LC 75-27887. (Renaissance & the Gods Ser.: Vol. 42). (Illus.). 1976. Repr. of 1748 ed. lib. bdg. 73.00 (ISBN 0-8240-2091-X). Garland Pub.
Blackwell, Vera, tr. see Havel, Vaclav.
Blackwell, William L. Industrialization of Russia: An Historical Perspective. LC 79-107304. (AHM Europe Since 1500 Ser.). 1970. pap. 5.95x (ISBN 0-88295-703-1). AHM Pub.
Blackwood, Andrew W. The Funeral. (Source Book for Ministers Ser.). 1972. pap. 4.95 (ISBN 0-8010-0576-0). Baker Bk.
Blackwood, Andrew W., Jr. In All Your Ways: A Study of Proverbs. 1980. pap. 3.95 (ISBN 0-8010-0770-4). Baker Bk.
--The Voice from the Cross. (Minister's Paperback Library Ser.). 1978. pap. 1.95 (ISBN 0-8010-0742-9). Baker Bk.
Blackwood, B. G. The Lancashire Gentry & the Great Rebellion 1640-60. (Illus.). 1978. text ed. 33.75x (ISBN 0-7190-1334-8). Humanities.
Blackwood, Caroline. The Fate of Mary Rose. 256p. 1981. 11.95 (ISBN 0-671-42321-5). Summit Bks.
--The Stepdaughter. LC 77-3500. 1977. 6.95 o.p. (ISBN 0-684-14934-6, ScribT). Scribner.
Blackwood, George, jt. auth. see Levin, Murray B.
Blackwood, R. T., jt. ed. see Herman, A. L.
Blade, Melinda K. The Education of Women in the Italian Renaissance. Ide, Arthur F., ed. LC 79-19011. (Woman in History Ser.: Vol. 21). (Illus.). 90p. (Orig.). 1981. 20.00 (ISBN 0-86663-024-4); pap. 14.95 (ISBN 0-86663-050-3). Ide Hse.
Bladel, Roderick. Walter Kerr: An Analysis of His Criticism. LC 76-3721. 216p. 1976. 10.00 (ISBN 0-8108-0917-6). Scarecrow.
Blades, Dudley. Spiritual Healing. 128p. (Orig.). 1980. pap. 4.95 o.s.i. (ISBN 0-686-65587-7). Newcastle Pub.
Blades, James. Orchestral Percussion Technique. 2nd ed. 94p. 1973. pap. 7.75x (ISBN 0-19-318803-1). Oxford U Pr.
--Percussion Instruments & Their History. new ed. (Illus.). 1978. 46.00 (ISBN 0-571-04832-3, Pub. by Faber & Faber); pap. 15.95 o.p. (ISBN 0-571-10360-X). Merrimack Bk Serv.
Blades, William. Books in Chains & Other Bibliographical Papers. LC 68-30610. 1968. Repr. of 1892 ed. 15.00 (ISBN 0-8103-3298-1). Gale.
Blagowidow, George. Optimum Book Marketing of Trade Books. (Illus.). 222p. 1980. pap. cancelled (ISBN 0-88254-522-1). Hippocrene Bks.
Blagrove, Luanna C. Business Problems & Solutions for Proprietors & Partnerships. 160p. 1981. 24.95; pap. 19.95 (ISBN 0-9604466-9-9). Blagrove Pubns.
--How to Have an Ideal Business Client in Four Months. (Illus.). 67p. (Orig.). 1981. pap. 9.95 (ISBN 0-9604466-6-4). Blagrove Pubns.
--How to Start & Operate a Business Manual. (Illus.). 175p. 1981. 24.95 (ISBN 0-9604466-4-8). Blagrove Pubns.
--Introduction to Proprietor & Partnership Businesses. 160p. 1981. 24.95; pap. 19.95. Blagrove Pubns.
--Management for Proprietors & Partnerships. (Illus.). 165p. 1981. text ed. 24.95 (ISBN 0-9604466-7-2). Blagrove Pubns.
--The Professional's Business Guide for Proprietor & Partnerships. rev. ed. (Illus.). 185p. 1981. 29.95 (ISBN 0-9604466-5-6). Blagrove Pubns.
--Strategy for Minority Businesses. 67p. (Orig.). 1980. pap. 5.95. Blagrove Pubns.
--Untapped Profits by Professionals in the Small Business Field. (Illus.). 169p. 1980. 29.95 (ISBN 0-9604466-2-1). Blagrove Pubns.
--Untold Facts About the Small Business Game. (Illus.). 171p. (Orig.). 1980. 24.95 (ISBN 0-9604466-1-3); pap. 19.95 (ISBN 0-9604466-0-5). Blagrove Pubns.
Blaguy, John. The Foundation of Moral Goodness, 2 vols. in 1. Wellek, Rene, ed. LC 75-11194. (British Philosophers & Theologians of the 17th & 18th Centuries: Vol. 1). 1976. Repr. of 1729 ed. lib. bdg. 42.00 (ISBN 0-8240-1750-1). Garland Pub.
Blaikie, M. P., et al. The Struggle for Basic Needs in Nepal. (Illus.). 100p. (Orig.). 1980. pap. 6.50 (ISBN 92-64-12101-3). OECD.
Blaikie, W. G. & Matthews, C. D. A Manual of Bible History. rev. ed. 432p. 1940. 13.95 (ISBN 0-471-07008-4). Wiley.
Blaikie, Walter B. Itinerary of Prince Charles Edward Stuart. 1976. 12.50x (ISBN 0-7073-0103-3, Pub. by Scottish Academic Pr Scotland). Columbia U Pr.
Blaikie, William G. The Book of Joshua. 1978. 14.00 (ISBN 0-686-12943-1). Klock & Klock.
--David, King of Israel. Date not set. 14.50 (ISBN 0-86524-054-X). Klock & Klock.
--The First Book of Samuel. 1978. 13.50 (ISBN 0-686-12946-6). Klock & Klock.
--The Second Book of Samuel. 1978. 13.50 (ISBN 0-686-12947-4). Klock & Klock.
Blaiklock, E. M. Acts of the Apostles. (Tyndale New Testament Commentary). 1959. pap. 2.65 o.p. (ISBN 0-8028-1404-2). Eerdmans.
--Blaiklock's Handbook to the Bible. 1981. pap. 5.95 (ISBN 0-8007-5055-1). Revell.
--The Pastoral Epistles. 128p. 1972. pap. 3.50 (ISBN 0-310-21233-2). Zondervan.
Blaiklock, E. M. & Wood, A. S. Bathsheba to Rehoboam - Man & Sin. (Bible Characters & Doctrines). 1972. pap. 1.75 o.p. (ISBN 0-8028-1461-1). Eerdmans.
Blaiklock, E. M., tr. see Thomas a Kempis.
Blain, A. N. Pilots & Management. 1972. 21.00x o.p. (ISBN 0-8464-0720-5). Beekman Pubs.
Blain, Daniel & Barton, Michael, eds. The History of American Psychiatry: A Teaching & Research Guide. LC 78-78396. (Task Force Reports: 15). 44p. 1979. pap. 5.00 (ISBN 0-685-95863-9, P146-0). Am Psychiatric.
Blaine, Harry R., jt. auth. see Sandver, Marcus H.
Blaine, Marge. The Terrible Thing That Happened at Our House. LC 80-15280. (Illus.). 40p. (ps-3). 1980. Repr. of 1975 ed. 8.95 (ISBN 0-590-07780-5, Four Winds). Schol Bk Serv.
Blaine, Tom R. Prevent That Heart Attack. 6.95 (ISBN 0-8065-0299-1). Citadel Pr.
Blainey, Geoffrey. The Causes of War. LC 73-2016. 1975. pap. 6.95 (ISBN 0-02-903590-2). Free Pr.
Blair, Adam. History of the Waldenses: 1832 Ed, 2 vols. Set. 185.00 (ISBN 0-686-12404-9). Church History.
Blair, Alan, tr. see Bergman, Ingmar.
Blair, Alan, tr. see Lagerkvist, Par.
Blair, Alex. Blood Is Not Enough: Stories of One Sq. Mile. (Illus.). 172p. (Orig.). 1981. pap. 3.50 (ISBN 0-938918-00-1). Chong-Donnie.
Blair, Alpha. Through Eyes of Evil. 1981. pap. 2.50 (ISBN 0-8439-0865-3, Leisure Bks). Nordon Pubns.
Blair, Carole L. & Salerno, Elizabeth M. The Expanding Family: Childbearing. LC 75-30278. 1976. pap. text ed. 11.95 (ISBN 0-316-09915-5). Little.
Blair, Carvel H. Seamanship: A Handbook for Oceanographers. LC 76-56349. (Illus.). 1977. 9.00x (ISBN 0-87033-228-7). Cornell Maritime.
Blair, Carvel H. & Ansel, Willits D. Chesapeake Bay: Notes & Sketches. LC 76-124311. (Illus.). 1970. 6.00 (ISBN 0-87033-148-5, Pub. by Tidewater). Cornell Maritime.
--A Guide to Fishing Boats & Their Gear. LC 68-19048. (Illus.). 1968. 6.00 (ISBN 0-87033-002-0). Cornell Maritime.
Blair, Clay, Jr. The Search for JFK. 1977. pap. 2.25 o.p. (ISBN 0-425-03354-6, Medallion). Berkley Pub.
--Survive! pap. 1.95 o.p. (ISBN 0-425-03309-0). Berkley Pub.
Blair, Clay, Jr. & Blair, Joan. The Search for JFK. LC 76-8257. (Illus.). (YA) 1976. 12.95 o.p. (ISBN 0-399-11418-1). Berkley Pub.
Blair, Clay, Jr., jt. auth. see Blair, Joan.
Blair, Cynthia. Once There Was a Fat Girl. 1981. pap. 1.95 (ISBN 0-449-14394-5, GM). Fawcett.
Blair, Dorothy, tr. see Bhely-Quenum, Olympe.
Blair, Dorothy S. African Literature in French. LC 75-39374. (Illus.). 1976. 49.50 (ISBN 0-521-21195-6). Cambridge U Pr.
Blair, Edward P. Deuteronomy, Joshua. LC 59-10454. (Layman's Bible Commentary Ser: Vol. 5). 1964. pap. 4.25 (ISBN 0-8042-3005-6). John Knox.
Blair, Eulalia. Breakfast & Brunch Dishes for Food Service Menu Planning. LC 74-34100. (Foodservice Menu Planning Ser.). 256p. 1975. 16.50 (ISBN 0-8436-2057-9). CBI Pub.
--Dishes for Special Occasions. LC 75-4684. (Foodservice Menu Planning Ser.). 1975. 16.50 (ISBN 0-8436-2058-7). CBI Pub.
Blair, Eulalia, ed. Salads & Salad Dressings for Food Service Menu Planning. LC 73-89528. (Foodservice Menu Planning Ser.). 1974. 16.50 (ISBN 0-8436-0576-6). CBI Pub.
Blair, Eulalia, ed. see Atkinson, Alta.
Blair, Eulalia C. Casseroles & Vegetables for Foodservice Menu Planning. LC 76-29357. (Cahners Foodservice Menu Planning Ser). 1976. 16.50 (ISBN 0-8436-2121-4). CBI Pub.
--Garnishes, Relishes & Sauces for Foodservice Menu Planning. LC 77-3292. (Foodservice Menu Planning Ser.). 1977. 16.50 (ISBN 0-8436-2173-7). CBI Pub.
--Luncheon & Supper Dishes for Foodservice Menu Planning. LC 72-92379. (Foodservice Menu Planning Ser.). 1973. 16.50 (ISBN 0-8436-0559-6). CBI Pub.
--Meat & Poultry Entrees for Foodservice Menu Planning. LC 78-9126. (Foodservice Menu Planning Ser.). (Illus.). 1978. 16.50 (ISBN 0-8436-2152-4). CBI Pub.
--Mini Meals for Food Service Menu Planning. LC 76-7073. (Foodservice Menu Planning Ser.). 1976. 16.50 (ISBN 0-8436-2102-8). CBI Pub.
--Quick to Fix Desserts. LC 80-13124. (Foodservice Menu Planning Ser.). 1980. 16.50 (ISBN 0-8436-2183-4). CBI Pub.
Blair, Eulilia C. Fish & Seafood Dishes for Foodservice Menu Planning. LC 75-25636. (Foodservice Menu Planning Ser.). 240p. 1975. 16.50 (ISBN 0-8436-2086-2). CBI Pub.
Blair, George S. Government at the Grass-Roots. 3rd ed. LC 80-84554. (Illus.). 1981. 15.95 (ISBN 0-913530-25-5); pap. 10.95x (ISBN 0-913530-24-7). Palisades Pub.
Blair, Gerry, jt. auth. see Musgrove, Bill.
Blair, Gertrude, jt. auth. see Engle, Fannie.
Blair, H., ed. see Nekrasov, V.
Blair, H. A., ed. Biological Effects of External Radiation. (Illus.). 1967. Repr. of 1954 ed. 21.75 o.s.i. (ISBN 0-02-841430-6). Hafner.
Blair, Hugh. Lectures on Rhetoric & Belles Lettres, 2 Vols. Harding, Harold F., ed. LC 65-13061. (Landmarks in Rhetoric & Public Address Ser). 1965. Set. 19.50x o.p. (ISBN 0-8093-0169-5). S Ill U Pr.
Blair, J. Allen. Living Obediently: Jonah. LC 63-18265. 1963. pap. 2.25 (ISBN 0-87213-050-9). Loizeaux.
--Living Peacefully: First Peter. 1959. pap. 3.50 (ISBN 0-87213-052-5). Loizeaux.
--Living Victoriously: Philippians. LC 62-290. 1962. pap. 2.75 (ISBN 0-87213-056-8). Loizeaux.
Blair, J. Antony & Johnson, Ralph H., eds. Informal Logic: The First International Symposium. LC 80-67674. 175p. (Orig.). 1980. pap. 9.95 (ISBN 0-918528-09-7). Edgepress.
Blair, J. W. Coleccion Navidena, No. 1. 1980. Repr. of 1977 ed. pap. 1.30 (ISBN 0-311-08201-7). Casa Bautista.
Blair, Jane N. The Gourmet's Bland Diet Cookbook. (Orig.). 1974. pap. 1.25 (ISBN 0-515-03306-5, V3306). Jove Pubns.
Blair, Joan & Blair, Clay, Jr. Return from the River Kwai. 320p. 1981. pap. 2.75 (ISBN 0-345-29007-0). Ballantine.
Blair, Joan, jt. auth. see Blair, Clay, Jr.
Blair, John. The Control of Oil. 1978. pap. 4.95 (ISBN 0-394-72532-8, V-532, Vin). Random.
Blair, Karen. The Club Woman As Feminist: True Womanhood Redefined, 1868 to 1914. LC 79-26390. 1980. text ed. 29.50x (ISBN 0-8419-0538-X). Holmes & Meier.
Blair, Karin. Meaning in Star Trek. LC 77-7438. (Illus.). 1978. 9.95 (ISBN 0-89012-010-2). Anima Pubns.
Blair, Lawrence. Rhythms of Vision. 1977. pap. 2.50 o.s.i. (ISBN 0-446-81232-3). Warner Bks.
Blair, Louis H., et al. Monitoring the Inpacts of Prison & Parole Services: An Initial Examination. (An Institute Paper). 88p. 1977. pap. 3.95 (ISBN 0-87766-201-0, 16900). Urban Inst.
Blair, P. H. An Introduction to Anglo-Saxon England. 2nd ed. LC 77-71404. (Illus.). 1977. 47.95 (ISBN 0-521-21650-8); pap. 10.95x (ISBN 0-521-29219-0). Cambridge U Pr.
Blair, Patricia, ed. Development in the People's Republic of China: A Selected Bibliography. LC 76-53149. (Occasional Papers: No. 8). 94p. 1976. 2.50 (ISBN 0-686-28696-0). Overseas Dev Council.
Blair, Robert. Tales of the Superstitions: Origins of the Lost Dutchman Legend. LC 35-35054. 1975. 8.95 (ISBN 0-685-67970-5); pap. 4.95 (ISBN 0-685-67971-3). AZ Hist Foun.
Blair, Robert W. & Vermont-Salas, Refugio. Spoken (Yucatec) Maya, Bk. 1, Lessons 1-12. 1979. pap. text ed. 19.00x (ISBN 0-87543-147-X). Lucas.
Blair, Roger D. & Vogel, Ronald J. The Cost of Health Insurance Administration. 128p. 1975. 21.95 (ISBN 0-669-00165-1). Lexington Bks.
Blair, Roger D. & Lanzillotti, Robert F., eds. The Conglomerate Corporation: An Antitrust Law & Economics Symposium. LC 80-22093. 288p. 1981. lib. bdg. 25.00 (ISBN 0-89946-051-8). Oelgeschlager.
Blair, Sam. Earl Campbell: The Driving Force. 1980. 8.95 (ISBN 0-8499-0259-2). Word Bks.
Blair, Susan, illus. The Three Billy-Goats Gruff. (Illus.). (gr. k-3). 1970. pap. 1.25 (ISBN 0-590-01613-X, Schol Pap); pap. 3.95 three billy goats gruff & gingerbread man (2 bks.) & 1 record (ISBN 0-590-04405-2). Schol Bk Serv.
Blair, T. & Fite, R. Weather Elements: Text in Elementary Meteorology. 5th ed. 1965. ref. ed. 17.95 (ISBN 0-13-947721-7). P-H.
Blair, Thomas. Oqua. LC 79-15861. Date not set. 10.95 (ISBN 0-87949-163-9). Ashley Bks.
Blair, Thomas L. Retreat to the Ghetto: The End of a Dream? 263p. 1977. 10.00 o.p. (ISBN 0-8090-8078-8); pap. 5.95 (ISBN 0-8090-0127-6). Hill & Wang.
Blair, Walter. Mark Twain & Huck Finn: 1855-1873. Frank, Michael B. & Sanderson, Kenneth M, eds. (California Library Reprint). 1974. 24.50x (ISBN 0-520-02521-0). U of Cal Pr.
Blair, Walter & Chandler, W. K. Approaches to Poetry. 2nd ed. LC 52-13690. 1953. 38.00x (ISBN 0-89197-027-4); pap. text ed. 18.95x. Irvington.
Blair, Walter, ed. see Twain, Mark.
Blair, Walter, et al. American Literature: A Brief History. rev. ed. 1974. pap. 6.95x o.p. (ISBN 0-673-05931-6). Scott F.
--Better Reading One: Factual Prose. 5th ed. 1963. 7.95x o.p. (ISBN 0-673-05209-5). Scott F.
--The Literature of the United States. 3rd ed. (Single volume edition). 1970. 17.95x (ISBN 0-673-05928-6). Scott F.
Blair, William & Hunt, Bruce. The Korean Pentecost & the Sufferings Which Followed. 1977. pap. 2.50 (ISBN 0-85151-244-5). Banner of Truth.
Blaisdell, Donald C. Government & Agriculture: Growth of Federal Farm Aid. LC 72-2365. (FDR & the Era of the New Deal Ser.). 217p. 1974. Repr. of 1940 ed. lib. bdg. 27.50 (ISBN 0-306-70488-9). Da Capo.
Blaisdell, Gus. Park City. LC 80-65768. (Illus.). 252p. 1981. 75.00. Aperture.
Blaisdell, Gus, jt. auth. see Baltz, Lewis.
Blaisdell, Gus, ed. see Connell, Evan S.
Blaisdell, Paul H. Three Centuries on Winnipesaukee. LC 75-10740. (Illus.). 16p. 1975. 2.95 (ISBN 0-912274-96-4). NH Pub Co.
Blakar, Rolv M. Studies of Familial Communication & Psychopathology: A Socio-Developmental Approach to Deviant Behavior. 192p. 1980. pap. 18.00x (ISBN 8-20001-999-3). Universitet.
Blake, Antonia. Lasting Love. (Orig.). 1981. pap. 1.50 (ISBN 0-440-14968-1). Dell.
Blake, B. J., jt. auth. see Dixon, R. M.
Blake, B. J., jt. ed. see Dixon, R. M.
Blake, Barbara. Good Morning, World. 40p. 1981. 3.50 (ISBN 0-8059-2777-8). Dorrance.
Blake, C. D. Fundamentals of Modern Agriculture. 516p. 1974. 14.00 o.p. (ISBN 0-424-05290-3, Pub. by Sydney U Pr); pap. 12.75x (ISBN 0-424-06930-X, Pub. by Sydney U Pr). Intl Schol Bk Serv.
Blake, C. Fred. Ethnic Groups & Social Change in a Chinese Market Town. (Asian Studies at Hawaii: No. 27). 192p. (Orig.). 1981. pap. 10.50x (ISBN 0-8248-0720-0). U Pr of Hawaii.
Blake, Claire. Greenhouse Gardening for Fun. (Illus.). 1967. pap. 3.95 (ISBN 0-688-06737-9). Morrow.
Blake, Daniel B. Ossicle Morphology of Some Recent Asteroids & Descriptions of Some West American Fossil Asteroids. (U. C. Publ. in Geological Sciences: Vol. 104). 1973. pap. 10.50x (ISBN 0-520-09472-7). U of Cal Pr.
Blake, David H., et al. Social Auditing: Evaluating the Impact of Corporate Programs. LC 76-2901. (Illus.). 1976. text ed. 18.95 o.p. (ISBN 0-275-56700-1); pap. text ed. 9.95 o.p. (ISBN 0-275-85710-7). Praeger.
Blake, Duane L. Dynamics of Human Relations in Vocational Education: The Development of Self-Confidence & a Sense of Mastery. LC 77-9416. 152p. 1979. pap. 10.00 (ISBN 0-910328-26-9). Carroll Pr.
Blake, Edith. Making of the Movie "Jaws". 1975. pap. 1.50 o.p. (ISBN 0-345-24882-1). Ballantine.
Blake, Fay M. The Strike in the American Novel. LC 72-623. 1972. 10.00 (ISBN 0-8108-0481-6). Scarecrow.
Blake, G. H. & Lawless, R. I., eds. The Changing Middle Eastern City. (Illus.). 273p. 1980. 28.50x. B&N.
Blake, Gary. The Status Book. LC 77-94863. 1978. pap. 3.95 (ISBN 0-385-13549-1, Dolp). Doubleday.
Blake, Henry. Talking with Horses. 1976. 9.95 (ISBN 0-87690-196-8). Dutton.
Blake, James N. Monty Monkey-Shines with Speech Sounds. (Illus.). 80p. 1973. pap. 8.75 (ISBN 0-398-02791-9). C C Thomas.
--Run Your Car on Sunshine: Using Solar Energy for a Solar Powered Car. LC 80-82734. (Illus.). 64p. 1981. lib. bdg. 12.95 (ISBN 0-915216-64-7); pap. 4.95 (ISBN 0-915216-65-5). Love Street.
--Speech Education Activities for Children. (Illus.). 136p. 1970. text ed. 14.50 photocopy ed. spiral (ISBN 0-398-00165-0). C C Thomas.
--Speech, Language & Learning Disorders: Education & Therapy. (Illus.). 172p. 1971. 12.75 (ISBN 0-398-00166-9). C C Thomas.
--Word Clowns & Sentence Circuses. (Illus.). 48p. 1973. pap. 5.75 (ISBN 0-398-02790-0). C C Thomas.
Blake, James Neal. A B C Phonics & Faces. (Illus.). 84p. 1972. pap. 9.75 (ISBN 0-398-02528-2). C C Thomas.
Blake, Jennifer. Golden Fancy. 1980. pap. 2.75 (ISBN 0-449-14369-4, GM). Fawcett.
Blake, John E., ed. Education in the History of Medicine. 1968. 14.25 o.s.i. (ISBN 0-02-841460-8). Hafner.
Blake, K., jt. auth. see McBee, M.
Blake, Kathryn. Educating Exceptional Pupils: An Introduction to Contemporary Practices. LC 80-15222. (Illus.). 528p. 1981. text ed. 15.95 (ISBN 0-201-00083-0). A-W.

--The Mentally Retarded: An Educational Psychology. (Special Education Ser.). (Illus.). 416p. 1976. 18.95x (ISBN 0-13-576280-4). P-H.
--Teaching the Retarded. LC 73-13719. (Special Education Ser.). (Illus.). 384p. 1974. 17.95 (ISBN 0-13-895276-0). P-H.
Blake, Kathryn A. College Reading Skills. (Illus.). 304p. 1973. pap. text ed. 9.95 (ISBN 0-13-150003-1). P-H.
Blake, Kathryn A. & McBee, Mary L. Essays. 1978. pap. text ed. 7.95 (ISBN 0-02-472160-3). Macmillan.
Blake, L. J. Antennas. (Electronic Technlogy Ser.). 1966. pap. 15.95 (ISBN 0-471-07928-6). Wiley.
Blake, Lamont V. Transmission Lines & Waveguides. LC 69-16039. (Electronic Engineering & Technology Ser). 1969. text ed. 17.95x (ISBN 0-471-07929-4). Wiley.
Blake, Maurice C. & Davis, Wilbur W. Boston Postmaks to Eighteen Ninety. LC 72-85120. (Illus.). 392p. 1974. Repr. of 1949 ed. 35.00x (ISBN 0-88000-040-6). Quarterman.
Blake, Michael. Natural Healer's Acupressure Handbook: G-Jo Fingertip Technique. (Illus.). 1977. 9.95 (ISBN 0-916878-06-6). Falkynor Bks.
Blake, Michael P. & Mitchell, William S., eds. Vibration & Acoustic Measurement Handbook. (Illus.). 1972. 34.50 (ISBN 0-8104-9195-8). Hayden.
Blake, N. F., ed. see Caxton, William.
Blake, Nicholas. The Dreadful Hollow. LC 53-7730. 1979. pap. 1.95 (ISBN 0-06-080493-9, P 493, PL). Har-Row.
--Minute for Murder. lib. bdg. 13.95x (ISBN 0-89966-246-3). Buccaneer Bks.
--The Morning After Death. LC 66-22042. 212p. 1980. pap. 1.95 (ISBN 0-06-080520-X, P 520, PL). Har-Row.
--The Private Wound. LC 68-15980. 224p. 1981. pap. 2.25 (ISBN 0-06-080531-5, PL). Har-Row.
--The Sad Variety. LC 64-18086. 1979. pap. 2.25 (ISBN 0-06-080495-5, P 495, PL). Har-Row.
Blake, O. & Walters, R. Politics of Global Economic Relations. (Illus.). 272p. 1976. pap. 9.95x (ISBN 0-13-684712-9). P-H.
Blake, Pamela. Peep-Show. LC 72-80750. (Illus.). 32p. (ps-3). 1973. 3.95g o.s.i. (ISBN 0-02-710700-0). Macmillan.
Blake, Patricia, ed. see Mayakovsky, Vladimir.
Blake, Quentin. Mister Magnolia. (gr. k-3). 1980. 8.95 (ISBN 0-224-01612-1, Pub. by Chatto Bodley Jonathan). Merrimack Bk Serv.
--Patrick. (Illus.). 32p. (gr. 4-7). 1980. 8.95 (ISBN 0-224-61463-0, Pub. by Chatto-Bodley-Jonathan). Merrimack Bk Serv.
Blake, Quentin, jt. auth. see Yeoman, John.
Blake, Ralph M., et al. Theories of Scientific Method: The Renaissance Through the Nineteenth Century. Madden, Edward H., ed. LC 60-8577. 350p. 1966. pap. 2.95 (ISBN 0-295-74010-8, WP2). U of Wash Pr.
Blake, Reed. Zion Trails. (Illus.). 1977. pap. 1.50 o.s.i. (ISBN 0-915272-09-1). Wasatch Pubs.
Blake, Reed H., jt. auth. see Harris, John S.
Blake, Robert. A Choice of Blake's Verse. Raines, Kathleen, ed. 1970. pap. 5.95 (ISBN 0-571-09268-3, Pub. by Faber & Faber). Merrimack Bk Serv.
--One Hundred & One Elephant Jokes. (Orig.). (YA) (gr. 7-12). 1964. pap. 0.95 (ISBN 0-515-01090-1, N1090). Jove Pubns.
Blake, Robert & Patten, John, eds. The Conservative Opportunity. 1976. text ed. 20.75x (ISBN 0-333-19971-5); pap. text ed. 10.50x (ISBN 0-333-19972-3). Humanities.
Blake, Robert R. & Mouton, Jane S. Building a Dynamic Corporation Through Grid Organization Development. Schein, Edgar, et al, eds. (Organization Development Ser). 1969. pap. text ed. 6.50 (ISBN 0-201-00612-X). A-W.
--Grid Approaches for Managerial Leadership in Nursing. Tapper, Mildred, ed. LC 80-21583. (Illus.). 158p. 1980. pap. text ed. 9.95 (ISBN 0-8016-0696-9). Mosby.
--Grid Approaches to Managing Stress. (Illus.). 196p. 1980. 15.50 (ISBN 0-398-04093-1). C C Thomas.
--Productivity & Creativity: A Social Dynamics Approach. 143p. 1981. 9.95 (ISBN 0-8144-5692-8). Am Mgmt.
--The Versatile Manager: A Grid Profile. LC 80-68466. 215p. 1981. 13.95 (ISBN 0-87094-222-0). Dow Jones-Irwin.
Blake, Robert R., et al. The Academic Administrator Grid: A Guide to Developing Effective Management Teams. LC 80-8908. (Higher Education Ser.). 1981. text ed. price not set (ISBN 0-87589-492-5). Jossey-Bass.
Blake, Roland P. Industrial Safety. 3rd ed. 1963. ref. ed. 15.95 (ISBN 0-13-463133-1). P-H.
Blake, S. F. Geographical Guide to Floras of the World. (Landmark Reprints in Plant Science). 1961. text ed. 40.00 (ISBN 0-86598-006-3). Allanheld.
Blake, Sidney F. & Atwood, A. C. Geographical Guide to Floras of the World: Pt. 1; Africa, Australia, North America, South America & Islands. 1967. Repr. of 1942 ed. 13.75 o.s.i. (ISBN 0-02-841470-5). Hafner.
Blake, Stephanie. Scarlet Kisses. LC 81-80079. 368p. (Orig.). 1981. pap. 2.95 (ISBN 0-87216-847-6). Playboy Pbks.
--Unholy Desires. LC 80-82849. 368p. (Orig.). 1981. pap. 2.95 (ISBN 0-87216-785-2). Playboy Pbks.
Blake, Stewart P. Managing for Responsive Research & Development. LC 77-26120. (Illus.). 1978. text ed. 21.95x (ISBN 0-7167-0036-0). W H Freeman.
Blake, Thomas M. The Practice of Electrocardiography. LC 80-13084. 1980. 18.95 (ISBN 0-87488-903-0); pap. 12.00 (ISBN 0-87488-997-9). Med Exam.
Blake, Vernon. The Way to Sketch: With Special Reference to Water Color. (Illus.). 144p. (Unabridged replication of 2nd ed.). 1981. pap. price not set (ISBN 0-486-24119-X). Dover.
Blake, Viola, jt. auth. see Christenson, Evelyn.
Blake, W. A., et al, eds. Spinning. (Engineering Craftsmen: No. D4). (Illus.). 1968. spiral bdg. 15.95x (ISBN 0-85083-009-5). Intl Ideas.
Blake, Wendon. The Color Book. (Illus.). 256p. 25.00 (ISBN 0-8230-0694-8). Watson-Guptill.
--Creative Color: A Practical Guide for Oil Painters. LC 79-1905. (Illus.). 176p. 1972. 21.95 o.p. (ISBN 0-8230-1035-X). Watson-Guptill.
Blake, William. Blake: Selected Poems & Letters. Bronowski, J., ed. (Poets Ser.). 1958. pap. 2.95 (ISBN 0-14-042042-8). Penguin.
--Blake's Illustrations to the Grave. 1978. pap. 7.50 o.s.i. (ISBN 0-913668-22-2). Ten Speed Pr.
--Blake's Job: William Blake's Illustrations of the Book of Job. Damon, S. Foster, ed. LC 66-13155. (Illus.). 66p. 1972. Repr. of 1966 ed. 10.00 (ISBN 0-87057-096-X, Pub. by Brown U Pr). Univ Pr of New England.
--Book of Thel: A Facsimile & a Critical Text. Bogen, Nancy, ed. LC 74-155857. (Illus.). 82p. 1971. 15.00 (ISBN 0-87057-127-3, Pub. by Brown U Pr). Univ Pr of New England.
--Complete Writings of William Blake, with Variant Readings. Keynes, Geoffrey, ed. (Oxford Standard Authors Ser.). 1966. 34.00 (ISBN 0-19-254157-9); pap. 9.95x (ISBN 0-19-281050-2). Oxford U Pr.
--The Marriage of Heaven & Hell. (Illus.). 82p. 1975. 19.95 (ISBN 0-19-212588-5). Oxford U Pr.
--Poems & Prophecies. Plowman, Max, ed. 1954. 6.00x (ISBN 0-460-00792-0, Evman); pap. 4.50 (ISBN 0-460-01792-6). Dutton.
--Prophetic Writings of William Blake, 2 Vols. Sloss, D. J. & Wallis, J. P., eds. (Oxford English Texts Ser). (Illus.). 1926. Set. 74.00x set (ISBN 0-19-811801-5). Oxford U Pr.
--Selected Poems. Gardner, Stanley, ed. 1973. pap. 3.75 (ISBN 0-340-08199-6). Dufour.
--Songs of Innocence & Experience. Bottrall, Margaret, ed. LC 70-127566. (Casebook Ser). 1970. pap. text ed. 2.50 o.s.i. (ISBN 0-87695-037-3). Aurora Pubs.
--William Blake's Writings, 2 vols. Bentley, G. E., ed. (Oxford English Texts Ser.). (Illus.). 1979. 185.00x (ISBN 0-19-811885-6). Oxford U Pr.
Blake, William, jt. ed. see Keynes, Geoffrey.
Blake, William D. My Time or Yours? (Orig.). 1979. pap. 1.95 (ISBN 0-532-23286-0). Manor Bks.
Blakeborough, Richard. Legends of Highwaymen & Others. LC 75-154493. (Illus.). 1971. Repr. of 1924 ed. 18.00 (ISBN 0-8103-3373-2). Gale.
Blakeley, Brian L. & Collins, Jacquelin. Documents in English History: Early Times to the Present. LC 74-18264. 448p. 1975. pap. text ed. 12.95 (ISBN 0-471-07946-4). Wiley.
Blakeley, Robert W. The Practice of Speech Pathology: A Clinical Diary. (Illus.). 240p. 1973. 14.75 (ISBN 0-398-02575-4). C C Thomas.
Blakeley, Walter R. Calculus for Engineering Technology. LC 67-29017. 1968. text ed. 20.95 (ISBN 0-471-07931-6). Wiley.
Blakely, Edward J., jt. auth. see Bradshaw, Ted K.
Blakely, Jack. Introduction to the Properties of Crystal Surfaces. 1973. text ed. 22.00 (ISBN 0-08-017641-0). Pergamon.
Blakely, James. Horses & Horse Sense: The Practical Science of Horse Husbandry. 1981. 17.95 (ISBN 0-8359-2887-X); text ed. 14.95 (ISBN 0-8359-2887-X); instr's. manual free (ISBN 0-8359-2888-8). Reston.
Blakely, Leslie. Teach Yourself Old English. (Teach Yourself Ser). pap. 2.95 o.p. (ISBN 0-679-10192-6). McKay.
Blakely, Mary K., jt. ed. see Kaufman, Gloria.
Blakely, Pat. What's Skin for? (Creative Question & Answer Library). 32p. (gr. 3-4). Date not set. PLB 5.75 (ISBN 0-87191-745-9); pap. 2.75 (ISBN 0-89812-214-7). Creative Ed. Postponed.
Blakely, Pat, ed. see Haislet, Barbara.
Blakely, Robert J. To Serve the Public Interest: Educational Broadcasting in the United States. 1979. 16.00x (ISBN 0-8156-2198-1); pap. 7.95x (ISBN 0-8156-0153-0). Syracuse U Pr.
Blakely, Robert L., ed. Biocultural Adaptation in Prehistoric America. LC 76-49155. (Southern Anthropological Society Ser: No. 11). 144p. 1977. pap. 6.50x (ISBN 0-8203-0417-4). U of Ga Pr.
Blakely, W. A., ed. American State Papers Bearing on Sunday Legislation. LC 79-122165. (Civil Liberties in American History Ser). 1970. Repr. of 1911 ed. lib. bdg. 75.00 (ISBN 0-306-71973-8). Da Capo.
Blakeman, John, et al. IPC: Interpersonal Communication Skills for Correctional Management. 118p. (Orig.). 1977. pap. text ed. 8.95x (ISBN 0-914234-69-2); Trainer Guide. pap. text ed. 12.95x (ISBN 0-914234-70-6). Human Res Dev Pr.
Blakemore, Colin. Mechanics of the Mind. LC 76-53515. (BBC Reith Lectures: 1976). 1977. 34.95 (ISBN 0-521-21559-5); pap. 8.95x (ISBN 0-521-29185-2). Cambridge U Pr.
Blakemore, Harold. British Nitrates & Chilean Politics, 1886-1896: Balmaceda & North. (Institute of Latin American Studies Monograph Ser: No. 4). (Illus.). 256p. 1974. text ed. 25.75x (ISBN 0-485-17704-8, Athlone Pr). Humanities.
Blaker, Alfred A. Field Photography: Beginning & Advanced Techniques. LC 75-33382. (Illus.). 1976. text ed. 26.95x (ISBN 0-7167-0518-4); field supplement incl. W H Freeman.
--Handbook for Scientific Photography. LC 77-24661. (Illus.). 1977. text ed. 28.95x (ISBN 0-7167-0285-1). W H Freeman.
--Photography: Art & Technique. LC 79-23536. (Illus.). 1980. text ed. 28.95x (ISBN 0-7167-1115-X); pap. text ed. 16.95x (ISBN 0-7167-1116-8); reference manual incl. W H Freeman.
Blaker, Charles W. The College Matchmaker. LC 80-67604. (Illus.). 56p. (Orig.). (gr. 11-12). 1980. pap. text ed. 3.25 (ISBN 0-9604614-0-X). Rekalb Pr.
Blaker, J. W., ed. see Rogers, R. R., et al.
Blaker, Michael. Japanese International Negotiating Behavior. LC 77-8056. (Studies of the East Asian Institute). 1977. 17.50x (ISBN 0-231-04130-6). Columbia U Pr.
Blaker, Richard. The Needle-Watcher: The Will Adams Story, British Samurai. LC 72-89743. 1973. pap. 7.95 (ISBN 0-8048-1094-X). C E Tuttle.
Blakeslee, Berton, ed. The Limb-Deficient Child. (Illus.). 1963. 32.50x (ISBN 0-520-00125-7). U of Cal Pr.
Blakeslee, David W. & Chinn, William G. Introductory Statistics & Probability: A Basis for Decision-Making. (gr. 11-12). 1975. text ed. 16.28 (ISBN 0-395-19992-1); instrs' guide 5.44 (ISBN 0-395-19991-3). HM.
Blakeslee, Grace. Wings O'er the Sea. 1980. 5.50 (ISBN 0-8233-0323-3). Golden Quill.
Blakeslee, Richard, et al. Dental Technology: Theory & Practice. LC 80-157. (Illus.). 1980. text ed. 24.95 (ISBN 0-8016-0695-0). Mosby.
Blakey, Ellen S., ed. see DeMers, Donald O., Jr. & Beilharz, Edwin A.
Blakey, Ellen S., ed. see Engstrand, Iris W.
Blakey, Ellen S., ed. see Garrett, Betty.
Blakey, Ellen S., ed. see Kratt, Mary.
Blakey, Ellen S., ed. see Lavender, David.
Blakey, Ellen S., ed. see Noel, Thomas.
Blakey, Ellen S., ed. see Pirtle, Caleb.
Blakey, G. Robert & Billings, Richard N. The Plot to Kill the President. 320p. 1981. 12.95 (ISBN 0-8129-0929-1). Times Bks.
Blakey, George T. Historians on the Homefront: American Propagandists for the Great War. LC 79-132825. 176p. 1970. 9.50x (ISBN 0-8131-1236-2). U Pr of Ky.
Blakstad, Michael. Risk Business: British Industrial Design Innovation. 1979. 10.00x (ISBN 0-85072-098-2). Nichols Pub.
Blalock, H., Jr. Theory Construction: From Verbal to Mathematical Formulations. LC 69-17478. 1969. pap. text ed. 10.95 (ISBN 0-13-913343-7). P-H.
Blalock, H. M., Jr., ed. Causal Models in the Social Sciences. LC 70-133304. 1971. text ed. 26.95x (ISBN 0-202-30076-5); pap. text ed. 13.95x (ISBN 0-202-30228-8). Aldine Pub.
--Measurement in the Social Sciences: Theories & Strategies. LC 73-89514. 512p. 1974. pap. text ed. 13.95x (ISBN 0-202-30272-5). Aldine Pub.
Blalock, Hubert M., Jr. Black-White Relations in the Nineteen Eighties: Towards a Long-Term Policy. LC 79-10224. 1979. 22.95 (ISBN 0-03-050461-9). Praeger.
Blalock, Hubert M., Jr. & Wilken, Paul H. Intergroup Processes: A Micro-Macro Perspective. LC 78-19856. 1979. 24.95 (ISBN 0-02-903620-8). Free Pr.
Blalock, Hubert M., Jr., ed. Sociological Theory & Research: A Critical Appraisal. LC 80-754. (Illus.). 1980. 24.95 (ISBN 0-02-903630-5). Free Pr.
Blalock, Jack E., Jr. It's All There If You Want It: And Here Is the Map. LC 80-69519. 250p. (Orig.). 1980. 12.95 (ISBN 0-9605156-1-5); pap. 10.95 (ISBN 0-9605156-1-5). Better Am Corp.
Blalock, Jane & Nettind, Dwayne. The Guts to Win. LC 77-7311. (Illus.). 158p. 1977. 7.95 (ISBN 0-914178-12-1). Golf Digest Bks.
Blalock, Joyce. Civil Liability of Law Enforcement Officers. 248p. 1974. photocopy ed. spiral 15.75 (ISBN 0-398-02864-8). C C Thomas.
Blamires, David. Characterization & Individuality in Wolfram's Parzival. 1966. 78.00 (ISBN 0-521-04271-2). Cambridge U Pr.
Blamires, Harry. The Secularist Heresy. 160p. 1980. pap. 4.95 (ISBN 0-89283-095-6). Servant.
Blanc, Albert D. So You Have Asthma! (Illus.). 280p. 1966. 11.50 (ISBN 0-398-00168-5). C C Thomas.
Blanc, Charles. Art in Ornament & Dress. LC 77-156923. (Tower Bks). (Illus.). 1971. Repr. of 1876 ed. 20.00 (ISBN 0-8103-3922-6). Gale.
Blanc, Charles Le see Bodde, Derk.
Blanc, F. L., jt. auth. see Foote, Richard H.
Blanc, Jacques Le see LeBlanc, Jacques.
Blance, Ellen, et al. Monster Books: Set 1, 12 bks. Incl. Monster Comes to the City (ISBN 0-8372-0826-2); Monster Looks for a House (ISBN 0-8372-0827-0); Monster Cleans His House (ISBN 0-8372-0828-9); Monster Looks for a Friend (ISBN 0-8372-0829-7); Monster on the Bus (ISBN 0-8372-0830-0); Monster Meets Lady Monster (ISBN 0-8372-0831-9); Monster Goes to the Museum (ISBN 0-8372-0832-7); Monster Goes to School (ISBN 0-8372-0833-5); Monster at School (ISBN 0-8372-0834-3); Monster & the Magic Umbrella (ISBN 0-8372-0835-1); Monster Has a Party (ISBN 0-8372-0836-X); Monster Goes to the Zoo (ISBN 0-8372-0837-8). (Illus., Avail. in Spanish). (ps-3). 1973. pap. 1.38 ea.; pap. 141.60 set of 10 ea. of 12 titles & tchr's. guide (ISBN 0-8372-0300-7, 300); pap. 15.00 set of monster bks. - 1 ea. title & tchr's. guide (ISBN 0-8372-0301-5, 301). Bowmar-Noble.
--More Monster Books: Set 2, 12 bks. Incl. Monster & the Mural (ISBN 0-8372-2124-2); Monster, Lady Monster & the Bike Ride (ISBN 0-8372-2125-0); Lady Monster Helps Out (ISBN 0-8372-2126-9); Monster Goes to the Circus (ISBN 0-8372-2127-7); Monster Goes to the Hospital (ISBN 0-8372-2128-5); Monster Goes to the Beach (ISBN 0-8372-2129-3); Monster Gets a Job (ISBN 0-8372-2130-7); Monster & the Surprise Cookie (ISBN 0-8372-2131-5); Monster Goes Around the Town (ISBN 0-8372-2132-3); Monster Buys a Pet; Lady Monster Has a Plan (ISBN 0-8372-2135-8). (Illus., Avail in spanish). (ps-3). 1976. pap. 1.56 ea.; pap. text ed. 16.92 12 bks. 1 of ea. & tchr's guide (ISBN 0-8372-2122-6, 2122); pap. text ed. 160.20 120 bks 10 of ea. & tchr's guide (ISBN 0-8372-2123-4, 2123). Bowmar-Noble.
Blanch, Jose M., tr. see Dunnett, W. M.
Blanch, Jose M., tr. see Ford, Leighton.
Blanch, Jose M., tr. see Lebar, Lois & Berg, Miguel.
Blanch, Lesley. Journey into the Mind's Eye. 1977. pap. 1.95 o.p. (ISBN 0-445-08581-9). Popular Lib.
Blanch, Miguel, tr. see Collins, Gary.
Blanch, Miguel, tr. see Ladd, George E.
Blanch, Miguel, tr. see Morris, Leon.
Blanch, Robert J., ed. Style & Symbolism in Piers Plowman: A Modern Critical Anthology. LC 69-20115. (Illus., Orig.). 1969. 12.50x (ISBN 0-87049-093-1); pap. text ed. 5.95x (ISBN 0-87049-101-6). U of Tenn Pr.
Blanch, Stuart. The Trumpet in the Morning. 1979. 12.95 (ISBN 0-19-520167-1). Oxford U Pr.
Blanchard, Edward B. & Epstein, Leonard H. Biofeedback Primer. LC 76-74321. (Clinical & Professional Psychology Ser.). 1978. pap. text ed. 7.50 (ISBN 0-201-00338-4). A-W.
Blanchard, Homer D. The Bach Organ Book. (The Little Organ Books Ser.: No. 3). (Illus.). Date not set. pap. price not set. Praestant.
Blanchard, Homer D., jt. auth. see Lindow, Ch. W.
Blanchard, Homer D., ed. Organs of Our Time Two. 154p. write for info. Praestant.
Blanchard, Homer D., tr. see Klais, Hans G.
Blanchard, Homer D., tr. see Lindow, Ch. W.
Blanchard, Howard L. Organization & Administration of Pupil Personnel Services. (Illus.). 148p. 1974. photocopy ed. spiral 14.75 (ISBN 0-398-03142-8). C C Thomas.
Blanchard, Jay, jt. auth. see Mason, George E.

Blanchard, John. Aceptado Por Dios. 2.50 (ISBN 0-686-12564-9). Banner of Truth.
Blanchard, Ken, jt. auth. see Hersey, Paul.
Blanchard, Marc E. Description: Sign, Self, Desire. (Approaches to Semiotics Ser.: No. 43). 1979. text ed. 40.00x (ISBN 0-686-27019-3). Mouton.
Blanchard, Marjorie. Sauce It! Making Sauces, Purees & Gravies from Fruits & Vegetables. (Illus.). 160p. (Orig.). 1980. pap. 5.95 (ISBN 0-88266-149-3). Garden Way Pub.
Blanchard, Marjorie P. The Outdoor Cookbook. (Cooking Plus Ser). (Illus.). (gr. 6 up). 1977. PLB 5.90 s&l o.p. (ISBN 0-531-00381-7). Watts.
Blanchard, Nina. How to Break into Motion Pictures, Television Commercials & Modeling. 272p. 1979. pap. 2.50 (ISBN 0-380-47118-3, 47118). Avon.
Blanchard, Rae, ed. see Steele, Richard.
Blanchard, Roberta R. Traditional Tole Painting: With Authentic Antique Designs & Working Diagrams for Stenciling & Brush-Stroke Painting. LC 77-78208. (Illus.). 1977. pap. 3.50 (ISBN 0-486-23531-9). Dover.
Blanche, Ella. Sidereality. (Illus.). 240p. (Orig.). 1980. pap. 6.00 (ISBN 0-9601542-4-8). Ivy Hill.
Blanche, R. Axiomatics. Keene, G. B., tr. (Monographs in Modern Logic). 1967. pap. 5.00 (ISBN 0-7100-3802-X). Routledge & Kegan.
Blanchette, Jean-Francois, jt. auth. see Boily, Lise.
Blanck, Gertrude, jt. auth. see Blanck, Rubin.
Blanck, Rubin & Blanck, Gertrude. Marriage & Personal Development. LC 68-9577. 1968. 17.50x (ISBN 0-231-03150-5). Columbia U Pr.
Blanco, Ignacio M. The Unconscious As Infinite Sets: An Essay in Bi-Logic. 1976. text ed. 35.00x o.p. (ISBN 0-7156-0718-9). Humanities.
Blanco, Miquel A., jt. auth. see Watson, E. W.
Blanco, Ralph F. Prescriptions for Children with Learning & Adjustment Problems. 320p. 1980. 13.75 (ISBN 0-685-02633-7). C C Thomas.
Blanco, V. M. & McCuskey, S. W. Basic Physics of the Solar System. 1961. 17.95 (ISBN 0-201-00615-4). A-W.
Bland, Alexander. The Royal Ballet: The First Fifty Years. LC 80-2403. (Illus.). 288p. 1981. 35.00 (ISBN 0-385-17043-2). Doubleday.
Bland, Carole J. Faculty Development Through Workshops. 232p. 1980. text ed. 15.50 (ISBN 0-398-03940-2); pap. 11.50 (ISBN 0-398-04002-8). C C Thomas.
Bland, Hamilton. Competitive Swimming. (EP Sport Ser.). (Illus.). 1979. 12.95 (ISBN 0-8069-9108-9, Pub. by EP Publishing England). Sterling.
Bland, Jeffrey. Your Health Under Siege: Using Nutrition to Fight Back. 256p. 1981. 12.95 (ISBN 0-8289-0415-4). Greene.
Bland, Randall W. Private Pressure on Public Law: Legal Career of Justice Thurgood Marshall. LC 72-91170. 1973. 15.00 (ISBN 0-8046-9035-9, Natl U). Kennikat.
--Private Pressure on Public Law: The Legal Career of Justice Thurgood Marshall. LC 72-91170. (Illus.). 220p. 1973. pap. 7.50 (ISBN 0-8046-9048-0, Natl U). Kennikat.
Bland, Randall W., jt. auth. see Pettus, Beryl E.
Bland, Robert. The Four Slaves of Cythera, a Romance in Ten Cantos. Reiman, Donald H., ed. LC 75-31160. (Romantic Context Ser.: Poetry 1789-1830: Vol. 15). 1978. Repr. of 1809 ed. lib. bdg. 47.00 (ISBN 0-8240-2114-2). Garland Pub.
Bland, Salem. New Christianity. LC 72-95815. (Social History of Canada Ser.). 1973. pap. 2.50 (ISBN 0-8020-6179-6). U of Toronto Pr.
Blandford, Percy. The Woodturner's Bible. (Illus.). 1979. 15.95 (ISBN 0-8306-9820-5); pap. 9.95 (ISBN 0-8306-1044-8, 1044). TAB Bks.
Blandford, Percy W. Build Your Own Boats. (Illus.). 160p. 1972. 17.50x o.p. (ISBN 0-09-080020-6, SpS). Soccer.
--Knots & Splices. LC 65-25270. (Illus.). 80p. 1965. lib. bdg. 4.50 o.p. (ISBN 0-668-01330-3). Arco.
--Old Farm Tools & Machinery: An Illustrated History. LC 75-44376. 1976. 26.00 (ISBN 0-8103-2019-3). Gale.
Blandy, John. Lecture Notes on Urology. 2nd ed. (Illus.). 1978. softcover 17.50 o.p. (ISBN 0-397-60457-2). Lippincott.
Blandy, Thomas & Lamoureux, Denis. All Through the House: A Guide to Home Weatherization. (Illus., Orig.). 1980. pap. 6.95 (ISBN 0-07-005871-7). McGraw.
Blandy, William. Castle or Picture of Policy. LC 71-38157. (English Experience Ser.: No. 436). 68p. 1972. Repr. of 1581 ed. 9.50 (ISBN 90-221-0436-2). Walter J Johnson.
Blane, Andrew, ed. Russia & Orthodoxy: Essays in Honor of Georges Florovsky. Vol. One: Georges Florovsky: Russian Intellectual & Orthodox Churchman. (Slavistic Printings & Reprintings Ser.: No. 260-1). 1979. 65.80. Mouton.
Blane, Patrica. Escape to Athena. 1979. pap. 1.95 o.p. (ISBN 0-425-04066-6). Berkley Pub.
Blanford, Charles J., jt. auth. see Spencer, Leland.
Blank, Florence W. & Guertin, Carolyn W. Sound Skill Builder: Use with Sure Steps to Reading & Spelling, 3 bks. Incl. Bk. 1. price not set (ISBN 0-916720-04-7); Bk. 2. price not set (ISBN 0-916720-05-5); Bk. 3. price not set (ISBN 0-916720-06-3). (gr. 1-7). 1981. Weiss Pub.
Blank, Joseph P. Nineteen Steps up the Mountain. 1977. pap. 1.95 (ISBN 0-515-04442-3). Jove Pubns.
Blank, Marion. Teaching Learning in the Preschool: A Dialogue Approach. LC 72-97007. 1973. pap. text ed. 11.95 (ISBN 0-675-08971-9). Merrill.
Blank, Marion, et al. Preschool Language Assessment Instrument: Language of Learning in Practice. 1978. 17.00 (ISBN 0-8089-1072-8); record forms 9.75 (ISBN 0-8089-1107-4). Grune.
Blank, Mark Van see Van Blank, Mark.
Blank, Martin, ed. Bioelectrochemistry: Ions, Surfaces, Membranes. LC 80-18001. (Advances in Chemistry Ser.: No. 188). 1980. 58.00 (ISBN 0-8412-0473-X). Am Chemical.
Blank, Phillip E., Jr., ed. Lyric Forms in the Sonnet Sequences of Barnabe Barnes. LC 72-94447. (De Proprietatibus Litterarum, Series Practica, No. 18). 162p. (Orig.). 1974. pap. text ed. 27.05x (ISBN 90-2793-062-7). Mouton.
Blank, R. Political Parties: An Introduction. 1980. 16.95 (ISBN 0-13-684761-7). P-H.
Blank, Raymond. Playing the Game: A Psychopolitical Strategy for Your Career. (Illus.). 224p. 1981. 10.95 (ISBN 0-688-00354-0). Morrow.
Blank, Robert H. The Political Implications of Human Genetic Technology. (Special Studies in Science, Technology, & Public Policy). 209p. (Orig.). 1981. lib. bdg. 24.00x (ISBN 0-89158-975-9); pap. text ed. 12.00x (ISBN 0-86531-193-5). Westview.
--Regional Diversity of Political Values: Idaho Political Culture. LC 78-62742. 1978. pap. text ed. 8.75 (ISBN 0-8191-0590-2). U Pr of Amer.
Blank, Stephen, jt. auth. see LaPalombara, Joseph.
Blank, Stuart J., jt. auth. see Hobbs, Donald A.
Blankenbaker, E. Keith. Modern Plumbing. LC 77-15954. (Illus.). 1978. text ed. 14.00 (ISBN 0-87006-245-X). Goodheart.
Blankenship, Albert B., jt. auth. see Heidingsfield, Myron S.
Blankenship, Martha L. & Moerchen, Barbara D. Home Economics Education. LC 78-69595. (Illus.). 1979. text ed. 16.95 (ISBN 0-395-26700-5); inst. manual 1.80 (ISBN 0-395-26699-8); self instruction module 9.25 (ISBN 0-395-26698-X). HM.
Blankenship, Ralph L., ed. Colleagues in Organization: The Social Construction of Professional Work. LC 80-18149. 442p. (Orig.). 1980. Repr. of 1977 ed. lib. bdg. 22.00 (ISBN 0-89874-233-1). Krieger.
Blankenship, Samuel M. A Backpacking Guide to the Southern Mountains. rev. ed. (Orig.). 1975. pap. 1.95 o.p. (ISBN 0-89176-472-0, 6472). Mockingbird Bks.
Blankenship, William. Tiger Ten. 1978. pap. 1.95 o.p. (ISBN 0-425-03674-X, Medallion). Berkley Pub.
Blankenship, William D. Brotherly Love. LC 80-70212. 1981. 11.95 (ISBN 0-87795-301-5). Arbor Hse.
--Yukon Gold. LC 76-55733. 1977. 9.95 (ISBN 0-525-23945-6, Henry Robbins Bks.). Dutton.
Blankstein, Kirk R., et al, eds. Assessment & Modification of Emotional Behavior. (Studies of Communication & Effect Ser.: Vol. 6). (Illus.). 235p. 1980. 25.00 (ISBN 0-306-40502-4, Plenum Pr). Plenum Pub.
Blanning, T. C. Reform & Revolution in Mainz, 1743-1803. (Studies in Early Modern History). 384p. 1974. 41.95 (ISBN 0-521-20418-6). Cambridge U Pr.
Blanshard, Brand. Reason & Analysis. 2nd ed. LC 62-9576. (Paul Carus Lectures Ser.). 505p. 1962. 22.50 (ISBN 0-87548-104-3); pap. 8.95 o.p. (ISBN 0-87548-112-4). Open Court.
Blanshard, Frances. Frank Aydelotte of Swarthmore. LC 70-108646. (Illus.). 1970. 22.50x (ISBN 0-8195-4023-4, Pub. by Wesleyan U Pr). Columbia U Pr.
Blanshard, J. M. & Mitchell, J. R. Polysaccharides in Food. new ed. LC 79-40370. (Studies in the Agricultural & Food Sciences). (Illus.). 1979. text ed. 55.95 (ISBN 0-408-10618-2). Butterworths.
Blanshard, Paul. Personal & Controversial: An Autobiography. LC 72-6225. 320p. 1973. 7.95 o.p. (ISBN 0-8070-0514-2). Beacon Pr.
Blansitt, Edward L., Jr. & Teschner, Richard V. A Festschrift for Jacob Ornstein: Studies in General Linguistics & Sociolinguistics. (Orig.). 1980. pap. text ed. 16.95 (ISBN 0-88377-172-1). Newbury Hse.
Blansitt, Edward L., Jr., ed. see Linguistic Association of Canada & the U.S.
Blanton, Alma E. God & Mrs. Adam. (Illus.). 152p. (Orig.). 1978. pap. 4.95 (ISBN 0-938134-00-0, G-1). Loving Pubs.
--Our Gospel's Women. (Illus.). 114p. (Orig.). 1979. pap. 3.00 (ISBN 0-938134-01-9). Loving Pubs.
Blanton, J. Neal. Game of the Century. (Illus.). 1970. 12.50 (ISBN 0-8363-0034-3). Jenkins.
Blanton, Linda L. Intermediate Composition Practice, Bk I. (Illus., Orig.). (gr. 7-12). 1981. pap. text ed. 5.95 (ISBN 0-88377-194-2). Newbury Hse.
Blaquiere, A., et al, eds. Dynamical Systems & Microphysics. (CISM - International Centre for Mechanical Sciences Courses & Lectures: Vol. 261). (Illus.). ix, 412p. 1980. pap. 39.00 (ISBN 0-387-81533-3). Springer-Verlag.
Blasberg, Robert & Bohdan, Carol L. Fulper Art Pottery: An Aesthetic Appreciation, 1909-1929. (Jordan-Volpe Gallery Ser.). (Illus.). 88p. pap. 14.95 (ISBN 0-87905-069-1). Peregrine Smith.
Blaschke, Wilhelm. Differentialgeometrie, 2 Vols. in 1. LC 62-11596. (Ger). 24.95 (ISBN 0-8284-0202-7). Chelsea Pub.
Blasecki. Mechanisms of Immunity to Virus-Induced Tumors. 376p. 1981. 49.50. Dekker.
Blaser, Robin, ed. see Spicer, Jack.
Blaser, Werner. Chinese Pavilion Architecture. Date not set. 45.00 o.p. (ISBN 0-8038-0043-6). Hastings.
--The Rock Is My Home: Structures in Stone. (Illus.). 224p. (Eng., Fr. & Ger.). 1976. text ed. 15.00 (ISBN 0-89192-299-7). Interbk Inc.
--Wood Houses: Form in Rural Architecture. (Illus.). 216p. (Eng., Fr. & Ger.). 1980. text ed. 19.00 (ISBN 0-89192-300-4). Interbk Inc.
Blashfield, Jean. Hellraisers, Heroines, & Holy Women. 256p. 1981. 14.95 (ISBN 0-312-36736-8); pap. 7.95. St Martin.
Blasi, Anthony J. Segregationist Violence & Civil Rights Movements in Tuscaloosa. LC 79-3714. 1980. text ed. 14.50 (ISBN 0-8191-0913-4); pap. text ed. 9.00 (ISBN 0-8191-0914-2). U Pr of Amer.
Blasi, Anthony J., et al. Toward an Interpretive Sociology. 1978. pap. text ed. 13.75x (ISBN 0-8191-0382-9). U Pr of Amer.
Blasier, Cole. The Hovering Giant: U. S. Responses to Revolutionary Change in Latin America. LC 75-9130. (Pitt Latin American Ser.). (Illus.). 1976. 15.95 (ISBN 0-8229-3304-7); pap. 6.95x (ISBN 0-8229-5264-5). U of Pittsburgh Pr.
Blasing, Randy, tr. see Hikmet, Nazim.
Blasingame, Ike. Dakota Cowboy: My Life in the Old Days. LC 58-11667. (Illus.). 1964. 12.95x (ISBN 0-8032-0906-1); pap. 3.45 (ISBN 0-8032-5015-0, BB 191, Bison). U of Nebr Pr.
Blasis, Celeste De see De Blasis, Celeste.
Blass, Friedrich. Philology of the Gospels. 1969. Repr. of 1898 ed. text ed. 28.50x (ISBN 90-6032-391-2). Humanities.
Blass, Thomas. Contemporary Social Psychology: Representative Readings. LC 75-17318. 1976. pap. text ed. 10.50 (ISBN 0-87581-190-6, 190). Peacock Pubs.
Blassingame, John W. The Slave Community: Plantation Life in the Ante-Bellum South. 2nd rev. enl. ed. (Illus.). 1979. 15.00x (ISBN 0-19-502562-8); pap. text ed. 5.95x (ISBN 0-19-502563-6). Oxford U Pr.
Blassingame, Wyatt. Combat Nurses of World War Two. (Landmark Ser: No, 116). (gr. 4 up). 1967. PLB 5.99 o.p. (ISBN 0-394-90416-8). Random.
--Look-It-Up Book of Presidents. LC 68-23656. (Look-It-up Book No. 5). (Illus.). (gr. 3-5). 1968. PLB 5.99 o.p. (ISBN 0-394-90748-5, BYR). Random.
--Skunks. LC 80-21555. (A Skylight Bk.). (Illus.). 64p. (gr. 2-5). 1981. PLB 5.95 (ISBN 0-396-07909-1). Dodd.
--Wonders of Alligators & Crocodiles. (Illus.). (gr. 4-6). 1974. pap. 1.25 (ISBN 0-590-04842-2, Schol Pap). Schol Bk Serv.
Blatch, Mervyn. Cathedrals. (Illus.). 176p. 1980. 12.95 (ISBN 0-7137-0943-X, Pub. by Blandford Pr England); pap. 6.95 (ISBN 0-7137-1081-0, Pub. by Blandford Pr England). Sterling.
Blatcher, Marjorie. Court of Kings Bench Fourteen Fifty to Fifteen Fifty: A Study in Self-Help. (University of London Legal Ser.: No. 12). 1978. text ed. 36.50x (ISBN 0-485-13412-8, Athlone Pr). Humanities.
Blate, Michael. The Natural Healer's Acupressure Handbook: G-Jo Fingertip Technique. LC 76-45282. (Illus.). 1977. 8.95 o.p. (ISBN 0-03-020631-6); pap. 4.95 (ISBN 0-03-020626-X). HR&W.
Blatt, A. H. Organic Synthesis Collective Volumes, Vol. 2. 1943. 32.50 (ISBN 0-471-07986-3). Wiley.
Blatt, Burton, et al. The Family Papers: A Return to Purgatory. (Illus., Orig.). 1980. pap. 8.95 (ISBN 0-582-28154-7). Longman.
Blatt, Gloria T. It's Your Move: Expressive Movement in the Language Arts Reading Class. (Orig.). 1981. pap. 8.95 (ISBN 0-8077-2640-0). Tchrs Coll.
Blatt, H., et al. Origin of Sedimentary Rock. 2nd ed. 1980. 30.95 (ISBN 0-13-642710-3). P-H.
Blatt, Sidney J. & Wild, Cynthia. Schizophrenia: A Developmental Analysis. 1976. 25.00 (ISBN 0-12-105050-5). Acad Pr.
Blattner, Barbara. Holistic Nursing. (Illus.). 400p. 1981. text ed. 15.95 (ISBN 0-13-392571-4); pap. text ed. 12.95 (ISBN 0-686-68605-5). P-H.
Blattner, E. F., tr. El Tabernaculo. (Spanish Bks.). 1977. 0.75 (ISBN 0-8297-0601-1). Life Pubs Intl.
Blattner, Elsie & Walker, Luisa, trs. Bosquejos Homileticos. (Spanish Bks.). 1979. 1.75 (ISBN 0-8297-0511-2). Life Pubs Intl.
Blatty, William P. John Goldfarb, Please Come Home! 160p. (Orig.). 1980. pap. 2.25 (ISBN 0-553-14251-8). Bantam.
--The Ninth Configuration. LC 78-4741. 1978. 7.95 o.s.i. (ISBN 0-06-010359-0, HarpT). Harrow.
Blau, Esther, ed. The Spice & Spirit of Kosher-Jewish Cooking. LC 77-72116. (Illus.). 1977. 13.95 (ISBN 0-8197-0455-5). Bloch.
Blau, Joseph L. Modern Varieties of Judaism. LC 66-10732. 1966. 17.50x (ISBN 0-231-02867-9); pap. 5.00 (ISBN 0-231-08668-7). Columbia U Pr.
Blau, Joseph L., ed. Social Theories of Jacksonian Democracy, 1825-1850: Representative Writings of the Period, 1825-1850. LC 55-169. (Social Theories of Jacksonian Democracy). 1954. pap. 8.45 o.p. (ISBN 0-672-60001-3, AHS1). Bobbs.
Blau, Joseph L., jt. ed. see Baron, Salo W.
Blau, Joseph L., et al, eds. Essays on Jewish Life & Thought. LC 57-11757. 1959. 22.50x (ISBN 0-231-02171-2). Columbia U Pr.
--Jews of the United States, 1790-1840: A Documentary History, 3 Vols. LC 64-10108. 1964. Set. 75.50x (ISBN 0-231-02651-X). Columbia U Pr.
Blau, Melinda. First Over the Oceans. LC 78-12960. (Famous Firsts Ser.). (Illus.). 1978. lib. bdg. 7.35 (ISBN 0-686-51103-4). Silver.
--Killer Bees. LC 77-10010. (Great Unsolved Mysteries of Our Time Ser.). (Illus.). (gr. 4-5). 1977. PLB 9.65 (ISBN 0-8172-1055-5). Raintree Pubs.
--What Ever Happened to Amelia Earhart? LC 77-22173. (Great Unsolved Mysteries Ser.). (Illus.). (gr. 4-5). 1977. PLB 9.65 (ISBN 0-8172-1057-1). Raintree Pubs.
Blau, Peter M. Bureaucracy in Modern Society. 2nd ed. (Orig.). 1971. pap. text ed. 3.95x (ISBN 0-394-31452-2, RanC). Random.
--The Dynamics of Bureacracy. 2nd. rev. ed. LC 63-22822. xiv, 322p. 1973. text ed. 6.95 (ISBN 0-226-05726-7, P500, Phoen). U of Chicago Pr.
--Exchange & Power in Social Life. LC 64-23827. 1964. 23.95 (ISBN 0-471-08030-6). Wiley.
--Inequality & Heterogeneity: A Primitive Theory of Social Structure. LC 77-70272. (Illus.). 1977. 15.95 (ISBN 0-02-903660-7). Free Pr.
--On the Nature of Organizations. LC 74-7392. 358p. 1974. 28.95 (ISBN 0-471-08037-3, Pub. by Wiley-Interscience). Wiley.
Blau, Peter M. & Duncan, Otis D. The American Occupational Structure. LC 78-50657. 1978. pap. text ed. 8.95 (ISBN 0-02-903670-4). Free Pr.
Blau, Peter M., ed. Approaches to the Study of Social Structure. LC 75-2809. 1975. 14.95 (ISBN 0-02-903650-X). Free Pr.
Blau, Richard M. The Body Impolitic: A Reading of Four Novels by Herman Melville. 219p. 1979. pap. text ed. 42.75x (ISBN 90-6203-571-X). Humanities.
Blau, Sheldon Paul, M.D. & Schultz, Dodi. Lupus-The Body Against Itself. LC 76-40881. 1977. 7.95 (ISBN 0-385-04562-X). Doubleday.
Blau, Zena S. Black Children-White Children: Competence, Socialization & Social Structure. LC 80-1643. 1981. 19.95 (ISBN 0-02-903640-2). Free Pr.
--Old Age in a Changing Society. 285p. 1973. 9.95 o.p. (ISBN 0-531-06354-2). Watts.
Blauer, Stephen. Rejuvenation: Dr. Ann Wigmore's Complete Diet & Health Program. 197p. pap. 4.95. Hippocrates.

Blaug, M. Economic Theory in Retrospect. LC 77-7899. 1978. 24.95x (ISBN 0-521-21733-4). Cambridge U Pr.
Blaug, Mark. The Methodology of Economics: Or How Economists Explain. LC 80-13802. (Cambridge Surveys of Economic Literature). 325p. 1980. 29.50 (ISBN 0-521-22288-5); pap. 9.95 (ISBN 0-521-29437-1). Cambridge U Pr.
Blaug, Mark, ed. The Economics of the Arts. LC 76-5889. 1976. 27.50 o.p. (ISBN 0-89158-613-X). Westview.
Blaustein, Albert P., ed. Fundamental Legal Documents of Communist China. 1962. 20.00x (ISBN 0-8377-0300-X). Rothman.
Blaustein, Ancel. Interpretation of Biopsy of Endometrium. (Biopsy Interpretation Ser.). 1979. text ed. 27.00 (ISBN 0-89004-370-1). Raven.
Blauth, W. & Schneider-Sickert, F. R. Congenital Deformities of the Hand: An Atlas of Their Surgical Treatment. (Illus.). 394p. 1980. 259.60 (ISBN 0-387-10084-9). Springer-Verlag.
Blauvelt, Euan & Durlacher, Jennifer, eds. Sources of Asian-Pacific Economic Information, 2 vols. LC 80-28645. 1981. Set. lib. bdg. 125.00 (ISBN 0-313-22963-5). Greenwood.
Blavatsky, Helena P. Collected Writings of H. P. Blavatsky. Incl. Vol. 1. 1874-1878. rev. ed (ISBN 0-8356-0082-3); Vol. 2. 1879-1880 (ISBN 0-8356-0091-2); Vol. 3. 1881-1882 (ISBN 0-8356-0099-8); Vol. 4. 1882-1883 (ISBN 0-8356-0106-4); Vol. 5. 1883 (ISBN 0-8356-0117-X); Vol. 6. 1883-1884-1885 (ISBN 0-8356-0125-0); Vol. 7. 1886-1887 (ISBN 0-8356-0222-2); Vol. 8. 1887 (ISBN 0-8356-7166-6); Vol. 9. 1888 (ISBN 0-8356-0217-6); Vol. 10. 1888-1889 (ISBN 0-8356-0218-4). (Illus.). 14.50 ea. Theos Pub Hse.
--Esoteric Writings of H. P. Blavatsky. LC 79-6547. (Illus.). 500p. (Orig.). 1980. pap. 8.75 (ISBN 0-8356-0535-3, Quest). Theos Pub Hse.
--H. P. Blavatsky Collected Writings, Vol. XII. De Zirkoff, Boris, ed. LC 80-53953. (Illus.). 849p. 1981. cloth 18.95 (ISBN 0-8356-0228-1). Theos Pub Hse.
--H. P. Blavatsky to the American Conventions: 1888-1891, with a Historical Perspective. LC 78-74256. 1979. softcover 3.75 (ISBN 0-911500-88-X). Theos U Pr.
--Isis Unveiled, 2 vols. LC 72-186521. 1976. Repr. of 1877 ed. Set. 17.00 (ISBN 0-911500-02-2); Set. softcover 12.50 (ISBN 0-911500-03-0). Theos U Pr.
--Isis Unveiled: A Master-Key to the Mysteries of Ancient & Modern Science & Theology, 2 vols. in 1. (Illus.). xlix, 1260p. 1931. Repr. of 1877 ed. 12.50 (ISBN 0-938998-01-3). Theosophy.
--The Key to Theosophy. 12.25 o.p. (ISBN 0-7229-5006-3). Theos Pub Hse.
--The Key to Theosophy. xii, 310p. 1930. Repr. of 1889 ed. 6.00 (ISBN 0-938998-03-X). Theosophy.
--The Key to Theosophy: Verbatim with 1889 Edition. LC 72-95701. 1972. 8.00 (ISBN 0-911500-06-5); pap. 5.00 (ISBN 0-911500-07-3). Theos U Pr.
--The Secret Doctrine, 2 vols. facsimile of 1888 ed. LC 74-76603. 1977. Repr. of 1888 ed. Set. 17.00 (ISBN 0-911500-00-6); Set. softcover 12.50 (ISBN 0-911500-01-4). Theos U Pr.
--The Secret Doctrine: The Synthesis of Science, Religion, & Philosophy, 2 vols. in 1. xci, 1474p. 1925. Repr. of 1888 ed. 14.00 (ISBN 0-938998-00-5). Theosophy.
--The Theosophical Glossary: A Photographic Reproduction of the Original Edition, As First Issued at London, England, 1892. Mead, G. R., ed. & intro. by. vi, 389p. 1930. Repr. of 1892 ed. 8.50 (ISBN 0-938998-04-8). Theosophy.
--Transactions of the Blavatsky Lodge of the Theosophical Society. xxiv, 149p. 1923. Repr. of 1890 ed. 5.00 (ISBN 0-938998-05-6). Theosophy.
--Voice of the Silence. LC 73-7619. 1970. pap. 2.50 (ISBN 0-8356-0380-6, Quest). Theos Pub Hse.
--The Voice of the Silence: Verbatim with 1889 Original Ed. LC 76-25345. 1976. 4.00 (ISBN 0-911500-04-9); pap. 2.25 (ISBN 0-911500-05-7). Theos U Pr.
Blavatsky, Helena P., tr. & intro. by. The Voice of the Silence: Chosen Fragments from the Book of the Golden Precepts. iv, 110p. 1928. Repr. of 1889 ed. 3.00 (ISBN 0-938998-06-4). Theosophy.
Blavatsky, Helene P. Theosophical Glossary. LC 74-142546. 1971. Repr. of 1892 ed. 22.00 (ISBN 0-8103-3679-0). Gale.
Blaxland, Gregory. J. H. Thomas: A Life for Unity. 14.95 (ISBN 0-392-07986-0, SpS). Soccer-
Blaze, Francois H. L' Academie Imperiale De Musique: Histoire Litteraire, Musicale, Politique et Galant De Ce Theater, De 1645 a 1855, 2 vols. LC 80-2258. 1981. Repr. of 1855 ed. 95.00 (ISBN 0-404-18804-4). AMS Pr.
--De l'Opera En France, 2 vols. LC 80-2259. 1981. Repr. of 1820 ed. Set. 82.50 (ISBN 0-404-18810-9). AMS Pr.
--L' Opera-Italien de 1548 a 1856. LC 80-2260. 1981. Repr. of 1856 ed. 52.00 (ISBN 0-686-69547-X). AMS Pr.
Blaze De Bury, Ange H. Meyerbeer et Son Temps. LC 80-2257. 1981. Repr. of 1865 ed. 40.50 (ISBN 0-404-18813-3). AMS Pr.
Blazevic, Donna J. & Ederer, Grace M., eds. Principles of Biochemical Tests in Diagnostic Microbiology. LC 75-17591. (Techniques in Pure & Applied Microbiology Ser.). 136p. 1975. 19.95 (ISBN 0-471-08040-3, Pub. by Wiley Medical). Wiley.
Blazier, Kenneth D. Una Escuela Biblica 002a: A Growing Church School. De Olivieri, Evelyn R., tr. from Eng. 64p. (Span.). 1981. pap. 3.25 (ISBN 0-8170-0928-0). Judson.
Blazier, William H. Lights! Action! Camera! Learn! LC 74-80347. 1974. 10.00 (ISBN 0-686-10561-3). Allison Pubs.
Blazynski, T. Z. Metal Forming: Tool Profiles & Flow. LC 75-42156. 1976. 47.95 (ISBN 0-470-15003-3). Halsted Pr.
Bleakney, Thomas. Retirement Systems for Public Employees. 1972. text ed. 9.75x (ISBN 0-256-01407-8). Irwin.
Bleaney, B., jt. auth. see Abragam, A.
Bleaney, B., jt. auth. see Bleaney, B. I.
Bleaney, B. I. & Bleaney, B. Electricity & Magnetism. 3rd ed. (Illus.). 1976. pap. 32.50x (ISBN 0-19-851141-8). Oxford U Pr.
Bleasdale, J. K. Plant Physiology in Relation to Horticulture. 1978. text ed. 11.00 (ISBN 0-87055-239-2). AVI.
Bleasdale, J. K., jt. ed. see Salter, P. J.
Bleazard, G. B. Why Packet Switching. (Illus.). 174p. (Orig.). 1979. pap. 32.50 (ISBN 0-85012-194-9). Intl Pubns Serv.
Blecher, George, tr. see Kullman, Harry.
Blecher, Lone T., tr. see Kullman, Harry.
Blecher, Melvin & Barr, Robert S. Receptors & Human Disease. (Illus.). 350p. 1981. write for info. (0609-6). Williams & Wilkins.
Blecher, W. No End of Nonsense. 1968. 3.95g o.s.i. (ISBN 0-02-710900-3). Macmillan.
Blechman, Barry M. Guide to Far Eastern Navies. LC 77-87942. 1978. 32.95 (ISBN 0-87021-235-4). Naval Inst Pr.
Blechman, Barry M. A. The Changing Soviet Navy. (Studies in Defense Policy). 1973. pap. 3.95 (ISBN 0-8157-0995-1). Brookings.
Blechman, Barry M. B. The Control of Naval Armaments: Prospects & Possibilities. (Studies in Defense Policy). 1975. 3.95 (ISBN 0-8157-0987-0). Brookings.
Blechman, Barry M. C. & Kaplan, Stephen S. Force Without War: U. S. Armed Forces As a Political Instrument. 1978. 21.95 (ISBN 0-8157-0986-2); pap. 11.95 (ISBN 0-8157-0985-4). Brookings.
Blechman, Barry M. D., jt. auth. see Quanbeck, Alton H.
Blechman, Barry M. E., et al. Setting National Priorities: F the 1975 Budget. LC 74-282. 1974. 11.95 (ISBN 0-8157-0994-3); pap. 4.95 (ISBN 0-8157-0993-5). Brookings.
Blechman, Barry M. F., et al. Setting National Priorities: G the 1976 Budget. 200p. 1975. 11.95 (ISBN 0-8157-0992-7); pap. 4.95 (ISBN 0-8157-0991-9). Brookings.
Blechman, Barry M. G., et al. The Soviet Military Buildup & U.S. Defense Spending. (Studies in Defense Policy). 1977. pap. 3.95 (ISBN 0-8157-0989-7). Brookings.
Blechman, Elaine A., ed. Feminist Issues in Behavior Therapy. (Women: Counseling, Therapy & Mental Health Services Ser.: Vol. 1, No. 1). 112p. 1980. text ed. cancelled (ISBN 0-917724-24-0). Haworth Pr.
Blechman, R. O. R. O. Blechman: Behind the Lines. LC 80-15191. (Illus.). 192p. 1980. 32.50 (ISBN 0-933920-07-5). Hudson Hills.
Blecka, Lawrence J. Concise Medical Parasitology. 1980. cancelled (ISBN 0-201-00756-8). A-W.
Bledsoe, Caroline H. Women & Marriage in Kpelle Society. LC 78-66170. (Illus.). 233p. 1980. 16.50x (ISBN 0-8047-1019-8). Stanford U Pr.
Bledsoe, Jerry. Just Folks: Visitin' with Carolina People. LC 80-36880. (Illus.). 208p. 1980. 9.95 (ISBN 0-914788-31-0). East Woods.
Bledsoe, Terry & Sanders, Peter. Line Drive. LC 75-22007. (The Venture Ser, a Reading Incentive Program). (Illus.). 76p. (gr. 7-12,RL 4.5-6.5). 1975. text ed. 23.25 ea. pack of 5 (ISBN 0-8172-0241-2). Follett.
Bledsoe, Thomas. Meanwhile Back at the Henhouse. LC 66-25670. 185p. 1966. 4.95 (ISBN 0-8040-0197-9). Swallow.
Bleecker, Ann E. The History of Maria Kittle, Repr. Of 1797 Ed. Bd. with Miscellanies in Prose & Verse. Morris, Thomas. Repr. of 1791 ed. LC 75-7041. (Indian Captivities Ser.: Vol. 20). 1976. lib. bdg. 44.00 (ISBN 0-8240-1644-0). Garland Pub.
Bleeker, Sonia. The Apache Indians: Raiders of the Southwest. (Illus.). (gr. 4-7). 1951. PLB 6.48 (ISBN 0-688-31046-X). Morrow.
--The Ashanti of Ghana. (Illus.). (gr. 4-7). 1966. PLB 6.67 (ISBN 0-688-31052-4). Morrow.
--The Cherokee: Indians of the Mountains. (Illus.). (gr. 3-6). 1952. PLB 6.67 (ISBN 0-688-31160-1). Morrow.
--The Chippewa Indians: Rice Gatherers of the Great Lakes. (Illus.). (gr. 3-6). 1955. PLB 6.67 (ISBN 0-688-31167-9). Morrow.
--The Delaware Indians: Eastern Fishermen & Farmers. (Illus.). (gr. 3-6). 1953. PLB 6.67 (ISBN 0-688-31230-6). Morrow.
--The Eskimo: Arctic Hunters & Trappers. (Illus.). (gr. 3-6). 1959. PLB 6.67 (ISBN 0-688-31275-6). Morrow.
--The Inca: Indians of the Andes. (Illus.). (gr. 3-6). 1960. PLB 6.67 (ISBN 0-688-31417-1). Morrow.
--Indians of the Longhouse. (Illus.). (gr. 3-6). 1950. PLB 6.67 (ISBN 0-688-31453-8). Morrow.
--The Masai: Herders of East Africa. (Illus.). (gr. 3-6). 1963. PLB 6.67 (ISBN 0-688-31460-0). Morrow.
--The Maya: Indians of Central America. (Illus.). (gr. 3-6). 1961. PLB 6.67 (ISBN 0-688-31461-9). Morrow.
--The Navajo: Herders, Weavers & Silversmiths. (Illus.). (gr. 3-6). 1958. PLB 6.67 (ISBN 0-688-31456-2). Morrow.
--The Pueblo Indians: Farmers of the Rio Grande. (Illus.). (gr. 3-6). 1955. PLB 6.67 (ISBN 0-688-31454-6). Morrow.
--The Pygmies: Africans of the Congo Forest. LC 68-25481. (Illus.). (gr. 3-6). 1968. PLB 6.67 (ISBN 0-688-31462-7). Morrow.
--The Sea Hunters: Indians of the Northwestern Coast. (Illus.). (gr. 3-6). 1951. PLB 6.67 (ISBN 0-688-31451-1). Morrow.
--The Seminole Indians. (Illus.). (gr. 3-6). 1954. PLB 6.67 (ISBN 0-688-31455-4). Morrow.
--The Sioux Indians: Hunters & Warriors of the Plains. (Illus.). (gr. 3-6). 1962. PLB 6.67 (ISBN 0-688-31457-0). Morrow.
--The Zulu of South Africa, Cattlemen, Farmers, & Warriors. (Illus.). (gr. 3-6). 1970. PLB 6.67 (ISBN 0-688-31451-1). Morrow.
Blegen, C. W. & Rawson, M. Palace of Nestor at Pylos in Western Messehia, 3 vols. Incl. Vol. 1. The Buildings & Their Contents, 2 pts. 1966. o.p. (ISBN 0-691-03525-3); Vol. 2. The Frescoes. Lang, M. 1969. 45.00 (ISBN 0-691-03531-8); Vol. 3. Acropolis & Lower Town, Tholoi, Grave Circle, & Chamber Tombs, Discoveries Outside the Citadel. 1973. 50.00 (ISBN 0-691-03529-6). LC 65-17131. (Cincinnati Classical Studies Ser.). Princeton U Pr.
Blegvad, Erik, jt. auth. see Livingston, Myra C.
Blegvad, Erik, illus. The Three Little Pigs. LC 80-10410. (Illus.). 32p. (ps-4). 1980. 8.95 (ISBN 0-689-50139-0, McElderry Bk). Atheneum.
Bleher, Petra, tr. see Nicolai, Jurgen.
Blei, Norbert. The Door Way. 240p. 1980. 16.95 (ISBN 0-933180-22-5). Ellis Pr.
Bleibtreu, Hermann, jt. auth. see Downs, James F.
Bleibtreu, Hermann K. & Downs, James F. Human Variation. (gr. 4-9). 1971. pap. text ed. 7.95x (ISBN 0-02-473200-1). Macmillan.
Bleibtreu, Hermann K., jt. auth. see Howells, W. W.
Bleibtreu, John N. Parable of the Beast. 1967. 6.95 o.s.i. (ISBN 0-02-511500-6). Macmillan.
Bleich, Friedrich. Buckling Strength of Metal Structures. (Engineering Societies Monographs Ser). 1952. 37.50 o.p. (ISBN 0-07-005890-3, P&RB). McGraw.
Bleich, J. David. With Perfect Faith: The Foundations of Jewish Belief. 1980. write for info. (ISBN 0-88482-924-3). Hebrew Pub.
Bleier, Rocky & O'Neil, Terry. Fighting Back. (Illus.). 288p. 1976. pap. 2.75 (ISBN 0-446-95704-6). Warner Bks.
--Fighting Back. rev. ed. LC 75-12865. (Illus.). 240p. 1980. 12.95 (ISBN 0-8128-2767-8). Stein & Day.
Bleifeld, Maurice. Modern Biology at a Glance. LC 78-154424. (Illus.). 122p. (Orig., Prog. Bk.). (YA) 1971. pap. 3.95 o.p. (ISBN 0-8120-0238-5). Barron.
Bleifeld, Maurice, jt. auth. see Edwards, Gabrielle.
Bleile, C. Roger. American Engravers. (Illus.). 191p. 1980. 29.95 (ISBN 0-917714-29-6). Beinfeld Pub.
Bleiler, E. F. His New Steam Man in Mexico; or Hot Work Among the Greasers. Electric Air Canoe; or the Search for the Valley of Diamonds. (The Frank Reade Library: Vol. 1). 1979. lib. bdg. 44.00 (ISBN 0-8240-3540-2). Garland Pub.
Bleiler, E. F., ed. Afloat in a Sunken Forest; or, with Frank Reade Jr. on a Submarine Cruise. (The Frank Reade Library: Vol. 8). 1980. lib. bdg. 44.00 (ISBN 0-8240-3547-X). Garland Pub.
--Below the Sahara. (The Frank Reade Library: Vol. 9). 1980. lib. bdg. 44.00 (ISBN 0-8240-3547-X). Garland Pub.
--Frank Reade Jr.'s New Electric Terror "The Thunderer"; or, the Search for the Tartar's Captive. (The Frank Reade Library: Vol. 2). 1980. lib. bdg. 44.00 (ISBN 0-8240-3541-0). Garland Pub.
--Lost in the Great Atlantic Valley. (Frank Reade Library: Vol. 6). 1980. lib. bdg. 44.00 (ISBN 0-8240-3545-3). Garland Pub.
Bleiler, E. F., ed. see Andrews, R. V.
Bleiler, E. F., ed. see Brauchli, Jakob.
Bleiler, E. F., ed. see Conan Doyle, Arthur.
Bleiler, E. F., ed. & intro. by see Hoffman, E. T.
Bleiler, E. F., ed. see Sweerts, Emmanuel.
Bleiler, E. F., ed. see Tarr, Sr. Mary.
Bleiler, E. F., ed. see Woelcken, Fritz.
Bleiler, E. G., ed. see Orczy, Emmuska.
Bleiler, Ellen, ed. & tr. see Bizet, Georges.
Blendermann, Louis. Controlled Storm Water Drainage. LC 78-15080. (Illus.). 200p. 1979. 27.00 (ISBN 0-8311-1123-2). Indus Pr.
--Design of Plumbing & Drainage Systems. 2nd ed. (Illus.). 1963. 20.00 (ISBN 0-8311-3004-0). Indus Pr.
Blenkin, Geva & Kelly, A. V. The Primary Curriculum. 1981. text ed. 21.00 (ISBN 0-06-318121-5, IntlDept); pap. text ed. 11.90 (ISBN 0-06-318121-5). Har-Row.
Blenkinsopp, J. Gibeon & Israel: The Role of Gibeon & the Gibeonites in the Political and Religious History of Early Israel. LC 74-171672. (Society for Old Testament Studies Monographs). 1972. 29.50 (ISBN 0-521-08368-0). Cambridge U Pr.
Blesh, Rudi. Classic Piano Rags. (Orig.). 1973. pap. 8.95 (ISBN 0-486-20469-3). Dover.
--Keaton. 1971. pap. 3.95 o.s.i. (ISBN 0-02-012090-7, Collier). Macmillan.
--Shining Trumpets: A History of Jazz. rev. 2nd ed. LC 75-31664. (Roots of Jazz Ser). (Illus.). xxxii, 412p. 1975. lib. bdg. 27.50 (ISBN 0-306-70658-X); pap. 7.95 (ISBN 0-306-80029-2). Da Capo.
Blessing, Richard. A Closed Book. LC 80-50865. 80p. 1980. 8.95 (ISBN 0-295-95757-3). U of Wash Pr.
Blessing, Richard, ed. see Oberg, Arthur.
Blessington, Francis C. Paradise Lost & the Classical Epic. 1979. 18.00 (ISBN 0-7100-0160-6). Routledge & Kegan.
Blessington, John P. Let My Children Work. LC 72-79377. 200p. 1975. pap. 2.95 (ISBN 0-385-00875-9, Anch). Doubleday.
Blessitt, Arthur. Tell the World: A Jesus People Manual. LC 78-177397. (Spire Bk). 64p. (Orig.). 1973. pap. 0.95 o.p. (ISBN 0-8007-8113-9). Revell.
Blessman, Lyle. The Blessman Approach. LC 78-64483. 1978. 9.95 (ISBN 0-87863-175-5). Farnswth Pub.
Bletter, Rosemarie H. Bruno Taut & Paul Scheerbart's Vision: Utopian Aspects of German Expressionist Architecture. LC 78-74362. (Outstanding Dissertations in the Fine Arts Ser.). (Illus.). 660p. 1979. lib. bdg. 55.00 (ISBN 0-8240-3951-3). Garland Pub.
Bletzer, Keith V. Selected References in Medical Anthropology. (Public Administration Ser.: Bibliography P-551). 59p. 1980. pap. 6.50. Vance Biblios.
Blevin, Margo & Ginder, Geri. The Low Blood Sugar Cookbook. LC 72-79378. 384p. 1973. 10.95 (ISBN 0-385-05174-3). Doubleday.
Blew, Genevieve S; see Mead, Robert G., Jr.
Blewett, George J. The Christian View of the World. 1912. 32.50x (ISBN 0-685-89741-9). Elliots Bks.
Blewitt, Mary. Celestial Navigation for Yachtsmen. LC 67-25097. 1967. 6.95 (ISBN 0-8286-0028-7). De Graff.
Blewitt, Phyllis, tr. see Doblin, Alfred.
Blewitt, Trevor, tr. see Doblin, Alfred.
Bley, Edgar S. Best Singing Games for Children of All Ages. rev. ed. LC 57-1014. (Illus.). (gr. k-6). 1959. 8.95 (ISBN 0-8069-4450-1); PLB 8.29 (ISBN 0-8069-4451-X). Sterling.
Bley, Helmut. South-West Africa Under German Rule, 1894-1914. Ridley, Hugh, tr. from Ger. 1971. 13.95k o.s.i. (ISBN 0-8101-0346-X). Northwestern U Pr.
Bley, Nancy S. & Thornton, Carol A. Teaching Mathematics to the Learning Disabled. 350p. 1981. text ed. price not set (ISBN 0-89443-357-1). Aspen Systems.
Bleyer, Willard G. Main Currents in the History of American Journalism. LC 70-77720. (American Scene Ser). (Illus.). v, 464p. 1973. Repr. of 1927 ed. lib. bdg. 45.00 (ISBN 0-306-71358-6). Da Capo.
Blicher, Adolph. Field-Effect & Bipolar Power Transistor Physics. 1981. write for info. (ISBN 0-12-105850-6). Acad Pr.
Blickle, Calvin & Corcoran, Frances. Sports: A Multimedia Guide for Children and Young Adults. (Selection Guide Ser.: No. 6). 245p. 1980. 16.50 (ISBN 0-87436-283-0). ABC Clio.

Blickle, Katrinka. Dark Beginnings. LC 77-80877. 1978. 8.95 o.p. (ISBN 0-385-12750-2). Doubleday.
--The Vain & the Vainglorious. LC 80-2324. 384p. 1981. 12.95 (ISBN 0-385-15182-9). Doubleday.
Blicq, Ronald S. Technically Write: Communication for the Technical Man. LC 77-177394. (Illus.). 384p. 1972. pap. text ed. 11.95 (ISBN 0-13-898676-2). P-H.
Bliek, Ruth De see Pena, Alberto & De Bliek, Ruth.
Bliese, Loren. A Generative Grammar of Afar. (SIL Publications on Linguistics Ser.). 315p. 1980. write for info. (ISBN 0-88312-083-6); price not set microfiche (ISBN 0-88312-483-1). Summer Inst Ling.
Bligh, A. S., et al. Radioisotopes in Radiodiagnosis. 256p. 1975. 29.95 (ISBN 0-407-00036-4). Butterworths.
Bligh, J., ed. Environmental Physiology of Animals. LC 76-25459. 1977. pap. text ed. 24.95 (ISBN 0-470-98925-4). Halsted Pr.
Bligh, William. An Account of the Mutiny on H. M. S. Bounty. Bowman, Robert, ed. 224p. 1980. text ed. write for info. (ISBN 0-391-02095-1). Humanities.
Blij, Harm J., jt. auth. see Best, Alan C.
Blij, Harm J. De see De Blij, Harm J.
Blij, Harm J. de see De Blij, Harm J.
Blij, Harm J. De see De Blij, Harm J.
Blinder, Alan S. & Solow, Robert M. The Economics of Public Finance. (Studies of Government Finance). 14.95 (ISBN 0-8157-0998-6); pap. 6.95 (ISBN 0-8157-0997-8). Brookings.
Blinder, Martin. Psychiatry in the Everyday Practice of Law. LC 72-95085. 305p. 1973. 40.00 (ISBN 0-686-05454-7). Lawyers Co-Op.
Blinderman, Abraham. American Writers on Education After 1865. (World Leader Ser.: No. 54). 1976. lib. bdg. 10.95 (ISBN 0-8057-7654-0). Twayne.
Bling, M. see Von Wiesner, J. & Von Regel, C.
Blinkhorn, M. Carlism & Crisis in Spain: 1931-1939. LC 75-2727. (Illus.). 408p. 1975. 51.50 (ISBN 0-521-20729-0). Cambridge U Pr.
Blinkhorn, S., jt. auth. see Saville, P.
Blinn, Lynn. Decisions: What to Eat. (Home Economics Ser.). (Illus.). 300p. (Orig.). 1981. pap. text ed. price not set (ISBN 0-8273-1853-7); price not set instr's guide (ISBN 0-8273-1854-5). Delmar.
--Making Decisions. LC 79-54910. 1981. pap. 5.28 (ISBN 0-8273-1712-3); instr's manual 1.50 (ISBN 0-8273-1711-5). Delmar.
Bliokh, P. V., et al. Schumann Resonances in the Earth Ionosphere Cavity. Jones, D. Llanwyn, ed. Chomer, S., tr. (Iee Electromagnetic Waves Ser.). (Illus.). 176p. 1980. softcover 62.00 (ISBN 0-906048-33-8, Pub. by Peregrinus London). Inst Elect Eng.
Blish, James. Black Easter - the Day After Judgment. (Science Fiction Ser.). 1980. lib. bdg. 16.95 (ISBN 0-8398-2644-3). Gregg.
--Cities in Flight. 1970. pap. 2.50 (ISBN 0-380-00998-6, 49908). Avon.
--Galactic Cluster. 176p. 1972. pap. 0.95 (ISBN 0-451-05441-5, Q5441, Sig). NAL.
--The Seedling Stars. 160p. 1972. pap. 1.25 (ISBN 0-451-06977-3, Y6977, Sig). NAL.
--Torrent of Faces. 1977. pap. 1.95 (ISBN 0-441-81782-3). Ace Bks.
Blishen, Edward. A Nest of Teachers. 186p. 1980. 19.95 (ISBN 0-241-10145-X, Pub. by Hamish Hamilton England). David & Charles.
--Sorry Dad: An Autobiography. 1979. 15.95 (ISBN 0-241-89849-8, Pub. by Hamish Hamilton England). David & Charles.
--The Thorny Paradise: Writers on Writing for Children. 1975. 8.50 (ISBN 0-7226-5463-4). Horn Bk.
Blishen, Edward, ed. Junior Pears Encyclopaedia. 20th ed. (Illus.). 704p. 1980. 11.95 (ISBN 0-7207-1263-7, Pub. by Michael Joseph). Merrimack Bk Serv.
--Junior Pears Encyclopedia. 19th ed. (Illus.). 704p. 1980. 9.95 o.p. (ISBN 0-7207-1158-4, Pub. by Michael Joseph). Merrimack Bk Serv.
--Oxford Book of Poetry for Children. LC 63-19091. (Illus.). (gr. k-3). 1964. PLB 7.90 o.p. (ISBN 0-531-01537-8). Watts.
Bliss. Bliss Bibliography, Second Class H: Anthropology, Human Biology & Health Sciences. 1981. price not set (ISBN 0-408-70828-X). Butterworth.
Bliss, Alan, ed. Spoken English in Ireland Sixteen Hundred to Seventeen Forty: Twenty Seven Representative Texts Assembled & Analysed. (Dolmen Texts: No. 5). 1979. text ed. 36.50x (ISBN 0-391-01119-7, Dolmen Pr). Humanities.
Bliss, Ann & Cohen, Eva. The New Health Professionals: Nurse Practitioners & Physician's Assistants. LC 76-46831. 1977. 29.95 (ISBN 0-912862-35-1). Aspen Systems.
Bliss, Anne. Handbook of Dyes. (Illus.). 180p. 1980. 15.95 (ISBN 0-684-16502-3, ScribT). Scribner.
Bliss, Betsy, jt. auth. see Ahern, Dee Dee.
Bliss, Betsy, jt. auth. see Gersten, Irene.
Bliss, Betsy L., jt. auth. see Brody, Eugene D.
Bliss, Bill, jt. auth. see Molinsky, Steven J.
Bliss, C. J. & Stern, N. H. Palanpur: The Economy of an Indian Village. (Illus.). 464p. 1981. 37.50 (ISBN 0-19-828419-5). Oxford U Pr.
Bliss, Christopher. Economic Growth & Resources: Natural Resources, Vol III. LC 79-4430. 1979. 37.50x (ISBN 0-312-23316-7). St Martin.
Bliss, Edward, Jr. & Patterson, John M. Writing News for Broadcast. 2nd ed. 1978. 17.50x (ISBN 0-231-04372-4). Columbia U Pr.
Bliss, George R. see Hovey, Alvah.
Bliss, Gilbert A. Lectures on the Calculus of Variations. LC 46-5369. 304p. 1980. 9.00x (ISBN 0-226-05896-4, Phoen). U of Chicago Pr.
Bliss, Gilbert A; see Evans, Griffith C.
Bliss, Jane, jt. auth. see Lerch, Constance.
Bliss, Michael. Confederation, 1867: Creating the Dominion of Canada. LC 75-9721. (World Focus Bks). (Illus.). 72p. (gr. 6 up). 1975. PLB 4.90 o.p. (ISBN 0-531-02173-4). Watts.
Bliss, Michael, jt. ed. see Grayson, Linda M.
Bliss, Sands & Co. The Magic Moving Picture Book. Orig. Title: The Motograph Moving Picture Book. 32p. (gr. 4 up). 1975. Repr. of 1898 ed. pap. 2.50 (ISBN 0-486-23224-7). Dover.
Bliss, Virginia, jt. auth. see Lerch, Constance.
Bliss, William R. Side Glimpses from the Colonial Meeting House. LC 70-140410. 1970. Repr. of 1894 ed. 18.00 (ISBN 0-8103-3594-8). Gale.
Blistein, Elmer M., ed. Drama of the Renaissance: Essays for Leicester Bradner. LC 72-91653. 199p. 1970. 8.50x (ISBN 0-87057-117-6, Pub. by Brown U Pr). Univ Pr of New England.
Blit, Lucjan. Origins of Polish Socialism: The History & Ideas of the First Polish Socialist Party, 1878-1886. LC 70-152642. (International Studies). 1971. 23.50 (ISBN 0-521-08192-0). Cambridge U Pr.
Blitstein, Dorothy. World of the Family: A Comparative Study of Family Organization in Their Social & Cultural Settings. 1963. text ed. 5.95 o.p. (ISBN 0-394-30072-6). Random.
Blitt, jt. auth. see Adair, J.
Blitzer, Charles. Age of Kings. LC 67-23412. (Great Ages of Man). (Illus.). (gr. 6 up). 1967. PLB 11.97 (ISBN 0-8094-0376-5, Pub. by Time-Life). Silver.
Blitzer, Charles, ed. see Harrington, James.
Blitzer, Charles, et al, eds. Economy-Wide Models & Development Planning. (World Research Bank Publications Ser). (Illus.). 1975. pap. 7.95x (ISBN 0-19-920074-2). Oxford U Pr.
Blitzer, Richard. Basic Electricity for Electronics. LC 73-20102. 727p. 1974. text ed. 21.95 (ISBN 0-471-08160-4). Wiley.
Bliven, B. Book Publishing & Selling. 1981. 28.50 o.p. (ISBN 0-686-68302-1). Porter.
Bliven, Bruce, Jr. The American Revolution. LC 80-20813. (Landmark Bks.). (Illus.). 160p. (gr. 5-9). 1981. pap. 2.95 (ISBN 0-394-84696-6). Random.
--The Finishing Touch. LC 78-1356. (Illus.). 1978. 8.95 (ISBN 0-396-07534-7). Dodd.
--From Casablanca to Berlin. (Landmark Ser, No. 112). (gr. 5-9). 1965. 2.95 o.p. (ISBN 0-394-80412-0, BYR); PLB 5.99 (ISBN 0-394-90412-5). Random.
--From Pearl Harbor to Okinawa. (Landmark Ser.: No. 94). (Illus.). (gr. 5-9). 1960. PLB 5.99 (ISBN 0-394-90394-3, BYR). Random.
--New York: The States & the Nation. (Illus.). 1981. 12.95 (ISBN 0-393-05665-1). Norton.
Blixrud, Julia C. A Manual of AACR 2 Examples for Serials. Snesrud, Janet E. & McClaskey, Marilyn J., eds. 50p. 1980. pap. 6.00 (ISBN 0-936996-04-8). Soldier Creek.
Bloch, Alfred, ed. see John Paul, Pope.
Bloch, Alice. Lifetime Guarantee. (Orig.). 1981. pap. price not set (ISBN 0-930436-09-1). Persephone.
Bloch, Barbara. If It Doesn't Pan Out: How to Cope with Cooking Disasters. LC 80-26508. 1981. 8.95 (ISBN 0-934878-02-1). Dembner Bks.
Bloch, Carolyn C. Coal Information Sources & Data Bases. LC 80-22344. 128p. 1981. 24.00 (ISBN 0-8155-0830-1). Noyes.
Bloch, Chayim. The Golem: Mystical Tales of the Ghetto. LC 75-183055. 288p. 1972. pap. 2.95 (ISBN 0-8334-1726-6). Steinerbks.
Bloch, Cheree, jt. auth. see Putterill, Martin.
Bloch, E. Atheism in Christianity. 12.50 (ISBN 0-8164-9102-X). Continuum.
Bloch, Ernst. A Philosophy of the Future. LC 79-110785. 1970. 5.95 o.p. (ISBN 0-8164-9134-8). Continuum.
Bloch, George, tr. see Mesmer, Franz A.
Bloch, Herbert & Niederhoffer, Arthur. Gang: A Study in Adolescent Behavior. 1958. 6.00 o.p. (ISBN 0-8022-0143-1). Philos Lib.
Bloch, Konrad E., et al, eds. Membranes, Molecules, Toxins, & Cells. LC 80-16595. 292p. 1981. 33.50 (ISBN 0-88416-309-1, 309). PSG Pub.
Bloch, Lolla, tr. see Taubes, Hella.
Bloch, Louis M., Jr. The Gas Pipe Networks: The Early History of College Radio, 1936-1946. (Illus.). 156p. 1981. 12.95 (ISBN 0-914276-02-6). Bloch & Co OH.
Bloch, Marc. French Rural History: An Essay on Its Basic Characteristics. Sondheimer, Janet, tr. (Illus.). 1966. 20.00x (ISBN 0-520-00127-3); pap. 6.95x (ISBN 0-520-01660-2, CAMPUS28). U of Cal Pr.
--Memoirs of War, Nineteen Fourteen to Nineteen Fifteen. Fink, Carole, tr. from Fr. LC 79-6849. Orig. Title: Souvenirs De Guerre. (Illus.). 184p. 1980. 15.00 (ISBN 0-8014-1220-X). Cornell U Pr.
Bloch, Mark. Slavery & Serfdom in the Middle Ages: Selected Papers by Marc Bloch. Beer, William R., tr. 320p. 1975. 25.75x (ISBN 0-520-01767-6). U of Cal Pr.
Bloch, Maurice, ed. Marxist Analysis & Social Anthropology. LC 75-4109. (Association of Social Anthropologists Studies: No. 3). 240p. 1975. 19.95 (ISBN 0-470-08205-4). Halsted Pr.
Bloch, Peter B. Equality of Distribution of Police Services: A Case Study of Washington, D.C. 27p. 1974. pap. 1.50 o.p. (ISBN 0-87766-113-8, 65000). Urban Inst.
Bloch, Peter B. & Specht, David I. Evaluation of Operation Neighborhood. 1973. pap. 7.00 o.p. (ISBN 0-87766-089-1, 26000). Urban Inst.
Bloch, R. Howard. Medieval French Literature & Law. LC 76-7754. 1977. 19.50x (ISBN 0-520-03230-6). U of Cal Pr.
Bloch, Robert. Pleasant Dreams: Nightmares. 1979. pap. 1.75 o.s.i. (ISBN 0-515-04743-0). Jove Pubns.
--Strange Eons. 1979. pap. 1.95 o.p. (ISBN 0-523-40447-6). Pinnacle Bks.
Bloch, Sidney, ed. An Introduction to the Psychotherapies. 1979. pap. text ed. 11.95x (ISBN 0-19-261217-4). Oxford U Pr.
Bloch, Stuart M. & Ingersoll, William B. Timesharing. LC 77-88799. (Illus.). 136p. 1977. pap. text ed. 19.50 (ISBN 0-87420-575-1). Urban Land.
Blocher, D. H. Developmental Counseling. 2nd ed. 320p. 1974. 17.50 (ISBN 0-471-06894-2). Wiley.
Blocher, Donald H. Developmental Counseling. 2nd ed. (Illus.). 371p. 1974. 17.50 (ISBN 0-8260-1131-4). Ronald Pr.
Bloch-Hoell, Nils. The Pentecostal Movement: Its Origin, Development & Distinctive Character. 1964. text ed. 19.00x (ISBN 8-200-06004-7, Dist. by Columbia U Pr). Universitet.
Blochman, Lawrence G. Understanding Your Body. LC 68-20263. (Illus.). (gr. 4-8). 1968. 3.95g o.s.i. (ISBN 0-02-710930-5, CCPr). Macmillan.
Block & Roering. Essentials of Cons. Behavior. 1979. 19.95 (ISBN 0-03-041961-1). Dryden Pr.
Block, A. The Changing World in Plays & Theatre. LC 73-77721. 448p. 1971. Repr. of 1939 ed. lib. bdg. 37.50 (ISBN 0-306-71359-4). Da Capo.
Block, Adrienne F. The Early French Parody Noel. Buelow, George, ed. (Studies in Musicology). 430p. 1981. 39.95 (ISBN 0-8357-1123-4, Pub. by UMI Res Pr). Univ Microfilms.
Block, Allan. In Noah's Wake. 1972. 5.95 o.p. (ISBN 0-87233-025-7). Bauhan.
Block, Gloria & Nolan, Joellen. Health Assessment for Professional Nursing: A Developmental Approach. 496p. 1981. 24.95 (ISBN 0-8385-3660-3). ACC.
Block, Haskell & Shedd, Robert, eds. Masters of Modern Drama. 1962. 29.95 (ISBN 0-394-40625-7); text ed. 27.95 (ISBN 0-394-30084-X). Random.
Block, Haskell M., ed. see Moliere, Jean B.
Block, Herb. Herblock on All Fronts. 1981. pap. 7.95 (ISBN 0-452-25266-0, Z5266, Plume). NAL.
Block, Irvin. The Lives of Pearl Buck: A Tale of China & America. Meltzer, Milton, ed. LC 73-8891. (Women of America Ser.). (gr. 5-9). 1973. 8.95 o.p. (ISBN 0-690-00165-7, TYC-J). T Y Crowell.
Block, J. Bradford. The Signs & Symptoms of Chemical Exposure. 164p. 1980. text ed. 12.75 lexotone (ISBN 0-398-03958-5). C C Thomas.
Block, J. L. Back in Circulation. 1969. 5.95 o.s.i. (ISBN 0-02-511580-4). Macmillan.
Block, Jerome B. Oncology: UCLA Postgraduate Medicine for the Internist. (Illus.). 1981. price not set (ISBN 0-89289-376-1). HM.
Block, Judy R. The First Woman in Congress: Jeanette Rankin. LC 78-14490. (Famous Firsts Ser.). (Illus.). 1978. lib. bdg. 7.35 (ISBN 0-686-51110-7). Silver.
--The World's First Police Detective. LC 78-16169. (Famous Firsts Ser.). (Illus.). 1978. lib. bdg. 7.35 (ISBN 0-686-51116-6). Silver.
Block, Julian. Tax Saving. LC 80-70260. 224p. 1981. 12.95 (ISBN 0-686-69525-9); pap. 7.95 (ISBN 0-686-69526-7). Chilton.
Block, Lawrence. Burglar in the Closet. 1981. pap. write for info. (ISBN 0-671-83581-5). PB.
--Burglars Can't Be Choosers. 1978. pap. 1.75 o.s.i. (ISBN 0-515-04584-5). Jove Pubns.
--Me Tanner, You Jane. LC 79-93176. (Cock Robin Mystery Ser). 1970. 4.50 o.s.i. (ISBN 0-02-511610-X). Macmillan.
Block, Lee F., ed. Marketing for Hospitals in Hard Times. 200p. 1981. text ed. 17.95 (ISBN 0-931028-16-7); pap. 13.95 (ISBN 0-931028-15-9). Teach'em.
Block, Marilyn. Women Over Forty: Visions & Realities. LC 80-20774. (Focus on Women Ser.: No. 4). 176p. 1980. text ed. 19.95 (ISBN 0-8261-3000-3); pap. text ed. 11.95 (ISBN 0-8261-3001-1). Springer Pub.
Block, Ned J., ed. Imagery. LC 81-24732. 192p. 1981. text ed. 15.00 (ISBN 0-89706-006-7); pap. text ed. 7.50 (ISBN 0-89706-007-5). Bradford Bks.
Block, Peter. Fifty-Fifty Consultation: A Guide to Getting Your Expertise Used. (Illus.). 200p. 1981. text ed. price not set (ISBN 0-89384-052-1). Learning Concepts.
Block, Richard. Violent Crime. LC 76-40818. (Illus.). 1977. 15.95 (ISBN 0-669-01044-8). Lexington Bks.
Block, Richard A., ed. Able Seaman & Lifevoatman: All Grades. rev. ed. (Illus.). 338p. 1978. pap. 21.00 (ISBN 0-934114-04-8). Marine Educ.
--Engineer-Chief & Assistant Engineer & Oiler: Limited to Service in the Mineral & Oil Industry. rev. ed. (Illus.). 82p. 1975. pap. text ed. 12.00 (ISBN 0-934114-07-2). Marine Educ.
--Motorboat Operator License Preparation Course. rev. ed. (Illus.). 269p. 1980. pap. text ed. 18.00 (ISBN 0-934114-29-3). Marine Educ.
--Ocean & Inland Operator License Preparation Course. rev. ed. (Illus.). 499p. 1979. pap. text ed. 42.00 (ISBN 0-934114-21-8). Marine Educ.
--Radiotelephone Operator. (Illus.). 70p. Date not set. pap. 9.00 (ISBN 0-934114-27-7). Marine Educ.
--Tankerman: All Grades. rev. ed. (Illus.). 250p. 1981. pap. 21.00 (ISBN 0-934114-30-7). Marine Educ.
--Understanding T-Boat Regulations. (Illus.). 143p. 1979. pap. text ed. 12.00 (ISBN 0-934114-22-6). Marine Educ.
Block, Richard A. & Collins, Charles B., eds. The M&O Master's Handbook. (Illus.). 271p. (Orig.). 1979. pap. text ed. 18.00 (ISBN 0-934114-16-1). Marine Educ.
--Standard Operations Manual for the Marine Transportation Sector of the Offshore Mineral & Oil Industry. 61p. (Orig.). 1979. pap. text ed. 7.50 (ISBN 0-934114-09-9). Marine Educ.
Block, Stanley B. & Hirt, Geoffrey A. Foundations of Financial Management. 1978. text ed. 20.95x (ISBN 0-256-02033-7). Irwin.
Block, Stanley B. & Louderback, Joseph G. Problems in Basic Business Finance. LC 73-9359. 240p. 1973. pap. text ed. 13.50 scp o.p. (ISBN 0-06-380585-5, HarpC); tchrs. ed. avail. o.p. (ISBN 0-06-371067-6). Har-Row.
Block, Thomas H. Mayday. 1980. pap. 2.95 (ISBN 0-425-04729-6). Berkley Pub.
Block, Toni. Yvette. (Orig.). 1978. pap. 1.95 o.p. (ISBN 0-523-40211-2). Pinnacle Bks.
Block, Walter. Defending the Undefendables: The Pimp, Prostitute, Scab, Usurer, Libeler, & Other Scapegoats in the Rogue's Gallery of American Society. new ed. LC 74-21359. 1976. 9.95 (ISBN 0-8303-0136-4); pap. 5.95 (ISBN 0-8303-0183-6). Fleet.
Blockcolsky, Valeda & Frazer, Joan. Star Trails, "CH". 1980. 20.00 (ISBN 0-88450-726-2, 3150-B). Communication Skill.
--Star Trails,"SH". 1980. 20.00 (ISBN 0-88450-727-0, 3140-B). Communication Skill.
--Star Trails,"TH". 1980. 20.00 (ISBN 0-88450-725-4, 3131-B). Communication Skill.
Blocker, H. Gene. The Metaphysics of Absurdity. LC 78-78399. 1979. pap. text ed. 9.00 (ISBN 0-8191-0712-3). U Pr of Amer.
Blocker, H. Gene & Smith, Elizabeth H., eds. John Rawls' Theory of Social Justice: An Introduction. LC 80-11272. xxiii, 520p. 1980. 22.95x (ISBN 0-8214-0445-8, 0445E); pap. 11.95x (ISBN 0-8214-0593-4). Ohio U Pr.
Blocker, William P., Jr. & Cardus, David, eds. Rehabilitation in Ischemic Heart Disease. 624p. 1981. text ed. 80.00 (ISBN 0-89335-096-6). Spectrum Pub.
Blockhaus, Arthur P. Grievance Arbitration Case Studies. LC 74-8433. 416p. 1974. 19.95 (ISBN 0-8436-0722-X). CBI Pub.
Blockhus, Wanda A., jt. auth. see Stewart, Jeffrey R., Jr.
Blockley, J., jt. auth. see Fraser, G. M.

Blockley, John. Creative Watercolour Techniques. (Leisure Arts Painting Ser.). (Illus.). 1980. pap. 2.50 (ISBN 0-8008-2005-3, Pentalic). Taplinger.

Blocksom, Claudia. It's Your World. (Illus.). 40p. (gr. 1-8). 1979. pap. 2.25 (ISBN 0-912300-19-1). Troubador Pr.

Blockson, Charles. Pennsylvania's Black History. (Illus.). 1981. pap. 5.95 (ISBN 0-933184-15-8). Flame Intl.

Blockson, Charles L. The Underground Railroad in Pennsylvania. LC 80-69847. (Illus.). 1981. 12.95 (ISBN 0-933184-21-2); pap. 6.95 (ISBN 0-933184-22-0). Flame Intl.

Blodgett, Harold W., ed. see Whitman, Walt.

Blodgett, Jean. The Coming & Going of the Shaman: Eskimo Shamanism & Art. (Illus.). 246p. 1981. pap. 17.50 (ISBN 0-88915-068-0, 08913-4, Pub. by Canadian Artic Producers Ltd). U of Chicago Pr.

Blodi, Frederick C., jt. auth. see Nover, Arno.

Bloemendal, Hans. Molecular & Cellular Biology of the Eye Lens. LC 80-26815. 400p. 1981. 45.00 (ISBN 0-471-05171-3, Pub. by Wiley-Interscience). Wiley.

Bloesch, Donald G. Faith & Its Counterfeits. 108p. (Orig.). 1981. pap. 3.95 (ISBN 0-87784-822-X). Inter Varsity.

--The Struggle of Prayer. LC 79-3589. 192p. 1980. 9.95 (ISBN 0-06-060797-1, HarpR). Har-Row.

Blofeld, J. Bangkok. (The Great Cities Ser.). (Illus.). 1979. lib. bdg. 11.97 (ISBN 0-8094-3101-7); kivar bdg. 11.49 (ISBN 0-8094-3102-5). Silver.

Blofeld, John. Beyond the Gods: Taoist & Buddhist Mysticism. 1974. 9.25 (ISBN 0-04-294084-2); pap. 6.95 (ISBN 0-04-294085-0). Allen Unwin.

--Gateway to Wisdom: Taoist & Buddhist Contemplative & Healing Yogas Adapted for Western Students of the Way. LC 79-67685. (Illus.). 1980. pap. 6.95 (ISBN 0-394-73878-0). Shambhala Pubns.

--Mantras: Sacred Words of Power. 1977. pap. 4.50 o.p. (ISBN 0-525-47451-X). Dutton.

--Taoism: The Road to Immortality. LC 77-90882. 1979. pap. 6.95 (ISBN 0-394-73582-X). Shambhala Pubns.

Blofeld, John, tr. I Ching, the Book of Change. 1968. pap. 3.95 (ISBN 0-525-47212-6). Dutton.

Blofeld, John, tr. see Huang Po.

Blois, K. J. & Cowell, D. W. Short Cases in Marketing Management. 1973. text ed. 16.50x (ISBN 0-7002-0207-2). Intl Ideas.

Blok, D. P., ed. Proceedings of the Eighth International Congress of Onomastic Sciences, Amsterdam, 1963. (Janua Linguarum Series Major: No. 17). 1966. 135.30x (ISBN 90-2790-609-2). Mouton.

Blom, Eric. Beethoven's Pianoforte Sonatas Discussed. LC 68-21092. (Music Ser). 1968. Repr. of 1938 ed. 22.50 (ISBN 0-306-71059-5). Da Capo.

--Classics: Major & Minor. LC 74-166098. 212p. 1972. Repr. of 1958 ed. lib. bdg. 19.50 (ISBN 0-306-70293-2). Da Capo.

--A General Index to Modern Musical Literature in the English Language: Including Periodicals for the Years 1915-1926. LC 71-108736. (Music Ser). 1970. Repr. of 1927 ed. lib. bdg. 17.50 (ISBN 0-306-71898-7). Da Capo.

--Romance of the Piano. LC 69-15608. (Music Ser). (Illus.). 1969. Repr. of 1928 ed. 19.50 (ISBN 0-306-71060-9). Da Capo.

Blom, Eric, tr. see Deutsch, Otto E.

Blom, Margaret. Charlotte Bronte. (English Authors Ser.: No. 203). 1977. lib. bdg. 10.95 (ISBN 0-8057-6673-1). Twayne.

Blomberg, Thomas G. Juvenile Court Reform: Widening the Social Control Net. 256p. 1981. lib. bdg. 20.00 (ISBN 0-89946-087-9). Oelgeschlager.

Blomberg, Thomas G., jt. ed. see Brantingham, Patricia L.

Blom-Cooper, L. Law & Morality: A Reader. Dreway, Gavin, ed. 265p. 1976. 40.50x (ISBN 0-7156-0805-3, Pub. by Duckworth England); pap. 13.50x (ISBN 0-7156-0804-5). Biblio Dist.

Blom-Cooper, Louis, ed. Progress in Penal Reform. 296p. 1975. 36.00x (ISBN 0-19-825325-7). Oxford U Pr.

Blomfield, Lady. The Chosen Highway. Hofman, David, ed. LC 67-16026. (Illus.). 7.95 o.p. (ISBN 0-87743-015-2, 7-31-07); pap. 4.95 o.p. (ISBN 0-87743-037-3, 7-31-08). Baha'i.

Blommers, Paul J. & Forsyth, Robert A. Elementary Statistical Methods in Psychology & Education. 2nd ed. LC 76-11983. (Illus.). 608p. 1976. text ed. 18.95 (ISBN 0-395-24340-8); study manual 8.50 (ISBN 0-395-24339-4); solutions manual 1.35 (ISBN 0-395-24341-6). HM.

Blomquist, Kathleen B., et al. Community Health Nursing Continuing Education Review. 1979. pap. 9.50 (ISBN 0-87488-401-2). Med Exam.

Blomquist, Laura L., jt. auth. see Dougherty, Richard M.

Blomstrom, Robert, jt. auth. see Davis, Keith.

Blond, Georges. Dreams of France. (Illus.). 120p. 1969. 13.50x (ISBN 0-8002-0756-4). Intl Pubns Serv.

Blondal, S. The Varangians of Byzantium. Benedikz, S., tr. LC 77-82486. (Illus.). 1979. 49.95 (ISBN 0-521-21745-8). Cambridge U Pr.

Blonde, Allan. The Complete Guide to Researching & Writing the English Term Paper. LC 78-63036. (Orig.). 1978. pap. text ed. 3.95x (ISBN 0-87936-013-5). Scholium Intl.

Blondel, J., jt. auth. see Ridley, F.

Blondel, Jean. Comparative Legislatures. (Contemporary Comparative Politics Ser.). (Illus.). 176p. 1973. ref. ed. 7.95 (ISBN 0-13-153874-8); pap. text ed. 7.95 (ISBN 0-13-153866-7). P-H.

--Thinking Politically. LC 75-38746. 1976. 19.50x (ISBN 0-89158-536-2). Westview.

--World Leaders. LC 79-63826. (Illus.). 1980. 20.00x o.p. (ISBN 0-8039-9830-9); pap. 9.95x o.p. (ISBN 0-8039-9831-7). Sage.

Blondel De Nesle. Der Lieder Des Blondel De Nesle. LC 80-2157. 1981. Repr. of 1904 ed. 35.50 (ISBN 0-404-19023-5). AMS Pr.

Blondis, Marion N. & Jackson, Barbara. Nonverbal Communication with Patients: Back to the Human Touch. LC 76-30732. 1977. 8.95 (ISBN 0-471-01753-1, Pub. by Wiley Medical). Wiley.

Blonk, W. A. Transport & Regional Development. 1979. text ed. 43.25x (ISBN 0-566-00285-X, Pub. by Gower Pub Co England). Renouf.

Blonsky, Marshal, ed. A Semiotics Reader: The Manipulation of Signs & Symbols in Culture. Date not set. 17.50 (ISBN 0-89396-008-X); pap. 7.95 (ISBN 0-89396-009-8). Urizen Bks.

Blood, Bob & Blood, Margaret. Marriage. 3rd ed. LC 77-3847. 1978. text ed. 15.95 (ISBN 0-02-904180-5). Free Pr.

Blood, Charles L. & Link, Martin. The Goat in the Rug. LC 80-17315. (Illus.). 40p. (ps-3). 1980. Repr. of 1976 ed. 8.95 (ISBN 0-590-07763-5, Four Winds). Schol Bk Serv.

Blood, F. R., ed. Essays in Toxicology, Vols. 1-7. Incl. Vol. 1. 1969. o. p. 22.50 (ISBN 0-12-107601-6); pap. 11.50 (ISBN 0-12-107651-2); Vol. 2. 1970. 31.50 (ISBN 0-12-107602-4); pap. 11.50 (ISBN 0-12-107652-0); Vol. 3. Hayes, Wayland J., Jr. 1972. 19.00 (ISBN 0-12-107603-2); pap. 11.50 (ISBN 0-12-107653-9); Vol. 4. 1973. 31.50 (ISBN 0-12-107604-0); pap. write for info. o. p.; Vol. 5. 1974. 31.00 (ISBN 0-12-107605-9); Vol. 6. 1975. 31.50 (ISBN 0-12-107606-7); lib ed. 46.00 (ISBN 0-12-107674-1); microfiche 23.00 (ISBN 0-12-107675-X); Vol. 7. 1976. 36.00 (ISBN 0-12-107607-5); lib ed. 44.00 (ISBN 0-12-107676-8); microfiche 27.00 (ISBN 0-12-107677-6). Acad Pr.

Blood-Horse, ed. Principal Winners Abroad of 1979. (Annual Supplement, the Blood-Horse). (Orig.). 1980. pap. 10.00 (ISBN 0-936032-07-3). Thoroughbred Own & Breed.

--Sires of Runners of 1979. (Annual Supplement). 1980. lib. bdg. 20.00 (ISBN 0-936032-19-7); pap. 10.00 (ISBN 0-936032-20-0). Thoroughbred Own & Breed.

--Stakes Winners of 1979. (Annual Supplement, the Blood-Horse). 1980. lib. bdg. 20.00 (ISBN 0-936032-23-5); pap. 10.00 (ISBN 0-936032-24-3). Thoroughbred Own & Breed.

Blood Horse, ed. Stallion Register, 1981. (Illus.). 900p. 1980. 20.00 (ISBN 0-936032-33-2); pap. 10.00 (ISBN 0-936032-34-0). Thoroughbred Own & Breed.

Blood-Horse Editors. Auctions of 1980. (Annual Supplement of the Blood-Horse). (Illus.). 190p. (Orig.). 1981. pap. 10.00 (ISBN 0-936032-36-7). Thoroughbred Own & Breed.

--Principal Winners Abroad of 1980. (Annual Supplement of the Blood-Horse). (Orig.). 1981. pap. 10.00 (ISBN 0-936032-38-3). Thoroughbred Own & Breed.

--Sires of Runners, 1980. 1981. pap. 10.00 (ISBN 0-936032-37-5). Thoroughbred Own & Breed.

--Stakes Winners of 1980. (Annual Supplement of the Blood-Horse). 1981. lib. bdg. 20.00 (ISBN 0-936032-39-1); pap. 10.00 (ISBN 0-936032-40-5). Thoroughbred Own & Breed.

Blood-Horse-Thoroughbred Owners & Breeders Assn., ed. The Breeder's Guide for 1979. (Bound Supplements of the Blood-Horse). 1980. 51.75 (ISBN 0-936032-01-4). Thoroughbred Own & Breed.

Blood, Margaret, jt. auth. see Blood, Bob.

Blood, Marie. If Once You Have Lived in Alaska. 1981. 6.95 (ISBN 0-533-04715-3). Vantage.

Blood, Marje. Exploring the Oregon Coast by Car. LC 80-25484. (Illus.). 224p. (Orig.). 1980. pap. 6.95 (ISBN 0-916076-41-5). Writing.

Blood, Robert O., Jr. The Family. LC 71-161235. 1972. text ed. 15.95 (ISBN 0-02-904150-3). Free Pr.

Blood, Robert O., Jr. & Wolfe, D. M. Husbands & Wives: The Dynamics of Married Living. LC 59-6824. 1965. pap. text ed. 5.95 (ISBN 0-02-904070-1). Free Pr.

Bloodstein, Oliver. Speech Pathology: An Introduction. LC 78-69600. (Illus.). 1979. text ed. 17.75 (ISBN 0-395-27048-0). HM.

Bloodworth, Dennis. Any Number Can Play. LC 72-79865. 1972. 6.95 o.p. (ISBN 0-374-10537-5). FS&G.

--The Chinese Looking Glass. rev. ed. 1980. 15.00 (ISBN 0-374-12241-5); pap. 8.95 (ISBN 0-374-51493-3). FS&G.

Bloodworth, Dennis & Ching Ping. Heirs Apparent: What Happens When Mao Dies? 272p. 1973. 7.95 (ISBN 0-374-16898-9). FS&G.

Bloodworth, J. M., Jr. Endocrine Pathology: General & Surgical. 2nd ed. (Illus.). 950p. 1981. write for info. (0854-4). Williams & Wilkins.

Bloodworth, William, Jr. Upton Sinclair. (United States Authors Ser.: No. 294). 1977. lib. bdg. 10.95 (ISBN 0-8057-7197-2). Twayne.

Bloom. The Language of Medicine in English. (English for Careers Ser.). (gr. 10 up). 1981. pap. text ed. 3.25 (ISBN 0-88345-351-7). Regents Pub.

Bloom, Alan. Moisture Gardening. (Illus.). 1966. 8.95 o.p. (ISBN 0-8231-6020-3). Branford.

--Perennials for Your Garden. LC 75-4057. (Encore Edition). (Illus.). 1974. 3.95 o.p. (ISBN 0-684-15236-3, ScribT). Scribner.

--Your Book of Traction Engines. (Your Book Ser.). (Illus.). 1975. 6.95 (ISBN 0-571-10413-4, Pub. by Faber & Faber). Merrimack Bk Serv.

Bloom, Alfred. Tannisho: A Resource for Modern Living. LC 80-39523. 112p. (Orig.). 1981. pap. 4.95 (ISBN 0-938474-00-6). Buddhist Study.

Bloom, Alfred H. Linguistic Shaping of Thought: A Study in the Impact of Language on Thinking in China & the West. 128p. 1981. prof. & reference 16.50 (ISBN 0-89859-089-2). L Erlbaum Assocs.

Bloom, Allan, ed. see Kojeve, Alexandre.

Bloom, Anthony. Living Prayer. 1975. pap. 4.95 (ISBN 0-87243-054-5). Templegate.

Bloom, Arnold. Toohey's Medicine for Nurses. 13th ed. (Illus.). 1981. pap. text ed. 17.50 (ISBN 0-443-02201-1). Churchill.

Bloom, Barbara. Utilization Patterns and Financial Characteristics of Nursing Homes in the United States: 1977 Nnhs. Shipp, Audrey, ed. (Series Thirteen: No. 53). 50p. 1981. pap. 1.75 (ISBN 0-8406-0215-4). Natl Ctr Health Stats.

Bloom, Benjamin S. & Krathwohl, David R. Taxonomy of Educational Objectives: Handbook 1: Cognitive Domain. LC 64-12369. 1977. pap. 7.95x (ISBN 0-582-28010-9). Longman.

Bloom, Benjamin S. & Madaus, George F. Evaluation to Improve Learning. (Illus.). 352p. (Orig.). 1981. pap. text ed. 13.95 (ISBN 0-07-006109-2). McGraw.

Bloom, Bernard, ed. Psychological Stress in the Campus Community. LC 74-6184. (Community Psychology Ser: No. 3). 282p. 1975. text ed. 22.95 (ISBN 0-87705-145-3). Human Sci Pr.

Bloom, D. M. Linear Algebra & Geometry. LC 77-26666. 1979. 41.50 (ISBN 0-521-21959-0); pap. 21.95x (ISBN 0-521-29324-3). Cambridge U Pr.

Bloom, Edward A. & Bloom, Lillian D. Joseph Addison's Sociable Animal: In the Market Place, On the Hustings, In the Pulpit. LC 73-111455. (Illus.). 276p. 1971. 12.50x (ISBN 0-87057-120-6, Pub. by Brown U Pr). Univ Pr of New England.

Bloom, Edward A., ed. Shakespeare 1564-1964: A Collection of Modern Essays by Various Hands. LC 64-17777. 226p. 1967. Repr. of 1964 ed. 10.00x (ISBN 0-87057-083-8, Pub. by Brown U Pr). Univ Pr of New England.

Bloom, Edward A. & Bloom, Lillian D., eds. The Variety of Fiction: A Critical Anthology. LC 65-79102. 1969. pap. 7.50 (ISBN 0-672-63137-7). Odyssey Pr.

Bloom, Edward A., ed. see Burney, Fanny.

Bloom, Edward A., ed. see Burney, Frances.

Bloom, Edward A., et al, eds. The Order of Poetry: An Introduction. (Orig.). 1961. pap. 4.95 (ISBN 0-672-63078-8). Odyssey Pr.

--The Variety of Poetry: An Anthology. LC 64-13149. (Orig.). 1964. pap. 5.50 (ISBN 0-672-63138-5). Odyssey Pr.

Bloom, Edward A., et al, eds. see Burney, Fanny.

Bloom, Floyd E., ed. Peptides: Integrators of Cell & Tissue Function, Vol. 35. (Society of General Physiologists Ser.). 250p. 1980. text ed. 25.00 (ISBN 0-89004-485-6). Raven.

Bloom, George F. & Harrison, Henry S. Appraising the Single Family Residence. 1978. 20.00 (ISBN 0-911780-40-8). Am Inst Real Estate Appraisers.

Bloom, Gordon F. & Northrup, Herbert R. Economics of Labor Relations. 8th ed. 1977. text ed. 19.50x (ISBN 0-256-01910-X). Irwin.

Bloom, Harold. The Flight to Lucifer: A Gnostic Fantasy. LC 79-22095. 1980. pap. 3.95 (ISBN 0-394-74323-7, V-323, Vin). Random.

--A Map of Misreading. 218p. 1980. pap. 4.95 (ISBN 0-19-502809-0, GB 623). Oxford U Pr.

--Wallace Stevens: The Poems of Our Climate. 416p. 1980. pap. 8.95 (ISBN 0-8014-9185-1). Cornell U Pr.

Bloom, Harold, ed. Romanticism & Consciousness. (Orig.). 1970. pap. text ed. 7.95x (ISBN 0-393-09954-7, NortonC). Norton.

Bloom, Harold, ed. see Ruskin, John.

Bloom, J. Harvey. Folk Lore, Old Customs & Superstitions in Shakespeare Land. LC 73-2830. viii, 167p. 1973. Repr. of 1930 ed. 10.00 (ISBN 0-8103-3269-8). Gale.

--Shakespeare's Garden: Being a Compendium of Quotations & References from the Bard to All Manner of Flower, Tree, Bush, Vine & Herb. LC 78-77000. (Tower Bks). (Illus.). 1971. Repr. of 1903 ed. 22.00 (ISBN 0-8103-3916-1). Gale.

Bloom, Jack D. Biology Experiments. LC 78-19643. (Pegasus Books: No. 14). 1968. 7.50x (ISBN 0-234-77998-5). Intl Pubns Serv.

Bloom, Kathleen, ed. Prospective Issues in Infancy Research. LC 80-17479. 208p. 1981. text ed. 19.95 (ISBN 0-89859-059-0). L Erlbaum Assocs.

Bloom, L. Z., et al. The New Assertive Woman. 1976. pap. 2.25 (ISBN 0-440-16393-5, LE). Dell.

Bloom, Lillian D., jt. auth. see Bloom, Edward A.

Bloom, Lillian D., jt. ed. see Bloom, Edward A.

Bloom, Lillian D., ed. see Burney, Fanny.

Bloom, Lois. One Word at a Time: The Use of Single Word Utterances Before Syntax. LC 72-94445. (Janua Linguarum, Ser. Minor: No. 154). 262p. 1973. pap. text ed. 21.20x (ISBN 90-2793-375-8). Mouton.

Bloom, Lois & Lahey, Margaret. Language Development & Language Disorders. LC 77-21482. (Communication Disorders Ser.). 1978. text ed. 22.95 (ISBN 0-471-08220-1). Wiley.

Bloom, Lois, ed. Readings in Language Development. LC 77-10717. (Communications Disorders Ser.). 1978. text ed. 19.95 (ISBN 0-471-08221-X). Wiley.

Bloom, Lynda. The Horse of Course! Guide to Winning at Western Trail Riding. LC 78-13541. (Illus.). 1980. 12.95 (ISBN 0-668-04569-8, 4569). Arco.

Bloom, Lynn Z. & Coburn, Karen. The New Assertive Woman. 1975. 7.95 o.s.i. (ISBN 0-440-06439-2). Delacorte.

Bloom, M. H., ed. see Symposium on Computers in Aerodynamics at the Aerodynamics Laboratories Polytechnic Institute of New York, 1979.

Bloom, Marc. Cross-Country Running. LC 77-84523. 193p. 1978. pap. 3.95 (ISBN 0-89037-092-3); write for info. handbk. (ISBN 0-89037-091-5). Anderson World.

--The Marathon: What It Takes to Go the Distance. LC 80-18859. (Illus.). 304p. 1981. 15.95 (ISBN 0-03-052476-8); pap. 8.95 (ISBN 0-686-69124-5). HR&W.

Bloom, Martin. The Paradox of Helping: Introduction to the Philosophy of Scientific Practice. LC 74-13524. 283p. 1975. text ed. 20.95 (ISBN 0-471-08235-X). Wiley.

--Primary Prevention: The Possible Science. (P-H Ser. in Social Work). (Illus.). 288p. 1981. pap. text ed. 7.95 (ISBN 0-13-700062-6). P-H.

Bloom, Michael V. Adolescent-Parental Separation. LC 79-13928. 177p. 1980. 22.95 (ISBN 0-470-26739-X). Halsted Pr.

Bloom, Murray T. The Thirteenth Man. 1977. 10.95 (ISBN 0-02-511770-X). Macmillan.

Bloom, Naomi. Contributions of Women: Religion. LC 77-20034. (Contributions of Women Ser.). (Illus.). (gr. 6 up). 1978. PLB 8.95 (ISBN 0-87518-123-6). Dillon.

Bloom, Samuel W. Doctor & His Patient: A Sociological Interpretation. LC 66-1994. 1965. pap. text ed. 4.95 (ISBN 0-02-903890-1). Free Pr.

--Power & Dissent in the Medical School. LC 73-8356. 1973. pap. text ed. 4.95 (ISBN 0-02-904250-X). Free Pr.

Bloom, Ursula. Prelude to Yesterday. 1978. pap. 1.95 o.p. (ISBN 0-523-40212-0). Pinnacle Bks.

Bloomberg, Marty & Evans, G. Edward. Introduction to Technical Services for Library Technicians. 4th ed. (Library Science Text Ser.). (Illus.). 325p. 1981. lib. bdg. 19.50 (ISBN 0-87287-228-9); pap. text ed. 14.50x (ISBN 0-87287-248-3). Libs Unl.

--Introduction to Technical Services for Library Technicians. 3rd ed. LC 76-43294. (Library Science Text Ser.). 1976. lib. bdg. 15.00x (ISBN 0-87287-125-8). Libs Unl.

Bloomberg, Marty & Weber, Hans. An Introduction to Classification & Number Building in Dewey. LC 76-26975. 200p. 1976. lib. bdg. 18.50x (ISBN 0-87287-115-0). Libs Unl.

Bloomberg, Warner, Jr. & Schmandt, Henry J., eds. Power, Poverty & Urban Policy. LC 68-24710. (Urban Affairs Annual Reviews: Vol. 2). 1968. 25.00x (ISBN 0-8039-0006-6); pap. 9.95x (ISBN 0-8039-0031-7). Sage.

Bloomenthal, Harold. Securities & Federal Corporate Law, 3 vols. LC 72-90956. 1972. Set. looseleaf with 1979 rev. pages 215.00 (ISBN 0-87632-086-8). Boardman.

Bloomenthal, Harold S. Securities Law Handbook, 1979. 1979. pap. 11.75 (ISBN 0-87632-273-9). Boardman.

--Securities Law in Perspective. 1977. pap. text ed. 6.95 (ISBN 0-316-09988-0). Little.

Bloomenthal, Harold S., ed. Securities Law Review Annual. Incl. 1976 (ISBN 0-87632-177-5); 1977 (ISBN 0-87632-178-3); 1978 (ISBN 0-87632-179-1). LC 72-96215. 47.50 ea. Boardman.

Bloomer, M. & Shaw, K. E. Constraint & Innovation: The Content & Organization of Schooling. 1979. 33.00 (ISBN 0-08-022994-8); pap. 15.75 (ISBN 0-08-022993-X). Pergamon.

Bloomfield, tr. see Mueller, F. Max.

Bloomfield, Arthur. The Changing Climate. LC 77-80427. 1977. pap. 1.95 (ISBN 0-87123-060-7, 200060). Bethany Fell.

Bloomfield, Arthur E. All Things New. LC 42-5300. 1959. pap. 5.95 (ISBN 0-87123-007-0); study guide .95 (ISBN 0-87123-520-X). Bethany Fell.

--End of the Days. LC 51-9505. 1961. 5.95 (ISBN 0-87123-122-0, 210122). Bethany Fell.

--How to Recognize the Antichrist. LC 75-29424. 1975. pap. 3.50 (ISBN 0-87123-225-1, 210225). Bethany Fell.

--Signs of His Coming. LC 57-8724. 1962. pap. 3.95 (ISBN 0-87123-513-7, 210513). Bethany Fell.

--Where Is the Ark of the Covenant? LC 76-2257. 1976. pap. 1.75 (ISBN 0-87123-004-6, 200004). Bethany Fell.

Bloomfield, Dennis A. & Simon, Hansjorg. Cardio Active Drugs: Pharmachlogical Basis for Practice. 1981. price not set. Urban & S.

Bloomfield, Derek. From Arithmetic to Algebra. (Illus.). 1976. pap. 12.95 (ISBN 0-87909-289-0); instrs'. manual avail. Reston.

Bloomfield, Gerald. The World Automotive Industry. LC 77-91774. 1978. 38.00 (ISBN 0-7153-7539-3). David & Charles.

Bloomfield, Harold H., et al. TM: Discovering Inner Energy & Overcoming Stress. 1975. 8.95 o.s.i. (ISBN 0-440-06048-6). Delacorte.

Bloomfield, Irirangi C., jt. auth. see Bloomfield, Lincoln P.

Bloomfield, Janet. The Concise Dictionary of Cats. LC 76-51527. (Funk & W Bk.). (Illus.). 1977. 9.95 o.s.i. (ISBN 0-308-10278-9, TYC-T). T Y Crowell.

Bloomfield, Leonard. The Menominio Language. 1962. 47.50x (ISBN 0-686-50049-0). Elliots Bks.

--Spoken Dutch. LC 75-15107. (Spoken Language Ser.). (Prog. Bk.). 1975. pap. 9.00x (ISBN 0-87950-054-9); cassettes 5 dual track 50.00x (ISBN 0-87950-060-3); cassettes with course-bk. 55.00x (ISBN 0-87950-061-1). Spoken Lang Serv.

Bloomfield, Lincoln P. & Bloomfield, Irirangi C. The U. S., Interdependence & World Order. LC 75-36296. (Headline Ser.: 228). (Orig.). 1975. pap. 2.00 (ISBN 0-87124-033-5). Foreign Policy.

Bloomfield, Louis M. & FitzGerald, Gerald F. Crimes Against Internationally Protected Persons: Prevention & Punishment - an Analysis of the UN Convention. LC 74-33031. 296p. 1975. text ed. 28.95 (ISBN 0-275-05350-4). Praeger.

Bloomfield, Morton, jt. ed. see Haugen, Einar.

Bloomfield, Morton W. & Black, Max, eds. In Search of Literary Theory. (Studies in Humanities Ser.). 272p. 1972. 16.50x o.p. (ISBN 0-8014-0714-1). Cornell U Pr.

Bloomfield, P. L. P. Hartley. pap. 2.95 (ISBN 0-685-31890-7, WTW217, WTW217). British Bk Ctr.

Bloomfield, Paul. Benjamin Disraeli. Dobree, Bonamy, et al, eds. Bd. with William Makepeace Thackeray. Brander, Laurence A; Charles Dickens. Fielding, K. J; Anthony Trollope. Davies, Hugh S. LC 63-63096. (British Writers & Their Work Ser: Vol. 9). 1965. pap. 3.25x (ISBN 0-8032-5659-0, BB 452, Bison). U of Nebr Pr.

Bloomfield, Peter. Fourier Analysis of Time Series: An Introduction. LC 75-34294. (Probability & Mathematical Statistics Ser.). 258p. 1976. 25.95 (ISBN 0-471-08256-2, Pub. by Wiley-Interscience). Wiley.

Bloomfield, Robert. Robert Bloomfield (Seventeen Sixty-Six to Eighteen Twenty-Three) Rural Tales, Ballads & Songs. Reiman, Donald H., ed. LC 75-31161. (Romantic Context Ser.: Poetry 1789-1830). 1977. lib. bdg. 47.00 (ISBN 0-8240-2115-0). Garland Pub.

--Robert Bloomfield: Wild Flowers; or, Pastoral & Local Poetry. 1806. Reiman, Donald H., ed. LC 75-31162. (Romantic Context Ser.: Poetry 1789-1830). 1977. lib. bdg. 47.00 (ISBN 0-8240-2116-9). Garland Pub.

Bloomfield, Victor A. & Harrington, Rodney E.intro. by. Biophysical Chemistry: Physical Chemistry in the Biological Sciences, Readings from Scientific American. LC 75-8748. (Illus.). 1975. text ed. 19.95x (ISBN 0-7167-0513-3); pap. text ed. 9.95x (ISBN 0-7167-0512-5). W H Freeman.

Bloomingdale, Teresa. I Should Have Seen It Coming When the Rabbit Died. 208p. 1980. pap. 2.25 (ISBN 0-553-13744-1). Bantam.

Bloomstein, Morris J. Consumer's Guide to Fighting Back. LC 76-12428. 1976. 7.95 (ISBN 0-396-07321-2). Dodd.

Bloor, Byron M. Cerebral Hemodynamics in Man & Monkey: Some Considerations in Cerebrovascular Disease, Subarachnoid Hemorrhage, & Intracranial Pressure. (Illus.). 132p. 1981. 19.75 (ISBN 0-398-04066-4). C C Thomas.

Bloor, C. H. Pathology. (Illus.). 1981. pap. text ed. write for info. (ISBN 0-443-08073-9). Churchill.

Bloor, Colin M. & Liebow, Averill A. The Pulmonary & Bronchial Circulations in Congenital Heart Disease. (Topics in Cardiovascular Disease Ser.). (Illus.). 284p. 1980. 32.50 (ISBN 0-306-40383-8, Plenum Pr). Plenum Pub.

Blos, Peter. On Adolescence: A Psychoanalytic Interpretation. LC 61-14110. 1962. 15.95 (ISBN 0-02-904320-4); pap. 4.95 (ISBN 0-02-904330-1). Free Pr.

--Young Adolescent. LC 73-125597. 1970. 15.95 (ISBN 0-02-904310-7); pap. 3.95 (ISBN 0-02-904300-X). Free Pr.

Bloss, Donald F. The Spindle Stage: Principles & Practice. LC 80-21488. (Illus.). 416p. Date not set. price not set (ISBN 0-521-23292-9). Cambridge U Pr.

Bloss, F. Donald, jt. auth. see Fang, Jen-Ho.

Blossey, E. C. & Neckers, D. C., eds. Solid Phase Synthesis. (Benchmark Papers in Organic Chemistry Ser: Vol. 2). 400p. 1975. 43.50 (ISBN 0-12-786165-3). Acad Pr.

Blot, David, jt. auth. see Davidson, David.

Blotner, Joseph. Faulkner: A Biography, 2 vols. (Illus.). 1974. Boxed Set. 30.00 (ISBN 0-394-47452-X). Random.

Blotner, Joseph, ed. see Faulkner, William.

Blotner, Joseph L., jt. ed. see Gwynn, Frederick L.

Blotnick, Elihu. Blue Turtle Moon Queen. (Illus.). 120p. (gr. 8-12). 1980. pap. 4.95 (ISBN 0-915090-20-1). Calif Street.

Blotnick, Elihu & Robinson, Barbara. Free-for-All: The Reds, the Whites & the Blues. (Illus.). 64p. (Orig.). 1981. pap. 6.95 (ISBN 0-915090-02-3). Calif Street.

Blouch, Ralph I., ed. see International Association of Fish & Wildlife Agencies.

Blouet, Brian. The Story of Malta. (Story Ser.). (Illus., Orig.). 1972. pap. 6.95 (ISBN 0-571-09654-9, Pub. by Faber & Faber). Merrimack Bk Serv.

Blouet, Brian W. & Stitcher, Teresa L., eds. The Origins of Academic Geography in the United States. 1981. 37.50 (ISBN 0-208-01881-6, Archon). Shoe String.

Blough, Roger M. The Washington Embrace of Business. 160p. 1975. 12.50x (ISBN 0-915604-03-5). Columbia U Pr.

Blouin, Francis X., ed. see Geda, Carolyn L., et al.

Blouin, Lenora P. May Sarton: A Bibliography. (Author Bibliography Ser.: No. 34). 1978. 12.00 (ISBN 0-8108-1054-9). Scarecrow.

Blount, Charles. Miscellaneous Works. LC 75-11197. (British Philosophers & Theologians of the 17th & 18th Centuries: Vol. 4). 1976. Repr. of 1695 ed. lib. bdg. 42.00 (ISBN 0-8240-1753-6). Garland Pub.

Blount, Charles, et al. A Just Vindication of Learning. Berkowitz, David S. & Thorne, Samuel E., eds. LC 77-86655. (Classics of English Legal History in the Modern Era Ser.: Vol. 39). 109p. 1979. lib. bdg. 40.00 (ISBN 0-8240-3088-5). Garland Pub.

Blount, James. Equations. 1981. 5.75 (ISBN 0-8062-1653-0). Carlton.

Blount, Paul G. George Sand & the Victorian World. LC 78-4274. 200p. 1979. 15.00x (ISBN 0-8203-0451-4). U of Ga Pr.

Blow, Suzanne K. A Study of Rhetoric in the Plays of Thomas Dekker. (Salzburg Studies in English Literature, Jacobean Drama Studies: No. 3). 1972. pap. text ed. 25.00x (ISBN 0-391-01327-0). Humanities.

Blower, J. G., et al. Estimating the Size of Animal Populations. 1st ed. 96p. (Orig.). 1981. text ed. 22.50x (ISBN 0-04-591017-0); pap. text ed. 9.95x (ISBN 0-04-591018-9). Allen Unwin.

Blowers & Smith. How to Read an ECG. 1977. pap. 6.00 (ISBN 0-8273-1307-1). Delmar.

Blowers, Andrew. The Limits of Power: The Politics of Local Planning Policy. (Urban & Regional Planning Ser.: Vol. 21). (Illus.). 23.00 (ISBN 0-08-023016-4). Pergamon.

Blowers, G. H., jt. ed. see Dawson, J. L.

Bloxsom, Peter, jt. auth. see Schollick, Nigel.

Bloy, Colin H. A History of Printing Ink, Balls & Tollers: 1440-1850. (Illus.). 17.50 (ISBN 0-913720-07-0). Sandstone.

Bloy, Myron B., Jr., jt. ed. see Hodgkinson, Harold L.

Bloy, Myron B., Jr., et al. The Recovery of Spirit in Higher Education. Rankin, Robert, ed. 1980. 14.95 (ISBN 0-8164-0469-0). Seabury.

Bluck, R. S., ed. see Plato.

Bluck, R. S., tr. see Plato.

Blue, Rose. Bed-Stuy Beat. LC 75-117178. (Illus.). (gr. 4-6). 1970. PLB 5.90 (ISBN 0-531-01940-3). Watts.

--Grandma Didn't Wave Back. LC 79-189568. 64p. (gr. 3-5). 1972. PLB 6.90 (ISBN 0-531-02557-8). Watts.

--I Am Here: Yo estoy acqui. LC 79-117183. (Illus.). (gr. k-3). 1971. PLB 4.33 o.p. (ISBN 0-531-01943-8). Watts.

--A Month of Sundays. LC 72-182293. (Illus.). 64p. (gr. 3-5). 1972. PLB 6.90 (ISBN 0-531-02037-1). Watts.

--My Mother the Witch. LC 79-23950. (gr. 6-8). 1980. 8.95 (ISBN 0-07-006169-6). McGraw.

--Nikki 108. LC 72-6071. (Illus.). 64p. (gr. 4-8). 1973. PLB 4.90 o.p. (ISBN 0-531-02602-7). Watts.

--The Preacher's Kid. LC 74-19154. (gr. 4-6). 1975. PLB 5.90 o.p. (ISBN 0-531-02804-6). Watts.

--Quiet Place. LC 69-1123. (Illus.). (gr. 4-6). 1969. PLB 4.33 o.p. (ISBN 0-531-01773-7). Watts.

--Seven Years from Home. LC 75-42105. (Values in Fiction Ser.). (Illus.). (gr. 5 up). 1976. 7.75 (ISBN 0-8172-0076-2). Raintree Pubs.

--The Thirteenth Year. (Illus.). (gr. 5 up). 1977. PLB 5.90 s&l (ISBN 0-531-00382-5). Watts.

--Wishful Lying. LC 79-21806. (Children's Ser.). 32p. 1980. 8.95 (ISBN 0-87705-473-8). Human Sci Pr.

--The Yo-Yo Kid. LC 76-17623. (Values in Fiction Ser.). (Illus.). 64p. (gr. 5 up). 1976. PLB 7.75 (ISBN 0-8172-0078-9). Raintree Pubs.

Blue, Shelley & Snow, Deborah. The Fourteenth Witch. 1977. pap. 5.50 o.p. (ISBN 0-930436-00-8). Persephone.

Bluem, A. William & Manvell, Roger, eds. Television: The Creative Experience: A Survey of Anglo-American Progress. (Communication Arts Bks.). 1967. 9.95 o.p. (ISBN 0-8038-7039-6). Hastings.

Bluem, A. William, et al. Television in the Public Interest. (Communication Arts Bks.). (Illus.). 1961. 8.95 o.p. (ISBN 0-8038-7044-2). Hastings.

Bluestein. Amphoteric Surfactants. Date not set. price not set (ISBN 0-8247-1277-3). Dekker.

Bluestein, Bill & Bluestein, Enid. The Year Santa Got Thin. (Illus.). 48p. (gr. k-4). 1981. 6.95 (ISBN 0-89638-045-9). CompCare.

Bluestein, Enid, jt. auth. see Bluestein, Bill.

Bluestein, Sheldon. Hiking Trails of Southern Idaho. LC 79-52543. (Illus.). 235p. (Orig.). 1981. pap. 7.95 (ISBN 0-87004-280-7). Caxton.

Bluestone, Barry & Jordan, Peter. Aircraft Industry Dynamics: An Analysis of Competition, Capital & Labor. 180p. 1981. 19.95 (ISBN 0-86569-053-7). Auburn Hse.

Bluestone, Barry, et al. The Retail Revolution: Market Transformation, Investment, & Labor in the Modern Department Store. LC 80-26036. (Illus.). 192p. 1980. 19.95 (ISBN 0-86569-052-9). Auburn Hse.

Bluestone, Max. From Story to Stage: The Dramatic Adaptation of Prose Fiction in the Period of Shakespeare & His Contemporaries. (Studies in English Literature: No. 70). 1974. pap. 40.00x (ISBN 90-2792-697-2). Mouton.

Bluestone, Morton D. Accounting: A Self-Instruction Guide to Procedures & Theory. (Illus.). 208p. 1973. pap. 2.95 o.s.i. (ISBN 0-02-008160-X, Collier). Macmillan.

Bluestone, Rodney, ed. Rheumatology. (UCLA Postgraduate Medicine Ser.). 1980. 30.00 (ISBN 0-89289-375-3). HM Prof Med Div.

Bluh, Bonnie. Banana: A Novel. LC 75-28030. 288p. 1976. 8.95 o.s.i. (ISBN 0-02-511900-1, 51190). Macmillan.

Bluhm, Donna L. Teaching the Retarded Visually Handicapped: Indeed They Are Children. LC 68-23679. (Illus.). 1968. 4.50 o.p. (ISBN 0-7216-1760-3). Saunders.

Bluhm, William T. Theories of the Political System: Classics of Political Thought & Modern Political Analysis. 3rd ed. 1978. ref. ed. 17.95 (ISBN 0-13-913327-5). P-H.

Blum, et al, eds. Pharmaceuticals & Health Policy: An International Perspective on Provision & Control. 387p. 1981. text ed. 38.00x (ISBN 0-8419-0682-3). Holmes & Meier.

Blum, Alan F. Socrates: The Original & Its Image. 1978. 20.00x (ISBN 0-7100-8766-7). Routledge & Kegan.

Blum, Albert A., ed. International Handbook of Industrial Relations: Contemporary Developments & Research. LC 79-8586. (Illus.). 640p. 1981. 45.00 (ISBN 0-313-21303-8, BLH/). Greenwood.

Blum, Alexander. Russian Dialogues. 1968. 15.00 (ISBN 0-08-012519-0); pap. 7.00 (ISBN 0-08-012518-2). Pergamon.

--Russkie Perezvony: An Album of Soviet Russian Recordings. LC 71-136569. 155p. 1972. 21.00 (ISBN 0-08-006878-2). Pergamon.

Blum, Arlene. Annapurna: A Woman's Place. LC 80-13288. (Illus.). 272p. 1980. 14.95 (ISBN 0-87156-236-7). Sierra.

Blum, Barbara L., ed. Psychological Aspects of Pregnancy, Birthing, & Bonding. (New Directions in Psychotherapy Ser.: Vol. IV). 336p. 1980. 25.95 (ISBN 0-87705-210-7). Human Sci Pr.

Blum, Daniel. A Pictorial History of the American Theatre 1860-1980. rev. ed. Aymar, Brandt, ed. 464p. 1981. 19.95 (ISBN 0-517-54262-5). Crown.

--Screen World, 10 vols. 1949, 1951-1959. LC 70-84068. (Illus.). 1969. Set. 165.00x (ISBN 0-8196-0255-8); 18.00x ea. Biblo.

Blum, David. Casals & the Art of Interpretation. LC 77-1444. text ed. 24.50x o.p. (ISBN 0-8419-0307-7). Holmes & Meier.

Blum, Ethel. Miami Alive. 1981. pap. 5.95 (ISBN 0-935572-09-0). Alive Pubns.

--Miami Alive. (Span.). 1981. pap. 5.95 (ISBN 0-935572-06-6). Alive Pubns.

Blum, Etta. The Space My Body Fills. LC 80-26565. 68p. (Orig.). 1980. pap. 4.95 (ISBN 0-913270-93-8). Sunstone Pr.

Blum, Jeffrey. Pseudoscience & Mental Ability: The Origins & Fallacies of the IQ Controversy. LC 77-81371. 1978. 13.95 o.p. (ISBN 0-85345-420-5, CL 4205). Natl Rail Hist Soc DC Chap.

Blum, John. PSRO & the Law. LC 77-70436. 1977. 24.95 (ISBN 0-912862-39-4). Aspen Systems.

Blum, John M. V Was for Victory: Politics & American Culture During World War 2. LC 75-38730. 384p. 1976. 12.95 o.p. (ISBN 0-15-194080-0). HarBraceJ.

--V Was for Victory: Politics & American Culture During World War II. LC 77-3426. 1977. pap. 5.95 (ISBN 0-15-693628-3, Harv). HarBraceJ.

Blum, Lawrence. Friendship, Altruism & Morality. (International Library of Philosophy). 256p. 1980. 20.00 (ISBN 0-7100-0582-2). Routledge & Kegan.

Blum, Lawrence P. & Kujoth, Richard K. Job Placement of the Emotionally Disturbed. LC 75-185399. 1972. 14.50 (ISBN 0-8108-0468-9). Scarecrow.

Blum, Milton L. & Naylor, James C. Industrial Psychology: Its Theoretical & Social Foundations. 3rd ed. 1968. text ed. 22.95 scp o.p. (ISBN 0-06-040781-6, HarpC); tchrs' manual avail. o.p. (ISBN 0-06-360781-6). Har-Row.

Blum, Peter. Everybody Counts: A T. A. Self-Help Book for Math Aversion. 54p. (Orig.). 1981. pap. 6.95 (ISBN 0-9605756-0-X). Math Counsel Inst.

Blum, Richard, et al. Pharmaceuticals & Health Policy: International Perspectives on Provision & Control of Medicine. 1981. write for info. (ISBN 0-312-60402-5). St Martin.

Blum, Richard H. Deceivers & Deceived: Observations on Confidence Men & Their Victims, Informants & Their Quarry, Political & Industrial Spies & Ordinary Citizens. (Illus.). 340p. 1972. 24.50 (ISBN 0-398-02235-6). C C Thomas.

Blum, Richard H., et al. The Dream Sellers: Perspectives on Drug Dealers. LC 79-184960. (Social & Behavioral Science Ser.). 1972. 16.95x o.p. (ISBN 0-87589-119-5). Jossey-Bass.

--Drug Dealers - Taking Action: Options for International Response. LC 76-187065. (Social & Behavioral Science Ser.). 1973. 15.95x o.p. (ISBN 0-87589-166-7). Jossey-Bass.

--Drug Education: Results & Recommendations. LC 75-45821. (Illus.). 1976. 21.50 (ISBN 0-669-00575-4). Lexington Bks.

--Horatio Alger's Children: The Role of the Family in the Origin & Prevention of Drug Risk. LC 72-186580. (Social & Behavioral Science Ser.). 1972. 15.95x o.p. (ISBN 0-87589-120-9). Jossey-Bass.

--Society & Drugs, Social & Cultural Observations. Incl. Vol. 2. Students & Drugs, College & High School Observations. LC 73-75936. (Social & Behavioral Science Ser.). 1969. 2 vol. set 37.50x (ISBN 0-87589-424-0); Vol. 1. (ISBN 0-87589-033-4); Vol. 2. (ISBN 0-87589-034-2). Jossey-Bass.

--Controlling Drugs: International Handbook for Psychoactive Drug Classification. LC 73-9070. (Social & Behavioral Science Ser.). 544p. 1974. 25.00x o.p. (ISBN 0-87589-203-5). Jossey-Bass.

Blum, Ronald, jt. auth. see Roller, Duane.

Blum, Ronald, jt. auth. see Roller, Duane, Sr.

Blum, S., ed. see Erte.

Blum, Shirley N. Early Netherlandish Triptychs: A Study in Patronage. LC 68-10902. (California Studies in the History of Art: No. XIII). (Illus.). 1969. 65.00x (ISBN 0-520-01444-8). U of Cal Pr.

Blum, Walter J. & Kalven, Harry, Jr. The Uneasy Case for Progressive Taxation. LC 53-3592. (Midway Reprint Ser.). 90p. 1963. pap. 6.00x (ISBN 0-226-06152-3). U of Chicago Pr.

Blum, William & Hogaboom, George B. Principles of Electroplating & Electroforming. 3rd ed. (Illus.). 1949. 32.50 o.p. (ISBN 0-07-006179-3, P&RB). McGraw.

Blumberg, Abraham S. Current Perspectives on Criminal Behavior. 2nd ed. 442p. 1981. pap. text ed. 10.95 (ISBN 0-394-32156-1). Knopf.

Blumberg, Albert. Logic: A First Course. 1976. text ed. 14.95 (ISBN 0-394-31442-5); tchr's manual free (ISBN 0-394-31178-7). Knopf.

Blumberg, Arthur. Current Perspectives. 1974. text ed. 10.95 (ISBN 0-394-31123-X, RanC). Knopf.

--Supervisors & Teachers: A Private Cold War. 2nd ed. LC 79-89771. 1980. 16.60 (ISBN 0-8211-0133-1); text ed. 15.00 in copies of 10 (ISBN 0-686-66218-0). McCutchan.

Blumberg, Harris M. A Program of Sequential Language Development: A Theoretical & Practical Guide for Remediation of Language, Reading & Learning Disorders. (Illus.). 108p. 1975. 12.75 (ISBN 0-398-03320-X). C C Thomas.

Blumberg, Herbert H., jt. auth. see Hare, A. Paul.

Blumberg, Paul. Inequality in an Age of Decline. 250p. 1980. 15.95 (ISBN 0-19-502804-X). Oxford U Pr.

Blumberg, Phillip I. The Megacorporation in American Society: The Scope of Corporate Power. LC 75-6667. 1975. pap. text ed. 9.95 (ISBN 0-13-574053-3). P-H.

Blumberg, Phyllis, jt. auth. see Gibson, Janice T.

Blumberg, Rhoda. Famine. LC 78-6837. (Impact Bks.). (Illus.). (gr. 9 up). 1978. PLB 6.90 s&l (ISBN 0-531-02201-3). Watts.

--Fire Fighters. rev. ed. (First Bks. Ser). (Illus.). 72p. (gr. 4). 1976. PLB 6.45 (ISBN 0-531-00850-9). Watts.

--First Ladies. LC 77-2617. (First Bks.). (gr. 4-6). 1977. PLB 6.45 (ISBN 0-531-01286-7). Watts.

--The First Travel Guide to the Moon: What to Pack, How to Go, & What to See When You Get There. LC 80-66244. (Illus.). 80p. (gr. 5 up). 1980. 7.95 (ISBN 0-590-07663-9, Four Winds). Schol Bk Serv.

--Sharks. (First Bks.). (Illus.). 72p. (gr. 4 up). 1976. PLB 6.45 (ISBN 0-531-00846-0). Watts.

--Sharks. 1980. pap. 1.75 (ISBN 0-380-49247-4, 49247, Camelot). Avon.

--The Truth About Dragons. LC 79-19589. (Illus.). 64p. (gr. 5 up). 1980. 8.95 (ISBN 0-590-07570-5, Four Winds). Schol Bk Serv.

--UFO. (First Books). (Illus.). (gr. 4-6). 1977. PLB 6.45 (ISBN 0-531-00397-3). Watts.

Blume, Eli. Cours superieur de francais. (Orig.). (gr. 11-12). 1970. pap. text ed. 5.75 (ISBN 0-87720-460-8); wkbk. 6.75 (ISBN 0-87720-462-4). AMSCO Sch.

--Douze Contes De Maupassant. (Fr.). (gr. 10-12). 1973. pap. text ed. 5.17 (ISBN 0-87720-468-3). AMSCO Sch.

--French Workbook, Book 1. (gr. 9 up). 1977. wkbk. 6.00 (ISBN 0-87720-993-6). AMSCO Sch.

--French Workbook, Book 2. (gr. 10-11). 1977. wkbk. 6.25 (ISBN 0-87720-994-4). AMSCO Sch.

--Review Text in French First Year. 2nd ed. (Illus., Orig.). (gr. 7-12). 1967. pap. text ed. 4.83 (ISBN 0-87720-451-9). AMSCO Sch.

--Review Text in French Three Years. (Illus., Orig.). (gr. 7-12). 1963. pap. text ed. 4.92 o.p. (ISBN 0-87720-457-8). AMSCO Sch.

--Review Text in French Three Years. 2nd ed. (Orig.). (gr. 11-12). 1980. pap. text ed. 6.33 (ISBN 0-87720-471-3). AMSCO Sch.

--Review Text in French Two Years. 2nd ed. (Illus., Orig.). (gr. 7-12). 1966. pap. text ed. 5.33 (ISBN 0-87720-454-3). AMSCO Sch.

--Workbook in French First Year. 2nd ed. (Illus., Orig.). (gr. 8-11). 1967. wkbk. 6.00 (ISBN 0-87720-452-7). AMSCO Sch.

--Workbook in French Three Years. 2nd. ed. (Illus., Orig.). (gr. 10-12). 1978. wkbk. 6.75 (ISBN 0-87720-459-4). AMSCO Sch.

--Workbook in French Two Years. (Illus., Orig.). (gr. 9-12). 1966. wkbk 5.83 o.p. (ISBN 0-87720-455-1). AMSCO Sch.

--Workbook in French Two Years. 3rd ed. (Orig.). (gr. 10-11). 1979. pap. text ed. 7.92 (ISBN 0-87720-470-5). AMSCO Sch.

Blume, Friedrich. Two Centuries of Bach. Godman, Stanley, tr. (Music Reprint Ser., 1978). 1978. Repr. of 1950 ed. lib. bdg. 14.50 (ISBN 0-306-77567-0). Da Capo.

Blume, H. Fund-Raising. (Orig.). 1977. pap. 6.95 (ISBN 0-7100-8549-4). Routledge & Kegan.

Blume, Helmut. The Caribbean Islands. Maczewski, J. & Norton, A. V., trs. from Ger. Orig. Title: Die Westindischen Inseln. (Illus.). 448p. 1977. pap. text ed. 14.95x (ISBN 0-582-48574-6). Longman.

Blume, Judy. Blubber. LC 73-94116. 160p. (gr. 4-6). 1974. 8.95 (ISBN 0-87888-072-0). Bradbury Pr.

--Deenie. LC 73-80197. 192p. (gr. 6-8). 1973. 8.95 (ISBN 0-87888-061-5). Bradbury Pr.

--Forever. LC 74-22850. 1975. 8.95 (ISBN 0-87888-079-8). Bradbury Pr.

--Freckle Juice. LC 74-161016. (Illus.). 40p. (gr. 2-5). 1971. 5.95 (ISBN 0-590-07242-0, Four Winds). Schol Bk Serv.

--Freckle Juice. 1978. pap. 1.25 (ISBN 0-440-42813-0, YB). Dell.

--It's Not the End of the World. (gr. 4-6). 1980. pap. 1.95 (ISBN 0-553-15090-1, Skylark). Bantam.

--It's Not the End of the World. LC 70-181739. 160p. (gr. 6-8). 1972. 8.95 (ISBN 0-87888-042-9). Bradbury Pr.

--The One in the Middle Is the Green Kangaroo. (Illus.). 40p. (ps-3). 1981. 7.95 (ISBN 0-87888-182-4). Bradbury Pr.

--Then Again, Maybe I Won't. LC 77-156548. (gr. 5-7). 1971. 8.95 (ISBN 0-87888-035-6). Bradbury Pr.

Blume, Marshall E. & Friend, Irwin. The Changing Role of the Individual Investor: A Twentieth Century Fund Report. LC 78-18303. 1978. 24.95 (ISBN 0-471-04547-0, Pub. by Wiley-Interscience). Wiley.

Blume, Stuart S. Toward a Political Sociology of Science. LC 73-5291. 1974. text ed. 16.95 (ISBN 0-02-904350-6). Free Pr.

Blumenau, Lili. Creative Design in Wall Hangings. 1967. 16.00 o.p. (ISBN 0-87245-035-X). Textile Bk.

Blumenberg, Werner. August Bebels Briefwechsel Mit Friedrich Engels. (Quellen und Untersuchungen Zur Geschichte der Deutschenund Osterreichischen Arbeiterbewegung: No. 6). 1965. 123.50x (ISBN 90-2790-155-4). Mouton.

Blumenfeld, Arthur. Heart Attack: Are You a Candidate? (Illus.). 1971. pap. 1.50 o.s.i. (ISBN 0-515-04302-8). Jove Pubns.

Blumenfeld, Gerry & Blumenfeld, Harold. Naughty but Nice. 1976. pap. 1.25 o.p. (ISBN 0-685-69508-5, LB374ZK, Leisure Bks). Nordon Pubns.

--Sex Over Lightly. 1976. pap. 1.25 o.p. (ISBN 0-685-72355-0, LB381ZK, Leisure Bks). Nordon Pubns.

Blumenfeld, Hans. Metropolis...& Beyond: Selected Essays. LC 78-17955. 1979. 28.50 (ISBN 0-471-04281-1, Pub. by Wiley-Interscience). Wiley.

Blumenfeld, Harold, jt. auth. see Blumenfeld, Gerry.

Blumenfeld, Harold, tr. see Praetorius, Michael.

Blumenfeld, L. A. Problems of Biological Physics. (Springer Series in Synergetics: Vol. 7). (Illus.). 300p. 1981. 36.00 (ISBN 0-387-10401-1). Springer-Verlag.

Blumenfeld, Samuel L. Is Public Education Necessary. 1981. 10.00 (ISBN 0-8159-5826-9). Devin. Postponed.

Blumenson, John J. Identifying American Architecture: A Pictorial Guide to Styles & Terms, 1600-1945. rev. ed. (Illus.). 1981. 12.95 (ISBN 0-393-01428-2). Norton.

Blumenson, Martin. Liberation. (World War Two Ser.). (Illus.). 1979. 12.95 (ISBN 0-8094-2510-6). Time-Life.

--Liberation. (World War II Ser.). (Illus.). 1979. lib. bdg. 14.94 (ISBN 0-686-51051-8). Silver.

Blumenstein, R., jt. auth. see Basmajian, John V.

Blumenthal, Arthur. Process of Cognition. (Illus.). 1977. ref. ed. 14.95 (ISBN 0-13-722983-6). P-H.

Blumenthal, Arthur L. Language & Psychology: Historical Aspects of Psycholinguistics. LC 80-12611. 262p. 1980. Repr. of 1970 ed. lib. bdg. write for info. (ISBN 0-89874-167-X). Krieger.

Blumenthal, Arthur R. Theater Art of the Medici. LC 80-22452. (Illus.). 243p. 1981. 15.00 (ISBN 0-87451-191-7). U Pr of New Eng.

Blumenthal, H. T., ed. see International Association Of Gerontology - 5th Congress.

Blumenthal, Henry. France & the United States: Their Diplomatic Relations, 1789-1914. 1972. pap. 2.95 o.p. (ISBN 0-393-00625-5, Norton Lib). Norton.

Blumenthal, Howard J. Complete Guide to Electronic Games. 1981. pap. price not set (ISBN 0-452-25268-7, Z5268, Plume). NAL.

Blumenthal, Leonard M. A Modern View of Geometry. (Illus.). 1980. pap. text ed. 4.00 (ISBN 0-486-63962-2). Dover.

--Theory & Applications of Distance Geometry. 2nd ed. LC 79-113117. 1970. text ed. 13.95 (ISBN 0-8284-0242-6). Chelsea Pub.

Blumenthal, Leonard M. & Menger, Karl. Studies in Geometry. LC 74-75624. (Illus.). 1970. text ed. 25.95x (ISBN 0-7167-0437-4). W H Freeman.

Blumenthal, Michael. Sympathetic Magic. LC 80-50812. (Illus.). 96p. (Orig.). 1980. 25.00 (ISBN 0-931956-04-8); pap. 6.50 (ISBN 0-931956-03-X); handbound 60.00. Water Mark.

Blumenthal, Monica D., et al. Justifying Violence: Attitudes of American Men. LC 74-169101. (Orig.). 1972. cloth 12.00 (ISBN 0-87944-005-8); pap. 7.50 (ISBN 0-87944-004-X). U of Mich Soc Res.

Blumenthal, Sherman S. Management Information Systems: A Framework for Planning & Development. 1969. ref. ed. 17.95 (ISBN 0-13-548636-X). P-H.

Blumenthal, Shirley. Black Cats & Other Superstitions. LC 77-10623. (Myth, Magic & Superstition Ser.). (Illus.). (gr. 4-5). 1977. PLB 9.65 (ISBN 0-8172-1036-9). Raintree Pubs.

Blumenthal, Shirley & Ozer, Jerome S. Coming to America: Immigrants from the British Isles. LC 80-65841. 192p. (gr. 9-12). 1980. 9.95 (ISBN 0-440-01071-3). Delacorte.

Blumenthal, Walter H. Brides from Bridewell: Female Felons Sent to Colonial America. LC 73-7307. (Illus.). 139p. 1973. Repr. of 1962 ed. lib. bdg. 15.00x (ISBN 0-8371-6924-0, BLBB). Greenwood.

Blumenthal, Warren B. The Creator & Man. LC 80-5843. 139p. 1980. lib. bdg. 15.75 (ISBN 0-8191-1340-9); pap. text ed. 7.50 (ISBN 0-8191-1341-7). U Pr of Amer.

Blumer, Herbert. Symbolic Interactionism: Perspective & Method. 1969. text ed. 13.95 (ISBN 0-13-879924-5). P-H.

Blumer, Rodney, tr. see Deane, Forbes, et al.

Blumler, Jay G. & Katz, Elihu. The Uses of Mass Communications: Current Perspectives on Gratifications Research. LC 73-90713. (Sage Annual Reviess of Communication Research: Vol. 3). 1975. 20.00x (ISBN 0-8039-0340-5); pap. 9.95x (ISBN 0-8039-0494-0). Sage.

Blumler, Jay G. & McQuail, Denis. Television in Politics: Its Uses & Influences. LC 69-12843. 1969. 15.00x o.s.i. (ISBN 0-226-06175-2). U of Chicago Pr.

Blumrosen, Alfred W. Black Employment & the Law. 1971. 30.00 (ISBN 0-8135-0682-4). Rutgers U Pr.

Blumstein, Sheila E. A Phonological Investigation of Aphasic Speech. (Janua Linguarum Ser. Minor: No. 153). 1973. pap. text ed. 20.50x (ISBN 90-2792-448-1). Mouton.

Blundell, Peter S. Marketplace Guide to Oak Furniture Styles & Values. (Illus.). 1980. 17.95 (ISBN 0-89145-141-2). Collector Bks.

Blundell, T. L., jt. ed. see Noble, D.

Blunden, Godfrey & Blunden, Maria. Impressionists & Impressionism. (Illus.). 1980. pap. 14.95 (ISBN 0-686-68748-5). Rizzoli Intl.

Blunden, Maria, jt. auth. see Blunden, Godfrey.

Blundeville, Thomas. The True Order & Method of Wryting & Reading Hystories. LC 79-84088. (English Experience Ser.: No. 908). 68p. (Eng.). 1979. Repr. of 1574 ed. lib. bdg. 7.00 (ISBN 90-221-0908-9). Walter J Johnson.

Blunt, Anthony. The Art of William Blake. (Icon Editions). (Illus.). 208p. 1974. pap. 5.95x o.s.i. (ISBN 0-06-430045-5, IN-45, HarpT). Har-Row.

--Artistic Theory in Italy, 1450-1600. 1956. 22.50x (ISBN 0-19-817106-4); pap. 4.95x (ISBN 0-19-881050-4, OPB). Oxford U Pr.

--Nicholas Poussin. 2 Vols. (Bollinger Ser.: No. 35). (Illus.). 1966. 60.00x, boxed o.p. (ISBN 0-691-09791-7). Princeton U Pr.

Blunt, Anthony F. Art of William Blake. LC 75-173034. (Illus.). 1959. 22.50x (ISBN 0-231-02364-2). Columbia U Pr.

Blunt, John H. Dictionary of Sects, Heresies, Ecclesiastical Parties & Schools of Religious Thought. LC 74-9653. 1974. Repr. of 1874 ed. 42.00 (ISBN 0-8103-3751-7). Gale.

Blunt, M. A New Approach to Teaching & Learning Anatomy: Objectives & Learning Activities for the Anatomy Course. 1976. 9.95 (ISBN 0-407-00098-4). Butterworths.

Blunt, Wilfred. England's Michelangelo: A Biography of George Frederic Watts. (Illus.). 1978. 25.00 (ISBN 0-241-89174-4, Pub. by Hamish Hamilton England). David & Charles.

Blunt, Wilfred S. Secret History of the English Occupation of Egypt. 1967. 18.50 (ISBN 0-86527-179-8). Fertig.

Blunt, Wilfrid. In for a Penny: A Prospect of Kew Gardens. (Illus.). 1978. 24.00 (ISBN 0-241-89823-4, Pub. by Hamish Hamilton England). David & Charles.

--Isfahan: Pearl of Persia. 1966. 21.95 (ISBN 0-236-31026-7, Pub. by Paul Elek). Merrimack Bk Serv.

Blurton-Jones, N. & Reynolds, V., eds. Human Behavior & Adaptation, Vol. 18. (Symposium of the Society for the Study of Human Biology). 1979. 39.95x (ISBN 0-470-26578-7). Halsted Pr.

Bluske, Margaret K. & Walther, Elizabeth K. Das Erste Jahr. 4th ed. (Illus.). 1980. text ed. 16.50 scp (ISBN 0-06-040788-3, HarpC); Programmed Assisant Bk. scp 8.50 (ISBN 0-06-040795-6); instructor's manual free; scp tapes 260.00 (ISBN 0-686-65944-9). Har-Row.

Blust, Robert A. The Proto-Oceanic Palatals. 1979. text ed. 15.00x (ISBN 0-8248-0684-0, Pub. by Polynesian Soc). U Pr of Hawaii.

Blustein, Lotte & Geary, Rosemary J. Writing the Research Paper. rev. ed. (Illus.). 60p. (gr. 7-12). 1980. pap. text ed. 4.45 (ISBN 0-9605248-2-7). Blustein-Geary.

Bluth, B. J. & McNeal, S. R., eds. Update on Space, Vol. 1. (Illus., Orig.). 1981. pap. 7.95 (ISBN 0-937654-00-0). Natl Behavior.

Bly, et al. Walt Whitman: The Measure of His Song. 1st ed. Perlman, Jim & Campion, Dan, eds. LC 80-85268. (Illus.). 288p. (Orig.). 1981. 13.95 (ISBN 0-930100-09-3); pap. 7.95 (ISBN 0-930100-08-5). Holy Cow.

Bly, Carol. Letters from the Country. LC 80-8194. 192p. 1981. 9.95 (ISBN 0-06-010357-4, HarpT). Har-Row.

Bly, Robert. Leaping Poetry: An Idea with Poems & Translations. LC 73-6243. (A Seventies Press Bk). 112p. 1975. pap. 4.50 (ISBN 0-8070-6393-2, BP462). Beacon Pr.

--Light Around the Body. 1967. 8.95 (ISBN 0-06-010388-4, HarpT); pap. 3.95 (ISBN 0-06-010389-2, CN-786, HarpT). Har-Row.

--The Morning Glory. LC 74-15811. 96p. 1975. 8.95 (ISBN 0-06-010368-X, HarpT); pap. 3.95 (ISBN 0-06-010367-1, CN-784, HarpT). Har-Row.

--News of the Universe. 320p. 1980. 15.95 o.p. (ISBN 0-87156-198-0); pap. 7.95 o.p. (ISBN 0-87156-199-9). Sierra.

--Silence in the Snowy Fields. LC 62-18340. (Wesleyan Poetry Program: Vol. 15). (Orig.). 1962. 10.00x (ISBN 0-8195-2015-2, Pub. by Wesleyan U Pr); pap. 4.95 (ISBN 0-8195-1015-7). Columbia U Pr.

--Sleepers Joining Hands. LC 72-123916. 96p. 1973. 8.95 (ISBN 0-06-010381-7, HarpT); pap. 3.95 o.p. (ISBN 0-06-010382-5, TD-139, HarpT). Har-Row.

--Talking All Morning. (Poets on Poetry Ser.). 316p. 1980. pap. 5.95 (ISBN 0-472-15760-4). U of Mich Pr.

Bly, Robert, ed. Seventies No. 1: An Anthology of Leaping Poetry. pap. 1.50 (ISBN 0-685-31525-8). Eighties Pr.

Bly, Robert, ed. see Jacosen, Rolf.

Bly, Robert, tr. see Ekelof, Gunnar.

Bly, Robert, tr. see Kabir.

Bly, Robert, tr. see Machado, Antonio.

Bly, Robert, tr. see Rilke, Rainer M.

Bly, Robert, tr. see Transtromer, Tomas.

Bly, Stephen. Radical Discipleship. 128p. (Orig.). 1981. pap. 3.95 (ISBN 0-8024-8219-8). Moody.

Bly, Tacey, compiled by. Poems & Hymns of Christ's Sweet Singer: Frances Ridley Havergal. LC 77-86549. 1977. 7.95 (ISBN 0-87983-163-4); pap. 3.95 (ISBN 0-87983-164-2). Keats.

Blyden, Edward. Christianity, Islam, & the Negro. Fyfe, C., ed. 1967. 24.50x (ISBN 0-85224-085-6, Pub. by Edinburgh U Pr Scotland). Columbia U Pr.

Blyth, Chay & Blyth, Maureen. Innocent Abroad. 196p. 1980. 6.00x (Pub. by Nautical England). State Mutual Bk.

Blyth, Hugh, jt. auth. see Stevenson, Don.

Blyth, Maureen, jt. auth. see Blyth, Chay.

Blyth, R. H. Haiku, 4 vols. Date not set. pap. 8.95 ea. Vol. 1 (ISBN 0-89346-158-X). Vol. 2 (ISBN 0-89346-159-8). Vol. 3 (ISBN 0-89346-160-1). Vol. 4 (ISBN 0-89346-161-X). Heian Intl.

Blyth, T. S. Module Theory: An Approach to Linear Algebra. (Illus.). 1977. 39.00x (ISBN 0-19-853162-1). Oxford U Pr.

Blyth, T. S. & Janowitz, M. F. Residuation Theory. LC 77-142177. 380p. 1972. text ed. 60.00 (ISBN 0-08-016408-0). Pergamon.

Blyth, W. A. English Primary Education: A Sociological Description, 2 vols. Incl. Vol. 1. Schools. text ed. 8.75x o.p. (ISBN 0-7100-3462-8); pap. text ed. 4.25x (ISBN 0-7100-6164-1); Vol. 2. Background. text ed. 6.00x (ISBN 0-7100-3485-7); pap. text ed. 4.25x (ISBN 0-7100-6165-X). (International Library of Sociology & Social Reconstruction). 1965. Humanities.

Blyth, W. A. & Derricott, R. The Social Significance of Middle Schools. 1977. 32.00 (ISBN 0-7134-0488-4, Pub. by Batsford England); pap. 16.95 (ISBN 0-686-63737-2). David & Charles.

Blythe, A. R. Electrical Properties of Polymers. LC 77-85690. (Cambridge Solid State Science Ser.). (Illus.). 201p. 1980. pap. text ed. 13.95x (ISBN 0-521-29825-3). Cambridge U Pr.

--Electrical Properties of Polymers. LC 77-85690. (Solid State Science Ser.). 1979. 49.50 (ISBN 0-521-21902-7). Cambridge U Pr.

Blythe, L. N., ed. see Ebel, Jurgen.

Blythe, L. N., ed. see Hasan, Khaja S.

Blythe, Leonora. Felicia. (Regency Romance Ser.). 1978. pap. 1.75 o.p. (ISBN 0-449-23754-0, Crest). Fawcett.

Blythe, Ronald, ed. Places: An Anthology of Britain. (Illus.). 270p. 1981. 19.95 (ISBN 0-19-211575-8). Oxford U Pr.

Blythe, Ronald, ed. see Austen, Jane.

Blyton, Carey. Bananas in Pyjamas. 28p. 1973. 7.50 (ISBN 0-571-10138-0). Transatlantic.

--Bananas in Pyjamas: A Book of Nonsense. (Orig.). (ps-5). 1976. pap. 3.95 (ISBN 0-571-10671-4, Pub. by Faber & Faber). Merrimack Bk Serv.

Blyton, Enid. Five Go to Demon's Rock. 1980. pap. 1.95 (ISBN 0-689-70478-X, Aladdin). Atheneum.

--Five on a Secret Trail. 1980. pap. 1.95 (ISBN 0-689-70477-1, Aladdin). Atheneum.

BNA Editorial Staff of Labor Relations Reporter. Labor Relations Yearbook--1979. 560p. 1980. 16.00 (ISBN 0-87179-334-2). BNA.

Boa, Kenneth. Cults, World Religions, & You. 1977. pap. 3.95 (ISBN 0-88207-752-X). Victor Bks.

--God I Don't Understand. 156p. 1975. pap. 3.95 (ISBN 0-88207-722-8). Victor Bks.

Boa, Kenneth & Proctor, William. Return of the Star of Bethlehem. LC 79-8548. 216p. 1980. 8.95 (ISBN 0-385-15454-2, Galilee). Doubleday.

Boadt, Lawrence, et al, eds. Biblical Studies: Meeting Ground of Jews & Christians. LC 80-82812. (Stimulus Bk). 220p. (Orig.). 1981. pap. 7.95 (ISBN 0-8091-2344-4). Paulist Pr.

Boadway, R. W. & Treddenick, J. M. The Impact of the Mining Industries on the Canadian Economy. 117p. (Orig.). 1977. pap. text ed. 4.50x (ISBN 0-686-63141-2, Pub. by Ctr Resource Stud Canada). Renouf.

Boahen, A. A., jt. auth. see Webster, J. B.

Boahen, A. Adu, et al. The Horizon History of Africa, 2 vols. Josephy, Alvin M., Jr., ed. LC 75-149732. (Illus.). 544p. 1971. 25.00 (ISBN 0-8281-0271-6, Dist. by Scribner); deluxe ed. 35.00 slipcased (ISBN 0-8281-0329-1, Dist. by Scribner). Am Heritage.

Boak, Denis. Andre Malraux. 1968. 12.95x o.p. (ISBN 0-19-815379-1). Oxford U Pr.

Boal, Augusto. The Theater of the Oppressed. McBride, Charles, tr. 1979. 12.95 (ISBN 0-916354-59-8); pap. 5.95 (ISBN 0-916354-60-1). Urizen Bks.

Boalt, G., et al, eds. Communication & Communication Barriers in Sociology. LC 75-44623. 1976. 29.95 (ISBN 0-470-15016-5). Halsted Pr.

Board of Cooperative Education Services, Nassau County. Two Hundred Ways to Help Children Learn While You're at It. 1976. 12.95 (ISBN 0-87909-845-7). Reston.

Board of Publication of the Reorganized Church of Jesus Christ of Latter Day Saints, ed. Doctrine & Covenants. LC 78-134922. 1978. 9.00 (ISBN 0-8309-0204-X). Herald Hse.

Board of Regents of IIA. Certified Internal Auditor Examination--May 1979: Questions & Suggested Solutions. 1979. pap. text ed. 3.00 (ISBN 0-89413-081-1). Inst Inter Aud.

--Certified Internal Auditor Examination, May 1980: Questions & Suggested Solutions, No. 7. (Illus.). 57p. 1980. pap. text ed. 3.00 (ISBN 0-89413-089-7). Inst Inter Aud.

Board on Agriculture & Renewable Resources. African Agricultural Research Capabilities. LC 74-22370. 1974. pap. 9.00 o.p. (ISBN 0-309-02241-X). Natl Acad Pr.

--Agricultural Production Efficiency. LC 74-28314. 1975. pap. 9.00 (ISBN 0-309-02310-6). Natl Acad Pr.

Board on Agriculture & Renewable Resources, National Research Council. Climate & Food: Climatic Fluctuation & U. S. Agricultural Production. LC 76-46195. 1976. pap. 7.75 (ISBN 0-309-02522-2). Natl Acad Pr.

--Enhancement of Food Production for the United States: World Food & Nutrition Study. LC 75-37121. xiii, 174p. 1975. pap. 6.00 (ISBN 0-309-02435-8). Natl Acad Pr.

--Genetic Improvement of Seed Proteins. LC 76-17097. 1976. pap. 15.25 (ISBN 0-309-02421-8). Natl Acad Pr.

Board on Agriculture & Renewable Resources. Nutrient Requirements of Non Human Primates. 1978. pap. 5.00 (ISBN 0-309-02786-1). Natl Acad Pr.

--Nutrient Requirements of Swine. 8th rev. ed. (Nutrient Requirements of Domestic Animals Ser). (Illus.). 64p. 1979. pap. 3.75 (ISBN 0-309-02870-1). Natl Acad Pr.

Board on Agriculture and Renewable Resources, National Research Council. Renewable Resources for Industrial Materials. LC 76-44604. 1976. pap. 8.25 (ISBN 0-309-02528-1). Natl Acad Pr.

Board on Energy Studies. Implications of Environmental Regulations for Energy Production & Consumption. 1977. pap. 8.25 (ISBN 0-309-02632-6). Natl Acad Pr.

Board on Mineral & Energy Resources. Radioactive Wastes at the Hanford Reservation. 1978. pap. 8.50 (ISBN 0-309-02745-4). Natl Acad Pr.

--Redistribution of Accessory Elements in Mining & Mineral Processing: Coal & Oil Shale, Pt. I. 1979. pap. 9.25 (ISBN 0-309-02897-3). Natl Acad Pr.

--Redistribution of Accessory Elements in Mining & Mineral Processing: Uranium, Phosphate, & Alumina, Pt. II. 1979. pap. 12.25 (ISBN 0-309-02899-X). Natl Acad Pr.

--Surface Mining of Non-Coal Minerals. LC 79-91887. xxiii, 339p. 1979. pap. 11.50 (ISBN 0-309-02942-2). Natl Acad Pr.

--Technological Innovation & Forces for Change in the Mineral Industry. 1978. pap. 5.50 (ISBN 0-309-02768-3). Natl Acad Pr.

Board on Mineral Resources. Concepts of Uranium Resources & Producibility. 1978. pap. 7.25 (ISBN 0-309-02864-7). Natl Acad Pr.

Board on Renewable Resources. Aquaculture in the United States: Constraints & Opportunities. 1978. pap. 7.50 (ISBN 0-309-02740-3). Natl Acad Pr.

--Interactions of Mycotoxins in Animal Production. 1979. pap. 9.25 (ISBN 0-309-02876-0). Natl Acad Pr.

Board on Toxicology & Environmental Health Hazards. Odors from Stationary & Mobile Sources. 1979. pap. 20.50 (ISBN 0-309-02877-9). Natl Acad Pr.

Board on Toxicology & Environmental Health, National Research Council. Sulfur Oxides. pap. text ed. 9.00x (ISBN 0-309-02862-0). Natl Acad Pr.

Board, Stephen, et al. HIS Guide to Life on Campus. LC 73-75893. 128p. 1973. pap. 1.75 o.p. (ISBN 0-87784-355-4). Inter-Varsity.

Boardman, A. D. Physics Programs. Incl. Applied Physics. LC 80-40121. 136p (ISBN 0-471-27740-1); Magnetism. LC 80-40124. 106p (ISBN 0-471-27733-9); Optics. LC 80-40123. 134p (ISBN 0-471-27729-0); Solid State Physics. LC 80-40125. 144p (ISBN 0-471-27734-7). 1980. 13.50 ea. Wiley.

Boardman, Allan D., et al. Symmetry & Its Applications in Science. LC 72-13908. 305p. 1973. pap. 24.95 (ISBN 0-470-08412-X). Halsted Pr.

Boardman, Elliot B. see Hill, Richard F., et al.

Boardman, Fon, Jr. Tyrants & Conquerors. (Illus.). (gr. 7 up). 1977. 8.95 o.p. (ISBN 0-8098-0010-1). Walck.

Boardman, J. & Robertson, C. M. Corpus Vasorum Antiquorum, Great Britain: Vol. 15: Castle Ashby. (Corpus Vasorum Antiquorum Ser.). (Illus.). 1979. 145.00 (ISBN 0-19-725981-2). Oxford U Pr.

Boardman, John. Archaic Greek Gems: Schools & Artists in the Sixth & Early Fifth Centuries. LC 68-25581. (Illus.). 1968. 16.75x o.s.i. (ISBN 0-8101-0029-0). Northwestern U Pr.

--Athenian Black Figure Vases. LC 73-89034. (World of Art Ser.). (Illus.). 253p. 1975. pap. 9.95 (ISBN 0-19-519760-7). Oxford U Pr.

--Athenian Red Figure Vases: The Archaic Period, a Handbook. (World of Art Ser.). (Illus.). 1979. pap. 9.95x (ISBN 0-19-520155-8). Oxford U Pr.

--Engraved Gems: The Ionides Collection. LC 68-17325. (Illus.). 1968. 16.95x o.s.i. (ISBN 0-8101-0048-7). Northwestern U Pr.

--Greek Art. (World of Art Ser.). (Illus.). 1973. pap. 9.95 (ISBN 0-19-519917-0). Oxford U Pr.

--Greek Sculpture: The Archaic Period. LC 77-25202. (World of Art Ser.). (Illus.). 1978. 17.95 (ISBN 0-19-520046-2); pap. 9.95 (ISBN 0-19-520047-0). Oxford U Pr.

Boardman, John & Vollenweider, Marie-Louise. Catalogue of the Engraved Gems & Finger Rings in the Ashmoleaw Museum, Vol. I: Green & Etruscan. (Illus.). 1978. 79.00 (ISBN 0-19-813195-X). Oxford U Pr.

Boardman, Philip. The Worlds of Patrick Geddes: Biologist, Town Planner, Re-Educator, Peace-Warrior. (Illus.). 1978. 40.00 (ISBN 0-7100-8548-6). Routledge & Kegan.

Boardman, R. S. Roger Sherman: Signer & Statesman. LC 75-168671. (Era of the American Revolution Ser.). 396p. 1972. Repr. of 1938 ed. lib. bdg. 37.50 (ISBN 0-306-70412-9). Da Capo.

Boardroom Reports Editors, ed. The Tax Avoidance Strategies. LC 80-18256. 178p. 1980. 50.00 (ISBN 0-932648-09-6). Boardroom.

Boarman, Patrick M. & Mugar, Jayson. Trade with China: Assessments by Leading Businessmen & Scholars. LC 74-1727. 208p. 1974. text ed. 23.95 (ISBN 0-275-08830-8). Praeger.

Boarman, Patrick M. & Schollhammer, Hans, eds. Multinational Corporations & Governments: Business-Government Relations in an International Context. LC 75-8402. (Illus.). 256p. 1975. text ed. 24.95 (ISBN 0-275-00900-9). Praeger.

Boas, F. S., ed. see Fletcher, Giles & Fletcher, Phineas.

Boas, Franz. Central Eskimo. LC 64-63593. (Illus.). 1964. pap. 3.75 (ISBN 0-8032-5016-9, BB 196, Bison). U of Nebr Pr.

--Mind of Primitive Man. rev. ed. 1965. pap. text ed. 3.50 o.s.i. (ISBN 0-02-904500-2). Free Pr.

--Primitive Art. (Illus.). 1962. 8.75 (ISBN 0-8446-1695-8). Peter Smith.

--Race & Democratic Society. LC 70-86641. 1969. Repr. of 1945 ed. 10.50x (ISBN 0-8196-0248-5). Biblo.

--Race, Language & Culture. 1966. pap. text ed. 6.95 o.s.i. (ISBN 0-02-904490-1). Free Pr.

Boas, Frederick S. Queen Elizabeth in Drama & Related Studies. 212p. 1980. Repr. lib. bdg. 25.00 (ISBN 0-8492-3588-X). R West.

Boas, George. History of Ideas: An Introduction. LC 74-85278. 1969. 6.95 o.p. (ISBN 0-684-10032-0, ScribT). Scribner.

--Rationalism in Greek Philosophy. 504p. 1961. 25.00x o.p. (ISBN 0-8018-0079-X). Johns Hopkins.

Boas, George, tr. see Bonaventura, Saint.

Boas, Maurits I. Etudes. LC 80-70949. 160p. 1981. 9.95 (ISBN 0-8119-0344-3). Fell.

--Preludes. LC 78-855. 1978. 8.95 (ISBN 0-8119-0305-2). Fell.

Boase, Paul H., ed. The Rhetoric of Protest & Reform, 1878-1898. LC 80-11631. 354p. 1980. 16.95x (ISBN 0-8214-0421-0, 0421E). Ohio U Pr.

Boase, Roger. The Troubador Revival: A Study of Social Change & Traditionalism in Late Medieval Spain. (Illus.). 1978. 28.00 (ISBN 0-7100-8956-2). Routledge & Kegan.

Boase, T. S. Kingdoms & Strongholds of the Crusaders. LC 73-157118. 1971. 15.00 o.p. (ISBN 0-672-51606-3). Bobbs.

Boase, T. S., ed. Cilician Kingdom of Armenia. LC 74-22291. 1979. text ed. 20.00 (ISBN 0-312-13895-4). St Martin.

Boase, Thomas S. English Art, 1100-1216. (Oxford History of English Art Ser.). (Illus.). 1953. 37.50x (ISBN 0-19-817202-8). Oxford U Pr.

Boase, Wendy. Ancient Egypt. (Civilization Library). (Illus.). (gr. 5-8). 1978. PLB 6.90 s&l (ISBN 0-531-01402-9). Watts.

--Early China. (Civilization Library). (Illus.). (gr. 5-8). 1978. PLB 6.90 s&l (ISBN 0-531-01426-6). Watts.

Boasson, C. Approaches to the Study of International Relations. 2nd ed. (Polemological Studies: No. 2). (Illus.). 112p. 1972. pap. text ed. 9.25x (ISBN 90-232-0923-0). Humanities.

Boasson, Charles & Nurock, Max, eds. The Changing International Community: Some Problems of Its Laws, Structures, & Peace Research & the Middle East Conflict. (New Babylon Studies in Social Sciences: No. 18). 1973. text ed. 37.75x (ISBN 90-2797-292-3). Mouton.

Boast, Carol, jt. auth. see Foster, Lynn.

Boateng, E. A. Geography of Ghana. 17.95 (ISBN 0-521-04272-0); pap. 8.95x (ISBN 0-521-04273-9). Cambridge U Pr.

--A Political Geography of Africa. LC 77-80828. 1978. 37.95 (ISBN 0-521-21764-4); pap. 12.95x (ISBN 0-521-29269-7). Cambridge U Pr.

Boatman, Don E. Helps from Hebrews. (The Bible Study Textbook Ser.). (Illus.). 1960. 13.50 (ISBN 0-89900-044-4). College Pr Pub.

Boatman, Don E. & Boles, Kenny. Galatians. rev. ed. LC 70-1141. (The Bible Study Textbook Ser.). (Illus.). 1976. 11.50 (ISBN 0-89900-039-8). College Pr Pub.

Boatman, Don E., ed. Out of My Treasure: Special Alumni Edition, Vol. V. LC 80-71104. (Out of My Treasure Ser.). 260p. 1981. pap. 4.95 (ISBN 0-89900-121-1). College Pr Pub.

Boatner, ed. see Makkai, Adam.

Boatner, Mark M., 3rd. The Civil War Dictionary. (Illus., Maps & diagrams). 22.50 (ISBN 0-679-50013-8). McKay.

Boatright, M. C. Folk Laughter on the American Frontier. 7.50 (ISBN 0-8446-0035-0). Peter Smith.

Boatright, Mody C. Folklore of the Oil Industry. LC 63-21186. 228p. 1980. Repr. of 1963 ed. 6.95 (ISBN 0-87074-007-5). SMU Press.

Boatwright, Howard. Introduction to the Theory of Music. (Illus.). 1956. 16.95x (ISBN 0-393-02057-6, NortonC). Norton.

Boatwright, Mody C., et al, eds. Madstones & Twisters. LC 58-9269. (Texas Folklore Society Publication Ser.: No. 28). 180p. 1980. Repr. of 1958 ed. 5.95 (ISBN 0-87074-017-2). SMU Press.

Boaz, Martha. Strategies for Meeting the Information Needs of Society in the Year 2000. 250p. 1981. lib. bdg. price not set (ISBN 0-87287-249-1). Libs Unl.

Boaz, Martha, ed. Current Concepts in Library Management. LC 79-20734. 1979. lib. bdg. 25.00x (ISBN 0-87287-204-1). Libs Unl.

Bobak, Irene, jt. auth. see Jensen, Margaret.

Bobango, Gerald S. The Emergence of the Romanian Nation State. (East European Monographs: No. 58). 1979. 17.00x (ISBN 0-914710-51-6, Dist. by Columbia U Pr). East Eur Quarterly.

Bobart, Henry H. Basketwork Through the Ages. LC 72-171354. 188p. 1971. Repr. of 1936 ed. 15.00 (ISBN 0-8103-3400-3). Gale.

Bobath, Berta. Abnormal Postural Reflex Activity Caused by Brain Lesions. 2nd ed. (Illus.). 1976. pap. 7.50 (ISBN 0-433-03332-0). Heinman.

--Abnormal Postural Reflex Activity Caused by Brain Lesions. 2nd ed. 1973. pap. 11.00x (ISBN 0-433-03332-0). Intl Ideas.

--Adult Hemiplegia. 2nd ed. 1978. pap. 11.00x (ISBN 0-433-03334-7). Intl Ideas.

Bobath, Berta & Bobath, Karel. Motor Development in the Different Types of Cerebral Palsy. (Illus.). 1978. pap. 7.50 (ISBN 0-685-79638-8). Heinman.

--Motor Development in the Different Types of Cerebral Palsy. (Illus.). 1975. pap. 11.00x (ISBN 0-433-03333-9). Intl Ideas.

Bobath, Karel. Motor Deficit in Patients with Cerebral Palsy. (Clinics in Developmental Medicine Ser. No. 23). 54p. 1966. Repr. of 1969 ed. 6.50 o.p. (ISBN 0-685-24722-8). Lippincott.

--A Neurophysical Basis for the Treatment of Cerebral Palsy. (Clinics in Developmental Medicine Ser.: No. 75). 106p. 1980. 19.50. Lippincott.

Bobath, Karel, jt. auth. see Bobath, Berta.

Bobbitt. Indiana Appellate Practice & Procedure, 2 vols. 1972. 59.50, with 1977 suppl (ISBN 0-672-81526-5, Bobbs-Merrill Law); 1977 suppl 10.00 (ISBN 0-672-82813-8). Michie.

Bobbitt, H. R., et al. Organizational Behavior: Understanding & Prediction. 2nd ed. LC 77-25383. 1978. ref. 19.95 (ISBN 0-13-641209-2). P-H.

Bobbitt, Richard. Harmonic Technique in the Rock Idiom. 1976. text ed. 16.95x o.p. (ISBN 0-534-00474-1); wkbk. 6.95x o.p. (ISBN 0-534-00478-4). Wadsworth Pub.

Bobek, Joanne R. Math for Medical Techs. 1973. 8.00 o.p. (ISBN 0-87488-964-2). Med Exam.

Bober, Anne M. Attention & Achievement. 32p. 1977. pap. 8.00 o.p. (ISBN 0-686-00903-7, D-102). Essence Pubns.

Bober, Anne M., jt. auth. see Halsted, Donald L.

Bober, Harry, jt. auth. see Winston, Richard.

Bober, Natalie S. A Restless Spirit: The Story of Robert Frost. LC 80-23930. (Illus.). 224p. (gr. 6 up). 1981. PLB 10.95 (ISBN 0-689-30801-9). Atheneum.

Bober, William & Kenyon, Richard A. Fluid Mechanics. LC 79-12977. 1980. 26.95 (ISBN 0-471-04886-0); solutions manual avail. (ISBN 0-471-04999-9). Wiley.

Bober, Wolffgang On see On Bober, Wolffgang.

Bobillier, P. A., et al. Simulation with Gpss & Gpssv. LC 75-40316. 1976. 25.95 (ISBN 0-13-810549-9). P-H.

Bobker, Lee R. Flight of a Dragon. LC 80-22670. 256p. 1981. 9.95 (ISBN 0-688-03759-3). Morrow.

Bobkins, Denk. The Compassionate Deathmakers. (Orig.). 1980. pap. 2.25 (ISBN 0-532-23209-7). Manor Bks.

Bobo, Benjamin F. & Osborne, Alford E., Jr. Emerging Issues in Black Economic Development. LC 76-10500. (Illus.). 1976. 12.95 (ISBN 0-669-00718-8). Lexington Bks.

Bobo, Sheilah. Potential Problems for Second Language & Second Dialect Speakers in Mastering Standard English. LC 79-54950. 1979. pap. text ed. 7.25 o.p. (ISBN 0-8191-0871-5). U Pr of Amer.

Bobri, Vladimir & Miller, Carl. A Musical Voyage with Two Guitars. LC 73-10568. (Illus.). 176p. 1974. 8.95 o.s.i. (ISBN 0-02-512000-X). Macmillan.

--Two Guitars: A Galaxy of Duets for Guitar. LC 78-181572. 176p. 1972. 7.95 o.s.i. (ISBN 0-02-511980-X). Macmillan.

Bobrick, Benson. Labyrinths of Iron: A History of the Subways. Bobrick, Danielle, ed. LC 80-80046. (Illus.). 400p. 1981. 12.95 (ISBN 0-88225-299-2). Newsweek.

Bobrick, Danielle, ed. see Bobrick, Benson.

Bobroff, Arthur. Acne: And Related Disorders of Complexion & Scalp. 136p. 1964. pap. 12.75 photocopy ed. spiral (ISBN 0-398-00183-9). C C Thomas.

--Eczema: Its Nature, Cure & Prevention. (Illus.). 264p. 1962. pap. 22.75 photocopy ed. spiral (ISBN 0-398-00184-7). C C Thomas.

Bobrow, David B., et al. Understanding Foreign Policy Decisions: The Chinese Case. LC 78-24667. (Illus.). 1979. 19.95 (ISBN 0-02-904410-3). Free Pr.

Bobrow, Davis B. International Relations: New Approaches. LC 72-77282. 1972. pap. text ed. 3.95 (ISBN 0-02-904370-0). Free Pr.

Bobrow, Jerry & Covino, William A. ACT (American College Testing) Date not set. pap. text ed. cancelled. Cliffs.

--GMAT (Graduate Management Admissions Test) Date not set. pap. text ed. cancelled. Cliffs.

--Graduate Management Admissions Test Preparation Guide. (Cliffs Test Preparation Ser.). (Illus.). 342p. 1980. wkbk. 5.25 (ISBN 0-8220-2006-8). Cliffs.

--Preliminary Scholastic Aptitude Test Preparation Guide. (Cliffs Test Preparation Guide). (Illus.). (gr. 10-11). 1979. pap. 2.50 (ISBN 0-8220-2002-5). Cliffs.

--PSAT (Preliminary Scholastic Aptitute Test) Date not set. pap. text ed. cancelled. Cliffs.

--SAT (Scholastic Apitute Test) Date not set. pap. text ed. cancelled. Cliffs.

--Scholastic Aptitude Test Preparation Guide. (Cliffs Test Preparation Ser.). (Illus.). (gr. 11-12). 1979. pap. 3.50 wkbk. (ISBN 0-8220-2000-9). Cliffs.

Bobrow, Jerry, et al. American College Testing Preparation Guide. (Cliffs Test Preparation Ser.). (Illus.). (gr. 10-12). 1979. pap. 3.50 wkbk. (ISBN 0-8220-2004-1). Cliffs.

Bobrow, Leonard S. & Arbib, Michael A. Discrete Mathematics: Applied Algebra for Computer & Information Science. LC 73-77936. (Illus.). 1974. 24.50 (ISBN 0-7216-1768-9). Hemisphere Pub.

Bobrowski, Johannes. Shadow Land: Selected Poems. Mead, Ruth & Mead, Matthew, trs. (Poetry in Europe: No. 1). 1966. 4.95 o.p. (ISBN 0-8040-0273-8). Swallow.

Bocca, Geoffrey. Best-Seller: A Nostalgic Celebration of the Less Than Great Books You Have Always Been Afraid to Admit You Loved. 1981. 12.95 (Wyndham Bks). S&S.

Boccaccio. Andreuccio de Perugia. (Easy Reader, A). pap. 2.90 (ISBN 0-88436-049-0, ITA110051). EMC.

Boccaccio, Giovanni. De Casibus Illustrium Virorum. LC 62-7017. 1962. Repr. of 1520 ed. 26.00x (ISBN 0-8201-1005-1). Schol Facsimiles.

--Decameron, 2 vols. 1953. 10.50x ea. (Evman). Vol. 1 (ISBN 0-460-00845-5). Vol. 2 (ISBN 0-460-00846-3). pap. 1.95 o.p.; Vol. 1. pap. o.p.; Vol. 2. pap. o.p. Dutton.

--The Decameron. Musa, Mark & Bondanella, Peter, eds. LC 77-5664. (Norton Critical Editions). 1977. pap. 4.95x (ISBN 0-393-04458-0); pap. 4.95 (ISBN 0-393-09132-5). Norton.

--Genealogia. LC 75-27843. (Renaissance & the Gods Ser.: Vol. 2). (Illus.). 1976. Repr. of 1494 ed. lib. bdg. 73.00 (ISBN 0-8240-2051-0). Garland Pub.

--Genealogie. LC 75-27847. (Renaissance & the Gods Ser.: Vol. 5). (Illus., Fr.). 1976. Repr. of 1531 ed. lib. bdg. 73.00 (ISBN 0-8240-2054-5). Garland Pub.

--On Poetry. Osgood, Charles G., tr. 1956. pap. 5.80 o.p. (ISBN 0-672-60265-2, LLA82). Bobbs.

Bocchi, Achille. Symbolicarum Quaestionum de Universo Genere. Orgel, Stephen, ed. LC 78-68188. (Philosophy of Images Ser: Vol. 5). 1979. lib. bdg. 66.00 (ISBN 0-8240-3679-4). Garland Pub.

Bocchino, Anthony J. & Tanford, J. Alexander. North Carolina Trial Evidence Manual. LC 76-29099. 1976. with 1978 suppl 20.00 (ISBN 0-87215-188-3); 1978 suppl. 7.50 (ISBN 0-87215-277-4). Michie.

Bochenski, Innocenty M. History of Formal Logic. 2nd ed. LC 72-113118. 1970. text ed. 16.95 (ISBN 0-8284-0238-8). Chelsea Pub.

Bochenski, Joseph M., et al, eds. Guide to Marxist Philosophy: An Introductory Bibliography. LC 76-188168. 1972. pap. 4.95x (ISBN 0-8040-0561-3). Swallow.

Bochkov, A. E. & Zaikov, G. E. Chemistry of the O-Glycosidic Bond: Formation & Cleavage. 1979. 45.00 (ISBN 0-08-022949-2). Pergamon.

Bochner, Salomon. Fouriersche Integrale. LC 49-22695. (Ger). 8.95 (ISBN 0-8284-0042-3). Chelsea Pub.

Bochner, Stephen, ed. The Meditating Person: Bridges Between Cultures. 380p. 1981. text ed. 22.50x (ISBN 0-686-64398-4); pap. text ed. 11.25x (ISBN 0-87073-893-3). Schenkman.

Bock, Bruno & Bock, Klaus. Soviet Bloc Merchant Ships. LC 80-81092. (Illus.). 272p. 1981. 29.95 (ISBN 0-87021-669-4). Naval Inst Pr.

Bock, Carolyn E; see Levy, Harold L.

Bock, Emil. The Apocalypse. 1980. pap. 12.50 (ISBN 0-903540-42-8, Pub. by Floris Books). St George Bk Serv.

--The Three Years. 1980. pap. 12.50 (ISBN 0-903540-41-X, Pub. by Floris Books). St George Bk Serv.

Bock, G. De see Vokaer, R. & De Bock, G.

Bock, Janet L. The Jesus Mystery: Of Lost Years & Unknown Travels. LC 80-67420. (Illus.). 231p. (Orig.). 1980. pap. 6.95 (ISBN 0-937736-00-7). Aura Bks.

Bock, Kenneth. Human Nature & History: A Response to Sociobiology. 192p. 1980. 18.95 (ISBN 0-231-05078-X). Columbia U Pr.

Bock, Klaus, jt. auth. see Bock, Bruno.

Bock, Maria P. Von see Von Bock, Maria P.

Bock, Philip K. Continuities in Psychological Anthropology: A Historical Introduction. LC 79-23200. (Illus.). 1980. text ed. 15.95x (ISBN 0-7167-1136-2); pap. text ed. 7.95x (ISBN 0-7167-1137-0). W H Freeman.

--Modern Cultural Anthropology. 2nd ed. 512p. 1974. text ed. 14.95 o.p. (ISBN 0-394-31778-5). Random.

Bock, Rudolf & Marr, Iain L. A Handbook of Decomposition Methods in Analytical Chemistry. LC 78-70559. 1979. 79.95 (ISBN 0-470-26501-9). Halsted Pr.

Bockarev, S. V. The Method of Averaging in the Theory of Orthogonal Series, & Some Questions in the Theory of Bases. (Trudy Steklov: No. 146). 1980. 26.00 (ISBN 0-8218-3045-7). Am Math.

Bockhoff, Frank J. Elements of Quantum Theory. rev. enl. 2nd ed. LC 76-41769. 1976. text ed. 24.50 (ISBN 0-201-00799-1, Adv Bk Prog). A-W.

Bockhoff, K. H., ed. see Specialists Meeting Held at the Central Bureau for Nuclear Measurements, Geel, Belgium, 5-8 Dec. 1977.

Bockle, Franz. Fundamental Moral Theology. Smith, N. D., tr. from Ger. (Orig.). 1980. pap. 17.50 (ISBN 0-916134-42-3). Pueblo Pub Co.

Bockle, Franz & Pohier, Jacques-Marie. Power & the Word of God. LC 73-6431. (Concilium Ser.: Religion in the Seventies: Vol. 90). 156p. (Orig.). 1973. pap. 4.95 (ISBN 0-8164-2574-4). Crossroad NY.

Bockle, Franz, ed. Future of Marriage As an Institution. LC 70-113057. (Concilium Ser.: Religion in the Seventies: Vol. 55). 1970. pap. 4.95 (ISBN 0-8164-2511-6). Crossroad NY.

--Man in a New Society. (Concilium Ser.: Religion in the Seventies: Vol. 75). 1972. pap. 4.95 (ISBN 0-8164-2531-0). Crossroad NY.

--Manipulated Man. (Concilium Ser.: Religion in the Seventies: Vol. 65). 1971. pap. 4.95 (ISBN 0-8164-2521-3). Crossroad NY.

Bockle, Franz & Pohier, Jacques, eds. The Death Penalty & Torture. (Concilium: Vol. 120). (Orig.). 1978. pap. 4.95 (ISBN 0-8164-2200-1). Crossroad NY.

Bockle, Franz & Pohier, Jacques-Marie, eds. Moral Foundation & Christianity Concilium, Vol. 110. 1978. pap. 4.95 (ISBN 0-8164-2169-2). Crossroad NY.

Bockle, Franz & Pohier, Jean-Marie, eds. Sexuality in Contemporary Catholicism. (Concilium Ser.: Religion in the Seventies: Vol. 100). 1977. pap. 4.95 (ISBN 0-8164-2097-1). Crossroad NY.

Bockmuehl, Klaus. The Challenge of Marxism. LC 79-9701. 1980. pap. 4.95 (ISBN 0-87784-816-5). Inter-Varsity.

Bockmuehl, Klaus, ed. see Court, John H.

Bocknek, Gene. The Young Adult: Development After Adolescence. LC 80-15148. 250p. 1980. text ed. 9.95 (ISBN 0-8185-0387-4). Brooks-Cole.

Bockris, jt. ed. see Conway.

Bockris, J., et al. An Introduction to Electrochemical Science. (Wyckeham Science Ser.: Vol. 29). pap. 8.30 o.p. (ISBN 0-387-91116-2). Springer Verlag.

--An Introduction to Electrochemical Science. (Wykeham Science Ser.: No.29). 1974. 9.95x (ISBN 0-8448-1156-4). Crane Russak Co.

Bockris, J. O. Energy: The Solar Hydrogen Alternative. LC 75-19125. 1976. 34.95 (ISBN 0-470-08429-4). Halsted Pr.

Bockris, John O. Energy Options: Real Economics & the Solar-Hydrogen System. 441p. 1980. 32.95x (ISBN 0-470-26915-4). Halsted Pr.

Bockris, John O'M., jt. auth. see McGown, Linda B.

Bockris, Victor. With William Burroughs. 288p. 1981. 14.95 (ISBN 0-394-51809-8); pap. 7.95 (ISBN 0-394-17828-9). Seaver Bks.

Bockus, Frank. Couple Therapy. LC 80-66923. 300p. 1980. 27.50 (ISBN 0-87668-412-6). Aronson.

Bockus, William. Check List for Better Tennis. LC 72-97268. 160p. 1973. pap. 1.95 (ISBN 0-385-04612-X, Dolp). Doubleday.

Bodaken, Edward, jt. auth. see Sereno, Kenneth.

Bodak-Gyovai, L. Z. & Manzione, J. V., Jr. Oral Medicine: Patient Evaluation & Management. (Illus.). 208p. 1980. softcover 16.95 (ISBN 0-683-00901-X). Williams & Wilkins.

Bodansky, Oscar & Latner, eds. Advances in Clinical Chemistry, Vol. 20. 1978. 42.50 (ISBN 0-12-010320-6); lib ed. 47.25 (ISBN 0-12-010380-X); microfiche 27.00 (ISBN 0-12-010381-8). Acad Pr.

Bodanszky, M. & Ondetti, Miklos A. Peptide Synthesis. (Interscience Monographs on Chemistry, Organic Chemistry Section). 1966. text ed. 15.75 (ISBN 0-470-08450-2, Pub. by Wiley). Krieger.

Bodard, Lucien. The French Consul. 1977. 10.00 o.p. (ISBN 0-394-49321-4). Knopf.

Bodde, Derk. Essays on Chinese Civilization. Le Blanc, Charles & Borei, Dorothy, eds. LC 80-8586. (Princeton Ser. of Collected Essays). 504p. 1981. 25.00x (ISBN 0-691-03129-0); pap. 8.95x (ISBN 0-691-00024-7). Princeton U Pr.

Bodde, Derk, jt. auth. see Morris, Clarence.

Bodde, Derk, tr. see Tun Li-Ch'En.

Boddewyn, J. J. & Marton, Katherin. Comparison Advertising: A Worldwide Study. (Illus.). 1978. pap. 9.50 (ISBN 0-8038-1249-3). Hastings.

Boddy, Frederick A. Ground Cover & Other Ways to Weed-Free Gardens. LC 74-78251. (Illus.). 176p. 1974. 13.50 (ISBN 0-7153-6575-4). David & Charles.

Boddy, John. Brain Systems & Psychological Concepts. LC 77-21203. 1978. 39.75 (ISBN 0-471-99601-7); pap. 18.95 (ISBN 0-471-99600-9, Pub. by Wiley-Interscience). Wiley.

Boddy, Michael & Beckett, Richard. Surviving in the Eighties. (Illus.). 192p. (Orig.). 1980. text ed. 28.50 (ISBN 0-86861-106-9, 2515); pap. text ed. 14.95 (ISBN 0-86861-114-X, 2516). Allen Unwin.

Bode, Carl. Antebellum Culture. LC 59-8759. (Illus.). 1970. Repr. of 1959 ed. lib. bdg. 7.00x o.p. (ISBN 0-8093-0464-3). S Ill U Pr.

--Maryland. (States & the Nation Ser.). (Illus.). 1978. 12.95 (ISBN 0-393-05672-4, Co-Pub by AASLH). Norton.

--Mencken. LC 72-11997. (Arcturus Books Paperbacks). (Illus.). 1973. pap. 8.95 (ISBN 0-8093-0627-1). S Ill U Pr.

--Practical Magic: Poems. LC 80-17597. 52p. 1981. 8.95 (ISBN 0-8040-0362-9); pap. 4.95 (ISBN 0-8040-0373-4). Swallow.

Bode, Carl, ed. Best of Thoreau's Journals. LC 67-15321. 1971. Repr. of 1967 ed. 8.95x o.p. (ISBN 0-8093-0475-9). S Ill U Pr.

Bode, Frederick A. Protestantism & the New South: North Carolina Baptists & Methodists in Political Crisis, 1894-1903. LC 75-1289. 300p. 1976. 10.95x (ISBN 0-8139-0597-4). U Pr of Va.

Bode, Hans. Lead Acid Batteries. LC 76-58418. (The Electrochemical Society Ser). 1977. 41.50 (ISBN 0-471-08455-7, Pub. by Wiley-Interscience). Wiley.

Bode, Hendrik W. Network Analysis & Feedback Amplifier Design. rev. ed. LC 74-23514. 596p. 1975. Repr. of 1945 ed. 29.50 o.p. (ISBN 0-88275-242-1). Krieger.

Bode, Janet. Fighting Back: How to Cope with the Medical, Emotional, Legal Consequences of Rape. 1978. 12.95 (ISBN 0-02-512050-6). Macmillan.

--Kids Having Kids. (gr. 9 up). 1980. PLB 7.90 (ISBN 0-531-02882-8, B19). Watts.

--Rape: Preventing It; Coping with the Legal, Medical, & Emotional Aftermath. (Impact Ser.). (gr. 7 up). 1979. PLB 6.90 s&l (ISBN 0-531-02289-7). Watts.

Bode, Richard. Blue Sloop at Dawn. LC 79-1439. 1979. 8.95 (ISBN 0-396-07658-0). Dodd.

Bode, Wilhelm. The Italian Bronze Statuettes of the Renaissance. Draper, James D., ed. Gretor, William, tr. LC 80-82165. (Illus.). 1980. 295.00 (ISBN 0-937370-00-2). MAS De Reinis.

Bodecker, N. M. The Lost String Quartet. LC 80-1106. (Illus.). 32p. (gr. 1 up). 1981. 9.95 (ISBN 0-689-50200-1, McElderry Bk). Atheneum.

--A Person from Britain: Whose Head Was the Shape of a Mitten & Other Limericks. (Illus.). (gr. 8 up). 1980. PLB 6.95 (ISBN 0-689-50152-8, McElderry Bk). Atheneum.

--Quimble Wood. LC 80-24042. (Illus.). 32p. (ps-4). 1981. 9.95 (ISBN 0-689-50190-0, McElderry Bk). Atheneum.

Bodeen, DeWitt. From Hollywood. LC 73-15158. (Illus.). 512p. 1976. 15.00 o.p. (ISBN 0-498-01346-4). A S Barnes.

--More from Hollywood! LC 77-3213. (Illus.). 512p. 1977. 15.00 (ISBN 0-498-01533-5). A S Barnes.

Bodelsen, Anders. Think of a Number. 1978. pap. 1.75 o.s.i. (ISBN 0-685-87091-X). Jove Pubns.

Boden, Margaret. Artificial Intelligence & Natural Man. LC 76-8117. (Illus.). 537p. 1981. pap. 8.95 (ISBN 0-465-00453-9). Basic.

Boden, Margaret A. Jean Piaget. (The Modern Masters Ser.). 1980. pap. 4.95 (ISBN 0-14-005327-1). Penguin.

Bodenheimer, Edgar. Philosophy of Responsibility. LC 79-26020. x, 147p. 1980. text ed. 18.50x (ISBN 0-8377-0309-3). Rothman.

Bodenheimer, Edgar, et al. An Introduction to the Anglo-American Legal System, Readings & Cases. LC 80-18757. (American Casebook Ser.). 185p. 1980. pap. text ed. 6.95 (ISBN 0-8299-2103-6). West Pub.

Bodenhofer, Marita. Pala. 1981. 8.95 (ISBN 0-8062-1715-4). Carlton.

Bodet, Jaime T. Selected Poems of Jaime Torres Bodet. Karsen, Sonja, tr. LC 64-10832. 160p. (Fr. & Eng.). 1964. 7.50x o.p. (ISBN 0-253-17890-8). Ind U Pr.

Bodger, Lorraine & Ephron, Delia. Crafts for All Seasons. LC 79-6410. (Illus.). 112p. 1980. 9.95 o.s.i. (ISBN 0-87663-318-1); pap. 5.95 (ISBN 0-87663-996-1). Universe.

Bodian, Nat G. Book Marketing Handbook: Tips & Techniques for the Sale & Promotion of Scientific, Technical, Professional, & Scholarly Books & Journals. 482p. 1980. 45.00 (ISBN 0-8352-1286-6). Bowker.

Bodie, Idella. The Secret of Telfair Inn. LC 79-177909. (Illus.). 112p. (gr. 5-9). 1971. 3.95 o.p. (ISBN 0-87844-015-1). Sandlapper Store.

Bodie, Idella F. Biography of Archibald Rutledge. Roberts, Del, ed. LC 80-50789. (gr. 5-12). 1981. 9.95 (ISBN 0-87844-046-1). Sandlapper Store.

Bodin, Jean. Method for Easy Comprehension of History. Reynolds, Beatrice, tr. (Columbia University Records of Civilization Ser). 1969. pap. 5.95x (ISBN 0-393-09863-X, NortonC). Norton.

Bodin, Jeanne, jt. auth. see Millstein, Beth.

Bodin, Svante. Weather & Climate. (Illus.). 1978. 13.95 (ISBN 0-7137-0858-1, Pub. by Blandford Pr England). Sterling.

Bodine, Walter R. The Greek Text of Judges: Recensional Developments. LC 80-12578. (Harvard Semitic Monographs: No. 23). 15.00x (ISBN 0-89130-400-2). Scholars Pr CA.

Bodington, Stephen. Science & Social Action. 192p. 1980. 14.00x (ISBN 0-85031-270-1, Pub. by Allison & Busby England); pap. 7.95 (ISBN 0-85031-349-X, Pub. by Allison & Busby England). Schocken.

Bodini, Vittorio. The Hands of the South. Feldman, Ruth & Swann, Brian, trs. LC 80-68879. 1980. 7.50 (ISBN 0-686-62253-7). Charioteer.

Bodker, Cecil. Silas & the Black Mare. La Farge, Sheila, tr. LC 77-86303. (gr. 5-9). 1978. 7.95 (ISBN 0-440-07921-7, Sey Lawr); PLB 7.45 (ISBN 0-440-07922-5). Delacorte.

Bodman, N. C. & Su-Chu, Wu. Spoken Taiwanese. (Spoken Language Ser.). 208p. (Taiwanese.). 1980. pap. 10.00x (ISBN 0-87950-460-9); cassettes 9 dual track 60.00x (ISBN 0-87950-461-7); text & cassettes 65.00x (ISBN 0-87950-462-5). Spoken Lang Serv.

Bodman, Nicholas C. Spoken Amoy Hokkien: Units 1-30. (Spoken Language Series). 450p. (Amoy Hokkien.). 1981. pap. text ed. 12.00x (ISBN 0-87950-450-1); cassettes, 48 dual track 200.00x (ISBN 0-87950-451-X); bk. & cassettes combined 210.00 (ISBN 0-87950-452-8). Spoken Lang Serv.

Bodmer, W. F. & Cavalli-Sforza, L. L. Genetics, Evolution, & Man. LC 75-33990. (Illus.). 1976. 23.95x (ISBN 0-7167-0573-7). W H Freeman.

Bodmer, Walter F., jt. auth. see Cavalli-Sforza, L. L.

Bodmer, Walter F., jt. auth. see Jones, Alun.

Bodnar, John. Immigration & Industrialization: Ethnicity in an American Mill Town, 1870-1940. LC 77-74549. 1977. 11.95 (ISBN 0-8229-3348-9). U of Pittsburgh Pr.

Bodnar, M. J. Durability of Adhesive Bonded Structures: Journal of Applied Polymer Science. (Applied Polymer Symposium: No. 32). 1977. 33.50 (ISBN 0-471-04564-0, Pub. by Wiley-Interscience). Wiley.

Bodo, Peter & Harrison, June. Inside Tennis: A Season on the Pro Tour. (Illus.). 1979. 17.95 o.s.i. (ISBN 0-440-04297-6). Delacorte.

Bodoczky, Caroline, tr. see Lesznai, Anna.

Bodor, G. B. Orientation Effects in Solid Polymers. (Journal of Polymer Science Symposium: No. 58). 1978. 27.95 (ISBN 0-471-04658-2, Pub. by Wiley-Interscience). Wiley.

Bodtke, Richard. Tragedy & the Jacobean Temper: The Major Plays of John Webster. (Salzburg Studies in English Literature, Jacobean Drama Studies: No. 2). 1972. pap. text ed. 25.00x (ISBN 0-391-01328-9). Humanities.

Bodwell, C. E. Evaluation of Proteins for Humans. (Illus.). 1977. lib. bdg. 37.50 (ISBN 0-87055-215-5). AVI.

Bodwell, C. E. & Adkins, J. S. Protein Quality for Humans: Assessment & in Vitro Estimation. (Illus.). 1981. lib. bdg. price not set (ISBN 0-87055-388-7). AVI.

Bodwell, Dorothy. Baked Potatoes in My Pockets. 1977. 6.95 o.p. (ISBN 0-685-81417-3). Vantage.

Boe, Alfred. From Gothic to Functional Form. (Architecture & Decorative Art Ser.). 1979. Repr. of 1957 ed. 22.50 (ISBN 0-306-77544-1). Da Capo.

Boeck, P., et al. Peroxisomes & Related Particles in Animal Tissues. (Cell Biology Monographs: Vol. 7). (Illus.). 250p. 1980. 79.00 (ISBN 0-387-81582-1). Springer-Verlag.

Boecker, Hans J. Law & the Administration of Justice in the Old Testament & Ancient East. Moiser, Jeremy, tr. LC 80-65556. 224p. 1980. pap. 12.50 (ISBN 0-8066-1801-9, 10-3761). Augsburg.

Boeder, Robert B. Malawi. (World Bibliographical Ser.). 165p. 1980. 28.50 (ISBN 0-903450-22-4). ABC Clio.

Boegehold, Betty. Chipper's Choices. (Illus.). 64p. (gr. 6-9). 1981. PLB 6.99 (ISBN 0-698-30725-9). Coward.

--Education Before Five. 1978. pap. 7.50x (ISBN 0-8077-2557-9). Tchrs Coll.

--Hurray for Pippa! LC 79-19105. (Illus.). 64p. (gr. k-3). 1980. 4.95 (ISBN 0-394-84067-4); PLB 5.99 (ISBN 0-394-94067-9). Knopf.

--In the Castle of Cats. LC 80-22144. (Illus.). (ps-5). 1981. PLB 9.95 (ISBN 0-525-32541-7). Dutton.

--What the Wind Told. LC 73-22184. (Illus.). 48p. (ps-3). 1974. 5.95 o.s.i. (ISBN 0-8193-0756-4, Four Winds); PLB 5.41 o.s.i. (ISBN 0-8193-0757-2). Schol Bk Serv.

Boeghold, Betty. Pippa Mouse. 64p. 1976. pap. 1.25 (ISBN 0-440-47148-6, YB). Dell.

Boegli, A. Karst Hydrology & Physical Speleology & Physical Speleology. (Illus.). 300p. 1980. 38.00 (ISBN 0-387-10098-9). Springer-Verlag.

Boeheim, W. & Koetschau, K., eds. Zeitschrift Fur Historische Waffen-und Kostumkunde: Eighteen Ninety Seven to Nineteen Twenty, 10. (Illus.). 3000p. 1973. Repr. 925.00 o.p. (ISBN 3-201-00782-X). Arma Pr.

Boehlke, Neal A. Man Who Met Jesus at Bethesda. (Arch Bk.). (gr. k-4). 1981. pap. 0.79 (ISBN 0-570-06143-1, 59-1260). Concordia.

Boehm, Ann E. & Slater, Barbara R. Cognitive Skills Assessment Battery. 1974. complete kit 23.50 (ISBN 0-8077-5959-7); refill 8.25 (ISBN 0-8077-5960-0); interpretive manual 0.50 (ISBN 0-8077-5961-9); sampler 2.15 (ISBN 0-8077-5962-7). Tchrs Coll.

Boehm, Ann E. & Weinberg, Richard A. The Classroom Observer: Guide to Developing Observation Skills. LC 77-4316. (Illus.). 1977. pap. text ed. 7.50x (ISBN 0-8077-2506-4). Tchrs Coll.

Boehm, Barry W., jt. ed. see Sackman, Harold.

Boehm, K. H. & Silberston, A. British Patent System. (Cambridge Dept. of Applied Economics Monographs: No. 13). 1967. 32.50 (ISBN 0-521-04274-7). Cambridge U Pr.

Boehm, Klaus & Morris, Brian. Who Decides What in Europe. 256p. 1981. lib. bdg. 27.50 (ISBN 0-87196-388-4). Facts on File.

Boehm, Laszlo. Modern Music Notation. 1961. pap. 5.95 (ISBN 0-02-870490-8). Schirmer Bks.

Boehm, Sylvia L., ed. After-Dinner Laughter. LC 76-51166. 1977. 7.95 (ISBN 0-8069-0102-0); lib. bdg. 7.49 (ISBN 0-8069-0103-9). Sterling.

Boehme, Jacob. Signature of All Things. 1968. 12.95 (ISBN 0-227-67733-1). Attic Pr.

Boehme, S., et al, eds. Astronomy & Astrophysics Abstracts: Literature 1979, Pt. 2, Vol. 26. 794p. 1980. 69.70 (ISBN 0-387-10134-9). Springer-Verlag.

Boehme, S, et al, eds. Astronomy & Astrophysics Abstracts, Vol. 27: Literature 1980, Pt. 1. 939p. 1981. 69.70 (ISBN 0-387-10479-8). Springer-Verlag.

Boehmer, Heinrich. Die Falschungen Erzbischof Lanfranks Von Canterbury. LC 80-2233. 1981. Repr. of 1902 ed. 29.50 (ISBN 0-404-18754-4). AMS Pr.

--Kirche und Staat in England und in Normandie Im XI. und XII. Jahrhundert: Eine Historische Studie. LC 80-2234. 1981. Repr. of 1899 ed. 57.50 (ISBN 0-404-18755-2). AMS Pr.

Boehn, Max Von see Von Boehn, Max.

Boehner, Philotheus, tr. see William Of Ockman.

Boeke, Kees. Cosmic View: The Universe in Forty Jumps. LC 57-14500. (Illus.). (gr. 5 up). 1957. 8.95 (ISBN 0-381-98016-2, A16260, JD-J). John Day.

Boekman. Surviving Your Parent's Divorce. (gr. 7 up). 1980. PLB 7.90 (ISBN 0-531-02869-0, B51). Watts.

Boelen, Bernard J. Existential Thinking. LC 68-5783. 1971. pap. 6.95 (ISBN 0-8164-2546-9). Crossroad NY.

Boelhower, William Q., tr. see Goldmann, Lucien.

Boell. Erzaehlungen. (Easy Reader, D). pap. 3.75 (ISBN 0-88436-108-X, GEA301052). EMC.

Boeman, John. Morotai: A Memoir of War. LC 80-697. 288p. 1981. 12.95 (ISBN 0-385-15586-7). Doubleday.

Boeni, Franz. Hospiz. (Edition Suhrkamp: Neue Folge). 100p. (Orig.). 1980. pap. text ed. 3.25 (ISBN 3-518-11004-7, Pub. by Insel Verlag Germany). Suhrkamp.

Boenig, Robert W., ed. Research in Science Education: 1938-1947. LC 69-12581. 1969. text ed. 12.75x (ISBN 0-8077-1093-8). Tchrs Coll.

Boening, John, ed. & intro. by. The Reception of Classical German Literature in England, 1760-1860: A Documentary History from Contemporary Periodicals, 10 vols. Incl. Vol. 1. General Introduction & Reviews from 1760 to 1813 (ISBN 0-8240-0990-8); Vol. 2. Reviews from 1813 to 1835 (ISBN 0-8240-0991-6); Vol. 3. Reviews from 1835 to 1860 (ISBN 0-8240-0992-4); Vol. 4. Authors from Bodmer to Klopstock (ISBN 0-8240-0993-2); Vol. 5. Authors from Lavater to Novalis (ISBN 0-8240-0994-0); Vol. 6. The Reception of Early German Romantics: Richter, the Brothers Schlegel, Tieck & Hoffmann (ISBN 0-8240-0995-9); Vol. 7. General Critical Articles on Goethe & Reviews Which Discuss Goethe & Schiller Together, Arranged in Order of Appearance (ISBN 0-8240-0996-7); Vol. 8. Reviews of Werther, Goethe's Early Works, His Poems & Faust (ISBN 0-8240-0997-5); Vol. 9. The Works of Goethe's Midcareer, Wilhelm Meister & Such Works As Dichtung und Wahrheit, Etc (ISBN 0-8240-0998-3); Vol. 10. The English Reception of Specific Works of **Schiller, from the Early Plays to the Historical Works (ISBN 0-8240-0999-1). 1977. Set. lib. bdg. 110.00 each. Garland Pub.**

Boeninger, Hildegard R. & Pietschmann, D., eds. Ich Lausche Dem Leben. (Orig., Ger.). 1963. pap. 6.95x (ISBN 0-393-09558-4, NortonC); tapes 30.00 (ISBN 0-393-09911-3). Norton.

Boer, Charles. Charles Olson in Connecticut. LC 73-13214. (Illus.). 146p. 1975. 8.95 (ISBN 0-8040-0649-0). Swallow.

--An Epic Poem on the Life of William Clarke Quantrill: An Epic on the Life of William Clarke Quantrill. LC 74-189194. 148p. 1972. 8.00 (ISBN 0-8040-0572-9); pap. 4.50 (ISBN 0-8040-0573-7). Swallow.

--Odes. LC 70-75737. (New Poetry Ser: No. 36). 51p. 1969. 5.50 (ISBN 0-8040-0229-0). Swallow.

Boer, Charles, tr. from Gr. Homeric Hymns. LC 73-132581. 184p. 1971. 9.00x (ISBN 0-8040-0524-9); pap. 3.95x o.s.i. (ISBN 0-8040-0525-7). Swallow.

--The Homeric Hymns. rev. ed. (Dunquin Ser.). 1979. pap. text ed. 8.50 (ISBN 0-88214-210-0). Spring Pubns.

Boer, Charles, tr. see Ficino, Marsilio.

Boer, Den W. Private Morality in Greece & Rome: Some Historical Aspects. 1980. text ed. 45.75x (ISBN 90-04-05976-8). Humanities.

Boer, Dena, jt. auth. see Maino, Jeanette.

Boer, Germain B. Direct Cost & Contribution Accounting: An Integrated Management Accounting System. LC 73-17324. (Systems & Controls for Financial Managment Ser). 256p. 1974. 26.95 (ISBN 0-471-08505-7, Pub. by Wiley-Interscience). Wiley.

Boer, Jan De see De Boer, Jan & Baillie, Thomas W.

Boer, Jan H. Missionary Messengers of Liberation in a Colonial Context: A Case Study of the Sudan United Mission. 542p. 1979. pap. text ed. 51.50x (ISBN 90-6203-561-2). Humanities.

Boer, K. W., ed. Sharing the Sun, Vols. 1-10. Incl. Vol. 1. International & US Programs Solar Flux. pap. text ed. 33.00 (ISBN 0-08-021686-2); Vol. 2. Solar Collectors. pap. text ed. 33.00 (ISBN 0-08-021687-0); Vol. 3. Solar Heating & Cooling Buildings. pap. text ed. 33.00 (ISBN 0-08-021688-9); Vol. 4. Solar System, Simulation, Design. pap. text ed. 38.50 (ISBN 0-08-021689-7); Vol. 5. Solar Thermal & Ocean Thermal. pap. text ed. 44.00 (ISBN 0-08-021690-0); Vol. 6. Photovoltaics & Materials. pap. text ed. 33.00 (ISBN 0-08-021691-9); Vol. 7. Agriculture, Biomass, Wind, New Developments. pap. text ed. 33.00 (ISBN 0-08-021692-7); Vol. 8. Storage, Water Heater, Data Communication, Education. pap. text ed. 33.00 (ISBN 0-08-021693-5); Vol. 9. Socio-Economics & Cultural. pap. text ed. 27.50 (ISBN 0-08-021694-3); Vol. 10. Business & Commercial Implications. pap. text ed. 22.00 (ISBN 0-08-021695-1). 1976. Set. pap. text ed. 350.00 (ISBN 0-08-021696-X). Pergamon.

Boer, P. de see Searle, A. G. & De Boer, P.

Boer-Hoff, Louise E., tr. see Schuurman, C. J.

Boeri, David & Gibson, James. Tell It Goodbye, Kiddo: The Decline of the New England Offshore Fishing Industry. LC 75-37368. (Illus.). 144p. 1976. 9.95 o.p. (ISBN 0-87742-063-7). Intl Marine.

Boericke, Arthur, jt. auth. see Shapiro, Barry.

Boerma, Conrad. The Rich, the Poor - & the Bible. rev. ed. Bowden, John, tr. from Dutch. LC 80-15337. 1980. write for info. (ISBN 0-664-24349-5). Westminster.

Boersma, Frederic J. & Muir, Walter. Eye Movements & Information Processing in Mentally Retarded Children. (Modern Approaches to the Diagnosis & Instruction of Multi-Handicapped Children Ser.: Vol. 14). 100p. 1975. text ed. 21.50 (ISBN 90-237-4125-0, Pub. by Swets Pub Serv Holland). Swets North Am.

Boersma, Frederic J., jt. auth. see Chapman, James W.

Boersma, Frederic J., jt. auth. see Wilton, Keri M.

Boersner, Demetrio. The Bolsheviks & the National & Colonial Question, 1917-1928. LC 79-2894. 285p. 1981. Repr. of 1957 ed. write for info. (ISBN 0-8305-0062-6). Hyperion Conn.

Boeschen, John. Successful Bed Book. Case, Virginia A., ed. (Successful Ser.). (Illus.). 200p. 1981. 18.95 (ISBN 0-89999-030-4); pap. 8.95 (ISBN 0-89999-031-2). Structures Pub.

--Successful Playhouses. LC 79-16230. (Successful Ser.). (Illus.). 1979. 13.95 (ISBN 0-912336-91-9); pap. 6.95 (ISBN 0-912336-92-7). Structures Pub.

Boese, A., ed. Search for the Cause of Multiple Sclerosis & Other Chronic Diseases of the Central Nervous System. (Illus.). 516p. (Orig.). pap. text ed. 55.00 (ISBN 3-527-25875-2). Verlag Chemie.

Boese, Jannik, et al. Ujamaa - Socialism from Above. (Scandinavian Institute of African Studies, Uppsala). (Illus.). 1978. text ed. 25.25x (ISBN 0-8419-9730-6). Holmes & Meier.

Boesen, Victor & Graybill, Florence C. Edward S. Curtis: Photographer of the North American Indian. LC 76-53435. (gr. 7 up). 1977. 6.95 (ISBN 0-396-07430-8). Dodd.

Boesen, Victor, jt. auth. see Graybill, Florence C.

Boesler, K. A. Geography & Capital. 1976. pap. text ed. 28.00 (ISBN 0-08-019712-4). Pergamon.

Boethius. The Consolation of Philosophy. Green, Richard H., tr. LC 62-11788. 1962. pap. 3.95 (ISBN 0-672-60273-3, LLA86). Bobbs.

--On the Consolation of Philopsophy. 1981. pap. 3.95 (ISBN 0-89526-885-X). Regnery-Gateway.

Boettinger, Henry M. Moving Mountains: The Art & Craft of Letting Others See Things Your Way. (Illus.). 1969. 7.95 o.s.i. (ISBN 0-02-512100-6). Macmillan.

Boewe, Charles. Prairie Albion: An English Settlement in Pioneer Illinois. LC 62-15000. (Illus.). 1962. 10.00x o.p. (ISBN 0-8093-0074-5). S Ill U Pr.

Boewering, Gerhard. The Mystical Vision of Existence in Islam Classical. (Studien zur Sprache, Geschichte und Kultur desislamischen Orients, Beihefte zur "der Islam"). 296p. 1979. text ed. 79.00x (ISBN 3-11-007546-6). De Gruyter.

Boeynaems, J. M. & Herman, A. G., eds. Prostaglandins, Prostacyclin, Thromboxanes Measurement. (Developments in Pharmacology Ser.: No. 1.). (Illus.). 209p. 1981. PLB 34.00 (ISBN 90-247-2417-1, Pub. by Martinus Nijhoff). Kluwer Boston.

Bogan, Aleta R. Nolan Nutria's Story. 1979. 4.00 o.p. (ISBN 0-8062-1192-X). Carlton.

Bogan, Louise, ed. see Renard, Jules.

Bogardus, LaDonna. Adventures in Christian Living & Learning, Pt. 2. (Orig.). 1970. pap. 2.50 tchrs' bk. (ISBN 0-687-00904-9); pap. 2.25 pupils' bk (ISBN 0-687-00905-7). Abingdon.

Bogart. Home, How to Run Effectively-Save Money. 1980. pap. cancelled (ISBN 0-8120-0685-2). Barron.

Bogart, Carlotta L., jt. auth. see Houk, Annelle S.

Bogart, Doris Van De see Van De Bogart, Doris.

Bogart, John L. Orthodox & Heretical Perfectionism in the Johannine Community As Evident in the First Epistle of John. LC 77-5447. (Society of Biblical Literature. Dissertation Ser.). 1977. pap. 7.50 (ISBN 0-89130-138-0, 060133). Scholars Pr Ca.

Bogart, Leo. The Press & Public. LC 80-18357. 304p. 1980. text ed. 24.95 (ISBN 0-89859-077-9). L Erlbaum Assocs.

Bogart, Lois S. Life Can Be Beautiful. 1981. 4.95 (ISBN 0-8062-1589-5). Carlton.

Bogart, Marcel J. Ammonia Absorption Refrigeration. (Illus.). 320p. 1981. 32.95 (ISBN 0-87201-027-9). Gulf Pub.

Bogart, Max, ed. Jazz Age. LC 69-11435. (American Character Ser). (Illus.). (gr. 9-12). 1969. pap. text ed. 5.95 (ISBN 0-684-51500-8, SSP18, ScribC). Scribner.

Bogart, Ralph, jt. auth. see Jones, William E.

Bogason, Sigurdur O. English-Icelandic Dictionary (1976) 1978. 75.00 (ISBN 0-685-29251-7). Heinman.

Bogason, Sigurdur O., jt. auth. see Sigurdsson, Angrimur.

Bogatyrev, Petr. The Functions of Folk Costume in Moravian Slovakia. LC 78-149915. (Approaches to Semiotics Ser: No. 5). (Illus.). 107p. 1971. text ed. 25.90x (ISBN 90-2791-756-6). Mouton.

Bogdan, A. V. Tropical Pasture & Fodder Plants. LC 76-14977. (Tropical Agriculture Ser.). (Illus.). 1977. text ed. 48.00x (ISBN 0-582-46676-8). Longman.

Bogdan, Robert & Taylor, Steven J. An Introduction to Qualitative Research Methods: A Phenomenological Approach to the Social Sciences. LC 75-19407. 266p. 1975. 21.95 (ISBN 0-471-08571-5, Pub. by Wiley-Interscience). Wiley.

Bogdan W., tr. see Wesolowski, Wlodzimierz, et al.

Bogdanor, Vernon, ed. see Disraeli, Benjamin.

Bogdanova, A. V., ed. see Shostakovskii, M. F.

Bogdanovich, Peter. Allan Dwan. (A Belvedere Bk.). 220p. 1981. pap. 5.95 (ISBN 0-87754-320-8). Chelsea Hse.

Bogel, Fredric V. Acts of Knowledge: Pope's Later Poems. LC 78-75194. 285p. 1981. 18.50 (ISBN 0-8387-2380-2). Bucknell U Pr.

Bogen, J. I. & Shipman, S. S. Financial Handbook. 4th ed. 1208p. 1968. 40.95 (ISBN 0-471-06556-0). Wiley.

Bogen, James. Wittgenstein's Philosophy of Language: Some Aspects of Its Development. (International Library of Philosophy & Scientific Method). 1972. text ed. 15.00x (ISBN 0-391-00227-9). Humanities.

Bogen, Jules I., et al, eds. Financial Handbook. rev. 4th ed. (Illus.). 1250p. 1968. 40.95 (ISBN 0-8260-1160-8). Ronald Pr.

Bogen, Nancy, ed. see Blake, William.

Boger, Louise. Complete Guide to Furniture Styles. rev. ed. LC 59-6239. (Encore Editions). (Illus.). 1969. 35.00 (ISBN 0-684-15020-4, ScribT). Scribner.

Bogert, Joan, jt. auth. see Bogert, John.

Bogert, John & Bogert, Joan. The Hundred Best Restaurants in the Valley of the Sun: 1981. 4th ed. LC 77-79784. 160p. 1980. pap. 2.25 (ISBN 0-937974-00-5). ADM Co.

Boggess, Louise. How to Write Fillers & Short Features That Sell. 2nd ed. LC 80-8682. 256p. 1981. 10.95 (ISBN 0-06-010492-9, HarpT). Har-Row.

Boggess, William R., ed. Lead in the Environment. (Illus.). 272p. 1979. 45.00x (ISBN 0-7194-0024-4). Intl Pubns Serv.

Boggs & Dixson. English Step by Step with Pictures. new ed. (gr. 7-12). 1980. pap. text ed. 3.75 (ISBN 0-88345-416-5, 18186). Regents Pub.

Boggs, Carl. The Impasse of European Communism. 1981. lib. bdg. 20.00x (ISBN 0-89158-784-5). Westview.

Boggs, Joseph M. The Art of Watching Films: Film Analysis. LC 77-87343. 1978. 9.95 (ISBN 0-8053-0970-5). Benjamin-Cummings.

Boggs, R. F. Radiological Safety Aspects of the Operation of Neutron Generators. (Safety Ser.: No. 42). (Illus.). 1976. pap. 6.00 (ISBN 92-0-123076-1, ISP427, IAEA). Unipub.

Boggs, R. S., jt. auth. see Jagendorf, Moritz A.

Boggs, Ralph S. Basic Spanish Pronunciation. (Orig., Span.). (gr. 9-11). 1969. pap. 2.95 (ISBN 0-88345-012-7, 17442); tapes o.p. 40.00 (ISBN 0-685-19784-0); cassettes 60.00 (ISBN 0-685-19785-9). Regents Pub.

Boggs, Ralph S., jt. auth. see Dixson, Robert J.

Boggs, Sue H. Is a Job Really Worth It? 1979. pap. 2.25 (ISBN 0-89137-522-8). Quality Pubns.

Boggs, William E., jt. auth. see Koob, Derry D.

Boggs, Winthrop S. Postage Stamps & Postal History of Newfoundland. LC 75-1791. (Illus.). 288p. 1975. Repr. 35.00x (ISBN 0-88000-066-X). Quarterman.

Bogitsh, Burton J., jt. auth. see Nunnally, David A.

Bogle, Kate, jt. auth. see Cutler, Katherine N.

Bognar, Desi K. Hungarians in America. LC 72-97113. (East-European Biographies & Studies Ser.: No. 3). 240p. 1972. 8.50x (ISBN 0-912460-01-6). AFI Pubns.

Bognar, Desi K., ed. Hungarians in America: A Biographical Directory of Professionals of Hungarian Origin. rev. ed. LC 79-53801. (East European Biographies & Studies Ser: Nos. 4 & 5). 1979. 25.00 (ISBN 0-685-71858-1). AFI Pubns.

Bognar, G., ed. see Colloquium of Microwave Communication, 5th, Budapest, 1970.

Bogner, Norman. California Dreamers. 1981. 13.95 (ISBN 0-671-42877-2, Wyndham Bks). S&S.

Bogolubov, Nikolai N., et al. Introduction to Axiomatic Quantum Field Theory. Fulling, Stephen & Popova, Ludmila G., trs. from Rus. LC 72-5554. (Mathematical Physics Monographs: No. 18). 700p. 1975. text ed. 39.50 (ISBN 0-8053-0982-9, Adv Bk Prog). Benjamin-Cummings.

Bogolyubov, N. N. A Method for Studying-Model Hamiltonians. 180p. 1972. text ed. 37.00 (ISBN 0-08-016742-X). Pergamon.

Bogolyubov, N. N., ed. Particles & Nuclei. Incl. Vol. 1, Pt. 1. 189p (ISBN 0-306-17191-0); Vol. 1, Pt. 2. 191p (ISBN 0-306-17192-9); Vol. 2, Pt. 1. 171p (ISBN 0-306-17193-7); Vol. 2, Pt. 2. 138p (ISBN 0-306-17194-5); Vol. 2, Pt. 3. 178p (ISBN 0-306-17195-3); Vol. 2, Pt. 4. 178p (ISBN 0-306-17196-1). LC 72-83510. 1972. 45.00 ea. (Consultants). Plenum Pub.

Bogorodskii, N. The Doctrine of St. John Damascene on the Procession of the Holy Spirit. LC 80-2351. 1981. Repr. of 1879 ed. 28.50 (ISBN 0-404-18903-2). AMS Pr.

Bogosh, R., ed. see Ravich, M. G. & Kamenev, E. N.

Bogue, Allan G. Money at Interest: The Farm Mortgage on the Middle Border. LC 55-1350. 1969. pap. 4.50x (ISBN 0-8032-5018-5, BB 396, Bison). U of Nebr Pr.

Bogue, Allan G., ed. Emerging Theoretical Models in Social & Political History. LC 73-87857. (Sage Contemporary Social Science Issues: No. 9). 4.95x (ISBN 0-8039-0321-9). Sage.

Bogue, Donald J. & Beale, Calvin L. Economic Areas of the United States. LC 61-9161. (Illus.). 1961. 35.00 (ISBN 0-02-904400-6). Free Pr.

Bogue, Grant. Basic Sociological Research Design. 1981. pap. text ed. 8.95x (ISBN 0-673-15349-5). Scott F.

Bogue, Lucile. Bloodstones: Lines from a Marriage. 1980. 5.50 (ISBN 0-8233-0324-1). Golden Quill.

Bogue, Margaret B., ed. The New American State Papers: Public Lands Subject Set, 8 vols. LC 72-95582. 1972. Set. lib. bdg. 450.00 (ISBN 0-8420-1643-0). Scholarly Res Inc.

Bogus, Ronald, jt. ed. see Landau, Sidney.

Bogus, S. Diane. Her Poems: An Anniversaric Chronology. (Illus., Orig.). 1980. pap. cancelled (ISBN 0-934172-02-1). WIM Pubns.

--Madness Beyond Belief. 300p. (Orig.). Date not set. price not set (ISBN 0-934172-05-6); pap. price not set. WIM Pubns.

Bogus, S. Diane, ed. The Fifty Best WIM Reviews. (Illus.). Date not set. pap. cancelled (ISBN 0-934172-04-8). WIM Pubns.

Boguslaw, Robert. New Utopians: A Study of System Design & Social Change. enl. ed. 1981. pap. text ed. 7.95x (ISBN 0-8290-0115-8). Irvington.

--Systems Analysis & Social Planning. 1981. text ed. 18.50x (ISBN 0-8290-0111-5). Irvington.

Bohachevska-Chomiak, Martha, tr. see Struk, Danylo S.

Bohan, Anthony. Rheumatology Continuing Education Review. 1980. spiral bdg. 14.00 (ISBN 0-87488-333-4). Med Exam.

Bohannan, Harry M. see Morris, Alvin L.

Bohannan, John. Your Guide to Boating: Power or Sail. (Illus., Orig.). 1965. pap. 2.50 o.p. (ISBN 0-06-463238-5, 238, EH). Har-Row.

Bohannan, Paul, ed. Law & Warfare: Studies in the Anthropology of Conflict. (Texas Press Sourcebooks: No. 1). (Illus.). 439p. 1976. pap. 7.95x (ISBN 0-292-74617-2). U of Tex Pr.

Bohannon C0., Locks Catalog. (Illus.). Repr. of 1911 ed. 15.00 (ISBN 0-87556-350-3). Saifer.

Bohannon, Laura, ed. see Pettengill, Samuel B.

Bohart, R. M. & Grissell, E. E. California Wasps of the Subfamily Philanthinae (Hymenoptera-Specidae) (Bulletin of the California Insect Survey: Vol. 19). 1975. pap. 9.00x (ISBN 0-520-09523-5). U of Cal Pr.

Bohart, R. M. & Horning, D. S. California Bembecine Sand Wasps in the Genera Bembix, Bicyrtes & Microbembex (Hymenoptera Sphecidae) (Bulletin of the California Insect Survey: Vol. 13). 1971. pap. 9.00x (ISBN 0-520-09387-9). U of Cal Pr.

Bohart, R. M. & Menke, A. S. A Reclassification of the Sphecinae, with a Revision of the Nearctic Species of the Tribes Sceliphronini & Sphecini (Hymenoptera, Sphecidae) (U. C. Publ. in Entomology: Vol. 30.2). 1963. pap. 6.50x (ISBN 0-520-09098-5). U of Cal Pr.

--Sphecid Wasps of the World: A Generic Revision. 1976. 62.50x (ISBN 0-520-02318-8). U of Cal Pr.

Bohart, R. M. & Stange, L. A. A Revision of the Genus Zethus Fabricius in the Western Hemisphere (Hymenoptera: Eumenidae) (U. C. Publ. in Entomology: Vol. 40). 1965. pap. 9.00x (ISBN 0-520-09112-4). U of Cal Pr.

Bohdan, Carol L., jt. auth. see Blasberg, Robert.

Bohen, Halcyone H. & Viveros-Long, Anamaria. Balancing Jobs & Family Life: Do Flexible Work Schedules Help? (Illus.). 328p. 1981. 19.50 (ISBN 0-87722-199-5). Temple U Pr.

Bohinski, Robert C. Modern Concepts in Biochemistry. 3rd ed. 1979. text ed. 27.95 (ISBN 0-205-06521-X, 6865216); answerbook avail. (ISBN 0-205-06542-2, 6865429). Allyn.

Bohl, Marilyn. Computer Concepts. LC 75-101499. (Illus.). 1970. text ed. 17.95 (ISBN 0-574-16080-9, 13-0751); instr's guide avail. (ISBN 0-574-16082-5, 13-0753); problems & exercises 6.50 (ISBN 0-574-16081-7, 13-0752); transparency masters 33.00 (ISBN 0-574-16083-3, 13-0754); problem-set master tape 57.50 (ISBN 0-574-16084-1, 13-0755). SRA.

--Introduction to IBM Direct Access Storage Devices. 320p. 1981. text ed. 12.95t (ISBN 0-574-21140-3, 13-4140). SRA.

Bohle, Bruce, ed. see Thompson, Oscar.

Bohle, Bruce W., ed. Human Life: Controversies & Concerns. (Reference Shelf Ser.). 1979. 6.25 (ISBN 0-8242-0636-3). Wilson.

Bohlen, Charles E. Transformation of American Foreign Policy. 1969. 3.95x (ISBN 0-393-05385-7, NortonC); pap. text ed. 2.95x (ISBN 0-393-09878-8). Norton.

--Witness to History. 1973. pap. 6.95x (ISBN 0-393-09287-9, 9287). Norton.

Bohler, Jorg, jt. auth. see Bohler, Lorenz.

Bohler, Lorenz & Bohler, Jorg. The Treatment of Fractures, 3 Vols. Tretter, tr. LC 55-5445. (Illus.). 1956-58. Set. 177.00 (ISBN 0-685-11775-8); Vol. 1. 70.00 o.p. (ISBN 0-8089-0064-1); Vol. 2. 48.00 (ISBN 0-8089-0065-X); Vol. 3. 59.00 (ISBN 0-8089-0066-8). Grune.

Bohlmann, Otto. Yeats & Nietzsche: An Exploration of Major Nietzschean Echoes in the Writings of William Butler Yeats. 390p. 1980. 28.50x (ISBN 0-389-20065-4). B&N.

Bohlool, Janet. Library Orientation: Syllabus. 1970. pap. text ed. 5.45 (ISBN 0-89420-080-1, 216720); cassette recordings 101.35 (ISBN 0-89420-161-1, 140800). Natl Book.

Bohm, David. Causality & Chance in Modern Physics. LC 57-28894. 1971. pap. 4.95x (ISBN 0-8122-1002-6, Pa Paperbks). U of Pa Pr.

Bohm, Peter. Social Efficiency: A Concise Introduction to Welfare Economics. LC 73-9379. 150p. 1975. pap. 11.95 (ISBN 0-470-08636-X). Halsted Pr.

Bohman, Raynard F., Jr. Guide to Maximizing Recovery of Loss & Damage Claims. 1976. spiral 14.95 o.p. (ISBN 0-8436-1408-0). CBI Pub.

Bohman, Sven-Olof, jt. ed. see Mandal, Anil K.

Bohme, H. & Viehe, H. G. Imminium Salts in Organic Chemistry. LC 76-16155. (Advances in Organic Chemistry Ser.: Vol. 9, Pt. 2). 1979. 85.00 (ISBN 0-471-90693-X, Pub. by Wiley-Interscience). Wiley.

Bohme, H. & Viehe, H. G., eds. Iminium Salts in Organic Chemistry. LC 76-16155. (Advances in Organic Chemistry Ser: Vol. 9, Pt. 1). 544p. 1976. 65.00 (ISBN 0-471-90692-1, Pub. by Wiley-Interscience). Wiley.

Bohmer, Gunter. Wonderful World of Puppets. LC 76-107968. (Illus.). 1971. 9.95 (ISBN 0-8238-0084-9). Plays.

Bohn, Dave & Petschek, Rodolfo. Kinsey, Photographer. LC 78-1029. (Illus.). 1978. pap. 24.95 (ISBN 0-87701-107-9). Chronicle Bks.

Bohn, Henry G., ed. Hand-Book of Games. LC 73-84610. 1969. Repr. of 1850 ed. 20.00 (ISBN 0-8103-3570-0). Gale.

--Polyglot of Foreign Proverbs - with English Translations. LC 67-23915. (Polyglot). 1968. Repr. of 1857 ed. 22.00 (ISBN 0-8103-3197-7). Gale.

Bohn, Hiebert & Ungurait. Mass Media: An Introduction to Modern Communication. 2nd ed. LC 77-17721. (Illus.). 1979. pap. text ed. 12.95x (ISBN 0-582-28070-2). Longman.

Bohn, Hinrich, et al. Soil Chemistry. LC 79-14515. 1979. 22.95 (ISBN 0-471-04082-7, Pub. by Wiley-Interscience). Wiley.

Bohn, Martin J., Jr., jt. auth. see Megargee, Edwin I.

Bohn, Ralph C., jt. auth. see Silvius, G. Harold.

Bohn, Robert F. Budget Book & Much More: Your Money, Goals, Time, Assets, Vital Records. 2nd ed. 128p. pap. text ed. 5.95 (ISBN 0-8403-2185-6). Kendall-Hunt.

Bohn, Thomas W., et al. Light & Shadows: A History of Motion Pictures. 2nd ed. LC 77-25909. 1978. pap. text ed. 11.50x (ISBN 0-88284-057-6). Alfred Pub.

Bohner, Charles H. Robert Penn Warren. (U. S. Authors Ser.: No. 69). 1964. lib. bdg. 9.95 (ISBN 0-8057-0772-7). Twayne.

Bohner, Olive. Demon of Padeng. LC 77-20928. (Nova Ser.). 1977. pap. 5.95 (ISBN 0-8127-0150-X). Southern Pub.

Bohr, Harald. Almost Periodic Functions. LC 47-5500. 1980. 8.50 (ISBN 0-8284-0027-X). Chelsea Pub.

Bohrer, Stanley P., ed. Bone Infarction in Sickle Cell Disease. (Illus.). 400p. 1981. 39.50 (ISBN 0-87527-188-X). Green.

Boice, J. Montgomery. God & History. (Foundations of the Christian Faith: Vol 4). 292p. (Orig.). 1981. pap. 6.95 (ISBN 0-87784-746-0). Inter-Varsity.

Boice, James M. Can You Run Away from God? 1977. pap. 1.95 (ISBN 0-88207-501-2). Victor Bks.

--God the Redeemer. LC 77-14880. (Foundations of the Christian Faith: Vol. 2). 1978. pap. 5.95 (ISBN 0-87784-744-4). Inter-Varsity.

--The Gospel of John: An Expositional Commentary, Vol. 4. 1978. 12.95 (ISBN 0-310-21460-2). Zondervan.

--The Gospel of John: An Expositional Commentary, 5 vols. 1979. Set. 62.75 (ISBN 0-310-21458-0). Zondervan.

--The Gospel of John: An Expositional Commentary, Vol. 5. 1979. 12.95 (ISBN 0-310-21470-X). Zondervan.

--The Gospel of John: Vol. 2 (5: 1-8: 59)(Christ & Judaism) 1976. 11.95 (ISBN 0-310-21430-0). Zondervan.

--The Gospel of John (1: 1-4: 54, Vol. 1. 416p. 1975. 12.95 (ISBN 0-310-21420-3). Zondervan.

--How God Can Use Nobodies. LC 74-91026. 160p. 1974. pap. 1.95 o.p. (ISBN 0-88207-027-4). Victor Bks.

--Philippians: An Expositional Commentary. LC 79-146573. 1971. 12.95 (ISBN 0-310-21500-5). Zondervan.

--The Sermon on the Mount. 328p. (Orig.). 1981. pap. 7.95 (ISBN 0-310-21511-0). Zondervan.

--The Sermon on the Mount. LC 72-83882. 256p. 1972. 14.95 (ISBN 0-310-21510-2). Zondervan.

Boikess, Robert S. & Edelson, Edward. Chemical Principles. (Illus.). 1978. pap. text ed. 22.95 scp (ISBN 0-06-040807-3, HarpC); scp lab manual 8.95 (ISBN 0-06-044626-9); scp solution manual 5.50 (ISBN 0-06-040806-5); scp student guide & glossary 7.50 (ISBN 0-06-044572-6); inst. manual avail. (ISBN 0-06-360790-5); ans. bk. free (ISBN 0-06-360791-3). Har-Row.

Boikess, Robert S. & Sorum, C. Harvey. How to Solve General Chemistry Problems. 6th ed. (Illus.). 1981. pap. text ed. 10.95 (ISBN 0-13-434126-0). P-H.

Boiko, Claire. Creative Plays & Programs for Girls & Boys. (gr. 3-6). 1972. 9.95 (ISBN 0-8238-0134-9). Plays.

Boillot, G. Geology of the Continental Margins. Scarth, Alwyn, tr. from Fr. (Illus.). 160p. 1981. pap. text ed. 14.50 (ISBN 0-582-30036-3). Longman.

Boillot, Michel. Understanding FORTRAN. 2nd ed. (Illus.). 500p. 1981. pap. text ed. 11.16 (ISBN 0-8299-0355-0). West Pub.

Boily, Lise & Blanchette, Jean-Francois. The Bread Ovens of Quebec. (Illus.). 1979. pap. 8.95 (ISBN 0-660-00120-9, 56284-0, Pub. by Natl Mus Canada). U of Chicago Pr.

Boim, L. & Morgan, G. G., eds. The Soviet Procuracy Protests: 1937-1973. (Law in Eastern Europe Ser.: No. 21). 324p. 1978. 95.00x (ISBN 90-286-0138-4). Sijthoff & Noordhoff.

Bois, Edward Du see Du Bois, Edward.

Bois, William E. Du see Du Bois, William E.

Bois, William Pene Du see Pene Du Bois, William.

Bois, William Pene Du see Pene du Bois, William.

Boise, Anne C. Adventures of a Roving Playhouse. 1981. 4.95 (ISBN 0-533-04550-9). Vantage.

Boiselle, Arthur H., et al. Using Mathematics in Business. LC 80-16710. (Illus.). 384p. 1981. pap. price not set (ISBN 0-201-00098-9). A-W.

Boisen, Anton T. Exploration of the Inner World: A Study of Mental Disorder and Religious Experience. 1971. pap. 6.50x (ISBN 0-8122-1020-4, Pa Paperbks). U of Pa Pr.

Boisen, Monte B., Jr. & Larsen, Max D. Understanding Basic Calculus: With Application from the Managerial, Social & Life Sciences. (Mathematics Ser.). 1978. text ed. 18.95 (ISBN 0-675-08430-X); manual 3.95 (ISBN 0-686-67993-8). Merrill.

Boissard, Janine. A Matter of Feeling. 256p. 1981. pap. 2.25 (ISBN 0-449-70001-1, Juniper). Fawcett.

Boissel, Francois. Le Cathechisme Du Genre Humain. 2nd ed. (Fr.). 1977. lib. bdg. 30.50x o.p. (ISBN 0-8287-0102-4); pap. text ed. 20.50x o.p. (ISBN 0-685-74920-7). Clearwater Pub.

Boissevain, Jeremy. Saints & Fireworks, Religion & Politics in Rural Malta. (Monographs on Social Anthropology Ser: No. 30). 1969. pap. text ed. 3.25x (ISBN 0-391-00756-4, Athlone Pr). Humanities.

Boissevain, Jeremy & Mitchell, J. Clyde, eds. Network Analysis: Studies in Human Interaction. LC 72-77471. (Change & Continuity in Africa Monographs). 1973. 24.70x (ISBN 90-2797-187-0). Mouton.

Boissier, Gaston. Great French Writers: Madame De Sevigne. 154p. 1980. Repr. of 1887 ed. lib. bdg. 25.00 (ISBN 0-8495-0476-7). Arden Lib.

Boissier, J. R., et al, eds. Advances in Pharmacology & Therapeutics, 10 vols. new ed. (Illus.). 1979. Set. text ed. 650.00 o.p. (ISBN 0-08-022680-9). Pergamon.

--International Congress of Pharmacology, 7th, Paris, 1978: Abstracts. 1979. text ed. 150.00 (ISBN 0-08-023768-1). Pergamon.

Boisson, M., jt. ed. see Chalazonitis, N.

Boissoneau, Robert. Continuing Education in the Health Professions. LC 80-19748. 322p. 1980. text ed. 27.50 (ISBN 0-89443-325-3). Aspen Systems.

Boit, John. The Log of the Union: John Boit's Remarkable Voyage, 1794-1796. Hayes, Edmund, Sr., intro. by. LC 80-83181. (North Pacific Studies: No. 6). (Illus.). 250p. 1981. 14.95 (ISBN 0-87595-068-X); pap. 9.95 (ISBN 0-87595-089-2). Oreg Hist Soc.

Bojarski, Richard. The Films of Bela Lugosi. 1980. 16.95 (ISBN 0-8065-5071-6). Lyle Stuart.

Bojer, Johan. The Emigrants. Jayne, A. G., tr. from Norwegian. LC 78-9813. 1978. pap. 4.95 (ISBN 0-8032-6051-2, BB 673, Bison). U of Nebr Pr.

Bojtar, Endre. Slavic Structuralism. (Linguistic & Literary Studies in Eastern Europe). 130p. 1980. text ed. 28.50x (ISBN 90-272-1507-3). Humanities.

Bok, Bart J. & Bok, Priscilla F. The Milky Way. 5th ed. LC 80-22544. (Harvard Books on Astronomy Ser.). (Illus.). 384p. 1981. text ed. 20.00 (ISBN 0-674-57503-2). Harvard U Pr.

--The Milky Way. 4th ed. LC 73-83418. (Books on Astronomy Ser.). 288p. 1974. 16.50x (ISBN 0-674-57501-6); pap. 7.95 (ISBN 0-674-57502-4). Harvard U Pr.

Bok, Priscilla F., jt. auth. see Bok, Bart J.

Bok, Sissela. Lying: Moral Choice in Public & Private Life. LC 78-21949. 1979. pap. 3.95 (ISBN 0-394-72804-1, Vin). Random.

Bok, Sissela, jt. ed. see Behnke, John A.

Bok, Sissela, jt. ed. see Callahan, Daniel.

Bokenkotter, Thomas. A Concise History of the Catholic Church. LC 78-20269. 1979. pap. 4.95 (ISBN 0-385-13015-5, Im). Doubleday.

--A Concise History of the Catholic Church. LC 77-75382. 1977. 10.00 o.p. (ISBN 0-385-13014-7). Doubleday.

Bokov, Nikolai. Nobody. Fitzlyon, April, tr. 1979. 9.95 (ISBN 0-7145-0975-2); pap. 4.95 (ISBN 0-7145-3551-6). Riverrun NY.

Bokser, Ben Z. The Jewish Mystical Tradition. 280p. 1981. 14.95 (ISBN 0-8298-0435-8); pap. 9.95 (ISBN 0-8298-0451-X). Pilgrim NY.

Bokser, Ben Zion. The Jewish Mystical Tradition. 1980. 15.00 (ISBN 0-88482-922-7); pap. 6.95 (ISBN 0-88482-923-5). Hebrew Pub.

Bokser, Ben Zion, tr. Abraham Isaac Kook: The Lights of Penitance, Lights of Holiness. the Moral Principles. Essays, Letters & Poems. (Classics of Western Spirituality). 1978. 11.95 (ISBN 0-8091-0278-1); pap. 7.95 (ISBN 0-8091-2159-X). Paulist Pr.

Bolam, R. & Smith, G. Local Education Authority Advisers & the Mechanisms of Innovation. (NFER General). (Orig.). 1979. pap. text ed. 22.00x (ISBN 0-85633-175-9, NFER). Humanities.

Boland, Bridget, jt. auth. see Boland, Maureen.

Boland, D. J., et al. Eucalyptus Seed. (Illus.). 191p. 1980. 25.00x (ISBN 0-643-02586-3, Pub. by Timber Pr.). Intl Schol Bk Serv.

Boland, Eavan. Introducing Eavan Boland: Poems. LC 80-84833. (Ontario Review Press Poetry Ser.). 80p. 1981. 9.95 (ISBN 0-86538-009-0); pap. 4.95 (ISBN 0-86538-010-4). Ontario Rev NJ.

Boland, Eavan, jt. auth. see MacLiammoir, Micheal.

Boland, Ian, tr. see Ginzburg, Eugenia.

Boland, Maureen & Boland, Bridget. Old Wives' Lore for Gardeners. (Illus.). Date not set. pap. 3.25 (ISBN 0-374-51639-1). FS&G.

Bolande, Robert P., jt. ed. see Rosenberg, Harvey S.

Bold, Harold C. & Hundell, C. L. The Plant Kingdom. 4th ed. (Foundation of Modern Biology Ser.). (Illus.). 1977. pap. 12.95 (ISBN 0-13-680389-X). P-H.

Bold, Harold C. & Wynne, Michael J. Introduction to the Algae: Structure & Reproduction. (P-H Biology Ser.). (Illus.). 1978. ref. ed. 28.95 (ISBN 0-13-477786-7). P-H.

Bolden, Theodore E., et al. Dental Hygiene Examination Review Book, Vol. 1. 3rd ed. 1973. spiral bdg. 9.50 (ISBN 0-87488-461-6). Med Exam.

Bolding, Amy. Easy Devotions to Give. (Paperback Program Ser.). 96p. (Orig.). 1981. pap. 2.95 (ISBN 0-8010-0794-1). Baker Bk.

--Fingertip Devotions. 1970. 2.95 (ISBN 0-8010-0798-4). Baker Bk.

--Please Give a Devotion for All Occasions. 1967. pap. 2.95 (ISBN 0-8010-0519-1). Baker Bk.

--Please Give a Devotion: For Women's Groups. (Paperback Program Ser.). 108p. 1976. pap. 2.95 (ISBN 0-8010-0583-3). Baker Bk.

--Simple Welcome Speeches & Other Helps. (Pocket Pulpit Library). 1973. pap. 2.25 (ISBN 0-8010-0612-0). Baker Bk.

--Words of Welcome. (Preaching Helps Ser). (Orig.). 1965. pap. 2.95 (ISBN 0-8010-0550-7). Baker Bk.

Boldizsar, Ivan. Hungary: A Guidebook. rev. 6th ed. (Illus.). 1969. 6.95 o.p. (ISBN 0-8038-3006-8). Hastings.

Boldy, Stephen. The Novels of Julio Cortazar. LC 79-41579. (Cambridge Iberian & Latin American Studies). 320p. 1980. 29.50 (ISBN 0-521-23097-7). Cambridge U Pr.

Bolen, Frances E. Irony & Self-Knowledge in the Creation of Tragedy. (Salzburg Studies in English Literature, Elizabethan & Renaissance Studies: No. 18). 379p. 1973. pap. text ed. 25.00x (ISBN 0-391-01330-0). Humanities.

Bolen, Jean S. The Tao of Psychology: Synchronicity. LC 79-1778. 1979. 7.95 (ISBN 0-06-250080-5, HarpR). Har-Row.

Bolen, William H. Advertising. LC 80-18915. (Wiley Ser in Marketing). 600p. 1981. text ed. 19.95 (ISBN 0-471-03486-X). Wiley.

--Contemporary Retailing. (Illus.). 1978. ref. ed. 18.95 (ISBN 0-13-170290-4). P-H.

Boles, Harold W. Leaders, Leading, & Leadership. LC 80-65616. 170p. 1981. cancelled (ISBN 0-86548-023-0). Century Twenty One.

Boles, Janet K. The Politics of the Equal Rights Amendment: Conflict & the Decision Process. LC 78-11052. 1979. pap. text ed. 8.95 (ISBN 0-582-28090-7). Longman.

Boles, John B. Great Revival, Seventeen Eighty-Seven to Eighteen Five: The Origins of the Southern Evangelical Mind. LC 77-183349. (Illus.). 260p. 1972. 14.00x (ISBN 0-8131-1260-5). U Pr of Ky.

Boles, John B., ed. Maryland Heritage: Five Baltimore Institutions Celebrate the Bicentennial. LC 76-10079. (Illus.). 1976. 16.00 (ISBN 0-938420-10-0); pap. 7.50 (ISBN 0-686-16684-1). Md Hist.

Boles, Kenny, jt. auth. see Boatman, Don E.

Boles, Paul D. The Mississippi Run. LC 76-27875. 1977. 10.00 o.s.i. (ISBN 0-690-01158-X, TYC-T). T Y Crowell.

Boleslavsky, Richard. Acting: The First Six Lessons. 1949. 5.95 (ISBN 0-87830-000-7). Theatre Arts.

Boley, Bruno A. Crossfire in Professional Education. LC 76-47033. 1977. 14.00 (ISBN 0-08-021429-0). Pergamon.

Boley, Bruno A. & Weiner, Jerome H. Theory of Thermal Stresses. LC 60-6446. 1960. 39.50 (ISBN 0-685-22215-2, 471-08679-7, Pub. by Wiley-Interscience). Wiley.

Boley, Robert E., ed. Land: Recreation & Leisure. LC 78-123466. (Special Report Ser). (Orig.). 1970. pap. 4.75 (ISBN 0-87420-554-9). Urban Land.

Bolgar, R. R. The Classical Heritage & Its Beneficiaries. LC 54-13284. 1977. 74.00 (ISBN 0-521-04277-1); pap. 17.50x (ISBN 0-521-09812-2). Cambridge U Pr.

--Classical Influences on Western Thought A.D. 1650-1870. LC 77-91078. 1979. 65.00 (ISBN 0-521-21964-7). Cambridge U Pr.

Bolgar, R. R., ed. Classical Influence on European Culture, A.D. 500-1500. LC 77-113599. (Illus.). 1971. 54.00 (ISBN 0-521-07842-3). Cambridge U Pr.

--Classical Influences on European Culture: 1500-1700. (Illus.). 300p. 1976. 63.00 (ISBN 0-521-20840-8). Cambridge U Pr.

Bolger, Philip C. The Folding Schooner: And Other Adventures in Boat Design. LC 76-8779. (Illus.). 1976. 17.50 (ISBN 0-87742-083-1). Intl Marine.

Bolger, Steve, et al, eds. Towards Socialist Welfare Work: Working in the State. (Critical Texts in Social Work & the Welfare State). 176p. 1980. text ed. 32.50x (ISBN 0-333-28905-6); pap. text ed. 10.50x (ISBN 0-333-28906-4). Humanities.

Bolian, Polly. Symbols: The Language of Communication. LC 74-22464. (First Bks.). (Illus.). 96p. (gr. 5 up). 1975. PLB 4.90 o.p. (ISBN 0-531-00833-9). Watts.

Bolian, Polly & Hinds, Shirley. First Book of Safety. LC 76-93222. (First Bks). (Illus.). (gr. 4-6). 1970. PLB 4.90 o.p. (ISBN 0-531-00694-8). Watts.

Bolick, James H. Sermon Outlines on Paul & His Message. (Dollar Sermon Library). 1976. pap. 1.00 o.p. (ISBN 0-8010-0658-9). Baker Bk.

--Sermons for Revival Preaching. (Pocket Pulpit Library Ser). pap. 1.45 (ISBN 0-8010-0551-5). Baker Bk.

Bolin, T. D., jt. auth. see Davis, A. E.

Boling, Katherine. A Piece of the Fox's Hide. 1974. pap. 1.75 o.p. (ISBN 0-89176-871-8, 6871). Mockingbird Bks.

Bolingbroke, Henry Viscount. The Philosophical Works, 5 vols. Wellek, Rene, ed. LC 75-11198. (British Philosophers & Theologians of the 17th & 18th Centuries: Vol. 5). 1976. Repr. of 1777 ed. Set. lib. bdg. 165.00 (ISBN 0-8240-1754-4); lib. bdg. 42.00 ea. Garland Pub.

Bolinger, Dwight. Degree Words. (Janua Linguarum, Ser. Major: No. 53). 1972. text ed. 51.75x (ISBN 0-686-22528-7). Mouton.

--Language: The Loaded Wagon. (Illus.). 240p. (Orig.). 1980. text ed. 25.00 (ISBN 0-582-29107-0); pap. text ed. 11.95 (ISBN 0-582-29108-9). Longman.

--Meaning & Form. (English Language Ser.). (Illus.). 1979. pap. text ed. 10.50x (ISBN 0-582-29104-6). Longman.

--Meaning & Form. LC 76-44857. (English Language Ser.). (Illus.). 1977. text ed. 18.95x (ISBN 0-582-55103-X). Longman.

--That's That. (Janua Linguarum, Ser. Minor: No. 155). 79p. (Orig.). 1972. pap. text ed. 12.95x (ISBN 90-2792-319-1). Mouton.

Bolinger, Judith & English, Jane. Water Child. LC 80-80650. (Orig.). 1980. pap. 6.95 (ISBN 0-89793-023-1). Hunter Hse.

Bolinger, Willeta R. You & Your World. (Special Education Ser. for slow learners). (gr. 7-12,RL 2.3). 1964. pap. 3.40 (ISBN 0-8224-7650-9); tchrs' manual free (ISBN 0-8224-7651-7). Pitman Learning.

Bolino. Development of the American Economy. 2nd ed. LC 66-20200. 1966. text ed. 13.95 (ISBN 0-675-09974-9). Merrill.

Bolis, Liana, jt. ed. see Straub, Ralph W.

Bolis, Liana, et al, eds. Membranes & Disease. LC 75-30235. 1976. 39.00 (ISBN 0-89004-082-6). Raven.

Bolitho, A. R. & Sandler, P. L. Learn English for Science. pap. text ed. 3.50x student bk. (ISBN 0-582-55247-8); pap. text ed. 2.50x tchr's bk. (ISBN 0-582-55482-9). Longman.

--Study English for Science. 1977. pap. text ed. 3.50x (ISBN 0-582-55248-6); tchr's ed. 2.50x (ISBN 0-582-74821-6). Longman.

Bolitho, H. Meiji Japan. LC 76-54130. (History of Mankind Ser.). (Illus.). 1977. 3.95 (ISBN 0-521-20922-6). Cambridge U Pr.

Bolitho, Hector. The House in Half Moon Street, & Other Stories. LC 79-53450. (Short Story Index in Reprint Ser.). Date not set. Repr. of 1936 ed. 23.75x (ISBN 0-8486-5005-0). Core Collection. Postponed.

Bolitho, Red & Tomlinson, Brian. Discover English. (Illus.). 168p. (Orig.). 1980. pap. text ed. 9.95x (ISBN 0-04-371076-X, 2586). Allen Unwin.

Bolivar, Josefa V., ed. see Bolivar, Jossy Ann.

Bolivar, Jossy Ann. With Love, from Jo. Bolivar, Josefa V., ed. LC 80-13999. (Illus.). 120p. (Orig.). 1980. pap. 5.95 (ISBN 0-914598-01-5). Padre Prods.

Bolker, Ethan D. & Kitchen, Joseph W. First Year Calculus. LC 73-14350. 1974. pap. text ed. 13.95 (ISBN 0-201-00645-6). A-W.

Bolkestein, A. M. Problems in the Description of Modal Verbs: An Investigation of Latin. (Studies in Greek & Latin Linguistics). 180p. 1980. pap. text ed. 21.00x (ISBN 90-232-1764-0). Humanities.

Boll, Heinrich. Abenteuer Eines Brotbeutels und Andere Geschichten. Plant, Richard, ed. (Ger). 1958. pap. 2.25x o.p. (ISBN 0-393-09459-6, NortonC). Norton.

--Billiards at Half-Past Nine. 1975. pap. 2.95 (ISBN 0-380-00280-9, 51383, Bard). Avon.

--The Clown. 1975. pap. 2.25 (ISBN 0-380-00333-3, 37523, Bard). Avon.

--Eighteen Stories. Vennewitz, Leila, tr. from Ger. 1966. 6.95 o.p. (ISBN 0-07-006403-2, GB); pap. 3.95 o.p. (ISBN 0-07-006416-4). McGraw.

Boll, Heinrich, et al. New Writing & Writers Fifteen. 1980. pap. 6.00 (ISBN 0-7145-3561-3). Riverrun NY.

Boll, Thomas J., jt. auth. see Filskov, Susan B.

Bollack, C. G. & Clavert, A., eds. Epididymis & Fertility: Biology & Pathology. (Progress in Reproductive Biology Ser.: Vol. 8). (Illus.). viii, 192p. 1981. 58.75 (ISBN 3-8055-2157-X). S Karger.

Bollard, Alan. Agricultural Project Design & Evaluation in an Island Community. (Development Studies Centre - Monograph: No. 15). (Illus., Orig.). 1980. pap. 13.95 (ISBN 0-7081-1071-1, 0537, Pub. by ANUP Australia). Bks Australia.

Bolle, H. J., ed. see Committee on Space Research.

Bolleme, Genevieve. Les Almanachs Populaires Aux XVIIe et XVIIIe Siecles: Essai D'histoire Sociale. (Livre et Societes: No. 3). 1969. pap. 16.50x (ISBN 90-2796-265-0). Mouton.

Bollens, John C. & Geyer, Grant B. Yorty: Politics of a Constant Candidate. LC 72-95289. 250p. 1973. 6.95 (ISBN 0-913530-00-X). Palisades Pub.

Bollens, John C., jt. auth. see Berman, David R.

Bollens, John C., ed. Exploring the Metropolitan Community. 1961. 21.50x (ISBN 0-520-00141-9). U of Cal Pr.

Boller, Henry A. Among the Indians: Four Years on the Upper Missouri, 1858-1862. Quaife, Milo M., ed. LC 76-100810. (Illus.). 370p. 1972. pap. 4.50 (ISBN 0-8032-5714-7, BB 514, Bison). U of Nebr Pr.

Bolles, R. N. What Color Is Your Parachute? 1981 Ed. (Illus.). 1981. 14.95 (ISBN 0-89815-047-7); pap. 6.95 (ISBN 0-89815-046-9). Ten Speed Pr.

Bolles, R. N. & Crystal, John. Where Do I Go from Here with My Life. LC 78-61867. (Illus.). 1980. pap. 9.95 (ISBN 0-89815-028-0). Ten Speed Pr.

Bolles, Richard. Quick Job-Hunting Map, Beginning Version. 1977. pap. 1.25x (ISBN 0-913668-59-1). Ten Speed Pr.

--Tea Leaves: A New Look at Resumes. 1976. pap. 0.50x (ISBN 0-913668-72-9). Ten Speed Pr.

Bolles, Richard H. The Quick Job Hunting Map. (Orig.). 1976. pap. 1.25x (ISBN 0-913668-60-5). Ten Speed Pr.

Bolles, Richard N. The Quick Job-Hunting Map: Advanced Version Trade. pap. 1.50 (ISBN 0-89815-008-6). Ten Speed Pr.

--What Color Is Your Parachute? rev. ed. 352p. 1981. 14.95 (ISBN 0-89815-047-7); pap. 6.95 (ISBN 0-89815-046-9). Ten Speed Pr.

--What Color Is Your Parachute? 5th.rev. ed. (Illus.). 1979. 11.95 o.p. (ISBN 0-89815-002-7); pap. 5.95 o.p. (ISBN 0-687-01211-2). Ten Speed Pr.

Bollet, Alfred J., ed. Harrison's Principles of Internal Medicine Patient Management Cases PreTest Self-Assessment & Review. (Illus.). 248p. (Orig.). 1980. 25.00 (ISBN 0-07-051647-2). McGraw Pretest.

Bolliger, Max. Noah & the Rainbow: An Ancient Story. Bulla, Clyde R., tr. LC 72-76361. (Illus.). (gr. k-3). 1972. 8.79 (ISBN 0-690-58448-2, TYC-J); pap. text ed. 2.95 (ISBN 0-690-03814-3). T Y Crowell.

Bolliger-Savelli, Antonella. The Knitted Cat. LC 72-163240. (Illus.). 28p. (ps-2). 1972. 5.95 o.s.i. (ISBN 0-02-711700-6). Macmillan.

Bollinger, Edward T. & Bauer, Frederick. Moffat Road. 2nd ed. LC 62-12397. (Illus.). 359p. 1967. 33.95 (ISBN 0-8040-0207-X, SB). Swallow.

Bollinger, G. A. Blast Vibration Analysis. LC 79-22421. 149p. 1980. pap. 6.95 (ISBN 0-8093-0951-3). S Ill U Pr.

Bollinger, L. L. & Tully, J. R. Personal Aircraft Business at Airports. 1970. Repr. of 1946 ed. 28.00 (ISBN 0-08-018742-0). Pergamon.

Bollinger, L. L., et al. Terminal Airport Financing & Management. 1970. Repr. of 1946 ed. 31.00 (ISBN 0-08-018746-3). Pergamon.

Bollinger, Lee C., jt. auth. see Jackson, John H.

Bollinger, Max. The Wooden Man. LC 74-1141. (Illus.). 24p. (ps-3). 1974. 6.95 (ISBN 0-395-28769-3, Clarion). HM.

Bollinger, William H., et al. Project Design & Recommendations for Watershed Reforestation & Fuelwood Development in Sri Lanka. (Illus.). 122p. 1979. pap. 15.00 (ISBN 0-936130-03-2). Intl Sci Tech.

Bollinger-Savelli, Antonella. Mouse & the Knitted Cat. LC 72-93303. (Illus.). 28p. (ps-2). 1974. 7.95 (ISBN 0-02-711710-3). Macmillan.

Bollitier, Nick & Anthony, Julie. Awinning Combination. (Illus.). 224p. 1980. 12.50 o.p. (ISBN 0-684-16710-7, ScribT). Scribner.

Bollitieri, Nick, jt. auth. see Anthony, Julie.

Bollobas, Bella, ed. Survey in Combinatorics. LC 79-51596. (London Mathematical Society Lecture Note Ser.: No. 38). 1979. pap. 23.95x (ISBN 0-521-22846-8). Cambridge U Pr.

Bolloten, Burnett. The Spanish Revolution: The Left & the Struggle for Power During the Civil War. LC 78-5011. 1979. 29.00x (ISBN 0-8078-1297-8); pap. 14.00x (ISBN 0-8078-4077-7). U of NC Pr.

Bolodeau, Michel L., jt. auth. see Mackenzie, Brian W.

Bologh, Roslyn W. Dialectical Phenomenology: Marx's Method. (International Library of Phenomenology & Moral Sciences). 1979. 23.50x (ISBN 0-7100-0335-8). Routledge & Kegan.

Bologna, Joseph V. A Mental Walk Through Life in Poetry. 1977. 5.50 o.p. (ISBN 0-533-02399-8). Vantage.

Bolognese, Don. Drawing Horses & Foals. (How to Draw Ser.). (gr. 4-6). 1977. PLB 6.90 (ISBN 0-531-00379-5). Watts.

Bolognese, Don, jt. auth. see Raphael, Elaine.

Bolooki, H. Thoracic Surgery. 2nd ed. (Medical Examination Review Book: Vol. 18). 1972. spiral bdg. 16.50 (ISBN 0-87488-118-8). Med Exam.

Bolotin, David. Plato's Dialogue on Friendship: An Interpretation of the "Lysis," with a New Translation. LC 79-4041. 1979. 15.00x (ISBN 0-8014-1227-7). Cornell U Pr.

Bolsby, Clare, jt. auth. see Berglund, Berndt.

Bolsby, Clare E., jt. auth. see Berglund, Berndt.

Bolshakoff, Sergius. Russian Mystics. (Cistercian Studies: No. 26). Orig. Title: I Mistici Russi. 303p. 1981. pap. 6.95 (ISBN 0-87907-926-6). Cistercian Pubns.

Bolster, Evelyn. A History of the Diocese of Cork from Earliest Times to the Reformation. (Illus.). 548p. 1972. 27.00x (ISBN 0-686-28339-2, Pub. by Irish Academic Pr). Biblio Dist.

Bolster, John. Lotus Elan & Europa: A Collector's Guide. (Collector's Guide Ser.). (Illus.). 138p. 1980. 18.95 (ISBN 0-900549-48-3, Pub. by Motor Racing England). Motorbooks Intl.

--Rolls-Royce Silver Shadow. (AutoHistory Ser.). (Illus.). 1979. 12.95 (ISBN 0-85045-324-0, Pub. by Osprey Pubns. England). Motorbooks Intl.

Bolsterli, Margaret J. The Early Community at Bedford Park: The Pursuit of "Corporate Happiness" in the First Garden Suburb. LC 76-8299. (Illus.). xii, 133p. 1977. 14.00x (ISBN 0-8214-0224-2). Ohio U Pr.

Bolt, Albert B. & Wardle, M. E. Communicating with a Computer. LC 73-85713. (Illus.). 1970. 11.50 (ISBN 0-521-07633-1); pap. 5.75x (ISBN 0-521-09587-5). Cambridge U Pr.

Bolt, Bruce A. Earthquakes: A Primer. LC 77-12908. (Geology Ser.). (Illus.). 1978. pap. text ed. 9.95x (ISBN 0-7167-0057-3). W H Freeman.

--Nuclear Explosions & Earthquakes: The Parted Veil. LC 75-28295. (Illus.). 1976. text ed. 18.95x (ISBN 0-7167-0276-2). W H Freeman.

Bolt, Bruce A., intro. by. Earthquakes & Volcanoes: Readings from Scientific American. LC 79-21684. (Illus.). 1980. text ed. 16.95x (ISBN 0-7167-1163-X); pap. text ed. 8.95x (ISBN 0-7167-1164-8). W H Freeman.

Bolt, Christine & Dresher, Seymour. Anti-Slavery, Religion & Reform. 275p. 1980. 27.50 (ISBN 0-208-01783-6, Archon). Shoe String.

Bolt, Christine, jt. auth. see Barbrook, Alec.

Bolt, Robert. Man for All Seasons. 1962. 8.95 (ISBN 0-394-40623-0). Random.

Boltax, Robert S., jt. auth. see Kra, Siegfried J.

Bolten, J. & Bolten-Rempt, H. The Hidden Rembrandt. LC 77-70249. (Illus.). 1977. 19.95 o.p. (ISBN 0-528-81044-8). Rand.

Bolten, Steven E. Managerial Finance: Principles & Practice. LC 75-31036. (Illus.). 896p. 1976. text ed. 20.95 (ISBN 0-395-20462-3); instr's. manual 2.00 (ISBN 0-395-20461-5). HM.

Bolten, Steven E. & Conn, Robert L. Essentials of Managerial Finance: Principles & Practice. LC 80-80961. (Illus.). 800p. 1981. text ed. 17.95 (ISBN 0-395-20462-3); write for info. instr's manual (ISBN 0-395-20461-5). HM.

Bolten-Rempt, H., jt. auth. see Bolten, J.

Boltho, Andrea. Foreign Trade Criteria in Socialist Economies. LC 78-121366. (Soviet & East European Studies). 1970. 25.50 (ISBN 0-521-07883-0). Cambridge U Pr.

--Japan: An Economic Survey 1953-1973. (Economies of the World). (Illus.). 220p. 1975. 24.00x (ISBN 0-19-877036-7). Oxford U Pr.

Boltin, Lee. Closed on Account of Death, Not Sam. 1977. pap. 2.95 o.p. (ISBN 0-345-27211-0). Ballantine.

Boltman, Brigid. Cook-Freeze Catering Systems. (Illus.). 1978. text ed. 42.60x (ISBN 0-85334-768-9, Pub. by Applied Science). Burgess-Intl Ideas.

Bolton, Brian, jt. auth. see Hinman, Sukit.

Bolton, Dale. Selection & Evaluation of Teachers. LC 72-10648. 260p. 1973. 16.00x (ISBN 0-8211-0123-4); text ed. 14.50x (ISBN 0-685-28805-6). McCutchan.

Bolton, David. Kukulcan - Rainman: A Legend of the Maya. Platt, Deborah, ed. (Illus.). 240p. 1980. 12.95 (ISBN 0-934506-02-7). Westminster Co.

Bolton, E. J. Verse Writing in Schools. 1966. 11.25 (ISBN 0-08-011993-X); pap. 5.75 (ISBN 0-08-011992-1). Pergamon.

Bolton, Edmund. The Cities Advocate: Whether Apprentiship Extinguisheth Gentry? LC 74-28834. (English Experience Ser.: No. 715). 1975. Repr. of 1629 ed. 7.00 (ISBN 90-221-0715-9). Walter J Johnson.

Bolton, Ethel S. Wax Portraits & Silhouettes. LC 71-164115. 88p. 1974. Repr. of 1914 ed. 18.00 (ISBN 0-8103-3168-3). Gale.

Bolton, Evelyn. Dream Dancer. LC 74-9571. (Evelyn Bolton's Horse Stories Ser). (Illus.). 32p. (gr. 3-7). 1974. PLB 5.95 (ISBN 0-87191-371-2); pap. 2.95 (ISBN 0-89812-128-0). Creative Ed.

--Goodbye Charlie. LC 74-9572. (Evelyn Bolton's Horse Stories Ser). (Illus.). 32p. (gr. 2-6). 1974. PLB 5.95 (ISBN 0-87191-369-0); pap. 2.95 (ISBN 0-89812-127-2). Creative Ed.

--Lady's Girl. LC 74-9528. (Evelyn Bolton's Horse Stories Ser). (Illus.). 32p. (gr. 3-7). 1974. PLB 5.95 (ISBN 0-87191-372-0); pap. 2.95 (ISBN 0-89812-125-6). Creative Ed.

--Ride When You're Ready. LC 74-9763. (Evelyn Bolton's Horse Stories Ser). (Illus.). 32p. (gr. 3-7). 1974. PLB 5.95 (ISBN 0-87191-373-9); pap. 2.95 (ISBN 0-89812-130-2). Creative Ed.
--Stable of Fear. LC 74-9704. (Evelyn Bolton's Horse Stories Ser). (Illus.). 32p. (gr. 3-7). 1974. PLB 5.95 (ISBN 0-87191-370-4); pap. 2.95 (ISBN 0-89812-129-9). Creative Ed.
--The Wild Horses. LC 74-9530. (Evelyn Bolton's Horse Stories Ser). (Illus.). 32p. (gr. 3-7). 1974. PLB 5.95 (ISBN 0-87191-374-7); pap. 2.95 (ISBN 0-89812-126-4). Creative Ed.
Bolton, G. C. The Passing of the Irish Act of Union: A Study in Parliamentary Politics. (Oxford Historical Ser.). 1966. 8.50x o.p. (ISBN 0-19-821827-3). Oxford U Pr.
Bolton, Henry C. Counting-Out Rhymes of Children. LC 68-23139. 1969. Repr. of 1888 ed. 15.00 (ISBN 0-8103-3475-5). Gale.
Bolton, Herbert E. Bolton & the Spanish Borderlands. Bannon, John F., ed. 1964. 12.95 (ISBN 0-8061-0612-3); pap. 5.95 (ISBN 0-8061-1150-X). U of Okla Pr.
--Coronado: Knight Pueblos & Plains. LC 64-17854. 491p. 1974. Repr. of 1964 ed. 12.95. U of NM Pr.
--Texas in the Middle Eighteenth Century: Studies in Spanish Colonial History and Administration. (Texas History Paperbacks Ser.: No. 8). 1970. 17.95x (ISBN 0-292-70056-3); pap. 7.95 (ISBN 0-292-70034-2). U of Tex Pr.
Bolton, Malcolm. A Guide to Soil Mechanics. 439p. 1980. 37.95x (ISBN 0-470-26929-4). Halsted Pr.
Bolton, Neil. Concept Formation. 1977. text ed. 13.75 (ISBN 0-08-021493-2); pap. text ed. 8.25 (ISBN 0-08-021494-0). Pergamon.
Bolton, Robert. A Discourse About the State of True Happinesse. LC 79-84089. (English Experience Ser.: No. 909). 184p. 1979. Repr. of 1611 ed. lib. bdg. 14.00 (ISBN 90-221-0909-7). Walter J Johnson.
Bolton, Robert H. People Skills: How to Assert Yourself, Listen to Others & Resolve Conflicts. (Illus.). 1979. 13.95 (ISBN 0-13-655779-1, Spec); pap. 4.95 (ISBN 0-13-655761-9). P-H.
Bolton, Robert J. Treasure Island: Church Growth Among Taiwan's Urban Minnan Chinese. LC 76-20828. (Illus.). 1976. pap. 8.95 (ISBN 0-87808-315-4). William Carey Lib.
Bolton, Theodore. Early American Portrait Draughtsmen in Crayons. LC 74-77724. (Library of American Art Ser). (Illus.). 1970. Repr. of 1923 ed. lib. bdg. 25.00 (ISBN 0-306-71362-4). Da Capo.
Bolton, W. Atoms and Quanta, Book 7. LC 80-41395. (Study Topics in Physics Ser.). 96p. 1980. pap. text ed. write for info. (ISBN 0-408-10658-1). Butterworths.
--Electronic Systems, Bk. 8. LC 80-41394. (Study Topics in Physics Ser.). 96p. 1980. pap. text ed. write for info. (ISBN 0-408-10659-X). Butterworths.
--Fields, Bk. 5. LC 80-41166. (Study Topics in Physics Ser.). 96p. 1980. pap. text ed. write for info. (ISBN 0-408-10656-5). Butterworths.
--Mechanical Science for Technicians, No. 3. (Technician Ser.). (Illus.). 128p. 1980. pap. text ed. 12.50. Butterworths.
--Patterns in Physics. 1974. 12.95 o.p. (ISBN 0-07-094396-6, C). McGraw.
--Study Topics in Physics, 4 vols. 1980. pap. text ed. 4.50 ea. Vol. 1, 79-41764 (ISBN 0-408-10652-2). Vol. 2, 79-41775 (ISBN 0-408-10653-0). Vol. 3, 80-40009 (ISBN 0-408-10654-9). Vol. 4, 80-40151 (ISBN 0-408-10655-7). Butterworths.
--Waves, Rays & Oscillations, Bk. 6. LC 80-41396. (Study Topics in Physics). 96p. 1980. pap. text ed. write for info. (ISBN 0-408-10657-3). Butterworths.
Bolton, W. F. Alcuin & Beowulf: An Eighth-Century View. 1978. 16.00 (ISBN 0-8135-0865-7). Rutgers U Pr.
Bolton, W. F. & Crystal, D. J. English Language, 2 vols. Incl. Vol. 1. 1490-1839. 39.00 (ISBN 0-521-04280-1); pap. 10.50x (ISBN 0-521-09379-1); Vol. 2. 1858-1964. 1965. 49.00 (ISBN 0-521-07325-1); pap. 12.50x (ISBN 0-521-09545-X). 1966. Cambridge U Pr.
Boltovskoy, E., et al, eds. Atlas of Benthic Shelf Foraminfera of the Southwest Atlantic. (Illus.). v, 153p. 1980. lib. bdg. 57.90 (ISBN 90-6193-604-7). Kluwer Boston.
Boltyanskii, V. G. Optimal Control of Discrete Systems. LC 78-67814. 1979. 69.95 (ISBN 0-470-26530-2). Halsted Pr.
Boltyanskiy, Vladimir G. Hilbert's Third Problem. LC 77-19011. (Scripta Mathematics Ser.). 1978. 19.95 (ISBN 0-470-26289-3). Halsted Pr.
Boltz, Carol & Thompson, Merle O. Language & Reality: A Rhetoric & Reader. LC 78-32080. (Illus.). 1979. pap. text ed. 9.95 (ISBN 0-88284-074-6). Alfred Pub.
Boltzmann, Ludwig. Wissenschaftliche Abhandlungen, 3 Vols. Hasenohrl, Fritz, ed. LC 66-26524. (Ger). 1969. Set. 89.50 (ISBN 0-8284-0215-9). Chelsea Pub.
Bolz, Harold A., et al, eds. Materials Handling Handbook. LC 57-11291. 1958. 60.00 (ISBN 0-8260-1175-6, Pub. by Wiley-Interscience). Wiley.
Bolz, Roger W. Multiple Thread Mills. 1950. 18.50 (ISBN 0-930220-02-1). Conquest.
Bolz, Roger W., ed. How to Automate Your Plant Successfully. LC 80-67334. (Illus.). 184p. (Orig.). 1980. pap. 28.50 (ISBN 0-930220-03-X). Conquest.
Bolza, Oskar. Lectures on the Calculus of Variations. 3rd ed. LC 73-16324. 9.95 (ISBN 0-8284-0145-4). Chelsea Pub.
--Vorlesungen Ueber Variationsrechnung. LC 62-8228. 19.95 (ISBN 0-8284-0160-8). Chelsea Pub.
Bolzano, Bernhard. The Theory of Science, (Die Wissenschaftslehre Oder Versuch Einer Neuen Darstellung der Logik) George, Rolf, ed. & tr. LC 71-126765. 1972. 27.50x (ISBN 0-520-01787-0). U of Cal Pr.
Boman, Thorleif. Hebrew Thought Compared with Greek. Moreau, Jules L., tr. from Ger. 1970. pap. 4.95 (ISBN 0-393-00534-8, Norton Lib). Norton.
Bomans, Godfried. The Wily Witch & All the Other Fairy Tales & Fables. Crampton, Patricia, tr. from Dutch. LC 76-54196. (Illus.). 208p. (gr. 3 up). 1977. 9.95 (ISBN 0-916144-09-7). Stemmer Hse.
Bombal, Maria L. New Islands. Cunningham, Richard, tr. from Span. 1981. 10.95 (ISBN 0-374-22118-9). FS&G.
Bombard, Alain. Doctor Bombard Goes to Sea. LC 57-7890. (gr. 7 up). 3.95 (ISBN 0-8149-0272-3). Vanguard.
Bombaugh, Charles C. Gleanings for the Curious from the Harvest Fields of Literature: A Melange of Excerpta. LC 68-23465. 1970. Repr. of 1875 ed. 30.00 (ISBN 0-8103-3086-5). Gale.
Bombaugh, Charles C., ed. Facts & Fancies for the Curious from the Harvest-Fields of Literature. LC 68-23464. 1968. Repr. of 1905 ed. 15.00 (ISBN 0-8103-3085-7). Gale.
Bombeck, Erma. At Wit's End. 1979. pap. 2.25 (ISBN 0-449-23784-2, Crest). Fawcett.
--Aunt Erma's Cope Book. 1980. pap. 2.75 (ISBN 0-449-24334-6, Crest). Fawcett.
--I Lost Everything in the Post-Natal Depression. 1978. pap. 2.25 (ISBN 0-449-23785-0, Crest). Fawcett.
Bombeck, Erma & Keane, Bil. Just Wait till You Have Children of Your Own! 1979. pap. 2.25 (ISBN 0-449-23786-9, Crest). Fawcett.
Bombwall, K. R. Foundations of Indian Federalism. 1967. 10.00x (ISBN 0-210-22721-4). Asia.
Bomford, G. Geodesy. 4th ed. 840p. 1980. 139.00 (ISBN 0-19-851946-X). Oxford U Pr.
Bomford, R. R., et al. Hutchinson's Clinical Methods. 16th ed. (Illus.). 362p. 1975. 9.25 o.p. (ISBN 0-397-58154-8). Lippincott.
Bomhard, jt. ed. see Arbeitman.
Bommel, W. J. Van see Van Bommel, W. J. & DeBoer, J. B.
Bomoma, Thomas V. & Slevin, Dennis P. Executive Survival Manual. LC 78-16130. 1978. pap. 11.95 (ISBN 0-8436-2137-0). CBI Pub.
Bompois, H. F. Examen Chronologique des Monnais Frappes par la Communaute des Macedoniens Avant, Pendant et Apes la Conquete Romaine. (Illus.). 102p. (Fr.). 20.00 (ISBN 0-916710-77-7). Obol Intl.
Bomse, Marguerite D. Practical Spanish Dictionary & Phrasebook. new ed. 1978. pap. text ed. 7.50 (ISBN 0-08-023020-2). Pergamon.
—Practical Spanish Grammar. 1978. pap. 7.50 (ISBN 0-08-021859-8). Pergamon.
Bomse, Marguerite D. & Alfaro, Julian H. Practical Spanish for Medical & Hospital Personnel. 2nd ed. 1978. pap. text ed. 16.55 (ISBN 0-08-023001-6). Pergamon.
--Practical Spanish for School Personnel, Firemen, Policemen & Community Agencies. 2nd ed. 1978. pap. text ed. 6.55 (ISBN 0-08-023002-4). Pergamon.
Bon, Gustave Le see Le Bon, Gustave.
Bonaparte, Felicia. The Triptych & the Cross: A Key to George Eliot's Poetic Imagination. LC 78-20542. 1979. 15.00x (ISBN 0-8147-1012-3); pap. 6.00x (ISBN 0-8147-1013-1). NYU Pr.
--Will & Destiny: Morality & Tragedy in George Eliot's Novels. LC 74-16832. 221p. 1975. 15.00x (ISBN 0-8147-0983-4); pap. 7.00x (ISBN 0-8147-1030-1). NYU Pr.
Bonaparte, Tony H. & Flaherty, John E., eds. Peter Drucker: Contributions to Business Enterprise. LC 70-133013. 1970. 15.00x (ISBN 0-8147-0951-6). NYU Pr.
Bonar, Andrew. Leviticus. (Banner of Truth Geneva Series Commentaries). 1978. 14.95 (ISBN 0-85151-086-8). Banner of Truth.
--The Life of R. M. M'Cheyne. 1978. pap. 2.50 (ISBN 0-85151-085-X). Banner of Truth.
Bonar, Andrew, jt. auth. see Tyler, Bennet.
Bonar, Andrew A. Memoirs & Remains of R. M. M'Cheyne. 1978. 14.95 (ISBN 0-85151-084-1). Banner of Truth.
Bonar, Ann. Shrubs for All Seasons. (Leisure Plan Books in Color). pap. 2.95 (ISBN 0-600-44175-X). Transatlantic.
Bonar, Ann & MacCarthy, Daphne. How to Grow & Use Herbs. (Orig.). 1980. pap. 6.95x (ISBN 0-8464-1024-9). Beekman Pubs.
Bonar, Horatius. How Shall I Go to God? (Summit Bks). 1977. pap. 1.95 (ISBN 0-8010-0713-5). Baker Bk.
--Thoughts on Genesis. LC 79-2516. 1979. 8.95 (ISBN 0-8254-2235-3). Kregel.
--When God's Children Suffer. LC 80-84441. (Shepherd Classics Ser.). 144p. 1981. pap. 5.95 (ISBN 0-87983-245-2). Keats.
--Words to Winners of Souls. (Summit Bks.). 1979. pap. 1.65 (ISBN 0-8010-0773-9). Baker Bk.
Bonar, James. Malthus & His Work. 2nd ed. LC 66-9610. Repr. of 1924 ed. 24.00x (ISBN 0-678-05029-5). Kelley.
--Philosophy & Political Economy: In Some of Their Historical Relations. 3rd ed. (Muirhead Library of Philosophy). 1967. Repr. of 1922 ed. 15.00x (ISBN 0-04-320056-7). Humanities.
--Theories of Population from Raleigh to Arthur Young. LC 66-5245. Repr. of 1931 ed. 22.50x (ISBN 0-678-05149-6). Kelley.
Bonar, Jeanne R. Diabetes - A Clinical Guide. 2nd ed. 1980. pap. 19.50 (ISBN 0-87488-710-0). Med Exam.
Bonarevsky, I. Combinations in the Middle Game. (Chess Player Ser.). 1977. pap. 3.95 o.p. (ISBN 0-900928-93-X, H-1189). Hippocrene Bks.
Bonaventura, Saint The Mind's Road to God. Boas, George, tr. 1953. pap. 2.50 (ISBN 0-672-60195-8, LLA32). Bobbs.
Bonavia, David. Peking. Time-Life Books, ed. (Great Cities Ser.). (Illus.). 1978. 14.95 (ISBN 0-8094-2327-8). Time-Life.
--Vienna. (The Great Cities Ser.). (Illus.). 1978. lib. bdg. 14.94 (ISBN 0-686-51009-7). Silver.
Bonavia, M. R. Economics of Transport. (Cambridge Economic Handbook Ser). 1954. 10.95x (ISBN 0-521-08752-X). Cambridge U Pr.
Bonavia, Michael R. British Rail: The First Twenty-Five Years. LC 80-68687. (Illus.). 208p. 1981. 18.50 (ISBN 0-7153-8002-8). David & Charles.
--The Four Great Railways. LC 79-91498. (Illus.). 1980. 17.95 (ISBN 0-7153-7842-2). David & Charles.
Bonazzi, Robert & Swann, Brian, eds. Border Crossings: International Fiction in Translation. (New Departures in Fiction: Vol. 3). 1980. pap. write for info. Latitudes Pr.
Bonbright, James C. Principles of Public Utility Rates. LC 61-6569. 1961. 24.00x (ISBN 0-231-02441-X). Columbia U Pr.
--Public Utilities & the National Power Policies. LC 73-172007. (FDR & the Era of the New Deal Ser.). 1972. Repr. of 1940 ed. lib. bdg. 14.50 (ISBN 0-306-70424-2). Da Capo.
Bonchek, Lawrence I. & Brooks, Harold L. Medical & Surgical Management of Heart Disease: A Concise Guide for Non-Cardiologists. 1981. text ed. price not set. Little.
Boncompagno, Signa Da see Boncompagno da Signa.
Boncompagno da Signa. Rota Veneris. Purkart, Josef, ed. LC 74-18250. 128p. 1975. Repr. of 1474 ed. lib. bdg. 20.00x (ISBN 0-8201-1137-6). Schol Facsimiles.
Bonczek, Robert H., et al. Foundations of Decision Support Systems. LC 80-1779. (Operations Research & Industrial Engineering Ser.). 1981. price not set (ISBN 0-12-113050-9). Acad Pr.
Bond, et al. New Writing & Writers, No. 14. text ed. 13.00x. Humanities.
Bond, A. M. & Hefter, G. T., eds. Critical Survey of Stability Constants & Related Thermodynamic Data of Flouride Complexes in Aqueous Solution. (Chemical Data Ser.: No. 27). 80p. 1980. 29.00 (ISBN 0-08-022377-X). Pergamon.
Bond, Beverley W. The Quit-Rent System in the American Colonies. 1919. 7.50 (ISBN 0-8446-1082-8). Peter Smith.
Bond, Brian. British Military Policy Between the Two World Wars. 480p. 1980. 48.00x (ISBN 0-19-822464-8). Oxford U Pr.
--France & Belgium, Nineteen Thirty-Nine to Nineteen Forty. Frankland, Noble & Dowling, Christopher, eds. LC 79-52237. (The Politics & Strategy of the Second World War Ser.). 1979. 13.50 (ISBN 0-87413-157-X). U Delaware Pr.
--Liddell Hart: A Study of His Military Thought. (Illus.). 1977. 20.00 (ISBN 0-8135-0846-0). Rutgers U Pr.
Bond, Clara-Beth Young, et al. Low Fat, Low Cholesterol Diet. rev. ed. LC 76-103741. 1971. 9.95 (ISBN 0-385-03905-0). Doubleday.
Bond, D., jt. auth. see Shearer, R.
Bond, D., jt. auth. see Thompson, Francis.
Bond, Donald F., jt. auth. see Sherburn, George.
Bond, Donald F., ed. see Addison, Joseph.
Bond, G. C. Heterogeneous Catalysis: Principles & Applications. new ed. (Oxford Chemistry Ser). 132p. 1978. pap. text ed. 11.50x (ISBN 0-19-855412-5). Oxford U Pr.
Bond, G. D. Corporate Finance for Management. 1974. 19.95 (ISBN 0-408-70560-4). Butterworths.
Bond, Gladys. The Magic Friend-Maker. (Illus.). 24p. (ps-4). 1966. PLB 5.00 (ISBN 0-307-60137-4, Golden Pr). Western Pub.
Bond, Godfrey W., ed. Euripides: Heracles: With Introduction & Commentary. 448p. 1981. 45.00 (ISBN 0-19-814012-6). Oxford U Pr.
Bond, Guy L., et al. Reading Difficulties: Their Diagnosis & Correction. 4th ed. (Illus.). 1979. ref. 18.95 (ISBN 0-13-754978-4). P-H.
Bond, Harold Lewis. An Encyclopedia of Antiques. LC 74-31297. (Illus.). 389p. 1975. Repr. of 1945 ed. 30.00 (ISBN 0-8103-4206-5). Gale.
Bond, James E. Plea Bargaining & Guilty Pleas. LC 75-15655. 1975. looseleaf with 1978 rev. pages & supplement 45.00 (ISBN 0-87632-105-8). Boardman.
Bond, Jenny T., et al, eds. Infant & Child Feeding. (Nutrition Foundation Ser.). 1981. write for info. (ISBN 0-12-113350-8). Acad Pr.
Bond, Mary W. To James Bond with Love. LC 80-17134. (Illus.). 224p. 1980. 10.95 (ISBN 0-915010-28-3). Sutter House.
Bond, Michael. Bear Called Paddington. LC 60-9096. (Illus.). (gr. 3-7). 1968. pap. 1.50 (ISBN 0-440-40483-5, YB). Dell.
--J. D. Polson & the Liberty Head Dimme. (Illus.). 48p. 1980. 6.95 (ISBN 0-7064-1381-4). Mayflower Bks.
--Olga Carries on: More Tales of Olga Da Polga. (Illus.). (gr. 3-6). 1977. 6.95 (ISBN 0-8038-5380-7). Hastings.
--Olga Meets Her Match: More Tales of Olga Da Polga. (Illus.). 128p. (Orig.). (gr. 3-6). 1975. 6.95g (ISBN 0-8038-5377-7). Hastings.
--Paddington at Large. (Illus.). (gr. 1-5). 1963. 8.95 (ISBN 0-395-06641-7). HM.
--Paddington Goes to Town. LC 68-28043. (Illus.). (gr. 1-5). 1968. 7.95 (ISBN 0-395-06635-2). HM.
--Paddington Marches On. (Illus.). (gr. 4-6). 1965. 8.95 (ISBN 0-395-06642-5). HM.
--The Tales of Olga Da Polga. LC 72-89048. (Illus.). 128p. (gr. 3-7). 1973. 4.95g o.s.i. (ISBN 0-02-711730-8). Macmillan.
--Tales of Olga De Polga. (gr. 3-7). 1974. pap. 1.95 (ISBN 0-14-030500-9, Puffin). Penguin.
Bond, Otto, jt. ed. see Bauer, Camille.
Bond, P. S., jt. auth. see Garber, Max B.
Bond, Richmond, ed. Studies in the Early English Periodical. 1957. text ed. 20.00x (ISBN 0-391-01609-1). Humanities.
Bond, Robert D., ed. Contemporary Venezuela & Its Role in International Affairs. LC 77-76055. (A Council on Foreign Relations Book). 267p. 1977. 15.00x (ISBN 0-8147-0991-5); pap. 7.00x (ISBN 0-8147-0992-3). NYU Pr.
Bond, Ruskin. Grandfather's Private Zoo. (Illus.). 95p. (gr. 3-5). 1.00 (ISBN 0-88253-345-2). Ind-US Inc.
--It Isn't Time That's Passing. 8.00 (ISBN 0-89253-461-3); flexible cloth 4.00 (ISBN 0-89253-462-1). Ind-US Inc.
--Lone Fox Dancing. 8.00 (ISBN 0-89253-497-4); flexible cloth 4.00 (ISBN 0-89253-498-2). Ind-US Inc.
--Love Is a Sad Song. 104p. 1976. pap. 1.80 (ISBN 0-89253-027-8). Ind-US Inc.
--The Man Eater of Manjari. 112p. 1975. pap. 2.15 (ISBN 0-88253-734-2). Ind-US Inc.
--Panther's Moon. (Illus.). (gr. 3-5). 1969. PLB 4.69 o.p. (ISBN 0-394-91497-X). Random.
--The Road to the Bazaar. (gr. 2-6). 1980. PLB 6.90 (ISBN 0-531-04181-6). Watts.
--Tales Told at Twilight. 166p. (gr. 4-6). 1970. 1.25 (ISBN 0-88253-394-0). Ind-US Inc.
Bond, W. H., ed. Eighteenth-Century Studies: In Honor of Donald F. Hyde. LC 77-123045. (Illus.). xv, 424p. 1970. 30.00x (ISBN 0-8139-0446-3, Grolier Club). U Pr of Va.
Bond, W. L. Crystal Technology. LC 75-23364. (Pure & Applied Optics Ser). 342p. 1976. 32.95 (ISBN 0-471-08765-3, Pub. by Wiley-Interscience). Wiley.
Bondanella, Peter, ed. see Boccaccio, Giovanni.
Bondanella, Peter E. Francesco Guicciardini. LC 75-41388. (World Authors Ser.,: Italy: No.389). 1976. lib. bdg. 10.95 (ISBN 0-8057-6231-0). Twayne.
--Machiavelli & the Art of Renaissance History. LC 73-9729. 200p. 1973. text ed. 12.95x (ISBN 0-8143-1499-6). Wayne St U Pr.
Bonderoff, Jason. Barbara Walters: Today's Woman. 1975. pap. 1.50 o.p. (ISBN 0-8439-0306-6, Leisure Bks). Nordon Pubns.

Bondi, H. Assumption & Myth in Physical Theory. 1967. 10.95 (ISBN 0-521-04282-8). Cambridge U Pr.
Bondi, Hermann. Relativity & Common Sense: A New Approach to Einstein. (Illus.). 177p. 1980. pap. 3.00 (ISBN 0-486-24021-5). Dover.
Bondi, Joseph, jt. auth. see Wiles, Jon.
Bondi, Joseph, Jr., jt. auth. see Wiles, Jon.
Bondi, Joseph, Jr., jt. auth. see Wiles, Jon W.
Bondo, Ulla. Ida: Life with My Handicapped Child. (Illus.). 128p. 1981. 23.00 (ISBN 0-571-11589-6, Pub. by Faber & Faber); pap. 8.95 (ISBN 0-571-11590-X). Merrimack Bk Serv.
Bonds, Joy, et al. Our Roots Are Still Alive: The Story of the Paliesinian People. LC 77-10952. (Illus.). 182p. pap. 5.45 (ISBN 0-917654-12-9). IISJ.
Bondurant, Joan V. Conquest of Violence: The Gandhian Philosophy of Conflict. rev. ed. (gr. 9 up). 1965. 16.50x (ISBN 0-520-00143-5); pap. 4.95x (ISBN 0-520-00145-1, CAMPUS243). U of Cal Pr.
Bone, Arthur H., ed. see Pierce, Walter M.
Bone, Hugh A. & Ranney, Austin. Politics & Voters. 5th ed. Munson, Eric M., ed. (Harris Ser.). 144p. 1981. pap. text ed. 6.95 (ISBN 0-07-006492-X, C). McGraw.
Bone, Hugh A., jt. auth. see Ogden, Daniel M., Jr.
Bone, Richard W. Maverick Guide to New Zealand: 1981 Edition. LC 80-25250. (Illus., Orig.). 1981. pap. 9.95 (ISBN 0-88289-269-X). Pelican.
Bone, Robert A. Negro Novel in America. rev. ed. (Publications in American Studies: No. 3). 1965. 21.00x o.p. (ISBN 0-300-00316-1). Yale U Pr.
Bone, Robert O., jt. auth. see Ocvirk, Otto G.
Bone, Robert W. Maverick Guide to Australia. rev. ed. (The Maverick Guide Ser.). (Illus.). 324p. (Orig.). 1981. pap. 9.95 (ISBN 0-88289-278-9). Pelican.
--Maverick Guide to Hawaii: 1981 Edition. LC 80-25076. (Illus.). 437p. (Orig.). 1981. pap. 8.95 (ISBN 0-88289-277-0). Pelican.
Bone, Roger C. Pulmonary Disease Review, Vol. 1. 600p. 1980. 35.00 (ISBN 0-471-05736-3, Pub. by WileyMed). Wiley.
Bone, Woutrina A. Children's Stories & How to Tell Them. LC 75-28363. (Illus.). xviii, 200p. 1975. Repr. of 1924 ed. 18.00 (ISBN 0-8103-3747-9). Gale.
Bonechi, Editore, ed. All Paris. LC 76-23572. (Encore Edition). (Illus.). 1976. 4.95 o.p. (ISBN 0-684-15936-8, ScribT). Scribner.
Boneck, John, ed. see Bakker, Jim.
Boneck, John, ed. see Miles, Austin.
Boneck, John, ed. see Vicker, Denise.
Bonell, Harold C. Sparks for the Kindling. 1968. 3.95 o.p. (ISBN 0-8170-0400-9). Judson.
Bonelli, Robert A. The Executive Handbook to Minicomputers. (Illus.). text ed. 14.00 (ISBN 0-89433-090-X). Petrocelli.
Bonello, Frank J. & Swartz, Thomas R., eds. Alternative Directions in Economic Policy. LC 77-17422. 1978. 3.95x (ISBN 0-268-00584-2); pap. 3.95 o.p. (ISBN 0-268-00585-0). U of Notre Dame Pr.
Bones, Jim, Jr. & Graves, John. Texas Heartland: A Hill Country Year. LC 75-16352. (Illus.). 104p. 1975. 21.50 (ISBN 0-89096-002-X). Tex A&M Univ Pr.
Bonewit, Kathy. Clinical Procedures for Medical Assistants. 1979. text ed. 18.50 (ISBN 0-7216-1846-4). Saunders.
Bonfanti, Joe. Italian Jokes. 1976. pap. 1.25 o.p. (ISBN 0-685-69147-0, LB356ZK, Leisure Bks). Nordon Pubns.
Bonfort, Lisa. Baby Animals. (Illus.). (ps-1). 1980. 2.95 (ISBN 0-525-69409-9, Gingerbread). Dutton.
Bonforte, Lisa, illus. Farm Animals. LC 80-53106. (Board Bks.). (Illus.). 14p. (ps). 1981. boards 2.95 (ISBN 0-394-84767-9). Random.
Bongard-Levin, G. M. Origin of Aryans: From Scythis to India. Gupta, H. C., tr. 124p. 1980. text ed. cancelled (ISBN 0-8426-1663-2). Verry.
Bongert, Yvonne. Recherches Sur les Cours Laiques Du Xe Au XIIIe Siecle. LC 80-1996. 1981. Repr. of 1949 ed. 34.00 (ISBN 0-404-18554-1). AMS Pr.
Bonghan, Kim, et al. Acupuncture- the Scientific Evidence & Far-Eastern Medicine. (Illus.). pap. write for info. (ISBN 0-916508-15-3). Happiness Pr.
Bonham. The Rascals from Haskell's Gym. (gr. 3-5). 1980. pap. 1.25 (ISBN 0-590-30231-0, Schol Pap). Schol Bk Serv.
Bonham, Barbara. Battle of Wounded Knee: The Ghost Dance Uprising. LC 71-125374. (gr. 6-8). 1970. 6.95 o.p. (ISBN 0-8092-8761-7); PLB avail o.p. (ISBN 0-685-04779-2). Contemp Bks.
Bonham, Frank. Blood on the Land. 1978. pap. 1.75 o.p. (ISBN 0-425-04809-8). Berkley Pub.
--Burma Rifles: A Story of Merrill's Marauders. LC 60-11535. (gr. 5 up). 1960. 7.95 o.p. (ISBN 0-690-16147-6, TYC-J). T Y Crowell.
--Chief. (gr. 6 up). 1971. PLB 7.95 o.p. (ISBN 0-525-27673-4). Dutton.
--Cool Cat. LC 77-133110. 160p. (gr. 7 up). 1971. PLB 7.95 o.p. (ISBN 0-525-28210-6). Dutton.
--Defiance Mountain. rev. ed. 1981. pap. 1.95 (ISBN 0-425-04932-9). Berkley Pub.
--Defiance Mountain. 1979. pap. 1.50 o.p. (ISBN 0-425-03955-2). Berkley Pub.
--A Dream of Ghosts. 160p. (gr. 3-6). 1973. PLB 7.95 o.p. (ISBN 0-525-28923-2). Dutton.
--Durango Street. (gr. 7 up). 1967. PLB 7.95 (ISBN 0-525-28950-X). Dutton.
--The Feud at Spanish Ford. 1981. pap. 1.95 (ISBN 0-425-04837-3). Berkley Pub.
--The Feud at Spanish Ford. 1978. pap. 1.50 o.p. (ISBN 0-425-03771-1). Berkley Pub.
--Fort Hogan. 1980. pap. 1.75 o.p. (ISBN 0-425-04562-5). Berkley Pub.
--Gimme an H, Gimme an E, Gimme an L, Gimme a P. LC 80-23926. 192p. (YA) (gr. 7 up). 1980. 9.95 (ISBN 0-684-16717-4). Scribner.
--Last Stage West. 1979. pap. 1.75 o.p. (ISBN 0-425-03884-X). Berkley Pub.
--Lost Stage Valley. 1981. pap. 1.75 (ISBN 0-425-04813-6). Berkley Pub.
--Lost Stage Valley. 1978. pap. 1.50 o.p. (ISBN 0-425-03752-5, Medallion). Berkley Pub.
--The Loud, Resounding Sea. LC 63-15082. (gr. 6 up). 1963. 6.95 o.p. (ISBN 0-690-51082-9, TYC-J). T Y Crowell.
--Mystery of the Fat Cat. (Illus.). (gr. 5-9). 1968. PLB 7.95 o.p. (ISBN 0-525-35588-X). Dutton.
--Night Raid. 1978. pap. 1.50 o.p. (ISBN 0-425-03770-3, Medallion). Berkley Pub.
--Rawhide Guns. rev. ed. (Orig.). 1981. pap. 1.95 (ISBN 0-425-04815-2). Berkley Pub.
--Snaketrack. (Frank Bonham Ser.). 1978. pap. 1.50 o.p. (ISBN 0-425-03760-6, Medallion). Berkley Pub.
--Tough Country. 1979. pap. 1.95 o.p. (ISBN 0-425-03873-4). Berkley Pub.
Bonham, Marilyn. Laughter & Tears of Children. 1967. 4.95 o.s.i. (ISBN 0-02-512890-6). Macmillan.
Bonham, Russell A. & Fink, Manfred. High Energy Electron Scattering. LC 73-12400. (ACS Monograph: No. 169). 1974. 33.00 (ISBN 0-442-30891-4). Am Chemical.
Bonham, Tal D. The Treasury of Clean Jokes. LC 80-67639. (Orig.). 1981. pap. 2.95 (ISBN 0-8054-5703-8). Broadman.
Bonham-Carter, Victor. Authors by Profession, Vol. 1. 1979. 12.95 (ISBN 0-913232-59-9). W Kaufmann.
Bonheim, Helmut. Joyce's Benefictions. (Perspectives in Criticism: No. 16). 1964. 16.75x (ISBN 0-520-00147-8). U of Cal Pr.
Bonhoeffer, Dietrich. Christ the Center: A New Translation. new ed. LC 78-4747. (Harper's Ministers Paperback Library Ser.). 1978. pap. 3.95 (ISBN 0-06-060815-3, RD 285, HarpR). Har-Row.
--Cost of Discipleship. 2nd ed. 1967. 4.95 (ISBN 0-02-512920-1); pap. write for info. (ISBN 0-685-14934-X). Macmillan.
--Cost of Disciplineship. 1963. pap. 3.95 (ISBN 0-02-083850-6, Collier). Macmillan.
--Letters & Papers from Prison. enl. ed. 448p. 1972. 12.95 (ISBN 0-02-513110-9). Macmillan.
--Prayers from Prison. Hampe, Johann C., tr. from Ger. LC 77-15228. 1978. pap. 3.50 (ISBN 0-8006-1334-1, 1-1334). Fortress.
Bonic, Robert, et al. Freshman Calculus. 2nd ed. 1976. text ed. 21.95x (ISBN 0-669-96727-0); wkbk. 7.95x (ISBN 0-669-97774-8). Heath.
Bonica, John J., ed. International Symposium on Pain. LC 72-93317. (Advances in Neurology Ser.: Vol. 4). 874p. 1974. 56.50 (ISBN 0-911216-57-X). Raven.
--Pain. (Association for Research in Nervous & Mental Disease Publications Ser.: Vol. 58). 1979. text ed. 38.00 (ISBN 0-89004-376-0). Raven.
Bonica, John J. & Ventafridda, Vittorio, eds. International Symposium on Pain of Advanced Cancer. LC 78-55811. (Advances in Pain Research & Therapy Ser.: Vol. 2). 1979. text ed. 73.50 (ISBN 0-89004-271-3). Raven.
Bonica, John J., ed. see World Congress on Pain, 1st, Florence, 1975.
Bonica, John J., et al, eds. Recent Advances on Pain: Pathophysiology & Clinical Aspects. (Illus.). 352p. 1974. 32.50 (ISBN 0-398-02964-4). C C Thomas.
Bonica, John J., et al, eds. see World Congress on Pain, 2nd, Montreal, Aug. 1978.
Boniface, St., et al. English Correspondence of Saint Boniface & His Friends in England. Kylie, Edward, tr. LC 66-30729. (Medieval Library). (Illus.). 209p. 1966. Repr. of 1926 ed. 19.50x (ISBN 0-8154-0028-4). Cooper Sq.
Bonifazi, Conrad. The Soul of the World: An Account of Inwardness of Things. LC 78-64826. 1978. pap. text ed. 10.25 (ISBN 0-8191-0638-0). U Pr of Amer.
Bonilla, Frank & Silva-Michelena, Jose A. The Politics of Change in Venezuela, 3 vols. Incl. Vol. 1. A Strategy for Research on Social Policy. 1967. o.p. (ISBN 0-262-02028-9); Vol. 2. The Failure of Elites. 1970. 23.00x (ISBN 0-262-02058-0); Vol. 3. The Illusion of Democracy in Dependent Nations. 1971. (ISBN 0-262-19069-9). 23.00x ea. MIT Pr.
Bonilla, Plutarco. Los Milagros Tambien Son Parabolas. LC 78-59240. 166p. (Orig., Span.). 1978. pap. 3.50 (ISBN 0-89922-114-9). Edit Caribe.
Bonin, Jane F. Major Themes in Prize-Winning American Drama. LC 74-34492. 205p. 1975. 10.00 (ISBN 0-8108-0799-8). Scarecrow.
--Prize-Winning American Drama: A Bibliographical & Descriptive Guide. LC 73-3111. 1973. 10.00 (ISBN 0-8108-0607-X). Scarecrow.
Boning, Richard A. Multiple Skills Series: Levels Picture Level Through I. Incl. E1 (ISBN 0-8484-0041-0); E2 (ISBN 0-8484-0042-9); E3 (ISBN 0-8484-0043-7); E4 (ISBN 0-8484-0044-5); F1 (ISBN 0-8484-0045-3); F2 (ISBN 0-8484-0046-1); F3 (ISBN 0-8484-0047-X); F4 (ISBN 0-8484-0048-8). (Also available in Span. edition-levels Picture through C). (YA) 1976. pap. 19.35 set (ISBN 0-685-69056-3); pap. 2.10 ea. Lowell & Lynwood.
--Picto-Cabulary Series, 7 sets. Incl. Basic Word Set-A. (gr. 1-2). 104.45 (ISBN 0-87965-409-0); Words to Eat. (gr. 4-6). 77.95 (ISBN 0-87965-401-5); Words to Wear. (gr. 4-6). 77.95 (ISBN 0-87965-402-3); Words to Meet. (gr. 4-6). 77.95 (ISBN 0-87965-403-1); Descriptive Words. (gr. 5-9). 77.95 (ISBN 0-87965-421-X); Words Around the House. (gr. 4-6). 54.95 (ISBN 0-87965-405-8); Words Around the Neighborhood. (gr. 4-6). 54.95 (ISBN 0-87965-404-X). 1976. B Loft.
--Specific Skill Reading Series: New 1976-1978. Incl. Detecting the Sequence, 14 bks. (gr. 1-12); Drawing Conclusions, 14 bks. (gr. 1-12); Following Directions, 14 bks. (gr. 1-12); Getting the Facts, 14 bks. (gr. 1-12); Getting the Main Idea, 14 bks. (gr. 1-12); Locating the Answer, 14 bks. (gr. 1-12); Using the Context, 14 bks. (gr. 1-12); Working with Sounds, 14 bks. (gr. 1-12). per bk. 1.95 (ISBN 0-685-39281-3); tchr's manuals 3.00ea. (ISBN 0-685-39282-1); Set. spirit masters 6.95 (ISBN 0-685-39283-X); complete elementary set 127.55 (ISBN 0-685-39284-8); complete midway set (4-9) 98.95 (ISBN 0-685-39285-6); complete secondary set (7-12) 98.95 (ISBN 0-685-39286-4). B Loft.
Bonini, Charles P. Computer Models for Decision Analysis. (Illus.). 148p. (Orig.). 1980. pap. text ed. 13.50x (ISBN 0-89426-042-1); tchrs'. ed. 12.50x (ISBN 0-89426-043-X). Scientific Pr.
Bonini, Charles P., jt. auth. see Spurr, William A.
Bonino, Jose M. Doing Theology in a Revolutionary Situation. Lazareth, William H., ed. LC 74-80424. (Confrontation Bks). 208p. 1975. pap. 4.50 (ISBN 0-8006-1451-8, 1-1451). Fortress.
Bonk, Wallace J. & Magrill, Rose M. Building Library Collections. 5th ed. LC 79-11151. 1979. 12.50 (ISBN 0-8108-1214-2). Scarecrow.
Bonn, M. J. The Crisis of Capitalism in America. Ray, Winifred, tr. Date not set. Repr. of 1932 ed. lib. bdg. 25.00 (ISBN 0-89760-030-4). Telegraph Bks.
Bonnat, Yves see Hainaux, Rene.
Bonne, Alfred. The Economic Development of the Middle East: An Outline of Planned Reconstruction After the War. LC 79-51856. 1981. Repr. of 1945 ed. 17.50 (ISBN 0-88355-949-8). Hyperion Conn.
--State & Economics in the Middle East. LC 72-11325. (Illus.). 452p. 1973. Repr. of 1955 ed. lib. bdg. 35.00x (ISBN 0-8371-6661-6, BOSE). Greenwood.
Bonneau, B. Lee & Smith, Billy A., eds. Astronomy Illustrated. 3rd ed. 1980. pap. text ed. 13.95 (ISBN 0-8403-2168-6). Kendall-Hunt.
Bonnecarrere, Paul. Ultimatum. 1976. pap. 1.75 o.p. (ISBN 0-345-25101-6). Ballantine.
Bonnefoy, Claude, et al. Dictionaire De Literature Contemporaire. 22.50 (ISBN 2-7113-0077-3). Gaylord Prof Pubns.
Bonnefoy, Yves. On the Motion & Immobility of Douve. Kinnell, Galway, tr. LC 67-24284. (Fr. & Eng.). 1968. 10.00x (ISBN 0-8214-0035-5). Ohio U Pr.
Bonnell, Howard. How to Give Yourself a Raise in Selling. LC 80-7845. 144p. 1980. 9.95 (ISBN 0-8119-0340-0). Fell.
Bonnell, Peter & Sedwick, Frank. Conversation in French: Points of Departure. 3rd ed. (Orig.). 1981. pap. text ed. write for info. (ISBN 0-442-24468-1). D Van Nostrand.
--Conversation in German: Points of Departure. 3rd ed. (Orig.). 1981. pap. text ed. write for info. (ISBN 0-442-24466-5). D Van Nostrand.
--German for Careers: Conversational Perspectives. (Orig.). 1980. pap. text ed. 8.95 (ISBN 0-442-20563-5). D Van Nostrand.
Bonnelle, C. & Mande, C., eds. Advances in X-Ray Spectroscopy: A Reference Text in Honour of Professor Y Cauchois. (Illus.). 400p. 1981. 60.00 (ISBN 0-08-025266-4). Pergamon.
Bonner, C. E. Index Hepaticarum: An Index to the Liverworts of the World. Incl. Pt. 2. Achiton to Balantiopsis. 37.50 (ISBN 3-7682-0092-2); Pt. 3. Barbilophozia to Ceranthus. 37.50 (ISBN 3-7682-0093-0); Pt. 4. Ceratolejeunea to Crystolejeunea. 37.50; Pt. 5. Delavayella to Geothallus. 50.00; Pt. 6. Goebelliella to Jubula. 37.50 (ISBN 3-7682-0096-5). 1963-66. Lubrecht & Cramer.
Bonner, James S., et al. Basic Driver Education. (gr. 7-12). 1966. pap. text ed. 3.25x o.p. (ISBN 0-8134-1125-4, 1125); tchrs' manual 3.25x o.p. (ISBN 0-8134-1126-2, 1126); study cards 6.95x o.p. (ISBN 0-8134-1339-7, 1339). Interstate.
Bonner, John T., ed. see Thompson, D'Arcy W.
Bonner, Marie T. Vermont Reflections. 62p. 1980. 3.95 (ISBN 0-8059-2740-9). Dorrance.
Bonner, Mary G. Wonders of Inventions. (Illus.). (gr. 4-9). 1961. 4.25 o.p. (ISBN 0-8313-0007-8); PLB 6.19 o.p. (ISBN 0-685-13790-2). Lantern.
Bonner, Nigel. Whales. (Illus.). 248p. 1980. 24.95 (ISBN 0-7137-0887-5, Pub. by Blandford Pr England). Sterling.
Bonner, Stanley F. Education in Ancient Rome. (Campus Ser: No. 198). (Illus.). 1977. 25.00x (ISBN 0-520-03439-2); pap. 10.95x (ISBN 0-520-03501-1). U of Cal Pr.
Bonner, Thomas, Jr. & Falcon, Guillermo N. William Faulkner, the William B. Wisdom Collection: A Descriptive Catalog. LC 79-26556. (Illus.). 1980. pap. 13.00 (ISBN 0-9603212-2-5). Tulane Univ.
Bonner, William H. Communicating Clearly: The Effective Message. 384p. 1980. pap. text ed. 8.95 (ISBN 0-574-20605-1, 13-3605); instr's. guide avail. (ISBN 0-574-20606-X, 13-3606). SRA.
Bonner, William H. & Voyles, Jean. Communicating in Business: Key to Success, Vol. 1. rev. ed. LC 79-84832. (Illus.). 388p. 1980. text ed. 14.95x (ISBN 0-931920-07-8); study guide 4.95 (ISBN 0-686-63215-X); letter writing wkbk. 4.50 (ISBN 0-686-63216-8); report writing wkbk. 3.95 (ISBN 0-686-63217-6). Dame Pubns.
Bonnerjea, Biren. Dictionary of Superstitions & Mythology. LC 69-17755. 1969. Repr. of 1927 ed. 20.00 (ISBN 0-8103-3572-7). Gale.
Bonners, Susan. A Penguin Year. LC 79-53595. (Illus.). 48p. (gr. 1-3). 1981. 9.95 (ISBN 0-440-00166-8); PLB 9.43 (ISBN 0-440-00170-6). Delacorte.
Bonnesen, T. & Fenchel, W. Theorie der Konvexen Koerper. LC 49-29452. (Ger). 9.95 (ISBN 0-8284-0054-7). Chelsea Pub.
Bonnet, Mireille. Microsurgery of Retinal Detachment. (Illus.). 1980. text ed. 27.00 (ISBN 0-89352-067-5). Masson Pub.
Bonnet, Pierre. Bibliographia Araneorum: Analyse Methodique De Toute la Litterature Araneologique Jusqu'en 1939. LC 57-58745. 832p. 1968. Repr. 40.00 (ISBN 0-686-09299-6). Entomol Soc.
Bonnett, Aubrey W. Institutional Adaptation of West Indian Immigrants to America: An Analysis of Rotating Credit Associations. LC 80-69054. 160p. 1981. lib. bdg. 16.50 (ISBN 0-8191-1500-2); pap. text ed. 7.50 (ISBN 0-8191-1501-0). U Pr of Amer.
Bonneville, J. F., et al. Radiology of the Sella Turcica. (Illus.). 262p. 1981. 116.80 (ISBN 0-387-10319-8). Springer-Verlag.
Bonney, Lorraine G., jt. auth. see Bonney, Orrin H.
Bonney, Lorraine G., jt. ed. see Bonney, Orrin H.
Bonney, Orrin H. & Bonney, Lorraine G. Field Book Wind River Range. rev. ed. (Illus.). 1968. pap. 5.95 with 1975 supp. (ISBN 0-685-07191-X). Bonney.
Bonney, Orrin H. & Bonney, Lorraine G., eds. Battle Drums & Geysers, 3 vols. Incl. Vol. I. Lt. Gustavus C. Doane: His Life & Remarkable Military Career; Vol. II. Exploration of Yellowstone Park, Lt. Doane's Yellowstone Journal; Vol. III. Lt. G. C. Doane's Snake River Journal of 1876. (Illus.). 1978. Vols. I & III. pap. 3.95; pap. 4.95. Bonney.
Bonney, Richard. Political Change in France Under Richelieu & Mazarin, 1624-1661. (Illus.). 1977. text ed. 49.95x (ISBN 0-19-822537-7). Oxford U Pr.
Bonnheim, Walter. From Dude to Cowman. 180p. 1975. 5.95 (ISBN 0-914330-05-5). Western Tanager.
Bonnie, Fred, jt. auth. see Thompson, H. C.

Bonnie, Richard J. Marijuana Use & Criminal Sanctions: Essays on the Theory & Practice of Law Reform. 264p. 1980. 20.00 (ISBN 0-87215-244-8). Michie.

Bonnie, Richard J. & Whitebread, Charles H. The Marihuana Conviction: A History of Marihuana Prohibition in the United States. LC 73-89907. 395p. 1974. 17.50x (ISBN 0-8139-0417-X). U Pr of Va.

Bonnin, J. Grant. Injuries to the Ankle. (Illus.). Repr. of 1970 ed. 25.25 o.s.i. (ISBN 0-02-841630-9). Hafner.

Bonnington, S. T., jt. auth. see Bain, A. G.

Bonnington, S. T. & King, A. L., eds. Jet Pumps & Ejectors: A State of the Art Review & Bibliography. 2nd ed. (BHRA Fluid Engineering Ser.: Vol. 1). 1977. pap. 36.00 (ISBN 0-900983-63-9, Dist. by Air Science Co.). BHRA Fluid.

Bonnot De Condillac, Etienne see Condillac, Etienne Bonnot de.

Bono, E. De see De Bono, E.

Bono, Edward De see De Bono, Edward.

Bono, Philip & Gatland, Kenneth. Frontiers of Space. rev. ed. LC 76-2028. (Macmillan Color Ser.). 288p. 1976. 9.95 (ISBN 0-02-542810-1, 54281). Macmillan.

Bono, Phillip & Gatland, Kenneth. Frontiers of Space: Pocket Encyclopedia of Space in Color. (gr. 8 up). 1969. 5.95 o.s.i. (ISBN 0-02-513500-7). Macmillan.

Bonomi, Patricia U. Factious People: Politics & Society in Colonial New York. LC 74-156803. 1971. 20.00x (ISBN 0-231-03509-8); pap. 7.50x (ISBN 0-231-08329-7). Columbia U Pr.

Bonomo, Michael, jt. auth. see Finacchiaro, Mary.

Bonsall, Crosby. The Case of the Double Cross. LC 80-7768. (I Can Read Bks.). (Illus.). 64p. (gr. k-3). 1980. 6.95 (ISBN 0-06-020602-0, HarpJ); PLB 7.89 (ISBN 0-06-020603-9). Har-Row.

--Goodbye Summer. LC 78-23245. (gr. 4-7). 1979. 7.50 (ISBN 0-688-80202-8); PLB 7.20 (ISBN 0-688-84202-X). Greenwillow.

Bonsall, F. F. & Duncan, J. Numerical Ranges, No. 2. (London Mathematical Society Lecture Note Ser.: No. 10). (Illus.). 192p. 1973. pap. text ed. 20.50x (ISBN 0-521-20227-2). Cambridge U Pr.

--Numerical Ranges of Operators on Normed Spaces & of Elements of Normed Algebras. LC 71-128498. (London Mathematical Society Lecture Note Ser.: No. 2). 1971. 16.95x (ISBN 0-521-07988-8). Cambridge U Pr.

Bonsall, Thomas E. The Linclon Motorcar: Sixty Years of Excellence. 325p. 1981. 32.95 (ISBN 0-934780-05-6). Bookman Dan.

--The Lincoln Motorcar: Sixty Years of Excellence. (Illus.). 1981. 32.95 (ISBN 0-934780-05-6). Bookman Dan.

--Pontiac: The Complete History, 1926-79. LC 79-56550. (Illus.). 1980. 26.95 (ISBN 0-934780-02-1). Bookman Dan.

Bonsall, Thomas E., ed. GTO: A Source Book. (Illus.). 142p. (Orig.). 1980. pap. 12.95 (ISBN 0-934780-03-X). Bookman Dan.

Bonser, Wilfred. A Prehistoric Bibliography. Troy, June, ed. 1976. 155.00x (ISBN 0-631-17090-1, Pub. by Basil Blackwell England). Biblio Dist.

Bonser, Wilfrid. Romano-British Bibliography: 55B.C.-449A.D, Vol. 1 & 2. 1977. Set. 225.00x (ISBN 0-631-08380-4, Pub. by Basil Blackwell). Biblio Dist.

Bonsignore, John J., et al. Before the Law: An Introduction to the Legal Process. 2nd ed. LC 78-69606. (Illus.). 1979. pap. text ed. 12.50 (ISBN 0-395-27514-8). HM.

Bonstingl, John J. Introduction to the Social Sciences. (gr. 7-12). 1980. text ed. 16.96 (ISBN 0-205-05886-8, 8058865); tchrs'. guide 12.00 (ISBN 0-205-05887-6). Allyn.

Bonta, I. L., et al, eds. Inflammation Mechanisms & Their Impact on Therapy. (Agents & Actions Supplements: No. 3). (Illus.). 192p. 1977. pap. text ed. 60.00 (ISBN 3-7643-0913-X). Birkhauser.

Bontemps, Arna, ed. Golden Slippers: An Anthology of Negro Poetry. (Illus.). 1941. 10.00 (ISBN 0-06-010395-7, HarpT); PLB 8.97 o.s.i. (ISBN 0-06-010404-X). Har-Row.

--The Harlem Renaissance Remembered. LC 72-723. (Illus.). 1972. 6.95 o.p. (ISBN 0-396-06517-1). Dodd.

Bontemps, Arna, et al, eds. Five Black Lives: The Autobiographies of Venture Smith, James Mars, William Grimes, the Rev. G. W. Offley, & James L. Smith. LC 74-108647. 1971. 17.50x (ISBN 0-8195-4036-6, Pub. by Wesleyan U Pr). Columbia U Pr.

Bonthius, R. H. Christian Paths of Self Acceptance. 20.00x o.p. (ISBN 0-231-09863-4). Columbia U Pr.

Bonvechio, Richard, jt. auth. see Smolensky, Jack.

Bonville, Frank. The Little Secrets. (Gambler's Book Shelf). 1976. pap. 2.95 (ISBN 0-89650-570-7). Gamblers.

Bonwick, G. Automation on Shipboard. 1967. 25.00 (ISBN 0-312-06195-1). St Martin.

Bonzon, Paul J. The Runaway Flying Horse. LC 76-2525. (Illus.). 40p. (gr. k-4). 1976. 5.95 o.s.i. (ISBN 0-8193-0875-7, Four Winds); PLB 5.41 o.s.i. (ISBN 0-8193-0876-5). Schol Bk Serv.

Boochever, Florence & Jackson, Raymond, eds. Writings from the Beaver Trail. (Illus.). 312p. (Orig.). 1979. pap. 5.50 (ISBN 0-9605090-0-3). Albany Pub Lib.

Boocock, Sarane S. Introduction to the Sociology of Learning. LC 72-7924. (Illus.). 1972. text ed. 17.50 o.p. (ISBN 0-395-12565-0, 3-04930). HM.

--Sociology of Education: An Introduction. 2nd ed. LC 79-88445. (Illus.). 1980. text ed. 17.95 (ISBN 0-395-28524-0). HM.

Boocock, Sarane S. & Schild, E. O., eds. Simulation Games in Learning. LC 68-21913. 1978. pap. 9.95x (ISBN 0-8039-1002-9). Sage.

Boodberg, Peter A. Selected Works of Peter A. Boodberg. Cohen, Alvin P., ed. LC 76-24580. 1979. 22.75x (ISBN 0-520-03314-0). U of Cal Pr.

Boodley, James W. The Commercial Greenhouse. LC 78-74806. (Agriculture Ser.). 576p. 1981. 16.40 (ISBN 0-8273-1719-0); instr's. guide 1.45 (ISBN 0-8273-1718-2). Delmar.

--The Commerical Greenhouse Handbook. 544p. 1981. 24.95 (ISBN 0-442-23146-6). Van Nos Reinhold.

Boodt, M. De see De Boodt, M.

Boogman, J. C. & Van Der Plaat, G. N., eds. Federalism: History & Current Significance of a Form of Government. (Illus.). 307p. 1980. pap. 16.90 (ISBN 90-247-9003-4, Pub by Martinus Nijhoff). Kluwer Boston.

Booher, Dianna D. Coping-When Your Family Falls Apart. LC 79-17342. 192p. (gr. 7 up). 1979. PLB 8.29 (ISBN 0-671-33083-7). Messner.

--Not Yet Free. LC 80-69005. (gr. 9 up). 1981. 5.95 (ISBN 0-8054-7315-7). Broadman.

--Rape: What Woud You Do If...? 192p. (gr. 7 up). 1981. PLB price not set (ISBN 0-671-42201-4). Messner.

Booij, G. E. Dutch Morphology: A Study of Word Formation in Generative Grammar. (PdR Press Dutch: No. 2). (Illus.). 1977. pap. text ed. 14.25x (ISBN 90-316-0150-0). Humanities.

Booij, H. L. & Bungenberg De Jong, H. G. Biocolloids & Their Interactions with Special Reference to Coacervates & Related Systems. (Protoplasmatologia: Vol. 1, Pt. 2). (Illus.). 1956. 46.70 o.p. (ISBN 0-387-80421-8). Springer-Verlag.

Book, Albert C., jt. auth. see Schick, C. Dennis.

Book Div. Research Staff. SN Distribution Study of Grocery Store Sales - 1981. 250p. 1981. pap. 30.00 (ISBN 0-87005-370-1). Fairchild.

Book Division Research. SN Distribution Study Grocery Store Sales - 1980. 1980. pap. text ed. 27.50 (ISBN 0-87005-313-2). Fairchild.

Book Division Research Staff. Fairchild's Textile & Apparel Financial Directory: 1980. 260p. 1980. text ed. 45.00 (ISBN 0-87005-361-2). Fairchild.

--Fairchild's Textile & Apparel Financial Directory: 1979. (Illus.). 230p. 1979. pap. text ed. 40.00 (ISBN 0-87005-309-4). Fairchild.

Book Division Staff. Fairchild's Financial Manual of Retail Stores: 1979. (Illus.). 1979. pap. text ed. 40.00 o.p. (ISBN 0-87005-310-8). Fairchild.

Book, Michael. Danger UXB. 1981. pap. 2.95 (ISBN 0-14-005852-4). Penguin.

Book Research Staff. Electronic News Financial Fact Book & Directory: 1980. (Illus.). 640p. 1980. pap. text ed. 90.00 (ISBN 0-87005-360-4). Fairchild.

--Electronic News Financial Fact Book & Directory: 1979. (Illus.). 616p. 1979. pap. text ed. 80.00 (ISBN 0-87005-308-6). Fairchild.

Book Review Committee. Family Life & Child Development: Selective Bibliography Cumulative Through 1979. (Jewish Board of Family & Children Services). 1979. pap. 3.00 (ISBN 0-87183-187-2). Jewish Bd Family.

Book, Ronald V., ed. Formal Language Theory: Perspectives & Open Problems. 1980. 25.00 (ISBN 0-12-115350-9). Acad Pr.

Booker, Christopher. The Booker Quiz. (Illus., Orig.). 1976. pap. 6.95 (ISBN 0-7100-8504-4). Routledge & Kegan.

--The Games War: A Moscow Journal. 208p. 1981. 18.50 (ISBN 0-571-11755-4, Pub. by Faber & Faber); pap. 8.95 (ISBN 0-571-11763-5). Merrimack Bk Serv.

--The Seventies: The Decade That Changed the Future. LC 80-5389. 350p. 1980. 16.95 (ISBN 0-8128-2757-0). Stein & Day.

Booker, Frank. The Great Western Railway: A New History. 1977. 14.95 (ISBN 0-7153-7455-9). David & Charles.

Booker, John, jt. auth. see Alderton, David.

Booker, Louise. Tar Heel Stories. (Illus.). 1968. 4.95 (ISBN 0-930230-34-5). Johnson NC.

Booker, Richard. The Miracle of the Scarlet Thread. (Orig.). (YA) 1981. pap. 4.95 (ISBN 0-88270-499-0). Logos.

Bookspan, Martin & Yockey, Ross. Andre Previn: A Biography. LC 80-2746. (Illus.). 384p. 1981. 14.95. Doubleday.

Bookstaber, Richard M. Option Pricing & Strategies in Investing. LC 80-15013. 256p. 1981. text ed. 18.95 (ISBN 0-201-00123-3). A-W.

Bookstein, Abraham, jt. ed. see Swanson, Don R.

Bookstein, Abraham, et al, eds. Prospects for Change in Bibliographic Control. (University of Chicago Studies in Library Science). 1977. lib. bdg. 10.00x (ISBN 0-226-06365-8). U of Chicago Pr.

Bookstein, Joseph J. & Clark, Richard L. Renal Microvascular Disease. 1980. text ed. 42.50 (ISBN 0-316-10237-7). Little.

Boole, George. Investigation of the Laws of Thought. 9.50 (ISBN 0-8446-1699-0). Peter Smith.

--Logical Works, 2 vols. Incl. Vol. 1. Studies in Logic & Probability. 500p. 22.50 (ISBN 0-87548-038-1); Vol. 2. Laws of Thought. xvi, 448p. 22.50 (ISBN 0-87548-039-X). 1952. Open Court.

--Treatise on the Calculus of Finite Differences. 5th ed. LC 76-119364. text ed. 10.95 (ISBN 0-8284-1121-2). Chelsea Pub.

Boolootian, Richard A. Elements of Human Anatomy & Physiology. LC 76-3681. 550p. 1976. text ed. 17.95 (ISBN 0-8299-0086-1); instrs.' manual avail. (ISBN 0-8299-0460-3). West Pub.

Boolos, G. The Unprovability of Consistency. LC 77-85710. (Illus.). 1979. 26.95 (ISBN 0-521-21879-9). Cambridge U Pr.

Boolos, G. S. & Jeffrey, R. Computability & Logic. 2nd ed. LC 77-85710. (Illus.). 280p. 1981. 39.95 (ISBN 0-521-23479-4); pap. 13.95 (ISBN 0-521-29967-5). Cambridge U Pr.

Boolos, G. S. & Jeffrey, R. C. Computability & Logic. LC 73-90811. 300p. 1974. 23.95x (ISBN 0-521-20402-X). Cambridge U Pr.

Boom, Corrie T. Amazing Love. (Orig.). pap. 1.50 (ISBN 0-515-04898-4). Jove Pubns.

--Amazing Love. 1976. pap. 1.25 (ISBN 0-89129-183-0). Jove Pubns.

--Amor, Asombroso Amor. Orig. Title: Amazing Love. 1980. pap. 1.80 (ISBN 0-311-40035-3, Edit Mundo). Casa Bautista.

--A Prisoner & Yet. (Orig.). pap. 1.95 (ISBN 0-515-05334-1). Jove Pubns.

--Tramp for the Lord. (Orig.). pap. 2.25 (ISBN 0-515-05828-9). Jove Pubns.

--Tramp for the Lord. 1976. pap. 1.50 (ISBN 0-89129-027-3). Jove Pubns.

Boom, Corrie T., tr. O Esconderiho. (Portuguese Bks.). 1979. 1.00 (ISBN 0-8297-0779-4). Life Pubs Intl.

--Na Casa De Meu Pai. (Portuguese Bks.). 1979. 1.50 (ISBN 0-8297-0894-4). Life Pubs Intl.

Boon, Gerard K. Technology & Employment in Footwear Manufacturing: A Study Prepared for the Int'l Labour Office Within the Framework of the World Employment Programme. LC 80-50458. 232p. 1980. 45.00x (ISBN 90-286-0170-8). Sijthoff & Noordhoff.

Boon, J. A. The Anthropological Romance of Bali 1597-1972. LC 76-19626. (Geertz Ser.). (Illus.). 1977. 29.95 (ISBN 0-521-21398-3); pap. 7.95x (ISBN 0-521-29226-3). Cambridge U Pr.

Boon, Jean P. & Yip, Sidney. Molecular Hydrodynamics. (Illus.). 440p. 1980. text ed. 49.95 (ISBN 0-07-006560-8). McGraw.

Boone & Johnson. Marketing Channels. 2nd ed. 1977. 14.95 (ISBN 0-87814-026-3). Pennwell Pub.

Boone & Kurtz. Sales Management Game. (Orig.). 1978. pap. 10.95 (ISBN 0-686-28581-6). Pennwell Pub.

Boone, Cheri, ed. Proceedings of the Eleventh International Conference on Underwater Education. Date not set. pap. 17.00 (ISBN 0-916974-32-4); addendum to proceedings, 147 pp. incl. NAUI.

Boone, Daniel. Cerebral Palsy. LC 76-190708. (Studies in Communicative Disorders Ser). 1972. text ed. 2.50 (ISBN 0-672-61290-9). Bobbs.

Boone, Daniel R. The Voice & Voice Therapy. 2nd ed. (Illus.). 1977. 18.95 (ISBN 0-13-943100-4). P-H.

Boone, Edna, jt. auth. see Boone, Tom.

Boone, Gene. Classics in Consumer Behavior. new ed. (Orig.). 1977. pap. 11.95 (ISBN 0-87814-092-1). Pennwell Pub.

Boone, Gray. Gray Boone on Antiques. LC 80-84408. (Illus.). 160p. 1981. 12.95 (ISBN 0-8487-0519-X). Oxmoor Hse.

Boone, J. Allen. Kinship with All Life. LC 54-6901. 160p. 1976. pap. 4.95 (ISBN 0-06-060912-5, RD128, HarpR). Har-Row.

Boone, L. V, et al. Producing Farm Crops. 2nd ed. 1981. 16.65 o.p. (ISBN 0-8134-2151-9); text ed. 12.50x o.p. (ISBN 0-685-64715-3, 2151). Interstate.

Boone, L. V., et al, eds. Producing Farm Crops. 3rd ed. 1981. 14.60 (ISBN 0-8134-2151-9); text ed. 10.95x. Interstate.

Boone, Louis E. & Hackleman, Edwin C. Marketing Strategy: A Marketing Decision Game. 2nd ed. LC 74-27870. (Illus.). 224p. 1975. pap. text ed. 11.95 (ISBN 0-675-08713-9); manual 3.95 (ISBN 0-686-67124-4); card deck 3.95 (ISBN 0-686-67125-2). Merrill.

Boone, Louis E. & Kurtz, David L. Contemporary Business. 2nd ed. 1979. 18.95 (ISBN 0-03-043646-X). Dryden Pr.

--Contemporary Marketing. 3rd ed. 640p. 1980. 19.95 (ISBN 0-03-051391-X). Dryden Pr.

Boone, Louis E., jt. auth. see Kurtz, David L.

Boone, Michele L., ed. Southern Appalachian Resource Catalog, Vol. I. rev. ed. (Illus.). 84p. 1980. pap. 4.00 (ISBN 0-937208-00-0). S Appalachian Res.

--Southern Applachian Resource Catalog, Vol. II. (Illus.). 76p. 1981. 4.00. S Appalachian Res.

Boone, Pat. Coming Out. 1978. pap. 2.50 (ISBN 0-89728-001-6, 693880). Omega Pubns OR.

--Get Your Life Together. pap. 3.95 (ISBN 0-89728-032-6, 578516). Omega Pubns OR.

--My Brothers Keeper? Orig. Title: Dr. Balaam's Talking Mule. 1975. pap. 1.50 (ISBN 0-89129-028-1). Jove Pubns.

--Pat Boone Devotional Book. 7.95 (ISBN 0-89728-050-4, 678753). Omega Pubns OR.

--Pray to Win: God Wants You to Succeed. 1980. 8.95 (ISBN 0-399-12494-2). Putnam.

--Twixt Twelve & Twenty. 1973. pap. 1.25 o.s.i. (ISBN 0-89129-147-4, FV2933). Jove Pubns.

Boone, Pat, jt. auth. see Boone, Shirley.

Boone, Patricia Z. Laboratory Procedures for the Medical Assistant. 1981. 15.00 (ISBN 0-8036-1003-3). Davis Co.

Boone, Shirley & Boone, Pat. The Honeymoon Is Over. 192p. 1980. pap. 4.95 (ISBN 0-8407-5721-2). Nelson.

Boone, Tom & Boone, Edna. Prayer & Action. (Prayer in My Life Ser.: Ser. II). 1974. pap. 1.00x (ISBN 0-8358-0309-0). Upper Room.

Boor, W. De see De Boor, W. & Kohlmann, G.

Boorer, Michael. The Life of Monkeys & Apes. LC 78-56603. (Easy Reading Edition of Introduction to Nature Ser.). (Illus.). 1978. lib. bdg. 7.95 (ISBN 0-686-51143-3). Silver.

--The Life of Strange Mammals. LC 78-56571. (Easy Reading Edition of Introduction to Nature Ser.). (Illus.). 1978. lib. bdg. 7.95 (ISBN 0-686-51147-6). Silver.

Boorkman, JoAnne, jt. auth. see Roper, Fred.

Boorman, Howard L. & Howard, Richard C., eds. Biographical Dictionary of Republican China, 4 vols. Incl. Vol. 1. Ai-Ch'u. 1967. 35.00x (ISBN 0-231-08955-4); Vol. 2. Dalai-Ma. 1968. 35.00x (ISBN 0-231-08956-2); Vol. 3. Mao-Wu. 1970. 35.00x (ISBN 0-231-08957-0); Vol. 4. Yang-Bibliography. 1971. 40.00x (ISBN 0-231-08958-9). LC 67-12006. 1967. Columbia U Pr.

Boorman, John T. & Havrilesky, Thomas M. Money Supply, Money Demand & Macroeconomic Models. LC 79-167998. 1972. pap. 11.95x (ISBN 0-88295-400-8). AHM Pub.

Boorman, John T., jt. auth. see Havrilesky, Thomas M.

Boorman, John T., jt. ed. see Havrilesky, Thomas M.

Boorman, Linda. The Giant Trunk Mystery. 96p. (gr. 6-12). 1981. pap. 2.25 (ISBN 0-686-69419-8). Victor Bks.

Boorman, Scott A. Protracted Game: A Wei-Ch'i Interpretation of Maoist Revolutionary Strategy. LC 70-83039. 1969. 14.95 (ISBN 0-19-500490-6). Oxford U Pr.

Boorman, Scott A. & Levitt, Paul R. The Genetics of Altruism. LC 79-52792. 1980. 29.50 (ISBN 0-12-115650-8). Acad Pr.

Boorstein, Seymour & Speeth, Kathleen, eds. Explorations in Transpersonal Psychotherapy. LC 80-51704. 1980. 19.95 (ISBN 0-8314-0060-9). Sci & Behavior.

Boorstin, Daniel. The Exploring Spirit: America & the World, Then & Now. LC 77-4454. 1977. pap. 2.45 (ISBN 0-394-72423-2, V-423, Vin). Random.

Boorstin, Daniel J. The Americans: The National Experience. 1967. pap. 5.95 (ISBN 0-394-70358-8, V-358, Vin). Random.

--Democracy & Its Discontents: Reflections on Everyday America. LC 74-20812. pap. 2.45 (ISBN 0-394-71501-2, V-501, Vin). Random.

--Genius of American Politics, 1958. (Walgreen Foundation Lectures). 10.50 (ISBN 0-226-06490-5, Phoen). U of Chicago Pr.

--The Lost World of Thomas Jefferson. LC 80-26835. 320p. 1981. pap. 6.95 (ISBN 0-226-06496-4). U of Chicago Pr.

Boorstin, Paul. The Accursed. 1977. pap. 1.75 o.p. (ISBN 0-451-07745-8, E7745, Sig). NAL.

Boorstin, Paul & Boorstin, Sharon. The Glory Hand. 320p. 1981. 12.95 (ISBN 0-399-90100-0). Marek.

Boorstin, Sharon, jt. auth. see Boorstin, Paul.

Boos, Robert V., jt. auth. see Jancura, Elise G.

Booss, Bernhelm & Niss, Mogens. Mathematics & the Real World. (Interdisciplinary Systems Research: No. 68). 1979. pap. 22.00 (ISBN 3-7643-1079-0). Birkhauser.

Boot, John C. & Cox, Edwin. Statistical Analysis for Managerial Decisions. 2nd ed. (Illus.). 672p. 1973. text ed. 18.95 (ISBN 0-07-006518-7, C); instructor's manual 4.95 (ISBN 0-07-006519-5). McGraw.

Booth, Alice L. Careers in Politics for the New Woman. (Choosing Careers & Life-Styles Ser.). (Illus.). (gr. 7 up). 1978. PLB 7.90 s&l (ISBN 0-531-01313-8). Watts.

Booth, Arthur J. Saint-Simon & Saint-Simonism: A Chapter in the History of Socialism in France. 202p. 1970. Repr. of 1871 ed. text ed. 34.25x (ISBN 90-6090-161-4). Humanities.

Booth, Charles. The Aged Poor in England & Wales, London 1894. LC 79-56948. (The English Working Class Ser.). 1980. lib. bdg. 40.00 (ISBN 0-8240-0103-6). Garland Pub.

Booth, Cindy. Getting Your Child into TV Commercials. LC 79-26106. 1980. pap. 2.95 (ISBN 0-87576-087-2). Pilot Bks.

Booth, David. Eura & Zephrya...with Poetical Pieces, Repr. Of 1816. Bd. with Elizabeth Hitchener (1783?-1822) The Fire-Side Bagatelle, Containing Enigmas on the Chief Towns of England & Wales. Hitchener, Elizabeth. Repr. of 1818 ed; The Weald of Sussex, a Poem. Repr. of 1822 ed. LC 75-31163. (Romantic Context Ser.: Poetry 1789-1830: Vol. 18). 1978. lib. bdg. 47.00 (ISBN 0-8240-2117-7). Garland Pub.

Booth, Edwin. Ambush at Adams Crossing. 192p. (YA) 1976. 4.95 o.p. (ISBN 0-685-64243-7, Avalon). Bouregy.

--The Colt-Packin' Parson. 192p. (YA) 1976. 5.95 (ISBN 0-685-57546-2, Avalon). Bouregy.

--Crossfire. 1977. pap. 1.75 (ISBN 0-441-12270-1). Ace Bks.

Booth, Eugene. At the Beach. LC 77-7659. (A Raintree Spotlight Book). (Illus.). (gr. k-3). 1977. PLB 8.25 (ISBN 0-8393-0111-1). Raintree Child.

--At the Circus. LC 77-7946. (A Raintree Spotlight Book). (Illus.). (gr. k-3). 1977. PLB 8.25 (ISBN 0-8393-0112-X). Raintree Child.

--At the Fair. LC 77-7961. (A Raintree Spotlight Book). (Illus.). (gr. k-3). 1977. PLB 8.25 (ISBN 0-8393-0114-6). Raintree Child.

--At the Zoo. LC 77-7627. (A Raintree Spotlight Book). (Illus.). (gr. k-3). 1977. PLB 8.25 (ISBN 0-8393-0107-3). Raintree Child.

--In the Air. LC 77-7984. (A Raintree Spotlight Book). (Illus.). (gr. k-3). 1977. PLB 8.25 (ISBN 0-8393-0105-7). Raintree Child.

--In the City. LC 77-7949. (A Raintree Spotlight Book). (Illus.). (gr. k-3). 1977. PLB 8.25 (ISBN 0-8393-0109-X). Raintree Child.

--In the Garden. LC 77-7628. (A Raintree Spotlight Book). (Illus.). (gr. k-3). 1977. PLB 8.25 (ISBN 0-8393-0115-4). Raintree Child.

--In the Jungle. LC 77-7947. (A Raintree Spotlight Book). (Illus.). (gr. k-3). 1977. PLB 8.25 (ISBN 0-8393-0104-9). Raintree Child.

--In the Park. LC 77-7622. (A Raintree Spotlight Book). (Illus.). (gr. k-3). 1977. PLB 8.25 (ISBN 0-8393-0106-5). Raintree Child.

--On the Farm. LC 77-7965. (A Raintree Spotlight Book). (Illus.). (gr. k-3). 1977. PLB 8.25 (ISBN 0-8393-0113-8). Raintree Child.

--Under the Ground. LC 77-8037. (A Raintree Spotlight Book). (Illus.). (gr. k-3). 1977. PLB 8.25 (ISBN 0-8393-0110-3). Raintree Child.

--Under the Ocean. LC 77-7983. (A Raintree Spotlight Book). (Illus.). (gr. k-3). 1977. PLB 8.25 (ISBN 0-8393-0108-1). Raintree Child.

Booth, George. Pussycats Need Love, Too. LC 80-17198. 128p. 1980. 8.95 (ISBN 0-396-07906-7). Dodd.

--Rehearsal's Off. LC 78-41380. (Illus.). 1976. 7.95 (ISBN 0-396-07389-1). Dodd.

--Think Good Thoughts About a Pussycat. LC 75-12929. (Illus.). 128p. 1975. 6.95 (ISBN 0-396-07224-0). Dodd.

Booth, George, et al, eds. Animals, Animals, Animals. LC 79-1653. (Illus.). 256p. 1981. pap. 8.95 (ISBN 0-06-090853-X, C*N 853, CN). Har-Row.

Booth, Grayce M. The Distributed System Environment. (Illus.). 288p. 1980. 21.95 (ISBN 0-07-006507-1, P&RB). McGraw.

--Functional Analysis of Information Processing. LC 80-11247. 288p. 1981. Repr. of 1973 ed. lib. bdg. write for info. (ISBN 0-89874-135-1). Krieger.

Booth, J. E. Textile Mathematics, Vol. 3. 18.00 (ISBN 0-87245-588-2). Textile Bk.

Booth, James. Writers & Politics in Nigeria. LC 80-17670. (Writers & Politics Ser.). 128p. 1981. text ed. 23.75x (ISBN 0-8419-0650-5, Africana); pap. text ed. 13.95x (ISBN 0-8419-0651-3). Holmes & Meier.

Booth, John A. The End & the Beginning: The Nicaraguan Revolution. (Special Studies on Latin America & the Caribbean). (Illus.). 225p. (Orig.). 1981. lib. bdg. 20.00x (ISBN 0-89158-939-2); pap. text ed. 10.00x (ISBN 0-86531-148-X). Westview.

Booth, John A. & Seligson, Mitchell A., eds. Citizen & State: Vol. 1 of Political Participation in Latin America. LC 77-16666. 260p. 1978. 27.00x (ISBN 0-8419-0334-4); pap. text ed. 10.50x (ISBN 0-8419-0376-X). Holmes & Meier.

Booth, Julianne. Books of the New Testament. (Arch Book Supplement Ser.). 1981. pap. 0.79 (ISBN 0-570-06150-4, 59-1305). Concordia.

--Books of the Old Testament. (Arch Book Supplement Ser.). 1981. pap. 0.79 (ISBN 0-570-06151-2, 59-1306). Concordia.

Booth, K. M. Dictionary of Refrigeration & Air Conditioning. 1970. 29.90x (ISBN 0-444-20069-X, Pub. by Applied Science). Burgess-Intl Ideas.

Booth, Ken & Wright, Moorhead, eds. American Thinking About Peace & War: New Essays on American Thought & Attitudes. 1978. text ed. 18.50x (ISBN 0-06-490581-0). B&N.

Booth, Martin. Devils' Wine. 112p. 1980. text ed. 16.25x (ISBN 0-86140-044-5); pap. text ed. 8.50x (ISBN 0-86140-044-5). Humanities.

Booth, Martin, jt. ed. see Macbeth, George.

Booth, Martin, et al. Bismarck. Yapp, Martin & Killingray, Margaret, eds. (Greenhaven World History Ser.). (Illus.). 32p. (gr. 10). 1980. lib. bdg. 5.95 (ISBN 0-89908-048-0); pap. text ed. 1.95 (ISBN 0-89908-023-5). Greenhaven.

Booth, Michael R. Victorian Spectacular Theatre, Eighteen Fifty Yo Nineteen Ten. (Theatre Production Studies). (Illus.). 190p. 1981. price not set (ISBN 0-7100-0739-6). Routledge & Kegan.

Booth, Norman. Industrial Gases. LC 72-10293. 1973. pap. text ed. 9.25 (ISBN 0-08-016860-4). Pergamon.

Booth, Philip. Before Sleep. 96p. 1980. 11.95 (ISBN 0-670-15529-2). Viking Pr.

--Before Sleep. 1980. pap. 5.95 (ISBN 0-14-042286-2). Penguin.

Booth, Philip, jt. auth. see Reid, Donald.

Booth, S., et al, eds. Inspection & Measurement. (Engineering Craftsmen: No. H26). (Illus.). 1969. spiral bdg. 18.50x (ISBN 0-685-90149-1). Intl Ideas.

Booth, Sally S. Women of Seventy-Six. (gr. 4 up). 1974. 9.95g (ISBN 0-8038-8066-9). Hastings.

Booth, Stanley. A Centenary Tribute Sir Alfred Munnings 1878-1959: An Appreciation of the Artist & a Selection of His Paintings. (Illus.). 218p. 1978. 120.00 (ISBN 0-85667-043-X, Pub. by Sotheby Parke Bernet England). Biblio Dist.

Booth, Sterling R., Jr. Allergy Cures Your Allergist Never Mentioned. 1981. 12.95 (ISBN 0-87949-191-4). Ashley Bks.

Booth, Stuart, ed. The Aerofilms Book of England from the Air. (Illus.). 1979. 14.95 (ISBN 0-7137-0965-0, Pub by Blandford Pr England). Sterling.

Booth, Taylor L. Digital Network & Computer Systems. 2nd ed. LC 77-10832. 1978. text ed. 26.95 (ISBN 0-471-08842-0); tchrs. manual avail. (ISBN 0-471-03049-X). Wiley.

--Sequential Machines & Automata Theory. 608p. 1981. Repr. of 1967 ed. text ed. price not set (ISBN 0-89874-269-2). Krieger.

Booth, Taylor L. & Chien, Yi-Tzuu. Computing Fundamentals & Applications. LC 73-20157. 1974. 22.95 (ISBN 0-471-08847-1). Wiley.

Booth, Timothy A., ed. Planning for Welfare: Social Policy & the Expenditure Process. (Aspects of Social Policy Ser.). 1979. 29.50x (ISBN 0-631-19560-2, Pub. by Basil Blackwell); pap. 12.95 (ISBN 0-631-11571-4). Biblio Dist.

Booth, W. L. Police Management of Traffic Accident Prevention Programs. 384p. 1980. 29.50 (ISBN 0-398-04008-7). C C Thomas.

Booth, Wayne C. A Rhetoric of Irony. LC 73-87298. xviii, 292p. 1975. 14.00x (ISBN 0-226-06552-9); pap. 5.95 (ISBN 0-226-06553-7, P641). U of Chicago Pr.

Boothby, Guy. Dr. Nikola Returns. LC 80-22358. (Dr. Nikola, Master of Occult Mystery: No. 2). 256p. 1980. Repr. of 1976 ed. lib. bdg. 9.95x (ISBN 0-89370-634-5). Borgo Pr.

--Enter Dr. Nikola! LC 80-22357. (Dr. Nikola, Master of Occult Mystery: No. 1). 256p. 1980. Repr. of 1975 ed. lib. bdg. 9.95x (ISBN 0-89370-632-9). Borgo Pr.

Booth-Clibborn, Edward, ed. Design & Art Direction Nineteen Seventy-Nine. 17th ed. Date not set. 42.50 o.p. (ISBN 0-8038-1567-0). Hastings.

--Design & Art Direction One Hundred Eighty: The 18th Annual of British Graphics, Advertising, Television & Editorial Design. (Visual Communications Bks.). (Illus.). 440p. 1980. cancelled o.p. (ISBN 0-8038-1574-3). Hastings.

Boothe, Joan N., jt. auth. see Council on Economic Priorities.

Boothroyd & Poli. Applied Engineering Mechanics: Statistics & Dynamics. 23.50 (ISBN 0-8247-6945-7). Dekker.

--Statistics & Dynamics. 472p. 1980. 23.50 (ISBN 0-8247-6945-7). Dekker.

Boothroyd, Carl W., jt. auth. see Roberts, Daniel A.

Boothroyd, Hylton. Articulate Intervention: The Interface of Science, Mathematics & Administration. LC 78-13026. (ORASA Text Ser.: No. 1). 1978. pap. 19.95 (ISBN 0-470-26536-1). Halsted Pr.

Boots, Andrew, et al. Inequality in Local Government Services: A Case Study of Neighborhood Roads. 1972. pap. 1.50 o.p. (ISBN 0-87766-063-8, 15000). Urban Inst.

Boots, B., jt. auth. see Getis, A.

Booty, John E. The Church in History. (Church's Teaching Ser.: Vol. 3). 1979. 9.50 (ISBN 0-8164-0420-8); pap. 3.95 (ISBN 0-8164-2216-8). Crossroad NY.

Booz, Elisabeth B. Seal of Jai. (Illus.). (gr. 4-6). 1968. 4.50g o.s.i. (ISBN 0-02-711760-X). Macmillan.

Booz, J., ed. see Symposium on Microdosimetry, Sixth, Brussels, Belgium, May 1978.

Bopp, William J. O. W. O. W. Wilson & the Search for a Police Profession. (National University Publications Interdisciplinary Urban Ser.). 1977. 12.95 (ISBN 0-8046-9179-7); pap. 7.95 (ISBN 0-8046-9201-7). Kennikat.

Bopp, William J. & Schultz, Donald O. A Short History of American Law Enforcement. (Illus.). 192p. 1977. pap. 8.75 (ISBN 0-398-02479-0). C C Thomas.

Bor, Josef. The Terezin Requiem. 1978. pap. 1.95 (ISBN 0-380-01673-7, 33449, Bard). Avon.

Bor, Walter. Making of Cities. (Illus.). 1972. 24.00x (ISBN 0-249-44071-7). Intl Ideas.

Borah, William E., jt. auth. see Baumbach, Richard O., Jr.

Borah, Woodrow, jt. auth. see Cook, Sherburne F.

Boraks, Jagna, tr. see Busza, Andrzej.

Boraston, Ian, et al. Workplace & Union. 1975. text ed. 11.95x o.p. (ISBN 0-435-85090-3). Heinemann Ed.

Borawska, Sr. M. Albertine. How to Have Fun Making a Rug. LC 74-14521. (Creative Craft Bks). (Illus.). 32p. (gr. 2-6). 1974. PLB 5.25 o.p. (ISBN 0-87191-359-3). Creative Ed.

Borba, Craig & Borba, Michele. The Good Apple Guide to Learning Centers. (gr. k-6). 1978. 11.95 (ISBN 0-916456-33-1, GA86). Good Apple.

Borba, Michele, jt. auth. see Borba, Craig.

Borch, Karl. The Mathematical Theory of Insurance. LC 73-11670. 352p. 1974. 24.95 (ISBN 0-669-86942-2). Lexington Bks.

Borchard, David C., et al. Your Career: Choices, Chances, Changes. 368p. 1980. pap. text ed. 15.95 (ISBN 0-8403-2293-3). Kendall-Hunt.

Borchard, Edwin M. Convicting the Innocent: Errors of Criminal Justice. LC 74-107406. (Civil Liberties in American History Ser). 1970. Repr. of 1932 ed. lib. bdg. 29.50 (ISBN 0-306-71886-3). Da Capo.

Borchardt, D. H. How to Find Out in Philosophy & Psychology. 1968. 11.25 (ISBN 0-08-012596-4); pap. 5.75 (ISBN 0-08-012595-6). Pergamon.

Borchardt, D. H. & Horacek, J. Librarianship in Australia, New Zealand & Oceania. 1976. 10.25 (ISBN 0-08-019920-8); pap. text ed. write for info. (ISBN 0-08-019752-3). Pergamon.

Borchardt, Jack & Redman, William, eds. Sludge & Its Ultimate Disposal. (Illus.). 1981. 37.50 (ISBN 0-250-40386-2). Ann Arbor Science.

Borchers, Elisabeth. Dear Sarah. Shub, Elisabeth, tr. from Ger. LC 80-14512. (Illus.). 32p. (gr. k-3). 1981. 9.95 (ISBN 0-688-80277-X); PLB 9.55 (ISBN 0-688-84277-1). Greenwillow.

Borchers, Mary, jt. auth. see Poole, Lon.

Borchert, Gerald L. Dynamics of Evangelism. LC 76-2866. 1976. 5.95 o.p. (ISBN 0-87680-468-7, 80468). Word Bks.

Borchert, H., ed. see Prokop, F. W.

Borchert, Wolfgang. Selected Short Stories. Hornsey, A. W., ed. 1964. 3.35 (ISBN 0-08-010714-1); pap. 3.00 (ISBN 0-08-010713-3). Pergamon.

Borchgrave, Arnaud de see De Borchgrave, Arnaud & Moss, Robert.

Borchgrevink, C. E. First on the Antarctic Continent. (Illus.). 333p. 1980. Repr. of 1901 ed. 49.00x (ISBN 0-7735-0515-6). McGill-Queens U Pr.

Borck, Leslie E. & Fawcett, Stephen B. Learning Counseling & Problem-Solving Skills. 350p. (Orig.). 1981. text ed. 26.00 (ISBN 0-917724-30-5); pap. text ed. 13.95 (ISBN 0-917724-35-6). Haworth Pr.

Bord, Colin, jt. auth. see Bord, Janet.

Bord, Janet & Bord, Colin. Alien Animals: A Worldwide Investigation. 248p. Date not set. pap. 6.95 (ISBN 0-13-021998-3). P-H. Postponed.

--The Secret Country. 1978. pap. 2.50 o.s.i. (ISBN 0-446-81648-5). Warner Bks.

Bordeau, Elvi L., tr. see Cancrinus, Franz L.

Bordeau, Kenneth V., tr. see Cancrinus, Franz L.

Bordeaux, Michael. Evidencia que Condeno a Aida Skripnikova. Vega, Pedro, tr. from Eng. 123p. (Orig., Span.). 1975. pap. 1.50 (ISBN 0-89922-060-6). Edit Caribe.

Bordelon, Abbe L. A History of the Ridiculous Extravagancies of Monsieur Oufle Occasion'd by His Reading Books Treating of Magick, the Black-Art Demoniacks... & Other Superstitious Practices. LC 76-170524. (Foundations of the Novel Ser.: Vol. 17). lib. bdg. 50.00 (ISBN 0-8240-0529-5). Garland Pub.

Borden, G. & Stone, J. Human Communication: The Process of Relating. LC 75-27821. 1976. 8.95 (ISBN 0-8465-0615-7). Benjamin-Cummings.

Borden, Gloria J. & Harris, Katherine S. Speech Science Primer: Physiology, Acoustics & Perception of Speech. (Illus.). 312p. 1980. pap. 20.95 (ISBN 0-683-00941-9). Williams & Wilkins.

Borden, Morton & Graham, Otis. The American Profile. 2nd ed. 1978. pap. text ed. 11.95x (ISBN 0-669-84822-0); inst. manual free (ISBN 0-669-99994-6). Heath.

Borden, Morton & Graham, Otis L. Speculations on American History. 1977. pap. text ed. 5.95x (ISBN 0-669-00488-X). Heath.

Borden, Morton & Borden, Penn, eds. The American Tory. LC 73-168739. (Great Lives Observed). 160p. 1972. 8.95 (ISBN 0-13-031393-9, Spec); pap. 2.45 o.p. (ISBN 0-13-031385-8, Spec). P-H.

Borden, Penn, jt. ed. see Borden, Morton.

Borden, Weston T. Modern Molecular Orbital Theory for Organic Chemists. (Illus.). 336p. 1975. 22.95 (ISBN 0-13-595983-7). P-H.

Bordet, E., jt. auth. see Vaquez, H.

Bordewijk, Ferdinand. Character: A Novel of Father & Son. Price, E. M., tr. 1966. 12.95 (ISBN 0-7206-1611-5). Dufour.

Bordin, Edward S. Research Strategies in Psychotherapy. LC 74-11272. (Personality Processes Ser). 272p. 1974. 24.95 (ISBN 0-471-08885-4, Pub. by Wiley-Interscience). Wiley.

Bordin, Ruth. Woman & Temperance: The Quest for Power & Liberty, 1873 to 1900. Davis, Allen F., ed. (American Civilization Ser.). 220p. 1980. 17.50 (ISBN 0-87722-157-X). Temple U Pr.

Bordman, Gerald. American Operetta: From H.M.S. Pinafore to Sweeney Todd. (Illus.). 240p. 1981. 15.95 (ISBN 0-19-502869-4). Oxford U Pr.

Bordman, Marcia Beth, et al. Practical English Structure. (Practical English Structure Ser: ol. 1). (Illus.). 224p. 1981. text ed. 6.95 (ISBN 0-913580-65-1). Gallaudet Coll.

Bordow, Allan, ed. The Worker in Australia: A Behavioral Science Perspective. (Illus.). 1978. text ed. 21.75x (ISBN 0-7022-1473-6); pap. text ed. 12.75x (ISBN 0-7022-1474-4). U of Queensland Pr.

Bordow, Joan W., jt. auth. see Rosenberg, Sharon.

Bordwell, David. Filmguide to la Passion de Jeanne d'arc. LC 72-88634. (Filmguide Ser: No. 1). 96p. 1973. 5.00x (ISBN 0-253-39301-9); pap. 1.75 (ISBN 0-253-39302-7). Ind U Pr.

--The Films of Carl-Theodor Dreyer. 1981. 23.50 (ISBN 0-520-03987-4). U of Cal Pr.

Bordwell, Sally, jt. auth. see Sussman, Les.

Borei, Dorothy, ed. see Bodde, Derk.

Borek, Carmia & Williams, Gary M., eds. Differentiation & Carcinogenesis in Liver Cell Cultures. new ed. LC 80-20918. (Vol. 349). 429p. 1980. 83.00 (ISBN 0-89766-087-0). NY Acad Sci.

Borek, Ernest. Atoms Within Us. LC 61-6159. (Illus.). (gr. 9 up). 1961. 17.00x (ISBN 0-231-02391-X); pap. 5.00x (ISBN 0-231-08535-4). Columbia U Pr.

--The Atoms Within Us. rev. ed. LC 80-19010. 272p. 1980. text ed. 20.00x (ISBN 0-231-04386-4); pap. text ed. 6.00x (ISBN 0-231-04387-2). Columbia U Pr.

--Code of Life. LC 65-10944. 1965. 16.00x o.p. (ISBN 0-231-02634-X); pap. 5.00x o.p. (ISBN 0-231-08630-X). Columbia U Pr.

--The Sculpture of Life. LC 73-6831. (Illus.). 192p. 1973. 17.50x (ISBN 0-231-03425-3); pap. 4.00x (ISBN 0-231-08334-3). Columbia U Pr.

Borek, Ernest, jt. ed. see Monod, Jacques.

Borel, A., ed. Automorphic Forms, Representations & L-Functions, 2 vols. LC 78-21184. (Proceedings of Symposia in Pure Mathematics: Vol. 33). 1980. 34.00 set (ISBN 0-686-52415-2, PSPUM-33); Pt. 1. 20.00 (ISBN 0-8218-1435-4); Pt. 2. 20.00 (ISBN 0-685-99018-4). Am Math.

Borelli, Luigi & Borelli, Mary. Leggende E Racconti Italiani E Quindici Canzoni Popolavi Tradizionali: An Easy Reader for Beginners. 1979. pap. 3.95 (ISBN 0-913298-03-4). S F Vanni.

Borelli, Marianne & Heidt, Patricia. Therapeutic Touch: A Book of Readings. LC 80-14109. 1980. pap. text ed. 14.95 (ISBN 0-8261-3111-5). Springer Pub.

Borelli, Mary, jt. auth. see Borelli, Luigi.
Boreman, Thomas. Gigantick Histories of the Two Famous Giants of Guildhall. Lurie, Alison & Schiller, Justin G., eds. LC 75-32140. (Classics of Children's Literature Ser.: 1621-1932). PLB 38.00 (ISBN 0-8240-2256-4). Garland Pub.
Boren, et al. Apple Tree: Pre-Post Test Booklet. 52p. (gr. 1 up). 1972. 4.95 (ISBN 0-86575-026-2). Dormac.
Boren, Henry C. The Ancient World: An Historical Perspective. (Illus.). 384p. 1976. ref. ed. 16.95x (ISBN 0-13-036442-8). P-H.
Boresi, Arthur P. & Lynn, Paul P. Elasticity in Engineering Mechanics. (Civil Engineering & Engineering Mechanics Ser.). 1974. 31.95 (ISBN 0-13-247080-2). P-H.
Boresi, Arthur P., et al. Advanced Mechanics of Materials. 3rd ed. LC 77-28283. 1978. text ed. 35.50 (ISBN 0-471-08892-7). Wiley.
Boretz, Benjamin. Language, As a Music: Six Marginal Pretexts for Composition. LC 80-80807. (Illus.). 88p. 1980. lib. bdg. 15.75. Lingua Pr.
Boreus, Lars O. Principles of Paediatric Clinical Pharmacology. (Monographs in Clinical Pharmacology). (Illus.). 1981. text ed. write for info. (ISBN 0-443-08006-2). Churchill.
Borevich, Z. I. & Shafarevich, I. R. Number Theory. (Pure and Applied Mathematics: Vol. 20). 1966. text ed. 22.50 (ISBN 0-12-117850-1). Acad Pr.
Borg, Alan. Architectural Sculpture in Romanesque Provence. (Oxford Studies in the History of Art & Architecture). 210p. 1972. 37.50x (ISBN 0-19-817192-7). Oxford U Pr.
Borg, Dorothy & Okamoto, Shumpei, eds. Pearl Harbor As History: Japanese-American Relations, 1931-1941. 830p. 1973. 35.00x (ISBN 0-231-03734-1); pap. 14.00x (ISBN 0-231-03890-9). Columbia U Pr.
Borg, Gunnar, ed. Physical Work Effort. LC 76-45405. 1977. text ed. 49.00 (ISBN 0-08-021373-1). Pergamon.
Borg, John. Descriptive Flora of the Maltese Islands Including the Ferns & Flowering Plants. 846p. 1976. pap. text ed. 108.90 (ISBN 3-87429-104-9). Lubrecht & Cramer.
Borg, Susan O. & Lasker, Judith. When Pregnancy Fails: Families Coping with Miscarriage, Stillbirth & Infant Death. LC 80-68167. 224p. 1981. 12.95 (ISBN 0-8070-3226-3, BP 613); pap. 6.95 (ISBN 0-8070-3227-1). Beacon Pr.
Borg, Walter R. Applying Educational Research: A Practical Guide for Teachers. 368p. (Orig.). 1981. text ed. 14.50 (ISBN 0-582-28145-8). Longman.
Borg, Walter R. & Gall, Meredith D. Educational Research: An Introduction. 3rd ed. LC 77-17723. 1978. text ed. 17.95x (ISBN 0-582-28056-7); instrs' manual free (ISBN 0-582-28120-2). Longman.
Borgaonkar, Digamber S. Chromosomal Variations in Man: A Catalog of Chromosomal Variants & Anomalies. 3rd ed. LC 80-81466. 846p. 1980. 58.00x (ISBN 0-8451-0206-0). A R Liss.
Borgatta, Edgar F. & Jackson, David J., eds. Aggregate Data: Analysis & Interpretation. LC 79-23909. 1980. 18.50 (ISBN 0-8039-1428-8); pap. 8.95 (ISBN 0-8039-1429-6). Sage.
Borgatta, Edgar F., jt. ed. see Jackson, David J.
Borgatta, Edgar F., et al. Social Workers' Perceptions of Clients: A Study of the Caseload of a Social Agency. LC 80-27204. 92p. 1981. Repr. of 1960 ed. lib. bdg. 17.50x (ISBN 0-313-22812-4, BOSW). Greenwood.
Borge, Victor. My Favorite Intermissions. 1971. 5.95 o.p. (ISBN 0-385-02651-X). Doubleday.
Borgella, F. F. Justice! Par un Officier De l'Armee De Paris. (Commune De Paris En 1871). (Fr.). 1977. lib. bdg. 13.75x o.p. (ISBN 0-8287-0119-9); pap. text ed. 3.75x o.p. (ISBN 0-685-74928-2). Clearwater Pub.
Borgen, C. Winston, jt. auth. see Miller, Gary A.
Borgen, Joe, jt. auth. see Davis, Dwight.
Borger, Gary A. Naturals: Foods Organisms of the Trout. (Illus.). 224p. 1980. 15.95 (ISBN 0-8117-1006-8). Stackpole.
Borger, R. & Cioffi, F., eds. Explanation in the Behavioural Sciences. LC 71-105497. 1970. 57.50 (ISBN 0-521-07820-2); pap. 16.95x (ISBN 0-521-09905-6). Cambridge U Pr.
Borges, J. L. Irish Strategies. (Dolmen Editions: No. XXI). (Illus.). 87p. 1975. text ed. 39.00x (ISBN 0-85105-277-0, Dolmen Pr). Humanities.
Borges, Jorge L. Borges on Writing. Di Giovanni, Norman T., et al, eds. 1973. pap. 2.95 o.p. (ISBN 0-525-47352-1). Dutton.
--Ficciones. Kerrigan, Anthony, ed. & intro. by. 1962. pap. 3.45 (ISBN 0-394-17244-2, E368, Ever). Grove.
--The Gold of the Tigers: Selected Later Poems. Reid, Alastair, tr. (Bilingual ed.). 1977. 8.95 o.p.; pap. 3.95 (ISBN 0-525-03465-X). Dutton.
--In Praise of Darkness. Di Giovanni, Norman T., tr. LC 73-79553. 1974. 8.95 o.p.; pap. 4.95 (ISBN 0-525-03635-0). Dutton.
--Introduction to American Literature. Evans, Robert O. & Keating, L. Clark, eds. Evans, Robert O. & Keating, L. Clark, trs. from Span. LC 73-147854. 108p. 1971. 8.00x (ISBN 0-8131-1247-8). U Pr of Ky.
--An Introduction to English Literature. Evans, Robert O. & Keating, L. Clark, eds. Evans, Robert O. & Keating, L. Clark, trs. from Span. LC 73-86401. 88p. 1974. 7.00x (ISBN 0-8131-1307-5). U Pr of Ky.
--Labyrinths, Selected Stories & Other Writings. Yates, Donald A. & Irby, James E., eds. LC 64-25440. (Fr). 1969. pap. 3.95 (ISBN 0-8112-0012-4, NDP186). New Directions.
--Six Problems for Don Isidro Parodi. Skedgell, Marian, ed. 160p. 1981. 10.95 (ISBN 0-525-20480-6). Dutton.
Borgese, Elisabeth M., jt. auth. see Adizes, Ichak.
Borgese, Elisabeth M. & Ginsburg, Norton, eds. Ocean Yearbook Two. LC 79-642855. 1981. 35.00x (ISBN 0-226-06603-7). U of Chicago Pr.
Borgese, Elisabeth M., jt. ed. see Adizes, Ichak.
Borgese, Elizabeth M., tr. see Schenker, Heinrich.
Borgeson, Paul W., tr. see Cardenal, Ernesto.
Borghese, Anita. The Down to Earth Cookbook. rev. ed. LC 80-21483. (Illus.). 128p. (gr. 3 up). 1980. 8.95 (ISBN 0-684-16618-6). Scribner.
--Foods from Harvest Festivals & Folk Fairs. LC 77-968. (Illus.). 1977. 9.95 o.s.i. (ISBN 0-690-01655-7, TYC-T). T Y Crowell.
Borglum, Lincoln & DenDooven, Gweneth R. Mount Rushmore: The Story Behind the Scenery. LC 76-57455. (Illus.). 1977. 7.95 (ISBN 0-916122-45-X); pap. 3.00 (ISBN 0-916122-20-4). K C Pubns.
Borgo, Ludovico. The Works of Mariotto Abertinelli. LC 75-23781. (Outstanding Dissertations in the Fine Arts - 16th Century). (Illus.). 1976. lib. bdg. 60.50 (ISBN 0-8240-1978-4). Garland Pub.
Borgo, S. Del see Del Borgo, S.
Borgstedt, Doug & Borgstedt, Jean. The Pet Set, Bk II. 1979. pap. 2.00 (ISBN 0-87666-637-3, PS-766). TFH Pubns.
Borgstedt, Jean, jt. auth. see Borgstedt, Doug.
Borgstrom, Georg. Focal Points. (Illus.). 288p. 1973. pap. 8.95 o.s.i. (ISBN 0-02-513650-X). Macmillan.
Borgstrom, George. Too Many: The Biological Limitations of Our Earth. 1969. 7.95 o.s.i. (ISBN 0-02-513660-7). Macmillan.
Borhek, James T. & Curtis, Richard F. A Sociology of Belief. LC 80-12472. 216p. 1981. Repr. of 1975 ed. lib. bdg. write for info. (ISBN 0-89874-177-7). Krieger.
--Sociology of Belief. LC 74-26584. 192p. 1975. 11.50 o.p. (ISBN 0-471-08895-1, Pub. by Wiley-Interscience). Wiley.
Borich, Gary D. Appraisal of Teaching: Concepts & Process. LC 76-6007. (Illus.). 1977. text ed. 14.95 (ISBN 0-201-00841-6). A-W.
Borich, Gary D. & Madden, Susan K. Evaluating Classroom Instruction: A Source-Book of Instruments. LC 76-2953. 1977. text ed. 18.95 (ISBN 0-201-00842-4). A-W.
Borich, Gary D., jt. auth. see Kash, Marilynn M.
Boring, Edwin G. Sensation & Perception in the History of Experimental Psychology. (Century Psychology Ser). 1977. 34.50x (ISBN 0-89197-491-1); pap. text ed. 19.50x (ISBN 0-89197-933-6). Irvington.
Boring, Edwin G., jt. ed. see Herrnstein, Richard J.
Boring, M. Eugene, tr. see Lohse, Eduard.
Boring, Mel. Clowns: The Fun Makers. LC 80-17193. (Illus.). 128p. (gr. 7 up). 1980. PLB 8.29 (ISBN 0-671-33059-4). Messner.
--Wovoka. LC 80-24003. (Story of an American Indian Ser.). (Illus.). 64p. (gr. 5 up). 1981. PLB 6.95 (ISBN 0-87518-179-1). Dillon.
Boring, Phyllis L. Elena Quiroga. (World Authors Ser.: No.459). 1977. lib. bdg. 12.50 (ISBN 0-8057-6296-5). Twayne.
Borish, Irving, jt. auth. see Brooks, Clifford F.
Borisoff, Norman. Bird Seed & Lightning. LC 72-75125. (Mystery & Adventure Ser.). (gr. 2-4). 1973. PLB 6.75 (ISBN 0-87191-206-6). Creative Ed.
--Unknown Avenues. LC 72-77224. (Mystery & Adventure Ser.). (gr. 2-4). 1973. PLB 6.75 (ISBN 0-87191-205-8). Creative Ed.
--Walkie-Talkie Patrol. LC 72-75122. (Mystery & Adventure Ser.). (gr. 2-4). 1973. PLB 6.75 (ISBN 0-87191-097-7). Creative Ed.
--Who's There. LC 72-75123. (Mystery & Adventure Ser.). (gr. 2-4). 1973. PLB 6.75 (ISBN 0-87191-098-5). Creative Ed.
Bork, Albert W. & Maier, Georg. Historical Dictionary of Ecuador. LC 73-11256. (Latin-American Historical Dictionaries Ser.: No. 10). 1973. 10.00 (ISBN 0-8108-0638-X). Scarecrow.
Bork, Alfred. Learning with Computers. (Illus.). 250p. 1981. 24.00 (ISBN 0-932376-11-8). Digital Pr.
Bork, Paul F. The World of Moses. LC 78-5022. (Horizon Ser.). 1978. pap. 4.95 (ISBN 0-8127-0166-6). Southern Pub.
Borka, H., jt. ed. see Slamecka, V.
Borkenau, Franz. World Communism: A History of the Communist International. 1962. pap. 6.50 (ISBN 0-472-06067-8, 67, AA). U of Mich Pr.
Borkowski, John G. & Anderson, D. Chris. Experimental Psychology: Tactics of Behavioral Research. 1977. pap. 11.95x (ISBN 0-673-15085-2). Scott F.
Borkowski, John G., jt. auth. see Anderson, D. Chris.
Borkowski, L., jt. auth. see Slupecki, J.
Borland, D. M. Homeopathy in Practice. Priestman, Kathleen, ed. 230p. 1980. 25.00x (Pub. by Beaconsfield England). State Mutual Bk.
Borland, Hal. A Countryman's Flowers. LC 80-2698. (Illus.). 208p. 1981. 22.50 (ISBN 0-394-51893-4). Knopf.
--The Golden Circle: A Book of Months. LC 77-23560. (Illus.). (gr. 5 up). 1977. 10.95 (ISBN 0-690-03803-8, TYC-J). T Y Crowell.
--Penny: The Story of a Free-Soul Basset Hound. LC 74-37927. (Illus.). (YA) 1972. 7.95 (ISBN 0-397-00864-3). Lippincott.
--Seasons. LC 73-5988. (Illus.). 1973. 14.95 o.s.i. (ISBN 0-397-00996-8). Lippincott.
Borland, Hal G. When the Legends Die. LC 63-11753. (gr. 10 up). 1963. 9.95 (ISBN 0-397-00303-X). Lippincott.
Borland, Marie, ed. Violence in the Family. 1976. text ed. 19.50x (ISBN 0-391-00610-X). Humanities.
Borlick, Martha M., et al. Community Health Nursing. 2nd ed. (Nursing Examination Bk.: Vol. 9). 1974. spiral bdg. 5.00 o.p. (ISBN 0-87488-509-4). Med Exam.
Borman, Lorraine, jt. auth. see Mittman, Benjamin.
Bormann, E., et al. Interpersonal Communication in the Modern Organization. 1969. text ed. 15.95 (ISBN 0-13-475038-1). P-H.
Bormuth, Robert, jt. auth. see Usher, Michael.
Bormuth, Robert, jt. auth. see Usher, Michael A.
Born, Anne, tr. see Dinesen, Isak.
Born, M. Physics in My Generation. 2nd rev. ed. LC 68-59281. (Heidelberg Science Lib: Vol. 7). (Illus.). 1969. pap. 7.30 (ISBN 0-387-90008-X). Springer-Verlag.
Born, M. & Wolf, E. Principles of Optics: Electromagnetic Theory of Propagation, Interference & Diffraction of Light. 6th ed. (Illus.). 808p. 1980. 50.00 (ISBN 0-08-026482-4); pap. 27.50 (ISBN 0-08-026481-6). Pergamon.
Born, Max. Einstein's Theory of Relativity. rev. ed. 1962. pap. 4.95 (ISBN 0-486-60769-0). Dover.
Born, Warren C., ed. The Foreign Language Teacher in Today's Classroom Environment. 1979. pap. 7.95x (ISBN 0-915432-79-X). NE Conf Teach.
--Goals Clarification: Curriculum, Teaching, Evaluation. 1975. pap. 7.95x. NE Conf Teach.
--Language: Acquisition, Application, Appreciation. Incl. Language Acquisition. Cintas, Pierre F; Language Application. Elaster, Kenneth; Language Appreciation. Bure, Germaine. 1977. pap. 7.95x (ISBN 0-915432-77-3). NE Conf Teach Foreign.
--Language & Culture: Heritage & Horizons. 1976. pap. 7.95x (ISBN 0-915432-76-5). NE Conf Teach Foreign.
Born, Warren C. & Geno, Thomas H., eds. New Contents, New Teachers, New Publics. 1978. pap. 7.95x (ISBN 0-915432-78-1). NE Conf Teach.
Born, Wina. Famous Dishes of the World. Powell, Marian, tr. (Illus.). 1973. pap. 3.95 o.s.i. (ISBN 0-02-009240-7, Collier). Macmillan.
Borneman, Henry S. Pennsylvania German Illuminated Manuscripts: A Classification of Fraktur-Schriften & an Inquiry into Their History & Art. (Illus.). 8.50 (ISBN 0-685-56779-6). Peter Smith.
Bornkamm, Gunther. Jesus of Nazareth. LC 61-5256. 240p. 1975. pap. 6.95 (ISBN 0-06-060932-X, RD113, HarpR). Har-Row.
--Paul. Stalker, D. M., tr. from Ger. LC 70-85068. 1971. 12.95x (ISBN 0-06-060933-8, HarpR). Har-Row.
Bornoff, Jack, ed. Music Theatre in a Changing Society: The Influence of the Technical Media. 1968. pap. 6.00 (ISBN 92-3-100709-2, U397, UNESCO). Unipub.
Bornstedt, Marianne Von see Von Bornstedt, Marianne & Prytz, Ulla.
Bornstein. Little Gorilla. (ps-3). pap. 1.50 (ISBN 0-590-11869-2, Schol Pap). Schol Bk Serv.
Bornstein, Harry. The Holiday Book. (Signed English Ser.). 48p. 1974. pap. 3.50 (ISBN 0-913580-30-9). Gallaudet Coll.
--Mouse's Christmas Eve. (Signed English Ser.). 44p. pap. 3.50 (ISBN 0-913580-28-7). Gallaudet Coll.
--The Signed English Dictionary. Miller, Ralph, tr. (Signed English Ser.). (Illus.). 300p. 1975. 17.50 (ISBN 0-913580-46-5). Gallaudet Coll.
--Stores. (Signed English Ser.). 56p. 1974. pap. 4.00 (ISBN 0-913580-33-3). Gallaudet Coll.
--Three Little Kittens. (Signed English Ser.). 32p. 1974. pap. 3.00 (ISBN 0-913580-16-3). Gallaudet Coll.
Bornstein, Morris, ed. Comparative Economic Systems: Models & Cases. 4th ed. 1979. text ed. 18.50x (ISBN 0-256-02152-X). Irwin.
--The Soviet Economy: Continuity & Change. 532p. (Orig.). 1981. lib. bdg. 26.50x (ISBN 0-89158-958-9); pap. text ed. 12.00x (ISBN 0-89158-959-7). Westview.
Bornstein, Richard, jt. ed. see Yarbro, John.
Bornstein, Ruth. Annabelle. LC 77-20059. (Illus.). (gr. k-1). 1978. 5.89 (ISBN 0-690-03804-6, TYC-J); PLB 4.79 (ISBN 0-690-03810-0). T Y Crowell.
--The Dancing Man. LC 77-29124. (Illus.). (gr. 1-4). 1978. 6.95 (ISBN 0-395-28770-7, Clarion). HM.
--The Dream of the Little Elephant. LC 76-27748. (Illus.). (ps-3). 6.95 (ISBN 0-395-28771-5, Clarion). HM.
--Jim. LC 77-12712. (Illus.). (ps-3). 1978. 7.95 (ISBN 0-395-28772-3, Clarion). HM.
--Little Gorilla. LC 75-25508. (Illus.). 32p. (ps-2). 1976. 6.95 (ISBN 0-395-28773-1, Clarion). HM.
Boroch, Rose M. Elements of Rehabilitation in Nursing: An Introduction. LC 76-4590. (Illus.). 1976. pap. text ed. 13.95 (ISBN 0-8016-1425-2). Mosby.
Borodin, A., jt. auth. see Gotlieb, C. C.
Boron, Leon F., tr. see Gnedenko, Boris V. & Khinchin, Alexander Y.
Boros, Julius. Swing Easy, Hit Hard. 192p. 1968. pap. 2.95 (ISBN 0-346-12305-4). Cornerstone.
Boros, L. The Hidden God. 132p. 1973. 5.95 (ISBN 0-8164-1042-9). Crossroad NY.
Boros, Ladislaus. Angels & Men. 1976. 6.95 (ISBN 0-8164-0329-5). Crossroad NY.
--Being a Christian Today. Davies, M. Benedict, tr. LC 79-13607. 124p. 1979. 7.95 (ISBN 0-8164-0440-2). Crossroad NY.
--Christian Prayer. 1976. 5.95 (ISBN 0-8164-1199-9). Crossroad NY.
--The Closeness of God. 1978. pap. 3.95 (ISBN 0-8164-2175-7). Crossroad NY.
--The Mystery of Death. 216p. 1973. pap. 3.95 (ISBN 0-8164-9157-7). Crossroad NY.
--Pain & Providence. 132p. 1975. pap. 2.95 (ISBN 0-8164-2110-2). Crossroad NY.
Boros, Ladislaus, S.J. Living in Hope. 120p. 1973. pap. 1.45 (ISBN 0-385-00133-9, Im). Doubleday.
--Meeting God in Man. 1971. pap. 1.45 (ISBN 0-385-05377-0, Im). Doubleday.
Boros, Laszlo, tr. see Turanszky, Ilona.
Boross, L., jt. auth. see Kremmer, T.
Borow, Henry, et al. Career Guidance for a New Age. (Illus.). 336p. 1973. text ed. 17.75 (ISBN 0-395-14362-4, 3-05191). HM.
Borow, Maxwell. Fundamentals of Homeostasis. 2nd ed. 1977. spiral bdg. 8.50 o.p. (ISBN 0-87488-758-5). Med Exam.
Borowiec, Andrew. Yugoslavia After Tito. LC 77-83466. (Praeger Special Studies). 1977. 24.95 (ISBN 0-03-040916-0). Praeger.
Borowitz, Albert I. The Woman Who Murdered Black Satin: The Bermondsey Horror. 347p. 1981. 17.50 (ISBN 0-8142-0320-5). Ohio St U Pr.
Borowitz, Eugene B. Contemporary Christologies: A Jewish Response. LC 80-81051. 224p. (Orig.). 1980. pap. 7.95 (ISBN 0-8091-2305-3). Paulist Pr.
Borradaile, B. & Borradaile, R. Strasburg Manuscript: A Medieval Painters Handbook. 10.00 (ISBN 0-685-20636-X). Transatlantic.
Borradaile, L. A. & Potts, F. A. Invertebrata. 4th ed. 1961. text ed. 29.95x (ISBN 0-521-04285-2). Cambridge U Pr.
Borradaile, R., jt. auth. see Borradaile, B.
Borras, F. M. Russian Syntax: Aspects of Modern Russian Syntax & Vocabulary. 2nd ed. 1971. 27.50x (ISBN 0-19-815634-0); pap. 22.50x (ISBN 0-19-872029-7). Oxford U Pr.
Borras, F. M. & Christian, R. F. Russian Prose Composition: Annotated Passages for Translation into Russian. 1964. 4.50 o.p. (ISBN 0-19-815618-9); pap. 11.95x (ISBN 0-19-815646-4). Oxford U Pr.
Borras, Jose. El Inmenso Amor De Dios. 96p. (Span.). Date not set. pap. price not set (ISBN 0-311-43038-4). Casa Bautista.
Borras, Maria L. Sert: Mediterranean Architecture. LC 75-9108. (Illus.). 1975. 19.50 o.p. (ISBN 0-8212-0675-3). NYGS.
Borrello, Alfred. E. M. Forster: An Annotated Bibliography of Secondary Materials. LC 73-7990. (Author Bibliographies Ser.: No. 11). 1973. 10.00 (ISBN 0-8108-0668-1). Scarecrow.
--E. M. Forster Dictionary. LC 72-151091. 1971. 8.00 o.p. (ISBN 0-8108-0392-5). Scarecrow.
--An E. M. Forster Glossary. LC 74-188548. 1972. 12.00 (ISBN 0-8108-0475-1). Scarecrow.

--Gabriel Fielding. (English Authors Ser.: No. 162). 1974. lib. bdg. 10.95 (ISBN 0-8057-1194-5). Twayne.
Borri, Christoforo. Cochin-China: Containing Many Admirable Rarities of That Countrey. LC 71-25710. (English Experience Ser.: No. 223). 1970. Repr. of 1633 ed. 9.50 (ISBN 90-221-0223-8). Walter J Johnson.
Borrie, John. Management of Thoracic Emergencies. 3rd ed. (Illus.). 500p. 1979. 39.50x (ISBN 0-8385-6124-1). ACC.
Borrie, Y. M., jt. auth. see Burghes, D. N.
Borroff, Edith. Music in Europe & the United States: A History. (Illus.). 1971. text ed. 20.95 (ISBN 0-13-608083-9). P-H.
--The Music of the Baroque. LC 77-17401. (Music Reprint Ser.: 1978). (Illus.). 1978. Repr. of 1970 ed. lib. bdg. 20.00 (ISBN 0-306-77438-0). Da Capo.
--Notations & Editions. (Music Reprint Series). 1977. Repr. of 1974 ed. lib. bdg. 25.00 (ISBN 0-306-70867-1). Da Capo.
Borror, Donald & Glitz, Maurice L. Florida Bird Songs. 1980. pap. 4.50 record & booklet (ISBN 0-486-23956-X). Dover.
Borror, Donald J. Bird Song & Bird Behavior. 1971. pap. 4.50 booklet with record (ISBN 0-486-22779-0). Dover.
Borrowman, Merle L., ed. Teacher Education in America: A Documentary History. LC 65-17004. 1965. text ed. 9.75 (ISBN 0-8077-1104-7); pap. text ed. 5.25x (ISBN 0-8077-1101-2). Tchrs Coll.
Borsch, Frederick. Introducing the Lessons of the Church Year: A Guide for Lay Readers & Congregations. 1978. 8.95 (ISBN 0-8164-0396-1). Crossroad NY.
Borsch, Frederick H. Coming Together in the Spirit. 1981. 1.75 (ISBN 0-8358-0426-7). Forward Movement.
Borsch, Frederick H. & Napier, Davie. Advent-Christmas. Achtemeier, Elizabeth, et al, eds. LC 79-7377. (Proclamation 2: Aids for Interpreting the Lessons of the Church Year, Ser. A). 64p. (Orig.). 1980. pap. 2.50 (ISBN 0-8006-4091-8, 1-4091). Fortress.
Borsenik, Frank D. The Management of Maintenance & Engineering Systems in Hospitality Industries. LC 78-13677. (Service Management Ser.). 1979. text ed. 22.95 (ISBN 0-471-03213-1); solutions manual avail. (ISBN 0-471-05185-3); tchrs. manual (ISBN 0-471-05374-0). Wiley.
Borsheim, Roger. Earth Watch. 64p. 1980. 8.00 (ISBN 0-682-49634-0). Exposition.
Borsook, Eve. The Mural Painters of Tuscany: From Cimabue to Andrea Del Sarto. (Oxford Studies in the History of Art & Architecture Ser.). (Illus.). 400p. 1981. 165.00 (ISBN 0-19-817301-6). Oxford U Pr.
Borsook, Henry. Vitamins: What They Are. (Orig.). pap. 1.75 (ISBN 0-515-05132-2). Jove Pubns.
Borsos, Tibor, jt. auth. see Rapp, Herbert J.
Borst, Diane, jt. ed. see Montana, Patrick H.
Borsten, Orin, jt. auth. see Wilde, Meta C.
Borsuk, Karol. Multidimensional Analytic Geometry. 1969. 19.25 (ISBN 0-02-841690-2). Hafner.
--Theory of Shape. LC 76-359585. 379p. 1975. 37.50x (ISBN 0-8002-2343-8). Intl Pubns Serv.
Borten, Helen. Halloween. LC 65-16184. (Holiday Ser.). (Illus.). (gr. 1-3). 1965. PLB 7.89 (ISBN 0-690-36314-1, TYC-J). T Y Crowell.
Borthwick, Bruce M. Comparative Politics of the Middle East: An Introduction. 1980. pap. text ed. 10.50 (ISBN 0-13-154088-2). P-H.
Borthwick, J. D. Gold Hunters. LC 70-146785. 1971. Repr. of 1917 ed. 21.00 (ISBN 0-8103-3635-9). Gale.
Bortin, Virginia. Publicity for Volunteer Groups: A Handbook. 128p. 1981. 10.95 (ISBN 0-8027-0685-1); pap. 5.95 (ISBN 0-8027-7176-9). Walker & Co.
Borton, Hugh. Japan's Modern Century--from Perry to 1970. 2nd ed. 610p. 1970. 18.95 (ISBN 0-8260-1220-5). Wiley.
Borts, George H. & Stein, Jerome L. Economic Growth in a Free Market. LC 64-13735. 1964. 20.00x (ISBN 0-231-02666-8). Columbia U Pr.
Bortstein, Larry, jt. auth. see Berger, Phil.
Boruch, Robert F. & Cecil, Joe S. Assuring the Confidentiality of Social Research Data. LC 78-65113. (Illus.). 1979. 19.95x (ISBN 0-8122-7761-9). U of Pa Pr.
Boruch, Robert F., ed. see Social Science Research Council Conference on Social Experiments.
Boruvka, Otakar. Foundations of the Theory of Groupoids & Groups. LC 75-8625. 215p. 1976. Repr. of 1960 ed. 37.95 (ISBN 0-470-08965-2). Halsted Pr.
Borwick, Beverly. Catskill Country Cooking. LC 75-40761. (Illus.). 192p. 1976. pap. 4.95 o.s.i. (ISBN 0-8027-0528-6). Walker & Co.
Borys, Jurij. The Russian Communist Party & the Sovietization of Ukraine: A Study in the Communist Doctrine of the Self-Determination of Nations. LC 79-2895. 374p. 1981. Repr. of 1960 ed. 29.50 (ISBN 0-8305-0063-4). Hyperion Conn.
Borysenko, Myrin, et al. Functional Histology. 1978. text ed. 17.95 (ISBN 0-316-10303-9); pap. text ed. 12.95 (ISBN 0-316-10302-0). Little.
Borza, Eugene N., ed. see Wilcken, Ulrich.
Bos, A. P. On the Elements: Aristotle's Early Cosmology. 168p. 1972. text ed. 23.25x (ISBN 90-232-1027-1). Humanities.
Bos, H. J., et al, eds. see Symposium on the Life and Work of Christiaan Huygens, Amsterdam, 22-25 August 1979.
Bosanquet, Helen. The Strength of the People: A Study in Social Economics, London Nineteen Three. 2nd ed. LC 79-56950. (The English Working Class Ser.). 1980. lib. bdg. 30.00 (ISBN 0-8240-0104-4). Garland Pub.
Bosch, H. G., jt. auth. see DeHaan, M. R.
Bosch, H. G., jt. auth. see De Haan, Martin R.
Bosch, Paul. The Paschal Cycle. 1979. pap. 6.75 (ISBN 0-570-03796-4, 12-2778). Concordia.
--The Sermon As Part of the Liturgy. (Preacher's Workshop Ser.). 48p. 1977. pap. 2.25 (ISBN 0-570-07405-3, 12-2677). Concordia.
Bosch, Robert & Society of Automotive Engineers. Automotive Handbook. 1979. 10.95 (ISBN 0-89883-510-0). Soc Auto Engineers.
Boschke, F., et al, eds. Inorganic & Analytical Chemistry. LC 51-5497. (Topics in Current Chemistry: Vol. 14, Pt. 1). (Illus.). 1970. pap. 27.20 (ISBN 0-387-04816-2). Springer-Verlag.
Boschke, F. L., ed. Analytical Problems. (Topics in Current Chemistry Ser.: Vol. 95). (Illus.). 210p. 1981. 56.70 (ISBN 0-387-10402-X). Springer-Verlag.
--Van der Waals Systems. (Topics in Current Chemistry: Vol. 93). (Illus.). 140p. 1980. 40.20 (ISBN 0-387-10058-X). Springer-Verlag.
Bosco, F. J. & Lolli, F. Incontro Con l'Italiano: Primo Corso. 1967. text ed. 16.95 (ISBN 0-471-00040-X); tapes avail. (ISBN 0-471-00041-8). Wiley.
Bosco, James S. Encyclopedia of Physical Education, Fitness & Sports: Philosophy, History, Programs Administration, & Related Organizations, Vol. I. Turner, Mary A. & Cureton, Thomas K., Jr., eds. (Illus.). 850p. Date not set. 38.00 (ISBN 0-89832-018-6). Brighton Pub Co. Postponed.
Bosco, Ronald A., ed. The Puritan Sermon in America, 1630-1750, 4 vols. LC 78-114749. 1978. Repr. 200.00x set (ISBN 0-8201-1320-4). Schol Facsimiles.
Bose, Aurobindo, tr. see Tagore, Rabindranath.
Bose, Buddladeva. Rain Through the Night. Seely, Clinton B., tr. from Bengali. (Orient Paperbacks). 139p. 1974. pap. 1.80 (ISBN 0-88253-285-5). Ind-US Inc.
Bose, N. K. Multidimensional Systems: Theory & Applications. (IEEE Reprint Ser.). 1978. 29.95 (ISBN 0-471-05214-0); pap. 19.50 (ISBN 0-471-05215-9, Pub. by Wiley-Interscience). Wiley.
Bose, Nemai S., ed. Calcutta: People & Empire. LC 75-907962. 1976. 12.50x o.p. (ISBN 0-88386-721-4). South Asia Bks.
Bose, Nirmal K., ed. Multidimensional Systems: Theory & Applications. LC 78-55096. 1979. 29.95 (ISBN 0-87942-109-6). Inst Electrical.
Bose, Prabodh C. Introduction to Juristic Psychology. (Historical Foundations of Forensic Psychiatry & Psychology Ser.). 426p. 1980. Repr. of 1917 ed. lib. bdg. 39.50 (ISBN 0-686-68561-X). Da Capo.
Bose, S. K. Introduction to General Relativity. LC 80-19150. 120p. 1981. pap. 9.95 (ISBN 0-470-27054-3). Halsted Pr.
Bose, S. K., ed. see International Congress on Asian Pediatrics.
Bose, Tarun C. American Soviet Relations 1921-1933. 228p. 1967. 7.50 (ISBN 0-8002-2398-5). Intl Pubns Serv.
--The Superpowers & the Middle East. 208p. 1972. lib. bdg. 7.50x (ISBN 0-210-22345-6). Asia.
Boselovic, Len, ed. Metric Editorial Guide. 3rd rev. ed. 1979. pap. text ed. 3.00 (ISBN 0-916148-13-0). Am Natl.
Boselovic, Len, jt. ed. see Perica, Lou.
Boseman, Glenn F., jt. auth. see Schellenberger, Robert E.
Boserup, Ester. Conditions of Agricultural Growth: The Economics of Agrarian Change Under Population Pressures. LC 65-19513. 1965. 12.95x (ISBN 0-202-07003-4). Aldine Pub.
--Population & Technological Change: A Study of Long-Term Trends. LC 80-21116. (Illus.). 1981. lib. bdg. 17.50x (ISBN 0-226-06673-8). U of Chicago Pr.
Bosha, Francis J. John Cheever: A Reference Guide. (Reference Books Ser.). 1981. 20.00 (ISBN 0-8161-8447-X). G K Hall.
Boshear, Walton C. & Albrecht, Karl G. Understanding People: Models & Concepts. LC 75-41686. (Illus.). 276p. 1977. pap. 15.50 (ISBN 0-88390-115-3). Univ Assocs.
Boshell, Buris R. Diabetes Mellitus Case Studies. 1976. spiral bdg. 14.00 (ISBN 0-87488-031-9). Med Exam.
Bosher, J. F. French Finances, 1770-95: From Private Enterprise to Public Administration. LC 73-111124. (Studies in Early Modern History). (Illus.). 1970. 46.50 (ISBN 0-521-07764-8). Cambridge U Pr.
Boshes, Louis D. & Gibbs, Frederic A. Epilepsy Handbook. 2nd ed. (Illus.). 206p. 1972. 17.50 (ISBN 0-398-02194-5). C C Thomas.
Bosich, Joseph F. Corrosion Prevention for Practicing Engineers. LC 74-109530. 1970. pap. 10.95 (ISBN 0-8436-0325-9). CBI Pub.
Bosk, Charles L. Forgive & Remember: Managing Medical Failure. LC 78-16596. 1979. 15.00x (ISBN 0-226-06679-7). U of Chicago Pr.
--Forgive & Remember: Managing Medical Failure. LC 78-16596. 248p. 1981. pap. 5.95 (ISBN 0-226-06680-0). U of Chicago Pr.
Boskin, Joseph. Humor & Social Change in Twentieth-Century America. pap. 8.00 (ISBN 0-89073-061-X). Boston Public Lib.
--Humor & Social Change in Twentieth Century America. pap. 8.00 (ISBN 0-89073-061-X). Boston Public Lib.
--Issues in American Society. 1978. pap. text ed. 8.95 (ISBN 0-02-472330-4). Macmillan.
--Opposition Politics: The Anti-New Deal Tradition. (Insight Series: Studies in Contemporary Issues). 1968. pap. text ed. 4.95x (ISBN 0-02-473770-4). Macmillan.
--Urban Racial Violence in the Twentieth Century. Krinsky, Fred, ed. LC 78-75964. (Insight Ser: Studies in Contemporary Issues). (Orig.). 1969. pap. 3.95x (ISBN 0-02-473780-1). Macmillan.
--Urban Racial Violence, in the Twentieth Century. 2nd ed. 1976. pap. 4.95x (ISBN 0-02-470890-9). Macmillan.
Boskin, Joseph & Krinsky, Fred. Oppenheimer Affair: A Political Play in Three Acts. (Insight Series: Studies in Contemporary Issues). 1968. pap. text ed. 4.95x (ISBN 0-02-473760-7). Macmillan.
Boskin, Joseph, jt. auth. see Krinsky, Fred.
Boskin, Joseph & Rosenstone, Robert A., eds. Seasons of Rebellion: Protest & Radicalism in Recent America. LC 79-9678. 349p. 1980. text ed. 19.25 (ISBN 0-8191-0976-2); pap. text ed. 10.50 (ISBN 0-8191-0977-0). U Pr of Amer.
Boskin, Joseph, ed. see Brown, Michael.
Boskin, Joseph, ed. see Hickman, Martin.
Boskin, Joseph, ed. see McGrath, Edward.
Boskin, Joseph, ed. see Rosenstone, Robert A.
Boskin, Joseph, ed. see Wolf, Jerome.
Boskin, Michael, et al. The Impact of Inflation on U.S. Productivity & International Competiveness. LC 80-83144. 69p. 1980. 7.00 (ISBN 0-89068-055-8). Natl Planning.
Boskoff, Alvin. Sociology of Urban Regions. 2nd ed. (Illus.). 1970. pap. text ed. 17.95 (ISBN 0-13-821751-3). P-H.
Boskovits, Miklos. Italian Panel Painting of the Fourteenth & Fifteenth Centuries. Hoch, Elisabeth, tr. from Hungarian. (Illus.). 70p. 1980. 25.00 (ISBN 0-937832-02-2). Dante Univ Bkshlf.
--Italian Panel Paintings. (Illus.). 12.50x (ISBN 0-89918-309-3, H309). Various.
Bosley, Keith, tr. see Jouve, Pierre J.
Boslooper, Thomas. Image of Women. LC 79-57637. (Illus.). 228p. 1980. 19.95 (ISBN 0-932894-04-6). Unif Theol Seminary.
Bosly, Caroline. Rugs to Riches: An Insider's Guide to Oriental Rugs. (Illus.). 1980. 15.95 (ISBN 0-394-50039-3). Pantheon.
Bosmajian, Haig & Bosmajian, Hamida. This Great Argument: The Rights of Women. LC 73-162463. (Speech Ser). 1972. pap. text ed. 7.50 (ISBN 0-201-00611-1). A-W.
Bosmajian, Haig A., ed. Rhetoric of the Speaker: Speeches & Criticism. (Uses of English Ser.). 1967. pap. text ed. 2.95x o.p. (ISBN 0-669-20982-1). Heath.
Bosmajian, Hamida, jt. auth. see Bosmajian, Haig.
Bosquet, Alain. Selected Poems. Beckett, Samuel, et al, trs. from Fr. & Eng. LC 71-181687. 189p. 1972. 10.00 (ISBN 0-8214-0111-4); pap. 5.95 (ISBN 0-8214-0112-2). Ohio U Pr.
--Speech Is Plurality. Yoken, Melvin B. & Lapointe, Juliet G., trs. from Fr. LC 78-61914. 1978. pap. text ed. 7.50 (ISBN 0-8191-0626-7). U Pr of Amer.
Bosquet, Michel. Capitalism in Crisis & Everyday Life. (Marxist Theory & Contemporary Capitalism: No. 6). 1977. text ed. 22.75x (ISBN 0-391-00670-3); pap. text ed. 9.25x (ISBN 0-391-01061-1). Humanities.
Boss, Bert G. Tall Are the Hills. 1972. 7.50 o.p. (ISBN 0-682-47448-7). Exposition.
Boss, Judith A. Newport: A Pictorial History. Friedman, Donna R., ed. (Illus.). 208p. 1981. pap. price not set (ISBN 0-89865-097-6). Donning Co.
Boss, Peter. Social Policy & the Young Delinquent. (Library of Social Policy & Administration). (Orig.). 1967. text ed. 5.25x (ISBN 0-7100-4030-X); pap. text ed. 2.75x (ISBN 0-7100-4029-6). Humanities.
Boss, Richard W. Grant Money & How to Get It: A Handbook for Librarians. 1st ed. 138p. 1980. 19.95 (ISBN 0-8352-1274-2). Bowker.
Boss, Richard W. & Maranjian, Lorig. Fee-Based Information Services: The Commercial Sector. 199p. 1980. 24.95 (ISBN 0-8352-1287-4). Bowker.
Bossanji, J., jt. ed. see Helliwell, P. R.
Bossart, Donald E. Creative Conflict in Religious Education & Church Administration. LC 80-12704. 284p. (Orig.). 1980. pap. 9.95 (ISBN 0-89135-048-9). Religious Educ.
Bossart, Jane, jt. auth. see Wasserman, Paul.
Bossart, Jane, jt. ed. see Wasserman, Paul.
Bosse, Abraham. Sentimens sur la Distinction Des Manieres de Peinture, des Sein et Graveure. (Documents of Art & Architectural History Series 2: Vol. 5). 142p. (Fr.). 1981. Repr. of 1649 ed. 27.50x (ISBN 0-89371-205-1). Broude Intl Edns.
Bosse, Malcolm. The Seventy Nine Squares. (YA) (gr. 7-12). pap. 1.95 (ISBN 0-440-98901-9, LE). Dell.
Bosselman, Beulah C. Neurosis & Psychosis. 3rd ed. 216p. 1969. pap. 14.75 photocopy ed. spiral (ISBN 0-398-00195-2). C C Thomas.
Bosselman, Fred, et al. The Permit Explosion. LC 76-55844. (Management & Control of Growth Ser.). 86p. 1976. pap. text ed. 11.00 (ISBN 0-87420-570-0). Urban Land.
Bossert, T. & Dunlop, D., eds. Selected Issues in Health Policies in Africa & Latin America. 82p. 1981. 17.50 (ISBN 0-08-024723-7). Pergamon.
Bossert, William H., jt. auth. see Wilson, Edward O.
Bossom, Naomi. Scale Full of Fish: And Other Turnabouts. LC 78-13293. (gr. k-3). 1979. 7.50 (ISBN 0-688-80203-6); PLB 7.20 (ISBN 0-688-84203-8). Greenwillow.
Bossone, Richard M. & Ashe, Amy E. English Proficiency: Developing Your Reading & Writing Power, Bk. 1. 320p. (gr. 7-9). 1980. 10.32 (ISBN 0-07-006589-6, W); tchrs. manual 6.00 (ISBN 0-07-006590-X). McGraw.
Bossone, Richard M. & Reid, James M., Jr. Handbook of Basic English Skills. 2nd ed. LC 77-20017. 1977. pap. text ed. 10.95 (ISBN 0-471-02196-2); tchrs. manual avail. (ISBN 0-471-04048-7). Wiley.
Bossong, Ken. A Guide to Community Energy Self-Reliance, Vol. 1. (Illus.). 100p. (Orig.). 1981. pap. 2.50 (ISBN 0-89988-023-1). Citizens Energy.
--Passive Solar Retrofit for Homeowners & Apartment Dwellers. (Illus.). 100p. (Orig.). 1981. pap. text ed. 5.00 (ISBN 0-89988-068-1). Citizens Energy.
Bossong, Ken & Denman, Scott. Nuclear Power & Civil Liberties: Can We Have Both? 2nd ed. 150p. 1981. 7.50 (ISBN 0-89988-071-1). Citizens Energy.
Bossong, Ken & Simpson, Jan. Appropriate Community Technologies Sourcebook. (Illus.). 180p. (Orig.). 1981. pap. text ed. 7.50 (ISBN 0-89988-055-X). Citizens Energy.
--Appropriate Community Technologies Sourcebook, Vol. I. (Illus., Orig.). 1980. pap. 3.00 (ISBN 0-89988-056-8). Citizens Energy.
Bossong, Ken, et al. Solar Compendium, 2 vols. (Illus.). 1980. 8.00 (ISBN 0-89988-013-4). Citizens Energy.
--A Solar Critique. 75p. (Orig.). 1981. 4.00 (ISBN 0-89988-070-3). Citizens Energy.
--Pioneers of Alcohol Fuels. 125p. (Orig.). 1981. 7.50 (ISBN 0-89988-067-3). Citizens Energy.
Bosstick, Maurice & Cable, John L. Patterns in the Sand: An Exploration in Mathematics. 1971. text ed. 10.95x o.p. (ISBN 0-02-473720-8); ans. bklt free o.p. (ISBN 0-685-03675-8). Glencoe.
--Patterns in the Sand: An Exploration in Mathematics. 2nd ed. (Illus.). 1975. text ed. 13.95x (ISBN 0-02-471960-9); ans. bk free (ISBN 0-02-471970-6). Macmillan.
Bossuet, Jacques-Benigne. Oraisons funebres. new ed. (Nouveaux Classiques Larousse Ser.). (Illus.). 168p. (Fr.). 1975. pap. 2.95 (ISBN 0-685-62360-2, 33). Larousse.
Bossy, John. The English Catholic Community, 1570-1850. (Illus.). 1976. 29.95x (ISBN 0-19-519847-6). Oxford U Pr.
Bostelmann, Clarissa S., tr. see De Crevecoeur, Michel-Guillanme St. J.
Bostock, David. Logic & Arithmetic: Natural Numbers. 229p. 1974. 29.95x (ISBN 0-19-824366-9). Oxford U Pr.
Bostock, J. Knight. A Handbook on Old High German Literature. 2nd ed. King, K. C. & McLintock, D. R., eds. (Illus.). 1976. 49.95x (ISBN 0-19-815392-9). Oxford U Pr.

Bostock, William. I, Cleopatra. 1977. pap. 2.50 o.p. (ISBN 0-446-81379-6). Warner Bks.

Boston Children's Medical Center Staff, jt. auth. see Simont, Marc.

Boston Children'S Medical Center Staff, jt. ed. see Gregg, Elizabeth M.

Boston, David M. Pre-Columbian Pottery of the Americas. Charleston, Robert J., ed. LC 78-55079. (Masterpieces of Western & Near Eastern Ceramics Ser.: Vol. 3). (Illus.). 318p. 1980. thru dec. 31 165.00 (ISBN 0-87011-344-5); thereafter 200.00 (ISBN 0-87011-344-5). Kodansha.

Boston, Eric, ed. Jersey Cattle. (Illus.). 1954. 8.50 o.p. (ISBN 0-571-02213-8, Pub. by Faber & Faber). Merrimack Bk Serv.

Boston, L. M. Nothing Said. LC 70-137756. (Illus.). (gr. 2-5). 1971. 4.95 o.p. (ISBN 0-15-257580-4, HJ). HarBraceJ.

--The Stones of Green Knowe. LC 75-44143. (Illus.). (gr. 5-9). 1976. 7.95 (ISBN 0-689-50058-0, McElderry Bk). Atheneum.

Boston, Lucy M. Memory in a House. LC 73-10690. (Illus.). 152p. 1974. 6.95 o.s.i. (ISBN 0-02-513730-1, 51373). Macmillan.

--Strongholds. LC 68-24383. 1969. 4.95 o.p. (ISBN 0-15-185988-4, HJ). HarBraceJ.

Boston, Richard. Baldness Be My Friend. 1978. 14.95 (ISBN 0-241-89732-7, Pub. by Hamish Hamilton England). David & Charles.

Boston, Thomas. Human Nature in Its Fourfold State. 1964. pap. 4.45 (ISBN 0-686-12519-3). Banner of Truth.

Boston, Virginia. Punk Rock. (Large Format Ser.). (Illus.). 1978. pap. 7.95 o.p. (ISBN 0-14-004985-1). Penguin.

Boston Women's Collective. The New York Women's Yellow Pages 1978-1979 Edition. LC 76-5369. (Illus.). 1978. 12.95 (ISBN 0-312-57120-8); pap. 5.95 o.p. (ISBN 0-312-57155-0). St Martin.

Bostrom, Christopher J. Philosophy of Religion. 1962. 32.50x (ISBN 0-685-69791-6). Elliots Bks.

Bostrom, Roald. Cameras. LC 80-17413. (A Look Inside Ser.). (Illus.). 48p. (gr. 4-12). 1981. PLB 10.25 (ISBN 0-8172-1404-6). Raintree Pubs.

Bostwick, Burdette. One Hundred One Proven Techniques for Getting the Job Interview. 256p. 1981. 12.95 (ISBN 0-471-07762-3, Pub. by Wiley-Interscience). Wiley.

Bostwick, Burdette E., ed. Resume Writing: A Comprehensive How-to-Do-It Guide. 2nd ed. LC 80-18100. 256p. 1980. 12.95 (ISBN 0-471-08067-5, Pub. by Wiley-Interscience). Wiley.

Boswell, Bryan. Skiing Fundamentals. (Fundamentals: A Series on Getting It Right the First Time). (Illus.). 80p. (Orig.). 1979. pap. 8.95 (ISBN 0-589-50085-6, Pub. by Reed Books Australia). C E Tuttle.

Boswell, G. G., jt. auth. see Faires, R. A.

Boswell, Hal. The Fourth Floor. 1981. 8.95 (ISBN 0-533-04772-2). Vantage.

Boswell, J. S. Social & Business Enterprises. (Economics & Society Ser.). 1976. text ed. 17.95x (ISBN 0-04-338078-6); pap. text ed. 13.50x (ISBN 0-04-338079-4). Allen Unwin.

Boswell, James. Dorando: A Spanish Tale, 1767. Shugrue, Michael F., ed. Bd. with The History of Nourjahad, 1767. Sheridan, Frances. LC 74-17301. (The Flowering of the Novel, 1740-1775 Ser: Vol. 78). 1974. lib. bdg. 50.00 (ISBN 0-8240-1177-5). Garland Pub.

--Life of Johnson, 2 vols. in 1. 1976. 23.00x (ISBN 0-460-00001-2, Evman). Dutton.

--Life of Johnson. (English Library Ser.). 1979. pap. 2.95 (ISBN 0-14-043116-0). Penguin.

Boswell, Jeanetta. Herman Melville & the Critics: A Checklist of Criticism, 1900-1978. LC 80-25959. (Author Bibliographies Ser.: No. 53). 259p. 1981. 13.50 (ISBN 0-8108-1385-8). Scarecrow.

--Ralph Waldo Emerson & the Critics: A Checklist of Criticism, 1900-1977. LC 79-4670. (Author Bibliographies Ser.: No. 39). 1979. 10.00 (ISBN 0-8108-1211-8). Scarecrow.

--Walt Whitman & the Critics: A Checklist of Criticism, 1900-1978. LC 80-20528. (The Scarecrow Author Bibliographies Ser.: No. 51). 270p. 1980. 14.50 (ISBN 0-8108-1355-6). Scarecrow.

Boswell, John. Christianity, Social Tolerance, & Homosexuality. LC 79-11171. 1980. 27.50 (ISBN 0-226-06710-6). U of Chicago Pr.

Boswell, Kathryn, jt. auth. see O'Connor, Francine M.

Boswell, Patricia M., ed. see Storm, Theodor.

Boswirth, L., jt. auth. see Plint, M. A.

Bosworth, A. B. A Historical Commentary on Arrian's History of Alexander, Vol. I: Bks. I-III. 416p. 1980. 89.00 (ISBN 0-19-814828-3). Oxford U Pr.

Bosworth, Allan R. America's Concentration Camps. (Illus.). 1967. 12.95x (ISBN 0-393-05338-5). Norton.

--Lovely World of Richi-San. (Illus.). 1960. 6.95 o.p. (ISBN 0-06-010400-7, HarpT). Har-Row.

Bosworth, Barry, et al. Capital Needs in the Seventies. 70p. 1975. pap. 3.95 (ISBN 0-8157-1031-3). Brookings.

Bosworth, Bruce. Programs in BASIC, a Lecture Notebook. 2nd ed. 1978. pap. text ed. 5.95 (ISBN 0-8403-1210-5). Kendall-Hunt.

Bosworth, Bruce & Nagel, Harry. Programming in BASIC for Business. 2nd ed. 256p. 1981. text ed. 10.95 (ISBN 0-574-21325-2, 13-4325); instr's. guide avail. (ISBN 0-574-21326-0, 13-4326). SRA.

Bosworth, C. E. The Islamic Dynasties. 245p. 1980. pap. 9.00x (ISBN 0-85224-402-9, Pub. by Edinburgh U Pr Scotland). Columbia U Pr.

--The Islamic Dynasties. 1967. 14.50x (ISBN 0-85224-110-0, Pub. by Edinburgh U Pr Scotland). Columbia U Pr.

--The Medieval History of Iran, Afghanistan & Central Asia. 374p. 1980. 75.00x (ISBN 0-86078-000-7, Pub. by Variorum England). State Mutual Bk.

Bosworth, C. E., jt. ed. see Schacht, Joseph.

Bosworth, Clifford. The Ghaznavids. (Arab Background Ser.). 1973. 15.00x (ISBN 0-685-77091-5). Intl Bk Ctr.

Bosworth, Clifford E. The Later Ghaznavids: Splendor & Decay. LC 77-7879. 1977. text ed. 17.50x (ISBN 0-231-04428-3). Columbia U Pr.

Bosworth, Fred. The Sparrows Fall. (gr. 7 up). 1975. pap. 1.50 o.p. (ISBN 0-451-08504-3, W8504, Sig). NAL.

Bosworth, J. Allan. White Water, Still Water. (gr. 5-7). pap. 1.25 (ISBN 0-671-29923-9). Archway.

Bosworth, Joseph, et al, eds. An Anglo-Saxon Dictionary. 2066p. 1972. Repr. of 1898 ed. 98.00x (ISBN 0-19-863101-4); 1921 supplement & addenda 79.00x (ISBN 0-19-863112-X); addenda 1972 pap. 14.50x (ISBN 0-19-863110-3). Oxford U Pr.

Bosworth, R. J. Italy, the Least of the Great Powers. LC 78-18090. (Illus.). 532p. 1980. 69.50 (ISBN 0-521-22366-0). Cambridge U Pr.

Botein, Bernard. Trial Judge: The Candid, Behind the Bench Story of Justice Bernard Botein. (American Constitutional & Legal History Ser.). 337p. 1974. Repr. of 1952 ed. lib. bdg. 32.50 (ISBN 0-306-70630-X). Da Capo.

Botein, Michael & Rice, David, eds. Network Television & the Public Interest: A Preliminary Inquiry. LC 79-1751. 320p. 1980. 19.95x (ISBN 0-669-02927-0). Lexington Bks.

Botel, Morton. Multi-Level Speller for Grades 3-12. (gr. 3-12). 4.10 (ISBN 0-931992-15-X); pap. 3.00 (ISBN 0-931992-16-8). Penns Valley.

--Multi-Level Speller Guidebook for Teachers. 1961. 4.95 (ISBN 0-931992-17-6). Penns Valley.

--Primary Multi-Level Speller & First Dictionary. (gr. k-2). 1959. pap. 3.00 (ISBN 0-931992-14-1). Penns Valley.

Botel, Morton, jt. auth. see Preston, Ralph C.

Botero, Giovanni. A Treatise, Concerning the Causes of the Magnificence & Greatness of Cities. LC 79-84090. (English Experience Ser.: No. 910). 128p. (Eng.). 1979. Repr. of 1606 ed. lib. bdg. 13.00 (ISBN 90-221-0910-0). Walter J Johnson.

Botez, M. I. & Reynolds, E. H., eds. Folic Acid in Neurology, Psychiatry, & Internal Medicine. LC 78-57243. 1979. text ed. 49.50 (ISBN 0-89004-338-8). Raven.

Botfield, Beriah. Notes on the Cathedral Libraries of England. LC 68-23138. 1969. Repr. of 1849 ed. 32.00 (ISBN 0-8103-3174-8). Gale.

Botha, F. M., ed. The Advertising & Press Annual of Sothern Africa, 1980. LC 52-41681. (Illus.). 278p. 1980. 62.50x (ISBN 0-8002-2727-1). Intl Pubns Serv.

Botha, Rudolf B. Methodological Status of Grammatical Argumentation. LC 79-126050. (Janua Linguarum Ser.Maior: No. 105). (Orig.). 1970. pap. text ed. 12.95x (ISBN 90-2790-714-5). Mouton.

Botha, Rudolf P. Function of the Lexicon in Transformational Generative Grammar. (Janua Linguarum, Ser. Major: No. 38). 1968. text ed. 44.10x (ISBN 90-2790-688-2). Mouton.

--The Justification of Linguistic Hypotheses. (Janua Linguarum Ser.Maior: No. 84). 1973. text ed. 57.65x (ISBN 90-2792-542-9). Mouton.

Botha, Rudolph P. Methodological Aspects of Transformational Generative Phonology. (Janua Linguarum, Ser. Minor: No. 112). 266p. 1971. pap. text ed. 24.70x (ISBN 90-2791-761-2). Mouton.

Bothe, H. & Trebst, A., eds. Biochemistry & Physiology of Nitrogen & Sulfur Metabolism. (Proceedings in Life Sciences Ser.). (Illus.). 370p. 1981. 49.80 (ISBN 0-387-10486-0). Springer-Verlag.

Botheroyd, Paul F. Ich und Er: First & Third-Person Self-Reference & Problems of Identity in Three Contemporary German-Language Novels. (De Proprietatibus Litterarum Series Practica: No.67). 143p. (Orig.). 1976. pap. text ed. 28.25x (ISBN 90-2793-214-X). Mouton.

Bothmer, B. V., ed. see Holz, R. K., et al.

Bothmer, Gerry, tr. see Wallin, Marie-Louise.

Bothner, Gerry, tr. see Lindgren, Astrid.

Bothra, Pushpa. Jaina Theory of Perception. 1976. 7.50 (ISBN 0-89684-229-0). Orient Bk Dist.

Bothwell, Dick. Bum Stories. (Illus.). 60p. (Orig.). 1980. pap. 3.95x (ISBN 0-9605382-0-8). St Petersburg Times.

Bothwell, Jean. Dancing Princess. LC 65-18726. (gr. 7 up). 4.50 o.p. (ISBN 0-15-221637-5, HJ). HarBraceJ.

--First Book of India. rev. ed. LC 66-10129. (First Bks). (Illus.). (gr. 4-6). 1971. PLB 6.45 (ISBN 0-531-00559-3). Watts.

--India. 2nd rev. ed. Whipple, Jane, ed. LC 78-2511. (First Bks). (Illus.). (gr. 4-6). 1978. PLB 6.45 s&l (ISBN 0-531-02229-3). Watts.

Bothwell, Sr. Mary D. We Believe. (Christ Our Life Ser.). (Illus.). (gr. 4). 1981. pap. text ed. 3.80 (ISBN 0-8294-0367-1); tchr's ed. 6.95 (ISBN 0-8294-0368-X). Loyola.

Bothwell, Sr. Mary. God Guides Us. (Christ Our Life Ser). (Illus.). (gr. 3). 1981. pap. text ed. 3.80 (ISBN 0-8294-0365-5); tchr's ed. 6.95 (ISBN 0-8294-0366-3). Loyola.

Bothwell, Reece B. La Ciudadania en Puerto Rico. 2nd ed. LC 78-24031. (Sp.). 1979. pap. 1.85 (ISBN 0-8477-2451-4). U of PR Pr.

Bothwell, Robert, et al. Canada Since Nineteen Forty-Five: Power, Politics, & Provincialism. 496p. 1981. 19.95 (ISBN 0-8020-2417-3). U of Toronto Pr.

Botkin, B. A. A Treasury of American Folklore. 640p. 1981. pap. 3.95 (ISBN 0-553-14149-X). Bantam.

Botkin, James W., et al. No Limits to Learning: Bridging the Human Gap: the Club of Rome Report. LC 79-40911. 1979. 17.00 (ISBN 0-08-024705-9); pap. 7.75 (ISBN 0-08-024704-0). Pergamon.

Botrom, Alice C. Bible Word Puzzles. (Illus.). 30p. (Orig.). 1980. pap. 1.50 (ISBN 0-89323-005-7). BMA Pr.

Botsch, Robert E. We Shall Not Overcome: Populism & Southern Blue-Collar Workers. LC 80-11567. 312p. 1981. 19.50x (ISBN 0-8078-1444-X). U of NC Pr.

Botsford, George W. A Brief History of the World. (Illus.). 518p. 1980. Repr. of 1917 ed. lib. bdg. 35.00 (ISBN 0-8492-3591-X). R West.

Botsio Utete, C. Munhamu. The Road to Zimbabwe: The Political Economy of Settler Colonialism, National Liberation & Foreign Intervention. LC 78-57669. 1978. pap. text ed. 9.00 (ISBN 0-8191-0536-8). U Pr of Amer.

Bott, Alan. Our Fathers (Eighteen Seventy to Nineteen Hundred) 249p. 1980. Repr. lib. bdg. 35.00 (ISBN 0-89987-061-9). Darby Bks.

Bott, Alan, ed. Our Mothers. 220p. 1980. Repr. of 1932 ed. lib. bdg. 30.00 (ISBN 0-8495-0461-9). Arden Lib.

Bott, Edmund. A Collection of Decisions of the Court of the King Bench Upon the Poor Laws. Berkowitz, David S. & Thorne, Samuel E., eds. LC 77-89222. (Classics of English Legal History in the Modern Era: Vol. 67). 399p. 1979. lib. bdg. 40.00 (ISBN 0-8240-3166-0). Garland Pub.

Bott, Raymond & Morrison, Stanley. Discovering Chess. 1975. 10.00 (ISBN 0-571-04834-X). Transatlantic.

--Junior Chess Games. 1966. 6.95 (ISBN 0-685-52088-9). Transatlantic.

--Junior Chess Puzzles. (Illus., Orig.). 1975. pap. 3.95 (ISBN 0-571-10688-9, Pub. by Faber & Faber). Merrimack Bk Serv.

--Your Book of Chess. (gr. 7 up). 1968. 6.25 (ISBN 0-571-08112-6). Transatlantic.

Bott, Ross, et al. Study Guide for Human Information Processing. 2nd ed. Lindsay, Norman, ed. 1977. 6.95 (ISBN 0-12-450962-2). Acad Pr.

Botterill, Cal, jt. auth. see Orlick, Terry.

Botterill, G. S. & Harding, T. D. The Scotch. 1977. 16.95 (ISBN 0-7134-0224-5, Pub. by Batsford England). David & Charles.

Botterill, G. S., jt. auth. see Keene, R. D.

Botterweck, G. Johannes & Ringgren, Helmer, eds. Theological Dictionary of the Old Testament, 3 vols. Incl. Vol. I. 21.00 (ISBN 0-8028-2325-4); Vol. II. 21.00 (ISBN 0-8028-2326-2); Vol. III. 21.00 (ISBN 0-8028-2327-0). 1978. Eerdmans.

--Theological Dictionary of the Old Testament, Vol. 4. 560p. 1981. 21.00 (ISBN 0-8028-2328-9). Eerdmans.

Bottiglia, William F., ed. Current Issues in Language Teaching. Incl. Linguistics & Language Teaching. Hall, Robert A., Jr; Programmed Learning. Hayes, Alfred S; A Survey of FLES Practices. Alkons, Nancy V. & Biophy, Mary A.. 1962. 7.95x (ISBN 0-915432-62-5). NE Conf Teach Foreign.

--The Language Classroom. Incl. The Drop-Out of Students After the Second Year. Fulton, Renee J; The Philosophy of the Language Laboratory. Archer, John B; The Place of Grammar & the Use of English in the Teaching of Foreign Languages. Grew, James H; Spoken Language Tests. Brooks, Nelson; Teaching Aids & Techniques. Pleasants, Jeanne V; Teaching Literature for Admission to College with Advanced Standing. Price, Blanche A. 84p. 1957. pap. 7.95x (ISBN 0-915432-57-9). NE Conf Teach Foreign.

--Language Learning: The Intermediate Phase. Incl. The Continuum: Listening & Speaking. Belasco, Simon; Reading for Meaning. Sherer, George; Writing an Expression. Prochoroff, Marina. 85p. 1963. pap. 9.95 (ISBN 0-915432-63-3). NE Conf Teach Foreign.

Botting, D. The Second Front. Time-Life Books, ed. (World War II). (Illus.). 1979. 12.95 (ISBN 0-8094-2498-3). Time-Life.

Botting, Douglas. The Pirates. new ed. Time-Life Books, ed. (Seafarers Ser.). (Illus.). 1978. 13.95 (ISBN 0-8094-2650-1). Time-Life.

--The Pirates. LC 77-91928. (The Seafarers Ser.). (Illus.). 1978. lib. bdg. 11.97 (ISBN 0-686-50988-9). Silver.

--Rio. (The Great Cities Ser.). (Illus.). 1978. lib. bdg. 14.94 (ISBN 0-686-51006-2). Silver.

--Rio De Janeiro. Time-Life Books, ed. (The Great Cities Ser). 1978. 14.95 (ISBN 0-8094-2294-8). Time-Life.

--The Second Front. LC 78-3405. (World War II Ser.). (Illus.). 1978. lib. bdg. 13.95 (ISBN 0-686-51050-X). Silver.

--Wilderness Europe. (The World's Wild Places Ser.). (Illus.). 1976. lib. bdg. 11.97 (ISBN 0-686-51025-9). Silver.

--Wilderness Europe. (The World's Wild Places). (Illus.). 1976. 12.95 (ISBN 0-8094-2062-7). Time-Life.

Botting, Douglas, jt. auth. see Time-Life Books Editors.

Bottle, E. K. Fractional Horse-Power Electric Motors: A Guide to Types & Applications. 209p. 1948. 10.95x (ISBN 0-85264-051-X, Pub. by Griffin England). State Mutual Bk.

Bottle, R. T. Use of Chemical Literature. 3rd ed. LC 79-41061. 1979. 42.50 (ISBN 0-408-38452-2). Butterworths.

Bottner, Barbara. Myra. LC 78-10417. (Illus.). (gr. k-3). 1979. 7.95 (ISBN 0-02-711740-5). Macmillan.

Botto, Ken. Past Joys. Vandenburgh, Jane, ed. LC 78-7999. (Illus.). 1978. ltd. signed ed. 45.00 o.p. (ISBN 0-87701-116-8, Prism Editions); pap. 12.95 o.p. (ISBN 0-87701-115-X). Chronicle Bks.

Bottomley, A. Keith. Prison Before Trial. 117p. 1970. pap. text ed. 5.00x (ISBN 0-7135-1816-2, Pub. by Bedford England). Renouf.

Bottomley, A. Keith, jt. ed. see Baldwin, John.

Bottomley, Gillian. After the Odyssey. (Studies in Society & Culture). 1980. 22.95x (ISBN 0-7022-1399-3). U of Queensland Pr.

Bottomley, Tom. Cruising for Fun. (Illus.). 1977. 8.95 o.p. (ISBN 0-8096-1913-X, Assn Pr); pap. 4.95 o.p. (ISBN 0-8096-1908-3). Follett.

Bottomore, Tom, ed. Crisis & Contention in Sociology. LC 75-24787. (Sage Studies in International Sociology: Vol. 1). 1976. 18.00x (ISBN 0-8039-9955-0); pap. 9.95x (ISBN 0-8039-9962-3). Sage.

--Karl Marx. 194p. 1979. 29.00x (ISBN 0-631-10961-7, Pub. by Basil Blackwell); pap. 10.50x (ISBN 0-631-11061-5). Biblio Dist.

Bottomore, Tom & Goode, Patrick, eds. Austro-Marxism. 1978. text ed. 29.95x (ISBN 0-19-827229-4); pap. text ed. 8.50x (ISBN 0-19-827230-8). Oxford U Pr.

Bottomore, Tom & Nisbet, Robert, eds. A History of Sociological Analysis. 717p. 1981. pap. text ed. 10.95x (ISBN 0-465-03024-6). Basic.

Bottomore, Tom, tr. see Hilferding, Rudolf.

Bottomore, Tom, tr. see Simmel, Georg.

Bottoms, A. E. & McClean, J. D. Defendants in the Criminal Process. (International Library of Social Policy). 250p. 1975. 27.75x (ISBN 0-7100-8274-6). Routledge & Kegan.

Bottone, Edward J., ed. Yersinia Enterocolitica. 240p. 1981. 69.95 (ISBN 0-8493-5545-1). CRC Pr.

Bottorff, William K. Thomas Jefferson. (United States Authors Ser.: No. 327). 1979. lib. bdg. 9.95 (ISBN 0-8057-7260-X). Twayne.

Bottrall, Margaret, ed. William Blake: Songs of Innocence & Experience. (Casebook Ser.). 1970. 2.50 o.s.i. (ISBN 0-87695-037-3). Aurora Pubs.

Bottrall, Margaret, ed. see Blake, William.

Bottrell, Donna, ed. see Wine Advisory Board.

Bottrell, Donna, et al, eds. see California Winemakers.

Botvinnik, M. M. Achieving the Aim. (Illus.). 230p. 1981. 19.00 (ISBN 0-08-024120-4); pap. cancelled (ISBN 0-08-024119-0). Pergamon.

--Mikhail Botvinnik: Soviet Chess Patriarch. LC 80-40437. (Pergamon Russian Chess Ser.). (Illus.). 230p. 1981. pap. 19.00 (ISBN 0-08-024120-4). Pergamon.
--Selected Games Nineteen Sixty-Seven to Nineteen Seventy. Neat, K. P., tr. (Pergamon Russian Chess Ser.). (Illus.). 150p. 1981. 29.00 (ISBN 0-08-024124-7); pap. 13.95 (ISBN 0-08-024123-9). Pergamon.
--Selected Games: 1967-1970. LC 80-40181. (Pergamon Russian Chess Ser.). (Illus.). 318p. 1981. 29.00 (ISBN 0-08-024124-7); pap. 13.95 (ISBN 0-08-024123-9). Pergamon.
Botwin, Carol & Fine, Jerome. The Love Crisis: Hit & Run Lovers, Sexual Stingies, Unreliables, Kinkies, & Other Typical Men of Today. 256p. 1980. pap. 2.50 (ISBN 0-553-13814-6). Bantam.
Botwinick, Aryeh. Ethics, Politics & Epistemology: A Study in the Unity of Hume's Thought. LC 80-5809. 197p. 1980. lib. bdg. 17.50 (ISBN 0-8191-1288-7); pap. text ed. 9.00 (ISBN 0-8191-1289-5). U Pr of Amer.
--Wittgenstein & Historical Understanding. LC 80-5968. 65p. (Orig.). 1981. pap. text ed. 5.00 (ISBN 0-8191-1431-6). U Pr of Amer.
Botwinick, Jack. We Are Aging. 1981. text ed. cancelled (ISBN 0-8261-3380-0); pap. text ed. 11.95 (ISBN 0-8261-3381-9). Springer Pub.
Botwinick, Jack & Storandt, Martha. Memory, Related Functions & Age. (Illus.). 208p. 1974. 18.75 (ISBN 0-398-03143-6). C C Thomas.
Botzow, Hermann S. Auto Fleet Management. LC 67-30632. 1968. 23.95 (ISBN 0-471-09100-6, Pub. by Wiley-Interscience). Wiley.
Boubat, Edward. Woman. LC 72-86679. (Illus.). 143p. 1973. 15.00 (ISBN 0-8076-0664-2). Braziller.
Bouce, P. G. The Novels of Tobias Smollett. LC 75-31687. 1976. text ed. 32.00x (ISBN 0-582-50023-0). Longman.
Bouce, P. G., jt. ed. see Rousseau, G. S.
Bouchard, Donald F., ed. see Foucault, Michel.
Bouchard, Rene, ed. Culture Populaire et Litteratures Au Quebec. (Stanford French & Italian Studies: Vol. 19). 308p. (Fr.). 1980. pap. 20.00 (ISBN 0-915838-20-6). Anma Libri.
Bouchard, Robert F., ed. Guidebook to the Freedom of Information & Privacy Acts. LC 79-27406. 1980. 35.00 (ISBN 0-87632-310-7). Boardman.
Bouchard, Rosemary & Owens, Norma F. Nursing Care of the Cancer Patient. 4th ed. LC 80-21708. (Illus.). 496p. 1981. pap. text ed. 19.95 (ISBN 0-8016-0720-5). Mosby.
Bouche, Claude. Lautreamont: Du lieu commun a la parodie. new ed. (Collection themes et textes). 253p. (Orig.). 1974. pap. 6.75 (ISBN 2-03-035024-9, 2615). Larousse.
Boucher, Carl O., ed. Current Clinical Dental Terminology: A Glossary of Accepted Terms in All Disciplines of Dentistry. 2nd ed. LC 73-4651. 1974. 27.50 (ISBN 0-8016-0719-1). Mosby.
Boucher, John & Paris, Robert L. Debuts. (Orig.). (gr. 10-12). 1975. text ed. 14.80 (ISBN 0-205-04148-5, 3641481); tchrs'. guide 5.12 (ISBN 0-205-04149-3, 364149X); workbook 4.92 (ISBN 0-205-04150-7, 3641503); cassettes 280.00 (ISBN 0-205-04151-5, 3641511); tests-dup masters 38.00 (ISBN 0-205-05402-1, 3654028). Allyn.
Boucher, John G. & Hurtgen, Andre O. Encore. (Allyn & Bacon French Program Ser.). (gr. 9-12). 1976. text ed. 15.12 (ISBN 0-205-04903-6, 3649032); tchrs'. guide 5.12 (ISBN 0-205-04904-4, 3649040). Allyn.
--Reprise. (Orig.). (gr. 10-12). 1975. text ed. 15.12 (ISBN 0-205-04171-X, 3641716); tchrs'. guide 5.12 (ISBN 0-205-04172-8, 3641724); wkbk. 5.60 (ISBN 0-205-04173-6, 3641732); cassettes 296.00 (ISBN 0-205-04174-4, 3641740); dup. masters 38.00 (ISBN 0-205-05404-8, 3654044). Allyn.
Boucher, John G. & Paris, Robert L. Contrastes. (Fr.). (gr. 7-12). 1972. text ed. 14.80 (ISBN 0-205-03368-7, 3633683); tchrs'. guide 5.12 (ISBN 0-205-03369-5, 3633691); wkbk. 5.60 (ISBN 0-205-03370-9, 3633705); ans. bk. 2.40 (ISBN 0-205-03371-7, 3633713). Allyn.
Boucher, Madeleine I. The Parables. (New Testament Message Ser.). 9.95 (ISBN 0-89453-130-1); pap. 5.95 (ISBN 0-89453-195-6). M Glazier.
Boucher, Sharon, jt. auth. see Burchard, Florence.
Bouchet, Jean. Epistres Morales et Familieres Du Traverseur (Poitiers, 1545) (Classiques De la Renaissance En France: No. 4). 1970. 35.90x (ISBN 90-2796-345-2). Mouton.
Bouchez, L. J., et al, eds. Netherlands Yearbook of International Law: State Immunity from Attachment & Execution, Vol. X. 650p. 1980. 40.00x (ISBN 90-286-0710-2). Sijthoff & Noordhoff.
Bouchier, Ian A., ed. Recent Advances in Gastroenterology, No. 4. (Illus.). 352p. 1980. text ed. 39.50x (ISBN 0-443-01748-4). Churchill.
Bouchot, Henri. Book: Its Printers, Illustrators, & Binders, from Gutenberg to the Present Time. Grevel, H., ed. LC 77-155741. (Illus.). 1971. Repr. of 1890 ed. 26.00 (ISBN 0-8103-3392-9). Gale.
Boucot, Arthur J., ed. see Biology Colloquium, 37th, Oregon State University, 1976.
Boudard, J. B. Iconologie. LC 75-27888. (Renaissance & the Gods Ser.: Vol. 43). (Illus.). 1976. Repr. of 1766 ed. lib. bdg. 73.00 (ISBN 0-8240-2092-8). Garland Pub.
Boudart, M., tr. see Semenov, N. N.
Boudinot, Elias. The Life & Public Services, Addresses & Letters of Elias Boudinot, President of the Continental Congress, 2 Vols. Boudinot, Jane J., ed. LC 72-119059. (Era of the American Revolution Ser). 1971. Repr. of 1896 ed. 75.00 (ISBN 0-306-71946-0). Da Capo.
Boudinot, Jane J., ed. see Boudinot, Elias.
Boudon, Raymond. The Crisis in Sociology: Problems of Sociological Epistemology. (European Perspectives Ser.). 272p. 1981. 25.00x (ISBN 0-231-05178-6). Columbia U Pr.
--Education, Opportunity & Social Inequality: Changing Prospects in Western Society. LC 73-14646. (Urban Research Ser.). 208p. 1974. 20.95 (ISBN 0-471-09105-7, Pub. by Wiley-Interscience). Wiley.
Boudon, Raymond & Lazarsfeld, Paul. Vocabulaire Des Sciences Sociales: Concepts et Indices. (Methodes De la Sociologie: No. 1). 1971. pap. text ed. 20.50x (ISBN 90-2796-891-8). Mouton.
Boudon, Raymond & Lazarsfeld, Paul, eds. L' Analyse Empirique De la Causalite. 3rd ed. (Methodes De la Sociologie: No. 2). 1976. pap. 20.50x (ISBN 90-2796-158-1). Mouton.
Boudreau, E. Buying Country Land. 1973. 4.95 o.s.i. (ISBN 0-02-513930-4). Macmillan.
Boudreaux, E. A. & Mulay, L. N. Theory & Applications of Molecular Paramagnetism. LC 75-28418. 1976. 55.00 (ISBN 0-471-09106-5, Pub. by Wiley-Interscience). Wiley.
Boudreaux, H. Bruce. Arthropod Phylogeny with Special Reference to Insects. LC 78-16638. 1979. 24.95 (ISBN 0-471-04290-0, Pub. by Wiley-Interscience). Wiley.
Bougainville, Louis A. De. Adventure in the Wilderness: The American Journals of Louis Antoine De Bougainville 1756-1760. Hamilton, Edward P., tr. (American Exploration & Travel Ser.: No. 42). 1964. 18.95 o.p. (ISBN 0-8061-0596-8). U of Okla Pr.
Boughey, Arthur S. Strategy for Survival. LC 75-44541. (Orig.). 1976. pap. text ed. 9.50 (ISBN 0-8053-1095-9). Benjamin-Cummings.
Boughey, Howard. Insights of Sociology: An Introduction. 1978. pap. text ed. 11.95 (ISBN 0-205-06011-0); instr's man. avail. (ISBN 0-205-06012-9). Allyn.
Boughton, Brian. Reinforced Concrete Detailer's Manual. 1979. pap. text ed. 16.25x (ISBN 0-258-97128-2, Pub. by Granada England). Renouf.
Boughton, James M. & Wicker, Elmus R. The Principles of Monetary Economics. 1975. text ed. 15.95x o.p. (ISBN 0-256-01667-4). Irwin.
Bouhours, Dominique. Art of Criticism. Repr. of 1705 ed. write for info. Schol Facsimil.
Bouhuys, Mies, jt. auth. see Ridge, Antonia.
Bouillon, Jo, jt. auth. see Baker, Josephine.
Bouis, Antonina, et al, trs. see Shefner, Vadim.
Bouis, Antonina W., tr. see Beliaev, Alexander.
Bouis, Antonina W., tr. see Okudjava, Boulat.
Bouis, Antonina W., tr. see Rasputin, Valentin.
Bouis, Antonina W., tr. see Strugatsky, Arkady & Strugatsky, Boris.
Bouis, Antonina W., tr. see Tolstoy, Alexei.
Bouissac, Paul. La Mesure Des Gestes: Prolegomenes a la Semiotique Gestuelle. (Approaches to Semiotics, Paperback Ser.: No. 3). 1973. pap. 42.35x (ISBN 90-279-2377-9). Mouton.
Boulanger, jt. auth. see Newman.
Boulay, G. H., ed. Atlas of Normal Vertebral Angiograms. 144p. 1976. 54.95 (ISBN 0-407-00042-9). Butterworths.
Boulay, G. H. Du see Du Boulay, G. H.
Boulay, George Du see Du Boulay, George.
Boulden, James. The Dance of Creation. (Illus.). 96p. (Orig.). 1981. pap. cancelled (ISBN 0-87516-416-1). De Vorss.
Boulding, Elise. The Underside of History: A View of Women Through Time. LC 75-30558. 750p. 1976. lib. bdg. 32.50x (ISBN 0-89158-009-3); text ed. 15.00 (ISBN 0-89158-056-5). Westview.
--Women: The Fifth World. LC 80-65602. (Headline Ser.: No. 248). (Illus.). 64p. (Orig.). 1980. pap. 2.00 (ISBN 0-87124-059-9). Foreign Policy.
Boulding, Elise, et al. Bibliography on World Conflict & Peace. (Special Studies in Peace, Conflict & Conflict Resolution). 1979. lib. bdg. 19.50x (ISBN 0-89158-374-2). Westview.
Boulding, K. E. Primer on Social Dynamics. LC 70-123192. 1970. 8.95 o.s.i. (ISBN 0-02-904580-0); pap. text ed. 3.50 o.s.i. (ISBN 0-02-904570-3). Free Pr.
Boulding, Kenneth E. The Image: Knowledge in Life & Society. 1956. pap. 4.50 (ISBN 0-472-06047-3, AA). U of Mich Pr.
--The Impact of the Social Sciences. (Brown & Haley Lecture Ser.). 1966. 8.00 (ISBN 0-8135-0525-9). Rutgers U Pr.
Boulding, Kenneth E. & Stahr, Elvis J. Economics of Pollution. LC 70-179973. (The Charles C. Moskowitz Lectures). 158p. 1971. 10.00x (ISBN 0-8147-0967-2). NYU Pr.
Boulding, Kenneth E. & Wilson, Thomas F., eds. Redistribution Through the Financial System: The Grants Economics of Money & Credit. LC 78-18017. 1978. 32.95 (ISBN 0-03-045341-0). Praeger.
Boulding, Kenneth E., et al. Social System of the Planet Earth. LC 79-21022. (Economics Ser.). 1980. text ed. 10.95 o.p. (ISBN 0-201-00207-8). A-W.
Boule, Marcellin. Fossil Men: Elements of Human Paleontology. LC 78-72691. 1980. Repr. of 1923 ed. 69.50 (ISBN 0-404-18262-3). AMS Pr.
--L' Homme Fossilede la Chapelle aux Saints. LC 78-72692. 1980. Repr. of 1913 ed. 46.50 (ISBN 0-404-18263-1). AMS Pr.
Bouleau, Charles. The Painter's Secret Geometry: A Study of Composition in Art. LC 79-91815. 268p. 1980. Repr. of 1963 ed. lib. bdg. 30.00 (ISBN 0-87817-259-9). Hacker.
Boulenger, G. A. Fishes of the Nile. 1964. Repr. of 1907 ed. 185.00 (ISBN 3-7682-0241-0). Lubrecht & Cramer.
Boulet, Jean. Magoumaz: Pays Mafa (Nord Cameroun) (Etude D'un Terroir De Montagne) (Atlas des Structures Agraires au Sud de Shara: No. 11). (Illus.). 92p. (Fr.). 1975. pap. text ed. 34.10x (ISBN 90-279-7575-2). Mouton.
Bouley, Alan. From Freedom to Formula: The Evolution of the Eucharistic Prayer from Oral Improvisation to Written Text. (Studies in Christian Antiquity: Vol. 21). 288p. 1980. 25.00x (ISBN 0-8132-0554-9, Pub. by Cath U of America Pr). Intl Schol Bk.
Boulger, James D. The Calvinistic Temper in English Poetry. (De Proprietatibus Litterarum, Ser. Major: No. 21). 1980. text ed. 70.50x (ISBN 90-279-7575-2). Mouton.
Boullata, Issa, ed. Critical Perspectives on Modern Arabic Literature. LC 78-13851. (Orig.). 1980. 22.00x (ISBN 0-89410-007-6); pap. 10.00x (ISBN 0-89410-008-4). Three Continents.
Boulle, Pierre. Because It Is Absurd. LC 74-164984. 8.95 (ISBN 0-8149-0697-4). Vanguard.
--Bridge Over the River Kwai. LC 54-11508. 8.95 (ISBN 0-8149-0072-0). Vanguard.
--Ears of the Jungle. LC 72-83350. 230p. 1972. 8.95 (ISBN 0-8149-0720-2). Vanguard.
--Executioner. LC 61-15474. 1961. 8.95 (ISBN 0-8149-0065-8). Vanguard.
--Face of a Hero. LC 56-12030. 1956. 8.95 (ISBN 0-8149-0070-4). Vanguard.
--Garden on the Moon. LC 65-10229. 1964. 8.95 (ISBN 0-8149-0063-1). Vanguard.
--The Good Leviathan. LC 78-57255. 1979. 8.95 (ISBN 0-8149-0807-1). Vanguard.
--The Marvelous Palace & Other Stories. LC 77-77035. 1978. 8.95 (ISBN 0-8149-0788-1). Vanguard.
--My Own River Kwai. LC 67-29216. 1967. 8.95 (ISBN 0-8149-0061-5). Vanguard.
--Noble Profession. LC 60-15063. 1960. 8.95 (ISBN 0-8149-0066-6). Vanguard.
--Other Side of the Coin. LC 58-13675. 1958. 8.95 (ISBN 0-8149-0068-2). Vanguard.
--Photographer. Fielding, Xan, tr. LC 68-8085. 1968. 8.95 (ISBN 0-8149-0060-7). Vanguard.
--Planet of the Apes. LC 63-21843. 1963. 8.95 (ISBN 0-8149-0064-X). Vanguard.
--S. O. P. H. I. A. LC 59-12392. 1959. 8.95 (ISBN 0-8149-0067-4). Vanguard.
--Test. LC 57-12252. 8.95 (ISBN 0-8149-0069-0). Vanguard.
--Time Out of Mind. LC 66-26792. 1966. 8.95 (ISBN 0-8149-0062-3). Vanguard.
--The Virtues of Hell. Wolf, Patricia, tr. from Fr. LC 74-81811. 224p. 1974. 8.95 (ISBN 0-8149-0744-X). Vanguard.
Boullin, David J. Cerebral Vasospasm. LC 79-40735. 1980. 51.75 (ISBN 0-471-27639-1, Pub. by Wiley-Interscience). Wiley.
Boulmetis, John. Job Competancy: Adult Vocational Instruction. LC 80-82711. (CBE Forum Ser.: Bk.2). 1981. pap. 5.95 (ISBN 0-8224-4014-8). Pitman Learning.
Boulougouris, John C. & Rabalivas, Andreas D., eds. The Treatment of Phobic & Obsessive Compulsive Disorders. 1977. text ed. 23.00 (ISBN 0-08-021472-X); pap. text ed. 11.25 o.p. (ISBN 0-08-021471-1). Pergamon.
Boulting, William. Woman in Italy: From the Introduction of the Chivalrous Service of Love to the Appearance of the Professional Actress. LC 79-2932. (Illus.). 356p. 1981. Repr. of 1910 ed. 27.50 (ISBN 0-8305-0099-5). Hyperion Conn.
Boulton, A. J. see Katritzky, A. R.
Boulton, A. J., jt. ed. see Katritzky, A. R.
Boulton, J. T., ed. The Letters of D. H. Lawrence, Vol. 1. LC 78-7531. (Illus.). 1979. 39.50 (ISBN 0-521-22147-1). Cambridge U Pr.
Boulton, James T. Edmund Burke: A Philosophical Enquiry into the Origin of Our Ideas of the Sublime & Beautiful. 1967. 11.50x (ISBN 0-7100-1140-7). Humanities.
Boulton, Jane & Whitely, Opal. Opal. 152p. 1976. 6.95 o.s.i. (ISBN 0-02-513970-3). Macmillan.
Boulton, John. Basic Steps in Astronomy. (Illus.). 100p. 1980. 9.95 (ISBN 0-7137-1012-8, Pub. by Blandford Pr England). Sterling.
Boulton, Marjorie. The Anatomy of Drama. 1968. pap. 8.95 (ISBN 0-7100-6090-4). Routledge & Kegan.
--The Anatomy of Language: Saying What We Mean. 1971. pap. 7.95 (ISBN 0-7100-6351-2). Routledge & Kegan.
--The Anatomy of Poetry. 1970. pap. 7.95 (ISBN 0-7100-6091-2). Routledge & Kegan.
--The Anatomy of Prose. 1968. pap. 7.95 (ISBN 0-7100-6089-0). Routledge & Kegan.
--Anatomy of the Novel. 1975. pap. 7.95 (ISBN 0-7100-8136-7). Routledge & Kegan.
Bouma, J. L. The Avenging Gun. 1978. pap. 1.50 (ISBN 0-505-51327-7). Tower Bks.
--Burning Valley. 1976. pap. 0.95 o.p. (ISBN 0-685-69511-5, LB378NK, Leisure Bks). Nordon Pubns.
--Hell on Horseback. 1981. pap. 1.75 (ISBN 0-8439-0893-9, Leisure Bks). Nordon Pubns.
--Mediterranean Caper. 1981. pap. 2.25 (ISBN 0-8439-0873-4, Leisure Bks). Nordon Pubns.
Bouma, Lowell. The Semantics of the Modal Auxiliaries in Contemporary German. (Janua Linguarum Ser. Practica: No. 146). 1973. pap. text ed. 28.25x (ISBN 90-279-2390-6). Mouton.
Bouma, Mary L. The Creative Homemaker. LC 73-17234. 1973. pap. 2.45 (ISBN 0-87123-078-X, 210508); study guide 0.95 (ISBN 0-87123-508-0). Bethany Fell.
Bouma, Mary La Grand. Divorce in the Parsonage. LC 79-16157. 1979. pap. 3.95 (ISBN 0-87123-109-3, 210109). Bethany Fell.
Bouman, Helen H., tr. see Chander, Krishan.
Boumans, P. W. Atomic Absorption Spectroscopy-Past, Present & Future: To Commemorate the 25th Anniversary of Alan Walsh's Landmark Paper in Spectrochimica Acta. 248p. 1981. pap. 32.50 (ISBN 0-08-026267-8). Pergamon.
--Line Coincidence Tables for Inductively Coupled Plasma Atomic Emission Spectrometry, 2 vols. LC 80-41344. (Illus.). 941p. 1980. 250.00 set (ISBN 0-08-026243-0). Pergamon.
Bounds, E. M. The Essentials of Prayer. (E. M. Bounds Ser. on Prayer). 144p. 1980. pap. 1.95 (ISBN 0-8024-6723-7). Moody.
--Power Through Prayer. pap. 0.95 (ISBN 0-8024-6721-0). Moody.
--Prayer & Praying Men. (Direction Bks). 1977. pap. 1.95 (ISBN 0-8010-0721-6). Baker Bk.
Bounds, E. M., ed. Power Through Prayer. 1979. mass 1.95 (ISBN 0-8024-6722-9). Moody.
Bounds, Edward M. Power Through Prayer. pap. 1.95 (ISBN 0-310-21612-5). Zondervan.
Boundy, Suzanne S. & Reynolds, Nancy J. Current Concepts in Dental Hygiene, Vol. 2. LC 76-40164. (Illus.). 1979. pap. text ed. 17.95 (ISBN 0-8016-0747-7). Mosby.
Bounton, A. P. Bridge Across Jordan. 6.95 o.p. (ISBN 0-8062-1202-0). Carlton.
Bouquet, A. C. Hinduism. 1949. pap. text ed. 5.25x (ISBN 0-09-030672-4, Hutchinson U Lib). Humanities.
Bouquet, Henry. The Papers of Henry Bouquet: Sept 1, 1759 to August 31, 1760, Vol. 4. 1978. 20.00 (ISBN 0-911124-99-3). Pa Hist & Mus.
Bourbaki, N. Elements of Mathematics: Commutative Algebra. 1972. 57.50 (ISBN 0-201-00644-8, Adv Bk Prog). A-W.
Bourbaki, Nicholas. Algebra, Part One: Elements of Mathematics. (Chapters 1-3). 1973. 57.50 (ISBN 0-201-00639-1, Adv Bk Prog). A-W.
Bourbaki, Nocolas. Elements of Mathematics: Lie Groups & Lie Algebras, Part 1. 1975. pap. 57.50 (ISBN 0-201-00643-X, Adv Bk Prog). A-W.
Bourbousson & Ashworth. Mechanical Engineering Craft Studies, Vol. I. 1974. 5.95 (ISBN 0-408-00120-8). Butterworths.
--Mechanical Engineering Craft Studies, Vol. 2. 1974. text ed. 9.95 (ISBN 0-408-00112-7). Butterworths.
Bourchier, J., tr. see Froissart, Jean.
Bourcier, S. Spectroscopic Data Relative to Diatomic Molecules. 1971. 145.00 (ISBN 0-08-016546-X). Pergamon.

Bourdeaux, Kenneth J. & Long, Hugh W. The Basic Theory of Corporate Finance. LC 76-27895. (Illus.). 1977. pap. text ed. 19.95 (ISBN 0-13-069435-5). P-H.
Bourdeaux, Michael & Murray, Katharine. Young Christians in Russia. LC 76-57846. 1977. pap. 1.95 (ISBN 0-87123-663-X, 200663). Bethany Fell.
Bourdeaux, Michael, ed. see Vins, Georgi.
Bourdieu, P. Outline of a Theory of Practice. LC 76-11073. (Studies in Social Anthropology: No. 16). (Illus.). 1977. 29.95 (ISBN 0-521-21178-6); pap. 9.95x (ISBN 0-521-29164-X). Cambridge U Pr.
Bourdieu, Pierre, et al. Travail et Travailleurs En Algerie. (Recherches Mediterraneennes Documents). 1963. pap. text ed. 40.50x (ISBN 90-279-6224-3). Mouton.
Bourdieu, Pierre, et al, eds. Rapport Pedagogique et Communication. 2nd ed. (Cahiers Du Centre De Sociologie Europeenne: No. 2). 1968. pap. 12.35x (ISBN 90-279-6254-5). Mouton.
Bourdieu, Pierre J., et al, eds. Le Metier De Sociologue: Prealables Epistemologiques. 2nd ed. (Textes De Sciences Sociales: No. 1). 1973. pap. 20.50x (ISBN 0-686-20919-2). Mouton.
Bourdillon, F. W. Aucassin et Nicolete. 128p. 1919. 9.00x (ISBN 0-7190-0387-3, Pub. by Manchester U Pr England). State Mutual Bk.
Bourdillon, F. W., ed. Aucassin et Nicolette Cest Daucasi&De Nicolete. LC 80-2241. (Illus.). 1981. Repr. of 1896 ed. 17.50 (ISBN 0-404-19036-7). AMS Pr.
Bourdoux, Michael. Religious Minorities in the Soviet Union. (Minority Rights Group: No. 1). 1975. pap. 2.50 (ISBN 0-89192-091-9). Interbk Inc.
Bouressa, LaVonne J. Genealogy My Way. LC 77-95808. 1977. 8.95 (ISBN 0-686-12309-3). Genealogy Res.
Bourgeau, Art. The Most Likely Suspects. 196p. (Orig.). 1981. pap. 7.65 (ISBN 0-441-54376-6). Charter Bks.
Bourgeois, Jacques. Animating Films Without a Camera. LC 74-82324. (Little Craft Bk.). (Illus.). 48p. (gr. 7-9). 1974. 5.95 (ISBN 0-8069-5304-7); PLB 6.69 (ISBN 0-8069-5305-5). Sterling.
Bourgeois, Patrick L., jt. auth. see Rosenthal, Sandra.
Bourget, Paul. Disciple. (Classiques Larousse). (Illus., Fr.). pap. 1.95 o.p. (ISBN 0-685-13888-7, 36). Larousse.
--The Disciple. xvii, 341p. 1976. Repr. of 1901 ed. 17.50 (ISBN 0-86527-238-7). Fertig.
Bourgue, R., jt. auth. see Green, C.
Bourguignon, Erika, ed. A World of Women: Anthropological Studies of Women in the Societies of the World. LC 79-11844. 384p. 1980. 24.95 (ISBN 0-03-051221-2); pap. 9.95 (ISBN 0-03-051226-3). Praeger.
Bourguina, A. M. Russian Social Democracy: The Menshevik Movement-A Bibliography. LC 68-21035. (Bibliographical Ser.: No. 36). (Rus). 1968. 10.00 (ISBN 0-8179-2361-6). Hoover Inst Pr.
Bourinot, J. G., et al. Our Intellectual Strength & Weakness; English-Canadian Literature; French-Canadian Literature. LC 72-91693. (Literature of Canada Ser.). 1973. pap. 5.00 (ISBN 0-8020-6175-3). U of Toronto Pr.
Bourinot, John G. Parliamentary Procedure & Practice in the Dominion of Canada. 785p. 1980. Repr. 70.00x (ISBN 0-7165-2021-4, Pub. by Irish Academic Pr). Biblio Dist.
Bourke, John. Baroque Churches of Central Europe. (Illus.). 1978. pap. 10.95 (ISBN 0-571-10689-7, Pub. by Faber & Faber). Merrimack Bk Serv.
Bourke, John G. The Medicine Man of the Apache. 1979. 10.00 (ISBN 0-87026-049-9). Westernlore.
--On the Border with Crook. LC 74-155699. 1971. pap. 8.50 (ISBN 0-8032-5741-4, BB 535, Bison). U of Nebr Pr.
Bourke, Linda. Handmade ABC: A Manual Alphabet. LC 80-27007. (Illus.). 64p. (gr. 1-9). 1981. PLB 6.95 (ISBN 0-201-00016-4, A-W Childrens); pap. 3.95 (ISBN 0-201-00015-6). A-W.
--Making Soft Dinos. LC 79-56337. (Illus.). 76p. (gr. 5 up). 1980. lib. bdg. 6.99 (ISBN 0-8178-0012-3). Harvey.
Bourke, Linda, jt. auth. see Sullivan, Mary Beth.
Bourke, S. F., et al. Oracy in Australian Schools. (Australian Council for Educational Research Ser.: No. 9). 258p. 1980. pap. text ed. 21.00x (ISBN 0-85563-212-7). Verry.
Bourke, Vernon J., jt. ed. see Miethe, Terry L.
Bourliere, Francois. Land & Wildlife of Eurasia. rev. ed. LC 63-21615. (Life Nature Library). (Illus.). 1967. PLB 8.97 o.p. (ISBN 0-8094-0628-4, Pub. by Time-Life). Silver.
Bourne, A. J., jt. auth. see Green, A. E.
Bourne, Eleanor. The Heritage of Flowers. (The Leprechaun Library). (Illus.). 64p. 1980. 3.95 (ISBN 0-399-12544-2). Putnam.
Bourne, G. H. & Danielli, J. F. International Review of Cytology, Vol. 69. (Serial Publications Ser.). 1981. 38.00 (ISBN 0-12-364469-0). Acad Pr.
Bourne, G. H; see Metzner, H.
Bourne, G. H., ed. Human Nutrition & Diet. (World Review of Nutrition & Dietetics Ser.: Vol. 36). (Illus.). x, 226p. 1980. 115.00 (ISBN 3-8055-1347-X). S Karger.
--Human Nutrition & Nutrition & Pesticides in Cattle, Vol. 35. (World Review of Nutrition & Dietetics: Vol. 35). (Illus.). 238p. 1980. 115.00 (ISBN 3-8055-0442-X). S Karger.
--Muscular Dystrophy in Man & Animals. (Illus.). 1963. 37.25 o.s.i. (ISBN 0-02-841750-X). Hafner.
--World Review of Nutrition & Dietetics, Vol. 37. (Illus.). x, 240p. 1981. 115.00 (ISBN 3-8055-2143-X). S Karger.
Bourne, G. H. & Danielli, J. F., eds. International Review of Cytology. Incl. Vol. 1. 1952. 49.50 (ISBN 0-12-364301-5); Vol. 2. 1953. 49.50 (ISBN 0-12-364302-3); Vol. 3. 1954. 49.50 (ISBN 0-12-364303-1); Vol. 4. 1955. 49.50 (ISBN 0-12-364304-X); Vol. 5. 1956. 49.50 (ISBN 0-12-364305-8); Vol. 6. 1957. 49.50 (ISBN 0-12-364306-6); Vol. 7. 1958. 49.50 (ISBN 0-12-364307-4); Vol. 8. 1959. 49.50 (ISBN 0-12-364308-2); Vol. 9. 1960. 49.50 (ISBN 0-12-364309-0); Vol. 10. 1960. 49.50 (ISBN 0-12-364310-4); Vol. 11. 1961. 49.50 (ISBN 0-12-364311-2); Vol. 12. 1961. 49.50 (ISBN 0-12-364312-0); Vol. 13. 1962. 49.50 (ISBN 0-12-364313-9); Vol. 14. 1963. 49.50 (ISBN 0-12-364314-7); Vol. 15. 1963. 49.50 (ISBN 0-12-364315-5); Vol. 16. 1964. 49.50 (ISBN 0-12-364316-3); 49.50 (ISBN 0-12-364317-1); Vol. 18. 1965. 49.50 (ISBN 0-12-364318-X); Vol. 19. 1966. 49.50 (ISBN 0-12-364319-8); Vol. 20. 1966. 49.50 (ISBN 0-12-364320-1); Vol. 21. 1967. 49.50 (ISBN 0-12-364321-X); Vol. 22. Jeon, K., ed. 1967. 46.50 (ISBN 0-12-364322-8); Vol. 23. 1968. **49.50 (ISBN 0-12-364323-6); Vol. 24. 1968. 49.50 (ISBN 0-12-364324-4); Vol. 25. 1969. 49.50 (ISBN 0-12-364325-2); Vol. 26. 1969. 49.50 (ISBN 0-12-364326-0); Vol. 27. 1970. 49.50 (ISBN 0-12-364327-9); Vol. 28. 1970. 49.50 (ISBN 0-12-364328-7); Vol. 29. 1970. 49.50 (ISBN 0-12-364329-5). Acad Pr.**
--International Review of Cytology. Incl. Vol. 30. 1971. 49.50 (ISBN 0-12-364330-9); Vol. 31. 1971. 49.50 (ISBN 0-12-364331-7); Vol. 32. 1972. 49.50 (ISBN 0-12-364332-5); Vol. 33. 1972. 49.50 (ISBN 0-12-364333-3); Vol. 34. 1973. 49.50 (ISBN 0-12-364334-1); Vol. 35. 1973. 49.50 (ISBN 0-12-364335-X); Vol. 36. 1973. 49.50 (ISBN 0-12-364336-8); Vol. 37. 1974. 49.50 (ISBN 0-12-364337-6); Vol. 38. 1974. 49.50 (ISBN 0-12-364338-4); Vol. 39. 1974. 49.50 (ISBN 0-12-364339-2); Vol. 40. Jones, R. N., ed. 1975. 49.50 (ISBN 0-12-364340-6); Vol. 41. Leibowitz, Paul J. & Schaechter, Moselio, eds. 1975. 49.50 (ISBN 0-12-364341-4); Vol. 42. Lozzio, Bismarck B. & Lozzio, Carmen, eds. 1975. 49.50 (ISBN 0-12-364342-2); Vol. 43. Mahler, Henry R. & Raff, Rudolf A., eds. 1975. 49.50 (ISBN 0-12-364343-0); Vol. 44. 1976. 49.50 (ISBN 0-12-364344-9); Vol. 45. 49.50 (ISBN 0-12-364345-7); Vol. 46. 1976. 52.50 (ISBN 0-12-364346-5); Vol. 47. 1976. 46.00 (ISBN 0-12-364347-3); Vol. 48. 1977. 52.75 (ISBN 0-12-364348-1); Vol. 49. 1977. 47.00 (ISBN 0-12-364349-X); Vol. 50. 1977. 44.00 (ISBN 0-12-364350-3). Acad Pr.
--International Review of Cytology, Vol. 71. 1981. write for info. (ISBN 0-12-364471-2). Acad Pr.
Bourne, G. H. & Muggleton-Harris, Audrey L., eds. International Review of Cytology: Supplement 12. (Serial Publication). 1981. price not set (ISBN 0-12-364373-2). Acad Pr.
Bourne, Geoffrey & Danielli, James, eds. International Review of Cytology, Vol. 72. (Serial Publication). 1981. price not set (ISBN 0-12-364472-0). Acad Pr.
Bourne, Geoffrey H. The Structure & Function of Muscle. 2nd ed. Vol. 1, 1972. 67.00 (ISBN 0-12-119101-X); Vol. 2, 1973. 72.50 (ISBN 0-12-119102-8); Vol. 3, 1973. 67.00 (ISBN 0-12-119103-6); Vol. 4, 1974. 67.00 (ISBN 0-12-119104-4); 223.25 set (ISBN 0-685-36103-9). Acad Pr.
Bourne, Geoffrey H., ed. Hearts & Heart-Like Organs: Comparative Anatomy & Development, Vol. I. LC 80-760. 1980. 51.00 (ISBN 0-12-119401-9). Acad Pr.
--Hearts & Heart-Like Organs, Vol. 2: Physiology. LC 80-18121. 1980. 57.00 (ISBN 0-12-119402-7). Acad Pr.
--Hearts & Heart-Like Organs: Vol. 3, Physiology. 1980. 53.00 (ISBN 0-12-119403-5). Acad Pr.
Bourne, Geoffrey H. & Danielli, James F., eds. International Review of Cytology, Vol. 64. LC 52-5203. 1980. 36.50 (ISBN 0-12-364464-X). Acad Pr.
--International Review of Cytology, Vol. 65. 1980. 39.50 (ISBN 0-12-364465-8). Acad Pr.
--International Review of Cytology, Vol. 66. (Serial Pub.). 1980. 39.00 (ISBN 0-12-364466-6). Acad Pr.
--International Review of Cytology, Vol. 68. 1980. 38.00 (ISBN 0-12-364468-2). Acad Pr.
--International Review of Cytology, Vol. 70. (Serial Publication). 1981. price not set (ISBN 0-12-364470-4). Acad Pr.
Bourne, Gordon, jt. auth. see Hector, Winifred.
Bourne, Kenneth. Britain & the Balance of Power in North America, 1815-1908. 1967. 26.00x (ISBN 0-520-00153-2). U of Cal Pr.
Bourne, Kenneth, ed. The Letters of the Third Viscount Palmerston to Laurence & Elizabeth Sulivan: 1804-1863. (Royal Historical Society: Camden Society Fourth Ser.: Vol. 23). 350p. 1979. 20.00x (ISBN 0-8476-3306-3). Rowman.
Bourne, L. S. Urban Systems-Strategies for Regulation. (Illus.). 284p. 1975. text ed. 29.95x (ISBN 0-19-874054-9); pap. text ed. 14.50x (ISBN 0-19-874055-7). Oxford U Pr.
Bourne, L. S., et al, eds. Urban Futures for Central Canada: Perspectives on Forecasting Urban Growth & Form. LC 73-92297. 1974. pap. 7.50x (ISBN 0-8020-6243-1). U of Toronto Pr.
Bourne, Larry S. Geography of Housing. (Scripta Series in Geography). 290p. 1981. 27.95 (ISBN 0-470-27058-6); pap. 19.95 (ISBN 0-470-27059-4). Halsted Pr.
Bourne, Larry S., ed. Internal Structure of the City: Readings on Space & Environment. 1971. pap. text ed. 8.95x (ISBN 0-19-501321-2). Oxford U Pr.
Bourne, Larry S. & Simmons, James W., eds. Systems of Cities: Readings on Structure Growth & Policy. (Illus.). 1978. pap. text ed. 10.95x (ISBN 0-19-502264-5). Oxford U Pr.
Bourne, Lyle E., Jr., et al. Psychology of Thinking. LC 79-135409. 1971. ref. ed. 19.95 (ISBN 0-13-736702-3). P-H.
Bourne, Miriam A. The Children of Mount Vernon: A Guide to George Washington's Home. LC 80-974. (Illus.). 64p. (gr. 4-6). 1981. PLB 8.95 (ISBN 0-385-15535-2); pap. 4.95 (ISBN 0-385-15534-4). Doubleday.
Bourne, R., ed. Handbook on Serials Librarianship. 1980. 33.00x (ISBN 0-85365-631-2, Pub. by Lib Assn England); pap. text ed. 15.95x (ISBN 0-85365-721-1). Oryx Pr.
Bourne, Randolph. History of a Literary Radical & Other Essays. LC 69-17713. 1969. Repr. of 1920 ed. 12.00x (ISBN 0-8196-0225-6). Biblo.
Bourne, Randolph S. Towards an Enduring Peace. LC 73-147574. (Library of War & Peace; Int'l. Organization, Arbitration & Law). lib. bdg. 38.00 (ISBN 0-8240-0340-3). Garland Pub.
Bourne, Richard & Newberger, Eli H., eds. Critical Perspectives on Child Abuse. LC 77-18565. (Illus.). 1978. 19.95 (ISBN 0-669-02109-1). Lexington Bks.
Bourne, Russell, ed. see Hay, Keith, et al.
Bourne, Russell, ed. see Johnson, Fred.
Bourne, Russell, ed. see LaBastille, Anne.
Bourne, William. A Booke Called the Treasure for Travellers. LC 77-25950. (English Experience Ser.: No. 911). 276p. 1979. Repr. of 1578 ed. lib. bdg. 26.00. Walter J Johnson.
Bournonville, August. My Theatre Life. McAndrew, Patricia, tr. LC 78-27349. (Illus.). 1979. 40.00 (ISBN 0-8195-5035-3, Pub. by Wesleyan U Pr). Columbia U Pr.
Bournot, K. see Von Wiesner, J. & Von Regel, C.
Bouscaren, Anthony T. Comparative Government: Europe & Asia. LC 79-64098. 1979. pap. text ed. 9.00 (ISBN 0-8191-0754-9). U Pr of Amer.
--Government in American Society. LC 78-62171. 1978. pap. text ed. 10.25 (ISBN 0-8191-0506-6). U Pr of Amer.
Bousfield, E. L. Shallow-Water Gammaridean Ampphipoda of New England. LC 72-4636. (Illus.). 1973. 35.00x (ISBN 0-8014-0726-5). Comstock.
Bousfield, Shirley, jt. auth. see Wallace, Arthur.
Boustead, Hugh. The Wind of Morning. (Illus.). 1979. 9.95 (ISBN 0-7011-1314-6, Pub. by Chatto Bodley Jonathan). Merrimack Bk Serv.
Boustead, I. & Hancock, G. F. Handbook of Industrial Energy Analysis. LC 78-40636. 1979. 76.95 (ISBN 0-470-26492-6). Halsted Pr.
Boutell, Charles. Boutell's Heraldry. rev. ed. LC 73-75030. (Illus.). 368p. 1978. 30.00 (ISBN 0-7232-2096-4). Warne.
Bouterse, Wesley. Scriptural Light on Speaking in Tongues. 1980. pap. 0.85 (ISBN 0-86544-010-7). Salvation Army.
Boutet de Monvel, Maurice. Joan of Arc. LC 80-5169. (Illus.). 64p. (gr. 7). 1980. Repr. of 1897 ed. 12.95 (ISBN 0-670-40735-6, Studio). Viking Pr.
Boutiere, Jean, ed. see De Sestero, Albertet.
Boutilier, Mary A., jt. auth. see Kelly, Rita M.
Bouton, Jim. Ball Four, Plus Ball Five. rev. ed. LC 80-6165. 432p. 1981. 12.95 (ISBN 0-8128-2771-6). Stein & Day.
Bouvard, Marguerite. The Intentional Community Movement: Building a New Moral World. LC 74-80593. 1975. 15.00 (ISBN 0-8046-9100-2, Natl U). Kennikat.
Bouvier, Jacqueline & Bouvier, Lee. One Special Summer. (Illus.). 70p. 1974. 7.95 o.s.i. (ISBN 0-440-06037-0, E Friede). Delacorte.
Bouvier, Jean & Girault, Rene. L' Imperialisme Francais d'Avant 1914: Recueil De Textes. (Savoir Historique Ser.: No. 10). (Fr.). 1976. pap. text ed. 34.10x (ISBN 90-279-7992-8). Mouton.
Bouvier, Jean, et al. Le Mouvement Du Profit En France Au XIXe Siecle: Materiaux et Etudes. (Industrie et Artisanat: No. 1). 1965. pap. 40.50x (ISBN 90-279-6132-8). Mouton.
Bouvier, Lee, jt. auth. see Bouvier, Jacqueline.
Bouwmeester, H. Winning Chess Combinations. 1977. 15.95 (ISBN 0-7134-0419-1, Pub. by Batsford England); pap. 12.50 (ISBN 0-7134-0420-5). David & Charles.
Bouwsma, William J. Venice & the Defense of Republican Liberty: Renaissance Values in the Age of the Counter Reformation. (Illus.). 1968. 30.00x (ISBN 0-520-00151-6). U of Cal Pr.
Bouyer, Louis. A History of Christian Spirituality, 3 vols. 1977. Set. 45.00 (ISBN 0-8164-0349-X); Vol. 1. 17.50 (ISBN 0-8164-0325-2); Vol. 2. 19.50 (ISBN 0-8164-0326-0); Vol. 3. 12.50 (ISBN 0-8164-0327-9). Crossroad NY.
--Woman in the Church. Teichert, Marilyn, tr. from Fr. LC 79-84878. Orig. Title: Mystere et Ministeres De la Femme Dans L'eglise. 132p. (Orig.). 1979. pap. 4.95 (ISBN 0-89870-002-7). Ignatius Pr.
Bouza, Anthony V. Police Administration: Organization & Performance. LC 77-24748. 1978. text ed. 18.25 (ISBN 0-08-022220-X). Pergamon.
Bova, Ben. Exiled from Earth. LC 74-133120. (gr. 5-12). 1971. PLB 9.95 (ISBN 0-525-29425-2); pap. 0.95 o.p. (ISBN 0-525-45016-5). Dutton.
--Forward in Time. 256p. 1974. pap. 1.25 o.p. (ISBN 0-445-08310-7). Popular Lib.
--In Quest of Quasars: An Introduction to Stars & Starlike Objects. (Surveyor Books Ser). (Illus.). (gr. 7 up). 1970. 7.95g o.s.i. (ISBN 0-02-711750-2, CCPr). Macmillan.
--Kinsman. 1981. pap. 2.95 (ISBN 0-440-14527-9). Dell. Postponed.
--Millennium. (A Del Rey Bk.). 1977. pap. 1.95 (ISBN 0-685-75021-3, 345-25556-9-195). Ballantine.
--The Starcrossed. 1979. pap. 1.75 (ISBN 0-515-05133-0). Jove Pubns.
Bova, Ben, ed. Analog Science Fact Reader. LC 73-87398. 1976. pap. 8.95 (ISBN 0-312-03220-X). St Martin.
Bovay, H. E., Jr. Handbook of Mechanical & Electrical Systems for Buildings. (Illus.). 1981. 49.50 (ISBN 0-07-006718-X). McGraw.
Bovbjerg, Dana, jt. auth. see Iggers, Jeremy.
Bove, Arthur. First Over Germany: A Story of the 306th Bombardment Group. LC 80-69557. (Aviation Ser.: No. 4). (Illus.). 138p. Repr. 20.00 (ISBN 0-89839-038-9). Battery Pr.
Bove, Paul A. Destructive Poetics: Heidegger & Modern American Poetry. 1980. text ed. 17.50x (ISBN 0-231-04690-1). Columbia U Pr.
Boverie, Edward. Audio Service in Public Libraries. (Illus.). 175p. (Orig.). Date not set. spiral 7.50 (ISBN 0-913578-21-5). Inglewood CA. Postponed.
Bovet, Theodore. Handbook to Marriage. rev. ed. LC 74-82958. 1969. pap. 1.95 (ISBN 0-385-09505-8, C23, Dolp). Doubleday.
Bovey, Frank, jt. ed. see Woodward, Arthur E.
Bovey, Frank A. NMR Data Tables for Organic Compounds, Vol. 1. LC 67-20258. 1967. 149.00 (ISBN 0-470-09210-6, Pub. by Wiley-Interscience). Wiley.
--Nuclear Magnetic Resonance Spectroscopy. LC 68-23485. 1969. 20.95 o.p. (ISBN 0-12-119750-6). Acad Pr.
Bovey, John. Desirable Aliens: Stories. LC 80-18596. (Illinois Short Fiction Ser.). 147p. 1980. 10.00 (ISBN 0-252-00837-5); pap. 3.95 (ISBN 0-252-00838-3). U of Ill Pr.
Bovey, Rodney W. & Young, Alvin L. The Science of Two, Four, Five-T & Associated Phenoxy Herbicides. 1980. 37.50 (ISBN 0-471-05134-9, Pub. by Wiley-Interscience). Wiley.
Bovie, Smith P., tr. see Horace.
Bovie, Smith P., tr. see Virgil.
Bovill, Edward W. & Hallet, Robin. Golden Trade of the Moors. 2nd ed. 1968. 13.50x (ISBN 0-19-215630-6); pap. 6.95x (ISBN 0-19-285045-8). Oxford U Pr.
Bovis, H. Eugene. Jerusalem Question: 1917-1968. LC 73-149796. (Studies Ser.: No. 29). (Illus.). 175p. 1971. 6.95 (ISBN 0-8179-3291-7). Hoover Inst Pr.
Bowan, John T. & Jones, P. Teach Yourself Welsh. (Teach Yourself Ser). pap. 4.50 o.p. (ISBN 0-679-10825-4). McKay.

Bowden, David K. The Execution of Isaac Hayne. new ed. LC 76-20850. (Illus.). 1977. 9.95 (ISBN 0-87844-037-2); ltd signed ed 12.95 (ISBN 0-87844-014-3). Sandlapper Store.

Bowden, Edwin T., ed. Satiric Poems of John Trumbull: The Progress of Dulness & M'Fingal. LC 61-15829. 1971. Repr. of 1962 ed. 12.50x (ISBN 0-292-73366-6). U of Tex Pr.

Bowden, Ernestine L. History of the Sunnyside Community: This Land We Hold. 12.95 o.p. (ISBN 0-685-48808-X). Nortex Pr.

Bowden, Frank P. & Tabor, D. Friction & Lubrication of Solids, 2 Vols. (International Ser. of Monographs on Physics). Vol. 1. 36.00x o.p. (ISBN 0-19-851204-X). Oxford U Pr.

Bowden, Gerald. Coastal Aquaculture Law & Policy: A Case Study of California. (Special Studies in Agricultural Science & Policy). 300p. 1981. lib. bdg. 25.00x (ISBN 0-86531-108-0). Westview.

Bowden, Henry W. & Ronda, James P. John Eliot's Indian Dialogues: A Study in Cultural Interaction. Eliot, John, ed. LC 80-542. (Contributions in American History: No. 88). (Illus.). 173p. 1980. lib. bdg. 22.95 (ISBN 0-313-21031-4, RID/). Greenwood.

Bowden, Joan. Bear's Surprise Party. (Eager Readers Ser). (gr. k-3). 1975. PLB 5.00 (ISBN 0-307-60809-3, Golden Pr). Western Pub.

--Bouncy Baby Bunny Finds His Bed. (Illus.). (gr. k-3). 1977. PLB 5.00 (ISBN 0-307-60029-7, Golden Pr). Western Pub.

--Ginghams & the Backward Picnic. (A Young Reader Ser.). (Illus.). (gr. k-3). 1979. PLB 5.00 (ISBN 0-307-60148-X, Golden Pr). Western Pub.

--A New Home for Snow Ball. (Eager Readers Ser.). (Illus.). (gr. k-3). 1975. PLB 5.00 (ISBN 0-307-60800-X, Golden Pr). Western Pub.

--Who Took the Top Hat Trick. (Eager Readers Ser.). (Illus.). (gr. k-3). 1975. PLB 5.00 (ISBN 0-307-60805-0, Golden Pr). Western Pub.

--Why the Tides Ebb & Flow. (gr. k-3). 1979. PLB 7.95 (ISBN 0-395-28378-7). HM.

Bowden, Joan C. The Bean Boy. LC 78-12150. (Ready-to-Read Ser.). (Illus.). (gr. 1-4). 1979. 7.95 (ISBN 0-02-711800-2). Macmillan.

--Little Grey Rabbit. (Tell-a-Tale Readers). (Illus.). (gr. k-3). 1979. PLB 4.77 (ISBN 0-307-68651-5, Whitman). Western Pub.

--My Measuring Book. (Golden Play & Learn Bk). (Illus.). 14p. (ps). 1980. pap. 2.95 (ISBN 0-307-10729-9). Western Pubs OH.

--Something Wonderful Happened. LC 77-6325. (I Can Read a Bible Story Ser.: No. 2). (Illus.). (gr. 2-4). 1977. 4.95 (ISBN 0-570-07324-3, 56-1515); pap. 1.95 (ISBN 0-570-07318-9, 56-1415). Concordia.

Bowden, John, tr. see Boerma, Conrad.

Bowden, John, tr. see Hengel, Martin.

Bowden, John, tr. see Herrmann, Siegfried.

Bowden, John, tr. see Soggin, J. Alberto.

Bowden, John, et al, trs. see Jeremias, Joachim.

Bowden, John S., tr. see Grillmeier, Aloys.

Bowden, Ken, jt. auth. see Nicklaus, Jack.

Bowden, M. L. & Feller, I., eds. The Psycho-Social Aspects of a Severe Burn: a Review of the Literature: Supplement to International Bibliography on Burns 1979. Jones, C. A. LC 79-89259. 1979. pap. text ed. 16.00 (ISBN 0-917478-34-7). Natl Inst Burn.

Bowden, M. L., et al. Progress in Rehabilitation: A Review of Three Studies. Jones, C., ed. LC 80-83417. (Illus.). 1981. 35.00 (ISBN 0-917478-35-5). Natl Inst Burn.

Bowden, Martyn J., jt. ed. see Lowenthal, David.

Bowden, Mary W. Philip Freneau. (U. S. Authors Ser.: No. 260). 1976. lib. bdg. 9.95 (ISBN 0-8057-7161-1). Twayne.

--Washington Irving. (United States Authors Ser.: No. 397). 1981. lib. bdg. 9.95 (ISBN 0-8057-7314-2). Twayne.

Bowder, Diana, ed. Who Was Who in the Roman World. LC 80-67821. (Illus.). 256p. 1980. 25.00 (ISBN 0-8014-1358-3). Cornell U Pr.

Bowdich, Thomas E. An Account of the Discoveries of the Portuguese in the Interior of Angola & Mozambique. LC 74-15013. Repr. of 1824 ed. 21.00 (ISBN 0-404-12008-3). AMS Pr.

Bowditch, James L., jt. auth. see Huse, Edgar F.

Bowditch, John & Ramsland, Clement, eds. Voices of the Industrial Revolution: Selected Readings from the Liberal Economists & Their Critics. 1961. pap. 4.50 (ISBN 0-472-06053-8, 53, AA). U of Mich Pr.

Bowditch, Nancy. George De Forest Brush: A Joyous Painter. 1970. 12.50x (ISBN 0-87233-008-7). Bauhan.

Bowditch, Nathaniel. Bowditch for Yachtsmen: Piloting. 1980. pap. 7.95 (ISBN 0-679-50930-5). McKay.

Bowdler, G. W. Measurements in High-Voltage Test Circuits. LC 72-86488. 192p. 1973. text ed. 30.00 (ISBN 0-08-016838-8). Pergamon.

Bowdler, Lucy. Janis Hall, Nurse Instructor. (YA) 1977. 4.95 o.p. (ISBN 0-685-73811-6, Avalon). Bouregy.

--Nurse Sandra's Choice. (YA) 1978. 5.95 (ISBN 0-685-85781-6, Avalon). Bouregy.

Bowe, Frank. Handicapping America: Barriers to Disabled People. LC 77-11816. 1978. 14.95 (ISBN 0-06-010422-8, HarpT). Har-Row.

Bowe, Nicola G. Harry Clarke: His Graphic Art. (Illus.). 120p. 1980. text ed. 39.00x (ISBN 0-85105-359-9, Dolmen Pr). Humanities.

Bowe, Richard J. Pictorial History of Florida. 3rd ed. 1970. 10.00 (ISBN 0-913122-14-9). Mickler Hse.

Bowen. Thoroughbreds of 1976. Date not set. 46.25 (ISBN 0-936032-14-6). Thoroughbred Own & Breed.

--Thoroughbreds of 1978. Date not set. 36.25 (ISBN 0-936032-15-4). Thoroughbred Own & Breed.

Bowen & Behr. The Logical Design of Multiple Microprocessor Systems. (Illus.). 272p. 1980. text ed. 21.50 (ISBN 0-13-539908-4). P-H.

Bowen, Barbara C., ed. Four Farces: L'obstination Des Femmes; le Cuvier: le Paste et la Tarte; Maistre Pierre Pathelin. (French Texts Ser.). 1967. pap. 10.00x (ISBN 0-631-00670-2, Pub. by Basil Blackwell). Biblio Dist.

Bowen, Bruce D. & Weisberg, Herbert F. An Introduction to Data Analysis. LC 79-27870. (Illus.). 1980. text ed. 15.95x (ISBN 0-7167-1173-7); pap. text ed. 7.95x (ISBN 0-7167-1174-5). W H Freeman.

Bowen, Bruce D., jt. auth. see Weisberg, Herbert F.

Bowen, Catherine & Von Meck, Barbara. Beloved Friend: The Story of Tchaikowsky & Nadejda Von Meck. LC 73-3923. 1976. Repr. of 1961 ed. lib. bdg. 32.00x (ISBN 0-8371-6861-9, BOBF). Greenwood.

Bowen, D. Q. Inqua Field Guides, 16 vols. Incl. Vol. 1. East Anglia. West, R. G., ed; Vol. 2. The English Midlands. Shotton, F. W., ed; Vol. 3. The Isle of Man: Lancashire Coast & Lake District. Tooley, M. J., ed; Vol. 4. South East England & the Thames Valley. Shepherd-Thorn, E. R. & Wymer, J. J., eds.; Vol. 5. Yorkshire & Lincolnshire. Catt, J. A., ed; Vol. 6. South West England. Mottershead, D. N., ed; Vol. 7. Wales & the Cheshire Shropshire Lowland. Bowen, D. Q., ed; Vol. 8. Mid & North Wales. Watson, E., ed; Vol. 9. The Northern Highlands of Scotland. Clapperton, C. M., ed; Vol. 10. The Scottish Highlands. Sissons, J. B., ed; Vol. 11. Western Scotland I. Price, R. J., ed; Vol. 12. Western Scotland II. Dickson, J. H., ed; Vol. 13. South East Ireland. Huddart, D., ed; Vol. 14. South & Southwest Ireland. Lewis, C. A., ed; Vol. 15. Western Ireland. Finch, T; Vol. 16. Southern Shores of the North Sea. Paepe, R., ed. 1980. Set. pap. text ed. 112.00 (ISBN 0-686-64925-7, Pub. by GEO Abstracts England); **pap. text ed. 8.00 ea. State Mutual Bk.**

--Quaternary Geology. (Illus.). 224p. 1978. 39.00 (ISBN 0-08-020601-8); pap. 13.75 (ISBN 0-08-020409-0). Pergamon.

Bowen, Dana T. Lore of the Lakes. 1940. 9.50 (ISBN 0-685-11634-4). Freshwater.

--Memories of the Lakes. 1946. 9.50 (ISBN 0-685-11635-2). Freshwater.

--Shipwrecks of the Lakes. 1952. 9.50 (ISBN 0-685-11636-0). Freshwater.

Bowen, David. Picture Book of San Antonio. 32p. (English & Spanish.). pap. 2.50 (ISBN 0-931722-02-0). Corona Pub.

Bowen, Denise M., jt. auth. see Darby, Michele L.

Bowen, Douglas J., jt. ed. see Keylin, Arlene.

Bowen, Earl K. Mathematics: With Applications in Management & Economics. 5th ed. 1980. 19.95x (ISBN 0-256-02349-2). Irwin.

--Mathematics: With Applications in Management & Economics. 4th ed. 1976. text ed. 16.95x o.p. (ISBN 0-256-01839-1). Irwin.

Bowen, Edward L., jt. auth. see Wharton, Mary E.

Bowen, Elizabeth. The Collected Stories of Elizabeth Bowen. LC 80-8729. 784p. 1981. 17.95 (ISBN 0-394-51666-4). Knopf.

--The Death of the Heart. 352p. Date not set. pap. 2.45 (ISBN 0-394-70021-X, Vin). Random.

--The House in Paris. 1979. pap. 2.50 (ISBN 0-380-44602-2, 44602). Avon.

Bowen, Ezra. The High Sierra. (The American Wilderness Ser). (Illus.). 1972. 12.95 (ISBN 0-8094-1140-7). Time-Life.

--The High Sierra. (American Wilderness Ser). (Illus.). (gr. 6 up). 1972. lib. bdg. 11.97 (ISBN 0-8094-1141-5, Pub. by Time-Life). Silver.

--Knights of the Air. Time-Life Books, ed. (Epic of Flight Ser.). (Illus.). 1980. 12.95 (ISBN 0-8094-3250-1). Time-Life.

Bowen, Francis. The Principles of Political Economy, Applied to the Condition, the Resources, & the Institutions of the American People. (The Neglected American Economists Ser.). 1974. lib. bdg. 50.00 (ISBN 0-8240-1011-6). Garland Pub.

Bowen, Gary. A Special Gift for Mother. LC 80-68234. (Illus.). (gr. 4 up). 1981. 6.95 (ISBN 0-374-37147-4). FS&G.

Bowen, H. R., ed. see Carnegie Commission on Higher Education.

Bowen, Harbison, Lester & Somers, et al. Princeton Symposium of Social Insurance: Its Philosophy, Impact & Future Development. 1968. text ed. 16.95 o.p. (ISBN 0-07-006730-9, C). McGraw.

Bowen, Howard. Toward Social Economy. LC 76-43973. (Political & Social Economy Ser.). 367p. 1977. Repr. of 1948 ed. 19.95x (ISBN 0-8093-0813-4). S Ill U Pr.

Bowen, I. Population. (Cambridge Economic Handbook Ser.). 1954. pap. 10.95x (ISBN 0-521-08753-8). Cambridge U Pr.

Bowen, Ian. Economics & Demography. (Studies in Economics). 1976. text ed. 19.95x (ISBN 0-04-330268-8); pap. text ed. 8.95x (ISBN 0-04-330269-6). Allen Unwin.

Bowen, Irene. Suddenly - a Witch. LC 74-117234. (Illus.). (gr. 4-6). 1970. 3.95 o.p. (ISBN 0-397-31164-8). Lippincott.

Bowen, J. David. The Land & People of Chile. LC 75-41364. (Portraits of the Nations). (gr. 7 up). 1976. 8.95 o.s.i. (ISBN 0-397-31557-0). Lippincott.

Bowen, J. Donald, ed. Beginning Tagalog: A Course for Speakers of English. (Orig.). 1965. pap. 17.75x (ISBN 0-520-00156-7). U. of Cal Pr.

--Intermediate Readings in Tagalog. (Orig.). 1968. pap. 15.50x (ISBN 0-520-00157-5). U of Cal Pr.

Bowen, James K., ed. Classic Short Fiction: An International Collection. Vanderbeets, Richard. LC 70-183111. 1972. pap. 6.95 (ISBN 0-672-61240-2). Bobbs.

Bowen, James K. & VanDerBeets, Richard, eds. American Short Fiction: Readings & Criticism. LC 74-115055. (Orig.). 1970. pap. 9.50 (ISBN 0-672-60648-8). Bobbs.

Bowen, John. These Primal Years. 240p. 1981. 10.00 (ISBN 0-682-49719-3). Exposition.

Bowen, K. C. Research Games: An Approach to the Study of Decision Processes. (ORASA Text Ser.: No. 3). 1978. pap. 19.95 (ISBN 0-470-26535-3). Halsted Pr.

Bowen, Majorie. Peter Porcupine. LC 78-145715. 1971. Repr. of 1935 ed. 20.00 (ISBN 0-8103-3677-4). Gale.

Bowen, Mary, jt. auth. see Petty, Walter T.

Bowen, Norman L. The Evolution of Igneous Rocks. 1928. pap. 5.00 (ISBN 0-486-60311-3). Dover.

Bowen, Owen. Tales from the Mabinogion. LC 78-155665. (Illus.). 1974. 6.95 (ISBN 0-8149-0706-7). Vanguard.

Bowen, Peter. Social Control in Industrial Organisations. (Direct Edition Ser.). (Orig.). 1976. pap. 17.95x (ISBN 0-7100-8312-2). Routledge & Kegan.

Bowen, Ralph, tr. see Diderot, Denis.

Bowen, Robert. Geothermal Resources. LC 79-41547. 243p. 1980. 59.95x (ISBN 0-470-26917-0). Halsted Pr.

--Grouting in Engineering Practice. LC 75-20111. 186p. 1975. 42.95 (ISBN 0-470-09221-1). Halsted Pr.

Bowen, Robert & Gunatilaka, Ananda. Copper: Its Geology & Economics. LC 77-5877. 1977. 99.95 (ISBN 0-470-99156-9). Halsted Pr.

Bowen, Robert S. Infield Flash. LC 69-14320. (gr. 7-12). 1969. 6.75 o.p. (ISBN 0-688-41007-3); PLB 6.48 (ISBN 0-688-51007-8). Lothrop.

--Lightning Southpaw. (gr. 7-12). 1967. 7.25 o.p. (ISBN 0-688-40992-X). Lothrop.

Bowen, Roger W. Rebellion & Democracy in Meiji Japan: A Study of Commoners in the Popular Rights Movement. 450p. 1980. 25.00x (ISBN 0-520-03665-4). U of Cal Pr.

Bowen, Van. Vestryman's Guide. pap. 1.95 (ISBN 0-8164-2136-6). Crossroad NY.

Bowen, William G. & Ashenfelter, Orley, eds. Labor & the National Economy. rev. ed. (Problems of the Modern Economy Ser). 1975. 8.95x (ISBN 0-393-05456-X); pap. 4.95x (ISBN 0-393-09996-2). Norton.

Bowen, Zack, ed. Irish Renaissance Annual I. (Irish Renaissance Annual Ser.). 192p. 1980. 8.00 (ISBN 0-87413-168-5). U Delaware Pr.

--Irish Renaissance Annual II. 192p. 1981. 12.00 (ISBN 0-87413-185-5). U Delaware Pr.

Bowen Jones, John, jt. auth. see Evans, D. MacLean.

Bower, B. D., jt. auth. see Jeavons, P. M.

Bower, B. M. Border Vengeance. (YA) 1971. 5.95 (ISBN 0-685-03333-3, Avalon). Bouregy.

Bower, Blair T., jt. auth. see Kneese, Allen V.

Bower, Eli M. Early Identification of Emotionally Handicapped Children in School. 2nd ed. (American Lecture in Psychology). (Illus.). 276p. 1974. pap. 14.75 photocopy ed., spiral (ISBN 0-398-00202-9). C C Thomas.

Bower, Eli M., jt. auth. see Shears, Loyda M.

Bower, F. L. Nursing & the Concept of Loss. 214p. 1980. 10.95 (ISBN 0-471-04790-2). Wiley.

Bower, Fay L. & Bevis, Em O. Fundamentals of Nursing Practice: Concepts, Roles & Functions. LC 77-26885. (Illus.). 1978. text ed. 16.95 (ISBN 0-8016-0732-9). Mosby.

Bower, Fay L., ed. Distortions in Body Image in Illness & Disability. LC 77-4429. (Nursing Concept Modules Ser.). 1977. pap. 10.95 (ISBN 0-471-02169-5, Pub. by Wiley Medical). Wiley.

--Normal Development of Body Image. LC 77-3487. (Nursing Concept Modules Ser.). 1977. pap. 10.95 (ISBN 0-471-02170-9, Pub. by Wiley Medical). Wiley.

Bower, Fay L. & Wheeler, Robinetta T., eds. The Nursing Assessment. LC 77-5160. (Wiley Nursing Concept Modules). 1977. pap. 10.95 (ISBN 0-471-02167-9, Pub. by Wiley Medical). Wiley.

Bower, Frederick O. Botany of the Living Plant. 4th ed. (Illus.). 1969. Repr. of 1947 ed. 21.25 (ISBN 0-02-841800-X). Hafner.

Bower, Gordon H. & Hilgard, Ernest J. Theories of Learning. 5th ed. (Illus.). 640p. 1981. text ed. 20.95 (ISBN 0-13-914432-3). P-H.

Bower, Gordon H., jt. auth. see Hilgard, Ernest R.

Bower, Joseph L. Managing the Resource Allocation Process. 1972. pap. text ed. 5.95x o.p. (ISBN 0-256-00457-9). Irwin.

Bower, Joseph L. & Christenson, Charles J. Public Management: Text & Cases. 1978. text ed. 19.95x (ISBN 0-256-02070-1). Irwin.

Bower, Kathleen A., jt. ed. see Zander, Karen S.

Bower, Lewis L., jt. auth. see Sands, Gary.

Bower, Muriel. Foil Fencing. 4th ed. (Physical Education Ser.). 112p. 1980. pap. text ed. write for info. (ISBN 0-697-07097-2). Wm C Brown.

Bower, Robert T. & De Gasparis, Priscilla. Ethics in Social Research: Protecting the Interests of Human Subjects. LC 78-19452. 1978. 24.95 (ISBN 0-03-046406-4). Praeger.

Bower, T. G. Human Development. LC 78-27223. (Psychology Ser.). (Illus.). 1979. text ed. 18.95x (ISBN 0-7167-0058-1). W H Freeman.

--A Primer of Infant Development. LC 76-27827. (Psychology Ser.). (Illus.). 1977. text ed. 16.95x (ISBN 0-7167-0499-4); pap. text ed. 7.95x (ISBN 0-7167-0498-6). W H Freeman.

Bower, T. G. R. Development in Infancy. LC 73-19995. (Psychology Ser.). (Illus.). 1974. text ed. 20.95x (ISBN 0-7167-0777-2); pap. text ed. 10.95x (ISBN 0-7167-0776-4). W H Freeman.

Bower, Wilma & Willard, Hildegard. Growing & Thinking Slim. 2nd expd. ed. (Illus., Orig.). 1978. pap. text ed. 10.00 (ISBN 0-686-12310-7). Willard-Bower.

Bowering, George. Burning Water: A Novel About George Vancouver, Pacific Explorer. LC 80-21755. 272p. 12.95 (ISBN 0-8253-0005-3). Beaufort Bks NY.

Bowerman. Radiology & Injury in Sport. (Illus.). 1977. 28.50 (ISBN 0-8385-8250-8). ACC.

Bowerman, Bill & Moore, Bobbie. Sports Illustrated Track: Field Events. LC 76-8268. (Illus.). 1977. 5.95 (ISBN 0-397-01172-5); pap. 2.95 (ISBN 0-397-01171-7). Lippincott.

Bowerman, J. E., jt. auth. see Trapnell, D. H.

Bowerman, Melissa. Early Syntactic Development: A Cross Linguistic Study with Special Reference to Finnish. (Cambridge Studies in Linguistics: No. 11). 42.50 (ISBN 0-521-20019-9); pap. 10.95x (ISBN 0-521-09797-5). Cambridge U Pr.

Bowerman, William J. Coaching Track & Field. 1974. text ed. 18.25 (ISBN 0-395-17834-7). HM.

Bowers, Arden C., jt. auth. see Thompson, June M.

Bowers, Carolyn O., et al. Judging & Coaching Women's Gymnastics. 2nd ed. 360p. 1981. pap. text ed. price not set (ISBN 0-87484-391-X). Mayfield Pub.

Bowers, Christine, jt. auth. see Bowers, Q. David.

Bowers, D., jt. auth. see Burkitt, B.

Bowers, David G. & Franklin, Jerome L. Survey-Guided Development I: Data-Based Organizational Change. rev. ed. LC 77-75523. 146p. 1977. pap. 11.50 (ISBN 0-88390-137-4). Univ Assocs.

Bowers, Edgar. Witnesses. 22p. (Orig.). 1981. pap. 22.50 (ISBN 0-936576-05-7). Symposium Pr.

Bowers, Ethel M., jt. auth. see Solomon, Ben.

Bowers, F., ed. see Marlowe, Christopher.

Bowers, Faubion. The World of Asif Currimbhoy. 4.80 (ISBN 0-89253-664-0); flexible cloth 3.00 (ISBN 0-89253-665-9). Ind-US Inc.

Bowers, Faubion, tr. see Champdor, Albert.

Bowers, Fredson. Textual & Literary Criticism. 1959. 28.50 (ISBN 0-521-04290-9); pap. 6.95x (ISBN 0-521-09407-0, 407). Cambridge U Pr.

Bowers, Fredson, ed. Studies in Bibliography, Vol. 34. LC 49-3353. 1981. 20.00x (ISBN 0-8139-0898-1). U Pr of Va.

Bowers, Fredson, ed. see Dekker, Thomas.

Bowers, Fredson, ed. see Fielding, Henry.

Bowers, Fredson, ed. see Hoy, Cyrus.

Bowers, Garvey B. My Brother Will Take the Blame. 1981. 10.00 (ISBN 0-533-04929-6). Vantage.

Bowers, J. The Anatomy of Regional Activity Rates. Bd. with Regional Social Accounts for the U.K. Woodward, V. H. (Economic & Social Research Ser: No. 1). 1971. 13.95 (ISBN 0-521-07719-2). Cambridge U Pr.

Bowers, James C. & Sedore, Stephen. Sceptre: A Computer Program for Circuit & System Analysis. (Illus.). 1971. ref. ed. 22.95 o.p. (ISBN 0-13-791590-X). P-H.

Bowers, John S. The Theory of Grammatical Relations. LC 80-21018. 304p. 1981. 24.50x (ISBN 0-8014-1079-7). Cornell U Pr.

Bowers, John Z. When the Twain Meet: The Rise of Western Medicine in Japan. LC 80-22356. (Henry E. Sigerist Supplement to the Bulletin of the History of Medicine Ser.: No. 5). 192p. 1981. text ed. 14.00x (ISBN 0-8018-2432-X). Johns Hopkins.

Bowers, Larry D., jt. auth. see Carr, Peter.

Bowers, Laverne E. Sterile. 1981. 6.95 (ISBN 0-533-04732-3). Vantage.

Bowers, Malcolm B., Jr. Retreat from Sanity: The Structure of Emerging Psychosis. LC 73-20296. 248p. 1974. 19.95 (ISBN 0-87705-134-8). Human Sci Pr.

Bowers, Margaretta, et al. Counseling the Dying. LC 74-33146. 192p. 1975. 17.50x (ISBN 0-87668-198-4). Aronson.

Bowers, Margaretta K., et al. Counseling the Dying. LC 80-8903. (Harper's Ministers Paperback Library). 208p. 1981. pap. 4.95 (ISBN 0-06-061020-4). Har-Row.

Bowers, Mary B., ed. Stories About Birds & Bird Watchers: From Bird Watcher's Digest. LC 80-7925. (Illus.). 192p. 1981. 12.95 (ISBN 0-689-11093-6). Atheneum.

Bowers, Melvyn K. Easy Bulletin Boards - Number 2. LC 73-21798. (Illus.). 1974. 10.00 (ISBN 0-8108-0695-9). Scarecrow.

--Library Instruction in the Elementary School. LC 72-155283. 1971. 10.00 (ISBN 0-8108-0391-7). Scarecrow.

Bowers, Peter. Guide to Homebuilts. 1974. pap. 3.95 o.p. (ISBN 0-8306-2214-4, 2214). TAB Bks.

Bowers, Peter M. Fortress in the Sky: B-17 Bombers. LC 76-17145. 256p. 1976. 18.95 (ISBN 0-913194-04-2, Pub. by Sentry). Aviation.

--Yesterday's Wings: Eighty-Two Historical Aircraft. pap. 7.95x o.p. (ISBN 0-911720-87-1). Aviation.

Bowers, Q. David & Bowers, Christine. Robert Robinson: American Illustator. (Illus.). 68p. 1981. pap. 9.95 (ISBN 0-911572-19-8). Vestal.

Bowers, Q. David & Martin, Mary L. The Postcards of Alphonse Mucha. (Illus.). 100p. 1980. 9.95 (ISBN 0-911572-18-X). Vestal.

Bowers, Q. David, jt. auth. see Reblitz, Arthur A.

Bowers, Richard. Track & Field Events. LC 73-83432. 1974. pap. 5.95 (ISBN 0-675-08893-3). Merrill.

Bowers, Ronald L. The Selznick Players. LC 74-9278. (Illus.). 288p. 1976. 17.50 o.p. (ISBN 0-498-01375-8). A S Barnes.

Bowers, Thomas A., jt. auth. see Fletcher, Alan D.

Bowers, Warner F. Self Assessment of Current Knowledge in Surgery for Family Physicians. 1972. spiral bdg. 12.00 o.p. (ISBN 0-87488-259-1). Med Exam.

Bowers, Warner F. & Dimendberg, David C. Emergency Medical Technician Examination Review Book, Vol. 1. 1969. spiral bdg. 9.50 (ISBN 0-87488-465-9). Med Exam.

Bowers, Warner F & Dimendberg, David C. Emergency Medical Technician Examination Review, Vol. 2. 1972. spiral bdg. 9.50 (ISBN 0-87488-466-7). Med Exam.

Bowers, Warner F., et al. ECFMG Examination Review, Pt. 1. 4th ed. LC 76-9880. 1976. Pt. 1. pap. 11.75 (ISBN 0-87488-120-X); Pt. 2. pap. 11.75 (ISBN 0-87488-121-8). Med Exam.

Bowers, William L. The Country Life Movement in America. LC 74-80587. 1974. 13.00 (ISBN 0-8046-9074-X, Natl U). Kennikat.

Bowersox, Donald J., et al. Introduction to Transportation. 1981. 14.95 (ISBN 0-02-313030-X). Macmillan.

Bowerstock, Glen W., et al, eds. Arctouros: Hellenic Studies Presented to Bernard M. Knos on the Occasion of His 65th Birthday. 462p. 1980. 99.00x (ISBN 3-1100-7798-1). De Gruyter.

Bowes, D. R. & Leake, B. E. Crustal Evolution in Northwestern Britain & Adjacent Regions: Geological Journal Special Issue, No. 10. (Liverpool Geological Society & the Manchester Geological Association). 508p. 1980. 97.50 (ISBN 0-471-27757-6, Pub. by Wiley-Interscience). Wiley.

Bowes, Florence. Interlude in Venice. LC 80-1720. (Starlight Romance Ser.). 192p. 1981. 9.95 (ISBN 0-385-17316-4). Doubleday.

--The Macorvan Curse. LC 79-48086. (Romantic Suspense Ser). 192p. 1980. 8.95 (ISBN 0-385-15844-0). Doubleday.

Bowes, P. Hindu Intellectual Tradition. 1977. 12.50 (ISBN 0-8364-0121-2). South Asia Bks.

Bowes, Pratima. The Hindu Religious Tradition: A Philosophical Approach. 1978. 24.00 (ISBN 0-7100-8668-7). Routledge & Kegan.

Bowes, W. H. & Russell, Leslie T. Stress Analysis by the Finite Element Method for Practically Engineers. 128p. 1975. 22.95 (ISBN 0-669-99903-2). Lexington Bks.

Bowey, Angela. Guide to Manpower Planning. 1977. text ed. 13.50x (ISBN 0-333-15555-6). Verry.

Bowhill, S. A., ed. Review Papers: International Solar-Terrestrial Physics Symposium, Sao-Paolo, June, 1974. 212p. 1976. pap. 55.00 (ISBN 0-08-019959-3). Pergamon.

Bowie, Donald. Cable Harbor. 300p. 1981. 11.95 (ISBN 0-87131-347-2). M Evans.

--Cable Harbor: A Novel. Graver, Fred, ed. 300p. 1981. 10.95 (ISBN 0-87131-347-2). M Evans.

--Station Identification: Confessions of a Video Kid. 216p. 1980. 9.95 (ISBN 0-87131-300-6); pap. 5.95 (ISBN 0-87131-310-3). M Evans.

Bowie, Henry P. The Techniques & Laws of Japanese Painting. (Illus.). 129p. 1981. 47.45 (ISBN 0-930582-91-8). Gloucester Art.

Bowie, Lemuel J. Automated Instrumentation for Radioimmunoassay. 240p. 1980. 59.95 (ISBN 0-8493-5747-0). CRC Pr.

Bowie, M. Mallarme & the Art of Being Difficult. LC 77-82488. 1978. 29.95 (ISBN 0-521-21813-6). Cambridge U Pr.

Bowie, Malcolm. Henri Michaux: A Study of His Literary Works. (Illus.). 224p. 1973. 24.00x (ISBN 0-19-815740-1). Oxford U Pr.

Bowie, Norman E. & Simon, R. L. The Individual & the Political Order: An Introduction to Social & Political Philosophy. 1977. pap. text ed. 11.95 (ISBN 0-13-457143-6). P-H.

Bowie, Norman E., jt. ed. see Beauchamp, Tom L.

Bowie, Robert. The Damning Owl Tree. LC 78-63430. (Orig.). 1980. pap. cancelled o.p. (ISBN 0-930138-05-8). Harold Hse.

Bowie, Robert R. Suez Nineteen Fifty-Six. (International Crisis & the Role of Law Ser). 164p. 1974. 9.95x (ISBN 0-19-519805-0); pap. 4.95x (ISBN 0-19-519804-2). Oxford U Pr.

Bowie, S. H., ed. see Royal Society of London, et al.

Bowie, Theodore, ed. East-West In Art. LC 66-12723. (Illus.). 192p. (Orig.). 1966. pap. 6.50x (ISBN 0-253-11901-4). Ind U Pr.

Bowie, Tom. Jamie, The Adventures of. LC 78-62815. (Illus.). 1978. 12.50 (ISBN 0-932508-00-6); pap. 3.95 (ISBN 0-932508-01-4). Seven Oaks.

--Three Plays for Reading. LC 79-64092. 1979. 12.50 (ISBN 0-932508-04-9); pap. 3.95 (ISBN 0-932508-05-7). Seven Oaks.

Bowker, John. Jesus & the Pharisees. 240p. 1973. 32.00 (ISBN 0-521-20055-5). Cambridge U Pr.

--Problems of Suffering in the Religions of the World. LC 77-93706. 1975. 39.50 (ISBN 0-521-07412-6); pap. 9.95x (ISBN 0-521-09903-X). Cambridge U Pr.

--Targums & Rabbinic Literature. LC 71-80817. 1969. 47.50 (ISBN 0-521-07415-0). Cambridge U Pr.

--Uncle Bolpenny Tries Things Out. (Illus.). (ps-5). 1973. 5.95 (ISBN 0-571-09973-4, Pub. by Faber & Faber). Merrimack Bk Serv.

Bowker, Lee H. Prisoner Subcultures. LC 77-6182. 1977. 17.95 (ISBN 0-669-01429-X). Lexington Bks.

--Women, Crime, & the Criminal Justice System. LC 78-57180. (Illus.). 1978. 23.95 (ISBN 0-669-02374-4). Lexington Bks.

Bowle, John. A History of Europe. xii, 626p. 1981. lib. bdg. write for info. (06856-0, Pub. by Secker & Warburg). U of Chicago Pr.

--John Evelyn & His Cracked World. (Illus.). 256p. 1981. price not set (ISBN 0-7100-0721-3). Routledge & Kegan.

--Unity of European History: A Political & Cultural Survey. rev. ed. 1970. pap. 6.95 (ISBN 0-19-501249-6, GB329, GB). Oxford U Pr.

Bowler, C., et al. New Writers Eight. (New Writing & Writers). 1968. text ed. 13.00x (ISBN 0-7145-0014-3). Humanities.

Bowler, Christine, et al. New Writers Eight. 1980. pap. 6.00 (ISBN 0-7145-0015-1). Riverrun NY.

Bowler, M. G. Nuclear Physics. 444p. 1973. text ed. 42.00 (ISBN 0-08-016983-X); pap. text ed. 24.00 (ISBN 0-08-018990-3). Pergamon.

Bowler, Peter J. Fossils & Progress: Paleontology & the Idea of Progressive Evolution in the Nineteenth Century. LC 75-40005. 1976. lib. bdg. 14.00 o.p. (ISBN 0-88202-043-9). N Watson.

Bowles, Chester. Promises to Keep: My Years in Public Life 1941-1969. LC 76-123917. (Illus.). 1971. 15.00 o.s.i. (ISBN 0-06-010421-X, HarpT). Har-Row.

Bowles, Ella S. About Antiques. LC 70-174011. (Tower Bks). (Illus.). 1971. Repr. of 1929 ed. 18.00 (ISBN 0-8103-3921-8). Gale.

Bowles, F., ed. see Carnegie Commission On Higher Education.

Bowles, Jane. Collected Works of Jane Bowles. 431p. 1966. 8.50 (ISBN 0-374-12576-7). FS&G.

Bowles, John B. Distribution & Biogeography of Mammals of Iowa. (Special Publications: No. 9). (Illus., Orig.). 1975. pap. 8.00 (ISBN 0-89672-034-9). Tex Tech Pr.

Bowles, K. L. Microcomputer: Problem Solving Using Pascal. LC 77-11959. 1977. pap. 9.80 (ISBN 0-387-90286-4). Springer-Verlag.

Bowles, Ken. The Beginner's Manual for the Pascal System. (Orig.). 1980. pap. 11.95 (ISBN 0-07-006745-7, BYTE Bks). Macgraw.

Bowles, Larry L., jt. auth. see Brumgardt, John R.

Bowles, Michael. The Art of Conducting. LC 74-23419. (Music Ser.). 210p. 1975. Repr. of 1959 ed. lib. bdg. 19.50 (ISBN 0-306-70718-7). Da Capo.

Bowles, Paul. Collected Stories of Paul Bowles. 419p. 1980. 14.00 (ISBN 0-87685-397-1); pap. 7.50 (ISBN 0-87685-396-3). Black Sparrow.

--The Delicate Prey. LC 72-80780. 307p. 1981. pap. 7.95 (ISBN 0-912946-01-6). Ecco Pr.

--Hundred Camels in the Courtyard. (Orig.). 1962. pap. 2.00 (ISBN 0-87286-002-7). City Lights.

--Let It Come Down. 300p. 1980. 14.00 (ISBN 0-87685-480-3); signed ed. o.p. 20.00 (ISBN 0-87685-481-1); pap. 7.50 (ISBN 0-87685-479-X). Black Sparrow.

--Midnight Mass. 120p. 1981. 14.00 (ISBN 0-87685-477-3); signed ed. 20.00 (ISBN 0-87685-478-1); pap. 5.00 (ISBN 0-87685-476-5). Black Sparrow.

--Next to Nothing: Collected Poems 1926-1977. 80p. (Orig.). 1981. 14.00 (ISBN 0-87685-505-2); pap. 4.00 (ISBN 0-87685-504-4); signed edition 20.00 (ISBN 0-87685-506-0). Black Sparrow.

--Three Tales. LC 75-18063. 24p. 1975. pap. 3.50 (ISBN 0-916228-10-X); pap. 3.50 (ISBN 0-685-16636-8). Phoenix Bk Shop.

Bowles, Samuel. Life & Times of Samuel Bowles, 2 Vols. Merriam, George S., ed. LC 75-87417. (American Scene Ser). 1970. Repr. of 1885 ed. lib. bdg. 75.00 (ISBN 0-306-71562-7). Da Capo.

Bowles, William L. William Lisle Bowles. Reiman, Donald H., ed. LC 75-31166. (Romantic Context Ser.: Poetry 1789-1830). 1978. lib. bdg. 47.00 (ISBN 0-8240-2119-3). Garland Pub.

--William Lisle Bowles: Poems, Never Before Published. 1813. Reiman, Donald H., ed. LC 75-31168. (Romantic Context Ser.: Poetry 1789-1830). 1978. lib. bdg. 47.00 (ISBN 0-8240-2121-5). Garland Pub.

Bowley, A. L. & Burnett-Hurst, A. R. Livelihood & Poverty: A Study in the Economic Conditions of Working-Class Households in Northampton, Warrington, Stanley, & Reading, London, 1915. LC 79-59651. (The English Working Class Ser.). 1980. lib. bdg. 22.00 (ISBN 0-8240-0105-2). Garland Pub.

Bowley, M. E. British Building Industry. 1966. 59.50 (ISBN 0-521-04292-5). Cambridge U Pr.

Bowman, jt. auth. see Canfield, D. T.

Bowman, Arthur G. & Milligan, W. D. Real Estate Law in California. 5th ed. 1978. ref. ed. 18.95 (ISBN 0-13-764043-9). P-H.

Bowman, Bruce. Shaped Canvas: Constructing, Stretching, Painting. LC 76-1183. (Illus.). 64p. (YA) 1976. 6.95 o.p. (ISBN 0-8069-5360-8); PLB 6.69 o.p. (ISBN 0-8069-5361-6). Sterling.

--Toothpick Sculpture & Ice-Cream Stick Art. LC 76-19808. (Illus.). (gr. 5 up). 1976. 7.95 (ISBN 0-8069-5372-1); PLB 7.49 (ISBN 0-8069-5373-X). Sterling.

Bowman, Claude C., ed. Humanistic Sociology: Readings. LC 72-13116. 1973. pap. text ed. 6.95x (ISBN 0-89197-221-8). Irvington.

Bowman, Daniel. Lift Trucks: A Practical Guide for Buyers & Users. LC 72-83304. (Illus.). 1973. 19.95 (ISBN 0-8436-1007-7). CBI Pub.

Bowman, Frank & Gerard, F. A. Higher Calculus. 1967. 48.00x (ISBN 0-521-04293-3). Cambridge U Pr.

Bowman, Fred. Reorientation of African Beliefs: A Prime Necessity. 1981. 4.95 (ISBN 0-8062-1566-6). Carlton.

Bowman, George M. How to Succeed with Your Money. pap. 1.95 (ISBN 0-8024-3656-0). Moody.

Bowman, Gerald. Let's Look at Ships. LC 68-22910. (Let's Look Series). (Illus.). (gr. 4-8). 1965. 4.95g o.p. (ISBN 0-8075-4501-5). A Whitman.

Bowman, Hank W. Famous Guns from the Smithsonian Collection. LC 67-16180. (Illus.). 1966. lib. bdg. 3.50 o.p. (ISBN 0-668-01606-X). Arco.

--Famous Old Cars. LC 57-14442. (Illus.). 1957. lib. bdg. 6.95 o.p. (ISBN 0-668-00597-1). Arco.

--Famous Old Cars. LC 57-14442. (Illus.). 1978. pap. 2.95 o.p. (ISBN 0-668-04311-3, 4311). Arco.

Bowman, James C. Contemporary American Criticism. 330p. 1980. Repr. of 1926 ed. lib. bdg. 35.00 (ISBN 0-8495-0457-0). Arden Lib.

Bowman, Jim R., jt. auth. see Pulliam, John P.

Bowman, John W. Unless I See. LC 76-42859. (Illus.). 1977. pap. 4.00 (ISBN 0-89430-002-4). Morgan-Pacific.

Bowman, Kathleen. New Women in Art & Dance. LC 76-5457. (New Women Ser.). (Illus.). (gr. 4-12). 1976. PLB 6.95 (ISBN 0-87191-512-X). Creative Ed.

--New Women in Entertainment. LC 76-4940. (New Women Ser.). (Illus.). (gr. 4-12). 1976. PLB 6.95 (ISBN 0-87191-510-3). Creative Ed.

--New Women in Media. LC 76-6061. (New Women Ser.). (Illus.). (gr. 4-12). 1976. PLB 6.95 (ISBN 0-87191-511-1). Creative Ed.

--New Women in Medicine. LC 76-4873. (New Women Ser.). (Illus.). (gr. 4-12). 1976. PLB 6.95 (ISBN 0-87191-508-1). Creative Ed.

--New Women in Politics. LC 76-5513. (New Women Ser.). (Illus.). (gr. 4-12). 1976. PLB 6.95 (ISBN 0-87191-507-3). Creative Ed.

--New Women in Social Sciences. LC 76-5508. (New Women Ser.). (Illus.). (gr. 4-12). 1976. PLB 6.95 (ISBN 0-87191-509-X). Creative Ed.

Bowman, Larry G. Captive Americans: Prisoners During the American Revolution. LC 75-36984. viii, 146p. 1976. 9.00x (ISBN 0-8214-0215-3); pap. 4.50x (ISBN 0-8214-0229-3). Ohio U Pr.

Bowman, Larry W. & Clark, Ian, eds. The Indian Ocean in Global Politics. (Westview Special Studies in International Relations). 270p. 1980. lib. bdg. 25.00x (ISBN 0-86531-038-6); pap. 12.00x (ISBN 0-86531-191-9). Westview.

Bowman, Lea, jt. auth. see Stringer, Leslea.

Bowman, Lewis & Boynton, G. R. Political Behavior & Public Opinion: Comparative Analysis. 512p. 1974. pap. text ed. 13.95 (ISBN 0-13-685065-0). P-H.

Bowman, Malcom C., ed. Reprints of Selected Articles on the Analysis of Pesticides by Chromatographic Methods. 1977. 25.00 (ISBN 0-912474-08-4). PolyScience.

Bowman, Martin. The B-Twenty-Four Liberator. LC 80-50342. (Illus.). 128p. 1980. 14.95 (ISBN 0-528-81538-5). Rand.

Bowman, Mary J. Educational Choice Second Labor Markets in Japan. LC 80-25557. 320p. 1981. lib. bdg. 19.00x (ISBN 0-226-06923-0). U of Chicago Pr.

Bowman, Mary J., jt. auth. see Plunkett, H. Dudley.

Bowman, Paul H. Adventurous Future. 296p. 1959. 3.75 o.p. (ISBN 0-87178-011-9). Brethren.

Bowman, Robert, ed. see Bligh, William.

Bowman, Ronald C., ed. see Glennon, Michael J & Franck, Thomas M.

Bowman, W. Graphic Communication. LC 67-29931. (Human Communication Ser.). 1968. 22.95 (ISBN 0-471-09290-8, Pub. by Wiley-Interscience). Wiley.

Bowman, Walter P. & Ball, Robert H. Theatre Language, a Dictionary. LC 60-10495. 1976. pap. 6.95 (ISBN 0-87830-551-3). Theatre Arts.

Bowman, William D. Story of Surnames. LC 68-8906. 1968. Repr. of 1932 ed. 19.00 (ISBN 0-8103-3110-1). Gale.

Bown, Derick, illus. Robin Hood & His Merrie Men. LC 78-4201. (Raintree's Illustrated Classics). (Illus.). (gr. 5-8). 1978. PLB 9.65 (ISBN 0-8393-6201-3). Raintree Child.

Bownas, G., jt. auth. see Norbury, Paul.

Bownas, Geoffrey, jt. ed. see Norbury, Paul.

Bowra, C. M. Classical Greece. LC 65-17305. (Great Ages of Man). (Illus.). (gr. 6 up). 1965. PLB 11.97 (ISBN 0-8094-0363-3, Pub. by Time-Life). Silver.

--Classical Greece. (Great Ages of Man Ser). (Illus.). 1965. 12.95 (ISBN 0-8094-0341-2); lib. bdg. avail. (ISBN 0-685-20546-0). Time-Life.

Bowra, C. M., ed. see Pindar.

Bowra, C. Maurice. The Romantic Imagination. (Oxford Paperbook Bks). 1961. pap. 8.95x (ISBN 0-19-281006-5). Oxford U Pr.

Bowra, M. Poetry & Politics. 1966. 29.95x (ISBN 0-521-04294-1). Cambridge U Pr.

Bowring, C. S. Radionuclide Tracer Techniques in Hematology. 1981. text ed. price not set (ISBN 0-407-00183-2). Butterworth.

Bowring, R. J. Mori Ogai & the Modernization of Japanese Culture. LC 76-11074. (Oriental Publications Ser.: No. 28). (Illus.). 1979. 44.00 (ISBN 0-521-21319-3). Cambridge U Pr.

Bowse, Robert A., ed. United States Coin Prices, 1980 to 1981. (Illus.). 304p. (Orig.). 1980. pap. 3.95 (ISBN 0-937458-04-X). Harris & Co.

Bowsher, Alice M. Design Review in Historic Districts. LC 78-61513. (Illus.). 138p. 1978. pap. 6.95 (ISBN 0-89133-080-1). Preservation Pr.

Bowsher, J. M., ed. see Wood, Alexander.

Bowyer, Chaz. Guns in the Sky: The Air Gunners of World War Two. (Illus.). 1979. 14.95 (ISBN 0-684-16262-8, ScribT). Scribner.

Bowyer, Jack. Building Technology Three. (Newnes-Butterworths Technician Ser.). 96p. 1980. pap. 9.95 (ISBN 0-408-00411-8). Butterworths.

Bowyer, John. Central Heating. LC 76-40808. (Illus.). 1977. 13.50 (ISBN 0-7153-7037-5). David & Charles.

Bowyer, John W. & Brooks, John L., eds. Victorian Age: Prose, Poetry & Drama. 2nd ed. 1954. text ed. 20.95 (ISBN 0-13-941724-9). P-H.

Bowyer, Michael J. Two Group R. A. F: A Complete History, 1936-1945. (Illus.). 1974. 21.95 o.p. (ISBN 0-571-09491-0, Pub. by Faber & Faber). Merrimack Bk Serv.

Bowyer, Michael J. & Philpott, Bryan. Mosquito: Classic Aircraft, No. 7. (Illus.). 128p. 1980. 29.95 (ISBN 0-85059-432-4). Aztex.

Bowyer, Michael J. & Sharp, C. Martin. Mosquito. 2nd ed. (Illus.). 1971. 18.95 o.p. (ISBN 0-571-04750-5, Pub. by Faber & Faber); pap. 6.95 o.p. (ISBN 0-571-09531-3). Merrimack Bk Serv.

Bowyer, Michael J. F. Aircraft for the Royal Air Force. (Illus.). 160p. 1980. 27.00 (ISBN 0-571-11515-2, Pub. by Faber & Faber). Merrimack Bk Serv.

Bowyer, P. J. Boat Engines: A Manual for Work & Pleasure Boats. LC 79-5369. (Illus.). 1979. 22.50 (ISBN 0-7153-7776-0). David & Charles.

Bowyer, R. The Lowenfeld World Technique: Studies in Personality. 1970. 27.00 (ISBN 0-08-013029-1); pap. 15.00 (ISBN 0-08-013028-3). Pergamon.

Box, Edgar. Death Before Bedtime. LC 79-10248. 1979. pap. 1.95 (ISBN 0-394-74053-X, V-53, Vin). Random.

Box, George E. & Draper, Norman R. Evolutionary Operation: A Statistical Method for Process Improvement. LC 68-56159. (Applied Probability & Mathematical Statistics Ser). 1969. 27.50 (ISBN 0-471-09305-X, Pub. by Wiley-Interscience). Wiley.

Box, George E. & Jenkins, Gwilym. Time Series Analysis, Forecasting & Control. rev. ed. LC 76-8713. 500p. 1976. text ed. 38.50x (ISBN 0-8162-1104-3). Holden-Day.

Box, George E. & Tiao, George C. Bayesian Inference in Statistical Analysis. LC 78-172804. 1973. text ed. 24.95 (ISBN 0-201-00622-7). A-W.

Box, George E., et al. Statistics for Experimenters: An Introduction to Design, Data Analysis & Model Building. LC 77-15087. (Wiley Ser. in Probability & Mathematical Statistics). 1978. 26.95 (ISBN 0-471-09315-7, Pub. by Wiley-Inerscience). Wiley.

Box, George H. Judaism in the Greek Period, from the Rise of Alexander the Great to the Intervention of Rome. LC 73-109712. Repr. of 1932 ed. lib. bdg. 21.50x (ISBN 0-8371-4288-1, BOJG). Greenwood.

Box, Joan F. R. A. Fisher: The Life of a Scientist. LC 78-1668. (Probability & Mathematical Statistics Ser.). 1978. 28.95 (ISBN 0-471-09300-9, Pub. by Wiley-Interscience). Wiley.

Boxall, V. E. Drawing & Materials. 2nd ed. (Illus.). 1975. pap. 16.50x (ISBN 0-7131-3320-1). Intl Ideas.

Boxer, C. R. The Dutch Seaborne Empire, Sixteen Hundred to Eighteen Hundred. 1980. pap. text ed. 11.75x (ISBN 0-09-131051-2, Hutchinson U Lib). Humanities.

--The Golden Age of Brazil, 1695-1750: Growing Pains of a Colonial Society. 1962. 17.50x (ISBN 0-520-00162-1); pap. 7.50x (ISBN 0-520-01550-9, CAMPUS78). U of Cal Pr.

Boxer, Charles R. Papers on Portugese, Dutch, & Jesuit Influences in 16th & 17th Century Japan: Studies in Japanese History & Civilization. 1979. 29.50 (ISBN 0-89093-255-7). U Pubns Amer.

--Portuguese Embassy to Japan (1644-1647) Bd. with Embassy of Captain Concalo de Siqueria de Souza to Japan in 1644-7. (Studies in Japanese History & Civilization). 172p. 22.00 (ISBN 0-89093-256-5). U Pubns Amer.

Boxer, Ray. Along the Edges: Special Issue 19. pap. 1.00 o.p. (ISBN 0-685-78393-6). The Smith.

Boxx, W. Randy, jt. auth. see Johnson, Jerry W.

Boy Scouts Of America. American Business. LC 19-600. (Illus.). 48p. (gr. 6-12). 1975. pap. 0.70x (ISBN 0-8395-3325-X, 3325). BSA.

Boy Scouts, of America. American Cultures. LC 19-600. (Illus.). 32p. (gr. 6-12). 1980. pap. 0.70x (ISBN 0-8395-3388-8, 3388). BSA.

Boy Scouts of America. American Heritage. LC 19-600. 48p. 1976. pap. 0.70x (ISBN 0-8395-3398-5). BSA.

--Animal Science. LC 19-600. (Illus.). 64p. (gr. 6-12). 1975. pap. 0.70x (ISBN 0-8395-3395-0, 3395). BSA.

--Archery. LC 19-600. (Illus.). 48p. (gr. 6-12). 1978. pap. 0.70x (ISBN 0-8395-3381-0, 3381). BSA.

--Architecture. LC 19-600. (Illus.). 48p. (gr. 6-12). 1966. pap. 0.70x (ISBN 0-8395-3321-7, 3321). BSA.

--Art. LC 19-600. (Illus.). 48p. (gr. 6-12). 1968. pap. 0.70x (ISBN 0-8395-3320-9, 3320). BSA.

--Astronomy. LC 19-600. (Illus.). 80p. (gr. 6-12). 1971. pap. 0.70x (ISBN 0-8395-3303-9, 3303). BSA.

--Athletics. LC 19-600. (Illus.). 24p. (gr. 6-12). 1964. pap. 0.70x (ISBN 0-8395-3324-1, 3324). BSA.

--Atomic Energy. LC 19-600. (Illus.). 72p. (gr. 6-12). 1965. pap. 0.70x (ISBN 0-8395-3275-X, 3275). BSA.

--Aviation. LC 19-600. (Illus.). 72p. (gr. 6-12). 1968. pap. 0.70x (ISBN 0-8395-3293-8, 3293). BSA.

--Basketry. LC 19-600. (Illus.). 32p. (gr. 6-12). 1968. pap. 0.70x (ISBN 0-8395-3313-6, 3313). BSA.

--Bear Cub Scout Book. rev. ed. LC 67-14538. (Illus.). 192p. (gr. 4). 1973. flexible bdg. 1.75x (ISBN 0-8395-3231-8, 3231). BSA.

--Beekeeping. LC 19-600. (Illus.). 48p. (gr. 6-12). 1975. pap. 0.70x (ISBN 0-8395-3362-4, 3362). BSA.

--Bird Study. LC 19-600. (Illus.). 64p. (gr. 6-12). 1967. pap. 0.70x (ISBN 0-8395-3282-2, 3282). BSA.

--Bookbinding. LC 19-600. (Illus.). 24p. (gr. 6-12). 1969. pap. 0.70x (ISBN 0-8395-3378-0, 3378). BSA.

--Botany. LC 19-600. (Illus.). 64p. (gr. 6-12). 1964. pap. 0.70x (ISBN 0-8395-3379-9, 3379). BSA.

--Camping. LC 19-600. (Illus.). 64p. (gr. 6-12). 1966. pap. 0.70x (ISBN 0-8395-3256-3, 3256). BSA.

--Canoeing. LC 19-600. (Illus.). 72p. (gr. 6-12). 1977. pap. 0.70x (ISBN 0-8395-3308-X, 3308). BSA.

--Citizenship in the Community. LC 19-600. (Illus.). 48p. (gr. 6-12). 1972. pap. 0.70x (ISBN 0-8395-3253-9, 3253). BSA.

--Citizenship in the Nation. LC 19-600. (Illus.). 64p. (gr. 6-12). 1972. pap. 0.70x (ISBN 0-8395-3252-0, 3252). BSA.

--Citizenship in the World. LC 19-600. (Illus.). 64p. (gr. 6-12). 1972. pap. 0.70x (ISBN 0-8395-3254-7, 3254). BSA.

--Coin Collecting. LC 19-600. (Illus.). 32p. (gr. 6-12). 1975. pap. 0.70x (ISBN 0-8395-3390-X, 3390). BSA.

--Communications. LC 19-600. (Illus.). 32p. (gr. 6-12). 1976. pap. 0.70x (ISBN 0-8395-3258-X, 3258). BSA.

--Community Living Skill Book. 1976. pap. 0.50x (ISBN 0-8395-6583-6); tchr's guide 0.30 (ISBN 0-685-73154-5, 18-323). BSA.

--Computers. LC 19-600. (Illus.). 64p. (gr. 6-12). 1973. pap. 0.70x (ISBN 0-8395-3338-1, 3338). BSA.

--Consumer Buying. LC 19-600. (Illus.). 64p. (gr. 6-12). 1975. pap. 0.70x (ISBN 0-8395-3387-X, 3387). BSA.

--Cooking. LC 19-600. (Illus.). 80p. (gr. 6-12). 1967. pap. 0.70x (ISBN 0-8395-3257-1, 3257). BSA.

--Cooking Skill Book. (Illus.). 32p. (gr. 6-12). 1975. pap. 0.50x (ISBN 0-8395-6585-2, 6585); cookings tchr's guide 0.30x (ISBN 0-685-53701-3, 18-325). BSA.

--Crafts for Cub Scouts. (Illus.). 80p. 1963. pap. 1.25x (ISBN 0-8395-3843-X, 3843). BSA.

--Cub Scout Family Book. (Illus.). 32p. (gr. 6-12). 1975. pap. 0.50x (ISBN 0-8395-3846-4, 3846). BSA.

--Cub Scout Fun Book. LC 67-23384. (Illus.). 96p. (gr. 3-5). 1967. pap. 2.45x (ISBN 0-8395-3215-6, 3215). BSA.

--Cub Scout Magic. LC 68-9493. (Illus.). 152p. (gr. 3-5). 1960. pap. 3.75x (ISBN 0-8395-3219-9, 3219). BSA.

--Cub Scout Songbook. (Illus.). (gr. 3-5). 1969. pap. 0.85x (ISBN 0-8395-3222-9, 3222). BSA.

--Cubmaster's Packbook. LC 67-26305. (Illus.). 352p. 1967. pap. 3.45x (ISBN 0-8395-3210-5, 3210). BSA.

--Cycling. LC 19-600. (Illus.). 40p. (gr. 6-12). 1971. pap. 0.70x (ISBN 0-8395-3277-6, 3277). BSA.

Boy Scouts, of America. Den Chief Handbook. LC 79-55446. (Illus.). 128p. (gr. 6-12). 1980. flexible bdg. 1.75x. BSA.

Boy Scouts Of America. Den Chief Handbook. LC 33-3848. (Illus.). 128p. (gr. 6-12). 1968. flexible bdg. 1.50 o.p. (ISBN 0-8395-3211-3, 3211). BSA.

--Den Leader's Book. LC 38-16321. (Illus.). 208p. 1967. pap. 1.75x (ISBN 0-8395-3212-1, 3212). BSA.

--Dentistry. LC 19-600. (Illus.). 32p. (gr. 6-12). 1975. pap. 0.70x (ISBN 0-8395-3394-2, 3394). BSA.

--Dog Care. LC 19-600. (Illus.). 64p. (gr. 6-12). 1972. pap. 0.70x (ISBN 0-8395-3289-X, 3289). BSA.

--Drafting. LC 19-600. (Illus.). 32p. (gr. 6-12). 1965. pap. 0.70x (ISBN 0-8395-3273-3, 3273). BSA.

--Electricity. LC 19-600. (Illus.). 48p. (gr. 6-12). 1974. pap. 0.70x (ISBN 0-8395-3206-7, 3206). BSA.

--Electronics. LC 19-600. (Illus.). 72p. (gr. 6-12). 1977. pap. 0.70x (ISBN 0-8395-3279-2, 3279). BSA.

--Emergency Preparedness. LC 19-600. (Illus.). 64p. (gr. 6-12). 1974. pap. 0.70x (ISBN 0-8395-3366-7, 3366). BSA.

--Engineering. LC 19-600. (Illus.). 48p. (gr. 6-12). 1978. pap. 0.70x (ISBN 0-8395-3376-4, 3376). BSA.

--Environmental Science. LC 19-600. (Illus.). 64p. (gr. 6-12). 1972. pap. 0.70x (ISBN 0-8395-3363-2, 3363). BSA.

--Exploring Emergency Service. (Illus.). 64p. 1971. pap. 3.00x (ISBN 0-8395-6609-3, 6609). BSA.

--Family Living Skill Book. (Illus.). 32p. (gr. 3-4). 1974. pap. 0.50x (ISBN 0-8395-6587-9, 6587); tchr's guide 0.30 (ISBN 0-685-41688-7, 18-327). BSA.

--Farm & Ranch Management. (Illus.). 32p. (gr. 6-12). 1980. pap. 0.70x (3348). BSA.

--Farm Mechanics. LC 19-600. (Illus.). 64p. (gr. 6-12). 1958. pap. 0.70x (ISBN 0-8395-3346-2, 3346). BSA.

--Fieldbook. LC 67-14537. (Illus.). 576p. (gr. 6-12). 1967. flexible bdg. 3.95x (ISBN 0-8395-3201-6, 3201). BSA.

--Fingerprinting. LC 19-600. (Illus.). 36p. (gr. 6-12). 1964. pap. 0.70x (ISBN 0-8395-3287-3, 3287). BSA.

--Firemanship. LC 19-600. (Illus.). 64p. (gr. 6-12). 1968. pap. 0.70x (ISBN 0-8395-3317-9, 3317). BSA.

--First Aid. (Illus.). 56p. (gr. 6-12). 1981. pap. 0.70x. BSA.

--First Aid. LC 19-600. (Illus.). 64p. (gr. 6-12). 1972. pap. 0.55x o.p. (ISBN 0-8395-3276-8, 3276). BSA.

--First Aid Skill Book. (Illus.). 32p. (gr. 3-4). 1974. pap. 0.50x (ISBN 0-8395-6588-7, 18-328); tchr's guide 0.30 (ISBN 0-685-41687-9). BSA.

--Fish & Wildlife Management. LC 19-600. (Illus.). 64p. (gr. 6-12). 1972. pap. 0.70x (ISBN 0-8395-3307-1, 3307). BSA.

--Fishing. LC 19-600. (Illus.). 64p. (gr. 6-12). 1974. pap. 0.70x (ISBN 0-8395-3295-4, 3295). BSA.

--Food Systems. LC 19-600. (Merit Badge Ser.). (Illus.). 48p. (gr. 6-12). 1978. pap. 0.70x (ISBN 0-8395-3399-3). BSA.

--Forestry. LC 19-600. (Illus.). 64p. (gr. 6-12). 1971. pap. 0.70x (ISBN 0-8395-3302-0, 3302). BSA.

--Games for Cub Scouts. (Illus.). 96p. 1963. pap. 1.25x (ISBN 0-8395-3844-8, 3844). BSA.

--Gardening. LC 19-600. (Illus.). 48p. (gr. 6-12). 1976. pap. 0.70x (ISBN 0-8395-3240-7, 3240). BSA.

--Genealogy. LC 19-600. (Illus.). 32p. (gr. 6-12). 1973. pap. 0.70x (ISBN 0-8395-3383-7, 3383). BSA.

--General Science. LC 19-600. (Illus.). 48p. (gr. 6-12). 1972. pap. 0.70x (ISBN 0-8395-3332-2, 3332). BSA.

--Geology. LC 19-600. (Illus.). 88p. (gr. 6-12). 1953. pap. 0.70x (ISBN 0-8395-3284-9, 3284). BSA.

--Group Meeting Sparklers. (Illus.). Repr. of 1962 ed. pap. text ed. 0.50x (ISBN 0-8395-3122-2). BSA.

--Hiking. LC 19-600. (Illus.). 36p. (gr. 6-12). 1962. pap. 0.70x (ISBN 0-8395-3380-2, 3380). BSA.

--Home Repairs. LC 19-600. (Illus.). 48p. (gr. 6-12). 1961. pap. 0.70x (ISBN 0-8395-3329-2, 3329). BSA.

--Horsemanship. LC 19-600. (Illus.). 56p. (gr. 6-12). 1974. pap. 0.70x (ISBN 0-8395-3298-9, 3298). BSA.

--Indian Lore. LC 19-600. (Illus.). 96p. (gr. 6-12). 1959. pap. 0.70x (ISBN 0-8395-3358-6, 3358). BSA.

--Insect Life. LC 19-600. (Illus.). 64p. (gr. 6-12). 1973. pap. 0.70x (ISBN 0-8395-3353-5, 3353). BSA.

--Journalism. LC 19-600. (Illus.). 40p. (gr. 6-12). 1976. pap. 0.70x (ISBN 0-8395-3350-0, 3350). BSA.

--Knots & How to Tie Them. (Illus.). pap. text ed. 0.55x (ISBN 0-8395-3170-2). BSA.

--Landscape Architecture. LC 19-600. (Illus.). 48p. (gr. 6-12). 1969. pap. 0.70x (ISBN 0-8395-3355-1, 3355). BSA.

--Law. LC 19-600. (Illus.). 64p. (gr. 6-12). 1975. pap. 0.70x (ISBN 0-8395-3389-6, 3389). BSA.

--Leatherwork. LC 19-600. (Illus.). 48p. (gr. 6-12). 1970. pap. 0.70x (ISBN 0-8395-3310-1, 3310). BSA.

--Lifesaving. LC 19-600. (Illus.). 56p. (gr. 6-12). 1965. pap. 0.55x o.p. (ISBN 0-8395-3278-4, 3278). BSA.

--Machinery. LC 19-600. (Illus.). 64p. (gr. 6-12). 1962. pap. 0.70x (ISBN 0-8395-3337-3, 3337). BSA.

--Mammals. LC 19-600. (Illus.). 48p. (gr. 6-12). 1972. pap. 0.70x (ISBN 0-8395-3271-7, 3271). BSA.

--Masonry. LC 19-600. (Illus.). 64p. (gr. 6-12). 1952. pap. 0.55x o.p. (ISBN 0-8395-3339-X, 3339). BSA.

--Metals Engineering. LC 19-600. (Illus.). 64p. (gr. 6-12). 1972. pap. 0.70x (ISBN 0-8395-3269-5, 3269). BSA.

--Metalwork. LC 19-600. (Illus.). 36p. (gr. 6-12). 1969. pap. 0.70x (ISBN 0-8395-3312-8, 3312). BSA.

--Model Design & Building. LC 19-600. (Illus.). 44p. (gr. 6-12). 1964. pap. 0.70x (ISBN 0-8395-3280-6, 3280). BSA.

--Motorboating. LC 19-600. (Illus.). 64p. (gr. 6-12). 1962. pap. 0.70x (ISBN 0-8395-3294-6, 3294). BSA.

--Music & Bugling. LC 19-600. (Illus.). 48p. (gr. 6-12). 1968. pap. 0.70x (ISBN 0-8395-3336-5, 3336). BSA.

--Nature. LC 19-600. (Illus.). 48p. (gr. 6-12). 1973. pap. 0.70x (ISBN 0-8395-3285-7, 3285). BSA.

--Oceanography. LC 19-600. (Illus.). 48p. (gr. 6-12). 1965. pap. 0.70x (ISBN 0-8395-3306-3, 3306). BSA.

--Orienteering. LC 19-600. (Illus.). 32p. (gr. 6-12). 1974. pap. 0.70x (ISBN 0-8395-3385-3, 3385). BSA.

--Painting. LC 19-600. (Illus.). 32p. (gr. 6-12). 1973. pap. 0.70x (ISBN 0-8395-3372-1, 3372). BSA.

--Patrol & Troop Activities. (gr. 6-12). pap. 3.85x (ISBN 0-8395-6543-7). BSA.

--Personal Fitness. LC 19-600. (Illus.). 48p. (gr. 6-12). 1971. pap. 0.70x (ISBN 0-8395-3286-5, 3286). BSA.

--Personal Management. LC 19-600. (Illus.). 32p. (gr. 6-12). 1972. pap. 0.70x (ISBN 0-8395-3270-9, 3270). BSA.

--Pets. LC 19-600. (Illus.). 48p. (gr. 6-12). 1969. pap. 0.70x (ISBN 0-8395-3281-4, 3281). BSA.

--Photography. LC 19-600. (Illus.). 64p. (gr. 6-12). 1971. pap. 0.70x (ISBN 0-8395-3334-9, 3334). BSA.

--Physical Fitness Skill Book. (Illus.). 32p. (gr. 3-4). 1975. pap. 0.50x (ISBN 0-8395-6590-9, 6590); tchr's guide 0.30x (ISBN 0-685-51280-0, 18-330). BSA.

--Pioneering. LC 19-600. (Illus.). 48p. (gr. 6-12). 1974. pap. 0.70x o.p. (ISBN 0-8395-3382-9, 3382). BSA.

--Plant Science. LC 19-600. (Illus.). 48p. (gr. 6-12). 1975. pap. 0.70x (ISBN 0-8395-3396-9, 3396). BSA.

--Plumbing. LC 19-600. (Illus.). 40p. (gr. 6-12). 1965. pap. 0.70x (ISBN 0-8395-3386-1, 3386). BSA.

--Pottery. LC 19-600. (Illus.). 64p. (gr. 6-12). 1969. pap. 0.70x (ISBN 0-8395-3314-4, 3314). BSA.

--Printing. LC 19-600. (Illus.). 64p. (gr. 6-12). 1965. pap. 0.70x (ISBN 0-8395-3377-2, 3377). BSA.

--Public Health. LC 19-600. (Illus.). 64p. (gr. 6-12). 1969. pap. 0.70x (ISBN 0-8395-3251-2, 3251). BSA.

--Public Speaking. LC 19-600. (Illus.). 44p. (gr. 6-12). 1969. pap. 0.70x (ISBN 0-8395-3373-X, 3373). BSA.

--Pulp & Paper. LC 19-600. (Illus.). 40p. (gr. 6-12). 1974. pap. 0.70x (ISBN 0-8395-3343-8, 3343). BSA.

--Rabbit Raising. LC 19-600. (Illus.). 32p. (gr. 6-12). 1974. pap. 0.70x (ISBN 0-8395-3375-6, 3375). BSA.

--Radio. LC 19-600. (Illus.). 48p. (gr. 6-12). 1965. pap. 0.70x (ISBN 0-8395-3333-0, 3333). BSA.

--Railroading. LC 19-600. (Illus.). 48p. (gr. 6-12). 1973. pap. 0.70x (ISBN 0-8395-3292-X, 3292). BSA.

--Reptile Study. LC 19-600. (Illus.). 64p. (gr. 6-12). 1972. pap. 0.70x (ISBN 0-8395-3342-X, 3342). BSA.

--Rifle & Shotgun Shooting. LC 19-600. (Illus.). 80p. (gr. 6-12). 1967. pap. 0.70x (ISBN 0-8395-3311-X, 3311). BSA.

--Rowing. LC 19-600. (Illus.). 44p. (gr. 6-12). 1964. pap. 0.70x (ISBN 0-8395-3392-6, 3392). BSA.

--Safety. LC 19-600. (Illus.). 48p. (gr. 6-12). 1971. pap. 0.70x (ISBN 0-8395-3347-0, 3347). BSA.

--Salesmanship. LC 19-600. (Illus.). 32p. (gr. 6-12). 1971. pap. 0.70x (ISBN 0-8395-3351-9, 3351). BSA.

--Scholarship. LC 19-600. (Illus.). 64p. (gr. 6-12). 1970. pap. 0.70x (ISBN 0-8395-3384-5, 3384). BSA.

--Scout Songbook. 128p. (gr. 6-12). 1972. pap. 0.90x (ISBN 0-8395-3224-5, 3224). BSA.

--Scouting for the Physically Handicapped. 96p. 1971. pap. 2.00x (ISBN 0-8395-3039-0, 3039). BSA.

--Scoutmaster's Handbook. (Illus.). 384p. 1972. flexible bdg 3.45x (ISBN 0-8395-6504-6, 6504). BSA.

--Sculpture. LC 19-600. (Illus.). 24p. (gr. 6-12). 1969. pap. 0.70x (ISBN 0-8395-3322-5, 3322). BSA.
--Sea Exploring Manual. LC 66-19112. 456p. (gr. 6-12). 1966. flexible bdg. 5.95x (ISBN 0-8395-3229-6, 3229). BSA.
--Signaling. LC 19-600. (Illus.). 32p. (gr. 6-12). 1974. pap. 0.70x (ISBN 0-8395-3237-7, 3237). BSA.
--Skating. LC 19-600. (Illus.). 32p. (gr. 6-12). 1973. pap. 0.70x (ISBN 0-8395-3250-4, 3250). BSA.
Boy Scouts, of America. Skiing. (Illus.). 56p. (gr. 6-12). 1980. pap. 0.70x. BSA.
Boy Scouts Of America. Skiing. LC 19-600. (Illus.). 64p. (gr. 6-12). 1965. pap. 0.55x o.p. (ISBN 0-8395-3364-0, 3364). BSA.
--Skits & Puppets. (Illus.). 68p. 1967. pap. 1.25x (ISBN 0-8395-3842-1). BSA.
--Small-Boat Sailing. LC 19-600. (Illus.). 96p. (gr. 6-12). 1965. pap. 0.70x (ISBN 0-8395-3319-5, 3319). BSA.
--Soil & Water Conservation. LC 19-600. (Illus.). 96p. (gr. 6-12). 1968. pap. 0.70x (ISBN 0-8395-3291-1). BSA.
--Space Exploration. LC 19-600. (Illus.). 64p. (gr. 6-12). 1966. pap. 0.70x (ISBN 0-8395-3354-3, 3354). BSA.
--Sports. LC 19-600. (Illus.). 72p. (gr. 6-12). 1972. pap. 0.70x (ISBN 0-8395-3255-5, 3255). BSA.
--Stamp Collecting. LC 19-600. (Illus.). 48p. (gr. 6-12). 1974. pap. 0.70x (ISBN 0-8395-3359-4, 3359). BSA.
--Surveying. LC 19-600. (Illus.). 56p. (gr. 6-12). 1960. pap. 0.70x (ISBN 0-8395-3327-6, 3327). BSA.
--Swimming. (Illus.). 48p. (gr. 6-12). 1980. pap. 0.70x. BSA.
--Swimming. LC 19-600. (Illus.). 48p. (gr. 6-12). 1960. pap. 0.55x o.p. (ISBN 0-8395-3299-7, 3299). BSA.
--Textile. LC 19-600. 64p. (gr. 6-12). 1972. pap. 0.70x (ISBN 0-8395-3344-6, 3344). BSA.
--Theater. LC 19-600. 64p. (gr. 6-12). 1968. pap. 0.70x (ISBN 0-8395-3328-4, 3328). BSA.
--Traffic Safety. LC 19-600. (Illus.). 64p. (gr. 6-12). 1975. pap. 0.70x (ISBN 0-8395-3391-8, 3391). BSA.
--Truck Transportation. LC 19-600. (Illus.). 32p. (gr. 6-12). 1973. pap. 0.70x (ISBN 0-8395-3371-3, 3371). BSA.
--Veterinary Science. LC 19-600. (Illus.). 40p. (gr. 6-12). 1973. pap. 0.70x (ISBN 0-8395-3261-X, 3261). BSA.
--Water Skiing. LC 19-600. (Illus.). 48p. (gr. 6-12). 1969. pap. 0.70x (ISBN 0-8395-3357-8, 3357). BSA.
--Weather. LC 19-600. 60p. (gr. 6-12). 1963. pap. 0.70x (ISBN 0-8395-3274-1, 3274). BSA.
--Webelos Den Activities. (Illus.). 1969. pap. 0.85x (ISBN 0-8395-3853-7, 3853). BSA.
--Webelos Den Leader's Book. LC 67-23387. (Illus.). 1967. pap. 1.75x (ISBN 0-8395-3217-2, 3217). BSA.
--Webelos Scout Book. LC 67-14536. (Illus.). (gr. 5). 1973. flexible bdg. 1.75x (ISBN 0-8395-3232-6, 3232). BSA.
--Wilderness Survival. LC 19-600. (Illus.). 40p. (gr. 6-12). 1974. pap. 0.70x (ISBN 0-8395-3265-2, 3265). BSA.
--Wolf Cub Scout Book. rev. ed. LC 67-14539. (Illus.). 192p. (gr. 3). 1973. flexible bdg. 1.75x (ISBN 0-8395-3207-5, 3207). BSA.
--Wood Carving. LC 19-600. (Illus.). 48p. (gr. 6-12). 1966. pap. 0.70x (ISBN 0-8395-3315-2, 3315). BSA.
--Woodwork. LC 19-600. (Illus.). 48p. (gr. 6-12). 1970. pap. 0.70x (ISBN 0-8395-3316-0, 3316). BSA.
--Your Flag. LC 19-600. (Illus.). 64p. (gr. 6-12). 1972. pap. 1.35x (ISBN 0-8395-3188-5, 3188). BSA.
Boy Scouts of America & Boys Scout of America. Handicapped Awareness. (Illus.). 48p. (gr. 6-12). 1981. pap. 0.70x (ISBN 0-8395-3370-5, 3370). BSA.
Boy Scouts of America, Exploring Division. Exploring Techniques: Exploring for the Handicapped. (Exploring Techniques Ser.). (gr. 9-12). pap. text ed. 0.60x o.s.i. (ISBN 0-8395-6675-1). BSA.
Boy Socuts of America. Chemistry. LC 19-600. (Illus.). 48p. (gr. 6-12). 1973. pap. 0.70x (ISBN 0-8395-3367-5, 3367). BSA.
Boyajian, Lee G. The Comprehensive Verbal Graduate Record Exam Study Guide. 1981. 6.95 (ISBN 0-533-04508-8). Vantage.
Boyan. Institute Supervision Training Program. 1978. text ed. 10.95 (ISBN 0-675-08415-6); video 695.00 (ISBN 0-675-08350-8); 16 mm film 395.00 (ISBN 0-675-08414-8). Merrill.
Boyan, Douglas R., ed. Open Doors Nineteen Seventy-Eight to Nineteen Seventy-Nine: Report on International Educational Exchange. rev. ed. LC 55-4594. 125p. 1980. pap. text ed. 15.00 o.p. (ISBN 0-87206-098-5). Inst Intl Educ.
--Open Doors Nineteen Seventy-Nine to Nineteen Eighty: Report on International Educational Exchange. LC 55-4594. 160p. 1981. pap. 20.00 o.p. (ISBN 0-87206-106-X). Inst Intl Educ.
Boyan, Norman & Copeland, Willis. Instructional Supervision Training Program. 1978. pap. text ed. 8.50 o.p. (ISBN 0-686-67368-9). Merrill.
Boyar, Burt, jt. auth. see Boyar, Jane.
Boyar, Jane & Boyar, Burt. World Class. LC 75-10257. 512p. 1975. 10.00 o.p. (ISBN 0-394-46053-7). Random.
Boyar, Jay. Be a Magician! How to Put on a Magic Show & Mystify Your Friends. (Illus.). 160p. (gr. 7 up). 1981. PLB price not set (ISBN 0-671-42273-1). Messner.
Boyarsky & Labay. Uretheral Dynamics. 503p. 1972. 23.00 o.p. (ISBN 0-683-00951-6, Pub. by Williams & Wilkins). Krieger.
Boyarsky, Bill. The Rise of Ronald Reagan. (Illus.). 1981. Repr. of 1964 ed. price not set. Random.
Boyarsky, Saul & Polakoski, Kenneth, eds. Goals in Male Reproductive Research: Proceedings of Conference on Future Goals in Reproductive Medicine & Surgery, 20 September, 1979, Bethesda, Md. 144p. 1981. 30.00 (ISBN 0-08-025910-3). Pergamon.
Boyarsky, Saul, et al. Care of the Patient with Neurogenic Bladder. 1978. text ed. 13.95 (ISBN 0-316-10431-0). Little.
Boyce, jt. auth. see Bacon.
Boyce, A. J. Chromosome Variation in Human Evolution. LC 75-25643. (Symposia for the Study of Human Biology Ser: Vol. 14). 131p. 1976. 24.95 (ISBN 0-470-09330-7). Halsted Pr.
--Chromosome Variation in Human Evolution, Vol. 14. 131p. 1975. 24.95 (ISBN 0-470-09330-7). Wiley.
Boyce, A. J., jt. ed. see Harrison, G. A.
Boyce, Byrl N., ed. Real Estate Appraisal Terminology. 2nd ed. 1980. 14.50 (ISBN 0-88410-597-0). Ballinger Pub.
Boyce, Chris. Catchworld. 1978. pap. 1.75 o.p. (ISBN 0-449-23635-8, Crest). Fawcett.
Boyce, Everett R., ed. see Hooper, Ben W.
Boyce, George A., ed. Some People Are Indians. LC 75-190224. (Illus.). (gr. 4-6). 1974. 5.95 (ISBN 0-8149-0714-8). Vanguard.
Boyce, Jefferson. Microprocessor & Microcomputer Basics. (Illus.). 1979. text ed. 18.95 (ISBN 0-13-581249-6). P-H.
Boyce, Jefferson C. Digital Computer Fundamentals. LC 76-11768. (Illus.). 1977. 19.95 (ISBN 0-13-214114-0). P-H.
Boyce, John C., et al. Mathematics for Technical & Vocational Schools. 6th ed. LC 74-10539. 572p. 1975. text ed. 18.95 (ISBN 0-471-09340-8); solutions manual avail. (ISBN 0-471-09341-6). Wiley.
Boyce, Mary. Zoroastrians: Their Religious Beliefs & Practices. (Library of Beliefs & Practices). 1979. 24.00 (ISBN 0-7100-0121-5). Routledge & Kegan.
Boyce, P. R. Human Factors in Lighting. (Illus.). xiii, 420p. 1981. 52.00x (ISBN 0-686-28903-X). Burgess-Intl Ideas.
Boyce, Ronald R., ed. see Ullman, Edward L.
Boyce, Sheila, jt. auth. see Dowding, Howard.
Boyce, Terry V. Chevy Super Sports. (Illus.). 1981. pap. 13.95 (ISBN 0-87938-096-9). Motorbooks Intl.
Boyce, William D. & Jensen, Larry C. Moral Reasoning: A Psychological-Philosophical Integration. LC 78-5935. 1978. 15.95x (ISBN 0-8032-0982-7). U of Nebr Pr.
Boyce, William E. & Di Prima, Richard C. Elementary Differential Equations. 3rd ed. LC 75-35565. 1977. text ed. 20.95x (ISBN 0-471-09339-4). Wiley.
Boyce, William E. & DiPrima, Richard C. Elementary Differential Equations & Boundary Value Problems. 3rd ed. LC 75-45093. 1977. 20.95x (ISBN 0-471-09334-3). Wiley.
--Introduction to Differential Equations. 1970. text ed. 18.50x (ISBN 0-471-09338-6). Wiley.
Boyd. The How. 32p. 1980. 8.95 (ISBN 0-87705-176-3). Human Sci Pr.
Boyd, jt. auth. see Garrard.
Boyd, A., jt. auth. see Kimber, Richard T.
Boyd, Alvin, tr. The Narrative Bible. 256p. 1981. 8.95 (ISBN 0-89490-047-1). Enslow Pubs.
Boyd, Anne. The Monks of Durham. LC 74-14438. (Introduction to the History of Mankind Ser). (Illus.). 48p. (gr. 6-11). 1975. text ed. 3.95 (ISBN 0-521-20647-2). Cambridge U Pr.
Boyd, Blanche M. Mourning the Death of Magic. LC 77-2343. 1977. 10.95 (ISBN 0-02-514270-4). Macmillan.
Boyd, Carl. The Extraordinary Envoy: General Hiroshi Oshima & Diplomacy in the Third Reich 1934-1939. LC 79-9600. 246p. 1980. text ed. 18.50 (ISBN 0-8191-0957-6); pap. text ed. 9.75 (ISBN 0-8191-0958-4). U Pr of Amer.
Boyd, Charles M. & Dalrymple, Glenn V., eds. Basic Science Principles of Nuclear Medicine. LC 74-664. (Illus.). 1974. text ed. 26.50 o.p. (ISBN 0-8016-0729-9). Mosby.
Boyd, Claude E. Water Quality in Warmwater Fish Ponds. (Illus.). 366p. 1979. pap. 9.95x (ISBN 0-8173-0055-4, Pub. by Ag Experiment). U of Ala Pr.
Boyd, Daniel. How to Double Your Sex Drive. 160p. 1980. 12.95 (ISBN 0-917224-09-4). Gregory Pubns.
Boyd, David. Elites & Their Education. (General Ser). 160p. 1973. pap. text ed. 12.00x (ISBN 0-85633-025-6, NFER). Humanities.
Boyd, Doug. Swami. 1976. 10.00 o.p. (ISBN 0-394-49603-5). Random.
Boyd, Edith. The Growth of the Surface Area of the Human Body. LC 75-14249. (Univ. of Minnesota, the Institute of Child Welfare Monograph: No. 10). (Illus.). 145p. 1975. Repr. of 1935 ed. lib. bdg. 14.00x (ISBN 0-8371-8069-4, CWBS). Greenwood.
Boyd, Eldon M. Protein Deficiency & Pesticide Toxicity. (Illus.). 480p. 1972. 42.50 (ISBN 0-398-02476-6). C C Thomas.
--Respiratory Tract Fluid. (Illus.). 336p. 1972. 29.75 (ISBN 0-398-02239-9). C C Thomas.
Boyd, Elizabeth. The Happy-Unfortunate: or the Female-Page. LC 76-170583. (Foundations of the Novel Ser.: Vol. 56). lib. bdg. 50.00 (ISBN 0-8240-0568-6). Garland Pub.
Boyd, Elizabeth F. Byron's Don Juan: A Critical Study. 1975. Repr. of 1945 ed. 12.50x (ISBN 0-391-00439-5). Humanities.
Boyd, Fannie L. & Stovall, Ruth. Handbook of Consumer Education: A Guide for Teaching Process & Content. new ed. 1978. pap. text ed. 17.95 (ISBN 0-205-05890-6). Allyn.
Boyd, G. W. The Will to Live: Five Steps to Officer Survival. 144p. 1980. 12.50 (ISBN 0-398-04020-6). C C Thomas.
Boyd, Gavin, ed. Region Building in the Pacific. (Pergamon Policy Studies). 400p. Date not set. price not set (ISBN 0-08-025985-5). Pergamon.
Boyd, Gavin & Pentland, Charles, eds. Issues in Global Politics. LC 80-69282. 1981. pap. text ed. 9.95 (ISBN 0-02-904470-7). Free Pr.
Boyd, Gavin, jt. ed. see Feld, Werner.
Boyd, George, ed. see Mann, Thomas.
Boyd, Hamish. Introduction to Homeopathic Medicine. 240p. 1980. 49.00x (Pub. by Beaconsfield England). State Mutual Bk.
Boyd, Harper W., Jr., et al. Marketing Management Casebook. rev. ed. 1976. 17.50x o.p. (ISBN 0-256-01837-5). Irwin.
--Marketing Research: Text & Cases. 4th ed. 1977. text ed. 19.95x (ISBN 0-256-01838-3). Irwin.
Boyd, J., jt. auth. see Darling, F.
Boyd, J. D. Sound Doctrine Briefs & Radio Sermons. 3.95 (ISBN 0-89315-258-7). Lambert Bk.
Boyd, J. P., et al, eds. see Jefferson, Thomas.
Boyd, Jack. Leading the Lord's Singing. 1981. pap. write for info. (ISBN 0-89137-603-8). Quality Pubns.
Boyd, James, jt. auth. see Anderson, Jack.
Boyd, Jessie, et al. Books, Libraries & You. 3rd ed. (Illus.). (gr. 7-12). 1965. text ed. 3.96 o.p. (ISBN 0-684-51501-6, ScribC). Scribner.
Boyd, John. Community Education & Urban Schools. LC 77-5912. 1977. pap. text ed. 6.95x (ISBN 0-582-48945-8). Longman.
--The Girl with the Jade Green Eyes. 1978. 8.95 o.p. (ISBN 0-670-34164-9). Viking Pr.
Boyd, John D. The Function of Mimesis & Its Decline. 2nd ed. LC 68-28691. 1980. pap. 8.00 (ISBN 0-8232-1046-4). Fordham.
Boyd, K., ed. The Ethics of Resource Allocations. 128p. 1980. text ed. 12.00x (ISBN 0-85224-368-5, Pub. by Edinburgh U Pr Scotland). Columbia U Pr.
Boyd, K. T. ATP-GA. (Illus.). 96p. 1981. pap. 9.25 (ISBN 0-8138-0510-4). Iowa St U Pr.
Boyd, Kenneth M. Scottish Church Attitudes to Sex, Marriage & the Family 1850-1914. 410p. 1980. text ed. 47.00x (ISBN 0-85976-056-1). Humanities.
Boyd, L. M. Boyd's Book of Odd Facts. 1980. pap. 1.75 (ISBN 0-451-09415-8, E9415, Sig). NAL.
--Boyd's Book of Odd Facts. LC 78-66296. (Illus.). 1979. 9.95 (ISBN 0-8069-0166-7); lib. bdg. 9.89 (ISBN 0-8069-0167-5). Sterling.
Boyd, Lawrence H. & Iversen, Gudmund R. Contextual Analysis: Concepts & Statistical Techniques. 1979. text ed. 25.95x (ISBN 0-534-00693-0). Wadsworth Pub.
Boyd, Malcolm. Human Like Me, Jesus. 1973. pap. 1.25 (ISBN 0-89129-148-2). Jove Pubns.
--Look Back in Joy: Celebration of Gay Lovers. 128p. (Orig.). 1981. 20.00 (ISBN 0-917342-85-2, Pub. by Gay Sunshine); pap. 6.95 (ISBN 0-917342-77-1). Bookpeople.
Boyd, Margaret A. Catalog Sources for Creative People: Where to Buy Craft, Needlework & Hobby Supplies by Mail. (Orig.). 1981. pap. 10.95 (ISBN 0-938814-01-X). Barrington.
Boyd, Margaret A. & Scott-Martin, Sue. Directory of Shop-by-Mail Bargain Sources. rev. ed. LC 77-17778. 1981. pap. 3.50 (ISBN 0-87576-063-5). Pilot Bks.
Boyd, Marilyn S. Women's Liberation Ideology & Union Participation: A Study. LC 79-65257. 135p. 1981. perfect bdg. 10.95 (ISBN 0-86548-024-9). Century Twenty One.
Boyd, Martin. Lucinda Brayford. 14.95 (ISBN 0-392-08085-0, SpS). Soccer.
Boyd, Maurice & Worcester, Donald B. American Civilization: An Introduction to the Social Sciences. 3rd ed. 800p. 1973. text ed. 10.95x o.p. (ISBN 0-205-03821-2, 8138214). Allyn.
Boyd, Morrison C. Elizabethan Music & Musical Criticism. LC 73-1837. 392p. 1974. pap. 4.95x o.p. (ISBN 0-8122-1071-9). U of Pa Pr.
Boyd, Nathaniel W., III. How to Stay Out of the Hospital. LC 76-39730. 1979. pap. 4.95 (ISBN 0-8119-0404-0). Fell.
Boyd, Neil. Bless Me, Father. LC 77-9169. 1978. 8.95 o.p. (ISBN 0-312-08379-3). St Martin.
--Father in a Fix. LC 80-15258. 256p. 1980. 9.95 (ISBN 0-688-03643-0). Morrow.
Boyd, R. L. Space Physics: The Study of Plasmas in Space. (Oxford Physics Ser). (Illus.). 112p. 1975. text ed. 15.50x (ISBN 0-19-851807-2). Oxford U Pr.
Boyd, Robert D., et al. Redefining the Discipline of Adult Education. LC 80-8006. (Higher Education Ser.). 1980. text ed. 15.95x (ISBN 0-87589-482-8). Jossey-Bass.
Boyd, Robert F. & Marr, J. Joseph. Medical Microbiology. 1980. text ed. 24.95 (ISBN 0-316-10432-9). Little.
Boyd, Robert N., jt. auth. see Morrison, Robert T.
Boyd, Robert R. & Hoerl, Bryan G. Basic Medical Microbiology. 2nd ed. 1981. text ed. write for info (ISBN 0-316-10433-7). Little.
--Laboratory Manual to Accompany Basic Medical Microbiology. 1981. write for info. lab manual (ISBN 0-316-10434-5). Little.
Boyd, Robin. Kenzo Tange. LC 62-16267. (Makers of Contemporary Architecture Ser). 1962. 4.95 o.p. (ISBN 0-8076-0196-9). Braziller.
--Victorian Modern. 1980. write for info. (ISBN 0-522-84156-2, Pub. by Melbourne U Pr). Intl Schol Bk Serv.
Boyd, Rogene & Schumacher, Margaret. Wyoming's People Activity Book. 1978. 4.00x (ISBN 0-933472-37-4). Johnson Colo.
Boyd, Shylah. American Made. 384p. 1976. pap. 1.95 o.p. (ISBN 0-449-22861-4, C2861, Crest). Fawcett.
Boyd, Sterling M; see O'Neal, William B.
Boyd, T. Gardner. Metal Working. LC 77-89986. (Illus.). 1978. text ed. 4.80 (ISBN 0-87006-258-1). Goodheart.
Boyd, T. Gardner, jt. auth. see Miller, W. R.
Boyd, T. J., jt. auth. see Coulson, C. A.
Boyd, William. Emile of Jean Jacques Rousseau. (No. 11). 1962. text ed. 8.50 (ISBN 0-8077-1110-1); pap. text ed. 3.95x (ISBN 0-8077-1107-1). Tchrs Coll.
--The Spontaneous Regression of Cancer. 112p. 1966. pap. 12.75 photocopy ed. spiral (ISBN 0-398-00209-6). C C Thomas.
Boyd, William & King, Edmund J. The History of Western Education. 11th ed. LC 65-789. 1980. pap. 13.50x (ISBN 0-389-20131-6). B&N.
Boyd, William & Sheldon, Huntington. Introduction to the Study of Disease. 8th ed. LC 80-23487. (Illus.). 660p. 1980. 19.75 (ISBN 0-8121-0729-2). Lea & Febiger.
Boyd, William C. Fundamentals of Immunology. 4th ed. LC 66-20389. 1967. 38.95 (ISBN 0-470-09342-0, Pub. by Wiley-Interscience). Wiley.
Boyd, William H., ed. Minor Educational Writings of Jean-Jacques Rousseau. LC 62-21561. 1962. pap. text ed. 3.50x (ISBN 0-8077-1113-6). Tchrs Coll.
Boyd, William L., jt. ed. see Immegart, Glenn L.
Boyd-Barrett, Oliver. The International News Agencies. LC 80-51779. (Communication & Society Ser.: Vol. 13). (Illus.). 284p. 1980. 25.00 (ISBN 0-8039-1511-X); pap. 12.50 (ISBN 0-8039-1512-8). Sage.
Boyde, P. Dante: Philomythes & Philosopher. LC 80-40551. (Illus.). 520p. Date not set. 55.00 (ISBN 0-521-23598-7). Cambridge U Pr.
Boyden, A. A. Perspectives in Zoology. LC 73-1279. 294p. 1973. text ed. 32.00 (ISBN 0-08-017122-2). Pergamon.
Boydston, Jo Ann, ed. Guide to the Works of John Dewey. LC 70-112383. (Arcturus Books Paperbacks). 413p. 1972. pap. 7.95 (ISBN 0-8093-0561-5). S Ill U Pr.
Boydston, Jo Ann & Poulos, Kathleen, eds. Checklist of Writings About John Dewey, 1887-1977. 2nd, enl. ed. LC 77-17136. 488p. 1978. 19.95x (ISBN 0-8093-0842-8). S Ill U Pr.
Boydston, Jo Ann, ed. see Dewey, John.
Boydston, Jo Ann see Dewey, John.
Boydston, Jo Ann, et. see Dewey, John.
Boydston, Jo Ann, et al, eds. see Dewey, John.
Boye, Henry. How to Make Money Selling the Songs You Write. rev. ed. LC 75-124473. 1975. pap. 4.95 (ISBN 0-8119-0381-8). Fell.

Boyen, J. L. Practical Heat Recovery. LC 75-17735. 254p. 1975. 21.95 o.p. (ISBN 0-471-09376-9, Pub. by Wiley-Interscience). Wiley.
Boyen, John L. Thermal Energy Recovery. 2nd ed. LC 79-19704. 1980. 27.50 (ISBN 0-471-04981-6, Pub. by Wiley-Interscience). Wiley.
Boyer. Safety on Wheels. LC 73-87802. (Safety Ser). (Illus.). (gr. k-5). 1974. prebound 7.99 (ISBN 0-87783-133-5); pap. 2.75 deluxe ed. (ISBN 0-87783-134-3); cassette 5.95 (ISBN 0-685-42417-0). Oddo.
Boyer, Bathyah. Material Relics of Music in Ancient Palestine and Its Environs. LC 64-251. 1963. pap. 9.00 (ISBN 0-913932-33-7). Boosey & Hawkes.
Boyer, Bruce H. The Solstice Cipher. 1981. pap. 2.75 (ISBN 0-440-18096-1). Dell.
Boyer, Calvin J. The Doctoral Dissertation As an Information Source: A Study of Scientific Information Flow. 1973. 8.00 o.p. (ISBN 0-8108-0623-1). Scarecrow.
Boyer, Carl B. History of Mathematics. LC 68-16506. 1968. 26.95 (ISBN 0-471-09374-2). Wiley.
Boyer, Carl, 3rd. Ancestral Lines Revised. 1981. 40.00 (ISBN 0-936124-05-9). C Boyer.
Boyer, Carl, 3rd, et al. Brown Families of Bristol Counties, Massachusetts & Rhode Island & Descendants of Jared Talbot. LC 80-68755. (New England Colonial Families: Vol. 1). 219p. 1980. 18.35 (ISBN 0-936124-04-0). C Boyer.
Boyer, David L., et al, eds. The Philosopher's Annual, 1978, Vol. 1. 223p. 1978. 22.50x (ISBN 0-8476-6105-9); pap. 10.95x (ISBN 0-8476-6106-7). Rowman.
--The Philosopher's Annual 1980, Vol. III. xii, 225p. (Orig.). 1980. lib. bdg. 22.00 (ISBN 0-917930-38-X); pap. text ed. 8.50x (ISBN 0-917930-18-5). Ridgeview.
Boyer, Dwight. Ships & Men of the Great Lakes. LC 77-5901. (Illus.). 1977. 8.95 (ISBN 0-396-07446-4). Dodd.
Boyer, Elizabeth. Freydis & Gudrid. 1978. pap. 1.95 o.p. (ISBN 0-445-04278-8). Popular Lib.
Boyer, James L. For a World Like Ours. (New Testament Studies Ser.). pap. 2.95 o.p. (ISBN 0-8010-0553-1). Baker Bk.
--For a World Like Ours: Studies in I Corinthians. pap. 3.95 (ISBN 0-88469-057-1). BMH Bks.
Boyer, John W. Political Radicalism in Late Imperial Vienna: Origins of the Christian Social Movement, 1848-1897. LC 80-17302. (Illus.). 1981. lib. bdg. price not set (ISBN 0-226-06957-5). U of Chicago Pr.
Boyer, Mary G. Arizona in Literature. LC 74-145714. 1971. Repr. of 1935 ed. 32.00 (ISBN 0-8103-3703-7). Gale.
Boyer, Maryjoan. Old Gravois Coal Diggings. 4.00 o.p. (ISBN 0-911208-12-7). Ramfre.
Boyer, Orlando, tr. Esforca-Te Para Ganhar Almas. (Portugese Bks.). (Port.). 1979. 1.60 (ISBN 0-8297-0662-3). Life Pubs Intl.
Boyer, Paul & Nissenbaum, Stephen, eds. The Salem Witchcraft Papers: Verbatim Transcripts, 3 vols. 1977. lib. bdg. 125.00 (ISBN 0-306-70655-5). Da Capo.
Boyer, Paul D., ed. The Enzymes. Incl. Vol. 1. Enzyme Structure, Control. 3rd. ed. 1970. 51.00 (ISBN 0-12-122701-4); Vol. 2. Kinetics, Mechamisms. 3rd. ed. 1970. 51.00 (ISBN 0-12-122702-2); Vol. 3. Peptide Bond Hydrolysis. 3rd ed. 1971. 62.50 (ISBN 0-12-122703-0); Vol. 4. 1971. 62.50 (ISBN 0-12-122704-9); Vol. 5. 1971. 62.50 (ISBN 0-12-122705-7); Vol. 6. 1972. 62.50 (ISBN 0-12-122706-5); Vol. 7. 1972. 62.50 (ISBN 0-12-122707-3); Vol. 8. 1973. 55.00 (ISBN 0-12-122708-1); Vol. 9. 1973. 55.00 (ISBN 0-12-122709-X); Vol. 10. 1974. 62.50 (ISBN 0-12-122710-3); Vol. 11. 1975. 62.50 (ISBN 0-12-122711-1); Vol. 12. 1975. 59.00 (ISBN 0-12-122712-X); Vol. 13. 1976. 62.50 (ISBN 0-12-122713-8). 629.00 set (ISBN 0-685-23119-4); student ed. 1973 22.50 (ISBN 0-12-122750-2). Acad Pr.
Boyer, R. & Keinath, S., eds. Molecular Motion in Polymers by ESR. (MMI Press Symposium Ser.: Vol. 1). 352p. 1980. lib. bdg. 44.00 (ISBN 3-7186-0012-9). Harwood Academic.
Boyer, R. E. Field Guide to Rock Weathering. (Earth Science Curriculum Project Pamphlet Ser). 1971. pap. 3.20 (ISBN 0-395-02615-6, 2-14601). HM.
Boyer, Ralph E. Survey of the Law of Property. 3rd ed. 737p. 1981. text ed. write for info. (ISBN 0-8299-2128-1). West Pub.
Boyer, Richard, jt. auth. see London, Barbara.
Boyer, Robert M. Z & Zahorski, Kenneth J., eds. The Fantastic Imagination. 1976. pap. 2.25 (ISBN 0-380-00956-0, 32326). Avon.
Boyer, Walter E., et al. Songs Along the Mahantonga: Pennsylvania Dutch Folksongs. 231p. 1964. Repr. of 1951 ed. 15.00 (ISBN 0-8103-5002-5). Gale.
Boyer Argens, Jean Baptiste De see Baptiste De Boyer Argens, Jean.
Boyers, Robert. Excursions: Selected Literary Essays. (Literary Criticism Ser). 1976. 15.00 (ISBN 0-8046-9148-7, Natl U). Kennikat.
Boyes, Geoffrey, ed. Synchro & Resolver Conversion. (Illus.). 196p. (Orig.). 1980. pap. 11.50 (ISBN 0-916550-06-0). Analog Devices.
Boyes, John & Russell, Ronald. The Canals of Eastern England. 1977. 22.50 (ISBN 0-7153-7415-X). David & Charles.
Boyes, R. L., et al. Introduction to Electronic Computing. 1971. 17.00 (ISBN 0-471-09380-7, Pub. by Wiley). Krieger.
Boyes, William E., ed. Jigs & Fixtures. LC 79-64915. (Manufacturing Update Ser.). (Illus.). 1979. 29.00 (ISBN 0-87263-051-X). SME.
Boyet, Howard. Eight Thousand Eighty Microcomputer Experiments. 416p. 1979. pap. 16.95 (ISBN 0-918398-08-8). Dilithium Pr.
Boykin, James H. Financing Real Estate. LC 77-205. (Special Ser. in Real Estate & Urban Land Economics). (Illus.). 1979. 28.95 (ISBN 0-669-01449-4); price not set instrs' manual (ISBN 0-669-03998-5). Lexington Bks.
--World Blacks: Self Help & Achievement. LC 19-53631. ix, 193p. 1980. pap. 6.25 (ISBN 0-9603342-0-3). Boykin.
Boykin, Lorraine S. Nutrition in Nursing. (Nursing Outline Ser.). 1975. spiral bdg. 6.00 o.p. (ISBN 0-87488-375-X). Med Exam.
Boyko, Walter N. Guidebook for the Smart Investor: How to Analyze Real Estate Investment Returns. Rand, Elizabeth H., ed. LC 80-52879. (Illus.). 72p. (Orig.). 1981. pap. 6.95 (ISBN 0-914488-24-4). Rand-Tofua.
Boylan, Brian R., jt. auth. see Weller, Charles.
Boylan, James, jt. auth. see Davison, W. Phillips.
Boyle, Andrew. The Fourth Man. 464p. 1980. pap. 3.50 (ISBN 0-553-14245-3). Bantam.
Boyle, Ann. Beyond the Wall. 192p. (YA) 1976. 4.95 o.p. (ISBN 0-685-57547-0, Avalon). Bouregy.
--The Snowy Hills of Innocence. (YA) 1977. 4.95 o.p. (ISBN 0-685-73807-8, Avalon). Bouregy.
--Veil of Sand. (YA) 1977. 5.95 (ISBN 0-685-81425-4, Avalon). Bouregy.
Boyle, Charles A. Speak Out with Clout. LC 77-17265. 196p. 1977. 6.95 (ISBN 0-89709-020-9). Liberty Pub.
Boyle, D. G. Language & Thinking in Human Developement. 1971. text ed. 8.00x (ISBN 0-09-109590-5, Hutchinson U Lib). Humanities.
Boyle, D. J. A Student's Guide to Piaget. LC 77-94056. 1969. 11.25 (ISBN 0-08-006407-8); pap. 5.75 (ISBN 0-08-006406-X). Pergamon.
Boyle, Donzella C. Quest of a Hemisphere. LC 71-113036. (Illus.). (gr. 7 up). 1970. PLB 15.00 (ISBN 0-88279-218-0). Western Islands.
Boyle, Elisabeth L. & Delbridge, Pauline N. Spoken Cantonese, Bk I. 410p. 1980. pap. 10.00x (ISBN 0-87950-675-X); cassettes 1 dual track 75.00x (ISBN 0-87950-677-6); book 1 & cassettes 1 80.00x (ISBN 0-87950-679-2). Spoken Lang Serv.
--Spoken Cantonese, Bk. II. 410p. 1980. pap. 10.00x (ISBN 0-87950-676-8); cassettes iI 75.00x (ISBN 0-87950-678-4); book iI & cassettes iI 80.00x (ISBN 0-686-66052-8); books i & iI & cassettes i & iI 150.00x (ISBN 0-87950-681-4). Spoken Lang Serv.
Boyle, G., et al. The Politics of Technology. LC 77-5678. (Open University Set Book). (Illus.). 1978. pap. text ed. 11.95x (ISBN 0-582-44373-3). Longman.
Boyle, Godfrey. Living on the Sun: Harnessing Renewable Energy for an Equitable Society. (Ideas in Progress Ser.). (Illus.). 1978. 11.95 (ISBN 0-7145-1094-7, Pub. by M Boyars); pap. 5.95 (ISBN 0-7145-0862-4). Merrimack Bk Serv.
Boyle, J. A. The Mongol World Empire, 1206-1370. 316p. 1980. 60.00x (ISBN 0-86078-002-3, Pub. by Variorum England). State Mutual Bk.
Boyle, J. David, jt. auth. see Radocy, Rudolf E.
Boyle, James. Practical Therapeutics for Nursing & Related Professions. 3rd ed. Orig. Title: Lectures Notes in Pharmacology & Therapeutics for Nurses. 288p. 1980. pap. text ed. 14.00x (ISBN 0-443-01540-6). Churchill.
Boyle, John A., tr. from Pers. Successors of Genghis Khan. LC 70-135987. (Illus.). 1971. 20.00x (ISBN 0-231-03351-6). Columbia U Pr.
Boyle, John H. China & Japan at War, 1937-1945: The Politics of Collaboration. LC 76-183886. (Illus.). 416p. 1972. 18.50x (ISBN 0-8047-0800-2). Stanford U Pr.
Boyle, Joseph M., Jr., jt. auth. see Grisez, Germain.
Boyle, Kay. Pinky in Persia. LC 68-18472. (Illus.). (gr. 1-3). 1968. 3.50g o.s.i. (ISBN 0-02-711820-7, CCPr). Macmillan.
--Pinky, the Cat Who Liked to Sleep. (Illus.). (gr. 1-3). 1968. 4.50g o.s.i. (ISBN 0-02-711770-7, CCPr). Macmillan.
Boyle, Marjorie O. Christening Pagan Mysteries: Erasmus in Pursuit of Wisdom. (Erasmus Studies). 168p. 1981. 15.00x (ISBN 0-8020-5525-7). U of Toronto Pr.
Boyle, Patrick G. Planning Better Programs. Pardoen, Alan & Seaman, Don, eds. (Adult Education Association Professional Development Ser.). (Illus.). 272p. 1980. text ed. 13.95 (ISBN 0-07-000552-4, C). McGraw.
Boyle, Patrick J., jt. auth. see Smith, Karl J.
Boyle, Raelene, jt. auth. see Clarke, Ron.
Boyle, Robert. Origin of Forms & Qualities: The Theorical Part. Barger, Bill, ed. (Orig.). 1976. pap. 5.95x o.p. (ISBN 0-917044-02-9). Sheffield Pr.
--Sceptical Chymist. 1964. 5.00x o.p. (ISBN 0-460-00559-6, Evman). Dutton.
Boyle, Robert H. & Ciampi, Elgin. Bass. (Illus.). 144p. 1980. 27.50 (ISBN 0-393-01379-0). Norton.
Boyle, Robert H. & Whitlock, Dave. The Second Fly-Tyer's Almanac. (Illus.). 1978. 14.95 o.s.i. (ISBN 0-397-01286-1). Lippincott.
Boyle, Robert H., jt. auth. see Environmental Defense Fund.
Boyle, Sean O. The Irish Song Tradition. 2nd ed. (Illus.). 1976. 12.95 (ISBN 0-9505173-0-5); pap. 4.95 (ISBN 0-9505173-1-3). Irish Bk Ctr.
Boyle, T. Coraghessan. Descent of Man & Other Stories. 228p. 1980. pap. 3.95 (ISBN 0-07-006956-5, SB). McGraw.
Boyle, Ted E. Brendan Behan. (English Authors Ser.: No. 91). lib. bdg. 10.95 (ISBN 0-8057-1036-1). Twayne.
Boyle, Terry. Under This Roof: Family Homes of Southern Ontario. LC 79-8925. (Illus.). 160p. 1980. 19.95 (ISBN 0-385-15636-7). Doubleday.
Boyle, William C. Design Production Safety Systems. 276p. 1979. 30.00 (ISBN 0-87814-096-4). Pennwell Pub.
Boyles, Marcia V., et al. The Health Professions. LC 77-11331. (Illus.). 465p. Date not set. price not set (ISBN 0-7216-1904-5). Saunders. Postponed.
Boyles, Tiny & Nuwer, Hank. The Deadliest Profession. LC 80-83561. 224p. (Orig.). 1981. pap. 2.50 (ISBN 0-87216-804-2). Playboy Pbks.
Boylestad, R. & Nashelsky, L. Electronic Devices & Circuit Theory. 2nd ed. 1978. 21.95 (ISBN 0-13-250340-9). P-H.
Boylestad, Robert L. & Nashelsky, L. Electricity, Electronics & Electromagnetics: Principles & Applications. (Illus.). 1977. text ed. 20.95 (ISBN 0-13-248310-6). P-H.
Boyne, D. A. & Wright, Lance, eds. Architect's Working Details, 15 vols. Incl. Repr. of 1953 ed. Vol. 1 (ISBN 0-85139-022-6); Repr. of 1954 ed. Vol. 2 (ISBN 0-85139-023-4); Repr. of 1955 ed. Vol. 3 (ISBN 0-85139-024-2); Repr. of 1957 ed. Vol. 4 (ISBN 0-85139-025-0); Repr. of 1958 ed. Vol. 5 (ISBN 0-85139-026-9); Repr. of 1959 ed. Vol. 6; Repr. of 1960 ed. Vol. 7 (ISBN 0-85139-028-5); Vol. 8. Repr. of 1961 ed (ISBN 0-85139-029-3); Repr. of 1962 ed. Vol. 9 (ISBN 0-85139-030-7); Repr. of 1954 ed. Vol. 10 (ISBN 0-85139-031-5); Repr. of 1965 ed. Vol. 11 (ISBN 0-85139-032-3); Repr. of 1965 ed. Vol. 12 (ISBN 0-85139-033-1); Repr. of 1969 ed. Vol. 13 (ISBN 0-85139-034-X); Repr. of 1971 ed. Vol. 14 (ISBN 0-85139-035-8); Repr. of 1973 ed. Vol. 15. 17.50 (ISBN 0-85139-036-6). 1978. 275.00 set (ISBN 0-685-38821-2, Pub. by Architectural); 25.00 ea. Nichols Pub.
Boyne, Walter J. Messerschmitt Me 262: Arrow to the Future. (Illus.). 192p. (Orig.). 1980. 19.95 (ISBN 0-87474-276-5); pap. 9.95 (ISBN 0-87474-275-7). Smithsonian.
Boyne, Walter J. & Lopez, Donald S., eds. The Jet Age: Forty Years of Jet Aviation. LC 79-20216. (Illus.). 190p. 1979. 19.50 (ISBN 0-87474-248-X); pap. 8.95 (ISBN 0-87474-247-1). Smithsonian.
Boynton, G. R., jt. auth. see Bowman, Lewis.
Boynton, John. Nuclear War: Can You Survive? (Illus.). 64p. pap. 4.95. Astroart Ent.
Boynton, Percy H. Some Contemporary Americans. LC 66-23516. 1924. 9.00x (ISBN 0-8196-0181-0). Biblo.
Boynton, Robert F. & Mack, Maynard. Whodunits, Farces, & Fantasies: Ten Short Plays. (Literature Ser.). 192p. 1976. pap. 5.95x (ISBN 0-8104-5503-X). Hayden.
Boynton, Robert S. Chemistry & Technology of Lime & Limestone. 2nd ed. LC 79-16140. 1980. 54.00 (ISBN 0-471-02771-5, Pub. by Wiley-Interscience). Wiley.
Boynton, Robert W. & Mack, Maynard. Introduction to the Play: In the Theater of the Mind. rev., 2nd ed. (Series in Literature). 1976. pap. text ed. 6.10x (ISBN 0-8104-5731-8); tchr's guide 1.75 (6048). Hayden.
--Introduction to the Short Story. rev. 2nd ed. (Introduction to Ser.). 304p. (gr. 10-12). 1972. text ed. 10.20x (ISBN 0-8104-5051-8); pap. text ed. 6.70x (ISBN 0-8104-5050-X). Hayden.
--Sounds & Silences: Poems for Performing. (Literature Ser.). 128p. 1975. pap. text ed. 5.95x (ISBN 0-8104-5501-3). Hayden.
Boynton, Robert W. & Mack, Maynard, eds. Introduction to the Poem. rev. 2nd ed. (Introduction to Ser.). (gr. 10-12). 1972. text ed. 8.50x o.p. (ISBN 0-8104-5517-X); pap. text ed. 7.45x (ISBN 0-8104-5516-1). Hayden.
Boynton, Robert W., ed. see Shakespeare, William.
Boynton, Robert W., et al. English One & Two: A Contemporary Approach, 2 Bks. (gr. 7-9). 1971. Bk. 1. 6.50x o.p. (ISBN 0-8104-5611-7); Bk. 2. text ed. 7.50x o.p. (ISBN 0-8104-5613-3); tchrs.' manual, bk. 1 o.p. (ISBN 0-8104-5612-5); tchrs.' manual, bk. 2 free o.p. (ISBN 0-8104-5614-1); transparencies, bk. 1 o.p. 125.95 o.p. (ISBN 0-8104-5615-X); transparencies, bk. 2 o.p. 112.15 o.p. (ISBN 0-8104-5616-8); lp record, bk. 2 o.p. 5.95 o.p. (ISBN 0-8104-5617-6). Hayden.
Boynton, Sandra. Gopher Baroque, & Other Beastly Conceits. (Thomas Congdon Bk.). (Illus.). 1979. 13.95 o.p.; pap. 6.95 (ISBN 0-525-03469-2). Dutton.
Boys' Clubs of America, et al. Alcohol Abuse Prevention: A Comprehensive Guide for Youth Organization. (Illus., Orig.). Date not set. pap. 10.00 (ISBN 0-9604288-0-1). Boys Clubs.
Boys' Life Magazine Editors. Boys' Life Book of Baseball Stories. (Boys' Life Library, No. 6). (gr. 5-9). 1964. PLB 3.99 o.p. (ISBN 0-394-91017-6, BYR). Random.
Boys' Life Magazine Editors, ed. Boys' Life Book of Basketball Stories. (Boys' Life Library, No. 11). (Illus.). (gr. 5-9). 1966. 2.95 o.p. (ISBN 0-394-81546-7, BYR). Random.
--Boys' Life Book of Wild Animal Stories. (Boys' Life Library, No. 9). (gr. 5-9). 1965. 2.95 o.p. (ISBN 0-394-81067-8, BYR). Random.
Boys, Mary C. Biblical Interpretation in Religious Education. LC 80-10249. 367p. (Orig.). 1980. pap. 10.95 (ISBN 0-89135-022-5). Religious Educ.
Boys, Mary C., ed. Ministry & Education in Conversation. LC 80-53204. 160p. (Orig.). 1981. pap. 6.95 (ISBN 0-88489-126-7). St Mary's.
Boys Scout of America, jt. auth. see Boy Scouts of America.
Boys Scouts of America. Communications Skill Book. 1976. pap. 0.50x (ISBN 0-8395-6582-8); tchr's guide 0.30 (ISBN 0-685-73153-7, 18-322). BSA.
--Reading. LC 19-600. (Illus.). 32p. (gr. 6-12). 1974. pap. 0.70x (ISBN 0-8395-3393-4, 3393). BSA.
--Scouting for the Mentally Retarded. (Illus.). 1967. pap. 0.95x (ISBN 0-8395-3058-7). BSA.
Boyte, Harry C. The Backyard Revolution: Understanding the New Citizen Movement. 264p. 1980. 14.95 (ISBN 0-87722-192-8). Temple U Pr.
Boyum, Burton H. Saga of Iron Mining in Michigan's Upper Peninsula. 1977. pap. 3.75 (ISBN 0-938746-03-0). Marquette Cnty Hist.
Boyum, Burton H., ed. The Mather Mine, Negaunee & Ishpeming Michigan. 87p. 1980. 18.95. Longyear Res.
--The Mather Mine, Negaunee & Ishpeming Michigan. LC 79-89638. 1979. 18.95 (ISBN 0-938746-04-9). Marquette Cnty.
Bozhilov, Bozhidar. American Pages. Bozhilova, Cornelia, tr. LC 80-83427. (International Poetry: Vol. 5). 40p. 1981. 10.95 (ISBN 0-8214-0596-9); pap. 6.95 (ISBN 0-8214-0597-7). Ohio U Pr.
Bozhilova, Cornelia, tr. see Bozhilov, Bozhidar.
Bozic, S. M., et al. Electronic & Switching Circuits. (Illus.). 1975. pap. 17.95x (ISBN 0-7131-3339-2). Intl Ideas.
Bozo, Dominique, jt. ed. see Rubin, William.
Bozza, Charles M. Criminal Investigation. LC 77-9896. (Nelson-Hall Law Enforcement Ser.). 1977. 21.95 (ISBN 0-88229-183-1). Nelson-Hall.
Bozzola, Angelo, jt. auth. see Tisdall, Caroline.
Bozzoli, Belinda. The Political Nature of a Ruling Class Capital & Ideology in South Africa, 1890-1933. (International Library of Sociology). 356p. 1981. price not set (ISBN 0-7100-0722-1). Routledge & Kegan.
Braak, H. Architectonics of the Human Telencephalic Cortex. (Studies of Brain Functions: Vol. 4). (Illus.). 147p. 1981. 27.50 (ISBN 0-387-10312-0). Springer-Verlag.
Braaten, Carl E., tr. see Kahler, Martin.
Braatoy, Bjarne. Labour & War: The Theory of Labour Action to Prevent War. LC 77-147508. (Library of War & Peace; Labor, Socialism & War). lib. bdg. 38.00 (ISBN 0-8240-0303-9). Garland Pub.
Brabander, M. De see De Brabander, M., et al.
Brabazon, Francis. Four & Twenty Blackbirds. (Illus.). 52p. 1975. pap. 2.25x (ISBN 0-913078-22-0). Sheriar Pr.
--The Word at World's End. 88p. 1971. 5.95 (ISBN 0-686-05767-8); pap. 2.95 (ISBN 0-686-05768-6). Meher Baba Info.
Brabazon, James. Biography of Dorothy L. Sayers. (Illus.). 320p. 1981. 15.95 (ISBN 0-684-16864-2, ScribT). Scribner.

--Dorothy L. Sayers: A Biography. (Illus.). 320p. 1981. 15.95 (ISBN 0-684-16864-2, ScribT). Scribner.

Brabb. Computers & Information Systems. 1976. 17.50 o.p. (ISBN 0-395-20657-X); instrs'. manual 1.75 o.p. (ISBN 0-395-24065-4). HM.

Brabb, George. Computers & Information Systems in Business. 2nd ed. LC 79-88716. (Illus.). 1980. text ed. 18.50 (ISBN 0-395-28671-9); inst. manual .90 (ISBN 0-395-28670-0). HM.

Brabec, Barbara. Creative Cash: How to Sell Your Crafts, Needlework, Designs, & Know-How. LC 79-64792. (Illus.). 1979. pap. 9.95 (ISBN 0-88453-017-5). Barrington.

Bracciolini, Francisco, tr. Alceste: The Tradgeie of Alceste & Eliza. LC 79-84082. (English Experience Ser.: No. 902). 80p. 1979. Repr. of 1638 ed. lib. bdg. 9.00 (ISBN 90-221-0902-X). Walter J Johnson.

Brace, Beverly W. Humboldt Years: 1930-39. 1977. pap. 3.50 (ISBN 0-686-19169-2). B W Brace.

Brace, C. The Stages of Human Evolution. 2nd ed. 1979. 9.95 (ISBN 0-13-840157-8); pap. 6.95 (ISBN 0-13-840140-3). P-H.

Brace, C. Loring & Metress, James F., eds. Man in Evolutionary Perspective. LC 72-14184. 496p. 1973. pap. text ed. 15.50 (ISBN 0-471-09420-X). Wiley.

Brace, Gerald, jt. ed. see Moureau, Magdaleine.

Brace, Pam & Jones, Peggy. Sidetracked Home Executives: From Pigpen to Paradise. LC 79-56324. (Illus.). 1979. pap. 5.95 (ISBN 0-8323-0355-0); 10.95 o.p. (ISBN 0-8323-0349-6). Binford.

Bracegirdle, Brian & Miles, Patricia H. Thomas Telford. (Great Engineers & Their Works Ser). (Illus.). 112p. 1973. 14.95 (ISBN 0-7153-5933-9). David & Charles.

Bracegirdle, Brian, jt. auth. see Freeman, W. H.

Bracewell-Milnes, Barry. The Economics of International Tax Avoidance: Political Power Versus Economic Law. (International Taxation Ser.: No. 2). 120p. 1980. lib. bdg. 29.00 (ISBN 90-2000-633-9, Pub. by Kluwer Law & Taxation Publishers). Kluwer Boston.

Bracey, Howard E. Neighbours: Subdivision Life in England & the United States. LC 64-15877. 1964. 12.50 (ISBN 0-8071-0329-2). La State U Pr.

Bracey, Hyler J. & Sanford, Aubrey. Basic Management: An Experience Based Approach. 1977. pap. 11.95x (ISBN 0-256-01933-9). Business Pubns.

Bracey, John H., et al. Black Nationalism in America. LC 79-99161. 1969. 10.00 o.p. (ISBN 0-672-51241-6, AHS89); pap. 10.95 (ISBN 0-672-60150-8, AHS89). Bobbs.

Bracher, Karl D. The German Dictatorship: The Origins, Structure, and Effects of National Socialism. Steinberg, Jean, tr. from German. LC 70-95662. Orig. Title: Die Deutsche Diktatur: Enstehung, Struktur, & Folgen Des Nationalsozialismus. 553p. 1972. pap. text ed. 8.95x. Praeger.

Brachet, Jean & Mirsky, A. E., eds. The Cell: Biochemistry, Physiology, Morphology, 6 vols. Incl. Vol. 1. Methods: Problems of Cell Biology. 1959. 62.00 (ISBN 0-12-123301-4); Vol. 2. Cells & Their Component Parts. 1961. 62.00 (ISBN 0-12-123302-2); Vol. 3. Meiosis & Mitosis. 1961. 47.00 (ISBN 0-12-123303-0); Vol. 4. Specialized Cells, Part 1. 1960. 51.00 (ISBN 0-12-123304-9); Vol. 5. Specialized Cells, Part 2. 1961. 55.50 (ISBN 0-12-123305-7); Vol. 6. Supplementary Volume. 1964. 55.50 (ISBN 0-12-123306-5). Set. 281.00 (ISBN 0-685-23120-8). Acad Pr.

Brack, Alan. The Wirral. LC 79-56465. (Illus.). 176p. 1980. 30.00 (ISBN 0-7134-1378-6, Pub. by Batsford England). David & Charles.

Brackbill, Yvonne & Thompson, G. G. Behavior in Infancy & Early Childhood. LC 67-15056. 1967. text ed. 14.95 (ISBN 0-02-904530-4). Free Pr.

Bracken, Carolyn. Super Stickers for Kids: One Hundred & Twenty-Eight Fun Labels. (Illus.). 16p. (Orig.). 1981. pap. price not set (ISBN 0-486-24092-4). Dover.

Bracken, Carolyn, illus. Bunny. (Floppies Ser.). (Illus.). 6p. (ps-k). Date not set. 2.95 (ISBN 0-671-42531-5, Little Simon). S&S.

--Panda. (Floppies Ser.). (Illus.). 6p. (ps-k). Date not set. 2.95 (ISBN 0-671-42530-7, Little Simon). S&S.

Bracken, Harry M. Berkeley. LC 74-15569. 176p. 1975. 15.95 (ISBN 0-312-07595-2). St Martin.

Bracken, Jeanne & Wigutoff, Sharon, eds. Books for Today's Children. 1979. pap. 3.00x (ISBN 0-912670-53-3). Feminist Pr.

Bracken, John & Stone, Linda. Restoring the Victorian House. (Illus.). 192p. 1981. pap. 8.95 (ISBN 0-87701-222-9). Chronicle Bks.

Bracken, Joseph A. What Are They Saying About the Trinity? LC 78-70819. 1979. pap. 2.45 (ISBN 0-8091-2179-4). Paulist Pr.

Bracken, Peg. The I Hate to Cook Almanack. 1977. pap. 2.50 (ISBN 0-449-23370-7, Crest). Fawcett.

--The I Hate to Housekeep Book. 1977. pap. 1.75 o.p. (ISBN 0-449-23358-8, Crest). Fawcett.

--A Window Over the Sink: A Mainly Affectionate Memoir. 1981. 10.95 (ISBN 0-15-196986-8). HarBraceJ.

Brackenbury, M. C., et al, eds. Dealing on the London Metal Exchange & Commodity Markets. 1976. 22.50 (ISBN 0-9504936-0-0, Pub. by Kogan Pg). Nichols Pub.

Brackenridge, Hugh H. see Washburn, Wilcomb E.

Brackenridge, R. Douglas. Eugene Carson Blake: Prophet with Portfolio. LC 77-25281. (Illus.). 1978. 12.95 (ISBN 0-8164-0383-X). Crossroad NY.

Bracker, Jon, jt. auth. see Wallach, Mark I.

Brackert, Helmut, ed. Und Wenn Sie Nicht Gestorben Sind... Maerchenim Spiegel Heutigen Bewusstseins. (Edition Suhrkamp: No. 973). (Orig.). 1980. pap. text ed. 6.50 (ISBN 3-518-10973-1, Pub. by Insel Verlag Germany). Suhrkamp.

Brackett, Leigh. The Long Tomorrow. 256p. 1975. pap. 1.50 o.p. (ISBN 0-345-24833-3). Ballantine.

--The Sword of Rhiannon. 1975. pap. 1.95 (ISBN 0-441-79142-5). Ace Bks.

Brackett, Leigh, ed. The Best of Edmond Hamilton. LC 77-574. 1977. pap. 1.95 o.p. (ISBN 0-345-25900-9). Ballantine.

Brackman, Arnold C. The Luck of Nineveh. 352p. 1981. pap. 8.95 (ISBN 0-442-28260-5). Van Nos Reinhold.

Bracton, Henry. Bracton on the Laws & Customs of England, Vols. 1-4. Thorne, Samuel E., ed. LC 68-28697. Orig. Title: Legibus et Consuetudinibus Angliae. 1400p. 1968. Vols. 1 & 2. 60.00x (ISBN 0-674-08035-1, Belknap Pr); Vols. 3 & 4. 70.00 (ISBN 0-674-08038-6, Belknap Pr). Harvard U Pr.

Bracy, Jane, et al. Read to Succeed. 2nd ed. (Illus.). 192p. 1980. pap. text ed. 9.95x (ISBN 0-07-007035-0); cassettes & tapes 60.00 (ISBN 0-07-007037-7); instructor's manual 6.95 (ISBN 0-07-007036-9). McGraw.

Brada, Josef C. & Somanath, V. S., eds. East-West Trade: Theory & Evidence. LC 78-16941. (Studies in East European & Soviet Planning, Development & Trade Ser.: No. 27). (Illus.). 1978. pap. text ed. 10.00 o.p. (ISBN 0-89249-025-X). Intl Development.

Bradach, Wilfrid, tr. see Johnson, Thomas M.

Bradbard, Marilyn, jt. auth. see Endsley, Richard.

Bradbrook, M. C. The Living Monument. LC 76-7142. (Illus.). 1976. 38.00 (ISBN 0-521-21255-3); pap. 10.95 (ISBN 0-521-29530-0). Cambridge U Pr.

--T. S. Eliot. Dobree, Bonamy, et al, eds. Bd. with W. H. Auden. Hoggart, Richard; Dylan Thomas. Fraser, G. S. LC 64-17226. (British Writers & Their Work Ser: Vol. 5). 1965. pap. 2.95x (ISBN 0-8032-5655-8, BB 454, Bison). U of Nebr Pr.

Bradbrook, M. C; see Coghill, Nevill.

Bradbrook, Muriel C. Growth & Structure of Elizabethan Comedy. 1955. text ed. 15.75x (ISBN 0-391-00319-4). Humanities.

--The Growth & Structure of Elizabethan Comedy. LC 79-2313. (History of Elizabethan Drama Ser.: Vol. 2). 1979. pap. 10.95 (ISBN 0-521-29526-2). Cambridge U Pr.

--Malcolm Lowry: His Art & Early Life. (Illus.). 170p. 1975. 28.50 (ISBN 0-521-20473-9); pap. 7.95x (ISBN 0-521-09985-4). Cambridge U Pr.

--Shakespeare: The Poet in His World. 272p. 1980. pap. 5.95 (ISBN 0-231-04649-9). Columbia U Pr.

--Themes & Conventions of Elizabethan Tragedy. 1952-1960. 34.50 (ISBN 0-521-04302-6); pap. 10.95 (ISBN 0-521-09108-X, 108). Cambridge U Pr.

--Themes & Conventions of Elizabethan Tragedy. 2nd ed. (A History of Elizabethan Drama Ser.). 270p. 1980. 44.50 (ISBN 0-521-22770-4); pap. 12.95 (ISBN 0-521-29695-1). Cambridge U Pr.

Bradbury. History of Kennebunkport. 10.00 o.s.i. (ISBN 0-911764-01-1). Durrell.

Bradbury, Bianca. Boy on the Run. LC 74-22486. 160p. (gr. 4-7). 1975. 5.95 (ISBN 0-395-28848-7, Clarion). HM.

--Where's Jim Now. (gr. 5-9). 1978. 7.95 (ISBN 0-395-27160-6). HM.

Bradbury, J. S., et al, eds. Turbulent Shear Flows, Two. (Illus.). 480p. 1980. 68.00 (ISBN 0-387-10067-9). Springer-Verlag.

Bradbury, M. & Palmer, D., eds. American Theatre. (Stratford-Upon-Avon Studies: No. 10). 228p. 1967. pap. text ed. 11.75x (ISBN 0-8419-5816-5). Holmes & Meier.

Bradbury, Malcolm & McFarlane, James, eds. Modernism: 1890-1930. (Pelican Guides to European Literature). 1978. Repr. of 1974 ed. text ed. 28.50x (ISBN 0-391-00818-8). Humanities.

Bradbury, Malcolm & Palmer, David, eds. The American Novel & the Nineteen Twenties. (Stratford -Upon-Avon Ser.: No. 13). 269p. 1971. pap. text ed. 13.50x (ISBN 0-8419-5819-X). Holmes & Meier.

--Contemporary Criticism. (Stratford-Upon-Avon Studies: No. 12). 219p. 1970. pap. text ed. 14.25x (ISBN 0-8419-5818-1). Holmes & Meier.

--The Contemporary English Novel. LC 79-20447. (Stratford-Upon-Avon Studies: No. 18). 1980. text ed. 31.75x (ISBN 0-8419-0570-3); pap. text ed. 13.95x (ISBN 0-8419-0571-1). Holmes & Meier.

--Metaphysical Poetry. (Stratford-Upon-Avon Studies: No. 11). 280p. 1970. text ed. 19.50x (ISBN 0-8419-5823-8). Holmes & Meier.

--Shakespearian Comedy. (Stratford-Upon-Aon Studies: No. 14). 247p. 1972. pap. text ed. 11.50x (ISBN 0-8419-5820-3). Holmes & Meier.

--Victorian Poetry. (Stratford-Upon-Avon Studies: No. 15). 304p. 1972. text ed. 19.50x (ISBN 0-8419-5821-1); pap. text ed. 12.50x (ISBN 0-8419-5821-1). Holmes & Meier.

Bradbury, Nicola. Henry James: The Later Novels. 236p. 1979. text ed. 36.00x (ISBN 0-19-812096-6). Oxford U Pr.

Bradbury, Peggy F. Transcriber's Guide to Medical Terminology. 1973. spiral bdg. 7.00 (ISBN 0-87488-972-3). Med Exam.

Bradbury, Ray. The Haunted Computer & the Android Pope. LC 80-2724. 128p. 1981. 8.95 (ISBN 0-394-51444-0). Knopf.

--The Martian Chronicles. LC 72-94171. 288p. 1973. 8.95 o.p. (ISBN 0-385-03862-3). Doubleday.

--The Mummies of Guanajuato. LC 77-16022. (Illus.). 1978. 17.50 o.p. (ISBN 0-8109-1325-9); pap. 8.95 o.p. (ISBN 0-8109-2150-2). Abrams.

--Vintage Bradbury. 1965. pap. 1.95 (ISBN 0-394-70294-8, Vin, V294). Random.

Bradbury, Ray, intro. by. The Best of Henry Kuttner. 416p. 1975. pap. 1.95 o.p. (ISBN 0-345-24415-X). Ballantine.

Bradbury, S. The Microscope Past & Present. 1969. 15.00 (ISBN 0-08-012848-3); pap. text ed. 7.75 (ISBN 0-08-013249-9). Pergamon.

Bradbury, Samuel, ed. Source Book on Powder Metallurgy. 1979. 38.00 (ISBN 0-87170-030-1). ASM.

Bradbury, Ted C. Theoretical Mechanics. 656p. 1981. Repr. of 1968 ed. text ed. price not set (ISBN 0-89874-235-8). Krieger.

Bradbury, Wilbur. The Adult Years. LC 75-18649. (Human Behavior). (Illus.). (gr. 5 up). 1975. PLB 11.97 (ISBN 0-8094-1942-4, Pub. by Time-Life). Silver.

Bradby, David, et al, eds. Performance & Politics in Popular Drama: Aspects of Popular Entertainment in Theatre, Film & Television, 1800-1976. LC 79-12036. (Illus.). 1980. 32.50 (ISBN 0-521-22755-0). Cambridge U Pr.

Braddock, David. Opening Closed Doors: The Deinstitutionalization of Disabled Individuals. LC 77-72050. 1977. pap. text ed. 7.50 o.p. (ISBN 0-86586-059-9). Coun Exc Child.

Braddock, Karen S., jt. auth. see Guthrie, Helen A.

Braddy, Haldeen. Mexico & the Old Southwest: People, Palaver, & Places. LC 71-141307. 1971. 12.50 (ISBN 0-8046-9001-4, Natl U); pap. 4.95 (ISBN 0-8046-9046-4). Kennikat.

Braden. Community Health: A Systems Approach. 1976. pap. 11.00 (ISBN 0-8385-1184-8). ACC.

Braden, Charles S. Spirits in Rebellion: The Rise & Development of New Thought. LC 63-13245. 584p. 1980. Repr. of 1963 ed. 10.00 (ISBN 0-87074-025-3). SMU Press.

--World's Religions. rev. ed. (Series C). 1958. pap. 3.95 o.p. (ISBN 0-687-46374-2, Apex). Abingdon.

Braden, George D. Citizens Guide to the Proposed New Texas Constitution. LC 75-25764. (Orig.). 1975. 3.25 o.p. (ISBN 0-88408-026-9). Sterling Swift.

Braden, Spruille, III. Graphic Standards of Solar Energy. LC 77-12217. (Illus.). 1977. 19.95 o.p. (ISBN 0-8436-0165-5). CBI Pub.

Braden, Vic & Bruns, Bill. Teaching Children Tennis the Vic Braden Way. (A Sports Illustrated Bk). (Illus.). 1980. 16.95 (ISBN 0-316-10512-0). Little.

--Vic Braden's Tennis for the Future. 1977. 15.95 (ISBN 0-316-10510-4, Sports Illustrated Book); pap. 6.95 (ISBN 0-316-10511-2). Little.

Bradford. A Better Guide Than Reason. 12.95 (ISBN 0-89385-006-3); pap. 4.95. Green Hill.

--A Year of Growing. (gr. 3-5). pap. 1.25 o.p. (ISBN 0-590-05411-2, Schol Pap). Schol Bk Serv.

Bradford, Alden. Speeches of the Governors of Massachusetts from 1765 to 1775. LC 71-119048. (Era of the American Revolution Ser). 1971. Repr. of 1818 ed. 45.00 (ISBN 0-306-71947-9). Da Capo.

Bradford, Ann & Gezi, Kal. The Mystery at the Tree House. LC 80-15654. (The Maple Street Five Ser.). (Illus.). 32p. (gr. k-4). 1980. PLB 5.50 (ISBN 0-89565-148-3). Childs World.

--The Mystery at the Treehouse. (The Maple Street Five Ser.). (Illus.). 1980. 7.95g (ISBN 0-516-06494-0). Childrens.

--The Mystery of the Missing Dogs. (The Maple Street Five Ser.). (Illus.). 1980. 7.95g (ISBN 0-516-06492-4). Childrens.

Bradford, Ann, jt. auth. see Gezi, Kal.

Bradford, Ann L. & Murai, Harold M. Pocket Patches. 2nd ed. (Cornerstone Ser.). (gr. 1). 1978. pap. text ed. 4.52 (ISBN 0-201-41020-6, Sch Div); tchr's. ed. 5.56 (ISBN 0-201-41021-4). A-W.

Bradford, Barbara T. Luxury Designs for Apartment Living. LC 77-16899. (Illus.). 352p. 1981. 29.95 (ISBN 0-385-12769-3). Doubleday.

--A Woman of Substance. 1980. pap. 2.95 (ISBN 0-380-49163-X, 49163). Avon.

Bradford, Colin I., Jr. Forces for Change in Latin America: U. S. Policy Implications. LC 70-181831. (Monographs: No. 5). 80p. 1971. 2.00 (ISBN 0-686-28690-1). Overseas Dev Council.

Bradford, Curtis. Yeats's Last Poems Again. (Yeats Cent. Papers: Vol. 8). 1966. pap. text ed. 1.75x (ISBN 0-85105-471-4, Dolmen Pr). Humanities.

Bradford, Dennis E. The Concept of Existence: A Study of Nonexistent Particulars. LC 80-5526. 142p. 1980. lib. bdg. 16.75 (ISBN 0-8191-1124-4); pap. text ed. 7.50 (ISBN 0-8191-1127-9). U Pr of Amer.

Bradford, John. Ancient Landscapes: Studies in Field Archaeology. LC 80-23204. (Illus.). xvii, 297p. 1980. Repr. of 1957 ed. lib. bdg. 49.75x (ISBN 0-313-22849-3, BRAL). Greenwood.

--A Sermon of Repentance. LC 74-28835. (English Experience Ser.: No. 716). 1975. Repr. of 1553 ed. 6.00 (ISBN 90-221-0716-7). Walter J Johnson.

--Writings of Bradford. 1979. Set. 28.95. Banner of Truth.

Bradford, Leland P. Making Meetings Work: A Guide for Leaders & Group Members. LC 76-16886. 122p. 1976. pap. 12.50 (ISBN 0-88390-122-6). Univ Assocs.

--Preparing for Retirement: A Program for Survival - A Participants Workbook. LC 80-52897. 106p. 1981. pap. write for info. (ISBN 0-88390-160-9). Univ Assocs.

--Preparing for Retirement: A Program for Survival - A Trainers Kit. LC 80-2897. 196p. 1981. looseleaf bdg. 39.95 (ISBN 0-88390-161-7). Univ Assocs.

Bradford, Leland P., ed. Group Development. 2nd, rev, enl. ed. LC 78-51283. 234p. 1978. pap. 12.50 (ISBN 0-88390-144-7). Univ Assocs.

Bradford, Leland P., et al, eds. T-Group Theory & Laboratory Method: Innovation in Re-Education. LC 64-11499. 1964. 26.50 (ISBN 0-471-09510-9). Wiley.

Bradford, Lowell W., jt. auth. see Kirk, Paul L.

Bradford, M. Gerald, jt. auth. see Baker, James C.

Bradford, M. Gerald, ed. see Santucci, James A.

Bradford, Peter & Prete, Barbara, eds. Chair: The Complete State of the Art. LC 78-60172. (Illus.). 1978. 19.95 o.p. (ISBN 0-690-01783-9, TYC-T). T Y Crowell.

Bradford, Richard. Red Sky at Morning. LC 68-11272. 1968. 10.95 (ISBN 0-397-00549-0). Lippincott.

--So Far from Heaven. LC 73-7885. 276p. 1973. 6.95 o.s.i. (ISBN 0-397-00853-8). Lippincott.

Bradford, Richard H. The Virginius Affair. LC 80-520000. 1980. 12.50x (ISBN 0-87081-080-4). Colo Assoc.

Bradford, Robert. Mathematics for Carpenters. LC 75-19525. 1975. pap. 9.40 (ISBN 0-8273-1116-8); instructor's guide 1.60 (ISBN 0-8273-1117-6). Delmar.

Bradford, Sarah. Cesare Borgia. (Illus.). 352p. 1976. 10.95 o.s.i. (ISBN 0-02-514400-6). Macmillan.

Bradford, Thomas L. Bibliographer's Manual of American History, 5 Vols. Henkels, Stan V., ed. LC 67-14023. 1968. Repr. of 1907 ed. 92.00 (ISBN 0-8103-3319-8). Gale.

Bradford, William. Of Plymouth Plantation: The Pilgrims in America. 8.75 (ISBN 0-8446-1718-0). Peter Smith.

Bradford, William, jt. auth. see Bates, Timothy.

Bradford, Winifred, tr. see Baudin, Louis.

Bradie, Michael & Brand, Myles, eds. Action & Responsibility. (Bowling Green Studies in Applied Philosophy: Vol. 2). 140p. 1980. text ed. 15.00 (ISBN 0-935756-02-7); pap. text ed. 10.00 (ISBN 0-935756-03-5). BGSU Dept Phil.

Brading, D. Miners & Merchants in Bourbon Mexico, 1763-1810. LC 74-123666. (Cambridge Latin American Studies: No. 10). (Illus.). 1971. 44.50 (ISBN 0-521-07874-1). Cambridge U Pr.

Brading, D. A. Haciendas & Ranchos in the Mexican Bajio Leon 1700-1860. LC 77-90203. (Cambridge Latin American Studies: No. 32). (Illus.). 1979. 41.50 (ISBN 0-521-22200-1). Cambridge U Pr.

Bradlee, Ben, Jr. The Ambush Murders: The True Account of the Killing of Two California Policemen. LC 79-10418. (Illus.). 1979. 12.95 (ISBN 0-396-07624-6). Dodd.

Bradlee, Ben, Jr. & Van Atta, Dale. Prophet of Blood: The Story of the "Mormon Manson". (Illus.). 384p. 1981. 12.95 (ISBN 0-399-12371-7). Putnam.

Bradley & Hanson, eds. Machine Interpretations of Patterson Functions & Alternative Direct Approaches & the Austin Symposium on Gas Phase Molecular Structure. pap. 5.00 (ISBN 0-686-60373-7). Polycrystal Bk Serv.

Bradley, A. W. & Wade, E. C. S., eds. Wade & Phillips Constitutional & Administrative Law. 9th ed. LC 77-5941. 1978. text ed. 34.00x (ISBN 0-582-48826-5); pap. text ed. 19.95x (ISBN 0-582-48827-3). Longman.

Bradley, Andrew C. Shakespearean Tragedy. 1977. pap. 1.95 o.p. (ISBN 0-449-30817-0, Prem). Fawcett.

Bradley, Anthony, ed. Contemporary Irish Poetry: An Anthology. 1980. 17.95 (ISBN 0-520-03389-2). U of Cal Pr.

Bradley, Bert E. Fundamentals of Speech Communication. 3rd ed. 430p. 1981. pap. text ed. write for info. (ISBN 0-697-04177-8); instr's manual avail. (ISBN 0-697-04184-0). Wm C Brown.

Bradley, Bill. The Last of the Great Stations. Walker, Jim, ed. LC 79-84387. (Special Ser.: No. 72). (Illus.). 1979. pap. 9.95 (ISBN 0-916374-36-X). Interurban.

Bradley, Bill, ed. Days of Commerce. (Special Ser.: No.X-8). 1981. pap. write for info. (ISBN 0-916374-45-9). Interurban.

Bradley, Buff. Growing from Word Play into Poetry. LC 76-29235. (Learning Handbooks Ser.). 1976. pap. 3.95 (ISBN 0-8224-1904-1). Pitman Learning.

Bradley, C. J. & Cracknell, A. P. The Mathematical Theory of Symmetry in Solids: Representation Theory for Point Groups & Space Groups. (Illus.). 762p. 1971. 125.00x (ISBN 0-19-851920-6). Oxford U Pr.

Bradley, C. Paul. The Camp David Peace Process: A Study of Carter Administration Policies (1977-1980) LC 81-50100. (Illus.). viii, 79p. 1981. pap. text ed. 4.50 (ISBN 0-936988-03-7). Tompson & Rutter.

Bradley, D & Milton, David. Somerset & Dorset Locomotive History. (Illus.). 1973. 11.50 (ISBN 0-7153-5956-8). David & Charles.

Bradley, D. L. Drummond Greyhounds of the LSWR. 1977. 14.95 (ISBN 0-7153-7329-3). David & Charles.

Bradley, David. The Chaneysville Incident. LC 80-8225. 480p. 1981. 12.95 (ISBN 0-06-010491-0, HarpT). Har-Row.

--Proto-Lolish. (Scandanavian Institute of Asian Studies Monograph: No. 39). (Orig.). 1980. pap. text ed. 18.00x (ISBN 0-7007-0128-1). Humanities.

Bradley, Edward J. The Child & Family Genealogy Reporting System. 2nd ed. 1979. 9.95 (ISBN 0-935202-01-3). Child & Family Ent.

Bradley, Ernestine S. Hermann Broch: World Author Ser. 1978. 12.95 (ISBN 0-8057-6326-0). Twayne.

Bradley, Francis H. Ethical Studies: Selected Essays. 1951. pap. 4.95 (ISBN 0-672-60189-3, LLA28). Bobbs.

Bradley, Gerald L. A Primer of Linear Algebra. (Illus.). 448p. 1975. text ed. 17.95 (ISBN 0-13-700328-5). P-H.

Bradley, Glenn D. The Story of the Pony Express. LC 75-141793. 1974. Repr. of 1913 ed. 15.00 (ISBN 0-8103-3632-4). Gale.

Bradley, Henry, ed. see Stratmann, Francis H.

Bradley, Ian. Marking-Out Practice for Engineers. LC 78-670183. (Illus.). 1977. pap. 7.50x (ISBN 0-85242-595-3). Intl Pubns Serv.

--The Optimists: Themes & Personalities in Victorian Liberalism. LC 80-670269. 301p. 1980. 37.00 (ISBN 0-571-11495-4, Pub. by Faber & Faber). Merrimack Bk Serv.

Bradley, Ian C. The Call to Seriousness: The Evangelical Impact on the Victorians. LC 75-44282. (Illus.). 288p. 1976. 12.95 o.s.i. (ISBN 0-02-514420-0, 51442). Macmillan.

Bradley, Iver F. & South, John B. Introductory Statistics for Business Economics. LC 80-65789. 640p. 1981. text ed. 18.95 (ISBN 0-03-053026-1). Dryden Pr.

Bradley, J. Mach's Philosophy of Science. (Illus.). 240p. 1971. text ed. 17.25x (ISBN 0-485-11124-1, Athlone Pr). Humanities.

--Probability, Decision, Statistics. 1976. 23.95 (ISBN 0-13-711556-3). P-H.

Bradley, J. D. & Fletcher, D. S. British Butterflies & Moths. 1980. 6.00x (ISBN 0-902068-08-3, Pub. by Curwen England). State Mutual Bk.

Bradley, J. D., et al. British Tortricoid Moths. Incl. Vol.1. Cochylidae & Tortricidae: Tortricinae. viii, 251p. 1973. 50.00x (ISBN 0-903874-01-6); Vol. 2. Tortrkidae: Olethreutinae. viii, 336p. 1979. 100.00x (ISBN 0-903874-06-7). (Illus., Pub. by Brit Mus Nat Hist England). Sabbot-Natural Hist Bks.

Bradley, J. E., tr. see Nikolskii, G. V.

Bradley, J. F., jt. auth. see Black, J.

Bradley, J. H. Programmer's Guide to the IBM System-360. 1969. 34.50 o.p. (ISBN 0-07-007063-6, P&RB). McGraw.

Bradley, J. N. Fast Reactions. (Oxford Chemistry Ser). (Illus.). 128p. 1975. 16.95x (ISBN 0-19-855456-7). Oxford U Pr.

Bradley, Jack I. & McClelland, James N. Basic Statistical Concepts: A Self-Instructional Text. 2nd ed. 1978. pap. 7.95x (ISBN 0-673-15075-5). Scott F.

Bradley, James, jt. auth. see Taylor, Dawson.

Bradley, James J. Aim for a Job in Automotive Service. LC 76-114140. (Career Guidance Ser.). 138p. 1971. pap. 3.50 (ISBN 0-668-02226-4). Arco.

Bradley, James V. Elementary Microstudies of Human Tissues. (Illus.). 376p. 1972. pap. 36.50 (ISBN 0-398-02240-2). C C Thomas.

Bradley, James W. & Korn, Donald H. Acquisition & Corporate Development: A Contemporary Perspective for the Manager. LC 79-7719. (An Arthur D. Little Bk.). (Illus.). 1981. price not set (ISBN 0-669-03170-4). Lexington Bks.

Bradley, John. Civil War in Russia, 1917-20. LC 75-18594. 200p. 1975. 19.95 (ISBN 0-312-14140-8). St Martin.

Bradley, Judy & Silverleaf, Jane. Making the Grade: Careers in E. E. Teaching. 1979. text ed. 20.75x (ISBN 0-85633-179-1, NFER); pap. text ed. 15.25x (ISBN 0-85633-177-5, NFER). Humanities.

Bradley, K., jt. auth. see Sumner, R.

Bradley, L. A., jt. ed. see Prokop, Charles.

Bradley, Larry C. Jesse James: The Making of a Legend. LC 80-81622. (Illus.). 228p. (Orig.). 1980. pap. 8.95 (ISBN 0-9604370-0-2). Larren Pubs.

Bradley, Lonnie, jt. auth. see Isakson, Marne.

Bradley, Marion. Drums of Darkness (Leo) (Zodiac Ser.). (Orig.). 1976. pap. 1.25 o.p. (ISBN 0-345-25108-3). Ballantine.

--Hunters of the Red Moon. (Science Fiction Ser). pap. 1.75 (ISBN 0-87997-407-9, UE1568). DAW Bks.

Bradley, Marion Z. The Bloody Sun. 192p. (Orig.). 1975. pap. 2.50 (ISBN 0-441-06855-3). Ace Bks.

--The Catch Trap. 1979. 10.95 (ISBN 0-345-28090-3). Ballantine.

--The Planet Savers. (Science Fiction Ser.). 1979. lib. bdg. 8.95 (ISBN 0-8398-2514-5). Gregg.

--The Shattered Chain. (Science Fiction Ser.). 1976. pap. 2.25 (ISBN 0-87997-327-7, UE1566). DAW Bks.

--The Web of Darkness. 1981. pap. 4.95 (ISBN 0-89865-032-1, Starblaze). Donning Co.

--The Winds of Darkover. 1977. pap. 1.95 (ISBN 0-441-89253-1). Ace Bks.

Bradley, Matt. Arkansas...Its Land & People. LC 80-81993. (Illus.). 112p. 1980. 25.00 (ISBN 0-9604642-0-4); limited gift edition 55.00 (ISBN 0-9604642-1-2). Mus Sci & Hist.

Bradley, Melvin. Horses: A Pactical & Scientific Approach. (Illus.). 560p. 1980. text ed. 19.95x. McGraw.

Bradley, Michael. Mantouche Factor. (Orig.). 1981. pap. 2.50 (ISBN 0-446-91546-7). Warner Bks.

--The Norwood Tor. LC 79-24215. (gr. 5 up). 1980. 6.95 (ISBN 0-396-07790-0). Dodd.

--The Shaping Room. LC 77-16877. (gr. 5 up). 1978. 5.95 (ISBN 0-396-07540-1). Dodd.

Bradley, Michael E. Macroeconomics. 1980. pap. text ed. 11.95x (ISBN 0-673-15336-3); study guide 5.95x (ISBN 0-673-15423-8). Scott F.

--Microeconomics. 1980. pap. text ed. 11.95x (ISBN 0-673-15335-5); study guide 5.95x (ISBN 0-673-15286-3). Scott F.

Bradley, Omar N. Bradley: A Soldier's Story. (Illus.). 1978. pap. 6.95 (ISBN 0-528-88133-7). Rand.

Bradley, P. B., ed. Methods in Brain Research. LC 74-404. 557p. 1975. 84.25 (ISBN 0-471-09514-1, Pub. by Wiley-Interscience). Wiley.

Bradley, Pat. Golf. (Burns Sports Ser.). 156p. Date not set. pap. 4.95 o.p. (ISBN 0-695-81569-5). Follett.

Bradley, Philip. An Index to the Waverley Novels. LC 75-6838. 695p. 1975. 30.00 (ISBN 0-8108-0812-9). Scarecrow.

Bradley, Philip D. Constitutional Limits to Union Power. 1976. pap. 10.00 (ISBN 0-685-79963-8). Coun Am Affairs.

Bradley, Raymond S. Precipitation History of the Rocky Mountains. Ives, Jack, ed. LC 75-45279. (Special Studies in High Altitude Geo-Ecology Ser). 1976. 25.50x (ISBN 0-89158-026-3). Westview.

Bradley, Richard. The Country Housewife & Lady's Director. 500p. 1980. Repr. of 1736 ed. 37.50x (ISBN 0-907325-01-7, Pub. by Prospect England). U Pr of Va.

--The Prehistoric Settlement of Britain. (The Archaeology of Britain Ser.). (Illus.). 1978. 24.00 (ISBN 0-7100-8993-7). Routledge & Kegan.

Bradley, Robert A. Husband Coached Childbirth. 3rd ed. LC 80-8683. (Illus.). 256p. 1981. 9.95 (ISBN 0-06-014850-0, HarpT). Har-Row.

Bradley, Ronald J., jt. auth. see Smythies, John R.

Bradley, Rusty. Bridlewise & Otherwise. 4.95 o.p. (ISBN 0-685-48789-X). Nortex Pr.

Bradley, Sculley, ed. see Clemens, Samuel L.

Bradley, Sculley, ed. see Whitman, Walt.

Bradley, Sculley, et al, eds. see Hawthorne, Nathaniel.

Bradley, Sculley, et al, eds. see Whitman, Walt.

Bradley, Stephen P. & Crane, Dwight B. Management of Bank Portfolios. LC 75-23030. 299p. 1975. 29.95 (ISBN 0-471-09522-2, Pub. by Wiley-Interscience). Wiley.

Bradley, Stephen P., et al. Applied Mathematical Programming. LC 76-10426. (Illus.). 1977. text ed. 23.95 (ISBN 0-201-00464-X). A-W.

Bradley, Steve. The Candy Man. (Pacesetters Ser.). (Illus.). 64p. (gr. 4 up). 1978. PLB 7.95 (ISBN 0-516-02152-4). Childrens.

Bradley, Van A., ed. see Crane, Stephen.

Bradley, William. Art: Magic, Impulse & Control-a Guide to Viewing. (Illus.). 208p. 1973. 12.95 (ISBN 0-13-046664-6); pap. text ed. 7.50 (ISBN 0-13-046656-5). P-H.

Bradley, William A. Dutch Landscape Etchers of the Seventeenth Century. (Illus.). 1919. 27.50x (ISBN 0-685-89748-6). Elliots Bks.

Bradner, Leicester, ed. see Elizabeth First.

Bradshaw, A. D. & Chadwick, M. J. The Restoration of the Land. (Blackwell Ecology Ser.: Vol. 6). 1980. 27.50 (ISBN 0-520-03961-0). U of Cal Pr.

Bradshaw, B. The Dissolution of the Religious Orders in Ireland Under Henry Eighth. LC 73-83104. (Illus.). 248p. 1974. 41.50 (ISBN 0-521-20342-2). Cambridge U Pr.

Bradshaw, Brendan. The Irish Constitutional Revolution in the Sixteenth Century. LC 78-58785. 1979. 41.50 (ISBN 0-521-22206-0). Cambridge U Pr.

Bradshaw, David N., tr. see Oki, Masahiro.

Bradshaw, Gillian. Hawk of May. 1981. pap. 2.75 (ISBN 0-451-09765-3, E9765, Sig). NAL.

--Kingdom of Summer. 1981. 12.95 (ISBN 0-671-25472-3). S&S.

Bradshaw, Jon, jt. auth. see Cooke, Barclay.

Bradshaw, Michael J. Earth: The Living Planet. LC 77-946. 1977. text ed. 19.95x (ISBN 0-470-99107-0). Halsted Pr.

Bradshaw, Michael J., et al. The Earth's Changing Surface. LC 77-25024. 1978. pap. text ed. 18.95 (ISBN 0-470-99365-0). Halsted Pr.

Bradshaw, P. An Introduction to Turbulance & Its Measurements. Woods, W. A., ed. 218p. 1975. text ed. 25.00 (ISBN 0-08-016620-2); pap. text ed. 13.25 (ISBN 0-08-016621-0). Pergamon.

Bradshaw, P., jt. auth. see Cebeci, T.

Bradshaw, P., ed. Turbulence. (Topics in Applied Physics: Vol. 12). 1976. 43.80 o.p. (ISBN 0-387-07705-7). Springer-Verlag.

Bradshaw, Pete. The Management of Self-Esteem: How People Can Feel Good About Themselves & Better About Their Organizations. (Illus.). 368p. 1981. 10.95 (ISBN 0-13-549535-0, Spec); pap. 4.95 (ISBN 0-13-549527-X). P-H.

Bradshaw, Ralph & Schneider, Diana, eds. Proteins of the Nervous System. 2nd ed. 407p. 1980. 39.00 (ISBN 0-89004-327-2). Raven.

Bradshaw, Ralph A., et al, eds. Surface Membrane Receptors: Interface Between Cells & Their Environment. LC 76-25821. (NATO Advanced Study Institutes Ser., Series A: Life Sciences: Vol. 11). 482p. 1976. 39.50 (ISBN 0-306-35611-2, Plenum Pr). Plenum Pub.

Bradshaw, Ted K. & Blakely, Edward J. Rural Communities in Advanced Industrial Society: Development & Developers. LC 78-19736. 1979. 21.95 (ISBN 0-03-041626-4). Praeger.

Bradshaw, Terry & Diles, Dave L. Terry Bradshaw: Man of Steel. (Illus.). 1979. 7.95 o.p. (ISBN 0-310-39460-0). Zondervan.

Bradshaw, Terry & Diles, David. Man of Steel. 1980. pap. 4.95 (ISBN 0-310-39461-9). Zondervan.

Bradshaw, Terry, jt. auth. see Diles, Dave L.

Bradshaw, Thornton & Vogel, David. Corporations & Their Critics. 1980. 14.95 (ISBN 0-07-007075-X). McGraw.

Bradshaw, William S., Jr. The Big Yellow Bus Is a Good Friend of Mine. LC 80-54535. (Illus.). 24p. (gr. k-5). 1981. pap. 6.95 (ISBN 0-935054-03-0). Webb-Newcomb.

Bradt, G. W. Michigan Wildlife Sketches. rev., 6th ed. (Illus.). 1971. pap. 2.75 (ISBN 0-910726-71-X). Hillsdale Educ.

Bradt, George. South America: River Trips. LC 80-69523. (Illus.). 128p. (Orig.). 1981. pap. 7.95 (ISBN 0-933982-13-5). Bradt Ent.

Bradt, George & Bradt, Hilary. Backpacking in Venezuela, Colombia & Equador. (Backpacking Ser). (Illus.). 1979. pap. 6.95 (ISBN 0-9505797-6-9). Bradt Ent.

Bradt, George, jt. auth. see Bradt, Hilary.

Bradt, Hilary & Bradt, George. Backpacking & Trekking in Peru & Bolivia. 3 rd rev. & enl ed. LC 80-115. (Backpacker Guide Ser.). (Illus.). 1980. pap. 7.95 (ISBN 0-9505797-6-9). Bradt Ent.

--Backpacking in Mexico & Central America, Including the Darien Gap. (Backpacker Guide Ser.). (Illus.). 1978. pap. 6.95 (ISBN 0-9505797-3-4). Bradt Ent.

Bradt, Hilary & Pilkington, John. Backpacking & Trekking in Chile & Argentina Plus the Falkland Islands. LC 80-68116. (Backpacker Guide Ser.). (Illus.). 144p. 1980. pap. 7.95 (ISBN 0-9505797-7-7). Bradt Ent.

Bradt, Hilary, jt. auth. see Bradt, George.

Brady & Richardson. Plaid for Basic Programming Language. rev. ed. 1981. write for info. (ISBN 0-256-02124-4, 14-1037-02). Learning Syst.

Brady, Allen H. & Richardson, James T. Plaid for Basic Programming Language. 1974. pap. 4.95 (ISBN 0-256-01485-X, 08-1037-00). Learning Syst.

Brady, Ann P. Lyricism in the Poetry of T. S. Eliot. LC 77-788. (National Univ. Publications Literary Criticism Ser.). 1977. 9.95 o.p. (ISBN 0-8046-9183-5). Kennikat.

Brady, Charles. Paints & Materials. LC 77-82985. (Teaching Primary Science Ser.). (Illus.). 1977. pap. text ed. 6.95 (ISBN 0-356-05075-0). Raintree Child.

Brady, Christine. Cooking in Season. (Illus.). 1978. 16.95 (ISBN 0-241-89451-4, Pub. by Hamish Hamilton England). David & Charles.

--Flour Power: The Art of Cooking with Flour. 1979. 16.95 (ISBN 0-241-10168-9, Pub. by Hamish Hamilton). David & Charles.

Brady, Cyrus T. Indian Fights & Fighters. LC 74-156373. (Illus.). 1971. 16.50x (ISBN 0-8032-1152-X); pap. 6.50 (ISBN 0-8032-5743-0, BB 538, Bison). U of Nebr Pr.

--Northwestern Fights & Fighters. LC 79-15171. (Illus.). 1979. 18.50x (ISBN 0-8032-1156-2); pap. 5.50 (ISBN 0-8032-6053-9, BB 713, Bison). U of Nebr Pr.

Brady, Darlene & Serban, William, eds. Stained Glass: A Guide to Information Sources. LC 79-23712. (Art & Architecture Information Guide Ser.: Vol. 10). 1980. 30.00 (ISBN 0-8103-1445-2). Gale.

Brady, Donald, ed. Green Words: A Handbook. LC 79-92506. 91p. 1980. pap. text ed. 2.50 (ISBN 0-8191-0965-7). U Pr of Amer.

Brady, Elizabeth. Eric Gill: Twentieth Century Book Designer. rev. ed. LC 73-18453. 150p. 1974. lib. bdg. 10.00 (ISBN 0-8108-0640-1). Scarecrow.

Brady, F. A Singular View. rev. ed. (Illus.). 1979. 16.50 (ISBN 0-87489-224-4). Med Economics.

Brady, Frank. Chess: How to Improve Your Technique. LC 74-4103. (Career Concise Guides Ser.). (Illus.). 72p. (gr. 5 up). 1974. PLB 4.90 o.p. (ISBN 0-531-02730-9). Watts.

--Hefner. (Illus.). 300p. 1974. 8.95 o.s.i. (ISBN 0-02-514600-9). Macmillan.

--Onassis: An Extravagant Life. 1978. pap. 1.95 o.s.i. (ISBN 0-515-04746-5). Jove Pubns.

--Playboy's Hefner. 230p. 1980. 28.50 (ISBN 0-686-68307-2). Porter.

Brady, Frank & Lawless, Joann. Brady & Lawless's Favorite Bookstores. (Illus.). 1978. 12.95 o.p. (ISBN 0-8362-7902-6). Andrews & McMeel.

Brady, Frank, ed. Twentieth Century Interpretations of Gulliver's Travels. LC 68-23699. 8.95 (ISBN 0-13-371575-2, Spec); pap. 1.25 (ISBN 0-13-371567-1, Spec). P-H.

Brady, Frank & Wimsatt, W. K., eds. Samuel Johnson: Selected Poetry & Prose. 1978. 30.00x (ISBN 0-520-02929-1); pap. 6.95 (ISBN 0-520-03552-6). U of Cal Pr.

Brady, Frank, ed. see Pope, Alexander.

Brady, Gerald P., jt. auth. see Thompson, George C.

Brady, I. A. & Isaac, B. L., eds. Reader in Culture Change, 2 vols. Incl. Vol. 1. Theories. pap. text ed. 5.95 o.p. (ISBN 0-470-09533-4); Vol. 2. Case Studies. pap. text ed. 6.95 o.p. (ISBN 0-470-09534-2). 1975. Halsted Pr.

Brady, Irene. Elephants on the Beach. (Illus.). 32p. (gr. 2-5). 1979. 7.95 (ISBN 0-684-16115-X). Scribner.

Brady, Ivan A., jt. ed. see Laughlin, Charles D., Jr.

Brady, J. & Nauta, W. J. Principles, Practices & Positions in Neuropsychiatric Research. 320p. 1973. text ed. 59.00 (ISBN 0-08-017007-2). Pergamon.

Brady, J. E. & Humiston, G. General Chemistry: Principles & Structures. 1975. 16.00 o.p. (ISBN 0-471-09530-3). Krieger.

Brady, J. E., jt. auth. see Beran, J. A.

Brady, James E. & Humiston, Gerard E. General Chemistry: Principles & Structure. 2nd ed. LC 77-11045. 1978. text ed. 23.95 (ISBN 0-471-01910-0); write for info tchr's manual (ISBN 0-471-03666-8); wkbk. 6.50x (ISBN 0-471-03498-3). Wiley.

Brady, John P. & Brodie, H. Keith, eds. Controversy in Psychiatry. LC 77-77097. (Illus.). 1978. text ed. 19.50 (ISBN 0-7216-1912-6). Saunders.

Brady, Katherine. Father's Days. 1981. pap. 2.95 (ISBN 0-440-12475-1). Dell.

Brady, Lillian. Saga of a Whitetail Deer. LC 77-77113. (Illus.). 182p. 1980. 12.50 (ISBN 0-86533-004-2). Amber Crest.

Brady, Luther W., ed. Radiation Sensitizers: Their Use in the Clinical Management of Cancer, Vol. 5. LC 80-81987. (Cancer Management Series). (Illus.). 544p. 1980. 58.50 (ISBN 0-89352-112-4). Masson Pub.

Brady, M. Michael. Nordic Touring & Cross Country Skiing. 4th, rev. ed. LC 77-77159. (Illus.). 92p. (Orig.). 1977. pap. 4.50x (ISBN 0-8277-7715-9, N395). Vanous.

Brady, Mari. Please Remember Me. (YA) 1978. pap. 1.50 (ISBN 0-686-68479-6). PB.

Brady, Marion T., ed. Numismatic Literature, No. 103. lix, 193p. 1980. pap. 4.00x o.p. (ISBN 0-89722-185-0). Am Numismatic.

Brady, Mary L., et al. Woman Power! (Illus.). 156p. 1981. pap. 4.95. J P Tarcher.

Brady, Maxine, jt. auth. see Hasegawa, Goro.

Brady, Michael. American Surrender. 1979. 9.95 o.s.i. (ISBN 0-440-00469-1). Delacorte.

--The Coda Alliance. (Orig.). Date not set. pap. 2.50 (ISBN 0-440-11415-2). Dell.

Brady, N. C., ed. Advances in Agronomy, Vol. 33. 1980. write for info. (ISBN 0-12-000733-9); lib. ed. 54.00 (ISBN 0-12-000786-X); microfiche 29.00 (ISBN 0-12-000787-8). Acad Pr.

Brady, Nicholas. Bad Guy. 1977. pap. 1.50 (ISBN 0-505-51202-5). Tower Bks.

--The Homecoming. 1977. pap. 1.50 (ISBN 0-505-51216-5). Tower Bks.

--The Microwave Factor. 1977. pap. 1.75 (ISBN 0-505-51170-3). Tower Bks.

Brady, Nick. The Doom Platoon. 1978. pap. 1.75 (ISBN 0-505-51302-1). Tower Bks.

Brady, Patrick. Marcel Proust. (World Authors Ser.: France: No. 404). 1977. lib. bdg. 12.50 (ISBN 0-8057-6307-4). Twayne.

Brady, R. J. Anatomy & Physiology: A Programmed Approach to, 15 bks. Incl. The Cell. 1972. pap. 6.95 (ISBN 0-87618-031-4); The Cardiovascular System. 1970. pap. 6.95 (ISBN 0-87618-037-3); The Digestive System. 1972. pap. 6.95 (ISBN 0-87618-040-3); The Endocrine System. 1972. pap. 6.95 (ISBN 0-87618-042-X); The Lymphatic & Reticuloendothelial System. 1973. pap. 6.95 (ISBN 0-87618-038-1); The Muscular System. 1972. pap. 6.95 (ISBN 0-87618-034-9); The Nervous System. 1972. pap. 6.95 (ISBN 0-87618-035-7); Nutrition, Metabolism, Fluid, & Electrolyte Balance. 1972. pap. 6.95 (ISBN 0-87618-043-8); Reproduction in Humans. 1973. pap. 6.95 (ISBN 0-87618-045-4); The Reproductive System. 1972. pap. 6.95 (ISBN 0-87618-044-6); The Respiratory System. 1972. pap. 6.95 (ISBN 0-87618-039-X); The Skeletal System. 1972. pap. 6.95 (ISBN 0-87618-033-0); The Skin. 1972. pap. 6.95 (ISBN 0-87618-032-2); The Special Senses. 1972. pap. 6.95 (ISBN 0-87618-036-5); The Urinary System. 1974. pap. 6.95 (ISBN 0-87618-041-1). **(Illus.). Set. 89.95 (ISBN 0-87618-635-5). R J Brady.**

--Medical Terminology: A Programmed Orientation to. (Illus.). 1970. pap. 9.95 (ISBN 0-87618-074-8). R J Brady.

--Microbiology: A Programmed Introduction to. (Illus.). 1969. pap. 9.95 (ISBN 0-87618-075-6). R J Brady.

Brady, Robert A. The Spirit & Structure of German Fascism. LC 68-9629. 1970. Repr. of 1937 ed. 19.00 (ISBN 0-86527-189-5). Fertig.

Brady, Robert N. Diesel Fuel Systems. (Illus.). 640p. 1981. text ed. 21.95 (ISBN 0-8359-1293-0). soln. manual avail. (ISBN 0-8359-1294-9). Reston.

Brady, Ryder. Instar. 1977. pap. 1.75 o.p. (ISBN 0-345-25658-1). Ballantine.

Brae, G., ed. see Camus, A.

Brafman, Morris & Schimel, David. Trade for Freedom. LC 75-26371. 96p. 1975. 5.95 (ISBN 0-88400-044-3). Shengold.

Braga, Joseph & Braga, Laurie. Children & Adults: Activities for Growing Together. (Human Development Bks.). (Illus.). 1978. 15.95 (ISBN 0-13-130351-1, Spec); pap. 7.95 (ISBN 0-13-130344-9). P-H.

Braga, Joseph, jt. auth. see Braga, Laurie.

Braga, Laurie & Braga, Joseph. Learning & Growing: A Guide to Child Development. 192p. 1975. 8.95 (ISBN 0-13-527614-4, Spec); pap. 3.95 (ISBN 0-13-527606-3, Spec). P-H.

Braga, Laurie, jt. auth. see Braga, Joseph.

Braga, Meg. Make & Tell: Christmas Holiday Book of Family Fun & Crafts. (Illus.). 1978. Repr. of 1974 ed. saddlestitched 1.95 (ISBN 0-87788-535-4). Shaw Pubs.

Braga de Macedo, Jorge. Portugal Since the Revolution: Economic & Political Perspectives. Serfaty, Simon, ed. (Westview Special Studies in West European Politics & Society). 128p. 1981. lib. bdg. 12.50x (ISBN 0-89158-972-4). Westview.

Bragadin, Marc'Antonio. The Italian Navy in World War II. Hoffman, Gale, tr. LC 79-6102. (Navies & Man Ser.). (Illus.). 1980. Repr. of 1957 ed. lib. bdg. 32.00x (ISBN 0-405-13031-7). Arno.

Bragdon, Claude. More Lives Than One. 368p. 1980. Repr. of 1938 ed. lib. bdg. 35.00 (ISBN 0-89984-063-9). Century Bookbindery.

Bragdon, Clifford R. Noise Pollution: The Unquiet Crisis. LC 70-157049. (Illus.). 1972. 16.95x (ISBN 0-8122-7638-8). U of Pa Pr.

Bragdon, Clifford R., ed. Noise Pollution: A Guide to Information Sources. LC 73-17535. (Man & the Environment Information Guide Ser.: Vol. 5). 600p. 1979. 30.00 (ISBN 0-8103-1345-6). Gale.

Bragdon, Henry W. & Eliot, Thomas H. The Bright Constellation: Documents of American Democracy. rev. ed. (Illus.). 277p. (gr. 10-12). 1980. pap. text ed. 4.95x (ISBN 0-88334-129-8). Ind Sch Pr.

Bragdon, Lillian J. The Land & People of France. rev. ed. LC 78-37605. (Portraits of the Nations Ser.). (Illus.). (gr. 6 up). 1972. 8.95 (ISBN 0-397-31297-0). Lippincott.

Brager, George & Holloway, Stephen. Changing Human Service Organizations: Politics & Practice. LC 77-87572. 1978. text ed. 15.95 (ISBN 0-02-904620-3). Free Pr.

Brager, George & Specht, Harry. Community Organizing. (Social Work & Social Issues Ser). 1973. 17.50x (ISBN 0-231-03393-1). Columbia U Pr.

Bragg, Arthur N. Gnomes of the Night. LC 64-24504. 1965. 7.00x o.p. (ISBN 0-8122-7472-5). U of Pa Pr.

Bragg, Bill. Enemy in Sight. (Orig.). 1980. pap. 1.75 (ISBN 0-505-51530-X). Tower Bks.

--The War Horses. (Orig.). 1980. pap. 1.75 (ISBN 0-505-51511-3). Tower Bks.

Bragg, Gordon M. Principles of Experimentation & Measurement. (Illus.). 192p. 1974. 18.95 (ISBN 0-13-701169-5). P-H.

Bragg, Gordon M. & Strauss, Jennifer. Strauss Air Pollution Control, Pt. 4. LC 79-23458. (Environmental Science & Technology Ser.). 416p. 1981. 30.00 (ISBN 0-471-07957-X, Pub. by Wiley-Interscience). Wiley.

Bragg, R. J. & Turner, Roy. Parachute Badges & Insignia of the World. (Illus.). 1979. 12.95 (ISBN 0-7137-0882-4, Pub. by Blandford Pr England). Sterling.

Bragg, W. F. Buckskin Rider. 1981. pap. 1.75 (ISBN 0-8439-0881-5, Leisure Bks). Nordon Pubns.

--Bullet Proof. 1981. pap. 1.95 (ISBN 0-8439-0909-9, Leisure Bks). Nordon Pubns.

--Bullet Song. 1981. pap. 1.75 (ISBN 0-8439-0880-7, Leisure Bks). Nordon Pubns.

--Ghost Mountain Guns. 1981. pap. 1.75 (ISBN 0-8439-0896-3, Leisure Bks). Nordon Pubns.

--Maverick Showdown. 1981. pap. 1.75 (ISBN 0-8439-0910-2, Leisure Bks). Nordon Pubns.

--Shotgun Gap. 1981. pap. 1.75 (ISBN 0-8439-0895-5, Leisure Bks). Nordon Pubns.

--Starr of Wyoming. 1981. pap. 2.25 (ISBN 0-8439-0860-2, Leisure Bks). Nordon Pubns.

--Texas Fever. 1981. pap. 1.75 (ISBN 0-8439-0864-5, Leisure Bks). Nordon Pubns.

Bragg, W. L., ed. see Royal Institution Library of Science.

Bragg, William, Jr. Wyoming Wealth: A History of Wyoming. Sancher, Amir, ed. LC 76-47108. (Illus.). 1977. text ed. 14.95 (ISBN 0-89100-006-2); pap. text ed. 9.95 (ISBN 0-89100-001-1). Aviation Maint.

Bragg, William L. & Porter, George, eds. Physical Sciences: The Royal Institution Library of Science, 10 vols. plus index. (Illus.). 1969. Set. 396.00x (ISBN 0-444-20048-7); Set. pap. 216.00x (ISBN 0-85334-615-1). Intl Ideas.

Bragg, Yana, ed. see Harvey, Bill.

Braham, Allan. The Architecture of the French Enlightenment. 1980. 55.00 (ISBN 0-520-04117-8). U of Cal Pr.

Braham, Raymond L. & Morris, Merle E. Textbook of Pediatric Dentistry. (Illus.). 568p. 1980. pap. text ed. 26.95 (ISBN 0-683-01012-3). Williams & Wilkins.

Brahe, Tycho. Learned Tico Brahe His Astronomicall Conjectur of the New & Much Admired Star Which Appeared in the Year 1572. LC 74-6157. (English Experience Ser.: No. 86). 28p. 1969. Repr. of 1632 ed. 14.00 (ISBN 90-221-0086-3). Walter J Johnson.

Brahmachari, Dhirenda. Yoga: Yogic Suksma Vyayama. (Illus.). 232p. 1975. 8.95 (ISBN 0-88253-802-0). Ind-US Inc.

Brahms, Johannes. Complete Shorter Works for Piano. Mandyczewski, Eusebius, ed. LC 70-116828. 1970. pap. 5.50 (ISBN 0-486-22651-4). Dover.

--Complete Symphonies; in Full Orchestral Score. Gal, Hans, ed. LC 73-92635. 352p. 1974. pap. 8.95 (ISBN 0-486-23053-8). Dover.

Brahs, Stuart J. An Album of Puerto Ricans in the United States. LC 73-5936. (Picture Albums Ser). (Illus.). 96p. (gr. 4-6). 1973. PLB 5.90 o.p. (ISBN 0-531-01517-3). Watts.

Brahtz, J. Peel. Coastal Zone Management: Multiple Use with Conservation. LC 74-178141. (University of California Engineering & Physical Sciences Extension Ser.). 384p. 1972. 34.00 o.p. (ISBN 0-471-09575-3, Pub. by Wiley-Interscience). Wiley.

Braidwood, Robert J. Prehistoric Men. 8th ed. 213p. 1975. pap. 7.95x (ISBN 0-673-07851-5). Scott F.

Braiker, Harriet B., ed. see Polich, J. Michael & Armor, David J.

Brailow, Michele. Cellars & Attics. 48p. 1981. 6.95 (ISBN 0-87881-099-4). Mojave Bks.

Brailsford, D. F. & Walker, A. N. Introductory ALGOL Sixty-Eight Programming. LC 79-40241. 1979. 34.95x (ISBN 0-470-26746-1); pap. text ed. 17.95x (ISBN 0-470-26799-2). Halsted Pr.

Brailsford, Henry N. The War of Steel & Gold: A Study of the Armed Peace. 3rd ed. (The Development of the Industrial Society Ser.). 340p. 1980. Repr. 25.00x (ISBN 0-7165-1767-1, Pub. by Irish Academic Pr). Biblio Dist.

--War of Steel & Gold: Study of the Armed Peace. LC 75-147545. (Library of War & Peace; Control & Limitation of Arms). lib. bdg. 38.00 (ISBN 0-8240-0326-8). Garland Pub.

--Why Capitalism Means War. LC 70-147494. (Library of War & Peace; the Political Economy of War). lib. bdg. 38.00 (ISBN 0-8240-0287-3). Garland Pub.

Brain. Brain's Diseases of the Nervous System. 8th ed. Walton, John N., ed. (Illus.). 1977. text ed. 35.00x (ISBN 0-19-261309-X). Oxford U Pr.

--My Mother Made Me. (gr. 6). 1979. pap. 1.25 (ISBN 0-590-05801-0, Schol Pap). Schol Bk Serv.

Brain, Elizabeth, ed. see Smith, E. Kinsey.

Brain, James L. Basic Structure of Swahili. (African Special Publications: No. 1). 151p. (Orig.). 1977. pap. text ed. 4.50x (ISBN 0-915984-58-X). Syracuse U Foreign Comp.

--The Last Taboo--Sex & the Fear of Death. LC 78-20060. (Illus.). 1979. 9.95 (ISBN 0-385-14581-0, Anchor Pr). Doubleday.

Brain, Jeffrey P. Tunica Treasure. (Peabody Museum Papers: Vol. 71). (Orig.). 1979. pap. 35.00 (ISBN 0-87365-196-0). Peabody Harvard.

Brain, Paul F. Hormones & Aggression, Vol. I. Horrobin, D. F., ed. (Hormone Research Review Ser.). 126p. 1980. Repr. of 1977 ed. 16.95x (ISBN 0-87705-963-2). Human Sci Pr.

--Hormones, Drugs & Aggression, Vol. III. (Hormone Research Review Ser.). 173p. 1980. Repr. of 1979 ed. 21.95x (ISBN 0-87705-959-4). Human Sci Pr.

Brain, R., tr. see Godelier, M.

Brain Sciences Committee - Division Of Medical Sciences. Early Experience & Visual Information Processing Perceptual & Reading Disorders. LC 72-605763. (Illus.). 1970. text ed. 10.75 o.p. (ISBN 0-309-01765-3). Natl Acad Pr.

Brainard, Joe. I Remember. LC 75-23153. 1975. 14.95 (ISBN 0-916190-02-1); pap. 6.00 (ISBN 0-916190-03-X). Full Court NY.

Brainard, William C. & Perry, George L., eds. Brookings Papers on Economic Activity. 1981. pap. subscription on 2 issues (ISBN 0-8157-1110-7). Brookings.

Braine, John. Writing a Novel. 224p. 1975. pap. 4.95 (ISBN 0-07-007112-8, SP). McGraw.

Brainerd, Charles J. The Origins of the Number Concept. LC 78-21223. 1979. 22.60 (ISBN 0-275-24310-9). Praeger.

--Piaget's Theory of Intelligence. (Illus.). 1978. 17.95 (ISBN 0-13-675108-3). P-H.

Brainerd, John W. Working with Nature: A Practical Guide. (Illus.). 550p. 1973. 24.95x (ISBN 0-19-501667-X). Oxford U Pr.

Brainerd, Walter S. & Landweber, Lawrence H. Theory of Computation. LC 73-12950. 336p. 1974. 27.95 (ISBN 0-471-09585-0). Wiley.

Brainina, K. Z. Stripping Voltammetry in Chemical Analysis. Shelnitz, P., tr. from Rus. LC 74-13974. 222p. 1974. 29.50 (ISBN 0-470-09590-3). Halsted Pr.

Braiott, Louis, Jr. The Audit Director's Guide: How to Serve Effectively on the Corporate Audit Committee. LC 80-23989. 250p. 1980. 24.95 (ISBN 0-471-05866-1, Pub. by Ronald Pr). Wiley.

Braisted, William R. United States Navy in the Pacific, 1909-1922. 1971. 25.00 (ISBN 0-292-70037-7). U of Tex Pr.

Braitenbach, E. H., tr. from Ger. On the Texture of Brains: An Introduction to Neuroanatomy for the Cybernetically Minded. LC 77-21351. (Illus.). 1977. pap. 8.70 (ISBN 0-387-08391-X). Springer-Verlag.

Braithwaite, Althea. Life in a Castle. (Illus.). 32p. 1980. 3.50 o.p. (ISBN 0-85122-172-6, Pub. by Dinosaur Pubns). pap. 1.75 o.p. (ISBN 0-85122-172-6, Pub. by Dinosaur Pubns); pap. in 5 pk. avail. o.p. Merrimack Bk Serv.

--Life in a Castle. (Dinosaur Ser.). (Illus.). (gr. 5 up). 1978. pap. 8.75 pack of 5 o.p. (ISBN 0-85933-009-5, Pub. by Paul Elek). Merrimack Bk Serv.

--Man Flies on. (Dinosaur Ser.). (Illus.). (gr. 5 up). 1978. pap. 1.75 ea. (ISBN 0-85933-155-5, Pub. by Paul Elek); pap. 8.75 pack of 5. Merrimack Bk Serv.

--Man in the Sky. (Dinosaur Ser.). (Illus.). (gr. 5 up). 1978. pap. 1.75 ea. (ISBN 0-85933-011-7, Pub. by Paul Elek); pap. 8.75 pack of 5. Merrimack Bk Serv.

--Peter Pig. (Dinosaur Ser.). (Illus.). (gr. k-3). 1978. pap. 7.25 pack of 5 o.p. (ISBN 0-85122-036-3, Pub. by Dino Pub); pap. 1.45 ea. o.p. Merrimack Bk Serv.

Braithwaite, Bruce. The Films of Jack Nicholson. Castell, David, ed. (The Films of...Ser.). (Illus.). (gr. 7-12). 1978. Repr. PLB 5.95 (ISBN 0-912616-76-8). Greenhaven.

--The Films of Marlon Brando. Castell, David, ed. (The Films of...Ser.). (Illus.). (gr. 7-12). 1978. Repr. of 1974 ed. PLB 5.95 (ISBN 0-912616-86-5). Greenhaven.

Braithwaite, E. R. To Sir, with Love. (gr. 9-12). 1973. pap. 1.95 (ISBN 0-515-05823-8). Jove Pubns.

Braithwaite, Edward. To Sir, with Love. 1960. 7.95 o.p. (ISBN 0-13-923037-8). P-H.

Braithwaite, Richard B. Theory of Games As a Tool for the Moral Philosopher. 1955. 15.50 (ISBN 0-521-04307-7). Cambridge U Pr.

Brake, J. R., ed. Farm & Personal Finance. LC 68-13437. (gr. 9-12). 1968. pap. 3.50 (ISBN 0-8134-0115-1, 115). Interstate.

Braly, Malcolm. The Protector. (Orig.). 1979. pap. 2.25 (ISBN 0-515-05178-0). Jove Pubns.

Bram, Elizabeth. A Dinosaur Is Too Big. LC 76-22669. (Illus.). (gr. k-3). 1977. PLB 6.00 (ISBN 0-688-84071-X). Greenwillow.

--I Don't Want to Go to School. LC 76-51274. (Illus.). (ps-3). 1977. 6.25 (ISBN 0-688-80095-5); PLB 6.00 (ISBN 0-688-84095-7). Greenwillow.

Bramah, Ernest, pseud. Kai Lung's Golden Hours. LC 79-53463. (Short Story Index in Reprint Ser.). Date not set. Repr. of 1922 ed. 24.75x (ISBN 0-8486-5011-5). Core Collection. Postponed.

Brambell Symposium 2nd, Wales, July 1978. Protein Transmission Through Living Membranes: Proceedings. Hemmings, W. A., ed. LC 79-15662. 1979. 88.00 (ISBN 0-444-80112-X, North Holland). Elsevier.

Brambilla, F. & Bridges. Perspectives in Endocrine Psychobiology. LC 76-27305. 650p. 1977. 55.00 o.p. (ISBN 0-471-99434-0, Pub. by Wiley-Interscience). Wiley.

Brambilla, Robert. Learning from Atlanta. (Learningfrom the U. S. A. Ser.). 150p. (Orig.). 1981. pap. text ed. 6.95 (ISBN 0-87855-835-7). Transaction Bks.

Brambilla, Roberto & Longo, Gianni. Learning from Atlanta. (Learning from the USA Ser.). (Illus.). 150p. Date not set. pap. 6.95 (ISBN 0-936020-04-0). Inst for Environ Action. Postponed.

--Learning from Minneapolis, St. Paul. (Learning from the USA Ser.). (Illus.). 150p. (Orig.). Date not set. pap. 6.95 (ISBN 0-936020-03-2). Inst for Environ Action. Postponed.

Bramble, J. C. Persius & the Programmatic Satire. LC 72-83579. (Cambridge Classical Studies). 192p. 1973. 19.95 (ISBN 0-521-08703-1). Cambridge U Pr.

Brame, Michael. Essays on Binding & Fusion. (Linguistics Research Monograph: Vol. 4). 1981. text ed. 32.00 (ISBN 0-932998-04-6). Noit Amrofer.

Brame, Michael, jt. auth. see Bettembourg, Georges.

Brame, Michael K. Essays Toward Realistic Syntax. new ed. LC 79-67347. (Linguistics Research Monograph: Vol. 2). 1979. text ed. 32.00x (ISBN 0-932998-01-1). Noit Amrofer.

Bramer, George R. Process One: A Multi-Media College Writing Program. 1976. pap. text ed. 10.95 (ISBN 0-675-08682-5); Set. cassettes & filmstrips 495.00 (ISBN 0-675-08683-3); 2-4 sets 300.00, 5-9 sets 250.00, 10 or more 195.00 (ISBN 0-686-67251-8). test 3.95 (ISBN 0-686-67253-4). Merrill.

Bramer, George R. & Sedley, Dorothy. Writing for Readers. (Illus.). 500p. 1981. text ed. price not set (ISBN 0-675-08045-2); write for info. tchr's. ed (ISBN 0-675-08038-X); instr's. manual 3.95 (ISBN 0-686-69504-6). Merrill.

Bramhall, John. Castigations of Mr. Hobbes. Wellek, Rene, ed. LC 75-11199. (British Philosophers & Theologians of the 17th & 18th Centuries: Vol. 6). 1976. Repr. of 1658 ed. lib. bdg. 42.00 (ISBN 0-8240-1755-2). Garland Pub.
--A Defence of True Liberty from Ante-Cedent & Extrinsical Necessity. an Answer to Hobbes' a Treatise of Liberty & Necessity. Wellek, Rene, ed. LC 75-11200. (British Philosophers & Theologians of the 17th & 18th Centuries: Vol. 7). 1976. Repr. of 1655 ed. lib. bdg. 42.00 (ISBN 0-8240-1756-0). Garland Pub.
Bramhall, William. The Literary Engagement Calendar. (Illus.). 112p. 1981. spiral 6.95 (ISBN 0-525-93196-1). Dutton.
Bramham, Peter. How Staff Rule: Structures of Authority in Two Community Schools. 213p. 1980. text ed. 29.50x (ISBN 0-566-00321-X, Pub. by Gower Pub Co England). Renouf.
Bramlette, Carl A., Jr., jt. ed. see Mescon, Michael H.
Brammer, L. & Shostrum, Everett. Therapeutic Psychology: Fundamentals of Counseling & Psychotherapy. 3rd ed. (Clinical & Social Psych. Ser.). (Illus.). 1977. 19.95 (ISBN 0-13-914622-9). P-H.
Brammer, Lawrence M. The Helping Relationship: Process & Skills. 2nd ed. (P-H Ser. in Counseling & Human Development). (Illus.). 1979. ref. ed. 14.95 (ISBN 0-13-386268-2); pap. 9.95 ref. ed. (ISBN 0-13-386250-X). P-H.
Brammer, Miriam, jt. ed. see Miller, Lynne G.
Brams, Steven J. Game Theory & Politics. LC 74-15370. (Illus.). 1975. pap. text ed. 9.95 (ISBN 0-02-904550-9). Free Pr.
--Paradoxes in Politics: An Introduction to the Nonobvious in Political Science. LC 75-28568. (Illus.). 1976. pap. text ed. 9.95 (ISBN 0-02-904590-8). Free Pr.
Brams, William A. Managing Your Coronary. 4th ed. LC 73-13869. 1975. 6.95 o.p. (ISBN 0-397-01010-9). Lippincott.
Bramsen, Michele B. A Portrait of Elie Halevy. 1978. pap. text ed. 28.50x (ISBN 90-6032-100-6). Humanities.
Bramsen, Michelle B., jt. ed. see Tinker, Irene.
Bramson, A. E., jt. auth. see Birch, N. H.
Bramson, Alan. Be a Better Pilot. LC 80-13401. (Illus.). 256p. 1980. 14.95 (ISBN 0-668-04901-4, 4901-4). Arco.
Bramson, Ann. Soap. rev. ed. LC 75-7286. 1975. pap. 3.50 (ISBN 0-911104-57-7). Workman Pub.
Bramson, Morris. Algebra: An Introductory Course. (gr. 9 up). 1978. wkbk 7.25 (ISBN 0-87720-240-0). AMSCO Sch.
--Mathematics: Level Two Achievement Test. LC 66-18139. (College Board Achievement Tests Ser). (Orig.). 1966. pap. 0.95 o.p. (ISBN 0-668-01456-3). Arc Bks.
Bramson, Robert M. Coping with Difficult People. 240p. 1981. 11.95 (ISBN 0-385-17362-8, Anchor Pr). Doubleday.
Bramsted, E. K. & Melhuish, K. J., eds. Western Liberalism: A History in Documents from Locke to Croce. 1978. text ed. 31.00x (ISBN 0-582-48830-3); pap. text ed. 16.95x (ISBN 0-582-48831-1). Longman.
Bramwell, A. R. Helicopter Dynamics. LC 76-4944. 1976. 59.95 (ISBN 0-470-15067-X). Halsted Pr.
Bramwell, James. Lost Atlantis. LC 80-19561. 288p. 1980. Repr. of 1974 ed. lib. bdg. 10.95x (ISBN 0-89370-623-X). Borgo Pr.
Brana-Shute, Gary, jt. ed. see Brana-Shute, Rosemary.
Brana-Shute, Rosemary & Brana-Shute, Gary, eds. Crime & Punishment in the Caribbean. LC 80-21078. (Illus.). x, 146p. 1980. pap. 6.00 (ISBN 0-8130-0685-6). U Presses Fla.
Brancato, Robin F. Don't Sit Under the Apple Tree. 128p. 1980. pap. 1.75 (ISBN 0-553-12966-X). Bantam.
Branch, Ben. Fundamentals of Investing. LC 75-26703. 1976. 21.50 (ISBN 0-471-09650-4); instructor's manual avail. (ISBN 0-471-09651-2). Wiley.
Branch, C. Hardin, pref. by. Aspects of Anxiety. 2nd ed. LC 68-27538. 1968. 4.50 o.p. (ISBN 0-397-59024-5). Lippincott.
Branch, Diana, ed. Tools for Homesteaders, Gardeners, & Small Scale Farmers. 1978. pap. 12.95 (ISBN 0-87857-235-X). Rodale Pr Inc.
Branch, E. Douglas. Hunting of the Buffalo. LC 62-8408. (Illus.). 1962. pap. 4.25 (ISBN 0-8032-5021-5, BB 130, Bison). U of Nebr Pr.
Branch, Melville C. Comparative Urban Design-Rare Engravings: 1830-1843. 108p. 49.50 (ISBN 0-686-69145-8, Co Pub by U of Cal Pr). Arno.
--Continuous City Planning: Integrating Municipal & City Planning. 192p. 1980. 21.95 (ISBN 0-471-08943-5, Pub. by Wiley-Interscience). Wiley.
Branch, Melville C. & Mazza, Eliane G. Selected Annotated Bibliography on New Town Planning & Development. (Architecture Ser.: Bibliography a-216). 133p. 1980. pap. 14.00. Vance Biblios.
Branch, Newton, tr. see Defourneaux, Mercelin.
Branch, Taylor. Empire Blues. 1981. 14.95 (ISBN 0-671-23096-4). S&S.
Branch, Watson G., ed. Melville: The Critical Heritage. (The Critical Heritage Ser.). 1974. 38.00x (ISBN 0-7100-7774-2). Routledge & Kegan.
Brand, Charles P. Torquato Tasso. 1965. 57.50 (ISBN 0-521-04311-5). Cambridge U Pr.
Brand, Christianna. Nurse Matilda. (Children's Literature Ser.). 1980. PLB 7.95 (ISBN 0-8398-2604-4). Gregg.
Brand, Edward A. Modern Supermarket Operation. 2nd ed. LC 62-19750. (Illus.). 1965. 15.00 o.p. (ISBN 0-87005-047-8). Fairchild.
Brand, J. C. & Speakman, J. C. Molecular Structure: The Physical Approach. 2nd ed. Tifer, J. K., ed. LC 75-8507. 1975. 31.95 (ISBN 0-470-09795-7). Halsted Pr.
Brand, J. P. Cretaceous of Llano Estacado of Texas. (Illus.). 59p. 1953. 0.70 (RI 20). Bur Econ Geology.
Brand, John. Observations on the Popular Antiquities of Great Britain: Chiefly Illustrating the Origin of Our Vulgar & Provincial Customs, Ceremonies & Superstitions. LC 67-23896. 1969. Repr. of 1849 ed. 42.00 (ISBN 0-8103-3256-6). Gale.
Brand, Larry. Birthpyre. 288p. (Orig.). 1980. pap. 2.25 (ISBN 0-380-76539-X, 76539). Avon.
Brand, Max. Ambush at Torture Canyon. 1981. pap. write for info. (ISBN 0-671-41557-3). PB.
--The Big Trail. 1974. pap. 1.75 (ISBN 0-446-94333-9). Warner Bks.
--The Border Bandit. 192p. 1973. pap. 0.75 o.p. (ISBN 0-446-74218-X). Warner Bks.
--Border Guns. 1975. pap. 1.95 (ISBN 0-446-90888-6). Warner Bks.
--Brothers on the Trail. 1972. pap. 1.95 (ISBN 0-446-86392-0). Warner Bks.
--Bull Hunter. LC 80-20858. 192p. 1981. 8.95 (ISBN 0-396-07916-4). Dodd.
--Dan Barry's Daughter. 256p. 1976. pap. 1.95 (ISBN 0-446-90665-4). Warner Bks.
--Devil Horse. 1974. pap. 1.75 (ISBN 0-446-94289-8). Warner Bks.
--The Gambler. 208p. 1976. pap. 1.75 (ISBN 0-446-94328-2). Warner Bks.
--The Gentle Desperado. (Max Brand Popular Classics Ser.). 160p. (Orig.). 1981. pap. 6.95 (ISBN 0-88496-157-5). Capra Pr.
--Gentle Gunman. 1976. pap. 1.75 (ISBN 0-446-94291-X). Warner Bks.
--Gunman's Gold. 1974. pap. 1.95 (ISBN 0-446-88337-9). Warner Bks.
--Guns of Dorking Hollow. 1976. pap. 1.75 (ISBN 0-446-94204-9). Warner Bks.
--Happy Jack. 224p. 1972. pap. 1.95 (ISBN 0-446-90303-5). Warner Bks.
--The Happy Valley. 240p. 1972. pap. 1.95 (ISBN 0-446-90304-3). Warner Bks.
--The Invisible Outlaw. 1974. pap. 1.75 (ISBN 0-446-94343-6). Warner Bks.
--King Bird Rides. 1972. pap. 1.95 (ISBN 0-446-90305-1). Warner Bks.
--The Last Showdown. 192p. 1975. 5.95 o.p. (ISBN 0-396-07082-5). Dodd.
--Lucky Larribee. 1975. pap. 1.75 (ISBN 0-686-58223-3). Warner Bks.
--The Man from Savage Creek. 208p. 1980. pap. 1.95 (ISBN 0-446-90815-0). Warner Bks.
--Marbleface. 240p. 1981. pap. 1.95 (ISBN 0-446-90307-8). Warner Bks.
--Mistral. 224p. 1971. pap. 1.95 (ISBN 0-446-90316-7). Warner Bks.
--Mountain Riders. 160p. 1972. pap. 1.95 (ISBN 0-446-90308-6). Warner Bks.
--Mystery Ranch. 1976. pap. 1.75 (ISBN 0-446-94102-6). Warner Bks.
--Ride the Wild Trail. 1981. pap. 1.75 (ISBN 0-671-41556-5). PB.
--Rustlers of Beacon Creek. 1976. pap. 1.75 (ISBN 0-446-94541-2). Warner Bks.
--Six-Gun Country. LC 79-24209. 180p. 1980. 7.95 (ISBN 0-396-07805-2). Dodd.
--Slow Joe. 240p. 1972. pap. 1.95 (ISBN 0-446-90311-6). Warner Bks.
--Smiling Charlie. 224p. 1971. pap. 1.95 (ISBN 0-446-90319-1). Warner Bks.
--The Smiling Desperado. 1979. pap. 1.50 o.p. (ISBN 0-446-98128-1). Warner Bks.
--Smoking Land: A Novel of Super-Science & Amazing Adventure. (Max Brand Popular Classics Ser.). 112p. 1980. pap. 5.95 (ISBN 0-88496-155-9). Capra Pr.
--Steve Train's Ordeal. 1980. pap. write for info. (ISBN 0-671-41489-5). PB.
--Storm on the Range. 1980. pap. 1.75 (ISBN 0-446-94300-2). Warner Bks.
--The Stranger. 208p. 1976. pap. 1.75 (ISBN 0-446-94508-0). Warner Bks.
--Tenderfoot. Orig. Title: Outlaw's Gold. 1976. pap. 1.95 (ISBN 0-446-90653-0). Warner Bks.
--Timbal Gulch Trail. 1972. pap. 1.95 (ISBN 0-446-90312-4). Warner Bks.
--Timbul Gulch Trail. 224p. (Orig.). 1981. pap. 1.95 (ISBN 0-446-90312-4). Warner Bks.
--Torture Trail. 1975. pap. 1.75 (ISBN 0-446-94344-4). Warner Bks.
--Trail Partners. 1974. pap. 1.50 (ISBN 0-446-98138-9). Warner Bks.
--Trouble Trail. 1972. pap. 1.95 (ISBN 0-446-90314-0). Warner Bks.
--War Party. 1975. pap. 1.50 (ISBN 0-446-88933-4). Warner Bks.
--Way of the Lawless. (gr. 7-12). 1979. lib. bdg. 12.95 (ISBN 0-8161-6747-8). G K Hall.
--Way of the Lawless. 1980. pap. 1.75 (ISBN 0-446-94301-0). Warner Bks.
--White Wolf. 1975. pap. 1.75 (ISBN 0-446-94605-2). Warner Bks.
Brand, May. Six-Gun Country. 1981. pap. 1.95 (ISBN 0-686-69453-8). PB.
Brand, Myles, jt. ed. see Bradie, Michael.
Brand, Paul & Yancey, Phillip. Fearfully & Wonderfully Made. 224p. 8.95 (ISBN 0-310-35450-1). Zondervan.
Brand, Raymond H., jt. auth. see Sheaffer, John R.
Brand, Reinhard, ed. Locke: Symposium Wolfenbuttel, Nineteen Hundred Seventy-Nine. 288p. 1980. text ed. 48.75x (ISBN 3-11-008266-7). De Gruyter.
Brand, Richard W. & Isselhard, Donald E. Anatomy of Orofacial Structures. LC 77-14586. 1977. pap. text ed. 19.95 (ISBN 0-8016-0740-X). Mosby.
Brand, Stewart, ed. The Next Whole Earth Catalog: Access to Tools. (Illus.). 608p. 1980. pap. 12.95 (ISBN 0-394-73951-5). Random.
Brand, Susan. Shadows on the Tor. 1978. pap. 1.50 o.s.i. (ISBN 0-515-04630-2). Jove Pubns.
Brand, T., jt. auth. see Morse, P.
Branda, Eldon S. see Webb, Walter P. & Carroll, H. Bailey.
Brandauer, Frederick P. Tung Yueh. (World Authors Ser.: No. 498 (China)). 1978. 13.95 (ISBN 0-8057-6339-2). Twayne.
Brande, Dorothea. Becoming a Writer. LC 80-53146. 256p. 1981. pap. 5.95 (ISBN 0-87477-164-1). J P Tarcher.
Brandejs, Jan F. & Pace, Graham. Physician's Primer on Computers: Private Practice. LC 75-39315. (Illus.). 1979. 18.50 (ISBN 0-669-00431-6). Lexington Bks.
Brandel, Marc. The Hand. 1981. pap. 2.50 (ISBN 0-425-04838-1). Berkley Pub.
Brandel, R., jt. auth. see Reese, Gustave.
Brandell, Gunnar. Freud-A Man of His Century. White, Iain, tr. LC 78-5347. 1979. text ed. 18.25x (ISBN 0-391-00871-4). Humanities.
Brandell, Raymond E., jt. auth. see Brandell, Raymond J.
Brandell, Raymond J. & Brandell, Raymond E. The Dynamics of Making a Fortune in Mail Order. (Illus.). 360p. 1980. 19.95 (ISBN 0-8119-0325-7). Fell.
Branden, Nathaniel. Nathaniel Branden Anthology: The Psychology of Self-Esteem, Breaking Free the Disowned Self. LC 80-51879. 723p. 1980. 17.50 (ISBN 0-87477-142-0). J P Tarcher.
Brandenberg, Franz. Fresh Cider & Pie. LC 73-585. (Illus.). 32p. (gr. k-3). 1973. 4.95g o.s.i. (ISBN 0-02-711910-6). Macmillan.
--I Once Knew a Man. (Illus.). (gr. k-2). 1970. 4.95g o.s.i. (ISBN 0-02-711900-9). Macmillan.
--I Wish I Was Sick, Too. LC 75-46610. (Illus.). (gr. k-3). 1976. 8.25 (ISBN 0-688-80047-5); PLB 7.92 (ISBN 0-688-84047-7). Greenwillow.
--Leo & Emily. LC 80-19657. (Read-Alone Bk.). (Illus.). 56p. (gr. 1-3). 1981. 5.95 (ISBN 0-688-80292-3); PLB 5.71 (ISBN 0-688-84292-5). Greenwillow.
--No School Today! LC 74-13186. (Illus.). 32p. (gr. 1-3). 1975. 7.95 o.s.i. (ISBN 0-02-711930-0). Macmillan.
--A Robber! a Robber! LC 75-26999. (Illus.). 32p. (gr. k-3). 1976. 7.25 (ISBN 0-688-80027-0); PLB 7.92 (ISBN 0-688-84027-2). Greenwillow.
--A Secret for Grandmother's Birthday. LC 75-10606. (Illus.). 32p. (ps-3). 1975. 7.92 (ISBN 0-688-84012-4). Greenwillow.
Brandenburg, D., ed. Insulin: Chemistry, Structure & Function of Insulin & Related Hormones. text ed. 112.00 (ISBN 3-11-008156-3). De Gruyter.
Brandenburg, M. M., tr. see Baegert, Johann J.
Brandenderg. Nice New Neighbors. (ps-3). 1980. pap. 1.50 (ISBN 0-590-30070-9, Schol Pap). Schol Bk Serv.
Brander, Laurence, ed. E. M. Forster: A Critical Study. 1979. 16.95x (ISBN 0-8464-0080-4); pap. 9.95 (ISBN 0-8464-0081-2). Beekman Pubs.
Brander, Laurence A; see Bloomfield, Paul.
Brander, Michael. The Goergian Gentleman. (Saxon House Bks.). 1974. 8.95 o.p. (ISBN 0-347-00020-7). Gordon-Cremonesi.
--The Victorian Gentleman. 1976. 15.95 o.p. (ISBN 0-86033-004-4). Gordon-Cremonesi.
Brandes, David, ed. Male Accessory Sex Organs: Structure & Function in Mammals. 1974. 60.00 (ISBN 0-12-125650-2). Acad Pr.
Brandes, Joseph & Douglas, Martin. Immigrants to Freedom: Jewish Communities in Rural New Jersey Since 1882. LC 76-122384. 1971. 15.00x (ISBN 0-8122-7620-5). U of Pa Pr.
Brandes, Juergen, compiled by. Electron Microscopy of Plant Viruses: Bibliography 1939-1965. 91p. (Orig.). 1967. pap. 16.00x (ISBN 3-489-12200-3). Intl Pubns Serv.
Brandes, Paul D. & Brewer, Jeutonne. Dialect Clash in America: Issues & Answers. LC 76-41248. 1977. 25.00 o.p. (ISBN 0-8108-0936-2). Scarecrow.
Brandes, Stanley. Metaphors of Masculinity: Sex & Status in Andalusian Folklore. LC 79-5258. (American Folklore Society Ser.). 224p. 1980. 19.95x (ISBN 0-8122-7776-7); pap. 9.95. U of Pa Pr.
Brandeth, Gyles. Pears All-the-Year-Round Quiz Book. (Illus.). 1978. 10.95 (ISBN 0-7207-1018-9, Pub. by Michael Joseph); pap. 5.95 (ISBN 0-7207-1019-7). Merrimack Bk Serv.
Brandis, Royall & Cox, Steven R., eds. Current Economic Problems: A Book of Readings. 1972. pap. text ed. 8.50x o.p. (ISBN 0-256-00239-8). Irwin.
Brandl, Albert. Improve Your Riding: Dressage, Jumping, Cross-Country. 116p. 1980. 12.95 (ISBN 0-8069-9120-8, Pub. by EP Publishing England). Sterling.
--Modern Riding. (EP Sports Ser.). (Illus.). 142p. 1981. 12.95 (ISBN 0-8069-9133-X, Pub. by EP Publishing England). Sterling.
Brandlen, David. In Search of Harmony, Vol. 2. 112p. 1980. pap. text ed. cancelled (ISBN 0-87881-093-5). Mojave Bks.
Brandlen, David L. In Search of Harmony, Vol. I. 1980. cancelled (ISBN 0-87881-092-7). Mojave Bks.
Brandly, C. A. & Jungherr, E. L., eds. Advances in Veterinary Science & Comparative Medicine. Incl. Vol. 13. 1969. 52.00 (ISBN 0-12-039213-5); Vol. 14. 1970. 52.00 (ISBN 0-12-039214-3); Vol. 15. 1971. 52.00 (ISBN 0-12-039215-1); Vol. 16. 1972. 52.50 (ISBN 0-12-039216-X); Vol. 17. 1973. 55.50 (ISBN 0-12-039217-8); Vol. 18. 1974. 47.00 (ISBN 0-12-039218-6); Vol. 19. 1976. 48.00 (ISBN 0-12-039219-4); lib. ed. 61.50 (ISBN 0-12-039274-7); microfiche 34.50 (ISBN 0-12-039275-5); Vol. 20. 1976. 47.00 (ISBN 0-12-039220-8); lib ed. 60.25 (ISBN 0-12-039276-3); microfiche 34.00 (ISBN 0-12-039277-1); Vol. 21. 1977. 52.75 (ISBN 0-12-039221-6); lib ed. 67.75 (ISBN 0-12-039278-X); microfiche 38.00 (ISBN 0-12-039279-8); Vol. 22. 1978. 43.50 (ISBN 0-12-039222-4); lib ed. 50.00 (ISBN 0-12-039280-1); microfiche 31.50 (ISBN 0-12-039281-X). LC 53-7098. Acad Pr.
Brandner, John H. Mammoth Vehicles of the World: Land-Sea-Air. (Illus.). Date not set. pap. 16.95 (ISBN 0-89404-009-X). Aztex. Postponed.
Brandom, Robert, jt. auth. see Rescher, Nicholas.
Brandon, Belinda B., ed. The Effect of the Demographics of Individual Households on Their Telephone Useage. 432p. 1980. write for info. (ISBN 0-88410-695-0). Ballinger Pub.
Brandon, David. Zen in the Art of Helping. 1976. 12.50 (ISBN 0-7100-8428-5). Routledge & Kegan.
Brandon, David & Jordan, Bill, eds. Creative Social Work. (Practice of Social Work Ser.: Vol. 3). 1979. 29.50x (ISBN 0-631-11831-4, Pub. by Basil Blackwell); pap. 10.00x (ISBN 0-631-11841-1). Biblio Dist.
Brandon, Dick H. & Segelstein, Sidney. Business Computers: How to Select Hardware, Software, Services. LC 80-26751. 302p. 1981. write for info. (ISBN 0-932648-18-5). Boardroom.
Brandon, Dick H. & Siegelstein, Sidney. The Business User's Guide to Minicomputers. 300p. 1980. 50.00 (ISBN 0-932648-18-5). Boardroom.
Brandon, Frances, jt. auth. see Gupta, Marie.
Brandon, Frances L. Bits & Pieces. 4.00 o.p. (ISBN 0-8062-0545-8). Carlton.
Brandon, James R., jt. auth. see Baumer, Rachel.
Brandon, James R., ed. The Performing Arts in Asia. 168p. 1972. pap. 6.00 (ISBN 92-3-100902-8, U445, UNESCO). Unipub.
--Theatre Perspectives One: Asian Theatre. 198p. 1980. 10.00. Am Theatre Assoc.
Brandon, Peter, ed. The South Saxons. (Illus.). 262p. 1978. 29.50x (ISBN 0-8476-6154-7). Rowman.
Brandon, Robin. The Good Crewman. 1979. 12.95x (ISBN 0-8464-0077-4). Beekman Pubs.
Brandon, Ruth. The Dollar Princesses. LC 80-7627. (Illus.). 224p. 1980. 12.95 (ISBN 0-394-50403-8). Knopf.
Brandon, Samuel G., ed. The Saviour God: Comparative Studies in the Concept of Salvation Presented to Edwin Oliver James. LC 80-14924. xxii, 242p. 1980. Repr. of 1963 ed. lib. bdg. 22.50x (ISBN 0-313-22416-1, BRSG). Greenwood.

Brandreth, Giles. Pears Book of Words. Oxford English Dict., ed. 204p. 1981. 13.95 (ISBN 0-7207-1186-X). Merrimack Bk Serv.
Brandreth, Giles, et al, eds. Pears Shilling Cyclopaedia. (Illus.). 1978. 12.95 (ISBN 0-7207-1032-4, Pub. by Michael Joseph). Merrimack Bk Serv.
Brandreth, Gyles. Amazing Facts About Animals. (Amazing Facts Books Ser.). (Illus.). 32p. (gr. 5-8). pap. 2.95 (ISBN 0-385-17017-3). Doubleday.
--Amazing Facts About Our Earth. LC 80-1087. (Amazing Facts Books Ser.). (Illus.). 32p. (gr. 5-8). 1981. pap. 2.95 (ISBN 0-385-17016-5). Doubleday.
--Amazing Facts About Prehistoric Animals. LC 80-1085. (Amazing Facts Books Ser.). (Illus.). 32p. 1981. pap. 2.95 (ISBN 0-385-17019-X). Doubleday.
--Amazing Facts About the Body. LC 80-1088. (Amazing Facts Books Ser.). (Illus.). 32p. (gr. 5-8). 1981. pap. 2.95. Doubleday.
--Biggest Tongue Twister Book in the World. LC 78-7784. (Illus.). 123p. (gr. 3 up). 1980. pap. 2.95 (ISBN 0-8069-8972-6). Sterling.
--The Biggest Tongue-Twister Book in the World. LC 78-57784. (Illus.). (gr. 2 up). 1978. 5.95 (ISBN 0-8069-4594-X); PLB 6.69 (ISBN 0-8069-4595-8). Sterling.
--Brain-Teasers & Mind-Benders. LC 78-66297. (Illus.). (gr. 3 up). 1979. 5.95 (ISBN 0-8069-4596-6); PLB 6.69 (ISBN 0-8069-4597-4). Sterling.
--Game a Day Book. LC 79-91386. (Illus.). 192p. (gr. 2-12). 1980. 6.95 (ISBN 0-8069-4610-5); PLB 7.49 (ISBN 0-8069-4611-3). Sterling.
--Home Entertainment for All the Family. LC 76-50266. (Illus.). 1977. 10.00 o.p. (ISBN 0-8289-0297-6); pap. 5.95 (ISBN 0-8289-0298-4). Greene.
--A Joke-a-Day Book. LC 78-66298. (Illus.). (gr. 3 up). 1979. 6.69 (ISBN 0-8069-4598-2); PLB 5.89 (ISBN 0-8069-4599-0). Sterling.
--The Little Red Darts Book. (Illus.). 1979. 6.50 (ISBN 0-370-30136-6, Pub. by Chatto Bodley Jonathan). Merrimack Bk Serv.
--Pranks, Tricks & Practical Jokes. LC 79-65291. (Illus.). (gr. 3 up). 1979. 5.95 (ISBN 0-8069-4606-7); PLB 6.69 (ISBN 0-8069-4607-5). Sterling.
--Seeing Is Not Believing. LC 79-91401. (Illus.). 96p. (gr. 3-12). 1980. 5.95 (ISBN 0-8069-4615-6); PLB 6.69 (ISBN 0-8069-4615-6). Sterling.
--This Is Your Body. LC 79-65078. (Illus.). (gr. 3-7). 1979. 6.95 (ISBN 0-8069-3112-4); PLB 7.49 (ISBN 0-8069-3113-2). Sterling.
--Total Nonsense Z to A. LC 80-54349. (Illus.). 96p. (gr. 4 up). 1981. 5.95; lib. bdg. 6.69 (ISBN 0-8069-4645-8). Sterling.
Brandrup, Johannes & Immergut, E. H., eds. Polymer Handbook. 2nd ed. LC 74-11381. 1408p. 1975. 50.50 (ISBN 0-471-09804-3, Pub. by Wiley-Interscience). Wiley.
Brandstadt, Wayne, jt. ed. see Zackler, Jack.
Brandstatter, A. F. & Hyman, A. A. Fundamentals of Law Enforcement. (Criminal Justice Ser). 1972. text ed. 14.95x (ISBN 0-02-473740-2). Macmillan.
Brandstatter, Hermann, et al, eds. Dynamics of Group Decisions. LC 78-19143. (Sage Focus Editions: Vol. 5). 1978. 18.95x (ISBN 0-8039-0872-5); pap. 9.95x (ISBN 0-8039-0873-3). Sage.
Brandt, A., et al. Cost-Sharing in Health Care: Proceedings. (Illus.). 184p. 1981. pap. 22.50 (ISBN 0-387-10325-2). Springer-Verlag.
Brandt, Andres von. Fish Catching Methods of the World. 2nd ed. (Illus.). 256p. 19.50 (ISBN 0-85238-026-7, FN). Unipub.
Brandt, Babette. Curator's Choice: Western Edition. Aymar, Brant, ed. 1981. pap. 6.95 (ISBN 0-517-54200-5). Crown.
Brandt, George, ed. British Television Drama. LC 80-41031. (Illus.). 300p. Date not set. price not set (ISBN 0-521-22186-2); pap. price not set (ISBN 0-521-29384-7). Cambridge U Pr.
Brandt, Henry & Landrum, Phil. I Want Happiness Now! 1978. 6.95 (ISBN 0-310-21640-0); pap. 4.95 (ISBN 0-310-21641-9). Zondervan.
--I Want to Enjoy My Children. 160p. 1975. 5.95 (ISBN 0-310-21630-3); pap. 4.95 (ISBN 0-310-21631-1). Zondervan.
Brandt, Henry R. & Dowdy, Homer E. Building a Christian Home. LC 60-53591. 158p. 1960. pap. 2.25 o.p. (ISBN 0-88207-051-7). Victor Bks.
Brandt, Jane L. La Chingada. 1980. pap. write for info. PB.
Brandt, John C. Introduction to the Solar Wind. LC 75-89919. (Illus.). 1970. text ed. 20.95x (ISBN 0-7167-0328-9). W H Freeman.
Brandt, John C. & Maran, Stephen P. New Horizons in Astronomy. 2nd ed. LC 78-11717. (Illus.). 1979. text ed. 21.95x (ISBN 0-7167-1043-9). W H Freeman.
Brandt, John C. & Maran, Stephen P., eds. The New Astronomy & Space Science Reader. LC 76-54316. (Illus.). 1977. text ed. 19.95x (ISBN 0-7167-0350-5); pap. text ed. 9.95x (ISBN 0-7167-0349-1). W H Freeman.
Brandt, Leonore. Raccoon Family Pets. pap. 2.50 (ISBN 0-87666-216-5, AP7500). TFH Pubns.
Brandt, Leslie. Praise the Lord. 48p. 1976. pap. 1.50 (ISBN 0-570-03042-0, 6-1165). Concordia.
--Psalms-Now. LC 73-78108. 1973. 7.50 (ISBN 0-570-03230-X, 15-2125). Concordia.
--Psalms of Strength. (Psalms Now Gift Books). 1977. pap. 1.75 (ISBN 0-570-07450-9, 12-2684). Concordia.
--Why Did This Happen to Me? 1978. pap. 2.25 (ISBN 0-570-03777-8, 12-2724). Concordia.
Brandt, Leslie, tr. Psalms of Comfort. (Psalms Now Gift Books). 1977. pap. 1.75 (ISBN 0-570-07452-5, 12-2686). Concordia.
--Psalms of Joy. (Psalms Now Gift Books). 1977. pap. 1.75 (ISBN 0-570-07451-7, 12-2685). Concordia.
--Psalms of Praise. (Psalms Now Gift Books). 1977. pap. 1.75 (ISBN 0-570-07453-3, 12-2687). Concordia.
Brandt, Leslie F. Prophets Now. 1979. 7.50 (ISBN 0-570-03278-4, 15-2722). Concordia.
Brandt, Patricia, et al. Current Practice in Pediatric Nursing, Vol. 2. LC 75-22183. (Current Practice Ser.). 1978. 12.50 (ISBN 0-8016-0750-7); pap. 9.50 (ISBN 0-8016-0751-5). Mosby.
Brandt, Patricia A. & Chinn, Peggy L. Current Practice in Pediatric Nursing, Vol. 1. LC 75-22183. (Illus.). 242p. 1976. 11.95 o.p. (ISBN 0-8016-0962-3); pap. 8.95 o.p. (ISBN 0-8016-0745-0). Mosby.
Brandt, Richard B., jt. auth. see Alston, William P.
Brandt, Robert L. One Way. (Radiant Life Ser.). 1977. pap. 1.50 (ISBN 0-88243-909-X, 02-0909); teacher's ed 2.50 (ISBN 0-88243-179-X, 32-0179). Gospel Pub.
Brandt, Ronald S., ed. Partners: Parents & Schools. LC 79-90730. 1979. pap. text ed. 4.75 (ISBN 0-87120-096-1, 611-79168). Assn Supervision.
Brandt, Ronald S., ed. see Remy, Richard C.
Brandt, Sue R. Facts About the Fifty States. rev. ed. (First Bks.). (Illus.). (gr. 4 up). 1979. PLB 6.45 s&l (ISBN 0-531-02899-2). Watts.
--First Book of How to Write a Report. LC 68-17702. (First Bks). (Illus.). (gr. 4-6). 1968. PLB 6.45 (ISBN 0-531-00554-2); pap. 0.95 o.p. (ISBN 0-685-21862-7). Watts.
Brandt, W., et al. Craft of Writing. 1969. pap. text ed. 7.95 (ISBN 0-13-188797-1). P-H.
Brandt, Walter I. & Lehmann, Helmut T., eds. Luther's Works: The Christian in Society II, Vol. 45. LC 55-9893. 1962. 15.95 (ISBN 0-8006-0345-1, 1-345). Fortress.
Brandt, William, et al. The Comprehensive Study of Music: Basic Principles of Music Theory, Vol. II. 1980. scp 16.50 (ISBN 0-06-040921-5, HarpC). Har-Row.
Brandys, Kazimierz. A Question of Reality: A Novel of Poland. Barzun, Isabel, tr. 1980. 8.95 (ISBN 0-684-16599-6). Scribner.
Branford, William. Elements of English: An Introduction to the Principles of the Study of Language. 1967. text ed. 7.25x (ISBN 0-7100-1106-7). Humanities.
Brangham, A. N. Provence. (History, People & Places Ser.). (Illus.). 1978. 12.50 o.p. (ISBN 0-904978-15-X). Hippocrene Bks.
Brangwyn, Frank & Preston, Hayter. Windmills. LC 70-176821. (Illus.). 126p. 1975. Repr. of 1923 ed. 20.00 (ISBN 0-8103-4077-1). Gale.
Branham, Richard L. & Stuhr, David D. A Language of Form: The Isometric Theory. LC 80-82996. 496p. 1980. pap. text ed. 22.95 (ISBN 0-8403-2291-7). Kendall-Hunt.
Branica, M., ed. see International Experts Discussion on Lead Occurrence, Fate & Pollution in the Marine Environment, Rovinj, Yugoslavia, 18-22 October 1977.
Branick, Vincent. Mary, the Spirit & the Church. LC 80-82856. 128p. (Orig.). 1981. pap. 4.95 (ISBN 0-8091-2343-6). Paulist Pr.
Branigan, Keith. Atlas of Ancient Civilizations. LC 75-22115. (John Day Bk.). (Illus.). 1976. 12.95 o.s.i. (ISBN 0-381-98284-X, TYC-T). T Y Crowell.
Branigan, Keith, et al. Hellas: The Civilization of Ancient Greece. LC 80-18306. (Illus.). 224p. 1980. 39.95 (ISBN 0-07-007229-9). McGraw.
Brankon, Robin. Good Crewman. (Illus.). 1979. 7.95 o.p. (ISBN 0-229-11502-0). Scribner.
Branley, Franklyn. Air Is All Around You. LC 62-7738. (A Let's-Read-&-Find-Out Science Bk). (Illus.). (gr. k-3). 1962. PLB 7.89 (ISBN 0-690-05356-8, TYC-J). T Y Crowell.
Branley, Franklyn M. The Beginning of the Earth. LC 79-184979. (A Let's-Read-&-Find-Out Science Book). (Illus.). (gr. k-3). 1972. 6.95 o.p. (ISBN 0-690-12987-4, TYC-J); PLB 7.89 (ISBN 0-690-12988-2). T Y Crowell.
--Big Dipper. LC 62-10999. (A Let's-Read-&-Find-Out Science Bk). (Illus.). (gr. k-3). 1962. PLB 7.89 (ISBN 0-690-01116-4, TYC-J). T Y Crowell.
--Book of Mars for You. LC 68-11058. (Illus.). (gr. 3-6). 1968. 8.95 o.p. (ISBN 0-690-15295-7, TYC-J); PLB 8.79 (ISBN 0-690-15296-5). T Y Crowell.
--Book of Planet Earth for You. LC 74-30408. (Illus.). 96p. (gr. 3-6). 1975. 8.79 (ISBN 0-690-00754-X, TYC-J). T Y Crowell.
--Book of Venus for You. LC 73-78256. (Illus.). (gr. 3-6). 1969. 8.95 (ISBN 0-690-15792-4, TYC-J); PLB 8.79 o.p. (ISBN 0-690-15793-2). T Y Crowell.
--Color: From Rainbows to Lasers. LC 76-46304. (Illus.). (gr. 6 up). 1978. 8.95 o.p. (ISBN 0-690-01256-X, TYC-J); PLB 8.79 (ISBN 0-690-03847-X). T Y Crowell.
--Comets, Meteoroids & Asteroids: Mavericks of the Solar System. LC 73-16043. (Exploring Our Universe Ser.). (Illus.). (gr. 7 up). 1974. 8.95 (ISBN 0-690-20176-1, TYC-J). T Y Crowell.
--The Earth: Planet Number Three. LC 66-12668. (Exploring Our Universe Ser.). (Illus.). (gr. 7 up). 1966. 8.95 (ISBN 0-690-25022-3, TYC-J). T Y Crowell.
--Eclipse: Darkness in Daytime. LC 73-3492. (A Let's-Read-&-Find-Out Science Bk). (Illus.). (gr. k-3). 1973. PLB 7.89 (ISBN 0-690-25414-8, TYC-J). T Y Crowell.
--Feast or Famine? The Energy Future. LC 79-7817. (Illus.). 128p. (gr. 5 up). 1980. 7.95 (ISBN 0-690-04040-7, TYC-J); PLB 7.89 (ISBN 0-690-04041-5). T Y Crowell.
--Flash, Crash, Rumble, & Roll. LC 64-18161. (A Let's-Read-&-Find-Out Science Bk). (Illus.). (gr. k-3). 1964. PLB 7.89 (ISBN 0-690-30563-X, TYC-J). T Y Crowell.
--Floating and Sinking. LC 67-15396. (A Let's-Read-&-Find-Out Science Bk). (Illus.). (gr. k-3). 1967. bds. 6.95 o.p. (ISBN 0-690-30917-1, TYC-J); PLB 7.89 (ISBN 0-690-30918-X). T Y Crowell.
--Gravity Is a Mystery. LC 70-101922. (A Let's-Read-and-Find-Out Science Bk). (Illus.). (gr. k-3). 1970. 7.95 (ISBN 0-690-35071-6, TYC-J); PLB 7.89 (ISBN 0-690-35072-4). T Y Crowell.
--Guide to Outer Space. LC 59-13620. (Illus.). (gr. 4-6). 1960. PLB 6.95 (ISBN 0-87396-002-5). Stravon.
--High Sounds, Low Sounds. LC 67-23662. (A Let's-Read-&-Find-Out Science Bk). (Illus.). (gr. k-3). 1967. 6.95 o.p. (ISBN 0-690-38017-8, TYC-J); PLB 7.89 (ISBN 0-690-38018-6); filmstrip with record 11.95 (ISBN 0-690-38019-4); filmstrip with cassette 14.95 (ISBN 0-690-38021-6). T Y Crowell.
--How Little, & How Much: A Book About Scales. LC 75-43643. (Young Math Ser.). (Illus.). 40p. (gr. k-3). 1976. PLB 7.89 (ISBN 0-690-01058-3, TYC-J). T Y Crowell.
--Lodestar: Rocket Ship to Mars. LC 51-764. (gr. 5-9). 1951. 7.95 o.p. (ISBN 0-690-50443-8, TYC-J). T Y Crowell.
--Measure with Metric. LC 74-4056. (Young Math Ser.). (Illus.). 40p. (gr. k-3). 1975. PLB 7.89 (ISBN 0-690-01117-2, TYC-J); pap. 2.95 (ISBN 0-690-01265-9, TYC-J); filmstrip with record 11.95 (ISBN 0-690-00996-8); filmstrip with cassette 14.95 (ISBN 0-690-00997-6). T Y Crowell.
--Moon Seems to Change. LC 60-8796. (A Let's-Read-&-Find-Out Science Bk). (Illus.). (gr. k-3). 1960. PLB 7.89 (ISBN 0-690-55485-0, TYC-J). T Y Crowell.
--North, South, East, & West. LC 66-14486. (A Let's-Read-&-Find-Out Science Bk). (Illus.). (gr. k-3). 1966. PLB 7.89 (ISBN 0-690-58609-4, TYC-J). T Y Crowell.
--Oxygen Keeps You Alive. LC 73-139093. (A Let's-Read-&-Find-Out Science Bk). (Illus.). (gr. k-3). 1971. 7.95 (ISBN 0-690-60702-4, TYC-J); PLB 7.89 (ISBN 0-690-60703-2); filmstrip with record 11.95 (ISBN 0-690-60704-0); filmstrip with cassette 14.95 (ISBN 0-690-60706-7). T Y Crowell.
--Pieces of Another World: The Story of Moon Rocks. LC 71-158684. (Illus.). (gr. 5-8). 1972. PLB 9.89 (ISBN 0-690-62566-9, TYC-J). T Y Crowell.
--Rain & Hail. LC 63-12649. (A Let's-Read-&-Find-Out Science Bk). (Illus.). (gr. k-3). 1963. 6.95 o.p. (ISBN 0-690-66844-9, TYC-J). T Y Crowell.
--Rockets & Satellites. rev. ed. LC 73-101923. (A Let's-Read-&-Find-Out Science Bk). (Illus.). (gr. k-3). 1970. 6.95 o.p. (ISBN 0-690-70820-3, TYC-J). T Y Crowell.
--Roots Are Food Finders. LC 74-23924. (A Let's Read & Find Out Bk). (Illus.). 40p. (gr. k-3). 1975. PLB 7.89 (ISBN 0-690-00703-5, TYC-J). T Y Crowell.
--Snow Is Falling. LC 63-15084. (A Let's-Read-&-Find-Out Science Bk). (Illus.). (gr. k-3). 1963. bds. 7.95 (ISBN 0-690-74299-1, TYC-J); PLB 7.89 (ISBN 0-690-74300-9). T Y Crowell.
--Sun Dogs & Shooting Stars: A Skywatcher's Calendar. (gr. 5 up). 1980. 6.95 (ISBN 0-395-29520-3). HM.
--Sun: Our Nearest Star. LC 60-13241. (A Let's-Read-&-Find-Out Science Bk). (Illus.). (gr. k-3). 1961. PLB 7.89 (ISBN 0-690-79483-5, TYC-J). T Y Crowell.
--Sunshine Makes the Seasons. LC 73-19694. (A Let's Read & Find Out Science Bk). (Illus.). 40p. (ps-3). 1974. PLB 7.89 (ISBN 0-690-00438-9, TYC-J). T Y Crowell.
--Think Metric! LC 72-78279. (Illus.). (gr. 3-6). 1973. 7.95 (ISBN 0-690-81861-0, TYC-J); PLB 7.89 (ISBN 0-690-81862-9). T Y Crowell.
--Weight & Weightlessness. LC 70-132292. (A Let's-Read-and-Find-Out Science Bk). (Illus.). (gr. k-3). 1972. PLB 7.89 (ISBN 0-690-87329-8, TYC-J). T Y Crowell.
--What Makes Day & Night. LC 60-8258. (A Let's-Read-&-Find-Out Science Bk). (Illus.). (gr. k-3). 1961. PLB 7.89 (ISBN 0-690-87790-0, TYC-J). T Y Crowell.
Branley, Franklyn M. & Vaughan, Eleanor K. Rusty Rings a Bell. LC 57-7492. (Illus.). (gr. k-3). 1957. 3.95 o.p. (ISBN 0-690-71601-X, TYC-J); PLB 5.79 (ISBN 0-690-71602-8). T Y Crowell.
Branley, Franklyn M., jt. auth. see Beeler, Nelson F.
Brann, Donald R. Brann's Guide to Home Improvement. LC 63-9605. (Illus.). 1963. 8.95 (ISBN 0-8303-0053-8). Fleet.
--Bricklaying Simplified. LC 77-140968. 1979. pap. 5.95 (ISBN 0-87733-668-7). Easi-Bild.
--Carpeting Simplified. LC 72-91055. (Illus.). 1980. pap. 5.95 (ISBN 0-87733-683-0). Easi-Bild.
--Concrete Work Simplified. LC 66-24876. 1980. pap. 5.95 (ISBN 0-87733-617-2). Easi-Bild.
--How to Add an Extra Bathroom. rev. ed. LC 68-18108. 1976. lib. bdg. 5.95 (ISBN 0-87733-082-4); pap. 5.95 (ISBN 0-87733-682-2). Easi-Bild.
--How to Build a Kayak. LC 75-2652. 1978. pap. 5.95 (ISBN 0-87733-757-8). Easi-Bild.
--How to Build a One Car Garage-Carport-Stable. rev. ed. LC 72-88709. 1973. lib. bdg. 5.95 (ISBN 0-87733-800-0); pap. 5.95 (ISBN 0-87733-680-6). Easi-Bild.
--How to Build a Patio, Porch, & Sundeck. LC 78-55238. 1979. pap. 5.95 (ISBN 0-87733-781-0). Easi-Bild.
--How to Build a Stable & a Red Barn Tool House. LC 72-88710. (Illus.). 1973. lib. bdg. 5.95 (ISBN 0-87733-079-4); pap. 5.95 (ISBN 0-87733-679-2). Easi-Bild.
--How to Build & Enclose a Porch. rev. ed. LC 65-18912. 1978. pap. 3.00 o.p. (ISBN 0-87733-613-X). Easi-Bild.
--How to Build Bars. LC 67-15263. 1979. pap. 5.95 (ISBN 0-87733-690-3). Easi-Bild.
--How to Build Bookcases & Stereo Cabinets. LC 79-56769. (Illus.). 194p. 1980. pap. 5.95 (ISBN 0-87733-804-3). Easi-Bild.
--How to Build Collectors' Display Cases. LC 78-57773. (Illus.). 194p. 1979. pap. 6.95 (ISBN 0-87733-792-6). Easi-Bild.
--How to Build Greenhouses - Walk-in, Window, Sun House, Garden Tool House. LC 80-67650. 210p. 1980. pap. 5.95 (ISBN 0-87733-811-6). Easi-Bild.
--How to Build Outdoor Projects. 210p. 1981. pap. 5.95 (ISBN 0-87733-807-8). Easi-Bild.
--How to Build Patios & Sundecks. rev. ed. LC 66-24279. 1976. lib. bdg. 5.95 (ISBN 0-87733-031-X); pap. 3.50 o.p. (ISBN 0-87733-631-8). Easi-Bild.
--How to Build Storage Units. rev. ed. LC 65-19666. 1965. lib. bdg. 5.95 (ISBN 0-87733-034-4); pap. 3.00 o.p. (ISBN 0-87733-634-2). Easi-Bild.
--How to Find a Job, Start a Business, Learn to Offer What Others Want to Buy. LC 80-65878. 194p. 1981. pap. 6.95 (ISBN 0-87733-850-7). Easi-Bild.
--How to Install Paneling, Make Valances, Cornices. LC 65-25756. 1979. pap. 5.95 (ISBN 0-87733-605-9). Easi-Bild.
--How to Install Protective Alarm Devices. rev ed. LC 72-89141. (Illus.). 1975. lib. bdg. 5.95 (ISBN 0-87733-095-6); pap. 5.95 (ISBN 0-87733-695-4). Easi-Bild.
--How to Modernize a Kitchen. rev. ed. LC 67-16947. 1976. lib. bdg. 5.95 (ISBN 0-87733-008-5); pap. 3.50 (ISBN 0-87733-608-3). Easi-Bild.
--How to Rehabilitate an Abandoned Building. Bk. 685. LC 73-87513. 258p. 1974. lib. bdg. 6.95 (ISBN 0-87733-085-9); pap. 5.95 o.p. (ISBN 0-87733-685-7). Easi-Bild.
--How to Transform a Garage into Living Space. Bk. 684. LC 72-92125. (Illus.). 128p. 1974. lib. bdg. 5.95 (ISBN 0-87733-084-0); pap. 5.95 (ISBN 0-87733-684-9). Easi-Bild.
--Plumbing Repairs Simplified. rev. ed. LC 67-27691. 1976. pap. 5.95 (ISBN 0-87733-750-0). Easi-Bild.
Brannen, Noah, jt. auth. see Thorlin, Eldora.

Brannen, William H. Practical Marketing for Your Small Retail Business. (Illus.). 272p. 1981. 16.95 (ISBN 0-13-692764-5, Spec); pap. 8.95 (ISBN 0-13-692756-4). P-H.

Branner, Robert. Manuscript Painting in Paris During the Reign of St. Louis. LC 73-78514. (Studies in the History of Art). (Illus.). 1977. 65.00x (ISBN 0-520-02462-1). U of Cal Pr.

Branner, Robert, ed. Chartres Cathedral. (Norton Critical Studies in Art History). (Illus.). 1969. pap. 7.95x (ISBN 0-393-09851-6, NortonC). Norton.

Brannigan, Gary, jt. auth. see Tolor, Alexander.

Branningan, Marilyn, jt. auth. see Biklen, Sari K.

Brannon, Robert, jt. auth. see David, Deborah S.

Branover, H. MHD Flows & Turbulence: Proceedings. 1977. 39.95 (ISBN 0-470-99061-9). Halsted Pr.

Branover, Herman. Magnetohydrodynamic Flow in Ducts. LC 78-67721. 1979. 54.95x (ISBN 0-470-26539-6). Halsted Pr.

Branscum, Robbie. Toby & Johnny Joe. 80p. 1981. pap. 1.75 (ISBN 0-380-52670-0, 52670). Avon.

Bransford, John D. Human Cognition: Learning, Understanding & Remembering. 1979. pap. text ed. 12.95x (ISBN 0-534-00699-X). Wadsworth Pub.

Bransome, Edwin D., Jr., jt. auth. see McFarland, Kay F.

Branson, Branley A. & Batch, Donald L. Fishes of the Red River Drainage, Eastern Kentucky. LC 73-80459. (Illus.). 76p. 1974. pap. 4.50x (ISBN 0-8131-1295-8). U Pr of Ky.

Branson, Dorothy. Methods in Clinical Bacteriology: A Manual of Tests & Procedures. (American Lectures in Clinical Microbiology Ser.). 240p. 1972. pap. 14.75 (ISBN 0-398-02241-0). C C Thomas.

Branson, Gary D. Home Maintenance & Repair: Walls, Ceilings, & Floors. (Illus.). 1977. pap. 6.95 (ISBN 0-672-23281-2, 23281). Audel.

Branson, Joan C. & Lennox, Margaret. Hotel, Hostel & Hospital Housekeeping. 3rd ed. (Illus.). 1976. pap. 12.95x (ISBN 0-7131-1974-8). Intl Ideas.

Branson, Karen. Streets of Gold. 160p. (gr. 10 up). 1981. 7.95 (ISBN 0-399-20791-0). Putnam.

Branson, O. T. Indian Jewelry Making, Vol. 1. (Illus.). 1977. pap. 7.95 (ISBN 0-918080-15-0). Treasure Chest.

Branson, Oscar T. What You Need to Know About Your Gold & Silver. (Illus.). 56p. (Orig.). 1980. pap. 4.95 (ISBN 0-918080-44-4). Treasure Chest.

Branston, A. J. Thematic & Topical Stamp Collecting. (Illus.). 192p. 1980. 24.00 (ISBN 0-7134-1974-1, Pub. by Batsford England). David & Charles.

Branston, Brian. Gods, & Heroes from Viking Mythology. (Illus.). 1978. 12.95 (ISBN 0-85654-029-3, Pub. by Two Continents). Hippocrene Bks.

Brant, Carroll. Transistor Ignition Systems. LC 76-43635. (Illus.). 1976. 8.95 o.p. (ISBN 0-8306-6882-9); pap. 5.95 (ISBN 0-8306-5882-3, 882). TAB Bks.

Brant, David A., ed. Solution Properties of Polysaccharides. (ACS Symposium Ser.: No. 150). 1981. price not set (ISBN 0-8412-0609-0). Am Chemical.

Brant, George. Introductory Animal Science. 1980. perfect binding 7.95 (ISBN 0-88252-112-8). Paladin Hse.

Brant, Henry & Lamdrum, Phil, trs. Quero Melhorar Meu Casamento. (Portuguese Bks.). 1979. 1.25 (ISBN 0-8297-0669-0). Life Pubs Intl.

Brant, Henry & Landrum, Phil, trs. Quiero Mejorar Mi Matrimonio. (Spanish Bks.). (Span.). 1977. 1.90 (ISBN 0-8297-0778-6). Life Pubs Intl.

Brant, Sandra & Cullman, Elissa. Small Folk: A Celebration of Childhood in America. (Illus.). 192p. 1981. 29.95 (ISBN 0-525-93131-7). Dutton.

Brant, Sebastian. Shyp of Folys of the Worlde. Barcley, Alexander, tr. LC 74-25743. (English Experience Ser.: No. 229). 1970. Repr. of 1509 ed. 76.00 (ISBN 90-221-0229-7). Walter J Johnson.

Brantingham, Patricia L. & Blomberg, Thomas G., eds. Courts & Diversion: Policy & Operations Studies. (Sage Research Progress Ser. in Criminology: Vol. 14). (Illus.). 1979. 12.95x (ISBN 0-8039-1321-4); pap. 6.50x (ISBN 0-8039-1322-2). Sage.

Brantingham, Paul J. & Kress, Jack M., eds. Structure, Law, & Power: Essays in the Sociology of Law. LC 79-18127. (Sage Research Progress Ser. in Criminology: Vol. 13). (Illus.). 1979. 12.95x (ISBN 0-8039-1318-4); pap. 6.50x (ISBN 0-8039-1319-2). Sage.

Brantley, C. Owen. One Hundred & Forty Four Ways to Sell Printing by Mail. LC 72-6609. 1972. 24.50 (ISBN 0-912920-23-8). North Am Pub Co.

Branton, D. & Deamer, D. W. Membrane Structure. Alfert, M., et al, eds. (Protoplasmatologia: Vol. 2, Pt. E1, 2, 3). (Illus.). 70p. 1972. 24.80 o.p. (ISBN 0-387-81031-5). Springer-Verlag.

Branton, Danialle. The Great Lover. 1978. pap. 1.95 o.p. (ISBN 0-449-14039-3, GM). Fawcett.

Branwood. Diagnosis & Interpretations of Changing Patterns in Multiple Disease States. 1981. price not set (ISBN 0-89352-025-X). Masson Pub.

Branyan, Robert L. The Eisenhower Administration, Nineteen Fifty-Three to Nineteen Sixty-One: A Documentary History, 2 vols. LC 71-164935. 1971. Set. lib. bdg. 85.00 (ISBN 0-313-20126-9). Greenwood.

Branyon, Brenda. Outstanding Women Who Promoted the Concept of the Unified School Library & Audio Visual Program. 375p. 1981. 20.00 (ISBN 0-686-69458-9). Hi Willow.

Brasch, Charles. Indirections. (Illus.). 450p. 1980. 33.00x (ISBN 0-19-558050-8). Oxford U Pr.

Brasch, Thomas. Der Schoene 27. September. 100p. (Ger.). 1980. pap. 6.50 (ISBN 3-518-02264-4, Pub. by Insel Verlag Germany). Suhrkamp.

Brascho, Donn J. & Shawker, Thomas H. Abdominal Ultrasound in the Cancer Patient. LC 80-15838. (Diagnostic & Therapeutic Radiology Ser.). 380p. 1980. 39.50 (ISBN 0-471-01742-6, Pub. by WileyMed). Wiley.

Brase, Charles H., jt. auth. see Brase, Corrinne P.

Brase, Corrinne P. & Brase, Charles H. Basic Algebra for College Students. LC 75-26093. (Illus.). 480p. 1976. text ed. 14.25 (ISBN 0-395-20656-1); options guide & solutions manual 1.75 (ISBN 0-395-20655-3). HM.

Brasel, jt. auth. see Kretchmer.

Brashear, H. Robert & Raney, R. Beverly. Shand's Handbook of Orthopaedic Surgery. 9th ed. LC 78-65. 1978. text ed. 29.95 (ISBN 0-8016-4082-2). Mosby.

Brashear, Richard E. & Rhodes, Mitchell L. Chronic Obstructive Lung Disease: Clinical Treatment & Management. new ed. LC 77-18551. (Illus.). 1978. text ed. 37.50 (ISBN 0-8016-0753-1). Mosby.

Brashear, William R. The Gorgon's Head: A Study in Tragedy & Despair. LC 76-491558. 164p. 1977. 12.00x (ISBN 0-8203-0417-4). U of Ga Pr.

Brasher, N. H. Arguments in History: Britain in the 19th Century. LC 68-10753. (Illus.). 1969. 15.95 (ISBN 0-312-04900-5). St Martin.

Brasher, Rex. Birds & Trees of North America, 2 vols. McGaw, Lisa, ed. (Illus.). 1962. Set. 115.00x o.p. (ISBN 0-87471-299-8). Rowman.

Brasher, Ruth E. & Garrison, Carolyn L. Modern Household Equipment. Date not set. 11.50 (ISBN 0-02-313540-9). Macmillan. Postponed.

Brasher, Thomas L., ed. see Whitman, Walt.

Brashers, H. C. Other Side of Love: Two Novellas. LC 63-11820. 88p. (Orig.). 1963. pap. 2.65 (ISBN 0-8040-0237-1, 49). Swallow.

Brashler, William. The Don: The Life & Death of Sam Giancana. LC 76-5113. 1977. 10.95 o.p. (ISBN 0-06-010447-3, HarpT). Har-Row.

--Josh Gibson: A Life in the Negro Leagues. LC 77-83861. (Illus.). 1978. 9.95 o.s.i. (ISBN 0-06-010446-5, HarpT). Har-Row.

Brashler, William, jt. auth. see Janus, Christopher G.

Brasier, M. D. Microfossils. (Illus., Orig.). 1980. text ed. 27.50x (ISBN 0-04-562001-6); pap. text ed. 14.95x (ISBN 0-04-562002-4). Allen Unwin.

Brasil, Emanuel, jt. ed. see Bishop, Elizabeth.

Brass, George A., jt. auth. see Castaldi, C. R.

Brass, Paul R. Factional Politics in an Indian State: The Congress Party in Uttar Pradesh. 1965. 20.00x (ISBN 0-520-00167-2). U of Cal Pr.

Brasseur, R. International Legislation & Fiscality of Hydrocarbons, Parts 1-8. Incl. Pt. 1 (ISBN 0-87201-950-0); Pt. 2 (ISBN 0-87201-951-9); Pt. 3 (ISBN 0-87201-952-7); Pt. 4; Pt. 5 (ISBN 0-87201-954-3); Pt. 6 (ISBN 0-87201-955-1); Pt. 7 (ISBN 0-87201-956-X); Pt. 8 (ISBN 0-87201-957-8). write for info. Gulf Pub.

Brasseur De Bourbourg, E. Ch. Histoire De Canada, De Son Eglise et De Ses Missions. (Canadiana Avant 1867: No. 4). 1968. 65.25x (ISBN 90-2796-333-9). Mouton.

Brasunas, Anton, ed. see Symposium on Corrosion Fundamentals.

Braswell, Michael, jt. auth. see Taylor, William.

Braswell, Michael, et al, eds. Approaches to Counseling & Psychotherapy: A Brief Overview of Issues, Systems, & Applications. LC 79-6845. 154p. 1980. pap. text ed. 7.75 (ISBN 0-8191-0964-9). U Pr of Amer.

Brata, Sashthi. A Search for Home. 152p. 1975. pap. 2.50 (ISBN 0-88253-771-7). Ind-US Inc.

Bratcher, R. G. A New Testament Wordbook for Translators, Pt. 2. (Exegetical Articles Ser.). 1964. pap. 2.00 (ISBN 0-8267-0019-5, 08637). United Bible.

Bratcher, R. G. & Nida, E. A. Translators Handbook on Mark. (Helps for Translators Ser.). 1976. Repr. of 1961 ed. soft cover 4.60 (ISBN 0-8267-0135-3, 08501). United Bible.

Bratcher, R. G., ed. Marginal Notes for the New Testament. 1980. softcover 2.30 (ISBN 0-8267-0026-8, 08558). United Bible.

--Marginal Notes for the Old Testament. 1980. softcover 2.50 (ISBN 0-8267-0025-X, 08557). United Bible.

--New Testament Index. 1963. pap. 0.50 (ISBN 0-8267-0003-9, 08507). United Bible.

--Old Testament Quotations in the New Testament. rev. ed. 1980. Repr. of 1967 ed. softcover 1.25 (ISBN 0-8267-0000-4, 08503). United Bible.

--Section Headings for the New Testament. 1961. pap. 0.85 (ISBN 0-8267-0001-2, 08505). United Bible.

--Short Bible Reference System. 1961. soft cover 2.85 (ISBN 0-686-14410-4, 08506). United Bible.

Bratcher, R. G. & Thompson, J. A., eds. Bible Index. 1970. pap. 1.00 (ISBN 0-8267-0005-5, 08511). United Bible.

--A Short Index to the Bible. 1973. pap. 1.15 (ISBN 0-8267-0007-1, 08519). United Bible.

Bratcher, R. G., et al. A New Testament Wordbook for Translators, Pt. 1. (Translational Articles Ser.). 1966. pap. 1.00 (ISBN 0-8267-0020-9, 08638). United Bible.

Bratcher, Robert G. & Nida, Eugene A. A Translators Handbook on Paul's Letters to the Colossians & to Philemon. (Helps for Translators Ser.). 1977. softcover 2.40 (ISBN 0-8267-0145-0, 08529). United Bible.

Brater, E. F., jt. auth. see Wisler, Chester O.

Brathwait, Richard. The English Gentleman: Containing Sundry Excellent Rules - How to Demeane or Accomodate Himselfe in the Manage of Publike or Private Affairs. LC 74-28836. (English Experience Ser.: No. 717). 1975. Repr. of 1630 ed. 35.00 (ISBN 90-221-0717-5). Walter J Johnson.

Brathwaite, Edward. Mother Poem. 1977. pap. text ed. 9.95x (ISBN 0-19-211859-5). Oxford U Pr.

Braton, Norman R. Cryogenic Recycling & Processing. 272p. 1980. 67.95 (ISBN 0-8493-5779-9). CRC Pr.

Braton, Norman R., jt. auth. see Lindberg, Roy A.

Bratos, S. & Pick, R. M., eds. Vibrational Spectroscopy of Molecular Liquids & Solids. (NATO Advanced Study Institutes Ser., Ser. B: Physics: Vol. 56). 475p. 1980. 49.50 (ISBN 0-306-40445-1, Plenum Pr). Plenum Pub.

Bratteli, O. & Robinson, D. W., eds. Operators Algebra & Quantum Statistical Mechanics, Vol. II: Equilibrium States; Models. (Texts & Monographs in Physics Ser.). 496p. 1981. 46.00 (ISBN 0-387-10381-3). Springer-Verlag.

Bratton, Esther C., jt. auth. see Steidl, Rose E.

Bratton, Fred G. History of the Bible. 1959. pap. 5.25 o.p. (ISBN 0-8070-1353-6, BP239). Beacon Pr.

Bratton, Michael. The Local Politics of Rural Development: Peasant & Party-State in Zambia. LC 79-56775. (Illus.). 350p. 1980. text ed. 17.50x (ISBN 0-87451-178-X). U Pr of New Eng.

Bratus, B. V. Russian Intonation. LC 78-82443. 149p. 1972. text ed. 28.00 (ISBN 0-08-012535-2). Pergamon.

Brau, M. M. Island in the Crossroads: The History of Puerto Rico. LC 68-17802. (gr. 6 up). 1968. 4.95 o.p. (ISBN 0-385-06170-6); pap. 2.50 o.p. (ISBN 0-385-06171-4). Doubleday.

Brauchli, Jakob. Der Englische Schauerroman um 1880 unter Berucksichtigung der unbekannten Bucher. Bleiler, E. F., ed. LC 78-60913. (The Fiction of Popular Culture Ser.: Vol. 2). 260p. 1979. lib. bdg. 26.00 (ISBN 0-8240-9666-5). Garland Pub.

Braude, Benjamin & Lewis, Bernard, eds. Christians & Jews in the Ottoman Empire, Vol. 1: The Central Lands. LC 80-11337. 1981. text ed. 40.00x (ISBN 0-8419-0519-3). Holmes & Meier.

--Christians & Jews in the Ottoman Empire, Vol. 2: The Arabic-Speaking Lands. LC 80-11337. 1981. text ed. 30.00x (ISBN 0-8419-0520-7). Holmes & Meier.

Braude, Lee. A Sense of Sociology. rev. ed. LC 79-20785. 160p. 1981. Repr. of 1974 ed. write for info. (ISBN 0-89874-016-9). Krieger.

--Work & Workers: A Sociological Analysis. rev. ed. LC 79-20996. 240p. 1981. Repr. of 1975 ed. lib. bdg. write for info. (ISBN 0-89874-017-7). Krieger.

Braude, M. C., et al, eds. Narcotic Antagonists. LC 73-84113. (Advances in Biochemical Psychopharmacology Ser.: Vol. 8). (Illus.). 580p. 1974. 48.00 (ISBN 0-911216-55-3). Raven.

Braude, Michael. Bruce Learns About Life Insurance. (Career Guidance Ser.). (Illus.). (gr. 3-6). PLB 2.00 o.p. (ISBN 0-513-00312-6). Denison.

Braude, Monique, ed. Substance Abuse: Genetic, Perinatal, & Developmental Aspects. Date not set. text ed. write for info. (ISBN 0-89004-413-9). Raven.

Braude, Monique C. & Szara, Stephen, eds. Pharmacology of Marihuana, 2 vols. LC 75-14562. (National Institute on Drug Abuse Monograph). 901p. 1976. Set. 68.50 (ISBN 0-89004-067-2). Raven.

Braude, William G. & Kapstein, Israel J., trs. from Heb. Tanna Debe Eliyyahu. 660p. 1980. 27.50 (ISBN 0-8276-0174-3). Jewish Pubn.

Braudel, Fernand. The Mediterranean & the Mediterranean World in the Age of Philip Second, 2 vols. rev. 2nd ed. Reynolds, Sian, tr. from Fr. (Illus.). 1418p. 1976. Vol. 1. pap. 8.95 (ISBN 0-06-090566-2, CN566, CN); Vol. 2. pap. 9.95 (ISBN 0-06-090567-0, CN567, CN). Har-Row.

--The Mediterranean & the Mediterranean World in the Age of Philip II, Vol. 1. Reynolds, Sian, tr. from Fr. LC 72-138708. (Illus.). 640p. 1972. 20.00 o.s.i. (ISBN 0-06-010452-X, HarpT). Har-Row.

--The Mediterranean & the Mediterranean World in the Age of Philip II, Vol. 2. Reynolds, Sian, tr. from Fr. LC 72-138708. (Illus.). 656p. 1974. 20.00 o.s.i. (ISBN 0-06-010456-2, HarpT). Har-Row.

--On History. Matthews, Sarah, tr. from Fr. LC 80-11201. 1980. lib. bdg. 15.00x (ISBN 0-226-07150-2). U of Chicago Pr.

Braudy, Leo. World in a Frame: What We See in Films. LC 75-6151. 1977. pap. 3.95 (ISBN 0-385-03605-1, Anchor Pr). Doubleday.

Braudy, Leo, ed. Norman Mailer: A Collection of Critical Essays. 1972. pap. 1.95 (ISBN 0-13-545541-3, STC101, Spec). P-H.

Braue, Frederick, jt. auth. see Hugard, Jean.

Brauer, Barbara S. Steam Cooking Now! LC 80-82174. (Illus.). 1980. pap. 2.50 (ISBN 0-915942-15-1). Owlswood Prods.

Brauer, Bil, jt. auth. see Fox, Siv C.

Brauer, Carl M. John F. Kennedy & the Second Reconstruction. 1979. pap. 8.00x (ISBN 0-231-08367-X). Columbia U Pr.

--John F. Kennedy & the Second Reconstruction. LC 76-57686. (Contemporary American History Ser.). 1977. 20.00x (ISBN 0-231-03862-3). Columbia U Pr.

Brauer, D. R. Harold, the Easter Rat. 1981. 4.95 (ISBN 0-8062-1631-X). Carlton.

Brauer, F. & Nohel, J. A. Ordinary Differential Equations: A First Course. 2nd ed. 1973. 15.75 o.p. (ISBN 0-8053-1208-0). Benjamin-Cummings.

Brauer, Jerald C. Images of Religion in America. Wolf, Richard C., ed. LC 67-22984. (Facet Bks). 48p. 1967. pap. 1.00 (ISBN 0-8006-3040-8, 1-3040). Fortress.

Brauer, Richard. Richard Brauer: Collected Papers, 3 vols. Wong, Warren & Fong, Paul, eds. 888p. 1980. Vol. 1. text ed. 55.00x (ISBN 0-262-02135-8); Vol. 2. text ed. 55.00x (ISBN 0-262-02148-X); Vol. 3. text ed. 55.00x (ISBN 0-262-02149-8). MIT Pr.

Brauer, W. Net Theory & Applications Proceedings: Proceedings. (Lecture Notes in Computer Science Ser.: Vol. 84). 537p. 1980. pap. 29.50 (ISBN 0-387-10001-6). Springer-Verlag.

Brault, Gerard J. Early Blazon: Heraldic Terminology in the Twelfth & Thirteenth Centuries; with Special Reference to Arthurian Literature. (Illus.). 328p. 1972. text ed. 45.00x (ISBN 0-19-822337-4). Oxford U Pr.

Braum, Myron, jt. auth. see Jacobs, Jack.

Braun & Collingridge. Technology & Survival. (Sicon Bks.). 1977. 3.95 (ISBN 0-408-71301-1). Butterworths.

Braun, A. C. & Stonier, T. Morphology & Physiology of Plant Tumors. (Protoplasmatologia: Vol. 10, Pt. 5a). (Illus.). 1958. 24.80 o.p. (ISBN 0-387-80492-7). Springer-Verlag.

Braun, Armin C. Cancer Problem. LC 77-90432. (Molecular Biology Ser). (Illus.). 1969. 20.00x (ISBN 0-231-02938-1). Columbia U Pr.

--Story of Cancer: On Its Nature, Causes, & Treatment. LC 77-13936. 1978. text ed. 24.50 (ISBN 0-201-00318-X, Adv Bk Prog); pap. text ed. 12.50 (ISBN 0-201-00319-8). A-W.

Braun, Aurel. Romanian Policy Since 1965: The Political & Military Limits of Autonomy. LC 78-9516. (Praeger Special Studies). 1978. 25.95 (ISBN 0-03-043471-8). Praeger.

Braun, D., et al. Techniques of Polymer Synthesis & Characterization. 282p. 1972. 24.50 o.p. (ISBN 0-471-09805-1, Pub. by Wiley). Krieger.

Braun, D. Duane. Sociology. (Cliffs Course Outlines Ser.). (Orig.). 1971. pap. 4.95 (ISBN 0-8220-1502-1). Cliffs.

--Sociology & History of American Music & Dance, 1920-1968. 1969. pap. 3.00 o.p. (ISBN 0-89039-152-1). Ann Arbor FL.

--Toward a Theory of Popular Culture: The Sociology & History of American Music & Dance 1920-1968. (gr. 10-12). 1969. pap. text ed. 3.00x o.p. (ISBN 0-89039-152-1). Ann Arbor Pubs.

Braun, E. & Macdonald, S. Revolution in Miniature. LC 77-82489. (Illus.). 1978. 29.95 (ISBN 0-521-21815-2). Cambridge U Pr.

Braun, E., et al. Assessment of Technological Decisions: Case Studies. (Science in a Social Context Ser.). 1979. pap. text ed. 3.95 (ISBN 0-408-71313-5). Butterworths.

Braun, E. L. The Woody Plants of Ohio. 1969. 35.00 (ISBN 0-02-841890-5). Hafner.

Braun, Eunice. From Strength to Strength: The First Half Century of the Formative Age of the Baha'i Faith. LC 78-9424. 1978. pap. 4.00 (ISBN 0-87743-125-6, 7-32-30). Baha'i.

Braun, Frederick G., jt. auth. see Whitman, Nancy C.

Braun, H. Cathedral Architecture. LC 72-86608. (Illus.). 272p. 1972. 19.50x (ISBN 0-8448-0100-3). Crane-Russak Co.

Braun, Harold A. & Diettert, Gerald A. Coronary Care Unit Nursing: A Workbook in Clinical Aspects. (Illus.). 1980. pap. text ed. 11.95 (ISBN 0-8359-1051-2). Reston.

Braun, Harold A., et al. Introduction to Respiratory Physiology. 2nd ed. 1980. pap. 9.95 (ISBN 0-316-10699-2). Little.

Braun, Herbert. Jesus of Nazareth: The Man & His Time. Kalin, Everett R., tr. from Ger. LC 78-14664. 160p. 1979. 6.95 (ISBN 0-8006-0531-4, 1-531). Fortress.

Braun, Hugh. Elements of English Architecture. (Illus.). 212p. 1980. Repr. 22.50 (ISBN 0-7153-5775-1). David & Charles.

--An Introduction to English Mediaeval Architecture. 2nd ed. 1968. 14.95 o.p. (ISBN 0-571-08331-5, Pub. by Faber & Faber). Merrimack Bk Serv.

--Parish Churches. 1974. pap. 7.95 (ISBN 0-571-10553-X, Pub. by Faber & Faber). Merrimack Bk Serv.

Braun, Hugo, jt. auth. see Page, Daniel.

Braun, J. R. Is This My Neighbor? The Union Gospel Mission. (Illus.). 60p. (Orig.). 1980. pap. text ed. 8.95 (ISBN 0-933656-08-4). Trinity Pub Hse.

--Male Sexual Fantasies: The Destruction of the Feminine Personality; The Christian Mandate Against Pornography. 48p. (Orig.). 1980. pap. 1.95 (ISBN 0-933656-05-X). Trinity Pub Hse.

Braun, K., et al. Deutsch Als Fremdsprache: Ein Unterrichtswerk Fuer Auslaender. Incl. Pt. 1. Grundkurs. text ed. 9.25x lehrbuch (ISBN 3-12-554100-X); strukturuebungen und tests 7.55x (ISBN 3-12-554150-6); dialogische uebungen 8.20x (ISBN 3-12-554160-3); glossar deutsch-englisch 2.10x (ISBN 3-12-556110-8); sprechuebungen fuer das elektronische klassenzimmer, textband. 8.60x, 8 tonbaender, 9.5 cm/s, tapes, 405.00x (ISBN 3-12-554120-4); 4 schallplatten, lektion 1-19 des grundkurses, 17 cm, 33 1/3 rpm, records 16.95x (ISBN 3-12-554110-7); compact-cassette, lektion 1-19 des grundkurses 16.65x (ISBN 0-685-47448-8); 16 tonba 200.00x (ISBN 0-685-47449-6); Pt. 1B. Ergaenzungskurs. text ed. 9.25x lehrbuch (ISBN 3-12-554500-5); glossar deutsch-englisch 2.20x (ISBN 3-12-556510-3); schallplatten, records 16.65x (ISBN 0-685-47450-X); Pt. 2. Aufbaukurs. text ed. 9.25x lehrbuch (ISBN 3-12-554200-6); strukturuebungen und tests 7.25x (ISBN 0-686-66995-9); dialogische uebungen 8.60x (ISBN 0-686-66996-7); **glossar deutsch-englisch 2.20x (ISBN 3-12-556210-4); 3 schallplatten, lektion 1-17 des aufbaukurses,17 cm, 33 1/3 rpm, records 16.65x (ISBN 3-12-554210-3); compact-cassette, lektion 1-17 des aufbaukurses 16.65x (ISBN 0-685-47451-8); 12 tonbaender, dialoge und hoer-sprechuebungen, 9.5 cm/s, tapes 221.00x (ISBN 3-12-990430-1). Schoenhof.**

Braun, M. Differential Equations & Their Applications: An Introduction to Applied Mathematics. LC 74-31123. (Applied Mathematics Sciences Ser.: Vol. 15). (Illus.). xiv, 718p. 1975. pap. 15.60 o.p. (ISBN 0-387-90114-0). Springer-Verlag.

Braun, Matt. The Spoilers. (Orig.). 1981. pap. 1.95 (ISBN 0-671-82034-6). PB.

--Tombstone. 1981. pap. 1.95 (ISBN 0-671-82033-8). PB.

Braun, Matthew. The Kincaids. 1977. pap. 1.95 o.p. (ISBN 0-425-03442-9, Medallion). Berkley Pub.

--The Save-Your-Life Defense Handbook. (Illus.). 1977. 10.00x (ISBN 0-8159-5711-4); pap. 7.95x (ISBN 0-8159-5712-2). Devin.

Braun, Rainer. Kohelet und die fruehhellenistische Popularphilosphie. LC 72-76043. (Beiheft 130 Zur Zeitschrift Fuer Die Alttestamentliche Wissenschaft Ser.). 187p. 1973. text ed. 41.75x (ISBN 3-11-004050-6). De Gruyter.

Braun, Richard, tr. see Sophocles.

Braun, Richard E., tr. see Euripides.

Braun, Robert J. Dentist's Manual of Emergency Medical Treatment. (Illus.). 1979. text ed. 13.95 (ISBN 0-8359-1263-9). Reston.

Braun, Samuel J. & Lasher, Miriam G. Are You Ready to Mainstream: Helping Preschoolers with Learning & Behavior Problems. 1978. pap. text ed. 7.95 (ISBN 0-675-08443-1). Merrill.

Braun, Susan, jt. ed. see Kitching, Jessie.

Braun, Thomas. Football's Powerful Runner: Franco Harris. (The Allstars Ser.). (Illus.). (gr. 2-6). 1977. PLB 5.95 o.p. (ISBN 0-87191-585-5). Creative Ed.

--Franco Harris. (Creative Superstars Ser.). (Illus.). (gr. 3-9). 1975. PLB 5.95 (ISBN 0-87191-473-5); pap. 2.75 o. p. (ISBN 0-89812-169-8). Creative Ed.

--The Hitters. LC 76-8422. (Stars of the Nl & Al Ser.). (Illus.). (gr. 4-12). 1976. PLB 7.95 (ISBN 0-87191-515-4). Creative Ed.

--John Havlicek. LC 75-34489. (Sports Superstars Ser.). (Illus.). (gr. 3-9). 1976. PLB 5.95 o.p. (ISBN 0-87191-498-0). Creative Ed.

--Julius Erving. LC 75-37584. (Sports Superstars Ser.). (Illus.). (gr. 3-9). 1976. PLB 5.95 (ISBN 0-87191-499-9); pap. 2.95 (ISBN 0-89812-181-7). Creative Ed.

--Meet the Hitters. (Meet the Players: Baseball). (Illus.). (gr. 2-4). 1977. PLB 5.95 o.p. (ISBN 0-87191-579-0). Creative Ed.

--Nadia Comaneci. (Sports Superstars Ser.). (Illus.). (gr. 3-9). 1977. PLB 5.95 (ISBN 0-87191-592-8); pap. 2.95 (ISBN 0-89812-195-7). Creative Ed.

--Richard Petty. LC 75-37887. (Sports Superstars Ser.). (Illus.). (gr. 3-9). 1976. PLB 5.50 o.p. (ISBN 0-87191-500-6). Creative Ed.

--Sonny & Cher. (Rock 'n Pop Stars Ser.). (Illus.). (gr. 4-12). 1978. PLB 5.95 (ISBN 0-87191-620-7); pap. 2.95 (ISBN 0-685-81994-9). Creative Ed.

Braun, Thomas, ed. see Rosenthal-Schneider, Ilse.

Braun, W., ed. see Symposium of the Institute of Microbiology, Rutgers University, 1967.

Braun, Werner. Bacterial Genetics. 2nd ed. LC 65-12318. (Illus.). 1965. 10.95 o.p. (ISBN 0-7216-1921-5). Saunders.

Braunberg, Rudolf & Brownjohn, John M. Betrayed Skies. LC 79-7860. 384p. 1980. 12.95 (ISBN 0-385-15183-7). Doubleday.

Braund, H. E., ed. Calling to Mind: An Account of the First Hundred Years of Steel Brothers & Company Ltd. (Illus.). 1976. 25.00 (ISBN 0-08-017415-9). Pergamon.

Braunfels, Wolfgang. Monasteries of Western Europe: The Architecture of the Orders. LC 73-2472. (Illus.). 263p. 1980. 35.00x; pap. 15.00x (ISBN 0-691-00313-0). Princeton U Pr.

Braungart, Richard G. Society & Politics: Readings in Political Sociology. (Illus.). 624p. 1976. 21.95 (ISBN 0-13-820555-8). P-H.

Braunstein & Copenhaver. Environmental, Health & Control Aspects of Coal Conversion: An Information Overview, 2 vols. 1338p. 1981. Set. text ed. 90.00 (ISBN 0-250-40445-1). Ann Arbor Science.

Braunstein, Joseph. Musica Aeterna: Program Notes, 1961-1967. LC 72-8420. (Music Ser). 332p. 1973. Repr. of 1968 ed. lib. bdg. 32.50 (ISBN 0-306-70554-0). Da Capo.

Braunstein, Mark. Radical Vegetarianism: A Dialectic of Diet & Ethic. 250p. (Orig.). 1980. 12.95 (ISBN 0-915572-52-4); pap. 6.95 (ISBN 0-915572-37-0). Panjandrum.

Brautigan, Richard. Confederate General from Big Sur. 1975. pap. 1.95 o.p. (ISBN 0-345-24213-0). Ballantine.

--Dreaming of Babylon. 1977. 7.95 o.s.i. (ISBN 0-440-02146-4, Sey Lawr). Delacorte.

--The Toyko-Montana Express. 1980. 10.95 (ISBN 0-440-08770-8, Sey Lawr); pap. 2.50 (ISBN 0-440-03725-5). Delacorte.

Brave, John R. Uncle John's Original Bread Book. 1976. pap. 2.25 (ISBN 0-515-05830-0). Jove Pubns.

Braverman, J. Probability, Logic & Management Decisions. text ed. 17.95 o.p. (ISBN 0-07-007345-7, C); solutions manual 4.95 o.p. (ISBN 0-07-007346-5). McGraw.

Braverman, Jerome D. Fundamentals of Business Statistics. 597p. 1979. tchrs' ed. 17.95 (ISBN 0-12-128050-0); instrs'. manual 3.00 (ISBN 0-12-128052-7); solutions manual 5.50 (ISBN 0-12-128054-3). Acad Pr.

Braverman, Jerome D. & Stewart, William C. Statistics for Business & Economics. 500p. 1973. 17.50 (ISBN 0-471-06610-9). Wiley.

Braverman, Jordan. A Consumer's Book of Health: Advice on Stretching Your Health Care Dollar. LC 80-53186. 256p. (Orig.). 1981. 11.95 (ISBN 0-7216-1930-4); pap. 6.95 (ISBN 0-7216-1935-5). Saunders.

Braverman, Kate. Lithium for Medea. 288p. 1981. pap. 2.75 (ISBN 0-523-41185-5). Pinnacle Bks.

Braverman, Sydell, jt. auth. see Chevigny, Hector.

Bravery, H. E. The Complete Book of Winemaking. 160p. 1973. pap. 1.50 o.s.i. (ISBN 0-02-009250-4, Collier). Macmillan.

--Home Brewing Without Failures. LC 66-17178. (Orig.). 1967. pap. 0.95 o.p. (ISBN 0-668-01436-9). Arc Bks.

Bravmann, R. A. Islam & Tribal Art in West Africa. (African Studies: No. 11). (Illus.). 180p. 1974. 36.00 (ISBN 0-521-20192-6). Cambridge U Pr.

Brawer, Florence B. New Perspectives on Personality Development in College Students. LC 73-7150. (Higher Education Ser). 256p. 1973. 14.95x o.p. (ISBN 0-87589-189-6). Jossey-Bass.

--Personality Characteristics of College & University Faculty: Implications for the Community College. 1968. 3.00 (ISBN 0-87117-076-0). Am Assn Comm Jr Coll.

Brawer, Florence B., jt. auth. see Cohen, Arthur M.

Brawley, Benjamin G. Negro Genius. LC 66-17517. 1966. Repr. of 1937 ed. 10.50x (ISBN 0-8196-0184-5). Biblo.

Brawley, James S. Rowan County: A Brief History. (Illus.). 1977. pap. 2.00 (ISBN 0-86526-129-6). NC Archives.

Brawner, Charles O., ed. First International Conference on Uranium Mine Waste Disposal. LC 80-69552. (Illus.). 626p. 1980. 22.00x (ISBN 0-89520-279-4). Soc Mining Eng.

Brawner, Julie R., et al. From the Kudzu to the Ivy: How to Find Your College: a Southerner's Guide to Northeastern Colleges. 256p. (Orig.). (YA) (gr. 11-12). 1980. pap. 5.95. Kudzu-Ivy.

Brax, Ralph S. The First Student Movement: Student Activism in the United States During the Nineteen Thirties. (National University Publications, Political Science Ser.). 1981. 17.50 (ISBN 0-8046-9266-1). Kennikat.

Braxton, Bernard. Women, Sex, & Race: A Realistic View of Sexism & Racism. LC 72-91049. 228p. 1973. 7.95 (ISBN 0-930876-01-6); pap. 3.95 (ISBN 0-930876-02-4). Verta Pr.

Braxton, Edward K. The Wisdom Community. LC 80-81053. 224p. (Orig.). 1980. pap. 7.95 (ISBN 0-8091-2307-X). Paulist Pr.

Braxton, Hank. The Committee. (Orig.). 1979. pap. 2.25 (ISBN 0-89083-484-9). Zebra.

Braxton, Virginia A. A Very Important Person's Workbook. (Illus.). 16p. (gr. 1-5). 1980. pap. 1.75 (ISBN 0-935322-08-6). C J Frompovich.

Bray, Barbara, tr. see Caron, Francois.

Bray, Barbara, tr. see Pinget, Robert.

Bray, Frank S. The Accounting Mission. LC 73-84525. 1973. Repr. of 1951 ed. text ed. 10.00 (ISBN 0-914348-01-9). Scholars Bk.

Bray, Frank T. & Moodie, Michael. Defense Technology & the Atlantic Alliance: Competition or Collaboration? LC 77-80297. (Foreign Policy Report Ser.). 5.00 (ISBN 0-89549-000-5). Inst Foreign Policy Anal.

Bray, G. A., jt. ed. see Hershman, Jerome M.

Bray, George A., jt. ed. see Hershman, Jerome M.

Bray, Jacqueline H., jt. auth. see Cohen, Theodore J.

Bray, Jean & Wright, Sheila, eds. The Use of Technology in the Care of the Elderly & the Disabled. LC 80-17847. xii, 267p. 1980. lib. bdg. 29.95 (ISBN 0-313-22616-4, BTC/). Greenwood.

Bray, Jennifer, tr. see Beaujeu-Garnier, J.

Bray, John. Theodore Beza's Doctrine of Predestination. (Bibliotheca Humanistica & Reformatorica Ser.: No. 12). 1975. text ed. 38.50x o.p. (ISBN 90-6004-334-0). Humanities.

Bray, John, jt. auth. see Barker, John N.

Bray, Martha C. Joseph Nicollet & His Map. LC 79-54278. (Memoirs Ser.: Vol. 140). 1980. 15.00 (ISBN 0-87169-140-X). Am Philos.

Bray, R. N. Dredging: A Handbook for Engineers. (Illus.). 276p. 1979. 75.00x (ISBN 0-7131-3412-7). Intl Ideas.

Bray, Reginald A. Boy Labour & Apprenticeship, London Nineteen Eleven. LC 79-56952. (The English Working Class Ser.). 1980. lib. bdg. 22.00 (ISBN 0-8240-0106-0). Garland Pub.

Bray, Reginald G. De see De Bray, Reginald G.

Bray, Ruth G. De, tr. see Reymond, Arnold.

Braybon, Gail. Women Workers in the First World War: The British Experience. 224p. 1981. 24.50x (ISBN 0-389-20100-6). B&N.

Braybrooke, David. Traffic Congestion Goes Through the Issue-Machine: A Case-Study in Issue Processing, Illustrating a New Approach. 74p. 1974. 16.50x (ISBN 0-7100-7749-1). Routledge & Kegan.

Braybrooke, David & Lindblom, Charles E. A Strategy of Decision: Policy Evaluation As a Social Process. LC 63-13537. 1970. 10.95 o.s.i. (ISBN 0-02-904600-9); pap. text ed. 7.95 (ISBN 0-02-904610-6). Free Pr.

Brayer, K. Data Communications Via Fading Channels. LC 74-33060. (IEEE Press Selected Reprint Ser.). 1975. 23.95 o.p. (ISBN 0-471-09815-9, Pub. by Wiley-Interscience); pap. text ed. 11.95x (ISBN 0-471-09816-7). Wiley.

Braymer, Daniel H. & Roe, A. C. Rewinding Small Motors. 3rd ed. LC 80-29580. 432p. 1981. Repr. of 1949 ed. lib. bdg. price not set (ISBN 0-89874-291-9). Krieger.

Brayton, R. K., et al. Modern Network Theory: An Introduction. Moschytz, G. S. & Neirynck, J., eds. 1978. text ed. 42.00 (ISBN 2-604-00034-2). Renouf.

Brazee, Edward, ed. Index to the Sierra Club Bulletin, 1950-1976. (Bibliographic Ser.: No. 16). 1978. pap. 4.00 (ISBN 0-87071-136-9). Oreg St U Pr.

Brazell, D. Edmunds. Licensing Check Lists. 49p. (Orig.). 1981. pap. 12.50x (ISBN 0-911378-36-7). Sheridan.

Brazell, James. Shelley & the Concept of Humanity: A Study of His Moral Vision. (Salzburg Studies in English Literature, Romantic Reassessment: No. 7). 1972. pap. text ed. 25.00x (ISBN 0-391-01331-9). Humanities.

Brazelton, T. Berry. Neonatal Behavioral Assessment Scale. (Illus.). 1974. 12.95x (ISBN 0-433-04030-0). Intl Ideas.

--On Becoming a Family: The Growth of Attachment. 1981. 14.95 (ISBN 0-440-06712-X, Sey Lawr). Delacorte.

Brazer, Clarence. Essays of U. S. Adhesive Postage Stamps. LC 75-40503. 1977. 35.00x (ISBN 0-88000-081-3). Quarterman.

Brazier, L. R., et al, eds. Die & Mould Making. (Engineering Craftsmen: No. H22). (Illus.). 1970. spiral bdg. 18.50x (ISBN 0-85083-126-1). Intl Ideas.

Brazier, M. A., ed. Growth & Development of the Brain: Nutritional, Genetic, & Environmental Factors. LC 75-14565. (International Brain Research Organization Ser.: Vol. 1). 412p. 1975. 39.00 (ISBN 0-89004-037-0). Raven.

Brazier, M. A., ed. see Conferences on Brain & Behavior, los Angeles.

Brazier, Mary, jt. ed. see Sigman, David S.

Brazier, Mary A. & Coceani, Flavio. Brain Dysfunction in Infantile Febrile Convulsions. LC 75-14564. (International Brain Research Organization Monograph: Vol. 2). 1976. 37.50 (ISBN 0-89004-068-0). Raven.

Brazier, Mary A., jt. auth. see Meisami, Esmail.

Brazier, Mary A., ed. Brain Mechanisms in Memory & Learning: From the Single Neuron to Man. LC 78-67019. (International Brain Research Organization Monograph Ser.: Vol. 4). 1978. 34.50 (ISBN 0-89004-160-1). Raven.

Brazier, Mary A. & Petsche, Hellmuth, eds. Architectonics of the Cerebral Cortex. LC 77-83694. (International Brain Research Organization (IBRO) Monograph Ser.: Vol. 3). 1978. 47.00 (ISBN 0-89004-140-7). Raven.

Brazier, Mary A., jt. ed. see Hobson, J. Allan.

Brazier, Shelley, ed. Fourth National Congress on Child Abuse & Neglect. 350p. 1981. casebound 27.00 (ISBN 0-88416-313-X, 313). PSG Pub.

Brazil, Diane. South Bay Bargain Guide. (Illus.). 96p. (Orig.). 1981. pap. 4.95 (ISBN 0-87701-142-7). Chronicle Bks.

Brazleton, T. B., ed. A Neonatol Behavioral Assessment Scale. (Clinics in Developmental Medicine Ser.: Vol. 50). 66p. 1973. 13.00 (ISBN 0-685-59044-5). Lippincott.

Breach, jt. auth. see Baker.

Break, George F. Financing Government in a Federal System. (Studies of Government Finance). 1980. 17.95 (ISBN 0-8157-1068-2); pap. 6.95 (ISBN 0-8157-1067-4). Brookings.

--Intergovernmental Fiscal Relations in the United States. (Studies of Government Finance). 14.95 (ISBN 0-8157-1074-7); pap. 5.95 (ISBN 0-8157-1073-9). Brookings.

Break, George F., ed. Metropolitan Financing: Principles & Practice. LC 77-77437. 1978. 25.00 (ISBN 0-299-07280-0). U of Wis Pr.

Brealy, jt. auth. see Love.

Brean, Herbert. How to Stop Smoking. LC 73-156224. (Rev, Ed). 1958. 5.95 (ISBN 0-8149-0027-5). Vanguard.

Brearley, C. Residential Work with the Elderly. (Library of Social Work Ser.). 1977. 13.50x (ISBN 0-7100-8587-7); pap. 7.95 (ISBN 0-7100-8588-5). Routledge & Kegan.

Brearley, C. Paul. Social Work, Ageing & Society. (Library of Social Work Ser.). 1975. 12.25x (ISBN 0-7100-8184-7); pap. 6.95 (ISBN 0-7100-8185-5). Routledge & Kegan.

Brearley, Joan. Ibizan Hounds. (Illus.). 128p. 1980. 2.95 (ISBN 0-87666-694-2, KW-060). TFH Pubns.

Brearley, Joan M. All About Himalayan Cats. (Illus.). 96p. (Orig.). 1976. 3.95 (ISBN 0-87666-756-6, PS736). TFH Pubns.

--Book of the Afghan Hound. (Illus.). 1978. 20.00 (ISBN 0-87666-665-9, H-991). TFH Pubns.

--The Book of the Pug. (Illus.). 320p. 1980. 20.00 (ISBN 0-87666-683-7, H-1021). TFH Pubns.

Brearley, Joan M. & Easton, Allen. Book of the Shih Tzu. (Illus.). 304p. 1980. 30.00 (ISBN 0-87666-664-0, H-996). TFH Pubns.

Brearley, Joan M., jt. auth. see Nicholas, Anna K.

Brearley, Joan McD. & Anderson, Marlene. This Is the Old English Sheepdog. (Illus.). 320p. 1974. 12.95 (ISBN 0-87666-345-5, PS-702). TFH Pubns.

Brearley, K. & McBride, R. Nouvelles Du Quebec. 2nd ed. (Fr). 1977. pap. text ed. 8.95 o.p. (ISBN 0-13-625467-5). P-H.

Brearley, M., et al. Fundamentals in the First School. (Illus.). 1974. Repr. of 1969 ed. 9.50x (ISBN 0-631-11840-3, Pub. by Basil Blackwell). Biblio Dist.

Brearley, Paul, et al. The Social Context of Health Care. (Aspects of Social Policy Ser.). 1978. 36.00x (ISBN 0-631-18110-5, Pub. by Basil Blackwell); pap. 14.00x (ISBN 0-631-18120-2). Biblio Dist.

Breasted, James H. Development of Religion & Thought in Ancient Egypt. LC 58-7111. 406p. 1972. pap. 6.95x (ISBN 0-8122-1045-X, Pa Paperbks). U of Pa Pr.

Breatnach, Riobard P., tr. see O'Siochain, Conchur.

Breault, William. Power & Weakness. LC 73-86209. 1973. 4.50 o.s.i. (ISBN 0-8198-0270-0); gift edition 6.00 o.s.i. (ISBN 0-8198-0271-9). Dghtrs St Paul.

Brebbia, C. A. The Boundary Element Method for Engineers. LC 78-9625. 1978. 39.95x (ISBN 0-470-26438-1). Halsted Pr.

Brebbia, C. A. & Ferrante, A. J. Computational Methods for the Solution of Engineering Problems. LC 76-53093. 1977. 34.50x (ISBN 0-8448-1079-7). Crane-Russak Co.

Brebbia, C. A., ed. Applied Numerical Modeling: Proceedings of the International Conference, University of Southampton, 11-15 July, 1977. LC 77-11141. 1978. 49.95 (ISBN 0-470-99271-9). Halsted Pr.

--Mathematical Models for Environmental Problems: Proceedings of the University of Southampton, England, 8-12 September, 1975. LC 75-41453. 1976. 49.95 (ISBN 0-470-15206-0). Halsted Pr.

Brebbia, C. A., et al, eds. Environmental Forces on Engineering Structures. LC 79-16733. 1979. 59.95x (ISBN 0-470-26820-4). Halsted Pr.

Breccia, A. & Breccia, A. Radiosensitizers of Hypoxic Cells: Proceedings. 1979. 44.00 (ISBN 0-444-80124-3, Biomedical Pr). Elsevier.

Brech, E. F. Management: Its Nature & Significance. 1967. 15.00x o.p. (ISBN 0-8464-0590-3). Beekman Pubs.

Brecheen, Carl & Faulkner, Paul. What Every Family Needs or Whatever Happened to Mom, Dad, & the Kids. LC 78-68726. (Journey Bks.). 1979. pap. 2.60 (ISBN 0-8344-0104-5). Sweet.

Brecher, Charles & Horton, Raymond D., eds. Setting Municipal Priorities, Nineteen Eighty-One. LC 80-67392. 212p. 1981. text ed. 25.00 (ISBN 0-86598-010-1). Allanheld.

Brecher, Charles, jt. ed. see Horton, Raymond D.

Brecher, Kenneth & Setti, Ginancarlo. High Energy Astrophysics & Its Relation to Elementary Particle Physics. LC 74-19794. 1974. 34.50x (ISBN 0-262-52035-4); pap. 12.50x o.p. (ISBN 0-262-52035-4). MIT Pr.

Brechner, Irv. The College Survival Kit. 96p. 1980. pap. 2.95. Bantam.

Brecht see Bentley, Eric.

Brecht, Bertold. Brecht: Mutter Courage und Ihre Kinder. Sander, Volkmar, ed. (Illus., Ger.). (gr. 9-12). 1964. pap. text ed. 4.95x (ISBN 0-19-500835-9). Oxford U Pr.

Brecht, Bertolt. Bertolt Brecht Gesammelte Prosa in Vier Baenden: Dreigroschenroman, Vol. 3. (Edition Suhrkamp: Bd. 184). (Ger.). 1980. pap. text ed. 4.55 (ISBN 3-518-10184-6, Pub. by Insel Verlag Germany). Suhrkamp.

--Bertolt Brecht, Gesammelte Prosa in Vier Baenden: Die Geschafte Des Herrn Julius Caesar, Fluechtlingsgesprache, Register. (Edition Suhrkamp: 185). (Ger.). 1980. pap. text ed. 4.55 (ISBN 3-518-10185-4, Pub. by Insel Verlag Germany). Suhrkamp.

--Bertolt Brecht, Gesammelte Prosa in Vier Baenden: Geschichten Vom Herrn Keuner Me-Ti - Buch der Wendungen der Tui-Roman, Vol. 2. (Edition Suhrkamp: 183). (Ger.). 1980. pap. text ed. 4.55 (ISBN 3-518-10183-8, Pub. by Insel Verlag Germany). Suhrkamp.

--Bertolt Brecht: Gesammelte Prosa in Vier Baenden, Vol. 1. (Edition Suhrkamp: 182). (Ger.). 1980. pap. text ed. 4.55 (ISBN 3-518-10182-X, Pub. by Insel Verlag Germany). Suhrkamp.

--Brecht, Gesammelte Prosa in Vier Baenden. (Edition Suhrkamp: 182 to 185). 1600p. (Ger.). 1980. pap. text ed. 15.60 (ISBN 3-518-09519-6, Pub. by Insel Verlag Germany). Suhrkamp.

--Edward the Second: A Chronicle Play. Bentley, Eric, tr. from German. & intro. by. (Orig.). 1970. pap. 1.95 (ISBN 0-394-17111-X, B119, BC). Grove.

--Leben Des Galilei. Brookes, H. F. & Fraenkel, C. E., eds. 1958. pap. text ed. 4.50x (ISBN 0-435-38110-5). Heinemann Ed.

--Mutter Courage und Ihre Kinder. Brookes, H. F. & Fraenkel, C. E., eds. 1960. pap. text ed. 3.95x (ISBN 0-435-38112-1). Heinemann Ed.

--Der Ozeanflug, Die Horatier und Die Kuriater, Die Massnahme. (Edition Suhrkamp: Bd. 222). 112p. (Ger.). pap. text ed. 3.90 (ISBN 3-518-10222-2, Pub. by Insel Verlag Germany). Suhrkamp.

Brechter, Jeremy & Costello, Tom. Common Sense for Hard Times. 277p. 1979. 12.50 o.p. (ISBN 0-686-63874-3); pap. 5.00 (ISBN 0-89758-026-5). Inst Policy Stud.

Breck, Donald W. Zeolite Molecular Sieves: Structure, Chemistry & Use. LC 73-11028. 1974. 56.50 (ISBN 0-471-09985-6, Pub. by Wiley-Interscience). Wiley.

Breck, Flora E. Choir Ideas. (Interlude Bks). 1971. pap. 1.95 o.p. (ISBN 0-8010-0545-0). Baker Bk.

Breck, Louis W. An Atlas of the Osteochondhoses. (Illus.). 192p. 1971. pap. 16.00 photocopy ed. spiral (ISBN 0-398-00218-5). C C Thomas.

Breckenridge, James D. Likeness: A Conceptual History of Ancient Portraiture. LC 68-29325. (Illus.). 1969. 18.25x o.s.i. (ISBN 0-8101-0024-X). Northwestern U Pr.

Breckenridge, James F. The Theological Self-Understanding of the Catholic Charismatic Movement. LC 79-6198. 154p. 1980. pap. text ed. 8.00 (ISBN 0-8191-1006-X). U Pr of Amer.

Breckinridge, John, jt. auth. see Hughes, John.

Breckinridge, Mary. Wide Neighborhoods: A Story of the Frontier Nursing Service. (Illus.). 400p. 1981. 18.50 (ISBN 0-8131-1453-5); pap. 8.50 (ISBN 0-8131-0149-2). U Pr of Ky.

Breckman, Brigid. Stoma Care. 230p. 1980. 40.00x (Pub. by Beaconsfield England). State Mutual Bk.

Breckon, Bill, ed. see Smith, Tony & Lee, Richard V.

Breda, A. Van see Van Breda, A.

Bredemeier, Harry C. & Toby, Jackson. Social Problems in America. 2nd ed. LC 72-1137. (Illus.). 1972. pap. text ed. 11.50x o.p. (ISBN 0-471-10006-4). Wiley.

Bredemeyer, Hans G. & Bullock, Kathleen. Orthoptics: Theory & Practice. LC 68-31415. (Illus.). 1968. 21.50 o.p. (ISBN 0-8016-0762-0). Mosby.

Bredes, Don. Hard Feelings. 352p. 1981. pap. price not set. Bantam.

Bredsdorff, Elias. Danish: An Elementary Grammar & Reader. 1959. 17.50x (ISBN 0-521-09821-1). Cambridge U Pr.

--Hans Christian Andersen. LC 75-23827. 344p. 1975. 10.00 o.p. (ISBN 0-684-14457-3, ScribT). Scribner.

Bredvold, L. I., ed. The Best of Dryden. 1933. 14.95 (ISBN 0-8260-1265-5). Wiley.

Bredvold, L. I., et al, eds. Eighteenth Century Poetry & Prose. 3rd ed. 1493p. 1973. text ed. 21.95 (ISBN 0-8260-1281-7). Wiley.

Bredvold, Louis I. Brave New World of the Enlightenment. 1961. 3.95 o.p. (ISBN 0-472-17755-9). U of Mich Pr.

Bredvold, Louis I., ed. Literature of the Restoration & Eighteenth Century, Vol. 3. rev. ed. (Orig.). 1962. pap. 0.95 o.s.i. (ISBN 0-02-048800-9, Collier). Macmillan.

Bree, G., ed. see Camus, A.

Bree, Germaine. Camus & Sartre: Crisis & Commitment. 256p. 1972. 7.95 o.s.i. (ISBN 0-440-01138-8). Delacorte.

--Women Writers in France: Variations on a Theme. 104p. 1973. 7.00 (ISBN 0-8135-0771-5). Rutgers U Pr.

Bree, Germaine, ed. Culture, Literature, & Articulation. Incl. Classical & Modern Foreign Languages: Common Areas & Problems. McCarthy, Barbara P; Foreign Language Instruction in Elementary Schools. Thompson, Mary P; Foreign Language Instruction in the Secondary School. Mead, Robert G., Jr; The Place of Culture & Civilization in Foreign Language Teaching. Wylie, Laurence; The Preparation of Foreign Language Teachers. Grace, Alonzo G; The Role of Foreign Languages in American Life. Starr, Wilmarth H; The Role of Literature in Language Teaching. MacAllister, Archibald T; Teaching Aids & Techniques: Principle Demonstrations. Pleasants, Jeanne V; Tests: All Skills, Speaking Test. Brooks, Nelson. 188p. 1955. pap. 7.95x (ISBN 0-915432-55-2). NE Conf Teach Foreign.

Bree, Josephine P; see Eddy, Frederick D.

Breed, C. B. Surveying. 3rd ed. 495p. 1971. 22.95 (ISBN 0-471-10070-6). Wiley.

Breed, C. B. & Hosmer, G. L. Principles & Practice of Surveying, 2 vols. Incl. Vol. 1. Elementary Surveying. 11th ed. 717p. 1977. 23.95 (ISBN 0-471-02979-3); Vol. 2. Higher Surveying. 8th ed. 543p. 1962. 22.95 (ISBN 0-471-10164-8). Wiley.

Breed, Paul F. & Sniderman, Florence M. Dramatic Criticism Index: Bibliography of Commentaries on Playwrights from Ibsen to the Avant-Garde. LC 79-127598. 1972. 40.00 (ISBN 0-8103-1090-2). Gale.

Breed, Warren. Self-Guiding Society. LC 75-128472. 1971. 8.95 (ISBN 0-02-904640-8); pap. text ed. 4.95 (ISBN 0-02-904650-5). Free Pr.

Breeden, James O. Joseph Jones, M.D. Scientist of the Old South. LC 73-80462. (Illus.). 320p. 1975. 17.00x (ISBN 0-8131-1296-6). U Pr of Ky.

Breeden, James O., ed. Advice Among Masters: The Ideal in Slave Management in the Old South. LC 79-54054. (Contributions in Afro-American & African Studies: No. 51). (Illus.). xxvi, 350p. 1980. lib. bdg. 25.00 (ISBN 0-313-20658-9, BRS/). Greenwood.

Breeden, Kay, jt. auth. see Breeden, Stanley.

Breeden, Stanley & Breeden, Kay. Australia's North. (A Natural History of Australia Ser.: No. 3). 208p. 1980. 34.95x (ISBN 0-00-211441-0, Pub. by W Collins Australia). Intl Schol Bk Serv.

Breen. Convexity & Related Combinatorial Geometry. Date not set. price not set (ISBN 0-8247-1278-1). Dekker.

Breen, T. H. & Innes, Stephen. Myne Owne Ground: Race & Freedom on Virginia's Eastern Shore, 1640-1676. (Illus.). 200p. 1980. 12.95 (ISBN 0-19-502727-2). Oxford U Pr.

Breen, Walter, jt. auth. see Swiatek, Anthony.

Breene, R. G., Jr. Theories of Spectral Line Shape. LC 80-20664. 384p. 1981. 35.00 (ISBN 0-471-08361-5, Pub. by Wiley-Interscience). Wiley.

Breese, Burtis B. & Hall, Caroline. Beta Hemolytic Streptococcal Diseases. (Illus.). 1978. 29.00x (ISBN 0-89289-400-8). HM Prof Med Div.

Breese, Dave. Know the Marks of Cults. LC 74-21907. 128p. 1975. pap. 2.95 (ISBN 0-88207-704-X). Victor Bks.

Breese, Gerald. Urbanization in Newly Developing Countries. (Illus., Orig.). 1966. pap. 8.95 ref. ed. (ISBN 0-13-939181-9). P-H.

Breeze, Paul. While My Guitar Gently Weeps: A Novel. LC 80-22065. 222p. 1981. 9.95 (ISBN 0-8008-8247-4). Taplinger.

Breffney, Brian de see De Breffney, Brian & Folliott, Rosemary.

Breger, Louis. Freud's Unfinished Journey. 220p. write for info. (ISBN 0-7100-0613-6). Routledge & Kegan.

--From Instinct to Identity: The Development of Personality. LC 73-5766. (P-H Personality Ser). (Illus.). 400p. 1974. ref. ed. 18.95x (ISBN 0-13-331637-8). P-H.

Breger, Louis, ed. Clinical Cognitive Psychology. LC 70-85956. 1969. 24.50x (ISBN 0-13-137620-9). Irvington.

Breggin, Peter R. The Psychology of Freedom: Liberty & Love As a Way of Life. LC 80-7459. 242p. 1980. 12.95 (ISBN 0-87975-132-0). Prometheus Bks.

Bregman. Mechanical Support of the Failing Heart & Lungs. (Illus.). 1977. 19.50 (ISBN 0-8385-6196-9). ACC.

Bregman, Alice, compiled by. Concise Encyclopedia of Psychology & Psychiatry. (Reference Collection Ser.). (Illus.). (gr. 6 up). 1977. PLB 9.90 s&l (ISBN 0-531-01332-4). Watts.

Brehaut, Ernest, tr. see Gregory - Bishop Of Tours.

Brehier, Emile. History of Philosophy, 7 vols. Incl. Vol. 1. The Hellenic Age. Thomas, Joseph, tr. LC 63-20912. 1963. pap. text ed. 5.00x (ISBN 0-226-07217-7); Vol. 2. The Hellenistic & Roman Age. Baskin, Wade, tr. LC 63-20913. 1965. pap. text ed. 7.00x (ISBN 0-226-07221-5, P199); Vol. 3. The Middle Ages & the Renaissance. Baskin, Wade, tr. LC 63-20912. 1965. pap. text ed. 5.00x (ISBN 0-226-07219-3); Vol. 4. The Seventeenth Century. Baskin, Wade, tr. LC 63-20912. 1966. pap. text ed. 5.00x (ISBN 0-226-07225-8); Vol. 5. The Eighteenth Century. Baskin, Wade, tr. LC 63-20912. 1971. pap. text ed. 5.00x (ISBN 0-226-07227-4); Vol. 6. The Nineteenth Century: Period of Systems 1800-1850. Baskin, Wade, tr. LC 63-20912. 1973. pap. text ed. 5.00x (ISBN 0-226-07229-0); Vol. 7. Contemporary Philosophy - Since 1850. Baskin, Wade, tr. LC 63-20912. 1973. pap. text ed. 5.00x (ISBN 0-226-07231-2, P538). Phoen). U of Chicago Pr.

Brehier, L. L' Art Chretien, son Developement Iconographique des Origines a nos Jours. 2nd ed. (Illus.). 480p. (Fr.). 1981. Repr. of 1928 ed. lib. bdg. 125.00 (ISBN 0-89241-138-4). Caratzas Bros.

Brehm, Henry P. & Coe, Rodney M. Medical Care for the Aged. LC 78-19786. 1980. 19.95 (ISBN 0-03-046306-8). Praeger.

Brehm, Henry P. & Lopata, Helena Z. Widowhood. LC 78-19789. 200p. 1981. price not set (ISBN 0-03-046301-7). Praeger.

Brehm, Henry P., jt. auth. see Lopata, Helena Z.

Brehm, Sharon S., et al, eds. Developmental Social Psychology: Theory & Research. (Illus.). 352p. 1981. text ed. 19.95x (ISBN 0-19-502840-6); pap. text ed. 11.95x (ISBN 0-19-502841-4). Oxford U Pr.

Brehme, Robert W., jt. auth. see Sears, Francis W.

Breide, Ole. Three Weeks on - Three Weeks off. Date not set. 9.95 (ISBN 0-533-04801-X). Vantage.

Breidenbach, Monica E., jt. auth. see Hover, Margot K.

Breidenbarn, Monica E., jt. auth. see Hover, Margot K.

Breig, Alf. Adverse Mechanical Tension of the Central Nervous System: An Analysis of Cause & Effect. LC 77-88852. 1978. 84.50 (ISBN 0-471-04137-8, Pub. by Wiley Medical). Wiley.

Breig, James. Hail Mary: Woman, Wife, Mother of God. (Today Paperback Ser.). (Illus.). 40p. (Orig.). 1980. pap. 1.95 (ISBN 0-89570-197-9). Claretian Pubns.

Breiham, Carl W. Quantrill & His Civil War Guerrillas. LC 59-8213. 174p. 1959. 6.95 (ISBN 0-8040-0256-8, SB). Swallow.

Breihan, Carl W. & Montgomery, Wayne. Forty Years on the Wild Frontier. (Illus.). Date not set. 15.00 (ISBN 0-8159-5518-9). Devin. Postponed.

Breiman, Leo. Probability. (Illus.). 1968. text ed. 23.95 (ISBN 0-201-00646-4). A-W.

--Probability & Stochastic Processes, with a View Toward Applications. LC 78-3566. (Illus.). 1969. text ed. 22.50 (ISBN 0-395-04231-3, 3-05970). HM.

--Statistics: With a View Toward Applications. LC 72-3131. 480p. 1973. text ed. 22.50 (ISBN 0-395-04232-1, 3-05972). HM.

Breinburg, Petronella. Sally-Ann in the Snow. (Illus.). 1979. 6.50 (ISBN 0-370-01809-5, Pub. by Chatto Bodley Jonathan). Merrimack Bk Serv.

--Sally-Ann's Umbrella. (Illus.). 1979. 6.95 (ISBN 0-370-10752-7, Pub. by Chatto Bodley Jonathan). Merrimack Bk Serv.

--Shawn's Red Bike. LC 73-40362. (Illus.). 32p. (gr. k-3). 1976. 5.95 (ISBN 0-685-63197-4, TYC-J); PLB 7.89 o.p. (ISBN 0-690-01115-6). T Y Crowell.

Breipohl, Arthur M. Probabilistic System Analysis: An Introduction to Probabilistic Models, Decisions & Applications of Random Processes. LC 77-94920. 1970. 28.95 (ISBN 0-471-10181-8). Wiley.

Breisacher, E. H., ed. Last Resting Places, Being a Compendium of Fact Pertaining to the Mortal Remains of the Famous & Infamous. LC 79-52704. (Illus.). 320p. 1981. 16.95 (ISBN 0-87850-032-4). Darwin Pr.

Breise, Frederic H. Fifty Years of Aviation Knowledge. 108p. 1981. 9.75 (ISBN 0-938576-00-3). F H Breise.

Breitbart, M., jt. auth. see Kasperson, R. E.

Breiter, Herta S. Fuel & Energy. LC 77-18560. (Read About Sciences Ser.). (Illus.). (gr. k-3). 1978. PLB 9.95 (ISBN 0-8393-0083-2). Raintree Child.

--Pollution. LC 77-26886. (Read About Science Ser.). (Illus.). (gr. k-3). 1978. PLB 9.95 (ISBN 0-8393-0081-6). Raintree Child.

--Time & Clocks. LC 77-19007. (Read About Science Ser.). (Illus.). (gr. k-3). 1978. PLB 9.95 (ISBN 0-8393-0088-3). Raintree Child.

--Weather. LC 77-27239. (Read About Science Ser.). (Illus.). (gr. k-3). 1978. PLB 9.95 (ISBN 0-8393-0079-4). Raintree Child.

Breithaupt, Herman A. How We Started Students on Successful Foodservice Careers. LC 72-75296. 256p. 1972. 11.95 (ISBN 0-8436-0544-8). CBI Pub.

Breitmaier, E. & Bauer, G. C-13 NMR Spectroscopy: A Working Manual with Exercises. Cassels, B. K., tr. from Ger. (Mmi Press Polymer Monographs). 400p. 1981. 80.00 (ISBN 3-7186-0022-6). Harwood Academic.

Breitmaier, E. & Bauer, G. C. NMR Spectroscopy: A Working Manual with Exercises. Cassels, B. K., tr. from Ger. 400p. 1981. 80.00 (ISBN 3-7186-0022-6). Harwood Academic.

Breitman, George. Fighting Racism in World War Ii. 1980. 20.00 (ISBN 0-913460-81-8); pap. 5.95 (ISBN 0-913460-82-6). Monad Pr.

Breitman, Richard. German Socialism & Weimar Democracy. LC 80-21412. 296p. 1981. 20.00x (ISBN 0-8078-1462-8). U of NC Pr.

Breitmeyer, Lois, jt. auth. see Leithauser, Gladys.

Breitung, Joan. Care of the Older Adult. LC 80-51870. (Illus.). 344p. (gr. 12). 1981. pap. text ed. 9.90 (ISBN 0-913292-05-2). Tiresias Pr.

Brejcha, M. F. & Samuels, C. L. Automotive Chassis & Accessory Circuits. LC 76-14835. (Illus.). 1977. 17.95 (ISBN 0-13-055475-8). P-H.

Brekhman, I. I. Man & Biologically Active Substances: Introduction to the Pharmacology of Health. 2nd ed. 90p. 1980. 18.25 (ISBN 0-08-023169-1); pap. 5.95 (ISBN 0-08-025524-8). Pergamon.

Brekke, Asgeir, ed. see EISCAT School.

Brekle, Herbert E., ed. Wortbildung Syntax & Morphologie: Festchrift Zum 60 Geburstag Von Hans Marchand Am, Oktober 1967. (Janua Linguarum, Ser. Major: No. 36). 1968. text ed. 51.75x (ISBN 90-2790-687-4). Mouton.

Brelje, Terry B., jt. ed. see Irvine, Lynn M., Jr.

Brelsford, William M. & Relles, Daniel A. Statlib: A Statistical Computing Library. 448p. 1981. text ed. 17.50 (ISBN 0-13-846220-8). P-H.

Brem, M. M. La Historia de Maria. (Libros Arco Ser.). (Illus.). 32p. (Orig., Span.). (gr. 1-3). 1979. pap. 0.95 (ISBN 0-89922-145-9). Edit Caribe.

Breman, Jan. Patronage & Exploitation: Changing Agrarian Relations in South Gujarat, India. 1974. 23.50x (ISBN 0-520-02197-5). U of Cal Pr.

Brembeck, Cole S. Social Foundations of Education: A Book of Readings. LC 77-76051. text ed. 10.95x o.p. (ISBN 0-471-10191-5). Wiley.

--Social Foundations of Education: Environmental Influences in Teaching & Learning. 2nd ed. LC 79-135886. 1971. text ed. 19.95x o.p. (ISBN 0-471-10185-0). Wiley.

Brembeck, Winston L. & Howell, William S. Persuasion: A Means of Social Influence. 2nd ed. (Illus.). 384p. 1976. 15.95 (ISBN 0-13-661090-0). P-H.

Bremer. Skills in Spelling: 1973 Ed, Bks. A-H. Incl. Bk. A. (gr. 1). pap. text ed. 3.44 (ISBN 0-8009-0551-2); tchr's ed. 5.04 (ISBN 0-8009-0555-5); 1967 ed. of text & tchr's. ed. also avail. Write for further info.; Bk. B. (gr. 2). text ed. 6.88 (ISBN 0-8009-0649-7); pap. text ed. 3.44 (ISBN 0-8009-0564-4); tchr's. ed. for hardcover text 5.04 (ISBN 0-8009-0651-9); tchr's. ed. for pap. text 4.56 (ISBN 0-8009-0568-7); 1967-68 eds. of texts & tchr's ed. also avail. Write for further info.; Bk. C. (gr. 3). text ed. 6.88 (ISBN 0-8009-0653-5); pap. text ed. 3.44 (ISBN 0-8009-0576-8); tchr's. ed. for hardcover text 6.04 (ISBN 0-8009-0655-1); tchr's. ed. for pap. text 4.56 (ISBN 0-8009-0580-6); 1964 & 1967-68 eds. of texts & tchr's. ed. avail. Write for further info.; Bk. D. (gr. 4). text ed. 6.88 (ISBN 0-8009-0657-8); pap. text ed. 3.44 (ISBN 0-8009-0588-1); tchr's. ed. for hardcover text 5.04 (ISBN 0-8009-0659-4); tchr's. ed. for pap. text 4.56 (ISBN 0-8009-0593-8); 1964 & 1967-68 eds. **of texts & tchr's. eds. also avail. Write for further info.; Bk. E. (gr. 5). text ed. 6.88 (ISBN 0-8009-0661-6); pap. text ed. 3.44 (ISBN 0-8009-0601-2); tchr's. ed. for hardcover text 5.04 (ISBN 0-8009-0663-2); tchr's. ed. for pap. text 4.56 (ISBN 0-8009-0605-5); 1967-68 eds. of texts & tchr's. eds. also avail. Write for further info.; Bk. F. (gr. 6). text ed. 6.88 (ISBN 0-8009-0665-9); pap. text ed. 3.44 (ISBN 0-8009-0614-4); tchr's. ed. for hardcover text 5.04 (ISBN 0-8009-0667-5); tchr's. ed. for pap. text 4.56 (ISBN 0-8009-0618-7); 1967-68 eds. also avail. Write for further info.; Bk. G. (gr. 7). text ed. 6.88 (ISBN 0-8009-0669-1); pap. text ed. 3.44 (ISBN 0-8009-0626-8); tchr's. ed. for hardcover text 5.04 (ISBN 0-8009-0671-3); tchr's. ed. for pap. text 4.56 (ISBN 0-8009-0630-6); 1964 & 1967-68 eds. also avail. Write for further info.; Bk. H. (gr. 8). text ed. 6.88 (ISBN 0-8009-0674-8); pap. text ed. 3.44 (ISBN 0-8009-0638-1); tchr's. ed. for hardcover text 5.04 (ISBN 0-8009-0676-4); tchr's. ed. for pap. text 4.56 (ISBN 0-8009-0643-8); 1964 & 1967-68 eds. also avail. Write for further info.. (gr. 1-8). McCormick-Mathers.**

Bremer, Fredrika. The Home; or, Family Cares & Family Joys. Howitt, M., tr. from Swedish. LC 76-28470. 1978. Repr. of 1850 ed. 19.75 (ISBN 0-86527-259-X). Fertig.

Bremer, Hans J., et al. Disturbances of Amino Acid Metabolism: Clinical Chemistry & Diagnosis. LC 78-31995. (Illus.). 430p. 1981. text ed. 54.00 (ISBN 0-8067-0251-6). Urban & S.

Bremer, Maura. And Send the Sun Tomorrow: A Journal of My Father's Last Days. 1979. pap. 2.95 (ISBN 0-03-049396-X). Winston Pr.

Bremm, M. M. Un Hombre Tragado por un Pez. Villalobos, Fernando, tr. from Eng. (Libros Arco). (Illus.). 32p. (Orig., Span.). (gr. 1-3). 1970. pap. 0.95 o.s.i. (ISBN 0-89922-047-9). Edit Caribe.

Bremner, Robert H. American Philanthropy. LC 60-7246. (Chicago History of American Civilization Ser). (Illus.). 1960. 5.00x (ISBN 0-226-07326-2); pap. 2.25 o.s.i. (ISBN 0-226-07327-0, CHAC2). U of Chicago Pr.

--From the Depths: The Discovery of Poverty in the United States. LC 56-7622. (Illus.). 364p. 1956. 10.95x (ISBN 0-8147-0054-3); pap. 6.00x (ISBN 0-8147-0055-1). NYU Pr.

Bremner, Robert H., compiled by. American Social History Since 1860. LC 70-146848. (Goldentree Bibliographies in American History Ser). (Orig.). 1971. 14.95x (ISBN 0-88295-504-7); pap. 10.95x (ISBN 0-88295-503-9). AHM Pub.

Brems, Hans. Inflation, Interest, & Growth: A Synthesis. LC 78-19226. 192p. 1980. 18.95 (ISBN 0-669-02466-X). Lexington Bks.

--Quantitative Economic Theory: A Synthetic Approach. LC 77-17202. 514p. 1979. Repr. of 1968 ed. lib. bdg. 19.00 o.p. (ISBN 0-88275-646-X). Krieger.

Brems, Marianne. Swim for Fitness. LC 78-32033. (Illus.). 1979. pap. 6.95 (ISBN 0-87701-124-9). Chronicle Bks.

Brena, Steven. Pain & Religion: A Psychophysiological Study. (Illus.). 176p. 1972. 14.75 (ISBN 0-398-02242-9). C C Thomas.

Brenan, G. St. John of the Cross: His Life & Poetry. Nicholson, Lynda, tr. LC 72-83577. (Illus.). 224p. 1973. 38.50 (ISBN 0-521-20006-7); pap. 8.95x (ISBN 0-521-09953-6). Cambridge U Pr.

--Thoughts in a Dry Season. LC 78-4508. 1978. 17.95 (ISBN 0-521-22006-8). Cambridge U Pr.

Brenan, Gerald. Literature of the Spanish People. 2nd ed. 1953. 52.00 (ISBN 0-521-04313-1); pap. 12.95 (ISBN 0-521-29043-0). Cambridge U Pr.

--South from Granada. LC 80-40376. (Illus.). 282p. 1980. pap. 8.95 (ISBN 0-521-28029-X). Cambridge U Pr.

Brenan, J. P. see Jackson, B. D., et al.

Brenchley, Julius, jt. auth. see Remy, Jules.

Brenci, Gianni, jt. auth. see Gedda, Luigi.

Brend, Ruthm M. & Pike, Kenneth L., eds. Tagemics: Theoretical Discussion Trends in Linguistics, Vol. 2. (Studies & Monographs: No. 2). 1976. pap. 27.05x (ISBN 90-2793-425-8). Mouton.

Brendel, Otto J. Etruscan Art. 1979. pap. 15.00 (ISBN 0-14-056143-9, Pelican). Penguin.

Brendel, W. & Zink, R. A., eds. High Altitude Physiology & Medicine I: Physiology of Adaptation. (Topics in Environmental Physiology & Medicine Ser.). (Illus.). 190p. 1981. 39.80 (ISBN 0-387-90482-4). Springer-Verlag.

Brendhel-Lamhout, Claire, tr. see Baczko, Bronislaw.

Brendtro, Larry K., jt. auth. see Vorrath, Harry H.

Breneman, David W. & Finn, D. Chester E., eds. Public Policy & Private Higher Education. (Studies in Higher Education Policy). 1978. 18.95 (ISBN 0-8157-1066-6); pap. 8.95 (ISBN 0-8157-1065-8). Brookings.

Breneman, James C. Basics of Food Allergy. (Illus.). 296p. 1978. 35.75 (ISBN 0-398-03670-5). C C Thomas.

Breneman, Mervin, ed. Biblia con Notas. 1696p. (Span.). 1981. 14.95 (ISBN 0-89922-164-5); imitation leather 18.95 (ISBN 0-686-69098-2). Edit Caribe.

Brener, David. The Jews of Lancaster, Pennsylvania: A Story with Two Beginnings. LC 79-21690. (Illus.). 200p. 1979. 18.00 (ISBN 0-686-28857-2); pap. 12.00 (ISBN 0-686-28858-0). Cong Shaarai.

Brener, David A. The Jews of Lancaster, Pennsylvania: A Story with Two Beginnings. (Illus.). 188p. (Orig.). 1981. 18.00 (ISBN 0-9605482-1-1); pap. 12.00 (ISBN 0-9605482-0-3). Shaarai Shomayim.

Brenet, Michel. Les Concerts en France Sous l'Ancien Regime. LC 68-16224. (Music Ser). 1970. Repr. of 1900 ed. lib. bdg. 35.00 (ISBN 0-306-71061-7). Da Capo.

Brengelman, Fred. Shaping Sentences & Paragraphs: A Systematic Approach to Sentence & Paragraph Construction. 128p. 1980. pap. 6.95 (ISBN 0-8403-2292-5). Kendall-Hunt.

--Understanding Words: Systematic Spelling & Vocabulary Building. 112p. 1980. pap. 6.95 (ISBN 0-8403-2252-6). Kendall-Hunt.

Brengelmann, J. C. Effect of Repeated Electroshock on Learning in Depressives. (Monographien Aus Dem Gesamtgebiete der Neurologie: Vol. 84). (Illus.). 1959. 12.40 o.p. (ISBN 0-387-02447-6). Springer-Verlag.

Brengle, Kenneth G. Principles & Practices of Dryland Farming. 1981. price not set (ISBN 0-87081-095-2). Colo Assoc.

Brengle, Richard L., ed. Arthur, King of Britain: History, Romance, Chronicle & Criticism. (Orig.). 1964. pap. 9.50 (ISBN 0-13-049270-1). P-H.

Brengle, Samuel L. Guest of the Soul. 1978. pap. 3.25 (ISBN 0-86544-001-8). Salvation Army.

--Heart Talks on Holiness. 1978. pap. 3.25 (ISBN 0-86544-002-6). Salvation Army.

--Helps to Holiness. 1978. pap. 3.25 (ISBN 0-86544-003-4). Salvation Army.

--Love Slaves. 1960. Repr. of 1923 ed. 3.25 (ISBN 0-86544-004-2). Salvation Army.

--Resurrection Life & Power. 1978. Repr. of 1925 ed. 3.25 (ISBN 0-86544-005-0). Salvation Army.

--Soul Winner's Secret. 1978. pap. 3.25 (ISBN 0-86544-007-7). Salvation Army.

--Way of Holiness. 1966. Repr. of 1902 ed. 3.25 (ISBN 0-86544-008-5). Salvation Army.

Brenig, W., jt. ed. see Stuke, J.

Brenman-Gibson, Margaret. Clifford Odets. LC 80-7927. 1981. 25.00 (ISBN 0-689-10827-3). Atheneum.

Brennan, Alice. Castle Mirage. 1976. pap. 1.25 o.p. (ISBN 0-685-72570-7, LB392, Leisure Bks). Nordon Pubns.

--Devil Take All. 256p. (Orig.). 1974. pap. 0.95 o.p. (ISBN 0-445-00612-9). Popular Lib.

Brennan, Andrew, ed. see Elder, Crawford.

Brennan, Andrew, ed. see Tiles, J. E.

Brennan, Bernard P. William James. (U. S. Authors Ser.: No. 131). 1968. lib. bdg. 10.95 (ISBN 0-8057-0408-6). Twayne.

Brennan, Dan. One of Our Bombers Is Missing. 1977. pap. 1.50 (ISBN 0-505-51140-1). Tower Bks.

Brennan, E. J., ed. Education for National Efficiency: The Contribution of Sidney & Beatrice Webb. 218p. 1975. text ed. 20.75x (ISBN 0-485-11151-9, Athlone Pr). Humanities.

Brennan, G. & Buchanan, J. The Power to Tax. LC 79-56862. (Illus.). 300p. 1980. 22.50 (ISBN 0-521-23329-1). Cambridge U Pr.

Brennan, Gale. Dugan the Duck. (Illus.). 1980. 5.95g (ISBN 0-516-09101-8). Childrens.

--Elihu the Elephant. (Illus.). 1980. 5.95g (ISBN 0-516-09102-6). Childrens.

--Here Come the Clowns. (Illus.). 32p. (Orig.). (gr. 1-4). 1980. pap. 1.95 (ISBN 0-89542-931-4). Ideals.

--In the Land of Sniggl-dee Sloop. (Illus.). 1980. 7.95g (ISBN 0-516-09172-7). Childrens.

--In the Land of Sniggle-Dee-Bloop. (Illus.). 48p. (Orig.). (ps-3). 1980. pap. 2.95 (ISBN 0-89542-936-5). Ideals.

--My Best Friend Ever. (Illus.). 48p. (Orig.). (ps-3). 1980. pap. 2.95 (ISBN 0-89542-937-3). Ideals.

--What If.... (Illus.). 32p. (Orig.). (ps-2). 1980. pap. 1.95 (ISBN 0-89542-932-2). Ideals.

Brennan, Gale & LaFleur, Tom. What If? (Illus.). 1980. 7.35g (ISBN 0-516-09154-9). Childrens.

Brennan, Hill. The Near Death Experience: A Christian Approach. 64p. (Orig.). 1981. pap. 3.50 (ISBN 0-697-01758-3). Wm C Brown.

Brennan, Irene J. Fort Mojave, Eighteen Fifty-Nine to Eighteen Ninety: Letter of the Commanding Officers. 1980. pap. 26.00 (ISBN 0-89126-083-8). Military Aff Aero.

Brennan, J. H. Dark Moon. LC 80-20034. 264p. 1981. 13.95 (ISBN 0-03-058013-7). HR&W.

Brennan, Jennifer. The Original Thai Cookbook. (Illus.). 276p. 1981. 12.95 (ISBN 0-399-90110-8). Marek.

Brennan, Joe. Hot Rod Thunder. LC 62-8928. (gr. 6-9). 1962. 5.95 o.p. (ISBN 0-385-01650-6). Doubleday.

Brennan, John M., ed. Buying Guide to California Wines. 3rd ed. (Illus.). 1981. 25.00 (ISBN 0-916040-53-4). Wine Consul Calif.

Brennan, Joseph P. The Shapes of Midnight. 1980. pap. 2.25 o.p. (ISBN 0-425-04567-6). Berkley Pub.

Brennan, Louis A. American Dawn: A New Model of American Prehistory. LC 71-93718. (Illus.). 1970. 14.95 (ISBN 0-02-514910-5). Macmillan.

Brennan, M. Theory of Economic Statics. 2nd ed. 1970. 18.95 (ISBN 0-13-913624-X). P-H.

Brennan, Martin. The Boyne Valley Vision. 1981. text ed. 26.00x (ISBN 0-85105-362-9, Dolmen Pr). Humanities.

Brennan, Mary E., ed. Canadian Conference, 12th Annual, October 27-31, 1979: Proceedings. 177p. 1980. pap. 10.00 (ISBN 0-89154-129-2). Intl Found Employ.

--EDP Institute, Los Angeles, Nov. 4-7, 1979: Proceedings. 95p. 1980. pap. 10.00 (ISBN 0-89154-127-6). Intl Found Employ.

--Pulic Employees Conference, Dec. 5-8, 1979, Hollywood, Fla. Proceedings. 160p. 1980. pap. 10.00 (ISBN 0-89154-126-8). Intl Found Employ.

Brennan, Mary E. & Heib, Elizabeth A., eds. Investment Institute Hollywood, Florida, April 27 to 30, 1980: Proceedings. 137p. 1980. pap. 10.00 (ISBN 0-89154-134-9). Intl Found Employ.

Brennan, Michael. The War in Clare Nineteen Eleven-Nineteen Twenty-One: Personal Memoirs of the Irish War of Independence. 112p. 1981. 12.50x (ISBN 0-906127-26-2, Pub. by Irish Academic Pr Ireland). Biblio Dist.

Brennan, Michael J., ed. Patterns of Market Behavior: Essays in Honor of Philip Taft. LC 65-12932. 258p. 1965. 10.00x (ISBN 0-87057-087-0, Pub. by Brown U Pr). Univ Pr of New England.

Brennan, Neil. Anthony Powell. (English Authors Ser.: No. 158). 1974. lib. bdg. 10.95 (ISBN 0-8057-1454-5). Twayne.

Brennan, Peter. Razorback. 384p. (Orig.). 1981. pap. price not set (ISBN 0-515-05392-9). Jove Pubns.

--Sudden Death. 1979. pap. 2.25 o.s.i. (ISBN 0-515-04851-8). Jove Pubns.

Brennan, Rory. The Sea on Fire. (Orig.). 1980. pap. text ed. 8.00x (ISBN 0-85105-308-4, Dolmen Pr). Humanities.

Brennan, Tim, et al. The Social Psychology of Runaways. LC 75-42947. 1978. 26.95 (ISBN 0-669-00565-7). Lexington Bks.

Brennan, W. K. Shaping the Education of Slow Learners. (Special Needs in Education Ser.). 1974. 9.50 (ISBN 0-7100-7984-2); pap. 4.50 (ISBN 0-7100-7985-0). Routledge & Kegan.

Brennan, William. Medical Holocausts I: Exterminative Medicine in Nazi Germany & Contemporary America. LC 80-82305. (The Nordland Series in Contemporary American Social Problems). 375p. 1980. pap. 12.95 (ISBN 0-913124-39-7). Nordland Pub.

--Medical Holocausts II: The Language of Exterminative Medicine in Nazi Germany & Contemporary America. LC 80-82305. (The Nordland Series in Contemporary American Social Problems). 320p. 1980. pap. 12.95 (ISBN 0-913124-40-0). Nordland Pub.

Brennan, William T. & Crowe, James W. Guide to Problems & Practices in First Aid & Emergency Care. 4th ed. 192p. 1981. wire coil 7.95x (ISBN 0-697-07390-4). Wm C Brown.

Brennecke, John H. & Amick, Robert G. Psychology & Human Experience. 2nd ed. 1978. pap. text ed. 9.95x (ISBN 0-02-471030-X); wkbk 5.95x (ISBN 0-02-471060-1); readings to accompany 6.95x (ISBN 0-02-471050-4). Macmillan.

--Significance: The Struggle We Share. 2nd ed. 1975. pap. text ed. 7.95x (ISBN 0-02-471020-2, 47102). Macmillan.

--Struggle for Significance. 1971. pap. text ed. 5.95x (ISBN 0-02-473360-1). Macmillan.

--The Struggle for Significance. 2nd ed. 1975. pap. text ed. 9.95x (ISBN 0-02-471000-8, 47100); tchrs' manual free (ISBN 0-02-471010-5). Macmillan.

Brenneman, H. G. Meditaciones Para la Nueva Madre. 1978. 2.20 (ISBN 0-311-40032-9). Casa Bautista.

Brenneman, Helen G. Morning Joy. LC 80-26449. 80p. 1981. pap. 3.95 (ISBN 0-8361-1942-8). Herald Pr.

Brenneman, Walter L., Jr. Spirals: A Study in Symbol, Myth & Ritual. LC 77-26365. 1978. pap. text ed. 7.50x (ISBN 0-8191-0463-9). U Pr of Amer.

Brennen, Mary, ed. Employee Contributions & Delinqukidncies Under ERISA Institute, las Vegas, Nov. 12-15, 1978. (Orig.). 1979. pap. 7.50 (ISBN 0-89154-097-0). Intl Found Employ.

Brennenstuhl, W., jt. auth. see Ballmer, T.

Brenner, Alfred. TV Scriptwriter's Handbook. LC 80-23700. 288p. 1980. 10.95 (ISBN 0-89879-024-7). Writers Digest.

Brenner, Anita. Idols Behind Altars. LC 67-19527. (Illus.). 1929. 18.00x (ISBN 0-8196-0190-X). Biblo.

--Wind That Swept Mexico: The History of the Mexican Revolution of 1910-1942. new ed. (Texas Pan American Ser). (Illus.). 310p. 1971. 17.95 (ISBN 0-292-70106-3). U of Tex Pr.

Brenner, Barbara. Cunningham's Rooster. LC 74-12285. (Illus.). 1975. 5.95 o.s.i. (ISBN 0-8193-0783-1, Four Winds); PLB 5.41 o.s.i. (ISBN 0-8193-0784-X). Schol Bk Serv.

--A Killing Season. LC 80-69993. 160p. (gr. 7 up). 1981. 8.95 (ISBN 0-590-07674-4, Four Winds). Schol Bk Serv.

--Mystery of the Plumed Serpent. LC 80-17316. (Capers Ser.). (Illus.). 128p. (gr. 3-6). 1981. PLB 4.99 (ISBN 0-394-94531-X); pap. 1.95 (ISBN 0-394-84531-5). Knopf.

--Ostrich Feathers. LC 77-24284. (Illus.). 32p. (gr. k-4). 1978. lib. bdg. 5.95 (ISBN 0-590-07718-X, Four Winds). Schol Bk Serv.

--The Prince & the Pink Blanket. LC 80-10950. (Illus.). 32p. (gr. k-3). 1980. 8.95 (ISBN 0-590-07614-0, Four Winds). Schol Bk Serv.

--A Snake-Lover's Diary. LC 79-98113. (Illus.). (gr. 3-7). 1970. PLB 6.95 (ISBN 0-201-09349-9, A-W Chidrens). A-W.

--Walt Disney's the Penguin That Hated the Cold. (Disney's Wonderful World of Reading Ser.: No. 7). (Illus.). (ps-3). 1973. 3.95 (ISBN 0-394-82628-0, BYR); PLB 4.99 (ISBN 0-394-92628-5). Random.

--Walt Disney's the Three Little Pigs. (Disney's Wonderful World of Reading Ser.: No. 6). (Illus.). (ps-3). 1974. 3.95 (ISBN 0-394-82522-5, BYR); PLB 4.99 (ISBN 0-394-92522-X). Random.

--We're off to See the Lizard. LC 76-10350. (Read to Myself Ser.). (Illus.). 32p. (gr. k-2). 1977. PLB 7.75 (ISBN 0-8172-0151-3). Raintree Pubs.

--A Year in the Life of Rosie Bernard. (gr. 3-7). 1975. pap. 1.50 (ISBN 0-380-01630-3, 43380, Camelot). Avon.

Brenner, Barbara, ed. see Turner, Edward & Turner, Clive.

Brenner, Barbara, ed. see Whitlock, Ralph.

Brenner, Barry M. & Stein, Jay H. Acute Renal Failure. (Contemporary Issues in Nephrology: Vol. 6). (Illus.). 320p. 1980. text ed. 35.00 (ISBN 0-443-08116-6). Churchill.

Brenner, Barry M. & Stein, Jay H., eds. Sodium & Water Homeostasis. (Contemporary Issues in Nephrology: Vol. 1). (Illus.). 1978. text ed. 25.00x o.p. (ISBN 0-443-08005-4). Churchill.

Brenner, Charles, M.D. An Elementary Textbook of Psychoanalysis. rev. ed. 280p. 1974. pap. 3.50 (ISBN 0-385-09884-7, Anch). Doubleday.

Brenner, Egon & Javid, M. Analysis of Electric Circuits. 2nd ed. (Electrical & Electronic Engineering Ser.). 1967. text ed. 29.95 (ISBN 0-07-007630-8, C); instructor's manual 2.75 (ISBN 0-07-007636-7); answers bk. 2.50 (ISBN 0-07-007635-9). McGraw.

Brenner, Eleanor P. Gourmet Cooking Without Salt. LC 79-6856. (Illus.). 416p. 1981. 15.95 (ISBN 0-385-14821-6). Doubleday.

Brenner, H., jt. ed. see Happel, J.

Brenner, Joel L., tr. see Faddeev, D. K. & Sominskii, I. S.

Brenner, Marie. Going Hollywood. 1977. 8.95 o.s.i. (ISBN 0-440-03018-7). Delacorte.

--Tell Me Everything. 1977. pap. 1.95 o.p. (ISBN 0-451-07685-0, J7685, Sig). NAL.

Brenner, Michael J. The Politics of International Monetary Reform: The Exchange Crisis. LC 75-45458. 128p. 1976. text ed. 16.50 o.p. (ISBN 0-88410-292-0). Ballinger Pub.

Brenner, Paul. Health Is a Question of Balance. 143p. 1980. pap. 4.95 (ISBN 0-87516-415-3). De Vorss.

Brenner, Paul H. Health Is a Question of Balance. 1978. 5.95 o.p. (ISBN 0-533-03513-9). Vantage.

Brenner, S., et al, eds. New Horizons in Industrial Microbiology: Philosophical Transactions of the Royal Society, 1980. rev. ed. (Ser. B: Vol. 290). (Illus.). 152p. text ed. 47.50x (ISBN 0-85403-146-4, Pub. by Dechema Germany). Scholium Intl.

Brenner, Y. S. Agriculture & the Economic Development of Low Income Countries. LC 77-146701. (Publications of the Institute of Social Studies Paperbacks: No. 2). 254p. 1972. pap. text ed. 12.25x (ISBN 90-2791-713-2). Mouton.

--Short History of Economic Progress. LC 68-21447. (Illus.). 1969. 24.00x (ISBN 0-678-05014-7). Kelley.

Brenni, Vito J. The Bibliographic Control of American Literature: Nineteen Twenty to Nineteen Seventy-Five. LC 79-12542. 484p. 1979. 11.00 (ISBN 0-8108-1221-5). Scarecrow.

--Essays on Bibliography. LC 75-14082. 1975. 18.00 (ISBN 0-8108-0826-9). Scarecrow.

--William Dean Howells: A Bibliography. LC 73-4855. (Author Bibliographies Ser.: No. 9). 1973. 10.00 (ISBN 0-8108-0620-7). Scarecrow.

Brenni, Vito J., compiled by. Book Illustration & Decoration: A Guide to Research. LC 80-1701. (Art Reference Collection Ser.: No. 1). viii, 191p. 1980. lib. bdg. 27.50 (ISBN 0-313-22340-8, BBI/). Greenwood.

Brent, Allen. Philosophical Foundations for the Curriculum. (Unwin Education Books). 1978. text ed. 19.50x (ISBN 0-04-370084-5); pap. text ed. 8.95x (ISBN 0-04-370085-3). Allen Unwin.

Brent, Audrey. Snowflakes in the Sun. 192p. 1981. pap. 1.50 (ISBN 0-671-57063-3). S&S.

Brent, Carol D. Fondue: The Fine Art of Fondue, Chinese Wok & Chafing Dish Cooking. LC 77-95289. 4.95 o.p. (ISBN 0-385-00606-3). Doubleday.

Brent, Joanna. A Few Days in Weasel Creek. LC 80-84368. 224p. 1981. pap. 2.50 (ISBN 0-87216-818-2). Playboy Pbks.

Brent, Kurt, jt. auth. see Batchelor, Kay.

Brent, Madeleine. Tregaron's Daughter. LC 78-150878. 1971. 6.95 o.p. (ISBN 0-385-00323-4). Doubleday.

--Tregaron's Daughter. 320p. 1981. pap. 2.50 (ISBN 0-449-24391-5, Crest). Fawcett.

Brent, Patricia. Crafts Careers. (Career Concise Guides Ser.). (Illus.). (gr. 7 up). 1977. PLB 6.45 s&l (ISBN 0-531-01304-9). Watts.

--Haircutting. LC 75-34251. (Career Concise Guides Ser.). (Illus.). 72p. (gr. 7 up). 1976. PLB 6.45 (ISBN 0-531-01127-5). Watts.

Brent, R. Spencer. Pattern Play Tennis. LC 72-89295. 144p. 1974. 6.95 o.p. (ISBN 0-385-05874-8). Doubleday.

Brentano, jt. auth. see Tiek, Ludwig.

Brentano, Clemens see Scher, Helene, et al.

Brentano, Franz. Aristotle & His World View. George, Rolf & Chisholm, Roderick, trs. from Ger. 1978. 15.50x (ISBN 0-520-03390-6). U of Cal Pr.

--On the Several Senses of Being in Aristotle. LC 72-89796. 210p. 1976. 16.75x (ISBN 0-520-02346-3). U of Cal Pr.

--The Origin of Our Knowledge of Right & Wrong. Chisholm, R. & Schneewind, E., trs. (International Library of Philosophy & Scientific Method). 1976. Repr. of 1969 ed. 14.50x (ISBN 0-391-00980-X). Humanities.

--Psychology from an Empirical Standpoint. Kraus, Oskar & McAlister, Linda L., eds. Rancurello, Antos C., et al, trs. from Ger. (International Library of Philosophy & Scientific Method). 520p. 1973. text ed. 32.50x (ISBN 0-391-00253-8). Humanities.

--The Psychology of Aristotle: In Particular His Doctrine of the Active Intellect with an Appendix Concerning the Activity of Aristotle's God. George, Rolf, tr. LC 75-17303. 1977. 16.75x (ISBN 0-520-03081-8). U of Cal Pr.

--Sensory & Noetic Consciousness (Psychology from an Empirical Standpoint III) Schattle, Margaret & McAlister, Linda L., trs. 1980. text ed. 20.75x (ISBN 0-391-01175-8). Humanities.

Brentano, Robert. Early Middle Ages. LC 64-21204. 1964. pap. text ed. 6.95 (ISBN 0-02-904670-X). Free Pr.

Brentano, Ron, pref. by. Ballou-Wright Automobile Supplies Catalog, 1906. LC 74-635336. (Illus.). 90p. 1971. pap. 2.95 (ISBN 0-87595-028-0). Oreg Hist Soc.

Brenton, Myron. How to Survive Your Child's Rebellious Teens: New Solutions for Troubled Parents. 1979. 9.95 (ISBN 0-397-01340-X). Lippincott.

--Lasting Relationships: How to Recognize the Man or Woman Who's Right for You. 224p. 1981. 10.95 (ISBN 0-89479-078-1). A & W Pubs.

Brereton, Bridget. Race Relations in Colonial Trinidad Eighteen Seventy to Nineteen Hundred. LC 78-72081. (Illus.). 1980. 41.50 (ISBN 0-521-22428-4). Cambridge U Pr.

Brereton, Georgine E. & Ferrier, Janet M., eds. Le Menagier De Paris: A Critical Edition. 600p. 1981. 99.00 (ISBN 0-19-815748-7). Oxford U Pr.

Brereton, Lewis. The Brereton Diaries. (Politics & Strategy of World War II Ser.). 1976. Repr. of 1946 ed. lib. bdg. 35.00 (ISBN 0-306-70766-7). Da Capo.

Bresciani, Francesco, ed. Perspectives in Steroid Receptor Research. 334p. 1980. text ed. 30.00 (ISBN 0-89004-490-2). Raven.

Bresher, David & Trubo, Richard. Free Yourself from Pain. 1980. pap. write for info. (ISBN 0-671-81683-7). PB.

Breslauer, S. Daniel. The Ecumenical Perspective & the Modernization of Jewish Religion: A Study in the Relationship Between Theology & Myth. 1978. pap. 7.50 (ISBN 0-89130-236-0, 140005). Scholars Pr Ca.

Bresler, B., et al. Design of Steel Structures. 2nd ed. 1968. 34.50 (ISBN 0-471-10297-0). Wiley.

Bresler, Boris. Reinforced Concrete Engineering, Vol. 1. LC 73-19862. 576p. 1974. 35.00 (ISBN 0-471-10279-2, Pub. by Wiley-Interscience). Wiley.

Bresler, Fenton. The Chinese Mafia. LC 80-5797. (Illus.). 256p. 1981. 12.95 (ISBN 0-8128-2752-X). Stein & Day.

Bresler, J., ed. Genetics & Society. LC 72-2650. 1973. pap. text ed. 7.95 (ISBN 0-201-00600-6). A-W.

Breslin, Catherine. Unholy Child. 1980. pap. 3.50 (ISBN 0-451-09477-8, E9477, Sig). NAL.

Breslin, Patrick. Interventions: A Cold War Novel of Love & Death. LC 79-6091. 264p. 1980. 10.95 (ISBN 0-385-15816-5). Doubleday.

Breslow, Aron. Hello Equal Rights! 1981. 2.00 (ISBN 0-918430-01-1). Happy History.

--Nothing Stops a Determined Being! 1981. 4.00 (ISBN 0-918430-03-8). Happy History.

--Save the Inch! 1981. 2.00 (ISBN 0-918430-02-X). Happy History.

Breslow, Kay & Breslow, Paul. Charles Gwathmey & Robert Siegel: Residential Works Nineteen Sixty-Six to Nineteen Seventy-Seven. (Illus.). 172p. 1980. 49.95 (ISBN 0-8038-0045-2). Architectural.

--Charles Gwathmey & Robert Siegel: Residential Works Nineteen Sixty-Six to Nineteen Seventy-Seven. 1980. 49.95 (ISBN 0-8038-0045-2). Hastings.

Breslow, Lester, et al, eds. Annual Review of Public Health, Vol. 1. (Illus.). 1980. text ed. 17.00 (ISBN 0-8243-2701-2). Annual Reviews.

--Annual Review of Public Health, Vol 2. 1981. text ed. 20.00 (ISBN 0-8243-2702-0). Annual Reviews.

Breslow, Paul, jt. auth. see Breslow, Kay.

Bresnan, Joan, ed. The Mental Representation of Grammatical Relations. (Cognitive Theory & Mental Representation Ser.: Vol. 1). 700p. 1981. text ed. 35.00x (ISBN 0-262-02158-7). MIT Pr.

Bresnan, Joan W. Theory of Complementation in English Syntax. Hankamer, Jorge, ed. LC 78-66551. (Outstanding Dissertations in Linguistics Ser.). 1979. lib. bdg. 36.00 (ISBN 0-8240-9689-4). Garland Pub.

Bresnan, Michael J., et al. Pediatric Neurology. (Medical Examination Review Book: Vol. 35). 1976. spiral bdg. 15.00 o.p. (ISBN 0-87488-175-7). Med Exam.

Bresnick, Edward & Schwartz, Arnold. Functional Dynamics of the Cell. LC 68-14640. 1968. text ed. 20.95 (ISBN 0-12-132650-0). Acad Pr.

Bress, Helene. The Weaving Book: Patterns & Ideas. (Illus.). Date not set. 40.00 (ISBN 0-684-15664-4, ScribT). Scribner. Postponed.

Bressler, M. N., et al. Criteria for Nuclear Safety Related Piping & Component Support Snubbers. (PVP: No. 45). 40p. 1980. 6.00 (H00173). ASME.

Bressler, R., jt. ed. see Brodie, Bernard B.

Bressler, Rubin & Conrad, Kenneth. Drug Therapy for the Elderly. (Illus.). 300p. 1981. pap. text ed. 13.95 (ISBN 0-8016-0782-5). Mosby.

Bressler, Rubin, ed. Management of Diabetes Mellitus. LC 80-10866. 325p. 1981. 29.50 (ISBN 0-88416-259-1, 259). PSG Pub.

Bresson, Robert. The Complete Screenplays, Vol. I: A Prisoner Escaped. Michelson, Annette, ed. Burch, Noel, tr. 1981. 15.00 (ISBN 0-89396-033-0); pap. 7.95 (ISBN 0-89396-034-9). Urizen Bks. Postponed.

Bressoud, David M. Analytical & Combinational Generalizations of the Rogers-Ramanujan Identities. LC 79-27622. (Memoirs Ser.). 1980. 6.00 (ISBN 0-8218-2227-6, MEMO-227). Am Math.

Brest, Albert N., ed. see Rackley, Charles E.

Brest, Paul. Processes of Constitutional Decisionmaking: Cases & Materials. 1375p. 1975. 27.50 (ISBN 0-316-10790-5); Suppl., 1980. pap. write for info. (ISBN 0-316-10791-3). Little.

Brestin, Dee. Proverbs & Parables: God's Wisdom for Living. (Fisherman Bible Studyguides). 1975. saddle-stitch 1.95 (ISBN 0-87788-694-6). Shaw Pubs.

Brestin, Dee & Brestin, Steve. Higher Ground. (Fisherman Bible Study Guide). 1978. pap. 1.95 saddle stitch (ISBN 0-87788-345-9). Shaw Pubs.

Brestin, Dee, jt. auth. see Brestin, Steve.

Brestin, Steve & Brestin, Dee. Building Your House on the Lord. LC 76-43127. (Fisherman Bible Study Guides). 87p. 1976. pap. 1.45 (ISBN 0-87788-098-0). Shaw Pubs.

Brestin, Steve, jt. auth. see Brestin, Dee.

Brestyanszky, I. Margit Kovacs. (Illus.). 1977. 25.00 (ISBN 0-912728-22-1). Newbury Bks Inc.

Breth, Robert D. Dynamic Management Communications. (Orig.). 1969. pap. 8.95 (ISBN 0-201-00702-9). A-W.

Brethower, Dale M. Behavior Analysis in Business & Industry: A Total Performance System. (Illus.). 130p. (Orig.). 1972. pap. 10.00 (ISBN 0-914474-06-5); instr's. manual avail. F Fournies.

Breton, Andre. Magritte. (Illus.). 1964. pap. 3.50 o.p. (ISBN 0-913456-87-X). Interbk Inc.

--Magritte. (Illus.). 1964. pap. 3.50 (ISBN 0-914412-24-8). Inst for the Arts.

--Young Cherry Trees Secured Against Hares. bilingual ed. LC 69-15847. Orig. Title: Jeunes Cerisiers Garantis Contre les Lievres. (Illus., Fr. & Eng.). 1969. 5.00 o.p. (ISBN 0-472-17910-1). U of Mich Pr.

Breton, Anne-Marie. To Flee from Eagles. 288p. (Orig.). 1981. pap. 2.75 (ISBN 0-523-40405-0). Pinnacle Bks.

Breton, Raymond. The Canadian Condition: A Guide to Research in Public Policy. 65p. 1977. pap. text ed. 2.95x (ISBN 0-920380-00-X, Pub. by Inst Res Pub Canada). Renouf.

Breton, Raymond & Akian, Gail G. Urban Institutions & People of Indian Ancestry. 52p. 1978. pap. text ed. 3.00x (ISBN 0-920380-14-X, Pub. by Inst Res Pub Canada). Renouf.

Bretonne, Anne-Marie. A Gallows Stands in Salem. 256p. 1975. pap. 1.25 o.p. (ISBN 0-445-00276-X). Popular Lib.

Brett, Barbara. Love After Hours. 352p. 1981. pap. 2.50 (ISBN 0-380-76257-9, 76257). Avon.

Brett, Jan. Fritz & the Beautiful Horses. (gr. k-3). 1981. pap. 8.95 (ISBN 0-395-30850-X). HM.

Brett, John. Who'd Hire John Brett. 176p. 1981. 9.95 (ISBN 0-312-87038-8). St Martin.

Brett, Lewis E. Nineteenth-Century Spanish Plays. (Span.). 1935. text ed. 18.95 (ISBN 0-13-622704-X). P-H.

Brett, Lionel, jt. auth. see Beazley, Elizabeth.

Brett, M. The English Church Under Henry I. (Oxford Historical Monographs). 288p. 1975. 37.50x (ISBN 0-19-821861-3). Oxford U Pr.

Brett, R. I. & Grant, G. F., eds. Andrew Marvell: Essays on the Tercentenary of His Death. 1979. 19.95x (ISBN 0-19-713435-1). Oxford U Pr.

Brett, R. L., ed. Writers & Their Background: Samuel Taylor Coleridge. LC 72-85533. (Writers & Their Background Ser.). xvii, 296p. 1975. 15.00x (ISBN 0-8214-0109-2); pap. 6.50x (ISBN 0-8214-0110-6). Ohio U Pr.

Brett, Simon. An Amateur Corpse. 1978. 7.95 o.p. (ISBN 0-684-15571-0, ScribT). Scribner.

--Cast in Order of Disappearance. 1979. pap. 2.25 (ISBN 0-425-04934-5). Berkley Pub.

--The Dead Side of the Mike. 1980. 8.95 (ISBN 0-684-16729-8, ScribT). Scribner.

--So Much Blood. 1981. pap. 2.25 (ISBN 0-425-04935-3). Berkley Pub.

--So Much Blood. LC 76-42083. (Encore Editions). 1977. 2.95 (ISBN 0-684-16535-X, ScribT). Scribner.

--Star Trap. 1981. pap. 2.25 (ISBN 0-425-04936-1). Berkley Pub.

--Star Trap. LC 77-78114. 1978. 7.95 o.p. (ISBN 0-684-15190-1, ScribT). Scribner.

Brett, Walter S. Planning Your Garden. (Illus.). 14.95x o.p. (ISBN 0-392-04148-0, SpS). Soccer.

Brett, William & Sentlowitz, Michael. Elementary Algebra by Example. LC 76-11979. (Illus.). 1977. pap. text ed. 14.95 (ISBN 0-395-24425-0); inst. manual 1.75 (ISBN 0-395-24426-9). HM.

Brettell, Richard & Lloyd, Christopher, eds. Catalogue of Drawings by Camille Pissarro in the Ashmolean Museum, Oxford. (Illus.). 440p. 1980. 115.00x (ISBN 0-19-817357-1). Oxford U Pr.

Brett-James, Antony. Life in Wellington's Army. 1972. text ed. 13.50x (ISBN 0-04-940042-8). Allen Unwin.

Bretung, Joan. Geriatric Procedure Manual. 192p. 1980. write for info. o.p. (ISBN 0-913292-05-2). Tiresias Pr.

Breuer, Georg. Air in Danger: Ecological Perspectives of the Atmosphere. Fabian, P., tr. from Ger. LC 79-18820. (Illus.). 180p. 1980. 24.95 (ISBN 0-521-22417-9); pap. 7.95 (ISBN 0-521-29483-5). Cambridge U Pr.

--Weather Modification, Prospect & Problems. Morth, H. T., tr. from Ger. LC 79-73236. (Illus.). 1980. 29.95 (ISBN 0-521-22453-5); pap. 8.95 (ISBN 0-521-29577-7). Cambridge U Pr.

Breuer, H., jt. ed. see Von Kleist, Sabine.

Breuer, M., ed. Cosmetic Science. Vol. 1, 1978. 49.00 (ISBN 0-12-133001-X); Vol. 2, 1980. 53.00 (ISBN 0-12-133002-8). Acad Pr.

Breuer, Melvin A. Design Automation of Digital Systems: Theory & Techniques, Vol. 1. (Illus.). 1972. ref. ed. 25.95 (ISBN 0-13-199893-5). P-H.

Breugelmans, Rene. Jacques Perk. LC 74-8658. (World Authors Ser.: Netherlands: No. 328). 1974. lib. bdg. 12.50 (ISBN 0-8057-2688-8). Twayne.

Breul, Frank R. & Diner, Steven J., eds. Compassion & Responsibility: Readings in the History of Social Welfare Policy in the United States. LC 79-56040. 1980. pap. text ed. 9.95x (ISBN 0-226-07413-7). U of Chicago Pr.

Breunig, Charles. Age of Revolution & Reaction, 1789-1850. (Illus.). 1977. 12.95 (ISBN 0-393-05612-0); pap. 5.95x (ISBN 0-393-09143-0). Norton.

Breunig, LeRoy C. Guillaume Apollinaire. LC 79-92030. (Columbia Essays on Modern Writers Ser.: No. 46). 1969. pap. 2.00 (ISBN 0-231-02995-0). Columbia U Pr.

Breva-Claramonte, Manuel. Sanctius' Theory of Language: A Contribution to the History of Renaissance Linguistics. (Studies in the History of Linguistics). 1980. text ed. 42.75x (ISBN 0-391-01673-3). Humanities.

Brew, Margaret W. The Burtons of Dunroe, 3 vols. Wolff, Robert L., ed. (Ireland-Nineteenth Century Fiction, Ser. Two: Vol. 69). 1979. Set. lib. bdg. 138.00 (ISBN 0-8240-3518-6). Garland Pub.

--Chronicles of Castles Cloyne: Pictures of Munster Life, 3 vols. Wolff, Robert L., ed. (Ireland-Nineteenth Century Fiction, Ser. Two: Vol. 70). 1979. lib. bdg. 46.00 (ISBN 0-8240-3519-4); lib. bdg. 42.00 (ISBN 0-686-66181-8). Garland Pub.

Brewer. Cellular Pathology. (Postgraduate Pathology Ser.). 1981. price not set (ISBN 0-407-00050-X). Butterworths. Postponed.

Brewer, Allen A. & Morrow, Robert M. Overdentures. LC 74-28500. (Illus.). 270p. 1975. 37.50 o.p. (ISBN 0-8016-3515-2). Mosby.

--Overdentures. 2nd ed. LC 80-19356. (Illus.). 426p. 1980. text ed. 47.50 (ISBN 0-8016-0785-X). Mosby.

Brewer, Annie, jt. auth. see Geiser, Elizabeth.

Brewer, Annie, ed. Popular Biographies Master Index. (Gale Biographical Index Ser.: No. 8). 1000p. 1980. write for info. (ISBN 0-8103-1076-7). Gale.

Brewer, Annie & Geiser, Elizabeth, eds. Book Publishers Directory: Supplement to Second Edition. 200p. 1980. 45.00 (ISBN 0-8103-0190-3). Gale.

Brewer, Annie M., ed. Dictionaries, Encyclopedias & Other Word-Related Books, 2 vols. 2nd ed. LC 78-31449. 1979. Set. 70.00 (ISBN 0-8103-1131-3); Vol. 1. 92.00 (ISBN 0-8103-1129-1); Vol. 2. 84.00 (ISBN 0-8103-1130-5). Gale.

Brewer, Annie M., jt. ed. see Geiser, Elizabeth A.

Brewer, Anthony. Marxist Theories of Imperialism. 304p. 1980. 35.00 (ISBN 0-7100-0531-8); pap. 16.50 (ISBN 0-7100-0621-7). Routledge & Kegan.

Brewer, D. S. Chaucer in His Time. LC 74-159930. 244p. (Orig.). 1973. pap. text ed. 11.50x (ISBN 0-582-48511-8). Longman.

Brewer, D. S., ed. see Chaucer, Geoffrey.

Brewer, David J., ed. World's Best Orations, 2 Vols. LC 75-15323. 1970. Repr. of 1901 ed. Set. 99.50 (ISBN 0-8108-0341-0). Scarecrow.

Brewer, Derek. Chaucer & His World. LC 77-10790. (Illus.). 1978. 20.00 (ISBN 0-396-07519-3). Dodd.

--Symbolic Stories: Traditional Narratives of the Family Drama in English Literature. 190p. 1980. 31.50x (ISBN 0-8476-6900-9). Rowman.

Brewer, Derek, ed. Chaucer-the Critical Heritage, 2 vols. Incl. Vol. 1. 1385-1837. 27.00 (ISBN 0-7100-8497-8); Vol. 2. 1837-1933. 35.00 (ISBN 0-7100-8498-6). (Critical Heritage Ser.). 1978. Set. 50.00 (ISBN 0-685-86576-2). Routledge & Kegan.

Brewer, Derek S., ed. Writers & Their Background: Geoffrey Chaucer. LC 74-84295. (Writers & Their Background Ser.). xiv, 401p. 1974. 17.00x (ISBN 0-8214-0183-1); pap. 7.00x (ISBN 0-8214-0184-X). Ohio U Pr.

Brewer, Donald D., jt. auth. see Truitt, John O.

Brewer, E. Cobham. Authors & Their Works, with Dates. LC 71-134907. 1970. Repr. of 1898 ed. 36.00 (ISBN 0-8103-3025-3). Gale.

--A Dictionary of Miracles, Imitative, Realistic, & Dogmatic. LC 66-29783. 1966. Repr. of 1885 ed. 24.00 (ISBN 0-8103-3000-8). Gale.

--Historic Note-Book. LC 66-23191. 1966. Repr. of 1891 ed. 38.00 (ISBN 0-8103-0152-0). Gale.

--Reader's Handbook: Famous Names in Fiction, Allusions, References, Proverbs, Plots, Stories, & Poems, 3 vols. LC 71-134907. 1966. Repr. of 1899 ed. Set. 70.00 (ISBN 0-8103-0153-9). Gale.

Brewer, Edward S. & Betts, Jim. Understanding Boat Design. 3rd ed. LC 70-147872. (Illus.). 1980. pap. 7.95 (ISBN 0-87742-015-7). Intl Marine.

Brewer, G., jt. auth. see Brunner, R.

Brewer, G. C. Medley on the Music Question. 1976. 2.50 (ISBN 0-89225-121-2). Gospel Advocate.

--Model Church. 6.50 o.p. (ISBN 0-89225-167-0). Gospel Advocate.

Brewer, Gail S. & Greene, Janice P. Right from the Start: Meeting the Challenges of Mothering Your Unborn & Newborn Baby. Gerras, Charlie, ed. (Illus.). 256p. (Orig.). 1981. pap. 11.95 (ISBN 0-87857-273-2). Rodale Pr Inc.

Brewer, Gail S., ed. Pregnancy After Thirty Workbook. 1978. pap. 10.95 (ISBN 0-87857-215-5). Rodale Pr Inc.

Brewer, Garry D. & Brunner, Ronald D., eds. Political Development & Change. LC 74-482. (Illus.). 1975. 25.00 (ISBN 0-02-904710-2). Free Pr.

Brewer, George, ed. see International Conference on Red Cell Metabolism & Function, 3rd, Ann Arbor, Michigan, Oct., 1974.

Brewer, George D. The Fighting Editor; or, Warren & the Appeal. (American Newspapermen 1790-1933 Ser.). 211p. 1974. Repr. of 1910 ed. 14.50x o.s.i. (ISBN 0-8464-0030-8). Beekman Pubs.

Brewer, Ingrid, jt. auth. see Palm, Septima.

Brewer, J. Party Ideology & Popular Politics at the Accession of George Third. (Illus.). 400p. 1916. 39.00 (ISBN 0-521-21049-6). Cambridge U Pr.

Brewer, James H. Confederate Negro: Virginia's Craftsmen & Military Laborers, 1861-1865. LC 75-86479. 1969. 9.75 o.p. (ISBN 0-8223-0204-7). Duke.

Brewer, Jeutonne, jt. auth. see Brandes, Paul D.

Brewer, John C., jt. ed. see Rea, Kenneth W.

Brewer, L. E., ed. see Chaucer, Geoffrey.

Brewer, Lucy. The Female Marine: Adventures of Miss Lucy Brewer. 2nd ed. LC 65-23390. 1966. Repr. of 1817 ed. 14.95 (ISBN 0-306-70913-9). Da Capo.

Brewer, Mary. What Floats? LC 75-34107. (Illus.). (ps-3). 1976. PLB 5.50 (ISBN 0-913778-25-7); pap. 2.75 (ISBN 0-89565-065-7). Childs World.

--Which Is Biggest? LC 75-35970. (Illus.). (ps-3). 1976. PLB 5.50 (ISBN 0-913778-26-5); pap. 2.75 (ISBN 0-89565-067-3). Childs World.

--Wind Is Air. LC 75-34141. (Illus.). (ps-3). 1976. PLB 5.50 (ISBN 0-913778-27-3); pap. 2.75 (ISBN 0-89565-068-1). Childs World.

Brewer, Robert S., jt. auth. see Curtis, Dan B.

Brewer, Roy. An Approach to Print: A Basic Guide to the Printing Process. (Illus.). 165p. 1972. 7.50 o.p. (ISBN 0-7137-0531-0). Transatlantic.

Brewer, Stephen. Solving Problems in Analytical Chemistry. LC 79-17164. 1980. pap. text ed. 13.95x (ISBN 0-471-04098-3). Wiley.

Brewer, Thomas L. American Foreign Policy: A Contemporary Introduction. (Illus.). 1980. pap. text ed. 10.50 (ISBN 0-13-026740-6). P-H.

Brewer, W. Karl. Armed with the Spirit: Missionary Experiences in Samoa. LC 75-15553. (Illus.). 237p. 1975. pap. 4.95 o.p. (ISBN 0-8425-0817-1). Brigham.

Brewer, Warren, jt. auth. see Antilla, Raimo.

Brewer, William H. Up & Down California: The Journal of William H. Brewer. Farquhar, Francis P., ed. (California Library Reprint Ser: No. 59). (Illus.). 1974. 25.00x (ISBN 0-520-02803-1); pap. 5.95 (ISBN 0-520-02762-0). U of Cal Pr.

Brewer, Wilmon. Life & Poems of Brookes More. (Illus.). 1980. 3.00. M Jones.

Brewin, Robert, jt. auth. see Hughes, Richard.

Brewington, Doyle W. The Parables of the Kingdom. 64p. 1981. 4.95 (ISBN 0-8059-2774-3). Dorrance.

Brewster, Albert H., Jr. How to Convert Gasoline Lawn Mower for Cordless Electric Mowing. LC 76-48500. (Illus.). 1979. pap. 10.00x o.p. (ISBN 0-918166-02-0). Amonics.

--How to Convert Gasoline Lawn Mowers for Cordless Electric Mowing. 3rd ed. LC 76-48500. (Illus.). 1981. pap. 10.00x (ISBN 0-918166-03-9). Amonics.

--How to Convert Salvage Auto Starter to Powerful DC Motor. 2nd ed. (Illus.). 1981. pap. 6.00x (ISBN 0-918166-04-7). Amonics.

--How to Convert Salvage Auto Starter to Powerful DC Motor. LC 76-48495. (Illus.). 1977. pap. 6.00x o.p. (ISBN 0-918166-01-2). Amonics.

Brewster, Ben, tr. see Mauss, Marcel.

Brewster, Benjamin. Baseball. 6th rev. ed. Gutman, Bill, ed. (First Bks.). (Illus.). (gr. 4-6). 1979. PLB 6.45 s&l (ISBN 0-531-00479-1). Watts.

--First Book of Baseball. rev. ed. (First Bks). (Illus.). (gr. 4-6). 1963. PLB 6.45 (ISBN 0-531-00479-1). Watts.

Brewster, Beverly J. American Overseas Library Technical Assistance, 1940-1970. LC 75-23006. 1976. 21.00 (ISBN 0-8108-0827-7). Scarecrow.

Brewster, Charles. Rambles About Portsmouth, Vol. 2. LC 70-181350. 445p. 1972. Repr. 22.50x o.p. (ISBN 0-912274-21-2). NH Pub Co.

Brewster, Charles W. Rambles About Portsmouth, Vol. 1. LC 70-181350. 1971. Repr. 22.50x o.p. (ISBN 0-912274-12-3). NH Pub Co.

Brewster, David. Conversations with Henry Moore. 1978. 2.50 (ISBN 0-686-63617-1). Jawbone Pr.

--A Poultice for Each Season. 1979. 2.00 (ISBN 0-918116-16-3). Jawbone Pr.

Brewster, David & Earnest, Rebecca, eds. The Seattle Book: The Weekly's Guide to Seattle. (Illus.). 1978. pap. 4.95 (ISBN 0-914842-27-7). Madrona Pubs.

Brewster, Dorothy. Virginia Woolf. LC 62-19050. (Gotham Library). 184p. (Orig.). 1962. 8.95x (ISBN 0-8147-0056-X); pap. 5.00 (ISBN 0-8147-0057-8). NYU Pr.

Brewster, Harold P. Saints & Festivals of the Christian Church. LC 73-159869. (Illus.). xiv, 558p. 1975. Repr. of 1904 ed. 24.00 (ISBN 0-8103-3992-7). Gale.

Brewster, Jennifer, tr. see Fujiwara no Nagako.

Brewster, John W. & Gentry, Deborah. Index to Book Reviews in Historical Periodicals 1977. LC 75-18992. 411p. 1979. 22.00 (ISBN 0-8108-1192-8). Scarecrow.

Brewster, John W. & McLeod, Joseph A. Index to Book Reviews in Historical Periodicals, 1973. LC 75-18992. 1976. 18.00 (ISBN 0-8108-0893-5). Scarecrow.

--Index to Book Reviews in Historical Periodicals 1972. LC 75-18992. 393p. 1976. 15.50 (ISBN 0-8108-0894-3). Scarecrow.

--Index to Book Reviews in Historical Periodicals 1975. LC 75-18992. 1977. 27.50 (ISBN 0-8108-0977-X). Scarecrow.

--Index to Book Reviews in Historical Periodicals 1974. LC 75-18992. 1975. 21.00 (ISBN 0-8108-0818-8). Scarecrow.

--Index to Book Reviews in Historical Periodicals 1976. LC 75-18992. 1977. 22.00 (ISBN 0-8108-1078-6). Scarecrow.

Brewster, Marge A. Self-Assessment of Current Knowledge in Clinical Biochemistry. 2nd ed. 1976. 9.50 (ISBN 0-87488-266-4). Med Exam.

Brewster, Marge A. & Naito, Herbert K., eds. Nutritional Elements & Clinical Biochemistry. 450p. 1980. 45.00 (ISBN 0-306-40569-5, Plenum Pr). Plenum Pub.

Brewster, Patience. Ellsworth & the Cats from Mars. (Illus.). 32p. (gr. 1-5). 1981. 9.95 (ISBN 0-395-29612-9, Clarion). HM.

Brewster, R. & McEwen, W. Organic Chemistry. 3rd ed. 1961. 26.95 (ISBN 0-13-640292-5). P-H.

Brewton, J. L., jt. auth. see McGowen, J. H.

Brewton, John E. & Brewton, Sara W. Index to Children's Poetry. 1942. 22.00 (ISBN 0-8242-0021-7); first suppl. 1954 12.00 (ISBN 0-8242-0022-5); second suppl. 1965. 12.00 (ISBN 0-8242-0023-3). Wilson.

Brewton, John E., jt. auth. see Brewton, Sara.

Brewton, John E., ed. Under the Tent of the Sky. (Illus.). (gr. 4-6). 1937. 8.95 (ISBN 0-02-712470-3). Macmillan.

Brewton, John E. & Blackburn, Lorraine A., eds. They've Discovered a Head in the Box for the Bread & Other Laughable Limericks. LC 77-26598. (Illus.). (gr. 3-7). 1978. 7.95 (ISBN 0-690-01388-4, TYC-J); PLB 7.89 (ISBN 0-690-03883-6). T Y Crowell.

Brewton, John E., jt. ed. see Brewton, Sara.

Brewton, John E., et al. In the Witch's Kitchen: Poems for Halloween. LC 79-7822. (Illus.). 96p. (gr. 2-5). 1980. 8.95 (ISBN 0-690-04061-X, TYC-J); PLB 8.79 (ISBN 0-690-04062-8). T Y Crowell.

Brewton, Sara & Brewton, John E. Birthday Candles Burning Bright. (Illus.). (gr. 4-6). 1960. 4.95g o.s.i. (ISBN 0-02-712560-2). Macmillan.

--Bridled with Rainbows. (Illus.). (gr. 4-6). 1949. 4.95g o.s.i. (ISBN 0-02-712680-3). Macmillan.

--Christmas Bells Are Ringing. (Illus.). (gr. 4-6). 1964. 4.95g o.s.i. (ISBN 0-02-712790-7). Macmillan.

--Gaily We Parade. (Illus.). (gr. 4-6). 1967. 8.95 (ISBN 0-02-712340-5). Macmillan.

--Sing a Song of Seasons. (Illus.). (gr. 4-6). 1955. 5.95g o.s.i. (ISBN 0-02-712890-3). Macmillan.

Brewton, Sara & Brewton, John E., eds. Laughable Limericks. LC 65-16179. (Illus.). (gr. 2 up). 1965. 8.95 (ISBN 0-690-48667-7, TYC-J). T Y Crowell.

--Shrieks at Midnight: Macabre Poems, Eerie & Humorous. LC 69-11824. (Illus.). (gr. 4 up). 1969. 8.95 (ISBN 0-690-73518-9, TYC-J). T Y Crowell.

Brewton, Sara, et al. Of Quarks, Quasars & Other Quirks: Quizzical Poems for the Supersonic Age. LC 76-54747. (Illus.). (gr. 4 up). 1977. 8.95 (ISBN 0-690-01286-1, TYC-J). T Y Crowell.

Brewton, Sara, et al, eds. My Tang's Tungled & Other Ridiculous Situations. LC 73-254. (Illus.). (gr. 4 up). 1973. 8.95 (ISBN 0-690-57223-9, TYC-J). T Y Crowell.

Brewton, Sara W., jt. auth. see Brewton, John E.

Brey, Wallace. Physical Chemistry & Its Biological Applications. 589p. 1978. tchrs' ed. 18.95 (ISBN 0-12-133150-4); solutions manual 4.95 (ISBN 0-12-133152-0). Acad Pr.

Breyer, Donald E. & Ank, John A. Design of Wood Structures. (Illus.). 1980. 27.50 (ISBN 0-07-007671-5). McGraw.

Breyer, Siegfried. Battleships of the World. (Illus.). 570p. 1980. 50.00 (ISBN 0-686-65674-1). Mayflower Bks.

Breyer, Stephen G. & MacAvoy, Paul W. Energy Regulation by the Federal Power Commission. LC 74-273. (Studies in the Regulation of Economic Activity). 163p. 1974. 10.95 (ISBN 0-8157-1076-3). Brookings.

Breyfogle, Newell D. The Common Sense Medical Guide & Outdoor Reference. McGraw, Robert P., ed. (Illus.). 416p. 1981. text ed. 11.95 (ISBN 0-07-007672-3, HP); pap. text ed. 6.95 (ISBN 0-07-007673-1). McGraw.

Brezhnev, Leonid I. How It Was: The War & Post-War Reconstruction in the Soviet Union. LC 78-41080. (Illus.). 1979. 13.25 (ISBN 0-08-023579-4); pap. 5.50 (ISBN 0-08-023578-6). Pergamon.

--Selected Speeches & Writings on Foreign Affairs. LC 78-40614. 1978. text ed. 45.00 (ISBN 0-08-023569-7). Pergamon.

--A Short Biography. LC 77-30493. 1978. text ed. 15.00 (ISBN 0-08-022266-8); pap. text ed. 5.00 o.p. (ISBN 0-08-022265-X). Pergamon.

--Socialism Democracy & Human Rights. LC 79-42659. 256p. 1981. 50.00 (ISBN 0-08-023605-7). Pergamon.

--Virgin Lands: Two Years in Kazakhstan Nineteen Fifty-Four to Nineteen Fifty-Five. LC 79-42773. (Illus.). viii, 100p. 1979. 16.50 (ISBN 0-08-023584-0); pap. 6.75 (ISBN 0-08-023583-2). Pergamon.

Brezina, Dennis W. & Overmyer, Allen. Congress in Action: The Environmental Education Act. LC 73-6492. 1974. 10.95 (ISBN 0-02-904900-8). Free Pr.

Breznitz, Shlomo. The Denial of Stress. 1981. write for info. (ISBN 0-8236-1185-X). Intl Univs Pr.

Brian, Denis. The Enchanted Voyager: The Life of J. B. Rhine, an Authorized Biography. 1981. 15.00 (ISBN 0-13-275107-0). P-H.

Brian, M. V., ed. Production Ecology of Ants & Termites. LC 76-54061. (International Biological Programme Ser.: No. 13). (Illus.). 1977. 72.50 (ISBN 0-521-21519-6). Cambridge U Pr.

Brian, P. L. Staged Cascades in Chemical Processing. (International Ser. in the Physical & Chemical Engineering Sciences). (Illus.). 272p. 1972. ref. ed. 25.95 (ISBN 0-13-840280-9). P-H.

Brian, Robert, jt. auth. see Eyongetah, Tambi.

Briar, Scott & Miller, Henry. Problems & Issues in Social Casework. LC 79-170924. 1971. 17.50x (ISBN 0-231-02771-0). Columbia U Pr.

Briard, Jacques. The Bronze Age in Barbarian Europe. (Illus.). 1979. 25.00 (ISBN 0-7100-0086-3). Routledge & Kegan.

Briault, Eric & Smith, Frances. Falling Rolls in Secondary Schools, Pt. 1. 1980. pap. text ed. 16.00x (ISBN 0-85633-207-0, NFER). Humanities.

--Falling Rolls in Secondary Schools, Pt. 2. 403p. 1980. pap. text ed. 27.50x (ISBN 0-85633-208-9, NFER). Humanities.

Briazack, Norman J. & Mennick, Simon. The UFO Guidebook. 1978. 10.00 (ISBN 0-8065-0636-9). Citadel Pr.

Brice, David K. Ion Implantation Range & Energy Deposition Distributions, Vol. 1: High Incident Ion Energies. LC 74-34119. 590p. 1975. 79.50 (ISBN 0-306-67401-7). IFI Plenum.

Brice, William C., ed. The Environmental History of the Near & Middle East Since the Last Ice Age. 1978. 52.00 o.s.i. (ISBN 0-12-133850-9). Acad Pr.

Brice-Wojciechowska, Susan, tr. see Maka, Henryk.

Brichant, Colette D. Premier Guide de France: The First Year Reader. (Illus.). 1978. pap. text ed. 10.50 (ISBN 0-13-695460-X). P-H.

Brichta, A. & Sharp, P. E. From Project to Production. LC 79-97830. 1970. 25.00 (ISBN 0-08-006638-0); pap. 13.25 (ISBN 0-08-006639-9). Pergamon.

Brichta, A. M., ed. & tr. see Gobel, E. F.

Brichto, Herbert. The Problem of "Curse" in the Hebrew Bible. (Society of Biblical Literature, Monographs). 1963. pap. 9.00 (ISBN 0-89130-183-6, 060013). Scholars Pr Ca.

Brick Development Association. Bricks: Their Properties & Use. 1974. pap. text ed. 25.00x (ISBN 0-904406-04-0). Longman.

Brickbauer, Elwood A. & Mortenson, William P. Approved Practices in Crop Production. LC 77-89853. (Illus.). (gr. 9-12). 1978. 14.00 (ISBN 0-8134-1975-1, 1975); text ed. 10.50x (ISBN 0-685-03864-5). Interstate.

Bricker, Charles. Landmarks of Mapmaking. LC 76-23570. (Illus.). 1976. 40.00 o.s.i. (ISBN 0-690-01177-6, TYC-T). T Y Crowell.

Bricker, George H., ed. see Schaff, Philip.

Bricker, George H., jt. ed. see Yrigoyen, Charles, Jr.

Bricker, George H, jt. ed. see Yrigoyen, Charles, Jr.

Bricker, George M., ed. see Nevin, John W.

Bricker, George W. Bricker's International Directory of University-Sponsored Executive Development Programs: 1979. LC 73-110249. 1978. 65.00 o.p. (ISBN 0-916404-04-8). Bricker's Intl.

Bricker, George W. & Pond, Samuel A. Bricker's International Directory of University Sponsored Executive Development Programs: 1980. 11th ed. LC 73-110249. 1979. 75.00x o.p. (ISBN 0-916404-05-6). Bricker's Intl.

Bricker, George W., jt. ed. see Pond, Samuel A.

Bricker, Victoria R. The Indian Christ, the Indian King: The Historical Substrate of Maya Myth & Ritual. (Illus.). 624p. 1981. text ed. 45.00x (ISBN 0-292-73824-2). U of Tex Pr.

--Ritual Humor in Highland Chiapas. LC 73-6501. (Texas Pan American Ser). (Illus.). 257p. 1973. 15.00x (ISBN 0-292-77004-9). U of Tex Pr.

Brickhill, Paul. The Great Escape. 1978. pap. 2.25 (ISBN 0-449-23717-6, Crest). Fawcett.

--Reach for the Sky. 1954. 6.95 o.p. (ISBN 0-393-07376-9). Norton.

Bricklin, Barry, et al. Hand Test: A New Projective Test with Special Reference to the Prediction of Overt Aggressive Behavior. (American Lecture in Psychology Ser.). 112p. 1978. 12.75 (ISBN 0-398-00223-1). C C Thomas.

Bricklin, Mark & Claessens, Charon. Natural Healing Cookbook: Over Four Hundred Fifty Delicious Ways to Get Better & Stay Healthy. (Illus.). 416p. 1981. 16.95 (ISBN 0-87857-338-0). Rodale Pr Inc.

Brickman, William & Lehrer, Stanley, eds. Automation, Education, & Human Values. (Illus.). 7.00 (ISBN 0-8446-0037-7). Peter Smith.

Brickman, William W. Two Millenia of International Relations in Higher Education. 263p. 1980. Repr. of 1976 ed. lib. bdg. 25.00 (ISBN 0-8414-1660-5). Folcroft.

Brickman, William W., ed. Educational Imperatives in a Changing Culture. LC 67-24846. 1967. 8.00 o.p. (ISBN 0-8122-7563-2). U of Pa Pr.

Brickman, William W. & Lehrer, Stanley, eds. Education & the Many Faces of the Disadvantaged: Cultural & Historical Perspectives. LC 74-37166. 380p. 1972. pap. text ed. 11.95x o.p. (ISBN 0-471-10355-1). Wiley.

Brickner, Balfour. Searching the Prophets for Values. 1981. 6.95 (ISBN 0-8074-0047-5). UAHC.

Brickner, Balfour & Saperstein, Marc. As Driven Sands: The Arab Refugees 1948-1969. (Issues of Conscience Ser). (Orig.). 1969. pap. 0.50 (ISBN 0-8074-0090-4, 707925). UAHC.

Brickner, Dwight. From Hell to Texas. 1977. pap. 1.50 (ISBN 0-505-51207-6). Tower Bks.

Brickner, Philip W. Home Health Care for the Aged: How to Help Older People Stay in Their Homes & Out of Institutions. (Illus.). 1978. 16.75 (ISBN 0-8385-3809-6). ACC.

Brickner, Richard P. Bringing Down the House. 1977. pap. 1.75 (ISBN 0-505-51139-8). Tower Bks.

--Tickets. 1981. 12.95 (ISBN 0-671-41209-4). S&S.

Bricq, Ron S. Technically Write! Communicating in a Technological Era. 2nd ed. (Illus.). 448p. 1981. pap. text ed. 11.95 (ISBN 0-13-898700-9). P-H.

Bridaham, Lester B. Gargoyles, Chimeres, & the Grotesque in French Gothic Sculpture. enl. & 2nd ed. LC 68-27724. (Architecture & Decorative Art Ser.: Vol. 22). (Illus.). 1969. Repr. of 1930 ed. lib. bdg. 55.00 (ISBN 0-306-71152-4). Da Capo.

Briden, J. C., jt. auth. see Smith, A. G.

Bridenbaugh, Carl. Cities in Revolt: Urban Life in America, 1743-1776. (Illus.). 1970. pap. 6.95 (ISBN 0-19-501362-X, GB). Oxford U Pr.

--Cities in the Wilderness: The First Century of Urban Life in America, 1625-1742. (Illus.). 1971. pap. 6.95 (ISBN 0-19-501361-1, GB). Oxford U Pr.

--Early Americans. (Illus.). 256p. 1981. 19.95 (ISBN 0-19-502788-4). Oxford U Pr.

--Myths & Realities: Societies of the Colonial South. LC 52-13024. 1963. pap. text ed. 2.95x (ISBN 0-689-70023-7, 17). Atheneum.

--Myths & Realities: Societies of the Colonial South. LC 80-25280. (The Walter Lynwood Fleming Lectures in Southern History Ser., Louisiana State University). x, 208p. 1981. Repr. of 1952 ed. lib. bdg. 19.75x (ISBN 0-313-22770-5, BRMR). Greenwood.

--Seat of Empire. LC 58-13522. (Williamsburg in America Ser: Vol. I). (Illus.). 1958. 3.95 o.p. (ISBN 0-910412-51-0). Williamsburg.

--Spirit of Seventy-Six: The Growth of American Patriotism Before Independence. 192p. 1975. 12.95x (ISBN 0-19-501931-8). Oxford U Pr.

--Spirit of Seventy-Six: The Growth of American Patriotism Before Independence, 1607-1776. LC 75-4323. 1977. pap. 3.95 (ISBN 0-19-502179-7, 488, GB). Oxford U Pr.

--Vexed & Troubled Englishman 1590-1642. LC 68-17604. 512p. 1976. pap. 6.95 (ISBN 0-19-502020-0, GB453, GB). Oxford U Pr.

Bridenbaugh, Phillip O., jt. auth. see Cousins, Michael J.

Bridenthal, Renate & Koonz, Claudia. Becoming Visible: Women in European History. LC 76-11978. 1977. pap. text ed. 9.50 (ISBN 0-395-24477-3). HM.

Bride's Magazine Editors & Calderone, Mary. Questions & Answers About Love & Sex. 144p. (Orig.). 1980. pap. 1.95 (ISBN 0-380-52977-7, 52977). Avon.

Bridge, Carl J. Alcoholism & Driving. (Illus.). 96p. 1972. 10.75 (ISBN 0-398-02243-7). C C Thomas.

Bridge, Donald & Phypers, David. Spiritual Gifts & the Church. LC 73-89303. pap. 1.95 o.p. (ISBN 0-87784-672-3). Inter-Varsity.

Bridge, F. R. From Sadowa to Sarajevo: The Foreign Policy of Austria-Hungary 1866-1914. (Foreign Policies of Great Powers Ser). (Illus.). 496p. 1972. 32.00x (ISBN 0-7100-7269-4). Routledge & Kegan.

Bridge, J. & Dodds, J. C. Managerial Decision Making. LC 75-18977. 309p. 1975. 15.95 (ISBN 0-470-10365-5). Halsted Pr.

Bridge, Jane. Beginning Model Theory: The Completeness Theorem & Some Consequences. (Oxford Logic Guides Ser.). 1977. 19.50x (ISBN 0-19-853157-5). Oxford U Pr.

Bridge, Raymond. America's Backing Guide. rev. ed. 448p. 1981. 14.95 (ISBN 0-684-16872-3, ScribT). Scribner.

--The Runner's Book. LC 78-18747. (Encore Editions). (Illus.). 1978. pap. 1.45 o.p. (ISBN 0-684-16698-4, ScribT). Scribner.

--Running Through the Wall: A Guide for the Serious Runner. (Illus.). 220p. 1980. pap. 7.95 (ISBN 0-8037-7609-8). Dial.

Bridge, Roy, jt. auth. see Bullen, Roger.

Bridge, William. A Lifting up for the Downcast. 1979. pap. 3.95 (ISBN 0-85151-298-4). Banner of Truth.

Bridgeman, Harriet & Drury, Elizabeth. Society Scandals. 1977. 8.95 (ISBN 0-7153-7413-3). David & Charles.

Bridgeman, Jon M. The Revolt of the Hereros. (Perspectives on Southern Africa Ser.). 200p. 1980. 12.50 (ISBN 0-520-04113-5). U of Cal Pr.

Bridgeman, Leonard, jt. ed. see Grey, C. G.

Bridgeman, William & Hazard, Jacqueline. The Lonely Sky. Gilbert, James, ed. LC 79-7232. (Flight: Its First Seventy-Five Years Ser.). (Illus.). 1979. Repr. of 1955 ed. lib. bdg. 24.00x (ISBN 0-405-12148-2). Arno.

Bridges, jt. auth. see Brambilla, F.

Bridges, Bill. The Great American Chili Book. LC 78-5384. 224p. 1981. 12.95 (ISBN 0-89256-074-6); pap. 6.95 (ISBN 0-89256-130-0). Rawson Wade.

Bridges, Charles. The Christian Ministry. 1980. 11.95 (ISBN 0-85151-087-6). Banner of Truth.

--Proverbs. (Geneva Commentaries Ser.). 1979. 14.95 (ISBN 0-85151-088-4). Banner of Truth.

--Psalm One Hundred Nineteen. 1977. 11.95 (ISBN 0-85151-176-7). Banner of Truth.

Bridges, David. Education Democracy & Discussion. (General Ser.). 1979. pap. text ed. 18.75 (ISBN 0-85633-176-7, NFER). Humanities.

Bridges, E. M. World Soils. 2nd ed. LC 77-90204. (Illus.). 1979. 23.95 (ISBN 0-521-21956-6); pap. 7.95x (ISBN 0-521-29339-1). Cambridge U Pr.

Bridges, F., et al. Management Decisions & Organizational Policy: Text, Cases & Readings. 2nd ed. 1977. text ed. 20.95 (ISBN 0-205-05793-4, 0857939); instructor's manual o.p. incl. (ISBN 0-205-05794-2). Allyn.

Bridges, F. J., jt. auth. see Chapman, James E.

Bridges, J. W. & Chasseaud, L. F. Progress in Drug Metabolism, Vol. 5. LC 80-40128. 384p. 1980. 72.00 (ISBN 0-471-27776-2, Pub. by Wiley-Interscience). Wiley.

Bridges, J. W. & Chasseaud, L. F., eds. Progress in Drug Metabolism, Vols. 1-4. Incl. Vol. 1. 1977. 46.00 (ISBN 0-471-10370-5); Vol. 2. 1977. 48.50 (ISBN 0-471-99442-1); Vol. 3. LC 75-19446. 1979. 52.95 (ISBN 0-471-99711-0); Vol. 4. LC 79-42723. 304p. 1980. 72.00 (ISBN 0-471-27702-9). Pub. by Wiley-Interscience). Wiley.

Bridges, Jerry. The Pursuit of Holiness. LC 78-18109. 1978. pap. 2.95 (ISBN 0-89109-430-X, 14308). NavPress.

Bridges, John H. The Life & Work of Roger Bacon. Jones, H. Gordon, ed. LC 79-8597. Repr. of 1914 ed. 21.50 (ISBN 0-404-18450-2). AMS Pr.

Bridges, Julian C. Guia De Estudios Sobre Bases Biblicas De la Etica. 1978. Repr. of 1973 ed. 2.75 (ISBN 0-311-43505-X). Casa Bautista.

Bridges, Robert, et al. Preliminary Announcement. Commager, Steele, ed. Incl. On English Homophones; A Few Practical Suggestions; The Pronunciation of English Words; The Englishing of French Words; On Hyphens & Shall & Will, Should & Would; English Influence on the French Vocabulary; What Is Pure French; The Language of Anatomy; On Grammatical Inversion. (Society for Pure English Ser.: Vol. 1). 1979. lib. bdg. 42.00 (ISBN 0-8240-3665-4). Garland Pub.

--The Society's Work. Commager, Steele, ed. Incl. The Nature of Human Speech; English Handwriting; Notes on Relative Clauses; On Some Disputed Points in English Grammar; English Vowel Sounds; The Study of American English; English Handwriting; Shakespeares English; American Pronunciation. (Society for Pure English: Vol. 3). 1979. lib. bdg. 42.00 (ISBN 0-8240-3667-0). Garland Pub.

Bridges, Thomas. Adventures of a Bank-Note, Seventeen Seventy to Seventeen Seventy-One, 4 vols. in 2. Shugrue, Michael F., ed. (The Flowering of the Novel, 1740-1775 Ser: Vol. 90). 1974. lib. bdg. 50.00 ea. (ISBN 0-8240-1189-9). Garland Pub.

Bridges, William. Gathering of Animals: An Unconventional History of the New York Zoological Society. LC 74-1793. (Illus.). 480p. (YA) 1974. 12.50 o.s.i. (ISBN 0-06-010472-4, HarpT). Har-Row.

--Transitions: Making Sense of Life's Changes. 160p. 1980. 10.95 (ISBN 0-201-00081-4); pap. 6.95 (ISBN 0-201-00082-2). A-W.

--Zoo Babies. (Illus.). (gr. k-3). 1953. PLB 6.48 o.p. (ISBN 0-688-31498-8). Morrow.

--Zoo Doctor. (Illus.). (gr. 3-6). 1957. 7.95 (ISBN 0-688-21499-1). Morrow.

Bridgewater, Alan & Bridgewater, Gill. The Craft of Wood Carving. LC 80-18562. (Illus.). 160p. 1981. 15.95 (ISBN 0-668-04985-5, 4985). Arco.

Bridgewater, Gill, jt. auth. see Bridgewater, Alan.

Bridgewater, Patrick. Nietzsche in Anglosaxony: A Study of Nietzsche's Impact on English & American Literature. 250p. 1972. text ed. 10.50x (ISBN 0-7185-1104-2, Leicester). Humanities.

Bridgman, Eiizabeth. If I Were a Horse. LC 77-6079. (Illus.). (gr. 3-6). 1977. PLB 5.95 (ISBN 0-396-07464-2). Dodd.

Bridgman, George B. Bridgman's Complete Guide to Drawing from Life. (Illus.). 1970. 20.00 o.p. (ISBN 0-8069-5000-5); lib. bdg. 17.59 o.p. (ISBN 0-8069-5001-3). Sterling.

Bridgman, P. W. The Nature of Thermodynamics. 8.50 (ISBN 0-8446-0512-3). Peter Smith.

Bridgman, Peter. Tree Surgery: The Complete Guide. LC 75-31320. (Illus.). 160p. 1976. 19.95 (ISBN 0-7153-7050-2). David & Charles.

Bridgman, Raymond. World Organization. LC 77-147575. (Library of War & Peace; Int'l. Organization, Arbitration & Law). 38.00 (ISBN 0-8240-0341-1). Garland Pub.

Bridgman, Richard. Gertrude Stein in Pieces. 1970. 18.95x (ISBN 0-19-501280-1). Oxford U Pr.

Bridson, Gavin D., et al, eds. Natural History Manuscript Resources in the British Isles. LC 79-92886. 1980. 100.00 (ISBN 0-8352-1281-5). Bowker.

Bridston, Keith R., et al, eds. Casebook on Church & Society. LC 74-13419. 224p. (Orig.). 1974. pap. 5.95 o.p. (ISBN 0-687-04709-9). Abingdon.

Bridwell. Clifford's Good Deeds. (ps-3). pap. 1.25 (ISBN 0-590-01379-3, Schol Pap). Schol Bk Serv.

--Ghost Charlie. (Illus.). (gr. 2-3). 1980. pap. 3.50 incl. record (ISBN 0-590-24002-1, Schol Pap). Schol Bk Serv.

--The Witch Grows up. (ps-3). 1980. pap. 1.25 (ISBN 0-590-30045-8, Schol Pap). Schol Bk Serv.

Bridwell, Norman. Clifford the Big Red Dog. (Illus.). (gr. k-3). 1969. pap. 1.25 (ISBN 0-590-08028-8, Schol Pap); pap. 3.95 clifford the big red dog & witch's christmas (2 bks.) & 1 record (ISBN 0-590-04385-4). Schol Bk Serv.

--Clifford, the Small Red Puppy. (Illus.). (gr. k-3). 1973. pap. 0.95 (ISBN 0-590-09349-5, Schol Pap); pap. 3.50 bk. & record (ISBN 0-590-20696-6). Schol Bk Serv.

--Clifford's Good Deeds. LC 75-15463. (Illus.). 48p. (gr. k-3). 1976. 5.95 (ISBN 0-590-07439-3, Four Winds). Schol Bk Serv.

--Clifford's Good Deeds. pap. 3.50 incl. record (ISBN 0-590-20792-X, Schol Pap). Schol Bk Serv.

--Clifford's Halloween. (Illus.). (gr. k-3). 1970. pap. 1.25 (ISBN 0-590-01466-8, Schol Pap); pap. 3.50 bk. & record (ISBN 0-590-20603-6). Schol Bk Serv.

--Clifford's Tricks. (Illus.). (gr. k-3). 1971. pap. 1.25 (ISBN 0-590-04439-7, Schol Pap); pap. 3.50 bk. & record (ISBN 0-590-04395-1). Schol Bk Serv.

--The Witch Next Door. (Illus.). (gr. k-3). 1971. pap. 1.25 (ISBN 0-590-00342-9, Schol Pap); pap. 3.95 witch next door & indian two feet (2 bks.) & 1 record (ISBN 0-590-04394-3). Schol Bk Serv.

--The Witch's Christmas. (Illus.). (gr. k-3). 1972. pap. 1.25 (ISBN 0-590-09216-2, Schol Pap); pap. 3.95 witch's christmas & clifford the big red dog (2 bks.) & 1 record (ISBN 0-590-04385-4). Schol Bk Serv.

--The Witch's Vacation. (Illus.). (gr. k-3). 1975. pap. 1.25 (ISBN 0-590-09839-X, Schol Pap); pap. 3.50 bk & record (ISBN 0-590-20697-4). Schol Bk Serv.

Bridwell, Randall & Whitten, Ralph U. The Constitution & the Common Law. LC 77-5281. 1977. 20.95 (ISBN 0-669-01601-2). Lexington Bks.

Bridwell, Raymond. Hydroponic Gardening: The Magic of Hydroponics for the Home Gardener. LC 72-86151. (Illus.). 224p. 1972. 7.95 (ISBN 0-912800-00-3); pap. 5.95 (ISBN 0-912800-09-7). Woodbridge Pr.

Bridwell, Tom. Anacoluthon. (Orig.). 1980. limited signed ed. 20.00x (ISBN 0-915316-79-X); pap. 5.00x (ISBN 0-915316-78-1). Pentagram.

Brie, G. A. De see De Brie, G. A.

Brief, et al. Managing Job Stress. (Orig.). 1981. pap. text ed. 8.95 (ISBN 0-316-10799-9). Little.

Brief, Arthur, jt. auth. see Aldag, Ramon.

Brieger, Peter. English Art, 1216-1307. (Oxford History of English Art Ser.). 1957. 33.00x (ISBN 0-19-817203-6). Oxford U Pr.

Brieland, Donald, et al. Contemporary Social Work: An Introduction to Social Work & Social Welfare. 2nd ed. Munson, Eric M., ed. (Illus.). Date not set. text ed. 16.95x (ISBN 0-07-007767-3); instr's manual 4.95 (ISBN 0-07-007768-1). McGraw.

Brier, Alan, et al. Computers & the Social Sciences. 285p. 1974. 17.50x (ISBN 0-231-03914-X); pap. 7.50x (ISBN 0-231-03915-8). Columbia U Pr.

Brier, Bob. Ancient Egyptian Magic. LC 80-15608. (Illus.). 320p. 1980. 14.95 (ISBN 0-688-03654-6). Morrow.

--Precognition & the Philosophy of Science: An Essay on Backward Causation. LC 73-12754. 105p. 1974. text ed. 6.50x (ISBN 0-391-00325-9). Humanities.

Brier, Herbert S. & Orr, William I. VHF Handbook for Radio Amateurs. LC 74-75450. (Illus.). 336p. 1974. 6.95 (ISBN 0-933616-00-7). Radio Pubns.

Brierley, Harry. Transvestism: A Handbook for Psychologists, Psychiatrists & Counsellors. (Illus.). 160p. 1979. 36.00 (ISBN 0-08-022268-4); pap. 15.50 (ISBN 0-08-024686-9). Pergamon.

Brierley, John. Children's Well-Being. 171p. 1981. pap. text ed. 18.75x (ISBN 0-85633-218-6, NFER). Humanities.

--The Growing Brain: Childhood's Crucial Years. (General Ser.). (Illus., Orig.). 1976. pap. text ed. 10.75x (ISBN 0-85633-099-X, NFER). Humanities.

Brierly, J. B. & Meldrum, B. S., eds. Brain Hypoxia. (Clinics in Developmental Medicine, Vol. 39-40). 1971. 25.50 (ISBN 0-685-27035-1). Lippincott.

Brierly, John E., jt. auth. see David, Rene.

Briffault, Herma, tr. see Colette.

Briffault, Herma, tr. see Mallet-Joris, Francoise.

Briffault, Herma, tr. see Racine, Jean B.

Brigance, William N. Jeremiah Sullivan Black, a Defender of the Constitution & the Ten Commandments. LC 72-139196. (American Scene Ser). (Illus.). 1971. Repr. of 1934 ed. lib. bdg. 32.50 (ISBN 0-306-70078-6). Da Capo.

Brigden, Raymond J. Operating Theatre Technique. 4th ed. (Illus.). 840p. 1980. text ed. 87.50x (ISBN 0-443-01999-1). Churchill.

Briggaman, Joan. Practical Problems in Mathematics for Office Workers. LC 76-54051. 1977. pap. text ed. 4.20 (ISBN 0-8273-1612-7); instructor's guide 1.60 (ISBN 0-8273-1613-5). Delmar.

Briggs. Soils. (Sources & Methods in Geography). 1977. pap. 6.95 (ISBN 0-408-70911-1). Butterworths.

--Sources & Methods in Geography: Sediments. 1977. 6.95 (ISBN 0-408-70815-8). Butterworths.

Briggs, A. D., tr. see Medvedev, R. A.

Briggs, Asa. Chartist Studies. 1959. pap. 9.95 (ISBN 0-312-13125-9, Papermac). St Martin.

Briggs, Asa, ed. History of the Elementary School Contest in England. Incl. The Struggle for National Education. 1975. Repr. text ed. 45.00x o.p. (ISBN 0-8277-4327-0). British Bk Ctr.

Briggs, C. A. & Briggs, E. G. Psalms. LC 6-26084. (International Critical Commentary). 22.00x (ISBN 0-567-05011-4). Attic Pr.

Briggs, Carole S. Skin Diving Is for Me. (Sports for Me Bks.). (Illus.). (gr. 2-5). 1981. PLB 5.95 (ISBN 0-8225-1132-0). Lerner Pubns.

Briggs, Charles L. The Wood Carvers of Cordova, New Mexico: Social Dimensions of an Artistic "Revival". LC 79-20883. 1980. 19.95 (ISBN 0-87049-275-6). U of Tenn Pr.

Briggs, Charlie, jt. auth. see Collett, Rosemary K.

Briggs, D., jt. ed. see Morgan, Michael.

Briggs, Dinus M., jt. auth. see Briggs, Hilton M.

Briggs, E. G., jt. auth. see Briggs, C. A.

Briggs, G. A. Audio Biographies. LC 65-1434. 1963. 12.50 o.p. (ISBN 0-89046-020-5). Herman Pub.

Briggs, Garrett, ed. Carboniferous of the Southeastern United States. LC 73-87234. (Special Paper: No. 148). (Illus., Orig.). 1974. pap. 10.00x (ISBN 0-8137-2148-2). Geol Soc.

Briggs, Hilton M. & Briggs, Dinus M. Modern Breeds of Livestock. 4th ed. (Illus.). 1980. text ed. 22.95 (ISBN 0-02-314730-X). Macmillan.

Briggs, K. M. Hobberdy Dick. LC 76-39896. (gr. 5-9). 1977. 8.25 (ISBN 0-688-80079-3); PLB 7.92 (ISBN 0-688-84079-5). Greenwillow.

Briggs, Katharine M. Abbey Lubbers, Banshees & Boggarts: An Illustrated Encyclopedia of Fairies. LC 79-1897. 1979. 10.00 (ISBN 0-394-50806-8). Pantheon.

--British Folktales. LC 77-2384. 1977. 10.00 (ISBN 0-394-41589-2). Pantheon.

--An Encyclopedia of Fairies: Hobgoblins, Brownies, Bogies, & Other Supernatural Creatures. LC 76-12939. (Illus.). (gr. 4 up). 1978. pap. 4.95 (ISBN 0-394-73467-X). Pantheon.

--Personnel of Fairyland: A Short Account of the Fairy People of Great Britain for Those Who Tell Stories to Children. LC 70-147084. (Illus.). 1971. Repr. of 1953 ed. 15.00 (ISBN 0-8103-3372-4). Gale.

--The Vanishing People: Fairy Lore & Legends. LC 78-53523. (Illus.). 1978. 8.95 (ISBN 0-394-50248-5). Pantheon.

--The Vanishing People: Fairy Lore & Legends. 1979. pap. 3.95 (ISBN 0-394-73740-7). Pantheon.

Briggs, Katherine M. British Folktales. (Fairy Tale & Folklore Library). 1980. pap. 5.95 (ISBN 0-394-73993-0). Pantheon.

--The Folklore of the Cotswolds. 1974. 19.95 (ISBN 0-7134-2831-7, Pub. by Batsford England). David & Charles.

Briggs, L. Cabot. Archaeological Investigations Near Tipasa, Algeria. LC 63-5554. (ASPR Bulletin: No. 21). 1963. pap. text ed. 10.00 (ISBN 0-87365-522-2). Peabody Harvard.

--The Stone Age Races of Northwest Africa. LC 55-1179. (American School of Prehistoric Research Bulletin Ser.: No. 18). (Orig.). 1955. pap. 10.00 (ISBN 0-87365-519-2). Peabody Harvard.

Briggs, Leslie J. & Wager, Walter W. Handbook of Procedures for the Design of Instruction. LC 80-20920. 270p. pap. 19.95 (ISBN 0-87778-177-X). Educ Tech Pubns.

Briggs, M. H. Vitamins in Human Biology & Medicine. 304p. 1981. 69.95 (ISBN 0-8493-5673-3). CRC Pr.

Briggs, M. H. & Christie, G. A., eds. Advances in Steroid Biochemistry & Pharmacology, Vols. 1-7. Incl. Vol. 1. 71.50 (ISBN 0-12-037501-X); Vol. 2. 66.50 (ISBN 0-12-037502-8); Vol. 3. 1972. 35.50 (ISBN 0-12-037503-6); Vol. 4. 1974. 45.00 (ISBN 0-12-037504-4); Vol. 5. 1976. 51.50 (ISBN 0-12-037505-2); Vol. 6. 1978. 24.50 (ISBN 0-12-037506-0); Vol. 7. 1980. 23.00 (ISBN 0-12-037507-9). Acad Pr.

Briggs, Martin S. The Architect in History. LC 69-15613. (Architecture & Decorative Art Ser.). (Illus.). 400p. 1974. Repr. of 1927 ed. lib. bdg. 29.50 (ISBN 0-306-70584-2). Da Capo.

--Baroque Architecture. LC 67-23634. (Architecture & Decorative Art Ser). 1967. Repr. of 1913 ed. 29.50 (ISBN 0-306-70960-0). Da Capo.

--Muhammadan Architecture in Egypt & Palestine. LC 74-1287. (Architecture & Decorative Arts Ser.). (Illus.). 255p. 1974. Repr. of 1924 ed. lib. bdg. 25.00 (ISBN 0-306-70590-7). Da Capo.

Briggs, Maxine, jt. auth. see Briggs, Michael.

Briggs, Michael & Briggs, Maxine. Oral Contraceptives, Vol. 1. LC 77-670169. (Annual Research Reviews Ser.). 1977. 14.40 (ISBN 0-88831-005-6). Eden Med Res.

--Oral Contraceptives, Vol. 2. LC 77-670169. (Annual Research Reviews Ser.). 1978. 19.20 (ISBN 0-88831-020-X). Eden Med Res.

Briggs, Michael & Corbin, Alan, eds. Progress in Hormone Biochemistry & Pharmacology, Vol. 1. (Endocrinology Ser.). (Illus.). 300p. 1980. 34.95 (ISBN 0-88831-076-5). Eden Med Res.

Briggs, Michael, ed. see Elstein, Max & Sparks, Richard.

Briggs, Raymond. The Mother Goose Treasury. (gr. k-6). 1980. pap. 7.95 (ISBN 0-440-46408-0, YB). Dell.

--The Snowman. LC 78-55904. (Illus.). (ps-2). 1978. 4.95 (ISBN 0-394-83973-0, BYR); PLB 5.99 (ISBN 0-394-93973-5). Random.

Briggs, S. R. & Elliott, J. H. Six Hundred Bible Gems & Outlines. LC 75-42955. 1976. pap. 3.95 (ISBN 0-8254-2255-8). Kregel.

Briggs, Sam. Essays, Humor, & Poems of Nathaniel Ames. LC 77-75945. (Illus.). 1969. Repr. of 1891 ed. 21.00 (ISBN 0-8103-3826-2). Gale.

Briggs, T., et al, eds. Mechanical Fitting, Vol. 1. (Engineering Craftsmen: No. H3). 1968. spiral bdg. 13.50x (ISBN 0-85083-012-5). Intl Ideas.

Briggs, Thomas L., jt. auth. see Barker, Robert L.

Briggs, Vernon M., Jr. & Foltman, Felician F., eds. Apprenticeship Research: Emerging Findings & Future Trends. 1981. pap. price not set (ISBN 0-87546-085-2). NY Sch Indus Rel.

Briggs, W. R., et al, eds. Annual Review of Plant Physiology, Vol 32. (Illus.). 1981. text ed. 20.00 (ISBN 0-8243-0632-5). Annual Reviews.

Briggs, Wallace A. & Benet, William R., eds. Great Poems of the English Language, 2 vols. enl. ed. LC 79-51965. (Granger Poetry Library). 1981. Repr. of 1941 ed. Set. 94.50x (ISBN 0-89609-178-3). Granger Bk.

Brigham, et al. Cases in Managerial Finance. 4th ed. 1980. pap. 9.95 (ISBN 0-03-054786-5). Dryden Pr.

Brigham, Amariah. Observations on the Influence of Religion Upon the Health & Physical Welfare of Mankind, 1835: Remarks on the Influence of Mental Cultivation & Mental Excitement Upon Health, 2 vols. in 1. LC 73-17271. (Hist. of Psych. Ser.). 1973. 48.00x (ISBN 0-8201-1125-2). Schol Facsimiles.

Brigham, Clarence S. History & Bibliography of American Newspapers, 1690-1820, 2 vols. LC 75-40215. (Special supplement of corrections & additions). 1976. Repr. of 1947 ed. Set. lib. bdg. 102.00x (ISBN 0-8371-8677-3, BRAN). Greenwood.

Brigham, Eugene F. Financial Management. 2nd ed. LC 78-56209. 1979. text ed. 22.95 (ISBN 0-03-045401-8). Dryden Pr.

--Fundamentals of Financial Management. 2nd ed. 627p. 1980. 20.95 (ISBN 0-03-054771-7). Dryden Pr.

Brigham, Eugene F. & Johnson, Ramon E. Issues in Managerial Finance. 2nd ed. 1980. pap. text ed. 9.95 (ISBN 0-03-055241-9). Dryden Pr.

Brigham, Eugene F., jt. auth. see Pappas, James L.

Brigham, Eugene F., jt. auth. see Weston, J. Fred.

Brigham, James A., ed. see Durrell, Lawrence.

Brigham, John. Constitutional Language: An Interpretation of Judicial Decision. LC 78-4020. (Contribution in Political Science: No. 17). 1978. lib. bdg. 17.50 (ISBN 0-313-20420-9, BCO/). Greenwood.

Brigham, John & Brown, Don W., eds. Policy Implementation: Penalties or Incentives? LC 80-16765. (Sage Focus Editions: Vol. 25). (Illus.). 284p. 1980. 18.95 (ISBN 0-8039-1350-8). Sage.

--Policy Implementation: Penalties or Incentives? LC 80-16765. (Sage Focus Editions: Vol. 25). (Illus.). 284p. 1980. pap. 9.95 (ISBN 0-8039-1351-6). Sage.

Brigham, T. A., jt. ed. see Catania, A. Charles.

Bright. Jorgoto (Goergie) (ps-3). 1980. pap. 1.50 (ISBN 0-590-30048-2, Schol Pap). Schol Bk Serv.

Bright, Bill. The Holy Spirit: The Key to Supernatural Living. 200p. 1980. 8.95 (ISBN 0-918956-67-6); pap. 4.95 (ISBN 0-918956-66-8). Campus Crusade.

Bright, Donald E. Biology & Taxonomy of the Bark Beetle Species in the Genus Pseudohylesinus Swaine (Coleoptera: Scolytidae). (U. C. Publ. in Entomology: Vol. 54). 1969. pap. 6.50x (ISBN 0-520-09127-2). U of Cal Pr.

Bright, Elizabeth. Reap the Wind. (Orig.). 1981. pap. write for info. (ISBN 0-671-41782-7). PB.

Bright, Elizabeth S. A Word Geography of California & Nevada. (U. C. Publ. in Linguistics: Vol. 69). 1971. pap. 8.50x (ISBN 0-520-09367-4). U of Cal Pr.

Bright, F. T., et al, eds. Jig Boring. (Engineering Craftsmen: No. H27). (Illus.). 1969. spiral bdg. 16.95x (ISBN 0-85083-043-5). Intl Ideas.

Bright, Hazel M. Out in the Back Forty: A Voice from the Field. (Illus.). 1978. pap. 17.50 (ISBN 0-686-26607-2). Redwood Pub Co.

Bright, James L. Outdoor Recreation Projects. LC 77-28410. 1978. 13.95 (ISBN 0-912336-62-5); pap. 6.95 (ISBN 0-912336-63-3). Structures Pub.

--The Tennis Court Book: A Player's Guide to Home Tennis Courts. LC 79-51373. (Illus.). 1979. 12.50x o.p. (ISBN 0-933122-02-0); pap. 7.50 o.p. (ISBN 0-933122-01-2); customized ed. 7.50x o.p. (ISBN 0-933122-03-9). Brick Hse Pub.

Bright, John. A History of Israel. 3rd ed. LC 80-22774. Date not set. price not set (ISBN 0-664-21381-2). Westminster.

--Kingdom of God. (Series A). 1957. pap. 2.95 o.p. (ISBN 0-687-20907-2, Apex). Abingdon.

--Teaching English As a Second Language. 1975. text ed. 8.75x (ISBN 0-582-54003-8). Longman.

Bright, Robert. Friendly Bear. 1971. Repr. of 1957 ed. Softbound 1.49 o.p. (ISBN 0-385-04470-4). Doubleday.

--Georgie. (gr. k-6). 1959. 6.95 (ISBN 0-385-07307-0); Softbound 1.95 (ISBN 0-385-08030-1). Doubleday.

--Georgie to the Rescue. LC 56-5582. (ps-1). 6.95a (ISBN 0-385-07308-9); PLB (ISBN 0-385-07613-4); Softbound 1.95 (ISBN 0-385-08067-0). Doubleday.

--Georgie's Halloween. LC 58-7154. (ps-3). 1971. 6.95a (ISBN 0-385-07773-4, 58-7154); softbound 1.95 (ISBN 0-385-01017-6); PLB (ISBN 0-385-07778-5). Doubleday.

--Jorgito. LC 76-23789. (ps-k). 1977. PLB 5.95 (ISBN 0-385-12005-2). Doubleday.

--Mi Paraguas Rojo. Redfield, Marion H., tr. LC 68-20836. Orig. Title: My Red Umbrella. (Illus., Span.). (ps-1). 1968. PLB 6.00 (ISBN 0-688-31788-X). Morrow.

--My Red Umbrella. (Illus.). (ps-1). 1959. PLB 6.48 (ISBN 0-688-31619-0). Morrow.

Bright, Susan. Julia. Lomax, Joseph F. & Whitebird, J., eds. (Illus.). 1977. pap. 3.00 (ISBN 0-930324-01-3). Wings Pr.

Brightbill, Charles K. & Mobley, Tony A. Educating for Leisure-Centered Living. 2nd ed. LC 76-47010. 1977. pap. text ed. 10.50 (ISBN 0-471-94914-0). Wiley.

Brightfield, Glory, jt. auth. see Brightfield, Rick.

Brightfield, Rick & Brightfield, Glory. The Great Round the World Maze Trip. (Illus.). 1977. pap. 4.95 o.p. (ISBN 0-345-25678-6). Ballantine.

Brightman, Frank H. Oxford Book of Flowerless Plants: Ferns, Fungi, Mosses, & Liverworts, Lichens, & Seaweeds. Nicholson, B. E., ed. (Illus.). 1966. 27.00 (ISBN 0-19-910004-7). Oxford U Pr.

Brightman, Harvey J. Problem-Solving: A Logical & Creative Approach. LC 80-25078. 256p. 1980. 14.95 (ISBN 0-88406-131-0). Ga St U Busn Pub.

Brightman, Robert. Bernzomatic Torch Tips. 6.95 (ISBN 0-916752-16-X). Green Hill.

--Fix It. 7.95 (ISBN 0-916752-18-6). Green Hill.

--Fix-It Duro-Loctite Guide to Home & Auto Care & Repair. LC 77-89550. (Illus.). 1978. 7.95 (ISBN 0-916752-18-6). Dorison Hse.

--One-Hundred One Practical Uses for Propane Torches. (Illus.). 1978. 6.95 o.p. (ISBN 0-8306-9976-7); pap. 3.95 (ISBN 0-8306-1030-8, 1030). TAB Bks.

Brigley, Catherine M. Pediatrics for the Practical Nurse. LC 72-9384. (Illus.). 224p. 1973. pap. 7.40 (ISBN 0-8273-0332-7); instructor's guide 1.60 (ISBN 0-8273-0333-5). Delmar.

Brigman, William E., jt. auth. see Buell, Erwin C.

Brignell, J. & Rhodes, G. Laboratory On-Line Computing: An Introduction for Engineers & Physics. LC 75-6261. 1975. 28.95 (ISBN 0-470-10400-7). Halsted Pr.

Brijbhushan, Jamila. Muslim Women: A in Purdah & Out of It. 150p. 1980. text ed. 17.50 (ISBN 0-7069-1074-5, Pub. by Vikas India). Advent Bk.

Brij Mohan. Social Psychiatry in India. LC 73-905946. 1973. 10.00x o.p. (ISBN 0-88386-185-2). South Asia Bks.

Brik, Lily, jt. auth. see Mayakovsky, Vladimir.

Briles, Judith. The Woman's Guide to Financial Savvy. 192p. 1981. 10.95 (ISBN 0-312-88649-7). St Martin.

Brilhart, John K., jt. auth. see Edwards, Barba J.

Brill, Abraham A., tr. see Freud, Sigmund.

Brill, Chip & Glenn, Peter, eds. The New York Casting-Survival Guide & Datebook, 1981. 124p. 1980. pap. 10.00 (ISBN 0-87314-036-2). Peter Glenn.

Brill, E. L. & Kilts, D. F. Foundations for Nursing. 813p. 1980. text ed. 24.95 (ISBN 0-8385-2687-X). ACC.

Brill, Earl H. The Future of the American Past. LC 73-17890. 1974. pap. 2.95 (ISBN 0-8164-2086-6). Crossroad NY.

Brill, Edith. Portrait of the Cotswolds. LC 66-4352. (Portrait Bks.). (Illus.). 1964. 10.50x (ISBN 0-7091-2498-8). Intl Pubns Serv.

Brill, Ernie. I Looked Over Jordan & Other Stories. LC 80-51042. 344p. (Orig.). 1980. 15.00 (ISBN 0-89608-118-4); pap. 6.00 (ISBN 0-89608-117-6). South End Pr.

Brill, Harry. Why Organizers Fail: The Story of a Rent Strike. LC 76-104103. 1971. 14.50x (ISBN 0-520-01672-6). U of Cal Pr.

Brill, Leon. The De-Addiction Process: Studies in the De-Addiction of Confirmed Heroin Addicts. 180p. 1972. 18.75 (ISBN 0-398-02532-0). C C Thomas.

Brill, Leon & Winick, Charles. The Yearbook of Substance Use & Abuse. LC 70-174271. 360p. 1980. 32.95 (ISBN 0-87705-487-8). Human Sci Pr.

Brill, Peter L. & Hayes, John P. Taming Your Turmoil: Managing the Transitions of Adult Life. (Illus.). 256p. 1981. 15.95 (ISBN 0-13-884445-3, Spectrum); pap. 6.95 (ISBN 0-13-884437-2). P-H.

Brill, Thomas B. Light: Its Interaction with Art & Antiquities. (Illus.). 300p. 1980. 29.50 (ISBN 0-306-40416-8, Plenum Pr). Plenum Pub.

Brilliant, Ashleigh. I Have Abandoned My Search for Truth, & Am Now Looking for a Good Fantasy. LC 80-22852. (Illus.). 160p. (Orig.). 1980. 8.95 (ISBN 0-912800-66-6); pap. 4.95 (ISBN 0-912800-90-9). Woodbridge Pr.

--I May Not Be Totally Perfect, but Parts of Me Are Excellent. LC 79-10052. (Illus.). 1979. 7.95 (ISBN 0-912800-66-6); pap. 4.95 (ISBN 0-912800-67-4). Woodbridge Pr.

Brilliant, Livia, jt. auth. see Rothschild, Eric.

Brilliantor, A. I. Ioann Skot Erigena. LC 80-2358. 1981. Repr. of 1898 ed. 64.50 (ISBN 0-404-18904-0). AMS Pr.

Brillinger, David R. Time Series: Data Analysis & Theory. enl. ed. (Illus.). 552p. 1980. Repr. of 1975 ed. text ed. 25.00 (ISBN 0-8162-1150-7); foreign ed. 29.95 (ISBN 0-686-69028-1). Holden-Day.

Brillinger, Peter C., jt. auth. see Cohen, Doron J.

Briloff, Abraham J. The Truth About Corporate Accounting. LC 80-7584. (Illus.). 416p. 1981. 17.95 (ISBN 0-06-010479-1, HarpT). Har-Row.

Brim, O. C., Jr., jt. ed. see Baltes, P. B.

Brim, Orville G., Jr., jt. auth. see Harman, David.

Brim, Orville G., Jr., et al. The Dying Patient. 390p. (Orig.). 1981. pap. 7.95 (ISBN 0-87855-684-2). Transaction Bks.

Brim, Q. G. & Wheeler, S. Socialization After Childhood: Two Essays. 1966. pap. text ed. 10.95 (ISBN 0-471-10418-3). Wiley.

Brimer, A., et al. Sources of Difference in School Achievement. (General Ser.). (Illus.). 1979. text ed. 33.75x (ISBN 0-85633-168-6, NFER); pap. text ed. 20.00x (ISBN 0-85633-155-4). Humanities.

Brimer, John B. Homeowner's Complete Outdoor Building Book. (Popular Science Bk.). (Illus.). 1971. 12.50 o.s.i. (ISBN 0-06-010473-2, HarpT). Har-Row.

Brimmer, Frances M. Histological Methods & Terminology. (Orig., In Dictionary Form). 1979. pap. text ed. 14.95x (ISBN 0-934696-00-4). Mosaic Pr.

Brin, Andre. Energy & the Oceans. 1981. pap. text ed. write for info. (ISBN 0-86103-024-9, Westbury Hse). Butterworth.

Brin, Ruth F. Contributions of Women: Social Reform. LC 77-9585. (Contributions of Women Ser.). (Illus.). (gr. 6 up). 1977. PLB 8.95 (ISBN 0-87518-145-7). Dillon.

Brinch-Hanson, P. Architecture of Concurrent Programs. 1977. 24.95 (ISBN 0-13-044628-9). P-H.

Brinckle, Gertrude, jt. auth. see Morse, Willard S.

Brinckloe, Julie. Gordon's House. LC 75-33189. 48p. (ps-3). 1976. 5.95 o.p. (ISBN 0-385-06886-7); PLB write for info. o.p. (ISBN 0-385-06905-7). Doubleday.

Brinckloe, William D. & Coughlin, Mary T. Managing Organizations. 1977. text ed. 14.95x (ISBN 0-02-471200-0). Macmillan.

Brincklow, William D., jt. auth. see Deep, Samuel D.

Brindle, Melbourne & May, Phil. Twenty Silver Ghosts: The Incomparable Pre-World War 1 Rolls-Royce. LC 78-8806. 1978. 17.95 o.p. (ISBN 0-385-14668-X). Doubleday.

Brindle, Reginald S., ed. see Bartolozzi, Bruno.

Brindze, Ruth. Charting the Oceans. LC 77-134674. (Illus.). 128p. (gr. 6-12). 1972. 6.95 (ISBN 0-8149-0002-X). Vanguard.

--Not to Be Broadcast: The Truth About the Radio. LC 73-19802. (Civil Liberties in American History Ser.). 310p. 1974. Repr. of 1937 ed. lib. bdg. 29.50 (ISBN 0-306-70598-2). Da Capo.

--Story of Gold. LC 55-11840. (Illus.). (gr. 4-8). 1954. 6.95 (ISBN 0-8149-0276-6). Vanguard.

Brine, Jenny, et al, eds. Home School & Leisure in the Soviet Union. (Illus.). 304p. 1980. text ed. 28.50x (ISBN 0-04-335040-2, 2537). Allen Unwin.

Brines, Steven F., ed. see Willcutt, J. Robert & Ball, Kenneth R.

Bringham, Madeleine. The Making of Kew. (Folio Miniature Ser.). 1975. 4.95 (ISBN 0-7181-1304-7, Pub. by Michael Joseph). Merrimack Bk Serv.

Bringhurst, Robert. Bergschrund. (Sono Nis Ser.). 104p. 1975. 10.95 o.s.i. (ISBN 0-913600-40-7). Kanchenjunga Pr.

--Bergschrund. (Sono Nis Ser). (Illus.). 104p. 1975. pap. 5.95 (ISBN 0-913600-50-4). Kanchenjunga Pr.

Bringle, Jerald, ed. see Shaw, George B.

Bringle, Mary. Eskimos. LC 72-10431. (Illus.). 96p. (gr. 4-7). 1973. PLB 3.90 o.p. (ISBN 0-531-00785-5). Watts.

Brings, Allen, et al. A New Approach to Keyboard Harmony. (Illus.). 1979. pap. text ed. 9.95x (ISBN 0-393-95001-8). Norton.

Brinig, Robert, jt. auth. see Reese, Terence.

Brininstool, E. A., ed. see Standing Bear, Luther.

Brink, Andre. Looking on Darkness. LC 75-4515. 408p. 1975. 8.95 o.p. (ISBN 0-688-02924-8). Morrow.

Brink, Carol. Harps in the Wind: The Story of The Singing Hutchinsons. (The Story of the Singing Hutchinsons). (Illus.). v, 312p. 1980. Repr. of 1947 ed. lib. bdg. 27.50 (ISBN 0-306-76024-X). Da Capo.

Brink, Carol R. The Bad Times of Irma Baumlein. LC 76-182018. (Illus.). (gr. 4-6). 1972. 8.95 (ISBN 0-02-714220-5). Macmillan.

--The Bad Times of Irma Baumlein. LC 76-182018. (Illus.). 144p. (gr. 4-6). 1974. pap. 2.95 (ISBN 0-02-041900-7, Collier). Macmillan.

--Caddie Woodlawn. rev. ed. (gr. 4-6). 1970. pap. 2.25 (ISBN 0-02-041880-9). Macmillan.

--Caddie Woodlawn. new ed. LC 73-588. (Illus.). 240p. (gr. 4-7). 1973. 8.95 (ISBN 0-02-713670-1). Macmillan.

--Louly. LC 73-21885. (Illus.). 208p. (gr. 4-7). 1974. 5.95g o.s.i. (ISBN 0-02-713680-9). Macmillan.

--Magical Melons. (Illus.). (gr. 5-7). 1963. 8.95 (ISBN 0-02-714210-8). Macmillan.

--Pink Motel. LC 59-12838. 224p. (gr. 4-6). 1972. pap. 1.95 (ISBN 0-02-041940-6, Collier). Macmillan.

--Snow in the River. 1964. 12.95 (ISBN 0-02-515890-2). Macmillan.

--Two Are Better Than One. LC 68-20615. (Illus.). (gr. 4-6). 1968. 6.95g o.s.i. (ISBN 0-02-714320-1). Macmillan.

Brink, D. M. Nuclear Forces. 1965. 19.50 (ISBN 0-08-011034-7); pap. 9.75 (ISBN 0-08-011033-9). Pergamon.

Brink, David M. & Satchler, George R. Angular Momentum. 2nd ed. (Oxford Library of the Physical Sciences). (Orig.). 1968. pap. 14.95x (ISBN 0-19-851419-0). Oxford U Pr.

Brink, G. Van den see International Symposium on Hearing, Fifth, Noordwijkerhout, the Netherlands, April 8-12, 1980.

Brink, J. M. Van see Van Brink, J. M. & Vorontsov, N. N.

Brink, Jeanie R., ed. Female Scholars: A Tradition of Learned Women Before 1800. (Illus.). 1980. 17.95 (ISBN 0-920792-02-2). EPWP.

Brink, Joseph, jt. auth. see Shreve, R. Norris.
Brink, P. J. Transcultural Nursing: A Book of Readings. (Illus.). 320p. 1976. pap. 11.95 (ISBN 0-13-928101-0). P-H.
Brink, R. Alexander, ed. see Mendel Centennial Symposium - Fort Collins - 1965.
Brink, Raymond W. Plane Trigonometry. 3rd ed. (Century Mathematics Ser.). 1959. 32.50x (ISBN 0-89197-627-2). Irvington.
Brink, V. Z., et al. Modern Internal Auditing: An Operational Approach. 3rd ed. 795p. 1973. 34.50 (ISBN 0-471-06524-2). Wiley.
Brink, Victor Z. Understanding Management Policy--& Making It Work. new ed. (Illus.). 1978. 19.95 (ISBN 0-8144-5455-0). Am Mgmt.
Brink, Victor Z., et al. Modern Internal Auditing: An Operational Approach. 3rd ed. (Illus.). 1973. 34.50 (ISBN 0-8260-1311-2). Ronald Pr.
Brink, William P. & DeRidder, Richard R. Manual of Christian Reformed Church Government: 1980 Edition. rev. ed. LC 80-24129. 1980. pap. text ed. 4.45 (ISBN 0-933140-19-3). Bd of Pubns CRC.
Brinker, Helmut & Fischer, Eberhard. Treasures from the Rietberg Museum. LC 80-12528. (Illus.). 176p. 1980. 19.95 (ISBN 0-87848-055-2). Asia Soc.
Brinker, Helmut, jt. ed. see Armbruster, Gisela.
Brinker, R. & Wolf, P. Topografia. (Span.). 1980. pap. text ed. 14.00 (ISBN 0-06-310064-9, HarLA Mexico). Har-Row.
Brinker, Russell C. & Barry, Austin. Noteforms for Surveying Measurements. 93p. 1957. pap. text ed. 3.50 scp o.p. (ISBN 0-685-01024-4, HarpC). Har-Row.
Brinkerhoff, Dericksen M. Hellenistic Statues of Aphrodite: Studies in the History of Their Stylistic Development. LC 77-94688. (Outstanding Dissertations in the Fine Arts Ser.). 1978. lib. bdg. 24.00 (ISBN 0-8240-3217-9). Garland Pub.
Brinkhurst, Ralph O. & Cook, David G., eds. Aquatic Oligochaete Biology. 530p. 1980. 55.00 (ISBN 0-306-40338-2). Plenum Pub.
Brinkley. A Family Is... (gr. 9-12). 1981. text ed. 7.92 (ISBN 0-87002-320-9). Bennett IL.
Brinkley, Jeanne, jt. auth. see Aletti, Ann.
Brinkman, Grover. Night of the Blood Moon. 200p. (gr. 4-6). 1976. 8.00 o.p. (ISBN 0-8309-0149-3). Independence Pr.
Brinkman, Karl-Heinz & Schmidt, Rudolf. Data Systems Dictionary: English-German & German-English. 1974. pap. 40.00x (ISBN 3-87097-095-2). Intl Learn Syst.
Brinkman, Richard L. Cultural Economics. LC 78-62056. 450p. 1981. pap. text ed. 15.95 (ISBN 0-913244-15-5). Hapi Pr.
Brinkmann, H. W. & Klotz, E. A. Linear Algebra & Analytic Geometry. LC 79-132056. (Mathematics Ser). 1971. text ed. 17.95 o.p. (ISBN 0-201-00648-0). A-W.
Brinkworth, E. R. Shakespeare & the Bawdy Court of Stratford. (Illus.). 184p. 1972. 16.50x (ISBN 0-87471-642-X). Rowman.
Brinnin, John M. Skin Diving in the Virgins & Other Poems. 1970. 4.50 o.p. (ISBN 0-440-08031-2, Sey Lawr). Delacorte.
Brinser, Marlin. Dictionary of Twentieth Century Italian Violin Makers & Import Dealers Scrapbook. 1978. pap. 12.50 (ISBN 0-9602298-1-7). M Brinser.
Brinsmead, Edgar. History of the Pianoforte. LC 79-76136. (Music Story Ser.). (Illus.). 1969. Repr. of 1879 ed. 18.00 (ISBN 0-8103-3559-X). Gale.
Brinton, et al. History of Civilization: Vol. 1, Prehistory to 1715. 5th ed. 1976. pap. 15.95 (ISBN 0-13-389007-4); study guide 5.95 (ISBN 0-13-389833-4). P-H.
Brinton, Anna C. Maphaeus Vegius & His Thirteenth Book of the "Aeneid". Commager, Steele, ed. LC 77-70765. (Latin Poetry Ser.). 1978. lib. bdg. 22.00 (ISBN 0-8240-2963-1). Garland Pub.
Brinton, C., et al. A History of Civilization: Prehistory to 1300. 5th ed. (Illus.). 352p. 1976. pap. text ed. 12.95 (ISBN 0-13-389791-5). P-H.
--A History of Civilization: Thirteen Hundred to Eighteen-Fifteen. 5th ed. (Illus.). 288p. 1976. pap. text ed. 12.95 (ISBN 0-13-389817-2). P-H.
--A History of Civilization: 1715 to Present. 5th ed. (Illus.). 528p. 1976. pap. text ed. 15.95 (ISBN 0-13-389809-1). P-H.
Brinton, Crane. Anatomy of Revolution. 7.75 (ISBN 0-8446-1740-7). Peter Smith.
--Ideas & Men: The Story of Western Thought. 2nd ed. 1963. ref. ed. 17.95 (ISBN 0-13-449249-8). P-H.
Brinton, Daniel G. The Myths of the New World: A Treatise on the Symbolism & Mythology of the Red Race in America. LC 74-1038. 360p. 1974. Repr. of 1896 ed. 15.00 (ISBN 0-8103-3959-5). Gale.
--Myths of the New World Indians. LC 72-81594. (Illus.). 334p. pap. 6.50 (ISBN 0-8334-1742-8). Steinerbks.
Brinton, Henry. Man in Space. (Junior Ref. Ser). (Illus.). (gr. 7 up). 1969. 7.95 (ISBN 0-7136-1504-4). Dufour.
Brinton, Henry, jt. auth. see Moore, Patrick.
Brion, John M. Corporate Marketing Planning. LC 67-19446. (Marketing Ser.). 1967. 27.95 (ISBN 0-471-10440-X). Wiley.
Brion, Marcel. The Medici. 1969. 25.00 (ISBN 0-236-17727-3, Pub. by Paul Elek). Merrimack Bk Serv.
--Venice: The Masque of Italy. 1962. 21.95 (ISBN 0-236-31030-5, Pub. by Paul Elek). Merrimack Bk Serv.
Brion de Latour, Louis. Tableau de la Population de la France. (Principal French Demographic Works of the 18th Century Ser.). (Illus., Fr.). 1977. lib. bdg. 22.50x o.p. (ISBN 0-8287-0140-7); pap. text ed. 12.50x o.p. (ISBN 0-685-75759-5). Clearwater Pub.
Briquet de Limos, Antonio A. Librarianship in Developing Societies. (Occasional Papers: No. 148). 1981. pap. 3.00 (ISBN 0-686-69073-7). U of Ill Lib Sci.
Brisbane. Developing Child. rev. ed. (gr. 9-12). 1980. text ed. 13.72 (ISBN 0-87002-312-8); tchr's guide avail. (ISBN 0-87002-324-1); student guide 3.20 (ISBN 0-87002-325-X). Bennett IL.
Brisbane, Holly E. Developing Child. rev. ed. (Illus.). (gr. 9-12). 1980. text ed. 11.96 (ISBN 0-87002-312-8); tchr guide avail. (ISBN 0-685-03307-4). Bennett IL.
Brisbin, James S., ed. Belden, the White Chief: Or, Twelve Years Among the Wild Indians of the Plains from the Diaries & Manuscripts of George P. Belden. facsimile ed. LC 73-92900. (Illus.). xxvi, 513p. 1974. Repr. of 1870 ed. 15.00 (ISBN 0-8214-0150-5). Ohio U Pr.
Brisco. Too Much in Love. (gr. 7-12). 1980. pap. 1.25 (ISBN 0-590-30910-2, Schol Pap). Schol Bk Serv.
Brisco, Patty. Merry's Treasure. (YA) 1970. 5.95 (ISBN 0-685-07447-1, Avalon). Bouregy.
Briscoe & Leonardson. Experiences in Public Administration. 1980. pap. text ed. 7.95 (ISBN 0-87872-248-3). Duxbury Pr.
Briscoe, Alan. Cooking with Wild Plants: How to Recognize & Prepare Edible Wilderness Plants of the Rocky Mountains. LC 78-52405. (Illus.). 1979. pap. 1.95 (ISBN 0-88290-091-9). Horizon Utah.
Briscoe, D. Stuart. Getting into God. 128p. 1975. pap. 2.95 (ISBN 0-310-21722-9). Zondervan.
--Let's Get Moving. LC 77-91773. 1978. pap. 2.50 (ISBN 0-8307-0538-4, S322-1-02). Regal.
--Patterns for Power. LC 78-68850. (Bible Commentary for Laymen Ser.). 1979. pap. 2.50 (ISBN 0-8307-0701-8, S331101). Regal.
--What Works When Life Doesn't. 144p. 1976. pap. 3.50 (ISBN 0-88207-725-2). Victor Bks.
Briscoe, Jill. Here I Am--Send Aaron. 1978. pap. 2.95 (ISBN 0-88207-767-8). Victor Bks.
Briscoe, Laurel. Lectura & Lengua. LC 77-83324. (Illus.). 1977. text ed. 16.05 (ISBN 0-395-25545-7); instructor's annotated edition 17.15 (ISBN 0-395-25539-2). HM.
Briscoe, Leonard R., jt. auth. see Briscoe, W. S.
Briscoe, Mary L., jt. auth. see Adams, Elsie.
Briscoe, Stuart. All Things Weird & Wonderful. 1977. pap. text ed. 3.50 (ISBN 0-88207-749-X). Victor Bks.
Briscoe, W. S. & Briscoe, Leonard R. Wildlife Adventure Ser, 8 vols. (gr. 3-7). 1966. pap. text ed. 6.52 ea. (Sch Div); tchr's. manual 3.72 (ISBN 0-201-40712-4). A-W.
Brisk, Maria E., et al. Working with the Bilingual Community. LC 79-84372. 90p. (Orig.). 1979. pap. 4.50 (ISBN 0-89763-013-0). Natl Clearinghse Bilingual Ed.
Briskey, Ernest J., et al, eds. Physiology & Biochemistry of Muscle As a Food: Proceedings, 1965, 2 vols. (Illus.). 1966. Vol. 1. 35.00x (ISBN 0-299-04110-7); Vol. 2. 50.00 (ISBN 0-299-05680-5). U of Wis Pr.
Briskin, Jacqueline. California Generation. 1980. pap. 2.75 (ISBN 0-446-95146-3). Warner Bks.
--Rich Friends. 468p. 1976. 8.95 o.p. (ISBN 0-440-07367-7). Delacorte.
Brisley, Joyce L. Milly-Molly-Mandy Again. LC 76-48834. (Illus.). (gr. k-3). 1977. 4.95 o.p. (ISBN 0-679-20398-2). McKay.
--Milly-Molly-Mandy & Billy Blunt. LC 76-48835. (Illus.). (gr. k-3). 1977. 4.95 o.p. (ISBN 0-679-20399-0). McKay.
--The Six in One Complete Milly-Molly-Mandy Stories. (gr. k-3). 1980. pap. cancelled o.p. (ISBN 0-679-20955-7). McKay.
Brislin, R. W., et al, eds. Cross Cultural Perspectives on Learning. LC 73-91353. 366p. 1975. 18.95 (ISBN 0-470-10471-6). Halsted Pr.
Brislin, Richard W. Crosscultural Encounters: Face-to-Face Interaction. LC 80-20202. (Pergamon General Psychology Ser.: No. 94). 350p. 1981. 35.01 (ISBN 0-08-026313-5); pap. 12.91 (ISBN 0-08-026312-7). Pergamon.
Brislin, Richard W. see Hamnett, Michael P.
Brislin, Richard W., et al. Cross-Cultural Research Methods. LC 73-772. (Comparative Studies in Behavioral Sciences). 1973. 18.95 (ISBN 0-471-10470-1, Pub. by Wiley-Interscience). Wiley.
Brisoff, Norman. Don't Give up. LC 72-75126. (Mystery & Adventure Ser.). (gr. 2-4). 1973. PLB 6.75 (ISBN 0-87191-207-4). Creative Ed.
Brisolara, Ashton. The Alcoholic Employee: A Handbook of Helpful Guidelines. LC 78-15763. 318p. 1978. text ed. 18.95 (ISBN 0-87705-327-8). Human Sci Pr.
Brissenden, R. F. The Whale in Darkness. LC 79-56757. 71p. 1980. 14.95 (ISBN 0-7081-1083-5, 0576). Bks Australia.
Brissenden, T. H. F. Mathematics Teaching. 1980. text ed. 21.00 (ISBN 0-06-318159-2, IntlDept); pap. text ed. 11.90 (ISBN 0-06-318160-6). Har-Row.
Brissett, Dennis & Edgley, Charles. Life As Theater: A Dramaturgical Sourcebook. LC 74-82604. 392p. 1975. 21.95x (ISBN 0-202-30277-6). Aldine Pub.
Brisson, David W. Hypergraphics: Visualizing Complex Relationships in Art, Science & Technology. (Illus.). 1979. lib. bdg. 22.00x (ISBN 0-89158-292-4). Westview.
Brisson, Jean P. Problemes De la Guerre a Rome. (Civilisations et Societes: No. 12). 1969. pap. 14.10x (ISBN 0-686-20921-4). Mouton.
Brissot, Jean-Pierre. Recherches Philosophiques Sur le Droit De Propriete Considere Dans la Nature, Pour Servir De Premier Chapitre a la Theorie Des Loix De M. Linguet, Par un Jeune Philosophe. (Fr.). 1977. lib. bdg. 21.25x o.p. (ISBN 0-8287-0143-1); pap. text ed. 11.25x o.p. (ISBN 0-685-74932-0). Clearwater Pub.
Brister, C. W. El Cuidado Pastoral De la Iglesia. Tinao, D., et al, trs. Orig. Title: Pastoral Care in the Church. 226p. (Span.). 1980. pap. 4.75 (ISBN 0-311-42040-0). Casa Bautista.
Brister, C. W., et al. Beginning Your Ministry. LC 80-25763. 160p. (Orig.). 1981. pap. 6.95 (ISBN 0-687-02780-2). Abingdon.
Bristle, Mable C., jt. auth. see Johnston, Louisa.
Bristol, James D. & Penner, David A. Exercises in Plane Geometry. (Illus., Orig.). (gr. 9-10). 1976. pap. text ed. 4.75x (ISBN 0-88334-086-0). Ind Sch Pr.
Bristol, Lee H. The Big Picnic & Other Meals in the New Testament. LC 75-13455. (Illus.). 96p. 1975. 4.95 o.p. (ISBN 0-8042-2286-X). John Knox.
Bristol, Lee H., Jr. Renewal from Within. 1978. 1.00 (ISBN 0-686-28790-8). Forward Movement.
Briston, J. H. & Katan, L. L. Plastic Films. LC 74-2295. 1974. 30.95 (ISBN 0-470-10472-4). Halsted Pr.
Briston, John. Plastics. LC 75-19357. (Pegasus Books: No. 23). 1969. 7.50x (ISBN 0-234-77186-0). Intl Pubns Serv.
Bristow, Allen P. Field Interrogation. 2nd ed. (Illus.). 168p. 1980. 9.75 (ISBN 0-398-00226-6). C C Thomas.
--Police Disaster Operations. (Illus.). 240p. 1972. 18.50 (ISBN 0-398-02244-5); pap. 18.50 o.p. (ISBN 0-398-02244-5). C C Thomas.
--Police Supervision Readings. 488p. 1971. pap. 29.75 photocopy ed. spiral (ISBN 0-398-00227-4). C C Thomas.
Bristow, Allen P., jt. auth. see Roberts, Willis J.
Bristow, Eugene K., ed. Anton Chekov's Plays. (Norton Critical Edition Ser.). 1978 12.95 (ISBN 0-393-04432-7); pap. 6.95 1977 (ISBN 0-393-09163-5). Norton.
Bristow, George. Rip Van Winkle. (Early American Music Ser.: No. 25). 297p. 1980. 39.50. Da Capo.
Bristow, Gwen. Calico Palace. LC 72-106584. 1970. 10.95 (ISBN 0-690-16608-7, TYC-T). T Y Crowell.
--Celia Garth. LC 59-10435. 1959. 10.95 (ISBN 0-690-18348-8, TYC-T). T Y Crowell.
--Deep Summer. LC 37-1118. 1964. 10.95 (ISBN 0-690-23318-3, TYC-T). T Y Crowell.
--Handsome Road. LC 38-27336. 1968. 7.95 o.s.i. (ISBN 0-690-36810-0, TYC-T). T Y Crowell.
--Jubilee Trail. 1969. pap. 2.75 (ISBN 0-445-08306-9). Popular Lib.
--Jubilee Trail. LC 50-5268. 1969. 10.95 o.s.i. (ISBN 0-690-46750-8, TYC-T). T Y Crowell.
--Plantation Trilogy: Incl. Deep Summer, the Handsome Road, This Side of Glory. LC 62-9363. 812p. 1962. 9.95 o.s.i. (ISBN 0-690-62868-4, TYC-T). T Y Crowell.
--This Side of Glory. LC 40-27259. 1968. 9.95 o.s.i. (ISBN 0-690-81896-3, TYC-T). T Y Crowell.
Bristow, Philip. Down the Spanish Coast. 196p. 1980. 12.00x (ISBN 0-245-52935-7, Pub. by Nautical England). State Mutual Bk.
--Round the Italian Coast. 256p. 1980. 15.00x (ISBN 0-245-52648-X, Pub. by Nautical England). State Mutual Bk.
--Through the Belgian Canals. 160p. 1980. 9.00x (ISBN 0-245-50975-5, Pub. by Nautical England). State Mutual Bk.
--Through the Dutch Canals. 250p. 1980. 15.00x (Pub. by Nautical England). State Mutual Bk.
--Through the French Canals. 200p. 1980. 18.00 (ISBN 0-245-53403-2, Pub. by Nautical England). State Mutual Bk.
--Through the German Waterways. 168p. 1980. 15.00x (ISBN 0-245-51000-1, Pub. by Nautical England). State Mutual Bk.
Britan, Gerald M. & Cohen, Ronald, eds. Hierarchy & Society: Anthropological Perspectives on Bureaucracy. LC 80-10835. 1980. text ed. 16.00x (ISBN 0-89727-009-6); pap. text ed. 6.95x (ISBN 0-89727-010-X). Inst Study Human.
Britan, Halbert H., tr. see De Spinoza, Benedictus.
Britchky, Seymour. Seymour Britchky's New Revised Guide to the Restaurants of New York: An Irreverent Appraisal of the Best, Most Interesting, Most Famous, Most Underated or Worst Restaurants in New York City. 1976. pap. 5.95 o.p. (ISBN 0-394-73222-7). Random.
--Seymour Britchky's Restaurants of New York, 1977-1978. (Illus.). 1977. pap. 5.95 o.p. (ISBN 0-394-73414-9). Random.
Brite, Robert L. Introduction to Business Statistics. LC 76-17717. (Illus.). 1977. text ed. 13.95 (ISBN 0-201-00593-X). A-W.
British Academy, 1979. Proceedings, Vol. LXV. (Illus.). 500p. 1981. 175.00 (ISBN 0-19-725998-7). Oxford U Pr.
British Association for the Advancement of Science, ed. Energy in the Balance. 260p. 1980. pap. text ed. 23.40 (ISBN 0-86103-031-1). Butterworths.
British Broadcasting Corporation. B B C Hymn Book. 1951. words only 3.75x (ISBN 0-19-231302-9); words & music 9.95x (ISBN 0-19-231301-0). Oxford U Pr.
British Columbia Institute of Technology, jt. auth. see Currie, John M.
British Council. Higher Education in the United Kingdom: 1980-1982. (Illus.). 308p. 1980. pap. 11.95 (ISBN 0-582-49710-8). Longman.
British Council, jt. ed. see Scott-Kilvert, Ian.
British Daily Mirror Children's Lit. Competitions. Children As Writers, No. 5. Longland, Ed J., ed. 1979. pap. text ed. 4.95 o.p. (ISBN 0-686-60336-2). Heinemann Ed.
British European Centre, Paris. Explorations: The English Language Course of the British European Centre. (Pergamon Institute of English Courses Ser.). 160p. 1981. pap. 5.95 (ISBN 0-08-025358-X). Pergamon.
British Geotechnical Society. Field Instrumentation in Geotechnical Engineering. LC 73-9535. 720p. 1974. 49.95 (ISBN 0-470-10475-9). Halsted Pr.
--Settlement of Structures. LC 74-9514. 730p. 1975. 71.95 o.p. (ISBN 0-470-10476-7). Halsted Pr.
British Horse Society & Pony Club. Aids & Their Application. 1976. pap. 3.25 (ISBN 0-8120-0760-3). Barron.
--Basic Training for Young Horses & Ponies. LC 76-54933. 1977. pap. 1.95 (ISBN 0-8120-0757-3). Barron.
--Bits & Bitting. LC 76-55354. 1976. pap. 1.50 (ISBN 0-8120-0759-X). Barron.
--The Foot & Shoeing. LC 76-55015. 1976. pap. 1.95 (ISBN 0-8120-0758-1). Barron.
--A Guide to the Purchase of Children's Ponies. 1979. pap. 1.95 (ISBN 0-8120-0786-7). Barron.
--The Instructors' Handbook. LC 76-55317. 1977. 5.75 (ISBN 0-8120-5125-4). Barron.
--Mounted Games & Gymkhanas. LC 76-56448. 1977. 5.75 (ISBN 0-8120-5124-6). Barron.
--Polo for the Pony Club. LC 76-54905. 1977. pap. 1.95 (ISBN 0-8120-0785-9). Barron.
--Riding to Hounds. 1976. pap. 1.95 (ISBN 0-8120-0756-5). Barron.
British Institute of International & Comparative Law. Selected Documents on International Environmental Law. 1977. 15.00 (ISBN 0-379-00348-1). Oceana.
British Leyland Motors. Complete Official Austin-Healey 100-Six & 3000, 1956-1968. LC 77-72588. (Illus.). 416p. 1977. pap. 25.00 (ISBN 0-8376-0133-9). Bentley.
--Complete Official MGB, Model Years 1975-1980: Comprising the Official Driver's Handbook & Workshop Manual. LC 80-65229. (Illus.). 304p. 1980. pap. 17.50 (ISBN 0-8376-0112-6). Bentley.
--Complete Official Sprite-Midget 948 & 1098cc: Comprising the Official Driver's Handbook, Workshop Manual, Special Tuning Manual. LC 67-28432. (Illus.). 384p. (Orig.). 1968. pap. 17.50 (ISBN 0-8376-0023-5). Bentley.
--Complete Official Triumph GT6, GT6 Plus &GT6 Mk 3 1967-1973: Official Driver's Handbook & Official Workshop Manual. LC 74-21353. (Illus.). 480p. 1975. pap. 25.00 (ISBN 0-8376-0120-7). Bentley.

--The Complete Official Triumph Spitfire MK III, MK IV & 1500, Model Years 1968-1974: Comprising the Official Driver's Handbook & Workshop Manual. LC 74-20004. (Illus.). 480p. 1975. pap. 25.00 (ISBN 0-8376-0123-1). Bentley.
--The Complete Official Triumph Tr6 & Tr250, 1967-1976: Comprising the Official Driver's Handbook & Workshop Manual. LC 77-91592. (Illus.). 608p. 1978. pap. 25.00 (ISBN 0-8376-0108-8). Bentley.
--The Complete Official Trump Spitfire Fifteen Hundred, Model Years 1975-1980: Comprising the Official Driver's Handbook & Workshop Manual. LC 79-53184. (Illus.). 1980. pap. 17.50 (ISBN 0-8376-0122-3). Bentley.
--The Complete Official 1275 cc Sprite-Midget 1967-1974: Comprising the Official Driver's Handbook, Workshop Manual, Emission Control Supplement. LC 75-37232. (Illus.). 400p. 1975. pap. 17.50 (ISBN 0-8376-0127-4). Bentley.
British Mechanical Engineering Confederation in Association with 'Engineering' The European Economic Community & United Kingdom Engineering Companies. 57p. 1980. 78.75x (ISBN 0-89771-002-9). State Mutual Bk.
British Medical Association, jt. auth. see Times Bks.
British Museum. Human Biology-an Exhibition of Ourselves. LC 76-53266. (Illus.). 1977. 18.95 (ISBN 0-521-21589-7); pap. 5.95 (ISBN 0-521-29193-3). Cambridge U Pr.
--Man's Place in Evolution. (Natural History Ser.). (Illus.). 120p. 1981. 22.50 (ISBN 0-521-23177-9); pap. 7.95 (ISBN 0-521-29849-0). Cambridge U Pr.
British Museum & Metropolitan Museum of Art. The Vikings. LC 79-25486. (Illus.). 192p. 1980. 22.95 (ISBN 0-688-03603-1). Morrow.
British Museum Natural History. Dinosaurs & Their Living Relatives. LC 79-14504. 1980. 17.95 (ISBN 0-521-22887-5); pap. 6.95 (ISBN 0-521-29698-6). Cambridge U Pr.
British Museum, Natural History. Life Before Birth. LC 78-60029. (Illus.). 1979. 7.95 (ISBN 0-521-22382-2); pap. 3.95 (ISBN 0-521-29464-9). Cambridge U Pr.
British Museum Natural History. Nature at Work. LC 78-66795. (Illus.). 1978. 18.95 (ISBN 0-521-22390-3); pap. 6.95 (ISBN 0-521-29469-X). Cambridge U Pr.
British Occupational Hygiene Society. Hygiene Standards of Chrysotile Asbestos Dust. 1968. pap. text ed. 3.05 o.p. (ISBN 0-08-012995-1). Pergamon.
British Postgraduate Medical Federation. The Scientific Basis of Medicine: Annual Reviews. Incl. 1966. text ed. 6.50x (ISBN 0-685-37476-9); 1967, 1968 & 1970. text ed. 8.25x ea.; 1973. text ed. 13.50x (ISBN 0-685-37478-5). Athlone Pr). Humanities.
British Pumps Manufacturers Association, 6th Technical Conference. Proceedings. 270p. 1979. pap. 60.00 (ISBN 0-906085-27-6, Dist. by Air Science Co.). BHRA Fluid.
British Schools Council. Project Technology Briefs. (Project Technology Ser.). 1975. pap. text ed. 16.25x (ISBN 0-435-75898-5). Heinemann Ed.
British Shippers' Council. Shipping Two Thousand: The Evolution of Maritime Trade in the Next 10 to 25 Years: An International Conference Held Under the Auspices of the British Shipper's Council, London Hilton-June 19th & 20th, 1979. 124p. 1979. 85.00x (ISBN 0-7099-0212-3, Pub. by Croom Helm Ltd England). Biblio Dist.
British Theatre Institute, jt. ed. see John Offord Pubns.
British Tourist Authority. AA Motorists' Atlas of Great Britain. (Illus.). 1979. 12.95 (ISBN 0-09-211480-6, Pub. by BTA). Merrimack Bk Serv.
--AA Motorists' Map of Northern England. 1979. pap. 2.50 (ISBN 0-905522-31-1, Pub. by B T a). Merrimack Bk Serv.
--AA Touring Guide to England. (Illus.). 1979. 23.95 (ISBN 0-09-125890-1, Pub. by B T A). Merrimack Bk Serv.
--AA Touring Guide to Ireland. (Illus.). 1979. 23.95 (ISBN 0-09-127020-0, Pub. by B T A). Merrimack Bk Serv.
--AA Touring Guide to Scotland. (Illus.). 1979. 23.95 (ISBN 0-09-125870-7, Pub. by B T A). Merrimack Bk Serv.
--AA Touring Guide to Wales. (Illus.). 1979. 23.95 (ISBN 0-09-125880-4, Pub. by B T A). Merrimack Bk Serv.
--Bed & Breakfast Stops Nineteen Eighty-One. (Illus.). 96p. 1981. pap. write for info. (Pub. by Auto Assn-British Tourist Authority England). Merrimack Bk Serv.
--Discovering Cathedrals. (Illus.). 80p. 1981. pap. write for info. (ISBN 0-85263-472-2, Pub. by Auto Assn-British Tourist Authority England). Merrimack Bk Serv.
--Discovering English Customs & Traditions. (Illus.). 80p. Date not set. pap. price not set (Pub. by Auto Assn-British Tourist Authority). Merrimack Bk Serv.
--Discovering Gardens in Britain. (Illus.). 80p. Date not set. pap. price not set (ISBN 0-85263-456-0, Pub. by Auto Assn-British Tourist Authority England). Merrimack Bk Serv.
--Discovering Kings & Queens. (Illus.). 88p. 1981. pap. write for info. (ISBN 0-85263-439-0, Pub. by Auto Assn-British Tourist Authority England). Merrimack Bk Serv.
--Discovering London's Villages. (Illus.). 72p. 1981. pap. write for info. (ISBN 0-85263-451-X, Pub. by Auto Assn-British Tourist Authority England). Merrimack Bk Serv.
--Discovering Preserved Railways. (Illus.). 72p. Date not set. pap. price not set (ISBN 0-85263-515-X, Pub. by Auto Assn-British Tourist Authority England). Merrimack Bk Serv.
--East Anglia. rev. ed. (Illus.). 114p. Date not set. pap. price not set (ISBN 0-86143-044-1, Pub. by Auto Assn-British Tourist Authority England). Merrimack Bk Serv.
--East Midlands. rev. ed. (Illus.). 66p. Date not set. pap. price not set (ISBN 0-86143-042-5, Pub. by Auto Assn-British Tourist Authority England). Merrimack Bk Serv.
--English Lakeland: Cumbria. rev. ed. (Illus.). 114p. 1981. pap. write for info. (ISBN 0-86143-037-9, Pub. by Auto Assn-British Tourist Authority England). Merrimack Bk Serv.
--Heart of England: Shakespeare Country. rev. ed. (Illus.). 122p. 1981. pap. write for info. (ISBN 0-86143-041-7, Pub. by Auto Assn-British Tourist Authority England). Merrimack Bk Serv.
--North West England. rev. ed. (Illus.). 74p. 1981. pap. write for info. (ISBN 0-86143-039-5, Pub. by Auto Assn-British Tourist Authority England). Merrimack Bk Serv.
--Northumbria. rev. ed. (Illus.). 82p. 1981. pap. write for info. (ISBN 0-86143-038-7, Pub. by Auto Assn-British Tourist Authority England). Merrimack Bk Serv.
--Seeing Britain on a Budget. (Illus.). 1981. pap. write for info. (ISBN 0-906318-07-6, Pub. by Auto Assn-British Tourist Authority England). Merrimack Bk Serv.
--South East England. rev. ed. (Illus.). 114p. 1981. pap. write for info. (ISBN 0-86143-048-4, Pub. by Auto Assn-British Tourist Authority England). Merrimack Bk Serv.
--South of England. rev. ed. (Illus.). 114p. 1981. pap. write for info. (ISBN 0-86143-047-6, Pub. by Auto Assn-British Tourist Authority). Merrimack Bk Serv.
--Thames & Chilterns. rev. ed. (Illus.). 66p. 1981. pap. write for info. (ISBN 0-86143-043-3, Pub. by Auto Assn-British Tourist Authority England). Merrimack Bk Serv.
--West Country. rev. ed. (Illus.). 274p. 1981. pap. write for info. (ISBN 0-86143-046-8, Pub. by Auto Assn-British Tourist Authority England). Merrimack Bk Serv.
--Yorkshire & Humberside. rev. ed. (Illus.). 106p. 1981. pap. write for info. (ISBN 0-86143-040-9, Pub. by Auto Assn-British Tourist Authority England). Merrimack Bk Serv.
British Tourist Authority, jt. auth. see Automobile Association.
Britnell, G. E. Wheat Economy. LC 39-25982. 1974. 19.50x o.p. (ISBN 0-8020-7034-5). U of Toronto Pr.
Britt, George, jt. auth. see Broun, Heywood.
Britt, George L. When Dust Shall Sing. 1958. 4.95 (ISBN 0-87148-901-5). Pathway Pr.
Britt, Katrina. Island for Dreams. (Harlequin Romances Ser.). 192p. 1980. pap. 1.25 (ISBN 0-373-02371-5, Pub. by Harlequin). PB.
--The Wrong Man. (Harlequin Romances). 192p. 1981. pap. 1.25 (ISBN 0-373-02397-9, Pub. by Harlequin). PB.
Britt, Rose & Ceely, Doris. Tom, the Poet & Gadgetmaker. 64p. 1980. 6.00 (ISBN 0-682-49622-7). Exposition.
Brittain, Bill. Devil's Donkey. LC 80-7907. (Illus.). 128p. (gr. 3-7). 1981. 8.95 (ISBN 0-06-020682-9, HarpJ); PLB 8.79g (ISBN 0-06-020683-7). Har-Row.
Brittain, Joan T. Laurence Stallings. LC 74-23831. (U. S. Authors Ser.: No. 250). 1975. lib. bdg. 10.95 (ISBN 0-8057-0686-0). Twayne.
Brittain, John A. Corporate Dividend Policy. (Studies of Government Finance). (Orig.). 1966. 11.95 (ISBN 0-8157-1078-X); pap. 4.95 (ISBN 0-8157-1077-1). Brookings.
--Inheritance & the Inequality of Material Wealth. LC 77-91814. (Studies in Social Economics). 1978. 9.95 (ISBN 0-8157-1084-4); pap. 3.95 (ISBN 0-8157-1083-6). Brookings.
--The Inheritance of Economic Status. LC 76-56369. (Studies in Social Economics). 1977. 11.95 (ISBN 0-8157-1082-8); pap. 4.95 (ISBN 0-8157-1081-X). Brookings.
--The Payroll Tax for Social Security. LC 72-142. (Studies of Government Finance). 336p. 1972. 11.95 (ISBN 0-8157-1080-1). Brookings.
Brittain, Vera. Testament of Youth. 1980. 13.95 (ISBN 0-686-68866-X). Seaview Bks.
--Testament of Youth. 1980. 13.95 (ISBN 0-686-68995-X); pap. 7.45 (ISBN 0-686-68996-8). Wideview Bks.
Brittan, Arthur. Meanings & Situations. (International Library of Sociology). 222p. 1973. 18.50 (ISBN 0-7100-7509-X); pap. 6.00 (ISBN 0-7100-7551-0). Routledge & Kegan.
--The Privatised World. (International Library of Sociology Ser.). 1978. 18.50x (ISBN 0-7100-8769-1); pap. 8.95 (ISBN 0-7100-8768-3). Routledge & Kegan.
Brittan, Gordon G., Jr., jt. auth. see Lambert, Karel.
Brittan, John. Electronics for Appliances. Sabin, A. Ross, ed. (Illus.). 172p. (gr. 11). 1979. 20.00 (ISBN 0-938336-09-6). Whirlpool.
Brittan, Martin. Rasbora. (Illus.). 1972. 9.95 (ISBN 0-87666-136-3, PS-681). TFH Pubns.
Brittin, Burdick H. International Law for Seagoing Officers. 4th ed. LC 80-81095. (Illus.). 624p. 1981. 22.95x (ISBN 0-87021-304-0). Naval Inst Pr.
Brittin, Burdick H. & Watson, Liselotte B. International Law for Seagoing Officers. 3rd ed. LC 77-172513. 1972. 17.00x o.p. (ISBN 0-87021-303-2). Naval Inst Pr.
Brittin, Norman A. Edna St. Vincent Millay. (U. S. Authors Ser.: No. 116). 1967. lib. bdg. 9.95 (ISBN 0-8057-0496-5). Twayne.
--Thomas Middleton. (English Authors Ser.: No. 139). lib. bdg. 10.95 (ISBN 0-8057-1388-3). Twayne.
Britting, Kenneth R. Inertial Navigation Systems Analysis. LC 70-168635. 1971. 27.50 (ISBN 0-471-10485-X, Pub. by Wiley-Interscience). Wiley.
Brittingham, Barbara E., jt. auth. see Pezzullo, Thomas R.
Brittle, Gerald. The Demonologist: The Extraordinary Career of Ed & Lorraine Warren. LC 80-21065. (Illus.). 216p. 1981. 10.95 (ISBN 0-13-198333-4). P-H.
Britton, Anne. Blackie: The Biography of Blackbird. 6.95 (ISBN 0-392-07664-0, SpS). Soccer.
Britton, Burt. Self Portrait: Book People Picture Themselves. 1976. 12.50 o.p. (ISBN 0-394-49648-5); pap. 6.95 (ISBN 0-394-73104-2). Random.
Britton, D. K. Cereals in the United Kingdom. 1969. 104.00 o.p. (ISBN 0-08-013896-9). Pergamon.
Britton, Dorothy. National Parks of Japan. LC 75-30181. 144p. 1981. 17.95 (ISBN 0-87011-250-3). Kodansha.
Britton, Dorothy, tr. see Akutagawa, Ryunosuke.
Britton, Dorothy G., tr. see Basho, Matsuo.
Britton, Frances. Basic Nursing Skills. (Illus.). 224p. 1981. pap. text ed. 7.95 (ISBN 0-87619-921-X). R J Brady.
Britton, Frank L. Behind Communism. 97p. (Orig.). 1979. pap. 1.75x (ISBN 0-911038-82-5). Noontide.
Britton, Jack & Washington, George. U. S. Military Shoulder Patches of the U.S. Armed Forces. rev ed. LC 79-112480. (Illus.). 1978. pap. 6.50 o.p. (ISBN 0-912958-04-9). Military Coll.
Britton, Jack L. Uniform Insignia of the United States Military Forces. (Illus.). 1980. pap. 6.50 (ISBN 0-912958-06-5). Military Coll.
Britton, K. Philosophy & the Meaning of Life. LC 69-12926. 1969. 27.95 (ISBN 0-521-07456-8); pap. 7.95x (ISBN 0-521-09593-X, 593). Cambridge U Pr.
Britvec, S. J. The Stability of Elastic Systems. 480p. 1973. text ed. 38.00 (ISBN 0-08-016859-0). Pergamon.
Britz, Richard, et al. The Edible City Resource Manual. (Illus.). 320p. (Orig.). 1981. pap. 11.50 (ISBN 0-913232-97-1). W Kaufmann.
Britz-Crecelius, Heidi. Children at Play. (Illus.). 1979. 12.50 (ISBN 0-903540-24-X, Pub. by Floris Books); pap. 6.95 (ISBN 0-903540-27-4, Pub. by Floris Books). St George Bk Serv.
Briwtow, Gwen. Golden Dreams. 224p. 1980. 11.50 (ISBN 0-686-62597-8). Lippincott.
Brizzee, Ken, jt. ed. see Ordy, J. Mark.
Brizzi, Mary. Philip Jose Farmer. LC 80-19171. (Starmont Reader's Guide Ser.: No. 3). 80p. 1980. Repr. of 1980 ed. lib. bdg. 9.95x (ISBN 0-89370-034-7). Borgo Pr.
Brizzi, Mary T. Reader's Guide to Philip Jose Farmer. Schlobin, Roger C., ed. LC 79-17691. (Starmont Reader's Guides to Contemporary Science Fiction & Fantasy Authors Ser.: Vol. 3). (Illus., Orig.). 1980. pap. text ed. 3.95 (ISBN 0-916732-05-3). Starmont Hse.
Brizzolara, Andrew, compiled by. A Directory of Italian & Italian American Organizations & Community Services in the Metropolitan Area of Greater New York: in the Metropolitan Area of Greater New York, Vol. II. rev. ed. 1980. 9.95x (ISBN 0-913256-44-7). Ctr Migration.
Bro, Bernard. The Little Way. pap. 5.95 (ISBN 0-87061-052-X). Chr Classics.
Bro, Harmon H. Edgar Cayce on Dreams. 224p. 1968. pap. 2.25 (ISBN 0-446-92687-6). Warner Bks.
--Edgar Cayce on Religion & Psychic Experience. Cayce, Hugh L., ed. (Orig.). 1970. pap. 2.25 (ISBN 0-446-92696-5). Warner Bks.
Bro, Lu. Drawing: A Studio Guide. (Illus.). 1978. pap. text ed. 8.95x (ISBN 0-393-95018-2). Norton.
Broad, C. D. Five Types of Ethical Theory. 8th ed. (International Library of Philosophy & Scientific Method). 1930. text ed. 25.00x (ISBN 0-7100-3080-0). Humanities.
--Lectures on Psychical Research. (International Library of Philosophy & Scientific Method). 1962. text ed. 31.25x (ISBN 0-7100-3611-6). Humanities.
--Religion, Philosophy & Psychical Research. (International Library of Psychology, Philosophy & Scientific Method Ser.). 1969. Repr. of 1953 ed. text ed. 10.00x (ISBN 0-391-00441-7). Humanities.
Broad, C. D. & Lewy, C. Leibniz: An Introduction. LC 74-31784. 192p. 1975. 26.95 (ISBN 0-521-20691-X); pap. 7.95x (ISBN 0-521-09925-0). Cambridge U Pr.
Broad, Delia. Space Adventures Reading Series Sampler. 1980. pap. 19.95 (ISBN 0-88450-723-8, 4520-B). Communication Skill.
Broad, Lyn. Alternative Schools. 1977. pap. 7.95 o.p. (ISBN 0-87545-009-1). Natl Sch Pr.
Broad, O. D. Kant: An Introduction. Lewy, C., ed. LC 77-80829. 1978. 47.50 (ISBN 0-521-21755-5); pap. 11.50 (ISBN 0-521-29265-4). Cambridge U Pr.
Broadbent, et al, eds. see Milton, John.
Broadbent, D. E. Decision & Stress. 1971. 46.00 o.s.i. (ISBN 0-12-135550-0). Acad Pr.
Broadbent, Geoffrey, et al. Signs, Symbols & Architecture. LC 78-13557. 1980. 54.25 (ISBN 0-471-99718-8, Pub. by Wiley-Interscience). Wiley.
Broadbent, Geoffrey, et al, eds. Meaning & Behaviour in the Built Environment. LC 79-41490. 336p. 1980. 55.00 (ISBN 0-471-27708-8, Pub. by Wiley-Interscience). Wiley.
Broadbent, J., ed. John Milton: Introductions. LC 72-93144. (Milton for Schools & Colleges Ser.). (Illus.). 350p. 1973. 42.00 (ISBN 0-521-20172-1); pap. 11.50 (ISBN 0-521-09799-1). Cambridge U Pr.
Broadbent, John. Introduction to Paradise Lost. (Milton for Schools & Colleges Ser). (Illus.). 1971. 28.50 (ISBN 0-521-08068-1); pap. 7.95x (ISBN 0-521-09639-1). Cambridge U Pr.
Broadbent, Michael. Wine Tasting. 5th ed. (Christie Wine Publications). 68p. 1977. 8.50x o.p. (ISBN 0-903432-11-0). Intl Pubns Serv.
Broadbent, Simon. Spending Advertising Money. 3rd ed. 381p. 1979. pap. 12.25x (ISBN 0-220-67020-X, Pub. by Busn Bks England). Renouf.
Broadhouse, John. How to Make a Violin. Repr. lib. bdg. 29.00 (ISBN 0-403-03872-3). Scholarly.
Broadhurst, A., jt. auth. see Feldman, M. P.
Broadley, Gwen. The Retriever Owner's Encyclopedia. 1968. 9.95 (ISBN 0-7207-0172-4, Pub. by Michael Joseph). Merrimack Bk Serv.
Broadman, Muriel, jt. auth. see Suib, Leonard.
Broadribb, Violet. Foundations of Pediatric Nursing. 2nd ed. (Illus., Orig.). 1973. pap. 9.50 o.p. (ISBN 0-397-54135-X). Lippincott.
Broadribb, Violet & Corliss, Charlotte. Maternal-Child Nursing. 600p. 1973. text ed. 12.50 o.p. (ISBN 0-397-54140-6). Lippincott.
Broadus, John A. see Hovey, Alvah.
Broadwell, Bruce, jt. auth. see Edwards, Perry.
Broadwell, Lucile & Milutnovic, Barbara. Medical-Surgical Nursing Procedures. LC 76-4305. 1977. pap. text ed. 12.40 (ISBN 0-8273-0353-X); instructor's guide 1.60 (ISBN 0-8273-0354-8). Delmar.
Broadwell, Lucile, jt. auth. see Von Gremp, Zella.
Broadwell, Martin M. Moving up to Supervision. LC 78-21995. 1978. pap. 8.95 (ISBN 0-8436-0749-1). CBI Pub.
--New Supervisor. 2nd ed. 1979. pap. text ed. 8.95 (ISBN 0-201-00565-4). A-W.
--The Practice of Supervising: Making Experience Pay. LC 76-23982. (Illus.). 1977. pap. text ed. 8.95 (ISBN 0-201-00789-4). A-W.
--Supervising Today: A Guide for Positive Leadership. LC 79-12751. 1979. pap. 8.95 (ISBN 0-8436-0775-0). CBI Pub.
--Supervisor & on the Job Training. 2nd ed. LC 74-30695. (Illus.). 176p. 1975. text ed. 8.95 (ISBN 0-201-00754-1). A-W.
--Supervisor As an Instructor: A Guide for Classroom Training. 3rd ed. LC 77-81201. (Illus.). 1978. pap. text ed. 8.95 (ISBN 0-201-00329-5). A-W.
Broadwell, Martin M. & Simpson, William F. New Insurance Supervisor. 168p. 1981. pap. text ed. cancelled (ISBN 0-201-00568-9). A-W.
Broadwell, Martin M., jt. auth. see Diekelmann, Nancy.
Broadwell, William E., Jr. The Management of Work: A Workbook. (Business Ser). (Illus.). 1971. 8.95 (ISBN 0-201-00672-3). A-W.

Broady, Maurice. Planning for People. 119p. 1968. pap. text ed. 4.00x (ISBN 0-7199-0765-9, Pub. by Bedford England). Renouf.
--Tomorrow's Community- the Development of Neighborhood Organisations. 86p. 1979. pap. text ed. 7.40x (ISBN 0-7199-0966-X, Pub. by Bedford England). Renouf.
Broccoletti, Pete. Building up: The Young Athlete's Guide to Weight Training. (Illus.). 160p. 1981. 13.95 (ISBN 0-89651-053-0); pap. 8.95 (ISBN 0-89651-054-9). Icarus.
Broccoletti, Pete & Hunter, Rich. Shape up for Soccer. (Illus.). 256p. 1981. 14.95 (ISBN 0-89651-750-0); wirebd. 9.95 (ISBN 0-89651-751-9). Icarus.
Broccoletti, Peter P. & Scanlon, Pat. The Notre Dame Weight Training Program for Football. LC 78-20947. (Illus.). 1979. 12.95 (ISBN 0-89651-502-8); pap. 9.95 (ISBN 0-89651-503-6). Icarus.
Broch, Hermann. Broch, Dramen: Kommentierte Werkausgabe, Bd. 7. (Suhrkamp Taschenbuecher: No. 538). 448p. (Ger.). 1980. pap. text ed. 6.50 (ISBN 3-518-37038-3, Pub. by Insel Verlag Germany). Suhrkamp.
--Death of Virgil. 8.75 (ISBN 0-8446-1742-3). Peter Smith.
--Hermann Broch, Gedichte. Lutzeler, Paul M., ed. (Suhrkamp Taschenbuecher: Vol. 8). 240p. (Orig.). 1980. pap. text ed. 4.55 (ISBN 3-518-37072-3, Pub. by Insel Verlag Germany). Suhrkamp.
Brochner, Jessie, tr. see Reumert, Elith.
Brock, Bernard L. & Scott, Robert L., eds. Methods of Rhetorical Criticism: A Twentieth-Century Perspective. rev. 2nd ed. 520p. 1980. 16.95 (ISBN 0-8143-1648-4). Wayne St U Pr.
Brock, Betty. The Shades. (gr. 3-5). 1973. pap. 1.25 o.s.i. (ISBN 0-380-01545-5, 27888, Camelot). Avon.
Brock, Bill, jt. auth. see Muskie, Edmund S.
Brock, D. Heyward & Welsh, James M. Ben Jonson: A Quadricentennial Bibliography, 1947-1972. LC 74-2424. (Author Bibliography Ser.: No. 16). 1974. 10.00 (ISBN 0-8108-0710-6). Scarecrow.
Brock, Dee & Howard, C. Jeriel. Writing for a Reason. LC 77-12617. 1978. pap. text ed. 8.50x (ISBN 0-471-03017-1); tchrs. manual 1.00 (ISBN 0-471-04052-5). Wiley.
Brock, Emma. Drusilla. (Illus.). (gr. 4-6). 1937. 3.95g o.s.i. (ISBN 0-02-714440-2). Macmillan.
Brock, Horace, et al. Cost Accounting: Principles & Applications. 3rd ed. (Accounting Instructional System). (Illus.). 1978. text ed. 11.95 (ISBN 0-07-008051-8, G); course management manual 9.95 (ISBN 0-07-008054-2); individualized performance guide 5.75 (ISBN 0-07-008052-6). McGraw.
Brock, Horace R. & Palmer, Charles E. Accounting: Principles & Applications, 3 pts. 4th ed. LC 80-16713. (College Accounting Instructional System Ser.). (Illus.). 1981. One Vol. Ed. text ed. 16.95x (ISBN 0-07-008090-9, G); Pt. 1. pap. text ed. 9.50x (ISBN 0-07-008092-5); Pt. 2. pap. text ed. 9.50x (ISBN 0-07-008093-3); Pt. 3. pap. text ed. 9.50x (ISBN 0-07-008094-1); wkbk. 5.45 (ISBN 0-07-008096-8); Pt. 2, Individualized Performance Guide. 5.95 (ISBN 0-07-008096-8); Course Management & solutions manual 10.00 (ISBN 0-07-008101-8); tests avail. (ISBN 0-07-008098-4). McGraw.
Brock, Katherine M., jt. auth. see Brock, Thomas D.
Brock, Michael. The Great Reform Act. Hurstfield, Joel, ed. (Illus.). 411p. 1974. text ed. 18.25x (ISBN 0-09-115910-5, Hutchinson U Lib); pap. text ed. 11.75x (ISBN 0-09-115911-3, Hutchinson U Lib). Humanities.
Brock, Peter. The Political & Social Doctrines of the Unity of Czech Brethren in the Fifteenth & Early Sixteenth Centuries. (Slavistic Printings & Reprintings). 1957. text ed. 34.25x (ISBN 0-391-01607-5). Humanities.
Brock, Raymond T. The Christ-Centered Family. (Radiant Life Ser.). 1977. pap. 1.95 (ISBN 0-88243-903-0, 02-0903); teacher's ed 2.50 (ISBN 0-88243-173-0, 32-0173). Gospel Pub.
Brock, Richards, et al. Ready or Not. 1977. 6.95 (ISBN 0-8027-0586-3); pap. 3.95 (ISBN 0-8027-7121-1). Walker & Co.
Brock, Sebastian. Syriac Version of the Ps. Nonnos Mythological Scholia. LC 79-139712. (Oriental Publications: No. 20). 1971. 62.00 (ISBN 0-521-07990-X). Cambridge U Pr.
Brock, Stuart. Double-Cross Ranch. 256p. (YA) 1974. 5.95 (ISBN 0-685-49064-5, Avalon). Bouregy.
Brock, T. E., ed. Fluidics Applications Bibliography. 1968. text ed. 24.00 (ISBN 0-900983-00-0, Dist. by Air Science Co.). BHRA Fluid.
Brock, Ted & Campbell, Jim. First Official NFL Trivia Book. 1980. pap. 1.95 (ISBN 0-451-09541-3, J9541, Sig). NAL.
Brock, Th. D. Thermophilic Microorganisms & Life at High Temperatures. LC 78-6110. (Springer Ser. in Microbiology). (Illus.). 1978. 27.10 (ISBN 0-387-90309-7). Springer-Verlag.
Brock, Thomas D. & Brock, Katherine M. Basic Microbiology with Applications. 2nd ed. (Illus.). 1978. 20.95 (ISBN 0-13-065284-9). P-H.
Brock, Thomas D., ed. Milestones in Microbiology. 1975. Repr. of 1961 ed. 7.00 (ISBN 0-914826-06-9). Am Soc Microbio.
Brock, W. H., ed. H. E. Armstrong & the Teaching of Science 1880-1930. LC 72-87179. (Cambridge Texts & Studies in the History of Education: No. 14). 168p. 1973. 23.95 (ISBN 0-521-08679-5). Cambridge U Pr.
Brock, W. R. Character of American History. 2nd ed. (Illus.). 1965. 18.95 (ISBN 0-312-12985-8). St Martin.
Brocke, Michael, jt. auth. see Petuchowski, Jakob L.
Brockel, Harry C., jt. ed. see Schenker, Eric.
Brockelman, Paul T., tr. see Gusdorf, Georges.
Brockelmann, C. History of the Islamic Peoples. 1980. 15.00 (ISBN 0-7100-1118-0); pap. cancelled (ISBN 0-7100-0521-0). Routledge & Kegan.
Brocker, T. H. Differentiable Germs & Catastrophes. Lander, L., tr. from Ger. LC 74-17000. (London Mathematical Society Lecture Note Ser.: No. 17). 160p. (Eng.). 1975. pap. text ed. 19.95 (ISBN 0-521-20681-2). Cambridge U Pr.
Brockett, O. & Findlay, R. Century of Innovation: A History of European & American Theatre & Drama, 1870-1970. (Theater & Drama Ser.). 1973. 24.95 (ISBN 0-13-122747-5). P-H.
Brockett, Oscar G., ed. & frwd. by. Studies in Theatre & Drama. (De Proprietatibus Litterarum, Ser. Major: No. 23). 217p. 1972. text ed. 43.50 (ISBN 90-2792-112-1). Mouton.
Brockett, Paul. Bibliography of Aeronautics. LC 66-25692. 1966. Repr. of 1910 ed. 50.00 (ISBN 0-8103-3320-1). Gale.
Brockett, W. A., et al. Elements of Applied Thermodynamics. 4th ed. LC 77-73341. 1978. text ed. 23.95x (ISBN 0-87021-169-2). Naval Inst Pr.
Brockington, Dave, jt. auth. see White, Roger.
Brockington, L. H., ed. see Robinson, Theodore H.
Brocklehurst, John C. & Hanley, Thomas. Geriatric Medicine for Students. LC 76-8473. (Livingstone Medical Texts Ser.). (Illus.). 1976. pap. text ed. 9.75 (ISBN 0-443-01470-1). Churchill.
Brockman, Ellis. Laboratory Manual for Microbiology. new ed. LC 74-28777. 1980. pap. 15.00 (ISBN 0-87812-085-8). Pendell Pub.
Brockman, H. L. Theory of Fashion Design. 1965. 22.50 (ISBN 0-87245-041-4). Textile Bk.
Brockman, Helen L. Theory of Fashion Design. LC 65-25852. 1965. 22.50 (ISBN 0-471-10586-4). Wiley.
Brockman, John. By the Late John Brockman. 1969. 6.95 o.s.i. (ISBN 0-02-516390-6). Macmillan.
Brockman, John, jt. auth. see Schlossberg, Edwin.
Brockman, Ross. An Adventure with Foods & Health. 1978. 4.95 (ISBN 0-533-02994-5). Vantage.
Brockopp, Gene W., jt. auth. see Lester, David.
Brockriede, W., jt. auth. see Darnell, D. K.
Brod, J., jt. ed. see Bahlmann, J.
Brod, J., jt. ed. see Eisenbach, G. M.
Brod, Richard I., ed. Language Study for the Nineteen Eighties: Reports of the MLA-ACLS Language Task Forces. LC 79-87582. 106p. 1980. pap. 8.50x (ISBN 0-87352-088-2). Modern Lang.
Brod, Ruth H., jt. auth. see Reilly, Harold J.
Broda, E. Evolution of Bioenergetic Processes. LC 75-6847. 220p. 1975. text ed. 30.00 o.p. (ISBN 0-08-018275-5); pap. text ed. 18.00 (ISBN 0-08-022651-5). Pergamon.
Broda, Paul. Plasmids. LC 79-10665. (Illus.). 1979. text ed. 19.95x (ISBN 0-7167-1111-7). W H Freeman.
Brodal, A. Neurological Anatomy in Relation to Clinical Medicine. 3rd ed. (Illus.). 1072p. 1981. 35.00 (ISBN 0-19-502694-2). Oxford U Pr.
Brodal, A. & Kawamura, K. The Olivocerebellar Projection: A Review. (Advances in Anatomy, Embryology & Cell Biology Ser.: Vol. 64). (Illus.). 144p. 1981. pap. 46.10 (ISBN 0-387-10305-8). Springer-Verlag.
Brodatz, Phil. Wood & Wood Grains: A Photographic Album for Artists & Designers. (Illus.). 8.75 (ISBN 0-8446-0040-7). Peter Smith.
Brodbeck, V. Enzyme Inhibitors. 270p. (Orig.). Date not set. pap. price not set. Verlag Chemie.
Broder, David S. Changing of the Guard. 1980. 14.95 (ISBN 0-671-24566-X). S&S.
--The Party's Over: The Failure of Politics in America. 265p. 1972. pap. 5.95x (ISBN 0-06-131919-8, TB1919, Torch). Har-Row.
--Party's Over: The Failure of Politics in Amer. LC 77-181608. 1972. 10.00 o.s.i. (ISBN 0-06-010483-X, HarpT). Har-Row.
Broder, Patricia J. American Indian Painting & Sculpture. LC 80-66526. (Illus.). 160p. 1981. 29.95 (ISBN 0-89659-147-6). Abbeville Pr.
--Great Paintings of the Old American West. LC 79-2401. (Illus.). 160p. 1979. 17.95 (ISBN 0-89659-068-2). Abbeville Pr.
Broderick, Carlfred B. Marriage & the Family. (Illus.). 1979. text ed. 17.95 (ISBN 0-13-559112-0). P-H.
Broderick, Francis, et al, eds. Black Protest Thought in the Twentieth Century. 2nd ed. LC 79-119007. (American Heritage Ser). 1971. pap. 10.95 (ISBN 0-672-61178-3, AHS-56R). Bobbs.
Broderick, Francis L. W. E. B. DuBois: Negro Leader in a Time of Crisis. 1959. 10.00x (ISBN 0-8047-0558-5); pap. 2.95 o.p. (ISBN 0-8047-0559-3). Stanford U Pr.
Brodhead, Michael J., jt. auth. see Cutright, Paul R.
Brodie, Benjamin. Psychological Inquiries: A Series of Essays Intended to Illustrate the Mutual Relations of the Physical Organization & the Mental Faculties. Bd. with On Animal Electricity. DuBois-Reymond, E. (Contributions to the History of Psychology Ser., Vol. VI, Pt. E). 1980. Repr. of 1854 ed. 30.00 (ISBN 0-89093-325-1). U Pubns Amer.
Brodie, Bernard B. & Bressler, R., eds. Minireviews of the Neurosciences from Life Sciences, Vols. 13-15. LC 75-8733. 493p. 1975. text ed. 32.00 combined ed. (ISBN 0-08-019724-8); pap. text ed. 16.00 combined ed. (ISBN 0-08-019723-X). Pergamon.
Brodie, Eugene D. When Your Name Is on the Door: The Independent Businessowner's Guide to Survival, Profits & Happiness. LC 80-66756. 225p. 1981. 24.95 (ISBN 0-916728-45-5). Bks in Focus.
Brodie, H. Keith, jt. ed. see Brady, John P.
Brodie, Iain. Ferrets & Ferreting. (Illus.). 1979. 9.95 (ISBN 0-7137-0903-0, Pub. by Blandford Pr England). Sterling.
Brodie, Ian. Steamers of the Forth. LC 76-11099. (Illus.). 168p. 1976. 5.95 (ISBN 0-7153-7155-X). David & Charles.
Brodie, Keith H., jt. auth. see Arieti, Silvano.
Brodin, Dorothy. Marcel Ayme. LC 68-54455. (Columbia Essays on Modern Writers Ser.: No. 38). (Orig.). 1968. pap. 2.00 (ISBN 0-231-03128-9). Columbia U Pr.
Brodin, Dorothy see Levy, Harold L.
Brodine, ed. see Wong, Nellie, et al.
Brodman, Estelle. The Development of Medical Bibliography. 226p. 1981. Repr. of 1954 ed. 8.25 (ISBN 0-912176-00-8). Med Lib Assn.
Brodnick, Max. Fun & Games. (Illus.). 1976. pap. 1.25 o.p. (ISBN 0-685-72565-0, LB394, Leisure Bks). Nordon Pubns.
--Indoor Sports. 1976. pap. 1.25 o.p. (ISBN 0-685-73455-2, LB396, Leisure Bks). Nordon Pubns.
--The International Joke Book, No. 2. 1976. pap. 1.25 o.p. (ISBN 0-685-69150-0, LB349ZK, Leisure Bks). Nordon Pubns.
--The Sex Joke Book. (Illus., Orig.). 1975. pap. 1.25 o.p. (ISBN 0-685-52937-1, LB264ZK, Leisure Bks). Nordon Pubns.
Brodskii, M. S., et al. Nine Papers on Number Theory & Theory of Operators. LC 51-5559. (Translations Ser.: No. 2, Vol. 13). 1980. Repr. of 1964 ed. 35.60 (ISBN 0-8218-1713-2, TRANS 2-13). Am Math.
Brodsky, Allen. Handbook of Radiation Measurement & Protection, CRC: Selection A-General Scientific & Engineering Information, 2 vols. Vol. 1, 1979. 74.95 (ISBN 0-8493-3756-9); Vol. 2, 1980, 448p. 54.95 (ISBN 0-8493-3757-7). CRC Pr.
Brodsky, Annette M., ed. The Female Offender. LC 75-27014. (Sage Contemporary Social Science Issues: Vol. 19). 1975. 4.95x (ISBN 0-8039-0568-8). Sage.
Brodsky, Annette M. & Hare-Mustin, Rachel, eds. Women & Psychotherapy. 428p. 1980. 22.50 (ISBN 0-89862-605-6). Guilford Pr.
Brodsky, Bernard. The Will to Go on. 64p. (Orig.). 1981. pap. 3.75 (ISBN 0-931896-01-0). Cove View.
Brodsky, Beverley. Secret Places. LC 77-16391. (Illus.). (gr. 1-3). 1979. 9.95 (ISBN 0-397-31790-5). Lippincott.
Brodsky, Beverly. Jonah: An Old Testament Story. LC 77-5925. (gr. 3 up). 1977. 9.95 (ISBN 0-397-31733-6). Lippincott.
Brodsky, Carroll M. The Harassed Worker. LC 76-43115. 1976. 17.95 (ISBN 0-669-01041-3). Lexington Bks.
Brodsky, Carroll M. & Platt, Robert T. Rehabilitaion Environment. LC 77-26370. 1978. 16.95 (ISBN 0-669-02168-7). Lexington Bks.
Brodsky, Jean. Swipe File 2. (NonProfit-Ability Ser.). 1976. pap. 9.95 o.s.i. (ISBN 0-914756-11-7). Taft Corp.
Brodsky, Jean, ed. The Directory of Management Training Opportunities for Nonprofit Executives. 1976. 35.00 o.s.i. (ISBN 0-914756-13-3). Taft Corp.
Brodsky, K. A. Mountain Torrent of the Tien Shan: An Ecology-Faunistic Essay. (Monographiae Biologicae: No. 39). (Illus.). 311p. 1980. lib. bdg. 79.00 (ISBN 90-6193-091-X). Kluwer Boston.
Brodsky, Michael. Flesh. Date not set. Vol. I & Ii. 10.00 ea. (ISBN 0-89396-027-6). Urizen Bks. Postponed.
--Wedding Feast & Two Novellas. 1981. 15.00 (ISBN 0-916354-81-4); pap. 6.95 (ISBN 0-89396-002-0). Urizen Bks.
Brodsky, Mimi. House at Twelve Rose Street. (gr. 4-6). 1969. pap. 0.95 (ISBN 0-671-29717-1). PB.
Brodsky, Stanley L., jt. auth. see Walker, Marcia J.
Brodsky, Stanley L., jt. ed. see Walker, Marcia J.
Brodsky, William A., ed. Anion & Proton Transport, Vol. 341. new ed. LC 80-15917. 610p. 1980. 107.00 (ISBN 0-89766-070-6). NY Acad Sci.
Brodtkorb, Reidar. Gold Coin. Kingsland, L. W., tr. LC 66-11198. (Illus.). (gr. 5-9). 1966. 4.95 o.p. (ISBN 0-15-231155-6, HJ). HarBraceJ.
Brody & Snider. Current Topics in Management of Respiratory Diseases, Vol. 1. 1981. pap. text ed. price not set (ISBN 0-443-08104-2). Churchill.
--Current Topics in Management of Respiratory Diseases, Vol. 2. 1981. pap. text ed. price not set (ISBN 0-443-08103-4). Churchill.
Brody, Alan. English Mummers & Their Plays: Traces of Ancient Mystery. LC 77-92855. (Folklore & Folklife Ser). (Illus.). 1971. 12.00x (ISBN 0-8122-7611-6). U of Pa Pr.
--Hey Lenny, Hey Jack. LC 77-24389. 1976. 8.95 o.p. (ISBN 0-688-03249-4). Morrow.
Brody, Arnold G., jt. auth. see Stuhlman, Daniel D.
Brody, Baruch, ed. Readings in the Philosophy of Religion: An Analytic Approach. LC 73-20485. 608p. 1974. text ed. 19.95 (ISBN 0-13-759340-6). P-H.
Brody, Baruch A. Identity & Essence. LC 80-7511. 1980. 16.50 (ISBN 0-691-07256-6); pap. 5.95 (ISBN 0-691-02013-2). Princeton U Pr.
Brody, Baruch A. & Englehardt, H. Tristram. Mental Illness: Law & Public Policy. (Philosophy & Medicine Ser.: No. 5). 276p. 1980. lib. bdg. 28.95 (ISBN 0-686-27528-4). Kluwer Boston.
Brody, Boruch. Readings in the Philosophy of Science. LC 71-98091. (Philosophy Ser). 1970. text ed. 19.95 (ISBN 0-13-760702-4). P-H.
Brody, David. Workers in Industrial America: Essays on the 20th Century Struggle. 1979. text ed. 14.95x (ISBN 0-19-502490-7); pap. text ed. 3.95x (ISBN 0-19-502491-5). Oxford U Pr.
Brody, David E. The American Legal System. 1978. text ed. 16.95x (ISBN 0-669-01439-7); instructor's manual free (ISBN 0-669-01840-6). Heath.
Brody, Elaine & Brook, Claire. The Music Guide to Austria & Germany. LC 75-30822. (Music Guides Ser.). 350p. 1976. 10.00 (ISBN 0-396-07217-8). Dodd.
--The Music Guide to Belgium, Luxembourg, Holland & Switzerland. LC 77-6446. (Music Guides Ser.). (Illus.). 1977. 10.00 (ISBN 0-396-07437-5). Dodd.
--The Music Guide to Great Britain. LC 75-30809. (Music Guides Ser.). 350p. 1976. 10.00 (ISBN 0-396-06955-X). Dodd.
--The Music Guide to Italy. LC 78-6846. (Music Guides Ser.). 1978. 10.00 (ISBN 0-396-07436-7). Dodd.
Brody, Elaine & Fowkes, Robert A. The German Lied & Its Poetry. LC 76-124520. 1971. 15.00 (ISBN 0-8147-0958-3). NYU Pr.
Brody, Eugene D. & Bliss, Betsy L. Odds on Investing: Survival & Success in the New Stock Market. LC 78-18222. 1978. 19.95 (ISBN 0-471-04478-4, Pub. by Wiley-Interscience). Wiley.
Brody, Garry S., jt. ed. see Fredricks, Simon.
Brody, Howard. Ethical Decisions in Medicine. 2nd ed. 1981. pap. text ed. write for info (ISBN 0-316-10899-5). Little.
Brody, Ilene, jt. ed. see Vardin, Patricia.
Brody, J. A., et al see Arber, W., et al.
Brody, Jane. Jane Brody's Nutrition Book: A Lifetime Guide to Good Eating for Better Health & Weight Conrol by the Personal Health Columnist for the New Yok Times. (Illus.). 1981. 17.95 (ISBN 0-393-01429-0). Norton.
Brody, Jerome S. & Snider, Gordon, eds. Current Topics in the Management of Respiratory Diseases. (Illus.). 200p. 1981. pap. text ed. 12.50 (ISBN 0-443-08104-2). Churchill.
--Current Topics in the Management of Respiratory Disease, Vol II. (Illus.). 200p. 1981. pap. text ed. 12.50 (ISBN 0-443-08103-4). Churchill.

Brody, Jules, jt. ed. see Cabeen, David C.
Brody, Steve. How to Break Ninety Before You Reach It. 4.95 (ISBN 0-88427-040-8). Green Hill.
--How to Break Ninety Before You Reach It. 3rd ed. LC 80-10704. 1980. pap. 4.95 (ISBN 0-88427-040-8, Dist. by Caroline Hse). North River.
--How to Break Ninety Before You Reach It: A Collection of Verse About Golf & Other Sports. 1980. pap. 4.95. Caroline Hse.
Brodzinsky, David M., jt. auth. see Ambron, Sueann R.
Broeg, R. & Ewbank, Weeb. Football Greats. (Illus.). 1977. pap. 4.95 (ISBN 0-8272-1007-8). Bethany Pr.
Broehl, Wayne G., Jr; see Friedman, Leon.
Broek, D. Elementary Engineering Fracture Mechanics. rev. ed. 450p. 1978. 60.00x (ISBN 90-286-0208-9); pap. 20.00x (ISBN 90-286-0218-6). Sijthoff & Noordhoff.
Broek, Jacobus Ten see TenBroek, Jacobus.
Broek, Jan O., et al. The Study & Teaching of Geography. 2nd ed. (Social Science Seminar, Secondary Education Ser.: No. C28). 120p. 1980. pap. text ed. 5.95 (ISBN 0-675-08163-7). Merrill.
Broekel, Ray, jt. auth. see White, Laurence B., Jr.
Broekhuizen, Richard. Graphic Communications. 380p. 1979. text ed. 15.72 (ISBN 0-87345-246-1); study guide 3.96 (ISBN 0-87345-247-X); ans. key free (ISBN 0-87345-248-8). McKnight.
Broer, Jill S., et al. Governors of Tennessee, Seventeen Ninety to Eighteen Thirty-Five: I. Crawford, Charles W., ed. LC 79-129790. (The Tennessee Ser.: Vol. 3). (Illus.). 1979. 12.95 (ISBN 0-87870-075-7). Memphis St Univ.
Broer, M. R. & Wilson, R. M. Fundamentals of Marching. (Illus.). 1965. 9.95 (ISBN 0-8260-1340-6). Wiley.
Broerse, J. J., ed. Ion Chambers for Neutron Dosimetry Workshop, Rijswijk, the Netherlands, Sept. 1979. (European Applied Research Reports Special Topics). 351p. 1980. 57.00 (ISBN 0-686-63373-3). Harwood Academic.
Broesamle, John J. William Gibbs McAdoo: A Passion for Change, 1863-1917. LC 73-83261. 320p. 1974. 12.50 (ISBN 0-8046-9043-X). Kennikat.
Broeshart, Hans, jt. auth. see Fried, Maurice.
Brofoss, Karl E., jt. auth. see Cowart, Andrew T.
Brofsky, Howard, jt. auth. see Bamberger, Jeanne S.
Brogan, D. W. Abraham Lincoln. rev. ed. 145p. 1974. 16.00x (ISBN 0-7156-0865-7, Pub. by Duckworth England). Biblio Dist.
Brogan, Denis W see Johnson, Allen & Nevins, Allan.
Brogan, Peggy, ed. see Domjan, Evelyn A.
Brogan, T. V., ed. English Versification: 1570-1980: a Reference Guide with a Global Appendix. LC 80-8861. 832p. 1981. text ed. 47.50x (ISBN 0-8018-2541-5). Johns Hopkins.
Broger, Achim. Bruno. Van Stockum, Hilda, tr. from Ger. LC 75-15800. (Illus.). 160p. (gr. 3-6). 1975. 6.25 (ISBN 0-688-22051-7); PLB 6.00 (ISBN 0-688-32051-1). Morrow.
--Bruno Takes a Trip. Gueritz, Caroline, tr. from Ger. LC 78-3878. (Illus.). (gr. k-3). 1978. 7.50 (ISBN 0-688-22138-6); PLB 7.20 (ISBN 0-688-32138-0). Morrow.
--Good Morning, Whale. LC 74-9762. (Illus.). 28p. (gr. 1-3). 1975. 7.95 (ISBN 0-02-714460-7). Macmillan.
--Little Harry. Crawford, Elizabeth D., tr. from Ger. LC 78-26028. (Illus.). (gr. 4-6). 1979. 7.50 (ISBN 0-688-22185-8); PLB 7.20 (ISBN 0-688-32185-2). Morrow.
--Outrageous Kasimir. Van Stockum, Hilda, tr. (Illus.). (gr. 5-9). 1976. 8.25 (ISBN 0-688-22085-1); PLB 7.92 (ISBN 0-688-32085-6). Morrow.
--Running in Circles. Crampton, Patricia, tr. from Germ. (gr. 7 up). 1977. 8.25 (ISBN 0-688-22119-X); PLB 7.92 (ISBN 0-688-32119-4). Morrow.
Broggcr, Jan. Montevarese: A Study of Peasant Society & Culture in Southern Italy. 160p. 1971. 19.50x (ISBN 8-200-06143-4, Dist. by Columbia U Pr). Universitet.
Brogger, Suzanne. Deliver Us from Love. 1976. 8.95 o.p. (ISBN 0-440-01851-X, Sey Lawr). Delacorte.
Brogger, W. W. & Shetelig, Hakon. The Viking Ships. (Illus.). 196p. 1980. 27.50 (ISBN 0-906191-40-8, Pub. by Thule Pr England). Intl Schol Bk Serv.
Broglio, John, tr. see Paque, Boris.
Brohaugh, William. Songwriter's Market 1980. 2nd ed. (Illus.). 1979. 10.95 o.p. (ISBN 0-89879-003-4). Writers Digest.
Brohaugh, William, ed. Writer's Market 1980. 50th ed. (Illus.). 1979. 14.95 o.p. (ISBN 0-89879-000-X). Writers Digest.
Broida, H. P., jt. ed. see Badash, Lawrence.
Broida, Helen. Coping with Stroke. LC 79-220. 136p. 1979. text ed. 14.95 (ISBN 0-933014-50-3). College-Hill.
Broida, Patricia, jt. auth. see Colgate, Craig, Jr.
Broido, Arnold & Davis, Marilyn K. Music Dictionary. LC 54-9837. (gr. 1-9). 1956. 5.95 o.p. (ISBN 0-385-07594-4). Doubleday.
Broido, Lucy, jt. auth. see Cheret, Jules.
Brokensha, D. & Crowder, M. Africa in the Wider World. 1967. 25.00 (ISBN 0-08-012673-1); pap. 13.25 (ISBN 0-08-012672-3). Pergamon.
Brokering, Lois. Odds & Ends. (A Nice Place to Live Ser.). 1978. pap. 2.25 (ISBN 0-570-07754-0, 12-2713). Concordia.
Brokering, Mark, jt. ed. see Flugaur, Florence.
Brokhoff, Barbara, jt. auth. see Brokhoff, John.
Brokhoff, John & Brokhoff, Barbara. Advent & Event. 88p. (Orig.). 1980. pap. text ed. 3.65 (ISBN 0-89536-453-0). CSS Pub.
--There's Always Hope! Advent Christmas Sermons, Ser. A. 1980. pap. text ed. 3.95 (ISBN 0-89536-452-2). CSS Pub.
Brokhoff, John R. Lectionary Preaching Workbook: Series A. 300p. (Orig.). 1980. pap. text ed. 17.25 (ISBN 0-89536-442-5). CSS Pub.
Brokke, Harold J. A Guide to Understanding Romans. 284p. 1980. pap. 3.95 (ISBN 0-87123-193-X, 210193). Bethany Fell.
--Ten Steps to the Good Life. LC 75-44926. 1976. pap. 1.50 (ISBN 0-87123-332-0, 200332). Bethany Fell.
Brolin, Don E. Vocational Preparation of Retarded Citizens. (Illus.). 320p. 1976. text ed. 18.95 (ISBN 0-675-08667-1). Merrill.
Brolin, Donn E. & Kokaska, Charles J. Career Education for Handicapped Children & Youth. (Special Education Ser.). 1979. text ed. 19.50 (ISBN 0-675-08278-1). Merrill.
Brolin, S. E., ed. Structure & Metabolism of the Pancreatic Islets. 1964. 64.00 (ISBN 0-08-010758-3). Pergamon.
Bromage, Bernard. Tibetan Yoga. 192p. (Orig.). 1980. pap. 7.95 o.s.i. (ISBN 0-85030-199-8). Newcastle Pub.
Bromage, Mary C. Writing for Business. (Orig.). 1965. pap. 2.95 o.p. (ISBN 0-472-06108-9, 108, AA). U of Mich Pr.
--Writing for Business. 176p. (Orig.). 1965. 4.95 o.p. (ISBN 0-472-09108-5). U of Mich Pr.
Bromage, Mary C. & Nelson, Bruce A. Cases in Written Communication II. (Michigan Business Cases Ser.: No. 2). 1967. pap. 5.50 o.p. (ISBN 0-87712-131-1). U Mich Busn Div Res.
Bromberg, Murray & Katz, Milton. Getting Your Words Across. 256p. (gr. 7-12). 1981. pap. text ed. 3.95 (ISBN 0-8120-2082-0). Barron.
Bromberg, Murray & Liebb, Julius. You Can Succeed in Reading & Writing: 30 Steps in Mastering English. (gr. 8-12). 1981. pap. text ed. 4.95 (ISBN 0-8120-2081-2). Barron.
Bromberg, Walter, jt. auth. see Halleck, Seymour.
Brombert, Beth A. A Concert of Hells. 205p. 1980. 17.95 (ISBN 0-241-10303-7, Pub. by Hamish Hamilton England). David & Charles.
Brome, Richard. Antipodes. Haaker, Ann, ed. LC 66-13403. (Regents Renaissance Drama Ser.). 1966. 8.95x (ISBN 0-8032-0253-9); pap. 1.65x (ISBN 0-8032-5254-4, BB 219, Bison). U of Nebr Pr.
--Jovial Crew. Haaker, Ann, ed. LC 68-10433. (Regents Renaissance Drama Ser.). 1968. 9.50x (ISBN 0-8032-0254-7); pap. 2.45x (ISBN 0-8032-5255-2, BB 228, Bison). U of Nebr Pr.
--A Mad Couple Well Match'd. Spove, Steen H. & Orgel, Stephen, eds. LC 78-13873. (Renaissance Drama Ser.). 1979. lib. bdg. 31.00 (ISBN 0-8240-9730-0). Garland Pub.
--The Weeding of Covent Garden & the Sparagus Garden. McClure, Donald S. & Orgel, Stephen, eds. LC 79-54351. (Renaissance Drama Second Ser.). 438p. 1980. lib. bdg. 50.00 (ISBN 0-8240-4468-1). Garland Pub.
Brome, Vincent. Havelock Ellis: Philosopher of Sex. (Illus.). 1979. 24.00 (ISBN 0-7100-0019-7). Routledge & Kegan.
--Jung: Man & Myth. LC 80-25159. 327p. 1981. pap. 6.95 (ISBN 0-689-70588-3). Atheneum.
Bromfield, Andrew, tr. see Mendelson, Maurice.
Bromfield, Louis. The Farm. 1979. pap. 2.50 (ISBN 0-380-41715-4, 41715). Avon.
Bromhead, Peter. Britain's Developing Constitution. LC 74-82270. 227p. 1974. 20.00 (ISBN 0-312-09905-3). St Martin.
Bromige, Iris. An April Girl, No. 4. 192p. 1974. pap. 0.95 o.p. (ISBN 0-345-26663-3). Ballantine.
--A Chance for Love: No. 36. 224p. (Orig.). 1975. pap. 0.95 o.p. (ISBN 0-345-26712-5). Ballantine.
--Rough Weather. (Aston Hall Romances Ser.). 192p. (Orig.). 1981. pap. 1.75 (ISBN 0-523-41133-2). Pinnacle Bks.
Bromiley, G. W. see Barth, Karl.
Bromiley, G. W., tr. see Barth, Karl.
Bromiley, Geoffrey, tr. see Thielicke, Helmut.
Bromiley, Geoffrey W., ed. see Barth, Karl.
Bromiley, Geoffrey W., tr. see Barth, Karl.
Bromiley, Geoffrey W., tr. see Kasemann, Ernst.
Bromley, Daniel W., jt. auth. see Sfeir-Younis, Alfredo.
Bromley, David G., jt. auth. see Shupe, Anson D., Jr.
Bromley, Dudley. North to Oak Island. (Pacesetters Ser.). (Illus.). 64p. (gr. 4 up). PLB 7.95 (ISBN 0-516-02171-0). Childrens.
Bromley, Ida. Tetraplegia & Paraplegia. 2nd ed. (Illus.). 264p. 1981. pap. text ed. 15.00 (ISBN 0-443-01992-4). Churchill.
Bromley, J. S. & Kossma, E. H., eds. Britain & the Netherlands in Europe & Asia. LC 68-17096. (Illus.). 1968. text ed. 18.95x (ISBN 0-312-10395-6). St Martin.
Bromley, John, ed. The Clockmakers' Library: The Catalogue of the Books & Manuscripts in the Library of the Worshipful Company of Clockmakers. (Illus.). 136p. 1977. 52.50x (ISBN 0-85667-033-2, Pub. by Sotheby Parke Bernet England). Biblio Dist.
Bromley, Willard S., ed. Pulpwood Productions. 3rd ed. LC 75-14771. (Illus.). 1976. text ed. 14.65 (ISBN 0-8134-1738-4, 1738); pap. text ed. 11.00x (ISBN 0-685-71184-6). Interstate.
Bromley, Yu, ed. Soviet Ethnology & Anthropology Today. (Studies in Anthropology Ser.: No. 1). 401p. 1974. pap. text ed. 64.70x (ISBN 90-2792-725-1). Mouton.
Brommelle, N. S. & Smith, P. Conservation & Restoration of Pictorial Art. LC 75-32570. 340p. 1976. 59.95 (ISBN 0-408-70712-7). Butterworths.
Brommer, Gerald F. Discovering Art History. LC 79-57018. (Illus.). 384p. 1981. 24.95 (ISBN 0-87192-121-9). Davis Mass.
Bromwich, Rachel. Medieval Celtic Literature: A Select Bibliography. LC 74-82287. 1974. 10.00x o.p. (ISBN 0-8020-2170-0); pap. 5.00x (ISBN 0-8020-6252-0). U of Toronto Pr.
Bronaugh, Mitch. How to Find Out What's Wrong with Your Car. 160p. 1980. pap. 6.95 (ISBN 0-442-29731-9). Van Nos Reinhold.
Bronaugh, Richard, ed. Philosophical Law: Authority, Equality, Adjudication, Privacy. (Contributions in Legal Studies: No. 2). 1978. lib. bdg. 19.95 (ISBN 0-8371-9809-7, BPL/). Greenwood.
Brondfield. Great Sports Photos. (gr. 3-5). 1980. pap. 1.50 (ISBN 0-590-30369-4, Schol Pap). Schol Bk Serv.
Brondolo, Barbara. Small Patchwork Projects. (Illus.). 64p. (Orig.). 1981. pap. write for info. (ISBN 0-486-24030-4). Dover.
Broneer, Oscar. Terracotta Lamps. LC 76-362971. (Isthmia Ser: Vol. 3). 1977. 25.00x (ISBN 0-87661-933-2). Am Sch Athens.
Broner, E. M. Her Mothers. pap. 1.75 o.p. (ISBN 0-425-03206-X). Berkley Pub.
Bronfenbrenner, Martin. Income Distribution Theory. LC 77-131045. (Treatises in Modern Economics Ser). 1971. 31.95x (ISBN 0-202-06037-3). Aldine Pub.
--Macroeconomic Alternatives. LC 79-50880. (Illus.). 1979. text ed. 16.50x (ISBN 0-88295-404-0). AHM Pub.
Bronheim, David, ed. Brazil 1969. LC 71-113454. 1970. pap. 1.50 o.p. (ISBN 0-913456-77-2). Interbk Inc.
Bronner, Edwin. The Encyclopedia of the American Theatre. LC 45-2439. (Illus.). 1980. 30.00 (ISBN 0-498-01219-0). A S Barnes.
Bronner, Felix, jt. ed. see Comar, C. L.
Bronner, Felix, et al, eds. Current Topics in Membranes & Transport, Vol. 14. 1980. 49.50 (ISBN 0-12-153314-X). Acad Pr.
Bronner, Stephen, ed. The Letters of Rosa Luxemburg. 1979. lib. bdg. 24.00x (ISBN 0-89158-186-3); pap. text ed. 9.50 (ISBN 0-89158-188-X). Westview.
Bronner, Stephen & Kellner, Douglas, eds. Passion & Rebellion: The Expressionist Movement & Its Heritage. 400p. 1981. lib. bdg. price not set (ISBN 0-89789-016-7); pap. text ed. price not set (ISBN 0-89789-017-5). J F Bergin.
Bronowski, J., ed. see Blake, William.
Bronowski, Jacob. Magic, Science & Civilization. (Bamptom Lectures in America Ser.: No. 20). 104p. 1981. pap. 4.95 (ISBN 0-231-04485-2). Columbia U Pr.
--Magic, Science, & Civilization. (Bampton Lectures in America: No. 20). 1978. 10.00 (ISBN 0-231-04484-4). Columbia U Pr.
--The Origins of Knowledge & Imagination. LC 77-13209. (Silliman Lectures Ser.). 1978. 10.00 (ISBN 0-300-02192-5); pap. 3.95 (ISBN 0-300-02409-6). Yale U Pr.
--Science & Human Values. enl. ed. pap. 3.50 (ISBN 0-06-090468-2, CN468, CN). Har-Row.
Bronson, Bertrand H. The Ballad as Song. LC 74-84045. (Illus.). 1969. 22.50x (ISBN 0-520-01399-9). U of Cal Pr.
--Facets of the Enlightenment: Studies in English Literature & Its Contexts. 1968. 19.50x (ISBN 0-520-00176-1). U of Cal Pr.
Bronson, Edgar B. Reminiscences of a Ranchman. LC 62-8407. xvi, 370p. 1962. 15.00x (ISBN 0-8032-0886-3); pap. 4.50 (ISBN 0-8032-5023-1, BB 127, Bison). U of Nebr Pr.
Bronson, R. Matrix Methods: An Introduction. 1970. text ed. 19.95 (ISBN 0-12-135250-1). Acad Pr.
Bronson, Wilfrid S. Horns & Antlers. LC 42-7882. (Illus.). (gr. 3-7). 1942. 4.95 o.p. (ISBN 0-15-235942-7, HJ). HarBraceJ.
--Wonder World of Ants. LC 37-27454. (Illus.). (gr. 3-7). 1937. 5.25 o.p. (ISBN 0-15-299287-1, HJ). HarBraceJ.
Bronson, William. Earth Shook, the Sky Burned. LC 59-6893. 1959. 14.95 (ISBN 0-385-05379-7). Doubleday.
Bronstein, Arthur J. Pronunciation of American English. (Illus.). 1960. 14.95 (ISBN 0-13-730887-6). P-H.
Bronstein, Daniel J., et al. Basic Problems of Philosophy. 4th ed. LC 79-179449. 656p. 1972. text ed. 17.95 (ISBN 0-13-067637-3). P-H.
Bronstein, David. Two Hundred Open Games. (Illus.). 256p. 1975. 11.95 (ISBN 0-02-516500-3). Macmillan.
Bronstein, Herbert, ed. A Passover Haggadah. (Illus.). 1974. 50.00 set (ISBN 0-916694-66-6); 7.95 (ISBN 0-916694-71-2); lib. bdg. 17.50 (ISBN 0-916694-06-2); pap. 4.00 (ISBN 0-916694-05-4). Central Conf.
Bronstein, I. U. Extensions of Minimal Transformation Groups. 327p. 1979. 47.50x (ISBN 90-286-0368-9). Sijthoff & Noordhoff.
Bronstein, Leo. El Greco. (Library of Great Painters Ser). (Illus.). 1950. 35.00 (ISBN 0-8109-0155-2). Abrams.
Bronstein, Raphael. Science of Violin Playing. 2nd ed. 288p. 1980. 20.00 (ISBN 0-87666-601-2, Z-10). Paganiniana Pubns.
Bronstein, Russell, jt. auth. see Maidment, Robert.
Bronte, Charlotte. Jane Eyre. pap. 1.75. Bantam.
--Jane Eyre. Dunn, Richard J., ed. (Critical Editions Ser). (gr. 9-12). 1971. pap. text ed. 5.95x (ISBN 0-393-09966-0). Norton.
--Jane Eyre. (Classics Ser). (gr. 9 up). 1964. pap. 1.95 (ISBN 0-8049-0017-5, CL-17). Airmont.
--Jane Eyre. (Literature Ser). (gr. 7-12). 1969. pap. text ed. 3.75 (ISBN 0-87720-706-2). AMSCO Sch.
--Jane Eyre. 1963. 10.50x (ISBN 0-460-00287-2, Evman); pap. 2.95 (ISBN 0-460-01287-8). Dutton.
--Jane Eyre. (Illus.). (gr. 9 up). 1962. 6.95g o.s.i. (ISBN 0-02-714760-6). Macmillan.
--Jane Eyre. Jack, Jane & Smith, Margaret, eds. (Clarendon Editions of the Novels of the Brontes Ser.). 1969. 45.00x (ISBN 0-19-811490-7). Oxford U Pr.
--Jane Eyre. Leavis, Q. D., ed. (English Library Ser.). pap. 2.25 (ISBN 0-14-043011-3). Penguin.
--Jane Eyre. LC 80-14426. (Raintree Short Classics). (Illus.). 48p. (gr. 4 up). 1981. PLB 9.95 (ISBN 0-8172-1661-8). Raintree Pubs.
--Jane Eyre. (The Zodiac Press Ser.). 1978. 9.95 (ISBN 0-7011-1239-5, Pub. by Chatto Bodley Jonathan). Merrimack Bk Serv.
--Jane Eyre. LC 78-3388. (Raintree's Illustrated Classics). (Illus.). (gr. 5-8). 1978. PLB 9.65 (ISBN 0-8393-6202-1). Raintree Child.
--Professor. 1954. 10.50 (ISBN 0-460-00417-4, Evman); pap. 8.95 (ISBN 0-460-01417-X). Dutton.
--Shirley: A Tale. (World's Classics Ser.). 14.95 (ISBN 0-19-250014-7). Oxford U Pr.
--Villette. (World's Classics Ser.). 1954. 14.95 (ISBN 0-19-250047-3). Oxford U Pr.
Bronte, Emily. Peculiar Music. Lewis, Naomi, ed. (gr. 5 up). 1972. 4.95 o.s.i. (ISBN 0-02-714750-9). Macmillan.
--Wuthering Heights. pap. 1.75. Bantam.
--Wuthering Heights. rev. ed. Sale, William M., Jr., ed. (Critical Editions Ser.). (Annotated). (gr. 9-12). 1972. pap. text ed. 4.95x (ISBN 0-393-09400-6, 9601). Norton.
--Wuthering Heights. (gr. 9 up). 1963. 4.95g o.s.i. (ISBN 0-02-714820-3). Macmillan.
--Wuthering Heights. 320p. (RL 10). 1973. pap. 1.95 (ISBN 0-451-51388-6, CJ1388, Sig Classics). NAL.
--Wuthering Heights. (Literature Ser). (gr. 9-12). 1969. pap. text ed. 3.92 (ISBN 0-87720-720-8). AMSCO Sch.
--Wuthering Heights. (The Zodiac Press Ser.). 1978. 9.95 (ISBN 0-7011-1241-7, Pub. by Chatto Bodley Jonathan). Merrimack Bk Serv.
--Wuthering Heights. Marsden, Hilda & Jack, Ion, eds. (Clarendon Edition of the Novels of the Brontes Ser.). 1976. 45.00x (ISBN 0-19-812511-9). Oxford U Pr.
--Wuthering Heights. LC 78-4049. (Raintree's Illustrated Classics). (Illus.). (gr. 5-8). 1978. PLB 9.65 (ISBN 0-8393-6203-X). Raintree Child.

--Wuthering Heights with Reader's Guide. (AMSCO Literature Program). (gr. 10-12). 1970. pap. text ed. 4.50 (ISBN 0-87720-809-3); with model ans. s.p. 2.90 (ISBN 0-87720-909-X). AMSCO Sch.

Bronte, Emily J. Complete Poems. Hatfield, C. W., ed. LC 41-21750. 1941. 17.50x (ISBN 0-231-01222-5). Columbia U Pr.

--Gondal's Queen: A Novel in Verse. Ratchford, Fannie E., ed. LC 54-10044. (Illus.). 1977. pap. text ed. 9.95x o.p. (ISBN 0-292-72711-9). U of Tex Pr.

Bronte, Louisa. Casino Greystone, No. 4. 256p. (Orig.). 1976. pap. 1.50 o.p. (ISBN 0-345-24962-3). Ballantine.

--Freedom Trail to Greystone. 240p. (Orig.). 1976. pap. 1.50 o.p. (ISBN 0-345-24860-0). Ballantine.

--Gathering at Greystone, No. 2. 256p. (Orig.). 1976. pap. 1.50 o.p. (ISBN 0-345-24766-3). Ballantine.

--Greystone Heritage. 1976. pap. 1.50 o.p. (ISBN 0-345-25161-X). Ballantine.

--Greystone Tavern. 256p. (Orig.). 1975. pap. 1.50 o.p. (ISBN 0-345-24642-X). Ballantine.

--The Gunther Heritage. 384p. (Orig.). 1981. pap. 2.75 (ISBN 0-515-04311-7). Jove Pubns.

--Moonlight at Greystone, No. 5. (Greystone Series). 240p. 1976. pap. 1.50 o.p. (ISBN 0-345-25060-5). Ballantine.

--The Vallette Heritage. 1978. pap. 2.25 (ISBN 0-515-04309-5). Jove Pubns.

--The Van Rhyne Heritage. (Orig.). 1979. pap. 2.25 (ISBN 0-515-04310-9). Jove Pubns.

Bronte, Patrick. Cottage Poems: A Miscellany of Descriptive Poems, Repr. Of 1811 Ed. Bd. with The Rural Minstrel: A Miscellany of Descriptive Poems. Repr. of 1813 ed. LC 75-31169. (Romantic Context Ser.: Poetry 1789-1830: Vol. 23). 1977. lib. bdg. 47.00 (ISBN 0-8240-2122-3). Garland Pub.

Bronthon. Heating Service Design. 1981. text ed. 53.95 (ISBN 0-408-00380-4). Butterworth.

Bronwell, Nancy. Lubbock: A Pictorial History. Friedman, Donna R., ed. (Illus.). 208p. 1980. pap. write for info. (ISBN 0-89865-076-3). Donning Co.

Bronwen, Meredith. Natural Health & Beauty. (Illus.). 304p. 1981. 19.95 (ISBN 0-03-057976-7). HR&W.

Bronzan, Robert T. Public Relations, Promotions, & Fund-Raising for Athletic & Physical Education Programs. LC 76-10950. 580p. 1977. text ed. 23.50 (ISBN 0-471-01540-7). Wiley.

Bronzo, Mary L., et al. An Introduction to Black Nonstandard English for Teachers. Smith, Donald E., ed. (Michigan Learning Modules Ser.: No. 30). 56p. (Orig.). 1979. pap. text ed. 2.95 (ISBN 0-914004-33-6). Ulrich.

Broodus, Robert N. Selecting Materials for Libraries. 2nd ed. 1981. write for info. (ISBN 0-8242-0510-3). Wilson.

Brook, Alan J. The Biology of Desmids. LC 80-26374. (Botanical Monographs Ser.: Vol. 16). (Illus.). 1981. 36.50x (ISBN 0-520-04281-6). U of Cal Pr.

Brook, Barry S., ed. see D'Ordonez, Carlo.

Brook, Barry S., jt. ed. see Jenkins, Newell.

Brook, Christopher. Saxon & Norman Kings. 1978. 28.00 (ISBN 0-7134-1534-7, Pub. by Batsford England). David & Charles.

Brook, Claire, jt. auth. see Brody, Elaine.

Brook, G. L. Books & Bookcollecting. (Grafton Books on Library & Information Science). 175p. 1980. lib. bdg. 25.00x (ISBN 0-233-97154-8, Pub. by Andre Deutsch). Westview.

--English Dialects. (Andre Deutsch Language Library). 1972. PLB 13.50x (ISBN 0-233-95641-7). Westview.

--English Sound Changes. 175p. 6.00x (ISBN 0-7190-0111-0, Pub.by Manchester U Pr England). State Mutual Bk.

--A History of the English Language. (Andre Deutsch Language Library). 1977. lib. bdg. 20.50 o.p. (ISBN 0-233-95910-6). Westview.

--Language of Shakespeare. (Andre Deutsch Language Library). 1978. 25.00x (ISBN 0-233-96762-1). Westview.

--Varieties of English. 2nd ed. 1977. text ed. 18.25x (ISBN 0-333-14284-5). Humanities.

Brook, George L., ed. see Layamon.

Brook, Jocelyn see Brooke, Jocelyn.

Brook, Judy. Noah's Ark. LC 73-2024. (Illus.). (gr. k-3). 1973. PLB 5.90 o.p. (ISBN 0-531-02630-2). Watts.

Brook, K. M., jt. auth. see Murdock, L. J.

Brook, Peter. Cosmopolitan Tales. 1980. pap. cancelled (ISBN 0-87881-087-0). Mojave Bks.

Brook, Robert & Whitehead, Paul. Drug-Free Therapeutic Community. 158p. 1980. 14.95 (ISBN 0-87705-383-9). Human Sci Pr.

Brooke, A. E. The Johannine Epistles. LC 13-170. (International Critical Commentary Ser.). 336p. 1912. text ed. 17.50x (ISBN 0-567-05037-8). Attic Pr.

Brooke, Anabel. Natalya. 352p. (Orig.). 1981. pap. 2.75 (ISBN 0-345-29254-5). Ballantine.

Brooke, Avery. As Never Before. 1976. 5.95 (ISBN 0-8164-0905-6). Crossroad NY.

--Doorway to Meditation. 1976. pap. 4.95 (ISBN 0-8164-0903-X). Crossroad NY.

--Hidden in Plain Sight: The Practice of Christian Meditation. LC 77-17548. (Illus., Orig.). 1978. pap. 5.95 (ISBN 0-8164-2176-5). Crossroad NY.

--How to Meditate Without Leaving the World. 1976. pap. 4.95 (ISBN 0-8164-0906-4). Crossroad NY.

Brooke, Avery, ed. The Vineyard Bible: A Central Narrative & Index. 416p. 1980. 12.95 (ISBN 0-8164-0144-6). Seabury.

Brooke, Bryan N. Understanding Cancer. LC 72-89655. 128p. 1973. 4.95 o.p. (ISBN 0-03-006181-4). HR&W.

Brooke, C. Europe in the Central Middle Ages 962-1154. 2nd ed. LC 75-308112. (General History of Europe Ser.). 404p. 1975. pap. text ed. 11.95 (ISBN 0-582-48476-6). Longman.

Brooke, C., et al, eds. Church & Government in the Middle Ages. LC 75-41614. (Illus.). 1977. 55.00 (ISBN 0-521-21172-7). Cambridge U Pr.

Brooke, C. N., jt. auth. see Morey, Adrian.

Brooke, Charlotte, ed. Reliques of Irish Poetry, 1789. Bd. with A Memoir of Miss Brooke, 1816. Seymour, A. C. LC 76-133327. 544p. 1970. 54.00x (ISBN 0-8201-1082-5). Schol Facsimiles.

Brooke, Christopher. London, Eight Hundred to Twelve Sixteen: The Shaping of a City. LC 73-92620. (The History of London Ser). (Illus.). 1975. 32.50x (ISBN 0-520-02686-1). U of Cal Pr.

--The Monastic World. (Illus.). 1978. 49.00 (ISBN 0-236-31059-3, Pub. by Paul Elek). Merrimack Bk Serv.

Brooke, Dinah. Death Games. LC 75-37524. 180p. 1976. 6.95 o.p. (ISBN 0-15-124093-0). HarBraceJ.

Brooke, Frances. The History of Emily Montague, 1769, 4 vols. in 2. Shugrue, Michael F., ed. (The Flowering of the Novel, 1740-1775 Ser: Vol. 85). 1974. lib. bdg. 50.00 ea. (ISBN 0-8240-1184-8). Garland Pub.

Brooke, Henry. The Fool of Quality, 5 vols. Paulson, Ronald, ed. LC 78-60842. (Novel 1720-1805 Ser.: Vol. 6). 1979. Set. lib. bdg. 155.00 (ISBN 0-8240-3655-7). Garland Pub.

Brooke, I. English Costume of the Early Middle Ages. (English Costume Ser.). 1977. Repr. of 1936 ed. text ed. 10.00x (ISBN 0-7136-0154-X). Humanities.

Brooke, Iris. Footwear. LC 79-109116. (Illus.). 1971. 5.95 (ISBN 0-87830-047-3). Theatre Arts.

--History of English Costume. LC 72-85476. (Illus.). 1973. pap. 7.45 (ISBN 0-87830-569-6). Theatre Arts.

--Medieval Theatre Costume. LC 67-25699. (Illus.). 1967. 8.95 (ISBN 0-87830-081-3). Theatre Arts.

Brooke, Jame T. A Viewer's Guide to Looking at Photographs. LC 77-74181. (Illus.). 1977. 7.95 o.p. (ISBN 0-918844-02-9); pap. 4.95 o.p. (ISBN 0-918844-01-0). Aurelian Pr.

Brooke, Jocelyn. Ronald Firbank. Incl. John Betjeman. Brook, Jocelyn. pap. 2.95 (ISBN 0-8277-6153-8). British Bk Ctr.

Brooke, Leslie L. Johnny Crow's Garden. (Peter Possum Paperbacks Ser). 1967. pap. 0.95 o.p. (ISBN 0-531-05110-2). Watts.

Brooke, Michael H., jt. auth. see Dubowitz, Victor.

Brooke, Michael Z. & Remmers, H. Lee. International Management & Business Policy. LC 78-69612. (Illus.). 1978. Repr. of 1977 ed. text ed. 20.95 (ISBN 0-395-26505-3). HM.

Brooke, Rosalind. Information & Advice Services. 181p. 1972. pap. text ed. 5.65x (ISBN 0-7135-1709-3, Pub. by Bedford England). Renouf.

Brooke, Rupert. The Collected Poems of Rupert Brooke. LC 80-16869. 1980. pap. 4.95 (ISBN 0-396-07894-X). Dodd.

--The Poetical Works of Rupert Brooke. 1970. 13.95 (ISBN 0-571-04708-4, Pub. by Faber & Faber); pap. 6.95 (ISBN 0-571-04704-1). Merrimack Bk Serv.

Brooke, Zachary N. The English Church & the Papacy, from the Conquest to the Reign of John. LC 80-2228. 1981. Repr. of 1931 ed. 37.50 (ISBN 0-404-18756-0). AMS Pr.

Brooke-Little, John. The British Monarchy in Color. (Color Ser.). (Illus.). 1976. 9.95 (ISBN 0-7137-0774-7, Pub by Blandford Pr England). Sterling.

Brooker, et al, eds. Current Methodology. LC 78-55806. (Advances in Cyclic Nucleotide Research Ser.: Vol. 10). 1979. 38.00 (ISBN 0-89004-265-9). Raven.

Brooker, Donald B., et al. Drying Cereal Grains. (Illus.). 1974. text ed. 26.00 (ISBN 0-87055-161-2); pap. 17.50 (ISBN 0-87055-303-8). AVI.

Brooke-Rose, Christine. A ZBC of Ezra Pound. LC 75-138284. 1971. 17.50x (ISBN 0-520-01848-6); pap. 4.95x (ISBN 0-520-03041-9). U of Cal Pr.

Brookes, A. M. Advanced Electric Circuits. 1966. text ed. 17.50 (ISBN 0-08-011610-8); pap. text ed. 7.75 (ISBN 0-08-011609-4). Pergamon.

--Basic Electric Circuits. 2nd ed. LC 75-8774. 368p. 1975. text ed. 27.00 (ISBN 0-08-018310-7); pap. text ed. 13.25 (ISBN 0-08-018309-3). Pergamon.

--Basic Instrumentation for Engineers & Physicists. 1968. text ed. 15.00 (ISBN 0-08-012538-7); pap. 6.50 (ISBN 0-08-012537-9). Pergamon.

Brookes, B. C. & Dick, W. F. Introduction to Statistical Method. 1969. pap. text ed. 7.50x o.p. (ISBN 0-435-53124-7). Heinemann Ed.

Brookes, Edgar. Apartheid. (World Studies Ser.). 1968. cased 13.00x o.s.i. (ISBN 0-7100-2994-2). Routledge & Kegan.

Brookes, Edgar H. & Vandenbosch, Amry. The City of God & the City of Man in Africa. LC 64-13998. (Illus.). 144p. 1964. 7.00x (ISBN 0-8131-1091-2). U Pr of Ky.

Brookes, Gerry H. The Rhetorical Form of Carlyle's Sartor Resartus. LC 71-185974. 208p. 1972. 17.00x (ISBN 0-520-02213-0). U of Cal Pr.

Brookes, H. F., ed. see Brecht, Bertolt.

Brookes, H. F., ed. see Grass, Gunter.

Brookes, John. Room Outside: A New Approach to Garden Design. (Large Format Ser.). (Illus.). 1979. pap. 6.95 o.p. (ISBN 0-14-005077-9). Penguin.

--The Small Garden. (Illus.). 1978. 10.95 o.s.i. (ISBN 0-02-516700-6). Macmillan.

Brookes, M. The Blood Supply of Bone. 1971. 29.95x (ISBN 0-407-11900-0). Butterworths.

Brookfield, Charles & Glover, J. M. The Poet & the Puppets: A Travestie Suggested by "Lady Windermere's Fan". Fletcher, Ian & Stokes, John, eds. Bd. with Aristophanes at Oxford. LC 76-20012. (Decadent Consciousness Ser.). 1978. lib. bdg. 38.00 (ISBN 0-8240-2784-1). Garland Pub.

Brookings, jt. auth. see Institute for Research on Public Policy, Canada.

Brookins, Dana. Alone in Wolf Hollow. LC 77-13118. (gr. 3-6). 1978. 7.95 (ISBN 0-395-28849-5, Clarion). HM.

--Rico's Cat. LC 76-8841. (Illus.). (gr. 3-6). 1976. 6.95 (ISBN 0-395-28850-9, Clarion). HM.

Brookins, Douglas G. Earth Resources, Energy & the Environment. (Illus.). 160p. (Orig.). 1981. pap. text ed. 6.95 (ISBN 0-675-08113-0). Merrill.

Brookner, Anita. The Debut. 1981. 11.95 (ISBN 0-671-42626-5, Linden). S&S.

--Jacques-Louis David. LC 79-3386. (Icon Editions). (Illus.). 1981. 35.00 (ISBN 0-06-430507-4, HarpT). Har-Row.

Brookover, Wilbur. School Systems & Student Achievement. LC 79-10758. 1979. 25.95 (ISBN 0-03-052721-X). Praeger.

Brookover, Wilbur & Ericksen, Edsel L. Sociology of Education. 1975. 18.50x (ISBN 0-256-01674-7). Dorsey.

Brooks & Brooks. The Human Body: Structure & Function in Health & Disease. 2nd ed. LC 79-24085. (Illus.). 1980. pap. text ed. 17.95 (ISBN 0-8016-0808-2). Mosby.

Brooks, A. E. Australian Native Plants for Home Gardens. 6th rev. ed. (Illus.). 1979. 13.95x (ISBN 0-85091-091-9, Pub. by Lothian). Intl Schol Bk Serv.

Brooks, A. Russell. James Boswell. (English Authors Ser.: No. 122). lib. bdg. 10.95 (ISBN 0-8057-1048-5). Twayne.

Brooks, Alfred. From Holbein to Whistler: Notes on Drawing & Engraving. (Illus.). 1920. 75.00x (ISBN 0-685-69792-4). Elliots Bks.

Brooks, Anita. Picture Book of Fisheries. (Picture Aids to World Geography Ser). (Illus.). (gr. 4-7). 1961. 6.89 (ISBN 0-381-99935-1, A61210, JD-J). John Day.

--Picture Book of Metals. LC 78-147271. (Pictures Aids to World Geography Ser). (Illus.). (gr. 4-7). 1972. 6.89 (ISBN 0-381-99933-5, A61225, JD-J). John Day.

--Picture Book of Oil. LC 65-19738. (Picture Aids to World Geography Ser.). (Illus.). (gr. 4-7). 1965. 6.89 (ISBN 0-381-99932-7, A61230, JD-J). John Day.

--Picture Book of Salt. LC 64-10451. (Picture Aids to World Geography Ser). (Illus.). (gr. 4-7). 1964. 6.89 (ISBN 0-381-99931-9, A61240, JD-J). John Day.

--Picture Book of Timber. LC 67-14617. (Picture Aids to World Geography Ser). (Illus.). (gr. 4-7). 1967. 6.89 (ISBN 0-381-99929-7, A61250, JD-J). John Day.

Brooks, Anne T. Point Virtue. 1979. pap. 1.95 (ISBN 0-505-51370-6). Tower Bks.

Brooks, Anton. Making People Laugh. (Illus.). 1980. pap. 12.95 o.p. (ISBN 0-930490-18-5). Future Shop.

Brooks, B. A. & Bajandas, F. J., eds. Eye Movements: ARVO Symposium, 1976. 223p. 1977. 22.50 (ISBN 0-306-31082-1, Plenum Pr). Plenum Pub.

Brooks, Barbara, ed. see Reynolds, Lloyd G.

Brooks, Charles, ed. Best Editorial Cartoons of the Year: Nineteen Eighty-One Edition. (Best Editorial Cartoons of the Year Ser.: Vol. 9). (Illus.). 160p. 1981. pap. 7.95 (ISBN 0-88289-280-0); pap. 5.95 (ISBN 0-88289-281-9). Pelican.

--Best Editorial Cartoons of the Year: 1978 Edition. LC 73-643645. (Best Editorial Cartoon Ser.). (Illus.). 1978. 11.95 o.p. (ISBN 0-88289-192-8); pap. 5.95 (ISBN 0-88289-193-6). Pelican.

--Best Editorial Cartoons of the Year: 1979 Edition. (Best Editorial Cartoon Ser.). (Illus.). 1979. 11.95 (ISBN 0-88289-229-0); pap. 5.95 o.p. (ISBN 0-88289-230-4). Pelican.

Brooks, Charles V. Sensory Awareness: The Study of Living As Experience. LC 73-7432. (Esalen Books). (Illus.). 320p. 1974. 12.95 o.p. (ISBN 0-670-63391-7). Viking Pr.

Brooks, Cleanth & Warren, Robert P. Scope of Fiction. 1960. text ed. 11.95 (ISBN 0-13-796656-3). P-H.

Brooks, Cleanth, jt. auth. see Warren, Robert P.

Brooks, Cleanth, et al. American Literature: The Makers & the Making, 2 vols. 1200p. 1973. Vol. 1. text ed. 16.95x (ISBN 0-312-02625-0); Vol. 2. text ed. 17.95x (ISBN 0-312-02695-1); Vol. 1. pap. text ed. 12.95 (ISBN 0-312-02590-4); Vol. 2. pap. text ed. 14.95 (ISBN 0-312-02660-9). St Martin.

--American Literature, the Makers & the Making, 4 vols. Incl. Bk. A. The Beginnings to 1826. 364p. pap. text ed. 8.95x (ISBN 0-312-02765-6); Bk. B. 1826 to 1861. 920p. pap. text ed. 10.95x (ISBN 0-312-02800-8); Bk. C. 1861 to 1914. 656p. pap. text ed. 9.95x (ISBN 0-312-02835-0); Bk. D. 1914 to the Present. 1216p. pap. text ed. 11.95 (ISBN 0-312-02870-9). 1974. St Martin.

--American Literature: The Makers & the Making. 1856p. (Shorter edition). 1974. text ed. 16.95 (ISBN 0-312-02730-3). St Martin.

--An Approach to Literature. 5th ed. 832p. 1975. ref. ed. 18.95x (ISBN 0-13-043802-2). P-H.

Brooks, Clifford F. & Borish, Irving. System for Ophthalmic Dispensing. 1979. 48.00 (ISBN 0-87873-025-7). Prof Press.

Brooks, Daniel F. Numerology. (Concise Guides Ser.). (Illus.). (gr. 7 up). 1978. PLB 6.45 s&l (ISBN 0-531-02248-X). Watts.

Brooks, Daniel T., ed. Computer Law: Purchasing, Leasing, & Licensing Hardware, Software & Services. LC 80-82741. (Nineteen Eighty to Nineteen Eighty-One Commercial Law & Practice Course Handbook Ser.). 382p. 1981. pap. 25.00 (ISBN 0-686-69165-2, A4-3089). PLI.

Brooks, David. How to Control & Use Photographic Lighting. (Orig.). 1980. pap. 7.95 (ISBN 0-89586-059-7). H P Bks.

Brooks, Douglas. Number & Pattern in the Eighteen-Century Novel: Defoe, Fielding, Smollett & Sterne. 208p. 1973. 16.50 (ISBN 0-7100-7598-7). Routledge & Kegan.

Brooks, Edwin, et al. Tribes of the Amazon Basin in Brazil, 1972: Report for the Aborigines Protection Society. 201p. 1974. 12.50x o.p. (ISBN 0-85314-210-6). Transatlantic.

Brooks, Elston. I've Heard Those Songs Before: The Weekly Top Ten Tunes from 1930 Through 1980. 448p. (Orig.). Date not set. 12.95 (ISBN 0-688-00379-6). Morrow.

Brooks, Frederick P. & Iverson, Kenneth E. Automatic Data Processing, System 360 Edition. LC 68-31293. 1969. 30.00 (ISBN 0-471-10605-4, Pub. by Wiley-Interscience). Wiley.

Brooks, Frederick P., Jr. The Mythical Man-Month: Essays on Software Engineering. (Illus.). 200p. 1974. pap. text ed. 9.95 (ISBN 0-201-00650-2). A-W.

Brooks, G. F., et al, eds. Immunobiology of Neisseria Gonorrhoeae. (Illus.). 1978. text ed. 15.00 (ISBN 0-914826-18-2). Am Soc Microbio.

Brooks, G. T. Chlorinated Insectides, 2 vols. Incl. Vol. 1. Technology & Applications. 249p (ISBN 0-8493-5062-X); Vol. 2. Biological & Environmental Aspects (ISBN 0-8493-5063-8). LC 73-90535. (Uniscience Ser.). 1974. 49.95 ea. CRC Pr.

Brooks, George A., ed. Perspectives on the Academic Discipline of Physical Education. 1981. text ed. 17.95 (ISBN 0-931250-18-8). Human Kinetics.

Brooks, Glenwood C., Jr., jt. auth. see Sedlacek, William E.

Brooks, Gregory. Monroe's Island. LC 79-1568. (Illus.). (ps-1). 1979. 7.95 (ISBN 0-87888-140-9). Bradbury Pr.

Brooks, Gwendolyn. World of Gwendolyn Brooks. LC 74-160646. 1971. 15.00 (ISBN 0-06-010538-0, HarpT). Har-Row.

Brooks, H. Leon, ed. Scoliosis & Allied Deformities of the Spine. 1981. write for info. (ISBN 0-88416-270-2). PSG Pub.

Brooks, Harold L., jt. auth. see Bonchek, Lawrence I.

Brooks, Hugh C., jt. auth. see Lees, Francis.

Brooks, J. L., ed. Benito Perez Galdos: Torquemada en la Hoguera. 100p. 1973. text ed. 5.90 (ISBN 0-08-016917-1); pap. text ed. 4.10 (ISBN 0-08-016918-X). Pergamon.
Brooks, James A. & Winbery, Carlton L. Syntax of New Testament Greek. LC 78-51150. 1978. pap. text ed. 7.50x (ISBN 0-8191-0473-6). U Pr of Amer.
Brooks, Jane B. The Process of Parenting. (Illus.). 460p. (Orig.). 1981. write for info (ISBN 0-87484-474-6). Mayfield Pub.
Brooks, Jerome. Make Me a Hero. LC 79-20269. 176p. (gr. 5-9). 1980. PLB 8.95 (ISBN 0-525-34475-6). Dutton.
Brooks, Joe. Saltwater Game Fishing. (Illus.). 1968. 15.95 o.p. (ISBN 0-06-070547-7, HarpT). Har-Row.
Brooks, John. Once in Golconda: A True Dream of Wall Street, Nineteen Twenty - Nineteen Thirty Eight. 1981. 15.95 (ISBN 0-393-01375-8). Norton.
Brooks, John, ed. South American Handbook, 1981. 57th ed. (Illus.). 1981. 29.95 (ISBN 0-528-84534-9). Rand.
Brooks, John B. & Orgel, Stephen, eds. The Phoenix by Thomas Middleton: A Critical, Modernized Edition. LC 78-66762. (Renaissance Drama Ser.). 424p. 1980. lib. bdg. 44.00 (ISBN 0-8240-9750-5). Garland Pub.
Brooks, John L., jt. ed. see Bowyer, John W.
Brooks, Juanita. Mountain Meadows Massacre. (Illus.). 1979. Repr. of 1962 ed. 14.95 (ISBN 0-8061-0549-6). U of Okla Pr.
Brooks, Juanita, ed. Journal of the Southern Indian Mission: Diary of Thomas D. Brown. 1972. pap. 5.00 (ISBN 0-87421-047-X). Utah St U Pr.
Brooks, Kate. The Immaculate Murders. (Orig.). 1979. pap. 1.95 (ISBN 0-532-23268-2). Manor Bks.
Brooks, Keith L. Acts, Adventures of the Early Church. (Teach Yourself the Bible Ser). 1961. pap. 1.75 (ISBN 0-8024-0125-2). Moody.
--Basic Bible Study for New Christians. (Teach Yourself the Bible Ser). 1961. pap. 1.75 (ISBN 0-8024-0478-2). Moody.
--Colossians & Philemon. (Teach Yourself the Bible Ser). 81p. (Orig.). 1961. pap. 1.75 (ISBN 0-8024-1525-3). Moody.
--Ephesians, the Epistle of Christian Maturity. (Teach Yourself the Bible Ser). 1944. pap. 1.75 (ISBN 0-8024-2333-7). Moody.
--First & Second Thessalonians. (Teach Yourself the Bible Ser). 1961. pap. 1.75 (ISBN 0-8024-2645-X). Moody.
--First Corinthians. (Teach Yourself the Bible Ser). 1964. pap. 1.75 (ISBN 0-8024-2649-2). Moody.
--Galatians, the Epistle of Christian Liberty. (Teach Yourself the Bible Ser). 1963. pap. 1.75 (ISBN 0-8024-2925-4). Moody.
--Great Prophetic Themes. (Teach Yourself the Bible Ser). 1962. pap. 1.50 (ISBN 0-8024-3320-0). Moody.
--Hebrews. (Teach Yourself the Bible Ser). 1961. pap. 1.75 (ISBN 0-8024-3507-6). Moody.
--How to Pray. (Teach Yourself the Bible Ser). 1961. pap. 1.75 (ISBN 0-8024-3708-7). Moody.
--James: Belief in Action. (Teach Yourself the Bible Ser). 1961. pap. 1.75 (ISBN 0-8024-4227-7). Moody.
--Luke, the Gospel of God's Man. (Teach Yourself the Bible Ser). 1964. pap. 1.75 (ISBN 0-8024-5047-4). Moody.
--Mark. (Teach Yourself the Bible Ser). 64p. 1961. pap. 1.75 (ISBN 0-8024-5183-7). Moody.
--Matthew, the Gospel of God's King. (Teach Yourself the Bible Ser). 1963. pap. 1.75 (ISBN 0-8024-5212-4). Moody.
--Philippians, the Epistle of Christian Joy. (Teach Yourself the Bible Ser). 1964. pap. 1.75 (ISBN 0-8024-6506-4). Moody.
--Practical Bible Doctrine Course. (Teach Yourself the Bible Ser). 1962. pap. 1.75 (ISBN 0-8024-6733-4). Moody.
--Revelation, the Future Foretold. (Teach Yourself the Bible Ser). 1962. pap. 1.75 (ISBN 0-8024-7308-3). Moody.
--Romans: The Gospel for All. (Teach Yourself the Bible Ser). 1962. pap. 1.75 (ISBN 0-8024-7372-5). Moody.
--The Summarized Bible. (Direction Bks.). 296p. 1980. pap. cancelled (ISBN 0-8010-0669-4). Baker Bk.
Brooks, Lee. First Ladies of the White House: Washington Thru Nixon. LC 76-86857. (Illus.). 156p. 1981. 12.50 (ISBN 0-87319-022-X). C Hallberg.
Brooks, Leonard. Painting & Understanding Abstract Art. 144p. 1980. pap. 9.95 (ISBN 0-442-24334-0). Van Nos Reinhold.
Brooks, Leroy D. Financial Management Decision Game (Fingame) 1975. pap. text ed. 9.50x (ISBN 0-256-01668-2). Irwin.
Brooks, Lucy. The Nurse Assistant. LC 77-73939. 1978. pap. text ed. 7.40 (ISBN 0-8273-1620-8); instructor's guide 1.60 (ISBN 0-8273-1621-6). Delmar.
Brooks, Mel. Silent Movie. 1976. pap. 1.75 o.p. (ISBN 0-345-23918-0). Ballantine.
Brooks, Nancy J. The Golden Leprechaun. 124p. (gr. 3-6). 1980. 5.95 (ISBN 0-8059-2767-0). Dorrance.
Brooks, Natalie & Brooks, Stewart M. Turner's Personal & Community Health. 15th ed. LC 78-31647. (Illus.). 1979. text ed. 15.95 (ISBN 0-8016-5536-6). Mosby.
Brooks, Nelson see Bottiglia, William F.
Brooks, Nelson see Bree, Germaine.
Brooks, Nelson see Eddy, Frederick D.
Brooks, Noah. Henry Knox, a Soldier of the Revolution. LC 74-8496. (Era of the American Revolution Ser). (Illus.). xiv, 286p. 1974. Repr. of 1900 ed. lib. bdg. 25.00 (ISBN 0-306-70617-2). Da Capo.
Brooks, Owen. The Inheritance. 1981. pap. write for info. (ISBN 0-671-41398-8). PB.
Brooks, Pat. Climb Mount Moriah. 1974. pap. 1.25 o.p. (ISBN 0-88368-024-6). Whitaker Hse.
Brooks, Patrice M. How to Get Any Job You Really Want. 1980. write for info. Unique Ent.
Brooks, Patricia. Best Restaurants New England. LC 80-16277. 211p. (Orig.). 1980. pap. 3.95 (ISBN 0-89286-178-9). One Hund One Prods.
Brooks, Paul. Speaking for Nature: How Our Literary Naturalists Have Shaped America. (Illus.). 288p. 1980. 12.95 (ISBN 0-395-29610-2). HM.
Brooks, Peter. Novels of Worldliness, Crebillon, Marivaux, Laclos, Stendhal. LC 68-56303. 1969. 18.00x (ISBN 0-691-06154-8). Princeton U Pr.
Brooks, Peter N., ed. Reformation Principle & Practice: Essays in Honour of A. G. Dickens. 256p. 1980. 40.00x (ISBN 0-85967-579-3, Pub. by Scolar Pr England). Biblio Dist.
Brooks, R. A., ed. see Floy, Michael.
Brooks, R. R., jt. auth. see Reeves, R. D.
Brooks, Reid M. & Olmo, Harold P. Register of New Fruit & Nut Varieties. 2nd rev. & enl. ed. LC 76-100017. 512p. 1972. 23.75x (ISBN 0-520-01638-6). U of Cal Pr.
Brooks, Richard & Warfield, Gerald. Layer Dictation: A New Approach to the Bach Chorales. LC 77-17720. (Music Ser.). 1978. pap. text ed. 11.95x (ISBN 0-582-28046-X). Longman.
Brooks, Richard A., ed. The Selected Letters of Voltaire. LC 72-96429. 349p. 1973. 18.50x (ISBN 0-8147-0972-9). NYU Pr.
Brooks, Robert. Bright Delinquents: The Story of a Unique School. (General Ser.). 184p. (Orig.). 1972. pap. text ed. 11.50x (ISBN 0-901225-97-5, NFER). Humanities.
Brooks, Robert F. Childrens Stories for Teenage Adults. rev. ed. (Illus.). 32p. (Orig.). (gr. 5-9). pap. 3.00 (ISBN 0-936868-05-8). Freeland Pubns.
--Nwandu's Child of Life Reader. (Illus.). 20p. (Orig.). (gr. k-4). Date not set. pap. 2.00 (ISBN 0-936868-00-7). Freeland Pubns.
Brooks, Ron. Timothy & Gramps. LC 78-17389. (gr. k-2). 1979. 7.95 (ISBN 0-87888-139-5). Bradbury Pr.
Brooks, Rose-Marie. Sunbeam Great Crepe Recipes. 7.95 (ISBN 0-916752-03-8). Green Hill.
Brooks, Shirley M. Fundamentals of Operating Room Nursing. 2nd ed. LC 79-500. (Illus.). 1979. pap. 11.50 (ISBN 0-8016-0814-7). Mosby.
--Instrumentation for the Operating Room: A Photographic Manual. LC 78-3622. 1978. pap. text ed. 17.95 (ISBN 0-8016-0816-3). Mosby.
Brooks, Stewart & Norton, Cynthia. Basic Chemistry. 3rd ed. LC 75-37515. (Illus.). 102p. 1976. pap. 8.50 (ISBN 0-8016-0797-3). Mosby.
Brooks, Stewart M. The Cancer Story. LC 71-39355. (Illus.). 176p. 1973. 7.95 o.p. (ISBN 0-498-01180-1). A S Barnes.
--Integrated Basic Science. 4th ed. LC 78-24430. (Illus.). 1979. 17.95 (ISBN 0-8016-0805-8). Mosby.
--Laboratory Manual & Workbook for Integrated Basic Science. 2nd rev. ed. (Illus., Orig.). 1971. text ed. 8.95 (ISBN 0-8016-0811-2). Mosby.
--Our Murdered Presidents: The Medical Story. (Illus.). 234p. 1966. 8.95. Fell.
--A Programmed Introduction to Microbiology. 2nd ed. LC 72-88509. (Illus.). 120p. 1973. pap. text ed. 8.50 (ISBN 0-8016-0819-8). Mosby.
Brooks, Stewart M., jt. auth. see Brooks, Natalie.
Brooks, Stewart M., et al. Handbook of Infectious Diseases. 1980. 9.95 (ISBN 0-316-10968-1). Little.
Brooks, Terry. The Sword of Shannara. (A Del Rey Bk.). 1978. pap. 3.50 o.p. (ISBN 0-345-29024-0). Ballantine.
Brooks, Thomas. Works of Brooks, 6 vols. 1980. Set. 90.00. Banner of Truth.
Brooks, Van Wyck. The Life of Emerson. LC 80-2528. 1981. Repr. of 1932 ed. 37.00 (ISBN 0-404-19252-1). AMS Pr.
Brooks, Van Wyck & Bettman, Otto L. Our Literary Heritage: A Pictorial History of the Writer in America. (gr. 9 up). 1956. 12.50 o.p. (ISBN 0-525-17275-0). Dutton.
Brooks, W. D. & Vogel, R. A., eds. Business Communication. LC 76-44138. (Series in Speech Communication). 1977. pap. text ed. 5.95 (ISBN 0-8465-7600-7); instr's guide 3.95 (ISBN 0-8465-7607-4). Benjamin-Cummings.
--Interpersonal Communication. LC 76-44141. (Ser. in Speech Communication). 1977. pap. text ed. 5.95 (ISBN 0-8465-7603-1); instr's. guide 3.95 (ISBN 0-8465-7607-4). Benjamin-Cummings.
Brooks, W. D., ed. see Kelley, Robert.
Brooks, W. D., ed. see Leth, Pamela C. & Leth, Steven A.
Brooks, Walter, ed. Creative Ways with Acrylic Painting. 1974. pap. 1.25 o.p. (ISBN 0-307-40054-9, Golden Pr). Western Pub.
--Creative Ways with Drawing. 1974. pap. 1.25 o.p. (ISBN 0-307-40052-2, Golden Pr). Western Pub.
--Creative Ways with Drawing Dogs & Cats. 1974. pap. 1.25 o.p. (ISBN 0-307-40053-0, Golden Pr). Western Pub.
--Creative Ways with Flower Painting. 1974. pap. 1.25 o.p. (ISBN 0-307-40055-7, Golden Pr). Western Pub.
--Creative Ways with Oil Painting. 1974. pap. 1.25 o.p. (ISBN 0-307-40051-4, Golden Pr). Western Pub.
--Creative Ways with Watercolor Painting. 1974. pap. 1.25 o.p. (ISBN 0-307-40050-6, Golden Pr). Western Pub.
Brooks, Walter R. Freddie Goes to Florida. (gr. k-6). 1980. pap. 1.75 (ISBN 0-440-42577-8, YB). Dell.
Brooks, William D. Speech Communication. 4th ed. 425p. 1981. pap. text ed. write for info. (ISBN 0-697-04178-6); instr's manual avail. (ISBN 0-697-04190-5); student activities wkbk. avail. (ISBN 0-697-04185-9). Wm C Brown.
Brooks, William D. & Emmert, Philip. Interpersonal Communication. 2nd ed. 1980. pap. text ed. 9.95x (ISBN 0-697-04172-7); instr's manual 2.00 (ISBN 0-697-04180-8). Wm C Brown.
Brooks, William D. & Friedrich, Gustav W. Teaching Speech Communication in the Secondary School. 368p. 1973. text ed. 19.50 (ISBN 0-395-12629-0, 3-06400). HM.
Brooks, William D., jt. auth. see Emmert, Philip.
Brooks, Wyck Van, tr. see Bazalgette, Leon.
Brooksbank, Kenneth, ed. see Society of Education Officers.
Brookshire, Annette, ed. see Wallower, Lucille.
Brookshire, Michael L. & Rogers, Michael. Collective Bargaining in Public Employment: The TVA Experience. LC 76-53867. (Illus.). 1977. 22.95 (ISBN 0-669-01291-2). Lexington Bks.
Brookstone, Jeffrey M. The Multinational Businessman & Foreign Policy: Entrepreneurial Politics in East-West Trade & Investment. LC 76-12845. (Illus.). 1976. text ed. 22.95 (ISBN 0-275-23360-X). Praeger.
Broom, H. Business Policy & Strategic Action: Text, Cases, Management Game. 1969. text ed. 21.95 (ISBN 0-13-107540-3). P-H.
Broom, L., et al. Investigating Social Mobility. (ANU Department of Sociology Monograph: No. 1). (Illus.). 220p. (Orig.). 1980. pap. text ed. 11.95 (ISBN 0-909851-32-8, 1561). Bks Australia.
Broom, Leonard & Kitsuse, John I. The Managed Casualty: The Japanese-American Family in World War II. (Library Reprint Ser.: No. 40). 1974. Repr. 20.00x (ISBN 0-520-02523-7). U of Cal Pr.
Broom, Leonard & Riemer, Ruth. Removal & Return: The Socio-Economic Effects of the War on Japanese Americans. (California Library Reprint). 1974. 20.00x (ISBN 0-520-02522-9). U of Cal Pr.
Broom, Leonard & Selznick, Philip. Essentials of Sociology, Second Edition: From "Sociology: A Text with Adapted Readings". 6th ed. 324p. 1979. pap. text ed. 14.95 scp (ISBN 0-06-040976-2, HarpC); instructor's manual free (ISBN 0-06-361496-0); doing essentials of sociology: chapter guides, projects, tool kits scp 7.50 (ISBN 0-06-040979-7). Har-Row.
--Sociology: A Text with Adapted Readings. 6th, rev. ed. (Illus.). 1977. text ed. 19.50 scp (ISBN 0-06-040965-7, HarpC); instructor's manual avail. (ISBN 0-06-360956-8); study guide scp 6.95x (ISBN 0-06-040978-9). Har-Row.
Brooman, Frederick & Jacoby, Henry D. Macroeconomics: An Introduction to Theory & Policy. LC 73-75979. 1970. 22.95x (ISBN 0-202-06026-8). Aldine Pub.
Broome, Connie. Vessels Unto Honor. LC 76-22242. 1977. pap. 3.25 (ISBN 0-87148-879-5). Pathway Pr.
Broome, P. & Chesters, G., eds. An Anthology of Modern French Poetry. LC 75-40769. 224p. 1976. 36.00 (ISBN 0-521-20793-2); pap. 8.95x (ISBN 0-521-20929-3). Cambridge U Pr.
Broome, Peter. Henri Michaux. (Athlone French Poets Ser). 1977. text ed. 19.75x (ISBN 0-485-14605-3, Athlone Pr); pap. text ed. 11.75x (ISBN 0-485-12205-7). Humanities.
Broome, Peter, ed. see Michaux, Henri.
Broome, Richard. Treasure in Earthen Vessels: Protestant Christianity in New South Wales Society 1900-1914. 216p. 1981. text ed. 36.25x (ISBN 0-7022-1525-2). U of Queensland Pr.
Broome, Susannah. The Pearl Pagoda. 1980. 12.95 (ISBN 0-671-25535-5). S&S.
Broomfield, Robert. Animal Babies. (Illus.). (ps). 1979. 1.25 (ISBN 0-370-02008-1, Pub. by Chatto Bodley Jonathan). Merrimack Bk Serv.
--Baby Animal ABC. (Picture Ser). (Orig.). 1968. pap. 1.95 (ISBN 0-14-050006-5, Puffin). Penguin.
--Toys. (Illus.). (ps). 1979. 1.25 (ISBN 0-370-02009-X, Pub. by Chatto Bodley Jonathan). Merrimack Bk Serv.
Brooten, Dorothy, jt. auth. see Miller, Mary Anne.
Brooten, Dorothy A., et al. Leadership for Change: A Guide for the Frustrated Nurse. LC 78-8661. pap. 7.50 (ISBN 0-397-54218-6). Lippincott.
Brophy, Ann. Flash & the Swan. LC 80-14513. (Illus.). (gr. 5 up). 1981. 8.95g (ISBN 0-7232-6190-3). Warne.
Brophy, James P. W. H. Auden. LC 70-126545. (Columbia Essays in Modern Writers Ser.: No. 54). (Orig.). 1970. pap. 2.00 (ISBN 0-231-03265-X, MW54). Columbia U Pr.
Brophy, Jere, et al. Student Characteristics & Teaching. (Professional Ser.). 224p. 1981. text ed. 22.50 (ISBN 0-582-28152-0). Longman.
Brophy, Jere E. & Evertson, Carolyn M. Learning from Teaching: A Developmental Perspective. 228p. 1976. text ed. 10.95 o.p. (ISBN 0-685-57480-6); pap. text ed. 7.95x o.p. (ISBN 0-205-05488-9). Allyn.
Brophy, Paul C., jt. auth. see Ahlbrandt, Roger S.
Brophy, William S. The Krag Rifle. 258p. 1978. 24.95 (ISBN 0-917714-21-0). Beinfeld Pub.
--L. C. Smith Shotguns. LC 77-84338. 244p. 1977. 24.95 (ISBN 0-917714-09-1). Beinfeld Pub.
Brosche, Susan L., jt. auth. see Fegan, Richard C.
Brosche, Susan L., jt. auth. see Fegan, Richard G.
Broschek, Anja. Michel Erhart: Ein Beitrag zur schwaebischen Plastik der Spaetgotik. LC 72-81548. (Beitraege Zur Kunstgeschichte: Vol. 8). 1973. 91.20x (ISBN 3-11-001765-2). De Gruyter.
Brose, Olive J. Frederick Denison Maurice: Rebellious Conformist, 1805-1872. LC 74-141380. xxiii, 308p. 1971. 16.00x (ISBN 0-8214-0092-4). Ohio U Pr.
Brosius, Jack & LeRoy, Dave. Canoes & Kayaks: A Complete Buyer's Guide. 1979. 12.95 o.p. (ISBN 0-8092-7691-7); pap. 5.95 o.p. (ISBN 0-8092-7690-9). Contemp Bks.
Brosnac, Donald. The Steel String Guitar: Its History & Construction. 2nd rev ed. (Illus.). 112p. 1976. pap. 6.95 (ISBN 0-915572-26-5). Panjandrum.
Brosnahan, L. F. & Malmberg, B. Introduction to Phonetics. LC 75-26277. (Illus.). 243p. 1975. 34.50 (ISBN 0-521-21100-X); pap. 9.95x (ISBN 0-521-29042-2). Cambridge U Pr.
Brosnan, Jim. Great Rookies of the Major Leagues. (Major League Baseball Library: No. 3). (Illus.). (gr. 5-9). 1966. PLB 3.69 (ISBN 0-394-90186-X, BYR). Random.
--Little League to Big League. (Major League Baseball Library: No. 10). (Illus.). 1968. PLB 3.69 (ISBN 0-394-90190-8, BYR). Random.
Brosnan, John. James Bond in the Cinema. 2nd rev. ed. LC 80-26573. (Illus.). 200p. 1981. 9.95 (ISBN 0-498-02546-2). A S Barnes.
Bross, Irwin D. Design for Decision. 1965. pap. text ed. 5.95 (ISBN 0-02-904740-4). Free Pr.
Brossard, Chandler. Raging Joys: Sublime Variations. 1981. 12.50x (ISBN 0-916156-58-3); pap. 6.00x (ISBN 0-916156-57-5); signed & lettered ed. 25.00x (ISBN 0-916156-59-1). Cherry Valley.
Brossi, A. Organic Synthesis. LC 21-17747. (Organic Synthesis Ser.: Vol. 53). 1973. 15.95 (ISBN 0-471-10615-1). Wiley.
Brost, Fred B. & Coale, Robert D. Guide to Shell Collecting in the Kwajalein Atoll. LC 78-130418. (Illus.). 1971. pap. 11.00 (ISBN 0-8048-0942-9). C E Tuttle.
Brosterman, Robert. The Complete Estate Planning Guide. rev. ed. 1981. pap. 2.95 (ISBN 0-451-61962-5, ME1692, Ment). NAL.
--Complete Estate Planning Guide: For Business & Professional Men & Women & Their Advisers. 1964. 24.95 o.p. (ISBN 0-07-008123-9, P&RB). McGraw.

Brostoff, Laya. Duble Weave: Theory & Practice. LC 79-91202. (Illus.). 54p. 1979. 4.95 (ISBN 0-934026-01-7). Interweave.

Brostrom, Anders, jt. auth. see Abrahamsson, Bengt.

Broszat, Martin. The Hitler State: The Foundation & Development of the Internal Structure of the Third Reich. Hiden, John, tr. from Ger. (Illus.). 400p. 1981. text ed. 22.00x (ISBN 0-582-49200-9); pap. text ed. 12.95x (ISBN 0-582-48997-0). Longman.

Brotchie, J. F., et al. TOPAZ - General Planning Technique & Its Applications at the Regional, Urban, & Facility Planning Levels. (Lecture Notes in Economics & Mathematical Systems: Vol. 180). (Illus.). 356p. 1980. pap. 29.00 (ISBN 0-387-10020-2). Springer-Verlag.

Brother Aloysius. Comfort to the Sick: A Recipe Book of Medicinal Herbs. 416p. 1981. pap. 8.95 (ISBN 0-87728-525-X). Weiser.

Brother Andrew. Building in a Broken World. 1981. pap. 3.95 (ISBN 0-8423-0184-4). Tyndale.

Brother Lawrence. The Practice of the Presence of God. Demaray, Donald E., ed. (Devotional Classics Ser). 64p. 1975. pap. 1.95 (ISBN 0-8010-2844-2). Baker Bk.

Brother Nectario M. Juan Colon Alias Christopher Columbus. Josephson, Emanuel M., ed. LC 72-166573. (Blacked-Out History Ser.). 1971. pap. 5.00 (Pub. by Chedney). Alpine Ent.

Brothers. Better Than Ever. Date not set. 2.98 (ISBN 0-686-69201-2). Bonanza.

Brothers, Dwight S. & Solis, M. Leopoldo. Mexican Financial Development. 1965. 12.95x (ISBN 0-292-73304-6). U of Tex Pr.

Brothers Grimm. The Bremen Town Musicians. LC 79-16944. (Illus.). 32p. (gr. k-3). 1980. 7.95 (ISBN 0-688-80233-8); PLB 7.63 (ISBN 0-688-84233-X). Greenwillow.

--Snow White. Heins, Paul, tr. LC 73-13585. (Illus.). (gr. k-3). 1979. pap. 3.95 o.p. (ISBN 0-316-35451-1, Pub. by Atlantic-Little Brown); 7.95 o.p. (ISBN 0-316-35450-3). Little.

Brothers, J., ed. Readings in the Sociology of Religion. 1967. 22.00 (ISBN 0-08-012186-1); text ed. 10.75 (ISBN 0-08-012187-X). Pergamon.

Brothers Grimm. Cinderella. LC 80-15394. (Illus.). 32p. (gr. k-3). 1981. 7.95 (ISBN 0-688-80299-0); PLB 7.63 (ISBN 0-688-84299-2). Greenwillow.

--The Fisherman & His Wife. Shub, Elizabeth, tr. from Ger. LC 78-8133. (Illus.). (gr. k-3). 1979. 9.50 (ISBN 0-688-86003-6). Greenwillow.

--The Seven Ravens. Crawford, Elizabeth D., tr. from Ger. LC 80-25365. (Illus.). 24p. (gr. k-3). 1981. 8.95 (ISBN 0-688-00371-0); PLB 8.59 (ISBN 0-688-00372-9). Morrow.

--The Shoemaker & the Elves. (Illus.). 32p. (gr. k-3). Repr. of 1960 ed. pap. 2.95 (ISBN 0-689-70480-1, A-107, Aladdin). Atheneum.

Brotherson, Mary Lound. A Handbook for Aides. 1981. pap. write for info (ISBN 0-8134-2177-2, 2177). Interstate.

Brotherston, G. Latin American Poetry. LC 75-2734. (Illus.). 256p. 1975. 36.00 (ISBN 0-521-20763-0); pap. 9.95x (ISBN 0-521-09944-7). Cambridge U Pr.

Brotherston, G., ed. Spanish American Modernista Poets. LC 68-31793. 1968. 17.00 (ISBN 0-08-012858-0); pap. 8.00 (ISBN 0-08-012857-2). Pergamon.

Brotherston, G. & Llosa, M. V., eds. Seven Stories from Spanish America. 1968. 5.40 (ISBN 0-08-012676-6); pap. 4.10 (ISBN 0-08-012675-8). Pergamon.

Brotherston, J. Gordon. Manuel Machado: A Revaluation. LC 68-11281. (Illus.). 1968. 32.00 (ISBN 0-521-04334-4). Cambridge U Pr.

Brotherton, Roy O. Me 'n' Steve. (Illus.). (gr. 4-7). 1965. 4.75g o.s.i. (ISBN 0-02-715050-X). Macmillan.

Brotherus, V. F. Die Laubmoose Fennoskansias. (Flora Fennica Ser.: Vol. 1). (Illus.). 635p. (Ger.). 1974. Repr. of 1923 ed. lib. bdg. 102.95x (ISBN 3-87429-078-6). Lubrecht & Cramer.

Brothwell, C., et al, eds. Maintenance of Numerically Controlled Machine Tools, 2 vols. 2nd ed. (Engineering Craftsmen: No. J27). (Illus.). 1973. Set. sprial bdg. 52.00x (ISBN 0-85083-155-5). Intl Ideas.

Brothwell, Don & Sandison, A. T. Diseases in Antiquity: A Survey of the Diseases, Injuries & Surgery of Early Populations. (Illus.). 792p. 1967. 74.50 (ISBN 0-398-00233-9). C C Thomas.

Broudy, Harry S., et al, eds. Philosophy of Educational Research. LC 72-2332. (Readings in Educational Research Ser.). 1973. 25.00 (ISBN 0-471-10625-9); text ed. 22.50 10 or more copies (ISBN 0-686-67151-1). McCutchan.

Brough, Ian, jt. auth. see Hyman, Richard.

Brough, James. The Vixens. 1981. 12.95 (ISBN 0-671-22688-6). S&S.

Brough, John, ed. Gandhari Dharmapada. (London Oriental Ser.). 1962. 34.50x o.p. (ISBN 0-19-713519-6). Oxford U Pr.

Brough, John B., ed. Philosophical Knowledge. LC 80-69505. (Proceedings: Vol. 54). 250p. (Orig.). 1981. pap. 8.00 (ISBN 0-918090-14-8). Am Cath Philo.

Brough, R. Clayton. His Servants Speak: Statements by Latter-day Saint Leaders on Contemporary Topics. LC 75-17101. 298p. 1975. 8.95 (ISBN 0-88290-054-4). Horizon Utah.

--The Lost Tribes: History Doctrine, Prophecies & Theories About Israel's Lost Ten Tribes. LC 79-89351. 1979. 5.95 (ISBN 0-88290-123-0). Horizon Utah.

Brough, Walter & Sutton, Michael. Explosion: The Day Texas City Died. 1980. pap. 2.75 (ISBN 0-686-69244-6, 75838). Avon.

Broughtn, Geoffrey, et al, eds. Teaching English As a Foreign Language. 2nd ed. (Routledge Education Bks.). 256p. 1980. write for info. (ISBN 0-7100-0642-X); pap. write for info. (ISBN 0-7100-0643-8). Routledge & Kegan.

Broughton, jt. auth. see Mills.

Broughton, Diane. Confessions of a Compulsive Eater. LC 78-1483. 1978. 8.95 o.p. (ISBN 0-525-66581-1). Elsevier-Nelson.

Broughton, Geoffrey, et al. Teaching English As a Foreign Language. (Education Bks). 1978. 20.00x (ISBN 0-7100-8950-3); pap. 9.50 (ISBN 0-7100-8951-1). Routledge & Kegan.

Broughton, James. Odes for Odd Occasions. 1977. signed ed. 12.00 o.p. (ISBN 0-686-19030-0). Man-Root.

--The Water Circle. 1977. pap. 1.50 (ISBN 0-686-28712-6). Man-Root.

Broughton, John M. & Freeman-Moir, D. John, eds. The Foundation of Cognitive-Development Psychology: James Mark Baldwin's Theory & Its Contemporary Meaning. 300p. 1981. text ed. price not set (ISBN 0-89391-043-0). Ablex Pub.

Broughton, L. N., jt. auth. see Baldwin, Dane L.

Broughton, Panthea R. William Faulkner: The Abstract & the Actual. LC 74-77324. 222p. 1974. 12.50 (ISBN 0-8071-0083-8). La State U Pr.

Broughton, Rhoda. Not Wisely, but Too Well. Van Thal, Herbert, ed. 1867-1967. 5.25 (ISBN 0-304-92524-1); pap. 3.95 (ISBN 0-685-09188-0). Dufour.

Broughton, Roger, jt. auth. see Gastaut, Henri.

Broughton, Roger, ed. see Roth, B.

Broughton, T. A. Winter Journey. 1980. 10.95 (ISBN 0-525-23515-9). Dutton.

Broughton, T. Alan. Family Gathering. 1977. 7.95 o.p. (ISBN 0-525-10310-4). Dutton.

--Winter Journey. 320p. 1981. pap. 2.95 (ISBN 0-449-24369-9, Crest). Fawcett.

Broughton, V., jt. ed. see Mills, J.

Broughton, W. B., ed. Biology of Brains. LC 74-178. 1974. 28.95 (ISBN 0-470-10630-1). Halsted Pr.

Broughton, W. J. Nitrogen Fixation, Vol. 1: Ecology. (Illus.). 350p. 1981. 59.00 (ISBN 0-19-854540-1). Oxford U Pr.

Broun, Heywood & Britt, George. Christians Only: A Study in Prejudice. LC 73-19688. (Civil Liberties in American History Ser). 333p. 1974. Repr. of 1931 ed. lib. bdg. 29.50 (ISBN 0-306-70599-0). Da Capo.

Broun, Heywood H. A Studied Madness. LC 79-84436. 1979. 15.95 (ISBN 0-933256-00-0); pap. 7.95 (ISBN 0-933256-03-5). Second Chance.

Broun, Kenneth S. & Meisenholder, Robert. Problems in Evidence. 2nd ed. (American Casebook Ser.). 1981. pap. text ed. 6.95 (ISBN 0-8299-2125-7). West Pub.

Brounstein, Sidney H. & Kamrass, Murray, eds. Operations Research in Law Enforcement & Societal Security. (Illus.). 1976. 21.95 (ISBN 0-669-00732-3). Lexington Bks.

Broussard, Louis. Measure of Poe. LC 69-16715. 1969. 5.95 o.p. (ISBN 0-8061-0859-2). U of Okla Pr.

Brouwer, A. De see De Brouwer, A.

Brow, Dix. A Trailerboater's Guide to the Sea of Cortez. (Illus.). 1980. pap. 12.95 o.p. (ISBN 0-89404-027-8). Aztex.

Brow, Thea J. The Secret Cross of Lorraine. (gr. 5-8). 1981. 8.95 (ISBN 0-395-30344-3). HM.

Browder, et al. Family Property Settlements Future Interest. 2nd ed. (Contemporary Legal Education Ser.). 1973. 19.00 o.p. (ISBN 0-672-81869-8, Bobbs-Merrill Law). Michie.

Browder, F., ed. Nonlinear Functional Analysis, Pts. 1 & 2. LC 74-3414. (Proceedings of Symposia in Pure Mathematics Ser.). 1968. Set. 44.80. Am Math.

Browder, F. E., ed. see Symposia in Pure Mathematics-Northern Illinois Univ., May 1974.

Browder, Lesley H., et al. Developing an Educationally Accountable Program. LC 72-83476. (Illus.). 350p. 1973. 16.25x o.p. (ISBN 0-8211-0121-8); text ed. 14.60x o.p. (ISBN 0-685-26755-5). McCutchan.

Browder, Lesley, Jr. Emerging Patterns of Administrative Accountability. LC 73-146309. 1971. 21.00x (ISBN 0-8211-0117-X); text ed. 19.00x (ISBN 0-685-04197-2). McCutchan.

Browder, Olin L., et al. Basic Property Law. 3rd ed. LC 79-11898. (American Casebook Ser.). 1979. text ed. 24.95 (ISBN 0-8299-2037-4). West Pub.

Browder, Robert P. Origins of Soviet-American Diplomacy. 1953. 16.50x (ISBN 0-691-05627-7); pap. o.p. (ISBN 0-691-01053-6). Princeton U Pr.

Brower, Brock. The Late Great Creature. 288p. 1974. pap. 1.25 o.p. (ISBN 0-445-00187-9). Popular Lib.

Brower, Charles D. Fifty Years Below Zero. LC 42-22432. (Illus.). 1942. 8.95 (ISBN 0-396-02379-7). Dodd.

Brower, Daniel, ed. The Russian Revolution. LC 78-67917. (Problems in Civilization Ser.). (Orig.). 1979. pap. text ed. 3.95x (ISBN 0-88273-406-7). Forum Pr MO.

Brower, David & Kauffman, Richard, eds. Headlands. (Gallery Format Ser.). (Illus.). 1976. 125.00 o.p. (ISBN 0-913890-15-4). Friends Earth.

Brower, David J., et al. Urban Growth Management Through Development Timing. LC 75-19766. (Special Studies). 1976. text ed. 21.95 (ISBN 0-275-55530-5). Praeger.

Brower, David R., ed. & pref. by see Collins, Lawrence & Schweitzer, Martin.

Brower, David R., ed. see Lappe, Marc & McCurdy, John C.

Brower, David R., ed. & pref. by see Lovins, Amory & Evans, Philip H.

Brower, Gary L. Haiku in Western Languages: An Annotated Bibliography (with Some Reference to Senryu) LC 70-187878. 1972. 10.00 (ISBN 0-8108-0472-7). Scarecrow.

Brower, Kenneth, ed. see Wenkam, Robert.

Brower, Reuben A. The Fields of Light: An Experiment in Critical Reading. LC 80-19289. xii, 218p. 1980. Repr. of 1951 ed. lib. bdg. 23.50x (ISBN 0-313-22653-9, BRFI). Greenwood.

Brower, Reuben A., et al, eds. Beginning with Poems. (Orig.). 1966. 10.95x (ISBN 0-393-09685-8); pap. 8.95x (ISBN 0-393-09509-6). Norton.

Browman, D. L., ed. Early Native Americans. (World Anthropology Ser.). 1979. text ed. 48.25x (ISBN 90-279-7940-5). Mouton.

Browman, David L., ed. Spirits, Shamans, & Stars: Perspectives from South America. Scwartz, Ronald A. (World Anthropology Ser.). 1979. text ed. 31.75x (ISBN 90-279-7890-5). Mouton.

Browman, David L. & Schwartz, Ronald A., eds. Peasants, Primitives, & Proletariats: The Struggle for Identity in South America. (World Anthropology Ser.). 1979. text ed. 48.25x (ISBN 90-279-7880-8). Mouton.

Brown. Desert Biology, 2 vols. 102.00 set; Vol. 1, 1968. 63.00 (ISBN 0-12-135901-8); Vol. 2. 63.00 (ISBN 0-12-135902-6). Acad Pr.

--Skitterbrain. (gr. 3-5). 1980. pap. 1.25 (ISBN 0-590-30906-4, Schol Pap). Schol Bk Serv.

--Transfer Station Techniques Manual. 1981. text ed. 39.95 (ISBN 0-250-40426-5). Ann Arbor Science.

Brown & Brown. Applied Finite Mathematics. 1977. 18.95x o.p. (ISBN 0-534-00499-7). Wadsworth Pub.

Brown, jt. auth. see Farmer.

Brown, A. Great Ideas in Communications. 1968. 7.00 (ISBN 0-08-007073-6). Pergamon.

Brown, A. C. & Crounse, Robert G., eds. Hair, Trace Elements & Human Illness. LC 80-10280. 320p. 1980. 42.95 (ISBN 0-03-055441-1). Praeger.

Brown, A. E. & Jeffcott, H. A., Jr. Absolutely Mad Inventions. Orig. Title: Beware of Imitations. (Illus.). 1970. pap. 2.00 (ISBN 0-486-22596-8). Dover.

Brown, A. G., jt. auth. see Hillis, W. E.

Brown, A. J. The Framework of Regional Economics in the United Kingdom. LC 72-83665. (Publications of the National Institute of Economic & Social Studies: No. 27). (Illus.). 384p. 1972. 42.50 (ISBN 0-521-08743-0). Cambridge U Pr.

Brown, A. Lee. Rules & Conflicts: An Introduction to Political Life & Its Study. (Illus.). 384p. 1981. pap. text ed. 9.95 (ISBN 0-13-783738-0). P-H.

Brown, A. Theodore. Frontier Community: Kansas City to 1870. LC 63-14768. 1963. 15.00x o.p. (ISBN 0-8262-0023-0). U of Mo Pr.

Brown, A. Theodore & Dorsett, Lyle W. K.C. A History of Kansas City, Missouri. (Western Urban History Ser.). (Illus.). 320p. 1980. pap. 6.95 (ISBN 0-87108-563-1). Pruett.

Brown, A. Theordore & Dorsett, Lyle W. K.C. A History of Kansas City, Missouri. (Western Urban History Ser.). (Illus.). 1978. 13.50 (ISBN 0-87108-526-7); pap. 6.95 (ISBN 0-87108-563-1). Pruett.

Brown, Adah. The Heavenly Computer. 1979. 4.50 o.p. (ISBN 0-8062-1212-8). Carlton.

Brown, Aileen, jt. ed. see Shaw, Stephen M.

Brown, Alan. Skoolplay. 1980. pap. 3.95 (ISBN 0-7145-3672-5). Riverrun NY.

--Wheelchair Willie & Other Plays. 1980. pap. 4.95 (ISBN 0-7145-3655-5). Riverrun NY.

--Wind up the Willow. 1981. 9.95 (ISBN 0-7145-3808-6); pap. 4.95 (ISBN 0-686-68791-4). Riverrun NY.

Brown, Alan, tr. see Giono, Jean.

Brown, Alan A. & Neuberger, Egon, eds. International Trade & Central Planning: An Analysis of Economic Interactions. 1968. 30.00x (ISBN 0-520-00187-7). U of Cal Pr.

Brown, Alan R., ed. Prejudice in Children. 224p. 1972. text ed. 17.50 (ISBN 0-398-02247-X). C C Thomas.

Brown, Alan R. & Avery, Connie, eds. Modifying Children's Behavior: A Book of Readings. (Illus.). 296p. 1974. 16.00 (ISBN 0-398-02953-9). C C Thomas.

Brown, Albert J., Jr. Branch Manager's Workbook. LC 75-36011. 1975. plastic comb 10.00 (ISBN 0-87267-023-6); wkbk, 3 ring bdg. o.p. 15.00 (ISBN 0-87267-032-5). Bankers.

Brown, Alexander. Juniper Waterway: A History of the Albemarle & Chesapeake Canal. LC 80-14093. 1981. price not set (ISBN 0-917376-35-8). U Pr of Va.

Brown, Alexander C. The Good Ships of Newport News. LC 76-12100. (Illus.). 1976. 12.75 (ISBN 0-87033-220-1, Pub. by Tidewater). Cornell Maritime.

--Longboat to Hawaii. LC 74-22317. (Illus.). 254p. 1974. 12.50 (ISBN 0-87033-201-5). Cornell Maritime.

Brown, Alexis, tr. see Keller, Horst.

Brown, Alfred G. From Buggy Whips to Moon Walks. 1978. 7.00 o.p. (ISBN 0-682-49037-7). Exposition.

Brown, Allen R. English Castles. 1976. 33.00 (ISBN 0-7134-3119-9). David & Charles.

Brown, Allen W. The Inner Fire. 1977. 3.95 o.p. (ISBN 0-87680-516-0, 80516). Word Bks.

Brown, Allison L. Ecology of Soil Organisms. LC 78-313368. 1978. text ed. 16.95 o.p. (ISBN 0-435-60620-4); pap. text ed. 8.95x (ISBN 0-435-60621-2). Heinemann Ed.

Brown, Andrew J. Community Health. 255p. (Orig.). 1981. pap. text ed. write for info. (ISBN 0-8087-4040-7). Burgess.

Brown, Ann L., jt. ed. see Lamb, Michael E.

Brown, Anne E. Wonders of Sea Horses. LC 78-22439. (Wonder Ser.). (Illus.). (gr. 5 up). 1979. 5.95 (ISBN 0-396-07664-5). Dodd.

Brown, Annice H. Thank You, Lord, for Little Things. LC 72-11166. (Illus.). 1973. 2.95 (ISBN 0-8042-2580-X). John Knox.

Brown, Anthony C., ed. The Secret War Report of the O.S.S. pap. 1.95 o.p. (ISBN 0-425-03253-1). Berkley Pub.

Brown, Arch. News Boy. LC 80-84131. (Illus.). 80p. (Orig.). 1980. pap. 3.95 (ISBN 0-935672-02-8). JH Pr.

Brown, Archie & Kaser, Michael, eds. The Soviet Union Since the Fall of Khrushchev. LC 75-39856. 1976. 17.95 (ISBN 0-02-904870-2). Free Pr.

Brown, Arlen D. Tractor & Small Engine Maintenance. 4th ed. LC 72-95181. 1973. 12.00 (ISBN 0-8134-1546-2); text ed. 9.00x (ISBN 0-685-34828-8). Interstate.

Brown, Arlen D. & Morrison, Ivan G. Farm Tractor Maintenance. LC 62-13066. 256p. 1962. 5.50 o.p. (ISBN 0-8134-0032-5); text ed. 4.25x o.p. (ISBN 0-685-57258-7). Interstate.

Brown, Arthur W., et al, eds. see Kiraly, Bela.

Brown, Ashley & Kimmey, John L., eds. Satire: An Anthology. 1978. pap. 8.50 scp (ISBN 0-690-01524-0, HarpC). Har-Row.

Brown, Ashley, jt. ed. see Kimmey, John.

Brown, Audrey K., jt. ed. see Aladjem, Silvio.

Brown, Barbara. Disaster Preparedness & the United Nations: Advance Planning for Disaster Relief. LC 79-179. (Pergamon Policy Studies). 120p. 1979. 17.75 (ISBN 0-08-022486-5). Pergamon.

--Nurse Staffing: A Practical Guide. 200p. 1980. 23.95 (ISBN 0-89443-291-5). Aspen Systems.

Brown, Barbara, jt. ed. see Rose, James M.

Brown, Barbara A. Aging: A Christian Approach. 1980. 0.65 (ISBN 0-686-28771-1). Forward Movement.

--Hematology: Principles & Procedures. 3rd ed. LC 80-16943. (Illus.). 358p. 1980. text ed. 22.00 (ISBN 0-8121-0707-1). Lea & Febiger.

Brown, Barbara A., et al. Women's Rights & the Law: The Impact of the ERA on State Laws. LC 77-9961. (Praeger Special Studies). 1977. text ed. 39.95 (ISBN 0-03-022316-4); pap. 11.95 (ISBN 0-03-022311-3). Praeger.

Brown, Barbara B. The Biofeedback Syllabus: A Handbook for the Psychophysiological Study of Biofeedback. 516p. 1975. 45.50 (ISBN 0-398-03268-8); pap. 31.75 (ISBN 0-685-57029-0). C C Thomas.

Brown, Barbara B. & Klug, Jay, eds. The Alpha Syllabus: A Handbook of Human EEG Alpha Activity. 368p. 1974. text ed. 34.50 (ISBN 0-398-03020-0); pap. text ed. 28.50 (ISBN 0-398-03021-9). C C Thomas.
Brown, Beatrice C. Jonathan Bing. LC 68-14074. (gr. k-3). 1968. 5.75 (ISBN 0-688-40989-X); PLB 5.00 o.p. (ISBN 0-688-50989-4). Lothrop.
Brown, Ben H. Death of Odysseus. LC 77-74291. 1977. 5.95 o.p. (ISBN 0-533-02426-9). Vantage.
Brown, Bernard, ed. Found: Long-Term Gains from Early Intervention. LC 78-3120. (AAAS Selected Symposium Ser.: No. 8). 1978. lib. bdg. 22.50x (ISBN 0-89158-436-6). Westview.
Brown, Bernard E., ed. Eurocommunism & Eurosocialism: The Left Confronts Modernity. 400p. text ed. 22.50x (ISBN 0-8290-0394-0); pap. text ed. 12.95x (ISBN 0-8290-0395-9). Irvington.
Brown, Bernard E., jt. ed. see Macridis, Roy C.
Brown, Bernard L. Risk Management for Hospitals: A Practical Approach. LC 78-31925. 1979. text ed. 28.00 (ISBN 0-89443-090-4). Aspen Systems.
Brown, Beth. Dogs. rev. ed. LC 68-9405. (Illus.). (gr. 3 up). 1981. PLB 6.87 (ISBN 0-87460-095-2). Lion.
Brown, Beth, compiled by. Fairy Tales of Birds & Beasts, Vol. 1. (Illus.). 128p. (gr. 3-7). 1981. PLB 8.95 (ISBN 0-87460-375-7). Lion.
Brown, Betty B. Speech Therapy: Principles & Practice. (Illus.). 288p. 1981. pap. 15.00 (ISBN 0-443-02099-X). Churchill.
Brown, Beverly S., illus. Key Soup. LC 78-73538. (Illus.). (gr. 1-5). Date not set. price not set (ISBN 0-89799-155-9); pap. price not set (ISBN 0-89799-073-0). Dandelion Pr. Postponed.
Brown, Bob. Six Hundred Sixty Six Science Tricks & Experiments. pap. 7.95 (ISBN 0-8306-6881-0, 881). TAB Bks.
Brown, Brenda W., jt. auth. see Brown, Robert F.
Brown, Brendan. Money Hard & Soft on the International Currency Markets. LC 78-16929. 1978. 21.95 (ISBN 0-470-26466-7). Halsted Pr.
Brown, Burnell R., Jr. Fluid, Blood, and Blood Component Administration. (Contemporary Anesthesia Practice Ser.: Vol. 5). 1981. write for info. (ISBN 0-8036-1271-0). Davis Co.
Brown, Burnell R., Jr., ed. Anesthesia & the Obese Patient. (Contemporary Anesthesia Practice Ser.: Vol. 6). 1981. write for info. (ISBN 0-8036-1273-7). Davis Co.
--Anesthesia & the Patient with Endocrine Disease. LC 80-13067. (Contemporary Anesthesia Practice Ser.: Vol. 3). (Illus.). 210p. 1980. text ed. 24.00 (ISBN 0-8036-1264-8). Davis Co.
--Anesthesia & the Patient with Liver Disease. LC 80-22088. (Contemporary Anesthesia Practice Ser.: Vol. 4). 190p. 1980. 25.00 (ISBN 0-8036-1268-0). Davis Co.
Brown, C. A., jt. auth. see Blackler, F. H.
Brown, C. H. Structural Materials in Animals. LC 75-1293. 1975. 38.95 o.p. (ISBN 0-470-10641-7). Halsted Pr.
Brown, C. Reynolds. Clara Weaver Parrish. LC 80-82147. (Illus.). 1980. pap. 4.00 (ISBN 0-89280-016-X). Montgomery Mus.
--Montgomery Museum of Fine Arts: A Handbook to the Collection. LC 80-80053. (Illus.). 68p. 1980. pap. 3.00 (ISBN 0-89280-014-3). Montgomery Mus.
Brown, C. V. Taxation & the Incentive to Work. (Illus.). 128p. 1980. 29.95 (ISBN 0-19-877134-7); pap. 12.00 (ISBN 0-19-877135-5). Oxford U Pr.
Brown, C. V. & Jackson, P. M. Public Sector Economics. 452p. 1978. 48.50x (ISBN 0-85520-134-7, Pub by Martin Robertson England); pap. 21.95x (ISBN 0-85520-133-9). Biblio Dist.
Brown, C. V., ed. Economic Principles Applied. 192p. 1980. pap. text ed. cancelled (ISBN 0-85520-001-4, Pub. by Martin Robertson England). Biblio Dist.
Brown, Carol W. The Minicomputer Simplified: An Executive's Guide to the Basics. LC 80-1031. (Illus.). 1980. 12.95 (ISBN 0-02-905130-4). Free Pr.
Brown, Carter. The Brazen. Bd. with The Stripper. Date not set. pap. 1.95 (ISBN 0-451-09575-8, J575, Sig). NAL.
--Busted Wheeler. 1979. pap. 1.50 (ISBN 0-505-51414-1). Tower Bks.
--Donavan's Delight. 1979. pap. 1.50 (ISBN 0-505-51382-X). Tower Bks.
--The Dream Is Deadly. Bd. with Savage Salome. 1981. pap. price not set (ISBN 0-451-09776-9, Sig). NAL.
--Model for Murder. (Orig.). 1980. pap. 1.50 (ISBN 0-505-51527-X). Tower Bks.
--The Phantom Lady. (Orig.). 1980. pap. 1.50 (ISBN 0-505-51516-4). Tower Bks.
--The Rip-Off. 1979. pap. 1.50 (ISBN 0-505-51425-7). Tower Bks.
--See It Again, Sam. 1979. pap. 1.50 (ISBN 0-505-51415-X). Tower Bks.
Brown, Catherine, ed. see Damon, S. Foster.
Brown, Cecil. Life & Loves of Mr. Jiveass Nigger. 1978. pap. 1.25 o.p. (ISBN 0-449-22975-0, Crest). Fawcett.
Brown, Charles B. Arthur Mervyn, or Memoirs of the Year Seventeen Ninety-Three. Krause, Sydney J. & Reid, S. W., eds. LC 79-92808. (The Novels & Related Works of Charles Brockden Brown Ser.: Vol. 3). 590p. 1980. 27.50x (ISBN 0-87338-241-2). Kent St U Pr.
--Jane Talbot. 237p. 1980. Repr. of 1857 ed. lib. bdg. 40.00 (ISBN 0-89987-062-7). Century Bookbindery.
Brown, Charles B., jt. auth. see Castellano, Juan R.
Brown, Charles Brockden. Wieland: Or, the Transformation. pap. 2.50 (ISBN 0-385-03100-9, C320, Anch). Doubleday.
Brown, Charles C. Small Church Library. 1980. 0.75 (ISBN 0-686-28794-0). Forward Movement.
Brown, Charles T. & Keller, Paul T. Monologue to Dialogue: An Exploration of Interpersonal Commuication. 2nd ed. LC 78-16541. (Special Communication Ser.). 1979. pap. 11.95 (ISBN 0-13-600825-9). P-H.
Brown, Charles W. Hybridization Among the Subspecies of the Plethodontid Salamander Ensatina Eschscholtzi. (U. C. Publ. in Zoology: Vol. 98). pap. 9.00x (ISBN 0-520-09442-5). U of Cal Pr.
Brown, Cheryl L. & Olson, Karen, eds. Feminist Criticism: Essays on Theory, Poetry & Prose. LC 78-8473. 1978. 18.00 (ISBN 0-8108-1143-X). Scarecrow.
Brown, Christopher, jt. auth. see Turner, Anthony.
Brown, Christopher P. The Political & Social Economy of Commodity Control. LC 79-88568. 394p. 1979. 39.95 (ISBN 0-03-053351-1). Praeger.
Brown, Clara L. Beating Around the Bush. (Illus.). 1967. 3.95 o.p. (ISBN 0-8158-0060-6). Chris Mass.
--One for the Road. 1970. 4.95 o.p. (ISBN 0-8158-0232-3). Chris Mass.
--Voyage into Danger. (Illus.). 150p. 1972. 4.95 o.p. (ISBN 0-8158-0291-9). Chris Mass.
Brown, Clarence. Mandelstam. LC 72-90491. (Illus.). 400p. 1973. 38.50 (ISBN 0-521-20142-X); pap. 9.95 (ISBN 0-521-29347-2). Cambridge U Pr.
Brown, Claude. Manchild in the Promised Land. (RL 7). 1971. pap. 2.25 (ISBN 0-451-08206-0, E9282, Sig). NAL.
--Manchild in the Promised Land. (gr. 8 up). 1965. 12.95 (ISBN 0-02-517320-0). Macmillan.
Brown, Clifton F., jt. auth. see Williams, Ethel L.
Brown, Clifton F., compiled by. Ethiopian Perspectives: A Bibliographical Guide to the History of Ethiopia. LC 77-89111. (African Bibliographic Center, Special Bibliographic Series, New Series: No. 5). lib. bdg. 22.50 (ISBN 0-8371-9850-X, BET/). Greenwood.
Brown, Colin. The New International Dictionary of New Testament Theology, 3 vols. Set. 92.00 (ISBN 0-310-21928-0). Zondervan.
Brown, Colin, ed. The New International Dictionary of New Testament Theology, Vol. 2. 1977. 29.95 (ISBN 0-310-21900-0). Zondervan.
Brown, Cora, et al. The South American Cookbook: Including Central America, Mexico, & the West Indies. 8.00 (ISBN 0-8446-0041-5). Peter Smith.
Brown, Curtis M. Boundary Control & Legal Principles. 2nd ed. LC 68-8712. 1969. 27.50 (ISBN 0-471-10660-7, Pub. by Wiley-Interscience). Wiley.
Brown, Curtis M. & Eldridge, Winfield H. Evidence & Procedures for Boundary Location. LC 62-18988. (Illus.). 1962. 32.50 (ISBN 0-471-10663-1, Pub. by Wiley-Interscience). Wiley.
Brown, D. Soviet Russian Literature Since Stalin. LC 77-73275. 1978. 36.00 (ISBN 0-521-21694-X); pap. 9.95 (ISBN 0-521-29649-8). Cambridge U Pr.
Brown, D., jt. auth. see Clark, R.
Brown, D. A., tr. see Fedorov, K. N.
Brown, D. E. Principles of Social Structure: Southeast Asia. LC 76-25889. 1977. lib. bdg. 26.75x (ISBN 0-89158-643-1). Westview.
Brown, D. S. W., et al. The Geological Evolution of Australia & New Zealand. 1968. 26.00 (ISBN 0-08-012278-7); pap. 14.50 (ISBN 0-08-012277-9). Pergamon.
Brown, Dale. American Cooking. LC 68-9172. (Foods of the World Ser). (Illus.). (gr. 6 up). 1968. PLB 14.94 (ISBN 0-8094-0060-X, Time-Life). Silver.
--American Cooking. (Foods of the World Ser). (Illus.). 1968. 14.95 (ISBN 0-8094-0033-2). Time-Life.
--American Cooking: The Northwest. LC 73-138262. (Foods of the World Ser.). (Illus.). (gr. 6 up). 1970. lib. bdg. 14.94 (ISBN 0-8094-0077-4, Pub. by Time-Life). Silver.
--Cooking of Scandinavia. LC 68-21587. (Foods of the World Ser). (Illus.). (gr. 6 up). 1968. PLB 14.94 (ISBN 0-8094-0058-8, Pub. by Time-Life). Silver.
--Cooking of Scandinavia. (Foods of the World Ser). (Illus.). 1968. 14.95 (ISBN 0-8094-0031-6). Time-Life.
--Wild Alaska. (The American Wilderness Ser.). (Illus.). 1972. 12.95 (ISBN 0-8094-1152-0). Time-Life.
--Wild Alaska. LC 74-190658. (American Wilderness Ser). (Illus.). (gr. 6 up). 1972. lib. bdg. 11.97 (ISBN 0-8094-1153-9, Pub. by Time-Life). Silver.
--World of Velazquez. (Library of Art). (Illus.). 1969. 15.95 (ISBN 0-8094-0252-1). Time-Life.
--World of Velazquez. LC 77-84575. (Library of Art Ser.). (Illus.). (gr. 6 up). 1969. 12.96 (ISBN 0-8094-0281-5, Pub. by Time-Life). Silver.
Brown, Dale, et al. American Cooking: The Melting Pot. LC 76-173191. (Foods of the World Ser.). (Illus.). (gr. 6 up). 1971. lib. bdg. 14.94 (ISBN 0-8094-0082-0, Pub. by Time-Life). Silver.
Brown, Daniel P. The Protectorate & The Northumberland Conspiracy: Political Intrigue in the Reign of Edward VI. LC 80-65156. (European History: Ser. I-1001). (Illus.). 60p. (Orig.). (gr. 11-12). 1980. pap. 3.15 (ISBN 0-930860-02-0). Golden West Hist.
Brown, Daphne M. Mother Tongue in English. LC 77-83987. 1979. 24.50 (ISBN 0-521-21873-X); pap. 7.95x (ISBN 0-521-29299-9). Cambridge U Pr.
Brown, David. Carrier Fighters. 1981. 8.95 (ISBN 0-356-08095-1, Pub. by MacDonald & Jane's England). Hippocrene Bks.
--Carrier Operations in World War II: The Royal Navy, Vol. 1. LC 74-33800. 1975. Vol. 1. 12.95 o.s.i. (ISBN 0-87021-814-X). Naval Inst Pr.
--The Four Gospels. 15.95 (ISBN 0-85151-016-7). Banner of Truth.
--Meet the Bible. 1980. 1.25 (ISBN 0-686-28784-3). Forward Movement.
--Thomas Weelkes. 1979. Repr. of 1969 ed. lib. bdg. 22.50 (ISBN 0-306-79523-X). Da Capo.
--Walter Scott & the Historical Imagination. 1979. 26.00x (ISBN 0-7100-0301-3). Routledge & Kegan.
--Wilbye. (Oxford Studies of Composers). 72p. 1974. pap. 7.95x (ISBN 0-19-315220-7). Oxford U Pr.
Brown, David B., ed. Mixed-Valence Compounds: Theory & Applications in Chemistry, Physics, Geology & Biology. (NATO Advanced Study Institute, C. Mathematical & Physical Sciences Ser.: No. 58). 525p. 1980. lib. bdg. 60.50 (ISBN 90-277-1152-6, Pub. by D. Reidel). Kluwer Boston.
Brown, David L. & Wardwell, John M., eds. New Directions in Urban-Rural Migration: The Population Turnaround in Rural America. (Studies in Population). 1980. 29.50 (ISBN 0-12-136380-5). Acad Pr.
Brown, David S. Freshwater Snails of Africa & Their Medical Importance. (Illus.). 450p. 1980. 55.00 (ISBN 0-85066-145-5). Am Malacologists.
Brown, Deborah, jt. auth. see Fawdry, Marguerite.
Brown, Dee. Creek Mary's Blood. 1981. pap. 3.50 (ISBN 0-671-42028-3). PB.
--Fort Phil Kearny: An American Saga. LC 62-10963. (Illus.). 1971. pap. 5.25 (ISBN 0-8032-5730-9, BB 523, Bison). U of Nebr Pr.
--The Year of the Century. LC 66-18538. 1975. 4.95 o.p. (ISBN 0-684-12730-X, SL338, ScribT). Scribner.
Brown, Dee & Schmitt, Martin F. Fighting Indians of the West. 256p. 1975. pap. 1.95 o.p. (ISBN 0-345-24538-5). Ballantine.
Brown, Deena, ed. American Yoga. LC 79-6156. (Illus.). 144p. (Orig.). 1981. pap. 9.95 (ISBN 0-394-17649-9, E751, Ever). Grove.
Brown, Delmer M. & Lishida, Ichiro, eds. The Future & the Past: A Translation of the Gukansko, an Interpretive History of Japan Written in 1219. LC 77-73493. 1979. 29.50x (ISBN 0-520-03460-0). U of Cal Pr.
Brown, Delwin. To Set at Liberty: Christian Faith & Human Freedom. LC 80-21783. 144p. (Orig.). 1981. pap. 6.95 (ISBN 0-88344-501-8). Orbis Bks.
Brown, Delwin, et al. Process Philosophy & Christian Thought. LC 74-127586. 1971. pap. 14.95 (ISBN 0-672-60799-9). Bobbs.
--Process Philosophy & Christian Thought. LC 74-127586. 1971. 38.50x (ISBN 0-672-51529-6). Irvington.
Brown, Deming O. Soviet Attitudes Toward American Writing. 1962. 19.00x o.p. (ISBN 0-691-08712-1). Princeton U Pr.
Brown, Dennis, ed. The Complete Indoor Gardener. rev. ed. LC 79-4799. (Illus.). 1979. 19.95 (ISBN 0-394-50748-7); pap. 9.95 (ISBN 0-394-73813-6). Random.
Brown, Derald E. Time to Pause & Reflect. 1981. 4.95 (ISBN 0-8062-1632-8). Carlton.
Brown, Diana. The Emerald Necklace. 1981. pap. 1.95 (ISBN 0-451-09727-0, J9727, Sig). NAL.
Brown, Diana L. Developmental Handicaps in Babies & Young Children: A Guide for Parents. 100p. 1972. 11.75 (ISBN 0-398-02534-7). C C Thomas.
Brown, Diana M. Building Codes & Residential Construction: An Annotated Bibliography. (Architecture Ser.: Bibliography A-334). 60p. 1980. pap. 6.50. Vance Biblios.
Brown, Diane. Notemaking. 245p. 1977. text ed. 10.20 (ISBN 0-7715-0858-1). Forkner.
Brown, Dik, jt. auth. see Walker, Mort.
Brown, Don W., jt. ed. see Brigham, John.
Brown, Donald. Basic Metallurgy. LC 80-68584. (Mechanical Ser.). (Illus.). 272p. (Orig.). 1981. pap. text ed. 10.40 (ISBN 0-8273-1769-7); price not set instr's. guide (ISBN 0-8273-1770-0). Delmar.
Brown, Donald, et al. Role & Status of Women in the Soviet Union. LC 68-27326. 1968. text ed. 8.75x (ISBN 0-8077-1128-4); pap. 5.75x (ISBN 0-8077-2466-1). Tchrs Coll.
Brown, Donald R. Neurosciences for Allied Health Therapies. LC 79-19685. (Illus.). 1980. text ed. 17.95 (ISBN 0-8016-0827-9). Mosby.
Brown, Donald R., jt. auth. see Harvey, D.
Brown, Doris M. Poems for All Occasions. Date not set. 5.95 (ISBN 0-533-04888-5). Vantage.
Brown, Doris S. & Senning, Hillyer. Psychiatric Guide to Iodine Trichloride Therapy. 4th ed. (Illus.). 1979. pap. text ed. 20.00 (ISBN 0-931918-02-2, D-3). Busn Psych.
Brown, Dorothy F. Button Parade. rev. ed. 1969. 14.95 o.p. (ISBN 0-87069-011-6). Wallace-Homestead.
Brown, Dorothy H. God & the Tree & Me. LC 79-66196. 1979. pap. 4.25x (ISBN 0-8358-0386-4). Upper Room.
Brown, Dort F. Souvenir Buildings: A Collection of Identified Miniatures, 2 vols. (Illus.). 203p. (Orig., Vol. 1, 1977, Vol. 2, 1979). pap. 5.00 set (ISBN 0-9603420-0-1). Indisota Pubs.
Brown, Douglas M. Introduction to Urban Economics. 301p. 1974. tchrs' ed. 17.95 (ISBN 0-12-136650-2). Acad Pr.
Brown, Douglas V., et al. The Economics of the Recovery Program. LC 70-163644. (FDR & the Era of the New Deal Ser). 1971. Repr. of 1934 ed. lib. bdg. 22.50 (ISBN 0-306-70197-9). Da Capo.
Brown, Duane, et al. Consultation: Strategy for Improving Education. new ed. 1979. text ed. 18.95 (ISBN 0-685-96341-1). Allyn.
Brown, E. Badminton. (Illus., Orig.). 1975. pap. 5.50 (ISBN 0-571-10659-5, Pub. by Faber & Faber). Merrimack Bk Serv.
Brown, E. Evan. World Fish Farming Cultivation & Economics. (Illus.). 1977. lib. bdg. 20.50 (ISBN 0-87055-234-1). AVI.
Brown, E. Evan & Gratzek, J. B. Fish Farming Handbook. (Illus.). 1980. 19.50 (ISBN 0-87055-341-0). AVI.
Brown, E. H., jt. auth. see Mead, W. R.
Brown, E. K. Rhythm in the Novel. LC 77-14165. 1978. 8.50x (ISBN 0-8032-1150-3); pap. 2.25x (ISBN 0-8032-6050-4, BB 667, Bison). U of Nebr Pr.
Brown, E. K. & Edel, Leon. Willa Cather: A Critical Biography. 304p. 1980. pap. 2.95 (ISBN 0-380-49676-3, 49676, Discus). Avon.
Brown, E. K. & Miller, J. E. Syntax: A Linguistic Introduction to Sentence Structure. 394p. 1981. text ed. 33.75x (ISBN 0-686-69131-8, Hutchinson U Lib); pap. text ed. 15.50x (ISBN 0-686-69132-6). Humanities.
Brown, E. M. The Helicopter in Civil Operations. 208p. 1981. 17.95 (ISBN 0-442-24528-9). Van Nos Reinhold.
Brown, E. T., ed. Rock Characterization, Testing & Monitoring: ISRM Suggested Methods. LC 80-49711. 200p. 1981. 40.00 (ISBN 0-08-027308-4); pap. 20.00 (ISBN 0-08-027309-2). Pergamon.
Brown, E. T., jt. ed. see Jenkins, J. P.
Brown, Edward E. Tassajara Cooking. LC 73-86144. (Illus.). 1980. 11.95 (ISBN 0-394-49523-3). Shambhala Pubns.
Brown, Edward F., et al. A Bibliography of Malawi. (Foreign & Comparative Studies-Eastern African Bibliographic Ser.: No. 1). 161p. 1965. pap. 3.50x. Syracuse U Foreign Comp.
Brown, Edward K. Foundations of Educational Evaluation: Its Technology, Management, Economicas, & Futurology. (Illus.). 200p. 1978. 10.00 (ISBN 0-8059-2519-8). Dorrance.
Brown, Edward K. & Edel, Leon. Willa Cather. (YA) 1953. 6.95 o.p. (ISBN 0-394-45196-1). Knopf.
Brown, Edward K. & Bailey, J. O., eds. Victorian Poetry. 2nd ed. 1962. 19.95 (ISBN 0-8260-1400-3). Wiley.

Brown, Eleanor F. Bibliotherapy & Its Widening Applications. LC 74-28187. 1975. 14.50 (ISBN 0-8108-0782-3). Scarecrow.
--Cutting Library Costs: Increasing Productivity & Raising Revenues. LC 79-19448. 274p. 1979. 13.50 (ISBN 0-8108-1250-9). Scarecrow.
--Library Service to the Disadvantaged. LC 78-162668. (Illus.). 1971. 18.50 (ISBN 0-8108-0437-9). Scarecrow.
Brown, Elizabeth. The Candle of the Wicked. 1976. pap. 2.25 (ISBN 0-310-21952-3). Zondervan.
Brown, Elizabeth G. British Statutes in American Law. LC 73-21605. (American Constitutional & Legal History Ser). 1974. Repr. of 1964 ed. lib. bdg. 35.00 (ISBN 0-306-70610-5). Da Capo.
Brown, Eric. Wings of the Luftwaffe. LC 77-14891. 1978. 10.95 o.p. (ISBN 0-385-13521-1). Doubleday.
Brown, Esther M., jt. ed. see Dellmann, Horst-Dieter.
Brown, Everett S. Ratification of the Twenty-First Amendment to the Constitution of the United States. LC 78-114757. (American Constitutional & Legal History Ser). 1970. Repr. of 1938 ed. 65.00 (ISBN 0-306-71928-2). Da Capo.
Brown, Everett S., ed. Missouri Compromises & Presidential Politics, 1820-1825: From the Letters of William Plumer. Jr. LC 76-103942. (American Constitutional & Legal History Ser). 1970. Repr. of 1926 ed. lib. bdg. 17.50 (ISBN 0-306-71869-3). Da Capo.
--William Plumer's Memorandum of Proceedings in the United States Senate 1803-1807. LC 74-94626. (Law, Politics & History Ser). 1969. Repr. of 1923 ed. 65.00 (ISBN 0-306-71823-5). Da Capo.
Brown, Ewen D., jt. auth. see Hock, Tan K.
Brown, F., et al, eds. Vehicle Painting, Pt. 1. (Engineering Craftsmen: No. E1). (Illus.). 1968. spiral bdg. 22.95x (ISBN 0-85083-032-X). Intl Ideas.
--Vehicle Painting, Pt. 2. (Engineering Craftsmen: No. E21). 1970. spiral bdg. 22.95x (ISBN 0-85083-116-4). Intl Ideas.
Brown, F. Christine. Hallucinogenic Drugs. (Amer. Lec. Living Chemistry Ser.). (Illus.). 164p. 1972. 19.75 (ISBN 0-398-02249-6). C C Thomas.
Brown, F. E. Marketing Research: A Structure for Decision Making. LC 79-25541. 1980. text ed. 18.95 (ISBN 0-201-00205-1). A-W.
Brown, F. K., jt. auth. see Frazier, Claude A.
Brown, F. Martin, jt. ed. see Ferris, Clifford D.
Brown, Fern. Behind the Scenes at the Horse Hospital. Tucker, Kathleen, ed. (Behind the Scenes Ser.). (Illus.). 48p. (gr. 3-9). 1981. 7.50 (ISBN 0-8075-0610-9). A Whitman.
--Bugs Bunny, Pioneer. (A Young Reader Ser.). (Illus.). (gr. k-3). 1979. PLB 5.00 (ISBN 0-307-60144-7, Golden Pr). Western Pub.
--Hard Luck Horse. Rubin, Caroline, ed. LC 75-31939. (Pilot Bks Ser). (Illus.). 128p. (gr. 4-7). 1975. 6.95g (ISBN 0-8075-3159-6). A Whitman.
--Racing Against the Odds: Robyn C. Smith. LC 75-42320. (Sports Profiles Ser.). (Illus.). 48p. (gr. 4-11). 1976. PLB 8.50 (ISBN 0-8172-0118-1). Raintree Pubs.
Brown, Fern G. Jockey-or Else. Pacini, Kathy, ed. LC 78-1715. (Pilot Bks.). (Illus.). (gr. 4-7). 1978. 6.95g (ISBN 0-8075-3944-9). A Whitman.
--You're Somebody Special on a Horse. LC 77-7506. (Pilotbooks). (Illus.). (gr. 4-8). 1977. 6.95g (ISBN 0-8075-9447-4). A Whitman.
Brown, Forman. Small Wonder: The Story of the Yale Puppeteers & the Turnabout Theatre. LC 80-17815. 288p. 1980. 12.50 (ISBN 0-8108-1334-3). Scarecrow.
Brown, Frances A. & Forkner, Hamden L. Study Guide & Test Manual for Correlated Dictation & Transcription. 2nd. ed. 1974. pap. 5.64x (ISBN 0-912036-19-2). Forkner.
Brown, Francis, et al. Bible Object Talks with Paper & Scissors. Shely, Patricia, ed. (Illus.). 1976. pap. 2.25 (ISBN 0-87239-116-7, 2747). Standard Pub.
Brown, Francis A. & Forkner, Hamden L. Correlated Dictation & Transcription. 2nd. ed. (Forkner Shorthand). 1974. 12.80x (ISBN 0-912036-15-X); pap. 9:96x (ISBN 0-912036-16-8). Forkner.
Brown, Francis F. Priests in Council: Initiatives Toward a Democratic Church. 1979. 20.00 o.p. (ISBN 0-8362-3301-8). Andrews & McMeel.
Brown, Frank & Stent, Madelon D. Minorities in U. S. Institutions of Higher Education. LC 75-19768. (Special Studies). 1977. text ed. 18.95 o.p. (ISBN 0-275-55540-2). Praeger.
Brown, Frank B. The Transition of Youth to Adulthood: A Bridge Too Long. 1980. lib. bdg. 24.50x (ISBN 0-89158-675-X); pap. text ed. 11.00 (ISBN 0-89158-756-X). Westview.
Brown, Frank E. Cosa: The Making of a Roman Town. (Illus.). 150p. 1980. 20.00x (ISBN 0-472-04100-2). U of Mich Pr.
--The House in Block E4, Block F3, the Roman Baths, Discoveries in the Temple of Artemis-Manaia, Arms & Armor, New & Revised Material from the Temple of Azzanathkona. (Illus.). 1936. pap. 47.50x (ISBN 0-686-52157-9). Elliots Bks.
Brown, Frederic J. Chemical Warfare: A Study in Restraints. LC 80-27993. xix, 355p. 1981. Repr. of 1968 ed. lib. bdg. 31.75x (ISBN 0-313-22823-X, BRCHW). Greenwood.
Brown, G. Listening to Spoken English. (Applied Linguistics & Language Study Ser.). 1978. pap. text ed. 8.50x (ISBN 0-582-55077-7). Longman.
--Phonological Rules & Dialect Variation: A Study of the Phonology of Lumasaaba. LC 70-184904. (Studies in Linguistics: No. 7). (Illus.). 200p. 1972. 34.50 (ISBN 0-521-08485-7); pap. 10.95x (ISBN 0-521-29063-5). Cambridge U Pr.
Brown, G. C. & Mussett, A. E. The Inaccessible Earth. (Illus.). 272p. 1981. text ed. 41.00x (ISBN 0-04-550027-4, 2538); pap. text ed. 22.50x (ISBN 0-04-550028-2, 2539). Allen Unwin.
Brown, G. H. see Weissberger, A.
Brown, G. M., jt. auth. see Wager, L. R.
Brown, G. N. Turning Complaints into Money. 1979. 12.50 o.p. (ISBN 0-685-67819-9). Porter.
Brown, G. W., jt. auth. see Wing, J. K.
Brown, G. W. see Halpenny, Francess.
Brown, Gabrielle. The New Celibacy: Why More Men & Wonen Are Abstaining from Ex & Enjoying It. 300p. 1980. 10.95 (ISBN 0-07-008430-0). McGraw.
Brown, Gail, jt. auth. see Dillon, Karen.
Brown, Gardner M., jt. auth. see Johnson, Ralph W.
Brown, Gary D. Beyond Cobol: Survival in Business Applications Programming. 225p. 1981. 17.50 (ISBN 0-471-09030-1, Pub. by Wiley-Interscience). Wiley.
--System-360 Job-Control Language. 1970. pap. 16.50 (ISBN 0-471-10870-7, Pub. by Wiley-Interscience). Wiley.
--System-370 Job Control Language. LC 77-24901. 1977. 14.95 (ISBN 0-471-03155-0, Pub. by Wiley-Interscience). Wiley.
Brown, Geoff. Sabotage: A Study in Industrial Conflict. 1977. 26.00x o.p. (ISBN 0-8476-2321-1). Rowman.
Brown, George, jt. auth. see Flanders, Helen H.
Brown, George E. The Pruning of Trees, Shrubs & Conifers. 1977. 24.95 o.p. (ISBN 0-571-09853-3, Pub. by Faber & Faber); pap. 9.95 (ISBN 0-571-11084-3). Merrimack Bk Serv.
Brown, George M. Hawkfall, & Other Stories. 1979. 8.95 (ISBN 0-7012-0391-9, Pub. by Chatto Bodley Jonathan). Merrimack Bk Serv.
--Pictures in the Cave. (Illus.). 136p. (gr. 4-7). 1980. 9.95 (ISBN 0-7011-5081-5, Pub. by Chatto Bodley Jonathan). Merrimack Bk Serv.
--Portrait of Orkney. (Illus.). 128p. 1981. 23.00 (ISBN 0-7012-0513-X, Pub. by Chatto-Bodley-Jonathan). Merrimack Bk Serv.
Brown, Gerald A. Green Ice. 1978. 9.95 o.p. (ISBN 0-440-03034-X). Delacorte.
Brown, Glenn. History of the United States Capitol, 2 Vols. in 1. LC 71-77734. (Architecture & Decorative Art Ser.: Vol. 34). (Illus.). 1970. Repr. of 1903 ed. lib. bdg. 75.00 (ISBN 0-306-71372-1). Da Capo.
Brown, Gwen, et al. Educating Adolescents with Behavior Disorders. (Special Education Ser.). 448p. Date not set. text ed. 18.95 (ISBN 0-675-08056-8). Merrill.
Brown, H., jt. auth. see Harvey, D.
Brown, H. C., Jr. & Brown, Velma. Preparing for Effective Bible Teaching. LC 76-157404. 1971. pap. 2.50 o.p. (ISBN 0-8054-3417-8). Broadman.
Brown, H. Douglas, jt. ed. see Wardhaugh, Ronald.
Brown, H. M. Thought-Patterns for Compositions. (Illus.). 400p. 1976. pap. 9.95 (ISBN 0-13-919985-3). P-H.
Brown, H. Miles. Cornish Clocks & Clockmakers. (Illus.). 102p. 1980. Repr. 14.95 (ISBN 0-7153-4999-6). David & Charles.
Brown, Harold. Most Splendid Men. (Illus.). 192p. 1981. 12.50 (ISBN 0-7137-1107-8, Pub. by Blandford Pr England). Sterling.
Brown, Harold, et al. Crystallographic Groups of Four-Dimensional Space. (Wiley Monographs in Crystallography). 1978. 55.50 (ISBN 0-471-03095-3, Pub. by Wiley-Interscience). Wiley.
Brown, Harold O. Death Before Birth. LC 77-13884. 1977. 5.95 o.p. (ISBN -08407-5119-2). Nelson.
Brown, Harriet C. Grandmother Brown's Hundred Years: 1827-1927. Baxter, Annette K., ed. LC 79-8778. (Signal Lives Ser.). (Illus.). 1980. Repr. of 1929 ed. lib. bdg. 36.00x (ISBN 0-405-12827-4). Arno.
Brown, Harriette J. Handweaving: For Pleasure & Profit. (Illus.). 1952. 7.95 o.p. (ISBN 0-06-030990-3, HarpT). Har-Row.
Brown, Harry G. Selected Articles by Harry Gunnison Brown: The Case for Land Value Taxation. 320p. 1980. 12.50x (ISBN 0-911312-50-1). Schalkenbach.
Brown, Harry W., tr. see Azevedo, Aluisio.
Brown, Henry, ed. Protein Nutrition. (Illus.). 256p. 1974. 27.50 (ISBN 0-398-02897-4). C C Thomas.
Brown, Henry C., Jr., et al. Steps to the Sermon. LC 63-19068. 1963. 8.50 (ISBN 0-8054-2103-3). Broadman.
Brown, Herbert P. & Schanzer, Stephan N. Female Sterilization by Vaginal Tubal Ligation. 200p. 1981. text ed. 15.00 (ISBN 0-88416-356-3). PSG Pub.
Brown, Howard M. Music in the Renaissance. (History of Music Ser.). (Illus.). 368p. 1976. pap. text ed. 12.95x (ISBN 0-13-608497-4). P-H.
Brown, Howard M., ed. Italian Opera Librettos. LC 76-20993. (Italian Opera 1640-1770 Ser.: Vol. 52). 1979. lib. bdg. 75.00 (ISBN 0-8240-2651-9). Garland Pub.
--Italian Opera Librettos. LC 76-20993. (Italian Opera Ser. 1640 to 1770: Vol. 60). 1979. lib. bdg. 75.00 (ISBN 0-8240-2659-4); lib. bdg. 3700.00 set of 60 vols. (ISBN 0-686-60104-1). Garland Pub.
Brown, Howard M., ed. see Albinoni, Tomaso.
Brown, Howard M., ed. see Cavalli, Francesco.
Brown, Howard M., ed. see Cesti, Antonio.
Brown, Howard M., ed. see Latilla, Gaetano.
Brown, Howard M., ed. see Mancini, Francesco.
Brown, Howard M., ed. see Pasquini, Bernardo.
Brown, Howard M., ed. see Vinci, Leonardo.
Brown, Hugh A. Cataclysms of the Earth. (Illus.). 288p. pap. 5.50 (ISBN 0-8334-1778-9). Steinerbks.
Brown, Ida M., jt. auth. see Snyder, Louis L.
Brown, Imogene E. American Aristides: A Biography of George Wythe. LC 77-89776. 1980. 28.50 (ISBN 0-8386-2142-2). Fairleigh Dickinson.
Brown, Ira L. Georgia Colony. LC 73-95174. (Forge of Freedom Ser). (Illus.). (gr. 5-8). 1970. 8.95 (ISBN 0-02-714900-5, CCPr). Macmillan.
Brown, Irene B. Morning Glory Afternoon. LC 80-18495. 224p. (gr. 5-9). 1981. PLB 9.95 (ISBN 0-689-30802-7). Atheneum.
--Run from a Scarecrow. (Midwestern Memories Ser.). (Illus.). (gr. 5-9). 1978. 5.95 (ISBN 0-570-07806-7, 39-1001); pap. 3.50 (ISBN 0-570-07801-6, 39-1011). Concordia.
--Skitterbrain. LC 78-18349. (gr. 5 up). 1978. 6.95 (ISBN 0-525-66587-0). Elsevier-Nelson.
Brown, Irving H. Gypsy Fires in America. LC 74-1035. Repr. of 1924 ed. 18.00 (ISBN 0-8103-3942-0). Gale.
Brown, Ivan W., ed. see International Conference On Hyperbaric Medicine - 3rd - Durham - N. C. - 1965.
Brown, Ivor. A Rhapsody of Words. 1972. 5.95 (ISBN 0-370-00333-0). Transatlantic.
--A Ring of Words. 1972. 5.95 (ISBN 0-370-00426-4). Transatlantic.
Brown, J. Recall & Recognition. LC 75-8770. 1976. 43.75 (ISBN 0-471-11229-1, Pub. by Wiley-Interscience). Wiley.
--A Socioeconomic History of Argentina: Seventeen Seventy-Six to Eighteen Sixty. LC 78-6800. (Latin American Studies: No. 35). (Illus.). 1979. 35.50 (ISBN 0-521-22219-2). Cambridge U Pr.
Brown, J., jt. auth. see Finkel, L.
Brown, J. A., jt. auth. see Aitchison, John.
Brown, J. Guthrie, ed. Hydro-Electric Engineering Practice: Mechanical & Electrical Engineering, Vol. 2. 2nd ed. (Illus.). 1970. 95.00x (ISBN 0-216-89056-X). Intl Ideas.
Brown, J. H. see Kenedi, R. M.
Brown, J. L., jt. auth. see Owler, L. W.
Brown, J. W., jt. auth. see Wilson, Paul R.
Brown, James & Seib, Philip M. The Art of Politics: Electoral Strategies & Campaign Management. LC 76-1872. (Illus.). 225p. 1976. pap. 7.95x (ISBN 0-88284-036-3). Alfred Pub.
Brown, James A. Techniques of Persuasion. (Orig.). 1963. pap. 2.95 o.p. (ISBN 0-14-020604-3, Pelican). Penguin.
Brown, James A., jt. auth. see Phillips, Philip.
Brown, James D. & Stratton, Stephen S. British Musical Biography: A Dictionary of Musical Artists, Authors & Composers, Born in Britain & Its Colonies. LC 76-139197. (Music Ser). 1971. Repr. of 1897 ed. lib. bdg. 42.50 (ISBN 0-306-70076-X). Da Capo.
Brown, James F., jt. ed. see King, Robert R.
Brown, James I. Programmed Vocabulary. 3rd ed. (The CPD Approach). 1980. pap. text ed. 8.95 (ISBN 0-13-729707-6). P-H.
--Reading Power. 1975. pap. 9.95x (ISBN 0-669-85571-5). Heath.
--Reading Power. alternate ed. 1978. pap. text ed. 9.95x (ISBN 0-669-00774-9). Heath.
Brown, James M. see Brown, O. Z.
Brown, James W. Heriberto Frias. (World Authors Ser.: No. 486). 1978. lib. bdg. 12.50 (ISBN 0-8057-6327-9). Twayne.
--New Media in Public Libraries: A Survey of Current Practices. pap. 12.50 (ISBN 0-88432-003-0). Gaylord Prof Pubns.
Brown, James W. & Brown, Shirley N., eds. Educational Media Yearbook 1980. 6th ed. LC 73-4891. 400p. 1980. lib. bdg. 25.00x (ISBN 0-87287-223-8). Libs Unl.
Brown, James W. & Lewis, Richard B., eds. Audio-Visual Instruction: Technology, Media & Methods. 5th ed. (Illus.). 1976. text ed. 19.95 (ISBN 0-07-008165-4, C); instructor's manual 5.95 (ISBN 0-07-008171-9); transparencies 25.00 (ISBN 0-07-008172-7). McGraw.
Brown, Jamieson-Fausett. Comentario Exegetico y Explicativo De la Biblia Tomo II. Quarles, Jaime C. & Quarles, Lemuel C., trs. 1979. pap. 8.95 (ISBN 0-311-03005-X). Casa Bautista.
Brown, Jan. Buy It Right. 1974. pap. 2.95 o.p. (ISBN 0-531-02753-8). Watts.
Brown, Janet. Feminist Drama: Definition & Critical Analysis. LC 79-22382. 167p. 1979. 10.00 (ISBN 0-8108-1267-3). Scarecrow.
Brown, Jason W., ed. Jargonaphasia. (Perspectives in Neurolinguistics & Psycholinguistics Ser.). 1981. price not set (ISBN 0-12-137580-3). Acad Pr.
Brown, Jean. A Song to Sing & a Tale to Tell. 174p. 1980. 14.95 (ISBN 0-906191-43-2, Pub. by Thule Pr England). Intl Schol Bk Serv.
Brown, Jeffrey L. Telephone Medicine: The Use of the Telephone & the Management of Pediatric Patients. LC 80-16674. (Illus.). 154p. 1980. pap. text ed. 11.95 (ISBN 0-8016-0856-2). Mosby.
Brown, Jerald. Instant BASIC. LC 77-70966. (Illus., Orig.). 1977. pap. 10.95 (ISBN 0-918398-21-5). Dilithium Pr.
Brown, Jerald R., jt. auth. see Finkel, Leroy.
Brown, Jeremy, jt. auth. see Power, John.
Brown, Jerram. The Evolution of Behavior. 900p. 1975. text ed. 19.95x (ISBN 0-393-09295-X). Norton.
Brown, Jerry E. Under the City of Angels. 304p. (Orig.). 1981. pap. 1.95 (ISBN 0-553-14605-X). Bantam.
Brown, Jim. Tennis Without Lessons. (Illus.). 1977. 12.95 (ISBN 0-13-903252-5); pap. 6.95 (ISBN 0-13-903245-2). P-H.
Brown, Jo G. The Good Food Compendium. LC 78-22306. (Illus.). 336p. 1981. pap. 10.95 (ISBN 0-385-13523-8, Dolp). Doubleday.
Brown, Joan W, compiled by. Dia-Tras-Dia Con Billy Graham. Orig. Title: Day by Day with Billy Graham. 1978. 2.70 (ISBN 0-311-40039-6). Casa Bautista.
Brown, Joan W., compiled by. Dia-Tras-Dia Con Billy Graham. Orig. Title: Day by Day with Billy Graham. 1978. 2.70 (ISBN 0-311-40039-6, Edit Mundo). Casa Bautista.
Brown, John. Discourses & Sayings of Our Lord Jesus Christ, 3 vols. Date not set. Set. 45.00 (ISBN 0-88469-142-X). BMH Bks.
--First Peter, 2 vols. 1980. 29.95 (ISBN 0-85151-204-6); Vol. 1, 577 Pp. (ISBN 0-85151-205-4); Vol. 2, 640 Pp. (ISBN 0-85151-206-2). Banner of Truth.
--Hebrews. (Geneva Commentaries Ser.). 1976. 12.95 (ISBN 0-85151-099-X). Banner of Truth.
--The Intercessory Prayer of Our Lord Jesus Christ. 1978. 10.50 (ISBN 0-686-12961-X). Klock & Klock.
--Letters Upon the Poetry & Music of the Italian Opera: Addressed to a Friend. LC 80-2261. 1981. Repr. of 1789 ed. 22.50 (ISBN 0-404-18814-1). AMS Pr.
--Life, Trial & Execution of Captain John Brown, Known As "Old Brown of Ossawatomie". LC 69-18827. (Law, Politics & History Ser). 1969. Repr. of 1859 ed. lib. bdg. 17.50 (ISBN 0-306-71250-4). Da Capo.
--Parting Counsels: Exposition of II Peter 1. (Banner of Truth Geneva Series Commentaries). 1980. 11.50 (ISBN 0-85151-301-8). Banner of Truth.
--Peter One, 2 vols. (Geneva Commentaries Ser.). 1980. Set. 29.95 (ISBN 0-85151-204-6). Vol. 1 (ISBN 0-85151-205-4). Vol. 2 (ISBN 0-85151-206-2). Banner of Truth.
--The Ressurection of Life. 1978. 13.25 (ISBN 0-686-12962-8). Klock & Klock.
--The Sufferings & the Glories of the Messiah. (Giant Summit Bks.). 352p. 1981. pap. 5.95 (ISBN 0-8010-0792-5). Baker Bk.
Brown, John, jt. auth. see Clarke, R. H.
Brown, John A., jt. auth. see Ruby, Robert H.
Brown, John H. History of Texas, from Sixteen Eighty-Five to Eighteen Ninety-Two, 2 vols. (Illus.). Set. 45.00 (ISBN 0-8363-0045-9). Jenkins.
Brown, John H. & Grant, Steven A. The Russian Empire & Soviet Union: A Guide to Manuscripts & Archival Materials in the United States. (Libary Catalogs Supplement). 1981. lib. bdg. 75.00 (ISBN 0-8161-1300-9). G K Hall.
Brown, John M., jt. auth. see Carr, Joseph J.

Brown, John R. Shakespeare's Dramatic Style. 1970. 7.95x o.p. (ISBN 0-435-18081-9); pap. text ed. 2.95x (ISBN 0-435-18082-7). Heinemann Ed.

Brown, John R., ed. Drama & the Theatre: With Radio, Film & Television; an Outline for the Student. (Outlines Ser). 1971. 14.00x (ISBN 0-7100-6971-5); pap. 7.95 (ISBN 0-7100-7053-5). Routledge & Kegan.

Brown, John R. & Harris, Bernard, eds. American Poetry. (Stratford-Upon-Avon Studies: No. 7). 244p. 1973. pap. text ed. 9.75x (ISBN 0-8419-5814-9). Holmes & Meier.

--Contemporary Theatre. (Stratford-Upon-Avon Studies: No. 4). 208p. 1962. pap. text ed. 15.00x (ISBN 0-8419-5811-4). Holmes & Meier.

--Hamlet. (Stratford - Upon -Avon Studies: No. 5). 212p. 1963. pap. text ed. 10.75x (ISBN 0-8419-5812-2). Holmes & Meier.

--Later Shakespeare. (Stratford-Upon-Avon Studies: No. 8). 264p. 1966. pap. text ed. 9.95x (ISBN 0-8419-5815-7). Holmes & Meier.

Brown, John R., ed. see Shakespeare, William.

Brown, Jonathan. History & Present Condition of St. Domingo, 2 vols. 1972. Repr. of 1837 ed. 65.00x (ISBN 0-7146-2704-6, F Cass Co). Biblio Dist.

--Zurbaran. LC 73-10481. (Library of Great Painters Ser.). (Illus.). 160p. 1974. 28.50 o.p. (ISBN 0-8109-0549-3). Abrams.

Brown, Jonathan & Elliott, John H. A Palace for a King: The Buen Retiro & the Court of Philip IV. LC 80-13659. (Illus.). 320p. 1980. 29.95x (ISBN 0-300-02507-6). Yale U Pr.

--A Palace for a King: The Buen Retiro & the Court of Philip IV. LC 79-24393. (Illus.). 320p. 1980. 29.95x (ISBN 0-300-02507-6). Yale U Pr.

Brown, Jonathan, jt. auth. see Enggass, Robert.

Brown, Joseph E. Oil Spills: Danger in the Sea. LC 78-7743. (Illus.). (gr. 5 up). 1978. 5.95 (ISBN 0-396-07607-6). Dodd.

--The Sea's Harvest: The Story of Aquaculture. LC 75-9646. (Illus.). 96p. (gr. 5 up). 1975. PLB 5.95 (ISBN 0-396-07153-8). Dodd.

Brown, Joseph E., ed. The Sacred Pipe: Black Elk's Account of the Seven Rites of Oglala Sioux. (Civilization of the American Indian Ser.: No. 36). (Illus.). 1953. 9.95 (ISBN 0-8061-0272-1). U of Okla Pr.

--Sacred Pipe: Black Elk's Account of the Seven Rites of the Oglala Sioux. (Metaphysical Library Ser.). 1971. pap. 3.25 (ISBN 0-14-003346-7). Penguin.

Brown, Joseph F. Diabetes Dictionary & Guide. LC 77-92938. (Illus.). 1978. 13.95 (ISBN 0-9601484-1-8). Press West.

Brown, Judith R. Back to the Beanstalk: Enchantment & Reality for Couples. LC 79-89476. 1980. 6.95 (ISBN 0-930626-03-6); pap. 3.95 (ISBN 0-930626-04-4). Psych & Consul Assocs.

Brown, Judson S. & Cole, James K., eds. Nebraska Symposium on Motivation, 1953. LC 53-11655. (Nebraska Symposia on Motivation Ser: Vol. 1). 1953. pap. 3.95x (ISBN 0-8032-5600-0). U of Nebr Pr.

Brown, K. C., jt. auth. see Dickinson, W. C.

Brown, Karen A., ed. see Hammell, Grandin K.

Brown, Karl. Adventures of D. W. Griffith. Brownlow, Kevin, ed. (Illus.). 251p. 1973. 10.00 (ISBN 0-374-10093-4). FS&G.

Brown, Kenneth S. & ReVelle, Jack B. Quantitative Methods for Managerial Decisions. LC 76-10408. (Illus.). 1978. text ed. 17.95 (ISBN 0-201-06448-0). A-W.

Brown, Kermit. Technology of Artificial Lift Methods, Vols. 2a & 2b. 1980. 55.00 ea. Vol. 2a, 736 P (ISBN 0-87814-119-7). Vol. 2b, 607 P (ISBN 0-87814-133-2). Pennwell Pub.

Brown, L. B. Psychology in Contemporary China. 320p. 1981. 45.00 (ISBN 0-08-026063-2). Pergamon.

Brown, L. Dave, jt. auth. see Alderfer, Clayton P.

Brown, L. F., et al. Pennsylvanian Depositional Systems in North-Central Texas: A Guide for Interpreting Terrigenous Clastic Facies in a Cratonic Basin. (Illus.). 122p. 1973. Repr. 3.50 (GB 14). Bur Econ Geology.

Brown, L. M. Aims of Education. LC 76-120600. 1970. pap. text ed. 8.75x (ISBN 0-8077-1129-2). Tchrs Coll.

Brown, Larry, jt. auth. see Bing, Stephen.

Brown, Laura. English Dramatic Form, Sixteen-Sixty to Seveenteen-Sixty: An Essay in Generic History. LC 80-25702. 264p. 1981. 19.50x (ISBN 0-300-02585-8). Yale U Pr.

Brown, Lennox see Harrison, Paul C.

Brown, Leslie, jt. auth. see Weick, Friedhelm.

Brown, Lester R. Human Needs & the Security of Nations. LC 78-51516. (Headline Ser.: 238). (Illus.). 1978. pap. 2.00 (ISBN 0-87124-045-9). Foreign Policy.

--The Interdependence of Nations. (Development Papers: No. 10). 70p. 1972. pap. 1.00 (ISBN 0-686-28679-0). Overseas Dev Council.

--Our Daily Bread. LC 75-851. (Headline Ser.: No. 225). (Illus.). 1975. pap. 2.00 (ISBN 0-87124-030-0). Foreign Policy.

Brown, Lewis S., ed. see Ellenberger, W., et al.

Brown, Lloyd. Amiri Baraka. (United States Author Ser.: No. 383). 1980. lib. bdg. 9.95 (ISBN 0-8057-7137-9). Twayne.

Brown, Lloyd A. The Story of Maps. LC 79-52395. (Illus.). 417p. 1980. Repr. of 1949 ed. 11.95 (ISBN 0-938164-00-7). Vintage Bk Co.

Brown, Lloyd A. & Peckham, Howard H., eds. Revolutionary War Journals of Henry Dearborn, 1775-1783. LC 74-146143. (Era of the American Revolution Ser). 1971. Repr. of 1939 ed. lib. bdg. 29.50 (ISBN 0-306-70107-3). Da Capo.

Brown, Lloyd L. Paul Robeson Rediscovered. 1976. 1.00 (ISBN 0-89977-028-2). Am Inst Marxist.

Brown, Lloyd W. West Indian Poetry. (World Authors Ser.: No. 422). 1978. lib. bdg. 12.50 (ISBN 0-8057-6262-0). Twayne.

--Women Writers in Black Africa. LC 80-1710. (Contributions in Women's Studies: No. 21). 256p. 1981. lib. bdg. 23.95 (ISBN 0-313-22540-0, BRW/). Greenwood.

Brown, Lorraine, jt. auth. see O'Connor, John.

Brown, Louise C. Elephant Seals. LC 78-25623. (Skylight Bks.). (Illus.). (gr. 2-5). 1979. 4.95 (ISBN 0-396-07665-3). Dodd.

Brown, Lucy M. & Christie, Ian R. Bibliography of British History Seventeen Eighty-Nine to Eighteen Fifty-One. 1977. 89.00x (ISBN 0-19-822390-0). Oxford U Pr.

Brown, M. Resistance of Pseudomonas Aeruginosa. 335p. 1975. 60.50 (ISBN 0-471-11210-0). Wiley.

Brown, M., et al. American Art: Painting, Sculpture, Architecture, Decorative Arts, Photography. 1979. 21.95 (ISBN 0-13-024653-0). P-H.

Brown, M. B., jt. ed. see Dixon, W. J.

Brown, M. L. Firearms in Colonial America: The Impact of History & Technology 1492-1792. LC 80-27221. (Illus.). 450p. 1980. 45.00 (ISBN 0-87474-290-0). Smithsonian.

Brown, M. Ralph. Legal Psychology. (Historical Foundations of Forensic Psychiatry & Psychology Ser.). (Illus.). 346p. 1980. Repr. of 1926 ed. lib. bdg. 35.00 (ISBN 0-306-76065-7). Da Capo.

Brown, M. T. New Juice. (Illus.). 1980. pap. 9.95 o.p. (ISBN 0-930490-32-0). Future Shop.

--The Sidlatches Are Coming. (Illus.). 1980. pap. 9.95 o.p. (ISBN 0-930490-29-0). Future Shop.

Brown, MacAlister, jt. auth. see Zasloff, Joseph J.

Brown, MacKenzie, jt. auth. see Easton, Robert.

Brown, Malcolm. The Politics of Irish Literature: From Thomas Davis to W. B. Yeats. LC 72-152328. (Washington Paperback Ser.: No. 67). 443p. 1972. 12.00 (ISBN 0-295-95170-2); pap. 3.95 (ISBN 0-295-95280-6). U of Wash Pr.

Brown, Malcolm & Webb, John N. Seven Stranded Coal Towns: A Study of an American Depressed Area. LC 76-165680. (FDR & the Era of the New Deal Ser). 1971. Repr. of 1941 ed. lib. bdg. 19.50 (ISBN 0-306-70355-6). Da Capo.

Brown, Malcolm M., jt. auth. see McGovern, Vincent J.

Brown, Marc. Arthur's Eyes. 32p. (gr. 1-3). 1981. pap. 1.95 (ISBN 0-380-53389-8, Camelot). Avon.

--Arthur's Nose. 32p. (gr. 1-3). 1981. pap. 1.95 (ISBN 0-380-53397-9, Camelot). Avon.

--Arthur's Valentine. (Illus.). (gr. 1-3). 1980. 7.95g (ISBN 0-316-11062-0, Pub. by Atlantic-Little Brown). Little.

--Finger Rhymes. LC 80-10173. (Illus.). 32p. (ps-3). 1980. PLB 8.95 (ISBN 0-525-29732-4, Unicorn). Dutton.

--Lenny & Lola. (ps-3). 1978. 6.95 o.p. (ISBN 0-525-33465-3). Dutton.

--Moose & Goose. (Illus.). (ps-3). 1978. PLB 6.95 o.p. (ISBN 0-525-35175-2). Dutton.

--One Two Three: An Animal Counting Book. 32p. (gr. k-3). 1976. PLB 6.95 (ISBN 0-316-11064-7, Pub. by Atlantic Monthly Pr). Little.

--The True Francine. (Illus.). 32p. (gr. 1-3). 1981. 8.95 (ISBN 0-316-11212-7, Atlantic). Little.

--Witches Four. LC 79-5263. (Illus.). 48p. (ps-3). 1980. 4.95 (ISBN 0-8193-1013-1); PLB 5.95 (ISBN 0-8193-1014-X). Parents.

Brown, Marcia. All Butterflies. (Illus.). 32p. (ps-2). pap. 2.95 (ISBN 0-689-70483-6, A-110, Aladdin). Atheneum.

--Once a Mouse. LC 61-14769. (Illus.). (ps-5). 1961. reinforced bdg. 9.95 (ISBN 0-684-12662-1, ScribJ). Scribner.

--Stone Soup. (Illus.). (gr. k-3). 1947. reinforced bdg. 8.95 (ISBN 0-684-92296-7, ScribJ); pap. 2.95 (ISBN 0-684-16217-2, SBF1, ScribJ). Scribner.

--Touch Will Tell. (Marcia Brown Concept Library Ser.). (Illus.). (gr. 1-4). 1979. 4.95 (ISBN 0-531-02384-2); PLB 7.90 s&l (ISBN 0-531-02931-X). Watts.

--Walk with Your Eyes. (Marcia Brown Concept Library). (Illus.). (gr. 1-4). 1979. 4.95 (ISBN 0-531-02385-0); PLB 7.90 s&l (ISBN 0-531-02925-5). Watts.

Brown, Marcia & Andersen, Hans C. The Snow Queen. LC 72-168499. (Encore Ser.). (Illus.). 96p. (gr. 1-5). 1972. 9.95 (ISBN 0-684-16564-3, ScribJ). Scribner.

Brown, Marcia & Perrault, Charles. Cinderella. (Illus.). 32p. (gr. k-3). pap. 2.95 (ISBN 0-689-70484-4, A-111, Aladdin). Atheneum.

Brown, Margaret. Coloring the Smithsonian. pap. 1.50 o.p. (ISBN 0-445-08302-6). Popular Lib.

--Wheel on the Chimney. (Illus.). (gr. k-3). 1954. 9.95 (ISBN 0-397-30288-6). Lippincott.

Brown, Margaret W. Christmas in the Barn. LC 52-7858. (Illus.). (gr. k-3). 1949. 7.95 (ISBN 0-690-19272-X, TYC-J); pap. 7.89 (ISBN 0-686-68499-0). T Y Crowell.

--Color Kittens. (Illus.). (ps-3). 1949. PLB 7.62 (ISBN 0-307-60546-9, Golden Pr). Western Pub.

--The Friendly Book. (ps-1). 1954. PLB 5.00 (ISBN 0-307-60592-2, Golden Pr). Western Pub.

--The Golden Egg Book. (Illus.). 32p. (ps-1). 1976. 2.95 (ISBN 0-307-12045-7, Golden Pr); PLB 7.62 (ISBN 0-307-60462-4). Western Pub.

--The Golden Egg Book. (Illus.). (ps-2). 1947. PLB 5.00 (ISBN 0-307-60456-X, Golden Pr). Western Pub.

--The Golden Sleepy Book. (Illus.). (ps-2). 1971. PLB 7.15 o.p. (ISBN 0-307-62038-7, Golden Pr). Western Pub.

--Home for a Bunny. (Illus.). 32p. (ps-2). 1975. 1.95 (ISBN 0-307-10446-X, Golden Pr); PLB 7.62 (ISBN 0-307-60446-2). Western Pub.

--Playtime to Bedtime, 6 bks. (Illus.). (ps). Date not set. boxed set 4.95 (ISBN 0-307-15515-3, Golden Pr). Western Pub.

--Pussy Willow. (Illus.). (ps-3). 1951. PLB 7.62 (ISBN 0-307-62448-X, Golden Pr). Western Pub.

--The Steamroller: A Fantasy. LC 74-78107. (Illus.). 32p. (gr. k-3). 1974. 5.95 o.s.i. (ISBN 0-8027-6191-7); PLB 5.85 o.s.i. (ISBN 0-8027-6192-5). Walker & Co.

--Train to Timbuctoo. (A Young Reader Ser.). (Illus.). (gr. k-3). 1979. PLB 5.00 (ISBN 0-307-60118-8, Golden Pr). Western Pub.

--Where Have You Been? (Illus.). (gr. k-2). 1963. 3.50 o.s.i. (ISBN 0-8038-8018-9). Hastings.

--Wonderful Storybook. 1974. PLB 10.69 o.p. (ISBN 0-307-65777-9, Golden Pr). Western Pub.

Brown, Margaret W. & Strugnell, Ann. Once Upon a Time in a Pig Pen. LC 77-5077. (Illus.). 64p. (ps-4). 1980. PLB 10.95 (ISBN 0-201-00343-0, A-W Childrens). A-W.

Brown, Marguerite. Magnificent Muslims. 1981. write for info. (ISBN 0-911026-10-X). New World Press NY.

Brown, Marie & Murphy, Mary A. Ambulatory Pediatrics for Nurses. 2nd ed. (Illus.). 624p. 1980. text ed. 17.95 (ISBN 0-07-008291-X, HP). McGraw.

Brown, Marie S. & Murphy, Mary A. Ambulatory Pediatrics for Nurses. (Illus.). 480p. 1975. 15.95 o.p. (ISBN 0-07-008290-1, HP). McGraw.

Brown, Marilyn M. An Exchange of Gifts. (Illus.). (gr. 10-12). 1980. pap. 6.95 (ISBN 0-938536-00-1). Wilton.

Brown, Marion. Marion Brown's Southern Cook Book. rev. ed. 489p. 1968. 12.95 (ISBN 0-8078-1065-7); pap. 8.50 (ISBN 0-8078-4078-5). U of NC Pr.

Brown, Marion & Crone, Ruth. Silent Storm. (gr. 6-8). 1963. 7.95 o.p. (ISBN 0-687-38453-2). Abingdon.

Brown, Marion M. Homeward the Arrow's Flight. LC 80-11957. (Illus.). 176p. (gr. 7 up). 1980. 7.95g (ISBN 0-687-17300-0). Abingdon.

Brown, Mark. Left Handed: Right Handed. LC 80-66094. (Illus.). 160p. 1980. 14.95 (ISBN 0-7153-7510-5). David & Charles.

--Memory Matters. LC 77-71252. (Illus.). 1977. 14.50x (ISBN 0-8448-1091-6). Crane-Russak Co.

Brown, Mark H. The Plainsmen of the Yellowstone: A History of the Yellowstone Basin. LC 60-5262. (Illus.). 1969. pap. 8.75 (ISBN 0-8032-5026-6, BB 397, Bison). U of Nebr Pr.

Brown, Marshall. The Shape of German Romanticism. LC 79-14313. 1979. 15.00x (ISBN 0-8014-1228-5). Cornell U Pr.

--Wit & Humor of Well-Known Quotations. LC 70-146919. 1971. Repr. of 1905 ed. 20.00 (ISBN 0-8103-3644-8). Gale.

Brown, Marshall G. & Stein, Gordon. Freethought in the United States: A Descriptive Bibliography. LC 77-91103. 1978. lib. bdg. 17.50 (ISBN 0-313-20036-X, BFT/). Greenwood.

Brown, Martin, ed. Social Responsibility of the Scientist. LC 75-143503. 1971. 9.95 o.s.i. (ISBN 0-02-904790-0); pap. text ed. 5.95 (ISBN 0-02-904730-7). Free Pr.

Brown, Mary L. Occupational Health Nursing. LC 80-21024. 368p. 1981. text ed. 21.95 (ISBN 0-8261-2250-7); pap. text ed. cancelled (ISBN 0-8261-2251-5). Springer Pub.

Brown, Maurice J. Chopin: An Index of His Works in Chronological Order. 2nd ed. LC 70-39498. (Music Ser.). 1972. Repr. of 1960 ed. 22.50 (ISBN 0-306-70500-1). Da Capo.

--Essays on Schubert. LC 77-22216. (Music Reprint Ser.). (Illus.). 1977. Repr. of 1966 ed. lib. bdg. 25.00 (ISBN 0-306-77439-9). Da Capo.

--Schubert: A Critical Biography. LC 77-4160. (Music Reprint Ser., 1977). (Illus.). 1977. Repr. of 1958 ed. lib. bdg. 29.50 (ISBN 0-306-77409-7). Da Capo.

Brown, Max & Shinn, Duane. One Hundred & One Creative Uses for Yesterday's Newspaper. 1978. pap. 3.95 o.p. (ISBN 0-912732-48-2). Duane Shinn.

Brown, Meta. Basic Drug Calculations for Nurses. LC 79-10785. 1979. pap. 9.50 (ISBN 0-8016-4488-7). Mosby.

Brown, Michael. Food & Wine of Southwest France. (Illus.). 216p. 1981. 35.00 (ISBN 0-7134-1847-8, Pub. by Batsford England). David & Charles.

--Laying Waste: The Poisoning of America by Toxic Chemicals. 1981. pap. 3.50. WSP.

--Politics & Anti-Politics of the Young. Krinsky, Fred & Boskin, Joseph, eds. LC 71-75965. (Insight Ser: Studies in Contemporary Issues). (Orig.). 1969. pap. text ed. 3.95x (ISBN 0-02-473640-6, 47364). Macmillan.

--Working the Street: Police Discretion & the Dilemmas of Reform. LC 80-69175. 380p. 1981. text ed. 15.00 (ISBN 0-87154-190-4). Russell Sage.

Brown, Michael & Woolams, Stan. TA: The Total Handbook of Transcendental Analysis. (Illus.). 1979. 15.95 (ISBN 0-13-881920-3, Spec); pap. 6.95 (ISBN 0-13-881912-2). P-H.

Brown, Michael B. Essays on Imperialism. (Illus.). 1972. pap. text ed. 5.25x (ISBN 0-85124-110-7). Humanities.

--What Economics Is About. 368p. 1970. pap. 7.95x o.p. (ISBN 0-8464-0966-6). Beekman Pubs.

Brown, Michael H. The Case for Polygamy. 1976. pap. 4.95 (ISBN 0-685-63906-1). Madison Pub.

Brown, Michael J. Itinerant Ambassador: The Life of Sir Thomas Roe. LC 77-94064. (Illus.). 324p. 1970. 12.00x (ISBN 0-8131-1192-7). U Pr of Ky.

Brown, Michael T. In & Out of Your Mind. LC 78-55992. (Illus.). 1978. softcover 7.95 o.p. (ISBN 0-930490-09-6). Future Shop.

--The Order of Melchisedech. LC 78-55995. 1980. softcover 7.95 o.p. (ISBN 0-930490-13-4). Future Shop.

--Suzy & the Rembrandt Kid. LC 78-55986. 1980. softcover 7.95 o.p. (ISBN 0-930490-12-6). Future Shop.

--You Are Creative! Become an Endless Producer of Good Ideas. LC 77-84036. (Illus.). 1978. 12.95 o.p. (ISBN 0-930490-02-9). Future Shop.

Brown, Michele. Food by Appointment: Royal Recipes 1066. (Illus.). 1978. 17.95 (ISBN 0-241-89635-5, Pub. by Hamish Hamilton England). David & Charles.

Brown, Mike. The New Nineteen Eighty Suppressed Inventions & How They Work. 2nd ed. 106p. 1974. pap. 11.95. Madison Pub.

--P. K. A Report on the Power of Psychokinesis, Mental Energy That Moves Matter. LC 76-21121. (Illus.). 320p. pap. 5.95 (ISBN 0-8334-1776-2). Steinerbks.

--Suppressed Inventions & How They Work. 1974. 5.95 o.p. (ISBN 0-913808-03-2); pap. 1.95 o.p. (ISBN 0-913808-04-0). Madison Pub.

Brown, Mollie, ed. Readings in Gerontology. 2nd ed. LC 77-14088. (Illus.). 1978. pap. text ed. 8.00 (ISBN 0-8016-0734-5). Mosby.

Brown, Montague & Lewis, Howard L. Hospital Management Systems: Multi-Unit Organization & Delivery of Health Care. LC 76-15769. 1976. 25.95 (ISBN 0-912862-22-X). Aspen Systems.

Brown, Montague & McCool, Barbara P. Multihospital Systems: Strategies for Organization & Management. LC 79-23439. (Illus.). 564p. 1979. text ed. 36.00 (ISBN 0-89443-169-2). Aspen Systems.

Brown, Montague, ed. Health Care Management Review. LC 75-45767. annual subscription 44.50 (ISBN 0-912862-50-5). Aspen Systems.

Brown, Muriel. Introduction to Social Administration in Britain. 1969. text ed. 4.00x (ISBN 0-09-110271-5, Hutchinson U Lib); pap. text ed. 2.75x (ISBN 0-09-084093-3, Hutchinson U Lib). Humanities.

Brown, Muriel & Baldwin, Sally, eds. The Year Book of Social Policy in Britain, 1977. 1978. 36.50 (ISBN 0-7100-0066-9). Routledge & Kegan.

--The Year Book of Social Policy in Britain 1979. 272p. (Orig.). 1980. pap. 45.00 (ISBN 0-7100-0690-X). Routledge & Kegan.

Brown, Nigel. Notes on Gogol's "The Government Inspector". 1974. pap. text ed. 1.50x o.p. (ISBN 0-435-18375-3). Heinemann Ed.

Brown, Norman D., ed. One of Cleburne's Command. LC 80-16447. 224p. 1980. 14.95 (ISBN 0-292-76014-0). U of Tex Pr.

Brown, Norman L., ed. Renewable Energy Resources & Rural Applications in the Developing World. (AAAS Selected Symposium Ser: No. 6). (Illus.). 1978. lib. bdg. 20.00x (ISBN 0-89158-433-1). Westview.

Brown, Norman O. Life Against Death: The Psychoanalytical Meaning of History. LC 59-5369. 1959. 20.00x (ISBN 0-8195-3005-0, Pub. by Wesleyan U Pr); pap. 8.95 (ISBN 0-8195-6010-3). Columbia U Pr.

Brown, Norman O., tr. see Hesiod.

Brown, O. Z. O. Z. Brown: A True Narrative of Daniel McCollum, a Captive Among the Indians During the Revolutionary War, Repr. Of 1853. Washington, Wilcomb E., ed. Incl. James Moore Brown: The Captives of Abb's Valley, a Legend of Frontier Life. By a Son of Mary Moore. Brown, James M. Repr. of 1854 ed; Jane A. Wilson: Narrative of Sufferings...Among Comanche. in "Supplement to the Courant," XIX, No. 3, p.p. 2021, Feb. 11, 1854. Wilson, Jane A; Joseph Barney: Eighteen Years a Captive Among the Indians. A Very Interesting Narrative. In: "America's Own..."New York, 1855, VII, No. 18. Barney, Joseph. (Narratives of North American Indian Captivities Ser.: Vol. 65). 1978. lib. bdg. 44.00 (ISBN 0-8240-1689-0). Garland Pub.

Brown, Olen R. Laboratory Manual for Basic Veterinary Microbiology. (Lucas Text Ser). 1973. spiral bdg. 5.95x (ISBN 0-87543-087-2). Lucas.

Brown, Oliver B. Vital Records of Falmouth, Mass. to Eighteen Fifty. LC 76-3955. 1976. 8.00x (ISBN 0-930272-01-3). RI Mayflower.

Brown, P. J., ed. Software Portability. LC 76-40835. (Illus.). 1977. 32.95 (ISBN 0-521-21485-8); pap. 12.95x (ISBN 0-521-29725-7). Cambridge U Pr.

Brown, Palmer. Beyond the Paw-Paw Trees. (gr. 3-5). 1973. pap. 0.95 o.s.i. (ISBN 0-380-01055-0, 14605, Camelot). Avon.

Brown, Paul & Faulder, Carolyn. Learning to Love: How to Make Bad Sex Good & Good Sex Better. LC 78-52202. 188p. (Orig.). 1981. pap. 4.95 (ISBN 0-87663-559-1, Pica Pr). Universe.

Brown, Paul B., ed. Computer Technology in Neuroscience. LC 76-6884. 1976. 28.95 (ISBN 0-470-15061-0). Halsted Pr.

Brown, Paula. Highland Peoples of New Guinea. LC 77-80830. (Illus.). 1978. 29.95 (ISBN 0-521-21748-2); pap. 7.95x (ISBN 0-521-29249-2). Cambridge U Pr.

Brown, Peter. Augustine of Hippo: A Biography. 1967. 15.00 o.p. (ISBN 0-520-00186-9); pap. 4.95 o.p. (ISBN 0-520-01411-1, CAL179). U of Cal Pr.

--The Book of Kells: A Selection from the Irish Medieval Manuscripts. LC 80-7973. (Illus.). 96p. 1980. pap. 10.95 (ISBN 0-394-73960-4). Knopf.

--The Cult of the Saints: Its Rise & Function in Latin Christianity. LC 80-11210. 1980. lib. bdg. 15.00x (ISBN 0-226-07621-0). U of Chicago Pr.

--The Real Oscar. (Illus.). 256p. 1981. 15.95 (ISBN 0-87000-498-0). Arlington Hse.

Brown, Peter, ed. see D'Ordonez, Carlo.

Brown, Peter G. & MacLean, Douglas, eds. Human Rights & U. S. Foreign Policy: Principles & Applications. Principles & Applications. 1979. 18.95 (ISBN 0-669-02807-X); pap. 10.95 (ISBN 0-669-04326-5). Lexington Bks.

Brown, Peter G. & Shue, Henry, eds. Food Policy: The Responsibility of the United States in the Life & Death Choices. LC 76-57803. (Illus.). 1979. pap. text ed. 8.95 (ISBN 0-02-905170-3). Free Pr.

Brown, Peter G., et al, eds. Income Support: Conceptual & Policy Issues. (Maryland Studies in Public Philosophy Ser.). 400p. 1981. 27.50x (ISBN 0-8476-6969-6). Rowman.

Brown, Peter L. Megaliths & Masterminds. (Illus.). 1979. 14.95 o.p. (ISBN 0-684-15908-2, ScribT). Scribner.

--Star & Planet Spotting: A Field Guide to the Night Sky. (Illus.). 1974. 6.95 (ISBN 0-7137-0655-4, Pub by Blandford Pr England). Sterling.

Brown, Peter Lancaster, jt. auth. see Hickling, C. F.

Brown, Peter M. Lionardo Salvati: A Critical Biography. (Oxford Modern Language & Literature Monographs). 297p. 1974. text ed. 37.50x (ISBN 0-19-815523-9). Oxford U Pr.

Brown, Philip. The Cat That Came in from the Cold. 1978. 7.95 o.p. (ISBN 0-684-15909-0, ScribJ). Scribner.

--Uncle Whiskers. 1976. pap. 1.95 (ISBN 0-685-96256-3). Warner Bks.

Brown, Philip L., ed. Clyde Company Papers. Incl. Vol. 2. 1836-40. 1952. 8.00x (ISBN 0-19-711411-3); Vol. 5. 1851-53. 1963. 11.25x (ISBN 0-19-711594-2); Vol. 6. 1854-58. 1968. 12.00x (ISBN 0-19-711627-2); Vol. 6. 1854-58. 1968. 12.00x (ISBN 0-19-711627-2). Oxford U Pr.

Brown, Pia T., compiled by. O. S. U. Theses & Dissertations, Nineteen Seventy-One to Nineteen Seventy-Seven. (Bibliographic Ser.: No. 17). 128p. 1980. pap. 4.00 (ISBN 0-87071-137-7). Oreg St U Pr.

Brown, R. & Campbell, G. A. How to Find Out About the Chemical Industry. 1969. pap. 14.00 (ISBN 0-08-013050-X). Pergamon.

Brown, R. Allen. Origins of English Feudalism. (Historical Problems; Studies & Documents). 1973. pap. text ed. 8.95x o.p. (ISBN 0-04-901021-2). Allen Unwin.

Brown, R. Allen, ed. Castles: A History & a Guide. (Illus.). 196p. 1980. 24.95 o.p. (ISBN 0-7137-0953-7, Pub. by Blandford Pr England). Sterling.

--Proceedings of the Battle Conference on Anglo-Norman Studies II: 1979. (Illus.). 210p. 1980. 49.50x (ISBN 0-8476-3455-8). Rowman.

Brown, R. Craig, jt. auth. see Careless, James M.

Brown, R. Don & Daigneault, Ernest A. Pharmacology of Hearing: Experimental & Clinical Bases. 360p. 1980. 45.00 (ISBN 0-471-05074-1, Pub. by Wiley-Interscience). Wiley.

Brown, R. G. The Male Nurse. 139p. 1973. pap. text ed. 5.00x (ISBN 0-7135-1878-2, Pub. by Bedford England). Renouf.

--Re-Organizing the National Health Service: A Case Study in Administrative Change. (Aspects of Social Policy Ser.). 232p. 1979. 24.50x (ISBN 0-631-18130-X, Pub. by Basil Blackwell). Biblio Dist.

Brown, R. H. A Poetics for Sociology. LC 75-35454. (Illus.). 1977. 34.50 (ISBN 0-521-21121-2); pap. 8.95x (ISBN 0-521-29391-X). Cambridge U Pr.

Brown, R. Hanbury. The Intensity Interferometer: Its Application to Astronomy. LC 74-14878. 184p. 1974. 26.95 (ISBN 0-470-10797-9). Halsted Pr.

Brown, R. I. & Hughson, E. A. Training of the Developmentally Handicapped Adult. (Illus.). 214p. 1980. 14.75 (ISBN 0-398-03993-3). C C Thomas.

Brown, R. W. Resistance of Pseudomonas Aeruginosa. LC 74-30224. 335p. 1975. 60.50 o.p. (ISBN 0-471-11210-0, Pub. by Wiley-Interscience). Wiley.

Brown, Ralph H. Mirror for Americans: Likeness of the Eastern Seaboard, 1810. LC 67-27449. (American Scene Ser). 1968. Repr. of 1943 ed. 35.00 (ISBN 0-306-70974-0). Da Capo.

Brown, Ralph S., Jr. Loyalty & Security: Employment Tests in the United States. LC 79-151417. (Civil Liberties in American History Ser). 522p. 1972. Repr. of 1958 ed. lib. bdg. 47.50 (ISBN 0-306-70218-5). Da Capo.

Brown, Ramona A. Memories of Abdu'l-Baha: Recollections of the Early Days of the Baha'i Faith in California. LC 79-16412. (Illus.). 1980. 10.00 (ISBN 0-87743-128-0, 7-32-10); pap. 5.00 (ISBN 0-87743-139-6, 7-32-11). Baha'i.

Brown, Ray. Characteristics of Local Media Audiences. 1978. text ed. 23.00x (ISBN 0-566-00218-3, Pub. by Gower Pr England). Renouf.

Brown, Ray, ed. Children & Television. LC 76-50500. (Illus.). 1976. 20.00x (ISBN 0-8039-0821-0); pap. 9.95x (ISBN 0-8039-0822-9). Sage.

--Children Australia. 320p. 1981. text ed. 22.50x (ISBN 0-86861-186-7, 2567); pap. text ed. 12.50x (ISBN 0-86861-194-8, 2568). Allen Unwin.

Brown, Ray E. Judgment in Administration. (Management Ser). 1966. 16.95 o.p. (ISBN 0-07-008175-1, C). McGraw.

Brown, Ray H. Robert Stewart Hyer, the Man I Knew. (Illus.). 1957. 8.00 (ISBN 0-685-05005-X). A Jones.

Brown, Raymond. The Virginal Conception & Bodily Resurrection of Jesus. LC 72-97399. 1973. pap. 2.95 (ISBN 0-8091-1768-1). Paulist Pr.

Brown, Raymond B. Marcos Presenta Al Salvador. Lerin, Olivia Y Alfredo, tr. Orig. Title: Mark - the Saviour for Sinners. 1978. pap. 1.95 (ISBN 0-311-04346-1). Casa Bautista.

Brown, Raymond E. Biblical Reflections on Crises Facing the Church. LC 75-18961. 1975. pap. 3.45 (ISBN 0-8091-1891-2). Paulist Pr.

--Priest & Bishop. LC 78-139594. 1970. pap. 2.95 (ISBN 0-8091-1661-8). Paulist Pr.

Brown, Raymond E., et al, eds. Jerome Biblical Commentary. 1969. 43.95 (ISBN 0-13-509612-X). P-H.

--Mary in the New Testament: A Collaborative Assessment by Protestant & Roman Catholic Scholars. LC 78-8797. 336p. 1978. pap. 3.95 (ISBN 0-8006-1345-7, 1-1345). Fortress.

Brown, Raymond E., S.S. New Testament Essays. 1968. pap. 1.95 (ISBN 0-385-05276-6, D251, Im). Doubleday.

Brown, Richard & Robbins, David. Advanced Mathematics: An Introductory Course. (gr. 11-12). 1978. text ed. 16.28 (ISBN 0-395-25553-8); instrs'. guide & solns. 9.40 (ISBN 0-395-25554-6). HM.

Brown, Richard, jt. auth. see Stokes, Eric.

Brown, Richard, ed. see Smith, Linda, et al.

Brown, Richard, illus. Sesame Street Do-It-Yourself Alphabet Book. (Golden Play & Learn Ser.). 14p. (ps). Date not set. pap. 2.95 (ISBN 0-307-13647-7, Golden Pr). Western Pub.

Brown, Richard C., jt. auth. see Nishiyama, Hidetaka.

Brown, Richard D. & Petrello, George J. Introduction to Business: An Integrated Approach. 1976. text ed. 14.95x (ISBN 0-02-471230-2). Macmillan.

Brown, Richard H., ed. see Baker, G.

Brown, Richard H., ed. see Bennett, P.

Brown, Richard H., ed. see Buffinton, Thomas.

Brown, Richard H., ed. see Casey, Dayle A.

Brown, Richard H., ed. see Cohan, G.

Brown, Richard H., ed. see Guttmann, Allen.

Brown, Richard H., ed. see Harris, Jonathan.

Brown, Richard H., ed. see Traverso, E.

Brown, Richard M. Strain of Violence: Historical Studies of American Violence & Vigilantism. LC 75-7351. 1977. pap. 6.95 (ISBN 0-19-502247-5, GB513, GB). Oxford U Pr.

Brown, Richard M., jt. ed. see Olson, Alison G.

Brown, Robert B. & Luby, Barry J. Visiones de Hoy. 228p. 1971. pap. text ed. 8.95 (ISBN 0-15-594930-6, HC); tapes 60.00 (ISBN 0-15-594931-4). HarBraceJ.

Brown, Robert C. Anesthesiology. 4th ed. (Medical Examination Review Book Ser.: Vol. 12). 1980. spiral bdg. 8.50 o.p. (ISBN 0-87488-112-9). Med Exam.

--Perchance to Dream: The Patient's Guide to Anesthesia. 96p. 1981. 10.95 (ISBN 0-686-69375-2). Nelson-Hall.

Brown, Robert D. Industrial Education Facilities: A Handbook for Organization & Management. 1979. text ed. 19.95 (ISBN 0-205-06171-0). Allyn.

Brown, Robert F. & Brown, Brenda W. Mathematics Applied to Business & the Social Sciences. 640p. 1980. text ed. 19.95x (ISBN 0-534-00754-6). Wadsworth Pub.

Brown, Robert G. Materials Management Systems: A Modular Library. LC 77-8281. 436p. 1977. 31.50 (ISBN 0-471-11182-1). Ronald Pr.

Brown, Robert H. Wyoming: A Geography. (Geographies of the United States Ser.). (Illus.). 375p. 1980. lib. bdg. 35.00 (ISBN 0-89158-560-5); text ed. 20.00 (ISBN 0-89158-560-5). Westview.

Brown, Robert K., jt. auth. see Mallin, Jay.

Brown, Robert K., ed. see Levy, Bert Y.

Brown, Robert K., ed. see Moyer, Frank A. & Scroggie, Robert J.

Brown, Robert K., ed. see Thomas, Donald G.

Brown, Robert L. Saloons of the American West. (Illus.). 144p. 16.50 (ISBN 0-913582-24-7). Sundance.

Brown, Robert M. Brother, Which Drummer. LC 60-7426. 1960. 4.50 o.p. (ISBN 0-15-114423-0). HarBraceJ.

--Creative Dislocation: The Movement of Grace. LC 80-16433. (Journey in Faith Ser.). 144p. 1980. 7.95 (ISBN 0-687-09826-2). Abingdon.

--The Electronic Invasion. rev. 2nd ed. (Illus.). 192p. 1975. pap. 7.15 (ISBN 0-8104-0825-2). Hayden.

--Gustavo Gutierrez. LC 80-82185. (Makers of Contemporary Theology Ser.). 75p. 1981. pap. 3.45 (ISBN 0-8042-0651-1). John Knox.

--Making Peace in the Global Village. LC 80-27213. (Orig.). 1981. pap. 5.95 (ISBN 0-664-24343-6). Westminster.

--Spirit of Protestantism. (YA) (gr. 9 up). 1965. pap. 5.95 (ISBN 0-19-500724-7, GB). Oxford U Pr.

Brown, Robert M. & Lawrence, Paul. How to Read Electronic Circuit Diagrams. LC 72-105970. 1970. 9.95 (ISBN 0-8306-0510-X); pap. 7.95 (ISBN 0-8306-9510-9, 510). TAB Bks.

Brown, Robert M., tr. see Casalis, George.

Brown, Robert W., et al. Africa & International Crisis. LC 77-17820. (Foreign & Comparative Studies-Eastern Africa Ser.: No. 22). 106p. 1976. pap. text ed. 4.50x (ISBN 0-915984-19-9). Syracuse U Foreign Comp.

Brown, Roger. Social Psychology. LC 65-11321. 1965. text ed. 14.95 (ISBN 0-02-904820-6). Free Pr.

--Travellers Survival Kit Europe. 2nd ed. 1980. pap. 6.95 o.p. (ISBN 0-901205-72-9). Writers Digest.

--Words & Things. LC 58-9395. 1968. 15.95 (ISBN 0-02-904800-1); pap. text ed. 7.95 (ISBN 0-02-904810-9). Free Pr.

Brown, Roger, ed. Psycholinguistics: Selected Papers. LC 73-95296. 1972. pap. text ed. 7.95 (ISBN 0-02-904840-0). Free Pr.

Brown, Roger L. Wilhelm Von Humboldt's Conception of Linguistic Relativity. LC 67-30542. (Janua Linguarum, Ser. Minor: No. 65). (Orig.). 1967. pap. text ed. 20.00x (ISBN 90-2790-593-2). Mouton.

Brown, Roland W. Composition of Scientific Words. LC 78-14717. 882p. 1978. Repr. of 1956 ed. 15.00x (ISBN 0-87474-286-2). Smithsonian.

Brown, Ronald D. From Selling to Managing. (AMACOM Executive Books). 1978. pap. 5.95 (ISBN 0-8144-7500-0). Am Mgmt.

Brown, Rosellen. The Autobiography of My Mother. LC 75-36581. 288p. 1976. 7.95 o.p. (ISBN 0-385-09896-0). Doubleday.

--Cora Fry. 1977. 9.95 (ISBN 0-393-04455-6); pap. 2.95 (ISBN 0-393-04461-0). Norton.

Brown, Rosellen, et al. Banquet: 5 Short Stories. LC 78-56621. (Illus.). 1978. 12.00x (ISBN 0-915778-24-6); pap. 4.00 (ISBN 0-915778-25-4); deluxe ed. 85.00x deluxe ed (ISBN 0-915778-23-8). Penmaen Pr.

Brown, Roxanna M. Legend & Reality: Early Ceramics from South-East Asia. (Oxford in Asia Studies in Ceramics). (Illus.). 246p. 1977. 43.00x (ISBN 0-19-580383-3). Oxford U Pr.

Brown, Roy. Battle of Saint Street. LC 74-152287. (gr. 5-8). 1971. 4.95 o.s.i. (ISBN 0-02-714920-X). Macmillan.

--The Cage. LC 77-1586. (gr. 6 up). 1977. 6.95 (ISBN 0-395-28892-4, Clarion). HM.

--Day of the Pigeons. LC 72-78079. (gr. 4-7). 1969. 4.50g o.s.i. (ISBN 0-02-714910-2). Macmillan.

--Escape the River. LC 76-179440. 160p. (gr. 6 up). 1972. 5.95 (ISBN 0-395-28893-2, Clarion). HM.

--Find Debbie! LC 75-25511. (gr. 7-12). 1976. 7.95 (ISBN 0-395-28894-0, Clarion). HM.

--Flight of Sparrows. LC 72-92432. 160p. (gr. 5-8). 1973. 7.95 (ISBN 0-02-714860-2). Macmillan.

--No Through Road. LC 74-3484. 192p. (gr. 6 up). 1974. 5.95 (ISBN 0-395-28896-7, Clarion). HM.

--Suicide Course. 128p. (gr. 6 up). 1980. 7.95 (ISBN 0-395-29436-3, Clarion). HM.

--The Swing of the Gate. LC 78-6422. (gr. 6 up). 1978. 6.95 (ISBN 0-395-28895-9, Clarion). HM.

--Viaduct. LC 68-23061. (gr. 5-7). 1968. 4.50g o.s.i. (ISBN 0-02-714890-4). Macmillan.

--The White Sparrow. LC 74-19352. 192p. (gr. 6 up). 1975. 6.95 (ISBN 0-395-28897-5, Clarion). HM.

Brown, Roy I. Psychology & Education of Slow Learners. 1978. pap. 6.50 (ISBN 0-7100-0046-4). Routledge & Kegan.

--Psychology & Education of Slow Learners. (Students Library of Education). 1976. 10.00x (ISBN 0-7100-8410-2). Routledge & Kegan.

Brown, Roy I., jt. auth. see Gibson, David.

Brown, Ruben S. Hydro for the Eighties: Bringing Hydroelectric Power to Poor People. (Orig.). 1980. 15.00 (ISBN 0-936130-01-6). Intl Sci Tech.

Brown, Rustie. The Titanic, the Psychic & the Sea. LC 80-70551. (Illus.). 176p. 1981. 12.95 (ISBN 0-9605278-0-X). Blue Harbor.

Brown, Sam E. Activities for Teaching Metrics in Kindergarden. LC 77-95155. 1978. pap. text ed. 7.00 (ISBN 0-8191-0462-0). U Pr of Amer.

--Bubbles, Rainbows & Worms: Science Experiments for Pre-School Children. LC 80-84598. (Illus.). 1981. pap. 5.95 (ISBN 0-87659-100-4). Gryphon Hse.

Brown, Sanborn C. Electron Molecule Scattering. LC 79-12705. (Wiley Series in Plasma Physics). 1980. 24.95 (ISBN 0-471-05205-1, Pub. by Wiley-Interscience). Wiley.

Brown, Scott S. Bounds on Transfer Principles for Algebraically Closed & Complete Discretely Valued Fields. LC 78-9121. 1978. 7.60 (ISBN 0-8218-2204-7, MEMO-204). Am Math.

Brown, Seyom. The Crises of Power: Foreign Policy in the Kissinger Years. LC 79-15796. 1979. 12.50 (ISBN 0-231-04264-7). Columbia U Pr.

--The Faces of Power: Constancy & Change in U.S. Foreign Policy from Truman to Johnson. 1968. 20.00x (ISBN 0-231-03089-4); pap. 7.50x (ISBN 0-231-08597-4). Columbia U Pr.

Brown, Seyom, et al. Regimes for the Ocean, Outer Space, & Weather. 1977. 14.95 (ISBN 0-8157-1156-5); pap. 5.95 (ISBN 0-8157-1155-7). Brookings.

Brown, Shirley N., jt. ed. see Brown, James W.

Brown, Stanley H., jt. auth. see Girard, Joe.

Brown, Stephen. Ireland in Fiction. 382p. Repr. of 1919 ed. 13.00x (ISBN 0-686-28347-3, Pub. by Irish Academic Pr). Biblio Dist.

Brown, Sterling. Negro in American Fiction. 1969. Repr. of 1937 ed. 12.50 (ISBN 0-87266-002-8). Argosy.

Brown, Stuart E., Jr. The Guns of Harpers Ferry. LC 77-746. (Illus.). 157p. 1968. 20.00 o.p. (ISBN 0-685-65063-4). Va Bk.

Brown, T. A., tr. see Rosenzweig, Mark R. & Brown, T. A.

Brown, T. A., jt. ed. see Rosenzweig, Mark R.

Brown, T. C., jt. auth. see Hunter, R. H.

Brown, T. E., et al. Field Excursions, East Texas: Clay, Glauconite, Ironstone Deposits. (Illus.). 48p. 1969. 1.00 (GB 9). Bur Econ Geology.

Brown, T. L. & LeMay, H. Eugene, Jr. Chemistry: The Central Science. LC 76-22159. (Illus.). 1977. text ed. 21.95 (ISBN 0-13-128769-9); students guide 7.95 (ISBN 0-13-128512-2); lab. exp. 9.95 (ISBN 0-13-128751-6); solutions 4.95 (ISBN 0-13-128793-1); pap. 9.95 lab manual (ISBN 0-13-128520-3). P-H.

Brown, T. M. & Millar, Robert. Put It in Writing. 1968. pap. text ed. 3.50x o.p. (ISBN 0-435-10130-7). Heinemann Ed.

Brown, Terence, jt. auth. see Rafroidi, Patrick.

Brown, Terence & Reid, Alec, eds. Time Was Away: The World of Louis MacNeice. (Illus.). 151p. 1974. text ed. 12.00x (ISBN 0-85105-237-1, Dolmen Pr). Humanities.

Brown, Terry & Hunter, Rob. The Concise Book of Orienteering. 1979. pap. 2.95. Vanguard.

--Map & Compass. rev. ed. (Venture Guides Ser.). (Illus.). 1978. pap. 2.95 o.p. (ISBN 0-902875-99-X). Hippocrene Bks.

Brown, Theodore L. & LeMay, H. E. Chemistry, The Central Science: Solutions to Exercises. 272p. 1980. 6.96 (ISBN 0-13-128538-6). P-H.

Brown, Theodore L. & LeMay, H. Eugene. Chemistry: The Central Science. 2nd ed. 832p. 1981. text ed. 22.95 (ISBN 0-13-128504-1). P-H.

Brown, Theodore L., jt. auth. see Drago, Russell S.

Brown, Thomas. Inquiry into the Relation of Cause & Effect. 4th ed. LC 77-16224. 1977. Repr. of 1835 ed. lib. bdg. 49.00 (ISBN 0-8201-1301-8). Schol Facsimiles.

--Sketch of a System of the Philosophy of the Human Mind. Bd. with Logic of Condillac. (Contributions to the History of Psychology Ser., Pt. A: Orientations). 1978. Repr. of 1820 ed. 30.00 (ISBN 0-89093-150-X). U Pubns Amer.

Brown, Thomas, jt. auth. see Holladay, Sylvia.

Brown, Thomas H. La Fontaine & Cupid & Psyche Tradition. (Charles E. Merrill Monograph Series in the Humanities & Social Sciences: Vol. 1, No. 3). 105p. 1968. pap. 1.50 o.p. (ISBN 0-8425-0016-2). Brigham.

--Langue et Litterature: A Second Course in French. 2nd ed. (Illus.). 448p. 1974. text ed. 18.00x (ISBN 0-07-008400-9, C); instructor's manual 3.95 (ISBN 0-07-008401-7); 6.50x (ISBN 0-07-008402-5). McGraw.

Brown, Thomas S. & Wallace, Patricia. Physiological Psychology. 1980. tchrs' ed. 20.95 (ISBN 0-12-136660-X). Acad Pr.

Brown, Tom & Watkins, William J. The Tracker. 1979. pap. 2.50 (ISBN 0-425-04222-7). Berkley Pub.

Brown, Tom, Jr. & Owen, William. The Search: The Continuing Story of the Tracker. LC 80-20588. 1980. 10.95 (ISBN 0-13-796953-8). P-H.

Brown University Library. Contribution to a Union Catalog of Sixteenth Century Imprints in Certain New England Libraries. 466p. 1953. 15.00x (ISBN 0-87057-032-3, Pub. by Brown U Pr). Univ Pr of New England.

--Life & Works of John Hay, 1838-1905: A Commemorative Catalogue. (Illus.). 51p. 1961. 5.00x (ISBN 0-87057-063-3, Pub. by Brown U Pr). Univ Pr of New England.

Brown, V. Backyard Wild Birds of the Pacific Northwest & California. pap. 2.50 (ISBN 0-87666-411-7, M521). TFH Pubns.

Brown, Velma, jt. auth. see Brown, H. C., Jr.

Brown, Vinson. The Amateur Naturalist's Handbook. (Illus.). 432p. 1980. 15.95 (Spec); pap. 6.95. P-H.

--Backyard Birds of the East & Middle West. (Illus.). 1971. pap. 2.50 (ISBN 0-87666-412-5, M-540). TFH Pubns.

--Great Upon the Mountain: The Story of Crazy Horse, Legendary Mystic & Warrior. LC 74-13458. 1975. 9.95 (ISBN 0-02-517350-2, 51735). Macmillan.

--Knowing the Outdoors in the Dark. LC 71-179605. (Illus.). 192p. 1973. pap. 2.95 o.s.i. (ISBN 0-02-062260-0, Collier). Macmillan.

--Sea Mammals & Reptiles of the Pacific Coast. (Illus.). 1976. 10.95 o.s.i. (ISBN 0-02-517310-3). Macmillan.

Brown, Vinson, et al. Handbook of California Birds. 3rd rev. ed. LC 73-6326. (Illus.). 1979. 11.95 (ISBN 0-911010-17-3); pap. 7.95 (ISBN 0-911010-16-5). Naturegraph.

Brown, Virginia S., jt. auth. see Phillips, Billie M.

Brown, W. Psychological Care During Pregnancy & the Postpartum Period. 1979. 18.00 (ISBN 0-89004-371-X); pap. 11.00 (ISBN 0-686-66187-7). Raven.

Brown, W. Norman. India & Indology. Rocher, Rosane, ed. 1979. 52.00x (ISBN 0-8364-0362-2). South Asia Bks.

--Man in the Universe: Some Cultural Continuities in Indian Thought. (Rabindranath Tagore Memorial Lectures). 1966. 14.00x (ISBN 0-520-00185-0). U of Cal Pr.

--Manuscript Illustrations of the Uttaradhyayana Sutra. (American Oriental Ser.: Vol. 21). (Illus.). 1941. 8.00x o.p. (ISBN 0-686-00010-2). Am Orient Soc.

Brown, W. Norman, ed. India, Pakistan, Ceylon. rev. ed. LC 61-15205. (Illus.). 1964. 10.00x o.p. (ISBN 0-8122-7428-8). U of Pa Pr.

Brown, Wallace. Good Americans: The Loyalists in the American Revolution. LC 69-11500. 1969. pap. 4.95 (ISBN 0-688-27754-3). Morrow.

--King's Friends: The Composition & Motives of the American Loyalist Claimants. LC 66-10179. (Illus.). 411p. 1965. 16.00 (ISBN 0-87057-092-7, Pub. by Brown U Pr). Univ Pr of New England.

Brown, Wallace C. The Triumph of Form. LC 73-13452. 212p. 1973. Repr. of 1948 ed. lib. bdg. 16.50x (ISBN 0-8371-7135-0, BRTF). Greenwood.

Brown, Walter & Anderson, Norman. Sea Disasters. LC 80-27156. (Illus.). 112p. (gr. 4-7). 1981. PLB 7.95 (ISBN 0-201-09154-2, 9154, A-W Childrens). A-W.

Brown, Walter C. Basic Mathematics. 96p. (Combination text & workbook). 1980. pap. 4.80 (ISBN 0-87006-315-4). Goodheart.

--Basic Mathematics. rev. ed. 128p. 1981. pap. text ed. 4.80 (ISBN 0-87006-317-0). Goodheart.

--Blueprint Reading for Construction. LC 79-23958. 1980. pap. text ed. 13.92 spiral. Goodheart.

--Blueprint Reading for Construction. LC 79-23958. (Illus.). 338p. (Orig.). 1980. pap. text ed. 13.92 (ISBN 0-87006-286-7). Good Heart.

--Drafting. (Illus.). 1978. text ed. 4.80 (ISBN 0-87006-256-5). Goodheart.

--Drafting for Industry: 1978 Ed. LC 77-25196. (Illus.). 616p. 1980. 16.56 (ISBN 0-87006-247-6); wkbk. 4.80 (ISBN 0-87006-306-5). Goodheart.

Brown, Walter C., et al. Modern General Shop. LC 74-23595. (Illus.). 1978. text ed. 12.40 (ISBN 0-87006-260-3). Goodheart.

Brown, Walter L. Up Front with U. S. Day by Day in the Life of a Combat Infantryman in General Patton's Third Army. LC 79-54035. (Illus.). 744p. 1979. 12.95x (ISBN 0-9604822-0-2); lib. bdg. write for info. (ISBN 0-9604822-0-2). Brown's Studio.

Brown, Walter R., et al. Catastrophies. LC 79-19141. (Illus.). (gr. 5 up). 1979. pap. 6.95 (ISBN 0-201-00791-6, 0791, A-W Childrens). A-W.

Brown, Walter V. & Bertke, Eldridge M. Textbook of Cytology. 2nd ed. LC 73-14625. 1974. text ed. 21.95 (ISBN 0-8016-0831-7). Mosby.

Brown, Warren J. Florida's Aviation History. 1980. pap. 6.95 (ISBN 0-912522-70-4). Aero-Medical.

Brown, Warren J., ed. Patients' Guide to Medicine: From the Drugstore Through the Hospital. 9th ed. 1981. pap. 7.95 (ISBN 0-912522-71-2). Aero-Medical.

Brown, Warrren B. & Moberg, Dennis G. Organization Management: A Macro Approach. LC 79-18709. (Wiley Ser. in Management). 1980. text ed. 21.95 (ISBN 0-471-02023-0); tchrs'. manual avail. (ISBN 0-471-02024-9). Wiley.

Brown, Weldon A. The Last Chopper: The Denouement of the American Role in Vietnam, 1964-1975. 1976. 17.50 (ISBN 0-8046-9121-5, Natl U). Kennikat.

--Prelude to Disaster: The American Role in Vietnam, 1940-1963. 1975. 18.50 (ISBN 0-8046-9122-3, Natl U). Kennikat.

Brown, Wenzell. Dark Drums. (Orig.). 1977. pap. 1.95 o.s.i. (ISBN 0-446-89292-0). Warner Bks.

Brown, Wesley. Tragic Magic. 1978. 7.95 (ISBN 0-394-50224-8). Random.

Brown, Wilburt S. Amphibious Campaign for West Florida & Louisiana, 1814-1815: A Critical Review of Strategy & Tactics at New Orleans. LC 68-10992. (Illus.). 253p. 1969. 15.95 o.p. (ISBN 0-8173-5100-0). U of Ala Pr.

Brown, William. Piecework Bargaining. 1973. text ed. 8.95x o.p. (ISBN 0-435-85125-X). Heinemann Ed.

Brown, William A., jt. auth. see Dobler, Lavinia.

Brown, William D. Families Under Stress. 154p. 1977. pap. text ed. 7.95 (ISBN 0-87619-844-2). R J Brady.

Brown, William E., ed. Testing of Polymers. LC 65-14733. (Testing of Polymers Ser.: Vol. 4). 1969. 42.50 (ISBN 0-470-11175-5, Pub. by Wiley-Interscience). Wiley.

Brown, William F. National Field Trial Champions, 1956-1966. (Illus.). 1966. 12.00 o.p. (ISBN 0-498-06387-9). A S Barnes.

Brown, William G. Life of Oliver Ellsworth. LC 76-118028. (American Constitutional & Legal History Ser). 1970. Repr. of 1905 ed. lib. bdg. 37.50 (ISBN 0-306-71940-1). Da Capo.

Brown, William G., ed. Manual for Authors: Reviews in Graph Theory, 4 vols. Set. write for info. o.p. (ISBN 0-8218-0214-3); Vol. 1. write for info. o.p. (ISBN 0-8218-0210-0); Vol. 2. write for info. o.p. (ISBN 0-8218-0211-9); Vol. 3. write for info. o.p. (ISBN 0-8218-0212-7); Vol. 4. write for info. o.p. (ISBN 0-8218-0213-5). Am Math.

--Reviews in Graph Theory, 4 vols. 1980. Set. 200.00 (ISBN 0-8218-0214-3); Vol. 1. 68.00 (ISBN 0-8218-0210-0); Vol. 2. 68.00 (ISBN 0-8218-0211-9); Vol. 3. 68.00 (ISBN 0-8218-0212-7); Vol. 4. 40.00 (ISBN 0-8218-0213-5). Am Math.

Brown, William T. Architecture Evolving: An Illinois Saga. Hasbrouck, Marilyn, ed. LC 76-45690. (Illus.). 1976. 25.00x (ISBN 0-931028-02-7); pap. 15.00x (ISBN 0-931028-01-9). Teach'em.

Brown, Willis M. How I Got Faith. 199p. 2.00. Faith Pub Hse.

Brown, Wilson H., jt. auth. see Hogendorn, Jan S.

Brown, Wm. A., Jr. Groping Giant: Russia. 1920. 22.50x (ISBN 0-685-69793-2). Elliots Bks.

Browne, A. L. The General Problem of Rolling Contact. Tsai, N. T., ed. (AMD: Vol. 40). 176p. 1980. 28.00 (G00173). ASME.

Browne, Anthony. Through the Magic Mirror. LC 76-13024. (Illus.). (gr. k-3). 1977. 9.25 (ISBN 0-688-80064-5); PLB 8.88 (ISBN 0-688-84064-7). Greenwillow.

Browne, Art, Jr., jt. auth. see Paulsen, Gary.

Browne, Corinne. Casualty: A Memoir of Love & War. 1981. 12.95 (ISBN 0-393-01422-3). Norton.

Browne, Corinne & Munroe, Robert. The Dragon's Tail: America's Continuing Nuclear Experiment. (Illus.). 288p. 1981. 10.95 (ISBN 0-688-03691-0). Morrow.

Browne, Dan. Simplified Home Appliance Repairs. LC 76-4732. (Illus.). 1978. 12.95 o.p. (ISBN 0-03-042636-7); pap. 6.95 o.p. (ISBN 0-03-015621-1). HR&W.

Browne, Dik. Hagar the Horrible: Born Leader. 128p. (gr. 3 up). 1981. pap. 1.50 (ISBN 0-448-12653-2, Tempo). G&D.

--Hagar the Horrible: Bring Em Back Alive. 1981. pap. 1.50 (ISBN 0-448-12650-8, Tempo). G&D.

--Sack Time. Wallace, Wendy, ed. (Hagar the Horrible Ser.: No. 6). 128p. (gr. 2 up). 1981. pap. 1.50 (ISBN 0-448-12623-0, Tempo). G&D.

Browne, Dik B. Hagar the Horrible: On the Rack, No. 5. (Hagar the Horrible Cartoons). 128p. (gr. 8-12). 1981. pap. text ed. 1.50 (ISBN 0-448-12649-4, Tempo). G&D.

Browne, E. Martin, ed. Religious Drama, Vol. 2: 21 Medieval Mystery & Morality Plays. 8.00 (ISBN 0-8446-2793-3). Peter Smith.

Browne, Edward G. Arabian Medicine. LC 79-2852. (Illus.). 138p. 1981. Repr. of 1962 ed. 16.00 (ISBN 0-8305-0028-6). Hyperion Conn.

--Literary History of Persia, 4 Vols. 1928. 62.00 ea. Vol. 1 (ISBN 0-521-04344-1). Vol. 2 (ISBN 0-521-04345-X). Vol. 3 (ISBN 0-521-04346-8). Vol. 4. Cambridge U Pr.

Browne, Edward G., tr. see Abdu'l-Baha.

Browne, Frances G. Pests & Diseases of Forest Plantation Trees: An Annotated List of the Principle Species Occurring in the British Commonwealth. 1968. 89.00x (ISBN 0-19-854367-0). Oxford U Pr.

Browne, Fred, ed. Machinery Buyers Guide 1980. 1499p. (Orig.). 1980. pap. 47.50x (ISBN 0-8002-2472-8). Intl Pubns Serv.

Browne, Gerald. Eleven Harrow House. 1979. pap. 2.25 o.s.i. (ISBN 0-440-12315-1). Dell.

Browne, Harry. How I Found Freedom in an Unfree World. 1974. pap. 2.75 (ISBN 0-380-00423-2, 47837). Avon.

--You Can Profit from a Monetary Crisis. LC 73-16686. (Illus.). 288p. 1974. 8.95 o.s.i. (ISBN 0-02-517460-6). Macmillan.

Browne, J. S. Basic Theory of Structures. 1966. 25.00 (ISBN 0-08-011654-X); pap. 12.75 (ISBN 0-08-011653-1). Pergamon.

Browne, John. The Marchants Aviso, 1589. McGrath, Patrick, ed. (Kress Library of Business & Economics: No. 13). 1957. pap. 5.00x (ISBN 0-678-09906-5, Baker Lib). Kelley.

Browne, Lawrence E. The Eclipse of Christianity in Asia. 1967. Repr. 15.75 (ISBN 0-86527-049-X). Fertig.

Browne, Lewis. This Believing World. 1944. 9.95 (ISBN 0-02-517600-5); pap. 2.95 (ISBN 0-02-084050-0). Macmillan.

Browne, M. Neil & Keely, Stuart M. Asking the Right Questions. 224p. 1981. pap. text ed. 6.95 (ISBN 0-13-049395-3). P-H.

Browne, Martha G. Autobiography of a Female Slave. LC 71-92745. Repr. 22.50x (ISBN 0-8371-2194-9). Negro U Pr.

Browne, Miriam. Pewter Jewellery. 1979. 19.95 (ISBN 0-7134-1608-4, Pub. by Batsford England). David & Charles.

Browne, Peter. Procedure, Extent & Limits of the Human Understanding. Wellek, Rene, ed. LC 75-11201. (British Philosophers & Theologians of the 17th & 18th Centuries: Vol. 8). 1976. Repr. of 1728 ed. lib. bdg. 42.00 (ISBN 0-8240-1757-9). Garland Pub.

--Things Divine & Supernatural Conceived by Analogy with Things Natural & Human. Wellek, Rene, ed. LC 75-11203. (British Philosophers & Theologians of the 17th & 18th Centuries: Vol. 9). 1976. Repr. of 1733 ed. lib. bdg. 42.00 (ISBN 0-8240-1758-7). Garland Pub.

Browne, Peter S. Securtiy: Checklist for Computer Center Self-Audits. LC 79-56012. (Illus.). 189p. 1979. pap. 35.00 (ISBN 0-88283-024-4). AFIPS Pr.

Browne, Ray, ed. A Night with the Hants & Other Alabama Experiences. LC 76-43449. 1976. 12.95 (ISBN 0-87972-075-1); pap. 6.95 (ISBN 0-87972-167-7). Bowling Green Univ.

Browne, Ray B. Popular Abstracts. 1978. 12.95 (ISBN 0-87972-166-9); pap. 6.95 (ISBN 0-87972-165-0). Bowling Green Univ.

Browne, Scribner. Tidal Swings of the Stock Market. (Illus.). 115p. 1980. 59.50 (ISBN 0-918968-75-5). Inst Econ Finan.

Browne, Terry. Playwrights' Theatre: The English State Company at the Royal Court. 1975. 8.00x (ISBN 0-273-00757-2, Pitman Pub); pap. 5.00 (ISBN 0-273-00758-0). Columbia U Pr.

Browne, Thomas. Religio Medici & Other Works. Martin, Leonard C., ed. 1964. 37.50x (ISBN 0-19-811429-X). Oxford U Pr.

Browne, William P. Politics, Programs, & Bureaucrats. (National University Publications, Political Science Ser.). 184p. 1980. 17.50 (ISBN 0-8046-9263-7). Kennikat.

Brownell, Blaine A., jt. auth. see Goldfield, David R.

Brownell, Blaine A. & Goldfield, David R., eds. The City in Southern History: The Growth of Urban Civilization in the South. (Interdisciplinary Urban Ser.). 1976. pap. 8.50 (ISBN 0-8046-9160-6, Natl U). Kennikat.

Brownell, Blaine A. & Stickle, Warren E., eds. Bosses & Reformers: Urban Politics in America, 1880-1920. LC 72-4798. (New Perspectives in History Ser.). 250p. (Orig.). 1973. pap. text ed. 7.25 (ISBN 0-395-14050-1, 3-41025). HM.

Brownell, Blaine E., jt. auth. see Mowry, George E.

Brownell, David W., ed. Vintage Auto Almanac. 4th ed. LC 76-649715. 256p. 1981. pap. 8.95 (ISBN 0-917808-04-5). Hemmings.

--The Vintage Auto Almanac. 3rd, annual ed. LC 76-649715. 1980. pap. 4.95 o.p. (ISBN 0-917808-03-7). Hemmings.

Brownell, J. A., jt. auth. see King, A. R., Jr.

Brownell, Lloyd E. & Young, Edwin H. Process Equipment Design: Vessel Design. LC 59-5882. 1959. 45.00 (ISBN 0-471-11319-0, Pub by Wiley-Interscience). Wiley.

Brownell, William A. Arithmetical Abstractions: The Movement Toward Conceptual Maturity Under Differing Systems of Instructions. (U. C. Publ. in Education: Vol. 17). 1967. pap. 10.00x (ISBN 0-520-09063-2). U of Cal Pr.

Brownfeld, Allan C. The Price of Detente. 180p. 1981. 10.00 (ISBN 0-8159-6517-6). Devin.

Browning. The Loss Rate Concept in Safety Engineering. 176p. 1980. 27.50 (ISBN 0-8247-1249-8). Dekker.

Browning, David. El Salvador: Landscape & Society. (Illus.). 350p. 1971. 29.95x (ISBN 0-19-823208-X). Oxford U Pr.

Browning, Dixie. Chance Tomorrow. 192p. 1981. pap. 1.50 (ISBN 0-671-57053-6). S&S.

--Tumbled Wall. 192p. (Orig.). 1980. pap. 1.50 (ISBN 0-671-57038-2). S&S.

--Unreasonable Summer. 192p. (Orig.). 1980. pap. 1.50 (ISBN 0-671-57012-9). S&S.

Browning, Don S. Pluralism & Personality: William James & Some Contemporary Cultures of Psychology. LC 78-75196. 280p. Date not set. 22.50 (ISBN 0-8387-2265-2). Bucknell U Pr.

Browning, Edgar K. & Johnson, William R. Distribution of the Tax Burden. 1979. pap. 4.25 (ISBN 0-8447-3349-0). Am Enterprise.

Browning, Elizabeth B. Casa Guidi Windows. Markus, Julia, ed. LC 77-24944. (Illus.). 1977. 11.50x (ISBN 0-930252-00-4, Pub by Browning Inst). Pub Ctr Cult Res.

Browning, Elizabeth Barrett. Sonnets from the Portuguese & Other Love Poems. LC 54-10779. 5.95 (ISBN 0-385-01463-5). Doubleday.

Browning, Freddie Melton, jt. auth. see Byrd, Ronald James.

Browning, Harley L., jt. ed. see Portes, Alejandro.

Browning, Iben, jt. auth. see Winkless, Nels, III.

Browning, Iben, jt. auth. see Winklessless, Nels.

Browning, J. D. Biography in the Eighteenth Century: Publications of the McMaster University Association for 18th Century Studies. LC 80-14652. (Vol. 8). 207p. 1980. 27.50 (ISBN 0-8240-4007-4). Garland Pub.

Browning, John, ed. Education in the Eighteenth Century. LC 79-18182. (The Eighteenth Century Ser.). 145p. 1979. lib. bdg. 27.50 (ISBN 0-8240-4006-6). Garland Pub.

Browning, John & Morton, Richard, eds. Religion in the Eighteenth Century. LC 79-17715. (The Eighteenth Century Ser.). 145p. 1979. lib. bdg. 20.00 (ISBN 0-8240-4005-8). Garland Pub.

Browning, Mary H., jt. auth. see Lewis, Edith P.

Browning, Mary H. & Lewis, Ruth P., eds. Maternal & Newborn Care: Nursing Interventions. 258p. 1973. 6.50 o.p. (ISBN 0-686-11198-2, C07). Am Journal Nurse.

Browning, Philip L. Mental Retardation: Rehabilitation & Counseling. (Illus.). 464p. 1974. 24.75 (ISBN 0-398-03006-5). C C Thomas.

--Rehabilitation & the Retarded Offender. (Illus.). 360p. 1976. 22.50 (ISBN 0-398-03481-8). C C Thomas.

Browning, Preston M., Jr. Flannery O'Connor. LC 74-8849. (Crosscurrents-Modern Critiques Ser.). 160p. 1974. 7.95 (ISBN 0-8093-0672-7). S Ill U Pr.

Browning, Robert. Browning: The Poems. (Penguin Poets Ser.). 1981. Vol. 1. pap. 4.95 (ISBN 0-14-042259-5); Vol. 2. pap. 4.95 (ISBN 0-14-042260-9). Penguin.

--Byzantine Empire. 224p. 1980. 25.00 o.p. (ISBN 0-684-16652-6, ScribT). Scribner.

--Byzantium & Bulgaria: A Comparative Study Across the Early Medieval Frontier. LC 73-91665. (Illus.). 1975. 20.00x (ISBN 0-520-02670-5). U of Cal Pr.

--The Complete Works of Robert Browning: With Variant Readings & Annotations, Vol. V. King, Roma A., Jr., et al, eds. LC 68-18389. (Illus.). 400p. 1981. 35.00x (ISBN 0-8214-0220-X). Ohio U Pr.

--The Emperor Julian. LC 75-13159. 1976. 15.00 o.p. (ISBN 0-520-03034-6); pap. 4.95 o.p. (ISBN 0-520-03731-6). U of Cal Pr.

--Medieval & Modern Greek. (Illus.). 1969. pap. text ed. 6.00x (ISBN 0-09-099601-1, Hutchinson U Lib). Humanities.

--Men & Women. Turner, Paul, ed. 1972. pap. 6.95x (ISBN 0-19-911019-0). Oxford U Pr.

--Poems, Eighteen Thirty-Five to Eighteen Eighty-Nine. Milford, Humphrey, ed. (World's Classics Ser.). 1954. 10.95 (ISBN 0-19-250513-0). Oxford U Pr.

--The Poetry of Robert Browning. Korg, Jacob, ed. LC 77-122683. (Library of Literature Ser). (Illus.). 630p. 1971. pap. 7.50 (ISBN 0-672-61002-7, LL25). Bobbs.

--Studies on Byzantine History, Literature & Education. 390p. 1980. 60.00x (ISBN 0-86078-003-1, Pub. by Variorum England). State Mutual Bk.

Browning, Robert J. Fisheries of the North Pacific: History, Species, Gear & Processes. rev. ed. (Illus.). 432p. 1980. pap. 24.95 (ISBN 0-88240-128-9). Alaska Northwest.

Brownjohn, John M., jt. auth. see Braunberg, Rudolf.

Brownlee, Ann T. Community, Culture & Care: A Cross-Cultural Guide for Health Workers. LC 77-16253. (Illus.). 1978. pap. text ed. 12.95 (ISBN 0-8016-0829-5). Mosby.

Brownlee, Harriet. The Low-Carbohydrate Gourmet: A Cookbook for Hungry Dieters. LC 74-14657. 320p. 1975. 8.95 o.p. (ISBN 0-688-02874-8). Morrow.

Brownlee, Kenneth A. Statistical Theory & Methodology in Science & Engineering. 2nd ed. 1965. 37.95 (ISBN 0-471-11355-7). Wiley.

Brownlee, Michael. Handbook of Diabetes Mellitus, 5 vols. Incl. Vol. 1. Etiology-Hormone Physiology. 450p. lib. bdg. 65.00 (ISBN 0-8240-7030-5); Vol. 2. Islet Cell Function-Insulin Action. 250p. lib. bdg. 37.50 (ISBN 0-8240-7214-6); Vol. 3. Intermediary Metabolism & Its Regulation. 340p. lib. bdg. 50.00 (ISBN 0-8240-7215-4); Vol. 4. Biochemical Pathology. 325p. lib. bdg. 45.00 (ISBN 0-8240-7223-5); Vol. 5. Current & Future Therapies. 420p. lib. bdg. 60.00 (ISBN 0-8240-7224-3). LC 79-26703. 1980. Garland Pub.

--Handbook of Diabetes Mellitus: Vol. 1, Etiology-Hormone Physiology. LC 79-26703. 450p. 1980. lib. bdg. 65.00 (ISBN 0-8240-7030-5). Garland Pub.

--Handbook of Diabetes Mellitus: Vol. 3, Intermediary Metabolism & Its Regulation. LC 79-26703. 340p. 1980. lib. bdg. 50.00 (ISBN 0-8240-7215-4). Garland Pub.

--Handbook of Diabetes Mellitus: Vol. 5, Current & Future Therapies. LC 79-26703. 420p. 1981. lib. bdg. 60.00 (ISBN 0-8240-7224-3). Garland Pub.

Brownlee, Oswald H. Taxing the Income from U. S. Corporate Investment Abroad. 1979. pap. 3.25 (ISBN 0-8447-3367-9). Am Enterprise.

Brownlee, W. The First Ships Round the World. LC 73-91815. (Cambridge Introduction to the History of Mankind Ser.). (Illus.). 48p. 1974. 3.95 (ISBN 0-521-20438-0). Cambridge U Pr.

Brownlee, W. Elliot, Jr. Progressivism & Economic Growth: The Wisconsin Income Tax, 1911-1929. LC 74-80065. 1974. 13.50 (ISBN 0-8046-9091-X, Natl U). Kennikat.

Brownlee, Walter. The Navy That Beat Napoleon. LC 78-18091. (Cambridge Introduction to the History of Mankind Ser.). 1981. 3.95 (ISBN 0-521-22145-5). Cambridge U Pr.

Brownlee, William H. The Midrash Pesher of Habakkuk. LC 76-30560. (Society of Biblical Literature Monograph Ser.). 1979. 10.50 (ISBN 0-89130-096-1, 060024); pap. 9.00 (ISBN 0-89130-147-X). Scholars Pr Ca.

Brownlie, Ian. African Boundaries: A Legal & Diplomatic Encyclopedia. 1979. 160.00x (ISBN 0-520-03795-2). U of Cal Pr.

Brownlie, Ian, jt. auth. see Jennings, R. Y.

Brownlie, Ian, ed. Basic Documents of Human Rights. 2nd ed. 450p. 1981. 67.50 (ISBN 0-19-876124-4); pap. 24.95 (ISBN 0-19-876125-2). Oxford U Pr.

Brownlie, Ian, jt. ed. see Jennings, R. Y.

Brownlow, Arthur H. Geochemistry. (Illus.). 1979. text ed. 23.95 (ISBN 0-13-351064-6). P-H.

Brownlow, Kevin, ed. see Brown, Karl.

Brownlow, Margaret. Herbs & the Fragrant Garden. 1980. 30.00x (ISBN 0-232-51396-1, Pub. by Darton-Longman-Todd England). State Mutual Bk.

Brownlow, William G. Sketches of the Rise, Progress, & Decline of Secession. 2nd ed. LC 68-23813. (American Scene Ser). 1968. Repr. of 1862 ed. 42.50 (ISBN 0-306-71137-0). Da Capo.

Brownridge, Linda, jt. auth. see Thorne-Thomsen, Kathleen.

Brownrigg, Ronald. The Twelve Apostles. (Illus.). 248p. 1974. 12.95 o.s.i. (ISBN 0-02-517400-2). Macmillan.

--Who's Who in the New Testament. 1971. 18.95 o.p. (ISBN 0-03-086262-0). HR&W.

Brownrigg, W. Grant. Corporate Fund Raising: A Practical Plan of Action. LC 76-58748. (Illus.). 74p. (Orig.). 1978. pap. text ed. 12.50 (ISBN 0-915400-10-3). Am Council Arts.

Brownsberger, Susan, tr. see Saltykov-Shchedrin, Mikhail.

Brownson, Anna L., ed. Election Index: Nineteen Eighty. LC 59-13987. 1980. pap. 8.00 (87289). Congr Staff.

Brownson, Anna L., jt. ed. see Brownson, Charles B.

Brownson, Charles B., ed. Advance Locator for Capital Hill, 1981: With Biographical Material. 19th ed. LC 59-13987. (Congressional Staff Directory Ser.). 1981. pap. 9.00. Congr Staff.

--Congressional Staff Directory. LC 59-13987. 1981. Repr. of 1978 ed. 25.00. Congr Staff.

--Congressional Staff Directory, 1981. 23rd ed. 1096p. 1981. pap. 25.00. Congr Staff.

Brownson, Charles B. & Brownson, Anna L., eds. Federal Staff Directory, 1981. 960p. 1981. casebound 25.00 (ISBN 0-686-69484-8). Congr Staff.

Brownstein. Mathematics Workbook for College Entrance Examinations. rev. ed. (gr. 10-12). 1976. pap. text ed. 5.95 (ISBN 0-8120-0654-2). Barron.

Brownstein & Weiner. Barron's How to Prepare for College Entrance Examinations. LC 80-330. 1980. 15.00 (ISBN 0-8120-5323-0); pap. 5.95 (ISBN 0-8120-2191-6). Barron.

--Basic Word List. 1981. pap. 2.50 (ISBN 0-8120-0709-3). Barron.

--Como Preparase Para la Prueba De Aptitud Academia y la Prueba De Aprovechamiento Academico, De Barron. (Span. ed.). Date not set. pap. 4.95 (ISBN 0-8120-0593-7). Barron.

Brownstein, A. M. U. S. Petrochemicals: Technologies, Markets & Economics. LC 77-184571. 1972. 25.50 o.p. (ISBN 0-87814-008-5). Pennwell Pub.

Brownstein, Michael. Highway to the Sky: "The Frank O'Hara Award Series". LC 79-93499. (A Full Court Rebound Bk.). 1978. pap. 6.00 (ISBN 0-231-03339-7). Full Court NY.

Brownstein, Michael, ed. see Jacob, Max.

Brownstein, Oscar L. & Daubert, Darlene M. Analytical Sourcebook of Concepts in Dramatic Theory. LC 80-1200. 584p. 1981. lib. bdg. 45.00 (ISBN 0-313-21309-7, BRN/). Greenwood.

Brownstein, Samuel C. & Weiner, Mitchel. Barron's How to Prepare for College Entrance Examinations. 9th rev ed. LC 78-9661. (gr. 11-12). 1978. 15.00 o.p. (ISBN 0-8120-5323-0); pap. 5.95 o.p. (ISBN 0-8120-2025-1). Barron.

--Barron's How to Prepare for the College Entrance Examinations (SAT) 10th ed. 704p. (gr. 11-12). 1980. text ed. 19.00 (ISBN 0-8120-5402-4); pap. text ed. 5.95 (ISBN 0-8120-2191-6). Barron.

--Barron's How to Prepare for the Graduate Record Examination. rev. ed. LC 78-15175. 1979. 12.95 (ISBN 0-8120-5164-5); pap. 6.95 (ISBN 0-8120-2032-4). Barron.

--Barron's Vocabulary Builder: A Systematic Plan for Building a Vocabulary, Testing Progress & Applying Knowledge. rev. ed. LC 75-14340. (Orig.). (gr. 9-12). 1975. pap. 3.25 (ISBN 0-8120-0964-9). Barron.

--You Can Win a Scholarship. (gr. 10-12). 1981. pap. text ed. price not set. Barron.

--You Can Win a Scholarship. rev. ed. LC 64-24871. (Orig.). (gr. 10-12). 1972. pap. text ed. 6.50 o.p. (ISBN 0-8120-2073-1). Barron.

Brownstone, D. L. How to Run a Successful Speccialty Food Store. 124p. 1978. pap. 5.95 (ISBN 0-471-04031-2). Wiley.

Brownstone, D. M. Successful Selling Skills for Small Business. 112p. 1978. 4.95 (ISBN 0-471-04029-0). Wiley.

Brownstone, David, ed. see Doyle, Dennis M.

Brownstone, David M. Sell Your Way to Success. 224p. 1981. 12.95 (ISBN 0-471-09257-6); pap. 7.95 (ISBN 0-471-09242-8). Wiley.

Brownstone, David M., jt. auth. see Hawes, Gene R.

Browrigg, W. Grant. Corporate Fund Raising a Practical Plan of Action. 1978. pap. 12.50 o.p. (ISBN 0-915400-10-3). Interbk Inc.

Browse, Lillian. William Nicholson. (Illus.). 1956. 15.00 o.p. (ISBN 0-246-63804-4). Dufour.

Browse, Norman L. Physiology & Pathology of Bed Rest. (Illus.). 240p. 1965. 22.50 (ISBN 0-398-00243-6). C C Thomas.

Broxon, Mildred D. Too Long a Sacrifice. (Orig.). 1981. pap. 2.50 (ISBN 0-440-18603-X). Dell.

Broyles, J. Frank & Hay, Robert D. Administration of Athletic Programs: A Managerial Approach. (Illus.). 1979. ref. 17.95 (ISBN 0-13-005249-3). P-H.

Broyles, R. L. The Man Who Could Read Cards. (Orig.). 1980. pap. 1.95 (ISBN 0-532-23310-7). Manor Bks.

Broyles, Robert. Financial & Managerial Accounting in Health Care Facilities. 600p. Date not set. text ed. price not set (ISBN 0-89443-340-7). Aspen Systems.

Broyles, Robert & Lay, Colin. Statistics in Health Administration, 2 vols. Incl. Vol. 1. Basic Concepts & Applications. 1979. 47.50 (ISBN 0-89443-153-6); Vol. II. Advanced Concepts & Applications. 1980. 48.00 (ISBN 0-89443-166-8). LC 79-23280. Aspen Systems.

Broyles, William, ed. Best of Texas Monthly. limited ed. (Illus.). 379p. 1978. 50.00 (ISBN 0-932012-01-9). Texas Month Pr.

Brozek, Josef, ed. see Watson, Robert I.

Brozen, Yale. Is Government the Source of Monopoly? And Other Essays. LC 80-14176. (Cato Paper Ser.: No. 9). 80p. 1980. pap. 2.00 (ISBN 0-932790-09-7). Cato Inst.

Brubacker, Earl R. Individual Values & Global Sharing. 192p. 1980. 17.50x (ISBN 0-8147-1031-X). NYU Pr.

Brubaker, Dale L. Creative Leadership in Elementary Schools. LC 76-15719. 1976. pap. text ed. 6.95 (ISBN 0-8403-1494-9). Kendall-Hunt.

Brubaker, Dale L. & Nelson, Roland H., Jr. Creative Survival in Education Bureaucracies. LC 73-17608. 1974. 16.00 (ISBN 0-8211-0125-0); text ed. 14.50x (ISBN 0-685-42627-0). McCutchan.

Brubaker, Ray. What in the World Is Happening? 1981. pap. 3.95 (ISBN 0-8407-5767-0). Nelson.

Brubaker, Sterling. To Live on Earth. pap. 1.50 o.p. (ISBN 0-451-61137-3, MW1137, Ment). NAL.

Brubaker, Susan H. Workbook for Aphasia: Exercises for the Redevelopment of Higher Level Language Functioning. LC 78-5305. 1978. 9.95 (ISBN 0-8143-1595-X). Wayne St U Pr.

Brucan, Silviu. The Dialectic of World Politics. LC 77-85349. 1978. 19.95 (ISBN 0-02-904680-7). Free Pr.

Bruccoli, Matthew. Reconquest of Mexico: An Amiable Journey in Persuit of Cortes. LC 74-76440. 1974. 8.95 (ISBN 0-8149-0742-3). Vanguard.

--Scott & Ernest: The Authority of Failure & the Authority of Success. LC 79-26848. 192p. 1980. pap. 7.95 (ISBN 0-8093-0977-7). S Ill U Pr.

Bruccoli, Matthew & Clark, C. Frazer, Jr., eds. Fitzgerald-Hemingway Annual. Incl. 1969. 18.00 (ISBN 0-685-60247-8); 1970. 18.00 (ISBN 0-910972-03-6); 1971. 22.00 (ISBN 0-910972-12-5); 1972. 22.00 (ISBN 0-910972-34-6); 1973. 22.00 (ISBN 0-910972-38-9); 1974. o.s.i. (ISBN 0-910972-49-4); 1975. o.s.i. (ISBN 0-910972-54-0); 1976. 24.00 (ISBN 0-910972-62-1). LC 75-83781. IHS-PDS.

Bruccoli, Matthew, ed. & intro. by see Cozzens, James G.

Bruccoli, Matthew J. Apparatus for F. Scott Fitzgerald's The Great Gatsby: Under the Red, White & Blue. LC 74-4142. (S. C. Apparatus of Definitive Editions: No. 1). 1974. 14.95x (ISBN 0-87249-313-X); deluxe ed. 95.00x (ISBN 0-87249-323-7). U of SC Pr.

--James Gould Cozzens: A Descriptive Bibliography. LC 80-53553. (Pittsburgh Ser in Bibliography). (Illus.). 256p. 1981. 32.95x (ISBN 0-8229-3435-3). U of Pittsburgh Pr.

--Some Kind of Epic Grandeur: The Life of F. Scott Fitzgerald. LC 80-8740. (Illus.). 384p. 1981. 17.50 (ISBN 0-15-183242-0). HarBraceJ.

--Supplement to F. Scott Fitzgerald: A Descriptive Bibliography. LC 79-21728. (Pittsburgh Ser. in Bibliography). (Illus.). 235p. 1980. 19.95x (ISBN 0-8229-3409-4). U of Pittsburgh Pr.

Bruccoli, Matthew J., ed. The Chief Glory of Every People: Essays on Classic American Writers. LC 73-1783. 310p. 1973. 14.95x (ISBN 0-8093-0615-8). S Ill U Pr.

--James Gould Cozzens: New Acquist of True Experience. LC 79-14581. (Crosscurrents-Modern Critiques-New Ser.). 158p. 1979. 17.95 (ISBN 0-8093-0930-0). S Ill U Pr.

Bruccoli, Matthew J. & Clark, C. E., Jr., eds. First Printings of American Authors, 4 vols. LC 74-11756. (Illus.). 1978. Set. 220.00 (ISBN 0-8103-0933-5). Gale.

--First Printings of American Authors: Supplement, Vol. 5. (Illus.). 1980. 55.00 (ISBN 0-8103-0934-3, Bruccoli Clark Bk). Gale.

Bruccoli, Matthew J. & Layman, Richard, eds. Fitzgerald-Hemingway Annual, 3 vols. Incl. 1977 Annual. 1978 (ISBN 0-8103-0909-2); 1978 Annual. 1979 (ISBN 0-8103-0910-6); 1979 Annual. 1980 (ISBN 0-8103-0911-4). LC 75-83781. (Illus.). 44.00 ea. (Bruccoli Clark). Gale.

Bruccoli, Matthew J., ed. see Fitzgerald, F. Scott.

Bruccoli, Matthew J., ed. see Lardner, Ring.

Bruccoli, Matthew J., ed. see Sayre, Joel & Faulkner, William.

Bruccoli, Matthew J., et al, eds. Conversations with Jazz Musicians. LC 77-9143. (Conversations Ser.: Vol. 2). 1977. 30.00 (ISBN 0-8103-0944-0, A Bruccoli Clark Book). Gale.

--Conversations with Writers. LC 77-9142. (Conversations Ser.: Vol. 1). 1977. 30.00 (ISBN 0-8103-0943-2, Bruccoli Clark Book). Gale.

--Conversations with Writers II. LC 77-27992. (Conversations Ser.: Vol. 3). 1978. 30.00 (ISBN 0-8103-0945-9, Bruccoli Clark Book). Gale.

Bruce, jt. auth. see Huffman.

Bruce, A. B. The Miracles of Christ. Date not set. 17.25 (ISBN 0-86524-060-4). Klock & Klock.

Bruce, Alice. The Guidance Function: Research & Precptions. 1977. pap. 10.00 o.p. (ISBN 0-686-00909-6, D-105). Essence Pubns.

--Use & Effect of School Psychological Services. 42p. 1978. pap. 10.00 o.p. (ISBN 0-686-00915-0, D-113). Essence Pubns.

Bruce, Carol, ed. see NASSP.

Bruce, Colin R., ed. see Krause, Chester L. & Mishler, Clifford.

Bruce, David L. Functional Toxicity of Anesthesia. LC 80-82766. (The Scientific Basis of Clinical Anesthesia Ser.). 1980. 15.50 (ISBN 0-8089-1276-3). Grune.

Bruce, David L., jt. auth. see Applebaum, Edward L.

Bruce, Dickson D., Jr. And They All Sang Hallelujah: Plain-Folk Camp-Meeting Religion, 1800-1845. LC 74-11344. (Illus.). 1974. 8.50x (ISBN 0-87049-157-1); pap. 4.75 (ISBN 0-87049-310-8). U of Tenn Pr.

Bruce, Errol. Cape Horn to Port. (Nautical). (Illus.). Date not set. cancelled (ISBN 0-679-50951-8). McKay.

Bruce, Erroll. This Is Rough Weather Cruising. (Illus.). 1980. 17.50 (ISBN 0-393-03245-0). Norton.

Bruce, F. F. Answers to Questions. 2nd ed. 1978. pap. 7.95 (ISBN 0-310-21991-4). Zondervan.

--Commentary on First & Second Corinthians. Black, Matthew, ed. (New Century Bible Commentary Ser.). 224p. 1980. pap. 6.95 (ISBN 0-8028-1839-0). Eerdmans.

--In Retrospect: Remembrance of Things Past. 272p. 1980. 13.95 (ISBN 0-8028-3537-6). Eerdmans.

--New Testament History. LC 78-144253. 462p. 1972. pap. 5.95 (ISBN 0-385-02533-5, Anch). Doubleday.

--Paul: Apostle of the Heart Set Free. LC 77-26127. 1978. 15.95 (ISBN 0-8028-3501-5). Eerdmans.

--Promise & Fulfilment: Present to Professor S. H. Hooke, by the Society for O. T. Study. 224p. 1963. text ed. 12.95x (ISBN 0-567-02055-X). Attic Pr.

Bruce, Frederick F. Epistle to the Ephesians. 1962. 7.95 (ISBN 0-8007-0083-X). Revell.

Bruce, Frederick F., jt. auth. see Simpson, E. K.

Bruce, Frederick F., ed. Second Thoughts on the Dead Sea Scrolls. 1956. pap. 4.95 (ISBN 0-8028-1026-8). Eerdmans.

Bruce, George. Harbottle's Dictionary of Battles. 3rd rev. ed. 304p. 1981. 14.95 (ISBN 0-442-22336-6); pap. 7.95 (ISBN 0-442-22335-8). Van Nos Reinhold.

Bruce, Harry J. Distribution & Transportation Handbook. LC 76-132669. (Illus.). 1971. 17.50 (ISBN 0-8436-1400-5). CBI Pub.

Bruce, Harry J. & Burke, Frederick J. How to Apply Statistics to Physical Distribution. 1967. 12.95 (ISBN 0-8436-1402-1). CBI Pub.

Bruce, Helen F. Your Guide to Photography. 2nd ed. (Orig.). 1974. pap. 3.95 (ISBN 0-06-463342-X, EH 342, EH). Har-Row.

Bruce, I. A. Historical Commentary on the Hellenica Cxyrhynchia. (Cambridge Classical Studies). 1967. 19.95 (ISBN 0-521-04352-2). Cambridge U Pr.

Bruce, J. M., intro. by. British Aviation Colours of World War Two. LC 76-13821. (R.A.F. Museum Ser.: Vol. 3). (Illus.). 1977. 11.95 o.p. (ISBN 0-88254-407-1). Hippocrene Bks.

Bruce, J. M., frwd. by. The Spitfire V Manual. LC 76-393. (RAF Museum Ser.: Vol 1). (Illus.). 336p. 1976. 12.50 o.p. (ISBN 0-88254-376-8). Hippocrene Bks.

Bruce, J. P. & Clark, R. H. Introduction to Hydrometeorology. 1966. 25.00 (ISBN 0-08-011715-5); pap. 12.00 (ISBN 0-08-011714-7). Pergamon.

Bruce, Jeannette. Judo: A Gentle Beginning. LC 74-26503. (Illus.). 160p. (gr. 3 up). 1975. 8.95 (ISBN 0-690-00557-1, TYC-J). T Y Crowell.

Bruce, John. Breathing Space. LC 74-76302. (Anansi Fiction Ser.: No. 31). 120p. 1974. 10.95 (ISBN 0-88784-432-4, Pub. by Hse Anansi Pr Canada); pap. 5.95 (ISBN 0-88784-330-1). U of Toronto Pr.

Bruce, John C. & Stokoe, John. Northumbrian Minstrelsy: A Collection of the Ballads, Melodies, & Small-Pipe Tunes of Northumbria. LC 65-4143. xxxiv, 197p. 1965. Repr. of 1882 ed. 10.00 (ISBN 0-8103-5042-4). Gale.

Bruce, Marjory. The Book of Craftsmen: The Story of Man's Handiwork Through the Ages. LC 70-185352. (Illus.). 283p. 1974. Repr. of 1937 ed. 18.00 (ISBN 0-8103-3960-9). Gale.

Bruce, Martin M. A Guide to Human Relations in Business & Industry. LC 73-6907. 1969. pap. 11.05 (ISBN 0-935198-00-8). M M Bruce.

Bruce, Maurice. The Coming of the Welfare State. 1974. 33.00 (ISBN 0-7134-1351-4, Pub. by Batsford England); pap. 14.95 (ISBN 0-7134-1359-X). David & Charles.

Bruce, Maye. Common Sense Compost Making. (Illus., Orig.). 1973. pap. 3.95 (ISBN 0-571-09990-4, Pub. by Faber & Faber). Merrimack Bk Serv.

Bruce, Neil. Portugal: The Last Empire. LC 75-1034. 160p. 1975. 11.95 o.p. (ISBN 0-470-11366-9). Halsted Pr.

Bruce, Nigel. Teamwork for Preventive Care, Vol. 1. (Social Policy Research Monographs). 264p. 1980. 55.00 (ISBN 0-471-27883-1, Pub. by Wiley-Interscience). Wiley.

Bruce, Peter H. Memoirs of Peter Henry Bruce: A Military Officer in the Services of Prussia, Russia, & Great Britian. (Russia Through European Eyes Ser). 1970. Repr. of 1782 ed. 49.50 (ISBN 0-306-77029-6). Da Capo.

Bruce, Robert. Software Debugging for Microcomputers. (Illus.). 1980. text ed. 18.95 (ISBN 0-8359-7021-3); pap. text ed. 10.95 (ISBN 0-8359-7020-5). Reston.

Bruce, V. Awakening the Slower Mind. 1969. 22.00 (ISBN 0-08-006387-X); pap. 10.75 (ISBN 0-08-006386-1). Pergamon.

Bruce, W. R. & Johns, H. E. The Spectra of X Rays Scattered in Low Atomic Number Materials. 1980. 10.00x (Pub. by Brit Inst Radiology). State Mutual Bk.

Bruce, W. Robert, et al, eds. Banbury Report 7-the Carcinogen & Mutagen Formation in the Gastrointestinal Tract. (Banbury Report Ser.). (Illus.). 1981. 60.00x (ISBN 0-87969-206-5). Cold Spring Harbor.

Bruce-Briggs, B. New Class. 252p. 1981. pap. 5.95 (ISBN 0-07-008573-0). McGraw.

Bruce-Mitford, Rupert, ed. Recent Archaeological Excavations in Europe. 1975. 35.00x o.p. (ISBN 0-7100-7963-X). Routledge & Kegan.

Brucer, et al, eds. The Heritage of Nuclear Medicine. LC 79-65338. (Illus.). 1979. soft cover 17.00 (ISBN 0-932004-02-4). Soc Nuclear Med.

Bruch, Charles D. Mechanics for Technology. LC 75-31719. 400p. 1976. text ed. 20.95 (ISBN 0-471-11369-7); instructor's manual avail. (ISBN 0-471-11373-5). Wiley.

--Strength of Materials for Technology. LC 77-27629. 1978. text ed. 19.95 (ISBN 0-471-11372-7); sol. manual (ISBN 0-471-04513-6). Wiley.

Bruchac, Joseph. How to Start & Sustain a Literary Magazine: Practical Strategies for Publications of Lasting Value. LC 80-80568. 150p. (Orig.). 1980. pap. 12.95 (ISBN 0-935446-01-X). Provision.

--Translator's Son. Barkan, Stanley H., ed. (Cross-Cultural Review Chapbook 10). 40p. 1980. pap. 3.50 (ISBN 0-89304-809-7). Cross Cult.

--Turkey Brother & Other Tales: Iroquois Folk Stories. LC 75-35580. (Illus.). 64p. (gr. 3-6). 1975. 6.95 o.p. (ISBN 0-912278-68-4); pap. 3.95 o.p. (ISBN 0-912278-85-4). Crossing Pr.

Bruchard, Gisele De see Corbasson, Nadine & De Bruchard, Gisele.

Bruchey, Stuart, ed. Small Business in American Life. LC 80-10994. 450p. 1980. 25.00x (ISBN 0-231-04872-6). Columbia U Pr.

Bruchez, Dardo. Mensaje a la Conciencia. 128p. (Orig., Span.). 1979. pap. 2.50 (ISBN 0-89922-143-2). Edit Caribe.

Bruchez, Dardo, tr. see Tozer, A. W.

Bruck, Axel. Creative Camera Techniques. LC 80-41402. (Illus.). 144p. 1981. 19.95 (ISBN 0-240-51106-9). Focal Pr.

--Practical Composition. LC 80-40759. (Practical Photography Ser.). (Illus.). 164p. 1981. 19.95 (ISBN 0-240-51060-7). Focal Pr.

Bruck, Lilly. Access: The Guide to a Better Life for Disabled Americans. 252p. 1978. 12.95 (ISBN 0-394-50133-0); pap. 5.95 (ISBN 0-394-73455-6). Random.

Bruck, Peter, ed. The Black American Short Story in the 20th Century: A Collection of Critical Essays. 1977. pap. text ed. 25.25x (ISBN 90-6032-085-9). Humanities.

Bruck, Stephen D. Blood Compatible Synthetic Polymers: An Introduction. (Illus.). 144p. 1974. 14.75 (ISBN 0-398-02931-8). C C Thomas.

Brucker, Gene. People & the Communities in the Western World, 2 vols. 1979. pap. text ed. 9.95x ea.; Vol. 1. (ISBN 0-256-02111-2); Vol. 2. (ISBN 0-256-02186-4). Dorsey.

Brucker, Gene A. Renaissance Florence. (New Dimensions in History-Historical Cities Ser.). 306p. 1969. pap. text ed. 9.95 (ISBN 0-471-11371-9). Wiley.

Brucker, Jerry. Horsethief Canyon. 1981. pap. 1.95 (ISBN 0-8439-0911-0, Leisure Bks). Nordon Pubns.

Bruckl, Renate. Structural & Thematic Analysis of George Meredith's Novel "Diana of the Crossways". (Salzburg Studies in English Literature: Romantic Reassessment Ser.: No. 73). 1978. pap. text ed. 25.00x (ISBN 0-391-01332-7). Humanities.

Bruckmann, G., ed. Input-Output Approaches in Global Modeling: Proceedings of the Fifth IIASA Symposium on Global Modeling, Sept. 26-29,1977. (IIASA Proceedings: Vol. 9). (Illus.). 518p. 1980. 115.00 (ISBN 0-08-025663-5). Pergamon.

Bruckner, D. J., ed. Politics & Language: Spanish & English in the United States. (Orig.). 1980. pap. 4.00x (ISBN 0-686-28732-0). U Chi Ctr Policy.

Bruckner, Dwight. Hot Lead. 1977. pap. 1.25 (ISBN 0-505-51217-3). Tower Bks.

Bruckner, Ira. Hardon. (Illus.). 1980. pap. 6.00 (ISBN 0-916906-30-2). Konglomerati.

Bruckner, J. A Bibliographical Catalogue of Seventeenth-Century German Books Published in Holland. (Anglica Germanica: No. 13). 1971. text ed. 95.30x (ISBN 0-686-20922-2). Mouton.

Bruckner, Steven, jt. auth. see Bergman, Samuel.

Brudney, jt. auth. see Meier.

Brue, Nordahl L. Retailer's Guide to Understanding Leases. 200p. 1980. 26.00 (C6580). Natl Ret Merch.

Brue, Stanley L. & Wentworth, Donald R. Economic Scenes: Theory in Today's World. 2nd ed. (Illus.). 1980. text ed. 11.95 (ISBN 0-13-233510-7). P-H.

Bruegel, J. W. Czechoslovakia Before Munich: The German Minority Problem & British Appeasement Policy. 41.95 (ISBN 0-521-08687-6). Cambridge U Pr.

Brueggeman, Walter, ed. see Westermann, Claus.

Brueggemann, Walter. Living Toward a Vision: Biblical Reflections on Shalom. LC 76-22172. (Shalom Resource Ser.). 1976. pap. 5.95 (ISBN 0-8298-0322-X). Pilgrim NY.

--The Prophetic Imagination. LC 78-54546. 128p. 1978. pap. 4.95 (ISBN 0-8006-1337-6, 1-1337). Fortress.

--Tradition for Crisis: A Study in Hosea. LC 68-21008. 1981. pap. 6.95 (ISBN 0-8042-0181-1). John Knox.

Brueggemann, Walter, ed. see Hamerton-Kelly, Robert.

Brueggemann, Walter, ed. see Harrelson, Walter.

Brueggemann, Walter, ed. see Harrington, Daniel J.

Brueggemann, Walter, ed. see Johnson, Luke T.

Brueggemann, Walter, ed. see Patrick, Dale.

Bruell, jt. auth. see Schneider.

Bruening, William H. Introduction to the Philosophy of Law. LC 78-62249. 1978. pap. text ed. 9.00 (ISBN 0-8191-0570-8). U Pr of Amer.

--The Is-Ought Problem: Its History, Analysis, & Dissolution. LC 77-18569. 1978. pap. text ed. 8.75x (ISBN 0-8191-0364-0). U Pr of Amer.

Bruford, W. H. The German Tradition of Self-Cultivation. LC 74-79143. 336p. 1974. 47.50 (ISBN 0-521-20482-8). Cambridge U Pr.

Bruford, Walter H. Germany in the Eighteenth Century. 1935. 38.50 (ISBN 0-521-04354-9); pap. 11.50x (ISBN 0-521-09259-0, 259). Cambridge U Pr.

--Theatre, Drama, & Audience in Goethe's Germany. LC 73-10579. 388p. 1974. Repr. of 1950 ed. lib. bdg. 26.25x (ISBN 0-8371-7016-8, BRTD). Greenwood.

Brugger, Bill. China: Liberation & Transformation 1942-1962. (Illus.). 288p. 1981. 27.50x (ISBN 0-389-20086-7). B&N.

--China: Radicalism to Revisionism 1962-1979. (Illus.). 275p. 1981. 27.50x (ISBN 0-389-20087-5). B&N.

Brugger, Robert. Nickel Plating. LC 70-523834. 1970. 32.50x (ISBN 0-85218-031-4). Intl Pubns Serv.

Brugger, Robert J., ed. Ourselves-Our Past: Psychological Approaches to American History. LC 80-81425. 448p. 1981. text ed. 26.50x (ISBN 0-8018-2312-9); pap. text ed. 8.95x (ISBN 0-8018-2382-X). Johns Hopkins.

Brugmann, Karl. Kurze Vergleichende Grammatik der Indogermanischen Sprachen. (Ger). 1969. Repr. of 1904 ed. 100.00x (ISBN 3-11-000179-9). De Gruyter.

Brugmann, Karl & Delbrueck, Berthold. Grundriss der Vergleichenden Grammatik der Indogermanischen Sprachen, 5 vols. (Ger). 1970. Repr. of 1893 ed. 576.00x (ISBN 3-11-000180-2). De Gruyter.

Bruhns, Karen O. Cihuatan: An Early Postclassic Town of El Salvador: the 1977-78 Excavations. Feldman, Lawrence, ed. (Monographs in Anthropology Ser.: No. 5). (Illus.). vii, 171p. (Orig.). 1980. pap. 8.60 (ISBN 0-913134-82-1). Mus Anthro MO.

Bruicker, S. De see Ward, S. & De Bruicker, S.

Bruins, Paul F., ed. Polyurethane Technology. LC 68-54598. (Polymer Engineering & Technology Ser). 1969. 30.00 (ISBN 0-471-11395-6, Pub by Wiley-Interscience). Wiley.

Brukoff, Barry, jt. auth. see Fowles, John.

Brumback, Carl. Holy Land Hymns. LC 73-93792. 1974. pap. 1.45 o.p. (ISBN 0-88270-087-1). Logos.

Brumbaugh. History of the German Baptist Brethren in Europe & America. Repr. 39.00 o.p. (ISBN 0-686-12346-8). Church History.

Brumbaugh, J. Frank. Mail Order....Starting up, Making It Pay. LC 78-14623. 1979. 13.95 o.p. (ISBN 0-8019-6804-6); pap. 7.95 (ISBN 0-8019-6805-4). Chilton.

Brumbaugh, James. Heating, Ventilating, & Air Conditioning Library, 3 vols. LC 76-29155. (Illus.). 1976. 11.95 ea. Vol. 1 (ISBN 0-672-23248-0, 23248). Vol. 2 (ISBN 0-672-23249-9, 23249). Vol. 3 (ISBN 0-672-23250-2, 23250). 32.95, set of 3 vols. (ISBN 0-672-23227-8). Audel.

--Upholstering. LC 72-83060. (Illus.). 400p. 1972. 9.95 (ISBN 0-672-23189-1). Audel.

--Welders Guide. 2nd ed. LC 72-97632. 736p. 1973. 12.95 (ISBN 0-672-23202-2). Audel.

Brumbaugh, James E. Wood Furniture: Finishing, Refinishing, Repairing. LC 73-91640. (Illus.). 352p. 1974. 9.95 (ISBN 0-672-23216-2). Audel.

Brumblay, Ray U. A First Course in Quantitative Analysis. LC 77-93982. (Chemistry Ser). 1970. text ed. cancelled (ISBN 0-201-00726-6). A-W.

--Qualitative Analysis. (Illus., Orig). 1964. pap. 3.95 (ISBN 0-06-460116-1, CO 116, COS). Har-Row.

--Quantitative Analysis. 2nd ed. (Orig.). 1972. pap. 4.50 (ISBN 0-06-460050-5, CO 50, COS). Har-Row.

Brumble, H. David, III. An Annotated Bibliography of American Indian & Eskimo Autobiographies. LC 80-23449. 190p. 1981. 10.95x (ISBN 0-8032-1175-9). U of Nebr Pr.

Brumfiel, Charles & Krause, Eugene. Mathematics I & II: Grade 8 Mathematics, 2 bks. 1975. Bk. 1. text ed. 11.20 (ISBN 0-201-00603-0, Sch Div); Bk. 2. text ed. 11.20 (ISBN 0-201-00605-7); Bk. 1. tchr's. ed. 14.52 (ISBN 0-201-00604-9); Bk. 2. tchr's. ed. 14.52 (ISBN 0-201-00606-5). A-W.

Brumfiel, Charles & Vance, Irvin. Algebra & Geometry for Teachers. LC 70-93983. (Mathematics Ser). 1970. text ed. 16.95 (ISBN 0-201-00667-7); instr's manual 1.25 (ISBN 0-201-00668-5). A-W.

Brumfield, Gregory W. Partially Ordered Rings & Semi-Algebraic Geometry. (London Mathematical Society Lecture Note Ser.: No. 37). 1980. pap. 23.95x (ISBN 0-521-22845-X). Cambridge U Pr.

Brumfit, Christopher. Problems & Principles in English Teaching. LC 79-40706. (Language Teaching Methodology Ser.). (Illus.). 168p. 1980. 13.95 (ISBN 0-08-024559-5); pap. 7.95 (ISBN 0-08-024558-7). Pergamon.

Brumfit, J. H., ed. & intro. by. see Voltaire.

Brumfitt, J. H., ed. see De Voltaire, Francois M.

Brumfitt, William & Asscher, A. W., eds. Urinary Tract Infection: National Symposium on Urinary, 2nd, London, March 1972. (Illus.). 310p. 1973. text ed. 19.00x o.p. (ISBN 0-19-261210-7). Oxford U Pr.

Brumgardt, John R. & Bowles, Larry L. People of the Magic Waters: The Cahuilla Indians of Palm Springs. (Illus.). 1981. 9.95 (ISBN 0-88280-060-4). ETC Pubns. Postponed.

Brumgardt, John R., ed. Civil War Nurse: The Diary & Letters of Hannah Ropes. LC 79-28372. 200p. 1980. 12.50x (ISBN 0-87049-280-2). U of Tenn Pr.

Brumhead, Derek. Geology Explained in the Yorkshire Dales & on the Yorkshire Coast. LC 78-660964. 1979. 17.95 (ISBN 0-7153-7703-5). David & Charles.

Brumm, Ursula. American Thought & Religious Typology. LC 76-97737. 1970. 18.00 (ISBN 0-8135-0621-2). Rutgers U Pr.

Brummitt, Wyatt. Kites. (Golden Guide Ser). (Illus.). 1971. PLB 9.15 (ISBN 0-307-64344-1, Golden Pr); pap. 1.95 (ISBN 0-307-64344-1). Western Pub.

Brun, Herbert & Gaburo, Kenneth. Collaboration One. 24p. 1976. soft cover saddle-stitched 15.00. Lingua Pr.

Brun, Kim, ed. see Federico, Pat A., et al.

Brun, Viggo. Sug, the Trickster Who Fooled the Monk: A Northern Thai Tale with Vocabulary. (Scandinavian Institute of Asian Studies Monographs: No. 27). (Orig.). 1976. pap. text ed. 9.25x (ISBN 0-7007-0095-1). Humanities.

Brundage, Anthony. The Making of the New Poor Law: The Politics of Inquiry, Enactment, & Implementation, 1832-1839. 1978. 15.00 (ISBN 0-8135-0855-X). Rutgers U Pr.

Brundage, D. J., jt. auth. see Strauch, K. P.

Brundage, Dorothy J. Nursing Management of Renal Problems. 2nd ed. LC 80-11720. (Illus.). 1980. pap. text ed. 9.95 (ISBN 0-8016-0849-X). Mosby.

Brundage, James, jt. auth. see Bullough, Vern.

Brundage, James, jt. ed. see Bullough, Vern.

Brundage, James A. Richard Lion Heart. LC 73-1361. (Illus.). 288p. 1974. 10.00 (ISBN 0-684-13802-6, ScribT). Scribner.

Brundage, Percival F. Changing Concepts of Business Income. LC 75-21163. 1975. Repr. of 1952 ed. text ed. 10.00 (ISBN 0-914348-18-3). Scholars Bk.

Brundritt, Alan. Elementary ALGOL. (Illus.). 80p. 1976. pap. text ed. 9.95 (ISBN 0-7121-0549-2, Pub. by Macdonald & Evans Engalnd). Intl Ideas.

Brune, Gunnar. Springs of Texas, Vol. 1. (Illus.). 534p. 1981. 35.00 (ISBN 0-9604766-0-1). G Brune.

Brune, K. & Baggiolini, M., eds. Arachidonic Acid Metabolism in Inflammation & Thrombosis: Proceedings of the First European Workshop on Inflammation, Basel, 1979. (Agents & Actions Supplements: No. 4). (Illus.). 1979. pap. 38.00 (ISBN 3-7643-1095-2). Birkhauser.

Bruneau, T. C. The Political Transformation of the Brazilian Catholic Church. LC 73-79318. (Perspectives on Development Ser.: No. 2). 302p. 1974. 41.50 (ISBN 0-521-20256-6); pap. 11.50x (ISBN 0-521-09848-3). Cambridge U Pr.

Brunell, R. Hydraulic & Pneumatic Cylinders. (Illus.). 27.95x o.p. (ISBN 0-85461-049-9). Intl Ideas.

Brunell, Richard, jt. auth. see Vazsonyi, Andrew.

Brunelle, Wallace & O'Neill, Robert. Constructional Geometry. Gray, Allan W., ed. 1972. pap. text ed. 8.25 (ISBN 0-89420-077-1, 350299); cassette recordings 107.95 (ISBN 0-89420-201-4, 350300). Natl Book.

Brunelli, B. Driven Magnetic Fusion Reactors: Proceedings. (Commission of the European Communities Ser.: EUR 6146). (Illus.). pap. 82.00 (ISBN 0-08-024459-9). Pergamon.

Brunenmeister, Susan L., jt. auth. see Fotheringham, Nick.

Bruner, Jerome S. & Garton, Alison, eds. Human Growth & Development: The Wolfson College Lectures, 1976. (Illus.). 1978. pap. text ed. 8.95x (ISBN 0-19-857518-1). Oxford U Pr.

Bruner, Jerome S., et al. Study of Thinking. LC 56-7999. 1956. pap. 13.95 o.p. (ISBN 0-471-11415-4). Wiley.

Brunet, Mario. All About Sailing: A Handbook for Juniors. 1976. pap. 7.95 (ISBN 0-8120-0699-2). Barron.

Brunet, Roger, ed. Bibliographie Geographique Internationale, 1977: International Geographical Bibliography, 1977, Vol. 82. 752p. (Fr.). 1979. Set, 5 Fasciculae. pap. 67.50x (ISBN 0-8002-2218-0). Intl Pubns Serv.

--Decouvrir la France, 7 vols. Incl. Vol. 1. Bretagne, Normandie, Poitou, Vendee, Charentes (ISBN 2-03-013351-5, 3578); Vol. 2. Paris, Bassin parisien, Pays de Loire (3579); Vol. 3. Nord, Alsace, Lorraine, Bourgogne (3581); Vol. 4. Franche-Comte, Auvergne, Lyonnais, Alpes (3582); Vol. 5. Languedoc, Provence, Cote d'azur, Corse (3583); Vol. 6. Limousin, Bassin aquitain, Pyrenees, Pays basque et catalan (3584); Vol. 7. La France d'outre-Mer, la France maintenant (3585). (Illus.). 336p. 1972. 78.25 ea. Larousse.

--Decouvrir la France, 18 vols, Vols. 1-5 & 10-22. Incl. Vol. 1. La Bretagne (ISBN 2-03-013801-0); Vol. 2. La Maine et la Normandie; Vol. 3. Poitou, Charentes, Vendee; Vol. 4. Paris (ISBN 2-03-013804-5); Vol. 5. Champagne, Picardie, Ile de France; Vol. 10. Bourgogne et Franche Comte; Vol. 11. L' Auvergne et le Boubonnais; Vol. 12. En Pays lyonnais (ISBN 2-03-013812-6); Vol. 13. Les Alpes (ISBN 2-03-013813-4); Vol. 14. Bas Languedoc, Cevennes, Causses, Languedoc (ISBN 2-03-013814-2); Vol. 15. La Provence; Vol. 16. Cote d'azur, la Corse (ISBN 2-03-013816-9); Vol. 17. Limousin, Perigord, Quercy, Bouergue; Vol. 18. L' Aquitaine (ISBN 2-03-013818-5); Vol. 19. Le Midi toulousain; Vol. 20. Pyrenees du Pays Basque au Pays Catalan; Vol. 21. La France d'outre-mer; Vol. 22. La France maintenant (ISBN 2-03-013822-3). (Illus.). 1972. 22.50 ea. Larousse.

Brungardt, Helen. Contemplation: The Activity of Mystical Consciousness. 2nd ed. 72p. 1980. pap. 3.00 (ISBN 0-87707-220-5). Red Earth.

--The Mystical Meaning of Jesus the Christ: Significant Episodes in the Life of the Master. 4.00 (ISBN 0-686-69472-4). Red Earth.

Brunhild, Gordon, jt. auth. see Burton, Robert H.

Brunhoff, Jean De see De Brunhoff, Jean.

Brunhoff, Laurent De see De Brunhoff, Laurent.

Brunhoff, Laurent de see De Brunhoff, Laurent.

Brunhouse, Robert L. The Counter-Revolution in Pennsylvania: 1776-1790. LC 42-5025. (Illus.). 1971. 8.00 (ISBN 0-911124-65-9). Pa Hist & Mus.

--Sylvanus G. Morley & the World of the Ancient Mayas. LC 78-160489. (Illus.). 1971. pap. 8.95 o.p. (ISBN 0-8061-1294-8). U of Okla Pr.

Bruni, C., ed. Systems Theory in Immunology. (Lecture Notes in Biomathematics: Vol. 32). 273p. 1980. pap. 16.00 (ISBN 0-387-09728-7). Springer-Verlag.

Bruni, J. Edward, jt. auth. see Montemurro, Donald G.

Bruni, Joseph, jt. auth. see Wilder, B. Joseph.

Bruning, Nancy P., jt. auth. see Katz, Jane.

Brunk, Jason W. Child & Adolescent Development. LC 74-16258. 464p. 1975. pap. text ed. 13.95x o.p. (ISBN 0-471-11430-8). Wiley.

Brunn, H. O. The Story of the Original Dixieland Jazz Band. LC 77-3791. (Roots of Jazz Ser.). (Illus.). 1977. Repr. of 1960 ed. lib. bdg. 22.50 (ISBN 0-306-70892-2). Da Capo.

Brunn, Stanley D. & Wheeler, James O. The American Metropolitan Systems: Present & Future. 250p. 1980. 27.95 (ISBN 0-470-27018-7, Pub. by Halsted Pr). Wiley.

Brunn, Stanley D., jt. auth. see Harries, Keith D.

Brunner & Gravas. Clinical Hypertension & Hypotension. Date not set. price not set (ISBN 0-8247-1279-X). Dekker.

Brunner, Bernard. Six Days to Sunday. 240p. 1976. pap. 1.75 o.p. (ISBN 0-345-25165-2). Ballantine.

Brunner, Calvin. Design of Sewage Sludge Incineration Systems. LC 80-21916. (Pollution Technology Review: No. 71). (Illus.). 380p. 1981. 48.00 (ISBN 0-8155-0825-5). Noyes.

Brunner, Emil. Our Faith. (Scribner Library Edition). 1936. pap. 2.45 o.p. (ISBN 0-684-71722-0, SL87, ScribT). Scribner.

--Scandal of Christianity. LC 65-12729. 1965. pap. 3.95 (ISBN 0-8042-0708-9). John Knox.

Brunner, Felix. Handbook of Graphic Reproduction Processes. (Visual Communication Bks.). (Illus.). 1962. 35.00 o.s.i. (ISBN 0-8038-2964-7). Hastings.

Brunner, Francis A., tr. see Jungmann, Josef A.

Brunner, Herb. Introduction to Microprocessors. 1981. text ed. 17.95 (ISBN 0-8359-3247-8); instr's. manual free (ISBN 0-8359-3248-6). Reston.

Brunner, John. Players at the Game of People. 1980. pap. 2.25 (ISBN 0-345-29235-9). Ballantine.

--The Productions of Time. (Science Fiction Ser.). 1977. pap. 1.50 o.p. (ISBN 0-87997-329-3, UW1329). DAW Bks.

--The Repairman of Cyclops. 1981. pap. 2.25 (ISBN 0-87997-638-1, UE1638). DAW Bks.

--The Sheep Look up. 192p. 1981. pap. 2.95 (ISBN 0-345-27503-9, Del Rey). Ballantine.

--Shockwave Rider. LC 74-1877. 304p. (YA) 1975. 8.95 o.p. (ISBN 0-06-010559-3, HarpT). Har-Row.

--Stand on Zanzibar. LC 79-19062. 1979. Repr. of 1968 ed. lib. bdg. 15.00x (ISBN 0-8376-0438-9). Bentley.

--Timescoop. 1981. pap. 2.25 (ISBN 0-440-18916-0). Dell.

--To Conquer Chaos. 1981. pap. 1.95 (ISBN 0-87997-596-2, JI596). Daw Bks.

Brunner, Joseph F. & Campbell, John J. Participating in Secondary Reading: A Practical Approach. (Illus.). 1978. ref. 15.95 (ISBN 0-13-651323-9). P-H.

Brunner, Karl, ed. The Great Depression Revisited. (Rochester Studies in Economics & Policy Issues: Vol. 2). 368p. 1980. lib. bdg. 20.00 (ISBN 0-89838-051-0, Pub by Martinus Nijhoff). Kluwer Boston.

Brunner, L. & Suddarth, D. Pediatric Nursing. 1981. pap. text ed. 18.35 (ISBN 0-06-318183-5, Pub. by Har-Row Ltd England). Har-Row.

Brunner, Lillian, intro. by. Diseases. (Reference Library). (Illus.). 1980. 19.95 (ISBN 0-916730-19-0). InterMed Comm.

Brunner, Lillian S. The Lippincott Manual of Nursing Practice. 2nd ed. LC 78-6987. 1978. text ed. 29.95 (ISBN 0-397-54212-7). Lippincott.

Brunner, Lillian S. & Suddarth, Doris S. Textbook of Medical-Surgical Nursing. 4th ed. LC 79-27506. 1500p. 1980. text ed. 33.95 (ISBN 0-397-54238-0). Lippincott.

Brunner, Lousene R. New Casserole Treasury. rev. enl. ed. LC 74-138711. (Illus.). 1971. 8.95 o.p. (ISBN 0-06-010557-7, HarpT). Har-Row.

Brunner, Marguerite A. Antiques for Amateurs on a Shoestring Budget. 1977. pap. 3.95 o.p. (ISBN 0-89104-063-3). A & W Pubs.

Brunner, Nancy A. Orthopedic Nursing: A Programmed Approach. 2nd ed. 1975. pap. text ed. 7.95 o.p. (ISBN 0-8016-0838-4). Mosby.

--Orthopedic Nursing: A Programmed Approach. 3rd ed. LC 78-32020. (Illus.). 1979. pap. text ed. 11.50 (ISBN 0-8016-0833-3). Mosby.

Brunner, R. & Brewer, G. Organized Complexity. LC 79-141936. 1971. 12.95 (ISBN 0-02-904850-8). Free Pr.

Brunner, Ronald D., jt. ed. see Brewer, Garry D.

Bruno, Agnes M. Formulaic & Non-Formulaic Style in the Nibelungenlied: A Computer-Based Analysis. (U. C. Publications in Modern Philology, Vol. 109). 1974. pap. 9.00x (ISBN 0-520-09499-9). U of Cal Pr.

Bruno, E. J., ed. High-Velocity Forming of Metals. rev. ed. LC 68-23027. (Manufacturing Data Ser). 1968. pap. 10.75x (ISBN 0-87263-009-5). SME.

Bruno, Frank J. Behavior & Life: An Introduction to Psychology. 1980. text ed. 18.95 (ISBN 0-471-02191-1); study guide 5.50 (ISBN 0-471-06340-1); tests avail. (ISBN 0-471-06342-8). Wiley.

--Think Yourself Thin. 265p. 1973. pap. 3.50 (ISBN 0-06-463348-9, EH 348, EH). Har-Row.

--Trends in Social Work, Eighteen Seventy-Four to Nineteen Fifty-Six: A History Based on the Proceedings of the National Conference of Social Work. 2nd ed. LC 80-19210. xviii, 462p. 1980. Repr. of 1957 ed. lib. bdg. 39.75x (ISBN 0-313-22665-2, BRTI). Greenwood.

Bruno, Giordano. The Ash Wednesday Supper. Jaki, Stanley L., tr. (Illus.). 174p. 1975. text ed. 28.90x (ISBN 90-2797-581-7). Mouton.

Bruno, Joseph. Baseball's Golden Dozen. 1976. 8.50 o.p. (ISBN 0-682-48564-0, Banner). Exposition.

Bruno, Michael S., jt. auth. see DePasquale, Nicholas P.

Bruno, Michael S., jt. ed. see DePasquale, Nicholas P.

Bruno, Vincent J., ed. The Parthenon. (Critical Studies in Art History Ser). (Illus.). 334p. 1974. 12.50 (ISBN 0-393-04373-8); pap. 6.95x (ISBN 0-393-09354-9). Norton.

Brunoff, Laurent De see De Brunoff, Laurent.

Brunotte, Hans. Dachshund Guide. 6.98 o.p. (ISBN 0-385-01574-7). Doubleday.

Bruns, Bill, jt. auth. see Braden, Vic.

Bruns, Bill, jt. auth. see Cochran, Mickey.

Bruns, Bill, jt. auth. see Wolf, Dave.

Bruns, Gerald L. Modern Poetry & the Idea of Language: A Critical & Historical Study. LC 73-86886. 1974. 20.00 o.p. (ISBN 0-300-01613-1). Yale U Pr.

Bruns, Roger & Vogt, George. Your Government Inaction. 80p. 1981. pap. 3.95 (ISBN 0-312-89814-2). St Martin.

Bruns, Roger, ed. Am I Not a Man & a Brother: The Antislavery Crusade of Revolutionary America, 1688-1788. LC 76-6118. (Illus.). 600p. 1981. pap. 11.95 (ISBN 0-87754-213-9). Chelsea Hse.

Bruns, Roger, jt. ed. see Schlesinger, Arthur M., Jr.

Bruns, W. J. Introduction to Accounting: Economic Measurement for Decisions. 1971. 16.95 (ISBN 0-201-00676-6); instructor's manual 2.95 (ISBN 0-201-00677-4). A-W.

Bruns, William, jt. auth. see Tutko, Thomas.

Brunsden, Denys, et al, eds. The Unquiet Landscape. LC 77-15583. (The Geographical Magazine Ser.). 1978. Repr. of 1972 ed. 17.95 (ISBN 0-470-99345-6). Halsted Pr.

Brunskill, R. W. Illustrated Handbook of Vernacular Architecture. new ed. (Illus.). 1979. 17.50 (ISBN 0-571-08636-5, Pub. by Faber & Faber); pap. 8.95 (ISBN 0-571-11244-7). Merrimack Bk Serv.

--Vernacular Architecture of the Lake Countries: A Field Handbook. (Illus.). 1978. pap. 8.95 (ISBN 0-571-09459-7, Pub. by Faber & Faber). Merrimack Bk Serv.

--Vernacular Architecture of the Lake Countries. 1978. 16.95 (ISBN 0-571-09460-0, Pub. by Faber & Faber). Merrimack Bk Serv.

Brunson, E., jt. auth. see Gearing, P.

Brunson, Madelon & Goodyear, Imogene. No Graven Images. LC 77-24081. 1977. 3.00 (ISBN 0-8309-0189-2). Herald Hse.

Brunson, Marion B. Our Bailey & Staggers History & Genealogy. 1980. 10.00 (ISBN 0-916620-51-4). Portals Pr.

Brunson, Nancy & Brunson, Wright A. Grieve Not for Wrightsie. 1978. pap. 3.95 o.p. (ISBN 0-88270-272-6). Logos.

Brunson, R. R. & Bass, Feris A., Jr. Fragile Empires: Correspondence of Samuel Swartwout & James Morgan 1836-1856. 1978. 7.50 (ISBN 0-88319-032-X). Shoal Creek Pub.

Brunson, Wright A., jt. auth. see Brunson, Nancy.

Brunt, H. L. Van see Van Brunt, H. L.

Brunt, John. Decisions. LC 79-16158. (Horizon Ser.). 1979. pap. 4.50 (ISBN 0-8127-0235-2). Southern Pub.

Brunt, P. A. Italian Manpower 225 B.C.-A.D. 14. 1971. 69.00x (ISBN 0-19-814283-8). Oxford U Pr.

--Social Conflicts in the Roman Republic. (Illus.). 1972. 6.00x (ISBN 0-393-04335-5); pap. 3.95 (ISBN 0-393-00586-0). Norton.

Brunt, P. A., ed. see Augustus.

Brunt, P. A., ed. see Jones, A. H.

Brunt, Samuel see Clarke, John.

Bruntjen, Carol R., jt. auth. see Bruntjen, Scott.

Bruntjen, Carol R., jt. ed. see Bruntjen, Scott.

Bruntjen, Scott & Bruntjen, Carol R. A Checklist of American Imprints for 1833: Items 17208-22795. LC 64-11784. (Checklist of American Imprints Ser.: Vol. 1833). 1979. lib. bdg. 27.50 (ISBN 0-8108-1191-X). Scarecrow.

--Checklist of American Imprints for 1831. LC 64-11784. (Checklist of American Imprints Ser.: Vol. 1831). 433p. 1975. 20.00 (ISBN 0-8108-0828-5). Scarecrow.

Bruntjen, Scott & Young, Melissa L. Douglas C. McMurtrie: Bibliographer & Historian of Printing. LC 78-25682. (The Great Bibliographers Ser.: No. 4). 1979. lib. bdg. 10.00 (ISBN 0-8108-1188-X). Scarecrow.

Bruntjen, Scott & Bruntjen, Carol R., eds. A Checklist of American Imprints for 1832. LC 64-11784. (Checklist of American Imprints Ser.: Vol. 1832). 1977. 22.50 (ISBN 0-8108-1019-0). Scarecrow.

Brunton, Mary. Self-Control: A Novel, 2 vols. Luria, Gina, ed. (The Feminist Controversy in England, 1788-1810 Ser.). 1974. Set. lib. bdg. 50.00 ea. (ISBN 0-8240-0852-9). Garland Pub.

Brunton, Paul. Search in Secret Egypt. LC 78-16641. 1980. pap. 4.50 (ISBN 0-87728-060-6). Weiser.

--Search in Secret India. (Illus.). 1981. pap. 4.50 (ISBN 0-87728-061-4). Weiser.

--Wisdom of the Overself. 1970. pap. 7.50 (ISBN 0-87728-062-2). Weiser.

Bruntz, George G. Children of the Volga. 144p. 1981. 6.95 (ISBN 0-8059-2763-8). Dorrance.

Brus, Wlodzimierz. The Market in a Socialist Economy. 1972. 19.00x (ISBN 0-7100-7276-7). Routledge & Kegan.

--Socialist Ownership & Political Systems Under Socialism. 256p. 1975. 20.00 (ISBN 0-7100-8247-9). Routledge & Kegan.

Brusca, Gary J. General Patterns of Invertebrate Development. (Illus.). 134p. 1975. pap. 7.15x (ISBN 0-916422-03-8). Mad River.

Brusca, Gary J. & Brusca, Richard C. A Naturalist's Seashore Guide: Common Marine Life Along the Northern California Coast & Adjacent Shores. 1978. pap. 8.50x (ISBN 0-916422-12-7). Mad River.

Brusca, Richard C., jt. auth. see Brusca, Gary J.

Brush, Elizabeth P. Guizot in the Early Years of the Orleanist Monarchy. LC 74-2319. (University of Illinois Studies in the Social Sciences). 236p. 1975. Repr. of 1929 ed. 15.25 (ISBN 0-86527-090-2). Fertig.

Brush, Lorelei R. Encouraging Girls in Mathematics. LC 79-55774. (Illus.). 1980. text ed. 16.00 (ISBN 0-89011-542-7). Abt Assoc.

Brush, Stephen B. Mountain, Field, & Family: The Economy & Human Ecology of an Andean Valley. LC 77-24364. 1977. 14.50x (ISBN 0-8122-7728-7). U of Pa Pr.

Brush, Stephen G., ed. see International Working Seminar on the Role of the History of Physics in Physics Education.

Brusher, Joseph S. Popes Through the Ages. 3rd rev. ed. (Illus.). 530p. 1980. 30.00 (ISBN 0-89141-110-0, Neff-Kane). Presidio Pr.

Brushwood, Carolyn, tr. see Aguilera-Malta, Demetrio.

Brushwood, Carolyn, tr. see Galindo, Sergio.

Brushwood, John, tr. see Aguilera-Malta, Demetrio.

Brushwood, John, tr. see Galindo, Sergio.

Brusick, David. Principles of Genetic Toxicology. 300p. 1980. 25.00 (ISBN 0-306-40414-1, Plenum Pr). Plenum Pub.

Brustein, Robert. Critical Moments: Reflecting on Theater & Society. 1980. 10.00 (ISBN 0-394-51093-3). Random.

--The Culture Watch: Essays on Theatre & Society, 1969-1974. 1975. 7.95 o.p. (ISBN 0-394-49814-3). Knopf.

Bruton, J. G. Ejercicios de espanol. (gr. 9 up). 1968. 5.15 (ISBN 0-08-012838-6); pap. 4.30 (ISBN 0-08-012837-8). Pergamon.

Brutus, Dennis. A Simple Lust: Collected Poems of South African Jail & Exile. 176p. 1973. 7.95 (ISBN 0-8090-8678-6); pap. 3.45 o.p. (ISBN 0-8090-1371-1). Hill & Wang.

Brutzkus, Boris. Economic Planning in Soviet Russia. Gardner, Gilbert, tr. from Ger. LC 79-51857. 1981. Repr. of 1935 ed. 19.75 (ISBN 0-88355-950-1). Hyperion Conn.

Bruun, Geoffrey, jt. auth. see Ferguson, Wallace K.

Bruun, Per. Port Engineering. 3rd ed. 750p. 1981. text ed. 50.00 (ISBN 0-87201-739-7). Gulf Pub.

Bruun-Rasmussen, Ole & Petersen, Grete. Make-up, Costumes & Masks for the Stage. LC 76-19803. (Illus.). 96p. (gr. 4-12). 1981. pap. 6.95 (ISBN 0-8069-8992-0). Sterling.

--Make up, Costumes & Masks for the Stage. LC 76-19803. (Illus.). (gr. 5 up). 1976. 10.95 (ISBN 0-8069-7024-3); PLB 9.87 (ISBN 0-8069-7025-1). Sterling.

Bruyere, Christain & Inwood, Robert. In Harmony with Nature. LC 74-22581. (Illus.). 200p. 1979. pap. 7.95 (ISBN 0-8069-8432-5). Sterling.

Bruyere, Christian & Inwood, Robert. Country Comforts. (Illus.). 224p. 1979. pap. 7.95 (ISBN 0-8069-8270-5). Sterling.

Bruyere, Christian, jt. auth. see Inwood, Robert.

Bruyere, Toni M. & Robey, Sidney J. For Gourmets with Ulcers. 224p. 1974. pap. 1.95 o.p. (ISBN 0-06-463395-0, 395, EH). Har-Row.

--For Gourmets with Ulcers. 224p. 1981. pap. 4.95 (ISBN 0-393-00984-X). Norton. Postponed.

Bruyn, Monica G. De see De Bruyn, Monica G.

Bruyn, S. T. The Social Economy: People Transforming Modern Business. 392p. 1977. 29.95 (ISBN 0-471-01985-2). Wiley.

Bruyn, Severyn T. The Social Economy: People Transforming Modern Business. LC 77-14597. 1977. 29.95 (ISBN 0-471-01985-2). Ronald Pr.

Bruyn, Severyn T. & Rayman, Paula, eds. Non-Violent Action & Social Change. (Orig.). 1980. pap. text ed. 8.95x (ISBN 0-8290-0271-5). Irvington.

Bruyn, Sevpryn. Quaker Testimonies & Economic Alternatives. LC 80-80915. 35p. pap. 1.25 (ISBN 0-87574-231-9). Pendle Hill.

Bry, Adelaide. T. A. Games: Using Transactional Analysis in Your Life. LC 74-10066. (Illus., Orig.). 1975. pap. 1.50 o.p. (ISBN 0-06-080334-7, P334, PL). Har-Row.

Bry, Doris. Alfred Steiglitz, Photographer. 1974. 15.00 (ISBN 0-87846-035-7); pap. 5.00 (ISBN 0-87846-147-7). Mus Fine Arts Boston.

Bry, Theodor De see De Bry, Theodor.

Bryan, Arthur H., et al. Bacteriology: Principles & Practice. 6th rev ed. (Orig.). 1962. pap. 3.95 (ISBN 0-06-460003-3, CO 3, COS). Har-Row.

Bryan, Ashley. Beat the Story-Drum, Pum-Pum. LC 80-12045. (Illus.). 80p. (gr. 4-6). 1980. 10.95 (ISBN 0-689-30769-1). Atheneum.

--Ox of the Wonderful Horns & Other African Folktales. LC 75-154749. (Illus.). (gr. 1-5). 1971. PLB 8.95 (ISBN 0-689-20690-9). Atheneum.

--Walk Together Children. (gr. 2 up). pap. 2.95 (ISBN 0-689-70485-2, A-112, Aladdin). Atheneum.

Bryan, Derek. Land & People of China. (gr. 7 up). 1965. 3.95g o.s.i. (ISBN 0-02-715110-7). Macmillan.

Bryan, Doris S. School Nursing in Transition. LC 73-11115. 1973. text ed. 11.95 o.p. (ISBN 0-8016-0840-6). Mosby.

Bryan, Dorothy & Bryan, Marguerite. Just Tammie. LC 51-13037. (Illus.). (gr. 1-3). 1951. 3.50 (ISBN 0-396-03314-8). Dodd.

Bryan, Frank M. Politics in Rural America: People, Parties, & Policy. (Special Study Ser.). 320p. (Orig.). lib. bdg. 26.50x (ISBN 0-89158-561-3); pap. text ed. 10.00x (ISBN 0-89158-984-8). Westview.

Bryan, George T., ed. Nitrofurans. LC 77-72824. (Carcinogenesis-A Comprehensive Survey Ser.: Vol. 4). 1978. 25.00 (ISBN 0-89004-250-0). Raven.

Bryan, Greyson. Taxing Unfair International Trade Practices: A Study of the U. S. Antidumping & Countervailing Duty Law. LC 80-7571. 1980. 34.95x (ISBN 0-669-03752-4). Lexington Bks.

Bryan, J., jt. auth. see Halsey, William.

Bryan, J. W. Development of the English Law of Conspiracy. LC 72-77737. (Law, Politics, & History Ser). 1970. Repr. of 1909 ed. lib. bdg. 20.00 (ISBN 0-306-71375-6). Da Capo.

Bryan, James & Murphy, Charles. The Windsor Story. 1981. pap. 3.95 (ISBN 0-440-19346-X). Dell.

Bryan, James, jt. auth. see Bryan, Tanis.

Bryan, James H. see Hetherington, E. Mavis.

Bryan, John. This Soldier Still at War. LC 74-5528. (Illus.). 352p. 1975. 9.95 o.p. (ISBN 0-15-190060-4). HarBraceJ.

Bryan, John & Castle, Coralie. Edible Ornamental Garden. LC 73-91941. (Illus.). 192p. (Orig.). 1974. pap. 4.95 (ISBN 0-912238-47-X) (ISBN 0-912238-46-1). One Hund One Prods.

Bryan, John E. Small World Vegetable Gardening. LC 76-58364. (Illus.). 144p. 1977. 4.95 (ISBN 0-912238-79-8); pap. 4.95 (ISBN 0-912238-78-X). One Hund One Prods.

Bryan, John L. Fire Suppression & Detection Systems. LC 73-7367. (Fire Science Ser). (Illus.). 320p. 1974. text ed. 14.95 (ISBN 0-02-473920-0, 47392). Macmillan.

Bryan, John L. & Picard, Raymond C., eds. Managing Fire Services. LC 79-10067. (Municipal Management Ser.). (Illus.). 1979. text ed. 34.00 (ISBN 0-87326-018-X). Intl City Mgt.

Bryan, Kay. Look! I Can Cook! A Simplified Guide to Cooking & Household Skills. LC 79-89358. 1979. pap. 7.95 (ISBN 0-88290-130-3). Horizon Utah.

Bryan, Lee. The Searching Years. 1981. pap. 2.25 (ISBN 0-8439-0871-8, Leisure Bks). Nordon Pubns.

Bryan, M. Leonard, ed. Remote Sensing of Earth Resources: A Guide to Information Sources. LC 79-22792. (Geography & Travel Information Guide Ser.: Vol. 1). (Illus.). 1979. 30.00 (ISBN 0-8103-1413-4). Gale.

Bryan, Marguerite, jt. auth. see Bryan, Dorothy.

Bryan, Mary C. Forrest Reid. (English Author Ser.: No. 199). 1976. lib. bdg. 12.50 (ISBN 0-8057-6661-8). Twayne.

Bryan, Nonobah G. & Young, Stella. Navajo Native Dyes. (Wild & Woolly West Ser: No. 34). (Illus.). 1978. 7.00 (ISBN 0-910584-49-4); pap. 2.50 (ISBN 0-910584-57-5). Filter.

Bryan, Tanis & Bryan, James. Understanding Learning Disabilities. 2nd ed. LC 77-25987. 1978. text ed. 15.95x (ISBN 0-88284-056-8). Alfred Pub.

Bryan, Thalia T. Poems of Inspiration. 1981. 5.95. Vantage.

Bryan, William F. & Dempster, G. C., eds. Sources & Analogues of Chaucer's Canterbury Tales. 1958. text ed. 35.00x (ISBN 0-391-00443-3). Humanities.

Bryan, William H. Standing Tall in Credit Management. (No. 6). 1977. pap. 1.90 (ISBN 0-934914-28-1). NACM.

Bryant, Al. Climbing the Heights. 1956. pocket ed. 5.95 o.p. (ISBN 0-310-22060-2). Zondervan.

--Daily Meditations with F. B. Meyer. 1979. 8.95 (ISBN 0-8499-0148-0). Word Bks.

--Keep in Touch. 1981. 8.95. Word Bks.

--New Compact Bible Dictionary. 1967. 8.95 (ISBN 0-310-22080-7); pap. 3.95 (ISBN 0-310-22082-3). Zondervan.

--A Pocket Treasury of Daily Devotions. LC 77-82183. 1978. pap. 1.75 (ISBN 0-87123-464-5, 200464). Bethany Fell.

--Religious Plays That Click. 1954. pap. 2.95 (ISBN 0-310-22101-3). Zondervan.

Bryant, Al, ed. Climbing Higher. LC 77-24978. 1977. 7.95 (ISBN 0-87123-052-6); pap. 4.95 (ISBN 0-87123-054-2, 210054). Bethany Fell.

--Climbing the Heights. 384p. 1981. pap. 4.95 (ISBN 0-310-22061-0). Zondervan.

--Favorite Poems. 96p. 1972. pap. 2.50 (ISBN 0-310-22072-6). Zondervan.

Bryant, Al, compiled by. A Pocket Treasury of Devotional Verse. (Orig.). 1980. pap. 2.95 (ISBN 0-87123-466-1, 200466). Bethany Fell.

Bryant, Al, ed. Poems That Bless. 96p. 1972. pap. 1.95 (ISBN 0-310-22092-0). Zondervan.

Bryant, Andrew. The Italians: How They Live & Work. LC 75-27493. 164p. 1976. text ed. 8.95 (ISBN 0-03-028511-9, HoltC). HR&W.

Bryant, Anita. Amazing Grace. 1971. 5.95 o.p. (ISBN 0-8007-0468-1). Revell.

--The Anita Bryant Story. 1977. 6.95 o.p. (ISBN 0-8007-0897-0). Revell.

--Bless This Food. 1976. pap. 1.95 o.p. (ISBN 0-345-24900-3). Ballantine.

--Mine Eyes Have Seen the Glory. (Illus.). 160p. 1970. 5.95 o.p. (ISBN 0-8007-0375-8); pap. 1.50 o.p. (ISBN 0-8007-8098-1, Spire Bks). Revell.

Bryant, Anita & Green, Bob. Fishers of Men. (Illus.). 1973. 5.95 o.p. (ISBN 0-8007-0612-9). Revell.

--Light My Candle. (Illus.). 160p. 1974. 5.95 o.p. (ISBN 0-8007-0690-0). Revell.

--Raising God's Children. 1979. 6.95 o.p. (ISBN 0-8007-0878-4). Revell.

Bryant, Arthur. Medieval Foundation of England. LC 67-12856. 1968. pap. 1.95 o.s.i. (ISBN 0-02-030710-1, Collier). Macmillan.

Bryant, Ben. Submarine Commander. (Bantam War Books). 272p. 1980. pap. 2.50 (ISBN 0-553-13665-8). Bantam.

Bryant, Bradford A. Special Foster Care: A History & Rationale. (Orig.). 1980. pap. text ed. 4.50 (ISBN 0-9604068-0-8). People Places.

Bryant, Carl. All About Repairing Major Household Appliances. (Illus.). 240p. (80 packages of sketches). 1974. pap. 4.95 (ISBN 0-8015-0158-X, Hawthorn). Dutton.

Bryant, Carlene F. We're All Kin: A Cultural Study of a Mountain Neighborhood. LC 81-473. 160p. 1981. 9.50x (ISBN 0-87049-312-4). U of Tenn Pr.

Bryant, Christopher. The Heart in Pilgrimage: Christian Guidelines for the Human Journey. 208p. 1980. 9.95 (ISBN 0-8164-0457-7). Seabury.

Bryant, Christopher G. Sociology in Action: A Critique of Selected Conceptions of the Role of Sociologist. LC 75-9120. 1976. 26.95 (ISBN 0-470-11470-3). Halsted Pr.

Bryant, Clifton D. Deviancy & the Family. LC 72-77588. pap. 10.95x (ISBN 0-88295-201-3). AHM Pub.

Bryant, Clifton D., ed. Social Problems Today: Dilemmas & Dissensus. LC 73-133948. 1971. pap. text ed. 6.95 o.p. (ISBN 0-685-04158-1). Lippincott.

Bryant, Coralie & White, Louise G. Managing Rural Development: Peasant Participation in Rural Development. LC 80-80681. (Kumarian Press Development Monographs). 62p. (Orig.). 1980. pap. 5.95x (ISBN 0-931816-50-5). Kumarian Pr.

Bryant, Cyril E. Presentamos Al Pueblo Bautista. Mariotti, Federico A., tr. (Illus.). 1976. pap. 0.40 (ISBN 0-311-17019-6). Casa Bautista.

Bryant, D. Physics. (Teach Yourself Ser.). 1974. pap. 2.95 (ISBN 0-679-10406-2). McKay.

Bryant, Darrol, ed. Proceedings of the Virgin Islands' Seminar on Unification Theology. LC 80-52594. (Conference Ser.: No. 6). (Illus.). xv, 323p. (Orig.). 1980. pap. text ed. 9.95 (ISBN 0-932894-06-2). Unif Theol Sem.

Bryant, Darrol & Foster, Durwood, eds. Hermeneutics & Unification Theology. LC 80-66201. (Conference Ser.: No. 5). (Illus., Orig.). 1980. pap. 7.95 (ISBN 0-932894-05-4). Unif Theol Seminary.

Bryant, Donald C. Edmund Burke & His Literary Friends. 323p. 1980. Repr. of 1939 ed. lib. bdg. 35.00 (ISBN 0-8482-0133-7). Norwood Edns.

Bryant, Donald C. & Wallace, Karl R. Fundamentals of Public Speaking. 5th ed. (Illus.). 640p. 1976. pap. 14.95 (ISBN 0-13-342725-0). P-H.

--Oral Communication: A Short Course in Speaking. 4th ed. (Illus.). 336p. 1976. pap. text ed. 11.95 (ISBN 0-13-638429-3). P-H.

Bryant, Dorothy. The Garden of Eros. LC 78-73215. 1979. pap. 6.00 (ISBN 0-931688-03-5). Ata Bks.

--Miss Giardino. LC 78-54280. 1978. pap. 6.00 (ISBN 0-931688-01-9). Ata Bks.

--Writing a Novel. LC 78-69766. 1978. pap. 5.00 (ISBN 0-931688-02-7). Ata Bks.

Bryant, E. H., jt. auth. see Atchley, W. R.

Bryant, Edward. Cinnabar. LC 75-20160. 1976. 7.95 o.s.i. (ISBN 0-02-518000-2, 51800). Macmillan.

--Wyoming Sun. (Illus.). 132p. 1980. deluxe ed. 12.95; pap. 6.00. Jelm Mtn.

Bryant, Edward, jt. auth. see Pennell, Joseph.

Bryant, Edward C., jt. auth. see King, Donald W.

Bryant, Gerald, jt. auth. see Hogins, Burl.

Bryant, Gerald A., jt. auth. see Hogins, J. Burl.

Bryant, Gerald A., Jr. Comment & Controversy. 1972. pap. text ed. 6.95x (ISBN 0-02-473350-4, 47335). Macmillan.

Bryant, Gerald A., Jr., jt. auth. see Hogins, J. Burl.

Bryant, Gerald, Jr., jt. auth. see Hogins, Burl.

Bryant, Gerald R., Jr., jt. auth. see Hogins, James B.

Bryant, J. A., ed. Molecular Aspects of Gene Expression in Plants. 1977. 46.50 (ISBN 0-12-138150-1). Acad Pr.

Bryant, J. A., Jr. Hippolyta's View: Some Christian Aspects of Shakespeare's Plays. LC 61-6555. 256p. 1961. 12.00x (ISBN 0-8131-1057-2). U Pr of Ky.

Bryant, J. H. Open Decision. LC 79-129473. 1970. 10.95 (ISBN 0-02-904860-5). Free Pr.

Bryant, Jacob. A New System, or, an Analysis of Ancient Mythology, 3 vols. Feldman, Burton & Richardson, Robert, eds. LC 78-60881. (Myth & Romanticism Ser.: Vol. 5). (Illus.). 1980. Set. lib. bdg. 198.00 (ISBN 0-8240-3554-2); lib. bdg. 66.00 ea. Garland Pub.

Bryant, James M. The Conquest. 1972. pap. 5.50 (ISBN 0-686-27963-8). J M Bryant.

--The Fulfillment. 1976. pap. 6.50 (ISBN 0-686-27964-6). J M Bryant.

--Loves & Tragedies. (Illus.). 1968. 22.00 (ISBN 0-686-27960-3). J M Bryant.

--Out of Darkness. 1971. pap. 6.50 (ISBN 0-686-27962-X). J M Bryant.

--The Reckless Era. 1968. pap. 5.50 (ISBN 0-686-27961-1). J M Bryant.

--The Timetable. (Illus.). 1981. 20.00 (ISBN 0-686-28942-0). J M Bryant.

Bryant, Jeannette, ed. Conservation Directory. 301p. 1981. 6.00 (ISBN 0-912186-39-9). Natl Wildlife.

--Conservation Directory 1980. rev. ed. 1980. 4.00 (ISBN 0-912186-34-8). Natl Wildlife.

Bryant, Keith L., Jr. History of the Atchison, Topeka, & Santa Fe Railway. LC 74-8250. (Railroads of America Ser). (Illus.). 512p. 1975. 12.95 o.s.i. (ISBN 0-02-517920-9). Macmillan.

Bryant, Kenneth E. Poems to the Child-God: Structures & Strategies in the Poetry of Surdas. LC 77-80467. (Center for South & Southeast Asian Studies). 1978. 20.00x (ISBN 0-520-03540-2). U of Cal Pr.

Bryant, M., tr. see Goncharov, Ivan.

Bryant, M. Darrol. Jonathan Edwards on God's Kingdom: Three Stages of Theological Development. (Studies in American Religion: Vol. 4). 1981. soft cover 24.95x (ISBN 0-88946-908-3). E Mellen.

Bryant, M. Darrol & Hodges, Susan, eds. Exploring Unification Theology. 2nd ed. LC 78-63274. (Conference Ser.: No. 1). 1978. pap. text ed. 7.95x (ISBN 0-932894-00-3). Unif Theol Seminary.

Bryant, Marcus D. & Kemp, Charles F. The Church and Community Resources. 96p. 1977. pap. 1.95 (ISBN 0-8272-0441-8). Bethany Pr.

Bryant, Margaret M., ed. Current American Usage: How Americans Say It & Write It. LC 62-9735. (Funk & W Bk.). 1965. 6.00 (ISBN 0-308-40056-9, TYC-T). T Y Crowell.

Bryant, Marjorie. Recall the Poppies. (Illus.). 1979. pap. 6.00 o.p. (ISBN 0-931832-14-4). No Dead Lines.

Bryant, Nellie L. Shades of Blue. 1981. 4.50 (ISBN 0-8062-1705-7). Carlton.

Bryant, Neville. Disputed Paternity. 1980. 24.00. Thieme Stratton.

Bryant, Neville J. An Introduction to Immunohematology. LC 75-25269. (Illus.). 320p. 1976. text ed. 14.95 (ISBN 0-7216-2170-8). Saunders.

Bryant, Paul T. H. L. Davis. (United States Authors Ser.: No. 306). 1978. lib. bdg. 12.50 (ISBN 0-8057-7211-1). Twayne.

Bryant, Ralph C. Financial Interdependence & Variability in Exchange Rates. 1980. pap. 2.50 (ISBN 0-8157-1127-1). Brookings.

--Money & Monetary Policy in Interdependent Nations. LC 80-19225. 584p. 1980. 29.95 (ISBN 0-8157-1130-1); pap. 12.95 (ISBN 0-8157-1129-8). Brookings.

Bryant, Sandra, jt. auth. see Tucker, Susan M.

Bryant, Sara C. How to Tell Stories to Children. LC 72-12693. 1973. Repr. of 1924 ed. 18.00 (ISBN 0-8103-3740-1). Gale.

Bryant, Steven, jt. auth. see Saltz, Daniel.

Bryant, Steven J., et al. Intermediate Algebra. 368p. 1968. text ed. 12.95x (ISBN 0-02-473860-3, 47386). Macmillan.

Bryant, Ted, ed. see Askins, Charles.

Bryant, Thelma H. Growing up in Church. LC 79-67524. 1980. 6.95 (ISBN 0-533-04474-X). Vantage.

Bryant, Traphes L. & Leighton, Frances S. Dog Days at the White House: The Outrageous Memoirs of the Presidential Kennel-Keeper Truman to Nixon. (Illus.). 288p. 1975. 9.95 o.s.i. (ISBN 0-02-517990-X). Macmillan.

Bryant, Victor & Postill, Ronald. Sunday Times Book of Brain Teasers, Bk. 1. (Unwin Paperbacks Ser.). (Illus.). 176p. (Orig.). 1980. pap. 4.95x (ISBN 0-04-793045-4, AU-452). Allen Unwin.

Bryant, Will. Blue Russell. 1979. pap. 1.95 o.p. (ISBN 0-449-23840-7, Crest). Fawcett.

Bryant, William C., II & Voss, Thomas G., eds. The Letters of William Cullen Bryant: Vol. III. LC 74-27169. (Illus.). 500p. 1981. 35.00 (ISBN 0-8232-0993-8). Fordham.

Bryce, Charles, ed. Biochemical Education. 208p. 1981. 33.00x (ISBN 0-7099-0600-5, Pub. by Croom Helm LTD England). Biblio Dist.

Bryce, D. P. Differential Diagnosis & Treatment of Hoarseness. (Illus.). 88p. 1974. 11.75 (ISBN 0-398-03166-5). C C Thomas.

Bryce, Felicia. Government Nurse. 192p. (YA) 1976. 4.95 o.p. (ISBN 0-685-66571-2, Avalon). Bouregy.

--Love Finds a Way. (YA) 1977. 4.95 o.p. (ISBN 0-685-73808-6, Avalon). Bouregy.

--Portia in Distress. (YA) 1977. 5.95 (ISBN 0-685-74267-9, Avalon). Bouregy.

--A Winter's Love. 192p. (YA) 1976. 4.95 o.p. (ISBN 0-685-59254-5, Avalon). Bouregy.

Bryce, Herrington J. Planning Smaller Cities. LC 78-14154. (Urban Round Table Ser.: No. 1). 1979. 23.95 (ISBN 0-669-02680-8). Lexington Bks.

Bryce, Herrington J., ed. Cities & Firms. LC 80-8367. (The Urban Roundtable Ser.). 272p. 1980. 18.95x (ISBN 0-669-04042-8). Lexington Bks.

--Revitalizing Cities. (Urban Round Table Ser.: No.2). (Illus.). 320p. 1979. 24.95 (ISBN 0-669-02846-0). Lexington Bks.

--Urban Governance & Minorities. LC 75-44875. (Illus.). 1976. text ed. 19.50 o.p. (ISBN 0-275-23500-9). Praeger.

Bryce, James. International Relations. LC 66-21391. Repr. of 1922 ed. 8.50 (ISBN 0-8046-0053-8). Kennikat.

--Public Opinion in the American Commonwealth. 1981. 18.95 (ISBN 0-87923-370-2); pap. 8.95 (ISBN 0-87923-371-0). Godine.

--South America: Observations & Impressions. (Latin America in the 20th Century Ser.). 1977. Repr. of 1912 ed. lib. bdg. 49.50 (ISBN 0-306-70835-3). Da Capo.

Bryce, Sr. M. Charles. Come Let Us Eat: Preparing for First Communion. rev. ed. LC 70-183075. (Illus.). (gr. 1-2). 1972. pap. 1.45 (ISBN 0-8164-6076-0); first communion, parent-teacher manual 1.95 (ISBN 0-8164-6077-9). Crossroad NY.

Bryce, Marvin & Lloyd, June C. Treating Families in the Home: An Alternative to Placement. (Illus.). 352p. 1980. text ed. 24.75 (ISBN 0-398-04085-0). C C Thomas.

Bryce, Marvin, jt. auth. see Maybanks, Sheila.

Bryce, W. A., tr. see Jelinek, Z. K.

Bryce-Laporte, Roy S. & Thomas, Claudewell S., eds. Alienation in Contemporary Society: A Multidisciplinary Examination. LC 76-18123. (Special Studies). (Illus.). 420p. 1976. text ed. 29.95 o.p. (ISBN 0-275-09800-1). Praeger.

Bryce-Smith, Roger, jt. auth. see Ostlere, Gordon.

Brycha, M. Automatic Transmissions. 2nd ed. 1981. 16.95 (ISBN 0-13-054577-5). P-H.

Brydall, John. Bastardy. Berkowitz, David & Thorne, Samuel, eds. LC 77-86581. (Classics of English Legal History in the Modern Era Ser.). 1979. lib. bdg. 55.00 (ISBN 0-8240-3064-8). Garland Pub.

--Lex Spuriorum; or the Law Relating to Bastardy, Collected from the Common, Civil & Ecclesiastical Laws. LC 77-86581. (Classics of English Legal History in the Modern Era Ser.: Vol. 17). 1978. Repr. of 1703 ed. lib. bdg. 55.00 (ISBN 0-8240-3064-8). Garland Pub.

Brydall, John & Highmore, Anthony. Non Compos Mentis. Berkowitz, David S. & Thorne, Samuel E., eds. LC 77-86669. (Classics of English Legal History in the Modern Era Ser.: Vol. 46). 471p. 1979. lib. bdg. 40.00 (ISBN 0-8240-3095-8). Garland Pub.

Bryden, J. M. Tourism & Development: A Case Study of the Commonwealth Caribbean. (Illus.). 280p. 1973. 42.50 (ISBN 0-521-20263-9). Cambridge U Pr.

Bryden, John & Houston, George. Agrarian Change in the Scottish Highlands: The Role of the Highlands & Islands Development Board in the Agricultural Economy of the Crofting Counties. 152p. 1976. bds. 24.50x (ISBN 0-85520-151-7, Pub. by Martin Robertson England). Biblio Dist.

Bryden, W. W. The Christian's Knowledge of God. 5.50 (ISBN 0-227-67434-0). Attic Pr.

Brydges, Samuel E. Poems. Fourth Edition, Repr. Of 1807. Bd. with Odo, Count of Lingen. A Poetical Tale: in Six Cantos. LC 75-31170. (Romantic Context Ser.: Poetry 1789-1830: Vol. 24). 1978. lib. bdg. 47.00 (ISBN 0-8240-2123-1). Garland Pub.

Brydges, Samuel E. & Quillinan, Edward. Bertram, a Poetical Tale, Repr. Of 1814. Bd. with Occasional Poems, Written in the Year 1811. Repr. of 1814 ed; Select Poems. Repr. of 1814 ed; Five Sonnets Addressed to Wootton, the Spot of the Author's Nativity. Repr. of 1819 ed; Edward Quillian: Dunluce Castle, a Poem, 4 pts. Repr. of 1814 ed. LC 75-31171. (Romantic Context Ser.: Poetry 1789-1830: Vol. 25). 1978. lib. bdg. 47.00 (ISBN 0-8240-2124-X). Garland Pub.

Brydson, J. A., ed. Developments with Natural Rubber. (Illus.). 1967. 22.30x (ISBN 0-85334-062-5). Intl Ideas.

Brydson, J. A., jt. ed. see Whelan, A.

Brydson, John A. Plastics Materials. 3rd ed. 744p. 1975. 49.50 (ISBN 0-88275-288-X). Krieger.
Brye, Joseph. Basic Principles of Music Theory. (Illus.). 1965. 18.95 (ISBN 0-8260-1460-7). Wiley.
Bryen, Diane, et al. Variant English: An Introduction to Language Variation. (Elementary Education Ser.). 1978. pap. text ed. 8.50 (ISBN 0-675-08353-2); instr. manual 3.95 (ISBN 0-686-67995-4). Merrill.
Bryen, Stephen D. The Application of Cybernetic Analysis to the Study of International Politics. 147p. 1971. 27.50x (ISBN 90-247-5076-8). Intl Pubns Serv.
Bryer, J. R. & Rees, R. A., eds. Emerson Bibliographies. LC 80-2526. (AMS Anthology Ser.). 1981. 34.50 (ISBN 0-404-19255-6). AMS Pr.
Bryers, R. W., ed. see Ash Deposit & Corrosion from Impurities in Combustion Gases Symposium, June 26-July 1, 1977, New England College, Henniker, New Hampshire.
Bryfogle, R. Charles. City in Print: An Urban Studies Bibliography. Incl. City in Print Supplement One. 1975. (ISBN 0-88874-046-8). 1974. 35.00 set (ISBN 0-88874-003-4). Dawson & Co.
--City in Print: An Urban Studies Bibliography, Supplement Three. 1979. pap. 15.00 (ISBN 0-918010-01-2). Dawson & Co.
--City in Print: An Urban Studies Bibliography, Supplement Two. 1977. pap. 12.00 (ISBN 0-918010-00-4). Dawson & Co.
Brym, Robert J. Intellectuals & Politics. (Controversies in Sociology Ser.: No. 9). (Orig.). 1980. text ed. 14.95x (ISBN 0-04-322005-3); pap. text ed. 6.95x (ISBN 0-04-322006-1). Allen Unwin.
Brymer, Jack. Clarinet. LC 77-275. (The Yehudi Menuhin Music Guides Ser.). (Illus.). 1977. 12.95 (ISBN 0-02-871430-X); pap. 6.95 (ISBN 0-02-871440-7). Schirmer Bks.
Bryne, Donn. Introduction to Personality. 2nd ed. LC 73-17157. (Personality, Clinical & Social Psychology Ser). (Illus.). 624p. 1974. ref. ed. 18.95 (ISBN 0-13-491597-6). P-H.
Brynn, Edward. Crown & Castle: British Rule in Ireland 1800-1830. (Illus.). 1978. text ed. 32.00x (ISBN 0-7705-1496-0). Humanities.
Brynner, Joseph F., jt. ed. see Schantz, Maria E.
Bryson & Bentley. Ability Grouping of Public School Students: Legal Aspects of Tracking Methods. 300p. 1980. 15.00 (ISBN 0-87215-332-0). Michie.
Bryson, A. E. & Ho, Y. C. Applied Optimal Control: Optimization, Estimation, & Control. rev. ed. LC 75-16114. (Illus.). 481p. 1981. pap. 15.95 (ISBN 0-89116-228-3). Hemisphere Pub.
Bryson, A. E. & Ho, Yu-Chi. Applied Optimal Control. rev. ed. LC 75-16114. 1979. pap. text ed. 15.95 (ISBN 0-470-26774-7). Halsted Pr.
Bryson, Carlton W. & Gray, Allan W. Numerical Trigonometry: Syllabus. 1973. pap. text ed. 7.35 (ISBN 0-89420-050-X, 355110); cassette recordings 70.50 (ISBN 0-89420-164-6, 355000). Natl Book.
Bryson, Harold T. & Taylor, James C. Building Sermons to Meet People's Needs. LC 78-74962. 1980. 5.95 (ISBN 0-8054-2109-2). Broadman.
Bryson, John, ed. Matthew Arnold: Poetry & Prose. 1979. 14.95 o.p. (ISBN 0-8464-0083-9). Beekman Pubs.
Bryson, L., et al, eds. see Conference On Science - Philosophy And Religion - 13th Symposium.
Bryson, L., et al, eds. see Conference On Science - Philosophy And Religion - 14th Symposium.
Bryson, L., et al, eds. see Conference On Science - Philosophy And Religion - 7th Symposium.
Bryson, Lyman, ed. see Institute for Religious & Social Studies.
Bryson, R. E. & Kutzbach, J. E., eds. Air Pollution. LC 68-54859. (CCG Resource Papers Ser.: No. 2). (Illus.). 1968. pap. text ed. 4.00 (ISBN 0-89291-049-6). Assn Am Geographers.
Bryson, Reid A. & Murray, Thomas J. Climates of Hunger: Mankind & the World's Changing Weather. (Illus.). 1979. pap. 6.95 (ISBN 0-299-07374-2). U of Wis Pr.
--Climates of Hunger: Mankind & the World's Changing Weather. LC 76-53649. 1977. 15.00 (ISBN 0-299-07370-X). U of Wis Pr.
Bryson, Thomas A. American Diplomatic Relations with the Middle East, 1784-1975: A Survey. LC 76-44344. 1977. 21.00 (ISBN 0-8108-0988-5). Scarecrow.
--Seeds of Mideast Crisis: The United States Diplomatic Role in the Middle East During World War II. LC 80-15896. 224p. 1981. lib. bdg. 15.95x (ISBN 0-89950-019-6). McFarland & Co.
--United States-Middle East Diplomatic Relations 1784-1978: An Annotated Bibliography. LC 78-26754. 1979. lib. bdg. 11.00 (ISBN 0-8108-1197-9). Scarecrow.
Bryson, W. H. The Equity Side of the Exchequer. LC 73-93394. (Cambridge Studies in English Legal History). 280p. 1975. 36.00 (ISBN 0-521-20406-2). Cambridge U Pr.
Brzezinski, Zbigniew. The Relevance of Liberalism. LC 77-8202. (Studies of the Research Institute on International Change, Columbia University: Vol. 2). 1978. lib. bdg. 22.50x (ISBN 0-89158-134-0). Westview.
Brzezinski, Zbigniew, ed. Africa & the Communist World. LC 63-17816. (Publications Ser.: No. 32). 272p. 1963. 10.00 (ISBN 0-8179-1322-X). Hoover Inst Pr.
Brzin, M., et al, eds. Synaptic Constituents in Health & Disease: Proceedings of the Third Meeting of the European Society for Neurochemistry, Bled, August 31st-Sept, 5th, 1980. (Illus.). 760p. 1980. 125.00 (ISBN 0-08-025921-9). Pergamon.
Brzozowski, J. A. & Yoeli, M. Digital Networks. (Illus.). 416p. 1976. ref. ed. 24.00 (ISBN 0-13-214189-2). P-H.
Buah, F. A., ed. see Davidson, Basil.
Bubani, Pietro. Flora Virgiliana. 134p. 1974. Repr. of 1869 ed. lib. bdg. 26.00x (ISBN 3-87429-075-1). Lubrecht & Cramer.
Bubber, Purobi. The Joys of Chinese Cooking. (Illus.). 1978. text ed. 10.00 (ISBN 0-7069-0553-9, Pub. by Vikas India). Advent Bk.
Bubel, Mike & Bubel, Nancy. Root Cellaring the Simple no-Processing Way to Store Fruits & Vegetables. (Illus.). 320p. 1979. 12.95 (ISBN 0-87857-277-5). Rodale Pr Inc.
Bubel, Nancy, jt. auth. see Bubel, Mike.
Buber, Martin. Eclipse of God: Studies in the Relation Between Religion & Philosophy. 1979. pap. text ed. 3.95x (ISBN 0-391-00902-8). Humanities.
--Good & Evil: Two Interpretations. 1953. pap. 3.95 o.p. (ISBN 0-684-71723-9, SL45, ScribT). Scribner.
--Writings of Martin Buber. Herberg, Will, ed. (Orig.). pap. 3.95 o.p. (ISBN 0-452-00407-1, F407, Mer). NAL.
Buber, Rafael, jt. ed. see Cohn, Margot.
Bubley, Esther & Knauth, Percy. A Mysterious Presence: The Inner Life of Plants. LC 77-79683. 1976. 9.95 (ISBN 0-911104-98-4); pap. 5.95 (ISBN 0-911104-99-2). Workman Pub.
Buccellati, G., ed. see Al-Khalesi, Yasin M.
Buccellati, Giorgio, ed. see Saporetti, Claudio.
Bucco, Martin. Rene Wellek. (United States Authors Ser.: No. 410). 1981. lib. bdg. 12.95 (ISBN 0-8057-7339-8). Twayne.
--Wilbur D. Steele. (U. S. Authors Ser. 198). lib. bdg. 10.95 (ISBN 0-8057-0688-7). Twayne.
Bucellati, G., ed. see Saporetti, C.
Buchan, Alastair. Change Without War: The Shifting Structure of World Power. LC 74-19962. 112p. 1975. 17.95 (ISBN 0-312-12880-0). St Martin.
--Europe's Futures Europe's Choices: Models of Western Europe in the 1970's. LC 77-83385. 1969. 20.00x (ISBN 0-231-03305-2). Columbia U Pr.
Buchan, Alice. A Scrap Screen. (Illus.). 1979. 24.00 (ISBN 0-241-10223-5, Pub. by Hamish Hamilton England). David & Charles.
Buchan, David. The Ballad & the Folk. 1972. 23.00 (ISBN 0-7100-7322-4). Routledge & Kegan.
Buchan, David, ed. Scottish Ballad Book. 244p. 1973. 16.00 (ISBN 0-7100-7566-9). Routledge & Kegan.
Buchan, John. The Magic Walking Stick. LC 75-32205. (Classics of Children's Literature, 1621-1932: Vol. 66). (Illus.). 1976. Repr. of 1932 ed. PLB 38.00 (ISBN 0-8240-2315-3). Garland Pub.
--Sir Walter Scott. LC 67-27580. Repr. of 1932 ed. 12.50 (ISBN 0-8046-0054-6). Kennikat.
Buchan, Perdita. Called Away. 1980. 10.95 (ISBN 0-316-11407-3, Pub. by Atlantic-Little Brown). Little.
Buchan, Roy M., jt. auth. see Beaulieu, Harry J.
Buchan, Tom. Dolphins at Cochin. LC 69-20017. 1969. 3.50 o.p. (ISBN 0-8090-3950-8). Hill & Wang.
Buchan, Vivian. Cat Sun Signs. LC 79-65117. (Illus.). 156p. 1981. pap. 5.95 (ISBN 0-8128-6097-7). Stein & Day.
Buchanan, A. Russell. Black Americans in World War II. LC 76-53577. 149p. 1977. pap. 6.95 (ISBN 0-87436-277-6). ABC-Clio.
Buchanan, Brian. Theory of Classification. (Outlines of Modern Librarianship Ser.). 141p. 1980. text ed. 12.00 (ISBN 0-89664-410-3, Pub. by K G Saur). Shoe String.
Buchanan, Briggs. Early Near Eastern Seals in the Yale Babylonian Collection. Kasten, Ulla, ed. LC 75-43309. (Illus.). 520p. 1981. text ed. 65.00 (ISBN 0-300-01852-5). Yale U Pr.
Buchanan, C. D. Spelling. (gr. 1). 1972. pap. text ed. 2.25 each incl. 8 texts, 4 tchrs' manuals & tests (ISBN 0-8449-2800-3). Learning Line.
Buchanan, Colin. The State of Britain. 1972. 4.95 o.p. (ISBN 0-571-10188-7, Pub. by Faber & Faber). Merrimack Bk Serv.
Buchanan, Cynthia D. Programed Introduction to Linguistics: Phonetics & Phonemics. 1963. pap. text ed. 15.95x (ISBN 0-669-20453-6). Heath.
Buchanan, D. Greek Athletics. (Aspects of Greek Life). (Illus.). 1977. pap. text ed. 2.95x (ISBN 0-582-20059-8). Longman.
--Roman Sport & Entertainment. (Aspects of Roman Life). (Illus.). 1976. pap. text ed. 2.95x (ISBN 0-582-31415-1). Longman.
Buchanan, Daniel, tr. One Hundred Famous Haiku. LC 72-95667. 1977. pap. 5.95 (ISBN 0-87040-222-6). Japan Pubns.
Buchanan, David A. The Development of Job Design Theories & Techniques. LC 79-83808. (Praeger Special Studies). 180p. 1979. 22.95 (ISBN 0-03-052376-1). Praeger.
Buchanan, Freda M. Land & People of Scotland. rev. ed. LC 58-10146. (Portraits of the Nations Ser). (Illus.). (gr. 7-9). 1962. 7.95 o.p. (ISBN 0-397-31554-6). Lippincott.
Buchanan, George W. The Prophet's Mantle in the Nation's Capital. LC 78-59167. 1978. pap. text ed. 5.75 (ISBN 0-8191-0545-7). U Pr of Amer.
Buchanan, Iain. Singapore in Southeast Asia: An Economic & Political Appraisal. LC 72-183727. (Illus.). 336p. 1972. 15.00x (ISBN 0-7135-1656-9). Intl Pubns Serv.
Buchanan, J., jt. auth. see Brennan, G.
Buchanan, James M. Freedom in Constitutional Contract: Perspectives of a Political Economist. LC 77-89513. (Texas A&M Univ. Economics Ser.: No. 2). 328p. 1977. 22.50x (ISBN 0-89096-038-0). Tex A&M Univ Pr.
--Public Finance in the Democratic Process. 1967. 16.00x (ISBN 0-8078-1014-2). U of NC Pr.
Buchanan, James M. & Flowers, Marilyn R. The Public Finances: An Introductory Textbook. 4th ed. 1975. text ed. 16.50x o.p. (ISBN 0-256-01633-X). Irwin.
--The Public Finances: An Introductory Textbook. 5th ed. 1980. 18.95x (ISBN 0-256-02333-6). Irwin.
Buchanan, James M. & Tullock, Gordon. Calculus of Consent: Logical Foundations of Constitutional Democracy. 1962. pap. 4.95 (ISBN 0-472-06100-3, 100, AA). U of Mich Pr.
Buchanan, James M. & Thirlby, G. F., eds. L.S.E Essays on Cost. (The Institute for Humane Studies Ser. in Economic Theory). 1981. text ed. 20.00x (ISBN 0-8147-1034-4); pap. text ed. 7.00x (ISBN 0-8147-1035-2). NYU Pr.
Buchanan, James W. Minnesota Walk Book: A Guide to Hiking & Cross-Country Skiing in the Pioneer Region. (Minnesota Walk Book Ser.: Vol. 5). (Illus.). 59p. (Orig.). 1979. pap. 4.50 (ISBN 0-931714-07-9). Nodin Pr.
Buchanan, Jerreal. Who's Calling My Name. LC 76-58063. 1977. pap. 3.50 (ISBN 0-8054-5418-7). Broadman.
Buchanan, Joseph. Philosophy of Human Nature. LC 71-90941. (History of Psychology Ser). (Illus.). 1969. Repr. of 1812 ed. 36.00x (ISBN 0-8201-1064-7). Schol Facsimiles.
Buchanan, Malcolm, et al. Transport Planning for Greater London. 315p. 1980. text ed. 42.75x (ISBN 0-566-00314-7, Pub. by Gower Pub Co England). Renouf.
Buchanan, Marie. The Dark Backward. 1976. pap. 1.75 o.p. (ISBN 0-345-25067-2). Ballantine.
Buchanan, N. J., jt. auth. see Young, J. M.
Buchanan, O. Lexton, Jr. Limits: A Transition to Calculus. Meder, Albert E., Jr., ed. (Modern Mathematics Ser). (gr. 9 up). 1974. pap. 6.08 (ISBN 0-395-17941-6); instr's. guide & solution key 3.12 (ISBN 0-395-17942-4). HM.
Buchanan, Patrick J., jt. auth. see Leach, Douglas E.
Buchanan, R. A. Technology & Social Progress. 1965. 10.50 (ISBN 0-08-011141-6); pap. 6.25 (ISBN 0-08-011140-8). Pergamon.
Buchanan, R. H., et al. Man & His Habitat: Essays Presented to Emyr Estyn Evans. 1971. 26.50 (ISBN 0-7100-6908-1). Routledge & Kegan.
Buchanan, R. Olgilvie, jt. auth. see Estall, R. C.
Buchanan, Robert. Foxglove Manor, Eighteen Eighty-Four. Wolff, Robert Lee, ed. LC 75-483. (Victorian Fiction Ser.). 1975. lib. bdg. 66.00 (ISBN 0-8240-1560-6). Garland Pub.
--The New Abelard: A Romance. Wolff, Robert L., ed. LC 75-483. (Victorian Fiction Ser.). 1975. lib. bdg. 66.00 (ISBN 0-8240-1603-3). Garland Pub.
Buchanan, Robert E. General Systematic Bacteriology: History, Nomenclature, Groups of Bacteria. 1970. Repr. of 1925 ed. 21.75 o.s.i. (ISBN 0-02-842140-X). Hafner.
Buchanan, Robert J. Health-Care Finance: An Analysis of Cost & Utilization Issues. LC 80-8362. 1981. write for info. (ISBN 0-669-04035-5). Lexington Bks.
Buchanan, Watson W. & Dick, Carson W. Recent Advances in Rheumatology, Pt. Two: Clinical Features & Treatment. LC 75-22434. (Regent Advances Ser.). (Illus.). 240p. 1976. text ed. 30.00x (ISBN 0-443-01362-4). Churchill.
Buchanan, William. Understanding Political Variables. 3rd ed. LC 80-23707. (Illus.). 1980. pap. text ed. 12.95x (ISBN 0-684-16673-9, ScribC). Scribner.
--Understanding Political Variables. 2nd ed. LC 73-1347. (Orig., Tables, Graphs). 1974. pap. text ed. 9.95x o.p. (ISBN 0-684-13654-6, ScribC). Scribner.
Buchanan, William, jt. auth. see Thompson, Joseph.
Buchanan-Brown, John. The Illustrations of William Makepeace Thackeray. (Illus.). 192p. 1980. 25.00 (ISBN 0-7153-7811-2). David & Charles.
--Phiz!: Illustrator of Dickens' World. (Encore Editions). (Illus.). 1978. 4.95 (ISBN 0-684-16675-5, ScribT). Scribner.
Buchannan, Daniel H. Development of Capitalistic Enterprise in India. LC 66-9611. Repr. of 1934 ed. 27.50x (ISBN 0-678-05032-5). Kelley.
Buchanon, C. A. & Buchanon, R. A. The Batsford Guide to the Industrial Archaeology of Central Southern England. (Illus.). 192p. 1980. 45.00 (ISBN 0-7134-1364-6, Pub. by Batsford England). David & Charles.
Buchanon, R. A., jt. auth. see Buchanon, C. A.
Buchard, O. Photochemistry of Heterocyclic Compounds. LC 75-33855. 1976. 80.95 (ISBN 0-471-11510-X). Wiley.
Buchdahl, G., ed. Changing Views About the Principles of Scientific Theory Evaluation. 90p. 1980. pap. 16.50 (ISBN 0-08-027408-0). Pergamon.
Buchdahl, H. A. Twenty Lectures on Thermodynamics. 1975. text ed. 21.00 (ISBN 0-08-018299-2); pap. text ed. 12.75 (ISBN 0-08-018951-2). Pergamon.
Buchdahl, Hans A. Concepts of Classical Thermodynamics. (Cambridge Monograph on Physics Ser). 1966. 35.50 (ISBN 0-521-04359-X). Cambridge U Pr.
--Introduction to Hamiltonian Optics. LC 69-19372. (Cambridge Monographs on Physics). (Illus.). 1970. 44.50 (ISBN 0-521-07516-5). Cambridge U Pr.
Buchele, Robert & Cohen, Howard. Equity & Efficiency in Public Policy. (Learning Packages in the Policy Sciences: No. 15). (Illus.). 30p. (Orig.). 1978. pap. text ed. 2.00 (ISBN 0-936826-04-5). Pol Stud Assocs.
Buchen, Irving H. Isaac Bashevis Singer & the Eternal Past. LC 68-29427. (Gotham Library). 1968. 15.00x (ISBN 0-8147-0062-4); pap. 3.95x (ISBN 0-8147-0063-2). NYU Pr.
Buchenholz, Bruce. Doctor in the Zoo. (Illus.). 192p. 1976. pap. 3.95 o.p. (ISBN 0-14-004238-5). Penguin.
Bucher, Charles & Olsen, Einar. Foundations of Health. 2nd ed. (Illus.). 448p. 1976. Ref. Ed. 15.95 (ISBN 0-13-329896-5). P-H.
Bucher, Charles A. Administration of Physical Education & Athletic Programs. 7th ed. LC 78-11952. (Illus.). 1979. text ed. 17.95 (ISBN 0-8016-0851-1). Mosby.
--Foundations of Physical Education. 8th ed. LC 78-17035. (Illus.). 1979. 17.95 (ISBN 0-8016-0867-8). Mosby.
Bucher, Charles A. & Bucher, Richard D. Recreation for Today's Society. (Illus.). 224p. 1974. 12.95 (ISBN 0-13-768721-4). P-H.
Bucher, Charles A. & Thaxton, Nolan A. Physical Education & Sport: Change & Challenge. LC 80-25237. (Illus.). 311p. 1981. pap. text ed. 11.95 (ISBN 0-8016-0876-7). Mosby.
Bucher, Charles A., ed. Dimensions of Physical Education. 2nd ed. LC 73-18169. (Illus.). 1974. pap. text ed. 8.95 o.p. (ISBN 0-8016-0879-1). Mosby.
Bucher, Francois. Architector, 2 vols. LC 77-86233. (Illus.). 1980. Set. 85.00 (ISBN 0-913870-47-1). Abaris Bks.
Bucher, L. Teaching of Art. 1963. 10.00 o.p. (ISBN 0-8022-0193-8). Philos Lib.
Bucher, Richard D., jt. auth. see Bucher, Charles A.
Buchheim, Hans. Totalitarian Rule: Its Nature & Characteristics. Hein, Ruth, tr. from Ger. LC 68-25417. 112p. 1968. 10.00x (ISBN 0-8195-3090-5, Pub. by Wesleyan U Pr); pap. 5.00 (ISBN 0-8195-6021-9). Columbia U Pr.
Buchheit, William & Truex, Raymond C., eds. Surgery of the Posterior Fossa. LC 78-73554. (Seminars in Neurological Surgery: Vol. 3). 1979. text ed. 24.00 (ISBN 0-89004-256-X). Raven.
Buchholz, Barbara & Gilberg, Laura S. Needlepoint Designs from Amish Quilts. (Encore Editions). (Illus.). 1977. 4.95 (ISBN 0-684-16536-8, ScribT). Scribner.
Buchi, George H. Organic Syntheses, Vol. 56. LC 22-17747. (Organic Synthesis Ser.). 1977. 16.95 (ISBN 0-471-02218-7, Pub. by Wiley-Interscience). Wiley.
Buchler, Justus, jt. auth. see Randall, John H., Jr.

Buchloh, Benjamin H. Dan Graham Video-Architecture-Television: Works, Propositions & Projects, Writings 1970-1978. LC 79-89645. (Illus.). 89p. 1979. 17.50x (ISBN 0-8147-1025-5); pap. 9.95x (ISBN 0-8147-1026-3). NYU Pr.
Buchner see Bentley, Eric.
Buchner, G. Danton's Tod & Woyzeck. Jacobs, M., ed. 220p. 1954. 9.00x (ISBN 0-7190-0456-X, Pub. by Manchester U Pr England). State Mutual Bk.
Buchner, Georg. Leonce & Lena. Hamburger, Michael, tr. from Ger. & intro. by. Bd. with Lenz; Woyzeck. LC 78-184507. (German Literary Classics in Translation Ser). 120p. 1972. text ed. 9.00 (ISBN 0-226-07841-8). U of Chicago Pr.
--Leonce & Lena. Hamburger, Michael, tr. from Ger. Incl. Lenz; Woyzeck. LC 78-184507. (German Literary Classics in Translation Ser). xiii, 99p. 1973. pap. 2.95 (ISBN 0-226-07842-6, P467, Phoen). U of Chicago Pr.
Buchner, Greet. Alternative Cooking. 1979. pap. 3.95 o.s.i. (ISBN 0-7225-0469-1). Newcastle Pub.
--Cooking with Flowers. (Illus.). 8.95 (ISBN 0-7225-0236-2). Dufour.
Bucholz, Hans & Gmelin, Wolfgang, eds. Science & Technology & the Future, 2 pts. 1439p. 1979. pap. text ed. 58.00 (ISBN 0-686-65493-5, Pub. by K G Saur). Shoe String.
Buchsbaum, Herbert, jt. auth. see Lifshitz, Samuel.
Buchsbaum, Herbert J. & Schmidt, Joseph D. Gynecologic & Obstetric Urology. LC 76-41535. (Illus.). 1978. text ed. 38.00 (ISBN 0-7216-2176-7). Saunders.
Buchsbaum, Mildred, ed. see Castro-Amaya, Rogelio A. & Kattan-Zablah, Jorge.
Buchsbaum, Ralph. Animals Without Backbones. rev., 2nd ed. LC 48-9508. (Illus.). 405p. 1975. pap. 9.50 (ISBN 0-226-07870-1). U of Chicago Pr.
--Animals Without Backbones: An Introduction to the Invertebrates. rev. ed. LC 48-9508. (Illus.). (gr. 9 up). 1948. text ed. 16.00 (ISBN 0-226-07869-8). U of Chicago Pr.
Buchsbaum, Steven, jt. auth. see Council on Economic Priorities.
Buchwald, Ann & Buchwald, Art. Seems Like Yesterday. 1981. pap. 2.75 (ISBN 0-425-04833-0). Berkley Pub.
Buchwald, Ann, jt. auth. see Stewart, Marjabelle Y.
Buchwald, Art. Washington Is Leaking. 1977. pap. 2.50 (ISBN 0-449-23294-8, Crest). Fawcett.
Buchwald, Art, jt. auth. see Buchwald, Ann.
Buchwald, Vagn F. Handbook of Iron Meteorites: Their History, Distribution, Composition & Structure. 1976. 225.00x (ISBN 0-520-02934-8). U of Cal Pr.
Buci-Glucksmann, Christine. Gramsci & the State. Fernbach, David, tr. from Fr. 485p. 1980. text ed. 36.50x (ISBN 0-85315-483-X). Humanities.
Buck, A. L. Brown Buck. (Illus.). 1976. 7.95 (ISBN 0-7181-1456-6, Pub. by Michael Joseph). Merrimack Bk Serv.
Buck, C. H. Problems of Product Design & Development. 1963. 13.75 (ISBN 0-08-009794-4); pap. 6.25 (ISBN 0-08-009793-6). Pergamon.
Buck, David C., tr. see Pampatti.
Buck, David D. Urban Change in China: Tsinan, Shantung, 1890-1949. 1978. 21.50 (ISBN 0-299-07110-3). U of Wis Pr.
Buck, Elizabeth H., jt. auth. see Buck, Solon J.
Buck, Ellen, jt. auth. see Buck, R. Creighton.
Buck, Frederick H. Glossary of Mongolian Technical Terms. LC 58-59834. (American Council of Learned Societies Publications). 79p. (Orig.). 1958. pap. 3.00x (ISBN 0-87950-257-6). Spoken Lang Serv.
Buck, George. The History of King Richard the Third (1619) Kincaid, A. N., ed. 512p. 1980. text ed. 60.50x (ISBN 0-904387-26-7). Humanities.
Buck, Harry M. People of the Lord. 1977. 8.95 o.p. (ISBN 0-89012-003-X). Anima Pubns.
Buck, Harry M. & Yocum, Glenn A., eds. Structural Approaches to South India Studies. LC 74-77412. 1974. pap. 5.95 (ISBN 0-89012-000-5). Anima Pubns.
Buck, James H., jt. auth. see Sarkesian, Sam C.
Buck, James H., ed. The Modern Japanese Military System. LC 75-14628. (Sage Research Progress Ser. on War, Revolution, & Peacekeeping: Vol. 5). 1975. 20.00x (ISBN 0-8039-0513-0); pap. 9.95x (ISBN 0-8039-0514-9). Sage.
Buck, John L. Three Essays on Chinese Farm Economy. LC 78-74308. (Modern Chinese Economy Ser.: Vol. 10). 155p. 1980. lib. bdg. 20.00 (ISBN 0-8240-4259-X). Garland Pub.
Buck, John N. & Hammer, Emanuel F., eds. Advances in the House-Tree-Person Technique: Variations & Applications. LC 66-29864. (Illus.). 1969. 22.50x o.p. (ISBN 0-87424-302-5). Western Psych.
Buck, Lewis A. Wetlands: Bogs, Marshes & Swamps. LC 73-5711. (Finding-Out Books for Science & Social Studies, Grades 1-4). 64p. (gr. 2-4). 1974. PLB 6.95 (ISBN 0-8193-0702-5, Pub. by Parents). Enslow Pubs.
Buck, Margaret W. Along the Seashore. (Illus., Orig.). (gr. 3-9). 1964. 5.95 (ISBN 0-687-01114-0). Abingdon.
--The Face: What It Means. LC 78-56844. 1980. 7.95 (ISBN 0-87212-138-0); pap. 4.95 (ISBN 0-87212-106-2). Libra.
Buck, N. Lewis, jt. auth. see Beckwith, Thomas G.
Buck, Pearl. The Good Earth. (Arabic.). pap. 7.95x (ISBN 0-686-63553-1). Intl Bk Ctr.
Buck, Pearl S. Child Who Never Grew. (Special Education Bks). 1950. 3.95 (ISBN 0-381-98020-0, A12200, JD-J). John Day.
--East Wind: West Wind. (John Day Bk.). 1930. 9.95 (ISBN 0-381-98026-X, A21660, TYC-T). T Y Crowell.
--Good Earth. (John Day Bk.). 1931. 12.95 (ISBN 0-381-98033-2, A30860, TYC-T). T Y Crowell.
--Good Earth. (Keith Jennison Large Type Bks). (gr. 6 up). PLB 9.95 o.p. (ISBN 0-531-00191-1). Watts.
--The Good Earth. (gr. 8-12). 1975. pap. 2.75 (ISBN 0-671-43342-3); 2.50 (ISBN 0-686-67106-6). PB.
--Little Fox in the Middle. (Illus.). (gr. 1-3). 1968. 3.95g o.s.i. (ISBN 0-02-715140-9, CCPr). Macmillan.
--The Lovers & Other Stories. LC 76-56819. (John Day Bk.). 1977. 9.95 (ISBN 0-381-97109-0, TYC-T). T Y Crowell.
--Man Who Changed China: The Story of Sun Yat-Sen. (World Landmark Ser.: No. 9). (Illus.). (gr. 7-9). 1953. PLB 5.99 (ISBN 0-394-90509-1). Random.
--Other Gods: An American Legend. (John Day Bk.). 1940. 8.95 o.s.i. (ISBN 0-381-98047-2, A58200, TYC-T). T Y Crowell.
--Secrets of the Heart. LC 76-6550. (John Day Bk.). 1976. 9.95 (ISBN 0-381-98287-4, TYC-T). T Y Crowell.
--Three Daughters of Madame Liang. (John Day Bk.). 1969. 9.95 (ISBN 0-381-98055-3, A79000, TYC-T). T Y Crowell.
--Time Is Noon. (John Day Bk.). 1967. 8.95 o.p. (ISBN 0-381-98056-1, A79800, TYC-T). T Y Crowell.
Buck, Pearl S., tr. All Men Are Brothers - Shui Huchuan, Vol. I. (John Day Bk.). 1968. Repr. of 1933 ed. 10.00 o.s.i. (ISBN 0-381-98017-0, A2000, TYC-T). T Y Crowell.
Buck, Peggy J. Tommy Learns About Time & Eternity. (Illus.). 68p. (Orig.). (gr. 1-3). 1980. pap. 2.50 (ISBN 0-89323-006-5). BMA Pr.
Buck, Peter. The Secret of San Felipe. (Mercenary Ser.: No. 2). (Orig.). 1981. pap. 1.95 (ISBN 0-451-09894-3, J9894, Sig). NAL.
--Thirteen for the Kill. (Mercenary Ser.: No. 1). (Orig.). 1981. pap. 1.95 (ISBN 0-451-09893-5, J9893, Sig). NAL.
Buck, R. Creighton & Buck, Ellen. An Introduction to Differential Equations. LC 75-25009. (Illus.). 416p. 1976. text ed. 19.50 (ISBN 0-395-20654-5). HM.
Buck, Ray. Dave Parker: The Cobra Swirl. LC 80-39987. (Sports Stars Ser.). (Illus.). 48p. (gr. 2-8). 1981. PLB 7.35 (ISBN 0-516-04310-2). Childrens.
Buck, Ray, jt. auth. see Phillips, O. A.
Buck, Robert N. Flying Know-How. 1975. 10.95 (ISBN 0-440-04931-8). Delacorte.
Buck, Robert T., et al, eds. Sonia Delaunay: A Retrospective. LC 79-57450. (Illus.). 236p. 1980. pap. 27.50 (ISBN 0-914782-32-0). Buffalo Acad.
Buck, Ross W. Human Motivation & Emotion. LC 75-37893. 1976. text ed. 21.95 (ISBN 0-471-11570-3); instructor's manual avail. (ISBN 0-471-02468-6). Wiley.
Buck, Solon J. Granger Movement: A Study of Agricultural Organization & Its Political, Economic, & Social Manifestations, 1870-1880. LC 63-9713. (Illus.). 1963. pap. 4.25x (ISBN 0-8032-5027-4, BB 166, Bison). U of Nebr Pr.
Buck, Solon J. & Buck, Elizabeth H. Planting of Civilization in Western Pennsylvania. LC 39-25307. (Illus.). 1939. 20.00 (ISBN 0-910294-28-3). Brown Bk.
Buck, Solon J see Johnson, Allen & Nevins, Allan.
Buck, Stratton. Gustave Flaubert. (World Authors Ser.: France: No. 3). 1966. pap. 10.95 (ISBN 0-8057-2312-9). Twayne.
Buck, William B., et al. Clinical & Diagnostic Veterinary Toxicology. 2nd ed. 1976. pap. 13.95 (ISBN 0-8403-0720-9). Kendall-Hunt.
Buckalew, Vardaman M. & Moore, Micahel A. Renal Tubular Dysfunction. LC 79-92915. (Discussions in Patient Management Ser.). 1980. pap. 13.50 (ISBN 0-87488-889-1). Med Exam.
Bucker, Bradley, jt. auth. see Lovaas, Ivar.
Buckett, M. An Introduction to Farm Organisation & Mamagement. (Illus.). 280p. 1981. 50.00 (ISBN 0-08-024433-5); pap. 21.00 (ISBN 0-08-024432-7). Pergamon.
Buckeye, Donald A. No Read Math Activities, 3vols. Incl. Vol. 1. One Hundred Ninety-Eight Activities on the Lower Elementary Level; Vol. 2. One Hundred Ninety-Eight Activities on the Upper Elementary Level; Vol. 3. One Hundred Ninety-Eight Activities on the Junior High Level (ISBN 0-910974-74-8). text ed. 35.00 ea. o.p.; Midwest Pubns.
Buckeye, Donald A., et al. Cloudburst of Math Lab Experiments. Incl. Vol. 1, Elementary. pap. o.p. (ISBN 0-910974-29-2); Vol. 2, Upper Elementary. pap. 6.95 (ISBN 0-910974-30-6); o.p. (ISBN 0-910974-60-8); Vol. 3, Junior High School. pap. 6.95 (ISBN 0-910974-61-6); o.p. (ISBN 0-910974-31-4); Vol. 4, High School. pap. 3.95 (ISBN 0-910974-32-2); card form o.p. 16.00 (ISBN 0-910974-62-4); Vol. 5, Lower College. pap. o.p. (ISBN 0-910974-40-3). tchrs. manual 3.50 (ISBN 0-910974-33-0). Midwest Pubns.
Buckholdt, David R. & Gubrium, Jaber F. Caretakers: Treating Emotionally Disturbed Children. LC 79-10000. (Sociological Observations: No. 7). 1979. 18.95x (ISBN 0-8039-1202-1); pap. 8.95x (ISBN 0-8039-1203-X). Sage.
Buckholz, Herbert, jt. auth. see Irving, Clifford.
Buckingham. International Review in Physical Chemistry. 1981. text ed. price not set (ISBN 0-408-12271-4). Butterworth.
Buckingham, Callie. Nurse at Orchard Hill. (YA) 1978. 5.95 (ISBN 0-685-87346-3, Avalon). Bouregy.
Buckingham, Hugh W. & Kertesz, Andrew. Neologistic Jargon Aphasia. (Neurolinguistics Ser.: Vol. 3). 100p. 1976. text ed. 21.50 (ISBN 90-265-0227-3, Pub. by Swets Pub Serv Holland). Swets North Am.
Buckingham, J., jt. auth. see Klyne.
Buckingham, J. E., Sr. Reminiscences & Souvenirs of the Assassination of Abraham Lincoln. LC 80-128964. (Illus.). 89p. 22.50 (ISBN 0-686-28744-4); pap. 17.50 (ISBN 0-686-28745-2). J L Barbour.
Buckingham, Jamie. Coping with Criticism. 1979. 6.95 (ISBN 0-88270-327-7). Logos.
--Daughter of Destiny. 1978. 7.95 o.p. (ISBN 0-88270-078-2); pap. 2.95 pocket ed. (ISBN 0-88270-318-8). Logos.
--The Last Word. 1978. pap. 3.95 (ISBN 0-88270-404-4). Logos.
Buckingham, Jamie, jt. auth. see Cruz, Nicky.
Buckingham, Jamie, jt. auth. see Riley, Jeannie C.
Buckingham, Jamie, jt. auth. see Robertson, Pat.
Buckingham, Margaret E. Development & Differentiation, Vol. III. (Biochemistry of Cellular Regulation Ser.). 240p. 1980. 59.95 (ISBN 0-8493-5456-0). CRC Pr.
Buckland, Charles E. Dictionary of Indian Biography. LC 68-23140. 1968. Repr. of 1906 ed. 34.00 (ISBN 0-8103-3156-X). Gale.
Buckland, Gail. First Photographs. (Illus.). 192p. 1980. 29.95 (ISBN 0-02-518070-3). Macmillan.
Buckland, Michael K. Book Availability & the Library User. LC 74-8682. 220p. 1975. text ed. 21.00 (ISBN 0-08-017709-3); pap. text ed. 11.50 (ISBN 0-08-018160-0). Pergamon.
Buckland, Patrick. James Craig. (Gill's Irish Lives Ser.). 143p. 1980. 20.00 (ISBN 0-7171-1078-8, Pub. by Gill & Macmillan Ireland); pap. 6.50 (ISBN 0-7171-0984-4). Irish Bk Ctr.
Buckland, William W. Textbook of Roman Law. 3rd ed. 1964. text ed. 86.50x (ISBN 0-521-04360-3). Cambridge U Pr.
Buckle, E., ed. Dams of National Hunt Winners, 1955-60. pap. 3.60 (ISBN 0-85131-076-1, Dist. by Sporting Book Center). J A Allen.
Buckle, E., compiled by. Dams of National Hunt Winners, 1963-64. pap. 3.60 (ISBN 0-85131-077-X, Dist. by Sporting Book Center). J A Allen.
--Dams of National Hunt Winners, 1966-73. (Illus.). pap. 18.35 (ISBN 0-85131-237-3, Dist. by Sporting Book Center). J A Allen.
Buckle, Esme. Dams of National Hunt Winners: 1973-1975. 17.50 (ISBN 0-85131-340-X). J A Allen.
Buckle, Henry T. History of Civilization in England. abr ed. Wood, Clement, ed. LC 64-15688. (Milestones of Thought Ser.). 8.50 (ISBN 0-8044-1125-5); pap. 3.45 (ISBN 0-8044-6062-0). Ungar.
Buckle, Leonard & Buckle, Suzann. Standards Relating to Planning for Juvenile Justice. (Juvenile Justice Standards Project Ser.). 1980. softcover 7.95; final casebound 16.50 (ISBN 0-88410-754-X). Ballinger Pub.
--Standards Relating to Planning for Juvenile Justice. LC 77-3938. (Juvenile Justice Standards Project Ser.). 1977. final casebound 12.50 o.p.; softcover 5.95 o.p. (ISBN 0-88410-763-9). Ballinger Pub.
Buckle, Leonard G., jt. auth. see Buckle, Suzann R.
Buckle, Mary, jt. auth. see Day, Lewis F.
Buckle, Suzann, jt. auth. see Buckle, Leonard.
Buckle, Suzann R. & Buckle, Leonard G. Bargaining for Justice: Case Disposition & Reform in the Criminal Courts. LC 75-19769. (Special Studies). 1977. text ed. 20.95 (ISBN 0-275-22830-4). Praeger.
Buckler, Beatrice. Living with a Mentally Retarded Child: A Primer for Parents. 1971. 7.95 o.p. (ISBN 0-8015-4614-1). Dutton.
Buckler, William E. The Victorian Imagination: Essays in Aesthetic Exploration. (The Gotham Library). 384p. 1980. 22.50x (ISBN 0-8147-1032-8); pap. 8.95x (ISBN 0-8147-1033-6). NYU Pr.
Buckler, William E., jt. auth. see Anderson, George K.
Buckley, A. & Swain, C. Retail Trade Developments in Great Britain. 4th ed. 1979. text ed. 82.25x (ISBN 0-566-02152-8, Pub. by Gower Pub Co England). Renouf.
Buckley, Ann, tr. see Baker, Theodore.
Buckley, Christopher. Pentimento. 1980. pap. 24.00x (ISBN 0-931460-10-7). Bieler.
Buckley, Earle A. How to Write Better Business Letters. 4th ed. (Illus.). 1957. 10.95 o.p. (ISBN 0-07-008778-4, P&RB); pap. 3.95 o.p. (ISBN 0-07-008779-2). McGraw.
Buckley, Edmund H. & Solkov, Arnold. A Conceptual Approach to College Writing. 2nd ed. 112p. 1980. pap. text ed. 6.95 (ISBN 0-8403-2308-5). Kendall-Hunt.
Buckley, Francis J. I Confess. the Sacrament of Penance Today. LC 72-80971. (Illus.). 96p. 1972. pap. 1.25 o.p. (ISBN 0-87793-048-1). Ave Maria.
Buckley, Helen E. Little Boy & the Birthdays. (Illus.). (gr. k-3). 1965. PLB 6.96 o.p. (ISBN 0-688-51202-X). Lothrop.
--Wonderful Little Boy. LC 73-101469. (Illus.). (gr. k-3). 1970. 8.25 o.p. (ISBN 0-688-41150-9); PLB 6.96 o.p. (ISBN 0-688-51150-3). Lothrop.
Buckley, J. W., et al. SEC Accounting. 1980. text ed. 20.95 (ISBN 0-471-01861-9); tchrs' manual (ISBN 0-471-07778-X). Wiley.
Buckley, John J., Jr., ed. Genetics Now: Ethical Issues in Genetic Research. LC 78-57577. 1978. pap. text ed. 9.50 (ISBN 0-8191-0528-7). U Pr of Amer.
Buckley, John W. & Buckley, Marlene H. The Accounting Profession. LC 74-8880. (Management, Accounting & Information Systems Ser.). 192p. 1974. 15.95 o.p. (ISBN 0-471-11610-6); pap. 8.95 (ISBN 0-471-11609-2). Wiley.
Buckley, John W. & Lightner, Kevin M. Accounting: An Information Systems Approach. LC 72-93646. text ed. 19.95 (ISBN 0-8221-0097-5). CBI Pub.
--Essentials of Accounting. 1975. pap. 17.95x (ISBN 0-685-70779-2). Dickenson.
Buckley, John W., ed. see Walton, Thomas F.
Buckley, Joseph P. & Ferrario, Carlos, eds. Central Nervous System Mechanisms in Hypertension. 425p. 1981. 39.95 (ISBN 0-89004-545-3). Raven.
Buckley, Julian, jt. auth. see Loll, Leo, Jr.
Buckley, Julian G., jt. auth. see Loll, Leo M., Jr.
Buckley, Larry. Easy-to-Make Slotted Furniture. (Illus.). 52p. (Orig.). 1980. pap. 2.25 (ISBN 0-486-23983-7). Dover.
Buckley, Lord. Hiparama of the Classics. 1980. pap. 3.00 (ISBN 0-87286-120-1). City Lights.
Buckley, Marlene H., jt. auth. see Buckley, John W.
Buckley, Mary & Baum, David, eds. Color Theory: A Guide to Information Sources. LC 73-17517. (Art & Architecture Information Guide Ser.: Vol. 2). x, 173p. 1975. 30.00 (ISBN 0-8103-1275-1). Gale.
Buckley, Michael. Why Are You Afraid. pap. 5.95 (ISBN 0-87061-060-0). Chr Classics.
Buckley, Patricia, jt. auth. see Maffei, Anthony C.
Buckley, Peter J. & Roberts, Brian R. European Direct Investment in the U.S.A. Before World War I. 1981. 25.00 (ISBN 0-312-26940-4). St Martin.
Buckley, Vincent. Late Winter Child. (Orig.). 1980. pap. text ed. 6.50x (ISBN 0-85105-358-0, Dolmen Pr). Humanities.
--The Pattern. (Orig.). 1979. pap. text ed. 8.00x (ISBN 0-85105-357-2, Dolmen Pr). Humanities.
Buckley, Walter, ed. Modern Systems Research for the Behavioral Scientist. LC 66-19888. (Illus.). 1968. 31.95x (ISBN 0-202-30011-0). Aldine Pub.
Buckley, Walter, jt. ed. see Burns, Tom R.
Buckley, William E. A New England Pattern: The History of Manchester, Connecticut. LC 73-79895. (Illus.). 376p. 1973. casebound 9.95 (ISBN 0-87106-116-3). Globe Pequot.
Buckley, William F., Jr. Airborne: A Sentimental Journey. (Illus.). 1976. 12.95 o.s.i. (ISBN 0-02-518040-1, 51804). Macmillan.
--Saving the Queen. 1977. pap. 2.25 o.p. (ISBN 0-446-89164-9). Warner Bks.

--Stained Glass. 1979. pap. 2.25 o.p. (ISBN 0-446-82323-6). Warner Bks.

Buckley, William F., Jr., ed. American Conservative Thought in the Twentieth Century. LC 76-99163. (American Heritage Ser: No. 82). 1970. pap. 7.95 (ISBN 0-672-51327-7, AHS82). Bobbs.

Buckley, William, Jr. Who's on First. 288p. 1981. pap. 2.75 (ISBN 0-380-52555-0, 52555). Avon.

Buckman, David L. Old Steamboat Days on the Hudson River: Tales & Reminiscences of the Stirring Times That Followed the Introduction of Steam Navigation. LC 77-156931. (Illus.). 1971. Repr. of 1909 ed. 18.00 (ISBN 0-8103-3737-1). Gale.

Buckman, Peter. Let's Dance: Social, Ballroom & Folk Dancing. (Illus.). 1979. pap. 8.95 o.p. (ISBN 0-14-005325-5). Penguin.

Buckman, Thomas R., jt. auth. see Lagerkvist, Par.

Buckman, William. Physics: Principles & Life Science Applications. Date not set. text ed. price not set (ISBN 0-442-20844-8). D Van Nostrand.

Buckmaster, Henrietta. Freedom Bound. 1967. pap. 1.25 o.s.i. (ISBN 0-02-030740-3, Collier). Macmillan.

--Walter Raleigh: Man of Two Worlds. (World Landmark Ser, No. 58). (Illus.). (gr. 5-8). 1964. PLB 4.39 o.p. (ISBN 0-394-90558-X, BYR). Random.

--Women Who Shaped History. (gr. 7 up). 1968. 8.95 (ISBN 0-02-715210-3, CCPr). Macmillan.

Buck-Morss, Susan. The Origin of Negative Dialectics: Theodor W. Adorno, Walter Benjamin, & the Frankfurt Institute. LC 76-55103. 1979. pap. text ed. 7.95 (ISBN 0-02-905150-9). Free Pr.

Bucknall, Barbara. Ursula le Guin. LC 80-53696. (Recognitions Ser.). 160p. 9.95 (ISBN 0-8044-2085-8). Ungar.

Bucknall, Benjamin, tr. see Viollet-Le-Duc, Eugene E.

Bucknall, Rixon. Our Railway History. 1970. pap. 7.95 o.p. (ISBN 0-04-385064-2). Allen Unwin.

Bucknell, jt. auth. see Hill, Hamilton.

Bucknell, Geoffrey. Fishing Days. 8.50x (ISBN 0-392-06580-0, SpS). Soccer.

Bucknell, Howard. Energy & the National Defense. Davis, Vincent, ed. LC 79-57566. (Essays for the Third Century). 256p. 1981. 19.50 (ISBN 0-8131-0402-5). U Pr of Ky.

Bucknell, Peter A. Entertainment & Ritual Six Hundred to Sixteen Hundred. (Illus.). 223p. 1979. 29.50x (ISBN 0-8476-6239-X). Rowman.

Buckner, H. Taylor. Deviance, Reality, & Change: Sex, Dope, & Cheap Thrills. 1971. text ed. 14.95 (ISBN 0-394-31002-0). Random.

Buckner, Ken. Available Light. Stensvold, Mike, ed. LC 76-15435. (Petersen's How.to Photographic Library). (Illus.). 80p. 1976. pap. 3.95 o.p. (ISBN 0-8227-4003-6). Petersen Pub.

Buckner, L. M. Customer Services. (Occupational Manuals & Projects in Marketing). 1971. 5.96 o.p. (ISBN 0-07-008821-7, G); tchr's manual & key 3.00 o.p. (ISBN 0-07-008822-5). McGraw.

Buckner, Michael, jt. auth. see Abrams, Natalie.

Bucknill, John C. Unsoundness of Mind in Relation to Criminal Acts. Bd. with Care of the Insane & Their Legal Control; Factors of the Unsound Mind. Guy, W. A. (Contributions to the History of Psychology Ser., Vol. IV Pt. F: Insanity & Jurisprudence). 1980. Repr. of 1854 ed. 30.00 (ISBN 0-89093-329-4). U Pubns Amer.

Buckroyd, Julia. Church & State in Scotland: Sixteen Sixty to Sixteen Eighty-One. 1980. text ed. 32.50x (ISBN 0-85976-042-1). Humanities.

Buckwalter, Len. Beginner's Guide to Ham Radio. LC 77-82931. 1978. pap. 4.95 (ISBN 0-385-11514-8, Dolp). Doubleday.

--The Complete CB Radio Handbook. LC 77-9300. (Illus.). 1977. 9.95 o.s.i. (ISBN 0-690-01442-2, TYC-T). T Y Crowell.

--The Homeowner's Handbook of Power Tools. LC 75-28061. (Funk & W Bk.). (Illus.). 256p. 1976. 9.95 o.s.i. (ISBN 0-308-10226-6, TYC-T). T Y Crowell.

--One Hundred Ways to Use Your Pocket Calculator. 128p. 1978. pap. 1.95 (ISBN 0-449-13356-7, GM). Fawcett.

Bucovetsky, Meyer W. Studies in Public Employment & Compensation in Canada. 177p. 1979. pap. text ed. 14.95x (ISBN 0-409-88601-7, Pub. by Inst Res Pub Canada). Renouf.

Bucy, R. S., et al. Stochastic Differential Equations. McKean, H. P. & Keller, J. B., eds. LC 72-13266. (SIAM-AMS Proceedings). 1973. 22.00 (ISBN 0-8218-1325-0). Am Math.

Buczkowski, Leopold. Black Torrent. Welsh, David, tr. 1970. 15.00x o.p. (ISBN 0-262-02064-5). MIT Pr.

Budak, Aram. Circuit Theory Fundamentals & Applications. LC 77-22344. (Illus.). 1978. 27.95 (ISBN 0-13-133975-3). P-H.

--Passive & Active Network Analysis & Synthesis. 600p. 1974. text ed. 26.95 (ISBN 0-395-17203-9); solutions manual 4.55 (ISBN 0-395-17835-5). HM.

Budassi, Susan A. & Barber, Janet. Emergency Nursing: Principles & Practice. LC 80-21629. (Illus.). 775p. 1980. pap. text ed. 24.95 (ISBN 0-8016-0451-6). Mosby.

Budassi, Susan A., jt. auth. see Barber, Janet M.

Buday, George. The History of the Christmas Card. LC 74-174012. (Tower Bks). (Illus.). xxiii, 304p. 1972. Repr. of 1954 ed. 26.00 (ISBN 0-8103-3931-5). Gale.

Budbill, David. Christmas Tree Farm. LC 73-6051. (Illus.). 32p. (gr. k-2). 1974. 5.95g o.s.i. (ISBN 0-02-715330-4, 71533). Macmillan.

Budd, Alan. The Politics of Economic Planning. LC 78-66341. 1978. 20.95 (ISBN 0-03-046211-8). Praeger.

Budd, Elaine. You & Your Hair. (gr. 7 up). 1978. pap. 1.25 o.p. (ISBN 0-590-03861-3, Schol Pap). Schol Bk Serv.

Budd, Elaine, jt. auth. see Place, Stan.

Budd, John, compiled by. Eight Scandanavian Novelists: Criticism & Reviews in English. LC 80-24895. 192p. 1981. lib. bdg. 25.00 (ISBN 0-313-22869-8, BSN/). Greenwood.

Budd, Lillian. April Snow. 1979. pap. 1.95 (ISBN 0-380-45401-7, 45401). Avon.

--Land of Strangers. 1979. pap. 2.25 (ISBN 0-380-48314-9, 48314). Avon.

Budd, Richard W. & Ruben, Brent D. Beyond Media: New Approaches to Mass Communication. (gr. 10 up). 1978. pap. text ed. 13.25x (ISBN 0-685-38877-8). Hayden.

Budd, Richard W., jt. auth. see Ruben, Brent D.

Buddee, Paul. Airways: The Call of the Sky. (Australian Life Ser.: No. 4). 1979. pap. 6.95x (ISBN 0-85091-055-2, Pub. by Lothian). Intl Schol Bk Serv.

Budden, Henry. Bulbous Flowers. (Illus.). 104p. 1980. 15.95x (ISBN 0-19-558055-9). Oxford U Pr.

Budden, Julian. The Operas of Verdi, Vol. 3: From Don Carlos to Falstaff. 1981. 39.95 (ISBN 0-19-520254-6). Oxford U Pr.

Buddensieg, Rudolf, et al, eds. see Wycliffe, John.

Buddhadharma. Upasaka Two & One. 1981. pap. 1.50 (ISBN 0-87881-078-1). Mojave Bks.

Buddhist Books International, tr. see Yamaguchi, Susumu.

Buder, et al. Where We Are: A Hard Look at Family & Society. 1970. pap. 3.50 (ISBN 0-686-12284-4). Jewish Bd Family.

Buder, Stanley. Pullman: An Experiment in Industrial Order & Community Planning, 1880-1930. (Urban Life in America). 1967. pap. 4.95x (ISBN 0-19-500838-3). Oxford U Pr.

Budevsky, Omortag. Foundations of Chemical Analysis. LC 79-40240. (Ellis Horwood Series in Analytical Chemistry). 372p. 1979. 59.95x (ISBN 0-470-26692-9). Halsted Pr.

Budge, B. P., jt. auth. see Hendrickson, E. S.

Budge, E. A. The Book of the Dead: An English Translation of the Chapters, Hymns, Etc., of the Theban Recension. 2nd ed. (Illus.). 1969. 35.00 (ISBN 0-7100-1128-8). Routledge & Kegan.

--Egyptian Book of the Dead: The Papyrus of Ani. 12.50 (ISBN 0-8446-1764-4). Peter Smith.

--Mummy. 2nd ed. LC 64-13391. (Illus.). 1894. 15.00x (ISBN 0-8196-0139-X). Biblo.

Budge, E. A. Wallis. Divine Origin of the Craft of the Herbalist. LC 78-174013. (Illus.). 1971. Repr. of 1928 ed. 18.00 (ISBN 0-8103-3794-0). Gale.

--Egyptian Book of the Dead: The Papyrus of Ani in the British Museum. 1967. pap. 5.95 (ISBN 0-486-21866-X). Dover.

Budge, E. Wallis. Egyptian Magic. (Illus.). 1979. pap. 6.95 (ISBN 0-7100-0135-5). Routledge & Kegan.

--Egyptian Religion. (Illus.). 1979. pap. 6.95 (ISBN 0-7100-0134-7). Routledge & Kegan.

Budge, Ernest A. Short History of the Egyptian People. 280p. 1980. lib. bdg. 30.00 (ISBN 0-8482-0148-5). Norwood Edns.

Budge, Ernest A. Wallis see Anan Isho.

Budge, Ian & O'Leary, Cornelius. Belfast: Approach to Crisis. LC 72-85194. 1973. 18.95 (ISBN 0-312-07420-4). St Martin.

Budinger, J. M., ed. Cardiovascular Pathology. (AP Slide Seminar Ser.). (Illus.). 1978. pap. text ed. 15.00 o.p. (ISBN 0-89189-051-3, 50-1-042-00); slides 75.00 o.p. (ISBN 0-686-67355-7, 01-1-076-01). Am Soc Clinical.

Budinger, John M. Dermatopathology. LC 77-95399. (Slide Seminar Ser.). (Illus.). 1978. text & slides 55.00 (ISBN 0-89189-049-1, 15-1-025-00); slides 5.50 (ISBN 0-89189-024-6, 50-1-041-00). Am Soc Clinical.

Budker, Paul. Life of Sharks. Whitehead, Peter, tr. LC 71-148462. (Illus.). 1971. 17.50x (ISBN 0-231-03551-9); pap. 5.95 (ISBN 0-231-08314-9). Columbia U Pr.

Budlong, John P. Shoreline & Sextant: Practical Coastline Navigation. 224p. 1980. pap. text ed. 9.95 (ISBN 0-442-21928-8). Van Nos Reinhold.

--Sky & Sextant. 232p. 1981. pap. text ed. 10.95 (ISBN 0-442-20460-4). Van Nos Reinhold.

Budman, Simon, ed. Forms of Brief Therapy. 500p. 1981. 25.00 (ISBN 0-89862-608-0). Guilford Pr.

Budnick, Frank S. Applied Mathematics for Business, Economics, & the Social Sciences. (Illus.). 1979. text ed. 18.50 (ISBN 0-07-008851-9, C); wkbk 6.96 (ISBN 0-07-008854-3); instructor's manual 7.95 (ISBN 0-07-008852-7). McGraw.

Budnick, Frank S., et al. Principles of Operations Research for Management. 1977. 21.95x (ISBN 0-256-01796-4). Irwin.

Budrys, A. J. The Life Machine. 1979. 9.95 o.p. (ISBN 0-399-12257-5). Berkley Pub.

--Michaelmas. LC 76-56214. (YA) 1977. 7.95 o.p. (ISBN 0-399-11653-2, Dist. by Putnam). Berkley Pub.

Budrys, Algis. Blood & Burning. 1978. pap. 1.75 o.p. (ISBN 0-425-03861-0, Medallion). Berkley Pub.

--The Falling Torch. 1978. pap. 1.50 o.s.i. (ISBN 0-515-04649-3). Jove Pubns.

--Michaelmas. 1978. pap. 1.95 o.p. (ISBN 0-425-03812-2, Medallion). Berkley Pub.

Budzik, Janet K. & Sims, Clarence A. Basic Data Processing. 1972. text ed. 16.95 (ISBN 0-201-00775-4). A-W.

Budzik, Richard. Precision Sheet Metal Shop Theory. LC 79-77586. 1969. 9.20 o.p. (ISBN 0-672-20679-X); pap. 5.00 instructor's guide o.p. (ISBN 0-672-20681-1); student wkbk 4.80 o.p. (ISBN 0-672-20680-3). Bobbs.

Budzik, Richard S. Precision Sheet Metal Mathematics. LC 71-83129. 1969. 9.70 o.p. (ISBN 0-672-97591-2); tchr's guide 6.67 o.p. (ISBN 0-672-97593-9); student wkbk 4.80 o.p. (ISBN 0-672-97592-0). Bobbs.

--Precision Sheet Metal Shop Practice. LC 78-97566. 1969. 4.55 o.p. (ISBN 0-672-97594-7); instructor's guide 6.67 o.p. (ISBN 0-672-97596-3); student guide 4.80 o.p. (ISBN 0-672-97595-5). Bobbs.

--Sheet Metal Technology. 2nd ed. 1981. 13.95 (ISBN 0-672-97360-X); instr's. guide 3.33 (ISBN 0-672-97361-8); students manual 6.55 (ISBN 0-672-97362-6). Bobbs.

--Short Course in Sheet Metal Shop Theory. 128p. 1980. 12.50 o.p. (ISBN 0-912914-05-X). Prakken.

Bue, Henri, tr. see Carroll, Lewis.

Bueche, Fred. Physical Science. LC 73-182927. (Illus.). 1972. 16.95x (ISBN 0-87901-019-3). Worth.

Buechel, T., et al, eds. Biological Chemistry of Organelle Formation: Proceedings. (Colloquium Mosbach Ser.: Vol. 31). (Illus.). 290p. 1981. 44.00 (ISBN 0-387-10458-5). Springer-Verlag.

Buechner, Artur. Abbreviations in National & International Standardization. LC 70-587455. 175p. 1971. pap. 30.00x (ISBN 3-486-33611-8). Intl Pubns Serv.

Buechner, Frederick. The Alphabet of Grace. (Orig.). 1977. pap. 3.95 (ISBN 0-8164-2163-3). Crossroad NY.

--Godric. 1980. 10.95 (ISBN 0-689-11086-3). Atheneum.

--Magnificent Defeat. (YA) (gr. 9-12). 1968. pap. 1.65 (ISBN 0-8164-2045-9, SP44). Crossroad NY.

--Wishful Thinking: A Theological ABC. LC 72-9872. 128p. 1973. 7.95 (ISBN 0-06-061155-3, HarpR). Har-Row.

Buechner, Howard A., ed. Management of Fungus Diseases of the Lungs. (Illus.). 248p. 1971. 22.50 (ISBN 0-398-00247-9). C C Thomas.

Buehler, Calvin A. & Pearson, Donald E. Survey of Organic Syntheses, 2 vols. LC 73-112590. Vol. 1, 1970. 49.50 (ISBN 0-471-11670-X); Vol. 2, 1977. 32.50 (ISBN 0-471-11671-8, Pub. by Wiley-Interscience). Wiley.

Buehner, William J. & Ambrose, John W. Preparatory Latin, 2 bks. (gr. 6-9). 1970. pap. text ed. 5.25x ea.; Bk. 1. (ISBN 0-88334-007-0); Bk. 2. (ISBN 0-88334-028-3) (ISBN 0-685-39239-2). Ind Sch Pr.

Buehner, William J. & Colby, John K. Comprehensive Second Year Latin. (Orig.). (gr. 9-10). 1977. pap. text ed. 5.50x (ISBN 0-88334-034-8). Ind Sch Pr.

Buehr, Walter. Automobiles, Past & Present. LC 68-12323. (Illus.). (gr. 5-9). 1968. PLB 6.96 (ISBN 0-688-31054-0). Morrow.

--Cloth, from Fiber to Fabric. (Illus.). (gr. 5-9). 1965. PLB 6.96 (ISBN 0-688-31176-8). Morrow.

--First Book of Machines. (First Bks). (Illus.). (gr. 4-6). 1962. PLB 4.90 o.p. (ISBN 0-531-00574-7). Watts.

--Meat, from Ranch to Table. (Illus.). (gr. 5-9). 1956. PLB 6.96 (ISBN 0-688-31557-7). Morrow.

--Storm Warning: The Story of Hurricanes & Tornadoes. LC 71-175815. (Illus.). 64p. (gr. 4-6). 1972 (ISBN 0-688-21921-7). PLB 6.96 (ISBN 0-688-31921-1). Morrow.

Bueker, E. D., jt. auth. see Butcher, Earl O.

Buel, Larry V., jt. ed. see Hanrieder, Wolfram F.

Buel, Richard, Jr. Dear Liberty: Connecticut's Mobilization for the Revolutionary War. 432p. 1980. 22.50x (ISBN 0-8195-5047-7). Wesleyan U Pr.

Bueler, Lois E. Wild Dogs of the World. LC 72-96435. (Illus.). 274p. (Orig.). 1980. pap. 6.95 (ISBN 0-8128-6075-6). Stein & Day.

Bueler, William. Mountains of the World. LC 74-87796. (Illus.). 1977. pap. 5.95 (ISBN 0-916890-49-X). Mountaineers.

Bueler, William M. Chinese Sayings. LC 79-182059. (YA) 1972. pap. 4.50 (ISBN 0-8048-1018-4). C E Tuttle.

Buelke-Sam, Judith, jt. ed. see Kimmel, Carole A.

Buell, Charles E. Physical Education for Blind Children. (Illus.). 244p. 1974. pap. 24.50 (ISBN 0-398-03141-X). C C Thomas.

Buell, Erwin C. & Brigman, William E. The Grass Roots: Readings in State & Local Government. 1968. pap. 7.95x (ISBN 0-673-05904-9). Scott F.

Buell, Frederick. Full Summer. LC 78-25914. (The Wesleyan Poetry Program: Vol. 95). 1979. 10.00x (ISBN 0-8195-2095-0, Pub. by Wesleyan U Pr); pap. 4.95 (ISBN 0-8195-1095-5). Columbia U Pr.

Buell, Hal. Viet Nam: Land of Many Dragons. LC 68-24027. (Illus.). (gr. 3 up). 1968. PLB 5.95 o.p. (ISBN 0-396-06466-3). Dodd.

Buell, John. Playground. 1977. pap. 1.75 o.p. (ISBN 0-345-25616-6). Ballantine.

Buell, Lawrence. Literary Transcendentalism: Style & Vision in the American Rennaisance. LC 73-8409. 336p. (Orig.). 1975. pap. 4.95 (ISBN 0-8014-9152-5). Cornell U Pr.

Buell, Lillian P. How to Raise & Train a Saint Bernard. (Orig.). pap. 2.00 (ISBN 0-87666-374-9, DS1125). TFH Pubns.

Buelow, George, ed. see Block, Adrienne F.

Buelow, George, ed. see Duffy, John.

Buelow, George, ed. see Friedland, Bea.

Buelow, George, ed. see Harriss, Ernest C.

Buelow, George, ed. see Johnson, Douglas P.

Buelow, George, ed. see McClymonds, Marita P.

Buelow, George, ed. see Moore, James H.

Buelow, George, ed. see Nicolaisen, Jay.

Buelow, George, ed. see Palmer, A. Dean.

Buelow, George, ed. see Pinnell, Richard T.

Buelow, George, ed. see Sadie, Julie A.

Buelow, George, ed. see Schmidt, John C.

Buelow, George, ed. see Stauffer, George B.

Buelow, George, ed. see Willis, Stephen C.

Buelow, George, ed. see Zuck, Barbara A.

Buelow, George J. Thorough Bass Accompaniment According to Johann David Heinichen. 1966. 28.50x (ISBN 0-520-00188-5). U of Cal Pr.

Bueltmann, A. J. Take the High Road. LC 67-24877. (Concordia Sex Education Ser). (gr. 7-9). 1967. pap. 4.50 (ISBN 0-570-06603-4, 14-1503); color filmstrips w. record 10.00 (ISBN 0-685-08641-0, 79-3102). Concordia.

Buening, Charles R. Communicating on the Job: A Practical Guide for Supervisors. 100p. 1974. text ed. 8.95 (ISBN 0-201-00855-6). A-W.

Buenker, John, et al, eds. Urban History...a Guide to Information Sources. LC 80-19643. (American Government & History Ser.,Part of the Gale Information Guide Library: Vol. 9). 400p. 1981. 30.00 (ISBN 0-8103-1479-7). Gale.

Buenker, John D. & Burckel, Nicholas C. Immigration & Ethnicity: A Guide to Information Sources. LC 74-11515. (American Government & History Information Guide Ser.: Vol. 1). 1977. 30.00 (ISBN 0-8103-1202-6). Gale.

Buenker, John D. & Burckel, Nicholas C., eds. Progressive Reform: A Guide to Information Sources. (The American Government & History Information Guide Ser.: Vol. 8). 300p. 1981. 30.00 (ISBN 0-8103-1485-1). Gale.

Bueno, Dorothy Del see Del Bueno, Dorothy.

Buergenthal, Thomas, ed. Human Rights, International Law & the Helsinki Accord. LC 77-11762. 215p. 1978. text ed. 17.00x (ISBN 0-916672-91-3). Allanheld.

Buerger, Alfred A. & Tobis, Jerome S. Approaches to the Validation of Manipulation Therapy. (Illus.). 352p. 1977. 34.50 (ISBN 0-398-03565-2). C C Thomas.

Buerger, Ing E., ed. Data Processing Programming: Datenerfassung Programmiering. (English-german-french-russian). 1978. 55.00 (ISBN 3-87144-264-X). Adler.

Buerger, Jane. Growing As Jesus Grew. LC 80-17187. (Illus.). 32p. (ps-2). 1980. PLB 4.95 (ISBN 0-89565-173-4). Childs World.

--Obedience. rev. ed. LC 80-39520. (What Is It? Ser.). (Illus.). 32p. (gr. k-3). 1981. PLB 5.50 (ISBN 0-89565-206-4). Childs World.

Buerger, Jane, ed. see Baker, Eugene.

Buerger, Jane, ed. see Colina, Tessa.

Buerger, Jane, ed. see Mancure, Jane B.

Buerger, Jane, ed. see Moncure, Jane B.

Buerger, Jane, ed. see Odor, Ruth.

Buerger, Jane, ed. see Ziegler, Sandy.

Buerger, M. J. X-Ray Crystallography. LC 80-12459. 554p. 1980. Repr. of 1942 ed. lib. bdg. 32.00 (ISBN 0-89874-176-9). Krieger.

Buerk, Charles A., jt. auth. see Van Way, Charles W.

Buerki, Frederick A. Stagecraft for Nonprofessionals. 3rd ed. (Illus., Orig.). 1972. pap. 5.95 (ISBN 0-299-06234-1). U of Wis Pr.

Buerkle, Jack V. & Barker, Danny. Bourbon Street Black: The New Orleans Black Jazzman. LC 73-77926. (Illus.). 254p. 1974. pap. 4.95 (ISBN 0-19-501832-X, GB415, GB). Oxford U Pr.

Buerlen, Wolfgang, tr. see Schubring, Walther.

Buero Vallejo, A. El Tragaluz: Experimento En Dos Partes. Pasquariello, Anthony & O'Connor, Patricia W., eds. 1977. pap. text ed. 6.95x (ISBN 0-684-14875-7, ScribC). Scribner.

Buero Vallejo, Antonio. Historia De una Escalera. Sanchez, Jose, ed. 196p. (Span.). 1955. pap. text ed. 6.95x (ISBN 0-684-41189-X, ScribC). Scribner.

Bueschel, Richard M. Nakajima Ki. 43, Hayabusha 1-3. (Arco-Aircam Aviation Ser. 15). 1970. pap. 2.95 o.p. (ISBN 0-668-02292-2). Arco.

Buescher, E. Stephen, jt. auth. see Hughes, Walter T.

Bueso, Alberto T., jt. auth. see O'Connor, Dennis J.

Buess, Lynn M. Synergy Session. LC 80-67932. (Illus.). 113p. (Orig.). 1980. pap. 4.95 (ISBN 0-87516-427-7). De Vorss.

Buettner-Janusch, John. Origins of Man: Physical Anthropology. LC 66-14128. 1966. 19.95 o.p. (ISBN 0-471-11790-0). Wiley.

--Physical Anthropology: A Perspective. LC 72-14093. (Illus.). 600p. 1973. text ed. 19.50x o.p. (ISBN 0-471-11785-4). Wiley.

Buettner-Janusch, John, ed. Evolutionary & Genetic Biology of Primates, 2 Vols. Set. 73.00 ea. o.p.; Vol. 1. 44.50 o.p. (ISBN 0-12-140201-0); Vol. 2. 44.50 o.p. (ISBN 0-12-140202-9). Acad Pr.

Buferd, Norma Bradley, jt. auth. see Cooper, Patricia.

Buffa & Newman. Plaid for Production & Operations Management. rev. ed. Date not set. price not set (ISBN 0-256-02222-4, 11-1035-02). Learning Syst.

Buffa, Elwood S. Basic Production Management, 2 vols. Incl. Vol. 1. A Short Course in Managing Day-to-Day Operations. LC 75-27388 (ISBN 0-471-11830-3); Vol. 2. A Short Course in Planning & Designing Productive Systems. LC 75-27389 (ISBN 0-471-11831-1). (Business Administration Ser.). 1975. Set. text ed. 37.90 (ISBN 0-471-11832-X, Pub. by Wiley-Interscience); text ed. 18.95 ea. Wiley.

--Basic Production Management. 2nd ed. LC 74-28396. (Management & Administration Ser.). 683p. 1975. text ed. 22.95x (ISBN 0-471-11801-X); instructor's guide avail. (ISBN 0-471-11804-4). Wiley.

--Elements of Production-Operations Management. 256p. 1981. pap. text ed. 10.95 (ISBN 0-471-08532-4). Wiley.

--Modern Production-Operations Management. 6th ed. LC 79-17788. (Wiley Ser. in Management). 1980. text ed. 23.50 (ISBN 0-471-05672-3); tchrs'. manual avail. (ISBN 0-471-06443-2). Wiley.

--Operations Management: Problems & Models. 3rd ed. LC 78-37167. (Management & Administration Ser). 1972. 24.95 (ISBN 0-471-11867-2); tchrs. manual avail. (ISBN 0-471-11880-X). Wiley.

--Operations Management: The Management of Productive Systems. LC 75-33179. (Management & Administration Ser.). 640p. 1976. text ed. 24.95 (ISBN 0-471-11890-7); instructor's manual avail. (ISBN 0-471-11891-5). Wiley.

--Plaid for Production & Operations Management. 1973. pap. 5.50 (ISBN 0-256-01481-7, 11-1035-00). Learning Syst.

Buffa, Elwood S. & Dyer, James S. Essentials of Management Science-Operations Research. LC 77-23799. (Manangement & Administration Ser.). 1978. text ed. 22.95 (ISBN 0-471-02003-6); tchrs. manual avail. (ISBN 0-471-02004-4). Wiley.

--Management Science - Operations Research: Model Formulation & Solution Methods. LC 76-25058. (Management & Administration Ser.). 1977. 25.50 (ISBN 0-471-11915-6); instructor's manual avail. (ISBN 0-471-02200-4). Wiley.

--Management Science-Operations Research: Formulation & Solution Methods. 2nd ed. LC 80-18082. 725p. 1981. text ed. 25.95 (ISBN 0-471-05851-3). Wiley.

Buffa, Elwood S. & Miller, Jeffrey G. Production-Inventory Systems: Planning & Control. 3rd ed. 1979. text ed. 20.95x (ISBN 0-256-02041-8). Irwin.

Buffa, Elwood S. & Pletcher, Barbara A. Understanding Business Today. 1980. 16.95x (ISBN 0-256-02257-7). Irwin.

Buffalo Fine Arts Academy & Cranbook Academy of Art-Museum. Donald Blumberg. LC 79-50455. (Illus.). Date not set. pap. 8.95 (ISBN 0-914782-24-X). Buffalo Acad.

Buffaloe, Neal D. & Ferguson, Dale V. Microbiology. LC 75-19538. (Illus.). 448p. 1976. text ed. 19.50 (ISBN 0-395-18712-5); inst. manual 1.25 (ISBN 0-395-18918-7). HM.

--Microbiology. 2nd ed. (Illus.). 752p. 1981. text ed. 20.95 (ISBN 0-395-29649-8); write for info. lab manual (ISBN 0-395-29652-8); write for info. instr's manual (ISBN 0-395-29650-1); write for info. set study guide (ISBN 0-395-29651-X). HM.

Buffet, Guy. Guy Buffet's Hawaii. LC 80-67292. 1981. 9.95 (ISBN 0-918684-11-0). Cameron & Co.

Buffet, Guy & Buffet, Pam. Adventures of Kama Pua'a. Tabrah, Ruth, ed. LC 72-76459. (Illus.). (gr. 1-7). 1972. 5.95 (ISBN 0-89610-003-0). Island Her.

Buffet, Pam, jt. auth. see Buffet, Guy.

Buffington, Audrey V., jt. auth. see Sohns, Marvin L.

Buffinton, Thomas. Imperialism & the Dilemma of Power. Brown, Richard H. & Halsey, Van R., eds. (Amherst Ser). (gr. 9-12). 1975. pap. text ed. 4.52 (ISBN 0-201-00757-6, Sch Div); tchr's. manual 1.92 (ISBN 0-201-00772-X). A-W.

Bufford, Rodger K. The Human Reflex: Behavioral Psychology in Biblical Perspective. LC 80-8900. (Illus.). 256p. 1981. 12.95 (ISBN 0-06-061165-0). Har-Row.

Bufithis, Philip H. Norman Mailer. LC 74-78438. (Modern Literature Ser.). 1978. 10.95 (ISBN 0-8044-2097-1); pap. 3.45 (ISBN 0-8044-6064-7). Ungar.

Bufkin, Don, jt. auth. see Walker, Henry P.

Bufkin, E. C. P. H. Newby. (English Authors Ser.: No. 176). 1975. lib. bdg. 10.95 (ISBN 0-8057-1414-6). Twayne.

Bugelski, B. R. An Introduction to the Principles of Psychology. 2nd ed. LC 73-323. 640p. 1973. pap. text ed. 4.95 (ISBN 0-672-61266-6); wkbk 4.65 (ISBN 0-672-61344-1). Bobbs.

--Principles of Learning & Memory. LC 78-19760. 1979. 21.95 (ISBN 0-03-046596-6). Praeger.

--The Psychology of Learning Applied to Teaching. 2nd ed. LC 79-149402. (Illus.). 1971. text ed. 13.95 (ISBN 0-672-60785-9). Bobbs.

Bugental, James F. Psychotherapy & Process: The Fundamentals of an Existential-Humanistic Approach. LC 77-83031. (Topics in Clinical Psychology). (Illus.). 1978. pap. text ed. 7.50 (ISBN 0-201-00333-3). A-W.

Bugg, Ralph. Job Power. 1977. pap. 1.75 o.s.i. (ISBN 0-685-75871-0). Jove Pubns.

Bugge, Thomas, jt. ed. see Crosland, Maruice P.

Buglass, Leslie J. Marine Insurance & General Average in the United States. 2nd ed. 1981. 22.50x (ISBN 0-87033-274-0). Cornell Maritime.

--Marine Insurance Claims: American Law & Practice. 2nd ed. LC 63-20544. 1972. 7.00x (ISBN 0-87033-045-4). Cornell Maritime.

Buglass, Leslie J., jt. auth. see Mullins, Hugh A.

Bugliarello, George & Simon, H. A., eds. Technology, the University, & the Community. 1975. 42.00 (ISBN 0-08-017872-3). Pergamon.

Bugliarello, George, et al. The Impact of Noise Pollution: A Socio-Technological Introduction. 475p. 1976. text ed. 39.50 (ISBN 0-08-018166-X). Pergamon.

Bugliosi, Vincent & Gentry, Curt. Helter Skelter: The True Story of the Manson Murders. (Illus.). 502p. 1974. 15.00 (ISBN 0-393-08700-X). Norton.

Buhler, tr. see Mueller, F. Max.

Buhler, Charlotte. From Birth to Maturity. 1968. text ed. 11.25x (ISBN 0-7100-6244-3). Humanities.

Buhler, Kathryn C. American Silver Sixteen Fifty-Five to Eighteen Twenty-Five. 1972. 45.00 (ISBN 0-87846-064-0); pap. 20.00 (ISBN 0-87846-148-5). Mus Fine Arts Boston.

--Colonial Silversmiths, Masters & Apprentices. (Illus.). 1956. pap. 2.50 (ISBN 0-87846-160-4). Mus Fine Arts Boston.

Buikema, Arthur L., Jr. & Hendricks, Albert C. Benzene, Xylene, & Toluene in Aquatic Systems: A Review. LC 80-67170. (Illus.). 69p. (Orig.). pap. 3.75 (ISBN 0-89364-038-7, API 847-86250). Am Petroleum.

Buila. Shoeshine Girl. (gr. 3-5). pap. 1.25 (ISBN 0-590-11897-8, Schol Pap). Schol Bk Serv.

Building Cost File. The Berger Building Cost File Unit Prices Central Edition, 1980. 1980. pap. text ed. 27.95 (ISBN 0-686-63069-6). Van Nos Reinhold.

--The Berger Building Cost File Unit Prices Eastern Edition, 1980. 1980. pap. text ed. 27.95 (ISBN 0-686-63070-X). Van Nos Reinhold.

--The Berger Building Cost File Unit Prices Southern Edition, 1980. 1980. pap. text ed. 27.95 (ISBN 0-686-63071-8). Van Nos Reinhold.

--The Berger Building Cost File Unit Prices Western Edition, 1980. 1980. pap. text ed. 27.95 (ISBN 0-686-63072-6). Van Nos Reinhold.

Building Cost File, compiled by. The Berger Building Cost File 1981: General Construction Trades with Comparative Building Systems & Costs, 4 editions, Vol. 1. Incl. Eastern Edition (ISBN 0-442-21240-2); Western Edition (ISBN 0-442-21238-0); Central Edition (ISBN 0-442-21237-2); Southern Edition (ISBN 0-442-21236-4). 210p. 1980. pap. text ed. 34.95 ea. Van Nos Reinhold.

--The Berger Building Cost File 1981: Mechanical & Electrical Trades with Comparative Building Systems Costs, 4 editions, Vol. II. Incl. Eastern Edition (ISBN 0-442-21235-6); Western Edition (ISBN 0-442-21234-8); Central Edition (ISBN 0-442-21232-1); Southern Edition (ISBN 0-442-21231-3). 105p. 1980. pap. text ed. 24.95 ea. Van Nos Reinhold.

Building Research Advisory Board. Criteria for Underground Heat Distribution Systems. LC 74-32581. 1975. pap. 4.75 (ISBN 0-309-02320-3). Natl Acad Pr.

--Expansion Joints in Buildings. LC 74-9845. 1974. pap. 3.75 (ISBN 0-309-02233-9). Natl Acad Pr.

--An Exploratory Study on Responsibility, Liability & Accountability for Risks in Construction. 1978. pap. 6.75 (ISBN 0-309-02791-8). Natl Acad Pr.

--Federal Agency Practices on Use of Piping. 1967. pap. 6.25 (ISBN 0-309-01572-3). Natl Acad Pr.

--Fire Resistance of Non-Loadbearing Exterior Walls. 1951. pap. 3.50 o.p. (ISBN 0-309-00076-9). Natl Acad Pr.

--High Frequency Lighting. (Federal Construction Council Technical Report, No. 53). 1968. pap. 4.00 (ISBN 0-309-01610-X). Natl Acad Pr.

--Impact of Air-Pollution Regulations on Design Criteria for Boiler Plants at Federal Facilities. (Illus.). 62p. 1972. pap. 5.00 (ISBN 0-309-02107-3). Natl Acad Pr.

--Permafrost. 2nd ed. (Illus.). 744p. 1973. 44.50 (ISBN 0-309-02115-4). Natl Acad Pr.

--Permafrost: Russian Papers. 1978. pap. 18.00 (ISBN 0-309-02746-2). Natl Acad Pr.

--Promotion of the Development & Use of the Subsystem Concept of Building Construction. LC 72-84109. 108p. 1972. pap. 3.75 (ISBN 0-309-02039-5). Natl Acad Pr.

--Supervision & Inspection of Federal Construction. (Federal Construction Council Technical Report No. 54). 1968. pap. 4.00 o.p. (ISBN 0-309-01609-6). Natl Acad Pr.

--Thermoplastic Piping for Potable Water Distribution Systems: BRAB Fcc Technical Report No. 61. LC 77-180651. 1971. pap. 3.00 (ISBN 0-309-01934-6). Natl Acad Pr.

--Underground Corrosion, Cathodic Protection & Required Field Measurements. 1962. pap. 3.00 o.p. (ISBN 0-309-00991-X). Natl Acad Pr.

--Value Engineering in Federal Construction Agencies. LC 75-603933. (Orig.). 1969. pap. 4.75 (ISBN 0-309-01756-4). Natl Acad Pr.

Building Research Advisory Board - Federal Housing Administration. Criteria for Compacted Fills. 1965. pap. 3.00 (ISBN 0-309-01281-3). Natl Acad Pr.

Building Research Advisory Board - Federal Construction Council. Criteria for the Acceptance of Cast Iron Soil Pipe. 1960. pap. 3.00 (ISBN 0-309-00836-0). Natl Acad Pr.

--Field Investigation of Underground Heat Distribution Systems. 1963. pap. 5.75 o.p. (ISBN 0-309-01144-2). Natl Acad Pr.

--High-Temperature Water for Heating & Light Process Loads. 1960. pap. 3.00 (ISBN 0-309-00753-4). Natl Acad Pr.

Building Research Advisory Board - Federal Housing Administration. Residential Building Sewers. 1960. pap. 3.00 o.p. (ISBN 0-309-00787-9). Natl Acad Pr.

Building Research Advisory Board For The Federal Construction Council. Dimensional Tolerances for Cast-In-Place Concrete. 1964. pap. 3.00 (ISBN 0-309-01227-9). Natl Acad Pr.

Building Research Advisory Board, National Research Council. Solar Radiation Considerations in Building Planning & Design. 1976. pap. 8.75 (ISBN 0-309-02516-8). Natl Acad Pr.

Building Research Establishment. Building Construction. 2nd ed. (BRE Digests Volumes). 1978. text ed. 20.00x (ISBN 0-904406-42-3). Longman.

--Building Defects & Maintenance. 2nd ed. (BRE Digests Volumes). (Illus.). 1978. text ed. 20.00x (ISBN 0-904406-45-8). Longman.

--Building Failure, Vol. 5. (Construction Press). 1978. 38.00 (ISBN 0-86095-800-0). Longman.

--Building Materials. 2nd ed. (BRE Digests Volumes). (Illus.). 1978. text ed. 20.00x (ISBN 0-904406-43-1). Longman.

--Energy, Heating & Thermal Comfort. (Building Research Ser.: Vol. 4). 1979. 38.00 (ISBN 0-904406-99-7). Longman.

--Fire Control, Vol. 8. 1978. 38.00x (ISBN 0-86095-805-1). Longman.

--Services & Environmental Engineering. 2nd ed (BRE Digests Volumes). (Illus.). 1977. text ed. 20.00x (ISBN 0-904406-44-X). Longman.

--The Strength Properties of Timber. 208p. 1974 24.50 (ISBN 0-89047-050-2). Herman Pub.

--Wind & Snow Load, Vol. 7. 1978. 38.00x (ISBN 0-86095-802-7). Longman.

Buist, Francis, jt. auth. see Tomasson, Katherine.

Buiten, J. A. Van see Van Buitenen, J. A.

Buitenen, J. A. Van see Van Buitenen, J. A.

Buitenhuis, Cornelius. Organization in Innovation, Innovation in Organization: The Matrix As a Stimulus to Renewal. (Mensen En Organisaties in Beweging: No. 2). 1978. pap. text ed. 15.00x (ISBN 90-232-1660-1). Humanities.

Buiter, Willem H. Temporary Equilibrium & Long-Run Equilibrium. LC 78-75046. (Outstanding Dissertations in Economics Ser.). 1979. lib. bdg. 30.00 (ISBN 0-8240-4125-9). Garland Pub.

Bukhari, Emil. Napoleon's Guards Cavalry. (Men-at-Arms Ser.). (Illus.). 48p. 1979. pap. 7.95 (ISBN 0-85045-288-0). Hippocrene Bks.

Bukhari, Emir. Napoleon's Line Chasseurs. (Men-at-Arms Ser.). (Illus.). 48p. 1977. pap. 7.95 (ISBN 0-85045-269-4). Hippocrene Bks.

Bukharin, Nicolai. Imperialism & World Economy. 1966. 15.50 (ISBN 0-86527-102-X). Fertig.

Bukharin, Nikolai I. The Politics & Economics of the Transition Period. Tarbuck, Kenneth J., ed. Field, Oliver, tr. from Russian. 1979. 30.00 (ISBN 0-7100-0114-2). Routledge & Kegan.

Bukkila, Laura, jt. auth. see Sandhu, Harpreet.

Bukofzer, Manfred, et al, eds. The Place of Musicology in American Institutions of Higher Learning, 2 vols. in one. Incl. Some Aspects of Musicology. LC 77-4226. (Music Reprint Ser.). 1977. Repr. of 1957 ed. lib. bdg. 19.50 (ISBN 0-306-77407-0). Da Capo.

Bukowski, Charles. Burning in Water, Drowning in Flame. 180p. (Orig.). 1980. 14.00 (ISBN 0-87685-192-8); pap. 6.00 (ISBN 0-87685-191-X). Black Sparrow.

--Days Run Away Like Wild Horses Over the Hills. 156p. (Orig.). 1979. 10.00 (ISBN 0-87685-006-9); pap. 5.00 (ISBN 0-87685-005-0). Black Sparrow.

--Factotum. 200p. 1980. 14.00 (ISBN 0-87685-264-9); pap. 6.00 (ISBN 0-87685-263-0). Black Sparrow.

--Legs, Hips, & Behind. 40p. 1978. pap. 2.00 (ISBN 0-935390-03-0). Wormwood Rev.

--Love Is a Dog from Hell: Poems 1974-1977. 260p. (Orig.). 1980. 14.00 (ISBN 0-87685-363-7); pap. 6.00 (ISBN 0-87685-362-9). Black Sparrow.

--Mockingbird Wish Me Luck. 160p. (Orig.). 1979. 10.00 (ISBN 0-87685-139-1); pap. 5.00 (ISBN 0-87685-138-3). Black Sparrow.

--Play the Piano Drunk Like a Percussion Instrument Until the Fingers Begin to Bleed a Bit. 140p. 1979. 14.00 (ISBN 0-87685-438-2); pap. 5.00 (ISBN 0-87685-437-4). Black Sparrow.

--South of No North. 189p. (Orig.). 1979. 14.00 (ISBN 0-87685-190-1); pap. 6.00 (ISBN 0-87685-189-8). Black Sparrow.

Bukstein, Edward J. Introduction to Biomedical Electronics. LC 73-83370. (Orig.). 1973. pap. 7.50 (ISBN 0-672-21005-3). Sams.

Bulani, W., jt. auth. see Dumas, T.

Bulatovic, Miodrag. Hero on a Donkey. 2.75 o.p. (ISBN 0-452-25025-0, Z5025, Plume). NAL.

Bulbring, E. & Shuba, M. F., eds. Physiology of Smooth Muscle. LC 75-14566. 440p. 1976. 41.50 (ISBN 0-89004-051-6). Raven.

Bulbrook, Mary Jo. Development of Theraputic Skills. 1979. text ed. 12.95 (ISBN 0-316-11472-3, Little Med Div). Little.

Bulbrook, R. D. & Taylor, D. Jane, eds. Commentaries on Research in Breast Disease, Vol. 2. 175p. 1981. price not set (ISBN 0-8451-1901-X). A R Liss.

Bulfinch, T., jt. auth. see Sewell, H.

Bulfinch, Thomas. Bulfinch's Mythology. 2nd rev. ed. LC 69-11314. (Illus.). 1970. 11.95 (ISBN 0-690-57260-3, TYC-T). T Y Crowell.

Bulgakov, M. Master & Margarita. pap. 0.95 o.p. (ISBN 0-451-50699-5, CQ699, Sig Classics). NAL.

Bulgakov, Mikhail. Master & Margarita. Ginsburg, Mirra, tr. from Russian. 1967. pap 4.95 (ISBN 0-394-17439-9, B147, BC). Grove.

--Sobranie Sochinenii, Vol. 3. 202p. (Rus.). 1981. 25.00 (ISBN 0-88233-698-3). Ardis Pubs.

--Sobranie Sochinenii: Tom. 1, Ranniaia Proza. Ranniaia, Tom I., tr. 300p. (Rus.). 1981. 25.00 (ISBN 0-88233-506-5). Ardis Pubs.

Bulgakov, Sergei. Karl Marx: As a Religious Type. Lang, Virgil, ed. Barna, Luba, tr. from Rus. LC 78-78117. 200p. 1980. 12.50 (ISBN 0-913124-34-6). Nordland Pub.

Bulgarian Academy of Sciences, ed. Nikola D. Obrechkoff: Opera, Vol. I. (Illus.). 431p. 1978. 61.50 (ISBN 3-7643-0988-1). Birkhauser.

Bulhof, Francis. Wortindex Zu Thomas Mann: Der Zauberberg. LC 75-42984. 614p. (Sponsored by The College of Humanities, The University of Texas at Austin). 1976. 39.00 (ISBN 0-8357-0159-X, SS-00006). Univ Microfilms.

Bulhof, Ilse N. Wilhelm Dilthey: A Hermeneutic Approach to the Study of History & Culture. (Martinus Nijhoff Philosophy Library: No. 2). 225p. 1980. lib. bdg. 37.00 (ISBN 90-247-2360-4, Pub. by Martinus Nijhoff). Kluwer Boston.

Bulka, Reuven P., ed. Mystics & Medics: A Comparison of Mystical & Psychotherapeutic Encounters. 120p. 1979. pap. 7.95 (ISBN 0-87705-377-4). Human Sci Pr.

Bulkeley, Houghton. Contributions to Connecticut Cabinetmaking. (Illus.). 1967. 7.50x (ISBN 0-686-26737-0). Conn Hist Soc.

Bulkin, Elly & Larkin, Joan, eds. Lesbian Poetry: An Anthology. (Orig.). 1981. pap. price not set (ISBN 0-930436-08-3). Persephone.

Bulkin, Elly, jt. ed. see Larkin, Joan.

Bulkley, Dwight H. Psycles: Using Your Circadian Rhythms to Control Accidents, Illness, & Psychological Problems. LC 80-692. 224p. 1981. 10.95 (ISBN 0-672-52651-4). Bobbs.

Bulkley, Gregory B., jt. auth. see Granger, Neil.

Bull, ed. see Lord Lugard, et al.

Bull, A. T., et al. Microbial Technology: Society for General Microbiology Symposium 29. LC 78-12206. (Illus.). 1979. 59.50 (ISBN 0-521-22500-0). Cambridge U Pr.

Bull, Alan T. & Meadow, Pauline M., eds. Companion to Microbiology: Selected Topics for Further Study. (Illus.). 1978. text ed. 33.00 (ISBN 0-582-46067-0). Longman.

Bull, Alan T., et al, eds. Companion to Biochemistry: Selected Topics for Further Study, Vol. 1. Lagnado, J. R. & Thomas, J. O. (Illus.). 432p. 1974. text ed. 26.00 (ISBN 0-582-46004-2). Longman.

--Companion to Biochemistry, Vol. 2. (Illus.). 1979. text ed. 35.00 (ISBN 0-582-46029-8). Longman.

Bull, Charlotte. Wild Foods: Treats for Your Table. (Illus.). 1981. 9.95 (ISBN 0-689-11031-6). Atheneum.

Bull, Clarence S. The Faces of Hollywood. LC 68-27205. (Illus.). 1968. 4.98 o.p. (ISBN 0-498-06844-7, Encore). A S Barnes.

Bull, D., jt. auth. see Friedrich, Manfred.

Bull, Donald, jt. auth. see Friedrich, Manfred.

Bull, G. M. Dartmouth Time-Sharing System. LC 80-41327. (Computers & Their Applications Ser.). 240p. 1980. 65.00 (ISBN 0-470-27082-9). Halsted Pr.

Bull, Geoffrey. I Hid in a Basket. (Hide & Seek Bks). 1975. 1.49 (ISBN 0-87508-881-3). Chr Lit.

Bull, George, tr. see Castiglione, Baldesar.

Bull, Hedley. The Anarchical Society. LC 76-21786. 1977. 22.50x (ISBN 0-231-04132-2). Columbia U Pr.

--The Anarchical Society: A Study of Order in World Politics. 1979. pap. 8.00 (ISBN 0-231-04133-0). Columbia U Pr.

Bull, Hedley, intro. by see Wight, Martin.

Bull, Hedley, et al. Greece & the European Community. 172p. 1979. text ed. 22.25x (ISBN 0-566-00232-9, Pub. by Gower Pub Co England). Renouf.

Bull, Inez. Ole Bull Returns to Pennsylvania: The Biography of a Norwegian Violin Virtuoso and Pioneer in the Keystone State. (Illus.). 1961. 5.00 o.p. (ISBN 0-686-67700-5). Exposition.

Bull, M. J., ed. Progress in Industrial Microbiology, Vol. 15. 1979. 63.00 (ISBN 0-444-41815-6, North Holland). Elsevier.

Bull, Neil, jt. ed. see Johannis, Theodore B., Jr.

Bull, Norman J. Moral Judgement from Childhood to Adolescence. LC 71-101420. 1970. 12.00x (ISBN 0-8039-0038-4). Sage.

Bull, Odd. War & Peace in the Middle East: The Experiences & Views of a U. N. Observer. (Illus., Stickered only). 1977. lib. bdg. 19.25x (ISBN 0-89158-706-3). Westview.

Bull, R. J. Accounting in Business. 4th ed. LC 80-49870. (Illus.). 448p. 1980. text ed. 34.95 (ISBN 0-408-10669-7); pap. text ed. 19.95 (ISBN 0-408-10670-0). Butterworths.

Bull, Ray, jt. auth. see Clifford, Brian.

Bull, Storm. Index to Biographies of Contemporary Composers. LC 64-11781. 1964. 15.50 (ISBN 0-8108-0065-9). Scarecrow.

--Index to Biographies of Contemporary Composers, Vol. 2. LC 64-11781. 1974. 22.50 (ISBN 0-8108-0734-3). Scarecrow.

Bull, T. R. & Cook, Joyce L. Speech Theraphy & ENT Surgery. (Blackwell Scientific Pubns.). (Illus.). 1976. 15.75 (ISBN 0-632-09410-9). Mosby.

Bull, William E. Spanish for Teachers: Applied Linguistics. 1965. 14.95 (ISBN 0-8260-1505-0). Wiley.

--Time, Tense, & the Verb: A Study in Theoretical & Applied Linguistics with Particular Attention to Spanish. (California Library Reprint Series: No. 5). 1971. 15.00x (ISBN 0-520-00189-3). U of Cal Pr.

Bulla, Clyde. What Makes a Shadow? (Illus.). (gr. k-3). 1971. pap. 1.25 o.p. (ISBN 0-590-03427-8, Schol Pap). Schol Bk Serv.

Bulla, Clyde R. The Beast of Lor. LC 77-6751. (Illus.). (gr. 3-7). 1977. 7.95 (ISBN 0-690-01377-9, TYC-J). T Y Crowell.

--Down the Mississippi. LC 54-5614. (Illus.). (gr. 2-5). 1954. 8.95 (ISBN 0-690-24383-9, TYC-J). T Y Crowell.

--Ghost of Windy Hill. LC 68-11059. (gr. 3-7). 1968. 6.95 (ISBN 0-690-32763-3, TYC-J); PLB 7.89 (ISBN 0-690-32764-1). T Y Crowell.

--Indian Hill. LC 63-15085. (Illus.). (gr. 2-5). 1963. 7.95 (ISBN 0-690-43626-2, TYC-J). T Y Crowell.

--John Billington, Friend of Squanto. LC 56-9797. (Illus.). (gr. 2-5). 8.95 (ISBN 0-690-46253-0, TYC-J). T Y Crowell.

--Johnny Hong of Chinatown. LC 52-7859. (Illus.). (gr. 2-5). 1952. 8.95 (ISBN 0-690-46466-5, TYC-J); PLB 6.49 (ISBN 0-690-46467-3). T Y Crowell.

--Jonah & the Great Fish. LC 69-13636. (Illus.). (gr. k-4). 1970. 9.95 (ISBN 0-690-46430-4, TYC-J). T Y Crowell.

--Keep Running, Allen! LC 77-23311. (Illus.). (gr. k-2). 1978. 6.95 (ISBN 0-690-01374-4, TYC-J); PLB 7.89 (ISBN 0-690-01375-2). T Y Crowell.

--Marco Moonlight. LC 75-33203. (Illus.). (gr. 3-7). 1976. 7.95 (ISBN 0-690-01011-7, TYC-J). T Y Crowell.

--More Stories of Favorite Operas. LC 65-18691. (Illus.). (gr. 4 up). 1965. 8.95 o.p. (ISBN 0-690-55910-0, TYC-J). T Y Crowell.

--New Boy in Dublin: A Story of Ireland. LC 77-78257. (Stories from Many Lands Ser). (Illus.). (gr. k-3). 1969. 7.95 (ISBN 0-690-57756-7, TYC-J). T Y Crowell.

--Open the Door & See All the People. LC 73-184980. (Illus.). (gr. 2-5). 1972. PLB 7.89 (ISBN 0-690-60046-1, TYC-J). T Y Crowell.

--Pirate's Promise. LC 58-8209. (Illus.). (gr. 2-5). 1958. PLB 7.89 (ISBN 0-690-62656-8, TYC-J). T Y Crowell.

--The Poppy Seeds. LC 55-5835. (Illus.). (gr. k-3). 1955. 8.95 (ISBN 0-690-64856-1, TYC-J). T Y Crowell.

--Riding the Pony Express. LC 48-8051. (Illus.). (gr. 2-5). 1948. PLB 7.89 (ISBN 0-690-70111-X, TYC-J). T Y Crowell.

--Saint Valentine's Day. LC 65-11643. (Holiday Ser.). (Illus.). (gr. 1-3). 1965. PLB 7.89 (ISBN 0-690-71744-X, TYC-J). T Y Crowell.

--Secret Valley. LC 49-10917. (Illus.). (gr. 2-5). 1949. PLB 7.95 o.p. (ISBN 0-690-72383-0, TYC-J). T Y Crowell.

--Song of Saint Francis. LC 52-6739. (Illus.). (gr. 2-5). 1952. 8.95 (ISBN 0-690-75222-9, TYC-J). T Y Crowell.

--Squanto, Friend of the Pilgrims. LC 54-9145. (Illus.). (gr. 2-5). 1954. 8.95 (ISBN 0-690-76642-4, TYC-J). T Y Crowell.

--The Stubborn Old Woman. LC 78-22506. (Illus.). 48p. (gr. 1-4). 1980. 7.95 (ISBN 0-690-03945-X, TYC-J); PLB 7.89 (ISBN 0-690-03946-8). T Y Crowell.

--Sword in the Tree. LC 56-5699. (Illus.). (gr. 2-5). 1956. 8.95 (ISBN 0-690-79908-X, TYC-J). T Y Crowell.

--Tree Is a Plant. LC 60-11540. (A Let's-Read-&-Find-Out Science Bk). (Illus.). (gr. k-3). 1960. PLB 7.89 (ISBN 0-690-83529-9, TYC-J). T Y Crowell.

--Viking Adventure. LC 63-9208. (Illus.). (gr. 3-6). 1963. PLB 7.89 (ISBN 0-690-86015-3, TYC-J). T Y Crowell.

--Washington's Birthday. LC 66-10504. (Holiday Ser.). (Illus.). (gr. 1-3). 1967. PLB 7.89 (ISBN 0-690-86796-4, TYC-J). T Y Crowell.

--What Makes a Shadow. LC 62-11001. (A Let's-Read-&-Find-Out Science Bk). (Illus.). (gr. k-3). 1962. PLB 7.89 (ISBN 0-690-87648-3, TYC-J). T Y Crowell.

--White Bird. LC 66-10505. (Illus.). (gr. 2-5). 1966. 7.95 (ISBN 0-690-88499-0, TYC-J). T Y Crowell.

--White Sails to China. LC 55-9207. (Illus.). (gr. 2-5). 1955. 8.95 (ISBN 0-690-88712-4, TYC-J); PLB 7.89 (ISBN 0-690-88713-2). T Y Crowell.

Bulla, Clyde R. & Syson, Michael. Conquista! LC 77-26585. (Illus.). (gr. 2-5). 1978. 7.95 (ISBN 0-690-03870-4, TYC-J); PLB 7.89 (ISBN 0-690-03871-2). T Y Crowell.

Bulla, Clyde R., tr. see Bolliger, Max.

Bullard, Ernie & Knuth, Larry. Triple Jump Encyclopedia. LC 77-4265. 1977. pap. 8.95 (ISBN 0-87095-057-6). Athletic.

Bullard, F. M. The Geology of Grayson County, Texas. (Illus.). 72p. 1931. 0.50 (BULL 3125). Bur Econ Geology.

Bullard, Fred M. Volcanoes of the Earth. rev. ed. LC 76-2560. (Illus.). 544p. 1976. 40.00 (ISBN 0-292-78701-4). U of Tex Pr.

Bullard, Melissa M. Filippo Strozzi & the Medici: Favour & Finance in Sixteenth-Century Florence & Rome. LC 79-51822. (Cambridge Studies in Early Modern History). 216p. 1980. 24.50 (ISBN 0-521-22301-6). Cambridge U Pr.

Bullard, Pamela & Stoia, Judith. The Hardest Lesson: Personal Stories of a School Desegregation Crisis. 252p. (gr. 7 up). 1980. 8.95 (ISBN 0-316-11477-4). Little.

Bullard, Scott R. & Collins, Michael. Who's Who in Sherlock Holmes. LC 79-66638. 1980. 14.95 (ISBN 0-8008-8281-4); pap. 7.95 (ISBN 0-8008-8282-2). Taplinger.

Bullard, William R., Jr., ed. Monographs & Papers in Maya Archaeology. LC 72-105721. (Peabody Museum Papers: Vol. 61). 1970. pap. text ed. 40.00 (ISBN 0-87365-175-8). Peabody Harvard.

Bullen, Anthony, jt. auth. see Rhymer, Joseph.

Bullen, K. E. Introduction to the Theory of Mechanics. 8th ed. 1971. 35.50 (ISBN 0-521-08291-9). Cambridge U Pr.

--An Introduction to the Theory of Seismology. LC 79-7707. (Illus.). 1979. 44.50 (ISBN 0-521-04367-0); pap. 15.95x (ISBN 0-521-29686-2). Cambridge U Pr.

Bullen, Mary S. L., ed. see Legare, H. S.

Bullen, Roger. Palmerston, Guizot & the Collapse of the Entente Cordiale. (University of London Historical Studies: No. 36). 380p. 1974. text ed. 30.00x (ISBN 0-485-13136-6, Athlone Pr). Humanities.

Bullen, Roger & Bridge, Roy. The Great Powers & the European States System: 1815-1914. (Illus.). 224p. (Orig.). 1980. text ed. 23.00 (ISBN 0-582-49134-7); pap. text ed. 11.95 (ISBN 0-582-49135-5). Longman.

Buller, Francis. An Introduction to the Law Relative to Trials at Nisi Prius. Berkowitz, David S. & Thorne, Samuel E., eds. LC 77-89211. (Classics of English Legal History in the Modern Era Ser.: Vol. 60). 670p. 1979. lib. bdg. 40.00 (ISBN 0-8240-3159-8). Garland Pub.

Bullett, Gerald, ed. Silver Poets of the Sixteenth Century. 1955. 12.95x (ISBN 0-460-00985-0, Evman); pap. 4.95 (ISBN 0-460-01985-6). Dutton.

Bullett, Gerald, ed. see Keats, John.

Bullied, H. A. The Aspinall Era. 17.95x (ISBN 0-392-07597-0, SpS). Soccer.

Bulliet, L. J. Servomechanisms. 1967. text ed. 16.95 (ISBN 0-201-00725-8). A-W.

Bullington, Bruce. Heroin Use in the Barrio. LC 76-40403. 1977. 19.95 (ISBN 0-669-01042-1). Lexington Bks.

Bullins, Ed see Hoffmann, William M.

Bullitt, Orville H. Phoenicia & Carthage: A Thousand Years to Oblivion. LC 78-67741. (Illus.). 260p. 1978. 10.00 (ISBN 0-8059-2562-7). Dorrance.

Bullivant, Roger. Fugue. 1971. pap. text ed. 3.00x (ISBN 0-09-108441-5, Hutchinson U Lib). Humanities.

Bullmer, Kenneth. The Art of Empathy: A Manual for Improving Accuracy of Interpersonal Perception. LC 74-11280. 140p. 1975. pap. text ed. 7.95 (ISBN 0-87705-228-X). Human Sci Pr.

Bullock, Alan. Hitler, a Study in Tyranny. rev. ed. (Illus.). pap. 8.95x (ISBN 0-06-131123-5, TB 1123, Torch). Har-Row.

Bullock, C. Hassell, jt. ed. see Inch, Morris A.

Bullock, C. L., jt. auth. see Petrillo, H. V.

Bullock, Charles S., 3rd, jt. auth. see Rodgers, Harrell R., Jr.

Bullock, Chris & Peck, David. Guide to Marxist Literary Criticism. LC 79-3627. 160p. 1980. 12.95x (ISBN 0-253-13144-8). Ind U Pr.

Bullock, Dorothy. Give Your Child Permission to Unfold. LC 80-70509. 64p. (Orig.). 1981. pap. 2.95 (ISBN 0-87516-438-2). De Vorss.

Bullock, G. William, Jr. & Conrad, Clifton F. Management: Perspectives from the Social Sciences. LC 80-6097. 343p. 1981. lib. bdg. 19.75 (ISBN 0-8191-1466-9); pap. text ed. 11.00 (ISBN 0-8191-1467-7). U Pr of Amer.

Bullock, Hazel J. Grammaire Francaise: Methode Orale. 1949. 22.50x (ISBN 0-89197-493-8); pap. text ed. 12.50x (ISBN 0-89197-775-9). Irvington.

Bullock, Henry M. & Peterson, Edward C., eds. Young Readers Bible. (Illus.). (gr. 3 up). 1978. pap. 6.95 (ISBN 0-687-46800-0). Abingdon.

Bullock, Hugh. Story of Investment Companies. LC 59-13778. (Illus.). 1959. 22.50x (ISBN 0-231-02378-2). Columbia U Pr.

Bullock, J. Benbow. Stars for Lincoln, Doctors & Dogs. LC 80-66936. (Illus.). 100p. (Orig.). 1981. pap. 4.95 (ISBN 0-937024-00-7). Gourmet Guides.

--Vaya Con Dios. (Illus.). 150p. 1981. pap. 6.95 (ISBN 0-937024-02-3). Gourmet Guides.

Bullock, James B. No More Dry Holes. LC 80-66936. (Illus.). 150p. 1981. pap. 9.95 (ISBN 0-937024-00-7). Gourmet Guides.

Bullock, John, jt. auth. see Carotenuto, Rosine.

Bullock, Kathleen, jt. auth. see Bredemeyer, Hans G.

Bullock, Mary B. An American Transplant: The Rockefeller Foundation & Peking Union Medical College. LC 77-83098. 280p. 1981. 17.50x (ISBN 0-520-03559-3). U of Cal Pr.

Bullock, Mary Brown. An American Transplant: The Rockefeller Foundation & Peking Union Medical College. 1980. 17.50 (ISBN 0-520-03559-3). U of Cal Pr.

Bullock, Micheal, tr. see Busza, Andrzej.

Bullock, Paul. How to Profit from Condominium Conversions. 1981. 17.95 (ISBN 0-913864-64-1). Enterprise Del.

Bullock, Paul, ed. Directory of Community Services Organizations in Greater Los Angeles. 255p. 1980. 6.50 (ISBN 0-89215-106-4). U Cal LA Indus Rel.

Bullock, Theodore H. & Horridge, G. Adrian. Structure & Function in the Nervous Systems of Invertebrates, 2 Vols. (Biology Ser.). (Illus.). 1965. 160.00x (ISBN 0-7167-0626-1). W H Freeman.

Bullock, Theodore H., et al. Introduction to Nervous Systems. LC 76-3735. (Illus.). 1977. pap. text ed. 23.95x (ISBN 0-7167-0030-1). W H Freeman.

Bullock, Waneta B. & Loveless, Ganelle. ABC Mazes. (Educational Ser.). (Illus.). (gr. k-1). 1979. pap. 3.50 (ISBN 0-89039-244-7). Ann Arbor FL.

Bullough, D. A. & Storey, R. L., eds. The Study of Medieval Records: Essays in Honour of Kathleen Major. (Illus.). 380p. 1971. 29.95x (ISBN 0-19-822347-1). Oxford U Pr.

Bullough, Geoffrey, ed. Narrative & Dramatic Sources of Shakespeare, 8 vols. Incl. Vol. 1. Early Comedies, Poems, Romeo & Juliet. 1957 (ISBN 0-231-08891-4); Vol. 2. The Comedies, 1597-1603. 1958 (ISBN 0-231-08892-2); Vol. 3. Earlier English History Plays: Henry Sixth, Richard Third, Richard Second. 1960 (ISBN 0-231-08893-0); Vol. 4. Later English History Plays: King John, Henry Fourth, Henry Fifth, Henry Eighth. 1962 (ISBN 0-231-08894-9); Vol. 5. The Roman Plays: Julius Caesar, Antony & Cleopatra, Coriolanus. 1964 (ISBN 0-231-08895-7); Vol. 6. Other Classical Plays: Titus Adronicus, Troilus & Cressida, Timon of Athens, Pericles, Prince of Tyre. 1966 (ISBN 0-231-08896-5); Vol. 7. Major Tragedies: Hamlet, Othello, King Lear, Macbeth (ISBN 0-231-08897-3). LC 57-9969. 30.00x ea. Columbia U Pr.

Bullough, Robert V. Creating Instructional Materials. 2nd ed. (Elementary Education Ser.). 1978. pap. text ed. 12.95x (ISBN 0-675-08361-3). Merrill.

Bullough, Sr. Robert V. Display Boards. Duane, James E., ed. LC 80-21332. (The Instructional Media Library: Vol. 3). (Illus.). 112p. 1981. 13.95 (ISBN 0-87778-163-X). Educ Tech Pubns.

--Multi-Image Media. Duane, James E., ed. LC 80-21341. (The Instructional Media Library: Vol. 9). (Illus.). 128p. 1981. 13.95 (ISBN 0-87778-169-9). Educ Tech Pubns.

--Photography. Duane, James E., ed. LC 80-21333. (The Instructional Media Library: Vol. 11). (Illus.). 104p. 1981. 13.95 (ISBN 0-87778-171-0). Educ Tech Pubns.

Bullough, Vern & Brundage, James. Sex in a Medieval Europe. (New Concepts in Human Sexuality Ser.). 250p. 1981. text ed. 17.95 (ISBN 0-87975-141-X); pap. text ed. 9.95 (ISBN 0-87975-151-7). Prometheus Bks.

Bullough, Vern & Brundage, James, eds. Sex in the Middle Ages. LC 80-85227. (New Concepts in Human Sexuality Ser.). 250p. 1980. 17.95 (ISBN 0-87975-141-X); pap. 9.95 (ISBN 0-87975-151-7). Prometheus Bks.

Bullough, William A. Cities & Schools in the Gilded Age: The Evolution of an Urban Institution. LC 74-80592. 1974. 14.50 (ISBN 0-8046-9094-4, Natl U). Kennikat.

Bullowa, Margaret, ed. Before Speech. LC 78-51671. (Illus.). 1979. 42.50 (ISBN 0-521-22031-9); pap. 9.95 (ISBN 0-521-29522-X). Cambridge U Pr.

Bullrich, Francisco. New Directions in Latin American Architecture. LC 71-85698. (New Directions in Architecture Ser). (Illus., Orig.). 1969. 7.95 o.s.i. (ISBN 0-8076-0524-7); pap. 3.95 o.s.i. (ISBN 0-8076-0528-X). Braziller.

Bulman, I., et al. Youth Service & Interprofessional Studies. 1970. 19.50 (ISBN 0-08-015736-X). Pergamon.

Bulman, Nathan, tr. see Kitov, A. E.

Bulman, Raymond F. A Blueprint for Humanity: Paul Tillich's Theology of Culture. LC 78-75208. 248p. 1981. 18.50 (ISBN 0-8387-5000-1). Bucknell U Pr.

Bulmer, Kenneth. City Under the Sea. 1979. pap. 1.95 (ISBN 0-380-48348-3, 48348, Discus). Avon.

Bulmer, M. G. The Mathematical Theory of Quantitative Genetics. (Illus.). 220p. 1980. 74.00 (ISBN 0-19-857530-0). Oxford U Pr.

Bulmer, Martin. Social Policy Research. 373p. 1978. text ed. 31.25x (ISBN 0-333-23142-2); pap. text ed. 13.00x (ISBN 0-333-23143-0). Humanities.
--Social Research & Royal Commissions. 224p. 1980. text ed. 27.50x (ISBN 0-04-351055-8, 2392). Allen Unwin.
Bulnheim, H. P., jt. auth. see Kinne, O.
Bulos, Afif. Handbook of Arabic Music. pap. 6.95x (ISBN 0-685-88938-6). Intl Bk Ctr.
Bulow, Edeltraud & Schmitter, Peter, eds. Integrale Linguistik. Festschrift Fur Helmut Gipper. 1979. text ed. 91.25x (ISBN 0-391-01264-9). Humanities.
Bulson, P. S., jt. auth. see Allen, H. G.
Bulter, J. R. & Doessel, D. P. The Economics of Natural Disaster Relief in Australia. LC 79-50570. (Centre for Research on Federal Financial Relations - Research Monograph: No. 27). 147p. (Orig.). 1980. pap. text ed. 14.95 (ISBN 0-7081-1073-8, 0565). Bks Australia.
Bultmann, Rudolf. The History of the Synoptic Tradition. 2nd ed. Marsh, John, tr. 1972. Repr. of 1968 ed. 48.00x (ISBN 0-631-11350-9, Pub. by Basil Blackwell). Biblio Dist.
--Jesus Christ & Mythology. 1958. 2.95 o.p. (ISBN 0-684-71727-1, ScribT). Scribner.
--The Johannine Epistles. Funk, Robert W., ed. O'Hara, R. Philip, et al, trs. from Gr. LC 75-171510. (Hermeneia: a Critical & Historical Commentary on the Bible). 158p. 1973. 14.95 (ISBN 0-8006-6003-X, 20-6003). Fortress.
Bulwer, John. Chirologia; or the Natural Language of the Hand. Chironomia; or the Art of Manual Rhetoric. Cleary, James W., ed. LC 76-132492. (Landmarks in Rhetoric & Public Address Ser.). 380p. 1974. 19.50x (ISBN 0-8093-0497-X). S Ill U Pr.
Bulwer-Lytton, E. Zanoni: A Rosicrucian Tale. LC 78-157505. 416p. 1971. pap. 8.95 (ISBN 0-8334-1723-1). Steinerbks.
Bulwer-Lytton, Edward. England & the English, 2 vols. 723p. 1971. Repr. of 1833 ed. 45.00x (ISBN 0-7165-1592-X, Pub. by Irish Academic Pr Ireland). Biblio Dist.
--G. E. Falkland. Thal, Herbert V., ed. (First Novel Library). 1964. 5.00 (ISBN 0-304-92027-4); pap. 2.95 (ISBN 0-685-09165-1). Dufour.
Bulychev, Kirill. Alice. Ginsburg, Mirra, tr. LC 76-47539. (Illus.). (gr. 3-6). 1977. 8.95 (ISBN 0-02-736520-4, 73652). Macmillan.
Bumagin & Hirn. Aging Is a Family Affair. 1981. 10.95 (ISBN 0-690-01823-1). Lippincott & Crowell.
Bumcrot, Robert J., jt. auth. see Althoen, Steven C.
Bumgarner, Marlene A. Organic Cooking for (Not-So-Organic) Mothers. Olson, Sue, ed. LC 80-23089. (Illus.). 160p. (Orig.). pap. 5.50 (ISBN 0-938006-01-0); spiral bdg. 4.95 (ISBN 0-938006-00-2). Chesbro.
Bumppo, Natalie, jt. auth. see Bumppo, Natty.
Bumppo, Natty. The Columbus Book of Euchre. (Illus.). 64p. 1981. pap. price not set (ISBN 0-9604894-2-8). Borf Bks.
Bumppo, Natty & Bumppo, Natalie. Ideas for a Better America. LC 80-66966. (Illus.). 80p. 1980. pap. 3.95 (ISBN 0-9604894-0-1). Borf Bks.
Bumpus, Jerry. Special Offer. LC 80-20671. 1981. pap. 5.00 (ISBN 0-914140-08-6). Carpenter Pr.
Bumpus, John S. Dictionary of Ecclesiastical Terms: Being a History & Explanation of Certain Terms Used in Architecture, Ecclesiology, Liturgiology, Music, Ritual, Cathedral, Constitution, Etc. LC 68-30653. 1969. Repr. of 1910 ed. 15.00 (ISBN 0-8103-3321-X). Gale.
Bumsted, J. M., ed. Documentary Problems in Canadian History, 2 Vols. 1969. pap. text ed. 8.95x ea.; Vol. I. pap. Pre-Confederation (ISBN 0-256-01061-7); Vol. II. pap. Post-Confederation (ISBN 0-256-01066-8). Dorsey.
Bunbury, E. H. A History of Ancient Geography: Among the Greeks & Romans from the Earliest Ages till the Fall of the Roman Empire, 2 vols. (Illus.). 1979. Repr. of 1879 ed. Set. text ed. 185.25x (ISBN 90-7026-511-7). Humanities.
Bunce, David, tr. see Bharati, Subramania.
Bunce, Richard. Television in the Corporate Interest. LC 75-23958. (Praeger Special Studies). 1976. 17.50 o.p. (ISBN 0-275-55950-5). Praeger.
Bunce, William K., ed. Religions in Japan. LC 59-9234. 216p. 1981. pap. 5.25 (ISBN 0-8048-0500-8). C E Tuttle.
Bunch, Clarence, ed. Art Education: A Guide to Information Sources. LC 73-17518. (Art & Architecture Information Guide Ser: Vol. 6). 1977. 30.00 (ISBN 0-8103-1272-7). Gale.
Bunch, Roger, jt. auth. see Bunch, Roland.
Bunch, Roland & Bunch, Roger. The Highland Maya: Patterns of Life & Clothing in Indian Guatemala. LC 77-77864. 1977. 8.95 (ISBN 0-930740-01-7). Indigenous Pubns.
Bunch, William A. Jean Mairet. (World Authors Ser.: France: No. 358). 1975. lib. bdg. 10.95 (ISBN 0-8057-2565-2). Twayne.
Buncke, Harry, jt. auth. see Serafin, Donald.
Bundesinstitut Fur Ostwissenschaftliche und Internationale Studien. The Soviet Union, Nineteen Seventy-Eight to Nineteen Seventy-Nine. (The Soviet Union Ser.: Vol. 5). 220p. 1980. text ed. 29.50x (ISBN 0-8419-0632-7). Holmes & Meier.
Bundick, Katherine E. Harrison Family Genealogy: Sixteen Seventy-Three to Nineteen Seventy-Six. (Illus.). 1977. 27.50x (ISBN 0-685-89824-5). Va Bk.
Bundt, Nancy. The Fire Station Book. LC 80-16617. (Illus.). 32p. (ps-3). 1981. PLB 5.95g (ISBN 0-87614-126-2). Carolrhoda Bks.
Bundy, Colin. The Rise & Fall of South African Peasantry. (Perspectives on Southern Africa Ser.: No. 28). 1979. 22.50x (ISBN 0-520-03754-5). U of Cal Pr.
Bundy, McGeorge & Muskie, Edmund S. Presidential Promises & Performance. LC 80-1855. (Charles C. Moskowitz Memorial Lectures). 1980. 10.95 (ISBN 0-02-904290-9). Free Pr.
Bundy, Mary Lee see Wasserman, Paul.
Bundy, William P., ed. America & the World Nineteen Seventy-Eight. (Pergamon Policy Studies). 260p. 1979. 31.00 (ISBN 0-08-023896-3); pap. 5.50 (ISBN 0-08-023895-5). Pergamon.
--America & the World Nineteen Seventy-Nine. (Pergamon Policy Studies). 281p. 1980. 31.00 (ISBN 0-08-025952-9); pap. 5.95 (ISBN 0-08-025951-0). Pergamon.
Bungay, Henry R. Energy, the Biomass Options. LC 80-19645. 448p. 1981. 22.50 (ISBN 0-471-04386-9, Pub. by Wiley-Interscience). Wiley.
Bungay, Stanley, jt. auth. see Leavell, Stuart.
Bunge, Hans. Mathematical Methods for Texture Analysis. 2nd ed. Morris, Peter, tr. from Ger. LC 79-40054. 1981. text ed. 79.00 (ISBN 0-408-10642-5). Butterworths.
Bunge, Mario. The Mind-Body Problem: A Psychobiological Approach. (Foundations & Philosophy of Science & Technology: Vol. 1). (Illus.). 245p. 1980. 33.00 (ISBN 0-08-024720-2); pap. 14.00 (ISBN 0-08-024719-9). Pergamon.
Bungenberg De Jong, H. G., jt. auth. see Booij, H. L.
Bunger, Robert L. Islamization Among the Upper Pokomo. 2nd ed. LC 80-242. (Foreign & Comparative Studies-African Ser.: No. XXXIII). 128p. (Orig.). 1979. pap. 8.00 (ISBN 0-915984-55-5). Syracuse U Foreign Comp.
Bunger, William B. see Weissberger, A.
Bunin, Ivan. Velga. Daniels, Guy, tr. from Rus. LC 74-120786. (Illus.). (gr. 7 up). 1970. 6.95 (ISBN 0-87599-177-7). S G Phillips.
--The Village. Hapgood, I., tr. from Rus. 291p. 1975. Repr. of 1923 ed. 17.50 (ISBN 0-86527-320-0). Fertig.
--The Well of Days. Struve, G. & Miles, H., trs. from Rus. 351p. 1976. Repr. of 1933 ed. 17.50 (ISBN 0-86527-326-X). Fertig.
Bunjes, Paul G. The Praetorius Organ. (Illus.). 1966. 57.00 (ISBN 0-570-01307-0, 99-1192). Concordia.
Bunker, Barbara, et al. Student's Guide to Conducting Social Science Research. LC 74-11814. 120p. 1975. pap. text ed. 6.95 (ISBN 0-87705-238-7). Human Sci Pr.
Bunker, Edward. Little Boy Blue. LC 80-16924. 324p. 1981. 13.95 (ISBN 0-670-43107-9). Viking Pr.
Bunker, M. N. Handwriting Analysis: The Science of Determining Personality by Graphoanalysis. 12.95 (ISBN 0-911012-68-0). Nelson-Hall.
--What Handwriting Tells You: About Yourself, Your Friends, & Famous People. 12.95 (ISBN 0-911012-02-8). Nelson-Hall.
Bunkle, Phillida, jt. ed. see Hughes, Beryl.
Bunn, John W. Art of Officiating Sports. 3rd ed. 1967. text ed. 16.50 (ISBN 0-13-047803-2). P-H.
Bunnell, C. A., jt. auth. see Fuchs, P. L.
Bunnell, David. Personal Computing: A Beginner's Guide. LC 77-99078. (Illus.). 1978. 11.95 o.p. (ISBN 0-8015-5843-3). Dutton.
Bunnell, Peter, ed. A Photographic Vision: Pictorial Photography. new ed. (Illus.). 124p. 1980. cancelled o.p. (ISBN 0-87905-075-6). Peregrine Smith.
Bunnell, Peter C., ed. A Photographic Vision: Pictorial Photography. (Illus.). 1980. pap. 17.50 (ISBN 0-87905-081-0). Peregrine Smith.
Bunnell, Peter C., ed. see Engrand, Bernard.
Bunnelle, Hasse R. Movable Feasts: The Backpacker Magazine Cookbook. Backpacker Magazine, ed. 1980. write for info. (ISBN 0-671-25032-9, Fireside); pap. write for info. (ISBN 0-671-25033-7). S&S.
Bunney, William E., jt. auth. see Usdih, Earl.
Bunsell, A. R., et al, eds. Advances in Composite Materials: Proceedings of the Third International Conference on Composite Materials, Paris, France, 26-29 August, 1980. LC 80-40997. 2000p. 1980. 200.00 (ISBN 0-08-026717-3). Pergamon.
Bunshah, R. F., ed. Measurement of Mechanical Properties. LC 67-20260. 1971. 45.00 (ISBN 0-685-55315-9). Krieger.
Bunshah, Rointan F. Films & Coatings for High Technology Applications. (Engineering Ser.). (Illus.). 600p. 1981. text ed. 60.00 o.p. (ISBN 0-686-69160-1). Lifetime Learn.
Bunt, Lucas N. H. & Jones, Phillip S. Historical Roots of Elementary Mathematics. (Illus.). 352p. 1976. Ref. Ed. 16.95 (ISBN 0-13-389015-5). P-H.
Bunt, Richard B., jt. auth. see Tremblay, Jean P.
Bunt, Richard B., jt. auth. see Tremblay, Jean-Paul.
Buntain, Ruth J. A Cross or a Ladder? (Uplook Ser.). 31p. 1970. pap. 0.75 (ISBN 0-8163-0069-0, 03654-1). Pacific Pr Pub Assn.
--Unbottled Poison. 32p. 1973. pap. 0.75 (ISBN 0-8163-0078-X, 21040-1). Pacific Pr Pub Assn.
Bunting. Iceberg! Orig. Title: High Tides for the Labrador. (gr. 5-6). Date not set. pap. cancelled (ISBN 0-590-30880-7, Schol Pap). Schol Bk Serv.
Bunting, et al. Taos Adobes. 1975. pap. 7.95 (ISBN 0-89013-088-4). Museum NM Pr.
Bunting, A. H., jt. ed. see Summerfield, R. J.
Bunting, Bainbridge. Early Architecture in New Mexico. LC 76-21511. (Illus.). 122p. 1976. 12.95 o.p. (ISBN 0-8263-0424-9); pap. 7.95 o.p. (ISBN 0-8263-0435-4). U of NM Pr.
Bunting, Basil, ed. Joseph Skipsey: Selected Poems. 96p. pap. 5.95x (ISBN 0-904461-08-4, Pub. by Ceolfrith Pr England). Intl Schol Bk Serv.
Bunting, Eve. Barney the Beard. LC 73-23111. (Illus.). 48p. (ps-3). 1975. 5.95 o.s.i. (ISBN 0-8193-0728-9, Four Winds); PLB 5.41 o.s.i. (ISBN 0-8193-0729-7). Schol Bk Serv.
--The Big Cheese. LC 76-45381. (gr. 2-5). 1977. 7.95 (ISBN 0-02-715370-3, 71537). Macmillan.
--The Day of the Earthlings. (Science Fiction Ser.). (Illus.). 32p. (gr. 3-9). 1978. PLB 5.95 (ISBN 0-87191-621-5); pap. 2.95 (ISBN 0-89812-054-3). Creative Ed.
--Fifteen. (Young Romance Ser.). (Illus.). (gr. 3-9). 1978. PLB 5.95 (ISBN 0-87191-632-0); pap. 2.95 (ISBN 0-89812-064-0). Creative Ed.
--The Followers. (Science Fiction Ser.). (Illus.). (gr. 3-9). 1978. PLB 5.95 (ISBN 0-87191-627-4); pap. 2.95 (ISBN 0-89812-055-1). Creative Ed.
--For Always. (Young Romance Ser.). (Illus.). (gr. 3-9). 1978. PLB 5.95 (ISBN 0-87191-636-3); pap. 2.95 (ISBN 0-89812-068-3). Creative Ed.
--The Girl in the Painting. (Young Romance Ser.). (Illus.). (gr. 3-9). 1978. PLB 5.95 (ISBN 0-87191-639-8); pap. 2.95 (ISBN 0-89812-069-1). Creative Ed.
--Island of One. (Science Fiction Ser.). (Illus.). (gr. 3-9). 1978. PLB 5.95 (ISBN 0-87191-626-6); pap. 2.95 (ISBN 0-89812-058-6). Creative Ed.
--Just Like Everyone Else. (Young Romance Ser.). (Illus.). (gr. 3-9). 1978. PLB 5.95 (ISBN 0-87191-630-4); pap. 2.95 (ISBN 0-89812-062-4). Creative Ed.
--Maggie the Freak. (Young Romance Ser.). (Illus.). (gr. 3-9). 1978. PLB 5.95 (ISBN 0-87191-633-9); pap. 2.95 (ISBN 0-685-59452-1). Creative Ed.
--The Mask. (Science Fiction Ser.). (Illus.). (gr. 3-9). 1978. PLB 5.95 (ISBN 0-87191-625-8); pap. 2.95 (ISBN 0-89812-056-X). Creative Ed.
--The Mirror Planet. (Science Fiction Ser.). (Illus.). (gr. 3-9). 1978. PLB 5.95 (ISBN 0-87191-628-2); pap. 2.95 (ISBN 0-89812-057-8). Creative Ed.
--Nobody Knows but Me. (Young Romance Ser.). (gr. 3-9). 1978. PLB 5.95 (ISBN 0-87191-635-5); pap. 2.95 (ISBN 0-89812-060-8). Creative Ed.
--Oh, Rick. (Young Romance Ser). (Illus.). (gr. 3-9). 1978. PLB 5.95 (ISBN 0-87191-634-7); pap. 2.95 (ISBN 0-89812-061-6). Creative Ed.
--A Part of the Dream. (Young Romance Ser.). (Illus.). (gr. 3-9). 1978. PLB 5.95 (ISBN 0-87191-638-X); pap. 2.95 (ISBN 0-89812-066-7). Creative Ed.
--The Robot People. (Science Fiction Ser.). (Illus.). (gr. 3-9). 1978. PLB 5.95 (ISBN 0-87191-622-3); pap. 2.95 (ISBN 0-89812-051-9). Creative Ed.
--The Skate Patrol. Tucker, Kathleen, ed. LC 80-18640. (First Read Alone Mysteries Ser.). (Illus.). 48p. (gr. 2-5). 1980. 5.50g (ISBN 0-8075-7393-0). A Whitman.
--The Skateboard Four. Rubin, Caroline, ed. LC 76-16115. (Springboard Sports Ser.). (Illus.). 64p. (gr. 3-6). 1976. 5.75g (ISBN 0-8075-7392-2). A Whitman.
--The Space People. (Science Fiction Ser.). (Illus.). (gr. 3-9). 1978. PLB 5.95 (ISBN 0-87191-623-1); pap. 2.95 (ISBN 0-89812-053-5). Creative Ed.
--The Spook Birds. Tucker, Kathleen, ed. (Illus.). 40p. (gr. 3-7). 1981. 5.50 (ISBN 0-8075-7587-9). A Whitman.
--Survival Camp. (Young Romance Ser.). (Illus.). (gr. 3-9). 1978. PLB 5.95 (ISBN 0-87191-631-2); pap. 2.95 (ISBN 0-89812-063-2). Creative Ed.
--Two Different Girls. (Young Romance Ser.). (Illus.). (gr. 3-9). 1978. PLB 5.95 (ISBN 0-87191-637-1); pap. 2.95 (ISBN 0-89812-067-5). Creative Ed.
--The Undersea People. (Science Fiction Ser.). (Illus.). (gr. 3-9). 1978. PLB 5.95 (ISBN 0-87191-624-X); pap. 2.95 (ISBN 0-89812-052-7). Creative Ed.
Bunting, James. Bavaria. (Batsford Countries of Europe Ser). 216p. 1972. 8.95 o.p. (ISBN 0-8038-0740-6). Hastings.
Bunton, John. World Markets for Construction. (Illus.). 1979. 33.50x (ISBN 0-7198-2720-5). Intl Ideas.
Bunuel. Las Tres de la Madrugada. (Easy Reader, A). pap. 2.90 (ISBN 0-88436-061-X, SPA112051). EMC.
Bunyan, John. A Book for Boys & Girls: Or Country Rhymes for Children. Lurie, Alison & Sciller, Justin G., eds. Incl. Divine Songs. Watts, Isaac; Moral Songs Composed for the Use of Children. Foxton, Thomas. LC 75-32136. (Classics of Children's Literature Ser., 1621-1932). 1978. PLB 38.00 (ISBN 0-8240-2253-X). Garland Pub.
--Grace Abounding. 1959. pap. 1.50 (ISBN 0-8024-3293-X). Moody.
--Grace Abounding to the Chief of Sinners. Sharrock, Roger, ed. (Oxford English Texts Ser). 1962. 29.95x (ISBN 0-19-811833-3). Oxford U Pr.
--Grace Abounding to the Chief of Sinners. Sharrock, Roger, ed. & intro. by. Bd. with The Pilgrim's Progress from This World to That Which Is to Come. (Oxford Standard Authors Ser). 1966. 24.95 (ISBN 0-19-254159-5). Oxford U Pr.
--Groans of a Lost Soul. LC 68-6571. 1967. pap. 3.25 (ISBN 0-685-19830-8). Reiner.
--The Holy War. Sharrock, Roger & Forrest, James F., eds. (Oxford English Texts Ser.). 344p. 1980. 72.00 (ISBN 0-19-811887-2). Oxford U Pr.
--Life of John Bunyan. (Summit Bks). 1977. pap. 1.95 (ISBN 0-8010-0717-8). Baker Bk.
--Light for Them That Sit in Darkness. pap. 3.50 (ISBN 0-685-19838-3). Reiner.
--Miscellaneous Works: Some Gospel Truths Opened,a Vindication of Some Gospel Truths Opened, & a Few Sighs from Hell, Vol 1. Underwood, T. L. & Sharrock, Roger, eds. (Oxford English Texts Ser.). (Illus.). 458p. 1980. 69.00x (ISBN 0-19-812730-8). Oxford U Pr.
--Pictorial Pilgrim's Progress. 1960. pap. 2.50 (ISBN 0-8024-0019-1). Moody.
--Pilgrim's Progress. 288p. 1981. pap. 2.95 (ISBN 0-88368-096-3). Whitaker Hse.
--Pilgrim's Progress. 1957. 10.50x (ISBN 0-460-00204-X, Evman); pap. 2.95 (ISBN 0-460-01204-5, Evman). Dutton.
--Pilgrim's Progress. abr. ed. (Illus.). (gr. 7-9). 1939. pap. 2.95 o.p. (ISBN 0-397-31705-0). Lippincott.
--Pilgrim's Progress. pap. 2.50 (ISBN 0-8024-0012-4). Moody.
--Pilgrim's Progress. 256p. 1973. pap. 2.25 (ISBN 0-310-22142-0). Zondervan.
--The Pilgrim's Progress. 1979. Repr. 16.95 (ISBN 0-85151-259-3). Banner of Truth.
--The Pilgrim's Progress. (Giant Summit Bks). pap. 6.95 (ISBN 0-8010-0732-1). Baker Bk.
--Pilgrims Progress. 1976. lib. bdg. 15.95x (ISBN 0-89968-156-5). Lightyear.
--Pilgrim's Progress: From This World to That Which Is to Come. 2nd ed. Wharey, James B. & Sharrock, Roger, eds. (Oxford English Texts Ser). 1960. 45.00x (ISBN 0-19-811802-3). Oxford U Pr.
--Pilgrim's Progress from This World, to That Which Is to Come. 2nd ed. 1974. 14.95x o.p. (ISBN 0-8277-2157-9); pap. text ed. 6.50x o.p. (ISBN 0-8277-3744-0). British Bk Ctr.
--The Pilgrim's Progress: From This World to That Which Is to Come. Wharey, James B., ed. (World's Classics Ser.: No. 12). 1902. 5.95 o.p. (ISBN 0-19-250012-0). Oxford U Pr.
--Upon a Penny Loaf: The Wisdom of John Bunyan. Palms, Roger C., compiled by. LC 78-12239. 1978. pap. 3.50 (ISBN 0-87123-573-0, 210573). Bethany Fell.
Bunyan, John & Goodwin, Thomas. La Oracion. (Span.). Date not set. pap. 2.50 (ISBN 0-686-28949-8). Banner of Truth.
Bunyan, John see Watson, Jean.
Bunyan, Juan. El Peregrino. 1966. 2.95x (ISBN 0-8361-1112-5). Herald Pr.

Bunyan, Juan & Leavell, L. P. El Progreso Del Peregrino. Duffer, Hiram F., Jr., tr. 1979. pap. 1.75 (ISBN 0-311-37006-3). Casa Bautista.
Bunyard, Peter, jt. auth. see Allaby, Michael.
Bunyard, R. S. Police: Organisation & Command. (Illus.). 400p. 1978. 21.95x (ISBN 0-7121-1671-0, Pub. by Macdonald & Evans England). Intl Ideas.
Buoncompagni, Marcellus. Educational Psychology. (The Library of Scientific Psychology). (Illus.). 1979. 27.50 (ISBN 0-89266-179-8). Am Classical Coll Pr.
Buoncristiano, S., et al. A Geometric Approach to Homology Theory. LC 75-22980. (London Mathematical Society Lecture Note Ser.: No. 18). (Illus.). 216p. 1976. pap. text ed. 17.95x (ISBN 0-521-20940-4). Cambridge U Pr.
Buonicore, Anthony & Theodore, Louis. Industrial Control Equipment for Gaseous Pollutants, 2 vols. new ed. LC 74-25260. (Uniscience Ser). 1975. Vol. 1, 209p. 49.95 (ISBN 0-87819-067-8); Vol. 2, 168p. 39.95 (ISBN 0-87819-068-6). CRC Pr.
Buono, Anthon, tr. see Pope John Paul II.
Buono, Carmen J. Dello see Dello Buono, Carmen J.
Buono, Dello & Joseph, Carmen. Rare Early Essays on George Eliot. 211p. 1980. lib. bdg. 25.00 (ISBN 0-8482-3660-2). R West.
--Rare Early Essays on the Brontes. 218p. 1980. lib. bdg. 17.50 (ISBN 0-8482-0646-0). Norwood Edns.
Bupp, Irvin C. & Derian, Jean-Claude. The Failed Promise of Nuclear Power: The Story of Light Water. LC 77-20419. (Illus.). 241p. 1981. pap. 5.95 (ISBN 0-465-02273-1). Basic.
Burack, A. S., ed. One Hundred Plays for Children. (gr. 1-6). 1970. 11.95 (ISBN 0-8238-0002-4). Plays.
--Skits, Comedies & Farces for Teen-Agers. (gr. 7-12). 1970. 10.95 (ISBN 0-8238-0001-6). Plays.
--The Writer's Handbook: 1980 Edition. new ed. 1980. 16.95 (ISBN 0-87116-119-2). Writer.
Burack, Elmer H. Personnel Management: Cases & Exercises. (Illus.). 1978. pap. text ed. 11.50 (ISBN 0-8299-0203-1); IM avail. (ISBN 0-8299-0461-1); exam questions avail. (ISBN 0-8299-0463-8). West Pub.
Burack, Elmer H. & Smith, Robert D. Personnel Management: A Human Resource Systems Approach. 500p. 1977. text ed. 18.95 (ISBN 0-8299-0130-2); IM avail. (ISBN 0-8299-0462-X). West Pub.
Buranelli, Vincent. Edgar Allan Poe. 2nd ed. (U.S. Authors Ser.: No. 4). 1977. lib. bdg. 9.95 (ISBN 0-8057-7189-1). Twayne.
--King & the Quaker. LC 61-6620. 1962. 9.00x o.p. (ISBN 0-8122-7343-5). U of Pa Pr.
Buranelli, Vincent, ed. Edgar Allan Poe. LC 77-7265. (Twaynes's U. S. Authors Ser.). 166p. 1977. pap. text ed. 4.95 (ISBN 0-672-61502-9). Bobbs.
Burbach, Roger & Flynn, Patricia. Agribusiness in the Americas: The Political Economy of Corporate Agriculture. LC 79-3869. 256p. 1980. 16.50 (ISBN 0-85345-535-X); pap. 6.50 (ISBN 0-85345-536-8). Monthly Rev.
Burbank, Garin. When Farmers Voted Red: The Gospel of Socialism in the Oklahoma Countryside, 1910-1924. LC 76-5259. (Contributions in American History Ser.: No. 53). (Illus.). 1976. lib. bdg. 15.00 (ISBN 0-8371-8903-9, BSO/). Greenwood.
Burbank, Rex. Sherwood Anderson. (U. S. Authors Ser.: No. 65). 1964. lib. bdg. 10.95 (ISBN 0-8057-0020-X). Twayne.
Burbank, Rex J. Thornton Wilder. 2nd ed. (United States Authors Ser.: No. 5). 1978. lib. bdg. 10.95 (ISBN 0-8057-7223-5). Twayne.
Burberry, Peter. Environment & Services. 2nd ed. (Mitchell's Building Construction Ser.). 1978. pap. 13.95 (ISBN 0-470-26352-0). Halsted Pr.
Burberry, Peter & Aldersey-Williams, Arthur. Guide to Domestic Central Heating Installation & Controls. LC 78-16062. 1979. 17.50 (ISBN 0-85139-207-5, Pub. by Architectural Pr). Nichols Pub.
Burbidge, Geoffrey & Burbidge, Margaret. Quasi-Stellar Objects. LC 67-17457. (Illus.). 1967. 18.95x (ISBN 0-7167-0321-1). W H Freeman.
Burbidge, Geoffrey, et al, eds. Annual Review of Astronomy & Astrophysics, Vol. 18. LC 63-8846. (Illus.). 1980. text ed. 20.00 (ISBN 0-8243-0918-9). Annual Reviews.
Burbidge, Margaret, jt. auth. see Burbidge, Geoffrey.
Burbidge, Peter & Sutton, Richard, eds. The Wagner Companion. LC 79-50099. 1979. 39.50 (ISBN 0-521-22787-9); pap. 9.95 (ISBN 0-521-29657-9). Cambridge U Pr.
Burbridge, John L. Production Planning. 427p. 1971. 29.50x (ISBN 0-8448-0182-8). Crane-Russak Co.
Burby, Raymond J. Communicating with People: The Supervisor's Introduction to Verbal Communication & Decision-Making. LC 78-109507. (Supervision Ser). (Prog. Bk.). 1970. pap. text ed. 8.95 (ISBN 0-201-00735-5). A-W.
--Fundamentals of Leadership: A Guide for the Supervisor. LC 72-2644. (Illus.). 128p. (Prog. Bk.). 1972. pap. text ed. 8.95 (ISBN 0-201-00744-4). A-W.
--Introduction to Basic Supervision of People. 1966. pap. 8.95 (ISBN 0-201-00719-3). A-W.
--Introduction to Creative Supervision. LC 79-13802. 1980. pap. text ed. 8.95 (ISBN 0-201-00836-X). A-W.
--Managing with People. 1968. pap. text ed. 8.95 (ISBN 0-201-00723-1). A-W.
Burcaw, George E. The Saxon House. LC 79-65600. (GEM Books Ser.). (Illus.). 122p. (Orig.). 1980. pap. 7.95 (ISBN 0-89301-065-0). U Pr of Idaho.
Burch. Training Thoroughbred Horses. 2nd rev. ed. 1973. lib. bdg. 10.75 (ISBN 0-936032-29-4). Thoroughbred Own & Breed.
Burch, Augustine. Thine Is the Glory. 1981. 4.50 (ISBN 0-8062-1626-3). Carlton.
Burch, Byron. Quality Brewing: A Guidebook for the Home Production of Fine Beers. pap. 2.50 (ISBN 0-9604284-0-2). Joby Bks.
Burch, George E. A Primer of Venous Pressure. (Illus.). 176p. 1972. 14.75 (ISBN 0-398-02556-8). C C Thomas.
Burch, John G., jt. auth. see Sardinas, Joseph.
Burch, John G., Jr. & Sardinas, Joseph L., Jr. Computer Control & Audit: A Total Systems Approach. 492p. 1978. 26.50 (ISBN 0-471-03491-6). Wiley.
Burch, Monte. Gun Care & Repair. 1978. 12.95 (ISBN 0-87691-256-0). Winchester Pr.
--The Home Cabinetmaker: Building Fine Furniture, Built-Ins, Millwork. LC 79-4747. (Popular Science Bk.). (Illus.). Date not set. 19.95 (ISBN 0-06-010349-3, HarpT). Har-Row. Postponed.
--Masonry & Concrete. Horowitz, Shirley & Kummings, Gail, eds. (Illus.). 144p. (Orig.). 1981. pap. 6.95 (ISBN 0-932944-30-2). Creative Homeowner.
--The Outdoorsman's Workshop. 1977. 12.95 (ISBN 0-87691-239-0). Winchester Pr.
--Tile: Indoors & Out. Horowitz, Shirley M. & Kummings, Gail, eds. (Illus.). 144p. (Orig.). 1980. 14.95 (ISBN 0-932944-27-2); pap. 5.95 (ISBN 0-932944-28-0). Creative Homeowner.
Burch, Monte, jt. auth. see Hedden, Jay W.
Burch, Monte, jt. auth. see Jones, Robert E.
Burch, Noel. Theory of Film Practice. Lane, Helen R., tr. from French. LC 80-8676. (Illus.). 172p. 1981. 18.50x (ISBN 0-691-03962-3); pap. 5.95 (ISBN 0-691-00329-7). Princeton U Pr.
--To the Distant Observer: Form & Meaning in Japanese Cinema. LC 77-20316. 1979. 21.50x (ISBN 0-520-03605-0); pap. 9.75 (ISBN 0-520-03877-0). U of Cal Pr.
Burch, Noel, tr. see Bresson, Robert.
Burch, Noel, tr. see Hodeir, Andre.
Burch, Pat. Rokudan: A Tale of Love in Six Movements. LC 80-29375. 192p. 1981. 8.95 (ISBN 0-8008-6818-8). Taplinger.
Burch, Philip H. Elites in American History: The Civil War to the New Deal. 300p. text ed. 20.00x (ISBN 0-8419-0595-9). Holmes & Meier.
Burch, Philip H., Jr. Elites in American History: The Federalist Years to the Civil War, Vol. 1. 320p. 1981. text ed. 20.00x (ISBN 0-8419-0594-0). Holmes & Meier.
--Elites in American History: The New Deal to the Carter Administration, Vol. 3. 1980. text ed. 19.50x (ISBN 0-8419-0565-7); pap. text ed. 14.50x (ISBN 0-8419-0566-5). Holmes & Meier.
Burch, Robert. Two That Were Tough. (Illus.). (gr. 6-8). 1976. 7.95 (ISBN 0-670-73684-8). Viking Pr.
Burch, Robert M. Colour Printing & Colour Printers. LC 78-74393. (Nineteenth Century Book Arts & Printing History Ser.: Vol. 8). 1980. lib. bdg. 33.00 (ISBN 0-8240-3882-7). Garland Pub.
Burch, Thomas K., ed. Demographic Behavior: Interdisciplinary Perspectives on Decision Making. (AAAS Selected Symposium: No. 45). 45p. 1980. lib. bdg. 22.00x (ISBN 0-89158-785-3). Westview.
Burch, Virginia M. How to Raise & Train a Saluki. (Illus.). (gr. 3-5). 1965. pap. 2.00 (ISBN 0-87666-377-3, DS1112). TFH Pubns.
Burchard, Christoph, ed. see Adam, Alfred.
Burchard, Florence & Boucher, Sharon. Someone Had to Hold the Lantern. LC 79-17836. (Crown Ser.). 1979. pap. 4.50 (ISBN 0-8127-0238-7). Southern Pub.
Burchard, Marshall. Sports Hero: Ron Guidry. (Sports Hero Ser.). (Illus.). 96p. (gr. 7-10). 1981. PLB 6.99 (ISBN 0-399-61178-9). Putnam.
--Sports Hero: Terry Bradshaw. (Sports Hero Ser.). (Illus.). (gr. 6-8). 1980. PLB 6.29 (ISBN 0-399-61133-9). Putnam.
Burchard, Peter. Balloons: From Paperbags to Skyhooks. (Illus.). (gr. 3-5). 1960. 5.95g o.s.i. (ISBN 0-02-715600-1). Macmillan.
--Digger. 128p. (gr. 5-12). 1980. 8.95 (ISBN 0-399-20717-1). Putnam.
Burchard, S. H. Sports Star: Tommy John. LC 80-8794. (Sports Star Ser.). (Illus.). 64p. (gr. 4-6). 1981. 6.95 (ISBN 0-15-278038-6, HJ). HarBraceJ.
--Sports Star: Tommy John. LC 80-8794. (Sports Star Ser.). (Illus.). 64p. (gr. 4-6). pap. 3.95 (ISBN 0-15-278039-4, VoyB). HarBraceJ.
Burchardt, Bill. Buck. LC 78-1188. 1978. 7.95 o.p. (ISBN 0-385-13439-8). Doubleday.
--The Lighthorsemen. LC 80-1986. (Double D Western Ser.). 192p. 1981. 9.95 (ISBN 0-385-17148-X). Doubleday.
Burchardt, Nellie. What Are We Going to Do, Michael? LC 73-5743. (gr. 4-6). 1973. PLB 4.90 o.p. (ISBN 0-531-02637-X). Watts.
Burchell, Mary. Elusive Harmony. (Alpha Books). 80p. (Orig.). 1978. pap. text ed. 2.25x (ISBN 0-19-424163-7). Oxford U Pr.
--Nightingales. (Harlequin Romances Ser.). 192p. 1980. pap. 1.25 (ISBN 0-373-02359-6, Pub. by Harlequin). PB.
--Yours with Love. (Harlequin Romances Ser.). 192p. (Orig.). 1981. pap. 1.25 (ISBN 0-373-02379-0, Pub. by Harlequin). PB.
Burchell, S. C. Building the Suez Canal. LC 66-21551. (Horizon Caravel Bks). (Illus.). 153p. 1966. 9.95 (ISBN 0-8281-0354-2, J028-0). Am Heritage.
Burchell, Samuel C. Age of Progress. (Great Ages of Man Ser). (Illus.). 1966. 12.95 (ISBN 0-8094-0351-X). Time-Life.
Burchenal, Joseph & Oettgen, Herbert. Cancer: Achievements, Challenges, & Prospects for the 1980's, Vol. 1. 1981. write for info. (ISBN 0-8089-1351-4). Grune.
Burchenal, Joseph, ed. Cancer: Achievements, Challenges, & Prospects for the 1980's, Vol. 2. Oettgen, Herbert. 1981. write for info. Grune.
Burchess, A., jt. auth. see Shapiro, Frank D.
Burchess, D. Specifications & Quantities. 2nd ed. (Illus.). 136p. 1980. pap. text ed. 12.95x (ISBN 0-7114-5640-2). Intl Ideas.
Burchett, Wilfred. Grasshoppers & Elephants. 1977. pap. 4.95 (ISBN 0-916354-65-2); pap. 5.95 (ISBN 0-916354-66-0). Urizen Bks.
Burchette, Dorothy. More Needlework Blocking & Finishing. (Illus.). 1979. 3.95 (ISBN 0-684-16892-8, ScribT). Scribner.
Burchfield, Joe D. Lord Kelvin & the Age of the Earth. 274p. 1975. pap. 8.95 o.p. (ISBN 0-88202-013-7, Sci Hist). N Watson.
Burck, H. D., et al. Counseling & Accountability: Methods & Critique. 224p. 1973. text ed. 27.00 (ISBN 0-08-017029-3); pap. text ed. 10.00 (ISBN 0-08-017684-4). Pergamon.
Burckel, Nicholas C., jt. auth. see Buenker, John D.
Burckel, Nicholas C., jt. ed. see Buenker, John D.
Burckhardt, C. H., et al. Das Gefieder des Huhnes: Abbild des Tieres und seiner Haltung. (Tierhaltung: No. 9). (Illus.). 67p. (Ger.). 1979. pap. 16.00 (ISBN 3-7643-1137-1). Birkhauser.
Burckhardt, J. K., tr. Arabic Proverbs: Or the Manners & Customs of the Modern Egyptian Illustrated from Their Proverbial Sayings Current at Cairo. 1972. Repr. text ed. 12.50x (ISBN 0-7007-0019-6). Humanities.
Burckhardt, Jakob. The Cicerone: An Art Guide to Painting in Italy for the Use of Travellers & Students. Freedberg, Sydney J., ed. LC 77-18677. (Connoisseurship, Criticism & Art History Ser.: Vol. 3). 305p. 1979. lib. bdg. 30.00. Garland Pub.
--Recollections of Rubens. Freedberg, Sydney J., ed. LC 77-18674. (Connoisseurship Criticism & Art History Ser.: Vol. 4). 374p. 1979. lib. bdg. 33.00 (ISBN 0-8240-3261-6). Garland Pub.
Burckhardt, John L. Travels in Arabia. (Arab Background Ser.). 25.00x (ISBN 0-685-77092-3). Intl Bk Ctr.
Burckhardt, Titus. Moorish Culture in Spain. Jaffa, Alisa, tr. (Illus.). 228p. 1972. 18.95x (ISBN 0-04-946008-0). Allen Unwin.
Burd, L. Arthur, ed. see Machiavelli, Niccolo.
Burda, ed. Whitework & Cutwork. (Burda Bks.). Date not set. 3.00x (ISBN 0-686-64667-3, B803). Toggitt.
Burda, Franz, jt. auth. see Friddell, Guy.
Burden, Charles, et al, eds. Business in Literature. LC 77-573. (English & Humanities Ser.). 1977. pap. text ed. 9.95x (ISBN 0-582-28160-1, Pub. by MacKay). Longman.
Burden, Ernest. Entourage: A Tracing File for Architecture & Interior Design Drawing. (Illus.). 256p. 1981. 15.95 (ISBN 0-07-008930-2). McGraw.
Burden, Ernest, ed. Living Barns: How to Find & Restore a Barn of Your Own. 1979. pap. 9.95 o.p. (ISBN 0-316-52886-2). NYGS.
Burden, J. Graphic Reproduction Photography. Date not set. 19.50 o.p. (ISBN 0-8038-5778-0). Hastings.
Burden, Shirley, ed. Presence. (Illus.). 92p. 1981. 20.00 (ISBN 0-89381-075-4). Aperture.
Burder, J. Technique of Editing Sixteen Mm. Films. 4th ed. (Illus.). 152p. 1979. 17.95 (ISBN 0-240-51019-4). Focal Pr.
Burder, John. Work of the Industrial Film Maker. (Library of Film & Television Practice). Date not set. 16.95 (ISBN 0-8038-8053-7). Hastings.
Burdett, Eric. The Craft of Bookbinding: A Practical Guide. 1977. 38.00 (ISBN 0-7153-6656-4). David & Charles.
Burdett, Jeremy K. Molecular Shapes: Theoretical Models of Inorganic Stereochemistry. 270p. 1980. 29.50 (ISBN 0-471-07860-3, Pub. by Wiley-Interscience). Wiley.
Burdette, A. C. An Introduction to Analytic Geometry & Calculus. rev. ed. 1973. text ed. 19.95 (ISBN 0-12-142252-6). Acad Pr.
Burdge, Rabel J., jt. auth. see Rogers, Everett M.
Burdic, William S. Radar Signal Analysis. 1967. ref. ed. 21.95 (ISBN 0-13-750018-1). P-H.
Burdick, Arthur J. Prospectors' Manual. (Illus.). 156p. pap. 7.50 (ISBN 0-8466-6018-0, SJU18). Shorey.
Burdick, Charles B., jt. ed. see Detwiler, Donald S.
Burdick, Donald J. A Taxonomic & Biological Study of the Genus Xyela Dalman in North America. (U. C. Publ. in Entomology: Vol. 17.3). 1961. pap. 5.00x (ISBN 0-520-09078-0). U of Cal Pr.
Burdick, E. & Lederer, W. Ugly American. 1977. pap. 2.25 (ISBN 0-449-24201-3, Crest). Fawcett.
Burdick, Elizabeth B., ed. Contemporary Stage Design - U.S.A. LC 74-26233. (Illus.). 1975. pap. 15.00x (ISBN 0-8195-8023-6, Pub. by Wesleyan U Pr). Columbia U Pr.
Burdick, Kenneth H. Electrosurgical Apparatus & Their Application in Dermatology. (American Lecture in Dermatology Ser.). (Illus.). 74p. 1966. 11.75 (ISBN 0-398-00259-2). C C Thomas.
Burdick, Loraine. The Shirley Temple Scrapbook. LC 74-31298. (Illus.). 1975. 12.95 o.p. (ISBN 0-8246-0195-5). Jonathan David.
--Shirley Temple's Dolls & Related Delights. rev. ed. 1977. pap. 5.50x o.p. (ISBN 0-87588-102-5). Hobby Hse.
Burdsall, Richard L. & Emmons, Arthur B., 3rd. Men Against the Clouds. LC 79-25369. (Illus.). 1980. pap. 9.95 (ISBN 0-916890-93-7). Mountaineers.
Bure, Germaine see Born, Warren C.
Bureau of Business Research, ed. Health Care Cost Containment: The Managerial Approach. 1978. 7.50 (ISBN 0-686-28414-3). Bur Busn Res U Nebr.
Buren, E. Ariane Van see Foley, Gerald & Van Buren, E. Ariane.
Buren, James Van see Van Buren, James & Dewett, Don.
Buren, Martin Van see Van Buren, Martin.
Buren, Paul M. Van see Van Buren, Paul M.
Buren, Paul Van see Chomsky, Noam.
Buren, Paul Van see Allen, J. P. & Van Buren, Paul.
Burfoot, J. C. & Taylor, G. W. Polar Dielectrics & Their Applications. 1979. 45.00x (ISBN 0-520-03749-9). U of Cal Pr.
Burford, E. J. Bawds & Lodgings: A History of the London Bankside Brothels, 100-1675. (Illus.). 208p. 1976. text ed. 14.75x (ISBN 0-7206-0144-4). Humanities.
--The Orrible Synne. LC 74-172023. (Illus.). 1979. 15.00 (ISBN 0-7145-0978-7, Pub. by M Boyars); pap. 5.95 (ISBN 0-7145-1126-9, Pub. by M Boyars). Merrimack Bk Serv.
--The Orrible Synne: A Look at London Lechery from Roman to Cromwellian Times. (Illus.). 256p. 1973. text ed. 12.50x (ISBN 0-7145-0978-7). Humanities.
Burford, Lolah. Alyx. LC 76-18883. 1977. 8.95 o.s.i. (ISBN 0-02-518100-9, 51810). Macmillan.
--Edward, Edward. LC 73-182446. 576p. 1973. 8.95 o.s.i. (ISBN 0-02-518200-5). Macmillan.
--MacLyon. LC 73-21292. 384p. 1974. 8.95 o.s.i. (ISBN 0-02-518190-4, 51819). Macmillan.
--The Vision of Stephen. LC 77-185142. 192p. 1972. 5.95 o.s.i. (ISBN 0-02-518120-3). Macmillan.
Burford, William, ed. see Proust, Marcel.
Burford, William, tr. see Proust, Marcel.
Burg, B. R. Richard Mather of Dorchester. LC 75-41987. 224p. 1976. 17.00x (ISBN 0-8131-1343-1). U Pr of Ky.
Burg, H., tr. see Bartknecht, W.
Burg, Leslie, et al. The Complete Reading Supervisor: Task & Roles. 1978. text ed. 15.95 (ISBN 0-675-08481-4); instr. manual 3.95 (ISBN 0-686-67972-5). Merrill.
Burg, Marie. Tales from Czechoslavakia. (gr. 3 up). 1967. 7.50 (ISBN 0-340-09142-8). Dufour.
Burgdorf, Arlene, jt. auth. see Barnes, Donald L.
Burgdorf, Robert L., ed. The Legal Rights of Handicapped Persons: Cases, Materials, & Text. 1178p. 1980. 24.50 (ISBN 0-933716-01-X). P H Brookes.

Burge, E. J. Atomic Nuclei & Their Particles. (Oxford Physics Ser.). (Illus.). 1977. pap. text ed. 14.95x (ISBN 0-19-851835-8). Oxford U Pr.

Burgee, John, jt. auth. see Johnson, Philip.

Burgen, Sir Arnold, et al. Neuroactive Peptides. (Proceedings of the Royal & Society, Series B.: Vol. 210). (Illus.). 192p. 1980. text ed. 35.00x (ISBN 0-85403-149-9, Pub. by Royal Soc London). Scholium Intl.

Burger. Sixteen MM Film Cutting. 158p. 1975. 7.95 (ISBN 0-240-50857-2). Focal Pr.

Burger, et al. Marxism, Science & the Movement of History. (Philosophical Currents Ser.: No. 27). 1981. pap. text ed. 34.25x. Humanities.

Burger, Angela S. Opposition in a Dominant-Party System: A Study of the Jan Sangh, the Praja Socialist & Socialist Parties in Uttar Pradesh, India. LC 77-76540. (Center for South & Southeast Asia Studies, UC Berkeley). 1969. 19.00x (ISBN 0-520-01428-6). U of Cal Pr.

Burger, Bob, jt. auth. see Morton, Craig.

Burger, Carl. All About Elephants. (Allabout Ser, No. 56). (Illus.). (gr. 5-10). 1965. 2.95 o.p. (ISBN 0-394-80256-X, BYR). Random.

Burger, Chester. The Chief Executive: Realities of Corporate Leadership. LC 77-2844. 1978. 19.95 (ISBN 0-8436-0747-5). CBI Pub.

--Creative Firing: Why Management Firings Happen & How to Reduce Them. Orig. Title: Walking the Executive Plank. 112p. 1973. pap. 1.50 o.s.i. (ISBN 0-02-008150-2, Collier). Macmillan.

--Survival in the Executive Jungle. 1966. pap. 1.95 o.s.i. (ISBN 0-02-008100-6, Collier). Macmillan.

Burger, Dionys. Sphereland. Rheinboldt, Cornelie J., tr. (Apollo Eds.). (Illus.). pap. 3.95 o.s.i. (ISBN 0-8152-0184-2, A184, TYC-T). T Y Crowell.

Burger, E. Technical Dictionary of Data Processing, Computers & Office Machines, English, German, French, Russian. 1970. 120.00 (ISBN 0-08-006425-6). Pergamon.

Burger, Edward J., Jr. Science at the White House: A Political Liability. LC 80-81425. 208p. 1981. text ed. 14.95x (ISBN 0-8018-2433-8). Johns Hopkins.

Burger, Henry & Dekretser, David, eds. The Testis. (Comprehensive Endocrinology Ser.). 450p. 1981. text ed. 40.00 (ISBN 0-89004-247-0). Raven.

Burger, Henry G. Wordtree: A Transitive Taxonomy for Solving Problems. 360p. 1981. 87.00 (ISBN 0-936312-00-9). Wordtree.

Burger, Isabel B. Creative Play Acting: Learning Through Drama. 2nd ed. (Illus.). 1966. 10.50 o.p. (ISBN 0-8260-1535-2). Wiley.

Burger, Joanna & Olla, Bori L., eds. Behavior of Marine Animals: Marine Birds, Vol. 4. (Behavior of Marine Animals: Current Perspectives in Research). (Illus.). 498p. 1980. 45.00 (ISBN 0-306-37574-5, Plenum Pr). Plenum Pub.

Burger, Joanna, et al, eds. Behavior of Marine Animals: Marine Birds, Vol. 4. 545p. 1980. 45.00 (ISBN 0-306-37574-5, Plenum Pr). Plenum Pub.

Burger, Joanne. SF Published in Nineteen Seventy-Five. LC 71-10701. 64p. 1980. Repr. of 1976 ed. lib. bdg. 9.95x (ISBN 0-89370-053-3). Borgo Pr.

--SF Published in Nineteen Seventy-Four. LC 71-10701. 64p. 1980. Repr. of 1975 ed. lib. bdg. 9.95x (ISBN 0-89370-052-5). Borgo Pr.

--SF Published in Nineteen Seventy-Seven. LC 71-10701. 64p. 1980. Repr. of 1979 ed. lib. bdg. 9.95x (ISBN 0-89370-055-X). Borgo Pr.

--SF Published in Nineteen Seventy-Six. LC 71-10701. 64p. 1980. Repr. of 1977 ed. lib. bdg. 9.95x (ISBN 0-89370-054-1). Borgo Pr.

--SF Published in Nineteen Seventy-Three. LC 71-10701. 64p. 1980. Repr. of 1974 ed. lib. bdg. 9.95x (ISBN 0-89370-051-7). Borgo Pr.

--SF Published in Nineteen Seventy-Two. LC 71-10701. 64p. 1980. Repr. of 1973 ed. lib. bdg. 9.95x (ISBN 0-89370-050-9). Borgo Pr.

Burger, K. Organic Reagents in Metal Analysis. 270p. 1973. text ed. 42.00 (ISBN 0-08-016929-5). Pergamon.

Burger, Max M., jt. ed. see Lash, James.

Burger, N. H. Executive's Wife. 1968. 5.95 o.s.i. (ISBN 0-02-518160-2). Macmillan.

Burger, Peter C. & Vogel, F. Stephen. Surgical Pathology of the Nervous System & Its Coverings. LC 76-6492. 1976. 65.50 (ISBN 0-471-12347-1, Pub. by Wiley Medical). Wiley.

Burger, Robert E., jt. auth. see Garvin, Richard M.

Burger, Warren E., frwd. by. The Bicentennial Conference on the United States Constitution. Incl. Vol. I. Conference Papers; Vol. II. Conference Discussions. LC 78-65110. (Illus.). 1979. 20.00 o.p. (ISBN 0-8122-7763-5). U of Pa Pr.

Burges, Bill. Facts & Figures: A Layman's Guide to Conducting Surveys. 125p. (Orig.). 1976. pap. text ed. 4.25 (ISBN 0-917754-02-6). Inst Responsive.

--Facts for a Change: Citizen Action Research for a Better Schools. 125p. (Orig.). 1976. pap. text ed. 5.00 (ISBN 0-917754-03-4). Inst Responsive.

Burges, James B. The Dragon Knight: A Poem in Twelve Cantos. Reiman, Donald H., ed. LC 75-31174. (Romantic Context Ser.: Poetry 1789-1830). 1977. lib. bdg. 47.00 (ISBN 0-8240-2126-6). Garland Pub.

--James Bland Burges Baronet (1752-1824) Richard the First, a Poem: in Eighteen Books. 1801. Reiman, Donald H., ed. LC 75-31172. (Romantic Context Ser.: Poetry 1789-1830). 1977. lib. bdg. 47.00 (ISBN 0-8240-2125-8). Garland Pub.

Burges, James B. see Reiman, Donald H.

Burgess. Elementary Electrochemistry. 3rd ed. 1981. text ed. price not set (ISBN 0-408-70931-6). Butterworth.

--Europe & America. 8.50 o.s.i. (ISBN 0-8027-0324-0). Walker & Co.

Burgess, A. W. & Lazare. Community Mental Health. LC 75-37561. 256p. 1976. 16.95x (ISBN 0-13-153148-4). P-H.

Burgess, Alan. Daylight Must Come. (Illus.). 288p. 1975. 8.95 o.p. (ISBN 0-440-03365-9). Delacorte.

--Daylight Must Come. 1978. pap. 2.50 (ISBN 0-87123-107-7, 200107). Bethany Fell.

Burgess, Alan, jt. auth. see Bergman, Ingrid.

Burgess, Andrew J. Passion, Knowing How, & Understanding: An Essay on the Concept of Faith. LC 75-31550. (American Academy of Religion. Dissertation Ser.). 1975. pap. 7.50 (ISBN 0-89130-044-9, 010109). Scholars Pr Ca.

Burgess, Ann W. & Baldwin, Bruce. Crisis Intervention Theory & Practice: A Clinical Guide. (Illus.). 288p. 1981. text ed. 14.95 (ISBN 0-13-193466-X); pap. text ed. 11.95 (ISBN 0-686-69274-8). P-H.

Burgess, Ann W. & Holmstrom, Lynda L. Rape: Crisis & Recovery. LC 79-51507. (Illus.). 350p. 1979. pap. 14.95 (ISBN 0-87619-433-1). R J Brady.

Burgess, Ann W. & Lazare, Aaron. Psychiatric Nursing in the Hospital & the Community. 3rd ed. (Illus.). 736p. 1981. text ed. 19.95 (ISBN 0-13-731927-4). P-H.

Burgess, Ann W., jt. auth. see Holmstrom, Lynda L.

Burgess, Ann W., ed. Nursing: Levels of Health Intervention. (P-H General Nursing Ser.). (Illus.). 1978. ref. 19.95 (ISBN 0-13-627687-3). P-H.

Burgess, Ann W., et al. Sexual Assault of Children & Adolescents. LC 77-10217. 1978. 22.95 (ISBN 0-669-01890-2); pap. 9.95 (ISBN 0-669-01892-9). Lexington Bks.

Burgess, Anne, jt. ed. see Gyorgy, Paul.

Burgess, Anthony. Clockwork Orange. 1963. 9.95 (ISBN 0-393-08519-8, Norton Lib); pap. 3.50 (ISBN 0-393-00224-1). Norton.

--Clockwork Orange. 1976. pap. 2.25 (ISBN 0-345-28411-9). Ballantine.

--Earthly Powers. 1980. 13.95 (ISBN 0-671-41490-9). Bobbs.

--Earthly Powers: A Novel. 1980. 15.95 (ISBN 0-671-41490-9). S&S.

--Ernest Hemingway & His World. LC 77-93899. (Illus.). 1978. 12.50 (ISBN 0-684-15661-X, ScribT). Scribner.

--The Eve of Saint Venus. 128p. 1979. pap. 1.95 (ISBN 0-393-00915-7). Norton.

--New York. (The Great Cities Ser.). (Illus.). (gr. 6 up). 1977. PLB 14.94 (ISBN 0-8094-2271-9, Pub. by Time-Life). Silver.

Burgess, Anthony & Haskell, Francis. The Age of the Grand Tour. 1967. ltd. ed. 50.00 o.p. (ISBN 0-236-30811-4, Pub. by Paul Elek). Merrimack Bk Serv.

Burgess, Anthony, ed. New York. (The Great Cities Ser.). 1977. 14.95 (ISBN 0-8094-2270-0). Time-Life.

Burgess, Chester F. The Fellowship of the Craft: Conrad on Ships & Seamen & the Sea. (Literary Criticism Ser.). 1976. 12.00 (ISBN 0-8046-9116-9, Natl U). Kennikat.

Burgess, Colin. The Age of Stonehenge. (History in the Landscape Ser.). (Illus.). 402p. 1980. 25.00x (ISBN 0-460-04254-8, Pub. by J M Dent England). Biblio Dist.

Burgess, Eric, jt. auth. see Murray, Bruce C.

Burgess, Ernest W., jt. auth. see Park, Robert E.

Burgess, Frederick W. Antique Jewelry & Trinkets. LC 74-178622. (Illus.). xvi, 399p. 1972. Repr. of 1919 ed. 21.00 (ISBN 0-8103-3863-7). Gale.

Burgess, G. Goops & How to Be Them. (Peter Possum Paperbacks Ser). 1967. pap. 0.95 o.p (ISBN 0-531-05130-7). Watts.

--More Goops & How Not to Be Them. (Peter Possum Paperbacks Ser). 1967. pap. 0.95 o.p (ISBN 0-531-05138-2). Watts.

Burgess, George. Ecclesiastical History of New England. 55.00 (ISBN 0-686-12406-5). Church History.

Burgess, Hovey. Circus Techniques. (Illus.). 1977. 11.95 o.s.i. (ISBN 0-690-01463-5, TYC-T); pap. 7.95 o.s.i. (ISBN 0-690-01464-3, TYC-T). T Y Crowell.

Burgess, John. Metal Ions in Solution. 1978. 65.95 o.p. (ISBN 0-470-26293-1). Halsted Pr.

--Metal Ions in Solutions. (Chemical Science). 481p. 1980. pap. 29.95x (ISBN 0-470-26987-1). Halsted Pr.

Burgess, John A. & Huber, Robert B. Persuasion in the Courtroom. (Orig.). 1981. text ed. write for info (ISBN 0-316-11635-1). Little.

Burgess, John A., jt. auth. see Everitt, Arthur V.

Burgess, John W. Reconstruction & the Constitution, 1866-1876. LC 70-99479. (American Constitutional & Legal History Ser.: Americana Ser). 1970. Repr. of 1902 ed. lib. bdg. 35.00 (ISBN 0-306-71849-9). Da Capo.

Burgess, Joseph A. & Winn, Albert C. Epiphany. Achtemeier, Elizabeth, et al, eds. LC 79-7377. (Proclamation 2: Aids for Interpreting the Lessons of the Church Year, Ser. A). 64p. (Orig.). 1980. pap. 2.50 (ISBN 0-8006-4092-6, 1-4092). Fortress.

Burgess, Joseph A., ed. The Role of the Augsburg Confession: Catholic & Lutheran Views. LC 79-7373. 224p. 1980. 13.95 (ISBN 0-8006-0549-7, 1-549). Fortress.

Burgess, Lorraine M. Garden Art: The Personal Pursuit of Artistic Refinements, Inventive Concepts, Old Follies, & New Conceits for the Home Gardener. (Illus.). 192p. 1980. 25.00 (ISBN 0-8027-0665-7). Walker & Co.

--The Garden Maker's Answer Book. (Illus.). 1975 (Assn Pr). pap. 6.95 o.p. (ISBN 0-686-67236-4). Follett.

Burgess, M. R. The House of the Burgesses. LC 80-10759. 64p. 1981. lib. bdg. 8.95x (ISBN 0-89370-801-1); pap. 2.95x (ISBN 0-89370-901-8). Borgo Pr.

Burgess, Mary A. The Wickiser Annals. LC 80-11075. 64p. 1981. lib. bdg. 8.95x (ISBN 0-89370-802-X); pap. 2.95x (ISBN 0-89370-902-6). Borgo Pr.

Burgess, Mary A., jt. auth. see Clarke, Boden.

Burgess, Mary A., jt. auth. see Reginald, R.

Burgess, Mary W. Contributions of Women: Education. LC 74-32070. (Contributions of Women Ser.). (Illus.). (gr. 6 up). 1975. PLB 8.95 (ISBN 0-87518-080-9). Dillon.

Burgess, Philip M., et al. International & Comparative Politics: A Handbook. 1978. pap. text ed. 13.60 (ISBN 0-205-06009-9). Allyn.

Burgess, R. A., et al, eds. The Construction Industry Handbook. 2nd ed. 1973. 29.95 (ISBN 0-8436-0119-1). CBI Pub.

Burgess, Robert, jt. ed. see Katz, William A.

Burgess, Robert F. The Cave Divers. LC 75-22130. (Illus.). 1976. 9.95 (ISBN 0-396-07204-6). Dodd.

--Exploring a Coral Reef. (Illus.). (gr. 3-5). 1972. 4.95g o.s.i. (ISBN 0-02-716130-7). Macmillan.

--Man: Twelve Thousand Years Under the Sea. LC 80-186. (Illus.). 448p. 1980. 12.95 (ISBN 0-396-07801-X). Dodd.

--Sharks. LC 75-107669. (gr. 4-9). 1971. PLB 5.95 (ISBN 0-385-04795-9). Doubleday.

Burgess, Robert F., jt. auth. see Royal, William R.

Burgess, Robert H. & Wood, H. Graham. Steamboats Out of Baltimore. LC 68-58859. (Illus.). 1968. 10.00 (ISBN 0-87033-120-5, Pub. by Tidewater). Cornell Maritime.

Burgess, Robert L. Behavioral Sociology: The Experimental Analysis of Social Process. LC 79-90821. (Illus.). 1969. 22.50x (ISBN 0-231-03203-X); pap. 10.00x (ISBN 0-231-08673-3). Columbia U Pr.

Burgess, Sara, jt. auth. see Ahnne, Marlene.

Burgess, Tyrrell. Education After School. 1977. 18.95x (ISBN 0-575-02237-X). Intl Ideas.

Burgess, Warren E. Butterflyfishes of the World. (Illus.). 1979. 20.00 (ISBN 0-87666-470-2, H-988). TFH Pubns.

--Corals. (Illus.). 1979. 2.95 (ISBN 0-87666-521-0, KW-053). TFH Pubns.

--Marine Aquaria. (Illus.). 96p. text ed. 2.95 (ISBN 0-87666-533-4, KW-088). TFH Pubns.

Burgess, Warren E. & Axelrod, Herbert R. Pacific Marine Fishes, Bk. 4. (Illus.). 272p. 1974. 20.00 (ISBN 0-87666-126-6, PS-720). TFH Pubns.

Burgess, William A. Recognition of Health Hazards in Industry: A Review of Materials & Processes. 372p. 1981. 28.00 (ISBN 0-471-06339-8, Pub. by Wiley-Interscience). Wiley.

Burgess, Yvonne. Life to Live: A Novel. LC 80-17914. 183p. 1981. 8.95 (ISBN 0-8008-4816-0). Taplinger.

Burgett, Gordon L. The Query Book. LC 80-24144. (Illus.). 120p. (Orig.). 1981. pap. 7.95 (ISBN 0-9605078-0-9). Write to Sell.

Burgh, James. Political Disquisitions, 3 Vols. LC 78-146144. (American Constitutional & Legal History Ser). 1971. Repr. of 1775 ed. lib. bdg. 135.00 (ISBN 0-306-70101-4). Da Capo.

Burghardt, Andrew F. Borderland: A Historical & Geographical Study of Burgenland, Austria. (Illus.). 1962. 25.00x (ISBN 0-299-02680-9). U of Wis Pr.

--Development Regions in the Soviet Union, Eastern Europe, & Canada. LC 74-31502. (Illus.). 175p. 1975. text ed. 24.95 (ISBN 0-275-09810-9). Praeger.

Burghardt, Erich. Early Histological Diagnosis of Cervical Cancer. LC 79-176203. (Major Problem in Obstetrics & Gynecology Ser.: Vol. 6). (Illus.). 1973. text ed. 27.00 (ISBN 0-7216-2175-9). Saunders.

Burghardt, W. J., et al, eds. Origen, Prayer, Exhortation to Martyrdom. (ACW Ser.: No. 19). 1954. 11.95 (ISBN 0-8091-0256-0). Paulist Pr.

Burghardt, Walter, ed. Why the Church. LC 77-74583. 1977. pap. 4.95 (ISBN 0-8091-2028-3). Paulist Pr.

Burghardt, Walter J. Tell the Next Generation: Homilies & Near Homilies. LC 79-91895. 256p. 1980. pap. 6.95 (ISBN 0-8091-2252-9). Paulist Pr.

Burghardt, Walter J., ed. Woman: New Dimensions. LC 76-50965. 1977. pap. 5.95 (ISBN 0-8091-2011-9). Paulist Pr.

Burghardt, Wolfgang & Hoelker, Klaus, eds. Text Processing. (Research in Text Theory Ser.). 466p. 1979. text ed. 92.00x (ISBN 3-11-007565-2). De Gruyter.

Burgher, Peter H. Changement: Understanding & Managing Business. 1979. 16.95 (ISBN 0-669-02569-0). Lexington Bks.

Burghes, D. N. Mathematical Models in the Social, Management & Life Sciences. LC 79-40989. 287p. 1980. pap. 19.95 (ISBN 0-470-27073-X). Halsted Pr.

Burghes, D. N. & Borrie, Y. M. Modelling with Differential Equations. (Mathematics & Its Applications Ser.). 160p. 1981. 29.95 (ISBN 0-470-27101-9). Halsted Pr.

Burghes, D. N. & Graham, M. A. Introduction to Control Theory, Including Optimal Control. 400p. 67.95x (ISBN 0-470-26998-7). Halsted Pr.

Burghes, D. N. & Wood, A. D. Mathematical Models in the Social, Management & Life Sciences. LC 79-40989. (Mathematics & Its Applications Ser.). 287p. 1980. 39.95x (ISBN 0-470-26862-X); pap. text ed. 19.95 (ISBN 0-470-27073-X). Halsted Pr.

Burghes, David N. & Downs, A. M. Modern Introduction to Classical Mechanics & Control Series: Mathematics & Its Applications. LC 75-16463. 300p. 1975. 43.95 (ISBN 0-470-12362-1). Halsted Pr.

Burgin, tr. see Chukovsky, Kornei.

Burgin, John C. Teaching Singing. LC 72-10594. 1973. 10.00 (ISBN 0-8108-0565-0). Scarecrow.

Burgin, Tricia, jt. auth. see Osler, Jack.

Burgis, Nina, ed. see Dickens, Charles.

Burglass, Milton E., jt. ed. see Shaffer, Howard.

Burgoon, Judee K. & Saine, Thomas. The Unspoken Dialogue: An Introduction to Nonverbal Communication. (Illus., LC 77-078913). 1978. text ed. 13.95 (ISBN 0-395-25792-1); inst. manual 0.75 (ISBN 0-395-25793-X). HM.

Burgoyne. Light of Egypt, 2 vol. (Illus.). 1980. pap. 15.00 (ISBN 0-89540-064-2). Sun Pub.

Burgoyne, Arthur G. The Homestead Strike of Eighteen Ninety-Two. LC 79-4702. (Illus.). 1979. 12.95 (ISBN 0-8229-3405-1); pap. 5.95 (ISBN 0-8229-5310-2). U of Pittsburgh Pr.

Burgoyne, J. & Stuart, R. Management Development: Context & Struggles. 160p. text ed. 24.00x (ISBN 0-566-02101-3, Pub. by Gower Pub Co England). Renouf.

Burgoyne, J. & Stuart, R., eds. Management Development: Context & Strategies. text ed. 24.00x (ISBN 0-566-02101-3, Pub. by Gower Pub England). Renouf.

Burgoyne, John. The Dramatic & Poetical Works of the Late Lieut. Gen. J. Burgoyne. LC 77-2932. 1977. Repr. of 1808 ed. 52.00x (ISBN 0-8201-1285-2). Schol Facsimiles.

Burgt, Robert J. Vanden see Vanden Burgt, Robert J.

Burhans, Clinton S., Jr. Would-Be Writer. 3rd rev. ed. LC 74-133494. 1971. text ed. 10.50 (ISBN 0-471-00058-2). Wiley.

Burhenne, H. Joachim, jt. auth. see Margulis, Alexander R.

Burhenne, H. Joachim, jt. ed. see Margulis, Alexander R.

Burian, Barbara J. A Simplified Approach to S-370 Assembly Language Programming. (Illus.). 1977. 17.95 (ISBN 0-13-810119-1); self study guide 7.50 (ISBN 0-13-810101-9). P-H.

Buritica, P. & Hennen, J. F. Pucciniosireae: Uredinales, Pucciniaceae. LC 79-27151. (Flora Neotropica Monograph: No. 24). (Illus.). 50p. 1980. pap. 7.75 (ISBN 0-89327-219-1). NY Botanical.

Burk, Bruce. Game Bird Carving. LC 72-79365. (Illus.). 1972. 19.95 (ISBN 0-87691-080-0). Winchester Pr.

Burk, Creighton A. & Drake, Charles, eds. Impact of the Geosciences on Critical Energy Resources. 1978. lib. bdg. 17.00x (ISBN 0-89158-293-2). Westview.

Burk, Dale A. A Brush with the West. (Illus.). 256p. 1980. 19.95 (ISBN 0-87842-133-5); limited ed. 60.00 (ISBN 0-87842-134-3). Mountain Pr.
Burk, Janet L. & Hayes, Stephen. Environmental Concerns: A Bibliography of U.S. Government Publications, 1971-1973. 1975. 4.00 (ISBN 0-932826-06-7). New Issues MI.
Burk, Janet L., jt. ed. see Kiraldi, Louis.
Burk, John N., ed. see Howe, M. De Wolfe.
Burk, M. C. Consumption Economics. 1968. prepub. 13.25 (ISBN 0-471-12370-6, Pub. by Wiley). Krieger.
Burk, Margaret T. Are the Stars Out Tonight? The Story of the Famous Ambassador & Cocoanut Grove... Hollywood's Hotel. (Illus.). 190p. 1980. text ed. 15.00 (ISBN 0-937806-00-5). M Burk.
Burk, Mary S. Doctor of the Hills. (YA) 1977. 4.95 o.p. (ISBN 0-685-71794-1, Avalon). Bouregy.
Burk, Tom. How to Photograph Weddings: Groups & Ceremonies. (Orig.). 1980. pap. 7.95 (ISBN 0-89586-057-0). H P Bks.
Burk, W. R. A Bibliography of North American Gasteromycetes I: Phalales. 200p. 1981. pap. text ed. 20.00x (ISBN 3-7682-1262-9, Pub. by Cramer Germany). Lubrecht & Cramer.
Burkan, Bruce, jt. auth. see Keyes, Ken, Jr.
Burkan, Bruce T., jt. auth. see Keyes, Ken, Jr.
Burkart, Adolf, jt. auth. see Helbing, Wolfgang.
Burke, Abbot G. Magnetic Therapy: Healing in Your Hands. LC 80-22941. (Illus.). 86p. (Orig.). 1980. pap. text ed. 4.95 (ISBN 0-932104-04-5). St George Pr.
Burke, Alan D. Fire Watch. 1980. 12.95 (ISBN 0-316-11683-1, Pub. by Atlantic-Little Brown). Little.
Burke, Arvid J. & Burke, Mary A. Documentation in Education. LC 67-17818. 1967. text ed. 14.95x (ISBN 0-8077-1134-9). Tchrs Coll.
Burke, C., jt. auth. see Levine, Gustav.
Burke, Catherine G. Innovation & Public Policy: The Case of Personal Rapid Transit. LC 79-2410. (Illus.). 416p. 1979. 23.95 (ISBN 0-669-03167-4). Lexington Bks.
Burke, Charles C. Woodworking for Cave Dwellers. (Illus.). 1978. pap. 6.95 (ISBN 0-8306-1022-7, 1022). TAB Bks.
Burke, Clifford. Printing It! (Illus.). 128p. 1974. pap. 3.95 (ISBN 0-914728-03-2). Wingbow Pr.
--Printing Poetry. LC 80-52171. 168p. 1980. 50.00 (ISBN 0-912962-01-1); unbound 37.50 (ISBN 0-686-63315-6). Scarab Pr.
Burke, D. Barlow. American Conveyance Patterns. LC 77-4628. (Real Estate & Urban Land Economics Ser.). 1978. 21.00 (ISBN 0-669-01731-0). Lexington Bks.
Burke, D. C. & Murray, D. D. Handbook of Spinal Cord Medicine. 100p. 1975. pap. 8.84 (ISBN 0-89004-066-4). Raven.
Burke, D. C. & Russell, W. C., eds. Control Processes in Virus Multiplication. (Society for General Microbiology Symposia Ser.: No. 25). (Illus.). 450p. 1975. 59.50 (ISBN 0-521-20728-2). Cambridge U Pr.
Burke, David G., ed. The Poetry of Baruch: A Reconstruction & Analysis of the Original Hebrew Text of Baruch 3: 9-5: 9. LC 80-10271. (Society of Biblical Literature, Septuagint & Cognate Studies: No. 10). 22.50x (ISBN 0-89130-381-2, 06 04 10); pap. 18.00x (ISBN 0-89130-382-0). Scholars Pr CA.
Burke, DeAnn, jt. auth. see Burke, Todd.
Burke, Diana. The Heart of the Matter. (Orig.). 1980. pap. 1.50 o.s.i. (ISBN 0-440-14208-3). Dell.
Burke, Doreen B. American Painting in the Metropolitan Museum of Art: A Catalogue of Works by Artists Born Between 1846 & 1864. LC 80-81074. 528p. 1980. 75.00x (ISBN 0-691-03961-5). Princeton U Pr.
Burke, Edmund. Archery. LC 62-12117. (Illus., Orig.). 1963. pap. 1.75 o.p. (ISBN 0-668-00862-8). Arc Bks.
--Reflections on the Revolution in France & Other Essays. 1953. 5.00x o.p. (ISBN 0-460-00460-3, Evman); pap. 2.75 o. p. o.p. (ISBN 0-460-01460-9). Dutton.
--Reflections on the Revolution in France. Mahoney, Thomas H., ed. 1955. pap. 6.95 (ISBN 0-672-60213-X, LLA46). Bobbs.
Burke, Edmund H. Archery Handbook. LC 54-9236. (Illus.). 1954. lib. bdg. 4.95 o.p. (ISBN 0-668-00336-7); pap. 2.95 o.p. (ISBN 0-668-04002-5). Arco.
Burke, Edmund M. A Participatory Approach to Urban Planning. LC 78-31107. 304p. 1979. text ed. 19.95 (ISBN 0-87705-393-6). Human Sci Pr.
Burke, Fred G. Tanganyika: Preplanning. (National Planning Ser.: No. 3). (Orig.). 1965. pap. 3.95x (ISBN 0-8156-2089-6). Syracuse U Pr.
Burke, Frederick J., jt. auth. see Bruce, Harry J.
Burke, Gill. Housing & Social Justice. 240p. 1981. pap. text ed. 12.95x (ISBN 0-582-29514-9). Longman.
Burke, J. E. Progress in Ceramic Science. 1961-1964. Vol. 3. 1964. 62.00 (ISBN 0-08-010026-0); Vol. 4. 1966. 62.00 (ISBN 0-08-011842-9). Pergamon.
Burke, J. J., jt. auth. see Kapany, N. S.
Burke, James. Connections. (Illus.). 312p. 1980. pap. 11.95 (ISBN 0-316-11685-8). Little.
--Connections. LC 78-21662. 1979. 17.95 (ISBN 0-316-11685-8). Little.
--A Forgotten Glory. (Illus.). 1979. 11.95 (ISBN 0-87244-049-4). Texian.
Burke, James D. Jan Both: Paintings, Drawings & Prints. LC 75-23783. (Outstanding Dissertations in the Fine Arts - 17th Century). (Illus.). 1976. lib. bdg. 45.00 (ISBN 0-8240-1980-6). Garland Pub.
Burke, James W. Arli. LC 78-66393. 1978. 8.95 o.p. (ISBN 0-916054-80-2). Caroline Hse.
Burke, Jim. The World of Jimmy Connors. (Illus., Orig.). 1976. pap. 1.50 o.p. (ISBN 0-685-64019-1, LB330DK, Leisure Bks). Nordon Pubns.
Burke, John. Czechoslovakia. 1976. 22.50 (ISBN 0-7134-3222-5). David & Charles.
--The Devil's Footsteps. 1978. pap. 1.75 o.p. (ISBN 0-445-04204-4). Popular Lib.
--England in Colour. 1972. 27.00 (ISBN 0-7134-0022-6, Pub. by Batsford England). David & Charles.
--English Villages. (Illus.). 200p. 1975. 11.50 o.s.i. (ISBN 0-7134-2932-1). Hippocrene Bks.
--Life in the Villa in Roman Britain. 1978. 19.95 (ISBN 0-7134-1013-2, Pub. by Batsford England). David & Charles.
--Origins of the Science of Crystals. 1966. 20.00x (ISBN 0-520-00198-2). U of Cal Pr.
Burke, John D. Advertising in the Marketplace. (Illus.). 454p. 1973. text ed. 16.95 (ISBN 0-07-009031-9, G); instructors' manual & key 4.00 (ISBN 0-07-009032-7). McGraw.
Burke, John J. & Weiss, Volker, eds. Risk & Failure Analysis for Improved Performance & Reliability. (Sagamore Army Materials Research Conference Ser.: Vol. 24). 365p. 1980. 42.50 (ISBN 0-306-40446-X, Plenum Pr). Plenum Pub.
Burke, John J., Jr., jt. auth. see Hermann, John P.
Burke, John P., et al, eds. Marxism & the Good Society. 224p. Date not set. price not set (ISBN 0-521-23392-5). Cambridge U Pr.
Burke, Joseph. English Art 1714-1800. (Oxford History of English Art). (Illus.). 620p. 1975. 39.95 (ISBN 0-19-817209-5). Oxford U Pr.
Burke, Ken & Doty, Walter. All About Vegetables. rev. ed. Ortho Books Editorial Staff, ed. LC 80-66344. (Illus.). 112p. 1981. pap. 4.95 (ISBN 0-917102-90-8). Ortho.
Burke, Kenneth. Collected Poems, 1915-1967. 1968. 16.50x (ISBN 0-520-00195-8). U of Cal Pr.
--A Grammar of Motives. LC 69-16741. 1969. 18.50x (ISBN 0-520-01543-6); pap. 6.95x (ISBN 0-520-01544-4). U of Cal Pr.
--Language As Symbolic Action: Essays on Life, Literature, & Method. 1966. 20.00x (ISBN 0-520-00191-5); pap. 8.95 (ISBN 0-520-00192-3, CAL166). U of Cal Pr.
--Permanence & Change: An Anatomy of Purpose. LC 64-66067. 1965. pap. 7.50 (ISBN 0-672-60452-3, LLA207). Bobbs.
--The Philosophy of Literary Form. 1974. pap. 7.95x (ISBN 0-520-02483-4). U of Cal Pr.
--A Rhetoric of Motives. LC 69-16742. 1969. 16.50x (ISBN 0-520-01545-2); pap. 6.95x (ISBN 0-520-01546-0, CAL178). U of Cal Pr.
--Towards a Better Life: Being a Series of Epistles, or Declamations. 1966. 15.95x (ISBN 0-520-00193-1). U of Cal Pr.
Burke, Kenneth B., ed. see Palmer, Derecke.
Burke, M. Desmond & Rock, Robert C. Chemical Pathology: A Progressive, Three Level Approach. 1980. pap. 8.50 study guide (ISBN 0-89189-075-0, 45-2-038-00). Am Soc Clinical.
Burke, Martyn. Laughing War. LC 77-16901. 312p. 1980. 10.95 (ISBN 0-385-13332-4). Doubleday.
Burke, Mary A., jt. auth. see Burke, Arvid J.
Burke, P., ed. The New Cambridge Modern History, Vol. XIII. LC 57-14935. (The New Cambridge Modern History Ser.). 384p. 1980. pap. 13.95 (ISBN 0-521-28017-6). Cambridge U Pr.
Burke, Peter. Culture & Society in Renaissance Italy, 1420-1540. LC 70-110682. (Illus.). 1972. 14.95 o.p. (ISBN 0-684-12576-5, ScribT). Scribner.
--Popular Culture in Early Modern Europe. 1978. pap. 7.95x (ISBN 0-06-131928-7, TB 1928, Torch). Har-Row.
--Sociology & History. (Controversies in Sociology Ser.: No. 10). 128p. (Orig.). 1980. text ed. 14.95x (ISBN 0-04-301114-4, 2409); pap. text ed. 5.95x (ISBN 0-04-301115-2, 2410). Allen Unwin.
Burke, Peter J., jt. auth. see Knoke, David.
Burke, Shirley R. The Composition & Function of Body Fluids. 3rd ed. LC 80-17952. (Illus.). 208p. 1980. pap. text ed. 8.95 (ISBN 0-8016-0903-8). Mosby.
Burke, Suzanne. Ollie Owl. Jordan, Alton, ed. (Elephant Ser.). (Illus.). (gr. k-3). 1975. PLB 3.50 (ISBN 0-89868-015-8, Read Res); text ed. 1.75 softbd. (ISBN 0-89868-048-4). ARO Pub.
--Our Parade. Jordan, Alton, ed. (Elephant Ser.). (Illus.). (gr. k-3). 1975. PLB 3.50 (ISBN 0-89868-017-4, Read Res); pap. text ed. 1.75 (ISBN 0-89868-050-6). ARO Pub.
Burke, Todd & Burke, DeAnn. Anointed for Burial. 1977. pap. 2.95 (ISBN 0-88270-485-0). Logos.
Burke, Vee, jt. auth. see Burke, Vincent.
Burke, Vincent & Burke, Vee. Nixon's Good Deed: Welfare Reform. 224p. 1974. 15.00x (ISBN 0-231-03850-X); pap. 6.00x (ISBN 0-231-08346-7). Columbia U Pr.
Burke, Virginia M., jt. ed. see Corbett, Edward P.
Burke, W. Warner. Current Issues & Strategies in Organization Development. LC 76-28755. 448p. 1977. 24.95 (ISBN 0-87705-270-0). Human Sci Pr.
Burke, W. Warner & Beckhard, Richard, eds. Conference Planning. 2nd ed. LC 76-124090. 174p. 1962. pap. 10.00 (ISBN 0-88390-118-8). Univ Assocs.
Burke, W. Warner & Goodstein, Leonard D., eds. Trends & Issues in OD: Current Theory & Practice. LC 80-52929. 351p. (Orig.). 1980. pap. 18.50 (ISBN 0-88390-162-5). Univ Assocs.
Burke, W. Warner, jt. ed. see Eddy, William B.
Burke, William J. Literature of Slang. LC 67-982. 1965. Repr. of 1939 ed. 15.00 (ISBN 0-8103-3243-4). Gale.
Burke, William P. The Irish Priests in Penal Times. 508p. 1968. Repr. of 1914 ed. 19.00x (ISBN 0-7165-0034-5, Pub. by Irish Academic Pr Ireland). Biblio Dist.
Burkert, H. & Nagel, G. A., eds. Neve Erfabrungen mit Oxazaphosphorinen Unter Bersonderer Bervecksichtigung des. (Beitraege zur Onkologie: Band 5). (Illus.). 120p. 1980. pap. 21.00 (ISBN 3-8055-1381-X). S Karger.
Burkert, Walter. Structure & History in Greek Mythology & Ritual. (Sather Classical Lectures: Vol. 47). 1980. 16.50x (ISBN 0-520-03771-5). U of Cal Pr.
Burkes, E. Jeff & Wood, Matthew T. Basic Sciences. 3rd ed. (Dental Assisting Manuals: No. 2). 120p. 1980. 7.00 (ISBN 0-8078-1376-1). U of NC Pr.
Burkes, Joyce M. The Music Machine: Level I. LC 79-92121. (The Music Machine Bks.). (Orig.). 1981. pap. 6.95 (ISBN 0-931218-07-1). Joybug.
--The Music Machine: Level 2. LC 79-92121. (The Music Machine Bks.). (Orig.). 1981. pap. 6.95 (ISBN 0-931218-08-X). Joybug.
--The Music Machine: Primer. LC 79-92121. (The Music Machine Bks.). 20p. (Orig.). 1981. pap. 6.95 (ISBN 0-931218-06-3). Joybug.
--The Spanish Word Machine: Book I. LC 79-2122. (The Spanish Word Machine Bks.). (Orig.). 1981. pap. 4.95 (ISBN 0-931218-09-8). Joybug.
--The Spanish Word Machine: Book II. LC 79-92122. (The Spanish Word Machine Bks.). 26p. (Orig.). 1981. pap. 4.95 (ISBN 0-931218-10-1). Joybug.
--The Spanish Word Machine: Book III. LC 79-2122. (The Spanish Word Machine Bks.). 26p. (Orig.). 1981. pap. 4.95 (ISBN 0-931218-11-X). Joybug.
--Word Machine, 3 vols. LC 79-67050. 1979. Set. 4.95. Bk. I (ISBN 0-931218-02-0). Bk. II (ISBN 0-931218-03-9). Bk. III (ISBN 0-931218-04-7). Liberty Pub.
--The Word Machine, Bk. 1. rev ed. LC 79-67050. (Illus.). (gr. k-1). 1978. pap. 4.95 (ISBN 0-931218-02-0, 1001). Joybug.
--The Word Machine, Bk. 2. LC 79-67050. (Illus.). (gr. 2-4). 1979. pap. 4.95 (ISBN 0-931218-03-9, 1002). Joybug.
--The Word Machine, Bk. 3. LC 79-67050. (Illus., Orig.). (gr. 2-6). 1979. pap. 4.95 (ISBN 0-931218-04-7, 1003). Joybug.
Burkett, David & Narcisco, John. Declare Yourself: Discovering the Me in Relationships. LC 75-11802. (Illus.). 1975. 9.95 (ISBN 0-13-197582-X, Spec); pap. 3.95 (ISBN 0-13-197574-9, Spec). P-H.
Burkett, Eva M. American Dictionaries of the English Language Before 1861. LC 78-11677. 1979. lib. bdg. 16.50 (ISBN 0-8108-1179-0). Scarecrow.
--American English Dialects in Literature. LC 78-17742. 1978. 12.00 (ISBN 0-8108-1151-0). Scarecrow.
--Writing in Subject-Matter Fields: A Bibliographic Guide, with Annotations & Writing Assignments. LC 76-30397. 1977. 10.00 (ISBN 0-8108-1012-3). Scarecrow.
Burkett, J., ed. Government & Related Library & Information Services in the U. K. 3rd rev. ed. 1974. pap. 15.50 (ISBN 0-85365-127-2, Pub. by Lib Assn England). Oryx Pr.
Burkett, J., jt. ed. see Ward, P. L.
Burkett, Larry. What Husbands Wish Their Wives Knew About Money. 1977. pap. 2.95 (ISBN 0-88207-758-9). Victor Bks.
Burkett, Randall K. Garveyism As a Religious Movement: The Institutionalization of a Black Civil Religion. LC 78-15728. (ATLA Monograph Ser.: No. 13). 1978. 13.50 (ISBN 0-8108-1163-4). Scarecrow.
Burkhard, Marianne. Conrad Ferdinand Meyer. (World Authors Ser.: No. 480 Spain). 1978. 11.95 (ISBN 0-8057-6321-X). Twayne.
Burkhard, R. E. & Derigs, U. Assignment & Matching Problems: Solution Methods with FORTRAN-Programs. (Lecture Notes in Economics & Mathematical Systems Ser.: Vol. 184). 148p. 1981. pap. 15.00 (ISBN 0-387-10267-1). Springer-Verlag.
Burkhart, F., ed. Neue Aspekte in der Behandlung der Herzinsuffizienz: Oberrheinisches Kardiologen - Symposium. (Cardiology: Vol.65, Suppl. 1,1980). (Illus.). 1980. pap. 11.50 (ISBN 3-8055-0652-X). S Karger.
Burkhead, Jesse. Governmental Budgeting. LC 56-8000. 1956. 26.95 (ISBN 0-471-12375-7). Wiley.
Burkhill, H., jt. auth. see Burkhill, J. C.
Burkhill, J. C. & Burkhill, H. Second Course in Mathematical Analysis. LC 69-16278. (Illus.). 1970. text ed. 35.50x (ISBN 0-521-07519-X). Cambridge U Pr.
Burkholder, Lloyd, Sr. Basic Pipe Estimating. 224p. (Orig.). 1981. pap. 15.50 (ISBN 0-910460-84-1). Craftsman.
Burkholder, Mark A. Politics of a Colonial Career: Jose Baquijano & the Audencia of Lima. 198p. 1981. 20.00 (ISBN 0-8263-0545-8). U of NM Pr.
Burkholz, Herbert, jt. auth. see Irving, Clifford.
Burkill, John C. First Course in Mathematical Analysis. 1962. 23.95x (ISBN 0-521-04381-6); pap. 13.95x (ISBN 0-521-29468-1). Cambridge U Pr.
--Lebesgue Integral. (Cambridge Tracts in Mathematics & Mathematical Physics). 1951. 14.50 (ISBN 0-521-04382-4). Cambridge U Pr.
Burkin, A. R. Topics in Non-Ferrous Extractive Metallurgy. (Critical Reports on Applied Chemistry Ser.: Vol. 1). 1980. 25.95 (ISBN 0-470-27016-0, Pub. by Halsted Pr). Wiley.
Burkitt, B. & Bowers, D. Trade Unions & the Economy. 1979. text ed. 23.75 (ISBN 0-8419-5064-4). Holmes & Meier.
Burkman, Katherine, jt. auth. see Auburn, Mark.
Burkman, Katherine H. Literature Through Performance: "Shakespeare's Mirror" & "a Canterbury Caper". LC 76-25615. (Illus.). xxvii, 104p. 1978. 10.00x (ISBN 0-8214-0365-6); pap. 3.50x (ISBN 0-8214-0384-2). Ohio U Pr.
Burks, Ardath W. Japan: Profile of a Postindustrial Power. (Nations of Contemporary Asia Ser.). (Illus.). 250p. 1980. lib. bdg. 22.00x (ISBN 0-89158-786-1); pap. 9.50x (ISBN 0-86531-040-8). Westview.
Burks, Julia M., jt. auth. see Wishon, George E.
Burks, Richard V. The Dynamics of Communism in Eastern Europe. LC 73-17027. (Illus.). 1976. Repr. of 1961 ed. lib. bdg. 20.25x (ISBN 0-8371-8961-6, BUDY). Greenwood.
Burland, Cottie. The Incas. LC 78-61225. (Peoples of the Past Ser.). (Illus.). 1979. lib. bdg. 7.95 (ISBN 0-686-51158-1). Silver.
--See Inside an Aztec Town. (gr. 5 up). 1980. PLB 6.90 (ISBN 0-531-09173-2, G18). Watts.
Burland, Cottie A. Adventuring in Archaeology. LC 63-11556. (Illus.). (gr. 4-8). 1963. 6.95 (ISBN 0-7232-6029-X). Warne.
--The Arts of the Alchemists. LC 79-8598. Repr. of 1968 ed. 27.50 (ISBN 0-404-18451-0). AMS Pr.
Burleigh, Robert. Basic Learning Skills: Base Words & Word Parts Learning Module. (gr. 2-3). 1978. pap. text ed. 215.00 (ISBN 0-89290-108-X, CM-38D). Soc for Visual.
--Basic Learning Skills: Consonant Sounds Learning Module. (gr. k-2). 1978. pap. text ed. 290.00 (ISBN 0-89290-106-3, CM-38B). Soc for Visual.
--Basic Learning Skills: Vowel Sounds Learning Module. (gr. 1-3). 1978. pap. text ed. 290.00 (ISBN 0-89290-107-1, CM-38C). Soc for Visual.
--Basic Reading Skills: Reading Readiness Learning Module. (gr. k-1). 1977. pap. text ed. 215.00 (ISBN 0-89290-105-5, CM-38A). Soc for Visual.
Burleigh, Robert & Gray, Mary Jane. Basic Writing Skills. LC 77-730072. (Illus.). (gr. 6-8). 1976. pap. text ed. 225.00 (ISBN 0-89290-115-2, CM-39). Soc for Visual.
Burleigh, Robert & Matlak, Raymond. Percent. LC 79-730248. (Illus.). 1979. pap. 99.00 (ISBN 0-89290-096-2, A512-SATC). Soc for Visual.
Burleson, Clyde, jt. auth. see McDonald, John.
Burleson, Donald R. Topics in Mathematics. LC 76-27301. (Illus.). 1977. 17.95 (ISBN 0-13-925305-X). P-H.

--Topics in Precalculus Mathematics. (Illus.). 544p. 1974. text ed. 17.95 (ISBN 0-13-925461-7); study guide 1.95 (ISBN 0-13-925214-2). P-H.
Burley, D. M. Studies in Optimization. LC 74-8454. 1974. text ed. 17.95 (ISBN 0-470-12410-5). Halsted Pr.
Burley, J. & Styles, B. T., eds. Tropical Forest Trees: Variation Breeding & Conservation. 1976. 34.00 o.s.i. (ISBN 0-12-145150-X). Acad Pr.
Burley, T. & Tregear, P. African Development & Europe. 1970. 19.50 (ISBN 0-08-006669-0); pap. 9.75 (ISBN 0-08-006670-4). Pergamon.
Burley, W. J. Guilt Edged. 1981. pap. 2.25 (ISBN 0-440-13082-4). Dell.
--Wycliffe in Paul's Court. LC 80-5449. (Crime Club Ser.). 192p. 1980. 8.95 (ISBN 0-385-17208-7). Doubleday.
Burlina, A. & Galzigna, L., eds. Clinical Enzymology Symposia, Vol. 2. (Illus.). 646p. 1980. text ed. 49.50 (ISBN 88-212-0772-2, Pub. by Piccin Italy). J K Burgess.
Burling, Robbins. Hill Farms & Padi Fields: Life in Mainland Southeast Asia. (Illus., Orig.). 1965. pap. 2.95 o.p. (ISBN 0-13-388926-2). P-H.
Burlingame, Anne E. Battle of the Books in Its Historical Setting. LC 68-54230. 1969. Repr. of 1920 ed. 9.00x (ISBN 0-8196-0224-8). Biblio.
Burlingame, Dwight F., et al. The College Learning Resource Center. LC 78-13716. 1978. lib. bdg. 18.50x (ISBN 0-87287-189-4). Libs Unl.
Burlingame, Hardin J. Leaves from Conjurors' Scrap Books, Or, Modern Magicians & Their Works. LC 74-148349. 1971. Repr. of 1891 ed. 18.00 (ISBN 0-8103-3371-6). Gale.
Burlingame, Helen, tr. see Trifonov, Yury V.
Burma, Ian, jt. auth. see Richie, Donald.
Burman, Ben L. High Treason at Catfish Bend. LC 76-52136. (Illus.). (gr. 6 up). 1977. 6.95 (ISBN 0-8149-0785-7). Vanguard.
--The Strange Invasion of Catfish Bend. LC 79-67487. (The Catfish Bend Stories). (Illus.). 160p. 1980. 8.95 (ISBN 0-8149-0828-4). Vanguard.
Burman, Bina R. Religion & Politics in Tibet. 1979. 14.00x (ISBN 0-7069-0801-5, Pub. by Croom Helm Ltd. England). Biblio Dist.
Burman, C. R. How to Find Out in Chemistry. 2nd ed. 1966. 15.00 (ISBN 0-08-011881-X); pap. 7.00 (ISBN 0-08-011880-1). Pergamon.
Burman, D., jt. auth. see McLaren, D.
Burman, P. J. Precedence Networks for Project Planning & Control. 20.00 (ISBN 0-686-27928-X). Blitz Pub Co.
Burman, Sandra. Chiefdom Politics & Alien Law. LC 79-25600. 1981. text ed. 38.00x (ISBN 0-8419-0591-6, Africana). Holmes & Meier.
Burmeister, E. Capital Theory & Dynamics. LC 79-28412. (Cambridge Surveys of Economic Literature Ser.). 224p. 1980. 37.00 (ISBN 0-521-22889-1); pap. 12.95 (ISBN 0-521-29703-6). Cambridge U Pr.
Burmeister, Edwin, jt. ed. see Klein, Lawrence R.
Burmeister, Eva E. Professional Houseparent. LC 60-6548. 1960. 20.00x (ISBN 0-231-02370-7). Columbia U Pr.
Burmeister, Jon. The Hard Men. LC 77-9170. 1978. 8.95 o.p. (ISBN 0-312-36196-3). St Martin.
Burmeister, Lou E. Words - From Print to Meaning: Classroom Activities. LC 74-20488. 176p. 1975. pap. text ed. 7.50 (ISBN 0-201-00770-3). A-W.
Burn, A. R. & Burn, Mary. The Living Past of Greece. (Illus.). 282p. 1980. 17.50 (ISBN 0-316-11710-2). Little.
Burn, Barbara. Complete Guide to Riding People's Horses. (Illus.). 256p. 1981. pap. 5.95 (ISBN 0-312-15746-0). St Martin.
--The Morris Approach: An Insider's Guide to Cat Care. LC 80-14051. (Illus.). 64p. 1980. 6.95 (ISBN 0-688-03693-7). Morrow.
Burn, Barbara, jt. auth. see Dolensek, Emil P.
Burn, Duncan & Epstein, Barbara. Realities of Free Trade. 1972. text ed. 12.95x (ISBN 0-04-382016-6). Allen Unwin.
Burn, Graham, jt. ed. see Loring, James.
Burn, June. Living High. rev. ed. (Illus.). 1962. 6.95 o.p. (ISBN 0-686-00955-X). Wellington.
Burn, Mary, jt. auth. see Burn, A. R.
Burn, R. P. Deductive Transformation Geometry. LC 74-82223. (Illus.). 152p. 1975. 19.95 (ISBN 0-521-20565-4). Cambridge U Pr.
Burnaby, John, ed. Augustine: Later Works. (Library of Christian Classics Ichthus Edition). 1980. pap. 9.95 (ISBN 0-664-24165-4). Westminster.
Burnam, Tom. The Dictionary of Misinformation. 1977. pap. 2.50 (ISBN 0-345-29534-X). Ballantine.
--More Misinformation. 1981. pap. 2.50 (ISBN 0-345-29251-0). Ballantine.
Burnand, F. C; see Gilbert, W. S.
Burnand, Tony. Dictionnaire chasse. (Dictionnaires de l'homme du vingtieme siecle). (Fr). 1970. 8.50 (ISBN 0-685-13859-3, 3711). Larousse.
Burnard, Francis C. My Time & What I've Done with It: An Autobiography, Compiled from the Diary, Notes & Personal Recollections of Cecil Colvin, 1874. (Victorian Fiction Ser.). 1975. lib. bdg. 66.00 (ISBN 0-8240-1535-5). Garland Pub.
Burne, Glenn S. Julian Green. (World Authors Ser.: France: No. 195). lib. bdg. 10.95 (ISBN 0-8057-2404-4). Twayne.
Burne, J. R. Caisse De Joseph. 1966. text ed. 2.25x (ISBN 0-521-04388-3). Cambridge U Pr.
Burne, Kevin G., et al. Functional English for Writers. 2nd ed. 1978. pap. 8.95x (ISBN 0-673-15105-0). Scott F.
Burne-Jones, Edward. The Pre-Raphaelite Drawings of Edward Burne-Jones. (Dover Art Library). (Illus.). 48p. (Orig.). 1981. pap. price not set (ISBN 0-486-24113-0). Dover.
Burnell, Diana P. Study Guide to Activities Therapy. LC 75-28928. 1976. 7.50 (ISBN 0-89004-081-8). Raven.
Burner, David & Marcus, Robert D. America Personified: Portraits from History, 2 vols. LC 74-76210. 224p. (Orig.). 1974. pap. text ed. 6.95 ea. Vol. 1 (ISBN 0-312-03010-X). Vol. 2 (ISBN 0-312-03045-2). St Martin.
Burner, David, jt. auth. see Marcus, Robert.
Burner, David, jt. ed. see Marcus, Robert D.
Burner, David, et al. The American People, 2 vols. Incl. Vol. I. To Eighteen Seventy-Seven. 342p (ISBN 0-9603726-2-8); Vol. II. From Eighteen Sixty. 440p (ISBN 0-9603726-3-6). (Illus., Orig.). 1980. Combined Edition. pap. text ed. 14.95 (ISBN 0-9603726-0-1); pap. text ed. 9.75 ea. Revisionary.
--The American People in the Twentieth Century: Nineteen Hundred to Nineteen Eighty. (Illus., Orig.). 1980. pap. 7.95x o.p. (ISBN 0-686-26623-4). Revisionary.
Burnes, Alan J., ed. see Williams, Elizabeth S.
Burness, Tad. American Car Spotter's Guide: 1966-1980. (Illus.). 432p. (Orig.). 1981. pap. 16.95 (ISBN 0-87938-102-7). Motorbooks Intl.
Burnet, F. M. Immunology, Aging, & Cancer. LC 76-16166. (Illus.). 1976. pap. text ed. 8.95x (ISBN 0-7167-0489-7). W H Freeman.
Burnet, F. M., intro. by. Immunology: Readings from Scientific American. LC 75-19356. (Illus.). 1976. text ed. 19.95x (ISBN 0-7167-0525-7); pap. text ed. 9.95x (ISBN 0-7167-0524-9). W H Freeman.
Burnet, F. Macfarlane. Cellular Immunology, 2 bks. in 1. LC 69-12162. (Illus.). 1969. 74.50 (ISBN 0-521-07217-4). Cambridge U Pr.
--Self & Not Self: Cellular Immunology, Bk. 1. (Illus.). 1969. 32.50 (ISBN 0-521-07521-1); pap. 14.50x (ISBN 0-521-09558-1, 558). Cambridge U Pr.
Burnet, F. Macfarlane & White, D. O. Natural History of Infectious Disease. 4th ed. LC 74-174264. (Illus.). 400p. 1972. 38.50 (ISBN 0-521-08389-3); pap. 12.95x (ISBN 0-521-09688-X). Cambridge U Pr.
Burnet, John. Early Greek Philosophy. 4th ed. 1963. Repr. of 1930 ed. 19.50x (ISBN 0-06-490783-X). B&N.
Burnet, John, ed. see Plato.
Burnet, Macfarlane. Endurance of Life. (Illus.). 1980. pap. 8.95 (ISBN 0-521-29783-4). Cambridge U Pr.
--Endurance of Life. LC 78-54323. (Illus.). 1978. 27.50 (ISBN 0-521-22114-5). Cambridge U Pr.
--Intrinsic Mutagenesis: A Genetic Approach to Aging. LC 74-6978. 236p. 1974. 36.95 (ISBN 0-471-12440-0, Pub. by Wiley-Medical). Wiley.
Burnet, Sir Thomas & Duckett, George. Second Tale of a Tub, or, the History of Robert Powel the Puppet-Show-Man. Shugrue, Michael, ed. LC 71-170539. (Foundations of the Novel Ser: Vol. 26). iv, 219p. 1973. Repr. of 1715 ed. lib. bdg. 50.00 (ISBN 0-8240-0538-4). Garland Pub.
Burnett, Alan D. & Taylor, Peter J. Political Studies from Spatial Perspectives: Anglo-American Essays on Political Geography. 1981. price not set (ISBN 0-471-27909-9, Pub. by Wiley-Interscience); pap. price not set (ISBN 0-471-27910-2). Wiley.
Burnett, Anne P. Catastrophe Survived: Euripides' Plays of Mixed Reversal. 244p. 1971. 23.50x o.p. (ISBN 0-19-814186-6). Oxford U Pr.
Burnett, Arthur C. Yankees in the Republic of Texas: Their Origin & Impact. 1952. wrappers 7.00 (ISBN 0-685-05007-6). A Jones.
Burnett, Ben G. Political Groups in Chile: The Dialogue Between Order & Change. (Latin American Monographs Ser.: No. 21). 1970. 14.95 (ISBN 0-292-70084-9). U of Tex Pr.
Burnett, Bernice. The First Book of Holidays. rev. ed. LC 74-3075. (First Bks. Ser.). (Illus.). 72p. (gr. 4-7). 1974. PLB 6.90 (ISBN 0-531-00548-8). Watts.
Burnett, C. W. The Anatomy & Physiology of Obstetrics. 1969. text ed. 8.95 o.p. (ISBN 0-571-04682-7, Pub. by Faber & Faber). Merrimack Bk Serv.
--The Anatomy & Physiology of Obstetrics. 1970. pap. text ed. 5.95 o.p. (ISBN 0-571-09236-5, Pub. by Faber & Faber). Merrimack Bk Serv.
--The Anatomy & Physiology of Obstetrics. 6th ed. Anderson, Mary, ed. (Illus.). 1979. 9.95 (ISBN 0-571-04682-7, Pub. by Faber & Faber); pap. 5.95 (ISBN 0-571-04992-3). Merrimack Bk Serv.
Burnett, Collins W., jt. auth. see White, Jane N.
Burnett, Constance B. Captain John Ericsson: Father of the Monitor. LC 60-15070. (gr. 7 up). 6.95 (ISBN 0-8149-0284-7). Vanguard.
--Five for Freedom: Lucretia Mott, Elizabeth Cady Stanton, Lucy Stone, Susan B. Anthony, Carrie Chapman Catt. LC 68-8734. (Illus.). 1968. Repr. of 1953 ed. lib. bdg. 17.50x (ISBN 0-8371-0034-8, BUFF). Greenwood.
--Happily Ever After: A Portrait of Frances Hodgson Burnett. LC 65-17370. (gr. 7 up). 6.95 (ISBN 0-8149-0283-9). Vanguard.
Burnett, D. & Cumming, E. E., eds. International Library & Information Programmes. 1979. pap. 11.50 (ISBN 0-85365-591-X, Pub. by Lib Assn England). Oryx Pr.
Burnett, Frances. Little Lord Fauntleroy. 1977. 10.95x (ISBN 0-89967-002-4). Harmony & Co.
Burnett, Frances H. Little Lord Fauntleroy. LC 75-32191. (Classics of Children's Literature, 1621-1932: Vol. 53). (Illus.). 1976. Repr. of 1886 ed. PLB 38.00 (ISBN 0-8240-2302-1). Garland Pub.
--The Secret Garden. LC 78-2914. (Raintree's Illustrated Classics). (Illus.). (gr. 5-8). 1978. PLB 9.65 (ISBN 0-8393-6204-8). Raintree Child.
Burnett, George W. & Schuster, George S. Pathogenic Microbiology. LC 73-16028. 1973. pap. text ed. 12.50 o.p. (ISBN 0-8016-0905-4). Mosby.
Burnett, Hallie & Burnett, Whit. Fiction Writer's Handbook. LC 74-1797. 1979. pap. 3.95 (ISBN 0-06-463492-2, EH 492, EH). Har-Row.
Burnett, J. H. & Trinci, A. P., eds. Fungal Walls & Hyphal Growth. LC 78-72082. (Illus.). 1980. 68.50 (ISBN 0-521-22499-3). Cambridge U Pr.
Burnett, John. Plenty & Want: A Social History of Diet in England from 1815 to the Present Day. 387p. 1979. Repr. of 1966 ed. 15.95 (ISBN 0-85967-461-4, Pub. by Scolar Pr England); pap. 7.95 (ISBN 0-85967-462-2). Biblio Dist.
--Social History of Housing. LC 77-91461. (Illus.). 1978. 38.00 (ISBN 0-7153-7524-5). David & Charles.
Burnett, John, jt. auth. see Pryor, Sam.
Burnett, John H., jt. auth. see Mayer, Lawrence C.
Burnett, Mary J. & Dollar, Alta. Business English: A Communications Approach. (gr. 7-12). 1979. pap. text ed. 14.80 (ISBN 0-205-06414-0, 1764144); tchrs'. ed. 4.80 (ISBN 0-205-06415-9). Allyn.
Burnett, Michael & Lawrence, Ian, eds. Music Education Review, Vol. 2. 226p. 1980. pap. text ed. 15.00x (ISBN 0-85633-196-1, NFER). Humanities.
Burnett, Millie & Cummins, Mary Ann. Texas Tales & Tunes: A Suite for Speech, Voices, & Orff Instruments. 1977. pap. 3.50 (ISBN 0-918812-00-3). Magnamusic.
Burnett, Peter H. Recollections & Opinions of an Old Pioneer. LC 76-87661. (American Scene Ser.). 1969. Repr. of 1880 ed. lib. bdg. 45.00 (ISBN 0-306-71765-4). Da Capo.
Burnett, Ruth. Dr. Galen's Dilemma. 192p. (YA) 1976. 5.95 (ISBN 0-685-59253-7, Avalon). Bouregy.
--The Picolata Treasure. 192p. (YA) 1974. 5.95 (ISBN 0-685-50326-7, Avalon). Bouregy.
--The Secret of Thundermyer House. (YA) 1976. 4.95 o.p. (ISBN 0-685-68912-3). Bouregy.
Burnett, W. R. Good-Bye Chicago. 182p. 1981. 9.95 (ISBN 0-686-69110-5). St Martin.
Burnett, Whit, jt. auth. see Burnett, Hallie.
Burnett, William. Clinical Science for Surgeons. 1981. text ed. price not set (ISBN 0-407-00181-6). Butterworth.
Burnett, William, ed. Views of Los Angeles. rev. ed. (Illus.). 1979. 24.95 (ISBN 0-9602274-1-5); pap. 14.95 (ISBN 0-9602274-0-7). Portriga Pubns.
Burnett-Hurst, A. R., jt. auth. see Bowley, A. L.
Burney, Charles. Memoirs of the Life & Writings of the Abate Metastasio, 3 Vols. LC 76-162295. (Music Ser). 1971. Repr. of 1796 ed. lib. bdg. 95.00 (ISBN 0-306-71110-9). Da Capo.
Burney, Eugenia, jt. auth. see Christensen, Gardell D.
Burney, Fanny. Evelina. 1958. 5.00x o.p. (ISBN 0-460-00352-6, Evman). Dutton.
--The Journals & Letters of Fanny Burney (Madame D'Arblay), Eighteen Twelve to Eighteen Fourteen: Vol. VII, Letters 632-834. Bloom, Edward A., et al, eds. (Illus.). 650p. 1978. 69.00x (ISBN 0-19-812468-6). Oxford U Pr.
--Journals of Fanny Burney (Madam D'Arblay, 4 vols. Incl. Vol. 1. Seventeen Ninety-One to Seventeen Ninety-Two, Letters 1-39. Hemlow, Joyce, et al, eds. 1972. 34.95x (ISBN 0-19-811498-2); Vol. 2. Courtship & Marriage Seventeen Ninety-Three, Letters 40-121. Hemlow, Joyce & Douglas, Althea, eds. 1972. 34.95x (ISBN 0-19-812421-X); Vol. 3. Great Bookham, 1793-1797. Hemlow, Joyce, et al, eds. (Illus.). 376p. (Letters 122-250). 1973. 37.50x (ISBN 0-19-812419-8); Vol. 4. West Humble, 1797-1801. Hemlow, Joyce, ed. (Illus.). 560p. (Letters 251-422). 1973. 42.00x (ISBN 0-19-812432-5); Vol. 5. West Humble & Paris 1801-1803, Letters 423-549. Hemlon, Joyce, ed. 1975. 55.00x (ISBN 0-19-812467-8); Vol. 6. France, 1803-1812, Letters 550-631. Hemlon, Joyce, ed. 1975. 49.50x (ISBN 0-19-812516-X). (Illus.). Oxford U Pr.
--The Letters & Journals of Fanny Burney: 1812-1814, Letters 632-834, Vol. VII. Bloom, Edward A. & Bloom, Lillian D., eds. 1979. 69.00x (ISBN 0-19-812468-6). Oxford U Pr.
Burney, Frances. Evelina: Or, the History of a Young Lady's Entrance into the World. Bloom, Edward A., ed. (Oxford English Novels Ser & Oxford Paperbacks Ser). 1968. pap. 4.95x (ISBN 0-19-281075-8). Oxford U Pr.
Burney, William. Wallace Stevens. (U. S. Authors Ser.: No. 127). 1968. lib. bdg. 10.95 (ISBN 0-8057-0696-8). Twayne.
Burnford, Sheila. The Incredible Journey. (Illus.). 1961. 8.95 (ISBN 0-316-11714-5, Pub. by Atlantic Monthly Pr). Little.
Burnham, Bonnie. Art Theft: Its Scope, Its Impact, & Its Control. LC 78-71095. 192p. 1978. pap. 8.00x (ISBN 0-89062-067-9, Pub. by Intl Found Art Res). Pub Ctr Cult Res.
--Index of Stolen Art: Nineteen Seventy-Seven. (Illus.). 72p. (Orig.). 1978. pap. 25.00x (ISBN 0-89062-082-2, Pub. by Intl Found Art Res). Pub Ctr Cult Res.
Burnham, Colin. Customizing Cars. LC 79-24124. (Illus.). 1980. 15.00 (ISBN 0-668-04888-3); pap. 7.95 (ISBN 0-668-04892-1). Arco.
Burnham, Daniel H. & Bennett, Edward H. Plan of Chicago Prepared Under the Direction of the Commercial Club During the Years 1906, 1907, 1908. Moore, Charles, ed. LC 71-75303. (Architecture & Decorative Art Ser.: Vol. 29). (Illus.). 1970. Repr. of 1909 ed. lib. bdg. 95.00 (ISBN 0-306-71261-X). Da Capo.
--Report on a Plan for San Francisco: A Facsimile Reprint of the 1906 Plan. facsimile ed. LC 77-182132. (Illus.). 217p. 1972. Repr. of 1905 ed. 25.00x o.p. (ISBN 0-686-02407-9). Urban Bks.
Burnham, David & Burnham, Sue. A Bible Study in My House? 1975. pap. 1.50 (ISBN 0-8024-0689-0). Moody.
Burnham, Don, intro. by. Manufacturing Productivity Solutions II. LC 80-54415. (Illus.). 161p. 1980. pap. text ed. 20.00 (ISBN 0-87263-106-0). SME.
Burnham, John C. Science in America, Historical Selections. 1971. text ed. 3.50 (ISBN 0-03-085288-9). N Watson.
Burnham, Linda F. Bob & Bob: The First Five Years. LC 80-67655. (Illus.). 100p. (Orig.). 1980. pap. 12.00 (ISBN 0-937122-00-9). Astro Artz.
Burnham, Patricia G. Playtraining Your Dog. (Illus.). 256p. 1980. 11.95 (ISBN 0-312-61689-9). St Martin.
Burnham, Paul S., jt. auth. see Crawford, Albert B.
Burnham, Philip & Lederer, Richard. Basic Verbal Skills. 2nd ed. 243p. (gr. 9-12). 1980. pap. text ed. 4.95x (ISBN 0-88334-134-4). Ind Sch Pr.
--Basic Verbal Skills. rev. ed. 245p. (gr. 9-12). 1975. pap. text ed. 4.75x (ISBN 0-88334-067-4); wkbk. 2.50x (ISBN 0-88334-130-1). Ind Sch Pr.
--Basic Verbal Skills for the Middle School. (gr. 6-9). 1976. pap. text ed. 5.25x (ISBN 0-88334-098-4); wkbk. 2.50x (ISBN 0-88334-074-7). Ind Sch Pr.
--Workbook for Basic Verbal Skills. 2nd ed. 74p. (gr. 9-12). 1980. 2.50 (ISBN 0-88334-130-1). Ind Sch Pr.
Burnham, Phillip & Lederer, Richard. Theme & Paragraph. Orig. Title: Basic Composition. (Illus.). 1976. pap. text ed. 3.50x (ISBN 0-88334-078-X). Ind Sch Pr.
Burnham, R., jt. auth. see Hogan, Robert.
Burnham, Robert, Jr. Burnham's Celestial Handbook: An Observer's Guide to the Universe Beyond the Solar System. (Illus.). 1980. Repr. of 1978 ed. 16.50x ea. Vintage Bk Co.

--Burnham's Celestial Handbook: An Observer's Guide to the Universe Beyond the Solar System, 3 vols. rev. ed. (Illus.). 2000p. 1980. 20.00 ea. Vol. 1 (ISBN 0-486-24063-0). Vol. 2 (ISBN 0-486-24064-9). Vol. 3 (ISBN 0-486-24065-7). Dover.

--Burnham's Celestial Handbook: An Observer's Guide to the Universe Beyond the Solar System, Vols. 1 & 2. LC 77-82888. (Illus.). 1978. pap. 8.95 ea. Vol. 1 (ISBN 0-486-23567-X). Vol. 2 (ISBN 0-486-23568-8). Dover.

Burnham, Sue, jt. auth. see Burnham, David.

Burnham, Tom. Dictionary of Misinformation. LC 75-15651. 352p. 1975. 12.95 (ISBN 0-690-00147-9, TYC-T). T Y Crowell.

Burnham, Walter D. Critical Elections & the Mainsprings of American Politics. (Illus.). 1971. pap. 5.95x (ISBN 0-393-09397-2). Norton.

Burnham, Walter D. & Weinberg, Martha W., eds. American Politics & Public Policy. (MIT Studies in American Politics & Public Policy). 432p. (Orig.). 1980. pap. text ed. 8.95 (ISBN 0-262-52061-3). MIT Pr.

--American Politics & Public Policy. (MIT Studies in American Politics & Public Policy: 4th). 1978. text ed. 20.00 (ISBN 0-262-02132-3). MIT Pr.

Burnham, Walter D., jt. ed. see Chambers, W. N.

Burnim, Kalman A. David Garrick: Director. LC 72-11834. (Arcturus Books Paperbacks). 250p. 1973. pap. 6.95 (ISBN 0-8093-0625-5). S Ill U Pr.

Burningham, John. Around the World in Eighty Days. (Illus.). (ps up). 1979. 14.95 (ISBN 0-224-00659-2, Pub. by Chatto Bodley Jonathan). Merrimack Bk Serv.

--The Baby. LC 75-4564. (Illus.). (ps-1). 1975. 3.95 (ISBN 0-690-00900-3, TYC-J); PLB 4.89 (ISBN 0-690-00901-1). T Y Crowell.

--The Blanket. LC 76-17630. (Illus.). (ps-1). 1976. 3.95 (ISBN 0-690-01269-1, TYC-J); PLB 4.89 (ISBN 0-690-01270-5). T Y Crowell.

--The Cupboard. LC 76-17797. (Illus.). (ps-1). 1976. 2.50 (ISBN 0-690-01300-0, TYC-J); PLB 4.89 (ISBN 0-690-01301-9). T Y Crowell.

--The Dog. LC 76-17626. (Illus.). (ps-1). 1976. 2.50 (ISBN 0-690-01271-3, TYC-J); PLB 4.89 (ISBN 0-690-01272-1). T Y Crowell.

--The Friend. LC 76-16436. (Illus.). (ps-1). 1976. 2.50 (ISBN 0-690-01273-X, TYC-J); PLB 4.89 (ISBN 0-690-01274-8). T Y Crowell.

--Jungleland Frieze. (Illus.). (ps-8). 1981. 4.95. Merrimack Bk Serv.

--Mr. Gumpy's Motor Car. LC 75-4582. (Illus.). 48p. (gr. k-3). 1976. 8.95 (ISBN 0-690-00798-1, TYC-J); PLB 8.79 (ISBN 0-690-00799-X). T Y Crowell.

--The Rabbit. LC 75-4566. (Illus.). (ps-1). 1975. 2.50 (ISBN 0-690-00906-2, TYC-J); PLB 4.89 (ISBN 0-690-00907-0). T Y Crowell.

--The School. LC 75-4611. (Illus.). (ps-1). 1975. 2.50 (ISBN 0-690-00902-X, TYC-J); PLB 4.89 (ISBN 0-690-00903-8). T Y Crowell.

--The Shopping Basket. LC 80-7987. (Illus.). 32p. (ps-2). 1980. 9.95 (ISBN 0-690-04082-2, TYC-J); PLB 9.79 (ISBN 0-690-04083-0). T Y Crowell.

--The Snow. LC 75-2492. (Illus.). (ps-1). 1975. 2.50 (ISBN 0-690-00904-6, TYC-J); PLB 4.89 (ISBN 0-690-00905-4). T Y Crowell.

--Time to Get Out of the Bath, Shirley. LC 76-58503. (Illus.). (gr. k-2). 1978. 8.95 (ISBN 0-690-01378-7, TYC-J); PLB 8.79 (ISBN 0-690-01379-5). T Y Crowell.

--Wonderland Frieze. (Illus.). (ps-3). 1981. 4.95 (ISBN 0-224-61537-8). Merrimack Bk Serv.

--Would You Rather... LC 78-7088. (Illus.). (ps-2). 1978. 8.95 (ISBN 0-690-03917-4, TYC-J); PLB 9.79 (ISBN 0-690-03918-2). T Y Crowell.

Burnley, I. H. Urbanization in Australia: The Post-War Experience. LC 73-77261. (Illus.). 1973. 32.95 (ISBN 0-521-20250-7). Cambridge U Pr.

Burnley, I. H., et al, eds. Mobility & Community Change in Australia. (Studies in Society & Culture). (Illus.). 286p. 1981. text ed. 30.25x (ISBN 0-7022-1446-9). U of Queensland Pr.

Burnley, Judith. The Wife. 1978. pap. 1.50 o.s.i. (ISBN 0-515-04568-3). Jove Pubns.

Burns. Great Ideas for Teaching Economics. 846p. 1981. pap. write for info. (ISBN 0-8302-2304-5). Goodyear.

Burns, A. E. & Watson, D. S. Government Spending & Economic Expansion. LC 75-173452. (FDR & the Era of the New Deal Ser). 174p. 1972. Repr. of 1940 ed. lib. bdg. 20.00 (ISBN 0-306-70368-8). Da Capo.

Burns, Aidan. Nature & Culture in D. H. Lawrence. 137p. 1980. 19.50x (ISBN 0-389-20091-3). B&N.

Burns, Alan. Babel. 1980. pap. cancelled (ISBN 0-7145-0011-9). Riverrun NY.

--Celebrations. 1980. pap. cancelled (ISBN 0-7145-0072-0). Riverrun NY.

--The Day Daddy Died. (Illus.). 192p. 1981. 13.95 (ISBN 0-8052-8086-3, Pub. by Allison & Busby England); pap. 5.95 (ISBN 0-8052-8085-5). Schocken.

--Europe After the Rain. 1980. pap. cancelled (ISBN 0-7145-0222-7). Riverrun NY.

--History of Nigeria. 1972. text ed. 17.95x o.p. (ISBN 0-04-966011-X); pap. text ed. 17.95x (ISBN 0-04-966014-4). Allen Unwin.

Burns, Alan & Sugnet, Charles. The Imagination on Trial: Conversations with the British & American Novelists. 192p. 1981. 16.95x (ISBN 0-8052-8084-7); pap. 7.95 (ISBN 0-8052-8083-9). Schocken.

Burns, Alan, et al. New Writers One. 1980. pap. 6.00 (ISBN 0-7145-0397-5). Riverrun NY.

Burns, Arthur & Williams, Edward. Federal Work, Security, & Relief Programs. LC 71-166956. (FDR & the Era of the New Deal Ser). 1971. Repr. of 1941 ed. lib. bdg. 15.00 (ISBN 0-306-70356-4). Da Capo.

Burns, Aubrey. First Book of Bird Watching. LC 68-11140. (First Bks). (Illus.). (gr. 4-6). 1968. PLB 4.90 o.p. (ISBN 0-531-00485-6). Watts.

Burns, C., et al. New Writers Six. (New Writing & Writers Ser.). 1967. pap. text ed. 6.00x (ISBN 0-391-02014-5). Humanities.

Burns, Carol, et al. New Writers Six. 1980. pap. 6.00 (ISBN 0-7145-0407-6). Riverrun NY.

Burns, D. G., ed. Commonwealth Bursars: Problems of Adjustment. Orig. Title: Travelling Scholars. 1965. pap. text ed. 5.75x (ISBN 0-901225-64-9, NFER). Humanities.

Burns, D. T. & Townshend, A. Inorganic Reaction Chemistry: Reactions of the Elements, Vol. 2. Carter, A. H., ed. (Ser. in Analytical Chemistry). 410p. 1981. 97.50 (ISBN 0-470-27105-1). Halsted Pr.

Burns, D. T., et al. Inorganic Reaction Chemistry: Systematic Chemical Separation, Vol. 1. LC 79-42957. 248p. 1980. 57.50x (ISBN 0-470-26895-6). Halsted Pr.

Burns, David. Feeling Good: The New Mood Therapy. LC 80-12694. (Illus.). 388p. 1980. 12.95 (ISBN 0-688-03633-3). Morrow.

Burns, David C., jt. auth. see Holmes, Arthur W.

Burns, David D. Feeling Good. 1981. pap. 3.95 (ISBN 0-451-09804-8, E9804, Signet Bks). NAL.

Burns, E. Applied Research & Statistics for Teachers. (Illus.). 264p. 1980. lexotone 12.00 (ISBN 0-398-03984-4). C C Thomas.

Burns, E. Bradford. Latin America: A Concise Interpretive History. 2nd ed. LC 76-21677. (Illus.). 1977. pap. text ed. 11.95 (ISBN 0-13-524314-9). P-H.

--Perspectives on Brazilian History. LC 67-13779. 1967. 17.50x (ISBN 0-231-02992-6). Columbia U Pr.

--The Poverty of Progress: Latin America in the Nineteenth Century. 224p. 1980. 12.95x (ISBN 0-520-04160-7). U of Cal Pr.

--Unwritten Alliance: Rio-Banco & Brazilian-American Relations. LC 65-25661. (Illus.). 1966. 20.00x (ISBN 0-231-02855-5). Columbia U Pr.

Burns, Edward M. & Ralph, Philip L. World Civilizations, 2 vols. 5th ed. (Illus.). 1974. 19.95x (ISBN 0-393-09276-3); Vol. 1. pap. text ed. 13.95x (ISBN 0-393-09266-6); Vol. 2. pap. text ed. 13.95x (ISBN 0-393-09272-0); Vol. 1. study guide 4.95x (ISBN 0-393-09277-1); Vol. 2. study guide 2.50x (ISBN 0-393-09285-2). Norton.

--World Civilizations. 6th ed. (Illus.). 1981. Two Vols. In 1. price not set (ISBN 0-393-95077-8); Vol. 1. pap. price not set (ISBN 0-393-95083-2); Vol. 2. pap. price not set (ISBN 0-393-95095-6). Norton. Postponed.

Burns, George. Living It Up. 1978. pap. 2.50 (ISBN 0-425-04811-X, Medallion). Berkley Pub.

Burns, George S. The Strange Adventures of Roger Ward. (Illus.). 48p. (gr. 9-12). 1981. 7.95 (ISBN 0-698-20495-6). Putnam.

Burns, George W. The Science of Genetics. 4th ed. (Illus.). 1979. text ed. 18.95 (ISBN 0-02-317140-5). Macmillan.

Burns, Henry. Corrections: Organization & Administration. (Criminal Justice Ser.). 1975. text ed. 16.50 (ISBN 0-685-99574-7); pap. instrs. manual avail. (ISBN 0-8299-0610-X); instrs. manual avail. West Pub.

Burns, J. H., ed. see Bentham, Jeremy.

Burns, J. T. Framing Pictures. LC 77-83674. (Illus.). 1978. 10.95 o.p. (ISBN 0-684-15509-5, ScribT); pap. 6.95 o.p. (ISBN 0-684-15508-7, ScribT). Scribner.

Burns, James M. Leadership. LC 76-5117. 1979. pap. 8.95 (ISBN 0-06-090697-9, CN 697, CN). Har-Row.

Burns, James M., et al. Government by the People, 3 pts. 11th ed. Incl. National, State, Local. 800p. text ed. 19.95 (ISBN 0-13-361253-8); Basic. 480p. text ed. 16.95 (ISBN 0-13-361238-4); National. 640p. text ed. 17.95 (ISBN 0-13-361246-5). (Illus.). 1981. P-H.

--Government by the People. 10th ed. Incl. Basic. rev. ed. LC 78-1264. text ed. 16.95 (ISBN 0-13-361162-0); study guide 3.95 (ISBN 0-13-361188-4); National. LC 78-1266. text ed. 17.95 (ISBN 0-13-361154-X); study guide 4.50 (ISBN 0-13-361220-1); National, State, Local. LC 78-1260. text ed. 19.95 (ISBN 0-13-361147-7); study guide 5.95 (ISBN 0-13-361196-5). 1978. P-H.

--State & Local Politics: Government by the People. 3rd ed. (Illus.). 1981. 9.95f (ISBN 0-13-843516-2). P-H.

--State & Local Politics: Government by the People. 2nd ed. 1978. pap. text ed. 9.50 (ISBN 0-13-843540-5). P-H.

Burns, John M. Biograffiti: A Natural Selection. 1980. pap. 3.95 (ISBN 0-393-00031-1). Norton.

Burns, Joseph M. Treatise on Markets: Spot, Futures, & Options. 1979. pap. 5.25 (ISBN 0-8447-3340-7). Am Enterprise.

Burns, Julie & Swan, Dorothy. Reading Without Books. LC 78-72078. 1979. pap. 4.95 (ISBN 0-8224-5830-6). Pitman Learning.

Burns, Ken, tr. see Ohsawa, George.

Burns, Kenneth R. & Johnson, Patricia J. Health Assessment in Clinical Practice. (Illus.). 1980. text ed. 26.95 (ISBN 0-13-385054-4). P-H.

Burns, L. S. & Grebler, L. The Housing of Nations: Analysis & Policy in a Comparative Framework. LC 76-43023. 1977. 29.95 (ISBN 0-470-98970-X). Halsted Pr.

Burns, Landon C. Pity & Fears: The Tragedies of Nicholas Rowe. (Salzburg Studies in English Literature, Poetic Drama & Poetic Theory: No. 8). 256p. 1974. pap. text ed. 25.00x (ISBN 0-391-01333-5). Humanities.

Burns, Lawrence D. Transportation, Temporal & Spatial Components of Accessibility. LC 79-1725. (Illus.). 176p. 1979. 19.95 (ISBN 0-669-02916-5). Lexington Bks.

Burns, Margaret A. & Morrissy, Lois E. Self-Assessment of Current Knowledge for the Operating Room Technician. 2nd ed. 1976. pap. 9.50 (ISBN 0-87488-474-8). Med Exam.

Burns, Ned H., jt. auth. see Lin, T. Y.

Burns, R. B. The Self Concept: Theory, Measurement, Development & Behaviour. (Illus.). 1979. pap. text ed. 12.95 (ISBN 0-582-48951-2). Longman.

Burns, R. G. Mineralogical Applications of Crystal Field Theory. LC 77-85714. (Earth Sciences Ser). (Illus.). 1969. 29.50 (ISBN 0-521-07610-2). Cambridge U Pr.

Burns, R. M. Conflict & Its Resolution in the Administration of Mineral Resources in Canada. 63p. (Orig.). 1976. pap. text ed. 3.50x (ISBN 0-88757-000-3, Pub. by Ctr Resource Stud Canada). Renouf.

--The Great Debate on Miracles: From Joseph Glanvill to David Hume. LC 78-75197. 300p. 1981. 20.00 (ISBN 0-8387-2378-0). Bucknell U Pr.

Burns, R. P., ed. see Leopold, Irving H.

Burns, Rex. The Alvarez Journal. LC 75-6365. (Harper Novel of Suspense). 208p. 1975. 8.95 o.p. (ISBN 0-06-010576-3, HarpT). Har-Row.

--The Farnsworth Score. 1978. pap. 1.75 o.p. (ISBN 0-425-03749-5, Medallion). Berkley Pub.

Burns, Richard C., jt. auth. see Cohen, Stephen.

Burns, Richard D. & Leitenberg, Milton. A Guide to the Vietnam Conflict. 2nd ed. LC 80-13246. (War Peace Bibliography Ser.: No. 3). 1981. write for info. (ISBN 0-87436-310-1). ABC Clio.

Burns, Richard D. & Bennett, Edward M., eds. Diplomats in Crisis: United States-Chinese-Japanese Relations, 1919-1941. LC 74-76444. 346p. 1974. text ed. 10.65 (ISBN 0-87436-135-4). ABC-Clio.

Burns, Richard D., ed. see Ball, Nicole.

Burns, Richard D., ed. see Smith, Myron J., Jr.

Burns, Robert. A Choice of Burns' Poems & Songs. Smith, Sydney G., ed. 1966. pap. 5.50 (ISBN 0-571-06835-9, Pub. by Faber & Faber). Merrimack Bk Serv.

--Poems & Songs. Kinsley, James, ed. (Oxford Standard Authors Ser). 1969. 29.50 (ISBN 0-19-254164-1); pap. 11.50x (ISBN 0-19-281114-2). Oxford U Pr.

Burns, Robert F. & Sands, Leo G. Citizens Band Radio Service Manual. LC 77-170665. 1971. 8.95 o.p. (ISBN 0-8306-1581-4); pap. 5.95 (ISBN 0-8306-0581-9, 581). TAB Bks.

Burns, Robert O. Innovation: The Management Connection. 160p. 1975. 17.95 (ISBN 0-669-00084-1). Lexington Bks.

Burns, Robert P., jt. auth. see Leopold, Irving H.

Burns, Robert P., ed. see Symposium on Ocular Therapy.

Burns, Sheila L. A Christmas Carol. LC 78-72141. (Illus.). (gr. 2-5). Date not set. price not set (ISBN 0-89799-093-5); pap. price not set (ISBN 0-89799-064-1). Dandelion Pr. Postponed.

Burns, Shelia L. Allergies & You. LC 79-26637. (Illus.). 64p. (gr. 3-7). 1980. PLB 6.97 (ISBN 0-671-33044-6). Messner.

Burns, Stuart L. Whores Before Descartes: Assorted Poetry & Sordid Prose. LC 80-54381. 96p. (Orig.). 1980. pap. 4.50 (ISBN 0-9605326-0-9). Wash Launderan.

Burns, Tom R. & Buckley, Walter, eds. Power & Control: Social Structures & Their Transformation. LC 76-22900. (Sage Studies in International Sociology: Vol. 6). 1976. 18.00x (ISBN 0-8039-9959-3); pap. 9.95x (ISBN 0-8039-9978-X). Sage.

Burns, William H. The Voices of Negro Protest in Amercia. LC 80-21197. 88p. 1980. Repr. of 1963 ed. lib. bdg. 17.50x (ISBN 0-313-22219-3, BUVN). Greenwood.

Burns Florey, Kitty. Family Matters. 1981. pap. 2.25 (ISBN 0-451-09667-3, 9667, Sig). NAL.

Burnshaw, Stanley. Mirages: Travel Notes in the Promised Land. LC 76-21513. 1977. 5.95 o.p. (ISBN 0-385-12500-3). Doubleday.

--The Seamless Web. LC 71-97603. 1970. 6.50 (ISBN 0-8076-0535-2); pap. 4.95 (ISBN 0-8076-0534-4). Braziller.

Burnside, C. D. Mapping from Aerial Photographs. LC 79-11497. 304p. 1979. 45.50 (ISBN 0-470-26690-2). Halsted Pr.

Burnside, Irene M. Nursing & the Aged. 2nd ed. (Illus.). 736p. 1980. text ed. 17.95 (ISBN 0-07-009211-7, HP). McGraw.

--Psychosocial Nursing Care of the Aged. (Illus.). 228p. 1972. pap. text ed. 8.95 o.p. (ISBN 0-07-009208-7, HP). McGraw.

Burnside, Irving L. The First American Circus Ever. LC 78-15552. (Famous Firsts Ser.). (Illus.). 1978. lib. bdg. 7.95 (ISBN 0-686-51099-2). Silver.

Burnside, John. Adams' Physical Diagnosis. 16th ed. (Illus.). 275p. 1981. write for info. soft cover (1137-5). Williams & Wilkins.

Burnstiner, Irving. Run Your Own Store: From Raising the Money to Counting the Profits. (Illus.). 304p. 1981. 19.95 (ISBN 0-13-784017-9, Spectrum); pap. 12.95 (ISBN 0-13-784009-8). P-H.

Burow, Daniel R. Plattertales. Incl. Bushy-Tailed Helper (ISBN 0-570-07021-X, 56-1162); Say & Do Thanks (ISBN 0-570-07022-8, 56-1163); Conrad the Cobbler (ISBN 0-570-07025-2, 56-1166); The Valley That Didn't Wake (ISBN 0-570-07026-0, 56-1167); Little King of All (ISBN 0-570-07024-4, 56-1165); Lester the Jester (ISBN 0-570-07023-6, 56-1164). 16p. (ps-3). 1974. pap. 2.69 ea.; record incl. Concordia.

Burows, D. R. Sound of the Bugle. 224p. (gr. 6-9). 1973. pap. 3.50 (ISBN 0-570-03145-1, 12-2529). Concordia.

Burpo, John H. Police Labor Movement: Problems & Perspectives. 224p. 1971. 14.75 (ISBN 0-398-00262-2). C C Thomas.

Burr, Aaron. Reports of the Trials of Colonel Aaron Burr, 2 Vols. LC 69-11321. (Law, Politics & History Ser). 1969. Repr. of 1808 ed. 69.50 (ISBN 0-306-71182-6). Da Capo.

Burr, Ann M., jt. auth. see Runkel, Philip J.

Burr, Betty J. Outer Limits of the Mind. (Pal Paperbacks Kit B Ser.). (Illus., Orig.). (gr. 7-12). 1974. pap. text ed. 1.25 (ISBN 0-8374-3515-3). Xerox Ed Pubns.

Burr, Gray. Choice of Attitudes. LC 69-17790. (Wesleyan Poetry Program: Vol. 44). 1969. 10.00x (ISBN 0-8195-2044-6, Pub. by Wesleyan U Pr); pap. 4.95x (ISBN 0-8195-1044-0). Columbia U Pr.

Burr, H. S. Classics in Neurology. 184p. 1963. pap. 14.50 photocopy ed. spiral (ISBN 0-398-00263-0). C C Thomas.

--The Neural Basis of Human Behavior. 272p. 1960. pap. 19.75 photocopy ed. spiral (ISBN 0-398-00264-9). C C Thomas.

Burr, Irving W. Applied Statistical Methods. (Operations Research & Industrial Engineering Ser.). 1973. 21.95 (ISBN 0-12-146150-5). Acad Pr.

Burr, John R., ed. Handbook of World Philosophy: Contemporary Developments Since 1945. LC 80-539. (Illus.). xxii, 639p. 1980. lib. bdg. 45.00 (ISBN 0-313-22381-5, BCD/). Greenwood.

Burr, Nelson R. A Narrative & Descriptive Bibliography of New Jersey. 1970. 12.50 (ISBN 0-8135-0639-5). Rutgers U Pr.

Burr, Nelson R., compiled by. Religion in American Life. LC 70-136219. (Goldentree Bibliographies in American History Ser.). (Orig.). 1971. pap. 6.95x (ISBN 0-88295-506-3). AHM Pub.

Burr, Robert N. By Reason or Force: Chile & the Balancing of Power in South America, 1830-1905. (California Library Reprint Ser.). 1974. 25.75x (ISBN 0-520-02644-6); pap. 6.95x (ISBN 0-520-02629-2). U of Cal Pr.

--Our Troubled Hemisphere: Perspectives on United States-Latin American Relations. 1967. 9.95 (ISBN 0-8157-1174-3). Brookings.

Burr, Wesley R. Successful Marriage: A Principles Approach. 1976. text ed. 17.95x (ISBN 0-256-01789-1). Dorsey.

Burrage, A. M. Some Ghost Stories. 1981. 8.50 (ISBN 0-686-69311-6). Bookfinger.

Burrage, Barbara. The Bible Quiz Book. (gr. 5 up). 1979. pap. 2.50 (ISBN 0-8192-1256-3). Morehouse.
--Bible Quizzerama Puzzle Book. 48p. (Orig.). (gr. 6 up). 1981. pap. 1.25 (ISBN 0-87239-446-8, 2836). Standard Pub.
Burrell, Arthur. Guide to Story Telling. LC 74-23577. 1971. Repr. of 1926 ed. 20.00 (ISBN 0-8103-3764-9). Gale.
Burrell, D. C., et al. Marine Environmental Studies in Boca de Quadra & Smeaton Bay: Physical & Chemical, Nineteen Seventy-Nine. (Science Technical Report Ser.: No. R80-1). (Illus.). 144p. pap. 10.50 (ISBN 0-914500-10-4). U of AK Inst Marine.
Burrell, D. J. In the Upper Room. (Short Course Ser.). 146p. 1913. text ed. 2.95 (ISBN 0-567-08317-9). Attic Pr.
Burrell, Jill & Burrell, Maurice. Arctic Mission. 1976. 1.55 (ISBN 0-08-017621-6). Pergamon.
Burrell, Lennette O., jt. auth. see Burrell, Zeb, Jr.
Burrell, Leonard F. Beginner's Guide to Home Coarse Tacklemaking. (Illus.). 134p. 1973. 12.95 (ISBN 0-7207-0548-7). Transatlantic.
--Make Your Own Sea-Angling Tackle. (Illus.). 108p. 1976. 12.00 (ISBN 0-7207-0894-X). Transatlantic.
Burrell, Maurice, jt. auth. see Burrell, Jill.
Burrell, Paul B., tr. see Dubois, Jacques, et al.
Burrell, Percival. Suttons Synagogue: Or the English Centurion (A Sermon) LC 74-28822. (English Experience Ser.: No. 647). 1974. Repr. of 1629 ed. 3.50 (ISBN 90-221-0647-0). Walter J Johnson.
Burrell, Philippa. The Golden Thread. 350p. 1980. 29.75x (ISBN 0-7050-0067-2, Pub. by Skilton & Shaw England). State Mutual Bk.
Burrell, R. Michael & Cottrell, Alvin J. Politics, Oil, & the Western Mediterranean. LC 73-638. (The Washington Papers: No. 7). 1973. write for info. (ISBN 0-8039-0259-X). Sage.
Burrell, Sidney A. Handbook of Western Civilization: 1700 to Present. 2nd ed. LC 76-37642. 1972. pap. text ed. 10.95 (ISBN 0-471-12516-4). Wiley.
Burrell, Zeb, Jr. & Burrell, Lennette O. Critical Care. 3rd ed. LC 76-53564. (Illus.). 1977. lib. bdg. 15.95 (ISBN 0-8016-0914-3). Mosby.
Burrello, Leonard C. & Sage, Daniel D. Leadership & Change in Special Education. (P-H Ser. in Special Education). 1979. 17.95 (ISBN 0-13-526921-0). P-H.
Burrells, W. Microscope Techniques: A Comprehensive Handbook for General & Applied Microscopy. LC 77-26687. 1978. 34.95 (ISBN 0-470-99376-6). Halsted Pr.
Burridge, Kenelm. Tangu Traditions: A Study of the Way of Life, Mythology & Developing Experience of a New Guinea People. 1969. 20.50x o.p. (ISBN 0-19-823136-9). Oxford U Pr.
Burridge, Kenelm O. Encountering Aborigines, a Case Study: Anthropology & the Australian Aboriginal. LC 72-1191. 272p. 1974. 23.00 (ISBN 0-08-017071-4); pap. 12.00 (ISBN 0-08-017646-1). Pergamon.
Burridge, Richard see Ames, William.
Burridge, T. D. British Labour & Hitler's War. 1977. 15.00 (ISBN 0-233-96714-1). Transatlantic.
Burright, Orrin U. The Sun Rides High: Pioneering Days in Oklahoma, Kansas & Missouri. 8.95 (ISBN 0-685-48814-4). Nortex Pr.
Burrill, Claude W. & Ellsworth, Leon W. Modern Project Management: Foundations for Quality & Productivity. LC 79-24457. (The Data Processing Handbook Ser.). (Illus.). 576p. 1980. text ed. 39.00x (ISBN 0-935310-00-2). Burrill-Ellsworth.
Burrill, Harry & Crist, Raymond F. Report on Trade Conditions in China. LC 78-74353. (The Modern Chinese Economy Ser.). 130p. 1980. lib. bdg. 16.50 (ISBN 0-8240-4265-4). Garland Pub.
Burrill, Richard. The Human Almanac: People Through Time. LC 79-92820. (Illus., Orig.). 1980. pap. cancelled (ISBN 0-915190-23-0). Jalmar Pr.
Burrington, Gillian. How to Find Out About the Social Sciences. LC 75-5809. 148p. 1975. text ed. 15.00 (ISBN 0-08-018289-5). Pergamon.
Burrington, John D. Pediatric Surgery Continuing Education Review. 1976. spiral bdg. 14.00 (ISBN 0-87488-332-6). Med Exam.
Burris, Barbara J. & Olson, Arne L. Badminton. 96p. 1974. pap. text ed. 2.95x o.p. (ISBN 0-205-04388-7). Allyn.
Burris, Russel W., et al. Teaching Law with Computers. (EDUCOM Series in Computing & Telecommunications in Higher Education). 1979. lib. bdg. 19.50x (ISBN 0-89158-193-6). Westview.
Burris-Meyer, Harold, et al. Sound in the Theatre. rev. ed. LC 78-66064. 1979. 12.95 (ISBN 0-87830-157-7). Theatre Arts.
Burro, Marian. Pure & Simple. 1979. pap. 3.50 (ISBN 0-425-04860-8). Berkley Pub.
Burron, Arnold & Claybaugh, Amos L. Basic Concepts in Reading Instruction. 2nd ed. (Elementary Education Ser.). 1977. pap. text ed. 8.95 (ISBN 0-675-08539-X). Merrill.
Burros, Marian & Levine, Lois. Freeze with Ease. LC 65-21466. 1968. pap. 2.95 (ISBN 0-02-009280-6, Collier). Macmillan.
Burrough, T. H. South German Baroque. (Illus.). 8.50 (ISBN 0-85458-698-9). Transatlantic.
Burroughs, Ben. Sketches. LC 56-11909. 160p. 1980. pap. 8.50 (ISBN 0-8303-0048-1). Fleet.
Burroughs, Edgar R. Apache Devil. 224p. 1975. pap. 1.25 o.p. (ISBN 0-345-24605-5). Ballantine.
--Apache Devil. 1976. Repr. of 1933 ed. lib. bdg. 14.20x (ISBN 0-89966-043-6). Buccaneer Bks.
--At the Earth's Core: Pellucidar, Tamar of Pellucidar. (Illus.). 9.00 (ISBN 0-8446-1778-4). Peter Smith.
--Back to the Stone Age. 192p. 1976. pap. 1.95 (ISBN 0-441-04636-3). Ace Bks.
--The Cave Girl. Wallace, Wendy, ed. 224p. 1981. pap. 1.95 (ISBN 0-448-17176-7, Tempo). G&D.
--Chessman of Mars. 1973. pap. 1.95 (ISBN 0-345-27838-0). Ballantine.
--The Eternal Savage. 192p. 1977. pap. 1.95 (ISBN 0-441-21805-9). Ace Bks.
--Fighting Man of Mars. 1976. pap. 1.95 (ISBN 0-345-27840-2). Ballantine.
--John Carter of Mars. 1973. pap. 1.95 (ISBN 0-345-27844-5). Ballantine.
--Jungle Tales of Tarzan, No. 6. 192p. 1975. pap. 1.95 (ISBN 0-345-29478-5). Ballantine.
--Llana of Gathol. 1973. pap. 1.95 o.p. (ISBN 0-345-25829-0). Ballantine.
--The Mad King. 256p. 1976. pap. 1.95 (ISBN 0-441-51404-9). Ace Bks.
--Moon Men. LC 62-8706. (Illus.). 1975. Repr. 8.95 (ISBN 0-686-10382-3). Canaveral.
--The Oakdale Affair. 1976. Repr. of 1937 ed. lib. bdg. 12.50x (ISBN 0-89966-041-X). Buccaneer Bks.
--The Outlaw of Torn. 1975. pap. 1.95 (ISBN 0-441-64513-5). Ace Bks.
--The Outlaw of Torn. 1976. Repr. of 1927 ed. lib. bdg. 10.55x (ISBN 0-89966-042-8). Buccaneer Bks.
--The People That Time Forgot. 1977. pap. 1.95 (ISBN 0-441-65947-0). Ace Bks.
--Swords of Mars. 1973. pap. 1.95 (ISBN 0-345-27841-0). Ballantine.
--Tarzan & the Ant Men, No. 10. Date not set. pap. 1.95 (ISBN 0-345-28997-8). Ballantine.
--Tarzan & the Castaways. Date not set. pap. 1.95 (ISBN 0-345-24980-1). Ballantine.
--Tarzan & the Forbidden City. Date not set. pap. 1.95 (ISBN 0-345-29106-9). Ballantine.
--Tarzan & the Foreign Legion. Date not set. pap. 1.95 (ISBN 0-345-24978-X). Ballantine.
--Tarzan & the Golden Lion, No. 9. Date not set. pap. 1.95 (ISBN 0-345-28998-6). Ballantine.
--Tarzan & the Jewels of Opar, No. 5. 160p. Date not set. pap. 1.95 (ISBN 0-345-28917-X). Ballantine.
--Tarzan & the Leopard Man. Date not set. pap. 1.95 (ISBN 0-345-28687-1). Ballantine.
--Tarzan & the Lion Men. Date not set. pap. 1.95 (ISBN 0-345-28988-9). Ballantine.
--Tarzan & the Lost Empire, No. 12. Date not set. pap. 1.95 (ISBN 0-345-29050-X). Ballantine.
--Tarzan at the Earth's Core. Date not set. pap. 1.95 (ISBN 0-345-24483-4). Ballantine.
--Tarzan Lord of the Jungle, No. 11. Date not set. pap. 1.95 (ISBN 0-345-28986-2). Ballantine.
--Tarzan of the Apes. 1976. Repr. of 1906 ed. lib. bdg. 17.30x (ISBN 0-89966-046-0). Buccaneer Bks.
--Tarzan of the Apes, No. 1. 256p. Date not set. pap. 1.95 (ISBN 0-345-28377-5). Ballantine.
--Tarzan the Magnificent. Date not set. pap. 1.95 (ISBN 0-345-25561-0). Ballantine.
--Tarzan the Terrible, No. 8. Date not set. pap. 1.95 (ISBN 0-345-28745-2). Ballantine.
--Tarzan the Triumphant. Date not set. pap. 1.95 (ISBN 0-345-28688-X). Ballantine.
--The War Chief. 1976. Repr. of 1927 ed. lib. bdg. 15.95x (ISBN 0-89966-044-4). Buccaneer Bks.
--The Warlord of Mars. 1976. Repr. of 1919 ed. lib. bdg. 13.95x (ISBN 0-89966-045-2). Buccaneer Bks.
Burroughs, Eliane. French Phonetics. (gr. 8-12). 1972. pap. text ed. 10.00 (ISBN 0-8449-1601-3). Learning Line.
--Modern French A, 2 bks. (gr. 8-12). 1966. pap. text ed. 7.00 each (ISBN 0-686-57756-6); tchr's manual & test avail. Learning Line.
--Modern French B, 3 bks. (gr. 8-12). 1966. pap. text ed. 7.00 each (ISBN 0-686-57757-4); tchr's manual & test avail. Learning Line.
--Programmed French Reading & Writing I. 1971. pap. text ed. 7.00 incl. tchrs' manual & test (ISBN 0-8449-1700-1). Learning Line.
--Programmed French Reading & Writing II. 1964. pap. text ed. 7.00 incl. tchrs' manual & test (ISBN 0-8449-1704-4). Learning Line.
--Programmed French Reading & Writing III. 1972. pap. text ed. 7.00 incl. tchrs' manual & test (ISBN 0-8449-1708-7). Learning Line.
Burroughs, Jean. On the Trail: The Life & Trail Stories of "Lead Steer" Potter. (Illus.). 1980. 12.95 (ISBN 0-89013-131-7). Museum NM Pr.
Burroughs, Jeremiah. The Rare Jewel of Christian Contentment. 1979. pap. 3.95 (ISBN 0-85151-091-4). Banner of Truth.
Burroughs, John. Return of the Birds: Selected Nature Essays of John Burroughs, Vol. 1. Bergon, Frank, ed. (Literature of the American Wilderness). 320p. 1981. pap. 4.45 (ISBN 0-87905-081-0). Peregrine Smith.
--A Sharp Lookout: Nature Essays of John Burroughs, Vol. II. Bergone, Frank, ed. (Literature of the American Wilderness). 320p. 1981. pap. 4.45 (ISBN 0-87905-082-9). Peregrine Smith.
--Signs & Seasons. (Nature Library Ser.). 300p. 1981. pap. 5.95 (ISBN 0-06-090840-8, CN 840, CN). Har-Row.
Burroughs, Polly. Guide to Nantucket. LC 74-76535. (Illus., Orig.). 1980. pap. 4.95 (ISBN 0-87106-144-9). Globe Pequot.
--Thomas Hart Benton: A Portrait. LC 77-16903. (Illus.). 208p. 1981. 29.95 (ISBN 0-385-12342-6). Doubleday.
--Zeb: A Celebrated Schooner Life. LC 72-80278. (Illus.). 1979. pap. 7.95 (ISBN 0-85699-050-7). Globe Pequot.
Burroughs, Wayne A., jt. auth. see Jaffee, Cabot J.
Burroughs, William. Cobble Stone Gardens. LC 76-40473. (Illus.). 1976. pap. 3.00x o.p. (ISBN 0-916156-14-1). Cherry Valley.
--Early Routines. Grauerholz, James & Miller, Jeffrey, eds. LC 79-54919. 1981. signed limited ed. 40.00 (ISBN 0-932274-03-X); pap. 10.00 (ISBN 0-932274-02-1). Cadmus Eds.
--Lasers. LC 77-88173. 1977. 9.95x (ISBN 0-8448-1088-6). Crane-Russak Co.
--The Soft Machine. Bd. with Nova Express; The Wild Boys. LC 80-8062. 544p. (Orig.). 1981. pap. 5.95 (ISBN 0-394-17749-5, B 446, BC). Grove.
Burroughs, William, et al. New Writing & Writers Sixteen. 1980. pap. 6.00 (ISBN 0-7145-3638-5). Riverrun NY.
Burroughs, William S. Book of Breeething. 2nd ed. LC 75-33858. (Illus.). 1980. 14.95 (ISBN 0-912652-72-1); signed 25.00 (ISBN 0-912652-73-X); pap. 4.95 (ISBN 0-912652-71-3). Blue Wind.
--Cities of the Red Night. LC 80-13637. 448p. 1981. 14.95 (ISBN 0-03-053976-5). HR&W.
--The Job: Interviews by Daniel Odier. LC 73-20496. 212p. 1974. pap. 4.95 (ISBN 0-394-17870-X, E642, Ever). Grove.
--Junky. 1977. pap. 2.95 (ISBN 0-14-004351-9). Penguin.
--The Last Words of Dutch Schultz. LC 80-54557. (Illus.). 128p. 1981. pap. 4.95 (ISBN 0-394-17852-1). Seaver Bks.
--The Last Words of Dutch Schultz. 128p. 1981. pap. 4.95 (ISBN 0-394-17852-1). Seaver Bks.
--Roosevelt After Inauguration. LC 79-21111. 1979. pap. 0.50 (ISBN 0-87286-115-5). City Lights.
Burrow, G. N., jt. ed. see Fisher, D. A.
Burrow, J. A. A Reading of Sir Gawain & the Green Knight. 1978. pap. 7.95 (ISBN 0-7100-8695-4). Routledge & Kegan.
Burrow, J. W. Evolution & Society. 1966. 29.95 (ISBN 0-521-04393-X); pap. 9.95x (ISBN 0-521-09600-6). Cambridge U Pr.
Burrow, J. W., jt. auth. see Karp, Walter.
Burrow, Jackie, jt. auth. see Seddon, George.
Burrow, John. English Verse 1300-1500. LC 76-7591. (Longman Annotated Anthologies of English Verse). 1977. text ed. 26.00x (ISBN 0-582-48367-0); pap. text ed. 12.95x (ISBN 0-582-48368-9). Longman.
Burrow, Paul. The Boys. LC 80-50129. 1980. 6.95 (ISBN 0-533-04598-3). Vantage.
Burrow, Thomas & Emeneau, Murray B. Dravidian Etymological Dictionary. 1961. 49.95x (ISBN 0-19-864310-1). Oxford U Pr.
Burroway, Janet. Material Goods. LC 80-12381. 77p. 1981. 7.95 (ISBN 0-8130-0670-8). U Presses Fla.
Burrowes, George. Song of Solomon. (Geneva Commentaries Ser.). 1977. 11.95 (ISBN 0-85151-157-0). Banner of Truth.
Burrows & Norman. Pschyotropic Drugs. 528p. 1980. 68.00 (ISBN 0-8247-1009-6). Dekker.
Burrows, Abe. Honest, Abe. (Illus.). 1980. 14.95 (ISBN 0-316-11771-4, Pub. by Atlantic-Little Brown). Little.
Burrows, David J., et al. Myths & Motifs in Literature. LC 72-90546. 448p. (Orig.). 1973. pap. text ed. 8.95 (ISBN 0-02-905030-8). Free Pr.
Burrows, David L., ed. see Gasparini, Francesco.
Burrows, E. H. & Leeds, Norman E. Neuroradiology, 2 vols. (Illus., Vol. 1, 800 p., vol. 2, 384 p.). 1980. text ed. 175.00x set (ISBN 0-443-08016-X). Churchill.
Burrows, Fredrika A., ed. see Rex, Percy F.
Burrows, G. D., et al, eds. Hypnosis Nineteen Hundred Seventy-Nine. LC 79-16095. 354p. 1979. 58.75 (ISBN 0-444-80142-1, North Holland). Elsevier.
Burrows, James C., jt. auth. see Woods, Douglas.
Burrows, L. A Grammar of the Ho Language. 194p. 1980. Repr. of 1915 ed. 20.00 o.p. (ISBN 0-89684-258-4, Pub. by Cosmo Pubns India). Orient Bk Dist.
Burrows, Lois M. & Myers, Laura G. Too Many Tomatoes...Squash, Beans, & Other Good Things: A Cookbook for When Your Garden Explodes. LC 75-34581. 1980. pap. 6.95 (ISBN 0-06-090765-7, CN 765, CN). Har-Row.
Burrows, Margaret, jt. auth. see Kurtz, Harold.
Burrows, Marion. Keep It Simple. 256p. 1981. 10.95 (ISBN 0-688-00450-4). Morrow.
Burrows, Paul. Economic Theory of Pollution Control. 240p. 1980. text ed. 25.00x (ISBN 0-262-02150-1); pap. text ed. 8.95 (ISBN 0-262-52056-7). MIT Pr.
Burrows, Stephen G. God's Daughter in Nassau. 1979. 8.50 (ISBN 0-682-49497-6). Exposition.
Burrows, William. Textbook of Microbiology. 20th ed. LC 72-88845. (Illus.). 1035p. 1973. text ed. 26.00 o.p. (ISBN 0-7216-2195-3). Saunders.
Burrows, William E. On Reporting the News. LC 76-16472. 345p. 1977. 15.00x (ISBN 0-8147-1009-3). NYU Pr.
Burrows, William R. New Ministries: The Global Context. LC 80-17261. 176p. 1980. pap. 7.95 (ISBN 0-88344-329-5). Orbis Bks.
Burrup. Financing Education in a Climate of Change. 2nd ed. 19.95x (ISBN 0-205-05696-2, 2256967). Allyn.
Burrus, Thomas L. & Spiegel, Herbert J. Earth in Crisis: An Introduction to the Earth Sciences. 2nd ed. LC 79-19596. (Illus.). 1980. 19.95 (ISBN 0-8016-0902-X). Mosby.
--Earth in Crisis: An Introduction to the Earth Sciences. LC 75-22029. (Illus.). 440p. 1976. 15.95 o.p. (ISBN 0-8016-0918-6). Mosby.
Bursill-Hall, G., ed. see Hunt, R. W.
Bursill-Hall, G. L., ed. Grammatica Speculativa of Thomas of Erfurt. (The Classics of Linguistics Ser). 340p. 1972. text ed. 25.00x (ISBN 0-582-52495-4). Longman.
Bursky, Dave. Components for Microcomputer System Design. 272p. 1980. pap. 11.95 (ISBN 0-8104-0975-5). Hayden.
--Memory Systems Design & Applications. 240p. pap. 11.95 (ISBN 0-8104-0980-1). Hayden.
--Microprocessor Systems Design & Applications. 192p. pap. 9.95 (ISBN 0-8104-0976-3). Hayden.
--The S-One Hundred Bus Handbook. 280p. 1980. pap. 14.50 (ISBN 0-8104-0897-X). Hayden.
Bursnall, W., ed. Planning Challenges of the 70's in the Public Domain. (Science & Technology Ser.: Vol. 22). (Illus.). 1969. lib. bdg. 40.00 (ISBN 0-87703-050-2); microfiche suppl 20.00 (ISBN 0-87703-131-2). Am Astronaut.
Burstall, Aubrey F. A History of Mechanical Engineering. (Illus.). 1963. 13.95 (ISBN 0-571-05343-2, Pub. by Faber & Faber). Merrimack Bk Serv.
Burstall, Clare. Primary French in the Balance: Main Report. (Research Reports Ser.). 304p. 1974. pap. text ed. 16.25x (ISBN 0-85633-052-3, NFER). Humanities.
Burstall, M. L., jt. auth. see Reuben, B. G.
Burstein. The Get Well Hotel. 113p. Date not set. lib. bdg. 4.95 (ISBN 0-07-009244-3). McGraw.
--Hotel & Motel Management. 240p. 1980. 29.50 (ISBN 0-8247-1002-9). Dekker.
Burstein, A. Religion, Cults & the Law. 1980. 5.95 (ISBN 0-379-11133-0). Oceana.
Burstein, Chaya. Rifka Bangs the Teakettle. LC 79-91068. (Illus.). (gr. 4-6). 1970. 4.95 o.p. (ISBN 0-15-266944-2, HJ). HarBraceJ.
Burstein, E., ed. see U. S.-Japan Seminar or Inelastic Light Scattering, Santa Monica, California. January 22-25, 1979.
Burstein, Elias & De Martini, Francesco, eds. Polaritons: Proceedings, Taormina Research Conference on the Structure of Matter, 1st, Taormina, Italy, Oct, 1972. LC 73-12845. 1974. text ed. 45.00 (ISBN 0-08-017825-1). Pergamon.
Burstein, Harvey. Hotel Security Management. LC 74-14039. 138p. 1975. text ed. 22.95 (ISBN 0-275-09820-6). Praeger.
--Industrial Security Management. LC 77-12762. 1977. 25.95 (ISBN 0-275-24050-9). Praeger.
Burstein, Herman. Questions & Answers About Tape Recording. LC 73-89813. 1974. pap. 5.95 (ISBN 0-8306-2681-6, 681). TAB Bks.
Burstein, John. Lucky You! LC 80-14641. (Illus.). 32p. (ps-3). 1980. 4.95 (ISBN 0-07-009243-5). McGraw.
Burstein, John, jt. auth. see Good Thing Inc.
Burstein, Jules Q. Conjugal Visits in Prison: Psychological & Social Consequences. LC 76-50485. (Illus.). 1977. 16.95 (ISBN 0-669-01287-4). Lexington Bks.

Burstein, Pat. Farrah: An Unauthorized Biography of Farrah Fawcett-Majors. (Illus.). (RL 7). 1977. pap. 1.50 o.p. (ISBN 0-451-07723-7, W7723, Sig). NAL.

Burstein, Stanley M. Outpost of Hellenism: The Emergence of Heraclea on the Black Sea. LC 74-620189. (Publications in Classical Studies: Vol. 14). 1975. 8.00x o.p. (ISBN 0-520-09530-8). U of Cal Pr.

Burstiner, Irving. Small Business Handbook: Comprehensive Guide to Starting & Running Your Own Business. (Illus.). 1979. text ed. 19.95 (ISBN 0-13-814202-5, Spec); pap. text ed. 10.95 (ISBN 0-13-814194-0). P-H.

Burstinger, Irving. Run Your Own Retail Store: From Raising the Money to Counting the Profits. (Illus.). 304p. 1981. 19.95 (ISBN 0-13-784017-9, Spec); pap. 12.95 (ISBN 0-13-784009-8). P-H.

Burston, W. H. James Mill on Philosophy & Education. 256p. 1973. text ed. 22.50x (ISBN 0-485-11138-1, Athlone Pr). Humanities.

Burston, W. H., ed. James Mill on Education. LC 69-11268. (Cambridge Texts & Studies in Education: No. 6). 1969. 22.95 (ISBN 0-521-07414-2). Cambridge U Pr.

Burstone, M. S. Enzyme Histochemistry & Its Application in the Study of Neoplasms. 1963. 62.00 o.s.i. (ISBN 0-12-146950-6). Acad Pr.

Burstyn, Ben. Bicycle Repair & Maintenance. LC 72-86242. (Illus.). 224p. 1974. o. p. 6.95 (ISBN 0-668-02706-1); pap. 2.95 (ISBN 0-668-02708-8). Arco.

Burstyn, Joan N. Victorian Education & the Ideal of Womanhood. (Illus.). 185p. 1980. 24.00x (ISBN 0-389-20103-0). B&N.

Bursynski, P. R., ed. To Be a Child: A Book of Photographic Essays on the Psychological Rights of the Child. 65p. 1979. 10.00 (ISBN 0-917668-03-0). Intl Schl Psych.

Bursztajn, Harold, et al. Medical Choices, Medical Chances: Decision Making for Patients, Families, & Physicians. 1981. 14.95 (ISBN 0-440-05750-7, Sey Lawr). Delacorte.

Burt, et al, eds. Viewpoints on English As a Second Language. 1977. text ed. 7.95 (ISBN 0-88345-298-7). Regents Pub.

Burt, Bruce C., compiled by. Calculators: Readings from the Arithmetic Teacher & the Mathematics Teacher. 1979. pap. 6.25 (ISBN 0-87353-144-2). NCTM.

Burt, Cyril. E.S.P. & Psychology. LC 75-16165. 179p. 1975. 19.95 (ISBN 0-470-12531-4). Halsted Pr.

--The Subnormal Mind. 1977. text ed. 14.95x o.p. (ISBN 0-19-261130-5). Oxford U Pr.

Burt, Donald X. Colors of My Days. 175p. (Orig.). 1980. pap. 3.95 (ISBN 0-8146-1198-2). Liturgical Pr.

Burt, Eugene C. Annotated Bibliography of the Visual Arts of East Africa. LC 80-7805. (Traditional Arts of Africa Ser.). 392p. 1980. 20.00x (ISBN 0-253-17225-X). Ind U Pr.

Burt, Forest D. & Want, E. Cleve. Invention & Design: Rhetorical Reader. 3rd ed. 406p. 1981. pap. text ed. 8.95 (ISBN 0-394-32557-5). Random.

Burt, John J., et al. Toward a Healthy Lifestyle: Through Elementary Education. 608p. 1980. text ed. 17.95x (ISBN 0-534-00776-7). Wadsworth Pub.

Burt, John R. From Phonology to Philology: An Outline of Descriptive & Historical Spanish Linguistics. LC 80-67212. 208p. 1980. lib. bdg. 17.50 (ISBN 0-8191-1310-7); pap. text ed. 9.50 (ISBN 0-8191-1311-5). U Pr of Amer.

Burt, McKinley, Jr. Black Inventors of America. 1969. pap. 6.85 (ISBN 0-89420-095-X, 296959). Natl Book.

Burt, Marvin R. Policy Analysis: Introduction & Applications to Health Programs. LC 74-81587. (Illus.). 136p. 1974. text ed. 18.00 (ISBN 0-87815-013-7). Info Resources.

Burt, Marvin R., jt. auth. see Sowder, Barbara J.

Burt, Olive. Sacajawea. LC 78-1572. (Visual Biography Ser.). (Illus.). (gr. 6 up). 1978. PLB 6.90 s&l (ISBN 0-531-00975-0). Watts.

Burt, Olive W. Old America Comes Alive: Our Restored Villages from Colonial Williamsburg to Dodge City. LC 65-20734. (Illus.). (gr. 5-8). 1966. PLB 7.95 o.p. (ISBN 0-381-99904-1, A57400, JD-J). John Day.

--Rescued! America's Endangered Wildlife on the Comeback Trail. LC 80-10638. (Illus.). 128p. (gr. 4-6). 1980. PLB 7.79 (ISBN 0-671-32984-7). Messner.

Burt, Richard, ed. Arms Control & Defense Postures in the Nineteen-Eighties. (Special Studies in National Security & Defense Policy Ser.). 220p. 1981. lib. bdg. 24.00x (ISBN 0-86531-162-5). Westview.

Burt, Robert A. & Wald, Michael. Standards Relating to Abuse & Neglect. (Juvenile Justice Standards Project Ser.). Date not set. softcover 7.95 (ISBN 0-88410-830-9); casebound 16.50 (ISBN 0-88410-242-4). Ballinger Pub.

--Standards Relating to Abuse & Neglect. LC 77-3279. (Juvenile Justice Standards Project Ser.). 1977. softcover 7.95 o.p. (ISBN 0-88410-764-7); 16.50, casebound o.p. (ISBN 0-88410-242-4). Ballinger Pub.

Burt, William A. A Key to the Solar Compass. 1978. pap. 8.50 (ISBN 0-686-25540-2, 512). CARBEN Survey.

Burtchaell, J. T. Catholic Theories of Biblical Inspiration, 1810 to the Present: A Review Critique. 1969. 44.50 (ISBN 0-521-07485-1). Cambridge U Pr.

Burtchaell, James T., ed. Abortion Parley. 420p. 1980. 20.00 (ISBN 0-8362-3600-9). Andrews & McMeel.

--Abortion Parley. 360p. 1980. cancelled. ACC.

Burtenshaw, D. The City in West Europe. 320p. 1981. 47.50 (ISBN 0-471-27929-3, Pub. by Wiley-Interscience). Wiley.

Burthogge, Richard. An Essay Upon Reason & the Nature of Spirits. LC 75-11204. (British Philosophers & Theologians of the 17th & 18th Centuries: Vol. 10). 1976. Repr. of 1694 ed. lib. bdg. 42.00 (ISBN 0-8240-1759-5). Garland Pub.

Burtle, James L., jt. auth. see Rolfe, Sidney E.

Burtle, Mary V. see Erulkar, Mary, pseud.

Burtness, James H., tr. see Harenberg, Werner.

Burton. All Color World of Farm Animals. (Illus.). 1980. 5.95 (ISBN 0-7064-1008-4). Mayflower Bks.

--Elementary Number Theory. rev. ed. 390p. 1980. text ed. 20.95 (ISBN 0-205-06965-7, 5669650). Allyn.

--Modeling of Differential Equations in Biology. 296p. 1980. 35.00 (ISBN 0-8247-1075-4). Dekker.

Burton, Alan. Police Telecommunications. (Illus.). 452p. 1973. 19.75 (ISBN 0-398-02251-8). C C Thomas.

Burton, Alexis L., ed. Cinematographic Techniques in Biology & Medicine. 1971. 49.00 o.p. (ISBN 0-12-147250-7). Acad Pr.

Burton, Anthony. Revolutionary Violence: The Theories. LC 77-83808. 1978. 14.00x (ISBN 0-8448-1262-5). Crane-Russak Co.

Burton, Anthony, jt. auth. see Pratt, Derek.

Burton, Arthur. Interpersonal Psychotherapy. LC 74-29379. 172p. 1975. Repr. of 1972 ed. 10.00x (ISBN 0-87668-192-5). Aronson.

--Modern Humanistic Psychotherapy. LC 67-27947. (Social & Behavioral Science Ser.). 1967. 11.95x o.p. (ISBN 0-87589-007-5). Jossey-Bass.

Burton, Arthur, ed. Encounter: Theory & Practice of Encounter Groups. LC 73-92889. (Social & Behavioral Science Ser.). 1969. 12.95x o.p. (ISBN 0-87589-044-X). Jossey-Bass.

Burton, Asa. Essays on Some of the First Principles of Metaphysicks, Ethicks, & Theology. LC 73-4839. (History of Psychology Ser). 440p. 1973. Repr. of 1824 ed. lib. bdg. 43.00x (ISBN 0-8201-1114-7). Schol Facsimiles.

Burton, D. M. Abstract & Linear Algebra. 1972. text ed. 16.95 o.p. (ISBN 0-201-00738-X). A-W.

--Introduction to Modern Abstract Algebra. 1967. 19.95 (ISBN 0-201-00722-3). A-W.

Burton, David H. American History - British Historians: A Cross-Cultural Approach to the American Experience. LC 76-8458. 328p. 1976. 17.95x (ISBN 0-88229-280-3); pap. 8.95x (ISBN 0-88229-584-5). Nelson-Hall.

--Oliver Wendell Holmes, Jr. (United States Authors Ser.). 1980. lib. bdg. 10.95 (ISBN 0-8057-7262-6). Twayne.

--Theodore Roosevelt. (World Leaders Ser). 1973. lib. bdg. 9.95 (ISBN 0-8057-3709-X). Twayne.

Burton, David H., ed. see Holmes, Oliver Wendell.

Burton, David M. Elementary Number Theory. 368p. 1976. text ed. 18.95x o.s.i. (ISBN 0-205-04814-5). Allyn.

Burton, Deirdre. Dialogue & Discourse: A Socio-Linguistic Approach to Modern Drama Dialogue & Naturally-Occurring Conversation. 220p. 1980. 30.00 (ISBN 0-7100-0560-1). Routledge & Kegan.

Burton, Dwight L., et al. Teaching English Today. 1975. text ed. 17.75 (ISBN 0-395-18616-1). HM.

Burton, E. Syntax of Moods & Tenses of New Testament Greek. 3rd ed. 240p. 1898. text ed. 11.50x (ISBN 0-567-01002-3). Attic Pr.

Burton, E. D. Galatians. LC 20-21079. (International Critical Commentary Ser.). 632p. 1920. text ed. 23.00x (ISBN 0-567-05029-7). Attic Pr.

Burton, Elizabeth. Pageant of Early Victorian England. LC 74-162746. (Encore Edition). 1971. 3.50 o.p. (ISBN 0-684-15393-9, ScribT). Scribner.

Burton, Elsie, jt. auth. see Werner, Peter H.

Burton, Elsie C. The New Physical Education for Elementary School Children. LC 76-11981. (Illus.). 1976. text ed. 16.75 (ISBN 0-395-20658-8). HM.

Burton, Frank. The Politics of Legitimacy: Struggles in a Belfast Community. (International Library of Sociology). 1978. 21.00 (ISBN 0-7100-8966-X). Routledge & Kegan.

Burton, H. & Corner, D. C. Investment & Unit Trust in Britain & America. 1970. 39.95 o.p. (ISBN 0-236-17603-X, Pub. by Paul Elek). Merrimack Bk Serv.

Burton, Hester. Beyond the Weir Bridge. LC 77-109906. (Illus.). (gr. 6 up). 1970. 4.95 o.p. (ISBN 0-690-14052-5, TYC-J). T Y Crowell.

--Kate Ryder. LC 75-8576. (Illus.). 160p. (gr. 7 up). 1975. 8.95 (ISBN 0-690-00978-X, TYC-J). T Y Crowell.

--Riders of the Storm. LC 73-4404. (Illus.). 256p. (gr. 5 up). 1973. 7.95 o.p. (ISBN 0-690-70074-1, TYC-J). T Y Crowell.

--To Ravensrigg. LC 76-54292. 1977. 8.95 (ISBN 0-690-01354-X, TYC-J). T Y Crowell.

Burton, Ian & Kates, Robert W. The Environment As Hazard. (Illus.). 1978. text ed. 12.95x (ISBN 0-19-502221-1); pap. text ed. 7.95x (ISBN 0-19-502222-X). Oxford U Pr.

Burton, Ian, jt. auth. see Whyte, Ann V.

Burton, Ian J. Out of Season. Baron, Carol, ed. 192p. 1981. 10.95 (ISBN 0-517-54334-6). Crown.

Burton, Isabel, ed. see Burton, Richard F.

Burton, J. The Collection of the Qur'an. LC 76-27899. 1977. 38.50 (ISBN 0-521-21439-4); pap. 12.95 (ISBN 0-521-29652-8). Cambridge U Pr.

Burton, J. A. Effective Warehousing. 2nd ed. LC 75-323434. (Illus.). 368p. 1973. 12.50x (ISBN 0-7121-0566-2). Intl Pubns Serv.

Burton, J. L. Aids to Undergraduate Medicine. 3rd ed. (Aids to... Ser.). (Illus.). 1980. pap. text ed. 7.50 (ISBN 0-443-02159-7). Churchill.

Burton, John. Ascanius; or, the Young Adventurer, 1746. Shugrue, Michael F., ed. (The Flowering of the Novel, 1740-1775 Ser: Vol. 17). 1974. lib. bdg. 50.00 (ISBN 0-8240-1116-3). Garland Pub.

--The Naturalist in London. LC 74-78247. (Regional Naturalist). (Illus.). 168p. 5.95 (ISBN 0-7153-6215-1). David & Charles.

Burton, John, et al. The Oxford Book of Insects. (Illus.). 216p. 1968. 19.50x (ISBN 0-19-910005-5). Oxford U Pr.

Burton, John C. A Revised Financial Reporting Model for Municipalities. (Government Auditing Ser.). 1980. pap. 6.00. Coun on Municipal.

Burton, John H. Book Hunter. Slater, Herbert J., ed. LC 79-78122. 1971. Repr. of 1895 ed. 20.00 (ISBN 0-8103-3607-3). Gale.

Burton, John W. Systems, States, Diplomacy & Rules. 256p. 1968. 28.95 (ISBN 0-521-07316-2). Cambridge U Pr.

--World Society. LC 71-176252. (Illus.). 250p. 1972. 26.50 (ISBN 0-521-08425-3); pap. 7.95x (ISBN 0-521-09694-4). Cambridge U Pr.

Burton, L. & Kuroda, K. Arts Play: Creative Activities in Art, Music, Dance & Drama for Young Children. (ps-3). 1981. write for info. spiral bdg. (ISBN 0-201-00201-9, Sch Div). A-W.

Burton, L. E., et al. Public Health & Community Medicine. 3rd ed. (Illus.). 616p. 1980. softcover 29.95 (ISBN 0-683-01236-3). Williams & Wilkins.

Burton, Leon & Hughes, William. Music Play--Learning Activities for Young Children. (gr. k-6). 1980. pap. text ed. 12.25 (ISBN 0-201-00883-1, Sch Div). A-W.

Burton, Leon, jt. auth. see University of Hawaii Music Project.

Burton, Leon, ed. see Gillett, Dorothy.

Burton, Lindy. The Family Life of Sick Children: A Study of Families Coping with Chronic Childhood Disease. 1975. 22.50x (ISBN 0-7100-8171-5); pap. 7.50 (ISBN 0-7100-8172-3). Routledge & Kegan.

Burton, Lindy, ed. Care of the Child Facing Death. 1974. 18.50 (ISBN 0-7100-7863-3). Routledge & Kegan.

Burton, Malcom K. Disorders in the Kingdom. 1981. 11.95 (ISBN 0-533-04751-X). Vantage.

Burton, Maurice. Deserts. (Illus.). 119p. (gr. 4 up). 1975. 8.50 (ISBN 0-584-62047-0). Transatlantic.

--Just Like an Animal. (Illus.). 1979. 12.50 o.p. (ISBN 0-684-15911-2, ScribT). Scribner.

--The Life of Birds. LC 77-88440. (Easy Reading Edition of Introduction to Nature Ser.). (Illus.). 1978. lib. bdg. 7.95 (ISBN 0-686-51139-5). Silver.

--The Life of Fishes. LC 77-88434. (Easy Reading Edition of Introduction to Nature Ser.). (Illus.). 1978. lib. bdg. 7.95 (ISBN 0-686-51140-9). Silver.

--The Life of Insects. LC 78-56576. (Easy Reading Edition of Introduction to Nature Ser.). (Illus.). 1979. lib. bdg. 7.95 (ISBN 0-686-51141-7). Silver.

--The Life of Reptiles & Amphibians. LC 77-88437. (Easy Reading Edition of Introduction to Nature Ser.). (Illus.). 1978. lib. bdg. 7.95 (ISBN 0-686-51145-X). Silver.

--Maurice Burton's Daily Telegraph Nature Book. LC 75-10701. (Illus.). 128p. 1975. 5.95 (ISBN 0-7153-7078-2). David & Charles.

Burton, Maurice & Burton, Robert. The Life of Meat Eaters. LC 77-88439. (Easy Reading Edition of Introduction to Nature Ser.). (Illus.). 1978. lib. bdg. 7.95 (ISBN 0-686-51142-5). Silver.

Burton, Philip. You, My Brother. 1973. 10.95 o.p. (ISBN 0-394-48478-9). Random.

Burton, Philip W. Advertising Copywriting. 4th ed. LC 77-81533. (Advertising Ser.). 1978. text ed. 20.95 (ISBN 0-88244-159-0). Grid Pub.

Burton, R. W. B. The Chorus in Sopocles Tragedies. 312p. 1980. 48.00x (ISBN 0-19-814374-5). Oxford U Pr.

Burton, Rebecca. The Loving Season. 1979. pap. 2.25 (ISBN 0-505-51413-3). Tower Bks.

Burton, Richard, ed. The Kama Sutra of Vatsyayana. Arbuthnot, F. F., tr. 1963. 8.50 (ISBN 0-04-891008-2). Allen Unwin.

Burton, Richard, tr. The Perfumed Garden. 1978. pap. 2.25 o.p. (ISBN 0-425-03657-X, Medallion). Berkley Pub.

Burton, Richard F. The Land of Midian, 2 vols. (Arabia Past & Present Ser.: No. 11). (Illus.). 1981. Set. 75.00 (ISBN 0-900891-55-6). Oleander Pr.

--Nile Basin. 2nd ed. LC 65-23403. 1967. Repr. of 1864 ed. 19.50 (ISBN 0-306-70926-0). Da Capo.

--Personal Narrative of a Pilgrimage to Al-Madinah & Meccah, 2 Vols. Burton, Isabel, ed. Set. 21.00 (ISBN 0-8446-1781-4). Peter Smith.

--Wit & Wisdom from West Africa: A Book of Proverbial Philosophy, Idioms, Enigmas, & Laconisms. LC 77-79952. 1969. Repr. of 1865 ed. 16.00x (ISBN 0-8196-0243-4). Biblo.

Burton, Sir Richard. The Look of the West, 1860. LC 63-17030. (Illus.). 1963. pap. 3.75 (ISBN 0-8032-5029-0, BB 148, Bison). U of Nebr Pr.

Burton, Rita. Reflections of My Spirit. LC 76-24042. 1977. pap. 2.95 o.p. (ISBN 0-89221-024-9). New Leaf.

Burton, Robert. The Anatomy of Melancholy. Jackson, Holbrook, ed. (Rowman & Littlefield University Library). 547p. 1972. 23.50x (ISBN 0-87471-672-1). Rowman.

--The Carnivores of Europe. 1979. 38.00 (ISBN 0-7134-0690-9, Pub. by Batsford England). David & Charles.

--The Cat Family. LC 78-64654. (Fact Finders Ser.). (Illus.). 1979. lib. bdg. 3.96 (ISBN 0-686-51125-5). Silver.

--The Language of Smell. (Illus.). 1976. 12.95 (ISBN 0-7100-8429-3). Routledge & Kegan.

--Seals. LC 79-13701. (New Biology Ser.). (Illus.). (gr. 4 up). 1980. 7.95 (ISBN 0-07-009285-0). McGraw.

Burton, Robert, jt. auth. see Burton, Maurice.

Burton, Robert E., ed. Travel in Oceania, Australia & New Zealand: A Guide to Information Sources. LC 80-15333. (Geography & Travel Information Guide Ser.: Vol. 2). 150p. 1980. 30.00 (ISBN 0-8103-1421-5). Gale.

Burton, Robert H. & Brunhild, Gordon. Macroeconomic Theory. (Illus.). 544p. 1973. ref. ed. 18.95x (ISBN 0-13-542639-1). P-H.

Burton, T. A., ed. Mathematical Biology-a Conference on Theoretical Aspects of Molecular Science: Proceedings of a Conference Held at Southern Illinois University at Carbondale, May 27-28, 1980. (Illus.). 241p. 1981. 30.00 (ISBN 0-08-026348-8). Pergamon.

Burton, Theodore E. The Constitution of the United States. 1923. 14.50x (ISBN 0-685-89744-3). Elliots Bks.

Burton, Thomas, tr. see Spiteris, Tony P.

Burton, Thomas G., ed. Tom Ashley, Sam McGee, Bukka White: Tennessee Traditional Singers. LC 79-19655. 1981. 14.50 (ISBN 0-87049-260-8). U of Tenn Pr.

Burton, Thomas L. & Cherry, G. E. Social Research Techniques for Planners. (Illus.). 1970. text ed. 15.95x (ISBN 0-04-711002-3). Allen Unwin.

Burton, Wayne. Alaska's Agriculture: An Analysis of Developmental Problems. LC 79-175624. (Institute of Social & Economic Research Ser.: No. 30). 276p. 1971. pap. 5.00 (ISBN 0-295-95198-2). U of Wash Pr.

Burton, William C. & DeCosta, Steven E. The Legal Thesaurus. LC 80-83803. 1980. 35.00 (ISBN 0-02-691000-4). Free Pr.

Burton, William H., et al. Developmental Reading Text Workbooks. Incl. Ready to Read. (readiness). text ed. 1.60 o.p. (ISBN 0-672-70588-5); Play Time. (primer). text ed. o.p. (ISBN 0-672-71285-7); Up & Away. (gr. 1). text ed. 2.00 (ISBN 0-672-71287-3); Animal Parade. (gr. 2). text ed. 2.00 (ISBN 0-672-71289-X); Picnic Basket. (gr. 3). text ed. 2.00 (ISBN 0-672-71291-1); Blazing New Trails. (gr. 6). text ed. 2.24 (ISBN 0-672-71293-8); Flying High. (gr. 5). text ed. 2.24 (ISBN 0-672-71295-4); Shooting Stars. (gr. 6). text ed. 2.24 (ISBN 0-672-71297-0). (readiness-6). 1975. tchrs' ed. 2.40 ea. Bobbs.

Burton, Wilma. Living Without Fear. 1981. pap. 3.95 (ISBN 0-89107-184-9). Good News.

--Sidewalk Psalms... & Some from Country Lanes. LC 79-92015. 119p. 1980. 6.95 (ISBN 0-89107-165-2). Good News.

Burton-Bradley, B. G., jt. auth. see Billig, O.

Burtschi, Mary, ed. see Hall, James.

Burtt, E. A. In Search of Philosophic Understanding. LC 65-26869. 350p. 1980. lib. bdg. 18.50 (ISBN 0-915145-06-5); pap. text ed. 6.95 (ISBN 0-915145-07-3). Hackett Pub.

Burtt, E. T. & Pringle, A. The Senses of Animals. LC 73-77794. (Wykeham Science Ser.: No. 26). 1974. 9.95x (ISBN 0-8448-1153-X). Crane-Russak Co.

Burtt, Edward H., Jr., ed. see Animal Behavior Society Symposium, 1977.

Burtt, Edwin A. Metaphysical Foundations of Modern Physical Science. 2nd ed. (International Library of Psychology, Philosophy & Scientific Method). 1967. Repr. of 1932 ed. text ed. 27.50x (ISBN 0-7100-3032-0); pap. text ed. 5.95x (ISBN 0-391-01633-4). Humanities.

Burtt, George. Stop Crying at Your Own Movies: How to Solve Personal Problems & Open Your Life to Its Full Potential Using the Vector Method. LC 75-4770. 206p. 1975. 12.95 (ISBN 0-911012-83-4). Nelson-Hall.

Burtt, Harold E. Psychology of Birds. 1967. 5.95 o.s.i. (ISBN 0-02-518550-0). Macmillan.

Burum, Linda. The Junk Food Alternative. LC 80-17799. (Illus.). 168p. (Orig.). 1980. pap. 5.95 (ISBN 0-89286-163-0). One Hund One Prods.

Burvill, G. H. Agriculture in Western Australia. 397p. 1980. 21.00x (ISBN 0-85564-154-1, Pub. by Univ Western Australia). Intl Schol Bk Serv.

Burwash, Peter & Tullius, John. Tennis for Life. 1981. 14.95 (ISBN 0-8129-0952-6). Times Bks.

Burwick, Frederick, ed. see De Quincey, Thomas.

Bury, Ange H. Blaze De see Blaze De Bury, Ange H.

Bury, Charles. Telephone Techniques That Sell. 1980. pap. 4.95 (ISBN 0-446-97453-6). Warner Bks.

Bury, George W. Pan-Islam. LC 80-1938. 1981. Repr. of 1919 ed. 30.00 (ISBN 0-404-18956-3). AMS Pr.

Bury, J. B. History of the Later Roman Empire from the Death of Theodosius Eight to the Death of Justinian, 2 vols. 11.00 ea. (ISBN 0-8446-1785-7). Peter Smith.

Bury, J. P. Gambetta & the National Defense. LC 70-80531. 1970. Repr. of 1936 ed. 17.50 (ISBN 0-86527-077-5). Fertig.

Buryn, Ed. Vagabonding in the U S A. LC 80-10966. (Illus.). 448p. 1980. pap. 9.95 (ISBN 0-915904-50-0). And-Or Pr.

Burzynski, Norbert J. see Melnick, Michael.

Busbecq, Ogier G. De. Turkish Letters of Ogier Ghiselin De Busbecq. Forster, Edward S., tr. 1927. 22.50x o.p. (ISBN 0-19-821473-1). Oxford U Pr.

Busbee, Jim. Riding Tough. 1981. pap. price not set (Leisure Bks). Nordon Pubns.

Busbee, Shirlee. Lady Vixen. 544p. 1979. pap. 2.75 (ISBN 0-380-75382-0, 75382). Avon.

Busby, F. M. All These Earths. 1978. pap. 1.75 o.p. (ISBN 0-425-03902-1, Medallion). Berkley Pub.

--Demu Trilogy. (gr. 10-12). 1980. pap. 3.50 (ISBN 0-671-43288-5). PB.

--The Long View: The Final Volume in the Saga of Rissa. LC 76-28472. 1976. 7.95 o.p. (ISBN 0-399-11875-6, Dist. by Putnam). Berkley Pub.

Busby, Horace W. Practical Sermons of Persuasive Power. pap. 3.50 (ISBN 0-89315-206-4). Lambert Bk.

Busby, Keith. Gauvain in Old French Literature. (Degre Second Ser.: No. 2). 425p. 1980. pap. text ed. 48.50x (ISBN 90-6203-831-X). Humanities.

Busby, Roy. British Music Hall. (Illus.). 1977. 28.00 o.p. (ISBN 0-236-40053-3, Pub. by Paul Elek). Merrimack Bk Serv.

Busby, Thomas. General History of Music from the Earliest Times, 2 Vols. LC 68-21091. (Music Ser). 1968. Repr. of 1819 ed. 55.00 (ISBN 0-306-71063-3). Da Capo.

--A Grammar of Music. LC 76-20711. (Music Reprint Ser). 1976. Repr. of 1818 ed. lib. bdg. 35.00 (ISBN 0-306-70789-6). Da Capo.

--A Musical Manual, or Technical Directory. LC 76-20708. (Music Reprint Ser). 1976. Repr. of 1828 ed. lib. bdg. 22.50 (ISBN 0-306-70788-8). Da Capo.

Buscaglia, Leo. Love. 1978. pap. 2.50 o.p. (ISBN 0-449-23452-5, Crest). Fawcett.

Buscaglia, Loe. Love. 208p. 1981. pap. 2.50 (ISBN 0-449-23452-5, Crest). Fawcett.

Busch & Wilkie Bros. Foundation. Fundamentals of Dimensional Metrology. LC 64-12593. 428p. 1966. 10.80 (ISBN 0-8273-0193-6); instructor's guide 1.60 (ISBN 0-8273-0197-9). Delmar.

Busch, Briton C. Britain & the Persian Gulf, 1894-1914. 1967. 20.00x (ISBN 0-520-00200-8). U of Cal Pr.

--Britain, India, & the Arabs, 1914-1921. LC 71-132421. 1971. 25.75x (ISBN 0-520-01821-4). U of Cal Pr.

--Hardinge of Penshurst: A Study in the Old Diplomacy. (British Biography Ser.: Vol. 1). (Illus.). 381p. 1980. 19.50 (ISBN 0-208-01830-1). Shoe String.

Busch, Briton C., ed. Master of Desolation: The Reminiscences of Capt. Joseph J. Fuller, Vol. 9. (American Maritime Library). 349p. 1980. 24.00 (ISBN 0-913372-21-8). Mystic Seaport.

Busch, Daryle H. Inorganic Syntheses, Vol. 20. (Inorganic Synthesis Ser.). 1980. 29.95 (ISBN 0-471-07715-1, Pub. by Wiley-Interscience). Wiley.

Busch, Daryle H., jt. auth. see Layde, Durwood C.

Busch, Daryle H., et al. Chemistry. 2nd ed. 1978. text ed. 21.95 (ISBN 0-205-05704-7); instr's manual (ISBN 0-205-05705-5). Allyn.

Busch, Frederick. The Mutual Friend. LC 77-11793. 1978. 8.95 o.s.i. (ISBN 0-06-010527-5, HarpT). Har-Row.

Busch, G. & Schade, D. Lectures on Solid State Physics. 1976. text ed. 64.00 (ISBN 0-08-016894-9); pap. text ed. 25.00 (ISBN 0-08-021653-6). Pergamon.

Busch, H. & Lohse, B. Baroque Sculpture. 1965. 14.95 o.s.i. (ISBN 0-02-518760-0). Macmillan.

--Pre-Romanesque Art. 1966. 14.95 o.s.i. (ISBN 0-686-66485-X). Macmillan.

Busch, H., ed. Mikrofiltration und andere Transfusions-Probleme in der Intensivmedizin. (Beitraege zu Infusionstherapie und klinische Ernaehrung: Band 3). (Illus.). 1979. pap. 12.00 (ISBN 3-8055-3057-9). S Karger.

Busch, H. Ted & Landeck, Terry. The Making of a Television Commercial. LC 80-23192. (Illus.). 228p. 1981. 10.95 (ISBN 0-02-518830-5). Macmillan.

Busch, Harris, ed. The Cell Nucleus: Nuclear Particles, Vol. 8. 1981. write for info. (ISBN 0-12-147608-1). Acad Pr.

Busch, Harris, et al, eds. Methods in Cancer Research. Incl. Vol. 1. 1967. 65.00, by subscription 53.00 (ISBN 0-12-147661-8); Vol. 2. 1967. 69.00, by subscription 56.00 (ISBN 0-12-147662-6); Vol. 3. 1967. 69.00, by subscription 56.00 (ISBN 0-12-147663-4); Vol. 4. 1968. 69.00, by subscription 56.00 (ISBN 0-12-147664-2); Vol. 5. 1970. 55.50, by subscription 45.00 (ISBN 0-12-147665-0); Vol. 6. 1971. 55.50, by subscription 45.00 (ISBN 0-12-147666-9); Vol. 7. 1973. 49.00, by subscription 40.00 (ISBN 0-12-147667-7); Vol. 8. 1973. 49.00, by subscription 40.00 (ISBN 0-12-147668-5); Vol. 9. 1973. 49.00, by subscription 40.00 (ISBN 0-12-147669-3); Vol. 10. 1974. 49.00, by subscription 40.00 (ISBN 0-12-147670-7); Vol. 11. 1975. 49.00, by subscription 40.00 (ISBN 0-12-147671-5); Vol. 12. 1976. 49.00, by subscription 40.00 (ISBN 0-12-147672-3); Vol. 13. 1976. 47.00, by subscription 39.00 (ISBN 0-12-147673-1). Acad Pr.

Busch, Lawrence, ed. Science & Agricultural Development. 220p. 1981. text ed. 28.00 (ISBN 0-86598-022-5). Allanheld.

Busch, Moritz. Travels Between the Hudson & the Mississippi, 1851-1952. Binger, Norman H., tr. LC 74-147857. 1971. 15.00x (ISBN 0-8131-1251-6). U Pr of Ky.

Busch, Niven. No Place for a Hero. (Illus.). 128p. Date not set. pap. 3.95 (ISBN 0-89395-027-0). Cal Living Bks.

Busch, Phillis S. Wildflowers & the Stories Behind Their Names. LC 73-1351. (Illus.). (gr. 3up). 1977. 10.00 (ISBN 0-684-14820-X, ScribT). Scribner.

Busch, Phyllis. Cactus in the Desert. LC 78-4771. (A Let's-Read-&-Find-Out Science Bk.). (Illus.). (gr. k-3). 1979. 7.95 (ISBN 0-690-00292-0, TYC-J); PLB 7.89 (ISBN 0-690-01336-1). T Y Crowell.

Busch, Phyllis S. A Walk in the Snow. (Illus.). 40p. (gr. k-3). 1971. 8.95 (ISBN 0-397-31233-4). Lippincott.

--What About VD? LC 75-45147. 128p. (gr. 7 up). 1976. 6.95 (ISBN 0-685-62043-3, Four Winds). Schol Bk Serv.

Busch, Robert L., jt. auth. see Hardin, Veralee.

Buschman, R. G., jt. auth. see Srivastava, H. M.

Buschow, Rosemarie. The Prince & I. LC 80-938. 264p. 1981. 12.95 (ISBN 0-385-17111-0). Doubleday.

Buscombe, et al. Film: Historical-Theoretical Speculations. Lawton, Ben & Staiger, Janet, eds. (Film Studies Annual, 1977: Pt. 2). (Orig.). 1977. pap. 6.00 (ISBN 0-913178-53-5). Redgrave Pub Co.

Buscombe, Ed, ed. & intro. by. MGM. (BFI Dossiers Ser.: No. 1). (Orig.). 1980. pap. 6.00 (ISBN 0-918432-33-2). NY Zoetrope.

Buscombe, Edward. Making "Legend of the Werewolf". (BFI Ser.). (Orig.). 1977. pap. 4.50 o.p. (ISBN 0-85170-057-8). NY Zoetrope.

Buscombe, Edward, ed. Football on Television. (BFI Television Monograph: No. 4). (Illus., Orig.). 1977. pap. 3.25 o.p. (ISBN 0-85170-046-2). NY Zoetrope.

Busemann, Herbert. Geometry of Geodesics. (Pure and Applied Mathematics: Vol. 6). 1955. 41.00 (ISBN 0-12-148350-9). Acad Pr.

Busemann, Herbert & Kelly, Paul J. Projective Geometry & Projective Metrics. (Pure and Applied Mathematics Ser.: Vol. 3). 1953. 36.50 o.s.i. (ISBN 0-12-148356-8). Acad Pr.

Busenbark, Robert, jt. auth. see Bates, Henry.

Busenkell, Richard L. BMW. (Modern Automobile Ser.). (Illus.). Date not set. 12.95 (ISBN 0-393-01342-1). Norton.

Busev, A. I. Analytical Chemistry of Molybdenum. (Analytical Chemistry of the Elements Ser.). 1971. 23.95 o.p. (ISBN 0-470-12601-9). Halsted Pr.

--A Handbook of the Analytical Chemistry of Rare Elements. LC 75-104379. 1972. 34.95 (ISBN 0-470-12620-5). Halsted Pr.

Busfield, Joan & Paddon, M. Thinking About Children. LC 76-22986. (Illus.). 1977. 29.95 (ISBN 0-521-21402-5). Cambridge U Pr.

Busfield, Roger M., ed. Theatre Arts Publications in the U. S., 1953-57. 188p. 1964. 5.00, ATA members 3.00 (ISBN 0-686-05077-0). Am Theatre Assoc.

Bush, B. M. Veterinary Laboratory Manual. 1975. pap. text ed. 27.50x (ISBN 0-433-04910-3). Intl Ideas.

Bush, B. M., jt. ed. see Roberts, A.

Bush, Barbara. I Can't Stand Cindy, Lord. 1976. 4.95 o.p. (ISBN 0-310-22150-1). Zondervan.

--A Woman's Workshop on Motherhood. (Women's Workshop Ser.). 144p. 1981. pap. 3.95 (ISBN 0-310-43031-3, 12013P). Zondervan.

Bush, Catharine S. Workshops for Parents & Teachers. (Language Remediation & Expansion Ser.). 1981. spiral 15.00 (ISBN 0-88450-738-6). Communication Skill.

Bush, Christine. Nurse at Deer Hollow. (YA) 1977. 5.50 o.p. (ISBN 0-685-81424-6, Avalon). Bouregy.

Bush, Christopher. Case of the Deadly Diamonds. 1969. 8.95 (ISBN 0-02-519280-9). Macmillan.

Bush, Clifford L. & Andrews, Robert C. Dictionary of Reading & Learning Disabilities. LC 79-57293. 179p. 1978. pap. 8.00x (ISBN 0-87424-153-7). Western Psych.

Bush, Douglas. English Literature in the Earlier Seventeenth Century: 1600-1660. 2nd ed. (Oxford History of English Literature Ser.). 1962. 37.50x (ISBN 0-19-812202-0). Oxford U Pr.

--Jane Austen. LC 73-18765. 256p. 1975. 10.95 (ISBN 0-02-519600-6, 51960). Macmillan.

--Jane Austen. 256p. 1975. pap. 6.95 o.s.i. (ISBN 0-02-049250-2, Collier). Macmillan.

--John Keats. 1967. pap. 1.95 o.s.i. (ISBN 0-02-049260-X, Collier). Macmillan.

--Matthew Arnold. (Masters of World Literature Ser.). 1971. 10.95 (ISBN 0-02-519630-8). Macmillan.

--Matthew Arnold. 1971. pap. 2.95 o.s.i. (ISBN 0-02-049280-4, Collier). Macmillan.

--Renaissance & English Humanism. LC 40-11006. 1939. pap. 3.50 (ISBN 0-8020-6008-0). U of Toronto Pr.

Bush, Frankie. A Time to Sing. 1978. pap. 2.95 (ISBN 0-89728-007-5). Omega Pubns OR.

Bush, George & Crane, Philip. Great Issues 79-80: A Forum on Important Questions Facing the American Public, Vol. 11. 1980. 14.95 (ISBN 0-916624-32-3). TSU Pr.

Bush, Grace & Young, John. The Mathematics of Business. LC 73-93624. (Illus.). 384p. 1974. pap. text ed. 11.95 (ISBN 0-574-19105-4, 13-2105); instr's guide avail. (ISBN 0-574-19106-2, 13-2106). SRA.

Bush, Grace A., jt. auth. see Young, John E.

Bush, Graham. Local Government & Politics in New Zealand. 200p. 1980. text ed. 22.95x (ISBN 0-86861-074-7, 2500); pap. text ed. 14.95x (ISBN 0-86861-082-8, 2501). Allen Unwin.

Bush, I. E., et al. The Chromatography of Steroids. 1961. 38.00 (ISBN 0-08-009544-5). Pergamon.

Bush, Jim & Weiskopf, Donald C. Dynamic Track & Field. 1978. text ed. 19.95 (ISBN 0-205-06004-8). Allyn.

Bush, Keith, tr. see Wadekin, Karl-Eugen.

Bush, Loren S. & McLaughlin, James. Introduction to Fire Science. Gruber, Harvey, ed. (Fire Science Ser.). 1970. text ed. 13.95x (ISBN 0-02-473900-6). Macmillan.

Bush, M. L. Renaissance, Reformation & the Outer World, 1450-1660. (History of Europe Ser.). 1967. text ed. 6.50x o.p. (ISBN 0-7137-0452-7). Humanities.

Bush, Martin H. Revolutionary Enigma: A Re-Appraisal of General Philip Schuyler of New York. LC 78-8329. (Empire State Historical Publications Ser). 1969. 12.95 (ISBN 0-8046-8080-9). Friedman.

Bush, Mary B. Black Secretary's Horror. 1981. 8.95 (ISBN 0-533-04698-X). Vantage.

Bush, Richard C. Religion in China. Swearer, Donald K., ed. (Major World Religion Ser.). pap. 3.95 (ISBN 0-913592-98-6). Argus Comm.

Bush, Richard C., jt. ed. see Townsend, James R.

Bush, Richardc., jt. ed. see Oxnam, Robert B.

Bush, Russ & Nettles, Tom. Baptists & the Bible. 1980. 10.95 (ISBN 0-8024-0466-9). Moody.

Bush, T., et al. Advances in School Management. 1980. text ed. 23.65 (ISBN 0-06-318167-3, IntlDept); pap. text ed. 13.10 (ISBN 0-06-318168-1). Har-Row.

Bush, Virginia. The Colossal Sculpture of the Cinquecento. LC 75-23785. (Outstanding Dissertations in the Fine Arts - 16th Century). (Illus.). 1976. lib. bdg. 48.00 (ISBN 0-8240-1981-4). Garland Pub.

Bush, Wilma J. & Giles, Marian T. Aids to Psycholinguistic Teaching. 2nd ed. (Special Education Ser.). 1977. text ed. 17.95 (ISBN 0-675-08525-X). Merrill.

Bush, Wilma J. & Waugh, Kenneth. Diagnosing Learning Disabilities. (Illus.). 300p. 1976. text ed. 16.95 (ISBN 0-675-08612-4). Merrill.

Busha, Charles H. Freedom Versus Suppression & Censorship. LC 72-91672. (Research Studies in Library Science: No. 8). 250p. 1972. lib. bdg. 15.00x (ISBN 0-87287-057-X). Libs Unl.

Busha, Charles H., ed. An Intellectual Freedom Primer. LC 77-7887. 1977. 20.00x (ISBN 0-87287-172-X). Libs Unl.

--A Library Science Research Reader & Bibliographic Guide. 210p. 1981. lib. bdg. 18.50 (ISBN 0-87287-237-8). Libs Unl.

Busha, Charles H. & Harter, Stephen P., eds. Research Methods in Librarianship: Techniques & Interpretation. LC 79-8864. (Library & Information Science Ser.). 432p. 1980. tchrs' ed. 19.50 (ISBN 0-12-147550-6). Acad Pr.

Bush-Brown, Albert. Louis Sullivan. LC 60-13306. (Masters of World Architecture Ser). 1960. 7.95 o.p. (ISBN 0-8076-0129-2); pap. 3.95 o.p. (ISBN 0-8076-0227-2). Braziller.

Bushell, S. W. Oriental Ceramic Art. (Illus.). 432p. 1980. 35.00 (ISBN 0-517-52581-X). Crown.

Bushell, Stephen W. Descryston of Chinese Poetry & Porcelain. (Oxford in Asia Studies in Ceramics). 1978. 24.95x (ISBN 0-19-580372-8). Oxford U Pr.

Bushkovitch, Paul. The Merchants of Moscow, Fifteen Eighty to Sixteen Fifty. LC 79-14491. (Illus.). 1980. 21.00 (ISBN 0-521-22589-2). Cambridge U Pr.

Bushman, Claudia, ed. see Bushman, Claudia L., et al.

Bushman, Claudia L. Harriet Hanson Robinson & Her Family: A Chronicle of Nineteenth-Century New England Life. LC 80-54470. 320p. 1981. 16.50 (ISBN 0-87451-193-3). U Pr of New Eng.

Bushman, Claudia L., et al. Mormon Sisters: Women in Early Utah. Bushman, Claudia, ed. LC 76-53854. (Illus.). 320p. 1980. pap. 5.95 (ISBN 0-918012-01-5). Olympus Pub Co.

Bushman, John H. & Jones, Sandra. Teaching English & the Humanities Through Thematic Units. LC 79-52998. 1979. pap. text ed. 4.50x (ISBN 0-87543-148-8). Lucas.

Bushman, Richard L. From Puritan to Yankee: Character & the Social Order in Connecticut, 1690-1765. 352p. 1980. pap. 4.95 (ISBN 0-674-32551-6). Harvard U Pr.

Bushman, Tanisse, ed. see Leonard, Anne & Terrell, John.

Bushnell, Eleanore & Driggs, Don W. The Nevada Constitution: Origin & Growth. 5th ed. LC 80-23682. (History & Political Science Ser.: No. 8). x, 221p. 1980. pap. text ed. 5.25x (ISBN 0-87417-060-5). U of Nev Pr.

Bushnell, Horace. Views of Christian Nurture & Subjects Related Thereto. LC 74-23297. 260p. 1975. Repr. of 1847 ed. lib. bdg. 26.00x (ISBN 0-8201-1147-3). Schol Facsimiles.

Bushnell, O. A. The Water of Kane. LC 80-5463. 472p. 1980. 12.95 (ISBN 0-8248-0714-6). U Pr of Hawaii.

Bushong, Ann B. A Guide to the Lectionary. 1978. pap. 5.95 (ISBN 0-8164-2156-0). Crossroad NY.

Bushong, Stewart. Radiologic Science for Technologists: Physics, Biology & Protection. LC 74-20847. 1975. 17.95 o.p. (ISBN 0-8016-0915-1). Mosby.

--Radiologic Science Workbook & Laboratory Manual. 2nd ed. (Illus.). 260p. 1980. pap. text ed. 11.95 (ISBN 0-8016-0927-5). Mosby.
Bushong, Stewart C. Radiologic Science for Technologists: Physics, Biology & Protection. 2nd ed. LC 80-19. (Illus.). 1980. 24.95 (ISBN 0-8016-0928-3). Mosby.
Bushrui. Gibran of Lebanon. 15.00x (ISBN 0-685-89877-6). Intl Bk Ctr.
Bushrui, S. B., ed. A Centenary Tribute to John Millington Synge 1871-1909: Sunshine & the Moon's Delight. 1972-1978. pap. text ed. 6.00x (ISBN 0-391-00854-4). Humanities.
Busi, Frederick. The Transformations of Godot. LC 79-4002. 160p. 1980. 12.00x (ISBN 0-8131-1392-X). U Pr of Ky.
Business Communication Co. Catalysis, C-023: New Directions. 1981. 800.00 (ISBN 0-89336-271-9). BCC.
Business Communications, ed. Analytical Instrumentation: Growth Markets, G-052. 1980. 750.00 (ISBN 0-89336-218-2). BCC.
--Biomass: How? What? Where, E-039. 1980. 850.00 (ISBN 0-89336-215-8). BCC.
--Distributed Processing, G-051. 1980. 700.00 (ISBN 0-89336-217-4). BCC.
--Energy Conservation & Home Improvements, E-024. 1980. cancelled (ISBN 0-89336-214-X, E-024). BCC.
--Fermentation Products: Processes & New Developments, C-018. 1980. 800.00 (ISBN 0-89336-222-0). BCC.
--Industrial Coatings: New Trends, Markets, C-017. 1979. 650.00 (ISBN 0-89336-221-2). BCC.
--Inks & Printing Chemicals: New Developments, C-025. 1981. 800.00 (ISBN 0-89336-212-3). BCC. Postponed.
--Low Energy & Radiation Cures, C-026. 1981. 800.00 (ISBN 0-89336-213-1, C-026). BCC. Postponed.
--New Consumer Product Electronics: Growth Trends, G-040r. 1980. 725.00 (ISBN 0-89336-224-7). BCC.
--New Directions in Robots for Manufacturing, G-053. 1979. 750.00 (ISBN 0-89336-219-0). BCC.
--New Markets for Small Business Computers, G-055. 1980. 750.00 (ISBN 0-89336-220-4, G-055). BCC.
--Polishes & Waxes: Shifts & Changes, C-024. 1981. 850.00 (ISBN 0-89336-211-5). BCC.
--Roadway Maintenance, E-027. 1981. 725.00 (ISBN 0-89336-224-7). BCC.
--Word Processing Markets, Where? Why?, G-050. 1979. 650.00 (ISBN 0-89336-216-6). BCC.
Business Communications Co. Advanced Metal Working Technologies, GB-052. 1979. 750.00 (ISBN 0-89336-230-1). BCC.
--Convenience Foods & Microwave, GA-044: Directions. 1980. 725.00 (ISBN 0-89336-227-1). BCC.
--Direct Marketing Business, GB-060: New Perspectives. 1980. cancelled (ISBN 0-89336-276-X). BCC.
--Future for Coal As a Fuel & Chemical, E-004. 1980. 825.00 (ISBN 0-89336-273-5). BCC.
--The Microwave Industry, G-020: Trends, Developments. 1981. 825.00 (ISBN 0-89336-275-1). BCC.
--Plastics Vs. Other Pipes, P-043R. 1980. 750.00 (ISBN 0-89336-270-0). BCC.
--Substitutes for Asbestos, Gb-061: What-Who-How Much. 1980. 850.00 (ISBN 0-89336-277-8). BCC.
--Sulfur Specialty Chemicals, C-031. 1981. 850.00 (ISBN 0-89336-272-7). BCC.
--Tapping Solar Markets in Developing Countries, E-041. 1981. 800.00 (ISBN 0-89336-274-3). BCC.
Business Communications Co., ed. Bulk Vitamins & Their Major Markets. 1980. 975.00 (ISBN 0-89336-235-2, GA-036R). BCC.
--Foods Under Glass, GA-046. 1980. 675.00 (ISBN 0-89336-229-8). BCC.
--Home Do-It Yourself Market. 1980. 675.00 (ISBN 0-89336-232-8, GB-054). BCC.
--New Trends in Food Retailing, GA-045. 1980. 825.00 (ISBN 0-89336-228-X). BCC.
--Retail Fast Foods, GA-038: Business Opportunities. 1980. 675.00 (ISBN 0-89336-236-0). BCC.
--Special Beverage Study. 1979. 1000.00 (ISBN 0-89336-237-9, MR-1). BCC.
--Specialty Agricultural Chemicals, GA-035r. 1980. 750.00 (ISBN 0-89336-225-5). BCC.
--Water Purification Processes, GB-053: A Technical Market Analysis. 1979. 750.00 (ISBN 0-89336-231-X). BCC.
Business Communications Co., Inc. The Changing Gas Industry: Good & Bad-E-019. 1976. 450.00 o.p. (ISBN 0-89336-018-X). BCC.
Business Communications Co. Staff. Synfuels: Equipment, Technology, Supplies, Money, People, E-042. 1981. 875.00 (ISBN 0-89336-281-6). BCC.
--Total Energy Systems, E-021, E-021. 1981. 875.00 (ISBN 0-89336-282-4). BCC.
Business Communications Staff. Alternate Energy Sources, E-007: A Study. rev. ed. 1977. 525.00 o.p. (ISBN 0-89336-009-0). BCC.
--Energy Conservation & Home Improvement, E-024. 1977. 525.00 o.p. (ISBN 0-89336-021-X). BCC.
Business Systems Research Group. The Pharmacy Computer Handbook. 141p. 1980. 29.95 (ISBN 0-9603584-1-2). Busn Systems Res.
--Small Business Computer Evaluation Program. 1978. ring bdg. 29.95x (ISBN 0-9603584-0-4). Busn Systems Res.
Business Traveler's Inc. The Business Traveler's Survival Guides. Incl. The Business Traveler's Survival Guide to New York. 9.95 (ISBN 0-531-09940-7); The Business Traveler's Survival Guide to Atlanta. 8.95 (ISBN 0-531-09941-5). (Illus.). 1981. Watts.
Business Week. The Decline of U. S. Power: & What We Can Do About It. 1980. 9.95 (ISBN 0-395-29248-4). HM.
Busing, ed. Intermolecular Forces & Packing in Crystals. pap. 5.00 (ISBN 0-686-60377-X). Polycrystal Bk Serv.
Busk, Hans. The Navies of the World: Their Present State & Future Capabilities. LC 73-82475. (Illus.). 440p. 1973. Repr. of 1859 ed. text ed. 11.00 o.s.i. (ISBN 0-87021-853-0). Naval Inst Pr.
Buske, Dorothea. The Last Romantic. LC 78-3966. 1979. 8.95 (ISBN 0-312-47135-1). St Martin.
Buskin, David. Outdoor Games. (Illus.). (gr. k-4). 1966. PLB 7.95 (ISBN 0-87460-090-1). Lion.
Buskin, Judith, jt. auth. see Singer, Laura J.
Buskin, Martin. Parent Power. 1977. pap. 1.95 o.s.i. (ISBN 0-346-12254-6). Cornerstone.
Buskirk, E. R., jt. ed. see Johnson, Warren R.
Buskirk, Richard. Cases & Readings in Marketing. LC 71-118233. 1976. text ed. 6.20 o.p. (ISBN 0-913310-47-6). Par Inc.
Buskirk, Richard H. Handbook of Management Tactics: Aggressive Strategies for Getting Things Done Your Way! LC 77-70138. (Orig.). 1978. pap. 4.95 (ISBN 0-8015-3489-5, Hawthorn). Dutton.
--Handbook of Managerial Tactics. LC 76-991. 1976. 12.95 (ISBN 0-8436-0745-9). CBI Pub.
--Modern Management & Machiavelli. LC 74-11194. 291p. 1974. 11.95 (ISBN 0-8436-0734-3). CBI Pub.
--Principles of Marketing. LC 74-29144. 1975. text ed. 17.45 (ISBN 0-913310-46-8). Par Inc.
--Your Career: How to Plan It-Manage It-Change It. 2nd ed. LC 80-15509. 168p. 1980. pap. 9.95 (ISBN 0-8436-0790-4). CBI Pub.
Buskirk, Richard H., jt. auth. see Stanton, William J.
Buskirk, Richard H., et al. Concepts of Business. LC 78-177981. text ed. 16.05 (ISBN 0-913310-45-X). Par Inc.
Buskirk, Steve. Mount McKinley: The Story Behind the Scenery. DenDooven, Gweneth R., ed. LC 78-57540. (Illus.). 1978. lib. bdg. 7.95 (ISBN 0-916122-52-2); pap. 3.50 (ISBN 0-916122-23-9). K C Pubns.
Buskirk, William R. Van see Fruchiger, Fritz & Van Buskirk, William R.
Busnar, Gene. It's Rock 'n' Roll. LC 79-10927. (Illus.). 256p. (gr. 7 up). 1979. PLB 9.29 (ISBN 0-671-32977-4). Messner.
--The Superstars of Rock: Their Lives & Their Music. LC 80-18912. (Illus.). 224p. (gr. 7 up). 1980. PLB 9.29 (ISBN 0-671-32967-7). Messner.
Busoni, Ferruccio. Letters to His Wife. Ley, Rosamond, tr. LC 74-34378. (Music Reprint Ser). (Illus.). 319p. 1975. Repr. of 1938 ed. lib. bdg. 25.00 (ISBN 0-306-70732-2). Da Capo.
Buss, Arnold H. Psychology: Behavior in Perspective. 2nd ed. LC 77-11676. 1978. text ed. 19.95 (ISBN 0-471-12646-2); tchrs. manual avail. (ISBN 0-471-01726-4); tests avail. (ISBN 0-471-03774-5); study guide 6.95 (ISBN 0-471-03060-0). Wiley.
--Self-Consciousness & Social Anxiety. LC 79-20890. (Psychology Ser.). (Illus.). 1980. text ed. 16.95x (ISBN 0-7167-1158-3); pap. text ed. 8.95x (ISBN 0-7167-1159-1). W H Freeman.
Buss, David H., et al. Clinical Pathology Continuing Education Review. LC 79-91972. 1980. pap. 14.75 (ISBN 0-87488-320-2). Med Exam.
Buss, Fran L. La Partera: Story of a Midwife. 1980. 10.95 (ISBN 0-472-09322-3); pap. 6.95 (ISBN 0-472-06322-7). U of Mich Pr.
Buss, Martin J. The Prophetic Words of Hosea: A Morphological Study. (Beiheft 111 Zur Zeitschrift Fuer Die alttestamentliche Wissenschaft). 1969. 28.50x (ISBN 3-11-002579-5). De Gruyter.
Buss, William G. & Goldstein, Stephen R. Standards Relating to Schools & Education. (Juvenile Justice Standards Project Ser.). Date not set. softcover 7.95 (ISBN 0-88410-841-4). Ballinger Pub.
Buss, William G & Goldstein, Stephen R. Standards Relating to Schools and Education. LC 77-1741. (Juvenile Justice Standards Project Ser.). 1977. soft cover 7.95 o.p. (ISBN 0-88410-765-5); 16.50, casebound o.p. (ISBN 0-88410-241-6). Ballinger Pub.
Bussabarger, Robert F. & Stack, Frank, eds. Selection of Etchings by John Sloan. LC 67-22228. (Illus.). 1967. pap. 10.00x o.p. (ISBN 0-8262-0059-1). U of Mo Pr.
Bussagli, Mario, et al. Oriental Architecture. Bussagli, Mario, ed. LC 74-4024. (History of World Architecture Ser.). (Illus.). 436p. 1975. 45.00 (ISBN 0-8109-1016-0). Abrams.
Busse, Ewald & Sussex, James N., eds. The Working Papers of the 1975 Conference on Education of Psychiatrists. 432p. 1976. 12.50 (ISBN 0-685-83185-X, P236-0). Am Psychiatric.
Busse, Ewald W. & Pfeiffer, Eric. Mental Illness in Later Life. 301p. 1973. casebound 12.00 (ISBN 0-685-38355-5, P188-1); pap. 9.00 (ISBN 0-685-38356-3, 188). Am Psychiatric.
Busse, Ewald W., et al, eds. see Rosenfeld, Anne H.
Busse, Heribert, tr. History of Persia Under Qajar Rule. LC 74-183229. 1972. 27.50x (ISBN 0-231-03197-1). Columbia U Pr.
Bussell, Jan. Puppets. Pringle, P., ed. LC 78-431256. (Pegasus Books: No. 16). 1968. 7.50x (ISBN 0-234-77154-2). Intl Pubns Serv.
Busselle, Michael. The Complete Book of Photographing People. 1980. 19.95 (ISBN 0-671-41257-4, Kenan Pr). S&S.
--Master Photography. LC 78-50818. 1978. 14.95 o.s.i. (ISBN 0-528-81079-0). Rand.
Bussey, Lynn E. The Economic Analysis of Industrial Projects. (International Ser. in Industrial & System Engineering). (Illus.). 1978. ref. 24.95 (ISBN 0-13-223388-6). P-H.
Bussy, Dorothy, tr. see Gide, Andre.
Bustad, Leo K. Animals, Aging, & the Aged. (Wesley W. Spink Lectures in Comparative Medicine Ser.). (Illus.). 224p. 1981. 19.50x (ISBN 0-8166-0966-7). U of Minn Pr.
Bustani, Addullah. Fakehat Al Bustan: Concise All Arabic Dictionary. 1970. 40.00x (ISBN 0-685-72029-2). Intl Bk Ctr.
Bustani, B. Qutr Al-Muhit: Concise Arabic-Arabic Dictionary, 2 vols. Repr. of 1869 ed. 50.00 (ISBN 0-685-72056-X). Intl Bk Ctr.
Bustanoby, Andre. But I Didn't Want a Divorce. 1978. o. p. 6.95 (ISBN 0-310-22170-6); pap. 3.95 (ISBN 0-310-22171-4). Zondervan.
Bustanoby, Andre & Bustanoby, Fay. Just Talk to Me. 192p. (Orig.). 1981. pap. text ed. 5.95 (ISBN 0-310-22181-1). Zondervan.
Bustanoby, Fay, jt. auth. see Bustanoby, Andre.
Busteed, H. E. Echoes from Old Calcutta. (Illus.). 454p. 1972. Repr. of 1908 ed. 31.00x (ISBN 0-7165-2115-6, Pub. by Irish Academic Pr Ireland). Biblio Dist.
Bustow, Sheldon M., jt. auth. see Deutsch, Henri.
Busvine, J. R. Insects, Hygiene & History. (Illus.). 1976. text ed. 23.75x (ISBN 0-485-11160-8, Athlone Pr). Humanities.
Busza, Andrzej. Astrologer in the Underground. Boraks, Jagna & Bullock, Micheal, trs. from Polish & Eng. LC 70-108331. 61p. 1970. 6.95 (ISBN 0-8214-0073-8). Ohio U Pr.
Busza, Andrzej, tr. see Bialoszewski, Miron.
Buszek, Beatrice R. The Blueberry Connection: Blueberry Cookery. LC 80-14623. (Illus.). 1980. pap. 7.95 (ISBN 0-8289-0394-8). Greene.
Butchart, Harvey. Grand Canyon Treks. rev. ed. (Illus.). 1976. 2.95 (ISBN 0-910856-38-9). La Siesta.
--Grand Canyon Treks II. 1976. 1.95 (ISBN 0-910856-61-3). La Siesta.
Butchart, Ronald E. Northern Schools, Southern Blacks, & Reconstruction: Freedmen's Education, 1862-1875. LC 79-8949. (Contributions in American History: No. 87). (Illus.). xiv, 309p. 1980. lib. bdg. 25.00 (ISBN 0-313-22073-5, BNS/). Greenwood.
Butcher, Earl O. & Bueker, E. D. Concepts of Neuroanatomy. (Illus.). 1969. Repr. of 1949 ed. 12.00 o.s.i. (ISBN 0-02-842360-7). Hafner.
Butcher, F., et al, eds. Electrical Maintenance & Installation: Part One. 2nd ed. (Engineering Craftsmen: No. J2). (Illus.). 1975. spiral bdg. 22.50x (ISBN 0-685-90134-3). Intl Ideas.
Butcher, Hugh, et al. Community Groups in Action. 272p. 1980. 30.00x (ISBN 0-7100-0617-9); pap. 15.00 (ISBN 0-7100-0618-7). Routledge & Kegan.
Butcher, James N. & Pancheri, Paolo. A Handbook of Cross-National MMPI Research. LC 75-28919. 1976. 22.50x (ISBN 0-8166-0758-3). U of Minn Pr.
Butcher, John G. The British in Malaya, Eighteen Eighty to Nineteen Forty-One: The Social History of a European Community in Colonial South-East Asia. (Illus.). 314p. 1979. 34.95x (ISBN 0-19-580419-8). Oxford U Pr.
Butcher, Lee. The Condominium Book: A Guide to Getting the Most for Your Money. rev. ed. LC 80-10497. 150p. (Orig.). 1980. pap. 8.95 (ISBN 0-87128-588-6). Dow Jones-Irwin.
Butcher, Norman. Radio Control Guide. 2nd ed. LC 77-359360. (Illus.). 250p. (Orig.). 1978. pap. 12.50x (ISBN 0-903676-07-9). Intl Pubns Serv.
Butcher, Phillip A., ed. see Wiener, Harvey S.
Butcher, S. H., tr. see Aristotle.
Butchvarov, Panayot. A Theory of Identity, Existence & Publication: A Theory of Identity, Existence & Predication. LC 78-13812. 288p. 1979. 15.00x (ISBN 0-253-13700-4). Ind U Pr.
Buteau, June D. Nonprint Materials on Communication: An Annotated Directory of Select Films, Videotapes, Videocassettes, Simulations & Games. LC 76-21857. 454p. 1976. 19.50 (ISBN 0-8108-0973-7). Scarecrow.
Butera, Josie. His First Piano Lesson. 1981. 4.75 (ISBN 0-8062-1596-8). Carlton.
Butkov, E. Mathematical Physics. 1968. 27.95 (ISBN 0-201-00727-4). A-W.
Butland, G. J. Latin America: A Regional Geography. 3rd ed. LC 72-5748. 1972. pap. 12.95 o.p. (ISBN 0-470-12658-2). Halsted Pr.
Butler, A. Lives of the Saints, 4 vols. Thurston, Attwater, ed. 1962. Set. 78.50 (ISBN 0-87061-045-7). Vol. 1 (ISBN 0-87061-046-5). Vol. 2 (ISBN 0-87061-047-3). Vol. 3 (ISBN 0-87061-048-1). Vol. 4 (ISBN 0-87061-049-X). Chr Classics.
Butler, A. R. & Perkins, J. M., eds. Organic Reaction Mechanism. Incl. Vol. 9. 1973. 96.95 (ISBN 0-471-12690-X); Vol. 10. 1974. 119.95 (ISBN 0-471-12693-4); Reprint A. 7.50 (ISBN 0-471-01531-8); Reprint B. 8.95 (ISBN 0-471-01532-6); Vol. 11. 1975. 115.95 (ISBN 0-471-01864-3); Vol. 12. 1976. 125.50 (ISBN 0-471-99523-1). LC 66-23143. 1975-1978 (Pub. by Wiley-Interscience). Wiley.
Butler, Addie J. The Distinctive Black College: Talladega, Tuskegee, & Morehouse. LC 77-22756. 1977. 10.00 (ISBN 0-8108-1055-7). Scarecrow.
Butler, Alan. The Law Enforcement Process. LC 74-6878. (Illus.). 300p. 1976. text ed. 9.95x o.p. (ISBN 0-88284-015-0). Alfred Pub.
Butler, Albert. Get Judge Parker! (Orig.). 1980. pap. 1.75 (ISBN 0-505-51500-8). Tower Bks.
--Mariposa Gold. (YA) 1977. 4.95 o.p. (ISBN 0-685-71790-9, Avalon). Bouregy.
Butler, Alfred B., jt. auth. see Slabaugh, Wendell H.
Butler, Alfred J. The Arab Conquest of Egypt & the Last Thirty Years of the Roman Dominion. Fraser, P. M., ed. 1978. text ed. 52.00x (ISBN 0-19-821678-5). Oxford U Pr.
Butler, Anne. Machine Stitches. 1976. 17.95 (ISBN 0-7134-3150-4). David & Charles.
Butler, Anne & Green, David. Pattern & Embroidery. LC 71-90357. (Illus.). 1970. 8.25 o.p. (ISBN 0-8231-4024-5). Branford.
Butler, Annie L., et al. Early Childhood Programs: Developmental Objectives & Their Uses. new ed. (Elementary Education Ser). 224p. 1975. text ed. 14.95 (ISBN 0-675-08725-2). Merrill.
--Play As Development. 1978. pap. text ed. 9.95 (ISBN 0-675-08422-9). Merrill.
Butler, Arthur, jt. ed. see Powell, Christopher.
Butler, Arthur J. Dante His Times & His Work. 201p. 1980. Repr. of 1895 ed. lib. bdg. 30.00 (ISBN 0-8495-0475-9). Arden Lib.
Butler, B. E. Soil Classification for Soil Survey: Monographs on Soil Survey. (Illus.). 144p. 1980. 22.50x (ISBN 0-19-854510-X). Oxford U Pr.
--A Soil Survey of the Horticultural Soils in the Murrumbidgee Irrigation Areas, New South Wales. 1980. 20.00x (ISBN 0-686-64952-4, Pub. by CSJRO Australia). State Mutual Bk.
Butler, Beverly. Captive Thunder. LC 69-16204. (gr. 8 up). 1969. 3.95 (ISBN 0-396-05880-9). Dodd.
--Gift of Gold. LC 72-3151. (gr. 4-8). 1972. 5.95 (ISBN 0-396-06636-4). Dodd.
--Gift of Gold. (YA) (gr. 7-9). 1973. pap. 1.95 (ISBN 0-671-41327-9). PB.
--Light a Single Candle. (YA) (gr. 7-9). 1970. pap. 1.75 (ISBN 0-671-41133-0). PB.
--My Sister's Keeper. LC 79-6637. (gr. 7 up). 1980. 6.95 (ISBN 0-396-07803-6). Dodd.
Butler, C. V. Domestic Service, London, Nineteen Sixteen. LC 79-56953. (The English Working Class Ser.). 1980. lib. bdg. 15.00 (ISBN 0-8240-0107-9). Garland Pub.
Butler, Charles. Principles of Musik, in Singing & Setting. LC 68-13273. (Music Ser). 1970. Repr. of 1636 ed. lib. bdg. 17.50 (ISBN 0-306-70939-2). Da Capo.
Butler, Charles, ed. see Fearne, Charles.
Butler, Christopher. After the Wake: An Essay on the Contemporary Avant-Garde. (Illus.). 192p. 1980. 24.00 (ISBN 0-19-815766-5). Oxford U Pr.
--Number Symbolism. (Ideas & Forms in English Literature Ser.). 1970. 15.00x (ISBN 0-7100-6766-6). Routledge & Kegan.

Butler, Clark. G. W. F. Hegel. (World Authors Ser.: Germany: No. 461). 1977. lib. bdg. 12.50 (ISBN 0-8057-6298-1). Twayne.

Butler, Cynthia. Michael Hendee. (N. H.-Vermont Historiettes). (Illus.). 56p. (gr. 2-3). 1976. 4.95x (ISBN 0-915892-05-7); pap. text ed. 1.95x (ISBN 0-915892-14-6). Regional Ctr Educ.

Butler, D. A., jt. auth. see Bathurst, P. E.

Butler, David. Disraeli: Portrait of a Romantic. (Orig.). 1980. pap. 2.75 (ISBN 0-446-85776-9). Warner Bks.

--Lillie. (Orig.). 1979. pap. 2.75 (ISBN 0-446-95818-2). Warner Bks.

Butler, David & Kavanagh, Dennis. British General Elections Nineteen Seventy-Nine. 416p. 1980. text ed. 50.00x (ISBN 0-8419-5081-4). Holmes & Meier.

Butler, David & Marquand, David. European Elections & British Politics. 208p. 1981. text ed. 25.00 (ISBN 0-582-29528-9); pap. text ed. 11.95 (ISBN 0-582-29529-7). Longman.

Butler, David & Halsey, A. H., eds. Policy & Politics: Essays in Honour of Norman Chester. 1978. text ed. 26.00x (ISBN 0-333-23561-4). Humanities.

Butler, David E. British General Election of 1959. Rose, Richard, ed. (Illus.). 293p. Repr. of 1970 ed. 27.50x (ISBN 0-7156-1549-1, F Cass Co). Biblio Dist.

--The Canberra Model: Essays on Australian Central Government. LC 73-93820. 200p. 1974. 22.50 (ISBN 0-312-11830-9). St Martin.

Butler, David H. An Income Tax Planning Model for Small Businesses. Dufey, Gunter, ed. (Research for Business Decisions). 178p. 1981. 24.95 (ISBN 0-8357-1131-5, Pub. by UMI Res Pr). Univ Microfilms.

Butler, Dorothy. Babies Need Books. LC 80-14027. 1980. 9.95 (ISBN 0-689-11112-6). Atheneum.

--Cushla & Her Books. LC 79-25695. (Illus.). 128p. 1980. Repr. 13.50 (ISBN 0-87675-279-2). Horn Bk.

Butler, E. M. The Fortunes of Faust. 1979. 42.00 (ISBN 0-521-22562-0); pap. 10.95 (ISBN 0-521-29552-1). Cambridge U Pr.

--The Myth of the Magus. LC 78-73950. 1979. 36.00 (ISBN 0-521-22564-7); pap. 8.95 (ISBN 0-521-29554-8). Cambridge U Pr.

--Ritual Magic. LC 80-19324. 329p. 1980. Repr. of 1971 ed. lib. bdg. 10.95x (ISBN 0-89370-601-9). Borgo Pr.

--Ritual Magic. LC 78-73949. 1979. 36.00 (ISBN 0-521-22563-9); pap. 9.95 (ISBN 0-521-29553-X). Cambridge U Pr.

--The Saint-Simonian Religion in Germany. 1968. Repr. of 1926 ed. 21.00 (ISBN 0-86527-177-1). Fertig.

Butler, Edgar. An Industry Survey of the Need for a Federal Grant-Assisted Geothermal Demonstration Power Plant. (Illus.). 36p. 1978. pap. 3.50 (ISBN 0-934412-75-8). Geothermal.

Butler, Eliot A., jt. auth. see Swift, Ernest H.

Butler, Eugenia, et al. Correct Wrtiting, Form One. 2nd ed. 384p. 1976. pap. text ed. 9.95x (ISBN 0-669-99655-6); answers free (ISBN 0-669-99663-7). Heath.

Butler, Francelia & Bakker, Jan. Marxism, Feminism & Free Love: The Story of the Ruskin Commonwealth. (Illus.). 140p. 1980. Repr. lib. bdg. 12.95x (ISBN 0-87991-034-8). Porcupine Pr.

Butler, Francelia, ed. Sharing Literature with Children: A Thematic Anthology. (English & Humanities Ser.). 1977. 22.50 (ISBN 0-679-30328-6, Pub. by McKay); pap. 12.95x (ISBN 0-582-28114-8); instr's manual free. Longman.

Butler, Francelia, ed. see Silvette, Herbert.

Butler, Francelia, et al, eds. Children's Literature: Annual of the Modern Language Association Division on Children's Literature Association, Vol. 9. LC 79-711. (Illus.). 272p. 1981. text ed. 27.50x (ISBN 0-300-02623-4); pap. 8.95 (ISBN 0-300-02642-0). Yale U Pr.

Butler, Frances. Colored Reading: The Graphic Art of Frances Butler. (Lancaster-Miller Art Ser.). (Illus.). 1980. 8.95 (ISBN 0-89581-011-5). Lancaster-Miller.

Butler, Francine. Biofeedback: A Survey of the Literature. LC 78-6159. 352p. 1978. 45.50 (ISBN 0-306-65173-4). IFI Plenum.

Butler, George, jt. auth. see Gaines, Charles.

Butler, George, ed. see Kerry, John F., Jr. & Vietnamese Veterans Against the War.

Butler, George D. Playgrounds: Their Administration & Operation. 3rd ed. (Illus.). 1960. 19.95 (ISBN 0-8260-1610-3). Wiley.

--Recreation Areas, Their Design & Equipment. 2nd ed. (Illus.). 1958. 18.95 (ISBN 0-8260-1625-1). Wiley.

Butler, Gwendoline. The Vesey Inheritance. 1977. pap. 1.50 o.p. (ISBN 0-449-23376-6, Crest). Fawcett.

Butler, H. E., ed. see Suetonius.

Butler, Hall. Inferno! Fourteen Fiery Tragedies of Our Time. (Illus.). 240p. 1975. 9.95 o.p. (ISBN 0-8092-8352-2). Contemp Bks.

Butler, Harold E. Post-Augustan Poetry. (Latin Poetry Ser.: Vol. 15). (LC 77-070766). 1977. Repr. of 1909 ed. lib. bdg. 33.00 (ISBN 0-8240-2964-X). Garland Pub.

Butler, Harry. Teeline Self-Taught. 1975. pap. 9.95x manual o.p. (ISBN 0-435-45340-8); pap. 19.95x kit with cassette o.p. (ISBN 0-435-45338-6). Heinemann Ed.

Butler, Ian S. & Grosse, Arthur E. Relevent Problems for Chemical Principles. 3rd ed. 1979. text ed. 10.95 (ISBN 0-8053-1587-X). Benjamin-Cummings.

Butler, Ivan. The War Film. LC 73-3765. (Illus.). 192p. 1973. 10.00 o.p. (ISBN 0-498-01395-2). A S Barnes.

Butler, J. A. Modern Biology & Its Human Implications. LC 76-27619. 1976. pap. 9.95x (ISBN 0-8448-1007-X). Crane-Russak Co.

Butler, J. D., jt. auth. see Barnard, Henry.

Butler, J. K. Semiconductor Injection Lasers. LC 79-91615. 400p. 1980. 36.95 (ISBN 0-471-08156-6, Pub. by Wiley Interscience); pap. 24.00 (ISBN 0-471-08157-4). Wiley.

Butler, J. K., ed. Semiconductor Injection Lasers. LC 79-91615. 1980. 36.95 (ISBN 0-87942-129-0). Inst Electrical.

Butler, James, ed. see Wordsworth, William.

Butler, James N. Ionic Equilibrium. (Illus.). 1964. 20.95 (ISBN 0-201-00730-4). A-W.

--Solubility & ph Calculations. LC 64-15563. (Chemistry Ser). (Orig.). (gr. 9 up). 1964. pap. 5.95 (ISBN 0-201-00733-9). A-W.

Butler, Jeffrey, ed. Boston University Papers in African History, 2 vols. LC 64-15197. (Pub. by Boston U Pr). Vol. 1. 1964. 12.50x (ISBN 0-8419-8709-2, Africana); Vol. 2. 1966. 15.00x (ISBN 0-8419-8710-6). Holmes & Meier.

Butler, Jerry. Swift to Hear, Slow to Speak. 1975. pap. 3.95 (ISBN 0-89137-511-2). Quality Pubns.

Butler, John. Family Doctors & Public Policy: A Study of Manpower Distribution. (International Library of Social Policy). 1973. 19.00 (ISBN 0-7100-7640-1). Routledge & Kegan.

Butler, John E. Natural Disasters. 1976. pap. text ed. 7.95x (ISBN 0-435-34068-9). Heinemann Ed.

Butler, John R. Who Goes Home? 75p. 1970. pap. text ed. 5.00x (ISBN 0-7135-1593-7, Pub. by Bedford England). Renouf.

Butler, Jonathan L. Latin-inus, -ina, -inus, & -ineus: From Proto-Indo-European to the Romance Languages. (U. C. Publ. in Linguistics: Vol. 68). 1971. pap. 7.00x (ISBN 0-520-09360-7). U of Cal Pr.

Butler, Joseph. Five Sermons: Preached at the Rolls Chapel & A Dissertation Upon the Nature of Virtue. LC 50-4922. 1950. pap. 2.95 (ISBN 0-672-60182-6, LLA21). Bobbs.

Butler, Joseph H. Economic Geography. LC 80-14542. 402p. 1980. 23.95 (ISBN 0-471-12681-0). Wiley.

Butler, Karen, jt. auth. see Butler, Pat.

Butler, L. J. Thomas Hardy. LC 77-23532. (British Authors Ser.). 1978. 23.95 (ISBN 0-521-21743-1); pap. 7.95x (ISBN 0-521-29271-9). Cambridge U Pr.

Butler, L. R., ed. The Analysis of Biological Materials: Proceedings of a Conference Held in Pretoria, South Africa, October 1977. (Illus.). 1979. 37.00 (ISBN 0-08-022853-4). Pergamon.

Butler, Margaret & Greves, Beryl. Fabric Furnishings. 1972. 27.00 (ISBN 0-7134-2754-X, Pub. by Batsford). David & Charles.

Butler, Margaret G. Clothes: Their Choosing, Making & Care. 1978. 25.50 (ISBN 0-7134-2700-0, Pub. by Batsford England); pap. 13.50 (ISBN 0-7134-3035-4). David & Charles.

Butler, Marilyn. Peacock Displayed: A Satirist in His Context. 1979. 30.00 (ISBN 0-7100-0293-9). Routledge & Kegan.

Butler, Matilda & Paisley, William. Women & the Mass Media: Sourcebook for Research & Action. 432p. 1979. text ed. 26.95 (ISBN 0-87705-409-6); pap. text ed. 9.95x (ISBN 0-87705-419-3). Human Sci Pr.

Butler, Michael & Shryack, Dennis. Gauntlet. 1977. pap. 1.95 o.s.i. (ISBN 0-446-89470-2). Warner Bks.

Butler, Octavia. Kindred. 1981. pap. write for info. (ISBN 0-671-83483-5). PB.

Butler, Octavia E. Patternmaster. 1978. pap. 1.75 (ISBN 0-380-41806-1, 41806). Avon.

--Patternmaster. LC 76-2759. 1976. 5.95 o.p. (ISBN 0-385-12197-0). Doubleday.

Butler, Pamela E. Self-Assertion for Women. rev. ed. LC 80-8904. (Illus.). 320p. (Orig.). 1981. pap. 7.95 (ISBN 0-06-250121-6, HarpR). Har-Row.

--Talking to Yourself: Learning to Communicate with the Most Important Person in Your Life. LC 80-6161. 192p. 1981. 12.95 (ISBN 0-8128-2779-1). Stein & Day.

Butler, Pat. Judo Complete. (Illus.). 1971. 8.95 (ISBN 0-571-05397-1, Pub. by Faber & Faber); pap. 4.95 (ISBN 0-571-09725-1). Merrimack Bk Serv.

--Your Book of Self-Defence. (Your Book Ser.). (Illus.). 1968. 5.95 o.p. (ISBN 0-571-08290-4, Pub. by Faber & Faber). Merrimack Bk Serv.

Butler, Pat & Butler, Karen. Judo and Self-Defence for Women & Girls. (Illus.). 1968. 10.95 (ISBN 0-571-08238-6, Pub. by Faber & Faber). Merrimack Bk Serv.

Butler, Paul. Daniel. (The Bible Study Textbook Ser.). (Illus.). 1971. 13.50 (ISBN 0-89900-025-8). College Pr Pub.

--Isaiah, Vol. I. LC 75-328170. (The Bible Study Textbook Ser.). (Illus.). 1975. 13.50 (ISBN 0-89900-020-7). College Pr Pub.

--Twenty-Six Lessons on Luke, Vol. 1. LC 79-57089. (Bible Student Study Guides Ser.). 220p. (Orig.). 1981. pap. 3.95 (ISBN 0-89900-166-1). College Pr Pub. Postponed.

Butler, Paul F. Exercises in Pre-Algebra. (gr. 6-8). 1977. pap. text ed. 4.75x (ISBN 0-88334-041-0) (ISBN 0-685-39243-0). Ind Sch Pr.

Butler, Paul T., jt. auth. see Ratzlaff, Ruben M.

Butler, Peter, ed. see Wagner, Richard.

Butler, Philip F., ed. see Racine, Jean B.

Butler, Phyllis. Woman's Guide. Leonard, Jan, ed. LC 80-66585. (Savvy San Francisco Ser.). (Illus.). 64p. (Orig.). 1980. pap. 2.50 (ISBN 0-89395-047-5). Cal Living Bks.

Butler, Phyllis & Gray, Dorothy. Everywoman's Guide to Political Awareness. LC 75-37073. 1976. pap. 3.95 o.p. (ISBN 0-89087-914-1). Les Femmes Pub.

Butler, Pierce. Judah P. Benjamin. LC 80-20134. (American Statesmen Ser.). 460p. 1981. pap. 6.95 (ISBN 0-87754-198-1). Chelsea Hse.

Butler, Raymond R. Captain Nash & the Wroth Inheritance. LC 76-29856. 1977. 7.95 o.p. (ISBN 0-312-11970-4). St Martin.

Butler, Rhoda. Doobled-up. 120p. 1980. pap. 11.95 (ISBN 0-906191-25-4, Pub. by Thule Pr England). Intl Schol Bk Serv.

Butler, Rick & Carrier, Jean-Guy. The Trudeau Decade. LC 78-22730. 1979. 16.95 o.p. (ISBN 0-385-14806-2); pap. 9.95 (ISBN 0-385-15543-3). Doubleday.

Butler, Robert B. The Ecological House. 256p. 1981. pap. 9.95 (ISBN 0-87100-175-6). Morgan.

Butler, Robert L. Wood for Wood-carvers & Craftsmen. LC 73-10513. (Illus.). 192p. 1975. 12.00 (ISBN 0-498-01376-6); pap. 4.95 o.p. (ISBN 0-498-02048-7). A S Barnes.

Butler, S. T., jt. ed. see Messel, H.

Butler, Samuel. The Fair Haven: A Work in Defence of the Miraculous Element in Our Lord's Ministry Upon Earth. Wolff, Robert L., ed. LC 75-1503. (Victorian Fiction Ser). 1975. Repr. of 1873 ed. lib. bdg. 66.00 (ISBN 0-8240-1578-9). Garland Pub.

--Hudibras. Wilders, John, ed. (Oxford English Texts Ser.). (Illus.). 1967. 54.00x (ISBN 0-19-811844-9). Oxford U Pr.

--Samuel Butler, Hudibras: Parts 1 & 2, & Selected Other Writings. Wilders, John & De Quehen, Hugh, eds. 1973. pap. 11.50x (ISBN 0-19-871067-1). Oxford U Pr.

--Way of All Flesh. 1954. 12.95x (ISBN 0-460-00895-1, Evman). Dutton.

--The Way of All Flesh. Wolff, Robert L., ed. LC 75-1540. (Victorian Fiction Ser.). 1975. Repr. of 1903 ed. lib. bdg. 66.00 (ISBN 0-8240-1611-4). Garland Pub.

Butler, Stanley. Guide to the Best in Contemporary Piano Music: An Annotated List of Graded Solo Piano Music Published Since 1950, 2 vols. Incl. Vol. 1. Levels 1-5. 10.00 (ISBN 0-8108-0628-2); Vol. 2. Levels 6-8. 10.00 (ISBN 0-8108-0669-X). LC 73-5693. 1973. Set. 17.95 o.p. (ISBN 0-685-34675-7). Scarecrow.

Butler, Stuart. Enterprise Zones. (Illus.). 192p. 1981. text ed. 12.50 (ISBN 0-87663-350-5). Universe.

Butler, U. Stars of God. 5.75 o.p. (ISBN 0-8062-1133-4). Carlton.

Butler, W. E. Collected Legislation of the U.S.S.R, Realeases 1 & 2. 1980. Set. looseleaf 300.00 (ISBN 0-379-20450-9). Oceana.

--International Law in Comparative Perspective. 324p. 1980. 42.50x (ISBN 90-286-0089-2). Sijthoff & Noordhoff.

Butler, William & Destiny, Warner. How to Read the Aura, Practice Psychometry, Telepathy, & Clairvoyancy. 2.25 (ISBN 0-446-82751-7). Inner Tradit.

Butler, William J. & Levasseur, Georges. Human Rights & the Legal System in Iran. 80p. (Orig.). 1976. pap. text ed. 2.50 (ISBN 0-89192-084-6). Interbk Inc.

Butlin, J. A., ed. The Economics of Environmental & Natural Resources Policy. 200p. 1981. lib. bdg. 27.50x (ISBN 0-86531-190-0); pap. text ed. 14.00x (ISBN 0-86531-196-X). Westview.

Butlin, Martin. The Paintings & Drawings of William Blake. LC 80-6221. (Paul Mellon Centre for Studies in British Art). (Hlus.). 1408p. 1981. 250.00x (ISBN 0-300-02550-5). Yale U Pr.

--Turner: Later Works. (Tate Gallery: Little Art Book Ser.). (Illus.). 1977. pap. 1.95 (ISBN 0-8120-0858-8). Barron.

--William Blake. (Tate Gallery: Little Art Book Ser.). (Illus.). 1977. pap. 1.95 (ISBN 0-8120-0855-3). Barron.

Butlin, Martin, jt. auth. see Rothenstein, John.

Butlin, R. A., jt. ed. see Baker, A. R.

Butlin, R. A., jt. ed. see Baker, Alan H.

Butnaurescu, Glenda F. Perinatal Nursing: Reproductive Health, Vol. 1. LC 77-25924. 1978. 19.95 (ISBN 0-471-04361-3, Pub. by Wiley Medical). Wiley.

Butner, Alfred N. Surgery Specialty Board Review. 5th ed. 1973. spiral bdg. 16.50 (ISBN 0-87488-302-4). Med Exam.

--Textbook Study Guide of Surgery. 2nd ed. (Medical Examination Review Book: Vol. 5A). 1975. pap. 8.50 (ISBN 0-87488-150-1). Med Exam.

Butot, Michel. Passing Time. Stewart, Jean, tr. 1980. pap. 4.95 (ISBN 0-7145-0438-6). Riverrun NY.

Butrick, Richard. Deduction & Analysis. rev. ed. LC 80-6177. 121p. 1981. lib. bdg. 15.75 (ISBN 0-8191-1410-3); pap. text ed. 6.75 (ISBN 0-8191-1411-1). U Pr of Amer.

Butrym, Zofia. Medical Social Work in Action. 128p. 1968. pap. text ed. 5.00x (Pub. by Bedford England). Renouf.

Butscher, Edward. Adelaide Crapsey. (United States Authors Ser.: No. 337). 1979. lib. bdg. 11.95 (ISBN 0-8057-7273-1). Twayne.

--Unfinished Sequence. Barkan, Stanley H., ed. (Cross-Cultural Review Chapbook 6). 16p. 1980. pap. 2.00 (ISBN 0-89304-805-4). Cross Cult.

Butscher, Edward, ed. Sylvia Plath: The Woman & the Work. LC 77-24700. 1977. 8.95 (ISBN 0-396-07497-9). Dodd.

Butt, Howard. Velvet Covered Brick. LC 72-111352. 200p. 1973. 7.95 o.p. (ISBN 0-06-061258-4, HarpR). Har-Row.

Butt, J. Reaction Kinetic & Reactor Design. 1980. 26.95 (ISBN 0-13-753335-7). P-H.

Butt, Jamshed. Shikar. 1967. pap. 2.35 (ISBN 0-88253-128-X). Ind-US Inc.

Butt, W. R. Hormone Chemistry, 2 vols. 2nd ed. Incl. Vol. 1. Protein, Polypeptides & Peptide Hormones. 272p. 1975. 54.95 (ISBN 0-470-12770-8); Vol. 2. Steroids, Thyroid Hormones, Biogenic Amines & Prostaglandins. 1977. 44.95 (ISBN 0-470-98961-0). LC 75-16158. Halsted Pr.

Butt, Wilfrid R., ed. Topics in Hormone Chemistry, Vol. I. LC 77-84147. 1978. 54.95 (ISBN 0-470-99310-3). Halsted Pr.

Buttel, Frederick H. & Newby, Howard, eds. The Rural Sociology of the Advanced Societies: Critical Perspectives. LC 79-5177. 538p. 1980. text ed. 20.50 (ISBN 0-916672-30-1); pap. text ed. 9.50 (ISBN 0-916672-34-4). Allanheld.

Buttel, Paula W., ed. see Hellyer, Barbara.

Buttenweiser, Paul. Free Association. 224p. 1980. 11.95 (ISBN 0-316-11899-0). Little.

Butter, P. H., ed. Shelly--Alastor & Other Poems, Prometheus Unbound with Other Poems,Adonais. (Illus.). 368p. 1980. pap. 13.95x (ISBN 0-7121-0145-4). Intl Ideas.

Butterfield, Herbert. Christianity & History. 1950. 5.95 o.p. (ISBN 0-684-12423-8, ScribT). Scribner.

--Englishman & His History. LC 76-121754. 1970. Repr. of 1944 ed. 9.50 o.p. (ISBN 0-208-00993-0, Archon). Shoe String.

--Herbert Butterfield: Writings on Christianity & History. 1979. 14.95 (ISBN 0-19-502454-0). Oxford U Pr.

--Man on His Past. 32.95 (ISBN 0-521-07265-4); pap. 8.50x (ISBN 0-521-09567-0). Cambridge U Pr.

--Origins of Modern Science. rev. ed. 1965. pap. text ed. 5.95 (ISBN 0-02-905070-7). Free Pr.

Butterfield, Jim, et al. The First Book of KIM. 1978. pap. 10.75 (ISBN 0-8104-5119-0); computer program tapes 9.95 ea.; no. 00700 tape 1; no. 00800 tape 2; no. 00900 tape 3. Hayden.

Butterfield, R., jt. ed. see Banerjee, P. K.

Butterfield, R. M., jt. auth. see Berg, R. T.

Butterfield, Sherri. Value Tales Teacher's Manual. (Illus.). 120p. 1981. 9.95 (ISBN 0-916392-49-X, Dist. by Oak Tree Pubns). Value Comm.

Butterick, George F., jt. ed. see Allen, Donald.

Butterick, George F., ed. see Olson, Charles & Creeley, Robert.

Butterick, George F., ed. see Olson, Charles F.

Butters, J. Keith, et al. Case Problems in Finance. 7th ed. 1975. text ed. 18.95x (ISBN 0-256-01756-5). Irwin.

Butterworth & Stockdale. Jim Hunter International Spy Stories. (gr. 6-12). 1975-1978. pap. 30.00 boxed set of 12 books with teacher's gd. (ISBN 0-8224-3780-5). Pitman Learning.

Butterworth, Bill. Materials Handling in Farm Production: A Guide to the Control of Handling Costs on the Farm. LC 78-21166. 1979. pap. 12.95x (ISBN 0-470-26589-2). Halsted Pr.

Butterworth, C. A. & Skidmore, D. Caring for the Mentally Ill in the Community. 160p. 1980. 27.00x (Pub by Croom Helm England). State Mutual Bk.

Butterworth, Charles E., ed. see Averroes.

Butterworth, D. & Hewitt, G. F. Two-Phase Flow & Heat Transfer. (Harwell Ser.). (Illus.). 1977. 49.50x (ISBN 0-19-851715-7); pap. 29.00x (ISBN 0-19-851718-1). Oxford U Pr.

Butterworth, Douglas & Chance, John K. Latin American Urbanization. LC 80-18486. (Urbanization in Developing Countries Ser.). (Illus.). 320p. 1981. text ed. 29.95 (ISBN 0-521-23713-0); pap. text ed. 8.95 (ISBN 0-521-28175-X). Cambridge U Pr.

Butterworth, E. & Weir, D. Social Problems of Modern Britain. 1972. pap. 2.75 o.p. (ISBN 0-531-06036-5, Fontana Pap). Watts.

Butterworth, E. A. Some Traces of the Pre-Olympian World in Greek Literature & Myth. (Illus.). 1966. 29.50x (ISBN 3-11-005010-2). De Gruyter.

Butterworth, Emma M. The Complete Book of Calligraphy. LC 79-7642. (Illus.). 164p. 1980. 14.95 (ISBN 0-690-01852-5). Lippincott & Crowell.

Butterworth, Eric. Discover the Power Within You. LC 68-17583. 1968. 9.95 (ISBN 0-06-061266-5, HarpR). Har-Row.

Butterworth, F. Edward. Pilgrims of the Pacific. LC 73-87643. 1974. 5.50 o.p. (ISBN 0-8309-0106-X). Herald Hse.

Butterworth, G. W., tr. see Origen.

Butterworth, Hezekiah. In Old New England. LC 73-19716. 1974. Repr. of 1895 ed. 15.00 (ISBN 0-8103-3686-3). Gale.

Butterworth, John H., 3rd. Tripper, the Sound Hound Book One: The Round Sounds. (Illus.). 1981. 4.50 (ISBN 0-533-04390-5). Vantage.

Butterworth, Michael. X Marks the Spot: A Symphony in Black in Four Movements. LC 77-92207. 1978. 7.95 o.p. (ISBN 0-385-13686-2). Doubleday.

Butterworth, Neil. Dvorak: His Life & Times. (Life & Times of the Composers Ser.). (Illus.). 1981. 16.95 (ISBN 0-8467-0583-4, Pub. by Midas Bks); pap. 7.95 cancelled (ISBN 0-8467-0584-2, Pub. by Midas Bks). Hippocrene Bks.

--Haydn: His Life & Times. (Illus.). 1978. 16.95 (ISBN 0-8467-0417-X, Pub. by Two Continents); pap. 5.95 (ISBN 0-8467-0418-8). Hippocrene Bks.

Butterworth, Oliver. The Enormous Egg. (gr. 4-6). 1956. 8.95 (ISBN 0-316-11904-0, Pub. by Atlantic Monthly Pr). Little.

--The Trouble with Jenny's Ear. (Illus.). (gr. 4-6). 1960. 8.95 (ISBN 0-316-11907-5, Pub. by Atlantic Monthly Pr). Little.

Butterworth, W. E. Careers in the Services. LC 76-9816. (Career Concise Guides Ser.). (Illus.). 72p. (gr. 7 up). 1976. PLB 6.45 (ISBN 0-531-00324-8). Watts.

--Hi-Fi: From Edison's Phonograph to Quadrophonic Sound. LC 76-56704. (Illus.). (gr. 7-11). 1977. 9.95g o.s.i. (ISBN 0-590-07365-6, Four Winds). Schol Bk Serv.

--Leroy & the Old Man. LC 79-6553. 160p. (gr. 7 up). 1980. 7.95 (ISBN 0-590-07638-8, Four Winds). Schol Bk Serv.

--Slaughter by Auto. LC 80-66245. 192p. (gr. 7 up). 1980. 8.95 (ISBN 0-590-07589-6, Four Winds). Schol Bk Serv.

--Under the Influence. LC 78-22127. 256p. (gr. 7 up). 1979. 8.95 (ISBN 0-590-07465-2, Four Winds). Schol Bk Serv.

Butterworth, William. An Album of Automobile Racing. (Picture Albums Ser.). (Illus.). 1977. PLB 7.90 s&l (ISBN 0-531-02909-3). Watts.

--Hot Wire. LC 80-84814. (Illus.). 128p. (gr. 7-9). 1981. lib. bdg. 5.89 (ISBN 0-8178-0018-2). Harvey.

--Next Stop, Earth. LC 77-18346. (Illus.). (gr. 2-4). 1978. 5.95 o.p. (ISBN 0-8027-6322-7); PLB 5.85 (ISBN 0-8027-6323-5). Walker & Co.

Buttery, P. J. & Lindsay, D. B. Protein Deposition in Animals. 29th ed. LC 80-49869. (Nottingham Easter School Ser.). (Illus.). 320p. 1980. text ed. 64.95 (ISBN 0-408-10676-X). Butterworths.

Butti, Ken & Perlin, John. The Golden Thread. LC 79-25095. (Illus.). 1980. 15.95 (ISBN 0-917352-07-6); pap. 9.95 (ISBN 0-917352-08-4). Cheshire.

Buttimer, Anne. Values in Geography. LC 74-76634. (CCG Resource Papers Ser.: No. 24). (Illus.). 1974. pap. text ed. 4.00 (ISBN 0-89291-071-2). Assn Am Geographers.

Buttimer, Anne & Seaman, David. The Human Experience of Space & Place. LC 80-12173. (Illus.). 1980. write for info. (ISBN 0-312-39910-3). St Martin.

Buttlar, Lois & Wynar, Lubomyr R. Building Ethnic Collections: An Annotated Guide for School Media Centers and Public Libraries. LC 76-55398. 1977. lib. bdg. 22.50x (ISBN 0-87287-130-4). Libs Unl.

Buttlar, Lois, jt. auth. see Wynar, Lubomyr R.

Buttle, J. W., et al. Chemistry: A Unified Approach. 1981. text ed. price not set (ISBN 0-408-70938-3). Butterworth.

Buttolph, Philip, tr. see Dibelius, Martin & Conzelmann, Hans.

Button, Kenneth. The Economics of Urban Transport. (Illus.). 1977. 21.95 (ISBN 0-566-00148-9, 00720-X, Pub. by Saxon Hse). Lexington Bks.

Button, Kenneth J., ed. Infrared & Millimeter Waves, Vol. 3: Submillimeter Techniques. 1980. 50.00 (ISBN 0-12-147703-7). Acad Pr.

Button, Leslie. Development Group Work with Adolescents. LC 74-26787. 208p. 1975. 15.95 (ISBN 0-470-12775-9). Halsted Pr.

Buttress, F. A., ed. World Guide to Abbreviations of Organizations. 6th ed. 500p. 1980. write for info. (ISBN 0-8103-2024-X). Gale.

Buttrey, T. V. Guide Book of Mexican Coins. (Whitman Coin Hobby Books). (Illus.). 1977. pap. 4.95 o.p. (ISBN 0-307-09098-1). Western Pub.

Buttrey, Theodore V., Jr. Coinage of the Americas. (Illus.). 139p. 1973. pap. 8.50 o.p. (ISBN 0-685-48744-X). Interbk Inc.

Buttrick, David, jt. auth. see Juel, Donald H.

Buttrick, George A. The Interpreter's Bible, 12 vols. Incl. Vol. 1. General Articles, Genesis, Exodus (ISBN 0-687-19207-2); Vol. 2. Leviticus - Samuel. 1953 (ISBN 0-687-19208-0); Vol. 3. Kings - Job. 1954 (ISBN 0-687-19209-9); Vol. 4. Psalms, Proverbs. 1955 (ISBN 0-687-19210-2); Vol. 5. Ecclesiates - Jeremiah. 1956 (ISBN 0-687-19211-0); Vol. 6. Lamentations - Malachi. 1956 (ISBN 0-687-19212-9); Vol. 7. General Articles, Matthew, Mark. 1951 (ISBN 0-687-19213-7); Vol. 8. Luke, John. 1952 (ISBN 0-687-19214-5); Vol. 9. The Acts, Romans. 1954 (ISBN 0-687-19215-3); Vol. 10. Corinthians, Ephesians. 1953 (ISBN 0-687-19216-1); Vol. 11. Philippians - Hebrews. 1955 (ISBN 0-687-19217-X); Vol. 12. James - Revelation. 1957 (ISBN 0-687-19218-8). 16.95; 185.00 (ISBN 0-687-19206-4). Abingdon.

Butts, David P. Teaching Science in the Elementary School. LC 72-86790. (Orig.). 1973. 8.95 (ISBN 0-02-905010-3); pap. text ed. 6.95 (ISBN 0-02-905060-X). Free Pr.

Butts, David P. & Hall, Gene E. Children & Science: The Process of Teaching & Learning. (Illus.). 368p. 1975. ref. ed. 15.95 (ISBN 0-13-132258-3); pap. text ed. 11.95 (ISBN 0-13-132241-9). P-H.

Butts, Hugh F., jt. auth. see Haskins, Jim.

Butts, Karen R. Breathing Exercises for Asthma. (Illus.). 66p. 1980. pap. 11.75 spiral (ISBN 0-398-04104-0). C C Thomas.

Butts, R. Freeman. The Revival of Civic Learning: A Rationale for Citizenship Education in American Schools. LC 80-81870. (Foundation Monograph Ser.). 170p. (Orig.). 1980. pap. 6.00 (ISBN 0-87367-423-5). Phi Delta Kappa.

Butts, R. Freeman, jt. ed. see Niblett, W. Roy.

Butts, Robert F., jt. auth. see Roberts, Jane.

Butwell, Richard. Foreign Policy & the Developing Nation. LC 68-55041. 244p. 1969. 13.00x (ISBN 0-8131-1185-4). U Pr of Ky.

Butwell, Richard, jt. auth. see Vandenbosch, Amry.

Butwin, Frances. Jews in America. rev. ed. LC 68-31501. (In America Bks.). (Illus.). (gr. 5-11). 1980. PLB 5.95. Lerner Pubns.

Butwin, Frances, jt. auth. see Butwin, Joseph.

Butwin, Joseph & Butwin, Frances. Sholom Aleichem. (World Authors Ser.: No. 460). 1977. lib. bdg. 10.95 (ISBN 0-8057-6297-3). Twayne.

Butz, A. R. The Hoax of the Twentieth Century. LC 77-778964. (Illus.). 1977. 10.00 (ISBN 0-911038-23-X, Inst Hist Rev); pap. 6.00 (ISBN 0-911038-00-0). Noontide.

Butzer, Karl. Environment & Archeology: An Ecological Approach to Prehistory. 2nd ed. LC 74-115938. (Illus.). 1971. 25.95x (ISBN 0-202-33023-0). Aldine Pub.

Buvinic, Mayra see Tinker, Irene & Bramsen, Michelle B.

Buvinic, Mayra, jt. ed. see Tinker, Irene.

Buxbaum, Richard M., jt. auth. see Jennings, Richard W.

Buxton, Barry. The Sustainable Society: Implications for Limited Growth. LC 76-24365. (Special Studies). 1977. text ed. 29.95 (ISBN 0-275-23890-3); pap. 10.95 (ISBN 0-275-64760-9). Praeger.

Buxton, Charles R., ed. Towards a Lasting Settlement. LC 78-147578. (Library of War & Peace; Int'l. Organization, Arbitration & Law). lib. bdg. 38.00 (ISBN 0-8240-0343-8). Garland Pub.

Buxton, Clyne W. This Way to Better Teaching. 1974. 4.50 (ISBN 0-87148-835-3); pap. 3.50 (ISBN 0-87148-836-1). Pathway Pr.

Buxton, Graham. Effective Marketing Logistics: The Analysis Planning & Control of Distribution Operations. 1975. 37.50x (ISBN 0-8419-5007-5). Holmes & Meier.

Buxton, Ian. Big Gun Monitors: The History of the Design, Construction & Operation of the Royal Navy's Monitors. LC 80-81901. (Illus.). 215p. 1980. 19.95 (ISBN 0-87021-104-8). Naval Inst Pr.

Buxton, Jean. Religion & Healing in Mandari. (Illus.). 446p. 1973. 45.00x (ISBN 0-19-823174-1). Oxford U Pr.

Buxton, Leonard H. China, the Land & the People: A Human Geography. LC 79-2818. (Illus.). 333p. 1981. Repr. of 1929 ed. 27.50 (ISBN 0-8305-0000-6). Hyperion Conn.

Buxton, N. K. & MacKay, D. I. British Employment Statistics: A Guide to Sources & Methods. 1977. 46.50x (ISBN 0-631-17240-8, Pub. by Basil Blackwell). Biblio Dist.

Buxton, Neil. The Economic Development of the British Coal Industry. 1979. 56.00 (ISBN 0-7134-1994-6, Pub. by Batsford England). David & Charles.

Buxton, Neil K. & Aldcroft, Derek H., eds. British Industry Between the Wars: Instability & Industrial Development 1919-1939. 308p. 1979. 40.00x (ISBN 0-85967-383-9, Pub. by Scolar Pr England). Biblio Dist.

Buyze, Jean. The Tenth Muse: Women Poets Before Eighteen Hundred. 1980. pap. 3.95 (ISBN 0-915288-39-7). Shameless Hussy.

Buzaljko, Grace, ed. see Kroeber, A. L. & Gifford, E. W.

Buzas, I., ed. see Analytical Chemical Conference, 3rd, Budapest, 1970.

Buzas, I., ed. see Conference on Applied Physical Chemistry, 2nd, Veszprem, Hungary, 1971.

Buzas, L., jt. ed. see Pungor, E.

Buzby, Beth. Data Entry: Concepts & Applications. 480p. 1980. pap. text ed. 14.95 (ISBN 0-574-21255-8, 13-4255); instructor's guide avail. (ISBN 0-574-21256-6, 13-4256). SRA.

Buzby, Walter J. & Paine, David. Hotel & Motel Security Management. LC 76-12555. 256p. 1976. 17.95 (ISBN 0-913708-24-0). Butterworths.

Buzzati, Dino. The Tartar Steppe. 1980. pap. 2.75 (ISBN 0-380-50252-6, 50252, Bard). Avon.

Buzzotta, V. R., et al. Effective Motivation Through Performance Appraisal. 1980. Repr. of 1977 ed. 18.50 (ISBN 0-88410-499-0). Ballinger Pub.

Byars. Personnel Management. 1979. 19.95. Dryden Pr.

--Readings & Cases in Personnel Management. 1979. 10.95 (ISBN 0-7216-2252-6). Dryden Pr.

Byars, Betsy. After the Goat Man. (gr. 3-5). 1975. pap. 1.75 (ISBN 0-380-00437-2, 53314, Camelot). Avon.

--The Cartoonist. (gr. k-6). 1981. pap. 1.25 (ISBN 0-440-41046-0, YB). Dell.

--The Cybil War. LC 80-26912. (Illus.). 144p. (gr. 8-12). 1981. 8.95 (ISBN 0-670-25248-4). Viking Pr.

--The Eighteenth Emergency. (gr. 4-6). 1974. pap. 1.75 (ISBN 0-380-00099-7, 51367, Camelot). Avon.

--The Midnight Fox. (gr. 3-7). 1975. pap. 1.50 o.s.i. (ISBN 0-380-00197-7, 46987, Camelot). Avon.

--Trouble River. (gr. 5-9). 1975. pap. 1.50 (ISBN 0-380-00345-7, 47001, Camelot). Avon.

Byars, Emma L. Witchcraft. 1981. 4.50 (ISBN 0-8062-1580-1). Carlton.

Byars, Lloyd L., jt. auth. see Rue, Leslie W.

Byatt, A. S. Wordsworth & Coleridge in Their Time. LC 73-82999. (Illus.). 288p. 1973. 19.50x (ISBN 0-8448-0040-6). Crane-Russak Co.

Byatt, I. C. The British Electrical Industry Eighteen Seventy-Five to Nineteen Fourteen. 1979. 29.95x (ISBN 0-19-828270-2). Oxford U Pr.

Bybee, Rodger W., jt. auth. see Sund, Robert B.

Bycer, Bernard B. Flowcharting: Programming, Software Design & Computer Problem Solving. LC 75-16175. 326p. 1975. pap. text ed. 16.95 (ISBN 0-471-12882-1). Wiley.

Byde, Alan. Canoe Building in Glass-Reinforced Plastic. (Illus.). 192p. 1974. 15.00 (ISBN 0-7136-1457-9). Transatlantic.

--Canoe Design & Construction. (Illus.). 176p. 1976. 16.50 (ISBN 0-7207-0862-1). Transatlantic.

--Canoeing (Kayaking) (Illus.). 1978. 8.95 (ISBN 0-7136-1826-4). Transatlantic.

--Living Canoeing. 3rd ed. (Illus.). 266p. 1979. 18.00 (ISBN 0-7136-1912-0). Transatlantic.

Byerly, Greg & Rubin, Rick. Pornography: The Conflict Over Sexually Explicit Materials in the United States. an Annotated Bibliography. LC 80-14336. (Garland Reference Library of Social Science). 162p. 1980. 20.00 (ISBN 0-8240-9514-6). Garland Pub.

Byerly, Wesley G. Nam Doc. 1980. 6.95 (ISBN 0-533-04499-5). Vantage.

Byers, A. L. Birth of a Reformation: Life & Labours of D. S. Warner. (Illus.). 496p. Repr. 5.50. Faith Pub Hse.

Byers, Cordia. Heather. (Orig.). 1979. pap. 1.95 o.p. (ISBN 0-449-14272-8, GM). Fawcett.

Byers, Edward E., jt. auth. see Place, Irene.

Byers, J. W. Parent & Child. 60p. pap. 0.50. Faith Pub Hse.

--Sanctification. 96p. 0.75. Faith Pub Hse.

Byers, Roland O. To the Sundown Side: The Mountain Man in Idaho. LC 79-65601. (GEM Books-Historical). (Illus.). 214p. (Orig.). 1979. pap. 8.95 (ISBN 0-89301-063-4). U Pr of Idaho.

Byers, Stephen & Sanders, Peter. Touchdown. LC 75-1127. (The Venture Ser, a Reading Incentive Program). (Illus.). 80p. (gr. 7-12,RL 4.5-6.5). 1975. In Packs Of 5. text ed. 23.25 ea. pack (ISBN 0-8172-0220-X). Follett.

Byerts, Thomas O., et al, eds. The Environmental Context of Aging. LC 78-20645. 256p. 1979. lib. bdg. 24.50 (ISBN 0-8240-7115-8). Garland Pub.

Byfield, Barbara Ninde. The Book of Weird. LC 73-79733. 160p. 1973. pap. 3.95 o.p. (ISBN 0-385-06591-4). Doubleday.

Byford, W. J., tr. see Verona, O. & Gambogi, P.

Bygott, Ursula M. With Pen & Tongue. 444p. 1980. 37.50x (ISBN 0-522-84150-3, Pub. by Melbourne U Pr Australia). Intl Schol Bk Serv.

Byham, C., jt. auth. see Moses, J. L.

Bykhovskii, B. E., ed. Bird Migrations: Ecological & Physiological Factors. Gordon, E. D., tr. from Rus. 298p. 1974. 42.95 (ISBN 0-470-12890-9). Halsted Pr.

Bylanski, P. & Ingram, D. G. Digital Transmission Systems. rev. ed. (IEE Telecommunications Ser.). 431p. pap. write for info. (ISBN 0-906048-37-0, Pub. by Peregrinus England). Inst Electrical.

Byles, Mather. The Works of Mather Byles. LC 78-6439. 1978. 56.00x (ISBN 0-8201-1309-3). Schol Facsimiles.

Bynner, John & Stribley, Keith M., eds. Social Research: Principles & Procedures. (Open University Set Bk.). (Illus.). 1979. pap. text ed. 14.50 (ISBN 0-582-29501-7). Longman.

Bynner, Wittter. Letters. Kraft, James, ed. 1981. 30.00 (ISBN 0-374-18504-2). FS&G.

Bynner, Wytter. Prose Pieces. Kraft, James, ed. LC 78-11441. 1979. 25.00 (ISBN 0-374-23833-2). FS&G.

Bynon, Theodora. Historical Linguistics. LC 76-62588. (Cambridge Textbooks in Linguistics). (Illus.). 1977. 39.95 (ISBN 0-521-21582-X); pap. 8.95 (ISBN 0-521-29188-7). Cambridge U Pr.

Bynum, Caroline W. Docere Verbo et Exemplo. LC 78-14025. (Harvard Theological Studies: No. 31). 1979. 15.00 (ISBN 0-89130-267-0, 020031); pap. 10.50 (ISBN 0-89130-298-0). Scholars Pr Ca.

Bynum, William. Drayton Hall: An Annotated Bibliography. LC 78-59288. (Research on Historic Properties Occasional Papers). (Illus.). 1978. 5.00 o.p. (ISBN 0-89133-068-2). Preservation Pr.

Byon, Jae-Hyon. Local Grazetteers of Southwest China: A Handbook. (Parerga Ser.: No. 5). 154p. 1979. pap. 5.50 (ISBN 0-295-95702-6). U of Wash Pr.

Byrd, Anita. Cooking with Fructose. LC 80-25086. 128p. 1981. 8.95 (ISBN 0-668-05138-8); pap. 4.95 (ISBN 0-668-05142-6). Arco.

Byrd, D. H. I'm an Endangered Species: The Autobiography of a Free Enterpriser. LC 78-62614. 1978. 6.95 (ISBN 0-88415-258-8). Pacesetter Pr.

Byrd, Donald R. Picture It. (Illus.). 232p. (gr. 10-12). 1981. pap. text ed. 5.95 (ISBN 0-88345-413-0). Regents Pub.

Byrd, Donald R. & Cabetas, Isis C. React & Interact: Situations for Communication. (Illus.). 100p. (gr. 10-12). 1980. pap. text ed. 4.95 (ISBN 0-88345-412-2). Regents Pub.

Byrd, Elizabeth. I'll Get By. 204p. (gr. 7up). 1981. 9.95 (ISBN 0-670-39134-4). Viking Pr.

Byrd, J. Jack. Operations Research Models for Public Administration. LC 74-31563. 192p. 1975. 19.95x o.p. (ISBN 0-669-98202-4). Lexington Bks.

Byrd, James F., jt. ed. see Carey, Floyd D.

Byrd, Larry, jt. auth. see Henrickson, Charles.

Byrd, Max. California Thriller. 224p. (Orig.). 1981. pap. 2.25 (ISBN 0-553-14508-8). Bantam.

Byrd, O. Medical Readings on Drug Abuse. (gr. 10-12). 1970. pap. text ed. 7.95 (ISBN 0-201-00749-5); pap. text ed. 7.25 (ISBN 0-201-00748-7). A-W.

Byrd, Peggy. Windy Lindy. (Illus.). 1981. pap. 4.50 (ISBN 0-8062-1702-2). Carlton.

Byrd, R. E. Assault on Eternity. 352p. 1980. 9.95 (ISBN 0-87021-085-8). Naval Inst Pr.

Byrd, Richard E. Discovery: The Story of the Second Byrd Antarctic Expedition. LC 76-159906. (Tower Bks). (Illus.). 1971. Repr. of 1935 ed. 28.00 (ISBN 0-8103-3904-8). Gale.
--A Guide to Personal Risk Taking. (AMACOM Executive Books). 1978. pap. 5.95 (ISBN 0-8144-7505-1). Am Mgmt.
Byrd, Ronald James & Browning, Freddie Melton. A Laboratory Manual for Exercise Physiology. (Illus.). 168p. 1972. 14.50 (ISBN 0-398-02459-6); pap. 9.75 (ISBN 0-398-02925-3). C C Thomas.
Byrd, Thomas L., Jr. The Early Poetry of W. B. Yeats: The Poetic Quest. (National University Pubns. Literary Criticism Ser.). 1978. 12.00 (ISBN 0-8046-9184-3). Kennikat.
Byrde, R. J. & Willetts, H. J. Brown Rot Fungi of Fruit: Their Biology & Control. 1977. text ed. 19.50 (ISBN 0-08-019740-X). Pergamon.
Byres, Terence. Adam Smith, Malthus & Marx. Yapp, Malcolm, et al, eds. (World History Ser.). (Illus.). 32p. (gr. 10). 1980. Repr. of 1977 ed. lib. bdg. 5.95 (ISBN 0-89908-046-4); pap. text ed. 1.95 (ISBN 0-89908-021-9). Greenhaven.
Byrkit & Shamma. Calculus for Business & Economics. 1981. text ed. write for info. (ISBN 0-442-21305-0). D Van Nostrand.
Byrne, jt. auth. see Martin, F. X.
Byrne, Betty. Fell's Beginner's Guide to Flower Arrangement. LC 75-583. 1976. pap. 4.95 (ISBN 0-8119-0363-X). Fell.
Byrne, Beverly. The Outcast. (The Griffin Saga Ser.: Vol. I). 512p. (Orig.). 1981. pap. 2.95 (ISBN 0-449-14396-1, GM). Fawcett.
Byrne, D. & Wright, A. What Do You Think? (Illus.). 1974. pap. text ed. 2.75x student bk. 1 (ISBN 0-582-52269-2); pap. text ed. 2.50x tchr's bk. 1 (ISBN 0-582-52270-6); pap. text ed. 2.75x student bk. 2 (ISBN 0-582-52271-4); pap. text ed. 2.50x tchr's bk. 2 (ISBN 0-582-52272-2). Longman.
Byrne, Don & Rixon, Shelagh. Communication Games. (English Language Teaching Institute Ser.: No. 1). 96p. 1980. pap. text ed. 14.50x (ISBN 0-85633-189-9, NFER). Humanities.
Byrne, Donald E. No Foot of Land: Folklore of American Methodist Itinerants. LC 75-1097. (ATLA Monograph: No. 6). (Illus.). 370p. 1975. 15.00 (ISBN 0-8108-0798-X). Scarecrow.
Byrne, Donn. English Teaching Perspectives. 1980. pap. text ed. 7.50x (ISBN 0-582-74604-3). Longman.
--Functional Comprehension. 1979. pap. text ed. 2.80x o.p. (ISBN 0-582-55242-7). Longman.
--Progressive Picture Compositions. 1975. pap. text ed. 2.00x (ISBN 0-582-52126-2); teacher's bk 3.00x (ISBN 0-582-52127-0); pictures-4 sets 28.00x (ISBN 0-582-52128-9). Longman.
--Teaching Oral English. (Longman Handbooks for Language Teachers). (Illus.). 192p. 1976. pap. text ed. 7.25x (ISBN 0-582-55081-5). Longman.
--Teaching Writing Skills. (Longman Handbooks for Language Teachers). (Illus.). 1980. pap. text ed. 7.50 (ISBN 0-582-74602-7). Longman.
Byrne, Donn & Cornelius, Edwin T. Thirty Passages: Comprehension Practice for High Intermediate & Advanced Students. (Illus.). 1978. pap. text ed. 2.95x (ISBN 0-582-79704-7). Longman.
Byrne, Donn, jt. auth. see Baron, Robert A.
Byrne, Donn, jt. auth. see Lindgren, Henry C.
Byrne, Eileen M. Planning & Educational Inequality. (General Ser.). 384p. 1974. pap. text ed. 22.50x (ISBN 0-85633-039-6, NFER). Humanities.
Byrne, Gerald E., Jr., et al. Granulocyte Identification. LC 78-720294. (Laboratory Learning Aids Ser.). (Illus.). 1977. binder 40.00 (ISBN 0-89189-062-9, 71-5-003-00). Am Soc Clinical.
Byrne, Herbert W. Christian Education for the Local Church. 14.95 (ISBN 0-310-22230-3). Zondervan.
Byrne, James, jt. auth. see Wood, Douglas.
Byrne, Janet, ed. Key Issues: Issues & Events of 1979. LC 80-1717. (News in Print Ser.). (Illus.). 1980. lib. bdg. 24.95x (ISBN 0-405-12877-0). Arno.
--The Middle East: Issues & Events of 1979. LC 80-1718. (News in Print Ser.). (Illus.). 1980. lib. bdg. 24.95x (ISBN 0-405-12878-9). Arno.
Byrne, John see Milne, John.
Byrne, John H. & Koester, John, eds. Molluscan Nerve Cells: From Biophysics to Behavior. (Cold Spring Harbor Reports in the Neurosciences Ser.: Vol. 1). 250p. 1980. 26.00x (ISBN 0-87969-135-2). Cold Spring Harbor.
Byrne, Julia. Curiosities of the Search-Room. LC 70-78117. 1969. Repr. of 1880 ed. 18.00 (ISBN 0-8103-3573-5). Gale.
Byrne, M. St. Clare, ed. see Pliny.
Byrne, Miles. Memoirs of Miles Byrne, 3 vols. in one. Repr. of 1863 ed. 36.00x (ISBN 0-686-28340-6, Pub. by Irish Academic Pr). Biblio Dist.
Byrne, Muriel S., ed. The Lisle Letters, 6 vols. LC 80-12019. 1981. Set. 250.00x (ISBN 0-226-08801-4). U of Chicago Pr.
Byrne, Patrick. Witchcraft in Ireland. 76p. 1967. pap. 3.25 o.p. (ISBN 0-85342-038-6). Irish Bk Ctr.
Byrne, Phil. Inside Skiing. LC 78-24074. 1979. 13.95 (ISBN 0-88229-455-5); pap. 7.95 (ISBN 0-88229-660-4). Nelson-Hall.
Byrne, Ralph. Out of the Mist. LC 69-11344. 1969. 5.95 o.p. (ISBN 0-8283-1007-6). Branden.
Byrne, Richard H. Guidance: A Behavioral Approach. (Illus.). 1977. lib. bdg. 17.95 (ISBN 0-13-368001-0). P-H.
Byrne, Robert. Byrne's Standard Book of Pool & Billiards. LC 78-53913. (Illus.). 1978. 17.95 (ISBN 0-15-115223-3). HarBraceJ.
--The Dam. LC 80-22109. 1981. 12.95 (ISBN 0-689-11123-1). Atheneum.
Byrnes, Christopher I., ed. see NATO ASI & AMS Summer Seminar in Applied Mathematics Held at Harvard University, Cambridge, Ma., June 18-29, 1979.
Byrnes, Joseph F. The Virgin of Chartres. LC 78-75174. 128p. 1981. 17.50 (ISBN 0-8386-2369-7). Fairleigh Dickinson.
Byrnes, W. G. & Chesterton, B. K. Decisions, Strategies & New Ventures: Modern Tools for Top Management. LC 73-18321. 195p. 1973. 14.95 o.p. (ISBN 0-470-12899-2). Halsted Pr.
Byrns, James H. Speak for Yourself. 329p. 1981. pap. text ed. 10.95 (ISBN 0-394-32410-2). Random.
Byrns, John H. Europe's Hidden Flea Markets & Budget Antique Shops. (Illus., Orig.). 1968. pap. 2.95 o.p. (ISBN 0-8038-1888-2). Hastings.
Byron & Hunt, Leigh. The Liberal Verse & Prose from the South: London, 4 vols. (Salzburger Studien zur Anglistik und Amerikanistik: No. 7). (Orig.). 1979. pap. text ed. 35.75x ea.; Bk. 1, 1822. pap. text ed. (ISBN 0-391-01334-3); Bk. 2, 1823. pap. text ed. (ISBN 0-391-01335-1); Bk. 3, 1823. pap. text ed. (ISBN 0-391-01336-X); Bk. 4, 1823. pap. text ed. (ISBN 0-391-01337-8). Humanities.
Byron, Brian. Loyalty in the Spirituality of St. Thomas More. (Bibliotheca Humanistica & Reformatorica: No. 4). 1972. text ed. 34.25x (ISBN 90-6004-293-X). Humanities.
Byron, F. W. & Fuller, R. W. Mathematics of Classical & Quantum Physics, 2 pts. (Physics Ser.). 1969. 16.95; Pt. 1. (ISBN 0-201-00745-2); Pt. 2. (ISBN 0-201-00746-0). A-W.
Byron, George G. Byron: A Self-Portrait, 2 Vols. Quennell, Peter, ed. 1967. Set. 30.00x (ISBN 0-391-00480-8). Humanities.
--The Poetical Works of Lord Byron. Coleridge, E. H., ed. (Illus.). 1120p. 1972. Repr. of 1905 ed. text ed. 18.25x (ISBN 0-7195-0171-7). Humanities.
--Selected Poems. (World's Classics Ser.). 5.95 o.p. (ISBN 0-19-250180-1). Oxford U Pr.
--Works, 13 vols. Coleridge, E. H. & Prothero, R. E., eds. 1967. lib. bdg. 450.00 (ISBN 0-374-91140-1). Octagon.
Byron, Gilbert. The Lord's Oysters. LC 74-9246. xiv, 330p. 1967. Repr. of 1957 ed. 15.00 (ISBN 0-8103-5032-7). Gale.
Byron, H. & Waksman, B. H., eds. Progress in Allergy, Vol. 29. (Illus.). 250p. 1981. 90.00 (ISBN 3-8055-2434-X). S Karger.
Byron, Lord. A Choice of Byron's Verse. Dunn, Douglas, ed. 1974. pap. 5.95 (ISBN 0-571-10589-0, Pub. by Faber & Faber). Merrimack Bk Serv.
Byron, Lord George G. Poetical Works. (Oxford Standard Authors). 936p. 1979. french morocco bdg. 45.00 o.p. (ISBN 0-19-192822-4). Oxford U Pr.
Byron, May C. A Day with Charlotte Bronte. 50p. 1980. Repr. lib. bdg. 8.50 (ISBN 0-8495-0462-7). Arden Lib.
Byron, Stuart & Weis, Elizabeth, eds. Movie Comedy. 1977. pap. 3.95 (ISBN 0-14-004578-3). Penguin.
Byron, William J. Toward Stewardship: An Interim Ethic of Poverty, Power & Pollution. LC 74-30806. (Topics in Moral Argument Ser.). 1975. pap. 1.95 (ISBN 0-8091-1865-3). Paulist Pr.
Byrum, E. E. The Secret of Salvation. 264p. pap. 2.50. Faith Pub Hse.
Byrum, Isabel. How John Became a Man. 64p. pap. 0.40; pap. 1.00 3 copies. Faith Pub Hse.
--The Pilot's Voice. (Illus.). 146p. pap. 1.50. Faith Pub Hse.
--The Poorhouse Waif & His Divine Teacher. 223p. pap. 2.00. Faith Pub Hse.
Byrum, R. R. Holy Spirit Baptism & the Second Cleansing. 108p. pap. 60.75; pap. 2.00 3 copies. Faith Pub Hse.
--Shadows of Good Things, or the Gospel in Type. (Illus.). 144p. pap. 1.50. Faith Pub Hse.
Bythell, Duncan. Handloom Weavers. LC 69-10487. (Illus.). 1969. 53.50 (ISBN 0-521-07580-7). Cambridge U Pr.
--The Sweated Trades: Outwork in the Nineteenth Century. 1978. 50.00 (ISBN 0-7134-1259-3, Pub. by Batsford England). David & Charles.
Bytheriver, Marylee, ed. see George, Llewellyn.
Bytyns'Kyi, Mykola. Mazepyntsi Po Poltávi. LC 75-561602. (Ukrainian.). 1974. 6.00 (ISBN 0-918884-19-5). Slavia Lib.
Bywater, R. Hardware-Software Design of Digital Systems. 1981. 28.00 (ISBN 0-13-383950-8). P-H.

C

C. B. S. News Staff. D-Day. Shapiro, William E., ed. (Illus.). (gr. 7 up). 1968. PLB 3.90 o.p. (ISBN 0-531-01136-4). Watts.
--Lenin & Trotsky. Shapiro, William E., ed. LC 67-25100. (Illus.). (gr. 7 up). 1967. PLB 3.90 o.p. (ISBN 0-531-01134-8). Watts.
C., E., tr. see Charnace, Guy.
C. S. Hammond & Co. The First Book Atlas. 2nd ed. (First Bks). (gr. 4 up). 1973. PLB 4.90 o.p. (ISBN 0-531-00473-2). Watts.
C. S. Peirce Bicentennial International Congress. Proceedings. Ketner, Kenneth, et al, eds. (Graduate Studies, Texas Tech Univ.: No. 23). 420p. (Orig.). 1981. price not set (ISBN 0-89672-075-6); pap. price not set (ISBN 0-89672-074-8). Tex Tech Pr.
Caballero, Jane A. Aerospace Projects for Young Children. (Illus.). 109p. (Orig.). 1979. pap. 9.95 (ISBN 0-89334-052-9). Humanics Ltd.
Cabana Committee of World Assoc. of Girl Guides & Girl Scouts. Canciones de Nuestra Cabana: Songs of Our Cabana. rev. ed. 112p. (Orig.). 1980. pap. 3.75x (ISBN 0-88441-366-7, 23-113). GS.
Cabanillas, B. Puerto Rican Dishes. 3rd ed. 1971. 9.75 (ISBN 0-8477-2776-9). Adler.
Cabanis, Pierre J; see Whytt, Robert.
Cabanne, Pierre. The Brothers Duchamp: Jacques Villon, Raymond Duchamp-Villon, Marcel Duchamp. LC 75-37285. (Illus.). 1976. 60.00 (ISBN 0-8212-0666-4, 109800). NYGS.
Cabasilas, Nicholas. Commentary on the Divine Liturgy. Hussey, J. M. & McNulty, P. A., trs. from Greek. LC 62-53410. 120p. 1977. pap. 4.95 (ISBN 0-913836-37-0). St Vladimirs.
Cabat, Louis & Cabat, Robert. Diga! Diga! (gr. 7-12). 1974. pap. text ed. 4.08 (ISBN 0-87720-510-8). AMSCO Sch.
Cabat, Louis, jt. auth. see Cabat, Robert.
Cabat, Louis, jt. auth. see Cabot, Robert.
Cabat, Louis, jt. auth. see Lopez, Juan E.
Cabat, Robert & Cabat, Louis. Un Verano En Mexico. (Orig.). (gr. 7-12). 1975. pap. text ed. 4.58 (ISBN 0-87720-504-3). AMSCO Sch.
Cabat, Robert, jt. auth. see Cabat, Louis.
Cabeceiras, James. The Multimedia Library: Materials Selection & Use. 275p. 1978. tchrs' ed. 14.00 (ISBN 0-12-153950-4). Acad Pr.
Cabeen, David C. & Brody, Jules, eds. Critical Bibliography of French Literature, Vol. 3: The Seventeenth Century. LC 47-3282. 1961. 25.00x (ISBN 0-8156-2007-1). Syracuse U Pr.
Cabeen, David C. & Holmes, Urban T., eds. Critical Bibliography of French Literature, Vol. 1: The Medieval Period. LC 47-3282. 1952. 25.00x (ISBN 0-8156-2005-5). Syracuse U Pr.
Cabeen, David C. & Schutz, Alexander H., eds. Critical Bibliography of French Literature, Vol. 2: The Sixteenth Century. LC 47-3282. 1956. 25.00x (ISBN 0-8156-2006-3). Syracuse U Pr.
Cabeen, Richard M. Standard Handbook of Stamp Collecting. 2nd ed. LC 75-15651. (Illus.). 1965. 14.95 o.s.i. (ISBN 0-690-76997-0, TYC-T). T Y Crowell.
Cabell, James B. Quiet, Please. 1952. 4.50 (ISBN 0-8130-0040-8). U Presses Fla.
Cabestrero, Teofilo. Mystic of Liberation: A Portrait of Bishop Pedro Casaldaliga of Brazil. Walsh, Donald D., tr. LC 80-25402. (Illus.). 176p. (Orig.). 1981. pap. 7.95 (ISBN 0-88344-324-4). Orbis Bks.
Cabetas, Isis C., jt. auth. see Byrd, Donald R.
Cabeza, Susana, tr. see Jones, Chris.
Cabeza De Baca, Fabiola. We Fed Them Cactus. LC 54-12881. (Zia Books). 208p. 1979. pap. 4.95 (ISBN 0-8263-0517-2). U of NM Pr.
Cabibbo, N. & Sertorio, L., eds. Hadronic Matter at Extreme Energy Density. (Ettore Majoana International Science Ser., Physical Sciences: Vol. 2). 365p. 1980. 42.50 (ISBN 0-306-40303-X, Plenum Pr). Plenum Pub.
Cable, jt. auth. see Nanney.
Cable, George W. The Grandissimes. 1957. pap. 5.95 o.p. (ISBN 0-8090-0025-3, AmCen). Hill & Wang.
--Old Creole Days. 234p. 1980. Repr. of 1897 ed. lib. bdg. 30.00 (ISBN 0-89987-111-9). Century Bookbindery.
Cable, James, tr. from Fr. Death of King Arthur. (Classics Ser.). 1972. pap. 2.95 (ISBN 0-14-044255-3). Penguin.
Cable, Sir James. The Royal Navy & the Siege of Bilbao. LC 78-73238. (Illus.). 1980. 21.50 (ISBN 0-521-22516-7). Cambridge U Pr.
Cable, John, jt. auth. see Nanney, Louis.
Cable, John L., jt. auth. see Bosstick, Maurice.
Cable, John L., jt. auth. see Nanney, J. Louis.
Cable, Mary. Avery's Knot. 248p. 1981. 11.95 (ISBN 0-399-12569-8). Putnam.
--Lost New Orleans. 256p. 1980. 21.95 (ISBN 0-395-27623-3). HM.
Cabot, A. Victor & Hartnett, Donald L. Introduction to Management Science. LC 76-20024. (Illus.). 1977. text ed. 18.95 (ISBN 0-201-02746-1). A-W.
Cabot, George. Life & Letters of George Cabot. Lodge, Henry C., ed. LC 71-124902. (American Public Figures Ser). xi, 617p. 1974. Repr. of 1877 ed. lib. bdg. 69.50 (ISBN 0-306-71001-3). Da Capo.
Cabot, Isabel. Come Summer, Come Love. (YA) 1977. 5.50 o.p. (ISBN 0-685-81422-X, Avalon). Bouregy.
Cabot, Richard C. Social Service & the Art of Healing. LC 73-84257. (NASW Classics Ser). 192p. 1973. pap. text ed. 3.50x (ISBN 0-87101-062-3, CBC-062-I). Natl Assn Soc Wkrs.
Cabot, Robert & Cabat, Louis. Momentos Hispanos. (gr. 11). 1978. pap. text ed. 3.92 (ISBN 0-87720-520-5). AMSCO Sch.
Cabral, Amilcar. Return to the Source: Selected Speeches of Amilcar Cabral. Africa Information Service, ed. LC 74-7788. (Illus.). 128p. 1974. 7.50 o.p. (ISBN 0-85345-345-4, CL-3454); pap. 2.95 (ISBN 0-85345-347-0, PB3470). Monthly Rev.
--Revolution in Guinea: Selected Texts. Handyside, Richard, ed. & tr. LC 73-124084. 144p. 1970. 4.95 o.p. (ISBN 0-85345-144-3, CL-1443); pap. 3.95 (ISBN 0-85345-222-9, PB-2229). Monthly Rev.
Cabral, Olga. In the Empire of Ice. LC 80-53808. (Illus.). 88p. (Orig.). 1980. pap. 3.25 (ISBN 0-931122-19-8). West End.
Cabral De Melo Neto, Joao. A Knife All Blade. 1980. pap. 10.00 (ISBN 0-930502-01-9). Pine Pr.
Cabrera, Vicente, jt. auth. see Gonzalez Del Valle, L.
Cachenmeyer, Charles. Organizational Politica. (Analysis Ser.). 74p. (Orig.). 1979. pap. text ed. 14.95 (ISBN 0-938526-00-6). Inst Analysis.
Cachia, Pierre. Al-Arif: A Dictionary of Grammatical Terms-Arabic-English, English-Arabic. 1974. 12.00x (ISBN 0-685-72025-X). Intl Bk Ctr.
Cada, Lawrence, et al. Shaping the Coming Age of Religious Life. 1979. 10.95x (ISBN 0-8164-0425-9); pap. 4.50x (ISBN 0-8164-2207-9). Crossroad NY.
Cadawallader, Sylvanus. Three Years with Grant: As Recalled by War Correspondent Sylvanus Cadwallader. Thomas, Benjamin P., ed. LC 80-21191. (Illus.). xiv, 361p. 1980. Repr. of 1955 ed. lib. bdg. 28.75x (ISBN 0-313-22576-1, CATY). Greenwood.
Cadbury, B. Bartram. Fresh & Salt Water. LC 60-6114. (Community of Living Things Ser). (Illus.). (gr. 4-8). 1967. PLB 7.45 (ISBN 0-87191-017-9). Creative Ed.
Cadbury, Edward, et al. Women's Work & Wages: London, Nineteen Nine. LC 79-56954. (The English Working Class). 1980. lib. bdg. 30.00 (ISBN 0-8240-0108-7). Garland Pub.
Caddell, Laurie. Modern Motor Bikes. (Illus.). 1979. 12.50 (ISBN 0-7137-0989-8, Pub by Blandford Pr England). Sterling.
Caddell, Laurie & Winfield, Mike. Superbikes. (Orig.). 1981. pap. 9.95 (ISBN 0-89586-067-8). H P Bks.
Caddell, Robert M. Deformation & Fracture of Solids. (Illus.). 1980. text ed. 26.95 (ISBN 0-13-198309-1). P-H.
Cade, Toni, ed. The Black Woman: An Anthology. 256p. 1974. pap. 1.95 (ISBN 0-451-61868-8, MJ1868, Ment). NAL.
Cadell, Elizabeth. Any Tow Can Play. 224p. 1981. 9.95. Morrow.
--The Cuckoo in Spring. 214p. 1976. Repr. of 1954 ed. lib. bdg. 13.95x (ISBN 0-89244-067-8). Queens Hse.
Cadenet, J. J. De see Castro, R. & De Cadenet, J. J.
Cadenhead, I. E., ed. see Hedley, John.
Cadet, Melissa L. Food Aid & Policy for Economic Development: An Annotated Bibliography & Directory. (Illus.). 187p. (Orig.). 1981. 24.95 (ISBN 0-938398-00-8); pap. 16.95. Trans Tech Mgmt.
Cadieux, Charles. These Are the Endangered. (Illus.). 228p. 1981. 15.00 (ISBN 0-913276-35-9). Stone Wall Pr.
Cadillac Publishing Company, jt. auth. see Shapiro, Max.
Cadiz, Luis M. de see De Cesarea, Eusebio.

Cadle, Richard D. The Measurement of Airborne Particles. LC 75-22121. (Environmental Science & Technology Ser.). 352p. 1975. 37.50 (ISBN 0-471-12910-0, Pub. by Wiley-Interscience). Wiley.
Cadman, Arthur. A Guide to Rough Shooting. LC 74-15791. (Illus.). 144p. 1975. 11.95 (ISBN 0-7153-6637-8). David & Charles.
Cadman, John. Hockey Rules Illustrated. (Illus.). 112p. 1980. 18.00 (ISBN 0-7207-1112-6). Transatlantic.
Cadmus, Robert R. Hospitals Are Us. 184p. (Orig.). 1979. 15.95 (ISBN 0-931028-12-4); pap. 12.95 (ISBN 0-931028-11-6). Teach'em.
Cadnum, Michael. The Morning of the Massacre. 1981. pap. price not set (ISBN 0-931460-19-0). Bieler.
Cadou, Jep, ed. see Hungness, Carl, et al.
Cadow, Harry W. Punched-Card Data Processing. LC 72-95421. (Illus.). 344p. 1973. pap. text ed. 13.95 (ISBN 0-574-18485-6, 13-1485); instr's guide avail. (ISBN 0-574-18486-4, 13-1486). SRA.
Cadrain, Linda A., adapted by. The Diary of Anne Frank. (Contemporary Motivators Ser.). (Illus.). 32p. (Orig.). (gr. 4-12). 1979. pap. text ed. 1.25 (ISBN 0-88301-308-8) (ISBN 0-686-65677-6). Pendulum Pr.
Cadwallader, Sharon. Savoring Mexico: A Travel Cookbook. (McGraw-Hill Paperbacks Ser.). (Illus.). 160p. (Orig.). 1980. 10.95 (ISBN 0-07-009532-9, GB); pap. 6.95 (ISBN 0-07-009531-0). McGraw.
--Whole Earth Cooking for the Eighties. (Illus.). 128p. 1981. 9.95 (ISBN 0-312-87050-7); pap. 5.95 (ISBN 0-312-87051-5). St Martin.
Cady, Blake, jt. auth. see Sedgwick, Cornelius E.
Cady, Dale R. Pilot's Bahamas Aviation Guide 1980. (Illus.). 442p. 1979. ring bdg. 16.95 (ISBN 0-911721-68-1). Pilot Pubns.
Cady, Edwin H. Stephen Crane. (U. S. Authors Ser.: No. 23). 1962. lib. bdg. 9.95 o.p. (ISBN 0-8057-0168-0). Twayne.
Cady, Jack. The Well. 1981. 11.95 (ISBN 0-87795-287-6). Arbor Hse.
Cady, John F. The History of Post War Southeast Asia: Independence Problems. LC 74-82497. xxii, 720p. 1974. pap. 20.00x (ISBN 0-8214-0160-2); pap. 10.00x (ISBN 0-8214-0175-0). Ohio U Pr.
Cady, Leo & Rotherham, E. R. Australian Native Orchids in Colour. (Reed Colourbook Ser.). (Illus.). 112p. 1970. 11.75 (ISBN 0-589-07011-8, Pub. by Reed Bks Australia). C E Tuttle.
Cadzow, James A. Discrete Time Systems: An Introduction with Interdisciplinary Applications. (Computer Applications in Electrical Engineering Ser.). (Illus.). 448p. 1973. ref. ed. 26.95 (ISBN 0-13-215996-1). P-H.
Cadzow, James A. & Martens, Hinrich R. Discrete Time & Computer Control Systems. (Electrical Engineering Ser). 1970. ref. ed. 26.95 (ISBN 0-13-216036-6). P-H.
Caelli, Terry. An Introduction to Modern Approaches in Visual Perception. LC 80-40167. (Illus.). 200p. 1981. 38.51 (ISBN 0-08-024420-3); pap. 18.71 (ISBN 0-08-024419-X). Pergamon.
Caemmerer, H. Paul. Life of Pierre Charles l'Enfant. LC 71-87546. (Architecture & Decorative Art Ser.: Vol. 33). 1970. Repr. of 1950 ed. lib. bdg. 45.00 (ISBN 0-306-71381-0). Da Capo.
Caenegem, R. C. Van see Van Caenegem, R. C.
Caesar. Commentarii, 2 Vols. Du Pontet, R. L., ed. (O. C. T). 1900-1901. Vol. 1. 14.95x (ISBN 0-19-814602-7); Vol. 2. 14.95x (ISBN 0-19-814603-5). Oxford U Pr.
Caesar, Julius. Caesar's Gallic War. Pearl, Joseph, tr. from Latin. (Orig.). (gr. 10 up). 1962. 5.50 (ISBN 0-8120-5014-2); pap. text ed. 3.95 (ISBN 0-8120-0037-4). Barron.
--The Civil War. Mitchell, Jane F., tr. (Classics Ser.). 1976. pap. 3.50 (ISBN 0-14-044187-5). Penguin.
--The Conquest of Gaul. Handford, S. A., tr. (Classics Ser). 1951. pap. 2.95 (ISBN 0-14-044021-6). Penguin.
Caesarius Of Arls, St. Sermons on to Eighty. (Fathers of the Church Ser.: Vol. 31). 20.00 (ISBN 0-8132-0031-8). Cath U Pr.
Cafarelli, Eugene J. Developing New Products & Repositing Mature Brands: A Risk-Reduction System That Produces Investment Alternatives. (Marketing Management Ser.). 1980. 21.95 (ISBN 0-471-04634-5, Pub by Ronald Pr). Wiley.
Cafferty. Chess Openings for You. 16.95 (ISBN 0-7134-1976-8, Pub. by Batsford England); pap. 10.95 (ISBN 0-7134-1977-6). David & Charles.
Cafferty, B., jt. auth. see Abramov, L.
Cafferty, B., jt. auth. see Lisitsyn, G. M.
Cafferty, Bernard. Chess Olympiad Skopje Nineteen Seventy-Two. 1979. 14.95 o.p. (ISBN 0-7134-1976-8); pap. 9.25 o.p. (ISBN 0-7134-1977-6). David & Charles.
--Spassky's One Hundred Best Games. 1973. pap. 17.95 (ISBN 0-7134-2409-5, Pub. by Batsford England). David & Charles.
Cafferty, Bernard & Hooper, David. A Complete Defence to 1d4: A Study of the Queen's Gambit Accepted. LC 79-41623. (Pergamon Chess Ser.). 160p. 1981. 15.75 (ISBN 0-08-024103-4); pap. 9.90 (ISBN 0-08-024102-6). Pergamon.
Cafferty, Bernard, jt. auth. see Lisitsyn, G. M.
Cafferty, Kathryn W. & Sugarman, Leone K. Steppingstones to Professional Nursing. 5th rev. ed. LC 76-158487. (Illus.). 1971. text ed. 12.95 o.p. (ISBN 0-8016-0929-1). Mosby.
Caffery, B., jt. auth. see Lisitsyn, G. M.
Cagan, Carl. Data Management Systems. LC 73-11036. 141p. 1973. 26.95 (ISBN 0-471-12915-1, Pub. by Wiley-Interscience). Wiley.
Cagan, Phillip. Persistent Inflation. LC 79-1017. 1979. 20.00x (ISBN 0-231-04728-2); pap. 10.00 (ISBN 0-231-04729-0). Columbia U Pr.
Cagan, Robert H. & Kare, Morley R., eds. Biochemistry of Taste & Olfaction. (Nutrition Foundation Ser.). 1981. write for info. (ISBN 0-12-154450-8). Acad Pr.
Cage, Bob N., jt. auth. see Wattenbarger, James L.
Cage, John. Empty Words. LC 78-27212. 1979. 17.50 (ISBN 0-8195-5032-9, Pub. by Wesleyan U Pr). Columbia U Pr.
--For the Birds. 220p. 1981. 20.00 (ISBN 0-7145-2690-8, Pub. by M. Boyars). Merrimack Bk Serv.
--M: Writings '67-'72. LC 72-11051. (Illus.). 224p. 1973. pap. 7.95 (ISBN 0-8195-6035-9, Pub. by Wesleyan U Pr). Columbia U Pr.
--Silence: Lectures & Writings. LC 61-14238. 1961. 15.00x o.p. (ISBN 0-8195-3021-2, Pub. by Wesleyan U Pr); pap. 7.95 (ISBN 0-8195-6028-6). Columbia U Pr.
--A Year from Monday: New Lectures & Writings. LC 67-24105. 1967. 10.00 o.p. (ISBN 0-8195-3081-6, Pub. by Wesleyan U Pr); pap. 6.95 (ISBN 0-8195-6002-2). Columbia U Pr.
Cagg, Richard D. The Clouds & the Sea. (Illus.). 80p. 1980. pap. 4.00. Cagg.
--The Clouds & the Sea. 80p. 1980. pap. 4.00 (ISBN 0-9605636-0-1). Cagg.
--The Clouds & the Sea. LC 80-67080. Date not set. write for info. Cagg.
Cagle, Charles V. Handbook of Adhesive Bonding. 1973. 43.50 o.p. (ISBN 0-07-009588-4, P&RB). McGraw.
Cagle, Malcolm W. The United States Navy of Tomorrow. LC 75-11444. (Illus.). 160p. (gr. 7 up). 1975. PLB 5.95 (ISBN 0-396-07228-3). Dodd.
Cagnac, B. & Pebay-Peyroula, J. C. Modern Atomic Physics. Incl. Vol. 1. Fundamentals & Principles. LC 74-28161. text ed. 24.95 (ISBN 0-470-12920-4); Vol. 2. Quantum Theory & Its Application. LC 74-26875. text ed. 17.95 o.p. (ISBN 0-470-12921-2). 1975. Halsted Pr.
Cagnat, R. & Chapot, V. Manuel D'archeologie Romaine, 2 vols. (Illus., Fr.). 1981. Repr. of 1920 ed. lib. bdg. 150.00x (ISBN 0-89241-139-2). Vol. 1. 735p. Vol. 2, 574p. Caratzas Bros.
Cagney, James. Cagney by Cagney. 1981. pap. 2.75 (ISBN 0-671-41757-6). PB.
Cahan, Abraham. Rise of David Levinsky. 7.50 (ISBN 0-8446-1794-6). Peter Smith.
Cahen, Claude. La Regime Feodal De l'Italie Normande. LC 80-1995. 1981. Repr. of 1923 ed. 22.00 (ISBN 0-404-18555-X). AMS Pr.
Cahen, Michel & Parker, Monique. Pseudo-Riemannian Symmetric Spaces. LC 79-27541. (Memoirs Ser.). 1980. 6.80 (ISBN 0-8218-2229-2, MEMO-229). Am Math.
Cahill, Audrey F. T. S. Eliot & the Human Predicament. 1967. 7.50x o.p. (ISBN 0-8426-1187-8). Verry.
Cahill, Daniel J. Harriet Monroe. (U. S. Authors Ser.: No. 222). 1973. lib. bdg. 10.95 (ISBN 0-8057-0515-5). Twayne.
Cahill, George F., jt. ed. see Skyler, Jay S.
Cahill, George F., Jr., ed. see American Physiological Society.
Cahill, Hope L. Old Age - a Balance Sheet. (Illus.). 102p. 1981. pap. 3.95 (ISBN 0-933174-13-6). Wide World.
Cahill, Kevin M., ed. Health & Development. LC 75-29504. 110p. 1976. 6.95x o.p. (ISBN 0-88344-178-0). Orbis Bks.
Cahill, P. Joseph, tr. see Leon-Dufour, Xavier.
Cahill, Robert B. & Herbic, Herbert J. Fan the Deck. rev. ed. 1980. pap. text ed. 4.55 (ISBN 0-933282-02-8). Stack the Deck.
Cahill, Susan. Earth Angels. 1978. pap. 1.95 o.p. (ISBN 0-445-04205-2). Popular Lib.
Cahill, Susan & Cahill, Thomas. A Literary Guide to Ireland. LC 72-1181. 1979. pap. 4.95 o.p. (ISBN 0-684-15892-2, ScribT). Scribner.
Cahill, Susan & Cooper, Michele. Urban Reader. LC 75-137898. (Illus.). 1971. pap. text ed. 10.50 (ISBN 0-13-939041-3). P-H.
Cahill, Thomas, jt. auth. see Cahill, Susan.
Cahlander, Adele, et al. Sling Braiding of the Andes. 96p. (Orig.). 1980. pap. text ed. 11.00 (ISBN 0-937452-03-3). Colo Fiber.
Cahm, Eric. Politics & Society in Contemporary France, 1789-1971: A Documentary History. 716p. 1972. 42.50x (ISBN 0-8448-0248-4). Crane-Russak Co.
Cahn, Ann F., ed. Women in the U. S. Labor Force. LC 78-22130. (Praeger Special Studies). 1979. 29.95 (ISBN 0-03-045646-0). Praeger.
Cahn, Edmond. Sense of Injustice. 7.50 (ISBN 0-8446-1795-4). Peter Smith.
Cahn, L. R., ed. see International Academy of Oral Pathology.
Cahn, Leonard, jt. auth. see Porter, Jean.
Cahn, Steven M. Eclipse of Excellence. 1.00 (ISBN 0-8183-0142-2). Pub Aff Pr.
--Education & the Democratic Ideal. LC 78-27155. 1979. 14.95 (ISBN 0-88229-589-6); pap. 8.95 (ISBN 0-88229-661-2). Nelson-Hall.
--Fate, Logic & Time. 1967. 10.50x o.p. (ISBN 0-300-00341-2). Yale U Pr.
Cahn, Steven M., jt. ed. see Tillman, Frank A.
Caianiello, E. R., ed. Lectures on Field Theory & the Many-Body Problem. (Spring School Lectures, 1961). 1961. 40.50 o.p. (ISBN 0-12-154556-3). Acad Pr.
Caiden, Gerald E. Police Revitalization. LC 77-3111. (Illus.). 1977. 23.95 (ISBN 0-669-01477-X). Lexington Bks.
Caiden, Naomi & Wildavsky, Aaron. Planning & Budgeting in Poor Countries. LC 73-12312. (Comparative Studies in Behavioral Science). 416p. 1974. 28.95 (ISBN 0-471-12925-9, Pub. by Wiley-Interscience). Wiley.
Caidin, Martin. Black Thursday. 272p. 1981. pap. 2.50 (ISBN 0-553-13582-1). Bantam.
--The Damocles Effect. Date not set. 12.95 (ISBN 0-525-08851-2). Dutton. Postponed.
--The Final Countdown. 240p. (Orig.). 1980. pap. 2.25 (ISBN 0-553-12155-3). Bantam.
--Fork-Tailed Devil: P-38. (Illus.). 1976. pap. 2.25 (ISBN 0-345-28301-5). Ballantine.
--Manfac. (Orig.). Date not set. pap. 2.95 (ISBN 0-440-15587-8). Dell.
--Six Million Dollar Man, No. 3: High Crystal. 1975. pap. 1.25 o.s.i. (ISBN 0-446-76408-6). Warner Bks.
Caifornia Energy Commission. Passive Solar Handbook. 330p. 1981. lib. bdg. 34.50 (ISBN 0-89934-101-2). Solar Energy Info.
Caiger, John, jt. auth. see Mason, Richard.
Caiger-Smith, Alan, tr. see Piccolpasso, Cipriano.
Cailliet, Emile. The Themes of Magic in Nineteenth Century French Fiction. (Studies in Comparative Literature: No. 2). 228p. Repr. of 1932 ed. lib. bdg. 16.00x (ISBN 0-87991-501-3). Porcupine Pr.
Cailliet, Rene. Shoulder Pain. 2nd ed. 1981. 9.95 (ISBN 0-8036-1613-9). Davis Co.
Caillois, Roger. Man, Play, & Games. LC 61-14109. 1961. 12.95 (ISBN 0-02-905200-9). Free Pr.
Caillois, Roger, jt. ed. see Von Grunebaum, Gustave E.
Caillou, Alan. Diamonds Wild. 1979. pap. 2.25 (ISBN 0-380-43588-8, 43588). Avon.
Cain, Albert C., ed. Survivors of Suicide. (Illus.). 324p. 1972. pap. 26.75 photocopy edition, spiral (ISBN 0-398-02252-6). C C Thomas.
Cain, Arthur H. Young People & Crime. LC 68-11297. (John Day Bk.). 1969. 5.95 o.s.i. (ISBN 0-381-98064-2, A93200, TYC-T). T Y Crowell.
--Young People & Drugs. LC 69-10816. (John Day Bk.). (YA) 1969. 4.95 o.s.i. (ISBN 0-381-98066-9, A93800, TYC-T). T Y Crowell.
--Young People & Work. LC 78-162597. (John Day Bk.). (YA) 1971. 4.95 o.s.i. (ISBN 0-381-98074-X, A94300, TYC-T). T Y Crowell.
Cain, Charles W. Fighters of World War Two. (Illus.). 128p. 1979. 16.50x (ISBN 0-85383-414-8). Intl Pubns Serv.
Cain, Harvey D. Flint's Emergency Treatment & Management. 6th ed. 1980. 19.95 (ISBN 0-7216-2312-3). Saunders.
Cain, J. Allan & Tyna, Eugene J. Geology: A Synopsis: Pt. 1, Physical Geology. (Orig.). 1980. pap. text ed. 7.95 (ISBN 0-8403-2162-7). Kendall-Hunt.
Cain, J. Allen, jt. auth. see Tynan, Eugene J.
Cain, Jack & Carman, Robert A. Mathematics for Business Careers. LC 79-21747. 1981. pap. text ed. 16.95 (ISBN 0-471-03163-1). Wiley.
Cain, Louis P. Sanitation Strategy for a Lakefront Metropolis: The Case of Chicago. LC 76-14711. 161p. 1979. 15.00 (ISBN 0-87580-064-5). N Ill U Pr.
Cain, Maureen E. Society & the Policeman's Role. (International Library of Sociology). (Illus.). 326p. 1973. 25.00x (ISBN 0-7100-7490-5). Routledge & Kegan.
Cain, Melinda, jt. ed. see Dauber, Roslyn.
Cain, Michael S. An Intelligent Guide to Book Distribution. 250p. 1981. 12.50 (ISBN 0-913218-77-4); pap. 5.95 (ISBN 0-913218-78-2). Dustbooks.
Cain, Peter J. Economic Foundations of British Overseas Expansion 1815-1914. (Studies in Economic & Social History). 1980. pap. text ed. 5.25x (ISBN 0-333-23284-4). Humanities.
Cain, Robert. Whole Lotta Shakin' Goin' on: Jerry Lee Lewis. (Illus.). 1981. pap. 9.95. Dial.
Cain, Sandra G. & Evans, Jack M. Sciencing: An Involvement Approach to Elementary Science Methods. 1979. 12.95 (ISBN 0-675-08364-8); instructor's manual 3.95 (ISBN 0-685-96162-1). Merrill.
Caine, Jeffrey. The Cold Room. 1977. 7.95 o.p. (ISBN 0-394-40903-5). Knopf.
Caine, Leslie. Bridge of Love. 192p. (Orig.). 1980. pap. 1.50 (ISBN 0-671-57010-2). S&S.
Caine, Thomas H. see Adderly, James G.
Caine, Tom, et al. Personal Styles in Neurosis: Implications for Small Group Psychotherapy & Behavior Therapy. (International Library of Group Psychotherapy & Group Process). 224p. write for info. (ISBN 0-7100-0617-9). Routledge & Kegan.
Caird, G. B. The Apostolic Age. (Studies in Theology). 1974. pap. 13.50x (ISBN 0-7156-0010-9, Pub. by Duckworth England). Biblio Dist.
--The Language & Imagery of the Bible. 1980. write for info. (ISBN 0-664-21378-2). Westminster.
Caird, James. English Agriculture in Eighteen Fifty & Eighteen Fifty-One. LC 67-16347. Repr. of 1852 ed. 20.00x (ISBN 0-678-05033-3). Kelley.
--Landed Interest & the Supply of Food. 4th ed. LC 67-16346. Repr. of 1880 ed. 15.00x (ISBN 0-678-05034-1). Kelley.
Caird, Kenneth A. Cameraready. 1973. 30.00 (ISBN 0-87703-066-9). Soc Tech Comm.
Cairncross. Introduction to Economics. 5th ed. 1973. pap. 7.95 (ISBN 0-408-70518-3). Butterworths.
Cairncross, Sir Alec. Control of Long-Term International Capital Movements. 1973. pap. 3.95 (ISBN 0-8157-1237-5). Brookings.
Cairncross, Andrew S., ed. see Kyd, Thomas.
Cairncross, John. After Polygamy Was Made a Sin: The Social History of Christian Polygamy. 1974. 18.00x (ISBN 0-7100-7730-0). Routledge & Kegan.
Cairncross, John, tr. see Corneille, Pierre.
Cairnes, Trevor. Europe Rules the World. LC 79-41598. (Cambridge Introduction to the History of Mankind: Bk. 9). (Illus.). 96p. (Orig.). Date not set. pap. price not set (ISBN 0-521-22710-0). Cambridge U Pr.
Cairns & Oswin. Packaging for Climatic Protection. 1975. text ed. 19.95 (ISBN 0-408-00146-1). Butterworths.
Cairns, Bill. Backpacking for Trout. (Illus.). 160p. 1980. 14.00 (ISBN 0-913276-32-4). Greene.
Cairns, Earle. Church History. pap. 1.50 (ISBN 0-8024-1483-4). Moody.
Cairns, Francis. Tibullus: A Hellenistic Poet at Rome. LC 79-50231. 1980. 57.00 (ISBN 0-521-22413-6); pap. 17.95 (ISBN 0-521-29683-8). Cambridge U Pr.
Cairns, G. O. Land & People of Australia. (gr. 5-9). 1954. 3.95g o.s.i. (ISBN 0-02-716410-1). Macmillan.
Cairns, H. & Hamilton, E., eds. The Collected Dialogues of Plato. (Bollingen Ser.: No. 71). 1961. 16.95 (ISBN 0-691-09718-6). Princeton U Pr.
Cairns, J., et al, eds. Phage & the Origins of Molecular Biology. LC 66-26455. (Illus.). 352p. 1966. 25.00 (ISBN 0-87969-104-2); pap. 8.50 o.p. (ISBN 0-87969-105-0). Cold Spring Harbor.
Cairns, John. Cancer: Science & Society. LC 78-16960. (Biology Ser.). (Illus.). 1978. pap. text ed. 8.50x (ISBN 0-7167-0097-2). W H Freeman.
Cairns, John, et al, eds. Banbury Report Four: Cancer Incidence in Defined Populations. LC 80-7676. (Banbury Report Ser.: Vol. 4). (Illus.). 458p. 1980. 45.00x (ISBN 0-87969-203-0). Cold Spring Harbor.
Cairns, John, Jr. & Dickson, K., eds. The Environment: Costs, Conflicts, Action. 180p. 1974. 22.50 o.p. (ISBN 0-8247-6121-9). Dekker.
Cairns, John, Jr., ed. see American Microscopical Society Symposium, 1980.
Cairns, Robert B. Social Development: The Origins & Plasticity of Interchanges. LC 78-12199. (Psychology Ser.). (Illus.). 1979. text ed. 19.95x (ISBN 0-7167-0195-2). W H Freeman.
Cairns-Malatt, Linda. Yang Khi: Vases of the Sea, an Exhibition of American China Trace Porcelain. (Illus.). 31p. (Orig.). 1979. pap. 4.00 o.s.i. (ISBN 0-89133-082-8). Preservation Pr.
Cairo International Workshop on Applications of Science & Technology for Desert Development September 9-15, 1978. Proceedings. Bishay, A. & McGinnies, W. B., eds. (Advances in Desert & Arid Land Technology & Development: Vol. 1). 630p. 1979. lib. bdg. 73.00 (ISBN 3-7186-0002-1). Harwood Academic.
Cajal, Santiago Ramon Y see Ramon Y Cajal, Santiago.
Cajori, F; see Ball, W. Rouse, et al.

Cajori, Florian. The Chequered Career of Ferdinand Rudolph Hassler: First Superintendent of the U. S. Coast Survey. Cohen, I. Bernard, ed. LC 79-7954. 1980. Repr. of 1929 ed. lib. bdg. 18.00x (ISBN 0-405-12535-6). Arno.

--History of Mathematical Notations, 2 vols. Incl. Vol. 1. Notations in Elementary Mathematics. xvi, 451p. 1951. 22.50 (ISBN 0-87548-171-X); pap. 5.95 o.p. (ISBN 0-87548-154-X); Vol. 2. Notations Mainly in Higher Mathematics. xviii, 367p. 1952. 19.95 (ISBN 0-87548-172-8). (Illus.). Open Court.

Cajori, Florian, rev. by see Newton, Sir Isaac.

Cakir, A., et al. Visual Display Terminals: A Manual Covering Ergonomics, Workplace Design, Health & Safety, Task Organization. LC 80-40070. 328p. 1980. 49.00 (ISBN 0-471-27793-2, Pub. by Wiley-Interscience). Wiley.

Calabrese, Edward J. Nutrition & Environmental Health: The Influence of Nutritional Status on Pollutant Toxicity & Carcinogenicity, 2 vols. Incl. Vol. 1. The Vitamins. 60.00 (ISBN 0-471-04833-X); Vol. 2. Minerals & Macronutrients. 544p. 35.00 (ISBN 0-471-08207-4). LC 79-21089. (Environmental Science & Technology Ser.). 1980 (Pub. by Wiley-Interscience). Wiley.

--Pollutants & High Risk Groups: The Biological Basis of Increased Human Susceptibility to Environmental & Occupational Pollutants. LC 77-13957. (Environmental Science & Technology: Wiley-Interscience Series of Texts & Monographs). 1977. 27.00 (ISBN 0-471-02940-8, Pub. by Wiley-Inerscience). Wiley.

Calahan, Harold A. Sailing Technique. (Illus.). 1950. 12.95 (ISBN 0-02-520670-2). Macmillan.

--Yachtsman's Omnibus. (Illus.). 1951. 12.00 o.s.i. (ISBN 0-02-520790-3). Macmillan.

Calamari, John D. & Perillo, Joseph M. Cases & Problems on Contracts. LC 78-18757. (American Casebook Ser.). 1061p. 1978. text ed. 21.95 (ISBN 0-8299-2010-2). West Pub.

Caland, W. Sankhyana Srauta Sutra. Chandra, L., tr. 483p. 1980. text ed. 45.00x (ISBN 0-8426-1646-2). Verry.

Calandra, Denis. Mother Courage & the Caucasian Chalk Circle Notes. 77p. 1975. pap. text ed. 1.25 o.s.i. (ISBN 0-8220-0858-0). Cliffs.

Calbe, jt. auth. see Nanney.

Calcagno, P. L., jt. ed. see Pascual, J. F.

Calcott, Peter H. Continuous Cultures of Cells, 2 vols. 1981. Vol. 1, 192p. 54.95 (ISBN 0-8493-5377-7); Vol. 2, 208p. 57.95 (ISBN 0-8493-5378-5). CRC Pr.

Caldarera, Claudio M., et al, eds. Advances in Polyamine Research, Vol. 3. 1981. text ed. price not set (ISBN 0-89004-621-2). Raven.

Calde, Mark A. Shadowboxer. 1977. pap. 1.75 o.p. (ISBN 0-345-25802-9). Ballantine.

Caldecott, illus. The House That Jack Built. (Peter Possum Paperbacks Ser). 1967. pap. 0.95 o.p. (ISBN 0-531-05100-5). Watts.

Caldecott, Randolph see Aesop.

Calder. A Gaelic Grammar. 352p. 12.50x (ISBN 0-686-27678-7). Colton Bk.

Calder, Angus. Revolutionary Empire. 1981. 35.00 (ISBN 0-525-19080-5). Dutton.

Calder, Angus & Calder, Jenni. Scott. (Literary Critiques Ser). (Illus.). 1970. lib. bdg. 4.95 o.p. (ISBN 0-668-02354-6). Arco.

Calder, Angus, ed. see Dickens, Charles.

Calder, Daniel C., ed. Old English Poetry: Essays on Style. (Contributions of the Center for Medieval & Renaissance Studies, UCLA: No. 10). 1979. 16.50x (ISBN 0-520-03830-4). U of Cal Pr.

Calder, Daniel G. & Forker, Charles. Edward Phillip's History of the Literature of England & Scotland. (Salzburg Studies in English Literature, Poetic Drama & Poetic Theory: No. 21). 134p. (A translation from the Compendios Enumeratio Poetarum). 1973. pap. text ed. 25.00x (ISBN 0-391-01338-6). Humanities.

Calder, G. The Principles & Techniques of Engineering Estimating. 180p. 1976. text ed. 23.00 (ISBN 0-08-019704-3); pap. 10.75 (ISBN 0-08-019703-5). Pergamon.

Calder, Grace J., ed. Carlyle's Dubliners. 1980. 22.50x (ISBN 0-85105-268-1, Dolmen Pr). Humanities.

Calder, Isabel M., ed. see Davenport, John.

Calder, J. M., tr. see Lange, Monique.

Calder, Jenni. Robert Louis Stevenson: A Life Study. (Illus.). 296p. 1980. 19.95 (ISBN 0-19-520210-4). Oxford U Pr.

--The Victorian & Edwardian Home from Old Photographs. 1979. 17.95 (ISBN 0-7134-0793-X). David & Charles.

Calder, Jenni, jt. auth. see Calder, Angus.

Calder, Jenni, ed. Robert Louis Stevenson: A Critical Celebration. (Illus.). 104p. 1981. 15.00x (ISBN 0-389-20145-6). B&N.

Calder, Jenni, ed. see Stevenson, Robert L.

Calder, John, intro. by. A Nouveau Roman Reader. 1979. 11.95 (ISBN 0-7145-3719-5); pap. 5.95 (ISBN 0-7145-3720-9). Riverrun NY.

Calder, Louisa & Konior, Mary. Louisa Calder's Creative Crochet. (Illus.). 144p. 1979. 12.95 o.p. (ISBN 0-670-44203-8, Studio). Viking Pr.

Calder, Nigel. The Comet Is Coming. 176p. 1981. 12.95 (ISBN 0-670-23216-5). Viking Pr.

--Nuclear Nightmares. 1981. pap. 3.95 (ISBN 0-14-005867-2). Penguin.

--Nuclear Nightmares: An Investigation into Possible Wars. (Illus.). 188p. 1980. 10.95 (ISBN 0-670-51820-4). Viking Pr.

Calder, Ritchie. The Evolution of the Machine. LC 68-17249. (Illus.). 160p. 1968. 4.95 (ISBN 0-8281-0342-9, J040-0, Co-Pub. by Smithsonian). Am Heritage.

Calder, Robert. The Dogs. 1976. 7.95 o.s.i. (ISBN 0-440-02050-6). Delacorte.

Caldera, Rafael. Andres Bello. 1977. text ed. 25.00x o.p. (ISBN 0-04-920049-6). Allen Unwin.

Calderbank, V. J. A Course in Programming in FORTRAN IV. 88p. 1969. pap. text ed. 6.95x o.p. (ISBN 0-412-20640-4, Pub. by Chapman & Hall). Methuen Inc.

--A Course on Programming in Fortran Four. 88p. 1969. pap. 8.95 o.p. (ISBN 0-470-12956-5). Halsted Pr.

Calder-Marshall, Arthur. The Grand Century of the Lady: 1720-1820. (Illus.). 1976. o. p. 29.95 (ISBN 0-86033-011-7); pap. 9.95 (ISBN 0-86033-049-4). Gordon-Cremonesi.

Calderon, Pedro. Life Is a Dream. Colford, William E., tr. from Span. 1958. pap. text ed. 2.25 (ISBN 0-8120-0127-3). Barron.

Calderon De La Barca, Pedro. Calderon: Four Plays. Honig, Edwin, tr. Incl. Secret Vengeance for Secret Insult; Phantom Lady; Mayor of Zalamea; Devotion to the Cross. (Orig.). 1961. pap. 2.95 o.p. (ISBN 0-8090-0721-5, Mermaid). Hill & Wang.

--Four Comedies by Pedro Calderon de la Barca. Muir, Kenneth, tr. LC 80-14570. 304p. 1980. 21.50x (ISBN 0-8131-1409-8). U Pr of Ky.

--Life's a Dream. Raine, Kathleen & Nadal, R. M., trs. LC 69-17967. 1.95x (ISBN 0-87830-072-4). Theatre Arts.

Calderone, Mary, jt. auth. see Bride's Magazine Editors.

Calderone, Mary S. & Johnson, Eric W. The Family Book About Sexuality. LC 79-2592. (Illus.). 320p. 1981. 14.95 (ISBN 0-690-01910-6, HarpT). Har-Row.

--The Family Book of Sexuality. 1981. 14.95 (ISBN 0-690-01910-6, H&R). Lippincott.

Calderwood, David. A Solution of Doctor Resolutus, His Resolutions for Kneeling. LC 79-84093. (English Experience Ser.: No. 913). 60p. 1979. Repr. of 1619 ed. lib. bdg. 8.00 (ISBN 90-221-0913-5). Walter J Johnson.

Calderwood, James L. Metadrama in Shakespeare's Henriad: Richard II to Henry V. LC 77-93467. 1979. 15.75x (ISBN 0-520-03652-2). U of Cal Pr.

Caldicott, C. E. Marcel Pagnol. (World Author Ser.: No. 391). 1977. lib. bdg. 12.50 (ISBN 0-8057-6233-7). Twayne.

Caldwell & Hegner. Health Assistant. LC 79-50661. (Illus.). 1980. pap. 8.60 (ISBN 0-8273-1337-3); instr's. guide 1.60 (ISBN 0-8273-1338-1). Delmar.

Caldwell & Utrecht. Indonesia: An Alternative History. 1978. 24.50 o.p. (ISBN 0-685-85435-3). Porter.

Caldwell, A. D. & Lambert, H. P., eds. Pneumonia & Pneumococcal Infections. (Royal Society of Medicine International Congress & Symposium Ser.: No. 27). 1980. 15.50 (ISBN 0-8089-1287-9). Grune.

Caldwell, A. D., jt. ed. see Neu, H. C.

Caldwell, A. D., jt. ed. see Parsonage, M. J.

Caldwell, Anne E. Origins of Psychopharmacology: From CPZ to LSD. (American Lecture in Objective Psychiatry Ser.). 240p. 1970. pap. 19.50 photocopy edition, spiral (ISBN 0-398-00271-1). C C Thomas.

Caldwell, Betty E. & Ricciuti, Henry N. Review of Child Development Research, 9 chapters, Vol. 3. Incl. Chap. 1. Development of Infant-Mother Attachment. pap. 30.00x ea, in packets of 10 (ISBN 0-226-09055-8); Chap. 2. Control of Aggression. pap. 20.00x ea, in packets of 10 (ISBN 0-226-09046-9); Chap. 3. Children in Fatherless Families. pap. 25.00x ea., in packets of 10 (ISBN 0-226-09047-7); Chap. 4. Social Class & Child Development. pap. 15.00x ea., in packets of 10 (ISBN 0-226-09048-5); Chap. 5. Operant Behavior Modification. pap. 15.00x ea., in packets of 10 (ISBN 0-226-09049-3); Chap. 7. Programs for Disadvantaged Parents. pap. 20.00 ea, in packets of 10 (ISBN 0-226-09051-5); Chap. 8. Adoption: A Policy Perspective. pap. 15.00x ea., in packets of 10 (ISBN 0-226-09052-3); Chap. 9. The Child & the Law. pap. 15.00x ea., in packets of 10 (ISBN 0-226-09053-1). 1975. pap. 20.00x (ISBN 0-226-09045-0). U of Chicago Pr.

Caldwell, Bettye & Stedman, Donald, eds. Infant Education. 1977. 9.95 (ISBN 0-8027-9042-9); pap. 8.95 (ISBN 0-8027-7110-6). Walker & Co.

Caldwell, Bill. Enjoying Maine. LC 77-78126. 1978. 9.95 (ISBN 0-930096-01-0). G Gannett.

Caldwell, Charles. Autobiography of Charles Caldwell, M. D. LC 67-27450. (Science & Medicine Ser.). 1968. Repr. of 1855 ed. 45.00 (ISBN 0-306-70978-3). Da Capo.

Caldwell, David, ed. Scottish Weapons & Fortifications, Eleven Hundred-Eighteen Hundred. (Illus.). 1980. text ed. 34.50x (ISBN 0-85976-047-2). Humanities.

Caldwell, E., jt. auth. see Dinkmeyer, D.

Caldwell, E. S. She's Gone. LC 75-43158. (Radiant Life Ser). 128p. (Orig.). 1976. pap. 1.95 (ISBN 0-88243-893-X, 020893); teacher's ed 2.50 (ISBN 0-88243-167-6, 32-0167). Gospel Pub.

Caldwell, Erskine. Deep South: Memory & Observation. LC 80-16013. (Brown Thrasher Ser.). 270p. 1980. pap. 5.95 (ISBN 0-8203-0525-1). U of Ga Pr.

Caldwell, Esther & Hegner, Barbara. Geriatrics: A Study of Maturity. 3rd ed. LC 79-55313. (Practical Nursing Ser.). (Illus.). 288p. 1981. pap. text ed. 8.80 (ISBN 0-8273-1935-5); instr's. guide 1.50 (ISBN 0-8273-1934-7). Delmar.

--Health Assistant. 288p. 1981. text ed. 13.95 (ISBN 0-442-21850-8). Van Nos Reinhold.

Caldwell, Genoa, ed. The Man Who Photographed the World: Burton Holmes (Travelogues 1892-1938) LC 77-8075. (Illus.). 1977. 30.00 o.p. (ISBN -08109-1059-4). Abrams.

Caldwell, Harry. Training Your Memory & Your Mind. (Illus.). 1980. pap. 12.95 o.p. (ISBN 0-930490-20-7). Future Shop.

Caldwell, Helen. Machado de Assis: The Brazilian Master & His Novels. LC 76-89891. 1970. 16.50x (ISBN 0-520-01608-4). U of Cal Pr.

--Michio Ito: The Dancer & His Dances. (Illus.). 1977. 19.50 (ISBN 0-520-03219-5). U of Cal Pr.

Caldwell, Helen, tr. see Machado de Assis, Joaquim M.

Caldwell, John. Amphetamines & Related Stimulants, Vol. 1. 1980. 59.95 (ISBN 0-8493-5347-5). CRC Pr.

Caldwell, John C. African Rural, Urban Migration, the Movement to Ghana's Towns. LC 69-17496. 1969. 16.00x (ISBN 0-231-03269-2). Columbia U Pr.

--Let's Visit Japan. rev ed. LC 59-7658. (Let's Visit Ser). (Illus.). (gr. 3-7). 1966. PLB 7.89 o.p. (ISBN 0-381-99889-4, A43010, JD-J). John Day.

Caldwell, M. Cambodia in the Southeast War. 1979. 24.50 o.p. (ISBN 0-685-67802-4). Porter.

Caldwell, Malcolm. Wealth of Some Nations. 192p. 1977. 10.00 (ISBN 0-905762-01-0); pap. 6.00. Lawrence Hill.

Caldwell, Malcolm & Tan, Lek. Cambodia in the Southeast Asian War. LC 79-147877. (Illus.). 1972. 15.00 o.p. (ISBN 0-85345-171-0, CL1710); pap. 4.95 o.p. (ISBN 0-85345-310-1, PB3101). Monthly Rev.

Caldwell, Margaret. Born to the Sun. 1980. pap. 2.50 (ISBN 0-446-91236-0). Warner Bks.

Caldwell, Patricia, jt. auth. see Clegg, Norma.

Caldwell, Robert G. Criminology. 2nd ed. 1965. 18.95 (ISBN 0-8260-1655-3). Wiley.

--Foundations of Law Enforcement & Criminal Justice. Nardini, William, ed. LC 76-46478. 1977. 16.95 (ISBN 0-672-61412-X). Bobbs.

Caldwell, Taylor. The Balance Wheel. 512p. 1980. pap. 2.75 (ISBN 0-515-05412-7). Jove Pubns.

--Captains & the Kings. 1977. pap. 2.95 (ISBN 0-449-24089-4, Crest). Fawcett.

--Ceremony of the Innocent. LC 75-36582. 1976. 10.95 o.p. (ISBN 0-385-07042-X). Doubleday.

--Ceremony of the Innocent. 1978. pap. 2.75 (ISBN 0-449-23977-2, Crest). Fawcett.

--Dear & Glorious Physician. LC 58-12032. 1959. 9.95 o.p. (ISBN 0-385-05215-4). Doubleday.

--Dear & Glorious Physician. 608p. 1981. pap. 3.50 (ISBN 0-553-14246-1). Bantam.

--Devil's Advocate. pap. 3.75 (ISBN 0-515-05092-X). Jove Pubns.

--Dynasty of Death. 1979. pap. 3.50 (ISBN 0-515-05981-1). Jove Pubns.

--The Eagles Gather. 1979. pap. 2.75 (ISBN 0-515-05093-8). Jove Pubns.

--The Earth Is the Lord's. 1979. pap. 2.75 (ISBN 0-515-05094-6). Jove Pubns.

--The Final Hour. 608p. 1978. pap. 2.95 (ISBN 0-449-24221-8, Crest). Fawcett.

--Glory & the Lightning. 1978. pap. 2.75 (ISBN 0-449-23972-1, Crest). Fawcett.

--Great Lion of God. LC 78-97653. 1970. 12.50 o.p. (ISBN 0-385-00042-1). Doubleday.

--Great Lion of God. 1977. pap. 2.75 (ISBN 0-449-24096-7, Crest). Fawcett.

--Let Love Come Last. 1977. pap. 2.75 (ISBN 0-515-05440-2). Jove Pubns.

--Melissa. 1979. pap. 2.95 (ISBN 0-515-05845-9). Jove Pubns.

--No One Hears But Him. 1977. pap. 2.25 (ISBN 0-449-24030-4, Crest). Fawcett.

--A Pillar of Iron. 768p. 1978. pap. 2.75 (ISBN 0-449-23952-7, Crest). Fawcett.

--A Prologue to Love. 768p. 1980. pap. 2.95 (ISBN 0-553-14238-0). Bantam.

--The Sound of Thunder. 576p. 1981. pap. 3.50 (ISBN 0-553-14255-0). Bantam.

--The Strong City. 544p. 1980. pap. 2.95 (ISBN 0-515-05629-4). Jove Pubns.

--Testimony of Two Men. 1978. pap. 2.95 (ISBN 0-449-23935-7, Crest). Fawcett.

--There Was a Time. 1979. pap. 2.75 (ISBN 0-515-05244-2). Jove Pubns.

--Time No Longer. 1976. pap. 2.75 o.p. (ISBN 0-515-05441-0). Jove Pubns.

--The Turnbulls. (Orig.). pap. 2.75 (ISBN 0-515-05291-4). Jove Pubns.

--The Wide House. 1974. Repr. of 1945 ed. lib. bdg. 19.55 (ISBN 0-88411-156-3). Amereon Ltd.

--The Wide House. 1979. pap. 2.75 (ISBN 0-515-05620-0). Jove Pubns.

Caldwell, Taylor & Stearn, Jess. The Romance of Atlantis. LC 74-17399. 320p. 1975. 7.95 o.p. (ISBN 0-688-00334-6). Morrow.

--The Romance of Atlantis. 272p. 1978. pap. 2.25 (ISBN 0-449-23787-7, Crest). Fawcett.

Caldwell, W. How to Save Urban America. pap. 1.50 (ISBN 0-451-05559-4, W5559, Sig). NAL.

Caldwell, William L. Cancer of the Urinary Bladder: With Emphasis on Treatment by Irradiation. LC 72-96980. (Illus.). 128p. 1970. 10.00 o.s.i. (ISBN 0-87527-003-4). Green.

Cale, David L. The Basics of Consequentialism. LC 80-82228. (Illus.). 160p. 1980. 12.95 (ISBN 0-87012-393-9); pap. 7.95 (ISBN 0-87012-389-0). Laurel Inst.

Calendar, Richard, jt. auth. see Stent, Gunther S.

Calenoff, Leonid. Radiology of Spinal Cord Injury. (Illus.). 500p. 1981. text ed. 42.50 (ISBN 0-8016-1114-8). Mosby.

Calero, Henry H., jt. auth. see Nierenberg, Gerard I.

Caley, Earle R., jt. ed. see Schwind-Belkin, Johanna.

Calhoon, Richard P. Personnel Management & Supervision. (Orig.). 1967. pap. text ed. 12.95 (ISBN 0-13-658260-5). P-H.

Calhoun. Vacation Time, Leisure Time, Any Time You Choose. 1974. pap. 2.25 (ISBN 0-687-43596-X). Abingdon.

Calhoun, Bruce. Council Fires: A Story of the Chippewa Indians in the Mid-1800s & the Treaties of the Great White Father. 158p. 1980. pap. 7.95 o.p. (ISBN 0-89404-004-9). Aztex.

Calhoun, Calfrey C. Managing the Learning Process in Business Education. 624p. 1980. text ed. 17.95x (ISBN 0-534-00834-8). Wadsworth Pub.

Calhoun, Calfrey C. & Finch, Alton V. Vocational & Career Education. text ed. 17.95x (ISBN 0-534-00437-7). Wadsworth Pub.

Calhoun, D. F. The United Front: The TUC & the Russians 1923-1928. (Soviet & East European Studies). 432p. 1976. 44.50 (ISBN 0-521-21056-9). Cambridge U Pr.

Calhoun, G. M & Delamere, C. A Working Bibliography of Greek Law. 1968. Repr. of 1927 ed. text ed. 23.00x (ISBN 90-6032-051-4). Humanities.

Calhoun, George M. The Growth of Criminal Law in Ancient Greece. LC 73-10874. 179p. 1974. Repr. of 1927 ed. lib. bdg. 15.00x (ISBN 0-8371-7043-5, CACL). Greenwood.

Calhoun, James, ed. Louisiana Sports Record Book. 104p. 1971. pap. 1.95 (ISBN 0-911116-55-9). Pelican.

Calhoun, James, ed. see Schlappi, Elizabeth.

Calhoun, James F. & Acocella, Joan. Psychology of Adjustment & Human Relationships. 1978. text ed. 14.95x (ISBN 0-394-31203-1); wkbk. 5.95x (ISBN 0-394-32125-1). Random.
Calhoun, John C. A Disquisition on Government. 1958. 6.00 (ISBN 0-8446-1099-2). Peter Smith.
Calhoun, John C. A. Disquisition on Government & Selections from the Discourse. Post, C. Gordon, ed. 1953. pap. 4.95 (ISBN 0-672-60014-5, AHS10). Bobbs.
Calhoun, Lawrence G. Dealing with Crisis: A Guide to Critical Life Problems. 1976. 14.95 (ISBN 0-13-197723-7, Spec); pap. 4.95 (ISBN 0-13-197715-6). P-H.
Calhoun, Lillian S. Desegregation Works: A Primer for Parents & Teachers. 1968. pap. 0.90 (ISBN 0-685-38478-0). Integrated Ed Assoc.
Calhoun, Marcus B., et al, eds. Suggested Pattern Jury Instructions: Civil Cases, Vol. 1. LC 80-14282. 335p. 1980. ring bind 35.000 (ISBN 0-89854-060-7). U of GA Inst Govt.
Calhoun, Mary. Audubon Cat. LC 80-16278. (Illus.). 32p. (gr. k-3). 1981. 7.95 (ISBN 0-688-22253-6); PLB 7.63 (ISBN 0-688-32253-0). Morrow.
--The Battle of Reuben Robin & Kite Uncle John. LC 72-12949. (Illus.). 32p. (gr. k-3). 1973. PLB 7.92 (ISBN 0-688-30075-8). Morrow.
--Cross-Country Cat. (Illus.). (gr. k-3). 1979. 7.50 (ISBN 0-688-22186-6); PLB 7.20 (ISBN 0-688-32186-0). Morrow.
--Euphonia & the Flood. LC 75-19274. (ps-4). 1976. 5.95 o.s.i. (ISBN 0-8193-0836-6, Four Winds); PLB 5.41 o.s.i. (ISBN 0-8193-0837-4); pap. 1.95 o.s.i. (ISBN 0-8193-0907-9, Pippin). Schol Bk Serv.
--The Flower Mother. LC 70-168469. (Illus.). 32p. (gr. k-3). 1972. PLB 6.96 o.p. (ISBN 0-688-31303-5). Morrow.
--Houn' Dog. (Illus.). (gr. k-3). 1959. 6.25 (ISBN 0-688-21406-1). Morrow.
--The House of Thirty Cats. (gr. 4-6). 1980. pap. 1.95 (ISBN 0-671-42064-X). Archway.
--Hungry Leprechaun. (Illus.). (gr. k-3). 1962. PLB 7.44 (ISBN 0-688-31713-8). Morrow.
--Jack the Wise & the Cornish Cuckoos. LC 77-22714. (Illus.). (gr. k-3). 1978. 7.95 (ISBN 0-688-22132-7); PLB 7.63 (ISBN 0-688-32132-1). Morrow.
--Katie John & Heathcliff. LC 80-7770. 160p. (gr. 3-6). 1980. 8.95 (ISBN 0-06-020931-3, HarpJ); PLB 8.79 (ISBN 0-06-020932-1). Har-Row.
--Katie John & Heathcliff. LC 80-7770. 160p. (gr. 3-6). 1981. pap. 1.95 (ISBN 0-06-440120-0, Trophy). Har-Row.
--The Last Two Elves in Denmark. LC 68-11572. (Illus.). (gr. k-3). 1968. 5.75 o.p. (ISBN 0-688-21468-1); PLB 5.52 (ISBN 0-688-31468-6). Morrow.
--The Witch of Hissing Hill. (Illus.). (gr. k-3). 1964. PLB 7.44 (ISBN 0-688-31762-6). Morrow.
--Wobble the Witch Cat. (Illus.). (gr. k-3). 1958. PLB 6.48 (ISBN 0-688-31621-2). Morrow.
Calhoun, Mary L., jt. auth. see Hawisher, Margaret F.
Calhoun, R. Cases in Personnel Management & Supervision. 2nd ed. 1971. pap. text ed. 10.95 (ISBN 0-13-120352-5). P-H.
Calhoun, Richard. Dina. 1978. pap. 1.95 o.p. (ISBN 0-425-03805-X, Medallion). Berkley Pub.
Calhoun, Robert & Schneider, Barry. The Power Profane. 1979. pap. 2.25 o.p. (ISBN 0-449-14113-6, GM). Fawcett.
Calhoun, Thomas O. Henry Vaughan: The Achievement of Silex Scintillans. LC 79-51851. 272p. Date not set. 22.50 (ISBN 0-87413-165-0). U Delaware Pr. Postponed.
--Henry Vaughan: The Achievement of Silex Scintillans. LC 79-51851. 272p. 1980. 22.50 (ISBN 0-87413-165-0). U Delaware Pr.
Cali, J. P., ed. Physicochemical Measurements: Catalogue of Reference Materials from National Laboratories. 1977. pap. text ed. 10.00 (ISBN 0-08-021578-5). Pergamon.
--Trace Analysis of Semiconductor Materials. 1963. 34.00 (ISBN 0-08-010031-7). Pergamon.
Cali, Santo. Yossiph Shyryn. Scammacca, Nat, ed. 132p. (Ital. & Eng.). 1980. 20.00 (ISBN 0-89304-563-2); pap. 10.00 (ISBN 0-89304-564-0). Cross Cult.
Calian, Carnegie S. Today's Pastor in Tommorrow's World. 1977. 6.95 o.p. (ISBN 0-8015-7761-6). Dutton.
Caliandro, Arthur. You Can Make Your Life Count. 192p. 1981. 8.95 (ISBN 0-916392-79-1). Oak Tree Pubns.
Calif, R. C. Rust. (Orig.). 1980. pap. 1.95 (ISBN 0-532-23198-8). Manor Bks.
Califano, Joseph. Crossfire. 15.95 (ISBN 0-671-25428-6). S&S.
Califano, Joseph A., jt. ed. see Simons, Howard.
Califano, Joseph, Jr. Presidential Nation. 1975. 5.95x (ISBN 0-393-09135-X). Norton.
California Academy of Sciences see Washburn, Dorothy.
California Dept. of Justice & Deukmejian. Law in the School: A Guide for California Teachers, Parents & Students. 3rd ed. LC 74-4146. 96p. 1980. pap. 3.95 (ISBN 0-87585-802-3). Patterson Smith.
California Energy Commission. California Renewable Energy Information Series, 6 vols. Incl. Vol. 1. Exploring New Energy Sources for California: The 1980-81 Report of the Legislature. 106p. pap. 17.95 (ISBN 0-89934-085-7); Vol. 2. Comparative Evaluation of Nontraditional Energy Sources. 122p. pap. 17.95 (ISBN 0-89934-086-5); Vol. 3. Wind Energy Overview: Wind-Elastic Power, Wind Energy Program Progress Report & Wind Resource Assessment. 104p. pap. 17.95 (ISBN 0-89934-087-3); Vol. 4. Impact of Large Wind Energy Systems in California. 200p. pap. 19.95 (ISBN 0-89934-088-1); Vol. 5. Solar & Wind Programs, Final Environmental Impact Reports. 195p. pap. 24.50 (ISBN 0-89934-110-1); Vol. 6. Program Plan for the Maximum Implementation of Solar Energy Through 1990. pap. 24.50 (ISBN 0-89934-109-8). 1981. pap. Solar Energy Info.
California Fertilizer Association. Western Fertilizer Handbook. 6th ed. 252p. 1980. pap. text ed. 5.50 (ISBN 0-8134-2122-5). Interstate.
California Medical Association, ed. see Thurber, Packard.
California Winemakers. Adventures in Wine Cookery. 2nd ed. Bottrell, Donna, et al, eds. (The Wine Cookbook Ser.). (Illus.). 128p. 1980. pap. 5.95 (ISBN 0-932664-10-5). Wine Appreciation.
Calin, Andrei & Fries, James F. Ankylosing Spondylitis. (Discussions in Patient Management Ser.). 1978. spiral 10.00 (ISBN 0-87488-887-5). Med Exam.
Calin, Harold. Dieppe. 1978. pap. 1.75 (ISBN 0-505-51231-9). Tower Bks.
Calin, William C., ed. Chanson de Roland. LC 67-29335. (Medieval French Literature Ser.). (Fr.). 1968. pap. text ed. 8.95x (ISBN 0-89197-071-1). Irvington.
Calkin, Ruth H. Lord, You Love to Say Yes. LC 75-18923. (Illus.). 160p. 1976. pap. 2.50 (ISBN 0-912692-81-2). Cook.
--Tell Me Again, Lord, I Forget. LC 74-76938. 96p. (Orig.). 1974. pap. 2.50 (ISBN 0-912692-37-5). Cook.
Calkins, Carroll. Gardening with Water, Plantings & Stone. 156p. 1975. pap. 1.95 o.s.i. (ISBN 0-346-12176-0). Cornerstone.
Calkins, Dick & Nowlan, Phil. Collected Works of Buck Rogers. Dille, Robert C., ed. LC 70-99585. (Illus.). 375p. 1981. pap. 12.50 (ISBN 0-87754-221-X). Chelsea Hse.
Calkins, Erling. Adventure at Beaver Falls. LC 79-15601. (Crown Ser.). (gr. 5-8). 1979. 4.50 (ISBN 0-8127-0223-9). Southern Pub.
Calkins, Frank. Jackson Hole. 1973. 7.95 o.p. (ISBN 0-394-47437-6). Knopf.
--The Tan-Faced Children. LC 78-18556. 1978. 7.95 o.p. (ISBN 0-385-14410-5). Doubleday.
Calkins, Gary N. & Summers, Francis M., eds. Protozoa in Biological Research. (Illus.). 1964. Repr. of 1941 ed. 38.50 o.s.i. (ISBN 0-02-842460-3). Hafner.
Calkins, Mary W., ed. & intro. by. Locke's Essay Concerning Human Understanding, Bks. II & IV. 1962. Repr. of 1905 ed. 19.95 (ISBN 0-87548-033-0). Open Court.
Calkins, Richard M. Anti-Trust: Guidelines for the Business Executive. 325p. 17.50 (ISBN 0-87094-231-X). Dow Jones-Irwin.
Call, Hughie. Golden Fleece. LC 80-38781. (Illus.). 1981. 17.95x (ISBN 0-8032-1413-8, Bison); pap. 5.25 (ISBN 0-8032-6308-2, BB 760, Bison). U of Nebr Pr.
Call, I. see Diffenderffer, Henry.
Call, Paul. Vasily I. Kelsiev: An Encounter Between the Russian Revolutionaries & the Old Believers. LC 78-78270. 350p. 1980. 33.50 (ISBN 0-913124-36-2). Nordland Pub.
Call, Steven T. & Holahan, William L. Microeconomics. 544p. 1980. text ed. 19.95x (ISBN 0-534-00804-6). Wadsworth Pub.
Calladine, G. R. Engineering Plasticity. 1969. 24.00 (ISBN 0-08-013970-1); pap. 13.25 (ISBN 0-08-013969-8). Pergamon.
Callaghan, Catherine A. Bodega-Miwok Dictionary. (U. C. Publ. in Linguistics: Vol. 60). 1970. pap. 6.00x (ISBN 0-520-09257-0). U of Cal Pr.
--Lake Miwok Dictionary. (U. C. Publ. in Linguistics: Vol. 39). 1965. pap. 10.50x (ISBN 0-520-09233-3). U of Cal Pr.
Callaghan, Dennis W., jt. auth. see Elkins, Arthur.
Callaghy, Thomas M., jt. ed. see Rosberg, Carl G.
Callaham, Ludmilla I. Russian-English Chemical & Polytechnical Dictionary. 3rd ed. LC 75-5982. 852p. 1975. 51.95 (ISBN 0-471-12998-4, Pub. by Wiley-Interscience). Wiley.
Callahan, Daniel, ed. Ethical Issues of Population Aid. 1980. text ed. 22.50x o.p. (ISBN 0-8290-0120-4). Irvington.
--The Teaching of Ethics in Higher Education: A Report by the Hastings Center. LC 80-10294. (The Teaching of Ethics Ser.). 103p. 1980. pap. 5.00 (ISBN 0-916558-09-6). Hastings Ctr Inst Soc.
Callahan, Daniel & Bok, Sissela, eds. Ethics Teaching in Higher Education. (Hastings Center Monograph Ser.). 275p. 1980. 19.50 (ISBN 0-306-40522-9). Plenum Pub.
Callahan, Daniel & Clark, Phillip G., eds. Ethical Issues of Population Aid: Culture, Economics & International Assistance. 1981. text ed. 24.50x (ISBN 0-8290-0364-9). Irvington.
Callahan, Dorothy. Under Christophers Hat. LC 79-37186. (Encore Ser.). (Illus.). (gr. k-1). 1972. write for info. (ISBN 0-684-12685-0, ScribJ). Scribner.
Callahan, Dorothy & Payne, Alma S. Young America's Cookbook. LC 59-5171. (Illus.). 320p. (gr. 7-9). 1959. 6.95 (ISBN 0-684-12358-4). Scribner.
Callahan, Harry. Harry Callahan: Color. Tow, Robert & Winsor, Ricker, eds. (Illus.). 144p. 1980. 85.00 (ISBN 0-936554-00-2). Matrix Pubns.
Callahan, James J., Jr. & Wallack, Stanley S., eds. Reforming the Long-Term-Care System: Financial & Organizational Options. LC 80-8366. (The University Health Policy Consortium Ser.). 272p. 1981. 24.95x (ISBN 0-669-04040-1). Lexington Bks.
Callahan, John W. & Lowden, J. Alexander, eds. Lysosomes & Lysosomal Storage Diseases. 455p. 1980. text ed. 42.00 (ISBN 0-89004-476-7). Raven.
Callahan, Kevin. Early American Furniture. LC 76-4519. (Illus.). 200p. 1976. pap. 5.95x (ISBN 0-8069-8290-X). Sterling.
Callahan, Neal & Young, David. Fill the Heavens with Commerce: Chicago Aviation 1855 to 1926. (Illus.). 250p. 1981. 15.00 (ISBN 0-914090-99-2). Chicago Review.
Callahan, North. Carl Sandburg: Lincoln of Our Literature: A Biography. LC 76-92521. (Illus.). 1970. 15.00x (ISBN 0-8147-0069-1); pap. 5.95x (ISBN 0-8147-0070-5). NYU Pr.
Callahan, Philip S. Soul of the Ghost Moth. (Illus.). 1980. 7.95 (ISBN 0-8159-6840-X). Devin.
Callahan, Robert, jt. ed. see Eron, Leonard D.
Callahan, S. The Magnificat: The Prayer of Mary. (Orig.). 1976. pap. 4.95 (ISBN 0-8164-2594-9). Crossroad NY.
Callahan, Sidney, jt. ed. see Berger, Brigitte.
Callahan, Thomas C. & Turner, Freda. Shadow of Death. LC 80-50008. (Illus.). 192p. 1980. 9.95 (ISBN 0-936354-01-1). Val-Hse Pub.
Callahan, W. J. & Higgs, D. Church & Society in Catholic Europe of the Eighteenth Century. LC 78-12165. 1979. 22.50 (ISBN 0-521-22424-1). Cambridge U Pr.
Callahan, William J. Honor, Commerce & Industry in Eighteenth-Century Spain. (Kress Library of Business & Economics: No. 22). 1972. pap. 5.00x (ISBN 0-678-09916-2, Baker Lib). Kelley.
Callan, Edward. Alan Paton. LC 67-25207. (World Authors Ser.: South Africa: No. 40). 1968. lib. bdg. 10.95 (ISBN 0-8057-2686-1). Twayne.
--Yeats on Yeats: The Last Introductions & 'Under Ben Bulben' (Illus.). 96p. 1980. pap. text ed. 16.50x (ISBN 0-85105-370-X, Dolmen Pr). Humanities.
Callan, Eileen T. Hardy Race of Men: America's Early Indians. LC 70-88111. (Curriculum Related Bks). (Illus.). (gr. 7 up). 1970. 4.95 o.p. (ISBN 0-15-233411-4, HJ). HarBraceJ.
Callan, Hilary. Ethology & Society: Towards an Anthropological View. 1970. 22.50x (ISBN 0-19-823161-X). Oxford U Pr.
Callan, Laurence B., jt. auth. see Eisner, Victor.
Callan, Richard J. Miguel Angel Asturias. (World Authors Ser.: Guatemala: No. 122). lib. bdg. 9.95 (ISBN 0-8057-2072-3). Twayne.
Callander, R. A., jt. auth. see Raudkivi, A. J.
Callander, R. A., jt. auth. see Stephenson, J.
Callarman, Frederick A. Paulevala: Land of Hurrahs. 88p. (Orig.). 1981. pap. 1.98 (ISBN 0-930092-01-5). Callarman Hse.
Callaway, Bob & Hughes, Michael. Platform Tennis. 1979. pap. 4.95 o.p. (ISBN 0-397-01198-9). Lippincott.
--Platform Tennis. (Illus.). 1977. 9.95 o.s.i. (ISBN 0-397-01183-0). Lippincott.
Callaway, Cason J., Jr. & Flowers, Charles M., eds. A Southern Collection. (Illus.). 318p. (Orig.). 1979. pap. 8.50. Jr League Columbus.
Callaway, Frank, ed. Australian Composition in the Twentieth Century. Tunley, David. 1979. 42.00x (ISBN 0-19-550522-0). Oxford U Pr.
Callaway, Joseph. Energy Band Theory. (Pure and Applied Physics: Vol. 16). 1964. 44.00 o.s.i. (ISBN 0-12-155250-0). Acad Pr.
Callaway, Sydney M. & Witherspoon, Gary. Grandfather Stories of the Navajos. rev. ed. Johnson, Broderick A., ed. LC 68-57898. (Illus.). 88p. 1974. 4.50 o.p. (ISBN 0-89019-006-2). Navajo Curr.
Callcott, George H., jt. auth. see Elkins, Wilson H.
Callcott, M. V. & Peters, Terry, eds. Mr. George, 2 pts. Incl. Pt. 1. In Victorian England; Pt. 2. In Pioneer Texas. (National History Ser.). (Illus.). Date not set. 16.95 (ISBN 0-89482-046-X); ltd. ed. 39.95 (ISBN 0-89482-048-6); pap. 8.95 (ISBN 0-89482-047-8); video cassette of Frank Callcott 165.00 (ISBN 0-89482-022-2). Stevenson Pr.
Callcott, Wilfrid H. Western Hemisphere: Its Influence on United States Policies to the End of World War Two. 1968. 25.00x (ISBN 0-292-78390-6). U of Tex Pr.
Calleley, A. & Forster, C. Treatment of Industrial Effluents. LC 76-54909. 1977. 27.95 (ISBN 0-470-98934-3). Halsted Pr.
Callen, Anna T. The Savory Pie. Behrman, Marion, ed. 288p. 1981. 15.95 (ISBN 0-517-54380-X). Crown.
Callen, Anthea. Courbet. (Oresko-Jupiter Art Bks). (Illus.). 96p. 1981. 17.95 (ISBN 0-933516-84-3, Pub. by Oresko-Jupiter England). Hippocrene Bks.
--Renoir. LC 77-10354. (Oresko Art Book). (Illus.). 1978. 15.95 (ISBN 0-8467-0377-7, Pub. by Two Continents); pap. 9.95 (ISBN 0-8467-0378-5). Hippocrene Bks.
Callen, Larry. Dashiel & the Night. LC 80-10948. (Illus.). (gr. 1-5). 1981. PLB 8.95 (ISBN 0-525-28540-7). Dutton.
--Muskrat War. 144p. (gr. 5 up). 1980. 8.95g (ISBN 0-316-12498-2, Pub. by Atlantic-Little Brown). Little.
Callenbach, Ernest. Ecotopia. LC 74-84366. 168p. (Orig.). 1975. 10.00 (ISBN 0-9604320-0-0); pap. 3.45 (ISBN 0-9604320-1-9). Banyan Tree.
Callenbach, Ernest, jt. auth. see Leefeldt, Christine.
Calleo, David. The German Problem Reconsidered. LC 78-9683. 208p. 1980. pap. 6.95 (ISBN 0-521-29966-7). Cambridge U Pr.
Calleo, David P, et al. Money & the Coming World Order. LC 75-34673. 120p. 1976. 8.95x (ISBN 0-8147-1367-X); pap. 5.00x (ISBN 0-8147-1368-8). NYU Pr.
Callery, Bernadette, et al. Kate Greenaway: Catalogue of an Exhibition of Original Artworks & Related Materials Selected from the Frances Hooper Collection at the Hunt Institute. Mosimann, Elizabeth, compiled by. (Illus.). 112p. 1981. 22.00x (ISBN 0-913196-33-9). Hunt Inst Botanical.
Callery, Bernadette G. & Mosimann, E. A., eds. The Tradition of Fine Bookbinding in the Twentieth Century. (Illus.). 120p. 1979. 25.00 (ISBN 0-913196-28-2); unbd. 22.00 (ISBN 0-686-65642-3). Hunt Inst Botanical.
Callewaert, Denis M. & Genyea, Julien. Fundamentals of College Chemistry. 1980. text ed. 15.95x (ISBN 0-87901-124-6). Worth.
Callicott, Catherine D. & Holderness, Lawson. In Praise of Dollhouses: The Story of a Personal Collection. LC 78-17316. (Illus.). 1978. 14.95 (ISBN 0-688-03328-8). Morrow.
Callies, Fritz A. Playing with Grown Ups. 1978. pap. 6.95 (ISBN 0-8100-0007-5, 11N0623). Northwest Pub.
Callison, Brian. An Act of War. 1977. 7.95 o.p. (ISBN 0-525-05023-X). Dutton.
--The Judas Ship. 1978. 7.95 o.p. (ISBN 0-525-13780-7). Dutton.
Callison, C. H., ed. America's Natural Resources. rev. ed. 1967. 14.95 (ISBN 0-8260-1685-5, Pub. by Wiley-Interscience). Wiley.
Callot, Jacques. Callot's Etchings. Daniel, Howard, ed. (Illus., Orig.). 1974. 10.00 (ISBN 0-486-23081-3); pap. 6.00 (ISBN 0-486-23073-2). Dover.
Calloud, Jean. Structural Analysis of Narrative. Beardslee, William A., ed. Patte, Daniel, tr. from Fr. LC 75-37158. (Semeia Studies). 128p. 1976. pap. 3.95 (ISBN 0-8006-1503-4, 1-1503). Fortress.
Calloway, jt. auth. see Igel.
Calloway, Barbara & Stone, Alan, eds. Turmoil & Consensus: A Reader in Basic Political Issues. 300p. 1981. 14.50 (ISBN 0-87073-868-2); pap. 7.95 (ISBN 0-87073-867-4). Schenkman.
Calloway, Northern J. & Hall, Carol. Super-Vroomer. LC 77-26512. (gr. k-3). 1978. PLB 5.95 (ISBN 0-385-14178-5). Doubleday.
Calloway, Stephen. English Prints for the Collector. LC 80-19370. (Illus.). 240p. 1981. 50.00 (ISBN 0-87951-120-6). Overlook Pr.
Callum, Myles. Body-Building & Self-Defense. 1962. pap. 2.95 (ISBN 0-06-463258-X, EH 258, EH). Har-Row.
--Body-Building & Self-Defense. LC 61-15729. (Illus.). (gr. 8-12). 1967. 7.95 (ISBN 0-8069-4031-X); PLB 6.69 (ISBN 0-8069-4007-7). Sterling.
Callus, D. A., ed. Robert Grosseteste: Scholar & Bishop. 1955. 22.50x (ISBN 0-19-821387-5). Oxford U Pr.
Callwood, June. Love, Hate, Fear, Anger, & the Other Lively Emotions. LC 80-19320. 168p. 1980. Repr. of 1971 ed. lib. bdg. 9.95x (ISBN 0-89370-602-7). Borgo Pr.

Calman, Kenneth C. & Paul, John. Introduction to Cancer Medicine. LC 77-91854. 1978. 21.95 (ISBN 0-471-04274-9, Pub. by Wiley Medical). Wiley.

Calmette, Joseph L. La Societe Feodale. LC 80-1994. 1981. Repr. of 1923 ed. 26.50 (ISBN 0-404-18556-8). AMS Pr.

Calmon, C. & Gold, H. Ion Exchange for Pollution Control, 2 vols. 1979. Vol. 1, 272p. 64.95 (ISBN 0-8493-5153-7); Vol. 2, 288p. 69.95 (ISBN 0-8493-5154-5). CRC Pr.

Calmus, Thomas W., jt. auth. see Sampson, Roy J.

Calne, D. B., ed. Progress in the Treatment of Parkinsonism. LC 72-93317. (Advances in Neurology Ser.: Vol. 3). (Illus.). 340p. 1973. 31.50 (ISBN 0-911216-49-9). Raven.

Calne, D. B., et al, eds. Dopaminergic Mechanisms. LC 74-13904. (Advances in Neurology Ser: Vol. 9). 1975. 41.50 (ISBN 0-911216-93-6). Raven.

Calter, Paul. Magic Squares. LC 77-1213. (Illus.). (gr. 7 up). 1977. 7.95 o.p. (ISBN 0-525-66433-5). Elsevier-Nelson.

Calveley, Christina. The Family Quiz Book. 1981. pap. 2.95 (ISBN 0-14-005507-X). Penguin.

Calverley, C. S. The English Poems of C. S. Calverley. Spear, Hilda D., ed. 116p. 1974. pap. text ed. 7.50x (ISBN 0-7185-1119-0, Leicester). Humanities.

Calverley, Edwin E., ed. see Al-Ghazzali.

Calvert. Introduction to Building Management. 4th ed. 1981. text ed. price not set (ISBN 0-408-00520-3); pap. price not set. Butterworth.

Calvert, Barbara. Role of the Pupil. (Students Library of Education Ser.). 1975. 12.00 (ISBN 0-7100-8065-4); pap. 6.00 (ISBN 0-7100-8066-2). Routledge & Kegan.

Calvert, D. R., jt. auth. see Simmons-Martin, A.

Calvert, Donald. Descriptive Phonetics. 1980. 16.00. Thieme Stratton.

Calvert, G. H. Spanish Dictionary. (Routledge Pocket Dictionaries Ser.). 560p. 1980. pap. 7.95 (ISBN 0-7100-0558-X). Routledge & Kegan.

Calvert, N. G. Windpower Principles: Their Applications on the Small Scale. LC 79-19706. 1980. 26.95x (ISBN 0-470-26867-0). Halsted Pr.

Calvert, Patricia. The Snowbird. LC 80-19139. 192p. (gr. 5 up). 1980. 8.95 (ISBN 0-686-62531-5). Scribner.

Calvert, Peter. Mexican Revolution Nineteen Ten - Nineteen Fourteen: The Diplomacy of Anglo-American Conflict. (Cambridge Latin American Studies: No. 3). (Illus.). 1968. 39.95 (ISBN 0-521-04423-5). Cambridge U Pr.

--The Mexicans: How They Live & Work. LC 74-17467. 168p. 1975. text ed. 8.95 (ISBN 0-03-029696-X, HoltC). HR&W.

--Mexico. (Nations of the Modern World Ser.). 1977. 17.25x (ISBN 0-510-37905-2). Westview.

Calvert, Robert A., jt. ed. see Wooster, Ralph A.

Calvert, Robert, Jr. Career Patterns of Liberal Arts Graduates. LC 73-84568. (gr. 12). 1973. 10.00x o.p. (ISBN 0-910328-00-5). Carroll Pr.

Calvert, Thomas H. Regulation of Commerce Under the Federal Constitution. (Studies in Constitutional Law). xiv, 380p. 1981. Repr. of 1907 ed. lib. bdg. 32.50x (ISBN 0-8377-0429-4). Rothman.

Calvin, Allen, ed. Perspectives on Education. LC 76-20019. (Illus.). 1977. pap. text ed. 9.95 (ISBN 0-201-00878-5). A-W.

Calvin, Jean. Aphorismes of Christian Religion or a Verie Compendious Abridgement of M I Calvins Institutions Set Forth by M I Piscator. Holland, H., tr. LC 73-6107. (English Experience Ser.: No. 575). 1973. Repr. of 1596 ed. 26.00 (ISBN 90-221-0575-X). Walter J Johnson.

--Opera Quae Supersunt Omnia, 59 Vols. in 58. Baum, G., et al, eds. 1863-1900. Set. 1715.00 (ISBN 0-384-07195-3); 42.00 ea. Johnson Repr.

--Three French Treatises. Higman, F. M., ed. (Athlone Renaissance Library). 1970. text ed. 10.75x (ISBN 0-485-13802-6, Athlone Pr); pap. text ed. 5.50x (ISBN 0-485-12802-0, Athlone Pr). Humanities.

Calvin, John. Calvin's Letters. pap. 4.95 (ISBN 0-686-28946-3). Banner of Truth.

--Concerning Scandals. Fraser, John W., tr. LC 78-8675. 1978. 6.95 o.p. (ISBN 0-8028-3511-2). Eerdmans.

--Concerning the Eternal Predestination of God. Reid, J. K., ed. 1961. 13.95 (ISBN 0-227-67438-3). Attic Pr.

--Genesis. (Geneva Commentaries Ser.). 1979. 17.95 (ISBN 0-85151-093-0). Banner of Truth.

--John Calvin's Sermons on the Ten Commandments. Farley, Benjamin W., ed. 544p. 1980. 12.95 (ISBN 0-8010-2443-9). Baker Bk.

--Letters of John Calvin. 261p. 1980. pap. 4.95 (ISBN 0-85151-323-9). Banner of Truth.

--On God & Political Duty. 2nd ed. LC 50-4950. 1956. pap. 3.95 (ISBN 0-672-60184-2, LLA23). Bobbs.

--On the Christian Faith: Selections from the Institutes, Commentaries & Tracts. McNeill, John T., ed. LC 58-7660. 1957. pap. 5.50 (ISBN 0-672-60283-0, LLA93). Bobbs.

--Sermons on Ephesians. 1979. 16.95 (ISBN 0-85151-170-8). Banner of Truth.

--Sermons on Isaiah's Prophecy of the Death & Passion of Christ. Parker, T. H., tr. write for info. (ISBN 0-227-67427-8). Attic Pr.

Calvin, Melvin & Pryor, William A.intro. by. Organic Chemistry of Life: Readings from Scientific American. LC 73-12475. (Illus.). 1973. text ed. 19.95x (ISBN 0-7167-0884-1); pap. text ed. 9.95x (ISBN 0-7167-0883-3). W H Freeman.

Calvin, Ross. Sky Determines: An Interpretation of the Southwest. rev ed. LC 48-6466. (Illus.). 1965. pap. 4.95 (ISBN 0-8263-0011-1). U of NM Pr.

Calvin, William H. & Ojemann, George A. Inside the Brain. (Illus., Orig.). 1980. pap. 2.50 (ISBN 0-451-61863-7, ME1863, Ment). NAL.

Calvino, Italo. The Baron in the Trees. Colquhoun, Archibald, tr. 1977. pap. 3.50 (ISBN 0-15-610680-9, HPL). HarBraceJ.

--Cosmicomics. Weaver, William, tr. LC 76-14795. 1976. pap. 2.95 (ISBN 0-15-622600-6). HarBraceJ.

--If on a Winter's Night a Traveler. Weaver, William, tr. from It. LC 80-8741. (Helen & Kurt Wolff Bk.). 288p. 1981. 12.95 (ISBN 0-15-143689-4). HarBraceJ.

--The Nonexistent Knight & the Clover Viscount. Ferrone, J. & Wolff, H., eds. 1977. pap. 3.95 (ISBN 0-15-665975-1, HPL). HarBraceJ.

--The Watcher & Other Stories. Weaver, William & Colquhoun, Archibald, trs. from It. LC 75-9829. 181p. 1975. pap. 2.95 (ISBN 0-15-694952-0, HPL65, HPL). HarBraceJ.

Calvo, Joraida, jt. auth. see Acosta, Antonio A.

Calvo, Juan A. & Del Prado, Carlos. La Veta Hispana: Panorama de la Civilizacion Espanola. LC 70-132804. (Illus.). 1972. 24.50 (ISBN 0-89197-494-6); pap. text ed. 14.95x (ISBN 0-89197-972-7). Irvington.

Calvocoressi, M. D. The Principles & Methods of Musical Criticism. (Music Reprint Ser.). 1979. Repr. of 1931 ed. 20.00 (ISBN 0-306-79557-4). Da Capo.

--A Survey of Russian Music. LC 73-6208. (Illus.). 142p. 1974. Repr. of 1944 ed. lib. bdg. 15.00x (ISBN 0-8371-6888-0, CARM). Greenwood.

Calvocoressi, M. D., tr. see Scherchen, Herman.

Calvocoressi, Peter. Top Secret Ultra. (Illus.). 1981. 10.95 (ISBN 0-394-51154-9). Pantheon.

--World Politics Since 1945. 3rd ed. 1978. pap. text ed. 11.95x (ISBN 0-582-48913-X). Longman.

Calvo-Sotelo, Joaquin. La Herencia. Klein, Richard B., ed. 112p. 1976. pap. text ed. 3.25x (ISBN 0-88334-075-5). Ind Sch Pr.

Cam, H. M., ed. see Maitland, Frederic W.

Camaione, David N. & Tillman, Kenneth G. Teaching & Coaching Wrestling: A Scientific Approach. 2nd ed. LC 79-18686. 1980. text ed. 17.95 (ISBN 0-471-05032-6). Wiley.

Camara, Dom H. Desert Is Fertile. 1976. pap. 1.50 (ISBN 0-89129-060-5). Jove Pubns.

Camarillo, Albert. Chicanos in a Changing Society: From Mexican Pueblos to American Barrios in Santa Barbara & Southern California, 1848-1930. LC 79-10687. 1979. 17.50x o.p. (ISBN 0-674-11395-0); pap. 7.95x (ISBN 0-674-11396-9). Harvard U Pr.

Camaro Editors. Official Visitors Guide: Los Angeles. 1980. 2.95 (ISBN 0-913290-30-0). Camaro Pub.

--Official Visitors Guide: San Francisco. 1980. 2.95 (ISBN 0-913290-32-7). Camaro Pub.

Camatini, E. & Kester, T., eds. Heat Pumps Their Contribution to Energy Conservation. 428p. 1976. 42.50x (ISBN 90-286-0056-6). Sijthoff & Noordhoff.

Cambanis, S. & Miller, Grady. Linear Problems in P-th Order & Stable Processes. 49p. 1980. pap. 1.60 (1272). U of NC Pr.

Cambanis, Stamatis & Simons, Gordon. Probability & Expectation Inequalities. 49p. 1980. pap. 1.60 (1263). U of NC Pr.

Cambel, A. B., ed. Energy Devices & Processes: Proceedings of a Workshop on the Second Law of Thermodynamics, Held at the George Washington University, Wash. D. C., 14-16 Aug. 1979. 300p. 1980. pap. 60.00 (ISBN 0-08-026704-1). Pergamon.

Cambell, Shep. Quick Tips from the Tennis Spot. LC 80-84952. (Illus.). 208p. 1981. pap. 6.95 (ISBN 0-914178-45-8, 42906-X). Golf Digest Bks.

Camberwell Council on Alcoholism. Women & Alcohol. LC 80-40370. 207p. 1980. 22.00 (ISBN 0-422-76960-6, 2007); pap. 10.95 (2007). Methuen Inc.

Cambitoglou, A., jt. auth. see Trendall, A. D.

Cambon, Glauco. Ugo Foscolo: Poet of Exile. LC 79-3193. 360p. 1980. 21.50x (ISBN 0-691-06424-5). Princeton U Pr.

Cambra, Ronald E., jt. auth. see Klopf, Donald W.

Cambrai, Fenelon De see De Cambrai, Fenelon.

Cambrensis, Giraldus. History & Topography of Ireland. O'Meara, John J., tr. (Dolmen Texts: No. 4). 1980. text ed. 31.25 (ISBN 0-391-01166-9, Dolmen Pr). Humanities.

Cambridge Consultants Training Ltd. Programmed Introduction to Critical Path Methods. 1975. pap. 6.25 (ISBN 0-08-014027-0). Pergamon.

Cambridge Research Institute & Teplitz, Paul V. Trends Affecting the U. S. Banking System. LC 75-37754. 1976. 17.50 o.p. (ISBN 0-88410-291-2). Ballinger Pub.

Cambridge School Classics Project. Cambridge Latin Course, 3 bklts, Unit 5, Pupils Books. Incl. Dido et Aeneas; Nero et Agrippina; Words & Phrases. (Illus.). 1974. pap. text ed. 4.50x (ISBN 0-521-08545-4). Cambridge U Pr.

Camden, Archie. Bassoon Technique. 1962. 7.75 (ISBN 0-19-318606-3). Oxford U Pr.

Camenzind, Hans R. Electronic Integrated Systems Design. LC 78-12195. (Illus.). 342p. 1980. Repr. of 1972 ed. lib. bdg. 18.50 (ISBN 0-88275-763-6). Krieger.

Cameron. The Future of British Conurbations. 1980. 38.00 o.p. (ISBN 0-582-44389-X). Longman.

Cameron, jt. auth. see Cohen.

Cameron, jt. ed. see Yerian.

Cameron, A. Principles of Lubrication. 2nd ed. Date not set. text ed. write for info. (ISBN 0-582-47000-5). Longman. Postponed.

Cameron, A. G. W., jt. ed. see Ponnamperuma, Cyril.

Cameron, A. J. Mathematical Enterprises for Schools. 1966. 7.50 (ISBN 0-08-011833-X). Pergamon.

Cameron, Alastair. Basic Lubrication Theory. 2nd ed. LC 76-48204. 1977. 34.95 (ISBN 0-470-99020-1). Halsted Pr.

Cameron, Allan. The Science of Food & Cooking. 3rd ed. (Illus.). 1973. pap. 13.95x (ISBN 0-7131-1791-5). Intl Ideas.

Cameron, Allan G. Food Facts & Fallacies. (Illus., Orig.). 1973. pap. 4.95 (ISBN 0-571-10290-5, Pub. by Faber & Faber). Merrimack Bk Serv.

Cameron, Allan G., jt. auth. see Fox, Brian A.

Cameron, Ann. The Angel Book. (Illus.). 1977. pap. 6.95 o.p. (ISBN 0-345-27263-3). Ballantine.

--The Stories Julian Tells. LC 80-18023. (Illus.). 96p. (gr. k-5). 1981. 7.95 (ISBN 0-394-84301-0); PLB 7.99 (ISBN 0-394-94301-5). Pantheon.

Cameron, Averil, ed. Flavius Cresconius Corippus: In Laudem Lustini Augusti Minoris. (Illus.). 235p. 1976. text ed. 52.00x (ISBN 0-485-11157-8, Athlone Pr). Humanities.

Cameron, Clare. Rustle of Spring: An Edwardian Childhood in London's East End. 288p. 1980. 19.75x (ISBN 0-7050-0074-5, Pub. by Skilton & Shaw England). State Mutual Bk.

Cameron, Cyril T. Public Relations in the Emergency Department. 126p. 1980. text ed. 14.95 (ISBN 0-87619-746-2). R J Brady.

Cameron, Derek. Audio Technology Systems: Principles, Applications & Troubleshooting. (Illus.). 1978. text ed. 17.95 (ISBN 0-87909-050-2). Reston.

--Handbook of Audio Circuit Design. (Illus.). 1978. text ed. 18.95 (ISBN 0-87909-362-5). Reston.

--Hi-Fi Stereo Installation Simplified. (Illus.). 1978. 15.95 (ISBN 0-8359-2842-X). Reston.

Cameron, Doug. How to Survive Being Committed to a Mental Hospital. LC 79-66488. 143p. 1980. 7.95 (ISBN 0-533-04399-9). Vantage.

Cameron, E. Hyaluronidase & Cancer. 1966. 15.95 o.p. (ISBN 0-08-011480-6). Pergamon.

Cameron, E., ed. see Valdes, Armando P.

Cameron, Eleanor. Beyond Silence. LC 80-10350. (gr. 5-9). 1980. PLB 9.95 (ISBN 0-525-26463-9). Dutton.

--The Court of the Stone Children. 208p. (gr. 5 up). 1973. PLB 9.95 (ISBN 0-525-28350-1). Dutton.

--Julia & the Hand of God. LC 77-4507. (Illus.). 1977. PLB 8.95 (ISBN 0-525-32910-2). Dutton.

--The Terrible Churnadryne. (Illus.). (gr. 4-6). 1959. 8.95 (ISBN 0-316-12535-0, Pub. by Atlantic Monthly Pr). Little.

Cameron, Elspeth. Hugh MacLennan: A Writers Life. 424p. 1981. 25.00 (ISBN 0-8020-5556-7). U of Toronto Pr.

Cameron, Ewan & Pauling, Linus. Cancer & Vitamin C. 1981. pap. 5.95 (ISBN 0-446-97735-7). Warner Bks.

Cameron, George G., ed. see Chiera, Edward.

Cameron, Gordon, ed. The Future of the British Conurbation Policies & Prescription for Change. 288p. 1980. lib. bdg. 38.00 (ISBN 0-582-44389-X). Longman.

Cameron, Iain. Scientific Images & Their Social Uses. (Science in a Social Context Ser.). 1979. pap. text ed. 3.95 (ISBN 0-408-71309-7). Butterworths.

Cameron, Ian. To the Farthest Ends of the Earth: One Hundred Fifty Years of World Exploration by the Royal Geographical Society. (Illus.). 304p. 1980. 27.00 (ISBN 0-525-22065-8). Dutton.

Cameron, Ivan L. & Padilla, George M., eds. Developmental Aspects of the Cell Cycle. (Cell Biology Ser.). 1971. 52.50 o.s.i. (ISBN 0-12-156960-8). Acad Pr.

Cameron, Ivan L. & Pool, Thomas B., eds. The Transformed Cell. (Cell Biology Ser.). 1981. price not set (ISBN 0-12-157160-2). Acad Pr.

Cameron, J. & Dodd, W. A. Society, Schools & Progress in Tanzania. 1970. 22.00 (ISBN 0-08-015564-2); pap. 11.25 (ISBN 0-08-015563-4). Pergamon.

Cameron, J. H., tr. see Girard, Paul F.

Cameron, J. Stewart, et al. Nephrology for Nurses - A Modern Approach to the Kidney. 2nd ed. 1977. spiral bdg. 9.50 (ISBN 0-87488-869-7). Med Exam.

Cameron, James B., et al. Advanced Accounting: Theory & Practice. LC 78-69529. (Illus.). 1979. text ed. 21.75 (ISBN 0-395-27446-X); inst. manual 3.00 (ISBN 0-395-27497-4); student check sheets 2.00 (ISBN 0-395-27497-4). HM.

Cameron, Jenks. The Development of Governmental Forest Control in the United States. LC 79-38096. (Law, Politics, & History Ser). 484p. 1972. Repr. of 1928 ed. lib. bdg. 45.00 (ISBN 0-306-70440-4). Da Capo.

Cameron, John. Development of Education in East Africa. LC 68-9320. (Illus.). 1970. pap. text ed. 5.75x (ISBN 0-8077-1137-3). Tchrs Coll.

Cameron, Judy. The Bolshoi Ballet. LC 74-25152. (Icon Editions, Helene Obolensky Enterprises Bk). (Illus.). 184p. 1975. 17.50 o.s.i. (ISBN 0-06-430600-3, HarpT). Har-Row.

Cameron, Kate. Kiss Me Kill Me. 1979. pap. 1.50 (ISBN 0-505-51384-6). Tower Bks.

--Music from the Past. (Holderly Hall Ser). (Orig.). 1975. pap. 1.25 o.p. (ISBN 0-685-53904-0, LB287ZK, Leisure Bks). Nordon Pubns.

--Voices in the Fog. (Holderly Hall Ser: No. 3). 1975. pap. 0.95 o.p. (ISBN 0-685-51410-2, LB230NK, Leisure Bks). Nordon Pubns.

Cameron, Keith. Agrippa D'aubigne. (World Authors Ser.: France: No. 443). 1977. lib. bdg. 12.50 (ISBN 0-8057-6280-9). Twayne.

Cameron, Ken see Bartram, George, pseud.

Cameron, Kenneth. English Place-Names. 1977. 22.50 (ISBN 0-7134-0841-3). David & Charles.

Cameron, Kenneth see Corrigan, Robert W.

Cameron, Kenneth M. The Father of Fires. (ARMS Saga Ser.: Bk. 1). 320p. 1981. pap. 2.95 (ISBN 0-445-04640-6). Popular Lib.

--Our Jo: A Chronicle of a Coming Man. LC 73-15145. 384p. 1974. 7.95 o.s.i. (ISBN 0-02-521010-6). Macmillan.

Cameron, Kenneth N. Shelley: The Golden Years. LC 73-80566. 1974. text ed. 22.50x (ISBN 0-674-80605-0). Harvard U Pr.

Cameron, Kenneth W. Emerson the Essayist: An Outline of His Philosophical Development Through 1836, 2 vols. LC 80-2529. 1981. Repr. of 1945 ed. Set. 92.00 (ISBN 0-404-19280-7). Vol. 1 (ISBN 0-404-19281-5). Vol. 2 (ISBN 0-404-19282-3). AMS Pr.

Cameron, Lou. The Big Lonely. 1978. pap. 2.25 (ISBN 0-445-04200-1). Popular Lib.

--Code Seven. 1977. pap. 1.25 o.p. (ISBN 0-425-03296-5). Berkley Pub.

--The Subway Stalker. (Orig.). 1980. pap. 2.50 (ISBN 0-440-17873-8). Dell.

Cameron, Mabel W., ed. The Biographical Cyclopaedia of American Women, 2 vols. LC 24-7615. 408p. 1975. Repr. of 1924 ed. 64.00 (ISBN 0-8103-3990-0). Gale.

Cameron, Miriam. Hello, I'm God & I'm Here to Help You. (Orig.). 1980. pap. 1.95 (ISBN 0-446-90063-X). Warner Bks.

Cameron, Nigel. China Today. LC 73-21234. (International Library). (Illus.). 128p. (gr. 7 up). 1974. PLB 6.90 o.p. (ISBN 0-531-02712-0). Watts.

--The Face of China As Seen by Photographers or Travelers: 1860-1930. LC 78-53932. (Illus.). 1978. 25.00 (ISBN 0-89381-029-0); pap. 14.95 (ISBN 0-89381-031-2). Aperture.

--Hong Kong: The Cultured Pearl. (Illus.). 1978. text ed. 29.50x (ISBN 0-19-580404-X). Oxford U Pr.

Cameron, Nigel, commentary by. The Face of China: As Seen by Photographers & Travelers, 1860 to 1912. (Illus.). 1980. pap. 14.95 o.p. (ISBN 0-89381-031-2). Aperture.

Cameron, Norman. Personality Development & Psychopathology: A Dynamic Approach. LC 63-6438. 1963. text ed. 20.95 (ISBN 0-395-04251-8, 3-08130); tchrs. manual by K.E.Renner 1.75 (ISBN 0-395-04252-6, 3-08131). HM.

Cameron, P. J. Parallelisms of Complete Designs. LC 75-32912. (London Mathematical Society Lecture Note Ser.: No. 23). (Illus.). 1976. 16.95x (ISBN 0-521-21160-3). Cambridge U Pr.

Cameron, P. J. & Van Lint, J. H. Graphs, Codes & Designs. (London Mathematical Society Lecture Notes Ser.: No. 43). 180p. 1980. 19.95x (ISBN 0-521-23141-8). Cambridge U Pr.

Cameron, R., jt. auth. see Cohen, D.

Cameron, Roderick. Australia: History & Horizons. LC 76-155154. (Illus.). 286p. 1971. 25.00x (ISBN 0-231-03559-4). Columbia U Pr.

Cameron, Ron & Dewey, Arthur J., trs. The Cologne Mani Codex. LC 79-14743. (Society of Biblical Literature Texts & Translations, 15. Early Christian Literature Ser.: No. 3). 1979. 10.50 (ISBN 0-89130-311-1, 060215); pap. 6.00 (ISBN 0-89130-312-X). Scholars Pr Ca.

Cameron, Sharon. LyricTime: Dickinson & the Limits of Genre. LC 78-9983. 1979. text ed. 15.00x (ISBN 0-8018-2171-1). Johns Hopkins.

Cameron, Stewart, et al. Nephrology for Nurses: A Modern Approach to the Kidney. 2nd ed. (Illus.). 330p. 1976. pap. 16.95x (ISBN 0-433-05111-6). Intl Ideas.

Cameron, W. M. & Pleasance, Peggy. Education in Movement Gymnastics. 1974. 4.00 o.p. (ISBN 0-8238-0166-7). Plays.

Cameron-Curry, U., tr. see Battezzati, M. & Donini, I.

Camiel, Reva & Michaelsen, Hila. First Time Out: Skills for Living Away from Home. LC 79-92821. (Illus., Orig.). (gr. 11-12). 1980. pap. 5.95 (ISBN 0-915190-26-5). Jalmar Pr.

Camiller, Patrick & Rothschild, Jon, eds. Power & Opposition in Post Revolutionary Societies. 288p. 1980. text ed. 17.50x (ISBN 0-906133-18-1); pap. text ed. 9.25x (ISBN 0-906133-19-X). Humanities.

Camilleri, Dorothy, jt. auth. see Grace, Helen K.

Camilleri, J. A. Civilization in Crisis. LC 76-4240. (Illus.). 1977. 28.95 (ISBN 0-521-21248-0); pap. 11.50x (ISBN 0-521-29078-3). Cambridge U Pr.

Cammack, Emerson, jt. auth. see Mehr, Robert I.

Camner, James. The Great Instrumentalists in Historic Photographs: 275 Portraits from 1850 to 1950. (Illus.). 1980. pap. 6.95 (ISBN 0-486-23907-1). Dover.

Camoens, Luis De see De Camoens, Luis.

Camp, Catherine C. de see De Camp, L. Sprague & De Camp, Catherine C.

Camp, Debbie. Gateway to the Heart. (Orig.). 1980. pap. 1.95 (ISBN 0-532-23208-9). Manor Bks.

Camp, Deborah. Tandem. (Orig.). 1980. pap. 1.95 (ISBN 0-532-23236-4). Manor Bks.

Camp, James, et al. Pegasus Descending: A Treasury of the Best Bad Poems in English. 1971. pap. 2.45 o.s.i. (ISBN 0-02-069280-3, Collier). Macmillan.

Camp, John M. Gods & Heroes in the Athenian Agora: Excavations of the Athenian Agora Picture Bks. (No. 19). (Illus.). 1980. pap. 1.50x (ISBN 0-87661-623-6). Am Sch Athens.

Camp, L. Sprague De see De Camp, L. Sprague.

Camp, L. Sprague de see DeCamp, L. Sprague.

Camp, L. Sprague de see De Camp, L. Sprague & De Camp, Catherine C.

Camp, L. Sprague De see Howard, Robert E. & Sprague De Camp, L.

Camp, Lewis, jt. auth. see Beaumier, John P.

Camp, Norman. Pensando Con Dios. 128p. (Span.). 1981. pap. 1.95 (ISBN 0-8024-6593-5). Moody.

Camp, William. The Jacobs Park Killings: A Police Procedural Mystery. LC 78-57257. 1979. 8.95 (ISBN 0-8149-0803-9). Vanguard.

Camp, William L. & Schwark, Bryan L. Guide to Periodicals in Education & Its Academic Disciplines. 2nd ed. LC 75-6784. 568p. 1975. 23.50 (ISBN 0-8108-0814-5). Scarecrow.

Campa, Arthur L. Treasure of the Sangre De Cristos: Tales & Traditions of the Spanish Southwest. (Illus.). 1963. 7.95 (ISBN 0-8061-0574-7); pap. 4.95 (ISBN 0-8061-1176-3). U of Okla Pr.

Campanella, Roy. Its Good to Be Alive. (RL 7). pap. 1.25 (ISBN 0-451-05952-2, Y5952, Sig). NAL.

Campanella, Tommaso. The City of the Sun: A Poetical Dialogue of Tommaso Campanella. Donno, Daniel J., ed. (Biblioteca Italiana Ser.). 1981. 12.50x (ISBN 0-520-04034-1); pap. 3.50x (ISBN 0-520-04036-8). U of Cal Pr.

Campardon, Emile. L'academie Royale de Musique au 18 Siecle, 2 Vols. LC 73-141152. (Music Ser). 1971. Repr. of 1884 ed. lib. bdg. 95.00 (ISBN 0-306-70090-5). Da Capo.

Campbell. Money & Banking. 3rd ed. 1978. 18.95 (ISBN 0-03-020806-8). Dryden Pr.

--The Monsters' Room. (gr. 3-5). pap. 1.25 (ISBN 0-590-02076-5, Schol Pap). Schol Bk Serv.

--Trixie Belden & the Mystery of the Velvet Gown. lib. bdg. 5.52 (ISBN 0-307-61550-2, Golden Pr); pap. 1.25 (ISBN 0-307-21550-4). Western Pub.

Campbell, A. Common Market Law, Vol. 3. 2nd ed. 1973. 65.00 (ISBN 0-379-16063-3). Oceana.

--Highland Dress, Arms & Ornament. 1969. Repr. of 1899 ed. 15.00 o.p. (ISBN 0-7129-0380-1, Dist by Shoe String). Dawson Pub.

Campbell, A. C. The Larousse Guide to the Seashore & Shallow Seas of Britain & Europe. LC 80-82755. (Larousse Nature Guides Ser.). (Illus.). 320p. (Orig.). 1981. 10.95 (ISBN 0-88332-251-X, 8068). Larousse.

Campbell, A. K. & Sacks, S. Metropolitan America. LC 67-14373. 1967. 12.95 (ISBN 0-02-905230-0). Free Pr.

Campbell, Ada M. & Penfield, Marjorie. Experimental Study of Food. 2nd ed. LC 78-69535. (Illus.). 1979. text ed. 19.95 (ISBN 0-395-26666-1). HM.

Campbell, Alan K. & Bahl, Roy W., eds. State & Local Government. LC 75-43361. 1976. 17.95 (ISBN 0-02-905180-0). Free Pr.

Campbell, Alex. Unbind Your Sons: The Captivity of America in Asia. LC 79-114382. (Illus.). 1970. 7.95 o.p. (ISBN 0-87140-500-8); pap. 2.45 o.p. (ISBN 0-87140-027-8). Liveright.

Campbell, Angus. The Sense of Well Being in America: Recent Patterns & Trends. 256p. 1980. 14.95 (ISBN 0-07-009683-X). McGraw.

--White Attitudes Toward Black People. LC 74-161548. 177p. 1971. cloth 10.00 (ISBN 0-87944-007-4); pap. 6.00 (ISBN 0-87944-006-6). U of Mich Soc Res.

Campbell, Angus, et al. American Voter: An Abridgement. LC 64-20076. (Illus.). 1964. pap. text ed. 11.95 (ISBN 0-471-13335-3). Wiley.

--The American Voter. LC 76-21115. (Midway Reprint Ser.). 576p. 1980. lib. bdg. 18.00x (ISBN 0-226-09254-2). U of Chicago Pr.

--The American Voter. LC 76-21115. 1976. Repr. of 1960 ed. lib. bdg. 15.00x o.s.i. (ISBN 0-226-09253-4). U of Chicago Pr.

Campbell, Ann. Let's Find Out About Color. LC 74-3302. (Let's Find Out Bks). (Illus.). 48p. (gr. k-3). 1975. PLB 4.90 o.p. (ISBN 0-531-00110-5). Watts.

--Start to Draw. LC 68-25727. (Illus.). (gr. k-3). 1968. PLB 4.90 o.p. (ISBN 0-531-01799-0). Watts.

Campbell, Ann R. Let's Find Out About Boats. LC 67-16966. (Let's Find Out Bks). (Illus.). (gr. k-3). 1967. PLB 4.47 o.p. (ISBN 0-531-00007-9). Watts.

Campbell, Anneke. Your Pregnancy Year. LC 77-94864. 1979. 5.95 o.p. (ISBN 0-385-14323-0, Dolp). Doubleday.

Campbell, Antony F. The Ark Narrative. LC 75-2361. (Society of Biblical Literature. Dissertation Ser.). vii, 282p. 1975. pap. 6.00 (ISBN 0-89130-218-2, 060116). Scholars Pr Ca.

Campbell, Arthur. Law of Sentencing, Vol.1. LC 78-18626. 1978. 47.50. Lawyers Co-Op.

Campbell, Ashley S. Thermodynamic Analysis of Combustion Engines. LC 78-16181. 1979. text ed. 27.95 (ISBN 0-471-03751-6); tchrs manual (ISBN 0-471-05498-4). Wiley.

Campbell, Bernard. Human Evolution: An Introduction to Man's Adaptations. 2nd ed. LC 72-140006. 404p. 1974. lib. bdg. 19.95x (ISBN 0-202-02012-6); pap. text ed. 11.95x (ISBN 0-202-02013-4). Aldine Pub.

Campbell, Bernard, jt. ed. see Oakley, Kenneth.

Campbell, Bonnie. The Time the Boat Came Back. (Hello World Ser.). 1976. pap. 1.65 (ISBN 0-8163-0268-5, 20475-0). Pacific Pr Pub Assn.

Campbell, Bruce F. Ancient Wisdom Revived: A History of the Theosophical Movement. 224p. 1980. 12.95 (ISBN 0-520-03968-8). U of Cal Pr.

Campbell, Byram. American Race Theorists. 1978. pap. 4.00x (ISBN 0-911038-33-7). Noontide.

Campbell, Charles, jt. auth. see Jahn, Penelope.

Campbell, Christopher. Aces & Aircraft of World War One. (Illus.). 128p. 1981. 24.95 (Pub. by Blandford Pr England). Sterling.

Campbell, Claire. Nursing Diagnosis & Intervention in Nursing Practice. LC 77-17095. 1978. text ed. 28.50 (ISBN 0-471-13307-8, Pub. by Wiley Medical). Wiley.

Campbell, Clyde. Toward Perfection in Learning. LC 68-59444. 142p. 1969. 5.50. Pendell Pub.

Campbell, Colin. Design of Racing Sports Cars. LC 73-85158. (Illus.). 268p. 1973. 12.50 (ISBN 0-8376-0081-2). Bentley.

--New Directions in Suspension Design: Making the Fast Car Faster. LC 80-24348. (Illus.). 224p. 1981. 18.50 (ISBN 0-8376-0150-9). Bentley.

Campbell, Colin & Campbell, Rosemary. Money & Banking. 4th ed. LC 80-65792. 608p. 1981. text ed. 18.95 (ISBN 0-03-058076-5). Dryden Pr.

Campbell, Colin D., ed. Financing Social Secutiy. 1979. 15.25 (ISBN 0-8447-2140-9); pap. 8.25 (ISBN 0-8447-2140-9). Am Enterprise.

Campbell, D. L. Comparative Law Yearbook, Vol. III. 294p. 1980. 47.50x (ISBN 90-286-0340-9). Sijthoff & Noordhoff.

Campbell, D. Ross. How to Really Love Your Child. 1977. pap. 3.50 (ISBN 0-88207-751-1). Victor Bks.

Campbell, David E., tr. from Fr. The Tale of Balain. LC 72-77830. (Medieval French Texts). 144p. 1972. text ed. 8.95x o.s.i. (ISBN 0-8101-0385-0). Northwestern U Pr.

Campbell, David P. Take the Road to Creatiity & Get off Your Dead End. 1977. pap. 2.95 (ISBN 0-913592-95-1). Argus Comm.

Campbell, Dennis, ed. see Mulville, Frank.

Campbell, Dennis, ed. see Woolf, Charlotte.

Campbell, Doak S. El Maestro Eficiente. Rodriguez, Jose M., tr. from Eng. Orig. Title: When Do Teachers Teach. 160p. (Span.). 1980. pap. 1.95 (ISBN 0-311-11029-0). Casa Bautista.

Campbell, Don. Police: The Exercise of Power. 128p. 1978. 13.95x (ISBN 0-7121-1678-8, Pub. by Macdonald & Evans Engalnd). Intl Ideas.

Campbell, Donald K. Daniel: Decoder of Dreams. 1977. pap. 2.95 (ISBN 0-88207-747-3). Victor Bks.

--Nehemiah: Man in Charge. 1979. pap. 2.50 (ISBN 0-88207-781-3) Victor Bks.

--No Time for Neutrality. 144p. 1981. pap. 3.95 (ISBN 0-88207-337-0) Victor Bks.

Campbell, Donald W. Archery. (Sports Ser). 1970. pap. 4.25x ref. ed. (ISBN 0-13-043992-4). P-H.

Campbell, Edward F., Jr., jt. auth. see Freedman, David Noel.

Campbell, Ernest T. Locked in a Room with Open Doors. LC 73-9 554. 1976. pap. 3.95 o.p. (ISBN 0-87680-852-6, 98082). Word Bks.

--Where Cross the Crowded Ways: Prayers of a City Pastor. 1973. pap. 2.95 o.p. (ISBN 0-8096-1861-3, Assn Pr). Follett.

Campbell, Eugene E., jt. auth. see Gowans, Fred R.

Campbell, Florence. Your Days Are Numbered. 21st ed. 246p. 1980. pap. 5.50 (ISBN 0-87516-422-6). De Vorss.

Campbell, Frank & Singer, George. Brain & Behaviour: Psychobiology of Everyday Life. (Illus.). 168p. 1980. 22.50 (ISBN 0-08-024788-1); pap. 11.25 (ISBN 0-08-024787-3). Pergamon.

Campbell, Frank R. God's Message in Troubled Times. 1981. pap. 3.95 (ISBN 0-8054-2239-0). Broadman.

Campbell, G. A., jt. auth. see Brown, R.

Campbell, Gail. Marathon: The World of Long Distance Athletes. LC 76-58625. (Illus.). (gr. 7). 1977. 9.95 (ISBN 0-8069-4114-6); PLB 9.29 (ISBN 0-8069-4115-4). Sterling.

--Salt-Water Tropical Fish in Your Home. LC 76-1175. (Illus.). 160p. (YA) 1976. 10.95 (ISBN 0-8069-3730-0); PLB 9.29 (ISBN 0-8069-3731-9). Sterling.

Campbell, George. Philosophy of Rhetoric. Bitzer, Lloyd F., ed. LC 63-14291. (Landmarks in Rhetoric & Public Address Ser.). 476p. 1963. 12.95x (ISBN 0-8093-0100-8). S Ill U Pr.

Campbell, Georgetta M. Extant Collections of Early Black Newspapers: A Research Guide to the Black Press, 1880-1915, with an Index to the Boston Guardian, 1902-1904. LC 80-51418. 433p. 1981. 28.50x (ISBN 0-87875-197-1). Whitston Pub.

Campbell, Gilbert L. Wet Plates & Dry Gulches. LC 71-41602. (Wild & Woolly West Ser., No. 8). (Illus., Orig.). 1975. 7.00 (ISBN 0-910584-94-X); pap. 2.00 (ISBN 0-910584-11-7). Filter.

Campbell, H. J. The Pleasure Areas: A New Theory of Behavior. 288p. 1973. 8.95 o.p. (ISBN 0-440-07226-3). Delacorte.

Campbell, Harry H. The Early History of Motley County. 6.95 (ISBN 0-685-48802-0). Nortex Pr.

Campbell, Helen. Darkness & Daylight: Or, Lights & Shadows of New York Life: A Pictorial Record of Personal Experiences by Day & Night in the Great Metropolis with Hundreds of Thrilling Anecdotes & Incidents. LC 76-81511. 1969. Repr. of 1895 ed. 24.00 (ISBN 0-8103-3566-2). Gale.

Campbell, Hilbert H. James Thomson. (English Authors Ser.: No. 269). 1979. lib. bdg. 10.95 (ISBN 0-8057-6715-0). Twayne.

Campbell, Hope. The Legend of Lost Earth. LC 76-48079. 160p. (YA) 1977. 6.95 (ISBN 0-590-07397-4, Four Winds). Schol Bk Serv.

--Mystery at Fire Island. LC 77-18311. (Illus.). 176p. (gr. 3-7). 1978. 7.95 (ISBN 0-590-07536-5, Four Winds). Schol Bk Serv.

--A Peak Beneath the Moon. LC 78-20427. 144p. (gr. 3-7). 1979. 6.95 (ISBN 0-590-07565-9, Four Winds). Schol Bk Serv.

--Peter's Angel: A Story About Monsters. LC 75-9517. (Illus.). 160p. (gr. 3-7). 1976. 6.95 (ISBN 0-590-07404-0, Four Winds). Schol Bk Serv.

Campbell, Hugh. Linear Algebra with Applications. 2nd ed. (Illus.). 1980. text ed. 18.95 (ISBN 0-13-536979-7). P-H.

Campbell, Hugh G. Introduction to Matrices, Vectors & Linear Programming. 2nd ed. LC 76-22757. (Illus.). 1977. text ed. 15.95 (ISBN 0-13-487439-0). P-H.

--Linear Algebra with Applications. LC 76-133903. (A-C Mathematics Ser). (Illus., Orig.). 1971. text ed. 17.95 (ISBN 0-13-536953-3). P-H.

--Linear Algebra with Applications: Including Linear Programming. LC 72-133902. (Mathematics Ser). (Illus., Orig.). 1971. text ed. 18.95 (ISBN 0-13-536946-0). P-H.

Campbell, I. R. Kudrun: A Critical Appreciation. LC 77-1721. (Anglica Germanica Ser.: No. 2). 1978. 55.00 (ISBN 0-521-21618-4). Cambridge U Pr.

Campbell, Ian M. Energy & the Atmosphere: A Physical-Chemical Approach. LC 76-57689. 1977. 50.75 (ISBN 0-471-99482-0); pap. 20.95 (ISBN 0-471-99481-2, Pub. by Wiley-Interscience). Wiley.

Campbell, Ivor E. & Sherwood, E. M. High-Temperature Materials & Technology. LC 67-13521. (Electrochemical Society Ser.). 1967. 52.95 o.p. (ISBN 0-471-13299-3, Pub. by Wiley-Interscience). Wiley.

Campbell, J. F. Leabhar Na Feinne. 272p. 1972. Repr. of 1872 ed. 36.00x (ISBN 0-7165-2060-5, Pub. by Irish Academic Pr Ireland). Biblio Dist.

Campbell, J. F. & Henderson, George. The Celtic Dragon Myth. (The Newcastle Mythology Library: Vol. 4). 1981. pap. 5.95 (ISBN 0-87877-048-8). Newcastle Pub.

Campbell, J. Gabriel. Saints & Householders: A Study of Hindu Ritual & Myth Among the Kangra Rajputs. (Illus.). 11.50x (ISBN 0-685-89506-8). Himalaya Hse.

Campbell, J. H. & Kameron, G. Simple Cooking for the Epicure. (Keith Jennison Large Type Bks). 7.95 o.p. (ISBN 0-531-00281-0). Watts.

Campbell, J. I., jt. auth. see Meadows, P. S.

Campbell, J. K. Honour, Family & Patronage: A Study of Institutions & Moral Values in a Greek Mountain Community. (Illus.). 406p. 1973. 29.95x (ISBN 0-19-823122-9); pap. text ed. 5.95x (ISBN 0-19-519756-9). Oxford U Pr.

Campbell, J. L. & Collinson, Francis, eds. Hebridean Folksongs, Vol. 3. 420p. 1980. 49.95 (ISBN 0-19-815215-9). Oxford U Pr.

Campbell, James. Bomber Raid. 1978. pap. 1.75 (ISBN 0-505-51272-6). Tower Bks.

--Greek Fathers. LC 63-10279. (Our Debt to Greece & Rome Ser). Repr. of 1930 ed. 16.50x (ISBN 0-8154-0046-2). Cooper Sq.

Campbell, James E., ed. Pottery & Ceramics: A Guide to Information Sources. LC 74-11545. (Art & Architecture Information Guide Ser.: Vol. 7). 1978. 30.00 (ISBN 0-8103-1274-3). Gale.

Campbell, James W. America in Her Centennial Year 1876. LC 79-6757. 272p. 1980. pap. text ed. 10.50 (ISBN 0-8191-0947-9). U Pr of Amer.

Campbell, Jean. Dreams Beyond Dreaming. LC 79-26131. 1980. pap. 5.95 (ISBN 0-89865-015-1, Unilaw). Donning Co.

Campbell, Jean, ed. see Lonik, Larry J.

Campbell, Jean M. Reaching Out with Love: Encounters with Troubled Youth. 144p. (Orig.). 1981. pap. 2.95 (ISBN 0-87239-453-0, 3652). Standard Pub.

Campbell, Jeffrey. The Homing. 256p. (Orig.). 1981. pap. 2.50 (ISBN 0-345-28793-2). Ballantine.

Campbell, Jim, jt. auth. see Brock, Ted.

Campbell, Joanna. The Films of Steve McQueen. Castell, David, ed. (The Films of... Ser.). (Illus.). (gr. 7-12). 1978. Repr. of 1973 ed. PLB 5.95 (ISBN 0-912616-84-9). Greenhaven.

Campbell, Joe B., jt. auth. see Campbell, June.

Campbell, John. The Travels & Adventures of Edward Brown, Esq. LC 75-170599. (Foundations of the Novel Ser.: Vol. 70). lib. bdg. 50.00 (ISBN 0-8240-0582-1). Garland Pub.

Campbell, John A. An Overview of Speech Preparation. Applbaum, Ronald & Hart, Roderick, eds. LC 13-5567. (Modcom, Modules in Speech Communication Ser.). 1980. pap. text ed. 2.25 (ISBN 0-574-22567-6, 13-5567). SRA.

Campbell, John B. The Upper Palaeolithic of Britain: A Study of Man & Nature in the Late Ice Age, Vols. I & II. (Illus.). 1978. 79.00 set (ISBN 0-19-813188-7). Oxford U Pr.

Campbell, John B., jt. auth. see Willson, James D.

Campbell, John C. Contemporary Japanese Budget Politics. 1977. 19.50x (ISBN 0-520-02573-3); pap. 6.95x (ISBN 0-520-04087-2, CAMPUS NO. 253). U of Cal Pr.

--Houses of Gold. (Illus.). 228p. (Orig.). 1980. pap. 15.00 (ISBN 0-8310-7121-4). Howell North.

Campbell, John F. Popular Tales of the West Highlands, 4 Vols. LC 67-23921. 1969. Repr. of 1890 ed. 92.00 (ISBN 0-8103-3458-5). Gale.

Campbell, John G. Superstitions of the Highlands & Islands of Scotland. 1970. 20.00 (ISBN 0-8103-3589-1). Gale.
Campbell, John J., jt. auth. see Brunner, Joseph F.
Campbell, John R. Introductory Treatise on Lie's Theory. LC 65-28441. 14.95 (ISBN 0-8284-0183-7). Chelsea Pub.
Campbell, Joseph. Poems of Joseph Campbell. 1963. 3.95 (ISBN 0-900372-66-4). Irish Bk Ctr.
Campbell, Joseph & Roberts, Richard. Tarot Revelations. (Illus., Orig.). 1980. pap. 8.95 (ISBN 0-931290-23-6). Alchemy Bks.
Campbell, Joseph & Robinson, Henry M. Skeleton Key to Finnegans Wake. 1977. pap. 5.95 (ISBN 0-14-004663-1). Penguin.
Campbell, Joseph, ed. Eranos Yearbooks, Papers from, 6 vols. Manheim, R. & Hull, R. F., trs. Incl. Vol. 1. Spirit & Nature. (Illus.). 1954. 18.50 o.p. (ISBN 0-691-09736-4); Vol. 2. The Mysteries. 1955. 20.00 (ISBN 0-691-09734-8); pap. 5.95 (ISBN 0-691-01823-5); Vol. 3. Man & Time. (Illus.). 1957. 17.50 (ISBN 0-691-09732-1); Vol. 4. Spirtual Disciplines. (Illus.). 1960. 25.00 (ISBN 0-691-09737-2); Vol. 5. Man & Transformation. (Illus.). 1964. 20.00 (ISBN 0-691-09733-X); pap. 5.95 (ISBN 0-691-01834-0); Vol. 6. Mystic Vision. 1969. 25.00 (ISBN 0-691-09735-6). (Bollingen Ser.: No. 30). Set. Princeton U Pr.
--Man & Transformation: Papers from the Eranosyears, Vol. 5. Manheim, Ralph, tr. from Fr. LC 72-1982. (Bollingen Ser.: Xxx). (Illus.). 452p. 1980. 20.00x (ISBN 0-691-09733-X); pap. 5.95 (ISBN 0-691-01834-0). Princeton U Pr.
Campbell, Joseph, ed. see Losang, Rato K.
Campbell, Judith. The World of the Horse. LC 76-49701. 1977. pap. 7.95 o.p. (ISBN 0-89104-056-0). A & W Pubs.
Campbell, Judy & Lowe, Susan. Twice the Heartache. 200p. (Orig.). 1981. 1.95 (ISBN 0-89896-050-9). Larksdale.
Campbell, Julie & Kenny, Katherine. Mystery of the Velvet Gown. (Trixie Belden Mystery Ser.). 236p. (gr. 4-6). 1980. PLB 5.52 (ISBN 0-307-61550-2, Golden Pr); pap. 1.25 (ISBN 0-307-21550-4). Western Pub.
Campbell, June & Campbell, Joe B. Laboratory Mathematics: Medical & Biological Applications. 2nd ed. LC 79-24996. (Illus.). 1980. pap. text ed. 12.95 (ISBN 0-8016-0702-7). Mosby.
Campbell, Katherine, ed. see Montgomery Museum of Fine Arts.
Campbell, Keith. Body & Mind. LC 79-123714. 1970. pap. 2.50 o.p. (ISBN 0-385-03022-3, Anch). Doubleday.
--Metaphysics: An Introduction. 1976. pap. text ed. 10.95x (ISBN 0-8221-0175-0). Dickenson.
Campbell, Kenneth D. New Opportunities in Realty Trusts. 1978. 35.00 (ISBN 0-912840-03-X); pap. 40.00 (ISBN 0-685-64945-8). Audit Investment.
Campbell, L. J. & Carlton, R. J. Atoms & Waves: Physics, Bk.2. (Secondary Science Ser.). (Illus., Orig.). (gr. 8-11). 1975. pap. text ed. 6.95 (ISBN 0-7100-7740-8). Routledge & Kegan.
--Force & Energy: Physics, Bk. 1. (Secondary Science Ser). (Illus., Orig.). (gr. 8-11). 1974. pap. text ed. 6.95 (ISBN 0-7100-7739-4). Routledge & Kegan.
Campbell, Leslie K. Architects of Destruction. 282p. (Orig.). 1980. pap. 4.95 (ISBN 0-9605164-4-1). Self.
Campbell, Lewis. The Theaetetus of Plato. 2nd ed. LC 78-66572. (Ancient Philosophy Ser.). 356p. 1980. lib. bdg. 35.00 (ISBN 0-8240-9606-1). Garland Pub.
Campbell, Lily B. Divine Poetry & Drama in Sixteenth-Century England. LC 59-3609. 1972. 16.75xx o.p. (ISBN 0-520-02108-8). U of Cal Pr.
Campbell, Lyle. Quichean Linguistic Pre-History. (Publications in Linguistics: Vol. 81). 1977. 11.50x (ISBN 0-520-09531-6). U of Cal Pr.
Campbell, M., jt. auth. see Petrie, W.
Campbell, M., ed. see Bennett, D. W.
Campbell, M., ed. see Murphy, Daniel.
Campbell, M. M. The New England Butt'ry Shelf Cookbook. 1968. 6.95 o.s.i. (ISBN 0-690-00362-5, TYC-T). T Y Crowell.
Campbell, Margaret, ed. see Aquilina, Alfred P.
Campbell, Margaret, ed. see Gordon, Julius & Weeks, Townsend E.
Campbell, Margaret, ed. see Stark, Raymond.
Campbell, Marjorie W. Fifty-Four-Forty or Fight. (Canadian Jackdaw Ser: No. C28). 1974. 5.95 o.s.i. (ISBN 0-670-31223-1, Grossman). Viking Pr.
Campbell, Mary C. & Stewart, Joyce L. The Medical Mycology Handbook. LC 80-11935. 436p. 1980. 25.00 (ISBN 0-471-04728-7, Pub. by Wiley Med). Wiley.
Campbell, Mary E. Attitude of Tennesseans Toward the Union, Eighteen Forty-Seven to Eighteen Sixty-One. LC 60-53338. 1961. 7.50 (ISBN 0-910294-15-1). Brown Bk.
Campbell, Mary J. My Experience Records in Homemaking. (gr. 7-12). 1963. pap. text ed. 2.60 (ISBN 0-87002-089-7). Bennett IL.
Campbell, Mary M. Kitchen Gardens. (Betty Crocker). 1974. pap. 4.95 (ISBN 0-307-09550-9, Golden Pr). Western Pub.
--New England Butt'ry Shelf Almanac. LC 76-128491. 1970. 9.95 o.s.i. (ISBN 0-690-00361-7, TYC-T). T Y Crowell.
Campbell, Mike. Capitalism in the UK: A Marxist Perspective. 216p. 1981. 28.00x (ISBN 0-7099-0089-9, Pub. by Croom Helm LTD England). Biblio Dist.
Campbell, Murdoch. From Grace to Glory: Meditations of the Psalms. 1979. pap. 3.95 (ISBN 0-85151-028-0). Banner of Truth.
Campbell, Oscar J. & Quinn, Edward G., eds. Reader's Encyclopedia of Shakespeare. LC 66-11946. (Illus.). 1966. 15.00 o.s.i. (ISBN 0-690-67412-0, TYC-T). T Y Crowell.
Campbell, P. J. In the Cannon's Mouth. 1979. 16.95 o.p. (ISBN 0-241-10166-2, Pub. by Hamish Hamilton England). David & Charles.
Campbell, Patricia. A History of the North Olympic Peninsula. Ducceschi, Frank, ed. (Illus.). 72p. 1979. pap. 6.95 (ISBN 0-918146-17-8). Peninsula WA.
Campbell, Patsy, et al. Seventy-Seven Dynamic Ideas for Teaching the Bible to Children. (Ideas Ser.). (Illus.). 1977. pap. text ed. 1.50 o.p. (ISBN 0-87239-130-2, 7966). Standard Pub.
Campbell, Paul N. & Greville, G. D., eds. Essays in Biochemistry, Vols. 1-5 & 8-15. Incl. Vol. 1. 1965 (ISBN 0-12-158101-2); Vol. 2. 1966 (ISBN 0-12-158102-0); Vol. 3. 1967 (ISBN 0-12-158103-9); Vol. 4. 1968 (ISBN 0-12-158104-7); Vol. 5. 1970 (ISBN 0-12-158105-5); Vol. 8. 1972 (ISBN 0-12-158108-X); Vol. 9. 1974 (ISBN 0-12-158109-8); Vol. 10. 1974 (ISBN 0-12-158110-1); Vol. 11. 1976 (ISBN 0-12-158111-X); Vol. 12. 1977 (ISBN 0-12-158112-8); Vol. 13. 1978 (ISBN 0-12-158113-6); Vol. 14. 1978 (ISBN 0-12-158114-4); Vol. 15. 1979 (ISBN 0-12-158115-2). (Illus.). pap. 13.00 ea. Acad Pr.
Campbell, Philip. Future Family. LC 80-84365. 1981. pap. 4.95 (ISBN 0-933350-39-2). Morse Pr.
Campbell, R. C. Statistics for Biologists. 2nd ed. (Illus.). 300p. 1974. 47.50 (ISBN 0-521-20381-3); pap. 9.95x (ISBN 0-521-09836-X). Cambridge U Pr.
Campbell, R. H. The Rise & Fall of Scottish Industry: Seventeen Seven to Nineteen Thirty-Nine. 217p. 1980. text ed. 32.50x (ISBN 0-85976-054-5). Humanities.
Campbell, R. H. & Dow, J. B. Source Book of Scottish Economic & Social History. 1968. 19.50x (ISBN 0-631-11080-1, Pub. by Basil Blackwell). Biblio Dist.
Campbell, R. H. & Wilson, R. G. Entrepreneurship in Britain, Seventeen Fifty to Nineteen Thirty-Nine. (Documents in Economic History). 1975. text ed. 13.00x (ISBN 0-7136-1524-9). Humanities.
Campbell, R. H., ed. see Smith, Adam.
Campbell, Ramsey. Démons by Daylight. pap. 1.75 o.s.i. (ISBN 0-515-04737-6). Jove Pubns.
--The Doll Who Ate His Mother. 1978. pap. 1.75 o.s.i. (ISBN 0-515-04483-0). Jove Pubns.
Campbell, Roald F. & Mazzoni, Tim L., Jr. State Policy Making for the Public Schools. new ed. LC 75-31311. 476p. 1976. 20.00 (ISBN 0-8211-0224-9); pap. text ed. 18.00x (ISBN 0-685-61059-4). McCutchan.
Campbell, Roald F., et al. Introduction to Educational Administration. 5th ed. 1977. text ed. 17.95 (ISBN 0-205-05678-4). Allyn.
Campbell, Robert. The Enigma of the Mind. LC 75-39976. (Human Behavior). (Illus.). (gr. 5 up). 1976. lib. bdg. 9.99 o.p. (ISBN 0-8094-1946-7, Pub. by Time-Life). Silver.
Campbell, Robert A., et al, eds. Advances in Polyamine Research, 2 vols. LC 77-83687. 1978. Vol. 1. 34.50 (ISBN 0-89004-189-X); Vol. 2. 41.00 (ISBN 0-89004-194-6). Raven.
Campbell, Robert G. The Panhandle Aspect of the Chaquaqua Plateau. (Graduate Studies: No. 11). (Illus., Orig.). 1976. pap. 5.00 (ISBN 0-89672-021-7). Tex Tech Pr.
Campbell, Robert J. Psychiatric Education & the Primary Physician. (Task Force Report: No. 2). 74p. 1970. pap. 5.00 (ISBN 0-685-24864-X, P241-0). Am Psychiatric.
Campbell, Robert J., ed. Psychiatric Dictionary. 800p. 1981. 29.50 (ISBN 0-19-502817-1). Oxford U Pr.
Campbell, Robert W. Soviet Energy Technologies. LC 80-7562. 288p. 1980. 22.50x (ISBN 0-253-15965-2). Ind U Pr.
--Soviet-Type Economies: Performance & Evolution. 3rd ed. 272p. 1974. pap. text ed. 9.95 (ISBN 0-395-17231-4). HM.
Campbell, Roger. Weight! A Better Way to Lose. 128p. 1976. pap. 2.95 (ISBN 0-88207-735-X). Victor Bks.
Campbell, Roger F., jt. auth. see Impe, Jack Van.
Campbell, Roger F., jt. auth. see Van Impe, Jack.
Campbell, Rosemary, jt. auth. see Campbell, Colin.
Campbell, Russell, compiled by. Photographic Theory for the Motion Picture Cameraman. (Illus.). 160p. 1981. pap. 6.95 (ISBN 0-498-07776-4). A S Barnes.
Campbell, Russell N., jt. auth. see King, Harold V.
Campbell, S. F. Piaget Sampler: An Introduction to Jean Piaget Through His Own Words. LC 75-34129. 154p. 1976. pap. text ed. 10.95 (ISBN 0-471-13344-2). Wiley.
Campbell, Sandy. B: Twenty-Nine Letters from Coconut Grove. 1974. wrappers, ltd. ed. 20.00x (ISBN 0-917366-03-4). S Campbell.
Campbell, Shep. Quick Tips from the CBS Tennis Spot. (Illus.). 208p. (Orig.). 1981. pap. 6.95 (ISBN 0-914178-45-8, 42906-X). Tennis Mag.
Campbell, Sid. Falcon Claw: The Motion Picture. Morales, Mahi, ed. 115p. 1980. pap. 7.50 (ISBN 0-937610-01-1). Dimond Pubs.
Campbell, Sid, et al. Two Thousand & One Martial Arts Questions, Kung Fu, Karate, Tae Kwon Do, Kenpo Students Should Know. LC 80-67769. (Illus.). 150p. 1980. pap. text ed. 8.95 (ISBN 0-686-28062-8). Dimond Pubs.
Campbell, Stafford. The Yachtsman Guide to Celestial Navigation. (Illus.). 1979. 9.95 (ISBN 0-87165-019-3, Yachting-Zd). Ziff-Davis Pub.
Campbell, Stuart D. & Reiss, Malcolm. Ski with the Big Boys. 1974. 11.95 (ISBN 0-87691-144-0). Winchester Pr.
Campbell, Stuart L. The Second Empire Revisited: A Study in French Historiography. LC 77-20247. 1978. 17.00 (ISBN 0-8135-0856-8). Rutgers U Pr.
Campbell, Susan. The Couple's Journey. LC 79-23836. 1980. pap. 5.95 (ISBN 0-915166-45-3). Impact Pubs Cal.
--Expanding Your Teaching Potential: A Role Clarification Guide for Educators & Human Service Workers. LC 76-58637. 1980. pap. 9.95 (ISBN 0-8290-0349-5). Irvington.
Campbell, Sydney S. Music in the Church. (Student's Music Library Ser). 1951. 6.95 (ISBN 0-234-77210-7). Dufour.
Campbell, Tessa. Children's Picture Atlas. LC 77-17968. (Children's Guides Ser.). (Illus.). (gr. 3 up). 1978. PLB 6.95 (ISBN 0-88436-465-8). EMC.
Campbell, Thomas C. & Reierson, Gary B. The Gift of Adminstration. LC 80-24594. 1981. soft cover 6.95 (ISBN 0-664-24357-6). Westminster.
Campbell, Toby H. & Bendick, Marc, Jr. A Public Assistance Data Book. (An Institute Paper). 344p. 1977. pap. 10.00 (ISBN 0-87766-207-X, 20300). Urban Inst.
Campbell, Viola, ed. Programas Para Reuniones Sociales y Banquetes. (Illus.). 1979. pap. 1.20 (ISBN 0-311-11011-8). Casa Bautista.
Campbell, Viola D. Recreacion Cristiana. (Illus.). 160p. (Span.). 1980. pap. 3.60 (ISBN 0-311-11037-1). Casa Bautista.
Campbell, Viola D., tr. see Ford, LeRoy.
Campbell, W. H., jt. ed. see Matsushita, S.
Campbell, Walter J., jt. auth. see Hawkins, David F.
Campbell, Walter S. Book Lover's Southwest: A Guide to Good Reading. 1955. 14.95x o.p. (ISBN 0-8061-0320-5). U of Okla Pr.
Campbell, William G. & Ballou, Stephen V. Form & Style: Theses, Reports, Term Papers. 5th ed. LC 77-75137. (Illus.). 1977. pap. text ed. 7.25 (ISBN 0-395-25442-6). HM.
Campbell-Johnson, Alan. Mission with Mountbatten. rev. ed. 1951. pap. 2.45 (ISBN 0-88253-129-8). Ind-US Inc.
Campderros, Daniel. Bosquejos Biblicos, Tomo 3. 96p. 1980. pap. 1.85 (ISBN 0-311-43033-3). Casa Bautista.
Campe, J. H. The New Robinson Crusoe, 4 vols. in 2. LC 75-32148. (Classics of Children's Literature, 1621-1932: Vol. 14). 1976. Repr. of 1788 ed. Set. PLB 70.00 (ISBN 0-8240-2262-9); PLB 38.00 ea. Garland Pub.
Campen, Joseph A. Van see Sholiton, Robert D. & Van Campen, Joseph A.
Campenhausen, Hans von see Von Campenhausen, Hans.
Campenhausen, Hansvon see Von Campenhausen, Hans.
Camper, Frank. Sand Castles. (Orig.). 1980. pap. 2.25 (ISBN 0-532-23132-5). Manor Bks.
Campert, Remco. In the Year of the Strike. Scott, John & Martin, Graham, trs. (Poetry Europe Ser.: No. 8). 60p. 1969. 4.95 o.p. (ISBN 0-8040-0163-4). Swallow.
Campillo, A. Algebroid Curves in Positive Characteristic. (Lecture Notes in Mathematics Ser.: Vol. 813). 168p. 1980. pap. text ed. 11.80 (ISBN 0-387-10022-9). Springer-Verlag.
Camping Club. Where to Camp in Spain. (Nicholson Leisure Guides). (Illus.). 1979. pap. 3.95 o.p. (ISBN 0-905522-38-9, ADON 8110-4, Pub. by R Nicholson). Barrie & Jenkins.
Campion, C. T., tr. see Schweitzer, Albert.
Campion, Dan, ed. see Bly, et al.
Campion, Edith. Back to Back. (Orig.). 1981. pap. 7.95 (ISBN 0-89407-041-X). Strawberry Hill. Postponed.
Campion, Gilbert F. European Parliamentary Procedure: A Comparative Handbook. LC 78-59009. (Illus.). 1981. Repr. of 1953 ed. 22.50 (ISBN 0-88355-684-7). Hyperion Conn.
Campion, Michael & Zehr, Wilmer. Especially for Husbands. (When Was the Last Time Ser.). (Illus.). 1978. pap. 4.95 (ISBN 0-87123-136-0, 210136). Bethany Fell.
--Especially for Parents. (When Was the Last Time Ser.). (Illus.). 1978. pap. 4.95 (ISBN 0-87123-137-9, 210137). Bethany Fell.
Campion, Michael A. Especially for Wives. (When Was the Last Time Ser.). 1979. pap. 4.95 (ISBN 0-87123-138-7, 210138). Bethany Fell.
Campion, Nardi R. & Reeder, Red. West Point Story. (Landmark Ser, No. 70). (Illus.). (gr. 4-6). 1956. PLB 4.39 o.p. (ISBN 0-394-90370-6, BYR). Random.
Campkin, T. V. & Turner, J. M. Neurosurgical Anesthesia & Intensive Care. LC 79-41659. (Illus.). 1980. text ed. 49.95 (ISBN 0-407-00185-9). Butterworths.
Campling, Elizabeth. Kennedy. (Leaders Ser.). (Illus.). 80p. (gr. 9-12). 1980. 16.95 (ISBN 0-7134-1920-2, Pub. by Batsford England). David & Charles.
Campling, Jo, ed. Image of Ourselves: Women with Disabilities Talking. 160p. 1981. price not set (ISBN 0-7100-0821-X); pap. price not set (ISBN 0-7100-0822-8). Routledge & Kegan.
Campo, Allan, jt. auth. see Bartlett, Lee.
Campolo, Anthony. The Success Fantasy. 1980. pap. 3.50 (ISBN 0-88207-796-1). Victor Bks.
Campos, Jules. The Sculpture of Jose De Creeft. LC 72-16688. (Illus.). 238p. 1972. lib. bdg. 45.00 (ISBN 0-306-70562-1); lib. bdg. 30.00 (ISBN 0-306-70294-0). Da Capo.
Campos Da Paz, Arthur, et al, eds. Human Reproduction. (Illus.). 1974. 18.00 o.p. (ISBN 0-89640-012-3). Igaku-Shoin.
Camps, jt. auth. see Gree.
Camps, Luis, jt. auth. see Gree, Alain.
Camps, Miriam. European Unification in the Sixties. (Council on Foreign Relations Ser). 1966. 8.95 o.p. (ISBN 0-07-009697-X, P&RB). McGraw.
Camps, W. A. An Introduction to Homer. 128p. 1980. 17.50x (ISBN 0-19-872099-8); pap. 7.50x (ISBN 0-19-872101-3). Oxford U Pr.
--An Introduction to Virgil's Aeneid. 174p. (Orig.). 1969. pap. 9.95x (ISBN 0-19-872024-6). Oxford U Pr.
Camps, W. A., ed. Propertius: Elegies Book 1. LC 77-82490. 1977. Bk. 1. 22.50 (ISBN 0-521-06000-1); Bk. 1. pap. 8.50 (ISBN 0-521-29210-7); Bk. 2. 22.50 (ISBN 0-521-06001-X); Bk. 3. 16.95 (ISBN 0-521-06002-8). Cambridge U Pr.
Camps, W. A., ed. see Propertius.
Campus Crusade for Christ Staff. Discovery II. 1980. pap. 2.25 saddlestitched (ISBN 0-918956-63-3). Campus Crusade.
--Game Plan II. 100p. (gr. 9-12). 1980. pap. text ed. 2.25 (ISBN 0-918956-64-1). Campus Crusade.
Camurati, Mireya & Rosenberg, Dorothy. Ideas y Motivos De Conversacion y Composicion En Espanol. 1974. 14.95x o.p. (ISBN 0-669-90845-2). Heath.
Camus, A. L' Etranger. Brae, G. & Lynes, C., eds. 1955. pap. 7.95 o.p. (ISBN 0-13-530790-2). P-H.
--L'etranger. Bree, G. & Lynes, C., eds. 1955. pap. 7.95 (ISBN 0-13-530790-2). P-H.
Camus, A. Le see Le Camus, A.
Camus, Albert see Otten, Anna.
Camus, Renaud. Tricks: Twenty-Five Encounters. 252p. 1981. pap. 10.95 (ISBN 0-312-81823-8). St Martin.
Camuti, Franklin. Dreams in a Wasteland. 156p. 1980. 7.95 (ISBN 0-8059-2733-6). Dorrance.
Camuti, Louis J. All My Patients Are Under the Bed. 1980. 10.95 (ISBN 0-671-24271-7). S&S.
Camuti, Louis J., et al. All My Patients Under the Bed. 1980. lib. bdg. 14.50 (ISBN 0-8161-3170-8, Large Print Bks). G K Hall.
Canada, Thomas. Accounting Systems of U. S. Government Agencies. 1980. 15.20 (ISBN 0-87771-013-9). Grad School.
Canaday, Downs. The Beer Drinker's Guide to Early Retirement. (Illus.). 96p. 1981. pap. 5.95 (ISBN 0-931896-03-7). Cove View.
Canaday, John. Culture Gulch: Notes on Art & Its Public in the 1960's. 1969. 5.95 o.p. (ISBN 0-374-13332-8). FS&G.
Canadian-American Conference on Parkinson's Disease, 2nd. Parkinson's Disease: Advances in Neurology, Vol. 5. McDowell, F. & Barbeau, A., eds. LC 72-93317. (Advances in Neurology Ser.: Vol. 5). 1974. 37.50 (ISBN 0-911216-63-4). Raven.
Canadian Manufacturers Association. Canadian Trade Index 1980. 70th ed. LC 14-21699. 1400p. 1980. pap. 70.00x (ISBN 0-919102-00-X). Intl Pubns Serv.

Canadian Royal Commission, ed. Violence in the Communications Industry, 7 vols. 1977. Set. pap. text ed. 85.00x o.p. (ISBN 0-685-87415-X). Renouf.

Canale, Andrew. Masters of the Heart. LC 78-58953. 1978. 9.95 (ISBN 0-8091-0271-4). Paulist Pr.

Canaletto, Antonio. Views of Venice by Canaletto. (Illus.). pap. 6.00 (ISBN 0-486-22705-7). Dover.

Canals, Salvatore. Jesus As Friend. 127p. 1979. 10.00x (ISBN 0-906127-11-4, Pub. by Irish Academic Pr). Biblio Dist.

Canarecci, T. Odds & Ends of Ward Wit. 1976. 7.50 (ISBN 0-87489-021-7). Med Economics.

Canario, Jack. The Big Hassle: Getting Along with Authority. (Read on! - Write on! Ser.). (Illus.). 64p. (gr. 6-12). 1980. 2.85 (ISBN 0-915510-38-3). Janus Bks.

--The Put-Down Pro: Getting Along with Friends. (Read on! - Write on! Ser.). (Illus.). 64p. (gr. 6-12). 1980. 2.85 (ISBN 0-915510-39-1). Janus Bks.

Canary, Brenda. Home to the Mountain. LC 74-82167. 192p. 1975. 11.95 o.p. (ISBN 0-8027-0578-2); pap. 7.95 (ISBN 0-8027-0474-3). Walker & Co.

Canary, Robert H. George Bancroft. (U. S. Authors Ser.: No. 226). 1974. lib. bdg. 10.95 (ISBN 0-8057-0034-X). Twayne.

Canary, Robert H. & Kozicki, Henry, eds. The Writing of History: Literary Form & Historical Understanding. LC 78-4590. 1978. 19.50 (ISBN 0-299-07570-2). U of Wis Pr.

Canavan, Michael M. Product Liability for Supervisors & Managers. 1981. text ed. 15.95 (ISBN 0-8359-5630-X). Reston.

Canavan, P. Joseph. The Effective Writer's Companion. 1981. pap. text ed. 8.95x (ISBN 0-673-15449-1). Scott F.

--Paragraphs & Themes. 3rd ed. 1979. pap. text ed. 9.95x (ISBN 0-669-01695-0); instructor's manual free (ISBN 0-669-01905-4). Heath.

Canavan-Gumpert, Donnah, et al. The Success Fearing Personality. LC 76-42853. 1978. 19.95 (ISBN 0-669-01075-8). Lexington Bks.

Canberra Nat'l. Library of Australia. Australian National Bibliography 1979, 2 vols. 19th ed. LC 63-33739. 1980. Set. 67.50x (ISBN 0-8002-1860-4). Intl Pubns Serv.

Canby, Henry S. Thoreau. 8.50 (ISBN 0-8446-1100-X). Peter Smith.

--Turn West, Turn East: Mark Twain & Henry James. LC 65-23485. 1951. 12.00x (ISBN 0-8196-0154-3). Biblo.

Canby, Vincent. Living Quarters. 1975. 6.95 o.p. (ISBN 0-394-49513-6). Knopf.

--Living Quarters. 224p. 1976. pap. 1.75 o.p. (ISBN 0-345-25205-5). Ballantine.

Cancer Care, Inc. & National Cancer Foundation, Inc. Listen to the Children: A Study of the Impact on the Mental Health of Children of a Parent's Catastrophic Illness. LC 77-94376. 1977. 2.50 (ISBN 0-686-26199-2). Cancer Care.

Canclini, Arnoldo, tr. see Geisler, Norman.

Canclini, Arnoldo, tr. see Jungel, Eberhard.

Canclini, Arnoldo, tr. see Ladd, George E.

Canclini, Arnoldo, tr. see Stagg, Frank.

Cancrinus, Franz L. First Principles of the Science of Mining & Salt Mining. Bordeau, Kenneth V. & Bordeau, Elvi L., trs. LC 80-65488. (Microform Publication: No. 10). 1980. 4.00 (ISBN 0-8137-6010-0). Geol Soc.

Cancro, R., et al, eds. Strategic Intervention in Schizophrenia: Current Developments in Treatment. LC 74-1201. 326p. 1974. text ed. 22.95 (ISBN 0-87705-133-X). Human Sci Pr.

Candler. Atlas of African Military Strategy. 102p. Date not set. 29.95 (ISBN 0-02-905750-7). Macmillan.

Candlin, A. Stanton. Psycho-Chemical Warfare. (Illus.). 1974. 14.95 o.p. (ISBN 0-87000-214-7). Arlington Hse.

Candlin, Enid S. The Breach in the Wall: A Memoir of the Old China. 306p. 1973. 8.95 o.s.i. (ISBN 0-02-521100-5). Macmillan.

Candlin, Enid Saunders. A Traveler's Tale: Memories of India. LC 73-16902. 360p. 1974. 12.95 o.s.i. (ISBN 0-02-521110-2). Macmillan.

Candrilli, Alfred J., et al. Law School Admission Test. rev. ed. LC 80-22181. 448p. 1981. lib. bdg. 10.95 (ISBN 0-668-05146-9); pap. 6.95 (ISBN 0-686-69096-6). Arco.

Candy, D. J. & Kilby, B. A., eds. Insect Biochemistry & Function. LC 74-26569. 314p. 1975. text ed. 29.95x o.p. (ISBN 0-412-21530-6, Pub. by Chapman & Hall). Methuen Inc.

--Insect Biochemistry & Function. LC 74-26569. 314p. 1975. 32.50 o.p. (ISBN 0-470-13347-3). Halsted Pr.

Candy, David S. Biological Functions of Carbohydrates. LC 80-18668. (Tertiary Level Biology Ser.). 197p. 1980. 34.95 (ISBN 0-470-27038-1). Halsted Pr.

Candy, Hugh C. Milton, the Individualist in Metre. 49p. 1980. Repr. lib. bdg. 8.50 (ISBN 0-89987-112-7). Darby Bks.

Cane, B. S., jt. auth. see Hilsum, S.

Cane, Brian & Schroeder, Colin. The Teacher & Research: A Study of Teachers' Priorities & Opinions on Educational Research & Development. (Research Reports Ser.). (Illus.). 130p. 1970. pap. text ed. 8.25x (ISBN 0-901225-53-3, NFER). Humanities.

Cane, Brian & Smithers, Jane. Roots of Reading: A Study of Twelve Infant Schools in Deprived Areas. Chanan, Gabriel, ed. (General Ser.). 1971. pap. text ed. 5.75x (ISBN 0-901225-74-6, NFER). Humanities.

Cane, M., et al. Structured Questions in "A" Level Chemistry. 1976. pap. text ed. 4.95x o.p. (ISBN 0-435-65098-X). Heinemann Ed.

Cane, Melville. To Build a Fire: Recent Poems & a Prose Piece. LC 64-14640. 1964. 3.75 (ISBN 0-15-190478-2). HarBraceJ.

Cane, Michael C., jt. auth. see Hillman, Robin A.

Caney, Steven. Steve Caney's Toybook. LC 75-8814. (Parents & Children Together Ser.). (Illus.). 176p. (gr. 3 up). 1972. 8.95 (ISBN 0-911104-15-1); pap. 4.95 (ISBN 0-911104-17-8). Workman Pub.

--Steven Caney's Playbook. LC 75-9816. (Parents & Children Together Ser). (Illus.). 240p. (ps-7). 1975. 9.95 (ISBN 0-911104-37-2); pap. 5.95 (ISBN 0-911104-38-0). Workman Pub.

Canfield, Bertrand R., jt. auth. see Moore, H. Frazier.

Canfield, Cass. Outrageous Fortunes: The Story of the Medici, the Rothschilds, & J. Pierpont Morgan. (Illus.). 1981. 10.95 (ISBN 0-15-170513-5). HarBraceJ.

Canfield, D. Lincoln. Spanish Pronunciation in the Americas. LC 80-23664. (Illus.). 1981. lib. bdg. 15.00x (ISBN 0-226-09262-3). U of Chicago Pr.

Canfield, D. Lincoln & Davis, J. Cary. An Introduction to Romance Linguistics. LC 74-34260. (Illus.). 230p. 1975. 13.95x (ISBN 0-8093-0677-8). S Ill U Pr.

Canfield, D. T. & Bowman. Business, Legal & Ethical Phases of Engineering. 2nd ed. 1954. text ed. 19.50 o.p. (ISBN 0-07-009729-1, C). McGraw.

Canfield, Jack, jt. auth. see Wells, Harold C.

Canfield, John V. Wittgenstein: Language & World. 256p. 1981. lib. bdg. 17.50x (ISBN 0-87023-318-1); pap. text ed. 7.50x (ISBN 0-87023-319-X). U of Mass Pr.

Canfield, Rosemary, ed. Perspectives: The Alabama Heritage. LC 78-64441. 1978. 15.00 (ISBN 0-916624-27-7). TSU Pr.

Canfield, William W. Legends of the Iroquois. LC 78-151808. (Empire State Historical Publications Ser., No. 93). 1971. Repr. of 1902 ed. 12.00 o.p. (ISBN 0-8046-8093-0). Kennikat.

Cangelosi, Vincent E., et al. Basic Statistics: A Real World Approach. 2nd ed. (Illus.). 1979. text ed. 17.95 (ISBN 0-8299-0194-9); pap. study guide 6.95 (ISBN 0-8299-0245-7); wkbk avail. (ISBN 0-8299-0464-6). West Pub.

--Basic Statistics: A Real World Approach. 2nd ed. (Illus.). 1979. pap. text ed. 15.95 (ISBN 0-8299-0268-6); international ed. avail. (ISBN 0-8299-0464-6). West Pub.

Cangemi, Joseph & Kowalski, Casimir. Perspectives in Higher Education. 1981. write for info. Philos Lib.

Cangemi, Joseph P., jt. auth. see Kowalski, Casimir J.

Canger, Raffaele, et al, eds. Advances in Epileptology: Eleventh International Epilepsy Symposium. 510p. 1980. text ed. 48.00 (ISBN 0-89004-510-0). Raven.

Canham, Don & Micoleau, T. The Track & Field Series. Incl. Vol. 1. Cross-Country Techniques Illustrated. 1953. 11.50 o.p. (ISBN 0-8260-1745-2); Vol. 2. Field Techniques Illustrated. 1952. o.p. (ISBN 0-8260-1760-6); Vol. 3. Track Techniques Illustrated. 1952. o.p. (ISBN 0-8260-1775-4). (Illus.). Ronald Pr.

Cannan, Edwin. Review of Economic Theory. Repr. of 1929 ed. 25.00x (ISBN 0-678-05040-6). Kelley.

--Wealth: A Brief Explanation of the Causes of Economic Welfare. LC 79-1575. 1981. Repr. of 1928 ed. 22.50 (ISBN 0-88355-881-5). Hyperion Conn.

Cannan, Edwin, ed. Review of Economic Theory. 2nd ed. 448p. 1964. 30.00x (ISBN 0-7146-1211-1, F Cass Co). Biblio Dist.

Cannata, F. & Ueberall, H. Giant Resonance Phenomena in Intermediate-Energy Nuclear Reactions. (Springer Tracts in Modern Physics: Vol. 89). (Illus.). 112p. 1980. 29.80 (ISBN 0-387-10105-5). Springer-Verlag.

Cannavale, Frank J., Jr. & Falcon, William. Witness Cooperation: With a Handbook of Witness Management. LC 75-28939. 1976. 21.95 (ISBN 0-669-00329-8). Lexington Bks.

Cannell, C. F., jt. auth. see Kahn, R. L.

Cannell, David & Leather, John. Modern Development in Yacht Design. LC 76-11397. (Illus.). 1976. 20.00 (ISBN 0-396-07355-7). Dodd.

Cannell, J. C. Secrets of Houdini. LC 74-10523. (Illus.). 1974. Repr. of 1931 ed. 24.00 (ISBN 0-8103-3725-8). Gale.

Canney, John, et al. Working on Words. vi, 250p. (Orig.). 1981. pap. text ed. 6.95 (ISBN 0-913580-72-4). Gallaudet Coll.

Canney, Maurice A. Encyclopaedia of Religions. LC 75-123370. 1970. Repr. of 1921 ed. 28.00 (ISBN 0-8103-3856-4). Gale.

Canning. Fifty Great Horror Stories. Date not set. 4.98 (ISBN 0-517-13671-6). Bonanza.

Canning, Connie, compiled by. State Constitutional Conventions, Revisions & Amendments, 1959-1976: A Bibliography, Supplement One. LC 76-57843. 1977. lib. bdg. 12.50 (ISBN 0-8371-9487-3, CSC/). Greenwood.

Canning, George. The Occasional Horseman. (Illus.). 8.05 (ISBN 0-85131-188-1, Dist. by Sporting Book Center). J A Allen.

Canning, Ray R. & Beeton, Beverly, eds. The Genteel Gentile: Letters of Elizabeth Cumming, 1857 - 1858. (Utah, The Mormons, & The West: No. 8). 1978. 12.50 (ISBN 0-87480-163-X, Tanner). U of Utah Pr.

Canning, Richard G. & Leeper, Nancy C. So You Are Thinking About a Small Business Computer. (Computing in Your Business Ser.). (Illus.). 100p. (Orig.). 1980. pap. 12.50 (ISBN 0-938516-01-9). Canning Pubns.

Canning, Victor. The Crimson Chalice. 1979. pap. 2.50 (ISBN 0-441-12190-X). Charter Bks.

--The Dragon Tree. 1980. pap. 2.25 (ISBN 0-441-16659-8). Charter Bks.

--Fall from Grace. LC 80-83325. 224p. 1981. 9.95 (ISBN 0-688-00195-5). Morrow.

--Runaways. (gr. 4-7). 1976. pap. 1.50 (ISBN 0-590-10231-1, Schol Pap). Schol Bk Serv.

--Scorpio Letter. 272p. 1981. pap. 2.25 (ISBN 0-441-75519-4). Charter Bks.

--The Scorpio Letters. 1964. 5.95 o.p. (ISBN 0-688-02436-X). Morrow.

Cannizzo, Cindy, ed. The Gun Merchants: Politics & Policies of the Major Arms Suppliers. (Pergamon Policy Studies). 1980. 27.00 (ISBN 0-08-024632-X). Pergamon.

Cannon, Albert, jt. auth. see Geschickter, Charles F.

Cannon, Bill. How to Cast Small Metal & Rubber Parts. (Illus.). 1979. 9.95 (ISBN 0-8306-9869-8); pap. 5.95 (ISBN 0-8306-1105-3, 1105). TAB Bks.

Cannon, Bryan J. Celebrate Yourself: The Secret to a Life of Hope & Joy. LC 76-48542. 1977. pap. 3.95 o.p. (ISBN 0-87680-802-X, 98107). Word Bks.

Cannon, Charles B. The O'Hare Story. LC 80-50072. 54p. 1981. 6.95 (ISBN 0-533-04585-1). Vantage.

Cannon, Dianne. Kathleen. LC 76-13241. 1977. 8.95 (ISBN 0-87949-072-1). Ashley Bks.

Cannon, Donald Q., jt. auth. see Cook, Lyndon W.

Cannon, Garland. An Integrated Transformational Grammar of the English Language. (Costerus New Ser.: No. 8). 1978. pap. text ed. 34.25x (ISBN 90-6203-400-4). Humanities.

--Sir William Jones: A Bibliography of Primary & Secondary Sources. (Library & Information Sourcesin Linguistics Ser.: No. 7). 1980. text ed. 17.25x (ISBN 90-272-0998-7). Humanities.

Cannon, H. Graham. Lamarck & Modern Genetics. LC 75-10211. 152p. 1975. Repr. of 1959 ed. lib. bdg. 16.50x (ISBN 0-8371-8173-9, CALA). Greenwood.

Cannon, Hal, compiled by. The Grand Beehive. (Illus.). 88p. (Orig.). 1980. pap. 9.50 (ISBN 0-87480-190-7). U of Utah Pr.

Cannon, Helen. A Better Place I Know. 1979. pap. 2.25 (ISBN 0-380-75009-0, 75009). Avon.

--Seasons Change. 320p. 1981. pap. 2.50 (ISBN 0-380-77164-0, 77164). Avon.

Cannon, J. Fox-North Coalition. LC 70-85715. 1970. 35.50 (ISBN 0-521-07606-4). Cambridge U Pr.

--Parliamentary Reform: 1640-1832. LC 72-83588. (Illus.). 288p. 1973. pap. 11.50x (ISBN 0-521-08697-3); pap. 11.50 (ISBN 0-521-09736-3). Cambridge U Pr.

Cannon, Jack & Cannon, Tom, eds. Nobody Asked Me, but... The World of Jimmy Cannon. LC 77-13832. (Illus.). 1978. 10.95 o.p. (ISBN 0-03-015381-6). HR&W.

Cannon, John. The Historian at Work. 216p. (Orig.). 1980. text ed. 25.00x (ISBN 0-04-901025-5, 2395); pap. text ed. 7.50x (ISBN 0-04-901026-3, 2396). Allen Unwin.

--The Road to Haworth. (Illus.). 176p. 1981. 10.95 (ISBN 0-670-60079-2). Viking Pr.

Cannon, Mary A. The Education of Women During the Renaissance. LC 79-2933. 182p. 1981. Repr. of 1916 ed. 16.00 (ISBN 0-8305-0100-2). Hyperion Conn.

Cannon, Melissa. Sister Fly Goes to Market. LC 80-21120. (Illus., Orig.). 1980. pap. 1.95 (ISBN 0-937212-01-6). Truedog.

Cannon, Minuha. The Fructose Cookbook. (Illus.). 128p. (Orig.). 1979. lib. bdg. 9.25 o.p. (ISBN 0-914788-18-3); pap. 5.95 (ISBN 0-914788-18-3). East Woods.

--Sweets Without Guilt. (Illus.). 128p. (Orig.). 1980. lib. bdg. 9.25 o.p. (ISBN 0-914788-30-2) (ISBN 0-686-27281-1). East Woods.

Cannon, R. D. Electron Transfer Reactions. LC 79-41278. 1980. text ed. 84.95 (ISBN 0-408-10646-8). Butterworths.

Cannon, Terence. Revolutionary Cuba. LC 77-26587. (Illus.). 368p. (gr. 9 up). 1980. 16.95 (ISBN 0-690-01307-8, TYC-J). T Y Crowell.

Cannon, Tim. Distribution Research. 1973. pap. text ed. 11.00x (ISBN 0-7002-0232-3). Intl Ideas.

Cannon, Tom. Advertising Research. 1973. pap. text ed. 11.00x (ISBN 0-7002-0220-X). Intl Ideas.

--Advertising: The Economic Implications. 1974. text ed. 16.95x (ISBN 0-685-83689-4). Intl Ideas.

Cannon, Tom, jt. ed. see Cannon, Jack.

Cannon, Trudy. Be Your Own Caterer: Recipes & Suggestions for Dinners, Buffets & Cocktail Parties. 216p. 1975. 9.95 o.s.i. (ISBN 0-02-521150-1). Macmillan.

Canny, M. J. Pholoem Translocation. 1973. 65.00 (ISBN 0-521-20047-4). Cambridge U Pr.

Cano, J., ed. see Valdes, Armando P.

Canon, Jack. Sable & Gold. 288p. (Orig.). 1981. pap. 2.50 (ISBN 0-523-41105-7). Pinnacle Bks.

Canonico & Margison, G. P., eds. Carcinogenesis. (Illus.). 1979. 68.00 (ISBN 0-08-024379-7). Pergamon.

Canonico, et al, eds. Cancer Control: International Cancer Congress, 12th, Buenos Aires, 1978, Vol. 2. LC 79-40704. (Advances in Medical Oncology, Research & Education: Vol. II). (Illus.). 68.00 (ISBN 0-08-024385-1). Pergamon.

Canovan, Margaret. G. K. Chesterton: Radical Populist. LC 77-73045. 1977. 10.95 o.p. (ISBN 0-15-135700-5). HarBraceJ.

Canright, D. M. El Adventismo Del Septimo Dia. Correa, F. G., tr. Date not set. pap. 1.20 (ISBN 0-311-05601-6). Casa Bautista.

Canright, David. Ships & the River. 32p. (gr. 5 up). 1975. pap. 2.00 o.s.i. (ISBN 0-913344-22-2). Interbk Inc.

Cant, Gilbert. Male Trouble. 1977. pap. 1.75 o.s.i. (ISBN 0-515-04378-8). Jove Pubns.

Cantarino, Vicente. Syntax of Modern Arabic Prose. Incl. Vol. 1. The Simple Sentence. 184p. 1974. 12.00x (ISBN 0-253-39504-6); Vol. 2. The Expanded Sentence. 544p. 1976. 17.50x (ISBN 0-253-39505-4); Vol. 3. The Compound Sentence. 424p. 1976. 15.00x (ISBN 0-253-39506-2). LC 69-16996. (Oriental Ser.: Vol. 4). Set. 37.50x (ISBN 0-253-39507-0). Ind U Pr.

Cantelon, Willard. The Day the Dollar Dies: Biblical Prophecy of a New World System in the End Times. LC 72-94186. 190p. 1973. 4.95 o.p. (ISBN 0-912106-92-1); pap. 2.50 (ISBN 0-88270-170-3). Logos.

Cantelon, Willard, tr. Le Bapteme Dans le Saint-Sprit. (French Bks.). (Fr.). 1979. 0.95 (ISBN 0-8297-0929-0). Life Pubs Intl.

--De Coracao Para Coracao. (Portuguese Bks.). 1979. 1.00 (ISBN 0-8297-0657-7). Life Pubs Intl.

--Morte Do Dolar. (Portuguese Bks.). 1979. 1.40 (ISBN 0-8297-0816-2). Life Pubs Intl.

Canter, David. Fires & Human Behaviour. LC 79-41489. 338p. 1980. 30.00 (ISBN 0-471-27709-6, Pub. by Wiley-Interscience). Wiley.

--Psychology for Architects. LC 74-30415. 171p. 1975. 24.95 (ISBN 0-470-13460-7). Halsted Pr.

--The Psychology of Place. LC 77-366169. (Illus.). 198p. 1977. 22.50x (ISBN 0-85139-532-5). Intl Pubns Serv.

Cantilli, Edmund J., jt. auth. see Horodniceanu, Michael.

Cantin, Donald W. Turn Your Ideas into Money. 1977. 6.95 o.p. (ISBN 0-8015-7996-1, Hawthorn); pap. 4.95 (ISBN 0-8015-7996-1, Hawthorn). Dutton.

Cantinieri, Joe. Honor Thy Teen. 1977. 5.95 o.p. (ISBN 0-533-02870-1). Vantage.

Cantlay, Jed, jt. auth. see Hoffman, Robert.

Canton, Frank M. Frontier Trails: The Autobiography of Frank M. Canton. Dale, Edward E., ed. LC 66-13415. (Western Frontier Library: Vol. 30). 258p. 1966. pap. 4.95 (ISBN 0-8061-1018-X). U of Okla Pr.

Cantonwine, Charles R. Battery Chargers & Testers: Operation, Repair, & Maintenance. LC 73-153135. (Illus.). 1971. 12.50 o.p. (ISBN 0-8019-5621-8). Chilton.

Cantor, Arthur, jt. auth. see Little, Stuart.

Cantor, Charles R. & Schimmel, Paul R. Biophysical Chemistry, Part I: The Conformation of Biological Macromolecules. LC 79-22043. (Illus.). 1980. 31.95x (ISBN 0-7167-1042-0); pap. text ed. 16.95x (ISBN 0-7167-1188-5). W H Freeman.

--Biophysical Chemistry, Part II: Techniques for the Study of Biological Structure & Function. LC 79-24854. (Illus.). 1980. text ed. 37.95x (ISBN 0-7167-1189-3); pap. text ed. 19.95x (ISBN 0-7167-1190-7). W H Freeman.

--Biophysical Chemistry, Part III: The Behavior of Biological Macromolecules. LC 79-27860. (Illus.). 1980. 39.95x (ISBN 0-7167-1191-5); pap. text ed. 21.95x (ISBN 0-7167-1192-3). W H Freeman.

Cantor, G. N. & Hodge, M. J. Conceptions of Ether: Studies in the History of Ether Theories 1740 to 1900. LC 80-21174. (Illus.). 350p. Date not set. price not set (ISBN 0-521-22430-6). Cambridge U Pr.

Cantor, Gilbert M. How to Avoid Estate Tax. LC 80-67503. 1980. 19.95 (ISBN 0-913864-57-9). Enterprise Del.

Cantor, Harold. Clifford Odets: Playwright-Poet. LC 77-27284. 1978. 12.00 (ISBN 0-8108-1107-3). Scarecrow.

Cantor, Leonard M. & Roberts, I. F. Further Education in England & Wales. 2nd rev. ed. (Illus.). 348p. 1972. 25.00 (ISBN 0-7100-7358-5). Routledge & Kegan.

Cantor, Lon. How to Select & Install Antennas. 2nd ed. 1978. pap. 5.95 (ISBN 0-8104-5745-8). Hayden.

Cantor, Milton, ed. Black Labor in America. LC 74-111265. (Contributions in Afro-American & African Studies, No. 2). 1969. 16.95x (ISBN 0-8371-4667-4). Negro U Pr.

Cantor, Milton & Laurie, Bruce, eds. Class, Sex, & the Woman Worker. LC 76-15304. (Contributions in Labor History Ser.: No. 1). 1977. lib. bdg. 16.95x (ISBN 0-8371-9032-0, CCS/). Greenwood.

Cantor, Milton, jt. ed. see Quint, Howard H.

Cantor, Muriel, jt. ed. see Stewart, Phyllis L.

Cantor, Muriel G. Prime-Time Television: Content & Control. LC 80-12288. (The Sage Commtext Ser: No. 3). 143p. 1980. 12.50 (ISBN 0-8039-1316-8); pap. 5.95 (ISBN 0-8039-1317-6). Sage.

Cantor, N. & Kihlstrom, J., eds. Personality, Cognition, & Social Interaction. 580p. 1981. text ed. 24.95 (ISBN 0-89859-057-4). L Erlbaum Assocs.

Cantor, Norman F. & Werthman, Michael S., eds. Ancient Civilizations: 4000 B.C. to 400 A.D. 2nd ed. LC 72-76355. (AHM Structure of European History Ser.: Vol. 1). 284p. 1972. pap. text ed. 5.95x (ISBN 0-88295-710-4). AHM Pub.

--Making of the Modern World: Eighteen Fifteen to Nineteen Fourteen. LC 67-16644. (AHM Structure of European History Ser.: Vol. 5). 240p. 1967. pap. text ed. 5.95x (ISBN 0-88295-714-7). AHM Pub.

--Medieval Society: 400-1450. 2nd ed. LC 72-76355. (AHM Structure of European History Ser.: Vol. 2). 303p. 1972. pap. text ed. 5.95x (ISBN 0-88295-711-2). AHM Pub.

--Renaissance, Reformation, & Absolutism: 1450 to 1650. 2nd ed. LC 72-76355. (AHM Structure of European History Ser.: Vol. 3). 319p. 1972. pap. text ed. 5.95x (ISBN 0-88295-712-0). AHM Pub.

--Twentieth Century: 1914 to the Present. LC 67-16644. (AHM Structure of European History Ser.: Vol. 6). 251p. 1967. pap. text ed. 5.95x (ISBN 0-88295-715-5). AHM Pub.

Cantor, Robert D. Introduction to International Politics. LC 75-17314. (Illus.). 1976. text ed. 12.95 (ISBN 0-87581-189-2, 189). Peacock Pubs.

Cantor, S. M. see Pigman, Ward & Wolfrom, Melville L.

Cantore, Virginia B., jt. auth. see Cantore, William J.

Cantore, William J. & Cantore, Virginia B. Creative Picture Framing. (Illus.). 128p. 1981. 12.95 (ISBN 0-13-190645-3, Spec); pap. 6.95 (ISBN 0-13-190637-2). P-H.

Cantori, Louis J. & Harik, Iliya, eds. Local Politics & Development in the Middle East. (Special Studies on the Middle East). 350p. 1981. lib. bdg. 24.50x (ISBN 0-86531-169-2). Westview.

Cantow, H. J., et al, eds. Polymer Products. (Advances in Polymer Science Ser.: Vol. 39). (Illus.). 230p. 1981. 57.80 (ISBN 0-387-10218-3). Springer-Verlag.

--Polymerization Processes. (Advances in Polymer Sciences Ser.: Vol. 38). (Illus.). 180p. 1981. 46.00 (ISBN 0-387-10217-5). Springer-Verlag.

--Advances in Polymer Science, Vols. 1-14. Incl. Vol. 1. (Illus.). iv, 612p. 1958-60. o.p. (ISBN 0-685-24350-8); Vol. 2. (Illus.). iv, 607p. 1960-61. o.p. (ISBN 0-685-24351-6); Vol. 3. (Illus.). iv, 711p. 1961-64. o.p. (ISBN 0-685-24352-4); Vol. 4. (Illus.). iv, 509p. 1965-67. o.p. (ISBN 0-685-24353-2); Vol. 5, 1 vol. ed. (Illus.). iv, 619p. 1967-68. 155.80 (ISBN 0-387-04034-X); Vol. 6, 1 vol. ed. (Illus.). iii, 574p. 1969-70. 147.00 (ISBN 0-387-04401-9); Vol. 7, 1 vol. ed. (Illus.). 600p. 1970. 155.80 (ISBN 0-387-05342-5); Vol. 8. (Illus.). 1971. 77.90 (ISBN 0-387-05838-9); Vol. 9. (Illus.). 1972. 93.30 (ISBN 0-387-05483-9); Vol. 9. (Illus.). 1972. 93.30 (ISBN 0-387-05484-7); Vol. 10. (Illus.). 1972. 56.70 (ISBN 0-387-05838-9); Vol. 11. 1973. 57.90 (ISBN 0-387-06054-5); Vol. 12. (Illus.). 1973. 50.80 (ISBN 0-387-06431-1); Vol. 13. (Illus.). 1974. 30.70 (ISBN 0-387-06552-0); Vol. 14. (Illus.). 1974. 37.80 (ISBN 0-387-06649-7). Springer-Verlag.

Cantrell, James R., jt. auth. see Miller, Robert H.

Cantrell, Leon, ed. The Eighteen Ninetys' Stories, Verses & Essays. (Portable Australian Authors Ser.). 1978. 12.75x (ISBN 0-7022-1037-4); pap. 8.50x (ISBN 0-7022-1038-2). U of Queensland Pr.

Cantril, Albert H., jt. auth. see Roll, Charles W., Jr.

Cantril, Hadley. Human Dimension: Experiences in Policy Research. 1967. 13.50 (ISBN 0-8135-0538-0). Rutgers U Pr.

--The Pattern of Human Concerns. 1966. 27.50 (ISBN 0-8135-0510-0). Rutgers U Pr.

--Pattern of Human Concerns Data, 1957-1963. 1977. codebk. 28.00 (ISBN 0-89138-115-5). ICPSR.

Cantril, Hadley, ed. see Ames, Adelbert, Jr.

Cantu, Connie & Steinberg, Peter. Roller Babies. LC 80-14071. (Illus.). 1980. pap. 7.95 (ISBN 0-13-782409-2). P-H.

Cantu, Rita. Great Smoky Mountains: The Story Behind the Scenery. DenDooven, Gweneth R., ed. LC 78-78123. (Illus.). 1979. 7.95 (ISBN 0-916122-60-3); pap. 3.00 (ISBN 0-916122-59-X). K C Pubns.

Cantu, Robert. Toward Fitness: Guided Exercise for Those with Health Problems. LC 79-27686. 256p. 1980. 12.95 (ISBN 0-87705-496-7). Human Sci Pr.

Cantu, Robert C. & Higdon, Hal. The Complete Diabetic Exercise & Diet Guide. (Illus.). 224p. Date not set. 12.95 (ISBN 0-8027-0670-3) (ISBN 0-8027-7170-X). Walker & Co.

Cantu, Robert C., ed. Health Maintenance Through Physical Conditioning. LC 80-15622. 275p. 1981. 12.50 (ISBN 0-88416-312-1). PSG Pub.

Cantwell, John D. Stay Young at Heart. LC 75-25958. (Illus.). 212p. 1975. 12.95 (ISBN 0-88229-247-1). Nelson-Hall.

Cantwell, Zita M. & Doyle, Hortense A. Instructional Technology: An Annotated Bibliography. LC 74-7394. 1974. 15.00 (ISBN 0-8108-0729-7). Scarecrow.

Canty, Donald J., jt. auth. see Smith, William S.

Canudo, Eugene R. Criminal Law of New York. 660p. (Supplemented annually). 1980. looseleaf 15.00 (ISBN 0-87526-201-5). Gould.

--Marriage, Divorce & Adoption: New York. 1979. pap. 5.50x (ISBN 0-87526-222-8). Gould.

Canzano, Dorthea & Canzano, Phyllis. A Practical Guide to Multi-Level Modular ESL. 1975. pap. 12.95 (ISBN 0-87789-130-3); cassettes intermediate 70.00; cassettes advanced 75.00. Eng Language.

Canzano, Phyllis, jt. auth. see Canzano, Dorthea.

Cao, Xueqin. Story of the Stone: The Dream of the Red Chamber, 2 vols. Hawkes, David, tr. from Chinese. Incl. Vol. 1. The Golden Days. 544p. Repr. of 1973 ed (ISBN 0-253-19261-7); Vol. 2. The Crab-Flower Club. 608p. Repr. of 1977 ed (ISBN 0-253-19262-5). LC 78-20279. (Chinese Literature in Translation Ser.). 1979. 25.00x ea. Ind U Pr.

Cao-Pinna, Vera & Shatalin, Stanislav S. Consumption Patterns in Eastern & Western Europe. 1979. 37.00 (ISBN 0-08-021808-3). Pergamon.

Caoursin, Guillaume see Aesopus.

Cap, Ferdinand, tr. see Karpman, V. I.

Capablanca, Jose R. Chess Fundamentals. (Illus.). 1967. pap. 4.95 (ISBN 0-679-14004-2, 27, Tartan). McKay.

Capacchione, Lucia. The Creative Journal: The Art of Finding Yourself. LC 78-51590. (Illus.). 180p. 1980. pap. 9.95 (ISBN 0-8040-0798-5). Swallow.

Capaccio, Albert, jt. auth. see Sloan, Annette.

Capaldi, Nicholas. The Art of Deception. 2nd ed. LC 75-21077. 200p. 1979. pap. text ed. 5.95 (ISBN 0-87975-058-8). Prometheus Bks.

--David Hume. LC 74-20931. (World Leaders Ser.: No. 48). 1975. lib. bdg. 9.95 (ISBN 0-8057-3685-9). Twayne.

--Monarch Notes on Hume's Philosophy. (Orig.). pap. 1.95 (ISBN 0-671-00529-4). Monarch Pr.

Capece, Raymond P., ed. see Electronics Magazine.

Capek, Karel. Letters from England. Selver, Paul, tr. 192p. 1980. Repr. of 1926 ed. lib. bdg. 25.00 (ISBN 0-8495-0952-1). Arden Lib.

--Letters from Spain. 192p. 1980. Repr. of 1931 ed. lib. bdg. 25.00 (ISBN 0-8495-0999-8). Arden Lib.

Capel, Evelyn. Making of Christianity & the Greek Spirit. 1980. pap. 10.75 (ISBN 0-903540-41-X, Pub. by Floris Books). St George Bk Serv.

Capell, Richard. Opera. LC 78-66894. (Encore Music Editions Ser.). 1981. Repr. of 1948 ed. 14.50 (ISBN 0-88355-730-4). Hyperion Conn.

--Schubert's Songs. LC 77-5524. (Music Reprint Ser.). 1977. Repr. of 1928 ed. lib. bdg. 25.00 (ISBN 0-306-77422-4). Da Capo.

Capella, Joseph N., jt. ed. see Monge, Peter R.

Capellanus, Andreas. Art of Courtly Love. abr ed. Locke, F. W., ed. Parry, John J., tr. LC 56-12400. (Milestones of Thought Ser.). 3.75 (ISBN 0-8044-2108-0); pap. 1.95 (ISBN 0-8044-6075-2). Ungar.

Capelle, J. Tomorrow's Education: The French Experience. 1967. 23.00 (ISBN 0-08-012517-4); pap. 12.25 (ISBN 0-08-012516-6). Pergamon.

Capellos, Christos & Bielski, Benon H. Kinetic Systems: Mathematical Description of Chemical Kinetics in Solution. LC 80-11940. 152p. 1980. pap. 7.75 (ISBN 0-89874-141-6). Krieger.

Caper, Janice M. Between the Bays: Somerset, Wicomico & Worcester Counties Maryland. LC 78-71245. (Illus.). 86p. 1979. pap. 13.00 (ISBN 0-935968-05-9). Holly Pr.

Capetti, Giselda, ed. Cronistoria, 5 vols. 400p. (Orig.). 1980. Set. pap. write for info. (ISBN 0-89944-043-6); Vol. 1. pap. (ISBN 0-89944-044-4); Vol. 2. pap. (ISBN 0-89944-045-2); Vol. 3. pap. (ISBN 0-89944-046-0); Vol. 4. pap. (ISBN 0-89944-047-9); Vol. 5. pap. (ISBN 0-89944-048-7). D Bosco Pubns.

Caplan, A. L., et al. Concepts of Health & Disease: Interdisciplinary Perspectives. McCartney, J. J., ed. 1980. pap. write for info. o.p. (ISBN 0-201-00973-0). A-W.

Caplan, Arthur L., jt. auth. see Rosen, Bernard.

Caplan, Arthur L., ed. The Sociobiology Debate. LC 77-3742. 1978. 14.95 o.p. (ISBN 0-06-010633-6, HarpT). Har-Row.

Caplan, Arthur L., et al. Concepts of Health & Disease: Interdisciplinary Perspectives. 608p. 1981. pap. text ed. write for info. (ISBN 0-201-00973-0). A-W.

Caplan, E. H. Management Accounting & Behavioral Science. 2nd ed. 1981. pap. 6.50 (ISBN 0-201-00952-8). A-W.

Caplan, Frank. The Quality System: A Sourcebook for Managers & Engineers. LC 80-969. 256p. 1980. 38.50 (ISBN 0-8019-6972-7). Chilton.

--Quality Systems Management & Engineering. LC 80-969. 256p. Date not set. 38.50x o.p. (ISBN 0-8019-6972-7). Chilton.

Caplan, Frank & Caplan, Theresa. The Power of Play. LC 68-10557. 336p. 1973. pap. 4.50 (ISBN 0-385-09935-5, Anch). Doubleday.

Caplan, Frank, ed. see Princeton Center for Infancy.

Caplan, Gerald L. The Elites of Barotseland, 1878-1969: A Political History of Zambia's Western Province. 1970. 22.50x (ISBN 0-520-01758-7). U of Cal Pr.

Caplan, H. H., ed. The Classified Directory of Artists' Signatures, Symbols, & Monograms. (Illus.). 1976. 110.00 (ISBN 0-8103-0985-8). Gale.

Caplan, Lionel. Land & Social Change in East Nepal: A Study of Hindu-Tribal Relations. LC 73-81801. 1970. 17.50x (ISBN 0-520-01400-6). U of Cal Pr.

Caplan, Paula. Barriers Between Women. 167p. 1981. 15.00 (ISBN 0-89335-103-2). Spectrum Pub.

Caplan, Theresa, jt. auth. see Caplan, Frank.

Caplan, Thomas. Line of Chance. 1981. pap. 2.95 (ISBN 0-671-83137-2). PB.

Caplen, R. H. A Practical Approach to Quality Control. 3rd ed. 310p. 1978. pap. text ed. 14.75x (ISBN 0-220-66368-8, Pub. by Busn Bks England). Renouf.

Capley, M. J. More Bible Puzzles & Games. 1978. pap. 1.95 (ISBN 0-8007-8320-4, Spire). Revell.

Caplin, Maxwell. The Tuberculin Test in Clinical Practice. (Illus.). 1980. pap. text ed. 18.50 (ISBN 0-02-857390-0). Macmillan.

Caplovitz, David. Making Ends Meet: How Families Cope with Inflation & Recession. LC 79-14438. (Sage Library of Social Research: No. 86). 1979. 18.00x (ISBN 0-8039-1292-7); pap. 8.95x (ISBN 0-8039-1293-5). Sage.

--Poor Pay More: Consumer Practices of Low Income Families. LC 63-18312. 1967. pap. text ed. 7.95 (ISBN 0-02-905250-5). Free Pr.

Caplow, Harriet M. Michelozzo. LC 76-23604. (Outstanding Dissertations in the Fine Arts - 2nd Series - 15th Century). (Illus.). 1977. Repr. of 1970 ed. lib. bdg. 115.50 (ISBN 0-8240-2678-0). Garland Pub.

Caplow, Theodore. Sociology. 2nd ed. LC 74-22417. (Illus.). 448p. 1975. text ed. 17.95 (ISBN 0-13-821363-1); study guide 5.95 (ISBN 0-13-821090-X). P-H.

Caplow, Theodore, jt. auth. see Bahr, Howard M.

Capno, A. De see De Capno, A.

Capon, Jack. Perceptual Motor Development Series, 5 bks. Incl. Balance Activities (ISBN 0-8224-5302-9); Ball, Rope, Hoop Activities (ISBN 0-8224-5301-0); Basic Movement Activities (ISBN 0-8224-5300-2); Beanbag, Rhythm-Stick Activities (ISBN 0-8224-5303-7); Tire, Parachute Activities (ISBN 0-8224-5304-5). (ps-3). 1975. pap. 3.95 ea. Pitman Learning.

--Successful Movement Challenges: Movement Activities for the Developing Child. Alexander, Frank & Alexander, Diane, eds. (Illus.). 129p. 1981. pap. 7.95 (ISBN 0-915256-07-X). Front Row.

Capon, Robert F. Exit Thirty Six: A Fictional Chronicle. 250p. 1975. 7.95 (ISBN 0-8164-0262-0). Crossroad NY.

--Hunting the Divine Fox. 1977. pap. 3.95 (ISBN 0-8164-2137-4). Crossroad NY.

--A Second Day: Reflections on Remarriage. LC 80-15750. 160p. 1980. 8.95 (ISBN 0-688-03680-5). Morrow.

Capon, Robert Farrar. The Third Peacock. LC 73-147357. 120p. 1972. pap. 1.95 (ISBN 0-385-03627-2, Im). Doubleday.

Capon, Robin. Introducing Drawing Techniques. LC 73-14367. (Illus.). 96p. 1974. 7.50 o.p. (ISBN 0-8008-4174-3). Taplinger.

--Introducing Graphic Techniques. 1979. 17.95 (ISBN 0-7134-2435-4, Pub. by Batsford England). David & Charles.

--Making Three-Dimensional Pictures. 1976. 16.95 o.p. (ISBN 0-7134-3109-1, Pub. by Batsford England). David & Charles.

--Paper Collage. (Illus.). 96p. 1975. 10.95 o.p. (ISBN 0-8231-7035-7). Branford.

Capon Springs Public Policy Conference, No. 1. Key Issues in Population: Problems, Options, & Recommendations for Action. Glassheim, Eliot, et al, eds. LC 78-50770. 1978. pap. text ed. 14.00x (ISBN 0-8191-0467-1). U Pr of Amer.

Capone. Your 14-Day Total Shape-up Plan. (gr. 7-12). 1980. pap. 1.25 (ISBN 0-590-30913-7, Schol Pap). Schol Bk Serv.

Caponi, Anthony. Boulders & Pebbles of Poetry & Prose. (Illus.). 96p. 1972. 2.50 o.p. (ISBN 0-8309-0085-3). Independence Pr.

Caponigri, A. Robert, tr. Major Trends in Mexican Philosophy. 1966. 10.95x o.p. (ISBN 0-268-00163-4). U of Notre Dame Pr.

Caporale, Rocco & Grumelli, Antonio, eds. The Culture of Unbelief: Studies & Proceedings from the First International Symposium on Belief, Held in Rome, March 22-27, 1969. LC 75-138513. 1971. 20.00x (ISBN 0-520-01856-7). U of Cal Pr.

Capote, Truman. Breakfast at Tiffany's. 1959. pap. 1.25 (ISBN 0-451-07483-1, Y7483, Sig). NAL.

--In Cold Blood. 1966. 8.95 (ISBN 0-394-43023-9). Random.

--Music for Chameleons. 1981. pap. 3.50 (ISBN 0-451-09800-5, E9800, Signet Bks). NAL.

--Music for Chameleons. 1980. 10.95 (ISBN 0-394-50826-2). Random.

Capote, Truman, et al. Trilogy: An Experiment in Multi-Media. (Illus.). 1969. 9.95 (ISBN 0-02-488810-9). Macmillan.

--Trilogy: An Experiment in Multimedia. (Illus.). 1971. pap. 2.95 o.s.i. (ISBN 0-02-079340-5, Collier). Macmillan.

Capotosto, John. Basic Carpentry. (Illus.). 544p. 1975. 15.95 o.p. (ISBN 0-87909-064-2). Reston.

Capotosto, John, et al. Workshop Ideas. LC 72-95384. (Illus.). 1977. 5.95 o.p. (ISBN 0-668-02940-4); pap. 2.95 o.p. (ISBN 0-668-04099-8). Arco.

Capozziello, Vincent, Jr. Planning My Career, Occupational Guidance. LC 75-20074. (gr. 7 up). 1979. 2.25 (ISBN 0-912486-43-0). Finney Co.

Capp, Al & Wallace, George. Great Issues: A Forum on Important Questions Facing the American Public. 1970. 5.95. Troy State Univ.

Capp, Bernard. English Almanacs: Fifteen Hundred to Eighteen Hundred: Astrology & the Popular Press. LC 78-74212. (Illus.). 1979. 38.50x (ISBN 0-8014-1229-3). Cornell U Pr.

Capp, Glenn R., et al. Basic Oral Communication. 3rd ed. (Illus.). 416p. 1981. pap. text ed. 12.95 (ISBN 0-13-065979-7). P-H.

Cappel, Robert P. S. W. A. T. Team Manual. (Illus.). 150p. 1979. pap. 10.00 (ISBN 0-87364-169-8). Paladin Ent.

Cappelli, Louis H. Gigi Bread, Gamblers & Friends. LC 79-67322. 195p. 1980. 7.95 (ISBN 0-533-04449-9). Vantage.

Cappon, Lester, ed. Atlas of Early American History: The Revolutionary Era, 1769-1790. 1976. 150.00 (ISBN 0-686-53820-X). Newberry.

Capponi, Attilio, jt. auth. see LeBoit, Joseph.

Capps, B. The Indians. LC 72-93991. (Old West Ser). (Illus.). (gr. 5 up). 1973. 12.96 o.p. (ISBN 0-8094-1455-4, Pub. by Time-Life). Silver.

Capps, Ben. The Indians. (The Old West Ser.). (Illus.). 1973. 12.95 (ISBN 0-8094-1454-6). Time-Life.

Capps, Benjamin. The Great Chiefs. LC 75-744. (The Old West). (Illus.). (gr. 5 up). 1975. kivar 12.96 (ISBN 0-8094-1494-5, Pub. by Time-Life). Silver.

--White Man's Road. LC 78-85926. 1969. 8.95 o.s.i. (ISBN 0-06-010602-6, HarpT). Har-Row.

Capps, Donald, et al. Encounter with Erikson: Historical Interpretation & Religious Biography. LC 76-44434. (American Academy of Religion, Formative Contemporary Thinkers Ser.: No. 2). 1977. pap. 9.00 (ISBN 0-685-85749-2, 010402). Scholars Pr Ca.

Capps, Donald, et al, eds. Psychology of Religion: A Guide to Information Sources. LC 73-17530. (Philosophy & Religion Information Guide Ser.: Vol. 1). vii, 380p. 1976. 30.00 (ISBN 0-8103-1356-1). Gale.

Capps, Walter H., ed. Seeing with the Native Eye: Contibutions to the Study of Native American Religion. LC 76-9980. 1976. pap. 4.95x (ISBN 0-06-061312-2, RD-177, HarpR). Har-Row.

Capra, L. G. Care of the Cancer Patient. (Illus.). 1972. pap. text ed. 21.00x (ISBN 0-433-05145-0). Intl Ideas.

Capri, Antonio. Il Settecento Musicale in Europa. LC 77-5523. (Music Reprint Ser). 1977. Repr. of 1936 ed. lib. bdg. 35.00 (ISBN 0-306-77413-5). Da Capo.

Caprini, Joseph A., et al. Gallstones. (Discussions in Surgical Management Ser.). 1979. pap. 10.50 (ISBN 0-87488-953-7). Med Exam.

Caprio, Anthony, jt. auth. see Carton, Dana.

Caprio, Betsy. Star Trek: Good News in Modern Images. 1978. 12.95 o.p. (ISBN 0-8362-3401-4); pap. 5.95 o.p. (ISBN 0-8362-3400-6). Andrews & McMeel.

Caprio, Frank S. & Leighton, Frances S. How to Avoid a Nervous Breakdown. 1969. pap. 2.95 o.p. (ISBN 0-8015-3798-3). Dutton.

Capron, Alexander M., jt. auth. see Katz, Jay.

Capron, Alexander M., et al, eds. Genetic Counseling: Fact, Values & Norms. LC 79-1736. (Alan R. Liss Ser.: Vol. 15, No. 2). 1979. write for info. (ISBN 0-8451-1025-X). March of Dimes.

Capron, J. Hugh. Wood Laminating. rev. ed. (gr. 11-12). 1972. 14.00 (ISBN 0-87345-046-9). McKnight.

Capron, William M., et al, eds. Technological Change in Regulated Industries. (Studies in the Regulation of Economic Activity). 1971. 11.95 (ISBN 0-8157-1282-0). Brookings.

Caproni, Gianni. Gli Aeroplani Caproni: Studi-Progetti-Realizzazioni dal 1908 al 1935. Gilbert, James, ed. LC 79-7234. (Flight: Its First Seventy-Five Years Ser.). (Illus.). 1979. Repr. of 1936 ed. lib. bdg. 54.00x (ISBN 0-405-12150-4). Arno.

Capstick, Peter. Death in the Silent Places. 320p. 1981. 13.95 (ISBN 0-312-18618-5). St Martin.

Capstick, Peter H. Death in the Long Grass. LC 77-9224. (Illus.). 1978. 10.95 (ISBN 0-312-18613-4). St Martin.

Capt, E. Raymond. The Great Pyramid Decoded. rev. ed. (Illus.). 96p. 1978. pap. 3.00 (ISBN 0-934666-01-6). Artisan Sales.

Captor, Renee S. Library Research for the Analysis of Public Policy. (Learning Packages in the Policy Sciences Ser.: No. 19). 36p. 1979. pap. text ed. 3.00 (ISBN 0-936826-08-8). Pol Stud Assocs.

Capurro, Luis R. Oceanography for Practicing Engineers. LC 71-126339. 1970. 11.95 (ISBN 0-389-00503-7); pap. 9.95 (ISBN 0-8436-0323-2). CBI Pub.

Caput, J. La Langue francaise: Histoire d'une institution, 842-1715, Vol. 1. new ed. (Collection L). 320p. (Orig., Fr.). 1972. pap. 12.75 o.p. (ISBN 2-03-036004-X, 3384). Larousse.

Caput, J., jt. auth. see Caput, J. P.

Caput, J. P. & Caput, J. Dictionnaire des verbes francais. (Fr). 27.50 (ISBN 0-685-13871-2, 3622). Larousse.

Caput, Jean-Pol. La Langue francaise, Vol. 2. (Collection "L"). 287p. (Orig., Fr.). 1975. pap. 13.95 (ISBN 2-03-036009-0). Larousse.

Caputi, Anthony, ed. Modern Drama: Annotated Texts. Bd. with Desire Under the Elms. O'Neill, Eugene; Devil's Disciple. Shaw, George B; Dream Play. Strindberg, August; Henry Fourth. Pirandello, Luigi; Three Sisters. Chekhov, Anton; Wild Duck. Ibsen, Henrik. (Critical Editions). 1966. pap. text ed. 9.95x (ISBN 0-393-09664-5). Norton.

Caputo, David A. Urban America: The Policy Alternatives. LC 76-7351. (Illus.). 1976. text ed. 17.95x (ISBN 0-7167-0556-7); pap. text ed. 9.95x (ISBN 0-7167-0565-6). W H Freeman.

Caputo, David A., ed. The Politics of Policy Making in America: Five Case Studies. LC 77-24516. (Illus.). 1977. text ed. 18.95x (ISBN 0-7167-0194-4); pap. text ed. 9.95x (ISBN 0-7167-0193-6). W H Freeman.

Caputo, John D. The Mystical Element in Heidegger's Thought. LC 77-92251. xvi, 292p. 1978. 18.00x (ISBN 0-8214-0372-9). Ohio U Pr.

Caputo, Rudolph R., jt. auth. see Aubry, Arthur S., Jr.

Caraboolad, Clemens J. Mysticism & Zen: An Introduction. LC 77-18492. 1978. pap. text ed. 7.50x (ISBN 0-8191-0422-1). U Pr of Amer.

Carafoli, E. Wing Theory in Supersonic Flow. 1969. 90.00 (ISBN 0-08-012330-9). Pergamon.

Carafoli, John & Carafoli, Marci. Look Who's Cooking. LC 73-93550. (Beginning-to-Read Bks). (Illus.). 32p. (gr. 2-4). 1974. 2.50 o.p. (ISBN 0-695-80475-8); lib. bdg. 3.39 o.p. (ISBN 0-695-40475-X); pap. 1.50 o.p. (ISBN 0-685-50751-3). Follett.

Carafoli, Marci, jt. auth. see Carafoli, John.

Caraley, Demetrios. City Governments & Urban Problems: A New Introduction to Urban Politics. LC 76-28327. (Illus.). 1977. 16.95 (ISBN 0-13-134973-2). P-H.

--Politics of Military Unification: A Study of Conflict & the Policy Process. LC 66-15762. 1966. 21.00x (ISBN 0-231-02885-7). Columbia U Pr.

Caraley, Demetrios, ed. American Political Institutions in the 1970's: A Political Science Quarterly Reader. LC 76-8494. 416p. 1976. 22.50x (ISBN 0-231-04106-3); pap. 10.00 (ISBN 0-231-04107-1). Columbia U Pr.

Caraman, Philip. The University of the Nations: The Story of the Geogorian University. (Illus.). 160p. (Orig.). 1981. pap. 6.95 (ISBN 0-8091-2355-X). Paulist Pr.

Caranfa, Angelo. Machiavelli Rethought: A Critique of Strauss' Machiavelli. LC 77-94393. 1978. pap. text ed. 7.00x (ISBN 0-8191-0421-3). U Pr of Amer.

Caras, Roger. The Roger Caras Pet Book. 1977. 7.95 o.p. (ISBN 0-03-017506-2). HR&W.

Caratheodory, Constantin. Theory of Functions. 2nd ed. LC 60-16838. Vol. 1. 12.95 (ISBN 0-8284-0097-0); Vol. 2. 12.95 (ISBN 0-8284-0106-3). Chelsea Pub.

Caravella, Joseph R. Minicalculators in the Classroom. 64p. 1977. pap. 3.50 (ISBN 0-686-63710-0, 1812-5-06). NEA.

Caraway, Caren. Beauty & the Beast. (A Stemmer House Story-to-Color Book). (Illus.). (ps up). 1980. 2.95 (ISBN 0-916144-46-1). Stemmer Hse.

--Beginners's Guide to Quilting. (gr. 7 up). 1980. 8.95 (ISBN 0-679-20532-2). McKay.

--Snow White & the Seven Dwarfs. (Stemmer House Story-to-Color Bks). (Illus.). 32p. (ps up). 1980. pap. 2.95 (ISBN 0-916144-57-7). Stemmer Hse.

Caraway, James E. God As Dynamic Actuality: A Preliminary Study of the Process Theologies of John B. Cobb, Jr. & Schubert M. Ogden. LC 78-61388. 1978. pap. text ed. 9.75 (ISBN 0-8191-0485-X). U Pr of Amer.

Carberry, Edward. Glassblowing: An Introduction to Artistic & Scientific Flameworking. rev. ed. LC 78-51569. (Illus.). 1980. 16.95 (ISBN 0-9601682-1-4). M G L S Pub.

Carbino, Rosemarie. Foster Parenting: An Updated Review of the Literature. 49p. (Orig.). 1980. pap. text ed. 4.25 (ISBN 0-87868-178-7). Child Welfare.

Carbo, Dorothy. Fix It Guide for Women. LC 76-21255. 1976. pap. 2.50 o.p. (ISBN 0-668-04016-5). Arco.

Carbon, Susan B. & Berkson, Larry C. Judicial Retention Elections in the United States. LC 80-69565. 96p. (Orig.). 1980. pap. 4.00 (8566). Am Judicature.

Carchedi, Guglielmo. On the Economic Identification of Social Classes. (Direct Editions Ser.). 1977. pap. 14.00 (ISBN 0-7100-8648-2). Routledge & Kegan.

Card, Josefina. Consequences of Adolescent Childbearing for the Young Parent's Future Personal & Professional Life. 1977. pap. 12.00 research report-paper (ISBN 0-89785-564-7). Am Inst Res.

Card, Orson S. Songmaster. (Quantum Science Fiction Ser.). 338p. 1980. 10.95 (ISBN 0-8037-7711-6). Dial.

--Unaccompanied Sonata & Other Stories. 288p. 1981. 10.95 (ISBN 0-8037-9175-5). Dial.

Cardamone, Tom. Advertising Agency & Studio Skills. 3rd ed. 160p. 1981. 10.95 (ISBN 0-8230-0151-2). Watson-Guptill.

--Advertising Agency & Studio Skills: A Guide to the Preparation of Art & Mechanicals for Reproduction. rev. ed. (Illus.). 1970. 9.95 o.p. (ISBN 0-8230-0150-4). Watson-Guptill.

Carden, Karen W. & Pelton, Robert W. The Persecuted Prophets. LC 74-10322. (Illus.). 192p. 1976. 9.95 o.p. (ISBN 0-498-01511-4). A S Barnes.

Cardenal, Ernesto. The Gospel in Solentiname, Vol. 1. Walsh, Donald, tr. from Spanish. LC 76-2681. Orig. Title: Elevangelio En Solentiname. 1976. 6.95x o.p. (ISBN 0-88344-168-3); pap. 4.95 o.p. (ISBN 0-88344-170-5). Orbis Bks.

--Love. 160p. (Span.). 1981. pap. 4.95 (ISBN 0-8245-0043-1). Crossroad NY.

--Psalms. 96p. (Span.). 1981. pap. 3.95 (ISBN 0-8245-0044-X). Crossroad NY.

--To Live Is to Love. 160p. 1974. pap. 1.45 (ISBN 0-385-03055-X, Im). Doubleday.

--Zero Hour & Other Documentary Poems. Walsh, Donald D., ed. Borgeson, Paul W. & Cohen, Jonathan, trs. from Span. LC 80-36817. 1980. 12.00 (ISBN 0-8112-0766-8); pap. 4.95 (ISBN 0-8112-0767-6, NDP502). New Directions.

Cardenas, Alfonso F., et al. Computer Science. LC 71-169162. 1972. 41.95 (ISBN 0-471-13468-6, Pub. by Wiley-Interscience). Wiley.

Carder, James N. Art Historical Problems of a Roman Land. LC 77-94730. (Outstanding Dissertations in the Fine Arts Ser.). 1979. lib. bdg. 33.00x (ISBN 0-8240-3218-7). Garland Pub.

Cardiff, Gray E. & English, John W. Coming Real Estate Crash. 1980. pap. 2.50 (ISBN 0-446-91575-0). Warner Bks.

Cardiff, Sara. The Bonaparte Kiss. (Orig.). 1979. pap. 1.75 o.p. (ISBN 0-449-24156-4, Crest). Fawcett.

--The Speaking Stones. 1978. pap. 1.75 o.p. (ISBN 0-449-23661-7, Crest). Fawcett.

Cardinal, Roger. Figures of Reality: A Perspective on the Poetic Imagination. (Illus.). 245p. 1980. 23.50x (ISBN 0-389-20064-6). B&N.

Carding, David K., ed. Family Medical Handbook. 2nd ed. 226p. 1981. 14.95 (ISBN 0-571-18027-2). Merrimack Bk Serv.

Cardon, Bartell, et al. Law & the School Psychologist. LC 68-52341. 105p. 1975. 12.95 (ISBN 0-87705-280-8). Human Sci Pr.

Cardona, Consuelo M., tr. see Lovato, Rebecca.

Cardona, Francisco J. & Cardona, Maria E. Handbook of Latin American Studies, Author Index to Numbers 1-28. LC 36-32633. 1968. 32.50x (ISBN 0-8130-0265-6). U Presses Fla.

Cardona, M., ed. Light Scattering in Solids. LC 75-20237. (Topics in Applied Physics Ser.: Vol. 8). (Illus.). 250p. 1975. 45.90 (ISBN 0-387-07354-X). Springer-Verlag.

Cardona, Maria E., jt. auth. see Cardona, Francisco J.

Cardona, Maria E., jt. ed. see Jose, Francisco.

Cardona, Rudolph, ed. see Perez Galdos, Benita.

Cardoso, Fernando E. & Faletto, Enzo. Dependency & Development in Latin America. Urquidi, Marjory M., tr. (Campus Ser.: No. 203). 1979. 22.75x (ISBN 0-520-03193-8); pap. 4.95x (ISBN 0-520-03527-5). U of Cal Pr.

Cardozo, Arlene R. Woman at Home. 1978. pap. 1.95 o.s.i. (ISBN 0-515-04501-2). Jove Pubns.

Cardozo, Benjamin N. The Growth of the Law. LC 73-8154. xvi, 145p. 1973. Repr. of 1963 ed. lib. bdg. 15.75x (ISBN 0-8371-6953-4, CAGL). Greenwood.

--Paradoxes of Legal Science. LC 76-104241. Repr. of 1928 ed. lib. bdg. 15.00x (ISBN 0-8371-3263-0, CALS). Greenwood.

Cardozo, Lida L., jt. auth. see Kindersley, David.

Cardozo, Paul L. Atlas of Clinical Cytology. (Illus.). 1979. text ed. 99.00 (ISBN 0-397-50456-X). Lippincott.

Cardozo, Richard N. Product Policy: Cases & Concepts. LC 78-67939. 1979. text ed. 17.95 (ISBN 0-201-00888-2). A-W.

Carducci, Giosue. Odi Barbare: Italian Text with English Prose. Smith, William F., tr. 1950. 6.50 o.p. (ISBN 0-913298-40-9). S F Vanni.

Carduner, Jean & Carduner, Sylvie. Contextes: A College Reader. 1974. pap. text ed. 7.95x o.p. (ISBN 0-669-73627-9). Heath.

Carduner, Jean, jt. auth. see Benamou, Michel.

Carduner, Sylvie, jt. auth. see Carduner, Jean.

Cardus, David, jt. ed. see Blocker, William P., Jr.

Cardwell, D. S., ed. Artisan to Graduate Essays Presented to Commemorate the Foundation in 1824 of the Manchester Mechanics Institution, Now the University of Manchester Institute of Science & Technology. 288p. 1974. 33.00x (ISBN 0-7190-1272-4, Pub. by Manchester U Pr England). State Mutual Bk.

Cardwell, Jerry D. Readings in Social Psychology: A Symbolic Interaction Perspective. LC 73-77106. pap. 5.95x (ISBN 0-88295-202-1). AHM Pub.

--The Social Context of Religiosity. LC 80-67216. 174p. 1980. lib. bdg. 17.50 (ISBN 0-8191-1135-X); pap. text ed. 8.75 (ISBN 0-8191-1136-8). U Pr of Amer.

Cardwell, Paul, Jr. Index of Model Periodicals: 1971 Through 1975. LC 77-1737. 1977. 32.50 (ISBN 0-8108-1027-1). Scarecrow.

Care, Norman S. & Grimm, Robert H., eds. Perception & Personal Identity: Proceedings of the 1967 Oberlin Colloquium in Philosophy. LC 68-9427. (Oberlin Colloquia in Philosophy Ser). 1969. 15.00 (ISBN 0-8295-0145-2). UPBS.

Careers Research & Advisory Centre, ed. Graduate Studies: The Guide to Postgraduate Study in the UK, 1980 to 1981. 7th ed. 1191p. 1980. 135.00x (ISBN 0-86021-342-0). Intl Pubns Serv.

--Graduate Studies (United Kingdom), Nineteen Eighty to Eighty-One. 1191p. 1980. 135.00x (ISBN 0-86021-342-0). Intl Pubns Serv.

Carek, Donald J. Principles of Child Psychotherapy. 240p. 1972. text ed. 19.75 (ISBN 0-398-02254-2). C C Thomas.

Careless, James M. Canada: A Story of Challenge. rev. ed. (Illus.). 1963. pap. 7.95 (ISBN 0-312-11620-9). St Martin.

Careless, James M. & Brown, R. Craig. Canadians: Eighteen Sixty-Seven to Nineteen Sixty-Seven, Pt. 1. (Illus.). 1969. pap. 9.95 (ISBN 0-312-11795-7). St Martin.

Carelli, M. Dino, ed. A New Look at the Relation Between School Education and Work: Second All-European Conference for Directors of Educational Research Institutions, Madrid 11-13 Sept. 79. (International Studies in Education Ser.: No. 37). vi, 164p. 1980. pap. text ed. 16.00 (ISBN 90-265-0355-5). Swets North Am.

Carelli, M. Dino, ed. see First All-European Conference for Directors of National Research Institutions in Education, Hamburg 26-29 April 1976.

Carelli, M. Dino, ed. see Third Colloquy for Directors of National Research Institutions in Education, Hamburg, 12-14 September 1978, Educational Research in Europe.

Carelli, Mario, tr. see Tucci, Giuseppe.

Carello, Claudia A., jt. auth. see Michaels, Claire F.

Carenas, F. & Ferrando, Jose. La Sociedad Espanola En la Novela de la Postguerra. 1971. 10.95 (ISBN 0-88303-997-4). E Torres & Sons.

Carens, James F. Surpassing Wit. LC 78-12644. 1979. 17.50x (ISBN 0-231-04642-1). Columbia U Pr.

Carens, James F., ed. & intro. by see Gogarty, Oliver S.

Carens, Joseph H. Equality, Moral Incentives, & the Market. LC 80-36774. (Illus.). 1981. lib. bdg. 19.00x (ISBN 0-226-09269-0). U of Chicago Pr.

Caress, Jay, jt. auth. see Hybels, Bill.

Carew, Bampfylde-Moore. The King of the Beggars, Bampfylde-Moore Carew. Wilkinson, C. H., ed. LC 80-2471. 1981. Repr. of 1931 ed. 39.50 (ISBN 0-404-19103-7). AMS Pr.

Carew, Dorothy. Portugal. LC 68-12087. (Nations Today Books). (Illus.). (gr. 7 up). 1969. 4.95 o.s.i. (ISBN 0-02-716490-X). Macmillan.

Carew, J. & Chan, I. Observing Intelligence in Young Children: Eight Case Studies. (Early Childhood Education Ser.). (Illus.). 192p. 1976. 11.95x (ISBN 0-13-628990-8); pap. 9.95 (ISBN 0-13-628982-7). P-H.

Carew, Jan. Black Midas. 2nd ed. 184p. 1981. 9.00x (ISBN 0-89410-124-2); pap. 5.00x (ISBN 0-89410-125-0). Three Continents.

--Children of the Sun. (Illus.). 40p. (gr. k up). 1980. 9.95 (ISBN 0-316-12848-1). Little.

Carew, Jocelyn. Crown of Passion. 416p. (Orig.). 1980. pap. 2.75 (ISBN 0-380-76414-8, 76414). Avon.

--Follow the Shadows. 480p. (Orig.). 1980. pap. 2.75 (ISBN 0-380-41921-1, 44776). Avon.

--The Golden Sovereigns. 408p. (Orig.). 1980. pap. 2.50 (ISBN 0-380-00845-9, 47381). Avon.

Carew, R., tr. see Huarte Navarro, Juan de Dios.

Carew, Thomas. Poems of Thomas Carew. Dunlap, Rhodes, ed. (Oxford English Texts Ser). 1949. 36.00x (ISBN 0-19-811804-X). Oxford U Pr.

Carey, Andrew G., jt. auth. see Carey, Jane P.

Carey, Bonnie, tr. from Rus. Baba Yaga's Geese & Other Russian Stories. LC 73-77852. (Midland Bks.: No. 222). (Illus.). 128p. (gr. 1-6). 1973. 10.00x o.s.i. (ISBN 0-253-10500-5); pap. 5.95x (ISBN 0-253-20222-1). Ind U Pr.

--Grasshopper to the Rescue. (Illus.). (gr. k-3). 1979. 7.50 (ISBN 0-688-22172-6); PLB 7.20 (ISBN 0-688-32172-0). Morrow.

Carey, Bonnie, tr. see Aleksin, Anatoli.

Carey, Ernestine G., jt. auth. see Gilbreth, Frank B.

Carey, Ernestine G., jt. auth. see Gilbreth, Frank B., Jr.

Carey, Floyd D. & Byrd, James F., eds. Manna: A Book of Table Devotions. 1973. pap. 3.25 (ISBN 0-87148-564-8). Pathway Pr.

Carey, Gary. All the Stars in Heaven: The Story of Louis B. Mayer & Metro-Goldwyn-Mayer. (Illus.). 1980. 15.00 (ISBN 0-525-05245-3). Dutton.

--Plague Notes. (Orig.). pap. 2.25 (ISBN 0-8220-1039-9). Cliffs.

Carey, George C. Maryland Folk Legends & Folk Songs. LC 75-180857. 1971. pap. 4.00 (ISBN 0-87033-158-2, Pub. by Tidewater). Cornell Maritime.
Carey, George G. Maryland Folklore & Folklife. LC 71-142189. (Illus.). 1971. pap. 5.00 (ISBN 0-87033-154-X, Pub. by Tidewater). Cornell Maritime.
Carey, George W., jt. ed. see Hyneman, Charles S.
Carey, Glenn O. Faulkner: the Unappeased Imagination: A Collection of Critical Essays. 290p. 1980. 18.50x (ISBN 0-87875-181-5). Whitston Pub.
Carey, Hugh. Duet for Two Voices. LC 78-62115. (Illus.). 1980. 24.95 (ISBN 0-521-22312-1). Cambridge U Pr.
Carey, Jane P. & Carey, Andrew G. Web of Modern Greek Politics. LC 68-28394. (Illus.). 1968. 18.00x (ISBN 0-231-03170-X). Columbia U Pr.
Carey, John. English Renaissance Studies: Presented to Dame Helen Gardner in Honour of Her Seventieth Birthday. (Illus.). 312p. 1980. 44.00x (ISBN 0-19-812093-1). Oxford U Pr.
--John Donne: Life, Mind & Art. 336p. 1981. 19.95 (ISBN 0-19-520242-2). Oxford U Pr.
--The Violent Effigy. LC 74-160359. 1979. pap. 4.95 (ISBN 0-571-11370-2, Pub. by Faber & Faber). Merrimack Bk Serv.
Carey, John, ed. John Milton: Complete Shorter Poems. (Longman Annotated English Poets Ser.). (Illus.). 1971. pap. text ed. 12.50x (ISBN 0-582-48456-1). Longman.
Carey, John J. Carlyle Marney: A Pilgrim's Progress. LC 80-82573. xii, 156p. 1980. 11.95 (ISBN 0-86554-001-2). Mercer Univ Pr.
Carey, John L. & Skousen, K. Fred. Getting Acquainted with Accounting. 2nd ed. LC 76-10904. (Illus.). 1977. pap. text ed. 6.25 (ISBN 0-395-24513-3). HM.
Carey, Lou, jt. auth. see Dick, Walter.
Carey, M. V. Alfred Hitchcock & the Three Investigators in the Mystery of the Flaming Footprints. Hitchcock, Alfred, ed. (Three Investigators Ser.: No. 15). (Illus.). (gr. 4-7). 1971. 2.95 (ISBN 0-394-82296-X, BYR); PLB 5.39 (ISBN 0-394-92296-4); pap. 1.95 (ISBN 0-394-83776-2). Random.
--Alfred Hitchcock & the Three Investigators in the Mystery of the Magic Circle. LC 78-55915. (Alfred Hitchcock & the Three Investigators Ser.: No. 27). (Illus.). (gr. 4-7). 1978. 2.95 (ISBN 0-394-83607-3, BYR); PLB 5.39 (ISBN 0-394-93607-8); pap. 1.95 (ISBN 0-394-84490-4). Random.
--Alfred Hitchcock & the Three Investigators in the Mystery of Monster Mountain. Hitchcock, Alfred, ed. (Three Investigators Ser.: No. 20). (Illus.). (gr. 4-7). 1973. 2.95 (ISBN 0-394-82664-7, BYR); PLB 5.39 (ISBN 0-394-92664-1); pap. 1.95 (ISBN 0-394-84259-6). Random.
--Alfred Hitchcock & the Three Investigators in the Mystery of the Invisible Dog. LC 75-8073. (Three Investigators Ser.: No. 23). (Illus.). 160p. (gr. 4-7). 1975. 2.95 (ISBN 0-394-83105-5, BYR); PLB 5.39 (ISBN 0-394-93105-X); pap. 1.95 (ISBN 0-394-84492-0). Random.
--Alfred Hitchcock & the Three Investigators in the Mystery of Death Trap Mine. LC 76-8135. (Illus.). (gr. 4-7). 1976. 2.95 (ISBN 0-394-83321-X, BYR); PLB 5.39 (ISBN 0-394-93321-4); pap. 1.95 (ISBN 0-394-84449-1). Random.
--Alfred Hitchcock & the Three Investigators in the Secret of the Haunted Mirror. LC 74-5750. (Alfred Hitchcock & the Three Investigators). (Illus.). 160p. (gr. 4-7). 1974. 2.95 (ISBN 0-394-82820-8, BYR); PLB 5.39 (ISBN 0-394-92820-2); pap. 1.95 (ISBN 0-394-84450-5). Random.
--The Mystery of the Invisible Dog. LC 79-27778. (Alfred Hitchcock & the Three Investigators Ser.). 160p. (gr. 4-7). 1981. pap. 1.95 (ISBN 0-394-84492-0). Random.
--The Mystery of the Magic Circle. LC 79-27657. (Alfred Hitchcock & the Three Investigators Ser.). 160p. (gr. 4-7). 1981. pap. 1.95 (ISBN 0-394-84490-4). Random.
Carey, Mary. Alonzo Purr: The Seagoing Cat. (Tell-a-Tale Readers). (Illus.). (gr. k-3). 1978. PLB 4.77 (ISBN 0-307-68569-1, Whitman). Western Pub.
--Happy, Healthy Pooh Book. (Look-Look Ser.). (Illus.). 1977. PLB 5.38 (ISBN 0-307-61832-3, Golden Pr); pap. 0.95 (ISBN 0-307-11832-0). Western Pub.
--Tawny Scrawny Lion & Clever Monkey. (ps-3). PLB 5.00 (ISBN 0-307-60128-5, Golden Pr). Western Pub.
--Walt Disney's Peter Pan & Captain Hook. (Disney's Wonderful World of Reading Ser.: No. 4). (Illus.). (ps-3). 1973. 3.95 (ISBN 0-394-82517-9, BYR); PLB 4.99 (ISBN 0-394-92517-3). Random.
Carey, Mary & Sherman, George. A Compendium of Bunk or How to Spot a Con Artist: A Handbook for Fraud Investigators, Bankers & Other Custodians of the Public Trust. 216p. 1976. 16.50 (ISBN 0-398-03498-2); pap. 11.50 (ISBN 0-398-03501-6). C C Thomas.
Carey, Mary, adapted by. Wizard of Oz. (Illus.). (gr. k-3). 1976. PLB 5.00 (ISBN 0-307-60119-6, Golden Pr). Western Pub.
Carey, Mathew. Addresses of the Philadelphia Society for the Promotion of National Industry. Hudson, Michael, ed. Bd. with Essay on Expediency & Practicability of Improving or Creating Home Markets for the Sale of Agricultural Productions & Raw Materials. Tibbits, George. (The Neglected American Economists Ser.). 1974. lib. bdg. 50.00 (ISBN 0-8240-1000-0). Garland Pub.
Carey, Michael J., jt. ed. see Balaam, David N.
Carey, Raymond G. Hospital Chaplains: Who Needs Them? 1974. pap. 6.00 (ISBN 0-87125-054-3). Cath Health.
Carey, Raymond G., jt. auth. see Posavac, Emile J.
Carey, Robin. Beautiful Mt. Hood. Shangle, Robert D., ed. LC 78-102323. (Illus.). 1977. 14.95 (ISBN 0-915796-27-9); pap. 7.95 (ISBN 0-915796-26-0). Beautiful Am.
Carey, Zenja & Habeeb, Virginia. The Complete Blender Cookbook. LC 78-52133. 1978. 9.95 (ISBN 0-87502-059-3); pap. 4.95 (ISBN 0-87502-060-7). Benjamin Co.
Carey-Jones, N. S., et al. Politics, Public Enterprise & the Industrial Development Agency: Industrialisation Policies & Practices. 248p. 1975. 22.50x (ISBN 0-8419-5500-X). Holmes & Meier.
Carfagno, V., tr. see Reich, Wilhelm.
Carfagno, Vincent R., tr. see Reich, Wilhelm.
Cargan, Leonard & Ballantine, Jeanne H. Sociological Footprints: Introductory Readings in Sociology. LC 78-69541. (Illus.). 1979. pap. text ed. 8.95 (ISBN 0-395-26718-8); inst. manual 0.45 (ISBN 0-395-26717-X). HM.
Cargas, Harry J. Encountering Myself: Contemporary Christian Meditations. LC 76-56519. 1977. 6.95 (ISBN 0-8164-0372-4). Crossroad NY.
Cargas, Harry J. & Radley, Roger J. Keeping a Spiritual Journal. LC 80-2072. 128p. (gr. 6 up). 1981. pap. 2.75 (ISBN 0-385-17439-X, Im). Doubleday.
Cargas, Harry J., jt. auth. see Erazmus, Edward T.
Cargile, J. Paradoxes. LC 78-67299. (Cambridge Studies in Philosophy). 1979. 32.95 (ISBN 0-521-22475-6). Cambridge U Pr.
Cargill, Jack. The Second Athenian League: Empire or Free Alliance. 325p. 1981. 17.50x (ISBN 0-520-04069-4). U of Cal Pr.
Cargill, Jennifer S. & Alley, Brian. Library Fiscal Controls. 1981. price not set (ISBN 0-912700-79-3). Oryx Pr.
--Library Technical Services Management: Alternatives for Technical Services Librarians. 1981. price not set postponed (ISBN 0-912700-55-6). Oryx Pr.
Cargill, Oscar, et al, eds. O'Neill & His Plays: Four Decades of Criticism. LC 61-17631. (Gotham Library). 1961. 15.00x o.p. (ISBN 0-8147-0075-6); pap. 6.95 (ISBN 0-8147-0076-4). NYU Pr.
Cargill, Thomas F. Money, the Financial System, & Monetary Policy. (Illus.). 1979. ref. 18.95 (ISBN 0-13-600346-X). P-H.
Cargille, Charles, jt. ed. see Glassheim, Eliot.
Carhart, Arthur H. Outdoorsman's Cookbook. rev. ed. 1962. pap. 0.95 o.s.i. (ISBN 0-02-009390-X, Collier). Macmillan.
Caribbean Archives Conf., 2nd. Proceedings: Special Volume Two. (Archivum Ser.). 200p. 1980. pap. 23.00 (ISBN 0-89664-134-1). K G Saur.
Caribbean Seminar on Science & Technology Policy & Planning, 2nd. Proceedings. (Studies on Scientific & Technological Development: No. 28). 1977. pap. text ed. 4.00 (ISBN 0-8270-6000-9). OAS.
Carico, Charles C. & Drooyan, Irving. Analytic Geometry. LC 79-21633. 1980. 16.95 (ISBN 0-471-06435-1); student supplement avail. (ISBN 0-471-06378-9). Wiley.
Caridi, R. Twentieth Century American Foreign Policy, Security, & Self Interest. 1974. 15.95 (ISBN 0-13-934935-9); pap. 12.95 (ISBN 0-13-934927-8). P-H.
Carin, Arthur A. & Sund, Robert B. Teaching Modern Science. 3rd ed. (Elementary Education Ser.: No. C22). 352p. 1980. pap. text ed. 12.95 (ISBN 0-675-08193-9). Merrill.
Carisella, P. J. & Ryan, James W. The Black Swallow of Death. LC 72-75762. (Illus.). 271p. 1972. 8.95 (ISBN 0-911721-87-8). Aviation.
--The Black Swallow of Death. 1972. 8.95 (Pub. by Carisella). Aviation.
Carkeet, David. Double Negative. 246p. 1980. 9.95 (ISBN 0-8037-1777-6). Dial.
Carkhuff, R. R., et al. Skills of Helping Student Workbook. 150p. pap. text ed. 5.95 o.p. (ISBN 0-914234-13-7, SHSW). Human Res Dev Pr.
Carkhuff, Robert, et al. The Skills of Helping: An Introduction to Counseling. LC 78-73987. 262p. 1979. text ed. 13.95x (ISBN 0-914234-09-9); pap. 10.95x (ISBN 0-914234-87-0). Human Res Dev.
--The Art of Helping, IV. 4th ed. LC 79-91075. (Life Skills). 243p. pap. text ed. 9.95x (ISBN 0-914234-10-2, CAH4); tchrs. guide 12.95 (ISBN 0-914234-11-0); wkbk. 6.95 (ISBN 0-914234-12-9). Human Res Dev Pr.
Carkhuff, Robert R. The Art of Problem Solving. LC 72-91238. (Life Skills Ser.). (Illus.). 143p. 1973. pap. text ed. 8.50x (ISBN 0-914234-01-3). Human Res Dev Pr.
--How to Help Yourself: The Art of Program Development. LC 74-18144. (Life Skills Ser.). (Illus.). 172p. 1974. pap. text ed. 8.50x (ISBN 0-914234-02-1). Human Res Dev Pr.
--The Skilled Teacher: A System Approach to Teaching Skills. (Illus.). 184p. 1981. pap. 10.95 (ISBN 0-914234-52-8). Human Res Dev Pr.
--Toward Actualizing Human Potential. (Illus.). 184p. 1981. 10.95x (ISBN 0-914234-15-3). Human Res Dev Pr.
Carkhuff, Robert R., jt. auth. see Friel, Theodore W.
Carkhuff, Robert R., et al. GETAJOB. LC 75-1498. (Career Skills Ser.). 178p. 1975. pap. text ed. 8.95x (ISBN 0-914234-44-7). Human Res Dev Pr.
Carl, Beverly M. International Economic Development Law. (Praeger Special Studies). 1981. write for info. (ISBN 0-03-022321-0). Praeger.
Carl, George E. First Among Equals: Great Britain & Venezuela, 1810-1910. Robinson, David J., ed. LC 80-17481. (Dellplain Latin American Studies: No. 5). (Illus.). 188p. (Orig.). 1980. pap. 17.75 (ISBN 0-8357-0574-9, SS-00142, Pub. by Syracuse U Dept Geog). Univ Microfilms.
Carl, Joseph B. Jesus in Our Affluent Society. 208p. 1981. 9.95 (ISBN 0-938234-01-3); pap. 5.95 (ISBN 0-938234-00-5). Ministry Pubns.
Carl, Linda. The Alumni College Movement. 1977. pap. 9.50 (ISBN 0-89964-001-X). CASE.
Carl, William J., III, jt. auth. see Pervo, Richard I.
Carl, William J., III, jt. auth. see Vawter, Bruce.
Carlbom, Hans. Horseshoe-Nail Crafting. LC 73-83450. (Little Craft Book Ser.). 48p. (gr. 7 up). 1973. 5.95 (ISBN 0-8069-5280-6); PLB 6.69 (ISBN 0-8069-5281-4). Sterling.
Carle, Cecil. Letters to Elderly Alcoholics. 1980. pap. 3.95. Hazelden.
Carle, Eric. The Grouchy Ladybug. LC 77-3170. (Illus.). (ps). 1977. 8.95 (ISBN 0-690-01391-4, TYC-J); PLB 8.79 (ISBN 0-690-01392-2). T Y Crowell.
--Have You Seen My Cat? LC 76-185324. (Illus.). 32p. (ps-2). 1973. PLB 5.95 o.p. (ISBN 0-531-02552-7). Watts.
--The Honeybee & the Robber: A Moving Picture Book. (Illus.). 16p. (gr. 4-8). 1981. 10.95 (ISBN 0-399-20767-8). Philomel.
--I See a Song. LC 72-9249. (Illus.). (ps-2). 1973. PLB 9.79 (ISBN 0-690-43307-7, TYC-J). T Y Crowell.
--The Mixed-up Chameleon. LC 75-5505. (Illus.). (gr. k-2). 1975. 8.95 (ISBN 0-690-00605-5, TYC-J); PLB 8.79 (ISBN 0-690-00924-0). T Y Crowell.
--My Very First Book of Colors. LC 72-83776. (Illus.). 10p. (ps-2). 1974. 3.95 (ISBN 0-690-57365-0, TYC-J). T Y Crowell.
--My Very First Book of Numbers. LC 72-83777. (Illus.). 10p. (ps-2). 1974. 3.95 (ISBN 0-690-57366-9, TYC-J). T Y Crowell.
--My Very First Book of Shapes. LC 72-83778. (Illus.). 10p. (ps-2). 1974. 3.95 (ISBN 0-690-57367-7, TYC-J). T Y Crowell.
--My Very First Book of Words. LC 72-83779. (Illus.). 10p. (ps-2). 1974. 3.95 (ISBN 0-690-57368-5, TYC-J). T Y Crowell.
--The Rooster Who Set Out to See the World. LC 78-171902. (Illus.). 32p. (gr. k-3). 1972. PLB 5.95 o.p. (ISBN 0-531-02042-8). Watts.
--Secret Birthday Message. LC 75-168726. (Illus.). (ps-3). 1972. 8.95 (ISBN 0-690-72347-4, TYC-J); PLB 6.85 (ISBN 0-690-72348-2). T Y Crowell.
--Seven Stories by Hans Christian Andersen. LC 78-2302. (Illus.). (gr. k-3). 1978. 5.95 (ISBN 0-531-02919-0); PLB 7.90 s&l (ISBN 0-531-02493-8). Watts.
Carlebach, Julius. Caring for Children in Trouble. (International Library of Sociology & Social Reconstruction). 1970. text ed. 8.50x (ISBN 0-7100-6564-7). Humanities.
Carlen, Claudia, ed. The Papal Encyclicals, 5 vols. 1981. Set. 400.00 (ISBN 0-8434-0765-4, Consortium). McGrath.
Carlen, Pat. Magistrate's Justice. 134p. 1976. 30.50x (ISBN 0-85520-121-5, Pub. by Martin Robertson England). Biblio Dist.
Carlen, Pat & Collison, Mike. Radical Issues in Criminology. 212p. 1980. 24.50x (ISBN 0-389-20083-2). B&N.
Carlen, Pat, ed. The Sociology of Law. (Sociological Review Monograph: No. 23). 250p. 1976. pap. 23.50x (ISBN 0-8476-2296-7). Rowman.
Carles, Riva. Thrall of Love. 1977. pap. 1.75 o.p. (ISBN 0-425-03405-4, Medallion). Berkley Pub.
Carleton, Ardis, ed. Guide to Microforms in Print: Author-Title 1980. LC 61-7082. 1980. 49.50 (ISBN 0-913672-35-1). Microform Rev.
--Guide to Microforms in Print: Subject. 1980. LC 62-21624. 1980. 49.50 (ISBN 0-913672-36-X). Microform Rev.
Carleton, Ardis V., ed. Guide to Microforms in Print: Supplement 1980. new ed. 320p. 1980. text ed. 35.00x (ISBN 0-913672-39-4). Microform Rev.
--Microform Market Place Nineteen Eighty to Nineteen Eighty-One. 4th ed. 250p. 1980. pap. text ed. 20.95 (ISBN 0-913672-37-8). Microform Rev.
Carleton, Frances B. The Dramatic Monologue: Vox Humana. (Salzburg Studies in English Literature: Romantic Reassessment: 64). 1977. pap. text ed. 25.00x (ISBN 0-391-01340-8). Humanities.
Carleton, H. M. Carleton's Histological Technique. 4th ed. Drury, R. A. & Wallington, E. A., eds. 1967. 46.50x o.p. (ISBN 0-19-261205-0). Oxford U Pr.
Carleton, H. M. & Drury, R. A., eds. Carleton's Histological Technique. 5th ed. (Illus.). 592p. 1980. text ed. 59.50 (ISBN 0-19-261310-3). Oxford U Pr.
Carleton, Ralph A. Biological & Ethical Deviations in Human Beings. (Illus.). 1980. 37.75 (ISBN 0-89920-007-9). Am Inst Psych.
Carleton, Robert H. The NST Story, 1944-1974. (Orig.). 1976. pap. 3.00 o.p. (ISBN 0-686-53818-8, 471-14700). Natl Sci Tchrs.
Carleton, William. The Black Prophet. 408p. 1972. Repr. of 1899 ed. 7.00x (ISBN 0-7165-1798-1, Pub by Irish Academic Pr). Biblio Dist.
--The Black Prophet: A Tale of the Irish Famine. Wolff, Robert L., ed. (Ireland Nineteenth Century Fiction Ser. Two: Vol. 41). 324p. 1979. lib. bdg. 32.00 (ISBN 0-8240-3490-2). Garland Pub.
--The Emigrants of Ahadarra: A Tale of Irish Life. Wolff, Robert L., ed. (Ireland Nineteenth Century Fiction Ser. Two: Vol. 42). 320p. 1979. lib. bdg. 32.00 (ISBN 0-8240-3491-0). Garland Pub.
--Fardorougha, the Miser; or, the Convicts of Lisnamona. Wolff, Robert L., ed. (Ireland Nineteenth Century Fiction - Ser. Two: Vol. 37). 481p. 1979. lib. bdg. 32.00 (ISBN 0-8240-3486-4). Garland Pub.
--Father Butler, the Lough Dearg Pilgrim. Wolff, Robert L., ed. (Ireland Nineteenth Century Fiction - Ser. Two: Vol. 33). 306p. 1979. lib. bdg. 32.00 (ISBN 0-8240-3482-1). Garland Pub.
--The Fawn of Spring-Vale, the Clarionet, & Other Tales, 3 vols. Wolff, Robert L., ed. (Ireland Nineteenth Century Fiction - Ser. Two: Vol. 38). 1068p. 1979. Set. lib. bdg. 96.00 (ISBN 0-8240-3487-2). Garland Pub.
--The Life of William Carleton. Wolff, Robert L., ed. (Ireland Nineteenth Century Fiction - Ser. Two: Vol. 44). 728p. 1979. lib. bdg. 32.00 (ISBN 0-8240-3493-7). Garland Pub.
--Tales of Ireland. Wolff, Robert L., ed. (Ireland Nineteenth Century Fiction - Ser. Two; Vol. 36). 384p. 1979. lib. bdg. 32.00 (ISBN 0-8240-3485-6). Garland Pub.
--The Tithe Proctor: Being a Tale of the Tithe Rebellion in Ireland. Wolff, Robert L., ed. (Ireland Nineteenth Century Proctor Fiction - Ser. Two: Vol. 43). 304p. 1979. lib. bdg. 32.00 (ISBN 0-8240-3492-9). Garland Pub.
--Traits & Stories of the Irish Peasantry, 2 vols. (Nineteenth Century Fiction Ser.: Ireland: Vol. 34). 596p. 1979. Set. lib. bdg. 46.00 (ISBN 0-8240-3483-X). Garland Pub.
--Traits & Stories of the Irish Peasantry: Second Series, 3 vols. Wolff, Robert L., ed. (Ireland Nineteenth Century Fiction - Ser. Two: Vol. 35). 1412p. 1979. lib. bdg. 96.00 (ISBN 0-8240-3484-8). Garland Pub.
--Valentine M'Clutchy, the Irish Agent: Chronicles of the Castle Cumber Property. Wolff, Robert L., ed. (Ireland Nineteenth Century Fiction - Ser. Two: Vol. 40). 480p. 1979. lib. bdg. 32.00 (ISBN 0-8240-3489-9). Garland Pub.
Carley, Maurine, jt. auth. see Trenholm, Virginia C.
Carlier, Robert, et al, eds. Larousse des citations: Francaises et etrangeres. new ed. 895p. (Fr.). 1975. 32.00x (ISBN 2-03-021001-3, 3932). Larousse.
Carlile, Clancy. Honkytonk Man. 1981. 12.95 (ISBN 0-671-41212-4). S&S.
--Spore Seven. 288p. 1979. pap. 2.25 (ISBN 0-380-49031-5, 49031). Avon.

Carlile, Clark S. Thirty-Eight Basic Speech Experiences. rev. ed. 1977. lib. bdg. 6.00 (ISBN 0-931054-03-6). Clark Pub.
Carlile, M. J. & Skehel, J. J., eds. Evolution in the Microbial World: Proceedings. (Illus.). 450p. 1974. 49.50 (ISBN 0-521-20416-X). Cambridge U Pr.
Carlile, R. E. & Gillett, B. E. Fortran & Computer Mathematics for the Engineer & Scientist. LC 72-95446. 1974. 23.00 (ISBN 0-87814-016-6). Pennwell Pub.
Carlin, Harriette L. Medical Secretary Medi-Speller: A Transcription Aid. 260p. 1973. pap. 11.50 (ISBN 0-398-02579-7). C C Thomas.
Carlin, Jerome E. Lawyers on Their Own: A Study of Individual Practitioners in Chicago. 1962. 15.00 (ISBN 0-8135-0412-0). Rutgers U Pr.
Carline, Richard. Stanley Spencer at War. (Illus.). 1978. 27.00 (ISBN 0-571-11028-2, Pub. by Faber & Faber). Merrimack Bk Serv.
Carlinsky, Dan, jt. auth. see Goodgold, Edwin.
Carlisle, Clark. Bugs Bunny's Carrot Machine. (Illus.). 24p. (gr. k-3). 1976. PLB 5.00 (ISBN 0-307-60127-7, Golden Pr). Western Pub.
Carlisle, Douglas H. Venezuelan Foreign Policy: Its Organization & Beginning. LC 78-57979. 1978. pap. text ed. 9.50 (ISBN 0-8191-0317-9). U Pr of Amer.
Carlisle, G. L., jt. auth. see Stanbury, Percy.
Carlisle, Howard M. Management: Concepts & Situations. LC 75-29382. (Illus.). 608p. 1976. text ed. 18.95 (ISBN 0-574-19230-1, 13-2230); instr's guide avail. (ISBN 0-574-19231-X, 13-2231). SRA.
--Management Essentials: Concepts & Applications. LC 78-16303. 1979. text ed. 16.95 (ISBN 0-574-19370-7, 13-2370); instr's guide avail. (ISBN 0-574-19371-5, 13-2371); study guide 5.95 (ISBN 0-574-19372-3, 13-2372); lecture suppl. 2.95 (ISBN 0-574-19373-1, 13-2373). SRA.
Carlisle, Olga. Poets on Street Corners. (YA) 1968. 7.95 o.p. (ISBN 0-394-44073-0). Random.
Carlisle, Olga A., tr. see Pasternak, Boris.
Carlisle, Rodney. The Roots of Black Nationalism. (National University Publications Ser. in American Studies). 1975. 11.50 (ISBN 0-8046-9098-7, Natl U). Kennikat.
Carlisle, Rodney P. Hearst & the New Deal - The Progressive As Reactionary. Freidel, Frank, ed. LC 78-62378. (Modern American History Ser.: Vol. 4). 1979. lib. bdg. 28.00 (ISBN 0-8240-3628-X). Garland Pub.
--Sovereignty for Sale. 336p. 1981. 19.95 (ISBN 0-87021-668-6). Naval Inst Pr.
Carlisle, Sarah. Penny Wise. 224p. 1981. pap. 1.95 (ISBN 0-449-50176-0, Coventry). Fawcett.
Carlisle, Thomas J. Journey with Job. LC 75-34230. 96p. 1976. pap. 2.25 o.p. (ISBN 0-8028-1617-7). Eerdmans.
Carlo & Murphy. Merchandising Mathmatics. 136p. 1981. pap. 6.60 (ISBN 0-8273-1416-7); instructor's guide 1.60 (ISBN 0-8273-1417-5). Delmar.
Carlo, Mona, jt. auth. see Scott, Gwendolyn D.
Carlon, Patricia, et al. Illinois Supplement for Real Estate Principles & Practices. (Business & Economics Ser.). 112p. 1976. 4.95 (ISBN 0-675-08583-7). Merrill.
Carlova, J., jt. auth. see Horsley, J. E.
Carlquist, Sherwin. Ecological Strategies of Xylem Evolution. LC 74-76382. (Illus.). 1975. 20.00x (ISBN 0-520-02730-2). U of Cal Pr.
--Island Biology. LC 73-4643. (Illus.). 656p. 1974. 32.50x (ISBN 0-231-03562-4). Columbia U Pr.
Carlsen, Darvey. Graphic Arts. new ed. (gr. 7-12). 1977. text ed. 10.48 (ISBN 0-87002-177-X); tchr's guide avail. (ISBN 0-685-57544-6). Bennett IL.
Carlsen, Melody A., jt. auth. see Cooper, Robert D.
Carlsmith, J. Merrill, et al. Methods of Research in Social Psychology. 352p. 1976. text ed. 18.95 (ISBN 0-201-00346-5). A-W.
Carlsnaes, Walter. The Concept of Ideology & Political Analysis: A Critical Examination of Its Usage by Marx, Lenin, & Mannheim. LC 80-1202. (Contributions in Philosophy Ser.: No. 17). 280p. 1981. lib. bdg. 32.50 (ISBN 0-313-22267-3, CCI/). Greenwood.
Carlson. Illinois: Government & Institutions. new ed. (gr. 9-12). 1973. pap. text ed. 4.20 o.p. (ISBN 0-205-03645-7, 7636458). Allyn.
--Sevinc Malaysia. LC 75-13846. (The Washington Papers: No. 25). 1975. 3.50x (ISBN 0-8039-0563-7). Sage.
--Springs: Troubleshooting & Failure Analysis. 216p. 1980. 27.50 (ISBN 0-8247-1003-7). Dekker.
Carlson & Lassey. Rural Society & Environment in America. (Agricultural Science Ser.). (Illus.). 448p. 1981. text ed. 15.95x (ISBN 0-07-009959-6, C). McGraw.
Carlson, A. Bruce & Gisser, David G. Electrical Engineering: Concepts & Applications. LC 80-21519. (Electrical Engineering Ser.). 640p. 1981. text ed. price not set (ISBN 0-201-03940-0). A-W.
Carlson, A. Bruce, jt. auth. see Frederick, Dean K.
Carlson, Andrew R. Anarchism in Germany, Vol. 1: The Early Movement. LC 78-186946. 1972. 16.50 (ISBN 0-8108-0484-0). Scarecrow.
--German Foreign Policy, 1890-1914 & Colonial Policy to 1914: A Handbook & Annotated Bibliography. 1970. 10.00 (ISBN 0-8108-0296-1). Scarecrow.
Carlson, Bernice W. Let's Pretend It Happened to You. LC 73-1488. (Illus.). 112p. (ps-3). 1973. 5.95 o.p. (ISBN 0-687-21503-X). Abingdon.
--Listen & Help Tell the Story. (Illus.). (gr. k-2). 1965. 8.95 o.p. (ISBN 0-687-22096-3). Abingdon.
Carlson, Bernice W., jt. auth. see Hunt, Kari.
Carlson, Bruce M. Patten's Foundations of Embryology. 4th, rev. ed. (Organismal Biology Ser.). (Illus.). 608p. 1981. text ed. 21.95 (ISBN 0-07-009875-1, C). McGraw.
Carlson, C. C., jt. auth. see Lindsey, Hal.
Carlson, Carole C. Established in Eden. 1978. 6.95 o.p. (ISBN 0-8007-0943-8). Revell.
Carlson, Dale. Boys Have Feelings Too. LC 80-12895. (Illus.). 160p. (gr. 6 up). 1980. 8.95 (ISBN 0-689-30770-5). Atheneum.
--Girls Are Equal Too. (Illus.). 1973. pap. 2.95 (ISBN 0-689-70433-X, Aladdin). Atheneum.
--Loving Sex for Both Sexes: Straight Talk for Teen-Agers. (gr. 9 up). 1979. PLB 9.90 s&l (ISBN 0-531-02872-0); pap. 5.95 (ISBN 0-531-02497-0). Watts.
--The Plant People. (Triumph Books). (Illus.). (gr. 4 up). 1977. PLB 6.90 s&l (ISBN 0-531-00380-9). Watts.
--A Wild Heart. (Triumph Bks.). 1977. PLB 6.90 (ISBN 0-531-01326-X). Watts.
Carlson, Dale Bick. Where's Your Head? LC 77-2292. (Illus.). (gr. 6-12). 1977. 8.95 (ISBN 0-689-30578-8). Atheneum.
Carlson, David B. & Heinberg, John D. How Housing Allowances Work: Integrated Findings to Date from the Experimental Housing Allowance Program. (An Institute Paper). 95p. 1978. pap. 4.00 (ISBN 0-87766-215-0, 21300). Urban Inst.
Carlson, Diane. Another Chance. Verdick, Mary, ed. (Beginning Pal Paperbacks Ser.). (Illus., Orig.). (gr. 7-12). 1977. pap. text ed. 1.25 (ISBN 0-8374-3460-2). Xerox Ed Pubns.
--You Can't Tell Me What to Do! Uhlich, Richard, ed. (Bluejeans Paperback Ser.). (Illus., Orig.). (gr. 7-12). 1978. pap. text ed. 1.25 (ISBN 0-8374-5006-3). Xerox Ed Pubns.
Carlson, Dwight L. Overcoming Hurts & Anger. LC 80-83852. 1981. pap. 4.95 (ISBN 0-89081-277-2). Harvest Hse.
Carlson, Edgar M. The Church & the Public Conscience. LC 79-8710. xii, 104p. 1981. Repr. of 1956 ed. lib. bdg. 17.50x (ISBN 0-313-22195-2, CACH). Greenwood.
Carlson, Elof Axel, ed. Modern Biology: Its Conceptual Foundations. LC 67-12476. (Science Ser). (Illus.). 1967. 7.50 o.s.i. (ISBN 0-8076-0405-4). Braziller.
Carlson, Estelle. The I'm Too Busy Cook Book: Recipes for Busy People Who Love to Cook. (Illus.). 59p. (Orig.). 1981. pap. write for info. Pot of Gold.
Carlson, G. R., tr. La Dynamique Spirituelle. (French Bks.). (Fr.). 1979. 1.80 (ISBN 0-8297-0777-8). Life Pubs Intl.
Carlson, G. Raymond. The Acts Story. (Radiant Life Ser). 1975. pap. 1.50 (ISBN 0-88243-913-8, 02-0913); teacher's ed 2.50 (ISBN 0-88243-184-6, 0184). Gospel Pub.
--The Life Worth Living. (Radiant Life Ser). 1975. pap. 1.95 (ISBN 0-88243-876-X, 02-0876); teacher's ed. 2.50 (ISBN 0-88243-160-9, 32-0160). Gospel Pub.
--Our Faith & Fellowship. LC 77-75023. (Radiant Life Ser). 1977. pap. 1.50 (ISBN 0-88243-908-1, 02-0908); teacher's ed. 2.50 (ISBN 0-88243-178-1, 32-0178). Gospel Pub.
--Prayer & the Christian's Devotional Life. (Radiant Life Ser.). 128p. (Orig.). 1981. write for info. Gospel Pub.
--Spiritual Dynamics. (Radiant Life Ser). 1976. pap. 1.95 (ISBN 0-88243-894-8, 02-0894); teacher's ed 2.50 (ISBN 0-88243-168-4, 32-0168). Gospel Pub.
Carlson, Gene & Orton, Carles, eds. Ground Cover Fire Fighting Practices. 2nd ed. (Illus.). 1981. pap. text ed. 7.00 (ISBN 0-87939-038-7, IFSTA 207). Intl Fire Serv. Postponed.
Carlson, Gene, ed. see IFSTA Committee.
Carlson, Gene, ed. see IFSTA Committee & Walker, Lorrin.
Carlson, Gene, ed. see ISTA Committee.
Carlson, Gene P., ed. see IFSTA Committee.
Carlson, Gordon. Bad Luck Stars of Sports. Mooney, Thomas J., ed. (Pal Paperbacks Ser., Kit A). (Illus., Orig.). (gr. 7-12). 1976. pap. text ed. 1.25 (ISBN 0-8374-3499-8). Xerox Ed Pubns.
--Cry for Help. Mooney, Thomas J., ed. (Beginning Pal Paperbacks Ser.). (Illus., Orig.). (gr. 7-12). 1977. pap. text ed. 1.25 (ISBN 0-8374-3452-1). Xerox Ed Pubns.
--Fire at Sea. Verdick, Mary, ed. (Beginning Pal Paperbacks Ser.). (Illus., Orig.). (gr. 7-12). 1977. pap. text ed. 1.25 (ISBN 0-8374-3461-0). Xerox Ed Pubns.
--Get Me Out of Here! Uhlich, Richard, ed. (Bluejeans Paperbacks Ser.). (Illus., Orig.). (gr. 7-12). 1978. pap. text ed. 1.25- (ISBN 0-8374-5005-5). Xerox Ed Pubns.
Carlson, Jack & Graham, Hugh. The Economic Importance of Exports to the United States, Vol. Ii. LC 80-66694. (Significant Issues Ser.: No. 6). 128p. 1980. 5.95 (ISBN 0-89206-019-0). CSI Studies.
Carlson, Jean. Enjoying Soccer. LC 76-9118. (Illus.). 1976. 6.95 (ISBN 0-914842-09-9); pap. 3.95 (ISBN 0-914842-10-2). Madrona Pubs.
Carlson, John G., jt. auth. see Minke, Karl A.
Carlson, Jon, jt. auth. see Dinkmeyer, Don.
Carlson, Jon, jt. auth. see Dinkmeyer, Don C.
Carlson, Karen & Meyers, Alan. Speaking with Confidence. 1977. pap. 9.95x (ISBN 0-673-15022-4). Scott F.
Carlson, Kenneth N. Manual for Travel Counsellors. 12th, rev. ed. LC 73-92320. (Illus.). 260p. 1981. 11.75x (ISBN 0-938428-00-4). Res Pubns WA.
Carlson, L. Neal. To Die Is Gain. (Contempo Ser.). pap. 0.95 (ISBN 0-8010-2357-2); dozen 9.50 (ISBN 0-686-66984-3). Baker Bk.
Carlson, Lars A. & Pernow, Bengt, eds. Metabolic Risk Factors in Ischemic Cardiovascular Disease. 1981. text ed. price not set (ISBN 0-89004-614-X). Raven.
Carlson, Leland H. Martin Marprelate, Gentleman. (Illus.). 400p. 1981. price not set (ISBN 0-87328-112-8). Huntington Lib.
--The Writings of Henry Barrow, 1587-1590. (Elizabethan Nonconformist Texts Ser.). 1962. text ed. 12.50x o.p. (ISBN 0-04-285001-0). Allen Unwin.
--The Writings of Robert Harrison & Robert Browne. (Elizabethan Nonconformist Text Ser.). 1953. text ed. 6.95x o.p. (ISBN 0-04-274002-9). Allen Unwin.
Carlson, Leland H., ed. Cartwrightiana. Peel, Albert. (Elizabethan Nonconformist Texts). 1951. text ed. 8.95x o.p. (ISBN 0-04-274001-0). Allen Unwin.
--The Writings of Henry Barrow, 1590-1591. (Elizabethan Nonconformist Texts Ser.). 1962. text ed. 16.50x o.p. (ISBN 0-04-285002-9). Allen Unwin.
--The Writings of John Greenwood & Henry Barrow, 1591-1593. (Elizabethan Nonconformist Texts Ser.). 1970. text ed. 17.95x o.p. (ISBN 0-04-809002-6). Allen Unwin.
--The Writings of John Greenwood, 1587-1590. (Elizabethan Nonconformist Texts Ser.). 1962. text ed. 8.95x o.p. (ISBN 0-04-285003-7). Allen Unwin.
Carlson, Leonard A. Indians, Bureaucrats, & Land: The Dawes Act & the Decline of Indian Farming. LC 80-1709. (Contributions in Economics & Economic History Ser.: No. 36). 280p. 1981. lib. bdg. 29.95 (ISBN 0-313-22533-8, CDA/). Greenwood.
Carlson, Lewis H. & Colburn, George A., eds. In Their Place: White America Defines Her Minorities, 1850-1950. LC 70-177881. 1972. pap. 9.95x o.p. (ISBN 0-471-13489-9). Wiley.
Carlson, Loraine. The TraveLeer Guide to Mexico City. 2nd ed. LC 80-26850. (Illus.). 220p. 1981. pap. 4.50 (ISBN 0-932554-02-4). Upland Pr.
--TraveLeer Guide to Yucatan & Guatemala. LC 79-53283. (Illus.). 365p. (Orig.). 1980. pap. 6.95 (ISBN 0-932554-01-6). Upland Pr.
Carlson, Marvin. The French Stage in the Nineteenth Century. LC 72-3981. 1972. 11.50 (ISBN 0-8108-0516-2). Scarecrow.
--Italian Stage from Goldoni to D'annunzio. LC 80-10554. 225p. 1981. lib. bdg. write for info. (ISBN 0-89950-000-5). McFarland & Co.
Carlson, Morry, jt. auth. see Anderson, Ken.
Carlson, Natalie S. Jaky or Dodo? (Illus.). 96p. (gr. 1-4). 1978. 6.95 (ISBN 0-684-15340-8). Scribner.
--Marie Louise & Christophe. LC 73-19365. (Illus.). 32p. (ps-3). 1974. 5.95 (ISBN 0-684-13736-4). Scribner.
--Marie Louise's Heyday. LC 75-8345. (Illus.). 32p. (ps-3). 1975. 6.95 (ISBN 0-684-14360-7). Scribner.
--Runaway Marie Louise. LC 77-9448. (Illus.). 32p. (gr. k-3). 1977. 9.95 (ISBN 0-684-15045-X). Scribner.
Carlson, Neal, jt. auth. see Crane, Dale.
Carlson, Neil. Physiology of Behavior. 1977. text ed. 19.95x (ISBN 0-205-05706-3, 7957068); instr's manual avail. (ISBN 0-205-05707-1, 7957676); wkbk 8.95 (ISBN 0-686-68513-X, 7957580). Allyn.
Carlson, Neil R. Physiology of Behavior. 2nd ed. 704p. 1981. text ed. 20.95 (ISBN 0-205-07262-3, 797262-8); free (ISBN 0-205-07263-1); write for info. study guide (ISBN 0-205-07264-X). Allyn.
Carlson, Norman & Peterson, Arthur, eds. Remember When-Trolley Wires Spanned the Country: Bullentin-119. LC 78-74495. (Illus.). 1980. 30.00 (ISBN 0-915348-20-9). Central Electric.
Carlson, Raymond, ed. National Directory of Budget Motels. LC 75-11992. 1981. pap. 3.50 (ISBN 0-87576-051-1). Pilot Bks.
--National Directory of Free Tourist Attractions. LC 77-3251. 1979. pap. 2.95 (ISBN 0-87576-057-0). Pilot Bks.
Carlson, Reynolds E., et al. Recreation & Leisure: The Changing Scene. 3rd ed. 1979. text ed. 17.95x (ISBN 0-534-00585-3). Wadsworth Pub.
Carlson, Rick J. The Dilemmas of Correction. LC 75-32223. 1976. 19.95 (ISBN 0-669-00346-8). Lexington Bks.
--The End of Medicine. LC 75-6856. (Health, Medicine & Society Ser). 1975. pap. 22.95 (ISBN 0-471-13494-5, Pub. by Wiley-Interscience). Wiley.
Carlson, Robert O., ed. Communications & Public Opinion: A Public Opinion Quarterly Reader. LC 75-11687. 660p. 1975. text ed. 26.95 (ISBN 0-275-07510-9); pap. text ed. 11.95 (ISBN 0-275-89330-8). Praeger.
Carlson, Robert S., et al. International Finance: Cases & Simulation. LC 80-81213. 400p. 1980. pap. text ed. 6.95 (ISBN 0-201-00903-X). A-W.
Carlson, Ronald L. Transcendental Meditation: Relation or Religion. 1978. pap. 2.50 (ISBN 0-8024-8800-5). Moody.
Carlson, Ruth. Writing Aids Through the Grades: One Hundred Eighty-Six Developmental Writing Activities. LC 77-108775. 1970. pap. 5.25x (ISBN 0-8077-1141-1). Tchrs Coll.
Carlson, Ruth K. Sparkling Words. 1979. 8.95 o.p. (ISBN 0-88252-009-1). Paladin Hse.
--Speaking Aids Through the Grades. LC 74-14719. 1975. pap. text ed. 4.50x (ISBN 0-8077-2421-1). Tchrs Coll.
Carlson, Sevinc. China's Oil: Problems & Prospects. LC 79-92159. (CSIS Monograph). 128p. 1979. 77.00 (ISBN 0-89206-010-7). CSI Studies.
Carlson, Steve & Schneider, Fred W. PCC: The Car That Fought Back. Sebree, Mac, ed. LC 80-81312. (Interurbans Special Ser.: No. 64). (Illus.). 256p. 1980. 29.95 (ISBN 0-916374-41-6). Interurban.
Carlson, Vada F. Great Migration: Emergence of the Americas, Indicated in the Readings of Edgar Cayce. (Orig.). 1970. pap. 1.95 (ISBN 0-87604-040-7). ARE Pr.
Carlson, Verne. The Cowboy Cookbook. LC 80-68342. (Illus.). 186p. 1981. 10.95 (ISBN 0-937844-00-4); pap. 6.95 (ISBN 0-937844-01-2). Caverne Pub.
Carlson, William. Sunrise West. LC 79-7043. (Science Fiction Ser.). 192p. 1981. 9.95 (ISBN 0-385-14498-9). Doubleday.
Carlsson, A., et al, eds. Current Topics in Extrapyramidal Disorders. (Journal of Neural Transmission Supplementum: No. 16). (Illus.). 240p. 1980. 57.90 (ISBN 0-387-81570-8). Springer-Verlag.
Carlstein, Tommy, et al, eds. Timing Space & Spacing Time, 3 vols. Incl. Vol. I. Making Sense of Time. 24.95 (ISBN 0-470-26511-6); Vol. II. Human Activity & Time Geography. 39.95 (ISBN 0-470-26513-2); Vol. III. Time & Regional Dynamics. 24.95 (ISBN 0-470-26512-4). 1979. Halsted Pr.
Carlton, Charles. Bigotry & Blood: Documents on the Ulster Crisis. LC 76-17018. 1977. 12.95 (ISBN 0-88229-278-1); pap. 7.95 (ISBN 0-88229-469-5). Nelson-Hall.
--The Court of Orphans. 1974. text ed. 10.50x (ISBN 0-7185-1125-5, Leicester). Humanities.
Carlton, D. & Schaerf, C., eds. International Terrorism & World Security. LC 75-16273. 1975. 24.95 (ISBN 0-470-13503-4). Halsted Pr.
Carlton, David & Schaerf, Carlo. Arms Control & Technological Innovation. LC 77-8790. 1977. 28.95 (ISBN 0-470-99274-3). Halsted Pr.
Carlton, David & Schaerf, Carlo, eds. The Dynamics of the Arms Race. LC 74-20106. 244p. 1975. 26.95 (ISBN 0-470-13480-1). Halsted Pr.
Carlton, Eric. Ideology & Social Order. (International Library of Sociology). 1976. 27.50 (ISBN 0-7100-8474-9). Routledge & Kegan.
--Sexual Anxiety: A Study of Male Impotence. 197p. 1980. 22.50x. B&N.

Carlton, Frank T. Economic Influences Upon Educational Progress in the United States 1820-1850. LC 66-11657. (Orig.). 1966. text ed. 8.75 (ISBN 0-8077-1143-8); pap. text ed. 4.00x (ISBN 0-8077-1140-3). Tchrs Coll.
Carlton, James T., jt. ed. see Smith, Ralph I.
Carlton, Joseph R. Carlton's Complete Reference Book of Music. LC 44-181. (Illus.). 729p. 1980. PLB 40.00 (ISBN 0-937348-00-7). Carlton Pubns CA.
Carlton, Malcolm. Music in Education. (New Education Ser.). 1978. 18.50x (ISBN 0-7130-0155-0, Woburn Pr England). Biblio Dist.
Carlton, Mitchell. Hot Oil. (Orig.). 1980. pap. 1.75 (ISBN 0-505-51477-X). Tower Bks.
Carlton, R. J., jt. auth. see Campbell, L. J.
Carlton, William M. Laboratory Studies in General Botany. (Illus., Orig.). 1961. pap. 12.95 (ISBN 0-8260-1805-X). Wiley.
Carluccio, Luigi. Domenico Gnoli. LC 74-82606. (Illus.). 168p. 1975. 40.00 (ISBN 0-87951-026-9). Overlook Pr.
Carlyle, Alexander J. Political Liberty: A History of the Conception in the Middle Ages & Modern Times. LC 80-18967. viii, 220p. 1980. Repr. of 1963 ed. lib. bdg. 19.75x (ISBN 0-313-21482-4, CAPL). Greenwood.
Carlyle, Ken. Challenging & Highly Profitable Business Careers for the New College Graduate Eager for Success & Adventure. (Illus.). 1977. 37.50 (ISBN 0-89266-078-3). Am Classical Coll Pr.
Carlyle, Thomas. Essays: Vol. 2, English & Other Critical Miscellanies. 1964. 5.00x (ISBN 0-460-00704-1, Evman); pap. 2.95 (ISBN 0-460-01704-7, Evman). Dutton.
--French Revolution, Vol. 2. 1955. 6.00x o.p. (ISBN 0-460-00032-2, Evman). Dutton.
--History of Friedrich 2nd of Prussia Called Frederick the Great. Clive, John, ed. LC 79-82375. (Classic European Histories Ser). 1969. text ed. 12.00x o.s.i. (ISBN 0-226-09296-8). U of Chicago Pr.
--The Nigger Question. August, Eugene R., ed. Bd. with The Negro Question. Mill, John S. LC 73-14584. (Crofts Classics Ser.). 1971. text ed. 5.95x (ISBN 0-88295-021-5); pap. text ed. 1.25x (ISBN 0-88295-020-7). AHM Pub.
--On Heroes, Hero-Worship & the Heroic in History. Niemeyer, Carl, ed. LC 66-12130. (Illus.). 1966. pap. 2.95x (ISBN 0-8032-5030-4, BB 334, Bison). U of Nebr Pr.
--On Heroes, Hero-Worship & the Heroic in History. (World's Classics Ser: No. 62). 320p. 1975. 10.95 (ISBN 0-19-250062-7). Oxford U Pr.
--Sartor Resartus. Incl. On Heroes & Hero Worship. 1954. 11.50x (ISBN 0-460-00278-3, Evman); pap. 2.95 (ISBN 0-460-01278-9, Evman). Dutton.
--Sartor Resartus: The Life & Opinions of Herr Teufelsdrockh. Harrold, C. F., ed. 1937. 8.95 (ISBN 0-672-63200-4). Odyssey Pr.
--Thomas Carlyle - Reminiscences. Norton, Charles E., ed. (Rowman & Littlefield Univerisity Library). 400p. 1972. 7.50x (ISBN 0-87471-656-X); pap. 3.50x (ISBN 0-87471-655-1). Rowman.
Carlyle, Thomas, jt. auth. see Emerson, Ralph W.
Carlyon, Richard. The Dark Lord of Pengersick. LC 80-13360. (Illus.). (gr. 4 up). 1980. 10.95 (ISBN 0-374-31700-3). FS&G.
Carmack, Robert M. The Quiche Mayas of Utatlan. LC 80-5241. (The Civilization of the American Indian Ser.: No. 155). (Illus.). 400p. 1981. 24.95 (ISBN 0-8061-1546-7). U of Okla Pr.
--Quichean Civilization: The Ethnohistoric, Ethnographic, & Archaelogical Sources. LC 70-149948. (Illus.). 1973. 25.75x (ISBN 0-520-01963-6). U of Cal Pr.
Carman, Bliss, ed. The World's Best Poetry, Vol. I: Home & Friendship. new ed. LC 80-84498. (The Granger Anthology Ser.: Ser. I). 480p. 1981. Repr. of 1904 ed. lib. bdg. 29.95x (ISBN 0-89609-202-X). Granger Bk.
Carman, John S. Obstacles to Mineral Development: A Pragmatic View. Varon, Benison, ed. LC 78-26807. (Illus.). 1979. 28.00 (ISBN 0-08-023904-8). Pergamon.
Carman, M. J., jt. auth. see Carman, R. A.
Carman, Marilyn J., jt. auth. see Carman, Robert A.
Carman, R. A. & Carman, M. J. Basic Mathematical Skills: A Guided Approach. 1975. 17.95 (ISBN 0-471-13495-3). Wiley.
Carman, Robert A. Algebra for the Trades: A Guided Approach. 1980. pap. text ed. write for info. (ISBN 0-471-05966-8). Wiley.
Carman, Robert A. & Carman, Marilyn J. Basic Mathematical Skills: A Guided Approach. 2nd ed. LC 80-19121. 560p. 1981. pap. text ed. 16.95 (ISBN 0-471-03608-0). Wiley.
--Quick Arithmetic. LC 74-2476. (Wiley Self-Teaching Guides). 275p. 1974. pap. text ed. 6.95 (ISBN 0-471-13496-1). Wiley.
Carman, Robert A. & Saunders, Hal M. Arithmetic for the Trades: A Guided Approach. 1980. pap. text ed. write for info. (ISBN 0-471-05968-4). Wiley.
Carman, Robert A. & Saunders, Hale. Geometry & Trigonometry for the Trades: A Guided Approach. 1981. 7.95 (ISBN 0-471-05969-2). Wiley.
Carman, Robert A., jt. auth. see Cain, Jack.
Carmel, M., ed. Handbook on Medical Librarianship. 1980. 33.00x (ISBN 0-85365-502-2, Pub. by Lib Assn England). Oryx Pr.
Carmel, Peter W. Clinical Neurosurgery, Vol. 27. (Illus.). 600p. 1981. write for info. (2022-6). Williams & Wilkins.
--Congress of Neurological Surgeons, Vol. 27. (CNS Ser.). (Illus.). 600p. 1981. lib. bdg. price not set (ISBN 0-683-02022-6). Williams & Wilkins.
Carmelite Sisters. St. Teresa of Avila. (gr. 4-8). 0.75 o.s.i. (ISBN 0-8198-0224-7). Dghtrs St Paul.
Carmer, Carl. The Hudson River. 1974. pap. 4.95 o.p. (ISBN 0-03-089387-9). HR&W.
Carmi, T. The Penguin Book of Hebrew Verse. 1981. 25.00 (ISBN 0-670-36507-6). Viking Pr.
Carmichael, A. Douglas. Ocean Engineering Power Systems. LC 74-4343. (Illus.). 1974. 8.00x (ISBN 0-87033-192-2). Cornell Maritime.
Carmichael, Alasdair. Kintyre. (Island Ser.). 1974. 16.95 (ISBN 0-7153-6317-4). David & Charles.
Carmichael, Alexander. The Sun Dances. 2nd ed. 1977. pap. 3.75 (ISBN 0-903540-07-X, Pub by Floris Books). St George Bk Serv.
Carmichael, Amy W. If. (Illus.). 64p. 1980. kivar 3.95 (ISBN 0-310-42202-7). Zondervan.
Carmichael, C. Women, Law, & the Genesis Tradition. 130p. 1979. 12.50x (ISBN 0-85224-364-2, Pub. by Edinburgh U Pr Scotland). Columbia U Pr.
Carmichael, C. see Kent, R. T.
Carmichael, Carrie. Big Foot: Man, Monster, or Myth? LC 77-21317. (Great Unsolved Mysteries Ser.). (Illus.). (gr. 4-5). 1977. PLB 9.65 (ISBN 0-8172-1052-0). Raintree Pubs.
--Secrets of the Great Magicians. LC 77-13297. (Myth, Magic & Superstition Ser.). (Illus.). (gr. 4-5). 1977. PLB 9.65 (ISBN 0-8172-1031-8). Raintree Pubs.
Carmichael, Douglas R., jt. auth. see Seidler, Lee J.
Carmichael, H. T. & Small, S. A. Prospects & Proposals: Lifetime Learning for Psychiatrists, 1972. 148p. 1972. pap. 3.50 o.p. (ISBN 0-685-31188-0, 178). Am Psychiatric.
Carmichael, Harry. The Motive. 1977. 6.95 o.p. (ISBN 0-525-16030-2). Dutton.
Carmichael, Hoagy & Longstreet, Stephen. Sometimes I Wonder. LC 76-7577. (Roots of Jazz Ser.). 1976. Repr. of 1965 ed. lib. bdg. 22.50 (ISBN 0-306-70809-4). Da Capo.
Carmichael, Joel. Arabs Today. LC 76-41554. 240p. 1977. pap. 2.95 (ISBN 0-385-11351-X, Anch). Doubleday.
Carmichael, Patrick H., ed. Understanding the Books of the New Testament. rev. ed. LC 61-9583. 1961. pap. 4.50 (ISBN 0-8042-3304-7). John Knox.
--Understanding the Books of the Old Testament. rev. ed. LC 61-9223. 1961. pap. 4.50 (ISBN 0-8042-3316-0). John Knox.
Carmichael, Ronald L., jt. auth. see Eckles, Robert W.
Carmines, Edward G. & Zeller, Richard A. Reliability & Validity Assessment. LC 79-67629. (Quantitative Applications in the Social Sciences: No. 17). (Illus.). 1979. pap. 3.50x (ISBN 0-8039-1371-0). Sage.
Carmo, Pamela B. Do. see Do Carmo, Pamela B. & Patterson, Angelo T.
Carmody, Denise L. The Oldest God: Archaic Religion Yesterday & Today. LC 80-25499. 192p. (Orig.). 1981. pap. 6.95 (ISBN 0-687-28813-4). Abingdon.
Carmody, John. Theology for the Nineteen-Eighties. LC 80-19349. 1980. pap. write for info. (ISBN 0-664-24345-2). Westminster.
Carmony, Marvin. Indiana Dialects in Their Historical Setting. (Illus.). 51p. 1979. pap. 2.95 (ISBN 0-936640-00-6). Sagamore Pr.
Carmony, Marvin, jt. auth. see Baker, Ronald L.
Carnac, Nicholas. Tournament of Shadows. 352p. 1981. pap. 2.75 (ISBN 0-345-28772-X). Ballantine.
--Tournament of Shadows. 1979. 9.95 o.p. (ISBN 0-684-16148-6, ScribT). Scribner.
Carnagie Commission on Higher Education. Black Elite: The New Market for Highly Educated Black Americans. LC 76-28702. (Carnegie Commission on Higher Education). (Illus.). 1977. 15.95 o.p. (ISBN 0-07-010116-7, P&RB). McGraw.
Carnahan Conference on Crime Countermeasures, May 14-16, 1980. Proceedings. 1980. 22.50 (ISBN 0-89779-030-8). U of Ky OES Pubns.
Carnap, Rudolf. The Logical Structure of the World & Pseudoproblems in Philosophy. George, Rolf A., tr. Orig. Title: Logische Aufbau der Welt. 1967. pap. 8.95x (ISBN 0-520-01417-0, CAL184). U of Cal Pr.
--Two Essays on Entropy. Shimony, Abner, ed. 1978. 18.00x (ISBN 0-520-02715-9). U of Cal Pr.
Carnap, Rudolf & Jeffrey, Richard C., eds. Studies in Inductive Logic & Probability, Vol. 1. LC 77-136025. 1971. 25.00x (ISBN 0-520-01866-4). U of Cal Pr.
Carnarius, Stanley E. Management Problems & Solution: A Guide to Problem Solving. LC 76-1741. 128p. 1976. pap. 8.95 (ISBN 0-201-00881-5). A-W.
Carnegie Commission on Higher Educaion. Demand & Supply in U. S. Higher Education. Radner, K. & Miller, L. S., eds. 1975. 22.95 o.p. (ISBN 0-07-010113-2, P&RB). McGraw.
Carnegie Commission On Higher Education. Academic Degree Structures: Innovative Approaches. 1970. 10.95 o.p. (ISBN 0-07-010010-1, P&RB). McGraw.
--The Academic Melting Pot: Catholics & Jews in American Higher Education. Steinberg, Stephen, ed. LC 73-9656. (Illus.). 208p. 1974. 10.95 o.p. (ISBN 0-07-010067-5, P&RB). McGraw.
--The Academic System in American Society. Touraine, Alain, ed. LC 73-3322. (Illus.). 336p. 1974. 15.95 o.p. (ISBN 0-07-010054-3, P&RB). McGraw.
--Academic Transformation: Seventeen Institutions Under Pressure. Riesman, David & Stadtman, Verne, eds. (Illus.). 512p. 1973. 16.95 o.p. (ISBN 0-07-010049-7, P&RB). McGraw.
--American College & American Culture. Handlin, O. & Handlin, M. F., eds. 1970. 8.95 o.p. (ISBN 0-07-010015-2, P&RB). McGraw.
--Antibias Regulations of Universities: Faculty Problems & Their Solutions. 1974. 5.95 o.p. (ISBN 0-07-010120-5, P&RB). McGraw.
--Any Person, Any Study: An Essay on Higher Education in the United States. Ashby, E., ed. 1971. 8.50 o.p. (ISBN 0-07-010022-5, P&RB). McGraw.
--Beginning of the Future: A Historical Approach to Graduation in the Arts & Sciences. Storr, Richard J., ed. 128p. 1973. 8.95 o.p. (ISBN 0-07-010056-X, P&RB). McGraw.
--Between Two Worlds: A Profile of Negro Higher Education. Bowles, F. & DeCosta, eds. 1971. 10.95 o.p. (ISBN 0-07-010024-1, P&RB). McGraw.
--Bridges to Understanding: International Programs of American Colleges & Universities. 1970. 9.95 o.p. (ISBN 0-07-010016-0, P&RB). McGraw.
--The Capitol & the Campus: State Responsibility for Postsecondary Education. 1971. 4.50 o.p. (ISBN 0-07-010025-X, P&RB). McGraw.
Carnegie Commission on Higher Education & Ben-David, Joseph. Centers of Learning: Britain, France, Germany, United States. LC 76-45798. (Illus.). 1977. 15.95 o.p. (ISBN 0-07-010133-7). McGraw.
Carnegie Commission on Higher Education. Change in University Organization: 1964-1971. Gross, Edward, ed. Grambsch, Paul V. LC 73-13634. (Illus.). 288p. 1974. 12.50 o.p. (ISBN 0-07-010066-7, P&RB). McGraw.
--College Graduates & Jobs: Adjusting to a New Labor Market Situation. LC 73-3288. (Illus.). 264p. 1973. 8.50 o.p. (ISBN 0-07-010061-6, P&RB). McGraw.
--Colleges of the Forgotten Americans: A Profile of State Colleges & Regional Universities. 1969. 8.95 o.p. (ISBN 0-07-010008-X, P&RB). McGraw.
--Content & Context: Essays on College Education. Kaysen, Carl, ed. LC 73-8858. (Illus.). 588p. 1973. 19.50 o.p. (ISBN 0-07-010048-9, P&RB). McGraw.
--Continuity & Discontinuity: Higher Education & the Schools. 1973. 3.95 o.p. (ISBN 0-07-010080-2, P&RB). McGraw.
--Degree & What Else? Correlates & Consequences of a College Education. 1971. 9.95 o.p. (ISBN 0-07-010035-7, P&RB). McGraw.
--A Digest of Reports of the Carnegie Commission on Higher Education. LC 73-22231. (Illus.). 416p. 1974. 19.50 o.p. (ISBN 0-07-010103-5, P&RB). McGraw.
--Dissent & Disruption: Proposals for Consideration by the Campus. 1971. 5.95 o.p. (ISBN 0-07-010031-4, P&RB). McGraw.
Carnegie Commission on Higher Education & Ladd, Everett C. The Divided Academy: Professors & Politics. LC 74-17247. (Illus.). 407p. 1975. 19.95 o.p. (ISBN 0-07-010112-4, P&RB). McGraw.
Carnegie Commission on Higher Education. Education & Evangelism: A Profile of the Protestant Colleges. Pace, C. Robert, ed. LC 70-39711. (Illus.). 129p. 1972. 6.95 o.p. (ISBN 0-07-010045-4, P&RB). McGraw.
--Education & Politics at Harvard. Lipset, S. M. & Riesman, D., eds. LC 75-34137. 448p. 1975. 18.50 o.p. (ISBN 0-07-010114-0, P&RB). McGraw.
--Education for the Professions of Medicine, Law, Theology, & Social Welfare. LC 73-6591. 304p. 1973. 12.95 o.p. (ISBN 0-07-010065-9, P&RB). McGraw.
--Education, Income & Human Behavior. Juster, T., ed. 1974. 21.95 o.p. (ISBN 0-07-010068-3, P&RB). McGraw.
--Efficiency in Liberal Education. Bowen, H. R. & Douglas, G. R., eds. 1971. 9.95 o.p. (ISBN 0-07-010034-9, P&RB). McGraw.
--The Emerging Technology: Instructional Uses of the Computer in Higher Education. Levien, Roger, ed. LC 72-2. (Illus.). 480p. 1972. 18.95 o.p. (ISBN 0-07-010041-1, P&RB). McGraw.
--Faculty Bargaining: Change & Conflict. 1975. 14.50 o.p. (ISBN 0-07-010111-6, P&RB). McGraw.
--The Fourth Revolution: Instructional Technology in Higher Education. LC 72-4363. (Illus.). 112p. 1972. 3.95 o.p. (ISBN 0-07-010050-0, P&RB). McGraw.
--From Isolation to Mainstream: Problems of the Colleges Founded for Negroes. 1971. 1.95 o.p. (ISBN 0-07-010028-4, P&RB). McGraw.
--Future of Higher Education: Some Speculation & Suggestions. Mood, Alexander, ed. LC 73-6533. 192p. 1973. 10.50 o.p. (ISBN 0-07-010064-0, P&RB). McGraw.
--Governance of Higher Education: Six Priority Problems. LC 73-4774. (Illus.). 272p. 1973. 8.50 o.p. (ISBN 0-07-010062-4, P&RB). McGraw.
--Higher Education & Earnings: College As an Investment & a Screening Device. Taubman, P. & Wales, T., eds. 1974. 21.50 o.p. (ISBN 0-07-010121-3, P&RB). McGraw.
--Higher Education & the Nation's Health: Policies for Medical & Dental Education. 1970. 5.50 o.p. (ISBN 0-07-010021-7, P&RB). McGraw.
--Higher Education: Who Pays? Who Benefits? Who Should Pay? LC 73-8856. (Illus.). 208p. 1973. 7.95 o.p. (ISBN 0-07-010079-9, P&RB). McGraw.
--The Home of Science: The Role of the University. Wolfle, Dael, ed. LC 78-39642. 209p. 1972. 8.95 o.p. (ISBN 0-07-010044-6, P&RB). McGraw.
--Institutions in Transition: A Profile of Change in Higher Education. 1971. 10.95 o.p. (ISBN 0-07-010033-0, P&RB). McGraw.
--Invisible Colleges: A Profile of Small, Private Colleges with Limited Resources. Astin, A. & Lee, C., eds. 1971. 8.95 o.p. (ISBN 0-07-010037-3, P&RB). McGraw.
--Leadership & Ambiguity: The American College President. Cohen, Michael D. & March, James G., eds. LC 73-7558. (Illus.). 304p. 1974. 13.50 o.p. (ISBN 0-07-010063-2, P&RB). McGraw.
--Less Time, More Options: Education Beyond the High School. 1971. 2.95 o.p. (ISBN 0-07-010026-8, P&RB). McGraw.
--Models & Mavericks: A Profile of Private Liberal Arts Colleges. 1971. 6.95 o.p. (ISBN 0-07-010029-2, P&RB). McGraw.
--The More Effective Use of Resources: An Imperative for Higher Education. 256p. 1972. 7.50 o.p. (ISBN 0-07-010051-9, P&RB). McGraw.
--New Depression in Higher Education: A Study of the Financial Conditions at 41 Colleges & Universities. 1971. 9.95 o.p. (ISBN 0-07-010027-6, P&RB). McGraw.
--New Directions in Legal Education. Packer, Herbert L. & Ehrlich, Thomas, eds. LC 72-5311. 416p. 1972. 13.95 o.p. (ISBN 0-07-010047-0, P&RB); pap. 2.95 o.p. (ISBN 0-07-010057-8). McGraw.
--The Nonprofit Research Institute: Its Origin, Operation, Problems & Prospects. Orlans, Harold, ed. LC 70-37532. 256p. 1972. 9.95 o.p. (ISBN 0-07-010040-3, P&RB). McGraw.
--Open Door Colleges: Policies for the Community Colleges. 1970. 2.95 o.p. (ISBN 0-07-010019-5, P&RB). McGraw.
--Opportunities for Women in Higher Education: Their Current Participation, Prospects for the Future & Recommendations for Action. LC 73-14726. (Illus.). 300p. 1973. 8.50 o.p. (ISBN 0-07-010102-7, P&RB). McGraw.
--Priorities for Action. (Illus.). 256p. 1973. 7.95 o.p. (ISBN 0-07-010072-1, P&RB); Brief Ed. pap. 3.95 o.p. (ISBN 0-07-010105-1). McGraw.
--Professional Education: Some New Directions. Schein, Edgar, ed. LC 76-38954. (Illus.). 176p. 1972. 10.95 o.p. (ISBN 0-07-010042-X, P&RB). McGraw.
--The Purposes & the Performance of Higher Education in the U. S. Approaching the Year 2000. (Illus.). 125p. 1973. 5.50 o.p. (ISBN 0-07-010071-3, P&RB). McGraw.
--Quality & Equality: New Levels of Federal Responsibility for Higher Education. 1969. text ed. 1.95 o.p. (ISBN 0-07-010002-0, P&RB). McGraw.

--Quality & Equality: Revised Recommendations: New Levels of Federal Responsibility for Higher Education. 1970. 1.95 o.p. (ISBN 0-07-010018-7, P&RB). McGraw.
--Reform on Campus: Changing Students, Changing Academic Programs. LC 72-4783. 160p. 1972. 4.50 o.p. (ISBN 0-07-010052-7, P&RB). McGraw.
--The Rise of the Arts on the American Campus. Morrison, Jack, ed. LC 72-10456. (Illus.). 244p. 1973. 12.50 o.p. (ISBN 0-07-010055-1, P&RB). McGraw.
--The Sponsored Research of the Carnegie Commission on Higher Education. LC 74-8975. (Illus.). 416p. 1975. 19.50 o.p. (ISBN 0-07-010073-X, P&RB). McGraw.
--A Statistical Portrait of Higher Education. Harris, E. J., ed. LC 72-38334. (Illus.). 1024p. 1972. 32.50 o.p. (ISBN 0-07-010039-X, P&RB). McGraw.
--Teachers & Students: Aspects of American Higher Education. Trow, Martin, ed. 1975. 21.50 o.p. (ISBN 0-07-010070-5, P&RB). McGraw.
--The University & the City: Eight Cases of Involvement. Nash, George, ed. LC 72-14182. 176p. 1973. 10.50 o.p. (ISBN 0-07-010059-4, P&RB). McGraw.
--The University As an Organization. Perkins, James A., ed. LC 72-8336. 352p. 1973. 14.50 o.p. (ISBN 0-07-010053-5, P&RB). McGraw.
--The Useful Arts & the Liberal Tradition. 1975. 13.50 o.p. (ISBN 0-07-010108-6, P&RB). McGraw.
Carnegie Commission on Higher Education & Anderson, C. Arnold. Where Colleges Are & Who Attends: Effects of Accessability on College Attendance. LC 72-2009. (Illus.). 352p. 1972. 10.95 o.p. (ISBN 0-07-010046-2, P&RB). McGraw.
Carnegie Commission on Higher Education. Women & the Power to Change. 224p. 1975. 10.95 o.p. (ISBN 0-07-010124-8, P&RB). McGraw.
Carnegie Council on Policy Studies in Higher Education. The Carnegie Council on Policy Studies in Higher Education: A Summary of Reports & Recommendations. LC 80-7999. (Carnegie Council Ser.). 1981. text ed. 25.00x (ISBN 0-87589-474-7). Jossey-Bass.
--Giving Youth a Better Chance: Options for Education, Work, & Service. LC 79-90851. (Carnegie Council Ser.). 1980. 14.95x (ISBN 0-87589-441-0). Jossey-Bass.
--Three Thousand Futures: The Next Twenty Years for Higher Education. LC 79-9675. (Carnegie Council Ser.). 1980. text ed. 17.95x (ISBN 0-87589-453-4). Jossey-Bass.
Carnegie Endowment for International Peace. American Labor in a Changing World Economy. LC 78-15545. (Praeger Special Studies). 1978. 31.95 (ISBN 0-03-045281-3). Praeger.
Carneiro, Jose, jt. auth. see Junqueira, Luis C.
Carnell, Corbin S. Huckleberry Finn. (Graded Readers for Students of English Ser.). (Illus.). 1979. pap. text ed. 3.50x o.p. (ISBN 0-89285-151-1). English Lang.
Carnell, Hilary, jt. auth. see Eagle, Dorothy.
Carnell, Hilary, jt. ed. see Eagle, Dorothy.
Carner, Chas. Tawny. LC 77-17411. (gr. 6-9). 1978. 8.95 (ISBN 0-02-716700-3, 71670). Macmillan.
Carner, Mosco, jt. auth. see Lenormand, Rene.
Carne-Ross, D. S. Instaurations: Essays in & Out of Literature, Pindar to Pound. 1979. 20.00x (ISBN 0-520-03619-0). U of Cal Pr.
Carnes, Lois, jt. auth. see Zakrajsek, Dorothy.
Carnes, Ralph & Carnes, Valerie. Bodysculpture. (Illus.). 192p. 1981. pap. 5.95 (ISBN 0-312-08735-7). St Martin.
--The Essential College Survival Handbook: An Insider's Guide to Making College Work for You. 224p. 1981. 12.95 (ISBN 0-87223-684-6); pap. 6.95 (ISBN 0-87223-694-3). Playboy.
Carnes, Valerie, jt. auth. see Carnes, Ralph.
Carnevale, Thomas & Shloming, Robert. Encounters with Arithmetic. 449p. 1979. pap. text ed. 14.95 (ISBN 0-15-522596-0, HC); instructor's manual avail. (ISBN 0-15-522597-9). HarBraceJ.
Carney, et al. Career Planning: Skills to Build Your Future. (Orig.). 1980. 8.95 (ISBN 0-442-23350-7); instr's. manual 2.50 (ISBN 0-442-25860-7). D Van Nostrand.
Carney, Andrew L. & Anderson, Evelyn M., eds. Diagnosis & Treatment of Brain Ischemia, Vol. 30. (Advances in Neurology). 450p. 1981. 43.00 (ISBN 0-89004-529-1). Raven.
Carney, Clarke G. & McMahon, Sarah Lynne, eds. Exploring Contemporary Male Female Roles: A Facilitator's Guide. LC 76-58237. 286p. 1977. pap. 15.50 (ISBN 0-88390-135-8). Univ Assocs.
Carney, Daniel. Under a Raging Sky. 322p. 1981. 10.95 (ISBN 0-312-83013-0). St Martin.
Carney, George O. The Sounds of People & Places: Readings in the Geography of Music. 1978. pap. text ed. 11.25x (ISBN 0-8191-0394-2). U Pr of Amer.
Carney, James. Medieval Irish Lyrics. 1967. 14.50x (ISBN 0-520-00210-5). U of Cal Pr.
Carney, John P. Nation of Change: The American Democratic System. 2nd ed. LC 74-26600. 416p. 1975. pap. text ed. 14.95 scp (ISBN 0-06-382347-0, HarpC); scp study guide 6.50 (ISBN 0-06-382348-9). Har-Row.
Carney, Matthew. Peripheral American: Destiny for the Coming Century. LC 80-68315. 278p. 1981. 16.95 (ISBN 0-937444-00-6); pap. 11.95 (ISBN 0-937444-01-4). Caislan Pr.
Carney, Otis. Chihuahua, Nineteen Sixteen. 1980. 9.95 (ISBN 0-13-130286-8). P-H.
Carney, Richard E., ed. Risk-Taking Behavior: Concepts, Methods, & Applications to Smoking & Drug Abuse. (Illus.). 224p. 1971. 19.75 (ISBN 0-398-00287-8). C C Thomas.
Carnicelli, Thomas A., ed. King Alfred's Version of St. Augustine's Soliloquies. LC 69-12719. 1969. 7.50x (ISBN 0-674-50360-0). Harvard U Pr.
Carnochan, W. B. Confinement & Flight: An Essay on English Literature of the Eighteenth Century. 1977. 14.50x (ISBN 0-520-03188-1). U of Cal Pr.
Carnochan, W. B., ed. see Etherege, George.
Carnoy, Martin. Education & Employment: A Critical Appraisal. (Fundamentals of Educational Planning Ser: No. 26). 1978. pap. 4.75 (ISBN 92-803-1078-X, U779, UNESCO). Unipub.
--Education As Cultural Imperialism. LC 73-93964. (Educational Policy, Planning, & Theory Ser.). 1978. 10.95 (ISBN 0-582-28021-4); pap. 9.95x (ISBN 0-582-28018-4). Longman.
--Industrialization in a Latin American Common Market. LC 73-161596. 1972. 11.95 (ISBN 0-8157-1294-4). Brookings.
Carnoy, Martin, et al. Can Educational Policy Equalise Income Distribution in Latin America. 1979. text ed. 16.25x (ISBN 0-566-00255-8, Pub. by Gower Pub Co England). Renouf.
Carns, Donald, jt. auth. see Walton, John.
Caro, Dennis. Man in the Dark Suit. 1980. pap. write for info. (ISBN 0-671-83153-4). PB.
Caro, J. P., ed. see American Society of Hospital Pharmacists Institute on Oncology Pharmacy Practice.
Caro, Ruth, et al. The Lake Is Always East. 128p. 1981. spiral bdg. 2.95 (ISBN 0-695-81566-0). Follett.
Caroe, Gwendolen M. William Henry Bragg, Eighteen Sixty-Two to Nineteen Forty-Two. LC 77-84799. (Illus.). 1978. 29.95 (ISBN 0-521-21839-X). Cambridge U Pr.
Caroe, Olaf. Wells of Power: The Oil Fields of South-Western Asia. (Middle East in the 20th Century Ser.). 1976. Repr. of 1951 ed. lib. bdg. 22.50 (ISBN 0-306-70825-6). Da Capo.
Caroff, Phyllis & Mailick, Mildred, eds. Social Work in Health Services: An Academic Practice Partnership. 1980. lib. bdg. 15.95 (ISBN 0-88202-131-1); pap. text ed. 9.95 (ISBN 0-88202-130-3). N Watson.
Carol, Estelle & Simpson, Bob. The Incredible Shrinking Dream: An Illustrated People's History of the United States. (Illus.). 180p. (Orig.). 1981. pap. 6.95 (ISBN 0-932870-07-4). Alyson Pubns.
Carola, Robert, jt. auth. see Ritchie, Donald.
Caroli, Betty B. Italian Repatriation from the United States, 1900-1914. LC 73-85825. (Illus.). 117p. 1974. pap. 9.95x (ISBN 0-913256-10-2, Dist. by Ozer). Ctr Migration.
Caroli, Betty B., commentaries by. We Italian Americans: A Pictorial History. (Illus.). 300p. Date not set. 25.00x (ISBN 0-913256-38-2). Ctr Migration.
Caroline, John, jt. auth. see Gooch, Ken.
Caroline, Nancy L. Ambulance Calls: Review Problems in Emergency Care. 1980. pap. text ed. 9.95 (ISBN 0-316-12871-6, Little Med Div). Little.
Caron, Francois. An Economic History of Modern France. Bray, Barbara, tr. from Fr. (Columbia Economic History of the Modern World). 1979. 18.50x (ISBN 0-231-03860-7). Columbia U Pr.
Caron, Roger. Go Boy! A Lifetime Behind Bars. 1978. 10.95 o.p. (ISBN 0-07-082535-1, GB). McGraw.
Carossa, Hans. Eine Kindheit. Bithell, Jethro, ed. 1965. Repr. of 1942 ed. pap. 4.50x o.p. (ISBN 0-631-01490-X, Pub. by Basil Blackwell). Biblio Dist.
Carosso, Vincent P. The California Wine Industry: A Study of the Formative Years, 1830-1895. (California Library Reprint Ser). 1976. 18.50x (ISBN 0-520-03178-4). U of Cal Pr.
--Investment Banking in America: A History. Sears, Martin V. & Katz, Irving, eds. LC 70-99515. (Studies in Business History: No. 25). 1970. 20.00x (ISBN 0-674-46574-1). Harvard U Pr.
Carotenuto, Rosine & Bullock, John. Physical Assessment of the Gerontologic Client. LC 80-15247. 1981. pap. text ed. 7.95 (ISBN 0-8036-1680-5). Davis Co.
Carothers, Doris. Chronology of the Federal Emergency Relief Administration: May 12, 1933 to December 31, 1935. LC 70-165681. (FDR & the Era of the New Deal Ser.). 1971. Repr. of 1937 ed. lib. bdg. 15.00 (ISBN 0-306-70338-6). Da Capo.
Carothers, Merlin, tr. La Alabanza En Accion. (Spanish Bks.). (Span.). 1979. 1.60 (ISBN 0-8297-0490-6). Life Pubs Intl.
--El Cielo Baja Al Infierno. (Spanish Bks.). (Span.). 1978. 1.75 (ISBN 0-8297-0766-2). Life Pubs Intl.
--De la Prision a la Alabanza. (Spanish Bks.). (Span.). 1979. 1.60 (ISBN 0-8297-0447-7). Life Pubs Intl.
--Louvor Em Acao. (Portugese Bks.). (Port.). 1979. 1.25 (ISBN 0-8297-0638-0). Life Pubs Intl.
Carpelan, Bo. Dolphins in the City. Lafarge, Sheila, tr. from Swedish. LC 75-8001. 128p. 1976. 5.95 o.s.i. (ISBN 0-440-05073-1, Sey Lawr). Delacorte.
Carpenter, et al. Plants in the Landscape. 1975. 18.50 (ISBN 0-7167-0778-0). Thomson Pub CA.
Carpenter, Allan. Enchantment of Chile. LC 79-8561. (Enchantment of South America Ser). (Illus.). (gr. 5 up). 1969. PLB 10.00 o.p. (ISBN 0-516-04505-9). Childrens.
--Enchantment of Costa Rica. LC 71-157829. (Enchantment of Central America Ser). (Illus.). (gr. 5 up). 1971. PLB 10.00 o.p. (ISBN 0-516-04515-6). Childrens.
Carpenter, Allan & Haan, Enno R. Enchantment of Venezuela. LC 70-85964. (Enchantment of South America Ser). (Illus.). (gr. 5 up). 1970. PLB 10.00 o.p. (ISBN 0-516-04511-3). Childrens.
Carpenter, Cal. The Walton War & Tales of the Great Smoky Mts. 4.95 (ISBN 0-932298-03-6). Green Hill.
Carpenter, Carole H., jt. auth. see Fowke, Edith.
Carpenter, Delores B., ed. The Life of Lidian Jackson Emerson by Ellen Tucker Emerson. (American Literary Manuscripts Ser.). 1980. lib. bdg. 25.00 (ISBN 0-8057-9651-7). Twayne.
Carpenter, Don. Turnaround. 13.95 (ISBN 0-671-25353-0). S&S.
Carpenter, Douglas. Mods I've Been. (Contemporary Poets of Dorrance Ser.). 36p. 1977. 2.95 (ISBN 0-8059-2402-7). Dorrance.
Carpenter, Edward. Animals & Ethics. 48p. 1980. 6.00x (ISBN 0-7224-0180-9, Pub. by Watkins England). State Mutual Bk.
--Civilization: Its Cause & Cure. 44p. pap. 1.50 (ISBN 0-934676-01-1). Greenlf Bks.
--Iolaus: An Anthology of Friendship. 3rd ed. LC 76-174018. 1971. Repr. of 1920 ed. 15.00 (ISBN 0-8103-3790-8). Gale.
Carpenter, F. Lynn. Ecology & Evolution of an Andean Hummingbird (Oreotrochilus Estella) (Publications in Zoology: Vol. 106). 1976. pap. 8.95x (ISBN 0-520-09545-6). U of Cal Pr.
Carpenter, Finley. The Skinner Primer: Behind Freedom & Dignity. LC 73-16603. 1974. 12.95 (ISBN 0-02-905290-4); pap. 2.95 (ISBN 0-02-905310-2). Free Pr.
Carpenter, Francis. Tales of a Chinese Grandmother. 293p. Repr. of 1937 ed. lib. bdg. 12.75x (ISBN 0-89190-481-6). Am Repr-Rivercity Pr.
Carpenter, Frederic I. Eugene O'neill. rev. ed. (United States Authors Ser.: No. 66). 1979. lib. bdg. 9.95 (ISBN 0-8057-7267-7). Twayne.
--Robinson Jeffers. (U. S. Authors Ser.: No. 22). lib. bdg. 10.95 (ISBN 0-8057-0412-4). Twayne.
Carpenter, H. J. Popular Christianity & the Early Theologians. Lee, Clarence L., ed. LC 66-12387. (Orig.). 1966. pap. 1.00 (ISBN 0-8006-3025-4, 1-3025). Fortress.
Carpenter, Humphrey. The Joshers. (Illus.). 1977. 10.50 (ISBN 0-04-823142-8). Allen Unwin.
Carpenter, Joseph E. Theism in Medieval India: London, 1921. LC 78-74266. (Oriental Religions Ser.: Vol. 2). 564p. 1980. lib. bdg. 60.50 (ISBN 0-8240-3901-7). Garland Pub.
Carpenter, Max H. & Waldo, Wayne M. Real Time Method of Radar Plotting. 2nd ed. (Illus.). 48p. 1981. pap. 8.00x (ISBN 0-87033-273-2). Cornell Maritime.
Carpenter, Michael A. Corporate Authorship: Its Role in Library Cataloging. LC 80-1026. (Contributions in Librarianship & Information Science Ser.: No. 34). 248p. 1981. lib. bdg. 27.50 (ISBN 0-313-22065-4, CAU/). Greenwood.
Carpenter, Nan Cooke. Music in the Medieval & Renaissance Universities. LC 70-171380. (Music Ser). (Illus.). 394p. 1972. Repr. of 1958 ed. lib. bdg. 29.50 (ISBN 0-306-70453-6). Da Capo.
Carpenter, Nathanael. Achitophel, or Toe Picture of a Wicked Politician. LC 79-84094. (English Experience Ser.: No. 914). 76p. 1979. Repr. of 1629 ed. lib. bdg. 9.00 (ISBN 90-221-0914-3). Walter J Johnson.
Carpenter, Philip L., et al. Plants in the Landscape. LC 74-32292. (Illus.). 1975. text ed. 24.95x (ISBN 0-7167-0778-0). W H Freeman.
Carpenter, R. E. A Comparison of Thermoregulation & Water Metabolism in the Kangaroo Rats Dypodomys agilis & Dipodomys merriami. (U. C. Publ. in Zoology: Vol. 78). 1966. pap. 4.50x (ISBN 0-520-09335-6). U of Cal Pr.
Carpenter, Rhys. Esthetic Basis of Greek Art. LC 59-13530. (Midland Bks.: No. 19). (Illus.). 1959. pap. 2.50x o.p. (ISBN 0-253-20019-9). Ind U Pr.
--Folk Tale, Fiction & Saga in the Homeric Epics. (Sather Classical Lectures Ser.: No. 20). 1974. 17.00x (ISBN 0-520-02808-2). U of Cal Pr.
Carpenter, Richard C. Thomas Hardy. (English Authors Ser.: No. 13). 1964. lib. bdg. 9.95 (ISBN 0-8057-1244-5). Twayne.
Carpenter, Robert, jt. auth. see Patten, Tom C.
Carpenter, Stanley B., jt. ed. see De Vore, R. William.
Carpenter, Stanley J. & Lacasse, Walter J. Mosquitoes of North America. (California Library Reprint Ser.). (Illus.). 1974. Repr. 40.00x (ISBN 0-520-02638-1). U of Cal Pr.
Carper, Don. Basic Electronics. new ed. (Technology Ser). (Illus.). 576p. 1975. text ed. 21.95x (ISBN 0-675-08779-1); instructor's manual 3.95 (ISBN 0-686-67095-7). Merrill.
Carper, Jean & Krause, Patricia A. The All-in-One Calorie Counter. rev. ed. 304p. (Orig.). 1980. pap. 2.50 (ISBN 0-553-13976-2). Bantam.
--The All-in-One Carbohydrate Gram Counter. rev. ed. 304p. 1980. pap. 2.50 (ISBN 0-553-13977-0). Bantam.
Carper, Jean, jt. auth. see Verrett, Jacqueline.
Carper, Robert S. America's New Railroads. LC 77-84563. (Illus.). 256p. 1980. 25.00 (ISBN 0-498-02179-3). A S Barnes.
Carpi, Amilcare, ed. The Pharmacology of Cerebral Circulation. LC 70-182263. 370p. 1972. text ed. 110.00 (ISBN 0-08-016209-6). Pergamon.
Carpozi, George, jt. auth. see Chiodo, Dan, Jr.
Carpozi, George, Jr. Frank Sinatra: Is This Man Mafia? (Orig.). 1979. pap. 2.25 (ISBN 0-532-23282-8). Manor Bks.
--Great Crimes of the Century: Murderers Leave Clues, No. 8. (Orig.). 1980. pap. 1.95 (ISBN 0-532-23130-9). Manor Bks.
--Great Crimes of the Century: The Savage Killers, No. 7. (Orig.). 1980. pap. 1.95 (ISBN 0-532-23129-5). Manor Bks.
--Great Crimes of the Century: The Senseless Slayers, No. 5. (Orig.). 1979. pap. 1.95 (ISBN 0-532-23165-1). Manor Bks.
--Great Crimes of the Century: The Weird Murderers, No. 6. (Orig.). 1979. pap. 1.95 (ISBN 0-532-23113-9). Manor Bks.
--Red Spies in the U. S. (Illus.). 256p. 1973. 8.95 o.p. (ISBN 0-87000-223-6). Arlington Hse.
--That's Hollywood: Beautiful & Special People, No. 7. (Orig.). 1980. pap. 1.95 (ISBN 0-532-23281-X). Manor Bks.
--That's Hollywood: The Clossal Cowboys, No. 6. (Orig.). 1980. pap. 1.95 (ISBN 0-532-23222-4). Manor Bks.
Carr, A., jt. ed. see Hails, J.
Carr, A. W. Angels & Principalities. (Society for the New Testament Studies Monographs: No. 42). 240p. Date not set. price not set (ISBN 0-521-23429-8). Cambridge U Pr.
Carr, Allan, jt. auth. see Sun Yun Chiang, Cecilia.
Carr, Anna & Olkowski, William. Rodale's Color Handbook of Garden Insects. (Illus.). 1979. 12.95 (ISBN 0-87857-250-3). Rodale Pr Inc.
Carr, Anne. The Theological Method of Karl Rahner. LC 76-51639. (American Academy of Religion. Dissertation Ser.). 1977. pap. 7.50 (ISBN 0-89130-129-1, 010119). Scholars Pr Ca.
Carr, Anne, ed. Academic Study of Religion: Proceedings. LC 74-14212. (American Academy of Religion. Section Papers). 1974. pap. 4.50 (ISBN 0-88420-115-5, 010911). Scholars Pr Ca.
Carr, Anne, et al. Academic Study of Religion: Nineteen Seventy-Five: Public Schools Religion-Studies: 1975. LC 75-26653. (American Academy of Religion. Section Papers). 1975. pap. 4.00 (ISBN 0-89130-023-6, 010917). Scholars Pr Ca.
Carr, Archie. The Everglades. (The American Wilderness Ser). (Illus.). 1973. 12.95 (ISBN 0-8094-1172-5). Time-Life.
--The Everglades. LC 72-96548. (American Wilderness Ser). (Illus.). 1973. lib. bdg. 11.97 (ISBN 0-8094-1173-3, Pub. by Time-Life). Silver.
--Land & Wildlife of Africa. rev. ed. LC 64-23586. (Life Nature Library). (Illus.). (gr. 5 up). 1967. PLB 8.97 o.p. (ISBN 0-8094-0631-4, Pub. by Time-Life). Silver.

--Reptiles. LC 63-12781. (Life Nature Library). (Illus.). (gr. 5 up). 1963. PLB 8.97 o.p. (ISBN 0-8094-0623-3, Pub. by Time-Life). Silver.
--The Reptiles. (Young Readers Library). (Illus.). 1977. lib. bdg. 7.98 (ISBN 0-686-51093-3). Silver.
Carr, Bruce, jt. ed. see Winter, Robert.
Carr, D. J., ed. see International Conference on Plant Growth Substances, 7th, Canberra, 1970.
Carr, David. The Beginners Guide to Good Gardening. (Illus.). 243p. 1980. 14.95 (ISBN 0-7137-0934-0, Pub. by Blandford Pr England). Sterling.
--Foreign Investment & Development in Egypt. LC 79-1250. 1979. 20.95 (ISBN 0-03-048351-4). Praeger.
--The Gardener's Handbook, 3 bks. Incl. Vol. 1. Broad-Leaved Trees. (Illus.). 144p. 24.00 (ISBN 0-7134-1306-9); pap. 14.50 o.p. (ISBN 0-7134-1306-9); Vol. 2. Conifers. (Illus.). 144p. 24.00 (ISBN 0-7134-1307-7); pap. 14.95 o.p. (ISBN 0-7134-1308-5); Vol. 3. Shrubs. (Illus.). 144p. 23.95 o.p. (ISBN 0-7134-1882-6); pap. 13.95 o.p. (ISBN 0-686-61986-2); Growing Fruit & Nuts. Carr, David. (Illus.). 1980. 23.95 o.p. (ISBN 0-7134-1883-4, Pub. by Batsford England); pap. 14.50 (ISBN 0-7134-1896-6). David & Charles. (Illus.). 1980 (Pub. by Batsford England). David & Charles.
Carr, David W. Foreign Investment & Development in the Southwest Pacific: With Special Reference to Austrailia & Indonesia. LC 78-8598. (Praeger Special Studies). 1978. 24.95 (ISBN 0-03-042271-X). Praeger.
Carr, E. H. Foundations of a Planned Economy, Vol IV Pt. 2. 1972. 19.95 (ISBN 0-02-522050-0). Macmillan.
--Foundations of a Planned Economy 1926-1929. LC 76-45527. (History of Soviet Russia Ser.: Vol. 3 Pts. 1 & 2). 1977. Pt. 1. 17.50 o.p. (ISBN 0-02-522060-8, 52206); Pt. 2. 17.50 (ISBN 0-02-522070-5, 52207). Macmillan.
--From Napoleon to Stalin & Other Essays. 1980. 20.00 (ISBN 0-312-30774-8). St Martin.
--The Soviet Impact on the Western World. 1973. 15.00 (ISBN 0-86527-187-9). Fertig.
Carr, E. H., ed. see Russell, Bertrand.
Carr, Edward H. A History of Soviet Russia, 7 vols. Incl. Vol. 1-3. The Bolshevik Revolution. 1951-53. 12.95 ea. Vol. 1 (52169). Vol. 2 (52175). Vol. 3 (52181); Vol. 4. The Interregnum. 1954. 12.95 (ISBN 0-685-22917-3, 52187); Vols. 5-6. Socialism in One Country. 1958-60. 12.95 ea. Vol. 5 (52193). Vol. 6 (52199); Vol. 7. Socialism in One Country. 1964. 14.95 (ISBN 0-685-22919-X). Pt. 2 (52202). Set. 29.95 (ISBN 0-686-66600-3, 52200). Macmillan.
--The Romantic Exiles. 392p. 1981. pap. 8.95 (ISBN 0-262-53040-6). MIT Pr.
Carr, Edwin. The Future's Advocate. LC 74-82187. 1975. 10.00 o.p. (ISBN 0-8309-0121-3). Herald Hse.
Carr, Francis. Ivan the Terrible. 1981. 18.50x (ISBN 0-389-20150-2). B&N.
Carr, George S. Formulas & Theorems in Pure Mathematics. LC 78-113122. Orig. Title: Synopsis of Pure Mathematics. 1970. text ed. 35.00 (ISBN 0-8284-0239-6). Chelsea Pub.
Carr, Gerald F., jt. ed. see Rauch, Irmengard.
Carr, Gwen B., ed. Marriage & Family in a Decade of Change: A Humanistic Reader. 1972. pap. text ed. 6.50 (ISBN 0-201-00899-8). A-W.
Carr, Herman Y. & Weidner, Richard T. Physics from the Ground up, 3 parts. LC 78-22000. 1980. Repr. of 1971 ed. Vol. 2. write for info. (ISBN 0-89874-021-5); Vol. 2. write for info. (ISBN 0-89874-213-7). Krieger.
Carr, Ian & Daems, W. T., eds. The Reticuloendothalial System--a Comprehensive Treatise: Morphology, Vol. 1. (Illus.). 771p. 1980. 49.50 (ISBN 0-686-62966-3, Plenum Pr). Plenum Pub.
Carr, Ian see Sbarra, Anthony J. & Strauss, Robert.
Carr, Ian, et al. Lymphoreticular Disease: An Introduction for the Pathologist & Oncologist. 1978. soft cover 26.00 (ISBN 0-397-60436-X, Pub. by Blackwell Scientific). Mosby.
Carr, J., jt. ed. see Yule, W.
Carr, J. G. Aroma & Flavour in Wine Making. (Illus.). 88p. 1975. 5.50 o.p. (ISBN 0-263-05594-9). Transatlantic.
Carr, Jacquelyn B. Communicating & Relating. LC 78-58969. 1979. pap. text ed. 12.95 (ISBN 0-8053-1820-8); instr's guide 3.95 (ISBN 0-8053-1821-6). Benjamin-Cummings.
Carr, Jan, jt. auth. see Flettrich, Terry.
Carr, Janet & Shepherd, Roberta. Early Care of the Stroke Patient: A Positive Approach. rev. ed. (Illus.). 1979. pap. 10.00 (ISBN 0-433-30140-6). Heinman.
Carr, Jayge, et al. Pandora, No. 5. Wickstrom, Lois, ed. (Illus.). 60p. (Orig.). 1980. pap. 2.50 (ISBN 0-916176-10-X). Sproing.
Carr, Jess. The Saint of the Wilderness. LC 74-77781. 441p. 1974. 8.95 (ISBN 0-89227-008-X); pap. 4.95 (ISBN 0-89227-026-8). Commonwealth Pr.
--A Star Rising. (Orig.). 1980. pap. 3.50 (ISBN 0-505-51575-X). Tower Bks.
Carr, Jo & Sorley, Imogene. Bless This Mess. 1976. pap. 1.50 (ISBN 0-89129-130-X). Jove Pubns.
--Plum Jelly & Stained Glass & Other Prayers. (Festival Bks). 1981. pap. 1.95 (ISBN 0-687-31660-X). Abingdon.
--Too Busy Not to Pray: A Homemaker Talks with God. 1966. 3.95 o.p. (ISBN 0-687-42379-1). Abingdon.
Carr, John C., et al. Pygmalion or Frankenstein? Alternative Schooling in American Education. LC 76-2929. 1977. pap. text ed. 7.95 (ISBN 0-201-00898-X). A-W.
Carr, John C., et al, eds. The Organization & Administration of Pastoral Counseling Centers. LC 80-22416. 304p. 1980. 15.95 (ISBN 0-687-29430-4). Abingdon.
Carr, John D. Crooked Hinge. 1964. pap. 2.95 (ISBN 0-02-018510-3, Collier). Macmillan.
--The Three Coffins. lib. bdg. 11.50x (ISBN 0-89966-048-7). Buccaneer Bks.
Carr, Sir John. Poems. 1809. Reiman, Donald H., ed. LC 75-31177. (Romantic Context Ser.: Poetry 1789-1830). 1977. lib. bdg. 47.00 (ISBN 0-8240-2129-0). Garland Pub.
Carr, Joseph. Elements of Electronic Instrumentation & Measurement. (Illus.). 1979. text ed. 18.95 (ISBN 0-8359-1650-2); students manual avail. (ISBN 0-8359-1651-0). Reston.
--Z-Eighty User's Manual. (Illus.). 352p. 1980. text ed. 17.95 (ISBN 0-8359-9517-8); pap. text ed. 10.95 (ISBN 0-8359-9516-X). Reston.
Carr, Joseph J. The Complete Book of Radio Transmitters. 350p. 1980. 8.95 o.p. (ISBN 0-8306-1224-6). Tab Bks.
Carr, Joseph J. & Brown, John M. Introduction to Biomedical Equipment Technology. LC 80-6218. 448p. 1981. text ed. 23.95 (ISBN 0-471-04143-2); solutions manual avail. (ISBN 0-471-04144-0). Wiley.
Carr, Larry. Four Fabulous Faces: Swanson, Garbo, Crawford, Dietrich. (Large Format Ser). (Illus.). 1978. pap. 12.95 o.p. (ISBN 0-14-004988-6). Penguin.
Carr, Micheline, jt. auth. see Crouch, James.
Carr, Oscar C., Jr., ed. Jesus, Dollars & Sense: An Effective Stewardship Guide for Clergy & Lay Leaders. 1976. pap. 3.95 (ISBN 0-8164-2132-3). Crossroad NY.
Carr, Patrick, ed. see Country Music Magazine Editors.
Carr, Peter & Bowers, Larry D. Immobilized Enzymes in Analytical & Clinical Chemistry: Fundamentals & Applications. LC 80-13694. (Chemical Analysis: a Series of Monographs on Analytical Chemistry & Its Applications). 454p. 1980. 45.00 (ISBN 0-471-04919-0, Pub. by Wiley-Interscience). Wiley.
Carr, Philippa. The Lion Triumphant. 384p. 1977. pap. 2.50 (ISBN 0-449-23233-6, Crest). Fawcett.
--The Song of the Siren. pap. 2.75 (Crest). Fawcett.
--Will You Love Me in September. 324p. 1981. 11.95 (ISBN 0-399-12590-6). Putnam.
Carr, Raymond. Modern Spain. 256p. 1981. 19.95 (ISBN 0-19-215828-7); pap. 11.50 (ISBN 0-19-289090-5). Oxford U Pr.
Carr, Robert K. Supreme Court & Judicial Review. LC 74-98215. Repr. of 1942 ed. lib. bdg. 19.75x (ISBN 0-8371-3261-4, CAJR). Greenwood.
Carr, Robyn. The Blue Falcon. 1981. 12.95 (ISBN 0-316-12972-0). Little.
Carr, Sam, ed. Hymns As Poetry. 1980. 17.95 (ISBN 0-7134-3447-3). David & Charles.
Carr, Samuel. The Batsford Book of Country Verse. 1979. 17.95 (ISBN 0-7134-2019-7, Pub. by Batsford England). David & Charles.
--The Poetry of Cats. 1979. 14.95 (ISBN 0-7134-2861-9, Pub. by Batsford England). David & Charles.
--The Poetry of Flowers. 1977. 14.95 (ISBN 0-7134-0427-2, Pub. by Batsford England). David & Charles.
--Poetry of the Railways. 1978. 14.95 (ISBN 0-7134-0222-9). David & Charles.
Carr, Samuel, ed. The Poetry of Horses. (Illus.). 128p. 1980. 17.95 (ISBN 0-7134-2594-6, Pub. by Batsford England). David & Charles.
Carr, Terry. Cirque. 1978. pap. 1.75 o.p. (ISBN 0-449-23556-4, Crest). Fawcett.
--Fantasy Annual III. (Orig.). 1981. pap. 2.95 (ISBN 0-671-41272-8). PB.
--Universe Ten. LC 79-6534. (Double Science Fiction Ser.). 1980. 8.95 (ISBN 0-385-15477-1). Doubleday.
--Universe Two. LC 80-2790. (Science Fiction Ser.). 192p. 1981. 9.95 (ISBN 0-385-17226-5). Doubleday.
Carr, Terry, ed. Best Science Fiction of the Year, No. 3. (Orig.). 1976. pap. 1.95 o.p. (ISBN 0-345-25015-X). Ballantine.
--The Best Science Fiction of the Year, No. 6. 1977. 9.95 o.p. (ISBN 0-03-020716-9). HR&W.
--The Best Science Fiction of the Year, No. 9. (Orig.). 1980. pap. 2.50 (ISBN 0-345-28601-4). Ballantine.
--Dream's Edge: Science Fiction Stories About the Future of Planet Earth. LC 80-13389. 320p. 1980. 14.95 (ISBN 0-87156-232-4); pap. 5.95 (ISBN 0-87156-238-3). Sierra.
--The Ides of Tomorrow: Original Science Fiction Tales of Horror. (gr. 7-12). 1976. 7.95 (ISBN 0-316-12970-4). Little.
--Into the Unknown: Eleven Tales of Imagination. LC 73-7826. 192p. 1973. 7.95 o.p. (ISBN 0-525-66342-8). Elsevier-Nelson.
--Worlds Near & Far: Nine Stories of Science Fiction & Fantasy. LC 74-10273. 224p. 1974. 7.95 o.p. (ISBN 0-525-66404-1). Elsevier-Nelson.
--Year's Finest Fantasy. (YA) 1979. 9.95 o.p. (ISBN 0-399-12146-3). Berkley Pub.
--Year's Finest Fantasy. 1978. pap. 1.95 o.p. (ISBN 0-425-03808-4, Medallion). Berkley Pub.
--The Year's Finest Fantasy. 1979. 9.95 o.p. (ISBN 0-399-12327-X). Berkley Pub.
--The Year's Finest Fantasy II. 1979. Repr. 9.95 o.p. (ISBN 0-425-04155-7). Berkley Pub.
Carr, Virginia M. The Drama As Propaganda: A Study of The Troublesome Reign of King John. (Salzburg Studies in English Literature, Elizabethan & Renaissance Studies: No. 28). 185p. 1974. pap. text ed. 25.00x (ISBN 0-391-01341-6). Humanities.
Carr, Virginia Spencer. The Lonely Hunter: A Biography of Carson McCullers. LC 74-9478. 1976. pap. 5.95 (ISBN 0-385-12289-6, Anch). Doubleday.
Carr, William. Arms, Autarky, & Agression. (Foundations of Modern History Ser.). 136p. 1973. 7.00 (ISBN 0-393-05486-1); pap. 3.95x (ISBN 0-393-09361-1). Norton.
Carr, William G. Collecting My Thoughts. LC 80-82881. (Foundation Monograph Ser.). 101p. (Orig.). 1980. pap. 5.00 (ISBN 0-87367-424-3). Phi Delta Kappa.
--Pawns in the Game. 1978. pap. 4.00x (ISBN 0-911038-29-9). Noontide.
--Red Fog Over America. 1978. pap. 4.00x (ISBN 0-911038-30-2). Noontide.
Carr, William H. Hollywood Tragedy. (Orig.). 1977. pap. 1.95 o.p. (ISBN 0-449-22889-4, Crest). Fawcett.
Carra, Andrew J., ed. The Complete Guide to Hiking & Backpacking. 1977. 10.95 (ISBN 0-87691-226-9). Winchester Pr.
Carra, J. L. Systeme De la Raison, Ou le Prophete Philosophe. (Fr.). 1977. Repr. of 1791 ed. lib. bdg. 20.50x o.p. (ISBN 0-8287-0162-8). Clearwater Pub.
Carra, Massimo, et al. Metaphysical Art. Tisdall, Caroline, tr. (World of Art Ser.). (Illus.). 1971. text ed. 9.95 (ISBN 0-19-520008-X). Oxford U Pr.
Carrabino, Victor, ed. The Power of Myth in Literature & Film. LC 80-21998. (A Florida State University Bk.). 136p. 1980. 12.25 (ISBN 0-8130-0673-2, IS-00116, Pub. by U Presses Fla). Univ Microfilms.
Carra de Vaux, Bernard. Les Penseurs de l'Islam, 5 vols. LC 80-2197. 1981. Repr. of 1926 ed. Set. 200.00 (ISBN 0-404-18990-3). AMS Pr.
Carraher, Ron & Chartier, Colleen. Electronic Flash Photography: A Complete Guide to the Best Equipment & Creative Techniques. 136p. 1980. 24.95 (ISBN 0-442-21463-4); pap. 14.95 (ISBN 0-442-23135-0). Van Nos Reinhold.
Carran, Eldon. Site Manual. 4th ed. (Illus.). 1975. 17.50x (ISBN 0-7198-2600-4). Intl Ideas.
Carrara, Antonio, jt. auth. see Frassica, Pietro.
Carrasco-Urgoiti, Maria S. The Moorish Novel: "El Abencerraje"& Gines Perez De Hita. LC 75-25977. (World Authors Ser.: No. 375). 1976. lib. bdg. 12.50 (ISBN 0-8057-6178-0). Twayne.
Carre, Jeffrey J., ed. see Reed, Muriel.
Carre, John le see Le Carre, John.
Carre, Marie-Rose, ed. see Reed, Muriel.
Carrell, Al. Do-It-Quick but Do-It Right Home Repair Hints. LC 80-24659. 1981. 9.95 (ISBN 0-13-875906-5). P-H.
Carrell, Mary J. Learning Math Skills. 1978. pap. text ed. 2.25x (ISBN 0-88323-139-5, 228). Richards Pub.
--Understanding the Metric System. 1978. pap. text ed. 2.25x (ISBN 0-88323-140-9, 229). Richards Pub.
Carrenno, Josephine & Larson, Diane. Spanish for Hospital Personnel. 1974. spiral bdg. 3.50 (ISBN 0-87488-722-4). Med Exam.
Carrera, Liane. Anna Held & Flo Ziegfeld. 1979. 10.00 o.p. (ISBN 0-682-49309-0). Exposition.
Carreras, J., et al. Shear Zones in Rocks: Papers Presented at the International Conference Held at the University of Barcelona, May 1979. 200p. 1980. pap. 40.00 (ISBN 0-08-026244-9). Pergamon.
Carreter, Fernando L. Diccionario de Terminos Filologicos. 3rd ed. 444p. (Espn.). 1977. 22.25 (ISBN 84-249-1112-1, S-50129, French & Eur). French & Eur.
Carretto, Carlo. God Who Comes. 1976. pap. 1.50 (ISBN 0-89129-062-1). Jove Pubns.
--In Search of the Beyond. LC 78-2048. 1978. pap. 2.45 (ISBN 0-385-14411-3, Im). Doubleday.
--Letters from the Desert. 1976. pap. 1.50 (ISBN 0-89129-061-3). Jove Pubns.
--Love Is for Living. Moiser, Jeremy, tr. from Ital. LC 76-49878. Orig. Title: Cio Che Conta E Amare. 1977. Repr. 6.95x (ISBN 0-88344-291-4); pap. 4.95 (ISBN 0-88344-293-0). Orbis Bks.
Carrey, John, jt. auth. see Conley, Cort.
Carrick, Carol. The Accident. LC 76-3532. (Illus.). 32p. (ps-3). 1976. 7.95 (ISBN 0-395-28774-X, Clarion). HM.
--Brook. (gr. k-2). 1967. 4.95g o.s.i. (ISBN 0-02-717330-5). Macmillan.
--The Climb. 32p. (gr. k-4). 1980. 8.95 o.p. (ISBN 0-395-29431-2, Clarion): HM.
--Dirt Road. LC 73-116758. (Illus.). (gr. k-2). 1970. 4.95g o.s.i. (ISBN 0-02-717300-3). Macmillan.
--The Empty Squirrel. LC 80-16475. (Read-Alone Bk.). (Illus.). 64p. (gr. 1-3). 1981. 5.95 (ISBN 0-688-80293-1); PLB 5.71 (ISBN 0-688-84293-3). Greenwillow.
--The Foundling. LC 77-1587. (Illus.). (ps-4). 1977. 6.95 (ISBN 0-395-28775-8, Clarion). HM.
--Lost in the Storm. LC 74-1051. (Illus.). 32p. (ps-3). 1974. 6.95 (ISBN 0-395-28776-6, Clarion). HM.
--Octopus. LC 77-12769. (Illus.). (gr. 1-4). 1978. 6.95 (ISBN 0-395-28777-4, Clarion). HM.
--Old Mother Witch. LC 75-4609. (Illus.). 32p. (ps-4). 1975. 7.95 (ISBN 0-395-28778-2, Clarion). HM.
--Paul's Christmas Birthday. LC 77-28408. (Illus.). (gr. k-3). 1978. 7.95 (ISBN 0-688-80159-5); PLB 7.63 (ISBN 0-688-84159-7). Greenwillow.
--Pond. (ps-2). 1970. 5.95g o.s.i. (ISBN 0-02-717310-0). Macmillan.
--A Rabbit for Easter. LC 78-15647. (Illus.). (gr. 4-8). 1979. 7.50 (ISBN 0-688-80195-1); PLB 7.20 (ISBN 0-688-84195-3). Greenwillow.
--Sand Tiger Shark. LC 76-40206. (gr. 1-5). 1977. 6.95 (ISBN 0-395-28779-0, Clarion). HM.
--Sleep Out. LC 72-88539. (Illus.). 32p. (gr. 1-3). 1973. 7.95 (ISBN 0-395-28780-4, Clarion). HM.
--Swamp Spring. LC 69-10497. (Illus.). (gr. k-2). 1969. 4.95g o.s.i. (ISBN 0-02-717320-8). Macmillan.
--The Washout. LC 78-8135. (Illus.). (gr. 1-4). 1978. 6.95 (ISBN 0-395-28781-2, Clarion). HM.
Carrick, Carol & Carrick, Donald. The Highest Balloon on the Common. LC 77-23309. (gr. k-3). 8.25 (ISBN 0-688-80100-5); PLB 7.92 (ISBN 0-688-84100-7). Greenwillow.
Carrick, Donald. The Deer in the Pasture. LC 75-23193. (Illus.). 32p. (gr. k-3). 1976. PLB 7.92 (ISBN 0-688-84023-X). Greenwillow.
--Drip, Drop. LC 73-4056. (Illus.). 32p. (ps-2). 1973. 5.95g o.s.i. (ISBN 0-02-717340-2). Macmillan.
--Tree. LC 70-133556. (Illus.). (gr. k-3). 1971. 4.95g o.s.i. (ISBN 0-02-717290-2). Macmillan.
Carrick, Donald, jt. auth. see Carrick, Carol.
Carrick, Peter. Great Moments in Sport: Motor Cycle Racing. (Illus.). 1977. 16.95 (ISBN 0-7207-0972-5). Transatlantic.
Carrico, Clayton H. Refrigeration Licenses: (Contractor-Journeyman-Operator) Unlimited. 1980. text ed. 25.00x (ISBN 0-912524-20-0). Busn News.
Carrie, Jacques. Bridge of Movie Producer Louis King. LC 80-67977. 204p. (Orig.). 1981. pap. 6.95 (ISBN 0-937578-00-2). Fablewaves.
Carrier, Barbara, jt. auth. see Carrier, Rick.
Carrier, Jean-Guy, jt. auth. see Butler, Rick.
Carrier, Rick & Carrier, Barbara. Dive: The Complete Book of Skin Diving. rev. ed. Berlitz, Charles, ed. LC 73-4513. (Funk & W Bk.). (Illus.). 304p. 1973. 7.95 o.s.i. (ISBN 0-308-10056-5, TYC-T). T Y Crowell.
Carrier, Rick & Carroll, David. Action! Camera! Super-Eight Cassette Film Making for Beginners. LC 78-162739. (Illus.). 78p. 1972. 7.95 (ISBN 0-684-12490-4). Scribner.
Carrier, Robert. Entertaining. LC 78-58768. (Illus.). 1978. 16.95 (ISBN 0-89479-034-X). A & W Pubs.
Carrier, Roch. Is It the Sun, Philibert? Fischman, Sheila, tr. from Fr. LC 75-190705. (Anansi Fiction Ser.: No. 20). 100p. 1972. pap. 3.95 (ISBN 0-88784-321-2, Pub. by Hse Anansi Pr Canada). U of Toronto Pr.
Carriere, Dean & Day, Fraser. Solar Houses for a Cold Climate. (Illus.). 1980. 20.00 (ISBN 0-684-16288-1, ScribT). Scribner.

Carrigan, Minnie B. Captured by the Indians: Reminiscences of Pioneer Life in Minnesota, Repr. Of 1907 Ed. Bd. with Eastern Kentucky Papers: The Founding of Harman's Station with an Account of the Indian Captivity of Mrs. Jennie Wiley. Connelley, William E. Repr. of 1910 ed. LC 75-7134. (Indian Captivities Ser.: Vol. 106). (Incl. rev. ed. of 1912). 1977. lib. bdg. 44.00 (ISBN 0-8240-1730-7). Garland Pub.

Carrighar, Sally. The Glass Dove. 1977. pap. 1.75 (ISBN 0-380-01829-2, 36194). Avon.

--One Day at Teton Marsh. 1975. pap. 1.75 o.p. (ISBN 0-345-24821-X). Ballantine.

--One Day at Teton Marsh. LC 78-26679. (Illus.). 1979. pap. 4.25 (ISBN 0-8032-6302-3, BB 692, Bison). U of Nebr Pr.

--One Day on Beetle Rock. (Walden Editions). 192p. 1976. pap. 1.50 o.p. (ISBN 0-345-24866-X). Ballantine.

--One Day on Beetle Rock. LC 78-18854. viii, 196p. 1978. pap. 3.25 (ISBN 0-8032-6301-5, BB 691, Bison). U of Nebr Pr.

Carril, Bonifacio Del see De Saint-Exupery, Antoine.

Carrington. Computers for Spectroscopists. LC 74-12526. 1975. 44.95 (ISBN 0-470-13581-6). Halsted Pr.

Carrington, Charles E. British Overseas. 2nd ed. LC 68-23176. (Illus.). 1968. 53.50 (ISBN 0-521-07174-7). Cambridge U Pr.

Carrington, Elsie R., jt. auth. see Willson, J. Robert.

Carrington, Glenda. Master of Greystone. 1977. pap. 1.50 o.p. (ISBN 0-425-03443-7, Medallion). Berkley Pub.

Carrington, Grant. Time's Fool. LC 79-8558. (Science Fiction Ser.). 192p. 1981. 9.95 (ISBN 0-385-15288-4). Doubleday.

Carrington, Hereward. American Seances with Eusapia Palladino. LC 54-7143. 1954. 3.75 o.p. (ISBN 0-912326-03-4). Garrett-Helix.

--Your Psychic Powers & How to Develop Them. LC 80-24076. 358p. 1980. Repr. of 1975 ed. lib. bdg. 11.95x (ISBN 0-89370-633-7). Borgo Pr.

Carrington, Hereward & Whitehead, Willis F. Keys to the Occult: Two Guides to Hidden Wisdom. LC 80-23835. 182p. 1980. Repr. of 1977 ed. lib. bdg. 10.95x (ISBN 0-89370-641-8). Borgo Pr.

Carrington, John C. & Edwards, George T. Financing Industrial Investment. LC 78-65708. 1979. 29.95 (ISBN 0-03-049761-2). Praeger.

Carrington, Leonora. The Oval Lady. Holt, Rochelle, tr. (Illus.). 1975. pap. 3.75 o.p. (ISBN 0-88496-037-4). Capra Pr.

--The Stone Door. LC 77-76629. 1977. 7.95 o.p. (ISBN 0-312-76210-0). St Martin.

Carrington, Noel. Industrial Design in Britain. 1976. text ed. 25.00x (ISBN 0-04-745006-1). Allen Unwin.

Carrington, Patricia, Ph.D. Freedom in Meditation. LC 76-6240. 1978. pap. 3.50 (ISBN 0-385-12407-4, Anch). Doubleday.

Carrington, Richard. Mammals. LC 63-20048. (Life Nature Library). (Illus.). (gr. 5 up). 1963. PLB 8.97 o.p. (ISBN 0-8094-0625-X, Pub. by Time-Life). Silver.

--The Mammals. (Young Readers Library). (Illus.). 1977. lib. bdg. 7.95 (ISBN 0-686-51091-7). Silver.

Carrino, Frank G., et al, trs. see Hernandez, Jose.

Carrithers, David W., ed. see Montesquieu.

Carrithers, T. W. How to Put on a Horse Show. LC 70-124197. (Illus.). 1971. 8.95 o.p. (ISBN 0-668-04204-4). Arco.

Carrol, Frieda. The Consumer Survival Notebook. LC 80-70456. 1980. pap. 5.95 (ISBN 0-9605246-2-2). Biblio Pr GA.

--Guide for the Unemployed: Keeping Busy Until... LC 80-70495. 103p. 1981. 16.95 (ISBN 0-9605246-5-7); pap. 12.95. Biblio Pr Ga.

--How to Get Something for Almost Nothing & More. LC 78-59909. 52p. (Orig.). 1981. pap. text ed. 5.00 (ISBN 0-9605246-0-6). Biblio Pr GA.

--Peple's Money Pages. 1st ed. LC 80-70419. 50p. 1980. 16.50 (ISBN 0-9605246-3-0); pap. 9.95. Biblio Pr GA.

--Prescriptions for Survival. LC 78-72312. 148p. 1981. pap. text ed. 14.95 (ISBN 0-9605246-1-4). Biblio Pr GA.

--Survival Handbook for Small Business. LC 80-70496. 73p. 1980. 16.95 (ISBN 0-9605246-4-9); pap. 12.95. Biblio Pr GA.

Carrol, Frieda, compiled by. The Woman's Index. LC 80-70675. 200p. 1981. 12.95 (ISBN 0-9605246-6-5); pap. 9.95. Biblio Pr Ga.

Carrol, Shana. Raven. (Orig.). pap. 2.25 (ISBN 0-515-04439-3). Jove Pubns.

Carroll. Learning God's Word, 3 bks. 1971. Bk. 1. pap. 1.65 (ISBN 0-87148-502-8); Bk. 2. pap. 1.25 (ISBN 0-87148-503-6); Bk. 3. pap. 1.25 (ISBN 0-87148-504-4). Pathway Pr.

--White Collar Crime. 1981. text ed. 18.95. Butterworth.

Carroll, Anne K., jt. auth. see Cooper, Darien B.

Carroll, Archie B. Business & Society: Managing Corporate Social Performance. text ed. 16.95 (ISBN 0-316-13010-9); training manual free (ISBN 0-316-13011-7). Little.

Carroll, Archie B., jt. ed. see Watson, Hugh J.

Carroll, B. H., et al. Introduction to Photographic Theory: The Silver Halide Process. LC 79-26802. 1980. 29.50 (ISBN 0-471-02562-3, Pub. by Wiley Interscience). Wiley.

Carroll, Betty De, ed. see Petter, Hugo M.

Carroll, Bonnie. Job Satisfaction. (Key Issues Ser.: No. 3). 1973. pap. 2.00 (ISBN 0-87546-206-5). NY Sch Indus Rel.

Carroll, Caroll. You May Quote Me. 1980. 4.95 (ISBN 0-87786-004-1). Gold Penny.

Carroll, Carroll. Carroll's First Book of Proverbs or Life Is a Fortune Cookie. (Illus.). 96p. 1981. pap. 4.95 (ISBN 0-87786-004-1). Gold Penny.

--Take My Wife... Please! My Life & Laughs. pap. 1.50 o.p. (ISBN 0-425-03241-8). Berkley Pub.

Carroll, Charles F. The Timber Economy of Puritan New England. LC 73-7122. (Illus.). 221p. 1973. 12.50 (ISBN 0-87057-142-7, Pub. by Brown U Pr). Univ Pr of New England.

Carroll, David. Chinua Achebe. (World Authors Ser.: Nigeria: No. 101). lib. bdg. 9.95 (ISBN 0-8057-2004-9). Twayne.

--The Complete Book of Natural Medicines. LC 80-11332. (Illus.). 416p. 1980. 17.95 (ISBN 0-671-24418-3); pap. 7.95 (ISBN 0-671-41623-5). Summit Bks.

--The Dictionary of Foreign Terms in the English Language. 1979. pap. 4.95 (ISBN 0-8015-2053-3, Hawthorn). Dutton.

Carroll, David, jt. auth. see Carrier, Rick.

Carroll, Donald. Why Didn't I Say That? The Art of Verbal Self-Defense. 1980. 7.95 (ISBN 0-531-09923-7, C37). Watts.

Carroll, Eugene A. The Drawings of Rosso Fiorentino, 2 vols. LC 75-23786. (Outstanding Dissertations in the Fine Arts - 16th Century). (Illus.). 1976. Set. lib. bdg. 121.00 (ISBN 0-8240-1982-2). Garland Pub.

Carroll, Frances, tr. see Szechter, Szymon.

Carroll, Francis M. American Opinion & the Irish Question: 1910-1923. LC 78-58897. 1978. 25.00x (ISBN 0-312-02890-3). St Martin.

Carroll, Frieda, compiled by. The People's Travel Book. LC 80-70869. 115p. 1981. 17.95; pap. 12.95. Biblio Pr Ga.

Carroll, H. Bailey, jt. ed. see Webb, Walter P.

Carroll, Herbert A. Mental Hygiene: Dynamics of Adjustment. 5th ed. 1969. text ed. 16.95x (ISBN 0-13-576314-2). P-H.

Carroll, J. S. & Payne, John W., eds. Cognition & Social Behavior. (Carnegie Mellon U. Cognition Studies). 1976. 16.50 o.p. (ISBN 0-470-99007-4). Halsted Pr.

Carroll, James. Fault Lines. 288p. 1980. 11.95 (ISBN 0-686-62569-2). Little.

--Forbidden Disappointments. LC 74-80349. 1975. 6.95 (ISBN 0-8091-0195-5); pap. 3.95 (ISBN 0-8091-1842-4). Paulist Pr.

--Mortal Friends. 1979. pap. 2.95 (ISBN 0-440-15789-7). Dell.

--A Terrible Beauty: Conversions in Prayers, Politics & Imagination. LC 72-97400. 1973. 4.95 (ISBN 0-8091-0182-3). Paulist Pr.

--Wonder & Worship. LC 70-133469. 1970. pap. 1.95 (ISBN 0-8091-1871-8). Paulist Pr.

Carroll, James L., ed. Contemporary School Psychology: Readings from Psychology in the Schools. 2nd ed. 1981. pap. 12.50x (ISBN 0-88422-014-1). Clinical Psych.

--Contemporary School Psychology: Readings from Psychology in the Schools. 2nd ed. 1981. pap. text ed. 12.95x (ISBN 0-88422-014-1). Clinical Psych.

Carroll, Jane, tr. see Paccagnini, Giovanni.

Carroll, Janet F., jt. auth. see Wolfart, H. Christoph.

Carroll, Jeffrey. Climbing to the Sun. LC 77-8617. (gr. 5 up). 1977. 6.95 (ISBN 0-395-28898-3, Clarion). HM.

Carroll, John. Break-Out from the Crystal Palace: The Anarcho-Psychological Critique-Stirner, Nietzsche, Dostoevsky. (International Library of Sociology). 1974. 18.00x (ISBN 0-7100-7750-5). Routledge & Kegan.

--Puritan, Paranoid, Remissive: A Sociology of Modern Culture. 1977. 15.00 (ISBN 0-7100-8622-9). Routledge & Kegan.

Carroll, John B. The Teaching of French As a Foreign Language in Eight Countries. LC 75-17945. (International Studies in Evaluation, Vol. 5). 1975. 17.95 (ISBN 0-470-13602-2). Halsted Pr.

Carroll, John E. & Logan, Roderick M. The Garrison Diversion Unit: A Case Study in Canadian-U.S. Environmental Relations. 56p. 1980. 5.00 (ISBN 0-88806-070-X). Natl Planning.

Carroll, John M. Computer Security. LC 77-10615. (Illus.). 1977. 19.95 (ISBN 0-913708-28-3). Butterworths.

--Confidential Information Sources: Public & Private. LC 74-20177. (Illus.). 320p. 1975. 18.95 (ISBN 0-913708-19-4). Butterworths.

Carroll, Kenneth. Quakerism on the Eastern Shore. LC 70-112986. (Illus.). 1970. 12.50x (ISBN 0-938420-15-1). Md Hist.

Carroll, L. Alice's Adventures in Wonderland. Bd. with Through the Looking Glass. (Illus.). 285p. 1966. 6.95 (ISBN 0-312-01821-5). St Martin.

--Alice's Adventures in Wonderland. (Illus.). 285p. (gr. 4 up). 1969. pap. 2.25 o.p. (ISBN 0-312-01785-5, Papermac). St Martin.

Carroll, L. Patrick & Dyckman, Katharine M. Inviting the Mystic, Supporting the Prophet: The Dynamics of Spiritual Direction. 128p. (Orig.). 1981. pap. 4.95 (ISBN 0-8091-2378-9). Paulist Pr.

Carroll, Lewis. Alice in Wonderland. Gray, Donald J., ed. (Critical Editions Ser). (Illus.). 1971. 10.00 (ISBN 0-393-04343-6); pap. 4.95x (ISBN 0-393-09977-6). Norton.

--Alice in Wonderland & Through the Looking Glass. 1965. 12.95x (ISBN 0-460-00836-6, Evman); pap. 2.95 (ISBN 0-460-01836-1). Dutton.

--Alice's Adventures in Wonderland. Bd. with Through the Looking Glass. (Classics Ser.). (gr. 5 up). pap. 1.50 (ISBN 0-8049-0079-5, CL-79). Airmont.

--Alice's Adventures in Wonderland & Through the Looking Glass. LC 78-3389. (Raintree's Illustrated Classics). (Illus.). (gr. 5-8). 1978. PLB 9.65 (ISBN 0-8393-6208-0). Raintree Child.

--Ania V Strane Chudes. Nabokov, Vladimir, tr. 1981. 15.00 (ISBN 0-88233-658-4); pap. 6.50 (ISBN 0-88233-659-2). Ardis Pubs.

--Aventures D'Alice au Pays des Merveilles. Bue, Henri, tr. from Eng. (Illus.). 196p. (Fr.). (gr. 4-8). 1972. pap. 3.25 (ISBN 0-486-22836-3). Dover.

--The Hunting of the Snark: Annotated by Martin Gardner. Gardner, Martin, ed. (Illus.). Date not set. 14.00 (ISBN 0-913232-98-X); collector's ed. 350.00 (ISBN 0-913232-98-X). W Kaufmann.

--The Letters of Lewis Carroll, 2 vols. Cohen, Morton H. & Green, Roger L., eds. (Illus.). 1979. Set. 65.00 (ISBN 0-19-520090-X). Oxford U Pr.

Carroll, Lewis, pseud. Lewis Carroll & the Kitchins. Cohen, Morton N., tr. LC 79-92406. (Carroll Studies: No. 4). (Illus.). 80p. (Orig.). pap. 15.00 (ISBN 0-930326-04-0). Lewis Carroll Soc.

Carroll, Lewis. Poems of Lewis Carroll. Livingston, Myra C., compiled by. LC 73-7914. (Poets Ser.). (Illus.). (gr. 6 up). 1973. 8.95 (ISBN 0-690-00178-9, TYC-J). T Y Crowell.

--Rhyme? & Reason? LC 75-32188. (Classics of Children's Literature, 1621-1932: Vol. 51). (Illus.). 1976. Repr. of 1883 ed. PLB 38.00 (ISBN 0-8240-2300-5). Garland Pub.

--Sylvia & Bruno. LC 75-32196. (Classics of Children's Literature, 1621-1932: Vol. 58). (Illus.). 1976. Repr. of 1889 ed. PLB 38.00 (ISBN 0-8240-2307-2). Garland Pub.

Carroll, Lewis & Tenniel, Sir John. Alice's Adventures in Wonderland. LC 77-77324. (Illus.). (gr. 5 up). 1977. 7.95 (ISBN 0-312-01821-5). St Martin.

Carroll, Malcolm E. Origins of the Whig Party: A Dissertation. LC 72-112705. (Law, Politics & History Ser). 1970. Repr. of 1925 ed. lib. bdg. 32.50 (ISBN 0-306-71917-7). Da Capo.

Carroll, Mary. Shadow & Sun. 192p. (Orig.). pap. 1.50 (ISBN 0-671-57002-1). S&S.

--Too Swift the Morning. 192p. (Orig.). 1980. pap. 1.50 (ISBN 0-671-57045-5). S&S.

Carroll, Mary-Jo & Sloane, Randy. Traveler's Guide to Running in Major American Cities. LC 79-949. 224p. (Orig.). 1979. pap. 6.95 (ISBN 0-8117-2091-8). Stackpole.

Carroll, Michael. Gates of the Wind. 8.95 (ISBN 0-7195-0197-0). Transatlantic.

Carroll, Peter N. Puritanism & the Wilderness: The Intellectual Significance of the New England Frontier, 1629-1700. LC 78-84673. 1969. 17.50x (ISBN 0-231-03253-6). Columbia U Pr.

Carroll, Shana. Paxton Pride. (Orig.). 1976. pap. 1.95 (ISBN 0-515-04019-3). Jove Pubns.

Carroll, Stephen J. & Tosi, Henry L. Organizational Behavior. (Illus.). 1977. 21.95 (ISBN 0-914292-08-0). Wiley.

Carroll, Stephen J., jt. auth. see Nash, Allan N.

Carroll, Stephen J., jt. auth. see Tosi, Henry L.

Carroll, Susanne, jt. auth. see Gregory, Michael.

Carroll, Theodus. Firsts Under the Wire: The World's Fastest Horses (1900-1950) LC 78-11476. (Famous Firsts Ser.). (Illus.). 1978. lib. bdg. 7.35 (ISBN 0-686-51108-5). Silver.

Carroll, W. H., et al. Reasons for Hope. 203p. (Orig.). 1978. pap. 5.95 (ISBN 0-931888-01-8, Chris. Coll. Pr.). Christendom Pubns.

Carroll, Walter J., ed. Hospital-Health Care Training Media Profiles, Vol. 8. 1981. 85.00 (ISBN 0-88367-206-5). Olympic Media.

--Olympic's Film Finder: Nineteen Eighty-One Business Edition. 1981. 24.00x (ISBN 0-88367-600-1). Olympic Media.

Carron, Harold & McLaughlin, Robert E. Office Management of Low Back Pain. 320p. 1981. 25.00 (ISBN 0-88416-317-2). PSG Pub.

Carrott, Richard G. The Egyptian Revival: Its Sources, Monuments, & Meaning, 1808-1858. (Illus.). 1978. 24.50 (ISBN 0-520-03324-8). U of Cal Pr.

Carrubba, Eugene R., et al. Assuring Product Integrity. 160p. 1975. 21.95 (ISBN 0-669-00088-4). Lexington Bks.

Carruth, Ella K. She Wanted to Read: The Story of Mary Bethune. (Illus.). (gr. 3-5). 1969. pap. 1.25 (ISBN 0-671-29861-5). PB.

--She Wanted to Read: The Story of Mary McLeod Bethune. (gr. 3-5). 1969. pap. 1.25 o.s.i. (ISBN 0-671-29861-5). Archway.

Carruth, J. H., jt. auth. see Eaves, Edgar D.

Carruth, William H. Verse Writing. 123p. 1980. Repr. of 1925 ed. lib. bdg. 15.00 (ISBN 0-8482-3554-1). Norwood Edns.

Carruthers, Ian, ed. Social & Economic Perspectives on Irrigation. 100p. 1980. pap. 22.00 (ISBN 0-08-026780-7). Pergamon.

Carruthers, M., ed. see Annual Conference for Psychosomatic Research, 20th, London, Nov. 15-16, 1976.

Carruthers, N. B., jt. auth. see Houghton, E. L.

Carruthers, W. Some Modern Methods of Organic Synthesis. 2nd ed. LC 77-77735. (Cambridge Texts in Chemistry & Biochemistry Ser.). (Illus.). 1978. 85.00 (ISBN 0-521-21715-6); pap. 19.95x (ISBN 0-521-29241-7). Cambridge U Pr.

Carsberg, Bryan. Current Issues in Accounting. Hope, Tony, ed. 304p. 1977. 34.50x (ISBN 0-86003-503-4, Pub. by Allan Pubs England); pap. 17.25x (ISBN 0-86003-603-0). State Mutual Bk.

Carse, Adam. The History of Orchestration. (Illus.). 1935. pap. 5.00 (ISBN 0-486-21258-0). Dover.

Carse, Stephen, et al. The Financing Procedures of British Foreign Trade. LC 79-18146. 160p. 1980. 24.95 (ISBN 0-521-22534-5). Cambridge U Pr.

Carsky, P. & Urban, M. Ab Initio Calculations: Methods & Applications in Chemistry. (Lecture Notes in Chemistry: Vol. 16). (Illus.). 247p. 1980. pap. 21.00 (ISBN 0-387-10005-9). Springer-Verlag.

Carslaw, Horatio S. & Jaeger, J. C. Conduction of Heat in Solids. 2nd ed. (Illus.). 1959. 39.50x (ISBN 0-19-853303-9). Oxford U Pr.

Carslaw, Horatio S; see Ball, W. Rouse, et al.

Carsley. This Ravished Rose. pap. 2.50 (ISBN 0-671-41293-0). PB.

Carsley, Anne. Griffin's Talon. (Orig.). 1980. pap. write for info. (ISBN 0-671-41293-0). PB.

Carson, Ada & Carson, Herbert. Royall Tyler. (United States Authors Ser.: No. 344). 1979. lib. bdg. 13.50 (ISBN 0-8057-7281-2). Twayne.

Carson, Alexander. Baptism: It's Mode & Subjects. Young, John, ed. LC 80-8067. 1981. 12.95 (ISBN 0-8254-2324-4). Kregel.

--The History of Providence As Explained in the Bible. (Summit Bks). 1977. pap. 2.95 (ISBN 0-8010-2402-1). Baker Bk.

Carson, Ann. The Memoirs of the Celebrated & Beautiful Mrs. Ann Carson, Daughter of an Officer of the U. S. Navy & Wife of Another, Whose Life Terminated in the Philadelphia Prison, 2 vols. in 1. Baxter, Annette K., ed. LC 79-8780. (Signal Lives Ser.). 1980. Repr. of 1838 ed. lib. bdg. 37.00x (ISBN 0-405-12829-0). Arno.

Carson, Ben, jt. auth. see Martin, Betty.

Carson, Bonnie L., jt. ed. see Smith, Ivan C.

Carson, C. Deane. Money & Finance: Readings in Theory, Policy & Institutions. 2nd ed. LC 70-37643. 1972. text ed. 18.95 (ISBN 0-471-13712-X). Wiley.

Carson, Charles R. Managing Employee Honesty. LC 76-51836. (Illus.). 1977. 16.95 (ISBN 0-913708-27-5). Butterworths.

Carson, Clarence B. Flight from Reality. 568p. 1969. 8.00 o.p. (ISBN 0-910614-33-4); pap. 4.00 (ISBN 0-910614-18-0). Foun Econ Ed.

Carson, D. A. Divine Sovereignty & Human Responsibility: Biblical Perspectives in Tension. Toon, Peter & Martin, Ralph, eds. LC 79-27589. (New Foundations Theological Library). 228p. 1981. 18.50 (ISBN 0-8042-3707-7); pap. 9.95 (ISBN 0-8042-3727-1). John Knox.

--The Farewell Discourse & the Final Prayer of Jesus: An Exposition of John 14-17. 196p. 1981. 9.95 (ISBN 0-8010-2460-9). Baker Bk.

Carson, E. W., Jr., ed. The Plant Root & Its Environment. LC 72-92877. 1974. 15.00x (ISBN 0-8139-0411-0). U Pr of Va.

Carson, Gordon B., et al, eds. Production Handbook. 3rd ed. (Illus.). 1470p. 1972. 45.95 (ISBN 0-8260-1820-3, 12602). Ronald Pr.

Carson, Herbert, jt. auth. see Carson, Ada.

Carson, J. W. & Rickards, T. Industrial New Product Development: A Manual for the 1980's. LC 79-65781. 1979. 32.95x (ISBN 0-470-26821-2). Halsted Pr.

Carson, Jane. James Innes & His Brothers of the F.H.C. LC 65-26594. (Williamsburg Research Studies). 171p. 1965. pap. 2.25x o.p. (ISBN 0-8139-0062-X). U Pr of Va.

Carson, Jo. X-Ray Diganosis Positioning Manual. 1971. pap. text ed. 4.95x (ISBN 0-02-473270-2, 47327). Macmillan.

Carson, Kit. Kit Carson's Autobiography. Quaife, Milo M., ed. LC 66-4130. (Illus.). 1966. pap. 3.95 (ISBN 0-8032-5031-2, BB 325, Bison). U of Nebr Pr.

Carson, Linwood. The Avenging Angels. 1976. pap. 1.50 o.p. (ISBN 0-685-72575-8, LB408, Leisure Bks). Nordon Pubns.

Carson, M. A. & Kirkby, M. J. Hillslope Form & Process. (Cambridge Geographical Studies). 49.50 (ISBN 0-521-08234-X). Cambridge U Pr.

Carson, Mary. Guide for Friends, Neighbors, & Relatives of Retarded Children. (Illus.). 1977. pap. 2.45 (ISBN 0-89570-107-3). Claretian Pubns.

Carson, Mary F. & Duba, Arlo D. Alabad a Dios. Gonzalez, Justo L., tr. from Eng. 86p. (Orig., Span.). 1979. pap. 2.50 (ISBN 0-89922-155-6). Edit Caribe.

Carson, Patricia. Materials for West African History in the Archives of Belgium & Holland. (Guides to Materials for West African History in European Archives: Vol. 1). 1962. 3.50x (ISBN 0-485-17201-1, Athlone Pr). Humanities.

--Materials for West African History in French Archives; Guides to Materials for West African History in European Archives. (Vol. 4). 1968. text ed. 7.00x (ISBN 0-485-17204-6, Athlone Pr). Humanities.

Carson, R. A. Coins of the World: Ancient, Medieval, Modern. (Illus.). 1962. 25.00x o.p. (ISBN 0-06-000750-8, HarpT). Har-Row.

Carson, R. A. & Kraay, C. M. Scripta Numaria Romana. 1979. 60.00 (ISBN 0-686-63876-X, Pub. by Spink & Son England). S J Durst.

Carson, Rachel. Edge of the Sea. 1971. pap. 0.95 o.p. (ISBN 0-451-04368-5, Q4368, Sig). NAL.

Carson, Rachel L. Sea Around Us. 1954. pap. 2.25 (ISBN 0-451-61873-4, ME1873, Ment). NAL.

Carson, Ray F. & Patterson, Buel R. Principles of Championship Wrestling. LC 73-169070. (Illus.). 192p. 1972. pap. 8.95 o.p. (ISBN 0-498-07930-9). A S Barnes.

Carson, Robert B. Main Line to Oblivion: The Disintegration of the New York Railroads in the Twentieth Century. LC 75-139352. (American Studies Ser). 1971. 15.00 (ISBN 0-8046-9003-0). Kennikat.

--Microeconomic Issues Today. 182p. (Orig.). 1980. text ed. 12.95 (ISBN 0-312-53175-3); write for info instrs'. manual (ISBN 0-312-53176-1); write for info. instructor's manual (ISBN 0-312-53177-X). St Martin.

Carson, Robert B. & Friesen, John W. Teacher Participation: A Second Look. LC 78-64522. 1978. pap. text ed. 7.25 (ISBN 0-8191-0634-8). U Pr of Amer.

Carson, Russell L. Tommy Strangeleaf & Bow. 116p. (gr. 4-6). 1979. 4.95 (ISBN 0-8059-2627-5). Dorrance.

Carson, S. M., ed. Environmental Studies: The Construction of an 'A' Level Syllabus. 1973. pap. text ed. 6.25x (ISBN 0-85633-029-9, NFER). Humanities.

Carson, Tom. Twisted Kicks. 264p. 1981. 11.95 (ISBN 0-934558-03-5); pap. 69.95 (ISBN 0-934558-05-1). Entwhistle Bks.

Carsten, F. L. Reichswehr & Politics: Nineteen Eighteen to Nineteen Thirty-Three. 1974. pap. 6.95x (ISBN 0-520-02492-3). U of Cal Pr.

--Revolution in Central Europe, 1918-1919. LC 78-165225. 1972. 25.00x (ISBN 0-520-02084-7). U of Cal Pr.

Carsten, F. L., et al, eds. The Hapsburg Monarchy, 2 vols. (Studies in Russian & East European History Ser.). 1981. text ed. 25.00x ea. Vol. 1, Austria & Bohemia 1835-1918 (ISBN 0-06-490991-3). Vol. 2, Hungary 1835-1918. B&N.

Carsten, Francis L. Fascist Movements in Austria: From Schonerer to Hitler. LC 76-22935. (Sage Studies in Twentieth Century History: Vol. 7). 1977. 20.00x (ISBN 0-8039-9992-5); pap. 9.95x (ISBN 0-8039-9857-0). Sage.

Carsten, Franz L. Reichswehr & Politics: Nineteen Eighteen to Nineteen Thirty-Three. 1966. 36.00x (ISBN 0-19-821457-X). Oxford U Pr.

Carstenpen, J. Thuro, jt. auth. see Leeson, Lewis J.

Carstens, A. L., jt. auth. see Cronkite, E. P.

Carstensen, Jens T. Solid Pharmaceutics: Mechanical Properties & Rate Phenomena. LC 79-6805. 1980. 35.00 (ISBN 0-12-161150-7). Acad Pr.

Carstensen, Vernon, ed. Public Lands: Studies in the History of the Public Domain. 1963. pap. 9.95 (ISBN 0-299-02754-6). U of Wis Pr.

Carstenson, Cecil C. The Craft & Creation of Wood Sculpture. (Illus.). 192p. 1981. pap. price not set (ISBN 0-486-24094-0). Dover.

Carswell, Catherine. Life of Robert Burns. LC 78-164157. (Illus.). 1971. Repr. of 1931 ed. 24.00 (ISBN 0-8103-3788-6). Gale.

Cartan, Elie. The Theory of Spinors. 160p. 1981. pap. price not set (ISBN 0-486-64070-1). Dover.

Cartan, Henri. Elementary Theory of Analytic Functions of One or Several Complex Variables. rev. ed. 1963. 23.50 (ISBN 0-201-00901-3, Adv Bk Prog). A-W.

Cartari, Vincenzo. Le Imagini...Degli Dei. LC 75-27855. (Renaissance & the Gods Ser.: Vol. 12). (Illus.). 1976. Repr. of 1571 ed. lib. bdg. 73.00 (ISBN 0-8240-2061-8). Garland Pub.

Carte, Elaine A., jt. auth. see Carte, Gene E.

Carte, Gene E. & Carte, Elaine A. Police Reform in the United States: The Era of August Vollmer, 1905-1932. LC 73-87248. 390p. 1976. 14.50x (ISBN 0-520-02599-7). U of Cal Pr.

Carter. The Changing World of Fashion: 1900 to the Present. Date not set. price not set (ISBN 0-517-31110-0). Bonanza.

--Chemotherapy of Cancer. 2nd ed. 400p. 1981. 15.75 (ISBN 0-471-08045-4, Pub. by Wiley Medical). Wiley.

--Metallic Coatings for Corrosion Control. 1977. text ed. 31.95 (ISBN 0-408-00270-0). Butterworths.

Carter, jt. auth. see Grinnell.

Carter, jt. auth. see Hubert, J. J.

Carter, jt. auth. see Packard.

Carter, A. E. Charles Baudelaire. (World Authors Ser.: No. 429). 1977. lib. bdg. 9.95 (ISBN 0-8057-6269-8). Twayne.

--Paul Verlaine. (World Authors Ser.: France: No. 158). lib. bdg. 10.95 (ISBN 0-8057-2944-5). Twayne.

Carter, A. H., jt. auth. see Speak, P.

Carter, A. H., ed. see Burns, D. T. & Townshend, A.

Carter, Albert E. The Miracles of Rebound Exercise. 188p. 1979. pap. 5.95 (ISBN 0-938302-00-0). NIRH.

--Rebound to Better Health: Includes Trampolining. 59p. 1977. pap. 2.95 (ISBN 0-938302-10-8). NIRH.

Carter, Alberta S. Fool's Proof. 256p. 1975. pap. 1.25 o.p. (ISBN 0-445-00261-1). Popular Lib.

Carter, Angela. The Bloody Chamber. LC 79-2645. 176p. 1981. pap. 3.95 (ISBN 0-06-090836-X, C*N 836, CN). Har-Row.

--Fireworks: Nine Stories in Various Disguises. LC 80-8706. 144p. 1981. 8.95 (ISBN 0-06-014852-7, HarpT). Har-Row.

--The Sadeian Woman: And the Ideaology of Pornography. LC 78-20412. 1980. pap. 3.50 (ISBN 0-06-090768-1, CN 768, CN). Har-Row.

Carter, Anne, tr. see Oldenbourg, Zoe.

Carter, Anne, tr. see Rodinson, Maxime.

Carter, Annette. Exploring from the Chesapeake Bay to the Poconos. rev. ed. LC 75-14092. (Illus.). 272p. 1975. 8.95 o.p. (ISBN 0-397-01099-0); pap. 4.95 o.p. (ISBN 0-397-01108-3). Lippincott.

Carter, Anthony. Bayonet: The History & Development of the Sword, Sabre, & Knife Bayonet. LC 74-5449. (Encore Edition). 1974. 3.95 o.p. (ISBN 0-684-15394-7, ScribT). Scribner.

Carter, April. Direct Action & Liberal Democracy. 1974. pap. 2.95x (ISBN 0-06-131816-7, TB1816, Torch). Har-Row.

Carter, C. M., ed. African One-Party States. LC 62-19165. 1962. 12.75 (ISBN 0-910294-14-3). Brown Bk.

Carter, C. O. & Fairbank, T. J. The Genetics of Locomotor Disorders. (Oxford Monographs on Medical Genetics). 230p. 1974. text ed. 18.95x o.p. (ISBN 0-19-264131-X). Oxford U Pr.

Carter, Candy & Rashkis, Zora, eds. Ideas for Teaching English in the Junior High & Middle School. LC 80-25921. 320p. 1980. 15.00 (ISBN 0-8141-2253-1). NCTE.

Carter, Charles F. The Wedding Day in Literature & Art: A Collection of the Best Descriptions of Wedding from the Works of the World's Leading Novelists & Poets. LC 74-86598. 1969. Repr. of 1900 ed. 15.00 (ISBN 0-8103-0154-7). Gale.

Carter, Charles H. Handbook of Mental Retardation Syndromes. 3rd ed. (Illus.). 432p. 1979. text ed. 26.25 (ISBN 0-398-03090-1). C C Thomas.

Carter, Chris, ed. Motocourse 1977-1978. (Ser. No. 2). (Illus.). 1978. 11.95 o.p. (ISBN 0-905138-04-X, Hazelton Securities Ltd.). Motorbooks Intl.

Carter, Codell K. A Contemporary Introduction to Logic with Applications. 1977. text ed. 9.95 (ISBN 0-02-471500-X). Macmillan.

Carter, Conrad, et al. The Production & Staging of Plays. LC 63-10203. (Illus.). 216p. 1963. lib. bdg. 4.50 o.p. (ISBN 0-668-01051-7). Arco.

Carter, Craig. How to Use the Power of Mind in Everyday Life. 96p. 1976. pap. 3.50 (ISBN 0-911336-65-6). Sci of Mind.

Carter, D. L. & Bate, R. T. Physics of Semimetals & Narrow-Gap Semiconductors. 1971. 105.00 (ISBN 0-08-016661-X). Pergamon.

Carter, Dan T. Scottsboro: A Tragedy of the American South. LC 79-1090. 1979. 24.95x (ISBN 0-8071-0568-6); pap. 7.95 (ISBN 0-8071-0498-1). La State U Pr.

Carter, David C. Action Techniques for the Take-Charge Sales Manager. 1974. 10.95 o.p. (ISBN 0-13-003376-6). P-H.

Carter, David E., ed. see Annual of Trade Mark Design.

Carter, David S. & Vogt, Andrew. Two Articles: Collinearity-Preserving Functions Between Affine Desarguesian Planes. LC 80-20427. (Memoirs: No. 235). 1980. 5.20 (ISBN 0-8218-2235-7). Am Math.

Carter, Dusty. Racing Planes & Air Races: Biennial 1979 to 1980, Vol. 14. LC 67-16455. (Illus.). 160p. 1981. pap. write for info. (ISBN 0-8168-7873-0). Aero.

Carter, E. Dale, Jr., ed. Antologia Del Realismo Magico: Ocho Cuentos Hispanoamericanos. LC 73-114674. (Span). 1970. pap. 4.50 (ISBN 0-672-63009-5). Odyssey Pr.

Carter, E. Eugene. Portfolio Aspects of Corporate Capital Budgeting: Method of Analysis, Survey of Applications and a Model. LC 74-4514. 1974. 19.95 (ISBN 0-669-93161-6). Lexington Bks.

Carter, E. Eugene & Rodriguez, Rita M. International Financial Management. 2nd ed. (Illus.). 1979. text ed. 21.95 (ISBN 0-13-472977-3). P-H.

Carter, E. F. Dictionary of Inventions and Discoveries. rev. 2nd ed. LC 75-37058. 214p. 1976. 14.50x (ISBN 0-8448-0867-9). Crane-Russak Co.

Carter, Edward C., et al, eds. The Journals of Benjamin Henry Latrobe, 1799-1820. LC 79-19001. (Papers of Benjamin Henry Latrobe Ser. 1: Vol. 3). (Illus.). 432p. 1981. text ed. 65.00x (ISBN 0-300-02383-9). Yale U Pr.

Carter, Eleanor-Jean. Doll Modes: Doll Fashions with Patterns. 105p. 1972. pap. 10.00x o.p. (ISBN 0-685-27933-2). Hobby Hse.

Carter, Elizabeth E. Valley of the Kings: A Novel of Tutankhamun. LC 77-5157. 1977. 7.95 o.p. (ISBN 0-525-22777-6). Dutton.

Carter, Ernest. Let's Look at Trains. 17.50x (ISBN 0-392-08037-0, SpS). Soccer.

Carter, Ernest F. Let's Look at Trains. LC 68-22191. (Let's Look Ser). (Illus.). (gr. 4-8). 1964. 4.95g o.p. (ISBN 0-8075-4507-4). A Whitman.

Carter, Ernestine. Magic Names of Fashion. LC 80-82524. 1980. 12.95 (ISBN 0-13-545426-3). P-H.

Carter, Ernestine R. Gymnastics for Girls & Women. (Illus.). 1968. text ed. 11.95 (ISBN 0-13-371781-X). P-H.

Carter, Everett & Homburger, Wolfgang S. Introduction to Transportation Engineering: Highways & Transit. (Illus.). 1978. ref. ed. 21.95 (ISBN 0-87909-388-9). Reston.

Carter, Forrest. The Education of Little Tree. (gr. 7-12). 1981. pap. 1.50 (ISBN 0-440-92200-3, LE). Dell.

--The Education of Little Tree. 1976. 9.95 (ISBN 0-440-02319-X). Delacorte.

Carter, Frank B., Jr. Mendacity Without Scruples. Ashton, Sylvia, ed. LC 77-78384. 1978. 8.95 (ISBN 0-87949-093-4). Ashley Bks.

Carter, G. & Grant, W. A. Ion Implantation of Semiconductors. LC 76-13558. (Contemporary Electrical Engineering Ser.). 1976. 24.50x o.p. (ISBN 0-470-15125-0). Halsted Pr.

Carter, G. A. J. L. Hobb's Local History & the Library. (Grafton Books on Library Science). (Illus.). 1977. lib. bdg. 17.75 o.p. (ISBN 0-233-95615-8). Westview.

Carter, G. R. Diagnostic Procedures in Veterinary Bacteriology & Mycology. 3rd. ed. (Illus.). 496p. 1979. 32.75 (ISBN 0-398-03792-2). C C Thomas.

Carter, G. W. & Richardson, A. Techniques of Circuit Analysis. LC 79-183222. (Illus.). 544p. 1972. 40.75x (ISBN 0-521-08435-0). Cambridge U Pr.

Carter, George F. Earlier Than You Think: A Personal View of Man in America. LC 79-5280. (4#368). 1980. 19.95 (ISBN 0-89096-091-7). Tex A&M Univ Pr.

Carter, Gwendolen & Morgan, E. Philip, eds. From the Frontline: Speeches of Sir Seretse Khama. (Special Project Ser.: 27). 252p. 1980. 26.95. Hoover Inst Pr.

Carter, Gwendolen M. Which Way Is South Africa Going? LC 79-3658. 256p. 1980. 12.95 (ISBN 0-253-10874-8). Ind U Pr.

Carter, Gwendolen M. & Morgan, E. Philip, eds. From the Frontline. (Special Project Ser.: No. 27). 252p. 1980. 26.95. Hoover Inst Pr.

Carter, Gwendolen M., ed. see Hess, Robert L.

Carter, Gwendolen M., et al. South Africa's Transkei: The Politics of Domestic Colonialism. (Northwestern African Studies Ser.). 1967. 9.95x o.s.i. (ISBN 0-8101-0062-2). Northwestern U Pr.

Carter, H. & Partington, I. Applied Economics in Banking & Finance. 1979. 29.00x (ISBN 0-19-877108-8). Oxford U Pr.

Carter, Harold. The Study of Urban Geography. 2nd ed. LC 76-22730. 1976. pap. text ed. 16.95 (ISBN 0-470-98911-4). Halsted Pr.

Carter, Harold A. Myths That Mire the Ministry. 1980. pap. 5.95 (ISBN 0-8170-0845-4); pap. 3.95 o.p. (ISBN 0-686-65909-0). Judson.

Carter, Hodding. The Commandos of World War II. LC 80-21142. (Landmark Bks.). (Illus.). 160p. (gr. 5-9). 1981. 2.95 (ISBN 0-394-84735-0, BYR); PLB 5.99 (ISBN 0-394-90561-X). Random.

--The Marquis De Lafayette: Bright Sword for Freedom. (World Landmark Ser. No. 34). (Illus.). (gr. 7-9). 1958. 4.39 o.p. (ISBN 0-394-90534-2). Random.

Carter, Hodding, ed. Louisiana Almanac, 1969. 1969. pap. 7.95 (ISBN 0-911116-49-4). Pelican.

Carter, Horace, jt. auth. see Hannon, Douglas.

Carter, Hugh & Leighton, F. Cousin Beedie & Cousin Hot: My Life with the Carter Family of Plains, Georgia. LC 78-4975. 1978. 12.50 o.p. (ISBN 0-13-185470-4). P-H.

Carter, Ian, ed. Aberdeenshire Peasant Life: William Alexander-Scottish Peasant Life. (Library of Peasant Studies: No. 5). 1981. 28.00x (ISBN 0-7146-3087-X, F Cass Co). Biblio Dist.

Carter, Irl, jt. auth. see Anderson, Ralph E.

Carter, J. Anthony. Allied Bayonets of World War Two. LC 69-13592. (Twentieth Century Arms Ser). (Illus.). 1969. 3.50 o.p. (ISBN 0-668-01862-3). Arco.

Carter, J. R., ed. see Desikachar, T. K.

Carter, James. Law: Law: Its Origin, Growth & Function. LC 74-6413. (American Constitutional & Legal History Ser.). 1974. Repr. of 1907 ed. lib. bdg. 35.00 (ISBN 0-306-70631-8). Da Capo.

Carter, James E. Christ & the Crowds. 1981. 3.25 (ISBN 0-8054-5181-1). Broadman.

--People Parables. (Pocket Pulpit Library). 128p. 1981. pap. 2.95 (ISBN 0-8010-2348-3). Baker Bk.

Carter, James J. Prose, Poetry, & Flows. (Orig.). 1979. pap. 2.95 (ISBN 0-937004-01-4). Carter.

--Self Analysis: The Book About Life. (Illus., Orig.). 1979. pap. 4.95 (ISBN 0-937004-00-6). Carter.

Carter, James L. & Rankin, Ernest H., eds. North to Lake Superior: Journal of Charles W. Penny, 1840. LC 74-80875. 1970. 4.50 (ISBN 0-938746-02-2). Marquette Cnty Hist.

Carter, James L., ed. see Castle, Beatrice H.

Carter, James M. The Norman Conquest in English Historiography. 1980. pap. 18.00 (ISBN 0-89126-085-4). Military Aff Aero.

Carter, James P., et al. Keeping Your Family Healthy Overseas. 1971. 6.95 o.s.i. (ISBN 0-440-04429-4, Sey Lawr). Delacorte.

Carter, Jan. Day Services for Adults Somewhere to Go. (National Institute Social Services Library: No. 40). 352p. 1981. text ed. 35.00x (ISBN 0-04-262035-X, 2620). Allen Unwin.

Carter, Jane R. Public Librarianship: A Reader. 400p. 1981. lib. bdg. price not set (ISBN 0-87287-246-7). Libs Unl.

Carter, Jared. Work, for the Night Is Coming. 64p. 1981. 12.95 (ISBN 0-02-522090-X); pap. 5.95 (ISBN 0-02-069290-0). Macmillan.

Carter, Jesse B. Religious Life of Ancient Rome. 270p. 1972. Repr. of 1911 ed. lib. bdg. 26.50x (ISBN 0-8154-0429-8). Cooper Sq.

Carter, John. The Eagle's Nest. 1978. pap. 1.50 o.p. (ISBN 0-425-03994-3, Dist. by Putnam). Berkley Pub.

Carter, John E., ed. see Annual Meeting of the Ohio Valley Philosophy of Educ. Society, August 1979.

Carter, John F. The New Dealers: By the Unofficial Observer. LC 74-23461. (Fdr & the Era of the New Deal Ser.). ix, 414p. 1975. Repr. of 1934 ed. lib. bdg. 35.00 (ISBN 0-306-70710-1). Da Capo.

Carter, John M. & Wyse, Lois. How to Be Outrageously Successful with Women. 160p. 1976. pap. 1.75 o.p. (ISBN 0-345-25206-3). Ballantine.

Carter, John R. Dhamma: Western Academic & Sinhalese Buddhist Interpretations: A Study of a Religious Concept. 1978. 32.50 (ISBN 0-89346-014-1, Pub. by Hokuseido Pr.). Heian Intl.

Carter, John S., ed. see Shirley, James.

Carter, Joseph, jt. auth. see LaMotta, Jake.

Carter, Judith Q. & Carter, Richard D., eds. Herbert L. Fink: Graphic Artist. (Illus.). Date not set. price not set (ISBN 0-8093-1016-3). S Ill U Pr.

Carter, L. R. & Huzan, E. A Practical Approach to Computer Simulation in Business. LC 73-11017. 1973. 25.95 (ISBN 0-470-13729-0). Halsted Pr.

Carter, Lanie. Congratulations! You're Going to Be a Grandmother. LC 80-1345. 1980. PLB 5.95 (ISBN 0-916392-48-1); pap. 4.95 (ISBN 0-916392-53-8). Oak Tree Pubns.

Carter, Lark P., jt. auth. see Chapman, Stephen R.

Carter, Lin. The City Outside the World. 1977. pap. 1.50 o.p. (ISBN 0-425-03549-2, Medallion). Berkley Pub.

--Hurok of the Stone Age. 1981. pap. 1.75 (ISBN 0-87997-597-0, UE1597). Daw Bks.

--Invisible Death. (Zarkon Ser.: No. 2). 1978. pap. 1.50 o.p. (ISBN 0-445-04256-7). Popular Lib.

--Lovecraft: A Look Behind the Cthulhu Mythos. 1976. pap. 1.50 o.p. (ISBN 0-345-25295-0). Ballantine.

--Thonger & the Dragon City. pap. 1.25 o.p. (ISBN 0-425-03572-7). Berkley Pub.

--Thongor & the Wizard of Lemuria. pap. 1.50 o.p. (ISBN 0-425-03435-6). Berkley Pub.

--Thongor at the End of Time. 1968. pap. 1.75 (ISBN 0-446-94332-0). Warner Bks.

--Thongor Fights the Pirates of Takakus. pap. 1.25 o.p. (ISBN 0-425-03147-0). Berkley Pub.

--Thongor in the City of Magicians. 1968. pap. 1.75 (ISBN 0-446-94208-1). Warner Bks.

Carter, Lin, jt. auth. see Sprague de Camp, L.

Carter, Lin, ed. Weird Tales, No. 1. 288p. (Orig.). 1981. pap. 2.50 (ISBN 0-89083-714-7). Zebra.

--Weird Tales, No. 2. 288p. (Orig.). 1981. pap. 2.50 (ISBN 0-89083-715-5). Zebra.

--The Year's Best Fantasy Stories, No. 4. (Science Fiction Ser.). 1978. pap. 1.75 o.p. (ISBN 0-87997-425-7, UE1425). DAW Bks.

Carter, Linda & Culinary Arts Institute Staff. The Food Processor Cookbook. Finnegan, Edward G., ed. LC 78-54620. (Adventures in Cooking Ser). (Illus.). 1980. cancelled (ISBN 0-8326-0608-1, 1517); pap. 3.95 (ISBN 0-8326-0607-3, 2517). Delair.

Carter, Lynn T., et al. The Thinking Skills Workbook: A Cognitive Skills Remediation Manual for Adults. (Illus.). 220p. 1980. pap. 13.75 (ISBN 0-398-04049-4). C C Thomas.

Carter, Lynne C. Guide to Cellular Energetics. LC 72-5397. (Illus.). 1973. pap. text ed. 6.95x (ISBN 0-7167-0598-2); tchr's manual avail. W H Freeman.

Carter, M. P. Education, Employment & Leisure. 1963. pap. 4.40 o.p. (ISBN 0-08-010321-9). Pergamon.

Carter, M. R. A Dictionary of Chess Openings. (Illus.). 320p. 1979. 15.00 o.p. (ISBN 0-498-01655-2). A S Barnes.

Carter, Mary E. Edgar Cayce on Prophecy. 208p. 1968. pap. 2.25 (ISBN 0-446-92694-9). Warner Bks.

Carter, Mary E. & McGarey, William A. Edgar Cayce on Healing. 208p. 1972. pap. 2.25 (ISBN 0-446-92692-2). Warner Bks.

Carter, Melvin W., et al, eds. Management of Low-Level Radioactive Waste, 2 vols. 1979. 155.00 (ISBN 0-08-023907-2). Pergamon.

Carter, Michael. Archaeology. (Illus.). 176p. 1980. 12.95 (ISBN 0-7137-0861-1, Pub. by Blandford Pr England); pap. 6.95 (ISBN 0-7137-1067-5, Pub. by Blandford Pr England). Sterling.

--Crafts of China. LC 76-51862. 1977. 9.95 o.p. (ISBN 0-385-13119-4). Doubleday.

Carter, Mildred C. & Dlugacz, Dorothy H. Improving Your Vocabulary. (gr. 7-12). 1980. pap. text ed. 5.95 (ISBN 0-671-18432-6). Monarch Pr.

Carter, Nicholas, ed. Development, Growth & Aging. 169p. 1980. 27.50x (ISBN 0-85664-861-2, Pub. by Croom Helm Ltd England). Biblio Dist.

--Development, Growth, & Aging. 176p. 1980. 25.00x (ISBN 0-85664-861-2, Pub. by Croom Helm England). State Mutual Bk.

Carter, Nick. Beirut Incident. (Nick Carter Ser.). 192p. (Orig.). 1981. pap. 1.95 (ISBN 0-441-05381-5). Charter Bks.

--The G Man. (Nick Carter Ser.). 224p. (Orig.). 1981. pap. 2.25 (ISBN 0-441-69656-2). Charter Bks.

--The Golden Bull. (Nick Carter Ser.). 224p. (Orig.). 1981. pap. 2.25 (ISBN 0-441-29782-X). Charter Bks.

--Katmandu Contract. (Nick Carter Ser.). 176p. (Orig.). 1981. pap. 2.25 (ISBN 0-441-43201-8). Charter Bks.

--The Ouster Conspiracy. (Nick Carter Ser.). 224p. (Orig.). 1981. pap. 2.25 (ISBN 0-441-16048-4). Charter Bks.

--Six Bloody Summer Days. (The Nick Carter Ser.). 174p. 1981. pap. 1.95 (ISBN 0-441-76839-3). Charter Bks.

--Society of Nine. (Nick Carter Ser.). 224p. (Orig.). 1981. pap. 2.25 (ISBN 0-441-77233-1). Charter Bks.

--Turkish Bloodbath. (Nick Carter Ser.). 224p. (Orig.). 1981. pap. 2.25 (ISBN 0-441-82726-8). Charter Bks.

--The Ultimate Code. (Nick Carter Ser.). 172p. 1981. pap. 2.25 (ISBN 0-441-84309-3). Charter Bks.

Carter, Noel V. The Lazarus Inheritance. 1976. pap. 1.25 o.p. (ISBN 0-445-00432-0). Popular Lib.

--Miss Hungerford's Handsome Hero. (Orig.). 1981. pap. 1.50 (ISBN 0-440-15312-3). Dell.

Carter, Pat H. Vivamos En el Espiritu Cada Dia. 160p. 1979. pap. 2.60 (ISBN 0-311-09089-3). Casa Bautista.

Carter, Paul A. Another Part of the Twenties. LC 76-27679. 1977. 13.50x (ISBN 0-231-04134-9); pap. 7.50x (ISBN 0-231-04135-7). Columbia U Pr.

--The Creation of Tomorrow: Fifty Years of Magazine Science Fiction. (Illus.). 330p. 1980. pap. 6.95 (ISBN 0-231-04211-6). Columbia U Pr.

--The Creation of Tomorrow: Fifty Years of Magazine Science Fiction. LC 77-5606. (Illus.). 1977. 16.00x (ISBN 0-231-04210-8). Columbia U Pr.

--Little America: Town at the End of the World. LC 79-13727. (Illus.). 1979. 16.95 (ISBN 0-231-04682-0). Columbia U Pr.

Carter, Peter. The Sentinels. 200p. (gr. 7 up). 1980. 10.95 (ISBN 0-19-271438-4). Oxford U Pr.

Carter, R. J., jt. auth. see Ronald, D. W.

Carter, Randolph. The World of Flo Ziegfeld. 1974. 9.95 o.p. (ISBN 0-236-31053-4, Pub. by Paul Elek). Merrimack Bk Serv.

Carter, Richard D., jt. ed. see Carter, Judith Q.

Carter, Robert E. Arson Investigation. 1978. text ed. 13.95x (ISBN 0-02-472400-9). Macmillan.

Carter, Robert G. Four Brothers in Blue. LC 78-56909. 1978. Repr. of 1913 ed. 16.95 (ISBN 0-292-72426-8). U of Tex Pr.

Carter, Robert M. & Klein, Malcolm. Back on the Street: The Diversion of Juvenile Offenders. (Illus.). 400p. 1976. pap. 12.95 (ISBN 0-13-055319-0). P-H.

Carter, Robert M., jt. auth. see Tubbs, Stewart L.

Carter, Robert M., ed. Communication in Organizations: An Annotated Bibliography & Sourcebook. LC 73-161194. (Management Information Guide Ser.: No. 25). 1972. 30.00 (ISBN 0-8103-0825-8). Gale.

Carter, Robert M. & Wilkins, Leslie T., eds. Probation, Parole, & Community Corrections. 2nd ed. LC 75-44332. 1976. text ed. 22.95 (ISBN 0-471-13845-2). Wiley.

Carter, Ronald L. & Hill, Kim Q. The Criminal's Image of the City. rev. ed. (Illus.). 1979. 13.75 (ISBN 0-08-024633-8). Pergamon.

Carter, Rosemary. Desert Dream. (Harlequin Presents Ser.). 192p. 1980. pap. 1.50 (ISBN 0-373-10397-2, Pub. by Harlequin). PB.

--Face in the Portrait. (Harlequin Presents Ser.). 192p. (Orig.). 1981. pap. 1.50 (ISBN 0-373-10410-3, Pub. by Harlequin). PB.

--Man in the Shadows. (Harlequin Romances Ser.). 192p. (Orig.). 1981. pap. 1.25 (ISBN 0-373-02380-4, Pub. by Harlequin). PB.

Carter, Roy. Classical Music Quiz with Richard Baker. LC 80-67581. 128p. 1980. 11.95 (ISBN 0-7153-7819-8). David & Charles.

Carter, Roy E., tr. see Schoenberg, Arnold.

Carter, Rubin. Sixteenth Round. (Illus.). 1975. pap. 2.50 o.s.i. (ISBN 0-446-91020-1). Warner Bks.

Carter, Samuel. The Cavalry: Confederate & Union Troops & Their Leaders in the Civil War. LC 76-62758. 1979. 15.00 o.p. (ISBN 0-685-96173-7). St Martin.

Carter, Samuel, III. Cherokee Sunset- Nation Betrayed. LC 74-33634. 336p. 1976. 9.95 o.p. (ISBN 0-385-06735-6). Doubleday.

--The Final Fortress: The Campaign for Vicksburg, 1862-1863. (Illus.). 384p. 1980. 19.95 (ISBN 0-312-28943-X). St Martin.

--Happy Dolphins. (Illus.). (YA) (gr. 7-9). 1972. pap. 1.25 (ISBN 0-671-29726-0). PB.

Carter, Samuel, 3rd. Incredible Great White Fleet. LC 77-129747. (Illus.). (gr. 7 up). 1971. 4.95 o.s.i. (ISBN 0-02-717770-X, CCPr). Macmillan.

--The Siege of Atlanta, 1864. 1976. pap. 1.95 o.p. (ISBN 0-345-24424-9). Ballantine.

Carter, Stanley N. Practical Instruction in Figure Drawing. (A Promotion of the Arts Library Book). (Illus.). 103p. 1981. 27.45 (ISBN 0-86650-002-2). Gloucester Art.

Carter, Stephen K., et al. Chemotherapy of Cancer. LC 77-8142. 1977. 17.95 (ISBN 0-471-02935-1, Pub by Wiley-Medical). Wiley.

Carter, T. Donald, jt. auth. see Mochi, Ugo.

Carter, Timothy J., et al, eds. Rural Crime: Integrating Research & Prevention. 1981. text ed. 25.00 (ISBN 0-86598-023-3). Allanheld.

Carter, Vernon G. & Dale, Tom. Topsoil & Civilization. rev. ed. (Illus.). 240p. 1974. pap. 5.95x (ISBN 0-8061-1107-0). U of Okla Pr.

Carter, Vertie Lee. How to Get a Career Job. 1978. pap. 4.00 o.p. (ISBN 0-682-49159-4). Exposition.

Carter, Virginia L., ed. Annual Fund Ideas. 48p. 1979. pap. 10.50 (ISBN 0-89964-016-8). CASE.

Carter, Virginia L. & Garigan, Catherine, eds. A Marketing Approach to Student Recruitment. 1979. pap. 10.50 (ISBN 0-89964-031-1). CASE.

Carter, W. Horace, jt. auth. see Hamlet, John N.

Carter, W. J. Papermachine Clothing. LC 74-28444. 227p. 1975. 31.95 o.p. (ISBN 0-470-13847-5). Halsted Pr.

Carter, Walter. Insects in Relation to Plant Disease. 2nd ed. LC 73-4362. 62.50 (ISBN 0-471-13849-5, Pub. by Wiley-Interscience). Wiley.

Carter, William E. First Book of Bolivia. (First Bks). (Illus.). (gr. 4-6). 1963. PLB 4.90 o.p. (ISBN 0-531-00486-4). Watts.

--The First Book of South America. rev. ed. LC 72-249. (First Bks). (Illus.). 96p. (gr. 4-6). 1972. PLB 4.90 o.p. (ISBN 0-531-00636-0). Watts.

Carter, William E., ed. Cannabis in Costa Rica: A Study of Chronic Marihuana Use. LC 80-14726. (Illus.). 1980. text ed. 17.50x (ISBN 0-89727-008-8). Inst Study Human.

Carter, William E., jt. ed. see Margolis, Maxine L.

Carter, William T. Soaring. Glines, Carroll V., ed. LC 72-92863. (Air Force Academy Ser.). 192p. 1973. 6.95 o.s.i. (ISBN 0-02-522480-8). Macmillan.

Carterette, Edward C. & Jones, Margaret H. Alphabetic & Phonetic Texts of Informal Speech with Statistical Analyses. 1975. 42.50x (ISBN 0-520-01476-6). U of Cal Pr.

Carterette, Edward C. & Friedman, Morton P., eds. Handbook of Perception. Incl. Vol. 1. 1974. 40.00 (ISBN 0-12-161901-X); Vol. 2. 1974. 48.00 (ISBN 0-12-161902-8); Vol. 4. Hearing. 1978. 49.50 (ISBN 0-12-161904-4); Vol. 5. 1975. 48.00 (ISBN 0-12-161905-2); Vol. 6, 2 pts. 1978. Pt. A, Testing & Smelling. 30.00 (ISBN 0-686-62060-7); Pt. B, Feeling & Hurting. 30.00 (ISBN 0-12-161922-2); Vol. 7. 1975. 48.00 (ISBN 0-12-161907-9); Vol. 8. Perceptual Coding. 1978. 40.00, by subscription 35.00 (ISBN 0-12-161908-7); Vol. 9. Perceptual Processing. 1978. 31.50, by subscription 25.00 (ISBN 0-12-161909-5); Vol. 10. Perceptual Ecology. 1978. 43.00, by subscription 34.00 (ISBN 0-12-161910-9). Acad Pr.

Carteron, Henri. La Notion De Force Dans le Systeme D' Aristote. LC 78-66622. (Ancient Philosophy Ser.). 293p. 1980. lib. bdg. 28.50 (ISBN 0-8240-9605-3). Garland Pub.

Cartes Tarides. Taride Guide of Paris & Its Suburbs. (Illus.). 368p. 1972. plastic 6.95 o.p. (ISBN 0-88332-014-2, 4896). Larousse.

Cartey, Wilfred. Black Images. LC 75-113096. 1970. text ed. 9.40x o.p. (ISBN 0-8077-1145-4); pap. 7.75x (ISBN 0-8077-1144-6). Tchrs Coll.

Carthew, John A. Physical Geography Workbook. rev. ed. (Illus.). 68p. 1981. pap. text ed. 4.70x (ISBN 0-89179-218-X). Tam's Bks.

Cartier, Dean, ed Ed Cartier: The Known & the Unknown. 1977. 15.00 (ISBN 0-938192-01-9). De La Ree.

Cartier, J. P., jt. auth. see Groueff, S.

Cartier, Jacques. A Shorte & Briefe Narration of the Two Navigations to Newe Fraunce. Florio, J., tr. LC 73-6110. (English Experience Ser.: No. 718). 1975. Repr. of 1580 ed. 8.00 (ISBN 90-221-0718-3). Walter J Johnson.

Cartier, John O. The Modern Deer Hunter. (Funk & W Bk.). (Illus.). 1977. 10.95 o.p. (ISBN 0-308-10270-3, TYC-T). T Y Crowell.

Cartier, John O., ed. Twenty Great Trophy Hunts. 1980. 17.95 (ISBN 0-679-51379-5). McKay.

Cartier, Raymond, ed. see Groueff, S. & Cartier, J. P.

Cartier-Bresson, Henri. Henri Cartier-Bresson: Photographer. LC 79-88493. (Illus.). 1979. 60.00 (ISBN 0-8212-0756-3, 357715). NYGS.

Cartland, Barbara. Afraid, No. 137. 160p. (Orig.). 1981. pap. 1.75 (ISBN 0-553-14509-6). Bantam.

--The Bitter Winds of Love, No. 76. 1978. pap. 1.50 o.s.i. (ISBN 0-515-04544-6). Jove Pubns.

--The Captive Heart. pap. 1.75 (ISBN 0-515-05566-2). Jove Pubns.

--The Coin of Love. pap. 1.75 (ISBN 0-515-05560-3). Jove Pubns.

--The Complacent Wife. (Barbara Cartland Ser.: No. 9). 272p. 1981. pap. 1.75 (ISBN 0-515-05568-9). Jove Pubns.

--Count the Stars. (Barbara Cartland Ser.: No. 10). 192p. (Orig.). 1981. pap. 1.75 (ISBN 0-515-05860-2). Jove Pubns.

--The Dawn of Love: No. 125. 192p. (Orig.). 1980. pap. 1.75 o.p. (ISBN 0-553-13830-8). Bantam.

--Debt of Honor: No. 16. 1978. pap. 1.50 o.s.i. (ISBN 0-515-04831-3). Jove Pubns.

--Desire of the Heart. 224p. 1980. pap. 1.75 (ISBN 0-515-05497-6). Jove Pubns.

--Dollars for the Duke. 160p. (Orig.). 1981. pap. 1.95 (ISBN 0-553-14650-5). Bantam.

--The Dream Within, No. 62. 1978. pap. 1.50 o.s.i. (ISBN 0-515-04593-4). Jove Pubns.

--Dreams Do Come True, No. 141. (Orig.). 1981. pap. 1.95 (ISBN 0-553-14750-1). Bantam.

--The Enchanting Evil: No. 5. 1978. pap. 1.50 o.s.i. (ISBN 0-515-04812-7). Jove Pubns.

--The Golden Gondola. (Barbara Cartland Ser.). (Orig.). pap. 1.75 (ISBN 0-515-05509-3). Jove Pubns.

--The Heart of the Clan. (Barbara Cartland Ser.: No. 13). 192p. (Orig.). 1981. pap. 1.75 (ISBN 0-515-05929-3). Jove Pubns.

--The Horizons of Love. (Barbara Cartland Ser.). (Orig.). pap. 1.75 (ISBN 0-515-05569-7). Jove Pubns.

--The Innocent Heiress, No. 15. 1979. pap. 1.50 o.p. (ISBN 0-685-63662-3, 04880-1). Jove Pubns.

--Journey to Paradise. 1979. 7.95 o.p. (ISBN 0-525-13756-4). Dutton.

--The Kiss of Life, No. 136. 144p. 1981. pap. 1.75 (ISBN 0-553-14504-5). Bantam.

--The Kiss of the Devil. (Barbara Cartland Ser.: No. 18). 1981. pap. 1.75 (ISBN 0-515-05957-9). Jove Pubns.

--The Light of Love: Lines to Live by, Day by Day. (Orig.). 1981. pap. 2.50 (ISBN 0-440-15402-2). Dell.

--Lights of Love, No. 46. 1978. pap. 1.50 o.p. (ISBN 0-685-86779-X). Jove Pubns.

--The Lioness & the Lily, No. 135. 144p. 1981. pap. 1.75 (ISBN 0-553-14503-7). Bantam.

--Lost Enchantment. (Barbara Cartland Ser.: No. 15). 256p. 1981. pap. 1.75 (ISBN 0-515-05942-0). Jove Pubns.

--Lost Laughter. 1980. 9.95 (ISBN 0-525-14891-4). Dutton.

--Lost Laughter, No. 131. 176p. 1980. pap. 1.75 (ISBN 0-553-13985-1). Bantam.

--Love for Sale. (Barbara Cartland Ser.: No. 129). (Orig.). 1980. pap. 1.75 (ISBN 0-553-13984-3). Bantam.

--Love for Sale. 1980. 9.95 (ISBN 0-525-14906-6). Dutton.

--Love Has His Way. LC 80-108. 1979. 6.95 (ISBN 0-87272-085-3, Duron Bks). Brodart.

--Love in the Moon, No. 138. 160p. (Orig.). 1981. pap. 1.95 (ISBN 0-553-14585-1). Bantam.

--Love Is the Enemy, No. 9. 1978. pap. 1.50 o.s.i. (ISBN 0-515-04565-9). Jove Pubns.

--Love on the Run. (Barbara Cartland Ser.: No. 17). 256p. (Orig.). 1981. pap. 1.75 (ISBN 0-515-05956-0). Jove Pubns.

--Money, Magic, & Marriage. (Orig.). pap. 1.75 (ISBN 0-515-05565-4). Jove Pubns.

--A Night of Gaiety, No. 142. (Orig.). 1981. pap. 1.95 (ISBN 0-553-14791-9). Bantam.

--Pride & the Poor Princes, No. 134. 160p. (Orig.). 1981. pap. 1.75 (ISBN 0-553-13032-3). Bantam.

--Punished with Love. 160p. (Orig.). 1980. pap. 1.75 (ISBN 0-553-13910-X). Bantam.

--The Secret Fear, No. 23. 1977. pap. 1.50 o.s.i. (ISBN 0-515-04461-X). Jove Pubns.

--Signpost to Love, No. 131. 144p. (Orig.). 1981. pap. 1.75 (ISBN 0-553-14360-3). Bantam.

--A Song of Love. 208p. 1980. pap. 1.75 (ISBN 0-515-05444-5). Jove Pubns.

--Stars in My Heart. 1978. pap. 1.50 o.p. (ISBN 0-515-04825-9). Jove Pubns.

--Stars in My Heart. (Barbara Carrtland Ser.: No. 12). 1981. pap. 1.75 (ISBN 0-515-05570-0). Jove Pubns.

--Sweet Adventure, No. 17. 1978. pap. 1.50 (ISBN 0-515-04137-8). Jove Pubns.

--Sweet Enchantress. 1979. pap. 1.50 (ISBN 0-515-05100-4). Jove Pubns.

--Theft of a Heart, No. 67. 1978. 1.50 o.s.i. (ISBN 0-515-04650-7). Jove Pubns.

--This Time It's Love. 1979. pap. 1.50 o.s.i. (ISBN 0-515-05101-2). Jove Pubns.

--Twists & Turns of Love. LC 78-486. 1978. 6.95 (ISBN 0-87272-036-5, Duron Bks). Brodart.

--The Unknown Heart. 1979. pap. 1.75 (ISBN 0-515-05859-9). Jove Pubns.

--The Unknown Heart. (Barbara Cartland Ser.: No. 11). 176p. (Orig.). 1981. pap. 1.75 (ISBN 0-515-05859-9). Jove Pubns.

--The Unpredictable Bride, No. 6. 1977. pap. 1.75 o.s.i. (ISBN 0-515-05567-0). Jove Pubns.

--A Virgin in Paris. (Barbara Cartland Ser.: No. 14). 208p. 1981. pap. 1.75 (ISBN 0-515-05571-9). Jove Pubns.

--The Waltz of Hearts, No. 139. 160p. (Orig.). 1981. pap. 1.95 (ISBN 0-553-14586-X). Bantam.

--Where Is Love, No. 71. 1978. pap. 1.50 o.s.i. (ISBN 0-515-04476-8). Jove Pubns.

--Who Can Deny Love. LC 79-28822. 1979. 6.95 (ISBN 0-87272-086-1, Duron Bks). Brodart.

--Wings of Ecstasy. (Barbara Cartland Ser.: No. 16). (Orig.). 1981. pap. 1.75 (ISBN 0-515-05955-2). Jove Pubns.

Cartledge, Paul. Sparta & Lakonia: A Regional History Thirteen Hundred to Three Sixty-Two B.C. (States & Cities of Ancient Greece Ser.). 1979. 25.00x (ISBN 0-7100-0377-3). Routledge & Kegan.

Cartlidge, David R. & Dungan, David L. Documents for the Study of the Gospels. LC 79-21341. 300p. (Orig.). 1980. 14.95 (1-640); pap. 8.95 (ISBN -08006-1640-5, 1-1640). Fortress.

Cartmell & Fowles. Valency & Molecular Structure. 4th ed. 1977. 16.95 (ISBN 0-408-70809-3). Butterworths.

Cartmell, Thomas K. Shenandoah Valley Pioneers & Their Descendants. LC 64-1062. (Illus.). 572p. Repr. of 1909 ed. 32.50 (ISBN 0-686-63647-3). Va Bk.

Cartmell, Van H., ed. Plot Outlines of One Hundred Famous Plays. 8.50 (ISBN 0-8446-0539-5). Peter Smith.

Cartmell, Van H. & Cerf, Bennett, eds. Twenty-Four Favorite One-Act Plays. LC 58-13274. pap. 3.95 (ISBN 0-385-06617-1, C423, Dolp). Doubleday.

Cartnal, Alan. California Crazy. LC 80-27315. 256p. 1981. 9.95 (ISBN 0-395-28213-6). HM.

Cartner, William. Fun with Fossils. (Learning with Fun Ser.). (Illus.). (gr. 5 up). 1977. 11.50x (ISBN 0-7180-0713-1, LTB). Soccer.

Cartographic Dept. of the Clarendon Pr. Oxford Economic Atlas of the World. 4th ed. (Illus.). 248p. 1972. 35.00 (ISBN 0-19-894106-4); pap. 9.95x (ISBN 0-19-894107-2). Oxford U Pr.

Carton, Dana & Caprio, Anthony. En Francais: Practical Conversational French. 2nd ed. 1980. text ed. write for info. (ISBN 0-442-21215-1); write for info. instr's. manual (ISBN 0-442-21218-6); write for info. tape (ISBN 0-442-21219-4); write for info. cassette (ISBN 0-442-21220-8). D Van Nostrand.

Carton, Jane. A Child's Garland. 1942. 6.95 o.p. (ISBN 0-571-05352-1, Pub. by Faber & Faber). Merrimack Bk Serv.

Cartoonists' Guild. The Art in Cartooning. (Illus.). 1979. pap. 9.95 o.p. (ISBN 0-684-16398-5, ScribT). Scribner.

Cartter, Allan M. Ph.D's & the Academic Labor Market. LC 75-38700. (Carnegie Commission on Higher Education Ser). 1976. 15.95 o.p. (ISBN 0-07-010132-9, P&RB). McGraw.

Cartwright, Ann. How Many Children? (Direct Editions Ser.). (Orig.). 1976. pap. 16.50x (ISBN 0-7100-8341-6). Routledge & Kegan.

--Patients & Their Doctors: A Study of General Practice. (Reports of the Institute of Community Studies). 1967. 23.50 (ISBN 0-7100-3919-0). Routledge & Kegan.

Cartwright, Ann, et al. Life Before Death. (Social Studies in Medical Care). 310p. 1973. 22.50x (ISBN 0-7100-7540-5). Routledge & Kegan.

Cartwright, Betty, jt. auth. see Cartwright, Raymond.

Cartwright, Carol & Forsberg, Sara J. Exceptional Previews: A Self-Evaluation Handbook for Special Education Students. 1979. pap. text ed. 8.95x (ISBN 0-534-00629-9). Wadsworth Pub.

Cartwright, Frederick F. A Social History of Medicine. LC 76-41898. (Themes in British Social History Ser.). 1977. pap. text ed. 10.95x (ISBN 0-582-48394-8). Longman.

Cartwright, John M. Farm & Ranch Real Estate Law. LC 70-189071. 1972. 45.00 (ISBN 0-686-14537-2). Lawyers Co-Op.

Cartwright, John R. Politics in Sierra Leone, Nineteen Forty-Seven to Nineteen Sixty-Seven. (Scholarly Reprint Ser.). 35.00x (ISBN 0-8020-7103-1). U of Toronto Pr.

Cartwright, Justin. The Horse of Darius. 1981. pap. 3.50 (ISBN 0-440-13761-6). Dell.

Cartwright, L. E., jt. auth. see Goodhew, P. J.

Cartwright, Nellie P. Bless the Nightingale: Ama Al ruisenor. LC 77-85799. 1977. 3.00 (ISBN 0-9601482-1-3). N P Cartwright.

Cartwright, Ralph & Russell, R. T. The Welshpool & Lanfair Light Railway. LC 80-70290. (Illus.). 208p. 1981. 19.95 (ISBN 0-7153-8151-2). David & Charles.

Cartwright, Raymond & Cartwright, Betty. Holy Island of Lindisfarne. (Island Ser.). (Illus.). 144p. 14.50 o.p. (ISBN 0-7153-7137-1). David & Charles.

Cartwright, Richard M. Design of Urban Space: A GLC Manual. 208p. 1981. 44.95 (ISBN 0-470-27066-7). Halsted Pr.

Cartwright, Rosalind D. Night Life: Explorations in Dreaming. (Illus.). 1977. 10.95 (ISBN 0-13-622324-9, Spec); pap. 4.95 (ISBN 0-13-622316-8). P-H.

--Primer on Sleep & Dreaming. LC 77-79453. (Topics in Clinical Psychology). (Illus.). 1978. pap. text ed. 7.50 (ISBN 0-201-00941-2). A-W.

Cartwright, Thomas. A Confutation of the Rhemists Translation, Glosses & Annotations on the New Testament. LC 71-171737. (English Experience Ser.: No. 364). 830p. 1971. Repr. of 1618 ed. 114.00 (ISBN 90-221-0364-1). Walter J Johnson.

Carty, Charles M. Padre Pio: The Stigmatist. (Illus.). 1977. pap. 6.00 (ISBN 0-89555-054-7, 115). TAN Bks Pubs.

Carty, T. & Smith, A. Power & Manoeuvrability. 1978. text ed. 18.25x (ISBN 0-905470-04-4). Humanities.

Caruana, Russell A. A Guide to Organizing a Health Care Fiscal Services Division with Job Descriptions for Key Functions. 2nd ed. 80p. 1981. pap. write for info. (ISBN 0-930228-13-8). Hospital Finan.

Carus, Paul. Karma; Nirvana: Two Buddhist Tales. LC 73-82781. (Illus.). 160p. 1973. 10.95 (ISBN 0-87548-249-X); pap. 4.95. Open Court.

Caruso, Dee, jt. auth. see Gardner, Gerald.

Caruso, Domenick & Weidenborner, Stephen. Creating Contexts: A Practical Approach to Writing. LC 76-55159. (Illus.). 1977. pap. text ed. 6.95x (ISBN 0-393-09101-5); tchrs manual gratis (ISBN 0-393-09107-4). Norton.

Caruso, Enrico & Tetrazzini, Louisa. How to Sing-Art of Singing, 2 vols. in 1. LC 74-23417. 1975. Repr. of 1909 ed. lib. bdg. 19.50 (ISBN 0-306-70674-1). Da Capo.

Caruso, Luiz A., ed. see Leenhouts, Keith.

Caruso, Luiz A., tr. see Nee, T. S.

Caruth, Donald L., et al. Office & Administrative Management. 3rd ed. 1970. text ed. 18.95 (ISBN 0-13-630996-8). P-H.

Caruthers, Clifford M., ed. see Lardner, Ring.

Carvell, Fred & Tadlock, Max. It's Not Too Late. 1971. pap. 4.95x (ISBN 0-02-472500-5, 47250). Macmillan.

Carver, Belford E. & Cloud, Charles D. Introduction to Business: A Programmed Approach. 1975. pap. text ed. 9.50 o.p. (ISBN 0-8403-1125-7). Kendall-Hunt.

Carver, C. C. Church of God Doctrines. 180p. 1948. pap. 2.00. Faith Pub Hse.

Carver, D. K. Introduction to Business Data Processing: With Basic, Fortran & Cobol Programming. 2nd ed. LC 78-19131. 1979. text ed. 21.95 (ISBN 0-471-03091-0); tchrs. manual (ISBN 0-471-03092-9); wkbk. 9.50 (ISBN 0-471-03998-5). Wiley.

Carver, D. Keith. Beginning Basic. LC 79-20457. 1980. pap. text ed. 12.95 (ISBN 0-8185-0368-8). Brooks-Cole.

Carver, Deenie B., jt. auth. see Dillow, Louise B.

Carver, Fred D., jt. auth. see Sergiovanni, Thomas J.

Carver, Humphrey. Compassionate Landscape. LC 75-22280. (Illus.). 1975. pap. 6.00 (ISBN 0-8020-6269-5). U of Toronto Pr.

Carver, Jeffrey. Star Riggers Way. 1978. pap. 1.75 o.s.i. (ISBN 0-440-17619-0). Dell.

Carver, Jeffrey A. Panglor. (Orig.). 1980. pap. 1.95 (ISBN 0-440-17310-8). Dell.

Carver, Jonathan. Travels Thru Interior Parts of North America. Repr. 15.00 o.p. (ISBN 0-87018-007-X). Ross.

Carver, Larry, ed. The Plays of Hugh Kelly. LC 78-66653. (Eighteenth Century English Drama Ser.). 1980. lib. bdg. 50.00 (ISBN 0-8240-3600-X). Garland Pub.

Carver, Michael. El Alamein. 1979. 24.00 (ISBN 0-7134-2148-7, Pub. by Batsford England). David & Charles.

Carver, Norman. Iberian Villages: Spain & Portugal. 26.95 (ISBN 0-932076-02-5); pap. 17.95 (ISBN 0-932076-03-3). Morgan.

Carver, Raymond. Furious Seasons & Other Stories. (Noel Young Bks.). 1977. cloth o.p. 10.00 (ISBN 0-88496-114-1); pap. 3.95 (ISBN 0-88496-113-3). Capra Pr.

--What We Talk About When We Talk About Love. LC 80-21752. 176p. 1981. 9.95 (ISBN 0-394-51684-2). Knopf.

Carver, Sally S. The American Postcard Guide to Tuck. rev. ed. (Illus.). 1980. pap. 7.95 (ISBN 0-686-18747-4). Carves.

Carver, Terrell, ed. see Zeleny, Jindrich.

Carver, Thomas N. Essential Factors of Social Evolution. 1935. 17.50 (ISBN 0-89020-007-6). Brown Bk.

Carver, Tina K. & Fotinos, S. Douglas. A Conversation Book: English in Everyday Life, Bk. 1. (Illus.). 1977. pap. text ed. 7.50 (ISBN 0-13-172239-5). P-H.

--A Conversation Book: English in Everyday Life, Bk. 2. (Illus.). 1977. pap. text ed. 7.50 (ISBN 0-13-172247-6). P-H.

Carvic, Heron. Odds on Miss Seeton. LC 75-9348. (Harper Novel of Suspense). 160p. (YA) 1975. 7.95 o.s.i. (ISBN 0-06-010654-9, HarpT). Har-Row.

Carvill. Famous Names in Engineering. 1981. text ed. price not set (ISBN 0-408-00536-X). Butterworth.

Carvill, J. Student Engineer's Companion: A Handbook for Engineers, Draftsmen & Students. Orig. Title: Mechanical Engineering Components. (Illus.). 1980. pap. 12.50 (ISBN 0-408-00438-X). Butterworths.

Cary & Weinberg. The Social Fabric: Volume 1. 3rd ed. (Orig.). 1980. pap. 8.95 (ISBN 0-316-13078-8). Little.

--The Social Fabric: Volume 2. 3rd ed. 1980. pap. text ed. 8.95 (ISBN 0-316-13074-5). Little.

Cary, Beth. The Greater Love. 1922. 3.00 o.p. (ISBN 0-685-88270-5). Metaphysical.

Cary, Bob. The Big Wilderness Canoe Manual. (Illus.). 1978. 12.95 o.p. (ISBN 0-679-50862-7); pap. 6.95 o.p. (ISBN 0-679-50864-3). McKay.

Cary, Emily. My High Love Calling. (YA) 1977. 5.95 (ISBN 0-685-80404-6, Avalon). Bouregy.

Cary, Howard B. Modern Welding Technology. LC 78-2966. (Illus.). 1979. 28.00 (ISBN 0-13-599290-7); text ed. 21.00 o.p. (ISBN 0-686-67267-4). P-H.

Cary, James, jt. auth. see Worcester, Tom.

Cary, Jane. Best Baths. LC 80-67154. (Illus., Orig.). 1980. 12.95 (ISBN 0-932944-19-1); pap. 5.95 (ISBN 0-932944-20-5). Creative Homeowner.

Cary, Joyce. The Captive & the Free. 369p. 1976. Repr. of 1959 ed. lib. bdg. 15.75x (ISBN 0-89244-071-6). Queens Hse.

--Herself Surprised. 275p. 1976. Repr. of 1948 ed. lib. bdg. 13.95x (ISBN 0-89244-070-8). Queens Hse.

--Herself Surprised. 1980. pap. 4.95 (ISBN 0-7145-0270-7). Riverrun NY.

--Prisoner of Grace. 301p. 1976. Repr. of 1952 ed. lib. bdg. 14.95x (ISBN 0-89244-072-4). Queens Hse.

Cary, M., ed. see Suetonius.

Cary, Norman R. Christian Criticism in the Twentieth Century. (National University Publications Literary Criticism Ser.). 1976. 11.50 (ISBN 0-8046-9104-5, Natl U). Kennikat.

Cary, Patrick. The Poems of Patrick Cary. Delany, Veronica, ed. 1978. 29.50x (ISBN 0-19-812566-6). Oxford U Pr.

Cary, Richard, ed. see Jewett, Sarah O.

Cary, William & Eisenberg, Melvin A. Cases & Materials on Corporations. 5th ed. LC 80-18042. (University Casebook Ser.). 1829p. pap. 2.50 (ISBN 0-88277-012-8). Foundation Pr.

Cary, William L. & Eisenberg, Melvin A. Cases & Materials on Corporations. abr. 5th ed. LC 80-68866. (University Casebook Ser.). 1085p. 1980. text ed. 21.50 (ISBN 0-88277-017-9). Foundation Pr.

Carynnk, Marco, tr. see Kotsiubynsky, Mykhailo.

Carynnk, Marco, tr. see Stern, August.

Carynnyk, Marco, tr. see Osadchy, Mykhaylo.

Carynnyk, Marco, tr. see Stern, August.

Casadio, Gian P. The Economic Challenge of the Arabs. LC 75-35111. 1976. 22.95 (ISBN 0-347-01067-9, 99390-5, Pub. by Saxon Hse). Lexington Bks.

Casady, Cort, jt. auth. see Davidson, John.

Casady, R. B. & Jawin, P. B. Commerical Rabbit Raising. (Illus.). 69p. pap. 3.00 (ISBN 0-8466-6054-7, SJU54). Shorey.

Casagrande, Peter J. Unity in Hardy's Novels: "Repetitive Symmetries". 272p. Date not set. 20.00x (ISBN 0-7006-0209-7). Regents Pr KS. Postponed.

Casalis, George. Portrait of Karl Barth. Brown, Robert M., tr. LC 80-25829. viii, 135p. 1981. Repr. of 1963 ed. lib. bdg. 17.50x (ISBN 0-313-22775-6, CAKB). Greenwood.

Casals, Felipe G. The Syncretic Society. Meyer, Alfred G., ed. Daniels, Guy, tr. from Fr. LC 80-5455. 100p. 1980. 15.00 (ISBN 0-87332-176-6). M E Sharpe.

Casanova, Giacomo. History of My Life, Vols. 1 & 2. Trask, Willard R., tr. LC 66-22274. (A Helen & Kurt Wolff Bk). (Illus.). 679p. 1967. slipcase 10.00 o.p. (ISBN 0-15-141080-1). HarBraceJ.

Casanova, Pablo G. The Fallacy of Social Science Research: A Critical Examination & New Qualitative Model. (PPS on Social Policy Ser.). 75p. 1981. 15.00 (ISBN 0-08-027549-4). Pergamon.

Casanova, Richard L. & Ratkevich, Ronald P. Illustrated Guide to Fossil Collecting. rev. ed. (Illus.). 212p. 1981. lib. bdg. 9.95 (ISBN 0-87961-112-X); pap. 5.95 (ISBN 0-87961-113-8). Naturegraph.

Casares. Diccionario Ideologico. (Span). 47.50x (ISBN 0-686-00066-8). Colton Bk.

Casares, Angel J. Carso de Filosofia. rev., 2nd ed. 238p. 1980. text ed. write for info. (ISBN 0-8477-2821-8); pap. text ed. write for info. (ISBN 0-8477-2822-6). U of PR Pr.

Casarett, George W. Radiation Histopathology, 2 vols. Vol. 1, 160p. 52.95 (ISBN 0-8493-5357-2); Vol. 2, 176p. 52.95 (ISBN 0-8493-5358-0). CRC Pr.

Casas, Myrna. Teatro De la Vanguardia. 288p. 1975. pap. text ed. 7.95x o.p. (ISBN 0-669-75408-0). Heath.

Casaubon, Meric. A Letter of Meric Casaubon to Peter du Moulin Concerning Natural Experimental Philosophie. LC 76-47045. 1976. Repr. of 1669 ed. 60.00x (ISBN 0-8201-1284-4). Schol Facsimiles.

--Treatise Concerning Enthusiasme. LC 77-119864. 1970. Repr. of 1656 ed. 32.00x (ISBN 0-8201-1077-9). Schol Facsimiles.

Casavant & Infanger. Agricultural Economics. 1981. text ed. 17.95 (ISBN 0-8359-0184-X); instr's. manual free (ISBN 0-8359-0184-X). Reston.

Casavola, Franco. Tommaso Traetta di Bitonto (1727-1779) La Vita e le Opere. LC 80-22630. 1981. Repr. of 1957 ed. 22.50 (ISBN 0-404-18816-8). AMS Pr.

Casberg, Melvin A. Death Stalks the Punjab. LC 80-23558. (Illus.). 240p. (Orig.). 1981. pap. 6.95 (ISBN 0-89407-045-2). Strawberry Hill.

Casce, Steward La see Balanger, Terry & La Casce, Steward.

Casciero, Albert J. & Roney, Raymond G. Introduction to AV for Technical Assistants. (Illus.). 300p. 1981. lib. bdg. price not set (ISBN 0-87287-232-7). Libs Unl.

Cascio, Vincenzo, ed. Italian Linguistics, Nineteen Seventy-Seven-One: Verbi 'modali' an Italiano, No. 3. 1977. pap. text ed. 8.75x (ISBN 0-391-01996-1). Humanities.

Cascio, Wayne F. & Awad, Elias M. Human Resources Management: An Information Systems Approach. 450p. 1981. text ed. 19.95 (ISBN 0-8359-3008-4); student activities guide 7.95 (ISBN 0-8359-3010-6); instr's. manual avail. (ISBN 0-8359-3009-2). Reston.

Casdorph, H. Richard. The Miracles. LC 76-2330. 1976. 5.95 o.p. (ISBN 0-88270-171-1); pap. 3.95 o.p. (ISBN 0-88270-172-X). Logos.

Case, Arthur E. Four Essays on Gulliver's Travels. 6.75 (ISBN 0-8446-1106-9). Peter Smith.

Case, Dave. Power Handtool Handbook. (Illus.). 1980. pap. 5.95 (ISBN 0-89586-027-9). H P Bks.

Case, David. Black Hats. (Orig.). 1981. pap. 1.95 (ISBN 0-440-10648-6). Dell.

--The Cell: Three Tales of Horror. 1969. 5.00 o.p. (ISBN 0-8090-3383-6). Hill & Wang.

--The Third Grave. (Illus.). 160p. 1981. 9.95 (ISBN 0-87054-089-0). Arkham.

--Wolf Tracks. (Orig.). 1980. pap. 1.95 (ISBN 0-505-51485-0). Tower Bks.

Case, Doug & Wilson, Ken. Off-Stage. (Orig.). 1979. pap. text ed. 5.95x (ISBN 0-435-28032-5); tchr's ed. 12.95x (ISBN 0-435-28033-3); tape 28.00x (ISBN 0-435-28035-X); cassette 24.00x (ISBN 0-686-65959-7). Heinemann Ed.

Case, Everett N. & Case, Josephine Y. Owen D. Young & American Enterprise: A Biography. 1981. 25.00 (ISBN 0-87923-360-5). Godine.

Case, Fred E. Investing in Real Estate. LC 78-3486. (Illus.). 1978. 15.95 o.p. (ISBN 0-13-503219-9); pap. 6.95 o.p. (ISBN 0-13-503201-6). P-H.

--The Investment Guide to Home & Land Purchase. LC 77-24751. (Illus.). 1977. 9.95 o.p. (ISBN 0-13-502674-1); pap. 3.95 o.p. (ISBN 0-13-502666-0). P-H.

Case, Frederick E. & Clapp, John M. Real Estate Financing. LC 77-27938. 1978. text ed. 23.50 (ISBN 0-471-07248-6). Wiley.

Case, Frederick E., jt. auth. see Kahn, Sanders A.

Case, Harry L. Commencement Address: A Talk to University Freshmen & Other Heretical Essays. Date not set. 7.95 (ISBN 0-533-04579-7). Vantage.

Case, John. Understanding Inflation. (Illus.). 224p. 1981. 9.95 (ISBN 0-688-00399-0). Morrow.

Case, John & Chilver, A. H. Strength of Materials & Structures: An Introduction to the Mechanics of Solids & Structures. 2nd ed. (Illus.). 1971. pap. text ed. 19.95x (ISBN 0-7131-3244-2). Intl Ideas.

Case, Josephine Y., jt. auth. see Case, Everett N.

Case, L. C. Water Problems in Oil Production: An Operator's Manual. 2nd ed. LC 75-118940. 1977. 23.00 (ISBN 0-87814-001-8). Pennwell Pub.

Case, Lynn M. & Spencer, Warren F. The United States & France: Civil War Diplomacy. LC 75-105108. 680p. 1974. 25.00x (ISBN 0-8122-7604-3). U of Pa Pr.

Case, Lynn M., jt. ed. see Thomas, Daniel H.

Case, Lynn M., tr. see De Bertier De Sauvigny, Guillaume.

Case, Paul F. Book of Tokens - Tarot Meditations. rev. ed. enl. ed. (Illus.). 1974. 6.50 (ISBN 0-938002-00-7). Builders of Adytum.

--The Great Seal of the United States. (Illus.). 1976. 2.25 (ISBN 0-938002-01-5). Builders of Adytum.

--Highlights of Tarot. rev. ed. 1970. 2.00 (ISBN 0-938002-02-3). Builders of Adytum.

--The Magical Language. 320p. pap. 9.95 (ISBN 0-87728-526-8). Weiser.

Case, Shirley J. Social Origins of Christianity. LC 74-84544. 263p. 1975. Repr. of 1923 ed. lib. bdg. 25.00x (ISBN 0-8154-0501-4). Cooper Sq.

Case, Virginia, ed. see Abrams, Kathleen & Abrams, Lawrence.

Case, Virginia, ed. see Keefe, William F.

Case, Virginia, ed. see Mueller, Larry.

Case, Virginia, ed. see Reschke, Robert C.

Case, Virginia, ed. see Ritchie, James D.

Case, Virginia, ed. see Schram, Joseph.

Case, Virginia, ed. see Taylor, Robert.

Case, Virginia A., ed. see Banov, Abel & Lytle, Marie-Jeanne.

Case, Virginia A., ed. see Boeschen, John.

Case, Virginia A., ed. see Derven, Ronald & Nichols, Carol.

Case, Virginia A., ed. see McClellan, Brenda.

Case, Virginia A., ed. see Scharff, Robert.

Casebier, Allen & Casebier, Janet J., eds. Social Responsibilities of the Mass Media. LC 78-58603. 1978. pap. text ed. 10.25 (ISBN 0-8191-0539-2). U Pr of Amer.

Casebier, Dennis G. The Mojave Road. new ed. LC 74-33063. (Illus.). 1975. 15.00 o.p. (ISBN 0-914224-04-2). Tales Mojave Rd.

Casebier, Dennis G., ed. Mojave Road in Newspapers. new ed. LC 75-31484. (Illus.). 1976. 7.50 o.p. (ISBN 0-914224-05-0). Tales Mojave Rd.

Casebier, Janet J., jt. ed. see Casebier, Allen.

Casebolt, Don E. Saturday or Sunday? Letter to a Sunday-Keeping Minister. LC 78-8672. (Flame Ser.). 1978. pap. 0.95 (ISBN 0-8127-0182-8). Southern Pub.

Caserta, John G. Take My Heart & Other Poems. 1981. 4.50 (ISBN 0-8062-1720-0). Carlton.

Casewit, Curtis. Graphology Handbook. (Illus.). 168p. (Orig.). 1980. pap. 6.95 (ISBN 0-914918-15-X). Para Res.

Casewit, Curtis W. The Complete Book of Mountain Sports. LC 78-15901. (Illus.). (gr. 7 up). 1978. PLB 7.79 o.p. (ISBN 0-671-32902-2). Messner.

--Freelance Photography: Advice from the Pros. 1980. 10.95 (ISBN 0-02-522400-X, Collier); pap. 5.95 (ISBN 0-02-079310-3, Collier). Macmillan.

--The Stop Smoking Book for Teens. LC 79-27933. (Illus.). 160p. (gr. 9-12). 1980. PLB 8.29 (ISBN 0-671-33015-2). Messner.

Casewit, Curtis W., tr. see Schranz, Karl.

Casey, Bill, jt. auth. see Paris, Claudine.

Casey, Clifford B. Alpine, Texas: Then & Now. (Illus.). 446p. 1980. 20.00 (ISBN 0-933512-33-3). Pioneer Bk Tx.

Casey, Daniel J. & Rhodes, Robert E., eds. Irish-American Fiction: Essays in Criticism. 1978. 24.50 (ISBN 0-404-16037-9); pap. 7.95 (ISBN 0-686-67216-X). AMS Pr.

Casey, Dayle A. Liberty & Law: The Nature of Individual Rights. Brown, Richard H. & Halsey, Van R., eds. (Amherst Ser). (gr. 9-12). 1972. pap. text ed. 4.52 (ISBN 0-201-00906-4, Sch Div). A-W.

Casey, Douglas. The International Man. 19.95 (ISBN 0-932496-01-6). Green-Hill.

Casey, Douglas R. International Investing. 1981. pap. 9.95. Everest Hse.

Casey, Genevieve. The Public Library in the Network Mode: A Preliminary Investigation. (Illinois Regional Council Occasional Papers Ser.: No. 3). 51p. 1978. soft cover 7.50 (ISBN 0-917060-01-6). Ill Regional Lib Coun.

Casey, J. The Kingdom of Valencia in the Seventeenth Century. LC 77-88669. (Cambridge Studies in Early Modern History). (Illus.). 1979. 38.50 (ISBN 0-521-21939-6). Cambridge U Pr.

Casey, James P., ed. Pulp & Paper: Chemistry & Chemical Technology, 2 vols. 3rd ed. LC 79-13435. 1980. Vol. 1. 55.00 (ISBN 0-471-03175-5, Pub. by Wiley-Interscience); Vol. 2. 50.00 (ISBN 0-471-03176-3). Wiley.

Casey, Juliana. Hebrews. (New Testament Message Ser.). 10.95 (ISBN 0-89453-141-7); pap. 5.95 (ISBN 0-89453-206-5). M Glazier.

Casey, M. Beth, jt. auth. see Abramson, David I.

Casey, Mary C., jt. auth. see Bate, Marjorie D.

Casey, R. & Rawson, P. F. The Boreal Lower Cretaceous Geological Journal Special Issue, No. 5. (Liverpool Geological Society & the Manchester Geological Association). 448p. 1973. 48.75 (ISBN 0-471-27752-5, Pub. by Wiley-Interscience). Wiley.

Cash, Alan. The Penguin Book of Daily Telegraph Quick Crosswords. 1980. pap. 2.95 (ISBN 0-14-005089-2). Penguin.

Cash, Anthony. Russian Revolution. (Jackdaw Ser: No. 42). (Illus.). 1968. 5.95 o.s.i. (ISBN 0-670-61366-5, Grossman). Viking Pr.

Cash, E. A. John A. Williams: The Evolution of a Black Writer. LC 73-92796. 1974. 10.00 (ISBN 0-89388-142-2). Okpaku Communications.

Cash, Harold C. & Crissy, W. J. The Psychology of Selling, 12 vols. Incl. Vol. 1. A Point of View for Salesman; Vol. 2. The Use of Appeals in Selling; Vol. 3. Motivation in Selling; Vol. 4. Personality & Sales Strategy; Vol. 5. Tactics for Conducting the Sales Call; Vol. 6. The Salesman As a Self-Manager; Vol. 7. Communication in Selling; Vol. 8. Logic & Creativity in Selling; Vol. 9. Managing Sales Resistance; Vol. 10. Guiding Buying Behavior; Vol. 11. Selling in Depth; Vol. 12. The Salesman's Role in Marketing. 4.00x ea. Personnel Dev.

Cash, J. Allan. The Complete Cotswolds. 2nd ed. (History, People & Places Ser.). (Illus.). 1978. pap. 10.95 (ISBN 0-902875-45-0). Hippocrene Bks.

Cash, Johnny. Man in Black: His Own Story in His Own Words. (Large Print Ser.). 1976. kivar 4.95 (ISBN 0-310-22327-X); pap. 2.95 (ISBN 0-310-22322-9). Zondervan.

Cash, June C. Among My Klediments. 160p. 1981. pap. 4.95 (ISBN 0-310-38171-1). Zondervan.

Cash, Phyllis. How to Write a Research Paper Step-by-Step. (How to Ser.). 128p. 1975. pap. 2.50 (ISBN 0-671-18752-X). Monarch Pr.

Cashdan, A. & Grugeon, E., eds. Language in Education: A Source Book. 1972. 13.95x (ISBN 0-7100-7430-1); pap. 8.95 (ISBN 0-7100-7431-X). Routledge & Kegan.

Cashdan, Sheldon. Abnormal Psychology. LC 70-39029. (Foundations of Modern Psychology). (Illus.). 160p. 1972. ref. ed. 12.95x (ISBN 0-13-000802-8); pap. 7.95x ref. ed. (ISBN 0-13-000794-3). P-H.

Cashell, G. T. & Durran, I. M. Handbook of Orthoptic Principles. 4th ed. (Illus.). 1981. pap. text ed. 13.75 (ISBN 0-443-02200-3). Churchill.

Cashen, Richard A. Solitude in the Thought of Thomas Merton. (Cistercian Studies: No. 40). 208p. 1981. 15.50 (ISBN 0-87907-840-5); pap. 5.50 (ISBN 0-87907-940-1). Cistercian Pubns.

Cashin, James & Polimeni, Ralph S. Cost Accounting. 1981. write for info. oHT's (ISBN 0-07-010213-9, C); write for info. instrs.' manual (ISBN 0-07-010214-7); study guide 5.95 (ISBN 0-07-010257-0); price not set OHT's (ISBN 0-07-075018-1); job order costing practice set 6.95 (ISBN 0-07-010258-9); process costing practice set 6.95 (ISBN 0-07-010259-7); exam questions avail. (ISBN 0-07-010215-5). McGraw.

Cashin, James A. & Lerner, Joel J. Schaum's Outline of Accounting I. 2nd ed. (Schaum's Outline Ser.). 1980. pap. 5.95 (ISBN 0-07-010251-1). McGraw.

--Schaum's Outline of Accounting II. 2nd ed. (Schaum's Outline Ser.). 288p. 1980. pap. 5.95 (ISBN 0-07-010252-X, SP). McGraw.

Cashin, James A. & Lerner, Joel L. Accounting Two. (Schaum's Outline Ser.). 1974. pap. text ed. 4.95 o.p. (ISBN 0-07-010212-0, SP). McGraw.

Cashman, John. The Gentlemen from Chicago. 288p. 1974. pap. 1.50 o.p. (ISBN 0-445-03050-X). Popular Lib.

--Kid Glove Charlie. LC 77-3786. 1978. 10.00 o.p. (ISBN 0-06-010698-0, HarpT). Har-Row.

Cashman, Richard I. The Myth of the Lokamanya: Tilak & Mass Politics in Maharashtra. LC 72-97734. 1975. 20.00x (ISBN 0-520-02407-9). U of Cal Pr.

Cashman, Seamus, jt. auth. see Quinn, Bridie.

Cashman, Sean D. Prohibition: The Life of the Land. LC 80-1853. (Illus.). 1981. 15.95 (ISBN 0-02-905730-2). Free Pr.

Cashman, Thomas J. & Keys, William J. Data Processing & Computer Programming: A Modular Approach. (Illus.). 1971. text ed. 20.50 scp o.p. (ISBN 0-06-382360-8, HarpC). Har-Row.

Cashman, Thomas J., jt. auth. see Keys, William J.

Cashman, Thomas J., jt. auth. see Shelly, Gary B.

Casida, L. E. Industrial Microbiology. LC 68-22302. 1968. 35.95 (ISBN 0-471-14060-0). Wiley.

Casier, Edgar. Faune Ichthyologique Du London Clay: Text & Atlas. (Illus.). xiv, 496p. 1966. 87.50x (ISBN 0-565-00654-1, Pub. by British Mus Nat Hist England). Sabbot-Natural Hist Bks.

Caskey, Clark. Balance in Management. LC 68-57174. 1968. 9.95 (ISBN 0-685-79073-8). Masterco Pr.

Caskey, Jefferson D. & Stapp, Melinda M., eds. Samuel Taylor Coleridge: A Selective Bibliography of Criticism, 1935-1977. LC 78-57765. 1978. lib. bdg. 17.95 (ISBN 0-313-20564-7, CCO/). Greenwood.

Caskey, Willie M. Secession & Restoration of Louisiana. LC 78-75302. (American Scene Ser). (Illus.). 1970. Repr. of 1938 ed. lib. bdg. 32.50 (ISBN 0-306-71263-6). Da Capo.

Casler, Lawrence. Is Marriage Necessary? 256p. 1976. pap. 1.50 o.p. (ISBN 0-445-03125-5). Popular Lib.

Casley, D. J. & Lury, D. A. Data Collection in Developing Countries. (Illus.). 1981. 45.00 (ISBN 0-19-877123-1); pap. 14.95 (ISBN 0-19-877124-X). Oxford U Pr.

Casmir, Fred L., ed. Intercultural & International Communication. LC 78-61912. 1978. pap. text ed. 19.75 (ISBN 0-8191-0625-9). U Pr of Amer.

Casner, A. James. American Law of Property: 1977 Supplement. 1977. pap. 65.00 (ISBN 0-316-13138-5). Little.

--Estate Planning, Vols. 1-6. 1980. text ed. 250.00 (ISBN 0-316-13148-2). Vol. 1. Vol. 2 (ISBN 0-316-13149-0). Vol. 3 (ISBN 0-316-13150-4). Vol. 4 (ISBN 0-316-13151-2). Vol. 5 (ISBN 0-316-13152-0). Vol. 6 (ISBN 0-316-13153-9). Little.

Caso, Adolph. America's Italian Founding Fathers: 1770-1780. 285p. 1975. 10.00 (ISBN 0-8283-1667-8). Dante U Am.

--Issues in Foreign Language & Biilingual Education. 125p. 1979. pap. 7.50 (ISBN 0-8283-1721-6). Dante U Am.

--Lives of the Italian Americans: Fifty Illustrated Biographies. (Illus.). 175p. 1980. 12.50 (ISBN 0-937832-00-6). Dante Univ Bkshlf.

--Mass Media Vs. the Italian Americans. 262p. 1980. 12.00 (ISBN 0-8283-1737-2). Dante U Am.

--The Straw Obelisk. 296p. 1971. 6.95 (ISBN 0-8283-1293-1). Dante U Am.

--They Too Made America Great. 175p. 1978. 12.50 (ISBN 0-8283-1699-6). Dante U Am.

--Water & Life. 94p. (Eng. & It.). 1976. pap. 5.00 (ISBN 0-8283-1682-1). Dante U Am.

Caso, Adolph, tr. see Alfieri, Vittorio.

Caso, Alfonso. Aztecs, People of the Sun. Dunham, Lowell, tr. (Civilization of the American Indian Ser.: No. 50). (Illus.). 1978. Repr. of 1958 ed. 16.95 (ISBN 0-8061-0414-7). U of Okla Pr.

Cason, James & Rapoport, Henry. Laboratory Text in Organic Chemistry. 3rd ed. (Chemistry Ser). 1970. pap. 16.95 ref. ed. (ISBN 0-13-521435-1). P-H.

Cason, Mabel E. Song of the Trail. LC 53-10772. (Destiny Ser.). 1979. pap. 4.95 (ISBN 0-8163-0245-6). Pacific Pr Pub Assn.

Casona, Alejandro. Corona De Amor Y Muerte. Balseiro, Jose & Owre, J. Riis, eds. (Orig., Span). 1960. pap. 5.95x (ISBN 0-19-500844-8). Oxford U Pr.

--Nuestra Natacha. Shoemaker, William H., ed. (Span.). (gr. 11 up). 1979. pap. text ed. 7.95x (ISBN 0-89197-541-1). Irvington.

Caspari, E. W. & Ravin, A. W., eds. Genetic Organization, Vol. 1. 1969. 56.00 (ISBN 0-12-163301-2); by subscription 56.00 (ISBN 0-12-163301-2). Acad Pr.

Caspari, E. W. see Demerec, M.

Caspari, Fritz. Humanism & Social Order in Tudor England. LC 68-29071. 1968. 9.40 o.p. (ISBN 0-8077-1149-7); pap. text ed. 5.25x (ISBN 0-8077-1146-2). Tchrs Coll.

Caspari, Irene E. Troublesome Children in Class. (Students Library of Education). 130p. 1975. 14.00x (ISBN 0-7100-8261-4); pap. 7.50 (ISBN 0-7100-8262-2). Routledge & Kegan.

Caspary, Gerard E. Politics & Exegesis: Origen & the Two Swords. 1979. 24.50x (ISBN 0-520-03445-7). U of Cal Pr.

Caspary, Vera. Laura. 224p. 1981. pap. 1.95 (ISBN 0-380-00043-1, 51565). Avon.

Casper, Barry M. & Wellstone, Paul D. Powerline: The First Battle of America's Energy War. 336p. 1981. lib. bdg. 18.50x (ISBN 0-87023-320-3); pap. 7.95 (ISBN 0-87023-321-1). U of Mass Pr.

Casper, Billy. Two-Hundred Ninety-Five Golf Lessons. 1973. pap. 2.95 o.p. (ISBN 0-695-80403-0). Follett.

Casper, Joseph A. Vincent Minelli & the Film Musical. LC 75-20614. (Illus.). 1977. 15.00 o.p. (ISBN 0-498-01784-2). A S Barnes.

Caspersz, D. A. The Scottish Terrier. LC 76-11027. (Illus.). 1976. bds. 2.25 o.p. (ISBN 0-668-03975-2). Arco.

Cass, Angelica. Reading Power. Bk. 1. pap. 4.95 (ISBN 0-671-18720-1); Bk. 2. pap. 5.95 (ISBN 0-671-18721-X); Bk. 3. pap. 5.95 (ISBN 0-671-18722-8); Bk. 4. pap. 5.95 (ISBN 0-671-18723-6). Monarch Pr.

Cass, Angelica W. Letters for Everyday Use. Date not set. pap. cancelled (ISBN 0-671-09224-3). Monarch Pr. Postponed.

Cass, David & Shell, Karl, eds. The Hamiltonian Approach to Dynamic Economics. (Economic Theory, Econometrics, & Mathematical Economics Ser.). 1976. 16.50 (ISBN 0-12-163650-X). Acad Pr.

Cass, James & Birnbaum, Max. Counselors' Comparative Guide to American Colleges, 1976. 2nd ed. LC 75-5789. 830p. 1975. pap. 12.50x o.s.i. (ISBN 0-06-010656-5, TD-225, HarpT). Har-Row.

Cass, Jeannette. Rudiments of Music: A Detailed Study in Music Essentials. (Illus., Orig.). 1956. pap. text ed. 14.95 (ISBN 0-13-783654-6). P-H.

Cass, Joan E. The Role of the Teacher in the Nursery School. 97p. 1975. 12.75 (ISBN 0-08-018282-8); pap. text ed. 7.00 (ISBN 0-08-018281-X). Pergamon.

--The Significance of Children's Play. 1977. 14.95 (ISBN 0-7134-0689-5, Pub. by Batsford England). David & Charles.

Cass, Zoe. Island of the Seven Hills. 1975. pap. 1.25 o.p. (ISBN 0-445-00277-8). Popular Lib.

Cassady, John M. & Douros, John D., eds. Anticancer Agents Based on Natural Product Models. LC 79-6802. (Medicinal Chemistry Ser.). 1980. 49.50 (ISBN 0-12-163150-8). Acad Pr.

Cassady, Ralph, Jr. Auctions & Auctioneering. 1967. 22.75x (ISBN 0-520-00216-4). U of Cal Pr.

Cassano, C. & Andreoli, M., eds. Current Topics in Thyroid Research. 1966. 88.00 (ISBN 0-12-163750-6). Acad Pr.

Cassara, Ernest. The Enlightenment in America. LC 74-20962. (World Leaders Ser: No. 50). 1975. lib. bdg. 10.95 (ISBN 0-8057-3675-1). Twayne.

--Universalism in America: A Documentary History. LC 77-136226. 1971. 10.00 o.p. (ISBN 0-8070-1664-0). Beacon Pr.

Cassara, Ernest, ed. History of the United States of America: A Guide to Information Sources. LC 73-17551. (American Studies Information Guide Series: Vol. 3). 1977. 30.00 (ISBN 0-8103-1266-2). Gale.

Cassard, Daniel W. & Juergenson, Elwood M. Approved Practices in Feeds & Feeding. 5th ed. LC 76-62743. (Illus.). (gr. 9-12). 1977. 14.00 (ISBN 0-8134-1901-8, 1901); text ed. 10.50x (ISBN 0-685-03868-8). Interstate.

Cassata, Mary B. & Palmer, Roger C., eds. Reader in Library Communication. LC 76-10123. (Reader in Librarianship & Information Science Ser.: Vol. 21). 1976. 20.00 o.s.i. (ISBN 0-910972-60-5). IHS-PDS.

Cassata, Mary B. & Totten, Herman L., eds. The Administrative Aspects of Education for Librarianship: A Symposium. LC 75-15726. 425p. 1975. 17.50 (ISBN 0-8108-0829-3). Scarecrow.

Cassebaum, John M., et al. China: A Workbook in World Cultures. LC 72-95839. (gr. 8-10). 1973. pap. 2.25 o.p. (ISBN 0-931992-29-X). Penns Valley.

Cassel & Swanson. Basic Made Easy: A Guide to Programming Microcomputers & Minicomputers. (Illus.). 272p. 1980. text ed. 14.95 (ISBN 0-8359-0399-0); pap. text ed. 10.95 (ISBN 0-8359-0398-2). Reston.

Cassel, Christine K., jt. auth. see Purtilo, Ruth B.

Cassel, Claes-Magnus, et al. Foundations of Inference in Survey Sampling. LC 77-5114. (Probability & Mathematical Statistics Ser., Probability & Statistics Section). 1977. 25.00 (ISBN 0-471-02563-1, Pub. by Wiley-Interscience). Wiley.

Cassel, Don. Programming Language One: A Structural Approach with PLC. 1978. pap. 12.95 (ISBN 0-87909-650-0). Reston.

Cassel, Don & Jackson, Martin. Introduction to Computers & Information Processing. (Orig.). 1980. study guide 7.95 (ISBN 0-8359-3154-4). Reston.

--Introduction to Computers & Information Processing: Language Free Editon. 1981. text ed. 17.95 (ISBN 0-8359-3155-2); study guide 7.95 (ISBN 0-8359-3157-9); instrs'. manual avail. (ISBN 0-8359-3156-0). Reston.

Cassel, Gustav. Downfall of the Gold Standard. LC 66-52921. Repr. of 1936 ed. 19.50x (ISBN 0-678-05160-7). Kelley.

Cassel, Virginia. The Juniata Valley. LC 80-25173. 336p. 1981. 13.95 (ISBN 0-670-41085-3). Viking Pr.

Cassell. Cassell's Colloquials, 4 bks. Incl. French. 160p. pap. 3.95 (ISBN 0-02-079420-7); German. 176p. pap. 3.95 (ISBN 0-02-079410-X); Spanish. 256p. pap. 4.95 (ISBN 0-02-079430-4); Italian. 192p. pap. 3.95 (ISBN 0-02-079440-1). 1981. Macmillan.

Cassell, Joan, jt. ed. see Wax, Murray L.

Cassells. French Concise Dictionary. 1977. 8.95 (ISBN 0-02-052267-3). Macmillan.

--German Concise Dictionary. 1977. 8.95 (ISBN 0-02-052265-7). Macmillan.

--Latin Concise Dictionary. 1977. 8.95 (ISBN 0-02-052263-0). Macmillan.

--Latin-English Dictionary. 1977. standard 14.95 (ISBN 0-686-63973-1); index 16.95 (ISBN 0-02-052258-4). Macmillan.

--Spanish Concise Dictionary. 1977. 8.95 (ISBN 0-02-052266-5). Macmillan.

Cassels, Alan. Fascism. LC 73-13716. (Illus.). 1975. pap. 9.95x (ISBN 0-88295-718-X). AHM Pub.

--Fascist Italy. LC 68-9740. (AHM Europe Since 1500 Ser.). (Illus.). 1968. pap. 5.95x (ISBN 0-88295-719-8). AHM Pub.

Cassels, B. K., tr. see Breitmaier, E. & Bauer, G.

Cassels, B. K., tr. see Breitmaier, E. & Bauer, G. C.

Cassels, Donald E. The Ductus Arteriosus. (Illus.). 356p. 1973. text ed. 32.50 (ISBN 0-398-02720-X). C C Thomas.

Cassels, Louis. Forbid Them Not. LC 73-75885. 1973. 2.00 o.p. (ISBN 0-8309-0097-7). Independence Pr.

Cassem, Ned H., jt. auth. see Hackett, Thomas P.

Casserley, H. C. Outline of Irish Railway History. (Illus.). 304p. 1974. 24.00 o.p. (ISBN 0-7153-6377-8). David & Charles.

Casserly, Johnston. Locomotives at the Grouping, Great Western Railway. 14.95x (ISBN 0-392-08054-0, SpS). Soccer.

Casserly, Michael D., et al. School Vandalism: Strategies for Prevention. LC 80-8118. 1980. 17.95 (ISBN 0-669-03956-X). Lexington Bks.

Cassetty, Judith. Child Support & Public Policy. LC 77-4541. (Illus.). 1978. 17.95 (ISBN 0-669-01486-9). Lexington Bks.

Cassian, Nina. Blue Apple. Feiler, Eve, tr. (Cross-Cultural Review Chapbook 13). 16p. (Romanian & Eng.). 1980. pap. 2.00 (ISBN 0-89304-812-7). Cross Cult.

Cassiday, Bruce. Home Guide to Lawns & Landscaping. LC 75-40601. (Popular Science Skill Bk.). 224p. 1976. 6.95 o.s.i. (ISBN 0-06-010689-1, HarpT). Har-Row.

--Home Guide to Lawns & Landscaping. LC 75-40601. (A Popular Science Skill Bk). (Illus.). 1977. pap. 3.95 o.p. (ISBN 0-06-010697-2, TD-275, HarpT). Har-Row.

Cassiday, Bruce, jt. auth. see Cassiday, Doris.

Cassiday, Doris & Cassiday, Bruce. Careers in the Beauty Industry. (Career Concise Guides Ser.). (Illus.). (gr. 7 up). 1978. PLB 6.45 s&l (ISBN 0-531-01419-3). Watts.

--Fashion Industry Careers. (Career Concise Guides Ser.). (gr. 7 up). 6.45 (ISBN 0-531-01303-0). Watts.

Cassidy, jt. auth. see Robertson.

Cassidy, Clara. We Like Kindergarten. (Illus.). 24p. (ps-k). 1965. PLB 4.57 o.p. (ISBN 0-307-60552-3, Golden Pr). Western Pub.

Cassidy, F. G. & Le Page, R. B., eds. Dictionary of Jamaican English. 2nd ed. LC 78-17799. 1980. 75.00 (ISBN 0-521-22165-X). Cambridge U Pr.

Cassidy, Harold G. Knowledge, Experience, & Action: An Essay on Education. LC 70-81590. 1969. pap. 6.50x (ISBN 0-8077-1150-0). Tchrs Coll.

Cassidy, Henry J. Using Econometrics: A Beginner's Guide. 1981. text ed. 18.95 (ISBN 0-8359-8135-5); instr's. manual free (ISBN 0-8359-8136-3). Reston.

Cassidy, John. A Station in the Delta. 320p. 1981. pap. 2.50 (ISBN 0-345-28846-7). Ballantine.

Cassidy, John & Rimbeaux, B. C. Juggling for the Complete Klutz. 2nd ed. (Illus.). 1980. pap. 7.95 (ISBN 0-932592-00-7). Klutz Enterprises.

Cassidy, John A. Algernon C. Swinburne. (English Authors Ser.: No. 10). lib. bdg. 10.95 (ISBN 0-8057-1524-X). Twayne.

Cassidy, Laurence L. Existence & Presence: The Dialectics of Divinity. LC 80-5881. 246p. 1981. lib. bdg. 16.50 (ISBN 0-8191-1486-3); pap. text ed. 7.50 (ISBN 0-8191-1487-1). U Pr of Amer.

Cassidy, Michael, jt. auth. see Lerrigo, Marion O.

Cassilis, Robert. Arrow of God. 184p. 1980. 16.95 (ISBN 0-241-10187-5, Pub. by Hamish Hamilton England). David & Charles.

--Winding Sheet. 222p. 1980. 16.95 (ISBN 0-241-89863-3, Pub. by Hamish Hamilton England). David & Charles.

Cassin, Maxine, et al, eds. The Maple Leaf Rag: An Anthology of New Orleans Poetry. (Illus.). 116p. (Orig.). 1980. pap. 4.95x (ISBN 0-938498-01-0). New Orleans Poetry.

Cassinelli, C. W. Total Revolution: A Comparative Study of Germany under Hitler, the Soviet union Under Stalin, & China Under Mao. Merkl, Peter H., ed. LC 76-10302. (Studies in International & Comparative Politics: No. 10). 1976. text ed. 26.50 o.p. (ISBN 0-87436-227-X); pap. 8.75 (ISBN 0-87436-228-8). ABC-Clio.

Cassin-Scott, Jack. Costumes & Settings for Historical Plays: Volume Five, The Nineteenth Century. LC 79-56537. (Illus.). 96p. 1980. 14.95 (ISBN 0-7134-1710-2, Pub. by Batsford England). David & Charles.

--The Greek & Persian Armies. (Men-at-Arms Ser.). (Illus.). 48p. 1978. pap. 7.95 (ISBN 0-85045-271-6). Hippocrene Bks.

--Making Historical Costume Dolls. LC 74-26667. (Illus.). 96p. 1975. 10.00 (ISBN 0-8231-3031-2). Branford.

Cassirer, Ernst. Essay on Man: An Introduction to a Philosophy of Human Culture. 1962. pap. 5.45 (ISBN 0-300-00034-0, Y52). Yale U Pr.

--Individual & the Cosmos in Renaissance Philosophy. Domandi, Mario, tr. 1972. pap. 6.95x (ISBN 0-8122-1036-0, Pa. Paperbacks). U of Pa Pr.

--Philosophy of Symbolic Forms, Vol. 2, Mythical Thought. Manheim, Ralph, tr. 1955. 19.50x (ISBN 0-300-00354-4); pap. 5.95 1965 (ISBN 0-300-00038-3, Y147). Yale U Pr.

--The Philosophy of Symbolic Forms, Vol. 3, The Phenomenolgy Of Knowledge. Manheim, Ralph, tr. 1965. pap. 7.95 (ISBN 0-300-00039-1, Y148). Yale U Pr.

--Symbol, Myth & Culture: Essays & Lectures of Ernst Cassirer 1935-45. Verne, Donald P., ed. LC 78-9887. 1979. 25.00x (ISBN 0-300-02306-5). Yale U Pr.

--Symbol, Myth & Culture: Essays & Lectures of Ernst Cassirer 1935-45. Verne, Donald P., ed. LC 78-9887. 368p. 1981. pap. 9.95x (ISBN 0-300-02666-8). Yale U Pr.

Cassirer, Thomas, tr. see Diderot, Denis.

Cassity, Turner. Watchboy, What of the Night? LC 66-23920. (Wesleyan Poetry Program: Vol. 31). (Orig.). 1966. 10.00x (ISBN 0-8195-2031-4, Pub. by Wesleyan U Pr); pap. 4.95x (ISBN 0-8195-1031-9). Columbia U Pr.

Cassola, Carlo. La Ragazza Di Bube. (Easy Readers, C). (Illus.). 1977. pap. text ed. 3.75 (ISBN 0-88436-284-1). EMC.

Casson, Lionel. Ancient Egypt. LC 65-28872. (Great Ages of Man). (Illus.). (gr. 6 up). 1965. PLB 11.97 (ISBN 0-8094-0367-6, Pub. by Time-Life). Silver.

--Ancient Egypt. (Great Ages of Man Ser). (Illus.). 1965. 12.95 (ISBN 0-8094-0345-5). Time-Life.

--Ancient Mariners. 1959. 9.95 (ISBN 0-02-522830-7). Macmillan.

Casson, Lionel, ed. & tr. Masters of Ancient Comedy: Selections from Aristophanes, Menander, Plautus & Terence. (Funk & W Bk.). 433p. 1967. pap. 2.95 o.s.i. (ISBN 0-308-60016-9, TYC-T). T Y Crowell.

Casson, Lionel, ed. The Plays of Menander. LC 76-171347. 1971. 12.00x (ISBN 0-8147-1353-X). NYU Pr.

Casson, Lionel, ed. see Plautus.

Casson, Lionel, et al. Mysteries of the Past. Thorndike, Joseph J., Jr., ed. LC 77-22838. (Illus.). 320p. 1977. 12.95 (ISBN 0-8281-0206-6, Dist. by Scribner); deluxe ed. 39.95 slipcased (ISBN 0-8281-0207-4, Dist. by Scribner). Am Heritage.

Casson-Scott, Jack. Fashion & Costume in Color: Fashion & Costume in Color: Seventeen Sixty to Nineteen Twenty. (Illus.). 1972. 10.95 (ISBN 0-02-522500-6). Macmillan.

Casstevens, Thomas B., jt. ed. see Shrivastava, B. K.

Cassuto, Alexander E., jt. auth. see Baird, Charles W.

Cast, David. The Calumny of Apelles: A Study in the Humanist Tradition. LC 80-26378. (Publication in the History of Art Ser.: No. 28). (Illus.). 320p. 1981. text ed. 32.50x (ISBN 0-300-02575-0). Yale U Pr.

Castagno, Margaret F. Historical Dictionary of Somalia. LC 75-25681. (African Historical Dictionary Ser.: No. 6). 1975. 11.50 (ISBN 0-8108-0830-7). Scarecrow.

Castagnoli, N., Jr., jt. ed. see Frigerio, A.

Castaing, D., et al. Hepatic & Portal Surgery in the Rat. (Illus.). 184p. 1980. 37.50 (ISBN 0-89352-101-9). Masson Pub.

Castaldi, C. R. & Brass, George A. Dentistry for the Adolescent Patient. new ed. LC 77-88308. (Illus.). 1979. text ed. 40.00 (ISBN 0-7216-2445-6). Saunders.

Castaldo, George, ed. see Doane, Jim.

Castaneda, Hector-Neri. Action, Knowledge & Reality: Studies in Honor of Wilfrid Sellars. LC 74-8419. 374p. 1975. text ed. 26.50 (ISBN 0-672-61213-5). Bobbs.

--The Structure of Morality. (American Lectures in Philosophy Ser.). (Illus.). 256p. 1974. 22.50 (ISBN 0-398-02794-3). C C Thomas.

Castaneda, James A. Agustin Moreto. (World Authors Ser.: Spain: No. 308). 1974. lib. bdg. 12.50 (ISBN 0-8057-2633-0). Twayne.

--Mira De Amescua. LC 77-1956. (World Authors Ser.: Spain: No. 449). 1977. lib. bdg. 12.50 (ISBN 0-8057-6285-X). Twayne.

Castaneda, Jorge. Legal Effects of United Nations Resolutions. LC 75-94629. (International Organization Ser). 1970. 17.00x (ISBN 0-231-03318-4). Columbia U Pr.

Castanien, Donald G. El Inca Garcilaso de la Vega. (World Authors Ser.: Peru: No. 61). lib. bdg. 10.95 (ISBN 0-8057-2928-3). Twayne.

Castano, Francis A. & Alden, Betsey, eds. Handbook of Clinical Dental Auxiliary Practice. 2nd ed. LC 79-18202. 290p. 1980. text ed. 17.50 (ISBN 0-397-54285-2). Lippincott.

Castano, John B. Naval Officers Uniform Guide. LC 74-82538. (Illus.). 1974. 10.50x o.p. (ISBN 0-87021-485-3); pap. 7.00x o.p. (ISBN 0-686-66912-6). Naval Inst Pr.

Castano, Wilf Redo. Soft Stones Cast Upon the Tender Earth. 1981. pap. 3.50 (ISBN 0-915016-28-1). Second Coming.

Castberg, A. Didrick, jt. ed. see Rosenblum, Victor G.

Castedo, Leopoldo. The Cuzco Circle. LC 76-381383. (Illus.). 144p. 1980. 16.50 (ISBN 0-295-95738-7); pap. 9.95 (ISBN 0-295-95739-5). U of Wash Pr.

Castel, Albert & Gibson, Scott L. The Yeas & the Nays: Key Congressional Decisions 1774-1945. 1975. 7.95 (ISBN 0-932826-15-6). New Issues MI.

Castel, Christine du see Du Castel, Christine.

Castelain, D., et al. New Writers Five. (New Writing & Writers Ser.). 1966. text ed. 13.00x (ISBN 0-7145-0404-1). Humanities.

Castelain, Daniel, et al. New Writers Five. 1980. pap. 6.00 (ISBN 0-7145-0405-X). Riverrun NY.

Castel de Sainte-Pierre & Abbe Charles-Irenee. Discours Sur la Polysynodie... (Utopias Ser.). 1976. Repr. of 1719 ed. lib. bdg. 34.00x o.p. (ISBN 0-8287-0165-2). Clearwater Pub.

Castell, Alburey, ed. see Huxley, Thomas H.

Castell, Alburey, ed. see Paine, Thomas.

Castell, David. The Films of Barbara Streisand. (The Films of...Ser.). (Illus.). (gr. 7-12). 1978. Repr. of 1974 ed. PLB 5.95 (ISBN 0-912616-78-4). Greenhaven.

--The Films of Robert Redford. (The Films of... Ser.). (Illus.). (gr. 7-12). 1978. Repr. of 1973 ed. PLB 5.95 (ISBN 0-912616-77-6). Greenhaven.

Castell, David, ed. Cinema Seventy Nine. (Illus.). 1978. pap. 7.95 (ISBN 0-8467-0504-4, Pub. by Two Continents). Hippocrene Bks.

Castell, David, ed. see Andrews, Emma.

Castell, David, ed. see Baxter, Brian.

Castell, David, ed. see Braithwaite, Bruce.

Castell, David, ed. see Campbell, Joanna.

Castell, David, ed. see D'Arcy, Susan.

Castell, David, ed. see McAsh, Iain F.

Castell, David, ed. see Thompson, Kenneth.

Castell, David, ed. see Whitman, Mark.

Castell, David, ed. see Williams, John.

Castell, Megan. Queen of a Lonely Country. 240p. 1980. pap. 2.25 (ISBN 0-671-82732-4). PB.

Castellan, Gilbert W. Physical Chemistry. 2nd ed. LC 75-133375. (Chemistry Ser). (Illus.). 1971. text ed. 23.95 (ISBN 0-201-00912-9). A-W.

Castellano, Carmine C. & Seitz, Clifford P. You Fix It: Insulation. LC 74-14206. (You Fix It Ser.). (Illus.). 1975. pap. 2.95 o.p. (ISBN 0-668-03614-1). Arco.

Castellano, Juan R. & Brown, Charles B. A New Shorter Spanish Review Grammar. LC 73-1349. 225p. 1975. text ed. 9.95x (ISBN 0-684-14482-4, ScribC). Scribner.

Castelli, James. What the Church Is Doing for Divorced & Remarried Catholics. (Illus.). 1978. pap. 1.95 (ISBN 0-89570-155-3). Claretian Pubns.

Castelli, Louis & Cleeland, Caryn L. David Lean: A Guide to References & Resources. 1980. lib. bdg. 18.50 (ISBN 0-8161-7933-6). G K Hall.

Castellino, Ronald A., jt. auth. see Parker, Bruce R.

Castells, Manuel. City, Class & Power. Lebas, Elizabeth, tr. from Fr. 1979. 20.00 (ISBN 0-312-13989-6). St Martin.

--The Economic Crisis & American Society. 285p. 20.00; pap. 7.50. Princeton U Pr.

Castells, Matilde & Lionetti, Harold E. La Lengua Espanola: Gramatica y Cultura. 2nd ed. LC 73-1315. (Illus.). 1978. 16.95x (ISBN 0-684-15333-5, ScribC); Teachers manual free (ISBN 0-684-15997-X); cuaderno de ejercicios workbook 6.95x (ISBN 0-684-15620-2); reel-reel tape 120.00 (ISBN 0-684-16053-6). Scribner.

Castells, Matilde O. Mundo Hispano: Lengua y Cultura. LC 80-23698. 416p. 1980. 13.95 (ISBN 0-471-03396-0); write for info. tapes (ISBN 0-471-03397-9); write for info. tapes (ISBN 0-471-05835-1). Wiley.

Castellucis, Richard L. Digital Circuits & Systems. 356p. 1981. text ed. 18.95 (ISBN 0-8359-1297-3); instrs. manual avail. (ISBN 0-8359-1298-1). Reston.

--Pulse & Logic Circuits. LC 75-27995. 1976. pap. 6.00 (ISBN 0-8273-1134-6); instructor's guide 1.00 (ISBN 0-8273-1135-4). Delmar.

Castenada Shular, A., et al. Literatura Chicana: Texto & Contexto. 1972. ref. ed. 12.95 (ISBN 0-13-537563-0); pap. text ed. 10.50 (ISBN 0-13-537555-X). P-H.

Caster, Lee E. Hunter's Folly. (Orig.). 1979. pap. 1.95 (ISBN 0-532-23288-7). Manor Bks.

Casterline, Gail F. Archives & Manuscripts: Exhibits. LC 80-80072. (Saa Basic Manual Ser.). 72p. (Orig.). 1980. pap. 7.00 (ISBN 0-931828-18-X). Soc Am Archivists.

Castiglione, Baldesar. The Book of the Courtier. Bull, George, tr. (Classics Ser.). 368p. 1976. pap. 2.95 (ISBN 0-14-044192-1). Penguin.

Castiglione, Pierina B. Italian Phonetics, Diction & Intonation. 103p. pap. 9.50x (ISBN 0-913298-48-4); castinglone tape set 20.00. S F Vanni.

Castille, Vernon De see De Castille, Vernon.

Castillejo, Irene Claremont De see Claremont De Castillejo, Irene.

Castillo, Adelaida Del see Mora, Magdalena & Del Castillo, Adelaida.

Castillo, Richard D. Del see Griswold del Castillo, Richard.

Castillo, Ronald Del see Del Castillo, Ronald.

Castillo Solorzano, Alonso De. The Spanish Pole-Cat: The Adventures of Seniora Rufina. L'Estrange, Roger & Ozell, John, eds. LC 80-2472. 1981. Repr. of 1717 ed. 62.50 (ISBN 0-404-19104-5). AMS Pr.

Castle, Barbara. Castle Diaries Nineteen Seventy-Four to Seventy-Six. 788p. 1981. text ed. 40.00 (ISBN 0-8419-0689-0). Holmes & Meier.

Castle, Beatrice H. The Grand Island Story. Carter, James L., ed. LC 71-11186. 1974. 4.50 (ISBN 0-938746-01-4). Marquette Cnty Hist.

Castle, Coralie, jt. auth. see Baylis, Maggie.

Castle, Coralie, jt. auth. see Bryan, John.

Castle, Courtney. Better Dancing. (Better Ser.). (Illus.). (gr. 7 up). 1976. 14.50x o.p. (ISBN 0-7182-0482-4, SpS). Soccer.

Castle, E. B., jt. auth. see Walters, Elsa H.

Castle, E. F. & Owens, N. P. Principles of Accounts. 5th ed. 448p. 1978. pap. text ed. 12.95x (ISBN 0-7121-1687-7, Pub. by Maconald & Evans England). Intl Ideas.

Castle, Frank. Dakota Boomtown. 1979. pap. 1.50 o.p. (ISBN 0-449-14180-2, GM). Fawcett.

Castle, Gladys C., jt. auth. see Gunn, Jack W.

Castle, Jayne. The Gentle Pirate. 1980. pap. 1.50 (ISBN 0-440-12981-8). Dell.

--Wagered Weekend. (Candlelight Romance Ser.). (Orig.). Date not set. pap. 1.50 (ISBN 0-440-19413-X). Dell.

Castle, M. Hospital Infection Control: Principles & Practices. LC 80-13424. 1980. 16.95 (ISBN 0-471-05395-3). Wiley.

Castle, Mary. Hospital Infection Control. LC 80-13424. 251p. 1980. 16.95 (ISBN 0-471-05395-3, Pub. by Wiley Med). Wiley.

Castle, Molly, jt. auth. see Tucker, W. E.

Castle, Sue. The Complete New Guide to Preparing Baby Foods. rev. ed. LC 79-6099. (Illus.). 336p. 1981. 12.95 (ISBN 0-385-15884-X). Doubleday.

Castle, Tony, ed. Through the Year with Pope John Paul II: Reading for Every Day of the Year. 288p. 1981. 12.95 (ISBN 0-8245-0041-5). Crossroad NY.

Castle, Wendell & Edman, David. Wendell Castle Book of Wood Lamination. 192p. 1980. 18.95 (ISBN 0-442-21478-2). Van Nos Reinhold.

Castleman, Kenneth R. Digital Image Processing. LC 78-27578. (Illus.). 1979. text ed. 32.95 (ISBN 0-13-212365-7). P-H.

Castleman, Michael. Sexual Solution. 1981. 11.95 (ISBN 0-671-24688-7). S&S.

Castleman, Riva. Printed Art: A View of Two Decades. LC 79-56089. (Illus.). 144p. 1979. 17.50 (ISBN 0-87070-531-8); pap. 9.95 (ISBN 0-87070-541-5). Museum Mod Art.

--Prints of the Twentieth Century: A History. LC 76-9219. (Illus.). 1976. 15.95 (ISBN 0-19-519887-5); pap. 9.95 (ISBN 0-19-519888-3). Oxford U Pr.

Castleman, Robbie. David: Man After God's Own Heart, 2 vols. (Fisherman Bible Studyguide Ser.). 72p. 1981. saddle stitched 2.25 ea. Vol. 1 (ISBN 0-87788-164-2). Vol. 2 (ISBN 0-87788-165-0). Shaw Pubs.

Castles, Francis G. Pressure Groups & Political Culture: A Comparative Study. (Library of Political Studies). (Orig.). 1967. pap. text ed. 2.50x (ISBN 0-7100-6526-4). Humanities.

--The Social Democratic Image of Society: A Study of the Achievements & Origins of Scandinavian Social Democracy in Comparative Perspective. 1978. 16.00x (ISBN 0-7100-8870-1). Routledge & Kegan.

Casto, Glendon, ed. see Casto, Helen & Hoagland, Victoria.

Casto, Helen & Hoagland, Victoria. CAMS Social-Emotional Program. Casto, Glendon, ed. LC 79-88182. (Curriculum & Monitoring System Ser.). 120p. (For use with early childhood handicapped). 1980. pap. text ed. 12.20 (ISBN 0-8027-9066-6). Walker Educ.

Castor, Henry. First Book of the War with Mexico. (First Bks). (Illus.). (gr. 4-6). 1964. PLB 4.90 o.p. (ISBN 0-531-00663-8). Watts.

--Teddy Roosevelt & the Rough Riders. (Landmark Ser: No. 41). (Illus.). (gr. 4-6). 1963. PLB 4.39 o.p. (ISBN 0-394-90341-2, BYR). Random.

Castoriadis, Cornelius. The Crossroads of the Labyrinth. Sozu, Kate & Ryle, Martin, trs. Date not set. 35.00 (ISBN 0-89396-032-2). Urizen Bks.

Castro, Americo. The Spaniards: An Introduction to Their History. King, Willard F. & Margaretten, Selma, trs. from Sp. LC 67-14000. 638p. 1980. 32.50x (ISBN 0-520-01617-3); pap. 14.95x (ISBN 0-520-01617-3). U of Cal Pr.

Castro, Carol C. Welcoming God's Forgiveness. 30p. (Orig.). 1978. pap. 1.05 adult resource bk.; pap. 10.25 (ISBN 0-697-01737-0). Wm C Brown.

--Welcoming God's Forgiveness. 120p. 1978. pap. text ed. 3.50 (ISBN 0-697-01681-1); 4.50 (ISBN 0-697-01682-X); classroom tchr's guide .75; adult resource book, pack/10,10.25 1.05 (ISBN 0-697-01685-4). Wm C Brown.
--Welcoming Jesus. 120p. 1979. pap. 3.50 (ISBN 0-697-01702-8); leader's guide 4.50 (ISBN 0-697-01703-6); classroom teacher's guide .75 (ISBN 0-697-01738-9); adult resource book, pack/10, 10.25 1.05 (ISBN 0-697-01704-4). Wm C Brown.
--Welcoming Jesus: Adult Resource Book. 30p. (Orig.). 1979. pap. 1.05 adult resource bk.; Set. tchr's manual 0.75 (ISBN 0-697-01738-9). Wm C Brown.
Castro, Daniel. Looking at Life, Bk. 1. LC 77-99081. (Orig.). 1978. pap. 2.00 o.p. (ISBN 0-918038-06-5). Journey Pubns.
Castro, Fernando J. De see De Castro, Fernando J., et al.
Castro, Josue De see De Castro, Josue.
Castro, Mercedes. Noche Callada (Poemas) (Illus.). 79p. (Orig., Span.). pap. 3.75 (ISBN 0-9604748-0-3). Castro.
Castro, Oscar. In Touch: A New American Series. Incl. students bk. 1, 1979 (ISBN 0-582-79742-X); tchr's manual 1 (ISBN 0-582-79743-8); workbook 1 (ISBN 0-582-79744-6); cassette 1; students bk. 2 (ISBN 0-582-79746-2); tchr's manual 2 (ISBN 0-582-79747-0); workbook 2 (ISBN 0-582-79748-9); cassette 2 (ISBN 0-582-79749-7); students bk. 3 (ISBN 0-582-79750-0); tchr's manual 3 (ISBN 0-582-79753-5); workbook 3 (ISBN 0-582-79752-7); cassette 3 (ISBN 0-582-79751-9). (Illus.). 1980. pap. text ed. 3.50x ea. student bk.; tchr's manual 4.50x ea.; wkbk. 1.95x ea.; cassette 18.95 ea. Longman.
Castro, R. & De Cadenet, J. J. Welding Metallurgy of Stainless & Heat-Resisting Steels. Jain, R. C., tr. from Fr. LC 74-76582. (Illus.). 200p. 1975. 29.95 (ISBN 0-521-20431-3). Cambridge U Pr.
Castro-Amaya, Rogelio A. & Kattan-Zablah, Jorge. Dos Amigos--Viajando por Hispanoamerica. Buchsbaum, Mildred, ed. (Illus., Span.). Date not set. pap. text ed. 5.95 (ISBN 0-910286-66-3). Boxwood. Postponed.
Castro De Davila, Maria D. Arquitectura En San Juan De Puerto Rico (Siglo XIX) LC 78-21582. (Illus.). 1979. 15.00 (ISBN 0-8477-2110-8). U of PR Pr.
Castroleal, jt. auth. see Suarez.
Castroleal, Alicia & Suarez, Diamantina V. Aprende En Espanol y En Ingles: Level 1-Reader B. 1979. pap. text ed. 2.50 (ISBN 0-88345-389-4); 5.25 o.p. (ISBN 0-88345-391-6). Regents Pub.
Casty, Alan. Act of Writing & Reading: A Combined Text. (Orig.). 1966. pap. text ed. 8.95x (ISBN 0-13-003780-X). P-H.
--A Mixed Bag: A New Collection for Understanding & Response. 2nd ed. (Illus.). 256p. 1975. pap. text ed. 8.95 (ISBN 0-13-586016-4). P-H.
Casty, Alan & Tighe, Donald J. Staircase to Writing & Reading. 3rd ed. (Illus.). 1979. pap. 10.95 (ISBN 0-13-840579-4). P-H.
Casty, Alan H. The Shape of Fiction. 2nd ed. 448p. 1975. pap. text ed. 9.95x (ISBN 0-669-91066-X); instructor's manual free (ISBN 0-669-91074-0). Heath.
Caswell, ed. Pesticide Handbook-Entoma. 1979. 9.00 (ISBN 0-686-23164-3); pap. 7.50 (ISBN 0-686-23165-1). Entomol Soc.
Catalano, Gary. The Years of Hope: Australian Art & Criticism 1959-1968. (Illus.). 224p. 1980. 33.50 (ISBN 0-19-554220-7). Oxford U Pr.
Catalano, Ralph. Health, Behavior & the Community: An Ecological Perspective. LC 78-23714. (Pergamon General Psychology Ser.: Vol. 76). (Illus.). 1979. text ed. 33.00 (ISBN 0-08-022972-7); pap. text ed. 11.00 (ISBN 0-08-022971-9). Pergamon.
Cataldo, Bernard F., et al. Introduction to Law & the Legal Process. 3rd ed. LC 79-13193. 1980. 26.50 (ISBN 0-471-14082-1); tchr's manual avail. (ISBN 0-471-02267-5). Wiley.
Cataldo, Everett F., et al. School Desegregation Policy. new ed. LC 77-6080. (Politics of Education Ser.). (Illus.). 1978. 14.95 (ISBN 0-669-01536-9). Lexington Bks.
Cataldo, Mary Ann, jt. auth. see Benvenuti, Judi.
Catalyst Staff. Making the Most of Your First Job. 288p. 1981. 11.95 (ISBN 0-399-12609-0). Putnam.
Catanese, Anthony J. & Farmer, W. Paul, eds. Personality, Politics & Planning: How City Planners Work. LC 77-17780. 1978. 17.50x (ISBN 0-8039-0961-6). Sage.
Catanese, Anthony J., et al. Urban Planning: A Guide to Information Sources. LC 78-13462. (Urban Studies Information Guide Ser.: Vol. 2). 1979. 30.00 (ISBN 0-8103-1399-5). Gale.
Catanese, Anthony James. Planners & Local Politics: Impossible Dreams. LC 73-94287. (Sage Library of Social Research: Vol. 7). 1974. 18.00x (ISBN 0-8039-0397-9); pap. 8.95x (ISBN 0-8039-0378-2). Sage.
Catania, A. Charles. Learning. (Century Psychology Ser.). (Illus.). 1979. text ed. 18.95 (ISBN 0-13-527432-X). P-H.
Catania, A. Charles & Brigham, T. A., eds. Handbook of Applied Behavior Analysis: Social & Instructional Processes. (Century Psychology Ser.). 1979. 39.50 (ISBN 0-470-99347-2). Halsted Pr.
Catania, Charles A. Contemporary Research in Operant Behavior. 1968. pap. 11.95x (ISBN 0-673-05496-9). Scott F.
Catanzariti, John, jt. ed. see Ferguson, E. James.
Catanzaro, Angela. Mama Mia Italian Cookbook. 1955. 5.95 o.p. (ISBN 0-87140-969-0). Liveright.
Catanzaro, Ronald J., ed. Alcoholism: The Total Treatment Approach. (Illus.). 528p. 1977. text ed. 34.50 (ISBN 0-398-00295-9). C C Thomas.
Catchpole, A. G., et al. Organic Chemistry. 1969. 17.95x (ISBN 0-245-58990-2). Intl Ideas.
Catchpole, Brian. A Map History of the British People Since 1700. 1975. pap. text ed. 8.95x (ISBN 0-435-31160-3). Heinemann Ed.
Catchpole, Joan M. Watercolour Painting: A Beginner's Guide. (Illus.). 1975. 15.95x (ISBN 0-7188-2162-9). Intl Ideas.
Cate, Curtis, tr. see De Saint-Exupery, Antoine.
Cate, Dick. Flying Free. LC 76-57722. (Illus.). (gr. 4-7). 1977. 6.95 o.p. (ISBN 0-525-66535-8). Elsevier-Nelson.
--Never Is a Long, Long Time. LC 77-10818. (Illus.). (gr. 4-7). 1977. 5.95 o.p. (ISBN 0-525-66563-3). Elsevier-Nelson.
--Nice Day Out? (Illus.). (gr. 3-6). 1981. 7.95 (ISBN 0-525-66700-8). Elsevier-Nelson.
--Old Dog, New Tricks. (Illus.). 96p. (gr. 3-6). 1981. 9.95 (ISBN 0-525-66730-X). Elsevier-Nelson.
Cate, Ten A. Richard see Ten Cate, A. Richard.
Cateora, Philip R. & Hess, John M. International Marketing. 4th ed. 1979. text ed. 19.50x (ISBN 0-256-02153-8). Irwin.
Cater, Douglass & Adler, Richard, eds. Television As a Social Force: New Approaches to Tv Criticism. LC 75-23951. (Special Studies). 1975. 23.95 (ISBN 0-275-01190-9). Praeger.
Cater, Douglass & Nyhan, Michael J., eds. The Future of Public Broadcasting. (Special Studies). 200p. 1976. text ed. 26.95 (ISBN 0-275-56990-X); pap. text ed. 10.95 (ISBN 0-275-64590-8). Praeger.
Cater, Douglass, jt. ed. see Adler, Richard.
Cater, Libby A., et al. Women & Men: Changing Roles, Relationships, & Perceptions. LC 76-14472. (Special Studies). 1977. text ed. 19.95 o.p. (ISBN 0-03-021476-9). Praeger.
Cates, Ann. Guilt Trips. (Illus.). 100p. (Orig.). 1980. pap. 2.95 (ISBN 0-937768-00-6). Expressions TX.
Cates, G. Truett & Swaffar, Janet K. Reading a Second Language. (Language in Education Ser.: No. 20). 1979. pap. 2.95 (ISBN 0-87281-106-9). Ctr Appl Ling.
Cates, Rosalie. Branded. Date not set. 10.95 (ISBN 0-87949-147-7). Ashley Bks.
Catford, Nancy. Making Nursery Toys. 1969. 6.95 (ISBN 0-236-17610-2, Pub. by Paul Elek). Merrimack Bk Serv.
Cath, Stanley H., et al. Love & Hate on the Tennis Court. LC 77-476. (Encore Edition). 1977. 3.50 o.p. (ISBN 0-684-15938-4, ScribT). Scribner.
Cathcart, Helen. Anne & the Princesses Royal. 2nd ed. 205p. 1975. 8.75 (ISBN 0-491-01321-3). Transatlantic.
Cathcart, Linda L. Nancy Graves: A Survey 1969 to 1980. LC 80-13227. (Illus.). 1980. pap. 15.00 (ISBN 0-914782-34-7). Buffalo Acad.
Cathcart, Richard B. Herman Sorgel. (Architecture Ser.: Bibliography A-181). 61p. pap. 6.50. Vance Biblios.
Cathcart, Robert. Post Communication: Criticism & Evaluation. LC 66-19701. (Orig.). 1966. pap. 5.95 (ISBN 0-672-61073-6, SC2). Bobbs.
--Post Communication: Rhetorical Analysis & Evaluation. LC 80-36842. (Speech Communication Ser.). 144p. 1981. pap. text ed. 5.95 (ISBN 0-672-61520-7). Bobbs.
Cathcart, Ruth & Strong, Michael. Beyond the Classroom. (Gateway to English Program). (Illus.). 208p. (Orig.). 1981. pap. text ed. 4.95 (ISBN 0-88377-170-5). Newbury Hse.
Cather, Willa. Alexander's Bridge. LC 76-56439. 1977. pap. 3.95 (ISBN 0-8032-5863-1, BB 635, Bison). U of Nebr Pr.
--April Twilights (1903) rev. ed. Slote, Bernice, ed. LC 76-14216. (Illus.). 1976. pap. 2.25 (ISBN 0-8032-5851-8, BB 629, Bison). U of Nebr Pr.
--A Lost Lady. 192p. 1972. pap. 2.45 o.p. (ISBN 0-394-71705-8, V705, Vin). Random.
--My Antonia. (Keith Jennison Large Type Bks). (gr. 7 up). PLB 9.95 o.p. (ISBN 0-531-00242-X). Watts.
--My Mortal Enemy. 1961. pap. 1.95 (ISBN 0-394-70200-X, V200, Vin). Random.
--O Pioneers. 10.95 (ISBN 0-395-07516-5); pap. 4.96 (ISBN 0-395-08365-6). HM.
--The Song of the Lark. 1915 ed. LC 77-15596. 1978. pap. 6.95 (ISBN 0-8032-6300-7, BB 670, Bison). U of Nebr Pr.
--Willa Cather's Collected Short Fiction, 1892-1912. rev. ed. Faulkner, Virginia, ed. LC 73-126046. 1970. 19.50x (ISBN 0-8032-0770-0). U of Nebr Pr.
Catherall, Arthur. Camel Caravan. LC 68-24733. (Illus.). (gr. 3-7). 1968. 5.95 o.p. (ISBN 0-8164-3009-8, Clarion). HM.
--Death of an Oil Rig. LC 70-77310. (Illus.). (gr. 5-8). 1969. 9.95 (ISBN 0-87599-159-9). S G Phillips.
Catherall, Ed, jt. auth. see Bird, John.
Catherine Of Genoa. Catherine of Genoa: Purgation & Purgatory, the Spiritual Dialogue. Hughes, Serge, tr. (Classics of Western Spirituality Ser). 1979. 11.95 (ISBN 0-8091-0285-4); pap. 7.95 (ISBN 0-8091-2207-3). Paulist Pr.
Cathers, David M. Furniture of the American Arts & Crafts Movement: Stickley & Roycroft Mission Oak. 1981. 9.95 (ISBN 0-453-00397-4, H397). NAL.
Catherwood, Frederick. First Things First. 128p. 1981. pap. 5.95 (ISBN 0-87784-472-0). Inter Varsity.
Catherwood, Mary H. Lower Illinois Valley Local Sketches of Long Ago. 55p. 1980. Repr. 3.00 (ISBN 0-686-27587-X). E S Cunningham.
Cathexis Institute, jt. auth. see Schiff, Jacqui L.
Cathey, W. Thomas. Optical Information Processing & Holography. LC 73-14604. (Pure & Applied Optics Ser). 398p. 1974. 29.95 (ISBN 0-471-14078-3, Pub. by Wiley-Interscience). Wiley.
Catholic Hospital Association. Math Primer for Students in Radiologic Technology. rev. ed. Barringhaus, Sr. Francita, ed. LC 73-86652. 44p. 1973. pap. text ed. 2.50 o.p. (ISBN 0-87125-009-8). Cath Health.
Catholic Polls Inc., ed. Bible in Pictures. (Illus.). 12.95 o.p. (ISBN 0-685-74102-8). Guild Bks.
Cathon, Laura E., et al, eds. Stories to Tell Children: A Selected List. LC 73-13317. (Illus.). 168p. 1974. pap. 3.95 (ISBN 0-8229-5246-7). U of Pittsburgh Pr.
Cativiela, A., tr. see Schroeder, L. Bonnetty A.
Catledge, Turner, jt. auth. see Alsop, Joseph.
Catlett, Cloe. Fifty More Hikes in Maine. LC 79-92571. (Fifty Hikes Ser.). (Illus., Orig.). 1980. pap. 8.95 (ISBN 0-89725-017-6). NH Pub Co.
Catlett, Joyce, jt. auth. see Firestone, Robert.
Catley, Robert. From Tweedledum to Tweedledee: The New Labor Government in Australia. LC 74-189120. 112p. 1974. pap. 6.00x (ISBN 0-85552-022-1). Intl Pubns Serv.
Catlin, Alberta P. & Bachand, Shirley. Practical Nursing: PreTest Self-Assessment & Review. LC 78-70622. (Nursing: Pretest Self-Assessment & Review Ser.). (Illus.). 1979. pap. 6.95 (ISBN 0-07-051571-9). McGraw-Pretest.
Catlin, George. Catlin's North American Indian Portfolio: A Reproduction. facs ed. LC 78-132585. (Reproduction). 1970. Repr. of 1845 ed. 250.00 (ISBN 0-8040-0029-8, SB). Swallow.
--George Catlin: Episodes from Life Among the Indians & Last Rambles. Ross, Marvin C., ed. 354p. 1980. pap. 12.50 (ISBN 0-8061-1693-5). U of Okla Pr.
--Letters & Notes on the Manners, Customs & Conditions of the North American Indians, Vol. 1. LC 64-18844. (Illus.). 264p. 1973. pap. 5.50 (ISBN 0-486-22118-0). Dover.
--Letters & Notes on the Manners, Customs & Conditions of the North American Indians, Vol. 2. LC 64-18844. (Illus.). 266p. 1973. pap. 5.50 (ISBN 0-486-22119-9). Dover.
--O-kee-pa: A Religious Ceremony & Other Customs of the Mandans. Ewers, John C., ed. LC 76-4522. (Illus.). 106p. 1976. pap. 7.95 (ISBN 0-8032-5845-3, BB 625, Bison). U of Nebr Pr.
Catlin, Stanton L. & Grieder, Terence, eds. Art of Latin America Since Independence. rev. ed. (Illus.). 246p. 1966. pap. 5.00 (ISBN 0-913456-01-2). Interbk Inc.
Catlin, Stanton L., intro. by. Pissarro in Venezuela. LC 68-21908. (Illus.). 1968. pap. 2.00 o.p. (ISBN 0-913456-05-5). Interbk Inc.
Catlin, Stanton L. Artists of the Western Hemisphere: Precursors of Modernism, 1860-1930. LC 67-29739. (Illus.). 60p. 1968. pap. 2.00 (ISBN 0-913456-02-0). Interbk Inc.
Catling, Patrick S. The Chocolate Touch. LC 78-31100. (Illus.). (gr. 4-6). 1979. Repr. of 1952 ed. 6.50 (ISBN 0-688-22187-4); PLB 6.24 (ISBN 0-688-32187-9). Morrow.
--The Chocolate Touch. (Skylark Ser.). 96p. 1981. pap. 1.75 (ISBN 0-553-15075-8). Bantam.
Cato, Ingemar, jt. auth. see Olausson, Eric.
Cato, Nancy. All the Rivers Run. 1979. pap. 2.95 (ISBN 0-451-08693-7, E8693, Sig). NAL.
Catoe, Lynn E., ed. UFOs & Related Subjects: An Annotated Bibliography. LC 78-26124. 1979. Repr. of 1969 ed. 38.00 (ISBN 0-8103-2021-5). Gale.
Catoir, John T. The Way People Pray: An Introduction to the History of Religions. LC 73-91369. (Orig.). 1974. pap. 1.95 (ISBN 0-8091-1805-X). Paulist Pr.
Caton, R. L., et al, eds. Rotating Electrical Equipment Testing, 2 vols. (Engineering Craftsmen: No. G22). (Illus.). 1969. Set. spiral bdg. 41.50x (ISBN 0-85083-072-9). Intl Ideas.
Catovsky, Daniel. The Leukemic Cell. (Methods in Haematology). (Illus.). 230p. 1981. lib. bdg. 35.00 (ISBN 0-443-01911-8). Churchill.
Catran, Jack. Is There Intelligent Life on Earth? LC 80-80016. 240p. 1981. 12.95 (ISBN 0-936162-29-5, L42). Lidiraven Bks.
Catsambas, Thanos. Regional Impacts of Federal Fiscal Policy. LC 77-12282. 1978. 16.95 (ISBN 0-669-01953-4). Lexington Bks.
Catsimpoolas, Nicholas. Immunological Aspects of Food. (Illus.). 1977. lib. bdg. 38.50 (ISBN 0-87055-203-1). AVI.
Catsimpoolas, Nicholas, ed. Methods of Cell Separation, 3 vols. LC 77-11018. (Biological Separations Ser.). (Illus.). 32.50 (ISBN 0-306-34604-4, Plenum Pr); Vol. 2, 315p, 1979. 32.50 (ISBN 0-306-40094-4); Vol. 3, 215p, 1980. 27.50 (ISBN 0-306-40377-3). Plenum Pub.
Catt, J. A. see Bowen, D. Q.
Cattabeni, Caball, et al, eds. Dioxin: Toxicological & Chemical Aspects. (Monographs of the Giovanni Lorenzini Foundation). 1978. 20.00 (ISBN 0-470-26361-X). Halsted Pr.
Cattabeni, F., et al, eds. Advances in Biochemical Psychopharmacology, Vol. 24. 680p. 1980. text ed. 62.50 (ISBN 0-89004-375-2). Raven.
Cattafi, Bartolo. Cattafi Selected Poems. Swann, Brian & Feldman, Ruth, trs. from Ital. 228p. 1981. 14.00 (ISBN 0-931556-04-X); pap. 6.00 (ISBN 0-931556-05-8). Translation Pr.
Cattan, Henry. Palestine & International Law: The Legal Aspects of the Arab-Israeli Conflict. 2nd ed. LC 75-42335. 1976. text ed. 22.00x (ISBN 0-582-78067-5). Longman.
Cattell, Psyche. Raising Children with Love & Limits. LC 77-187810. 232p. 1972. 12.95 (ISBN 0-911012-20-6). Nelson-Hall.
Cattell, Raymond B. A New Morality from Science: Beyondism. 1976. 35.00 (ISBN 0-08-016956-2). Pergamon.
Cattell, Raymond B. & Schuerger, James M. Personality Theory in Action: Handbook for the Objective-Analytic Test Kit. LC 78-50146. 1978. 26.50 (ISBN 0-918296-11-0). Inst Personality Ability.
Catterson, Joy S., ed. see Gibson, Karon W., et al.
Catterson, R. Smith. Drawing from Memory. (Illus.). 1979. deluxe ed. 34.45 (ISBN 0-930582-44-6). Gloucester Art.
Catterson, Robert A. How to Draw from Memory. (Illus.). 1980. 33.45 (ISBN 0-930582-58-6). Gloucester Art.
Catto, Max. Sam Casanova. 1977. pap. 1.75 o.p. (ISBN 0-451-07790-3, E7790, Sig). NAL.
Catton, Bruce. America Goes to War. LC 58-13602. (Illus.). 1971. pap. 5.00x (ISBN 0-8195-6016-2, Pub. by Wesleyan U Pr). Columbia U Pr.
--Banners at Shenandoah. 254p. 1976. Repr. of 1955 ed. lib. bdg. 13.95x (ISBN 0-89244-019-8). Queens Hse.
--Bruce Catton's America. Jensen, Oliver, ed. LC 79-17534. (Illus.). 224p. 1979. deluxe ed. 17.50 (ISBN 0-8281-0310-0, Dist. by Doubleday). Am Heritage.
--Coming Fury. LC 61-12502. (Centennial History of the Civil War: Vol. 1). 14.95 (ISBN 0-385-09813-8). Doubleday.
--Gettysburg: The Final Fury. LC 73-11896. (Illus.). 128p. 1974. slip cased 10.00 (ISBN 0-385-02060-0). Doubleday.
--Michigan. (States & the Nation Ser.). (Illus.). 224p. 1976. 12.95 (ISBN 0-393-05572-8, Co-Pub by AASLH). Norton.
Catton, William R., Jr. Overshoot: The Ecological Basis of Revolutionary Change. LC 80-13443. (Illus.). 250p. 1980. 16.50 (ISBN 0-252-00818-9). U of Ill Pr.
Catudal, Honore M. Kennedy & the Berlin Wall Crisis: A Case Study in U. S. Decision Making. (Illus.). 358p. (Orig.). 1980. pap. 20.00x (ISBN 3-87061-160-X). Intl Pubns Serv.
Catullus. The Catullus of William Hull. Hull, William, tr. 7.00 (ISBN 0-89253-791-4); flexible cloth 4.00 (ISBN 0-89253-792-2). Ind-US Inc.
--Odi Et Amo: The Complete Poetry of Latussus. Swanson, Roy A., tr. LC 59-11685. 1959. pap. 3.95 (ISBN 0-672-60314-4, LLA114). Bobbs.
Catz, Boris. Thyroid Case Studies. 1975. spiral bdg. 14.00 (ISBN 0-87488-038-6). Med Exam.
Caubang, Ted C. Readings on Production Planning & Control. 178p. 1972. 11.75 (ISBN 92-833-1017-9, APO51, APO). Unipub.

Cauchois, Y., et al, eds. Wavelengths of X-Ray Emission Lines & Absorption Edges. LC 78-40419. 1978. text ed. 150.00 (ISBN 0-08-022448-2); pap. text ed. 80.00 (ISBN 0-08-023392-9). Pergamon.

Caudill, Harry M. The Mountain, the Miner & the Lord: & Other Tales from a Country Law Office. LC 80-51012. 192p. 1980. 12.50 (ISBN 0-8131-1403-9). U Pr of Ky.

Caudill, Rebecca. Wind, Sand & Sky. (Illus.). 32p. (gr. k-6). 1976. PLB 7.95 (ISBN 0-525-42899-2). Dutton.

Caudill, William. Memos from Egypt: Joint U.S. Egyptian Study Group on Building Materials & Building Technology. LC 75-13629. 260p. 1975. pap. 9.95 (ISBN 0-8436-0157-4). CBI Pub.

Caudill, William W., et al. Architecture & You: How to Experience & Enjoy Buildings. (Illus.). 1978. 18.50 (ISBN 0-8230-7040-9, Whitney Lib); pap. 12.95 (ISBN 0-8230-7041-7). Watson-Guptill.

Caudle, Peggy. Manon & the Prince. 1979. 4.00 (ISBN 0-8062-1370-1). Carlton.

Caudy, Don W., jt. auth. see Hackman, Donald J.

Caufield, Don & Caufield, Joan. Incredible Detectives. 1980. pap. 1.50 (ISBN 0-380-01282-0, 50443, Camelot). Avon.

Caufield, Joan, jt. auth. see Caufield, Don.

Caughey, C. A. Depositional Systems in the Paluxy Formation (Lower Cretaceous) Northeast Texas-Oil, Gas, & Ground-Water Resources. (Illus.). 59p. 1977. 2.00 (GC 77-8). Bur Econ Geology.

Caughie, John, ed. Theories of Authorship. (B. F. I. Readers in Film Studies). (Illus.). 320p. 1981. 28.00 (ISBN 0-7100-0649-7); pap. 14.00 (ISBN 0-7100-0650-0). Routledge & Kegan.

Caulcott, Evelyn. Significance Tests. (Applied Statistics Ser). 1973. 16.00x (ISBN 0-7100-7406-9); pap. 8.00 (ISBN 0-7100-8385-8). Routledge & Kegan.

Cauley, Lorinda B. The Goose & the Golden Coins. LC 80-24591. (Illus.). 48p. (ps-3). 1981. pap. 5.95 (ISBN 0-15-232207-8, VoyB). HarBraceJ.

Cauley, Lorinda B., retold by. & illus. The Goose & the Golden Coins. LC 80-24591. (Illus.). 48p. (ps-3). 1981. 11.95 (ISBN 0-15-232206-X, HJ). HarBraceJ.

Caulfield, Sophia F. House Mottoes & Inscriptions. LC 68-21758. 1968. Repr. of 1908 ed. 15.00 (ISBN 0-8103-3322-8). Gale.

Caulfield, Sophia F. & Saward, Blanche C. Dictionary of Needlework. LC 75-172439. (Illus.). 1971. Repr. of 1882 ed. 54.00 (ISBN 0-8103-3404-6). Gale.

Cauman, Samuel, jt. auth. see Janson, H. W.

Cauro, Dominique, jt. auth. see Cauro, Roland.

Cauro, Roland & Cauro, Dominique. Stringcraft. LC 76-1181. (Little Craft Book Ser.). (Illus.). 48p. 1976. 4.95 o.p. (ISBN 0-8069-5364-0); PLB 5.89 o.p. (ISBN 0-8069-5365-9). Sterling.

Causby, Ralph E., jt. auth. see Baucom, Marta E.

Causer, H. Phillip. M.I.A. (Missing in Action) LC 77-88747. (Illus.). 1977. 9.95 (ISBN 0-918442-00-1). Phipps Pub.

Causey, Andrew. Paul Nash. (Illus.). 532p. 1980. 98.00x (ISBN 0-19-817348-2). Oxford U Pr.

Causey, Denzil Y. Accounting for Decision Making. LC 77-78479. (Accounting Ser.). 1978. text ed. 19.95 o.p. (ISBN 0-88244-156-6). Grid Pub.

Causey, Don. Killer Insects. (Illus.). (gr. 4-6). 1979. PLB 6.90 s&l (ISBN 0-531-02924-7). Watts.

Causley, Charles. The Batsford Book of Stories in Verse for Children. 1979. 17.95 (ISBN 0-7134-1529-0). David & Charles.

--Figgie Hobbin. 1974. 4.95 (ISBN 0-8027-6131-3); PLB 4.85 o.s.i. (ISBN 0-8027-6132-1). Walker & Co.

--Johnny Alleluia. 1962. 4.95 (ISBN 0-246-63643-2). Dufour.

Causly, Henry. Remedies for Positive Living. 1981. 4.75 (ISBN 0-8062-1690-5). Carlton.

Causton, Donald R. A Biologist's Mathematics. (Contemporary Biology Ser). 1978. pap. 18.95 (ISBN 0-7131-2605-1). Univ Park.

Caute, David, ed. Essential Writings of Karl Marx. 1970. pap. 2.95 o.s.i. (ISBN 0-02-072620-1, Collier). Macmillan.

Cautela, Joseph R. Organic Dysfunction Survey Schedules. LC 80-53910. 157p. (Orig.). 1981. pap. text ed. write for info. (ISBN 0-87822-223-5, 2235). Res Press.

Cautela, Joseph R., jt. ed. see Upper, Dennis.

Cauthen, Irby B., Jr., ed. see Sackville, Thomas & Norton, Thomas.

Cauthron, Michael, jt. auth. see Smith, Del.

Cautley, Patricia W. New Foster Parents. 288p. 1980. 19.95 (ISBN 0-87705-495-9). Human Sci Pr.

--New Foster Parents: The First Experience. LC 80-10937. 288p. 1980. 19.95x (ISBN 0-87705-495-9). Human Sci Pr.

Cauvin, Patrick. Blind Love. 1978. pap. 1.75 o.p. (ISBN 0-449-23483-5, Crest). Fawcett.

Cava, Ester, et al, eds. A Pediatrician's Guide to Child Behavior Problems. 1979. text ed. 21.50 (ISBN 0-89352-075-6). Masson Pub.

Cava, Ralph Della see Della Cava, Ralph.

Cavaiani, Mabel. The Low Cholesterol Cookbook. 272p. 1974. pap. 2.95 (ISBN 0-06-463408-6, EH 408, EH). Har-Row.

Cavaiani, Mabel, et al. Simplified Quantity Regional Recipes. 1979. 15.25 (ISBN 0-8104-9453-1). Hayden.

Cavalcanti, Pedro & Piccone, Paul, eds. History, Philosophy & Culture in the Young Gramsci. LC 74-82995. 160p. (Orig.). 1975. 9.50 (ISBN 0-914386-07-7); pap. 3.95 (ISBN 0-914386-05-0). Telos Pr.

Cavalcaselle, G. B., jt. auth. see Crowe, J. A.

Cavalchini, Mariella, ed. see Tasso, Torquato.

Cavalier, Julien. Classic American Railroad Stations. LC 78-69669. (Illus.). 1980. 17.50 (ISBN 0-498-02216-1). A S Barnes.

Cavalier, Robert J. Ludwig Wittgenstein's Tractatus Logico-Philosophicus: A Transcendental Critique of Ethics. LC 79-3724. 1980. text ed. 15.50 (ISBN 0-8191-0915-0); pap. text ed. 9.25 (ISBN 0-8191-0916-9). U Pr of Amer.

Cavaliere, Alfredo, ed. see Raimon, Peire.

Cavalieri, Grace, jt. auth. see Watkins, William J.

Cavalla, J. F. & Price, Jones D. The Chemist in Industry Two: Human Health & Plant Protection. (Oxford Chemistry Ser). (Illus.). 96p. 1974. pap. 4.95x o.p. (ISBN 0-19-855416-8). Oxford U Pr.

Cavallaro, Ann. Careers in Food Services. 160p. (YA) 1981. 9.95 (ISBN 0-525-66698-2). Elsevier-Nelson.

Cavalli, Francesco. Gli Amori d'Apollo e di Dafne. Brown, Howard M., ed. LC 76-21071. (Italian Opera 1640-1770 Ser.). 1978. lib. bdg. 70.00 (ISBN 0-8240-2600-4). Garland Pub.

--Scipione Africano. Brown, Howard M., ed. LC 76-20963. (Italian Opera 1640-1770 Ser.). 1978. lib. bdg. 70.00 (ISBN 0-8240-2604-7). Garland Pub.

Cavallini, D., et al, eds. Natural Sulfur Compounds: Novel Biochemical & Structural Aspects. 565p. 1980. 49.50 (ISBN 0-306-40335-8, Plenum Pr). Plenum Pub.

Cavalli-Sforza, L. L. Elements of Human Genetics. 2nd ed. LC 76-58969. 1977. pap. text ed. 8.95 (ISBN 0-8053-1874-7). Benjamin-Cummings.

Cavalli-Sforza, L. L. & Bodmer, Walter F. The Genetics of Human Populations. LC 79-120302. (Biology Ser.). (Illus.). 1978. pap. text ed. 21.95x (ISBN 0-7167-1018-8). W H Freeman.

Cavalli-Sforza, L. L. & Feldman, M. W. Cultural Transmission & Evolution: A Quantitative Approach. May, Robert M., ed. LC 80-8539. (Monographs in Population Biology: No. 16). (Illus.). 368p. 1981. 20.00x (ISBN 0-691-08280-4); pap. 8.95x (ISBN 0-691-08283-9). Princeton U Pr.

Cavalli-Sforza, L. L., jt. auth. see Bodmer, W. F.

Cavallito, C. J., ed. Structure-Activity Relationships & Theory. LC 72-13533. 1973. text ed. 75.00 (ISBN 0-08-016890-6). Pergamon.

Cavallo, Adolph S. Tapestries of Europe & Colonial Peru in the MFA. 1968. 17.50 (ISBN 0-87846-015-2). Mus Fine Arts Boston.

Cavallo, Diana. Lower East Side: A Portrait in Time. LC 75-127459. (gr. 5-9). 1971. 6.95 o.s.i. (ISBN 0-02-717880-3, CCPr). Macmillan.

Cavallo, Dominick. Muscles Morals & Team Sports: The Culture of City Playgrounds, Eighteen Eighty to Nineteen Twenty. LC 80-50689. 240p. 1980. 21.50x (ISBN 0-8122-7782-1). U of Pa Pr.

Cavallo, Dominick, jt. auth. see Albin, Mel.

Cavanagh. Honey. (gr. 7-12). 1980. pap. 1.25 (ISBN 0-590-30002-4, Schol Pap). Schol Bk Serv.

Cavanagh, Gerald, jt. auth. see Purcell, Theodore.

Cavanagh, J., jt. auth. see Clairmonte, F.

Cavanagh, Margery. The Custom of Living. LC 80-5487. 72p. (Orig.). 1980. pap. 3.95 (ISBN 0-931694-08-6). Wampeter Pr.

Cavanagh, Maura, jt. auth. see Smithies, Richard H.

Cavanagh, Michael E. Make Your Tomorrow Better: A Psychological Resource for Singles, Parents & the Entire Family. LC 80-80638. 320p. (Orig.). 1980. pap. 8.95 (ISBN 0-8091-2293-6). Paulist Pr.

Cavanagh, P. R., jt. auth. see Faria, I. E.

Cavanagh, Peter. The Running Shoe Book. LC 80-20365. (Illus.). 400p. 1980. pap. 11.95 (ISBN 0-89037-182-2). Anderson World.

Cavanagh, Ursula M. Cooking & Catering the Wholefood Way. 1970. 6.95 o.p. (ISBN 0-571-09283-7). Transatlantic.

--The Wholefood Cookery Book. (Orig.). 1971. 10.95 (ISBN 0-571-08871-6, Pub. by Faber & Faber); pap. 6.50 (ISBN 0-571-10617-X). Merrimack Bk Serv.

Cavanah, Frances. Jenny Lind & Her Listening Cat. LC 61-15483. (Illus.). (gr. 3-6). 1961. 6.95 (ISBN 0-8149-0289-8). Vanguard.

--Secret of Madame Doll. LC 65-26160. (Illus.). (gr. 4-7). 1965. 6.95 (ISBN 0-8149-0288-X). Vanguard.

Cavanaugh, Arthur, jt. ed. see Horn, Geoffrey.

Cavanaugh, G. M., et al. Formulae & Methods. 1964. 6.00 (ISBN 0-685-52858-8). Marine Bio.

Cavanaugh, Gerald J., jt. ed. see Gay, Peter.

Cavanaugh, Helen. Superflirt. 176p. (Orig.). (gr. 7 up). 1980. pap. 1.50 (ISBN 0-590-30951-X, Schol Pap). Schol Bk Serv.

Cavanaugh, J. Albert. Lettering & Alphabets. (Illus.). 8.50 (ISBN 0-8446-0541-7). Peter Smith.

Cavanaugh, Tom R. & Thomas, Payne E. Bannerstone House: A Frank Lloyd Wright House, Springfield, Illinois. 5th ed. 48p. 1977. pap. 3.75 (ISBN 0-398-00299-1). C C Thomas.

Cavandish, Marshall. Needleworker's Constant Companion. (Illus.). 1978. 29.95 o.p. (ISBN 0-670-50576-5, Studio). Viking Pr.

Cavanna, Betty. Almost Like Sisters. (gr. 7 up). 1963. 8.75 (ISBN 0-688-21014-7). Morrow.

--The Boy Next Door. (gr. 7 up). 1956. PLB 8.40 (ISBN 0-688-31116-4). Morrow.

--Country Cousin. (gr. 7 up). 8.75 (ISBN 0-688-21189-5). Morrow.

--Jenny Kimura. (gr. 7 up). 1964. PLB 7.92 (ISBN 0-688-31737-5). Morrow.

--Joyride. LC 74-5930. 224p. (gr. 7 up). 1974. 8.25 (ISBN 0-688-20125-3); PLB 7.92 (ISBN 0-688-30125-8). Morrow.

--Mystery at Love's Creek. (gr. 7 up). 1965. PLB 7.44 o.p. (ISBN 0-688-31791-X). Morrow.

--Mystery in the Museum. 240p. (gr. 7 up). 1972. PLB 7.92 (ISBN 0-688-31775-8). Morrow.

--Mystery of the Emerald Buddha. LC 76-21826. (gr. 7 up). 1976. 8.25 (ISBN 0-688-22086-X); PLB 7.92 (ISBN 0-688-32086-4). Morrow.

--Ruffles & Drums. LC 75-9630. (Illus.). (gr. 7-9). 1975. 7.75 (ISBN 0-688-22035-5); PLB 7.44 (ISBN 0-688-32035-X). Morrow.

--Runaway Voyage. (gr. 7-9). 1978. PLB 7.63 (ISBN 0-688-32152-6). Morrow.

--Six on Easy Street. pap. 0.95 o.p. (ISBN 0-425-03511-5, Highland). Berkley Pub.

--Spice Island Mystery. LC 72-83531. (gr. 7 up). 1969. 8.25 (ISBN 0-688-21706-0). Morrow.

--The Surfer & the City Girl. LC 80-25901. (A Hiway Bk.). (gr. 7-9). 1981. 8.95 (ISBN 0-664-32679-X). Westminster.

--Time for Tenderness. (gr. 7 up). 1962. PLB 7.63 (ISBN 0-688-31625-5). Morrow.

Cavanna, Roberto & Servadio, Emilio. ESP Experiments with LSD Twenty-Five & Psilocybin. LC 64-24271. (Parapsychological Monograph No. 5). 1964. pap. 3.00 (ISBN 0-912328-08-8). Parapsych Foun.

Cavanna, Roberto, ed. see International Conference on Hypnosis, Drugs, Dreams, & Psi, France, 1967.

Cavanna, Roberto, ed. see International Conference on Methodology in Psi Research, France, 1968.

Cave, C. H., tr. see Jeremias, Joachim.

Cave, Cyril & Maddison, Pamela. A Survey of Recent Research in Special Education. (General Ser.). 1979. text ed. 27.50x (ISBN 0-85633-148-1, NFER). Humanities.

Cave, Emma. The Blood Bond. 192p. 1981. pap. 2.50 (ISBN 0-449-24402-4, Crest). Fawcett.

Cave, F. H., tr. see Jeremias, Joachim.

Cave, Frank & Terrell, David. Digital & Microprocessor Technology. 448p. 1981. text ed. 18.95 (ISBN 0-8359-1326-0); instrs. manual avail. (ISBN 0-8359-1327-9). Reston.

Cave, Marion S. Chromosomes of the California Liliaceae. (U. C. Publ. in Botany: Vol. 57). 1970. pap. 5.50x (ISBN 0-520-09031-4). U of Cal Pr.

Cave, Martin. Computers & Economic Planning. LC 79-7659. (Soviet & East European Studies). 1980. 27.50 (ISBN 0-521-22617-1). Cambridge U Pr.

Cave, Oenone. Traditional Smocks & Smocking. (Illus.). 101p. (Orig.). 1979. pap. 14.00 (ISBN 0-263-06408-5). Transatlantic.

Cave, Peter. Foxbat. (Orig.). 1979. pap. 1.95 o.s.i. (ISBN 0-515-04878-X). Jove Pubns.

--House of Cards. (Avengers Ser.). 1978. pap. 1.50 o.p. (ISBN 0-425-03993-5, Medallion). Berkley Pub.

Cave, Richard, ed. see Moore, George.

Cave, Roy C. & Coulson, Herbert H. Source Book for Medieval Economic History. LC 64-25840. 1936. 12.00x (ISBN 0-8196-0145-4). Biblo.

Cave, Terence C. Devotional Poetry in France, Fifteen Seventy to Sixteen Thirteen. LC 68-23177. 1969. 58.00 (ISBN 0-521-07145-3). Cambridge U Pr.

Cave Brown, Anthony. Bodyguard of Lies. LC 72-9749. (Illus.). 962p. (YA) 1975. 19.95 o.s.i. (ISBN 0-06-010551-8, HarpT). Har-Row.

Cavell, S. Must We Mean What We Say? LC 75-32911. 365p. 1976. 38.50 (ISBN 0-521-21116-6); pap. 11.50 (ISBN 0-521-29048-1). Cambridge U Pr.

Cavell, Stanley. The World Viewed: Reflections on the Ontology of Film. enl. ed. (Paperback Ser.: No. 151). 1980. 12.50x (ISBN 0-674-96197-8); pap. 5.95 (ISBN 0-674-96196-X). Harvard U Pr.

Caven, R. M. Quantitative Chemical Analysis & Inorganic Preparations. 2nd ed. 1962. 19.95x (ISBN 0-686-63579-5). Intl Ideas.

Cavendish, George. Metrical Visions. Edwards, Anthony S., ed. (Renaissance English Text Society Ser.: Vol. 9). 1980. 15.00. Newberry.

Cavendish, George, jt. auth. see Renaissance English Text Society.

Caveney, Philip. The Sins of Rachel Ellis. 1979. pap. 2.25 o.p. (ISBN 0-425-04144-1). Berkley Pub.

--The Sins of Rachel Ellis. LC 77-16763. 1978. 8.95 o.p. (ISBN 0-312-72603-1). St Martin.

Cavert, Edward C., et al. Students Guide to Accounting, 2 vols. 512p. 1980. pap. text ed. 15.95 (ISBN 0-8403-2223-2). Kendall-Hunt.

Caves & Jones. World Trade & Payments: An Introduction. 3rd ed. 1981. text ed. 17.95 (ISBN 0-316-13226-8). Little.

Caves, Richard E. & Uekusa, Masu. Industrial Organization in Japan. 1976. 10.95 (ISBN 0-8157-1324-X); pap. 4.95 (ISBN 0-8157-1323-1). Brookings.

Caves, Richard E. & Krause, Lawrence B., eds. Britain's Economic Performance. 1980. 18.95 (ISBN 0-8157-1320-7); pap. 7.95 (ISBN 0-8157-1319-3). Brookings.

Caviani, Mabel, et al. Simplified Quantity Ethnic Recipies. (Ahrens Ser.). 272p. 1980. 15.95 (ISBN 0-8104-9474-4). Hayden.

Caviedes, Cesar. The Politics of Chile: A Socio-Geographical Assessment. (Special Studies on Latin America). 1979. lib. bdg. 27.50x (ISBN 0-89158-311-4). Westview.

Cavier, R., ed. Chemotherapy of Helminthiasis. LC 72-86179. 532p. 1973. text ed. 90.00 (ISBN 0-08-015755-6). Pergamon.

Cawa, Mary A. A Metapoetic of the Passage: Architextures in Surrealiam & After. LC 80-54468. 192p. 1981. 12.00x (ISBN 0-87451-194-1). U Pr of New Eng.

Cawelti, John. Six-Gun Mystique. 148p. 1970. 7.95 (ISBN 0-87972-007-7); pap. 4.95 (ISBN 0-87972-008-5). Bowling Green Univ.

Cawkwell, George. Philip of Macedon. (Illus.). 1978. 19.95 (ISBN 0-686-08751-8, Pub. by Faber & Faber). Merrimack Bk Serv.

Cawley, A. C. Pearl, Sir Gawain & Cleanness. 1977. pap. 4.50 (ISBN 0-686-63595-7, Everyman). Dutton.

Cawley, A. C., ed. Everyman Medieval Miracle Plays. pap. 3.25 (ISBN 0-525-47036-0, Evman). Dutton.

--Pearl. Incl. Sir Gawain & the Green Knight. 1962. 5.00x o.p. (ISBN 0-460-00346-1, Evman). Dutton.

Cawley, A. C., intro. by. The Towneley Cycle. Stevens, Martin. LC 75-42854. 250p. 1976. softcover 12.00 (ISBN 0-87328-113-6). Huntington Lib.

Cawley, J. C., et al, eds. Hairy Cell Leukaemia. (Recent Results in Cancer Research Ser.: Vol. 72). (Illus.). 180p. 1980. 33.00 (ISBN 0-387-09920-4). Springer-Verlag.

Cawley, James & Cawley, Margaret. Along the Old York Road. 1965. pap. 2.75 o.p. (ISBN 0-8135-0487-2). Rutgers U Pr.

--The First New York-Philadelphia Stage Road. LC 78-75175. (Illus.). 120p. 1980. 14.50 (ISBN 0-8386-2331-X). Fairleigh Dickenson.

Cawley, John F., et al. The Slow Learner & the Reading Problem. (Illus.). 328p. 1972. 24.75 (ISBN 0-398-02256-9). C C Thomas.

Cawley, Leo P., et al. Electrophoresis & Immunochemical Reactions in Gels: Techniques & Interpretation. LC 77-93631. (Illus.). 1978. pap. text ed. 20.00 (ISBN 0-89189-038-6, 45-2-035-00). Am Soc Clinical.

Cawley, Margaret, jt. auth. see Cawley, James.

Cawley, Rebecca E., jt. auth. see Mervine, Kathryn E.

Cawley, Robert & McLachlan, Gordon, eds. Policy for Action: A Symposium on the Planning of a Comprehensive District Psychiatric Service. 190p. 1973. pap. 9.50x (ISBN 0-19-721376-6). Oxford U Pr.

Caws, Mary A. The Eye in the Text: Essays on Perception, Mannerist to Modern. LC 80-8540. (Princeton Essays on the Arts Ser.: No. 11). (Illus.). 334p. 1981. 17.50x (ISBN 0-691-06453-9); pap. 6.95x (ISBN 0-691-01377-2). Princeton U Pr.

Caws, Mary Ann. Rene Char. (World Authors Ser.: No. 428). 1977. lib. bdg. 12.50 (ISBN 0-8057-6268-X). Twayne.

Caws, Mary Ann & Terry, Patricia, eds. Roof Slates & Other Poems of Pierre Reverdy. LC 80-26806. (Illus.). 340p. 1981. 17.95x (ISBN 0-930350-09-X). NE U Pr.

Caws, Peter, ed. Two Centuries of Philosophy: American Philosophy Since the Revolution -- Papers from the Bicentennial Symposium. (American Philosophical Quarterly Library of Philosophy). 381p. 1980. 30.00x (ISBN 0-8476-6249-7). Rowman.

Cawson, R. A. Aids to Oral Pathology & Diagnosis. (Dental Ser.). (Illus.). 144p. 1981. pap. text ed. 8.75 (ISBN 0-443-01871-5). Churchill.

Caxton, W., tr. Here Begynneth a Lityll Treatise Spekynge of the Arte & Crafte to Knowe Well to Dye. LC 72-169. (English Experience Ser.: No. 221). 28p. Repr. of 1490 ed. 14.00 (ISBN 90-221-0221-1). Walter J Johnson.

Caxton, W., tr. see Jerome, Saint.

Caxton, William. Begin Two A. LC 72-5980. (English Experience Ser.: No. 508). 1973. Repr. of 1480 ed. 61.00 (ISBN 90-221-0508-3). Walter J Johnson.

--Selections from William Caxton. Blake, N. F., ed. (Clarendon Medieval & Tudor Ser.). 1973. 13.00x o.p. (ISBN 0-19-871081-X). Oxford U Pr.

Caxton, William, tr. see Du Castel, Christine.

Caxton, William, tr. see Heraclius.

Caxton, William, tr. see Vincentius, Bellovacensis.

Cay, Donald F. Curriculum: Design for Learning. LC 63-16939. 1965. text ed. 7.50 (ISBN 0-672-60630-5). Bobbs.

Cayce, Edgar. Auras: An Essay on the Meaning of Colors. 1973. pap. 1.25 (ISBN 0-87604-012-1). ARE Pr.

Cayce, Edgar & Cayce, Hugh L. God's Other Door & the Continuity of Life. 1976. pap. 1.95 (ISBN 0-87604-007-5). ARE Pr.

Cayce, Edgar E. Atlantis, Fact or Fiction: From the Edgar Cayce Readings. 1962. pap. 1.50 (ISBN 0-87604-018-0). ARE Pr.

--Edgar Cayce on Atlantis. Cayce, Hugh L., ed. 176p. 1968. pap. 2.25 (ISBN 0-446-89918-6, 9918-6). Warner Bks.

Cayce, Hugh L. Earth Changes Update. 134p. (Orig.). 1980. pap. 4.95 (ISBN 0-87604-121-7). ARE Pr.

Cayce, Hugh L., jt. auth. see Cayce, Edgar.

Cayce, Hugh L., jt. auth. see Grof, Stanislav.

Cayce, Hugh L., ed. The Edgar Cayce Reader. 192p. 1969. pap. 2.25 (ISBN 0-446-92698-1). Warner Bks.

Cayce, Hugh L., ed. see Bro, Harmon H.

Cayce, Hugh L., ed. see Cayce, Edgar E.

Cayce, J. Gail. Osteopathy: Comparative Concepts - A. T. Still & Edgar Cayce. 61p. (Orig.). 1973. pap. 4.95 (ISBN 0-87604-080-6). ARE Pr.

Cayford, John E. Underwater Work: A Manual of Scuba Commercial Salvage & Construction Operations. 2nd ed. LC 66-28081. (Illus.). 1966. 10.00 (ISBN 0-87033-129-9). Cornell Maritime.

Cayford, John E. & Scott, Ronald E. Underwater Logging. LC 64-18585. (Illus.). 1964. pap. 3.00 (ISBN 0-87033-128-0). Cornell Maritime.

Cayley, E. S. On Commercial Economy. 280p. Repr. of 1830 ed. 30.00x (ISBN 0-686-28326-0, Pub. by Irish Academic Pr). Biblio Dist.

Cayne, Bernard S., ed. Encyclopedia Americana, 30 vols. LC 80-84517. (Illus.). 1981. write for info. (ISBN 0-7172-0112-0). Grolier Ed Corp.

--Encyclopedia Americana, 30 vols. LC 79-55176. (Illus.). 1980. write for info o.p. (ISBN 0-7172-0111-2). Grolier Ed Corp.

Cayton, Horace R. Long Old Road: An Autobiography. LC 64-24280. (Paperbacks Ser.: No. 53). 412p. 1970. pap. 3.95 (ISBN 0-295-95069-2, WP53). U of Wash Pr.

Cazacu, C. A., et al, eds. Romanian-Finnish Seminar on Complex Analysis. (Lecture Notes in Mathematics: Vol. 743). 713p. 1980. pap. 33.00 (ISBN 0-387-09550-0). Springer-Verlag.

Cazalas, Mary W. Nursing & the Law. 3rd ed. LC 78-24253. 1978. text ed. 17.50 (ISBN 0-89443-075-0). Aspen Systems.

Cazalet-Keir, Thelma, ed. Homage to P. G. Wodehouse. (Illus.). 146p. 1973. text ed. 9.00x (ISBN 0-214-66880-0). Humanities.

Cazamian, Louis. The Social Novel in England 1830-1850: Dickens, Disraeli, Mrs. Gaskell, Kingsley. Fido, Martin, ed. & tr. 1973. 22.00 (ISBN 0-7100-7282-1). Routledge & Kegan.

Cazden, Courtney B., ed. Language in Early Childhood Education. rev. ed. (Illus.). 144p. 1980. pap. text ed. write for info. (ISBN 0-912674-74-1). Natl Assn Child Ed.

Cazden, Courtney B., et al, eds. Functions of Language in the Classroom. LC 78-173091. 1972. text ed. 14.25x o.p. (ISBN 0-8077-1147-0); pap. 10.95x (ISBN 0-8077-1142-X). Tchrs Coll.

Cazeau, Charles. Earthquakes. LC 73-93549. (Beginning Science Ser.). (Illus.). 32p. (gr. 2-4). 1974. 2.50 o.p. (ISBN 0-695-80474-X); lib. bdg. 2.97 o.p. (ISBN 0-695-40474-1). Follett.

Cazeau, Charles J. & Scott, Stuart D., Jr. Exploring the Unknown: Great Mysteries Reexamined. (Da Capo Quality Paperbacks Ser.). (Illus.). 1981. pap. 8.95 (ISBN 0-306-80139-6). Da Capo.

Cazeaux, Isabelle, tr. see De Commynes, Philippe.

Cazet, Denys. The Duck with Squeaky Feet. LC 80-18018. (Illus.). 32p. (ps-2). 7.95 (ISBN 0-87888-171-9). Bradbury Pr.

--Mud Baths for Everyone. (Illus.). 32p. (ps-2). 1981. 8.95 (ISBN 0-87888-178-6). Bradbury Pr.

Cazort, Mimi, intro. by see Jackson, H. A.

Cazziol, R. J. Paul et Remi. (Illus.). 40p. (Fr.). 1974. pap. text ed. 2.25x (ISBN 0-521-20433-X). Cambridge U Pr.

--Safari En Cote d'Ivoire. (Illus.). 40p. 1974. pap. 2.25x (ISBN 0-521-20434-8). Cambridge U Pr.

Cazziol, Roger J. Gloire D'Afrique. (Illus.). 1971. text ed. 2.25x (ISBN 0-521-08181-5). Cambridge U Pr.

--Kone. (Illus.). 1971. text ed. 2.25x (ISBN 0-521-07955-1). Cambridge U Pr.

--Vacances Au Senegal. (Illus.). 1971. text ed. 2.25x (ISBN 0-521-08180-7). Cambridge U Pr.

Ceadel, Martin. Pacifism in Britain Nineteen Fourteen to Nineteen Forty Five: The Defining of a Faith. 352p. 1980. 37.50x (ISBN 0-19-821882-6). Oxford U Pr.

Cebeci, T. & Bradshaw, P. Momentum Transfer in Boundary Layers. LC 76-57750. (Thermal & Fluids Engineering Ser.). (Illus.). 1977. text ed. 23.95 (ISBN 0-07-010300-3, C); solutions manual 4.95 (ISBN 0-07-010301-1). McGraw.

Cebeci, Tuncer & Smith, A. M. Analysis of Turbulent Boundary Layers. 1974. 51.00 (ISBN 0-12-164650-5); lib. ed. 65.00 (ISBN 0-12-164651-3); microfiche 37.00 (ISBN 0-12-164652-1). Acad Pr.

Cebik, L. B. Concepts, Events, & History. LC 78-64825. 1978. pap. text ed. 9.00 (ISBN 0-8191-0639-9). U Pr of Amer.

Cebula, J., jt. auth. see Bertrand, A.

Cebula, Joseph P., jt. auth. see Bertrand, Arthur.

Cebula, Richard J. The Determinants of Human Migration. LC 79-2271. 160p. 1979. 18.95 (ISBN 0-669-03096-1). Lexington Bks.

Cebulak, W., et al, eds. see National Powder Metallurgy Conferenes, Los Angeles & Cincinnati, 1978 & 1979.

Cebulash, Mel. The Ball That Wouldn't Bounce. (Illus.). (gr. k-3). 1972. pap. 1.25 (ISBN 0-590-09297-9, Schol Pap); pap. 3.50 bk. & record (ISBN 0-686-68502-4). Schol Bk Serv.

--Benny's Nose. (Illus.). (gr. k-3). 1972. pap. 1.25 (ISBN 0-590-09298-7, Schol Pap); pap. 3.50 bk. & record (ISBN 0-590-04352-8). Schol Bk Serv.

Cebulash, Mel, jt. ed. see Hasinbiller, Dolly.

Ceccarelli, B., ed. see International Symposium on Cell Biology & Cytopharmacology, First.

Ceccarelli, B., et al, eds. see Nato Advanced Study Institution, et al.

Ceccarelli, Bruno & Clementi, Francesco, eds. Neurotoxins: Tools in Neurobiology. LC 78-57244. (Advances in Cytopharmacology Ser.: Vol. 3). 1979. text ed. 49.00 (ISBN 0-89004-303-5). Raven.

Ceccherini, Silvano. The Transfer. Quigley, Isabel, tr. LC 66-20533. 1966. 6.00 o.s.i. (ISBN 0-8076-0399-6). Braziller.

Cecchetti, Giovanni. Giovanni Verga. (World Authors Ser.: No. 489 Italy). 1978. 12.95 (ISBN 0-8057-6330-9). Twayne.

Ceccio, Joseph F., ed. Medicine in Literature: An Anthology for Reading & Writing. LC 77-17721. (English & Humanities Ser.). 1978. pap. text ed. 9.95x (ISBN 0-582-28051-6). Longman.

Cecco, Marcello De see De Cecco, Marcello.

Cecelski, Elizabeth, et al. Household Energy & the Poor in the Third World: Domestic Energy Consumption for Low-Income Groups in Development Areas. LC 79-4863. (Resources for the Future Ser.). 1979. 6.75x (ISBN 0-8018-2283-1). Johns Hopkins.

Cecil, Anthony C., Jr. The Theological Development of Edwards Amasa Park: Last of the "Consistent Calvinists". LC 74-83338. (American Academy of Religion. Dissertation Ser.). 1974. pap. 9.00 (ISBN 0-88420-118-X, 010101). Scholars Pr Ca.

Cecil, David. Poets & Story-Tellers. 201p. 1980. Repr. of 1968 ed. lib. bdg. 30.00 (ISBN 0-8495-0852-5). Arden Lib.

--A Portrait of Jane Austen. 208p. 1980. text ed. 25.00 (ISBN 0-8090-7811-2); pap. text ed. 9.95 (ISBN 0-8090-1392-4). Hill & Wang.

Cecil, David, ed. Modern Biography. 229p. 1980. Repr. of 1938 ed. lib. bdg. 15.00 (ISBN 0-8492-3971-0). R West.

Cecil, David, ed. see Tennyson, Alfred L.

Cecil, Edward. A Journall & Relation of the Action Which E. Lord Cecil Did Vndertake Vpon the Coast of Spaine. LC 68-54643. (English Experience Ser.: No. 27). 1968. Repr. of 1625 ed. 7.00 (ISBN 90-221-0027-8). Walter J Johnson.

Cecil, George. Digging. (Easy-Read Fact Book Ser.). (Illus.). 48p. (gr. 2-4). 1976. PLB 4.47 o.p. (ISBN 0-531-01218-2). Watts.

--Salt. (Easy-Read Fact Bks.). (Illus.). 48p. (gr. 2-4). 1976. PLB 4.47 o.p. (ISBN 0-531-00359-0). Watts.

Cecil, Joe S., jt. auth. see Boruch, Robert F.

Cecil, Martin. Being Where You Are. 1974. 2.95 (ISBN 0-686-27650-7). Cole-Outreach.

--On Eagle's Wing. 1977. 2.95 (ISBN 0-686-27653-1). Cole-Outreach.

Cecil, Michael, et al. Spirit of Sunrise. 1979. 7.00 (ISBN 0-686-27655-8); pap. 2.95 (ISBN 0-686-27656-6). Cole-Outreach.

Cecil, Mirabel. Spiky the Hedgehog. LC 79-26358. (Illus.). 32p. (gr. k-3). 1980. 3.95 (ISBN 0-07-010322-4). McGraw.

Cecil, P. B. Word Processing in the Modern Office. 2nd ed. 1980. pap. 10.95 (ISBN 0-8053-1758-9); instrs manual 3.95 (ISBN 0-8053-1760-0); student wkbk 3.95 (ISBN 0-8053-1761-9). A-W.

Cecil, Paula B. IG for Management of Word Processing Operations. 1980. 3.95 (ISBN 0-8053-1762-7). Benjamin Cummings.

--Management of Word Processing Operations. 1980. 18.95 (ISBN 0-8053-1759-7). Benjamin-Cummings.

--Word Processing in the Modern Office: Student Workbook. 1980. 3.95 o.p. (ISBN 0-8053-1761-9). Benjamin Cummings.

Cecil, William. A Declaration of the Fauourable Dealing of Her Maiesties Commissioners Appointed for the Examination of Certaine Traitours. LC 73-25637. (English Experience Ser.: No. 113). 1969. Repr. of 1583 ed. 7.00 (ISBN 90-221-0113-4). Walter J Johnson.

Cedar, Paul A. Seven Keys to Maximum Communication. 1980. pap. 2.95 (ISBN 0-8423-5875-7). Tyndale.

Cedarbaum, Sophia. Chanukah: The Festival of Lights. (Illus.). (gr. k-2). 1960. 2.00 o.p. (ISBN 0-685-20730-7, 301572). UAHC.

--Passover: Festival of Freedom. (Illus.). (gr. k-2). 1960. 3.50 (ISBN 0-8074-0147-1, 301592). UAHC.

Cedarbaum, Sophia N. Purim: A Joyous Holiday. (Illus.). (gr. k-2). 1960. 3.50 (ISBN 0-8074-0148-X, 301562). UAHC.

--Sabbath: A Day of Delight. (Illus.). (gr. k-2). 1960. 3.50 o.p. (ISBN 0-685-20757-9, 301582). UAHC.

Cedeno, et al. The Exercise Plus Pregnancy Program: Exercises for Before, During & After Pregnancy. LC 80-14278. (Illus.). 192p. 1980. 10.95 (ISBN 0-688-03697-X, Quill); pap. 4.95 (ISBN 0-686-68533-4, Quill). Morrow.

Ceder, Jack. Trigonometry: A Modern Approach. LC 77-21688. 224p. 1978. text ed. 11.95 (ISBN 0-03-020901-3, HoltC). HR&W.

Ceder, Jack G. & Outcalt, David L. Calculus. 1977. text ed. 27.25 (ISBN 0-205-05560-5); instr's manual avail. (ISBN 0-205-05561-3); study guide 5.95 (ISBN 0-685-74024-2). Allyn.

Cederbaums, Juris. Wiretapping & Electronic Eavesdropping, the Law & Its Implications: A Comparative Study. (New York University Criminal Law Education & Research Center Monograph: No. 2). 77p. (Orig.). 1969. pap. text ed. 8.50x (ISBN 0-8377-0402-2). Rothman.

Cedering, Siv, tr. see Aspenstrom, Werner.

Cedrins, Inara, tr. see Bels, Albert.

Cedrins, Inara, tr. see Ivask, Astrid.

Ceely, Doris, jt. auth. see Britt, Rose.

Cegelka, Patricia T., jt. auth. see Berdine, William H.

Cehelsky, Marta. Land Reform in Brazil: The Management of Social Change. (Westview Replica Edition Ser.). 1979. lib. bdg. 23.00 o.p. (ISBN 0-89158-075-1). Westview.

Ceidigh, P. O., jt. ed. see Keegan, B. F.

Cela, C., et al, eds. La Familia De Pascula Duarte. 1961. pap. 7.95 o.p. (ISBN 0-13-528307-8). P-H.

Celant, Germano, jt. auth. see D'Harnoncourt, Anne.

Celebrity Kitchen & United Fresh Fruit & Vegetable Association. The Fresh Fruit & Vegetable Book: A Complete Guide to Enjoying Fresh Fruits & Vegetables. LC 80-8390. (Illus.). 320p. 1981. pap. 3.95 (ISBN 0-06-463527-9, EH 527). Har-Row.

Celenza, Frank V. Occlusal Morphology. 110p. 1980. pap. 18.00 (ISBN 0-931386-33-0). Quint Pub Co.

Celenza, Frank V. & Nasedkin, John N. Occlusion, the State of the Art. (Illus.). 165p. 1978. 32.00 (ISBN 0-931386-00-4). Quint Pub Co.

Celeste, Emily, jt. auth. see Courtney, Elise.

Celine, Louis-Ferdinand. North. 1972. 10.00 o.p. (ISBN 0-440-06420-1, Sey Lawr). Delacorte.

--Rigadoon. 273p. 1974. 8.95 o.p. (ISBN 0-440-07364-2, Sey Lawr). Delacorte.

Celis, J. E., et al, eds. Transfer of Cell Constituents into Eukaryotic Cells. (NATO Advanced Study Institutes Ser., A: Life Sciences: Vol. 31). 450p. 1980. 45.00 (ISBN 0-306-40425-7, Plenum Pr). Plenum Pub.

Celletti, Rodolfo. Marta. LC 62-9936. 1962. 4.95 o.s.i. (ISBN 0-8076-0177-2). Braziller.

Celli, Elisa & Krech, Inez M. Naturally Italian: A Treasury of Original Stay-Slim Dishes Prepared in Minutes. 1978. 12.95 o.p. (ISBN 0-87690-305-7). Dutton.

Cellier, Elizabeth. The Matchless Rogue: A Brief Account of the Life of Don Thomazo, the Unfortunate Son. LC 80-2473. 1981. Repr. of 1680 ed. 23.50 (ISBN 0-404-19105-3). AMS Pr.

Cellini. Autobiography. (Classic Ser). 1956. pap. 4.50 (ISBN 0-14-044049-6). Penguin.

Cellini, Benvenuto. Life of Benvenuto Cellini. 1979. 5.00x o.p. (ISBN 0-460-00051-9, Evman). Dutton.

--Treatises of Benvenuto Cellini on Goldsmithing & Sculpture. Ashbee, C. R., tr. (Illus.). 10.00 (ISBN 0-8446-1828-4). Peter Smith.

Celms, Theodor. Der Phanomenologische Idealismus Husserls. Natanson, ed. LC 78-66733. (Phenomenology: Vol. 3). 192p. 1979. lib. bdg. 20.00 (ISBN 0-8240-9567-7). Garland Pub.

Cencov, N. N. Statistical Decision Rules & Optimal Inference. (Mathematical Monographs: Vol. 53). Date not set. cancelled (ISBN 0-8218-4502-0). Am Math.

Cendrars, Blaise. The Astonished Man. LC 80-9056. 260p. 1981. 12.95 (ISBN 0-8128-2814-3). Stein & Day.

--Complete Postcards from the Americas: Poems of Road & Sea. LC 73-94445. 1976. 15.95x (ISBN 0-520-02716-7). U of Cal Pr.

--Lice. LC 80-9058. 189p. 1981. 12.95 (ISBN 0-8128-2815-1). Stein & Day.

--Lice. Rootes, Nina, tr. from Fr. 1979. 18.00x (ISBN 0-8464-0045-6). Beekman Pubs.

--Pathe Baby. (Pocket Poets Ser.: No. 39). 1980. pap. 3.50 o.p. (ISBN 0-87286-108-2). City Lights.

--Planus. LC 80-9057. 220p. 1981. 12.95 (ISBN 0-8128-2816-X). Stein & Day.

--Planus. Rootes, Nina, tr. from Fr. 1979. 18.00x (ISBN 0-8464-0046-4). Beekman Pubs.

Cenini, S., jt. auth. see Malatesta, Li.

Centeno, Augusto, jt. auth. see Tarr, F. C.

Center, Allen H. Public Relations Practices: Case Studies. (Illus.). 416p. 1975. 15.95 (ISBN 0-13-738682-6); pap. text ed. 12.95 (ISBN 0-13-738674-5). P-H.

Center, Allen H. & Cutlip, Scott H. Effective Public Relations. 5th ed. (Illus.). 1978. ref. 19.95 (ISBN 0-13-245035-6). P-H.

Center, Allen H., jt. auth. see Walsh, Frank E.

Center, Elizabeth M., jt. ed. see Wessels, N. K.

Center for Academic Publications Japan, ed. Current Contents of Academic Journals in Japan, 1978. 18th ed. LC 72-623679. 392p. (Orig.). 1980. pap. 55.00x (ISBN 0-8002-2740-9). Intl Pubns Serv.

Center for Academic Publications Japan. Current Contents of Academic Journals in Japan, 1977: The Humanities & Social Sciences. LC 72-623679. 344p. (Orig.). 1979. pap. 50.00x (ISBN 0-8002-2322-5). Intl Pubns Serv.

Center for Academic Publications, Japan. Current Contents of Academic Journals in Japan 1974-75. LC 72-623679. 1973. pap. 45.00x (ISBN 0-8002-0311-9). Intl Pubns Serv.

Center for Applied Linguistics. Bilingual Education, Current Perspectives No.5: Synthesis. LC 77-80381. (Orig.). 1978. pap. 7.95 (ISBN 0-87281-076-3). Ctr Appl Ling.

--Bilingual Education, Current Perspectives: Synthesis. LC 77-80381. 1978. pap. text ed. 7.95x o.p. (ISBN 0-87281-076-3). Ctr Appl Ling.

Center for Arts Information. Directory for the Arts. LC 78-18486. 1978. 10.00 (ISBN 0-89062-048-2, Pub. by Ctr for Arts Info); pap. 6.00 (ISBN 0-89062-061-X). Pub Ctr Cult Res.

Center for Curriculum Design, ed. Somewhere Else: A Living-Learning Catalog. LC 72-91916. 214p. 1972. pap. 5.95 (ISBN 0-8040-0610-5). Swallow.

Center for Design Planning. Streetscape Equipment Sourcebook, No. 2. LC 79-56221. (Illus.). 244p. 1979. pap. text ed. 19.50 (ISBN 0-87420-589-1). Urban Land.

Center for Environmental & Consumer Justice. Discrimination in Private Employment in Puerto Rico (Color, Sex & National Origin) LC 79-16965. 450p. 1980. pap. write for info. (ISBN 0-8477-2454-9). U of PR Pr.

Center for Equal Education. Covering the Desegregation Story. LC 76-45286. 1976. 3.00 (ISBN 0-912008-12-1). Integrated Ed Assoc.

--Whites in Desegregated Schools. LC 76-24186. 1976. 4.50 (ISBN 0-685-84406-4). Integrated Ed Assoc.

Center for Equal Education & Egerton, John. Education & Desegregation in Eight Schools. LC 77-80528. 1977. pap. 3.60 (ISBN 0-912008-14-8). Integrated Ed Assoc.

Center for Inter-American Relations & American Federation of Arts. El Dorado: The Gold of Ancient Columbia. LC 74-175969. (Illus.). 150p. 1980. pap. 14.95 (ISBN 0-295-95736-0). U of Wash Pr.

Center for Ocean Management Studies. Comparative Marine Policy. 288p. 1981. 24.95 (ISBN 0-03-058307-1). J F Bergin.
Center for Ocean Management Studies, ed. Comparative Marine Policy. 336p. 1980. 26.95 (ISBN 0-03-058307-1). Praeger.
Center for Science in the Public Interest. Household Pollutant Guide. Fritsch, Al, ed. LC 77-76269. 1978. pap. 3.50 (ISBN 0-385-12494-5, Anch). Doubleday.
Center for Strategic & International Studies, Georgetown University. Future of Business - Annual Review 1980-81: Practical Issues. Slappey, G. Sterling, ed. LC 79-24081. (Pergamon Policy Studies). 110p. 1980. 16.50 (ISBN 0-08-025585-X); pap. 6.25 (ISBN 0-08-025584-1). Pergamon.
Center for the American Woman & Politics, compiled by. Women in Public Office: A Biographical Directory & Statistical Analysis. 2nd ed. LC 78-7463. 1978. 35.00 (ISBN 0-8108-1142-1). Scarecrow.
Center for the Study of the American Experience, ed. Energy in America: Fifteen Views. 300p. 1981. 22.50 (ISBN 0-88474-103-6). Transaction Bks.
Center for Theoretical Studies. Energy for Developed & Developing Countries: Proceedings. Kursunogl, Behram & Perlmutter, Arnold, eds. 1981. price not set (ISBN 0-88410-634-9). Ballinger Pub.
Centlivre, Susannah. Bold Stroke for a Wife. Stathas, Thalia, ed. LC 67-12640. (Regents Restoration Drama Ser). 1968. 7.95x (ISBN 0-8032-0351-9); pap. 1.65x (ISBN 0-8032-5351-6, BB 267, Bison). U of Nebr Pr.
Centner, Leon, ed. La Revolution Francaise et L'emancipation Des Juifs, 8 vols. 1900p. (Fr.). 1976. Set. lib. bdg. 195.00 o.p. (ISBN 0-8287-0724-3); Set. pap. text ed. 135.00 o.p. (ISBN 0-685-64325-5). Clearwater Pub.
Central Bureau of Statistics, Indonesia. Statistical Pocketbook of Indonesia 1976. LC 60-18985. 1976. pap. 25.00x o.p. (ISBN 0-686-65036-0). Intl Pubns Serv.
Central Electricity Generating Board, ed. Phraseology for Civil Engineers, 2 vols. 1970. Set. ring binder 58.00x (ISBN 0-685-83867-6). Intl Ideas.
Central Intelligence Agency. CIA Energy Information Reprint Series, 5 vols. Bereny, J. A., ed. Incl. Vol. I. The International Energy Situation: Outlook to 1985; Vol. 2. Prospects for Soviet Oil Production; Vol. 3. Prospects for Soviet Oil Production: A Supplemental Analysis; Vol. 4. China: Oil Production Prospects; Vol. 5. World Petroleum Outlook. 89p. 1979. 49.00 (ISBN 0-930978-57-9); pap. 38.00 (ISBN 0-89934-000-8). Solar Energy Info.
Central State University Dept. of Mathematics. Essential Mathematics for College Freshmen. 1978. pap. text ed. 10.95 (ISBN 0-8403-1518-X). Kendall-Hunt.
Central Statistical Office of Finland. Statistical Yearbook of Finland, 1978. 75th ed. Laakso, Elia, ed. LC 59-42150. (Illus.). 577p. (Eng, Finnish, Swed.). 1980. vinyl bnd. 38.00x (ISBN 0-8002-2731-X). Intl Pubns Serv.
Centre De Creation Industrielle, Paris, France, ed. World Design Sources Directory 1980: An ICOGRADA ICSID Publication. LC 79-41455. 192p. 1980. 29.00 (ISBN 0-08-025676-7). Pergamon.
Centre, F. C. Practical Larder Work. 15.00x (ISBN 0-392-06305-0, LTB). Soccer.
Centre National De la Recherche Scientifique, ed. Annuaire Francais De Droit International, Vol. 25. LC 57-28515. 1288p. 1979. 125.00x (ISBN 2-222-02737-3). Intl Pubns Serv.
Centre National De la Recherche Scientifique, Paris, ed. International Directory of Medievalists, 2 vols. 5th ed. 1979. 140.00 (ISBN 0-89664-046-9, Pub. by K G Saur). Gale.
Centro Studi e Laboratori Telecomumicazioni. Optical Fibre Communication. (Illus.). 928p. 1980. 39.50 (ISBN 0-07-014882-1, P&RB). McGraw.
Ceram, C. W. The First American: A Story of North American Archaeology. 1972. pap. 2.95 (ISBN 0-451-61862-9, ME1862, Ment). NAL.
Cerami & Washington. Sickle Cell Anemia. LC 72-93681. 1973. 8.95 (ISBN 0-89388-068-X). Okpaku Communications.
Ceravolo, Joseph. Spring in This World of Poor Mutts: "the Frank O'Hara Award Series". LC 68-56371. (A Full Court Rebound Bk.). 1978. 14.95 (ISBN 0-685-60027-0); pap. 6.00 (ISBN 0-685-60028-9). Full Court NY.
Cercignani, Fausto. Shakespeare's Works & Elizabethan Pronunciation. 448p. 1981. 74.00 (ISBN 0-19-811937-2). Oxford U Pr.
Cerda, Rodolfo De la see DeHaan, Richard.
Cerepak, John R. Accounting for Business. 2nd ed. LC 73-85889. 832p. 1974. text ed. 18.95 (ISBN 0-675-08881-X); Vols. 1-14 Ea. 6.50 ea. (ISBN 0-675-08823-2); Vols. 15-27. 6.50 ea. (ISBN 0-675-08822-4). Merrill.
Ceres. Herbs & Fruit for Dieting. LC 80-53452. (Everybodys Home Herbal Ser.). 64p. 1981. pap. 1.95 (ISBN 0-394-74837-9). Shambhala Pubns.
--Herbs for First-Aid & Minor Ailments. LC 80-53453. (Everybodys Home Herbal Ser.). (Illus.). 64p. 1981. pap. 1.95 (ISBN 0-394-74925-1). Shambhala Pubns.
--Herbs for Healthy Hair. LC 80-50747. (Everybody's Home Herbal Ser.). (Illus.). 62p. (Orig.). 1980. pap. 1.95 (ISBN 0-394-73947-7). Shambhala Pubns.
--Herbs for Indigestion. LC 80-53451. (Everybody's Home Herbal Ser.). (Illus.). 63p. (Orig.). 1981. pap. 1.95 (ISBN 0-394-74833-6). Shambhala Pubn.
--Herbs to Help You Sleep. LC 80-50749. (Everybody's Home Herbal Ser.). (Illus.). 62p. (Orig.). 1980. pap. 1.95 (ISBN 0-394-73946-9). Shambhala Pubns.
Cerf, Bennett. Bennett Cerf's Houseful of Laughter. (Illus.). (gr. 6-9). 1963. 4.95 (ISBN 0-394-80956-4, BYR); PLB 6.99 (ISBN 0-394-90956-9). Random.
Cerf, Bennett, jt. ed. see Cartmell, Van H.
Cerf, Jonathon, jt. auth. see Cerf, Roseanne.
Cerf, Roseanne & Cerf, Jonathon. Big Bird's Red Book. (Illus.). (gr. k-3). 1977. PLB 5.00 (ISBN 0-307-60157-9, Golden Pr). Western Pub.
Cerling, Charles E., Jr. Holy Boldness. LC 80-65435. 160p. 1980. pap. 5.95 (ISBN 0-915684-67-5). Christian Herald.
Cermack, Laird S. Human Memory & Amnesia. 400p. 1981. ref. ed. 24.95 (ISBN 0-89859-095-7). L Erlbaum Assocs.
Cermak, J. E., ed. Wind Engineering: Proceedings of the 5th International Conference, Colorado State University, USA, July 8-14, 1979, 2 vols. LC 80-40753. (Illus.). 1400p. 1981. Set. 200.00 (ISBN 0-08-024745-8). Pergamon.
Cerminara, Gina. Insights for the Age of Aquarius. LC 76-6173. 314p. 1976. pap. 5.75 (ISBN 0-8356-0483-7, Quest). Theos Pub Hse.
Cerney, Joseph, ed. Nuclear Spectroscopy & Reactions, 4 pts. Set. 199.50 (ISBN 0-685-48719-9); Pt. A 1974. 67.00 (ISBN 0-12-165201-7); Pt. B 1974. 68.00 o.s.i. (ISBN 0-12-165202-5); Pt. C 1974. 68.00 (ISBN 0-12-165203-3); Pt. D 1975. 43.50 (ISBN 0-12-165204-1). Acad Pr.
Cernica, John N. Fundamentals of Reinforced Concrete. (Illus.). 1964. 19.95 (ISBN 0-201-00945-5). A-W.
Cernuda, Luis. Selected Poems of Luis Cernuda. Gibbons, Reginald, tr. from Span. LC 75-3767. 1976. 14.95x (ISBN 0-520-02984-4). U of Cal Pr.
Cerny, Jaroslav. Coptic Etymological Dictionary. LC 69-10192. 350p. 1976. 160.00 (ISBN 0-521-07228-X). Cambridge U Pr.
Cerny, Ladislav. Statics & Strength of Materials. (Illus.). 382p. 1981. text ed. 21.95 (ISBN 0-07-010339-9, C). McGraw.
Cerny, Philip & Schain, Martin, eds. French Politics & Public Policy. 1980. write for info. (ISBN 0-312-30509-5). St Martin.
Cerny, Phillip G. The Politics of Grandeur. LC 79-50232. 1980. 35.50 (ISBN 0-521-22863-8). Cambridge U Pr.
Certo, Dominic N. The Valor of Francesco D'amini. (Orig.). 1979. pap. 2.25 (ISBN 0-532-23111-2). Manor Bks.
Certon, M. J. & Davidson, H. F. Industrial Technology Transfer. 480p. 1977. 45.50x (ISBN 90-286-0426-X). Sijthoff & Noordhoff.
Cerutti, Toni. Guide to Composition in Italian. 1966. text ed. 6.50x (ISBN 0-521-04593-2). Cambridge U Pr.
Cervantes. Don Quixote. (Easy Reader, D). pap. 3.75 (ISBN 0-88436-056-3, SPA301051). EMC.
Cervantes, Alex & Cervantes, E. DeMichael. Saturday with Daddy. LC 78-73527. (Illus.). (gr. k-4). Date not set. pap. price not set (ISBN 0-89799-079-X); pap. text ed. price not set (ISBN 0-89799-161-3). Dandelion Pr. Postponed.
Cervantes, E. DeMichael, jt. auth. see Cervantes, Alex.
Cervantes, Lorna D. Emplumada. LC 80-54063. (Pitt Poetry Ser.). 1981. 9.95 (ISBN 0-8229-3436-1); pap. 4.50 (ISBN 0-8229-5327-7). U of Pittsburgh Pr.
Cervantes, Miguel De. Aventuras de Don Quijote: Relatos Ilustrados. (Span.). 9.00 (ISBN 84-241-5412-6). E Torres & Sons.
--Don Quixote. (Oxford Progressive English Readers Ser.). (Illus.). 1973. pap. text ed. 2.95x (ISBN 0-19-638224-6). Oxford U Pr.
--Novelas Ejemplares. (Span.). 7.95 (ISBN 84-241-5613-7). E Torres & Sons.
--Rinconete & Cortadillo. pap. 2.00 (ISBN 0-8283-1453-5, IPL). Branden.
Cervantes, Miguel De see De Cervantes, Miguel.
Cervantes, Miguel De see De Cervantes Saavedra, Miguel.
Cervantes-Saavedra, Miguel De. Miguel De Cervantes-Saavedra: Two Cervantes Short Novels: El Curioso impertinente & El Celoso extremeno. Pierce, F. F., ed. 1970. pap. 4.30 (ISBN 0-08-015781-5). Pergamon.
Cervantes Saavedra, Miguel De. Two Humorous Novels: A Diverting Dialogue Between Scipio & Bergansa & the Comical History of Rinconete & Cortadillo. Goadby, Robert, tr. LC 80-2474. 1981. Repr. of 1741 ed. 39.50 (ISBN 0-404-19106-1). AMS Pr.
Cervenka, Jaroslav & Koulischer, Lucien. Chromosomes in Human Cancer. (Illus.). 212p. 1973. 19.75 (ISBN 0-398-02629-7). C C Thomas.
Cervenka, Zdenek. The Nigerian War: 1967-70. LC 73-885548. (Illus.). 459p. 1971. pap. 40.00x (ISBN 3-7637-0210-5). Intl Pubns Serv.
Cervera, Joseph P. Modernismo: the Catalan Renaissance of the Arts. LC 75-23787. (Outstanding Dissertations in the Fine Arts - 19th Century). (Illus.). 1976. lib. bdg. 48.00 (ISBN 0-8240-1983-0). Garland Pub.
Cerveri De Girona. Obras Completas. LC 80-2175. 1981. Repr. of 1947 ed. 59.50 (ISBN 0-404-19005-7). AMS Pr.
Cervos-Navarro, H., et al, eds. The Cerebral Vessel Wall. LC 75-25110. 1976. 31.50 (ISBN 0-89004-071-0). Raven.
Cervos-Navarro, J. & Fritschka, E., eds. Cerebral Microcirculation & Metabolism. 1981. text ed. price not set (ISBN 0-89004-590-9). Raven.
Cervos-Navarro, J., et al, eds. Pathology of Cerebrospinal Microcirculation. LC 77-84125. (Advances in Neurology Ser.: Vol. 20). 1978. 56.00 (ISBN 0-89004-237-3). Raven.
Cerwinske, Laura. Tropical Deco: The Architecture & Design of Old Miami Beach. LC 80-51596. (Illus.). 96p. (Orig.). 1981. pap. 14.95 (ISBN 0-8478-0345-7). Rizzoli Intl.
Cesaire, Aime. Discourse on Colonialism. Pinkham, Joan, tr. LC 72-178714. 96p. 1972. 4.95 o.p. (ISBN 0-85345-205-9, CL-2059); pap. 2.95 (ISBN 0-685-23743-5, PB-2266). Monthly Rev.
Cesaire, Aime see Harrison, Paul C.
Cesare, Mario Di see Di Cesare, Mario.
Cesare, Marion Di see Di Cesare, Marion.
Cesarea, Eusebio de see De Cesarea, Eusebio.
Cesaretti, C. A., ed. The Prometheus Question: A Moral and Theological Perspective on the Energy Crisis. 176p. 1980. pap. 3.95 (ISBN 0-8164-2285-0). Seabury.
Cesari, Isotta, tr. see Balabanoff, Angelica.
Cesari, Lamberto, et al, eds. Dynamical Systems: An International Symposium, Vol. 2. 1975. 51.50 (ISBN 0-12-164902-4); Set. 84.50 (ISBN 0-685-99221-7). Acad Pr.
Cescinsky, Herbert. English Furniture: From Gothic to Sheraton. (Illus.). 1968. pap. 10.00 (ISBN 0-486-21929-1). Dover.
Ceserani, Victor & Kinton, Ronald. Practical Cookery. 4th ed. 1974. 16.50x (ISBN 0-7131-1853-9). Intl Ideas.
Ceserani, Victor, jt. auth. see Kinton, Ronald.
Cess, R. D., jt. auth. see Sparrow, E. M.
Cesti, Antonio. L' Argia. Brown, Howard M., ed. LC 76-21082. (Italian Opera 1640-1770 Ser.: Vol. 3). 1978. lib. bdg. 75.00 (ISBN 0-8240-2602-0). Garland Pub.
Cetin. Stamp Collecting for Fun & Profit. pap. 2.00 o.p. (ISBN 0-87980-149-2). Wilshire.
Cey, Ron, jt. auth. see Auker, Jim.
Chabaud, Jacqueline. Education & Advancement of Women. (Orig.). 1971. pap. 6.00 (ISBN 92-3-100842-0, U182, UNESCO). Unipub.
Chabner, Davi-Ellen. The Language of Medicine: A Worktext Explaining Medical Terms. LC 75-38150. (Illus.). 350p. 1976. pap. text ed. 14.95 (ISBN 0-7216-2480-4). Saunders.
--The Language of Medicine: A Write-in Text Explaining Medical Terms. 2nd ed. (Illus.). 600p. 1981. text ed. 16.95 (ISBN 0-7216-2479-0). Saunders.
Chabod, Federico. A History of Italian Fascism. Grindrod, Muriel, tr. from It. 192p. 1975. Repr. of 1963 ed. 15.50 (ISBN 0-86527-095-3). Fertig.
Chabot, G., jt. auth. see Beaujeu-Garnier, J.
Chabrol, Claude, jt. auth. see Marin, Louis.
Chabrowe, Leonard see Smith Experimental Fiction Project.
Chace, G. Earl. Wonders of Prairie Dogs. LC 76-12510. (Wonders Ser.). (gr. 5 up). 1976. 5.95 o.p. (ISBN 0-396-07366-2). Dodd.
Chacholiades, Miltiades. Principles of International Economics. (Illus.). 656p. 1980. text ed. 19.95 (ISBN 0-07-010345-3, C). McGraw.
Chacko, David. Price. LC 78-21360. 1979. pap. 3.95 o.p. (ISBN 0-312-64211-3). St Martin.
Chacko, G. K., ed. Health Handbook: An International Reference on Care & Cure. 1979. 146.50 (ISBN 0-444-85254-9, North Holland). Elsevier.
Chacko, George K. Management Information Systems. (Illus.). 454p. text ed. 27.00 (ISBN 0-89433-095-0). Petrocelli.
Chacksfield, E. M., et al. Music & Language with Young Children. 192p. 1981. pap. 6.50x (Pub. by Basil Blackwell England). Biblio Dist.
--Music & Language with Young Children. (Illus.). 1975. 18.50x (ISBN 0-631-15330-6, Pub. by Basil Blackwell). Biblio Dist.
Chacon, R., ed. see International Cancer Congress, 12th, Buenos Aires, 5-11 October 1978.
Chadbourne, Ava H. Cumberland County. (Maine County Place - Name Ser.). Date not set. pap. 4.95 (ISBN 0-87027-115-6). Wheelwright. Postponed.
Chadbourne, Richard M. Charles-Augustin Sainte Beuve. (World Authors Ser.: No. 453). 1978. lib. bdg. 12.50 (ISBN 0-8057-6290-6). Twayne.
Chadderdon, H. Determining Effectiveness of Teaching Home Ec. LC 74-78396. 1971. pap. 2.50 (ISBN 0-686-00147-8, 261-08408). Home Econ Educ.
Chaddick, Ron. Love's Labor Lost. LC 80-82093. (Understand Ye Shakespeare Ser.). 1980. pap. 8.95 deluxe ed. (ISBN 0-933350-35-X). Morse Pr.
Chaddock, D. H. Introduction to Fastening Systems. (Engineering Design Guides Ser.). (Illus.). 1974. pap. 5.95x o.p. (ISBN 0-19-859128-4). Oxford U Pr.
Chaddock, Ron. As You Like It. LC 80-82091. (Understand Ye Shakespeare Ser.). 1980. pap. 8.95 deluxe ed. (ISBN 0-933350-34-1). Morse Pr.
--Tragedy of Macbeth. LC 80-82092. (Understand Ye Shakespeare Ser.). 1980. pap. 8.95 deluxe ed. (ISBN 0-933350-33-3). Morse Pr.
--Tragedy of MacBeth: Armchair Exposition. 1979. pap. 3.85 (ISBN 0-933350-20-1). Morse Pr.
Chadeayne, Lee, tr. see Luthi, Max.
Chadwell, David. Christian Perspectives on Dating & Marriage. 1980. pap. 3.95 (ISBN 0-89137-523-6). Quality Pubns.
Chadwich, Philip & Smith, Foster, eds. Seafaring in Colonial Massachusetts. LC 80-51256. (Illus.). xvii, 240p. 1981. 25.00x (ISBN 0-8139-0897-3, Colonial Soc MA). U Pr of Va.
Chadwick, Bill. Illustrated Ice Hockey Rules. LC 76-2834. 160p. 1976. pap. 2.50 (ISBN 0-385-11408-7, Dolp). Doubleday.
Chadwick, C. Verlaine. 1973. text ed. 16.25x (ISBN 0-485-14603-7, Athlone Pr); pap. text ed. 8.75x (ISBN 0-485-12203-0). Humanities.
Chadwick, Charles. Arthur Rimbaud. (French Poets Ser.). 1978. text ed. 26.00x (ISBN 0-485-14610-X, Athlone Pr); pap. text ed. 13.00x (ISBN 0-485-12210-3). Humanities.
Chadwick, Charles, ed. see Verlaine, Paul.
Chadwick, Donna see Clark, Cynthia.
Chadwick, French E., ed. The Graves Papers & Other Documents Relating to the Naval Operations of the Yorktown Campaign, July to October 1781: New York Historical Society. LC 16-19248. (Illus.). 1916. 8.00x o.p. (ISBN 0-685-73899-X). U Pr of Va.
Chadwick, George W. Judith: Lyric Drama for Soli, Chorus, & Orchestra. LC 70-169727. (Earlier American Music Ser.: Vol. 3). 176p. 1972. Repr. of 1901 ed. lib. bdg. 22.50 (ISBN 0-306-77303-1). Da Capo.
--Songs to Poems by Arlo Bates, 1892-1897. LC 73-170928. (Earlier Amer. Music Ser.: Vol. 16). 1976. Repr. of 1897 ed. 18.50 (ISBN 0-306-77316-3). Da Capo.
--Symphony No. Two: In B Flat, Opus 21. facsimile ed. LC 71-170930. (Earlier American Music Ser.: No. 4). 216p. 1972. Repr. of 1888 ed. 22.50 (ISBN 0-306-77304-X). Da Capo.
Chadwick, J. The Mycenaean World. (Illus.). 224p. 1976. 39.50 (ISBN 0-521-21077-1); pap. 9.95x (ISBN 0-521-29037-6). Cambridge U Pr.
Chadwick, J., jt. auth. see Ventris, M.
Chadwick, John. Decipherment of Linear B. (Illus.). 1970. 29.95 (ISBN 0-521-04599-1); pap. 7.50x (ISBN 0-521-09596-4, 596). Cambridge U Pr.
Chadwick, John, et al. Knossos Tables: A Transliteration. 4th ed. (Illus.). 1971. 53.00 (ISBN 0-521-08085-1). Cambridge U Pr.
Chadwick, K. H. & Leenhouts, H. P. The Molecular Theory of Radiation Biology. (Monographs on Theoretical & Applied Genetics: Vol. 5). (Illus.). 450p. 1981. 67.50 (ISBN 0-387-10297-3). Springer-Verlag.
Chadwick, Lee. Cuba Today. LC 75-43185. (Illus.). 224p. 1976. 7.95 (ISBN 0-88208-065-2); pap. 5.95 (ISBN 0-88208-066-0). Lawrence Hill.
Chadwick, M. H., jt. ed. see Goodman, G. T.
Chadwick, M. J. & Goodman, G. T. The Ecology of Resource Degradation & Renewal. LC 75-5776. (British Ecological Society Symposia Ser.). 450p. 1976. 50.95 (ISBN 0-470-14295-2). Halsted Pr.
Chadwick, M. J., jt. auth. see Bradshaw, A. D.
Chadwick, Mary, jt. auth. see Lennox, Stanley C.
Chadwick, Nora K. & Zhirmunsky, Victor. Oral Epics of Central Asia. LC 68-21189. 1969. 78.00 (ISBN 0-521-07053-8). Cambridge U Pr.

Chadwick, O. Catholicism & History. LC 77-77740. 1978. 18.95 (ISBN 0-521-21708-3). Cambridge U Pr.

--The Secularization of the European Mind in the Nineteenth Century. LC 77-88670. (The Gifford Lectures in the University of Edinburgh Ser.: 1973-1974). 278p. 1976. 33.50 (ISBN 0-521-20892-0); pap. 9.95x (ISBN 0-521-29317-0). Cambridge U Pr.

Chadwick, Owen. Acton & Gladstone. 1976. pap. text ed. 6.50x (ISBN 0-485-14122-1, Athlone Pr). Humanities.

--John Cassian. 2nd ed. 1968. 26.50 (ISBN 0-521-04607-6). Cambridge U Pr.

--The Victorian Church, Pt. I. 3rd ed. (Ecclesiastical History of England Ser.). 1971. text ed. 22.50x (ISBN 0-06-491025-3). B&N.

--The Victorian Church, Pt. II. 2nd ed. (Ecclesiastical History of England Ser.). 1972. text ed. 22.50x (ISBN 0-06-491026-1). B&N.

Chadwick, P. Continuum Mechanics: Concise Theory & Problems. LC 75-26519. 1976. text ed. 16.95 o.p. (ISBN 0-470-14303-7). Halsted Pr.

Chae. Lebesque Integration. 352p. 1980. 35.00 (ISBN 0-8247-6983-X). Dekker.

Chafe, Wallace, ed. American Indian Languages & American Linguistics. 1976. pap. text ed. 9.25x (ISBN 90-316-0086-5). Humanities.

Chafe, William H. American Woman: Her Changing Social, Economic & Political Roles, 1920-1970. 336p. 1974. pap. 5.95 (ISBN 0-19-501785-4, GB406). Oxford U Pr.

--Civilities & Civil Rights: Greensboro, North Carolina, & the Black Struggle for Freedom. (Illus.). 1980. 15.95 (ISBN 0-19-502625-X). Oxford U Pr.

--Civilities & Civil Rights: Greensboro, North Carolina, & the Black Struggle for Freedom. (Illus.). 320p. 1981. pap. 5.95 (ISBN 0-19-502919-4, GB 644, GB). Oxford U Pr.

Chafee, Zechariah. The Inquiring Mind. LC 74-699. (American Constitutional & Legal History Ser.). 276p. 1974. Repr. of 1928 ed. lib. bdg. 27.50 (ISBN 0-306-70641-5). Da Capo.

Chafer, Lewis S. Grace. pap. 6.95 (ISBN 0-310-22331-8). Zondervan.

--He That Is Spiritual. 1918. 6.95 (ISBN 0-310-22340-7, Pub. by Dunham). Zondervan.

--Salvation. 160p. 1972. pap. 3.95 (ISBN 0-310-22351-2). Zondervan.

--Systematic Theology, 8 vols. 2700p. 1981. Repr. 89.95 (ISBN 0-310-22378-4). Zondervan.

Chafer, Lewis S. & Walvoord, John F. Major Bible Themes. rev. ed. 10.95 (ISBN 0-310-22390-3). Zondervan.

Chafetz, Janet S. Masculine-Feminine or Human. 2nd ed. LC 77-83425. 1978. pap. text ed. 7.50 (ISBN 0-87581-231-7). Peacock Pubs.

Chafetz, Morris E. & Demone, Harold W., Jr. Alcoholism & Society. 1962. 14.95 (ISBN 0-19-500504-X). Oxford U Pr.

Chaff, Sandra L., et al. Women in Medicine: An Annotated Bibliography of the Literature on Women Physicians. LC 77-24914. 1977. 40.00 (ISBN 0-8108-1056-5). Scarecrow.

Chaffee, Allen, ed. see Baum, L. Frank.

Chaffee, Dorcas, jt. ed. see Goodwin, Del.

Chaffee, Ellen, et al. Laboratory Manual for Basic Physiology & Anatomy. 4th ed. 222p. 1980. text ed. 8.95 (ISBN 0-397-54228-3). Lippincott.

Chaffee, Ellen E. Laboratory Manual in Physiology & Anatomy. 3rd rev. ed. 250p. 1974. pap. text ed. 8,95 o.p. (ISBN 0-397-47313-3). Lippincott.

Chaffee, John & Culbertson, Judi. Games America Played. (Illus.). 192p. Date not set. 16.95 o.p. (ISBN 0-686-61465-8, ScribT). Scribner. Postponed.

Chaffee, John, Jr. Business-School Partnerships: A Plus for Kids. 1980. pap. 11.95 (ISBN 0-87545-018-0). Natl Sch PR.

Chaffee, Steven H., ed. Political Communication. LC 75-14629. (Sage Annual Reviews of Communication Research: Vol. 4). 1975. 20.00x (ISBN 0-8039-0505-X); pap. 9.95x (ISBN 0-8039-0507-6). Sage.

Chaffetz, David. A Journey Through Afghanistan: Amemonal. LC 80-51565. 350p. 1981. 13.00 (ISBN 0-89526-675-X). Regnery-Gateway.

--On the Eve of Invasion: A Journey Through Afghanistan. 12.95 (ISBN 0-686-68743-4). Regnery-Gateway.

Chaffin, James B. The Wolfer. 1980. pap. 1.50 (ISBN 0-505-51461-3). Tower Bks.

Chaffin, Lillie D. Bear Weather. LC 69-10498. (Illus.). (gr. k-2). 1969. 4.95g o.s.i. (ISBN 0-02-717890-0). Macmillan.

--John Henry McCoy. (Illus.). 169p. (gr. 4-6). 1971. 4.95 o.s.i. (ISBN 0-02-717920-6). Macmillan.

Chaffurin, L. & De Quericize, F. Parfait Secretaire. (Fr). pap. 10.95 (ISBN 0-685-14021-0, 3922). Larousse.

Chaffurin, L. & Mergault, J. Dictionnaire bilingue Larousse, francais-anglais, anglais-francais. (Apollo). (Fr. & Eng.). 10.50 (ISBN 0-685-13856-9, 3767). Larousse.

Chafin, Kenneth. Help! I'm a Layman. LC 66-22155. 1966. pap. 0.95 o.p. (ISBN 0-87680-908-5, 90008). Word Bks.

Chagall, David. Diary of a Deaf Mute. 1971. pap. 3.50 (ISBN 0-916538-01-X). Millenium Hse.

Chagla, M. C. Individual & the State. 4.50x o.p. (ISBN 0-210-33676-5). Asia.

Chagsuchinda, Pensak. Nang Loi: The Floating Maiden. (Scandinavian Institute of Asian Studies Monograph: No. 18). 80p. (Orig.). 1973. pap. text ed. 6.00x (ISBN 0-7007-0067-6). Humanities.

Chai, Ch'U & Chai, Winberg. Changing Society of China. (Orig.). 1962. pap. 1.50 (ISBN 0-451-61205-1, MW1205, Ment). NAL.

Chai, Henry, jt. auth. see Chai, Winchung.

Chai, Winberg, jt. auth. see Chai, Ch'U.

Chai, Winchung & Chai, Henry. Progamming Standard Cobol. 1976. 13.95 (ISBN 0-12-166550-X). Acad Pr.

Chaij, Fernando. The Impending Drama. LC 78-22061. (Horizon Ser.). 1979. pap. 4.50 (ISBN 0-8127-0208-5). Southern Pub.

--Key to Victory. LC 79-548. (Horizon Ser). 1979. pap. 4.50 (ISBN 0-8127-0224-7). Southern Pub.

Chaiken, William E. & Harper, Mary J. Mainstreaming the Learning Disabled Adolescent: A Staff Development Guide. (Illus.). 162p. 1979. text ed. 14.75 (ISBN 0-398-03871-6). C C Thomas.

Chaikin, Alan L. & Derlega, Valerian J. Sharing Intimacy: What We Reveal to Others & Why. 1975. 12.95 (ISBN 0-13-807867-X, Spec); pap. 3.45 (ISBN 0-13-807859-9). P-H.

Chaikin, Joseph. The Presence of the Actor. LC 70-175287. (Illus.). 1972. pap. text ed. 4.95x (ISBN 0-689-70338-4, 194). Atheneum.

Chaikin, Joseph, jt. auth. see Malpede, Karen.

Chaikin, Miriam. Finders Weepers. LC 79-9608. (Illus.). 128p. (gr. 3-6). 1980. 8.95 (ISBN 0-06-021176-8, HarpJ); PLB 8.79 (ISBN 0-06-021177-6). Har-Row.

--I Should Worry, I Should Care. (gr. k-6). 1981. pap. price not set (ISBN 0-440-44149-8, YB). Dell.

--Ittki Pittki. LC 75-137000. (Illus.). (gr. k-3). 1971. 5.95 o.s.i. (ISBN 0-8193-0463-8, Four Winds); PLB 5.41 o.s.i. (ISBN 0-8193-0464-6). Schol Bk Serv.

Chaikin, Richard. Elements of Surgical Treatment in the Delivery of Periodontal Therapy. (Illus.). 177p. 1978. 54.00 (ISBN 3-87652-661-2). Quint Pub Co.

Chaikin, Sol C. A Labor Viewpoint. LC 80-12784. (Illus.). 250p. (Orig.). 1980. pap. 10.95 (ISBN 0-912526-26-2). Lib Res.

Chailley, Jacques. Forty Thousand Years of Music: Man in Search of Music. Myers, Rollo, tr. from Fr. LC 74-31227. (Music Reprint Ser). (Illus.). xiv, 229p. 1975. Repr. of 1964 ed. lib. bdg. 25.00 (ISBN 0-306-70661-X). Da Capo.

Chaillu, Paul B. Du see Du Chaillu, Paul.

Chaillu, Paul Du see Du Chaillu, Paul.

Chaisson, Eric. Cosmic Dawn: The Origins of Matter & Life. (Illus.). 320p. 1981. 14.95 (ISBN 0-316-13590-9, Pub. by Atlantic Monthly Pr). Little.

Chaitanya, Krishna see Nair, K. K., pseud.

Chaithiraphan, S. Current Concept in the Therapy of Hypertension with Beta-Blockers. (Journal: Cardiology Ser.: Vol. 66, Suppl. 1). (Illus.). vi, 62p. 1980. pap. 19.50 (ISBN 3-8055-0912-X). S Karger.

Chajes, Alexander. Principles of Structural Stability Theory. (Civil Engineering & Engineering Mechanics Ser.). (Illus.). 288p. 1974. 25.95 (ISBN 0-13-709964-9). P-H.

Chakeres, John A. Traces: An Investigation in Reason. LC 76-47816. (Illus., Orig.). 1977. pap. 7.95 (ISBN 0-917924-00-2). Nuance Pr.

Chakerian, Don, et al. Geometry: A Guided Inquiry. LC 71-179132. 1972. text ed. 18.50 (ISBN 0-395-13148-0, 3-53528); tchrs. ed. 19.95 (ISBN 0-395-13149-9, 3-53529); sample test questions 1.90 (ISBN 0-395-18003-1, 3-53531); solution key pap. 4.55 (ISBN 0-685-02024-X, 3-53530). HM.

Chakrabarti, C. L. Progress in Analytical Atomic Spectroscopy, 2 vols. (Illus.). 282p. 1980. 76.00 (ISBN 0-08-027126-X). Pergamon.

Chakrabarti, Nirendranath. The Naked King & Other Poems. Mukherjee, Sujit & Mukherjee, Meenakshi, trs. from Bengali. (Saffronbird Bk). 53p. 8.00 (ISBN 0-88253-833-0); pap. 4.80 (ISBN 0-88253-834-9). Ind-US Inc.

Chakraborty, A. K. Jawaharlal Nehru's Writings. 1981. 15.00x (ISBN 0-685-59378-9). South Asia Bks.

Chakraborty, J. & Dhande, S. G. Kinematics & Geometry of Planer & Spatial CAM Mechanisms. LC 76-50585. 1977. 14.95 (ISBN 0-470-15069-6). Halsted Pr.

Chakraborty, S. K. Management by Objectives. LC 76-901892. 1976. 12.00x o.p. (ISBN 0-333-90112-6). South Asia Bks.

Chakravarti, Aravinda & Morizot, Donald C. Not Everything We Eat Is Curry. LC 78-52255. (Illus., Orig.). 1978. pap. 8.95 o.p. (ISBN 0-930138-01-5). Harold Hse.

Chakravarti, D., jt. ed. see Agrawal, D.

Chakravarti, P. C. Integrals & Sums. 1970. text ed. 22.50x (ISBN 0-485-11114-4, Athlone Pr). Humanities.

Chakravarti, Prithvindra. Prettier Than the Black Pea Flower. (Redbird Bk.). 1976. lib. bdg. 8.00 (ISBN 0-89253-092-8); flexible bdg. 4.80 (ISBN 0-89253-147-9). Ind-US Inc.

Chakravarty, A. S. Introduction to the Magnetic Properties of Solids. LC 80-12793. 736p. 1980. 65.00 (ISBN 0-471-07737-2, Pub. by Wiley-Interscience). Wiley.

Chakravorty, U. N. Anglo-Maratha Relations & Malcolm Seventeen Ninety-Eight to Eighteen Thirty. 1979. text ed. 15.00x (ISBN 0-210-40623-2). Asia.

Chalazonitis, N. & Boisson, M., eds. Abnormal Neuronal Discharges. LC 76-58750. 1978. 38.00 (ISBN 0-89004-238-1). Raven.

Chalef, Morton N. PSRO Journal Articles. 1977. spiral bdg. 18.00 o.p. (ISBN 0-87488-792-5). Med Exam.

Chaleff, R. S. Genetics of Higher Plants: Applications of Cell Culture. (Development & Cell Biology Monographs: No. 9). 208p. Date not set. price not set (ISBN 0-521-22731-3). Cambridge U Pr.

Chalek, Lenore F., et al. Speed-Script Secretarial Shorthand, 3 bks. LC 73-93436. (Speed-Script Secretarial Shorthand Program Ser.). 440p. 1974. Set. text ed. 24.75 set (ISBN 0-913310-23-9). PAR Inc.

Chalfant. Religion in Contemporary Society. 1981. 14.95 (ISBN 0-88284-126-2). Alfred Pub.

Chalfant, H. Paul, compiled by. Social & Behavioral Aspects of Female Alcoholism: An Annotated Bibliography. LC 80-1021. 168p. 1980. lib. bdg. 22.50 (ISBN 0-313-20947-2, CAL/). Greenwood.

Chalfant, James C., jt. auth. see Van Dusen Pysh, Margaret.

Chalfant, W. A. Gold, Guns & Ghost Towns. 12.95 (ISBN 0-912494-32-8); pap. 6.95 (ISBN 0-686-63864-6). Chalfant Pr.

--The Story of Inyo. 1980. 18.95 (ISBN 0-912494-34-4); pap. 12.50 (ISBN 0-912494-35-2). Chalfant Pr.

Chalfont, Lord, ed. Waterloo. LC 79-3499. (Illus.). 1980. 17.95 o.p. (ISBN 0-394-51119-0). Knopf.

Chaliand, Gerard, ed. & intro. by. People with Out a Country: The Kurds & Kurdistan. 292p. (Orig.). 1980. 19.95 (ISBN 0-905762-69-X, Pub. by Zed Pr); pap. 8.50 (ISBN 0-905762-74-6). Lawrence Hill.

Chalk, L., jt. ed. see Metcalfe, C. R.

Chalk, W. C. Brainbox. (Instant Readers Ser.). 1971. pap. text ed. 2.50x o.p. (ISBN 0-435-11193-0). Heinemann Ed.

--Conquest of Mars. 1971. pap. text ed. 2.75x o.p. (ISBN 0-435-11200-7). Heinemann Ed.

--Escape from Bondage. pap. text ed. 2.75x o.p. (ISBN 0-435-11228-7). Heinemann Ed.

--The Firebirds. 1971. pap. text ed. 2.50x o.p. (ISBN 0-435-11198-1). Heinemann Ed.

--The Gnomids. pap. text ed. 2.75x o.p. (ISBN 0-435-11229-5). Heinemann Ed.

--The Gomez Story. pap. text ed. 2.75x o.p. (ISBN 0-435-11224-4). Heinemann Ed.

--H.M.S. Thing. pap. text ed. 2.75x o.p. (ISBN 0-435-11225-2). Heinemann Ed.

--The Iron Man. 1971. pap. text ed. 2.95x o.p. (ISBN 0-435-11195-7). Heinemann Ed.

--Jim Silent. 1971. pap. text ed. 2.95x o.p. (ISBN 0-435-11196-5). Heinemann Ed.

--The Man from Mars. pap. text ed. 2.75x o.p. (ISBN 0-435-11220-1). Heinemann Ed.

--Mask of Dust. pap. text ed. 2.75x o.p. (ISBN 0-435-11227-9). Heinemann Ed.

--The Moonlanders. 1971. pap. text ed. 2.50x o.p. (ISBN 0-435-11199-X). Heinemann Ed.

--Old Ugly. pap. text ed. 2.75x o.p. (ISBN 0-435-11222-8). Heinemann Ed.

--Pontius the Pilot. 1971. pap. text ed. 2.95x o.p. (ISBN 0-435-11194-9). Heinemann Ed.

--School at Ash Green. 1971. pap. text ed. 2.50x o.p. (ISBN 0-435-11192-2). Heinemann Ed.

--Secret Factory. pap. text ed. 2.95x o.p. (ISBN 0-435-11221-X). Heinemann Ed.

--Skinny Willy. 1971. pap. text ed. 2.50x o.p. (ISBN 0-435-11191-4). Heinemann Ed.

--The Spider Bomb. pap. text ed. 2.75x o.p. (ISBN 0-435-11226-0). Heinemann Ed.

--The Talking Machine. pap. text ed. 2.75x o.p. (ISBN 0-435-11223-6). Heinemann Ed.

--Terrible Things. 1971. pap. text ed. 2.50x o.p. (ISBN 0-435-11197-3). Heinemann Ed.

Chalk, William, jt. auth. see Levens, Alexander.

Chalker, J., ed. see Swift, Jonathan.

Chalker, Jack L. The Devil's Voyage. LC 79-7841. 336p. 1981. 11.95 (ISBN 0-385-15284-1). Doubleday.

--A Jungle of Stars. 1976. pap. 2.25 (ISBN 0-345-28960-9). Ballantine.

Chalker, Kenneth W. Dare to Defy: Challenging Sterotypes & Looking at Relationships in a Christian Context. LC 80-54478. 144p. 1981. pap. 4.50x (ISBN 0-8358-0418-6). Upper Room.

Chall, Jeanne S. Learning to Read: The Great Debate. 1967. 12.50 (ISBN 0-07-010390-9, C); pap. 4.95 (ISBN 0-07-010391-7). McGraw.

Challem, Jack & Challem, Renate. What Herbs Are All About. LC 80-82913. 150p. (Orig.). 1980. pap. 2.95 (ISBN 0-87983-242-8). Keats.

Challem, Renate, jt. auth. see Challem, Jack.

Challener, Richard D., ed. Economic Assistance to China & Korea: 1949-50 (March, June, June, July 1949; January 1950) (Legislative Origins of American Foreign Policy Ser.: Vol. 7). 1979. lib. bdg. 31.00 (ISBN 0-8240-3036-2). Garland Pub.

--The Legislative Origins of American Foreign Policy, 5 vols. Incl. Vol. 1. Proceedings, April 7, 1913 to March 7, 1923. 415p. lib. bdg. 40.00 (ISBN 0-8240-3030-3); Vol. 2. Proceedings, December 3, 1923 to March 3, 1933. 279p. lib. bdg. 28.00 (ISBN 0-8240-3031-1); Vol. 3. Legislative Origins of the Truman Doctrine, March to April, 1947. 235p. 23.00 (ISBN 0-8240-3032-X); Vol. 4. Foreign Relief Aid, 1947. 401p. lib. bdg. 36.00 (ISBN 0-8240-3033-8); Vol. 5. Foreign Relief Assistance Act of 1948. 809p. lib. bdg. 65.00 (ISBN 0-8240-3034-6). (The Senate Foreign Relations Committee's Historical Ser.). 1979. Garland Pub.

--Nineteen Twenty (Feb. Seventh - April Ninth, 1920) (United States Military Intelligence 1917-1927 Ser.). 1979. lib. bdg. 60.50 (ISBN 0-8240-3011-7). Garland Pub.

--Reviews of the World Situation: 1949-50. (Legislative Origins of American Foreign Policy Ser.: Vol. 8). 1979. lib. bdg. 55.00 (ISBN 0-8240-3037-0). Garland Pub.

--Weekly Summary: April Twentieth to August Third, Nineteen Eighteen. LC 77-17413. (United Ststes Military Intelligence 1917-1927 Ser.). 1978. lib. bdg. 60.50 (ISBN 0-8240-3003-6). Garland Pub.

--Weekly Summary: December Thirteenth, Nineteen Nineteen to January Thirty-First, Nineteen Twenty. LC 77-17413. (United States Military Intelligence 1917-1927 Ser.). 1978. lib. bdg. 60.50 (ISBN 0-8240-3010-9). Garland Pub.

--Weekly Summary: February Eighth to May Seventeenth, Nineteen Nineteen. LC 77-17413. (United States Military Intelligence 1917-1927 Ser.). 1978. lib. bdg. 60.50 (ISBN 0-8240-3006-0). Garland Pub.

--Weekly Summary: January Twenty-Sixth to April Thirteenth, Nineteen Eighteen. LC 77-17413. (United States Military Intellegence 1917-1927 Ser.). 1978. lib. bdg. 60.50 (ISBN 0-8240-3002-8). Garland Pub.

--Weekly Summary: July Ninth to September Twenty-Seventh, Nineteen Nineteen. LC 77-17413. (United States Military Intelligence 1917-1927 Ser.). 1978. lib. bdg. 60.50 (ISBN 0-8240-3008-7). Garland Pub.

--Weekly Summary: May Twenty-Fourth to July Second, Nineteen Nineteen. LC 77-17413. (United States Military Intelligence 1917-1927 Ser.). 1978. lib. bdg. 60.50 (ISBN 0-8240-3007-9). Garland Pub.

--Weekly Summary: November Second, Nineteen Eighteen to February First, Nineteen Nineteen. LC 77-17413. (United States Military Intelligence 1917-1927 Ser.). 1978. lib. bdg. 60.50 (ISBN 0-8240-3005-2). Garland Pub.

--Weekly Summary: October Fourth to December Sixth, Nineteen Nineteen. LC 77-17413. (United States Military Intelligence 1917-1927 Ser.). 1978. lib. bdg. 60.50 (ISBN 0-8240-3009-5). Garland Pub.

--World War I, June Second, Nineteen Seventeen to October Thirteenth, Nineteen Seventeen. (United States Military Intelligence 1917-1927 Ser.: Vol. 1). 1978. lib. bdg. 60.50 (ISBN 0-8240-3000-1). Garland Pub.

--World War One, Oct. 20, 1917-Jan. 19, 1918. (United States Military Intelligence 1917-1927 Ser.). 1979. lib. bdg. 60.50 (ISBN 0-8240-3001-X). Garland Pub.

Challenge, Jack. St. Mick. 270p. 1981. 13.95 (ISBN 0-915520-41-9); pap. 6.95 (ISBN 0-915520-41-9). Ross-Erikson.

Challenor, Bernard, et al. Physician's Assistant Examination Review Book. 1975. pap. 12.50 (ISBN 0-87488-422-5). Med Exam.

Challinor, Joan R., jt. auth. see Lichtman, Allan J.

Challinor, John, jt. auth. see Platt, John.

Challis, Aidan J. Motueka: An Archaeological Survey. (New Zealand Archaeological Assn. Monographs). (Illus.). 1978. pap. text ed. 12.50x (ISBN 0-582-71758-2). Longman.

Chalmers, A. F. What Is This Thing Called Science? An Assessment of the Nature & Status of Science & Its Methods. 1976. pap. text ed. 10.50x (ISBN 0-7022-1341-1). Humanities.

Chalmers, Amanda J., jt. auth. see McCormack, James E.
Chalmers, B., ed. Progress in Materials Science, Vol. 23. 280p. 1980. 85.00 (ISBN 0-08-024846-2). Pergamon.
Chalmers, Edlen. Making the Most of Family Living. LC 79-84303. 1979. pap. 5.95 (ISBN 0-8163-0244-8). Pacific Pr Pub Assn.
Chalmers, George. An Introduction to the History of the Revolt of the American Colonies, 2 Vols. LC 75-119049. (Era of the American Revolution Ser). 1971. Repr. of 1845 ed. lib. bdg. 65.00 (ISBN 0-306-71948-7). Da Capo.
Chalmers, Helena. Clothes, on & off the Stage: A History of Dress from the Earliest Times to the Present Day. LC 73-180965. (Illus.). xx, 292p. 1976. Repr. of 1928 ed. 22.00 (ISBN 0-8103-4033-X). Gale.
Chalmers, Mary. Come to the Doctor, Harry. LC 80-7910. (Illus.). 32p. (ps-1). 1981. 5.95 (ISBN 0-06-021178-4, HarpJ); PLB 5.89g (ISBN 0-06-021179-2). Har-Row.
Chalmers, Thomas C., jt. ed. see Berk, Paul D.
Chalmers-Hunt, J. M., ed. Natural History Auctions, Seventeen Hundred to Nineteen Seventy-Two: A Register of Sales in the British Isles. 192p. 1976. 45.00x (ISBN 0-85667-021-9, Pub. by Sotheby Parke Bernet England). Biblio Dist.
Chalon, Jack, jt. auth. see Turndorf, Herman.
Chalon, Jack, et al. Humidification of Anesthetic Gases. (Illus.). 120p. 1981. price not set (ISBN 0-398-04461-9). C C Thomas.
Chaloner, W. H. The Movement for the Extension of Owens College, Manchester, Eighteen Sixty-Three to Seventy-Three. 136p. 1973. 9.00x (ISBN 0-7190-0552-3, Pub by Manchester U Pr England). State Mutual Bk.
Chaloner, W. H., ed. & intro. by see Bamford, Samuel.
Chalpin, Lila. A New Look at Microwave Cooking. 1981. 8.95 (ISBN 0-916752-04-6). Green Hill.
Chamala, Shankarish, jt. auth. see Crouch, Bruce L.
Chamala, Shankarish, jt. auth. see Crouch, Bruce R.
Chambadal, L. Dictionnaire mathematiques modernes. (Illus., Fr.). pap. 7.75 o.p. (ISBN 0-685-13875-5). Larousse.
Chamberlain, Basil H. Japanese Things: Being Notes on Various Subjects Connected with Japan. LC 76-87791. 1970. pap. 8.50 (ISBN 0-8048-0713-2). C E Tuttle.
Chamberlain, C. C., et al. Animal Science. 1982. text ed. 17.95 (ISBN 0-8359-0224-2); instr's. manual free (ISBN 0-8359-0225-0). Reston.
Chamberlain, Edward M. Freud's Incredible Conception of the Contemporary Female. (Illus.). 1979. deluxe ed. 47.45 (ISBN 0-930582-38-1). Gloucester Art.
Chamberlain, G. H. Trading in Options. 144p. 1980. 30.00x (ISBN 0-85941-168-0, Pub. by Woodhead-Faulkner England). State Mutual Bk.
Chamberlain, Houston S. Foundations of the Nineteenth Century, 2 vols. LC 67-29735. 1968. Repr. Set. 85.00 (ISBN 0-86527-069-4). Fertig.
Chamberlain, J. The Principals of Interferometric Spectroscopy. LC 78-13206. 360p. 1979. 58.00 (ISBN 0-471-99719-6). Wiley.
Chamberlain, John, jt. auth. see Kirk, Russell.
Chamberlain, Joseph P. Legislative Processes: National & State. LC 73-95087. Repr. of 1936 ed. lib. bdg. 19.75x (ISBN 0-8371-2580-4, CHLP). Greenwood.
Chamberlain, Judi. On Our Own: Patient Controlled Alternatives to the Mental Health System. LC 76-56520. 1978. 12.00 o.p. (ISBN 0-8015-5523-X). Dutton.
Chamberlain, Mildred & Clarenbach, Laura. Descendants of Hugh Mosher & Rebecca Maxson Through Seven Generations. LC 80-51754. 808p. 1980. 22.50 (ISBN 0-9604142-0-7). M M Chamberlain.
Chamberlain, N. H. Samuel Sewall & the World He Lived in. 319p. 1980. Repr. of 1897 ed. lib. bdg. 30.00 (ISBN 0-89987-110-0). Darby Bks.
Chamberlain, Narcissa. Old Rooms for New Living. (Illus.). 1977. 12.95 (ISBN 0-8038-5346-7). Hastings.
Chamberlain, Neil W. & Cullen, D. E. The Labor Sector. 2nd ed. Orig. Title: The Firm: Microeconomic Planning & Action. 1972. 17.95 (ISBN 0-07-010428-X, C). McGraw.
Chamberlain, Neil W., ed. Contemporary Economic Issues. rev. ed. 1973. pap. text ed. 8.95x (ISBN 0-256-01427-2). Irwin.
Chamberlain, Newell D. The Call of Gold. (Illus.). 185p. 1981. pap. 5.95 (ISBN 0-934136-12-2). Western Tanager.
Chamberlain, Peter, jt. auth. see Jones, Ken.
Chamberlain, Russell. Rome. (Great Cities Ser.). (Illus.). 1976. 14.95 (ISBN 0-8094-2258-1). Time-Life.
--Rome. (The Great Cities Ser.). (Illus.). (gr. 6 up). 1976. PLB 14.94 (ISBN 0-8094-2259-X, Pub by Time-Life). Silver.
Chamberlain, Samuel. Domestic Architecture in Rural France. (Illus.). 64p. (Orig.). 1981. pap. 7.95 (ISBN 0-8038-1578-6). Hastings.
--Soft Skies of France. (Illus.). 1953. 12.50 (ISBN 0-8038-6662-3). Hastings.
--Stroll Through Historic Salem. LC 78-79738. (Illus.). 1969. 8.95 (ISBN 0-8038-6689-5). Hastings.
Chamberlain, Samuel & Flynt, Henry N. Historic Deerfield: Houses & Interiors. Date not set. 16.95 (ISBN 0-8038-3027-0). Hastings.
Chamberlain, V. B., 3rd, jt. ed. see Rogers, Robert S.
Chamberlain, Valerie & Kelly, Joan. Creative Home Economics Instruction. 2nd ed. O'Neill, Martha, ed. (Illus.). 256p. 1980. pap. text ed. 10.95 (ISBN 0-07-010424-7, W). McGraw.
Chamberlain, Valerie M. & Kelly, Joan. Creative Home Economics Instruction. (Illus.). 272p. 1974. pap. text ed. 10.95 (ISBN 0-07-010423-9, W). McGraw.
Chamberlain, Von Del, jt. ed. see Hanle, Paul A.
Chamberlain, W. H. & Taylerson, A. W. Adams' Revolvers. 1978. 29.95 o.p. (ISBN 0-214-20089-2, 8011, Dist. by Arco). Barrie & Jenkins.
Chamberlain, Wilt & Shaw, David. Wilt. (Illus.). 368p. 1975. pap. 1.95 o.s.i. (ISBN 0-446-79621-2). Warner Bks.
--Wilt: Just Like Any Other 7-Foot Black Millionaire Who Lives Next Door. (Illus.). 362p. 1973. 6.95 o.s.i. (ISBN 0-02-523360-2). Macmillan.
Chamberlin, E. R. The Awakening Giant: Britain in the Industrial Revolution. 1976. 30.00 (ISBN 0-7134-3053-2, Pub. by Batsford England). David & Charles.
--Preserving the Past. (Illus.). 205p. 1979. 17.50x (ISBN 0-460-04364-1, Pub. by J. M. Dent England). Biblio Dist.
--The Sack of Rome. (Illus.). 1980. 25.00 (ISBN 0-7134-1645-9, Pub. by Batsford England). David & Charles.
Chamberlin, Geoffrey. Contemporary Obstetrics & Gynaecology. (Illus.). 1977. 46.50x (ISBN 0-7198-2546-6). Intl Ideas.
Chamberlin, Hope. A Minority of Members: Women in the U.S. Congress. 408p. (RL 10). 1974. pap. 2.25 o.p. (ISBN 0-451-61316-3, ME1316, Ment). NAL.
Chamberlin, J. Gordon. The Educating Act: A Phenomenological View. LC 80-6076. 202p. 1981. lib. bdg. 17.75 (ISBN 0-8191-1449-9); pap. text ed. 8.75 (ISBN 0-8191-1450-2). U Pr of Amer.
Chamberline. Forces of Change in Western Europe. (Illus.). 352p. 1980. text ed. 24.50 (ISBN 0-07-084107-1). McGraw.
Chambers, A. B., et al see Dryden, John.
Chambers, Aidan. Seal Secret. LC 80-8456. 128p. (gr. 5 up). 1981. 8.95 (ISBN 0-06-021258-6, HarpJ); PLB 8.79g (ISBN 0-06-021259-4). Har-Row.
Chambers, Bradford. How to Hypnotize. LC 57-6582. (Illus.). 1957. 9.95 (ISBN 0-87396-004-1). Stravon.
Chambers, Carl D. & Heckman, Richard D. Employee Drug Abuse: A Manager's Guide for Action. LC 73-183372. 1972. 15.95 (ISBN 0-8436-0718-1). CBI Pub.
Chambers, Clarke A., ed. New Deal at Home & Abroad, 1929-1945. LC 65-11896. (Orig.). 1965. pap. text ed. 3.50 o.s.i. (ISBN 0-02-905300-5). Free Pr.
Chambers, David, ed. Private Press Books, 1975. LC 60-31492. (Illus.). 1978. pap. 13.50x (ISBN 0-900002-53-0). Intl Pubns Serv.
--Private Press Books, 1976. LC 60-31492. (Illus.). 117p. (Orig.). 1979. pap. 13.50x (ISBN 0-900002-83-2). Intl Pubns Serv.
Chambers, David & Sandford, Christopher, eds. Cock-a-Hoop. LC 76-10113. (Illus.). 128p. 1976. 15.00 o.p. (ISBN 0-498-01986-1); ltd. ed 50.00 o.p. (ISBN 0-498-01987-X). A S Barnes.
Chambers, Dewey W. The Oral Tradition: Storytelling & Creative Drama. 2nd ed. (Literature for Children Ser). 1977. pap. text ed. 3.50x (ISBN 0-697-06210-4). Wm C Brown.
Chambers, Frances. France. (World Bibliographical Ser.: No. 13). 175p. 1980. 31.50 (ISBN 0-903450-25-9). ABC Clio.
Chambers, Francis T., Jr. The Drinker's Addiction: Its Nature & Practical Treatment. 164p. 1968. pap. 14.75 photocopy ed. spiral (ISBN 0-398-00301-7). C C Thomas.
Chambers, Frank. Prosateurs Francais XVIE Siecle. 1976. pap. 12.95x (ISBN 0-669-00016-7). Heath.
Chambers, G. B. Folksong-Plainsong: A Study in Origins & Musical Relationships. 2nd ed. 1972. Repr. of 1956 ed. 9.50x (ISBN 0-85036-178-8). Humanities.
Chambers, Ginger. The Kindred Spirit. (Orig.). 1981. pap. 1.50 (ISBN 0-440-14395-0). Dell.
Chambers, Harry T. The Management of Small Offset Print Departments. 2nd ed. 217p. 1979. text ed. 22.00x (ISBN 0-220-67007-2, Pub. by Busn Bks England). Renouf.
Chambers, Henry A., ed. Treasury of Negro Spirituals. (gr. 7 up). 1963. 10.95 o.s.i. (ISBN 0-87523-145-4). Emerson.
Chambers, J. D. Conflict & Community: Europe Since 1750. LC 68-107879. (Illus.). 492p. 1968. 8.75x (ISBN 0-540-00005-1). Intl Pubns Serv.
Chambers, J. D. & Mingay, G. E. The Agricultural Revolution. 1975. 22.50 (ISBN 0-7134-1350-6, Pub. by Batsford England); pap. 14.50 (ISBN 0-7134-1358-1). David & Charles.
Chambers, J. K. & Trudgill, P. Dialectology. LC 79-41604. (Cambridge Textbooks in Linguistics). (Illus.). 210p. 1980. 34.50 (ISBN 0-521-22401-2); pap. 11.95 (ISBN 0-521-29473-8). Cambridge U Pr.
Chambers, Jane. Burning. 1978. pap. 1.50 o.s.i. (ISBN 0-515-04450-4). Jove Pubns.
Chambers, Jessie. D. H. Lawrence: A Personal Record, by E. T. LC 80-40254. 223p. 1980. pap. 8.95 (ISBN 0-521-29919-5). Cambridge U Pr.
Chambers, John. Finder. LC 80-23928. 168p. (gr. 4-6). 1981. PLB 8.95 (ISBN 0-689-30803-5). Atheneum.
--United States Government Documents & Reports Pertaining to Conscription & Conscientious Objection, 1917-1968. LC 76-147694. (Library of War & Peace: Documentary Anthologies). 1974. lib. bdg. 38.00 (ISBN 0-8240-0450-7). Garland Pub.
Chambers, John C., et al. An Executive's Guide to Forecasting. LC 74-2433. (Managers Guide Ser.). 320p. 1974. 27.50 (ISBN 0-471-14335-9, Pub. by Wiley-Interscience). Wiley.
Chambers, John M. Computational Methods for Data Analysis. LC 77-9493. (Wiley Ser. in Probability & Mathematical Statistics: Applied Section). 1977. 21.50 (ISBN 0-471-02772-3, Pub. by Wiley-Interscience). Wiley.
Chambers, John W. The Tyranny of Change: America in the Progressive Era, 1900-1917. (The St. Martin's Series in Twentieth Century United States History). 280p. Date not set. text ed. 12.95x (ISBN 0-312-82757-1); pap. text ed. 5.95x (ISBN 0-312-82758-X). St Martin.
Chambers, Jonathan D. Nottinghamshire in the Eighteenth Century. LC 65-5293. Repr. of 1932 ed. 22.50x (ISBN 0-678-05036-8). Kelley.
Chambers, Kenneth A. A Country Lover's Guide to Wildlife. (Illus.). 1980. pap. 8.95 (ISBN 0-452-25239-3, Plume). NAL.
Chambers, Kenton L., ed. see Biology Coloquium, 29th, Oregon State Univ.
Chambers, Lyn, ed. see Wallach, Harold C.
Chambers, Marilyn. Marilyn Chambers: My Story. (Illus., Orig.). 1975. pap. 1.95 o.s.i. (ISBN 0-446-79827-4). Warner Bks.
Chambers, Marilyn, jt. auth. see Hollander, Xaviera.
Chambers, Melvin T. Born Out of Season. 1978. 5.50 o.p. (ISBN 0-682-49063-6). Exposition.
--A Dog Named Sam. 1978. 6.00 o.p. (ISBN 0-682-49064-4). Exposition.
Chambers, Oswald. Daily Thoughts for Disciples. 251p. 1976. 6.95. Chr Lit.
--Still Higher for His Highest. 192p. 1970. 5.95. Chr Lit.
Chambers, P. L. & Klinger, W., eds. Further Studies in the Assessment of Toxic Actions: Proceedings. (Archives of Toxicology Supplementum Ser.: No. 4). (Illus.). 507p. 1981. pap. 57.80 (ISBN 0-387-10191-8). Springer-Verlag.
Chambers, Quintin, jt. auth. see Draeger, Donn F.
Chambers, R. Buyers Handbook: A Guide to Defensive Shopping. 1976. 7.95 o.p. (ISBN 0-13-109579-X, Spec); pap. 2.45 o.p. (ISBN 0-13-109561-7). P-H.
Chambers, R., ed. Twentieth Century Interpretations of All the Kings Men. 1977. 8.95 (ISBN 0-13-022434-0, Spec); pap. 3.45 (ISBN 0-13-022426-X, Spec). P-H.
Chambers, Raymond J. Accounting, Evaluation & Economic Behavior. LC 66-13944. 1975. Repr. of 1966 ed. text ed. 13.00 (ISBN 0-914348-15-9). Scholars Bk.
Chambers, Raymond W. Thomas More. 1958. pap. 4.95x (ISBN 0-472-06018-X, 18, AA). U of Mich Pr.
Chambers, Raymond W., ed. Beowulf: An Introduction. 1959. 55.00 (ISBN 0-521-04615-7). Cambridge U Pr.
Chambers, Richard D. Fluorine in Organic Chemistry. 410p. 1981. Repr. of 1973 ed. lib. bdg. price not set (ISBN 0-89874-345-1). Krieger.
Chambers, Robert. Cyclopedia of English Literature: A History, Critical & Biographical, of British Authors, from the Earliest to the Present Times, 3 vols. (Illus.). 1979. Repr. of 1938 ed. Set. 130.00 (ISBN 0-8103-4213-8). Gale.
--Popular Rhymes of Scotland. LC 68-58902. 1969. Repr. of 1870 ed. 18.00 (ISBN 0-8103-3828-9). Gale.
--Vestiges of the Natural History of Creation. (Victorian Library). 1969. Repr. of 1844 ed. text ed. 10.00x (ISBN 0-7185-5001-3, Leicester). Humanities.
Chambers, Robert, ed. Book of Days: A Miscellany of Popular Antiquities in Connection with the Calendar, Including Anecdote, Biography & History, Curiosities of Literature, & Oddities of Human Life & Character, 2 Vols. LC 67-13009. (Illus.). 1967. Repr. of 1862 ed. 64.00 (ISBN 0-8103-3002-4). Gale.
Chambers, Robert & King, Carlyle, eds. Book of Essays. 1963. pap. text ed. 5.50 (ISBN 0-312-08855-8). St Martin.
Chambers, Selma. Words. (Illus.). (ps-3). 1948. PLB 5.00 (ISBN 0-307-60045-9, Golden Pr). Western Pub.
Chambers, W. N. & Burnham, Walter D., eds. The American Party Systems. rev. 2nd ed. (Illus.). 380p. 1975. pap. 5.95x (ISBN 0-19-501917-2). Oxford U Pr.
Chambers, William E. Death Toll. 1976. pap. 1.25 o.p. (ISBN 0-445-00385-5). Popular Lib.
Chamblain De Marivaux, Pierre C. De see De Chamblain De Marivaux, Pierre C.
Chambless-Rigie, Jane, illus. My First Mother Goose Book. (Golden Storytime Bk. of Learning). 24p. (ps). 1980. 1.50 (ISBN 0-307-11981-5); PLB 6.08 s&l (ISBN 0-307-61981-8). Western Pub.
Chambliss, Glenn & Vary, James C., eds. Spores VII: Papers Presented at the 7th International Spore Conference, Madison, Wisc., Oct. 1977. LC 57-14449. (Illus.). 1978. text ed. 20.00 (ISBN 0-914826-17-4). Am Soc Microbio.
Chambliss, William J. Criminal Law in Action. LC 74-32149. 480p. 1975. text ed. 17.95 (ISBN 0-471-14474-6). Wiley.
Chambliss, William J. & Mankoff, Milton. Whose Law? What Order? A Conflict Approach to Criminology. LC 75-23220. 256p. 1976. pap. text ed. 11.95x (ISBN 0-471-14476-2). Wiley.
Chambliss, William J. & Seidman, Robert B. Law, Order & Power. 1971. text ed. 18.95 (ISBN 0-201-00957-9). A-W.
Chambliss, William J., ed. Problems of Industrial Society. LC 72-578. 1973. pap. text ed. 8.95 (ISBN 0-201-00958-7). A-W.
--Sociological Readings in the Conflict Perspective. LC 72-579. 1973. pap. text ed. 9.95 (ISBN 0-201-00959-5). A-W.
Chambrun, Adolphe De see De Chambrun, Adolphe.
Chambry, Pierre. Your First Book of Riding. Date not set. price not set (ISBN 0-8120-5193-9). Barron.
Chamie, Joseph. Religion & Fertility: Arab Christian-Muslim Differentials. LC 80-19787. (ASA Rose Monograph Ser.). (Illus.). 176p. Date not set. price not set (ISBN 0-521-23677-0); pap. price not set (ISBN 0-521-28147-4). Cambridge U Pr.
Chamier, John. Safety & Seamanship. (Illus.). 1979. 13.95 (ISBN 0-229-11501-2, ScribT). Scribner.
--Safety & Seamanship. 1979. 14.95x (ISBN 0-8464-0067-7). Beekman Pubs.
Chamier, John, tr. see Grout, Jack.
Chamisso, Adelbert von see Von Chamisso, Adelbert.
Chamling, Dhiraj R. India & the United Nations. 1979. text ed. 15.00x (ISBN 0-210-40617-8). Asia.
Chamot, E. M. & Mason, C. W. Handbook of Chemical Microscopy, Vol. 2. 2nd ed. 1940. 37.50 (ISBN 0-471-04122-X). Wiley.
Chamot, Mary. Turner: Early Works. (Tate Gallery: Little Art Book Ser.). (Illus.). 1977. pap. 1.95 (ISBN 0-8120-0857-X). Barron.
Champdor, Albert. Book of the Dead: Based on the Ani, Hunefer & Anhai Papyri in the British Museum. Bowers, Faubion, tr. LC 66-17862. (Illus.). 1966. 10.00 o.p. (ISBN 0-912326-17-4). Garrett-Helix.
Champernowne, D. G. The Distribution of Income Between Persons. LC 73-75859. (Illus.). 316p. 1973. 47.50 (ISBN 0-521-08546-2). Cambridge U Pr.
Champigny, Robert. Pagan Hero: An Interpretation of Meursault in Camus' the Stranger. Portis, Rowe, tr. LC 79-83139. 1970. 8.00 o.p. (ISBN 0-8122-7597-7). U of Pa Pr.
Champion, Dean J., jt. auth. see Black, James A.
Champion, John M. & James, John H. Critical Incidents in Management. 3rd ed. (Ser. in Management). (Orig.). 1975. pap. text ed. 7.95x o.p. (ISBN 0-256-01557-0). Irwin.
--Critical Incidents in Management. 4th ed. 1980. pap. 10.95x (ISBN 0-256-02269-0). Irwin.
Champion, Larry S. Ben Jonson's "Dotages": A Reconsideration of the Late Plays. LC 67-29338. 168p. 1967. 10.00x (ISBN 0-8131-1143-9). U Pr of Ky.
--King Lear: An Annotated Bibliography. LC 80-8489. (The Garland Shakespeare Bibliographies). 900p. 1980. lib. bdg. 100.00 (ISBN 0-8240-9498-0). Garland Pub.

Champion, Richard G. Go on Singing. (Radiant Life). 128p. 1976. pap. 1.95 (ISBN 0-88243-895-6, 02-0895); teacher's ed 2.50 (ISBN 0-88243-169-2, 32-0169). Gospel Pub.

Champion, Robert H., jt. auth. see Warin, Robert P.

Champion, Sara. Dictionary of Terms & Techniques in Archeology. 1980. 15.95 (ISBN 0-87196-445-7). Facts on File.

Champlin, Charles. The Movies Grow up, Nineteen Forty to Nineteen Eighty. rev. ed. Orig. Title: The Flicks; or Whatever Became of Andy Hardy? (Illus.). 300p. 1981. 19.95 (ISBN 0-8040-0363-7); pap. 10.00 (ISBN 0-8040-0364-5). Swallow.

Champlin, Connie, jt. auth. see Champlin, John.

Champlin, John & Champlin, Connie. Books, Puppets & the Mentally Retarded Student. (Illus.). 162p. (Orig.). 1981. pap. 9.95 (ISBN 0-938594-00-1). Spec Lit Pr.

Champlin, Joseph M. An Important Office of Immense Love: A Handbook for Eucharistic Ministers. LC 80-80085. 128p. (Orig.). 1980. pap. 2.95 (ISBN 0-8091-2287-1). Paulist Pr.

--The Sacraments in a World of Change. LC 73-83347. (Know Your Faith Ser.). 144p. (Orig.). 1973. pap. 1.65 (ISBN 0-87793-085-6). Ave Maria.

Champney, Benjamin. Sixty Years' Memories of Art & Artists. Weinberg, H. Barbara, ed. LC 75-28887. (Art Experience in Late 19th Century America Ser.: Vol. 20). (Illus.). 1976. Repr. of 1900 ed. lib. bdg. 37.00 (ISBN 0-8240-2244-0). Garland Pub.

Chan, E. C. S., jt. auth. see Pelczar, Michael, Jr.

Chan, Gilbert F., ed. Nationalism in East Asia: An Annotated Bibliography of Selected Works. LC 80-8490. 180p. 1981. lib. bdg. 22.00 (ISBN 0-8240-9497-2). Garland Pub.

Chan, I., jt. auth. see Carew, J.

Chan, K. C. More Precious Than Rubies. 1981. 8.95 (ISBN 0-533-04287-9). Vantage.

Chan, Lois M. Cataloging & Classification: An Introduction. (Library Education Ser.). (Illus.). 416p. 1980. text ed. 18.95 (ISBN 0-07-010498-0, C). McGraw.

--Library of Congress Subject Headings: Principles & Application. LC 78-9497. (Research Studies in Library Science: No. 15). 1978. lib. bdg. 22.50x (ISBN 0-87287-187-8). Libs Unl.

Chan, Marie. Kao Shih. (World Authors Ser.: No. 476). 1978. lib. bdg. 12.50 (ISBN 0-8057-6317-1). Twayne.

Chan, Mary. Music in the Theatre of Ben Jonson. (Illus.). 344p. 1980. 69.00x (ISBN 0-19-812632-8). Oxford U Pr.

Chan, Ming K. Historiography of the Chinese Labor Movement. LC 80-8323. (Bibliographical Ser.: No. 60). 1981. 35.00 (ISBN 0-8179-2601-1). Hoover Inst Pr.

Chan, Pedro. Finger Acupressure. 1976. pap. 1.95 (ISBN 0-345-27868-2). Ballantine.

Chan, Shu-Park, et al. Analysis of Linear Networks & Systems: A Matrix-Oriented Approach with Computer Applications. LC 70-156589. 1972. text ed. 25.95 (ISBN 0-201-00953-6). A-W.

Chan, Titus. The Chan-Ese Way. LC 74-16221. 1974. 12.95 (ISBN 0-87909-117-7). Reston.

Chan, Wing-Tsit, tr. see Lao Tzu.

Chan, Wing Tstit. Instructions for Practical Living, & Other Neo-Confucian Writings. LC 62-16688. (Records of Civilization, Sources & Studies: No. 68). 1963. 22.50x (ISBN 0-231-02484-3). Columbia U Pr.

Chan, Wing Tstit, tr. Reflections on Things at Hand: The Neo-Cunfucian Anthology. LC 65-22548. (Records of Civilization Sources Studies). xli, 441p. 1967. 27.50x (ISBN 0-231-02819-9). Columbia U Pr.

Chanaiwa, David. Zimbabwe Controversy-a Case of Colonial Historiography. (Foreign & Comparative Studies-Eastern African Ser.: No. 8). 142p. 1973. pap. 4.50x (ISBN 0-915984-05-9). Syracuse U Foreign Comp.

Chanan, G., jt. auth. see Ross, J. M.

Chanan, Gabriel, ed. Towards a Science of Teaching. (General Ser.). 144p. 1973. pap. text ed. 17.00x (ISBN 0-85633-001-9, NFER). Humanities.

Chanan, Gabriel & Delamont, Sara, eds. Frontiers of Classroom Research. (General Ser.). 266p. 1975. pap. text ed. 20.75x (ISBN 0-85633-075-2, NFER). Humanities.

Chanan, Gabriel, ed. see Cane, Brian & Smithers, Jane.

Chanan, Michael, ed. Santiago Alvarez. (BFI Dossier Ser.: No. 2). 71p. (Orig.). 1980. pap. 7.50 (ISBN 0-918432-35-9). NY Zoetrope.

Chanan, Michael, tr. see Mattelart, Armand.

Chanarin, Israel, et al. Blood & Its Diseases. 2nd ed. (Illus.). 320p. 1980. text ed. 18.00x (ISBN 0-443-02191-0). Churchill.

Chance, Burton. Ophthalmology. (Illus.). 1962. Repr. of 1939 ed. pap. 9.75 o.s.i. (ISBN 0-02-842700-9). Hafner.

Chance, John K., jt. auth. see Butterworth, Douglas.

Chance, M. R. & Larsen, R. R. The Social Structure of Attention. 339p. 1976. 46.00 (ISBN 0-471-01573-3). Wiley.

Chancellor, Betty. A Child's Christmas Cookbook. (Illus.). 32p. (gr. 4-7). 1974. PLB 5.79 (ISBN 0-8178-5362-6). Harvey.

Chancellor, John. Audubon. (Illus.). 1978. 17.95 o.p. (ISBN 0-670-14053-8, Studio). Viking Pr.

Chancellor, Philip, tr. see Lavier, J.

Chancellor, Philip, tr. see Wu Wei-P'Ing.

Chancellor, Phillip. Handbook on the Bach Flower Remedies. LC 79-93435. 254p. (Orig.). 1980. pap. 5.95 (ISBN 0-87983-196-0). Keats.

Chancler, A. Bertram. Star Loot. (Science Fiction Ser.). 1980. pap. 1.75 (ISBN 0-87997-564-4, UE1564). Daw Bks.

Chandaman, C. D. English Public Revenue Sixteen Sixty to Sixteen Eighty-Eight. (Illus.). 400p. 1975. 55.00x (ISBN 0-19-828268-0). Oxford U Pr.

Chandavarkar, Sumana. Children of India. LC 74-120167. (Illus.). (gr. 4-6). 1971. 7.75 (ISBN 0-688-41291-2); PLB 6.96 o.p. (ISBN 0-688-51291-7). Lothrop.

Chander, Krishan. The Dreamer & Other Stories. Ratan, Jai, tr. 160p. 1970. pap. 2.50 (ISBN 0-88253-025-9). InterCulture.

--Mr. Ass Comes to Town. Bouman, Helen H., tr. 167p. 1968. pap. 1.60 o.p. (ISBN 0-88253-026-7). Ind-US Inc.

Chander, M., jt. auth. see Ravindranath, B.

Chandler, A. Bertram. Far Traveller. (Science Fiction Ser). (Orig.). 1979. pap. 1.50 o.p. (ISBN 0-87997-444-3, UW1444). DAW Bks.

--The Rim of Space. 192p. 1981. 12.95 (ISBN 0-8052-8090-1, Pub. by Allison & Busby England). Schocken.

--When the Dream Dies. 160p. 1981. 12.95 (ISBN 0-8052-8089-8, Pub. by Allison & Busby, England). Schocken.

Chandler, Alfred D., Jr. The Visible Hand: The Managerial Revolution in American Business. 1980. pap. 8.95 (ISBN 0-674-94052-0). Harvard U Pr.

Chandler, Allison. When Oklahoma Took the Trolley. Sebree, Mac, ed. LC 79-92539. (Special Ser.: No. 71). 1980. 21.95 (ISBN 0-916374-35-1). Interurban.

Chandler, Arthur B. Old Tales of San Francisco. LC 77-78491. (History Ser.). (Illus.). 1977. pap. text ed. 7.95 (ISBN 0-8403-1746-8). Kendall-Hunt.

Chandler, Asa C. & Read, C. P. Introduction to Parasitology: With Special References to the Parasites of Man. 10th ed. LC 61-5670. 1961. 29.95 (ISBN 0-471-14487-8). Wiley.

Chandler, B. V. see Mrak, E. M. & Stewart, G. F.

Chandler, Billie T. Geisha Story: With Doll & Flower Arrangements. LC 63-8717. (Illus.). 1963. brocade 5.50 o.p. (ISBN 0-8048-0205-X). C E Tuttle.

Chandler, C., ed. see Durey, Peter.

Chandler, C. K. God Told Me to. 1976. pap. 1.75 (ISBN 0-345-28580-8). Ballantine.

Chandler, Charles L., et al. Philadelphia: Port of History 1609-1837. (Illus.). 82p. 1976. pap. 3.25 (ISBN 0-913346-02-0). Phila Maritime Mus.

Chandler, D. C., ed. Selections from Tacitus Annals II-III, Germanicus & Piso. (Latin Texts Ser.). (Illus., Orig.). 1980. pap. 3.95 (ISBN 0-521-22650-3). Cambridge U Pr.

Chandler, David. The Campaigns of Napoleon: The Mind & Method of History's Greatest Soldier. 1216p. 1973. 35.00 (ISBN 0-02-523660-1). Macmillan.

--Marlbouough As Military Commander. 1979. 30.00 (ISBN 0-7134-2075-8, Pub. by Batsford England). David & Charles.

--The Middleman. LC 80-66504. 1981. 12.95 (ISBN 0-87795-279-5). Arbor Hse.

--Waterloo: The Hundred Days. LC 80-36696. 224p. 1981. 18.95. Macmillan.

Chandler, David G. Atlas of Military Strategy. (Illus.). 1980. Repr. 29.95 (ISBN 0-02-905750-7). Free Pr.

Chandler, E. M. Educating Adolescent Girls. (Unwin Education Books Ser.). 240p. (Orig.). 1980. text ed. 27.50x (ISBN 0-04-370096-9); pap. text ed. 10.50x (ISBN 0-04-370097-7). Allen Unwin.

Chandler, Edna W. Lifestyles for the Aging. 160p. 1980. 9.95 (ISBN 0-525-66685-0). Elsevier-Nelson.

--Women in Prison. LC 72-88765. (gr. 9 up). 7.95 o.p. (ISBN 0-672-51702-7). Bobbs.

Chandler, G. How to Find Out. rev. 4th ed. 216p. 1974. text ed. 16.00 (ISBN 0-08-017781-6). Pergamon.

--How to Find Out About the Novel. 4th ed. 1974. write for info. (ISBN 0-685-25212-4). Pergamon.

Chandler, Harry E. How to Write What. 1978. 10.95 (ISBN 0-87170-001-8). ASM.

Chandler, Kathleen. Les Belles Lettres. (Illus.). 160p. 1981. 7.95 (ISBN 0-89962-204-6). Todd & Honeywell.

Chandler, Lester. Inflation in the United States 1940-1948. (Fdr & the Era of the New Deal). 1976. Repr. of 1951 ed. lib. bdg. 29.50 (ISBN 0-306-70804-3). Da Capo.

Chandler, Linda S. Davids Asks, "Why?". (gr. 3-7). 1981. 4.95 (ISBN 0-8054-4266-9). Broadman.

Chandler, Lotus H. The Book of Proverbs in Rhyme from the Holy Bible. LC 79-56329. 1981. 6.95 (ISBN 0-533-04528-2). Vantage.

Chandler, Murray. Sicilian 2c3. (Algebraic Chess Openings Ser.). (Illus.). 96p. 1981. pap. 11.50 (ISBN 0-7134-1933-4, Pub. by Batsford England). David & Charles.

Chandler, Raymond. The Big Sleep. 224p. 1975. pap. 1.50 o.p. (ISBN 0-345-24565-2). Ballantine.

--The Long Goodbye. 1977. pap. 2.25 (ISBN 0-345-28859-9). Ballantine.

--Trouble Is My Business. pap. 2.25 (ISBN 0-345-27671-X). Ballantine.

Chandler, Richard E. & Schwartz, Kessel. New History of Spanish Literature. LC 61-15756. (Illus.). 1961. text ed. 30.00x (ISBN 0-8071-0343-8). La State U Pr.

Chandler, Robert, tr. see Afanasyev, Alexander.

Chandler, Robert F., Jr. Rice in the Tropics: A Guide to Development of National Programs. (IADS Development-Oriented Literature Ser.). 1979. lib. bdg. 22.00x (ISBN 0-89158-361-0). Westview.

Chandler, Robert W. War of Ideas: The U. S. Propaganda Compaign in Vietnam. (Westview Special Studies in National Defense & Security Ser.). 301p. 1981. lib. bdg. 25.00x (ISBN 0-86531-082-3). Westview.

Chandler, Russell. The Overcomers. 1978. 6.95 o.p. (ISBN 0-8007-0944-6). Revell.

Chandler, Sue P., jt. ed. see Shockley, Ann A.

Chandler, T. J. The Air Around Us. LC 70-78676. (gr. 4-9). 5.95 o.p. (ISBN 0-385-06766-6). Doubleday.

Chandler, T. J. & Gregory, S. The Climate of the British Isles. (Illus.). 1977. text ed. 24.00x (ISBN 0-582-48558-4). Longman.

Chandler, W. K., jt. auth. see Blair, Walter.

Chandoha, Walter. The Literary Cat. (Illus.). 1977. 10.00 o.p. (ISBN 0-397-01213-6). Lippincott.

Chandra, C., jt. auth. see Consul, S. C.

Chandra, L., tr. see Caland, W.

Chandra, Prakash. International Politics. 1980. text ed. 12.50x (ISBN 0-7069-0773-6, Pub by Vikas India). Advent Bk.

Chandrasekhar, S. Abortion in a Crowded World: The Problem of Abortion with Special Reference to India. LC 73-19750. (John Danz Lecture Ser.). 150p. 1974. 10.50 (ISBN 0-295-95317-9). U of Wash Pr.

--Hydrodynamic & Hydromagnetic Stability. (Illus.). 704p. pap. write for info. (ISBN 0-486-64071-X). Dover.

--Liquid Crystals. LC 75-32913. (Cambridge Monographs in Physics). (Illus.). 1977. 71.50 (ISBN 0-521-21149-2). Cambridge U Pr.

Chandrasekhar, S. & Elbert, Donna D. Illumination & Polarization of the Sunlit Sky on Rayleigh Scattering. LC 54-12909. (Transactions Ser.: Vol. 44, Pt. 6). (Illus.). 1954. pap. 1.00 o.p. (ISBN 0-87169-446-8). Am Philos.

Chandrasekhar, Sripati. A Dirty Filthy Book: The Writings of Charles Knowlton & Annie Besant. 1981. 12.50 (ISBN 0-520-04168-2). U of Cal Pr.

Chandrasekharan, K. R. Bhabani Bhattacharya. (Indian Writers Ser.). 1976. 8.50 (ISBN 0-89253-505-9). Ind-US Inc.

Chandrasenkhar, S. Liquid Crystals. (Cambridge Monographs in Physics). (Illus.). 352p. 1980. pap. 22.95 (ISBN 0-521-29841-5). Cambridge U Pr.

Chandy, K. & Yeh, Raymond T., eds. Current Trends in Programming Methodology: Software Modeling, Vol. 3. (Illus.). 1978. ref. 21.95 (ISBN 0-13-195727-9). P-H.

Chandy, Mani K., jt. auth. see Sauer, Charles.

Chaney & Ciepiy. The Hearsts. 1981. 16.95 (ISBN 0-671-24765-4). S&S.

Chaney, Charles & Skee, Stanley. Plaster Mold & Model Making. 144p. 1981. Repr. of 1973 ed. text ed. write for info. (ISBN 0-89874-282-X). Krieger.

Chaney, Lindsay & Ciepi, Michael. The Hearst: Family & Empire, the Later Years. 1981. 14.95 (ISBN 0-671-24765-4). S&S.

Chaney, M. L. Successful Garage-Yard Sale. 1.00 o.p. (ISBN 0-686-17207-8). Sandollar Pr.

Chaney, Margaret S., et al. Nutrition. 9th ed. LC 78-69546. (Illus.). 1979. text ed. 18.95 (ISBN 0-395-25448-5); o.p. inst. manual (ISBN 0-395-25449-3). HM.

Chaney, Otto P., Jr. Zhukov. LC 74-145505. (Illus.). 1971. 19.95 o.p. (ISBN 0-8061-0951-3). U of Okla Pr.

Chaney, Warren H. & Beech, Thomas R. The Union Epidemic: A Prescription for Supervisors. LC 76-24132. 1976. 24.00 (ISBN 0-912862-28-9). Aspen Systems.

Chaney, William A. The Cult of Kingship in Anglo-Saxon England: The Transition from Paganism to Christianity. LC 72-79041. 1970. 18.50x (ISBN 0-520-01401-4). U of Cal Pr.

Chang. Tumors of the Central Nervous System. 1981. write for info. Masson Pub.

Chang, Charlotte M., jt. ed. see Livingston, G. E.

Chang, Chun-shu. The Making of China: Main Themes in Premodern Chinese History. (Illus.). 352p. 1975. Repr. 17.95 (ISBN 0-13-545640-1). P-H.

Chang, Chung-Li, jt. auth. see Michael, Franz.

Chang, Constance D. Chinese Cooking at Home. (Illus., Orig.). 1977. pap. 4.95 (ISBN 0-87040-408-3). Japan Pubns.

--Chinese Cooking Lessons. LC 76-21508. 1977. 6.95 o.p. (ISBN 0-385-12455-4). Doubleday.

Chang, Diana. A Perfect Love. (Orig.). 1978. pap. 1.95 (ISBN 0-515-04355-9). Jove Pubns.

Chang, Florence C. Believe It or Not: An Anthology of Ancient Tales Retold. LC 80-68258. (Chinese Can Be Fun Ser.: Bk. 3). (Illus.). 80p. (gr. 10-12). 1980. pap. text ed. 3.75 (ISBN 0-936620-02-1). Ginkgo Hut.

--China Is Farther Than the Sun? A Beginning Chinese-English Reader. LC 80-68256. (Chinese Can Be Fun Ser.: Bk. 1). (Illus.). 51p. (gr. 3-5). 1980. pap. 3.00 (ISBN 0-936620-00-5). Ginkgo Hut.

--With Sound & Color: An Intermediate Chinese-English Reader. LC 80-68257. (Chinese Can Be Fun Ser.: Bk. 2). (Illus.). 71p. (Orig.). (gr. 6-9). 1980. pap. text ed. 3.50 (ISBN 0-936620-01-3). Ginkgo Hut.

Chang, Frederic Ming & Faurot, Albert. Team Piano Repertoire: A Manual of Music for Multiple Players at One or More Pianos. LC 76-14927. 201p. 1976. 10.00 (ISBN 0-8108-0937-0). Scarecrow.

Chang, H. C., ed. Chinese Literature: Popular Fiction & Drama, Vol. 1. LC 73-79265. 1973. text ed. 27.50x (ISBN 0-85224-240-9). Columbia U Pr.

Chang, H. C., tr. from Chinese. Chinese Literature: Nature Poetry, Vol. 2. LC 73-79265. (Chinese Literature Ser.). 1977. 12.50x (ISBN 0-231-04288-4). Columbia U Pr.

Chang, Huan-Yang & Over, Ira Earl. Selected Numerical Methods & Computer Programs for Chemical Engineers. 235p. (Orig.). 1981. pap. text ed. 11.95 (ISBN 0-88408-131-1). Sterling Swift.

Chang, Paul see Aisner, Joseph.

Chang, Raymond. Basic Principles of Spectroscopy. LC 77-10971. 314p. 1978. lib. bdg. 19.50 (ISBN 0-88275-613-3). Krieger.

--Chemistry. Incl. Losey, Eugene. wkbk. 6.95 (ISBN 0-394-32447-1); Goldwhite, Harold & Spielman, John. solutions to problem sets 4.95 (ISBN 0-394-32519-2). 815p. 1981. text ed. 23.95 (ISBN 0-394-31224-4). Random.

Chang, Roy, jt. auth. see Li, Tze-Chung.

Chang, Sung-wen, jt. auth. see Bennett, Frances C.

Chang, T. M., jt. ed. see Sideman, Samuel.

Chang, Thomas Ming Swi. Artificial Cells. (Illus.). 224p. 1972. pap. 24.50 photocopy ed. spiral (ISBN 0-398-02257-7). C C Thomas.

Chang, Wallace H. J. Fundamentals of Plastic & Reconstructive Surgery. (Illus.). 424p. 1980. softcover 32.50 (ISBN 0-683-01515-X). Williams & Wilkins.

Chang, Yu-Chuan. Wang Shou-Jen As a Statesman. (Studies in Chinese History & Civilization). 517p. 1977. Repr. of 1940 ed. 21.00 (ISBN 0-89093-094-5). U Pubns Amer.

Chang, Yu-Kon, et al, trs. from Chinese. Civil Code of the Republic of China. Hsia, Ching-Lin. (Studies in Chinese Government & Law). 400p. 1977. Repr. of 1930 ed. 26.50 (ISBN 0-89093-055-4). U Pubns Amer.

Change Magazine Editors. The Communications Revolution & the Education of Americans. LC 80-66849. 64p. (Orig.). 1980. pap. 6.95 (ISBN 0-915390-24-8). Change Mag.

--Educating for the World View. LC 80-68195. 80p. 1980. pap. 3.00 (ISBN 0-915390-26-4). Change Mag.

Chang Kia-ngau, pseud. China's Struggle for Railroad Development. LC 74-34331. (China in the 20th Century Ser). (Illus.). vii, 340p. 1975. Repr. of 1943 ed. lib. bdg. 29.50 (ISBN 0-306-70689-X). Da Capo.

Chang Shu-Ting. The Chinese Mushroom (Volvariella volvacea) Morphology, Cytology, Genetics, Nutrition, & Cultivation. (Illus.). 118p. 1972. 8.95 (ISBN 0-295-95743-3, Pub by Chinese Univ Hong Kong). U of Wash Pr.

Chanh, Amos I. The Tao of Existence. 2nd ed. LC 80-8677. (Illus.). 88p. 1981. 14.50x (ISBN 0-691-03963-1); pap. 4.95 (ISBN 0-691-00330-0). Princeton U Pr.

Chanin, Leah F. Reference Guide to Georgia Legal History & Legal Research. 175p. 1980. 20.00 (ISBN 0-87215-315-0). Michie.

Chanin, Myra. The Secret Life of Mother Wonderful. LC 80-22904. 192p. 1980. 9.95 (ISBN 0-8253-0021-5). Beaufort Bks NY.

Ch'An Master Hua, commentary by. Flower Adornment (Avatamsaka) Sutra: Chapter Fifteen, The Ten Dwellings. Bhikshuni Heng Hsien, et al, trs. from Chinese. (Orig.). 1981. pap. write for info. (ISBN 0-917512-30-8). Buddhist Text.
Ch'An Master Hua, ed. see Ch'An Master Yung Chia.
Ch'An Master Yung Chia. The Song of Enlightenment. Ch'An Master Hua, ed. Bhikshu Heng Yo, et al, trs. from Chin. (Illus., Orig.). 1981. pap. write for info. (ISBN 0-917512-20-0). Buddhist Text.
Channa, V. C. Caste: Identity & Continuity. 1979. text ed. 10.00x (ISBN 0-391-01871-X). Humanities.
Channan, Krishan K. The Lure of Politics. 64p. 1980. 6.00 (ISBN 0-682-49641-3). Exposition.
Channappa, K. H., et al. Introductory Physics. 1977. 12.50 (ISBN 0-7069-0571-7, Pub. by Vikas India). Advent Bk.
Channels, Vera & Vestermark, Mary. Freedom Is an Inside Job. LC 77-15745. 1978. 5.95 o.p. (ISBN 0-8042-2060-3). John Knox.
Channing, Edward & Coolidge, Archibald C. The Barrington-Bernard Correspondence, & Illustrative Matter, 1760-1770. LC 75-109612. (Era of the American Revolution Ser). 1970. Repr. of 1912 ed. lib. bdg. 32.50 (ISBN 0-306-71909-6). Da Capo.
Channing, Justin. Southern Blood. 400p. 1980. pap. 2.50 (ISBN 0-553-13132-X). Bantam.
Channing, Marion L. The Textile Tools of Colonial Homes. 6th ed. LC 75-229981. (Illus.). 64p. 1971. pap. 2.75 (ISBN 0-9600496-1-4). Channing Bks.
Channing, Steven A. Kentucky. (The States & the Nation Ser.). (Illus.). 1977. 12.95 (ISBN 0-393-05654-6, Co-Pub by AASLH). Norton.
Channing, William E. Thoreau, Poet-Naturalist. new & enl. ed. Sanborn, F. B., ed. LC 65-27095. (Illus.). 1902. 15.00x (ISBN 0-8196-0173-X). Biblo.
--Thoreau the Poet-Naturalist: With Memorial Verses. LC 80-2679. 1981. Repr. of 1873 ed. 37.50 (ISBN 0-404-19073-1). AMS Pr.
Channon, Derek F. The Service Industries: Strategy, Structure & Financial Performance. 1978. text ed. 53.75x (ISBN 0-8419-5032-6). Holmes & Meier.
Channon, Howard. Portrait of Liverpool. LC 72-550617. (Portrait Books Ser). 1970. 10.50x (ISBN 0-7091-5575-1). Intl Pubns Serv.
Chanover, E. Pierre. The Marquis De Sade: A Bibliography. LC 72-10288. (Author Bibliographies Ser.: No. 12). 1973. 8.00 o.p. (ISBN 0-8108-0561-8). Scarecrow.
Chant, Barry. Straight Talk About Sex. (Illus.). (gr. 10-12). 1977. pap. 1.95 (ISBN 0-88368-078-5). Whitaker Hse.
Chant, Chris. Armed Forces of the United Kingdom. LC 80-66428. (Illus.). 80p. 1980. 14.95 (ISBN 0-7153-8024-9). David & Charles.
Chant, Colin & Fauvel, John. Darwin to Einstein: Historical Studies in Science & Belief. (Illus.). 352p. 1981. text ed. 25.00 (ISBN 0-582-49156-8). Longman.
Chanticleer Press. Encyclopedia of American Art. Nelson, Cy, ed. 670p. 1981. 39.95 (ISBN 0-525-93164-3). Dutton.
Chantikian, Kosrof, ed. Octavio Paz: Homage to the Poet. LC 80-82167. 256p. (Orig.). 1981. 15.00 (ISBN 0-916426-03-3); pap. 7.95 (ISBN 0-916426-04-1). Kosmos.
Chantikian, Kosrof, ed. see Alberti, Rafael.
Chantry, G. W. Submillimetre Spectroscopy. 1972. 53.00 (ISBN 0-12-170550-1). Acad Pr.
Chantry, Walter. Signs of the Apostles. 1979. pap. 3.45 (ISBN 0-85151-175-9). Banner of Truth.
--Today's Gospel. 1980. pap. 2.45. Banner of Truth.
Chantry, Walter J. God's Righteous Kingdom. 151p. (Orig.). 1980. pap. 3.50 (ISBN 0-85151-310-7). Banner of Truth.
Chantz, N. E. Just Pick a Hurricane? 1.25 (ISBN 0-902675-11-7). Oleander Pr.
Chao, Kang. Agricultural Production in Communist China, Nineteen Forty-Nine to Nineteen Sixty-Five. LC 70-121766. (Illus.). 1970. 27.50 (ISBN 0-299-05770-4). U of Wis Pr.
--Capital Formation in Mainland China, 1952-1965. 1974. 23.75x (ISBN 0-520-02304-8). U of Cal Pr.
Chao, L. Statistics: Methods & Analyses. 2nd ed. 1974. text ed. 18.95 (ISBN 0-07-010525-1, C); solutions manual 5.95 (ISBN 0-07-010526-X). McGraw.
Chao, Lincoln & Rodich, G. Study Guide for Stat. for Management. 272p. 1980. pap. text ed. 7.95 (ISBN 0-8185-0409-9). Brooks-Cole.
Chao, Lincoln L. Introduction to Statistics. LC 79-13686. 1979. text ed. 17.95 (ISBN 0-8185-0321-1); study guide 6.95 (ISBN 0-8185-0410-2). Brooks-Cole.
--Statistics for Management. LC 79-22706. 1980. text ed. 20.95 (ISBN 0-8185-0367-X); study guide 6.95 (ISBN 0-8185-0409-9). Brooks-Cole.
Chao, Yuen Ren. A Grammar of Spoken Chinese. 1968. 35.00x (ISBN 0-520-00219-9). U of Cal Pr.
Chao, Yuen-Ren. Language & Symbolic Systems. (Orig.). 1968. 29.95 (ISBN 0-521-04616-5); pap. 10.95x (ISBN 0-521-09457-7, 457). Cambridge U Pr.
Chao Pu-Wei. Autobiography of a Chinese Woman, Buwei Yang Chao. Chao Yuen-Ren, tr. LC 72-100225. Repr. of 1947 ed. lib. bdg. 22.50x (ISBN 0-8371-3712-8, CHCW). Greenwood.
Chao Yuen-Ren, tr. see Chao Pu-Wei.
Chapalay & Mottier, ed. Swiss Watchmaking Year-Book, 1980-1981. 83rd ed. LC 46-34872. Orig. Title: Quid Horloger: Annuaire De L'Horlogerie Suisse. 602p. (Orig.). 1980. pap. write for info. (ISBN 0-8002-2751-4). Intl Pubns Serv.
Chapanis, Alphonse. Man-Machine Engineering. LC 65-15099. (Behavioral Science in Industry Ser). (Orig.). 1966. pap. text ed. 6.95x (ISBN 0-8185-0306-8). Brooks-Cole.
Chapelot, Pierre, jt. auth. see Sternberg, Jacques.
Chapeville, F. & Haenni, A. O., eds. Chemical Recognition in Biology. (Molecular Biology, Biochemistry & Biophysics: Vol. 32). (Illus.). 430p. 1980. 57.80 (ISBN 0-387-10205-1). Springer-Verlag.
Chapey, Roberta. Language Intervention Strategies in Adult Aphasia. (Illus.). 381p. 1981. 32.00 (ISBN 0-686-69565-8, 1511-7). Williams & Wilkins.
Chapian, Marie. Free to Be Thin. LC 79-15656. (Illus.). 192p. 1979. pap. 3.95 (ISBN 0-87123-560-9, 210560); study guide by Neva Coyle 64 pgs. 1.95 (ISBN 0-87123-163-8, 210163). Bethany Fell.
--Of Whom the World Was Not Worthy. LC 78-769. (Illus.). 1978. pap. 3.95 (ISBN 0-87123-250-2, 210417). Bethany Fell.
Chapian, Marie & Sadler, Robert. Help Me Remember, Lord--Help Me Forget. (Illus.). 256p. 1981. pap. 2.95 (ISBN 0-87123-203-0, 200203). Bethany Fell.
Chapian, Marie, jt. auth. see Backus, William.
Chapian, Marie, jt. auth. see Sadler, Robert.
Chapin, Anna Alice. The Story of the Rhinegold: Der Ring Des Nibelungen. 138p. 1980. Repr. of 1897 ed. lib. bdg. 25.00 (ISBN 0-89760-119-X). Telegraph Bks.
Chapin, Bradley. Provincial America, 1600-1763. LC 65-11895. (Orig.). 1966. pap. text ed. 3.50 o.s.i. (ISBN 0-02-905320-X). Free Pr.
Chapin, Charles. Charles Chapin Story. (American Newspapermen 1790-1933 Ser.). xxv, 334p. 1974. Repr. of 1920 ed. 17.50x o.s.i. (ISBN 0-8464-0028-6). Beekman Pubs.
Chapin, F. Stuart, Jr. Human Activity Patterns in the City: Things People Do in Time & in Space. LC 74-5364. (Urban Research Ser). 272p. 1974. 21.95 (ISBN 0-471-14563-7, Pub. by Wiley-Interscience). Wiley.
Chapin, F. Stuart, Jr. & Kaiser, Edward J. Urban Land Use Planning. 3rd ed. LC 64-18666. (Illus.). 1979. 22.50 (ISBN 0-252-00580-5); wkbk 6.95 (ISBN 0-252-00791-3). U of Ill Pr.
Chapin, Harry. Looking....Seeing. LC 77-11564. (Illus.). 1978. pap. 4.95 o.p. (ISBN 0-690-01657-3, TYC-T). T Y Crowell.
Chapin, Henry. Poems Chosen. 1981. pap. 5.95 (ISBN 0-87233-056-7). Bauhan.
Chapin, Kim. Fast As White Lightning: The Story of Stock Car Racing. (Illus.). 1981. 11.95. Dial.
Chapin, Suzy. The Adjustable Diet Cookbook. rev. ed. LC 75-26762. (Funk & W Bk.). 1976. 8.95 (ISBN 0-308-10222-3, TYC-T). T Y Crowell.
Chapin-Park, Sue, jt. auth. see Park, William R.
Chaplin, A. H., ed. The British Library & AACR, Nineteen Sixty-Seven: A Study. 1973. pap. 11.00x (ISBN 0-85365-286-4, Pub. by Lib Assn England). Oryx Pr.
--The Organization for the Library Profession. 2nd ed. (IFLA Ser.: Vol. 6). 132p. 1976. text ed. 15.00 (ISBN 3-7940-4309-X, Pub. by K G Saur). Shoe String.
Chaplin, Hamako I., jt. auth. see Jorden, Eleanor H.
Chaplin, Jack W. Metal Manufacturing Technology. (gr. 10 up). 1976. text ed. 15.72 (ISBN 0-87345-132-5). McKnight.
Chaplin, James P. & Demers, Aline. Primer of Neurology & Neurophysiology. LC 78-6680. 1978. pap. text ed. 10.95 (ISBN 0-471-03027-9, Pub. by Wiley Medical). Wiley.
Chaplin, Mary. Gardening for the Physically Handicapped & Elderly. 1978. 13.50 (ISBN 0-7134-1081-7). David & Charles.
Chaplin, R., et al. Centralia Case: Three Views of the Armistice Day Tragedy at Centralia, Washington, November 11, 1919. LC 77-160845. (Civil Liberties in American History Ser). 1971. Repr. of 1924 ed. lib. bdg. 29.50 (ISBN 0-306-70211-8). Da Capo.
Chaplin, Ralph. Wobbly. LC 70-166089. (Civil Liberties in American History Ser). 1972. Repr. of 1948 ed. lib. bdg. 37.50 (ISBN 0-306-70212-6). Da Capo.
Chaplin, Raymond E. Deer. (Illus.). 1978. 17.50 (ISBN 0-7137-0796-8, Pub by Blandford Pr England). Sterling.
Chaplin, Stewart. Suspension of the Power of Alienation, & Postponement of Vesting, Under the Laws of New York, Mich Igan, Minnesota & Wisconsin. xxxix, 370p. 1981. Repr. of 1891 ed. lib. bdg. 30.00x (ISBN 0-8377-0428-6). Rothman.
Chaplina, Vera. True Stories from the Moscow Zoo. Titiev, Estelle & Pargment, Lila, trs. (Illus.). (gr. 5 up). 1970. PLB 4.50 o.p. (ISBN 0-13-930990-X). P-H.
Chapman. Medical Dictionary for the Lay Person. 1981. pap. 2.95 (ISBN 0-8120-2247-5). Barron.
Chapman, A. H. Put-Offs & Come-Ons. 1977. pap. 1.50 o.p. (ISBN 0-425-03382-1, Medallion). Berkley Pub.
Chapman, Alexandra, jt. auth. see Oakes, George.
Chapman, Alexandra, jt. auth. see Oakes, George W.
Chapman, Anne. Using a Textbook As a Primary Source. Date not set. cancelled (ISBN 0-934402-07-8). BYLS Pr.
Chapman, Annie B., jt. auth. see Hart, Albert B.
Chapman, Antoine, ed. Acute Renal Failure. (Clinics in Critical Care Medicine). 224p. 1980. text ed. 29.50x (ISBN 0-443-01930-4). Churchill.
Chapman, Antony J. & Foot, Hugh C. It's a Funny Thing Humour: The International Conference on Humor & Laughter. LC 76-53731. 400p. 1976. text ed. 45.00 (ISBN 0-08-021376-6). Pergamon.
Chapman, Antony J., jt. auth. see McGhee, Paul E.
Chapman, Arthur H. Physician's Guide to Managing Emotional Problems. (Illus.). 1969. 13.95 o.p. (ISBN 0-397-50238-9, 70-78609). Lippincott.
Chapman, B. N., jt. auth. see Leaver, K. D.
Chapman, Berlin B. Oto & Missouri Indians. Horr, David A., ed. (American Indian Ethnohistory Ser.). 1978. lib. bdg. 42.00 (ISBN 0-8240-0746-8). Garland Pub.
Chapman, Brian. Glow Discharge Processes: Sputtering & Plasma Etching. LC 80-17047. 432p. 1980. 31.50 (ISBN 0-471-07828-X, Pub. by Wiley-Interscience). Wiley.
Chapman, Carl H. Osage Indians, Vol. Three: The Origin of the Osage Indian Tribe: an Ethnographical, Historical & Archaeological Study. (American Indian Ethnohistory Ser.: Plains Indians). (Illus.). lib. bdg. 42.00 (ISBN 0-8240-0749-2). Garland Pub.
Chapman, Carol. Herbie's Troubles. LC 80-21848. (Illus.). (ps-1). 1981. PLB 9.95 (ISBN 0-525-31645-0). Dutton.
--The Tale of Meshka the Kvetch. LC 80-11225. (Illus.). 32p. (gr. k-3). PLB 8.95 (ISBN 0-525-40745-6). Dutton.
Chapman, Carol J. & Mouret, Francois J., eds. Michel de Montaigne: Essais. (Athlone Renaissance Library). 1978. text ed. 26.50x (ISBN 0-485-13810-7, Athlone Pr); pap. text ed. 12.50x (ISBN 0-485-12810-1). Humanities.
Chapman, Caroline & Roben, Paul, eds. Queen Victoria's Jubillees Eighteen Eighty-Seven & Eighteen Ninety-Seven. (Illus.). 1978. 15.95 o.p. (ISBN 0-670-58417-7, Debrett's Peerage, Ltd.). Viking Pr.
Chapman, Charles F. & Maloney, E. S. Piloting, Seamanship & Small Boat Handling. 54th ed. (Illus.). 13.95 (ISBN 0-910990-46-8); Presentation ed. 19.95 (ISBN 0-910990-47-6). Hearst Bks.
Chapman, Christopher. The Right Side of the Hedge. LC 77-89372. 1977. 8.95 (ISBN 0-7153-7342-0). David & Charles.
Chapman, Clark R. Inner Planets. LC 76-58914. (Illus.). 1977. 9.95 (ISBN 0-684-14898-6, ScribT). Scribner.
Chapman, D. J., jt. auth. see Chapman, V. J.
Chapman, David, jt. auth. see Visser, John.
Chapman, David W., ed. Improving College Information for Prospective Students. 70p. 1980. pap. 10.50 (ISBN 0-89964-162-8). CASE.
Chapman, E. N. Getting into Business. LC 75-20279. 1976. 17.95 (ISBN 0-471-14600-5). Wiley.
Chapman, Edward M. New England Village Life. LC 72-143643. 1971. Repr. of 1937 ed. 18.00 (ISBN 0-8103-3699-5). Gale.
Chapman, Elizabeth K. Visually Handicapped Children & Young People. (Special Needs in Education Ser.). 1978. 16.00 (ISBN 0-7100-8878-7). Routledge & Kegan.
Chapman, Elwood. College Survival. 2nd ed. 230p. 1980. pap. text ed. 6.95 (ISBN 0-574-20615-9, 13-3615); instr's. guide avail. (ISBN 0-574-20616-7, 13-3616). SRA.
--Dynamic Retailing. 416p. 1980. pap. text ed. 15.50 (ISBN 0-574-20610-8, 13-3610); instr's. guide avail. (ISBN 0-574-20611-6, 13-3611). SRA.
Chapman, Elwood N. Career Search. LC 75-35758. (Illus.). 200p. 1976. pap. text ed. 6.50 (ISBN 0-574-20005-3, 13-3005); instr's guide avail. (ISBN 0-574-20006-1, 13-3006). SRA.
--College Survival: Find Yourself. Find a Career. LC 73-93239. (Illus.). 168p. 1974. pap. text ed. 6.50 (ISBN 0-574-19108-9, 13-2108); instr's guide avail. (ISBN 0-574-20006-1, 13-3006). SRA.
--From Campus to Career Success. LC 78-9085. 304p. 1978. pap. text ed. 6.95 (ISBN 0-574-20580-2, 13-3580); instr's guide avail. (ISBN 0-574-20581-0, 13-3581). SRA.
--Scrambling: Zig-Zagging Your Way to the Top. 192p. 1981. 8.95 (ISBN 0-87477-129-3). J P Tarcher.
--Supervisor's Survival Kit: A Mid-Management Primer. 2nd ed. LC 75-26903. (Illus.). 192p. 1975. pap. text ed. 7.95 (ISBN 0-574-20000-2, 13-3000); instr's guide avail. (ISBN 0-574-20001-0, 13-3001). SRA.
Chapman, F. B. Flute Technique. 4th ed. 1973. pap. 7.75 (ISBN 0-19-318609-8). Oxford U Pr.
Chapman, G., tr. see Hesoid.
Chapman, Geoff & Young, Bob. Box Hill. (Illus., Orig.). 1979. pap. 7.95 (ISBN 0-9504143-1-X). Bradt Ent.
Chapman, George. All Fools. Manley, Frank, ed. LC 68-10664. (Regents Renaissance Drama Ser). 1968. 6.95x (ISBN 0-8032-0255-5); pap. 1.65x (ISBN 0-8032-5256-0, BB 229, Bison). U of Nebr Pr.
--Bussy D'ambois. Lordi, Robert J., ed. LC 64-11358. (Regents Renaissance Drama Ser.). 1964. 8.95x (ISBN 0-8032-0256-3); pap. 1.85x (ISBN 0-8032-5257-9, BB 205, Bison). U of Nebr Pr.
--Gentleman Usher. Smith, John H., ed. LC 69-12399. (Regents Renaissance Drama Ser). 1970. 9.95x (ISBN 0-8032-0285-7); pap. 2.75x (ISBN 0-8032-5286-2, BB 232, Bison). U of Nebr Pr.
--Widow's Tears. Smeak, Ethel M., ed. LC 65-24305. (Regents Renaissance Drama Ser). 1966. 8.50x (ISBN 0-8032-0257-1); pap. 1.65x (ISBN 0-8032-5258-7, BB 217, Bison). U of Nebr Pr.
Chapman, Harry H., jt. auth. see Chapman, Jane E.
Chapman, Hester W. Last Tudor King. (Illus.). 1959. 9.95 (ISBN 0-02-523790-X). Macmillan.
Chapman, J. C., et al. Principles of Education. Cubberley, Ellwood P., ed. 645p. 1980. Repr. of 1924 ed. lib. bdg. 25.00 (ISBN 0-8495-0851-7). Arden Lib.
Chapman, James E. & Bridges, F. J. Critical Incidents in Organizational Behavior & Administration: With Selected Readings. (Illus.). 1977. pap. text ed. 12.95 (ISBN 0-13-193896-7). P-H.
Chapman, James W. & Boersma, Frederic J. Affective Correlates of Learning Disabilities. (Modern Approaches to the Diagnosis & Instruction of Multihandicapped Children Ser.: Vol. 15). 108p. 1980. text ed. 22.50 (ISBN 90-265-0341-5, Pub. by Swets Pub Serv Holland). Swets North Am.
Chapman, Jane E. & Chapman, Harry H. Behavior & Health Care: A Humanistic Helping Process. LC 75-15579. 194p. 1975. pap. 8.50 o.p. (ISBN 0-8016-0947-X). Mosby.
Chapman, Jane R. Economic Realities & Female Crime: Program Choices & Economic Rehabilitation. LC 79-3785. 240p. 1980. 21.95x (ISBN 0-669-03515-7). Lexington Bks.
Chapman, Jeffrey I. Proposition Thirteen & Land Use: A Case Study of Fiscal Limits in California. LC 79-3749. 1981. 22.95x (ISBN 0-669-03471-1). Lexington Bks.
Chapman, Joan & Smith, Jeffrey. Multiple-Choice Questions in Economics. 1973. pap. text ed. 2.95 with ans. o.p. (ISBN 0-435-84271-4); pap. text ed. 2.50 text only o.p. (ISBN 0-435-84270-6). Heinemann Ed.
Chapman, John. Adult English One. (Illus.). 1978. pap. 7.50 (ISBN 0-13-008821-8). P-H.
--Adult English Three. 1978. pap. 7.50 (ISBN 0-13-008862-5). P-H.
--Adult English Two. (Illus.). 1978. pap. 7.50 (ISBN 0-13-008839-0). P-H.
--Welcome to English: Let's Begin. new ed. (Welcome to English Ser.). (Illus.). 48p. 1980. pap. 2.50 (ISBN 0-88345-379-7); tchr's manual 1.95 (ISBN 0-88345-448-3). Regents Pub.
--Welcome to English: Let's Begin - A. (gr. 3-6). 1978. pap. text ed. 1.25 o.p. (ISBN 0-88345-354-1); tchr's manual, 1-3 4.95 (ISBN 0-88345-355-X). Regents Pub.
Chapman, John, et al. Talk It Over: Discussion Topics for Intermediate Students. (Illus.). 1978. pap. text ed. 2.50x (ISBN 0-582-79719-5); cassette 7.95 (ISBN 0-582-79720-9). Longman.
Chapman, John J. William Lloyd Garrison. (American Newspapermen 1790-1933 Ser.). 1974. Repr. 17.50x (ISBN 0-8464-0027-8). Beekman Pubs.
Chapman, John W., jt. ed. see Pennock, J. Roland.

Chapman, John W., jt. ed. see Penrock, J. Roland.

Chapman, Joseph I. First Things First. LC 74-22523. 96p. (Orig.). 1975. pap. 2.50 o.p. (ISBN 0-8170-0649-4). Judson.

Chapman, Keith. North Sea Oil & Gas. (Problems in Modern Geography). (Illus.). 240p. 1976. 18.95 (ISBN 0-7153-7183-5). David & Charles.

--People, Pattern & Processes: An Introduction to Human Geography. LC 79-18917. 334p. 1980. 44.95x (ISBN 0-470-26719-4); pap. 18.95x (ISBN 0-470-26806-9). Halsted Pr.

Chapman, Kenneth G. Graded Readings & Exercises in Old Icelandic. 1970. pap. 8.75x (ISBN 0-520-00221-0, CAMPUS25). U of Cal Pr.

Chapman, Kenneth M. & Harlow, Francis H. The Pottery of San Ildefonso Pueblo. LC 76-99565. (School of American Research). (Illus.). 260p. 1977. Repr. of 1970 ed. 29.95x o.p. (ISBN 0-8263-0157-6). U of NM Pr.

Chapman, Kim W. The Magic Hat. 2nd ed. LC 76-20842. (Illus.). 47p. (gr. k-4). 1976. pap. 3.00 (ISBN 0-914996-10-X). Lollipop Power.

Chapman, L. Disordered Thought in Schizophrenia. 1974. 19.95 (ISBN 0-13-216192-3). P-H.

Chapman, L. J. & Putnam, D. F. Physiography of Southern Ontario. 2nd ed. LC 66-6736. (Illus.). 1966. 20.00x (ISBN 0-8020-1944-7); pap. 5.95 (ISBN 0-8020-6071-4); maps 7.50x (ISBN 0-8020-2107-7). U of Toronto Pr.

Chapman, L. R. The Process of Learning Mathematics. LC 71-178683. 405p. 1972. text ed. 51.00 (ISBN 0-08-016623-7); pap. text ed. 17.00 (ISBN 0-08-017357-8). Pergamon.

Chapman, Marie. Fun with Bible Geography. LC 80-65055. (Teaching Aid Ser.). 65p. 1980. plastic spiral 3.75 (ISBN 0-89636-044-X). Accent Bks.

--Successful Teaching Ideas. LC 74-82558. (Illus.). 96p. 1975. pap. 5.50 (ISBN 0-87239-032-2, 3195). Standard Pub.

Chapman, Paul. Unmet Needs & the Delivery of Care. 110p. 1979. pap. text ed. 9.90x (ISBN 0-7199-0962-7, Pub. by Bedford England). Renouf.

Chapman, R. A. Decision Making: A Case Study of the Decision to Raise the Bank Rate in September 1957. (Library of Political Studies). 1969. text ed. 5.75x (ISBN 0-7100-6302-4). Humanities.

Chapman, R. W. Marketing Today. 2nd ed. 1973. 17.50x (ISBN 0-7002-0202-1). Intl Ideas.

Chapman, R. W., ed. see Austen, Jane.

Chapman, Raymond, jt. ed. see Gottlieb, Nora.

Chapman, Renate. Mystic Island. 1980. 5.95 (ISBN 0-686-59793-1, Avalon). Bouregy.

Chapman, Richard, ed. The Role of Commissions in Policy Making. 1973. pap. text ed. 9.50x o.p. (ISBN 0-04-350043-9). Allen Unwin.

Chapman, Richard A. & Greenaway, J. R. The Dynamics of Administrative Reform. 249p. 1980. 37.50x (ISBN 0-85664-107-3, Pub. by Croom Helm Ltd England). Biblio Dist.

Chapman, Richard A. & Dunsire, A., eds. Style in Administration: Readings in British Public Administration. (Royal Institute of Public Administration). 1971. text ed. 14.50x o.p. (ISBN 0-04-350027-7). Allen Unwin.

Chapman, Robert, jt. auth. see Clarke, David L.

Chapman, Robert D. Discovering Astronomy. LC 77-16024. (Illus.). 1978. text ed. 26.95x (ISBN 0-7167-0034-4); pap. text ed. 16.95x (ISBN 0-7167-0033-6); instructors' guide avail. W H Freeman.

Chapman, Roger, jt. auth. see Landon, Robbins H.

Chapman, S. & Cowling, T. G. Mathematical Theory of Non-Uniform Gases. 3rd ed. LC 70-77285. (Illus.). 1970. 47.95 (ISBN 0-521-07577-7). Cambridge U Pr.

Chapman, S. B., ed. Methods in Plant Ecology. LC 75-37570. 1977. pap. 19.95 o.p. (ISBN 0-470-99201-8). Halsted Pr.

Chapman, Samuel. The Postage Stamps of Mexico 1856-1868. LC 75-40501. (Illus.). 1976. Repr. 35.00x (ISBN 0-88000-079-1). Quarterman.

Chapman, Samuel G. Police Patrol Readings. 2nd. ed. (Illus.). 788p. 1972. pap. 49.75 photocopy ed. spiral (ISBN 0-398-00304-1). C C Thomas.

Chapman, Samuel G., jt. auth. see Eastman, George D.

Chapman, Sidney, jt. auth. see Akasofu, Syun-Ichi.

Chapman, Stephen R. & Carter, Lark P. Crop Production: Principles & Practices. LC 75-40318. (Illus.). 1976. text ed. 23.95x (ISBN 0-7167-0581-8). W H Freeman.

Chapman, Suzanne E. see Dunham, Dows.

Chapman, V. J. & Chapman, D. J. The Algae. 2nd ed. 500p. 1975. 19.95 (ISBN 0-312-01715-4). St Martin.

Chapman, Vera. Blaedud the Birdman. 1980. pap. 1.95 (ISBN 0-380-45070-4, 45070). Avon.

--The Green Knight. 1977. pap. 1.50 (ISBN 0-380-01704-0, 33795). Avon.

Chapman, W. A. Workshop Technology, Pt. 1. 5th ed. (Illus.). 1976. pap. 14.95x (ISBN 0-7131-3269-8). Intl Ideas.

--Workshop Technology, Pt. 2. 4th ed. (Illus.). 1972. pap. 14.95x (ISBN 0-7131-3272-8). Intl Ideas.

Chapmann, John. Welcome to English: Teacher's Manual 4-5. (Welcome to English Ser.). 134p. 1980. pap. text ed. 4.95 (ISBN 0-88345-368-1, 18499). Regents Pub.

Chapot, V., jt. auth. see Cagnat, R.

Chapot, Victor. The Roman World. 449p. 1980. Repr. of 1928 ed. lib. bdg. 50.00 (ISBN 0-89760-118-1). Telegraph Bks.

Chappel, Bernice M. A Time for Learning: A Self-Instructional Handbook for Parents & Teachers of Young Children. 144p. 1974. pap. text ed. 5.00x (ISBN 0-89039-059-2). Ann Arbor Pubs.

Chappel, T. J. Decorated Gourds in North-Eastern Nigeria. 1977. text ed. 55.00x (ISBN 0-905788-02-8). Humanities.

Chappell, Clovis G. Faces About the Cross. (Glovis Chappell Library). pap. 3.95 (ISBN 0-8010-2364-5). Baker Bk.

--The Seven Words: The Words of Jesus on the Cross Reveal the Heart of the Christian Faith. (Procket Pulpit Library). 80p. 1976. pap. 1.75 (ISBN 0-8010-2387-4). Baker Bk.

--Ten Rules for Living. (Clovis G. Chappell Library). 1976. pap. 2.95 o.p. (ISBN 0-8010-2385-8). Baker Bk.

Chappell, D. J. An Economic History of England. 320p. 1980. pap. 12.95x (ISBN 0-7121-0587-5). Intl Ideas.

Chappell, Duncan & Monahan, John, eds. Violence & Criminal Justice. LC 74-31912. 1975. 16.95 (ISBN 0-669-98194-X). Lexington Bks.

--Violence & Criminal Justice. 1977. pap. text ed. 6.95x o.p. (ISBN 0-669-01064-2). Heath.

Chappell, Duncan, et al. Forcible Rape. The Crime, the Victim, & the Criminal. LC 77-3377. 1977. 22.50x (ISBN 0-231-03839-9); pap. 10.00x (ISBN 0-231-04641-3). Columbia U Pr.

Chappell, Fred. Moments of Light. LC 80-81219. 195p. 1980. 12.95 (ISBN 0-917990-05-6). New South Co.

Chappell, James D. Cobol Demand Processing Manual. 80p. 1981. pap. text ed. 6.95 (ISBN 0-8403-2376-X). Kendall-Hunt.

Chappell, R. T. & Read, W. L. Business Communications. 4th ed. 232p. (Orig.). 1979. pap. text ed. 13.95x (ISBN 0-7121-0272-8, Pub. by Macdonald & Evans England). Intl Ideas.

Chappell, V. C., ed. Ordinary Language: Essays in Philosophical Method. 128p. 1981. pap. 2.75 (ISBN 0-486-24082-7). Dover.

Chappell, Warren. Short History of the Printed Word. LC 72-127091. (Illus.). 1970. 12.50 o.p. (ISBN 0-394-44534-1). Knopf.

--A Short History of the Printed Word. LC 79-90409. (Nonpareil Bks.). (Illus.). 288p. 1980. pap. 9.95 (ISBN 0-87923-312-5). Godine.

Chapple, Eliot D. The Biological Foundations of Individuality & Culture. LC 79-23284. 388p. (Orig.). 1980. lib. bdg. 17.50 (ISBN 0-89874-041-X). Krieger.

Chapple, Jonathan, jt. auth. see Porter, Jimathan.

Chapple, M. A-Level Physics: Electricity & Semiconducters, Vol.3. 2nd ed. (Illus.). 288p. (Orig.). 1980. pap. text ed. 11.95x (ISBN 0-7121-0158-6). Intl Ideas.

--A Level Physics: Mechanics & Heat, Vol. 1. 2nd ed. (Illus.). 336p. (Orig.). 1979. pap. text ed. 10.95x (ISBN 0-7121-0154-3, Pub. by Macdonald & Evans England). Intl Ideas.

--A Level Physics: Wave Motion-Sound & Light, Vol. 2. 2nd ed. (Illus.). 240p. (Orig.). 1979. pap. text ed. 10.95x (ISBN 0-7121-0155-1, Pub. by Macdonald & Evans England). Intl Ideas.

Chapple, Steve, jt. auth. see Garofalo, Reebee.

Chapuis, Alfred. History of the Musical Box & of Mechanical Music. Fitch, Howard M. & Fitch, Helen F., eds. Roesch, Joseph E., tr. from Fr. LC 80-12449. (Illus.). xvi, 304p. 1980. 27.50 (ISBN 0-915000-01-6). Musical Box Soc.

Chaput, Donald. The Cliff, America's First Great Copper Mine. LC 75-146505. (Illus.). 116p. 1971. 14.95 (ISBN 0-910726-90-6). Hillsdale Educ.

Char, John K. Holistic Dentistry. Date not set. cancelled (ISBN 0-9601978-3-4). G A Eversaul.

Char, S. V. Desika see Desika Char, S. V.

Charalambous, George, ed. Analysis & Control of Less-Desirable Flavors in Foods & Beverages. 1980. 24.50 (ISBN 0-12-169065-2). Acad Pr.

Charbeneau, Gerald T., et al, eds. Principles & Practice of Operative Dentistry. 2nd ed. LC 80-21029. (Illus.). 500p. 1981. text ed. write for info. (ISBN 0-8121-0775-6). Lea & Febiger.

Charboneau, Joe, et al. Super Joe: The Life & Legend of Joe Charboneau. LC 80-6169. 256p. 1981. 12.95 (ISBN 0-8128-2806-2). Stein & Day.

Charbonneau, Gerard & Seguin, Hubert. Workbook in Everyday French, 2 bks. rev. ed. 213p. (gr. 9-11). 1971. Bk. 1. pap. text ed. 3.75 (ISBN 0-88345-167-0, 17479); Bk. 2. pap. text ed. 3.75 (ISBN 0-88345-168-9, 17480); answer key 2.75 (ISBN 0-685-38985-5). Regents Pub.

Charbonneau, Manon P. Learning to Think in a Math Lab. (Illus.). 1971. pap. 5.75 (ISBN 0-934338-12-4). NAIS.

Charbonneaux, Jean, et al. Classical Greek Art. LC 72-80015. (Arts of Mankind Ser). (Illus.). 422p. 1973. 45.00 o.s.i. (ISBN 0-8076-0627-8). Braziller.

--Hellenistic Art. LC 72-89850. (Arts of Mankind Ser). 35.00 o.s.i. (ISBN 0-8076-0666-9). Braziller.

Chard, Chester S. Northeast Asia in Prehistory. LC 73-2040. 1974. 15.00x (ISBN 0-299-06430-1). U of Wis Pr.

Chardin, Pierre Teilhard De see Teilhard De Chardin, Pierre.

Charell, Ralph. How to Make Things Go Your Way. 192p. 1981. pap. 4.95 (ISBN 0-346-12518-9). Cornerstone.

Chargaff, Erwin. Heraclitean Fire. 1980. pap. 6.95 (ISBN 0-446-97659-8). Warner Bks.

Chari, S. M. Advaita & Visistadvaita. 2nd ed. 1976. 7.50 (ISBN 0-8426-0886-9). Orient Bk Dist.

Charite, Raymond La see La Charite, Raymond C. & La Charite, Raymond.

Chariton, Igumen. The Art of Prayer. Kadloubovsky, Palmer, tr. 1966. 21.95 (ISBN 0-571-06899-5, Pub. by Faber & Faber). Merrimack Bk Serv.

Charitos, Minas, jt. auth. see Livadeas, Themistocles.

Charity, A. C. Events & Their Afterlife. 1966. 39.95 (ISBN 0-521-04622-X). Cambridge U Pr.

Charke, Charlotte C. Narrative of the Life of Mrs. Charlotte Charke. LC 70-81365. (Illus.). 1969. Repr. of 1755 ed. 32.00x (ISBN 0-8201-1065-5). Schol Facsimiles.

Charles, Allegra. How to Win at Ladies Doubles. LC 75-3780. (Illus.). 1975. pap. 2.95 o.p. (ISBN 0-668-03794-6). Arco.

Charles, C. M. Educational Psychology: The Instructional Enedeavor. 2nd ed. LC 75-43611. 1976. pap. text ed. 12.00 (ISBN 0-8016-0952-6). Mosby.

--Individualizing Instruction. LC 75-22246. (Illus.). 304p. 1976. pap. text ed. 11.50 o.p. (ISBN 0-8016-0967-4). Mosby.

--Individualizing Instruction. 2nd ed. LC 79-26645. (Illus.). 1980. pap. 11.95 (ISBN 0-8016-0974-7). Mosby.

Charles, C. M. & Malian, Ida. The Special Student: Practical Help for the Classroom Teacher. LC 80-13053. (Illus.). 1980. pap. text ed. 9.95 (ISBN 0-8016-1132-6). Mosby.

Charles, C. M., ed. Learning Centers That Teach. 1978. pap. 10.75 (ISBN 0-8191-0367-5). U Pr of Amer.

Charles, Carole. The Boston Tea Party. LC 75-33156. (Stories of the Revolution Ser.). (Illus.). (gr. 2-6). 1975. PLB 5.50 (ISBN 0-913778-18-4). Childs World.

--General George at Yorktown. LC 75-33158. (Stories of the Revolution Ser.). (Illus.). (gr. 2-6). 1975. PLB 5.50 (ISBN 0-913778-23-0). Childs World.

--John Paul Jones, Victory at Sea. LC 75-33157. (Stories of the Revolution Ser.). (Illus.). (gr. 2-6). 1975. PLB 5.50 (ISBN 0-913778-21-4). Childs World.

--Martha Helps the Rebel. LC 75-33126. (Stories of the Revolution). (Illus.). (gr. 2-6). 1975. PLB 5.50 (ISBN 0-913778-22-2). Childs World.

--Paul Revere & the Minutemen. LC 75-33204. (Stories of the Revolution Ser.). (Illus.). (gr. 2-6). 1975. PLB 5.50 (ISBN 0-913778-19-2). Childs World.

--Survival at Valley Forge. LC 75-33159. (Stories of the Revolution Ser.). (Illus.). (gr. 2-6). 1975. PLB 5.50 (ISBN 0-913778-20-6). Childs World.

Charles, David. Self-Assessment of Current Knowledge in Obstetrics & Gynecology. 3rd ed. LC 79-91970. 1980. pap. 16.50 (ISBN 0-87488-260-5). Med Exam.

Charles, Donald. Calico Cat at the Zoo. LC 80-26380. (Calico Cat Storybooks). (Illus.). 32p. (ps-3). 1981. PLB 7.95 (ISBN 0-516-03443-X). Childrens.

Charles, Edgar D. & Kronenfeld, Jennie J., eds. Social & Economic Impacts of Coronary Artery Disease. LC 79-1554. 160p. 1980. 18.95 (ISBN 0-669-02912-2). Lexington Bks.

Charles, Elizabeth. The Bertram Family. Wolff, Robert L., ed. LC 75-494. (Victorian Fiction Ser.). 1975. Repr. of 1876 ed. lib. bdg. 66.00 (ISBN 0-8240-1570-3). Garland Pub.

--How to Keep Your Pet Healthy. LC 79-180464. (Illus.). 176p. 1974. pap. 1.50 o.s.i. (ISBN 0-02-062400-X, Collier). Macmillan.

Charles, H. P. & Knight, B. C., eds. Organization & Control in Prokaryotic & Eukaryotic Cells: Proceedings. (Illus.). 1970. 49.50 (ISBN 0-521-07815-6). Cambridge U Pr.

Charles Hall Page & Assocs., ed. see Foundation for San Francisco's Architectural Heritage.

Charles, Iona. Draw a Dark Circle. 1977. pap. 1.50 o.p. (ISBN 0-445-03191-3). Popular Lib.

--Grenencourt. 256p. 1975. pap. 1.25 o.p. (ISBN 0-445-00264-6). Popular Lib.

Charles, J. Norman & Charles, Sharon. Heaven on Earth, Family Style. (Orig.). 1980. pap. 4.95 (ISBN 0-88270-495-8). Logos.

Charles, John. Research & Public Health. 1961. text ed. 3.00x (ISBN 0-485-26312-2, Athlone Pr). Humanities.

Charles, R. H. Divorce & the Roman Doctrine of Nullity. 100p. 1927. text ed. 2.95 (ISBN 0-567-22067-2). Attic Pr.

--Gambling & Betting: Their Origin & Their Relation to Morality & to Religion. 3rd ed. 92p. 1928. text ed. 2.95 (ISBN 0-567-22066-4). Attic Pr.

--Revelation, Vol. I. LC 21-5413. (International Critical Commentary Ser.). 568p. 1920. text ed. 22.00x (ISBN 0-567-05038-6). Attic Pr.

--Revelation, Vol. II. LC 21-5413. (International Critical Commentary Ser.). 506p. 1920. text ed. 22.00x (ISBN 0-567-05039-4). Attic Pr.

Charles, R. H., et al. Apocrypha & Pseudepigrapha of the Old Testament, 2 Vols. Vol. 1. 74.00x (ISBN 0-19-826155-1); Vol. 2. 69.00x (ISBN 0-19-826152-7). Oxford U Pr.

Charles River Assoc. International Cartels: Policy Implications for the United States. 1979. write for info. o.p. Praeger.

Charles, Robert. The Hour of the Wolf. 192p. (Orig.). 1975. pap. 1.25 o.p. (ISBN 0-523-00638-1). Pinnacle Bks.

Charles, Robert J. Broken Vows: A Novel of Betrayal. LC 80-25321. 1981. 10.95 (ISBN 0-934878-00-5). Dembner Bks.

Charles, Sharon, jt. auth. see Charles, J. Norman.

Charles, Sydney R. Handbook of Music & Music Literature: In Sets & Series. LC 71-143502. 1972. 17.95 (ISBN 0-02-905400-1). Free Pr.

Charles-Dominique, P. & Martin, R. D. Behavior & Ecology of Nocturnal Prosimians: Field Studies in Gabon & Madagascar. (Advances in Ethology Ser.: Vol. 9). (Illus.). 91p. (Orig.). 1972. pap. text ed. 23.50. Parey Sci Pubs.

Charles-Dominique, P., et al. Nocturnal Malagasy Primates: Ecology, Physiology & Behavior. LC 89-6799. (Communication & Behavior: an Interdisciplinary Ser.). 1980. 27.50 (ISBN 0-12-169350-3). Acad Pr.

Charles-Dominique, Pierre. Ecology & Behavior of Nocturnal Primates: Prosimians of Equatorial West Africa. Martin, R. D., tr. LC 77-1227. 1977. 20.00x (ISBN 0-231-04362-7). Columbia U Pr.

Charles-Edwards, Imelda & Nixon, Harold. Nursing Care of the Pediatric Surgical Patient. 1981. text ed. price not set. Butterworth.

Charles-Picard, Colette, jt. auth. see Charles-Picard, Gilbert.

Charles-Picard, Gilbert & Charles-Picard, Colette. Daily Life in Carthage at the Time of Hannibal. (Illus.). 1961. 10.95 (ISBN 0-02-523970-8). Macmillan.

Charles-Roux, Francois. Bonaparte: Governor of Egypt. Dickes, E. W., tr. LC 80-1932. (Illus., Fr.). 1981. Repr. of 1937 ed. 47.50 (ISBN 0-404-18958-X). AMS Pr.

Charleston, R. J., jt. auth. see Cook, R. M.

Charleston, Robert J. Islamic Pottery. LC 78-55079. (Masterpieces of Western & Near Eastern Ceramics: Vol. IV). (Illus.). 1980. thru. sept. 1980 165.00 (ISBN 0-87011-345-3); thereafter 200.00 (ISBN 0-87011-345-3). Kodansha.

Charleston, Robert J., ed. see Boston, David M.

Charleston, Robert J., ed. see Cook, R. M. & Charleston, R. J.

Charleston, Robert J., ed. see Liverani, Giuseppe.

Charlesworth, Andrew. Social Portrait in a Rural Society. (Historical Geography Research Ser.). 1980. pap. 3.50x (ISBN 0-686-27387-7, Pub. by GEO Abstracts England). State Mutual Bk.

Charlesworth, B. Evolution in Age-Structured Populations. LC 79-8909. (Cambridge Studies in Mathematical Biology: No. 1). 250p. 1980. 44.50 (ISBN 0-521-23045-4); pap. 13.50 (ISBN 0-521-29786-9). Cambridge U Pr.

Charlesworth, Edward A., jt. auth. see Nathan, Ronald G.

Charlesworth, James C., ed. Contemporary Political Analysis. LC 67-14374. (Orig.). 1967. 9.95 (ISBN 0-02-905460-5); pap. text ed. 9.95 (ISBN 0-02-905470-2). Free Pr.

Charlesworth, Maria L. Ministering Children. Lurie, Alison & Schiller, Justin G., eds. LC 75-32166. (Classics of Children's Literature Ser.: 1621-1932). PLB 38.00 (ISBN 0-8240-2279-3). Garland Pub.

Charlesworth, Martin P., jt. auth. see Tarn, William W.

Charlesworth, R. & Radeloff, D. J. Experiences in Math for Young Children. LC 77-80039. 1978. pap. text ed. 7.20 (ISBN 0-8273-1660-7); instructor's guide 1.60 (ISBN 0-8273-1661-5). Delmar.

Charley, Helen. Food Science. LC 80-17047. 530p. 1970. 19.50 (ISBN 0-8260-1925-0). Wiley.

--Food Study Manual. 2nd ed. LC 79-75636. (Illus.). 275p. (Orig.). 1971. 14.50 (ISBN 0-8260-1940-4, 14195). Wiley.

Charlier, C. V. & Greenwood, J. A. Elements of Mathematical Statistics. 1947. pap. 5.25 o.s.i. (ISBN 0-02-842770-X). Hafner.

Charlier, Roger. Harnessing Ocean Energies: Tapping Ocean Energies to Produce Inexhaustible, Pollution-Free Electricity. 1977. Repr. soft cover 8.00 (ISBN 0-686-21178-2). Maple Mont.

Charlier, Roger H. & Gordon, Bernard L. Ocean Resources: An Introduction to Economic Oceanography. LC 78-61393. (Illus.). 1978. pap. text ed. 9.00 (ISBN 0-8191-0599-6). U Pr of Amer.

Charlip, Remy. Arm in Arm. LC 80-18091. (Illus.). 48p. (gr. 1-5). 1980. Repr. of 1969 ed. 9.95 (ISBN 0-590-07758-9, Four Winds). Schol Bk Serv.

--Fortunately. LC 80-36956. (Illus.). 48p. (ps-3). 1980. Repr. of 1964 ed. 8.95 (ISBN 0-590-07762-7, Four Winds). Schol Bk Serv.

Charlip, Remy & Joyner, Jerry. Thirteen. LC 75-8875. (Illus.). 40p. (gr. 1 up). 1975. 7.95 (ISBN 0-590-17712-5, Four Winds); PLB 7.95 (ISBN 0-590-07712-0). Schol Bk Serv.

Charlip, Remy & Moore, Lilian. Hooray for Me! LC 80-15285. (Illus.). 40p. (ps-3). 1980. Repr. of 1975 ed. 8.95 (ISBN 0-590-07768-6, Four Winds). Schol Bk Serv.

Charlip, Remy & Supree, Burton. Harlequin & the Gift of Many Colors. LC 76-136999. (Illus.). 48p. (ps-3). 1973. 7.95 (ISBN 0-590-17710-9, Four Winds); lib. bdg. 7.95 (ISBN 0-590-07710-4). Schol Bk Serv.

--Mother Mother I Feel Sick Send for the Doctor Quick Quick Quick. LC 80-17029. (Illus.). 48p. (ps-3). 1980. Repr. of 1966 ed. 8.95 (ISBN 0-590-07772-4, Four Winds). Schol Bk Serv.

Charlot, G. & Tremillon, B. Chemical Reactions in Solvents & Melts. 1969. 79.00 (ISBN 0-08-012678-2). Pergamon.

Charlot, Jean. The Gaullist Phenomenon: The Gaullist Movement in the Fifth Republic. (Studies in Political Science). 1971. text ed. 32.50x (ISBN 0-04-320069-9). Allen Unwin.

Charlton, Elizabeth. Terrible Tyrannosaurus. (Illus.). 32p. (ps-2). 1981. 5.95 (ISBN 0-525-66724-5). Elsevier-Nelson.

Charlton, Henry B. Hamlet. 50p. 1980. Repr. of 1942 ed. lib. bdg. 6.00 (ISBN 0-8492-3865-X). R West.

Charlton, James & Gilson, Barbara, eds. The Christmas Feast: A Delightful Treasury of Yuletide Stories and Poems for the Whole Family. LC 76-20833. 1976. 7.95 o.p. (ISBN 0-385-12512-7). Doubleday.

Charlton, Jim & Thompson, Bill. Croquet. LC 76-56089. (Encore Edition). (Illus.). 1977. 9.95 o.p. (ISBN 0-916844-01-3, ScribT); pap. 2.45 o.p. (ISBN 0-684-16369-1, ScribT). Scribner.

Charlton, Leigh & Swanberg, Annette. Glad Rags II. (Illus.). 168p. (Orig.). 1981. pap. 7.95 (ISBN 0-87701-178-8). Chronicle Bks.

Charlton, T. M. Model Analysis of Plane Structures. 1966. 9.90 o.p. (ISBN 0-08-011304-4); pap. 6.00 o.p. (ISBN 0-08-011303-6). Pergamon.

Charm, Stanley E. Fundamentals of Food Engineering. 3rd ed. 1978. pap. text ed. 22.50 (ISBN 0-87055-313-5). AVI.

Charman, Sarah, jt. auth. see Kraus, Richard.

Charmatz, Bill. Cat's Whiskers. LC 75-78085. (Illus.). (gr. k-2). 1969. 5.95g o.s.i. (ISBN 0-02-718170-7). Macmillan.

--Little Duster. (gr. k-2). 1967. 5.95g o.s.i. (ISBN 0-02-718180-4). Macmillan.

Charmaz, Kathleeen C. Social Reality of Death... (Sociology Ser.). 1980. text ed. 9.95 (ISBN 0-201-01033-X). A-W.

Charmet, Raymond. Dictionnaire art contemporain. (Illus., Fr.). pap. 8.50 (ISBN 0-685-13851-8, 3704). Larousse.

Charnace, Guy. A Star of Song: The Life of Christina Nilsson. M., J. C. & C., E., trs. LC 80-2264. 1981. Repr. of 1870 ed. 14.50 (ISBN 0-404-18818-4). AMS Pr.

Charnas, Suzy. The Vampire Tapestry. 1980. 11.95 (ISBN 0-671-25415-4). S&S.

Charnas, Suzy M. Walk to the End of the World. Date not set. pap. 2.50 (ISBN 0-345-27946-8). Ballantine.

Charnay, David B. Target Sixteen Hundred. 1980. 10.00 (ISBN 0-8184-0290-3). Lyle Stuart.

Charnego, Michael, jt. auth. see Indiana University.

Charney, Hanna. The Detective Novel of Manners: Hedonism, Morality, & the Life of Reason. LC 79-17634. 160p. 1981. 16.50 (ISBN 0-8386-3004-9). Fairleigh Dickinson.

Charney, I. Marital Love & Hate. 1972. 5.95 o.s.i. (ISBN 0-02-523990-2). Macmillan.

Charney, Jonathan I., ed. The New Nationalism & the Use of Common Spaces: Issues in Marine Pollution & the Exploitation of Antarctica. 420p. 1981. text ed. 29.00 (ISBN 0-86598-012-8). Allanheld.

Charney, Len. Build a Yurt: The Low Cost Mongolian Round House. (Illus.). 160p. 1974. pap. 3.95 o.s.i. (ISBN 0-02-079320-0, Collier). Macmillan.

--Build a Yurt: The Low-Cost Mongolian Round House. LC 73-11837. (Illus.). 160p. 1974. 7.95 o.s.i. (ISBN 0-02-523980-5). Macmillan.

Charney, Maurice, ed. Shakespearean Comedy: Theories & Traditions. LC 79-52616. (The New York Literary Forum). 320p. 1980. lib. bdg. 22.50x (ISBN 0-931196-07-8). NY Lit Forum.

Charnock, Joan. Land & People of Poland. (gr. 5-9). 1968. 3.95g o.s.i. (ISBN 0-02-718190-1). Macmillan.

Charnock, Richard S. Ludus Patronymicus: Or, the Etymology of Curious Surnames. LC 68-23141. 1968. Repr. of 1868 ed. 15.00 (ISBN 0-8103-3122-5). Gale.

Charnwood, J. R. Essays in Binocular Vision. 1970. Repr. of 1950 ed. 8.75 o.s.i. (ISBN 0-02-842790-4). Hafner.

Charny, Israel W. Strategies Against Violence: Design for Nonviolent Change. LC 78-3135. 1978. lib. bdg. 26.50x (ISBN 0-89158-151-0). Westview.

Charon, J. Symbolic Interactionism: An Introduction, an Interpretation, an Integration. 1979. pap. 9.95 (ISBN 0-13-870105-9). P-H.

Charon, Joel M. The Meaning of Sociology. LC 79-24396. 1980. pap. 7.95 (ISBN 0-88284-097-5). Alfred Pub.

Charosh, Mannis. The Ellipse. LC 73-132293. (Young Math Ser). (Illus.). (gr. 1-4). 1971. 7.95 (ISBN 0-690-25856-9, TYC-J). T Y Crowell.

--Mathematical Games for One or Two. LC 74-187934. (Young Math Ser.). (Illus.). (gr. 1-5). 1972. 7.95 (ISBN 0-690-52324-6, TYC-J); PLB 7.89 (ISBN 0-690-52325-4). T Y Crowell.

--Number Ideas Through Pictures. LC 73-4370. (Young Math Ser.). (Illus.). 40p. (gr. 1-5). 1974. PLB 7.89 (ISBN 0-690-00156-8, TYC-J). T Y Crowell.

--Straight Lines, Parallel Lines, Perpendicular Lines. LC 76-106569. (Young Math Ser). (Illus.). (gr. 1-4). 1970. 7.95 (ISBN 0-690-77992-5, TYC-J); PLB 7.89 (ISBN 0-690-77993-3). T Y Crowell.

Charques, Richard D. Short History of Russia. 1958. pap. 3.95 o.p. (ISBN 0-525-47015-8). Dutton.

Charran, R. & Maharaj, B. Va De Cuento. (Illus.). 1977. pap. text ed. 2.50x (ISBN 0-582-76616-8). Longman.

Charrell, Ralph. The Magic of Thinking Rich. 11.95 (ISBN 0-671-42376-2). S&S.

Charriere, Henri. Papillon. 1970. 9.95 o.p. (ISBN 0-688-02269-3). Morrow.

Charriere, Jacques. S. M. Eisenstein. 1974. pap. 8.95 o.p. (ISBN 0-525-47371-8). Dutton.

Charron, C., et al. Behavior: A Guide for Managers. 1977. 14.95 (ISBN 0-87909-078-2). Reston.

Charroux, Robert. The Gods Unknown. (Orig.). 1974. pap. 1.25 o.p. (ISBN 0-425-02547-0, Medallion). Berkley Pub.

Charry, Dana. Mental Health Skills for Clergy. 160p. 1981. 10.95 (ISBN 0-8170-0886-1). Judson.

Chartered Financial Analysts, ed. C.F.A. Personal Trust Investment Management. (Illus.). 1968. text ed. 5.55x o.p. (ISBN 0-256-00245-2). Irwin.

Charteris, Evan E. John Sargent...with Reproductions from His Paintings & Drawings. LC 70-164163. (Illus.). xii, 308p. 1972. Repr. of 1927 ed. 24.00 (ISBN 0-8103-3946-3). Gale.

Charteris, Leslie. Call for the Saint. (The Saint Ser.). 224p. 1981. pap. 2.25 (ISBN 0-441-09151-2). Charter Bks.

--Featuring the Saint. 1980. pap. 1.95 (ISBN 0-441-23155-1). Charter Bks.

--Leslie Charteris Count on the Saint: The Pastor's Problem & the Unsaintly Santa. LC 80-939. (Crime Club Ser.). 192p. 1980. 8.95 (ISBN 0-385-17191-9). Doubleday.

--Leslie Charteris' Send for the Saint: The Midas Double & the Pawn Gambit. LC 77-92210. 1978. 7.95 o.p. (ISBN 0-385-14138-6). Doubleday.

--Leslie Charteris' The Saint in Trouble: The Imprudent Professor & the Red Sabbath. LC 78-18551. 1978. 7.95 o.p. (ISBN 0-385-14612-4). Doubleday.

--The Saint & the People Importers. (Saint Ser.). 1979. pap. 1.95 (ISBN 0-441-74900-3). Charter Bks.

--The Saint & the Sizzling Saboteur. (The Saint Ser.). 160p. 1981. pap. 2.25 (ISBN 0-441-74908-9). Charter Bks.

--The Saint Errant. (The Saint Ser.). 224p. 1981. pap. 2.25 (ISBN 0-441-74888-0). Charter Bks.

--The Saint on the Spanish Main. (Saint Ser.). 224p. 1981. pap. 2.25 (ISBN 0-441-74889-9). Charter Bks.

--The Saint Overboard. 1976. Repr. of 1936 ed. lib. bdg. 12.85 (ISBN 0-89190-381-X). Am Repr-Rivercity Pr.

--The Saint Overboard. (The Saint Ser.). 288p. 1981. pap. 2.25 (ISBN 0-441-74895-3). Charter Bks.

Charters, Alexander N., et al. Comparing Adult Education Worldwide. LC 80-8911. (Higher Education Ser.). 1981. text ed. price not set (ISBN 0-87589-494-1). Jossey-Bass.

Charters, Ann & Charters, Samuel. I Love: The Story of Vladimir Mayakovsky & Lili Brik. 432p. 1979. 17.50 (ISBN 0-374-17406-7). FS&G.

Charters, Janet. The General. (Illus.). 1961. 7.95 (ISBN 0-7100-1173-3). Routledge & Kegan.

Charters, Samuel. The Legacy of the Blues: Art & Lives of Twelve Great Bluesmen. LC 76-51809. (Roots of Jazz Ser.). (Illus.). 1977. 21.50 (ISBN 0-306-70847-7); pap. 4.95 (ISBN 0-306-80054-3). Da Capo.

--Roots of the Blues: An African Search. 160p. 1981. 15.00 (ISBN 0-7145-2705-X). Merrimack Bk Serv.

Charters, Samuel & Kunstadt, Leonard. My Husband Gabrilowitsch: A History of the New York Scene. 27.50 (ISBN 0-306-76055-X). Da Capo.

Charters, Samuel, jt. auth. see Charters, Ann.

Charters, Samuel B. The Country Blues. LC 75-14122. (The Roots of Jazz Ser.). (Illus.). 288p. 1975. lib. bdg. 22.50 (ISBN 0-306-70678-4); pap. 4.95 (ISBN 0-306-80014-4). Da Capo.

Chartham, Robert. The Sensuous Couple. 2nd ed. 192p. 1981. pap. 2.50 (ISBN 0-345-29543-9); 12 copy counter display 30.00 (ISBN 0-345-29543-9). Ballantine.

Chartier, Armand B. Barbey D'Aurevilly. (World Authors Ser.: France: No. 468). 1977. lib. bdg. 12.50 (ISBN 0-8057-6305-8). Twayne.

Chartier, Colleen, jt. auth. see Carraher, Ron.

Chartier, Myron R. Preaching As Communication: An Interpersonal Perspective. LC 80-21304. (Abingdon Preacher Library). 128p. (Orig.). 1981. pap. 4.95 (ISBN 0-687-33826-3). Abingdon.

Chartier, P., jt. ed. see Palz, W.

Charton, Nancy, ed. The Ciskei: Economics & Politics of Dependence in a South African Homeland. 253p. 1980. 32.50x (ISBN 0-7099-0332-4, Pub. by Croom Helm Ltd England). Biblio Dist.

Charton, Nancy C. J., jt. ed. see Van Der Merwe, Hendrik W.

Chartrand, Gary, ed. & The Theory & Application of Graphs: Fourth International Conference, Western Michigan Univ., May 6-9, 1980. 500p. 1981. 30.00 (ISBN 0-471-08473-5, Pub. by Wiley-Interscience). Wiley.

Chartrand, René, jt. auth. see Summers, Jack L.

Chartrand, Robert L. & Morentz, James W. Information Technology Serving Society. (Illus.). 1979. 35.00 (ISBN 0-08-021979-9). Pergamon.

Chartrand, Robert L., ed. Computers in the Service of Society. LC 73-112401. 256p. 1972. text ed. 27.00 (ISBN 0-08-016332-7). Pergamon.

Chartrand, Robert Lee & Morentz, James W., Jr., eds. Information Technology Serving Society. 1979. 25.00 (ISBN 0-08-021979-9). Chartrand.

Chartridge Symposium on Real-Time Computing in Patient Management, 1975. Proceedings. Date not set. 28.50 (ISBN 0-901223-88-3, Pub. by Peregrinus England). Inst Elect Eng.

Chartridge Symposium on the Management of the Acutely Ill, 1976. Proceedings. Date not set. 29.50 (ISBN 0-901223-92-1, Pub. by Peregrinus England). Inst Elect Eng.

Charvat, William. Literary Publishing in America, 1790-1850. LC 59-12190. (Rosenbach Publication Ser). 1959. 7.50x o.p. (ISBN 0-8122-7214-5). U of Pa Pr.

--Origins of American Critical Thought, 1810-1835. 1961. pap. 1.65 o.p. (ISBN 0-498-04042-9, Prpta). A S Barnes.

Charwat, Andrew F., et al see Heat Transfer & Fluid Mechanics Institute.

Charyn, Jerome. Darlin' Bill. 1980. 11.95 (ISBN 0-87795-283-3). Arbor Hse.

--The Education of Patrick Silver. 208p. 1981. pap. 2.75 (ISBN 0-380-01698-2, 53603, Bard). Avon.

--Secret Isaac. 240p. 1980. pap. 2.75 (ISBN 0-380-47126-4, 47126). Avon.

Charyn, Jerome, ed. Troubled Vision: An Anthology of Contemporary Short Novels & Passages. 1970. pap. 2.95 o.s.i. (ISBN 0-02-049370-3, Collier). Macmillan.

Chasan, Daniel J. Up for Grabs: Inquiries into Who Wants What. LC 77-23881. 1977. 7.95 (ISBN 0-914842-18-8); pap. 4.95 (ISBN 0-914842-17-X). Madrona Pubs.

Chasco, Edmond De see De Chasca, Edmund.

Chase, Agnes. First Book of Grasses: The Structure of Grasses Explained for Beginners. 3rd ed. LC 76-48919. (Illus.). 127p. 1977. text ed. 8.95x (ISBN 0-87474-307-9). Smithsonian.

Chase, Alice E. Looking at Art. LC 66-11947. (Illus.). (gr. 7-9). 1966. 8.95 o.p. (ISBN 0-690-50869-7, TYC-J). T Y Crowell.

Chase, Alston H. A New Introduction to Latin. (gr. 9). text ed. 5.00x (ISBN 0-88334-001-1). Ind Sch Pr.

Chase, Bob. Diggs. 1981. 10.00 (ISBN 0-533-04670-X). Vantage.

Chase, Catherine. The Miracles at Cana. LC 78-64117. (Illus.). (gr. k-5). 1979. 3.50 (ISBN 0-89799-124-9); pap. 1.50 (ISBN 0-89799-033-1). Dandelion Pr.

Chase, Catherine, ed. The Birth of Moses. LC 78-73540. (Illus.). (gr. k-5). Date not set. price not set (ISBN 0-89799-151-6); pap. price not set (ISBN 0-89799-069-2). Dandelion Pr. Postponed.

Chase, Chris. How to Be a Movie Star. 1979. pap. write for info. o.p. (ISBN 0-425-04194-8). Berkley Pub.

Chase, Cleveland B. The Young Voltaire. 253p. 1980. Repr. of 1926 ed. lib. bdg. 35.00 (ISBN 0-8495-0799-5). Arden Lib.

Chase, Cora G. Glimpses of Gleams & Glooms. 32p. 1980. 2.95 (ISBN 0-8059-2757-3). Dorrance.

Chase, Don. They Came This Way: The Humboldt Valley, Highroad to the Gold Rush. (Illus.). 1973. velo-bind 3.50 (ISBN 0-918634-33-4); pap. 3.00 limited ed. (ISBN 0-685-73469-2). D M Chase.

Chase, Don M. Basket Maker Artists. (Illus.). 1978. pap. 2.50 (ISBN 0-918634-34-2). D M Chase.

Chase, Emma L., ed. see Chivers, Thomas H.

Chase, Ernest D. Romance of Greeting Cards: An Historical Account of the Origin, Evolution, & Development. LC 76-159914. (Tower Bks). (Illus.). 1971. Repr. of 1926 ed. 26.00 (ISBN 0-8103-3903-X). Gale.

Chase, Francis. Gathered Sketches from the Early History of New Hampshire & Vermont: Containing Vivid & Interesting Account of a Great Variety of the Adventures of Our Forefathers, & of Other Incidents of Olden Time. LC 75-7092. (Indian Captivities Ser.: Vol. 68). 1976. Repr. of 1856 ed. lib. bdg. 44.00 (ISBN 0-8240-1692-0). Garland Pub.

Chase, G. America's Music: From the Pilgrims to the Present. rev. ed. (Music Ser.). 1966. text ed. 15.95 o.p. (ISBN 0-07-010672-X, C). McGraw.

--Contemporary Art in Latin America. LC 70-78890. 1970. 9.95 o.s.i. (ISBN 0-02-905340-4). Free Pr.

Chase, Glen. Busted. (Cherry Delight Ser: No. 16). 1974. pap. 1.25 o.p. (ISBN 0-685-51409-9, LB214ZK, Leisure Bks). Nordon Pubns.

--Cherry Delight up Your Ante. 1976. pap. 1.25 o.p. (ISBN 0-685-72568-5, LB407, Leisure Bks). Nordon Pubns.

--Crack Shot. 1976. pap. 1.25 o.p. (ISBN 0-685-72569-3, LB400ZK, Leisure Bks). Nordon Pubns.

--Hang Loose. (Cherry Delight Ser.: No. 18). 1974. pap. 1.25 o.p. (ISBN 0-685-47977-3, LB233ZK, Leisure Bks). Nordon Pubns.

--I'm Cherry, Fly Me. 1976. pap. 1.25 o.p. (ISBN 0-685-69160-8, LB368ZK, Leisure Bks). Nordon Pubns.

--In a Bind. (Cherry Delight Ser: No. 19). (Orig.). 1975. pap. 1.25 o.p. (ISBN 0-685-52171-0, LB242ZK, Leisure Bks). Nordon Pubns.

--Lights! Action! Murder! (Cherry Delight Ser.). (Orig.). 1975. pap. 1.25 o.p. (ISBN 0-685-53127-9, LB274ZK, Leisure Bks). Nordon Pubns.

--Made in Japan. (Cherry Delight Ser.). 1976. pap. 1.25 o.p. (ISBN 0-685-74574-0, LB423ZK, Leisure Bks). Nordon Pubns.

--Mexican Standoff. (Cherry Delight Ser: No. 21). (Orig.). 1975. pap. 1.25 o.p. (ISBN 0-685-52941-X, LB260ZK, Leisure Bks). Nordon Pubns.

--Roman Candle. (Cherry Delight Ser.). (Orig.). 1975. pap. 1.25 o.p. (ISBN 0-685-54127-4, LB2932K, Leisure Bks). Nordon Pubns.

--Up Your Ante. (Cherry Delight Ser.: No. 4). 1975. pap. 1.25 o.p. (ISBN 0-685-46896-8, LB4072K, Leisure Bks). Nordon Pubns.

--What a Way to Go. (Cherry Delight Ser.: No. 15). 1974. pap. 1.25 o.p. (ISBN 0-685-47978-1, LB208ZK, Leisure Bks). Nordon Pubns.

Chase, Helen M., jt. auth. see Chase, William D.

Chase, Lawrence, et al. Practicing Management: A Guide to Accompany Tansik, Chase, & Aquilano's Management: a Life Cycle Approach. 1980. pap. 6.50x (ISBN 0-256-02354-9). Irwin.

Chase, Mary E. Bible & the Common Reader. rev. ed. 1962. pap. 2.95 (ISBN 0-02-084390-9, Collier). Macmillan.

--Mary Peters. 1944. 4.95 o.s.i. (ISBN 0-02-524330-6). Macmillan.

--Silas Crockett. 1943. 10.95 (ISBN 0-02-524450-7). Macmillan.

--Windswept. 1941. 10.95 (ISBN 0-02-524510-4). Macmillan.

Chase, Merrill W., jt. ed. see Williams, Curtis A.

Chase, Mildred P. Just Being at the Piano. LC 80-8999. 112p. (Orig.). 1981. 9.95 (ISBN 0-915238-44-6); pap. 5.95 (ISBN 0-915238-45-4). Peace Pr.

Chase, Nan E., ed. Bountiful: A Poetry Digest. (First Annual Ser.). (Illus.). 53p. pap. 4.25 (ISBN 0-938512-00-5). Brigadoon.

Chase, Richard, ed. see Harris, Joel C.

Chase, Richard B. & Aquilano, Nicholas J. Production & Operations Management: A Life Cycle Approach. rev. ed. 1977. text ed. 20.95x (ISBN 0-256-01919-3). Irwin.

Chase, Salmon P. Diary & Correspondence of Salmon P. Chase. LC 74-75301. (Law, Politics, & History Ser). 1971. Repr. of 1903 ed. lib. bdg. 49.50 (ISBN 0-306-71264-4). Da Capo.

Chase, Samuel. Trial of Samuel Chase, an Associate Justice of the Supreme Court Impeached by the House of Representatives, 2 Vols. LC 69-11324. (Law, Politics, & History Ser). Repr. of 1805 ed. 59.50 (ISBN 0-306-71181-8). Da Capo.

Chase, Samuel B., Jr., et al, eds. Problems in Public Expenditure Analysis. (Studies of Goverment Finance). 1967. 14.95 (ISBN 0-8157-1382-7); pap. 5.95 (ISBN 0-8157-1381-9). Brookings.

Chase, Samuel, Jr. Asset Prices in Economic Analysis. (California Library Reprint Series: No. 22). 1971. 18.50x (ISBN 0-520-01928-8). U of Cal Pr.

Chase, Stuart. Guides to Straight Thinking, with Thirteen Common Fallacies. 1956. 10.00 o.s.i. (ISBN 0-06-010710-3, HarpT). Har-Row.

Chase, Thomas N., et al, eds. Huntington's Disease. LC 78-68608. (Advances in Neurology Ser.: Vol. 23). 1979. text ed. 41.00 (ISBN 0-89004-374-4). Raven.

Chase, Virginia. One Crow, Two Crow. LC 78-8164. 1978. lib. bdg. 9.50 o.p. (ISBN 0-89621-009-X); pap. 4.95x (ISBN 0-89621-008-1). Thorndike Pr.

Chase, W. Linwood & John, Martha T. A Guide for the Elementary Social Studies Teacher. 3rd ed. 1978. pap. text ed. 11.50 (ISBN 0-205-05938-4). Allyn.

Chase, William D. & Chase, Helen M. Chase's Calendar of Annual Events: Special Days, Weeks & Months in 1981. rev. ed. (Illus., Orig.). 1980. pap. 12.95 (ISBN 0-913082-28-7). Apple Tree.

Chasen, Daniel Jack. Up for Grabs: Inquiries into Who Wants What. (Illus.). 133p. 7.95 (ISBN 0-914842-18-8); pap. 4.95 (ISBN 0-914842-17-X). Madrona Pubs.

Chasen, Sylvan H. Geometric Principles & Procedures for Computer Graphic Applications. LC 78-7998. (Illus.). 1978. 21.95 (ISBN 0-13-352559-7). P-H.

Chase-Riboud, Barbara. Sally Hemings. 1980. pap. 2.75 (ISBN 0-380-48686-5, 48686). Avon.

Chasin, Barbara, jt. auth. see Franke, Richard.

Chasseaud, L. F., jt. auth. see Bridges, J. W.

Chasseaud, L. F., jt. ed. see Bridges, J. W.

Chasseguet-Smirgel, J., et al. Female Sexuality: New Psychoanalytic Views. LC 79-107974. Orig. Title: Recherches Psychanalytiques Nouvelles Sur La Sexualite Feminine. 1970. 8.95 o.p. (ISBN 0-472-21900-6). U of Mich Pr.

Chassman, Neil A. & Murdock, Robert, eds. Poets of the Cities: New York & San Francisco, 1950-65. 150p. 1975. pap. 9.95 o.p. (ISBN 0-525-47388-2). Dutton.

Chastain, James G., tr. see Stadelmann, Rudolph.

Chastain, Madye L. Bright Days. LC 52-10063. (Illus.). (gr. 4-7). 4.50 o.p. (ISBN 0-15-212135-8, HJ). HarBraceJ.

--Plippen's Palace. LC 61-6346. (Illus.). (gr. 4-7). 1961. 4.50 o.p. (ISBN 0-15-262792-8, HJ). HarBraceJ.

Chastain, Sherry. Winning the Salary Game: Salary Negotiation for Women. 192p. 1980. text ed. 9.95 (ISBN 0-471-08433-6); pap. text ed. 6.95 (ISBN 0-471-08023-3). Wiley.

Chastain, Theron B. We Can Win Others. 1953. pap. 1.75 o.p. (ISBN 0-8170-0194-8). Judson.

Chastain, Thomas. The Diamond Exchange. LC 80-1118. 240p. 1981. 10.95 (ISBN 0-385-14438-5). Doubleday.

--High Voltage. 1981. pap. 2.50 (ISBN 0-425-04831-4). Berkley Pub.

Chasteen, Joseph E. Essentials of Clinical Dental Assisting. 2nd. ed. LC 80-372. (Illus.). 1980. 18.95 (ISBN 0-8016-0976-3). Mosby.

--Four-Handed Dentistry in Clinical Practice. LC 78-7436. 1978. text ed. 16.95 (ISBN 0-8016-0977-1). Mosby.

Chastel, Andre. Flowering of the Italian Renaissance. LC 65-27309. (Arts of Mankind Ser). 30.00 o.s.i. (ISBN 0-8076-0503-4). Braziller.

--Studios & Styles of the Italian Renaissance. LC 68-20093. (Arts of Mankind Ser). 30.00 o.s.i. (ISBN 0-8076-0504-2). Braziller.

Chastel, Andre, intro. by. The Vatican Frescoes of Michelangelo, 2 vols. Rosenthal, Raymond, tr. from Fr. LC 80-66646. (Illus.). 528p. 1980. ltd. ed. 6000.00 (ISBN 0-89659-158-1). Abbeville Pr.

Chastenet de Puysegur, A. M. Du Magnetisme Animal: Considere Dans Ses Rapports Avec Diverses Brances De la Physique Generale. 483p. (Fr.). Repr. of 1807 ed. text ed. 32.00x (ISBN 0-8290-0285-5). Irvington.

Chateaubriand, Francois R. Chateaubriand's Travels in America. Switzer, Richard, ed. & tr. LC 68-55043. (Illus.). 248p. 1969. 12.00x (ISBN 0-8131-1178-1). U Pr of Ky.

Chateaubriand, Francois R De see De Chateaubriand, Francois R.

Chateaubriand, Francois R. De see De Chateaubriand, Francois R.

Chatfield, Charles. For Peace & Justice: Pacifism in America, 1914-1941. LC 70-142143. (Illus.). 1971. 16.50x (ISBN 0-87049-126-1). U of Tenn Pr.

Chatfield, Susan. Leaves of Fire, Flame of Love. 1981. pap. 1.50 (ISBN 0-440-14937-1). Dell.

Chatfield-Taylor, Joan. Picnics. LC 79-64872. (Illus.). 1980. pap. 4.95 (ISBN 0-394-73760-1). Taylor & NG.

Chatham, James R. & Ruiz-Fornells, Enrique. Dissertations in Hispanic Languages & Literatures: 1876-1966. LC 70-80093. 136p. 1970. 15.50x (ISBN 0-8131-1183-8). U Pr of Ky.

Chatham, Russell, ed. Silent Seasons. 1978. 11.95 o.p. (ISBN 0-525-20456-3). Dutton.

Chatman, Seymour. Story & Discourse: Narrative Structure in Fiction & Film. 1978. pap. 5.95 1980 ed. (ISBN 0-8014-1131-9); pap. 5.95 (ISBN 0-8014-9186-X). Cornell U Pr.

Chatman, Seymour, ed. Approaches to Poetics. (Studies of the English Institute Ser.). 208p. 1973. text ed. 12.50x (ISBN 0-231-03781-3). Columbia U Pr.

Chatman, Seymour B. Story & Discourse: Narrative Structure in Fiction & Film. LC 78-9329. (Illus.). 1978. 17.50x o.p. (ISBN 0-8014-1131-9). Cornell U Pr.

Chatov, Robert. Corporate Financial Reporting: Public or Private Control? LC 74-15368. 1975. 17.95 (ISBN 0-02-905410-9). Free Pr.

Chattergy, R., jt. auth. see Pooch, U.

Chattergy, Rahul & Pooch, Udo. Sixteen-Bit Microprocessors. 256p. 1982. text ed. 19.95 (ISBN 0-8359-7003-5). Reston.

Chatterjee, Basant. Inside Bangladesh Today: An Eye-Witness Account. LC 73-906296. 159p. 1973. 6.00x (ISBN 0-8002-1568-0). Intl Pubns Serv.

Chatterjee, Biswanath. Pulse Circuits. 5.50x o.p. (ISBN 0-210-34015-0). Asia.

Chatterjee, Lata, jt. auth. see Lakshmanan, T. R.

Chatterjee, Margaret. At the Homeopath's. (Writers Workshop Greenbird Ser.). 87p. 1975. 12.00 (ISBN 0-88253-504-8); pap. text ed. 5.00 (ISBN 0-88253-503-X). Ind-US Inc.

--The Sandalwood Tree. 4.80 (ISBN 0-89253-457-5); flexible cloth 4.00 (ISBN 0-89253-458-3). Ind-US Inc.

--The Spring & the Spectacle. 4.80 (ISBN 0-89253-555-5); flexible cloth 4.00 (ISBN 0-89253-556-3). Ind-US Inc.

--Towards the Sun. (Writers Workshop Redbird Ser.). 1975. 8.00 (ISBN 0-88253-664-8); pap. text ed. 3.00 (ISBN 0-88253-663-X). Ind-US Inc.

Chatterjee, Nirmal C. & Rao, P. Parameswara. Emergency & Law, with Special Reference to India. 1966. 7.50x (ISBN 0-210-22741-9). Asia.

Chatterjee, Partha. Arms, Alliances & Stability. LC 73-20977. (Illus.). 1975. 24.95 (ISBN 0-470-14935-3). Halsted Pr.

Chatterjee, Pranab. Taste of a Rain Forest. (Redbird Bk.). 1976. lib. bdg. 10.00 (ISBN 0-89253-121-5); flexible bdg. 4.80 (ISBN 0-89253-137-1). Ind-US Inc.

Chatterjee, Samprit & Price, Bertram. Regression Analysis by Example. LC 77-24510. (Probability & Mathematical Statistics Ser.: Applied Probability Section). 1977. 21.95 (ISBN 0-471-01521-0, Pub. by Wiley-Interscience). Wiley.

Chatterjee, Satya N., ed. Renal Transplantation. 1980. 26.50 (ISBN 0-89004-308-6). Raven.

Chatterji, J. C. Wisdom of the Vedas. LC 80-51550. 100p. 1980. pap. 3.95 (ISBN 0-8356-0538-8, Quest). Theos Pub Hse.

Chatterji, Jagadish C. The Wisdom of the Vedas. LC 73-8889. Orig. Title: India's Outlook on Life. 100p. 1973. Repr. of 1931 ed. 3.95 o.p. (ISBN 0-8356-0214-1). Theos Pub Hse.

Chatterji, Suniti K. The Origin & Development of the Bengali Language, 3 vols. 1971. Set. text ed. 47.50x (ISBN 0-685-85182-6); Vol. 1. text ed. (ISBN 0-04-491007-X); Vol. 2. text ed. (ISBN 0-04-491008-8); Vol. 3. text ed. (ISBN 0-04-491009-6). Allen Unwin.

Chatterton, E. Keble. Whalers & Whaling: The Story of the Whaling Ships up to the Present Day. LC 79-178626. (Illus.). 248p. 1975. Repr. of 1925 ed. 18.00 (ISBN 0-8103-4028-3). Gale.

Chatterton, M., jt. ed. see Neville, A. M.

Chatterton, Mark. The Saab: The Innovator. (Illus.). 192p. 1980. 25.00 (ISBN 0-7153-7945-3). David & Charles.

Chatterton, Pauline. Scandinavian Knitting Designs. LC 76-27879. (Encore Edition). (Illus.). 1977. 5.95 (ISBN 0-684-16538-4, ScribT). Scribner.

Chatterton, Wayne. Alexander Woollcott. (United States Authors Ser.: No. 305). 1978. lib. bdg. 12.50 (ISBN 0-8057-7210-3). Twayne.

Chatterton, Wayne, jt. auth. see Heasley Cox, Martha.

Chatto, William A. Treatise on Wood Engraving, Historical & Practical. LC 69-16477. (Illus.). 1969. Repr. of 1861 ed. 32.00 (ISBN 0-8103-3531-X). Gale.

Chatton, Milton J., jt. ed. see Krupp, Marcus A.

Chattopadhyaya, Alalca, tr. see Chattopadhyaya, Debiprasad.

Chattopadhyaya, D., ed. see Stcherbatsky, T.

Chattopadhyaya, D. P., ed. Studies in the History of Indian Philosophy, 3 vols. 1981. text ed. 37.50x (ISBN 0-391-02084-6). Humanities.

Chattopadhyaya, Debiprasad. Science & Society in Ancient India. (Philosophical Currents Ser.: No. 22). 1978. text ed. 34.25x (ISBN 90-6032-098-0). Humanities.

Chattopadhyaya, Debiprasad, ed. Taranath's History of Buddhism in India. Lama Chimpa, Alaka Chattopadhyaya & Chattopadhyaya, Alalca, trs. from Tibetan. 500p. 1980. Repr. of 1608 ed. text ed. write for info. (ISBN 0-391-02176-1). Humanities.

Chattopadhyaya, Saratchandra. Chandranath. 101p. 1969. pap. 2.50 (ISBN 0-88253-027-5). Ind-US Inc.

--Shrikant. 168p. 1969. pap. 2.50 (ISBN 0-88253-028-3). Ind-US Inc.

Chattopadhyaya, Sudhakar. Reflections on the Tantras. 1978. 7.50 (ISBN 0-89684-028-X, Pub. by Motilal Banarsidass India). Orient Bk Dist.

Chatwin, Bruce. In Patagonia. LC 78-885. 1978. 8.95 (ISBN 0-671-40045-2); pap. 4.95 (ISBN 0-671-44857-9). Summit Bks.

--The Viceroy of Ouidah. LC 80-17896. 155p. 1980. 11.95 (ISBN 0-671-41253-1). Summit Bks.

Chau, Ta N. Demographic Aspects of Educational Planning. (Fundamentals of Educational Planning Ser., No. 9). (Illus., Orig.). 1969. pap. 6.00 (ISBN 92-803-1028-3, U153, UNESCO). Unipub.

Chaucer, Geoffrey. Canon's Yeoman's Tale. Hussey, M., et al, eds. (Selected Tales from Chaucer). 1965. text ed. 4.95x (ISBN 0-521-04623-8). Cambridge U Pr.

--The Canterbury Tales. pap. 2.50. Bantam.

--The Canterbury Tales. Halverson, John, ed. LC 79-153880. (Library of Literature Ser: No. 27). 1971. pap. text ed. 8.95 (ISBN 0-672-61006-X). Bobbs.

--Canterbury Tales. (Illus.). (gr. 7 up). 10.95 (ISBN 0-385-00028-6). Doubleday.

--Canterbury Tales. Skeat, Walter W., ed. (World's Classics Ser.). 14.95 (ISBN 0-19-250076-7). Oxford U Pr.

--The Canterbury Tales. LC 80-22141. (Raintree Short Classics). (Illus.). 48p. (gr. 4-8). 1981. PLB 9.95 (ISBN 0-8172-1666-9). Raintree Pubs.

--The Canterbury Tales: A Facsimile & Transcription of the Hengwrt Manuscript with Variants from the Ellesmere Manuscript. Ruggiers, Paul G., ed. LC 77-18611. (Illus.). 1979. 100.00x (ISBN 0-8061-1416-9). U of Okla Pr.

--Canterbury Tales (Selected) An Interlinear Translation. Hopper, Vincent F., ed. LC 70-99791. 1970. 6.00 (ISBN 0-8120-5015-0); pap. text ed. 4.95 (ISBN 0-8120-0039-0). Barron.

--Chanticleer & the Fox. LC 58-10449. (Illus.). (gr. k-3). 1958. 6.95 (ISBN 0-690-18561-8, TYC-J); PLB 7.89 (ISBN 0-690-18562-6). T Y Crowell.

--Chaucer's World: A Pictorial Companion. Hussey, M., ed. (Selected Tales from Chaucer). (Orig.). 1967. 23.95 (ISBN 0-521-05354-4); pap. 7.95x (ISBN 0-521-09430-5, 430). Cambridge U Pr.

--A Choice of Chaucer's Verse. Coghill, Nevill, ed. 1972. pap. 4.95 (ISBN 0-571-09691-3, Pub. by Faber & Faber). Merrimack Bk Serv.

--Clerk's Prologue & Tale. Winny, J., ed. (Selected Tales from Chaucer). 1966. text ed. 4.95x (ISBN 0-521-04632-7). Cambridge U Pr.

--Complete Works. Skeat, Walter W., ed. (Oxford Standard Authors). 1933. 27.50x (ISBN 0-19-254119-6). Oxford U Pr.

--Franklin's Prologue & Tale. Spearing, A. C., ed. (Selected Tales from Chaucer). text ed. 4.95x (ISBN 0-521-04624-6). Cambridge U Pr.

--General Prologue to the Canterbury Tales. Winny, J., ed. (Selected Tales from Chaucer). 1965. text ed. 5.75x (ISBN 0-521-04629-7). Cambridge U Pr.

--Geoffrey Chaucer: A Selection of His Works. Kee, Kenneth, ed. LC 66-13408. (College Classics in English Ser.). 1966. pap. 5.95 (ISBN 0-672-63017-6). Odyssey Pr.

--Knight's Tale. Spearing, A. C., ed. (Selected Tales from Chaucer). 1966. text ed. 7.95x (ISBN 0-521-04633-5). Cambridge U Pr.

--Literary Context of Chaucer's Fabliaux: Texts & Translations. Benson, Larry & Andersson, Theodore, eds. LC 70-138663. 1971. 13.85 o.p. (ISBN 0-672-51120-7); pap. 8.50 (ISBN 0-672-61008-6, LL28). Bobbs.

--Merchant's Prologue & Tale. Hussey, M., ed. (Selected Tales from Chaucer). 1966. text ed. 4.95x (ISBN 0-521-04631-9). Cambridge U Pr.

--Miller's Prologue & Tale. Winny, J., ed. LC 76-132283. (Selected Tales from Chaucer). 1970. text ed. 4.95x (ISBN 0-521-08033-9). Cambridge U Pr.

--Nun's Priest's Prologue & Tale. Hussey, M., ed. (Selected Tales from Chaucer). 1966. text ed. 4.95x (ISBN 0-521-04626-2). Cambridge U Pr.

--Pardoner's Prologue & Tale. Spearing, A. C., ed. (Selected Tales from Chaucer). 1966. text ed. 4.95x (ISBN 0-521-04627-0). Cambridge U Pr.

--The Tales of Canterbury: Complete. Pratt, Robert A., ed. LC 72-9380. (Illus.). 587p. 1974. text ed. 17.50 (ISBN 0-395-14052-8). HM.

--Troilus & Criseyde. Coghill, Nevill, tr. (Classics Ser). 1971. pap. 2.95 (ISBN 0-14-044239-1). Penguin.

--Troilus & Criseyde (Abridged) Brewer, D. S. & Brewer, L. E., eds. 1977. pap. 7.25 (ISBN 0-7100-8719-5). Routledge & Kegan.

--Wife of Bath's Prologue & Tale. Winny, J., ed. (Selected Tales from Chaucer). 1966. text ed. 5.75x (ISBN 0-521-04630-0). Cambridge U Pr.

--Works of Geoffrey Chaucer. 2nd ed. Robinson, F. N., ed. (New Cambridge Editions). xliv, 1002p. 1957. text ed. 15.50 (ISBN 0-395-05568-7). HM.

Chaudhuri, Asim. Private Economic Power in India: A Study in Genesis & Concentration. LC 76-900858. 1976. 10.00x (ISBN 0-88386-717-6). South Asia Bks.

Chaudhuri, Haridas. Integral Philosophy of Sri Aurobindo. Spiegelberg, Frederic, ed. 350p. 1980. 6.00 (ISBN 0-89744-992-4, Pub. by Cultural Integration). Auromere.

--Philosophy of Integralism. 184p. (Orig.). pap. 3.50 (ISBN 0-686-64766-1, Pub. by Sri). Auromere.

--Philosophy of Meditation. 2nd ed. 88p. 1974. pap. 3.50 (ISBN 0-89744-994-0, Pub. by Cultural Integration). Auromere.

--Sri Aurobindo: Prophet of Life Divine. 270p. (Orig.). 1973. pap. 3.50 (ISBN 0-89744-994-0, Pub. by Cultural Integration). Auromere.

Chaudhuri, Haridas & Frank, Leonard R. Mahatma Gandhi. (Orig.). 1969. pap. 1.00 (ISBN 0-89744-993-2, Pub. by Cultural Integration). Auromere.

Chaudhuri, Nirad C. The Autobiography of an Unknown Indian. 1968. 18.00x (ISBN 0-520-00224-5). U of Cal Pr.

--Hinduism: A Religion to Live by. 352p. 1980. pap. 4.95 (ISBN 0-19-520221-X, GB 612). Oxford U Pr.

Chaudhuri, Sukanta. The Glass King & Other Poems. (Writers Workshop Redbird Book Ser.). 32p. 1975. 6.00 (ISBN 0-88253-548-X); pap. text ed. 3.00 (ISBN 0-88253-547-1). Ind-US Inc.

--Poems. 8.00 (ISBN 0-89253-500-8); flexible cloth 4.00 (ISBN 0-89253-501-6). Ind-US Inc.

Chauffurin, L. Petit Dictionnaire bilingue Larousse, francais-anglais et English-French. (Adonis). (Fr. & Eng.). plastic bdg. 5.95 (ISBN 0-685-14032-6, 3768). Larousse.

Chauhan, S. S. Advanced Educational Psychology. 1978. 18.95 (ISBN 0-7069-0572-5, Pub. by Vikas India). Advent Bk.

--Principles & Techniques of Guidance. 300p. Date not set. text ed. 17.50 (ISBN 0-7069-1183-0, Pub. by Vikas India). Advent Bk.

Chauliaguet, Charles, et al. Solar Energy in Buildings. LC 78-27031. 1979. 30.50 (ISBN 0-471-27570-0, Pub. by Wiley-Interscience). Wiley.

Chauncey, Charles F. County Funding of the Arts in New York State. 24p. 1975. pap. 2.00x (ISBN 0-89062-033-4, Pub. by NYSCA). Pub Ctr Cult Res.

Chaussy, Charles, et al. Beruehrungsfreie Nierensteinzertruemmerung Durch Extrakorporal Erzeugte, Fokussierte Stosswellen. (Beitraege Zur Urology Ser.: Vol. 2). vi, 94p. 1980. pap. 36.00 (ISBN 3-8055-1901-X). S Karger.

Chavarria, Jesus. Jose Carlos Mariategui & the Rise of Modern Peru, 1890-1930. LC 78-21426. 1979. 14.95 (ISBN 0-8263-0507-5). U of NM Pr.

Chavchavadze, Paul, tr. see Alliluyeva, Svetlana.

Chaves, Jonathan. Mei Yao-Ch'en & the Development of Early Sung Poetry. (Studies in Oriental Culture Ser.). 240p. 1976. 15.00x (ISBN 0-231-03965-4). Columbia U Pr.

Chavez, Angelico. My Penitente Land. LC 79-63671. 1979. Repr. of 1974 ed. 27.50 (ISBN 0-88307-568-7); pap. 13.50 o.p. (ISBN 0-88307-569-5). Gannon.

--When the Santos Talked. LC 76-53086. 1977. Repr. of 1957 ed. 15.00 o.p. (ISBN 0-88307-528-8). Gannon.

Chavez, Carlos. Toward a New Music: Music & Electricity. Weinstock, Herbert, tr. from Span. LC 74-28308. (Illus.). 180p. 1975. Repr. of 1937 ed. lib. bdg. 19.50 (ISBN 0-306-70719-5). Da Capo.

Chavez, Moises. Enfoque Arqueologico del Mundo de la Biblia. LC 76-25325. 138p. (Orig., Span.). pap. 3.25 (ISBN 0-89922-076-2). Edit Caribe.

--Hebreo Biblico Texto Programado: Tomo 1. (Span.). Date not set. pap. price not set (ISBN 0-311-42068-0, Edit Mundo). Casa Bautista.

--Hermeneutica: El Arte de la Parafrasis Libre. 132p. (Orig., Span.). 1978. pap. 3.50 (ISBN 0-89922-142-4). Edit Caribe.

--La Ishah, la Mujer en la Biblia. LC 76-43123. 180p. (Orig., Span.). 1976. pap. 3.25 (ISBN 0-89922-078-9). Edit Caribe.

--Modelo de Oratoria. 144p. (Orig., Span.). 1979. pap. 3.50 (ISBN 0-89922-141-6). Edit Caribe.

--Proverbios: Reflexion de la Vida. 1976. pap. 2.75 (ISBN 0-311-46069-0, Edit Mundo). Casa Bautista.

Chavignerie, Emile B. De La see De La Chavignerie, Emile B. & Auvray, Louis.

Chavin, Walter. Responses of Fish to Environmental Changes. (Illus.). 472p. 1973. text ed. 36.75 (ISBN 0-398-02743-9). C C Thomas.

Chawla, Sudershan & SarDesai, D. R., eds. New Patterns of Defense & Development in Asia. LC 79-22977. 272p. 1980. 23.95 (ISBN 0-03-052416-4); pap. 9.95 (ISBN 0-03-052411-3). Praeger.

Chawla, Sudershan, et al, eds. Southeast Asia Under the New Balance of Power. LC 73-19441. (Special Studies). 225p. 1974. 19.95 o.p. (ISBN 0-275-28826-9); student ed. 8.95 o.p. (ISBN 0-275-88850-9). Praeger.

Chay, John. The Problems & Prospects of American East Asian Relations. LC 76-27694. (Special Studies on China & East Asia). 1977. lib. bdg. 24.50x (ISBN 0-89158-113-8). Westview.

Chayen, J. The Cytochemical Bioassay of Polypeptide Hormones. (Monographs on Endocrinology: Vol. 17). (Illus.). 230p. 1980. 46.00 (ISBN 0-387-10040-7). Springer-Verlag.

Chayet, Neil L. Legal Implications of Emergency Care. 1981. pap. 12.50 (ISBN 0-686-69605-0). ACC.

Chayken, Howard, jt. auth. see Delaney, Samuel R.

Chayne, G. J. Classified Spanish Vocabulary. LC 78-670001. 1964. text ed. 12.95x (ISBN 0-245-55575-7). Intl Ideas.

Chazal, Malcolm De see De Chazal, Malcolm.

Chazan, Maurice, ed. International Research in Early Education. (General Ser.). (Illus.). 1978. pap. text ed. 22.00x (ISBN 0-85633-143-0, NFER). Humanities.

Chazan, Maurice, et al. Deprivation & School Progress, Vol. 1. (Studies in Infant School Children). 1976. 65.00x o.p. (ISBN 0-631-17050-2, Pub. by Basil Blackwell England). Biblio Dist.

Cheadle, John R. Basic Greek Vocabulary. 1939. text ed. 4.50 (ISBN 0-312-06790-9). St Martin.

Cheatham, K. Follis. Bring Home the Ghost. LC 80-7981. 325p. (gr. 7 up). 1980. 8.95 (ISBN 0-15-212485-3, HJ). HarBraceJ.

Cheatham, Lillian. The Shadowed Reunion. 1981. pap. 1.50 (ISBN 0-440-18247-6). Dell.

Cheatle, Wayne C. Loss & Discovery. 1981. 4.95 (ISBN 0-8062-1658-1). Carlton.

Chebyshev, P. L. Oevres: Collected Papers, 2 Vols. LC 61-17956. (Fr). 69.50 set (ISBN 0-8284-0157-8). Chelsea Pub.

Checkland, Olive. Philanthropy in Victorian Scotland. (Illus.). 1980. text ed. 52.00x (ISBN 0-85976-041-3). Humanities.

Checkland, P. B. Systems Thinking, Systems Practice. 320p. 1981. 31.95 (ISBN 0-471-27911-0, Pub. by Wiley-Interscience). Wiley.

Checkland, S. G. Gladstones: A Family Biography. LC 72-134611. 1971. 44.50 (ISBN 0-521-07966-7). Cambridge U Pr.

Chedd, Graham. Sound: From Communications to Noise Pollution. LC 78-111152. 5.95 o.p. (ISBN 0-385-05992-2). Doubleday.

Chedid, Andree. Contemporary French Women Poets: A Bilingual Critical Anthology. Hermey, Carl W., ed. LC 76-3065. (Perivale Translation Series No. 4). 207p. 1977. pap. 6.95 (ISBN 0-912288-08-6). Perivale Pr.

Chedid, L., ed. Immunostimulation. (Illus.). 236p. 1981. 22.50 (ISBN 0-387-10354-6). Springer-Verlag.

Chee, Anthony N. Anatomy & Physiology - a Dynamic Approach. (Illus.). 287p. (Orig.). 1979. pap. text ed. 13.95x (ISBN 0-89641-020-X). American Pr.

Cheek, Earl H., Jr., jt. auth. see Cheek, Martha C.

Cheek, Logan. Zero-Base Budgeting Comes of Age. (Illus.). 1979. pap. 8.95 (ISBN 0-8144-7516-7). Am Mgmt.

Cheek, Logan M. Zero-Base Budgeting Comes of Age. LC 77-4362. (Illus.). 1977. 23.95 (ISBN 0-8144-5442-9). Am Mgmt.

Cheek, Logan M., jt. auth. see Austin, L. Allan.

Cheek, Martha C. & Cheek, Earl H., Jr. Diagnostic & Prescriptive Reading Instruction: A Guide for Classroom Teachers. 1980. text ed. 13.95x (ISBN 0-697-06019-5); inst. manual avail. (ISBN 0-697-06028-4). Wm C Brown.

Cheek, William F. Black Resistance Before the Civil War. 1970. pap. text ed. 4.95x (ISBN 0-02-473550-7, 47355). Macmillan.

Cheesman, John, et al. The Grace of God in the Gospel. 1976. pap. 2.45 (ISBN 0-85151-153-8). Banner of Truth.

Cheesman, Paul R. The World of the Book of Mormon. LC 77-18772. (Illus.). 1978. pap. text ed. 5.95 o.p. (ISBN 0-87747-649-7). Deseret Bk.

Cheetham, J. H. & Piper, John. Whiltshire: A Shell Guide. (Illus.). 1968. 12.95 (ISBN 0-571-04633-9, Pub. by Faber & Faber). Merrimack Bk Serv.

Cheetham, Juliet. Social Work with Immigrants. (Library of Social Work). 242p. 1972. 12.95x (ISBN 0-7100-7365-8); pap. 7.95 (ISBN 0-7100-7366-6). Routledge & Kegan.

--Unwanted Pregnancy & Counselling. 1978. pap. 8.95 (ISBN 0-7100-0044-8). Routledge & Kegan.

Cheetham, Nicholas. Mediaeval Greece. LC 80-13559. 352p. 1981. 27.50x (ISBN 0-300-02421-5). Yale U Pr.

Cheever, John. Falconer. 1978. pap. 2.75 (ISBN 0-345-28589-1). Ballantine.

Cheever, Mary. The Need for Chocolate: And Other Poems. LC 80-5390. 96p. 1980. 12.50 (ISBN 0-8128-2728-7). Stein & Day.

Cheever, Susan. Looking for Work. 256p. 1981. pap. 2.50 (ISBN 0-449-24389-3, Crest). Fawcett.

Chef Alexander. The Best of the Italian & Wall Street High Class Cuisine, 3 vols. Incl. Vol. 1. Soups, Fish, Meat (ISBN 0-89266-165-8); Vol. 2. Chicken, Eggs, Pasta & Rice, Vegetables (ISBN 0-89266-166-6); Vol. 3. Salads, Desserts, Coffees & Wines (ISBN 0-89266-167-4). (An Essential Knowledge Library Bk.). (Illus.). 1979. plastic spiral bdg. 4.00 ea. o.p. Am Classical Coll Pr.

Cheffers, John T. & Evual, Thomas. Introduction to Physical Education: Concepts of Human Movement. (Illus.). 1978. text ed. 16.50 (ISBN 0-13-493031-2). P-H.

Cheigh, Jhoong S., et al, eds. Manual of Clinical Nephrology of the Rogosin Kidney Center. (Developments in Nephrology: No. 1). (Illus.). 470p. 1981. PLB 65.00 (ISBN 90-247-2397-3, Pub. by Martinus Nijhoff). Kluwer Boston.

Cheilik, Michael. Ancient History: From Its Beginnings to the Fall of Rome. LC 79-76467. (Orig.). 1969. pap. 3.95 (ISBN 0-06-460001-7, CO 1, COS). Har-Row.

--Western Civilization Vol. II, Since 1715. LC 80-66627. (Cliffs Rapid Review Ser.). 112p. (Orig.). (gr. 10-12). 1980. pap. text ed. 3.95 (ISBN 0-8220-1742-3). Cliffs.

Chein, Orin, jt. auth. see Averbach, Bonnie.

Cheiro. Cheiro's Language of the Hand. LC 62-16458. (Illus.). 1968. pap. 1.95 (ISBN 0-668-01780-5). Arc Bks.

Che Kan Leong. Children with Specific Reading Disability. (Modern Approaches to the Diagnosis & Instruction of Mnulti-Handicapped Children Ser.). 160p. Date not set. text ed. price not set (Pub. by Swets Pub Serv Holland). Swets North Am.

Chekenian, Jane & Meyer, Monica. Shellfish Cookery. (Illus.). 1971. 12.50 o.s.i. (ISBN 0-02-524610-0). Macmillan.

Chekhov, Anton. Anton Chekhov: Four Plays. Magarshack, David, tr. Incl. Seagull; Uncle Vanya; Three Sisters; Cherry Orchard. 256p. (Orig.). 1969. pap. 5.95 (ISBN 0-8090-0743-6, Mermaid). Hill & Wang.

--Anton Chekhov's Short Stories. Matlaw, Ralph E., ed. Garnett, Constance, et al, trs. (Critical Edition). 1979. text ed. 24.95 (ISBN 0-393-04528-5); pap. text ed. 5.95x (ISBN 0-393-09002-7). Norton.

--Cherry Orchard. Gielgud, John, ed. (Orig.). 1963. pap. 3.25x (ISBN 0-87830-510-6, 10). Theatre Arts.

--In the Ravine & Other Stories. Wilks, Ronald, tr. Date not set. pap. 4.95 (ISBN 0-14-044336-3). Penguin. Postponed.

--The Oxford Chekhov. Hingley, Ronald, ed. & tr. Incl. Vol. 1. Short Plays. 222p. 1968. 27.50x (ISBN 0-19-211349-6); Vol. 2. Platonov, Ivanov, the Seagull. 376p. 1967. 37.50x (ISBN 0-19-211347-X); Vol. 5. Stories, 1889-1891. 270p. 1970. 32.00x (ISBN 0-19-211353-4); Vol. 6. Stories, 1892-1893. 330p. 1971. 37.50x (ISBN 0-19-211363-1); Vol. 8. Stories, 1895-1897. 300p. 1965. 28.50x (ISBN 0-19-211340-2). Oxford U Pr.

--The Oxford Chekhov, Vol. 9: Stories 1898 - 1904. Hingley, Ronald, ed. 346p. 1975. 37.50x (ISBN 0-19-211383-6). Oxford U Pr.

--Short Plays. Hingley, Ronald, tr. 1969. pap. 2.95x o.p. (ISBN 0-19-281057-X, OPB). Oxford U Pr.

Chekhov, Anton see Caputi, Anthony.

Chekhov, Anton see Watson, E. Bradlee & Pressey, Benfield.

Chekhover, V., jt. auth. see Averbakh, Yuri.

Chekijian, Vartan S. The Strange Dreams. 109p. 1980. 5.95 (ISBN 0-533-03227-X). Vantage.

Chekki, Dan A., ed. Community Development: Theory & Method of Planned Change. LC 79-907884. xiv, 258p. 1980. text ed. 18.95x (ISBN 0-7069-0819-8, Pub. by Vikas India). Advent Bk.

--Participatory Democracy in Action: International Profiles of Community Development. xvi, 306p. 1980. text ed. 20.00x (ISBN 0-7069-0923-2, Pub. by Vikas India). Advent Bk.

Chelf, Carl P. Congress in the American System. LC 77-1084. 1978. text ed. 15.95 (ISBN 0-88229-210-2); pap. 8.95 (ISBN 0-88229-517-9). Nelson-Hall.

--Public Policymaking in America: Difficult Choices, Limited Solutions. 1981. text ed. write for info. (ISBN 0-8302-7376-X). Goodyear.

Chelius, Carl R. & Frentz, Henry J. A Basic Meteorology Exercise Manual. rev. ed. (Illus.). 1978. 8.50 (ISBN 0-8403-1623-2). Kendall-Hunt.

Chell, G. G., ed. Developments in Fracture Mechanics-1. (Illus.). 1979. 57.00x (ISBN 0-85334-858-8, Pub. by Applied Science). Burgess-Intl Ideas.

Chellas, Brian F. Modal Logic. LC 76-47197. 1980. 50.50 (ISBN 0-521-22476-4); pap. 15.95x (ISBN 0-521-29515-7). Cambridge U Pr.

Chelminsk, Rudy. Paris. (The Great Cities Ser.). (Illus.). (gr. 6 up). 1977. 14.94 (ISBN 0-8094-2279-4, Pub. by Time-Life). Silver.

Chelminski, Rudolph. Paris. (Great Cities Ser.). 14.95 (ISBN 0-8094-2278-6). Time-Life.

Chemers, Martin M., jt. auth. see Fiedler, Fred E.

Chemical Engineering, compiled By. Industrial Waste Water & Solid Waste Engineering. LC 80-12608. 376p. 1980. pap. 23.50 (ISBN 0-07-010694-0, Chem Eng). McGraw.

Chemical Engineering Magazine. Fluid Movers: Pumps, Compressors, Fans & Blowers. (Chemical Engineering Bks.). (Illus.). 384p. 1980. 24.95 (ISBN 0-07-010769-6, P&RB). McGraw.

--Pneumatic Conveying of Bulk Materials. Kraus, Milton N., ed. (Chemical Engineering Bks). 352p. 1980. 24.50 (ISBN 0-07-010724-6, P&RB). McGraw.

--Process Heat Exchange. (Chemical Engineering Book Ser.). (Illus.). 624p. 1980. 34.50 (ISBN 0-07-010742-4, P&RB). McGraw.

--Process Technology & Flowsheets. LC 79-12117. (Chemical Engineering Bks). 384p. 1980. 24.95 (ISBN 0-07-010741-6, P&RB). McGraw.

--Safe & Efficient Plant Operation & Maintenance. LC 80-14762. (Chemical Engineering Ser.). 400p. 1980. 29.50 (ISBN 0-07-010707-6); pap. 24.50. McGraw.

--Selecting Materials for Process Equipment. (Chemical Engineering Ser.). 280p. 1980. 24.50 (ISBN 0-07-010692-4). McGraw.

--Separation Techniques I: Liquid-Liquid Systems. (Chemical Engineering Book Ser.). 384p. 1980. 29.50 (ISBN 0-07-010711-4). McGraw.

--Separation Techniques II: Gas-Liquid-Solid Systems. (Chemical Engineering Book Ser.). 400p. 1980. 29.50 (ISBN 0-07-010717-3). McGraw.

Chemical Engineering Magazine, jt. auth. see Matley, Jay.

Chemical Engineering Magazine, compiled By. Industrial Air Pollution Engineering. LC 80-12609. 304p. 1980. pap. 24.50 (ISBN 0-07-606664-9, Chem Eng). McGraw.

Chemical Engineering Magazine, jt. ed. see Deutsch, David J.

Chemsak, J. A. Taxonomy & Bionomics of the Genus Tetraopes (Cerambycidae Coleoptera). (U. C. Publ. in Entomology: Vol. 30.1). 1963. pap. 5.00x (ISBN 0-520-09097-7). U of Cal Pr.

Chen, et al. The Cuisine of China. 1981. 15.95 (ISBN 0-8120-5361-3). Barron.

Chen, C. H., ed. Pattern Recognition & Signal Processing. (NATO Advanced Study Institute Ser.). 666p. 1978. 46.00x (ISBN 90-286-0978-4). Sijthoff & Noordhoff.

Chen, C. J. Vertical Turbulent Buoyant Jets: A Review of Experimental Data. (Heat & Mass Transfer: Vol. 4). (Illus.). 94p. 1979. 28.00 (ISBN 0-08-024772-5). Pergamon.

Chen, Ching-Chih. Biomedical Scientific & Technical Book Reviewing. LC 76-20480. 1976. 10.00 (ISBN 0-8108-0939-7). Scarecrow.

--Sourcebook on Health Sciences Librarianship. LC 76-30263. 1977. 15.50 (ISBN 0-8108-1005-0). Scarecrow.

Chen, Jack. The Chinese of America. LC 80-7749. (Illus.). 288p. 1981. 15.95 (ISBN 0-06-250140-2, HarpR). Har-Row.

--Inside the Cultural Revolution. 512p. 1975. 15.95 o.s.i. (ISBN 0-02-524630-5). Macmillan.

--The Sinkiang Story. LC 77-22938. (Illus.). 1977. 17.95 o.s.i. (ISBN 0-02-524640-2). Macmillan.

--A Year in Upper Felicity. (Illus.). 384p. 1973. 12.95 (ISBN 0-02-524650-X). Macmillan.

Chen, James C., jt. auth. see Meade, George P.

Ch'en, Jerome. China & the West: Society & Culture 1815-1937. LC 79-2704. (Illus.). 488p. 1980. 22.50x (ISBN 0-253-12032-2). Ind U Pr.

--Mao & the Chinese Revolution. (Illus.). 1967. pap. 6.95 (ISBN 0-19-500270-9, GB). Oxford U Pr.

Chen, Jerome. State Economic Policies of the Ch'ing Government: 1840-1895. LC 78-24797. (The Modern Chinese Economy Ser.: Vol. 2). 250p. 1980. lib. bdg. 27.50 (ISBN 0-8240-4251-4). Garland Pub.

Chen, Jo-hsi. Execution of Mayor Yin & Other Stories from the Great Proletarian Cultural Revolution. Ing, Nancy & Goldblatt, Howard, trs. LC 78-1956. 248p. 1978. 10.95 (ISBN 0-253-12475-1); pap. 4.95 (ISBN 0-253-20231-0). Ind U Pr.

Chen, Joyce. Joyce Chen Cook Book. (Illus.). 1963. 13.95 o.s.i. (ISBN 0-397-00285-8); pap. 6.95 o.s.i. (ISBN 0-397-01278-0). Lippincott.

Ch'en, Kenneth K. Buddhism: The Light of Asia. LC 67-30496. 1968. 7.95 (ISBN 0-8120-6012-1); pap. text ed. 3.75 (ISBN 0-8120-0272-5). Barron.

Chen, L. T., ed. see Sun Yat-sen.

Ch'En, Li-Li. Master Tung's Western Chamber Romance: A Chinese Chantefable. LC 75-12469. (Studies in Chinese History, Literature, & Institutions Ser.). 268p. 1976. 42.50 (ISBN 0-521-20871-8). Cambridge U Pr.

Chen, P. S., jt. auth. see Chen, T. S.

Chen, Philip S. Chemistry: Inorganic, Organic & Biological. (Orig.). 1968. pap. 3.95 o.p. (ISBN 0-06-460082-3, 82, COS). Har-Row.

--Chemistry: Inorganic, Organic & Biological. 2nd ed. (College Outline Ser.). 288p. 1980. pap. text ed. 4.95 (ISBN 0-06-460182-X, CO 182, COS). Har-Row.

--The Joy of Being a Vegetarian. LC 76-44049. (Dimension Ser.). 1977. pap. 5.95 (ISBN 0-8163-0302-9, 10484-4). Pacific Pr Pub Assn.

Chen, Reuven & Kirsh, D. Y. The Analysis of Thermally Stimulated Processes. Date not set. 60.00 (ISBN 0-08-022930-1). Pergamon.

Chen, Ronald. Foreign Medical Graduates in Psychiatry: Issues & Problems. LC 79-17189. 448p. 1980. 22.95x (ISBN 0-87705-485-1). Human Sci Pr.

Chen, Shu-Jen, jt. auth. see Sawatzky, Jasper J.

Chen, T. P. Aquaculture Practices in Taiwan. (Illus.). 176p. 1976. 13.75 (ISBN 0-85238-080-1, FN). Unipub.

Chen, T. S. & Chen, P. S. Essential Hepatology. 1977. 29.95 (ISBN 0-409-95005-X). Butterworths.

Chen, T. T., ed. Research in Protozoology, Vol. 4. 1972. 64.00 (ISBN 0-08-016437-4). Pergamon.

Chen, T. Y., jt. auth. see Large, George E.

Chen, Ta-Chuan, jt. auth. see Nichols, Paul L.

Chen, Tony, illus. Wild Animals. LC 80-53105. (Board Bks.). (Illus.). 14p. (ps). 1981. boards 2.95 (ISBN 0-394-84748-2). Random.

Chen, Virginia, compiled by. The Economic Conditions of East & Southeast Asia: A Bibliography of English-Language Material, 1965 to 1977. LC 78-57762. 840p. 1978. lib. bdg. 45.00 (ISBN 0-313-20565-5, CEC/). Greenwood.

Chen, W. F. & Ting, E. C., eds. Fracture in Concrete. LC 80-69656. 110p. 1980. pap. text ed. 12.00 (ISBN 0-87262-259-2). Am Soc Civil Eng.

Chen, Wayne. Year of the Robot. 150p. 1981. pap. 7.95 (ISBN 0-918398-50-9). Robotics Pr.

Chen, Y. K. Tai-Chi Ch'uan: Its Effects & Practical Applications. LC 80-19810. 184p. 1980. Repr. of 1979 ed. lib. bdg. 10.95x (ISBN 0-89370-643-4). Borgo Pr.

Chen, Yuan-Tsung. The Dragon's Village. 1981. pap. 4.95 (ISBN 0-14-005811-7). Penguin.

Chen, Yung-Ping. Social Security in a Changing Society: An Introduction to Programs, Concepts, & Issues. new ed. LC 80-81652. (Illus.). 200p. (Orig.). 1980. pap. text ed. 6.00 (ISBN 0-937094-00-5). McCahan Found.

Chenard, Marcelle. Working Through Grief. (Thantology Service Ser.). 70p. 1980. 6.95 (ISBN 0-930194-05-5). Highly Specialized.

Ch'en Chieh-Hsien. Manchu Palace Memorials from the Palace Museum in Taipei. (Indiana University Uralic & Altaic Ser.: Vol. 139). 350p. write for info. Ind U Res Inst.

Chen Chih-Fan & Haas, J. Elements of Control Systems Analysis: Classical & Modern Approaches. 1967. ref. ed. 25.95 (ISBN 0-13-263509-7). P-H.

Chenevert, Melodie. Special Techniques in Assertive Training for Women in the Health Profession. LC 78-11635. (Illus.). 1978. pap. 9.50 (ISBN 0-8016-0971-2). Mosby.

Cheney, C. R. English Synodalia of the Thirteenth Century. 1968. Repr. of 1941 ed. 16.50x (ISBN 0-19-821396-4). Oxford U Pr.

--Medieval Texts & Studies. 382p. 1973. 33.00x (ISBN 0-19-822399-4). Oxford U Pr.

Cheney, Cora. The Case of the Iceland Dogs. LC 76-53635. (gr. 4 up). 1977. 5.95 (ISBN 0-396-07398-0). Dodd.

--Tales from a Taiwan Kitchen. LC 75-38364. (Illus.). (gr. 4 up). 1976. 5.95 (ISBN 0-396-07291-7). Dodd.

--Vermont: The State with the Storybook Past. 2nd ed. (Illus.). 256p. (gr. 3-6). 1981. pap. 9.95 (ISBN 0-8289-0440-5). Greene.

--Vermont: The State with the Storybook Past. LC 76-13804. (gr. 5-9). 1976. 9.95 o.p. (ISBN 0-8289-0283-6). Greene.

Cheney, David M. Son of Minos. LC 64-25838. (gr. 7). 8.50x (ISBN 0-8196-0142-X). Biblo.

Cheney, E. W., ed. Approximation Theory III. 1980. 59.00 (ISBN 0-12-171050-5). Acad Pr.

Cheney, Ednah D. Louisa May Alcott. LC 80-24025. (American Men & Women of Letters Ser.). 410p. 1981. pap. 5.95 (ISBN 0-87754-162-0). Chelsea Hse.

Cheney, Frances N. Fundamental Reference Sources. LC 73-151051. 1971. 12.00 o.p. (ISBN 0-8389-0081-X). ALA.

Cheney, Frances N. & Williams, Wiley J. Fundamental Reference Sources. 2nd ed. 300p. 1980. 12.50 (ISBN 0-8389-0308-8). ALA.

Cheney, Gay & Strader, Janet. Modern Dance. 2nd ed. 100p. 1975. pap. text ed. 6.50 (ISBN 0-205-04839-0, 624839X). Allyn.

Cheney, Lois A. God Is No Fool. (Orig.). pap. 1.50 (ISBN 0-89129-251-9). Jove Pubns.

Cheney, Margaret. The Coed Killer. LC 75-25196. 240p. 1976. 8.95 o.s.i. (ISBN 0-8027-0514-6). Walker & Co.

Cheney, Mary G. Roger, Bishop of Worcestor Eleven Sixty Four to Eleven Seventy Nine: An English Bishop of the Age of Becket. (Oxford Historical Monographs). (Illus.). 320p. 1980. 49.50 (ISBN 0-19-821879-6). Oxford U Pr.

Cheney, Ruth G., ed. Sharing the Vision: The Church Teaching Series Reader. 112p. (Orig.). 1980. pap. 3.95 (ISBN 0-8164-2044-0). Crossroad NY.

Cheney, Simeon P. The American Singing Book. (Earlier American Music Ser.). (Illus.). 1980. Repr. of 1879 ed. lib. bdg. 25.00 (ISBN 0-306-77322-8). Da Capo.

Cheney, Theodore. Camping by Backpack & Canoe. LC 69-19649. (Funk & W Bk.). 1970. 7.95 o.s.i. (ISBN 0-308-70404-5, 781340, TYC-T). T Y Crowell.

Cheney, Theodore A. Day of Fate. 288p. (Orig.). 1981. pap. 2.50 (ISBN 0-441-13908-6). Charter Bks.

Cheney, Ward & Kincaid, David. Numerical Analysis & Computing. LC 79-17230. 1980. text ed. 18.95 (ISBN 0-8185-0357-2). Brooks-Cole.

Cheng, Charles W. Altering Collective Bargaining: Citizen Participation in Educational Decision Making. LC 75-36415. (Special Studies). 192p. 1976. text ed. 22.95 (ISBN 0-275-56300-6). Praeger.

Cheng, D. G. Analysis of Linear Systems. 1959. 22.95 (ISBN 0-201-01020-8). A-W.

Cheng, F. T., tr. from Chinese. The Chinese Supreme Court Decisions: Relating to General Principles of Civil Law, Obligations & Commercial Law. 229p. 1979. Repr. of 1923 ed. 22.50 (ISBN 0-89093-065-1). U Pubns Amer.

Cheng, H. S. & Keer, L. M., eds. Solid Contact & Lubrication. (AMD: Vol. 39). 248p. 1980. 30.00 (G00172). ASME.

Cheng, H. S., jt. ed. see Rohde, S. M.

Cheng, J. Chester, tr. Documents of Dissent: Chinese Political Thought Since Mao. (Publication Ser.: No. 230). 120p. (Orig.). 1980. pap. 7.95 (ISBN 0-8179-7302-8). Hoover Inst Pr.

Cheng, Peter P. A Chronology of the People's Republic of China from October 1, 1949. LC 70-184667. (Quality Paperbacks Ser.: No. 250). 347p. (Orig.). 1972. pap. 4.95 (ISBN 0-8226-0250-4). Littlefield.

Cheng, Phillip C. Financial Management in the Shipping Industry. LC 79-15869. 1979. 27.50x (ISBN 0-87033-249-X, 249X). Cornell Maritime.

--Steamship Accounting. LC 70-80637. 1969. 11.00x (ISBN 0-87033-117-5). Cornell Maritime.

Cheng, T-K. Archaeological Studies in Szechwan. 1957. 47.50 (ISBN 0-521-04635-1). Cambridge U Pr.

Cheng, Thomas C. General Parasitology. 1973. text ed. 27.00 (ISBN 0-12-170750-4). Acad Pr.

Chenier, Blanche. Love in Exile. (A Regency Love Story Ser.). (Orig.). 1980. pap. 1.75 (ISBN 0-449-50046-2, Coventry). Fawcett.

--Summer Masquerade. (Regency Romance Ser.). 1978. pap. 1.75 o.p. (ISBN 0-449-23820-2, Crest). Fawcett.

Chennakesavan, S. & Rao, K. P., eds. Perception. 1966. 5.00x (ISBN 0-210-27196-5). Asia.

Chennakesavan, Sarasvati. Concepts of Mind in Indian Philosophy. 1980. 14.00x (ISBN 0-8364-0638-9). South Asia Bks.

Chennakesvan, Sarasvati. A Critical Study of Hinduism. 1980. 12.50x (ISBN 0-8364-0614-1). South Asia Bks.

Chennault, Stephen D. Re'lize Whut Ahm Talkin Bout? 7.95 (ISBN 0-912216-24-7). Green Hill.

Chenon, Emile. Etude sur l'Histoire des Alleux en France avec une Carte des Pays Allodiaux. LC 80-2036. 1981. Repr. of 1888 ed. 33.00 (ISBN 0-404-18557-6). AMS Pr.

Chenoweth, Don W. Soviet Civil Procedure: History & Analysis. LC 77-76427. (Transactions Ser.: Vol. 67, Pt. 7). 1977. pap. 6.00 o.p. (ISBN 0-87169-676-2). Am Philos.

Chenoweth, H., jt. auth. see Jensen, Alfred E.

Chenoweth, Patricia & Chenoweth, Thomas. How to Raise & Train a Lhasa Apso. (Orig.). pap. 2.00 (ISBN 0-87666-334-X, DS1097). TFH Pubns.

Chenoweth, Thomas, jt. auth. see Chenoweth, Patricia.

Chenu, M. D. Nature, Man & Society in the Twelfth Century: Essays on New Theological Perspectives in the Latin West. abr. ed. Taylor, Jerome, tr. LC 68-15574. 1968. 15.00x o.s.i. (ISBN 0-226-10254-8). U of Chicago Pr.

Chenuz, Frida J. Sealyham Terriers. Foyle, W. G., ed. (Foyle Handbks). (Illus.). 1973. 3.95 (ISBN 0-685-55795-2). Palmetto Pub.

Chen Wai-Kai. Theory & Design of Broadband Matching Networks. 360p. 1976. text ed. 64.00 (ISBN 0-08-019702-7); pap. text ed. 26.00 (ISBN 0-08-019918-6). Pergamon.

Cheny, David, jt. auth. see Sanders, Steven.

Chen-ying, Chow L., jt. auth. see Chien-chiu, Chow.

Cheong, W. E. Mandarins & Merchants: A China Agency of the Early Nineteenth Century. (Scandinavian Inst. of Asian Studies, Monographs: No. 26). (Illus.). 1977. pap. text ed. 13.00x (ISBN 0-7007-0094-3). Humanities.

Cheradame, H., jt. auth. see Gandini, A.

Cheraskin, E. & Ringsdorf, W. M., Jr. New Hope for Incurable Diseases. LC 72-3330. 192p. 1973. pap. 1.65 o.p. (ISBN 0-668-02671-5). Arc Bks.

Cherbonneau. French Arabic Dictionary, 2 vols. Set. 25.00x (ISBN 0-685-54027-8). Intl Bk Ctr.

Cherdyntsev, V. V. Uranium Two Thirty-Four. LC 73-184432. 1972. 23.95 o.p. (ISBN 0-470-15210-9). Halsted Pr.

Cheremisinoff. Process Level Instrumentation & Control. 200p. 1981. 29.75 (ISBN 0-8247-1212-9). Dekker.

Cheremisinoff, Nicholas P., et al. Chemical & Nonchemical Methods of Wastewater Disinfection. (Illus.). 170p. 1981. 29.50 (ISBN 0-250-40390-0). Ann Arbor Science.

Cheremisinoff, P., jt. ed. see Dickerson, W.

Cheremisinoff, Paul N. Bioconversion Sourcebook: (Abstracts) 1981. text ed. 29.95 (ISBN 0-250-40424-9). Ann Arbor Science.

Cheremisinoff, Paul N. & Cheremisinoff, Peter P. Industrial Noise Control Handbook. LC 76-46023. 1977. 37.50 (ISBN 0-250-40144-4). Ann Arbor Science.

Cheremisinoff, Paul N. & Perlis, Harlan J. Analytical Measurements & Instrumentation for Process & Pollution Control. LC 80-70319. 450p. 1981. text ed. 49.95 (ISBN 0-250-40405-2). Ann Arbor Science.

Cheremisinoff, Paul N., jt. auth. see Price, Elizabeth C.

Cheremisinoff, Paul N. & Perlis, Harlan J., eds. Automatic Process Control. 150p. 1981. text ed. write for info. (ISBN 0-250-40400-1). Ann Arbor Science.

Cheremisinoff, Peter P., jt. auth. see Cheremisinoff, Paul N.

Cheremisinopf, P. N. Gasohol Sourcebook: (Abstracts) 1981. text ed. 29.95 (ISBN 0-250-40425-7). Ann Arbor Science.

Cherepin, Valentin T. & Mallick, A. K. Experimental Techniques in Physical Metallurgy. 1967. 20.00x (ISBN 0-210-22503-3). Asia.

Cherescavich, Gertrude D. A Textbook for Nursing Assistants. 3rd ed. LC 72-12852. (Illus.). 1973. 15.95 (ISBN 0-8016-0957-7). Mosby.

Cheret, Jules & Broido, Lucy. Posters of Jules Cheret. (Illus.). 128p. (Orig.). 1980. pap. 8.95 (ISBN 0-486-24010-X). Dover.

Cherfas, Jeremy & Lewin, Roger, eds. Not Work Alone: A Cross-Cultural View of Activities Superfluous to Survival. LC 79-3805. (Illus.). 255p. 1980. 20.00x (ISBN 0-8039-1394-X). Sage.

Cherington, P. W. Airline Price Policy: A Study of Airline Passenger Fares. 1970. Repr. of 1958 ed. 40.00 (ISBN 0-08-018739-0). Pergamon.

Cherkin, Arthur, et al, eds. Physiology & Cell Biology of Aging. LC 77-94148. (Aging Ser.: Vol. 8). 1979. text ed. 26.00 (ISBN 0-89004-283-7). Raven.

Chermak, Gail D. Handbook of Audiological Rehabilitation. (Illus.). 480p. 1981. 43.75 (ISBN 0-398-04170-9). C C Thomas.

Chermayeff, Serge & Alexander, Christopher. Community & Privacy: Toward a New Architecture of Humanism. LC 63-10704. 1963. pap. 2.50 (ISBN 0-385-03476-8, A474, Anch). Doubleday.

Chernev, Irving. Capablanca's Best Chess Endings. (Illus.). 1978. 23.95 o.p. (ISBN 0-19-217553-X); pap. 8.95 o.p. (ISBN 0-19-217554-8). Oxford U Pr.

Cherniavsky, Michael, ed. Structure of Russian History. (Orig.). 1970. pap. text ed. 7.95x (ISBN 0-394-30112-9, RanC). Random.

Cherniavsky, Michael, et al, eds. Social Textures of Western Civilization: The Lower Depths, Vol. 1-2. (Orig.). 1972. pap. 8.95x o.p. (ISBN 0-685-03065-2). Vol. 1 (ISBN 0-471-00673-4). Vol. 2. 8.95x o.p. (ISBN 0-471-00674-2). Wiley.

Cherniavsky, O. F., jt. auth. see Gokhfeld, D. A.

Chernin, Dennis, et al. Ancient & Modern Medicine: A Preventive & Therapeutic Synthesis. 200p. (Orig.). Date not set. pap. price not set (ISBN 0-89389-068-5). Himalayan Intl.

Cherniss, Cary. Professional Burnout in the Human Services: Job Stress & the Loss of Commitment in the Novice. LC 80-12136. 318p. 1980. 22.95 (ISBN 0-03-056912-5). Praeger.

--Staff Burnout: Job Stress in the Human Services. LC 80-19408. (Sage Studies in Community Mental Health: Vol. 2). (Illus.). 200p. 1980. 20.00 (ISBN 0-8039-1338-9); pap. 9.95 (ISBN 0-8039-1339-7). Sage.

Chernoff, Goldie T. Clay-Dough, Play-Dough. LC 73-92449. (Illus.). 24p. (gr. k-3). 1974. 3.95 o.s.i. (ISBN 0-8027-6178-X). Walker & Co.

--Easy Costumes You Don't Have to Sew. LC 76-46428. (Illus.). 48p. (gr. 1-5). 1977. 6.95 (ISBN 0-590-07491-1, Four Winds). Schol Bk Serv.

--Puppet Party. LC 76-186171. 3.50 o.s.i. (ISBN 0-8027-6100-3). Walker & Co.

Chernoff, Herman & Moses, L. E. Elementary Decision Theory. LC 59-9337. (Illus.). 1959. 24.95 (ISBN 0-471-15213-7). Wiley.

Chernok, Norma B. Surgical Typists Handbook. 1972. spiral bdg. 6.00 o.p. (ISBN 0-87488-991-X). Med Exam.

Chernok, Norma B., ed. Radiology Typists Handbook. 150p. 1970. spiral bdg. 6.00 o.p. (ISBN 0-87488-981-2). Med Exam.

Chernov, A. A., ed. Growth of Crystals, Vol. 12. (Illus.). 400p. 1981. 47.50 (ISBN 0-306-18112-6, Consultants). Plenum Pub.

Chernov, Alexander, jt. auth. see Aksyonov, Andrei.

Cherns, Albert B., jt. ed. see Davis, Louis E.

Cherns, J. J. Official Publishing, an Overview: An International Survey & Review of the Role, Organization & Principles of Official Publishing. LC 78-41157. (Guides to Official Publication Ser.: Vol. 3). 1979. 60.00 (ISBN 0-08-023340-6). Pergamon.

Cherny, Robert W. Populism, Progressivism, & the Transformation of Nebraska Politics: 1885 - 1915. LC 80-11151. (Illus.). xviii, 227p. 1981. 17.50x (ISBN 0-8032-1407-3). U of Nebr Pr.

Chernyshevskii, Nikolai G. Selected Philosophical Essays. LC 79-2896. 610p. 1981. Repr. of 1953 ed. 37.50 (ISBN 0-8305-0064-2). Hyperion Conn.

Cheronis, Nicholas D., et al. Semimicro Qualitative Organic Analysis. 3rd ed. LC 80-461. (The Systematic Identification of Organic Compounds). 1072p. 1981. Repr. of 1965 ed. lib. bdg. write for info. (ISBN 0-89874-124-6). Krieger.

Cherrett, J. M. & Sager, G. R., eds. Origins of Pest, Parasite, Disease & Weed Problems. (British Ecological Society Symposia Ser.). 1977. 44.95 (ISBN 0-470-99121-6). Halsted Pr.

Cherrington, David J., jt. auth. see Jensen, Ronald.

Cherrington, Homer V. The Investor & the Securities Act. LC 78-173651. (FDR & the Era of the New Deal Ser.). 266p. 1973. Repr. of 1942 ed. lib. bdg. 27.50 (ISBN 0-306-70371-8). Da Capo.

Cherry, B. W. Polymer Surfaces. LC 80-40013. (Cambridge Solid State Science Ser.). (Illus.). 150p. Date not set. 37.50 (ISBN 0-521-23082-9); pap. 14.95 (ISBN 0-521-29792-3). Cambridge U Pr.

Cherry, C. God's New Israel: Religious Interpretations of American Destiny. 1971. pap. 11.95 (ISBN 0-13-357335-4). P-H.

--Theology of Jonathan Edwards: A Reappraisal. 7.50 (ISBN 0-8446-1849-7). Peter Smith.

Cherry, Caroline L. The Most Unvaluedst Purchase: Women in the Plays of Thomas Middleton. (Salzburg Studies in English Literature, Jacobean Drama Studies: No. 34). 114p. 1973. pap. text ed. 25.00x (ISBN 0-391-01342-4). Humanities.

Cherry, Clare. Think of Something Quiet. LC 80-82981. (Early Childhood Library). 1981. pap. 5.95 (ISBN 0-8224-6949-9). Pitman Learning.

Cherry, Clare, et al. Nursery School & Day Care Center Management Guide. rev ed. 1978. looseleaf bdg. 18.50 (ISBN 0-8224-4791-6). Pitman Learning.

Cherry, Colin. World Communications: Threat or Promise - A Socio-Technical Approach. rev. ed. LC 78-3761. 1978. 30.25 (ISBN 0-471-99616-5); pap. 13.00 (ISBN 0-471-99660-2, Pub. by Wiley-Interscience). Wiley.

Cherry, Conrad. Nature & Religious Imagination: From Edwards to Bushnell. LC 79-7374. 256p. 1980. 12.95 (ISBN 0-8006-0550-0, 1-550). Fortress.

Cherry, Conrad, ed. see Cohn, Robert L.

Cherry, Conrad, ed. see Wyllie, Robert W.

Cherry, David. Preparing Artwork for Reproduction. 1976. 24.00 (ISBN 0-7134-3097-4, Pub. by Batsford England). David & Charles.

Cherry, Eloise H. The Complete Chesapeake Bay Retriever. LC 80-25037. (Illus.). 288p. 1981. 14.95 (ISBN 0-87605-074-7). Howell Bk.

--Complete Chesapeake Bay Retriever. LC 80-25037. 1981. write for info. (ISBN 0-87605-074-7). Howell Bk.

Cherry, G. E. The Evolution of British Town Planning. LC 74-470. (Illus.). 275p. 1974. 24.95 (ISBN 0-470-15350-4). Halsted Pr.

Cherry, G. E., jt. auth. see Burton, Thomas L.

Cherry, George. ADA Programming Structures: With an Introduction to Structured Concurrent Programming. 400p. 1981. text ed. 15.95 (ISBN 0-8359-0151-3). Reston.

Cherry, Gordon E., ed. Shaping an Urban World: Planning in the Twentieth Century. LC 80-17276. 1980. 27.50 (ISBN 0-312-71618-4). St Martin.

Cherry, Joe H. Molecular Biology of Plants. 224p. 1973. text ed. 20.00x (ISBN 0-231-03642-6). Columbia U Pr.

Cherry, John P., ed. Protein Functionality in Foods. (ACS Symposium Ser.: No. 147). 1981. price not set (ISBN 0-8412-0605-8). Am Chemical.

Cherry, Mike. Steel Beams & Iron Men. LC 80-66246. (Illus.). 96p. (gr. 5 up). 1980. 9.95 (ISBN 0-590-07591-8, Four Winds). Schol Bk Serv.

--Train Whistle Blues. LC 77-11229. 1978. 7.95 o.p. (ISBN 0-385-11374-9). Doubleday.

Cherry, Raymond. General Plastics: Projects & Procedures. rev. ed. (Illus.). (gr. 10-12). 1967. text ed. 14.64 (ISBN 0-87345-162-7). McKnight.

--Leathercrafting: Procedures & Projects. LC 79-83885. (Illus.). 1979. pap. 5.00 (ISBN 0-87345-153-8, B81925). McKnight.

Cherry, Richard, et al. The Essay: Structure & Purpose. 1975. pap. text ed. 9.95 (ISBN 0-395-18610-2). HM.

Cherry, Richard L., et al, eds. A Return to Vision. 2nd ed. Conley, Robert J. & Hirsch, Bernard A. 432p. 1975. pap. text ed. 9.95 (ISBN 0-395-17836-3); instructors' manual 1.00x (ISBN 0-395-17869-X). HM.

Cherry, Robert D. Macroeconomics. LC 79-3130. (Economics Ser.). 1980. text ed. 16.95 (ISBN 0-201-00911-0). A-W.

Cherry, Sheldon H. The Menopause Myth. (Orig.). 1976. pap. 1.95 o.p. (ISBN 0-685-57525-X, 0-25355-8-150). Ballantine.

Cherryh, C. J. Downbelow Station. (Science Fiction Ser.). 1981. pap. 2.75 (ISBN 0-87997-594-6, UE1594). Daw Bks.

Cherryl, C. J. Sunfall. (Science Fiction Ser.). 1981. pap. 2.25 (ISBN 0-87997-618-7, UE1618). DAW Bks.

Chertkov, Aleksandr D. Opisanie Voiny Velikago Kniazia Sviatoslava Igorevicha Protiv Bolgar I Grekov V 967-971 Godakh. (Ukra.). 1972. 17.50 (ISBN 0-918884-24-1). Slavia Lib.

Chertoff, Mordecai, jt. ed. see Alexander, Yona.

Chertok, Leon. Hypnosis Between Biology & Psychoanalysis. 220p. cancelled (ISBN 0-87630-244-4). Brunner-Mazel.

--Hypnosis: The Psychobiological Crossroads. 224p. 1981. 36.00 (ISBN 0-08-026793-9); pap. 18.00 (ISBN 0-08-026813-7). Pergamon.

--Motherhood & Personality: Psychosomatic Aspects of Childbirth. 1969. 10.50 o.p. (ISBN 0-685-14245-0). Lippincott.

Chertow, Bruce S., et al. Patient Management Problems: Exercises in Decision Making & Problem Solving. 336p. 1979. pap. 28.95x (ISBN 0-8385-7769-5). ACC.

Cherubini, jt. auth. see Ragusa.

Cherubini, Maria L. Demophoon. Gossett, Philip & Rosen, Charles, eds. LC 76-49213. (Early Romantic Opera Ser.: Vol. 32). 1979. lib. bdg. 82.00 (ISBN 0-8240-2931-3). Garland Pub.

--Les Deux Journees. Gossett, Phillip & Rosen, Charles, eds. LC 76-49214. (Early Romantic Opera Ser.: No. 35). 1980. lib. bdg. 82.00 (ISBN 0-8240-2934-8). Garland Pub.

--Eliza Ou le Voyage Aux Glaciers Du Mont S. Bernard. Gossett, Philip & Rosen, Charles, eds. LC 76-49216. (Early Romantic Opera Ser.). 1979. lib. bdg. 82.00 (ISBN 0-8240-2933-X). Garland Pub.

--Lodoiska. Gossett, Philip & Rosen, Charles, eds. LC 76-49217. (Early Romantic Opera Ser.: Vol. 33). 1979. lib. bdg. 82.00 (ISBN 0-8240-2932-1). Garland Pub.

Chervin, Ronda. Why I Am a Catholic Charismatic: A Catholic Explains. 1978. pap. 2.95 (ISBN 0-89243-089-3). Liguori Pubns.

Chervin, Ronda & Neill, Mary. The Woman's Tale: A Journal of Inner Exploration. 160p. (Orig.). 1980. pap. 7.95 (ISBN 0-8164-2016-5). Crossroad NY.

Chesbro, George. An Affair of Sorcerers. 1980. pap. 2.25 (ISBN 0-451-09243-0, E9243, Sig). NAL.

Chesher, Debby, ed. Starart. (Illus.). 240p. 1979. 32.50 (ISBN 0-9690053-0-X, Pub by Starart Canada). New Glide.

Cheshire, P. D. Regional Unemployment Differences in Great Britain. Bd. with Interregional Migration Models & Their Application to Great Britain. Weeden, R. LC 73-86048. (National Institute of Economic & Social Research - Regional Studies: No. 2). (Illus.). 200p. 1973. 13.95 (ISBN 0-521-20376-7). Cambridge U Pr.

Cheska, Alyce T. Play As Context. (Illus., Orig.). 1981. pap. text ed. 12.95 (ISBN 0-918438-66-7). Leisure Pr.

Chesler, Phyllis. With Child. 1981. pap. 2.95 (ISBN 0-425-04834-9). Berkley Pub.

Cheslow, Melvyn. A Road Pricing & Transit Improvement Program in Berkeley, California: A Preliminary Analysis. (An Institute Paper). 73p. 1978. pap. 5.00 (ISBN 0-87766-233-9, 22300). Urban Inst.

Cheslow, Melvyn D. Industrial & Economic Impacts of Improving Automobile Fuel Efficiency: An Input-Output Analysis. (An Institute Paper). 77p. 1976. pap. 3.50 (ISBN 0-87766-163-4, 14200). Urban Inst.

Chesneaux, Jean. Chinese Labor Movement, 1919-1927. Wright, H. M., tr. 1968. 25.00x (ISBN 0-8047-0644-1). Stanford U Pr.

--Peasant Revolts in China 1840-1949. Barraclaugh, Geoffrey, ed. Curwen, C. A., tr. from Fr. LC 72-13015. (Library of the World Civilization). (Illus.). 180p. 1973. 7.95 (ISBN 0-393-05485-3); pap. 5.95x (ISBN 0-393-09344-1). Norton.

Chesney, D. Noreen & Chesney, Muriel O. Radiographic Anatomy of the Chest & Abdomen: A Student's Handbook. (Blackwell Scientific Pubns.). (Illus.). 1976. 23.00 (ISBN 0-632-09440-0). Mosby.

Chesney, Marion. Constant Companion. 224p. 1980. pap. 1.75 (ISBN 0-449-50114-0, Coventry). Fawcett.

--Quadrille. 224p. 1981. pap. 1.95 (ISBN 0-449-50174-4, Coventry). Fawcett.

Chesney, Muriel O., jt. auth. see Chesney, D. Noreen.

Chesnoff, Richard Z. The Philippines. LC 77-99197. (Illus.). 1978. 125.00 o.p. (ISBN 0-8109-1458-1). Abrams.

Chesnut, Roberta C. Three Monophysite Christologies: Severus of Antioch, Philoxenus of Mabbug, & Jacob of Sarug. (Oxford Theological Monographs). 1976. 24.95x (ISBN 0-19-826712-6). Oxford U Pr.

Chesnutt, Charles W. Marrow of Tradition. 1969. pap. 4.95 (ISBN 0-472-06147-X, 147, AA). U of Mich Pr.

--The Marrow of Tradition. 1969. 6.95 (ISBN 0-472-09147-6). U of Mich Pr.

--Wife of His Youth & Other Stories. (Illus.). 1968. pap. 5.95 (ISBN 0-472-06134-8, 134, AA). U of Mich Pr.

Chess, Stella & Thomas, Alexander, eds. Annual Progress in Child Psychiatry & Child Development, 12 vols. Incl. Vol. 1. 1968. o.p.; Vol. 2. 1969. (ISBN 0-685-57359-1); Vol. 3. 1970.; Vol. 4. 1971.; Vol. 5. 1972. o.p.; Vol. 6. 1973; Vol. 7. 1974; Vol. 8. 1975; Vol. 9. 1976; Vol. 10. 1977; Vol. 11. 1978; Vol. 12. 1979 (ISBN 0-87630-216-9). LC 68-23452. (Illus.). Vols. 2-4 & 6-12. 20.00 ea. Brunner-Mazel.

--Annual Progress in Child Psychiatry & Child Development 1980. LC 66-4030. 600p. 1980. 25.00 (ISBN 0-87630-248-7). Brunner-Mazel.

Chess, Stella, et al. Your Child Is a Person: A Psychological Approach to Parenthood Without Guilt. 224p. 1977. pap. 3.50 (ISBN 0-14-004439-6). Penguin.

Chess, Stella, et al, eds. Psychiatric Disorders of Children with Congenital Rubella. LC 71-173092. 1971. 12.50 o.p. (ISBN 0-87630-046-8). Brunner-Mazel.

Chess, Victoria, jt. auth. see Gorey, Edward.

Chesser, Edward S., jt. auth. see Meyer, Victor C.

Chessmore, Roy A. Profitable Pasture Management. LC 78-70056. 1979. 13.95 (ISBN 0-685-90887-9, 2056). Interstate.

Chesson, Michael B. Richmond After the War, Eighteen Sixty-Five to Eighteen Ninety. (Illus.). 1981. write for info. (ISBN 0-88490-085-1); pap. write for info. (ISBN 0-88490-086-X). VA State Lib.

Chester, Alfred. Jamie Is My Heart's Desire. LC 57-12253. 3.50 (ISBN 0-8149-0465-3). Vanguard.

Chester, C. Techniques in Partial Differential Equations. 1970. 22.50 o.p. (ISBN 0-07-010740-8, C). McGraw.

Chester, Carole. New York. 1977. 24.00 (ISBN 0-7134-0183-4, Pub. by Batsford England). David & Charles.

--New York. (Illus.). 1977. 10.95 o.s.i. (ISBN 0-7134-0183-4). Hippocrene Bks.

Chester, David. The Olympic Games. LC 75-18816. (Encore Edition). 1975. 3.50 o.p. (ISBN 0-684-15688-1, ScribT). Scribner.

Chester, Deborah. A Love So Wild. 1981. pap. 2.50 (ISBN 0-345-28773-8). Ballantine.

--The Sign of the Owl. LC 80-69998. 256p. (gr. 5-9). 1981. 9.95 (ISBN 0-590-07729-5, Four Winds). Schol Bk Serv.

Chester, Edward W. Clash of Titans: Africa & U. S. Foreign Policy. LC 73-80518. 320p. 1974. 12.95x o.p. (ISBN 0-88344-065-2). Orbis Bks.

--Sectionalism, Politics & American Diplomacy. LC 74-30418. 1975. 15.00 (ISBN 0-8108-0787-4). Scarecrow.

Chester, Giraud, et al. Television & Radio. 5th ed. (Illus.). 1978. ref. ed. 18.95 (ISBN 0-13-902981-8). P-H.

Chester, Laura & Barba, Sharon, eds. Rising Tides: Twentieth Century American Women Poets. (Orig.). 1973. pap. 2.50 o.s.i. (ISBN 0-671-48753-1). WSP.

Chester, Michael. Deeper Than Speech: Frontiers of Language & Communication. LC 75-14167. (Illus.). 96p. (gr. 6 up). 1975. 5.95 o.s.i. (ISBN 0-02-718310-6, 71831). Macmillan.

--Particles: An Introduction to Particle Physics. LC 77-12352. (Illus.). (gr. 7 up). 1978. 9.95 (ISBN 0-02-718240-1, 71824). Macmillan.

Chester, Robert D., jt. auth. see Otto, Wayne.

Chesterfield. Letters to His Son & Others. 1957. 12.95x (ISBN 0-460-00823-4, Evman). Dutton.

Chesterfield, Ray, jt. auth. see Ruddle, Kenneth.

Chester-Jones, I. & Henderson, I. W., eds. General, Comparative & Clinical Endocrinology of the Adrenal Cortex. Vol. 1, 1976. 63.50 (ISBN 0-12-171501-9); Vol. 2, 1978. 126.50 (ISBN 0-12-171502-7); Vol. 3, 1978. write for info. (ISBN 0-12-171503-5). Acad Pr.

Chesterman, John, jt. auth. see Marten, Michael.

Chesters, G., jt. ed. see Broome, P.

Chesterton, A. K. The New Unhappy Lords. 255p. (Orig.). 1970. pap. 4.50x (ISBN 0-911038-83-3, Christian Book Club of America). Noontide.

Chesterton, B. K., jt. auth. see Byrnes, W. G.

Chesterton, D. W., jt. auth. see Duff, Alan.

Chesterton, G. K. The Collected Poems of G. K. Chesterton. LC 80-16874. 1980. pap. 5.95 (ISBN 0-396-07896-6). Dodd.

--The Everlasting Man. 280p. 1974. pap. 2.95 (ISBN 0-385-07198-1, Im). Doubleday.

--Orthodoxy. 160p. 1973. pap. 1.95 (ISBN 0-385-01536-4, Im). Doubleday.

--Saint Francis of Assisi. LC 57-1230. 1957. pap. 1.95 (ISBN 0-385-02900-4, D50, Im). Doubleday.

--Selected Stories. Amis, Kingsley, ed. 1972. 9.95 (ISBN 0-571-09914-9, Pub. by Faber & Faber). Merrimack Bk Serv.

--What I Saw in America. 2nd ed. LC 68-16226. (American Scene Ser). 1968. Repr. of 1922 ed. 29.50 (ISBN 0-306-71009-9). Da Capo.

Chestnut, Harold. Systems Engineering Methods. LC 67-17336. (System Engineering & Analysis Ser.). 1967. 29.50 o.p. (ISBN 0-471-15448-2, Pub. by Wiley-Interscience). Wiley.

--Systems Engineering Tools. LC 65-19484. (System Engineering & Analysis Ser.). 1965. 39.50 o.p. (ISBN 0-471-15446-6, Pub. by Wiley-Interscience). Wiley.

Chetanananda, Swami. Swami Adbhutananda: Teachings & Reminiscences. LC 80-50962. (Illus.). 175p. 1980. pap. 6.95 (ISBN 0-916356-59-0). Vedanta Soc St Louis.

Chetham, Charles. The Role of Vincent Van Gogh's Copies in the Development of His Art. LC 75-23788. (Outstanding Dissertations in the Fine Arts - 19th Century). (Illus.). 1976. lib. bdg. 41.00 (ISBN 0-8240-1984-9). Garland Pub.

Chethimattam, John B. Consciousness & Reality. LC 73-164417. 1971. 5.95x o.p. (ISBN 0-88344-066-0). Orbis Bks.

--Patterns of Indian Thought. LC 77-164418. 1971. 4.95x o.p. (ISBN 0-88344-375-9). Orbis Bks.

Chetin, Helen. Cat. 1977. pap. 1.00 o.p. (ISBN 0-931832-06-3). No Dead Lines.

Chettle, Henry. Piers Plainnes Seauen Yeres Prentship. LC 80-2476. 1981. Repr. of 1595 ed. 32.50 (ISBN 0-404-19108-8). AMS Pr.

Chettle, Henry see Rankins, William.

Chetverikov, Sergii. Starets Paisii Velichkovskii: His Life, Teachings & Influence on Orthodox Monasticism. Janov, Carol, ed. Lickwar, Vasily & Lisenko, Alexander I., trs. from Rus. LC 75-29632. 340p. (Orig.). 1980. pap. 35.00 (ISBN 0-913124-22-2). Nordland Pub.

Chetwode, Penelope. Kulu: The End of the Habitable World. (Illus.). 233p. 1972. 12.00 o.p. (ISBN 0-7195-2431-8). Transatlantic.

Chetwood, William R. The Voyages, & Adventures of Captain Robert Boyle. LC 79-170565. (Foundations of the Novel Ser.: Vol. 46). lib. bdg. 50.00- (ISBN 0-8240-0558-9). Garland Pub.

--The Voyages, Dangerous Adventures & Imminent Escapes of Captain Richard Falconer. LC 77-170543. (Foundations of the Novel Ser.: Vol. 32). lib. bdg. 50.00 (ISBN 0-8240-0544-9). Garland Pub.

--The Voyages, Travels & Adventures of William Owen Gwin Vaughan, Esq, Pt. 1. LC 76-170591. (Foundations of the Novel Ser.: Vol. 61). lib. bdg. 50.00 (ISBN 0-8240-0573-2). Garland Pub.

--The Voyages, Travels & Adventures of William Owen Gwin Vaughan, Esq, Pt. 2. LC 76-170591. (Foundations of the Novel Ser.: Vol. 62). lib. bdg. 50.00 (ISBN 0-8240-0574-0). Garland Pub.

Chetwynd-Hayes, R. Dominique. 1979. pap. 1.50 (ISBN 0-505-51345-5). Tower Bks.

Cheuk, Shu L., jt. auth. see Weinberg, Roger.

Cheung, Dominic. Feng Chin. (World Authors Ser.: No. 515). 1979. lib. bdg. 13.95 (ISBN 0-8057-6356-2). Twayne.

Cheung, Steven. The Myth of Social Cost. LC 80-26083. (Cato Papers: No. 16). 150p. 1980. pap. 5.00 (ISBN 0-932790-21-6). Cato Inst.

Cheung, Wai Yiu, ed. Calcium & Cell Function: Vol. 1, Calmodulin. LC 80-985. (Molecular Biology Ser.). 1980. 46.50 (ISBN 0-12-171401-2). Acad Pr.

Cheung, Y. K. Finite Strip Method in Structural Analysis. Neal, B. G., ed. 130p. 1976. text ed. 32.00 (ISBN 0-08-018308-5). Pergamon.

Cheuse, Alan & Koffler, Richard, eds. The Rarer Action: Essays in Honor of Francis Fergusson. LC 70-127050. 1970. 23.00 (ISBN 0-8135-0670-0). Rutgers U Pr.

Chevalier, Francois. Land & Society in Colonial Mexico: The Great Hacienda. Eustis, Alvin, tr. Simpson, Lesley B., ed. & frwd. by. 1963. 19.50x o.p. (ISBN 0-520-00229-6); pap. 3.65 o.p. (ISBN 0-520-01665-3, CAL191). U of Cal Pr.

Chevalier, Jack. The Broad Street Bullies: The Incredible Story of the Philadelphia Flyers. (Illus.). 192p. 1974. pap. 5.95 o.s.i. (ISBN 0-02-028180-3, Collier). Macmillan.

Chevalier, Louis. Laboring Classes & Dangerous Classes in Paris During the First Half of the Nineteenth Century. Jellinek, Frank, tr. from Fr. 544p. 1973. 27.50 (ISBN 0-86527-114-3). Fertig.

Chevalier, Luois. Laboring Classes & Dangerous Classes in Paris During the First Half of the Nineteenth Century. Jellinek, Frank, tr. from Fr. LC 80-8678. 520p. (Orig.). 1981. pap. 8.95 (ISBN 0-691-00783-7). Princeton U Pr.

Chevalier, Paul. The Grudge. 352p. 1981. 11.95 (ISBN 0-312-35190-9). St Martin.

Chevalley, Claude C. Introduction to the Theory of Algebraic Functions of One Variable. LC 51-4714. (Mathematical Surveys Ser.: No. 6). 1979. Repr. of 1971 ed. 18.40 (ISBN 0-8218-1506-7, SURV-6). Am Math.

Chevallez, G. A., ed. International Tapestries. (Illus.). 1973. pap. 2.50 o.p. (ISBN 0-88397-054-6). Intl Exhibit Found.

Chevallier, Raymond. Roman Roads. LC 74-82845. 1976. 36.50x (ISBN 0-520-02834-1). U of Cal Pr.

Chevigny, Hector & Braverman, Sydell. Adjustment of the Blind. 1950. 37.50x (ISBN 0-685-89731-1). Elliots Bks.

Cheville, Lila R. & Cheville, Richard A. Festivals & Dances of Panama. (Illus.). 187p. (Orig.). 1981. pap. 8.50 (ISBN 0-913714-53-4). Legacy Bks.

Cheville, Richard A., jt. auth. see Cheville, Lila R.

Cheville, Roy A. Humor in Gospel Living. LC 77-27889. 1978. pap. 5.25 o.p. (ISBN 0-8309-0198-1). Herald Hse.

--Spiritual Resources Are Available Today, Vol. 1. LC 74-21216. 1975. 8.00 o.p. (ISBN 0-8309-0138-8). Herald Hse.

Cheviot, Andrew, ed. Proverbs, Proverbial Expressions, & Popular Rhymes of Scotland. LC 68-23144. 1969. Repr. of 1896 ed. 18.00 (ISBN 0-8103-3198-5). Gale.

Chevreul, M. E. The Principles of Harmony & Contrast of Colors & Their Applications to the Arts. Freedberg, Sydney J., ed. LC 77-18673. (Connoisseurship Criticism & Art History Ser.: Vol. 5). (Illus.). 1980. lib. bdg. 72.00 (ISBN 0-8240-3262-4). Garland Pub.

Chevy Chase Manuscripts, ed. see Johnson, Hubert R.

Chew. Trouble with Magic. (ps-3). pap. 1.50 (ISBN 0-590-10343-1, Schol Pap). Schol Bk Serv.

Chew, Al H., et al. Technical Mathematics. LC 75-25011. (Illus.). 576p. 1976. text ed. 17.50 (ISBN 0-395-24009-3); inst. manual 2.75 (ISBN 0-395-24010-7). HM.

Chew, Helena M. The English Ecclesiastical Tenants-in-Chief & Knight Service, Especially in the Thirteenth & Fourteenth Centuries. LC 80-2310. 1981. Repr. of 1932 ed. 32.50 (ISBN 0-404-18558-4). AMS Pr.

Chew, Paul, Jr., jt. auth. see Freiberger, Stephen.

Chew, Peter. The Inner World of the Middle-Aged Man. LC 76-7455. 1976. 8.95 o.s.i. (ISBN 0-02-525000-0, 52500). Macmillan.

Chew, Ruth. Witch in the House. (Illus.). (gr. 2-3). 1976. pap. 1.50 (ISBN 0-590-00093-4, Schol Pap). Schol Bk Serv.

--The Witch's Broom. (gr. k-3). 1978. pap. 1.50 (ISBN 0-590-05407-4, Schol Pap). Schol Bk Serv.

--Witch's Broom. LC 77-6090. (Illus.). (gr. 2-5). 1977. 5.95 (ISBN 0-396-07486-3). Dodd.

--The Witch's Garden. (gr. k-3). 1979. pap. 1.50 (ISBN 0-590-12107-3, Schol Pap). Schol Bk Serv.

Chew, W. Y., jt. auth. see Williams, C. N.

Chew Kang, Lee. Orchids. (Illus.). 1979. 15.00 (ISBN 0-89860-032-4). Eastview.

Chewning, Betty. Staff Manual for Teaching Patients About Hypertension. LC 78-27337. (Illus.). 340p. 1979. pap. 37.75 (ISBN 0-87258-251-5, 1319). Am Hospital.

Cheyfitz, Eric. The Trans-Parent: Sexual Politics in the Lanuage of Emerson. LC 80-25750. 224p. 1981. text ed. 13.50 (ISBN 0-8018-2450-8). Johns Hopkins.

Cheymol, J. Neuromuscular Blocking & Stimulating Agents, Vols. 1 & 2. 654p. 1972. text ed. 145.00 (ISBN 0-08-016277-0). Pergamon.

Cheyney, Arnold B. Teaching Children of Different Cultures in the Classroom: A Language Approach. (Elementary Education Ser.). 1976. pap. text ed. 8.50 (ISBN 0-675-08622-1). Merrill.

Cheyney, Edward P. Dawn of a New Era: 1250-1453. (Rise of Modern Europe Ser). (Illus.). 1936. 15.00x o.s.i. (ISBN 0-06-010760-X, HarpT). Har-Row.

--Dawn of a New Era: 1250-1453. (Rise of Modern Europe Ser). pap. 4.95x o.p. (ISBN 0-06-133002-7, TB3002, Torch). Har-Row.

--Modern English Reform: From Individualism to Socialism. 1962. pap. 3.95 o.p. (ISBN 0-498-04077-1, Prpta). A S Barnes.

Chhandler, Linda S. Uncle Ike. (gr. 1-6). 1981. 4.95 (ISBN 0-8054-4264-2). Broadman.

Chi, Ch'Ao-Ting. Wartime Economic Development in China: New York, 1939. LC 78-74328. (The Modern Chinese Economy Ser.: Vol. 36). 199p. 1980 (ISBN 0-8240-4284-0). lib. bdg. 22.00 (ISBN 0-686-62489-0). Garland Pub.

Chi, Sik R., jt. auth. see Pong, K. Lee.

Chia, C. Y. Nonlinear Analysis of Plates. (Illus.). 448p. 1980. text ed. 46.50 (ISBN 0-07-010746-7). McGraw.

Chia-Ao, see Chang Kia-ngau, pseud.

Chian, Nancy & Berkson, Larry. Literature on Judicial Selection. LC 80-69415. 112p. (Orig.). 1980. pap. 4.00 (8564). Am Judicature.

Chiang. Progressive Cantonese Reader. pap. 2.50x o.s.i. (ISBN 0-686-12049-3). Colton Bk.

Chiang, Chin Long. Stochastic Processes: Some Problems & Solutions. 1981. write for info. (ISBN 0-89874-214-5). Krieger.

Chiang Ker Chiu. Cantonese for Beginners, 2 vols. 5.00x (ISBN 0-686-00846-4). Colton Bk.

Chiang Ker-Chiu. Practical English-Cantonese Dictionary. 25.00x (ISBN 0-686-00881-2). Colton Bk.

--Practical English-Mandarin Dictionary. 8.50x o.s.i. (ISBN 0-686-00882-0). Colton Bk.

Chiang Young-Meng. Morphological Studies of Red Algae of the Family Cryptonemiaceae. (U. C. Publ. in Botany: Vol. 58). 1970. pap. 6.50x (ISBN 0-520-09354-2). U of Cal Pr.

Chiappelli, Fredi, ed. First Images of America: The Impact of the New World. LC 75-7191. 1976. 130.00x (ISBN 0-520-03010-9). U of Cal Pr.

Chiappetta, Vincent J., jt. auth. see Greulach, Victor A.

Chiapuris, John P. The Ait Ayash of the High Moulouya Plain: Rural Social Organization in Morocco. (Anthropological Papers Ser.: No. 69). 1980. pap. 6.00x (ISBN 0-932206-83-2). U Mich Mus Anthro.

Chiara, jt. auth. see Piero.

Chiara, M. L., ed. Italian Studies in the Philosophy of Science. Fawcett, Carolyn, tr. (Boston Studies in the Philosophy of Science Ser.: No. 47). 525p. 1980. lib. bdg. 73.50 (ISBN 90-277-0735-9); pap. 34.00 (ISBN 90-277-1073-2). Kluwer Boston.

Chiarelli, A. B., jt. ed. see Ciochon, Russell L.

Chiarelli, Brunetto, et al, eds. Comparative Karyology of Primates. (World Anthropology Ser.). text ed. 39.00x (ISBN 9-0279-7840-9). Mouton.

Chiarini, Marco. Selected Drawings of Claude Lorrain. (Illus.). 188p. 1969. 125.00x o.p. (ISBN 0-271-00077-5). Pa Hist & Mus.

Chiaro, Mario A. Del see Del Chiaro, Mario A.

Chiaromonte, Nicola. The Worm of Consciousness & Other Essays. LC 75-31868. 120p. 1976. 10.00 o.p. (ISBN 0-15-199440-4). HarBraceJ.

Chia-Sun Yih see Von Mises, Richard & Von Karman, Theodore.

Chiba, Reiko. Painted Fans of Japan: Fifteen Noh Drama Masterpieces. LC 62-20775. (Illus., Fr., Or Eng). 1962. 15.50 (ISBN 0-8048-0468-0). C E Tuttle.

Chibata, Ichiro, ed. Immobilized Enzymes: Research & Development. LC 78-13266. 1978. 42.95 (ISBN 0-470-26531-0). Halsted Pr.

Chibbett, D. G. The History of Japanese Printing & Book Illustration. LC 76-9362. (Illus.). 264p. 1977. 55.00 (ISBN 0-87011-288-0). Kodansha.

Chibbett, David, tr. see Kato, Shuichi.

Chibisova, O. I. & Kozar, L. A., eds. English-Russian Biological Dictionary. 3rd ed. LC 78-40145. 1980. text ed. 120.00 (ISBN 0-08-023163-2). Pergamon.

Chibnall, A. C. Sherington: Fiefs & Fields of a Buckinghamshire Village. 1966. 57.50 (ISBN 0-521-04637-8). Cambridge U Pr.

Chibnall, Marjorie, ed. The Ecclesiastical History of Orderic Vitalis, Vol. 1. (Oxford Medieval Texts Ser.). (Illus.). 416p. 1980. 79.00 (ISBN 0-19-822243-2). Oxford U Pr.

Chi-Bonnardel, Regine Van see Van Chi-Bonnardel, Regine.

Chibwe, E. C. Afro-Arab Relations in the New World Order. LC 77-90935. 1978. 19.95 (ISBN 0-312-01063-X). St Martin.

Chicago Center for Afro-American Studies & Research, ed. Black People & the Nineteen Eighty Census: Proceedings from a Conference on the Poplation Undercount, Vol. 1. LC 80-68927. (Black People & the Nineteen Eighty Census Ser.). (Illus.). 702p. 1980. pap. 20.00 (ISBN 0-937954-01-2); pap. 15.00. Chr Ctr Afro-Am Stud.

Chicago Dietetic Association & South Suburban Dietetic Association. Manual of Clinical Dietetics. 1981. text ed. price not set (ISBN 0-7216-2537-1). Saunders.

Chicago Institute for Psychoanalysis, ed. The Annual of Psychoanalysis, Vol. 7. LC 72-91376. (Annual of Psychoanalysis Ser.). 490p. 1980. text ed. 22.50x (ISBN 0-8236-0368-7, 00-0368). Intl Univs Pr.

Chicago Institute for Psychoanalysis. The Chicago Psychoanalytic Literature Index 1979. Miller, Glenn E., ed. LC 76-182629. 1980. lib. bdg. 50.00 (ISBN 0-918568-06-4). Chicago Psych.

Chicago, Judy. The Complete Dinner Party: The Dinner Party & Embroidering Our Heritage, 2 vols. 544p. 1981. pap. 28.90 boxed set (ISBN 0-385-17311-3, Anch). Doubleday.

Chicago, Judy & Hill, Susan. Embroidering Our Heritage: The Dinner Party Needlework. (Illus.). 1980. pap. 15.95 (ISBN 0-385-14569-1, Anch). Doubleday.

--Embroidering Our Heritage: The Dinner Party Needlework. LC 79-6645. (Illus.). 288p. 1980. 34.95 (ISBN 0-385-14568-3, Anchor Pr). Doubleday.

Chi Chen. Chen Chi Watercolors, Drawings, Sketches: Deluxe Edition. (Illus.). 108p. 1980. leather bound 100.00 (ISBN 0-9604652-1-9). Chen Chi Studio.

Chichester, C. O., et al, eds. Advances in Food Research, Vol. 26. LC 48-7808. 1980. 31.00 (ISBN 0-12-016426-4); lib. ed. 40.50 (ISBN 0-12-016494-9); microfiche 21.50 (ISBN 0-12-016495-7). Acad Pr.

Chichester, C. O., et al see Mrak, E. M., et al.

Chichester, O. see Mrak, E. M. & Stewart, G. F.

Chick, Victoria. The Theory of Monetary Policy. rev. ed. 1977. pap. 14.50x (ISBN 0-631-18210-1, Pub. by Basil Blackwell England). Biblio Dist.

Chicken, Betty. Introducing Design in Embroidery. (Illus.). 1971. 7.50 o.p. (ISBN 0-8231-4028-8). Branford.

Chicken, J. C. Nuclear Power Hazard Control Policy. LC 80-40992. (Illus.). 300p. 1981. 35.00 (ISBN 0-08-023254-X); pap. 17.50 (ISBN 0-08-023255-8). Pergamon.

Chicken, John C. Hazard Control Policy in Britain. LC 75-12900. 204p. 1975. text ed. 27.00 (ISBN 0-08-019739-6). Pergamon.

Chickering, A. Lawrence, ed. Public Employee Unions: A Study in the Crisis in Public Sector Labor Relations. LC 76-25771. 1976. 19.95 (ISBN 0-669-00980-6). Lexington Bks.

Chickering, Arthur W., et al. The Modern American College: Responding to the New Realities of Diverse Students & a Changing Society. LC 80-8010. (Higher Education Ser.). 1981. text ed. 29.95x (ISBN 0-87589-466-6). Jossey-Bass.

Chickering, Howell D., Jr., ed. Beowulf: A Dual Language Edition. LC 75-21250. pap. 4.95 (ISBN 0-385-06213-3). Doubleday.

Chickering, William H. Within the Sound of These Waves: The Story of the Kings of Hawaii Island, Containing a Full Account of the Death of Captain Cook, Together with the Hawaiian Adventures of George Vancouver & Sundry Other Mariners. LC 70-138584. (Illus.). 1971. Repr. of 1941 ed. lib. bdg. 21.75x (ISBN 0-8371-5783-8, CHSW). Greenwood.

Chickos, James S., et al. Chemistry: Its Role in Society. 1973. pap. text ed. 7.95x o.p. (ISBN 0-669-83030-5); instructor's guide free o.p. (ISBN 0-669-83048-8). Heath.

Chicorel, Marietta. Chicorel Abstracts to Reading & Learning Disabilities, 1976 Annual. annual ed. (Chicorel Index Ser.). 1000p. 1976. text ed. 85.00 ca. (ISBN 0-934598-15-0); Vol. 19. text ed. (ISBN 0-934598-15-0); Vol. 19A. text ed. o.p. Am Lib Pub Co.

--Chicorel Index to Abstracting & Indexing, Vols. 11 & 11a. 2nd ed. (Chicorel Index Ser.). 1978. text ed. 190.00x set (ISBN 0-934598-20-7). Am Lib Pub Co.

Chicorel, Marietta, ed. Chicorel Index to Mental Health Book Reviews, 1976, Vol. 26. annual ed. (Chicorel Index Ser). 1977. text ed. 85.00 ca. (ISBN 0-934598-08-8). Am Lib Pub Co.

--Chicorel Index to Poetry Nineteen Seventy Five - Nineteen Seventy Seven, 2 vols, Vols. 5 & 5a. (Chicorel Index Ser.). 1979. Set. text ed. 170.00 (ISBN 0-934598-13-4). Am Lib Pub Co.

--Chicorel Index to Urban Planning & Environmental Design, Vols. 17 & 17a. LC 75-30637. (Index Ser.). 1000p. 1975. Set. 170.00 (ISBN 0-934598-65-7). Am Lib Pub Co.

--Chicorel Theater Index to Plays for Young People, Vol. 9. 500p. 1974. 85.00 (ISBN 0-934598-34-7). Am Lib Pub Co.

Chidsey, Donald B. And Tyler Too. LC 78-807. 1978. 7.95 (ISBN 0-525-66585-4). Elsevier-Nelson.

--Mr. Hamilton & Mr. Jefferson. LC 74-34448. 160p. 1975. 7.95 o.p. (ISBN 0-525-66446-7). Elsevier-Nelson.

Chieffo, Clifford. Contemporary Oil Painters Handbook. LC 75-40302. (Illus.). 160p. 1976. 14.95 (ISBN 0-13-170167-3). P-H.

Chielens, Edward E. The Literary Journal in America, 1900-1950: A Guide to Information Sources. LC 74-11534. (American Literature, English Literature, & World Literature in English Information Guide Ser.: Vol. 16). 1977. 30.00 (ISBN 0-8103-1240-9). Gale.

Chielens, Edward E., ed. The Literary Journal in America to 1900: A Guide to Information Sources. LC 74-11533. (American Literature, English Literature & World Literatures in English Information Guide Ser.: Vol. 3). 228p. 1975. 30.00 (ISBN 0-8103-1239-5). Gale.

Chien, Robert I., ed. Issues in Pharmaceutical Economics. LC 78-19726. 1979. 18.95 (ISBN 0-669-02729-4). Lexington Bks.

Chien, Szuma. Selections from Records of the Historian. 1979. pap. 6.95 (ISBN 0-8351-0618-7). China Bks.

Chien, Yi-Tzuu, jt. auth. see Booth, Taylor L.

Chien-chiu, Chow & Chen-ying, Chow L. Chinese Painting: A Comprehensive Guide. (Illus.). 240p. 1980. 45.00 (ISBN 0-89955-139-4, Pub. by Art Bk Co Taiwan). Intl Schol Bk Serv.

Chi'en Chung-shu. Fortress Besieged. Kelly, Jeanne & Mao, Nathan K., trs. from Chinese. LC 78-24846. (Chinese Literature in Translation Ser.). 416p. 1980. 17.50x (ISBN 0-253-16518-0). Ind U Pr.

Chiera, Edward. They Wrote on Clay: The Babylonian Tablets Speak Today. Cameron, George G., ed. LC 38-27631. (Illus.). 1956. pap. 3.50 (ISBN 0-226-10425-7, P2, Phoen). U of Chicago Pr.

Chiesa, Carol D., tr. see Collodi, Carlo.

Chiesa, Carol Della see Collodi, C.

Chigier, N. A. Progress in Energy & Combustion Science, Vol. 4. 224p. 1980. 112.50 (ISBN 0-08-024257-X). Pergamon.

Chigier, N. A., ed. Energy & Combustion Science: Selected Papers from Progress in Energy & Combustion Science. LC 79-40860. (Illus.). 1979. 41.00 (ISBN 0-08-024781-4); pap. 15.75 (ISBN 0-08-024780-6). Pergamon.

--Progress in Energy & Combustion Science, Vol. 6, Pt. 2. 102p. 1980. pap. 24.50 (ISBN 0-08-026059-4). Pergamon.

Chigounis, Evans. Secret Lives. LC 74-185195. (Wesleyan Poetry Program: Vol. 60). 80p. (Orig.). 1972. 10.00x (ISBN 0-8195-2060-8, Pub. by Wesleyan U Pr); pap. 4.95 (ISBN 0-8195-1060-2). Columbia U Pr.

Chihabi. Agriculture & Allied Terminology Dictionary: English-Arabic with Arabic Glossary. Khatib, A., ed. 40.00x (ISBN 0-686-65470-6). Intl Bk Ctr.

Chi Han. Nan-fang ts'ao-mu chuang, a Fourth Century Flora of Southeast Asia: Introduction, Translation, Commentaries. Li Hui-Lin, tr. from Chinese. LC 80-100381. (Illus.). 178p. 1980. 15.00 (ISBN 0-295-95745-X, Pub. by Chinese Univ Hong Kong). U of Wash Pr.

Chihara, D. Borobudur: The Buddhist Monument of Java (1971) (Illus.). 1977. 75.00 (ISBN 0-685-79813-5). Heinman.

Chih-Liang, Na. Chinese Jades: Archaic & Modern. (Illus.). 1977. 25.00 o.p. (ISBN 0-685-67980-2). Minneapolis Inst Arts.

Chikashige, Masumi. Alchemy & Other Chemical Achievements of the Ancient Orient. LC 79-8602. Repr. of 1936 ed. 20.00 (ISBN 0-404-18456-1). AMS Pr.

Chilcote, Ronald H. Theories of Comparative Politics: The Search for a Paradigm. 492p. (Orig.). 1981. lib. bdg. 30.00x (ISBN 0-89158-970-8); pap. 15.00x (ISBN 0-89158-971-6). Westview.

Chilcote, Ronald H., ed. Brazil & Its Radical Left: An Annotated Bibliography on the Communist Movement & the Rise of Marxism, 1922-1972. LC 80-12617. 1981. lib. bdg. 60.00 (ISBN 0-527-16821-1). Kraus Intl.

Chilcote, Russell Q. Sharad: Camel Driver for the Kings. 1978. pap. 1.25x (ISBN 0-8358-0379-1). Upper Room.

Child, Charles G. Portal Hypertension: As Seen Today by Seventeen Authorities. LC 73-81829. (Major Problem in Clinical Surgery Ser.: Vol. 14). (Illus.). 283p. 1974. text ed. 17.00 (ISBN 0-7216-2541-X). Saunders.

Child, Irvin L. Humanistic Psychology & the Research Tradition: Their Several Virtues. LC 72-6595. 256p. 1973. text ed. 17.95 o.p. (ISBN 0-471-15570-5). Wiley.

--Humanistic Psychology & the Research Tradition: Their Several Virtues. 220p. 1981. Repr. of 1973 ed. text ed. write for info. (ISBN 0-89874-277-3). Krieger.

Child, Irvin L., jt. auth. see Zigler, Edward F.

Child, J., ed. Man & Organization. LC 73-8645. 261p. 1974. 16.95 (ISBN 0-470-15580-9). Halsted Pr.

Child, John. Australian Spider. pap. 6.50x (ISBN 0-392-07647-0, SpS). Soccer.

--Trees of the Sydney Region. pap. 6.50x (ISBN 0-392-06871-0, ABC). Soccer.

--Unequal Alliance: The Inter-American Military System, Nineteen Thirty-Eight to Nineteen Seventy-Nine. (A Westview Replica Edition Ser.). 254p. 1980. 24.00x (ISBN 0-89158-677-6). Westview.

Child, Lydia M. Over the River & Through the Wood. (Illus.). (gr. k-3). 1975. pap. 1.95 (ISBN 0-590-09937-X, Schol Pap). Schol Bk Serv.

Child, Mark. English Church Architecture. (Illus.). 120p. 1981. 19.95 (ISBN 0-7134-2776-0, Pub. by Batsford England). David & Charles.

Child, Reginald. Coconuts. 2nd ed. (Tropical Agriculture Ser.). (Illus.). 1974. text ed. 33.00x o.p. (ISBN 0-582-46675-X). Longman.

Child Study Association. Brothers & Sisters Are Like That: Stories to Read Yourself. LC 78-158703. (Illus.). (gr. 1-4). 1971. 6.95 (ISBN 0-690-16041-0, TYC-J); PLB 7.89 (ISBN 0-690-16042-9). T Y Crowell.

Child Study Association of America. Families Are Like That. LC 73-21647. (Illus.). 192p. (gr. 1-5). 1975. PLB 7.49 o.p. (ISBN 0-690-00433-8, TYC-J). T Y Crowell.

--Pets & More Pets. LC 69-11825. (Illus.). (gr. 1-5). 1969. 7.95 (ISBN 0-690-61661-9, TYC-J). T Y Crowell.

--Read Me More Stories. LC 51-6972. (Illus.). (ps-1). 1951. 5.95 o.p. (ISBN 0-690-68690-0, TYC-J). T Y Crowell.

--Read to Me Again. LC 60-11547. (Illus.). (ps-1). 1961. 7.95 (ISBN 0-690-68761-3, TYC-J). T Y Crowell.

--Read-To-Me Storybook. LC 47-31488. (Illus.). (ps-1). 1947. 7.95 (ISBN 0-690-68832-6, TYC-J). T Y Crowell.

--Round About the City: Stories You Can Read to Yourself. LC 66-10055. (Illus.). (gr. k-5). 1966. 7.95 (ISBN 0-690-71317-7, TYC-J); PLB 7.89 (ISBN 0-690-71318-5). T Y Crowell.

--What to Tell Your Child About Sex. rev. ed. (Illus.). 1968. 3.95 o.p. (ISBN 0-8015-8550-3). Dutton.

Childbearing Rights Information Project. For Ourselves, Our Families, & Our Future: The Struggle for Childbearing Rights. McDonald, Marian, ed. LC 80-52554. (Illus.). 165p. (Orig.). 1980. pap. 5.00 (ISBN 0-932728-03-0). Red Sun Pr.

Childe, Vere G. Bronze Age. LC 63-18050. 1930. 10.00x (ISBN 0-8196-0123-3). Biblo.

Childerhose, R. J. & Trim, Marj. Pacific Salmon & Steelhead Trout. LC 78-65830. (Illus.). 166p. 1979. 27.50 (ISBN 0-295-95642-9). U of Wash Pr.

Childers, N. F., jt. ed. see Eck, Paul.

Childers, Richard L. & Jones, Edwin R. General Physics Laboratory Manual. 3rd ed. 1978. pap. text ed. 4.50 o.p. (ISBN 0-8403-0034-4). Kendall-Hunt.

Children's Book Committee. Reading with Your Child Through Age 5. rev. ed. 44p. 1972. pap. 1.50 (ISBN 0-686-12288-7). Jewish Bd Family.

Children's Hospital Medical Center, Boston. Manual of Pediatric Therapeutics. 2nd ed. Graef, John W. & Cone, Thomas E., Jr., eds. 450p. 1980. 13.95 (ISBN 0-316-13911-4). Little.

Children's Hospital Medical Center, the Health Education Department, Boston, Mass. Your Child & Ilael Conduit Surgery: A Guidebook for Parents. (Illus.). 120p. 1970. pap. 11.75 (ISBN 0-398-00305-X). C C Thomas.

Children's TV Workshop, ed. Sesame Street Book of People & Things. (Illus.). (gr. k-2). 1971. pap. 0.75 (ISBN 0-451-04502-5, Q4502, Sig). NAL.

Childress, Alice. Rainbow Jordan. 160p. (gr. 7 up). 1981. 8.95 (ISBN 0-698-20531-6). Putnam.

--A Short Walk. 336p. 1981. pap. 3.50 (ISBN 0-380-54239-0, 54239, Bard). Avon.

Childress, Alice, ed. Black Scenes: Collection of Scenes from Plays Written by Black People About Black Experience. LC 70-150881. 4.95 o.p. (ISBN 0-385-01146-6). Doubleday.

Childress, James F. Priorities in Biomedical Ethics. (Orig.). 1981. pap. price not set (ISBN 0-664-24368-1). Westminster.

Childress, R. L. Fundamentals of Finite Mathematics. (Illus.). 1976. ref. ed. 17.95 (ISBN 0-13-339325-9). P-H.

Childress, Robert L. Calculus for Business & Economics. 2nd ed. LC 77-2855. (Illus.). 1978. text ed. 17.95 (ISBN 0-13-111534-0). P-H.

--Mathematics for Managerial Decisions. LC 73-17352. (Illus.). 656p. 1974. ref. ed. 19.95 (ISBN 0-13-562231-X). P-H.

Childress, Stephen. Mechanics of Swimming & Flying. LC 80-23364. (Cambridge Studies in Mathematical Biology: No. 2). (Illus.). 170p. Date not set. price not set (ISBN 0-521-23613-4); pap. price not set (ISBN 0-521-28071-0). Cambridge U Pr.

Childress, William. Burning the Years: Special Issue 13. pap. 1.00 o.p. (ISBN 0-685-78395-2). The Smith.

Childs, Barney, jt. ed. see Schwartz, Elliot.

Childs, Charles, intro. by. Some American History. LC 72-153088. (Illus.). 1971. pap. 3.00 o.p. (ISBN 0-913456-86-1). Interbk Inc.

Childs, Christopher, ed. see Thoreau, Henry D.

Childs, Corinne. Yasmina's Daughter. 1981. pap. 2.50 (ISBN 0-8439-0838-6, Leisure Bks). Nordon Pubns.

Childs, David & Johnson, Jeffrey. West Germany: Politics & Society. 1980. write for info. (ISBN 0-312-86300-4). St Martin.

Childs, David, ed. The Changing Face of Western Communism. 1980. 27.50 (ISBN 0-312-12951-3). St Martin.

Childs, Harwood L. Reference Guide to the Study of Public Opinion. LC 73-12777. Repr. of 1934 ed. 18.00 (ISBN 0-8103-3704-5). Gale.

Childs, James J. Numerical Control Part Programming. (Illus.). 340p. 1973. 21.00 (ISBN 0-8311-1099-6); answer bks. avail. (ISBN 0-685-30302-0). Indus Pr.

--Principles of Numerical Control. 2nd ed. (Illus.). (gr. 11 up). 1969. text ed. 18.00 (ISBN 0-8311-1051-1); ans. bks. avail. (ISBN 0-685-03852-1). Indus Pr.

Childs, James M., Jr. Christian Anthropology & Ethics. LC 77-78626. 192p. 1978. pap. 5.95 (ISBN 0-8006-1316-3, 1-1316). Fortress.

Childs, John. The Army, James II & the Glorious Revolution. 25.00 (ISBN 0-312-04949-8). St Martin.

Childs, John L. Education & the Philosophy of Experimentalism. 264p. 1980. Repr. of 1931 ed. lib. bdg. 25.00 (ISBN 0-89760-115-7). Telegraph Bks.

Childs, Marquis. The Farmer Takes a Hand: The Electric Power Revolution in Rural America. LC 73-19736. (Fdr & the Era of the New Deal Ser.). (Illus.). 256p. 1974. Repr. of 1952 ed. lib. bdg. 29.50 (ISBN 0-306-70478-1). Da Capo.

Childs, Marquis W. Yesterday, Today & Tomorrow: The Farmer Takes a Hand. rev. ed. LC 52-5629. 178p. 1980. pap. 2.25 (ISBN 0-686-28113-6). Natl Rural.

Childs, W. H. Physical Constants. 9th ed. 107p. 1972. pap. text ed. 7.95x o.p. (ISBN 0-412-21050-9, Pub. by Chapman & Hall). Methuen Inc.

--Physical Constants. 9th ed. 1972. pap. 7.95x o.p. (ISBN 0-470-15578-7). Halsted Pr.

Childs, William H. Consolidated Financial Statements: Principles & Procedures. 352p. 1949. 22.50x o.p. (ISBN 0-8014-0076-7). Cornell U Pr.

Childs World Editors. How Do You Feel? LC 73-4745. (Illus.). (ps-2). 1973. 5.95 (ISBN 0-913778-01-X). Childs World.

Chiles, L. B., et al, eds. Life (Elevator) Servicing & Maintenance. (Engineering Craftsmen: No. J25). (Illus.). 1974. spiral bdg. 16.50x (ISBN 0-85083-236-5). Intl Ideas.

--Lift (Elevator) Erection. (Engineering Craftsmen: No. J26). (Illus.). 1978. spiral bdg. 21.50x (ISBN 0-85083-414-7). Intl Ideas.

--Lift (Elevator) Practice. (Engineering Craftsmen Ser.: No. J5). (Illus.). 203p. 1979. spiral bdg. 28.95x (ISBN 0-85083-458-9). Intl Ideas.

Chill, Abraham. The Minhagim: The Customs & Ceremonies of Judaism, Their Origins & Rationale. 2nd corrected ed. LC 78-62153. (Illus.). 339p. 1980. 13.95 (ISBN 0-87203-076-8); pap. 7.95 (ISBN 0-87203-077-6). Hermon.

Chill, Dan S. The Arab Boycott of Israel: Economic Aggression and World Reaction. LC 76-14431. 1976. text ed. 24.95 (ISBN 0-275-56810-5). Praeger.

Chillingworth, H. R. Complex Variables. LC 72-86178. 280p. 1973. text ed. 32.00 (ISBN 0-08-016938-4); pap. text ed. 18.75 (ISBN 0-08-016939-2). Pergamon.

Chilson, Richard. Creed for a Young Catholic. 128p. (Orig.). (gr. 5-9). pap. 2.45 (ISBN 0-529-05780-8). Collins Pubs.

--Creed for a Young Catholic. LC 80-2073. 128p. 1981. pap. 2.75 (ISBN 0-385-17436-5, Im). Doubleday.

--Faith of Catholics: An Introduction. rev. ed. LC 72-81229. 192p. 1976. pap. 3.45 (ISBN 0-8091-1873-4, Deus). Paulist Pr.

--Way to Christianity: The Pilgrim. 1980. pap. 8.95 (ISBN 0-03-053426-7). Winston Pr.

Chilton Automotive Staff. Chilton's Easy Car Care. LC 78-7152. (Illus.). 1978. 9.95 (ISBN 0-8019-6784-8); pap. 8.95 o.p. (ISBN 0-8019-6729-5). Chilton.

Chilton Book Company Auto. Ed. Dept. Chilton's Motorcycle Troubleshooting Guide. 2nd ed. LC 77-121. 1977. pap. 7.95 (ISBN 0-8019-6587-X, 6587). Chilton.

Chilton Book Company. Automotive Editorial Dept. Chilton's Repair & Tune-up Guide: For Blazer-Jimmy, 1969-1977. LC 76-53144. (Chilton's Repair & Tune up Guides). 1977. pap. 8.95 (ISBN 0-8019-6558-6). Chilton.

Chilton, P. A. The Poetry of Jean de la Ceppede: A Study in Text & Content. (Oxford Modern Languages & Literature Monographs). 1977. 37.50x (ISBN 0-19-815529-8). Oxford U Pr.

Chilton Staff. Easy Car Care. 2nd ed. LC 78-7152. 384p. Date not set. 12.95 (ISBN 0-8019-6887-9); pap. 9.95 (ISBN 0-8019-6888-7). Chilton.

Chilton's Automotive Ed. Dept. Chilton's Repair & Tune-up Guide for Aspen-Volare, 1976-1978. (Chilton's Repair & Tune-up Guides). (Illus., Orig.). 1977. pap. 8.95 (ISBN 0-8019-6637-X, 6637). Chilton.

--Chilton's Repair & Tune-up Guide for Chevelle, el Camino, Monte Carlo 1964-1977. LC 76-57314. (Chilton's Repair & Tune-up Guides Ser.). (Illus., Orig.). 1977. pap. 8.95 (ISBN 0-8019-6611-6, 6611). Chilton.

--Chilton's Repair & Tune-Up Guide for Camaro 1967-1979. (Repair & Tune-up Guides Ser.). (Illus.). 1978. pap. 8.95 (ISBN 0-8019-6735-X). Chilton.

--Chilton's Repair & Tune-up Guide for Cutlass-442, 1970-1977. LC 77-89117. (Chilton's Repair & Tune-up Guides). (Illus., Orig.). 1978. pap. 8.95 (ISBN 0-8019-6597-7, 6597). Chilton.

--Chilton's Repair & Tune-up Guide for Dodge-Plymouth Vans 1967-1977. LC 77-71692. (Chilton's Repair & Tune-up Guides). (Illus., Orig.). 1977. pap. 8.95 (ISBN 0-8019-6599-3, 6599). Chilton.

--Chilton's Repair & Tune-up Guide for Dodge 1968-1977. LC 77-71635. (Chilton's Repair & Tune-up Guides Ser.). (Illus.). 1977. pap. 8.95 (ISBN 0-8019-6554-3). Chilton.

--Chilton's Repair & Tune-up Guide for Datsun 240-260-280z, 1970-1977. LC 77-85345. (Chilton's Repair & Tune-up Guides). (Illus., Orig.). 1977. pap. 8.95 (ISBN 0-8019-6638-8, 6638). Chilton.

--Chilton's Repair & Tune-up Guide for Ford Courier 1972-78. (Repair & Tune-up Guides Ser.). (Illus.). pap. 8.95 (ISBN 0-8019-6723-6). Chilton.

--Chilton's Repair & Tune-up Guide for Ford Vans 1966-1977. LC 76-57320. (Chilton's Repair & Tune-up Guides). (Illus., Orig.). 1977. pap. 8.95 (ISBN 0-8019-6585-3, 6585). Chilton.

--Chilton's Repair & Tune-up Guide for Fiat 1969-1978. (Repair & Tune-up Guides Ser.). (Illus.). 1978. pap. 8.95 (ISBN 0-8019-6734-1). Chilton.

--Chilton's Repair & Tune-up Guide for Granada-Monarch, 1975-1977. LC 77-89116. (Chilton's Repair & Tune-up Guides). (Illus., Orig.). 1977. pap. 8.95 (ISBN 0-8019-6636-1, 6636). Chilton.

--Chilton's Repair & Tune-Up Guide for Honda 350-550, 1972-1977. LC 77-89115. (Chilton's Repair & Tune-up Guides). (Illus., Orig.). 1977. pap. 8.95 (ISBN 0-8019-6603-5, 6603). Chilton.

--Chilton's Repair & Tune-up Guide for Honda 750 1969-1977. LC 76-57321. (Chilton's Repair & Tune-up Guides). (Illus., Orig.). 1977. pap. 8.95 (ISBN 0-8019-6589-6, 6598). Chilton.

--Chilton's Repair & Tune-up Guide for Jeep Wagoneer, Commando & Cherokee 1966-79. (Repair & Tune-up Guides Ser.). (Illus.). 1978. pap. 8.95 (ISBN 0-8019-6739-2). Chilton.

--Chilton's Repair & Tune-up Guide for Maverick & Comet 1970-1977. LC 77-75991. (Chilton's Repair & Tune-up Guides). (Illus., Orig.). 1977. pap. 8.95 (ISBN 0-8019-6634-5, 6634). Chilton.

--Chilton's Repair & Tune-up Guide for Mazda 1971-78. (Repair & Tune-up Guides Ser.). (Illus.). 1978. pap. 8.95 (ISBN 0-8019-6746-5). Chilton.

--Chilton's Repair & Tune-up Guide for Rabbit-Scirocco 1975-1978. (Repair & Tune-up Guides Ser.). (Illus.). 1978. pap. 8.95 (ISBN 0-8019-6736-8). Chilton.

--Chilton's Repair & Tune-up Guide for Toyota 1970-1977. LC 76-57318. (Chilton's Repair & Tune-up Guides). (Illus., Orig.). 1977. pap. 8.95 (ISBN 0-8019-6617-5, 6617). Chilton.

--Chilton's Repair & Tune-up Guide for Volkswagen 1970-1977. LC 76-57319. (Chilton's Repair & Tune-up Guides). (Illus., Orig.). 1977. pap. 8.95 (ISBN 0-8019-6619-1, 6619). Chilton.

--Chilton's Repair & Tune-up Guide for Vega 1971-1977. LC 76-53150. (Chilton's Repair & Tune-up Guides). (Illus., Orig.). 1977. pap. 8.95 (ISBN 0-8019-6609-4, 6609). Chilton.

--Chilton's Repair & Tune-up Guide for Yamaha 360-400 1976-78. (Repair & Tune-up Guides Ser.). (Illus.). 1978. pap. 8.95 (ISBN 0-8019-6738-4). Chilton.

Chilton's Automotive Editorial Department. Chevy Two & Nova, Nineteen Sixty-Two to Nineteen Seventy-Nine. LC 78-20253. (Chilton's Repair & Tune-up Guides). (Illus.). 1979. pap. 8.95 (ISBN 0-8019-6841-0, 6841). Chilton.

--Chilton's Auto Repair Manual, 1964-1971. LC 54-17274. (Illus.). 1536p. 1974. 19.95 (ISBN 0-8019-5974-8). Chilton.

--Chilton's Guide to Emission Controls & How They Work. LC 74-6332. (Illus.). 160p. 1974. pap. 8.95 (ISBN 0-8019-6084-3). Chilton.

--Chilton's Repair & Tune-up Guide, Bronco 1966-1973. LC 74-2472. (Illus.). 1974. 8.95 (ISBN 0-8019-5920-9); pap. 8.95 (ISBN 0-8019-5921-7). Chilton.

--Chilton's Repair & Tune-up Guide for Audi, 1970-1973. (Illus.). 190p. 1973. 8.95 (ISBN 0-8019-5864-4); pap. 8.95 (ISBN 0-8019-5902-0). Chilton.

--Chilton's Repair & Tune-up Guide for Barracuda & Challenger: 1965-1972. LC 72-7036. (Illus.). 128p. 1972. 8.95 (ISBN 0-8019-5721-4); pap. 8.95 (ISBN 0-8019-5807-5). Chilton.

--Chilton's Repair & Tune-up Guide for Bultaco, Montesa, & Ossa 1963-1972. LC 74-4029. (Illus.). 1974. 8.95 (ISBN 0-8019-5817-2); pap. 8.95 (ISBN 0-8019-5888-1). Chilton.

--Chilton's Repair & Tune-up Guide for Bmw Motorcycle Through 1972. LC 72-8340. (Illus.). 150p. 1973. 8.95 (ISBN 0-8019-5738-9); pap. 8.95 (ISBN 0-8019-6049-5). Chilton.

--Chilton's Repair & Tune-up Guide for BSA Thru 1972. LC 72-6147. (Illus.). 176p. 1972. 8.95 (ISBN 0-8019-5713-3); pap. 8.95 (ISBN 0-8019-6048-7). Chilton.

--Chilton's Repair & Tune-Up Guide for BMW: 1959-1970. LC 78-143690. (Illus.). 1971. 8.95 (ISBN 0-8019-5576-9). Chilton.

--Chilton's Repair & Tune-up Guide for BMW 2, 1969-1974. LC 74-17352. (Illus.). 224p. 1974. 8.95 (ISBN 0-8019-5979-9); pap. 8.95 (ISBN 0-8019-5980-2). Chilton.

--Chilton's Repair & Tune-up Guide for Charger, Coronet 1971-1975. (Illus.). 190p. 1975. 8.95 (ISBN 0-8019-6315-X); pap. 8.95 (ISBN 0-8019-6316-8). Chilton.

--Chilton's Repair & Tune-up Guide for Chevrolet-GMC Vans, 1967-1974. LC 74-12293. (Illus.). 256p. 1974. 8.95 (ISBN 0-8019-6011-8); pap. 8.95 (ISBN 0-8019-6012-6). Chilton.

--Chilton's Repair & Tune-up Guide for Capri, 1970-1976. (Illus.). 192p. 1975. 8.95 (ISBN 0-8019-6403-2); pap. 8.95 (ISBN 0-8019-6404-0). Chilton.

Chilton's Automotive Editorial Department, ed. Chilton's Repair & Tune-up Guide for Colt, 1971-1976. (Illus.). 1976. 8.95 (ISBN 0-8019-6474-1); pap. 8.95 (ISBN 0-8019-6475-X). Chilton.

Chilton's Automotive Editorial Department. Chilton's Repair & Tune-up Guide for Dasher, 1974-1975. (Illus.). 190p. 1975. 8.95 (ISBN 0-8019-6212-9); pap. 8.95 (ISBN 0-8019-6213-7). Chilton.

--Chilton's Repair & Tune-up Guide for Datsun 2, 1973-1975, Vol. 2. (Illus.). 224p. 1975. pap. 8.95 (ISBN 0-8019-6311-7). Chilton.

--Chilton's Repair & Tune-up Guide for Datsun, 240-260z, 1970-1974. (Illus.). 224p. 1975. 8.95 (ISBN 0-8019-6214-5); pap. 8.95 (ISBN 0-8019-6215-3). Chilton.

--Chilton's Repair & Tune-up Guide for Ford Courier, 1972-1975. (Illus.). 224p. 1975. 8.95 (ISBN 0-8019-6202-1); pap. 8.95 (ISBN 0-8019-6203-X). Chilton.

--Chilton's Repair & Tune-up Guide for Firebird, 1967-1974. LC 74-16191. (Illus.). 190p. 1974. 8.95 (ISBN 0-8019-5995-0, 16191); pap. 8.95 (ISBN 0-8019-5996-9). Chilton.

--Chilton's Repair & Tune-up Guide for Gremlin & Hornet, 1970-1974. 2nd ed. LC 74-10693. (Illus.). 224p. 1974. 8.95 (ISBN 0-8019-5993-4); pap. 8.95 (ISBN 0-8019-5994-2). Chilton.

--Chilton's Repair & Tune-up Guide for Honda Elsinores, 1973-1975. (Illus.). 152p. 1975. 8.95 (ISBN 0-8019-6283-8); pap. 8.95 (ISBN 0-8019-6284-6). Chilton.

--Chilton's Repair & Tune-up Guide for Honda Fours, 1969-1974. 2nd ed. (Illus.). 200p. 1974. 8.95 (ISBN 0-8019-6029-0); pap. 8.95 (ISBN 0-8019-6030-4). Chilton.

--Chilton's Repair & Tune-up Guide for Honda Singles, 1968-1975. (Illus.). 1975. 8.95 (ISBN 0-8019-6033-9); pap. 8.95 (ISBN 0-8019-6034-7). Chilton.

--Chilton's Repair & Tune-up Guide for Honda Twins, 1966-1972. LC 72-7035. (Illus.). 148p. 1972. 8.95 (ISBN 0-8019-5736-2); pap. 8.95 (ISBN 0-8019-5799-0). Chilton.

--Chilton's Repair & Tune-up Guide for Hodaka, 1964-1973. LC 74-8643. (Illus.). 220p. 1974. 8.95 (ISBN 0-8019-6026-6); pap. 8.95 (ISBN 0-8019-6027-4). Chilton.

--Chilton's Repair & Tune-up Guide for Honda 125-200 Twins, 1969-1976. LC 75-38656. (Illus.). 175p. 1975. 8.95 (ISBN 0-8019-6468-7); pap. 8.95 (ISBN 0-8019-6469-5). Chilton.

--Chilton's Repair & Tune-up Guide for Honda 350-360 Twins, 1968-1975. (Illus.). 1975. 8.95 (ISBN 0-8019-6037-1); pap. 8.95 (ISBN 0-8019-6038-X). Chilton.

--Chilton's Repair & Tune-up Guide for Inboard-Outdrives: 1968-1972. LC 73-1268. (Illus.). 251p. 1973. 8.95 (ISBN 0-8019-5781-8). Chilton.

--Chilton's Repair & Tune-up Guide for International Scout, 1967-1973: International Scout. LC 74-5077. (Illus.). 200p. 1974. 8.95 (ISBN 0-8019-5878-4); pap. 8.95 (ISBN 0-8019-5912-8). Chilton.

Chilton's Automotive Editorial Department, ed. Chilton's Repair & Tune-up Guide for Jeep Universal, 1953-1976. 1976. 8.95 (ISBN 0-8019-6555-1); pap. 8.95 (ISBN 0-8019-6556-X). Chilton.

Chilton's Automotive Editorial Department. Chilton's Repair & Tune-up Guide for Jaguar, 1969-1974. LC 74-10545. (Illus.). 220p. 1974. 8.95 (ISBN 0-8019-5997-7); pap. 8.95 (ISBN 0-8019-5998-5). Chilton.

--Chilton's Repair & Tune-up Guide for Kawasaki Triples, 1969-1975. Martinell, Charles, ed. (Illus.). 175p. 1975. 8.95 (ISBN 0-8019-6264-1); pap. 8.95 (ISBN 0-8019-6265-X). Chilton.

--Chilton's Repair & Tune-up Guide for Kawasaki, 1966-1972. LC 72-6444. (Illus.). 171p. 1972. 8.95 (ISBN 0-8019-5696-X); pap. 8.95 (ISBN 0-8019-6044-4). Chilton.

--Chilton's Repair & Tune-up Guide for Kawasaki 900 Z1, 1973-1974. LC 74-8628. (Illus.). 200p. 1974. 8.95 (ISBN 0-8019-6024-X); pap. 8.95 (ISBN 0-8019-6025-8). Chilton.

--Chilton's Repair & Tune-up Guide for Moto Guzzi, 1966-1972. LC 73-17292. (Illus.). 224p. 1973. 8.95 (ISBN 0-8019-5866-0); pap. 8.95 (ISBN 0-8019-5908-X). Chilton.

--Chilton's Repair & Tune-up Guide for Mazda Pick-up, 1972-1975. (Illus.). 1975. 8.95 (ISBN 0-8019-6273-0); pap. 8.95 o.p. (ISBN 0-8019-6274-9). Chilton.

--Chilton's Repair & Tune-up Guide for Mustang: 1965-1973. (Illus.). 271p. 1972. 8.95 o.p. (ISBN 0-8019-6541-1); pap. 8.95 (ISBN 0-8019-6542-X). Chilton.

--Chilton's Repair & Tune-up Guide for Mazda, 1971-1973. (Illus.). 190p. 1974. 8.95 (ISBN 0-8019-5862-8); pap. 8.95 (ISBN 0-8019-5906-3). Chilton.

--Chilton's Repair & Tune-up Guide for Norton 750 & 850, 1966-1973. LC 73-16164. (Illus.). 224p. 1973. 8.95 (ISBN 0-8019-5816-4); pap. 8.95 (ISBN 0-8019-5913-6). Chilton.

--Chilton's Repair & Tune-up Guide for Outboard Motors 30 Horsepower & Over: 1966-1972. LC 72-11533. (Illus.). 284p. 1973. 8.95 (ISBN 0-8019-5722-2); pap. 8.95 (ISBN 0-8019-5803-2). Chilton.

--Chilton's Repair & Tune-up Guide for Opel: 1964-1970. LC 72-153140. (Illus.). 170p. 1971. pap. 8.95 (ISBN 0-8019-5792-3). Chilton.

--Chilton's Repair & Tune-up Guide for Ramcharger - Trailduster, 1974-1975. (Illus.). 1975. 8.95 (ISBN 0-8019-6330-3); pap. 8.95 (ISBN 0-8019-6331-1). Chilton.

--Chilton's Repair & Tune-up Guide for Rebel-Matador, 1967-1974. LC 74-13402. (Illus.). 190p. 1974. 8.95 (ISBN 0-8019-5985-3); pap. 8.95 (ISBN 0-8019-5986-1). Chilton.

--Chilton's Repair & Tune-up Guide for Road Runner, Satellite, Belvedere, GTX, 1968-1973. LC 73-4347. (Illus.). 224p. 1973. 8.95 (ISBN 0-8019-5810-5); pap. 8.95 (ISBN 0-8019-5821-0). Chilton.

--Chilton's Repair & Tune-up Guide for Suzuki Triples, 1972-1974. LC 74-14579. (Illus.). 175p. 1974. 8.95 (ISBN 0-8019-6031-2); pap. 8.95 (ISBN 0-8019-6032-0). Chilton.

--Chilton's Repair & Tune-up Guide for Suzuki, 1963-1972. LC 72-8075. (Illus.). 247p. 1972. 8.95 (ISBN 0-8019-5695-1); pap. 8.95 (ISBN 0-8019-5800-8). Chilton.

--Chilton's Repair & Tune-up Guide for Snowmobiles, 1969-1976. (Illus.). 240p. 1975. 8.95 (ISBN 0-8019-6007-X); pap. 8.95 (ISBN 0-8019-6008-8). Chilton.

--Chilton's Repair & Tune-up Guide for Tempest, GTO & Le Mans, 1968-1973. LC 73-10219. (Illus.). 190p. 1973. 8.95 (ISBN 0-8019-5809-1); pap. 8.95 (ISBN 0-8019-5905-5). Chilton.

--Chilton's Repair & Tune-up Guide for Toyota Hi Lux, 1970-1974. (Illus.). 224p. 1974. 8.95 (ISBN 0-8019-6204-8); pap. 8.95 (ISBN 0-8019-6205-6). Chilton.

--Chilton's Repair & Tune-up Guide for Toyota Land Cruiser, 1966-1974. (Illus.). 224p. 1974. 8.95 (ISBN 0-8019-6275-7); pap. 8.95 (ISBN 0-8019-6276-5). Chilton.

--Chilton's Repair & Tune-up Guide for Triumph Motorcycle Through 1972. LC 72-5158. (Illus.). 201p. 1972. 8.95 (ISBN 0-8019-5712-5); pap. 8.95 (ISBN 0-8019-6046-0). Chilton.

--Chilton's Repair & Tune-up Guide for Triumph 2, 1969-1973. LC 73-18387. (Illus.). 224p. 1974. 8.95 (ISBN 0-8019-5863-6); pap. 8.95 (ISBN 0-8019-5910-1). Chilton.

--Chilton's Repair & Tune-up Guide for Volkswagen: 1949-1971. LC 74-154691. (Illus.). 212p. 1971. 8.95 (ISBN 0-8019-5624-2); pap. 8.95 (ISBN 0-8019-5796-6). Chilton.

--Chilton's Repair & Tune-up Guide for Volvo, 1970-1973. LC 73-3398. (Illus.). 224p. 1973. 8.95 o.p. (ISBN 0-8019-5813-X); pap. 8.95 (ISBN 0-8019-5850-4). Chilton.

--Chilton's Repair & Tune-up Guide for Winnebago Motor Homes, 1968-1974. LC 74-17354. (Illus.). 224p. 1974. 8.95 (ISBN 0-8019-6013-4); pap. 8.95 (ISBN 0-8019-6014-2). Chilton.

--Chilton's Repair & Tune-up Guide for Yamaha Enduros, 1968-1974. (Illus.). 1975. 8.95 (ISBN 0-8019-6085-1); pap. 8.95 (ISBN 0-8019-6086-X). Chilton.

--Chilton's Repair & Tune-up Guide for Yamaha Four-Strokes, 1970-1974. LC 74-16276. (Illus.). 200p. 1974. 8.95 (ISBN 0-8019-6087-8); pap. 8.95 (ISBN 0-8019-6088-6). Chilton.

--Guia Chilton Pare la Diagnosis De Averias En el Automovil. (Illus.). 130p. (Span.). 1975. 8.95 (ISBN 0-8019-6353-2); pap. 8.95 (ISBN 0-8019-6176-9). Chilton.

--Guia Pare la Reparacion y Afinacion Del Volkswagen 1, 1949-1971. 2nd ed. (Illus.). 222p. (Span.). 1975. 8.95 (ISBN 0-8019-6354-0); pap. 8.95 (ISBN 0-8019-6175-0). Chilton.

Chilton's Automotive Editorial Dept. Chevette, Nineteen Seventy-Six to Nineteen Eighty. LC 78-20248. (Chilton's Repair & Tune-Up Guides). (Illus.). 1128p. 1979. pap. 8.95 (ISBN 0-8019-6836-4, 6836). Chilton.

--Chevrolet Mid-Size Nineteen Sixty-Four to Nineteen Seventy-Nine. LC 78-20252. (Chilton's Repair & Tune-Up Guides). (Illus.). 1979. pap. 8.95 (ISBN 0-8019-6840-2, 6840). Chilton.
--Chevrolet, Nineteen Sixty-Eight to Nineteen Seventy-Nine. LC 78-20251. (Chilton's Repair & Tune-Up Guides). (Illus.). 1979. pap. text ed. 8.95 (ISBN 0-8019-6839-9, 6839). Chilton.
--Chilton's Chevrolet Luv: 1972-1979, Repair & Tune-up Guide. LC 78-20241. (Repair & Tune-up Guides Ser.). 1979. pap. 8.95 (ISBN 0-8019-6815-1). Chilton.
--Chilton's Datsun Pick-Ups: 1970-1979 Repair & Tune-up Guide. LC 78-20245. (Repair & Tune-up Guides Ser.). 1979. pap. 8.95 (ISBN 0-8019-6816-X). Chilton.
--Chilton's Jeep CJ: 1953-1979, Repair & Tune-up Guide. LC 78-19732. (Repair & Tune-up Guides Ser.). (Illus.). 1979. pap. 8.95 (ISBN 0-8019-6817-8). Chilton.
--Chilton's Motor Age Professional Truck & Van Repair Manual: Gasoline & Diesel Engines. (Illus.). 1980. 27.00x (ISBN 0-8019-6925-5). Chilton.
--Chilton's Motorcycle Owner's Handbook. (Illus.). 1979. 10.95 (ISBN 0-8019-6894-1); pap. 8.95 (ISBN 0-8019-6867-4, 795). Chilton.
--Chilton's Mustang II: 1974-1978, Repair & Tune-up Guide. LC 78-22143. (Repair & Tune-up Guides Ser.). (Illus.). 1979. pap. 8.95 (ISBN 0-8019-6812-7). Chilton.
--Chilton's Pinto-Bobcat: 1971-1979, Repair & Tune-up Guide. LC 78-22144. (Repair & Tune-up Guides Ser.). (Illus.). 1979. pap. 8.95 (ISBN 0-8019-6813-5). Chilton.
--Chilton's Repair & Tune-up Guide for Dodge Dart & Demon, 1968-1976. (Illus.). 190p. 1976. 8.95 (ISBN 0-8019-6323-0); pap. 8.95 (ISBN 0-8019-6324-9). Chilton.
--Chilton's Repair & Tune-up Guide for Fairlane & Torino, 1962-1975. (Illus.). 250p. 1975. 8.95 (ISBN 0-8019-6319-2); pap. 8.95 (ISBN 0-8019-6320-6). Chilton.
--Chilton's Repair & Tune-up Guide for Valiant & Duster, 1968-1976. (Illus.). 190p. 1975. 8.95 (ISBN 0-8019-6325-7); pap. 8.95 (ISBN 0-8019-6326-5). Chilton.
--Datsun Nineteen Seventy-Three to Nineteen Eighty. (Illus.). 1980. pap. 8.95 (ISBN 0-8019-6960-3). Chilton.
--Ford Bronco 1966-1980. (Illus.). 1980. pap. 8.95 (ISBN 0-8019-6961-1). Chilton.
--Ford Courier 1972-1980. (Illus.). 1980. pap. 8.95 (ISBN 0-8019-6983-2). Chilton.
--Ford Fiesta, 1978 to 1980. LC 78-20258. (Chilton's Repair & Tune-up Guides). (Illus.). 1979. pap. 8.95 (ISBN 0-8019-6846-1, 6846). Chilton.
--Ford, 1968 to 1979. LC 78-20254. (Chilton' Repair & Tune-up Guides). (Illus.). 1979. pap. 8.95 (ISBN 0-8019-6842-9). Chilton.
--Honda 1973-1980. (Illus.). 1980. pap. 8.95 (ISBN 0-8019-6980-8). Chilton.
--Honda 750 1969-1980. (Illus.). 1980. pap. 8.95 (ISBN 0-8019-6968-9). Chilton.
--Omni & Horizon, Nineteen Seventy-Eight to Nineteen Eighty. LC 78-20257. (Chilton's Repair & Tune-Up Guides). (Illus.). 1979. pap. 8.95 (ISBN 0-8019-6845-3, 6845). Chilton.
--Rabbit Scirocio, 1974-1980. (Illus.). 1980. pap. 8.95 (ISBN 0-8019-6962-X). Chilton.
--Toyota, 1970-1979. LC 78-20250. (Chilton's Repair & Tune-up Guides). (Illus., Orig.). 1979. pap. 8.95 (ISBN 0-8019-6838-0, 6838). Chilton.
--Volkswagen, Nineteen Seventy to Nineteeen Seventy-Nine. LC 78-20249. (Chilton's Repair & Tune-up Guides). (Illus.). 1979. pap. 8.95 (ISBN 0-8019-6837-2). Chilton.
--Yamaha XS 360-400 1976-1980. (Illus.). 1980. pap. 8.95 (ISBN 0-8019-6969-7). Chilton.
--Fairmont Zephyr 1978-1980. (Illus.). 1980. pap. 8.95 (ISBN 0-8019-6965-4). Chilton.
Chilton's Editorial Dept., ed. Chilton's Import Car Repair Manual. LC 78-20243. (Illus.). 1536p. 1981. 19.95 (ISBN 0-8019-7029-6). Chilton.
--Chilton's Mechanics' Handbook: Automobile Sheet Metal Repair, Vol. III. (Illus.). 300p. 1981. pap. 14.95 (ISBN 0-686-69516-X). Chilton.
--Chilton's Mechanics' Handbook: Engine Rebuilding, Engine Repair, Engine Theory, Vol. II. (Illus.). 300p. (Orig.). 1981. pap. text ed. 14.95 (ISBN 0-686-69515-1). Chilton.
Chilver, A. H., jt. auth. see Case, John.
Chilver, Peter. Teaching Improvised Drama. 1978. 17.95 (ISBN 0-7134-1036-1, Pub. by Batsford England). David & Charles.
Chimenti, Francesca. Night Falls Too Soon. 1978. pap. 1.50 o.s.i. (ISBN 0-515-04552-7). Jove Pubns.
Chimienti, Teresa, ed. see Schmitt, Conrad J.
Chin, Felix. Cable Television: A Comprehensive Bibliography. 279p. 1978. 45.00 (ISBN 0-306-65172-6). IFI Plenum.
--Regulatory Reform of Telecommunications: A Selected Bibliography. (Public Administration Ser.: Bibliography P-521). 50p. 1980. pap. 5.50. Vance Biblios.
Chin, Frank, et al. Aiiieeeee! 320p. 1975. pap. 3.95 o.p. (ISBN 0-385-01243-8, Anch). Doubleday.
China International Famine Relief Commission. Herr Raiffeisen Among Chinese Farmers. LC 78-74320. (The Modern Chinese Economy Ser.: Vol. 22). 140p. 1980. lib. bdg. 16.50 (ISBN 0-686-62487-4). Garland Pub.
China Travel & Tour Service. The Official Guidebook of China: 1980-1981 Edition. pap. 9.95 (ISBN 0-86519-000-3). Green Hill.
Chinaglia, Giorgio & Kane, Basil. Chinaglia. 1980. 11.95 (ISBN 0-671-25049-3). S&S.
Chinery, Michael. Picture Atlas of Animals. LC 79-29657. (Illus.). 48p. (gr. 3-7). 1980. 6.95 (ISBN 0-528-82371-X). Rand.
--Science Dictionary of the Animal World. LC 68-17109. (gr. 9 up). 1969. PLB 4.95 o.p. (ISBN 0-531-01784-2). Watts.
--Science Dictionary of the Plant World. LC 68-17110. (gr. 9 up). 1969. PLB 4.95 o.p. (ISBN 0-531-01785-0). Watts.
Chinery, Michael, jt. auth. see Dempsey, Michael.
Chinese Ministry of Information & Tong, Hollington K., eds. China Handbook, Nineteen Thirty-Seven to Nineteen Forty-Five: A Comprehensive Survey of Major Developments in China. rev. enl. ed. (China in the 20th Century Ser). (Illus.). xvi, 862p. 1975. Repr. of 1947 ed. lib. bdg. 75.00 (ISBN 0-306-70701-2). Da Capo.
Ching, Julia. To Acquire Wisdom: The Way of Wang Yang-Ming. LC 75-20038. (Studies in Oriental Culture). 367p. 1976. 22.50x (ISBN 0-231-03938-7). Columbia U Pr.
Ching-Chih, Chen. Applications of Operations Research Models to Libraries: A Case Study in the Use of Monographs in the Francis A. Countway Library of Medicine, Harvard University. LC 75-28210. 192p. 1976. text ed. 20.00x (ISBN 0-262-03056-X). MIT Pr.
Ching-Chih Chen. Health Sciences Information Sources. 608p. 1981. text ed. 50.00x (ISBN 0-262-03074-8). MIT Pr.
Ching Ping, jt. auth. see Bloodworth, Dennis.
Ching-Shan. Diary of His Excellency Ching-Shan: Being a Chinese Account of the Boxer Trouble. Duyvendak, Jan J., tr. from Chinese. (Studies in Chinese History & Civilization). 134p. 1977. Repr. of 1924 ed. 14.50 (ISBN 0-89093-074-0). U Pubns Amer.
Chinitz, Benjamin. The Declining Northeast: Demographic & Economic Analyses. LC 78-6137. (Praeger Special Studies). 1978. 22.95 (ISBN 0-03-043476-9). Praeger.
Chinitz, Jacob, ed. see Adler, Morris.
Chin-Kuei Cho. An Introdution to Software Quality Control. LC 80-15241. (Business Data Processing Ser.). 445p. 1980. 29.95 (ISBN 0-471-04704-X, Pub. by Wiley-Interscience). Wiley.
Chinmoy, Sri. Aspiration-Glow & Dedication-Flow, 2 pts. (Orig.). 1977. Pt. 1, 60p. pap. text ed. 2.00 (ISBN 0-88497-386-7); Pt. 2, 70p. pap. 2.00 (ISBN 0-686-68529-6). Aum Pubns.
--The Avatars & the Masters. 60p. (Orig.). 1979. pap. 2.00 o.p. (ISBN 0-88497-370-0). Aum Pubns.
--Commentaries on the Bhagavad Gita. LC 78-189999. (Illus.). 192p. pap. 1.95 o.s.i. (ISBN 0-8334-1731-2). Steinerbks.
--The Jewel of Humility. (Illus.). 56p. (Orig.). 1980. pap. 2.00 (ISBN 0-88497-493-6). Aum Pubns.
--Light of the Beyond. (Teachings of an Illumined Master). 221p. (Orig.). 1980. pap. 4.95 (ISBN 0-88497-481-2). Aum Pubns.
--Mother India's Lighthouse: India's Spiritual Leaders. LC 74-189998. 288p. 1973. pap. 2.95 (ISBN 0-8334-1732-0). Steinerbks.
--O My Pilot Beloved. 54p. (Orig.). 1980. pap. 2.00 (ISBN 0-88497-502-9). Aum Pubns.
--Perfection in the Head World. 55p. (Orig.). 1980. pap. 2.00 (ISBN 0-88497-492-8). Aum Pubns.
--Secrets of the Inner World. (Illus.). 54p. (Orig.). 1980. pap. 2.00 (ISBN 0-88497-499-5). Aum Pubns.
Chinn, Gary. The Garrett Wade Book of Woodworking Tools. LC 79-7082. (Illus.). 1980. 17.50 (ISBN 0-690-01840-1, TYC-T). T Y Crowell.
Chinn, Peggy L. Current Practice in Pediatric Nursing, Vol. 3. LC 75-22183. (Current Practice Ser.). (Illus.). 1980. pap. 12.95 (ISBN 0-8016-1111-3). Mosby.
Chinn, Peggy L. & Leitch, Cynthia J. Child Health Maintenance: A Guide to Clinical Assessment. 2nd ed. LC 78-11964. 1979. pap. text ed. 10.50 (ISBN 0-8016-0949-6). Mosby.
Chinn, Peggy L., jt. auth. see Brandt, Patricia A.
Chinn, Peggy L., jt. auth. see Goerzen, Janice L.
Chinn, Philip C., et al. Mental Retardation: A Life Cycle Approach. 2nd ed. LC 78-31835. 1979. text ed. 18.95 (ISBN 0-8016-0968-2). Mosby.
--Two-Way Talking with Parents of Special Children. LC 77-26980. (Illus.). 1978. pap. text ed. 12.95 (ISBN 0-8016-0973-9). Mosby.
Chinn, William G., jt. auth. see Blakeslee, David W.
Chinn, William G., et al. Arithmetic & Calculators: How to Deal with Arithmetic in the Calculator Age. LC 77-11111. (Illus.). 1978. text ed. 22.95x (ISBN 0-7167-0016-6); pap. text ed. 12.95x (ISBN 0-7167-0015-8); solutions manual avail. W H Freeman.
Chinnock, Frank. How to Break Ninety - Consistently! LC 76-22655. (Illus.). 1977. 8.95 o.p. (ISBN 0-397-01118-0). Lippincott.
Chinnock, Frank W. The Quiz Show Quiz Book. 1977. pap. 1.25 o.p. (ISBN 0-425-03542-5, Medallion). Berkley Pub.
Chinoy, Ely. Sociological Perspective. 2nd rev. & enl. ed. 9.00 (ISBN 0-8446-1855-1). Peter Smith.
Chinoy, Helen K. & Jenkins, Linda W. Women in American Theatre. Michelman, Herber, ed. (Illus.). 384p. 1981. 15.95 (ISBN 0-517-53729-X, Michaelman Books). Crown.
Chinoy, Helen K., ed. Reunion: A Self Portrait of the Group Theatre (1976) 77p. Repr. 4.00. Am Theatre Assoc.
--Reunion: A Self Portrait of the Group Theatre. 77p. 1976. Repr. 4.00; AA members 3.00. Am Theatre Assoc.
Chinoy, Helen K., jt. ed. see Cole, Toby.
Chintamani, Sir Shirroavoore Y. Indian Politics Since the Mutiny: Being an Account of the Development of Public Life & Political Institutions of Prominent Local Political Personalities. LC 79-4911. 1981. Repr. of 1947 ed. 19.50 (ISBN 0-88355-961-7). Hyperion Conn.
Chiodi, Pietro. Sartre & Marxism. Soper, Kate, tr. from It. (European Philosophy & the Human Sciences Ser.). 1976. text ed. 26.25x (ISBN 0-391-00590-1); pap. text ed. 10.50x (ISBN 0-391-00886-2). Humanities.
Chiodo, Dan, Jr. & Carpozi, George. The Velvet Jungle, Vol. 3. LC 78-71442. 1979. pap. 2.25 o.p. (ISBN 0-87216-543-4). Playboy Pbks.
Chioffi, Nancy & Mead, Gretchen. Keeping the Harvest. rev. ed. (Illus.). 208p. 1980. pap. text ed. 7.95 (ISBN 0-88266-247-3). Garden Way Pub.
Chipeta, Chinyamata. Indigenous Economics: A Cultural Approach. (Illus.). 64p. 1980. 12.50x (ISBN 0-682-49657-X). Exposition.
Chiplin, Brian, et al. Can Workers Manage? (Hobart Papers Ser.: No. 77). 1978. pap. 5.75 (ISBN 0-255-36103-3). Transatlantic.
Chipp, Sylvia A. & Green, Justin J., eds. Asian Women in Transition. LC 79-20517. (Illus.). 256p. 1980. text ed. 16.00x (ISBN 0-271-00251-4); pap. text ed. 8.95x (ISBN 0-271-00257-3). Pa St U Pr.
Chipperfield, Mary. Lions. LC 77-13039. (Animals of the World Ser.). (Illus.). (gr. 4-8). 1977. PLB 10.65 (ISBN 0-8172-1075-X). Raintree Pubs.
Chiranky, Gary, ed. see Colletti, Anthony B.
Chirgotis, William G. Two-Hundred Fifty Home Plans for Today's Living. LC 78-65787. (Illus.). 1979. 11.95 o.p. (ISBN 0-8069-7150-9); pap. 6.95 o.p. (ISBN 0-685-91095-4). Sterling.
Chirgwin, B. & Plumpton, C. A. Course of Mathematics for Engineers & Scientists. Vol. 1 2nd Ed. 1970. text ed. 34.00 (ISBN 0-08-006388-8); pap. text ed. 14.25 (ISBN 0-08-021678-1); Vol. 2. 2nd Ed. 1972. text ed. 16.50 (ISBN 0-08-015970-2); Vol. 3, 1st Ed. 1963. text ed. 34.00 (ISBN 0-08-009376-0); Vol. 3, 1978. pap. text ed. 14.00 (ISBN 0-08-023042-3); Vol. 4. 1st Ed. 1964. text ed. 12.00 (ISBN 0-08-009377-9); Vol. 4, 2nd Ed. pap. text ed. 11.25 (ISBN 0-08-021634-X); Vol. 5. 1st Ed. 1964. text ed. 9.00 (ISBN 0-08-009378-7); Vol. 6, 1st Ed. 1966. text ed. 18.00 (ISBN 0-08-009379-5). Pergamon.
--Elementary Classical Hydrodynamics. 1968. 19.50 (ISBN 0-08-012406-2); pap. 9.75 (ISBN 0-08-012405-4). Pergamon.
Chirichigno, F. Norma. Clave Para Identificar los Peces Del Peru. (Institut del Mar del Peru Ser.: Informe 44). (Illus.). 388p. (Span.). 1978. pap. text ed. 72.80x (ISBN 3-87429-131-6). Lubrecht & Cramer.
Chirigos, Michael A., ed. Control of Neoplasia by Modulation of the Immune System. LC 76-5665. (Progress in Cancer Research & Therapy Ser.: Vol. 2). 1977. 43.50 (ISBN 0-89004-125-3). Raven.
--Immune Modulation & Control of Neoplasia by Adjuvant Therapy. LC 76-5665. (Progress in Cancer Research & Therapy: Vol. 7). 1978. 48.50 (ISBN 0-89004-220-9). Raven.
Chirlian, Paul M. Analysis & Design of Integrated Electronic Circuits. (Illus.). 976p. 1981. text ed. 31.50 scp (ISBN 0-06-041266-6, HarpC); avail. Har-Row.
--Basic Network Theory. LC 68-25648. (Electrical & Electronic Eng. Ser). (Illus.). 1968. 24.50 (ISBN 0-07-010788-2, C); ans. bk. 1.50 (ISBN 0-07-010789-0); solutions manual 3.00 (ISBN 0-07-010792-0). McGraw.
--Beginning BASIC. 1978. pap. 10.95 (ISBN 0-918398-06-1). Dilithium Pr.
--Microsoft Fortran. 325p. 1981. pap. 14.95 (ISBN 0-918398-46-0). Dilithium Pr.
--Understanding Computers. LC 78-60611. 1978. pap. 9.95 (ISBN 0-918398-15-0). Dilithium Pr.
Chiro, Giovanni Di see Di Chiro, Giovanni, et al.
Chiro, Giovanni Di see Di Chiro, Giovanni.
Chirol, Valentine, jt. auth. see Eversley, George J.
Chironis, Nicholas P., ed. Machine Devices & Instrumentation: Mechanical; Electromechanical; Hydraulic; Thermal; Pneumatic; Photoelectric; Optical. 1966. 33.50 o.p. (ISBN 0-07-010785-8, P&RB). McGraw.
Chirot, D., tr. see Stahl, Henri.
Chirot, H. C., tr. see Stahl, Henri.
Chirovsky, Nicholas & Mott, Vincent. Philosophical Foundations of Economic Doctrines. 1978. 7.95 (ISBN 0-912598-18-2); pap. 4.50 (ISBN 0-912598-16-6). Florham.
Chirovsky, Nicholas L. An Introduction to Ukrainian History, Vol. 1. LC 79-84848. 1981. 19.95 (ISBN 0-8022-2248-X). Philos Lib.
Chiscon, J. Alfred, et al. The Laboratory Experience: A Principles of Biology Manual. 2nd ed. 1976. spiral ed. 7.95 o.p. (ISBN 0-8087-0362-5). Burgess.
Chisholm, Anne. Philosophers of the Earth: Talking with Ecologists. 1972. 8.95 o.p. (ISBN 0-525-17890-2). Dutton.
Chisholm, D., ed. Developments in Heat Exchanger Technology - One. (Illus.). x, 288p. 1980. 65.00x (ISBN 0-85334-913-4). Burgess-Intl Ideas.
Chisholm, Derrick M., et al. Introduction to Oral Medicine. (Illus.). 1979. text ed. 18.00 (ISBN 0-7216-2593-2). Saunders.
Chisholm, E. Operas of Leos Janacek. 1976. 23.00 (ISBN 0-08-012854-8); pap. 10.75 (ISBN 0-08-012853-X). Pergamon.
Chisholm, Francis P. Introductory Lectures on General Semantics. 1971. Repr. of 1944 ed. 5.00x (ISBN 0-910780-05-6). Inst Gen Semantics.
Chisholm, J. S. Vectors in Three-Dimensional Space. LC 77-82492. (Illus.). 1978. 63.50 (ISBN 0-521-21832-2); pap. 15.95 (ISBN 0-521-29289-1). Cambridge U Pr.
Chisholm, Jack M. My Life's Venture in Prayer. (Prayer in My Life Ser.: Ser. II). 1974. pap. 1.00x (ISBN 0-8358-0316-3). Upper Room.
Chisholm, James. South Pass, 1868: James Chisholm's Journal of the Wyoming Gold Rush. Homsher, Lola M., ed. LC 60-12692. (Pioneer Heritage Ser: Vol. 3). (Illus.). vi, 245p. 1960. pap. 2.95 (ISBN 0-8032-5824-0, BB 606, Bison). U of Nebr Pr.
Chisholm, M. & O'Sullivan, P. Freight Flows & Spatial Aspects of the British Economy. LC 72-83592. (Geographical Studies: No. 4). (Illus.). 140p. 1973. 27.50 (ISBN 0-521-08672-8). Cambridge U Pr.
Chisholm, M. & Manners, G., eds. Spatial Policy Problems of the British Economy. LC 70-160090. (Illus.). 1971. 38.50 (ISBN 0-521-08235-8). Cambridge U Pr.
Chisholm, Malcolm, ed. Reactivity of Metal-Metal Bonds. (ACS Symposium Ser.: No. 155). 1981. price not set (ISBN 0-8412-0624-4). Am Chemical.
Chisholm, Margery M., et al. Psychiatric Community Mental Health Nursing Case Studies. 1976. sprial bdg. 9.50 (ISBN 0-87488-391-1). Med Exam.
Chisholm, Michael. Rural Settlement & Land Use: An Essay in Location. 1966. text ed. 16.25x (ISBN 0-09-063001-7, Hutchinson U Lib). Humanities.
Chisholm, R. & Haller, R., eds. Die Philosophie Franz Brentanos: Beitrage Zur Brentano-Konferenz Graz 4-8, September 1977. (Grazer Philosophische Studien: No. 5). 1978. pap. text ed. 29.00x (ISBN 90-6203-692-9). Humanities.
Chisholm, R., tr. see Brentano, Franz.
Chisholm, Roderick. The First Person: An Essay on Reference & Intentionality. LC 80-24910. 192p. 1981. 22.50x (ISBN 0-8166-1045-2). U of Minn Pr.
--Theory of Knowledge. 2nd ed. (Foundations of Philosophy Ser.). 1977. text ed. 13.50 (ISBN 0-13-914168-5); pap. text ed. 7.95 (ISBN 0-13-914150-2). P-H.
Chisholm, Roderick, tr. see Brentano, Franz.
Chisholm, Roderick M., ed. Realism & the Background of Phenomenology. vii, 308p. 1981. lib. bdg. 22.00 (ISBN 0-917930-34-7); pap. text ed. 8.50x (ISBN 0-917930-14-2). Ridgeview.
Chisholm, Roger & McCarty, Marilu. Principles of Economics. 2nd ed. 1981. text ed. 18.95x (ISBN 0-673-15492-0). Scott F.
--Principles of Macroeconomics. 2nd ed. 1981. pap. text ed. 10.95x (ISBN 0-673-15493-9). Scott F.

--Principles of Microeconomics. 2nd ed. 1981. pap. text ed. 10.95x (ISBN 0-673-15402-5). Scott F.

Chisholm, Terry. A London Bibliography of the Social Sciences, Eleventh Supplement, 1976, Vol. 34. LC 31-9970. 1977. lib. bdg. 40.00 (ISBN 0-7201-0721-0, Pub. by Mansell England). Merrimack Bk Serv.

Chisick, Harvey. The Limits of Reform in the Enlightenment: Attitudes Toward the Education of the Lower Classes in Eighteenth Century France. LC 80-7512. 296p. 1981. 22.50 (ISBN 0-691-05305-7). Princeton U Pr.

Chisnall, Peter M. Effective Industrial Marketing. LC 76-54987. (Illus.). 1977. text ed. 20.00x (ISBN 0-582-45067-5). Longman.

Chisnell, R. F. Vibrating Systems. (Library of Mathematics). 1966. Repr. of 1960 ed. pap. 5.00 (ISBN 0-7100-4350-3). Routledge & Kegan.

Chisolm, J. J. & O'Hara, D. M. Lead Absorption in Children: Management, Clinical & Environmental Aspects. 1981. price not set. Urban & S.

Chisolm, M. & Ely, D. P. Media Personnel in Education: A Competency Approach. (Illus.). 1976. 18.95x (ISBN 0-13-572461-9). P-H.

Chissell, Joan. Schumann. rev. ed. (Master Musicians Ser.). (Illus.). 1981. cancelled (ISBN 0-460-03170-8, Pub. by J. M. Dent England). Biblio Dist.

Chissick, S. S. & Derricott, R. Occupational Health & Safety Management. LC 80-41218. 720p. 1981. 117.00 (ISBN 0-471-27646-4, Pub. by Wiley-Interscience). Wiley.

Chistensen, R. Entropy Minimax Sourcebook: General Description. 700p. 1981. text ed. 29.50 (ISBN 0-686-28918-8). Entropy Ltd.

Chiswell, B. & Grigg, E. C. S. I. Units: An Introduction. LC 74-139498. 1971. pap. 5.95 o.p. (ISBN 0-471-15588-8, Pub. by Wiley-Interscience). Wiley.

Chiswick, Barry R. & O'Neill, June, eds. Human Resources & Income Distribution. 1977. 12.50 (ISBN 0-393-05623-6); pap. 5.95x (ISBN 0-393-09131-7). Norton.

Chiswick, Malcolm L. Neonatal Medicine. (Illus.). 1978. text ed. 10.50x (ISBN 0-906141-01-X, Pub. by Update Pubns England). Kluwer Boston.

Chitayat, Gideon. Trade Union Mergers & Labor Conglomerates. LC 79-2966. (Praeger Special Studies Ser.). 240p. 1979. 23.95 (ISBN 0-03-051326-X). Praeger.

Chiteji, Frank M. The Development & Socio-Economic Impact of Transportation in Tanzania Eighteen Eighty-Four - Present. LC 80-5092. 151p. 1980. pap. text ed. 7.75 (ISBN 0-8191-1041-8). U Pr of Amer.

Chitrabhanu, Gurudev S. The Psychology of Enlightenment: Meditations on the Seven Energy Centers. LC 79-795. (Illus.). 1979. 6.95 (ISBN 0-396-07676-9). Dodd.

--Realize What You Are: The Dynamics of Jain Meditation. Marks, Leonard M., ed. LC 78-9461. (Illus.). 1978. 7.95 (ISBN 0-396-07579-7). Dodd.

Chitrabkanu, Gurudev S. Twelve Facets of Reality: The Jain Path to Freedom. Rosenfeld, Clare, ed. LC 80-16773. 200p. 1980. 8.95 (ISBN 0-396-07902-4). Dodd.

Chittenden, F. J. & Synge, P. M., eds. Dictionary of Gardening: A Practical & Scientific Encyclopedia of Horticulture, 4 Vols. 2nd ed. 1956. 195.00x (ISBN 0-19-869106-8). Oxford U Pr.

Chittenden, L. E., ed. see Peace Convention - Washington D.C. - Feb 1861.

Chittenden, Russel H. History of the Sheffield Scientific School of Yale, 2 vols. 1928. 150.00x (ISBN 0-685-69797-5). Elliots Bks.

Chittendon, Hiram M. The Yellowstone National Park. LC 64-11334. (Illus.). 208p. 1964. pap. 3.95 (ISBN 0-8061-0937-8). U of Okla Pr.

Chittock, Derek. Portrait Painting. 1979. 24.00 (ISBN 0-7134-3293-4, Pub. by Batsford England). David & Charles.

Chittock, J. World Directory of Stockshot & Film Production Libraries. 1969. 32.00 (ISBN 0-08-013246-4). Pergamon.

Chittum, Ida. Farmer Hoo & the Baboons. LC 77-132357. (Illus.). (ps-3). 1971. 4.95 o.s.i. (ISBN 0-440-02582-6); PLB 4.58 o.s.i. (ISBN 0-440-02584-2). Delacorte.

Chitty, Arthur, ed. see Green, Ely.

Chitty, Elizabeth, ed. see Green, Ely.

Chitty, Joseph. A Practical Treatise on the Criminal Law; Comprising the Practice, Pleadings & Evidence Which Occur in the Course of Criminal Prosecutions Whether by Indictment or Information; with a Copious Collection of Precedents, 5 vols, Vol.93. Berkowitz, David & Thorne, Samuel, eds. LC 77-86637. (Classics of English Legal History in the Modern Era Ser.). 1979. Repr. of 1816 ed. lib. bdg. 55.00 (ISBN 0-8240-3080-X). Garland Pub.

--A Treatise on the Game Laws & on Fisheries, 2 vols. Berkowitz, David S. & Thorne, Samuel E., eds. LC 77-86657. (Classics of English Legal History in the Modern Era Ser.: Vol. 41). 1662p. 1979. lib. bdg. 80.00 (ISBN 0-8240-3090-7). Garland Pub.

Chitty, Joseph, Jr. A Practical Treatise on the Law of Contracts. Berkowitz, David S. & Thorne, Samuel E., eds. LC 77-86636. (Classics of English Legal History in the Modern Era Ser.: Vol. 25). 807p. 1979. lib. bdg. 40.00 (ISBN 0-8240-3074-5). Garland Pub.

--A Treatise on the Law of the Prerogative of the Crown. Berkowitz, David S. & Thorne, Samuel E., eds. LC 77-89235. (Classics of the English Legal History in the Modern Era Ser.: Vol. 72). 515p. 1979. lib. bdg. 40.00 (ISBN 0-8240-3171-7). Garland Pub.

Chitwood, Frances, jt. auth. see Skwire, David.

Chitwood, Oliver P. Justice in Colonial Virginia. LC 72-87557. (American Constitutional & Legal History Ser). 1971. Repr. of 1905 ed. lib. bdg. 17.50 (ISBN 0-306-71388-8). Da Capo.

Chiu, Hungdah. China & the Taiwan Issue. LC 79-14270. (Praeger Special Studies Ser.). 1980. 27.95 (ISBN 0-03-048911-3). Praeger.

Chiu, Kwong Ki see Kwong Ki Chaou.

Chiu, Ray C. Myocardial Protection in Regional & Global Ischemia, Vol. 1. (Annual Research Reviews). 177p. 1981. 26.00 (ISBN 0-88831-097-8). Eden Med Res.

Chiu, Shui-Chen, jt. auth. see Townes, Henry.

Chivers, David J., ed. Malayan Forest Primates: Ten Years' Study in a Tropical Rain Forest. 375p. 1980. 42.50. Plenum Pub.

Chivers, Thomas H. Complete Works of Thomas Holley Chivers: Correspondence of Thomas Holley Chivers, 1838-1858, Vol. 1. Chase, Emma L. & Parks, Lois F., eds. LC 57-8677. 320p. 1957. 12.50x (ISBN 0-87057-047-1, Pub. by Brown U Pr). Univ Pr of New England.

--Path of Sorrow (1832), Eonchs of Ruby (1851), Memoralia (1849), Virginalia (1853), Sons of Usna (1858, 5 vols. in 1. LC 79-22103. 1979. 58.00x (ISBN 0-8201-1340-9). Schol Facsimiles.

--Unpublished Plays of Thomas Holley Chivers. LC 79-29747. 51.00x (ISBN 0-8201-1350-6). Schol Facsimiles.

Chi Wen-Shun, ed. Readings in Chinese Communist Documents. 1963. 20.00x o.p. (ISBN 0-520-00231-8). U of Cal Pr.

--Readings in Chinese Communist Ideology. 1968. 24.50x (ISBN 0-520-00232-6). U of Cal Pr.

--Readings in the Chinese Communist Cultural Revolution: A Manual for Students of the Chinese Language. LC 70-94988. (Center for Chinese Studies, UC Berkeley). 1971. 22.75x (ISBN 0-520-01593-2). U of Cal Pr.

Chi-Yen, Hsia. The Coldest Winter in Peking: A Novel from Inside Red China. LC 77-26522. 1978. 10.00 o.p. (ISBN 0-385-13402-9). Doubleday.

Chlupaty, Peter. Marine Aquarium Guide. (Orig.). pap. 1.79 o.p. (ISBN 0-87666-100-2, M519). TFH Pubns.

Chmiel, Horst & Walitza, Eckehard. Rheology of Blood & Synovial Fluids. 184p. 1981. 42.00 (ISBN 0-471-27858-0, Pub. by Wiley-Interscience). Wiley.

Chmielewski, Edward. The Polish Question in the Russian State Duma. LC 77-100411. 1970. 11.50x (ISBN 0-87049-110-5). U of Tenn Pr.

Chmura, Louis J., jt. auth. see Ledgard, Henry F.

Chmura, Louis J., Jr., jt. auth. see Ledgard, Henry F.

Cho, Cheng & Dudding, Burton. Pediatric Infectious Diseases. (Medical Outline Ser.). 1978. pap. 21.00 (ISBN 0-87488-659-7). Med Exam.

Cho, Paul Y. The Fourth Dimension. 1979. pap. 4.95 (ISBN 0-88270-380-3). Logos.

--Solucion Para los Problemas De la Vida. Marosi, Esteban & Whidden, Angela, eds. Julio, C. & Orozco, O., trs. from Chinese. 155p. (Span.). 1980. pap. 1.35 (ISBN 0-8297-0999-1). Vida Pubs.

--Solving Life's Problems. (Orig.). 1980. pap. 4.95 (ISBN 0-88270-450-8). Logos.

Cho, Sihak H. Korean Karate: Free Fighting Techniques. LC 68-18608. (Illus.). 1968. 22.50 (ISBN 0-8048-0350-1). C E Tuttle.

--Self-Defense Karate. LC 71-84824. (Illus.). 1969. 7.95 (ISBN 0-87396-005-X); pap. 3.95 (ISBN 0-87396-006-8). Stravon.

Choat, E. Mathematics & the Primary School Curriculum. 128p. 1980. pap. text ed. 18.75x (ISBN 0-85633-206-2, NFER). Humanities.

Choat, Ernest. Children's Acquisition of Mathemathics. (General Ser.). (Illus.). 1978. pap. text ed. 14.50x (ISBN 0-685-90799-6, NFER). Humanities.

Choate, Pat, jt. auth. see Schwartz, Gail G.

Choate, Robert A. & Francis, William H. Cases & Materials on Patent Law, Also Including Trade Secrets - Copyrights - Trademarks. 2nd ed. (American Casebook Ser.). 1100p. 1981. text ed. 23.95 (ISBN 0-8299-2124-9). West Pub.

Choay, Francoise. Le Corbusier. LC 60-6079. (Masters of World Architecture Ser). 1960. 7.95 o.p. (ISBN 0-8076-0104-7). Braziller.

Choca, James. Manual for Clinical Psychology Practicums. LC 80-18731. 172p. 1980. 15.00 (ISBN 0-87630-258-4); pap. 9.95 (ISBN 0-87630-240-1). Brunner-Mazel.

Chodes, John. Corbitt: The Story of Ted Corbitt, Long Distance Runner. LC 73-76246. (Illus.). 1974. 3.00 (ISBN 0-911520-45-7). Tafnews.

Chodorov, Frank. Fugitive Essays: Selected Writings of Frank Chodorov. LC 79-28720. 416p. 1980. 9.00 (ISBN 0-913966-72-X); pap. 4.00 (ISBN 0-686-63047-5). Liberty Fund.

Chodorow, M., et al, eds. see Gutfreund, H., et al.

Chodorow, Stanley. Christian Political Theory & Church Politics in the Mid-Twelfth Century: The Ecclesiology of Gratian's Decretum. (UCLA Center for Medieval & Renaissance Studies). 1972. 26.50x (ISBN 0-520-01850-8). U of Cal Pr.

Choi, H., jt. auth. see Rohsenow, Warren M.

Choi, Juliet. Teacher's Manual for Beginning Chinese for Intermediate Schools. xxii, 331p. 1980. tchrs' ed. 29.00x (ISBN 0-89644-641-7). Chinese Materials.

Choi, Juliet & Defrancis, John. Beginning Chinese for Intermediate Schools, 2 vols. viii, 145p. (Orig.). 1980. Set. pap. text ed. 15.45 (ISBN 0-89644-639-5). Chinese Materials.

--Character Workbook for Beginning Chinese for Intermediate Schools, 2 vols. viii, 115p. (Orig.). (gr. 7-12). 1980. Set. pap. text ed. 15.45x (ISBN 0-89644-640-9). Chinese Materials.

Choksey, R. D. Economic Life in the Bombay Gujerat: 1818-1939. 14.00x o.p. (ISBN 0-210-22648-X). Asia.

Choksi, Armeane, et al. The Planning of Investment Programs in the Fertilizer Industry. LC 78-8436. (World Bank Ser: No. 2). 1978. text ed. 19.50x (ISBN 0-8018-2138-X); pap. text ed. 6.95x (ISBN 0-8018-2153-3). Johns Hopkins.

Choksy, Lois. The Kodaly Method: Comprehensive Music Education from Infant to Adult. LC 73-18316. (Illus.). 224p. 1974. 15.95 (ISBN 0-13-516765-5); pap. 11.50 (ISBN 0-13-516757-4). P-H.

Cholmondely, Mary see Besant, Walter.

Chomei, Kano N. Notes of a Ten-Square Rush Mat Sized World. Rowe, Thomas & Kerrigan, Anthony, trs. 1980. text ed. 11.25x (ISBN 0-85105-343-2, Dolmen Pr). Humanities.

Chomer, S., tr. see Bliokh, P. V., et al.

Chomin, Nakae. Nakae Chomin & His Sansuijin Keirin Mondo, 1847-1901. Dardess, Margaret B., tr. from Jap. LC 76-58485. (Program in East Asian Studies Occasional Papers Ser.: No. 10). (Illus.). 1977. pap. 4.00 o.p. (ISBN 0-914584-10-3). West Wash Univ.

Chomsky, Noam. Questions of Form & Interpretation. (PDR Press Publication on Philosophy of Language: No. 4). 1975. pap. 2.25x (ISBN 90-316-0005-9). Humanities.

--Selected Readings. Allen, J. P. & Van Buren, Paul, eds. (Language & Learning Ser). 1971. text ed. 16.95x (ISBN 0-19-437046-1). Oxford U Pr.

Chomsky, Noam, et al. Explorations in the Biology of Language. Walker, Edward, ed. LC 78-18352. (Higher Mental Processes Ser.). (Illus.). 256p. 1978. text ed. 22.50 (ISBN 0-89706-000-8). Bradford Bks.

Chong & Marin. Cheech & Chong's Next Movie. 1980. pap. 2.50 (ISBN 0-515-05709-6). Jove Pubns.

Chong Sun Kim. Rev. Sun Myung Moon. LC 78-52115. 1978. pap. text ed. 7.75 (ISBN 0-8191-0494-9). U Pr of Amer.

Chopin, Frederic. Complete Preludes & Etudes for Solo Piano. Paderewski, Ignacy J., ed. 224p. 1980. pap. 6.50 (ISBN 0-486-24052-5). Dover.

--Waltzes for Piano. (Carl Fischer Music Library: No. 309). 80p. (gr. 9-12). 1902. pap. 3.00 (ISBN 0-686-64064-0, L 309). Fischer Inc NY.

Chopin, Frederick F. Chopin Preludes Opus. Higgins, Thomas, ed. (Critical Scores Ser). 1974. 7.95x (ISBN 0-393-02161-0); pap. 4.95x (ISBN 0-393-09699-8). Norton.

Chopin, Kate. The Awakening. new ed. Culley, Margaret, ed. (Critical Edition Ser.). 256p. 1977. 10.00 (ISBN 0-393-04434-3); pap. text ed. 4.95x (ISBN 0-393-09172-4). Norton.

Choppin, B., jt. auth. see Dean, J.

Choppin, B. & Postlethwaite, N., eds. Evaluation in Education: International Progress, Vol. 1. 1979. text ed. 56.00 (ISBN 0-08-023352-X). Pergamon.

Choppin, B. H. & Postlethwaite, T. N., eds. Evaluation in Education, Vol. 3. (Reviews in Educational Evaluation Ser.). 250p. 1980. 56.00 (ISBN 0-08-026066-7). Pergamon.

Choppin, B. H., et al. After a - Level? A Study of the Transition from School to Higher Education. (General Ser.). 1972. pap. text ed. 3.75x (ISBN 0-85633-008-6, NFER). Humanities.

Choppin, Bruce & Orr, Lea. Aptitude Testing at Eighteen Plus. (NFER Research Reports). 160p. (Orig.). 1976. pap. text ed. 13.75x (ISBN 0-85633-109-0, NFER). Humanities.

Choppin, Bruce & Fara, Patricia, eds. Admission to Higher Education: A Select Annotated Bibliography. 1972. pap. text ed. 3.25x (ISBN 0-901225-89-4, NFER). Humanities.

Choppin, G. & Ryberg, J., eds. Nuclear Chemistry: Theory & Applications. (Illus.). 1980. text ed. 87.00 (ISBN 0-08-023826-2); pap. text ed. 29.50 (ISBN 0-08-023823-8). Pergamon.

Choppin, Gregory R. Nuclei & Radioactivity: Elements of Nuclear Chemistry. (Orig.). (YA) (gr. 9-12). 1964. pap. 9.95 o.p. (ISBN 0-8053-2151-9). Benjamin-Cummings.

Chopra, H. S. De Gaulle & European Unity. LC 75-900442. 1974. 12.50 o.p. (ISBN 0-88386-551-3). South Asia Bks.

Chopra, H. S., jt. ed. see Lall, K. B.

Chopra, I. J. Triiodothyronines in Health & Disease. (Monographs in Endocrinology: Vol. 18). (Illus.). 160p. 1981. 46.00 (ISBN 0-387-10400-3). Springer-Verlag.

Chopra, M. G. & Kumar, Ram. Fortran IV Programming. 248p. 1980. text ed. 22.50 (ISBN 0-7069-1040-0, Pub. by Vikas India). Advent Bk.

Chopra, P. N. British Secret Reports: India's Major Non-Violent Movements, 1919-1934. 1980. 12.50x o.p. (ISBN 0-8364-0515-3). South Asia Bks.

Chopra, S. N. India: An Area Study. 1977. 26.00x (ISBN 0-7069-0494-X, Pub by Croom Helm Ltd. England). Biblio Dist.

Chorafas, Dimitris. Data Communication for Distributed Information Systems. (Illus.). 235p. 1980. 24.00 (ISBN 0-07-091061-8). McGraw.

--Interactive Videotex. (Illus.). 300p. 1981. text ed. 21.95 (ISBN 0-89433-127-2). Petrocelli.

Chorafas, Dimitris N. Computer in der Medizin. (IS-Informations-Systeme). (Illus.). 127p. 1973. 29.50x (ISBN 3-11-004031-X). De Gruyter.

Chorao, Kay. Ida Makes a Movie. LC 73-20147. (Illus.). 48p. (gr. 1-4). 1974. 5.95 (ISBN 0-395-28782-0, Clarion). HM.

--Magic Eye for Ida. LC 72-85337. (Illus.). 48p. (gr. 1-3). 1973. 6.95 (ISBN 0-395-28783-9, Clarion). HM.

--Molly's Lies. LC 78-12383. (Illus.). (gr. 1-3). 1979. 7.50 (ISBN 0-395-28951-3, Clarion). HM.

--Molly's Moe. LC 76-3526. (Illus.). (ps-3). 1976. 7.50 (ISBN 0-395-28784-7, Clarion). HM.

Chorley, Henry F. Modern German Music: Recollections & Criticisms, 2 vols. LC 79-110994. (Music Reprint Ser.). 1973. Repr. of 1854 ed. 57.50 (ISBN 0-306-71911-8). Da Capo.

Chorlton, Frank. Vector & Tensor Methods. LC 75-16460. 300p. 1976. 39.95x (ISBN 0-470-15604-X). Halsted Pr.

Chorlton, Frank, ed. Textbook of Dynamics. LC 77-85395. (Mathematics & Its Applications Ser.). 1978. Repr. of 1963 ed. 28.95 (ISBN 0-470-99325-1). Halsted Pr.

Choron, Jacques. Death & Western Thought. LC 62-17575. 320p. 1973. 6.95 o.s.i. (ISBN 0-02-525200-3). Macmillan.

--Suicide. LC 75-162757. 288p. 1972. pap. 3.95 o.p. (ISBN 0-684-13500-0, SL 457, ScribT). Scribner.

Chothia, J. Forging a Language. LC 78-73239. (Illus.). 1980. 29.50 (ISBN 0-521-22569-8). Cambridge U Pr.

Chotjewitz, Peter O. The Thirty Years Peace. Kimber, Robert & Kimber, Rita, trs. from Ger. LC 80-24472. 256p. 1981. 11.95 (ISBN 0-394-50182-9). Knopf.

Chotzinoff, Samuel. Toscanini: An Intimate Portrait. LC 76-7576. 1976. Repr. of 1956 ed. lib. bdg. 18.50 (ISBN 0-306-70777-2). Da Capo.

Chou, E. Statistical Analysis. 2nd ed. 1975. 24.95. Dryden Pr.

Chou, Eric. Mao Tse-Tung: The Man & the Myth. LC 80-22758. 304p. 1981. 16.95 (ISBN 0-8128-2769-4). Stein & Day.

Chou, Hung-hsiang. Oracle Bone Collections in the United States. LC 74-34551. (Publications, Occasional Papers, Archaeology: Vol. 10). 1976. pap. 16.50x (ISBN 0-520-09534-0). U of Cal Pr.

Chou, Marilyn, et al. World Food Prospects & Agriculture Potential. LC 76-24346. 1977. text ed. 28.95 (ISBN 0-275-23770-2). Praeger.

Chou, Marylin & Harmon, David P., Jr. Critical Food Issues of the Nineteen Eighties. LC 79-14718. (Pergamon Policy Studies). (Illus.). 1979. 44.00 (ISBN 0-08-024611-7); pap. 9.95 (ISBN 0-08-024639-7). Pergamon.

Chou, Shelley N. & Seljeskog, Edward L., eds. Spinal Deformities & Neurological Dysfunction. LC 76-5665. (Seminars in Neurological Surgery). 1978. 33.50 (ISBN 0-89004-183-0). Raven.

Chou Shun-Hsin. Chinese Inflation, Nineteen Thirty-Seven to Nineteen Forty-Nine. LC 62-18260. 1963. 18.50x (ISBN 0-231-02565-3). Columbia U Pr.

Choubey, B. N. Principles & Practice of Cooperative Banking in India. 12.50x o.p. (ISBN 0-210-22556-4). Asia.

Choucri, Nazli. International Energy Policy: Petroleum, Prices, Power & Payments. (Illus.). 352p. 1981. text ed. 35.00x (ISBN 0-262-03075-6). MIT Pr.

--Population Dynamics & International Violence: Propositions, Insights & Evidence. LC 74-11227. 1974. 22.95 (ISBN 0-669-94037-2). Lexington Bks.

Choucri, Nazli & North, Robert. Nations in Conflict: National Growth & International Violence. LC 74-23453. (Illus.). 1975. text ed. 24.95x (ISBN 0-7167-0773-X). W H Freeman.

Choucri, Nazli & Robinson, Thomas W., eds. Forecasting in International Relations: Theory, Methods, Problems, Prospects. LC 78-19169. (Illus.). 1978. text ed. 36.95x (ISBN 0-7167-0059-X). W H Freeman.

Choudhary, G., ed. Chemical Hazards in the Workplace: Measurement & Control. (ACS Symposium Ser.: No. 149). 1981. price not set (ISBN 0-8412-0608-2). Am Chemical.

Choudhry, L. P., jt. auth. see Sharma, B. M.

Choudhuri, A. D. Contemporary British Drama: An Outsider's View. 1976. 10.50 o.p. (ISBN 0-8426-0883-4). Verry.

Choudhury, G. W. Last Days of United Pakistan. LC 74-8977. 256p. 1975. 12.50x (ISBN 0-253-33260-5). Ind U Pr.

Choudhury, P. Roy see Heat Transfer & Fluid Mechanics Institute.

Choudhury, Rabindra N., tr. see Tagore, Rabindranath.

Choudhury, Sadananda. Economic History of Colonialism. 1979. text ed. 13.50x (ISBN 0-391-01852-3). Humanities.

Chouquet, Gustave. Histoire de la Musique Dramatique en Frane Depuis Ses Origines Jusqua Nos Jours. LC 80-2265. 1981. Repr. of 1873 ed. 45.00 (ISBN 0-404-18818-4). AMS Pr.

Chow, Chuen-Yen. An Introduction to Computational Fluid Mechanics. LC 78-27555. 1979. text ed. 25.95 (ISBN 0-471-15608-6). Wiley.

Chow, Chuen-Yen, jt. auth. see Kuethe, Arnold M.

Chow, David & Spangler, Richard. Kung Fu, History, Philosophy, & Techniques. LC 73-14043. (Illus.). 220p. 1980. pap. 10.95 (ISBN 0-86568-011-6). Unique Pubns.

Chow, Gregory C. Econometric Analysis by Control Methods. (Wiley Series in Probability & Mathematical Statistics). 325p. 1981. 31.95 (ISBN 0-471-08706-8, Pub. by Wiley-Interscience). Wiley.

Chow, Marilyn P., et al. Handbook of Pediatric Primary Care. LC 78-19731. 1979. 27.95 (ISBN 0-471-01771-X, Pub. by Wiley Medical). Wiley.

Chowan College Creative Writing Group & North Carolina Writers Conference. Strange Things Happen. Harris, Bernice K., ed. 1971. 7.50 (ISBN 0-930230-24-8). Johnson NC.

Chowdhary, Savitri. Indian Cooking. 2nd ed. 1976. pap. 3.25 (ISBN 0-89253-070-7). Ind-US Inc.

Chowdhuri, Satyabrata R. Leftist Movements in India, 1917-1947. LC 76-52206. 1976. 11.50x o.p. (ISBN 0-88386-803-2); pap. 8.50x o.p. (ISBN 0-685-71767-4). South Asia Bks.

Chowdhury, Nira P. Researches on Living Pteridophytes in India, Burma & Ceylon. (Illus.). 1971. text ed. 6.95x (ISBN 0-210-22349-9). Asia.

Chowdhury, R. H. Social Aspects of Fertility. 200p. 1980. text ed. 22.50x (ISBN 0-7069-1211-X, Pub by Vikas India). Advent Bk.

Chowdhury, Rabindra N., tr. see Tagore, Rabindranath.

Chown, John F. Taxation & Multinational Enterprise. 2nd ed. (International Business Ser.). (Illus.). 1977. text ed. 18.50x o.p. (ISBN 0-686-28509-3). Longman.

Chowning, Ann. An Introduction to the Peoples & Cultures of Melanesia. 2nd ed. LC 76-7651. 1977. pap. 4.95 o.p. (ISBN 0-8465-0931-8). Benjamin-Cummings.

Choy, Bong-Yong. Koreans in America. LC 79-9791. 1979. 18.95 (ISBN 0-88229-352-4). Nelson-Hall.

Chretien De Troyes. Arthurian Romances. Comfort, W. W., tr. 1955. 6.00x (ISBN 0-460-00698-3, Evman); pap. 3.95 (ISBN 0-460-01698-9). Dutton.

Chrimes, K. M. T. The Respublica Lacedaemoniorum Ascribed to Xenophon. 119p. 1948. 24.00x (ISBN 0-7190-1207-4, Pub. by Manchester U Pr England). State Mutual Bk.

Chrimes, S. B. Henry VII. LC 72-78947. (English Monarch Ser.). (Illus.). 400p. 1973. 27.50x (ISBN 0-520-02266-1). U of Cal Pr.

--An Introduction to the Administrative History of Mediaeval England. 3rd ed. 1966. 36.00x (ISBN 0-631-09170-X, Pub. by Basil Blackwell). Biblio Dist.

Chrimes, S. B., ed. Henry VII. (English Monarch Ser.). 1981. pap. 8.95 (ISBN 0-520-04414-2, CAL 506). U of Cal Pr.

Chrimes, S. B., intro. by see Fortescue, John.

Chrisman, Harry E. Lost Trails of the Cimarron. LC 61-14370. (Illus.). 313p. 1964. pap. 6.95 (ISBN 0-8040-0615-6, SB). Swallow.

Chrisman, Harrys E. & Herron, Jim. Fifty Years on the Owl Hoot Trail: Jim Herron, the First Sheriff of No Man's Land, Oklahoma Territory. LC 73-75735. (Illus.). 356p. 1969. 12.00 o.p. (ISBN 0-8040-0114-6, SB); pap. 7.95 (ISBN 0-8040-0614-8, Sb). Swallow.

Chrisman, Marilyn K. Respiratory Nursing Continuing Education Review. 1976. spiral bdg. 9.50 (ISBN 0-87488-396-2). Med Exam.

Chrisomalis, Marion. Day's End for Gunmen. 1979. pap. 1.50 (ISBN 0-505-51450-8). Tower Bks.

Chrispeels, Maarten J. & Sadava, David. Plants, Food, & People. LC 76-46498. (Illus.). 1977. text ed. 19.95x (ISBN 0-7167-0378-5); pap. text ed. 9.95x (ISBN 0-7167-0377-7). W H Freeman.

Christ, Carol P. Diving Deep & Surfacing: Women Writers on Spiritual Quest. LC 79-51153. 176p. 1980. pap. 4.95 (ISBN 0-8070-6363-0, BP 609). Beacon Pr.

Christ, Carol P. & Plaskow, Judith. Womanspirit Rising: A Feminist Reader in Religion. LC 78-3363. (Orig.). 1979. pap. 6.95 (ISBN 0-06-061385-8, RD 275, HarpR). Har-Row.

Christ, F. & Adams, R. You Can Learn to Learn. 695.00 (ISBN 0-13-976704-5). P-H.

Christ, William & Delone, Richard P. Introduction to Materials & Structure of Music. (Illus.). 390p. 1975. pap. text ed. 13.95 (ISBN 0-13-485532-9). P-H.

Christ, William, et al. Materials & Structures of Music, Vol. 1. 3rd ed. 1980. text ed. 16.95 (ISBN 0-13-540417-7); wkbk. 7.95 (ISBN 0-13-560425-7). P-H.

Christ, William B., et al. Materials & Structure of Music, Vol. 2. 3rd ed. 480p. 1981. text ed. 14.95 (ISBN 0-13-560433-8); pap. text ed. 10.95 wkbk. P-H.

Christakes, George. Albion W. Small. (World Leaders Ser.: No. 68). 1978. lib. bdg. 12.50 (ISBN 0-8057-7718-0). Twayne.

Christanand, M. P. The Philosophy of Indian Monotheism. 132p. 1980. text ed. 12.00x (ISBN 0-333-90313-7). Humanities.

Christen, Dorothy. How to Survive Belonging to a Club. 1979. pap. 1.95 (ISBN 0-916774-02-3). Tolvan Co.

Christensen. Experimental Methodology. 2nd ed. 432p. 1980. text ed. 17.95 (ISBN 0-205-06960-6, 7969600). Allyn.

Christensen, jt. auth. see Knudsen, Estelle H.

Christensen, Barbara see Garber, Janet.

Christensen, Barbara see Neuman, Pearl.

Christensen, Bernard, tr. see Steinberger, G.

Christensen, C. Explorando: Affective Learning Activities for Intermediate Practice in Spanish. 1977. pap. text ed. 9.50 (ISBN 0-13-295980-1). P-H.

Christensen, C. Roland, et al. Business Policy: Text & Cases. 4th ed. 1978. text ed. 19.95x (ISBN 0-256-01989-4). Irwin.

--Policy Formulation & Administration: A Casebook of Top-Management Problems in Business. 7th ed. 1976. text ed. 19.95x (ISBN 0-256-01820-0). Irwin.

Christensen, Chuck & Christensen, Winnie. James: Faith in Action. LC 75-33442. (Fisherman Bible Study Guides). 1975. pap. 1.95 saddle stitched (ISBN 0-87788-421-8). Shaw Pubs.

Christensen, Clyde M. Common Edible Mushrooms. (Illus.). 1969. 8.95x o.p. (ISBN 0-8166-0509-2); pap. 3.45 o.p. (ISBN 0-8166-0510-6, MP20). U of Minn Pr.

--Edible Mushrooms. 2nd, rev. ed. (Illus.). 136p. 1981. 12.95 (ISBN 0-8166-1049-5); pap. 6.95 (ISBN 0-8166-1050-9). U of Minn Pr.

Christensen, Daphne, jt. auth. see Pikarsky, Milton.

Christensen, Darrel E., ed. Contemporary German Philosophy, Vol. 1. 1980. text ed. 17.50x (ISBN 0-391-00983-4). Humanities.

Christensen, Deborah. God & Me. (Sunflower Bks. for Young Children: Bk. 3). (Illus., Orig.). (ps-2). 1980. pap. 2.00 (ISBN 0-87743-143-4, 7-53-03). Baha'i.

--My Baha'i Book. (Sunflower Bks. for Young Children: Bk. 1). (Illus., Orig.). (ps-2). 1980. pap. 2.00 (ISBN 0-87743-141-8, 7-53-01). Baha'i.

--My Favorite Prayers & Passages. (Sunflower Bks. for Young Children: Bk. 2). (Illus., Orig.). (ps-2). 1980. pap. 2.00 (ISBN 0-87743-142-6, 7-53-02). Baha'i.

--Our Baha'i Holy Places. (Sunflower Bks. for Young Children: Bk. 4). (Illus., Orig.). (ps-2). 1980. pap. 2.00 (ISBN 0-87743-144-2, 7-03-04). Baha'i.

Christensen, Devon, ed. see Holmes, Bill.

Christensen, Doris, jt. auth. see Feeney, Stephanie.

Christensen, Dorothea H. George the Alligator. 1979. 4.50 (ISBN 0-533-04149-X). Vantage.

Christensen, Duane L. Transformations of the War Oracle in Old Testament Prophecy. LC 75-34264. (Harvard Dissertations in Religion Ser.). 1975. pap. 9.00 (ISBN 0-89130-064-3, 020103). Scholars Pr Ca.

Christensen, Eli H., jt. auth. see Acosta-Belen, Edna.

Christensen, Erwin O. Index of American Design. (Illus.). 1950. 19.95 (ISBN 0-02-525240-2). Macmillan.

Christensen, G D. Buffalo Kill. (gr. 4-6). 1968. pap. 1.25 (ISBN 0-671-29821-6). Archway.

Christensen, Gardell D. & Burney, Eugenia. Colonial Delaware. LC 74-10265. (Colonial History Ser.). (Illus.). 160p. (gr. 5 up). 1975. 7.95 o.p. (ISBN 0-525-67118-8). Elsevier-Nelson.

Christensen, Howard B. Statistics: Step-by-Step. LC 76-10903. (Illus.). pap. text ed. 18.75 (ISBN 0-395-24527-3); manual with solutions 1.75 (ISBN 0-395-24528-1). HM.

Christensen, J. J., et al. Handbook of Proton Ionization Heats & Related Thermodynamic Quantities. LC 76-16511. 1976. 34.50 (ISBN 0-471-01991-7). Wiley.

Christensen, James E. & Fisher, Jamer E. Analytic Philosophy of Education As a Sub-Discipline of Educology: An Introduction to Its Techniques & Application. LC 79-66235. 1979. pap. text ed. 9.00 (ISBN 0-8191-0802-2). U Pr of Amer.

Christensen, James E., ed. Perspectives on Education As Educology. LC 80-6078. 396p. 1981. lib. bdg. 25.50 (ISBN 0-686-69075-3); pap. text ed. 14.75 (ISBN 0-8191-1394-8). U Pr of Amer.

Christensen, James J. & Hansen, Lee D. Handbook of Proton Ionization Heats. 286p. Repr. of 1976 ed. lib. bdg. write for info. (ISBN 0-89874-344-3). Krieger.

Christensen, James J., jt. auth. see Izatt, Reed M.

Christensen, James M., ed. Gastrointestinal Motility. 520p. 1980. 47.50 (ISBN 0-89004-503-8, 566). Raven.

Christensen, James R. Field Guide to the Butterflies of the Pacific Northwest. LC 80-52967. (GEM Bks. - Natural History). (Illus.). 200p. (Orig.). 1981. pap. 12.95 (ISBN 0-89301-074-X). U Pr of Idaho.

Christensen, Jo I. & Ashner, Sonie S. Needlepoint Simplified. LC 75-167666. (Little Craft Book Ser.). (Illus.). (gr. 6 up). 1971. 5.95 (ISBN 0-8069-5178-8); PLB 6.69 (ISBN 0-8069-5179-6). Sterling.

Christensen, Jo Ippolito. The Needlepoint Book: 303 Stitches with Patterns & Projects. (Illus.). 384p. 1976. 19.95 (ISBN 0-13-610980-2, Spec); pap. 10.95 (ISBN 0-13-610972-1). P-H.

Christensen, John B., jt. auth. see Langley, Lee.

Christensen, Kathleen. Social Impact of Land Development: An Initial Approach for Estimating Impacts on Neighborhood Usages & Perceptions. (Land Development Impact Ser.). 144p. 1966. pap. 3.95 (ISBN 0-87766-171-5, 15700). Urban Inst.

Christensen, Larry. Experimental Methodology. 1977. text ed. 15.95x o.p. (ISBN 0-205-05721-7); instr's manual avail. o.p. (ISBN 0-205-05722-5). Allyn.

Christensen, Mary L. Microbiology for Nursing & Allied Health Students. (Illus.). 624p. write for info. (ISBN 0-398-04176-8). C C Thomas.

Christensen, Nadia, tr. see Thorup, Kirsten.

Christensen, Nancy. Monsters: Creatures of Mystery. LC 79-55011. (Illus.). 48p. (gr. 2-8). 1980. 5.95 (ISBN 0-448-47485-9); PLB 11.85 (ISBN 0-448-13622-8). Platt.

Christensen, Parrish, et al. Missouri Heart of the Nation. LC 80-66209. 1980. text ed. 16.95x (ISBN 0-88273-237-4). Forum Pr MO.

Christensen, R. Entropy Minimax Sourcebook: Computer Implementation. x, 254p. 1980. 37.50. Entropy Ltd.

--Entropy Minimax Sourcebook: Philosophical Origins. x, 218p. 1980. 32.50. Entropy Ltd.

--Foundations of Inductive Reasoning. xii, 363p. 1964. 39.50 (ISBN 0-686-28748-7, 04-08-01). Entropy Ltd.

--Mathematical Analysis of Bluffing in Poker. 60p. 1981. 9.50 (ISBN 0-686-28920-X). Entropy Ltd.

--Thermal Mechanical Behavior of VO2 Nuclear Fuel: Multi-Cycle Test Description, Vol. IV. xiv, 325p. Date not set. 49.50. Entropy Ltd.

--Thermal Mechanical Behavior of VO2 Nuclear Fuel: Statistical Analysis of Acoustic Emission Axial Elagation, & Crack Characteristics. xii, 238p. 1981. 34.50. Entropy Ltd.

--Thermal Mechanical Behavior of VO2 Nuclear Fuel: Statistical Analysis of Acoustic Emission, Diametral Expansion,Anrol Elongation & Crash Characteristics. x, 238p. pap. 34.50. Entropy Ltd.

--Thermal Mechanical Behavior of VO2 Nuclear Fuel: Single Cycle Test Discription, Vol. III. x, 308p. Date not set. 46.50. Entropy Ltd.

--Thermal Mechanical Behavior of V02 Nuclear Fuel: Electrothermal Analysis, Vol. II. x, 122p. Date not set. 19.50. Entropy Ltd.

Christensen, R., ed. Entropy Minimax Sourcebook: Applications. 800p. 1981. 59.50 (ISBN 0-686-28919-6). Entropy Ltd.

Christensen, R., et al. Futuristic Community Development: East Central Florida Crime Impact 1974-1984. xxii, 390p. Date not set. pap. 15.00 (ISBN 0-686-28750-9, 04-80-04). Entropy Ltd.

Christensen, R. M. Mechanics of Composite Materials. LC 79-14093. 1979. 33.50 (ISBN 0-471-05167-5, Pub. by Wiley-Interscience). Wiley.

Christensen, Walter K. Upper Cretaceous Belemnites from the Kristianstad Area. (Fossils & Strata: No. 7). 1975. pap. text ed. 15.00x (ISBN 8-200-09374-3, Dist. by Columbia U Pr). Universitet.

Christensen, Winnie, jt. auth. see Christensen, Chuck.

Christenson, Charles J., jt. auth. see Bower, Joseph L.

Christenson, Charles J., et al. Managerial Economics: Text & Cases. rev ed. 1973. text ed. 18.95x (ISBN 0-256-00089-1). Irwin.

Christenson, Evelyn. Gaining Through Losing. 1980. 8.95 (ISBN 0-88207-795-3). Victor Bks.

--Lord, Change Me. 1977. pap. 3.50 (ISBN 0-88207-756-2). Victor Bks.

Christenson, Evelyn & Blake, Viola. What Happens When Women Pray. 144p. 1975. pap. 2.95 (ISBN 0-88207-715-5). Victor Bks.

Christenson, James A. & Robinson, Jerry W., Jr. Community Development in America. (Illus.). 256p. 1980. text ed. 8.95 (ISBN 0-8138-1475-8). Iowa St U Pr.

Christenson, Larry. The Charismatic Renewal Among Lutherans. 1976. pap. 3.95 (ISBN 0-87123-081-X, 210081). Bethany Fell.

--Christ & His Church. (Trinity Bible Ser.). 1973. pap. 4.95 spiral wkbk. (ISBN 0-87123-550-1, 240550). Bethany Fell.

--The Covenant. (Trinity Bible Ser.). 1973. pap. spiral wkbk. (ISBN 0-87123-551-X, 240551). Bethany Fell.

--Gift of Tongues. 1963. pap. 0.45 (ISBN 0-87123-184-0, 260184). Bethany Fell.

--How to Have a Daily Quiet Time. 1979. saddle stitch 0.60 (ISBN 0-87123-235-9, 200235). Bethany Fell.

--The Kingdom. (Trinity Bible Ser.). 1972. pap. 4.95 (ISBN 0-87123-548-X, 240548). Bethany Fell.

--Larry Christenson's Financial Record System for Families & Individuals. 160p. (Orig.). 1980. spiral bdg. 4.95 (ISBN 0-87123-344-4, 210344). Bethany Fell.

--A Message to the Charismatic Movement. 1972. pap. 1.75 (ISBN 0-87123-372-X, 200372). Bethany Fell.

--Social Action - Jesus Style. LC 75-44927. Orig. Title: Charismatic Approach to Social Action. 1974. pap. 1.50 (ISBN 0-87123-504-8, 200504). Bethany Fell.

--Speaking in Tongues. LC 97-5595. 1968. pap. 2.25 (ISBN 0-87123-518-8, 200518). Bethany Fell.

--Which Way the Family? 1973. pap. 0.75 (ISBN 0-87123-643-5, 260643). Bethany Fell.

Christenson, Larry & Christenson, Nordis. The Christian Couple. LC 77-24085. 1977. pap. 3.95 (ISBN 0-87123-051-8); 0.95 (ISBN 0-87123-046-1, 210046). Bethany Fell.

Christenson, Nordis, jt. auth. see Christenson, Larry.

Christesen, Barbara. The First Olympic Games. LC 78-15976. (Famous Firsts Ser.). (Illus.). 1978. lib. bdg. 7.35 (ISBN 0-686-51102-6). Silver.

--The Magic & Meaning of Voodoo. LC 77-12781. (Myth, Magic & Superstition Ser.). (Illus.). (gr. 4-5). 1977. PLB 9.65 (ISBN 0-8172-1030-X). Raintree Pubs.

--Myths of the Orient. LC 77-22199. (Myth, Magic & Superstition Ser.). (Illus.). (gr. 4-5). 1977. PLB 9.65 (ISBN 0-8172-1043-1). Raintree Pubs.

Christian, Barbara. Black Women Novelists: The Development of a Tradition, 1892-1976. LC 79-8953. (Contributions in Afro-American & African Studies: No. 52). xiv, 275p. 1980. lib. bdg. 25.00 (ISBN 0-313-20750-X, CBW/). Greenwood.

--Creative Escapes. LC 80-65477. 1980. pap. 5.50 (ISBN 0-8224-1631-X). Pitman Learning.

Christian, C. Donald, jt. ed. see Reid, Duncan E.

Christian, Catherine. The Pendragon. 624p. 1980. pap. 2.95 (ISBN 0-446-83820-9). Warner Bks.

Christian, Diane, jt. auth. see Jackson, Bruce.

Christian, Donna. Language Arts & Dialect Differences. (Dialects & Educational Equity Ser.: No. 5). 1979. pap. 2.50 (ISBN 0-87281-124-7). Ctr Appl Ling.

Christian, Donna, jt. auth. see Wolfram, Walt.

Christian, Harry, ed. The Sociology of Journalism & the Press. (Sociological Review Monograph: No. 29). 1981. pap. 9.95x (ISBN 0-8476-3257-1). Rowman.

Christian, J. H., jt. ed. see Hobbs, Betty C.

Christian, J. W. Theory of Transformations in Metals & Alloys., Part 1: Equilibrium & General Kinetic Theory. 2nd ed. LC 74-22470. 564p. 1975. text ed. 57.00 (ISBN 0-08-018031-0). Pergamon.

Christian, J. W., et al, eds. Progress in Material Science, Vol. 24. (Illus.). 346p. 1980. 85.00 (ISBN 0-08-027107-3). Pergamon.

Christian, John. Management, Machines & Methods in Civil Engineering. 375p. 1981. 34.95 (ISBN 0-471-06334-7, Pub. by Wiley-Interscience). Wiley.

--The Oxford Union Murals. LC 79-23664. (Illus.). 84p. 1981. incl. fiche 24.00 (ISBN 0-226-68922-0). U of Chicago Pr.

Christian, M. B. The Goosehill Gang, 4 bks. Incl. The Goosehill Gang & the Chocolate Cake Caper: Illustrating 1 John 3: 18 (ISBN 0-570-03606-2, 39DD1031); The Goosehill Gang & the Disappearing Dues: Illustrating Matthew 22: 39 (ISBN 0-570-03607-0, 39DD1032); The Goosehill Gang & the Test Paper Thief: Illustrating Matthew 5: 39 (ISBN 0-570-03608-9, 39DD1033); The Goosehill Gang & the Vanishing Sandwich: Illustrating Luke 10: 37 (ISBN 0-570-03609-7, 39DD1034). (Illus.). (gr. 1-4). 1977. pap. 3.55 set (ISBN 0-686-67954-7); pap. 0.95 ea. Concordia.

Christian, M. Blount. CB Convoy Caper. (The Goosehill Gang Series: No. 2). (gr. 2-5). 1981. pap. 1.10 (ISBN 0-570-07352-9, 39-1042). Concordia.

--The Pocket Park Problem. (The Goosehill Gang Series: No. 2). (gr. 2-5). 1977. pap. 1.10 (ISBN 0-570-07353-7, 39-1043). Concordia.

Christian, Marcus B. Negro Ironworkers in Louisiana. LC 72-85953. (Illus.). 64p. (Orig.). 1972. pap. 3.95 (ISBN 0-911116-74-5). Pelican.

Christian, Mary B. Christmas Reflections. 1980. pap. 3.50 (ISBN 0-570-03494-9, 56-1711). Concordia.

--The Devil Take You, Barnabas Beane! LC 79-7891. (Illus.). (ps-3). 1980. 6.95 (ISBN 0-690-03997-2, TYC-J); PLB 6.89 (ISBN 0-690-03998-0). T Y Crowell.

--The Doggone Mystery. Fay, Ann, ed. LC 80-10448. (A First Read-Alone Mystery Bk.). (Illus.). (gr. 1-3). 1980. 5.50g (ISBN 0-8075-1656-2). A Whitman.

--The First Sign of Winter. LC 73-1066. (Illus.). 48p. (gr. k-3). 1973. 5.95 o.s.i. (ISBN 0-8193-0671-1, Four Winds); PLB 5.41 o.s.i. (ISBN 0-8193-0672-X). Schol Bk Serv.

--The Lucky Man. LC 79-11024. (Ready-to-Read Ser.). (Illus.). (gr. 1-4). 1979. 7.95 (ISBN 0-02-718270-3, 71827). Macmillan.

--The Test Paper Thief. (Goosehill Gang Ser.). (Illus.). 32p. (gr. 1-4). 1976. pap. 1.10 (ISBN 0-570-03608-9, 39-1033). Concordia.

--Two-Ton Secret. Fay, Ann, ed. (First Read-Alone Mysteries Ser.). (Illus.). 32p. (gr. 1-3). 1981. 5.50 (ISBN 0-8075-8165-8). A Whitman.

--The Vanishing Sandwich. (Goosehill Gang Ser.). (Illus.). 32p. (gr. 1-4). 1976. pap. 1.10 (ISBN 0-570-03609-7, 39-1034). Concordia.

Christian, Paula. Amanda. 144p. 1981. pap. 6.50 (ISBN 0-931328-07-1). Timely Bks.

--Another Kind of Love. LC 79-92584. 144p. 1980. pap. 6.50 (ISBN 0-931328-06-3). Timely Bks.

--Edge of Twilight. LC 78-54182. 1978. pap. 6.50x (ISBN 0-931328-00-4). Timely Bks.

--The Other Side of Desire. 160p. 1981. pap. 6.50 (ISBN 0-931328-08-X). Timely Bks.

--This Side of Love. LC 78-54181. 1978. pap. 6.50 (ISBN 0-931328-01-2). Timely Bks.

Christian, Portia, ed. Agricultural Enterprises Management in an Urban-Industrial Society: A Guide to Information Sources. LC 76-27856. (Management Information Guide: No. 34). 1978. 30.00 (ISBN 0-8103-0834-7). Gale.

Christian, Portia & Hicks, Richard, eds. Ethics in Business Conduct: A Guide to Information Sources. LC 77-127411. (Management Information Guides Ser.: No. 21). 1970. 30.00 (ISBN 0-8103-0821-5). Gale.

Christian, R. F., jt. auth. see Borras, F. M.

Christian, R. F., ed. & tr. Tolstoy's Letters, 2 vols. LC 77-90494. (Encore Editions). (Illus.). 1978. 9.95 set (ISBN 0-684-15596-6, ScribT). Scribner.

Christian, Reginald F. Tolstoy: A Critical Introduction. LC 69-19373. 1970. 48.00 (ISBN 0-521-07493-2); pap. 10.95 (ISBN 0-521-09585-9, 585). Cambridge U Pr.

Christian, Roy. Derbyshire. 27.00 (ISBN 0-7134-1295-X, Pub. by Batsford England). David & Charles.

--Old English Customs. (Illus.). 1966. 7.50 o.p. (ISBN 0-8038-5342-4). Hastings.

--The Peak District. LC 75-26358. (British Topographical Ser.). (Illus.). 224p. 1976. 14.95 (ISBN 0-7153-7094-4). David & Charles.

--Vanishing Britain. 1977. 8.95 (ISBN 0-7153-7346-3). David & Charles.

Christian, W. P., et al. Schedule-Induced Behavior, Vol. 1. LC 77-307775. 1977. 14.40 (ISBN 0-904406-52-0). Eden Med Res.

Christian, William, ed. The Idea File of Harold Adam Innis. 1980. 20.00x (ISBN 0-8020-2350-9); pap. 7.50 (ISBN 0-8020-6382-9). U of Toronto Pr.

Christian, William A., Jr. Apparitions in Late Medieval & Renaissance Spain. LC 80-8541. (Illus.). 304p. 1981. 20.00x (ISBN 0-691-05326-X). Princeton U Pr.

--Local Religion in Sixteenth-Century Spain. LC 80-7513. 296p. 1981. 18.50x (ISBN 0-691-05306-5). Princeton U Pr.

Christiani, Adolph. The Principles of Expression in Pianoforte Playing. LC 74-1348. (Music Reprint Ser.). 303p. 1974. Repr. of 1886 ed. lib. bdg. 21.50 (ISBN 0-306-70623-7). Da Capo.

Christiani, Dounia B., ed. see Ibsen, Henrik.

Christianica Center. Christianica. LC 74-13005. (Illus.). 1975. 6.50 (ISBN 0-911346-02-3). Christianica.

--Scriptural Rosary. LC 64-66463. (Illus.). 1961. 4.50 (ISBN 0-911346-01-5). Christianica.

Christianica Ctr. Rosario Biblico. (Illus.). 1980. 4.50 (ISBN 0-911346-04-X). Christianica.

Christians, Clifford G. & Covert, Catherine L. Teaching Ethics in Journalism Education. LC 80-10426. (The Teaching of Ethics Ser.). 71p. 1980. pap. 4.00 (ISBN 0-916558-08-8). Hastings Ctr Inst Soc.

Christians, Clifford G., ed. see Ellul, Jacques, et al.

Christians, George F. The Compulsive Overeater: Seven Steps to Thin Sanity. LC 77-90808. 1978. 5.95 o.p. (ISBN 0-385-14038-X). Doubleday.

Christiansen, Donald, jt. auth. see Fink, Donald G.

Christiansen, Eric. The Northern Crusades: The Baltic & the Catholic Frontier, 1100-1525. (Illus.). xxii, 265p. 1981. 25.00x (ISBN 0-8166-0994-2); pap. 10.95x (ISBN 0-8166-1018-5). U of Minn Pr.

--Origins of Military Power in Spain, 1800-1854. (Oxford Historical Monographs). 1967. 7.95x o.p. (ISBN 0-19-821828-1). Oxford U Pr.

Christiansen, Harley D. Basic Background for Test Interpretation. (Illus.). 96p. (Orig.). 1981. pap. text ed. 8.95 (ISBN 0-915456-04-4). P Juul Pr.

--Casebook of Test Interpretation in Counseling. (Illus.). 96p. (Orig.). 1981. pap. text ed. 8.95 (ISBN 0-915456-05-2). P Juul Pr.

--Key Readings in Testing. 96p. (Orig.). 1981. pap. text ed. 8.95 (ISBN 0-915456-06-0). P Juul Pr.

--Self Relaxation: Comfort in Times of Tension. (Illus.). 96p. (Orig.). 1981. pap. 8.95 (ISBN 0-915456-02-8). P Juul Pr.

--Testing in Counseling, Uses & Misuses. (Illus.). 96p. (Orig.). 1981. pap. text ed. 8.95 (ISBN 0-915456-03-6). P Juul Pr.

Christiansen, Karl O., jt. auth. see Hurwitz, Stephan.

Christiansen, Larry K. & Strate, James W. Cases in Retail Management Attitude Development. (Gregg-McGraw-Hill Marketing Ser.). (Illus.). 256p. Date not set. wkbk. 5.75 (ISBN 0-07-010820-X, G). McGraw.

Christiansen, M. Skytte. The Pocket Encyclopedia of Wild Flowers. (European Ecology Ser.). (Illus.). 1965. 9.95 (ISBN 0-7137-0374-1, Pub by Blandford Pr England). Sterling.

Christiansen, Monty L. Park Planning Handbook: Fundamentals of Physical Planning for Parks & Recreation Areas. LC 77-51844. 1977. text ed. 24.95 (ISBN 0-471-15619-1). Wiley.

Christiansen, Rex. Forgotten Railways: North & Mid Wales. LC 75-31317. (Forgotten Railways Ser.). (Illus.). 144p. 1976. 14.95 (ISBN 0-7153-7059-6). David & Charles.

--A Regional History of the Railways of Great Britain: The West Midlands, Vol. 7. 1973. 19.95 (ISBN 0-7153-6093-0). David & Charles.

Christianson, Christopher. The Concise Gospel & the Acts. 1973. 4.95 o.p. (ISBN 0-88270-042-1). Logos.

Christianson, Christopher J., compiled by. New Life. pap. 3.95 o.p. (ISBN 0-88270-008-1). Logos.

Christianson, Victoria, jt. auth. see Laumark, Eleanor.

Christie, A. B. Infectious Diseases: Epidemiology & Clinical Practice. 3rd ed. (Illus.). 1981. text ed. 95.00 (ISBN 0-443-02263-1). Churchill.

Christie, A. B. & Christie, Mary C. Food Hygiene & Food Hazards. 2nd ed. (Illus.). 1977. 12.95 o.p. (ISBN 0-571-04949-4, Pub. by Faber & Faber); pap. 5.95 (ISBN 0-571-10902-0). Merrimack Bk Serv.

Christie, Agatha. And Then There Were None. (Enriched Classics Ser.). (YA) pap. 2.25 (ISBN 0-671-82683-2). WSP.

--Cards on the Table. 1980. pap. 2.25 (ISBN 0-440-11052-1). Dell.

--A Caribbean Mystery. 1980. pap. write for info. (ISBN 0-671-83052-X). PB.

--Come Tell Me How You Live. 1980. pap. 2.50 (ISBN 0-671-43282-6). PB.

--Crooked House. 1980. pap. 2.50 (ISBN 0-671-83319-7). PB.

--Death Comes As the End. 1977. pap. 2.50 (ISBN 0-671-43283-4). PB.

--Death on the Nile. 288p. 1981. pap. 2.50 (ISBN 0-553-14847-8). Bantam.

--Funerals Are Fatal. 1980. pap. 2.25 (ISBN 0-671-83173-9). PB.

--The Man in the Brown Suit. 1981. pap. 2.25 (ISBN 0-440-15230-5). Dell.

--The Mirror Crack'd. 1980. pap. 2.50. PB.

--Mister Parker Pyne, Detective. 1971. pap. 1.95 o.s.i. (ISBN 0-440-15888-5). Dell.

--Mr. Parker Pyne, Detective. 1981. pap. 2.25 (ISBN 0-440-15888-5). Dell.

--The Mousetrap & Other Plays. 720p. 1981. pap. 3.95 (ISBN 0-553-13024-2). Bantam.

--Murder in Retrospect. 192p. 1981. pap. 2.25 (ISBN 0-440-16030-8). Dell.

--Murder Is Announced. 1980. pap. 2.50 (ISBN 0-671-43284-2). PB.

--Murder of Roger Ackroyd. 1980. pap. 2.25 (ISBN 0-671-83050-3). PB.

--Murder on the Links. 1980. pap. 1.95 (ISBN 0-440-16102-9). Dell.

--The Mysterious Affair at Styles. 1980. pap. 8.95 (ISBN 0-8161-3105-8, Large Print Bks). G K Hall.

--N or M? Date not set. pap. 2.25 (ISBN 0-440-16254-8). Dell.

--Partners in Crime. 1981. pap. 2.25 (ISBN 0-440-16848-1). Dell.

--Postern of Fate. 288p. 1980. pap. 2.25 (ISBN 0-553-13775-1). Bantam.

--Remembered Death. 1980. pap. write for info. (ISBN 0-671-83442-8). PB.

--The Secret Adversary. 224p. 1981. pap. 2.25 (ISBN 0-553-13777-8). Bantam.

--Three Blind Mice & Other Stories. 1980. pap. 2.25 (ISBN 0-440-15867-2). Dell.

--Why Didn't They Ask Evans. 1981. pap. 2.25 (ISBN 0-440-10704-0). Dell.

Christie, F. M. Graded German Comprehension. 1968. pap. text ed. 2.50x (ISBN 0-435-38160-1). Heinemann Ed.

Christie, G. A., jt. ed. see Briggs, M. H.

Christie, Ian R. Myth & Reality in Late Eighteenth-Century British Politics & Other Papers. LC 73-104105. 1970. 23.50x (ISBN 0-520-01673-4). U of Cal Pr.

Christie, Ian R., jt. auth. see Brown, Lucy M.

Christie, John A. Thoreau As World Traveler. LC 65-24586. (Illus.). 1966. 22.50x (ISBN 0-231-02833-4). Columbia U Pr.

Christie, John D., ed. see Virgil.

Christie, Mary C., jt. auth. see Christie, A. B.

Christie, Nils. Limits to Pain. 96p. 1981. pap. 10.00x (ISBN 82-00-05528-0). Universitet.

Christie, Nils, ed. Scandinavian Studies in Criminology, Vol. 5. 125p. 1980. cancelled (ISBN 0-85520-095-2, Pub. by Martin Robertson England). Biblio Dist.

Christie, Tom & Holmes, Deb. Thumbs up. (gr. 5-12). 1978. 11.95 (ISBN 0-916456-34-X, GA88). Good Apple.

Christie, W. W. Lipid Analysis. 1973. text ed. 42.00 (ISBN 0-08-017753-0). Pergamon.

Christie, W. W., ed. Lipid Metabolism in Ruminant Animals. (Illus.). 464p. 1981. 70.00 (ISBN 0-08-023789-4). Pergamon.

Christie, William M., Jr. Preface to a Neo-Firthian Linguistics. LC 80-21016. (Edward Sapir Monograph Series in Language, Culture, & Cognition: No. 7). viii, 70p. (Orig.). 1980. pap. 6.00x (ISBN 0-933104-11-1). Jupiter Pr.

Christiensen, Ronald, ed. Entropy Minimax Sourcebook. (Entropy Minimax Sourcebook Ser.: Vol. IV). 1981. lib. bdg. 59.50 (ISBN 0-938876-07-4). Entropy Ltd.

Christie's. Christie's Review of the Season 1978. Herbert, John, ed. (Illus.). 1979. 45.00 (ISBN 0-02-525270-4). Macmillan.

Christin, Pierre, et al. Sejour En France. LC 73-1317. (Illus.). 1975. pap. 6.95x o.p. (ISBN 0-684-14019-5, ScribC). Scribner.

Christ-Janer, Albert, et al, eds. American Hymns Old & New. LC 79-4630. (Illus.). 833p. 1980. 45.00 (ISBN 0-231-03458-X); pre-december 19.95 (ISBN 0-686-61142-X). Columbia U Pr.

Christman, Elizabeth. A Broken Family. 256p. 1981. 10.95 (ISBN 0-688-00473-3). Morrow.

--Flesh & Spirit. 1980. pap. 2.25 (ISBN 0-686-69260-8, 52142). Avon.

Christman, Ernst H. Primer on Refraction. (Illus.). 128p. 1972. pap. 11.75 spiral bd. (ISBN 0-398-02258-5). C C Thomas.

Christman, H. K., jt. auth. see Gish, Ira M.

Christman, Luther, jt. auth. see Counte, Michael A.

Christodoulou, G. N., ed. Aspects of Preventive Psychiatry. (Bibliotheca Psychiatrica: No. 160). (Illus.). vi, 142p. 1980. soft cover 42.00 (ISBN 3-8055-1218-X). S Karger.

Christofalo, Vincent J., jt. ed. see Rothblat, George H.

Christoff, Nicholas B. Saturday Night, Sunday Morning. LC 77-7830. 1978. 7.95 o.p. (ISBN 0-06-061380-7, HarpR). Har-Row.

--Saturday Night, Sunday Morning: Singles of the Church. LC 77-7841. 160p. 1980. pap. 4.95 (ISBN 0-06-061381-5, RD 341, HarpR). Har-Row.

Christoph, H. J. Diseases of Dogs. LC 71-163386. 279p. 1974. text ed. 115.00 (ISBN 0-08-015800-5). Pergamon.

Christoph, S. G. Collision Theory & Statistical Theory of Chemical Reactions. (Lectures Notes in Chemistry: Vol. 18). (Illus.). 322p. 1980. pap. 27.70 (ISBN 0-387-10012-1). Springer-Verlag.

Christopher, Bob & Christopher, Ellen. America on Eight to Sixteen Dollars a Night 1978-79. 6th ed. LC 77-85277. 1978. pap. 5.95 o.p. (ISBN 0-688-08321-8). Morrow.

--America's Favorite Restaurants & Inns. 7th, rev. ed. LC 79-2034. 1019p. (Orig.). 1980. pap. 6.95 (ISBN 0-688-08550-4). Morrow.

Christopher, Ellen, jt. auth. see Christopher, Bob.

Christopher, John. Beyond the Burning Lands. LC 78-152288. (gr. 5-9). 1971. 8.95 (ISBN 0-02-718420-X). Macmillan.

--City of Gold & Lead. (gr. 7 up). 1967. 8.95 (ISBN 0-02-718380-7). Macmillan.

--The Death of Grass. (Alpha Books). 96p. (Orig.). 1979. pap. text ed. 2.25x (ISBN 0-19-424232-3). Oxford U Pr.

--Dom & Va. 176p. (gr. 5-8). 1973. 7.95 (ISBN 0-02-718320-3). Macmillan.

--Empty World. (gr. 7-9). 1978. PLB 10.95 (ISBN 0-525-29250-0). Dutton.

--Fireball. LC 80-22094. (gr. 5-7). 1981. PLB 9.95 (ISBN 0-525-29738-3). Dutton.

--Guardians. (gr. 6 up). 1970. 5.95g o.s.i. (ISBN 0-02-718370-X). Macmillan.

--Lotus Caves. LC 74-78074. (gr. 6-9). 1969. 7.95g o.s.i. (ISBN 0-02-718390-4). Macmillan.

--Pool of Fire. LC 68-23062. (gr. 5-7). 1968. 8.95 (ISBN 0-02-718350-5). Macmillan.

--Prince in Waiting. LC 70-119838. (gr. 5-9). 1970. 4.95 o.s.i. (ISBN 0-02-718410-2). Macmillan.

--Prince in Waiting. LC 70-119838. 224p. (gr. 5-9). 1974. pap. 2.75 (ISBN 0-02-042400-0, 04240, Collier). Macmillan.

--The Sword of the Spirits. LC 74-176419. (Illus.). 192p. (gr. 5-9). 1972. 4.95 o.s.i. (ISBN 0-02-718340-8). Macmillan.

--The Sword of the Spirits Trilogy, 3 bks. Incl. Beyond the Burning Lands; The Prince in Waiting; The Sword of the Spirits. (gr. 6 up). 1980. Boxed Set. pap. 7.95 (ISBN 0-02-042770-0, Collier). Macmillan.

--The Tripods Trilogy, 3 bks. Incl. The White Mountains; the City of Gold & Lead; The Pool of Fire; The White Mountains. (gr. 6 up). 1980. Boxed Set. pap. 7.95 (ISBN 0-02-042570-8, Collier). Macmillan.

--White Mountains. (gr. 7 up). 1967. 9.95 (ISBN 0-02-718360-2). Macmillan.

--Wild Jack. 192p. (gr. 5-9). 1974. 8.95 (ISBN 0-02-718300-9, 71830). Macmillan.

--Wild Jack. LC 77-16437. (gr. 5-9). 1978. pap. 1.95 o.s.i. (ISBN 0-02-042410-8, 04241, Collier). Macmillan.

Christopher, John B., et al. Civilization in the West, Pt. II. 4th ed. (Illus.). 512p. 1981. pap. text ed. 13.95 (ISBN 0-13-134932-5). P-H.

Christopher, Kenneth. The Merry Missionary: A Story About Philip Neri. (Stories About Christian Heroes Ser.). (Illus.). 32p. (gr. 6-9). pap. 1.95 (ISBN 0-686-63634-1). Winston Pr.

Christopher, Mark S., jt. auth. see Newman, Steven L.

Christopher, Martin, et al. Customer Service & Distribution Strategy. LC 79-24121. 191p. 1980. 34.95x (ISBN 0-470-26890-5). Halsted Pr.

--Distribution Planning & Control. LC 77-378813. 1979. 19.95 (ISBN 0-566-02013-0, 00314-X, Pub. by Saxon Hse England). Lexington Bks.

Christopher, Matt. Baseball Pals. (Illus.). (gr. 4-6). 1956. 6.95 (ISBN 0-316-13950-5). Little.

--The Basket Counts. (Illus.). (gr. 4-6). 5.95 o.p. (ISBN 0-316-14014-7). Little.

--Catch That Pass. (Illus.). (gr. 3-5). 1974. pap. 0.75 (ISBN 0-671-29612-4). PB.

--Jinx Glove. (Illus.). 48p. (gr. 1-3). 1974. 6.95 (ISBN 0-316-13965-3). Little.

--Kid Who Only Hit Homers. (gr. 4-6). 1972. 6.95 (ISBN 0-316-13918-1). Little.

--Run, Billy, Run. 156p. (gr. 3-6). 1980. 7.95 (ISBN 0-316-14020-1). Little.
--Tight End. 128p. (gr. 3 up). 1981. 6.95 (ISBN 0-316-32672-0). Little.
--Touchdown for Tommy. (Illus.). (gr. 4-6). 1959. 6.95 (ISBN 0-316-13938-6). Little.
--The Twenty-One Mile Swim. LC 79-15197. (gr. 3-7). 1979. 8.95g (ISBN 0-316-13979-3). Little.
Christopher, Milbourne. ESP, Seers & Physics. LC 78-127607. (Illus.). 1970. 10.95 o.s.i. (ISBN 0-690-26815-7, TYC-T); pap. 5.95 o.s.i. (ISBN 0-690-01674-3, TYC-T). T Y Crowell.
--Houdini: The Untold Story. LC 69-11829. (Illus.). 1969. 9.95 o.s.i. (ISBN 0-690-40431-X, TYC-T). T Y Crowell.
--Mediums, Mystics & the Occult. LC 74-26812. (Illus.). 288p. 1975. 9.95 (ISBN 0-690-00476-1, TYC-T). T Y Crowell.
--Milbourne Christopher's Magic Book. LC 77-9098. (Illus.). 1977. 10.95 o.s.i. (ISBN 0-690-01677-8, TYC-T). T Y Crowell.
--Search for the Soul. LC 78-3298. 1979. 10.95 (ISBN 0-690-01760-X, TYC-T). T Y Crowell.
Christopher, W. Management for the Nineteen Eighties. 1979. pap. 6.95 (ISBN 0-13-549154-1, Spec). P-H.
Christopherson, Ragnar, tr. see Madsen, Stephan T.
Christopherson, W. M., jt. auth. see Riotton, G.
Christopherson, W. M., jt. auth. see Vellios, Frank.
Christopherson, William, jt. auth. see Riotton, C.
Christophus, Mike, jt. auth. see Kenyon, Mel.
Christou, Evangelos. The Logos of the Soul. Hillman, James, ed. (Dunquin Ser.). 1963. pap. text ed. 6.50 (ISBN 0-88214-202-X). Spring Pubns.
Christovich, Mary Louise, jt. auth. see Toledano, Roulhac B.
Christy, Francis M. Transfer of Stock, 2 vols. 5th ed. LC 72-84858. 1972. 90.00 (ISBN 0-686-14484-8). Lawyers Co-Op.
Christy, Howard C. The American Girl. LC 76-4778. 1976. lib. bdg. 35.00 (ISBN 0-306-70854-X); pap. 9.95 (ISBN 0-306-80042-X). Da Capo.
Christy, John & Ludvigsen, Karl. The Complete MG Guide Model by Model. 2nd ed. (Illus.). 1979. cancelled (ISBN 0-8306-9783-7); pap. 4.95 (ISBN 0-8306-2056-7, 2056). TAB Bks.
Christy, Van A. Foundations in Singing: A Basic Text in the Fundamentals of Teaching & Song Interpretation - Medium-High Voice Edition. 250p. (Orig.). 1981. write for info. plastic comb bind. (ISBN 0-697-03483-6). Wm C Brown.
Chroman, Eleanor. The Potter's Primer. 1974. pap. 5.95 (ISBN 0-8015-5959-6, Hawthorn). Dutton.
Chromaster, W. W. House Plans Designed for Southern Families. LC 72-96463. (Illus.). 1973. pap. 2.95 o.p. (ISBN 0-8487-0242-5). Oxmoor Hse.
Chronicle Guidance Publications, Inc. Chronicle Two-Year College Databook Nineteen Eighty. 1980. pap. 11.00 (ISBN 0-912578-43-2). Chron Guide.
Chrysostomos, Archimandrite. The Ancient Fathers of the Church: Translated Narratives from the Evertinos on Passions & Perfection in Christ. (Illus.). 118p. 1980. 7.95 (ISBN 0-916586-77-4); pap. 4.95. Hellenic Coll Pr.
Chryssostomidis, Marjorie, ed. Offshore Petroleum Engineering: A Bibliographic Guide to Publications & Information Sources. 1978. 50.00x (ISBN 0-89397-045-X). Nichols Pub.
Chrystal, K. A. Controversies in British Macroeconomics. 1979. 21.00x (ISBN 0-86003-022-9, Pub. by Allan Pubs England); pap. 10.50x (ISBN 0-86003-123-3). State Mutual Bk.
Chrystie, Frances N. Pets. rev. 3rd ed. (Illus.). (gr. 4 up). 1974. 8.95 (ISBN 0-316-14051-1). Little.
Chu, Daniel & Chu, Samuel. Passage to the Golden Gate: A History of the Chinese in America to 1910. LC 67-10546. (Illus.). (gr. 7 up). 1967. pap. 2.50 o.p. (ISBN 0-385-05971-X, Z11, Zenith). Doubleday.
Chu, Daniel, et al. The Glorious Age in Africa: The Story of Three Great African Empires. LC 65-10280. 1965. 4.95 o.p. (ISBN 0-385-03763-5). Doubleday.
Chu, Donald, jt. ed. see Segrave, Jeffrey.
Chu, Godwin C. & Schramm, Wilbur. Learning from Television: What the Research Says. 116p. 1979. pap. 6.00 (Pub Telecomm). NAEB.
Chu, Samuel, jt. auth. see Chu, Daniel.
Chu, W. K., jt. auth. see Sherrill, W. A.
Chu, Wen-Kaung, jt. auth. see Melyan, Gary G.
Chu, Wesley W., ed. Advances in Computer Communications. rev. ed. LC 75-31381. (Illus.). 1977. pap. 27.00 o.p. (ISBN 0-685-79343-5). Artech Hse.
Chu, Y. Computer Organization & Microprogramming. (Illus.). 528p. 1972. ref. ed. 24.95 (ISBN 0-13-166025-X). P-H.
Chua, L. & Lin, P. Computer-Aided Analysis of Electronic Circuits: Algorathms & Computational Techniques. 1975. 32.95 (ISBN 0-13-165415-2). P-H.
Chuan, Helen, ed. Medical-Surgical Nursing: Pretest Self-Assessment & Review. Allman, Margaret. LC 78-50598. (PreTest Self-Assessment & Review). (Illus.). 1978. pap. 6.95 (ISBN 0-07-051567-0). McGraw-Pretest.
Chuang Shu Chi & Deisher, Joe. Chinese Secrets of Longevity. (Illus.). 126p. (Orig.). 1979. pap. 3.50 o.p. (ISBN 0-686-65533-8). C E Tuttle.
Chuang Shu Chih & Deisher, Joe. Chinese Secrets of Longevity. (Illus., Orig.). 1973. pap. 3.50 o.p. (ISBN 0-8048-1338-8, Pub. by Shufunotomo Co Ltd Japan). C E Tuttle.
Chuang Tzu. Chuang Tzu: Basic Writings. Watson, Burton, tr. LC 64-21079. pap. 5.00x (ISBN 0-231-08606-7). Columbia U Pr.
--Complete Works of Chuang Tzu. Watson, Burton, tr. LC 68-19000. (Translations from the Oriental Classics & Records of Civilization Ser.). 1968. 23.00x (ISBN 0-231-03147-5). Columbia U Pr.
Chubb, Michael. One Third of Our Time? An Introduction to Recreation, Behavior & Resources: An Introduction to Recreation Behavior & Resources. LC 80-25131. 600p. 1981. text ed. 16.95 (ISBN 0-471-15637-X); write for info. study guide (ISBN 0-471-02184-9). Wiley.
Chubb, Thomas. Comparative Excellence & Obligation of Moral & Positive Duties, 1731. Wellek, Rene, ed. LC 75-11205. (British Philosophers & Theologians of the 17th & 18th Centuries Ser.). 1978. lib. bdg. 42.00 (ISBN 0-8240-1760-9). Garland Pub.
Chubin, Daryl E., jt. auth. see Studer, Kenneth E.
Chudacoff, Edward, jt. auth. see Berry, Wallace.
Chudacoff, Howard P. The Evolution of American Urban Society. 2nd ed. (Illus.). 256p. 1981. pap. text ed. 10.95 (ISBN 0-13-293605-4). P-H.
Chudley. Construction Technology One: Checkbook. 1981. text ed. price not set (ISBN 0-408-00602-1, Westbury Hse). Butterworth.
Chugg, Brian. Devon: A Thematic Study. LC 79-56459. (Illus.). 208p. 1980. 27.00 (ISBN 0-7134-0417-5, Pub. by Batsford England). David & Charles.
--Victorian & Edwardian Devon. 1975. pap. 11.95 (ISBN 0-7134-2113-4, Pub. by Batsford England). David & Charles.
Chujoy, Anatole, et al, trs. see Vaganova, Agrippina.
Chu-Kia, Wang. Introductory Structural Analysis with Matrix Methods. LC 72-667. 240p. 1973. ref. ed. 26.95 (ISBN 0-13-501650-9). P-H.
Chukovsky, Kornei. Alexander Blok As Man & Poet. Burgin & O'Connor, trs. from Rus. 1981. 22.00 (ISBN 0-88233-491-3). Ardis Pubs.
--From Two to Five. Morton, Miriam, ed. & tr. (YA) (gr. 7 up). 1963. pap. 3.95 (ISBN 0-520-00238-5, CAL119). U of Cal Pr.
Chukuocha, Bessie. Accounting Methods for Non-Profit Organizations. 1981. 6.95 (ISBN 0-8062-1650-6). Carlton.
Chumbley, Lee C. Ophthalmology in Internal Medicine. (Illus.). 288p. 1980. write for info. (ISBN 0-7216-2578-9). Saunders.
Chun, Bong D., et al. Traditional Korean Legan Attitudes. (Korean Research Monographs: No. 2). 101p. 1980. pap. 8.00 (ISBN 0-912966-30-0). IEAS Ctr Chinese Stud.
Chun, Richard. Moo Duk Kwan Tae Kwon Do, Korean Art of Self-Defense. Johnson, Gilbert, et al, eds. LC 75-3784. (Ser. 120). (Illus.). 1975. pap. text ed. 6.95 (ISBN 0-89750-015-6). Ohara Pubns.
Chun-fang Yu. The Renewal of Buddhism in China: Chu-Hung & the Late Ming Synthesis. LC 79-28073. (Buddhist Studies). (Illus.). 1980. 25.00x (ISBN 0-231-04972-2). Columbia U Pr.
Chung, Edward K. Electrocardiography: Practical Applications with Vectorial Principles. 2nd ed. (Illus.). 693p. 1980. text ed. 42.50 (ISBN 0-06-140642-2, Harper Medical). Har-Row.
Chung, Edward K., ed. Cardiac Emergency Care. 2nd ed. LC 79-28235. (Illus.). 475p. 1980. text ed. 25.00 (ISBN 0-8121-0690-3). Lea & Febiger.
Chung, Kae H. Ventriloquism in a Nutshell. (Illus.). 1974. pap. 3.00 (ISBN 0-686-20905-2, 065). Maher Ventril Studio.
Chung, Kai L. A Course in Probability Theory. 2nd ed. (Probability & Mathematical Statistics: A Series of Monographs & Textbooks). 1974. 23.95 (ISBN 0-12-174650-X). Acad Pr.
Chung, Kyung C. New Korea. (Illus.). 1962. 6.00 o.s.i. (ISBN 0-02-525540-1). Macmillan.
Chung, Stanley M., ed. Hip Disorders in Infants & Children. (Illus.). 450p. 1981. text ed. price not set (ISBN 0-8121-0706-3). Lea & Febiger.
Chung, William K., jt. auth. see Denison, Edward F.
Chun-ming, Hwang. Drowning of an Old Cat & Other Stories. Goldblatt, Howard, tr. LC 80-7494. (Chinese Literature in Translation Ser.). 320p. 1980. 27.50x (ISBN 0-253-32452-1); pap. 9.95 (ISBN 0-253-20253-1). Ind U Pr.
Churacek, Jaroslov, ed. see Gasparic, Jiri.
Churba, Joseph. The Politics of Defeat: America's Decline in the Middle East. (Illus.). 1977. text ed. 12.50x (ISBN 0-8290-0391-6). Irvington.
Church & Schatz. Office Systems & Careers: A Resource for the Administrative Assistants. 780p. 1981. text ed. 18.95 (ISBN 0-205-07134-1, 087134-6); tchrs' ed. avail. (ISBN 0-205-07135-X). Allyn.
Church, Alfred J. Aeneid for Boys & Girls. (gr. 6 up). 1962. 4.95g o.s.i. (ISBN 0-02-718400-5). Macmillan.
--Lucius, Adventures of a Roman Boy. LC 60-16706. (gr. 7-11). 8.50x (ISBN 0-8196-0108-X). Biblo.
--Roman Life in the Days of Cicero. LC 61-24994. (gr. 7-11). 9.50x (ISBN 0-8196-0105-5). Biblo.
Church, Austin H. Mechanical Vibrations. 2nd ed. LC 63-14755. 1963. text ed. 34.95 (ISBN 0-471-15678-7). Wiley.
Church, Carol B. Billie Jean King: Queen of the Courts. Bender, David L. & Mc Cuen, Gary E., eds. (Focus on Famous Women Ser). (Illus.). (gr. 3-9). 1976. 6.95 (ISBN 0-912616-41-5); read-along cassette 9.95 (ISBN 0-89908-240-8). Greenhaven.
--Carol Burnett: Star of Comedy. Bender, David L. & Mc Cuen, Gary E., eds. (Focus on Famous Women Ser). (Illus.). (gr. 3-9). 1976. 6.95 (ISBN 0-912616-42-3); read-along cassette 9.95 (ISBN 0-89908-241-6). Greenhaven.
--Dorothy Day: Friend of the Poor. Bender, David L. & Mc Cuen, Gary E., eds. (Focus on Famous Women Ser). (Illus.). (gr. 3-9). 1976. 6.95 (ISBN 0-912616-45-8); read-along cassette 9.95 (ISBN 0-89908-244-0). Greenhaven.
--Indira Gandhi: Rose of India. Bender, David L. & McCuen, Gary E., eds. (Focus on Famous Women Ser). (gr. 3-9). 1976. 6.95 (ISBN 0-912616-43-1); read-along cassette 9.95 (ISBN 0-89908-242-4). Greenhaven.
--Margaret Mead: Student of the Global Village. Bender, David L. & McCuen, Gary E., eds. (Focus on Famous Women Ser). (Illus.). (gr. 3-9). 1976. 6.95 (ISBN 0-912616-46-6); read-along cassette 9.95 (ISBN 0-89908-245-9). Greenhaven.
--Rose Kennedy: No Time for Tears. Bender, David L. & Mc Cuen, Gary E., eds. (Focus on Famous Women Ser.). (Illus.). (gr. 3-9). 1976. 6.95 (ISBN 0-912616-44-X); read-along cassette 9.95 (ISBN 0-89908-243-2). Greenhaven.
Church, Charles F. Wisconsin Quantity Cuisine: The Foods That Make Wisconsin Famous. LC 76-43274. 1976. 14.95 (ISBN 0-685-74394-2). CBI Pub.
Church, Charles F. & Church, Helen N. Food Values of Portions Commonly Used. 12th ed. 195p. 1975. pap. text ed. 7.95 o.p. (ISBN 0-397-54172-4). Lippincott.
Church, D. C., ed. Digestive Physiology & Nutrition of Ruminants: Practical Nutrition, Vol. 3. 2nd ed. 1980. text ed. 25.00 (ISBN 0-9601586-7-7). O & B Bks.
Church, D. C., et al. Livestock Feeds & Feeding. 1977. 17.00 (ISBN 0-686-26680-3). Dairy Goat.
Church, E. D. Catalog of Books Relating to the Discovery & Early History of North & South America, 5 vols. Cole, G. W., compiled by. Set. 100.00 (ISBN 0-8446-1113-1). Peter Smith.
Church, F. J., tr. see Plato.
Church, Frank, intro. by. Atlantic Conference. LC 70-150596. 1971. pap. 1.25 o.p. (ISBN 0-913456-82-9). Interbk Inc.
Church, George B., Jr. The Life of Henry Laurens Mitchell: Florida's 16th Governor. 1978. 7.50 o.p. (ISBN 0-533-03070-6). Vantage.
Church, Helen N., jt. auth. see Church, Charles F.
Church, Helen N., jt. auth. see Pennington, Jean.
Church, Herbert, Jr. British & American Poetry. (gr. 9-11). 1970. pap. text ed. 4.25x (ISBN 0-88334-027-5). Ind Sch Pr.
Church, Horace K. Excavation Handbook. 1980. 49.50 (ISBN 0-07-010840-4). McGraw.
Church, Joseph. Understanding Your Child from Birth to Three: A Guide to Your Child's Psychological Development. 1973. 6.95 o.p. (ISBN 0-394-47314-0). Random.
Church, Joseph, jt. auth. see Stone, L. Joseph.
Church, Leslie F., ed. see Henry, Matthew.
Church, Margaret. Don Quixote: The Knight of La Mancha. LC 70-172419. 1971. 12.00x (ISBN 0-8147-1352-1). NYU Pr.
--No Way to Stop It. LC 80-27102. (Prime Time Adventures Ser.). (Illus.). 64p. (gr. 4 up). 1981. PLB 7.95 (ISBN 0-516-02107-9). Childrens.
Church of England. Articles to Be Inquired of, in the First Metropoliticall Visitation of the Most Reverend Father, Richarde...Archbishop of Canterbury. LC 74-28851. (English Experience Ser.: No. 732). 1975. Repr. of 1605 ed. 3.50 (ISBN 90-221-0732-9). Walter J Johnson.
--The Durham Book: Being the First Draft of the Revision of the Book of Common Prayer in 1661. Cuming, G. J., ed. LC 79-12674. 1979. Repr. of 1961 ed. lib. bdg. 27.50x (ISBN 0-313-21481-6, CEBC). Greenwood.
--A Parte of a Register, Contayninge Sundrie Memorable Matters, Written by Diuers Godly & Learned in Our Time, Which Stande for the Reformation of Our Church. LC 72-5981. (English Experience Ser.: No. 509). 1973. Repr. of 1593 ed. 67.00 (ISBN 90-221-0509-1). Walter J Johnson.
Church Of Scotland - General Assembly - Committee On Public Worship And Aids To Devotion. Prayers for the Christian Year. 2nd ed. 1952. 8.50x (ISBN 0-19-145602-0). Oxford U Pr.
Church Of South India. Book of Common Worship. 1962. 4.95x (ISBN 0-19-149906-4). Oxford U Pr.
--Order for the Lord's Supper or the Holy Eucharist. 3rd ed. 1962. 0.25x o.p. (ISBN 0-19-635177-4). Oxford U Pr.
Church, Olive. Office Dynamics Company: An Office Services & Temporary Help Practice Set. 250p. 1981. pap. text ed. 6.95 (ISBN 0-205-07136-8); free (ISBN 0-205-07361-1). Allyn.
Church, R. E., jt. auth. see Sneddon, I. B.
Church, R. J. West Africa. 8th ed. (Geographies for Advanced Study Ser.). (Illus.). 560p. 1980. pap. 28.00 (ISBN 0-582-30020-7). Longman.
Church, R. J., et al. Africa & the Islands. 4th ed. LC 77-3459. 1977. pap. text ed. 14.95 (ISBN 0-470-99085-6). Halsted Pr.
Church, Ralph W. Hume's Theory of the Understanding. LC 79-55608. 238p. 1980. Repr. of 1935 ed. lib. bdg. 19.75x (ISBN 0-313-20651-1, CHHU). Greenwood.
Church, Richard. Five Boys in a Cave. LC 51-10431. (gr. 7-9). 1951. 7.95 (ISBN 0-381-99854-1, A27660, JD-J). John Day.
--French Lieutenant: A Ghost Story. LC 71-147272. (gr. 6-8). 1972. 7.95 (ISBN 0-381-99853-3, A28920, JD-J). John Day.
--London in Color. (Illus.). 160p. 1980. 24.00 (ISBN 0-7134-0020-X, Pub. by Batsford England). David & Charles.
Church, Richard W. Spenser. LC 67-23879. 1968. Repr. of 1906 ed. 20.00 (ISBN 0-8103-3057-1). Gale.
Church, Robert. Turtles. (Illus., Orig.). pap. 2.00 (ISBN 0-87666-226-2, M515). TFH Pubns.
Church, Robert L. Education in the United States: An Interpretive History. LC 75-22764. 1976. text ed. 14.95 (ISBN 0-02-905490-7). Free Pr.
Church, Roy. Herbert Austin: The British Motor Car Industry to 1941. (Europa Library of Business Biography: No. 4). (Illus.). 233p. 1979. 30.00x (ISBN 0-905118-29-4). Intl Pubns Serv.
Church, Roy A. Economic & Social Change in a Midland Town: Victorian Nottingham, 1815-1900. LC 66-5409. (Illus.). 1966. 22.50x (ISBN 0-678-05038-4). Kelley.
Church, Ruth E. Wines of the Midwest. LC 77-83753. (Illus.). 207p. 1981. 14.95 (ISBN 0-8040-0779-9). Swallow.
Church, Thomas. Your Private World: A Study of Intimate Gardens. LC 74-99220. 1969. 9.95 o.p. (ISBN 0-87701-001-3). Chronicle Bks.
Church, W. H., compiled by. A Garland of Wisdom: From the Edgar Cayce Readings. (Edgar Cayce Readings). 36p. 1975. pap. 1.25 o.p. (ISBN 0-87604-081-4). ARE Pr.
Church, William F. Impact of Absolutism in France: National Experience Under Richelieu, Mazarin, & Louis XIV. 1969. pap. text ed. 8.95x o.p. (ISBN 0-471-15633-7). Wiley.
--Louis the Fourteenth in Historical Thought. (Historical Controversies Ser.). 128p. 1976. pap. text ed. 2.95x (ISBN 0-393-09211-9). Norton.
Churches Alive Inc. Communicating. (Love One Another Bible Study). 1979. wkbk. 1.50 (ISBN 0-934396-06-X). Churches Alive.
--Contributing. (Love One Another Bible Study). 1979. wkbk. 1.50 (ISBN 0-934396-05-1). Churches Alive.
--Esteeming. (Love One Another Bible Study). 1979. wkbk. 1.50 (ISBN 0-934396-03-5). Churches Alive.
--Forgiving. (Love One Another Bible Study). 1979. wkbk. 1.50 (ISBN 0-934396-01-9). Churches Alive.
Churches Alive, Inc. Growing by Discipling Pastor's Handbook. rev. ed. (Illus.). 150p. 1980. pap. text ed. 8.00 (ISBN 0-934396-09-4). Churches Alive.
--Growth Group Leader's Guide. rev. ed. (Illus.). 110p. 1980. pap. 6.50 (ISBN 0-934396-10-8). Churches Alive.

Churches Alive Inc. Growth Group Member's Notebook. (Illus.). 105p. (Orig.). 1980. pap. text ed. 5.00 (ISBN 0-934396-11-6). Churches Alive.

--Maintaining Unity. (Love One Another Bible Study). 1979. wkbk. 1.50 (ISBN 0-934396-07-8). Churches Alive.

--Submitting. (Love One Another Bible Study). 1979. wkbk. 1.50 (ISBN 0-934396-04-3). Churches Alive.

--Understanding. (Love One Another Bible Study). 1979. wkbk. 1.50 (ISBN 0-934396-02-7). Churches Alive.

Churchill, Charles. Poetical Works. Grant, Douglas, ed. 1956. 49.00x (ISBN 0-19-811316-1). Oxford U Pr.

Churchill, Charles, ed. The City of Beirut: A Socio-Economic Survey. 78p. 1954. pap. 10.00x (ISBN 0-8156-6023-5, Am U Beirut). Syracuse U Pr.

Churchill, Creighton. The World of Wine. (Illus.). 384p. 1980. pap. 6.95 (ISBN 0-02-009460-4, Collier). Macmillan.

Churchill, Don W. Infantile Autism: Proceedings. (Illus.). 360p. 1971. pap. 29.50 photocopy ed. (ISBN 0-398-00307-6). C C Thomas.

--Language of Autistic Children. LC 78-18860. 1978. 14.95 (ISBN 0-470-26417-9). Halsted Pr.

Churchill, E. Richard. Holiday Hullabaloo! Facts, Jokes, & Riddles. (Illus.). (gr. 4 up). 1977. PLB 7.90 (ISBN 0-531-00384-1). Watts.

--The McCartys. 1978. 2.00 (ISBN 0-913488-02-X). Timberline Bks.

Churchill, James E., jt. ed. see Humphrey, Edward.

Churchill, Kenneth. Italy & English Literature: Seventeen Sixty-Four to Nineteen Thirty. LC 79-55524. 230p. 1980. text ed. 25.00x (ISBN 0-06-491130-6). B&N.

Churchill, Linda R. & Richard, E. The Bionic Banana. LC 78-17512. (Illus.). (gr. 3 up). 1979. PLB 6.45 s&l (ISBN 0-531-02920-4). Watts.

Churchill, Linda R., jt. auth. see Richard, E.

Churchill, Peter. Horse Racing. (Illus.). 168p. 1981. 12.95 (ISBN 0-7137-1016-0, Pub. by Blandford Pr England); pap. 6.95 (ISBN 0-7137-1115-9). Sterling.

Churchill, Richard. The Six - Million Dollar Cucumber: Riddles & Fun for Children. LC 75-23103. (Illus.). 96p. (gr. 3 up). 1976. 2.95 o.p. (ISBN 0-531-02429-6); PLB 4.90 o.p. (ISBN 0-531-01106-2). Watts.

Churchill, Sam. Don't Call Me Ma. LC 77-70895. 1977. 7.95 o.p. (ISBN 0-385-08481-1). Doubleday.

Churchill, Stuart W. The Interpretation & Use of Rate Data: The Rate Concept. rev. ed. LC 78-23365. (Illus.). 1979. text ed. 24.50 (ISBN 0-89116-133-3); solutions man. avl. 5.95. Hemisphere Pub.

Churchill, Winston. Richard Carvel. (Illus.). 1914. 12.95 (ISBN 0-02-525660-2). Macmillan.

Churchill, Winston S. My Early Life: A Roving Commission. (Illus.). 1930. lib. rep. ed. 17.00x (ISBN 0-684-15154-5; ScribT). Scribner.

Churchill, Winston S. & Glubb, John. Great Issues 71: A Forum on Important Questions Facing the American Public. 1972. 5.95. TSU Pr.

Churchill-Taylor, Samuel E. Tea & Sects. 64p. (Orig.). 1975. pap. 1.95 (ISBN 0-686-10978-3). MTM Pub Co.

Churchland, P. M. Scientific Realism & the Plasticity of Mind. LC 78-73240. (Cambridge Studies in Philosophy). (Illus.). 1979. 22.50 (ISBN 0-521-22632-5). Cambridge U Pr.

Churchman, C. West, ed. see Singer, Edgar A.

Churchward, L. G. The Soviet Intelligentsia: An Essay on the Social Structure & Roles of the Soviet Intellectuals During the 1960's. (Illus.). 218p. 1973. 18.00 (ISBN 0-7100-7475-1). Routledge & Kegan.

Churchyard, Thomas. A Sparke of Frendship & Warme Goodwill. 40p. pap. 10.00 (ISBN 0-913720-18-6). Sandstone.

Churgin, Bathia D., ed. see Sammartini, Giovanni B.

Chused, Richard H. A Modern Approach to Property: Cases, Notes, Materials. LC 78-5110. (American Casebook Ser.). 1069p. 1978. text ed. 21.95 (ISBN 0-8299-2004-8). West Pub.

Chusid, Martin, ed. see Schubert, Franz.

Chute, B. J. Greenwillow. 1956. 5.95 o.p. (ISBN 0-525-11835-7). Dutton.

--Katie: An Impertinent Fairy Tale. 1978. 7.95 o.p. (ISBN 0-525-13826-9). Dutton.

Chute, Marchette. End of the Search. 1960. 6.95 o.p. (ISBN 0-525-09812-7). Dutton.

--Geoffrey Chaucer of England. 1946. 7.95 o.p. (ISBN 0-525-11257-X). Dutton.

--Search for God. rev. ed. 1949. 10.00 o.p. (ISBN 0-525-19842-3). Dutton.

--Shakespeare of London. 1950. 8.95 o.p. (ISBN 0-525-20182-3); pap. 4.95 (ISBN 0-525-47001-8). Dutton.

--Two Gentle Men: The Lives of George Herbert & Robert Herrick. 1959. 6.95 o.p. (ISBN 0-525-22528-5). Dutton.

--Wonderful Winter. (gr. 5-9). 1954. PLB 5.95 o.p. (ISBN 0-525-43208-6). Dutton.

Ch'u Tung-Tsu. Law & Society in Traditional China. LC 79-1602. 1981. Repr. of 1961 ed. 22.50 (ISBN 0-88355-905-6). Hyperion Conn.

Chwast, Seymour, jt. auth. see Suares, J. C.

Chwun, L. S. Wild Boar Forest. LC 75-13303. pap. 4.95 o.p. (ISBN 0-87359-008-2). Northwood Inst.

Chyet, Stanley F. Lopez of Newport: Colonial American Merchant Prince. LC 78-93898. 1970. 11.95x (ISBN 0-8143-1407-4). Wayne St U Pr.

Chyzhevskyi, Dmytro. History of Russian Literature from the Eleventh Century to the End of the Baroque. LC 79-3074. (Illus.). 451p. 1981. Repr. of 1960 ed. 35.00 (ISBN 0-8305-0067-7). Hyperion Conn.

CIA. Rote Kapelle: The CIA's History of Soviet Intelligence & Espionage Networks in Western Europe, 1936-1945. Kesaris, Paul, ed. 1979. 29.50 (ISBN 0-89093-203-4). U Pubns Amer.

Ciabotti, Patricia. Gaming It up with Shakespeare. Smith, Linda H., ed. 1980. pap. 3.95 (ISBN 0-936386-09-6). Creative Learning.

Ciampi, Elgin, jt. auth. see Boyle, Robert H.

Ciancio, June. Scat Cat Finds a Friend. (Make-a-Bk). (Illus.). 32p. (Orig.). (ps-6). 1975. pap. 1.95 (ISBN 0-8467-0047-6, Pub. by Two Continents). Hippocrene Bks.

Ciano, Edda M. My Truth. Finletter, Eileen, tr. from Fr. 1977. 8.95 o.p. (ISBN 0-688-03099-8). Morrow.

Ciarcia, Steve. Build Your Own Z-80 Computer. 473p. 1980. 21.95 (ISBN 0-07-010961-3, BYTE Bks); pap. 15.95 (ISBN 0-07-010962-1). McGraw.

--Circuit Cellar, Vol. II. 190p. 1981. pap. 11.95 (ISBN 0-07-010963-X). McGraw.

Ciardi, John. A Browser's Dictionary. LC 79-1658. 464p. 1980. 16.95 (ISBN 0-06-010766-9, HarpT). Har-Row.

--Man Who Sang the Sillies. LC 61-11734. (Illus.). (gr. 4-6). 1961. 8.95 (ISBN 0-397-30568-0). Lippincott.

Ciardi, John & Williams, Miller. How Does a Poem Mean. 2nd ed. LC 74-11592. 432p. 1975. 10.95 (ISBN 0-395-18605-6). HM.

Ciardi, John, jt. auth. see Asimov, Issac.

Ciardi, John, tr. see Alighiere, Dante.

Ciba Foundation. Chlorophyll Organization & Energy Transfer in Photosynthesis. (Ciba Foundation Symposium: No. 61). 1979. 42.00 (ISBN 0-444-90044-6, Excerpta Medica). Elsevier.

--Enzyme Defects & Immune Dysfunction. (Ciba Foundation Symposium Ser.: No. 68). 1979. 35.20 (ISBN 0-444-90088-8, Excerpta Medica). Elsevier.

--Human Genetics: Possibilities & Realities. LC 79-10949. (Ciba Foundation Symposium Ser.: No. 66). 1979. 51.25 (ISBN 0-444-90064-0, Excerpta Medica). Elsevier.

--Pregnancy Metabolism, Diabetes & the Fetus. (CIBA Foundation Symposium: No. 63). 1979. 39.50 (ISBN 0-444-90054-3, Excerpta Medica). Elsevier.

--Sex, Hormones & Behaviour. (CIBA Foundation Symposium: No. 62). 1979. 41.00 (ISBN 0-444-90045-4). Elsevier.

--Submolecular Biology & Cancer. LC 79-10949. (Ciba Foundation Ser.: No. 67). 360p. 1979. 42.50 (ISBN 0-444-90078-0, Excerpta Medica). Elsevier.

Cibber, Colley. Careless Husband. Appleton, William W., ed. LC 66-15482. (Regents Restoration Drama Ser). 1966. 8.50x (ISBN 0-8032-0352-7); pap. 1.65x (ISBN 0-8032-5352-4, BB 257, Bison). U of Nebr Pr.

Cibils, Luis A. Electronic Feto-Maternal Monitoring: Antepartum-Intrapartum. (Illus.). 600p. 1981. text ed. 56.00 (ISBN 0-88416-192-7). PSG Pub.

Cicco, Philip Di see Krutza, William J. & Dicicco, Philip P.

Cicco, Philip P. Di see Krutza, William J. & DiCicco, Philip P.

Cicellis, Kay, tr. see Tsirkas, Stratis.

Cicero. Cicero: Pro Archia. Nall, G. H., ed. (Elementary Classics Ser.). (Latin). 1962. Repr. of 1901 ed. 5.95 (ISBN 0-312-13685-4). St Martin.

--Cicero: Pro Milone. Colson, Francis M., ed. (Classical Ser.). (Latin). 1954. Repr. of 1893 ed. 5.95 (ISBN 0-312-13720-6). St Martin.

--Cicero's Letters to Atticus, 16 bks. in 6 vols. Bailey, D. R., ed. (Cambridge Classical Texts & Commentaries). (Lat.). Vol. 1, Bks. 1 & 2. 52.00 (ISBN 0-521-04643-2); Vol. 2, Bks. 3 & 4. 32.50 (ISBN 0-521-04644-0); Vol. 3, Bks. 5-7. 44.50 (ISBN 0-521-06927-0); Vol. 4, Bks. 8-10. 59.00 (ISBN 0-521-06928-9); Vol. 5, Bks. 11-13. 54.00 (ISBN 0-521-04645-9); Vol. 6, Bks. 14-16. 44.50 (ISBN 0-521-04646-7); Vol. 7, Indices To Vols. 1-6. 19.95 (ISBN 0-521-07840-7); 265.00 (ISBN 0-521-08773-2). Cambridge U Pr.

--Correspondence of M. Tullius Cicero, 7 Vols. Tyrell, R. Y. & Purser, L. C., eds. Repr. Set. 350.00 (ISBN 3-4870-2445-4). Adler.

--In L. Calpurnium Pisonem. Nisbet, R. G., ed. (Lat). 1961. 17.95x (ISBN 0-19-814427-X). Oxford U Pr.

--Murder at Larinum. Grose-Hodge, Humfrey, ed. (Latin). 1932. text ed. 5.75x (ISBN 0-521-04648-3). Cambridge U Pr.

--Offices. Cockman, Thomas, tr. Incl. Laelius, on Friendship; & Cato, on Old Age & Selected Letters. Melmouth, W., tr. 1953. 12.95x (ISBN 0-460-00345-3, Evman). Dutton.

--On Old Age. Bd. with On Friendship. LC 67-27680. 1967. pap. 3.50 (ISBN 0-672-60463-9, LLA213). Bobbs.

--On the Commonwealth. Sabine, George H & Smith, Stanley B, trs. LC 50-11678. 1929. pap. 5.95 (ISBN 0-672-60309-8). Bobbs.

--Orationes Philippicae: 1 & 2. Denniston, J. D., ed. & intro. by. 1926. 9.95x (ISBN 0-19-831778-6). Oxford U Pr.

--Pro M. Caelio Oratio. 3rd ed. Austin, R. G., ed. 1960. 11.95x (ISBN 0-19-814401-6). Oxford U Pr.

--Pro Milone. Reid, J. S., ed. 1895. text ed. 5.25x (ISBN 0-521-04650-5). Cambridge U Pr.

--Pro Roscio. Nicol, J. C., ed. (Latin). text ed. 5.75x (ISBN 0-521-04652-1). Cambridge U Pr.

--Select Letters, 2 vols. How, W. W., ed. Vol. 1. 1925 Text. 14.95x (ISBN 0-19-814403-2); Vol. 2. 1926 Notes. 24.00x (ISBN 0-19-814404-0). Oxford U Pr.

--Selected Political Speeches. Grant, Michael, tr. (Classics Ser). 1977. pap. 2.95 (ISBN 0-14-044214-6). Penguin.

--Selections from Cicero: Orations, Philosophical Writings & Letters. Pearl, Joseph, tr. LC 68-17258. 1968. pap. text ed. 2.95 (ISBN 0-8120-0301-2). Barron.

--Verres in Sicily. Grose-Hodge, Humfrey & Davies, E. W., eds. (Latin). text ed. 5.75x (ISBN 0-521-04653-X). Cambridge U Pr.

Cichy, F. C., et al. Corrosion of Steel & Aluminium Scuba Tanks. (Marine Technical Report Ser.: No. 62). 2.00 (ISBN 0-938412-05-1). URI MAS.

Cichy, Helen J. Defrosting of Minnesota. LC 77-86170. 1977. 8.00 (ISBN 0-9601852-0-8); pap. 4.75 (ISBN 0-9601852-1-6). H J Cichy.

--The Defrosting of Minnesota. LC 77-86170. 1977. 7.00 (ISBN 0-9601852-1-6); pap. 4.75 (ISBN 0-685-89498-3). H J Cichy.

Cicourel, Aaron V. Cognitive Sociology. LC 73-18771. 1973. 10.95 (ISBN 0-02-905440-8); pap. text ed. 5.95 (ISBN 0-02-905450-8). Free Pr.

--Method & Measurement in Sociology. LC 64-16970. 1964. 14.95 (ISBN 0-02-905480-X). Free Pr.

Ciechanowska, Paola. Le Pur-Sang Francais. (Illus.). 18.35 (ISBN 0-85131-003-6, Dist. by Sporting Book Center). J A Allen.

Ciechanowski, J. M. The Warsaw Rising of Nineteen Forty Four. LC 73-79315. (Soviet & East European Studies). 348p. 1974. 38.50 (ISBN 0-521-20203-5). Cambridge U Pr.

Cienkus, Robert, jt. auth. see Manoni, Mary H.

Ciepi, Michael, jt. auth. see Chaney, Lindsay.

Cieply, jt. auth. see Chaney.

Ciesielski, Stephen D. & Edison, Nancy, eds. Baltimore Renaissance: Poetry. (New Poets Ser.: Vol. 8). 50p. 1980. pap. 4.00 (ISBN 0-932616-06-2). New Poets.

Ciesla, William M., intro. by. Color Aerial Photography in the Pl Sc & Related Fields: Seventh Biennial Workshop. 255p. 1979. pap. 19.50 (ISBN 0-686-27663-9). ASP.

Cifelli, Edward M., jt. auth. see Zulauf, Sander W.

Cifre De Loubriel, Estela. Catalogo De Extranjeros Residentes En Puerto Rico En el Siglo XIX. 3.10 o.p. (ISBN 0-8477-0822-5); pap. 1.85 (ISBN 0-8477-0823-3). U of PR Pr.

Cigar, Norman, ed. Muhammad Al-Qadiris Nashr Al Mathani: The Chronicles. (Fontes Historiae Africanae Ser.). (Illus.). 400p. 1980. 89.00 (ISBN 0-19-725994-4). Oxford U Pr.

Cigno, Alessandro, tr. see Napoleoni, Claudio.

Ciklamini, Marlene. Snorri Sturluson. (World Authors Ser.: No. 493 (Iceland)). 1978. 13.95 (ISBN 0-8057-6334-1). Twayne.

Cikovsky, Nicolai, Jr. The Life & Work of George Inness. LC 76-23605. (Outstanding Dissertations in the Fine Arts - American). (Illus.). 1977. Repr. of 1965 ed. lib. bdg. 70.00 (ISBN 0-8240-2679-9). Garland Pub.

Cimarron Valley Historical Society. Journal, Nineteen Seventy-Three. 7.95 (ISBN 0-685-48813-6). Nortex Pr.

Cimbolic, Peter, jt. auth. see Hipple, John.

Ciminero, Anthony R., et al, eds. Handbook of Behavioral Assessment. LC 76-54170. (Personality Processes Ser). 1977. 39.50 (ISBN 0-471-15797-X, Pub. by Wiley-Interscience). Wiley.

Ciminillo, Lewis, jt. auth. see Ban, John.

Cimmino, Marion, jt. auth. see Edwards, Gabrielle I.

Cincerelli, Sr. Carol J. Opening Five: Art for Grade Five. LC 79-3013. 192p. (gr. 5). 1980. pap. text ed. 9.00x (ISBN 0-934902-10-0). Learn Concepts OH.

--Opening One: Art for Grade One. LC 79-3013. 174p. (gr. 1). 1979. pap. text ed. 9.00x (ISBN 0-934902-07-0). Learn Concepts OH.

--Opening Three: Art for Grade Three. LC 79-3013. 195p. (gr. 3). 1980. pap. text ed. 9.00x (ISBN 0-934902-09-7). Learn Concepts OH.

--Opening-Two: Art for Grade Two. LC 79-3013. (gr. 2). 1979. pap. text ed. 9.00x (ISBN 0-934902-06-2). Learn Concepts OH.

--Opening VII: Art for Grade Eight. LC 79-3013. 192p. (gr. 8). 1979. pap. text ed. 9.00x (ISBN 0-934902-13-5). Learn Concepts OH.

Cincinnato, Paul D. & Tursi, Joseph A. Italian Two & Three Years. (It.). (gr. 9-12). 1978. pap. text ed. 6.50 (ISBN 0-87720-594-9). AMSCO Sch.

Cini, Zelda, et al. Hollywood: Land & Legend. (Illus.). 192p. 1980. 19.95 (ISBN 0-87000-486-7). Arlington Hse.

Cinlar, E. Introduction to Stochastic Processes. (Illus.). 448p. 1975. ref. ed. 22.95 (ISBN 0-13-498089-1). P-H.

Cinnamon, Kenneth & Farson, Dave. Cults & Cons: The Exploitation of the Emotional Growth Consumer. 1979. 10.95 (ISBN 0-88229-456-3); pap. 6.95 (ISBN 0-88229-671-X). Nelson-Hall.

Cinnamon, Kenneth M., jt. auth. see Morris, Kenneth T.

Cintas, Pierre F; see Born, Warren C.

Ciochon, Russell L. & Chiarelli, A. B., eds. Evolutionary Biology of the New World Monkeys & Continental Drift. (Advances in Primatology Ser.). 500p. 1981. 49.50 (ISBN 0-306-40487-7, Plenum Pr). Plenum Pub.

Cioffari, Vincenzo. Beginning Italian. 3rd ed. 1979. text ed. 15.95x (ISBN 0-669-00580-0); wkbk. & lab manual 5.95x (ISBN 0-669-00581-9); tapes-reels 60.00 (ISBN 0-669-00582-7); cassettes 60.00 (ISBN 0-669-00583-5). Heath.

--Spoken Italian. LC 75-15151. (Spoken Language Ser.). 220p. (Prog. Bk.). 1976. pap. 8.00x (ISBN 0-87950-130-8); 12 inch lP records (33.3 rpm) 40.00x (ISBN 0-87950-133-2); records with course-bk. 45.00x (ISBN 0-87950-134-0); cassettes 60.00x (ISBN 0-87950-135-9); cassettes with course-bk. 65.00x (ISBN 0-87950-136-7). Spoken Lang Serv.

Cioffari, Vincenzo, et al. Graded Italian Reader: Prima Tappa. 2nd ed. 1979. pap. text ed. 6.95 (ISBN 0-669-01955-0). Heath.

Cioffi, F., jt. ed. see Borger, R.

Cipolla, C. M. Public Health & the Medical Profession in Renaissance Italy. LC 25-22984. (Illus.). 1976. 23.95 (ISBN 0-521-20959-5). Cambridge U Pr.

Cipolla, Carlo M. Before the Industrial Revolution: European Economy & Society, 1000-1700. 2nd ed. (Illus.). 1980. pap. text ed. 6.95x (ISBN 0-393-95115-4). Norton.

--Faith, Reason, & the Plague in Seventeenth-Century Tuscany. 128p. 1981. pap. 3.95 (ISBN 0-393-00045-1). Norton.

--Fighting the Plague in Seventeenth-Century Italy. (Curti Lecture Ser.). 168p. 1981. 13.50 (ISBN 0-299-08340-3); pap. 4.95 (ISBN 0-299-08344-6). U of Wis Pr.

--Guns, Sails & Empires: Technological Innovation & the Early Phases of European Expansion 1400-1700. (Funk & W Bk.). (gr. 9-12). pap. 1.95 o.s.i. (ISBN 0-308-60014-2, M14, TYC-T). T Y Crowell.

Cipolla, Carlo M., ed. The Economic History of World Population. 7th ed. (Illus.). 1978. text ed. 16.00x (ISBN 0-06-491138-1). B&N.

Cipolla, Wilma. Catalog of the Works of Arthur William Foote, Eighteen Fifty-Three to Nineteen Thirty-Seven. LC 79-92139. (Bibliographies in American Music: No. 6). 1980. 17.50 (ISBN 0-911772-99-5). Info Coord.

Cipriano, Robert E., jt. auth. see Ball, Edith L.

Circle Fine Art. Circle Fine Art: Editions Catalog. LC 80-54149. (Orig.). 1980. pap. write for info. (ISBN 0-932240-01-1). Circle Fine Art.

Circle, Sydney, jt. auth. see Smith, Allan K.

Cirlot, Juan-Eduardo. Picasso: Birth of a Genius. Penrose, Roland, ed. 1972. 29.95 o.p. (ISBN 0-236-15419-2, Pub. by Paul Elek). Merrimack Bk Serv.

Cirovic, Michael M. Integrated Circuits: A User's Handbook. (Illus.). 1977. text ed. 21.00 (ISBN 0-87909-356-0); students manual avail. Reston.

Cisek, James D. & George, Anthea, eds. Finding Solutions: Learning How to Deal with Life's Problems & Decisions. (Illus.). (gr. 6-10). 1980. wkbk 3.95 (ISBN 0-9604510-0-5); lab manual 4.95 (ISBN 0-9604510-1-3). Life Skills.

Ciske, Karen & Mayer, Gloria, eds. Primary Nursing. LC 79-90370. (Nursing Dimensions Ser.: Vol. VIII, No. 4). 1980. pap. text ed. 6.95 (ISBN 0-913654-60-4). Nursing Res.

CISM (International Center for Mechanical Sciences), Dept. for General Mechanics, Technical Univ. of Brunswick, 1970. Extremum & Variational Principles in Mechanics. Lippmann, H., ed. (CISM Pubns. Ser.: No. 54). (Illus.). ii, 239p. 1972. pap. 29.00 (ISBN 0-387-81115-X). Springer-Verlag.

CISM (International Center for Mechanical Sciences) Dept. of Mechanics of Solids. Rock Mechanics. Mueller, L., ed. (CISM Pubns. Ser.: Vol. 165). (Illus.). v, 390p. 1975. pap. 34.30 o.p. (ISBN 0-387-81301-2). Springer-Verlag.

CISM (International Center for Mechanical Sciences) Structural Dynamics Heat Conduction. De Veubeke, B. F., et al, eds. (CISM Pubns. Ser.: No. 126). (Illus.). 256p. 1974. pap. 25.60 (ISBN 0-387-81201-6). Springer-Verlag.

Cismaru, Alfred. Boris Vian. (World Authors Ser.: France: No. 293). 1974. lib. bdg. 10.95 (ISBN 0-8057-2951-8). Twayne.

--Marguerite Duras. (World Authors Ser.: France: No. 147). lib. bdg. 10.95 (ISBN 0-8057-2280-7). Twayne.

Cisneros, Jose, tr. see Simmons, Marc.

Cisneros, Louis. Good Mornin', Vietnam. 1981. 4.95 (ISBN 0-8062-1568-2). Carlton.

Cisneros, Sheran A. Poems for a Lazy Evening. 1981. 5.95 (ISBN 0-533-04823-0). Vantage.

Cissell, Robert, et al. Mathematics of Finance. 5th ed. LC 77-73993. (Illus.). 1977. text ed. 18.95 (ISBN 0-395-25807-3); inst. manual 1.00 (ISBN 0-395-25806-5). HM.

Ciszek, Walter J. & Flaherty, Daniel. He Leadeth Me. 240p. 1975. pap. 2.95 (ISBN 0-385-02805-9, Im). Doubleday.

Ciszek, Walter J., Fr., S.J. & Flaherty, Daniel L., Fr., S.J. With God in Russia. pap. 2.45 (ISBN 0-385-03954-9, D200, Im). Doubleday.

City Clerk's Office, ed. see City of Los Angeles, City Attorney's Office.

City of Los Angeles, City Attorney's Office. Los Angeles Municipal Code, 5 vols. 4th rev. ed. City Clerk's Office, ed. 3300p. 1972. looseleaf 275.00 (ISBN 0-911110-33-X); with current 1980 changes avail. (ISBN 0-685-26720-2). Parker & Son.

Ciucci, Giorgio, et al. Philip Johnson: Processes. (IAUS Exhibition Catalogues Ser.). (Illus.). 1979. pap. 10.00 (ISBN 0-932628-01-X). IAUS.

Ciupik, Larry A. The Universe. LC 77-27567. (Read About Science Ser.). (Illus.). (gr. k-3). 1978. PLB 9.95 (ISBN 0-8393-0089-1). Raintree Child.

Ciupik, Larry A. & Seevers, James A. Space Machines. LC 78-26991. (Machine World Ser.). (Illus.). (gr. 2-4). 1979. PLB 9.95 (ISBN 0-8172-1325-2). Raintree Pubs.

Civetta, Joseph M. Intensive Care Therapeutics. 400p. 1980. pap. 17.50x (ISBN 0-8385-4305-7). ACC.

Civikly, Jean. Messages: A Reader in Human Communication. 2nd ed. 1977. pap. text ed. 8.95x o.p. (ISBN 0-394-31268-6). Random.

Cixous, Helen. Portrait of Dora Simone Bennussa: The Singular Life of Albert Nobbs. Barrows, Anita & Wright, Barbara, trs. 1980. pap. 4.95 (ISBN 0-7145-3764-0). Riverrun NY.

Cixous, Helene & Benmussa, Simone. Benmussa Directs. 1981. pap. 4.75 (ISBN 0-7145-3764-0). Riverrun NY.

Cizankas, Victor I. & Hanna, Donald G. Modern Police Management Organization. (Illus.). 256p. 1977. text ed. 15.95 (ISBN 0-13-597104-7). P-H.

Cizelj, K. Yugoslav Coast: Atlas & Guide Book. (Illus.). 186p. 1975. pap. text ed. 13.50x (ISBN 0-89918-722-6, Y722). Vanous.

Clabaugh, Gary K. Thunder on the Right: The Protestant Fundamentalists. LC 74-9551. 283p. 1974. 13.95 (ISBN 0-88229-108-4). Nelson-Hall.

Clabburn, Pamela. The Needleworker's Dictionary. LC 75-45517. (Illus.). 228p. 1976. 19.95 o.p. (ISBN 0-688-03054-8). Morrow.

Clabby, D. A., jt. auth. see Attwell, Arthur A.

Clabby, J. The History of the RAVC, 1919-1961. (Illus.). 19.25 (ISBN 0-85131-082-6, Dist. by Sporting Book Center). J A Allen.

Clack, Doris H., ed. The Making of a Code: The Issues Underlying AACR2. LC 80-17496. 264p. 1980. pap. 15.00 (ISBN 0-8389-0309-6). ALA.

Claerbaut, David, ed. New Directions in Ethnic Studies: Minorities in America. LC 80-69329. 115p. 1981. perfect bdg. 8.50 (ISBN 0-86548-026-5). Century Twenty One.

Claessens, Charon, jt. auth. see Bricklin, Mark.

Claflin, Tennie C., et al. The Evolution of Womens' Rights, 16 vols. 1973. lib. bdg. 2500.00 o.p. (ISBN 0-686-66806-5). Gordon Pr.

Claflin, William E. Collecting, Culturing, & Caring for Living Materials: A Guide for the Teacher, Student & Hobbyist. LC 80-69329. 110p. 1981. perfect bdg. 8.50 (ISBN 0-86548-026-5). Century Twenty One.

Clagett, Marshall. Archimedes in the Middle Ages, Vol. 1. Arabo-Latin Tradition. (Medieval Science Pubns., No. 6). (Illus.). 1964. 50.00x (ISBN 0-299-03360-0). U of Wis Pr.

--Studies in Medieval Physics & Mathematics. 366p. 1980. 75.00x (ISBN 0-86078-048-1, Pub. by Variorum England). State Mutual Bk.

Clagett, Marshall, ed. Critical Problems in the History of Science. 1959. 25.00x (ISBN 0-299-01870-9); pap. 9.95x (ISBN 0-299-01874-1). U of Wis Pr.

Clagett, Marshall, tr. Nicole Oresme & the Medieval Geometry of Qualities & Motions. (Medieval Science Pubns., No. 12). (Illus.). 1968. 50.00x (ISBN 0-299-04880-2). U of Wis Pr.

Clagett, Marshall, et al, eds. Twelfth-Century Europe & the Foundations of Modern Society. (Illus.). 1961. pap. 7.50x (ISBN 0-299-02304-4). U of Wis Pr.

Clagett, Marshall, et al, eds. see University of Wisconsin, Division of Humanities.

Clague, Christopher, jt. auth. see Betancourt, Roger.

Clague, Ewan, jt. ed. see Kramer, Leo.

Claiborn, William, jt. ed. see Evans, Dorothy.

Claiborn, William, jt. ed. see Specter, Gerald.

Claiborne, Craig. Craig Claiborne's Favorites, Vol. 3. 1981. pap. 2.95 (ISBN 0-446-93808-4). Warner Bks.

--Craig Claiborne's Favorites from The New York Times, 2 vols. 1977. Vol. 1. pap. 2.95 (ISBN 0-446-93472-0); Vol. 2. pap. 2.95 (ISBN 0-446-93534-4). Warner Bks.

--Craig Claiborne's Gourmet Diet. 1981. pap. 2.95 (ISBN 0-345-29579-X). Ballantine.

--The New York Times Cook Book. Incl. The New York Times Menu Cook Book. (Illus.). 1975. boxed set 29.95 o.s.i. (ISBN 0-06-010775-8, HarpT). Har-Row.

Claiborne, Craig & Franey, Pierre. Classic French Cooking. LC 79-124640. (Foods of the World Ser.). (Illus.). (gr. 6 up). 1970. PLB 14.94 (ISBN 0-8094-0074-X, Pub. by Time-Life). Silver.

--Craig Claiborne's Gourmet Diet. 288p. 1980. 10.95 (ISBN 0-8129-0914-3). Times Bks.

Claiborne, Craig & Lee, Virginia. The Chinese Cookbook. 1976. pap. 9.95 (ISBN 0-397-01173-3). Lippincott.

Claiborne, Louis. Race & Law in Britain & the U. S. (Minority Rights Reports Ser.: No. 22). 1974. pap. 2.50 (ISBN 0-89192-108-7). Interbk Inc.

Claiborne, Robert. The First Americans. (Emergence of Man Ser). (Illus.). 170p. 1973. 9.95 (ISBN 0-8094-1267-5); lib. bdg. avail. (ISBN 0-685-31460-X). Time-Life.

--The First Americans. LC 73-75294. (Emergence of Man Ser). (Illus.). (gr. 6 up). 1973. lib. bdg. 9.63 o.p. (ISBN 0-8094-1268-3, Pub. by Time-Life). Silver.

--The Summer Stargazer: Astronomy for Beginners. 1981. pap. 3.95 (ISBN 0-14-046487-5). Penguin.

Claiborne, Robert & Goudsmit, Samuel. Time. LC 66-28543. (Life Science Library). (Illus.). (gr. 5 up). 1966. PLB 8.97 o.p. (ISBN 0-8094-0478-8, Pub. by Time-Life). Silver.

Clair, Daphne. The Jasmine Bride. (Harlequin Romance Ser.). (Orig.). 1980. pap. 1.25 o.p. (ISBN 0-373-02329-4, Pub. by Harlequin). PB.

--A Wilder Shore. (Harlequin Presents Ser.). 192p. 1980. pap. 1.50 (ISBN 0-373-10385-9, Pub. by Harlequin). PB.

Clair, Leonard St. see St. Clair, Leonard.

Clair, Rene see Otten, Anna.

Clair, Wilcox, jt. auth. see Shepherd, William G.

Claire, Anne. Andro, the Star of Bethlehem. (Illus.). 32p. (Orig.). (gr. k-6). 1981. pap. 1.95 (ISBN 0-87239-472-7, 2870). Standard Pub.

Claire, Elizabeth. A Foreign Student's Guide to Dangerous English. (Illus.). 92p. (Orig.). 1980. pap. 4.95 (ISBN 0-937630-00-4). Eardley Pubns.

Claire, Keith. The Otherwise Girl. LC 75-29789. 1976. 6.95 o.p. (ISBN 0-03-016681-0). HR&W.

Claire, Vivian. Linda Ronstadt: A Photo-Bio. 1979. pap. 2.25 (ISBN 0-515-05159-4). Jove Pubns.

Claire, William, ed. see Van Doren, Mark.

Clairmonte, F. & Cavanagh, J. The World in Their Web: The Textile Multi-Nationals To-Day. 300p. (Orig.). 1981. 22.95 (ISBN 0-905762-95-9, Pub. by Zed Pr); pap. cancelled (ISBN 0-905762-96-7). Lawrence Hill.

Clampett, Bob. Motorcycle Handbook. 1975. pap. 1.75 o.p. (ISBN 0-449-13270-6, X3270, GM). Fawcett.

Clancy, Charles J. Lava, Hock & Soda-Water: Byron's Don Juan. (Salzburg Studies in English Literature, Romantic Reassessment: No. 41). 1974. pap. text ed. 25.00x (ISBN 0-391-01344-0). Humanities.

Clancy, Charles J., jt. auth. see Hogg, James.

Clancy, John. The John Clancy Baking Book. 1975. pap. 3.95 o.p. (ISBN 0-445-08327-1). Popular Lib.

Clancy, Judith. Last Look at the Old Met. LC 79-103983. (Illus.). 1969. bds. 5.95 (ISBN 0-912184-02-7). Synergistic Pr.

Clancy, L. J. Aerodynamics. LC 73-15266. 1975. text ed. 27.95 (ISBN 0-470-15837-9). Halsted Pr.

Clancy, Paul R. Untitled Biography of Tip N'Neill. 1980. 10.95 (ISBN 0-02-525700-5). Macmillan.

Clanton, Bruce. Family ADVENTures. LC 80-51060. (ps-6). 1980. pap. 3.95 (ISBN 0-89390-018-4). Resource Pubns.

--In Season & Out. LC 80-54272. 80p. 1981. pap. 6.25 (ISBN 0-89390-025-7). Resource Pubns.

Clanton, Gordon & Downing, Chris. Face to Face to Face: An Experiment in Intimacy. 256p. 1976. pap. 1.95 o.p. (ISBN 0-345-25116-4). Ballantine.

Clapham, A. R., ed. The IBP Survey of Conservation Sites: An Experimental Study. LC 79-50233. (International Biological Programme Ser.: No. 24). (Illus.). 500p. 1980. 57.50 (ISBN 0-521-22697-X). Cambridge U Pr.

Clapham, A. R., et al. Excursion Flora of the British Isles. 3rd ed. LC 79-51679. 600p. Date not set. 29.95 (ISBN 0-521-23290-2). Cambridge U Pr.

Clapham, Arthur R., et al. Excursion Flora of the British Isles. 2nd ed. LC 68-20329. 1968. 28.95 (ISBN 0-521-04656-4). Cambridge U Pr.

--Flora of the British Isles. 2nd ed. 1962. 68.50 (ISBN 0-521-04657-2); illustrations, 4 pts. 28.50 ea. Cambridge U Pr.

Clapham, C. R. Introduction to Abstract Algebra. (Library of Mathematics). 1969. pap. 5.00 (ISBN 0-7100-6626-0). Routledge & Kegan.

--Introduction to Mathematical Analysis. (Library of Mathematics). (Illus.). 92p. 1973. pap. 5.00 (ISBN 0-7100-7529-4). Routledge & Kegan.

Clapham, Christopher. Foreign Policy Making in Developing States. LC 77-71401. (Praeger Special Studies). 1979. 23.95 (ISBN 0-03-046691-1). Praeger.

Clapham, Francis, ed. Our Human Ancestors. (Visual World Ser.). (Illus.). (gr. 9 up). 1977. 5.95 (ISBN 0-685-74307-1, Warwick Press Book); PLB 7.90 s&l (ISBN 0-531-01279-4). Watts.

Clapham, John. The Historie of Great Britannie - from the Romans First Entrance, Untill the Raigne of Egbert, the West-Saxon Prince. LC 74-28837. (English Experience Ser.: No. 719). 1975. Repr. of 1606 ed. 22.00 (ISBN 90-221-0719-1). Walter J Johnson.

Clapham, John H. Bank of England, 2 Vols. 1945. Set. 71.50 set (ISBN 0-521-04662-9). Cambridge U Pr.

--Economic Development of France & Germany 1815-1914. 4th ed. 1935. 50.50 (ISBN 0-521-04664-5); pap. 15.95 (ISBN 0-521-09150-0, 150). Cambridge U Pr.

Clapham, Michael. Multinational Enterprises & Nation States. (The Stamp Memorial Lectures). 1975. pap. text ed. 2.75x (ISBN 0-485-16429-9, Athlone Pr). Humanities.

Clapin, Sylvia. New Dictionary of Americanisms. LC 68-17985. 1968. Repr. of 1902 ed. 24.00 (ISBN 0-8103-3244-2). Gale.

Clapp, Andrew D. Merger Yearbook Nineteen Eighty. 1981. 68.00 (ISBN 0-939008-03-3). Cambridge Corp.

Clapp, Edwin J. Economic Aspects of the War. 1915. 42.50x (ISBN 0-685-69798-3). Elliots Bks.

Clapp, Jane. Art Censorship: A Chronology of Proscribed & Prescribed Art. LC 76-172789. (Illus.). 1972. 22.50 (ISBN 0-8108-0455-7). Scarecrow.

--Professional Ethics & Insignia. LC 74-10501. (Illus.). 1974. 32.50 (ISBN 0-8108-0735-1). Scarecrow.

--Sculpture Index: Sculpture of Europe & the Contemporary Middle East, Vol. 1. LC 79-9538. 1970. 35.00 o.p. (ISBN 0-8108-0249-X). Scarecrow.

--Sculpture Index: Sculpture of the Americas, the Orient, Africa, the Pacific Area & the Classical World, Vol. 2. LC 79-9538. 1970. 45.00 (ISBN 0-8108-0311-9). Scarecrow.

Clapp, Jeremy, jt. ed. see Langan, John.

Clapp, John M., jt. auth. see Case, Frederick E.

Clapp, Patricia. King of the Dollhouse. LC 74-21827. (Illus.). 96p. (gr. 1-5). 1974. 6.75 o.p. (ISBN 0-688-40982-2); PLB 6.96 (ISBN 0-688-50982-7). Lothrop.

--King of the Dollhouse. (gr. 2-3). 1976. pap. 1.25 o.p. (ISBN 0-590-02063-3, Schol Pap). Schol Bk Serv.

Clappe, Louise. Shirley Letters. LC 77-141468. (Illus.). 1970. pap. 4.95 (ISBN 0-87905-004-7). Peregrine Smith.

Clapper, Raymond. Watching the World. (FDR & the Era of the New Deal Ser.). 1975. Repr. of 1944 ed. 35.00 (ISBN 0-306-70730-6). Da Capo.

Clapper, Ronald. The Development of Walden: A Genetic Text. LC 80-2503. 1981. 75.00 (ISBN 0-686-28931-5). AMS Pr.

Clapperton, C. M. see Bowen, D. Q.

Clapperton, R. H. The Papermaking Machine. 1968. 120.00 (ISBN 0-08-010896-2). Pergamon.

Clar, C. Raymond. Out of the River Mist. new ed. LC 74-80008. (Illus.). 135p. 1974. pap. 3.50 (ISBN 0-89030-000-3). Forest Hist Soc.

Clar, Lawrence & Hart, James. Mathematics for the Technologies with Calculus. (P-H Ser. in Technical Mathematics). (Illus.). 1978. ref. ed. 21.95 (ISBN 0-13-562553-X). P-H.

Clar, Lawrence M. & Hart, James A. Mathematics for the Technologies. (Illus.). 1978. text ed. 18.95 (ISBN 0-13-565200-6). P-H.

Clar, Lawrence M, et al. Business Mathematics. Latham, Calvin, ed. 1980. text ed. 15.95x (ISBN 0-686-65089-1). Macmillan.

Clarborne, Robert. The Birth of Writing. LC 74-83646. (Emergence of Man Ser.). (gr. 6 up). 1974. PLB 11.49 o.p. (ISBN 0-8094-1282-9, Pub. by Time-Life). Silver.

Clardy, Andrea F., ed. Ithaca: A Book of Photographs. (Illus.). 96p. (Orig.). 1980. pap. 8.95 (ISBN 0-935526-03-X). McBooks Pr.

Clardy, Betty S., jt. auth. see Clardy, Jesse V.

Clardy, Jesse V. & Clardy, Betty S. The Superfluous Man in Russian Letters. LC 80-5080. 189p. 1980. text ed. 17.00 (ISBN 0-8191-1039-6); pap. text ed. 9.00 (ISBN 0-8191-1040-X). U Pr of Amer.

Clare, Andrea M., jt. auth. see Dickens, Charles.

Clare, John. Selected Poems. Hibble, S. W., ed. 1965. 6.00x (ISBN 0-460-00563-4, Evman); pap. 7.95 (ISBN 0-460-01563-X). Dutton.

--Selected Poems & Prose of John Clare. Robinson, Eric & Summerfield, Geoffrey, eds. (Illus.). 1967. 14.95x (ISBN 0-19-212164-2); pap. 8.95 (ISBN 0-19-281232-7). Oxford U Pr.

Clare, Paul & Kramer, John. Introduction to American Corrections. 1976. text ed. 15.95 (ISBN 0-205-05465-X, 825465-6); instructor's manual free (ISBN 0-205-05466-8, 8254664). Allyn.

Claremon, Neil. Borderland. 1975. 6.95 o.p. (ISBN 0-394-49619-1, 49619). Knopf.

--West of the American Dream. 1973. pap. 1.95 (ISBN 0-688-05164-2). Morrow.

Claremont De Castillejo, Irene. Knowing Woman: Feminine Psychology. 192p. 1974. pap. 3.50 (ISBN 0-06-090349-X, CN349, CN). Har-Row.

Clarenbach, Laura, jt. auth. see Chamberlain, Mildred.

Clarence-Smith, W. G. Slaves, Peasants, & Capitalists in Southern Angola: Eighteen Forty to Nineteen Twenty-Six. LC 78-67805. (African Studies: No. 27). (Illus.). 1979. 21.50 (ISBN 0-521-22406-3). Cambridge U Pr.

Clarey, Elizabeth M. & Dixson, Robert J. Pronunciation Exercises in English. (gr. 9 up). 1963. pap. text ed. 2.75 (ISBN 0-88345-135-2, 17418); with 3 records 18.00 (ISBN 0-685-02029-0). Regents Pub.

Clarey, M. Elizabeth & Dixson, Robert J. Curso Practico De Pronunciacion Del Ingles. Andujar, Julio I., ed. (gr. 10 up). 1967. pap. text ed. 2.95 (ISBN 0-88345-039-9, 17377); with 3 records 18.00 (ISBN 0-685-04773-3). Regents Pub.

Clarfield, Gerard H. Timothy Pickering & American Diplomacy 1795-1800. LC 69-13333. 1969. 6.00x o.p. (ISBN 0-8262-8414-0). U of Mo Pr.

--United States Diplomatic History, Vol. 1. LC 72-5519. 256p. 1973. pap. text ed. 8.25 (ISBN 0-395-14026-9). HM.

Claridge, Gordon S., et al. Personality Differences & Biological Variations: A Study of Twins. LC 72-10132. 1973. text ed. 28.00 (ISBN 0-08-017124-9). Pergamon.

Clarie, Thomas C. Occult Bibliography: An Annotated List of Books Published in English, 1971 Through 1975. LC 78-17156. 1978. 24.00 (ISBN 0-8108-1152-9). Scarecrow.

Claris, A. J. La Proscription Francaise En Suisse, 1871-1872. (Commune De Paris En 1871). (Fr.). 1976. lib. bdg. 15.00x o.p. (ISBN 0-8287-0201-2); pap. text ed. 5.00x o.p. (ISBN 0-685-74930-4). Clearwater Pub.

Clarizio, Harvey, et al. Contemporary Issues in Educational Psychology. 4th ed. 1981. pap. text ed. 9.95 (ISBN 0-205-07331-X). Allyn.

--Contemporary Issues in Educational Psychology. 3rd ed. 1977. pap. text ed. 8.95x o.p. (ISBN 0-205-05627-X). Allyn.

Clarizio, Harvey F. Toward Positive Classroom Discipline. 3rd ed. LC 75-25583. 183p. 1976. text ed. 10.50 o.p. (ISBN 0-471-15850-X). Wiley.

Clark. Lighthouse Boy. 1976. pap. 3.75 (ISBN 0-89272-043-3). Down East.
--Mystery at Star Lake. (gr. 3-5). pap. 1.25 o.p. (ISBN 0-590-11927-3, Schol Pap). Schol Bk Serv.

Clark, jt. ed. see Hahn.

Clark, A. F. & Reed, R. P., eds. Advances in Cryogenic Engineering (Materials, Vol. 26. 720p. 1981. 59.50 (ISBN 0-306-40531-8, Plenum Pr). Plenum Pub.

Clark, A. Kennedy. Man, Medicine & Morality. (Illus.). 1969. 5.95 o.p. (ISBN 0-571-09052-4, Pub. by Faber & Faber). Merrimack Bk Serv.

Clark, A. P. Advanced Data-Transmission Systems. LC 76-55018. 1977. 29.95 (ISBN 0-470-99029-5). Halsted Pr.
--Principles of Digital Data Transmission. LC 76-23217. 1976. 21.95 (ISBN 0-470-98913-0). Halsted Pr.

Clark, Admont G. The Real Imagination: An Introduction to Poetry. LC 70-190106. 480p. 1972. pap. text ed. 9.95 (ISBN 0-574-18560-7, 13-1560); instr's guide avail. (ISBN 0-574-18561-5, 13-1561). SRA.

Clark, Ailsa M. Starfishes. new ed. Orig. Title: Starfishes & Their Relations. (Illus.). 1977. pap. 4.95 (ISBN 0-87666-466-4, PS-750). TFH Pubns.

Clark, Ailsa M. & Rowe, Francis W. Monographs of the Shallow-Water Indo-West Pacific Echinoderms. (Illus.). ix, 238p. 1971. 46.00x (ISBN 0-565-00690-8, Pub. by Brit Mus Nat Hist England). Sabbot-Natural Hist Bks.

Clark, Alan F., jt. ed. see Suenaga, Masaki.

Clark, Alice, jt. auth. see Clark, Lincoln.

Clark, Alice S., jt. ed. see Hoadley, Irene B.

Clark, Andrew. Elizabethan Domestic Drama: A Survey of the Origins, Antecedents,& Nature of the Domestic Play in England, 1500-1640, 2 vols. (Salzburg Studies in English Literature, Jacobean Drama Studies: Vol. 49). 455p. (Orig.). 1975. Set. pap. text ed. 50.25x (ISBN 0-391-01345-9). Humanities.
--Minerals. (Illus.). 128p. 1979. 8.95 (ISBN 0-600-36313-9). Transatlantic.

Clark, Andrew H. Acadia: The Georgraphy of Early Nova Scotia to 1760. (Illus.). 470p. 1968. 27.50x (ISBN 0-299-05080-7). U of Wis Pr.

Clark, Ann L. Culture & Childrearing. LC 80-19481. (Illus.). 255p. 1980. 24.00 (ISBN 0-8036-1836-0). Davis Co.

Clark, Ann L. & Mandell, Steven L. A Short Course in PL-I PL-C. (Series in Data Processing & Information Systems). 1978. pap. text ed. 9.95 (ISBN 0-8299-0219-8); instrs.' manual avail. (ISBN 0-8299-0465-4). West Pub.

Clark, Ann N. Secret of the Andes. (Illus.). (gr. 4-8). 1952. 8.95 (ISBN 0-670-62975-8). Viking Pr.

Clark, Anne. Australian Adventure: Letters from an Ambassador's Wife. (Illus.). 1969. 12.95 (ISBN 0-292-70001-6). U of Tex Pr.

Clark, Anne & Rivin, Zelma. Homesteading in Urban U. S. A. LC 77-2939. (Special Studies). 1977. text ed. 22.95 (ISBN 0-275-24060-6). Praeger.

Clark, Arthur C. The Sands of Mars. (RL 7). pap. 1.75 (ISBN 0-451-08176-5, E8176, Sig). NAL.

Clark, Aubert J. The Movement for International Copyright in Nineteenth Century America. LC 73-9209. 215p. 1973. Repr. of 1960 ed. lib. bdg. 15.00x (ISBN 0-8371-6980-1, CLIC). Greenwood.

Clark, Audrey N., jt. auth. see Stamp, Dudley.

Clark, Barbara L. E. B. The Story of Elias Boudinot IV. (Illus.). 1977. 10.00 (ISBN 0-8059-2246-6). Dorrance.

Clark, Barkley & Fonseca, John R. Handling Consumer Credit Cases, 2 vols. LC 76-166148. (Criminal Law Library). 738p. 1972. 85.00 (ISBN 0-686-14480-5). Lawyers Co-Op.

Clark, Barkley, ed. Warranties in the Sale of Goods 1980: Course Handbook, 2 vols. LC 78-643376. (Nineteen Eighty to Nineteen Eighty-One Commercial Law & Practice Course Handbook Ser.). 1131p. 1980. pap. text ed. 25.00 (ISBN 0-686-69173-3, A6-3091). PLI.

Clark, Barrett H., ed. America's Lost Plays, 21 Vols. in 11. Incl. Vols. 1 & 2. 440p. 19.50x (ISBN 0-253-30650-7); Vols. 3 & 4. 500p. 15.00x (ISBN 0-253-30651-5); Vols. 9 & 10. 568p. 15.00x (ISBN 0-253-30654-X); Vols. 11 & 12. 480p. 15.00x (ISBN 0-253-30655-8); Vols. 13 & 14. 600p. 15.00x (ISBN 0-253-30656-6); Vols. 15 & 16. 492p. 15.00x (ISBN 0-253-30657-4); Vols. 17 & 18. 704p. 15.00x (ISBN 0-253-30658-2); Vols. 19 & 20. 768p. 15.00x (ISBN 0-253-30659-0); Vol. 21. 178p. 9.95x (ISBN 0-253-30660-4). LC 63-18068. 1963-69. Ind U Pr.

Clark, Bea. Centrist. 1981. 6.50 (ISBN 0-8062-1577-1). Carlton.

Clark, Bob, jt. auth. see Lewinski, Jorge.

Clark, Brian. Whose Life Is It Anyway? 160p. 1980. pap. 2.50 (ISBN 0-380-52407-4, 52407). Avon.

Clark, Brian D., et al. Environmental Impact Assessment: a bibliography with abstracts. LC 79-67626. 524p. 1980. 59.95 (ISBN 0-8352-1255-6, Co-Pub. by Mansell Info England). Bowker.

Clark, Buddy. Alone, Unarmed but Safe--the Woman's Judo Defense Book. (Illus.). 128p. 1981. 8.00 (ISBN 0-682-49712-6); pap. 6.00 (ISBN 0-682-49711-8). Exposition.

Clark, C. E., Jr., jt. ed. see Bruccoli, Matthew J.

Clark, C. Frazer, Jr. Nathaniel Hawthorne: A Descriptive Bibliography. LC 76-50885. (Pittsburgh Ser. in Bibliography). 1978. 30.00x (ISBN 0-8229-3343-8). U of Pittsburgh Pr.

Clark, C. Frazer, Jr., ed. Nathaniel Hawthorne Journal. LC 75-148262. (Illus.). 1971 ed. 22.00 (ISBN 0-910972-04-4); 1972 ed. o.s.i. 22.00 (ISBN 0-910972-33-8); 1973 ed. 22.00 (ISBN 0-910972-39-7); 1974 ed. 23.00 (ISBN 0-910972-50-8); 1975 o.s.i. 23.00 (ISBN 0-910972-55-9); 1976 24.00 (ISBN 0-910972-60-5). IHS-PDS.
--Nathaniel Hawthorne Journal Nineteen Seventy-Eight. (Bruccoli Clark Bk.). (Illus.). 400p. 1980. 28.00 (ISBN 0-8103-0929-7). Gale.

Clark, C. Frazer, Jr., jt. ed. see Bruccoli, Matthew.

Clark, C. Wells, ed. see Bigl, Joseph H., et al.

Clark, Campbell. Raiders of the Lost Ark: A Novelization Adapted from the Screenplay by Lawrence Kasden. 192p. 1981. pap. 2.50 (ISBN 0-345-29490-4). Ballantine.

Clark, Carl D. & Essary, Loris. Semi-Constructs of the Secretaire De Registre. 1980. pap. 2.00 signed ed. (ISBN 0-918406-07-2). Future Pr.

Clark, Carol R., jt. auth. see Schallert, William F.

Clark, Carolyn C. Enhancing Wellness. 1981. text ed. 26.95 (ISBN 0-8261-2950-1); pap. text ed. 16.95 (ISBN 0-8261-2951-X). Springer Pub.
--Nursing Concepts & Processes. LC 76-14095. 1977. pap. text ed. 11.60 (ISBN 0-8273-1318-7); instructor's guide 2.75 (ISBN 0-8273-1319-5). Delmar.

Clark, Champ. The Badlands. (The American Wilderness Ser.). (Illus.). 1975. 12.95 (ISBN 0-8094-1208-X). Time-Life.
--The Badlands. LC 74-18063. (American Wilderness). (Illus.). (gr. 6 up). 1974. PLB 11.97 (ISBN 0-8094-1209-8, Pub. by Time-Life). Silver.

Clark, Charles. Publishing Agreements: A Book of Precedents. 176p. 1980. text ed. 19.50x (ISBN 0-04-655015-1, 2481). Allen Unwin.

Clark, Charles A. Religions of Old Korea: New York, 1932. LC 78-74297. (Oriental Religions Ser.: Vol. 14). 295p. 1981. lib. bdg. 33.00 (ISBN 0-8240-3916-5). Garland Pub.

Clark, Charles E. Maine: A History. (State & the Nation Ser.). (Illus.). 1977. 12.95 (ISBN 0-393-05653-8, Co-Pub by AASLH). Norton.

Clark, Chris. Test Match Career of Freddie Trueman. LC 80-66089. (Illus.). 208p. 1980. 19.95 (ISBN 0-7153-7944-5). David & Charles.

Clark, Clara E. A Tangram Diary. (Illus.). 64p. (Orig.). (gr. 3-6). 1980. pap. 4.95 (ISBN 0-934734-05-4). Construct Educ.

Clark, Clara E. & Sternberg, Betty J. Math in Stride, Bk. 1. (Illus.). 166p. (Orig.). (gr. k-2). 1980. pap. 5.65 (ISBN 0-934734-06-2). Construct Educ.
--Math in Stride, Bk. 2. (Illus.). 203p. (Orig.). (gr. 1-3). 1980. pap. 5.80 (ISBN 0-934734-07-0). Construct Educ.
--Math in Stride, Bk. 3. (Illus.). 219p. (Orig.). (gr. 2-4). 1980. pap. 5.95 (ISBN 0-934734-08-9). Construct Educ.

Clark, Cline. Self-Programming Self-Hypnosis. (Orig.). 1980. pap. text ed. 17.95 (ISBN 0-937798-00-2). Packard Pub.

Clark, Colin. National Income & Outlay. LC 67-33059. Repr. of 1937 ed. 22.50x (ISBN 0-678-05162-3). Kelley.
--National Income Nineteen Twenty-Four to Nineteen Thirty-One. LC 67-33571. Repr. of 1932 ed. 24.00x (ISBN 0-678-05161-5). Kelley.
--Value of Agricultural Land. (Illus.). 124p. 1973. text ed. 11.75 o.p. (ISBN 0-08-017070-6). Pergamon.

Clark, Colin W. Mathematical Bioeconomics: The Optimal Management of Renewable Resources. LC 76-16473. (Pure & Applied Mathematics Ser.). 1976. 26.95 (ISBN 0-471-15856-9, Pub. by Wiley-Interscience). Wiley.

Clark, Cynthia & Chadwick, Donnacompiled by. Clinically Adapted Instruments for the Multiply Handicapped: A Sourcebook. rev. ed. 1980. Repr. of 1979 ed. 12.95 (ISBN 0-918812-13-5). Magnamusic.

Clark, D., ed. Twentieth Century Interpretations of Murder in the Cathedral. 1971. 7.95 o.p. (ISBN 0-13-606400-0, Spec). P-H.

Clark, David. Colne Valley: Radicalism to Socialism. (Illus.). 240p. text ed. 27.00 (ISBN 0-582-50293-4). Longman.

Clark, David Allen. Jokes, Puns, & Riddles. LC 67-19070. (gr. 3-7). 1968. 5.95a (ISBN 0-385-09018-8); PLB (ISBN 0-385-09019-6). Doubleday.

Clark, David L. Stratigraphy & Glacial-Marine Sediments of the Amerasian Basin,Central Arctic Ocean. LC 80-65270. (Special Paper Ser.: No. 181). (Illus., Orig.). 1980. pap. 13.00 (ISBN 0-8137-2181-4). Geol Soc.

Clark, David R. Computers for Image-Making. (Audio-Visual Media for Education & Research Ser.: Vol. 2). (Illus.). 166p. 1980. 29.00 (ISBN 0-08-024058-5); pap. 14.50 (ISBN 0-08-024059-3). Pergamon.
--Merrill Studies in The Bridge. 1970. pap. text ed. 2.95 (ISBN 0-675-09292-2). Merrill.
--That Black Day: The Manuscripts of 'Crazy Jane on the Day of Judgement' (New Years Papers Ser.: No. XVIII). (Illus.). 56p. 1980. pap. text ed. 11.75x (ISBN 0-85105-355-6, Dolmen Pr). Humanities.

Clark, David S., jt. auth. see Sharpe, Anthony N.

Clark, David W. & Kaiser, Robert L., eds. Guide to the Administration of Charitable Remainder Trusts. 3rd ed. 1978. pap. 38.50 (ISBN 0-89964-018-4). CASE.

Clark, Dennis J. Irish Blood: Northern Ireland and the American Conscience. LC 76-21808. (National University Publications Ser. in American Studies). 1977. 11.00 (ISBN 0-8046-9163-0). Kennikat.

Clark, Dennis J., ed. Philadelphia: Seventeen Seventy-Six to Two Thousand Seventy-Six, a Three Hundred Year View. (Interdisciplinary Urban Ser.). 130p. 1975. 11.50 (ISBN 0-8046-9141-X, Natl U). Kennikat.

Clark, Dennis R., jt. auth. see Kalman, Sumner M.

Clark, Diane. Diane Clark's Microwave Cookbook. 1981. 14.95 (ISBN 0-8015-2023-1, Hawthorn). Dutton.

Clark, Donald B. Alexander Pope. (English Authors Ser.: No. 41). 1966. lib. bdg. 10.95 (ISBN 0-8057-1452-9). Twayne.

Clark, Donald H., ed. Psychology of Education. LC 67-15144. 1967. pap. text ed. 4.50 o.s.i. (ISBN 0-02-905510-5). Free Pr.

Clark, Dorothy, jt. auth. see Clark, Michael.

Clark, Doug. They Saw the Second Coming: An Explosive Novel About the End of the World! LC 78-71427. 1979. 6.95 (ISBN 0-89081-196-2, 1903); pap. 3.95 (ISBN 0-89081-190-3). Harvest Hse.

Clark, Duncan W. & Macmahon, Brian, eds. Preventive & Community Medicine. 2nd ed. 1981. pap. text ed. price not set (ISBN 0-316-14596-3). Little.

Clark, Duvie. The Peculiar Truth. LC 78-55206. 1978. 9.95 o.p. (ISBN 0-689-10909-1). Atheneum.

Clark, E. Culpepper. Francis Warrington Dawson & the Politics of Restoration: South Carolina, Eighteen Seventy-Four to Eighteen Eighty-Nine. LC 79-27884. (Illus.). 256p. 1980. 18.95x (ISBN 0-8173-0039-2). U of Ala Pr.

Clark, Edith. My Mother Who Fathered Me: A Study of the Family in the Selected Communities in Jamaica. 1976. pap. text ed. 8.95x (ISBN 0-04-573010-5). Allen Unwin.

Clark, Edna M. Ohio Art & Artists. LC 74-13860. xvi, 509p. 1975. Repr. of 1932 ed. 32.00 (ISBN 0-8103-4058-5). Gale.

Clark, Edward W., jt. ed. see Vaughan, Alden T.

Clark, Edwin C. History of Roman Private Law, 3 vols in 4. Incl. Vol. 1. Source. 168p; Vol. 2. Jurisprudence, 2 vols. 1234p; Vol. 3. Regal. 634p. LC 64-13392. 230p. 1906. 50.00x set (ISBN 0-8196-0146-2). Biblo.

Clark, Eleanor D. When Mama Was a Little Girl: Memories of a Georgia Childhood. (Illus.). 64p. 1980. 6.00 (ISBN 0-682-49663-4). Exposition.

Clark, Elizabeth. John the Beloved: An Essene Understanding of the Book of Revelations. 1981. 6.95 (ISBN 0-533-04781-1). Vantage.

Clark, Elizabeth & Richardson, Herbert W., eds. Women & Religion: Readings in the Western Tradition from Aeschylus to Mary Daly. LC 76-9975. 1976. pap. 6.95 (ISBN 0-06-061398-X, RD-178, HarpR). Har-Row.

Clark, Elizabeth A. Jerome, Chrysostom, & Friends: Essays & Translations. LC 79-66374. (Studies in Women & Religion: Vol. 1). xi, 254p. 1979. soft cover 24.95x (ISBN 0-88946-548-7). E Mellen.

Clark, Ella E. Indian Legends of the Pacific Northwest. (Illus.). (YA) (gr. 9-12). 1953. pap. 3.95 (ISBN 0-520-00243-1, CAL18). U of Cal Pr.

Clark, Emery, illus. Recipes & Reminiscences of New Orleans. (Illus.). 237p. (Orig.). 1971. pap. 6.95 (ISBN 0-9604718-0-4). Old Ursuline.

Clark, Emily. Ingenue Among the Lions: The Letters of Emily Clark to Joseph Hergesheimer. Langford, Gerald, ed. 1965. 12.50x (ISBN 0-292-73274-0). U of Tex Pr.

Clark, Eric. Send in the Lions. LC 80-69371. 1981. 9.95 (ISBN 0-689-11125-8). Atheneum.

Clark, Erskine. Wrestlin Jacob: A Portrait of Religion in the Old South. LC 78-52453. 1979. 12.95 o.p. (ISBN 0-8042-1088-8); pap. 6.95 (ISBN 0-8042-1089-6). John Knox.

Clark, Floyd B. The Constitutional Doctrines of Justice Harlan. LC 74-87560. (Law, Politics & History Ser.). 1969. Repr. of 1915 ed. lib. bdg. 25.00 (ISBN 0-306-71391-8). Da Capo.

Clark, Francis I. The Position of Women in Contemporary France. LC 79-5210. 250p. 1981. Repr. of 1937 ed. 19.75 (ISBN 0-8305-0101-0). Hyperion Conn.

Clark, Frank. Contemporary Math. LC 64-12131. (Illus.). (gr. 7 up). 1964. PLB 3.90 o.p. (ISBN 0-531-01650-1). Watts.

Clark, Frank J. Mathematics for Data Processing. LC 73-8868. (Illus.). 432p. 1974. 17.95 (ISBN 0-87909-470-2); students manual avail. Reston.

Clark, Frank W., et al. The Pursuit of Competence in Social Work: Contemporary Issues in the Definition, Assessment, & Improvement of Effectiveness in the Human Services. LC 79-83570. (Social & Behavioral Science Ser.). (Illus.). 1979. text ed. 16.95x (ISBN 0-87589-404-6). Jossey-Bass.

Clark, G. B., jt. auth. see Lewis, Robert S.

Clark, G. Kitson. Expanding Society: Britain 1830-1900. 1967. 23.95 (ISBN 0-521-05897-X). Cambridge U Pr.

Clark, Gail. Bachelor's Fare. (Orig.). 1981. pap. price not set (ISBN 0-671-41276-0). PB.

Clark, Garth. American Potters: The Work of 20 Modern Masters. 144p. 1981. 24.50 (ISBN 0-8230-0213-6). Watson-Guptill.

Clark, Gary. The Clearing. (The Norwegian Trilolgy Ser.). 200p. (Orig.). Date not set. price not set (ISBN 0-913124-45-1). Nordland Pub.

Clark, George. Seventeenth Century. 2nd ed. 1961. pap. 5.95 (ISBN 0-19-500227-X, GB). Oxford U Pr.
--Staining Procedures. 3rd ed. 16.00 o.p. (ISBN 0-683-01706-3). Williams & Wilkins.
--Staining Procedures. 4th ed. (Illus.). 444p. 1980. softcover 39.95 (ISBN 0-683-01707-1). Williams & Wilkins.

Clark, George & Clark, Margaret P. Primer in Neurological Staining Procedures. (Illus.). 84p. 1971. text ed. 12.75 (ISBN 0-398-02176-7). C C Thomas.

Clark, George N. English History: A Survey. 1971. 21.95 o.p. (ISBN 0-19-822339-0). Oxford U Pr.
--Science & Social Welfare in the Age of Newton. 1949. 19.50x (ISBN 0-19-822326-9). Oxford U Pr.

Clark, Georgie W. & Newcomb, Duane. Georgie Clark: Thirty Years of River Running. LC 77-25448. (Illus.). 1978. 6.95 o.p. (ISBN 0-87701-105-2). Chronicle Bks.

Clark, Gerald R., jt. ed. see Rosen, Marvin.

Clark, Gertrude M., tr. see Kant, Immanuel.

Clark, Glenn. God's Reach. pap. 3.50 o.p. (ISBN 0-910924-48-1). Macalester.
--Living Prayer. 1980. pap. 0.50 (ISBN 0-910924-88-0). Macalester.

Clark, Glenn T., jt. auth. see Solberg, William K.

Clark, Gordon H. A Christian View of Men & Things. (Twin Brooks Ser.). 325p. 1981. pap. 8.95 (ISBN 0-8010-2466-8). Baker Bk.
--First & Second Peter. 1980. pap. 4.95. Presby & Reformed.
--First John: A Commentary. 1980. pap. 4.75 (ISBN 0-87552-166-5). Presby & Reformed.

Clark, Grahame. The Earlier Stone Age Settlement of Scandanavia. LC 73-94358. (Illus.). 304p. 1975. 42.50 (ISBN 0-521-20446-1). Cambridge U Pr.

Clark, Grover. Economic Rivalries in China. 1932. 37.50x (ISBN 0-685-69799-1). Elliots Bks.

Clark, H. B. Biblical Law. 1980. pap. cancelled o.p. (ISBN 0-8323-0326-7). Binford.

Clark, H. F. The English Landscape Garden. (Illus.). 128p. 1980. text ed. 16.50x (ISBN 0-904387-38-0). Humanities.

Clark, Harold. The New Creationism. LC 79-22250. (Horizon Ser.). 1980. pap. 6.95 (ISBN 0-8127-0247-6). Southern Pub.

Clark, Harry. A Venture in History: The Production, Publication, & Sale of the Works of Hubert Howe Bancroft. 1973. pap. 19.50x (ISBN 0-520-09417-4). U of Cal Pr.

Clark, Harry & Rathbun, John. American Literary Criticism: Vol. II, 1860-1905. (United States Authors Ser.: No. 340). 1979. lib. bdg. 12.50 (ISBN 0-8057-7264-2). Twayne.

Clark, Harry H., compiled by. American Literature: Poe Through Garland. LC 77-137641. (Goldentree Bibliographies in Language & Literature Ser). (Orig.). 1971. 10.95x (ISBN 0-88295-509-8); pap. 6.95x (ISBN 0-88295-508-X). AHM Pub.

Clark, Harry H., jt. ed. see Allen, Gay W.

Clark, Harry H., ed. see Freneau, Philip.

Clark, Homer H., Jr. Cases & Problems on Domestic Relations. 3rd ed. LC 80-19763. (American Casebook Ser.). 1193p. 1980. text ed. 22.95 (ISBN 0-8299-2104-4). West Pub.

Clark, Hubert L. Catalogue of the Recent Sea-Urchins (Echinoidea) in the Collection of the British Museum (Natural History) (Illus.). xxviii, 250p. 1925. 21.00x (ISBN 0-565-00165-5, Pub. by British Mus Nat Hist England). Sabbot-Natural Hist Bks.

Clark, Hyla M. The Tall Ships. LC 76-43112. (Illus.). 1976. pap. 8.95 (ISBN 0-8467-0236-3, Pub. by Two Continents). Hippocrene Bks.

Clark, Ian. Reform & Resistance in the International Order. LC 79-54017. 1980. 29.50 (ISBN 0-521-22998-7); pap. 8.95 (ISBN 0-521-29763-X). Cambridge U Pr.

Clark, Ian, jt. ed. see Bowman, Larry W.

Clark, Isobel. Practical Geostatistics. 1979. 28.50x (ISBN 0-85334-843-X). Intl Ideas.

--Practical Geostatistics. (Illus.). 1979. 28.50x (ISBN 0-85334-843-X, Pub. by Applied Science). Burgess-Intl Ideas.

Clark, J., et al. Global Simulation Models: A Comparative Study. LC 74-32231. 135p. 1975. 24.95 (ISBN 0-471-15899-2, Pub. by Wiley-Interscience). Wiley.

Clark, J., et al, eds. Engineering Woodworking, Vol. 1. 2nd ed. (Engineering Craftsmen: No. K1). (Illus.). 1975. spiral bdg. 31.50x (ISBN 0-85083-280-2). Intl Ideas.

Clark, J. Desmond. Excavations at Star Carr: An Early Mesolithic Site at Seamer Near Scarborough, Yorkshire. LC 75-172830. (Illus.). 226p. 1971. 65.00 (ISBN 0-521-08394-X). Cambridge U Pr.

--Kalambo Falls Prehistoric Site, 2 vols. LC 68-25084. (Illus.). 1973. Vol. 1. 75.00 (ISBN 0-521-06962-9); Vol. 2. 125.00 (ISBN 0-521-20009-1). Cambridge U Pr.

Clark, J. G. Audiology for the School Speech-Language Clinician. (Illus.). 208p. 1980. 14.75 (ISBN 0-398-04004-4). C C Thomas.

--Mesolithic Prelude: The Paleolithic-Neolithic Transition in Europe & the Near East. 100p. 1980. 15.00x (ISBN 0-85224-365-0, Pub. by Edinburgh U Pr Scotland). Columbia U Pr.

Clark, J. H., et al, eds. Hormone & Antihormone, Action at the Target Cell, LSRR 3. (Dahlem Workshop Reports Ser.). 1976. pap. 26.50 (ISBN 0-89573-087-1). Verlag Chemie.

Clark, J. W. The Language & Style of Anthony Trollope. (Andre Deutsch Language Library). 1977. lib. bdg. 19.00x (ISBN 0-233-96641-2). Westview.

Clark, James. Cars. LC 80-17876. (A Look Inside Ser.). (Illus.). 48p. (gr. 4-12). 1981. PLB 10.25 (ISBN 0-8172-1405-4). Raintree Child.

Clark, James, jt. auth. see Halbouty, Michel.

Clark, James A. An Oilman's Oilman. LC 75-5318. (Illus.). 1979. write for info. (ISBN 0-88415-633-8). Pacesetter Pr.

Clark, James D. & Orgel, Stephen, eds. The Bugbears. LC 78-66768. (Renaissance Drama Ser.). 1979. lib. bdg. 28.50 (ISBN 0-8240-9749-1). Garland Pub.

Clark, James H. Take AIM, Vol. 1. 416p. (Orig.). pap. text ed. 16.95 (ISBN 0-686-69549-6). Matrix Pubns.

Clark, James I. & Remini, Robert. We the People: A History of the U. S., Combined. 1975. pap. text ed. 11.95 (ISBN 0-02-471730-4, 47173); tchrs' manual free (ISBN 0-02-471740-1). Macmillan.

--We the People: A History of U. S, 2 vols. 1975. Vol. 1. pap. text ed. 8.95x (ISBN 0-02-471710-X, 47171); Vol. 2. pap. text ed. 8.95x (ISBN 0-02-471720-7, 47172). Macmillan.

Clark, James I. & Remini, Robert O. Freedom Frontiers: The Story of the American People. 1975. 13.95 (ISBN 0-02-640660-8, 64066); tchr's manual 3.48 (ISBN 0-02-640670-5, 64067). Macmillan.

Clark, James J., jt. ed. see Woodward, Robert H.

Clark, James L. & Clark, Lyn. How Two: A Handbook for Office Workers. 2nd ed. 1979. pap. text ed. 7.95x (ISBN 0-534-00635-3). Wadsworth Pub.

Clark, Jean. Untie the Winds. LC 75-31595. 340p. 1976. 9.95 o.s.i. (ISBN 0-02-525780-3, 52578). Macmillan.

Clark, Jerome & Coleman, Loren. Creatures of the Outer Edge. 1978. pap. 1.95 o.s.i. (ISBN 0-446-89150-9). Warner Bks.

Clark, John. Tether, Contracture, & Deformity. 1976. 27.50x (ISBN 0-685-83929-X). Intl Ideas.

Clark, John, jt. auth. see Ringold, Paul L.

Clark, John, et al. Small Seaports: Revitalization Through Conserving Heritage Resources. LC 79-67736. (Illus.). 64p. (Orig.). 1979. pap. 6.50 (ISBN 0-89164-059-2). Conservation Foun.

Clark, John G. New Orleans, 1718-1812: An Economic History. LC 77-119115. (Illus.). 1970. 25.00 (ISBN 0-8071-0346-2). La State U Pr.

--Three Generations in Twentieth Century America: Family, Community & Nation. 1977. 12.50x (ISBN 0-256-01932-0); pap. 12.50x (ISBN 0-256-02099-X). Dorsey.

Clark, John Grahame Douglas. World Prehistory in New Perspective. 3rd ed. LC 76-51318. (Illus.). 1977. 57.00 (ISBN 0-521-21506-4); pap. 12.95 (ISBN 0-521-29178-X). Cambridge U Pr.

Clark, John H., jt. auth. see Cohen, John.

Clark, John J., jt. auth. see Elgers, Pieter T.

Clark, John J., et al. Financial Management: A Capital Market Approach. 1976. text ed. 19.95 (ISBN 0-205-05445-5, 105445-7); instructor's manual free (ISBN 0-205-05447-1, 105447-3). Allyn.

Clark, John M. Studies in the Economics of Overhead Costs. 1980. pap. write for info. (ISBN 0-226-10851-1). U of Chicago Pr.

Clark, John M., Jr. & Switzer, Robert L. Experimental Biochemistry. 2nd ed. (Illus.). 1977. lab. manual 12.95x (ISBN 0-7167-0179-0). W H Freeman.

Clark, John R. Coastal Ecosystem Management: A Technical Manual for the Conservation of Coastal Zone Resources. LC 76-40125. 1977. 55.00 (ISBN 0-471-15854-2, Pub by Wiley-Interscience). Wiley.

Clark, John W. The Care of Books: An Essay on the Development of Libraries & Their Fittings, from the Earliest Times to the End of the 18th Century. 442p. 1980. 50.00x (ISBN 0-902089-78-1, Pub. by Variorum England). State Mutual Bk.

Clark, Jon, et al, eds. Culture & Crisis in Britain in the Thirties. 1980. text ed. 19.50x (ISBN 0-85315-491-0). Humanities.

Clark, Jon D. Data Base Selection: Design & Administration. LC 80-607121. 250p. 1980. 23.95 (ISBN 0-03-055891-3). Praeger.

Clark, Jon D. & Reisman, Arnold. Computer System Selection. (Praeger Special Studies). 250p. 1980. 19.95 (ISBN 0-03-057888-4). Praeger.

Clark, Joseph D. Beastly Folklore. LC 68-12617. 1968. 11.00 (ISBN 0-8108-0009-8). Scarecrow.

Clark, Joseph S., et al. The Senate Establishment. (Orig.). 1963. pap. 1.50 o.p. (ISBN 0-8090-0067-9, AmCen). Hill & Wang.

Clark, Katerina. The Soviet Novel: History As Ritual. LC 80-18758. 1981. lib. bdg. 20.00x (ISBN 0-226-10766-3). U of Chicago Pr.

Clark, Kenneth. Animals & Men. LC 76-52335. (Illus.). 1977. 19.95 o.p. (ISBN 0-688-03200-1). Morrow.

--Another Part of the Wood: A Self Portrait. 304p. 1976. pap. 2.25 o.p. (ISBN 0-345-24919-4). Ballantine.

--Civilisation: A Personal View. LC 75-97174. (Illus.). 1970. 25.00 (ISBN 0-06-090787-8, CN 787, HarpT); pap. 10.95 (ISBN 0-06-010801-0, TD-113, HarpT). Har-Row.

--Rembrandt & the Italian Renaissance. LC 66-13550. (Illus.). 1966. 19.95 (ISBN 0-8147-0080-2). NYU Pr.

--What Is a Masterpiece? (Illus.). pap. 2.95 (ISBN 0-500-27206-9). Thames Hudson.

Clark, Kenneth B. Dark Ghetto. LC 64-7834. 1965. 10.00 o.p. (ISBN 0-06-031470-2, HarpT). Har-Row.

--The Pathos of Power. LC 73-14250. 224p. 1974. 10.00 o.s.i. (ISBN 0-06-010799-5, HarpT). Har-Row.

--Prejudice & Your Child. 2nd ed. 6.75 (ISBN 0-8446-1863-2). Peter Smith.

Clark, Kenneth B. & Hopkins, Jeannette. Relevant War Against Poverty: A Study of Community Action Programs & Observable Social Change. LC 72-88633. 1969. 10.00 o.s.i. (ISBN 0-06-010798-7, HarpT). Har-Row.

Clark, Kenneth M. The Nude: A Study in Ideal Form. (Bollingen Series, No. 35: A. W. Mellon Lectures in the Fine Arts, Vol. 2). (Illus.). 458p. 1972. 50.00 (ISBN 0-691-09792-5); pap. 14.95 (ISBN 0-691-01788-3). Princeton U Pr.

Clark, Kenneth, Sir. The Best of Aubrey Beardsley. 1979. 16.95 o.p. (ISBN 0-385-14543-8). Doubleday.

Clark, L. D. The Minoan Distance: The Symbolism of Travel in D. H. Lawrence. LC 80-18844. 1980. text ed. 25.00x (ISBN 0-8165-0707-4); pap. 12.95 (ISBN 0-8165-0712-0). U of Ariz Pr.

Clark, L. H., jt. auth. see Ruttenber, E. M.

Clark, L. Roy & Locke, Sam. How to Survive Your Doctor's Care. (Illus.). 96p. 1981. pap. 4.95 (ISBN 0-87786-005-X). Gold Penny.

Clark, Larry V., ed. see Permanent International Altaistic Conference, 18th Meeting, Bloomington, June 29-July 5, 1975.

Clark, Lawrence P. Designs for Evaluating Social Programs. (Learning Packages in the Policy Sciences: No. 11). vi, 44p. (Orig.). 1979. pap. text ed. 3.00 (ISBN 0-936826-00-2). Pol Stud Assocs.

--Introduction to Surveys & Interviews. (Learning Packages in the Policy Sciences: No. 12). (Illus.). 56p. (Orig.). 1978. pap. text ed. 3.00 (ISBN 0-936826-01-0). Pol Stud Assocs.

Clark, LeMon. One Hundred & One Intimate Sexual Problems Answered. (Orig.). 1967. pap. 0.95 o.p. (ISBN 0-451-05519-5, Q5519, Sig). NAL.

Clark, Lincoln & Clark, Alice. A B C's of Small Boat Sailing. LC 63-13079. (YA) pap. 2.50 (ISBN 0-385-06690-2, C424, Dolp). Doubleday.

Clark, Linda. Get Well Naturally. LC 65-18927. 1968. pap. 2.75 (ISBN 0-668-01762-7). Arc Bks.

--Know Your Nutrition. rev. ed. LC 80-84437. 275p. 1981. pap. 4.95 (ISBN 0-87983-247-9). Keats.

--Secrets of Health & Beauty. 1979. pap. 1.95 (ISBN 0-515-05077-6). Jove Pubns.

--Stay Young Longer. (Orig.). pap. 1.95 (ISBN 0-515-05076-8). Jove Pubns.

Clark, Linda & Lee, Kay. Beauty Questions & Answers. 1977. pap. 2.25 (ISBN 0-515-05647-2). Jove Pubns.

Clark, Linda, et al. Image Breaking - Image Building. 148p. (Orig.). 1981. pap. 7.95 (ISBN 0-8298-0407-2). Pilgrim NY.

Clark, Lyn, jt. auth. see Clark, James L.

Clark, M. J. Politics in Camera: Film & Television for the Political Scientist & Historian. (Audio-Visual Media Education & Research: Vol. 1). 1979. 28.00 (ISBN 0-08-022483-0); pap. 14.00 (ISBN 0-08-022484-9). Pergamon.

Clark, Malcolm. The Need to Question: An Introduction to Philosophy. LC 72-5579. 304p. 1973. text ed. 13.95 (ISBN 0-13-610857-1). P-H.

Clark, Malcolm, Jr. The Eden Seekers. 320p. 1981. 15.00 (ISBN 0-686-69047-8). HM.

Clark, Malcolm, Jr., intro. by see Deady, Matthew P.

Clark, Marden J. Modern & Classic: The "Wooing Both Ways". (Charles E. Merrill Monograph Series in the Humanities & Social Sciences: Vol. 2, No. 2). 94p. 1973. pap. 2.00 o.p. (ISBN 0-8425-0808-2). Brigham.

Clark, Margaret. Health in the Mexican-American Culture: A Community Study. 2nd ed. 1970. 16.50x (ISBN 0-520-01666-1); pap. 3.85 (ISBN 0-520-01668-8, CAL192). U of Cal Pr.

Clark, Margaret G. The Mystery in the Flooded Museum. LC 77-16860. (Illus.). (gr. 5 up). 1978. 5.95 (ISBN 0-396-07550-9). Dodd.

--Who Stole Kathy Young? LC 80-1013. (gr. 5 up). 1980. 6.95g (ISBN 0-396-07888-5). Dodd.

Clark, Margaret P., jt. auth. see Clark, George.

Clark, Marjorie A. Captive on the Ho Chi Minh Trail. 160p. 1974. pap. 2.25 (ISBN 0-8024-1170-3). Moody.

Clark, Martin. Antonio Gramsci & the Revolution That Failed. LC 76-49754. 1977. 22.50x (ISBN 0-300-02077-5). Yale U Pr.

Clark, Marvin H., Jr. Pinnell & Talifson: Last of the Great Brown Bear Men. (Illus.). 224p. 1980. 15.00x (ISBN 0-937708-00-3). Great Northwest.

Clark, Mary E. Contemporary Biology. 2nd ed. LC 77-25553. (Illus.). 1979. 18.95 o.p. (ISBN 0-7216-2598-3). Saunders.

Clark, Mary H. The Cradle Will Fall. (Large Print Bks.). 1980. lib. bdg. 13.95 (ISBN 0-8161-3121-X). G K Hall.

--The Cradle Will Fall. 1981. pap. 3.50 (ISBN 0-440-11476-4). Dell.

--A Stranger Is Watching. 1979. pap. 2.50 o.s.i. (ISBN 0-440-18125-9). Dell.

Clark, Mary T., ed. An Aquinas Reader. LC 72-76709. pap. 3.50 (ISBN 0-385-02505-X, Im). Doubleday.

Clark, Mavis T. The Hundred Islands. LC 77-5353. (gr. 6-9). 1977. 8.95 (ISBN 0-02-718900-7, 71890). Macmillan.

--If the Earth Falls In. LC 75-4781. 176p. (gr. 6 up). 1975. 6.95 (ISBN 0-395-28900-9, Clarion). HM.

--Min-Min. (gr. 5-9). 1969. 8.95g (ISBN 0-02-718960-0). Macmillan.

--The Sky Is Free. LC 76-15171. (gr. 5-8). 1976. 8.95 (ISBN 0-02-718910-4, 71891). Macmillan.

--Wildfire. LC 73-19049. 224p. (gr. 6-9). 1974. 5.95g o.s.i. (ISBN 0-02-718970-8, 71897). Macmillan.

Clark, Merrian E. Ford's Freighter Travel Guide: Published Semi-Annually, March & September. 57th ed. D'Ascenzo, Juliann & Wilson, Bonnie, eds. LC 54-3845. (Illus.). 140p. pap. 4.95 (ISBN 0-916486-57-5). Fords Travel.

--Ford's International Cruise Guide. 26th ed. Wilson, Bonnie & D'Ascenzo, Juliann, eds. LC 75-29725. (Illus.). 160p. 1980. pap. 5.95 o.p. (ISBN 0-916486-53-2). M Clark.

--Ford's International Cruise Guide. 28th ed. Wilson, Bonnie & D'Ascenzo, Juliann, eds. LC 75-29725. (Illus.). 160p. 1981. pap. 5.95 (ISBN 0-916486-56-7). M Clark.

--Ford's International Cruise Guide: Summer 1981. 29th ed. Wilson, Bonnie & D'Ascenzo, Juliann, eds. LC 75-29725. (Illus.). 160p. 1981. pap. 5.95 (ISBN 0-916486-59-1). M Clark.

Clark, Michael & Clark, Dorothy. Sexual Joy in Marriage. (Illus.). 256p. (Orig.). 1980. pap. 7.95 (ISBN 0-523-41137-5). Pinnacle Bks.

Clark, Mollie. International Folktales Series. Incl. The Bird Catcher & the Crow-Peri: Turkey. LC 73-84508. (RL 3.7) (ISBN 0-8224-9300-4); The Buffalo Stone: North America. LC 73-84505. (RL 3.4) (ISBN 0-8224-9302-0); The Clever Jackal: India. LC 73-84503. (RL 3.3) (ISBN 0-8224-9304-7); Mac-the-Rascal from Mull: Scotland. LC 73-84504. (RL 3.3) (ISBN 0-8224-9306-3); Mink & the Fire: North America. LC 73-84501. (RL 3.2) (ISBN 0-8224-9308-X); The Monkey & the Roaring Rakhas: India. LC 73-84506. (RL 3.6) (ISBN 0-8224-9310-1); Rabbit & Fox: Canada. LC 73-84500. (RL 2.9) (ISBN 0-8224-9312-8); The Remarkable Rat: India. LC 73-84502. (RL 3.2) (ISBN 0-8224-9314-4); Three Marvelous Things: Italy. LC 73-84509. (RL 3.7) (ISBN 0-8224-9316-0); Wu & the Yellow Dragon: China. LC 73-84510. (RL 3.7) (ISBN 0-8224-9318-7). 1973. pap. text ed. 2.60 ea. Pitman Learning.

Clark, N. Introduction to Nepali. 1977. 22.00x (ISBN 0-88386-385-5). South Asia Bks.

Clark, N. E., et al, eds. Electronic Equipment Wiring & Assembling: Part Two. (Engineering Craftsmen: No. G25). (Illus.). 1969. spiral bdg. 24.95x (ISBN 0-685-90137-8). Intl Ideas.

Clark, Nancy. The Athlete's Kitchen: A Nutrition Guide & Cookbook. (Illus.). 276p. 1981. pap. 9.95 (ISBN 0-8436-2212-1). CBI Pub.

--Littleton: A Pictorial History. Friedman, Donna R., ed. (Illus.). 208p. 1981. pap. price not set (ISBN 0-89865-112-3). Donning Co.

Clark, Neil M., jt. auth. see Thorp, N. Howard.

Clark, Norma L. The Tynedale Daughters. LC 80-54482. 192p. 1981. 9.95 (ISBN 0-8027-0676-2). Walker & Co.

Clark, Norman H. Washington. (States & the Nation Ser). (Illus.). 1976. 12.95 (ISBN 0-393-05587-6, Co-Pub by AASLH). Norton.

Clark, Oliver. Never Catch Colds Again. 64p. 1979. pap. 6.95x (ISBN 0-8464-1035-4). Beekman Pubs.

Clark, P. M. & Kricka, L. J. Medical Consequences of Alcohol Abuse. LC 80-41993. (Chemical Science Ser.). 282p. 1980. 97.95 (ISBN 0-470-27076-4). Halsted Pr.

Clark, P. M., jt. auth. see Kricka, L. J.

Clark, Patrick. Sports Firsts. 320p. 1981. 14.95 (ISBN 0-87196-302-7). Facts on File.

Clark, Pauline. The Return of the Twelves. (Children's Literature Ser.). 1981. PLB 9.95 (ISBN 0-8398-2718-0). Gregg.

Clark, Peter, ed. The Early Modern Town. LC 76-7041. (Open University set book). 1976. text ed. 18.95x (ISBN 0-582-48404-9); pap. text ed. 8.95x (ISBN 0-582-48405-7). Longman.

Clark, Phillip G., jt. ed. see Callahan, Daniel.

Clark, Phyllis E., jt. auth. see Lehrman, Robert.

Clark, R. & Brown, D. The Chemistry of Vanadium, Niobium & Tantalum. (Pergamon Texts in Inorganic Chemistry: Vol. 20). 132p. 1975. text ed. 27.00 (ISBN 0-08-018866-4); pap. text ed. 14.00 (ISBN 0-08-018865-6). Pergamon.

Clark, R., jt. auth. see Son, Duk S.

Clark, R. see Kalven, H., Jr.

Clark, R., et al. The Chemistry of Titanium, Zirconium & Hafnium. (Pergamon Texts in Inorganic Chemistry: Vol. 19). 136p. 1975. text ed. 27.00 (ISBN 0-08-018864-8); pap. text ed. 14.00 (ISBN 0-08-018863-X). Pergamon.

Clark, R. Bradbury. California Corporation Laws: Including Current Changes to 1980, 6 vols. LC 63-47230. 1980. 350.00 (ISBN 0-911110-00-3). Parker & Son.

Clark, R. E. God Beyond Nature. LC 77-76108. (Redwood Ser.). 1978. pap. 3.95 (ISBN 0-8163-0002-X, 07345-2). Pacific Pr Pub Assn.

Clark, R. H., jt. auth. see Bruce, J. P.

Clark, R. H., jt. auth. see Mayneord, W. V.

Clark, R. L. & Spengler, J. J. The Economics of Individual & Population Aging. LC 79-19495. (Cambridge Surveys of Economic Literature Ser.). (Illus.). 1980. 24.95 (ISBN 0-521-22883-2); pap. 8.95 (ISBN 0-521-29702-8). Cambridge U Pr.

Clark, R. T., jt. auth. see Quigley, Hugh.

Clark, Raymond C. Language Teaching Techniques. LC 80-84109. (Pro Lingua Language Resource Handbook Ser.). (Illus.). 128p. (Orig.). 1980. pap. 5.50 (ISBN 0-86647-000-X). Pro Lingua.

Clark, Raymond J. Catabasis: Vergil & the Wisdom Tradition. 1979. pap. text ed. 34.25x (ISBN 9-0603-2104-9). Humanities.

Clark, Richard L., jt. auth. see Bookstein, Joseph J.

Clark, Robert B. Dynamics in Metazoan Evolution: The Origin of the Coelom & Segments. 1964. 29.95x (ISBN 0-19-854353-0). Oxford U Pr.

Clark, Robert D., ed. Australian Renewable Energy Resources Index: Issue No. 1. 1979. pap. 7.00x (ISBN 0-686-24273-4, Pub. by CSIRO). Intl Schol Bk Serv.

Clark, Robert L., ed. Retirement Policy in an Aging Society. LC 79-56502. (Illus.). vii, 215p. 1980. 16.75 (ISBN 0-8223-0441-4). Duke.

Clark, Robert P. The Basques: The Franco Years & Beyond. LC 79-24926. (Basque Bk.). xvii, 434p. 1980. 17.50 (ISBN 0-87417-057-5). U of Nev Pr.
Clark, Robert S. Fundamentals of Criminal Justice Research. (Illus.). 1977. 18.95 (ISBN 0-669-01005-7). Lexington Bks.
Clark, Rodney. The Japanese Company. 1979. 25.00x (ISBN 0-300-02310-3). Yale U Pr.
--The Japanese Company. LC 78-65480. 292p. 1981. pap. 7.95 (ISBN 0-300-02646-3). Yale U Pr.
Clark, Ronald. Sir Edward Appleton, C.B.E., K.C.B., F.R.S. 256p. 1972. text ed. 27.00 (ISBN 0-08-016093-X). Pergamon.
--Wonders of the World. LC 79-27835. (Illus.). 96p. 1980. 11.95 (ISBN 0-668-04932-4, 4932-4). Arco.
Clark, Ronald D. & Amai, Robert L. Chemistry: The Science & the Scene. LC 74-13782. 355p. 1975. text ed. 16.50x o.p. (ISBN 0-471-15857-7). Wiley.
Clark, Ronald W. Einstein: The Life & Times. (Illus.). 1972. pap. 3.95 (ISBN 0-380-01159-X, 44123). Avon.
--Einstein: The Life & Times. LC 71-149419. 1971. 15.00 o.s.i. (ISBN 0-690-00448-6, TYC-T). T Y Crowell.
--The Greatest Power on Earth: The International Race for Supremacy. LC 80-7899. (Illus.). 352p. 1981. 12.95 (ISBN 0-06-014846-2, HarpT). Har-Row.
--The Role of the Bomber. LC 77-11570. (Illus.). 1978. 15.95 o.p. (ISBN 0-690-01720-0, TYC-T). T Y Crowell.
--The Role of the Bomber. (Illus.). 1980. 14.95 (ISBN 0-690-01720-0). Quality Bks IL.
Clark, Roy P., ed. Best Newspaper Writing. 1979: Winners of the American Society of Newspaper Editors Competition. (Illus.). 176p. (Orig.). 1980. pap. 3.95 o.p. (ISBN 0-935742-01-8). Mod Media Inst.
Clark, Ruth M., jt. auth. see Vaughn, Gwenyth R.
Clark, Sabina. An Artful Lady. (Second Chance at Love, Regency Ser.: No. 6). (Orig.). 1981. pap. 1.75 (ISBN 0-515-05863-7). Jove Pubns.
Clark, Sam L., ed. see Ranson, Stephen W.
Clark, Sandra & Long, T. H., eds. The New Century Shakespeare Handbook. 304p. 1974. Repr. 13.95 (ISBN 0-13-612093-8). P-H.
Clark, Sarah. From Grammar to Paragraphs. 306p. 1981. pap. text ed. 8.95 (ISBN 0-394-32560-5). Random.
Clark, Stephen & Lyman, Daniel, eds. Incredible Illustrated Tool Book. (Illus.). 415p. Date not set. price not set (ISBN 0-89196-082-1, Domus Bks). Quality Bks IL. Postponed.
Clark, Stephen B. Building Christian Communities: Strategy for Renewing the Church. LC 75-189990. 192p. 1972. pap. 2.95 (ISBN 0-87793-043-0). Ave Maria.
--Man & Woman in Christ: An Examination of the Roles of Men & Women in the Light of Scripture & the Social Sciences. 754p. (Orig.). 1980. 15.95 (ISBN 0-89283-084-0). Servant.
Clark, Stephen R. The Moral Status of Animals. 1977. 26.50x (ISBN 0-19-824578-5). Oxford U Pr.
Clark, Steve. Illustrated Basketball Dictionary for Young People. (Illus.). 1978. pap. 2.50 (ISBN 0-13-450940-4). P-H.
Clark, Steve B. Baptized in the Spirit & Spiritual Gifts. new ed. 1967. pap. 1.50 (ISBN 0-89283-033-6). Servant.
--Growing in Faith. (Living As a Christian Ser.). 1972. pap. 1.50 (ISBN 0-89283-004-2). Servant.
--Knowing God's Will. (Living As a Christian Ser.). 1974. pap. 1.50 (ISBN 0-89283-005-0). Servant.
Clark, Steven B. Unordained Elders & Renewal Communities. LC 75-35329. 1976. pap. 3.50 (ISBN 0-8091-1916-1). Paulist Pr.
Clark, T. J. & Godfrey, S., eds. Asthma. LC 76-57835. (Illus.). 1977. text ed. 24.00 (ISBN 0-7216-2596-7). Saunders.
Clark, T. W., ed. The Novel in India: Its Birth & Development. LC 70-119719. 1970. 19.50x (ISBN 0-520-01725-0). U of Cal Pr.
Clark, Thomas A. Ways Through Bracken. 1980. signed ltd. ed. 20.00 (ISBN 0-912330-44-9); pap. 7.50 (ISBN 0-912330-44-9). Jargon Soc.
Clark, Thomas D. Historic Maps of Kentucky. LC 79-4003. (Illus.). 1979. 27.50 (ISBN 0-8131-0097-6). U Pr of Ky.
--Indiana University: Midwestern Pioneer, 3 vols. Incl. Vol. 1. The Early Years. (Illus.). 352p. 1970. 12.50x (ISBN 0-253-14170-2); Vol. 2. In Mid-Passage. (Illus.). 448p. 1973. 17.50x (ISBN 0-253-32995-7); Vol. 3. Years of Fulfillment. 704p. 1977. 19.95x (ISBN 0-253-32996-5). LC 74-126207. (Illus.). Set. 42.50x (ISBN 0-253-32997-3). Ind U Pr.
--Kentucky. LC 65-23498. 1965. pap. 2.95 (ISBN 0-8077-1164-0). Tchrs Coll.
--Kentucky: Land of Contrast. (Regions of America Ser). (YA) 1968. 11.95 o.s.i. (ISBN 0-06-010808-8, HarpT). Har-Row.
--Pills, Petticoats, & Plows: The Southern Country Store. (Illus.). 1964. 9.95 (ISBN 0-8061-0593-3); pap. 5.95 (ISBN 0-8061-1093-7). U of Okla Pr.
--Travels in the Old South: A Bibliography, 3 vols. Incl. Vol. 1. The Formative Years, 1527-1783: from the Spanish Explorations Through the American Revolution. (Illus.). 330p. 1956; Vol. 2. The Expanding South, 1750-1825: the Ohio Valley & the Cotton Frontier. (Illus.). 292p. 1959; Vol. 3. The Ante Bellum South, 1825-1860: Cotton, Slavery, & Conflict. (Illus.). 406p. 1969. (American Exploration & Travel Ser: No. 19). boxed set 52.50 (ISBN 0-8061-0878-9). U of Okla Pr.
Clark, Thomas D. & Kirwan, Albert D. The South Since Appomattox: A Century of Regional Change. LC 80-24023. (Illus.). vii, 438p. 1980. Repr. of 1967 ed. lib. bdg. 39.75x (ISBN 0-313-22698-9, CLSS). Greenwood.
Clark, Thomas D., ed. The Great American Frontier: A History of Western Pioneering. LC 74-28026. (No. 87). 376p. 1975. pap. 8.95 (ISBN 0-672-60146-X, AHS-87). Bobbs.
Clark, Thomas D., et al, eds. Travels in the New South, 2 vols. Incl. Vol. 1. The Postwar South, 1867-1900. (Illus.). xvi, 267p; Vol. 2. The Twentieth-Century South, 1900-1955. (Illus.). xiv, 301p. (American Exploration & Travel Ser: No. 36). 1962. Set. 37.50 (ISBN 0-8061-0524-0). U of Okla Pr.
Clark, Thomas E., ed. Above Every Name: The Lordship of Christ & Social Systems. LC 80-82082. (Woodstock Studies). 256p. (Orig.). 1980. pap. 7.95 (ISBN 0-8091-2338-X). Paulist Pr.
Clark, Tom. Blue. (Illus.). 80p. (Orig.). 1974. ltd. signed o.p. 15.00 (ISBN 0-87685-184-7); pap. 3.00 (ISBN 0-87685-183-9). Black Sparrow.
--The Great Naropa Poetry Wars. LC 79-55794. 1980. pap. 5.00 (ISBN 0-932274-06-4); signed ed. o.p. 20.00 (ISBN 0-932274-07-2). Cadmus Eds.
--The Last Gas Station & Other Stories. 200p. 1980. 14.00 (ISBN 0-87685-457-9); signed ed. 20.00 (ISBN 0-87685-458-7); pap. 6.00 (ISBN 0-87685-456-0). Black Sparrow.
--The Master. 1979. 17.50x (ISBN 0-915316-65-X); pap. 4.50x (ISBN 0-915316-66-8). Pentagram.
--A Short Guide to the High Plains, For Ed Dorn. Miller, Jeffrey, ed. 1981. signed limited ed. 15.00 (ISBN 0-932274-18-8); pap. 3.50 (ISBN 0-932274-17-X). Cadmus Eds.
Clark, Tom, ed. see Dorn, Edward.
Clark, Tom C., ed. see U. S. Department of Justice.
Clark, Ursula, jt. auth. see Allsop, Bruce.
Clark, Ursula, jt. auth. see Allsopp, Bruce.
Clark, Virginia A., jt. auth. see Dunn, Olive J.
Clark, Virginia A., jt. auth. see Gross, Alan J.
Clark, Vivian. God's Remedy for Depression. (Direction Bks.). (Orig.). 1980. pap. 3.50 (ISBN 0-8010-2444-7). Baker Bk.
Clark, Vivian V. Outpatient Services Journal Articles. 2nd ed. 317p. 1973. spiral bdg. 12.00 o.p. (ISBN 0-87488-797-6). Med Exam.
Clark, Vivian V., ed. Outpatient Services: Journal Articles. 2nd ed. 348p. 1973. 10.00 o.s.i. (ISBN 0-686-68575-X, 1498). Hospital Finan.
Clark, W. A. V. & Moore, Eric G., eds. Residential Mobility & Public Policy. LC 80-12624. (Urban Affairs Annual Reviews: Vol. 19). (Illus.). 320p. 1980. 20.00 (ISBN 0-8039-1447-4); pap. 9.95 (ISBN 0-8039-1448-2). Sage.
Clark, W. E. The Tissues of the Body. 6th ed. (Illus.). 1977. pap. text ed. 18.95x (ISBN 0-19-857163-1). Oxford U Pr.
Clark, Wallace. Sailing Round Ireland. 1976. 22.50 (ISBN 0-7134-3133-4, Pub. by Batsford England). David & Charles.
Clark, Walter H., et al. Religious Experience: Its Nature & Function in the Human Psyche. (Illus.). 168p. 1973. 11.75 (ISBN 0-398-02550-9). C C Thomas.
Clark, Walter V. Ox-Bow Incident. 6.75 (ISBN 0-8446-0060-1). Peter Smith.
--The Track of the Cat. LC 80-22458. 344p. 1981. 18.50x (ISBN 0-8032-1412-X); pap. 5.95 (ISBN 0-8032-6307-4, BB 734, Bison). U of Nebr Pr.
Clark, William, jt. auth. see Lewis, Meriwether.
Clark, William, ed. see Shane, Harold G.
Clark, William B. Lambert Wickes: Sea Raider & Diplomat-the Story of a Naval Captain of the Revolution. 1932. 42.50x (ISBN 0-685-69800-9). Elliots Bks.
Clark, William D. Conducting Technique. LC 78-66123. 1979. pap. text ed. 9.50 (ISBN 0-8191-0684-4). U Pr of Amer.
--Death Valley: The Story Behind the Scenery. rev. ed. Dendooven, Gweneth R., ed. LC 79-91050. (Illus.). 1980. 7.95 (ISBN 0-916122-37-9); pap. 3.00 (ISBN 0-686-60733-3). K C Pubns.
Clark, William J. Great American Sculptures. LC 75-28869. (Art Experience in Late 19th Century America Ser.: Vol. 5). (Illus.). 1976. Repr. of 1878 ed. lib. bdg. 44.00 (ISBN 0-8240-2229-7). Garland Pub.
Clark, William N. see Hovey, Alvah.
Clark, William R. The Experimental Foundations of Modern Immunology. LC 80-13565. 372p. 1980. text ed. 18.95 (ISBN 0-471-04088-6). Wiley.
Clark, William R., ed. Charles Dickens. (Discussions of Literature). 1961. pap. text ed. 2.95x o.p. (ISBN 0-669-21832-4). Heath.
Clark, Wilson. Energy for Survival: The Alternative to Extinction. LC 72-89297. (Illus.). 672p. 1974. 12.50 o.p. (ISBN 0-385-03501-2, Anchor Pr). Doubleday.
--Energy for Survival: The Alternative to Extinction. LC 72-89297. 672p. 1975. pap. 5.95 (ISBN 0-385-03564-0). Doubleday.
Clarke, A. B. & Disney, R. L. Probability & Random Processes for Engineers & Scientists. 1970. 24.95 (ISBN 0-471-15980-8). Wiley.
Clarke, A. D., jt. ed. see Clarke, Ann M.
Clarke, Adam. Bibliographical Dictionary Plus the Bibliographical Miscellany. 1971. Repr. of 1802 ed. 55.00 o.p. (ISBN 0-8108-0399-2). Scarecrow.
Clarke, Alfred C., jt. auth. see Curry, Timothy J.
Clarke, Allan. Soccer: How to Become a Champ. (Illus.). 1976. pap. 5.95 (ISBN 0-86002-131-9). Transatlantic.
Clarke, Amanda. Growing up in Ancient Britain. (Growing up Ser.). (Illus.). 72p. (gr. 6 up). 1981. 14.95 (ISBN 0-7134-3557-7, Pub. by Batsford England). David & Charles.
--Growing up in Elizabethan Times. LC 79-56439. (Growing up Ser.). (Illus.). 72p. (gr. 7 up). 1980. text ed. 14.95 (ISBN 0-7134-3364-7, Pub. by Batsford England). David & Charles.
--Growing up in Puritan Times. LC 79-56452. (Growing up Ser.). (Illus.). 72p. (gr. 7 up). 1980. text ed. 14.95 (ISBN 0-7134-3366-3, Pub. by Batsford England). David & Charles.
Clarke, Ann M. & Clarke, A. D., eds. Early Experience: Myth & Evidence. LC 76-21992. 1979. pap. text ed. 7.95 (ISBN 0-02-905690-X). Free Pr.
--Early Experience: Myth & Evidence. LC 76-21992. 1977. 13.95 o.s.i. (ISBN 0-02-905630-6). Free Pr.
Clarke, Anna. Letter from the Dead. LC 80-2043. (Crime Club Ser.). 192p. 1981. 9.95 (ISBN 0-385-17330-X). Doubleday.
Clarke, Arthur. The City & the Stars. 192p. (RL 7). 1973. pap. 1.75 (ISBN 0-451-09232-5, E9232, Sig). NAL.
--The Nine Billion Names of God. 204p. (RL 7). Date not set. pap. 1.75 o.p. (ISBN 0-451-08381-4, E8381, Sig). NAL.
--Starting Rock Climbing. (Illus.). 1979. 8.95 o.p. (ISBN 0-214-20488-X, 8050, Dist. by Arco, 8075). Barrie & Jenkins.
Clarke, Arthur C. Against the Fall of Night. 1978. pap. 1.75 o.s.i. (ISBN 0-515-04832-1). Jove Pubns.
--Challenge of the Spaceship. 1980. pap. 2.50 (ISBN 0-671-82139-3). PB.
--Dolphin Island. 1971. pap. 1.75 (ISBN 0-425-04302-9, Medallion). Berkley Pub.
--Earthlight. 1975. pap. 1.75 (ISBN 0-345-27273-0). Ballantine.
--Expedition to Earth. 1975. pap. 1.95 (ISBN 0-345-28467-4). Ballantine.
--Islands in the Sky. (RL 7). pap. 1.75 (ISBN 0-451-08382-2, E8382, Sig). NAL.
--Man & Space. LC 64-25368. (Life Science Library). (Illus.). (gr. 5 up). 1969. PLB 8.97 o.p. (ISBN 0-8094-0464-8, Pub. by Time-Life). Silver.
--Nine Billion Names of God. LC 67-16086. 1967. 7.95 o.p. (ISBN 0-15-165890-0). HarBraceJ.
--Profiles of the Future. 1977. pap. 2.25 (ISBN 0-445-04061-0). Popular Lib.
--Profiles of the Future: An Inquiry into the Limits of the Possible. rev. ed. LC 72-6714. 288p. 1973. 10.95 o.s.i. (ISBN 0-06-010792-8, HarpT). Har-Row.
--Promise of Space. LC 68-17042. (Illus.). 1968. 9.95 o.s.i. (ISBN 0-06-000931-4, HarpT). Har-Row.
--Report on Planet Three & Other Speculations. 1973. pap. 1.50 (ISBN 0-451-07864-0, W7864, Sig). NAL.
--Tales of Ten Worlds. (RL 7). 1973. pap. 1.50 (ISBN 0-451-08328-8, W8328, Sig). NAL.
Clarke, Arthur H. The Freshwater Molluscs of Canada, (Illus.). 416p. 1981. lib. bdg. 39.95x (ISBN 0-660-00022-9, 56350-2, Pub. by Natl Mus Canada). U of Chicago Pr.
Clarke, Austin. The Frenzy of Sweeney. (Dolmen Editions Ser.: No. XXIX). 1980. text ed. 26.00x (ISBN 0-85105-349-1, Dolmen Pr). Humanities.
--Liberty Lane: A Ballad Play of Dublin in Two Acts with a Prologue by Austin Clarke. (Dolmen Editions: No. XXVII). 1978. text ed. 22.25x (ISBN 0-85105-324-6, Dolmen Pr). Humanities.
--The Singing Men at Cashel. 320p. 1980. text ed. 15.75x (ISBN 0-85105-354-8, Dolmen Pr). Humanities.
--The Third Kiss. (Dolmen Editions: No. XxIV). 1976. text ed. 19.50x (ISBN 0-85105-292-4, Dolmen Pr). Humanities.
Clarke, Basil. Mental Disorder in Earlier Britain. 1975. 50.00 (ISBN 0-7083-0562-8). Verry.
Clarke, Basil F. Parish Churches of London. (Illus.). 30.00 o.s.i. (ISBN 0-8038-0205-6). Architectural.
Clarke, Bob, jt. auth. see De Bartolo, Dick.
Clarke, Bob, jt. auth. see Jacobs, Frank.
Clarke, Bob, jt. auth. see Koch, Tom.
Clarke, Boden. Lords Temporal & Lords Spiritual. LC 80-10979. (Stokvis Studies in Historical Chronology & Thought: No. 1). 64p. 1981. lib. bdg. 8.95x (ISBN 0-89370-800-3); pap. 2.95x (ISBN 0-89370-900-X). Borgo Pr.
Clarke, Boden & Burgess, Mary A. Eastern Churches Review: An Index to Volumes One Through Ten, 1966-1978. LC 80-2550. (Borgo Reference Library: Vol. 6). 64p. 1981. lib. bdg. 8.95x (ISBN 0-89370-812-7); pap. text ed. 2.95x (ISBN 0-89370-912-3). Borgo Pr.
Clarke, Brenna K., jt. auth. see Ferrar, Harold.
Clarke, Brian & Goddard, John. The Trout & the Fly. LC 80-493. 1980. 20.00 (ISBN 0-385-17141-2, NLB). Doubleday.
Clarke, C. Elementary General Relativity. 131p. 1980. pap. 19.95x (ISBN 0-470-26930-8). Halsted Pr.
Clarke, Carl D. Illustration, Its Technique & Application to the Sciences. 2nd ed. (Illus.). 258p. 1949. 18.00 (ISBN 0-685-25473-9). Standard Arts.
--Metal Casting of Sculpture & Ornament. 2nd ed. (Illus.). 250p. 1980. 18.00 (ISBN 0-685-50214-7). Standard Arts.
--Molding & Casting: Its Technique & Application. 3rd ed. (Illus.). 380p. 1972. 18.00 (ISBN 0-685-25470-4). Standard Arts.
--Pictures, Their Preservation & Restoration. (Illus.). 250p. 1959. 18.00 (ISBN 0-685-25472-0). Standard Arts.
--Prosthetics: Methods of Producing Facial & Body Restorations. (Illus.). 336p. 1965. 18.00 (ISBN 0-685-25471-2). Standard Arts.
Clarke, Charlotte L., jt. auth. see Farlie, Barbara L.
Clarke, Colin, ed. D. H. Lawrence: The Rainbow & Women in Love. (Casebook Ser.). 1970. 2.50 o.s.i. (ISBN 0-685-59923-X). Aurora Pubs.
Clarke, Colin G. Kingston, Jamaica: Urban Growth & Social Change, 1692-1962. (Illus.). 1976. 40.00x (ISBN 0-520-02025-1). U of Cal Pr.
Clarke, Cynthia A., et al. A Teacher's Notebook: Alternatives for Children with Learning Problems. 1975. pap. 5.75 (ISBN 0-934338-09-4). NAIS.
Clarke, D. & Grainger, J. F. Polarized Light & Optical Measurements. 1971. text ed. 28.00 (ISBN 0-08-016320-3). Pergamon.
Clarke, D., jt. auth. see Roy, A. E.
Clarke, D. B. & Barnes, A. D., eds. Intensive Care for Nurses. 2nd ed. (Illus.). 208p. 1975. 22.50 (ISBN 0-632-00696-X, Blackwell). Mosby.
Clarke, D. H. The Blue Water Dream. 1980. 14.95 (ISBN 0-679-51004-4). McKay.
--An Evolution of Singlehanders. 1976. 9.95 o.p. (ISBN 0-679-50706-X). McKay.
Clarke, D. V. & O'Connor, Anne, eds. From the Stone Age to the Forty-Five: Studies in Scottish Material Culture Presented to R. B. K. Stevenson, Former Keeper, National Museum of Antiquities of Scotland. 1980. text ed. 34.50x (ISBN 0-85976-046-4). Humanities.
Clarke, David, jt. auth. see Roy, Archie E.
Clarke, David H. & Clarke, H. Harrison. Research Processes in Physical Education, Recreation & Health. (Physical Education Ser). 1970. text ed. 17.95 (ISBN 0-13-774463-3). P-H.
Clarke, David H., jt. auth. see Clarke, H. Harrison.
Clarke, David L. Analytical Archaeology. 2nd ed. LC 78-16957. 1978. 27.50x (ISBN 0-231-04630-8). Columbia U Pr.
--Beaker Pottery of Great Britain & Ireland, 2 vols. LC 69-11269. (Illus.). 1969. Set. 160.00 set (ISBN 0-521-07249-2). Cambridge U Pr.
Clarke, David L. & Chapman, Robert. Analytical Archaeology. 2nd ed. 1981. pap. text ed. 12.50 (ISBN 0-231-04631-6). Columbia U Pr.
Clarke, David R., ed. see Yeats, William B.
Clarke, Desmond. Dublin. 1977. 19.95 (ISBN 0-7134-0146-X). David & Charles.
Clarke, Donald. The Encyclopedia of How It's Made. LC 78-58391. (Illus.). 1978. 16.95 (ISBN 0-89479-035-8). A & W Pubs.

Clarke, Donald, ed. The Encyclopedia of How It Works. LC 76-56962. (Illus.). 1977. 16.95 (ISBN 0-89479-002-1). A & W Pubs.
Clarke, Dorothy, jt. auth. see Clarke, Michael.
Clarke, Duncan L. Politics of Arms Control: The Role & Effectiveness of the U. S. Arms Control & Disarmament Agency. LC 79-1955. 1979. 17.95 (ISBN 0-02-905700-0). Free Pr.
Clarke, Dwight L., ed. see Turner, Henry S.
Clarke, Edward H. Demand Revelation & the Provision of Public Goods. 1980. 26.50 (ISBN 0-88410-686-1). Ballinger Pub.
Clarke, Edwin, ed. Modern Methods in the History of Medicine. 1971. text ed. 33.75x (ISBN 0-485-11121-7, Athlone Pr). Humanities.
Clarke, Elizabeth. The Darkening Green. (Illus.). 1964. 8.95 (ISBN 0-571-05680-6, Pub. by Faber & Faber). Merrimack Bk Serv.
--Secret. 1972. 6.50 (ISBN 0-571-09981-5, Pub. by Faber & Faber). Merrimack Bk Serv.
Clarke, Frank, tr. see Kasemann, Ernst.
Clarke, G. M. & Cooke, D. A Basic Course in Statistics. LC 78-10749. 1979. pap. text ed. 19.95 (ISBN 0-470-26527-2). Halsted Pr.
Clarke, Gerald E. McGregor School. 1980. 5.50 (ISBN 0-8233-0310-1). Golden Quill.
Clarke, H. C. Menu Terminology. 1969. pap. 5.25 (ISBN 0-08-006525-2). Pergamon.
Clarke, H. D. & Hamamura, Motoko. Colloquial Japanese. (Colloquial Ser.). (Orig.). 1981. pap. price not set (ISBN 0-7100-0595-4). Routledge & Kegan.
Clarke, H. Edwards. The Greyhound. rev., 7th ed. 222p. 1980. text ed. 24.95x (ISBN 0-09-141410-5, SpS). Soccer.
Clarke, H. Harrison. Application of Measurement to Health & Physical Education. 5th ed. (Illus.). 464p. 1976. 17.50x (ISBN 0-13-039024-0). P-H.
Clarke, H. Harrison & Clarke, David H. Developmental & Adapted Physical Education. 2nd ed. (Illus.). 1978. ref. ed. 15.95 (ISBN 0-13-208421-X). P-H.
Clarke, H. Harrison, jt. auth. see Clarke, David H.
Clarke, H. T. A Handbook of Organic Analysis: Qualitative & Quantitative. 5th ed. Haynes, B., ed. LC 74-83479. 1975. pap. 20.50x (ISBN 0-8448-0662-5). Crane-Russak Co.
Clarke, Heather F., jt. auth. see Robinson, Geoffrey C.
Clarke, Helen. Vikings. (Civilization Library). (Illus.). (gr. 5 up). 1979. PLB 6.90 s&l (ISBN 0-531-03412-7). Watts.
Clarke, Herman F. & Foote, Henry W. Jeremiah Dummer: Colonial Craftsman & Merchant 1645-1718. LC 75-87563. (Architecture & Decorative Art Ser). (Illus.). 1970. Repr. of 1935 ed. 27.50 (ISBN 0-306-71394-2). Da Capo.
Clarke, Howard. Homer's Readers: A Historical Introduction to the Iliad & the Odyssey. LC 78-66824. 328p. 1980. 26.50 (ISBN 0-87413-150-2). U Delaware Pr.
Clarke, J. A., ed. see Second European Conference on Mixing.
Clarke, J. I. Population Geography. 2nd ed. LC 70-183339. 187p. 1972. text ed. 18.00 (ISBN 0-08-016853-1); pap. text ed. 7.75 (ISBN 0-08-016854-X). Pergamon.
--Population Geography & Developing Countries. 1971. 17.25 (ISBN 0-08-016445-5); pap. 7.75 (ISBN 0-08-016446-3). Pergamon.
Clarke, James M. The Life & Adventures of John Muir. LC 79-64178. (Sierra Club Paperback Library Ser.). (Illus.). 326p. 1980. pap. 7.95 (ISBN 0-87156-241-3). Sierra.
Clarke, Jane. The Truth Machine. LC 77-70857. (Star Trek Bks.). (Illus.). (gr. 2-5). 1977. 2.95 (ISBN 0-394-83575-1); PLB 3.99 (ISBN 0-394-93575-6). Random.
Clarke, Jenny, ed. see Second International Conference on the Internal & External Protection of Pipes.
Clarke, John. The Price of Progress: Cobbett's England Seventeen Eighty to Eighteen Thirty-Five. 224p. 1980. text ed. 18.25x (ISBN 0-246-10604-2). Humanities.
--The Virgin Seducer. Bd. with The Batchelor-Keeper; A Voyage to Cacklagallinia. Brunt, Samuel; An Account of the State of Learning in the Empire of Lilliput. (Foundations of the Novel Ser.: Vol. 49). lib. bdg. 50.00 (ISBN 0-8240-0561-9). Garland Pub.
Clarke, John, tr. from Fr. St. Therese of Lisieux: Her Last Conversations. LC 76-27207. (Illus.). 1977. pap. 6.95x (ISBN 0-9600876-3-X). ICS Pubns.
Clarke, John H. Clinical Repertory. 346p. 1979. text ed. 24.95x (ISBN 0-8464-1000-1). Beekman Pubs.
--Malcolm X. 1969. 7.95 o.s.i. (ISBN 0-02-525850-8). Macmillan.
--The Prescriber. 11th ed. 382p. 1972. 11.95x (ISBN 0-8464-1041-9). Beekman Pubs.
Clarke, John H., ed. William Styron's Nat Turner: Ten Black Writers Respond. 1968. 4.95 o.p. (ISBN 0-8070-6426-2); pap. 1.95 o.p. (ISBN 0-8070-6427-0, BP304). Beacon Pr.
Clarke, Juanne N., jt. auth. see Eshleman, J. Ross.
Clarke, Katherine A., tr. see Giono, Jean.
Clarke, Kenneth & Clarke, Mary. The Harvest & the Reapers: Oral Traditions of Kentucky. LC 74-7872. (Kentucky Bicentennial Bookshelf Ser.). 112p. 1974. 5.95 (ISBN 0-8131-0201-4). U Pr of Ky.
Clarke, Kenneth & Kohn, Ira. Kentucky's Age of Wood. LC 76-4432. (Kentucky Bicentennial Bookshelf Ser.). (Illus.). 88p. 1976. 5.95 (ISBN 0-8131-0225-1). U Pr of Ky.
Clarke, Kenneth K. & Hess, Donald T. Communication Circuits: Analysis & Design. LC 78-125610. (Engineering Ser). 1971. text ed. 27.95 (ISBN 0-201-01040-2). A-W.
Clarke, Kenneth U. The Biology of the Arthropoda. LC 73-2309. (Contemporary Biology Ser.). 270p. 1975. 24.50 (ISBN 0-444-19559-9). Univ Park.
Clarke, L. Harwood. Additional Pure Mathematics. 1970. pap. text ed. 11.50x o.p. (ISBN 0-435-51177-7). Heinemann Ed.
--Hints for Ordinary Mathematics. 1971. pap. text ed. 2.95x o.p. (ISBN 0-435-50212-3). Heinemann Ed.
--Modern Mathematics at Ordinary Level. 1970. pap. text ed. 7.50x o.p. (ISBN 0-435-50180-1). Heinemann Ed.
--Ordinary Level Mathematics. 1978. pap. text ed. 11.95x with ans. o.p. (ISBN 0-435-50221-2). Heinemann Ed.
--Pure Mathematics at Advanced Level. 1967. pap. text ed. 10.95x o.p. (ISBN 0-435-51179-3). Heinemann Ed.
--Trigonometry at Ordinary Level. 1970. pap. text ed. 4.95x o.p. (ISBN 0-435-50207-7). Heinemann Ed.
Clarke, L. Harwood & Norton, F. G. Additional Applied Mathematics. 1972. pap. text ed. 6.25x o.p. (ISBN 0-435-51183-1). Heinemann Ed.
--Objective Tests in C. S. E. Mathematics. 1970. pap. text ed. 3.50x o.p. (ISBN 0-435-50208-5). Heinemann Ed.
Clarke, M. J. Anthropology, Psychology, Education, Language & Philosophy. 1966. pap. 6.00x o.p. (ISBN 0-19-437712-1). Oxford U Pr.
Clarke, M. P. Parliamentary Privilege in the American Colonies. LC 76-166322. (American Constitutional & Legal History Ser.). 304p. 1971. Repr. of 1943 ed. lib. bdg. 29.50 (ISBN 0-306-70237-1). Da Capo.
Clarke, M. W. David G. Burnett, First President of Texas. LC 77-79108. (Illus.). 12.50 (ISBN 0-8363-0024-6); limited ed. 85.00 (ISBN 0-685-13270-6). Jenkins.
Clarke, Mary & Crisp, Clement. Making a Ballet. (Illus.). 192p. 1975. 14.95 (ISBN 0-02-525790-0). Macmillan.
Clarke, Mary, jt. auth. see Clarke, Kenneth.
Clarke, Mary, et al. A History of Dance. 1981. 35.00 (ISBN 0-517-54282-X). Crown.
Clarke, Mary W. The Slaughter Ranches & Their Makers. (Illus.). Date not set. 12.95. Jenkins.
--Thomas J. Rusk: Soldier, Statesman, Jurist. LC 79-157043. (Illus.). 1971. 9.50 (ISBN 0-685-00320-5). Jenkins.
Clarke, Mary W., jt. ed. see Lemaster, J. R.
Clarke, Maude V. Fourteenth Century Studies. Sutherland, L. S. & McKisack, M., eds. 1937. 27.00x (ISBN 0-19-822303-X). Oxford U Pr.
Clarke, Michael & Clarke, Dorothy. Sexual Joy in Marriage. pap. 6.95 o.p. (ISBN 0-523-41137-5). Pinnacle Bks.
Clarke, Michael G., jt. ed. see Drucker, Henry M.
Clarke, Nita. The Mystery at Rancho Verde. (Illus.). (gr. 1-4). 1981. 6.95 (ISBN 0-933184-13-1); pap. 4.95 (ISBN 0-933184-14-X). Flame Intl.
--Timothy & the Blanket Fairy. (gr. k-6). 1981. 6.95 (ISBN 0-933184-06-9); pap. 4.95 (ISBN 0-933184-16-6). Flame Intl.
Clarke, P. Liberals & Social Democrats. LC 78-6970. 1978. 36.00 (ISBN 0-521-22171-4). Cambridge U Pr.
Clarke, P. H., ed. see Suetin, A. S.
Clarke, Patricia, ed. Paul of Venice: Logica Magna, Pt. 1, Fascicule 7. (Classical & Medieval Logic Texts Ser.). 232p. 1981. 149.00 (ISBN 0-19-726003-9). Oxford U Pr.
Clarke, Patti. Creative Jewelry. LC 77-90127. 1978. 13.95 (ISBN 0-8008-1995-0). Taplinger.
Clarke, Pauline. Torolv the Fatherless. (Illus.). (gr. 6-8). 1978. 6.95 (ISBN 0-571-03620-1, Pub. by Faber & Faber). Merrimack Bk Serv.
Clarke, Penny. Growing up During the Industrial Revolution. LC 79-56472. (Growing up Ser.). (Illus.). 72p. (gr. 7 up). 1980. text ed. 14.95 (ISBN 0-7134-3370-1, Pub. by Batsford England). David & Charles.
Clarke, Peter, jt. ed. see Kline, F. Gerald.
Clarke, Peter B., jt. auth. see Wilkinson, C. W.
Clarke, Peter J. Plastics for Schools: Applied Polymer Science. 191p. (gr. 9 up). 1973. pap. 9.95 (ISBN 0-263-05380-6). Transatlantic.
Clarke, Philip S. Calculus & Analytic Geometry. 1974. text ed. 21.95x o.p. (ISBN 0-669-75879-5); instructor's manual free o.p. (ISBN 0-669-85753-X); Vol. 1. study guide by James F. Hurley 7.95x o.p. (ISBN 0-669-94748-2); Vol. 2. study guide 7.95 o.p. (ISBN 0-669-94672-9); transparencies 175.00 o.p. (ISBN 0-669-94748-2). Heath.
Clarke, R. F. Growth & Nature of Drama. 1965. 4.95x (ISBN 0-521-04672-6). Cambridge U Pr.
Clarke, R. H. College Statistics. 1969. pap. 13.95x (ISBN 0-17-741010-8). Intl Ideas.
Clarke, R. H. & Brown, John. Diffraction Theory & Antennas. 320p. 1980. 97.50x (ISBN 0-470-27003-9). Halsted Pr.
Clarke, R. M. Austin-Healy 3000 1959-1967. (Brookland Bks). (Illus.). 100p. 1979. pap. text ed. 11.95 (ISBN 0-906589-64-9, Pub. by Enthusias England). Motorbooks Intl.
--Ferrari Cars: 1962-1966. (Brooklands Bks.). (Illus.). 100p. 1979. pap. 11.95 (ISBN 0-906589-57-6, Pub. by Enthusias England). Motorbooks Intl.
--Jaguar E-Type 1966-1971. (Brooklands Bks.). (Illus.). 100p. 1979. pap. 11.95 (ISBN 0-906589-58-4). Motorbooks Intl.
--Jaguar E Type 1971-1975. (Brooklands Bks). (Illus.). 100p. (Orig.). 1979. pap. 11.95 (ISBN 0-906589-77-0, Pub. by Enthusiast England). Motorbooks Intl.
--Pantera, 1970-1973. (Brooklands Bks.). (Illus., Orig.). 1979. pap. 8.95 (ISBN 0-906589-75-4, Pub. by Enthusiast Pubns England). Motorbooks Intl.
--Porsche Cars in the 60's. (Brooklands Bks.). (Illus.). 100p. (Orig.). 1980. pap. 11.95 (ISBN 0-906589-81-9, Pub. by Enthusiast England). Motorbooks Intl.
--Porsche Cars, 1964-1968. (Brooklands Bks.). (Illus., Orig.). 1979. pap. 11.95 (ISBN 0-906589-61-4, Pub. by Enthusiast Pubns. England). Motorbooks Intl.
--Porsche Cars 1968-1972. (Brooklands Bks.). (Illus., Orig.). 1979. pap. 11.95 (ISBN 0-906589-62-2, Pub. by Enthusiast England). Motorbooks Intl.
--Porsche Nine Fourteen: Nineteen Sixty-Nine to Nineteen Seventy-Five. (Brooklands Bks.). (Illus.). 100p. (Orig.). 1980. 11.95 (ISBN 0-906589-83-5). Motorbooks Intl.
--Porsche 914: 1969-1975. (Brooklands Bks.). (Illus.). 100p. (Orig.). 1980. pap. 11.95 (ISBN 0-906589-84-3, Pub. by Enthusiast Pubns England). Motorbooks Intl.
Clarke, R. M., ed. Ferrari Cars Nineteen Sixty-Nine to Nineteen Seventy-Three. (Brooklands Bks.). (Illus., Orig.). 1980. pap. 11.95. Motorbooks Intl.
--Lotus Elan Nineteen Sixty-Two to Nineteen Seventy-Three. (Brooklands Bks.). (Illus.). 100p. (Orig.). 1980. pap. 11.95. Motorbooks Intl.
--Pantera & Mangusta Nineteen Sixty-Nine to Nineteen Seventy-Four. (Illus.). 70p. (Orig.). 1980. pap. 8.95 (ISBN 0-907073-00-X). Motorbooks Intl.
Clarke, R. V. G. & Hough, J. M., eds. The Effectiveness of Policing. 184p. 1980. 19.95x (ISBN 0-566-00297-3, 03295-6, Pub by Gower Pub Co England). Lexington Bks.
Clarke, Rebecca. Trio for Piano, Violin & Cello. (Women Composer Ser.). (Illus.). 64p. 1980. 16.95 (ISBN 0-306-76053-3). Da Capo.
Clarke, Robert A., et al. Biology by Inquiry, 3 bks. Bk. 1. text ed. 6.95x o.p. (ISBN 0-435-59169-X); Bk. 2. text ed. 9.50x o.p. (ISBN 0-435-59171-1); Bk. 3. text ed. 7.95x o.p. (ISBN 0-435-59173-8); Bk. 3. tchr's guide 4.50 o.p. (ISBN 0-435-59174-6). Heinemann Ed.
Clarke, Robert C. Marijuana Botany. (Illus.). 224p. 1981. pap. 7.95 (ISBN 0-915904-45-4). And-or Pr.
Clarke, Robert F., et al. DNA Action Model. 1968. 2.95 o.p. (ISBN 0-8087-0324-2). Burgess.
Clarke, Robert L., ed. Afro-American History: Sources for Research. (Illus.). 450p. 1981. 19.50 (ISBN 0-88258-018-3). Howard U Pr.
Clarke, Robin, ed. see Gunston, Bill.
Clarke, Robin, ed. see Kilmeister, Clive W.
Clarke, Roger, jt. auth. see Hart, P. E.
Clarke, Ron & Boyle, Raelene. Successful Track & Field. LC 76-51186. (Illus.). (gr. 7 up). 1977. 9.95 (ISBN 0-8069-4116-2); PLB 9.29 (ISBN 0-8069-4117-0). Sterling.
Clarke, Samuel. The Works, 4 vols. LC 75-11207. (British Philosophers & Theologians of the 17th & 18th Centuries: Vol. 12). 1976. Repr. of 1742 ed. Set. lib. bdg. write for info. (ISBN 0-8240-1762-5); lib. bdg. 42.00 ea. Garland Pub.
Clarke, Simon. Foundations of Structuralism: A Critique of Levi-Strauss & the Structuralist Movement. 224p. 1981. 26.50x (ISBN 0-389-20156-1). B&N.
Clarke, Ted, jt. ed. see Jaffe, Dennis T.
Clarke, Theodore H., ed. Yearbook of Podiatric Medicine & Surgery 1981. (Illus.). 512p. 1980. 49.00 (ISBN 0-87993-129-9). Futura Pub.
--Yearbook of Podiatry: 1978-79. (Illus.). 1979. 28.50 (ISBN 0-87993-099-3). Futura Pub.
Clarke, Thurston. By Blood & Fire. 288p. 1981. 13.95 (ISBN 0-399-12605-8). Putnam.
Clarke, Tom & Clements, Laurie, eds. Trade Unions Under Capitalism. 1978. text ed. 24.75x (ISBN 0-391-00728-9). Humanities.
Clarke, Tom C., ed. An Index to Rolls-Royce & Bentley Periodicals. 43p. 1974. pap. 5.95 o.p. (ISBN 0-87938-023-3, Pub. by Transport Bkman England). Motorbooks Intl.
Clarke, W. K., tr. & intro. by see Basilius.
Clarke, W. M. Private Enterprise in Developing Countries. 1966. pap. 4.20 (ISBN 0-08-012142-X). Pergamon.
Clarke, W. N. An Outline of Christian Theology. 498p. 1898. text ed. 9.50x (ISBN 0-567-02069-X). Attic Pr.
Clarke, Wayne, et al. Cruising Nova Scotia. LC 79-11352. 1979. 12.95 (ISBN 0-396-07671-8). Dodd.
Clarke, William. Clarke Papers, 4 Vols. Firth, C. H., ed. Set. 89.50 (ISBN 0-384-09232-2); 22.50 ea. Johnson Repr.
Clarke, William C. Place & People: An Ecology of a New Guinean Community. LC 78-126764. (Illus.). 1971. 23.50x (ISBN 0-520-01791-9). U of Cal Pr.
Clarke, William K. The Robber Baroness. LC 78-21417. 1979. 2.95 (ISBN 0-312-68549-1). St Martin.
Clarke-Stewart, K. Alison, jt. auth. see Fein, Greta G.
Clark-Hall, John R. Beowulf & Finnesburg Fragment: A Translation into Modern English Prose. 1950. text ed. 10.50x o.p. (ISBN 0-04-829001-7). Allen Unwin.
Clarkson, Bayard, et al, eds. Differentiation of Normal & Neoplastic Hematopoietic Cells: Cold Spring Harbor Conferences on Cell Proliferation, 2 bks, Vol. 5. LC 78-60391. (Illus.). 994p. 1978. Set. text ed. 95.00 (ISBN 0-87969-121-2). Cold Spring Harbor.
Clarkson, D. Ion Transport & Cell Structure in Plants. LC 74-7132. 1974. text ed. 32.95 (ISBN 0-470-15985-5). Halsted Pr.
Clarkson, E. N. Invertebrate Palaeontology & Evolution. (Illus.). 1979. text ed. 40.00x (ISBN 0-04-560007-4); pap. text ed. 19.95x (ISBN 0-04-560008-2). Allen Unwin.
Clarkson, Ewan. Sylva the Mink. LC 68-25764. (Illus.). 1968. 4.95 o.p. (ISBN 0-525-21355-4). Dutton.
Clarkson, Kenneth, et al. West's Business Law: Text & Cases. (Illus.). 1980. text ed. 20.95 (ISBN 0-8299-0295-3); study guide 5.95 (ISBN 0-8299-0305-4); instrs.' manual avail. (ISBN 0-8299-0466-2). West Pub.
Clarkson, Kenneth, et al, eds. Economic Regulation & Consumer Welfare: The Federal Trade Commission Since 1970. (Illus.). 448p. Date not set. price not set (ISBN 0-521-23378-X). Cambridge U Pr.
Clarkson, Kenneth W., et al. Alternate Test Items to Accompany West's Business Law: Text & Cases. 169p. Date not set. price not set (ISBN 0-8299-0508-1). West Pub.
--West's Business Law: Alternate UCC Comprehensive Edition. 750p. 1981. text ed. 13.95 (ISBN 0-8299-0366-6). West Pub.
--West's Business Law: Alternate UCC Comprehensive Edition. write for info. alt. test items (ISBN 0-8299-0526-X). West Pub.
Clarkson, Margaret. Grace Grows Best in Winter. large print ed. 208p. 1975. kivar 5.95 (ISBN 0-310-22467-5). Zondervan.
Clarkson, Roy B., et al. Forest Plants of the Monangahela National Forest. 1980. pap. 8.95 (ISBN 0-910286-82-5). Boxwood.
Clarkson, Thomas W., jt. auth. see Miller, Morton W.
Clarneau, William. Do-It Yourselfer's Guide to Home Planning & Construction. LC 76-24781. 1976. 8.95 o.p. (ISBN 0-8306-6888-8); pap. 4.95 o.p. (ISBN 0-8306-5888-2, 888). TAB Bks.
Claro. Meatballs. (gr. 7-12). 1980. pap. 1.50 (ISBN 0-590-30920-X, Schol Pap). Schol Bk Serv.
--Snowball Express. (gr. 3-5). 1980. pap. 1.50 (ISBN 0-590-30359-7, Schol Pap). Schol Bk Serv.
Clarricoats, P. J., ed. Progress in Optical Communication. 1980. Repr. soft cover 35.00 (ISBN 0-906048-32-X). Inst Elect Eng.
Clary, Jack. The Gamemakers: Winning Philosophies of Eight NFL Coaches. (Illus.). 256p. 1976. 10.95 o.s.i. (ISBN 0-695-80630-0). Follett.
Clary, Raymond. The Making of Golden Gate Park: The Early Years, 1865-1906. LC 79-51159. (Illus.). 224p. 1980. 25.00 (ISBN 0-89395-024-6); pap. 10.95 (ISBN 0-89395-025-4). Cal Living Bks.
Clasing, Henry K., Jr., jt. auth. see Rudd, Andrew.
Clason, George S. Richest Man in Babylon. 1955. 8.95 (ISBN 0-8015-6360-7, Hawthorn); pap. 3.50 (ISBN 0-8015-6366-6, Hawthorn). Dutton.

Clasper, Paul D. The Yogi, the Commissar, & the Third-World Church. LC 78-183648. 96p. (Orig.). 1972. pap. 1.95 o.p. (ISBN 0-8170-0560-9). Judson.

Class, Robert A. & Koehler, Robert E., eds. Current Techniques in Architectural Practice. (Illus.). 1976. 27.50 o.p. (ISBN 0-07-002324-7, Architectural Res Bks). McGraw.

Classen, E., tr. see Bjerre, Andreas.

Clastres, Helene. The Land Without Evil: Tupi-Guarani Prophetism. Grenez-Brovender, Jacqueline, tr. 160p. 1981. 18.50x (ISBN 0-8476-6271-3). Rowman.

Clastres, Pierre. Chronicle of the Guayaki Indians. Auster, Paul & Davis, Lydia, trs. 1981. 20.00 (ISBN 0-89396-031-4). Urizen Bks.

--Society Against the State. Hurley, Robert, tr. 1977. 12.95 (ISBN 0-916354-38-5); pap. 7.95, 1981 (ISBN 0-916354-39-3). Urizen Bks.

Claude, Inis L., Jr. Power & International Relations. 1962. text ed. 10.95 (ISBN 0-394-30133-1). Random.

Claudel, Paul. The Satin Slipper or the Worst Is Not the Surest. 1931. 42.50x (ISBN 0-686-51305-3). Elliots Bks.

Claudine. The Flight of the Animals. LC 70-153788. (Illus.). (gr. k-3). 1971. 5.95 o.s.i. (ISBN 0-8193-0492-1, Four Winds); PLB 5.41 o.s.i. (ISBN 0-8193-0493-X). Schol Bk Serv.

Claudin-Urondo, Carmen. Lenin & the Cultural Revolution. Pearce, Brian, tr. from Fr. (Marxist Theory & Contemporary Capitalism Ser.). 1977. text ed. 13.00x (ISBN 0-391-00739-4). Humanities.

Claudon, Michael P. & Cornwall, Richard. Incomes Policy for the United States: New Approaches. 240p. 1980. lib. bdg. 18.00 (ISBN 0-89838-048-0). Kluwer Boston.

Claus, David B. Toward the Soul: A Inquiry into the Meaning of XUXN Before Plate. LC 80-13559. (Classical Monographs). 232p. 1981. text ed. 17.50x (ISBN 0-300-02096-1). Yale U Pr.

Claus, K. E., jt. auth. see Claus, R. J.

Claus, Karen E. & Bailey, June T. Living with Stress & Promoting Well Being: A Handbook for Nurses. LC 80-14605. (Illus.). 1980. pap. text ed. 9.95 (ISBN 0-8016-1148-2). Mosby.

Claus, Karen E., jt. auth. see Bailey, June T.

Claus, R., et al. Light Scattering by Phonon Polaritons. (Springer Tracts in Modern Physics Ser.: Vol. 75). (Illus.). 240p. 1975. 34.20 o.p. (ISBN 0-387-07423-6). Springer-Verlag.

Claus, R. J. & Claus, K. E. Sign User's Guide. (Illus.). 1978. 7.50 (ISBN 0-686-27783-X). Signs of Times.

Clausen, H. & Tipsen, E. Farm Animals in Color. (Illus.). 1970. 9.95 (ISBN 0-7137-0539-6, Pub by Blandford Pr England). Sterling.

Clausen, Jan. Mother, Daughter, Sister, Lover: A Collection of Short Stories Dealing with Woman's Relations to Woman. LC 80-16386. (The Crossing Press Feminist Ser.). (Orig.). 1980. 10.95 (ISBN 0-89594-034-5); pap. 4.95 (ISBN 0-89594-033-7). Crossing Pr.

Clausen, Jens. Plant Evolution Through Amphiploidy & Autoploidy, with Examples from the Madlinae. (Experimental Studies on the Nature of Species: Vol. 2). (Illus.). 564p. 1945. pap. 7.25 (ISBN 0-87279-575-6). Carnegie Inst.

Clausen, Muriel C. Menopause: Vitamins & You. 105p. (Orig.). 1980. pap. 4.75 (ISBN 0-9603664-1-5). M C Clausen.

Clausen, Robert T., ed. Sedum of North America North of the Mexican Plateau. LC 75-6084. (Illus.). 784p. 1975. 80.00x (ISBN 0-8014-0950-0). Comstock.

Clausen, W. V., ed. see Persius & Juvenal.

Clausewitz, Karl Von. The Campaign of Eighteen Hundred & Twelve in Russia. LC 79-84266. (Illus.). 1977. Repr. of 1843 ed. lib. bdg. 25.00x (ISBN 0-8371-5004-3, CLCA). Greenwood.

Clausewitz, Karl Von see Von Clausewitz, Karl.

Clausing, Don A. Nocturnal Learning: Theory & Practice of Sleep Learning. 64p. (Orig.). 1980. pap. text ed. 6.95 (ISBN 0-936214-02-3). Nat Learn Res.

Clauson, Gerard. An Etymological Dictionary of Pre-Thirteenth Century Turkish. 1040p. 1972. 125.00x (ISBN 0-19-864112-5). Oxford U Pr.

Clauss, J. E., ed. see Hill, Grace L.

Claussen, Claus F. & Desa, Joe V. Clinical Study of Human Equilibrium by Electonystagmography & Allied Tests. (Illus.). xiii, 437p. 1980. text ed. 50.00x (ISBN 0-86590-002-7). Apt Bks.

Clavel, Pierre & Goldsmith, William W., eds. Urban & Regional Planning in an Age of Austerity. LC 79-21416. (Pergamon Policy Studies in Urban Affairs). 402p. 1980. 39.50 (ISBN 0-08-025539-6); pap. 7.50 (ISBN 0-08-025540-X). Pergamon.

Clavell, James. Shogun. LC 74-77840. 1975. 19.95 (ISBN 0-689-10565-7). Atheneum.

--Shogun. 1980. pap. 3.50 (ISBN 0-440-17800-2). Dell.

--Tai-Pan. 1980. pap. 3.25 (ISBN 0-440-18462-2). Dell.

Clavell, James, frwd. by. The Making of James Clavell's Shogun. (Illus.). 1980. pap. 8.95 (ISBN 0-440-55709-7, Delta). Dell.

Clavert, A., jt. ed. see Bollack, C. G.

Claviere, Maude la & Rene de, Marie Alphonse. The Women of the Renaissance. 510p. 1980. Repr. of 1905 ed. lib. bdg. 50.00 (ISBN 0-8482-5077-X). Norwood Edns.

Clavigero, Francesco S. The History of Mexico, 2 vols. Feldman, Burton & Richardson, Robert D., eds. LC 78-60908. (Myth & Romanticism Ser.: Vol. 7). (Illus.). 1979. Set. lib. bdg. 132.00 (ISBN 0-8240-3556-9). Garland Pub.

Clawson, Elmer. Our Economy: How It Works. 1980. 12.64 (ISBN 0-201-01057-7, Sch Div); tchr's. ed. 8.24. A-W.

Clawson, George. Trapping & Tracking. (Illus.). 1977. 10.95 (ISBN 0-87691-198-X). Winchester Pr.

Clawson, Marion. Man, Land & the Forest Environment. LC 76-45999. (Geo. S. Long Publication Ser.). (Illus.). 86p. 1977. 8.95 (ISBN 0-295-95540-6). U of Wash Pr.

Clawson, Marion & Held, Burnell. Federal Lands: Their Use & Management. LC 57-12121. (Illus.). 1965. pap. 5.95x (ISBN 0-8032-5034-7, BB 318, Bison). U of Nebr Pr.

Clawson, Marion, ed. Research in Forest Economics & Forest Policy. LC 77-81676. (Research for the Future Research Paper Ser: No. 3). 1977. pap. text ed. 8.95x o.p. (ISBN 0-8018-2033-2). Johns Hopkins.

Clawson, Robert W., jt. auth. see Kaplan, Lawrence S.

Claxton, Guy. The Little Ed Book. 1978. pap. 6.00 (ISBN 0-7100-8868-X). Routledge & Kegan.

Claxton, Guy, ed. Cognitive Psychology: New Directions. (International Library of Psychology). 1980. 35.00 (ISBN 0-7100-0485-0); pap. 17.50 (ISBN 0-7100-0486-9). Routledge & Kegan.

Clay, Albert T. Empire of the Amorites. (Yale Oriental Researches Ser.: No. VI). 1919. 29.50x (ISBN 0-685-69801-7). Elliots Bks.

--Hebrew Deluge Story. (Yale Oriental Researches Ser.: No. V, Pt. III). 1922. 19.50x (ISBN 0-685-69802-5). Elliots Bks.

Clay, C. J. & Wheble, B. S., eds. Modern Merchant Banking: A Guide to the Workings of the Accepting Houses of the City of London & Their Services to Industry & Commerce. 160p. 1980. pap. 12.50 (ISBN 0-85941-044-7). Herman Pub.

Clay, Catherine L. Escape from Eden: A Novel. LC 77-77112. 232p. 1980. 9.95 (ISBN 0-86533-005-0). Amber Crest.

Clay, Charlotte N. The Role of Anxiety in English Tragedy, 1580-1642. (Salzburg Studies in English Literature, Jacobean Drama Studies: No. 23). 1974. pap. text ed. 25.00x (ISBN 0-391-01343-2). Humanities.

Clay, Christopher. Public Finance & Private Wealth: The Career of Sir Stephen Fox, 1627-1716. 1978. 45.00x (ISBN 0-19-822467-2). Oxford U Pr.

Clay, Clarence S. & Medwin, Herman. Acoustical Oceanography: Principles & Applications. LC 77-1133. (Ocean Engineering Ser.). 1977. text ed. 39.50 (ISBN 0-471-16041-5, Pub. by Wiley-Interscience). Wiley.

Clay, Diskin, tr. see Sophocles.

Clay, E. Jefferson. Aces Wild. Bd. with Badge for Brazos. 1980. pap. 2.25 (ISBN 0-505-51470-2). Tower Bks.

--Adios, Bandido! Bd. with Desparados on the Loose. 1980. pap. 2.25 (ISBN 0-505-51459-1). Tower Bks.

Clay, Edith. Lady Blessington at Naples. 1979. 25.00 (ISBN 0-241-89975-3, Pub. by Hamish Hamilton England). David & Charles.

Clay, Gervas. Your Friend, Lewanika: The Life & Times of Lubosi Lewanika Lituga of Barotseland 1842 to 1916. (Robins Ser: No. 7). (Illus.). 1968. text ed. 11.50x (ISBN 0-391-02072-2). Humanities.

Clay, Grady, ed. see Landscape Architecture Magazine.

Clay, Henry. The Papers of Henry Clay, 5 vols. Hopkins, James F. & Hargreaves, Mary W., eds. Incl. Vol. 1. The Rising Statesman, 1797-1814. 1060p. 1959 (ISBN 0-8131-0051-8); Vol. 2. The Rising Statesman, 1815-1820. 952p. 1961 (ISBN 0-8131-0052-6); Vol. 3. Presidential Candidate, 1821-1824. 944p. 1963 (ISBN 0-8131-0053-4); Vol. 4. Secretary of State, 1825. 1004p. 1972 (ISBN 0-8131-0054-2); Vol. 5. Secretary of State, 1826. 1104p. 1973 (ISBN 0-8131-0055-0). LC 59-13605. 35.00x ea. U Pr of Ky.

Clay, Marie. Stones. (Orig.). (gr. 1-2). 1980. pap. text ed. 2.50x (ISBN 0-686-63229-X, 00556). Heinemann Ed.

Clay, Marie M. Reading: The Patterning of Complex Behaviour. 2nd ed. 1980. pap. text ed. 11.95x (ISBN 0-686-64050-0, 00558). Heinemann Ed.

Clay, N. L. Eight Plays for Boys. pap. text ed. 3.25x o.p. (ISBN 0-435-21002-5). Heinemann Ed.

--Six Plays for Girls. pap. text ed. 3.25x o.p. (ISBN 0-435-21004-1). Heinemann Ed.

Clay, N. L., ed. see Dickens, Charles.

Clay, N. L., ed. see Trollope, Anthony.

Clay, Patrice. We Work with Horses. (Illus.). 160p. (YA) (gr. 7-12). 1980. 8.95 (ISBN 0-399-20735-X). Putnam.

Clay, Phillip L. Neighborhood Renewal: Trends & Strategies. LC 78-14153. 1979. 14.95 (ISBN 0-669-02681-6). Lexington Bks.

Clay, Rotha M. Hermits & Anchorites of England. LC 68-21759. (Illus.). 1968. Repr. of 1914 ed. 18.00 (ISBN 0-8103-3424-0). Gale.

Clay, Vidal S., jt. auth. see Loeb, Robert L.

Clay, William C. The Dow-Jones Irwin Guide to Estate Planning. 3rd ed. 176p. 1981. pap. 2.50 (ISBN 0-553-14913-X). Bantam.

Clay, William C., Jr. The Dow Jones-Irwin Guide to Estate Planning. rev. ed. LC 76-2113. 1977. 9.95 o.p. (ISBN 0-87094-138-0). Dow Jones-Irwin.

Claybaugh, Amos L., jt. auth. see Burron, Arnold.

Claycombe, W. Wayne, jt. auth. see Sullivan, William F.

Claycombe, William W. & Sullivan, William G. Foundations of Mathematical Programming. (Illus.). 304p. 1975. 16.95 (ISBN 0-87909-282-3); students manual avail. Reston.

Claydon, L. F. Renewing Urban Teaching. LC 73-77266. (Illus.). 180p. 1974. 23.50 (ISBN 0-521-20268-X); pap. 9.95x (ISBN 0-521-09844-0). Cambridge U Pr.

Clayette-Hugonnier, Suzanne, jt. auth. see Hugonnier, Rene.

Claypole, William & Robottom, John. Caribbean Story: Foundations, Bk. 1. (Longman Caribbean Ser.). (Illus.). 198p. (Orig.). 1981. pap. text ed. 9.95 (ISBN 0-582-76534-X). Longman.

Claypool, Bob. Saturday Night at Gilley's. LC 80-8061. (Illus.). 1980. pap. 8.95 (ISBN 0-394-17727-4, E758, Delilah-Ever). Grove.

Claypool, John. Tracks of a Fellow Struggler. 1976. pap. 1.25 (ISBN 0-89129-208-X). Jove Pubns.

Clayre, Alasdair, ed. Nature & Industrialization. (Illus.). 1977. 19.50x (ISBN 0-19-871096-8); pap. 6.95x (ISBN 0-19-871097-6). Oxford U Pr.

--The Political Economy of the Third Sector: Co-Operation & Participation. 240p. 1980. 29.50x (ISBN 0-19-877137-1); 29.50x (ISBN 0-19-877138-X). Oxford U Pr.

Clayton, et al. The Porcupine Book of Verse. (Illus.). 48p. (ps-2). 1974. 6.95 (ISBN 0-570-06995-5, 56-1186). Concordia.

Clayton, Anthony. Counter-Insurgency in Kenya, 1952-1960: A Study of Military Operations Against the Mau Mau. (Transafrica Historical Papers: No. 4). (Illus.). 1976. pap. 5.00x (ISBN 0-8002-0203-1). Intl Pubns Serv.

Clayton, Barbara & Whitley, Kathleen. Exploring Coastal New England: Gloucester to Kennebunkport. LC 79-624. (Illus.). 1979. 10.95 (ISBN 0-396-07572-X); pap. 6.95 (ISBN 0-396-07698-X). Dodd.

Clayton, Bernard. The Complete Book of Pastry. 17.95 (ISBN 0-671-24276-8). S&S.

Clayton, Bruce D. Life After Doomsday: A Survivalist Guide to Nuclear War & Other Disasters. (Illus.). 192p. 1981. pap. 8.95 (ISBN 0-8037-4752-7). Dial.

Clayton, Bruce D., jt. auth. see Ryan, Sheila A.

Clayton, Bruce D., jt. auth. see Squire, Jessie.

Clayton, E. S. Agrarian Development in Peasant Economies. 1964. 16.50 (ISBN 0-08-010562-9); pap. 7.25 o.p. (ISBN 0-08-010561-0). Pergamon.

Clayton, Ed. Martin Luther King: The Peaceful Warrior. (gr. 4-6). 1969. pap. 1.75 (ISBN 0-671-75986-8). Archway.

--Martin Luther King: The Peaceful Warrior. (gr. 4-6). 1969. pap. 1.50 (ISBN 0-671-29932-8). PB.

Clayton, F. E., jt. auth. see Clayton, G. D.

Clayton, Florence, jt. auth. see Clayton, George D.

Clayton, Florence E., jt. auth. see Clayton, George D.

Clayton, G. British Insurance. 1971. 39.95 o.p. (ISBN 0-236-17618-3, Pub. by Faber & Faber). Merrimack Bk Serv.

--Operational Amplifiers. 2nd ed. 1979. text ed. 26.95 (ISBN 0-408-00370-7). Butterworths.

Clayton, G. D. & Clayton, F. E. Pattys Industrial Hygiene & Toxicology, 4 vols. 3rd ed. 1981. 305.00 (ISBN 0-471-08431-X). Wiley.

Clayton, George B. Linear IC Applications Handbook. LC 77-7... 1977. 9.95 o.p. (ISBN 0-8306-7938-3); pap. 6.95 o.p. (ISBN 0-8306-6938-8, 938). TAB Bks.

Clayton, George D. & Clayton, Florence E. Patty's Industrial Hygiene & Toxicology: General Principles, Vol. 1. 3rd rev. ed. LC 77-17515. 1978. 99.50 (ISBN 0-471-16046-6, Pub. by Wiley-Interscience). Wiley.

Clayton, George D. & Clayton, Florence. Patty's Industrial Hygiene & Toxicology: Toxicology, Vol. IIA. 3rd rev. ed. LC 77-17515. 1675p. 1980. 100.00 (ISBN 0-471-16042-3, Pub. by Wiley Interscience). Wiley.

Clayton, J. P., jt. auth. see Sykes, S. W.

Clayton, J. P., ed. Ernst Troeltsch & the Future of Theology. LC 75-44576. 1976. 32.50 (ISBN 0-521-21074-7). Cambridge U Pr.

Clayton, John P. The Concept of Correlation: Paul Tillich & the Possibility of a Mediating Theology. (Theologische Bibliothek Topelmann: No. 37). 427p. 1979. text ed. 51.25x (ISBN 3-11007-914-3). De Gruyter.

Clayton, Michael. Cutting the Cost of Energy: A Practical Guide for the Householder. LC 80-67579. (Illus.). 160p. 1981. 16.95 (ISBN 0-7153-7927-5). David & Charles.

Clayton, Nanalee. Young Living. rev. ed. (Illus.). (gr. 7-8). 1970. text ed. 15.36 (ISBN 0-87002-011-0); tchr guide avail. (ISBN 0-685-06852-8). Bennett IL.

Clayton, Peter A., rev. by see Lurker, Manfred.

Clayton, Philip T., jt. auth. see Smolin, Pauline.

Clayton, R. F. Monitoring of Radioactive Contamination on Surfaces. (Technical Reports Ser.: No. 120). (Illus., Orig.). 1970. pap. 5.00 (ISBN 92-0-125570-5, IDC 120, IAEA). Unipub.

Clayton, R. K. Photosynthesis: Physical Mechanisms & Chemical Patterns. LC 79-27543. (IUPAB Biophysics Ser.: No. 4). 295p. Date not set. 32.50 (ISBN 0-521-22300-8); pap. 11.95 (ISBN 0-521-29443-6). Cambridge U Pr.

Clayton, Richard R. Family Marriage & Social Change. 2nd ed. 1979. text ed. 16.95x (ISBN 0-669-01957-7); inst. manual free (ISBN 0-669-01956-9). Heath.

Clayton, Robert. Western Europe. LC 71-135281. (Finding Out About Geography Ser). (Illus.). (gr. 3-6). 1972. 4.50 o.p. (ISBN 0-381-99847-9, A86820, JD-J). John Day.

Clayton, Robert D., jt. auth. see Torney, John A., Jr.

Clayton, Ross, et al. Managing Public Systems. 1980. text ed. 15.95 (ISBN 0-87872-249-1). Duxbury Pr.

Clayton, Thompson. What It Takes: Developing Skills for Contemporary Living. LC 70-186590. (Illus., Orig., Special education ser. for slow learners). (gr. 4-9). 1972. pap. 3.20 (ISBN 0-8224-7400-X); tchrs' manual free (ISBN 0-8224-7401-8). Pitman Learning.

--Young Wrestler. LC 77-1208. (Illus.). 125p. 1977. pap. 3.95 (ISBN 0-87095-064-9). Athletic.

Clayton, William R. Matter & Spirit. LC 80-81694. 1981. 8.75 (ISBN 0-8022-2368-0). Philos Lib.

Cleage, Albert B., Jr. Black Christian Nationalism: New Directions for the Black Church. 1972. pap. 5.95 (ISBN 0-688-06019-6). Morrow.

Clean Air Society. International Clean Air Conference, 7th, Australia. International Clean Air Conference, 1981: Proceedings. 1981. text ed. 49.95 (ISBN 0-250-40415-X). Ann Arbor Science.

Clear Creek Editors, ed. see Aigner, Hal, et al.

Clear, Val, ed. see Rogers, Cyril H.

Cleary, A. A. Men Homeward. 54p. 1980. pap. 5.95x (ISBN 0-904461-35-1, Pub. by Ceolfrith Pr England). Intl Schol Bk Serv.

Cleary, Alan. Instrumentation for Psychology. LC 77-1250. 1978. 31.25 (ISBN 0-471-99483-9, Pub by Wiley Interscience). Wiley.

Cleary, Beverly. Beezus & Ramona. (Illus.). (gr. 3-7). 1955. 7.75 (ISBN 0-688-21076-7); PLB 7.44 (ISBN 0-688-31076-1); pap. 1.50 (ISBN 0-688-25078-5). Morrow.

--Ellen Tebbits. (Illus.). (gr. 3-7). 1951. 7.75 (ISBN 0-688-21264-6); PLB 7.44 (ISBN 0-688-31264-0). Morrow.

--Emily's Runaway Imagination. (Illus.). (gr. 3-7). 1961. 8.25 (ISBN 0-688-21267-0); PLB 7.92 (ISBN 0-688-31267-5). Morrow.

--Fifteen. (Illus.). (gr. 6-9). 1956. 8.75 (ISBN 0-688-21285-9); PLB 8.40 (ISBN 0-688-31285-3). Morrow.

--Fifteen. (gr. 7-12). 1980. pap. 1.75 (ISBN 0-440-92559-2, LFL). Dell.

--Henry & Beezus. (Illus.). (gr. 3-7). 1952. 8.25 (ISBN 0-688-21383-9); PLB 7.92 (ISBN 0-688-31383-3). Morrow.

--Henry & Ribsy. (Illus.). (gr. 3-7). 1954. 8.25 (ISBN 0-688-21382-0); PLB 7.92 (ISBN 0-688-31382-5); pap. 1.50 (ISBN 0-688-25382-2). Morrow.

--Henry & the Clubhouse. (Illus.). (gr. 3-7). 1962. 7.75 (ISBN 0-688-21381-2); PLB 7.44 (ISBN 0-688-31381-7). Morrow.

--Henry & the Paper Route. (Illus.). (gr. 3-7). 1957. 8.25 (ISBN 0-688-21380-4); PLB 7.92 (ISBN 0-688-31380-9). Morrow.

--Henry Huggins. (Illus.). (gr. 3-7). 1950. 7.75 (ISBN 0-688-25385-7); PLB 7.44 (ISBN 0-688-31385-X). Morrow.

--Jean & Johnny. (Illus.). (gr. 6-9). 1959. 8.75 (ISBN 0-688-21740-0); PLB 8.40 (ISBN 0-688-31740-5). Morrow.
--The Luckiest Girl. (gr. 7 up). 1958. PLB 9.55 (ISBN 0-688-31741-3). Morrow.
--The Luckiest Girl. (gr. 7-12). 1980. pap. 1.75 (ISBN 0-440-94899-1, LFL). Dell.
--Mitch & Amy. (Illus.). (gr. 3-7). 1967. 8.25 (ISBN 0-688-21688-9); PLB 7.92 (ISBN 0-688-31688-3). Morrow.
--The Mouse & the Motorcycle. (Illus.). (gr. 2-6). 1965. 7.75 (ISBN 0-688-21698-6); PLB 7.44 (ISBN 0-688-31698-0). Morrow.
--Otis Spofford. (Illus.). (gr. 3-7). 1953. 7.75 (ISBN 0-688-21720-6); PLB 7.44 (ISBN 0-688-31720-0); pap. 1.50 (ISBN 0-688-26720-3). Morrow.
--Ramona & Her Father. LC 77-1614. (gr. 3-7). 1977. 7.75 (ISBN 0-688-22114-9); PLB 7.44 (ISBN 0-688-32114-3). Morrow.
--Ramona & Her Mother. LC 79-10323. (Illus.). 192p. (gr. 4-6). 1979. 7.95 (ISBN 0-688-22195-5); PLB 7.63 (ISBN 0-688-32195-X). Morrow.
--Ramona the Brave. LC 74-164968. (Illus.). 192p. (gr. 3-7). 1975. 7.75 (ISBN 0-688-22015-0); PLB 7.44 (ISBN 0-688-32015-5). Morrow.
--Ramona the Brave. (gr. 4-6). 1977. pap. 1.50 (ISBN 0-590-10316-4, Schol Pap). Schol Bk Serv.
--Ramona the Pest. (Illus.). (gr. 3-7). 1968. 7.75 (ISBN 0-688-21721-4); PLB 7.44 (ISBN 0-688-31721-9). Morrow.
--Ramona the Pest. (gr. 4-6). 1976. pap. 1.50 (ISBN 0-590-04493-1, Schol Pap). Schol Bk Serv.
--The Real Hole. (Illus.). (ps-1). 1960. PLB 6.96 (ISBN 0-688-31655-7). Morrow.
--Ribsy. (Illus.). (gr. 3-7). 1964. 7.75 (ISBN 0-688-21662-5); PLB 7.44 (ISBN 0-688-31662-X). Morrow.
--Ribsy. (gr. 3-5). 1975. pap. 1.75 o.s.i. (ISBN 0-671-56090-5). Archway.
--Risby. (Illus.). (gr. 3-5). 1975. pap. 1.75 (ISBN 0-671-56090-5). PB.
--Runaway Ralph. (Illus.). (gr. 3-7). 1970. 7.95 (ISBN 0-688-21701-X); PLB 7.63 (ISBN 0-688-31701-4). Morrow.
--Runaway Ralph. (gr. k-6). 1981. pap. 1.75 (ISBN 0-440-47519-8, YB). Dell.
--Runaway Ralph. (gr. 3-5). 1974. pap. 1.50 o.p. (ISBN 0-671-56017-4). Archway.
--Sister of the Bride. (Illus.). (gr. 7 up). 1963. PLB 8.48 (ISBN 0-688-31742-1). Morrow.
--Sister of the Bride. (gr. 7-12). 1981. pap. 1.75 (ISBN 0-440-97596-4, LE). Dell.
--Socks. LC 72-10298. (Illus.). 192p. (gr. 3-7). 1973. 7.75 (ISBN 0-688-20067-2); PLB 7.44 (ISBN 0-688-30067-7). Morrow.
--Two Dog Biscuits. (Illus.). (ps-1). 1961. PLB 7.92 (ISBN 0-688-31656-5). Morrow.
Cleary, David P. Great American Brands: The Success Formulas That Made Them Famous. (Illus.). 300p. 1980. text ed. 17.50 (ISBN 0-87005-338-8). Fairchild.
Cleary, Denis J. & Maher, Frank J. The Capricorn Run. LC 78-70355. 1979. pap. 1.50 o.p. (ISBN 0-87216-513-2). Playboy Pbks.
Cleary, Florence D. Discovering Books & Libraries. 2nd ed. 1977. pap. 4.00 (ISBN 0-8242-0594-4). Wilson.
Cleary, J. C., jt. auth. see Cleary, Thomas.
Cleary, James, tr. see White, Carol.
Cleary, James P., jt. auth. see Levenbach, Hans.
Cleary, James W., ed. see Bulwer, John.
Cleary, Jon. The Beaufort Sisters. 1980. pap. 2.50 (ISBN 0-445-04578-7). Popular Lib.
--The Sundowners. 288p. 1981. pap. 2.50 (ISBN 0-445-04642-2). Popular Lib.
Cleary, Thomas & Cleary, J. C. The Blue Cliff Record. LC 76-14202. 1978. 25.00 (ISBN 0-87773-706-1, Prajna). Great Eastern.
Cleary, Thomas, tr. from Japanese. Timeless Spring. 176p. 1980. pap. 7.95 (ISBN 0-8348-0148-5, Pub. by John Weatherhill Inc Japan). C E Tuttle.
Cleasby, Richard & Vigfusson, Gudbrand, eds. Icelandic-English Dictionary. 2nd ed. 1957. 65.00x (ISBN 0-19-863103-0). Oxford U Pr.
Cleave, Alan. Cartoon Animation for Everyone. 1977. pap. 8.95 o.p. (ISBN 0-85242-566-X, Pub. by Fountain). Morgan.
--Your Instant Guide to Movie Making. 1977. pap. 3.75 o.p. (ISBN 0-85242-499-X, Pub. by Fountain). Morgan.
Cleave Alexander, Michael Van see Van Cleave Alexander, Michael.
Cleaveland, Agnes M. No Life for a Lady. LC 77-6825. (Illus.). 1977. pap. 4.50 (ISBN 0-8032-5868-2, BB 652, Bison). U of Nebr Pr.
Cleaveland, Frederic N., et al. Congress & Urban Problems: A Casebook on the Legislative Process. 405p. 1969. 14.95 (ISBN 0-8157-1474-2); pap. 5.95 (ISBN 0-8157-1473-4). Brookings.
Cleaver. How the Chipmunk Got Its Stripes. (ps-3). pap. 1.25 (ISBN 0-590-11960-5, Schol Pap). Schol Bk Serv.
Cleaver, Bill, jt. auth. see Cleaver, Vera.
Cleaver, Eldridge. Soul on Fire. LC 77-83335. 1978. 8.95 o.p. (ISBN 0-8499-0046-8, 0046-8). Word Bks.
Cleaver, Vera & Cleaver, Bill. The Kissimmee Kid. LC 80-29262. 160p. (gr. 5 up). 1981. 8.95 (ISBN 0-688-41992-5); PLB 8.59 (ISBN 0-688-51992-X). Morrow.
--The Mimosa Tree. 140p. (RL 6). Date not set. pap. 1.25 o.p. (ISBN 0-451-07406-8, Y7406, Sig). NAL.
--Mock Revolt. LC 75-151467. 160p. (gr. 6 up). 1971. PLB 8.79 (ISBN 0-397-31238-5); pap. 1.95 (ISBN 0-397-31237-7). Lippincott.
Cleaves, A. B., jt. auth. see Schultz, John R.
Cleaves, Peter S. Bureaucratic Politics & Administration in Chile. 1974. 25.00x (ISBN 0-520-02448-6). U of Cal Pr.
Clebsch, William. Christianity in European History. 1979. 15.95 (ISBN 0-19-502471-0); pap. text ed. 4.95x (ISBN 0-19-502472-9). Oxford U Pr.
Clecak, Peter. Crooked Paths: Reflections on Socialism, Conservatism & the Welfare State. LC 76-5118. 1977. 10.95 o.s.i. (ISBN 0-06-010838-X, HarpT). Har-Row.
Cleckley, Franklin D. Handbook on Evidence for West Virginia Lawyers. 1978. 40.00, with 1979 suppl (ISBN 0-87215-202-2); 1979 suppl 15.00 (ISBN 0-87215-285-5). Michie.
Cleckley, Hervey M. Mask of Sanity. 5th ed. LC 75-31875. 544p. 1976. 23.50 (ISBN 0-8016-0985-2). Mosby.
Cleckley, Hervey M., jt. auth. see Thigpen, Corbett H.
Cleef, E. Van see Van Cleef, E.
Cleeland, Caryn L., jt. auth. see Castelli, Louis.
Cleeton, Claud E. Strategies for the Options Trader. LC 78-11230. 1979. 22.95 (ISBN 0-471-04973-5, Pub. by Wiley-Interscience). Wiley.
Cleeve, Brian. Judith. 1979. pap. 2.25 o.p. (ISBN 0-425-04168-9). Berkley Pub.
--Kate. 1978. pap. 2.25 o.p. (ISBN 0-425-03827-0, Medallion). Berkley Pub.
Cleeve, Brian, ed. see Yeats, William B., et al.
Cleeve, Richard. The Student Map Manual: Historical Geography of the Bible Landa. Monson, J., et al, eds. 168p. 1980. 34.95 (ISBN 0-310-42980-3). Zondervan.
Clegg, Alec. About Our Schools. (Illus.). 160p. 1981. 24.50x (ISBN 0-631-12881-6, Pub. by Basil Blackwell); pap. 9.95 (ISBN 0-631-12832-8). Biblio Dist.
Clegg, Ambrose A., Jr., jt. auth. see Banks, James A.
Clegg, Charles, jt. auth. see Beebe, Lucius.
Clegg, E. J. & Garlick, J. P., eds. Disease & Urbanization. (Symposia of the Society for the Study of Human Biology: Vol. 20). 1980. text ed. 22.25x (ISBN 0-85066-190-0). Humanities.
Clegg, H. A. Trade Unionism Under Collective Bargaining: A Theory Based on Comparisons of Six Countries. 1976. 13.75x o.p. (ISBN 0-631-17210-6, Pub. by Basil Blackwell); pap. 12.50x (ISBN 0-631-17220-3, Pub. by Basil Blackwell). Biblio Dist.
Clegg, Hugh, ed. see Mellish, Michael.
Clegg, Hugh, ed. see Rimmer, M.
Clegg, Hugh A. The Changing System of Industrial Relations in Great Britain: A Completely Rewritten Version of "the System of Industrial Relations in Great Britain". 1979. 45.50x (ISBN 0-631-11091-7, Pub. by Basil Blackwell England); pap. 21.00x (ISBN 0-631-11101-8). Biblio Dist.
Clegg, Hugh A., et al. History of British Trade Unions Since 1889 Vol. 1: 1889-1910. 1964. 37.50x (ISBN 0-19-828229-X). Oxford U Pr.
Clegg, James S., jt. ed. see Crowe, John H.
Clegg, Joan. Dictionary of Social Services- Policy & Practice. 147p. 1977. text ed. 12.50x (ISBN 0-7199-0932-5, Pub. by Bedford England). Renouf.
Clegg, John. Your Book of Freshwater Life. (Illus.). (gr. 7 up). 1968. 5.95 (ISBN 0-571-08399-4). Transatlantic.
Clegg, Norma & Caldwell, Patricia. Spanish Once a Week. rev. ed. 1977. pap. 5.25x (ISBN 0-631-94610-1, Pub. by Basil Blackwell). Biblio Dist.
Clegg, Reed K. Probation & Parole: Principles & Practices. 196p. 1979. pap. 11.75 (ISBN 0-398-03036-7). C C Thomas.
Clegg, Stewart. Power, Rule & Domination: A Critical & Empizical Understanding of Power in Sociological Theory & Organizational Life. (International Library of Sociology). 272p. 1975. pap. 12.95 (ISBN 0-7100-8238-X). Routledge & Kegan.
--The Theory of Power & Organization. 1979. 20.00x (ISBN 0-7100-0143-6). Routledge & Kegan.
Clegg, W. Paul & Styring, John S. Steamers of British Railways and Associated Companies. (Illus.). 140p. 1967. 4.95 o.p. (ISBN 0-7153-4202-9). David & Charles.
Cleghorn, William, jt. auth. see Keddie, James.
Cleland, Charles. Mental Retardation: A Developmental Approach. (Spec. Educ. Ser.). 1978. ref. ed. 18.95x (ISBN 0-13-576504-8). P-H.
Cleland, Charles C. The Profoundly Mentally Retarded. LC 79-1258. 1979. text ed. 17.95 (ISBN 0-13-729566-9). P-H.
Cleland, David I. & Kocaoglu, Dundar F. Engineering Management. (Industrial Engineering & Management Science Ser.). (Illus.). 528p. 1980. text ed. 21.95 (ISBN 0-07-011316-5, C). McGraw.
Cleland, John. The Memoirs of a Coxcomb. LC 74-14913. (Novel in England, 1700-1775 Ser). 1974. Repr. of 1751 ed. lib. bdg. 50.00 (ISBN 0-8240-1132-5). Garland Pub.
Cleland, Max. Strong at the Broken Places. 1980. 6.95 (ISBN 0-912376-55-4). Word Bks.
Cleland, Robert G. & Putnam, Frank B. Isaias W. Hellman & the Farmers & Merchants Bank. LC 65-12230. (Huntington Library Classics). 136p. 1980. Repr. of 1965 ed. softcover 4.00 (ISBN 0-87328-018-0). Huntington Lib.
Cleland, William, et al. Medical & Surgical Cardiology. (Illus.). 1168p. 1969. 38.50 (ISBN 0-397-60130-1, Blackwell). Mosby.
Clem, Alan. American Electoral Politics: Strategies for Renewal. 1980. pap. text ed. 9.95 (ISBN 0-442-24475-4). D Van Nostrand.
Clem, Mabeth. The Servant Story (Mark) Leader's Guide. (New Horizons Bible Study Ser.). 48p. 1980. pap. 1.75 (ISBN 0-89367-050-2). Light & Life.
Clem, Ralph S., et al, eds. No Room for Man: Population & the Future Through Science Fiction. 247p. 1979. 11.50x (ISBN 0-8476-6181-4). Rowman.
Clemen & Eigsti. Comprehensive Family & Community Health Nursing. (Illus.). 544p. 1981. text ed. 19.95 (ISBN 0-07-011324-6, HP). McGraw.
Clemens, Clara. My Husband Ggabrilowitsch. (Music Reprint Ser.). 1979. Repr. of 1938 ed. 25.00 (ISBN 0-306-79563-9). Da Capo.
Clemens, Dale P. Advanced Custom Rod Building. (Illus.). 1978. 16.95 (ISBN 0-87691-258-7). Winchester Pr.
--Fiberglass Rod Making. 1974. 14.95 (ISBN 0-87691-136-X). Winchester Pr.
Clemens, David A. God Encountered, Vol. 1. LC 79-52420. (Steps to Maturity Ser.). 1973. tchrs'. manual 14.95 (ISBN 0-86508-002-X); student's manual 12.50 (ISBN 0-86508-001-1); visuals packet 4.25 (ISBN 0-86508-007-0). BCM Inc.
--Living, Vol. 3. LC 79-55503. (Steps to Maturity Ser.). 1980. tchrs' manual 14.95 (ISBN 0-86508-006-2); students' manual 12.50 (ISBN 0-86508-005-4). BCM Inc.
Clemens, S., jt. auth. see O'Daffer, P.
Clemens, Samuel see Twain, Mark, pseud.
Clemens, Samuel L. Adventures of Huckleberry Finn. 2nd ed. Bradley, Sculley & Beatty, Richmond C., eds. LC 76-30648. (Critical Eidtions). 1977. 15.00 (ISBN 0-393-04454-8); pap. 4.95x (ISBN 0-393-09146-5). Norton.
--Adventures of Tom Sawyer. LC 58-13029. (Great Il. Classics). (Illus.). (gr. 7 up). 1979. 8.95 (ISBN 0-396-07743-9). Dodd.
--Mark Twain's Letters to Mary. Leary, Lewis, ed. 1961. pap. 5.00x (ISBN 0-231-08545-1). Columbia U Pr.
--Personal Recollections of Joan of Arc by the Sieur Louis De Conte. LC 80-23663. (Illus.). xiv, 461p. 1980. Repr. of 1906 ed. lib. bdg. 45.00x (ISBN 0-313-22373-4, CLPR). Greenwood.
--Pudd'nhead Wilson & Those Extraordinary Twins. Berger, Sidney E., ed. (Norton Critical Edition Ser.). 1980. text ed. 22.50 (ISBN 0-393-01337-5); pap. text ed. 5.95x (ISBN 0-393-95027-1). Norton.
Clemens, W. A., Jr. Fossil Mammals of the Type Lance Formation, Wyoming, Part II, Marsupialia. (U. C. Publ. in Geological Sciences: Vol. 62). 1966. pap. 8.00x (ISBN 0-520-09163-9). U of Cal Pr.
Clemens, Walter C., Jr. The Arms Race & Sino Soviet Relations. LC 68-21253. (Publication Ser.: No. 72). 1968. 7.50 (ISBN 0-8179-1722-5); pap. 3.95 (ISBN 0-8179-1722-5). Hoover Inst Pr.
Clemens, William A., Jr. Fossil Mammals of the Type Lance Formation, Wyoming, Part 3: Eutheria & Summary. (U. C. Publ. in Geological Sciences: Vol. 94). 1973. pap. 9.00x (ISBN 0-520-09418-2). U of Cal Pr.
Clemensen, Jessie. Mountainside Reflections. (Illus.). 64p. 1980. 5.95 (ISBN 0-89962-022-1). Todd & Honeywell.
Clement, Abigail. Christabel's Room. 176p. 1977. pap. 1.25 o.p. (ISBN 0-449-13820-8, GM). Fawcett.
Clement, Besse A., tr. see Le Tourneau, Roger.
Clement, Charles. Gericault: Etude Biographique et Critique, Averc Le Catalogue Raisonne De L'Oeuvre Du Maitre. rev ed. LC 73-83834. (Graphic Art Ser.). (Illus.). 550p. (Fr.). 1974. Repr. of 1879 ed. lib. bdg. 65.00 (ISBN 0-306-70643-1). Da Capo.
Clement, Clara E. Handbook of Christian Symbols & Stories of the Saints, As Illustrated in Art. LC 70-159863. 1971. Repr. of 1886 ed. 24.00 (ISBN 0-8103-3288-4). Gale.
--Handbook of Legendary & Mythological Art. LC 68-26616. (Illus.). 1969. Repr. of 1881 ed. 26.00 (ISBN 0-8103-3175-6). Gale.
--Saints in Art. LC 77-89303. 1976. Repr. of 1899 ed. 17.00 (ISBN 0-8103-3030-X). Gale.
Clement, Felix & Larousse, Pierre. Dictionnaire Des Operas, 2 Vols. LC 69-15617. (Music Reprint Ser). 1969. Repr. of 1905 ed. 95.00 (ISBN 0-306-71197-4). Da Capo.
Clement, Hal. Close to Critical. 192p. 1981. pap. 1.95 (ISBN 0-345-29168-9, Del Rey). Ballantine.
--Close to Critical. 192p. (Orig.). 1975. pap. 1.95 (ISBN 0-345-29168-9). Ballantine.
--Cycle of Fire. 192p. 1981. pap. 2.25 (ISBN 0-345-29172-7, Del Rey). Ballantine.
--Left of Africa. (Lost Manuscripts Ser.). 160p. 1976. 12.95. Manuscript Pr.
--Needle. 1979. pap. 1.95 (ISBN 0-380-00635-9, 44263). Avon.
Clement, Herb. Zoo Man. (Illus.). (gr. 7 up). 1969. 5.95 o.s.i. (ISBN 0-02-526100-2). Macmillan.
Clement, Jacqueline P. Sex Bias in School Leadership. LC 75-3712. 1975. 2.70 (ISBN 0-685-52790-5). Integrated Ed Assoc.
Clement, John A., jt. auth. see Stryker, John A.
Clement, Paul A., jt. auth. see Packard, Pamela M.
Clement, Roland C. The Living World of Audubon. (Illus.). 1980. 9.95 (ISBN 0-686-68770-1, Fireside). S&S.
Clemente, Carmine D. Anatomy - A Regional Atlas of the Human Body. 2nd ed. (Illus.). 392p. 1981. text ed. price not set (ISBN 0-8067-0322-9). Urban & S.
Clemente, F. F. Di see Di Clemente, F. F.
Clemente, Jose E., ed. Martin Fierro, un Siglo. limited ed. (Illus., Span., Special centennial vol., vols. no. 500-1000 only, for sale). 1972. 50.00 (ISBN 0-935738-03-7). US Comm UNICEF.
Clementi, E. Computational Aspects for Large Chemical Systems. (Lecture Notes in Chemistry: Vol. 19). (Illus.). 184p. 1980. pap. 17.50 (ISBN 0-387-10014-8). Springer-Verlag.
Clementi, F., ed. see International Symposium on Cell Biology & Cytopharmacology, First.
Clementi, Francesco, jt. ed. see Ceccarelli, Bruno.
Clements, Abigail. Highland Fire. 1977. pap. 1.50 o.p. (ISBN 0-449-13638-8, GM). Fawcett.
Clements, Bruce. Anywhere Else but Here. LC 77-10081. 208p. (gr. 4 up). 1980. 8.95 (ISBN 0-374-30371-1). FS&G.
--I Tell a Lie Every So Often. LC 73-22356. 160p. (gr. 7 up). 1974. 9.95 (ISBN 0-374-33619-9, 374-33619-9). FS&G.
Clements, Bruce & Clements, Hanna. Coming Home to a Place You've Never Been Before. LC 75-26716. 192p. (gr. 7 up). 1975. 6.95 (ISBN 0-374-31530-2). FS&G.
Clements, Christine. Slewfoot, the Despicable Monster. (Illus.). 100p. (ps-4). Date not set. pap. price not set. C Clements.
Clements, Edith S. Flowers of Mountain & Plain. 3rd ed. (Illus.). 1955. Repr. of 1926 ed. 9.75 o.s.i. (ISBN 0-02-842950-8). Hafner.
Clements, F. A. Oman: The Reborn Land. 1981. text ed. 25.00 (ISBN 0-582-78300-3). Longman.
Clements, Frank A. Saudi Arabia. (World Bibliographical Ser.: No. 5). 197p. 1979. 25.25 (ISBN 0-903450-15-1). ABC-Clio.
Clements, Hanna, jt. auth. see Clements, Bruce.
Clements, Harry F. Sugarcane Crop Logging & Crop Control: Principles & Practices. (Illus.). 540p. 1980. 30.00 (ISBN 0-8248-0508-9). U Pr of Hawaii.
Clements, James F. Birds of the World: A Checklist. rev. ed. LC 75-29874. 1978. Repr. of 1975 ed. 15.00 (ISBN 0-8467-0123-5, Pub. by Two Continents). Hippocrene Bks.
Clements, Julia. Flowers in Praise: Church Flower Arrangements & Festivals. LC 79-57312. (Illus.). 96p. 1980. 24.00 (ISBN 0-7134-3328-0, Pub. by Batsford England). David & Charles.
Clements, Laurie, jt. ed. see Clarke, Tom.
Clements, Millard, et al. Social Study: Inquiry in Elementary Classrooms. LC 63-12182. 1966. 28.95x (ISBN 0-672-60644-5). Irvington.
Clements, Patricia & Grindle, Juliet, eds. The Poetry of Thomas Hardy. (Critical Studies Ser.). 194p. 1980. 26.00x (ISBN 0-389-20057-3). B&N.
Clements, R. E. Isaiah & the New Jerusalem. (Journal for the Study of the Old Testament, Supplement Ser.: No. 13). 1980. text ed. 16.95 (ISBN 0-905774-23-X, Pub. by JSOT Pr England). Eisenbrauns.
--New Century Bible Commentary on Isaiah 1-39. rev. ed. 320p. 1980. pap. 7.95 (ISBN 0-8028-1841-2). Eerdmans.

Clements, Robert J. The Poetry of Michelangelo. LC 65-19514. (Gotham Library). 368p. (Orig.). 1965. 15.00x (ISBN 0-8147-0085-3); pap. 7.00 (ISBN 0-8147-0086-1). NYU Pr.
Clements, Robert J. & Gibaldi, Joseph. The Anatomy of the Novella: The European Tale Collection from Boccaccio & Chaucer to Cervantes. LC 76-52548. 1977. 15.00x (ISBN 0-8147-1369-6); pap. 7.00x (ISBN 0-8147-1370-X). NYU Pr.
Clements, Robert J. & Levant, Lorna, eds. Renaissance Letters: Revelations of a World Reborn. LC 75-21806. 469p. 1976. 20.00x o.p. (ISBN 0-8147-1362-9); pap. 9.50x (ISBN 0-8147-1363-7). NYU Pr.
Clements, Robert W., jt. auth. see Tetreault, Wilfred F.
Clements, Ronald E. God's Chosen People: A Theological Interpretation of the Book of Deuteronomy. 1968. pap. text ed. 2.50x o.p. (ISBN 0-8401-0422-7). Allenson.
Clements, Ronald E., ed. see Hyatt, J. P.
Clements, Ronald E., ed. see Mayes, A. D.
Clements, Ronald E., ed. see Rowley, H. H.
Clements, Ronald E., ed. see Whybray, R. N.
Clements, William M. Care & Counseling of the Aging. Clinebell, Howard J. & Stone, Howard W., eds. LC 78-54547. (Creative Pastoral Care & Counseling Ser). 96p. 1979. pap. 2.95 (ISBN 0-8006-0561-6, 1-1561). Fortress.
Clements, William M., ed. Ministry with the Aging. LC 80-7739. 288p. 1981. 11.95 (ISBN 0-06-061496-X, HarpR). Har-Row.
Clemes, Harris, jt. auth. see Bean, Reynold.
Clemhout, Simone. Perspectives for Public Policy: An Environmental View on Human Ecology. 1977. pap. text ed. 8.50x o.p. (ISBN 0-8191-0182-6). U Pr of Amer.
Cleminshaw, Clarence H. Beginner's Guide to the Skies. LC 76-28317. 1977. 9.95 (ISBN 0-690-01214-4, TYC-T). T Y Crowell.
Clemmens, jt. auth. see Kenny.
Clemmens, Raymond L., jt. auth. see Kenny, Thomas J.
Clemmensen, J., ed. Quantitative Aspects of Risk Assessment in Chemical Carcinogenesis. (Illus.). 350p. 1980. pap. 34.40 (ISBN 0-387-09584-5). Springer-Verlag.
Clemmow, P. C. An Introduction to Electromagnetic Theory. LC 73-77174. (Illus.). 320p. 1973. 42.00 (ISBN 0-521-20239-6); pap. 14.50x (ISBN 0-521-09815-7). Cambridge U Pr.
Clemoes, P. Anglo-Saxon England, Vol. 9. LC 78-190423. (Anglo-Saxon England Ser.). (Illus.). 330p. Date not set. 56.00 (ISBN 0-521-23449-2). Cambridge U Pr.
Clemoes, Peter & Hughes, Kathleen, eds. England Before the Conquest. LC 76-154508. (Illus.). 1971. 53.95 (ISBN 0-521-08191-2). Cambridge U Pr.
Clemoes, Peter A., ed. Anglo-Saxon England, 8 vols. Incl. Vol. 1. 320p. 1972. 47.50 (ISBN 0-521-08557-8); Vol. 2. 300p. 1973. 47.50 (ISBN 0-521-20218-3); Vol. 3. 320p. 1974. 47.50 (ISBN 0-521-20574-3); Vol. 4. 270p. 1975. 47.50 (ISBN 0-521-20868-8); Vol. 5. 1976. 47.50 (ISBN 0-521-21270-7); Vol. 6. 1977. 47.50 (ISBN 0-521-21701-6); Vol. 7. 1979. 47.50 (ISBN 0-521-22164-1); Vol. 8. 1980. 57.50 (ISBN 0-521-22788-7). LC 78-19043. (Illus.). Cambridge U Pr.
Clemons, Neil L., jt. auth. see Heinzen, Richard H.
Clendenen, C. C. Blood on the Border. 1969. 12.50 o.s.i. (ISBN 0-02-526110-X). Macmillan.
Clendenin, M. The Ghost of McDow Hole. 4.75 o.p. (ISBN 0-8062-1204-7). Carlton.
Clendenning, P. H. & Bartlett, R. Eighteenth Century Russia: A Select Bibliography of Works Published Since 1955. (Russian Bibliography Ser.: No. 3). (Illus.). 260p. 1981. 18.00 (ISBN 0-89250-110-3); pap. 8.95 (ISBN 0-89250-111-1). Orient Res Partners.
Clene, Inc., compiled by. Who's Who in Continuing Education. 304p. 1979. 40.00 (ISBN 0-89664-024-8, Pub. by K G Saur). Gale.
Cleobury, F. H. From Clerk to Cleric. 1977. pap. 3.00 (ISBN 0-227-67825-7). Attic Pr.
Clepper, Henry. Careers in Conservation: Opportunities in Natural Resource Management. 2nd ed. LC 78-21917. 1979. 15.50 (ISBN 0-471-05163-2). Ronald Pr.
Clepper, Henry, ed. Marine Recreational Fisheries, Vol. 5. LC 76-22389. 1980. 15.00. Sport Fishing.
Clepper, Henry, ed. see Stroud, Richard H.
Clepper, Henry E., ed. Origins of American Conservation. 1966. 18.50 (ISBN 0-8260-2060-7, Pub. by Wiley-Interscience). Wiley.
Clerk, William. An Epitome of Certaine Late Aspersions Cast at Civilians. LC 79-84095. (English Experience Ser.: No.915). 56p. 1979. Repr. of 1631 ed. lib. bdg. 7.00 (ISBN 90-221-0915-1). Walter J Johnson.
Clery, Val. Doors. (Illus.). 144p. 1979. 14.95 o.p. (ISBN 0-670-28039-9, Studio). Viking Pr.
--Windows. (Illus.). 168p. 1979. 14.95 o.p. (ISBN 0-670-77180-5, Studio). Viking Pr.
Clery, Val, jt. auth. see Hogarth, Peter.
Clet, Vince. Fire Related Codes, Laws & Ordinances. 1978. text ed. 12.95x (ISBN 0-02-471760-6). Macmillan.
Cleton, F. J & Simons, J. W., eds. Genetic Origins of Tumor Cells. (Developments in Oncology Ser.: Vol. 1). xv, 125p. 1980. lib. bdg. 26.30 (ISBN 90-247-2272-1, Pub. by Martinus Nijhoff). Kluwer Boston.
Cleve, John. The Crusader No. 1: The Accursed Tower. 1974. pap. 1.50 o.p. (ISBN 0-685-47910-2, D3444, Dist. by Dell). Grove.
--The Crusader No. 2: The Passionate Princess. 1974. pap. 1.50 o.p. (ISBN 0-685-47911-0, D6039, Dist. by Dell). Grove.
--The Crusader No. 3: Julanar the Lioness. 1975. pap. 1.50 o.p. (ISBN 0-685-56547-5, D4731, Dist. by Dell). Grove.
--The Crusader No. 4: My Lady Queen. 1975. pap. 1.50 o.p. (ISBN 0-685-56548-3, D5749, Dist. by Dell). Grove.
--The Crusader: The Accursed Tower the Passionate Princess, Bks. 1 & 2. LC 80-1000. 1980. pap. 2.95 (ISBN 0-394-17735-5, B440, BC). Grove.
--My Lady Queen. pap. 1.50 o.s.i. (ISBN 0-440-15749-8). Dell.
--The Passionate Princess. pap. 1.50 o.s.i. (ISBN 0-440-16039-1). Dell.
Cleve, Thomas C. Van see Van Cleve, Thomas C.
Cleveland, E. E. The Gates Shall Not. (Horizon Ser.). 96p. 1980. pap. write for info. (ISBN 0-8127-0325-1). Southern Pub.
--Living Soul. LC 73-91286. 219p. 1974. pap. text ed. 1.95 (ISBN 0-8127-0078-3). Southern Pub.
Cleveland, Harlan, ed. Energy Futures of Developing Countries: The Neglected Victims of the Energy Crisis. 1980. 19.95 (ISBN 0-03-058669-0). Praeger.
--The Management of Sustainable Growth. LC 80-24162. (Pergamon Policy Studies on International Development). 386p. 1981. 40.00 (ISBN 0-08-027171-5). Pergamon.
Cleveland, Harold, jt. auth. see Sanderson, Fred.
Cleveland, Hugh. Cattle Pricing Guide. 3rd rev. ed. (Illus.). 1980. pap. 7.95 (ISBN 0-89145-137-4). Collector Bks.
Cleveland, James O., jt. auth. see Peterson, Raymond M.
Cleveland, John. Poems of John Cleveland. Morris, Brian & Withington, Eleanor, eds. (Oxford English Texts Ser). 1967. 29.00x (ISBN 0-19-811839-2). Oxford U Pr.
Cleveland, John, jt. auth. see Gamow, G.
Cleveland Museum of Art Staff. Handbook of the Cleveland Museum of Art. LC 76-54618. (Illus.). 456p. 1978. pap. 20.00x vinyl cover (ISBN 0-910386-31-5, Pub. by Cleveland Mus Art). Ind U Pr.
--Selected Works: The Cleveland Museum of Art. LC 66-21226. (Illus.). 252p. 1966. slipcased 12.50x (ISBN 0-910386-12-9, Pub. by Cleveland Mus Art). Ind U Pr.
Cleveland, William A. Britannica Atlas. (YA) (gr. 9 up). 1980. write for info. (ISBN 0-85229-390-9). Ency Brit Ed.
Clevenger, Shobal V. A Treatise on the Method of Government Surveying. 1978. pap. 8.50 (ISBN 0-686-25541-0). CARBEN Survey.
Cleverley, Graham. The Fleet Street Disaster. LC 76-25733. (Communication & Society: Vol. 7). 1976. 17.50x (ISBN 0-8039-9989-5, Co-Pub with Constable). Sage.
Cleverley, William O. Essentials of Hospital Finance. LC 78-7447. (Illus.). 1978. text ed. 21.95 (ISBN 0-89443-035-1). Aspen Systems.
--Financial Management of Health Care Facilities. 394p. 1976. 18.75 (ISBN 0-686-68581-4, 14915). Hospital Finan.
--Financial Management of Health Care Facilities. LC 76-4034. 1976. 26.00 (ISBN 0-912862-20-3). Aspen Systems.
Clevett, Kenneth J. Handbook of Process Stream Analysis. LC 73-14416. (Ser. in Analytical Chemistry). (Illus.). 544p. 1974. 58.95 (ISBN 0-470-16048-9). Halsted Pr.
Clevin, Jorgen. Pete's First Day at School. (Illus.). (ps-k). 1973. PLB 4.69 (ISBN 0-394-92652-8, BYR). Random.
Clew, Kenneth R. The Kennet & Avon Canal. (Inland Waterways Histories Ser.). (Illus.). 1973. 16.95 (ISBN 0-7153-5939-8). David & Charles.
Clewell, David. Room to Breathe. LC 76-42865. 1976. pap. 4.00 (ISBN 0-915316-29-3); signed ltd. ed. 10.00x (ISBN 0-915316-30-7). Pentagram.
Clewlow, C. William, Jr., et al, eds. Archaeological Investigations at the Ring Brothers Site Complex, Thousand Oaks, California. (Institute of Archaeology Monographs: No. 13). (Illus.). 156p. 1979. pap. 7.00 (ISBN 0-917956-13-3). UCLA Arch.
Clewlow, Carol. Hong Kong & Macau. (Illus., Orig.). 1978. pap. 2.95 (ISBN 0-8467-0519-2, Pub. by Two Continents). Hippocrene Bks.
Clews, F. H. Heavy Clay Technology. 1969. 29.00 o.s.i. (ISBN 0-12-176350-1). Acad Pr.
Clews, Roderick. A Textbook of Insurance Broking. 224p. 1980. 27.00x (ISBN 0-85941-121-4, Pub. by Woodhead-Faulkner England). State Mutual Bk.
Cliatt, Mary J. & Shaw, Jean M. Junk Treasures: A Sourcebook for Using Recycled Materials with Children. (Illus.). 256p. 1981. pap. text ed. 14.95 (ISBN 0-13-512608-8). P-H.
Click, Phyllis. Administration of Schools for Young Children. (Early Childhood Education Ser.). 148p. 1975. pap. 7.20 o.p. (ISBN 0-8273-0575-3); instructor's guide 1.45 o.p. (ISBN 0-8273-0576-1). Delmar.
--Administration of Schools for Young Children. 2nd ed. LC 79-55235. (Early Childhood Education Ser.). 175p. 1981. pap. text ed. 10.60 (ISBN 0-8273-1575-9); instr's. guide 1.80 (ISBN 0-8273-1576-7). Delmar.
Clief, Sylvia Van see Heide, Florence P. & Van Clief, Sylvia.
Cliff, A. D., et al. Elements of Spatial Structure. LC 74-12973. (Geographical Studies: No. 6). (Illus.). 206p. 1974. 37.50 (ISBN 0-521-20689-8). Cambridge U Pr.
--Spatial Diffusion: An Historical Geography of Epidemics in an Island Community. (Cambridge Geographical Studies: No. 14). (Illus.). 244p. Date not set. price not set (ISBN 0-521-22840-9). Cambridge U Pr.
Cliff, Freda & Cliff, Philip. A Diary for Teachers of Young Children. pap. 1.95x (ISBN 0-8192-4036-2). Morehouse.
Cliff, Michelle. Claiming an Identity They Taught Me to Despise. LC 80-23137. (Orig.). 1980. pap. 4.00 (ISBN 0-930436-06-7). Persephone.
Cliff, Philip, jt. auth. see Cliff, Freda.
Cliff, W. J. Blood Vessels. LC 74-31789. (Biological Structure & Functions Ser.: No. 6). (Illus.). 224p. 1976. 50.00 (ISBN 0-521-20753-3). Cambridge U Pr.
Cliffe, A. E. Let Go & Let God. 1951. pap. 2.95 o.p. (ISBN 0-13-531509-3). P-H.
Clifford, A. H. & Preston, G. B. Algebraic Theory of Semigroups, 2 Vols. LC 61-15686. (Mathematical Surveys Ser.: Vol. 7). 1977. Repr. of 1961 ed. Vol. 1. with corrections 16.40 (ISBN 0-8218-0271-2, SURV-7-1); Vol. 2. with corrections 19.20 (ISBN 0-8218-0272-0, SURV-7.2). Am Math.
Clifford, Alan. The Middle Ages. Yapp, Malcolm, et al, eds. (World History Ser.). (Illus.). (gr. 10). 1980. Repr. of 1977 ed. lib. bdg. 5.95 (ISBN 0-89908-028-6); pap. text ed. 1.95 (ISBN 0-89908-003-0). Greenhaven.
Clifford, Alec, tr. see Sweeting, George.
Clifford, Alejandro, tr. see Ten Boom, Corrie.
Clifford, Brian & Bull, Ray. The Psychology of Person Identification. 1978. 22.50 (ISBN 0-7100-8867-1). Routledge & Kegan.
Clifford, E., jt. auth. see Hampton, C. W.
Clifford, Eth. The Killer Swan. (gr. 5-8). 1980. 6.95 (ISBN 0-395-29742-7). HM.
Clifford, Francis. Drummer in the Dark. 1977. pap. 1.50 o.p. (ISBN 0-345-25609-3). Ballantine.
Clifford, Frederick. History of Private Bill Legislation, 2 Vols. LC 70-350284. Repr. of 1885 ed. 55.00x (ISBN 0-678-05163-1). Kelley.
--A History of Private Bill Legislation, 2 vols. 1968. 75.00x (ISBN 0-7156-1563-7, F Cass Co). Biblio Dist.
Clifford, Gay. The Transformations of Allegory. 1974. 12.50 (ISBN 0-7100-7976-1). Routledge & Kegan.
Clifford, Geraldine J. The Shape of American Education. (Illus.). 288p. 1975. 16.95 (ISBN 0-13-807891-2). P-H.
Clifford, H. T. & Constantine, J. Ferns, Fern Allies & Conifers of Australia. (Illus.). 150p. 1980. text ed. 24.25x (ISBN 0-7022-1447-7). U of Queensland Pr.
Clifford, Howard. Rails North: The Story of the Railroads of Alaska & the Yukon. (Illus.). 176p. 1981. 19.95 (ISBN 0-87564-536-4). Superior Pub.
Clifford, James L. Young Sam Johnson. (McGraw-Hill Paperbacks Ser.). (Illus.). 400p. 1981. pap. 6.95 (ISBN 0-07-011381-5). McGraw.
Clifford, James L., ed. Eighteenth-Century English Literature: Modern Essays in Criticism. (Orig.). 1959. pap. 5.95 (ISBN 0-19-500682-8, GB). Oxford U Pr.
--Man Versus Society in Eighteenth Century Britain. LC 68-12057. 1968. 22.95 (ISBN 0-521-04675-0). Cambridge U Pr.
Clifford, John G. The Citizen Soldiers: The Plattsburg Training Camp Movement, 1913-1920. LC 71-183350. 336p. 1972. 14.00x (ISBN 0-8131-1262-1). U Pr of Ky.
Clifford, Joseph A. Workmen's Compensation New York. 1981 ed. 75p. 1978. 5.00 (ISBN 0-87526-214-7). Gould.
Clifford, Lucy L. Anyhow Stories, Repr. Of 1882 Ed. Bd. with Wooden Tony - an Anyhow Story. Repr. of 1892 ed. LC 75-32186. (Classics of Children's Literature, 1621-1932: Vol. 49). (Illus.). 1976. lib. bdg. 38.00 (ISBN 0-8240-2298-X). Garland Pub.
Clifford, Margaret M. Practicing Educational Psychology. (Illus.). 752p. 1981. pap. text ed. write for info. (ISBN 0-395-29921-7); write for info. set test bank (ISBN 0-395-29925-X); write for info. instr's manual (ISBN 0-395-29923-3). HM.
Clifford, Margaret M. & Grandgenett, Myrna. Activities & Readings in Learning & Development. LC 80-84892. (Illus.). 256p. 1981. pap. text ed. price not set (ISBN 0-395-29924-1). HM.
Clifford, Martin. Modern Electronics Math. LC 73-86767. (Illus.). 602p. 1976. pap. 11.95 (ISBN 0-8306-5655-3, 655). TAB Bks.
Clifford, Mary L. Bisha of Burundi. LC 72-83780. (Illus.). 160p. (gr. 5 up). 1973. 7.95 o.p. (ISBN 0-690-14596-9, TYC-J). T Y Crowell.
Clifford, Nicholas. Retreat from China: British Policy in the Far East, 1937-1941. (China in the 20th Century Ser.). 1976. Repr. of 1967 ed. lib. bdg. 22.50 (ISBN 0-306-70757-8). Da Capo.
Clifford, Ray T., jt. auth. see Lange, Dale L.
Clifford, Richard M., jt. auth. see Harms, Thelma.
Clifford, Sandy. The Roquefort Gang. (gr. 2-6). 1981. 5.95 (ISBN 0-395-29521-1). HM.
--The Smartest Person in the World. LC 79-14138. (Illus.). (gr. k-3). 1979. pap. 4.95 (ISBN 0-395-28411-2). Parnassus.
Clifford, Terry. The Diamond Healing: Tibetan Buddhist Medicine & Psychiatry. 196p. 1981. pap. 7.95 (ISBN 0-87728-528-4). Weiser.
Clifford, William. Crime Control in Japan. LC 75-22883. 224p. 1976. 19.95 (ISBN 0-669-00184-8). Lexington Bks.
--Planning Crime Prevention. LC 74-42910. (Illus.). 1976. 16.95 (ISBN 0-669-00560-6). Lexington Bks.
Clifford, William G. Books in Bottles: The Curious in Literature. LC 70-78125. 1971. Repr. of 1926 ed. 15.00 (ISBN 0-8103-3791-6). Gale.
Clifford, William K. Mathematical Papers. LC 67-28488. 1968. Repr. 29.50 (ISBN 0-8284-0210-8). Chelsea Pub.
Cliff's Notes Editors. Merchant of Venice Notes. (Orig.). pap. 1.95 (ISBN 0-8220-0052-0). Cliffs.
--Of Human Bondage Notes. (Orig.). pap. 1.95 (ISBN 0-8220-0930-7). Cliffs.
--Othello Notes. (Orig.). pap. 1.95 (ISBN 0-8220-0063-6). Cliffs.
Clift, Charles, III & Greer, Archie, eds. Broadcast Programming. 5th ed. LC 79-66407. (III). 1979. pap. text ed. 7.75 (ISBN 0-8191-0820-0). U Pr of Amer.
--Broadcast Programming: The Current Perspective. 6th ed. LC 80-8127. 249p. 1981. text ed. 8.50 (ISBN 0-8191-1429-4). U Pr of Amer.
Clift, G. Glenn, et al. Kentucky in Retrospect: Noteworthy Personages & Events in Kentucky History, 1792-1967. rev. ed. Ardery, Mrs. Wm. B. & McChesney, Harry V., eds. (Illus.). 1967. 5.00 o.p. (ISBN 0-916968-00-6). Kentucky Hist.
Clift, J. C. & Imrie, B. W. Assessing Students Appraising Teaching. 160p. 1981. 24.95 (ISBN 0-470-27098-5). Halsted Pr.
Clift, Phillip, et al. The Aims, Role & Deployment of Staff in the Nursery. (Report of the National Foundation for Educational Research in England & Wales). 224p. 1980. pap. text ed. 18.75x (ISBN 0-85633-197-X). Humanities.
Clift, S., jt. auth. see Greenfield, S.
Clifton & Di Grazia. My Friend Jacob. LC 79-19168. 32p. (gr. k-2). 1980. PLB 7.95 (ISBN 0-525-35487-5). Dutton.
Clifton & Lucey. Accounting & Computer Systems. 1977. 22.50x o.p. (ISBN 0-8464-0107-X). Beekman Pubs.
Clifton, A. Kay, jt. auth. see Lee, Dorothy E.
Clifton, D. Business Data Systems. 1979. pap. 16.95 (ISBN 0-13-093963-3). P-H.
Clifton, David S., Jr. & Fyffe, David E. Project Feasibility Analysis: A Guide to Profitable New Ventures. LC 76-51321. 1977. text ed. 26.95 (ISBN 0-471-01611-X, Pub. by Wiley-Interscience). Wiley.
Clifton, H. D. Systems Analysis for Business Data Processing. 3rd ed. 242p. 1978. text ed. 30.75x (ISBN 0-220-66369-6, Pub. by Busn Bks England). Renouf.
Clifton, Lucille. Black B C's. (Illus.). (ps-4). 1970. 5.95 o.p. (ISBN 0-525-26596-1). Dutton.
--Don't You Remember? (Illus.). 32p. (ps-2). 1973. PLB 8.50 (ISBN 0-525-28840-6). Dutton.
--Two-Headed Woman. LC 80-5379. 72p. 1980. lib. bdg. 8.00x (ISBN 0-87023-309-2); pap. 3.95 (ISBN 0-87023-310-6). U of Mass Pr.
Clifton, Merritt. Freedom Comes from Human Beings. 80p. (Orig.). 1980. pap. 4.00 (ISBN 0-686-28738-X). Samisdat.
Clifton, Nancy A. & Simmons, Pamela J. Basic Imaging Procedures in Nuclear Medicine. 192p. 1981. pap. 13.50 (ISBN 0-8385-0578-3). ACC.

Clifton, R. H. Principles of Planned Maintenance. 1974. pap. 14.95x (ISBN 0-7131-3317-1). Intl Ideas.
Clifton, Robert B. Murder by Mail: And Other Postal Investigations. LC 79-51377. (Illus.). 240p. 1979. 7.95 (ISBN 0-8059-2649-6). Dorrance.
Clifton, Robert T. Barbs, Prongs, Points, Prickers, & Stickers: Complete & Illustrated Catalogue of Antique Barbed Wire. LC 78-88140. (Illus.). 1970. 13.95 (ISBN 0-8061-0875-4); pap. 7.95 (ISBN 0-8061-0876-2). U of Okla Pr.
Clifton-Taylor, Alec. English Parish Churches As Works of Art. 1974. 24.00 (ISBN 0-7134-2776-0, Pub. by Batsford England). David & Charles.
--The Pattern of English Building. 1972. 32.00 o.p. (ISBN 0-571-09525-9, Pub. by Faber & Faber). Merrimack Bk Serv.
--The Pattern of English Building. 2nd ed. 1981. 41.00 (ISBN 0-571-09525-9, Pub. by Faber & Faber); pap. 27.50 (ISBN 0-571-09526-7, Pub. by Faber & Faber). Merrimack Bk Serv.
Clignet, Remi. The Africanization of the Labor Market: Educational & Occupational Segmentations in the Camerouns. LC 75-13145. 1976. 20.00x (ISBN 0-520-03019-2). U of Cal Pr.
Climatic Impact Committee. Environmental Impact of Stratospheric Flight. 1975. pap. 11.00 (ISBN 0-309-02346-7). Natl Acad Pr.
Climo, Shirley. Piskies, Spriggans, & Other Magical Beings: Tales from the Droll-Teller. LC 79-7839. (Illus.). 128p. (gr. 4-7). 1981. 8.95 (ISBN 0-690-04063-6, TYC-J); PLB 8.79 (ISBN 0-690-04064-4). T Y Crowell.
Clinard, M. B. Cities with Little Crime. LC 77-88672. (ASA Rose Monograph Ser.). 1978. 19.95 (ISBN 0-521-21960-4); pap. 6.95x (ISBN 0-521-29327-8). Cambridge U Pr.
Clinard, Marshall. Slums & Community Development. LC 66-10960. 1966. 14.95 (ISBN 0-02-905570-9); pap. text ed. 4.00 (ISBN 0-02-905580-6). Free Pr.
Clinard, Marshall B. Anomie & Deviant Behavior: A Discussion & Critique. LC 64-20314. (Illus.). 1964. 9.95 (ISBN 0-02-905560-1); pap. text ed. 4.95 (ISBN 0-02-905550-4). Free Pr.
Clinard, Marshall B. & Abbott, Daniel J. Crime in Developing Countries: A Comparative Perspective. LC 73-4031. 319p. 1973. 25.95 (ISBN 0-471-16060-1, Pub. by Wiley-Interscience). Wiley.
Clinard, Marshall B. & Yeager, Peter C. Corporate Crime. 1980. 16.95 (ISBN 0-02-905710-8). Macmillan.
--Corporate Crime. LC 80-2156. (Illus.). 352p. 1980. 16.95 (ISBN 0-02-905710-8). Free Pr.
Cline, C. L., ed. see Meredith, George.
Cline, C. T., Jr. Mindreader. LC 80-2737. 336p. 1981. 13.95 (ISBN 0-385-17372-5). Doubleday.
Cline, C. Terry, Jr. Damon. 320p. 1978. pap. 2.25 (ISBN 0-449-22702-2, Crest). Fawcett.
Cline, Gloria G. Exploring the Great Basin. LC 63-8988. (American Exploration & Travel Ser.: Vol. 39). (Illus.). 254p. 1963. pap. 6.95 (ISBN 0-8061-1014-7). U of Okla Pr.
Cline, Gloria S. & Baker, Jeffrey A. An Index to Criticisms of British & American Poetry. LC 73-15542. 1973. 12.00 (ISBN 0-8108-0684-3). Scarecrow.
Cline, Howard F. Florida Indians I. Horr, David A., ed. (American Indian Ethnohistory Ser.). 1978. lib. bdg. 42.00 (ISBN 0-8240-0766-2). Garland Pub.
--Florida Indians II. Horr, David A., ed. (American Indian Ethnohistory Ser.). 1978. lib. bdg. 42.00 (ISBN 0-8240-0767-0). Garland Pub.
Cline, Howard F., et al, eds. Handbook of Middle American Indians: Guide to Ethnohistorical Sources, Vols. 14 & 15, Pts. 3 & 4. LC 64-10316. 1975. 60.00x set (ISBN 0-292-70154-3). U of Tex Pr.
Cline, Hugh F. & Sinnott, Loraine T. Building Library Collections: Policies & Practices in Academic Libraries. LC 80-8602. (Illus.). 192p. 1981. 15.95x (ISBN 0-669-04321-4). Lexington Bks.
Cline, Linda. The Miracle Season. LC 76-18070. (YA) 1976. 6.95 o.p. (ISBN 0-399-11654-0, Dist. by Putnam). Berkley Pub.
--The Miracle Season. 1977. pap. 1.25 o.p. (ISBN 0-425-03447-X, Medallion). Berkley Pub.
Cline, Martin, ed. Leukocyte Function. (Methods in Hematology). (Illus.). 224p. 1981. lib. bdg. 25.00 (ISBN 0-686-28872-6). Churchill.
Cline, Martin J. & Haskell, Charles M. Cancer Chemotherapy. 3rd ed. (Illus.). 397p. 1980. text ed. 27.50 (ISBN 0-7216-2609-2). Saunders.
Cline, Ray S. U. S. Power in a World of Conflict, Vol. II. (Significant Issues Ser.: No. 7). 45p. 1980. 5.95 (ISBN 0-89206-021-2). CSI Studies.
--World Power Trends & U. S. Foreign Policy for the Nineteen Eighties. 206p. 1980. lib. bdg. 20.00x (ISBN 0-89158-917-1); pap. 8.95x (ISBN 0-89158-790-X). Westview.
Cline, Ray S., et al. Main Trends in World Power: Political Impact of Strategic Weapons. 1978. pap. text ed. 2.95 o.p. (ISBN 0-89206-004-2). CSI Studies.
Cline, Victor, et al. Between Ring & Temple: A Book for Engaged L.D.S. Couples. 1981. price not set (ISBN 0-913420-87-5). Olympus Pub Co.
Cline, Victor B. How to Make Your Child a Winner: Ten Keys to Rearing Successful Children. 320p. 1980. 14.95 o.p. (ISBN 0-8027-0658-4); pap. 8.95 o.p. (ISBN 0-8027-7165-3). Walker & Co.
Cline, William. Policy Alternatives for a New International Economic Order. LC 79-87553. 1979. 26.95 (ISBN 0-03-049471-0); pap. 9.95 (ISBN 0-03-049466-4). Praeger.
Cline, William R. International Monetary Reform & the Developing Countries. 1976. 9.95 (ISBN 0-8157-1476-9); pap. 3.95 (ISBN 0-8157-1475-0). Brookings.
Cline, William R. & Weintraub, Sidney. Economic Stabilization in Developing Countries. LC 80-70079. 514p. 1981. 26.95 (ISBN 0-8157-1466-1); pap. 11.95 (ISBN 0-8157-1465-3). Brookings.
Cline, William R., ed. Policy Alternatives for a New International Economic Order: An Economic Analysis. LC 79-87553. 410p. 1979. pap. 7.95 (ISBN 0-03-049466-4). Overseas Dev Council.
Cline, William R. & Delgado, Enrique, eds. Economic Integration in Central America. LC 78-60708. 1978. 21.95 (ISBN 0-8157-1470-X). Brookings.
Cline, William R., et al. Trade Negotiations in the Tokyo Round: A Quantitative Assessment. 1978. 12.95 (ISBN 0-8157-1472-6). Brookings.
Cline, William R. & Assocs. World Inflation & the Less-Developed Countries. 300p. 1981. 19.95 (ISBN 0-8157-1468-8); pap. 7.95 (ISBN 0-8157-1467-X). Brookings.
Clinebell, Howard. Contemporary Growth Therapies. LC 80-24368. 304p. 1981. 10.95 (ISBN 0-687-09502-6). Abingdon.
Clinebell, Howard J., ed. see Augsburger, David W.
Clinebell, Howard J., ed. see Clements, William M.
Clinebell, Howard J., ed. see Irwin, Paul B.
Clinebell, Howard J., ed. see Leas, Speed & Kittlaus, Paul.
Clinebell, Howard J., ed. see Pattison, E. Mansell.
Clinebell, Howard J., ed. see Stone, Howard W.
Clinebell, Howard J., Jr. Understanding & Counseling the Alcoholic. rev. ed. 1968. 8.95 (ISBN 0-687-42801-7). Abingdon.
Clines, David J. I, He, We & They: A Literary Approach to Isaiah Fifty-Three. (JSOT Supplement Ser.: No. 1). 65p. 1976. pap. text ed. 8.50x (ISBN 0-905774-00-0, Pub. by JSOT Pr England). Eisenbrauns.
--The Theme of the Pentateuch. (JSOT Supplement Ser.: No. 10). 152p. 1978. text ed. 29.95x (ISBN 0-905774-14-0, Pub. by JSOT Pr England); pap. text ed. 16.95x (ISBN 0-905774-15-9, Pub. by JSOT Pr England). Eisenbrauns.
Clines, Francis X. About New York. LC 80-16080. 288p. 1980. 12.95 (ISBN 0-07-011384-X). McGraw.
Clinevell, Howard J., ed. see Oates, Wayne E.
Clinic on Library Applications of Data Processing, 1980. Public Access to Library Automation: Proceedings. Divilbiss, J. L., ed. 1981. 10.00 (ISBN 0-87845-065-3). U of Ill Lib Sci. Postponed.
Clinkscale, Edward, ed. Les Oeuvres Completes d'antoine de Fevin. (Gesamtausgaben - Collected Works Ser.: Vol. XI, No. 1). xvi, 134p. (Eng. & Ger.). 1980. lib. bdg. 55.00 (ISBN 0-912024-68-2). Inst Mediaeval.
Clinton, Elizabeth. The Countesse of Lincolnes Nurserie. LC 74-28838. (English Experience Ser.: No. 720). 1975. Repr. of 1622 ed. 3.50 (ISBN 90-221-0720-5). Walter J Johnson.
Clinton, Jerome W. The Divan of Manuchihri Damghani: A Critical Study. LC 72-87873. (Studies in Middle Eastern Literatures Ser: No. 1). 1972. pap. 15.00x (ISBN 0-88297-001-1). Bibliotheca.
Clinton-Baddeley, V. C. Only a Matter of Time. Date not set. pap. price not set (ISBN 0-440-16055-3). Dell.
Clipman, William. Dog Light. (Wesleyan Poetry Program Ser.: No. 102). 72p. 1981. 8.00; pap. 3.95. Wesleyan U Pr.
Clipper, Lawrence J. G. K. Chesterton. (English Authors Ser.: No. 166). 1974. lib. bdg. 10.95 (ISBN 0-8057-1090-6). Twayne.
Clissold, Stephen. Spain. Roxburgh, Toby, ed. LC 69-11266. (Nations & Peoples Library). 1969. 8.50x o.s.i. (ISBN 0-8027-2116-8). Walker & Co.
Clissold, Stephen, et al, eds. Short History of Yugoslavia. LC 66-20181. (Illus.). 1968. 32.95 (ISBN 0-521-04676-9); pap. 11.95x (ISBN 0-521-09531-X, 531). Cambridge U Pr.
Clive, Geoffrey. The Broken Icon: Intuitive Existentialism in Classical Russian Fiction. LC 70-182019. 228p. 1972. 7.95 o.s.i. (ISBN 0-02-526170-3). Macmillan.
Clive, H. P. Pierre Louys Eighteen Seventy to Nineteen Twenty-Five: A Biography. 1978. 37.50x (ISBN 0-19-815751-7). Oxford U Pr.
Clive, H. P., ed. see De Navarre, Marguerite.
Clive, John. The Last Liberator. 1981. pap. 2.75 (ISBN 0-440-15071-X). Dell.
Clive, John, ed. see Carlyle, Thomas.
Cloar, Carroll. Hostile Butterflies & Other Paintings. LC 77-7549. (Illus.). 216p. 1980. Repr. of 1977 ed. 39.95 (ISBN 0-87870-040-4). Memphis St Univ.
Clodd, Edward. Magic in Names, & in Other Things. LC 67-23906. 1968. Repr. of 1920 ed. 15.00 (ISBN 0-8103-3024-5). Gale.
--Myths & Dreams. LC 70-159918. 1971. Repr. of 1891 ed. 18.00 (ISBN 0-8103-3776-2). Gale.
--Story of the Alphabet. LC 70-123369. (Illus.). 1970. Repr. of 1938 ed. 15.00 (ISBN 0-8103-3855-6). Gale.
--Tom Tit Tot. LC 67-23907. 1968. Repr. of 1898 ed. 15.00 (ISBN 0-8103-3459-3). Gale.
Clogan, P. M., ed. Medievalia et Humanistica, Vols. 1-3 & 6-9. Incl. Vol. 1. LC 75-32451. 251p. 1976 (ISBN 0-521-21032-1); Vol. 2. Medieval & Renaissance Studies in Review. LC 75-32452. 223p (ISBN 0-521-21033-X); Vol. 3. Social Dimension in Medieval & Renaissance Studies. LC 75-32453. 328p (ISBN 0-521-21034-8); Vol. 6. LC 75-16872. 1979 (ISBN 0-521-20999-4); Vol. 7. Studies in Medieval & Renaissance Culture: Medieval Poetics. LC 76-12914. 1977 (ISBN 0-521-21331-2); Vol. 8. Studies in Medieval & Renaissance Culture Transformation & Continuity. LC 75-32451. 1978 (ISBN 0-521-21783-0); Vol. 9. LC 75-32451. 1979 (ISBN 0-521-22446-2). 36.00 ea. Cambridge U Pr.
Clogan, Paul M. Medieval & Renaissance Spirituality. LC 70-99227. (Medievalia et Humanistica: Studies in Medieval & Renaissance Culture Ser.: No. 4). 1973. 24.95 (ISBN 0-913904-00-7). Medieval.
--Medievalia et Humanistica: Studies in Medieval & Renaissance Culture. (New Ser.: No. 10). 1981. 25.00x (ISBN 0-8476-6944-0). Rowman.
Clogg, Mary Jo & Clogg, Richard. Greece. (World Bibliographical Ser.: No. 17). 1981. write for info. (ISBN 0-903450-30-5). ABC Clio.
Clogg, R. A Short History of Modern Greece. LC 78-72083. (Illus.). 1979. 29.95 (ISBN 0-521-22479-9); pap. 9.95 (ISBN 0-521-29517-3). Cambridge U Pr.
Clogg, Richard, jt. auth. see Clogg, Mary Jo.
Clogg, Richard, ed. Balkan Society in the Age of Greek Independence. (Studies in Russian & East European History). 1981. 29.00x (ISBN 0-389-20024-7). B&N.
Cloherty, John P. & Stark, Ann B., eds. Manual of Neonatal Care. (Spiral Manual Ser.). 1980. 12.95 (ISBN 0-316-14749-4). Little.
Cloke, Richard. Yvar, Prince of Rus. LC 80-80543. 700p. (Orig.). 1981. pap. 6.75 (ISBN 0-917458-08-7). Kent Pubns.
Clooney, Rosemary & Strait, Raymond. This for Remembrance. 1979. pap. 2.25 (ISBN 0-87216-680-5). Playboy Pbks.
Clopton, Beverly B. Her Honor the Judge. 240p. 1980. 15.95 (ISBN 0-8138-0565-1). Iowa St U Pr.
Cloquhoun, Archibald, tr. see Manzoni, Alessandro.
Close, A. The Romantic Approach to Don Quixote. LC 76-57097. 1978. 47.50 (ISBN 0-521-21490-4). Cambridge U Pr.
Close, Arthur C. & Colgate, Craig, Jr., eds. Washington Representatives. 4th ed. LC 76-21152. 1980. pap. 30.00x o.p. (ISBN 0-910416-33-8). Columbia Bks.
--Washington Representatives. 5th ed. LC 76-21152. 1981. pap. 35.00 (ISBN 0-910416-35-4). Columbia Bks.
Close, Arthur C., jt. ed. see Colgate, Craig, Jr.
Close, Charles M. & Frederick, Dean K. Modeling & Analysis of Dynamic Systems. LC 77-74421. (Illus.). 1978. text ed. 27.95 (ISBN 0-395-25040-4); sol. manual 2.05 (ISBN 0-395-25031-5). HM.
Close, Frank A., et al. Study Guide to Accompany Principles of Economics. 2nd ed. 1981. pap. text ed. 6.95x (ISBN 0-673-15494-7). Scott F.
--Study Guide to Accompany Principles of Macroeconomics. 2nd ed. 1981. pap. text ed. 4.95x (ISBN 0-673-15496-3). Scott F.
--Study Guide to Accompany Principles of Microeconomics. 2nd ed. 1981. pap. text ed. 4.95x (ISBN 0-673-15495-5). Scott F.
Close, Guy C., Jr. Work Improvement. LC 60-9616. (Illus.). 1960. text ed. 21.95 (ISBN 0-471-16071-7). Wiley.
Close, John J., et al. Team Teaching Experiments. Taylor, Monica, ed. (Education Ser.). 156p. 1974. pap. text ed. 10.75x (ISBN 0-85633-045-0, NFER). Humanities.
Close, K. J. & Yarwood, Y. Experimental Electronics for Students. 227p. cancelled (ISBN 0-470-26767-4). Halsted Pr.
Close, R. A. English As a Foreign Language. 3rd ed. 224p. (Orig.). 1981. pap. text ed. 10.95x (ISBN 0-04-425025-8, 2638). Allen Unwin.
Close, Reg A. A Reference Grammar for Students of English. (Illus.). 384p. 1975. pap. text ed. 9.00x (ISBN 0-582-52277-3). Longman.
Close, Robert. Europe Without Defense? 48 Hours That Could Change the Face of the World. LC 79-4693. (Pergamon Policy Studies). (Illus.). 22.00 (ISBN 0-08-023108-X). Pergamon.
Close, Sylvia. Birth Report. 356p. 1980. pap. text ed. 16.50x (ISBN 0-85633-191-0, NFER). Humanities.
--The Toddler & the New Baby. 128p. 1980. 14.50 (ISBN 0-7100-0522-9); pap. 6.95 (ISBN 0-7100-0523-7). Routledge & Kegan.
Closen, Ludwig Von see Von Closen, Ludwig.
Closs, A., ed. see Von Strassburg, Gottfried.
Closs, Hannah. Silent Tarn. 1962. 10.00 o.s.i. (ISBN 0-8149-0038-0). Vanguard.
Closurdo, Janette S., ed. Library Management 1979. 1980. pap. 8.50. SLA.
Clotfelter, Cecil F. Hunting & Fishing. LC 73-90569. (Spare Time Guides Ser.: No. 2). 1974. lib. bdg. 7.50 o.p. (ISBN 0-87287-079-0). Libs Unl.
Clotfelter, Cecil F. & Clotfelter, Mary L., eds. Camping & Backpacking: A Guide to Information Sources. LC 79-84659. (Sports, Games, & Pastimes Information Guide Ser.: Vol. 2). 1978. 30.00 (ISBN 0-8103-1437-1). Gale.
Clotfelter, Mary L., jt. ed. see Clotfelter, Cecil F.
Clouard, Henri & Leggewie, Robert, eds. Anthologie De la Litterature Francaise, 2 vols. 2nd ed. 860p. 1975. Vol. 1. pap. text ed. 12.95x (ISBN 0-19-501877-X); Vol. 2. pap. text ed. 12.95x (ISBN 0-19-501878-8). Oxford U Pr.
--French Writers of Today. (Illus.). 336p. (Fr.). 1965. pap. 7.95x (ISBN 0-19-500853-7). Oxford U Pr.
Cloud, Charles D., jt. auth. see Carver, Belford E.
Cloud, Henry. Crusader in Pink. (Illus.). 176p. (Orig.). 1981. pap. 2.50 (ISBN 0-553-14996-2). Bantam.
Cloudesley-Thompson, J. D. Terrestrial Environments. 262p. 1980. 29.00x (ISBN 0-85664-001-8, Pub. by Croom Helm England). State Mutual Bk.
Cloudesley-Thompson, J. L. Man & the Biology of Arid Zones. LC 77-20663. (Contemporary Biology Ser). 1978. pap. 17.95 (ISBN 0-8391-1192-4). Univ Park.
Cloudsley-Thompson, J. L. Animal Twilight, Man & Game in Eastern Africa. (Illus.). 1967. 10.50 (ISBN 0-85429-062-1). Dufour.
--Terrestrial Environments. LC 74-16704. 1975. pap. text ed. 14.95x (ISBN 0-470-26743-7). Halsted Pr.
--Tooth & Claw: Defensive Strategies in the Animal World. (Illus.). 252p. 1980. 22.50x (ISBN 0-460-04360-9, Pub. by J M Dent England). Biblio Dist.
Cloudsley-Thompson, S. J. Terrestrial Environments. LC 74-16704. 350p. 1975. text ed. 16.95x o.p. (ISBN 0-470-16080-2). Halsted Pr.
Clough, Arthur H. A Choice of Clough's Verse. Thorpe, Michael, ed. 1969. pap. 5.95 (ISBN 0-571-08685-3, Pub. by Faber & Faber). Merrimack Bk Serv.
Clough, Gordon, tr. see Svirsky, Grigory.
Clough, Ralph N. Deterrence & Defense in Korea: The Role of U. S. Forces. (Studies in Defense Policy). 1976. pap. 3.95 (ISBN 0-8157-1481-5). Brookings.
Clough, Ralph N., et al. The United States, China & Arms Control. 153p. 1975. 11.95 (ISBN 0-8157-1478-5); pap. 4.95 (ISBN 0-8157-1477-7). Brookings.
Clough, Shepard B. The Life That I've Lived. LC 80-5503. 297p. 1981. lib. bdg. 19.75 (ISBN 0-8191-1116-3); pap. text ed. 10.75 (ISBN 0-8191-1117-1). U Pr of Amer.
--The Rise & Fall of Civilization. 1951. pap. 7.50x (ISBN 0-231-08521-4, 21). Columbia U Pr.
Clough, Shepard B., et al. Economic History of Europe. LC 68-27379. (Documentary History of Western Civilization Ser). 1968. 15.00x o.s.i. (ISBN 0-8027-2005-6). Walker & Co.
Clough, T. H., ed. Sylloge of Coins of the British Isles: Vol. 26, Museums of East Anglia. 1980. 99.00x (ISBN 0-19-725991-X). Oxford U Pr.

Clouse, Robert G., ed. War: Four Christian Views. 220p. 1981. pap. 5.95 (ISBN 0-87784-801-7). Inter Varsity.

Clouser, Joseph L. Keller Plan for Self-Paced Study Using Masterton & Slowinski's Chemical Principles. 2nd ed. LC 76-20081. 1977. pap. text ed. 9.95 o.p. (ISBN 0-7216-2611-4). Saunders.

Clouser, K. Danner. Teaching Bioethics: Strategies, Problems & Resources. LC 80-10492. (The Teaching of Ethics Ser.). 77p. 1980. pap. 4.00 (ISBN 0-916558-07-X). Hastings Ctr Inst Soc.

Clouston, Brian, ed. Landscape Design with Plants. (Illus.). 1977. 50.00x (ISBN 0-434-36650-1). Intl Ideas.

Clouston, Brian & Stansfield, Kathy, eds. After the Elm. (Illus.). 186p. 1980. text ed. 24.50x (ISBN 0-8419-6107-7). Holmes & Meier.

Clouston, William A. Book of Noodles: Stories of Simpletons. LC 67-24351. 1969. Repr. of 1888 ed. 15.00 (ISBN 0-8103-3519-0). Gale.

--Popular Tales & Fictions, Their Migrations & Transformations, 2 Vols. LC 67-23920. 1968. Repr. of 1887 ed. Set. 54.00 (ISBN 0-8103-3460-7). Gale.

Clout, Hugh. Agriculture in France on the Eve of the Railway Age. (Illus.). 239p. 1980. 28.50x (ISBN 0-389-20017-4). B&N.

Clout, Hugh, jt. ed. see Salt, John.

Clout, Hugh D. Agriculture. (Studies in Contemporary Europe). (Illus.). 64p. (Orig.). 1971. pap. text ed. 2.50x (ISBN 0-333-12293-3). Humanities.

--The Geography of Post-War France: A Social & Economic Approach. 180p. 1972. text ed. 18.50 (ISBN 0-08-016765-9); pap. text ed. 7.75 (ISBN 0-08-016766-7). Pergamon.

--Regional Development in Western Europe. 432p. 1981. 16.50 (ISBN 0-471-27846-7, Pub. by Wiley-Interscience); pap. 7.50 (ISBN 0-471-27845-9). Wiley.

--Rural Geography. 1972. 18.00 (ISBN 0-08-017041-2); pap. 9.95 (ISBN 0-08-017042-0). Pergamon.

Clout, Hugh D. & Dennis, Richard J. Social Geography of Great Britain: An Introduction. (Pergamon Oxford Geographies). Date not set. 33.75 (ISBN 0-08-021802-4); pap. 14.50 (ISBN 0-08-021801-6). Pergamon.

Cloutier, David. My Grandfather's House: Tlingit Songs of Death & Sorrow. LC 80-15499. (Illus.). 40p. (Orig.). 1980. pap. 3.00 (ISBN 0-914974-26-2). Holmgangers.

--Spirit Spirit: Shaman Songs. rev. enl. ed. (Illus.). 100p. 1980. pap. 4.50 (ISBN 0-914278-30-4). Copper Beech.

--Tongue & Thunder. (Illus.). 64p. (Orig.). 1980. pap. 4.50x (ISBN 0-914278-32-0). Copper Beech.

--Tongue & Thunder. (Illus., Orig.). 1980. pap. 4.50 (ISBN 0-914278-32-0). Cooper Beech.

Cloutier, David, tr. see Esteban, Claude.

Cloutier, James. Orygone III; or, Everything You Always Wanted to Know About Oregon but Were Afraid to Find Out. LC 77-90955. (Illus., Orig.). 1977. pap. 4.95 o.s.i. (ISBN 0-918966-02-7). Image West.

--Orygone, Too or, a Nice Place to Visit but You Wouldn't Want to Get Stuck There. LC 80-83718. (Illus.). 160p. (Orig.). (gr. 4 up). 1980. pap. 4.95 (ISBN 0-918966-05-1). Image West.

--This Day in Oregon. LC 80-83719. (Illus.). 128p. (gr. 4 up). 1981. pap. 6.95 (ISBN 0-918966-06-X). Image West.

Clover, Helen, ed. see Lanfranc.

Clover, Vernon T. & Balsley, Howard L. Business Research Methods. LC 78-50046. (Management Ser.). 1979. text ed. 20.95 (ISBN 0-88244-164-7). Grid Pub.

Clovis, Albert I., et al, eds. Consumer Protection: A Symposium. LC 72-6757. 1972. Repr. of 1968 ed. lib. bdg. 15.00 (ISBN 0-306-70524-9). Da Capo.

Clow, W. Bible Reader's Encyclopedia & Concordance. (Illus.). 6.95 (ISBN 0-00-512008-X, RT1, Pub. by Collins Pubs). World Bible.

Cloward, R. A., jt. ed. see Stein, Herman D.

Cloward, Richard A. & Ohlin, Lloyd E. Delinquency & Opportunity: A Theory of Delinquent Gangs. LC 60-10892. 1966. 17.95 (ISBN 0-02-905600-4); pap. text ed. 5.95 (ISBN 0-02-905590-3). Free Pr.

Clowdus, Bernard F., 2nd, jt. auth. see Steigmann, Frederick.

Clower, Robert W. & Due, John F. Microeconomics. 1972. text ed. 12.95x o.p. (ISBN 0-256-00453-6). Irwin.

Clowes, William. A Profitable & Necessarie Booke of Observations. LC 73-171740. (English Experience Ser.: No. 366). 1971. Repr. of 1596 ed. 33.50 (ISBN 90-221-0366-8). Walter J Johnson.

Cloyd, E. L. James Burnett, Lord Monboddo. (Illus.). 212p. 1972. 15.25x o.p. (ISBN 0-19-812437-6). Oxford U Pr.

Cloyd, Frances, ed. see National Association of College & University Food Services.

Club Managers Association & Duncan, Horace G. Club Management Operations. 320p. (Orig.). 1980. text ed. 19.95 (ISBN 0-8403-2188-0). Kendall-Hunt.

Clubb, Jerome, et al. Partisan Realignment: Voters, Parties, & Government in American History. LC 80-16474. (Sage Library of Social Research: Vol. 108). 320p. 1980. 18.00 (ISBN 0-8039-1445-8); pap. 8.95 (ISBN 0-8039-1446-6). Sage.

Clubb, Jerome M. Ecological Data in Comparative Research. (Reports & Papers in the Social Sciences Ser., No. 25). (Orig). 1970. pap. 2.50 (ISBN 92-3-100845-5, U174, UNESCO). Unipub.

Clubb, Louise G., tr. see Porta, Giambattista Della.

Clubb, O. Edmund. China & Russia: The Great Game. LC 72-155362. (Illus.). 1970. 22.50x (ISBN 0-231-02740-0); pap. 9.00x (ISBN 0-231-08305-X, 138). Columbia U Pr.

--Communism in China As Reported from Hankow in 1932. LC 68-56634. (Illus.). 1968. 17.50x (ISBN 0-231-03209-9). Columbia U Pr.

--Twentieth Century China. 3rd ed. 1978. 24.00x (ISBN 0-231-04518-2); pap. 9.00x (ISBN 0-231-04519-0). Columbia U Pr.

--The Witness & I. LC 74-11385. 240p. 1975. 16.00x (ISBN 0-231-03859-3). Columbia U Pr.

Clubbe, John, ed. see Hood, Thomas.

Cluett, Christopher, et al. Individual & Community Response to Energy Facility Siting: An Annotated Bibliography. (Public Adminstration Ser.: Bibliography P-493). 50p. 1980. pap. 5.50. Vance Biblios.

Cluff, E. Dale. Microforms. Duane, James E., ed. LC 80-21457. (The Instructional Media Library: Vol. 7). (Illus.). 104p. 1981. 13.95 (ISBN 0-87778-167-2). Educ Tech Pubns.

Cluff, Leighton E., et al. Clinical Problems with Drugs. (Major Problems in Internal Medicine Ser., Vol. 5). (Illus.). 308p. 1975. text ed. 18.00 (ISBN 0-7216-2613-0). Saunders.

Clugston, Donald. All That Money & No Cash. 128p. 1981. 7.50 (ISBN 0-682-49678-2). Exposition.

Clugston, George A. A Looking Glasse for London & England by Thomas Lodge & Robert Greene: A Critical Edition. Orgel, Stephen, ed. LC 79-3098. (Renaissance Drama Second Ser.). 300p. 1980. lib. bdg. 33.00 (ISBN 0-8240-4482-7). Garland Pub.

Clugston, Richard. Estimating Manufacturing Costs. LC 78-185563. (Illus.). 214p. 1971. 14.95 (ISBN 0-8436-0811-0). CBI Pub.

Cluley, J. C. Programming for Minicomputers. LC 77-83270. (Computer Systems Engineering Ser.). 1978. 19.50x (ISBN 0-8448-1259-5). Crane-Russak Co.

Cluley, John C. Computer Interfacing & On-Line Operation. LC 74-16952. (Computer Systems Engineering Ser.). (Illus.). 190p. 1975. 19.50x (ISBN 0-8448-0567-X). Crane-Russak Co.

Clulow, F. W. Colour: Its Principles & Their Applications. 1972. 16.95 o.p. (ISBN 0-85242-098-6, Pub. by Fountain). Morgan.

Clum, John M. Ridgely Torrence. (U. S. Authors Ser.: No. 212). lib. bdg. 10.95 (ISBN 0-8057-0740-9). Twayne.

Clum, Woodworth. Apache Agent: The Story of John P. Clum. LC 77-14135. (Illus.). 1978. 13.95x (ISBN 0-8032-0967-3); pap. 4.25 (ISBN 0-8032-5886-0, BB 654, Bison). U of Nebr Pr.

Clumpner, Mick. Outlaws' Gold. 224p. (Orig.). 1981. pap. 1.95 (ISBN 0-89083-712-0). Zebra.

Clumpner, Mike. The Broncbuster. 220p. (Orig.). 1980. pap. 1.95 (ISBN 0-89083-671-X). Zebra.

Clune, H. W. O'Shaughnessy's Cafe. 1969. 6.95 o.s.i. (ISBN 0-02-526370-6). Macmillan.

Clunie, J. G. & Hayman, W. K., eds. Symposium on Comples Analysis. LC 73-92787. (London Mathematical Society Lecture Note Ser.: No. 12). 200p. 1974. 21.50 (ISBN 0-521-20452-6). Cambridge U Pr.

Clunn, Patricia A., ed. see Payne, Dorris B.

Clure, Beth & Rumsey, Helen. I Can Do It: Manipulative Books. Incl. Come with Me (ISBN 0-8372-2169-2); Can You Guess (ISBN 0-8372-2170-6); What's Inside (ISBN 0-8372-2171-4); A Sailor Said (ISBN 0-8372-2172-2); Matching Hands (ISBN 0-8372-2173-0); Surprise Boxes (ISBN 0-8372-2174-9); What Can It Be (ISBN 0-8372-2175-7); Mirror Magic (ISBN 0-8372-2176-5); Things I Like to Do (ISBN 0-8372-0367-8); Me (ISBN 0-8372-0363-5); Cowboy Can (ISBN 0-8372-0372-4); Where Is Home (ISBN 0-8372-0364-3); Through the Day (ISBN 0-8372-0366-X); Telling Tails (ISBN 0-8372-0365-1). (Illus.). (gr. k-2). 1976. text ed. 6.24 ea.; text ed. 75.00 set o.p. (ISBN 0-8372-3721-1, 2168); tchr's guide 6.00 (ISBN 0-8372-9130-5). Bowmar-Noble.

Manipulative Books. (I Can Do It Ser.). (ps-2). 1969. set & tchrs. guide avail. o.p. (ISBN 0-685-28637-1); resource bk. & tchrs. guide 6.00 o.p. (ISBN 0-8372-0703-7). Bowmar-Noble.

Clurman, David. The Business Condominium: A New Form of Business Property Ownership. LC 73-10089. (Real Estate for Professional Practitioners Ser.). 185p. 1973. 28.95 (ISBN 0-471-16129-2). Wiley.

Clurman, David & Hebard, Edna L. Condominiums & Cooperatives. LC 73-106012. (Real Estate for Professional Practitioners Ser.). 1970. 31.50 (ISBN 0-471-16130-6, Pub. by Wiley-Interscience). Wiley.

Clurman, Harold. The Divine Pastime: Theatre Essays. LC 73-10551. 352p. 1974. 7.95 o.s.i. (ISBN 0-02-526150-9). Macmillan.

--Ibsen. (Masters of World Literature). 1977. 12.95 (ISBN 0-02-526420-6). Macmillan.

--On Directing. 320p. 1972. 12.95 (ISBN 0-02-526410-9). Macmillan.

--On Directing. (Illus.). 336p. 1974. pap. 6.95 (ISBN 0-02-013350-2, Collier). Macmillan.

Clurman, Harold, ed. Nine Plays of the Modern Theater. LC 79-52121. 912p. 1981. pap. text ed. 11.95 (ISBN 0-394-17411-9, E 773, Ever). Grove.

Clurman, Harold, ed. see Miller, Arthur.

Clute, P. D. The Legal Aspects of Prisons & Jails. 248p. 1980. 21.75- (ISBN 0-398-04005-2); pap. 14.95 (ISBN 0-398-04006-0). C C Thomas.

Clutten, Cecil, ed. Britten's Old Clocks & Watches & Their Makers. 8th ed. (Illus.). 1973. 50.00 (ISBN 0-525-93140-6). Dutton.

Clutterbock, Richard. Guerillas & Terrorists. 1977. 10.95 (ISBN 0-571-11027-4, Pub. by Faber & Faber). Merrimack Bk Serv.

Clutterbuck, Richard. Guerrillas & Terrorists. LC 80-83219. 125p. 1980. 12.00x (ISBN 0-8214-0590-X); pap. 5.95x (ISBN 0-8214-0592-6). Ohio U Pr.

Clutton, Cecil & Daniels, George. Watches: A Complete History of the Technical & Decorative Development of the Watch. 3rd rev. & enlarg. ed. (Illus.). 312p. 1979. 92.50 (ISBN 0-85667-05?-8, Pub by Sotheby Parke Bernet England). Biblio Dist.

Clutton, Cecil, jt. ed. see Daniels, George.

Clutton, Cecil, et al. Batsford Guide to Vintage Cars. 1976. 14.95 o.p. (ISBN 0-686-63854-9, Pub. by Batsford England). David & Charles.

Clutton-Brock, T. H. & Harvey, Paul H., eds. Readings in Sociobiology. LC 77-22283. (Illus.). 1978. text ed. 23.95x (ISBN 0-7167-0191-X); pap. text ed. 11.95x (ISBN 0-7167-0190-1). W H Freeman.

Cluysenaar, Anne, ed. see Singer, Burns.

Clyde, Paul H. & Beers, Burton F. Far East: A History of Western Impacts & Eastern Responses (1830 - 1975) 6th ed. (Illus.). 576p. 1976. 19.95 (ISBN 0-13-302968-9). P-H.

Clydesdale, F. M., jt. auth. see Francis, F. G.

Clydesdale, Fergus. Food Science & Nutrition: Current Issues & Answers. (Illus.). 1979. ref. 16.95 (ISBN 0-13-323162-3). P-H.

Clydesdale, Fergus S. & Francis, F. J. Food, Nutrition & You. (Illus.). 1977. lib. bdg. 12.95 (ISBN 0-13-323048-1); pap. text ed. 8.95 (ISBN 0-13-323030-9). P-H.

Clyman, Toby, tr. see Bitsilli, Peter.

Clymer. Luke Was There. (gr. 3-5). pap. 0.95 o.s.i. (ISBN 0-686-58477-X, 29790). Archway.

Clymer, Eleanor. The Get-Away Car. (gr. 4-7). 1978. PLB 8.95 (ISBN 0-525-30470-3). Dutton.

--The Get Away Car. 144p. (gr. 3-6). 1981. pap. 1.75 (ISBN 0-553-15092-8). Bantam.

--A Search for Two Bad Mice. LC 80-12789. (Illus.). 80p. (gr. 2-5). 1980. 7.95 (ISBN 0-689-30771-3). Atheneum.

Clymer Publications. Bultaco Service Repair Handbook: 125-370cc, Through 1977. (Illus.). 1977. pap. 9.95 (ISBN 0-89287-174-1, M303). Clymer Pubns.

--Corvette V-Eight, Nineteen Fifty-Five to Nineteen Sixty-Two: Complete Owner's Handbook. (Illus.). 1961. pap. 7.95 (ISBN 0-89287-247-0, A141). Clymer Pubns.

--Ford Fairmont, 1978-1979: Shop Manual. Jorgensen, Eric, ed. (Illus.). 328p. (Orig.). 1980. 10.95 (ISBN 0-89287-307-8, A174). Clymer Pubns.

--Harley-Davidson Service--Repair Handbook: Sportster Series, 1959-1980. Robinson, Jeff, ed. (Illus.). 1978. pap. 9.95 (ISBN 0-89287-126-1, M419). Clymer Pubns.

--Honda Service-Repair Handbook: 750cc Fours, 1969-1978. Jorgensen, Eric, ed. (Illus.). 1978. pap. 9.95 (ISBN 0-89287-167-9, M341). Clymer Pubns.

--Jeep Service, Repair Handbook: Covers Willy-Overland Model MB & Ford Model GPW. (Illus.). 1971. pap. 7.95 (ISBN 0-89287-250-0, A162). Clymer Pubns.

--Kawasaki 900 & 1000cc Fours, 1973-1979: Service, Repair, Performance. Robinson, Jeff, ed. (Illus.). 1978. pap. 8.50 (ISBN 0-89287-321-3, M359). Clymer Pubns.

--Montesa Service-Repair Handbook: 123-360cc Singles, 1965-1975. (Illus.). 1975. pap. text ed. 8.50 o.p. (ISBN 0-89287-020-6, M356). Clymer Pubns.

--Mustng II Service Repair Handbook All Models, 1974-1978. (Illus., Orig.). 1979. pap. text ed. 10.95 (ISBN 0-89287-119-9, A169). Clymer Pubns.

--Porsche Owners Handbook & Service Manual: Covers All Porsche Models up to 356c. (Illus.). 1967. pap. 7.95 (ISBN 0-89287-251-9, A181). Clymer Pubns.

--Toyota Service Repair Handbook: Corolla & Carina, 1968-78. 4th ed. 1978. pap. 9.95 o.p. (ISBN 0-89287-232-2, A198). Clymer Pubns.

--Yamaha Service Repair Handbook: 80-175cc Enduro & Motocross, 1968-1978. (Illus.). 1979. pap. text ed. 9.95 (ISBN 0-89287-235-7, M410). Clymer Pubns.

--Yamaha: 250-400cc, 2-Stroke Twins 1965-1978, Service, Repair, Performance. 3rd ed. Jorgensen, Eric, ed. (Illus.). 1978. pap. 9.95 (ISBN 0-89287-283-7, M401). Clymer Pubns.

--Yamaha: 250-500cc Enduro & Motocross, 1968-78, Service, Repair, Performance. 3rd ed. Jorgensen, Eric, ed. (Illus.). 1978. pap. 9.95 (ISBN 0-89287-276-4, M415). Clymer Pubns.

Clymer Publications, ed. Corvair Owners Handbook of Maintenance & Repair: 1960-1965. (Illus.). 1965. pap. 7.95 (ISBN 0-89287-246-2, A140). Clymer Pubns.

--Datsun Sports Car Handbook: 1600 & 2000cc. (Illus.). 1970. pap. 11.00 o.p. (ISBN 0-89287-248-9, A150). Clymer Pubns.

--Falcon Comet Fairlane Handbook of Maintenance & Repair: 1960-1965 Models. (Illus.). 1965. pap. 7.95 (ISBN 0-89287-249-7, A160). Clymer Pubns.

--Sunbeam Owners Handbook of Maintenance & Repair. (Illus.). 1965. pap. 8.95 (ISBN 0-89287-253-5, A189). Clymer Pubns.

--Triumph Spitfire Owner's Handbook: 1962-1970. (Illus.). 1971. pap. 8.95 (ISBN 0-89287-254-3, A215). Clymer Pubns.

Clymer Publications, ed. see Page, Victor W.

Clymer Publications Staff. Ducati Service-Repair Handbook: 160, 250,350, 450cc, Through 1974. (Illus.). 136p. 1974. pap. text ed. 9.95 (ISBN 0-89287-004-4, M306). Clymer Pubns.

--Honda Service-Repair Handbook: 250-305cc Twins, All Years. (Illus.). 184p. 1971. pap. text ed. 9.95 (ISBN 0-89287-010-9, M331). Clymer Pubns.

--Volvo Service-Repair Handbook: 122s Series & P 1800, All Years. (Illus.). 224p. 1972. pap. text ed. 10.95 (ISBN 0-89287-066-4, A220). Clymer Pubns.

Clymer Pubns. Suzuki: 380-750cc Triples, 1972-1977 Service, Repair, Maintenance. (Illus.). 1977. pap. 9.95 (ISBN 0-89287-285-3, M368). Clymer Pubns.

Clymer, Reuben S. Alchemy & the Alchemists, 3 vols. LC 79-8603. Repr. of 1907 ed. Set. 79.50 (ISBN 0-404-18457-X). AMS Pr.

Clyne, Densey. The Garden Jungle. 184p. 1980. 27.95x (ISBN 0-00-216411-6, Pub. by W Collins Australia). Intl Schol Bk Serv.

Clyne, Douglas G. A Concise Textbook for Midwives. 5th ed. (Illus.). 528p. 1980. pap. 17.95 (ISBN 0-571-18018-3, Pub. by Faber & Faber). Merrimack Bk Serv.

--A Concise Textbook for Midwives. 4th ed. 1975. pap. text ed. 11.50 o.p. (ISBN 0-571-04845-5, Pub. by Faber & Faber). Merrimack Bk Serv.

Clyne, Patricia. Ghostly Animals of America. LC 77-6487. (Illus.). (gr. 5 up). 1977. 5.95 (ISBN 0-396-07465-0). Dodd.

Clyne, Patricia E. The Curse of Camp Gray Owl. LC 80-2783. 176p. (gr. 5 up). 1981. PLB 7.95 (ISBN 0-396-07922-9). Dodd.

Clynes, Manfred, Dr. Sentics: The Touch of Emotions. LC 74-17608. 1978. pap. 3.95 (ISBN 0-385-08622-9, Anch). Doubleday.

Co, Francesco Dal see Tafuri, Manfredo & Dal Co, Francesco.

Coad, Brian W., jt. auth. see McAllister, D. E.

Coad, Oral S. see Gabriel, Ralph H.

Coakley, Carroll B., ed. Distributive Education Teacher-Coordinators' Handbook. LC 77-190664. 190p. 1972. pap. text ed. 4.25x o.p. (ISBN 0-8134-1467-9, 1467). Interstate.

Coakley, Davis. Acute Geriatric Medicine. 290p. 1981. pap. 27.50 (ISBN 0-88416-354-7). PSG Pub.

Coakley, Davis, ed. Acute Geriatric Medicine. 256p. 1980. 30.00 (Pub. by Croom Helm England). State Mutual Bk.

Coakley, Jay J. Sport in Society: Issues & Controversies. LC 77-23062. (Illus.). 1978. pap. text ed. 11.50 (ISBN 0-8016-0991-7). Mosby.

Coakley, Mary L. Sex, Sisterhood, & Self-Delusion: What Happened to Women's Magazines? 1980. 10.95 o.p. (ISBN 0-87000-452-2). Arlington Hse.

Coal Age Magazine. Coal Age Operating Handbook of Underground Mining, Vol. II. 2nd ed. (Coal Age Ser.). (Illus.). 430p. 1980. 19.50 (ISBN 0-07-011461-7, P&RB). McGraw.

Coale, Robert D., jt. auth. see Brost, Fred B.

Coale, Samuel. John Cheever. LC 77-4829. (Modern Literature Ser.). 1977. 10.95 (ISBN 0-8044-2126-9). Ungar.

Coan, Eugene. James Graham Cooper: Pioneer Western Naturalist. LC 80-52313. (GEM Books-Historical & Natural History Ser.). (Illus.). 210p. (Orig.). 1981. pap. 11.95 (ISBN 0-89301-071-5). U Pr of Idaho.

Coan, James S. Advanced BASIC: Applications & Problems. Haag, J., ed. (Computer Programming Ser.). 1976. text ed. 13.25x (ISBN 0-8104-5856-X); pap. text ed. 10.75x (ISBN 0-8104-5855-1). Hayden.

--Basic BASIC: An Introduction to Computer Programming in BASIC Language. 2nd ed. (gr. 10 up). 1978. text ed. 13.95x (ISBN 0-8104-5107-7); pap. text ed. 10.50x (ISBN 0-8104-5106-9); tchrs. guide 1.40 (ISBN 0-8104-5108-5). Hayden.

Coan, Otis W. & Lillard, Richard G. America in Fiction: An Annotated List of Novels That Interpret Aspects of Life in the United States, Canada, & Mexico. 6th ed. Date not set. price not set. Pacific Bks.

Coan, Richard W. Hero, Artist, Sage, or Saint? LC 76-57751. 1977. 22.50x (ISBN 0-231-03806-2); pap. 9.00x (ISBN 0-231-08355-6). Columbia U Pr.

--The Optimal Personality: An Empirical & Theoretical Analysis. LC 74-11498. 216p. 1974. 17.50x (ISBN 0-231-03807-0). Columbia U Pr.

Coastal Engineering International Conference, 11th, London, Sept. 1968. Coastal Engineering: Proceedings. American Society of Civil Engineers, compiled By. 1624p. 1969. pap. 39.50 (ISBN 0-87262-013-1). Am Soc Civil Eng.

Coastal Engineering International Conference, 12th, September, 1970. Coastal Engineering: Proceedings. American Society of Civil Engineers, compiled By. 2484p. 1971. pap. text ed. 59.00 o.p. (ISBN 0-87262-028-X). Am Soc Civil Eng.

Coastal Engineering International Conference, 16th, Hamburg, Germany, Aug. 1978. Coastal Engineering: Proceedings, 3 vols. American Society of Civil Engineers, compiled By. 3096p. 1979. pap. text ed. 110.00 (ISBN 0-87262-190-1). Am Soc Civil Eng.

Coastal Resources Center. An Environmental Study of a Nuclear Plant at Charlestown: Rhode Island. (Marine Technical Report Ser.: No. 33). 1974. pap. 5.00 (ISBN 0-938412-07-8). URI MAS.

Coates, Austin. Numerology. 1980. pap. 3.95 (ISBN 0-8065-0499-4). Lyle Stuart.

Coates, B. E., et al. Geography & Inequality. (Illus.). 1977. text ed. 29.95x (ISBN 0-19-874069-7); pap. text ed. 9.95x (ISBN 0-19-874070-0). Oxford U Pr.

Coates, C. R. Developing a Commanding Personality. LC 79-23634. 180p. 1981. 14.95 (ISBN 0-88229-414-8). Nelson-Hall.

Coates, D. The Labor Party & the Struggle for Socialism. LC 74-19526. 272p. 1975. 36.00 (ISBN 0-521-20740-1); pap. 11.50x (ISBN 0-521-09939-0). Cambridge U Pr.

Coates, D. S. Industrial Catering Management. 1971. 13.95x o.p. (ISBN 0-8464-0508-3). Beekman Pubs.

Coates, Donald, ed. Coastal Geomorphology. (Binghamton Symposia in Geomorphology International Ser.: No. 3). (Illus.). 416p. 1980. text ed. 20.00x (ISBN 0-04-551038-5, 2506). Allen Unwin.

Coates, Donald R. Environmental Geology. LC 80-21272. 736p. 1980. text ed. 23.00 (ISBN 0-471-06379-7). Wiley.

Coates, Donald R., ed. Environmental Geomorphology & Landscape Conservation, 3 vols. Incl. Vol. 1. Prior to 1900. 1972. 43.50 (ISBN 0-12-786241-2); Vol. 2. Urban Areas. 464p. 1974. 39.00 (ISBN 0-12-786242-0); Vol. 3. Non-Urban Regions. 496p. 1973. 43.50 (ISBN 0-12-786243-9). LC 72-77882. (Benchmark Papers in Geology Ser.). (Illus.). Acad Pr.

--Geomorphology & Engineering. (Binghamton Symposia in Geomorphology: International Ser.: No. 7). (Illus.). 384p. 1980. text ed. 30.00x (ISBN 0-04-551040-7, 2584). Allen Unwin.

Coates, Donald R. & Vitek, John D., eds. Thresholds in Geomorphology. (Binghamton Symposia in Geomorphology Ser.: Vol. 9). (Illus.). 512p. (Orig.). 1980. text ed. 35.00x (ISBN 0-04-551033-4, 2393). Allen Unwin.

Coates, Felicia & Howle, Harriet. The Texas Monthly Guidebooks: Houston. 3rd ed. 288p. 1980. pap. 5.95 (ISBN 0-932012-12-4). Texas Month Pr.

Coates, Gary. Resettling America: Energy, Ecology, & Community. (Illus.). 400p. 1981. pap. 10.95 (ISBN 0-931790-06-9). Brick Hse Pub.

Coates, J. B. Coates Brothers: A History, 1877-1977. (Illus.). 103p. 1980. 28.50 (ISBN 0-913720-12-7). Sandstone.

Coates, Margaret K. Perennials for the Western Garden. (Illus.). 1976. 9.95 o.p. (ISBN 0-87108-088-5). Pruett.

Coates, R. F. Modern Communication Systems. (Illus.). 1976. pap. text ed. 17.95x (ISBN 0-333-18560-9). Scholium Intl.

Coates, Robert M. The Outlaw Years: The History of the Land Pirates of the Natchez Trace. LC 74-1087. (Illus.). 307p. 1974. Repr. of 1930 ed. 24.00 (ISBN 0-8103-3961-7). Gale.

Coates, S. D., et al, eds. Electronic Maintenance, Vol. 1. (Engineering Craftsmen: No. J4). (Illus.). 1969. spiral bdg. 24.95x (ISBN 0-85083-027-3). Intl Ideas.

Coates, Sanford E. Psychical Research & Spiritualism. (Illus.). 1980. deluxe ed. 49.75 (ISBN 0-89920-006-0). Am Classical Coll Pr.

Coates, Thomas J., jt. auth. see Goodwin, Dwight L.

Coatesville-Jefferson Conference on Addiction, 1st, October 1977. Addiction Research & Treatment Converging Trends: Proceedings. Gottheil, E. L., et al, eds. LC 78-23703. 1978. 18.25 (ISBN 0-08-023025-3). Pergamon.

Coats, B. E. & Tawstron, E. M. Regional Variations in Britain: Studies in Economic & Social Geography. 1972. 40.00 (ISBN 0-7134-2103-7, Pub. by Batsford England). David & Charles.

Coats, Warren L. & Khatkhate, Deena R., Jr., eds. Money & Monetary Policy in Less Developed Countries: A Survey of Issues & Evidence. LC 79-42703. (Illus.). 834p. 1980. 105.00 (ISBN 0-08-024041-0); pap. 25.00 (ISBN 0-08-024042-9). Pergamon.

Coatsworth, jt. auth. see Beston.

Coatsworth, Elizabeth. Alice-All-By-Herself. (Illus.). (gr. 4-6). 1966. 4.95g o.s.i. (ISBN 0-02-719060-9). Macmillan.

--All-of-Sudden Susan. LC 74-6200. (Illus.). 80p. (gr. 3-5). 1974. 7.95g (ISBN 0-02-722610-7, 72261). Macmillan.

--Away Goes Sally. (Illus.). (gr. 4-6). 1934. 6.95g o.s.i. (ISBN 0-02-719300-4). Macmillan.

--Bess & the Sphinx. (Illus.). (gr. 3-5). 1967. 6.95 (ISBN 0-02-719420-5). Macmillan.

--Boy with the Parrot. (Illus.). (gr. 4-6). 1964. 3.95g o.s.i. (ISBN 0-02-721640-3). Macmillan.

--The Cat & the Captain. LC 73-6041. (Illus.). 64p. (gr. 1-3). 1974. 6.95 (ISBN 0-02-719070-6). Macmillan.

--The Cat Who Went to Heaven. LC 58-10917. (gr. 3-6). 1972. pap. 2.95 (ISBN 0-02-042580-5, Collier). Macmillan.

--Dancing Tom. (Illus.). (gr. 3-8). 1967. 4.25g o.s.i. (ISBN 0-02-720100-7). Macmillan.

--Down Half the World. (Illus.). (gr. 7 up). 1968. 4.50g o.s.i. (ISBN 0-02-721470-2). Macmillan.

--Fair American. (Illus.). (gr. 3-7). 1968. 3.95g o.s.i. (ISBN 0-02-720270-4). Macmillan.

--First Adventure. (Illus.). (gr. 4-6). 1950. 3.50 o.s.i. (ISBN 0-02-720380-8). Macmillan.

--Five Bushel Farm. (Illus.). (gr. 4-6). 1939. 4.95g o.s.i. (ISBN 0-02-720480-4). Macmillan.

--Fox Friend. (Illus.). (gr. k-2). 1966. 4.25g o.s.i. (ISBN 0-02-720510-X). Macmillan.

--George & Red. LC 69-11293. (Illus.). (gr. 4-6). 1969. 3.95g o.s.i. (ISBN 0-02-720260-7). Macmillan.

--Golden Horseshoe. LC 35-18415. (Illus.). (gr. 4-6). 1968. Repr. of 1935 ed. 4.95g o.s.i. (ISBN 0-02-720590-8). Macmillan.

--Grandmother Cat & the Hermit. LC 70-99786. (Illus.). (gr. 3-5). 1970. 4.95g o.s.i. (ISBN 0-02-720580-0). Macmillan.

--Jock's Island. (Viking Seafarer Ser). (Illus.). (gr. 7 up). 1969. pap. 0.65 o.p. (ISBN 0-670-05026-1, Puffin). Penguin.

--Littlest House. (Illus.). (gr. 3-5). 1967. 4.25g o.s.i. (ISBN 0-02-721050-2). Macmillan.

--Marra's World. LC 75-9520. (Illus.). 80p. (gr. 3-5). 1975. 7.25 (ISBN 0-688-80007-6); PLB 6.96 (ISBN 0-688-84007-8). Greenwillow.

--Poems. (Illus.). (gr. 4-6). 1957. 4.95g o.s.i. (ISBN 0-02-721490-7). Macmillan.

--Pure Magic. LC 72-92435. (Illus.). 96p. (gr. 3-6). 1973. 7.95 (ISBN 0-02-721500-8, 72150). Macmillan.

--Ronnie & the Chief's Son. (Illus.). (gr. 4-6). 1962. 6.95 (ISBN 0-02-721600-4). Macmillan.

--Sod House. 1967. 7.95 (ISBN 0-02-721690-X). Macmillan.

--Sword of the Wilderness. (Illus.). (gr. 7 up). 1966. 4.95g o.s.i. (ISBN 0-02-721910-0). Macmillan.

--Under the Green Willow. LC 73-123131. (Illus.). (gr. k-2). 1971. 4.50 o.s.i. (ISBN 0-02-722600-X). Macmillan.

Cobb, A. Beatrix. Medical & Psychological Aspects of Disability. (Amer. Lec. Social & Rehabilitation Psychology Ser.). (Illus.). 384p. 1977. 19.75 (ISBN 0-398-02653-X). C C Thomas.

Cobb, Alice, jt. auth. see Fahs, Sophia L.

Cobb, Betsy & Cobb, Hubbard. City People's Guide to Country Living. LC 72-85757. 224p. 1973. pap. 1.50 o.s.i. (ISBN 0-02-079360-X, Collier). Macmillan.

Cobb, Boughton, Jr. Fiberglass Boats. (Illus.). 1978. 9.95 (ISBN 0-87165-015-0, Yachting-Zd). Ziff-Davis Pub.

Cobb, Buell E., Jr. The Sacred Harp: A Tradition & Its Music. LC 76-12680. 248p. 1978. 12.50x (ISBN 0-8203-0426-3). U of Ga Pr.

Cobb, Carl W. Antonio Machado. (World Authors Ser.: Spain: No. 161). lib. bdg. 10.95 (ISBN 0-8057-2556-3). Twayne.

--Contemporary Spanish Poetry: 1898-1963. LC 75-23016. (World Authors Ser.: Spain: No. 373). 1976. lib. bdg. 9.95 (ISBN 0-8057-6202-7). Twayne.

--Federico Garcia Lorca. (World Authors Ser.: Spain: No. 23). 1968. lib. bdg. 9.95 (ISBN 0-8057-2544-X). Twayne.

Cobb, Charles E. Christian Counsellor. 3.00 o.p. (ISBN 0-89225-062-3). Gospel Advocate.

Cobb, David A. New Hampshire Maps to Nineteen Hundred: An Annotated Cartobibliography. LC 78-63588. 1981. text ed. 9.00x (ISBN 0-87451-166-6). U Pr of New Eng.

Cobb, H. How to Paint Anything. 1972. 6.95 o.s.i. (ISBN 0-02-526360-9). Macmillan.

Cobb, Henry V. The Forecast of Fulfillment: A Review of Research on Predictive Assessment of the Adult Retarded for Social & Vocational Adjustment. LC 72-3084. (Illus.). 176p. 1972. 5.00x (ISBN 0-8077-1168-3). Tchrs Coll.

Cobb, Hubbard, jt. auth. see Cobb, Betsy.

Cobb, Irvin S. Exit Laughing. LC 73-19798. 1974. Repr. of 1941 ed. 28.00 (ISBN 0-8103-3687-1). Gale.

Cobb, J. Stanley & Phillips, Bruce F., eds. The Biology & Management of Lobsters: Vol. 1, Physiology & Behavior. LC 79-6803. 1980. 55.00 (ISBN 0-12-177401-5). Acad Pr.

--The Biology & Management of Lobsters: Vol. 2, Ecology & Management. LC 79-6803. 1980. 45.00 (ISBN 0-12-177402-3) (ISBN 0-686-65861-2). Acad Pr.

Cobb, John B., Jr. The Structure of Christian Existence. (Library of Contempory Theology). 1979. pap. 6.95 (ISBN 0-8164-2229-X). Crossroad NY.

--To Pray or Not to Pray. (Prayer in My Life Ser.: Ser. I). 1974. pap. 1.00x (ISBN 0-8358-0310-4). Upper Room.

Cobb, John B., Jr. & Schroeder, W. Widick, eds. Process Philosophy & Social Thought. LC 80-70781. (Studies in Religion & Society). 250p. 1981. 19.95x (ISBN 0-913348-18-X). Ctr Sci Study.

Cobb, John B., Jr., jt. ed. see Griffin, David R.

Cobb, John W., III. Seagull Wind. LC 80-80556. (Illus.). 64p. (Orig.). 1980. pap. 4.95x (ISBN 0-9602968-0-8). Cobb Ent.

Cobb, Loren & Thrall, Robert M., eds. Mathematical Frontiers of the Social & Policy Sciences. (AAAS Selected Symposium Ser.: No. 54). 186p. 1980. lib. bdg. 22.00x (ISBN 0-89158-953-8). Westview.

Cobb, Richard. Promenades: An Historian's Appreciation of Modern French Literature. 160p. 1980. 16.95x (ISBN 0-19-211758-0). Oxford U Pr.

Cobb, Richard C. Death in Paris, 1795-1801: The Records of the Basse-Geole De la Seine. 1978. 19.50x (ISBN 0-19-215843-0). Oxford U Pr.

--Police & the People: French Popular Protest, 1789-1820. 414p. 1970. 34.50x (ISBN 0-19-821479-0); pap. 5.95x (ISBN 0-19-881297-3, OPB). Oxford U Pr.

Cobb, Roger W. & Elder, Charles D. Participation in American Politics: The Dynamics of Agenda-Building. LC 74-25268. 192p. 1975. pap. 4.95x (ISBN 0-8018-1716-1). Johns Hopkins.

Cobb, Sanford H. Rise of Religious Liberty in America: A History. LC 68-27517. 541p. 1968. Repr. of 1902 ed. 32.50x (ISBN 0-8154-0051-9). Cooper Sq.

Cobb, Stanley J. The American Lobster: The Biology of Homarus Americanus. (Marine Technical Report Ser: No. 49). 1976. pap. 2.00 (ISBN 0-938412-01-9). URI MAS.

Cobb, Stanwood. Tomorrow & Tomorrow. 1951. pap. 1.00 (ISBN 0-87743-059-4, 7-31-35). Baha'i.

Cobb, Vicki. First Book of Cells, the Basic Structure of Life. LC 79-101745. (First Bks). (Illus.). (gr. 7 up). 1970. PLB 4.90 o.p. (ISBN 0-531-00703-0). Watts.

--First Book of Gases. LC 74-114922. (First Bks). (gr. 4-6). 1970. PLB 4.90 o.p. (ISBN 0-531-00713-8). Watts.

--Heat. LC 68-17703. (First Bks). (Illus.). 72p. (gr. 5-8). 1973. PLB 4.90 o.p. (ISBN 0-531-00787-1). Watts.

--The Long & Short of Measurement. LC 72-4903. (Finding-Out Books for Science & Social Studies, Grades 1-4). (Illus.). 64p. (gr. 2-4). 1973. PLB 6.95 (ISBN 0-8193-0628-2, Pub. by Parents). Enslow Pubs.

--Making Sense of Money. LC 74-131256. (Finding-Out Books for Science & Social Studies, Grades 1-4). (Illus.). (gr. 2-4). 1971. PLB 6.95 (ISBN 0-8193-0439-5, Pub. by Parents). Enslow Pubs.

--More Science Experiments You Can Eat. LC 78-12732. (Illus.). 1979. 7.95 (ISBN 0-397-31828-6); pap. 3.95 (ISBN 0-397-31853-7). Lippincott.

--Science Experiments You Can Eat. LC 71-151474. (Illus.). (gr. 7 up). 1972. 7.95 (ISBN 0-397-31179-6); pap. 4.95 (ISBN 0-397-31253-9, LSC-14). Lippincott.

Cobban, A. The Nation State & National Self Determination. 1969. pap. 1.50 o.p. (ISBN 0-531-06014-4, Fontana Pap). Watts.

Cobban, Alfred. Aspects of the French Revolution. LC 68-24195. 1968. 6.95 o.p. (ISBN 0-8076-0454-2). Braziller.

--A History of Modern France. LC 65-14605. 1965. 10.00 o.s.i. (ISBN 0-8076-0310-4). Braziller.

--In Search of Humanity. LC 60-13305. 1960. 6.00 o.p. (ISBN 0-8076-0119-5). Braziller.

Cobban, Alfred B. Social Interpretation of the French Revolution. LC 64-21535. 1968. 24.95 (ISBN 0-521-04679-3); pap. 7.50xx (ISBN 0-521-09548-4). Cambridge U Pr.

Cobban, J. M. & Colebourn, R. Civis Romanus: Reader for the First Two Years of Latin. (Illus., Lat.). (gr. 8-10). 1969. text ed. 5.95 (ISBN 0-312-14175-0); key s.p. 3.95 (ISBN 0-312-14210-2). St Martin.

Cobbe, James. Governments & Mining Companies in Developing Countries. LC 79-4851. (Special Studies in Social, Political & Economic Development). (Illus.). 1979. lib. bdg. 25.00x (ISBN 0-89158-562-1). Westview.

Cobbett, William. Advice to Young Men. 352p. 1980. 16.50x (ISBN 0-19-212212-6). Oxford U Pr.

Cobbold, R. S. Theory & Application of Field-Effect Transistors. LC 75-91162. 1970. 35.00 o.p. (ISBN 0-471-16150-0; Pub. by Wiley-Interscience). Wiley.

Cobbold, Richard S. Transducers for Biomedical Measurements: Principles & Applications. LC 74-2480. (Biomedical Engineering & Health Systems Ser). 486p. 1974. 36.50 (ISBN 0-471-16145-4, Pub. by Wiley-Interscience). Wiley.

Cobbs, C. Glenn & Griffin, Frank M., Jr. Infectious Diseases Case Studies. 2nd ed. 1974. spiral bdg. 14.00 (ISBN 0-87488-011-4). Med Exam.

Cobden, J. C. The White Slaves of England. 498p. 1971. Repr. of 1860 ed. 31.00x (ISBN 0-686-28327-9, Pub. by Irish Academic Pr). Biblio Dist.

Cobden, Richard. England, Ireland, & America. LC 77-28350. 1980. text ed. 15.95x (ISBN 0-915980-44-4). Inst Study Human.

Cobden-Sanderson, et al. Art & Life: The Building & Decoration of Cities. Stansky, Peter & Shewan, Rodney, eds. LC 76-17778. (Aesthetic Movement & the Arts & Crafts Movement). 1978. Repr. of 1897 ed. lib. bdg. 44.00x (ISBN 0-8240-2484-2). Garland Pub.

Cobden-Sanderson, T. J. Ecce Mundus Industrial Ideals, the Book Beautiful, Repr. Of 1902. Stansky, Peter & Shewan, Rodney, eds. Incl. The Arts & Crafts Movement. Repr. of 1905 ed. LC 76-18325. (Aesthetic Movement & the Arts & Crafts Movement Ser.). 1977. lib. bdg. 44.00x (ISBN 0-8240-2479-6). Garland Pub.

Cobelli, E. & Bergman, R. N. Carbohydrate Metabolism: Quantitative Physiology & Mathematical Modelling. 432p. 1981. 77.00 (ISBN 0-471-27912-9, Pub. by Wiley Interscience). Wiley.

Coben, Stanley. A. Mitchell Palmer: Politician. LC 79-180787. (Civil Liberties in American History Ser). (Illus.). 352p. 1972. Repr. of 1963 ed. lib. bdg. 35.00 (ISBN 0-306-70208-8). Da Capo.

Cobes, Jon P., jt. auth. see Heck, Shirley.

Cobham, Claude D., et al, trs. see Mariti, Giovanni.

Cobham, Rosemary. Kaleidoscope-Plus. 160p. 1980. 25.00x (ISBN 0-85683-046-1, Pub. by Shepheard-Walwyn England). State Mutual Bk.

Cobin, Everettt J. Storm Over Nashville: A Case Against "Modern" Country Music. 202p. (Orig.). 1980. pap. text ed. 9.95 (ISBN 0-932534-01-5). Ashlar Pr.

Coblans, H., ed. The Use of Physics Literature. 320p. 1975. 27.95 (ISBN 0-408-70709-7). Butterworths.

Cobleigh, Ira & Dorfman, Bruce. The Dowbeaters: How to Buy Stocks That Go up. (Illus.). 1979. 10.95 (ISBN 0-02-526500-8). Macmillan.

Coblentz, Stanton. Lord of Tranerica. (YA) 5.95 (ISBN 0-685-07444-7, Avalon). Bouregy.

Coblentz, Stanton A. When the Birds Fly South. Reginald, R. & Menville, Douglas, eds. LC 80-23935. (Newcastle Forgotten Fantasy Library Ser.: Vol. 23). 223p. 1980. Repr. lib. bdg. 11.95x (ISBN 0-89370-522-5). Borgo Pr.

--When the Birds Fly South. (Newcastle Forgotten Fantasy Library: Vol. 23). 1980. lib. bdg. 10.95x o.p. (ISBN 0-87877-522-6); pap. 4.95 (ISBN 0-87877-122-0). Newcastle Pub.

Cobler, Sebastian. A Policeman's Utopia: An Interview with the Director of the West German FBI, with an Essay by Hans Magnus Enzensberger. Taubes, Tonia & Wilkins, Sophie, trs. from Ger. (Orig.). 1981. pap. 4.95 (ISBN 0-89396-044-6). Urizen Bks.

Cobley, L. S. An Introduction to the Botany of Tropical Crops. 2nd ed. LC 76-7447. (Longman Text Ser.). (Illus.). 1977. pap. text ed. 17.95x (ISBN 0-582-44153-6). Longman.

Coborn. Goldfish: Their Care & Breeding. (Illus.). 96p. 1981. 3.95 (ISBN 0-903264-24-2, 5215-5, Pub. by K & R Bks England). Arco.

Coburn, Alvin F. Commitment Total. LC 73-93939. 256p. 1975. 7.95 o.s.i. (ISBN 0-8027-0449-2). Walker & Co.

Coburn, Jewell R. Encircled Kingdom: Legends & Folktales of Laos. LC 79-53838. (Illus.). 100p. 1979. 8.95 (ISBN 0-918060-03-6). Burn-Hart.

--Khmers, Tigers, & Talismans: From the History & Legends of Mysterious Cambodia. LC 77-14887. (Illus.). 100p. 1978. 8.95 (ISBN 0-918060-02-8). Burn-Hart.

Coburn, Jewell R., jt. auth. see Van Duong, Quyen.

Coburn, John. A Life to Live - a Way to Pray. 160p. (Orig.). 1973. pap. 3.95 (ISBN 0-8164-2079-3, SP80). Crossroad NY.

Coburn, John B. Anne & the Sand Dobbies: A Story of Death for Children & Their Parents. 120p. 1980. pap. 3.95 (ISBN 0-686-60134-3). Crossroad NY.

--Christ's Life: Our Life. 1979. pap. 3.95 (ISBN 0-8164-2616-3). Crossroad NY.

--Christ's Life, Our Life. LC 77-17172. 1978. 6.95 (ISBN 0-8164-0384-8). Crossroad NY.

--Deliver Us from Evil: The Prayer of Our Lord. 1976. pap. 4.95 (ISBN 0-8164-2124-2). Crossroad NY.

--The Hope of Glory: Exploring the Mystery of Christ in You. 160p. 1976. 7.95 (ISBN 0-8164-1208-1); pap. 3.95 (ISBN 0-8164-2117-X). Crossroad NY.

Coburn, Karen, jt. auth. see Bloom, Lynn Z.

Coburn, Oliver, tr. see Sabet, Huschmand.

Coburn, Oliver, tr. see Schaefer, Udo.

Coburn, Patricia, jt. auth. see Becker, Mary K.

Coburn, Stephen P. The Chemistry & Metabolism of the Vitamin B6 Antagonist, 4' Deoxypyridoxine. 224p. 1981. 69.95 (ISBN 0-8493-5783-7). CRC Pr.

Coburn, Walt. Drift Fence. Orig. Title: Rope Law. 1978. pap. 1.25 (ISBN 0-505-51236-X). Tower Bks.

--Fast Gun. 1978. pap. 1.25 (ISBN 0-505-51227-0). Tower Bks.

--Invitation to a Hanging. 1977. pap. 1.25 (ISBN 0-505-51196-7). Tower Bks.

--The Night Branders. 1979. pap. 1.50 (ISBN 0-505-51348-X). Tower Bks.

--Pioneer Cattleman in Montana: The Story of the Circle C Ranch. LC 68-15691. (Illus.). 1972. 14.95 o.p. (ISBN 0-8061-0815-0). U of Okla Pr.

Coccari, Ronald L. see Ben-Horim, Moshe & Levy, Haim.

Cocchia, Aldo. The Hunters & the Hunted. Gwyer, M., tr. LC 79-6106. (Navies & Men Ser.). (Illus.). 1980. Repr. of 1958 ed. lib. bdg. 16.00x (ISBN 0-405-13035-X). Arno.

Cocchiara, Giuseppe. The History of Folklore in Europe. McDaniel, John N., tr. from Ital. LC 80-17823. (Translations in Folklore Studies Ser.). 1981. text ed. 19.50x (ISBN 0-915980-99-1). Inst Study Human.

Coceani, Flavio, jt. auth. see Brazier, Mary A.

Coceani, Flavio & Olley, Peter M., eds. Prostaglandins & Perinatal Medicine. LC 77-17758. (Advances in Prostaglandin & Thromboxane Research Ser.: Vol. 4). 1978. 43.50 (ISBN 0-89004-216-0). Raven.

Cochard, G. & Kessler, P., eds. Photon-Photon Collisions: Proceedings. (Lecture Notes in Physics Ser.: Vol. 134). 400p. 1981. pap. 27.70 (ISBN 0-387-10262-0). Springer-Verlag.

Coche, Richard. Veronese. (Oresko-Jupiter Art Bks). (Illus.). 1981. 17.95 (ISBN 0-933516-80-0, Pub. by Oresko-Jupiter England). Hippocrene Bks.

Cochran, Alan. Two Plus Two. LC 79-8964. (Illus.). 288p. 1980. 10.95 (ISBN 0-385-15603-0). Doubleday.

Cochran, Alastair & Stobbs, John. Search for the Perfect Swing. LC 68-9441. (Illus.). 1968. 19.95 o.s.i. (ISBN 0-397-00552-0). Lippincott.

Cochran, Alice C. Miners, Merchants & Missionaries: The Roles of Missionaries & Pioneer Churches in the Colorado Gold Rush & Its Aftermath, 1858-1870. LC 80-16895. (ATLA Monographs: No. 15). x, 287p. 1980. 15.00 (ISBN 0-8108-1325-4). Scarecrow.

Cochran, Charles L. Civil-Military Relations: Changing Concepts in the Seventies. LC 73-17646. 1974. 17.95 (ISBN 0-02-905670-5). Free Pr.

Cochran, E. E. Experimental Didactics of Ernst Otto. 1950. pap. 19.70x (ISBN 3-11-003210-4). De Gruyter.

Cochran, George Van B. Orthopaedic Biomechanics. (Illus.). 1981. text ed. write for info. (ISBN 0-443-08027-5). Churchill. Postponed.

Cochran, Hamilton & Nesmith, Robert I. Pirates of the Spanish Main. LC 61-10676. (American Heritage Junior Library). (Illus.). 153p. (gr. 5 up). 1961. 9.95 (ISBN 0-8281-0355-0, J005-0); PLB 6.89 o.p. (ISBN 0-06-021346-9). Am Heritage.

Cochran, Michael. Texas vs. Davis: The Only Complete Account of the Cullen Davis Murder Trials. LC 80-674. 400p. 1980. 12.95 (ISBN 0-672-52569-0). Bobbs.

Cochran, Mickey & Bruns, Bill. The Cochran Family Book of Ski Racing. LC 77-79914. (Illus.). 1977. 8.95 o.p. (ISBN 0-8015-1371-5). Dutton.

Cochran, Molly. Dressing Sexy. (Orig.). 1980. pap. (ISBN 0-671-41529-8, Fireside). S&S.

Cochran, Thomas C. Frontiers of Change: Early Industrialism in America. 175p. 1981. 15.00 (ISBN 0-19-502875-9). Oxford U Pr.

--Pennsylvania. (States & the Nation Ser.). (Illus.). 1978. 12.95 (ISBN 0-393-05635-X, Co-Pub by AASLH). Norton.

Cochran, Thomas C. & Reina, Reuben E. Capitalism in Argentine Culture: A Study of Torcuato Di Tella & S.I.A.M. LC 62-18996. Orig. Title: Entrepreneurship in Argentine Culture. (Illus.). 1971. pap. 4.95x o.p. (ISBN 0-8122-1005-0, Pa Paperbks). U of Pa Pr.

Cochran, Thomas C., ed. The New American State Papers: Complete Series, 179 vols. Set. 8125.00 (ISBN 0-8420-2161-2). Scholarly Res Inc.

Cochran, W. G. & Cox, G. M. Experimental Designs. 2nd ed. LC 57-5908. 1957. 28.95 (ISBN 0-471-16203-5). Wiley.

Cochran, William C. Western Reserve & the Fugitive Slave Law: A Prelude to the Civil War. LC 71-127273. 1972. Repr. of 1920 ed. 22.50 (ISBN 0-306-71212-1). Da Capo.

Cochran, William G. & Snedecor, George W. Statistical Methods. 7th ed. 507p. 1980. 21.50 (ISBN 0-8138-1560-6). Iowa St U Pr.

--Statistical Methods. 7th ed. (Illus.). 608p. 1980. text ed. 21.50 (ISBN 0-8138-1560-6). Iowa St U Pr.

Cochrane, Arthur C. The Church's Confession Under Hitler. 2nd ed. LC 76-57655. (Pittsburgh Reprint Ser.: No. 4). 1977. pap. text ed. 7.50 (ISBN 0-915138-28-X). Pickwick.

Cochrane, Carmie T. & Myers, David V. Children in Crisis: A Time for Caring, a Time for Change. LC 79-20132. (Sage Human Service Guides: Vol. 12). 95p. 1980. pap. 6.00 (ISBN 0-8039-1386-9). Sage.

Cochrane, Charles N. Christianity & Classical Culture: A Study of Thought & Action from Augustus to Augustine. 1957. pap. 7.95 (ISBN 0-19-500207-5, GB). Oxford U Pr.

Cochrane, D. Glynn. The Cultural Appraisal of Development Projects. LC 78-31130. 1979. 20.95 (ISBN 0-03-047586-4). Praeger.

Cochrane, Don & Manley-Casimir, Michael, eds. Development of Moral Reasoning: Practical Approaches. LC 80-17141. 352p. 1980. 27.95 (ISBN 0-03-056209-0). Praeger.

Cochrane, Eric. Historians & Historiography in the Italian Renaissance. LC 80-16097. 1981. lib. bdg. 35.00x (ISBN 0-226-11152-0). U of Chicago Pr.

Cochrane, Glynn, ed. What We Can Do for Each Other: An Interdisciplinary Approach to Development Anthropology. 1976. pap. text ed. 7.00x (ISBN 90-6032-069-7). Humanities.

Cochrane, James R., tr. see Rinker, Rosalind.

Cochrane, Tuovi S. International Gymnastics for Girls & Women. LC 69-15372. (Illus., Orig.). 1969. 12.25 o.p. (ISBN 0-201-01144-1). A-W.

Cock, Liliane De see De Cock, Liliane.

Cockburn, Aiden & Cockburn, Eve, eds. Mummies, Disease & Ancient Cultures. (Illus.). 352p. 1980. 49.95 (ISBN 0-521-23020-9). Cambridge U Pr.

Cockburn, Eve, jt. ed. see Cockburn, Aiden.

Cockburn, W., jt. auth. see Street, H. E.

Cockcroft, A. N. & Lameijer, J. N. A Guide to the Collision Avoidance Rules: International Regulations for Preventing Collision at Sea, 1972, in Force 1977 (1978) 2nd ed. (Illus.). 1978. 12.50 (ISBN 0-540-07272-9). Heinman.

Cockcroft, Eva, et al. Toward a People's Art. 1977. 12.95 o.p. (ISBN 0-525-22165-4); pap. 7.95 (ISBN 0-525-47426-9). Dutton.

Cockcroft, James D. Intellectual Precursors of the Mexican Revolution, 1900-1913. (Latin American Monographs: No. 14). 1969. pap. 7.95x (ISBN 0-292-73808-0). U of Tex Pr.

Cocke, Marian J. I Called Him Babe: Elvis Presley's Nurse Remembers. LC 79-124443. (Twentieth Century Reminiscences Ser.). (Illus.). 160p. 1979. 10.95 (ISBN 0-87870-053-6); deluxe ed. 25.00 (ISBN 0-87870-056-0). Memphis St Univ.

Cocke, William T., III, ed. see Day, John.

Cocker, Henry, jt. auth. see Pizzetti, Ippolito.

Cockerell, H. A. & Dickinson, G. M. Motor Insurance & the Consumer. 192p. 1980. 30.00x (ISBN 0-85941-146-X, Pub. by Woodhead-Faulkner England). State Mutual Bk.

Cockerham, Allan W. The Apostolic Succession in the Liberal Catholic Church. 2nd ed. (Illus.). 1980. pap. text ed. 2.80 (ISBN 0-918980-09-7). St Alban Pr.

Cockerham, H., ed. see Gautier, Theophile.

Cockerham, William C. Medical Sociology. LC 77-13162. (P-H Ser. in Sociology). (Illus.). 1978. ref. 17.95x (ISBN 0-13-573402-9). P-H.

--Sociology of Mental Disorder. (Ser. in Sociology). (Illus.). 300p. 1981. text ed. 17.95 (ISBN 0-13-820886-7). P-H.

Cockerill, A. & Silberton, A. The Steel Industry. (Department of Applied Economics, Occasional Papers Ser: No. 42). (Illus.). 128p. 1974. pap. 12.50x (ISBN 0-521-09878-5). Cambridge U Pr.

Cockett, A. H., et al. The Chemistry of Monatomic Gases. (Pergamon Texts in Inorganic Chemistry: Vol. 4). 192p. 1975. text ed. 28.00 (ISBN 0-08-018782-X); pap. text ed. 17.50 (ISBN 0-08-018781-1). Pergamon.

Cockett, Mary. Dolls & Puppets. LC 74-76185. (David & Charles Children's Books). (Illus.). 80p. (gr. 3-8). 1974. 4.95 o.p. (ISBN 0-7153-6311-5). David & Charles.

Cockfield, Jamie H., ed. Dollars & Diplomacy: Ambassador David Rowland Francis & the Fall of Tsarism, 1916-17. LC 80-19786. ix, 149p. 1981. 12.75 (ISBN 0-8223-2445-8). Duke.

Cockman, N. Live Like a King: Leader's Guide. 1979. pap. 3.25 (ISBN 0-8024-4906-9). Moody.

Cockman, Thomas, tr. see Cicero.

Cockman, Welda. Layman Looks at the Lord's Prayer: Leader's Guide. 1979. pap. 3.25 (ISBN 0-8024-4646-9). Moody.

Cockriel, Irwin W., jt. auth. see Pettit, Neila T.

Cockroft, John, jt. auth. see Craven, John.

Cocks, G., jt. auth. see Preis, S.

Cocks, Leonard R., jt. auth. see Bassett, Michael G.

Cocks, Paul M., jt. ed. see Triska, Jan G.

Cockshott, Gerald. Music & Nature: A Study of Aldous Huxley. (Salzburger Studien: No. 11). 1980. pap. text ed. 39.00x (ISBN 0-391-02158-3). Humanities.

Cockshut, A. O., intro. by. The Novel to Nineteen Hundred. 320p. 1981. pap. 7.95 (ISBN 0-312-57965-9). St Martin.

Coco, Charlene D. Intravenous Therapy: A Handbook for Practice. LC 79-19930. 1980. pap. text ed. 10.50 (ISBN 0-8016-0995-X). Mosby.

Cocoran, John, ed. see Norris, Chuck.

Cocozzoli, Gary, jt. ed. see Keresztesi, Michael.

Cocteau see Bentley, Eric.

Cocteau, Jean. Cocteau: Five Plays. Incl. Eagle with Two Heads; Antigone; Orphee; Intimate Relations; Holy Terrors. (Orig.). 1961. pap. 5.25 o.p. (ISBN 0-8090-0722-3, Mermaid). Hill & Wang.

--The Difficulty of Being. Sprigge, Elizabeth, tr. from Fr. (Illus.). 160p. 1980. text ed. 17.25x (ISBN 0-7206-2518-1). Humanities.

--Les Enfants Terribles. (Easy Readers, B). (Illus.). 1977. pap. text ed. 3.75 (ISBN 0-88436-286-8). EMC.

--The Grand Ecart. Galantiere, Lewis, tr. from Fr. LC 74-22403. 153p. 1977. Repr. of 1925 ed. 14.00 (ISBN 0-86527-257-3). Fertig.

--Le Livre Blanc. 10.95x (ISBN 0-8464-0576-8). Beekman Pubs.

--Opium: The Diary of a Cure. Crosland, Margaret & Road, Sinclair, trs. LC 58-5967. (Illus.). 176p. 1980. pap. 6.95 (ISBN 0-394-17737-1, E771, Ever). Grove.

--Orphee. Freeman, E., ed. (French Texts Ser.). (Illus.). 1976. pap. 10.25x (ISBN 0-631-00720-2, Pub. by Basil Blackwell). Biblio Dist.

Coda-Messerle, Margaret, jt. auth. see Covino, William A.

Codd, Clara M. Technique of the Spiritual Life. 2nd ed. 1963. 2.95 (ISBN 0-8356-7090-2). Theos Pub Hse.

Codding, George A., Jr. & Safran, William. Ideology & Politics: The Socialist Party of France. (Westview Special Studies in European Politics & Society). 1978. lib. bdg. 24.50 (ISBN 0-89158-182-0). Westview.

Coddington, Earl A. Introduction to Ordinary Differential Equations. 1964. ref. ed. 19.95 (ISBN 0-13-491316-7). P-H.

Coddington, Mary & Destiny, Warner. In Search of the Healing Energy. 2.25 (ISBN 0-446-82575-1). Inner Tradit.

Coddington, R. Dean, et al. Child Psychiatry Case Studies. 1973. spiral bdg. 14.00 (ISBN 0-87488-029-7). Med Exam.

Coddington, Robert H. Modern Radio Broadcasting. LC 68-56096. 288p. 1969. 12.95 o.p. (ISBN 0-8306-9482-X, 482). TAB Bks.

Coddon, Hal. Jai Alai-Walls & Balls. 1978. pap. 2.95 (ISBN 0-89650-772-6, Gambler's Book Shelf). Gamblers.

Coder, S. Maxwell. God's Will for Your Life. 1946. pap. 1.50 (ISBN 0-8024-3055-4). Moody.

Codrescu, Andrei. The Life & Times of an Involuntary Genius. LC 74-24906. 192p. 1976. pap. 3.95 o.p. (ISBN 0-8076-0773-8). Persea Bks.

Codrington, W. S. Know Your Horse. (Illus.). 14.75 (ISBN 0-85131-207-1, Dist. by Sporting Book Center); pap. 9.75 (ISBN 0-85131-208-X). J A Allen.

Cody, Al. The Black Rider. (YA) 1977. 5.95 (ISBN 0-685-81421-1, Avalon). Bouregy.

--Forbidden River. (YA) 1973. 5.95 (ISBN 0-685-29160-X, Avalon). Bouregy.

--The Fort at the Dry. (YA) 1977. 5.95 (ISBN 0-685-75640-8, Avalon). Bouregy.

--The Heart of Texas. 1981. pap. 1.95 (ISBN 0-8439-0861-0, Leisure Bks). Nordon Pubns.

--Powder Burns. 256p. (YA) 1973. 5.95 (ISBN 0-685-31777-3, Avalon). Bouregy.

--Return to Fort Yavapa. (YA) 1975. 5.95 (ISBN 0-685-52990-8, Avalon). Bouregy.

--Rimrock Vengeance. 1981. pap. 1.75 (ISBN 0-8439-0879-3, Leisure Bks). Nordon Pubns.

--The Sheriff of Singing River. 1981. pap. 1.75 (ISBN 0-8439-0862-9, Leisure Bks). Nordon Pubns.

--The Thundering Hills. 256p. (YA) 1973. 5.95 (ISBN 0-685-32413-3, Avalon). Bouregy.

Cody, D. Thane. Your Child's Ears, Nose & Throat: A Parent's Medical Guide. LC 73-22530. (Illus.). 192p. 1975. 10.95 o.s.i. (ISBN 0-02-526540-7). Macmillan.

Cody, Martin L. & Diamond, Jared M., eds. Ecology & Evolution of Communities. LC 74-27749. (Illus.). 838p. 1975. text ed. 29.50x (ISBN 0-674-22444-2, Belknap Pr); pap. 12.50x (ISBN 0-674-22446-9). Harvard U Pr.

Cody, William F. The Life of Hon. William F. Cody: Known As Buffalo Bill, the Famous Hunter, Scout, & Guide. LC 78-18732. (Illus.). 1978. 15.00x (ISBN 0-8032-1406-5); pap. 4.95 (ISBN 0-8032-6303-1, BB 686, Bison). U of Nebr Pr.

Cody, William J. & Porsild, A. Erling. Vascular Plants of Continental Northwest Territories. (Illus.). 676p. 1980. lib. bdg. 85.00x (ISBN 0-660-00119-5, 56546-7, Pub. by Natl Mus Canada). U of Chicago Pr.

Cody, William J., Jr. & White, William. Software Manual for the Elementary Functions. (Illus.). 288p. 1980. text ed. 17.95 (ISBN 0-13-822064-6). P-H.

Coe, Ben. Christian Churches at the Crossroads. 1980. pap. write for info. (ISBN 0-87808-178-X). William Carey Lib.

Coe, Charles. Understanding Risk Management: A Guide for Governments. 70p. (Orig.). 1980. pap. 7.50x. U of GA Inst Govt.

Coe, Charles K. Maximizing Revenue: Minimizing Expenditure. 76p. (Orig.). 1981. pap. 7.50 (ISBN 0-89854-070-4). U of GA Inst Govt.

Coe, Frances & Coe, Ivan. Insearch. 112p. 1981. 6.50 (ISBN 0-682-49713-4). Exposition.

Coe, Graham. Colloquial English. (Illus.). 192p. (Orig.). 1981. pap. 9.50 (ISBN 0-7100-0740-X). Routledge & Kegan.

Coe, Ivan, jt. auth. see Coe, Frances.

Coe, Linda, compiled by. Arts Management: An Annotated Bibliography. 1978. pap. 3.00x o.p. (ISBN 0-89062-062-8, Pub. by Natl Endow Arts). Pub Ctr Cultures.

Coe, Michael D. The Maya. rev. ed. (Ancient People & Places Ser.). (Illus.). 180p. 1980. 19.95 (ISBN 0-500-02097-3); pap. 9.95 (ISBN 0-500-27195-X). Thames Hudson.

Coe, Michael D. & Benson, Elizabeth P. Three Maya Relief Panels at Dumbarton Oaks. LC 66-30016. (Studies in Pre-Columbian Art & Archaeology: No. 2). (Illus.). 1966. pap. 2.00 (ISBN 0-88402-079-7, Ctr Pe-Columbian). Dumbarton Oaks.

Coe, Richard. Form & Substance: An Advance Rhetoric. 400p. 1981. text ed. 10.95 (ISBN 0-471-04585-3). Wiley.

Coe, Richard N. Eugene Ionesco. 1968. pap. 1.50 (ISBN 0-394-17161-6, B 235, BC). Grove.

Coe, Richard N., ed. see Stendhal.

Coe, Rodney M. & Pepper, Max. Community Medicine: Some New Perspectives. (Illus.). 1978. pap. text ed. 10.95 (ISBN 0-07-011548-6, HP). McGraw.

Coe, Rodney M., jt. auth. see Brehm, Henry P.

Coe, Stella. Free-Style Ikebana. (Modern Japanese Flower Arrangement Ser.). 1979. 11.95 o.p. (ISBN 0-214-65247-5, 8045, Dist. by Arco). Barrie & Jenkins.

Coe, William C., jt. auth. see Sarbin, Theodore R.

Coedes, G. The Making of Southeast Asia. Wright, H. M., tr. (gr. 9-12). 1969. 15.00x (ISBN 0-520-00248-2); pap. 3.95x (ISBN 0-520-01420-0, CAMPUS20). U of Cal Pr.

Coekin, J. A. High Speed Pulse Technique. Hammond, P., ed. 263p. 1975. text ed. 27.00 (ISBN 0-08-018774-9); pap. text ed. 14.50 (ISBN 0-08-018773-0). Pergamon.

Coel, Margaret. Chief Left Hand: Southern Arapaho. LC 80-5940. (The Civilization of the American Indian Ser.: Vol. 159). (Illus.). 482p. 1981. 15.95 (ISBN 0-8061-1602-1). U of Okla Pr.
Coelho, jt. ed. see Ahmed.
Coelho, George V., et al, eds. Uprooting & Development--Dilemmas of Coping with Modernization. (Current Topics in Mental Health Ser.). 500p. 1980. 27.50 (ISBN 0-306-40509-1, Plenum Pr). Plenum Pub.
Coen, Luciano & Duncan, Louise. The Oriental Rug. LC 76-5119. (Illus.). 1978. 35.00 o.s.i. (ISBN 0-06-010824-X, HarpT). Har-Row.
Coen, Sue H. Horseback Riding Made Easy & Fun. pap. 4.00 (ISBN 0-87980-194-8). Wilshire.
Coen, V. & Holtbecker, H. Post Accident Heat Removal. (European Applied Research Reports Special Topics Ser.). 402p. 1980. pap. text ed. 92.00 (ISBN 3-7186-0025-0). Harwood Academic.
Coes, Donald V. The Impact of Price Uncertainty: A Study of Brazilian Exchange Rate Policy. LC 78-75067. (Outstanding Dissertations in Economics Ser.). 1979. lib. bdg. 30.00 (ISBN 0-8240-4143-7). Garland Pub.
Coetzee, J. F., ed. Recommended Methods for Purification of Solvents. (International Union of Pure & Applied Chemistry). 1979. pap. text ed. 14.51 (ISBN 0-08-022370-2). Pergamon.
Cofer. Plaid for Introduction to Psychology. rev. ed. 1979. 5.50 (ISBN 0-256-02127-9, 11-0829-02). Learning Syst.
Cofer, Charles N. & Appley, M. H. Motivation: Theory & Research. LC 64-13214. (Illus.). 1964. 32.95 (ISBN 0-471-16317-1). Wiley.
Cofer, Charles N., ed. Human Motivation: A Guide to Information Sources. rev. ed. (The Psychology Information Guide Ser.: Vol. 4). 175p. 1980. 30.00 (ISBN 0-8103-1418-5). Gale.
--The Structure of Human Memory. LC 76-2581. (Psychology Ser.). (Illus.). 1976. pap. text ed. 9.95x (ISBN 0-7167-0715-2). W H Freeman.
Coffed, Frank. The Self-Sufficient House. LC 80-13434. (Illus.). 1981. 16.95 (ISBN 0-03-053611-1); pap. 8.95 (ISBN 0-686-69126-1). HR&W.
Coffelt, Kenneth & Combs, Bob. Basic Design & Utilization of Instructional Television. 2nd ed. (Bridges for Ideas Ser.). 1981. pap. text ed. 14.95 (ISBN 0-913648-13-2). U Tex Austin Film Lib.
Coffer, William E. Where Is the Eagle? 288p. 1981. 16.95 (ISBN 0-442-26163-2). Van Nos Reinhold.
Coffer, William E. & Hosh, Koi. Sleeping Giants. LC 79-64248. 1979. pap. text ed. 7.50 (ISBN 0-8191-0760-3). U Pr of Amer.
Coffey, Alan, jt. auth. see Eldefonso, Edward.
Coffey, Alan R. Correctional Administration: The Management of Institutions, Probation, & Parole. (Illus.). 320p. 1975. 15.95 (ISBN 0-13-188284-8). P-H.
--The Prevention of Crime & Delinquency. (Illus.). 400p. 1975. 16.95 (ISBN 0-13-699157-2). P-H.
Coffey, Alan R. & Eldefonso, Edward. Process & Impact of Justice. (Criminal Justice Ser.). 1975. pap. text ed. 7.95x (ISBN 0-02-471750-9, 47175). Macmillan.
Coffey, Alan R., jt. auth. see Eldefonso, Edward.
Coffey, Brian. The Face of Fear. 1978. pap. 1.95 o.p. (ISBN 0-345-27117-3). Ballantine.
--The Voice of the Night. LC 79-7327. 1980. 10.95 (ISBN 0-385-15258-2). Doubleday.
Coffey, G. New Grange & Other Incised Tumuli in Ireland. (Illus.). 1978. 9.95 o.p. (ISBN 0-85642-041-7, Pub. by Blandford Pr England). Sterling.
Coffey, Jane. His Promise. 1980. 5.95 (ISBN 0-533-04403-0). Vantage.
Coffey, Joseph I. Arms Control & European Security: A Guide to East-West Negotiations. LC 76-29615. (Praeger Special Studies). 1977. text ed. 29.95 (ISBN 0-275-24340-0). Praeger.
Coffey, P., jt. auth. see Miller, E.
Coffey, Richard A. A Midwestern Village. Deegan, Paul, ed. LC 70-156065. (World's People Ser.). (Illus.). (gr. 5-9). 1971. text ed. 6.95 (ISBN 0-87191-077-2). Creative Ed.
Coffey, Robert E., et al. Behavior in Organizations: A Multi-Dimensional View. 2nd ed. LC 74-12372. (Illus.). 608p. 1975. 21.95 (ISBN 0-13-073148-X). P-H.
Coffey, Thomas M. Agony at Easter: The Nineteen Sixteen Irish Uprising. (Illus.). 1969. 6.95 o.s.i. (ISBN 0-02-526650-0). Macmillan.
Coffin, Arthur B. Robinson Jeffers: Poet of Inhumanism. LC 74-121767. 1971. 25.00 (ISBN 0-299-05840-9). U of Wis Pr.
Coffin, Berton. Coffin's Overtones of Bel Canto: Phonetic Basis of Artistic Singing with One Hundred Chromatic Vowel-Chart Exercises. LC 80-21958. 254p. 1980. text ed. 20.00 (ISBN 0-8108-1370-X); Accompanying Chart. 7.50; Set. 27.50. Scarecrow.
--The Singer's Repertoire, 4 vols. 2nd ed. Incl. Vol. 1. Coloratura, Lyric & Dramatic Soprano (ISBN 0-8108-0188-4); Vol. 2. Mezzo Soprano & Contralto (ISBN 0-8108-0189-2); Vol. 3. Lyric & Dramatic Tenor (ISBN 0-8108-0190-6); Vol. 4. Baritone & Bass (ISBN 0-8108-0191-4). 1960. Set. 36.00 (ISBN 0-8108-0187-6); 11.00 ea. Scarecrow.
Coffin, Berton & Singer, Werner. Program Notes for the Singer's Repertoire. LC 60-7265. 1962. 11.00 (ISBN 0-8108-0169-8). Scarecrow.
Coffin, Berton, et al. Word-by-Word Translations of Songs & Arias, Pt. 1: German & French. LC 66-13746. 1966. 17.50 (ISBN 0-8108-0149-3). Scarecrow.
Coffin, Charles M. John Donne & the New Philosophy. 1958. Repr. of 1937 ed. text ed. 12.50x (ISBN 0-391-00444-1). Humanities.
Coffin, Frank. The Ways of a Judge: Reflections from the Federal Apellate Bench. 288p. 1980. 10.95 (ISBN 0-395-29461-4). HM.
Coffin, Harold G., jt. auth. see Wheeler, Ruth.
Coffin, Margaret M. Death in Early America: History & Folklore of Customs & Superstitions of Early Medicine, Funerals, Burial & Mourning. LC 76-7513. (Illus.). 224p. (gr. 8 up). 1976. Repr. 8.95 o.p. (ISBN 0-525-66482-3). Elsevier-Nelson.
Coffin, Patricia. One-Two-Three-Four-Five-Six: How to Understand & Enjoy the Years That Count. LC 72-76278. 160p. 1972. 8.95 o.s.i. (ISBN 0-02-526690-X). Macmillan.
Coffin, Patricia & Hansen, J. One Through Six: How to Understand & Enjoy the Years That Count. 1972. pap. 4.95 o.s.i. (ISBN 0-02-079380-4, Collier). Macmillan.
Coffin, Raymond. Poetry for Crazy Cowboys & Zen Monks. (Illus.). 128p. 1980. pap. 4.95 (ISBN 0-915520-26-5). Ross-Erikson.
Coffin, Robert P. Maine Doings. LC 78-26413. 1978. lib. bdg. 11.50 o.p. (ISBN 0-89621-025-1); pap. 4.95 (ISBN 0-89621-024-3). Thorndike Pr.
--Strange Holiness. LC 78-8151. 1978. lib. bdg. 8.50 o.p. (ISBN 0-89621-003-0); pap. 3.95x (ISBN 0-89621-002-2). Thorndike Pr.
Coffin, Royce A. The Communicator. LC 74-23481. (Illus.). 176p. 1975. 10.95 (ISBN 0-8144-5374-0). Am Mgmt.
--The Negotiator: A Manual for Winners. LC 73-75768. (Illus.). 1973. 10.95 (ISBN 0-8144-5327-9). Am Mgmt.
Coffin, Tristam P. The Female Hero in Folklore & Legend. LC 75-14412. (Illus.). 192p. 1975. 10.95 o.p. (ISBN 0-8164-9263-8). Continuum.
Coffin, Tristram P. The Illustrated Book of Baseball Folklore. LC 75-9968. (Illus.). 250p. 1975. 14.95 o.p. (ISBN 0-8164-9262-X). Continuum.
Coffin, Tristram P., ed. Indian Tales of North America: An Anthology for the Adult Reader. LC 61-11866. (American Folklore Soc. Bibliographical & Special Ser.: No. 13). 1961. pap. 4.00 (ISBN 0-292-73506-5). U of Tex Pr.
Coffin, Tristram P. & Cohen, Hennig, eds. Folklore in America. LC 79-97699. 1970. pap. 2.50 (ISBN 0-385-05071-2, A15, Anch). Doubleday.
Coffman, C. DeWitt. Hospitality for Sale: Techniques of Promoting Business for Hospitality Establishments. LC 79-28567. (Illus.). 339p. 1980. 17.56x (ISBN 0-86612-000-9); text ed. 21.95 (ISBN 0-686-28892-0). Educ Inst Am Hotel.
Coffman, Edward G., Jr. & Denning, Peter J. Operating Systems Theory. LC 73-491. 400p. 1973. ref. ed. 25.95 (ISBN 0-13-637868-4). P-H.
Coffman, Edward M. Hilt of the Sword: The Career of Peyton C. March. (Illus.). 1966. 25.00 (ISBN 0-299-03910-2). U of Wis Pr.
Coffman, James B. The Gospel in Gotham. 3.50 (ISBN 0-89315-077-0). Lambert Bk.
Coffman, Mary. Schaum's Outline of French Grammar. (Schaum's Outline Ser.). 288p. 1980. pap. 4.95 (ISBN 0-07-011553-2, SP). McGraw.
Coffman, Ralph J. Solomon Stoddard. (United States Authors Ser.: No. 295). 1978. lib. bdg. 12.50 (ISBN 0-8057-7198-0). Twayne.
Coffman, Sue E. Music of Finer Tone: Musical Imagery of the Major Romantic Poets. (Salzburg Studies in English Literature, Romantic Reassessment: No. 89). (Orig.). 1979. pap. text ed. 25.00x (ISBN 0-391-01672-5). Humanities.
Coffman, Virginia. Black Heather. Bd. with Night at Sea Abbey. 1980. pap. 1.95 (ISBN 0-451-09468-9, J9468, Sig). NAL.
--The Dark Palazzo. 1978. pap. 1.75 o.p. (ISBN 0-449-23545-9, Crest). Fawcett.
--Hyde Place. 1977. pap. 1.75 o.p. (ISBN 0-449-23351-0, Crest). Fawcett.
--Marsanne. 1977. pap. 1.75 o.p. (ISBN 0-449-23373-1, Crest). Fawcett.
--Of Love & Intrigue. Bd. with The Chinese Door. 1980. pap. 1.95 (J9313, Sig). NAL.
--Pacific Cavalcade. LC 80-66502. 1981. 12.95 (ISBN 0-87795-277-9). Arbor Hse.
Coffron, J. Understanding & Troubleshooting Microprocessors. 1980. 19.95 (ISBN 0-13-936625-3). P-H.
Coffron, James W. Practical Troubleshooting for Microprocessors. (Illus.). 256p. 1981. text ed. 19.95 (ISBN 0-13-694273-3). P-H.
Cogan, David G. Neurology of the Ocular Muscles. 2nd ed. (Illus.). 320p. 1978. 18.75 (ISBN 0-398-00321-1). C C Thomas.
--Ophthalmic Manifestations of Systemic Vascular Disease. LC 74-4556. (Major Problem in Internal Medicine Ser.: Vol. 3). (Illus.). 225p. 1974. 15.00 (ISBN 0-7216-2648-3). Saunders.
Cogan, Marc. The Human Thing: The Speeches & Principles of Thucydides' History. LC 80-24226. (Chicago Original Paperback Ser.). 248p. 1981. lib. bdg. 19.00x (ISBN 0-226-11194-6). U of Chicago Pr.
Cogan, Morris L. Clinical Supervision. LC 72-85906. 250p. 1973. text ed. 19.95 (ISBN 0-395-14027-7). HM.
Cogan, Morton. Imperialism & Religion: Assyria, Judah and Israel in the Eighth and Seventh Centuries B.C.E. LC 73-83723. (Society of Biblical Literature. Monograph). 1974. 9.00 (ISBN 0-89130-330-8, 060019); pap. 7.50 (ISBN 0-89130-331-6). Scholars Pr Ca.
Cogan, Robert & Escot, Pozzi. Sonic Design: Practice & Problems. (Illus.). 160p. 1981. text ed. 12.95 (ISBN 0-686-68608-X). P-H.
--Sonic Design: The Nature of Sound & Music. (Illus.). 544p. 1976. 19.95 (ISBN 0-13-822726-8). P-H.
Cogburn, Shirley B., jt. auth. see Hilt, Nancy E.
Coger, Leslie I. & White, Melvin R. Readers Theatre Handbook: A Dramatic Approach to Literature. rev. ed. 1973. pap. 9.95x (ISBN 0-673-07605-3). Scott F.
Coggeshall, John H. Management of Retirement Homes & Long Term Care Facilities. LC 73-4450. 1973. 13.95 o.p. (ISBN 0-8016-1008-7). Mosby.
Coggin, P. A. Education for the Future: The Case for Radical Change. 170p. 1979. 29.00 (ISBN 0-08-023729-0). Pergamon.
Coggins, George C. & Wilkinson, Charles F. Federal Public Land & Resources Law. (University Casebook Ser.). 1018p. 1981. text ed. write for info. (ISBN 0-88277-022-5). Foundation Pr.
Coggins, Jack. The Campaign for North Africa. LC 79-7585. (Illus.). 1980. 15.00 (ISBN 0-385-04351-1). Doubleday.
--Horseman's Bible. LC 66-17921. pap. 3.50 (ISBN 0-385-03167-X). Doubleday.
Coggins, Richard. Who's Who in the Bible: From Historic Sources. (Illus.). 232p. 1981. 16.50x (ISBN 0-686-69582-8). B&N.
Coghill, Mrs. H., ed. Autobiography & Letters of Mrs. Margaret Oliphant. (Victorian Library). 520p. 1974. Repr. of 1899 ed. text ed. 15.75x (ISBN 0-7185-5019-6, Leicester). Humanities.
Coghill, Mary A. Games & Simulatons in Industrial & Labor Relations Training. (Key Issues Ser.: No. 7). 1971. pap. 2.00 (ISBN 0-87546-207-3). NY Sch Indus Rel.
--Lie Detector in Employment. (Key Issues Ser.: No. 2). 1973. pap. 2.00 (ISBN 0-87546-208-1). NY Sch Indus Rel.
Coghill, Nevill. Geoffrey Chaucer. Dobree, Bonamy, et al, eds. Bd. with Sir Thomas Malory. Bradbrook, M. C. LC 63-63096. (British Writers & Their Work Ser: Vol. 1). 1964. pap. 1.60x (ISBN 0-8032-5650-7, BB 450, Bison). U of Nebr Pr.
--Shakespeare's Professional Skills. 1964. 42.00 (ISBN 0-521-04681-5). Cambridge U Pr.
Coghill, Nevill, ed. see Chaucer, Geoffrey.
Coghill, Nevill, tr. see Chaucer, Geoffrey.
Coghill, Nevill, tr. see Langland, William.
Coghlan, Brian. Hofmannsthal's Festival Dramas. 1964. 65.00 (ISBN 0-521-04682-3). Cambridge U Pr.
Coghlan, David A. Automotive Brake System. 1980. pap. text ed. 10.95 (ISBN 0-534-00822-4, Breton Pubs). Wadsworth Pub.
Coghlan, John P., jt. ed. see Denton, Derek A.
Coghlan, Richard. Money Credit & the Economy. (Illus.). 192p. 1981. text ed. 35.00x (ISBN 0-04-332079-1, 2649). Allen Unwin.
Coghland, Richard & Sykes, Carolyn. Managing the Money Supply. 224p. 1980. 21.00x (ISBN 0-85941-164-8, Pub. by Woodhead-Faulkner England). State Mutual Bk.
Cogley, John. A Canterbury Tale: Experiences & Reflections: 1916-1976. 1976. 8.95 (ISBN 0-8164-0322-8). Crossroad NY.
--Catholic America. 240p. 1974. pap. 2.95 (ISBN 0-385-08916-3, Im). Doubleday.
Cognia, Raymond & Elgar, Frank. Illustrated Dictionary of Impressionism. (Illus.). (gr. 10-12). 1979. pap. 3.95 (ISBN 0-8120-0986-X). Barron.
Cogniat, Raymond. Georges Braque. (Library of Great Painters). (Illus.). 1980. 35.00 (ISBN 0-8109-0703-8). Abrams.
Cogniaux, Alfredus. Orchidaceae, 4 vols. (Flora Brasiliensis Ser.: Vol. 3, Pts. 4-6). (Illus.). 970p. (Lat.). 1975. Repr. Set. lib. bdg. 325.00x (ISBN 3-87429-080-8). Lubrecht & Cramer.
Cogny, Pierre. L' Education sentimentale de Flaubert: Le Monde en creux. new ed. (Collection themes et textes). 270p. (Orig., Fr.). 1975. pap. 6.75 (ISBN 2-03-035030-3, 2685). Larousse.
Cogoli, John E. Photo-Offset Fundamentals. 4th ed. (Illus.). (gr. 10-12). 1980. text ed. 15.72 (ISBN 0-87345-235-6); study guide 4.48 (ISBN 0-87345-236-4); filmstrips & ans. avail. 336.00 (ISBN 0-685-42198-8). McKnight.
Cogswell, Philip, Jr. Capitol Names: Individuals Woven into Oregon's History. LC 76-56657. (Illus.). 144p. 1977. 4.95 (ISBN 0-87595-076-0); pap. 2.95 (ISBN 0-87595-054-X). Oreg Hist Soc.
Cogswell, Theodore. The Wall Around the World. 1973. pap. 1.25 (ISBN 0-515-03278-6, N3278). Jove Pubns.
Cohan & Yoshikawa. Nursery Management. 1982. text ed. 16.95 (ISBN 0-8359-5051-4); instr's. manual free (ISBN 0-8359-5052-2). Reston.
Cohan, A. S. Irish Political Elite. (Studies in Irish Political Culture). 128p. 1972. pap. 3.75 o.p. (ISBN 0-7171-0538-5). Irish Bk Ctr.
Cohan, Avery B. & Wyman, Harold E. Cases in Financial Management. LC 72-39508. (Illus.). 256p. 1972. pap. text ed. 10.95x (ISBN 0-13-118745-7). P-H.
Cohan, G. Collective Security in the 1930's: The Failure of Men or the Failure of Principle? Brown, Richard H. & Halsey, Van R., eds. (Amherst Ser.). (gr. 9-12). 1970. pap. text ed. 4.52 (ISBN 0-201-01161-5, Sch Div); tchr's. man. 1.92 (ISBN 0-201-01163-8). A-W.
Cohan, Tony. Canary. LC 80-2045. 336p. 1981. 13.95 (ISBN 0-385-17086-6). Doubleday.
Cohen. Jimmy Walker-the Dyn-O-Mite Kid. (gr. 3-5). pap. 1.25 (ISBN 0-590-10268-0, Schol Pap). Schol Bk Serv.
--Plaid for Personal Finance. 3rd ed. 1981. write for info. (ISBN 0-256-02126-0, 06-0117-03). Learning Syst.
--R My Name Is Rosie. (gr. 5). 1980. pap. 1.25 (ISBN 0-590-30331-7, Schol Pap). Schol Bk Serv.
--Special People: A Brighter Future for Everyone with Physical, Mental & Emotional Disabilities. (Psychology in Action Series). 1977. text ed. 9.95 (ISBN 0-13-826511-9, Spec); pap. text ed. 5.95 (ISBN 0-13-826503-8). P-H.
Cohen & Cameron. Elementary Algebra. 480p. 1981. pap. text ed. 16.95 (ISBN 0-205-07308-5, 5671728); free tchr's ed. (ISBN 0-205-07309-3). Allyn.
--Intermediate Algebra. 576p. 1980. pap. text ed. 17.80 (ISBN 0-205-07172-4, 5671728); free tchr's ed. (ISBN 0-205-07173-2). Allyn.
Cohen, A. K. Delinquent Boys. LC 55-7337. 1955. 14.95 (ISBN 0-02-905760-4); pap. text ed. 4.95 (ISBN 0-02-905770-1). Free Pr.
Cohen, Abner. Arab Border-Villages in Israel. 1965. text ed. 28.00x (ISBN 0-7190-0251-6). Humanities.
--Custom & Politics in Urban Africa: A Study of Hausa Migrants in Yoruba Towns. 1969. 18.50x (ISBN 0-520-01571-1); pap. 6.95x (ISBN 0-520-01836-2, CAMPUS43). U of Cal Pr.
--The Politics of Elite Culture: Explorations in the Dramaturgy of Power in a Modern African Society. 200p. 1981. 18.50x (ISBN 0-520-04120-8); pap. 6.95x (ISBN 0-520-04275-1, 270). U of Cal Pr.
--Two-Dimensional Man. 1974. pap. 4.95x (ISBN 0-520-03241-1). U of Cal Pr.
Cohen, Abraham. Hi-Fi Loudspeakers & Enclosures. 2nd, rev. ed. (Illus.). 1968. 10.60 (ISBN 0-8104-0721-3). Hayden.
Cohen, Alan, ed. see Pizzuto, Joseph.
Cohen, Alan, jt. ed. see Sherwood, William.
Cohen, Albert K., et al, eds. Prison Violence. LC 75-24561. 1976. 19.50 o.p. (ISBN 0-669-00185-6). Lexington Bks.
Cohen, Allan R. & Gadon, Herman. Alternative Work Schedules: Integrating Individual & Organizational Needs. LC 78-52506. 1978. pap. text ed. 6.50 (ISBN 0-201-01052-6). A-W.
Cohen, Allan R., et al. Effective Behavior in Organizations: Learning from the Interplay of Cases, Concepts & Student Experiences. 1976. text ed. 16.50x o.p. (ISBN 0-256-01773-5). Irwin.
--Effective Behavior in Organizations. rev. ed. 1980. 18.95x (ISBN 0-256-02283-6). Irwin.
Cohen, Alvin P., ed. see Boodberg, Peter A.
Cohen, Andrew D. Describing Bilingual Education Classrooms: The Role of the Teacher in Evaluation. LC 80-80307. 64p. (Orig.). 1980. pap. 3.00 (ISBN 0-89763-050-5). Natl Clearinghse Bilingual.
Cohen, Andrew D., et al. Evaluating Evaluation. LC 79-56013. (Bilingual Ed. Ser.: No. 6). 71p. 1979. pap. text ed. 5.75x (ISBN 0-87281-109-3). Ctr Appl Ling.

Cohen, Annabelle. Handbook of Cellular Chemistry. 2nd ed. LC 78-11881. (Illus.). 1979. pap. text ed. 11.00 (ISBN 0-8016-1006-0). Mosby.

--Handbook of Microscopic Anatomy for the Health Sciences. LC 74-13572. (Illus.). 1975. pap. text ed. 8.95 (ISBN 0-8016-1012-5). Mosby.

Cohen, Arnold W. Emergencies in Obstetrics & Gynecology. (Clinics in Emergency Medicine Ser.). (Illus.). 224p. 1981. lib. bdg. 20.00 (ISBN 0-443-08130-1). Churchill.

Cohen, Arthur, jt. auth. see Halverson, Marvin.

Cohen, Arthur A. Osip Emilievich Manelstam: An Essay in Antiphon. (Ardis Essay Ser.: No. 2). 82p. 1974. pap. 2.50 o.p. (ISBN 0-88233-076-4). Ardis Pubs.

--The Tremendum: A Theological Interpretation of the Holocaust. 144p. 1981. 9.95 (ISBN 0-8245-0006-7). Crossroad NY.

Cohen, Arthur A. & Halverson, Marvin, eds. A Handbook of Christian Theology. 382p. 1980. pap. 5.95 (ISBN 0-687-16567-9). Abingdon.

Cohen, Arthur M. & Brawer, Florence B. The Two-Year College Instructor Today. LC 77-83482. (Praeger Special Studies). 1977. 23.95 (ISBN 0-03-039706-5). Praeger.

Cohen, Arthur M. & Smith, R. Douglas. The Critical Incident in Growth Groups: A Manual for Group Leaders. LC 75-18139. 262p. 1976. 12.50 (ISBN 0-88390-107-2). Univ Assocs.

--The Critical Incident in Growth Groups: Theory & Technique. LC 75-22510. 286p. 1976. pap. 14.95 (ISBN 0-88390-102-1). Univ Assocs.

Cohen, Barbara. Fat Jack. LC 80-12510. 192p. (gr. 6 up). 1980. 8.95 (ISBN 0-689-30772-1). Atheneum.

--Queen for a Day. LC 80-28115. 160p. (gr. 5 up). 1981. 7.95 (ISBN 0-688-00437-7); PLB 7.63 (ISBN 0-688-00438-5). Morrow.

Cohen, Barbara, retold by. Lovely Vassilisa. LC 80-12494. (Illus.). 48p. (ps-4). 1980. 9.95 (ISBN 0-689-30773-X). Atheneum.

Cohen, Barry, jt. auth. see Quirin, Jim.

Cohen, Barry D., ed. see Jospe, Michael, et al.

Cohen, Ben & Lederer, Rhoda. Current Conventions Made Clear. 1973. 9.50 o.p. (ISBN 0-04-793020-9). Allen Unwin.

Cohen, Benjamin & Basagni, Fabio, eds. Private Lending for Balance of Payments Purpose. (Atlantic Institute for International Affairs Ser.: No. 4). 265p. 1981. text ed. 31.50 (ISBN 0-86598-038-1). Allanheld.

Cohen, Bernard. Deviant Street Networks: Prostitution in New York. LC 80-8039. 1980. 19.95 (ISBN 0-669-03949-7). Lexington Bks.

Cohen, Bernard C. Political Process & Foreign Policy: The Making of the Japanese Peace Settlement. LC 80-19832. x, 293p. 1980. Repr. of 1957 ed. lib. bdg. 37.50x (ISBN 0-313-22715-2, COPF). Greenwood.

--Press & Foreign Policy. 1963. 15.00 (ISBN 0-691-07519-0); pap. 5.95 o.p. (ISBN 0-691-02157-0). Princeton U Pr.

Cohen, Beth. Attic Bilingual Vases & Their Painters. LC 77-94689. (Outstanding Dissertations in the Fine Arts Ser.). 1978. lib. bdg. 80.00 (ISBN 0-8240-3220-9). Garland Pub.

Cohen, Carl. Civil Disobedience: Conscience, Tactics & the Law. LC 14-7897. 1971. 15.00x (ISBN 0-231-03470-9); pap. 5.00x (ISBN 0-231-08646-6). Columbia U Pr.

--Communism, Fascism, & Democracy. 2nd ed. 620p. 1972. pap. text ed. 8.95x (ISBN 0-394-31319-4, RanC). Random.

--Democracy. LC 77-142911. 1973. pap. text ed. 3.95 (ISBN 0-02-906100-8). Free Pr.

--Earth's Hidden Mysteries. McCarthy, Pat, ed. (Pal Paperbacks Ser., Kit B). (Illus., Orig.). (gr. 7-12). 1974. pap. text ed. 1.25 (ISBN 0-8374-3506-4). Xerox Ed Pubns.

Cohen, Chapman. Essays in Freethinking, Vol. 1. 1980. pap. 4.00. Am Atheist.

Cohen, Chester G. Shtetl Finder. 1980. pap. 8.25. Periday.

Cohen, D. & Cameron, R. Elementary Algebra. LC 75-27504. 1976. 16.95 o.p. (ISBN 0-8465-0950-4); instr's guide 2.95 o.p. (ISBN 0-8465-0951-2). Benjamin-Cummings.

Cohen, D. & Daniel, J. The Political Economy of Africa. (Illus.). 1981. text ed. 25.00x (ISBN 0-582-64284-1); pap. text ed. 11.95x (ISBN 0-582-64285-X). Longman.

Cohen, D. Walter, jt. auth. see Goldman, Henry M.

Cohen, Daniel. The Ancient Visitors. LC 75-21220. 224p. (gr. 4-7). 1976. 7.95 (ISBN 0-385-09786-7). Doubleday.

--Animal Territories. (Illus.). 96p. (gr. 4-8). 1975. 6.95g (ISBN 0-8038-0368-0). Hastings.

--Ceremonial Magic. LC 78-20429. (Illus.). 160p. (gr. 7 up). 1979. 7.95 (ISBN 0-590-07466-0, Four Winds). Schol Bk Serv.

--A Close Look at Close Encounters. LC 80-2784. (Illus.). 192p. (gr. 7 up). 1981. PLB 7.95 (ISBN 0-396-07927-X). Dodd.

--Creativity: What Is It? LC 77-23481. (Illus.). 160p. (gr. 7 up). 1977. 5.95 (ISBN 0-87131-245-X). M Evans.

--Creatures from the UFO's. LC 78-7730. (High Interest-Low Vocabulary Book). (Illus.). (gr. 4 up). 1978. 5.95 (ISBN 0-396-07582-7). Dodd.

--Creatures from UFO's. (gr. 4 up). 1979. pap. 1.50 (ISBN 0-671-29951-4). Archway.

--Dreams, Visions & Drugs: A Search for Other Realities. LC 75-33694. 160p. (gr. 7 up). 1976. PLB 7.45 (ISBN 0-531-01141-0). Watts.

--Everything You Need to Know About Monsters & Still Be Able to Get to Sleep. LC 79-6589. (Illus.). 128p. (gr. 4 up). 1981. 7.95a (ISBN 0-385-15803-3); PLB (ISBN 0-385-15804-1). Doubleday.

--Famous Curses. (gr. 3-6). pap. 1.75 (ISBN 0-671-41867-X). Archway.

--Frauds & Hoaxes & Swindles. (YA) (gr. 7-12). pap. 1.25 (ISBN 0-440-92699-8, LE). Dell.

--Ghostly Animals. LC 76-23751. (gr. 4-7). 1977. 6.95 o.p. (ISBN 0-385-11567-9); PLB (ISBN 0-385-11568-7). Doubleday.

--Greatest Monsters in the World. (Illus.). (gr. 4 up). 1977. pap. 1.50 (ISBN 0-671-29990-5). PB.

--The Headless Roommate & Other Tales of Terror. (Illus.). 128p. (gr. 8 up). 1980. 7.95 (ISBN 0-87131-327-8). M Evans.

--Intelligence: What Is It? LC 73-80178. (Illus.). 160p. (gr. 5 up). 1974. 7.95 (ISBN 0-87131-127-5). M Evans.

--Missing: Stories of Strange Disappearances. 1980. pap. write for info. (ISBN 0-671-56052-2). PB.

--Missing: Stories of Strange Disappearances. LC 78-25729. (High Interest-Low Vocabulary Ser.). (Illus.). (gr. 4 up). 1979. 5.95 (ISBN 0-396-07651-3). Dodd.

--Missing Stories of Strange Disappearances. (Illus.). 1980. pap. write for info. (ISBN 0-671-56052-2). PB.

--The Monsters of Star Trek. (Illus.). 1980. pap. 1.75 (ISBN 0-671-56057-3). PB.

--The Monsters of Star Trek. (Illus., Orig.). (gr. 4 up). 1980. pap. 1.75 (ISBN 0-671-56057-3, HI/LO). Archway.

--Mysterious Disappearances. LC 75-38352. (Illus.). (gr. 7 up). 1976. 5.95 (ISBN 0-396-07298-4). Dodd.

--Not of the World: A History of the Commune in America. (Illus.). 224p. (gr. 5 up). 1974. lib. ed. 5.97 o.p. (ISBN 0-695-40405-9). Follett.

--Real Ghosts. (Illus.). (gr. 4 up). 1979. pap. 1.50 (ISBN 0-671-29908-5). PB.

--Real Ghosts. LC 77-6502. (gr. 4-5). 1977. 5.95 (ISBN 0-396-07454-5). Dodd.

--Science Fiction's Greatest Monsters. LC 80-1087. (High Interest-Low Vocabulary Ser.). (Illus.). (gr. 4-9). 1980. 5.95g (ISBN 0-396-07859-1). Dodd.

--Supermonsters. (gr. 4 up). 1978. pap. 1.50 (ISBN 0-671-41190-X). Archway.

--Supermonsters. (Illus.). (gr. 4 up). 1978. pap. 1.50 (ISBN 0-671-41190-X, HI-LO). PB.

--Supermonsters. LC 76-48970. (gr. 4-9). 1977. 5.95 (ISBN 0-396-07399-9). Dodd.

--Superstitions. Liberty, Gene, ed. LC 74-125916. (Understanding Bks). (Illus.). (gr. 6-9). 1971. PLB 7.95 (ISBN 0-87191-069-1). Creative Ed.

--What Really Happened to the Dinosaurs? (gr. 3-5). 1977. PLB 8.95 (ISBN 0-525-42472-5). Dutton.

--The World's Most Famous Ghosts. (Illus.). (gr. 4 up). 1979. pap. 1.50 (ISBN 0-671-29962-X, HI-LO). PB.

Cohen, David. Fixed Base Operators - Management Handbook. Jones, David & Hurst, M. Dale, eds. (Aviation Management Ser.). 1980. pap. text ed. write for info. (ISBN 0-89100-148-4). Aviation Maintenance.

--J. B. Watson-the Founder of Behaviourism: A Biography. 1979. 22.00 (ISBN 0-7100-0054-5). Routledge & Kegan.

Cohen, David D. & Dillon, John B. Anesthesia for Outpatient Surgery. (Illus.). 84p. 1970. 11.75 (ISBN 0-398-00324-6). C C Thomas.

Cohen, Doron J. & Brillinger, Peter C. Introduction to Data Structures & Non-Numeric Computation. (Illus.). 656p. 1972. ref. ed. 22.95 (ISBN 0-13-479899-6). P-H.

Cohen, Dorothy. Consumer Behavior. 504p. 1981. pap. text ed. 19.95 (ISBN 0-394-31160-4). Random.

Cohen, Dorothy H. The Learning Child. 384p. 1973. pap. 3.95 (ISBN 0-394-71877-1, Vin). Random.

Cohen, Dorothy H. & Rudolph, Marguerita. Kindergarten & Early Schooling. (Illus.). 352p. 1977. text ed. 17.95 (ISBN 0-13-515239-9). P-H.

Cohen, Edward P. & Kohler, Heinz, eds. Membranes, Receptors, & the Immune Response: Eighty Years After Ehrich's Side Chain Theory. LC 80-7811. (Progress in Clinical & Biological Research Ser.: Vol. 42). 404p. 1980. 34.00 (ISBN 0-8451-0042-4). A R Liss.

Cohen, Edward R. Materials for a Basic Course in Property. LC 78-17714. (American Casebook Ser.). 526p. 1978. text ed. 17.95 (ISBN 0-8299-2008-0). West Pub.

Cohen, Eleanor, ed. Expanding the Environmental Responsibility of Local Government: Claremont's Environmental Task Force & Its Recommendations. LC 72-83451. (Environmental Studies Ser: No. 3). 1972. pap. 10.00x (ISBN 0-912102-07-1). Cal Inst Public.

Cohen, Elias, ed. see Symposium, Woods Hole, Mass., October, 1978.

Cohen, Eva, jt. auth. see Bliss, Ann.

Cohen, Fred. Cases & Materials on the Law of Deprivation of Liberty: A Study in Social Control. LC 79-26667. (American Casebook Ser.). 793p. 1980. text ed. 18.95 (ISBN 0-8299-2079-X). West Pub.

--Standards Relating to Dispositional Procedures. (Juvenile Justice Standards Project Ser.). 1980. softcover 5.95 (ISBN 0-88410-808-2); casebound 16.50 (ISBN 0-88410-233-5). Ballinger Pub.

--Standards Relating to Dispositional Procedures. LC 76-14414. (Juvenile Justice Standards Project Ser.). 1977. softcover 5.95 o.p. (ISBN 0-88410-766-3); 12.50, casebound o.p. Ballinger Pub.

Cohen, Fred, jt. auth. see Rutherford, Andrew.

Cohen, Gail A. Summer Study Abroad. LC 73-78423. 1979. pap. 6.00 o.p. (ISBN 0-87206-091-8). Inst Intl Educ.

Cohen, Gail A., ed. The Learning Traveler: Vacation Study Abroad, Vol. 2. rev. ed. 186p. 1981. pap. text ed. 8.00 (ISBN 0-87206-107-8). Inst Intl Educ.

--The Learning Traveler: Vol. I, U. S. College-Sponsored Programs Abroad-Academic Year. rev. ed. 186p. 1980. pap. text ed. 8.00 o.p. (ISBN 0-87206-102-7). Inst Intl Educ.

--The Learning Traveler: Vol. II, Vacation Study Abroad. rev. ed. 185p. 1981. pap. text ed. 8.00 o.p. (ISBN 0-87206-107-8). Inst Intl Educ.

--The Learning Traveler Vol. 1: U. S. College-Sponsored Programs Abroad: Academic Year. rev. ed. 186p. 1981. pap. text ed. 8.00 (ISBN 0-87206-108-6). Inst Intl Educ.

--U.S. College-Sponsored Programs Abroad: Academic Year. LC 73-75994. 1979. pap. text ed. 6.00 o.p. (ISBN 0-87206-087-X). Inst Intl Educ.

Cohen, Gene D., jt. ed. see Miller, Nancy.

Cohen, Gustav, tr. see Hanslick, Eduard.

Cohen, Gustav, tr. see Hanslick, Edward.

Cohen, H., et al. Gas Turbine Theory. 2nd ed. 1979. 19.95 o.p. (ISBN 0-470-26781-X). Halsted Pr.

Cohen, Habiba S. Elusive Reform: The New French Universities, 1968-1978. (Westview Replica Edition). 1978. lib. bdg. 23.75x (ISBN 0-89158-195-2). Westview.

Cohen, Helen A. The Nurse's Quest for a Professional Identity. 1980. 14.95 (ISBN 0-201-00956-0); pap. 9.95 (ISBN 0-201-01157-3). A-W.

Cohen, Hennig & Dillingham, William B., eds. Humor of the Old Southwest. 2nd ed. LC 74-13512. 455p. 1975. pap. text ed. 7.95x (ISBN 0-8203-0358-5). U of Ga Pr.

Cohen, Hennig, jt. ed. see Coffin, Tristram P.

Cohen, Henry. Brutal Justice: The Ordeal of an American City. 248p. 1980. lib. bdg. 10.00x (ISBN 0-89444-027-6). John Jay Pr.

--Why Judaism? a Search for Meaning in Jewish Identity. 192p. 1973. pap. 5.00 (ISBN 0-8074-0077-7, 161901). UAHC.

Cohen, Henry, ed. Criminal Justice History: An International Annual, 1980, Vol. I. (Criminal Justice History Ser.). (Illus.). 294p. 1980. lib. bdg. 20.00x (ISBN 0-686-28890-4). Crime & Justice Hist.

Cohen, Herb. You Can Negotiate Anything. 1980. 12.00 (ISBN 0-8184-0305-5). Lyle Stuart.

Cohen, Howard. Equal Rights for Children. 172p. 1981. 13.50x (ISBN 0-8476-6772-3). Rowman.

Cohen, Howard, jt. auth. see Buchele, Robert.

Cohen, I. B. The Newtonian Revolution. LC 79-18637. 1981. 37.50 (ISBN 0-521-22964-2). Cambridge U Pr.

Cohen, I. Bernard. The Birth of a New Physics. LC 78-25792. (Illus.). 200p. 1981. Repr. of 1960 ed. lib. bdg. 19.75x (ISBN 0-313-20773-9, COBN). Greenwood.

--Birth of a New Physics. LC 60-5918. 1960. pap. 2.50 (ISBN 0-385-09447-7, S10, Anch). Doubleday.

--The Birth of the New Physics. LC 78-25792. (Illus.). 200p. 1981. Repr. of 1960 ed. lib. bdg. 19.75x (ISBN 0-313-20773-9, COBN). Greenwood.

--Introduction to Newton's Principia. LC 76-28770. 1971. 30.00 o.p. (ISBN 0-674-46175-4); pap. 10.00x (ISBN 0-674-46193-2). Harvard U Pr.

Cohen, I. Bernard, ed. Cotton Mather & American Science & Medicine: With Studies & Documents Concerning the Introduction of Inoculation or Variolation, 2 vols. LC 79-7974. (Three Centuries of Science in America Ser.). (Illus.). 1980. lib. bdg. 65.00x (ISBN 0-405-12556-9). Arno.

--The Life & the Scientific & Medical Career of Benjamin Waterhouse: With Some Account of the Introduction of Vaccination in America. an Original Anthology, 2 vols. LC 79-8004. (Three Centuries of Science in America Ser.). (Illus.). 1980. Set. lib. bdg. 60.00x (ISBN 0-405-12591-7). Arno.

Cohen, I. Bernard, ed. see Beaumont, William.

Cohen, I. Bernard, ed. see Cajori, Florian.

Cohen, I. Bernard, ed. see Fulton, John F.

Cohen, I. Bernard, ed. see Organisation for Economic Co-Operation & Development.

Cohen, I. Bernard, ed. see U. S. House of Representatives, 55th Congress, 2nd Session, Doc. No. 575, Pt. 3.

Cohen, I. Bernard, ed. see U. S. National Resources Committee.

Cohen, J. Living Embryos. 2nd ed. 1967. 16.50 (ISBN 0-08-012317-1); pap. 7.75 (ISBN 0-08-012316-3). Pergamon.

Cohen, J. M. Stable Homotopy. LC 77-139950. (Lecture Notes in Mathematics: Vol. 165). 1970. pap. 7.80 (ISBN 0-387-05192-9). Springer-Verlag.

Cohen, J. M. & Cohen, M. J. Penguin Dictionary of Modern Quotations. Date not set. pap. 3.95 (ISBN 0-14-051038-9). Penguin. Postponed.

--The Penguin Dictionary of Quotations. 1978. 15.00 o.p. (ISBN 0-670-27226-4). Viking Pr.

Cohen, J. M., ed. see Fitzgerald, Edward.

Cohen, Jack. Reproduction. 1977. 14.95 (ISBN 0-408-70798-4). Butterworths.

Cohen, Jack, tr. see Marx, Karl.

Cohen, Jack S., jt. auth. see Portugal, Franklin H.

Cohen, Jacob, jt. auth. see Williams, Edward.

Cohen, Jamey. Dmitri. 1981. pap. 2.25 (ISBN 0-451-09663-0, E9663, Sig). NAL.

--The Night Chasers. 353p. 1981. 11.95 (ISBN 0-87223-685-4). Seaview Bks.

Cohen, Jane, jt. auth. see Miller, Elizabeth.

Cohen, Jane R. Charles Dickens & His Original Illustrators. LC 79-21570. (Illus.). 320p. 1980. 32.50 (ISBN 0-686-65921-X). Ohio St U Pr.

Cohen, Jean P. & Goirand, Roger. Your Baby: Pregnancy, Delivery, & Infant Care. (Illus.). 304p. 1981. 16.95 (ISBN 0-13-978130-7, Spec); pap. 8.95 (ISBN 0-13-978122-6). P-H.

Cohen, Jerome, et al, eds. Psychosocial Aspects of Cancer. Orig. Title: Research Issues in Psychological Dimensions of Cancer. 300p. 1981. text ed. 25.00 (ISBN 0-89004-494-5). Raven.

Cohen, Jerome B. Personal Finance. 6th ed. 1979. text ed. 17.95x (ISBN 0-256-02154-6). Irwin.

Cohen, Jerome B., et al. Guide to Intelligent Investing. LC 77-83590. 1978. 12.50 (ISBN 0-87094-152-6). Dow Jones-Irwin.

--Investment Analysis & Portfolio Management. 3rd ed. 1977. text ed. 18.95x (ISBN 0-256-01883-9). Irwin.

Cohen, Joan, et al. Hitting Our Stride: Good News About Women in Their Middle Years. 1980. 10.95 (ISBN 0-440-03656-9). Delacorte.

Cohen, Joe H. Equipped for Good Work: A/Guide for Pastorso. 1981. 14.95 (ISBN 0-88289-271-1). Pelican.

Cohen, Joel B. Behavioral Science Foundations of Consumer Behavior. LC 79-142357. 1972. 15.95 (ISBN 0-02-905860-0). Free Pr.

Cohen, John. The Lineaments of Mind. LC 79-21794. (Illus.). 1980. text ed. 19.95x (ISBN 0-7167-1175-3). W H Freeman.

Cohen, John & Clark, John H. Medicine, Mind, & Man: An Introduction to Psychology for Students of Medicine & Allied Professions. LC 78-27201. (Illus.). 1979. text ed. 21.95x (ISBN 0-7167-1089-7); pap. text ed. 11.95x (ISBN 0-7167-1090-0). W H Freeman.

Cohen, John, ed. Essential Lenny Bruce. 1974. pap. 1.75 o.p. (ISBN 0-345-24386-2). Ballantine.

--Psychology: An Outline for the Intending Student. (Outlines Ser). 1968. pap. 7.95 (ISBN 0-7100-2998-5). Routledge & Kegan.

Cohen, John M., tr. see De Cervantes, Miguel.

Cohen, Jonathan, jt. ed. see Keylin, Arleen.

Cohen, Jonathan, tr. see Cardenal, Ernesto.

Cohen, Kalman J. & Cyert, Richard M. Theory of the Firm: Resource Allocation in a Market Economy. 2nd ed. (Illus.). 640p. 1975. 20.95 (ISBN 0-13-913798-X). P-H.

Cohen, Kathleen R. Metamorphosis of a Death Symbol: The Changing Meaning of the Transi Tomb in the Late Middle Ages & the Renaissance. (California Studies in the History of Art: Vol. 15). 1974. 50.00x (ISBN 0-520-01844-3). U of Cal Pr.

Cohen, Kenneth P. Hospice: Prescription for Terminal Care. LC 79-13341. 1979. text ed. 27.95 (ISBN 0-89443-151-X). Aspen Systems.

Cohen, L. J. & Hesse, M. B., eds. Applications of Inductive Logic: Proceedings of a Conference at the Queen's College, Oxford, August 1978. (Illus.). 410p. 1980. 65.00x (ISBN 0-19-824584-X). Oxford U Pr.
Cohen, L. Jonathan. The Probable & the Provable. (Clarendon Library of Logic & Philosophy). 1977. 36.00x (ISBN 0-19-824412-6). Oxford U Pr.
Cohen, Lawrence S., et al. Physical Conditioning & Cardiovascular Rehabilitation. 344p. 1981. 25.00 (ISBN 0-471-08713-0, Pub. by Wiley-Med). Wiley.
Cohen, Leonard. Choosing to Work. 1979. case bdg. 11.95 (ISBN 0-8359-0764-3); pap. 6.95 (ISBN 0-8359-0762-7); instrs'. manual avail. Reston.
--The Energy of Slaves. LC 72-75749. 192p. 1973. pap. 2.95 o.s.i. (ISBN 0-670-00376-X). Penguin.
Cohen, Lester H. The Revolutionary Histories: Contemporary Narratives of the American Revolution. LC 80-11243. 1980. 15.00x (ISBN 0-8014-1277-3). Cornell U Pr.
Cohen, Louis. Educational Research in Classrooms & Schools. 1977. text ed. 25.10 (ISBN 0-06-318047-2, IntlDept). Har-Row.
Cohen, M., et al, eds. Central Axis Depth Dose Data for Use in Radiotherapy. 1980. 25.00x (Pub. by Brit Inst Radiology England). State Mutual Bk.
Cohen, M. J., jt. auth. see Cohen, J. M.
Cohen, Malcom S. On the Feasibility of a Labor Market Information System, 3 vols. 1974. pap. 10.95x set (ISBN 0-87736-331-5); pap. 3.95x ea. U of Mich Inst Labor.
Cohen, Margo P. & Foa, Piero P., eds. Special Topics in Endocrinology & Metabolism, Vol. 1. 154p. 1979. 18.00x (ISBN 0-8451-0700-3). A R Liss.
Cohen, Mark N. The Food Crisis in Prehistory: Over Population & Origins of Agriculture. LC 76-41858. 1979. 20.00x (ISBN 0-300-02016-3); pap. 7.95x (ISBN 0-300-02351-0). Yale U Pr.
Cohen, Mark R. Jewish Self-Government in Medieval Egypt: The Origins of the Office of Head of the Jews, ca. 1065-1126. LC 80-7514. (Princeton Studies on the Near East). 425p. 1980. 27.50 (ISBN 0-691-05307-3). Princeton U Pr.
Cohen, Marshall, jt. ed. see Mast, Gerald.
Cohen, Martin. In Quest of Telescopes. (Illus.). 131p. 1980. 10.95 (ISBN 0-933346-25-5, 6255). Sky Pub.
Cohen, Martin, jt. auth. see Anderson, James L.
Cohen, Maurice. Woodcutter's Companion: A Guide to Locating, Cutting, Transporting & Storing Your Own Firewood. Rowland, Amy, ed. (Illus.). 160p. (Orig.). 1981. 11.95 (ISBN 0-87857-328-3); pap. 7.95 (ISBN 0-87857-329-1). Rodale Pr Inc.
Cohen, Maynard M., ed. Biochemistry of Neural Disease. (Illus.). 1975. text ed. 27.50x (ISBN 0-06-140646-5, Harper Medical). Har-Row.
Cohen, Melvin R. Laparoscopy, Culdoscopy & Gynecography: Technique & Atlas. LC 72-126452. (Major Problems in Obstetrics & Gynecology: Vol. 1). (Illus.). 1970. 15.00 (ISBN 0-7216-2650-5). Saunders.
Cohen, Michael D., ed. see Carnegie Commission on Higher Education.
Cohen, Michael V. Correlative Atlas of Adult Cardiac Disorders: Noninvasive Diagnostic Techniques. LC 80-66333. (Illus.). 428p. 1980. 48.50 (ISBN 0-87993-149-3). Futura Pub.
Cohen, Miriam. Bee My Valentine. LC 77-21950. (Illus.). (gr. k-3). 1978. 7.95 (ISBN 0-688-80129-3); PLB 7.63 (ISBN 0-688-84129-5). Greenwillow.
--Best Friends. LC 70-146620. (Illus.). (ps-1). 1971. 6.95 (ISBN 0-02-722800-2). Macmillan.
--First Grade Takes a Test. LC 80-10316. (Illus.). 32p. (ps-3). 1980. 7.95 (ISBN 0-688-80265-6); PLB 7.63 (ISBN 0-688-84265-8). Greenwillow.
--Lost in the Museum. LC 78-16765. (Illus.). (gr. k-3). 1979. 7.75 (ISBN 0-688-80187-0); PLB 7.44 (ISBN 0-688-84187-2). Greenwillow.
--Tough Jim. LC 73-19065. (Illus.). 32p. (ps-1). 1974. 4.95g o.s.i. (ISBN 0-02-722760-X). Macmillan.
--When Will I Read? LC 76-28320. (ps-3). 1977. 8.25 (ISBN 0-688-80073-4); PLB 7.92 (ISBN 0-688-84073-6). Greenwillow.
--Will I Have a Friend. (Illus.). (gr. k-1). 1967. 7.95 (ISBN 0-02-722790-1). Macmillan.
Cohen, Mitch, ed. Berlin: Contemporary Writing from Berlin. LC 77-642342. (Rockbottom Specials Ser.). (Illus., Eng. & Ger.). Date not set. 15.00 o.p. (ISBN 0-930012-23-2); pap. 6.00 o.p. (ISBN 0-930012-22-4). Mudborn. Postponed.
Cohen, Monroe D., ed. Personal Liberty & Education. LC 76-2511. 288p. 1976. 8.95 (ISBN 0-590-07462-8, Citation); pap. text ed. 4.95 (ISBN 0-590-09406-8). Schol Bk Serv.
--Testing & Evaluation: New Views. LC 74-34211. 64p. 1980. Repr. of 1975 ed. 3.50x (ISBN 0-87173-000-6). ACEI.
--When Children Move. LC 72-83410. (Illus.). 47p. 1972. 1.50x o.p. (ISBN 0-87173-045-6). ACEI.
Cohen, Monroe D., ed. see ACEI Committee, et al.
Cohen, Mortimer T. From Prologue to Epilogue in Vietnam. LC 79-54798. (Illus.). 612p. 15.00 (ISBN 0-686-28498-4). Retriever.
--Poems of Morris Rosenfield Transliterated. LC 79-54799. 140p. pap. 7.50 (ISBN 0-686-28499-2). Retriever.
Cohen, Morton H., ed. see Carroll, Lewis.
Cohen, Morton N., tr. see Carroll, Lewis.
Cohen, Myer M. Notices of Florida & the Campaigns. Tyler, O. Z., Jr., ed. LC 64-19153. (Floridiana Facsimile & Reprint Ser). 1964. Repr. of 1836 ed. 10.75 (ISBN 0-8130-0048-3). U Presses Fla.
Cohen, Nicholas, jt. ed. see Marchalonis, John J.
Cohen, Norm. Long Steel Rail: The Railroad in American Folksong. LC 80-14874. (Music in American Life Ser.). (Illus.). 738p. 1981. 49.95 (ISBN 0-252-00343-8). U of Ill Pr.
Cohen, Patricia F., jt. auth. see Creighton, Margo N.
Cohen, Patricia F., jt. auth. see Neal, Margo C.
Cohen, Paul. Realm of the Submarine. LC 69-12176. 1969. 5.95 o.s.i. (ISBN 0-685-15803-9). Macmillan.
Cohen, Paul A. Between Tradition & Modernity: Wang T'ao & Reform in Late Ch'ing China. LC 74-75109. (East Asian Ser.: No. 77). 336p. 1974. text ed. 17.50x (ISBN 0-674-06875-0). Harvard U Pr.
Cohen, Percy S., jt. ed. see Shack, William A.
Cohen, Peter Z. Deadly Game at Stoney Creek. (Orig.). (gr. 6-12). 1980. pap. 1.25 (ISBN 0-440-91288-1, LFL). Dell.
Cohen, R. Economics of Agriculture. (Cambridge Economic Handbook Ser). 1949. 10.95x (ISBN 0-521-08754-6). Cambridge U Pr.
Cohen, R. B., et al, eds. see Hymer, S.
Cohen, Randy & Anderson, Alexandra. Why Didn't I Think of That. (Illus.). 1980. pap. 5.95 (ISBN 0-449-90037-1, Columbine). Fawcett.
Cohen, Richard L. Applications of Mossbauer Spectroscopy, Vol. 2. 1980. write for info (ISBN 0-12-178402-9). Acad Pr.
Cohen, Richard M., et al. The Notre Dame Football Scrapbook. LC 77-5262. (Illus.). 1977. pap. 6.95 o.p. (ISBN 0-672-52335-3). Bobbs.
Cohen, Robert. Color of Man. (gr. 5-9). 1968. pap. 1.95 o.p. (ISBN 0-394-82306-0, BYR). Random.
--The Theatre. (Illus.). 500p. (Orig.). 1981. pap. text ed. price not set (ISBN 0-87484-459-2). Mayfield Pub.
Cohen, Robert & Harrop, John. Creative Play Direction. (Theater & Drama Ser). (Illus.). 304p. 1974. ref. ed. 14.95 (ISBN 0-13-190918-5). P-H.
Cohen, Robert, et al, eds. Psych City. LC 72-11593. 348p. 1974. text ed. 21.00 (ISBN 0-08-017082-X); pap. text ed. 12.75 (ISBN 0-08-017083-8). Pergamon.
Cohen, Robert D. & Jody, Ruth. Freshman Seminar: A New Orientation. LC 77-1682. (Westview Special Studies in Higher Education Ser.). 1978. PLB 20.00x (ISBN 0-89158-098-0); pap. text ed. 9.75x (ISBN 0-89158-099-9). Westview.
Cohen, Robert J., jt. auth. see Gaines, Steven.
Cohen, Robert S., ed. Herbert Feigl: Inquiries & Provocations, Selected Writings. 1929 to 1974. (Vienna Circle Collection: No. 14). 450p. 1980. lib. bdg. 50.00 (ISBN 90-277-1101-1, Pub. by D. Reidel); pap. 23.50 (ISBN 90-277-1102-X). Kluwer Boston.
Cohen, Robin, jt. auth. see Sandbrook, Richard.
Cohen, Ronald, jt. ed. see Britan, Gerald M.
Cohen, Ronald, jt. ed. see Naroll, Raoul.
Cohen, Roy. Stand up for Your Rights. 14.95 (ISBN 0-671-25341-7). S&S.
Cohen, S., et al. Mechanisms of Immunopathology. LC 78-18290. (Basic & Clinical Immunologies Ser.). 1979. 32.95 (ISBN 0-471-16429-1, Pub. by Wiley Medical). Wiley.
Cohen, S. S. Advaitic Sadhana. 1976. 7.50 (ISBN 0-8426-0989-X). Orient Bk Dist.
Cohen, S. T. The Neutron Bomb: Political, Technological & Military Issues. LC 78-63388. (Special Reports Ser.). 1978. 6.50 (ISBN 0-89549-009-9). Inst Foreign Policy Anal.
Cohen, S. T., jt. auth. see Van Cleave, W. R.
Cohen, Sandee. All We Know of Heaven. (Orig.). 1981. pap. 2.50 (ISBN 0-451-09891-9, E9891, Sig). NAL.
Cohen, Sandra B. Resource Teaching: A Mainstreaming Simulation. 1978. pap. text ed. 4.95 (ISBN 0-675-08351-6); 125.00, 4 cassettes 4 filmstrips (ISBN 0-675-08444-X); 2-5 sets 75.00, 6 or more sets 60.00 (ISBN 0-686-67988-1). cards 3.95 (ISBN 0-686-67990-3). Merrill.
Cohen, Sandy. Norman Mailer's Novels. (Costerus Ser.: No. 20). 1979. pap. text ed. 14.25x (ISBN 90-6203-912-X). Humanities.
Cohen, Sanford. Labor in the United States. 5th ed. (Economics Ser.). 1979. text ed. 18.95 (ISBN 0-675-08299-4). Merrill.
Cohen, Sanford I. & Ross, Robert. Handbook of Clinical Psychobiology & Pathology, Vol. 1 & 2. LC 80-14321. (Clinical & Community Psychology Ser.). 1981. Set. text ed. 55.00 (ISBN 0-89116-172-4); Vol. 1. text ed. 25.00 (ISBN 0-89116-173-2); Vol. 2. text ed. 35.00 (ISBN 0-89116-174-0). Hemisphere Pub. Postponed.
Cohen, Saul B. Jerusalem: Bridging the Four Walls: a Geopolitical Perspective. LC 77-76665. (Illus.). 1978. lib. bdg. 12.00 o.p. (ISBN 0-685-91823-8). Westview.
--Jerusalem Undivided. 1980. pap. 3.00 (ISBN 0-930832-58-2). Herzl Pr.
Cohen, Selma J., ed. The Modern Dance: Seven Statements of Belief. LC 66-14663. (Illus.). 1969. pap. 5.95x (ISBN 0-8195-6003-0, Pub. by Wesleyan U Pr). Columbia U Pr.
Cohen, Seymour S. Virus-Induced Enzymes. LC 68-55418. (Biology Ser.: No. 24). (Illus.). 1968. 22.50x (ISBN 0-231-03053-3). Columbia U Pr.
Cohen, Sharleen C. Regina's Song. (Orig.). 1980. pap. 2.50 o.s.i. (ISBN 0-440-17414-7). Dell.
Cohen, Sherry S., jt. auth. see DuCoffe, Jean.
Cohen, Sidney. The Substance Abuse Problems. 416p. 1981. text ed. 22.95 (ISBN 0-917724-18-6); pap. text ed. 13.95 (ISBN 0-917724-22-4). Haworth Pr.
Cohen, Sidney, ed. Drug Abuse & Alcoholism: Current Critical Issues. LC 79-25648. (Collected Essay Ser.). 1981. pap. text ed. 6.95 (ISBN 0-917724-10-0). Haworth Pr.
Cohen, Sol, compiled by. Education in the United States: A Documentary History, 5 vols. LC 73-3099. 1974. Set. lib. bdg. 200.00 (ISBN 0-313-20141-2). Greenwood.
Cohen, Stan. The Tree Army: A Pictorial History of the Civilian Conservation Corps 1933-1943. LC 80-81071. 172p. 1980. 11.95 (ISBN 0-933126-11-5); pap. 7.95 (ISBN 0-933126-10-7). Pictorial Hist.
Cohen, Stan B. & Houde, Frank. Missoula-Bitterroot Memory Book: A Picture Post Card History. LC 79-90794. (Illus.). 96p. 1979. pap. 5.95 (ISBN 0-933126-09-3). Pictorial Hist.
Cohen, Stan B. & Miller, Don C. The University of Montana: A Pictorial History. LC 80-53616. (Illus.). 96p. 1980. pap. 5.95 (ISBN 0-933126-12-3). Pictorial Hist.
Cohen, Stanley. Law Enforcement Guide to United States Supreme Court Decisions. (Illus.). 232p. 1972. text ed. 19.75 (ISBN 0-398-02261-5). C C Thomas.
Cohen, Stanley, ed. Pediatric Emergency Management: Guidelines for Rapid Diagnosis. new ed. (Illus.). 250p. 1981. pap. text ed. 55.00 (ISBN 0-87619-665-2). R J Brady.
Cohen, Stanley & Young, Jock, eds. The Manufacture of News: Social Problems, Deviance & the Mass Media. LC 73-87747. (Communication & Society: Vol. 3). 1973. 20.00x (ISBN 0-8039-0325-1); pap. 9.95x (ISBN 0-8039-1174-2). Sage.
Cohen, Stephen & Burns, Richard C. Pathways of the Pulp. LC 76-15672. (Illus.). 592p. 1976. 36.50 o.p. (ISBN 0-8016-1014-1). Mosby.
--Pathways of the Pulp. 2nd ed. LC 79-15286. 1979. pap. 42.50 (ISBN 0-8016-1009-5). Mosby.
Cohen, Stephen D. The Making of United States International Economic Policy: Principles, Problems, & Proposals for Reform. LC 77-7469. (Praeger Special Studies). 1977. text ed. 24.95 (ISBN 0-03-021926-4); pap. 10.95 (ISBN 0-03-021921-3). Praeger.
Cohen, Stephen F., et al, eds. The Soviet Union Since Stalin. LC 79-3092. 352p. 1980. 22.50x (ISBN 0-253-32272-3); pap. 7.95x (ISBN 0-253-20236-1). Ind U Pr.
Cohen, Stephen P. The Indian Army: Its Contribution to the Development of a Nation. LC 77-111421. 1971. 20.00x (ISBN 0-520-01697-1). U of Cal Pr.
Cohen, Stephen P. & Park, Richard L. India: Emergent Power? LC 78-50920. (NSIC Strategy Paper Ser.). 1978. 7.50x o.p. (ISBN 0-8448-1351-6). Crane-Russak Co.
Cohen, Stephen S. Modern Capitalist Planning: The French Model. new ed. 1977. 24.00x (ISBN 0-520-02793-0); pap. 7.95x (ISBN 0-520-02892-9, CAMPUS 141). U of Cal Pr.
Cohen, Steve. Avalanche! 1980. pap. 2.50 (ISBN 0-89083-672-8, Kable News Co). Zebra.
Cohen, Steven & Gans, Bruce. The Other Generation Gap: You & Your Aging Parents. 336p. 1980. pap. 2.95 (ISBN 0-446-93756-8). Warner Bks.
Cohen, Stuart. Proceedings of Towing Tank Conference, 2 vols. 1275p. 1981. Set. text ed. 88.00 (ISBN 0-250-40444-3). Ann Arbor Science.
Cohen, Stuart E. Chicago Architects: A Revisionist View of Chicago Architecture. LC 76-2194. (Illus.). 1976. 25.00 o.s.i. (ISBN 0-8040-0732-2); pap. 10.00 o.s.i. (ISBN 0-8040-0731-4). Swallow.
Cohen, Stuart J., ed. New Directions in Patient Compliance. (Illus.). 1979. 16.95 (ISBN 0-669-02721-9). Lexington Bks.
Cohen, Sydney & Sadun, Elvio H. Immunology of Parasitic Infections. (Blackwell Scientific Pubns.). (Illus.). 1976. 48.75 (ISBN 0-632-00097-X). Mosby.
Cohen, Theodore J. & Bray, Jacqueline H. The Magic Machine. (Illus.). (ps-3). 1979. 2.00 (ISBN 0-931718-17-1, BYTE Bks). McGraw.
Cohen, W. I. America's Response to China: An Interpretive History of Sino-American Relations. (America & the World Ser.). 1971. pap. text ed. 8.95x o.p. (ISBN 0-471-16336-8). Wiley.
Cohen, Warren I. America's Response to China: An Interpretive History of Sino-American Relations. 2nd ed. LC 80-13383. (America & the World Ser.). 265p. 1980. pap. text ed. 8.95 (ISBN 0-471-06089-5). Wiley.
--The China Connection. (Studies of the East Asian Institute). 1978. 20.00x (ISBN 0-231-04444-5). Columbia U Pr.
--Dean Rusk. (The American Secretaries of State & Their Diplomacy: Vol. XIX). 375p. 1980. 22.50x (ISBN 0-8154-0519-7). Cooper Sq.
Cohen, Wilbur J. & Westoff, Charles F. Demographic Dynamics in America. LC 77-80227. 1977. 12.95 (ISBN 0-02-905780-9). Free Pr.
Cohen, William. European Empire Building. LC 79-57459. (Problems in Civilization Ser.). (Orig.). 1980. pap. text ed. 3.95x (ISBN 0-88273-410-5). Forum Pr MO.
--Roll Call. 1981. 14.95 (ISBN 0-671-25142-2). S&S.
Cohen, William A. The Executive's Guide to Finding a Superior Job. LC 78-7370. (Illus.). 1978. 13.95 (ISBN 0-8144-5475-5). Am Mgmt.
--How to Sell to the Government: A Step by Step Guide to Success. LC 80-2297. 375p. 1981. 14.95 (ISBN 0-471-08103-5, Pub. by Ronald Pr). Wiley.
Cohen, William A. & Reddick, Marshall E. Successful Marketing for Small Business. 364p. 1981. 17.95 (ISBN 0-8144-5611-1). Am Mgmt.
Cohen, Y. Radionuclides in Pharmacology, 2 Vols. 1971. Set. 160.00 (ISBN 0-08-016152-9). Pergamon.
Cohen, Yehudi A., ed. Man in Adaptation. Incl. Biosocial Background. 2nd ed. LC 74-169511. 1974. Vol. 1. lib. bdg. 24.95x (ISBN 0-202-01111-9); pap. 12.95x (ISBN 0-202-01112-7); Cultural Present. 2nd ed. 1974. Vol. 2. lib. bdg. 24.95x (ISBN 0-202-01109-7); pap. 12.95x (ISBN 0-202-01110-0); Institutional Framework. 1971. Vol. 3. 24.95x (ISBN 0-202-01095-3); pap. 9.95x (ISBN 0-202-01096-1). Aldine Pub.
Cohen-Tannoudji, Claude, et al. Quantum Mechanics, 2 vols. LC 76-5874. 1978. Vol. 1. 37.50 (ISBN 0-471-16432-1, Pub. by Wiley-Interscience); 34.50 (ISBN 0-471-16434-8); Vol. 1. pap. 21.95 (ISBN 0-471-16433-X); Vol. 2. pap. 20.50 (ISBN 0-471-16435-6). Wiley.
Cohler, Bertram J. & Grunebaum, Henry U. Mothers, Grandmothers & Daughters: Personality & Child-Care in Three Generation Families. LC 80-17979. (Personality Processes Ser.). 496p. 1981. 22.50 (ISBN 0-471-05900-5, Pub. by Wiley-Interscience). Wiley.
Cohler, David. Gamemaker. 1981. pap. 2.50 (ISBN 0-451-09766-1, E9766, Sig). NAL.
Cohn. Pancreatic Cancer: New Directions in Therapeutic Management. 1981. price not set (ISBN 0-89352-133-7). Masson Pub.
Cohn & Madrid. Coming Back: A Guide to Recovering from Heart Attack & Living Confidently. 10.95 (ISBN 0-201-04562-1). A-W.
Cohn, Adrian, jt. auth. see Bell, James K.
Cohn, Albert & Miller, Leta E. Music in the Paris Academy of Sciences. LC 78-70025. (Detroit Studies in Music Bibliography Ser.: No. 43). 1979. 8.50 (ISBN 0-911772-96-0). Info Coord.
Cohn, Alvin W., jt. auth. see Viano, Emilio.
Cohn, Alvin W., ed. Criminal Justice Planning & Development. LC 77-81154. (Sage Research Progress Series in Criminology: Vol. 5). 1977. 12.95x (ISBN 0-8039-0918-7); pap. 6.50x (ISBN 0-8039-0913-6). Sage.
--The Future of Policing. LC 77-92833. (Sage Criminal Justice System Annuals: Vol. 9). 1978. 20.00x (ISBN 0-8039-0702-8); pap. 9.95x (ISBN 0-8039-0703-6). Sage.
Cohn, Alvin W. & Ward, Benjamin, eds. Improving Management in Criminal Justice. LC 80-18331. (Sage Research Progress Ser. in Criminology: Vol. 17). (Illus.). 159p. 1980. 12.95 (ISBN 0-8039-1515-2); pap. 6.50 (ISBN 0-8039-1516-0). Sage.
Cohn, Angelo. First Book of the Netherlands. rev. ed. (First Bks). (Illus.). (gr. 4-6). 1971. PLB 4.90 o.p. (ISBN 0-531-00593-3). Watts.

Cohn, Arthur. The Collector's Twentieth-Century Music in the Western Hemisphere. LC 74-167848. (Music Ser.). 1972. Repr. of 1961 ed. 25.00 (ISBN 0-306-70404-8). Da Capo.

--Twentieth-Century Music in Western Europe: The Compositions & Recordings. LC 70-39297. 510p. 1972. Repr. of 1965 ed. lib. bdg. 37.50 (ISBN 0-306-70460-9). Da Capo.

Cohn, David L. & Melsa, James L. A Step by Step Introduction to 8080 Microprocessor Systems. 1977. pap. 8.95 (ISBN 0-918398-04-5). Dilithium Pr.

Cohn, Frederick & Moritz, C. Understanding Human Sexuality. (Illus.). 304p. 1974. 13.95 (ISBN 0-13-937425-6); pap. 11.95 (ISBN 0-13-937417-5). P-H.

Cohn, H. W. Else Lasker-Schuler, the Broken World. LC 73-80481. (Anglica Germanica Ser.: No. 2). 172p. 1974. 42.50 (ISBN 0-521-20292-2). Cambridge U Pr.

Cohn, Harvey. Advanced Number Theory. (Illus.). 1980. pap. 5.00 (ISBN 0-486-64023-X). Dover.

--Conformal Mapping on Riemann Surfaces. (Illus.). 352p. 1980. pap. text ed. 6.00 (ISBN 0-486-64025-6). Dover.

Cohn, Henry J. Government of the Rhine Palatinate in the Fifteenth Century. 1965. 24.00x (ISBN 0-19-821454-5). Oxford U Pr.

Cohn, Jan. Improbable Fiction: The Life of Mary Roberts Rinehart. LC 79-3997. 1980. 16.95 (ISBN 0-8229-3401-9). U of Pittsburgh Pr.

Cohn, Jeff. Saturday Night at Daisy's. LC 77-92055. 1978. 8.95 o.p. (ISBN 0-15-179412-X). HarBraceJ.

Cohn, Laurence S. Effective Use of ANS COBOL Computer Programming Language: A Supplemental Text for Programmers Working with IBM's OS & DOS Systems. LC 75-5584. (Business Data Processing Ser). 178p. 1975. 20.95 (ISBN 0-471-16436-4, Pub. by Wiley-Interscience). Wiley.

Cohn, M. Woerterbuch Des Juedischen Rechts. (Illus.). xii, 196p. 1981. 57.00 (ISBN 3-8055-2062-X). S Karger.

Cohn, M. M. Dictionnaire francais-hebreu. (Fr. & Heb.). 29.00 (ISBN 0-685-13874-7). Larousse.

Cohn, M. Z. Limit Design for Reinforced Concrete Structures. (Bibliography: No. 8). 1970. pap. 26.25 (ISBN 0-685-85146-X, B-8) (ISBN 0-685-85147-8). ACI.

Cohn, M. Z., ed. see NATO Advanced Study Institute, University of Waterloo, Canada 2-12, August 1977.

Cohn, Margot & Buber, Rafael, eds. Martin Buber: A Bibliography of His Writings, 1897-1978. 164p. 1980. 35.00 (ISBN 3-598-10146-5, Dist by Gale Research Co.). K G Saur.

Cohn, Marjorie B. Wash & Gouache: A Study of the Development of the Materials of Watercolor. LC 77-176. 120p. 1980. pap. 7.50 (ISBN 0-916724-06-9). Fogg Art.

Cohn, Marjorie B. & Siegfried, Susan L. Works by J. A. D. Ingres in the Collection of the Fogg Art Museum, Vol. III. Walsh, Peter & Kaliski, Andrea, eds. (Fogg Art Museum Handbooks). (Illus.). 190p. pap. write for info. Fogg Art.

Cohn, Marvin. Helping Your Teen-Age Student: What Parents Can Do to Improve Reading & Study Skills. 1980. pap. 2.50 (ISBN 0-451-09502-2, E9502, Sig). NAL.

Cohn, Michael & Platzer, Michael. Black Men of the Sea. LC 78-4873. (Illus.). 1978. 8.95 (ISBN 0-396-07546-0). Dodd.

Cohn, P. M. Algebra, 2 vols. LC 73-2780. Vol. 1, 1974, 384p. 34.25 (ISBN 0-471-16430-5, Pub. by Wiley-Interscience); Vol. 2, 1977. 29.95 (ISBN 0-471-01823-6); Vol. 1. pap. 15.95 (ISBN 0-471-16431-3). Wiley.

--Linear Equations. (Library of Mathematics). 1971. pap. 3.50 (ISBN 0-7100-6181-1). Routledge & Kegan.

--Skew Field Constructions. LC 76-46854. (London Mathematical Society Lecture Note Series: No. 27). (Illus.). 1977. limp bdg. 26.95x (ISBN 0-521-21497-1). Cambridge U Pr.

--Solid Geometry. (Library of Mathematics). 1968. pap. 3.00 (ISBN 0-7100-6343-1). Routledge & Kegan.

Cohn, Robert G. Toward the Poems of Mallarme. 1965. 12.50x (ISBN 0-520-00250-4, CAMPUS 221); pap. 5.95x (ISBN 0-520-03846-0). U of Cal Pr.

Cohn, Robert L. The Shape of Sacred Space: Four Biblical Studies. Cherry, Conrad, ed. LC 80-11086. (Studies in Religion: No. 23). 12.00x (ISBN 0-89130-383-9, 01 00 23); pap. 7.50x (ISBN 0-89130-384-7). Scholars Pr CA.

Cohn, Ruby. Samuel Beckett: The Comic Gamut. 1962. 18.00 (ISBN 0-8135-0402-3). Rutgers U Pr.

Cohn, Ruby & Dukore, Bernard, eds. Twentieth Century Drama: England, Ireland, the United States. 1966. pap. text ed. 9.95x (ISBN 0-394-30141-2, RanC). Random.

Cohn, S. H., ed. Non-Invasive Measurements of Bone Mass & Their Clinical Application. 240p. 1980. 64.95 (ISBN 0-8493-5789-6). CRC Pr.

Cohn, Samuel K., Jr. The Laboring Classes in Renaissance Florence. (Studies in Social Discontinuity). 1980. 29.50 (ISBN 0-12-179180-7). Acad Pr.

Cohn, Sidney A. & Gottlieb, Marvin. Anatomy Review. 6th ed. LC 80-20349. (Basic Science Review Bks.). 1980. pap. 8.50 (ISBN 0-87488-201-X). Med Exam.

Cohn, Sidney A. & Gottlieb, Marvin I. Head & Neck Anatomy Review. (Basic Science Review Bks.). 1976. spiral bdg. 8.50 (ISBN 0-87488-222-2). Med Exam.

Cohn, Stanley H. Economic Development in the Soviet Union. 1970. pap. text ed. 3.95x o.p. (ISBN 0-669-52688-6). Heath.

Cohn, W. The Gypsies. 1973. pap. 5.95 (ISBN 0-201-11362-7, 11362). A-W.

Cohn, Waldo E., ed. Progress in Nucleic Acid Research & Molecular Biology, Vol. 24. 1980. 32.50 (ISBN 0-12-540024-1); lib. ed. 42.50 (ISBN 0-12-540092-6); microfiche ed. 22.50 (ISBN 0-12-540093-4). Acad Pr.

--Progress in Nucleic Acid Research & Molecular Biology, Vol. 25. (Serial Publication). 1981. 29.50 (ISBN 0-12-540025-X); lib. bdg. 38.50 (ISBN 0-12-540094-2); microfiche ed. 20.00 (ISBN 0-12-540095-0). Acad Pr.

--Progress in Nucleic Acid Research & Molecular Biology: DNA: Multiprotein Interactions, Vol. 26. (Serial Publication Ser.). 1981. write for info. (ISBN 0-12-540026-8); lib. ed. (ISBN 0-12-540095-0); microfiche ed. (ISBN 0-12-540096-9). Acad Pr.

Cohn, Werner. The Gypsies. 1973. pap. text ed. 5.95 (ISBN 0-8461-1362-7). Benjamin-Cummings.

Cohn-Gilletly, Joanne. Ten Minutes with Me. 3rd ed. (Illus., Orig.). (gr. k-3). 1980. pap. 2.00 (ISBN 0-916634-05-1). Double M Pr.

Cohn-Vossen, Stephan, jt. auth. see Hilbert, David.

Cohodas, Marvin. The Great Ball Court of Chichen Itza, Yucatan, Mexico. LC 77-94690. (Outstanding Dissertations in the Fine Arts Ser.). 1978. lib. bdg. 48.50 (ISBN 0-8240-3221-7). Garland Pub.

Cohon, Beryl D. Come, Let Us Reason Together. LC 76-24330. 1977. 5.95x (ISBN 0-8197-0397-4). Bloch.

--Judaism in Theory & Practice. 3rd rev. ed. LC 68-57021. 1969. write for info. (ISBN 0-8197-0069-X). Bloch.

Cohu, J. R. Vital Problems of Religion. 304p. Repr. of 1914 ed. text ed. 2.95 (ISBN 0-567-02077-0). Attic Pr.

Coil, Ann P., jt. auth. see Andres, Ann A.

Coil, Henry W. Conversation on Freemasonry. 1980. Repr. soft cover 12.50 (ISBN 0-686-68272-6). Macoy Pub.

Coit, Margaret L. The Growing Years, 1789-1829. LC 63-8572. (Life History of the United States). (Illus.). (gr. 5 up). 1974. PLB 8.67 o.p. (ISBN 0-8094-0552-0, Pub. by Time-Life). Silver.

--The Sweep Westward, 1829-1849. LC 63-8572. (Life History of the United States). (Illus.). (gr. 5 up). 1974. PLB 9.93 (ISBN 0-8094-0553-9, Pub. by Time-Life). Silver.

Coke, Desmond. Art of Silhouette. LC 73-110809. (Illus.). 1970. Repr. of 1913 ed. 18.00 (ISBN 0-8103-3549-2). Gale.

Coke, Dorothy V. Mary Catherine & the Little Pig's Tail. (Illus.). 1981. 4.95 (ISBN 0-533-04761-7). Vantage.

Coke, Edward & Highmore, Anthony, Jr. A Little Treatise on Baile & Maineprize. Berkowitz, David S. & Thorne, Samuel E., eds. LC 77-86576. (Classics of English Legal History in the Modern Era Ser.: Vol. 13). 352p. 1979. lib. bdg. 40.00 (ISBN 0-8240-3062-1). Garland Pub.

Coke, Paul T. Mountain & Wilderness. 1978. pap. 3.95 (ISBN 0-8164-2177-3). Crossroad NY.

Coke, Tom S. Life in a Fishbowl. 1978. pap. 2.50 (ISBN 0-88207-764-3). Victor Bks.

--More Than Just You. 1979. pap. 2.50 (ISBN 0-88207-578-0). Victor Bks.

Coke, Van Deren. The Painter & the Photograph: From Delacroix to Warhol. rev ed. LC 75-129804. (Illus.). 324p. 1972. pap. 19.95 (ISBN 0-8263-0325-0). U of NM Pr.

Coker, Elizabeth B. Blood Red Roses. LC 77-1366. 1977. 9.95 o.p. (ISBN 0-525-06860-0). Dutton.

--The Grasshopper King. 1981. 13.95 (ISBN 0-525-10716-9). Dutton.

Coker, Lawrence T. & Gaddis, Robert S. Protective Coatings for Structural Steel in the Pulp & Paper Industry. (TAPPI PRESS Reports). 1980. pap. 44.95 (ISBN 0-89852-380-X, 01-01-R080). TAPPI.

Coker, Paul, jt. auth. see Hart, Stan.

Coker, Peter. Etching Techniques. 1976. 22.50 (ISBN 0-7134-3063-X, Pub. by Batsford England). David & Charles.

Coker, W. Music & Meaning. LC 72-142358. 1972. 12.95 (ISBN 0-02-906350-7). Free Pr.

Coladarci, Arthur P. & Coladarci, Theodore. Elementary Discriptive Statistics: For Those Who Think They Can't. 144p. 1979. pap. text ed. 6.95x (ISBN 0-534-00782-1). Wadsworth Pub.

Coladarci, Arthur P., jt. auth. see Koosis, Donald J.

Coladarci, Theodore, jt. auth. see Coladarci, Arthur P.

Colander, David, jt. auth. see Lerner, Abba.

Colangelo, Vito J. & Heiser, F. A. Analysis of Metallurgical Failures. LC 73-19773. (Science & Technology of Materials Ser). 384p. 1974. 33.00 (ISBN 0-471-16450-X, Pub. by Wiley-Interscience). Wiley.

Colasurdo, James F., jt. auth. see Weiner, Richard.

Colavita, Francis B. Sensory Changes in the Elderly. (Illus.). 152p. 1978. 14.50 (ISBN 0-398-03829-5). C C Thomas.

Colbeck, John, jt. auth. see Billington, Dora.

Colbeck, Maurice. Yorkshire. 1979. 19.95 (ISBN 0-7134-3059-1, Pub. by Batsford England). David & Charles.

--Yorkshire: The Dales. (Illus.). 160p. 1980. 19.95 (ISBN 0-7134-2236-X, Pub. by Batsford England). David & Charles.

Colberg, Marshall R. Social Security Retirement Test: Right or Wrong? 1978. pap. 4.25 (ISBN 0-8447-3307-5). Am Enterprise.

Colberg, Marshall R., jt. auth. see Greenhut, M. L.

Colberg, Marshall R., et al. Business Economics: Principles & Cases. 5th ed. 1975. text ed. 19.50x (ISBN 0-256-01547-3). Irwin.

Colbert, E. H., jt. ed. see Kay, Marshall.

Colbert, Edwin H. The Dinosaur World. LC 76-16586. (Illus.). 1977. 8.95 (ISBN 0-87396-081-5). Stravon.

--Evolution of the Vertebrates: A History of the Backboned Animals Through Time. 2nd ed. LC 67-84960. 1969. 21.50 o.p. (ISBN 0-471-16466-6, Pub. by Wiley-Interscience). Wiley.

--Evolution of the Vertebrates: A History of the Backboned Animals Through Time. 3rd ed. LC 79-27621. 544p. 1980. 25.00 (ISBN 0-471-04966-2, Pub. by Wiley Interscience). Wiley.

Colborne, C. L. Practical Boat Handling on Rivers & Canals. 1977. 8.95 (ISBN 0-7153-7061-8). David & Charles.

Colburn, Alan. Squash: The Ambitious Player's Guide. (Illus.). 112p. 1981. 19.95 (ISBN 0-571-11657-4, Pub. by Faber & Faber); pap. 8.95 (ISBN 0-571-11658-2). Merrimack Bk Serv.

Colburn, David R. & Sher, Richard K. Florida's Gubernatorial Politics in the Twentieth Century. LC 80-10277. 19.95 (ISBN 0-8130-0644-9). U Presses Fla.

Colburn, Francis. Letters Home & Further Indiscretions. 96p. 1978. 10.00 (ISBN 0-933050-00-3); pap. 6.95 (ISBN 0-933050-01-1). New Eng Pr VT.

Colburn, George A., jt. ed. see Carlson, Lewis H.

Colburn, William & Weinberg, Sanford. An Orientation to Listening & Audience Analysis. rev. ed. Applbaum, Ronald & Hart, Roderick, eds. (MODCOM, Modules in Speech Communication Ser.). 1980. pap. text ed. 2.25 (ISBN 0-574-22568-4, 13-5568). SRA.

Colby, Averil. Patchwork Quilts. 1965. 17.95 (ISBN 0-7134-3025-7, Pub. by Batsford England). David & Charles.

--Patchwork Quilts. (Encore Edition). 1975. 4.95 o.p. (ISBN 0-684-15240-1, ScribT). Scribner.

--Pincushions. 1975. 24.00 (ISBN 0-7134-3030-3, Pub. by Batsford England). David & Charles.

--Quilting. 1979. pap. 17.95 (ISBN 0-7134-2665-9, Pub. by Batsford England). David & Charles.

Colby, Benjamin N. & Colby, Lore M. The Daykeeper: The Life & Discourse of As IXII Deliver. (Illus.). 352p. 1981. text ed. 25.00 (ISBN 0-674-19409-8). Harvard U Pr.

Colby, Benjamin N. & Van Den Berghe, Pierre L. Ixil Country: A Plural Society in Highland Guatemala. 1969. 18.50x (ISBN 0-520-01515-0). U of Cal Pr.

Colby, C. B. First Book of Wild Bird World. (First Bks). (Illus.). (gr. 4-6). 1970. PLB 4.90 o.p. (ISBN 0-531-00698-0). Watts.

--Weirdest People in the World. (Illus.). 192p. (gr. 8 up). 1973. 5.95 o.p. (ISBN 0-8069-3922-2); PLB 5.89 o.p. (ISBN 0-8069-3923-0). Sterling.

Colby, Constance. A Skunk in the House. LC 73-497. (Illus.). 1973. 8.95 (ISBN 0-397-00978-X). Lippincott.

Colby, Constance T. The View from Morningside: One Family's New York. LC 78-4052. 1978. 8.95 o.s.i. (ISBN 0-397-01257-8). Lippincott.

Colby, Constance T., intro. by see Taber, Gladys.

Colby, Jean P. Building Wrecking. rev. & enl. ed. LC 72-5484. (Illus.). 96p. (gr. 5 up). 1972. 6.95g (ISBN 0-8038-0717-1). Hastings.

--Plimoth Plantation: Then & Now. (Famous Museum Ser). (Illus.). 1970. 6.95g (ISBN 0-8038-5757-8). Hastings.

Colby, John K. Latin Word Lists. 1978. pap. text ed. 1.50x (ISBN 0-88334-097-6). Ind Sch Pr.

--Lively Latin. (gr. 8-10). 1971. pap. text ed. 2.95x (ISBN 0-88334-035-6). Ind Sch Pr.

--Review Latin Grammar. (gr. 8-10). 1971. pap. text ed. 2.75x (ISBN 0-88334-034-8). Ind Sch Pr.

Colby, John K., jt. auth. see Buehner, William J.

Colby, K. M. Artificial Paranoia: A Computer Simulation of Paranoid Processes. 1976. text ed. 17.25 (ISBN 0-08-018162-7); pap. text ed. 9.00 (ISBN 0-08-018161-9). Pergamon.

Colby, Kenneth M., jt. ed. see Schank, Roger C.

Colby, Lore M., jt. auth. see Colby, Benjamin N.

Colby, Lydia. The Touch of Evil. LC 77-79429. 1977. pap. 1.50 o.p. (ISBN 0-87216-415-2). Playboy Pbks.

Colby, Robert A., et al. Color Atlas of Oral Pathology. 3rd ed. LC 73-147050. (Illus.). 200p. 1971. 27.50 (ISBN 0-397-50279-6). Lippincott.

Colby, Vineta. The Singular Anomaly: Women Novelists of the Nineteenth Century. LC 70-92522. (Gotham Library). 1970. 15.00x (ISBN 0-8147-0096-9); pap. 4.95x (ISBN 0-8147-0097-7). NYU Pr.

--Yesterday's Woman: Domestic Realism in the English Novel. 356p. 1974. text ed. 17.00 o.p. (ISBN 0-691-06263-3). Princeton U Pr.

Colby, William. Honorable Men. 1980. pap. write for info. PB.

Colclough, Christopher & McCarthy, Stephen. The Politocal Economy of Botswana: A Study of Growth & Distribution. (Illus.). 308p. 1980. 37.50 (ISBN 0-19-877136-3). Oxford U Pr.

Colcock, Bentley P. Diverticular Disease of the Colon. LC 79-158398. (Major Problems in Clinical Surgery: Vol. 11). (Illus.). 1971. 12.50 (ISBN 0-7216-2636-X). Saunders.

Colcord, Joanna C. Sea Language Comes Ashore. LC 45-966. 1945. pap. 5.00 (ISBN 0-87033-095-0). Cornell Maritime.

Cold Spring Harbor Conferences on Cell Proliferation. Origins of Human Cancer, 3 bk. set, Vol. 4. Hiatt, H. H., et al, eds. LC 76-57915. (Illus.). 1889p. 1977. 125.00 (ISBN 0-87969-119-0). Cold Spring Harbor.

Cold Spring Harbor Symposia on Quantitative Biology. Genetic Mechanisms: Proceedings, Vol. 21. LC 34-8174. (Illus.). 410p. 1957. 30.00 (ISBN 0-87969-020-8). Cold Spring Harbor.

--Heredity & Variation in Microorganisms: Proceedings, Vol. 11. Repr. of 1946 ed. 22.00 (ISBN 0-384-22475-X). Johnson Repr.

--Nucleic Acids & Nucleoproteins: Proceedings, Vol. 12. Repr. of 1947 ed. 19.50 (ISBN 0-384-42250-0). Johnson Repr.

--Relation of Hormones to Development: Proceedings, Vol. 10. Repr. of 1942 ed. 22.00 (ISBN 0-384-50250-4). Johnson Repr.

--Viral Oncogenes, Vol. 44. LC 34-8174. (Illus.). 1322p. 1980. 2 book set 130.00 (ISBN 0-87969-043-7). Cold Spring Harbor.

Colden, Cadwallader. History of the Five Indian Nations. 181p. (YA) (gr. 9-12). 1958. pap. 4.95 (ISBN 0-8014-9086-3, CP86). Cornell U Pr.

Coldham, Peter W. American Loyalist Claims. LC 80-8609. 615p. 24.00 (ISBN 0-915156-45-8). Natl Genealogical.

--Lord Mayor's Court of London: Depositions Relating to Americans Sixteen Forty-One to Seventeen Thirty-Six. Russell, George E., ed. LC 80-80349. 119p. Date not set. lib. bdg. price not set (ISBN 0-915156-23-7, SP 44); pap. price not set (ISBN 0-686-27217-X). Natl Genealogical.

Coldren, Sharon L., jt. auth. see Van Alstyne, Carol.

Coldrey, C. Courses for Horses. new ed. 1978. 20.10 (ISBN 0-85131-305-1, Dist. by Sporting Book Center). J A Allen.

Coldsmith, Don. Buffalo Medicine. LC 80-1690. (Double D Western Ser.). 192p. 1981. 9.95 (ISBN 0-385-15970-6). Doubleday.

Cole. Nungu & the Elephant. 117p. Date not set. lib. bdg. 6.95 (ISBN 0-07-011696-2). McGraw.

--USSR Geography. 1981. text ed. price not set. Butterworth.

Cole, ed. Instrumentation for Tomorrow's Crystallography. pap. 7.50 (ISBN 0-686-60382-6). Polycrystal Bk Serv.

Cole, A. J. Macro Processors. (Cambridge Computer Science Texts Ser.: No. 4). (Illus.). 200p. 1976. 12.95x (ISBN 0-521-29024-4). Cambridge U Pr.

Cole, A. R., et al, eds. The Role of Laboratory Teaching in University Courses. 1979. text ed. 15.00 (ISBN 0-08-023914-5). Pergamon.

Cole, Alan. The Epistle of Paul to the Galatians. (Tyndale Bible Commentaries). 1964. pap. 2.95 (ISBN 0-8028-1408-5). Eerdmans.

--Introduction to the Atmosphere Lab Manual. 1980. loose leaf shrink wrapped 4.75 (ISBN 0-88252-110-1). Paladin Hse.

Cole, Ann K. American Antiques. (Golden Guide Ser.). 1967. PLB 9.15 (ISBN 0-307-63537-6, Golden Pr); pap. 1.95 o.p. (ISBN 0-307-24013-4). Western Pub.

Cole, Arthur C. The Whig Party in the South. 1959. 7.50 (ISBN 0-685-24467-9). Peter Smith.

Cole, Arthur C., Jr. Pogonomyrmex Harvester Ants: A Study of the Genus in North America. LC 68-17144. (Illus.). 1968. 16.50x (ISBN 0-87049-085-0). U of Tenn Pr.

Cole, Arthur H. The Great Mirror of Folly. (Kress Library of Business & Economics: No. 6). 1949. pap. 5.00x (ISBN 0-678-09901-4, Baker Lib). Kelley.

--The Historical Development of Economic & Business Literature. (Kress Library of Business & Economics: No. 12). 1957. pap. 5.00x (ISBN 0-678-09907-3, Baker Lib). Kelley.

Cole, Arthur H. & Watts, George B. The Handicrafts of France As Recorded in the Description Des Arts et Metiers, 1761-1788. (Kress Library of Business & Economics: No. 8). (Illus.). 1952. pap. 5.00x (ISBN 0-678-09903-0, Baker Lib). Kelley.

Cole, Barry, ed. Television Today: A Close-up View, Readings from TV Guide. (Galaxy Book Ser.: No. 618). 448p. 1981. pap. 7.95 (ISBN 0-19-502799-X, GB). Oxford U Pr.

--Television Today: A Close-up View. Readings from TV Guide. 448p. 1981. 19.95 (ISBN 0-19-502798-1). Oxford U Pr.

Cole, Bruce. Agnolo Gaddi. (Oxford Studies in History of Art & Archetecture). (Illus.). 1977. 52.00x (ISBN 0-19-817339-3). Oxford U Pr.

Cole, C. Robert & Moody, Michael E., eds. The Dissenting Tradition: Essays for Leland H. Carlson. LC 74-27706. xxiii, 272p. 1975. 15.00x (ISBN 0-8214-0176-9). Ohio U Pr.

Cole, David. The Theatrical Event: A "Mythos," a Vocabulary, a Perspective. LC 74-21922. (Illus.). 1975. 15.00x (ISBN 0-8195-4078-1, Pub. by Wesleyan U Pr); pap. 5.95 (ISBN 0-8195-6047-2). Columbia U Pr.

Cole, David, et al. Three Places in New Inkland. 1977. pap. 5.95 (ISBN 0-9605610-1-3). Zartscorp.

Cole, Donald B. Immigrant City: Lawrence, Massachusetts Eighteen Forty Five to Nineteen Twenty One. LC 63-39156. 257p. 1980. Repr. of 1963 ed. 13.50x (ISBN 0-8078-0876-8). U of NC Pr.

Cole, Donald P. Nomads of the Nomads: The Al Murrah Bedouin of the Empty Quarter. LC 74-18211. (Worlds of Man Ser.). 192p. 1975. pap. 5.75x (ISBN 0-88295-605-1). AHM Pub.

Cole, Donald W. Professional Suicide. 256p. 1980. 12.95 (ISBN 0-07-011697-0, P&RB). McGraw.

Cole, Edward W. Racing Maxims & Methods of Pittsburg Phil. 1965. pap. 2.95 (ISBN 0-89650-506-5). Gamblers.

Cole, F. R. & Pritchard, A. E. The Genus Mallophora & Related Asilid Genera in North America (Diptera: Asilidae) (U. C. Publ. in Entomology: Vol. 36.2). 1964. pap. 5.00x o.p. (ISBN 0-520-09108-6). U of Cal Pr.

Cole, Frank R. & Schlinger, Evert L. The Flies of Western North America. LC 68-10687. (Illus.). 1969. 58.50x (ISBN 0-520-01516-9). U of Cal Pr.

Cole, Frank W., jt. auth. see McCray, Arthur W.

Cole, Franklyn W. Introduction to Meteorology. 3rd ed. LC 79-1212. 1980. text ed. 20.95 (ISBN 0-471-04705-8); tchr's manual avail. (ISBN 0-471-06224-3). Wiley.

Cole, G. D. A History of the Labour Party: New Impression. 1978. Repr. of 1958 ed. 40.00x (ISBN 0-7100-6628-7). Routledge & Kegan.

Cole, G. D., ed. William Morris: Prose, Verse, Lectures, & Essays. (Nonesuch Library). 1978. 11.95 (ISBN 0-370-00514-7, Pub. by Chatto Bodley Jonathan). Merrimack Bk Serv.

Cole, G. H. An Introduction to the Statistical Theory of Classical Simple Dense Fluids. 1967. 45.00 (ISBN 0-08-010397-9). Pergamon.

Cole, G. H., jt. auth. see Killingbeck, J.

Cole, G. T. & Kendrick, B. Biology of Conidial Fungi, 2 vols. 1981. Vol. 1. write for info. (ISBN 0-12-179501-2); Vol. 2. write for info. (ISBN 0-12-179502-0). Acad Pr.

Cole, G. W., compiled by see Church, E. D.

Cole, George D. Fabian Socialism. LC 68-21432. Repr. of 1943 ed. 21.00x (ISBN 0-678-05020-1). Kelley.

Cole, Gerald A. Textbook of Limnology. 2nd ed. LC 78-24532. (Illus.). 1979. text ed. 19.95 (ISBN 0-8016-1016-8). Mosby.

Cole, Guy, ed. Best of Uffa: Fifty Great Yacht Designs from the Uffa Fox Books. LC 78-55781. (Illus.). 1979. 20.00 (ISBN 0-87742-102-1). Intl Marine.

Cole, H. A., ed. see Royal Society.

Cole, H. H., ed. Introduction to Livestock Production: Including Dairy & Poultry. 2nd ed. LC 66-16377. (Illus.). 1966. 26.95x (ISBN 0-7167-0812-4). W H Freeman.

Cole, H. H. & Garrett, W. N., eds. Animal Agriculture: The Biology, Husbandry, & Use of Domestic Animals. 2nd ed. LC 79-18984. (Animal Science Ser.). (Illus.). 1980. text ed. 21.95x (ISBN 0-7167-1099-4). W H Freeman.

Cole, Harry B. The British Labour Party: A Functioning Participatory Democracy. 1977. pap. text ed. 5.75 (ISBN 0-08-021811-3). Pergamon.

Cole, Harry E. Stage Coach & Tavern Tales of the Old Northwest. Kellogg, Louise P., ed. LC 77-137353. 1972. Repr. of 1930 ed. 22.00 (ISBN 0-8103-3073-3). Gale.

Cole, Herbert. Heraldry & Floral Forms As Used in Decoration. LC 74-164180. (Tower Bks). (Illus.). 1971. Repr. of 1922 ed. 22.00 (ISBN 0-8103-3913-7). Gale.

Cole, Howard C. A Quest of Inquirie: Some Contexts of Tudor Literature. LC 73-91621. 1973. 9.80 (ISBN 0-672-63583-6). Pegasus.

Cole, Hubert. Josephine. 1979. pap. 1.95 (ISBN 0-505-51351-X). Tower Bks.

Cole, Hunter, jt. ed. see Wells, Dean F.

Cole, J. Ainsworth Rand Spofford: Bookman & Librarian. Harris, Michael H., ed. LC 75-31517. (Heritage of Librarianship: No. 2). 208p. 1975. PLB 20.00x (ISBN 0-87287-117-7). Libs Unl.

Cole, J. & Schepman, F. Rebel: His Moment & His Motives. 1971. pap. 8.95 (ISBN 0-13-767368-X). P-H.

Cole, J. D., jt. auth. see Kevorkian, J.

Cole, J. P. The Development Gap: A Spatial Analysis of World Poverty & Inequality. 416p. 1981. write for info. (ISBN 0-471-27796-7, Pub. by Wiley-Interscience). Wiley.

--The Development Gap: A Spatial Analysis of World Poverty & Inequality. LC 80-40284. 1981. write for info. (ISBN 0-471-16477-1). Wiley.

--Situations in Human Geography: A Practical Approach. pap. 15.00x (ISBN 0-631-16860-5, Pub. by Basil Blackwell). Biblio Dist.

Cole, Jack. Walk Softly on the Green. LC 80-52463. 288p. 1981. 8.95 (ISBN 0-938556-00-2). Taugus Hse.

Cole, Jack T., jt. auth. see Cole, Martha L.

Cole, Jackson. Crown for Azora. 1976. pap. 0.95 o.p. (ISBN 0-445-00695-1). Popular Lib.

--Dinero of Doom. 1975. pap. 0.95 o.p. (ISBN 0-445-00674-9). Popular Lib.

--The Land Pirates. 128p. 1976. pap. 0.95 o.p. (ISBN 0-445-00686-2). Popular Lib.

--Lost River Loot. 144p. 1975. pap. 0.95 o.p. (ISBN 0-445-00633-1). Popular Lib.

Cole, James K., jt. ed. see Arnold, William J.

Cole, James K., jt. ed. see Brown, Judson S.

Cole, James K., jt. ed. see Dienstbier, Richard.

Cole, Jean M. Exile in the Wilderness: The Life of Chief Factor Archibald McDonald, 1790-1853. LC 79-5361. (Illus.). 288p. 1980. 15.95 (ISBN 0-295-95704-2). U of Wash Pr.

Cole, Joan W., jt. auth. see Welch, Karen K.

Cole, Joanna. A Calf Is Born. LC 75-12408. (Illus.). 48p. (gr. k-3). 1975. PLB 6.48 (ISBN 0-688-32036-8). Morrow.

--A Chick Hatches. (Illus.). 48p. (gr. k-3). 1976. PLB 7.92 (ISBN 0-688-32087-2). Morrow.

--Dinosaur Story. LC 74-5931. (Illus.). 32p. (gr. k-3). 1974. PLB 6.48 (ISBN 0-688-31826-6). Morrow.

--A Fish Hatches. (Illus.). (gr. k-3). 1978. 7.95 (ISBN 0-688-22153-X); PLB 7.63 (ISBN 0-688-32153-4). Morrow.

--Fun on Wheels. (Illus.). (ps-1). 1977. 7.25 (ISBN 0-688-22102-5); PLB 6.96 (ISBN 0-688-32102-X). Morrow.

--A Horse's Body. LC 80-28147. (Illus.). 48p. (gr. k-3). 1981. 6.95 (ISBN 0-688-00362-1); PLB 6.67 (ISBN 0-688-00363-X). Morrow.

--My Puppy Is Born. LC 72-14201. (Illus.). 40p. (gr. k-3). 1973. PLB 6.48 (ISBN 0-688-30078-2). Morrow.

--Plants in Winter. LC 73-1771. (A Let's-Read-&-Find-Out Science Bk). (Illus.). (ps-3). 1973. 7.95 (ISBN 0-690-62885-4, TYC-J); PLB 7.89 (ISBN 0-690-62886-2). T Y Crowell.

--Saber-Toothed Tiger & Other Ice-Age Mammals. (Illus.). (gr. 1-5). 1977. 8.25 (ISBN 0-688-22120-3); PLB 7.92 (ISBN 0-688-32120-8). Morrow.

Cole, Joanna & Edmondson, Madeleine. Twins, the Story of Multiple Births. LC 75-168470. (Illus.). 64p. (gr. 3-7). 1972. PLB 6.00 (ISBN 0-688-31981-5). Morrow.

Cole, Johanna. Fleas. (Illus.). 64p. (gr. 3-7). 1973. PLB 6.48 (ISBN 0-688-31844-4). Morrow.

Cole, John. The Poor of the Earth. LC 75-46616. 1976. 22.00x (ISBN 0-89158-538-9). Westview.

--Sun Reflections: Images for a New Solar Age. Posner, Marcy, ed. (Illus.). 208p. 1981. 14.95 (ISBN 0-87857-318-6); pap. 10.95 (ISBN 0-87857-317-8). Rodale Pr Inc.

Cole, John N. The Amaranth: From the Past for the Future. (Illus.). 1979. 8.95 (ISBN 0-87857-240-6). Rodale Pr Inc.

Cole, Jonathan, et al. Peer Review in the National Science Foundation: Phase One of a Study. 1978. pap. text ed. 10.75 (ISBN 0-309-02788-8). Natl Acad Pr.

Cole, Jonathan O. Anxiety, Depression, & Organic Disease. (Illus.). 1976. pap. text ed. 18.50 (ISBN 0-89147-037-9). CAS.

--Mental Illness & Psychotropic Medications, 2 vols. (Illus.). 131p. 1977. Set. 43.00 (ISBN 0-685-62203-7); Bk. 1. 18.50 (ISBN 0-89147-036-0); Bk. 2. 24.50 (ISBN 0-89147-037-9). CAS.

Cole, Jonathan O., ed. Clinical Research in Alcoholism: PRR 24. 178p. 1968. pap. 5.00 (ISBN 0-685-24867-4, P024-0). Am Psychiatric.

--Psychopharmacology Update. LC 79-48064. 195p. 1980. 14.95 (ISBN 0-669-03695-1). Heath.

Cole, Jonathan O. & Barrett, James E., eds. Psychopathology in the Aged. (American Psychopathology Association Ser.). 320p. 1980. text ed. 32.00 (ISBN 0-89004-406-6). Raven.

Cole, Jonathan R. & Cole, Stephen. Social Stratification in Science. 1973. pap. 9.00 (ISBN 0-226-11339-6). U of Chicago Pr.

Cole, Kenneth S. Membranes, Ions & Impulses: A Chapter of Classical Biophysics. (Biophysics Series: No. 1). (Illus.). 1968. 30.00x (ISBN 0-520-00251-2). U of Cal Pr.

Cole, Lee, jt. auth. see Cuthbertson, Tom.

Cole, M. & Scribner, S. Culture & Thought: A Psychological Introduction. LC 73-16360. 1974. pap. 11.95 (ISBN 0-471-16477-1). Wiley.

Cole, Margaret, jt. auth. see H, G. D.

Cole, Marion & Cole, Olivia H. Things to Make & Do for Easter. LC 78-12457. (Things to Make & Do Ser.). (Illus.). (gr. k-3). 1979. PLB 7.90 (ISBN 0-531-01463-0). Watts.

Cole, Martha L. & Cole, Jack T. Language Training for the Nonverbal-Language Delayed Child. 275p. 1981. text ed. price not set (ISBN 0-89443-344-X). Aspen Systems.

Cole, Michel, ed. Soviet Developmental Psychology. Vale, Michel, et al, trs. from Rus. LC 77-85709. 1977. 30.00 o.p. (ISBN 0-87332-093-X). M E Sharpe.

Cole, Olivia H., jt. auth. see Cole, Marion.

Cole, Peter, ed. Radical Pragmatics. 1981. price not set (ISBN 0-12-179660-4). Acad Pr.

Cole, R. A. Industrial Safety Techniques. 1975. 23.95 o.p. (ISBN 0-471-01424-9). Wiley.

Cole, R. B. Drug Treatment of Respiratory Disease. (Monographs in Clinical Pharmacology). (Illus.). Date not set. text ed. price not set (ISBN 0-443-08012-7). Churchill. Postponed.

--Essentials of Respiratory Disease. LC 75-35316. (Illus.). 278p. 1976. 16.00 o.p. (ISBN 0-397-58187-4, Pub. by Blackwell Medical). Mosby.

Cole, R. Wellesley. Kossoh Town Boy. (Illus.). 1960. 4.95 (ISBN 0-521-04686-6). Cambridge U Pr.

Cole, Randal H. Theory of Ordinary Differential Equations. LC 68-13433. (Illus.). 1968. 32.50x (ISBN 0-8290-0132-8); pap. text ed. 18.50x (ISBN 0-8290-0132-8). Irvington.

Cole, Richard B. The Application of Security Systems & Hardware. 272p. 1970. pap. 27.95 photocopy ed. sprial (ISBN 0-398-00332-7). C C Thomas.

--Executive Security: A Corporate Guide to Effective Response to Abduction & Terrorism. LC 80-14662. 336p. 1980. 24.95 (ISBN 0-471-07736-4, Pub. by Wiley Interscience). Wiley.

Cole, Richard J. & Cox, Richard H., eds. Handbook of Toxic Fungal Metabolites. 1981. write for info. (ISBN 0-12-179760-0). Acad Pr.

Cole, Robert. The Book of Houses. LC 80-16931. 132p. 1980. 8.95 (ISBN 0-934558-04-3); pap. 4.95 (ISBN 0-934558-01-9). Entwhistle Bks.

Cole, Robert E. Japanese Blue Collar: The Changing Tradition. LC 77-107656. 1971. 12.75 o.p. (ISBN 0-520-01681-5); pap. 7.95x (ISBN 0-520-02354-4, CAMPUS86). U of Cal Pr.

--Work, Mobility, & Participation: A Comparative Study of American & Japanese Industry. LC 77-80468. 1979. 22.50x (ISBN 0-520-03542-9); pap. 6.95x (ISBN 0-520-04204-2). U of Cal Pr.

Cole, Robert H. Consumer & Commercial Credit Management. 6th ed. 1980. 20.95x (ISBN 0-256-02255-0). Irwin.

Cole, Robert S. The Practical Handbook of Public Relations. (Illus.). 224p. 1981. text ed. 18.95 (ISBN 0-13-691162-5, Spec); pap. text ed. 9.95 (ISBN 0-13-691154-4). P-H.

Cole, Roger W., ed. Current Issues in Linguistic Theory. LC 76-26427. (Illus.). 312p. 1977. 17.50x (ISBN 0-253-31608-1); pap. 9.95x (ISBN 0-253-11262-1). Ind U Pr.

Cole, Roland J. & Tegeler, Philip D. Government Requirements of Small Business. LC 79-3046. (Human Affairs Research Center Ser.). 192p. 1980. 18.95 (ISBN 0-669-03307-3). Lexington Bks.

Cole, Sam. Global Models & the International Economic Order. LC 77-30175. 1977. text ed. 13.50 (ISBN 0-08-022991-3); pap. text ed. 4.45 (ISBN 0-08-022025-8). Pergamon.

Cole, Sam, ed. Models, Planning & Basic Needs: Conference on the Applicability of Global Modelling to Integrated Planning & Developing Countries. (Illus.). 1979. text ed. 28.00 (ISBN 0-08-023732-0). Pergamon.

Cole, Sheila. Meaning Well. LC 73-12225. (Illus.). 72p. (gr. 4-7). 1974. PLB 5.90 (ISBN 0-531-02665-5). Watts.

--Working Kids on Working. (gr. 5 up). 1980. 8.95 (ISBN 0-688-41959-3); PLB 8.59 (ISBN 0-688-51959-8). Morrow.

Cole, Stephen, jt. auth. see Cole, Jonathan R.

Cole, Sylvan, Jr. Raphael Soyer: Fifty Years of Printmaking, 1917-1967. LC 67-29917. (Graphic Art Ser.). 1967. 27.50 (ISBN 0-306-70986-4). Da Capo.

Cole, Toby, ed. Venice. 288p. (Orig.). 1980. pap. 6.95 (ISBN 0-88208-107-1). Lawrence Hill.

Cole, Toby & Chinoy, Helen K., eds. Directors on Directing. rev. ed. LC 62-20686. Orig. Title: Directing the Play. 1963. pap. 8.95 (ISBN 0-672-60622-4). Bobbs.

Cole, Tom, ed. see Allen, Dorothy S.

Cole, W. A., jt. auth. see Deane, Phyllis.

Cole, W. Owen. World Faiths in Education. (Unwin Education Books). (Illus.). 1978. text ed. 22.50x (ISBN 0-04-371054-9); pap. text ed. 8.95x (ISBN 0-04-371055-7). Allen Unwin.

Cole, W. Owen & Sambhi, Piara S. The Sikhs: Their Religious Beliefs & Practices. (Library of Religious Beliefs & Practices). 1978. 22.50 (ISBN 0-7100-8842-6); pap. 9.00 (ISBN 0-7100-8843-4). Routledge & Kegan.

Cole, Wendell. Kyoto in the Momoyama Period. (Centers of Civilization Ser.: Vol. 22). 166p. 1967. 5.95x (ISBN 0-8061-0748-0). U of Okla Pr.

Cole, William. The Book of Giggles. (gr. k-6). 1980. pap. 1.25 (ISBN 0-440-40723-0, YB). Dell.

--A Boy Named Mary Jane & Other Silly Verse. (Illus.). (gr. 4-6). 1977. 6.45 (ISBN 0-531-00394-9). Watts.

--Give Up? LC 78-6842. (Illus.). (gr. 4-6). 1978. PLB 6.45 s&l (ISBN 0-531-02249-8). Watts.

--Knock Knocks: The Most Ever. LC 75-33205. (Illus.). 96p. (gr. 4 up). 1976. PLB 6.90 (ISBN 0-531-01142-9). Watts.

--Knock Knocks You've Never Heard Before. (Illus.). (gr. 4-6). 1977. PLB 6.90 s&l (ISBN 0-531-00385-X). Watts.

--Oh, How Silly. (Illus.). (gr. 4-6). 1970. PLB 3.95 o.p. (ISBN 0-670-52095-0). Viking Pr.

--Oh, Such Foolishness! LC 78-1622. (Illus.). (gr. 3-6). 1978. 8.95 (ISBN 0-397-31807-3). Lippincott.

Cole, William, ed. Good Dog Poems. (Illus.). 192p. (gr. 5 up). 1980. 9.95 (ISBN 0-684-16709-3). Scribner.

--Oh, What Nonsense. (Illus.). (gr. k-6). 1966. PLB 6.95 o.p. (ISBN 0-670-52117-5). Viking Pr.

--Pick Me Up: A Book of Short, Short Poems. LC 78-165103. (gr. 5 up). 1972. 4.95 o.s.i. (ISBN 0-02-722810-X). Macmillan.

--The Sea, Ships, & Sailors. (Illus.). 1967. 4.95 o.p. (ISBN 0-670-62642-2). Viking Pr.

Cole, William E., jt. auth. see Harris, Diana K.

Colebourn, R., jt. auth. see Cobban, J. M.

Colebrook, C. Spider, Egg, & Microcosm: Three Men & Three Worlds of Science. LC 55-9287. 1955. 6.50 (ISBN 0-9600476-1-1). E Kinkead.

Colebrook, Val. Shades of Jade. LC 80-52170. (Illus.). 52p. (Orig.). 1980. pap. 3.50 (ISBN 0-932384-11-0). Tashmoo.

Colecchia, Francesca. Repaso Oral. 1967. text ed. 9.95x o.p. (ISBN 0-669-31419-6); tapes. 5 reels o.p. 25.00 o.p. (ISBN 0-669-34140-1). Heath.

Coleiro, E. Introduction to Vergil's Bucolics. 1979. pap. text ed. 46.00x (ISBN 90-6032-117-0). Humanities.

Colella, Albert M., et al. Systems Simulation. LC 73-11645. 288p. 1974. 21.50 (ISBN 0-669-90308-6). Lexington Bks.

Coleman. Maurice Sceve: Poet of Love. LC 74-31794. 212p. 1975. 44.50 (ISBN 0-521-20745-2). Cambridge U Pr.

Coleman, Alexander. Eca De Queiros & European Realism. LC 79-3011. (The Gotham Library). 1980. 17.50x (ISBN 0-8147-1378-5); pap. 9.00x (ISBN 0-8147-1379-3). NYU Pr.

Coleman, Anne. Fabrics & Threads for Schools. 1977. 17.95 (ISBN 0-7134-0187-7, Pub. by Batsford England). David & Charles.

Coleman, Arthur & Tyler, Gary R. Drama Criticism, 2 vols. Incl. Vol. 1. A Checklist of Interpretation Since 1940 of English & American Plays. LC 66-30426. 1966. 18.00x (ISBN 0-8040-0069-7); Vol. 2. A Checklist of Interpretation Since 1940 of Classical & Continental Plays. LC 75-115031. 446p. 1970. 18.00x (ISBN 0-8040-0500-1). Swallow.

Coleman, Arthur P. & Coleman, Marion M. Wanderers Twain: Exploratory Memoir on Helen Modjeska & Henryk Sienkiewicz. LC 63-20948. (Illus.). 1964. 5.00 (ISBN 0-910366-23-3). Alliance Coll.

Coleman, B. D. Money: How to Save It, Spend It, & Make It. 1969. 22.00 (ISBN 0-08-012936-6); pap. text ed. 10.75 (ISBN 0-08-012935-8). Pergamon.

Coleman, B. I., ed. The Idea of the City in Nineteenth-Century Britain. (Birth of Modern Britain Ser). 256p. 1973. 16.00 (ISBN 0-7100-7591-X); pap. 7.95 (ISBN 0-7100-7592-8). Routledge & Kegan.

Coleman, Brian. Basketball: Techniques, Teaching & Training. 2nd rev. ed. LC 78-54017. (Illus.). 1978. 9.95 o.p. (ISBN 0-498-02275-7). A S Barnes.

Coleman, Mrs. Chapman. Life of John J. Crittenden, 2 Vols. LC 72-99469. (American Public Figures Ser). 1970. Repr. of 1871 ed. lib. bdg. 69.50 (ISBN 0-306-71843-X). Da Capo.

Coleman, Charles. Sergeant Back Again. LC 80-7061. 352p. 1980. 10.95 (ISBN 0-06-010864-9, HarpT). Har-Row.

Coleman, Charles G. Shining Sword. LC 56-31266. 1956. pap. 1.75 (ISBN 0-87213-086-X). Loizeaux.

Coleman, D. C. Courtaulds: An Economic & Social History, 2 Vols. 1969. Set. 45.00x o.p. (ISBN 0-19-920016-5). Oxford U Pr.

--Courtaulds: An Economic & Social History Vol. III: Crisis & Change 1940-65. (Illus.). 352p. 1980. 44.00x (ISBN 0-19-920111-0). Oxford U Pr.

Coleman, D. G. Rabelais: A Critical Study in Prose Fiction. LC 76-173822. 1971. 47.50 (ISBN 0-521-08125-4); pap. 10.50x (ISBN 0-521-29458-4). Cambridge U Pr.

Coleman, David. For the Long Term Investor. 12.95 (ISBN 0-930726-05-7). Green Hill.

--Management of the Firm. 13.95; pap. 9.95 (ISBN 0-930726-02-2). Green Hill.

Coleman, David W., jt. auth. see Zollinger, Robert M.

Coleman, Dorothy. The Gallo-Roman Muse. LC 79-71. 1979. 32.50 (ISBN 0-521-22254-0). Cambridge U Pr.

--Lenci Dolls. (Illus.). 1977. 13.95 (ISBN 0-686-68039-1); pap. 9.95 (ISBN 0-87588-119-X). Hobby Hse.

--Prices for Dolls 1977. (Illus.). 1976. pap. 3.00 o.p. (ISBN 0-87588-134-3). Hobby Hse.

Coleman, Dorothy S., et al. Doll Collectors' Manual, 1973, Vol. 8. LC 65-29362. 1978. 8.50 (ISBN 0-9603210-0-4). Doll Collect Am.

Coleman, Dulcie V., jt. auth. see Koss, Leopold G.

Coleman, Eric. Dinghies for All Waters: Safe Family Cruising & Day Sailing. (Illus.). 176p. 1976. 12.00 (ISBN 0-370-10459-5); pap. 9.95 (ISBN 0-685-69467-4). Transatlantic.

Coleman, F. Guide to Surgical Terminology. 3rd ed. 1978. pap. 13.95 (ISBN 0-87489-191-4). Med Economics.

Coleman, F. G., tr. see McDonald, Hope.

Coleman, Francis. Great Britain. LC 75-44870. (Macdonald Countries). (Illus.). (gr. 6 up). 1976. PLB 7.95 (ISBN 0-382-06102-0, Pub. by Macdonald Ed). Silver.

Coleman, Freada A., jt. ed. see McDermott, Beatrice S.

Coleman, Gary J. A Look at Mormonism. pap. 3.95 (ISBN 0-89036-142-8). Hawkes Pub Inc.

Coleman, J. R. & Kaminsky, F. C. Ambulatory Care Systems, Vol. 4: Designing Medical Services for Health Maintenance Organizations. LC 76-55865. (Illus.). 1977. 27.95 (ISBN 0-669-01327-7). Lexington Bks.

--Ambulatory Care Systems, Vol. 5: Financial Design & Administration of Health Maintenance Organizations. LC 76-55865. 1977. 26.95 (ISBN 0-669-01328-5). Lexington Bks.

Coleman, James C. Contemporary Psychology & Effective Behavior. 4th ed. 1979. text ed. 17.95x (ISBN 0-673-15202-2); student's guide 5.95x (ISBN 0-673-15203-0). Scott F.

Coleman, James C., et al. Abnormal Psychology & Modern Life. 6th ed. 1979. text ed. 21.95x (ISBN 0-673-15213-8); pap. 6.95x student's guide (ISBN 0-673-15283-9). Scott F.

Coleman, James J., Jr. Gilbert Antoine de St. Maxent: The Spanish-Frenchman of New Orleans. LC 68-54600. 136p. 1980. 10.00 (ISBN 0-911116-06-0). Pelican.

Coleman, James S. Adolescent Society. LC 61-14725. 1971. pap. text ed. 4.95 (ISBN 0-02-906410-4). Free Pr.

--Introduction to Mathematical Sociology. 1964. 19.95 (ISBN 0-02-906520-8). Free Pr.

--Longitudinal Data Analysis. LC 80-66309. Date not set. text ed. 15.00x (ISBN 0-465-04224-4). Basic. Postponed.

--Nigeria: Background to Nationalism. (California Library Reprint Series: No. 28). 1971. 32.50x (ISBN 0-520-02070-7). U of Cal Pr.

Coleman, James S. & Rosberg, Carl G., Jr., eds. Political Parties & National Integration in Tropical Africa. (African Studies Center, UCLA). 1964. 30.00x (ISBN 0-520-00253-9). U of Cal Pr.

Coleman, James S., et al. Trends in School Segregation: Nineteen Sixty-Eight to Seventy-Three. (An Institute Paper). 133p. 1975. pap. 3.50 o.p. (ISBN 0-685-99499-6, 12300). Urban Inst.

Coleman, John. Coleman's Drive. 1966. 4.95 (ISBN 0-685-52076-5). Transatlantic.

Coleman, John A. The Evolution of Dutch Catholicism, 1958-1974. LC 74-22958. 1979. 25.00x (ISBN 0-520-02885-6). U of Cal Pr.

--Other Voices: A Study of the Late Poetry of Luis Cernuda. (Studies in the Romance Languages & Literatures: No. 81). 1969. pap. 8.50x (ISBN 0-8078-9081-2). U of NC Pr.

Coleman, John C. Relationships in Adolescence. 1974. 22.50x (ISBN 0-7100-7868-4). Routledge & Kegan.

Coleman, John E. Kephala. LC 76-13187. (Keos Ser: Vol. 1). 1977. pap. 35.00x (ISBN 0-87661-701-1). Am Sch Athens.

Coleman, John F. The Disruption of the Pennsylvania Democracy, 1848-1860. LC 75-623874. (Illus.). 184p. 1975. 8.00 (ISBN 0-911124-82-9). Pa Hist & Mus.

Coleman, John R. Blue-Collar Journal: A College President's Sabbatical. LC 73-21902. 1974. 8.95 (ISBN 0-397-01030-3). Lippincott.

Coleman, Joseph. The First Witch. (Pal Paperbacks, - Pal Skills II Ser.). (Illus.). (gr. 5-12). 1980. pap. text ed. 1.25 (ISBN 0-8374-6812-4). Xerox Ed Pubns.

--Missing Papers. (Pal Paperbacks, - Pal Skills II Ser.). (Illus.). (gr. 5-12). 1980. pap. text ed. 1.25 (ISBN 0-8374-6802-7). Xerox Ed Pubns.

--Space Wars. (Pal Paperbacks, - Pal Skills II Ser.). (Illus.). (gr. 5-12). 1980. pap. text ed. 1.25 (ISBN 0-8374-6809-4). Xerox Ed Pubns.

Coleman, Juliet C. John Gordon: Invictus Georgia Love Story. 1980. 8.95 (ISBN 0-533-04441-3). Vantage.

Coleman, Kenneth. Georgia History in Outline. rev. ed. LC 78-14087. 142p. 1978. pap. text ed. 4.00x (ISBN 0-8203-0467-0). U of Ga Pr.

Coleman, Laurence V. Historic House Museums. LC 71-175318. (Illus.). xii, 187p. 1973. Repr. of 1933 ed. 20.00 (ISBN 0-8103-3118-7). Gale.

Coleman, Lonnie. The Legacy of Beulah Land. 1981. pap. 2.95 (ISBN 0-440-15085-X). Dell.

Coleman, Loren, jt. auth. see Clark, Jerome.

Coleman, M. M. Our Other World: A Polish Scrapbook. (Illus.). 1978. 6.00 (ISBN 0-685-63579-1). Alliance Coll.

Coleman, Marigold. North American Indians. (Jackdaw Ser: No. 145). (gr. 7 up). 1977. 5.95 o.s.i. (ISBN 0-670-51521-3, Grossman). Viking Pr.

Coleman, Marion M. Fair Rosalind: The American Career of Helena Modjeska, 1877-1907. LC 69-10370. (Illus.). 1969. 20.00 (ISBN 0-910366-07-1). Alliance Coll.

--The Polish Land. rev. ed. LC 74-81566. iv, 152p. 1974. pap. text ed. 5.00 (ISBN 0-910366-18-7). Alliance Coll.

--Vistula Voyage. LC 73-82795. (Pocket Folklore Ser.: No. 3). (Illus.). 95p. (Orig.). 1974. pap. 3.00 o.p. (ISBN 0-910366-16-0). Alliance Coll.

--Zosia & Thaddeus. 1st ed. LC 73-93707. 115p. 1974. pap. 4.00 (ISBN 0-910366-17-9). Alliance Coll.

Coleman, Marion M., jt. auth. see Coleman, Arthur P.

Coleman, Marion M., ed. see Modjeska, Helena.

Coleman, Marion M., ed. see Sienkiewicz, Henryk.

Coleman, Marion M., tr. see Dyboski, Roman.

Coleman, Matthew, ed. see Miller Freeman Publications, Inc.

Coleman, Richard. Is Your Prescription Killing You? Richards, Carolyn, ed. 1980. 9.95 (ISBN 0-87949-164-7). Ashley Bks.

Coleman, Richard J. Issues of Theological Conflict. rev. ed. 1980. pap. 5.95 o.p. (ISBN 0-8028-1806-4); 12.95 (ISBN 0-8028-3185-0). Eerdmans.

Coleman, Richard P., et al. Social Standing in America: New Dimensions of Class. LC 77-20426. 353p. 1981. pap. 6.95 (ISBN 0-465-07929-6). Basic.

Coleman, Robert E. Life in the Living Word. (Spire Bks). 1975. pap. 1.50 (ISBN 0-8007-8193-7). Revell.

--The Master Plan of Evangelism. 1978. pap. 2.95 (ISBN 0-8007-5007-1, Power Bks); pap. 1.75 o.p. (ISBN 0-8007-8303-4, Spire Bks). Revell.

--The Spirit & the Word. (Spire Bks). 1975. pap. 1.50 (ISBN 0-8007-8192-9). Revell.

Coleman, Rodney. Stochastic Processes. (Problem Solves Ser.). (Illus.). 1974. text ed. 12.50x o.p. (ISBN 0-04-519016-X); pap. text ed. 6.50x (ISBN 0-04-519017-8). Allen Unwin.

Coleman, Ron. Lady Luck Ain't No Lady. (Gambler's Book Shelf). 64p. 1975. pap. 2.95 (ISBN 0-89650-546-4). Gamblers.

Coleman, Satis N. Bells: Their History, Legends, Making, & Uses. LC 74-159919. (Illus.). 1971. Repr. of 1928 ed. 28.00 (ISBN 0-8103-3906-4). Gale.

Coleman, Sherman S. Congenital Dysplasia & Dislocation of the Hip. LC 78-59669. 1978. 44.50 (ISBN 0-8016-1018-4). Mosby.

Coleman, Thomas E. Successful Drugstore: How to Build a Million Dollar Business. 1973. 32.95 o.p. (ISBN 0-13-860734-6). P-H.

Coleman, Thomas G. Blood Pressure Control, Vol. 1. 248p. 1980. 32.50 (ISBN 0-88831-088-9). Eden Med Res.

Coleman, Vernon. Paper Doctors: A Critical Assessment of Medical Research. 1977. 12.95 (ISBN 0-85117-109-5). Transatlantic.

--Stress Control. 214p. 1979. 20.00 (ISBN 0-85117-167-2). Transatlantic.

Coleman, Dr. Vernon. Everything You Wanted to Know About Ageing. 1976. 9.95 o.p. (ISBN 0-86033-036-2). Gordon-Cremonesi.

Coleman, W. Biology in the Nineteenth Century. LC 77-83989. (History of Science Ser.). (Illus.). 1978. 22.50 (ISBN 0-521-21861-6); pap. 7.50x (ISBN 0-521-29293-X). Cambridge U Pr.

Coleman, Wanda. Mad Dog Black Lady. 138p. (Orig.). 1979. pap. 4.50 (ISBN 0-87685-411-0). Black Sparrow.

Coleman, William. Chesapeake Charlie & Blackbeard's Treasure. (Chesapeake Charlie Ser.). 112p. (Orig.). (gr. 5-9). 1981. pap. 2.50 (ISBN 0-87123-116-6, 200116). Bethany Fell.

--Chesapeake Charlie & the Bay Bank Robbers. (Chesapeake Charlie Ser.). 112p. (Orig.). 1980. pap. 2.50 (ISBN 0-87123-113-1, 200113). Bethany Fell.

--Counting Stars. LC 76-28973. 1976. 3.50 (ISBN 0-87123-055-0, 210055). Bethany Fell.

--Far Out Facts About the Bible. (gr. 4-9). 1980. pap. 2.50 (ISBN 0-89191-336-X). Cook.

--To Catch a Golden Ring. (gr. 4-9). 1980. pap. 2.50 (ISBN 0-89191-330-0). Cook.

Coleman, William, et al, eds. A Casebook of Grant Proposals in the Humanities. 350p. 1981. 24.95 (ISBN 0-918212-45-6). Neal-Schuman.

Coleman, William E. Grants in the Humanities: A Scholar's Guide to Funding Sources. LC 79-25697. 1980. pap. 12.95x (ISBN 0-918212-21-9). Neal-Schuman.

--On the Discrimination of Gothicisms. Varma, Devendra P., ed. LC 79-8447. (Gothic Studies & Dissertations Ser.). 1980. lib. bdg. 25.00x (ISBN 0-405-12651-4). Arno.

Coleman, William L. A Dozen Daring Christians. LC 79-50813. 1979. pap. 2.95 (ISBN 0-89636-023-7). Accent Bks.

--Listen to the Animals. LC 79-11312. (ps-6). 1979. pap. 3.95 (ISBN 0-87123-341-X, 210341). Bethany Fell.

--My Magnificient Machine. LC 78-5035. 1978. pap. 3.95 (ISBN 0-87123-381-9, 210381). Bethany Fell.

--Singing Penguins & Puffed-up Toads. 128p. (ps-4). 1981. pap. 3.95 (ISBN 0-87123-554-4, 210554). Bethany Fell.

Coleman, William V. & McLemore, Patricia R. God Believes in Me. Incl. Standard Edition-Family Bk. 24p. (gr. 4-6) (ISBN 0-87793-080-5); Simplified Edition-Classroom Bk. 32p. (gr. 2-3) (ISBN 0-87793-081-3); Standard Edition Classroom Book. 24p. (gr. 4-6) (ISBN 0-87793-079-1). (Illus., Orig.). (gr. 2-6). 1975. wkbk. 0.95 ea. o.p. Ave Maria.

--God Believes in Me, Director Guide. (Illus.). 24p. (Orig.). (gr. 2-6). 1975. pap. 1.25 o.p. (ISBN 0-87793-082-1); simplified family ed. gr. 2-3 0.95 o.p. (ISBN 0-87793-080-5). Ave Maria.

Colen, B. D. Born at Risk. (Illus.). 240p. 1981. 9.95 (ISBN 0-312-09291-1). St Martin.

Colenso, M., tr. see Vainshtein, Sevyan.

Coleridge, A. D., tr. see Von Dittersdorf, Karl D.

Coleridge, Christabel. Charlotte Mary Yonge, Her Life & Letters. LC 77-75961. (Library of Lives & Letters). 1969. Repr. of 1903 ed. 20.00 (ISBN 0-8103-3891-2). Gale.

Coleridge, E. H., ed. see Byron, George G.

Coleridge, E. H., ed. see Coleridge, Samuel T.

Coleridge, Herbert. A Dictionary of the First or Oldest Words in the English Language: From the Semi-Saxon Period of Ad 1250 to 1300, Consisting of an Alphabetical Inventory of Every Word Found in the Printed English Literature of the 13th Century. LC 74-19205. 103p. 1975. Repr. of 1863 ed. 20.00 (ISBN 0-8103-4119-0). Gale.

Coleridge, K. A. A Descriptive Catalogue of the Milton Collection in the Alexander Turnbull Library, Wellington, New Zealand. (Illus.). 544p. 1980. 98.00x (ISBN 0-19-920110-2). Oxford U Pr.

Coleridge, Samuel T. Biographia Literaria. Watson, George, ed. 1978. 6.50x (ISBN 0-460-10011-4, Evman); pap. 3.95 o.p. (ISBN 0-460-11011-X). Dutton.

--The Collected Works of Samuel Taylor Coleridge: Logic, Vol. 13. Jackson, J. R., ed. LC 68-10201. (Bollingen Ser.: No. LXXV). 1981. 30.00 (ISBN 0-691-09880-8). Princeton U Pr.

--Poems. Bierre, John, ed. 1963. 11.50 (ISBN 0-460-00043-8, Evman); pap. 4.50 (ISBN 0-460-01043-3). Dutton.

--Poems of Samuel Taylor Coleridge. Coleridge, E. H., ed. 1912. pap. 9.95x (ISBN 0-19-281051-0). Oxford U Pr.

--Poems of Samuel Taylor Coleridge. Coleridge, E. H., ed. (Oxford Standard Authors Ser.). 1912. 27.50 (ISBN 0-19-254120-X). Oxford U Pr.

--The Rime of the Ancient Mariner. (Illus.). 1979. 8.50 (ISBN 0-7011-2277-3, Pub. by Chatto Bodley Jonathan). Merrimack Bk Serv.

Coles, Alan. The Baralong Affair. 1981. write for info. Sheridan. Postponed.

Coles, Clarence & Young, Howard. Evinrude One & Two Cylinder Outboard Tune-up & Repair Manual. 1980. pap. 11.95 (ISBN 0-89330-008-X). Caroline Hse.

Coles, Flournoy A., Jr. Black Economic Development. LC 74-30495. 232p. 1975. 15.95 (ISBN 0-88229-176-9). Nelson-Hall.

Coles, J. M. & Simpson, D. D., eds. Studies in Ancient Europe: Essays Presented to Stuart Piggott. (Illus.). 1968. text ed. 14.00x (ISBN 0-7185-1079-8, Leicester). Humanities.

Coles, John. Archaeology by Experiment. (Illus.). 1974. pap. 3.50 o.p. (ISBN 0-684-14078-0, SL562, ScribT). Scribner.

Coles, K. A. Channel Harbours & Anchorages. 5th ed. 198p. 1980. 24.00 (ISBN 0-245-53086-X, Pub. by Nautical England). State Mutual Bk.

Coles, K. Adlard. North Brittainy Pilot. 1979. 34.95x (ISBN 0-8464-0071-5). Beekman Pubs.

Coles, K. Adlard & Black, A. N. North Biscay Pilot. 1979. 44.95x (ISBN 0-8464-0072-3). Beekman Pubs.

Coles, Richard N. Dynamic Chess: The Modern Style of Aggressive Play. rev. & enl. ed. (Illus.). 1966. pap. 3.50 (ISBN 0-486-21676-4). Dover.

Coles, Robert. The Darkness & the Light. LC 74-76878. (Illus.). 112p. 1974. 20.00 (ISBN 0-912334-60-6); pap. 12.50 (ISBN 0-912334-64-9). Aperture.

--Irony in the Mind's Life: Essays on Novels by James Agee, Elizabeth Bowen, & George Eliot. LC 74-5260. (University of Virginia Page-Barbour Lecture Ser.). 1974. 12.95x (ISBN 0-8139-0550-8). U Pr of Va.

Coles, Robert & Trachtenberg, Alan. Aperture Nineteen: Four, No. 76. (Illus.). 88p. 1975. pap. 9.50 (ISBN 0-912334-72-X). Aperture.

Coles, William E., Jr. Composing: Writing As a Self-Creating Process. 128p. (Orig.). 1974. pap. text ed. 5.95x (ISBN 0-8104-5838-1). Hayden.

Coleson, Ann see Wakefield, Sarah.

Coletta, Irene. From A to Z. (Illus.). (ps-2). 1979. 7.95g (ISBN 0-13-331678-5); pap. 2.95 (ISBN 0-13-331546-0). P-H.

Coletta, Paolo. American Secretaries of the Navy, 2 vols. LC 78-70967. (Illus.). 1750p. 1980. Set. slipcased 59.95x (ISBN 0-87021-073-4). Naval Inst Pr.

Coletta, Paolo E. The American Naval Heritage in Brief. 2nd ed. LC 79-6603. 689p. 1980. 22.50 (ISBN 0-8191-0927-4); pap. 11.00 (ISBN 0-8191-0928-2). U Pr of Amer.

--Bowman Hendry McCalla: A Fighting Sailor. LC 79-66975. (Illus.). 1979. pap. text ed. 10.50 (ISBN 0-8191-0863-4). U Pr of Amer.

--French Ensor Chadwick: Scholarly Warrior. LC 80-67240. 264p. 1980. lib. bdg. 18.75 (ISBN 0-8191-1153-8); pap. text ed. 10.75 (ISBN 0-8191-1154-6). U Pr of Amer.

Coletta, Paolo E., ed. A Bibliography of American Naval History. 453p. 1981. 14.95 (ISBN 0-87021-105-6). Naval Inst Pr.

Colette. The Complete Claudine. White, Antonia, tr. from French. Incl. Claudine at School; Claudine & Annie; Claudine in Paris; Claudine Married. 1976. 20.00 (ISBN 0-374-12691-7); pap. 9.95 (ISBN 0-374-51379-1). FS&G.

--Earthly Paradise: An Autobiography of Colette Drawn from Her Lifetime Writings. Phelps, Robert, ed. pap. 9.95 (ISBN 0-685-83818-8). FS&G.

--My Mother's House & Sido. Troubridge, Una V. & McLeod, Enid, trs. from Fr. Incl. Sido. 219p. 1975. 7.95 (ISBN 0-374-21735-1); pap. 3.95 (ISBN 0-374-51218-3). FS&G.

--The Pure & the Impure. Briffault, Herma, tr. 175p. 1967. 7.95 (ISBN 0-374-23920-7); pap. 4.95 (ISBN 0-374-50692-2). FS&G.

--The Tender Shoot & Other Stories. White, Antonia, tr. from Fr. 404p. 1975. 10.00 (ISBN 0-374-27310-3); pap. 6.95 (ISBN 0-374-51258-2). FS&G.

--The Vagabond. McLeod, Enid, tr. from Fr. LC 55-5832. 223p. 1975. 8.95 (ISBN 0-374-28233-1); pap. 4.95 (ISBN 0-374-51175-6). FS&G.

Coletti, Anthony. Handbook for Dairymen. (Illus.). 1963. 6.00x o.p. (ISBN 0-8138-0740-9). Iowa St U Pr.

Cole-Whittaker, Terry. What You Think of Me Is None of My Business. LC 79-21739. 1979. 9.95 (ISBN 0-916392-39-2). Oak Tree Pubns.

Coley, Chris & Wolfe, Sidney. Four Hundred Drugs That Don't Work. 6.95. Green Hill.

Coley, Ida L. Pediatric Assessment of Self Care Activities. LC 77-2252. (Illus.). 1978. pap. text ed. 13.95 (ISBN 0-8016-1022-2). Mosby.

Coley, Noel & Hall, Vance, eds. Darwin to Einstein: Primary Sources on Science & Belief. (Illus.). 368p. 1981. text ed. 25.00 (ISBN 0-582-49158-4). Longman.

Coley, William, ed. see Fielding, Henry.

Colford, William E., tr. from Span. Classic Tales from Modern Spain. LC 63-23445. 1964. 6.95 (ISBN 0-8120-5022-3); pap. text ed. 3.50 (ISBN 0-8120-0046-3). Barron.

--Classic Tales from Spanish America. LC 61-18356. 1963. pap. 3.50 (ISBN 0-8120-0045-5). Barron.

Colford, William E., tr. see Calderon, Pedro.

Colgate, Craig, Jr. & Broida, Patricia. National Trade & Professional Associations of the U. S. & Canada & Labor Unions. 16th ed. LC 74-647774. 624p. 1981. pap. 35.00 (ISBN 0-910416-34-6). Columbia Bks.

--National Trade & Professional Associations of the United States & Canada & Labor Unions 1980. 15th ed. LC 74-647774. 1980. pap. 30.00x o.p. (ISBN 0-910416-32-X). Columbia Bks.

Colgate, Craig, Jr. & Evans, Laurie. National Recreational, Sporting & Hobby Organizations of the United States. LC 80-70429. 1981. pap. 25.00 (ISBN 0-910416-36-2). Columbia Bks.

Colgate, Craig, Jr. & Close, Arthur C., eds. National Association Executives of the United States. LC 80-20428. 1981. pap. 37.50 (ISBN 0-910416-38-9). Columbia Bks.

Colgate, Craig, Jr., jt. ed. see Close, Arthur C.

Colgate, Isabele. The Shooting Party. 192p. 1981. 11.95 (ISBN 0-670-64064-6). Viking Pr.

Colgate, John A. Administration of Intramural & Recreational Activities: Everyone Can Participate. LC 77-9265. 1978. text ed. 18.95 (ISBN 0-471-01728-0). Wiley.

Colie, Rosalie. The Resources of Kind: Genre-Theory in the Renaissance. 1974. 15.00x (ISBN 0-520-02397-8). U of Cal Pr.

Colin, Patrick. Neon Gobies. (Illus.). 304p. 1976. 9.95 (ISBN 0-87666-450-8, H-957). TFH Pubns.

Colin, Patrick I. Caribbean Reef Invertebrates & Plants. (Illus.). 1978. 20.00 (ISBN 0-87666-460-5, H-971). TFH Pubns.

Colin, Sid. And the Bands Played on: An Informal History of British Dance Bands. (Illus.). 1978. 16.95 (ISBN 0-241-89589-8, Pub. by Hamish Hamilton England). David & Charles.

Colin, Sid & Stavearce, Tony. Al Bowlly. 1979. 24.00 (ISBN 0-241-10057-7, Pub. by Hamish Hamilton England). David & Charles.

Colina, Tessa. You & Me. Buerger, Jane, ed. (Illus.). 1980. 5.95 (ISBN 0-89565-179-3, 4936). Standard Pub.

Colinvaux, Paul. The Fates of Nations: A Biological Theory of History. 1980. 12.95 (ISBN 0-671-25204-6). S&S.

Colinvaux, Paul A. Introduction to Ecology. LC 72-3788. 621p. 1973. text ed. 25.95 (ISBN 0-471-16498-4). Wiley.

Colker, David. Running Away from Home: A Guide to Running Trails in 32 Cities Across America. (Orig.). 1979. pap. 2.50 (ISBN 0-515-05398-8). Jove Pubns.

Colker, Marvin L., ed. Analecta Dublinensia. 1975. 22.00 o.p. (ISBN 0-910956-56-1). Medieval.

Collange, J. F. Enigmes De la Deuxienne Epitre De Paul Aux Corinthiens: Etudes Exegetique De 2 Cor. LC 71-154504. (Society for New Testament Studies Monographs: No. 18). 1972. 49.50 (ISBN 0-521-08135-1). Cambridge U Pr.

Collard, David, et al. Income Distribution: The Limits to Redistribution. 267p. 1981. 34.95 (ISBN 0-470-27099-3). Halsted Pr.

Collard, Jean, jt. auth. see Thornes, Barbara.

Collard, Jean, jt. ed. see Prichard, Elizabeth.

Collarte, Juan, jt. auth. see Barraclough, Solon.

Collatz, L., et al, eds. Numerische Methoden bei Graphentheoretischen und Kombinatorishen Problemen: Vol. II. (International Series of Numerical Mathematics: No. 46). (Illus.). 255p. (Ger. & Eng.). 1979. pap. 32.50 (ISBN 3-7643-1078-2). Birkhauser.

Collatz, Lothar & Albrecht, Julius, eds. Constructive Methods for Nonlinear Boundary Value Problems & Nonlinear Oscillations. Kirchgassner, K., tr. (International Series of Numerical Mathematics: Vol. 48). 190p. 1979. pap. 19.50 (ISBN 3-7643-1098-7). Birkhauser.

Collcutt, Martin. Five Mountains: The Rinzai Zen Monastic Institution in Medieval Japan. (Harvard East Asian Monograph: Vol. 85). (Illus.). 450p. 1981. 20.00 (ISBN 0-674-30497-7). Harvard U Pr.

Colledge, Edmund, tr. see Guigo II.

Colledge, Edmund, et al, eds. Julian of Norwich, "Showings". (Classics of Western Spirituality). 1978. 11.95 (ISBN 0-8091-0234-X); pap. 7.95 (ISBN 0-8091-2091-7). Paulist Pr.

College & Education Division. Barron's Profiles of American Colleges: Regional Editions. (gr. 10-12). 1981. Northeast. pap. text ed. 5.75 (ISBN 0-8120-2271-8); West. pap. text ed. 4.95 (ISBN 0-8120-2272-6); South. pap. text ed. 5.75 (ISBN 0-8120-2273-4); Midwest. pap. text ed. 5.75 (ISBN 0-8120-2274-2). Barron.

College & University Archives Committee, ed. Directory of College & University Archives in the United States & Canada. LC 80-50627. 80p. 1980. pap. 10.00 (ISBN 0-931828-21-X). Soc Am Archivists.

College Division of Barron's Educational Ser., Inc. Barron's Compact Guide to Colleges. 2nd ed. LC 80-26124. (Illus.). 352p. (gr. 11-12). 1980. pap. 2.75 (ISBN 0-8120-2288-2). Barron.

College Entrance Examination Board. CLEP General & Subject Examinations: Descriptions & Sample Questions. 1980. pap. 1.00 (ISBN 0-87447-013-7, 200631). College Bd.

College Scholarship Service of the College Board. The College Cost Book 1980-81. 192p. (Orig.). 1980. pap. 7.50 (ISBN 0-87447-131-1, 001311). College Bd.

Collegium Internationale Neuro-Psychopharmacologium 11th Congress, Vienna, July 9-14 1978. Neuro-Psychopharmacology: Proceedings. Saletu, B., et al, eds. (Illus.). 1979. 140.00 (ISBN 0-08-023089-X). Pergamon.

Colleran, Joseph M., tr. see Augustine, St.

Colles, William M. & Cresswell, Henry. Success in Literature. 360p. 1980. Repr. of 1911 ed. lib. bdg. 20.00 (ISBN 0-89760-116-5): Telegraph Bks.

Collester, J. Bryan, ed. European Communities: A Guide to Information Sources. LC 73-17506. (International Relations Information Guide Ser.: Vol. 3). 1979. 30.00 (ISBN 0-8103-1322-7). Gale.

Collet, Andre, ed. see Wilen, Sam & Jacques, J.

Collet, Collet D. History of Taxes on Knowledge: Their Origin & Repeal. LC 75-142565. 1971. Repr. 18.00 (ISBN 0-8103-3615-4). Gale.

Collet, K., ed. Polygraph Dictionary for the Graphic Industries in Six Languages. 38th ed. LC 68-117537. (Ger. Eng. Fr. Span. It. Swedish.). 1967. 65.00x (ISBN 3-87641-150-5). Intl Pubns Serv.

Colleton, John. The Delights of Anna. (Orig.). 1980. pap. 2.75 (ISBN 0-451-09453-0, E9453, Sig). NAL.

--The Enjoyment of Amy. 1980. pap. write for info. (ISBN 0-671-83659-5). PB.

--On or About the First Day in June. (Orig.). 1978. pap. 2.25 (ISBN 0-451-09007-1, E9007, Sig). NAL.

--Trembling of a Leaf. 1981. pap. 2.50 (ISBN 0-671-41612-X). PB.

Collett, Rosemary K. My Orphans of the Wild: Rescue & Home Care of Native Wildlife. LC 74-1111. (Illus.). 1974. 9.95 (ISBN 0-397-01021-4). Lippincott.

Collett, Rosemary K. & Briggs, Charlie. Rescue & Home Care of Native Wildlife. 1976. pap. 5.95 (ISBN 0-8015-6292-9, Hawthorn). Dutton.

Collette, Jacques, ed. see Kierkegaard, Soren.

Colletti. The Art of Wood Carving. 160p. 1977. 10.95 o.p. (ISBN 0-13-049247-7, Spec); pap. 4.95 o.p. (ISBN 0-13-049239-6). P-H.

Colletti, Anthony B. Audio-Visual Program, No. 5. (Keystone Publications' Audio-Visual Program Ser.). 1979. 215.00 (ISBN 0-912126-39-6); instrs's. guide 7.07 (ISBN 0-912126-37-X); student wkbk. 1.79 (ISBN 0-912126-38-8). Keystone Pubns.

--A Complete Question & Answer Guide to Hairdressing & Cosmetology. 1978. text ed. 16.00 (ISBN 0-912126-48-5, 1258-01); pap. text ed. 14.21 (ISBN 0-912126-49-3, 1258-00). Keystone Pubns.

--La Cosmetologia, la Guia Keystone Para Aprender el Arte De Embellecer. rev. ed. (Span.). 1981. text ed. 16.78 (ISBN 0-912126-61-2, 1260-00); pap. text ed. 12.15 (ISBN 0-912126-62-0, 1261-00). Keystone Pubns.

--Cosmetology. (Illus.). 1980. 11.00x (ISBN 0-912126-29-9). Sheridan.

--Cosmetology Instructor's Guide, No. 1. (Keystone Publications' Audio-Visual Program Ser.). 88p. 1976. 7.10 (ISBN 0-912126-16-7). Keystone Pubns.

--Cosmetology Instructor's Guide, No. 2. (Keystone Publications' Audio-Visual Program Ser.). 80p. 1976. 7.10311 (ISBN 0-912126-17-5). Keystone Pubns.

--Cosmetology Instructor's Guide, No. 3. (Keystone's Publications' Audio-Visual Program Ser.). 136p. 1976. 7.10 (ISBN 0-912126-18-3). Keystone Pubns.

--Cosmetology Instructor's Guide, No. 4. (Keystone Publications' Audio-Visual Program Ser.). 112p. 7.10 (ISBN 0-912126-19-1). Keystone Pubns.

--Cosmetology Review Book. 1981. pap. text ed. 5.00 (ISBN 0-912126-56-6, 1267-00). Keystone Pubns.

--Cosmetology: The Keystone Guide to Beauty Culture. rev. ed. 1981. text ed. 10.00 (ISBN 0-912126-59-0, 1248-00); pap. text ed. 7.14 (ISBN 0-912126-60-4, 1249-00). Keystone Pubns.

--A Dictionary of Cosmetology & Related Services. Chiranky, Gary, ed. 1981. text ed. 23.57 (ISBN 0-912126-58-2, 1275-00). Keystone Pubns.

--Revista a los Examenes De Cosmetologia Que Hace la Junta Estatal (State Board Review Examinations in Cosmetology) 1976. pap. 6.00 (ISBN 0-912126-12-4, 1271-00). Keystone Pubns.

--Teacher's Reference Manual for Cosmetology. 1981. cancelled (ISBN 0-912126-33-7). Keystone Pubns.

--Trichology: The Keystone Guide to Hair Analysis As Related to the Practice of Cosmetology & Barbering. (Illus.). 1981. text ed. 11.36 (ISBN 0-912126-57-4). Keystone Pubns.

--Twenty-Four Practice Hairstyles. rev. ed. 1981. pap. text ed. 5.00 (ISBN 0-912126-47-7, 1265-00). Keystone Pubns.

Colley, Iain. Dos Passos & the Fiction of Despair. 170p. 1978. 25.00x (ISBN 0-8476-6020-6). Rowman.

Colley, John S. John Marston's Theatrical Drama. (Salzburg Studies in English Literature, Jacobean Drama Studies: No. 33). 202p. 1974. pap. text ed. 25.00x (ISBN 0-391-01347-5). Humanities.

Collias, Eugene E., et al. An Atlas of Physical & Chemical Properties of Puget Sound & Its Approaches. LC 74-10057. (Washoington Sea Grant). (Illus.). 248p. 1974. pap. 18.50 (ISBN 0-295-95345-4). U of Wash Pr.

Collias, Joe G. Mopac Power. (Illus.). 352p. 1980. 30.00 (ISBN 0-8310-7117-6). Howell-North.

Collie, David, ed. see Ssu Shu.

Collie, Erroll S. Quimby's Science of Happiness. 119p. (Orig.). 1980. pap. 5.50 (ISBN 0-87516-410-2). De Vorss.

Collie, Michael. Jules Laforgue. (Athlone French Poets Ser). 160p. 1977. text ed. 18.75x (ISBN 0-485-14606-1, Athlone Pr); pap. text ed. 6.25x (ISBN 0-485-12206-5). Humanities.

Collie, Michael, ed. see Laforgue, Jules.

Collier, et al. Kids' Stuff: Kindergarten - Nursery School. (ps-k). 1969. pap. 10.95 (ISBN 0-913916-00-5, IP005). Incentive Pubns.

Collier, Arthur. Clavis Universalis: New Inquiry After Truth, Being a Demonstration of the Non-Existence or Impossibility of an External World, 1713. Wellek, Rene, ed. LC 75-11208. (British Philosophers & Theologians of the 17th & 18th Centuries Ser.). lib. bdg. 42.00 (ISBN 0-8240-1763-3). Garland Pub.

Collier, Basil. Arms & the Men: The Arms Trade & Governments. (Illus.). 320p. 1980. 37.00 (ISBN 0-241-10308-8, Pub. by Hamish Hamilton England). David & Charles.

--Dunkirk. (Jackdaw Ser: No. 130). 1974. 5.95 o.p. (ISBN 0-670-28628-1, Grossman). Viking Pr.

--A History of Air Power. LC 73-20991. (Illus.). 331p. 1974. 14.95 o.s.i. (ISBN 0-02-527170-9). Macmillan.

Collier, C. Patrick. Geometry for Teachers. LC 75-25017. (Illus.). 352p. 1976. text ed. 17.50 (ISBN 0-395-20661-8). solutions manual 1.90 (ISBN 0-395-24219-3). HM.

Collier, Charles. Essay on the Principles of Education, Physiologically Considered. Bd. with Art of Instructing the Infant Deaf & Dumb. (Contributions to the History of Psychology, Vol. V, Pt. B: Psychometrics & Educational Psychology). 1980. Repr. of 1856 ed. 30.00 (ISBN 0-89093-319-7). U Pubns Amer.

Collier, Christopher, jt. auth. see Collier, James L.

Collier, Diana & Goff, Nancy. Frozen Delights. LC 75-42494. (Illus.). 256p. 1976. 8.95 o.s.i. (ISBN 0-690-01097-4, TYC-T). T Y Crowell.

Collier, Elsie, jt. auth. see Collier, John.

Collier, Eugenia W., jt. ed. see Long, Richard A.

Collier, Francis, et al. Quantitative Laboratory Experiments in General Chemistry. LC 75-26087. (Illus.). 288p. 1976. pap. 10.50 (ISBN 0-395-18982-9). HM.

Collier, G. Jazz. (Resources of Music Ser.). (Illus.). 200p. 1975. 19.95 (ISBN 0-521-20561-1); pap. 6.95 (ISBN 0-521-09887-4); tape 16.95 (ISBN 0-521-20560-3); record 11.95 (ISBN 0-521-20563-8). Cambridge U Pr.

Collier, G., et al, eds. Values & Moral Development in Higher Education. LC 74-1599. 225p. 1974. 18.95 (ISBN 0-470-16549-9). Halsted Pr.

Collier, Gordon. Make Your Own World. 9.95 (ISBN 0-912576-04-9). R Collier.

Collier, Graham. Art & the Creative Consciousness. (Illus.). 208p. 1973. pap. text ed. 7.95 (ISBN 0-13-046706-5). P-H.

--Form, Space & Vision. 3rd ed. LC 75-167911. 1972. pap. text ed. 18.95 (ISBN 0-13-329458-7). P-H.

Collier, J., jt. ed. see Phillips, I.

Collier, J. G. Convective Boiling & Condensation. 2nd ed. (Illus.). 460p. 1981. text ed. 59.50 (ISBN 0-07-011798-5). McGraw.

Collier, J. W. Wood Finishing. 1967. 13.75 (ISBN 0-08-011242-0). Pergamon.

Collier, James L. CB. (Career Concise Guides Ser.). (Illus.). (gr. 7 up). 1977. PLB 6.45 s&l (ISBN 0-531-00095-8). Watts.

--The Great Jazz Artists. LC 77-7212. (Illus.). 192p. (gr. 7 up). 1977. 7.95 (ISBN 0-590-07493-8, Four Winds). Schol Bk Serv.

--Making Music for Money. LC 75-31843. (Career Concise Guides Ser.). (Illus.). 72p. (gr. 7 up). 1976. PLB 6.45 (ISBN 0-531-02903-4). Watts.

Collier, James L. & Collier, Christopher. The Bloody Country. LC 75-34461. 192p. (gr. 7 up). 1977. 7.95 (ISBN 0-590-07411-3, Four Winds). Schol Bk Serv.

--My Brother Sam Is Dead. LC 74-8350. 224p. (gr. 7 up). 1974. 7.95 (ISBN 0-590-07339-7, Four Winds). Schol Bk Serv.

--The Winter Hero. LC 78-7609. 160p. (gr. 7 up). 1978. 7.95 (ISBN 0-590-07529-2, Four Winds). Schol Bk Serv.

Collier, Jeremy. Collier Tracts Seventeen Three to Seventeen Eight: Mr. Collier's Dissuasive from the Playhouse. Bd. with A Farther Vindication of the Short View of the English Stage. Collier, Jeremy; The Person of Quality's Answer to Mr. Colliers Letters Being a Disswasive from the Playhouse. Dennis, John; A Representation of the Impiety & Immorality of the English Stage; Some Thoughts Concerning the Stage in a Letter to a Lady. Collier, Jeremy; The Stage-Beaux Toss'd in a Blanket. Gildon, Charles. LC 70-170462. (The English Stage Theory: Vol. 35). lib. bdg. 50.00 (ISBN 0-8240-0618-6). Garland Pub.

--A Defence of the Short View off the Profaneness & Immorality of the English Stage. LC 72-170444. (The English Stage Ser.: Vol. 30). lib. bdg. 50.00 (ISBN 0-8240-0613-5). Garland Pub.

--A Second Defence of the Short View of the English Stage. LC 76-170445. (The English Stage Ser.: Vol. 34). lib. bdg. 50.00 (ISBN 0-8240-0617-8). Garland Pub.

--A Short View of the Immorality, & Profaneness of the English Stage. LC 70-170438. (The English Stage Ser.: Vol. 22). lib. bdg. 50.00 (ISBN 0-8240-0605-4). Garland Pub.

Collier, John. Indians of the Americas. abr. ed. (Orig.). 1952. pap. 1.95 (ISBN 0-451-61886-6, MJ1886, Ment). NAL.

--On the Gleaming Way: Navajos, Eastern Pueblos, Zunis, Hopis, Apaches & Their Land, & Their Meaning to the World. LC 62-12407. 163p. (Photos, Orig). 1962. pap. 4.95 (ISBN 0-8040-0232-0, 8, SB). Swallow.

Collier, John & Collier, Elsie. China's Socialist Revolution. LC 74-7782. 272p. 1975. 8.95 o.p. (ISBN 0-85345-336-5, CL3365). Monthly Rev.

Collier, John G., jt. auth. see Lauterpacht, Elihu.

Collier, K. G., ed. Innovation in Higher Education. (General Ser.). 140p. 1974. pap. text ed. 12.50x (ISBN 0-85633-032-9, NFER). Humanities.

Collier, Keith. Construction Contracts. (Illus.). 1979. ref. ed. 21.95 (ISBN 0-8359-0912-3); text ed. 16.95 (ISBN 0-8359-0912-3). Reston.

--Fundamentals of Construction Estimating & Cost Accounting. (Illus.). 400p. 1974. 21.95 (ISBN 0-13-335604-3). P-H.

Collier, Kenneth W., jt. auth. see Kalish, Richard A.

Collier, Raymond O., Jr. & Hummel, Thomas J., eds. Experimental Design & Interpretation. LC 76-18039. (Readings in Educational Research Ser.). 1977. 25.00 (ISBN 0-8211-0225-7); text ed. 22.50 10 or more copies (ISBN 0-685-71415-2). McCutchan.

Collier, Richard. War in the Desert. (World War II Ser.). 1977. 12.95 (ISBN 0-8094-2474-6). Time-Life.

--War in the Desert. LC 77-81945. (World War 11 Ser.). (gr. 6 up). 1977. PLB 11.97 (ISBN 0-8094-2475-4). Silver.

Collier, Richard B. Pleneurethic: Its Evolution & Scientific Basis, Vol. 2. 64p. 1980. 15.00 (ISBN 0-682-49623-5). Exposition.

Collier, Robert. The Amazing Secrets of the Masters of the Far East. 9.95 (ISBN 0-912576-02-2). R Collier.

--Be Rich. pap. 1.50 (ISBN 0-912576-05-7). R Collier.

--Prayer Works! 3.25 (ISBN 0-912576-01-4). R Collier.

--Riches Within Your Reach: The Law of the Higher Potential. 9.95 (ISBN 0-912576-00-6). R Collier.

--Robert Collier Letter Book. 6th ed. 1950. 14.95 o.p. (ISBN 0-13-781500-X). P-H.

--The Robert Collier Letter Book. 14.95 o.p. (ISBN 0-13-781500-X). R Collier.

--The Secret of the Ages. pocketbook ed. 4.00 (ISBN 0-912576-06-5); deluxe ed. 9.95 (ISBN 0-912576-07-3). R Collier.

Collier, Zena. Seven for the People: Public Interest Groups at Work. LC 79-136. 192p. (gr. 7 up). 1979. PLB 8.29 (ISBN 0-671-32926-X). Messner.
Collieu, A. & Powney, Derek J. The Mechanical & Thermal Properties of Materials. LC 72-85498. 240p. 1973. 19.50x (ISBN 0-8448-0074-0). Crane-Russak Co.
Collieu, A., jt. auth. see Hulme, H. R.
Colligan. The A Plus Guide to Good Grades. (gr. 7-12). 1980. pap. 1.50 (ISBN 0-590-30001-6, Schol Pap). Schol Bk Serv.
Colligan, Doug, jt. auth. see Teresi, Dick.
Collignon, Joseph. Patterns for Composition. 312p. (Orig.). 1969. text ed. 6.95x (ISBN 0-02-474020-9, 47402). Macmillan.
--Sound of Prose. 1971. pap. text ed. 5.95x (ISBN 0-02-474430-1, 47443); tchrs' manual free (ISBN 0-02-474440-9). Macmillan.
Collin, H. B., jt. auth. see Augusteyn, R. C.
Collin, Laure. Histoire Abregee De la Musique et Des Musiciens. (Music Reprint Series). (Fr.). 1977. Repr. of 1897 ed. lib. bdg. 29.50 (ISBN 0-306-70875-2). Da Capo.
Collin, Richard O. Imbroglio. 288p. 1980. 13.95 (ISBN 0-312-40938-9). St Martin.
Collin, Rodney. The Theory of Celestial Influence. 414p. 1980. 18.00x (ISBN 0-7224-0019-5, Pub. by Watkins England). State Mutual Bk.
Collin, W. E. White Savannahs. LC 73-92516. (Literature of Canada Ser.). 1975. pap. 5.95 (ISBN 0-8020-6241-5). U of Toronto Pr.
Collinder, Bjorn. An Introduction to the Uralic Languages. 1965. 20.00x (ISBN 0-520-00256-3). U of Cal Pr.
Colling, Russell L. Hospital Security. 2nd ed. 1981. text ed. price not set. Butterworths.
--Hospital Security. LC 75-46098. (Illus.). 384p. 1976. 19.95 (ISBN 0-913708-22-4). Butterworths.
Collingridge, jt. auth. see Braun.
Collingridge, David. The Social Control of Technology. 1980. 22.50 (ISBN 0-312-73168-X). St Martin.
Collingridge, Ruth & Sekowsky, JoAnne. Introduction to Praise. (Workshop Ser.). (Orig.). 1980. pap. write for info. (ISBN 0-930756-60-6, 4235-PW1). Women's Aglow.
Collings, jt. auth. see McBurney, D.
Collings, Ellsworth & England, Alma. The One Hundred & One Ranch. LC 73-167774. (Illus.). 255p. 1937. 9.95 (ISBN 0-8061-0986-6); pap. 5.95 (ISBN 0-8061-1047-3). U of Okla Pr.
Collings, Judith, jt. auth. see Collings, Michael.
Collings, Lawrence & Ruhen, Olaf. On & Around Sydney Harbour. 128p. 1980. 13.95x (ISBN 0-00-216407-8, Pub. by W Collins Australia). Intl Schol Bk Serv.
Collings, Merle D. Projects in Electricity. (gr. 9-12). 1941. pap. text ed. 5.00 (ISBN 0-685-04240-5). McKnight.
Collings, Michael & Collings, Judith. Whole Wheat Harvest-Recipes for Unground Wheat. pap. 2.95 (ISBN 0-89036-143-6). Hawkes Pub Inc.
Collingwood, Harris. Stripping the Trees. (Chapbook Ser.: No. 2). 48p. (Orig.). 1980. pap. 4.95 (ISBN 0-937672-01-7). Rowan Tree.
Collingwood, Robin G. An Essay on Metaphysics. 364p. 1940. 24.95x (ISBN 0-19-824121-6). Oxford U Pr.
--Idea of History. Knox, T. M., ed. 1956. pap. 5.95 (ISBN 0-19-500205-9, 1, GB). Oxford U Pr.
--Principles of Art. 1958. pap. 5.95 (ISBN 0-19-500209-1, GB). Oxford U Pr.
Collingwood, Robin G. & Myres, J. N. Roman Britain & the English Settlements. 2nd ed. (Oxford History of England Ser.). (Illus.). 1937. 34.50 (ISBN 0-19-821703-X). Oxford U Pr.
Collingwood, Stuart D. Life & Letters of Lewis Carroll. LC 67-23871. 1967. Repr. of 1899 ed. 18.00 (ISBN 0-8103-3061-X). Gale.
Collini, Stefan. Liberalism & Sociology: Lt. Hobhouse & Political Argument in English 1880-1914. LC 78-23779. 1979. 32.95 (ISBN 0-521-22304-0). Cambridge U Pr.
Collins, jt. auth. see Russell, Donald S.
Collins, A. C. Alphabet Soup. (Cornerstone Ser.). (gr. 1-6). 1970. pap. text ed. 4.12 o.p. (ISBN 0-201-41001-X, Sch Div); tchr's manual 5.04 o.p. (ISBN 0-201-41002-8). A-W.
Collins, Adela Y. Apocalypse. Harrington, Wilfrid & Senior, Donald, eds. (New Testament Message Ser.: Vol. 22). 172p. 1979. 9.00 (ISBN 0-89453-145-X); pap. 4.95 (ISBN 0-89453-210-3). M Glazier.
Collins, Adrian, tr. see Nietzsche, Friedrich W.
Collins, Alberta C. & Dawson, Mildred A. Alphabet Soup. rev. ed. (Cornerstone Ser.). (gr. 2-3). 1978. pap. text ed. 4.52 (ISBN 0-201-41022-2, Sch Div); tchr's. ed. 5.56 (ISBN 0-201-41023-0). A-W.
Collins, Alice. The Human Services: An Introduction. LC 72-10176. Orig. Title: People to People - an Introduction to the Human Services. 1973. pap. 5.50 (ISBN 0-672-63081-8). Odyssey Pr.
Collins, Alice H. The Lonely & Afraid: Counseling the Hard to Reach. LC 78-76614. 1969. pap. 8.50 (ISBN 0-672-63055-9). Odyssey Pr.
Collins, Anthony. A Discourse on the Grounds & Reasons of the Christian Religion. Wellek, Rene, ed. LC 75-11212. (British Philosophers & Theologians of the 17th & 18th Centuries: Vol. 15). 1976. Repr. of 1724 ed. lib. bdg. 41.00 (ISBN 0-8240-1766-8). Garland Pub.
Collins, Barry. Judgement. (Orig.). 1974. pap. 3.95 o.p. (ISBN 0-571-10649-8, Pub. by Faber & Faber). Merrimack Bk Serv.
Collins, Bobby & White, Fred. Elementary Forestry. 1981. text ed. 15.95 (ISBN 0-8359-1647-2); instr's. manual free (ISBN 0-8359-1646-4). Reston.
Collins, C. H. Microbiology Hazards. 1981. text ed. price not set (ISBN 0-408-10650-6). Butterworth.
Collins, Charles B., jt. ed. see Block, Richard A.
Collins, Charles W. The Fourteenth Amendment & the States. LC 74-5437. (American Constitutional & Legal History Ser.). 1974. Repr. of 1912 ed. lib. bdg. 25.00 (ISBN 0-306-70638-5). Da Capo.
Collins, Charles W., ed. Atlas of Illinois. (State Atlas Ser). (Illus.). 1976. lib. bdg. 26.95x o.p. (ISBN 0-89534-003-8). Am Pub Co WI.
--Atlas of Iowa, State Atlas Ser. (Illus.). 1974. lib. bdg. 19.95x o.p. (ISBN 0-89534-007-0). Am Pub Co WI.
--Atlas of New York. (State Atlas Ser). (Illus.). lib. bdg. 29.95x o.p. (ISBN 0-89534-002-X). Am Pub Co WI.
--Atlas of Ohio, State Atlas Ser. (Illus.). 1975. lib. bdg. 26.95x o.p. (ISBN 0-89534-008-9). Am Pub Co WI.
--Atlas of Wisconsin. (State Atlas Ser). (Illus.). 1972. lib. bdg. 15.95x o.p. (ISBN 0-89534-009-7). Am Pub Co WI.
Collins, Christine. Perfect Puddings. 1976. 5.95 (ISBN 0-571-10859-8, Pub. by Faber & Faber). Merrimack Bk Serv.
Collins, D. Aspects of British Politics, 1904-1919. 1965. 25.00 (ISBN 0-08-010987-X); pap. 12.75 (ISBN 0-08-010986-1). Pergamon.
Collins, David R. The One Bad Thing About Birthdays. LC 80-23104. (A Let Me Read Bk.). (Illus.). 32p. (ps-3). 1981. pap. 2.95 (ISBN 0-15-258289-4, VoyB). HarBraceJ.
--The One Bad Thing About Birthdays. LC 80-23104. (A Let Me Read Bk.). (Illus.). 32p. (gr. 4-6). 1981. 6.95 (ISBN 0-15-258288-6, HJ). HarBraceJ.
--The Wonderful Story of Jesus. 1980. 5.95 (ISBN 0-570-03490-6, 56-1344); pap. 1.50 (ISBN 0-570-03491-4, 56-1345). Concordia.
Collins, Desmond, ed. The Origins of Europe: Four New Studies in Archeology & History. (Apollo Eds.). (Illus.). 384p. 1976. pap. 6.95 o.s.i. (ISBN 0-8152-0396-9, TYC-T). T Y Crowell.
Collins, Doreen. The European Communities-The Social Policy of the First Phase: The European Coal & Steel Community 1951-1970, Vol. 1. 1975. 48.50x (ISBN 0-85520-083-9, Pub by Martin Robertson England). Biblio Dist.
--Social Policy of the European Economic Community. LC 75-22282. 286p. 1975. 27.95 (ISBN 0-470-16583-9). Halsted Pr.
Collins, Edward A., et al. Experiments in Polymer Science. LC 73-650. 530p. 1973. pap. text ed. 18.95 (ISBN 0-471-16585-9, Pub. by Wiley-Interscience). Wiley.
Collins, Edward, Jr. International Law in a Changing World. 1970. text ed. 14.95 (ISBN 0-394-30098-X, RanC). Random.
Collins, Emily C., jt. auth. see Karnes, Frances A.
Collins, Eric J., jt. auth. see Collins, Ian D.
Collins, Fletcher, Jr., ed. Medieval Church Music-Dramas: A Repertory of Complete Plays. LC 75-33896. 1976. 15.00x o.p. (ISBN 0-8139-0644-X). U Pr of Va.
Collins, Fletcher, Jr., jt. ed. see Collins, Margaret.
Collins, Floyd. Scarecrow. LC 79-19491. 1980. pap. 3.95 (ISBN 0-918518-06-7). St Luke TN.
Collins, Gary. Helping People Grow. (Orig.). 1980. pap. 6.95 (ISBN 0-88449-069-6). Vision Hse.
--Hombre in Transicion. Ingledew, Roberto, tr. from Eng. 220p. (Orig., Span.). 1978. pap. 4.50 (ISBN 0-89922-124-6). Edit Caribe.
--How to Be a People Helper. (Orig.). 1976. pap. 4.95 (ISBN 0-88449-055-6). Vision Hse.
--The Joy of Caring. 192p. 1980. pap. 5.95 (ISBN 0-8499-2928-8). Word Bks.
--Orientacion Sicologica Eficaz. Blanch, Miguel, tr. from Eng. 206p. (Orig., Span.). 1979. pap. 4.50 (ISBN 0-89922-136-X). Edit Caribe.
--People Helper Growthbook. 1976. pap. 4.95 (ISBN 0-88449-056-4). Vision Hse.
--Personalidades Quebrantadas. Flores, Jose, tr. from Eng. LC 78-62403. 215p. (Orig., Span.). 1978. pap. 4.50 (ISBN 0-89922-116-5). Edit Caribe.
Collins, Gary R. Psychology & Theology. 160p. (Orig.). 1981. pap. 5.95 (ISBN 0-687-34830-7). Abingdon.
Collins, Gary R., ed. Facing the Future: Church & Family Together. 1976. pap. 3.95 o.p. (ISBN 0-87680-845-3, 98086). Word Bks.
--Living & Growing Together: The Christian Family Today. LC 76-19525. 1976. pap. 4.25 o.p. (ISBN 0-87680-844-5, 98087). Word Bks.
Collins, George R. see O'Neal, William B.
Collins, Henry B., et al. The Far North: Two Thousand Years of American Eskimo & Indian Art. LC 77-3132. (Illus.). 320p. 1977. 22.50x (ISBN 0-253-32120-4); pap. 17.50x (ISBN 0-253-28105-9). Ind U Pr.
Collins, Henry G. Collin's Illustrated Atlas of London. (Victorian Library). 120p. 1973. Repr. of 1854 ed. 6.50x (ISBN 0-391-00156-6, Leicester). Humanities.
Collins, Henry H., Jr., ed. Harper & Row's Complete Field Guide to North American Wildlife: Eastern Edition. LC 80-8198. (Illus.). 810p. 1981. 17.50 (ISBN 0-690-01977-7, HarpT); flexible vinyl cover 12.95 (ISBN 0-690-01969-6). Har-Row.
Collins, Ian D. & Collins, Eric J. Window Selection: A Guide for Architects & Designers. (Illus.). 1977. text ed. 16.95 (ISBN 0-408-00285-9). Butterworths.
Collins, J. A. Failure of Materials in Mechanical Design: Analysis, Prediction, Prevention. 700p. 1981. 25.00 (ISBN 0-471-05024-5, Pub. by Wiley-Interscience). Wiley.
Collins, J. L. & Opitz, Glenn. Women Artists in America: Eighteenth Century to Present. rev. ed. (Illus.). 1981. 60.00 (ISBN 0-938290-00-2). Apollo.
Collins, Jackie. Love Killers. Orig. Title: Lovehead. 192p. 1975. pap. 2.25 (ISBN 0-446-92842-9). Warner Bks.
--Stronger Than Sin. Date not set. pap. price not set. Warner Bks.
--The World Is Full of Divorced Women. 416p. (Orig.). 1981. pap. 2.95 (ISBN 0-446-83183-2). Warner Bks.
Collins, Jacquelin, jt. auth. see Blakeley, Brian L.
Collins, Jean. She Was There: Stories of Pioneering Women Journalists. LC 80-36769. (Illus.). 192p. (gr. 7 up). 1980. PLB 8.79 (ISBN 0-671-33082-9). Messner.
Collins, Jim. The Bermuda Triangle. LC 77-21808. (Great Unsolved Mysteries Ser.). (Illus.). (gr. 4-5). 1977. PLB 9.65 (ISBN 0-8172-1050-4). Raintree Pubs.
--First to the Moon. LC 78-13611. (Famous Firsts Ser.). (Illus.). 1978. lib. bdg. 7.35 (ISBN 0-686-51106-9). Silver.
--The Strange Story of Uri Geller. LC 77-24501. (Myth, Magic & Superstition Ser.). (Illus.). (gr. 4-5). 1977. PLB 9.65 (ISBN 0-8172-1037-7). Raintree Pubs.
--Unidentified Flying Objects. LC 77-13040. (Great Unsolved Mysteries Ser.). (Illus.). (gr. 4-5). 1977. PLB 9.65 (ISBN 0-8172-1065-2). Raintree Pubs.
Collins, John, jt. auth. see Lovett, William.
Collins, John A., jt. auth. see Collins, Sheila D.
Collins, John J. Anthropology: Culture, Society & Evolution. (Illus.). 480p. 1975. text ed. 17.95 (ISBN 0-13-038596-4). P-H.
--The Apocalyptic Vision of the Book of Daniel. LC 77-23124. (Harvard Semitic Monograph). 1977. text ed. 9.00 (ISBN 0-89130-133-X, 040016). Scholars Pr Ca.
--Proverbs & Ecclesiastes. LC 79-92067. (Knox Preaching Guides Ser.). 117p. (Orig., John Hayes series editor). 1980. pap. 4.50 (ISBN 0-8042-3218-0). John Knox.
--The Sibylline Oracles of Egyptian Judaism. LC 74-81099. (Society of Biblical Literature. Dissertation Ser.). 1975. pap. 7.50 (ISBN 0-89130-260-3, 060113). Scholars Pr Ca.
Collins, John M. American & Soviet Military Trends: Since the Cuban Missile Crisis. LC 78-58310. (Illus.). 1978. text ed. 14.95 (ISBN 0-89206-003-4); pap. 10.95 (ISBN 0-89206-002-6). CSI Studies.
--Grand Strategy: Principles & Practices. LC 73-76606. 1973. 15.00 o.s.i. (ISBN 0-87021-683-X); pap. 7.50 o.p. (ISBN 0-686-66756-5). Naval Inst Pr.
Collins, John W. Maxims of Chess. 1978. 10.95 o.p. (ISBN 0-679-13066-7). McKay.
Collins, Joseph, jt. auth. see Lappe, Frances M.
Collins, Joseph T., ed. see Armstrong, Barry L. & Murphy, James B.
Collins, June M. Valley of the Spirits: The Upper Skagit Indians of Western Washington. LC 74-8719. (Illus.). 282p. 1974. pap. text ed. 8.50 (ISBN 0-295-95734-4). U of Wash Pr.
Collins, Larry & Lapierre, Dominique. The Fifth Horseman. 1980. 13.95 (ISBN 0-671-24316-0). S&S.
--O Jerusalem. 1980. pap. write for info. (ISBN 0-671-83684-6). PB.
Collins, Lawrence & Schweitzer, Martin. Only a Little Planet. Brower, David R., ed. & pref. by. LC 72-187904. (Celebrating the Earth Ser). (Illus.). 128p. 1974. 14.95 o.p. (ISBN 0-913890-27-8); pap. 6.95 o.p. (ISBN 0-685-56645-5, Co-Pub. by Ballantine). Friends Earth.
Collins, Lyndhurst, ed. The Use of Models in the Social Sciences. LC 75-22018. 227p. 1975. 19.75x (ISBN 0-89158-507-9). Westview.
Collins, M. B., et al, eds. Industrialised Embayments & Their Environmental Problems: a Case Study of Swansea Bay: Proceedings of an Interdisciplinary Symposium Held at University College, Swansea, 26-28 Sept. 1979. LC 80-40507. (Illus.). 608p. 1980. 84.00 (ISBN 0-08-023992-7). Pergamon.
Collins, M. E. Conquest & Colonisation. (History of Ireland Ser.: Vol. 2). (Illus.). 240p. 1969. pap. text ed. 8.50 (ISBN 0-7171-0256-4). Irish Bk Ctr.
--Ireland, Eighteen Hundred to Nineteen Seventy. (Illus.). 1976. pap. text ed. 6.95x (ISBN 0-582-22140-4). Longman.
Collins, Margaret & Collins, Fletcher, Jr., eds. Theater Wagon Plays of Place & Any Place. LC 73-84160. (Illus.). 297p. 1973. pap. 3.95x o.p. (ISBN 0-8139-0535-4). U Pr of Va.
Collins, Margaret S., et al, eds. Science & the Question of Human Equality. (AAAS Selected Symposium: No. 58). 180p. 1981. lib. bdg. 16.00x (ISBN 0-89158-952-X). Westview.
Collins, Marjorie A. Dedication: What It's All About. 1976. pap. 3.50 (ISBN 0-87123-103-4, 210103). Bethany Fell.
Collins, Mattie. Communication in Health Care: Understanding & Implementing Effective Human Relationships. (Illus.). 1977. pap. text ed. 10.00 (ISBN 0-8016-1021-4). Mosby.
Collins, Max. The Broker's Wife. (The Quarry Ser.). pap. 1.50 o.p. (ISBN 0-425-03187-X). Berkley Pub.
--Nolan: Bait Money, No. 1. 192p. pap. 1.95 (ISBN 0-523-41159-6). Pinnacle Bks.
--Nolan, Number Two: Blood Money. rev. ed. 192p. 1981. pap. 1.95 (ISBN 0-523-41160-X). Pinnacle Bks.
Collins, Michael. The Blood Red Dream. LC 80-83589. (Dan Fortune Detective Mystery Ser.). 192p. 1981. pap. 2.25 (ISBN 0-87216-812-3). Playboy Pbks.
--The Brass Rainbow. LC 79-57533. (A Dan Fortune Detective Mystery). 176p. 1980. pap. 1.95 (ISBN 0-87216-672-4). Playboy Pbks.
--The Nightrunners. LC 80-84369. 224p. 1981. pap. 2.25 (ISBN 0-87216-822-0). Playboy Pbks.
--The Slasher. LC 81-80081. (Dan Fortune Detective Mysteries Ser.). 208p. 1981. pap. 2.25 (ISBN 0-87216-855-7). Playboy Pbks.
Collins, Michael, jt. auth. see Bullard, Scott R.
Collins, Michael F. & Pharoah, Timothy M. Transport Organization in a Great City: The Case of London. LC 74-77339. 1974. 40.00x (ISBN 0-8039-0434-7). Sage.
Collins, Mildred. Students into Teachers: Experiences of Probationers in Schools. (Students Library of Education). 1969. text ed. 5.25x (ISBN 0-7100-6338-5); pap. text ed. 2.25x (ISBN 0-7100-6342-3). Humanities.
Collins, N. L. & Michie, D., eds. Machine Intelligence, 2 vols. (Machine Intelligence Ser.). 1975. Set. 45.95 (ISBN 0-470-59332-6). Halsted Pr.
Collins, Norman. Dulcimer Street. 1977. pap. 2.50 o.p. (ISBN 0-445-08588-6). Popular Lib.
Collins, P. D. An Introduction to Regge Theory & High-Energy Physics. LC 76-2233. (Cambridge Monographs on Mathematical Physics). (Illus.). 1977. 97.50 (ISBN 0-521-21245-6). Cambridge U Pr.
Collins, Patricia. My Friend Andrew. (Illus.). (ps-2). 1979. PLB 7.95 o.p. (ISBN 0-13-608844-9). P-H.
Collins, Patrick. Living in Troubled Lands. 190p. 1980. 12.95 (ISBN 0-87364-205-8). Paladin Ent.
Collins, Paul, jt. auth. see Harrison, Phyllis.
Collins, Peggie & Collins, Shirley. Putting It All Together, A Consumer's Guide to Home Furnishings. LC 77-1885. (Illus.). 1977. 10.00 (ISBN 0-684-14883-8, ScribT); pap. 6.95 o.p. (ISBN 0-684-14884-6, ScribT). Scribner.
Collins, Peter, tr. see Durkheim, Emile.
Collins, Philip. Dickens: The Critical Heritage. (Critical Heritage Ser.). 1971. 27.00x (ISBN 0-7100-6907-3). Routledge & Kegan.
Collins, Philip, ed. Charles Dickens: Interviews & Recollections, 2 vols. (Illus.). 1981. 26.50x ea. Vol. 1, 160pgs (ISBN 0-389-20042-5). Vol. 2, 160 Pgs (ISBN 0-389-20043-3). B&N.
Collins, R. & Van Der Werff, T. J. Mathematical Models of the Dynamics of the Human Eye. (Lecture Notes in Biomathematics: Vol. 34). 99p. 1980. pap. 9.80 (ISBN 0-387-09751-1). Springer-Verlag.
Collins, Randall. The Credential Society: A Historical Sociology of Education & Stratification. LC 78-20042. 1979. 13.50 (ISBN 0-12-181360-6). Acad Pr.

Collins, Ray. Everything's Great in Seventy-Eight. (Illus.). 1978. pap. 3.95 (ISBN 0-914842-30-7). Madrona Pubs.
Collins, Richard. Flying Safely. rev. ed. 1981. 10.95 (ISBN 0-440-02652-0, E Friede). Delacorte.
Collins, Richard, jt. auth. see Herpel, George.
Collins, Robert E. Theodore Parker: American Transcendentalist: A Critical Essay & a Collection of His Writings. LC 73-9593. 1973. 10.00 (ISBN 0-8108-0641-X). Scarecrow.
Collins, Sarah H. & Tuttle, Frederick B., Jr. Technical & Scientific Writing. 127p. 1979. pap. 4.75 (ISBN 0-686-63671-6, 1718-8-06). NEA.
Collins, Sheila D. & Collins, John A. In Your Midst: Perspectives on Christian Mission. (Orig.). 1980. pap. 3.25 (ISBN 0-377-00101-5). Friend Pr.
Collins, Shirley, jt. auth. see Collins, Peggie.
Collins, Stanley. Courage & Submission. 2nd ed. LC 74-32323. 1977. pap. 2.25 (ISBN 0-8307-0459-0, S292-1-22). Regal.
Collins, Stephen. Forest & Woodland. LC 60-6114. (Community of Living Things Ser). (Illus.). (gr. 4-8). 1967. PLB 7.45 (ISBN 0-87191-015-2). Creative Ed.
Collins, Steven, jt. auth. see Stone, A. Harris.
Collins, Susanna. Flamenco Nights. (Second Chance at Love, Contemporary Ser.: No. 1). 192p. (Orig.). 1981. pap. 1.75 (ISBN 0-515-05703-7). Jove Pubns.
Collins, Thomas. Nightside. (Orig.). 1979. pap. 2.25 (ISBN 0-532-23143-0). Manor Bks.
Collins, Thomas C., jt. auth. see Reynolds, Donald C.
Collins, Thomas W., ed. Cities in a Larger Context. LC 79-54361. (Southern Anthropological Society Proceedings Ser.: No. 14). (Illus.). 168p. 1980. 12.00x (ISBN 0-8203-0504-9); pap. 5.95x (ISBN 0-8203-0505-7). U of Ga Pr.
Collins, Val. Microwave Baking. (Illus.). 128p. 1980. 17.95 (ISBN 0-7153-8018-4). David & Charles.
Collins, Violet F. The Magical Maze. 100p. (Orig.). (gr. 1-8). 1981. write for info. (ISBN 0-9604578-0-1); write for info. tchr's ed. (ISBN 0-9604578-1-X). Baraka Bk.
Collins, W., jt. auth. see Leyden, D.
Collins, W. Andrew, ed. Aspects of the Development of Competence. LC 80-20568. (Minnesota Symposia on Child Psychology: Vol. 14). 288p. 1981. 19.95 (ISBN 0-89859-070-1). L Erlbaum Assocs.
Collins, W. P., ed. Perspectives on State & Local Politics. LC 74-5202. (Illus.). 288p. 1974. pap. text ed. 9.95 (ISBN 0-13-660548-6). P-H.
Collins, Wilkie. Armadale. (The Zodiac Press Ser.). 1978. 9.95 (ISBN 0-7011-1375-8, Pub. by Chatto Bodley Jonathan). Merrimack Bk Serv.
--Basil. 352p. 1980. pap. 4.50 (ISBN 0-486-24015-0). Dover.
--Moonstone. (World's Classics Ser.). 8.95 o.p. (ISBN 0-19-250316-2). Oxford U Pr.
--Moonstone: Abridged & Adapted to Grade 2 Reading Level. Laklan, Carli, ed. LC 67-25786. (Pacemaker Classics Ser.). (Illus., Orig.). 1967. pap. 3.80 (ISBN 0-8224-9220-2); tchrs' manual free (ISBN 0-8224-5200-6). Pitman Learning.
Collinson, Francis. The Bagpipe: The History of a Musical Instrument. (Illus.). 278p. 1975. 25.00 (ISBN 0-7100-7913-3). Routledge & Kegan.
--The Traditional & National Music of Scotland. (Illus.). 1970. Repr. of 1966 ed. 25.00 (ISBN 0-7100-1213-6). Routledge & Kegan.
Collinson, Francis, jt. ed. see Campbell, J. L.
Collinson, Patrick. Archbishop Grindal, 1519-1589: The Struggle for a Reformed Church in England. 1979. 30.00x (ISBN 0-520-03831-2). U of Cal Pr.
Collis, Eirene, tr. see Sand, George.
Collis, Harry. Colloquial English. 96p. 1981. pap. text ed. write for info. (ISBN 0-88345-428-9). Regents Pub.
Collis, John S. Shaw. LC 70-160748. 1971. Repr. of 1925 ed. 12.00 o.p. (ISBN 0-8046-1561-6). Kennikat.
Collis, Margaret. Early Explorations. LC 77-83012. (Using the Environment Ser.). (Illus.). 1977. pap. text ed. 9.30 (ISBN 0-356-04353-3). Raintree Child.
--Investigations, Pts. 1 & 2. LC 77-83013. (Using the Environment). (Illus.). 1977. Pt. 1. pap. text ed. 9.30 (ISBN 0-356-04354-1); Pt. 2. pap. text ed. 9.30 (ISBN 0-356-04355-X). Raintree Child.
--Tackling Problems, Pt. 1. LC 77-83014. (Using the Environment Ser.). (Illus.). 1977. pap. text ed. 9.30 (ISBN 0-356-04356-8). Raintree Child.
--Tackling Problems, Pt. 2. LC 77-83014. (Using the Environment Ser.). (Illus.). 1977. pap. text ed. 9.30 (ISBN 0-356-05000-9). Raintree Child.
--Ways & Means. LC 77-83015. (Using the Environment Ser.). (Illus.). 1977. pap. text ed. 9.30 (ISBN 0-356-05001-7). Raintree Child.
Collis, Martin & Kirchoff, William. Swimming. 96p. 1974. pap. text ed. 2.95x o.p. (ISBN 0-205-03853-0, 623853X). Allyn.
Collis, Maurice. Cortes & Montezuma. (Illus.). 1963. pap. 3.95 o.p. (ISBN 0-571-05626-1, Pub. by Faber & Faber). Merrimack Bk Serv.
--Foreign Mud. (Illus., Orig.). 1964. pap. 4.95 (ISBN 0-571-05797-7, Pub. by Faber & Faber). Merrimack Bk Serv.
--The Journey up. (Illus.). 1970. 9.95 (ISBN 0-571-09000-1, Pub. by Faber & Faber). Merrimack Bk Serv.
--Raffles. 1970. 4.95 (ISBN 0-571-09227-6, Pub. by Faber & Faber). Merrimack Bk Serv.
--Siamese White. (Orig.). 1965. pap. 4.95 (ISBN 0-571-06511-2, Pub. by Faber & Faber). Merrimack Bk Serv.
Collisn, W. Lucas. Lucian. 180p. 1981. Repr. lib. bdg. 30.00 (ISBN 0-89987-113-5). Darby Bks.
Collison. The Developers Dictionary & Handbook. 160p. 1974. 17.95 (ISBN 0-669-92882-8). Lexington Bks.
Collison, David. Stage Sound. LC 75-6799. (Illus.). 192p. 1976. text ed. 15.00x (ISBN 0-910482-65-9). Drama Bk.
Collison, Mary, jt. auth. see Collison, Robert.
Collison, Mike, jt. auth. see Carlen, Pat.
Collison, Robert & Collison, Mary. Dictionary of Foreign Quotations. 1980. 29.95 (ISBN 0-87196-428-7). Facts on File.
Collison, Robert L. Encyclopaedias: Their History Throughout the Ages. 2nd ed. (Illus.). 1966. 18.00 o.s.i. (ISBN 0-02-843100-6). Hafner.
--Library Assistance to Readers. 1963. 4.75 o.p. (ISBN 0-8022-0284-5). Philos Lib.
--Uganda. (World Bibliographical Ser.: No. 11). 1981. write for info. (ISBN 0-903450-17-8). ABC Clio.
Collister, Peter. The Sulivans & the Slave Trade. (Illus.). 199p. 1981. 14.95x (ISBN 0-8476-3611-9). Rowman.
Collman, James P. & Hegedus, Louis S. Principles & Applications or Organotransition Metal Chemistry. LC 79-57228. 725p. 1980. 24.00 (ISBN 0-935702-03-2). Univ Sci Bks.
Collman, Russ, ed. see Digerness, David S.
Collman, Russ, ed. see Jones, Robert C.
Collman, Russ, ed. see Le Massena, Robert A.
Collman, Russ, ed. see Mangan, Terry W.
Collman, Russ, ed. see Roberts, Jack.
Collman, Russ, ed. see Shoemaker, Len.
Collman, Russ, ed. see Wentworth, Frank L.
Collman, Russell, jt. auth. see McCoy, Dell.
Collmer, Candace W. see Hetherington, E. Mavis.
Collocott, T. C., jt. ed. see Thorne, J. O.
Collodi, C. The Adventures of Pinocchio. Della Chiesa, Carol, tr. (Illus.). (gr. 3-5). 1972. pap. 1.50 o.s.i. (ISBN 0-02-042740-9, Collier). Macmillan.
Collodi, Carlo. Adventures of Pinocchio. rev. ed. Chiesa, Carol D., tr. LC 25-26908. (Illus.). (gr. k-5). 1969. deluxe ed. 19.95 (ISBN 0-02-722820-7). Macmillan.
--Pinocchio. (Childrens Illustrated Classics Ser). (Illus.). 1975. Repr. of 1972 ed. 5.50x o.p. (ISBN 0-460-06923-3, Pub. by J. M. Dent England). Biblio Dist.
Collomb, Robin G. Alpine Guide, 2 vols. LC 75-455891. (Illus.). 1969. Vol. 1, Chamonix & Mont Blanc. Vol. 2, Zermatt & District. 10.00x ea.; 10.00x (ISBN 0-686-66323-3). Set (ISBN 0-09-456670-4). Intl Pubns Serv.
Collop, John. Poems of John Collop. Hilberry, Conrad, ed. 1962. 21.50x (ISBN 0-299-02490-3). U of Wis Pr.
Colloquium of Microwave Communication, 5th, Budapest, 1970. Proceedings, 5 vols. rev. ed. Bognar, G., ed. LC 65-40139. 1974. Set. 75.00x (ISBN 963-05-0300-X). Intl Pubns Serv.
Colloquium on Protides of the Biological Fluids, 27th, Brussels, Apr. 30-May 3, 1979. Protides of the Biological Fluids: Proceedings. Peeters, H., ed. LC 58-5908. (Illus.). 895p. 1980. 150.00 (ISBN 0-08-024933-7). Pergamon.
Colloquium on the Law of Outer Space - International Institute of Space Law of the International Astronautical Federation, 20th, 1977. Proceedings. Schwartz, Mortimer D., ed. v, 524p. 1978. pap. text ed. 32.50x (ISBN 0-8377-0439-1). Rothman.
Collu, Robert, et al, eds. Central Nervous System Effects of Hypothalamic Hormones. LC 77-94310. 1978. text ed. 41.00 (ISBN 0-89004-347-7). Raven.
--Pediatric Endocrinology. (Comprehensive Endocrinology Ser.). 1981. text ed. price not set (ISBN 0-89004-543-7). Raven.
Collyer, David J. Fly-Dressing. LC 74-20454. (Illus.). 280p. 1975. 25.00 (ISBN 0-7153-6719-6). David & Charles.
Collyer, Mary. Felicia to Charlotte, Seventeen Forty-Four to Seventeen Forty-Nine, 2 vols. in 1. (The Flowering of the Novel, 1740-1775 Ser: Vol. 13). 1974. lib. bdg. 50.00 (ISBN 0-8240-1112-0). Garland Pub.
--Virtuous Orphan; or, the Life of Marianne, Countess of ---, 4 vols. Paulson, Ronald, ed. LC 78-60843. (Novel 1720-1805 Ser.). 1979. lib. bdg. 31.00 ea. Garland Pub.
Colman. The Amazing Miss Laura. (gr. 9-12). 1980. pap. 1.25 (ISBN 0-590-30006-7, Schol Pap). Schol Bk Serv.
Colman, Arthur & Colman, Libby. Earth Father-Sky Father: The Changing Concept of Fathering. (Illus.). 224p. 1981. 12.95t (ISBN 0-13-223032-1, Spec); pap. 5.95b (ISBN 0-13-223024-0). P-H.
Colman, Bruce, jt. auth. see Hileman, Josephine.
Colman, David & Nixson, Fred. Economics of Change in Less Developed Countries. LC 78-9708. 1978. pap. 15.95 (ISBN 0-470-26436-5). Halsted Pr.
Colman, E. A., ed. King Lear. (The Challis Shakespeare Ser). 1981. pap. 3.50x (ISBN 0-686-68844-9, Pub. by Sydney U Pr Australia). Intl Schol Bk Serv.
Colman, George. Broad Grins: Comprising, with New Additional Tales in Verse, Those Formerly Published Under the Title of "My Nightgown & Slippers". Repr. Of 1802 Ed. Bd. with Eccentricities for Edinburgh. Repr. of 1816 ed. LC 75-31180. (Romantic Context: Poetry 1789-1830 Ser.: Vol. 33). 1977. lib. bdg. 47.00 (ISBN 0-8240-2132-0). Garland Pub.
--New Brooms! & The Manager in Distress. LC 80-14205. 25.00x (ISBN 0-8201-1353-0). Schol Facsimiles.
--Poetical Vagaries, Repr. Of 1812 Ed. Bd. with Vagaries Vindicated: Or, Hypocritick Hypocriticks: a Poem Addressed to the Reviewers. Repr. of 1813 ed. LC 75-31182. (Romantic Context: Poetry 1789-1830 Ser.: Vol. 34). 1976. lib. bdg. 47.00 (ISBN 0-8240-2133-9). Garland Pub.
Colman, Hila. Accident. LC 80-20509. 160p. (gr. 7-9). 1980. 7.95 (ISBN 0-688-22238-2); PLB 7.63 (ISBN 0-688-32238-7). Morrow.
--After the Wedding. LC 75-11587. 192p. (gr. 7 up). 1975. PLB 6.96 (ISBN 0-688-32043-0). Morrow.
--The Amazing Miss Laura. LC 76-17316. 192p. (gr. 7 up). 1976. PLB 6.48 (ISBN 0-688-32079-1). Morrow.
--Bride at Eighteen. (gr. 7 up). 1966. PLB 6.96 (ISBN 0-688-31122-9). Morrow.
--Chicano Girl. 192p. (gr. 7 up). 1973. 6.75 o.p. (ISBN 0-688-20082-6). Morrow.
--Claudia, Where Are You? (gr. 7 up). 1969. PLB 6.96 (ISBN 0-688-31174-1). Morrow.
--Claudia, Where Are You? (gr. 7-9). 1976. pap. 1.95 (ISBN 0-671-42450-5). Archway.
--Claudia, Where Are You? (YA) (gr. 7-9). 1976. pap. 1.75 (ISBN 0-671-56071-9). PB.
--Daughter of Discontent. LC 74-155995. (gr. 7 up). 1971. PLB 6.48 o.p. (ISBN 0-688-31215-2). Morrow.
--Diary of a Frantic Kid Sister. (gr. 4-6). 1975. pap. 1.75 (ISBN 0-671-42452-1, 29625-6). Archway.
--Diary of a Frantic Kid Sister. (gr. 4-6). 1975. pap. 1.50 (ISBN 0-671-29986-7). PB.
--The Happenings at North End School. LC 77-117224. (gr. 7 up). 1970. 7.25 (ISBN 0-688-21374-X). Morrow.
--Nobody Has to Be a Kid Forever. (gr. 5-7). 1977. pap. 1.75 (ISBN 0-671-56098-0). PB.
--The Secret Life of Harold the Bird Watcher. LC 77-11559. (Illus.). (gr. 3-6). 1978. 5.95 (ISBN 0-690-01306-X, TYC-J); PLB 7.89 (ISBN 0-690-03830-5). T y Crowell.
--Sometimes I Don't Love My Mother. (gr. 7 up). 1977. 8.25 (ISBN 0-688-22121-1); PLB 7.92 (ISBN 0-688-32121-6). Morrow.
--That's the Way It Is, Amigo. LC 74-30398. (Illus.). 96p. (gr. 6 up). 1975. 7.95 (ISBN 0-690-00750-7, TYC-J). T Y Crowell.
--Watch That Watch. (Illus.). (gr. k-3). 1962. PLB 6.48 o.p. (ISBN 0-688-31623-9). Morrow.
Colman, Itila. Tell Me No Lies. (YA) (gr. 7-9). 1979. pap. write for info. (ISBN 0-671-29920-4). PB.
Colman, Libby, jt. auth. see Colman, Arthur.
Colman, Morris. On Consciousness, Language, & Cognition: Three Studies in Materialism. (Occasional Papers: No. 31). 1978. 1.50 (ISBN 0-89977-027-4). Am Inst Marxist.
Colman, Raphael. How to Develop the Learning Powers of the Child & of the Teenager. (Illus.). 1977. 39.50 (ISBN 0-89266-086-4). Am Classical Coll Pr.
Colman, William G. Cities, Suburbs & States: Governing & Financing Urban America. LC 75-2810. (Illus.). 1975. 17.95 (ISBN 0-02-906490-2). Free Pr.
Colman-Porter, C. A. Science for Chemical Process Operators. 1972. pap. 7.24 (ISBN 0-08-015725-4). Pergamon.
Colmer, Michael. Calendar Girl. LC 76-6265. (Illus.). 1977. Repr. of 1976 ed. 19.95 o.p. (ISBN 0-89104-106-0). A & W Pubs.
Colodner, Solomon. Concepts & Values. LC 68-58503. 140p. 1968. 5.95 (ISBN 0-88400-020-6). Shengold.
Colodny, Robert G., ed. see Nalimov, V. V.
Colokathis, Jane. Comprehensive Index to CPL Exchange Bibliographies, No. 1-1565: A Numerical Index. (CPL Bibliographies: No. 3). 89p. 1979. pap. 9.00 (ISBN 0-86602-003-9). CPL Biblios.
--Comprehensive Index to CPL Exchange Bibliographies, No. 1-1565: A Subject Index. (CPL Bibliographies: No. 1). 119p. 1979. pap. 12.00 (ISBN 0-86602-001-2, Z5942). CPL Biblios.
--Comprehensive Index to CPL Exchange Bibliographies, Nos. 1-1565: An Author Index. (CPL Bibliographies: No. 2). 100p. 1979. pap. 10.00 (ISBN 0-86602-002-0). CPL Biblios.
Colombani, Alfredo. L Opera Italiana Nel Secolo Xix: Dono Agli Abbonati Des Corriere Della Sera. LC 80-2266. 1981. Repr. of 1900 ed. 61.00 (ISBN 0-404-18819-2). AMS Pr.
Colombe, Paul D. see De Sainte Colombe, Paul.
Colombe, Paul De Sainte see De Sainte Colombe, Paul.
Colombetti, Giuliano, jt. ed. see Lenci, Francesco.
Colombo, J. P., ed. see Eastham, R. C.
Colombo, J. P., ed. see Richterich, R.
Colonell, J. M. & Stockholm, H. K., eds. Port Valdez, Alaska: Environmental Studies, Nineteen Seventy-Six to Nineteen Seventy-Nine. (Occasional Publications Ser.: No. 5). (Illus.). 500p. 1980. write for info. (ISBN 0-914500-09-0). U of AK Inst Marine.
Colonias, John S. Particle Accelerator Design Computer Programs. 1974. 44.50 (ISBN 0-12-181550-1). Acad Pr.
Colonna, Francesco. Hypnerotomachia Poliphili. LC 75-27842. (Renaissance & the Gods Ser.: Vol. 1). 1976. Repr. of 1499 ed. lib. bdg. 73.00 (ISBN 0-8240-2050-2). Garland Pub.
--Hypnerotomachia: The Strife of Love in a Dreame. Dallington, R., tr. LC 73-6347. (English Experience Ser.: No. 87). 200p. 1969. Repr. of 1592 ed. 28.50 (ISBN 90-221-0087-1). Walter J Johnson.
--Hypnerotomachia, the Strife of Love in a Dreame. LC 75-27858. (Renaissance & the Gods Ser.: Vol. 15). (Illus.). 1976. Repr. of 1592 ed. lib. bdg. 73.00 (ISBN 0-8240-2064-2). Garland Pub.
Colorado, Antonio J. The First Book of Puerto Rico. 2nd ed. (First Bks.). (Illus.). (gr. 3-5). 1978. PLB 6.45 s&l (ISBN 0-531-01292-1). Watts.
Colorado Energy Research Institute, Colorado School of Mines. Water & Energy in Colorado's Future. 330p. 1981. lib. bdg. 25.00x (ISBN 0-86531-118-8). Westview.
Colorforms Books. Colorforms ABC Book. (Illus.). (ps-1). 1973. 2.95 (ISBN 0-394-82657-4, BYR). Random.
Colorni, Evelina. Singers' Italian: A Manual of Diction & Phonetics. 1970. pap. text ed. 7.95 (ISBN 0-02-870620-X). Schirmer Bks.
Colourmaster. Day Outings. (Travel in England Ser.). (Illus.). 96p. 1975. 7.95 (ISBN 0-85936-004-0). Transatlantic.
--Historic Buildings. (Travel in England Ser.). (Illus.). 64p. 1975. 7.95 (ISBN 0-85933-129-6). Transatlantic.
--Lake District (Cumberland, Lancashire, Westmoreland) (Travel in England Ser.). (Illus.). 96p. 1975. Repr. 7.95 (ISBN 0-85933-006-0). Transatlantic.
--London's Pageantry. (Travel in England Ser.). (Illus.). 64p. 1975. 7.95 (ISBN 0-85933-110-5). Transatlantic.
--Pubs & Pub Signs. (Travel in England Ser.). (Illus.). 64p. 1975. 7.95 (ISBN 0-85933-105-9). Transatlantic.
--Southern England (Kent, Sussex, Hampshire, Isle of Wight) (Travel in England Ser.). (Illus.). 96p. 1975. 7.95 (ISBN 0-85933-007-9). Transatlantic.
--West Country (Cornwall, Devon, Dorset, Somerset) (Travel in England Ser.). (Illus.). 96p. 1975. 7.95 (ISBN 0-685-51761-6). Transatlantic.
Colowick, S. P., et al, eds. Methods in Enzymology, Vol. 71: Lipids, Part C. 1981. write for info. (ISBN 0-12-181971-X). Acad Pr.
--Methos in Enzymology: Lipids, Pt. D, Vol. 72. (Serial Publications). 1981. price not set (ISBN 0-12-181972-8). Acad Pr.
Colquhoon, D. Lectures on Biostatistics: An Introduction to Statistics with Applications in Biology & Medicine. 1971. pap. 16.95x (ISBN 0-19-854119-8). Oxford U Pr.
Colquhoun, Archibald, tr. see Calvino, Italo.
Colquhoun, Archibald R. Amongst the Shans. (Illus.). 1968. Repr. of 1885 ed. 17.00 o.p. (ISBN 0-8188-0023-2). Paragon.
Colquhoun, Frank. Hymns That Live. 320p. 1981. pap. 6.95 (ISBN 0-87784-473-9). Inter Varsity.
Colquhoun, Frank, ed. Prayers for Every Occasion. Orig. Title: Parish Prayers. 445p. 1974. Repr. of 1967 ed. kival 12.95 (ISBN 0-8192-1280-6). Morehouse.
Colquhoun, John. Repentance. pap. 1.95 o.p. (ISBN 0-686-12536-3). Banner of Truth.

Colquhoun, P. A New & Appropriate System of Education for the Labouring People. 98p. 1971. Repr. of 1806 ed. 15.00x (ISBN 0-7165-1773-6, Pub. by Irish Academic Pr Ireland). Biblio Dist.

Colquitt, Betsy. Honor Card & Other Poems. 100p. 1980. 9.50 (ISBN 0-936830-01-8); pap. 4.50 (ISBN 0-936830-02-6). Saurian Pr.

Colson, Charles. Naci de Nuevo. Ward, Rhode, tr. from Eng. LC 77-81645. 419p. (Orig., Span.). 1977. pap. 3.95 (ISBN 0-89922-087-8). Edit Caribe.

Colson, Elizabeth. Plateau Tonga of Northern Rhodesia. (Rhodes Livingston Inst. Publications). 1970. text ed. 8.75x o.p. (ISBN 0-7190-1011-X). Humanities.

Colson, Elizabeth, jt. auth. see Scudder, Thayer.

Colson, Elizabeth & Gluckman, Max, eds. Seven Tribes of Central Africa. (Rhodes Livingston Institute Publications). 1968. text ed. 9.25x o.p. (ISBN 0-7190-1014-4). Humanities.

Colson, Francis M., ed. see Cicero.

Colson, Frank A. Kiln Building with Space-Age Materials. 127p. 1980. pap. 7.95 (ISBN 0-442-24423-1). Van Nos Reinhold.

Colson, Greta, jt. auth. see Colson, John.

Colson, Howard & Rigdon, Raymond. Understanding Your Churches Curriculum. LC 77-93915. 1970. pap. 3.00 o.p. (ISBN 0-8054-3201-9). Broadman.

Colson, Howard P. & Rigdon, Raymond M. Understanding Your Church's Curriculum. rev. ed. LC 80-67351. 1981. pap. 4.95. Broadman.

Colson, John & Colson, Greta. English. (Illus.). 212p. tape included 17.50x o.p. (ISBN 0-686-09303-8, Dist. by Hippocrene Books Inc.). Leviathan Hse.

Colt, C. F. & Miall, Anthony. The Early Piano. (Illus.). 160p. 1981. 75.00x (ISBN 0-389-20187-1). B&N.

Colt, Clem. Coyote Song. 1978. pap. 1.50 (ISBN 0-505-51317-X). Tower Bks.

Colter, Cyrus. The Hippodrome. 192p. 1976. pap. 1.50 o.p. (ISBN 0-445-03122-0). Popular Lib.

--The Hippodrome: A Novel. LC 72-96164. 213p. 1973. 9.95 (ISBN 0-8040-0625-3). Swallow.

--Night Studies: A Novel. LC 79-64295. 775p. 1980. 16.00 (ISBN 0-8040-0827-2). Swallow.

--Rivers of Eros. LC 73-189191. 219p. 1972. 9.95 (ISBN 0-8040-0563-X). Swallow.

Coltey, Roger W. Survey of Medical Technology. (Illus.). 1978. pap. text ed. 13.95 (ISBN 0-8016-1020-6). Mosby.

Coltheart, Max, et al, eds. Deep Dyslexia. (International Library of Psychology). 1980. 45.00x (ISBN 0-7100-0456-7). Routledge & Kegan.

Coltman, Charles A., Jr. & Golomb, Harvey, eds. Hodgkin's Disease & Non-Hodgkin's Lymphomas. (Seminars in Oncology Ser.). 1980. write for info. (ISBN 0-8089-1354-9). Grune.

Coltman, D., tr. see Mallet-Joris, Francoise.

Coltman, Derek, tr. see Leduc, Violette.

Coltman, Michael M. Cost Controls for the Hospitality Industry. 410p. 1980. text ed. 15.95 (ISBN 0-8436-2170-2). CBI Pub.

--Financial Management for the Hospitality Industry. LC 79-378. 1979. text ed. 16.95 (ISBN 0-8436-2141-9). CBI Pub.

--Hospitality Management Accounting. LC 77-16670. (Illus.). 1978. 15.95 (ISBN 0-8436-2170-2); paper student wkbk. 6.95 (ISBN 0-8436-2180-X). CBI Pub.

Colton, Calvin. The Junius Tracts. (The Neglected American Economists Ser.). 1974. lib. bdg. 50.00 (ISBN 0-8240-1009-4). Garland Pub.

--The Life & Times of Henry Clay, 2 vols. (The Neglected American Economists Ser.). 1974. Set. lib. bdg. 90.00 (ISBN 0-8240-1008-6); lib. bdg. 50.00 ea. Garland Pub.

Colton, Helen. Our Sexual Evolution. LC 70-71899. (gr. 7 up). 1971. PLB 6.90 (ISBN 0-531-01996-9). Watts.

Colton, Joel. Twentieth Century. LC 68-54204. (Great Ages of Man). (Illus.). (gr. 6 up). 1968. PLB 11.97 (ISBN 0-8094-0383-8, Pub. by Time-Life). Silver.

Colton, Kent W. IRP, Vol. III: Police Computer Technology. LC 77-9137. (Irp Ser.). 1978. 24.95 (ISBN 0-669-01786-8). Lexington Bks.

Colton, Kent W. & Kramer, Kenneth L., eds. Computers & Banking: Electronic Fund Transfer Systems & Public Policy. (Applications of Modern Technology in Business Ser.). (Illus.). 325p. 1980. 25.00 (ISBN 0-306-40255-6, Plenum Pr). Plenum Pub.

Colton, Raymond R., jt. auth. see Arkin, Herbert.

Colum, Padraic. Arabian Nights. (Illus.). (gr. 4-6). 1964. 4.95 o.s.i. (ISBN 0-02-722940-8). Macmillan.

--Children of Odin. (Illus.). (gr. 4-6). 1962. 6.95g o.s.i. (ISBN 0-02-723370-7). Macmillan.

--Golden Fleece & the Heroes Who Lived Before Achilles. (Illus.). (gr. 4-6). 1962. 9.95 (ISBN 0-02-723620-X). Macmillan.

--Irish Elegies. 4th ed. 1976. text ed. 11.75x (ISBN 0-85105-315-7, Dolmen Pr). Humanities.

--Roofs of Gold: Poems to Read Aloud. (gr. 7 up). 1964. 5.95g o.s.i. (ISBN 0-02-722920-3). Macmillan.

Colum, Padraic, ed. see Swift, Jonathan.

Columbetti, Lelio G., ed. Principles of Radiopharmacology, 2 vols. 1979. Vol. 1, 304p. 69.95 (ISBN 0-8493-5465-X); Vol. 2, 288p. 64.95 (ISBN 0-8493-5466-8). CRC Pr.

Columbia College - Contemporary Civilization Staff. Introduction to Contemporary Civilization in the West, 2 Vols. 3rd ed. LC 60-16650. 1960-61. Vol. 1. text ed. 22.50x (ISBN 0-231-02423-1); Vol. 2. text ed. 22.50x (ISBN 0-231-02477-0). Columbia U Pr.

--Man in Contemporary Society. student ed. LC 62-17503. (gr. 12 up). 1962. 22.50x (ISBN 0-231-02587-4). Columbia U Pr.

Columbia University. Avery Index to Architectural Periodicals: Third Supplement. (Library Catalogs-Bib. Guides). 1979. lib. bdg. 120.00 (ISBN 0-8161-0282-1). G K Hall.

--Catalog of the Avery Memorial Architectural Library, Second Edition, Fourth Supplement. 1979. lib. bdg. 325.00 (ISBN 0-8161-0283-X). G K Hall.

Columbia University Press. The New Columbia Encyclopedia. LC 74-26686. (Illus.). 1975. 79.50 o.p. (ISBN 0-397-03572-1); deluxe ed. 135.00 leather bdg. o.p. (ISBN 0-397-03977-8). Lippincott.

Columbo, Anita & Columbu, Franco. Firm up Your Thighs in Fifteen Minutes a Day. (Anita & Franco Columbu's Shape up in Minutes-a-Day Program). (Illus., Orig.). 1980. pap. 1.95 (ISBN 0-8092-7078-1); prepack 93.60 (ISBN 0-8092-7022-6). Contemp Bks.

--Flatten Your Stomach in Fifteen Minutes a Day. (Anita & Franco Columbu's Shape up in Minutes-a-Day Program). (Illus., Orig.). 1980. pap. 1.95 (ISBN 0-8092-7076-5); 93.60 (ISBN 0-8092-7022-6). Contemp Bks.

Columbo, Franco, jt. auth. see Columbu, Anita.

Columbu, Anita & Columbo, Franco. Shape up Your Bust in Ten Minutes a Day: "Anita & Franco Columbu's Shape up in Minutes-a-Day Program". (Anita & Franco Columbu's Shape up in Minutes-a-Day Program). (Illus., Orig.). 1980. pap. 1.95 (ISBN 0-8092-7074-9); 48-copy sorted prepack 93.60 (ISBN 0-686-65599-0). Contemp Bks.

Columbu, Franco, jt. auth. see Columbo, Anita.

Columbus, Christopher. Four Voyages to the New World. Major, R. H., tr. 1961. pap. 1.95 o.s.i. (ISBN 0-87091-004-3, AE). Corinth Bks.

Colver, A. Wayne, ed. see Hume, David.

Colver, Anne. Bad Jack & the Lincoln Boys. LC 76-17629. (Read to Myself Ser.). (Illus.). 48p. (gr. k-3). 1976. PLB 7.75 (ISBN 0-8172-0155-6). Raintree Pubs.

--Bread-&-Butter Indian. (gr. 3-6). 1972. pap. 1.75 (ISBN 0-380-00699-5, 52092, Camelot). Avon.

--Bread & Butter Journey. 1971. pap. 1.25 (ISBN 0-380-00708-8, 43802, Camelot). Avon.

--Florence Nightingale. (Illus.). (gr. 1-7). 1966. pap. 1.25 (ISBN 0-440-42620-0, YB). Dell.

Colvert, J., ed. see Crane, Stephen.

Colvig, Richard, jt. auth. see Coover, James.

Colville, John. Winston Churchill & His Inner Circle. 1981. 13.95 (ISBN 0-671-42583-8, Wyndham Bks). S&S.

Colvin. The Industrial Triangle. 5.50 o.p. (ISBN 0-686-00167-2). Columbia Graphs.

Colvin, Elaine W., jt. auth. see Gentz, William H.

Colvin, Howard. A Biographical Dictionary of British Architects, 1600-1840. 1978. write for info. (ISBN 0-7195-3328-7). Intl Pubns Serv.

Colvin, Howard & Newman, John. Of Building: Roger North's Writings on Architects. (Illus.). 200p. 1981. 45.00 (ISBN 0-19-817325-3). Oxford U Pr.

Colvin, Lucie G. Historical Dictionary of Senegal. LC 80-25466. (African Historical Dictionaries: No. 23). 355p. 1981. 17.50 (ISBN 0-8108-1369-6). Scarecrow.

Colvin, Sidney. English Men of Letters, Walter Savage Landor. Morley, John, ed. 224p. 1980. Repr. of 1881 ed. lib. bdg. 15.00 (ISBN 0-89760-117-3). Telegraph Bks.

Colvin, Thomas. Electrical Wiring: Residential, Utility Bldgs, & Service Areas. 10.95 (ISBN 0-89606-030-6). Green Hill.

Colvin, Thomas, jt. auth. see Klingel, Gilbert.

Colvin, Thomas E. Coastwise & Offshore Cruising Wrinkles. (Illus.). 1979. pap. 4.00 (ISBN 0-915160-14-5). McKay.

Colwell, Eileen, ed. Humblepuppy: And Other Stories for Telling. (Illus.). 176p. (gr. 3-5). 1980. 9.95 (ISBN 0-370-30127-7, Pub. by Chatto, Bodley Head & Jonathan). Merrimack Bk Serv.

Colwell, John A. Clinical Recognition & Treatment of Diabetic Vascular Disease. (Amer. Lec. Circulation Ser.). (Illus.). 104p. 1975. 12.75 (ISBN 0-398-03251-3). C C Thomas.

Colwell, John A. & Lizarralde, German. Diabetes & Metabolic Disorders Continuing Education Review. 1975. 12.00 o.p. (ISBN 0-87488-362-8). Med Exam.

Colwell, Richard J. Teaching of Instrumental Music. (Illus.). 1969. 16.95 (ISBN 0-13-893131-3). P-H.

Colwell, Rita R., ed. The Role of Culture Collections in the Era of Molecular Biology: Proceedings of the 50th Anniversary Symposium of the American Type, Culture Collection. LC 76-4273. (American Type Culture Collection Ser.). 1976. 12.00 (ISBN 0-914826-08-5). Am Soc Microbio.

Colwell, Stephen, ed. see List, Friedrich.

Colwill, Nina L., jt. auth. see Lips, Hilary M.

Colwin, Laurie. The Lone Pilgrim. LC 80-24572. 224p. 1981. 9.95 (ISBN 0-394-51453-X). Knopf.

--Shine on Bright & Dangerous Object. 1979. pap. 2.95 (ISBN 0-345-28415-1). Ballantine.

Coly, Lisette, ed. see International Conference, Montreal Canada, Aug. 24-25, 1978.

Coly, Lisette, ed. see Proceedings of the International Conference, Paris, France, 1977.

Coly, Lisette, jt. ed. see Shapin, Betty.

Colyer, Penrose. I Can Read Spanish. LC 76-6136. (Illus.). 118p. (gr. 2 up). 1976. 4.95 o.p. (ISBN 0-531-02437-7); PLB 6.90 o.p. (ISBN 0-531-00333-7). Watts.

Colyer, Penrose, ed. I Can Read French. LC 73-8788. 128p. (gr. 2 up). 1974. 6.90 o.p. (ISBN 0-531-02655-8); PLB 4.95 o.p. (ISBN 0-531-02654-X). Watts.

Comanor, William S. National Health Insurance in Ontario: Effects of a Policy Cost Control. 1980. pap. 4.25 (ISBN 0-8447-3379-2). Am Enterprise.

Comar, C. L. & Bronner, Felix, eds. Mineral Metabolism: An Advanced Treatise, 3 vols. Incl. Vol. 1, Pt. A. Principles, Processes & Systems. 1960. 49.00 (ISBN 0-12-183201-5); Vol. 1, Pt. B. Principles, Processes & Systems. 1961. 61.00 (ISBN 0-12-183241-4); Vol. 2, Pt. A. The Elements. 1964. 68.00 (ISBN 0-12-183202-3); Set. 52.00 (ISBN 0-686-66613-5); Vol. 2, Pt. B. The Elements. 1962. 64.00 (ISBN 0-12-183242-2); 41.00 (ISBN 0-686-66614-3); Vol. 3. Supplementary Volume. 1969. 55.00 (ISBN 0-12-183250-3). 240.75 set (ISBN 0-685-23116-X). Acad Pr.

Comaromi, John P. Book Numbers: A Historical Study & Practical Guide to Their Use. 250p. 1981. lib. bdg. price not set (ISBN 0-87287-251-3). Libs Unl.

--The Eighteen Editions of the Dewey Decimal Classification. LC 76-10604. 1976. 10.00x (ISBN 0-910608-17-2). Forest Pr.

Comay, Joan. The Hebrew Kings. (Illus.). 1977. 8.95 o.p. (ISBN 0-688-03139-0). Morrow.

Comay, Joan & Pearlman, Moshe. Israel. (Illus.). (gr. 7 up). 1964. 3.95 o.s.i. (ISBN 0-02-724190-4). Macmillan.

Combe, Andrew. Observations on Mental Derangement: Being an Application of the Principles of Phrenology to the Elucidation of the Causes, Symptoms, Nature, Treatment of Insanity. LC 72-161928. (History of Psychology Series). Repr. of 1834 ed. 35.00x (ISBN 0-8201-1089-2). Schol Facsimiles.

Combe, G. S., ed. see Harmer, Lewis.

Combe, George. The Constitution of Man Considered in Relation to External Objects. 2nd ed. LC 74-16109. (Hist. of Psych. Ser.). 313p. 1974. Repr. of 1833 ed. 25.00x (ISBN 0-8201-1136-8). Schol Facsimiles.

Combe, Iris. Border Collies. (Illus.). 1978. 15.95 (ISBN 0-571-11173-4, Pub. by Faber & Faber). Merrimack Bk Serv.

Combe, T. G. & Rickard, P. French Language: History, Practice, & Stylistics. 1970. 14.95x (ISBN 0-245-59995-9). Intl Ideas.

Comber, Chris, jt. auth. see Paris, Mike.

Comber, L. C. & Keeves, J. P., eds. Science Education in Eleven Countries: An Empirical Study. LC 73-8048. (International Studies in Evaluation Ser: Vol. 1). 403p. 1973. pap. 14.95 (ISBN 0-470-16682-7). Halsted Pr.

Comber, Leon. More Favourite Stories from Asia. (Favourite Stories Ser.). pap. text ed. 1.25 (ISBN 0-686-65637-7, 00301). Heinemann Ed.

Comber, Leon, tr. Favourite Stories from Asia. (Favourite Stories Ser.). 1971. pap. text ed. 1.25 (ISBN 0-686-65609-1). Heinemann Ed.

Comber, Leon, retold by. Further Favourite Stories from Asia. (Favourite Stories Ser.). 1978. pap. text ed. 1.25 (ISBN 0-686-60435-0, 00302). Heinemann Ed.

Combes, Angela, ed. The Vermont Symphony Cookbook. (Illus.). 128p. 1981. pap. cancelled (ISBN 0-8397-8571-2). Eriksson.

Combes, Sharon. Cherron. 336p. (Orig.). 1980. pap. 2.75 (ISBN 0-89083-700-7). Zebra.

Combs. Percussion Manual. 1977. 13.95x (ISBN 0-534-00504-7). Wadsworth Pub.

Combs, Ann. Smith College Never Taught Me How to Salute. LC 80-8227. 216p. 1981. 9.95 (ISBN 0-690-02012-0, HarpT). Har-Row.

Combs, Arthur W. Myths in Education: Beliefs That Hinder Progress & Their Alternatives. 1978. pap. text ed. 8.95 (ISBN 0-205-05984-8, 2359847). Allyn.

Combs, Arthur W., et al. Helping Relationships: Basic Concepts for the Helping Professions. 2nd ed. 1978. pap. text ed. 10.50 (ISBN 0-205-05959-7). Allyn.

--Professional Education of Teachers: A Humanistic Approach to Teacher Preparation. 2nd ed. 1974. pap. text ed. 10.95x (ISBN 0-205-04331-3, 2243318). Allyn.

--Perceptual Psychology: A Humanistic Approach to the Study of Persons. 492p. 1976. pap. text ed. 16.50 scp (ISBN 0-06-041346-8, HarpC). Har-Row.

Combs, Bert T. The Public Papers of Governor Bert T. Combs, 1959-1963. Robinson, George W. & Sexton, Robert F., eds. LC 78-58103. (The Public Papers of the Governors of Kentucky). 568p. 1980. 28.00x (ISBN 0-8131-0604-4). U Pr of Ky.

Combs, Bob, jt. auth. see Coffelt, Kenneth.

Combs, J., jt. auth. see Nimmo, D.

Combs, Jerald A. The Jay Treaty: Political Battleground of the Founding Fathers. LC 70-84044. 1970. 18.50x (ISBN 0-520-01573-8). U of Cal Pr.

Combs, Jim. BMW: Sixteen Hundred-Two Thousand & Two Series, 3rd ed. Robinson, Jeff, ed. (Illus.). 1978. pap. 10.95 (ISBN 0-89287-286-1, A138). Clymer Pubns.

--BMW Three Hundred Twenty i: Nineteen Seventy-Seven to Nineteen Eighty Shop Manual. Jorgensen, Eric, ed. (Illus.). 248p. (Orig.). 1980. pap. text ed. 10.95 (ISBN 0-89287-326-4, A139). Clymer Pubns.

--Camaro Service-Repair Handbook: All Models, 1967-1979. Jorgensen, Eric, ed. (Illus.). 1978. pap. 10.95 (ISBN 0-89287-226-8, A136). Clymer Pubns.

--Chevrolet Tune-up Maintenance: All Models, 1966-1980. Robinson, Jeff, ed. (Illus.). 152p. 1977. pap. text ed. 7.95 (ISBN 0-89287-191-1, A137). Clymer Pubns.

--Chevy Malibu Chevelle MonteCarlo: 1970-1980 Shop Manual. Jorgensen, Eric, ed. (Illus.). 360p. (Orig.). 1980. pap. text ed. 10.95 (ISBN 0-89287-319-1, A246). Clymer Pubns.

--Dodge & Plymouth Vans, 1971-1979: Shop Manual. Jorgensen, Eric, ed. (Illus.). 420p. (Orig.). 1980. pap. text ed. 10.95 (ISBN 0-89287-314-0, A244). Clymer Pubns.

--Dodge Aspen: 1976-1979 Shop Manual. Jorgensen, Eric, ed. (Illus.). 328p. (Orig.). 1980. pap. text ed. 10.95 (ISBN 0-89287-311-6, A199). Clymer Pubns.

--Dodge Omni: 1978-1980 Shop Manual. Jorgensen, Eric, ed. (Illus.). 1979. pap. 10.95 (ISBN 0-89287-297-7, A155). Clymer Pubns.

--Dodge Pickups: 1971-1979 Shop Manual. Jorgensen, Eric, ed. (Illus.). 400p. (Orig.). 1980. pap. text ed. 10.95 (ISBN 0-89287-313-2, A243). Clymer Pubns.

--Dodge Tune-up & Maintenance, Nineteen Sixty-Seven to Nineteen Seventy-Nine. new ed. Robinson, Jeff, ed. (Illus.). 1977. pap. 7.95 (ISBN 0-89287-143-1, A-153). Clymer Pubns.

--Fiat Service-Repair Handbook: 131 Series, 1975-1977. Jorgensen, Eric, ed. (Illus.). 1978. pap. 10.95 (ISBN 0-89287-197-0, A158). Clymer Pubns.

--Ford Fiesta 1978-1979 Shop Manual. Jorgensen, Eric, ed. (Illus.). 272p. 1979. pap. text ed. 10.95 (ISBN 0-89287-299-3, A173). Clymer Pubns.

--Honda Service Repair Handbook: Accord, 1976-79. Jorgensen, Eric, ed. 1978. pap. 10.95 (ISBN 0-89287-201-2, A228). Clymer Pubns.

--Mazda GLC Shop Manual: 1977-1979. Jorgensen, Eric, ed. (Illus.). 1978. pap. 10.95 (ISBN 0-89287-288-8, A262). Clymer Pubns.

--Oldsmobile Cutlass: Nineteen Seventy to Nineteen Eighty Shop Manual. Jorgensen, Eric, ed. (Illus.). 342p. (Orig.). 1980. pap. text ed. 10.95 (ISBN 0-89287-324-8, A285). Clymer Pubns.

--Plymouth Horizon: 1978 Shop Manual. Jorgensen, Eric, ed. (Illus.). 1979. pap. text ed. 10.95 (ISBN 0-89287-298-5, A177). Clymer Pubns.

--Plymouth Tune-up - Maintenance, 1967-1978 Models. Robinson, Jeff, ed. (Illus.). 1977. pap. 7.95 (ISBN 0-89287-142-3, A-179). Clymer Pubns.

--Plymouth Volare: 1976-1979 Shop Manual. Jorgensen, Eric, ed. (Illus.). 328p. (Orig.). 1980. pap. text ed. 10.95 (ISBN 0-89287-312-4, A236). Clymer Pubns.

--Pontiac Firebird Nineteen Seventy to Nineteen Eighty Shop Manual. Jorgensen, Eric, ed. (Illus., Orig.). 1980. pap. text ed. 10.95 (ISBN 0-89287-306-X, A235). Clymer Pubns.

--Triumph Service Repair Handbook: 500-750cc Twins, 1963-1979. Robinson, Jeff, ed. (Illus.). 1979. pap. 9.95 (ISBN 0-89287-195-4, M382). Clymer Pubns.

Combs, Jim & Robinson, Jeff. Vega Service, Repair Handbook 1971-1977 Models. 3rd ed. (Illus.). 1976. pap. 10.95 (ISBN 0-89287-130-X, A135). Clymer Pubns.

Combs, Paul H. Handbook of International Purchasing. 2nd ed. LC 75-31560. 224p. 1976. 15.95 (ISBN 0-8436-1309-2). CBI Pub.

Combs, Richard E. Authors: Critical & Biographical References. LC 73-16744. (A guide to 4,700 critical & biographical passages in books). 1971. 10.00 (ISBN 0-8108-0448-4). Scarecrow.

Combs, Tram. Saint Thomas: poems. LC 65-14050. (Wesleyan Poetry Program: Vol. 25). (Orig.). 1965. 10.00x (ISBN 0-8195-2025-X, Pub. by Wesleyan U Pr); pap. 4.95 (ISBN 0-8195-1025-4). Columbia U Pr.

Comden, Betty, et al. Comden & Green on Broadway. LC 80-18531. (Illus.). 320p. 1981. 16.95 (ISBN 0-89676-042-1). Drama Bk.

--On the Twentieth Century. LC 79-28365. (Illus.). 1981. 7.95 (ISBN 0-89676-033-2). Drama Bk.

Comenius, John A. Orbis Pictus of John Amos Comenius. Bardeen, Charles W., ed. LC 67-23933. (Illus., Eng. & Lat.). 1968. Repr. of 1887 ed. 18.00 (ISBN 0-8103-3476-3). Gale.

Comer, David J. Electronic Design with Integrated Circuits. LC 80-23365. (Electrical Engineering Ser.). (Illus.). 416p. 1981. text ed. 24.95 (ISBN 0-201-03931-1). A-W.

--Modern Electronic Circuit Design. LC 75-9008. 704p. 1976. text ed. 25.95 (ISBN 0-201-01008-9); solutions manual 2.00 (ISBN 0-201-01009-7). A-W.

Comer, James. How to Survive a Roommate. 240p. 1980. 7.95 (ISBN 0-531-09938-5). Watts.

Comer, James P. School Power: Implications of an Intervention Project. LC 80-757. 1980. 14.95 (ISBN 0-02-906550-X). Free Pr.

Comer, Joyce B. Pharmacology in Critical Care. Percy, R. Craig, ed. (The Fleschner Series in Critical Care Nursings). (Illus.). 175p. (Orig.). 1981. pap. text ed. 9.95 (ISBN 0-937878-03-0). Fleschner.

Comerchero, Victor, ed. Values in Conflict: Christianity, Marxism, Psychoanalysis & Existentialism. LC 74-111099. (Orig., Free booklet, "Suggestions for Instructors," available). 1970. pap. text ed. 12.95x (ISBN 0-89197-463-6). Irvington.

Comerci, George D., et al. Adolescent Medicine Case Studies. LC 78-61736. 1979. pap. 18.00 (ISBN 0-87488-053-X). Med Exam.

Comes, Natalis. Mythologiae. LC 75-27853. (Renaissance & the Gods Ser.: Vol. 11). (Illus.). 1976. Repr. of 1567 ed. lib. bdg. 73.00 (ISBN 0-8240-2060-X). Garland Pub.

Comfort, jt. auth. see Terrass.

Comfort, Alex. What Is a Doctor? LC 80-51834. 240p. 1980. text ed. 10.95 (ISBN 0-89313-022-2). G F Stickley Co.

Comfort, Daniel B., Jr. Through the Winds Rain. rev. ed. LC 80-53436. 64p. 1981. 7.95 (ISBN 0-938316-00-1). Bridges Sound.

Comfort, W. W., tr. see Chretien De Troyes.

Comfort, Will L. Apache. (Western Fiction Ser.). 1980. lib. bdg. 11.95 (ISBN 0-8398-2678-8). Gregg.

Comici, Luciano. The Heart Is No Stranger. (Orig.). 1981. pap. 2.50 (ISBN 0-515-04801-1). Jove Pubns.

Comings, Pamela. Widow's Walk. Baron, Carole, ed. 1981. 12.95 (ISBN 0-686-68920-8). Crown.

Comins, Ethel M. Under a Dancing Star. (YA) 1977. 4.95 o.p. (ISBN 0-685-75643-2, Avalon). Bouregy.

Comins, Jeremy. Eskimo Crafts & Their Cultural Backgrounds. LC 75-9573. (Illus.). 128p. (gr. 5 up). 1975. PLB 6.96 o.p. (ISBN 0-688-51705-6). Lothrop.

Comision Especial De Consulta Sobre Seguridad-15th-1971. Los Caminos Del Comunismo Internacional En las Americas. 50p. (Span.). 1971. pap. 1.00 o.p. (ISBN 0-8270-2920-9). OAS.

Comision Especial De Consulta Sobre Seguridad. Creacion y Organizacion: Sintesis De Informes y Estudios Especiales Presentados, 1962-1971. 140p. (Span.). 1971. pap. 1.00 o.p. (ISBN 0-8270-2925-X). OAS.

Comito, Terry. The Idea of the Garden in the Renaissance. 1978. 19.00 (ISBN 0-8135-0841-X). Rutgers U Pr.

Commager, A., ed. Documents of American History, 2 vols. 9th ed. 1974. Vol. 1. pap. 13.95 (ISBN 0-13-216994-0); Vol. 2. pap. 14.95 (ISBN 0-13-217000-0). P-H.

Commager, H. Steele, ed. see Knight, William F.

Commager, Henry S. Fifty Epic Paintings of American History. LC 79-88368. (Illus.). 104p. (Orig.). pap. 9.95 (ISBN 0-89659-064-X). Abbeville Pr.

--First Book of American History. (First Bks.). (Illus.). (gr. 4-6). 1957. PLB 4.90 (ISBN 0-531-00458-9); pap. 1.95 o.p. (ISBN 0-531-02305-2). Watts.

--Noah Webster's American Spelling Book. LC 62-21960. 1963. text ed. 8.75 (ISBN 0-8077-1179-9); pap. text ed. 4.00x (ISBN 0-8077-1176-4). Tchrs Coll.

--Study of History. 1966. pap. text ed. 4.95x (ISBN 0-675-09712-6). Merrill.

Commager, Henry S. & Muessig, Raymond H. The Study & Teaching of History. 2nd ed. (Social Science Seminar, Secondary Education Ser.: No. C28). 136p. 1980. pap. text ed. 5.95 (ISBN 0-675-08317-6). Merrill.

Commager, Henry S., jt. auth. see Nevins, Allan.

Commager, Henry S. & Morris, Richard B., eds. The Spirit of Seventy-Six. bicentennial ed. LC 75-9349. (Illus.). 1408p. 1975. 25.00 o.p. (ISBN 0-06-010834-7, HarpT). Har-Row.

Commager, Henry S., ed. see Hamilton, Madison.

Commager, Henry S., ed. see Smelser, Marshal L.

Commager, Henry S., ed. see Thomas, Emory M.

Commager, Steele, ed. see Bae Hrens, Aemilius.

Commager, Steele, ed. see Ball, Allan P.

Commager, Steele, ed. see Bentley, Richard.

Commager, Steele, ed. see Bridges, Robert, et al.

Commager, Steele, ed. see Brinton, Anna C.

Commager, Steele, ed. see Cousin, Jean.

Commager, Steele, ed. see Crump, Mary M.

Commager, Steele, ed. see Daryusl, A. A., et al.

Commager, Steele, ed. see Deutsch, Rosamund E.

Commager, Steele, ed. see Enk, P. J.

Commager, Steele, ed. see Ewbank, William W.

Commager, Steele, ed. see Fowler, H. W., et al.

Commager, Steele, ed. see Kroll, Wilhelm.

Commager, Steele, ed. see Lier, Bruno, et al.

Commager, Steele, ed. see Lilja, Saara.

Commager, Steele, ed. see Onions, C. T., et al.

Commager, Steele, ed. see Piwonka, Mario P.

Commager, Steele, ed. see Richardson, Lawrence.

Commager, Steele, ed. see Robinson, Ellis.

Commager, Steele, ed. see Smith, Logan P., et al.

Commager, Steele, ed. see Sparrow, John.

Commager, Steele, ed. see Taylor, Walt, et al.

Commager, Steele, ed. see Wagenvoort, Hendrik.

Commager, Steele, ed. see Winbolt, Samuel E.

Commentary Editors. Condition of Jewish Belief. (Orig.). 1967. 10.95 (ISBN 0-02-527260-8). Macmillan.

Commerce & Community Affairs Dept. Fire Protection Administration for Small Communities & Fire Protection Districts. LC 79-93086. (Illus.). 1980. pap. text ed. 15.00 (ISBN 0-87939-037-9). Intl Fire Serv.

Commerce Clearing House. Federal Tax Return Manual: 1981. 1980. ring binder 57.00 (ISBN 0-686-64882-X). Commerce.

--Guidebook to North Carolina Taxes. 1981. pap. 9.00 (ISBN 0-685-39507-3). Commerce.

--Guidebook to Ohio Taxes: 1981. 1981. pap. 9.00 (ISBN 0-685-39506-5). Commerce.

--Guidebook to Wisconsin Taxes: 1981. 1981. pap. 9.00 (ISBN 0-685-39504-9). Commerce.

Commire, Anne, ed. Something About the Author, Vol. 21. LC 72-27107. 300p. 1980. 38.00 (ISBN 0-8103-0093-1). Gale.

--Something About the Author, Vol. 22. LC 72-27107. (Illus.). 375p. 1981. 38.00 (ISBN 0-8103-0085-0). Gale.

--Something About the Author: Facts & Pictures About Contemporary Authors & Illustrators of Books for Young People. Incl. Vol. 1. 1971 (ISBN 0-8103-0050-8); Vol. 2. 1972 (ISBN 0-8103-0052-4); Vol. 3. 1972 (ISBN 0-8103-0054-0); Vol. 4. 1973 (ISBN 0-8103-0056-7); Vol. 5. 1973 (ISBN 0-8103-0058-3); Vol. 6. 1974 (ISBN 0-8103-0060-5); Vol. 7. 1975 (ISBN 0-8103-0062-1); Vol. 8. 1975. (ISBN 0-8103-0064-8); Vol. 9. 1976. (ISBN 0-8103-0066-4); Vol. 10. 1976. (ISBN 0-8103-0068-0); Vol. 11. 1977. (ISBN 0-8103-0070-2); Vol. 12. 1977. (ISBN 0-8103-0072-9); Vol. 13. 1978. (ISBN 0-685-43929-1); Vol. 14. 1978 (ISBN 0-8103-0095-8); Vol. 15. 1979 (ISBN 0-8103-0096-6); Vol. 16. 1979 (ISBN 0-8103-0097-4); Vol. 17. 1979 (ISBN 0-8103-0098-2); Vol. 18. 1980 (ISBN 0-8103-0099-0). LC 72-27107. (Illus.). (gr. 7-12). 38.00 ea. Gale.

--Yesterday's Authors of Books for Children: Facts & Pictures About Authors & Illustrators of Books for Young People, 2 vols. LC 76-17501. (Yesterday's Authors of Books for Children Ser.). (Illus.). (gr. 7-12). 38.00 ea.; Vol. 1, 1977. (ISBN 0-8103-0073-7); Vol. 2 1978. (ISBN 0-8103-0090-7). Gale.

Commisiion on Critical Choices. The Soviet Empire: Expansion & Detente. LC 75-44727. (Critical Choices for Americans Ser.: Vol. IX). 1976. 22.95 (ISBN 0-669-00421-9). Lexington Bks.

Commission For Christian Literature, ed. Is Evolutionism the Answer. (Truth Unchanging Series). (Illus.). 1968. pap. 2.50 (ISBN 0-8100-0023-7, 12-0331). Northwest Pub.

Commission for the European Communities, Directorate-General for Research, Science & Education, ed. Inventory of Major Research Facilities in the European Community, 2 vols. 1561p. 1977. text ed. 120.00 (ISBN 3-7940-3019-2, Pub. by K G Saur). Gale.

Commission of Architecture of AEA. Architecture for Adult Education. 74p. 1953. 2.30. Adult Ed.

Commission of European Communities Directorate-General for Research Science & Documentation, ed. Agricultural Economics & Rural Sociology: A Multilingual Thesaurus. 1979. 4 vols. & index 160.00 (ISBN 0-89664-035-3, Pub. by K G Saur). Gale.

Commission of European Communities, Directorate-Center for Research-Science & Education, ed. Food: Multilingual Thesaurus. 1979. 4 vols. & index 180.00 (ISBN 0-89664-036-1, Pub. by K G Saur). Gale.

Commission of the European Communities. Course in Diagnostics for Fusion Experiments: Proceedings, Varenna, Italy, 1978. Sindoni, E. & Wharton, C., eds. (Commission of the European Communities, EUR, 6123). (Illus.). 1979. pap. 110.00 (ISBN 0-08-023429-1). Pergamon.

--Criteria (Dose-Effect Relationships) for Radium. LC 77-30193. 1977. text ed. 28.00 (ISBN 0-08-022024-X). Pergamon.

Commission of the European Communities, Brussels, Belgium. Energy Research & Development Programme, 2 vols. in one. 1979. lib. bdg. 121.05 (ISBN 90-247-2220-9, Martinus Nijhoff Pubs). Kluwer Boston.

Commission of the European Communities, Luxembourg. Fusion Technology Nineteen Seventy-Eight: Proceedings, 2 vols. LC 79-40553. (Commission of the European Communities: Eur 6215). (Illus.). 1979. Set. pap. 235.00 (ISBN 0-08-023439-9). Pergamon.

--Fusion Technology: Proceedings of the 11th Symposium, Oxford, England, Sept. 15-19, 1980, 2 vols. (Illus.). 1000p. Date not set. Set. price not set (ISBN 0-08-025697-X). Pergamon.

Commission of the European Communities, Joint Varenna-Grenoble International Symposium on Heating in Toroidal Plasmas, Grenoble, July 1978. Heating in Toroidal Plasmas: Proceedings. 1978. text ed. 125.00 (ISBN 0-08-023400-3). Pergamon.

Commission of the European Communities. The Law & Practice Relating to Pollution Control in the Member States of the European Communities. Environmental Resources Ltd, ed. Incl. Vol. 1 (ISBN 0-86010-040-5); Vol. 2a (ISBN 0-86010-041-3); Vol. 3 (ISBN 0-86010-029-4); Vol. 4 (ISBN 0-86010-033-2); Vol. 4a (ISBN 0-86010-035-9); Vol. 5 (ISBN 0-86010-032-4); Vol. 5a (ISBN 0-86010-034-0); Vol. 6 (ISBN 0-86010-031-6); Vol. 7 (ISBN 0-86010-039-1); Vol. 7a (ISBN 0-86010-042-1); Vol. 8 (ISBN 0-86010-030-8); Vol. 9 (ISBN 0-86010-037-5); Vol. 11 (ISBN 0-86010-038-3). 1976. 16.00x ea. (Pub. by Graham & Trotman England). State Mutual Bk.

--Organophosphorus Pesticides Criteria (Dose-Effect Relationships) for Organophosphorus Compounds. Derache, R., ed. 1977. pap. text ed. 37.00 (ISBN 0-08-021993-4). Pergamon.

--Plasma Wall Interaction: Proceedings of the International Symposium EUR 5782e, Kernsfoschungsanlage Julich, 1976. LC 77-75794. 1977. pap. 110.00 (ISBN 0-08-021989-6). Pergamon.

--Public Health Risks of Exposure to Asbestos. Zielhuis, R. L., ed. LC 76-51964. 1977. pap. text ed. 21.00 (ISBN 0-08-021580-7). Pergamon.

Commission of the European Communities, ed. Veterinary Multilingual Thesaurus, 4 vols. 1122p. 1979. 4 vols. & index 325.00 (ISBN 3-598-07082-9, Pub. by K G Saur). Gale.

Commission on Chicago Historical & Architectural Landmarks. City House. LC 79-51990. (Illus.). 100p. (Orig.). 1979. pap. 4.95 (ISBN 0-934076-25-1). Comm Chi Hist & Arch.

Commission on Critical Choice. How Others See Us. LC 75-44720. (Critical Choices for Americans Ser.: Vol. 3). 1976. 14.95 (ISBN 0-669-00420-0). Lexington Bks.

Commission on Critical Choices. The Americans: Nineteen Seventy-Six. Kristol, Irving, ed. Weaver, Paul H. LC 75-44719. (Critical Choices for Americans Ser.: Vol. 2). 1976. 18.95 (ISBN 0-669-00415-4). Lexington Bks.

--Vital Resources, Vol. I. LC 75-44718. (Critical Choices for Americans Ser.). 1976. 17.95 (ISBN 0-669-00413-8). Lexington Bks.

--Western Europe: The Trials of Partnership. LC 75-44726. (Critical Choices of Americans Ser.: Vol. 8). 1976. 22.95 (ISBN 0-669-00423-5). Lexington Bks.

Commission on Critical Choices & Hellman, Donald C. China & Japan: A New Balance of Power. LC 75-44730. (Critical Choices for Americans Ser.: Vol. XII). 1976. 19.95 (ISBN 0-669-00426-X). Lexington Bks.

--Southern Asia: The Politics of Poverty & Peace. LC 75-44731. (Critical Choices for Americans Ser.: Vol. XIII). 1976. 19.95 (ISBN 0-669-00427-8). Lexington Bks.

Commission on Critical Choices & Kitchen, Helen. Africa: From Mystery to Maze, Vol. XI. LC 75-44729. (Critical Choices for Americans Ser.). 1976. 22.95 (ISBN 0-669-00425-1). Lexington Bks.

Commission on Education for Health Administration. Selected Papers of the Commission on Education for Health Administration, Vol. 2. LC 74-17537. 350p. 1975. 12.50 (ISBN 0-914904-05-1). Health Admin Pr.

Commission On Education In Agriculture And Natural Resources. Undergraduate Education in the Biological Sciences for Students in Agriculture & Natural Resources. 1967. pap. 4.25 (ISBN 0-309-01495-6). Natl Acad Pr.

--Undergraduate Education in the Plant & Soil Sciences. LC 71-600161. (Orig.). 1969. pap. 3.25 (ISBN 0-309-01704-1). Natl Acad Pr.

--Undergraduate Education in the Sciences for Students in Agriculture & Natural Resources. 1971. pap. text ed. 7.50 (ISBN 0-309-01921-4). Natl Acad Pr.

--Undergraduate Teaching in the Animal Sciences. 1967. pap. 4.25 (ISBN 0-309-01486-7). Natl Acad Pr.

Commission on Educational Issues. The Expanding School Environment. 1978. pap. 6.50 (ISBN 0-934338-38-8). NAIS.

Commission on Human Resources. A Century of Doctorates. LC 78-5644. 1978. pap. text ed. 10.50 (ISBN 0-309-02738-1). Natl Acad Pr.

Commission on Human Resources, Nat. Research Council. Climbing the Academic Ladder: Doctoral Women Scientists in Academe. 1979. pap. text ed. 8.00 (ISBN 0-309-02880-9). Natl Acad Pr.

Commission on International Relations. Astronomy in China. 1979. pap. 6.25 (ISBN 0-309-02867-1). Natl Acad Pr.

--Oral Contraceptives & Steroid Chemistry in People's Republic of China. 1977. pap. 8.00 (ISBN 0-309-02638-5). Natl Acad Pr.

--Wheat Studies in the People's Republic of China. 1977. pap. 10.00 (ISBN 0-309-02637-7). Natl Acad Pr.

Commission on International Relations, National Research Council. World Food & Nutrition Study: Interim Report. LC 75-37120. xix, 82p. 1975. pap. 5.50 (ISBN 0-309-02436-6). Natl Acad Pr.

Commission on International Relations. World Food & Nutrition Study: Supporting Papers, 5 vols. 1977. Vol. I. pap. 6.75 (ISBN 0-309-02647-4); Vol. II. pap. 6.75 (ISBN 0-309-02726-8); Vol. III. pap. 7.00 (ISBN 0-309-02730-6); Vol. IV. pap. 6.00 (ISBN 0-309-02727-6); Vol. V. pap. 6.00 (ISBN 0-309-02646-6). Natl Acad Pr.

Commission on Natural Resources. Environmental Monitoring. 1977. pap. 7.75 (ISBN 0-309-02639-3). Natl Acad Pr.

--Perspectives on Technical Information for Environmental Protection. 1977. pap. 6.25 (ISBN 0-309-02623-7). Natl Acad Pr.

Commission on Natural Resources, National Research Council. The Shallow Land Burial of Low-Level Radioactively Contaminated Solid Waste. LC 76-56928. 1976. pap. 7.00 (ISBN 0-309-02535-4). Natl Acad Pr.

Commission on Sociotechnical Systems. Cryogenic Preservation of Cell Cultures. 1975. pap. 5.75 (ISBN 0-309-02344-0). Natl Acad Pr.

Commission on Sociotechnical Systems, National Research Council. The Integrity of Frozen Spermatozoa. LC 77-940301. (Illus.). 1978. pap. text ed. 9.75 (ISBN 0-309-02645-8). Natl Acad Pr.

Commission on Sociotechnical Systems. N R C Trans-Bus Study. 1979. pap. 1.50 (ISBN 0-309-02929-5). Natl Acad Pr.

Commission on Sociotechnical Systems, National Research Council. A Program of Studies on Socioeconomic Effects of Earthquake Predictions. 1978. pap. text ed. 8.50x (ISBN 0-309-02789-6). Natl Acad Pr.

Commission to Study the Organization of Peace. Building Peace: Reports of the Commission to Study the Organization of Peace, 1939-1972, 2 vols. LC 73-4845. 1973. Repr. Set. 32.50 (ISBN 0-8108-0621-5). Scarecrow.

Commissioner of Education. Strengthening Bilingual Education. 1979. pap. 3.50 o.s.i. (ISBN 0-89763-017-3). Natl Clearing Bilingual Ed.

Commissiong, Florence, et al. Integrated Science for Caribbean Schools, 2 bks. 1976. Bk. 1. pap. text ed. 4.75x o.p. (ISBN 0-435-57579-1); Bk. 2. pap. text ed. 6.95x o.p. (ISBN 0-435-57580-5). Heinemann Ed.

Committee for Economic Development. Helping Insure Our Energy Future: A Program for Developing Synthetic Fuel Plants Now. (CED Statement on National Policy Ser.). 1979. lib. bdg. 6.00 (ISBN 0-87186-769-9); pap. 4.50 (ISBN 0-87186-069-4). Comm Econ Dev.

--Redefining Government's Role in the Market System. (CED Statement on National Policy Ser.). 1979. lib. bdg. 6.50 (ISBN 0-87186-768-0); pap. 5.00 (ISBN 0-87186-068-6). Comm Econ Dev.

--Stimulating Technological Progress. (CED Statement on National Policy Ser.). lib. bdg. 6.50 (ISBN 0-87186-770-2); pap. 5.00 (ISBN 0-87186-070-8). Comm Econ Dev.

Committee for International Environmental Programs. Institutional Arrangements for International Environmental Cooperation. LC 72-188498. 80p. 1972. pap. 3.75 (ISBN 0-309-01946-X). Natl Acad Pr.

Committee for Study of Environmental Manpower. Manpower for Environmental Pollution Control. 1977. 11.25 (ISBN 0-309-02634-2). Natl Acad Pr.

Committee for the Inauguration of Wendell R. Anderson. Governors of Minnesota: 1849-1971. (Illus.). 22p. 1971. pap. 2.00 (ISBN 0-685-47097-0). Minn Hist.

Committee For The Survey Of Chemistry. Basic Chemical Research in Government Laboratories. 1966. pap. 3.75 (ISBN 0-685-17304-6). Natl Acad Pr.

--Chemical Dynamics. 1966. pap. 4.00 (ISBN 0-309-01292-9). Natl Acad Pr.

--Chemistry: Opportunities & Needs. 1965. pap. 6.00 (ISBN 0-309-01292-9). Natl Acad Pr.

--Theoretical Chemistry. 1966. pap. 3.00 (ISBN 0-309-01292-9). Natl Acad Pr.

Committee of Community Social Researchers, 1976. Social Indicators in Community Research: Proceedings. 1976. 2.00 (ISBN 0-86671-034-5). Comm Coun Great NY.

Committee of London Clearing Banks. London Clearing Banks' Evidence to the Wilson Committee. (Illus.). 1978. text ed. 25.00x (ISBN 0-582-03029-3). Longman.

Committee of Scholarly Communication with the People's Republic of China, National Research Council. Herbal Pharmacology in the People's Republic of China: A Trip Report of the American Herbal Pharmacology Delegation. LC 75-39772. v, 169p. 1975. pap. 8.00 (ISBN 0-309-02438-2). Natl Acad Pr.

Committee on a Multimedium Approach to Municipal Sludge Management, National Research Council. Multimedium Management of Municipal Sludge. LC 77-93086. (Analytical Studies for the U. S. Environmental Protection Agency Ser.). (Illus.). 1978. pap. text ed. 8.00 (ISBN 0-309-02733-0). Natl Acad Pr.

Committee On Agricultural Land Use And Wildlife Resources. Land Use & Wildlife Resources. LC 70-607553. (Orig.). 1970. pap. 9.25 (ISBN 0-309-01857-9). Natl Acad Pr.

Committee on Animal Health. A Nationwide System for Animal Health Surveillance. LC 74-19048. 1974. pap. 4.25 (ISBN 0-309-02243-6). Natl Acad Pr.

--Prenatal & Postnatal Mortality in Cattle. (Orig.). 1968. pap. 5.75 o.p. (ISBN 0-309-01685-1). Natl Acad Pr.

Committee on Animal Nutrition. Effects of Fluorides in Animals. LC 74-4061. (Illus.). 76p. 1974. pap. 4.25 (ISBN 0-309-02219-3). Natl Acad Pr.

--Nutrient Requirements of Dairy Cattle, 1978. 5th ed. (Nutrient Requirements of Domestic Animals Ser). 1978. pap. text ed. 4.50 (ISBN 0-309-02749-7). Natl Acad Pr.

--Nutrient Requirements of Dogs. 1974. pap. 4.75 (ISBN 0-309-02315-7). Natl Acad Pr.

--Nutrient Requirements of Mink & Foxes. (Nutrient Requirements of Domestic Animals Ser.). 1968. pap. 3.50 (ISBN 0-309-01676-2). Natl Acad Pr.

--Nutrient Requirements of Rabbits. rev. 7th ed. LC 77-6318. 1977. pap. 4.50 (ISBN 0-309-02607-5). Natl Acad Pr.

--Selenium in Nutrition. LC 74-172093. 1971. pap. 3.75 (ISBN 0-309-01926-5). Natl Acad Pr.

Committee on Animal Nutrition, Agricultural Board. Atlas of Nutritional Data on United States & Canadian Feeds. LC 76-612077. 1972. 15.50 (ISBN 0-309-01919-2). Natl Acad Pr.

Committee on Animal Nutrition Board on Agriculture & Renewable Resources, Natl Research Council. Nutrient Requirements of Beef Cattle. new 5th rev. ed. LC 75-43977. (Nutrient Requirements of Domestic Animals Ser.). 56p. 1976. pap. 3.75 (ISBN 0-309-02419-6). Natl Acad Pr.

Committee on Animal Nutrition, National Research Council. Nutrient Requirements of Cats. LC 78-5976. (Nutrient Requirements of Domestic Animals Ser.). 1978. pap. text ed. 5.50 (ISBN 0-309-02743-8). Natl Acad Pr.

Committee On Atmospheric Sciences. Atmospheric Sciences & Man's Needs: Priorities for the Future. LC 70-611003. (Orig.). 1971. pap. text ed. 4.00 (ISBN 0-309-01912-5). Natl Acad Pr.

--Atmospheric Sciences: Problems & Applications. 1977. pap. 7.75 (ISBN 0-309-02626-1). Natl Acad Pr.

--Weather & Climate Modification. (Illus.). 256p. 1973. pap. 8.75 (ISBN 0-309-02121-9). Natl Acad Pr.

Committee on Atmospheric Sciences, ed. Severe Storms: Predicion, Detection & Warning. LC 77-77588. (Illus.). 1977. pap. text ed. 6.50 (ISBN 0-309-02613-X). Natl Acad Pr.

Committee on Biologic Effects of Atmosphere Pollutants. Particulate Polycyclic Organic Matter. (Biologic Effects of Atmospheric Pollutants Ser.). (Illus.). 336p. 1972. pap. 11.50 (ISBN 0-309-02027-1). Natl Acad Pr.

Committee On Biological Effects Of Atmospheric Pollutants. Fluorides. LC 70-169178. (Biological Effects of Atmospheric Pollutants Ser). 1971. pap. text ed. 7.75 (ISBN 0-309-01922-2). Natl Acad Pr.

--Lead: Airborne Lead in Perspective. LC 71-186214. (Biological Effects of Atmospheric Pollutants Ser.). (Illus.). 1972. pap. 9.50 (ISBN 0-309-01941-9). Natl Acad Pr.

Committee on Colorimetry of the Optical Society of America. The Science of Color. LC 52-7039. (Illus.). 340p. 1963. 20.00x (ISBN 0-9600380-1-9). Optical Soc.

Committee on Contingency Plans for Chromium Utilization, National Research Council. Contingency Plans for Chromium Utilization. LC 77-95193. (Illus.). 1978. pap. text ed. 10.50 (ISBN 0-309-02737-3). Natl Acad Pr.

Committee on Continuity in Academic Research Performance. Research Excellence Through the Year 2000. LC 79-67784. xiv, 241p. 1979. pap. 9.00 (ISBN 0-309-02938-4). Natl Acad Pr.

Committee On Data For Science And Technology Of The International Council Of Scientific Unions. International Compendium of Numerical Data Projects. 1969. 29.70 (ISBN 0-387-04570-8). Springer-Verlag.

Committee on Drinking Water, National Research Committee. Drinking Water & Health, Vol. 1. LC 77-89284. (Illus.). 1978. pap. text ed. 20.75 (ISBN 0-309-02619-9). Natl Acad Pr.

Committee on Economics Teaching Material for Asian Universities. Economic Theory & Practice in the Asian Setting, 4 vols. Incl. Vol. 1. Macroeconomics. LC 75-20408. o.p. (ISBN 0-470-14272-3); Vol. 2. Microeconomics. LC 75-20409 (ISBN 0-470-14273-1); Vol. 3. The Economics of Agriculture. LC 75-20412. o.p. (ISBN 0-470-14270-7); Vol. 4. The Economics of Development. LC 75-20411 (ISBN 0-470-14271-5). (Economic Theory & Practice in the Asian Setting Ser.). 1975. Vols. 2 & 4. pap. 9.95 ea. Halsted Pr.

Committee on Env. Geochem., National Research Council. Geochemistry & the Environment: Distribution of Trace Elements Related to the Occurrence of Certain Cancers, Cardiovascular Diseases, & Urolithiasis, Vol. III. (Geochemistry & the Environment Ser.). 1978. pap. text ed. 14.00x (ISBN 0-309-02795-0). Natl Acad Pr.

Committee on Environmental Pollutants, National Research Council. Nitrates: An Environmental Assessment. (Scientific & Technical Assessments of Environmental Pollutants Ser.). 1978. pap. text ed. 15.25 (ISBN 0-309-02785-3). Natl Acad Pr.

Committee on Evaluation of Poverty Research. Evaluating Federal Support for Poverty Research. 1979. pap. 6.50 (ISBN 0-309-02894-9). Natl Acad Pr.

Committee on Evaluation of Sound Spectrograms, National Research Council. On the Theory & Practice of Voice Identification. 1979. pap. text ed. 7.00 (ISBN 0-309-02873-6). Natl Acad Pr.

Committee on Federal Agency Evaluation Research, National Research Council. Protecting Individual Privacy in Evaluation Research. LC 75-18591. 133p. 1975. pap. 7.00 (ISBN 0-309-02406-4). Natl Acad Pr.

Committee on Fire Research. Directory of Fire Research in the United States, 1967-1969. 5th ed. LC 68-60084. 1970. pap. text ed. 14.25 (ISBN 0-309-01763-7). Natl Acad Pr.

--Directory of Fire Research in the U. S. 1969-1971. 6th ed. LC 68-60084. 800p. 1972. pap. 16.00 (ISBN 0-309-02033-6). Natl Acad Pr.

Committee on Fire Research & Committee on Toxicology. An Appraisal of Halogenated Fire Extinguishing Agents. (Illus.). 360p. 1972. pap. 7.75 (ISBN 0-309-02111-1). Natl Acad Pr.

Committee on Fire Research, National Research Council. Air Quality & Smoke from Urban & Forest Fires. LC 76-8356. (Illus.). 1976. pap. 10.25 (ISBN 0-309-02500-1). Natl Acad Pr.

--Directory of Fire Research. 8th ed. 1978. pap. text ed. 9.50x (ISBN 0-309-02799-3). Natl Acad Pr.

--Fire Detection for Life Safety. LC 76-53105. 1977. pap. 7.75 (ISBN 0-309-02600-8). Natl Acad Pr.

--Physiological & Toxicological Aspects of Combustion Products. LC 76-24955. 1976. pap. 8.00 (ISBN 0-309-02521-4). Natl Acad Pr.

Committee On Food Protection. Evaluation of Public Health Hazards from Microbiological Contamination of Foods. 1964. pap. 3.75 (ISBN 0-309-01195-7). Natl Acad Pr.

Committee on Food Protection, NRC. The Use of Chemicals in Food Production, Processing, Storage & Distribution. 40p. 1973. pap. 2.25 (ISBN 0-309-02136-7). Natl Acad Pr.

Committee on Food Stability, National Research Council. Objective Methods for Food Evaluation. LC 76-26723. 1976. pap. 8.75 (ISBN 0-309-02520-6). Natl Acad Pr.

Committee on Gas Production Opportunities. Potential for Increasing Production of Natural Gas from Existing Fields in the Near Term. 1978. pap. 6.25 (ISBN 0-309-02784-5). Natl Acad Pr.

Committee on Germplasm Resources. Conservation of Germplasm Resources: An Imperative. 1978. pap. 6.50 (ISBN 0-309-02744-6). Natl Acad Pr.

Committee on Hazardous Materials. Pressure Relieving Systems for Marine Bulk Liquid Cargo Containers. (Illus.). 168p. 1973. pap. 10.25 (ISBN 0-309-02122-7). Natl Acad Pr.

Committee on Impacts of Stratospheric Change, National Research Council. Halocarbons: Environmental Effects of Chlorofluoromethane Release. 1976. pap. 6.25 (ISBN 0-309-02529-X). Natl Acad Pr.

Committee on Impacts of Stratospheric Change, et al. Protection Against Depletion of Stratospheric Ozone by Chlorofluorocarbons. LC 79-57247. xvii, 392p. (Orig.). 1979. pap. text ed. 8.75 (ISBN 0-309-02947-3). Natl Acad Pr.

Committee on International Disaster Assistance. Assessing International Disaster Needs. 1979. pap. 6.00 (ISBN 0-309-02893-0). Natl Acad Pr.

Committee On Interplay Of Engineering With Biology And Medicine. Assessment of Industrial Activity in the Field of Biomedical Engineering. LC 79-171609. 1971. pap. text ed. 6.00 (ISBN 0-309-01925-7). Natl Acad Pr.

Committee on Interplay of Engineering with Biology & Medicine. Study of Engineering in Medicine & Health Care. LC 74-7253. 80p. 1974. pap. 3.50 (ISBN 0-309-02148-0). Natl Acad Pr.

Committee on Materials Specifications, Testing Methods & Standards, National Research Council. Materials & Process Specifications & Standards. LC 77-92433. (Illus.). 1977. pap. text ed. 8.50 (ISBN 0-309-02731-4). Natl Acad Pr.

Committee on Medical and Biologic Effects of Environmental Pollutants, National Research Council. Selenium. LC 76-40687. (Medical and Biologic Effects of Environmental Pollutants Ser). 1976. pap. 10.25 (ISBN 0-309-02503-6). Natl Acad Pr.

Committee on Medical & Biologic Effects of Environmental Pollutants, Division of Medical Science, National Research Council. Vapor-Phase Organic Pollutants. (Medical & Biologic Effects of Environmental Pollutants Ser.). 1976. pap. 13.00 (ISBN 0-309-02441-2). Natl Acad Pr.

Committee on Medical & Biological Effects of Environmental Pollutants. Nickel. 1975. pap. 15.00 (ISBN 0-309-02314-9). Natl Acad Pr.

Committee on Mineral Resources & Environment, National Research Council. Reserves & Resources of Uranium in the United States: Mineral Resources & the Environment Supplementary Report. ix, 236p. 1975. pap. 7.00 (ISBN 0-309-02423-4). Natl Acad Pr.

Committee on Mineral Resources & the Environment, National Research Council. Coal Workers' Pneumoconiosis-Medical Considerations, Some Social Implications: Mineral Resources & the Environment Supplementary Report. LC 75-39531. 149p. 1976. pap. 6.00 (ISBN 0-309-02424-2). Natl Acad Pr.

--Resource Recovery from Municipal Solid Wastes: Mineral Resources & the Environment Supplementary Report. 432p. 1975. pap. 9.25 (ISBN 0-309-02422-6). Natl Acad Pr.

Committee on National Statistics. Privacy & Confidentiality As Factors in Survey Response. 1979. pap. 12.75 (ISBN 0-309-02878-7). Natl Acad Pr.

Committee on National Statistics, National Research Council. Counting the People in 1980: An Appraisal of Census Plans. 1978. pap. text ed. 10.50 (ISBN 0-309-02797-7). Natl Acad Pr.

--Surveying Crime. Penick, Bettye, ed. LC 76-50120. 1976. pap. 11.00 (ISBN 0-309-02524-9). Natl Acad Pr.

Committee on Natural Resources, jt. auth. see Working Group Meeting on Energy Planning.

Committee on Nitrate Accumulation. Accumulation of Nitrate. vii, 106p. 1972. pap. text ed. 6.00 (ISBN 0-309-02038-7). Natl Acad Pr.

Committee on Nuclear & Alternative Energy Sources. Alternative Energy Demand Futures to 2010. 1979. pap. 10.00 (ISBN 0-309-02939-2). Natl Acad Pr.

Committee on Nuclear & Alternative Energy Systems, National Research Council. Controlled Nuclear Fusion: Current Research & Potential Progress. 1978. pap. text ed. 4.75x (ISBN 0-309-02863-9). Natl Acad Pr.

Committee on Nuclear & Alternative Energy Systems. Domestic Potential of Solar & Other Renewable Energy Sources. 1979. pap. 8.00 (ISBN 0-309-02927-9). Natl Acad Pr.

Committee on Nuclear & Alternative Energy Systems, National Research Council & National Academy of Sciences. Energy in Transition, Nineteen Eighty-Five to Two Thousand Ten. LC 79-27389. (Illus.). 1980. text ed. 25.95x (ISBN 0-7167-1227-X); pap. 12.95x (ISBN 0-7167-1228-8). W H Freeman.

Committee on Nuclear & Alternative Energy Systems, National Research Council. Geothermal Resources & Technology in the U. S. 1979. pap. text ed. 5.50 (ISBN 0-309-02874-4). Natl Acad Pr.

Committee on Nuclear & Alternative Energy Systems. Problems of U. S. Uranium Resources & Supply to the Year 2010. 1978. pap. 6.00 (ISBN 0-309-02782-9). Natl Acad Pr.

--U. S. Energy Supply Prospects to 2010. 1979. pap. 8.75 (ISBN 0-309-02936-8). Natl Acad Pr.

Committee On Nuclear Science. Source Material for Radiochemistry. rev. ed. LC 59-60042. (Nuclear Sciences Ser). 1971. pap. 3.50 (ISBN 0-309-01867-6). Natl Acad Pr.

Committee On Nuclear Sciences. Geochronology of North America. 1965. pap. 7.00 (ISBN 0-309-01276-7). Natl Acad Pr.

Committee on Occupational Classification & Analysis. Job Evaluation: An Analytical Review. 1979. pap. 7.00 (ISBN 0-309-02882-5). Natl Acad Pr.

Committee On Ocean Engineering, jt. auth. see Committee On Oceanography.

Committee on Ocean Engineering, jt. auth. see Committee On Oceanography.

Committee On Oceanography. Oceanography Nineteen Sixty-Six: Achievements & Opportunities. 1967. pap. 6.25 (ISBN 0-309-01492-1). Natl Acad Pr.

--Radioactivity in the Marine Environment. (Illus.). 1971. text ed. 15.75 o.p. (ISBN 0-309-01865-X). Natl Acad Pr.

--Recommended Procedures for Measuring Productivity of Plankton Standing Stock & Related Ocean Properties. (Orig.). 1970. pap. 4.00 (ISBN 0-309-01760-2). Natl Acad Pr.

--Scientific Exploration of the South Pacific. LC 72-603750. (Orig.). 1970. 11.50 (ISBN 0-309-01755-6). Natl Acad Pr.

Committee On Oceanography & Committee On Ocean Engineering. Oceanic Quest: The International Decade of Ocean Exploration. (Orig.). 1969. pap. 5.00 (ISBN 0-309-01709-2). Natl Acad Pr.

--Wastes Management Concepts for the Coastal Zone. (Orig.). 1970. pap. 4.25 (ISBN 0-309-01855-2). Natl Acad Pr.

Committee on Particulate Control Technology, National Research Council. Controlling Airborne Particles. xi, 114p. (Orig.). 1980. pap. text ed. 8.00 (ISBN 0-309-03035-8). Natl Acad Pr.

Committee On Patent Policy. Nonprofit Research & Patent Management in the United States. 1956. pap. 2.75 (ISBN 0-309-00371-7). Natl Acad Pr.

Committee on Pattern Jury Instructions of the Maryland Bar Association, Inc. Maryland Pattern Jury Instructions: Civil. LC 77-72007. 1977. 47.50 (ISBN 0-686-21281-9). Lawyers Co-Op.

Committee on Pesticide Decision Making, National Research Council. Pesticide Decision Making. LC 77-94524. (Analytical Studies for the U. S. Environmental Protection Agency Ser.). (Illus.). 1978. pap. text ed. 6.00 (ISBN 0-309-02734-9). Natl Acad Pr.

Committee On Pollution. Waste Management & Control. 1966. pap. 6.25 o.p. (ISBN 0-309-01400-X). Natl Acad Pr.

Committee on Population. Growth of U. S. Population. 1965. pap. 2.50 (ISBN 0-309-01279-1). Natl Acad Pr.

Committee on Power Plant Siting. Engineering for Resolution of the Energy-Environment Dilemma. LC 79-186370. (Illus.). 1972. pap. 10.75 (ISBN 0-309-01943-5). Natl Acad Pr.

Committee on Pre & Postoperative Care American College of Surgeons. Manual of Surgical Intensive Care. Kinney, John M., ed. LC 76-51009. (Illus.). 1977. text ed. 14.50 o.p. (ISBN 0-7216-1180-X). Saunders.

Committee on Private Sector Participation in Government Energy RD&D Planning. Private Sector Participation in Federal Energy RD&D Planning. 1978. pap. 6.50 (ISBN 0-309-02783-7). Natl Acad Pr.

Committee On Prosthetic-Orthotic Education. Geriatric Amputee: Principles of Management. LC 79-610527. (Illus., Orig.). 1971. pap. text ed. 4.25 (ISBN 0-309-01873-0). Natl Acad Pr.

Committee on Prosthetics Research & Development. The Child with an Acquired Amputation. (Illus.). 176p. 1972. pap. 7.75 (ISBN 0-309-02047-6). Natl Acad Pr.
--Comprehensive Management of Musculoskeletal Disorders in Hemophilia. (Illus.). 200p. 1973. pap. 8.75 (ISBN 0-309-02139-1). Natl Acad Pr.

Committee On Prosthetics Research And Development. Selected Lower-Limb Anomalies. LC 76-611159. 1971. pap. text ed. 3.50 (ISBN 0-309-01915-X). Natl Acad Pr.

Committee on Prototype Explicit Analysis for Pesticides. Regulating Pesticides. xiii, 288p. 1980. pap. text ed. 11.00 (ISBN 0-309-02946-5). Natl Acad Pr.

Committee on Radioactive Waste Management. An Evaluation of the Concept of Storing Radioactive Wastes in Bedrock Below the Savannah River Plant Site. (Illus.). 88p. 1972. pap. 3.50 (ISBN 0-309-02035-2). Natl Acad Pr.
--Implementation of Long-Term Environmental Radiation Standards? The Issue of Verification. ix, 65p. 1979. pap. text ed. 5.50 (ISBN 0-309-02879-5). Natl Acad Pr.
--Long-Term Environmental Radiation Standards. 1979. pap. 5.50 (ISBN 0-309-02879-5). Natl Acad Pr.
--A Review of the Swedish KBS-II Plan for Disposal of Spent Nuclear Fuel. Subcommittee for Review of the KBS-II Plan, ed. LC 80-80362. xiii, 91p. 1980. pap. text ed. 7.75 (ISBN 0-309-03036-6). Natl Acad Pr.

Committee On Research In The Life Sciences. Life Sciences. LC 71-606918. (Illus., Orig.). 1970. pap. 11.50 (ISBN 0-309-01770-X). Natl Acad Pr.

Committee on Research on Law Enforcement & Criminal Justice. Rehabilitation of Criminal Offenders: Problems & Prospects. 1979. pap. 13.75 (ISBN 0-309-02895-7). Natl Acad Pr.
--Understanding Crime. 1977. pap. 12.00 (ISBN 0-309-02635-0). Natl Acad Pr.

Committee on Research Priorities in Tropical Biology. Research Priorities in Tropical Biology. xii, 116p. 1980. pap. text ed. 8.25 (ISBN 0-309-03043-9). Natl Acad Pr.

Committee On Salmonella - Division Of Biology And Agriculture. Evaluation of the Salmonella Problem. LC 76-600461. (Illus., Orig.). 1969. pap. 7.00 (ISBN 0-309-01683-5). Natl Acad Pr.

Committee on Scholarly Communication with the People's Republic of China. Acupuncture Anesthesia in the People's Republic of China: A Trip Report of the American Acupuncture Anesthesia Study Group. LC 76-22856. 1976. pap. 5.75 (ISBN 0-309-02517-6). Natl Acad Pr.

Committee on Scholarly Communication with the People's Republic of China (CSCPRC) Insect Control in the People's Republic of China: A Trip Report of the American Insect Control Delegation. LC 76-52849. (CSCPRC Report: No. 2). 1977. pap. 11.25 (ISBN 0-309-02525-7). Natl Acad Pr.

Committee on Scholarly Communications with the Peoples Republic of China National Research Council. Pure & Applied Mathematics in the Peoples Republic of China. 1977. pap. 12.00 (ISBN 0-686-25566-6, PB279 509); microfiche 3.50 (ISBN 0-686-25567-4). Natl Tech Info.

Committee On Scientific And Technical Communication. Scientific & Technical Communication: A Pressing National Problem & Recommendations for Its Solution. LC 76-601241. (Illus., Orig.). 1969. pap. 8.25 o.p. (ISBN 0-309-01707-6). Natl Acad Pr.

Committee on Seismology, ed. Global Earthquake Monitoring: Its Uses, Potentials, & Support Requirements. LC 77-5219. 1977. pap. text ed. 6.25 (ISBN 0-309-02608-3). Natl Acad Pr.

Committee on Seismology-Division of Earth Sciences. Seismology: Responsibilities & Requirements of a Growing Science. Incl. Part 1. Summary & Recommendations. o.p.; Part 2. Problems & Prospects. o.p. (ISBN 0-309-01738-6). LC 70-602511. (Illus., Orig.). 1969. Set. pap. 6.75 (ISBN 0-686-66876-6). Natl Acad Pr.

Committee on Seismology, National Research Council. Predicting Earthquakes: A Scientific and Technical Evaluation--with Implications for Society. LC 76-40493. 1976. pap. 5.25 (ISBN 0-309-02527-3). Natl Acad Pr.

Committee On Social And Behavioral Urban Research - Division Of Behavioral Sciences. Strategic Approach to Urban Research & Development: Social & Behavioral Science Considerations. LC 73-601566. 1969. pap. 4.75 (ISBN 0-309-01728-9). Natl Acad Pr.

Committee on Space Research. Remote Sounding of the Atmosphere from Space: Proceedings of the 21st Plenary Meeting, Innsbruck, Austria, 1978. Bolle, H. J., ed. (Illus.). 1979. 63.00 (ISBN 0-08-023419-4). Pergamon.
--X-Ray Astronomy, Including a Catalogue & Bibliography of Galactic X-Ray Sources: Proceedings of the 21st Plenary Meeting, Innsbruck, Austria, 1978. Baity, W. A. & Peterson, L. E., eds. (Illus.). 1979. text ed. 63.00 (ISBN 0-08-023418-6). Pergamon.

Committee on Substance Abuse & Habitual Behavior. Issues in Controlled Substance Use. Maloff, Deborah R. & Levison, Peter K., eds. LC 80-81027. ix, 183p. 1980. pap. text ed. 8.25 (ISBN 0-309-03041-2). Natl Acad Pr.

Committee on Taxation Resources and Economic Development Symposium, 4th. Land & Building Taxes: Their Effect on Economic Development: Proceedings. Becker, Arthur P., ed. (Illus.). 1969. 25.00 (ISBN 0-299-05460-8). U of Wis Pr.

Committee On Taxation - Resources - And Economic Development Symposium - 1967. Property Tax & Its Administration: Proceedings. Lynn, Arthur D., Jr., ed. (Committee on Taxation, Resources & Economic Development Ser., No. 3). 1969. 20.00 (ISBN 0-299-05240-9); pap. 7.50x (ISBN 0-299-05214-1). U of Wis Pr.

Committee On Telecommunications. Reports on Selected Topics in Telecommunications. (Orig.). 1969. pap. 5.75 (ISBN 0-309-01751-3). Natl Acad Pr.

Committee on the Alaska Earthquake. The Great Alaska Earthquake of 1964: Biology. (Illus.). 320p. 1972. text ed. 21.95 (ISBN 0-309-01604-5). Natl Acad Pr.
--The Great Alaska Earthquake of 1964: Geology. (Illus.). 848p. 1972. text ed. 35.00 (ISBN 0-309-01601-0). Natl Acad Pr.
--Great Alaska Earthquake of 1964: Human Ecology. 1970. 29.50 (ISBN 0-309-01607-X). Natl Acad Pr.
--Great Alaska Earthquake of 1964: Hydrology. (Great Alaskan Earthquake Ser). (Illus.). 1968. 25.00 (ISBN 0-309-01603-7). Natl Acad Pr.
--The Great Alaska Earthquake of 1964: Oceanography & Coastal Engineering. LC 68-60037. (Illus.). 624p. 1972. 32.50 (ISBN 0-309-01605-3). Natl Acad Pr.
--The Great Alaska Earthquake of 1964: Seismology & Geodesy. LC 68-60037. (Illus.). 592p. 1972. 25.00 (ISBN 0-309-01602-9). Natl Acad Pr.
--The Great Alaska Earthquake of 1964: Summary & Recommendations Including Index to Series. (Illus.). 288p. 1973. 16.00 (ISBN 0-309-01608-8). Natl Acad Pr.

Committee on the Education & Employment of Women in Science & Engineering. Women Scientists in Industry & Government: How Much Progress in the 1970's. LC 80-80079. vii, 56p. 1980. pap. text ed. 5.00 (ISBN 0-309-03023-4). Natl Acad Pr.

Committee on the Great Alaska Earthquake of 1964. The Great Alaska Earthquake of 1964: Engineering. (The Great Alaska Earthquake of 1964 Ser.). (Illus.). 1210p. 1973. 37.50 (ISBN 0-309-01606-1). Natl Acad Pr.

Committee on the Judiciary, U. S. Senate, Eighty-Ninth Congress, First Session. Morgenthau Diary (China, 2 vols. LC 70-167844. (FDR & the Era of the New Deal Ser.). 1693p. 1974. Repr. of 1965 ed. Set. lib. bdg. 125.00 (ISBN 0-306-70332-7). Da Capo.

Committee on Toxicology, jt. auth. see Committee on Fire Research.

Committee on Transportation, Assembly of Engineering, Natl. Research Council. A Review of Short Haul Passenger Transportation. 1976. pap. 6.25 (ISBN 0-309-02445-5). Natl Acad Pr.

Committee On Underwater Telecommunications Division Of Physical Sciences. Present & Future Civil Uses of Underwater Sound. LC 76-606666. (Illus., Orig.). 1970. pap. 4.25 (ISBN 0-309-01771-8). Natl Acad Pr.

Committee On Urban Technology - Division Of Engineering. Long-Range Planning for Urban Research & Development: Technological Considerations. (Illus., Orig.). 1969. pap. 4.75 (ISBN 0-309-01729-7). Natl Acad Pr.

Committee on Urban Waterfront Lands. Urban Waterfront Lands. xii, 243p. 1980. pap. text ed. 11.50 (ISBN 0-309-02940-6). Natl Acad Pr.

Committee on Veterinary Medical Research & Education. New Horizons for Veterinary Medicine. LC 74-181827. 176p. (Orig.). 1972. pap. 5.50 (ISBN 0-309-01935-4). Natl Acad Pr.

Committee on Vision. Color Vision. (Illus.). 1973. pap. 7.00 (ISBN 0-309-02105-7). Natl Acad Pr.
--Visual Search. (Illus.). 152p. 1973. pap. 8.20 (ISBN 0-309-02103-0). Natl Acad Pr.

Committee on Vocational Education Research & Development, National Research Council. Assessing Vocational Education Research & Development. LC 76-46196. 1976. pap. 8.00 (ISBN 0-309-02526-5). Natl Acad Pr.

Committee to Defend Czech Socialists, ed. Voices of Czechoslovak Socialists. 1977. pap. 3.95 (ISBN 0-686-23504-5, Merlin Pr). Carrier Pigeon.

Committee to the Human Health Effects of Subtherapeutic Antibiotic Use in Animal Feeds. The Effects on Human Health of Subtherapeutic Use of Antimicrobials in Animal Feeds. LC 80-81486. 1980. pap. text ed. 10.25 (ISBN 0-309-03044-7). Natl Acad Pr.

Commitee on Animal Production. Plant & Animal Products in the U. S. Food System. 1978. pap. 10.75 (ISBN 0-309-02769-1). Natl Acad Pr.

Common, Alfred F. How to Repair Violins. Repr. lib. bdg. 19.00 (ISBN 0-403-03871-5). Scholarly.

Common, M. S. Basic Econometrics: An Introductory Text for Economists. LC 76-7466. (Modern Economics Ser.). (Illus.). 1976. pap. text ed. 16.95x (ISBN 0-582-44670-8). Longman.

Commons, Michael & Nevin, John A., eds. Discriminative Properties of Reinforcement Schedules. (The Quantitative Analysis of Behavior Ser.). 1981. price not set professional reference (ISBN 0-88410-377-3). Ballinger Pub.

Commons, Michael, et al. Quantitative Analysis of Behavior, 4 vols. 1980. write for info. (ISBN 0-88410-377-3). Ballinger Pub.

Commons, Michael L. & Nevin, John A. Quantitative Analysis of Behavior: Discriminative Properties of Reinforcement Schedules. (General Psychology Ser.). Date not set. cancelled (ISBN 0-08-024642-7). Pergamon.

Commune de Paris, 1789-1794. Actes de la Commune de Paris pendant la Revolution, 9 vols. (Second Ser.). Repr. of 1955 ed. Set. 479.25 (ISBN 0-404-52630-6); 53.25 ea. AMS Pr.
--Actes de la Commune de Paris pendant la Revolution, 10 vols. (First Ser.). Repr. of 1942 ed. Set. 532.50 (ISBN 0-404-52620-9); 53.25 ea. AMS Pr.

Communications Research Machines, Inc. Abnormal Psychology: Current Perspectives. 2nd ed. 1976. text ed. 18.95 o.p. (ISBN 0-394-31062-4). Random.
--Psychology Today: An Introduction. 4th ed. 1979. text ed. 16.95x (ISBN 0-394-32066-2); wkbk. 6.95 (ISBN 0-394-32313-0). Random.

Community Associations Institute. Creating a Community Association: The Developer's Role in Condominium & Homeowners Association. LC 76-56982. 1976. 12.00 (ISBN 0-87420-574-3). Urban Land.

Community Management Corporation. Financial Management of Condominium & Homeowner's Associations. LC 76-21960. (Special Report Ser.). 1976. 14.50 (ISBN 0-87420-569-7). Urban Land.

Community Service Editors. Pioneering in Education Requires Pioneering in Community. 1973. pap. 1.50 (ISBN 0-910420-15-7). Comm Serv.

Community Work Group. Current Issues in Community Work. 1973. 14.95 o.s.i. (ISBN 0-7100-7687-8); pap. 5.75 o.s.i. (ISBN 0-7100-7688-6). Routledge & Kegan.

Compaine, Benjamin M., ed. Who Owns the Media? Concentration of Ownership in the Mass Communications Industry. LC 79-15891. (Communications Library). 1979. 24.95x (ISBN 0-914236-36-9). Knowledge Indus.

Comparative Literature Symposium, No. 12. Shakespeare's Art from a Comparative Perspective: Proceedings. Aycock, Wendell M., ed. (Proceedings of the Comparative Literature Symposium). (Illus.). 197p. (Orig.). 1981. pap. write for info. (ISBN 0-89672-081-0). Tex Tech Pr.

Comper, W. D. Heparin (& Related Polysaccharides) Structural & Functional Properties. 1981. price not set (ISBN 0-677-05040-2). Gordon.

Compere, Newton L. How to Raise & Train a German Wirehaired Pointer. 1966. pap. 1.79 o.p. (ISBN 0-87666-304-8, DS1080). TFH Pubns.

Compressed Gas Association. Handbook of Compressed Gases. 2nd ed. 1981. text ed. 44.50 (ISBN 0-442-25419-9). Van Nos Reinhold.

Comprone, Joseph J. From Experience to Expression: A College Rhetoric. 2nd ed. LC 80-82348. (Illus.). 528p. 1981. pap. text ed. 11.50 (ISBN 0-395-29310-3); write for info. instr's manual (ISBN 0-395-29311-1). HM.

Compton, Al. Armonia Familiar. 1980. pap. 0.85 (ISBN 0-311-46078-X). Casa Bautista.

Compton, Alan. Comunicacion Cristiana. Date not set. Repr. of 1979 ed. 2.75 (ISBN 0-311-13833-0). Casa Bautista.

Compton, Beulah & Galaway, Burt. Social Work Processes. rev. ed. 1979. pap. text ed. 14.50x (ISBN 0-256-02194-5). Dorsey.

Compton, Beulah R. Introduction to Social Welfare & Social Work: Structure, Function, & Process. 1980. 17.95x (ISBN 0-256-02093-0). Dorsey.

Compton, D. G. Ascendancies. LC 80-7823. 1980. 12.95 o.p. (ISBN 0-399-12484-5). Berkley Pub.
--Synthajoy. 1979. pap. 1.95 o.p. (ISBN 0-425-04207-3). Berkley Pub.
--Windows. 1979. 9.95 o.p. (ISBN 0-399-12378-4). Berkley Pub.
--Windows. LC 79-921. 1979. 10.95 o.p. (ISBN 0-399-12378-4). Berkley Pub.

Compton, Eric N. Inside Commercial Banking. LC 80-13269. 191p. 1980. 19.95 (ISBN 0-471-07974-X, Pub. by Wiley-Interscience). Wiley.

Compton, Grant. What Does a Meteorologist Do? (What Do They Do Ser.). (Illus.). 80p. (gr. 5 up). 1981. PLB 5.95 (ISBN 0-396-07931-8). Dodd.

Compton, H. K. Supplies & Materials Management. 2nd ed. (Illus.). 512p. 1979. text ed. 45.00x (ISBN 0-7121-1964-7, Pub. by Macdonald & Evans England). Intl Ideas.

Compton, Hugh J. The Oxford Canal. LC 76-54077. (Inland Waterways History Ser.). (Illus.). 1977. 6.95 (ISBN 0-7153-7238-6). David & Charles.

Compton, Michael. Optical & Kinetic Art. (Tate Gallery: Little Art Book Ser.). 1977. pap. 1.95 (ISBN 0-8120-0859-6). Barron.

Compton, Michael & Sylvester, David. Robert Morris. (Tate Gallery Art Ser.). (Illus.). 1977. 4.50 (ISBN 0-8120-5143-2). Barron.

Compton, W. H. Special Day Sermons. 1972. 2.95 (ISBN 0-87148-752-7); pap. 2.25 (ISBN 0-87148-753-5). Pathway Pr.

Compton, W. V., jt. auth. see Quinlan, P. M.

Computer Consultants Ltd. British Commercial Computer Digest. 11th ed. 1970. 79.00 (ISBN 0-08-016279-7). Pergamon.
--European Computer Survey Nineteen Sixty-Nine to Seventy. 6th ed. LC 74-102635. 1970. 675.00 (ISBN 0-08-016026-3). Pergamon.
--European Computer Users Handbook, 1969-70. LC 63-25287. 1970. 46.00 (ISBN 0-08-016027-1). Pergamon.

Computer Information Services, Chicago Hospital Council. Shared Hospital Computer Services Evaluation. 165p. 1975. 15.00 (ISBN 0-686-68578-4, 14912). Hospital Finan.

Computer Partners, Inc. Handbook of COBOL Techniques. (Illus.). 86p. (Orig.). 1979. pap. 10.00 (ISBN 0-89435-037-4). QED Info Sci.

Computer Science and Engineering Board. Libraries & Information Technology: A System Challenge. 96p. (Orig.). 1972. pap. text ed. 3.50 (ISBN 0-309-01938-9). Natl Acad Pr.

Computerist Inc. All of Micro Vol. 2: The 6502 Journal No. 7-12 Oct-Nov 78 - May 79. Tripp, Robert M., ed. (Illus.). 8.00 (ISBN 0-938222-01-5). Computerist.
--The Best of Micro, Vol. 1. Tripp, Robert M., et al, eds. (Illus.). 176p. (Orig.). 1978. pap. 6.00 (ISBN 0-938222-00-7). Computerist.

Comrey, Andrew. Handbook of Interpretations for the Comrey Personality Scales. LC 80-67424. 1980. 7.95 (ISBN 0-912736-23-2). EDITS Pubs.

Comrey, Andrew L. Elementary Statistics: A Problem Solving Approach. 1975. text ed. 17.95x (ISBN 0-256-01676-5). Dorsey.

Comrie, B. Aspect. (Textbooks in Linguistics). 180p. 1976. 34.95 (ISBN 0-521-21109-3); pap. 9.95x (ISBN 0-521-29045-7). Cambridge U Pr.
--The Languages of the Soviet Union. (Cambridge Language Surveys Ser.: No. 2). (Illus.). 320p. Date not set. price not set (ISBN 0-521-23230-9); pap. price not set (ISBN 0-521-29877-6). Cambridge U Pr.

Comrie, Bernard & Stone, Gerald. The Russian Language Since the Revolution. 1978. 36.00x (ISBN 0-19-815648-0). Oxford U Pr.

Comstock, Anna B. Ways of the Six Footed. rev. ed. (Illus.). 176p. 1977. 7.95 (ISBN 0-8014-1081-9). Comstock.

Comstock, Craig, jt. auth. see Sanford, R. Nevitt.

Comstock, Craig, jt. auth. see Sanford, Nevitt.

Comstock, George. Television in America. LC 80-10891. (Sage Commtext Ser.: No. 1). 155p. 1980. 12.50x (ISBN 0-8039-1244-7); pap. 5.95 (ISBN 0-8039-1245-5). Sage.

Comstock, George, et al. Television & Human Behavior. 1978. 20.00 (ISBN 0-231-04420-8); pap. 10.00 (ISBN 0-231-04421-6). Columbia U Pr.

Comstock, John H. Introduction to Entomology. 9th ed. 1093p. 1940. text ed. 35.00x (ISBN 0-8014-0083-X). Comstock.

Comstock, Mary & Vermeule, Cornelius. Roman Medallions. 2nd enl. ed. (Illus.). 1975. Repr. of 1962 ed. 5.00 (ISBN 0-87846-177-9). Mus Fine Arts Boston.

Comstock, Mary B. & Vermeule, Cornelius C. Sculpture in Stone: The Greek, Roman & Etruscan Collections of the Museum of Fine Arts Boston. LC 76-40711. (Illus.). 1978. 35.00 (ISBN 0-87846-103-5, Pub. by Mus Fine Arts Boston); pap. 15.00 (ISBN 0-686-68049-9). C E Tuttle.

Comstock, Mary B., frwd. by. Greek Coins Supplement. (Illus.). 1964. 12.50 (ISBN 0-87846-165-5); pap. 4.50 (ISBN 0-87846-166-3). Mus Fine Arts Boston.

Comte, August. Introduction to Positive Philosophy. Ferre, Frederick, ed. LC 73-84164. (Library of Liberal Arts Ser). (Orig.). 1970. pap. 3.05 o.p. (ISBN 0-672-60284-9, LLA94). Bobbs.

--The Positive Analysis of Social Phenomena. (The Essential Library of the Great Philosophers). (Illus.). 129p. (Fr.). 1981. 37.85 (ISBN 0-89901-027-X). Found Class Reprints.

Comte, Edward Le see LeComte, Edward.

Comte, Edward Le see Le Comte, Edward.

Comte, Robert, jt. auth. see Lee, Leslie.

Comtois, M. F. & Miller, Lynn F. Contemporary American Theatre Critics: A Dictionary & Anthology of Their Works. LC 77-23063. 1977. 40.00 (ISBN 0-8108-1057-3). Scarecrow.

Comyn, J. & Johnson, R. Wills & Intestacies. LC 78-92109. 1970. 13.75 (ISBN 0-08-006691-7); pap. 6.25 (ISBN 0-08-006690-9). Pergamon.

Conacher, D. J. Aeschylus' "Prometheus Bound". A Literary Commentary. 128p. 1980. 20.00x (ISBN 0-8020-2391-6); pap. 7.50 (ISBN 0-8020-6416-7). U of Toronto Pr.

Conacher, J. B. Aberdeen Coalition, 1852-1855: A Study in Mid-Nineteenth-Century Party Politics. LC 68-10148. (Illus.). 1968. 64.00 (ISBN 0-521-04711-0). Cambridge U Pr.

Conan, Pierre. The Greatest Sports Stars. Mooney, Thomas J., ed. (Pal Paperbacks, Pal Skills Ser.). (Illus., Orig.). (gr. 7-12). 1978. pap. text ed. 1.25 (ISBN 0-8374-6713-6). Xerox Ed Pubns.

Conan Doyle, A. The Firm of Girdlestone. LC 80-65205. (Conan Doyle Centennial Ser.). (Illus.). 364p. 1981. 16.95 (ISBN 0-934468-42-7). Gaslight.

--The Mystery of Cloomber. LC 80-65206. (Conan Doyle Centennial Ser.). (Illus.). 195p. 1980. 11.95 (ISBN 0-934468-41-9). Gaslight.

Conan Doyle, Arthur. Adventures of Gerard. new ed. 15.95 (ISBN 0-7195-3226-4). Transatlantic.

--Adventures of Sherlock Holmes. (gr. 10 up). pap. 2.25 (ISBN 0-425-04869-1, Medallion). Berkley Pub.

--The Adventures of Sherlock Holmes. facsimile ed. (Illus.). 328p. 1975. pap. 3.95 o.p. (ISBN 0-89104-023-4). A & W Pubs.

--Case Book of Sherlock Holmes. (gr. 10 up). pap. 1.95 (ISBN 0-425-04822-5, Medallion). Berkley Pub.

--The Case of the Five Orange Pips. Pauk, Walter & Harris, Raymond, eds. (Classics Ser). (Illus.). (gr. 6-12). 1976. pap. text ed. 1.60x (ISBN 0-89061-062-2, 545); tchrs. ed. 3.00 (ISBN 0-89061-063-0, 547). Jamestown Pubs.

--The Case of the Six Napoleons. Pauk, Walter & Harris, Raymond, eds. (Classics Ser). (Illus.). (gr. 6-12). 1976. pap. text ed. 1.60x (ISBN 0-89061-058-4, 537); tchrs. ed. 3.00 (ISBN 0-89061-059-2, 539). Jamestown Pubs.

--Complete Professor Challenger Stories. 1952. 18.50 (ISBN 0-7195-0360-4). Transatlantic.

--Exploits of Brigadier Gerard. 15.95 (ISBN 0-7195-3227-2). Transatlantic.

--His Last Bow. (gr. 10 up). pap. 1.95 (ISBN 0-425-04870-5, Medallion). Berkley Pub.

--Hound of the Baskervilles. (Classics Ser). (gr. 8 up). pap. 1.25 (ISBN 0-8049-0062-0, CL-62). Airmont.

--Hound of the Baskervilles. (gr. 10 up). pap. 1.95 (ISBN 0-425-04421-1, Medallion). Berkley Pub.

--Hound of the Baskervilles. (gr. 7-12). 1972. pap. 1.50 o.p. (ISBN 0-590-01355-6, Schol Pap). Schol Bk Serv.

--Lost World. (Looking Glass Library: No. 10). 1959. PLB 4.39 o.p. (ISBN 0-394-90460-5, BYR). Random.

--Lost World. (gr. 10 up). pap. 0.95 o.p. (ISBN 0-425-03514-X, Medallion). Berkley Pub.

--Memoirs of Sherlock Holmes. (gr. 10 up). pap. 1.95 (ISBN 0-425-04821-7, Medallion). Berkley Pub.

--The Musgrave Ritual. Pauk, Walter & Harris, Raymond, eds. (Classics). (Illus.). (gr. 6-12). 1976. pap. text ed. 1.60x (ISBN 0-89061-056-8, 533); tchrs. ed. 3.00 (ISBN 0-89061-057-6, 535). Jamestown Pubs.

--The Red-Headed League. Pauk, Walter & Harris, Raymond, eds. (Classics Ser). (Illus.). (gr. 6-12). 1976. pap. text ed. 2.40x (ISBN 0-89061-060-6, 541); tchrs. ed. 3.00 (ISBN 0-89061-061-4, 543). Jamestown Pubs.

--Refugees: A Tale of Two Continents. 8.95 (ISBN 0-685-20618-1). Transatlantic.

--Return of Sherlock Holmes. (gr. 10 up). pap. 1.95 (ISBN 0-425-04871-3, Medallion). Berkley Pub.

--Sir Nigel. 15.95 (ISBN 0-7195-3228-0). Transatlantic.

--William Harrison Ainsworth & His Friends, 2 vols. Bleiler, E. F., ed. LC 78-60905. (Fiction of Popular Culture Ser.: Vol. 5). 1979. Set. lib. bdg. 88.00 (ISBN 0-8240-9663-0). Garland Pub.

Conan Doyle, Arthur see Doyle, Arthur Conan.

Conant, Howard & Randall, Arne. Art in Education. (YA) (gr. 9 up). 1963. 9.28 (ISBN 0-87002-064-1). Bennett IL.

Conant, James B. Thomas Jefferson & the Development of American Public Education. 1962. 7.50x o.p. (ISBN 0-520-00262-8). U of Cal Pr.

Conant, James C. All Dreams Never Die. 1977. 4.50 o.p. (ISBN 0-682-48920-4). Exposition.

Conant, Jonathan B. Cochran's German Review Grammar. 3rd ed. LC 73-21535. 384p. 1974. text ed. 13.95 (ISBN 0-13-139501-7). P-H.

Conant, Miriam B., ed. see Aron, Raymond.

Conant, Ralph W. Politics of Community Health. 2.00 (ISBN 0-8183-0193-7). Pub Aff Pr.

Conant, Roger. The Political Poetry & Idealogy of F. I. Tiutchev. (Ardis Essay Ser.: No. 6). 1981. 10.00. Ardis Pubs.

--The Political Poetry & Ideology of Fyodor Tyutchev. (Ardis Essay Ser.: No. 7). 82p. 1981. text ed. 10.00. Ardis Pubs.

Conant, Roger C. Electrical Circuits Problems & Laboratory Manual. (Illus.). 1980. 4.50x (ISBN 0-917974-33-6). Waveland Pr.

Conard, Howard L. Uncle Dick Wootton: The Pioneer Frontiersman of the Rocky Mountain Region. Quaife, Milo M., ed. LC 79-19038. (Illus.). xxiv, 462p. 1980. 22.50x (ISBN 0-8032-1408-1); pap. 7.50 (ISBN 0-8032-6306-6, BB 730, Bison). U of Nebr Pr.

Conarroe, Joel. John Berryman: An Introduction to the Poetry. LC 77-8461. (Columbia Introductions to Twentieth-Century American Poetry). 1977. 15.00x (ISBN 0-231-03811-9). Columbia U Pr.

--William Carlos Williams' Paterson: Language & Landscape. LC 73-92854. 1974. pap. 4.95x (ISBN 0-8122-1046-8). U of Pa Pr.

Conarroe, Richard R. Bravely, Bravely in Business. LC 72-78297. (Illus.). 1972. 10.95 (ISBN 0-8144-5304-X). Am Mgmt.

--Bravely, Bravely...in Business. (AMACOM Executive Bks). 1978. pap. 4.95 (ISBN 0-8144-7509-4). Am Mgmt.

Conatser, Dean. Bowhunting the White Deer. (Illus.). 1977. 12.95 (ISBN 0-87691-192-0). Winchester Pr.

Conaway, J. C. Deadlier Than the Male. 1977. pap. 1.50 (ISBN 0-505-51160-6). Tower Bks.

--Garden of Unicorns. 176p. (Orig.). 1976. pap. 1.25 o.p. (ISBN 0-345-25109-1). Ballantine.

--The Magician's Sleeve. 1979. pap. 1.75 o.p. (ISBN 0-449-14120-9, GM). Fawcett.

Conaway, James. World's End. 384p. 1980. pap. 2.50. Bantam.

Conaway, Jim. The Deadly Spring. 1976. pap. 1.50 o.p. (ISBN 0-685-72567-7, LB395). Nordon Pubns.

Conaway, Judith. The Discovery Book of Inside & Outside. LC 76-46347. (Discovery Ser.). (Illus.). (gr. k-3). 1977. PLB 8.65 (ISBN 0-8172-0250-1). Raintree Pubs.

--The Discovery Book of Size. LC 76-46471. (Discovery Ser.). (Illus.). (gr. k-3). 1977. PLB 8.65 (ISBN 0-8172-0252-8). Raintree Pubs.

--The Discovery Book of Time. LC 76-44236. (Discovery Ser). (Illus.). (gr. k-3). 1977. PLB 8.65 (ISBN 0-8172-0253-6). Raintree Pubs.

--The Discovery Book of Up & Down. LC 76-46470. (Discovery Ser.). (Illus.). (gr. k-3). 1977. PLB 8.65 (ISBN 0-8172-0251-X). Raintree Pubs.

--Garbage Mountain: A United States Community Solves a Problem. (A World of Our Own). (Illus.). 16p. (primer). 1977. 7 bks. & one cassette 15.00 (ISBN 0-89290-017-2). Soc for Visual.

--Great Indoor Games from Trash & Other Things. LC 77-7383. (Games & Activities Ser.). (Illus.). (gr. k-4). 1977. PLB 9.30 (ISBN 0-8172-0952-2). Raintree Pubs.

--Great Outdoor Games from Trash & Other Things. LC 77-7785. (Games & Activities Ser.). (Illus.). (gr. k-4). 1977. PLB 9.30 (ISBN 0-8172-0950-6). Raintree Pubs.

--I Dare You! LC 76-46432. (Moods & Emotions Ser.). (Illus.). (gr. k-3). 1977. PLB 8.95 (ISBN 0-8172-0062-2). Raintree Pubs.

--I'll Get Even. LC 77-23455. (Moods & Emotions Ser.). (Illus.). (gr. k-3). 1977. PLB 8.95 (ISBN 0-8172-0964-6). Raintree Pubs.

--Reading Workbook Four (Cowardly Lion's Book) (Funny Face Activity Bks.). (Illus.). 48p. (ps-1). 1981. pap. 1.95 saddle-stitched (ISBN 0-394-84695-8). Random.

--Reading Workbook Three (Rascal Raccoon's Book) (Funny Face Activity Bks.). (Illus.). 48p. (ps-1). 1981. pap. 1.95 saddle stitched (ISBN 0-394-84440-8). Random.

--Sometimes It Scares Me. LC 76-46342. (Moods & Emotions Ser.). (Illus.). (gr. k-3). 1977. PLB 8.95 (ISBN 0-8172-0060-6). Raintree Pubs.

--Unsolved Mysteries...with Sherlock Holmes & Dr. Watson. (gr. 7-9). 1976. 135.00 (ISBN 0-89290-113-6, CM-37). Soc for Visual.

--Will I Ever Be Good Enough? LC 76-45854. (Moods & Emotions Ser.). (Illus.). (gr. k-3). 1977. PLB 8.95 (ISBN 0-8172-0059-2). Raintree Pubs.

Conde, John A. The Cars That Hudson Built. (Illus.). 224p. 1980. 19.95 (ISBN 0-9605048-0-X). Arnold-Porter Pub.

Conde, Julian, jt. auth. see Zachariah, K. C.

Conde, Julien, et al. Mortality in Developing Countries. OECD Deveopment Centre, ed. (Development Centre Studies). (Orig.). 1980. Tome 1 & 2, 1266p. pap. 85.00 (ISBN 9-2640-2097-7, 41-80-05-3); Tome 3, 550p. pap. 30.00 (ISBN 9-2640-2120-5, 41-80-06-1). OECD.

Condemi, John J. & Schwartz, Robert. Allergy. (Medical Examination Review Book Ser.: No. 26). 1973. spiral bdg. 16.50 (ISBN 0-87488-132-3). Med Exam.

Conder, Peggy. Competency-Based Education. 1978. pap. 9.50 o.p. (ISBN 0-685-87370-6). Natl Sch Pr.

Condie, K. C. Plate Tectonics & Crustal Evolution. LC 75-4690. 35.00 (ISBN 0-08-019594-6). Pergamon.

Condillac, Etienne Bonnot de. Essay on the Origin of Human Knowledge. Nugent, Thomas, tr. from Fr. LC 76-161929. (Hist. of Psych. Ser.). 1971. Repr. of 1756 ed. 42.00x (ISBN 0-8201-1090-6). Schol Facsimiles.

Condit, Carl W. Chicago School of Architecture. LC 64-13287. (Illus.). xvii, 238p. 1973. pap. 9.95 (ISBN 0-226-11455-4, P540, Phoen). U of Chicago Pr.

Condominas, Georges. We Have Eaten the Forest: The Story of a Montagnard Village in the Central Highlands of Vietnam. Foulke, Adrienne, tr. 1977. 17.50 o.p. (ISBN 0-686-63835-2); pap. 10.95 (ISBN 0-8090-1386-X). Hill & Wang.

Condon, E. U. & Odabasi, H. Atomic Structure. LC 77-88673. (Illus.). 1980. 83.50 (ISBN 0-521-21859-4); pap. 26.00x (ISBN 0-521-29893-8). Cambridge U Pr.

Condon, Edward U. & Shortley, George H. Theory of Atomic Spectra. (Orig.). 1935. pap. 24.95x (ISBN 0-521-09209-4, 209). Cambridge U Pr.

Condon, John C. InterAct: Mexico-United States. Renwick, George W., ed. LC 80-83092. (Country Orientation Ser.). 80p. 1980. pap. text ed. 10.00 (ISBN 0-933662-13-0). Intercult Pr.

Condon, John C. & Yousef, Fathi S. An Introduction to Intercultural Communication. LC 74-14633. (No. 19). 326p. 1975. 7.50 (ISBN 0-672-61328-X, SC19). Bobbs.

Condon, Lorna, ed. see Harrison, Richard J.

Condon, Lorna, ed. see Hencken, Hugh.

Condon, Lorna, ed. see Linares, Olga F. & Ranere, Anthony J.

Condon, Lorna, ed. see Phillips, Philip & Brown, James A.

Condon, Lorna, ed. see Vogt, Evon.

Condon, Lorna, ed. see Von Euw, Eric.

Condon, Richard. Money Is Love. 320p. 1976. pap. 1.95 o.p. (ISBN 0-345-24971-2). Ballantine.

--The Whisper of the Axe. Date not set. pap. 2.25 (ISBN 0-345-28296-5). Ballantine.

Condon, Robert. Data Processing with Applications. abr. ed. 1981. pap. text ed. 12.95 (ISBN 0-8359-1259-0); instr's. manual free (ISBN 0-8359-1260-4). Reston.

Condon, Robert J. Data Processing Systems Analysis & Design. 2nd ed. (Illus.). 1978. ref. ed. 17.95 (ISBN 0-8359-1251-5); instrs'. manual avail. Reston.

--Data Processing with Applications. (Illus.). 1978. text ed. 15.95 (ISBN 0-87909-181-9); students manual avail. Reston.

Condorcet, Marie J. Essai sur l'Application de l'Analyse aux Probabilites des Decisions Rendues a la Pluralite des Voix. LC 75-113124. 495p. (Fr.). 1973. Repr. of 1785 ed. 27.50 (ISBN 0-8284-0252-3). Chelsea Pub.

Condry, William. Pathway to the Wild. (Illus.). 1975. 13.95 (ISBN 0-571-09934-3, Pub. by Faber & Faber). Merrimack Bk Serv.

Cone, Arthur L., Jr. Complete Guide to Hunting. LC 70-119124. (Illus.). 1970. 6.95 o.s.i. (ISBN 0-02-527270-5). Macmillan.

--Fishing Made Easy. (Illus.). 1968. 6.95 o.s.i. (ISBN 0-02-526270-X). Macmillan.

Cone, Edward T. The Composer's Voice. (Illus.). 1974. 16.95x (ISBN 0-520-02508-3). U of Cal Pr.

Cone, Edward T., ed. see Berlioz, Hector.

Cone, James. God of the Oppressed. 1978. pap. 4.95 (ISBN 0-8164-2607-4). Crossroad NY.

Cone, James H. Black Theology & Black Power. LC 70-76462. (Orig.). 1969. pap. 3.95 (ISBN 0-8164-2003-3, SP59). Crossroad NY.

--Black Theology of Liberation. LC 74-120333. 1970. pap. 4.50 (ISBN 0-397-10098-1). Lippincott.

--The Spirituals & the Blues. pap. 3.95 (ISBN 0-8164-2073-4, SP74). Crossroad NY.

Cone, Joan. Fish & Game Cooking. 1981. 10.95 o.p. (ISBN 0-914440-46-2); pap. 7.95 (ISBN 0-914440-45-4). EPM Pubns.

Cone, John D. & Hayes, Steven C. Environmental Problems - Behavioral Solutions. LC 80-12471. (Environment & Behavior Ser.). 280p. (Orig.). 1980. pap. text ed. 8.95 (ISBN 0-8185-0392-0). Brooks-Cole.

Cone, Mary. Fletcher Without Beaumont: A Study of the Independent Plays of John Fletcher. (Salzburg Studies in English Literature, Jacobean Drama Studies: No. 60). 1976. pap. 25.00x (ISBN 0-391-01348-3). Humanities.

Cone, Molly. About Belonging. (Shema Storybooks: No. 3). (Illus.). 64p. (Orig.). (gr. 1-2). 1972. pap. 5.00 (ISBN 0-8074-0125-0, 101083). UAHC.

--About God. (Shema Storybooks: No. 4). (Illus.). 64p. (gr. 1-2). 1973. pap. 5.00 (ISBN 0-8074-0126-9, 101084). UAHC.

--About Learning. (Shema Primary Ser: No. 2). (Illus., Orig.). (gr. 1). 1972. pap. 5.00 (ISBN 0-8074-0127-7, 101082). UAHC.

--The Amazing Memory of Harvey Bean. (gr. 3-6). 1980. 5.95 (ISBN 0-395-29181-X). HM.

--First I Say the Shema. (Shema Primary Ser: No. 1). (Illus., Orig.). (gr. 1). 1971. pap. text ed. 5.00 (ISBN 0-8074-0134-X, 101081). UAHC.

--Jewish New Year. LC 66-10056. (Holiday Ser.). (Illus.). (gr. k-3). 1966. PLB 7.89 (ISBN 0-690-46041-4, TYC-J). T Y Crowell.

--Mishmash. (Illus.). (gr. 3-5). 1971. pap. 1.50 (ISBN 0-671-56083-2). PB.

--Mishmash & the Robot. (gr. 2-5). 1981. 6.95 (ISBN 0-395-30345-1). HM.

--Mishmash & the Sauerkraut Mystery. (Illus.). (gr. 3-5). 1979. pap. 1.50 (ISBN 0-671-29935-2). PB.

--Mishmash & the Venus Flytrap. (Illus.). (gr. 3-5). 1979. pap. 1.50 (ISBN 0-671-29936-0). PB.

--Mishmash & Uncle Looey. (Illus.). (gr. 3-5). 1979. pap. 1.50 (ISBN 0-671-29937-9). PB.

--Purim. LC 67-10071. (Holiday Ser.). (Illus.). (gr. k-3). 1967. PLB 7.89 (ISBN 0-690-65922-9, TYC-J). T Y Crowell.

--Ringling Brothers. LC 70-132295. (Biography Ser). (Illus.). (gr. 2-5). 1971. 7.95 (ISBN 0-690-70287-6, TYC-J); PLB 7.89 (ISBN 0-690-70288-4). T Y Crowell.

--Who Knows Ten: Children's Tales of the Ten Commandments. LC 65-24639. (Illus.). (gr. 3-5). 1968. text ed. 5.00 (ISBN 0-8074-0080-7, 102551); record 5.95 (ISBN 0-8074-0081-5, 102552). UAHC.

Cone, Nancy, ed. see Zepke, Brent E.

Cone, Paul. Executive Decision Making Through Simulation. 2nd ed. LC 79-165985. pap. text ed. 9.95x (ISBN 0-675-09762-2). Merrill.

Cone, Polly, ed. The Imperial Style: Fashions of the Hapsburg Era. (Illus.). 168p. 1980. 25.00 (ISBN 0-87099-232-5). Metro Mus Art.

Cone, Richard A. & Dowling, John E., eds. Membrane Transduction Mechanisms. LC 78-65280. (Society of General Physiologists Ser.). 1979. text ed. 29.00 (ISBN 0-89004-236-5). Raven.

Cone, Thomas E., Jr. History of American Pediatrics. 1980. 18.95 (ISBN 0-316-15289-7). Little.

Cone, Thomas E., Jr., ed. see Children's Hospital Medical Center, Boston.

Cone, William F. Supervising Employees Effectively. (Illus.). 180p. 1974. 8.95 (ISBN 0-201-01154-9). A-W.

Coney, Peter J. see Crittenden, Max D., Jr., et al.

Confalonieri, Giulio. Prigionia Di un Artistaa: Il Romanzo Di Luigi Cherubini, 2 vols. LC 80-2267. 1981. Repr. of 1948 ed. 78.00 (ISBN 0-404-18820-6). AMS Pr.

Conference at Dumbarton Oaks, October 18 & 19, 1975. Pre-Columbian Metallurgy of South-America: Proceedings. Benson, Elizabeth P., ed. LC 79-49261. (Illus.). 107p. 1979. 11.00 (ISBN 0-88402-094-0, Ctr Pre-Columbian). Dumbarton Oaks.

Conference Board. Challenge to Leadership: Managing in a Changing World. LC 73-1861. (Orig.). 1973. pap. 5.95 (ISBN 0-02-906570-4). Free Pr.

Conference Held at Jackson Laboratory, Bar Harbor, Maine, Sept. 1976. Genetic Effects on Aging: Proceedings. Harrison, David E. & Bergsma, Daniel, eds. LC 77-20249. (Birth Defects Original Article Ser.: Vol. 14, No. 1). 550p. 1978. 58.00x (ISBN 0-8451-1016-0). A R Liss.

Conference of Economic Staff, jt. auth. see Keyserling, Leon H.

Conference of National Social Science Councils & Analogous Bodies. International Directory of Social Science Research Councils & Analogous Bodies 1978-79. 1979. pap. 22.00 (ISBN 0-89664-149-X, Pub. by K G Saur). Gale.

Conference of Socialist Economists, ed. Microelectronics: Capitalist Technology & the Working Class. (Illus.). 152p. 1981. text ed. write for info. (ISBN 0-906336-16-3); pap. text ed. write for info. (ISBN 0-906336-17-1). Humanities.

Conference on Applied Physical Chemistry, 2nd, Veszprem, Hungary, 1971. Proceedings, 2 vols. Buzas, I., ed. LC 73-155062. (Illus.). 1500p. 1971. Set. 32.50x (ISBN 0-8002-1841-8). Intl Pubns Serv.

Conference on Civil & Human Rights in Education, 11th. Student Displacement-Exclusion: Violations of Civil & Human Rights. LC 73-9751. 64p. 1973. pap. 1.50 (ISBN 0-8106-0543-0). NEA.

Conference on Computer in the Undergraduate Curricula, Second Annual, 1971. Proceedings. LC 79-165540. 1971. pap. 15.00 (ISBN 0-87451-084-8). U Pr of New Eng.

Conference on Confidentiality of Health Records, Key Biscayne, Fla., Nov. 6-9, 1974. Confidentiality: Report of the Conference on Confidentiality of Health Records. Springarn, Natalie D., ed. 58p. 1975. pap. 2.00 (ISBN 0-685-63944-4, P175-0). Am Psychiatric.

Conference on Electrical Insulation & Dielectric Phenomena. Annual Report. Incl. 1952. 61p. 3.00 (ISBN 0-309-00020-3); 1957. 69p. 3.00 (ISBN 0-309-00570-1); 1958. 57p. 3.00 (ISBN 0-686-64608-8); 1963. 144p. 5.00 (ISBN 0-309-01141-8); 1964. 146p. 5.00 (ISBN 0-309-01238-4); 1965. 139p. 5.00 (ISBN 0-686-64609-6); 1966. 129p. 10.00 (ISBN 0-309-01484-0); 1967. 201p. 10.00 (ISBN 0-309-01578-2); 1968. 204p. 10.00 (ISBN 0-309-01705-X); 1969. 193p. 15.00 (ISBN 0-309-01764-5); 1970. 258p. 15.00 (ISBN 0-309-01870-6); 1971. 289p. 15.00 (ISBN 0-309-02032-8); 1972. 496p. 20.00 (ISBN 0-309-02112-X); 1973. 638p. 25.00 (ISBN 0-309-02229-0); 1974. 706p. 25.00 (ISBN 0-309-02416-1); 1975. 544p. 22.00 (ISBN 0-686-64610-X); 1976. 576p. 25.00 (ISBN 0-686-64611-8); 1977. 596p. 25.00 (ISBN 0-309-02866-3); 1978. 405p. 25.00 (ISBN 0-309-02861-2); 1979. 25.00 (ISBN 0-309-02933-3). Natl Acad Pr.

--Digest of Literature on Dielectrics, Vols. 11-13, 18-42. Incl. Vol. 11. 1947. 5.00 (ISBN 0-309-00013-0); Vol. 12. 1948. 5.00 (ISBN 0-309-00014-9); Vol. 13. 1949. 5.00 (ISBN 0-309-00015-7); Vol. 18. 1954. 5.00 (ISBN 0-309-00383-0); Vol. 19. 1955. 5.00 (ISBN 0-309-00503-5); Vol. 20. 1956. 5.00 (ISBN 0-309-00562-0); Vol. 21. 1957. 5.00 (ISBN 0-309-00599-X); Vol. 22. 1958. 5.00 (ISBN 0-309-00713-5); Vol. 24. 1960. 10.00 (ISBN 0-309-00917-0); Vol. 25. 1961. 15.00 (ISBN 0-309-01034-9); Vol. 26. 1962. 15.00 (ISBN 0-309-01139-6); Vol. 27. 1963. 15.00 (ISBN 0-309-01230-9); Vol. 28. 1964. 27.00 (ISBN 0-309-01342-9); Vol. 29. 1965. 27.00 (ISBN 0-309-01461-1); Vol. 30. 1966. 27.00 (ISBN 0-309-01496-4); Vol. 31. 1967. 27.00 (ISBN 0-309-01595-2); Vol. 32. 1968. 35.00 (ISBN 0-309-01732-7); Vol. 33. 1969. 35.00 (ISBN 0-309-01856-0); Vol. 34. 1970. 35.00 (ISBN 0-309-01920-6); Vol. 35. 1971. 40.00 (ISBN 0-309-02049-2); Vol. 36. 1972. 40.00 (ISBN 0-309-02316-5); Vol. 37. 1973. 40.00 (ISBN 0-309-02437-4); Vol. 38, 1974. 40.00 (ISBN 0-686-66646-1); Vol. 39, 1975. 45.00 (ISBN 0-309-02748-9); Vol. 40, 1976. 45.00 (ISBN 0-309-02787-X); Vol. 41, 1979. 45.00 (ISBN 0-309-02886-8); Vol. 42, 1979. 45.00 (ISBN 0-309-02934-1). Natl Acad Pr.

--Digest of Literature on Dielectrics, Vols. 38-42. 1977. Vol. 38, 1977. 40.00 (ISBN 0-309-02643-1); Vol. 39. 1978 45.00 (ISBN 0-309-02748-9); Vol. 40. 1978 45.00 (ISBN 0-309-02787-X); Vol. 41, 1979. 45.00 (ISBN 0-309-02886-8); Vol. 42, 1979. 45.00 (ISBN 0-309-02934-1). Natl Acad Pr.

Conference on Graduate Psychiatric Education, 1962. Training the Psychiatrist to Meet Changing Needs. 1963. 3.00 o.p. (ISBN 0-685-24853-4, 150). Am Psychiatric.

Conference on Indo-European Studies, U. of Texas, Austin, Feb. 4-5, 1980. The Indo-Europeans in the Fourth & Third Millennia: Proceedings. Polome, Edgar C., ed. (Linguistica Extranea: Studia: No. 14). (Illus.). 245p. 1981. text ed. 21.50 (ISBN 0-89720-041-1). Karoma.

Conference on Mathematical Programming, 3rd, Matrafured, Hungary, 1975. Studies on Mathematical Programming: Proceedings. Prekopa, A., ed. (Mathematical Methods of Operations Research). 200p. 1980. 22.50x (ISBN 963-05-1854-6). Intl Pubns Serv.

Conference on Non-Fossil Fuel & Non-Nuclear Fuel Energy Strategies, Honolulu, USS, January 1979. Renewable Energy Prospects: Proceedings. Bach, W., et al, eds. 340p. 1980. 57.50 (ISBN 0-08-024252-9). Pergamon.

Conference on Psychiatry & Medical Education, Atlanta, 1967. Psychiatry & Medical Education Two. 1969. pap. 4.00 o.p. (ISBN 0-685-24857-7, 180). Am Psychiatric.

--Teaching Psychiatry in Medical School: Proceedings. 589p. 1969. pap. 5.00 o.p. (ISBN 0-685-65581-4, 213). Am Psychiatric.

Conference on Recombinant DNA, Committee on Genetic Experimentation (COGENE) & the Royal Society of London, Wye College, Kent, UK, April, 1979. Recombinant DNA & Genetic Experimentation: Proceedings. Morgan, Joan & Whelan, W. J., eds. LC 79-40962. (Illus.). 334p. 1979. 61.00 (ISBN 0-08-024427-0). Pergamon.

Conference On Science - Philosophy And Religion - 7th Symposium. Conflicts of Power in Modern Culture. Bryson, L., et al, eds. 703p. 1964. Repr. of 1947 ed. 35.00x (ISBN 0-8154-0037-3). Cooper Sq.

Conference On Science - Philosophy And Religion - 14th Symposium. Symbols & Society. Bryson, L., et al, eds. 1964. Repr. of 1955 ed. 19.50x (ISBN 0-8154-0039-X). Cooper Sq.

Conference On Science - Philosophy And Religion - 13th Symposium. Symbols & Values. Bryson, L., et al, eds. 1964. Repr. of 1954 ed. 35.00x (ISBN 0-8154-0038-1). Cooper Sq.

Conference on Space Science & Space Law. Proceedings. Schwartz, Mortimer D., ed. (Illus.). 176p. 1964. pap. text ed. 6.75x (ISBN 0-8377-1100-2). Rothman.

Conference On The Use Of Orbiting Spacecraft In Geographic Research - Houston - Tex 1965. Spacecraft in Geographic Research. 1966. pap. 4.00 o.p. (ISBN 0-309-01353-4). Natl Acad Pr.

Conference on Training in Child Psychiatry, 1963. Career Training in Child Psychiatry. 1964. 3.00 o.p. (ISBN 0-685-24854-2, 161). Am Psychiatric.

Conference Sponsored by ASCE Construction Division, May 1980, San Francisco, CA. Social & Economic Impact of Earthquakes on Utility Lifelines: Proceedings. Isenberg, J., ed. LC 80-69153. 250p. pap. text ed. 21.00 (ISBN 0-87262-254-1). Am Soc Civil Eng.

Conference Sponsored by National Foundation-March of Dimes, Key Biscayne, Florida, Nov. 1975. Iron Metabolism & Thalassemia: Proceedings. Bergsma, Daniel, et al, eds. LC 76-25835. (Birth Defects Original Article Ser.: Vol. 12, No. 8). 212p. 1976. 26.00x (ISBN 0-8451-1006-3). A R Liss.

Conferences on Brain & Behavior, los Angeles. Brain & Behavior: Proceedings, 2 vols. Brazier, M. A., ed. Incl. Vol. 1. Brain & Behavior. First Conference, 1961; Vol. 2. The Internal Environment & Alimentary Behavior. Second Conference, 1962. 7.75 ea. Lubrecht & Cramer.

Confod, Ellen. Luck of Pokey Bloom. (gr. 4-6). 1977. pap. 1.25 (ISBN 0-671-29841-0). PB.

Conford, Ellen. Alfred G. Graebner Memorial High School Handbook of Rules & Regulations: A Novel. (YA) (gr. 7-9). 1977. pap. 1.75 (ISBN 0-671-56043-3). PB.

--And This Is Laura. (gr. 5-7). 1980. pap. 1.75 (ISBN 0-671-56077-8). PB.

--Anything for a Friend. 1981. pap. 1.95 (ISBN 0-671-56069-7). Archway.

--Dreams of Victory. (Illus.). 144p. (gr. 4-6). 1973. 7.95 (ISBN 0-316-15294-3). Little.

--Felicia the Critic. (Illus.). (gr. 4-6). 1978. pap. 1.25 (ISBN 0-671-29883-6). PB.

--Felicia, the Critic. (gr. 4-6). 1978. pap. 1.75 (ISBN 0-671-42061-5). Archway.

--Hail, Hail Camp Timberwood. (Illus.). (gr. 4-6). 1980. pap. 1.75 (ISBN 0-671-56066-2). PB.

--Hail, Hail, Camp Timberwood. (Illus.). (gr. 4-6). 1980. pap. 1.95 (ISBN 0-671-42685-0). Archway.

--Just the Thing for Geraldine. (Illus.). 32p. (gr. 1-3). 1974. 7.95 (ISBN 0-316-15304-4). Little.

--The Luck of Pokey Bloom. (Illus.). 144p. (gr. 4-6). 1975. 7.95 (ISBN 0-316-15305-2). Little.

--The Luck of Pokey Bloom. (gr. 4-6). 1977. 1.75 (ISBN 0-671-41895-5). Archway.

--Me & the Terrible Two. (gr. 4-6). 1977. pap. 1.75 (ISBN 0-671-41769-X). Archway.

--Seven Days to a Brand-New Me. 96p. (gr. 5 up). 1981. 7.95 (ISBN 0-316-15311-7). Little.

Conforti, Joseph. Samuel Hopkins & the New Divinity Movement: Calvinism, the Congregational Ministry, & Reform in New England Between the Great Awakenings. 240p. (Orig.). 1981. pap. 12.95 (ISBN 0-8028-1871-4). Eerdmans.

Confucius. Sayings of Confucius. Ware, James R., tr. (Orig.). pap. 1.50 (ISBN 0-451-61885-8, MW1885, Ment). NAL.

Congar, Yves M. J. Catholic Church & the Race Question. 1966. pap. 2.50 (ISBN 92-3-100415-8, U68, UNESCO). Unipub.

Congdon, Kirby. Contemporary Poets in American Anthologies 1960-1977. LC 78-13772. 1978. 12.00 (ISBN 0-8108-1168-5). Scarecrow.

Congdon, S. Perry, 2nd. The Drama Reader: Full-Length Plays for the Secondary School. LC 62-13409. 1962. text ed. 4.40 o.p. (ISBN 0-672-73248-3); pap. text ed. 4.95 (ISBN 0-672-73220-3). Odyssey Pr.

Conger, Arthur L., ed. see De Purucker, G.

Conger, John. Adolescence: Generation Under Pressure. (Life Cycle Ser.). 1979. pap. text ed. write for info. (ISBN 0-06-384744-2, HarpC). Har-Row.

Conger, John J. Adolescence & Youth: Psychological Development in a Changing World. 2nd ed. (Illus.). 1977. text ed. 20.50 scp (ISBN 0-06-041362-X, HarpC). Har-Row.

--Contemporary Issues in Adolescent Development. 522p. 1975. pap. text ed. 11.50 scp (ISBN 0-06-041363-8, HarpC). Har-Row.

Conger, Shirley & Moore, Kay. Social Work in Long-Term Care Facilities. 160p. 1981. 15.95 (ISBN 0-8436-0850-1). CBI Pub.

Conger, Syndy M. Mathew G. Lewis, Charles Robert Maturin & the Germans: An Interpretive Study of the Influence of German Literature on Two Gothic Novels. (Salzburg Studies in English Literature, Romantic Reassessment: No. 67). 1977. pap. text ed. 25.00x (ISBN 0-391-01349-1). Humanities.

--Matthew G. Lewis, Charles Robert Maturin & the Germans: An Interpretative Study of the Influence of German Literature on Two Gothic Novels. Varma, Devendra P., ed. LC 79-8448. (Gothic Studies & Dissertations Ser.). 1980. Repr. of 1977 ed. lib. bdg. 28.00x (ISBN 0-405-12652-2). Arno.

Conger, Syndy M. & Welsch, Janice R., eds. Narrative Strategies: Original Essays in Film & Prose Fiction. (Essays in Literature Ser.: Bk. 4). 140p. (Orig.). 1981. pap. 8.00x (ISBN 0-934312-03-6). Western Ill Univ.

Congleton, Carol A. Navigational Applications of Plane & Spherical Trigonometry. LC 79-9431. (Illus.). 1980. pap. 8.50x (ISBN 0-87033-256-2). Cornell Maritime.

Congress, Elaine, jt. auth. see Pietropinto, Anthony.

Congress of the International Economic Association, 4th, Budapest, Hungary. Economic Integration: Worldwide, Regional, Sectoral: Proceedings. Machlup, Fritz, ed. LC 76-10281. 1977. 39.95 (ISBN 0-470-01381-8). Halsted Pr.

Congress of the U. S., Office of Technology Assessment. Nuclear Proliferation & Safeguards. LC 77-60024. (Praeger Special Studies). 1977. 29.95 (ISBN 0-03-041601-9). Praeger.

Congressional Information Service. CIS U.S. Congressional Committee Prints Index, 5 vols. 3172p. 1980. lib. bdg. 1475.00 (ISBN 0-912380-57-8). Cong Info.

Congressional Quarterley Staff. Congressional Ethics. 2nd ed. 220p. (Orig.). 1980. pap. text ed. 7.95 (ISBN 0-87187-154-8). Congr Quarterly.

Congressional Quarterly. Elections '80. Congressional Quarterly, ed. 250p. 1980. pap. text ed. 6.95 (ISBN 0-87187-199-8). Congr Quarterly.

--Health Policy. Congressional Quarterly, ed. 220p. 1980. pap. text ed. 6.95 (ISBN 0-87187-199-8). Congr Quarterly.

--Historic Documents: Nineteen Seventy-Nine. Congressional Quarterly, ed. 1000p. 1980. 44.00 (ISBN 0-87187-197-1). Congr Quarterly.

--Inside Congress. 2nd ed. 1979. pap. text ed. 7.95 (ISBN 0-87187-177-7). Congr Quarterly.

--Middle East: U. S. Policy, Israel, Oil & the Arabs. 4th ed. 1979. pap. text ed. 7.95 (ISBN 0-87187-176-9). Congr Quarterly.

--Spring Guide to Current American Government 1980. (Guide to Current American Government Ser.). 1979. pap. 6.95 (ISBN 0-87187-179-3). Congr Quarterly.

--Washington Lobby. 3rd ed. 1979. pap. text ed. 6.95 (ISBN 0-87187-178-5). Congr Quarterly.

Congressional Quarterly, ed. Defense Policy. 2nd ed. 200p. 1980. pap. text ed. 7.95 (ISBN 0-87187-158-0). Congr Quarterly.

--Politics in America. 1979. pap. text ed. 7.25 (ISBN 0-87187-148-3). Congr Quarterly.

Congressional Quarterly Inc. Candidates Nineteen Eighty. 1980. pap. text ed. 6.95 (ISBN 0-87187-190-4). Congr Quarterly.

--Congressional Quarterly Almanac, 1979. (Almanac Ser.). 1980. 82.00 (ISBN 0-87187-192-0). Congr Quarterly.

--Federal Regulatory Directory Nineteen Eighty to Eighty One. Congressional Quarterly Inc., ed. 931p. 1980. pap. text ed. 25.00 (ISBN 0-87187-153-X). Congr Quarterly.

--Guide to Current American Government Fall Nineteen Eighty. Congressional Quarterly Inc., ed. 190p. 1980. pap. text ed. 6.95 (ISBN 0-87187-151-3). Congr Quarterly.

--Nineteen Seventy Nine Guide to Current Amerian Government. 1979. pap. text ed. cancelled o.p. (ISBN 0-87187-175-0). Congr Quarterly.

--President Carter Nineteen Seventy Nine. Congressional Quarterly Inc., ed. (Presidency Ser.). 240p. 1980. pap. text ed. 7.95 (ISBN 0-87187-150-5). Congr Quarterly.

--Roll Call 1979. (Roll Call Ser.). 1980. pap. text ed. 12.00 (ISBN 0-87187-191-2). Congr Quarterly.

--Washington Information Directory Nineteen Eighty to Eighty One. Congressional Quarterly Inc., ed. 931p. 1980. pap. text ed. 25.00 (ISBN 0-87187-152-1). Congr Quarterly.

Congressional Quarterly Inc., ed. China. (Orig.). 1980. pap. text ed. 10.95 (ISBN 0-87187-188-2). Congr Quarterly.

Congressional Quarterly Staff. Guide to Current American Government: Spring 1981 Edition. 160p. 1980. pap. text ed. 6.95 (ISBN 0-87187-159-9). Congr Quarterly.

--Supreme Court & Individual Rights. Congressional Quarterly Staff, ed. 310p. (Orig.). 1980. pap. text ed. 6.95 (ISBN 0-87187-195-5). Congr Quarterly.

Congreve, William. Amendments of Mr. Collier's False & Imperfect Citations: From the Old Batchelour, Double Dealer, Love for Love, Mourning Bride, Vol. 23. LC 73-170439. (The English Stage Ser.). lib. bdg. 50.00 (ISBN 0-8240-0606-2). Garland Pub.

--Love for Love. Avery, Emmett L., ed. LC 66-20827. (Regents Restoration Drama Ser). 1966. 9.25x (ISBN 0-8032-0353-5); pap. 3.95x (ISBN 0-8032-5353-2, BB 259, Bison). U of Nebr Pr.

--Way of the World. Lynch, Kathleen M., ed. LC 65-10543. (Regents Restoration Drama Ser). 1965. 8.95x (ISBN 0-8032-0354-3); pap. 2.75x (ISBN 0-8032-5354-0, BB 251, Bison). U of Nebr Pr.

Coniaris, A. M. Christ's Comfort for Those Who Sorrow. 1978. pap. 2.95 (ISBN 0-937032-00-X). Light & Life Pub Co MN.

--Eighty Talks for Orthodox Young People. 1975. pap. 3.50 (ISBN 0-937032-16-6). Light&Life Pub Co MN.

--The Great I Came's of Jesus. 1980. pap. 5.95 (ISBN 0-686-27069-X). Light&Life Pub Co MN.

--Making God Real in the Orthodox Christian Home. 1977. pap. 4.95 (ISBN 0-937032-07-7). Light & Life Pub Co MN.

--No Man Ever Spoke As This Man. 1969. pap. 3.50 (ISBN 0-937032-18-2). Light&Life Pub Co MN.

--Orthodoxy: A Creed for Today. 1972. pap. 5.95 (ISBN 0-937032-19-0). Light&Life Pub Co MN.

--Sermons on the Major Holy Days of the Orthodox Church. 1978. pap. 4.95 (ISBN 0-937032-03-4). Light & Life Pub Co MN.

--Sixty-One Talks for Orthodox Funerals. 1969. pap. 4.95 (ISBN 0-937032-02-6). Light & Life Pub Co MN.

--These Are the Sacraments. 1981. pap. 5.95 (ISBN 0-686-69400-7). Light & Life.

--Treasures from Paul's Letters, Vol. I. 1978. pap. 5.95 (ISBN 0-937032-05-0). Light & Life Pub Co MN.

--Treasures from Paul's Letters, Vol. II. 1979. pap. 5.95 (ISBN 0-937032-06-9). Light & Life Pub Co MN.

Coninx, Raymond G. Foreign Exchange Dealer's Manual. 168p. 1980. 30.00x (ISBN 0-85941-152-4, Pub. by Woodhead-Faulkner England). State Mutual Bk.

--Foreign Exchange Today. rev. ed. 167p. 1980. 19.95 (ISBN 0-470-27025-X, Pub. by Halsted Pr). Wiley.

--Foreign Exchange Today. LC 77-11932. 1978. 19.95 (ISBN 0-470-99315-4). Halsted Pr.

Conkin, Paul K. Prophets of Prosperity. LC 79-3251. 352p. 1980. 25.00 (ISBN 0-253-30843-7). Ind U Pr.

Conkin, Paul K. & Stromberg, Roland N. The Heritage & Challenge of History. 1971. pap. text ed. 9.50 scp (ISBN 0-06-041342-5, HarpC). Har-Row.

Conklin, Gladys. Fairy Rings & Other Mushrooms. LC 73-76799. (Illus.). (gr. k-3). 1973. PLB 4.95 (ISBN 0-8234-0223-1). Holiday.

--Lucky Ladybugs. (Illus.). (gr. k-3). 1968. reinforced bdg. 7.95 (ISBN 0-8234-0072-7). Holiday.

Conklin, Groff, ed. Science Fiction Thinking Machines. LC 54-6995. 1954. 8.95 (ISBN 0-8149-0040-2). Vanguard.

--Supernatural Reader. 1962. pap. 1.50 o.s.i. (ISBN 0-02-019110-3, Collier). Macmillan.

--Thirteen Great Stories of Science Fiction. 1979. pap. 1.50 o.p. (ISBN 0-449-14228-0, GM). Fawcett.

Conklin, Groff, jt. ed. see Asimov, Isaac.

Conklin, Harold C. Ethnographic Atlas of Ifugao. LC 79-689774. (Illus.). 124p. 1980. text ed. 75.00x (ISBN 0-300-02529-7). Yale U Pr.
--Folk Classification: A Topically Arranged Bibliography of Contemporary & Background References Through 1971. LC 72-9400. 501p. 1972. pap. 4.00 o.p. (ISBN 0-913516-01-5). Yale U Anthro.
--Hanunoo Agriculture: A Report on an Integral System of Shifting Cultivation in the Phillipines Fao Forestry Development Paper No. 12. LC 75-28745. (Illus.). 209p. 1975. text ed. 14.50x scholars (ISBN 0-911830-22-7); pap. 24.50x institutions (ISBN 0-685-69785-1). Elliots Bks.
--Ifugao Bibliography. (Bibliography: No. 11). vi, 75p. 1980. 4.00 (ISBN 0-686-63731-3). Yale U Pr.
Conklin, John. Illegal but Not Criminal: Business Crime in America. LC 77-7621. 1977. 8.95 o.p. (ISBN 0-13-450890-4); pap. 3.95 o.p. (ISBN 0-13-450882-3). P-H.
Conklin, Mike. Inside Football. 1978. 9.95 o.p. (ISBN 0-685-25150-0); pap. 5.95 (ISBN 0-8092-7585-6). Contemp Bks.
Conklin, Mike, jt. auth. see Zolna, Ed.
Conklin, Paul. Michael of Wales. LC 76-53431. (gr. 4-7). 1977. 5.95 (ISBN 0-396-07415-4). Dodd.
--Tomorrow a New World. (FDR & the Era of the New Deal Ser.). 1976. Repr. of 1959 ed. lib. bdg. 32.50 (ISBN 0-306-70805-1). Da Capo.
Conklin, William, jt. auth. see Benson, Elizabeth.
Conley, Cort & Carrey, John. The Middle Fork & the Sheepeater War. LC 80-17367. 1977. pap. 9.95 (ISBN 0-9603566-1-4). Backeddy Bks.
--River of No Return. LC 78-52373. 1978. pap. 10.95 (ISBN 0-9603566-2-2). Backeddy Bks.
Conley, Darrell. First Corinthians (Adult Workbook) pap. 1.95 (ISBN 0-89315-052-5). Lambert Bk.
Conley, Ellen A. Soho Madonna. 1980. pap. 2.25 (ISBN 0-380-75614-5, 75614). Avon.
Conley, Herbert N. Living & Dying Gracefully. LC 79-65569. 70p. 1979. 4.95 (ISBN 0-8091-0298-6). Paulist Pr.
Conley, J., jt. auth. see Moldaver, J.
Conley, Lucy. Gone to the Zoo. 1979. 5.10 (ISBN 0-686-25258-6). Rod & Staff.
Conley, Patrick T. Providence: A Pictorial History. Friedman, Donna R., ed. (Illus.). 205p. 1981. pap. price not set (ISBN 0-89865-128-X). Donning Co.
Conley, Robert J. see Cherry, Richard L., et al.
Conley, William. Computer Optimization Techniques. 1980. 25.00 (ISBN 0-89433-111-6). Petrocelli.
--Optimization: A Simplified Approach. (Illus.). 272p. 1980. 20.00 (ISBN 0-89433-121-3). Petrocelli.
Conlin, Joseph R. American Anti-War Movements. (Insight Ser). 144p. (Orig.). 1968. 4.95x (ISBN 0-02-474030-6, 47403). Macmillan.
Conlin, Joseph R., ed. At the Point of Production: The Local History of the I.W.W. LC 80-1708. (Contributions in Labor History Ser.: No. 10). 328p. 1981. lib. bdg. 29.95 (ISBN 0-313-22046-8, CPP/). Greenwood.
Conlin, Mary Lou. Concepts of Communication: Reading, Ideas Module, Inferences Module. LC 77-78895. (Illus.). 1977. pap. text ed. 9.95 (ISBN 0-395-25492-2); instrs'. guide 0.65 (ISBN 0-395-25493-0). HM.
--Concepts of Communication: Reading Vocabulary Module. LC 77-78866. (Illus.). 1977. pap. text ed. 7.75 (ISBN 0-395-25494-9). HM.
--Concepts of Communication: Writing: Summary, Paragraph, Essay-Test, Theme Modules. 2nd ed. LC 79-49830. 1980. pap. text ed. 9.95 (ISBN 0-395-28735-9); inst. man. 1.00 (ISBN 0-395-28485-6). HM.
--Concepts of Communication: Writing: Writing Skills Module. 2nd ed. LC 79-49830. 1980. pap. text ed. 10.95 (ISBN 0-395-28484-8); instrs'. manual avail. (ISBN 0-395-28485-6). HM.
Conlon, Frank F. A Caste in a Changing World: The Chitrapur Saraswat Brahmans, 1700-1935. LC 75-7192. 1977. 20.00x (ISBN 0-520-02998-4). U of Cal Pr.
Conlon, Kathleen. A Forgotten Season. 177p. 1981. 9.95 (ISBN 0-312-29899-4). St Martin.
Conlon, V. M. Camera Techniques in Archaeology. LC 73-82631. (Illus.). 112p. 1973. 19.95 (ISBN 0-312-11445-1). St Martin.
Conn, Charles P. Julian Carroll of Kentucky. (Illus.). 1977. 5.95 o.p. (ISBN 0-8007-0838-5). Revell.
Conn, Charles P. & Miller, Barbara. Kathy. 1981. pap. 2.50 (ISBN 0-425-04825-X). Berkley Pub.
Conn, Charles P., jt. auth. see DeVos, Richard M.
Conn, Charles W. The Anatomy of Evil. 1981. 7.95 (ISBN 0-8007-1177-7). Revell.
--A Certain Journey. 152p. 1965. 2.95 (ISBN 0-87148-000-X); pap. 2.25 (ISBN 0-87148-001-8). Pathway Pr.
--The Evangel Reader. 1958. 3.25 (ISBN 0-87148-275-4). Pathway Pr.
--Highlights of Hebrew History. 1975. 4.50 (ISBN 0-87148-402-1); pap. 3.50 (ISBN 0-87148-401-3); instrs. guide 4.50 (ISBN 0-87148-834-5). Pathway Pr.
--Why Men Go Back. 1966. 5.95 (ISBN 0-87148-902-3). Pathway Pr.
Conn, Eric E. & Stumpf, P. K. Outlines of Biochemistry. 4th ed. LC 75-34288. 1976. text ed. 25.95 (ISBN 0-471-16843-2). Wiley.
Conn, George H. Horse Selection & Care for Beginners. pap. 4.00 (ISBN 0-87980-193-X). Wilshire.
Conn, Harry. Four Trojan Horses. 1978. pap. cancelled o.s.i. (ISBN 0-89728-031-8, 700212). Omega Pubns OR.
Conn, Herb & Conn, Jan. The Jewel Cave Adventure: Fifty Miles of Discovery Under South Dakota. (Speleologia Ser.). (Illus.). 240p. 1977. 12.95 o.s.i. (ISBN 0-914264-19-2, Dist. by Caroline Hse); pap. 6.95 o.s.i. (ISBN 0-914264-20-6). Zephyrus Pr.
Conn, Howard, ed. Current Therapy 1981. (Illus.). 1100p. 1981. pap. write for info. (ISBN 0-7216-2709-9). Saunders.
Conn, Howard F. & Conn, Rex B., Jr. Current Diagnosis Six. (Illus.). 1424p. 1980. text ed. 48.00 (ISBN 0-7216-2707-2). Saunders.
Conn, Howard F. & Conn, Rex B., eds. Current Diagnosis - 5. LC 66-15617. (Illus.). 1977. text ed. 35.00 (ISBN 0-7216-2674-2). Saunders.
Conn, Jack F. Non-Abelian Minimal Closed Ideals of Transitive Lie Algebras. LC 79-5479. (Mathematical Notes Ser.: 25). 216p. 1980. pap. 7.50x (ISBN 0-691-08251-0). Princeton U Pr.
Conn, Jan, jt. auth. see Conn, Herb.
Conn, Jerry D. Preston Smith: The Making of a Texas Governor. (Illus.). 173p. 8.50 (ISBN 0-8363-0078-5). Jenkins.
Conn, Martha O. Crazy to Fly. LC 77-23871. (Illus.). (gr. 4-8). 1978. 8.95 (ISBN 0-689-30616-4). Atheneum.
Conn, Rex B., jt. ed. see Conn, Howard F.
Conn, Rex B., Jr., jt. auth. see Conn, Howard F.
Conn, Robert L., jt. auth. see Bolten, Steven E.
Conn, Stewart. Ambush & Other Poems. LC 78-91030. 1970. 3.95 o.s.i. (ISBN 0-02-527300-0). Macmillan.
--The Aquarium. 1980. pap. 4.95 (ISBN 0-7145-3560-5). Riverrun NY.
Conn, Walter E. Conscience: Development & Self-Transcendence. LC 80-24043. 280p. (Orig.). 1981. pap. 11.95 (ISBN 0-89135-025-X). Religious Educ.
--Conversion: Perspectives on Personal & Social Transformation. LC 78-19079. 1978. pap. 7.95 (ISBN 0-8189-0368-6). Alba.
Connah, Graham. Three Thousand Years in Africa: Man & His Environment in the Lake Chad Region of Nigeria. LC 79-41508. (New Studies in Archaeology). (Illus.). 240p. Date not set. price not set (ISBN 0-521-22848-4). Cambridge U Pr.
Connally, Andrew M. & Hicks, Olan. Connally-Hicks Debate on Divorce & Remarriage. 1979. pap. 11.95 (ISBN 0-934916-31-4); pap. 8.95 (ISBN 0-686-23941-5). Natl Christian Pr.
Connaughton, Howard W. Craftsmen in Business: A Guide to Financial Management & Taxes. rev. ed. LC 79-64530. 73p. 1979. 7.20 (ISBN 0-88321-032-0). Am Craft.
Conneau, Theophilus. A Slaver's Log Book: Or, 20 Years' Residence in Africa. 1972. pap. 2.75 (ISBN 0-380-01773-3, 35063, Discus). Avon.
Connell, D. W. Water Pollution: Causes & Effects in Australia. 1974. 9.00x (ISBN 0-7022-0880-9); pap. 5.50x o.s.i. (ISBN 0-7022-0881-7). U of Queensland Pr.
Connell, D. W., jt. auth. see Vowles, P. D.
Connell, Donna. Teach Your Preschooler to Write. (Illus.). 132p. (Orig.). 1980. pap. 7.95 (ISBN 0-9604192-0-9). Can Do Bks.
Connell, Evan S. St. Augustine's Pigeon: The Selected Stories. Blaisdell, Gus, ed. 288p. 1980. 12.50 (ISBN 0-86547-013-8). N Point Pr.
--The White Latern. 1981. pap. 5.95 (ISBN 0-686-69130-X). HR&W.
Connell, G. Spanish Poetry of the Grupo Poetico De 1927. text ed. 13.75 (ISBN 0-08-016950-3). Pergamon.
Connell, J. H., jt. auth. see MacArthur, Robert H.
Connell, J. J. Advances in Fish Science & Technology. 77p. 1980. 100.00x (ISBN 0-686-64734-3, Pub. by Fishing News England). State Mutual Bk.
Connell, J. J., ed. Advances in Fish Science & Technology. 528p. 1980. cloth 118.50x (ISBN 0-85238-108-5, Pub. by Fishing News England). State Mutual Bk.
Connell, Maureen. Mary Lacey. LC 80-7893. 288p. 1981. 10.95 (ISBN 0-690-01950-5, HarpT). Har-Row.
Connell, Royal W., jt. auth. see Mack, William P.
Connell, W. F. A History of Education in the Twentieth Century World. 1981. text ed. 29.95x (ISBN 0-8077-8024-3). Tchrs Coll.
Connell, W. F., et al. A History of Education in Australia. 1981. write for info. (ISBN 0-686-16293-5, Pub. by Sydney U Pr). Intl Schol Bk Serv.
Connellan, Thomas K. The Brontosaurus Principle: A Manual for Corporate Survival. 1976. 12.95 o.p. (ISBN 0-685-67122-4). P-H.
--How to Improve Human Performance: Behaviorism in Business & Industry. 1978. text ed. 13.95 scp (ISBN 0-06-041349-2, HarpC). Har-Row.
Connelley, William E. see Carrigan, Minnie B.
Connell-Smith, Gordon & Lloyd, Howell A. The Relevance of History. 1972. text ed. 6.95x o.p. (ISBN 0-435-32805-0). Heinemann Ed.
Connelly, J. Campbell. A Manager's Guide to Speaking & Listening. LC 67-29357. 1967. 7.95 o.p. (ISBN 0-8144-5156-X). AM Mgmt.
Connelly, R. J. Whitehead Vs. Hartshorne: Basic Metaphysical Issues. LC 80-69053. 172p. (Orig.). 1981. lib. bdg. 17.75 (ISBN 0-8191-1420-0); pap. text ed. 9.00 (ISBN 0-8191-1421-9). U Pr of Amer.
Connelly, Thomas G., et al, eds. Morphogenesis & Pattern Formation. 325p. 1981. 29.50 (ISBN 0-89004-635-2). Raven.
Connelly, Will. The Musician's Guide to Independent Record Production. (Illus.). 1981. 12.95 (ISBN 0-8092-5969-9); pap. 6.95 (ISBN 0-8092-5968-0). Contemp Bks.
Conner, David A., jt. auth. see Vogt, Lawrence J.
Conner, J. Richard & Loehman, Edna, eds. Economics & Decision Making for Environmental Quality. LC 74-6056. 1974. pap. 4.95 (ISBN 0-8130-0508-6). U Presses Fla.
Conner, Mac, et al, illus. Cities & Suburbs. (Bowmar-Noble Social Studies Program). Orig. Title: Man & His World. (Illus.). (gr. 3). text ed. 7.86 (ISBN 0-8372-3684-3); tchrs. ed. 11.28 (ISBN 0-8372-3685-1); tests 9.30 (ISBN 0-8372-3727-0). Bowmar-Noble.
--Many Americans-One Nation. rev. ed. (Bowmar-Noble Social Studies Program). (Illus.). 469p. (gr. 5). 1979. text ed. 9.99 (ISBN 0-8372-3688-6); tchrs. ed. 12.75 (ISBN 0-8372-3689-4); tests 9.30 (ISBN 0-8372-3729-7). Bowmar-Noble.
--People & the Land. rev. ed. (Bowmar-Noble Social Studies Program). Orig. Title: Man & His World. (Illus.). 349p. (gr. 4). 1979. text ed. 7.98 (ISBN 0-686-64536-7); tchrs. ed. 11.55 (ISBN 0-8372-3687-8); test 9.00 (ISBN 0-8372-3728-9). Bowmar-Noble.
Conner, Macet Al & Contreras, Gerry, illus. You & Your Family. rev. ed. (Bowmar-Noble Social Studies Program). Orig. Title: Man & His World. (Illus.). 152p. (gr. 1). 1979. text ed. 6.24 (ISBN 0-8372-3680-0); tchrs. ed. 9.00 (ISBN 0-8372-3681-9). Bowmar-Noble.
Conner, P. E. Neumann's Problem for Differential Forms on Riemannian Manifolds. LC 52-42839. (Memoirs: No. 20). 1979. pap. 6.40 (ISBN 0-8218-1220-3, MEMO-20). Am Math.
Conner, Patrick. Oriental Architecture in the West. (Illus.). 1980. 30.00 (ISBN 0-500-34079-X). Thames Hudson.
Conner, Paul W. Poor Richard's Politicks: Benjamin Franklin & His New American Order. LC 80-21490. xiv, 285p. 1980. Repr. of 1965 ed. lib. bdg. 27.50x (ISBN 0-313-22695-4, COPRP). Greenwood.
Conner, Robert, jt. auth. see Ulrich, Heinz.
Conner, Ross F. & Huff, C. Ronald. Attorneys As Activists: Evaluating the American Bar Association's BASICS Program. LC 79-19830. (Contemporary Evaluation Research: Vol. 1). (Illus.). 263p. 1979. 18.95x (ISBN 0-8039-1363-X); pap. 9.95x (ISBN 0-8039-1364-8). Sage.
Conner, T. Doctrina Cristiana. Robleto, Adolfo, tr. Orig. Title: Christian Doctrine. 408p. (Span.). Date not set. pap. price not set (ISBN 0-311-09012-5). Casa Bautista.
Connerton, P. The Tragedy of Enlightenment. LC 79-16102. (Cambridge Studies in the History & Theory of Politics). 1980. 29.95 (ISBN 0-521-22842-5); pap. 7.95 (ISBN 0-521-29675-7). Cambridge U Pr.
Connery, Robert H., et al. Politics of Mental Health: Organizing Community Mental Health in Metropolitan Areas. LC 68-28396. (Illus.). 1968. 22.50x (ISBN 0-231-03029-0). Columbia U Pr.
Connery, Robert Howe. The Navy & the Industrial Mobilization in World War II. LC 73-166951. (FDR & the Era of the New Deal Ser). 526p. 1972. Repr. of 1951 ed. lib. bdg. 49.50 (ISBN 0-306-70322-X). Da Capo.
Connick, C. Milo. Jesus: The Man, the Mission, & the Message. 2nd ed. (Illus.). 512p. 1974. 17.95 (ISBN 0-13-509521-2). P-H.
Conniff, Michael, ed. Latin American Populism in Comparative Perspective. (Illus.). 272p. 1981. 19.95 (ISBN 0-8263-0580-6); pap. 9.95 (ISBN 0-8263-0581-4). U of NM Pr.
Conniff, Michael L. Urban Politics in Brazil: The Rise of Populism, 1925-1945. LC 80-54060. (Pitt Latin American Ser.). (Illus.). 280p. 1981. 19.95x (ISBN 0-8229-3438-8). U of Pittsburgh Pr.
Connolly, Cyril, tr. see Jarry, Alfred.
Connolly, Eileen. Tarot: A New Handbook for the Apprentice. LC 80-22271. 244p. 1980. Repr. of 1979 ed. lib. bdg. 16.95x (ISBN 0-89370-645-0). Borgo Pr.
--The Tarot: A New Handbook for the Apprentice. LC 79-15303. (Illus.). 1979. pap. 7.95 (ISBN 0-87877-045-3). Newcastle Pub.
Connolly, James M. Human History & the Word of God. 1965. 6.50 o.s.i. (ISBN 0-02-527360-4). Macmillan.
Connolly, John F., ed. DePalma's the Management of Fractures & Dislocations: An Atlas, 2 vols. 3rd ed. (Illus.). 2000p. Date not set. Set. text ed. price not set (ISBN 0-7216-2666-1); Vol. 1. price not set (ISBN 0-7216-2702-1); Vol. 2. price not set (ISBN 0-7216-2703-X). Saunders.
Connolly, John G., ed. Carcinoma of the Bladder. (Progress in Cancer Research & Therapy Ser.). 275p. 1981. 27.00 (ISBN 0-89004-536-4). Raven.
Connolly, John R. Dimensions of Belief & Unbelief. LC 80-67241. 373p. 1981. lib. bdg. 21.75 (ISBN 0-8191-1389-1); pap. text ed. 12.75 (ISBN 0-8191-1390-5). U Pr of Amer.
Connolly, Joseph. P. G. Wodehouse. (Illus.). 160p. 1980. text ed. 18.25x (ISBN 0-85613-235-7). Humanities.
Connolly, K. J., jt. auth. see Smith, P. K.
Connolly, Michael J., ed. see Black, Henry C.
Connolly, Myles. Mister Blue. pap. 0.75 (ISBN 0-385-02866-0, D5, Im). Doubleday.
--Mister Blue. 1928. 8.95 (ISBN 0-02-527460-0). Macmillan.
Connolly, Paul H. On Essays: A Reader for Writers. 352p. 1980. pap. text ed. 7.50 scp (ISBN 0-06-041345-X, HarpC). Har-Row.
Connolly, Ray. Newsdeath. LC 77-15840. 1978. 8.95 o.p. (ISBN 0-689-10872-9). Atheneum.
--Trick or Treat! 1977. pap. 1.75 o.p. (ISBN 0-345-26050-3). Ballantine.
Connolly, Robert D. The New Collector's Directory for the 1980's. rev. 2nd ed. (Illus.). 168p. 1980. pap. 5.95 (ISBN 0-914598-38-4). Padre Prods.
Connolly, Thomas J. Foundations of Nuclear Engineering. LC 77-26916. 1978. text ed. 27.95 (ISBN 0-471-16858-0); tchrs. manual 5.00 (ISBN 0-471-02971-8). Wiley.
Connolly, Vivian. Five Ports to Danger. (Orig.). 1980. pap. 1.75 (ISBN 0-505-51518-0). Tower Bks.
Connolly, W. E. Appearance & Reality in Politics. 224p. Date not set. price not set (ISBN 0-521-23026-8). Cambridge U Pr.
Connolly, William E., jt. auth. see Best, Michael H.
Connon, James. A Clear View - Guide to Industrial Pollution Control. LC 75-15321. 1975. pap. 4.00. Inform.
Connor, Anna T. Corncraft. LC 78-69664. (Illus.). 1980. 9.95 (ISBN 0-498-02256-0). A S Barnes.
Connor, Billie M., jt. auth. see Connor, John M.
Connor, Donald. Filing Practice Workbook. 3rd ed. (gr. 9-12). 1975. pap. 2.00 (ISBN 0-8224-2002-3); key 0.96 (ISBN 0-8224-2006-6). Pitman Learning.
Connor, F. R. Antennas. (Introductory Topics in Electronics & Telecommiunication). 99p. 1972. pap. 11.00x (ISBN 0-7131-3279-5). Intl Ideas.
--Modulation. (Introductory Topics in Electronics & Telecommunication Ser.). (Illus.). 1973. pap. text ed. 11.00x (ISBN 0-7131-3303-1). Intl Ideas.
--Networks. (Introductory Topics in Electronics & Telecommunication Ser.). (Illus.). 1972. pap. text ed. 11.00x (ISBN 0-7131-3258-2). Intl Ideas.
--Noise. (Introductory Topics in Electronics & Telecommunication Ser.). (Illus.). 1973. pap. text ed. 11.00x (ISBN 0-7131-3306-6). Intl Ideas.
--Signals. (Introductory Topics in Electronics & Telecommunications Ser.). (Illus.). 1972. pap. text ed. 11.00x (ISBN 0-7131-3262-0). Intl Ideas.
--Wave Transmission. (Introductory Topics in Electronics & Telecommunications Ser.). (Illus.). 1972. pap. text ed. 11.00x (ISBN 0-7131-3278-7). Intl Ideas.
Connor, Frances P. Education of Homebound or Hospitalized Children. LC 64-16622. (Orig.). 1964. pap. text ed. 4.25x (ISBN 0-8077-1185-3). Tchrs Coll.
Connor, Frances P., et al. Program Guide for Infants & Toddlers with Neuromotor & Other Developmental Disabilities. LC 77-28188. 1978. pap. 14.50x (ISBN 0-8077-2546-3). Tchrs Coll.

Connor, James E. Lenin on Politics & Revolution: Selected Writings. LC 68-21041. 1968. pap. 7.50 (ISBN 0-672-63553-4). Pegasus.

Connor, Jeannette T., tr. see Solis De Meras, Gonzalo.

Connor, Jerome J., Jr. Analysis of Structural Member Systems. LC 74-22535. 1976. 33.95 o.p. (ISBN 0-8260-2098-4). Wiley.

Connor, Jim. Ann Miller: Tops in Taps. (Illus.). 224p. (Orig.). 1981. 19.95 (ISBN 0-531-09949-0); pap. 10.95 (ISBN 0-531-09950-4). Watts.

Connor, John M. Market Power of Multinationals: A Quantitative Analysis of U. S. Corporations in Brazil & Mexico. LC 77-14302. (Praeger Special Studies). 1977. 28.95 (ISBN 0-03-023036-5). Praeger.

Connor, John M. & Connor, Billie M. Ottemiller's Index to Plays in Collections: An Author & Title Index to Plays Appearing in Collections Published Between 1900 & Early 1975. 6th. rev. enl. ed. LC 71-166073. 1976. 21.00 (ISBN 0-8108-0919-2). Scarecrow.

Connor, John N. Tradition & Change in Three Generations of Japanese Americans. LC 76-28999. 1977. 19.95 (ISBN 0-88229-288-9). Nelson-Hall.

Connor, Joseph. Marine Fire Prevention, Fire Fighting & Fire Safety. (Illus.). 404p. 1979. pap. text ed. 9.95 (ISBN 0-87618-994-X). R J Brady.

Connor, Larry J., et al. Managing Farm Business. (Illus.). 384p. 1981. text ed. 17.95 (ISBN 0-13-550376-0). P-H.

Connor, Patrick E. Dimensions in Modern Management. 2nd ed. LC 77-75692. (Illus.). 1977. pap. text ed. 10.95 (ISBN 0-395-25515-5). HM.

--Organizations: Theory & Design. 1979. text ed. 21.95 (ISBN 0-574-19380-4, 13-2380); instr's guide avail. (ISBN 0-574-19381-2, 13-2381). SRA.

Connor, Ralph. Black Rock: A Tale of the Selkirks. 1976. lib. bdg. 12.95x (ISBN 0-89968-014-3). Lightyear.

--The Doctor: A Tale of the Rockies. 1976. lib. bdg. 17.25x (ISBN 0-89968-015-1). Lighthouse Pr NY.

--The Major. 1976. lib. bdg. 16.75x (ISBN 0-89968-014-3). Lightyear.

--The Man from Glengarry. 1976. lib. bdg. 19.50x (ISBN 0-89968-017-8). Lightyear.

--The Sky Pilot, a Tale of the Foothills. 1976. lib. bdg. 14.25x (ISBN 0-89968-019-4). Lightyear.

--The Sky Pilot in No Man's Land. 1976. lib. bdg. 15.75x (ISBN 0-89968-018-6). Lightyear.

Connor, Robert. Walled-in: The True Story of a Cult. 1979. pap. 2.25 o.p. (ISBN 0-451-08662-7, E8662, Sig). NAL.

Connor, Seymour, ed. Dear America. LC 70-172388. 1971. 8.50 (ISBN 0-685-02299-4). Jenkins.

Connor, Seymour V. Texas: A History. LC 71-136037. (Illus., Orig.). 1971. text ed. 16.50x (ISBN 0-88295-724-4). AHM Pub.

Connor, W. Robert, ed. Greek Orations: Lysias, Isocrates, Demosthenes, Aeschines, Hyperides. (Orig.). 1966. pap. 5.95 (ISBN 0-472-06116-X, 116, AA). U of Mich Pr.

Connor, Walter D. Deviance in Soviet Society: Crime, Delinquency, Alcoholism. LC 71-180044. 1972. 22.50x (ISBN 0-231-03439-3). Columbia U Pr.

--Socialism, Politics, & Equality. (Illus.). 1979. 27.50x (ISBN 0-231-04318-X). Columbia U Pr.

--Socialism, Politics & Equality: Hierarchy & Change in Eastern Europe & the USSR. (Illus.). 1980. pap. 10.00x (ISBN 0-231-04319-8). Columbia U Pr.

Connor, Walter D., et al. Public Opinion in European Socialist Systems. LC 77-83471. (Praeger Special Studies). 1977. 21.95 (ISBN 0-03-040931-4). Praeger.

Connors, C. Keith. Food Additives for Hyperactive Children. 180p. 1980. 18.50 (ISBN 0-306-40400-1, Plenum Pr). Plenum Pub.

Connors, Joseph. Borromini & the Roman Oratory: Style & Society. (Illus.). 528p. 1980. text ed. 45.00x (ISBN 0-262-03071-3). MIT Pr.

Connors, Kenneth A. Reaction Mechanisms in Organic Analytical Chemistry. LC 72-5845. 1973. 34.50 o.p. (ISBN 0-471-16845-9, Pub. by Wiley-Interscience). Wiley.

--A Textbook of Pharmaceutical Analysis. 2nd ed. LC 74-34134. 611p. 1975. 29.50 (ISBN 0-471-16853-X, Pub. by Wiley-Interscience). Wiley.

Connors, Richard J. A Cycle of Power: The Career of Jersey City Mayor Frank Hague. LC 71-168603. 1971. 10.00 (ISBN 0-8108-0435-2). Scarecrow.

Conoley, Jane C., ed. Consultation in Schools: Theory, Research Procedures. LC 80-2329. (Educational Technology Ser.). 1981. price not set (ISBN 0-12-186020-5). Acad Pr.

Conolly, Brian. Lecture Notes in Queueing Systems. LC 75-7788. 176p. 1975. pap. 14.95 (ISBN 0-470-16857-9). Halsted Pr.

Conolly, John. On Some of the Forms of Insanity. Bd. with Inquiry Concerning the Indications of Insanity. (Contributions to the History of Psychology Ser.). 1980. Repr. of 1850 ed. 30.00 (ISBN 0-89093-315-4). U Pubns Amer.

Conolly, Leonard W. & Wearing, J. P., eds. English Drama & Theatre, 1800-1900: A Guide to Information Sources. LC 73-16975. (American Literature, English Literature, & World Literatures in English Information Guide Ser.: Vol. 12). 1978. 30.00 (ISBN 0-8103-1225-5). Gale.

Conover, Carole. The Cover Girls. LC 78-15686. 1978. 10.95 o.p. (ISBN 0-13-188300-3). P-H.

Conover, Chris. Six Little Ducks. LC 75-22155. (Illus.). 32p. (gr. k-2). 1976. 7.95 (ISBN 0-690-01036-2, TYC-J); PLB 7.89 (ISBN 0-690-01037-0). T Y Crowell.

Conover, Donald W., jt. auth. see Woodson, Wesley E.

Conover, Helen F., jt. auth. see Duignan, Peter.

Conover, Mary B. Understanding Electrocardiography: Physiological & Interpretive Concepts. 3rd ed. LC 80-14104. (Illus.). 254p. 1980. pap. text ed. 12.50 (ISBN 0-8016-5676-1). Mosby.

Conover, Mary H. Cardiac Arrhythmias: Exercises in Pattern Interpretation. 2nd ed. LC 77-24509. (Illus.). 1978. pap. text ed. 11.50 (ISBN 0-8016-1024-9). Mosby.

Conover, W. J. Practical Nonparametric Statistics. 2nd ed. LC 80-301. (Probability & Mathematical Statistics Ser.). 493p. 1980. 25.95 (ISBN 0-471-02867-3). Wiley.

Conover, William J. Practical Nonparametric Statistics. LC 74-126223. (Illus.). 1971. 23.95 o.p. (ISBN 0-471-16851-3). Wiley.

Conquest, Robert. Arias from a Love Opera: Other Poems. LC 71-79030. 1970. 4.95 o.s.i. (ISBN 0-02-527570-4). Macmillan.

--Present Danger: Towards a Foreign Policy. LC 79-2086. (Publication Ser.: 216). 170p. 1979. 12.00 (ISBN 0-8179-7161-0). Hoover Inst Pr.

Conrad, Barnaby. Fire Below Zero. (Orig.). 1981. pap. 2.75 (ISBN 0-440-12524-3). Dell.

Conrad, Clifton. The Undergraduate Curriculum: A Guide to Innovation & Reform. (Westview Special Studies in Higher Education). 1979. lib. bdg. 19.75x (ISBN 0-89158-196-0). Westview.

Conrad, Clifton F., jt. auth. see Bullock, G. William, Jr.

Conrad, Earl. Da Vinci Machine: Tales of the Population Explosion. LC 66-25986. 1969. 6.95 (ISBN 0-8303-0067-8). Fleet.

--Gulf Stream North. LC 80-50244. 256p. 1980. 15.95 (ISBN 0-933256-13-2); pap. 7.95 (ISBN 0-933256-17-5). Second Chance.

Conrad, Eva & Maul, Terry. Introduction to Experimental Psychology. 350p. 1981. text ed. 16.95 (ISBN 0-471-06005-4). Wiley.

Conrad, Jeff, ed. see Terres, John K.

Conrad, John. Joseph Conrad-Times Remembered. LC 79-41596. (Illus.). 212p. Date not set. price not set (ISBN 0-521-22805-0). Cambridge U Pr.

Conrad, John P. Crime & Its Correction: An International Survey of Attitudes & Practices. 1976. 16.50x o.p. (ISBN 0-520-03057-5). U of Cal Pr.

--Justice & Consequences. LC 78-348. (The Dangerous Offender Project Ser.). 1981. price not set (ISBN 0-669-02190-3). Lexington Bks.

Conrad, John P. & Dinitz, Simon. In Fear of Each Other: Studies of Dangerousness in America. LC 77-286. (The Dangerous Offender Project). 1977. 15.95 (ISBN 0-669-01478-8). Lexington Bks.

Conrad, John P., jt. ed. see Flynn, Edith E.

Conrad, John W. Ceramic Formulas: A Guide to Clay, Glaze, Enamel, Glass & Their Colours. 160p. 1973. 14.95 (ISBN 0-02-527610-7). Macmillan.

--Contemporary Ceramic Formulas. (Illus.). 256p. 1981. 17.95 (ISBN 0-686-65889-2). Macmillan.

--Contemporary Ceramic Techniques. 1979. 17.95 (ISBN 0-13-169540-1). P-H.

Conrad, Joseph. Almayer's Folly. lib. bdg. 13.95x (ISBN 0-89966-056-8). Buccaneer Bks.

--Great Short Works: The Lagoon, the Nigger of Narcissus, Youth, Heart of Darkness, Typhoon, the Secret Sharer. 6.75 (ISBN 0-8446-0068-7). Peter Smith.

--Heart of Darkness. 112p. Repr. of 1973 ed. lib. bdg. cancelled (ISBN 0-8376-0458-3). Bentley.

--Heart of Darkness & the Secret Sharer. 1978. Repr. of 1910 ed. lib. bdg. 12.50x (ISBN 0-89966-054-1). Buccaneer Bks.

--Joseph Conrad on Fiction. Wright, Walter F., ed. LC 64-11355. (Regents Critics Ser). 1964. 11.95x (ISBN 0-8032-0452-3); pap. 3.45x (ISBN 0-8032-5452-0, BB 400, Bison). U of Nebr Pr.

--Lord Jim. pap. 1.95. Bantam.

--Lord Jim. Moser, Thomas, ed. (Critical Editions Ser). (Annotated). (gr. 9-12). 1968. pap. text ed. 5.95x (ISBN 0-393-09656-4). Norton.

--Lord Jim. (Literature Ser). (gr. 7-12). 1969. pap. text ed. 3.75 (ISBN 0-87720-708-9). AMSCO Sch.

--Lord Jim. LC 44-22843. 1927. 12.95 (ISBN 0-385-04265-5). Doubleday.

--Lord Jim. lib. bdg. 11.95x (ISBN 0-89966-057-6). Buccaneer Bks.

--Lord Jim, with Reader's Guide. (Literature Program Ser.). (Orig.). (gr. 9-12). 1973. pap. text ed. 4.42 (ISBN 0-87720-820-4); tchr's ed. 2.85 (ISBN 0-87720-920-0). AMSCO Sch.

--The Nigger of the "Narcissus". Kimbrough, Robert, ed. (Norton Critical Editions). 1979. 12.95 (ISBN 0-393-04517-X); pap. 4.95 (ISBN 0-393-09019-1). Norton.

--Nigger of the Narcissus. lib. bdg. 12.95x (ISBN 0-89966-055-X). Buccaneer Bks.

--Secret Agent. 1953. pap. 2.95 (ISBN 0-385-09352-7, A8, Anch). Doubleday.

--The Secret Agent. lib. bdg. 12.95x (ISBN 0-89966-058-4). Buccaneer Bks.

--Victory. LC 32-26954. 1957. pap. 3.95 (ISBN 0-385-09314-4, A106, Anch). Doubleday.

--Youth, Heart of Darkness, Typhoon, the Secret Sharer. (Literature Ser). (gr. 10-12). 1970. pap. text ed. 3.83 (ISBN 0-87720-748-8). AMSCO Sch.

--Youth, Heart of Darkness, Typhoon, The Secret Sharer. with Reader's Guide. (AMSCO Literature Program). (gr. 9-12). 1974. pap. text ed. 5.08 (ISBN 0-87720-819-0); tchr's ed. 3.25 (ISBN 0-87720-919-7). AMSCO Sch.

Conrad, Joseph, et al. Fifty Great Sea Stories. 768p. 1980. Repr. lib. bdg. 30.00 (ISBN 0-686-68073-1). Arden Lib.

Conrad, Kenneth, jt. auth. see Bressler, Rubin.

Conrad, L. K., tr. see Guaresch, Giovanni.

Conrad, L. K., tr. see Guareschi, Giovanni.

Conrad, L. K., tr. see Servadio, Gaia.

Conrad, M., et al, eds. Physics & Mathematics of the Nervous Systems. (Lecture Notes in Biomathematics Ser.: Vol. 4). (Illus.). xii, 584p. 1975. pap. 22.40 (ISBN 0-387-07014-1). Springer-Verlag.

Conrad, Marion L. Allergy Cooking. (Orig.). pap. 2.25 (ISBN 0-515-05738-X). Jove Pubns.

Conrad, Pamela. Amanda. (Orig.). 1980. pap. 2.25 (ISBN 0-505-51554-7). Tower Bks.

Conrad, Peter. Romantic Opera & Literary Form. (Quantum Ser.). 1977. 14.00 (ISBN 0-520-03258-6). U of Cal Pr.

Conrad, Peter & Schneider, Joseph W. Deviance & Medicalization: From Badness to Sickness. LC 79-20333. 1980. pap. text ed. 11.50 (ISBN 0-8016-1025-7). Mosby.

Conrad, Peter F. Identifying Hyperactive Children: A Study in the Medicalization of Deviant Behavior. LC 75-44559. (Illus.). 1976. 15.95 (ISBN 0-669-00499-5). Lexington Bks.

Conrad, Robert. The Destruction of Brazilian Slavery, 1850-1888. 1972. pap. 6.50x (ISBN 0-520-02371-4, CAMPUS89). U of Cal Pr.

Conrad, Robert, ed. Taxation of Mineral Resources. Hool, Bryce. LC 80-8392. (Lincoln Institute of Land Policy Book). 1980. 14.95x (ISBN 0-669-04104-1). Lexington Bks.

Conrad, Sybil. Believe in Spring. LC 67-29446. (gr. 7 up). 1968. 5.95 (ISBN 0-8149-0290-1). Vanguard.

Conrad, William R., Jr. & Glenn, William E. The Effective Voluntary Board of Directors: What Is Is & How It Works. LC 76-13425. 186p. 1976. pap. 7.95x (ISBN 0-8040-0735-7). Swallow.

Conrader, Jay & Conrader, Constance, illus. Tokens from the Writings of Baha 'u'llah. LC 73-78441. (Illus.). 1973. 16.00 (ISBN 0-87743-074-8, 7-03-18); pap. 6.50 o.s.i. (ISBN 0-87743-094-2). Baha'i.

Conradt, David P. The German Polity. LC 77-17711. (Comparative Studies of Political Life Ser.). 1978. text ed. 15.95x (ISBN 0-582-28034-6); pap. text ed. 9.95x (ISBN 0-582-28033-8). Longman.

Conrat, Heinz F. & Wagner, Robert, eds. Comprehensive Virology: Methods Used in the Study of Viruses, Vol. 17. 425p. 1981. 39.50 (ISBN 0-306-40418-4). Plenum Pub.

Conron, John, ed. The American Landscape: A Critical Anthology of Prose & Poetry. (Illus.). 640p. 1974. pap. text ed. 14.95x (ISBN 0-19-501767-6). Oxford U Pr.

Conron, John P. Socorro: A Historic Study. LC 79-56821. (Illus.). 144p. 1980. 14.95 (ISBN 0-8263-0528-8). U of NM Pr.

Conroy, Barbara. Library Staff Development & Continuing Education: Principles & Practices. LC 78-18887. 1978. 23.50x (ISBN 0-87287-177-0). Libs Unl.

Conroy, Hilary. The Japanese Seizure of Korea, 1868-1910: A Study of Realism & Idealism in International Relations. LC 60-6936. 544p. 1974. pap. 7.50x (ISBN 0-8122-1074-3). U of Pa Pr.

Conroy, Hilary & Miyakawa, T. Scott, eds. East Across the Pacific. LC 72-77825. 322p. 1972. pap. 2.85 (ISBN 0-87436-087-0). ABC-Clio.

Conroy, Jack. The Disinherited. 1963. pap. 5.95 o.p. (ISBN 0-8090-0060-1, AmCen). Hill & Wang.

Conroy, Joseph F. Guide Terrestre, Ou La Terre et Ses Singes. (Orig.). (gr. 7-12). 1975. pap. text ed. 4.58 (ISBN 0-87720-461-6). AMSCO Sch.

--Le Monstre dans le Metro et d'Autres Merveilles. (gr. 7-12). 1974. wkbk. 4.58 (ISBN 0-87720-469-1). AMSCO Sch.

Conroy, Kathleen. Valuing the Timeshare Property. 97p. 1981. 15.00 (ISBN 0-911780-50-5). Am Inst Real Estate Appraisers.

Conroy, Mary & Ritvo, Edward R. Common Sense Self-Defense: A Practical Manual for Students & Teachers. LC 76-28533. (Illus.). 1977. pap. text ed. 8.50 o.p. (ISBN 0-8016-1027-3). Mosby.

Conroy, Pat. The Great Santini. 536p. Repr. of 1976 ed. 10.00 (ISBN 0-937036-00-5). Old NY Bk Shop.

--The Great Santini. 1979. pap. 2.50 (ISBN 0-380-00991-9, 44768). Avon.

--The Water Is Wide. 1979. pap. 2.25 (ISBN 0-380-46037-8, 46037). Avon.

Conroy, Patricia, tr. see Andersen, Hans C.

Conroy, Robert. Battle of Bataan: America's Greatest Defeat. LC 69-11294. (Battle Books Ser). (Illus.). (gr. 5-8). 1969. 4.95g o.s.i. (ISBN 0-02-724290-0). Macmillan.

Conroy, William T., Jr. Villiers De L'isle - Adam. (World Author Ser.: No. 491). 1978. 12.95 (ISBN 0-8057-6332-5). Twayne.

Conrwall, Judson. Let Us See Jesus. 1981. pap. 4.95 (ISBN 0-8007-5052-7). Revell.

Conseil International De la Langue Francaise. Glossary of the Environment. LC 76-19547. (Praeger Special Studies). 1977. 21.95 (ISBN 0-275-23760-5). Praeger.

Conservation Education Association. Education: Key to Conservation. Incl. Bk. 1. Important Characteristics of a Good Local Program. (Illus.). 8p. 1965. pap. text ed. o.p. (ISBN 0-685-22440-6, 869); Bk. 2. Planning a State Program in Conservation Education. (Illus.). 16p. 1965. pap. text ed. 0.30 (ISBN 0-8134-0870-9, 870); Bk. 3. Twenty-Five Key Guides for Preparing Conservation Education Publications & Visual Aids. (Illus.). 16p. 1965. pap. text ed. 0.30 (ISBN 0-8134-0871-7, 871); Bk. 5. A Selected List of Filmstrips on the Conservation of Natural Resources. (Illus.). 48p. 1968. pap. text ed. 0.50 (ISBN 0-685-22443-0, 1040). LC 65-23951. Interstate.

Conservation of Human Resources Staff, jt. auth. see Ginzberg, Eli.

Considine, Bob & Lawson, Ted. Thirty Seconds Over Tokyo. (Landmark Ser.: No. 35). (Illus.). (gr. 7-9). 1953. PLB 5.99 (ISBN 0-394-90335-8). Random.

Considine, Douglas M. Encyclopedia of Instrumentation & Control. 814p. 1981. Repr. text ed. write for info. (ISBN 0-89874-281-1). Krieger.

Consky, Susan B. Mischief on the Farm. (Childrens Bks). Orig. Title: Beanie and His Friends. (Illus.). 128p. (gr. 1-5). 1970. pap. 1.50 (ISBN 0-8024-1540-7). Moody.

Consolo, Dominick. Out of the Cradle, Endlessly Rocking. LC 70-138465. (Literary Casebook Ser.). 1971. pap. text ed. 2.95x (ISBN 0-675-09254-X). Merrill.

Constable, Benjamin. God & the "New" Psychology of Sex. (Illus.). 265p. 1976. 43.75 (ISBN 0-89266-043-0). Am Classical Coll Pr.

Constable, Betty, et al. Squash Basics for Men & Women. (Illus.). 1979. pap. 5.95 (ISBN 0-8015-7039-5, Hawthorn). Dutton.

Constable, George. The Neanderthals. (Emergence of Man Ser.). (Illus.). 1973. 9.95 (ISBN 0-8094-1263-2); lib. bdg. avail. (ISBN 0-685-30024-2). Time-Life.

--The Neanderthals. LC 72-96553. (Emergence of Man Ser). (Illus.). 1973. lib. bdg. 9.63 o.p. (ISBN 0-8094-1264-0, Pub. by Time-Life). Silver.

Constable, Giles. Monastic Tithes from Their Origins to the Twelfth Century. (Cambridge Studies in Medieval Life & Thought). 46.95 (ISBN 0-521-04715-3). Cambridge U Pr.

Constable, Ian J., jt. auth. see Lim, Arthur.

Constable, John. Correspondence & Discourses of John Constable, R.A, 8 vols. Beckett, R. B., ed. Incl. No. 1. The Family at East Bergholt, 1807-1837. (Illus.). 337p. 1976. Repr. 22.75x (ISBN 0-8476-1252-X); No. 2. Early Friends & Marie Bicknell (Mrs. Constable) (Illus.). 474p. 18.75x (ISBN 0-8476-1253-8); No. 3. The Correspondence with C.R. Leslie R.A. 12.50x (ISBN 0-8476-1254-6); No. 4. Patrons, Dealers & Fellow Artists. (Illus.). 481p. 18.75x (ISBN 0-8476-1255-4); No. 5. Various Friends with Charles Boner & the Artist's Children. (Illus.). 229p. 12.50x (ISBN 0-8476-1256-2); No. 6. The Fishers. Grigson, Geoffrey, pref. by. (Illus.). 294p. 18.50x (ISBN 0-8476-1257-0); No. 7. Discourses. (Illus.). 109p. 12.50x (ISBN 0-8476-1258-9); No. 8. Further Correspondence & Documents. Paris, Leslie, et al, eds. (Illus.). 371p. 1976. 30.00x (ISBN 0-8476-1259-7). Set. 145.00x (ISBN 0-8476-1260-0). Rowman.
Constable, Trevor, jt. auth. see Toliver, Raymond.
Constable, Trevor J. The Cosmic Pulse of Life: The Revolutionary Biological Power Behind UFO's. LC 77-72046. (Illus.). 446p. 1977. pap. 7.95 (ISBN 0-8334-1777-0). Steinerbks.
Constable, W. G. Canaletto: Giovanni Antonio Canal(1697-1768, 2 vols. 2nd ed. Links, J. G., ed. 1977. Set. 145.00x (ISBN 0-19-817324-5). Oxford U Pr.
Constance, Lincoln, jt. auth. see Mathias, Mildred E.
Constans, H. Philip, Jr. Fit for Freedom. LC 79-6405. 141p. 1980. pap. text ed. 7.50 (ISBN 0-8191-0945-2). U Pr of Amer.
Constans, Jacques A. Marine Sources of Energy. (Pergamon Policy Studies). (Illus.). 1980. 28.00 (ISBN 0-08-023897-1). Pergamon.
Constant, Alberta W. Does Anyone Care About Lou Emma Miller? LC 78-4774. (gr. 3-7). 1979. 7.95 (ISBN 0-690-01335-3, TYC-J); PLB 8.79 (ISBN 0-690-03890-9). T Y Crowell.
--Miss Charity Comes to Stay. LC 59-5250. (Illus.). (gr. 5-9). 1959. 8.95 o.p. (ISBN 0-690-54490-1, TYC-J). T Y Crowell.
--Paintbox on the Frontier: The Life & Times of George Caleb Bingham. LC 73-6954. (Illus.). 224p. (gr. 7-9). 1974. 9.95 (ISBN 0-690-60844-6, TYC-J). T Y Crowell.
--Willie & the Wildcat Well. LC 62-7741. (Illus.). (gr. 5-9). 1962. 8.95 o.p. (ISBN 0-690-89351-5, TYC-J). T Y Crowell.
Constant, Benjamin. Adolphe. (Classiques Larousse). (Illus., Fr.). pap. 2.95 (ISBN 0-685-13793-7, 59). Larousse.
Constant, Constantine. Earth Science: Intermediate Level. (gr. 7-10). 1972. wkbk. ed. 7.08 (ISBN 0-87720-154-4). AMSCO Sch.
--Review Text in Earth Science, Intermediate Level. (Orig.). (gr. 7-9). 1971. pap. text ed. 6.08 (ISBN 0-87720-152-8). AMSCO Sch.
Constant, Edward W., II. The Origins of the Turbo-Jet Revolution. LC 80-11802. (JH Studies in the History of Technology). 1981. 22.50x (ISBN 0-8018-2222-X). Johns Hopkins.
Constant, Jacques see Otten, Anna.
Constant, James N. Introduction to Defense Radar Systems Engineering. (Illus.). 1972. text ed. 22.95x (ISBN 0-8104-9194-X, 0-8104-9194-X). Hayden.
Constant, Jules. Learning Electrocardiography: A Complete Course. 2nd ed. (Illus.). 1981. text ed. write for info. (ISBN 0-316-15322-2). Little.
Constant, Stephen. Foxy Ferdinand: Tsar of Bulgaria. 352p. 1980. 17.50 (ISBN 0-531-09930-X). Watts.
Constantelos, D. J. Marriage, Sexuality & Celibacy: A Greek Orthodox Perspective. 1975. pap. 3.95 (ISBN 0-937032-15-8). Light&Life Pub Co MN.
Constantelos, Demetrios J. Greek Orthodox Church: Faith, History, & Practice. (Orig.). (YA) (gr. 9-12). 1967. pap. 1.95 (ISBN 0-8164-2029-7, SP38). Crossroad NY.
Constantian, Mark B., ed. Pressure Ulcers: Principles & Techniques in Management. 320p. 1980. text ed. 32.50 (ISBN 0-316-15330-3). Little.
Constantine & Hobbs. Know Your Woods. 1975. text ed. 19.80 (ISBN 0-87002-903-7). Bennett IL.
Constantine, Albert. Know Your Woods. rev. ed. 1975. 17.50 (ISBN 0-684-14115-9, ScribT). Scribner.
Constantine, J., jt. auth. see Clifford, H. T.
Constantine, Larry L., jt. auth. see Yourdon, Edward.
Constantine, Mildred & Larsen, Jack L. The Art Fabric. 240p. 1981. 39.95 (ISBN 0-442-21638-6). Van Nos Reinhold.
Constantine I. A Treatise of the Donation of Gyfts & Endowment of Possessyons Gyven & Graunted Unto Sylvester Pope of Rome by Constantyne Emperour of Rome. Marshall, William, tr. LC 79-84096. (English Experience Ser.: No. 916). 152p. (Eng.). 1979. Repr. of 1534 ed. lib. bdg. 24.00 (ISBN 90-221-0916-X). Walter J Johnson.
Constantinescu, F. & Magyari, E. Problems in Quantum Mechanics. 1971. 42.00 (ISBN 0-08-006826-X); pap. text ed. 18.50 (ISBN 0-08-019008-1). Pergamon.
Constantino, Renato. The History of the Philippines: From the Spanish Colonization to the Second World War. 459p. 1981. pap. 8.95 (ISBN 0-85345-579-1). Monthly Rev.
Constiner, Merle. Killer's Corral. 1978. pap. 1.25 (ISBN 0-505-51237-8). Tower Bks.
--Sumatra Alley. LC 79-140080. (gr. 6 up). 1971. 6.95 o.p. (ISBN 0-525-66126-3). Elsevier-Nelson.
Consul, S. C. & Chandra, C. Advocacy. 1967. 5.50x o.p. (ISBN 0-210-26934-0). Asia.
Consultant's Library Editors. The Successful Consultant's Guide to Winning Government Contracts. 122p. pap. write for info. leatherette (ISBN 0-930686-12-8). Bermont Bks.
Consultation on Church Union. World Bread Cup. 1978. 0.85 (ISBN 0-686-28801-7). Forward Movement.
Consumer-Aid Group. Successful Dieter's Sure-Fire Dieting Tips. Grooms, Kathe, ed. (A Consumer-Aid Bk.). (Illus.). 130p. 1981. pap. 3.95 (ISBN 0-915658-34-8). Meadowbrook Pr.
Consumer Guide. Add-a-Room. 1980. pap. 8.95 (ISBN 0-686-60943-3, 25270); pap. 7.95 (ISBN 0-686-60944-1, 25271). S&S.
--Complete Medicine Book. 1980. 11.95 (ISBN 0-671-25501-0). S&S.
--The Fastest, Cheapest, Best Way to Clean Everything. 1980. 10.95 (ISBN 0-686-62878-0, 25500). S&S.
--The Food Processor Bread Cookbook. (Illus.). 1980. 14.95 (ISBN 0-671-25201-1, 25201); pap. 7.95 (ISBN 0-671-25138-4, 25138). S&S.
Consumer Guide & Freeman, John. The Complete Book of War Games. 1980. pap. 8.95 (ISBN 0-671-25375-1, Fireside). S&S.
Consumer Guide, ed. The Complete Book of Walking. 1980. 5.95 (ISBN 0-671-41286-8, Fireside). S&S.
--The Consumer Guide Body Fitness & Shaping Program. (Illus.). 384p. 1981. pap. 8.95 (ISBN 0-89104-206-7). A & W Pubs.
--Consumer Guide: Nineteen Eighty-One Buying Guide. 1981. pap. 3.50 (ISBN 0-451-09623-1, E9623, Sig). NAL.
--Consumer Guide: Nineteen Eighty-One Cars. 1981. pap. 3.50 (ISBN 0-451-09625-8, Sig). NAL.
Consumer Guide Editors. The Complete Book of Prefabs, Kits & Manufactured Houses. 160p. 1981. pap. 7.95 (ISBN 0-449-90051-7, Columbine). Fawcett.
--The Dieter's Complete Guide to Calories, Carbohydrates, Sodium, Fats & Cholesterol. 192p. (Orig.). 1981. pap. 5.95 (ISBN 0-449-90050-9, Columbine). Fawcett.
--Gas Savers Guide. (Orig.). 1979. pap. 1.95 (ISBN 0-449-80000-8, Columbine). Fawcett.
--The Home Energy Saver. (Orig.). 1979. pap. 1.95 (ISBN 0-449-80002-4). Fawcett.
--Social Security Benefits. 1980. pap. 2.50 (ISBN 0-449-90029-0, Columbine). Fawcett.
--Special Report: How to Make Money During Inflation-Recession. LC 79-3669. (Illus.). 1980. pap. 4.95 (ISBN 0-06-090782-7, CN 782, CN). Har-Row.
--The Whole Bath Catalog. 1979. 14.95 (ISBN 0-671-25200-3, Fireside); pap. 7.95 (ISBN 0-671-24768-9). S&S.
Consumer Guide Editors & Ojakangas, Beatrice A. The Convection Oven Cookbook. (Illus.). 1980. pap. 6.95 (ISBN 0-449-90042-8, Columbine). Fawcett.
Consumer Guide Editors, jt. auth. see Kay, Sophie.
Consumer Guide Editors, ed. Complete Book of Mopeds. 1977. pap. 1.95 (ISBN 0-446-89475-3). Warner Bks.
--Complete Book of Video Games. 1977. pap. 1.95. Warner Bks.
Consumer Guide Magazine, ed. Spectators Guide to Sports: Rules, Scoring, Strategy & Competing. 1976. pap. 5.95 o.p. (ISBN 0-451-79975-5, G9975, Sig). NAL.
Consumer Liaison Committee of the American National Metric Council. Metric Reference for Consumers. 1976. pap. text ed. 2.50 (ISBN 0-916148-10-6). Am Natl.
Consumer Reports Editors. Consumer Reports: The 1980 Buying Guide. 1979. 3.50 o.p. (ISBN 0-385-15919-6). Doubleday.
--The Consumers Union Report on Life Insurance: A Guide to Planning & Buying the Protection You Need. 384p. 1981. 14.95 (ISBN 0-03-059109-0); pap. 7.95 (ISBN 0-03-059108-2). HR&W.
--Health Quackery: Consumer's Union's Report on False Health Claims, Worthless Remedies & Unproved Therapies. 252p. 1981. 13.95 (ISBN 0-03-058899-5); pap. 6.95x (ISBN 0-03-058898-7). HR&W.
--The Medicine Show. rev. & updated ed. 384p. 1980. 10.00 (ISBN 0-394-51106-9); pap. 5.95 (ISBN 0-394-73887-X). Pantheon.
Consumer's Guide Editors. Caring for Your Child: A Complete Medical Guide. (Illus.). 1979. 10.95 (ISBN 0-517-53957-8, Harmony); pap. 5.95 (ISBN 0-517-53910-1). Crown.
--The Complete Book of Mopeds. 1977. pap. 1.95 o.s.i. (ISBN 0-446-89475-3). Warner Bks.
Consumers Power Company. Fundamentals of Natural Gas. LC 74-100858. (Supervision Ser). 1970. pap. text ed. 10.95 (ISBN 0-201-01180-8). A-W.
Consumer's Union. Consumer's Union Guide to Consumer Service. 1981. write for info. Little.
Consumption, Location, & Occupational Patterns Resource Group Systhesis Panel of the Committee on Nuclear & Alternative Energy Systems. Energy Choices in a Democratic Society. LC 80-81335. (Study of Nuclear & Alternative Energy Systems Ser.). xvii, 136p. 1980. pap. text ed. 6.50 (ISBN 0-309-03045-5). Natl Acad Pr.
Conta, Marcia & Reardon, Maureen. Feelings Between Brothers & Sisters. LC 75-20172. (Identity I Ser.). (Illus.). 32p. (gr. k-3). 1975. Repr. of 1974 ed. PLB 7.95 o.p. (ISBN 0-8172-0039-8). Raintree Pubs.
--Feelings Between Friends. LC 75-19348. (Moods & Emotions Ser.). (Illus.). 32p. (gr. k-3). 1975. Repr. of 1974 ed. PLB 8.95 (ISBN 0-8172-0041-X). Raintree Pubs.
--Feelings Between Kids & Grownups. LC 75-19383. (Moods & Emotions Ser.). (Illus.). 32p. (gr. k-3). 1975. Repr. of 1974 ed. PLB 8.95 (ISBN 0-8172-0043-6). Raintree Pubs.
--Feelings Between Kids & Parents. LC 75-19398. (Identity I Ser.). (Illus.). 32p. (gr. k-3). 1975. Repr. of 1974 ed. PLB 7.95 o.p. (ISBN 0-8172-0045-2). Raintree Pubs.
Conte, John E., Jr. & Barriere, Steven L. Manual of Antibiotics & Infectious Diseases. 4th ed. (Illus.). 275p. 1981. text ed. price not set (ISBN 0-8121-0768-3). Lea & Febiger.
Conte, Sylvester B. & Kemmee, Douglas H. Positioning & Technique Handbook for Radiologic Technologists. LC 78-5245. 1978. pap. text ed. 13.50 (ISBN 0-8016-1031-1). Mosby.
Conte, William, jt. auth. see Murray, Diane.
Conti, C., et al. Research on Steroids, Vol. 4. 1971. 50.00 (ISBN 0-08-017573-2). Pergamon.
Conti, Natale & Tritonio, Antonio M. Mythologiae & Mythologia. Orgel, Stephen, ed. LC 78-68194. (Philosophy of Images Ser.: Vol. 13). (Illus.). 1980. lib. bdg. 66.00 (ISBN 0-8240-3687-5). Garland Pub.
Continho, O., jt. auth. see Sharma, T. C.
Continuing Library Education Network & Exchange, ed. Directory of Continuing Education Opportunities for Library, Information, Media Personnel. 2nd ed. 292p. 1979. text ed. 30.00 (ISBN 0-89664-064-7, Pub. by K G Saur). Gale.
Contosta, David R. Henry Adams & the American Experiment. (American Biography Library: Library of American Biography). 176p. (Orig.). 1980. 10.95 (ISBN 0-316-15401-6); pap. 4.95 (ISBN 0-316-15400-8). Little.
Contreras, Mamie M., tr. see Wade, Harlan.
Contruction Steel Research & Development Organization. Steel Designer's Manual. 4th ed. LC 75-19073. 1089p. 1975. 54.95 (ISBN 0-470-16865-X). Halsted Pr.
Converse, Gordon, et al. Fishers of Men: The Way of the Apostles. LC 80-23760. 1980. 14.95 (ISBN 0-13-319673-9). P-H.
Converse, John M., et al. Symposium on Diagnosis & Treatment of Craniofacial Anomalies, Vol. 20. LC 79-27063. 1979. text ed. 72.50 (ISBN 0-8016-1030-3). Mosby.
Converse, Philip E. The Dynamics of Party Support. LC 76-40523. (Sage Library of Social Research: Vol. 35). 1976. 18.00x (ISBN 0-8039-0727-3); pap. 8.95x (ISBN 0-8039-0728-1). Sage.
Conveyor Equipment Manufacturers Assoc. Belt Conveyors for Bulk Materials. 2nd ed. LC 78-31987. 1979. 32.50 (ISBN 0-8436-1008-5). CBI Pub.
Conway & Bockris, eds. Modern Aspects of Electrochemistry, No. 13. (Illus.). 1979. 42.50 (ISBN 0-306-40256-4, Plenum Pr). Plenum Pub.
Conway, Anne. The Conway Letters: Being the Correspondence of Anne, Viscountess Conway, Henry More & Their Friends. Nicolson, M. H., ed. 1930. 47.50x (ISBN 0-685-89745-1). Elliots Bks.
Conway, Barbara L. Carini & Owens' Neurological & Neurosurgical Nursing. 7th ed. 1978. text ed. 18.95 (ISBN 0-8016-0946-1). Mosby.
--Pediatric Neurologic Nursing. (Illus.). 1977. text ed. 16.95 o.p. (ISBN 0-8016-1029-X). Mosby.
Conway, Carle. The Joy of Soaring: A Training Manual. LC 73-98038. (Illus.). 134p. 1969. 14.95 (ISBN 0-911720-54-5, Pub. by Soaring). Aviation.
Conway, David. Magic: An Occult Primer. 1972. 11.95 o.p. (ISBN 0-525-15010-2). Dutton.
Conway, Flo & Siegelman, Jim. Snapping. LC 78-6627. 1978. 10.00 o.s.i. (ISBN 0-397-01258-6). Lippincott.
Conway, H. McKinley. Disaster Survival: How to Choose Secure Sites & Make Practical Escape Plans. LC 80-68816. (Illus.). 1980. 48.00 (ISBN 0-910436-17-7). Conway Pubns.
--Marketing Industrial Buildings & Sites. LC 78-74933. 358p. 1980. 35.00 (ISBN 0-910436-15-0). Conway Pubns.
--Pitfalls in Development. LC 78-62198. 1980. pap. 29.00 (ISBN 0-910436-19-3). Conway Pubns.
Conway, J. B. Functions of One Complex Variable. Halmos, P. R., ed. LC 72-96938. (Lecture Notes in Mathematics: Vol. 11). (Illus.). xiv, 314p. 1973. text ed. 18.30 o.p. (ISBN 0-387-90061-6). Springer-Verlag.
Conway, J. C. Death Style. 1977. pap. text ed. 1.50 (ISBN 0-505-51160-6, BT51160). Tower Bks.
Conway, Jack. Compass Course 180 Degrees. 1978. 7.50 (ISBN 0-8158-0367-2); pap. 4.95 (ISBN 0-686-68022-7). Chris Mass.
Conway, James A., et al. Understanding Communities. LC 73-22370. (Illus.). 288p. 1974. 14.95 (ISBN 0-13-936393-9). P-H.
Conway, James V. Evidential Documents. (Police Science Ser). (Illus.). 288p. 1978. 19.75 (ISBN 0-398-00342-4). C C Thomas.
Conway, John, tr. see Baumer, Franz.
Conway, John, tr. see Tank, Kurt L.
Conway, Laura. The Abbot's House. 256p. 1975. pap. 1.25 o.p. (ISBN 0-445-00328-6). Popular Lib.
--Cast a Long Shadow. 1978. 6.95 o.p. (ISBN 0-525-07790-1). Dutton.
--Too Well Beloved. 1979. 7.95 o.p. (ISBN 0-525-22086-0). Dutton.
Conway, Lynn, jt. auth. see Mead, Carver.
Conway, M. D. Omitted Chapters of History Disclosed in the Life & Papers of Edmund Randolph. LC 73-124041. (American Public Figures Ser). 1971. Repr. of 1888 ed. lib. bdg. 39.50 (ISBN 0-306-70995-3). Da Capo.
Conway, McKinley. The Airport City: Development Concepts for the Twenty-First Century. rev. ed. LC 80-65254. (Illus.). 227p. 1980. 29.00x (ISBN 0-910436-14-2). Conway Pubns.
Conway, McKinley, ed. see Myhra, David.
Conway, Madeleine & Kirk, Nancy. The Museum of Modern Art Artists' Cookbook. LC 77-82029. (Illus.). 1977. pap. 8.95 (ISBN 0-87070-219-X, Dist. by Harry N. Abrams, Inc.). Museum Mod Art.
Conway, Margaret M. & Feigert, Frank B. Political Analysis: An Introduction. 2nd ed. 1972. pap. text ed. 10.45 (ISBN 0-205-05512-5, 7655126). Allyn.
Conway Maritime Press, ed. All the World's Fighting Ships, 1922-1946. (Illus.). 448p. 1980. 65.00 (ISBN 0-8317-0303-2). Mayflower Bks.
Conway, Martin. Harpers Ferry: Time Remembered. Mehrkam, Deborah, ed. 160p. 1980. 13.95 (ISBN 0-938634-00-3). Carabelle.
Conway, Moncure. Autobiography: Memoirs, & Experiences of Moncure Daniel Conway, 2 Vols. LC 76-87495. (American Public Figures Ser). (Illus.). 1970. Repr. of 1904 ed. lib. bdg. 85.00 (ISBN 0-306-71402-7). Da Capo.
Conway, Moncure D. Travels in South Kensington. LC 76-17754. (Aesthetic Movement & the Arts & Crafts Movement Ser.: Vol. 8). 1977. Repr. of 1882 ed. lib. bdg. 44.00 (ISBN 0-8240-2457-5). Garland Pub.
Conway, R. S. see Livy.
Conway, R. S., et al see Livy.
Conway, Richard, et al. Programming for Poets: A Gentle Introduction Using Pascal. (Computer Science Ser.). 352p. 1980. pap. text ed. 11.95 (ISBN 0-87626-727-4). Winthrop.
Conway, Richard A. & Ross, Richard D. Handbook of Industrial Waste Disposal. 576p. 1980. text ed. 32.50 (ISBN 0-442-27053-4). Van Nos Reinhold.
Conway, Richard W., et al. Theory of Scheduling. 1967. 18.95 (ISBN 0-201-01189-1). A-W.
Conway, Robert S. Harvard Lectures on the Vergilian Age. LC 67-13861. 1928. 9.50x (ISBN 0-8196-0182-9). Biblo.
Conway, Sally. You & Your Husband's Mid-Life Crisis. (Orig.). 1980. pap. 4.95 (ISBN 0-89191-318-1). Cook.
Conway, Theresa. Crimson Glory. 1979. pap. 2.25 o.p. (ISBN 0-449-14112-8, GM). Fawcett.
--Gabrielle. 1978. pap. 1.95 o.p. (ISBN 0-449-13916-6, GM). Fawcett.
--Paloma. 672p. (Orig.). 1981. pap. 2.75 (ISBN 0-345-28706-1). Ballantine.
Conway, William M. The Woodcutters of the Netherlands in the Fifteenth Century. 1970. Repr. of 1884 ed. text ed. 31.50x (ISBN 90-6004-034-1). Humanities.
Conwell. Acres of Diamonds. 1975. 4.95 (ISBN 0-8007-1075-4). Revell.
Conwell, Russell H. Acres of Diamonds. 1972. pap. 1.75 (ISBN 0-515-05650-2, V2762). Jove Pubns.

Conybeare, C. E. B. Oil Search in Australia. LC 80-65047. (Illus.). 151p. 1980. pap. text ed. 14.95 (ISBN 0-7081-1164-5, 0593). Bks Australia.

Conybeare, Mrs. F. C., tr. see Scherer, W., et al.

Conybeare, Fred C. The Key of Truth. 55.00 (ISBN 0-686-12403-0). Church History.

Conybeare, Frederick C. & Stock, G. A Grammar of Septuagint Greek. 80p. 1980. pap. 5.95 (ISBN 0-310-43001-1). Zondervan.

Conybeare, William J. Perversion; or, the Causes & Consequences of Infidelity, 1856. Wolff, Robert L., ed. LC 75-497. (Victorian Fiction Ser.). 1975. lib. bdg. 66.00 (ISBN 0-8240-1572-X). Garland Pub.

Conyers, James E., jt. ed. see Medley, Morris L.

Conze, Edward. Buddhism: Its Essence & Development. 8.25 (ISBN 0-8446-1889-6). Peter Smith.

--Buddhist Thought in India. 1967. pap. 3.95 (ISBN 0-472-06129-1, 129, AA). U of Mich Pr.

--The Buddhist Wisdom Books: The "Diamond Sutra" & the "Heart Sutra". 1975. pap. 7.50 (ISBN 0-04-294090-7). Allen Unwin.

--Further Buddhist Studies: Selected Essays. 1976. text ed. 13.00x o.p. (ISBN 0-85181-009-8). Verry.

Conze, Edward, ed. & tr. The Large Sutra on Perfect Wisdom, with the Divisions of the Abhisamayalankara. 1975. 35.00x (ISBN 0-520-02240-8). U of Cal Pr.

Conze, Edward, tr. from Sanskrit. & pref. by. The Perfection of Wisdom in Eight Thousand Lines & Its Verse Summary. LC 72-76540. (Wheel Ser.: No. 1). 348p. 1973. 12.00 (ISBN 0-87704-023-0); pap. 6.00 (ISBN 0-87704-024-9). Four Seasons Foun.

Conzelmann, Hans, jt. auth. see Dibelius, Martin.

Coode, Thomas H. & Bauman, John F. People, Poverty, & Politics: Pennsylvanians During the Great Depression. LC 78-75198. 280p. 1981. 24.50 (ISBN 0-8387-2320-9). Bucknell U Pr.

Coogan, Michael D. West Semitic Personal Names in the Murasu Documents. LC 75-23246. (Harvard Semitic Monographs). 1976. 7.50 (ISBN 0-89130-019-8, 040007). Scholars Pr Ca.

Coogler, O. J. Structure Mediation in Divorce Settlements: A Handbook for Marital Mediators. LC 77-15814. 1978. 16.95 (ISBN 0-669-02343-4). Lexington Bks.

Cook. The Little Fish That Got Away. (ps-3). pap. 1.25 (ISBN 0-590-01503-6, Schol Pap). Schol Bk Serv.

Cook, et al. Family Mediation Workbook. Polk, Donice, ed. 90p. (Orig.). 1980. pap. 10.00. D Polk.

Cook, A. H. Celestial Masers. LC 76-14028. (Cambridge Monographs on Physics). (Illus.). 1977. 28.95 (ISBN 0-521-21344-4). Cambridge U Pr.

--Interference of Electromagnetic Waves. (International Series of Monographs on Physics). 264p. 1971. 25.75x o.p. (ISBN 0-19-851255-4). Oxford U Pr.

--Interiors of the Planets. (Cambridge Planetary Science Ser.: No. 1). (Illus.). 360p. 1981. 59.50 (ISBN 0-521-23214-7). Cambridge U Pr.

--The Physics of the Earth & the Planets. LC 72-12261. 316p. 1973. text ed. 34.95 (ISBN 0-470-16910-9). Halsted Pr.

Cook, A. H. & Saunders, V. T. Gravity & the Earth. (Wykeham Science Ser.: No. 6). 1969. 9.95x (ISBN 0-8448-1108-4). Crane Russak Co.

Cook, Adrian. The Armies of the Streets: The New York City Draft Riots of 1863. LC 73-80463. (Illus.). 336p. 1974. 17.50x (ISBN 0-8131-1298-2). U Pr of Ky.

Cook, Albert. Adapt the Living. LC 80-17828. 83p. 1981. 8.95 (ISBN 0-8040-0350-5); pap. 4.50 (ISBN 0-8040-0359-9). Swallow.

--Charges. LC 70-112872. 154p. 1970. 8.95 (ISBN 0-8040-0036-0); pap. 4.95 (ISBN 0-8040-0037-9). Swallow.

--Enactment: Greek Tragedy. LC 78-153076. 175p. 1971. 13.95 (ISBN 0-8040-0539-7). Swallow.

--French Tragedy: The Power of Enchantment. LC 80-39611. 136p. 1981. 12.00x (ISBN 0-8040-0548-6). Swallow.

--Meaning of Fiction. LC 60-9591. 1960. 8.95x o.p. (ISBN 0-8143-1136-9). Wayne St U Pr.

Cook, Albert, ed. & tr. see Homer.

Cook, Albert M. & Webster, John G., eds. Clinical Engineering: Principles & Practices. (Illus.). 1979. text ed. 27.95 (ISBN 0-13-137737-X). P-H.

--Therapeutic Medical Devices: Application & Design. (Illus.). 656p. 1981. 39.95 (ISBN 0-13-914796-9). P-H.

Cook, Albert S. Adapt the Living. LC 80-17828. 85p. 1981. 8.95 (ISBN 0-8040-0350-5); pap. 4.50 (ISBN 0-8040-0359-9). Swallow.

--Concordance to Beowulf. LC 68-23146. 1968. Repr. of 1911 ed. 18.00 (ISBN 0-8103-3169-1). Gale.

Cook, Albert S., ed. see Eglamour.

Cook, Arthur B. Zeus: A Study of Ancient Religion, 2 vols. Incl. Vol. 1. Zeus, God of the Bright Sky. LC 64-25839. (Illus.). 885p. Repr. of 1914 ed. 45.00x (ISBN 0-8196-0148-9); Vol. 2. Zeus, God of the Dark Sky: Thunder & Lightning, 2 pts. LC 64-25839. Repr. of 1925 ed. 90.00x set (ISBN 0-8196-0156-X); Vol. 2, Pt. 1. Text & Notes. xliii, 858p; Vol. 2, Pt. 2. Appendixes & Index. (Illus.). 539p. Biblo.

Cook, Arthur H., ed. Barley & Malt: Biology, Biochemistry, Technology. 1962. 68.00 o.s.i. (ISBN 0-12-186550-9). Acad Pr.

Cook, Barbara. How to Raise Good Kids. LC 78-7844. 1978. pap. 3.50 (ISBN 0-87123-233-2, 210233). Bethany Fell.

Cook, Bernadine. Looking for Susie. (ps-3). 1959. PLB 4.95 o.p. (ISBN 0-201-09267-0, A-W Childrens). A-W.

Cook, Blanche. Toward the Great Change: Crystal & Max Eastman on Feminism, Anti-Militarism, & Revolution. (Library of War & Peace: Documentary Anthologies). 1974. lib. bdg. 38.00 (ISBN 0-8240-0502-3). Garland Pub.

Cook, Blanche W. The Declassified Eisenhower: A Divided Legacy. LC 80-699. 360p. 1981. 15.95 (ISBN 0-385-05456-4). Doubleday.

Cook, Bob, jt. auth. see Berry, Henry.

Cook, Bridget M. & Stott, Geraldine. The Book of Bobbin Lace Stitches. (Illus.). 144p. 1980. 18.50 (ISBN 0-8231-5057-7). Branford.

Cook, Bruce. Listen to the Blues. LC 72-11126. (Encore Edition). 1975. pap. 0.95 o.p. (ISBN 0-684-15762-4, SL 533, ScribT). Scribner.

Cook, Charles C., intro. by. Land Valuation Methods: Urban Land. (Lincoln Institute Monograph: No. 80-1). (Illus.). 200p. 1980. pap. text ed. 10.00. Lincoln Inst Land.

Cook, Charles E., jt. auth. see Steinberg, Arthur G.

Cook, Charles L. Inventor's Guide in a Series of Four Parts: How to Protect, Search, Compile Facts & Sell Your Invention. (Illus.). 1979. 11.95 (ISBN 0-9604670-0-9). C L Cook.

Cook, Charles M. The American Codification Movement: A Study of Antebellum Legal Reform. LC 80-662. (Contributions in Legal Studies: No. 14). 272p. 1981. lib. bdg. 35.00 (ISBN 0-313-21314-3, CAC/). Greenwood.

Cook, Charles W., et al. The Valley of the Upper Yellowstone. 1965. 6.95 (ISBN 0-8061-0664-6). U of Okla Pr.

Cook, Chester L. Inventor's Guide in a Series of Four Parts: How to Protect, Search, Compile Facts & Sell Your Invention. rev. ed. (Illus.). 52p. 1981. Repr. of 1979 ed. saddle stitch 11.95 (ISBN 0-9604670-1-7). C L Cook.

Cook, Chris. The First European Elections: A Handbook & Guide. 1979. text ed. 20.75x (ISBN 0-391-00989-3); pap. text ed. 10.00x (ISBN 0-391-00990-7). Humanities.

Cook, Chris & Wroughton, John. English Historical Facts: Sixteen Hundred & Three to Sixteen Eighty-Eight. 231p. 1981. 32.50x (ISBN 0-8476-6295-0). Rowman.

Cook, Chris, ed. Pears Cyclopedia. 88th ed. (Illus.). 976p. 1980. 11.95 o.p. (ISBN 0-7207-1159-2, Pub. by Michael Joseph). Merrimack Bk Serv.

Cook, Chris, et al. British Historical Facts Seventeen Sixty to Eighteen Thirty. ix, 197p. 1980. 32.50 (ISBN 0-208-01868-9, Archon). Shoe String.

Cook, Christopher. History of the Great Trains. LC 77-73046. (Illus.). 1977. 14.95 o.p. (ISBN 0-15-140930-7). HarBraceJ.

Cook, Christopher & Stevenson, John. Longman Atlas of Modern British History: A Visual Guide to British Society & Politics, 1700-1970. (Illus.). 1978. text ed. 17.95x (ISBN 0-582-36485-X); pap. text ed. 10.95x (ISBN 0-582-36486-8). Longman.

Cook, Clarence. Art & Artists of Our Time: With Many Illustrations, 3 vols. Weinberg, H. Barbara, ed. LC 75-28881. (Art Experience in Late 19th Century America Ser.: Vol. 15). (Illus.). 1976. Repr. of 1888 ed. Set. lib. bdg. 250.00 (ISBN 0-8240-2239-4). Garland Pub.

--The House Beautiful: Essays on Beds & Tables, Stools & Candlesticks. LC 80-10704. (Illus.). 336p. 1980. Repr. of 1878 ed. 30.00 (Dist. by Caroline House). North River.

Cook, Clifford A. Essays of a String Teacher: Come Let Us Rosin Together. LC 73-77584. 1973. 7.50 o.p. (ISBN 0-682-47690-0). Exposition.

Cook, Cornelia. Joyce Cary: Liberal Principles. (Barnes & Noble Critical Studies). 240p. 1981. 28.50x (ISBN 0-389-20201-0). B&N.

Cook, Cynthia C. The Ages of Mathematics: Western Mathematics Comes of Age, Vol. 3. LC 76-10336. (Illus.). (YA) (gr. 10 up). 1977. 5.95 o.p. (ISBN 0-385-11218-1); PLB (ISBN 0-385-11219-X). Doubleday.

Cook, D. Keeping Warm with an Ax. LC 80-19295. (Illus.). 160p. 1981. 12.95x (ISBN 0-87663-347-5); pap. 6.50 (ISBN 0-87663-552-4). Universe.

Cook, D. B. Ab Initio Valence Calculations in Chemistry. LC 73-15144. 1974. 37.95 (ISBN 0-470-17000-X). Halsted Pr.

--Structures & Approximations for Electrons in Molecules. LC 77-15665. 1978. 44.95 (ISBN 0-470-99348-0). Halsted Pr.

Cook, D. J. Hands Up: Or Twenty Years of Detective Life in the Mountains & on the Plains. (Western Frontier Library: No. 11). (Illus.). 1958. pap. 4.95 (ISBN 0-8061-0934-3). U of Okla Pr.

Cook, David. African Literature: A Critical View. 1978. pap. text ed. 9.95x (ISBN 0-582-64211-6). Longman.

--Studies on Neotropical Water Mites. (Memoir Ser.: No. 31). (Illus.). 644p. 1980. 44.00 (ISBN 0-686-27979-4). Am Entom Inst.

--Water Mite Genera & Subgenera. (Memoris Ser: No. 21). (Illus.). 860p. 1974. 55.00 (ISBN 0-686-08749-6). Am Entom Inst.

Cook, David, jt. auth. see Pitt, Valerie.

Cook, David, jt. auth. see Prasad, Vikram.

Cook, David A. A History of Narrative Film. (Illus.). 1981. 24.95 (ISBN 0-393-01370-7). Norton.

Cook, David A., tr. see Henrichsen, Walter A.

Cook, David A., tr. see Stott, John R.

Cook, David A., tr. see Wagner, Maurice.

Cook, David G., jt. ed. see Brinkhurst, Ralph O.

Cook, David M. The Theory of the Electromagnetic Field. (Illus.). 560p. 1975. ref. ed. 23.95 (ISBN 0-13-913293-7). P-H.

Cook, David M. & Swauger, Craig G., eds. The Small Town in American Literature. 2nd ed. 1977. pap. text ed. 9.50 scp (ISBN 0-06-041354-9, HarpC). Har-Row.

Cook, David R. Water Mites from India. (Memoirs Ser: No. 9). (Illus.). 411p. 1967. 25.00 (ISBN 0-686-17145-4). Am Entom Inst.

--The Water Mites of Liberia. (Memoirs Ser: No. 6). (Illus.). 418p. 1966. 25.00 (ISBN 0-686-17144-6). Am Entom Inst.

Cook, David R. & LaFleur, N. Kenneth. Guide to Educational Research. 2nd ed. 192p. 1975. pap. text ed. 12.50x (ISBN 0-205-04747-5, 224747X). Allyn.

Cook, Don. Ten Men & History. LC 80-1062. 528p. 1981. 14.95 (ISBN 0-385-14908-5). Doubleday.

Cook, Earl. Energy: The Ultimate Resource? Natoli, Salvatore J., ed. LC 77-87402. (Resource Papers for College Geography). (Illus.). 1978. pap. 4.00 (ISBN 0-89291-127-1). Assn Am Geographers.

--Man, Energy, Society. LC 75-33774. (Illus.). 1976. text ed. 21.95x (ISBN 0-7167-0725-X); pap. text ed. 11.95x (ISBN 0-7167-0724-1). W H Freeman.

Cook, Edwin A. & O'Brien, Denise, eds. Blood & Semen: Kinship Systems of Highland New Guinea. LC 80-21559. (Anthropology Ser.: Studies in Pacific Anthropology). (Illus.). 532p. (Orig.). 1980. pap. 38.50 (ISBN 0-472-02710-7, IS-00117, Pub. by U of Mich Pr). Univ Microfilms.

Cook, Elizabeth. The Ordinary & the Fabulous. 2nd ed. LC 75-7213. 204p. 1976. 26.50 (ISBN 0-521-20825-4); pap. 7.95x (ISBN 0-521-09961-7). Cambridge U Pr.

Cook, Emilie C., jt. auth. see Quinn, Daniel.

Cook, Fred. Rise of American Political Parties. LC 77-161834. (First Bks). (Illus.). (gr. 7 up). 1971. PLB 4.90 o.p. (ISBN 0-531-00741-3). Watts.

Cook, Fred J. American Political Bosses & Machines. LC 73-6777. (gr. 7 up). 1973. PLB 5.90 o.p. (ISBN 0-531-02646-9). Watts.

--City Cop. (YA) (gr. 7-12). 1981. pap. 1.25 (ISBN 0-440-90974-0, LE). Dell.

--The Cuban Missile Crisis, October 1962: The U. S. & Russia Face a Nuclear Showdown. LC 76-39813. (World Focus Books). (Illus.). 72p. (gr. 7-12). 1972. PLB 4.90 o.p. (ISBN 0-531-02159-9). Watts.

--Lobbying in American Politics. LC 75-34286. 160p. (gr. 6 up). 1976. PLB 5.90 o.p. (ISBN 0-531-01143-7). Watts.

--Mob, Inc. (gr. 7 up). 1977. PLB 7.90 (ISBN 0-531-00124-5). Watts.

--New Jersey Colony. LC 69-10893. (Forge of Freedom Ser). (Illus.). (gr. 4-7). 1969. 8.95 (ISBN 0-02-724360-5, CCPr). Macmillan.

--The U-2 Incident, May, 1960: An American Spy-Plane Downed Over Russia Intensifies the Cold War. LC 73-6796. (World Focus Bks). (gr. 7 up). 1973. PLB 4.47 o.p. (ISBN 0-531-02170-X). Watts.

--Warfare State. 1964. pap. 1.50 o.s.i. (ISBN 0-02-072770-4, Collier). Macmillan.

Cook, Frederick A. Through the First Antarctic Night, Eighteen Ninety-Eight to Eighteen Ninety-Nine. (Illus.). 478p. 1980. 49.00x (ISBN 0-7735-0514-8). McGill-Queens U Pr.

Cook, G. C. & Phipps, Lloyd J. Six Hundred More Things to Make for the Farm & Home. (Illus.). (gr. 9-12). 1952. 16.65 (ISBN 0-8134-0198-4); text ed. 12.50x (ISBN 0-685-03923-4). Interstate.

Cook, Geoffrey, tr. see Fortunatus, Venantius.

Cook, Glenn C. Five Hundred More Things to Make for Farm & Home. (Illus.). (gr. 9-12). 1944. 16.65 (ISBN 0-8134-0038-4); text ed. 13.75x (ISBN 0-685-03891-2). Interstate.

Cook, Harold R. Introduction to Christian Missions. 1971. 7.95 o.p. (ISBN 0-8024-4132-7). Moody.

Cook, Herbert N. Shemya Island. 63p. 1980. 3.95 (ISBN 0-8059-2461-2). Dorrance.

Cook, Hettie M. A Bouquet of Laughter. LC 79-54023. 164p. 1980. 6.95 (ISBN 0-8059-2665-8). Dorrance.

Cook, Howard. Swifter Than Eagles: Bill White and the Battle of Athens-1946. (Illus.). 354p. 15.00x (ISBN 0-938212-00-1). Friendly City.

Cook, J. E. & Earlley, Elsie C. Remediating Reading Disabilities: Simple Things That Work. LC 79-20412. 1979. text ed. 27.00 (ISBN 0-89443-154-4). Aspen Systems.

Cook, James. Grace Upon Grace. 6.95. Eerdmans.

Cook, James D. Iron. (Methods in Hematology Ser.: Vol. 1). (Illus.). 224p. 1980. 32.00 (ISBN 0-443-08118-2). Churchill.

Cook, James E. see Ketner, Kenneth L.

Cook, James H. Fifty Years on the Old Frontier As Cowboy, Hunter, Guide, Scout, & Ranchman. LC 57-5951. 310p. 1957. 14.95 (ISBN 0-8061-0364-7). U of Okla Pr.

Cook, Jeffrey. The Architecture of Bruce Goff. LC 78-2135. (Icon Editions). (Illus.). 1978. 22.50 (ISBN 0-06-430950-9, HarpT). Har-Row.

Cook, Jerry & Baldwin, Stanley C. Love, Acceptance & Forgiveness. LC 79-63763. 128p. 1979. pap. 3.95 (ISBN 0-8307-0654-2, 5411106). Regal.

Cook, Jim & Lewington, Mike, eds. Images of Alcoholism. (BFI Ser.). (Orig.). 1980. pap. 7.95 (ISBN 0-85170-091-8). NY Zoetrope.

Cook, John & Cook, Maria. The Forest of Enchantment. (Illus.). 48p. (gr. 4-6). 1979. 3.95 (ISBN 0-8059-2670-4). Dorrance.

Cook, John L., et al. A New Way to Proficiency in English. 336p. 1980. pap. 9.95x (ISBN 0-631-12652-X, Pub. by Basil Blackwell). Biblio Dist.

--The Student's Book of English: A Complete Course-Book & Grammar to Advanced Intermediate Level. 448p. 1980. pap. 9.95x (ISBN 0-631-12812-3, Pub. by Basil Blackwell); tapes 35.00 (ISBN 0-631-12893-X); complete pack 40.00x (ISBN 0-631-12903-0). Biblio Dist.

Cook, John P. Composite Construction Methods. LC 76-26020. (Practical Construction Guides Ser.). 1977. 33.00 (ISBN 0-471-16905-6, Pub by Wiley-Interscience). Wiley.

Cook, John S., ed. Biogenesis & Turnover of Membrane Macromolecules. LC 75-25111. (Society of General Physiologists Ser: Vol. 31). 1976. 27.00 (ISBN 0-89004-092-3). Raven.

Cook, John W. & Winkle, Gary M. Auditing: Philosophy & Technique. LC 75-31033. (Illus.). 512p. 1976. text ed. 18.50 o.p. (ISBN 0-395-20660-X); inst. manual 3.25 o.p. (ISBN 0-395-20662-6). HM.

--Auditing: Philosophy & Technique. 2nd ed. LC 79-88718. (Illus.). 1980. text ed. 19.75 (ISBN 0-395-28660-3); instructor's manual 3.25 (ISBN 0-395-28661-1). HM.

Cook, Joseph G. Constitutional Rights of the Accused: Post-Trial. new ed. LC 75-160369. (Criminal Law Library). 1976. 47.50 (ISBN 0-686-20646-0). Lawyers Co-Op.

--Constitutional Rights of the Accused: Trial Rights. LC 75-160369. (Criminal Law Library). 1974. 47.50 (ISBN 0-686-14499-6). Lawyers Co-Op.

--Constitutional Rights of the Accused: Pretrial Rights. LC 75-160369. 1972. 47.50 (ISBN 0-686-14498-8). Lawyers Co-Op.

Cook, Joseph J. The Incredible Atlantic Herring. LC 78-24540. (Illus.). (gr. 4 up). 1979. 5.95 (ISBN 0-396-07647-5). Dodd.

Cook, Joseph J. & Wisner, William L. Coastal Fishing for Beginners. LC 77-6488. (Illus.). (gr. 5 up). 1977. PLB 5.95 (ISBN 0-396-07487-1). Dodd.

Cook, Joyce L., jt. auth. see Bull, T. R.

Cook, Kenneth. Play Little Victims. 1978. text ed. 7.75 (ISBN 0-08-023123-3). Pergamon.

Cook, Lewis. Beautiful Montana Country. Shangle, Robert D., ed. (Illus.). 72p. 1980. 12.95 (ISBN 0-89802-205-3); pap. 6.95 (ISBN 0-89802-206-1). Beautiful Am.

Cook, Louis. Beautiful Michigan, Vol. II. Shangle, Robert D., ed. LC 78-105527. (Illus.). 72p. 14.95 (ISBN 0-915796-89-9); pap. 7.95 (ISBN 0-915796-88-0). Beautiful Am.

Cook, Louis & Shangle, Robert D. Beautiful: Michigan Country. (Illus.). 72p. 1980. 14.95 (ISBN 0-89802-203-7); pap. 7.95 (ISBN 0-89802-204-5). Beautiful Am.

Cook, Lyndon W. & Cannon, Donald Q. A New Light Breaks Forth. pap. 7.95 (ISBN 0-89036-148-7). Hawkes Pub Inc.

Cook, M. Early Muslim Dogma. 256p. Date not set. 49.50 (ISBN 0-521-23379-8). Cambridge U Pr.

Cook, M., jt. auth. see Argyle, M.

Cook, M., jt. auth. see Crone, Patricia.

Cook, M. A., ed. The History of the Ottoman Empire 1730. LC 75-38188. (Illus.). 232p. 1976. 32.95 (ISBN 0-521-20891-2); pap. 10.50x (ISBN 0-521-09991-9). Cambridge U Pr.

Cook, Maria, jt. auth. see Cook, John.

Cook, Mariana R. Manhattan Island to My Self. (Illus.). 1978. 10.00 o.p. (ISBN 0-89396-005-5). Urizen Bks.

Cook, Mark & McHenry, R. Sexual Attraction. 1978. text ed. 21.00 (ISBN 0-08-022231-5); pap. text ed. 8.25 (ISBN 0-08-022230-7). Pergamon.

Cook, Mark & Wilson, Glenn, eds. Love & Attraction: An International Conference. LC 78-40286. 1979. text ed. 72.00 (ISBN 0-08-022234-X); pap. text ed. 22.00 o.p. (ISBN 0-08-022235-8). Pergamon.

Cook, Mary J. From My Heart to Yours. LC 77-86313. (Illus.). 1977. pap. 4.95 o.p. (ISBN 0-89769-006-0). Pine Mntn.

Cook, Mercer & Henderson, Stephen E. Militant Black Writer in Africa & the United States. LC 69-17324. 1969. pap. 5.25 (ISBN 0-299-05394-6). U of Wis Pr.

Cook, Mercer, tr. see Thiam, Djibi.

Cook, Michael. Archives & the Computer. LC 80-41286. 152p. 1980. text ed. 27.00 (ISBN 0-408-10734-0). Butterworths.

Cook, Micheal L. The Jesus of Faith: A Study in Christology. 192p. (Orig.). pap. 6.95 (ISBN 0-8091-2349-5). Paulist Pr.

Cook, Myra, jt. auth. see Piechowiak, Ann.

Cook, N. H. Manufacturing Analysis. 1966. 19.95 (ISBN 0-201-01211-1). A-W.

Cook, Olive. The English Country House: An Art & a Way of Life. (Illus.). 1979. 19.95 (ISBN 0-500-24090-6). Thames Hudson.

Cook, P. Lesley & Surrey, A. John. Energy Policy: Strategies for Uncertainty. 240p. 1977. 36.00x (ISBN 0-85520-213-0, Pub. by Martin Robertson England). Biblio Dist.

Cook, Patsy A., ed. New York Times Oral History Guide, No. 2. 134p. 1979. pap. 17.50 (ISBN 0-667-00620-6). Microfilming Corp.

Cook, Peter & Webb, Barbara, eds. The Complete Book of Sailing. LC 76-19620. 1977. 17.95 (ISBN 0-385-11531-8). Doubleday.

Cook, Philip J. & Lambert, Richard D., eds. Gun Control. (The Annals of the American Academy of Political & Social Science Ser.: No. 455). 250p. 1981. 7.50x (ISBN 0-87761-262-5); pap. 6.00x (ISBN 0-87761-263-3). Am Acad Pol Soc Sci.

Cook, R. M. Greek Art. (Illus.). 222p. 1976. 12.95 (ISBN 0-374-16670-6). FS&G.

Cook, R. M. & Charleston, R. J. Greek & Roman Pottery. Charleston, Robert J., ed. LC 78-55079. (Masterpieces & Western & Near Eastern Ceramics Ser.: Vol. 2). (Illus.). 1979. 200.00 (ISBN 0-87011-343-7) (ISBN 0-686-52652-X). Kodansha.

Cook, Ramsey. Politics of John W. Dafoe & The Free Press. 1963. 20.00x o.p. (ISBN 0-8020-5119-7). U of Toronto Pr.

Cook, Ray L. Soil Management for Conservation & Production. LC 62-8770. (Illus.). 1962. 24.95 (ISBN 0-471-16995-1). Wiley.

Cook, Ray M. The Complete Sing-for-Fun Book. Cook, Samuel, ed. (gr. 2-12). 1974. loose leaf 10.00 (ISBN 0-8074-0004-1, 583992). UAHC.

Cook, Richard I. Bernard Mandeville. (English Authors Ser.: No. 170). 1974. lib. bdg. 12.50 (ISBN 0-8057-1371-9). Twayne.

--Sir Samuel Garth. (English Authors Ser.: No. 276). 1980. lib. bdg. 12.50 (ISBN 0-8057-6775-4). Twayne.

Cook, Richard J. Super Power Steam Locomotives. LC 66-29787. (Illus.). 1966. 15.95 (ISBN 0-87095-010-X). Golden West.

Cook, Richard M. Carson McCullers. LC 75-2789. (Modern Literature Ser.). 160p. 1975. 10.95 (ISBN 0-8044-2128-5). Ungar.

Cook, Robert A. Now That I Believe. 1956. pap. 1.50 (ISBN 0-8024-5982-X). Moody.

Cook, Robert C., ed. see Population Reference Bureau.

Cook, Robert D. Concepts & Applications of Finite Element Analysis. 2nd ed. 576p. 1981. text ed. 31.95 (ISBN 0-471-03050-3); price not set tchr's ed (ISBN 0-471-08200-7). Wiley.

Cook, Robert F. Chanson D'Antioche, Chanson De Geste: Le Cycle de la Croisade Estil Epique? (Purdue University Monographs in Romance Languages: No. 2). 115p. 1980. text ed. 17.25x (ISBN 90-272-1712-2, Athlone Pr). Humanities.

Cook, Robert P., ed. Cholesterol: Chemistry, Biochemistry, & Pathology. 1958. 55.00 o.s.i. (ISBN 0-12-187350-1). Acad Pr.

Cook, Robin. Brain. 320p. 1981. 11.95 (ISBN 0-399-12563-9). Putnam.

--Sphinx: Movie Edition. 1981. pap. 2.95 (ISBN 0-451-09745-9, E9745, Sig). NAL.

Cook, Roger & Zimmerman, Karl. Western Maryland Railroad. (Illus.). 320p. 1981. 25.00 (ISBN 0-8310-7139-7). Howell-North.

Cook, S. F. Indian Population of New England in the 17th Century. (Publ. in Anthropology Ser: Vol. 12). 1977. pap. 6.75x o.p. (ISBN 0-520-09553-7). U of Cal Pr.

Cook, S. T. & Jackson, P. M., eds. Current Issues in Fiscal Policy. 230p. 1981. pap. 13.50x (ISBN 0-85520-352-8, Pub. by Martin Robertson England). Biblio Dist.

Cook, Samuel, ed. see Cook, Ray M.

Cook, Sherburne F. The Conflict Between the California Indian & White Civilization. LC 75-23860. 1976. 32.50x (ISBN 0-520-03142-3); pap. 6.95 (ISBN 0-520-03143-1, CAL332). U of Cal Pr.

--The Population of the California Indians 1769-1970. LC 74-27287. 1976. 18.50x (ISBN 0-520-02923-2). U of Cal Pr.

Cook, Sherburne F. & Borah, Woodrow. Essays in Population History, 3 vols. Incl. Vols. 1 & 2. Mexico & the Caribbean. 1971. 27.50x ea. Vol. 1 (ISBN 0-520-01764-1). Vol. 2 (ISBN 0-520-02272-6); Vol. 3. Mexico & California. 1979. 25.00x (ISBN 0-520-03560-7). U of Cal Pr.

--The Population of the Mixteca Alta, 1520-1960. (U. C. Publ in Ibero-Americana: Vol. 50). 1968. pap. 6.00x (ISBN 0-520-09203-1). U of Cal Pr.

Cook, Shirley. Building on the Back Forty. LC 78-53324. (Illus.). 1978. pap. 2.95 o.p. (ISBN 0-89636-003-2). Accent Bks.

Cook, Sue C. The Numbers Book: Student Syllabus, 2 vols. (gr. k-2). 1974. Vol. 1. pap. text ed. 11.85 ea. packs of 10 (ISBN 0-89420-081-X, 193050). Vol. 2 (ISBN 0-89420-082-8, 193051). cassette recordings 17.36 (ISBN 0-89420-208-1, 193000). Natl Book.

Cook, Susannah. A Closer Look at Oceans. (A Closer Look at Ser.). (Illus.). 32p. (gr. 5-8). 1976. 2.95 (ISBN 0-531-02434-2); PLB 6.90 (ISBN 0-531-01190-9). Watts.

Cook, T. C., Jr., jt. auth. see Thorson, J. A.

Cook, T. M. & Cullen, D. J. Chemical Plant & Its Operation (Including Safety & Health Aspects) 2nd ed. (Illus.). 1980. text ed. 19.00 (ISBN 0-08-023812-2); pap. text ed. 8.50 (ISBN 0-08-023813-0). Pergamon.

Cook, Thomas C., Jr., jt. auth. see Thorson, James A.

Cook, Thomas D. & Reichardt, Charles S., eds. Qualitative & Quantitative Methods in Evaluation Research. LC 79-20962. (Sage Research Progress Ser. in Evaluation: Vol. 1). (Illus.). 1979. 12.95x (ISBN 0-8039-1300-1); pap. 6.50x (ISBN 0-8039-1301-X). Sage.

Cook, Thomas J., jt. auth. see Scioli, Frank P.

Cook, Thomas M. & Russell, Robert A. Contemporary Operations Management: Texts & Cases. 1980. text ed. 21.95 (ISBN 0-13-170407-9). P-H.

--Introduction to Management Science. 2nd ed. (Illus.). 640p. 1981. text ed. 22.95 (ISBN 0-13-486092-6). P-H.

--Introduction to Management Science. 1977. text ed. 19.95 (ISBN 0-13-486084-5). P-H.

Cook, V. J. English for Life, Vol. I: People & Places. (Illus.). 144p. 1980. 3.95 (ISBN 0-08-024564-1). Pergamon.

Cook, W. A. Electrostatics in Reprography. (Reprographic Lib.). Date not set. 8.95 (ISBN 0-8038-1899-8). Hastings.

Cook, W. R., jt. auth. see McLean, R. C.

Cook, W. Robert. The Theology of John. 1979. 10.95 (ISBN 0-8024-8629-0). Moody.

Cook, Walter L. Table Prayers for Children. new ed. (Illus.). (gr. k-4). 1977. pap. 1.50 (ISBN 0-8272-3621-2). Bethany Pr.

--Worship Stories. (Object Lesson Ser.). 64p. 1980. pap. 2.95 (ISBN 0-8010-2445-5). Baker Bk.

Cook, Will. The Outcasts. 144p. (Orig.). 1981. pap. 1.75 (ISBN 0-553-14740-4). Bantam.

--The Tough Texan. 160p. 1980. pap. 1.75 o.p. (ISBN 0-553-13759-X). Bantam.

Cook, William J. Confidence in Fact. 1969. pap. 3.40 (ISBN 0-89137-700-X). Quality Pubns.

Cook, William J., Jr. Masks, Modes, & Morals: The Art of Evelyn Waugh. LC 73-118125. 1971. 18.00 (ISBN 0-8386-7707-X). Fairleigh Dickinson.

Cook Adams, Marjorie E. God in the Classroom. pap. 1.95 (ISBN 0-89107-116-4). Good News.

Cookbook Committee, 1979, ed. Indianapolis Collects & Cooks. (Illus.). 208p. 1980. pap. text ed. 11.75 (ISBN 0-936260-00-9). Ind Mus Art.

Cooke, Alistair. The English: Commentaries by Alistair Cooke from Masterpiece Theatre. LC 80-2701. (Illus.). 240p. 1981. cancelled (ISBN 0-394-51907-8). Knopf.

Cooke, Ann. Giraffes at Home. LC 79-158686. (A Let's-Read-&-Find-Out Science Bk.). (Illus.). (gr. k-3). 1972. 7.95 (ISBN 0-690-33082-0, TYC-J); PLB 7.89 (ISBN 0-690-33083-9). T Y Crowell.

Cooke, Arthur L., ed. see Stroup, Thomas B.

Cooke, Barclay & Bradshaw, Jon. Backgammon, the Cruelest Game: The Art of Winning. LC 74-8725. (Illus.). 1974. 15.00 (ISBN 0-394-48812-1); pap. 5.95 (ISBN 0-394-73243-X). Random.

Cooke, Bernard. Ministry to Word & Sacraments: History & Theology. LC 75-36459. 688p. 1980. pap. 14.95 (ISBN 0-8006-1440-2, 1-1440). Fortress.

Cooke, Blanche & Markowitz, Gerald. American Anti-Imperialism: 1895-1901. LC 78-147760. (Library of War & Peace; Documentary Anthologies). 1974. lib. bdg. 38.00 (ISBN 0-8240-0500-7). Garland Pub.

Cooke, Cynthia W. Handbook of Gynecologic Emergencies. 1975. spiral bdg. 10.00 o.s.i. (ISBN 0-87488-640-6). Med Exam.

Cooke, Cynthia W. & Dworkin, Susan. The Ms. Guide to a Woman's Health. 1981. pap. 3.95 (ISBN 0-425-04796-2). Berkley Pub.

Cooke, D., jt. auth. see Clarke, G. M.

Cooke, David C. Better Physical Fitness for Boys. LC 61-8310. (Illus.). (gr. 7-9). 1961. PLB 5.95 o.p. (ISBN 0-396-06586-4). Dodd.

--Tecumseh: Destiny's Warrior. LC 59-7011. (Biography Ser.). (gr. 6 up). 1959. PLB 4.29 o.p. (ISBN 0-671-32275-3). Messner.

Cooke, Deryck. I Saw the World End: A Study of Wagner's Ring. 1979. 19.95 (ISBN 0-19-315316-5). Oxford U Pr.

--Language of Music. 1959. pap. 8.95x (ISBN 0-19-284004-5, OPB). Oxford U Pr.

Cooke, Fred J. Ku Klux Klan: America's Recurring Nightmare. (Illus.). 160p. (YA) (gr. 7 up). 1980. PLB 8.29 (ISBN 0-671-34055-7). Messner.

Cooke, Frederick H. The Law of Trade & Labor Combinations As Applicable to Boycotts, Strikes, Trade Conspiracies, Monopolies, Pools, Trusts, & Kindred Topics. xxv, 214p. 1981. Repr. of 1898 ed. lib. bdg. 24.00x (ISBN 0-8377-0430-8). Rothman.

Cooke, G. A. Ezekiel. LC 38-12281. (International Critical Commentary Ser.). 608p. Repr. of 1936 ed. text ed. 23.00x (ISBN 0-567-05016-5). Attic Pr.

Cooke, George W. John Sullivan Dwight: A Biography. LC 79-90210. (Music Reprint Ser). 1969. Repr. of 1898 ed. 29.50 (ISBN 0-306-71818-9). Da Capo.

Cooke, Gillian. A Celebration of Christmas. 1980. 16.95 (ISBN 0-686-68353-6). Putnam.

Cooke, Grace. Meditation. 1955. 6.50 (ISBN 0-85487-011-3). De Vorss.

--The New Mediumship. 1965. 4.95 (ISBN 0-85487-013-X). De Vorss.

--Sun Men of the Americas. 6.95 (ISBN 0-85487-035-0). De Vorss.

Cooke, Grace & Cooke, Ivan. The Light in Britain. (Illus.). 1971. 5.50 (ISBN 0-85487-006-7). De Vorss.

--The Return of Arthur Conan Doyle. (Illus.). 1963. 12.00; pap. 6.50 o.p. De Vorss.

Cooke, H. Lester, Jr. Fletcher Martin. LC 75-2472. (Contemporary Artists Ser.). (Illus.). 1977. 65.00 o.p. (ISBN 0-8109-0319-9). Abrams.

Cooke, Hope. Time Change: An Autobiography. 1981. 12.95 (ISBN 0-671-41225-6). S&S.

Cooke, Ivan. Healing by the Spirit. 1955. 12.00 (ISBN 0-85487-039-3). De Vorss.

Cooke, Ivan, jt. auth. see Cooke, Grace.

Cooke, Jacob E., ed. The Federalist. LC 61-6971. 1961. 35.00x (ISBN 0-8195-3016-6, Pub. by Wesleyan U Pr). Columbia U Pr.

Cooke, James J., jt. ed. see Heggoy, Alf A.

Cooke, Joan, jt. auth. see Rowland-Entwistle, A. T.

Cooke, Katharine. Coleridge: An Author Guide. 1979. 19.00x (ISBN 0-7100-0141-X). Routledge & Kegan.

Cooke, Katherine. A. C. Bradley & His Influence in Twentieth-Century Shakespeare Criticism. 1972. 22.00x (ISBN 0-19-812024-9). Oxford U Pr.

Cooke, Kenneth, jt. auth. see Bellman, Richard.

Cooke, Nelson M. & Adams, Herbert F. Arithmetic Review for Electronics. 1968. 11.95 (ISBN 0-07-012516-3, G); answers to review problems 1.00 (ISBN 0-07-012517-1). McGraw.

--Basic Mathematics for Electronics. 4th ed. (Illus.). 1976. text ed. 17.25 (ISBN 0-07-012512-0, G); answers to even-numbered problems 2.95 (ISBN 0-07-012511-2); study guide 4.25 (ISBN 0-07-000305-X). McGraw.

Cooke, Peter N. Inflation Management in Motor Transport Operations. 192p. 1978. text ed. 25.25x (ISBN 0-566-02056-4, Pub. by Gower Pr England). Renouf.

Cooke, Philip. Dependent Development in United Kingdom Regions with Particular Reference to Wales. (Progress on Planning Ser.: Vol. 15, Part 1). 90p. 1980. pap. 13.50 (ISBN 0-08-026809-9). Pergamon.

Cooke, R. Gordon & Miller, Ann. A Summary of Medicine for Nurses & Medical Auxiliaries. 7th ed. 1978. pap. 4.95 (ISBN 0-571-04942-7, Pub. by Faber & Faber). Merrimack Bk Serv.

Cooke, R. J., jt. auth. see Trevena, D. H.

Cooke, R. V. & Johnson, J. H. Trends in Geography: An Introductory Survey. 1969. 13.75 (ISBN 0-08-006675-5); pap. 6.25 (ISBN 0-08-006674-7). Pergamon.

Cooke, Roderic C. Fungi, Man & His Environment. LC 77-1460. (Illus.). 144p. 1978. text ed. 20.00x (ISBN 0-582-46034-4); pap. text ed. 6.95 (ISBN 0-582-44262-1). Longman.

Cooke, Ronald U. & Doornkamp, John C. Geomorphology in Environmental Management: An Introduction. (Illus.). 348p. 1974. text ed. 29.50x (ISBN 0-19-874020-4); pap. text ed. 16.50x (ISBN 0-19-874021-2). Oxford U Pr.

Cooke, Ronald U. & Reeves, Richard W. Arroyos & Environmental Change in the American South-West. (Oxford Research Studies in Geography Ser.). (Illus.). 1976. 36.00x (ISBN 0-19-823213-6). Oxford U Pr.

Cooke, W. S. The Ottoman Empire & Its Tributary States(Expecting Egypt) With a Sketch of Greece. (Illus.). 1968. text ed. 34.25x (ISBN 90-6032-211-8). Humanities.

Cookey, S. J. Britain & the Congo Question, 1885-1913. (Ibadan History Ser). (Illus.). 1968. text ed. 8.00x (ISBN 0-582-64511-5, 67-16973). Humanities.

Cook-Gumperz, Jenny. Social Control & Socialization: A Study of Class Differences in the Language of Maternal Control. (Primary Socialization, Language & Education Ser.). 300p. 1973. 22.50 (ISBN 0-7100-7409-3). Routledge & Kegan.

Cooklin, Lawrence. Profitable Mail Order Marketing. 1976. 18.95x (ISBN 0-434-90259-4). Intl Ideas.

Cookridge, E. H. The Orient Express: The Life & Times of the World's Most Famous Train. LC 78-57119. (Illus.). 1980. pap. 5.95 (ISBN 0-06-090770-3, CN 770, CN). Har-Row.

Cookson, Catherine. The Cinder Path. LC 78-54993. 1978. 9.95 o.p. (ISBN 0-688-03339-3). Morrow.

--Feathers in the Fire. 288p. 1981. pap. 2.25 (ISBN 0-553-13936-3). Bantam.

--Go Tell It to Mrs. Golightly. LC 80-10308. 192p. (gr. 5 up). 1980. 7.95 (ISBN 0-688-41965-8); PLB 7.63 (ISBN 0-688-51965-2). Lothrop.

--Hannah Massey. 1973. pap. 1.50 (ISBN 0-451-06623-5, W6623, Sig). NAL.

--The Husband. 1976. pap. 1.75 (ISBN 0-451-07858-6, E7858, Sig). NAL.

--Katie Mulholland. 512p. 1981. pap. 2.75 (ISBN 0-553-13935-5). Bantam.

--Lanky Jones. LC 80-22676. 192p. (gr. 6 up). 1981. 7.95 (ISBN 0-688-00430-X); PLB 7.63 (ISBN 0-688-00431-8). Morrow.

--The Mallen Girl. 288p. 1981. pap. 2.50 (ISBN 0-553-13933-9). Bantam.

--The Mallen Streak. 288p. 1981. pap. 2.50 (ISBN 0-553-13932-0). Bantam.

--Tilly. LC 80-16627. 384p. 1980. 12.95 (ISBN 0-688-03715-1). Morrow.

--Tilly Wed. Orig. Title: Tilly Trotter Wed. 384p. 1980. 12.95 (ISBN 0-688-00188-2). Morrow.

Cookson, G. M., tr. see Aeschylus.

Cookson, William. Advanced Methods for Sheet Metal Work. 6th ed. (Illus.). 1975. 21.00x (ISBN 0-291-39427-2). Intl Ideas.

Coole, Arthur B. Ch'i Heavy Sword Coins of the Chou Dynasty, Vol. 5. LC 72-86801. (Encyclopedia of Chinese Coins Ser.: Vol. 5). (Illus.). 1976. 35.00x (ISBN 0-88000-014-7). Quarterman.

--The Earliest Round Coins of China. (Encyclopedia of Chinese Coins Ser.: Vol. 7). 325p. Date not set. lib. bdg. 35.00 (ISBN 0-88000-122-4). Quarterman.

--The Early Coins of the Chou Dynasty. LC 72-86804. (Encyclopedia of Chinese Coins: Vol. 2). (Illus.). 550p. 1973. 35.00x (ISBN 0-88000-010-4). Quarterman.

--Pointed Spade Coins of the Chou Dynasty. LC 72-86806. (Encyclopedia of Chinese Coins Ser: Vol. 4). (Illus.). 464p. 1975. 35.00x (ISBN 0-88000-012-0). Quarterman.

--Spade Coin Types of the Chou Dynasty. LC 76-86803. (Encyclopedia of Chinese Coins Ser.: Vol. 3). (Illus.). 1973. 35.00x (ISBN 0-88000-011-2). Quarterman.

--State of Ming Coin Knives & Minor Knife Coins. LC 72-86802. (Encyclopedia of Chinese Coins Ser.: Vol. 6). (Illus.). 1977. 35.00x (ISBN 0-88000-013-9). Quarterman.

Coolen, jt. auth. see Roddy.

Cooley, Everett L., ed. Diary of Brigham Young, 1857. (Utah, the Mormons, & the West Ser). 132p. 1981. 17.50 (ISBN 0-87480-195-8, Tanner). U of Utah Pr.

Cooley, H. B. Chartering & Charter Parties. 2nd ed. LC 47-27564. 1974. pap. 6.00x (ISBN 0-87033-012-8). Cornell Maritime.

Cooley, John. Savages & Naturals: Black Portraits by White Writers in Modern American Literature. Date not set. 12.00 (ISBN 0-87413-167-7). U Delaware Pr. Postponed.

Cooley, Leland. The Dancer. 1979. pap. 2.75 (ISBN 0-451-08651-1, E8651, Sig). NAL.

Cooley, Leland F. The Richest Poor Folks. LC 77-1267. 1977. 10.00 o.p. (ISBN 0-312-68225-5). St Martin.

Cooley, Marilyn. Checklist for a Working Wife. LC 78-8205. 1979. pap. 2.50 (ISBN 0-385-14205-6, Dolp). Doubleday.

Cooley, Thomas, ed. The Norton Sampler: Short Essays for Composition. 1978. pap. text ed. 5.45x (ISBN 0-393-09007-8); instructor's handbook free (ISBN 0-393-95047-6). Norton.

Cooley, Thomas M. A Treatise on the Constitutional Limitations. LC 78-87510. (American Constitutional & Legal History Ser). 720p. 1972. Repr. of 1868 ed. lib. bdg. 59.50 (ISBN 0-306-71403-5). Da Capo.

Cooley, W. C., ed. see Karasik, V. M., et al.

Cooley, W. C., ed. see Pokrovskaya, Vera N.

Cooley, W. C., ed. see Traynis, V. V.

Cooley, W. C., ed. see Turchaninov, S. P.

Cooley, W. W. & Lohnes, P. R. Evaluation Research in Education. LC 75-37696. 352p. 1976. 16.50 (ISBN 0-470-01398-2). Halsted Pr.

Cooley's Anemia Symposium, 4th, et al. Proceedings. Bank, Arthur, et al, eds. LC 80-17575. (N.Y. Academy of Sciences Annals: Vol. 344). 1980. 79.00x (ISBN 0-89766-076-5); pap. write for info. NY Acad Sci.

Coolican, Don & Lemoine, Serge. Charles: Royal Adventurer. (Illus.). 1978. 10.00 (ISBN 0-7207-1056-1, Pub. by Two Continents). Hippocrene Bks.

Coolidge, Archibald C., jt. auth. see Channing, Edward.

Coolidge, Archibald C., ed. see Harris, Joel C.

Coolidge, Calvin. Your Son, Calvin Coolidge: A Selection of Letters from Calvin Coolidge to His Father. Lathem, Edward C., ed. LC 68-57427. (Illus.). 255p. 1968. text ed. 12.50x (ISBN 0-87451-058-9). U Pr of New Eng.

Coolidge, Julian L. Treatise on the Circle & the Sphere. LC 78-128872. 1971. text ed. 19.50 o.p. (ISBN 0-8284-0236-1). Chelsea Pub.

Coolidge, Oliver. Golden Days of Greece. LC 68-21599. (Illus.). (gr. 5 up). 1968. 9.95 (ISBN 0-690-33473-7, TYC-J). T Y Crowell.

Coolidge, Olivia. Come by Here. LC 72-115451. (Illus.). (gr. 5 up). 1970. 6.95 (ISBN 0-395-10912-4). HM.

--Greek Myths. (Illus.). (gr. 7 up). 1949. 8.95 (ISBN 0-395-06721-9). HM.

--Tom Paine, Revolutionary. LC 69-17064. (gr. 9 up). 1969. lib. rep. ed. 10.00x o.p. (ISBN 0-684-15152-9, ScribJ). Scribner.

Coolidge, Usher, tr. see Sato, Masahiko.

Cooling, Benjamin F., ed. War, Business, & World Military-Industrial Complexes. (National University Publications, Political Science Ser.). 1981. 19.50 (ISBN 0-8046-9276-9). Kennikat.

Coomaraswamy, A. K. History of Indian & Indonesian Art. (Illus.). 432p. 1972. 25.00x o.p. (ISBN 0-8426-0393-X). Verry.

Coomaraswamy, Amanda K. Elements of Buddhist Iconography. (Illus.). 130p. 1972. Repr. of 1935 ed. 22.50x (ISBN 0-8002-1390-4). Intl Pubns Serv.

Coombe, D. E., tr. see Von Denffer, Dietrich, et al.

Coombes, B., ed. Vehicle Body Building, Pt. 2, 2 vols. (Engineering Craftsmen: No. E22). (Illus.). 1969. Set. spiral bdg. 52.00x (ISBN 0-85083-063-X). Intl Ideas.

Coombes, B., et al, eds. Vehicle Body Building: Pt. 1. (Engineering Craftsmen: Pt. 2). (Illus.). 1968. 26.50x (ISBN 0-686-65562-1). Intl Ideas.

Coombes, David. State Enterprise: Business or Politics? (Political & Economic Planning Ser.). 1971. text ed. 14.95x o.p. (ISBN 0-04-338047-6). Allen Unwin.

Coombes, David, ed. The Power of the Purse: A Symposium on the Role of European Parliaments in Budgetary Decisions. LC 75-23959. (Special Studies). (Illus.). 380p. 1976. text ed. 28.95 (ISBN 0-275-05790-9). Praeger.

Coombes, Susan E., jt. auth. see Simmons, Frank G.

Coombs, C. A. The Arena of International Finance. 1976. 22.95 (ISBN 0-471-01513-X, Pub. by Wiley-Interscience). Wiley.

Coombs, Charles. Auto Racing. LC 73-153770. (Illus.). (gr. 5-9). 1971. 7.25 (ISBN 0-688-21053-8); PLB 6.96 (ISBN 0-688-31053-2). Morrow.

--Be a Winner in Baseball. (Illus.). 128p. (gr. 5-9). 1973. PLB 7.44 (ISBN 0-688-30093-6). Morrow.

--Be a Winner in Basketball. LC 75-17778. (Illus.). 128p. (gr. 5-9). 1975. PLB 7.44 (ISBN 0-688-32039-2); pap. 2.45 (ISBN 0-688-27039-5). Morrow.

--Be a Winner in Football. LC 74-5932. 128p. (gr. 5-9). 1974. 7.44 (ISBN 0-688-30119-3); pap. 2.45 (ISBN 0-688-25119-6). Morrow.

--Be a Winner in Horsemanship. LC 76-17118. (Illus.). 128p. (gr. 5-9). 1976. 7.25 (ISBN 0-688-22080-0); PLB 6.96 (ISBN 0-688-32080-5). Morrow.

--Be a Winner in Ice Hockey. LC 73-10769. (Illus.). 128p. (gr. 5-9). 1974. PLB 6.50 (ISBN 0-688-30099-5); pap. 2.45 (ISBN 0-688-25099-8). Morrow.

--Be a Winner in Soccer. (gr. 5-9). 1977. 7.25 (ISBN 0-688-22099-1); PLB 6.96 (ISBN 0-688-32099-6). Morrow.

--Be a Winner in Soccer. (Illus.). (gr. 5-7). 1980. pap. write for info. (ISBN 0-671-41104-7). PB.

--Be a Winner in Tennis. LC 74-23262. (Illus.). 128p. (gr. 5-9). 1975. PLB 7.44 (ISBN 0-688-32020-1); pap. 2.45 (ISBN 0-688-27022-0). Morrow.

--Be a Winner in Track & Field. LC 75-33077. (Illus.). 128p. (gr. 5-9). 1976. 7.75 (ISBN 0-688-22064-9); PLB 7.44 (ISBN 0-688-32064-3). Morrow.

--Bicycling. (Illus.). (gr. 5-9). 1972. PLB 6.96 o.p. (ISBN 0-688-20032-X); PLB 6.96 (ISBN 0-688-30032-4). Morrow.

--Drag Racing. (Illus.). (gr. 5-9). 1970. PLB 6.96 (ISBN 0-688-31243-8). Morrow.

--Hot-Air Ballooning. LC 80-26704. (Illus.). 128p. (gr. 4-6). 1981. 7.95 (ISBN 0-688-00364-8); PLB 7.63 (ISBN 0-688-00365-6). Morrow.

--Mopeding. (Illus.). (gr. 4-6). 1978. 6.95 (ISBN 0-688-22155-6); PLB 6.67 (ISBN 0-688-32155-0). Morrow.

--Motorcycling. LC 68-23911. (gr. 5-9). 1968. PLB 7.25 (ISBN 0-688-21564-5); pap. 6.96 (ISBN 0-688-31564-X). Morrow.

--Passage to Space: The Shuttle Transportation System. LC 79-1176. (Illus.). (gr. 4-6). 1979. 7.50 (ISBN 0-688-22188-2); PLB 7.20 (ISBN 0-688-32188-7). Morrow.

--Pipeline Across Alaska. LC 77-28986. (Illus.). (gr. 5-9). 1978. 6.50 (ISBN 0-688-22139-4); PLB 6.24 (ISBN 0-688-32139-9). Morrow.

--Skyhooks: The Story of Helicopters. (Illus.). (gr. 5-9). 1967. 6.25 o.p. (ISBN 0-688-21556-4); PLB 6.00 o.p. (ISBN 0-688-31556-9). Morrow.

--Skylab. LC 79-168471. (Illus.). (gr. 5-9). 1972. PLB 6.96 (ISBN 0-688-31812-6). Morrow.

--Spacetrack, Watchdog of the Skies. LC 69-14233. (Illus.). (gr. 5-9). 1969. PLB 6.96 (ISBN 0-688-31561-5). Morrow.

--Water Sports. (Young Readers Bookshelf). (Illus.). (gr. 4-7). 4.25 o.p. (ISBN 0-8313-0022-1); PLB 6.19 (ISBN 0-685-23444-4). Lantern.

Coombs, Charles I. Be a Winner in Skiing. LC 77-2621. (gr. 5-9). 1977. 7.25 (ISBN 0-688-22131-9); PLB 6.96 (ISBN 0-688-32131-3). Morrow.

Coombs, Clyde, et al. Mathematical Psychology: An Elementary Introduction. 1969. text ed. 21.95 (ISBN 0-13-562157-7). P-H.

Coombs, Franklin. The Crows: A Study of the Corvids of Europe. 1978. 38.00 (ISBN 0-7134-1327-1, Pub. by Batsford England). David & Charles.

Coombs, L. F. Harrow Railway Disaster 1952. 1977. 14.95 (ISBN 0-7153-7409-5). David & Charles.

Coombs, Norman. The Black Experience in America. LC 73-186717. (The Immigrant Heritage of America Ser.). 1972. lib. bdg. 10.95 (ISBN 0-8057-3208-X). Twayne.

Coombs, Patricia. Dorrie & the Witchville Fair. LC 80-10189. (Illus.). 48p. (gr. 1-4). 1980. 6.95 (ISBN 0-688-41957-7); PLB 6.67 (ISBN 0-688-51957-1). Lothrop.

Coombs, Philip H. What Is Educational Planning? (Fundamentals of Educational Planning Ser). (Orig.). 1971. pap. 6.00 (ISBN 92-803-1037-2, U715, UNESCO). Unipub.

Coombs, Philip H. & Ahmed, Manzoor. Attacking Rural Poverty: How Non-Formal Education Can Help. LC 73-19350. (The World Bank Ser). (Illus.). 308p. 1974. 18.50x (ISBN 0-8018-1600-9); pap. 6.95x (ISBN 0-8018-1601-7). Johns Hopkins.

Coombs, Philip H. & Hallak, Jacques. Managing Educational Costs. (Illus.). 200p. 1972. pap. text ed. 5.95x (ISBN 0-19-501557-6). Oxford U Pr.

Coombs, Philip H., ed. Meeting the Basic Needs of the Rural Poor: The Integrated, Community-Based Approach. LC 80-19838. (Pergamon Policy Studies on International Development). 828p. 1980. 49.50 (ISBN 0-08-026306-2). Pergamon.

Coombs, Robert H. Mastering Medicine: Professional Socialization in Medical School. LC 77-85351. 1978. 17.95 (ISBN 0-02-906640-9). Free Pr.

Coombs, Robert H., ed. Junkies & Straights. LC 75-27250. (Illus.). 240p. 1975. 19.95 (ISBN 0-669-00320-4). Lexington Bks.

Coombs, Rod, jt. auth. see Green, K.

Coombs, Susan E., jt. auth. see Simmons, Frank G.

Coomer, James C., ed. Quest for a Sustainable Society. LC 80-24158. (Pergamon Policy Studies on International Development). 230p. 1981. 24.01 (ISBN 0-08-027168-5). Pergamon.

Coon, Carleton S. The Hunting Peoples. (Illus.). 1979. 10.95 (ISBN 0-224-00685-1, Pub. by Chatto Bodley Jonathan). Merrimack Bk Serv.

--The Seven Caves: Archaeological Explorations in the Middle East. LC 80-24503. (Illus.). xx, 354p. 1981. Repr. of 1957 ed. lib. bdg. 31.50x (ISBN 0-313-22824-8, COSCA). Greenwood.

Coon, Carleton S. & Gambit Editors. A North Africa Story: An Anthropologist As OSS Agent, 1941-1943. 1980. 10.95 (ISBN 0-87645-108-3). Gambit.

Coon, Carleton S., et al. Races: A Study of the Problems of Race Formation in Man. LC 80-24479. (American Lecture Ser.: No. 77). (Illus.). xiv, 153p. 1981. Repr. of 1950 ed. lib. bdg. 19.75x (ISBN 0-313-22878-7, CORA). Greenwood.

Coon, Caroline. Nineteen Eighty-Eight: The New Wave Punk Rock Explosion. (Illus.). 1978. pap. 4.95 o.p. (ISBN 0-8015-6129-9). Dutton.

Coon, Dennis L. Essentials of Psychology: Exploration & Application. (Illus.). 1979. pap. text ed. 14.50 (ISBN 0-8299-0241-4); study guide 6.50 (ISBN 0-8299-0244-9); instrs.' manual avail. (ISBN 0-8299-0468-9); study guide 6.50. West Pub.

--Introduction to Psychology Exploration & Application. 2nd ed. (Illus.). 1980. text ed. 17.95 (ISBN 0-8299-0303-8). study guide 5.95 (ISBN 0-8299-0304-6); instrs.' manual avail. (ISBN 0-8299-0467-0). West Pub.

Coon, Ethel, jt. auth. see Coon, Glenn.

Coon, Glenn. God's Promises Solve My Problems. (Harvest Ser.). 1979. pap. 3.95 (ISBN 0-8163-0334-7, 07550-7). Pacific Pr Pub Assn.

Coon, Glenn & Coon, Ethel. Lovely Lord of the Lord's Day. LC 75-464238. 1976. pap. 4.95 (ISBN 0-8163-0225-1, 12740-7). Pacific Pr Pub Assn.

Coon, Minor J., ed. Microsomes, Drug Oxidations & Chemical Carcinogenesis, Vol. I. LC 80-11363. 1980. 39.50 (ISBN 0-12-187701-9). Acad Pr.

Coon, Nelson. Using Plants for Healing. 1979. 9.95 (ISBN 0-87857-247-3); pap. 7.95 (ISBN 0-87857-313-5). Rodale Pr Inc.

--Using Wild & Wayside Plants. (Illus.). 288p. 1980. pap. 4.00 (ISBN 0-486-23936-5). Dover.

Coon, Susan. Cassilee. 1980. pap. 2.25 (ISBN 0-686-69246-2, 75887). Avon.

--Rahne. 1979. pap. 1.95 (ISBN 0-380-75044-9, 75044). Avon.

Cooney. Advances in Biomedical Engineering, Pt. I. 360p. 1980. 35.00 (ISBN 0-8247-6925-2). Dekker.

Cooney, Barbara. Christmas. LC 67-18510. (Holiday Ser.). (Illus.). (gr. k-3). 1967. PLB 7.89 (ISBN 0-690-19201-0, TYC-J). T Y Crowell.

--Garland of Games & Other Diversions. LC 69-15675. (Younger Reader Ser). (Illus., Orig.). (gr. k-3). 1969. 3.95 o.p. (ISBN 0-910412-01-4); pap. 1.95 o.p. (ISBN 0-910412-12-X). Williamsburg.

Cooney, Barbara, jt. auth. see Preston, Edna M.

Cooney, Caroline B. The Paper Caper. (Illus.). 64p. (gr. 9-12). 1981. 6.95 (ISBN 0-698-20506-5). Coward.

Cooney, David O., ed. Advances in Biomedical Engineering, Pt. 2. (Biomedical Engineering & Instrumentation Ser.: Vol. 6). (Illus.). 368p. 1980. 39.50 (ISBN 0-8247-6994-5). Dekker.

Cooney, Nancy E. The Blanket That Had to Go. (Illus.). 32p. (gr. 4-8). 1981. 7.95 (ISBN 0-399-20716-3). Putnam.

--The Wobbly Tooth. (Illus.). 32p. (Orig.). (gr. k-3). 1981. pap. 2.95 (ISBN 0-399-20776-7, Peppercorn). Putnam.

Cooney, Nancy H. Sex, Sexuality, & You: A Handbook for Growing Christians. 100p. (Orig.). 1980. pap. text ed. 3.50 (ISBN 0-697-01741-9); tchr's resource guide 0.75 (ISBN 0-697-01742-7). Wm C Brown.

Cooney, Seamus, jt. auth. see Morrow, Bradford.

Cooney, Seamus, ed. see Reznikoff, Charles.

Cooney, Thomas J., et al. Geometry. Date not set. text ed. price not set (ISBN 0-201-00974-9, Sch Div); price not set tchr's manual (ISBN 0-201-00975-7). A-W. Postponed.

--Dynamics of Teaching Secondary Mathematics. 1975. 17.95 (ISBN 0-395-18617-X). HM.

Coonfare, Clifford R. Luke Four-Eighteen: Sermons to Touch the Heart & Grip the Soul. 96p. 1980. pap. 5.95 (ISBN 0-8059-2747-6). Dorrance.

Coons. Trampolining for Women & Men. 1980. pap. 6.95 (ISBN 0-8015-7886-8, Hawthorn). Dutton.

Coons, John E. & Sugarman, Stephen D. Education by Choice: The Case for Family Control. LC 77-20318. 1978. 12.95 (ISBN 0-520-03613-1); pap. 4.95 (ISBN 0-520-03837-1). U of Cal Pr.

Coontz, Otto. Starring Rosa. (Illus.). 48p. (gr. 1-3). 1980. 7.95g (ISBN 0-316-15535-7). Little.

Coope, Christopher, et al. Wittgenstein Workbook. LC 79-135161. 1970. pap. 3.50x (ISBN 0-520-01840-0, CAMPUS48). U of Cal Pr.

Cooper. Introd. Operations Research Models. 1977. 18.95 (ISBN 0-7216-2688-2). Dryden Pr.

--Software Quality Management. 1979. 21.50 (ISBN 0-89433-093-4). Petrocelli.

--Surgery Annual: 1969, Vol. 1. (Illus.). 1969. 18.85 o.p. (ISBN 0-8385-8700-3). ACC.

--Surgery Annual: 1970, Vol. 2. (Illus.). 1970. 17.80 o.p. (ISBN 0-8385-8702-X). ACC.

--Surgery Annual: 1971, Vol. 3. (Illus.). 1971. 19.50 o.p. (ISBN 0-8385-8703-8). ACC.

--Surgery Annual: 1972, Vol. 4. (Illus.). 1972. 17.50 o.p. (ISBN 0-8385-8704-6). ACC.

Cooper, et al. Eli Whitney & the Whitney Armory. (Illus.). 95p. 8.95 (ISBN 0-9603662-0-2); pap. 4.95 (ISBN 0-686-63873-5). Arma Pr.

Cooper, A. A. Speeches of the Earl of Shaftesbury. 456p. Repr. of 1868 ed. 32.00x (ISBN 0-686-28328-7, Pub. by Irish Academic Pr). Biblio Dist.

Cooper, Al. Examining the Gospels. 1981. 4.75 (ISBN 0-8062-1601-8). Carlton.

Cooper, Alice C. & Palmer, Charles A., eds. Twenty Modern Americans. LC 42-1234. (gr. 7 up). 1942. 6.50 o.p. (ISBN 0-15-291590-7, HJ). HarBraceJ.

Cooper, Ann. Fool's Paradise. (Harlequin Romances Ser.). 192p. (Orig.). 1981. pap. 1.25 (ISBN 0-686-68820-1, Pub. by Harlequin). PB.

Cooper, Anthony R., ed. Ultrafiltration Membranes & Applications. (Polymer Science & Technology Ser.: Vol. 13). 700p. 1981. 75.00 (ISBN 0-306-40548-2, Plenum Pr). Plenum Pub.

Cooper, B. & Bartlett, A. Industrial Relations. 1976. pap. 14.95x (ISBN 0-434-90261-6). Intl Ideas.

Cooper, B. E. Statistics for Experimentalists. 1969. 19.50 (ISBN 0-08-012600-6). Pergamon.

Cooper, Barbara A. The Savage Passion. 400p. (Orig.). 1981. pap. 2.50 (ISBN 0-89083-707-4). Zebra.

Cooper, Barbara E., jt. auth. see Somer, John L.

Cooper, Barry. Merleau-Ponty & Marxism: From Terror to Reform. LC 78-16829. 1979. 20.00x (ISBN 0-8020-5435-8). U of Toronto Pr.

Cooper, Brian. Monsoon Murder. LC 68-8081. 1968. 6.95 (ISBN 0-8149-0042-9). Vanguard.

--Murder of Mary Steers. LC 66-16980. 5.95 (ISBN 0-8149-0043-7). Vanguard.

Cooper, Brian & Morgan, H. G. Epidemiological Psychiatry. (American Lectures Living Chemistry). (Illus.). 232p. 1973. 17.75 (ISBN 0-398-02581-9). C C Thomas.

Cooper, Bryan. E-Boat Threat. 1980. 12.95 (ISBN 0-356-08144-3, Pub. by MacDonald & Jane's England). Hippocrene Bks.

Cooper, C. Behavioral Problems in Organizations. 1979. 15.95 (ISBN 0-13-073080-7). P-H.

Cooper, C. L. & Payne, R. Stress at Work. (Studies in Occupational Stress). 293p. 1978. 36.50 (ISBN 0-471-99547-9, Pub. by Wiley-Interscience). Wiley.

Cooper, Carl, jt. auth. see Humble, Lance.

Cooper, Cary. Developing Managers for the Nineteen Eighties. LC 80-15212. 160p. 1981. text ed. 36.00x (ISBN 0-8419-0649-1). Holmes & Meier.

Cooper, Cary L. & Marshall, Judi. Understanding Executive Stress. LC 77-16077. 1978. text ed. 14.00 (ISBN 0-89433-059-4). Petrocelli.

Cooper, Cary L. & Payne, Roy. Current Concerns in Occupational Stress. LC 79-40641. (Wiley Ser. on Studies in Occupational Stress). 1980. 39.75 (ISBN 0-471-27624-3, Pub. by Wiley-Interscience). Wiley.

Cooper, Cary L., jt. auth. see Alderfer, Clayton P.

Cooper, Cary L., jt. auth. see Jones, Andrew N.

Cooper, Cary L., jt. auth. see Marshall, Judi.

Cooper, Cary L., ed. Developing Social Skills in Managers: Advances in Group Training. LC 75-30510. 140p. 1976. 18.95 o.p. (ISBN 0-470-17121-9). Halsted Pr.

Cooper, Charles. English Table in History & Literature. LC 68-21760. 1968. Repr. of 1929 ed. 15.00 (ISBN 0-8103-3520-4). Gale.

Cooper, Charles, ed. Science,Technology & Development: Political Economy of Technical Advance in Underdeveloped Countries. 204p. 1973. 27.50x (ISBN 0-7146-2999-5, F Cass Co). Biblio Dist.

Cooper, Christine & Hildesley, Angela. Carefree Cookbook. 1976. 8.95 (ISBN 0-600-31879-6). Transatlantic.

Cooper, Clare C. Easter Hill Village: Some Social Implications of Design. LC 74-10311. (Illus.). 1975. 17.95 (ISBN 0-02-906670-0). Free Pr.

Cooper, Dale, et al. The Outdoor Handbook. (Illus.). 1978. 13.95 (ISBN 0-600-36743-6). Transatlantic.

Cooper, Darien B. You Can Be the Wife of a Happy Husband. LC 74-77450. 156p. 1974. pap. 3.95 (ISBN 0-88207-711-2). Victor Bks.

Cooper, Darien B. & Carroll, Anne K. We Became Wives of Happy Husbands. 168p. 1976. pap. 3.50 (ISBN 0-88207-731-7). Victor Bks.

Cooper, David see Glastonbury, Bryan, et al.

Cooper, David, ed. To Free a Generation: The Dialectics of Liberation. LC 68-31275. (Orig.). 1969. pap. 1.95 o.s.i. (ISBN 0-02-095300-3, Collier). Macmillan.
Cooper, David D. The Lesson of the Scaffold: The Public Execution Controversy in Victorian England. LC 73-92901. (Illus.). xi, 212p. 1974. 12.95x (ISBN 0-8214-0148-3). Ohio U Pr.
Cooper, David E. International Bibliography of Discographies: Classical Music and Jazz & Blues 1962-1972. LC 75-4516. (Keys to Music Bibliography Ser.: No. 2). 272p. 1975. lib. bdg. 13.50x o.p. (ISBN 0-87287-108-8). Libs Unl.
--Knowledge of Language. 196p. 1975. text ed. 15.50x (ISBN 0-391-00382-8); pap. text ed. 10.50x (ISBN 0-391-00383-6). Humanities.
Cooper, Denis A., ed. Public Utilities Law Anthology, Vol. 5. LC 74-77644. (National Law Anthology Ser.). 1979. 59.95 (ISBN 0-914250-19-1). Intl Lib.
Cooper, Dennis. Idols. 1979. pap. 4.95 (ISBN 0-686-28355-4). Sea Horse.
Cooper, Derek. Guide to the Whiskies of Scotland. 1979. 2.95 (ISBN 0-346-12425-5). Cornerstone.
--Road to the Isles: Travellers in the Hebrides, 1770-1914. 1979. 18.00 (ISBN 0-7100-0256-4). Routledge & Kegan.
--Skye. (Illus.). 1970. 22.50 (ISBN 0-7100-6820-4). Routledge & Kegan.
Cooper, Douglas. Living God's Joy. LC 78-71158. (Redwood Ser.). 1979. pap. 3.95 (ISBN 0-8163-0241-3). Pacific Pr Pub Assn.
--Living God's Love. LC 74-27171. (Redwood Ser.). 1975. pap. 3.95 (ISBN 0-8163-0176-X, 12523-7). Pacific Pr Pub Assn.
--Toulouse-Lautrec. (Library of Great Painters Ser). (Illus.). 1956. 35.00 (ISBN 0-8109-0512-4). Abrams.
Cooper, E. Mary. Banking & Finance. (Australian Life Ser.: No. 6). 1980. pap. 6.95x (ISBN 0-686-26706-0, Pub. by Lothian). Intl Schol Bk Serv.
Cooper, E. S. The Language of Medicine: A Guide for Stenotypists. 1977. pap. 9.95 (ISBN 0-87489-045-4). Med Economics.
Cooper, Edmund. Let's Look at Costume. LC 67-17421. (Let's Look Ser). (Illus.). (gr. 4-8). 1965. 4.95g o.p. (ISBN 0-8075-4470-1). A Whitman.
Cooper, Edward L. Comparative Immunology. (Foundations of Immunology Ser.). (Illus.). 480p. 1976. 23.95x (ISBN 0-13-153429-7). P-H.
Cooper, Edwin L., ed. see International Symposium of the American Society of Zoologists, Toronto, December 27-30, 1977.
Cooper, Elizabeth. Harim & the Purdah: Studies of Oriental Women. LC 68-23147. 1975. Repr. of 1915 ed. 20.00 (ISBN 0-8103-3167-5). Gale.
--The Women of Egypt. LC 79-2934. (Illus.). 380p. 1981. Repr. of 1914 ed. 26.50 (ISBN 0-8305-0102-9). Hyperion Conn.
Cooper, Elizabeth I., jt. ed. see Bailey, N. Louise.
Cooper, Elizabeth K. Discovering Chemistry. LC 59-7281. (Illus.). (gr. 7-9). 1959. 5.50 o.p. (ISBN 0-15-223591-4, HJ). HarBraceJ.
--Insects & Plants: The Amazing Partnership. LC 63-7893. (Illus.). (gr. 4-6). 1963. 6.95 o.p. (ISBN 0-15-238701-3, HJ). HarBraceJ.
--Silkworms & Science: The Story of Silk. (Illus.). (gr. 5-9). 1961. 4.95 o.p. (ISBN 0-15-274241-7, HJ). HarBraceJ.
Cooper, Ella G., jt. auth. see Goodall, Helen S.
Cooper, Emanuel. The Potter's Book of Glaze Recipes. 1980. 15.95 (ISBN 0-684-16670-4, ScribT). Scribner.
Cooper, F. T., tr. see Donauer, Friedrich.
Cooper, Frank E. State Administrative Law, 2 vols. 1965. slip case 40.00 (ISBN 0-672-81444-7, Bobbs-Merrill Law). Michie.
--Writing in Law Practice. 1963. text ed. 17.00 (ISBN 0-672-81021-2, Bobbs-Merrill Law). Michie.
Cooper, Frederic T., jt. auth. see Maurice, Arthur B.
Cooper, Frederick. From Slaves to Squatters: Plantation Labor & Agriculture in Zanibar & Coastal Kenya, 1890-1925. LC 80-5391. (Illus.). 352p. 1981. text ed. 25.00 (ISBN 0-300-02454-1). Yale U Pr.
Cooper, Gayle. Checklist of American Imprints for 1830: Items 1-5609. (Checklist of American Imprints Ser.: Vol. 1830). 1972. 20.00 (ISBN 0-8108-0520-0). Scarecrow.
Cooper, Gayle, ed. see Shoemaker, Richard H.
Cooper, George. Voluntary Tax: New Perspectives on Sophisticated Estate Tax Avoidance. LC 78-20853. (Studies of Government Finance). 1979. 9.95 (ISBN 0-8157-1552-8); pap. 3.95 (ISBN 0-8157-1551-X). Brookings.
Cooper, H. H. The Hostage-Takers. 1st ed. (Illus.). 100p. (Orig.). 1981. pap. 12.00 (ISBN 0-87364-209-0). Paladin Ent.
Cooper, Harold. Living Jesus. (Illus.). 106p. pap. text ed. 1.50 (ISBN 0-89114-077-8); tchrs. ed. 1.00 (ISBN 0-89114-078-6). Baptist Pub Hse.
--True Service. (Illus.). 110p. 1978. pap. text ed. 1.50 (ISBN 0-89114-081-6); tchrs. ed. 1.25 (ISBN 0-89114-082-4). Baptist Pub Hse.
Cooper, Harry, jt. auth. see Hargrove, Jim.
Cooper, Helen. Great Grandmother Goose. LC 79-1081. (Illus.). (gr. k up). 1979. 7.95 (ISBN 0-688-80218-4); PLB 7.63 (ISBN 0-688-84218-6). Greenwillow.
Cooper, Henry. Boxing. (Pelham Pictorial Sports Instruction Ser). (Illus.). 1977. 10.95 (ISBN 0-7207-0790-0). Transatlantic.
Cooper, I. S. It's Hard to Leave While the Music's Playing. 1978. pap. 1.95 o.p. (ISBN 0-445-04267-2). Popular Lib.
Cooper, I. S., ed. Cerebellar Stimulation in Man. LC 77-76925. 1978. 28.00 (ISBN 0-89004-206-3). Raven.
Cooper, Irving S., et al. The Pulvinar-LP Complex. (Illus.). 312p. 1974. 29.50 (ISBN 0-398-02849-4). C C Thomas.
Cooper, J. Microprocessor Background for Management Personnel. 208p. 1981. 14.95 (ISBN 0-13-580829-4). P-H.
--Minolta Systems Handbook. 2nd ed. 1979. 34.95 (ISBN 0-13-584581-5, Spec). P-H.
Cooper, J., jt. auth. see Curtis, A.
Cooper, J., jt. ed. see Rose, J. W.
Cooper, J. David, et al. The What & How of Reading Instruction. 1979. pap. text ed. 13.50 (ISBN 0-675-08287-0); instructor's manual 3.95 (ISBN 0-686-67294-1). Merrill.
Cooper, J. E. & Eley, J. T. First Aid & Care of Wild Birds. 1979. 28.00 (ISBN 0-7153-7664-0). David & Charles.
Cooper, J. P., ed. Photosynthesis & Productivity in Different Environments. (International Biological Programme Ser.: No. 3). (Illus.). 550p. 1975. 99.00 (ISBN 0-521-20573-5). Cambridge U Pr.
Cooper, J. P., jt. ed. see Thirsk, Joan.
Cooper, J. R. Dental Problems in Medical Practice. 1976. pap. text ed. 21.00x (ISBN 0-433-06425-0). Intl Ideas.
Cooper, Jackie & Kleiner, Dick. Please Don't Shoot My Dog: The Autobiography of Jackie Cooper with Dick Kleiner. (Illus.). 288p. 12.95 (ISBN 0-688-03659-7). Morrow.
Cooper, James F. Afloat & Ashore: A Sea Tale. 549p. 1980. Repr. of 1844 ed. lib. bdg. 18.25x (ISBN 0-89968-212-X). Lightyear.
--The American Democrat. LC 80-83794. 280p. 1981. 9.00 (ISBN 0-913966-91-6); pap. 4.00 (ISBN 0-913966-92-4). Liberty Fund.
--Last of the Mohicans. (Literature Ser). (gr. 7-12). 1970. pap. text ed. 3.58 (ISBN 0-87720-731-3). AMSCO Sch.
--Last of the Mohicans: Abridged & Adapted to Grade 2 Reading Level. Hurdy, John M., ed. LC 67-25787. (Pacemaker Classics Ser.). (Illus., Orig.). 1967. pap. 3.80 (ISBN 0-8224-9215-6); tchr's manual free (ISBN 0-8224-5200-6). Pitman Learning.
--The Pathfinder. Dixson, Robert J., ed. (American Classics Ser.: Bk. 4). (gr. 9 up). 1973. pap. text ed. 2.75 (ISBN 0-88345-200-6, 18123); cassettes 40.00 (ISBN 0-685-38992-8); tapes 40.00 (ISBN 0-685-38993-6). Regents Pub.
--Pathfinder. 1976. lib. bdg. 14.95x (ISBN 0-89968-159-X). Lightyear.
--The Pioneers. 1976. lib. bdg. 15.95x (ISBN 0-89968-157-3). Lighthouse Pr NY.
--The Prairie. 1976. lib. bdg. 14.95x (ISBN 0-89968-160-3). Lightyear.
--The Red Rover. 1976. lib. bdg. 16.95x (ISBN 0-89968-158-1). Lightyear.
--Satanstoe. LC 62-9515. 1962. pap. 4.50x (ISBN 0-8032-5036-3, BB 138, Bison). U of Nebr Pr.
--The Spy. 1976. lib. bdg. 13.95x (ISBN 0-89968-161-1). Lightyear.
Cooper, James M. & DeVault, M. Vere. Competency Based Teacher Education. LC 72-83478. 123p. 1973. 16.60x (ISBN 0-8211-0010-6); text ed. 15.00 in copies of 10 (ISBN 0-686-66847-2). McCutchan.
Cooper, James M., jt. auth. see Ryan, Kevin.
Cooper, James M., et al. Classroom Teaching Skills: A Handbook. 1977. pap. text ed. 12.95x (ISBN 0-669-94722-9); instructor's manual free (ISBN 0-669-97899-X); wkbk. 8.95x (ISBN 0-669-94730-X). Heath.
Cooper, James R. & Guntermann, Karl L. Real Estate & Urban Land Analysis. LC 73-10397. (Special Ser. in Real Estate & Urban Land Economics). (Illus.). 544p. 1974. 32.95 (ISBN 0-669-90415-5). Lexington Bks.
Cooper, James W. Introduction to Pascal for Scientists. 304p. 1981. 17.50 (ISBN 0-471-08785-8, Pub. by Wiley-Interscience). Wiley.
--The Minicomputer in the Laboratory: With Examples Using the PDP-11. LC 76-44255. 1977. 22.50 (ISBN 0-471-01883-X, Pub. by Wiley-Interscience). Wiley.
Cooper, Jane. Maps & Windows. 1974. pap. 2.95 o.s.i. (ISBN 0-02-069300-1, Collier). Macmillan.
--Weather of Six Mornings: Poems. LC 68-29507. 1969. 9.95 (ISBN 0-02-528070-8). Macmillan.
Cooper, Janelle. Think & Link: An Advanced Course in Reading & Writing Skills. (Illus.). 1979. pap. 9.95x (ISBN 0-7131-0315-9). Intl Ideas.
Cooper, Jay S. & Pizzarello, Donald J. Concepts in Cancer Care: A Practical Explanation of Radiotherapy & Chemotherapy for Primary Care Physicians. LC 80-10334. (Illus.). 273p. 1980. text ed. 16.50 (ISBN 0-8121-0716-0). Lea & Febiger.
Cooper, Jeff. Fireworks: A Gunsite Anthology. LC 80-83992. 1981. 19.95 (ISBN 0-916172-07-4). Janus Pr.
Cooper, Jeremy. Nineteenth Century Romantic Bronzes. 1977. 23.95 o.p. (ISBN 0-7153-6346-8). David & Charles.
Cooper, Jilly. Class. LC 80-2718. (Illus.). 288p. 1981. 12.95 (ISBN 0-394-51414-9). Knopf.
--Prudence. 192p. 1981. pap. 1.95 (ISBN 0-449-24361-3, Crest). Fawcett.
Cooper, Jilly & Hartman, Tom, eds. Violets & Vinegar. LC 80-9059. 231p. 1981. 15.95 (ISBN 0-8128-2813-5). Stein & Day.
Cooper, Joan. The Ancient Teaching of Yoga & the Spiritual Evolution of Man. 218p. 1980. 14.75x (ISBN 0-7050-0064-8, Pub. by Skilton & Shaw England). State Mutual Bk.
Cooper, Joel, jt. auth. see Worchel, Stephen.
Cooper, John C. The Joy of the Plain Life. 200p. 1981. pap. 4.95 (ISBN 0-914850-62-8, 14015P). Impact Tenn.
Cooper, John C. & Wahlberg, Rachel C. Your Exciting Middle Years. LC 76-2858. 1976. pap. 3.95 o.p. (ISBN 0-87680-857-7, 98075). Word Bks.
Cooper, John E., et al. Endangered & Threatened Plants & Animals of North Carolina: Proceedings of a Symposium on Endangered & Threatened Biota of N. C., Biological Concerns. LC 76-18670. (Illus.). 1977. pap. text ed. 8.00 o.p. (ISBN 0-917134-01-X). NC Natl Hist.
Cooper, John L. The Anti-Gravity Force. LC 80-83402. 160p. 1981. pap. text ed. 9.95 (ISBN 0-8403-2300-X). Kendall-Hunt.
Cooper, John M. Analytical & Critical Bibliography of the Tribes of Tierra Del Fuego & Adjacent Territory. (Map). 1967. pap. text ed. 13.50x (ISBN 90-6234-005-9). Humanities.
Cooper, John M. & Glassow, Ruth B. Kinesiology. rev. 4th ed. LC 75-33991. (Illus.). 1976. 13.95 (ISBN 0-8016-1048-6). Mosby.
Cooper, John M. & Strong, Clinton. The Physical Education Curriculum. 8th ed. 1973. saddle stitched 2.95x (ISBN 0-87543-099-6). Lucas.
Cooper, John O. Measuring Behavior. 2nd ed. (Special Education Ser.). (Illus.). 224p. 1981. pap. text ed. 7.95 (ISBN 0-675-08078-9). Merrill.
Cooper, Kay. Journeys on the Mississippi. (Illus.). 96p. (gr. 4-6). 1981. PLB 7.29 (ISBN 0-686-69304-3). Messner.
Cooper, Ken. Nonverbal Communication for Business Success. new ed. (Illus.). 1979. 12.95 o.p. (ISBN 0-8144-5500-X). Am Mgmt.
Cooper, L. C. Horseshow Organization. new ed. 1978. 15.75 (ISBN 0-85131-310-8, Dist. by Sporting Book Center). J A Allen.
Cooper, Lane. Poetics of Aristotle. LC 63-10307. (Our Debt to Greece & Rome Ser). 157p. 1963. Repr. of 1930 ed. 16.50x (ISBN 0-8154-0053-5). Cooper Sq.
Cooper, Laura G. & Smith, Marilyn Z. Standard Fortran: A Problem-Solving Approach. LC 72-4395. 288p. (Orig.). 1973. pap. text ed. 13.95 (ISBN 0-395-14028-5). HM.
Cooper, Leo K. Ankle Fractures: Treatment Without Casts. (Illus.). 124p. 1974. 23.75 (ISBN 0-398-03155-X). C C Thomas.
Cooper, Lester. Pelicans. (Animals Animals Animals Library: Second Ser.). (Illus.). (gr. 1-9). 1979. 6.95 (ISBN 0-917080-11-4). Handel & Sons.
Cooper, Lettice. Blackberry's Kitten. LC 63-13798. (Illus.). (gr. 1-4). 1963. 3.00 (ISBN 0-8149-0291-X). Vanguard.
Cooper, Linn F. & Erickson, Milton H. Time Distortion in Hypnosis. (Illus.). 1981. Repr. of 1954 ed. text ed. 18.50x (ISBN 0-89197-967-0). Irvington.
Cooper, Lynn A., jt. auth. see Shepard, Roger N.
Cooper, Lynna. Inherit My Heart. (Orig.). 1981. pap. 1.95 (ISBN 0-451-09782-3, J9782, Sig). NAL.
--Portrait of Love. (Orig.). 1980. pap. 1.75 (ISBN 0-451-09495-6, E9495, Sig). NAL.
--Substitute Bride. Bd. with My Treasure, My Love. 1981. pap. 2.25 (ISBN 0-451-09739-4, E9739, Sig). NAL.
Cooper, M., et al, eds. B Lymphocytes in the Immune Response. (Developments in Immunology: Vol. 3). 1979. 45.00 (ISBN 0-444-00319-3, North Holland). Elsevier.
Cooper, M. Frances. A Checklist of American Imprints Eighteen Twenty to Eighteen Twenty-Nine: Title Index. (Checklist of American Imprints Ser.). 1972. 22.00 (ISBN 0-8108-0513-8). Scarecrow.
--A Checklist of American Imprints Eighteen Twenty to Eighteen Twenty-Nine: Author Index, Corrections & Sources. 1973. 11.00 (ISBN 0-8108-0567-7). Scarecrow.
Cooper, M. H. Prices & Profits in the Pharmaceutical Industry. 1967. 25.00 (ISBN 0-08-012178-0); pap. 12.75 (ISBN 0-08-012177-2). Pergamon.
Cooper, M. K. Private Lies. 1980. pap. 2.25 (ISBN 0-445-04566-3). Popular Lib.
Cooper, Marcia H., jt. auth. see Cooper, Morton.
Cooper, Margaret. Great Bone Hunt. (gr. 2-4). 1967. 2.95 o.s.i. (ISBN 0-02-724380-X). Macmillan.
--Inventions of Leonardo Da Vinci. (Illus.). (gr. 7 up). 1968. 9.95 (ISBN 0-02-724490-3). Macmillan.
Cooper, Margaret C. Solution: Escape. LC 80-50496. (Illus.). 94p. (gr. 3-7). 1981. 8.95 (ISBN 0-8027-6404-5); PLB 8.85 (ISBN 0-8027-6405-3). Walker & Co.
Cooper, Mario. Flower Painting in Watercolor. rev. ed. 144p. 1980. pap. 9.95 (ISBN 0-442-23137-7). Van Nos Reinhold.
--Watercolor by Design. (Illus.). 176p. 1980. 21.95 (ISBN 0-8230-5655-4). Watson-Guptill.
Cooper, Martin see Abraham, Gerald, et al.
Cooper, Max D. & Dayton, Delbert H., eds. Development of Host Defenses. LC 76-51866. 1977. 31.50 (ISBN 0-89004-117-2). Raven.
Cooper, Michael. Rationing Health Care. LC 74-32600. 150p. 1975. 19.95 (ISBN 0-470-17119-7). Halsted Pr.
--Things to Make & Do for George Washington's Birthday. (Things to Make & Do Ser.). (Illus.). (gr. k-3). 1979. PLB 7.90 s&l (ISBN 0-531-02294-3). Watts.
Cooper, Michael H., ed. Social Policy: A Survey of Recent Developments. (Aspects of Social Policy Series). 1973. 30.50x (ISBN 0-631-15300-4, Pub. by Basil Blackwell); pap. 10.00x (ISBN 0-631-16230-5). Biblio Dist.
Cooper, Michele, jt. auth. see Cahill, Susan.
Cooper, Michele F. Freshman Writer. (Illus.). 208p. (Orig.). 1972. pap. 2.95 (ISBN 0-06-460136-6, CO 136, COS). Har-Row.
Cooper, Miriam. Snap! Photography. (Illus.). (gr. 4-7). 1981. PLB price not set (ISBN 0-671-34021-2). Messner.
Cooper, Montgomery & Allyn, Jane. Dance for Life: Ballet in South Africa. (Illus.). 160p. 1981. 22.00x (ISBN 0-8476-3286-5). Rowman.
Cooper, Morton. Modern Techniques of Vocal Rehabilitation. (Amer. Lec. Speech & Hearing Ser.). (Illus.). 384p. 1977. 19.75 (ISBN 0-398-02451-0). C C Thomas.
Cooper, Morton & Cooper, Marcia H. Approaches to Vocal Rehabilitation. (Illus.). 420p. 1977. 29.75 (ISBN 0-398-03517-2). C C Thomas.
Cooper, Murray S., ed. Quality Control in the Pharmaceutical Industry, 3 vols. Vol. 1, 1972. 39.00 (ISBN 0-12-187601-2); Vol. 2, 1972. 48.00 (ISBN 0-12-187602-0); Vol. 3, 1979. 32.50 (ISBN 0-12-187603-9). Acad Pr.
Cooper, Patricia & Buferd, Norma Bradley. The Quilters - Women & Domestic Art. LC 76-2765. 1977. 12.95 o.p. (ISBN 0-385-11685-3); pap. 6.95 (ISBN 0-385-12039-7). Doubleday.
Cooper, Paul. Dimensions of Sight Singing: An Anthology. (Longman Music Ser.). (Orig.). 1981. pap. text ed. 12.95 (ISBN 0-582-28159-8). Longman.
--Perspectives in Music Theory: An Historical-Analytical Approach. 2nd ed. LC 78-26448. 1980. text ed. 15.50 scp (ISBN 0-06-041373-5, HarpC); Vol. 1. pap. text ed. 10.50 scp (ISBN 0-06-041374-3); Vol. 2. pap. text ed. 10.50 scp (ISBN 0-06-041375-1). Har-Row.
Cooper, Paulette. Let's Find Out About Halloween. LC 70-182290. (Let's Find Out Bks). (Illus.). 48p. (gr. k-2). 1972. PLB 4.47 o.p. (ISBN 0-531-00075-3). Watts.
Cooper, Paulette, ed. Growing up Puerto Rican. 144p. (RL 10). 1973. pap. 1.25 o.p. (ISBN 0-451-61233-7, MY1233, Ment). NAL.
Cooper, Peter. Style in Piano Playing. 1980. 11.95 (ISBN 0-7145-3512-5). Riverrun NY.
Cooper, Philip. The Craft of Surgery, 3 vols. 2nd ed. (Illus.). 1971. Set. 85.00 o.p. (ISBN 0-316-15554-3). Little.
--Health Care Marketing: Issues & Trends. LC 79-18447. 1979. text ed. 27.95 (ISBN 0-89443-162-5). Aspen Systems.
Cooper, Phyllis. Feminine Gymnastics. 3rd rev. ed. 1980. pap. 11.95 spiral bdg. (ISBN 0-8087-2962-4). Burgess.
Cooper, R. & Osselton, J. W. EEG Technology. 3rd ed. Shaw, J. C., ed. (Illus.). 304p. 1980. text ed. 29.95 (ISBN 0-407-16002-7). Butterworths.
Cooper, Richard & Uden, Grant. British Ships & Seamen. (Illus.). 591p. 1981. lib. bdg. 40.00x (ISBN 0-312-20028-5). St Martin.
Cooper, Richard N. Economics of Interdependence. (Council on Foreign Relations Ser.). 1980. pap. 6.50x (ISBN 0-231-05071-2, Pub. by Morningside). Columbia U Pr.

Cooper, Robert D. & Carlsen, Melody A. Pension Fund Operations & Expenses: The Technical Report. (Illus.). 149p. (Orig.). 1980. pap. 15.00 (ISBN 0-89154-139-X). Intl Found Employ.
Cooper, Robert M. Lost on Both Sides, Dante Gabriel Rossetti: Critic & Poet. LC 71-91957. 268p. 1970. 14.00x (ISBN 0-8214-0069-X). Ohio U Pr.
Cooper, Russell M. & Fisher, Margaret B. The Vision of a Contemporary University: A Case Study of Expansion & Development in American Higher Education, 1950-75. LC 80-29022. (Illus.). iv, 380p. 1981. 12.95 (ISBN 0-8130-0702-X). U Presses Fla.
Cooper, Signe S., jt. ed. see Neal, Margo C.
Cooper, Stephen. Graduate Theses & Dissertations in ESL: 1978-79. (Language in Education Ser.: No. 27). 1980. pap. text ed. 2.95 (ISBN 0-87281-127-1). Ctr Appl Ling.
--Graduate Theses Dissertations in E S L: Ninteen Seventy-Six to Nineteen Seventy-Seven. (Language in Education Ser.: No. 3). 1978. pap. text ed. 2.95 (ISBN 0-87281-079-8). Ctr Appl Ling.
Cooper, Susan, jt. auth. see Heenan, Cathy.
Cooper, T., et al. Sentence Combining in Second Language Construction. (Language in Education Ser.: No. 31). 1980. pap. text ed. 7.95 (ISBN 0-87281-130-1). Ctr Appl Ling.
Cooper, Ted. Guide to Bees & Honey. 1977. 10.95 o.p. (ISBN 0-87857-177-9). Rodale Pr Inc.
Cooper, Terry & Ratner, Marilyn. Many Friends Cookbook: An International Cookbook for Boys & Girls. LC 79-24832. (Illus.). 64p. (gr. 3-6). 1980. pap. 6.95 (ISBN 0-399-20755-4). Philomel.
Cooper, Terry Touff & Ratner, Marilyn. Many Friends Cooking. LC 79-24832. (gr. 3 up). spiral bdg. 6.00 (ISBN 0-935738-00-2, 5065). US Comm UNICEF.
Cooper, Thomas. The Life of Thomas Cooper. (Victorian Library). 408p. 1971. Repr. of 1872 ed. text ed. 13.00x (ISBN 0-391-00159-0, Leicester). Humanities.
--Treatise on the Law of Libel & the Liberty of the Press. LC 71-107408. (Civil Liberties in American History Ser). 1970. Repr. of 1833 ed. lib. bdg. 19.50 (ISBN 0-306-71892-8). Da Capo.
Cooper, Thomas & Hill, Paul. Dialogue with Photography. (Illus.). 448p. 1980. 12.95 (ISBN 0-374-13893-1); pap. 6.95 (ISBN 0-374-51544-1). FS&G.
Cooper, Thomas M. & DiBiaggio, John A. Applied Practice Management: A Strategy for Stress Control. LC 79-15266. (Illus.). 1979. text ed. 26.50 (ISBN 0-8016-1082-6). Mosby.
Cooper, Valerie. Diary of a Divorce. (Orig.). 1981. pap. 3.95 (ISBN 0-88449-054-8). Vision Hse.
Cooper, W. C. Physics of Selenium & Tellurium. 1969. 60.00 (ISBN 0-08-013895-0). Pergamon.
Cooper, W. F. & Fordham. Electrical Safety Engineering. 1977. 52.95 (ISBN 0-408-00289-1). Butterworths.
Cooper, W. W. & Ijiri, Yuji. Eric Louis Kohler: Accounting's Man of Principles. (Illus.). 1978. 14.95 (ISBN 0-8359-1773-8). Reston.
Cooper, William. The Poems of William Cowper, Vol. I: 1748 - 1782. Baird, John D. & Ryskamp, Charles, eds. (English Texts Ser.). (Illus.). 636p. 1980. 74.00 (ISBN 0-19-811875-9). Oxford U Pr.
Cooper, William, ed. see Pennsylvania University Bicentennial Conference.
Cooper, William D. Electronic Instrumentation & Measurement Techniques. 2nd ed. LC 77-24528. (Illus.). 1978. ref. ed. 20.95 (ISBN 0-13-251710-8). P-H.
Cooper, William E. & Paccia-Cooper, Jeanne. Syntax & Speech. LC 80-16614. (Cognitive Science Ser.: No. 3). 1980. text ed. 21.00x (ISBN 0-674-86075-6). Harvard U Pr.
Cooper, William F., tr. see Romero, Francisco.
Cooper, William J. Chemistry in Water Reuse, Vol. 2. 1981. text ed. 39.95 (ISBN 0-250-40391-9). Ann Arbor Science.
Cooper, William J., ed. Chemistry in Water Reuse, Vol. 1. 350p. 1981. text ed. 39.95 (ISBN 0-686-69578-X). Ann Arbor Science.
Cooper, William R. Archaic Dictionary. LC 73-76018. 1969. Repr. of 1876 ed. 40.00 (ISBN 0-8103-3885-8). Gale.
Cooper Madlener, Judith. The Sea Vegetable Gelatin Cookbook. (Illus., Orig.). 1981. pap. 7.95 (ISBN 0-912800-76-3). Woodbridge Pr.
Cooperman, Stanley. Monarch Notes on Fitzgerald's Tender Is the Night. (Orig.). pap. 1.95 (ISBN 0-671-00668-1). Monarch Pr.
--Monarch Notes on Hemingway's Major Novels. (Orig.). pap. 1.75 (ISBN 0-671-00621-5). Monarch Pr.
Cooper-Oakley, Isabel. Count of Saint-Germain: The Secret of Kings. LC 70-137422. 256p. 1970. pap. 6.50 (ISBN 0-8334-1702-9). Steinerbks.
Cooperrider, Edward A., tr. see Rommel, Kurt.
Cooperrider, Edward A., tr. see Thielicke, Helmut.
Cooper-Smith, John H., jt. auth. see Eatwell, David.
Cooperstein, Bruce & Mason, Geoffrey, eds. Proceedings of Symposia in Pure Mathematics, Vol. 37. 1981. cancelled (ISBN 0-8218-1440-0). Am Math.
Coopland, G. W., ed. Songe De Vieil Pelerin of Philippe De Mezieres, 2 Vols. LC 69-10194. (Illus.). 1969. Set. 220.00 (ISBN 0-521-07116-X). Cambridge U Pr.
Coordinating Committee for Continuing Education in Thoracic Surgery. Self-Education-Self Assessment in Thoracic Surgery. 208p. 1980. pap. text ed. 100.00 (ISBN 0-8403-2331-X). Kendall-Hunt.
Coortice, F. C., jt. auth. see Yoffey, J. M.
Coote, Robert B. Amos Among the Prophets: Composition & Theology. 144p. 1981. pap. 5.50 (ISBN 0-8006-1400-3, 1-1400). Fortress.
Cootes, R. J. & Snellgrove, L. E. The Ancient World. (Longman Secondary Histories). (Illus.). 1974. pap. text ed. 6.95x (ISBN 0-582-20503-4). Longman.
Coots, Max. Seasons of the Self. LC 71-158676. (Illus.). 1971. 3.50 (ISBN 0-687-37140-6). Unitarian.
Coover, James & Colvig, Richard. Medieval & Renaissance Music on Long-Playing Records: Supplement 1962-1971. (Detroit Studies in Music Bibliography: No. 26). 1973. 8.50 (ISBN 0-685-30212-1); pap. 7.00 (ISBN 0-685-30212-1). Info Coord.
Coover, Virginia, et al. Resource Manual for a Living Revolution. 351p. 1977. pap. 5.00 (ISBN 0-86571-008-2). Movement New Soc.
Copass, Michael, jt. auth. see Eisenberg, Mickey S.
Copass, Michael K. & Eisenberg, Mickey. The Paramedic Manual. (Illus.). 304p. 1980. text ed. 11.95 (ISBN 0-7216-2716-1). Saunders.
Cope, A. T., ed. see Fuze, M. M.
Cope, David. New Music Composition. LC 76-21376. 1977. pap. text ed. 10.95 (ISBN 0-02-870630-7). Schirmer Bks.
Cope, David H. New Directions in Music. 3rd ed. 200p. 1981. pap. text ed. 7.50x (ISBN 0-697-03448-8). Wm C Brown.
--New Directions in Music. 3rd ed. 286p. 1981. pap. text ed. price not set (ISBN 0-697-03448-8). Wm C Brown.
Cope, Dwight W. & Schoude, Lee E. Plastics. LC 77-21618. (Illus.). 1977. text ed. 4.80 (ISBN 0-87006-239-5). Goodheart.
Cope, E. M. The Rhetoric of Aristotle with a Commentary, 3 vols. Sandys, J. E., ed. (Classical Studies Ser.). (Gr. & Eng.). Repr. of 1877 ed. Set. lib. bdg. 76.00x (ISBN 0-89197-922-0); Vol. 1. lib. bdg. 29.00x (ISBN 0-697-00033-8); Vol. 2. lib. bdg. 27.00x (ISBN 0-697-00034-6); Vol. 3. lib. bdg. 32.00x (ISBN 0-697-00035-4). Irvington.
Cope, Emma E. How to Decipher & Study Old Documents: Being a Guide to the Reading of Ancient Manuscripts, the Key to the Family Deed Chest. 2nd ed. LC 73-18446. 1974. Repr. of 1903 ed. 20.00 (ISBN 0-8103-3701-0). Gale.
Cope, Esther. The Life of a Public Man: Edward, First Baron Montego of Boughton. LC 79-54279. (Memoirs Ser.: Vol. 142). 1980. 9.50 (ISBN 0-87169-142-6). Am Philos.
Cope, Herman see Hutchinson, K. M.
Cope, Jackson I. Joyce's Cities: Archaeologies of the Soul. LC 80-8056. 176p. 1981. text ed. 12.95x (ISBN 0-8018-2543-1). Johns Hopkins.
Cope, Ken. Fishing Canals. LC 79-55994. (Illus.). 1980. 17.95 (ISBN 0-7153-7887-2). David & Charles.
Cope, Robert & Hannah, William. Revolving College Doors: The Causes & Consequences of Dropping Out, Stopping Out & Transferring. LC 75-16472. 190p. 1975. 20.95 (ISBN 0-471-17124-7, Pub. by Wiley-Interscience). Wiley.
Cope, Robert S. Carry Me Back: Slavery & Servitude in Seventeenth Century Virginia. (Illus.). xv, 179p. 1973. 2.00. Pikeville Coll.
Copel, Sidney L. Psychodiagnostic Study of Children & Adolescents. 216p. 1967. pap. 14.75 photocopy ed. spiral (ISBN 0-398-00346-7). C C Thomas.
Copelan, Rachel. How to Hypnotize Yourself & Others. LC 80-70951. 386p. 1981. 10.95 (ISBN 0-8119-0418-0). Fell.
--The Sexually Fulfilled Man. 1973. pap. 1.50 (ISBN 0-451-05675-2, W5675, Sig). NAL.
Copeland, Adrian D. Textbook of Adolescent Psychopathology & Treatment. (Illus.). 152p. 1974. text ed. 14.75 (ISBN 0-398-03114-2); pap. text ed. 9.75 (ISBN 0-398-03115-0). C C Thomas.
Copeland, Benny R. & Sullivan, Nelson G. Cost Accounting: Accumulation, Analysis, & Control. 1977. text ed. 18.95 (ISBN 0-8299-0122-1); check figures bklt. avail. (ISBN 0-8299-0470-0); solutions manual avail. (ISBN 0-8299-0469-7). West Pub.
Copeland, Carolyn. Tankas from the Koelz Collection: Museum of Anthropology, University of Michigan. (Michigan Papers on South & Southeast Asia: No. 18). (Illus.). 100p. (Orig.). 1980. pap. 9.00x (ISBN 0-89148-018-8). Ctr S&SE Asian.
Copeland, E. L. El Cristianismo y Otras Religiones. Mora, Abdias A., tr. Orig. Title: Christianity & World Religious. (Illus.). 192p. (Span.). Date not set. pap. price not set (ISBN 0-311-05760-8, Edit Mundo). Casa Bautista.
Copeland, Irene. The Flea Market & Garage Sale Handbook. 1977. pap. 1.75 o.p. (ISBN 0-445-08624-6). Popular Lib.
Copeland, J. Isaac, jt. ed. see Green, Fletcher M.
Copeland, James E., ed. see Bennett, Michael, et al.
Copeland, John A. A Study of Daniel. 1973. pap. 3.45 (ISBN 0-89137-703-4). Quality Pubns.
--A Study of the Revelation. 1971. pap. 3.45 (ISBN 0-89137-702-6). Quality Pubns.
Copeland, Lewis, ed. Ten Thousand Jokes, Toasts & Stories. LC 66-737. 1965. 10.95 (ISBN 0-385-00163-0). Doubleday.
Copeland, Marks & Soeharjo, Mintari. The Indonesian Kitchen. LC 80-69385. 1981. write for info. (ISBN 0-689-11142-8). Atheneum.
Copeland, Melvin T. & Towl, Andrew R. Board of Directors & Business Management. LC 69-10079. 1969. Repr. lib. bdg. 20.25x (ISBN 0-8371-0052-6, COBD). Greenwood.
Copeland, Morris A. Essays in Socioeconomic Evolution. 1981. 10.00 (ISBN 0-533-04328-X). Vantage.
Copeland, Peter F. American Military Uniforms, 1639-1968: A Coloring Book. (Coloring Book Ser.). 48p. (Orig.). 1976. pap. 1.75 (ISBN 0-486-23239-5). Dover.
Copeland, R. M., et al. Financial Accounting. LC 79-18276. 1980. 19.95 (ISBN 0-471-17173-5); working papers & study guide avail. Wiley.
Copeland, Richard W. Math Activities for Children: A Diagnostic Approach. (Elementary Curriculum Ser.). 1979. pap. text ed. 8.95 (ISBN 0-675-08316-8). Merrill.
Copeland, Ronald M. & Dascher, Paul E. Managerial Accounting: An Introduction to Planning, Information Processing & Control. 2nd ed. LC 74-5147. 658p. 1978. text ed. 21.95 (ISBN 0-471-17171-9); study guide 7.95 (ISBN 0-471-02346-9). Wiley.
Copeland, Thomas E. & Weston, J. Fred. Financial Theory & Corporate Policy. LC 78-73366. 1979. text ed. 21.95 (ISBN 0-201-00971-4); solution manual 5.95 (ISBN 0-201-00972-2). A-W.
Copeland, Willis, jt. auth. see Boyan, Norman.
Copeman, W. S. C. A Short History of the Gout & the Rheumatic Diseases. 1964. 20.00x (ISBN 0-520-00267-9). U of Cal Pr.
Copenhaver, jt. auth. see Braunstein.
Copenhaver, Edward H. Surgery of the Vulva & Vagina: A Practical Guide. (Illus.). 100p. 1981. text ed. write for info. (ISBN 0-7216-2718-8). Saunders.
Copernicus, Nicholas. On the Revolution of the Heavenly Spheres. Duncan, Alistair M., ed. LC 76-7172. (Illus.). 1976. text ed. 26.50x o.p. (ISBN 0-06-491279-5). B&N.
Copes, Jane see Herron, Dudley.
Copestake, Tim. Editing Super Eight. (Illus.). 1980. cancelled o.p. (ISBN 0-8038-2387-8). Hastings.
Copestake, Timothy. Editing Super Eight. (Illus.). 288p. 1980. 19.95 (ISBN 0-240-50997-8). Focal Pr.
Copi. Eva Peron & Other Plays. 1980. pap. 4.95 (ISBN 0-7145-3563-X). Riverrun NY.
Copi, Irving M. The Theory of Logical Types. (Monographs in Modern Logic). 1971. 11.50 (ISBN 0-7100-7026-8). Routledge & Kegan.
Coplan, Rachel. The Sexually Fulfilled Woman. 1973. pap. 1.50 (ISBN 0-451-05676-0, W5676, Sig). NAL.
Copland, Aaron. Copland on Music. LC 76-13512. 1976. Repr. of 1960 ed. lib. bdg. 25.00 (ISBN 0-306-70775-6). Da Capo.
--What to Listen for in Music. rev. ed. (RL 9). 1964. pap. 1.95 (ISBN 0-451-61882-3, MJ1882, Ment). NAL.
Copland, Ian. Jawaharlal Nehru of India Eighteen Eighty-Nine to Nineteen Sixty-Four. (Leaders of Asia Ser.). 53p. (Orig.). 1980. pap. 3.00x (ISBN 0-7022-1506-6). U of Queensland Pr.
Copland, Robert, tr. see Aristotle.
Copland, Samuel. History of the Island of Madagascar. LC 72-106856. Repr. of 1822 ed. 19.75x (ISBN 0-8371-3478-1). Negro U Pr.
Copleston, F. W., et al, eds. Advanced Pipe & Tube Welding. (Engineering Craftsmen: No. F21). (Illus.). 1970. spiral bdg. 28.50x (ISBN 0-85083-131-8). Intl Ideas.
Copleston, Frederick. Contemporary Philosophy. rev. ed. Orig. Title: Contemporary Philosophy, Studies of Logical Positivism & Existentialism. 230p. 1972. pap. 4.95 (ISBN 0-8091-1757-6). Paulist Pr.
--History of Philosophy: Greece & Rome, 2 pts, Vol. 1. Pt. 1. pap. 2.95 (ISBN 0-385-00210-6, D134A, Im); Pt. 2. pap. 2.95 (ISBN 0-385-00211-4, D134B). Doubleday.
--Philosophers & Philosophies. 272p. 1976. Repr. of 1955 ed. 13.50x (ISBN 0-06-491278-7). B&N.
--Philosophies & Cultures. 208p. 1980. 16.95x (ISBN 0-19-213960-6). Oxford U Pr.
Copleston, Frederick J. A History of Philosophy-Maine De Biran to Sartre: Part I, the Revolution to Henri Bergson, Vol. 9. 1977. pap. 2.45 (ISBN 0-385-12910-6, Im). Doubleday.
--A History of Philosophy-Maine De Biran to Sartre: Part II Bengson to Sartre, Vol. 9. 1977. pap. 2.45 (ISBN 0-385-12926-2, Im). Doubleday.
Copley, A., ed. Biorheology: Abstracts of the Second International Congress, No. 2. 1976. pap. text ed. 23.50 (ISBN 0-08-019962-3). Pergamon.
--Biorheology: Proceedings of the Second International Congress. 1976. pap. text ed. 47.00 (ISBN 0-08-019963-1). Pergamon.
--Hemorheology: Proceedings of the First International Conference. 1968. 130.00 (ISBN 0-08-013171-9). Pergamon.
Copley, Frank O., ed. & tr. see Vergil.
Copley, Frank O., tr. Roman Drama: Nine Plays of Terence, Plautus & Seneca. LC 64-66074. (YA) (gr. 11 up). 1965. pap. 7.95 (ISBN 0-672-60455-8, LLA209). Bobbs.
Copley, Frank O., tr. see Plautus.
Copley, Frank O., tr. see Terence.
Copley, John S. Letters & Papers of John Singleton Copley & Henry Pelham, 1739-1776. LC 78-100615. (Library of American Art Ser.). (Illus.). 1970. Repr. of 1914 ed. lib. bdg. 39.50 (ISBN 0-306-71406-X). Da Capo.
Coplin, William D. Introduction to International Politics. 3rd ed. (Illus.). 1980. text ed. 16.95 (ISBN 0-13-485383-0). P-H.
Coplin, William D. & O'Leary, Michael K. Analyzing Public Policy Issues. (Learning Packages in the Policy Sciences: No. 17). (Illus.). 50p. 1980. pap. text ed. 3.00 (ISBN 0-936826-06-1). Pol Stud Assocs.
Coplin, William D., ed. Teaching Policy Studies: A Guide to What, How & Where. LC 77-9186. (Policy Studies Organization Ser.). 1978. 19.95 (ISBN 0-669-01829-5). Lexington Bks.
Coplin, William D., ed. see Rochester, J. Martin & Stern, Jean.
Copp, E. Anthony. Regulating Competition in Oil: Government Intervention in the U.S. Refining Industry, 1948-1975. LC 76-19795. (Texas A&M University Economics Ser.: No. 1). 304p. 1976. 22.50x (ISBN 0-89096-014-3). Tex A&M Univ Pr.
Coppa, Frank J. Pope Pius IX. (World Leaders Ser.: No. 81). 1979. lib. bdg. 14.95 (ISBN 0-8057-7727-X). Twayne.
Coppa, Frank J., jt. auth. see Curran, Thomas J.
Coppa, Frank J. & Dolce, Philip C., eds. Cities in Transition: From the Ancient World to Urban America. LC 73-84778. 1974. 17.95 (ISBN 0-911012-95-8). Nelson-Hall.
Coppel, Alfred. Between the Thunder & the Sun. LC 77-147228. 1971. 7.95 o.p. (ISBN 0-15-111950-3). HarBraceJ.
--The Hastings Conspiracy. LC 80-10366. 352p. 1980. 12.95 (ISBN 0-03-056058-6). HR&W.
Coppen, H. E. Aids to Teaching & Learning. 1969. 22.00 (ISBN 0-08-012905-6); pap. 10.75 (ISBN 0-08-012904-8). Pergamon.
Coppens, Peter R. de see De Coppens, Peter R.
Coppens, Peter Roche De see De Coppens, Peter R.
Coppens de Houthulst, Willy. Days on the Wing: Being the War Memoirs of Major the Chevalier Willy Coppens De Houthulst D.S.O., M.C., Etc., Etc. Gilbert, James, ed. Insall, A. J., tr. LC 79-7242. (Flight: Its First Seventy-Five Years Ser.). (Illus.). 1979. Repr. of 1931 ed. 22.00x (ISBN 0-405-12157-1). Arno.
Copper, John F. China's Foreign Aid: An Instrument of Peking's Foreign Policy. LC 75-39318. (Illus.). 1976. 21.95 (ISBN 0-669-00441-3). Lexington Bks.
--China's Global Role: An Analysis of Peking's National Power Capabilities in the Context of an Evolving International System. LC 79-88585. (Publication: No. 226). 1980. pap. 7.95 (ISBN 0-8179-7262-5). Hoover Inst Pr.
Copperfield, David, jt. ed. see Salat, Barbara.
Coppi, B., ed. Theory of Magnetically Confined Plasmas: Proceedings. (Commission of the European Communities Ser.: Eur 5737). (Illus.). 1979. pap. 92.00 (ISBN 0-08-023434-8). Pergamon.
Coppins, Richard, jt. auth. see Wu, Nesa.
Coppleson, M. & Reid, B. Pre-Clinical Carcinoma of the Cervix Uteri. 1967. 50.00 (ISBN 0-08-012433-X). Pergamon.

Coppleson, Malcolm, et al. Colposcopy: A Scientific & Practical Approach to the Cervix in Health & Disease. 2nd ed. (American Lecture in Gynecology & Obstetrics Ser.). (Illus.). 512p. 1978. 40.25 (ISBN 0-398-03761-2). C C Thomas.
Coppock, J. T. & Best, Robin H. The Changing Land Use in Britain. (Illus.). 1962. 9.95 (ISBN 0-571-05239-8, Pub. by Faber & Faber). Merrimack Bk Serv.
Coppock, J. T., ed. Second Homes: Curse or Blessing. 1977. text ed. 23.00 (ISBN 0-08-021371-5); pap. text ed. 8.50 (ISBN 0-08-021370-7). Pergamon.
Coppock, J. T. & Wilson, C. B., eds. Environmental Quality: With Emphasis on Urban Problems. 207p. 1974. 17.95 (ISBN 0-470-17205-3). Halsted Pr.
Coppock, J. T., jt. ed. see Maunder, W. F.
Coppock, Joseph D. International Trade Instability. 1977. 32.95 (ISBN 0-566-00154-3, 001276-9, Pub. by Saxon Hse). Lexington Bks.
Coppock, Paul R. Memphis Memoirs. LC 80-24019. (Illus.). 265p. 1980. 14.95 (ISBN 0-87870-110-9). Memphis St Univ.
Coppock, Thomas. The Genuine Dying Speech of the Reverend Parson Coppock, Pretended Bishop of Carlisle: Who Was Drawn, Hanged & Quartered There, Oct. 18, 1746, for High Treason & Rebellion, Etc. LC 80-2477. 1981. Repr. of 1746 ed. 23.50 (ISBN 0-404-19109-6). AMS Pr.
Coppolino, Carl A. The Crime That Never Was. LC 80-81163. (Illus.). 309p. 1980. 13.95 (ISBN 0-936802-00-6). Justice Pr.
Copps, Dale. The Savage Survivor: 300 Million Years of the Shark. (gr. 7 up). 1976. 5.95 o.p. (ISBN 0-685-78821-0, Dist. by Westwind Pr); lib. ed. 5.97 o.p. (ISBN 0-695-40663-9). Follett.
--The Sherlock Holmes Puzzle Book. (Illus.). 160p. 1980. pap. 3.95 (ISBN 0-385-14839-9, Dolp). Doubleday.
Copson, David A. Informational Bioelectromagnetics. 650p. 1981. text ed. 24.95 (ISBN 0-916460-09-6). Matrix Pubns.
--Microwave Heating. 2nd ed. (Illus.). 1975. lib. bdg. 49.00 (ISBN 0-87055-182-5). AVI.
Copson, E. T. Introduction to the Theory of Functions of a Complex Variable. (Illus.). 1935. pap. 19.95x (ISBN 0-19-853145-1). Oxford U Pr.
Copson, Edward T. Asymptotic Expansions. (Cambridge Tracts in Mathematics & Mathematical Physics). 1965. 21.50 (ISBN 0-521-04721-8). Cambridge U Pr.
--Metric Spaces. (Cambridge Tracts in Mathematics & Mathematical Physics). 1968. 23.95 (ISBN 0-521-04722-6). Cambridge U Pr.
Copy Club of N. Y., jt. auth. see Art Directors Club of N. Y.
Copyright Society Of The United States. Studies on Copyright, 2 vols. 1963. 35.00x (ISBN 0-8377-1101-0). Rothman.
Coquelin, Charles. The Art of the Actor. 1932. pap. 2.95 o.p. (ISBN 0-04-792005-X). Allen Unwin.
Coray, Henry W. J. Gresham Machen. 128p. (Orig.). 1981. pap. 4.95 (ISBN 0-8254-2327-9). Kregel.
--Rebel Prince. (Spire Bks.). 1975. pap. 1.50 o.p. (ISBN 0-8007-8225-9). Revell.
Corb, D. A., jt. auth. see Kent, Robert W.
Corballis, M. C. & Beale, I. L. The Psychology of Left & Right. LC 76-13233. 1976. text ed. 14.95 o.p. (ISBN 0-470-15104-8). Halsted Pr.
Corballis, R. & Harding, J. M. John Webster Concordance, Vol. 2, Pt. 3. (Jacobean Drama Studies: No. 70). 1979. pap. text ed. 25.00x (ISBN 0-391-01761-6). Humanities.
Corballis, Richard & Harding, J. M. A Concordance to the Works of John Webster, Vol. 1 Pt. 2. (Salzburg Studies in English Literature, Jacobean Drama: No. 70-1). (Orig.). 1980. pap. text ed. 25.00x (ISBN 0-391-01316-5). Humanities.
--A Concordance to the Works of John Webster, Vol. 1 Pt. 3. (Salzburg Studies in English Literature, Jacobean Drama Ser.: 70). (Orig.). 1979. pap. text ed. 25.00x (ISBN 0-391-01723-3). Humanities.
--A Concordance to the Works of John Webster, Vol. 1 Pt. 4. (Salzburg Studies in English Literature, Jacobean Drama Ser.). (Orig.). 1979. pap. text ed. 25.00x (ISBN 0-391-01717-9). Humanities.
--A Concordance to the Works of John Webster, Vol. 2, Pt. 4. (Salzburg Studies in English Literature, Jacobean Drama: No. 70-2). 1979. pap. text ed. 25.00x (ISBN 0-391-01317-3). Humanities.
--A Concordance to the Works of John Webster, Vol. 2 Pt. 1. (Salzburg Studies in English Literature, Jacobean Drame Ser.: 70). (Orig.). 1979. pap. text ed. 25.00x (ISBN 0-391-01724-1). Humanities.
--A Concordance to the Works of John Webster, Vol. 3 Pt. 1. (Salzburg Studies in English Literature, Jacobean Drama: No. 70-3). (Orig.). 1980. pap. text ed. 25.00x (ISBN 0-391-01318-1). Humanities.
--A Concordance to the Works of John Webster: Vol. 4, Appendix, Sir Thomas Wyatt. (Salzburg Studies in English Literature, Jacobean Drama Ser.: No. 70-4). (Orig.). 1979. pap. text ed. 25.00x (ISBN 0-391-01213-4). Humanities.
Corballis, Richard & Harding, John. A Concordance to the Works of John Webster, Vol. 2 Pt. 2. (Salzburg Studies in English Literature, Jacobean Drama Ser.: 70). (Orig.). 1979. pap. text ed. 25.00x (ISBN 0-391-01737-3). Humanities.
Corbally, Marguerite. The Partners. LC 77-74121. 1977. pap. text ed. 4.95x (ISBN 0-8134-1953-0). Interstate.
Corbasson, Nadine & De Bruchard, Gisele. La Beaute: From Head to Toe-a la Francais. Turley, Katherine, tr. from Fr. (Illus.). 64p. 1974. pap. 3.95 o.s.i. (ISBN 0-02-046100-3, Collier). Macmillan.
Corbeiller, Clara Le see Le Corbeiller, Clara.
Corbet, H. & Robertson, D. Europe's Free Trade Area Experiment. 1971. pap. 11.30 o.p. (ISBN 0-08-016233-9). Pergamon.
Corbet, H. & Jackson, R., eds. In Search of a New World Economic Order. LC 73-22724. 288p. 1974. 24.95 (ISBN 0-470-17221-5). Halsted Pr.
Corbett, E. V. The Fundamentals of Library Organisation & Administration: A Practical Guide. 1978. 24.50x (ISBN 0-85365-540-5, Pub. by Lib Assn England); pap. text ed. 15.50x (ISBN 0-85365-840-4). Oryx Pr.
Corbett, Edmund V. Illustrations Collection: Its Formation, Classification & Exploitation. LC 72-164185. (Illus.). 1971. Repr. of 1941 ed. 18.00 (ISBN 0-8103-3786-X). Gale.
Corbett, Edward E. & Jensema, Carl J. Teachers of the Deaf: Descriptive Profiles. xviii, 158p. 1981. 7.95 (ISBN 0-913580-64-3). Gallaudet Coll.
Corbett, Edward P. The Little English Handbook: Choices & Conventions. 3rd ed. 300p. 1981. pap. text ed. 5.95 (ISBN 0-471-07856-5). Wiley.
--The Little Rhetoric. LC 76-45081. 1977. pap. text ed. 8.50 (ISBN 0-471-17231-6). Wiley.
--The Little Rhetoric & Handbook. LC 76-45189. 1977. text ed. 10.95 (ISBN 0-471-17232-4); instructors manual avail. (ISBN 0-471-03048-1). Wiley.
Corbett, Edward P., ed. The Essay: Subjects & Stances. (English Literature Ser). (277). 1974. pap. text ed. 8.50 (ISBN 0-13-283515-0). P-H.
Corbett, Edward P. & Burke, Virginia M., eds. The New Century Composition-Rhetoric. LC 73-150594. 1971. 22.50x (ISBN 0-89197-315-X); pap. text ed. 14.95x (ISBN 0-89197-865-8). Irvington.
Corbett, Edward P., jt. ed. see Tate, Gary.
Corbett, J. Elliott. Prophets on Main Street. rev. ed. LC 77-79597. 1977. pap. 5.95 (ISBN 0-8042-0841-7). John Knox.
Corbett, J. Elliott & Smith, Elizabeth S. Becoming a Prophetic Community. LC 80-17618. 201p. (Orig.). 1980. pap. 7.95 (ISBN 0-8042-0784-4). John Knox.
Corbett, Jim. Jim Corbett's India: Stories Selected by R. E. Hawkins. Hawkins, R. E., ed. (Illus.). 1979. 14.95 (ISBN 0-19-212968-6). Oxford U Pr.
Corbett, John, ed. Basic Metric Style Manual for Secretaries. new ed. 1976. pap. 2.95x (ISBN 0-912702-04-4). Global Eng.
Corbett, Margery & Lightbown, R. W. The Comely Frontispiece: The Emblematic Title-Page in England, 1550-1660. (Illus.). 1979. 35.00x (ISBN 0-7100-8554-0). Routledge & Kegan.
Corbett, Michael N. A Better Place to Live: New Designs for Tomorrow's Communities. Stoner, Carol, ed. (Illus.). 256p. (Orig.). 1981. pap. 14.95 (ISBN 0-87857-348-8). Rodale Pr Inc.
Corbett, Percy E. Law in Diplomacy. 9.50 (ISBN 0-8446-1125-5). Peter Smith.
Corbett, Scott. The Big Joke Game. LC 78-179052. (Illus.). 128p. (gr. 3-6). 1972. 7.50 (ISBN 0-525-26515-5, Anytime Bks); PLB 7.50 o.p. (ISBN 0-525-45013-0, Anytime Bks). Dutton.
--Bridges. LC 77-13871. (Illus.). 128p. (gr. 3-7). 1978. 10.95 (ISBN 0-590-07464-4, Four Winds). Schol Bk Serv.
--The Case of the Silver Skull. (Illus.). 128p. (gr. 4-6). 1974. 5.95 (ISBN 0-316-15711-2, Pub. by Atlantic Monthly Pr). Little.
--The Deadly Hoax. LC 80-26552. (gr. 5 up). 1981. PLB 9.95 (ISBN 0-525-28585-7). Dutton.
--Diamonds Are Trouble. LC 67-17998. 1967. reinforced bdg. 4.95 o.p. (ISBN 0-03-089822-6). HR&W.
--The Great McGoniggle Rides Shotgun. (Illus.). (gr. 1-3). 1977. 6.95 (ISBN 0-316-15729-5, Atlantic-Little, Brown). Little.
--The Great McGoniggle Switches Pitches. (Illus.). 64p. (gr. 2 up). 1980. 6.95 (ISBN 0-316-15710-4, Pub. by Atlantic Monthly Pr). Little.
--Great McGonigle Rides Shotgun. (gr. k-6). 1980. pap. 0.95 (ISBN 0-440-43313-4, YB). Dell.
--Home Computers: A Simple & Informative Guide. (Illus.). 128p. (gr. 5 up). 1980. 7.95 (ISBN 0-316-15658-2, Pub. by Atlantic Monthly Pr); pap. 4.95 (ISBN 0-316-15712-0). Little.
--The Red Room Riddle. 1978. pap. 1.25 o.s.i. (ISBN 0-440-47524-4). Dell.
--Steady, Freddie. LC 78-116881. (Illus.). (gr. 3-6). 1970. 7.95 o.p. (ISBN 0-525-39951-8). Dutton.
--What About the Wankel Engine? LC 74-8593. (Illus.). 80p. (gr. 3-7). 1974. 6.95 (ISBN 0-590-07369-9, Four Winds). Schol Bk Serv.
Corbett, Thomas H. Cancer & Chemicals. LC 76-54270. 1977. 12.95 (ISBN 0-88229-305-2); pap. 6.95 (ISBN 0-88229-465-2). Nelson-Hall.
Corbiere, Tristan. Selections from Les Amours jaunes. MacIntyre, C. F., tr. (Fr & Eng). 1954. 15.00x (ISBN 0-520-00270-9). U of Cal Pr.
Corbiere-Gille, Gisele, jt. auth. see Waldinger, Renee.
Corbierre, Anne. Paris. LC 80-50996. (Rand McNally Pocket Guide Ser.). (Illus.). 1980. pap. 3.95 (ISBN 0-528-84308-7). Rand.
Corbin, et al. Spring '80: An Annual of Archetypal Psychology & Jungian Thought. Hillman, James, ed. 196p. (Orig.). 1980. pap. text ed. 10.00 (ISBN 0-88214-015-9). Spring Pubns.
Corbin, Alan, jt. ed. see Briggs, Michael.
Corbin, Charles B. & Dowell, J. Linus. Concepts in Physical Education with Laboratories & Experiments. 4th ed. 350p. 1981. pap. text ed. write for info. (ISBN 0-697-07177-4); instrs.' manual avail. (ISBN 0-697-07178-2). Wm C Brown.
Corbin, Cheryl. Nutrition. LC 80-11138. (Illus.). 208p. 1981. 13.95 (ISBN 0-03-048281-X, Owl Bks); pap. 7.95 (ISBN 0-03-048276-3). HR&W.
Corbin, David R. Discover Swaging. LC 78-22085. (Illus.). 288p. 1979. 16.95 (ISBN 0-8117-0497-1). Stackpole.
Corbin, H. Dan & Tait, William J. Education for Leisure. (Illus.). 160p. 1973. ref. ed. 9.50 o.p. (ISBN 0-13-240531-8). P-H.
Corbin, Henri. Avicenna & the Visionary Recital. Task, Willard R., tr. from French. 320p. 1980. pap. text ed. 12.50 (ISBN 0-88214-213-5). Spring Pubns.
Corbin, Henry. Creative Imagination in the Sufism of Ibn 'arabi. LC 68-20869. (Bollingen Ser.: XCI). (Illus.). 420p. 1980. pap. 6.95 (ISBN 0-691-01828-6). Princeton U Pr.
Corbin, John. Developing Computer-Based Library Systems. (Neal-Schuman Professional Bk). 1981. lib. bdg. 18.50 (ISBN 0-912700-10-6). Oryx Pr.
Corbin, John B. Technical Services Manual for Small Libraries. LC 70-156885. 1971. 10.00 (ISBN 0-8108-0388-7). Scarecrow.
Corbin, Patricia. Designers Design for Themselves. (Illus.). 96p. 1981. 19.95 (ISBN 0-525-93135-X). Dutton.
Corbit, Julia. Julia's Book. Sonnack, Iver & Hatchimonji, Mike, eds. LC 79-66049. (Illus.). 1979. 14.95 (ISBN 0-934724-00-8). Xenos Bks.
Corbman, B. P. & Krieger, M. Mathematics of Retail Merchandising. 2nd ed. 411p. 1972. 19.95 (ISBN 0-471-06587-0). Wiley.
Corbman, Bernard P. & Krieger, Murray. Mathematics of Retail Merchandising. 2nd ed. 450p. 1972. 19.95 (ISBN 0-8260-2150-6). Ronald Pr.
Corby, Jane. Riverwood. 1975. pap. 1.25 o.p. (ISBN 0-685-61049-7, LB317, Leisure Bks). Nordon Pubns.
--The Shadow & the Fear. 1977. pap. 1.50 (ISBN 0-505-51174-6). Tower Bks.
Corby, Michael. Postal Business Nineteen Sixty-Nine to Nineteen Seventy-Nine: A Study in Public Sector Management. 1979. 28.75x (ISBN 0-85038-227-0). Nichols Pub.
Corcoran, A. Wayne. Costs: Accounting, Analysis & Control. LC 77-18798. (Accounting & Information Systems Ser.). 1978. pap. text ed. 27.95 (ISBN 0-471-17251-0); solutions manual avail. (ISBN 0-471-03339-1). Wiley.
Corcoran, Barbara. Beloved Enemy. 160p. (Orig.). 1981. pap. 1.95 (ISBN 0-345-28667-7). Ballantine.
--The Call of the Heart. (Orig.). 1981. pap. 1.95 (ISBN 0-345-28668-5). Ballantine.
--Hey, That's My Soul You're Stepping on. (gr. 5-9). pap. 2.95 (ISBN 0-689-70486-0, A-113, Aladdin). Atheneum.
--Making It. 176p. (YA) (gr. 7 up). 1981. 8.95 (ISBN 0-316-15731-7, Pub. by Atlantic). Little.
--The Person in the Potting Shed. LC 80-12299. 132p. (gr. 5-9). 1980. 8.95 (ISBN 0-689-30774-8). Atheneum.
Corcoran, Eileen. Gaining Skills in Using the Library. (Illus.). 1980. pap. 2.25x (ISBN 0-88323-158-1, 247). Richards Pub.
--Meeting Basic Competencies in Communications. 1979. pap. 2.25x (ISBN 0-88323-152-2, 242); tchr's answer key 1.00x (ISBN 0-88323-156-5, 246). Richards Pub.
--Meeting Basic Competencies in Math. 1978. pap. text ed. 2.25x (ISBN 0-88323-138-7, 227); tchrs answer key free (ISBN 0-88323-141-7, 230). Richards Pub.
--Reading for Survival. 1978. pap. 2.25x (ISBN 0-88323-145-X, 234); tchr's. answer key free (ISBN 0-88323-151-4, 240). Richards Pub.
Corcoran, Eileen L. Meeting Basic Competencies in Practical Science & Health: A Workstudy Book to Improve Daily Living Skills. (Illus.). 1979. 2.25x (ISBN 0-88323-146-8, 237); tchrs answer key free (ISBN 0-88323-154-9, 245). Richards Pub.
--Meeting Basic Competencies in Reading. 1977. pap. text ed. 1.95 (ISBN 0-88323-134-4, 221); tchrs answer key 1.00 (ISBN 0-88323-144-1, 232). Richards Pub.
Corcoran, Frances, jt. auth. see Blickle, Calvin.
Corcoran, J. W., ed. Biosynthesis. (Antibiotics Ser.: Vol. 4). (Illus.). 500p. 1981. 97.00 (ISBN 0-387-10186-1). Springer-Verlag.
Corcoran, John, ed. see Tarski, Alfred.
Corcoran, John, ed. see Tulleners, Tonny.
Corcos, Lucille. The City Book. (Illus.). (gr. 1-6). 1972. PLB 10.69 o.p. (ISBN 0-307-65772-8, Golden Pr). Western Pub.
Cord, Alex. Sandsong. 224p. 1976. pap. 1.75 o.s.i. (ISBN 0-446-59772-4). Warner Bks.
Cord, Barry. Deadly Amigos: Two Graves for a Gunman. 1979. pap. 2.25 (ISBN 0-505-51419-2). Tower Bks.
--The Gun Shy Kid. 1979. pap. 1.25 (ISBN 0-505-51379-X). Tower Bks.
--The Guns of Hammer. 1979. pap. 1.25 (ISBN 0-505-51338-2). Tower Bks.
--Hell in Paradise Valley. 1978. pap. 1.25 (ISBN 0-505-51316-1). Tower Bks.
--Last Stage to Gomorrah. 1979. pap. 1.25 (ISBN 0-505-51339-0). Tower Bks.
--The Long Wire. 1978. pap. 1.25 (ISBN 0-505-51238-6). Tower Bks.
--Shadow Valley. 1978. pap. 1.25 (ISBN 0-505-51329-3). Tower Bks.
Cord, Robert L., et al. Political Science: An Introduction. 688p. 1974. Repr. text ed. 17.95 (ISBN 0-13-687889-X); study guide & access wkbk. 4.95 (ISBN 0-13-687913-6). P-H.
Cord, W., ed. see Romero, Jose R.
Cordasco, Francesco. Eighteenth Century Bibliographies. LC 70-8541. 1970. 9.50 o.p. (ISBN 0-8108-0288-0). Scarecrow.
--Italian Mass Emigration: The Exodus of a Latin People--A Bibliographical Guide to the "Bollettino Dell'Emigrazione, 1902-1927. (Illus.). 307p. 1980. 47.50x (ISBN 0-8476-6283-7). Rowman.
--Register of Eighteenth Century Bibliographies & References: A Chronological Quarter-Century Survey Relating to English Literature, Booksellers, Newspapers, Periodicals, Printing & Publishing, Aesthetics, Art & Music, Economics, History & Science, a Preliminary Contribution. LC 76-4182. 1968. Repr. of 1950 ed. 15.00 (ISBN 0-8103-3521-2). Gale.
--The Shaping of American Graduate Education: Daniel Coit Gilman & the Protean Ph. D. 164p. 1973. Repr. of 1959 ed. 10.00x o.p. (ISBN 0-87471-161-4). Rowman.
Cordasco, Francesco & Pitkin, Thomas M. The White Slave Trade & the Immigrants: A Chapter in American Social History. LC 80-25556. 1981. write for info. (ISBN 0-87917-077-8); pap. write for info. (ISBN 0-87917-076-X). Blaine Ethridge.
Cordasco, Francesco, ed. Bilingual Education in American Schools: A Guide to Information Sources. Bernstein, George. LC 79-15787. (Education Information Guide Ser.: Vol. 3). 1979. 30.00 (ISBN 0-8103-1447-9). Gale.
--Italian Americans: A Guide to Information Sources. LC 78-4833. (Ethnic Studies Information Guide Ser.: Vol. 2). 1978. 30.00 (ISBN 0-8103-1397-9). Gale.
Cordasco, Francesco & Alloway, David N., eds. Medical Education in the United States: A Guide to Information Sources. LC 79-24030. (Education Information Guide Ser.: Vol. 8). 1980. 30.00 (ISBN 0-8103-1458-4). Gale.
--Sociology of Education: A Guide to Information Sources. LC 78-10310. (Education Information Guide Ser.: Vol. 2). 1979. 30.00 (ISBN 0-8103-1436-3). Gale.
Cordasco, Francesco, ed. see Dissemination Center for Bilingual-Bicultural Education.
Cordasco, Francesco, et al, eds. History of American Education: A Guide to Information Sources. LC 79-23010. (Education Information Guide Ser.: Vol. 7). 1979. 30.00 (ISBN 0-8103-1382-0). Gale.
Cordeiro, Daniel R., ed. A Bibliography of Latin American Bibliographies: Social Sciences & Humanities, Vol. 1. LC 78-11935. 1979. lib. bdg. 13.00 (ISBN 0-8108-1170-7). Scarecrow.

Cordell, Brad. My Name on the Bullet. 1979. pap. 1.25 (ISBN 0-505-51411-7). Tower Bks.

Cordell, Geoffrey A. Introduction to Alkaloids: A Biogenetic Approach. 1056p. 1981. 50.00 (ISBN 0-471-03478-9, Pub. by Wiley-Interscience). Wiley.

Cordell, Linda S., ed. Tijeras Canyon: Analyses of the Past. (Illus.). 232p. 1980. 19.95 (ISBN 0-8263-0553-9, Pub. by Maxwell Mus Anthropology); pap. 9.95 (ISBN 0-8263-0565-2). U of NM Pr.

--Tijeras Canyon: Analyses of the Past. (Illus.). 232p. 1980. pap. 9.95 (ISBN 0-8263-0565-2). U of NM Pr.

Cordell, Linda S. & Beckerman, Stephen, eds. The Versatility of Kinship. LC 80-525. (Studies in Anthropology). 1980. 40.00 (ISBN 0-12-188250-0). Acad Pr.

Cordellos, Harry C. Breaking Through. LC 78-23270. (Illus.). 240p. (Orig.). 1981. pap. 6.95 (ISBN 0-89037-168-7). Anderson World.

Cordemoy, Geraud de. A Philosophicall Discourse Concerning Speech (1668) & a Discourse Written to a Learned Frier (1670) LC 72-6400. (History of Psychology Ser.). 224p. 1972. Repr. 23.00x (ISBN 0-8201-1106-6). Schol Facsimiles.

Corden, W. M. Inflation, Exchange Rates, & the World Economy: Lectures on International Monetary Economics. (Business & Society Studies). 1980. pap. write for info. (ISBN 0-226-11584-4). U of Chicago Pr.

--Theory of Protection. (Illus.). 1971. 17.95x (ISBN 0-19-828171-4). Oxford U Pr.

--Trade Policy & Economic Welfare. (Illus.). 400p. 1974. text ed. 39.00x (ISBN 0-19-828199-4); pap. text ed. 17.95x (ISBN 0-19-828401-2). Oxford U Pr.

Corden, W. M. & Fels, Gerhard, eds. Public Assistance to Industry: Protection & Subsidies in Britain & Germany. new ed. LC 76-19791. (Illus.). 1976. lib. bdg. 35.00x (ISBN 0-89158-632-6). Westview.

Corder, Brice W., et al. Health: Current Perspectives. 3rd ed. 403p. 1981. pap. text ed. write for info. (ISBN 0-697-07388-2); instructor's manual avail. (ISBN 0-697-07389-0). Wm C Brown.

Corder, E. M. The Deer Hunter. 1979. pap. 1.95 (ISBN 0-515-05321-X). Jove Pubns.

--Nickelodeon. 1976. pap. 1.50 o.p. (ISBN 0-345-25471-6). Ballantine.

Corder, Jim W. Handbook of Current English. 6th ed. 1981. pap. text ed. 8.95x (ISBN 0-673-15425-4). Scott F.

Corder, S. Pit. An Intermediate English Practice Book. 1974. pap. text ed. 4.25x (ISBN 0-582-52512-8); key 2.00x (ISBN 0-582-52513-6). Longman.

Corder, S. Pit, jt. ed. see Allen, J. P.

Corderman, Susan & McGarry, Jane, eds. College Admissions Data Service Handbook: National Edition, 1980-1981, 4 vols. rev. ed. 2256p. 1980. Set. text ed. 110.00x looseleaf (ISBN 0-933510-12-8); Set. pap. text ed. 95.00x (ISBN 0-933510-11-X). Orchard Hse MA.

--College Admissions Data Service Handbook, 1980-81: 1980-81 Edition. rev. ed. Incl. Northeast Regional. 628p. pap. text ed. 30.00x (ISBN 0-933510-07-1); Southeast Regional. 602p. pap. text ed. 30.00x (ISBN 0-933510-08-X); Mid-West Regional. 520p. pap. text ed. 25.00x (ISBN 0-933510-09-8); West Regional. 502p. pap. text ed. 25.00x (ISBN 0-933510-10-1). 1980. Orchard Hse MA.

Corderoy, Eileen. Dressmaking & Fashion. LC 68-95775. (Pegasus Books: No. 8). (Illus.). 1967. 10.50x (ISBN 0-234-77940-3). Intl Pubns Serv.

Cordes, Alfred. The Descent of the Doves: Camus's Journey to the Spirit. LC 79-3811. 1980. text ed. 18.50 (ISBN 0-8191-0931-2); pap. text ed. 10.25 (ISBN 0-8191-0932-0). U Pr of Amer.

Cordes, Eugene & Schaeffer, Riley S. Chemistry. (Rice Chemistry Ser.). (Illus.). 702p. 1973. text ed. 23.50 scp (ISBN 0-06-041359-X, HarpC); instructor's manual avail. (ISBN 0-06-361393-X). Har-Row.

Cordes, Lianne. The Reflecting Pond. 1980. pap. 6.95 (ISBN 0-89486-121-2). Hazelden.

Cordier, Andrew W., ed. Columbia Essays in International Affairs: The Dean's Papers, Vol. 2, 1966. LC 66-14078. 1967. 25.00x (ISBN 0-231-03047-9). Columbia U Pr.

--Columbia Essays in International Affairs: The Dean's Papers, Vol. 3, 1967. LC 66-14078. 1968. 25.00x (ISBN 0-231-03156-4). Columbia U Pr.

--Columbia Essays in International Affairs: The Dean's Papers, Vol. 4, 1968. LC 66-14078. 1969. 25.00x (ISBN 0-231-03270-6). Columbia U Pr.

--Columbia Essays in International Affairs: The Dean's Papers, Vol. 5, 1969. LC 66-14078. 1970. 25.00x (ISBN 0-231-03487-3). Columbia U Pr.

--Columbia Essays in International Affairs: The Dean's Papers, Vol. 6, 1970. LC 66-14078. 180p. 1971. 25.00x (ISBN 0-231-03550-0). Columbia U Pr.

--Columbia Essays in International Affairs: The Dean's Papers, Vol. 7, 1971. LC 66-14078. 304p. 1972. 25.00x (ISBN 0-231-03667-1). Columbia U Pr.

--Paths to World Order. (Orig.). 1967. pap. 4.00x (ISBN 0-231-08578-8). Columbia U Pr.

Cordier, Andrew W. & Foote, Wilder, eds. Public Papers of the Secretaries-General of the United Nations: Trygve Lie, 1946-1953, Vol. 1. LC 68-8873. 1969. 30.00x (ISBN 0-231-03137-8). Columbia U Pr.

--Public Papers of the Secretaries-General of the United Nations: Dag Hammarskjold, 1953-1956, Vol. 2. LC 68-8873. 650p. 1972. 30.00x (ISBN 0-231-03633-7). Columbia U Pr.

--Public Papers of the Secretaries-General of the United Nations: Dag Hammarskjold, 1956-1957, Vol. 3. 784p. 1973. 30.00x (ISBN 0-231-03735-X). Columbia U Pr.

--Public Papers of the Secretaries-General of the United Nations: Dag Hammarskjold, 1958-1960, Vol. 4. LC 68-8873. 736p. 1974. 30.00x (ISBN 0-231-03810-0). Columbia U Pr.

Cordier, Andrew W. & Harrelson, Max, eds. Public Papers of the Secretaries General of the United Nations, Vol. 7, U Thant, 1965-1967. 1976. 30.00 (ISBN 0-231-04098-9). Columbia U Pr.

Cording, Edward J., jt. ed. see American Society of Civil Engineers.

Cordle, Thomas. Andre Gide. (World Authors Ser.: France: No. 86). lib. bdg. 12.50 (ISBN 0-8057-2364-1). Twayne.

Cordon, Faustino. An Introduction to the Biological Basis of Feeding: Essential Biological Ideas Necessary to a Study of Living Beings from the Evolutionary Standpoint. LC 79-40933. (Illus.). 250p. 1980. pap. 34.00 (ISBN 0-08-025484-5). Pergamon.

Cordon, William A. Freezing & Thawing of Concrete: Mechanisms & Control. (Monograph: No. 3). 1966. 9.00 o.p. (ISBN 0-685-85136-2, M-3); members 7.25 o.p. (ISBN 0-685-85137-0). ACI.

Cordova, F. David, jt. auth. see Schenck, Jeanne M.

Cords, Nicholas & Gerster, Patrick. Myth & the American Experience, Vol. 1. 2nd ed. 1978. pap. text ed. 7.95x (ISBN 0-02-471880-7). Macmillan.

Cords, Nicholas, jt. auth. see Gerster, Patrick.

Corduneanu, Constantin. Principles of Differential & Integral Equations. 2nd ed. LC 77-2962. 1977. text ed. 10.95 (ISBN 0-8284-0295-7). Chelsea Pub.

Cordwell, Justine & Schwartz, Ronald A., eds. The Fabrics of Culture: The Anthology of Clothing & Adornment. (World Anthropology Ser.). 1979. text ed. 63.50x (ISBN 90-279-7910-3). Mouton.

Cordy-Collins, Alana, jt. auth. see Nicholson, H. B.

Core, Arthur C. Otterbein (Philip William) 1968. 4.00 (ISBN 0-687-30917-4); pap. 2.25 (ISBN 0-687-30918-2). Abingdon.

Corea, Gamani. Need for Change: Towards the New International Economic Order. LC 80-40800. 350p. 1980. 25.00 (ISBN 0-08-026095-0). Pergamon.

Corea, Gena. The Hidden Malpractice. 1978. pap. 1.95 (ISBN 0-515-04522-5). Jove Pubns.

Corelli, Marie. A Romance of Two Worlds. -Wolff, Robert L., ed. LC 75-484. (Victorian Fiction Ser.). 1975. Repr. of 1886 ed. lib. bdg. 66.00 (ISBN 0-8240-1561-4). Garland Pub.

Coren, Alan. The Best of Alan Coren. 424p. 1981. 15.95 (ISBN 0-312-07711-4). St Martin.

--Golfing for Cats. LC 75-21688. 176p. 1976. 7.95 o.p. (ISBN 0-312-33810-4). St Martin.

--A Rhinestone As Big As the Ritz. LC 79-83524. 1979. 8.95 o.p. (ISBN 0-312-68091-0). St Martin.

--The Sanity Inspector. 176p. 1975. 6.95 o.p. (ISBN 0-312-69930-1). St Martin.

Coren, Stanley, et al. Sensation & Perception. 439p. 1979. 19.95 (ISBN 0-12-188550-X). Acad Pr.

Corey, D. Q. & Maas, J. P. The Energy Couple. (Illus.). 160p. 1980. 9.95 (ISBN 0-398-03964-X). C C Thomas.

Corey, Dorothy. Everybody Takes Turns. Ann, Fay, ed. LC 79-18652. (Self-Starter Ser.). (Illus.). (ps-1). 1980. 6.50g (ISBN 0-8075-2166-3). A Whitman.

--Tomorrow You Can. Rubin, Caroline, ed. LC 77-12789. (Self-Starter Ser.). (Illus.). (ps-1). 1977. 6.50g (ISBN 0-8075-8015-5). A Whitman.

--We All Share. Fay, Ann, ed. LC 80-18988. (Self-Starter Bks.). (Illus.). 32p. (ps-1). 1980. 6.50 (ISBN 0-8075-8696-X). A Whitman.

--You Go Away. LC 75-33015. (Self Starter Bks.). (Illus.). 32p. (ps). 1975. 6.50g (ISBN 0-8075-9441-5). A Whitman.

Corey, E. Raymond. Procurement Management: Strategy, Organization & Decision-Making. LC 78-5826. 1978. 19.95 (ISBN 0-8436-0759-9). CBI Pub.

Corey, Gerald. Manual for Theory & Practice of Group Counseling. 150p. 1980. pap. text ed. 5.95 (ISBN 0-8185-0432-3). Brooks-Cole.

--Theory & Practice of Group Counseling. LC 80-18985. 500p. 1980. text ed. 15.95 (ISBN 0-8185-0400-5). Brooks-Cole.

Corey, Lee. Shuttle Down. 224p. (Orig.). 1981. pap. 2.25 (ISBN 0-345-29262-6, Del Rey). Ballantine.

--Space Doctor. 256p. (Orig.). 1981. pap. 2.50 (ISBN 0-345-29263-4, Del Rey). Ballantine.

Corey, Paul. Do Cats Think? 1978. pap. 1.75 (ISBN 0-515-04484-9). Jove Pubns.

--How to Build Country Homes on a Budget. LC 75-6854. (Funk & W Bk.). (Illus.). 245p. 1975. 8.95 o.s.i. (ISBN 0-308-10197-9, TYC-T); pap. 5.95 o.s.i. (ISBN 0-308-10198-7, F128, TYC-T). T Y Crowell.

Corey, Tom, ed. Field & Equipment Record Book. new ed. 1979. pap. 9.45 (ISBN 0-932250-07-6); ringed binder 15.95. Doane Agricultural.

Corfe, T. Archbishop Thomas & King Henry Second. LC 74-14442. (Introduction to the History of Mankind Ser). (Illus.). (gr. 6-11). 1975. pap. text ed. 3.95 (ISBN 0-521-20646-4). Cambridge U Pr.

--St. Patrick & Irish Christianity. LC 73-75862. (Introduction to the History of Mankind Ser.). 48p. 1973. 3.95 (ISBN 0-521-20228-0). Cambridge U Pr.

Cork, Dorothy. Barefoot Bride. (Harlequin Romances). 192p. 1981. pap. 1.25 (ISBN 0-373-02390-1, Pub. by Harlequin). P-H.

--Outback Runaway. (Harlequin Romances Ser.). 192p. 1980. pap. 1.25 (ISBN 0-373-02372-3, Pub. by Harlquin). PB.

Cork, Richard. The Social Role of Art. 128p. 1980. 19.95x (ISBN 0-86092-048-8, Pub. by Douglas & McIntyre Canada). Intl Schol Bk Serv.

Cork, Seamus. Irish Erotic Art. 96p. 1981. 5.95 (ISBN 0-312-43601-7). St Martin.

Corke, Helen. In Our Infancy: An Autobiography, Pt. 1, 1882-1912. LC 74-31799. (Illus.). 250p. 1975. 32.50 (ISBN 0-521-20797-5). Cambridge U Pr.

Corkill, W. A. Railway Modelling: An Introduction. 1979. 14.95 (ISBN 0-7153-7571-7). David & Charles.

Corkindale, David R. & Kennedy, Sherrel H. Measuring the Effect of Advertising. LC 75-35021. (Illus.). 1976. 26.95 (ISBN 0-347-01110-1, 00207-0). Lexington Bks.

Corkindale, David R., jt. auth. see Kennedy, Sherrie H.

Corle, Edwin. Gila: River of the Southwest. LC 51-6152. (Illus.). 1964. pap. 4.50 (ISBN 0-8032-5040-1, BB 305, Bison). U of Nebr Pr.

Corlett, P. N. Practical Programming. 2nd ed. LC 75-161295. (School Mathematics Project Handbooks). (Illus.). 1971. 23.95 (ISBN 0-521-08198-X); pap. 10.95x (ISBN 0-521-09740-1). Cambridge U Pr.

Corlett, William. The Dark Side of the Moon. LC 76-57890. (gr. 6-9). 1977. 6.95 (ISBN 0-87888-118-2). Bradbury Pr.

--Return to the Gate. LC 76-57889. 1977. 6.95 (ISBN 0-87888-112-3). Bradbury Pr.

Corlett, William & Moore, John. The Buddha Way. LC 79-15685. (Questions Ser.). 1980. 8.95 (ISBN 0-87888-153-0). Bradbury Pr.

--Christ Story. LC 79-15687. (Questions Ser.). 1980. 8.95 (ISBN 0-87888-150-6). Bradbury Pr.

--The Hindu Sound. LC 79-15815. (Questions Ser.). 1980. 8.95 (ISBN 0-87888-151-4). Bradbury Pr.

--The Islamic Space. LC 79-15204. (Questions Ser.). 1980. 8.95 (ISBN 0-87888-154-9). Bradbury Pr.

--The Judaic Law. LC 79-16432. (Questions Ser.). 1980. 8.95 (ISBN 0-87888-152-2). Bradbury Pr.

--The Question of Religion. LC 79-15140. (Questions Ser.). 1980. 8.95 (ISBN 0-87888-149-2). Bradbury Pr.

--Questions of Human Existence As Answered by Major World Religions, 6 bks. Incl. The Question of Religion (ISBN 0-87888-149-2); The Christ Story (ISBN 0-87888-150-6); The Hindu Sound (ISBN 0-87888-151-4); The Judaic Law (ISBN 0-87888-152-2); The Buddha Way (ISBN 0-87888-153-0); The Islamic Space (ISBN 0-87888-154-9). (Illus.). 1979. 8.95 ea. Bradbury Pr.

Corlew, Robert E. Tennessee: A Short History. 2nd ed. LC 80-13553. (Illus.). 568p. 1981. 22.50 (ISBN 0-87049-258-6); pap. text ed. 14.50x (ISBN 0-87049-302-7). U of Tenn Pr.

Corley & Smallwood. Speak English, Text 2. (Speak English Ser.). (Illus.). 96p. (Orig.). 1981. pap. 3.95 (ISBN 0-88499-653-0). Inst Mod Lang.

--Speak English, Workbook 2. (Speak English Ser.). (Illus.). 72p. (Orig.). 1981. pap. 3.95 (ISBN 0-88499-654-9). Inst Mod Lang.

Corley & Steurer. Basic Beginner Book. (Speak English! Ser.). (Illus.). 80p. 1980. pap. text ed. 3.95 (ISBN 0-88499-652-2). Inst Mod Lang.

Corley, Edwin. Air Force One. 1979. pap. 2.50 o.s.i. (ISBN 0-440-10063-1). Dell.

--Air Force One. LC 77-82618. 1978. 8.95 o.p. (ISBN 0-385-11402-8). Doubleday.

--The Genesis Rock. 1981. pap. 2.75 (ISBN 0-440-12877-3). Dell.

--Long Shots. LC 80-1089. 408p. 1981. 12.95 (ISBN 0-385-15922-6). Doubleday.

--Sargasso. 1981. pap. price not set o.p. (ISBN 0-440-17575-5). Dell.

Corley, Hugh. Organic Small Farming. Bargyla & Rateaver, Gylver, eds. LC 74-33122. (Conservation Gardening & Farming Ser: Ser. C). 1975. pap. 10.00 (ISBN 0-9600698-4-4). Rateavers.

Corley, Monte & Nichols, Roy. Creative Ideas for Bible Discovery. LC 79-67509. (Bible Discovery Bks.). 1979. pap. 4.25 (ISBN 0-8344-0109-6). Sweet.

--Games for Bible Discovery. LC 79-55019. (Bible Discovery Bks.). 1979. pap. 4.25 (ISBN 0-8344-0110-X). Sweet.

Corley, Robert, jt. auth. see Windal, Floyd.

Corley, Robert N. & Robert, William J. Principles of Business Law. 11th ed. 1979. 21.95 (ISBN 0-13-701318-3); pap. 7.95 student guide & wkbk., 3rd ed. (ISBN 0-13-701326-4). P-H.

Corley, Robert N., et al. The Legal Environment of Business. 5th ed. (Illus.). 608p. 1981. 19.95 (ISBN 0-07-013186-4, C); instr's manual 5.95 (ISBN 0-07-013187-2); test file 7.95 (ISBN 0-07-013189-9). McGraw.

Corley, T. A. Quaker Enterprises in Biscuits: Huntley & Palmers of Reading, 1822-1972. 1972. text ed. 10.50x (ISBN 0-09-111320-2). Humanities.

Corliss, Charlotte, jt. auth. see Broadribb, Violet.

Corliss, John O. The Ciliated Protozoa: Characterization, Classification & Guide to the Literature. 2nd ed. LC 78-41075. (Illus.). 1979. text ed. 49.50 (ISBN 0-08-018752-8). Pergamon.

Corliss, William R. Incredible Life: A Handbook of Biological Mysteries. LC 80-53971. (Illus.). 1050p. 1981. 22.50 (ISBN 0-915554-07-0). Sourcebook.

--Unknown Earth: A Handbook of Geological Enigmas. LC 80-50159. (Illus.). 839p. 1980. 19.95 (ISBN 0-915554-06-2). Sourcebook.

Cormack, A. J. German Small Arms. (Illus.). 160p. 1979. 20.00x (ISBN 0-85383-261-7). Intl Pubns Serv.

Cormack, David H., jt. auth. see Ham, Arthur W.

Cormack, M. Catalogue of Drawings & Watercolour in the Fitzwilliam Museum, Cambridge. M. W. Turner, R. A., 1775-1851. LC 75-12158. (Illus.). 132p. 1975. 32.50 (ISBN 0-521-20955-2). Cambridge U Pr.

Cormack, Maribelle B. First Book of Stones. (First Bks). (Illus.). (gr. 3-5). 1950. PLB 4.90 o.p. (ISBN 0-531-00644-1). Watts.

Corman, Avery. The Old Neighborhood. 1980. 10.95 (ISBN 0-686-68758-2, 41475, Linden). S&S.

--The Old Neighborhood. 1980. lib. bdg. 12.95 (ISBN 0-8161-3146-5, Large Print Bks). G K Hall.

Corman, Cid. Auspices. (Orig.). 1978. limited signed ed. 20.00x (ISBN 0-915316-59-5); pap. 5.00x (ISBN 0-915316-58-7). Pentagram.

Cormany, Christine. How to Raise & Train a Whippet. (Orig.). pap. 2.00 (ISBN 0-87666-409-5, DS1131). TFH Pubns.

Cormican, John & Stanford, Gene. A Guidebook for Teaching About the English Language. new ed. 1978. pap. text ed. 19.95 (ISBN 0-205-06119-2). Allyn.

Cormier, Patricia P. & Levy, Joyce I. Community Oral Health: A Systems Approach for the Dental Health Profession. 240p. 1980. pap. 14.95x (ISBN 0-8385-1184-8). ACC.

Cormier, Robert. Take Me Where the Good Times Are. 176p. 1981. pap. 2.25 (ISBN 0-380-52662-X, 52662). Avon.

Cormier, Sherilyn N., jt. auth. see Hackney, Harold L.

Corn, Alfred. The Various Light. 1980. pap. 7.95 (ISBN 0-14-042284-6). Penguin.

Corn, Ira G. Foreword by see Martin, Ira.

Corn, Ira G., Jr. A Businessman Answers Questions Asked by College Students. 1981. 7.95. Green Hill.

--The Story of the Declaration of Independence. 1980. 8.95 (ISBN 0-89474-010-5). Green Hill.

Corn, Wanda, ed. Art of Andrew Wyeth. LC 73-93900. (Illus.). 1975. pap. 12.95 (ISBN 0-8212-0685-0, 052280). NYGS.

Cornaby, W. Arthur. A String of Chinese Peach-Stones. LC 70-175730. (Illus.). xvi, 478p. 1974. Repr. of 1895 ed. 20.00 (ISBN 0-8103-3125-X). Gale.

Cornacchia, Harold J. & Barrett, Stephen. Consumer Health: A Guide to Intelligent Decisions. 2nd ed. LC 80-11515. (Illus.). 1980. pap. text ed. 12.95 (ISBN 0-8016-1037-0). Mosby.

Cornacchia, Harold J. & Staton, Wesley M. Health in the Elementary Schools. 5th ed. LC 78-21076. (Illus.). 1979. text ed. 15.95 (ISBN 0-8016-1062-1). Mosby.

Cornacchia, Harold J., et al. Drugs in the Classroom: A Conceptual Model for School Programs. 2nd ed. LC 77-22968. (Illus.). 1978. pap. text ed. 13.95 (ISBN 0-8016-1043-5). Mosby.

Corne, Michele F. American Neptune Pictorial Supplements, Vol. 14. pap. 2.50 (ISBN 0-87577-101-7). Peabody Mus Salem.

Cornehls, James V., jt. auth. see Taebel, Delbert A.

Corneille, Pierre. Le Cid. Lapp, John C., ed. & tr. LC 55-9014. (Crofts Classics Ser.). 1955. pap. text ed. 2.75x (ISBN 0-88295-026-6). AHM Pub.

--The Cid, Cinna, the Theatrical Illusion. Cairncross, John, tr. from Fr. (Penguin Classics). 1980. pap. 3.95 (ISBN 0-14-044312-6). Penguin.

--Mort de Pompee. (Nouveaux Classiques Larousse). (Illus., Fr). pap. 2.95 (ISBN 0-685-13995-6, 71). Larousse.

--Nicomede. (Documentation thematique). pap. 2.95 (ISBN 0-685-14000-8, 73). Larousse.

--Polyeucte. Sayce, R. A., ed. 1962. pap. 10.25x (ISBN 0-631-00480-7, Pub. by Basil Blackwell). Biblio Dist.

--Writings on the Theatre. Barnwell, H. T., ed. (French Texts Ser.). 1965. pap. text ed. 12.50x (ISBN 0-631-00640-0, Pub. by Basil Blackwell). Biblio Dist.

Cornelia, Elizabeth. Australia. LC 78-56592. (Countries Ser.). (Illus.). 1978. lib. bdg. 7.95 (ISBN 0-686-51148-4). Silver.

Cornelia, Marie. The Function of the Masque in Jacobean Tragedy & Tragicomedy. (Salzburg Studies in English Literature, Jacobean Drama Studies: No. 77). 1978. pap. text ed. 25.00x (ISBN 0-391-01350-5). Humanities.

Cornelison, Gayle, ed. Directory of Children's Theatre in the United States. 1980. pap. 9.00; ATA members 7.00. Am Theatre Assoc.

Cornelison, Isaac J. The Relation of Religion to Civil Government in the United States. LC 75-107409. (Civil Liberties in American History Ser). 1970. Repr. of 1895 ed. lib. bdg. 35.00 (ISBN 0-306-71890-1). Da Capo.

Cornelison, Kathy D., jt. auth. see Risser, Paul G.

Cornelius. Food Service Careers. 1979. text ed. 14.60 (ISBN 0-87002-206-7); avail. tchr's guide; student's guide 2.96 (ISBN 0-87002-165-6). Bennett IL.

Cornelius, C. E., jt. ed. see Kaneko, J. J.

Cornelius, E. T., Jr., jt. auth. see Alexander, L. G.

Cornelius, Edwin T., jt. auth. see Byrne, Donn.

Cornelius, Edwin T., Jr. New English Course, 6 bks. Incl. Book 1. pap. text ed. (ISBN 0-89285-125-2); tchr's. annotated ed. 5.95 (ISBN 0-89285-137-6); wkbk. 1.50 (ISBN 0-89285-131-7); cassette 110.00 (ISBN 0-89285-119-8); cassette tape 14.95 (ISBN 0-89285-113-9); Book 2. pap. text ed. (ISBN 0-89285-126-0); tchr's annotated ed. 5.95 (ISBN 0-89285-138-4); wkbk. 1.50 (ISBN 0-89285-132-5); cassette 110.00 (ISBN 0-89285-120-1); cassette tape 14.95 (ISBN 0-89285-114-7); Book 3. pap. text ed. (ISBN 0-89285-127-9); tchr's annotated ed. 5.95 (ISBN 0-89285-139-2); wkbk. 1.50 (ISBN 0-89285-133-3); cassette 110.00 (ISBN 0-89285-121-X); cassette tape 14.95 (ISBN 0-89285-115-5); Book 4. pap. text ed. (ISBN 0-89285-128-7); tchr's annotated ed. 5.95 (ISBN 0-89285-140-6); wkbk. 1.50 (ISBN 0-89285-134-1); cassette 110.00 (ISBN 0-89285-122-8); cassette tape 14.95 (ISBN 0-89285-116-3); Book 5. pap. text ed. (ISBN 0-89285-129-5); tchr's annotated ed. 5.95 (ISBN 0-89285-141-4); wkbk. 1.50 (ISBN 0-89285-135-X); cassette **110.00 (ISBN 0-89285-123-6); cassette tape 14.95 (ISBN 0-89285-117-1); Book 6. pap. text ed. (ISBN 0-89285-130-9); tchr's annotated ed. 5.95 (ISBN 0-89285-142-2); wkbk. 1.50 (ISBN 0-89285-136-8); cassette 110.00 (ISBN 0-89285-124-4); cassette tape 14.95 (ISBN 0-89285-118-X); progress quizzes & placement tests avail.. (Illus.). 1979. pap. text ed. 3.95 ea. English Lang.**

Cornelius, Patsy S. E. K.'s Commentary on The Shepheardes Calendar. (Salzburg Studies in English Literature, Elizabethan & Renaissance Studies: No. 31). 111p. 1974. pap. text ed. 25.00x (ISBN 0-391-01350-5). Humanities.

Cornelius, Wanda & Short, Thayne. Ding Hao: America's Air War in China, 1937-1945. LC 80-19337. (Illus.). 502p. 1980. 19.95 (ISBN 0-88289-253-3). Pelican.

Cornelius, Wayne A. & Kemper, Robert V., eds. Metropolitan Latin American: The Challenge & the Response. LC 77-79867. (Latin American Urban Research: Vol. 6). (Illus.). 1978. 20.00x (ISBN 0-8039-0661-7); pap. 9.95x (ISBN 0-8039-0662-5). Sage.

Cornelius, Wayne A. & Trueblood, Felicity M., eds. Anthropological Perspectives on Latin American Urbanization. LC 73-86706. (Latin American Urban Research: Vol. 4). 1974. 20.00x (ISBN 0-8039-0313-8); pap. 9.95x (ISBN 0-8039-0852-0). Sage.

Cornell, Elizabeth see Rose, Louisa, et al.

Cornell, F. M. & Hoffman, A. C. American Merchant Seamans Manual. 6th ed. Hayler, William B., ed. LC 56-12402. (Illus.). 1981. 25.00x (ISBN 0-87033-267-8). Cornell Maritime.

Cornell, George W., jt. auth. see Johnson, Douglas W.

Cornell, James. Ancient Visions. (Illus.). 288p. 1980. cancelled o.p. (ISBN 0-686-61460-7, ScribT). Scribner.

--The First Stargazers. (Illus.). 288p. 1981. 17.95 (ISBN 0-684-16799-9, ScribT). Scribner.

--The Great International Disaster Book. LC 76-20752. (Encore Editions). (Illus.). 432p. 1976. 5.95 (ISBN 0-684-16894-4, ScribT). Scribner.

Cornell, James C., Jr. Lost Lands & Forgotten People. LC 78-57795. (Illus.). (gr. 5 up). 1978. 8.95 (ISBN 0-8069-3926-5); PLB 8.29 (ISBN 0-8069-3927-3). Sterling.

Cornell, Jane. Successful Custom Interiors. Horowitz, Shirley M., ed. LC 79-15910. (Successful Ser.). (Illus.). 1979. 13.95 (ISBN 0-912336-87-0); pap. 6.95 (ISBN 0-912336-88-9). Structures Pub.

--Successful Family & Recreation Rooms. LC 77-719. (Illus.). 136p. 1977. 13.95 (ISBN 0-912336-42-0); pap. 6.95 (ISBN 0-912336-43-9). Structures Pub.

Cornell, John A. Experiments with Mixtures: Designs, Models & the Analysis of Mixtures Data. LC 80-22153. 275p. 1981. 21.95 (ISBN 0-471-07916-2, Pub. by Wiley-Interscience). Wiley.

Cornell, Richard. Your Career in Music. LC 77-13361. (Arco Career Guidance Ser.). 1979. lib. bdg. 6.95 (ISBN 0-668-04459-4); pap. 3.50 (ISBN 0-668-04461-6). Arco.

Cornell, Ross, jt. auth. see Dudick, Thomas S.

Cornell, Steven H. The Roentgenographic Diagnosis of Diseases of the Thoracic Aorta. (Illus.). 292p. 1973. 29.50 (ISBN 0-398-02687-4). C C Thomas.

Cornell University. Third Supplement to the Cumulation of the Library Catalogsupplements of the New York State School of Industrial & Labor Relations. (Library Catalogs-Bib. Guides). 1979. lib. bdg. 180.00 (ISBN 0-8161-0260-0). G K Hall.

Cornell, William A. & Altland, Millard. Our Pennsylvania Heritage. LC 78-50430. (gr. 7-12). 1978. 10.50 (ISBN 0-931992-21-4). Penns Valley.

Corner. Popular Entertainments. pap. write for info. (ISBN 0-914162-56-X). Knowles.

Corner, C. M., jt. auth. see Gunston, C. A.

Corner, D. C. & Stafford, D. C. Open-End Investment Funds in the European Economic Community & Switzerland. LC 76-17101. 1977. lib. bdg. 46.50x (ISBN 0-89158-620-2). Westview.

Corner, D. C., jt. auth. see Burton, H.

Corner, E. J. H. The Seeds of Dicotyledons, 2 vols. LC 74-14434. (Illus.). 860p. 1976. Vol. 1. 79.00 (ISBN 0-521-20688-X); Vol. 2. 115.00 (ISBN 0-521-20687-1). Cambridge U Pr.

Corner, George W. Anatomy. (Illus.). 1964. Repr. of 1930 ed. pap. 6.50 o.s.i. (ISBN 0-02-843150-2). Hafner.

Corner, Paul. Fascism in Ferrara Nineteen Fifteen to Nineteen Twenty-Five. (Oxford Historical Monographs). 312p. 1975. 36.00x (ISBN 0-19-821857-5). Oxford U Pr.

Cornes, Paul, jt. auth. see Jones, Howard.

Cornet, Joseph. Art of Zaire: 100 Works from the National Collection. (Illus.). 150p. 1975. 10.75 (ISBN 0-89192-061-7). Interbk Inc.

Cornett, Charles F., jt. auth. see Cornett, Claudia E.

Cornett, Claudia E. & Cornett, Charles F. Bibliotherapy: The Right Book at the Right Time. LC 80-82684. (Fastback Ser.: No. 151). (Orig.). 1980. pap. 0.75 (ISBN 0-87367-151-1). Phi Delta Kappa.

Corney, Estelle. Pa's Top Hat. LC 80-65663. (Illus.). 32p. (ps-3). 1980. 7.95 (ISBN 0-233-97255-2). Andre Deutsch.

Corney, G., jt. auth. see Strong, S. J.

Cornfield, Jim. Electronic Flash. LC 76-1544. (Petersen's How-to Photographic Library). (Illus.). 80p. 1976. pap. 4.50 o.p. (ISBN 0-8227-0126-X). Petersen Pub.

Cornford, A. J. The Market for Owned Houses in England & Wales Since Ninteen Forty-Five. 1979. text ed. 28.25x (ISBN 0-566-00195-0, Pub. by Gower Pub Co England). Renouf.

Cornford, Adam. Shooting Scripts. (Illus.). 1979. 25.00 (ISBN 0-686-28250-7); pap. 10.00 (ISBN 0-686-28251-5). Black Stone.

Cornford, F. M. From Religion to Philosophy. A Study of the Origins of Western Speculation. 1957-1979. text ed. o. p. (ISBN 0-391-01238-X); pap. text ed. 7.95x (ISBN 0-391-01239-8). Humanities.

--Microcosmographia Academia. 1980. pap. 2.95 (ISBN 0-370-00145-1, Pub. by Chatto, Bodley Head & Jonathan). Merrimack Bk Serv.

Cornford, Francis. Plato's Theory of Knowledge. (International Library of Psychology, Philosophy & Scientific Method). 1967. text ed. 21.00x (ISBN 0-7100-3119-X). Humanities.

Cornford, Francis M. Before & After Socrates. 23.95 (ISBN 0-521-04726-9); pap. 5.95x (ISBN 0-521-09113-6). Cambridge U Pr.

--Thucydides Mythistoricus. (Illus.). 1971. pap. 4.95x (ISBN 0-8122-1021-2, Pa. Paperbacks). U of Pa Pr.

--Unwritten Philosophy & Other Essays. Guthrie, William K., ed. 1967. 23.95 (ISBN 0-521-04727-7); pap. 7.95x (ISBN 0-521-09444-5). Cambridge U Pr.

Cornford, Francis M., tr. see Plato.

Cornforth, John. English Interiors: 1790-1848. (The Quest for Comfort Ser.). (Illus.). 1978. 29.95 o.p. (ISBN 0-686-01032-9, 8056, Dist. by Arco). Barrie & Jenkins.

--Pyne's Royal Residences. (Folio Miniature Ser.). 1976. 4.95 (ISBN 0-7181-1476-0, Pub. by Michael Joseph). Merrimack Bk Serv.

Cornforth, John, jt. auth. see Fowler, John.

Cornforth, Maurice. Communism & Human Values. LC 72-85924. 72p. 1972. pap. 1.00 o.p. (ISBN 0-7178-0378-3). Intl Pub Co.

--Communism & Philosophy: Contemporary Dogmas & Revisions of Marxism. 1980. text ed. 23.25x (ISBN 0-85315-430-9). Humanities.

--Dialectical Materialism, 3 vols. new ed. Incl. Vol. 1. Materialism & the Dialectical Method. pap. 1.45 (ISBN 0-7178-0326-0); Vol. 2. Historical Materialism. pap. 1.65 (ISBN 0-7178-0327-9); Vol. 3. The Theory of Knowledge. pap. 2.75 (ISBN 0-7178-0328-7). 1971. Intl Pub Co.

--Open Philosophy & the Open Society. LC 68-27395. (Orig.). 1968. pap. 3.45 o.p. (ISBN 0-7178-0142-X). Intl Pub Co.

Corngold, Stanley, et al. Thomas Mann, 1875-1955. (Illus.). 1975. pap. 3.00 (ISBN 0-87811-021-6). Princeton Lib.

Cornick, Delroy L. Auditing in the Electronic Environment: Theory, Practice & Literature. LC 80-81813. 300p. 1980. 19.75 (ISBN 0-912338-23-7); microfiche 14.75. Lomond.

Cornick, H. F. Dock & Harbour Engineering: The Design of Docks, Vol. 1. 338p. 80.00x (ISBN 0-85264-037-4, Pub. by Griffin England). State Mutual Bk.

Corning, Howard M. Willamette Landings: Ghost Towns of the River. 2nd ed. LC 73-81023. 272p. 1973. 8.95 (ISBN 0-87595-093-0); pap. 6.95 (ISBN 0-87595-042-6). Oreg Hist Soc.

Corning, Howard M., ed. Dictionary of Oregon History. 15.00 (ISBN 0-8323-0099-3). Binford.

Corning Museum of Glass. New Glass: A Worldwide Survey. (Illus.). 286p. 1981. pap. price not set (ISBN 0-486-24156-4). Dover.

Cornish, et al. Sampling Systems for Process Analyzers, 1981. write for info. Butterworths.

Cornish, John. The Raising of Lazarus. 1979. pap. 2.50 (ISBN 0-916786-36-6). St George Bk Serv.

Cornish, Roger & Kase, C. Robert, eds. Senior Adult Theatre: The American Theatre Association Handbook. LC 80-23485. (Illus.). 96p. 1981. 8.95x (ISBN 0-271-00275-1); pap. text ed. 5.95x (ISBN 0-271-00275-1). Pa St U Pr.

Cornish, Sam. Grandmother's Pictures. 1978. pap. 0.95 (ISBN 0-380-01912-4, 30163, Camelot). Avon.

--Sam's World. 1978. 7.95 o.p. (ISBN 0-916276-03-1). Decatur Hse.

Cornish, W. R., et al. Crime & Law in Nineteeth Century Britain. (Government & Society in 19th Century Britain Ser.). 232p. 1978. 25.00x (ISBN 0-7165-2213-6, Pub. by Irish Academic Pr Ireland). Biblio Dist.

Cornish-Bowden, Athel. Fundamentals of Enzyme Kinetics. LC 79-40116. (Illus.). 1979. text ed. 19.95 (ISBN 0-408-10617-4). Butterworths.

Cornog, Mary, ed. Growing & Cooking Potatoes. LC 80-52993. 1981. pap. 7.95 (ISBN 0-911658-15-7, 3076). Yankee Bks.

Corns, Albert R. Bibliography of Unfinished Books in the English Language. Sparke, Archibald, ed. LC 67-28093. 1968. Repr. of 1915 ed. 18.00 (ISBN 0-8103-3208-6). Gale.

Cornsweet, Tom N. Visual Perception. 1970. text ed. 22.95 (ISBN 0-12-189750-8). Acad Pr.

Cornwall Collective. Your Daughters Shall Prophesy: Feminist Alternatives in Theological Education. LC 80-14891. 155p. 1980. pap. 6.95 (ISBN 0-8298-0404-8). Pilgrim NY.

Cornwall, I. W. Prehistoric Animals & Their Hunters. (Illus.). 1968. 6.95 (ISBN 0-571-08340-4, Pub. by Faber & Faber). Merrimack Bk Serv.

Cornwall, John. Growth & Stability in a Mature Economy. 1976. pap. 28.00x (ISBN 0-85520-100-2, Pub. by Martin Robertson England). Biblio Dist.

Cornwall, Judson. Freeway Under Construction. 1978. bklt. 1.95 (ISBN 0-88270-304-8). Logos.

--Let Us Be Holy. 1979. pap. 4.95 (ISBN 0-88270-278-5). Logos.

--Let Us Draw Near. 1977. pap. 4.95 (ISBN 0-88270-226-2). Logos.

--Let Us Praise: A Prominent Charismatic Leader Tells How & Why to Praise God. LC 73-75957. 1973. pap. 4.95 (ISBN 0-88270-039-1). Logos.

--Profiles of a Leader. (Orig.). 1981. pap. 4.95 (ISBN 0-88270-503-2). Logos.

Cornwall, Rebecca & Arrington, Leonard J. Rescue of the Eighteen Fifty-Six Handcraft Companies. (Charles Redd Monographs in Western History: No. 11). (Illus.). 64p. 1981. pap. text ed. 4.95 (ISBN 0-8425-1941-6). Brigham.

Cornwall, Richard, jt. auth. see Claudon, Michael P.

Cornwell, Bernard. Sharpe's Eagle. LC 80-54081. 264p. 1981. 12.95 (ISBN 0-670-63944-3). Viking Pr.

Cornwell, Ethel F. The Still Point: Theme & Variations in the Writings of T. S. Eliot, Coleridge, Yeats, Henry James, Virginia Woolf, & D. H. Lawrence. 1962. 18.00 (ISBN 0-8135-0413-9). Rutgers U Pr.

Cornwell, John. The Super. 1972. pap. 2.25 (ISBN 0-8439-0682-0, Leisure Bks). Nordon Pubns.

Cornyn, William S. Spoken Burmese. Incl. Bk. 1, Units 1-12. pap. 8.00x (ISBN 0-87950-020-4); Bk. 2, Units 13-30. pap. 10.00x (ISBN 0-87950-021-2); Guides Manual (in Burmese) tchrs. guide 5.50x (ISBN 0-87950-022-0). LC 79-1552. (Spoken Language Ser.). (Prog. Bk.). 1979. cancelled cassettes with course book 1 5.50x (ISBN 0-87950-026-3); cancelled (ISBN 0-87950-025-5). Spoken Lang Serv.

Corominas. Breve Diccionario Etimologico De la Lengua Castellana. 25.00x o.s.i. (ISBN 0-686-00845-6). Colton Bk.

Corpron, Carlotta & Sandweiss, Martha A. Carlotta Corpron: Designer with Light. 64p. 1980. 14.95 (ISBN 0-292-71064-X); pap. 9.95 (ISBN 0-292-71065-8). U of Tex Pr.

Corr, Michael. Yarrow. 1981. 3.00 (ISBN 0-934834-20-2). White Pine.

Corran, H. S. Isle of Man. (Islands Ser.). 1977. 13.50 (ISBN 0-7153-7417-6). David & Charles.

Correa, Elsie G. Lluvia De Cuentos. (Illus.). 3.10 o.p. (ISBN 0-8477-3115-4). U of PR Pr.

Correa, F. G., tr. see Canright, D. M.

Correa, Gustavo, ed. Poesia Espanola Del Siglo Veinte: Antologia. (Span.). 1972. 17.95 (ISBN 0-13-684506-1). P-H.

Correa, Hector. Integrated Economic Accounting: Theory & Applications to National, Real, & Financial Economic Planning. LC 76-17445. 1976. 26.95 (ISBN 0-669-00779-X). Lexington Bks.

Correia-Alfonso, John. Jesuit Letters & Indian History 1542-1773. 1969. pap. 7.25x o.p. (ISBN 0-19-635280-0). Oxford U Pr.

Corren, Grace. Dark Threshold. 1977. pap. 1.50 o.p. (ISBN 0-445-03227-8). Popular Lib.

Correy, Lee. Star Driver. 1980. pap. 1.95 (ISBN 0-345-28994-3). Ballantine.

Corrie, Jane. Island Fiesta. (Harlequin Romances Ser.). 192p. (Orig.). 1981. pap. 1.25 (ISBN 0-373-02384-7, Pub. by Harlequin). PB.

--Tasmanian Tangle. (Harlequin Romances Ser.). (Orig.). 1980. pap. text ed. 1.25 o.p. (ISBN 0-373-02335-9, Pub. by Harlequin). PB.

Corriere, Richard & Hart, Joseph. The Dream Makers: Discovering Your Breakthrough Dreams. LC 76-47680. (Funk & W Bk.). 1977. 8.95 o.s.i. (ISBN 0-308-10276-2, TYC-T). T Y Crowell.

--Psychological Fitness: Twenty-One Days to Feeling Good. LC 78-14073. (Illus.). 1979. 9.95 o.p. (ISBN 0-15-175280-X). HarBraceJ.

Corriere, Richard, et al. Dreaming & Waking. LC 80-21876. 226p. 1980. pap. 6.95 (ISBN 0-915238-41-1). Peace Pr.

Corrigan, Barbara. How to Make Something Out of Practically Nothing: New Fashions from Old Clothes. LC 75-15774. 96p. (gr. 4-7). 1976. 5.95 o.p. (ISBN 0-385-11670-5). Doubleday.

--Of Course You Can Sew: Basics of Sewing for the Young Beginner. LC 77-110030. (gr. 5 up). 1971. 4.95 o.p. (ISBN 0-385-07697-5); PLB (ISBN 0-385-03241-2). Doubleday.

Corrigan, Dean C. & Howey, Kenneth R., eds. Special Education in Transition: Concepts to Guide the Education of Experienced Teachers with Implications for PL 94-142. LC 80-68281. 208p. 1980. pap. 12.95 (ISBN 0-86586-109-9). Coun Exc Child.

Corrigan, Eileen M., jt. auth. see Sauber, Mignon.

Corrigan, John T. Archives: The Light of Faith. (Catholic Library Association Studies in Librarianship: No. 4). 1980. 4.00 (ISBN 0-87507-008-6). Cath Lib Assn.

Corrigan, L. Luan, ed. APhA Drug Names. Shoff, Janet. LC 78-78275. 1979. softcover 18.00 (ISBN 0-917330-24-2). Am Pharm Assn.

Corrigan, Philip. Capitalism, State Formation & Marx Theory. 258p. 1980. 9.95 (ISBN 0-7043-3311-2, Pub. by Quartet England). Horizon.

Corrigan, Robert. The Theatre in Search of a Fix. 1973. 10.00 o.p. (ISBN 0-440-08662-0). Delacorte.

Corrigan, Robert W. Comedy: Meaning & Form. 2nd ed. 352p. 1980. pap. text ed. 10.95 scp (ISBN 0-06-041370-0, HarpC). Har-Row.

--The Making of Theatre: From Drama to Performance. 1980. pap. text ed. 8.95x (ISBN 0-673-15403-3). Scott F.

--Tragedy: Vision & Form. 2nd ed. 384p. 1980. pap. text ed. 10.95 scp (ISBN 0-06-041371-9, HarpC). Har-Row.

--The World of the Theatre. 1979. text ed. 14.95x (ISBN 0-673-15107-7). Scott F.

Corrigan, Robert W., ed. New American Plays, Vol. 1. Incl. Mister Biggs. Barlow, Anna M; The Hundred & First. Cameron, Kenneth; A Summer Ghost. Fredericks, Claude; Blood Money. Jasudowicz, Dennis; Socrates Wounded. Levinson, Alfred; Constantinople Smith. Mee, Charles L., Jr; Pigeons. Osgood, Lawrence; The Death & Life of Sneaky Fitch. Rosenberg, James L; Ginger Anne. Washburn, Deric; The Golden Bull of Boredom. Yerby, Lorees. 284p. (Orig.). 1965. pap. 5.95 (ISBN 0-8090-0734-7, Mermaid). Hill & Wang.

Corrigan, Robert W. & Loney, Glenn M., eds. Comedy: A Critical Anthology. LC 78-150137. (Orig.). 1971. pap. text ed. 9.75 (ISBN 0-395-04325-5). HM.

--Forms of Drama. LC 74-150136. 906p. (Orig.). 1972. pap. text ed. 9.75 (ISBN 0-395-04327-1). HM.

Corrin, Brownlee S; see Mead, Robert G., Jr.

Corrin, Sara, et al. Stories for Five Year-Olds & Other Young Readers. Corrin, Stephen, ed. (Illus.). (ps-5). 1973. 8.95 (ISBN 0-571-10162-3, Pub. by Faber & Faber). Merrimack Bk Serv.

--Stories for Tens & Over. Corrin, Stephen, ed. (Illus.). 1976. 9.95 (ISBN 0-571-10873-3, Pub. by Faber & Faber). Merrimack Bk Serv.

Corrin, Sara, et al, eds. Stories for Under-Fives. (Illus.). (ps-5). 1974. 9.95 (ISBN 0-571-10371-5, Pub. by Faber & Faber). Merrimack Bk Serv.

Corrin, Stephen, ed. see Corrin, Sara, et al.

Corrington, John W. The Southern Reporter & Other Stories. LC 80-26204. 168p. 1981. 9.95 (ISBN 0-8071-0869-3). La State U Pr.

Corris, Peter, jt. auth. see Kessing, Roger M.

Corry, Bernard, ed. see Rowley, J. C.

Corry, Grace, jt. auth. see Corry, John.

Corry, John & Corry, Grace. The Gardner's Kitchen. (Illus.). 128p. 1980. 9.95 (ISBN 0-87691-321-4). Winchester Pr.

Corry, John P. Indian Affairs in Georgia, 1732-1756. LC 76-43685. 1977. Repr. of 1936 ed. 21.50 (ISBN 0-404-15518-9). AMS Pr.

Corry, Robert J. & Thompson, John S. Renal Transplantation Case Studies. 1977. spiral bdg. 14.00 (ISBN 0-87488-015-7). Med Exam.

Cors, Paul B. Railroads. LC 74-31396. (Spare Time Guides Ser.: No. 8). 152p. 1975. lib. bdg. 10.00x o.p. (ISBN 0-87287-082-0). Libs Unl.

Corsaro, Frank. Maverick: A Director's Personal Experience in Opera & Theatre. LC 77-77036. (Illus.). 1978. 12.95 (ISBN 0-8149-0790-3). Vanguard.

Corse, Larry B. & Corse, Sandra B. Articles on American & British Literature: An Index to Selected Periodicals, 1950-1977. 450p. 1981. 30.00x (ISBN 0-8040-0408-0). Swallow.

Corse, Sandra B., jt. auth. see Corse, Larry B.

Corsini, Raymond. Handbook of Innovative Psychotherapies. 1100p. 1981. 40.00 (ISBN 0-471-06229-4, Pub. by Wiley-Interscience). Wiley.

Corsini, Raymond J. Current Psychotherapies. 2nd ed. LC 78-61880. 1979. pap. text ed. 13.95 (ISBN 0-87581-240-6). Peacock Pubs.

Corsini, Raymond J., jt. auth. see Ignas, Edward.

Corsini, Raymond J., ed. Current Personality Theories. 1977. text ed. 15.95 (ISBN 0-87581-204-X, 204). Peacock Pubs.

Corsini, Raymond J., jt. ed. see Ignas, Edward.

Corson. Fashions in Makeup. 1980. text ed. 78.00. Humanities.

Corson, Betty M., ed. The New Secretary's Deskbook. LC 78-78240. 1980. cancelled (ISBN 0-87100-160-8). Morgan.

Corson, Dale R., jt. auth. see Lorrain, Paul.

Corson, E. O'Leary, jt. auth. see Corson, S. A.

Corson, J. J. Business in the Humane Society. 1971. 24.95 o.p. (ISBN 0-07-013185-6, P&RB). McGraw.

Corson, John J. & Hodson, Harry V., eds. Philanthropy in the Seventies: An Anglo-American Discussion. 128p. 1973. pap. 3.00 (ISBN 0-913456-54-3). Interbk Inc.

Corson, Richard. Champions at Speed. LC 78-25853. (Illus.). (gr. 6 up). 1979. 5.95 (ISBN 0-396-07656-4). Dodd.

--Fashions in Eyeglasses: From the 14th Century to the Present Day. rev. ed. (Illus.). 1980. Repr. of 1967 ed. text ed. 70.00x (ISBN 0-7206-3282-X). Humanities.

--Fashions in Hair: The First Five Thousand Years. 3rd rev. ed. (Illus.). 1971. text ed. 75.00x (ISBN 0-391-00167-1). Humanities.

--Stage Makeup. 5th ed. (Illus.). 384p. 1975. 23.95 (ISBN 0-13-840496-8). P-H.

--Stage Makeup. 6th ed. (Illus.). 464p. 1981. text ed. 23.95 (ISBN 0-13-840512-3). P-H.

Corson, S. A. & Corson, E. O'Leary. Ethology & Nonverbal Communication in Mental Health: An Interdisciplinary Biopsychosocial Exploration. LC 79-41689. (International Ser. in Biopsychosocial Sciences). (Illus.). 290p. 1980. 48.00 (ISBN 0-08-023728-2). Pergamon.

Corson, Samuel A., tr. see Anokhin, Peter K.

Corsten, F. L. The Rise of Facism. 2nd ed. 1980. 18.50 (ISBN 0-520-04307-3). U of Cal Pr.

Cort, Stanton G. Perspectives on Retail Strategic Decision Making. 112p. 1979. pap. text ed. 30.00 (ISBN 0-686-60195-5, G28679). Natl Ret Merch.

Cortazar, Julio. A Change of Light & Other Stories. Rabassa, Gregory, tr. from Span. LC 80-7656. 288p. 1980. 11.95 (ISBN 0-394-50721-5). Knopf.

--Cronopios & Famas. Blackburn, Paul, tr. from Span. LC 69-15477. (Illus.). 1978. pap. 2.95 (ISBN 0-394-73616-8). Pantheon.

--End of the Game: And Other Stories. 1978. pap. 5.95 (ISBN 0-06-090637-5, CN 637, CN). Har-Row.

Cortazzo, Arnold D., jt. auth. see Allen, Robert M.

Corte, Andrea D., ed. Canto E Bel Canto P.F. Tosi: Opinioni De Cantori Antchi E Moderni Seventeen Twenty Three. LC 80-2268. 1981. Repr. of 1933 ed. 31.50 (ISBN 0-404-18823-0). AMS Pr.

Corte, Andrea Della. L' Opera Comica Italiana nel Settecento, Studi ed Appunti, 2 vols. LC 80-2269. 1981. Repr. of 1923 ed. Set. 62.50 (ISBN 0-404-18830-3). Vol. 1 (ISBN 0-404-18831-1). Vol. 2 (ISBN 0-404-18832-X). AMS Pr.

Cortes, F., et al. Systems Analysis for Social Scientists. LC 73-23061. 1974. 29.95 (ISBN 0-471-17509-9, Pub. by Wiley-Interscience). Wiley.

Cortes Conde, Roberto & Stein, Stanley J., eds. Latin America: A Guide to Economic History 1830-1930. LC 74-30534. 1977. 46.50x (ISBN 0-520-02956-9). U of Cal Pr.

Cortesi, Lawrence. Forty Fathoms Down. 1979. pap. 1.75 (ISBN 0-505-51445-1). Tower Bks.

--The Last Outlaw. (Orig.). 1980. pap. write for info. (ISBN 0-505-51560-1). Tower Bks.

--Mission Incredible. 1979. pap. 1.50 (ISBN 0-505-51346-3). Tower Bks.

--Operation Bodenplatte. 288p. (Orig.). 1981. pap. 2.50 (ISBN 0-89083-710-4). Zebra.

--Rogue Sergeant. 1979. pap. 1.75 (ISBN 0-505-51352-8). Tower Bks.

Cortey, Noel. Modern Elementary Linear Algebra. LC 78-57573. 1978. pap. text ed. 7.50 (ISBN 0-8191-0524-4). U Pr of Amer.

Cortez, Diego, ed. Private Elvis. (Illus.). 1978. pap. 6.00 (ISBN 0-8467-0537-0, Pub. by Two Continents). Hippocrene Bks.

Corti, V., tr. see Artaud, Antonin.

Cortina, Frank M. Face to Face. LC 76-184745. 250p. 1972. 20.00x (ISBN 0-231-03635-3). Columbia U Pr.

Cortissoz, Royal. John Lafarge,A Memoir &A Study. LC 70-87508. (Library of American Art Ser). (Illus.). 1971. Repr. of 1911 ed. lib. bdg. 25.00 (ISBN 0-306-71405-1). Da Capo.

Cortner, R. & Lytle, C. Modern Constitutional Law. LC 73-122280. 1971. text ed. 14.95 (ISBN 0-02-906740-5). Free Pr.

Cortner, Richard C. The Apportionment Cases. LC 75-100408. 296p. 1970. 15.50x (ISBN 0-87049-107-5). U of Tenn Pr.

Cortot, Alfred. French Piano Music. Andrews, Hilda, tr. from Fr. LC 77-4108. (Music Reprint, 1977 Ser.). 1977. Repr. of 1932 ed. 19.50 (ISBN 0-306-70896-5). Da Capo.

Corvisier, Andre. Armies & Societies in Europe: 1494-1789. Siddall, Abigail T., tr. from Fr. LC 78-62419. 224p. 1979. 12.95x (ISBN 0-253-12985-0). Ind U Pr.

Corwen, Leonard. Your Future in Publishing. LC 72-91800. 144p. 1975. pap. 3.50 (ISBN 0-668-03428-9). Arco.

--Your Job: Where to Find It---How to Get It. LC 80-22251. 256p. 1981. lib. bdg. 11.95 (ISBN 0-668-05129-9); pap. 6.95 (ISBN 0-668-05131-0). Arco.

Corwin, Charles, et al. A Dictionary of Japanese & English Idiomatic Equivalents. LC 68-11818. 302p. 1980. 15.00 (ISBN 0-87011-111-6). Kodansha.

Corwin, Edward S. Commerce Power Versus States Rrights. 1959. write for info. (ISBN 0-8446-1130-1). Peter Smith.

--Constitutional Revolution, Ltd. LC 77-805. 1977. Repr. of 1941 ed. lib. bdg. 15.00x (ISBN 0-8371-9498-9, COCO). Greenwood.

--The President: Office & Powers, 1787-1957: History & Analysis of Practice & Opinion. 4th rev. ed. LC 57-11573. (Stokes Lectureship on Politics Ser.). 1974. 14.50x (ISBN 0-8147-0100-0); pap. 7.00x (ISBN 0-8147-0101-9). NYU Pr.

Corwin, Harry O. & Jenkins, John B. Conceptual Foundation of Genetics: Selected Readings. LC 75-26092. (Illus.). 448p. 1976. pap. text ed. 11.50 (ISBN 0-395-24064-6). HM.

Corwin, Norman. A Date with Sandburg. (Santa Susana Press Ser.). 1981. 17.50 (ISBN 0-937048-30-5). CSUN.

Corwin, R. Sociology of Education: Emerging Patterns of Class Status & Power in the Public Schools. 1965. 17.95 (ISBN 0-13-821207-4). P-H.

Corwin, Ronald, jt. ed. see Nagi, Saad.

Corwin, Ronald G. Education in Crisis: A Sociological Analysis of Schools & Universities in Transition. LC 73-12844. 380p. 1974. pap. text ed. 16.95 (ISBN 0-471-17521-8). Wiley.

Corwin, Sheila. Marriage & the Family & Child-Rearing Practices. Zak, Therese A., ed. (Lifeworks Ser.). (Illus.). 160p. 1981. text ed. 4.56 (ISBN 0-07-013198-8). McGraw.

Cory, Beverly. Birdseye View of Language Arts: Worksheets in Spelling & Phonics, Word Structure, Word Meaning, Grammar & Usage. (Makemaster Bk.). (gr. 6-9). 1977. pap. 12.95 (ISBN 0-8224-0701-9). Pitman Learning.

Cory, Daniel. Santayana: The Later Years. LC 63-19573. 7.50 o.s.i. (ISBN 0-8076-0246-9). Braziller.

Cory, Hans. Sukuma Law & Customs. LC 70-106831. (Illus.). 194p. Repr. of 1953 ed. 15.00x (ISBN 0-8371-3453-6). Negro U Pr.

Cory, Irene. Pawdie. LC 68-21586. 1968. 5.95 (ISBN 0-8149-0047-X). Vanguard.

Cory, Lloyd. Quote Unquote. 1977. text ed. 6.95 o.p. (ISBN 0-88207-810-0); pap. 4.95 (ISBN 0-88207-803-8). Victor Bks.

Coryell, Julie & Friedman, Laura. Jazz Rock Fusion. 1978. 15.95 o.s.i. (ISBN 0-440-04187-2). Delacorte.

Cosand, Joseph P. Perspective: Community Colleges in the Nineteen Eighties. (ERIC Monographs Ser.). 60p. (Orig.). pap. 5.00 (ISBN 0-87117-049-3). Am Assn Comm Jr Coll.

Coscarelli, Diego. Italian Level Three, Comprehensive. LC 75-39381. (Regents Exams & Answers Ser.). 1977. pap. 3.95 (ISBN 0-8120-0663-1). Barron.

Coscia, Joseph F. Reincarnation of Bridgett. 160p. 1981. 6.00 (ISBN 0-682-49699-5). Exposition.

Cosentino, Andrew J. The Paintings of Charles Bird King. LC 77-608258. (Illus.). 214p. 1978. 25.00 (ISBN 0-87474-336-2). Smithsonian.

Cosentino, Geraldine. Bargello, Step by Step. (Step by Step Craft Ser). 1974. PLB 9.15 o.p. (ISBN 0-307-62011-5, Golden Pr); pap. 2.95 (ISBN 0-307-42011-6, Golden Pr). Western Pub.

Cosentino, Geraldine, jt. auth. see Stewart, Regina.

Cosentino, John, ed. Computer Graphics Marketplace. 1981. pap. 22.50 (ISBN 0-912700-91-2). Oryx Pr.

Cosentino, Rodolfo. Atlas of Anatomy & Surgical Approaches in Orthopaedic Surgery, Vol. 1: Upper Extremity. (Illus.). 208p. 1960. 19.75 (ISBN 0-398-00349-1). C C Thomas.

--Atlas of Anatomy & Surgical Approaches in Orthopaedic Surgery, Vol. 2: Lower Extremity. (Illus.). 276p. 1973. pap. 24.50 spiral bd. (ISBN 0-398-00350-5). C C Thomas.

Coser, Lewis, jt. auth. see Howe, Irving.

Coser, Lewis A. Continuities in the Study of Social Conflict. LC 67-25330. 1970. pap. text ed. 3.50 o.s.i. (ISBN 0-02-906760-X). Free Pr.

--Functions of Social Conflict. LC 56-6874. 1964. pap. text ed. 5.95 (ISBN 0-02-906810-X). Free Pr.

--Greedy Institutions. LC 73-10571. 1974. 12.95 (ISBN 0-02-906750-2). Free Pr.

--The Pleasures of Sociology. (Orig.). 1980. pap. 2.75 (ISBN 0-451-61825-4, ME1825, Ment). NAL.

Coser, Lewis A. & Larsen, Otto N., eds. The Uses of Controversy in Sociology. LC 76-7177. 1976. 17.95 (ISBN 0-02-906830-4). Free Pr.

Coser, Rose L. Life in the Ward. 1962. 7.50 o.p. (ISBN 0-87013-068-4). Mich St U Pr.

Coser, Rose L., jt. ed. see Epstein, Cynthia F.

Cosgrave, Gerald P. Choices for Tomorrow. 1978. pap. text ed. 4.25x (ISBN 0-8077-8065-0, Guidance Center). Tchrs Coll.

--Let's Think About You. 1978. pap. text ed. 4.25x (ISBN 0-8077-8064-2, Pub. by Guid Ctr U of Toronto). Tchrs Coll.

--Set Your Course. 1978. pap. text ed. 4.00x (ISBN 0-8077-8063-4, Pub. by Guid Ctr U of Toronto). Tchrs Coll.

Cosgriff, James H., Jr. & Anderson, Diann. The Practice of Emergency Nursing. 1975. 21.00 (ISBN 0-397-54169-4). Lippincott.

Cosgriff, John, jt. auth. see Welles, S. P.

Cosgrove, Ed, jt. auth. see Cosgrove, Irene.

Cosgrove, Francis M. Essentials of Discipleship. LC 79-93015. 1980. pap. 4.95 (ISBN 0-89109-442-3). NavPress.

Cosgrove, Irene & Cosgrove, Ed. My Recipes Are for the Birds. LC 76-23757. 62p. 1976. pap. 3.95 (ISBN 0-385-12634-4). Doubleday.

Cosgrove, Margaret. Animals Alone & Together. LC 77-12625. (gr. 7 up). 1978. 5.95 (ISBN 0-396-07520-7). Dodd.

--Its Snowing. LC 80-14254. (A Skylight Bk.). (Illus.). 48p. (gr. 2-5). 1980. PLB 5.95 (ISBN 0-396-07851-6). Dodd.

--Your Muscles & Ways to Exercise Them. LC 79-22936. (Illus.). (gr. 3-6). 1980. PLB 6.95 (ISBN 0-396-07787-0). Dodd.

Cosgrove, Richard A. The Rule of Law: Albert Venn Dicey, Victorian Jurist. LC 79-18027. (Studies in Legal History Ser.). 340p. 1980. 19.50x (ISBN 0-8078-1410-5). U of NC Pr.

Cosgrove, Stephen. Catundra. (Creative Fantasies Ser.). (Illus.). (gr. k-4). 1979. PLB 6.95 (ISBN 0-87191-692-4). Creative Ed.

--Creole. (Serendipity Bks). (Illus.). (gr. k-4). 1978. PLB 6.95 (ISBN 0-87191-655-X). Creative Ed.

--Flutterby. (Serendipity Bks). (Illus.). (gr. k-4). 1978. PLB 6.95 (ISBN 0-87191-664-9). Creative Ed.

--Kartusch. (Creative Fantasies Ser.). (Illus.). (gr. k-4). 1979. PLB 6.95 (ISBN 0-87191-689-4). Creative Ed.

--Little Mouse on the Prairie. (Creative Fantasies Ser.). (Illus.). (gr. k-4). 1979. PLB 6.95 (ISBN 0-87191-690-8). Creative Ed.

--Nitter Pitter. (Creative Fantasies Ser.). (Illus.). (gr. k-4). 1979. PLB 6.95 (ISBN 0-87191-691-6). Creative Ed.

--Snaffles. (Serendipity Bks.). (Illus.). 32p. 1980. pap. 1.50 (ISBN 0-8431-0576-3). Price Stern.

Cosgrove, Steve. Bangalee. (Serendipity Bks). (Illus.). (gr. k-4). 1978. PLB 6.95 (ISBN 0-87191-666-5). Creative Ed.

--Cap'n Smudge. (Serendipity Bks). (Illus.). (gr. k-4). 1978. PLB 6.95 (ISBN 0-87191-659-2). Creative Ed.

--Dream Tree. (Serendipity Bks). (Illus.). (gr. k-4). 1978. PLB 6.95 (ISBN 0-87191-665-7). Creative Ed.

--Gnome from Nome. (Serendipity Bks). (Illus.). (gr. k-4). 1978. PLB 6.95 (ISBN 0-87191-656-8). Creative Ed.

--Hucklebug. (Serendipity Bks). (Illus.). (gr. k-4). 1978. PLB 6.95 (ISBN 0-87191-657-6). Creative Ed.

--In Search of Saveopotomas. (Serendipity Bks). (Illus.). (gr. k-4). 1978. PLB 6.95 (ISBN 0-87191-661-4). Creative Ed.

--Jake O'Shawnasey. (Serendipity Bks). (Illus.). (gr. k-4). 1978. PLB 6.95 (ISBN 0-87191-654-1). Creative Ed.

--Leo the Lop. (Serendipity Bks). (Illus.). (gr. k-4). 1978. PLB 6.95 (ISBN 0-87191-658-4). Creative Ed.

--Leo the Lop. Tail Two. (Serendipity Bks). (Illus.). (gr. k-4). 1980. PLB 6.95 (ISBN 0-87191-779-3). Creative Ed.

--Maui-Maui. (Serendipity Bks). (Illus.). (gr. k-4). 1980. PLB 6.95 (ISBN 0-87191-778-5). Creative Ed.

--Morgan & Me. (Serendipity Bks). (Illus.). (gr. k-4). 1978. PLB 6.95 (ISBN 0-87191-660-6). Creative Ed.

--Muffin Muncher. (Serendipity Bks). (Illus.). (gr. k-4). 1978. PLB 6.95 (ISBN 0-87191-667-3). Creative Ed.

--Wheedle on the Needle. (Serendipity Bks). (Illus.). (gr. k-4). 1978. PLB 6.95 (ISBN 0-87191-663-0). Creative Ed.

Cosgrove-Twitchett, Carol. Europe & Africa. 212p. 1978. text ed. 25.50x (ISBN 0-566-00182-9, Pub. by Gower Pub Co England). Renouf.

Cosic, Dobrica. A Time of Death, Vol. 3. Heppell, Muriel, tr. write for info. HarBraceJ.

Cosio Villegas, Daniel. American Extremes. Paredes, Americo, tr. from Span. LC 64-11188. (Pan American Paperbacks Ser.: No. 1). Orig. Title: Extremos de America. 1964. pap. 4.95x (ISBN 0-292-70069-5). U of Tex Pr.

Cosman, Anna. How to Read & Write Poetry. (First Bks.). (Illus.). (gr. 5-8). 1979. PLB 6.45 s&l (ISBN 0-531-02261-7). Watts.

Cosman, Carol, tr. see Robert, Marthe.

Cosmi, Ermelando, jt. ed. see Scarpelli, Emilie.

Cosmi, Ermelando V. Obstetric Anesthesia & Perinatology. 500p. 1981. 33.50 (ISBN 0-8385-7196-4). ACC.
Cosmi, Ermelando V., jt. ed. see Scarpelli, Emile M.
Cosofret, V. V., jt. auth. see Baiulescu, G. E.
COSPAR-IAU-IUTAM Symposium, Paris, 1965. Trajectories of Artificial Celestial Bodies As Determined from Observations: Proceedings. Kovalevsky, J., ed. (Illus.). 1966. 52.00 (ISBN 0-387-03681-4). Springer-Verlag.
COSPAR, Twenty-Second Plenary Meeting, Bangalore, India, 1979. Low Latitude Aeronomical Processes: Proceedings. Mitra, A. P., ed. LC 79-41341. 1980. 69.00 (ISBN 0-08-024439-4). Pergamon.
--Non-Solar Gamma-Rays: Proceedings. Cowsik, R. & Wills, R. D., eds. 254p. 1980. 50.00 (ISBN 0-08-024440-8). Pergamon.
Cossa, Luigi. Introduction to the Study of Political Economy. Dyer, Louise, tr. from It. LC 79-1576. 1981. Repr. of 1893 ed. 37.50 (ISBN 0-88355-882-3). Hyperion Conn.
Cossart, Michael De see De Cossart, Michael.
Cossery, Albert. Proud Beggars. Cushing, Thomas, tr. from Fr. 230p. 1981. 14.00 (ISBN 0-87685-451-X); signed ed. 20.00 (ISBN 0-87685-452-8); pap. 6.50 (ISBN 0-87685-450-1). Black Sparrow.
Cossi, Olga. Fire Mate. LC 77-1334. (Illus.). 1977. 5.50 o.p. (ISBN 0-8309-0163-9). Independence Pr.
Cossman, E. Joseph. How to Get One Hundred Thousand Dollars Worth of Services Free, Each Year, from the U. S. Government. rev. ed. 1975. 9.95 o.s.i. (ISBN 0-8119-0257-9). Fell.
Cosson, Annie, ed. see LaHaye, Beverly.
Cossons, Neil. The BP Book of Industrial Archaeology. LC 74-20468. (Illus.). 1975. 19.95 (ISBN 0-7153-6250-X). David & Charles.
Cossons, Neil & Trinder, Barrie. The Iron Bridge: Symbol of the Industrial Revolution. (Illus.). 1979. text ed. 23.50 (ISBN 0-239-00187-7). Humanities.
Cost, March. After the Festival. LC 66-28883. 1966. 7.95 (ISBN 0-8149-0049-6). Vanguard.
--Countess. LC 63-13789. 1963. 6.95 (ISBN 0-8149-0076-3). Vanguard.
--Jubilee of a Ghost. LC 68-8080. 1968. 7.95 (ISBN 0-8149-0048-8). Vanguard.
--A Key to Laurels. LC 72-90476. 7.95 (ISBN 0-8149-0723-7). Vanguard.
--Two Guests for Swedenborg. LC 74-155664. 7.95 (ISBN 0-8149-0695-8). Vanguard.
Costa, Beverley Da see American Heritage Editors.
Costa, Beverly Da see American Heritage Editors.
Costa, C. D., ed. Seneca. (Greek & Latin Studies Ser.). 252p. 1974. 20.00x (ISBN 0-7100-7900-1). Routledge & Kegan.
Costa, C. D., ed. see Seneca.
Costa, Dennis. Irenic Apocalypse: Some Uses of Apocalyptic in Dante, Petrarch & Rebelais. (Stanford French & Italian Studies: Vol. 21). 160p. 1980. pap. 20.00 (ISBN 0-915838-18-4). Anma Libri.
Costa, E., jt. auth. see Mouly, J.
Costa, E. & Gessa, G. L., eds. Nonstriatal Dopaminergic Neurons. LC 76-5661. (Advances in Biochemical Psychopharmacology Ser.: Vol. 16). 1977. 59.50 (ISBN 0-89004-127-X). Raven.
Costa, E. & Greengard, P., eds. Mechanism of Action of Benzodiazepines. LC 75-10978. (Advances in Biochemical Psychopharmacology Ser.: Vol. 14). 190p. 1975. 23.00 (ISBN 0-89004-039-7). Raven.
Costa, E. & Holmstedt, B., eds. Gas Chromatography-Mass Spectrometry in Neurobiology. LC 73-84113. (Advances in Biochemical Psychopharmacology Ser.: Vol. 7). (Illus.). 183p. 1973. 24.50 (ISBN 0-911216-48-0). Raven.
Costa, E. & Sandler, M., eds. Monoamine Oxidases - New Vistas. LC 73-84113. (Advances in Biochemical Psychopharmacology Ser.: Vol. 5). (Illus.). 1972. 34.50 (ISBN 0-911216-19-7). Raven.
Costa, E. & Trabucchi, Marco, eds. The Endorphins. LC 77-18301. (Advances in Biochemical Psychopharmacology Ser.: Vol. 18). 1978. 35.00 (ISBN 0-89004-226-8). Raven.
Costa, E., jt. ed. see Ebadi, M.
Costa, E., jt. ed. see Greengard, P.
Costa, E., et al, eds. Serotonin, New Vistas: Biochemistry & Behavioral & Clinical Studies. LC 73-91166. (Advances in Biochemical Psychopharmacology Ser.: Vol. 11). 446p. 1974. 31.50 (ISBN 0-911216-69-3). Raven.
--Serotonin, New Vistas: Histochemistry & Pharmacology. LC 73-91165. (Advances in Biochemical Psychopharmacology Ser.: Vol. 10). 345p. 1974. 31.50 (ISBN 0-911216-68-5). Raven.
--First & Second Messengers: New Vistas. LC 75-14583. (Advances in Biochemical Psychopharmacology Ser: Vol. 15). 1976. 41.50 (ISBN 0-89004-084-2). Raven.
--Studies of Neurotransmitters at the Synaptic Level. LC 73-84113. (Advances in Biochemical Psychopharmacology: Vol. 6). 256p. 1972. 24.50 (ISBN 0-911216-20-0). Raven.
Costa, E., et al, eds. see Symposium of the Parkinson's Disease Information & Research Center, 2nd, Columbia University, 1965.
Costa, Erminio & Trabucchi, Marco, eds. Neural Peptides & Neural Communication. (Advances in Biochemical Psychopharmacology Ser.). 1980. text ed. 61.50 (ISBN 0-89004-375-2). Raven.
Costa, Francis D., ed. see Hopko, T., et al.
Costa, J. & Baker, V. Surficial Geology: Building with the Earth. LC 80-22644. 1981. write for info. (ISBN 0-471-03229-8). Wiley.
Costa, John E. & Baker, Victor R. Surficial Geology Building with the Earth. 608p. 1981. text ed. 19.95 (ISBN 0-471-03229-8). Wiley.
Costa, Joseph H. & Nelson, Gordon K. Child Abuse & Neglect: Legislation, Reporting & Prevention. LC 77-3836. 1978. 26.95 (ISBN 0-669-01670-5). Lexington Bks.
Costa, Leon Da. Freedom & Discipline in the Education of Young People. (Science of Man Library Bk). (Illus.). 176p. 1976. lib. bdg. 37.50 (ISBN 0-913314-68-4). Am Classical Coll Pr.
Costa, Louis, et al. Streetcar Guide to Uptown New Orleans. Swords, David, ed. (Illus.). 136p. (Orig.). 1980. pap. 5.00 (ISBN 0-939108-00-3). Transitour.
Costa, Margaret. Four Seasons Cookery Book. 1979. 28.00x (ISBN 0-8464-0423-0). Beekman Pubs.
Costa, Richard H. Edmund Wilson: Our Neighbor from Talcottville. (York State Bks.). (Illus.). 192p. 1980. 11.95 (ISBN 0-8156-0163-8). Syracuse U Pr.
--H. G. Wells. (English Authors Ser.: No. 43). 1966. lib. bdg. 9.95 (ISBN 0-8057-1568-1). Twayne.
--Malcolm Lowry. LC 75-185451. (World Authors Ser.: Canada: No. 217). lib. bdg. 10.95 (ISBN 0-8057-2548-2). Twayne.
Costain, Thomas B. The Conquering Family. (Plantagenets Ser: No. 1). 1976. pap. 2.75 (ISBN 0-445-08511-8). Popular Lib.
--White & the Gold. 5.95 (ISBN 0-385-04526-3); limited edition o.p. 35.00. Doubleday.
--William the Conqueror. (Landmark Ser.: No. 41). (Illus.). (gr. 7-10). 1959. PLB 4.39 o.p. (ISBN 0-394-90541-5, BYR). Random.
Costanza, Betty & Glossbrenner, Alfred. Women's Track & Field. LC 77-70120. 1978. pap. 5.95 (ISBN 0-8015-8795-6, Hawthorn). Dutton.
Costas, O. E. Theology of the Crossroads in Contemporary Latin America: Missiology in Mainline Proestantism 1969-1974. (Orig.). 1976. pap. text ed. 27.50x (ISBN 90-6203-259-1). Humanities.
Costas, Orlando. Compromiso y Mision. 159p. (Orig., Span.). 1979. pap. 3.50 (ISBN 0-89922-165-3). Edit Caribe.
Costas, Orlando E. Comunicacion Por Medio De la Predicacion. 255p. (Span.). 1978. pap. 4.75 (ISBN 0-89922-021-5). Edit Caribe.
Costello, Andrew. Cries - but Silent. 180p. 1981. 8.95 (ISBN 0-88347-126-4). Thomas More.
Costello, Anita C. Picasso's "Vollard Suite". LC 78-74365. (Outstanding Dissertations in the Fine Arts, Fourth Ser.). 1979. lib. bdg. 47.00 (ISBN 0-8240-3953-X). Garland Pub.
Costello, Bella, tr. see Kuschevsky, Ivan.
Costello, C. G. Psychology for Psychiatrists. 1966. 19.50 (ISBN 0-08-011729-5); pap. 10.50 (ISBN 0-08-011728-7). Pergamon.
--Symptoms of Psychopathology: A Handbook. LC 78-88309. 1970. 37.95 (ISBN 0-471-17520-X). Wiley.
Costello, D. P. & Henley, Catherine. Methods for Obtaining & Handling Marine Eggs & Embryos. LC 76-171320. 1971. 10.00 (ISBN 0-685-52860-X). Marine Bio.
Costello, David F. The Desert World. LC 77-184973. (Illus.). 256p. 1972. 9.95 (ISBN 0-690-23513-5, TYC-T). T Y Crowell.
--The Mountain World. LC 74-34369. (Illus.). 256p. 1975. 8.95 o.s.i. (ISBN 0-690-00695-0, TYC-T). T Y Crowell.
--Prairie World. LC 69-15413. (Illus.). 1969. 8.95 o.s.i. (ISBN 0-690-65211-9, TYC-T). T Y Crowell.
--World of the Gull. LC 74-159726. (Living World Bk. Ser.). (Illus.). 1971. 7.95 o.p. (ISBN 0-397-00730-2). Lippincott.
--World of the Porcupine. LC 66-16658. (Living World Books Ser). (Illus.). 1966. 8.95 (ISBN 0-397-00449-4); PLB 6.82 o.p. (ISBN 0-397-00934-8). Lippincott.
--World of the Prairie Dog. LC 70-110650. (Living World Bks Ser). (Illus.). 1970. 7.95 (ISBN 0-397-00679-9); PLB 7.82 o.p. (ISBN 0-397-00680-2, L). Lippincott.
Costello, Frank B. The Political Philosophy of Luis De Molina, S. J. 1974. pap. 12.00 (ISBN 0-8294-0360-4). Jesuit Hist.
Costello, Jacinta L., jt. auth. see Masterson, James F.
Costello, James A. The Underbelly Poems. 1981. pap. 2.95 (ISBN 0-9605098-0-1). En Passant Poet.
Costello, Peter. In Search of Lake Monsters. 1975. pap. 1.75 o.p. (ISBN 0-425-02935-2, Medallion). Berkley Pub.
--James Joyce. (Gill's Irish Lives Ser.). 135p. 1980. 20.00 (ISBN 0-7171-1077-X, Pub. by Gill & Macmillan Ireland); pap. 6.50 (ISBN 0-7171-0986-0). Irish Bk Ctr.
--Jules Verne: Inventor of Science Fiction. LC 78-57528. (Illus.). 1978. 10.95 o.p. (ISBN 0-684-15824-8, ScribT). Scribner.
Costello, Timothy & Zalkind, S. Psychology in Administration: Research Orientation Text with Integrated Readings. (Illus.). 1963. text ed. 19.95 (ISBN 0-13-732867-2). P-H.
Costello, Tom, jt. auth. see Brechter, Jeremy.
Costello, V. F. Urbanization in the Middle East. LC 76-11075. (Urbanization in Developing Countries Ser.). (Illus.). 1977. 19.95 (ISBN 0-521-21324-X); pap. 6.95x (ISBN 0-521-29110-0). Cambridge U Pr.
Costelloe, J., jt. auth. see Hemstock, H. F.
Costeloe, Michael P. Mexico State Papers: 1744-1843. (Institute of Latin American Studies Monograph Ser.: No. 6). 144p. 1976. text ed. 19.50x (ISBN 0-485-17706-4, Athlone Pr). Humanities.
Costich, Julia F. Antonin Artaud. (World Authors Ser.: No. 492). 1978. lib. bdg. 12.50 (ISBN 0-8057-6333-3). Twayne.
Costigan, Giovanni. A History of Modern Ireland: With a Sketch of Earlier Times. LC 69-15699. (Illus.). 1970. 7.50 (ISBN 0-672-63547-X). Pegasus.
--Sigmund Freud. 1965. 5.95 o.s.i. (ISBN 0-02-528450-9). Macmillan.
Costigan, James I., jt. auth. see Rothwell, J. Dan.
Costikyan, Edward N. How to Win Votes: The Politics of Nineteen Eighty. LC 79-3892. 1980. 12.95 (ISBN 0-15-142221-4). HarBraceJ.
Costin, Alec, et al. Kosciusko Alpine Flora. 408p. 1980. 35.00x (ISBN 0-643-02473-5, Pub. by CSIRO Australia). Intl Schol Bk Serv.
Costley, Bill. The War Stories. 30p. 1981. write for info. (ISBN 0-933292-03-1); pap. write for info. (ISBN 0-933292-02-3). Arts End.
Costley, Dan L. & Todd, Ralph. Human Relations in Organizations. (Management Ser.). (Illus.). 1978. pap. text ed. 13.95 (ISBN 0-8299-0211-2); instrs.' manual avail. (ISBN 0-8299-0471-9). West Pub.
Costner, Thomas E., ed. Patent Law Review: Annual. Incl. 1969 (ISBN 0-87632-040-X); 1970 (ISBN 0-87632-044-2); 1971 (ISBN 0-87632-047-7); 1972 (ISBN 0-87632-081-7); 1973 (ISBN 0-87632-091-4); 1974 (ISBN 0-87632-140-6); 1975 (ISBN 0-87632-141-4). LC 79-88703. except where noted 42.50 ea. o.p. Boardman.
Costonis, John & DeVoy, Robert. The Puerto Rico Plan: Environmental Protection Through Development Rights Transfer. LC 75-15460. (Illus.). 90p. 1975. 9.00 (ISBN 0-87420-561-1). Urban Land.
Cotchett, Joseph W. & Elkind, Arnold B. Federal Courtroom Evidence. LC 75-26155. 1980. incl. 1979 suppl. 29.50 (ISBN 0-911110-20-8). Parker & Son.
Cotchett, Joseph W., jt. auth. see Haight, Fulton.
Cote, Wilfred A., ed. Papermaking Fibers: A Photomicroscopic Atlas. (Renewable Materials Institute Ser.). (Illus.). 200p. 1980. pap. text ed. 12.00x (ISBN 0-8156-2228-7). Syracuse U Pr.
Cotera, Martha P., tr. see Hazen, Nancy.
Cotes, Peter, jt. auth. see Croft-Cooke, Rupert.
Cotgreave, Alfred. Contents-Subject Index to General & Periodical Literature. LC 74-31272. 1971. Repr. of 1900 ed. 42.00 (ISBN 0-8103-3778-9). Gale.
Cothren, Paige. Let None Deal Treacherously. 224p. (Orig.). 1981. pap. 4.95 (ISBN 0-937778-03-6). Fulness Hse.
Cotich, Felicia, et al. Primavera, V. Heller, Janet R., et al, eds. LC 76-647540. (Illus.). 1979. pap. 4.00 (ISBN 0-916980-05-7). Primavera.
Cotler, Sherwin B. & Guerra, Julio J. Assertion Training: A Humanistic-Behavioral Guide to Self-Dignity. LC 76-1704. (Illus., Orig.). 1976. pap. text ed. 8.95 (ISBN 0-87822-173-5). Res Press.
Cotlow, Lewis. The Twilight of the Primitive. (Walden Editions). 1973. pap. 1.65 o.p. (ISBN 0-685-32483-4, 345-23568-1-165). Ballantine.
Cotman, Carl W. & Jenson, Robert. Instructor's Manual for Behavioral Neuroscience: An Introduction. 1979. 3.00 (ISBN 0-12-191655-3). Acad Pr.
Cotman, Carl W. & McGaugh, James L. Behavioral Neuroscience: An Introduction. LC 79-50214. 1979. 21.95 (ISBN 0-12-191650-2). Acad Pr.
Cotman, Carl W., jt. auth. see Angevine, Jay B.
Cotman, Carl W., ed. Neuronal Plasticity. LC 77-72807. 1978. 31.50 (ISBN 0-89004-210-1). Raven.
Cotner, Robert C. Readings in American History, 2 vols. 4th ed. LC 75-37038. (Illus.). 1976. Vol. 1. 9.75 (ISBN 0-395-17810-X); Vol. 2. pap. text ed. 9.75 (ISBN 0-395-17811-8). HM.
Cotner, Robert C., ed. see Urbantke, Carl.
Cotner, Robert C., et al, eds. Texas State Capitol. (Illus.). 7.50 (ISBN 0-8363-0095-5). Jenkins.
Cotran, Ramzi, jt. auth. see Leaf, Alexander.
Cotsforde, Thomas, tr. see Zwingli, Ulrich.
Cott, Jonathan. Charms. 24p. 1980. pap. 4.00 (ISBN 0-915124-48-3). Toothpaste.
--Forever Young. (Illus.). 1978. 10.00 o.p. (ISBN 0-685-85032-3); pap. 5.95 (ISBN 0-394-73398-3). Random.
Cott, Jonathan, ed. Masterworks of Children's Literature, Fifteen Fifty to Nineteen Hundred, 7 vols. LC 78-56257. (Illus.). Date not set. Set. 225.00 (ISBN 0-87754-089-6). Chelsea Hse.
--Masterworks of English Children's Literature, 1550-1900, 5 vols. 3100p. 1979. Set. 150.00 (ISBN 0-88373-134-7). Stonehill Pub Co.
Cott, Jonathan & Gimbel, Mary, eds. Wonders: Writings & Drawings for the Child in Us All. LC 80-17146. (Rolling Stone Press Book). (Illus.). 1980. 17.95 (ISBN 0-671-40053-3). Summit Bks.
Cott, Nancy, ed. The Root of Bitterness: Documents of the Social History of American Women. 1972. pap. 8.50 (ISBN 0-525-47328-9). Dutton.
Cotte, Sabine, jt. auth. see Roger-Marx, Claude.
Cotten, Emmi. Clothes Make Magic. 2nd, rev. ed. Rateaver, Bargyla & Rateaver, Gylver, eds. LC 79-55932. (Conservation Gardening & Farming Ser. C: The Home). (Illus.). 223p. (gr. 9-10). 1980. pap. 10.00 (ISBN 0-915966-00-X). Rateavers.
Cotten, Nell. Piney Woods. LC 62-11221. (gr. 4-8). 3.50 (ISBN 0-8149-0292-8). Vanguard.
Cotter, Cornelius P., jt. auth. see Smith, John Malcolm.
Cotter, I. A., jt. auth. see Gurney, J. D.
Cotter, John & Frankle, Judith. Nights with Sasquatch. 1977. pap. 1.25 o.p. (ISBN 0-425-03393-7, Medallion). Berkley Pub.
Cotterell, Arthur, ed. Encyclopedia of Ancient Civilizations. Renfrew, Colin. 320p. 1980. 29.95 (ISBN 0-8317-2790-X). Mayflower Bks.
Cotterell, Howard H. Old Pewter: Its Makers & Marks in England, Scotland & Ireland; an Account of the Old Pewterer & His Craft. LC 29-22959. (Illus.). 1963. 87.50 (ISBN 0-8048-0443-5). C E Tuttle.
Cotterill, J. A., jt. auth. see Cunliffe, W. J.
Cotterill, Owen J., jt. auth. see Stadelman, William J.
Cotterill, P. & Mould, P. R. Recrystallization & Grain Growth in Metals. LC 75-33874. 1976. 34.95 (ISBN 0-470-17527-3). Halsted Pr.
Cotterill, R. S. The Southern Indians: The Story of the Civilized Tribes Before Removal. LC 54-5931. (Civilization of the American Indian Ser.: Vol. 38). 259p. 1954. 12.50 (ISBN 0-8061-0286-1); pap. 5.95 (ISBN 0-8061-1171-2). U of Okla Pr.
Cotterrell, G. P., tr. see Jakubke, H. D. & Jeschkeit, H.
Cottesloe, Gloria. The Story of the Battersea Dogs' Home. 1979. 16.95 (ISBN 0-7153-7704-3). David & Charles.
Cottin, Lin. All About Landscaping. Ortho Books Editorial Staff, ed. LC 80-66347. (Illus.). 96p. (Orig.). 1981. pap. 4.95 (ISBN 0-917102-87-8). Ortho.
Cottingham, Clive, Jr. Game of Billiards. LC 64-23471. (Illus.). 1967. 8.95 o.p. (ISBN 0-397-00322-6); pap. 5.95 (ISBN 0-397-00476-1, LP-11). Lippincott.
Cottle, Joseph. The Fall of Cambria, a Poem, 2 vols. in 1. LC 75-31186. (Romantic Context Ser.: Poetry 1789-1830: Vol. 38). 1978. Repr. of 1808 ed. lib. bdg. 47.00 (ISBN 0-8240-2137-1). Garland Pub.
--Messiah; a Poem. LC 75-31187. (Romantic Context Ser.: Poetry 1789-1830: Vol. 39). 1978. Repr. of 1815 ed. lib. bdg. 47.00 (ISBN 0-8240-2138-X). Garland Pub.
Cottle, Richard W., ed. see Society for Industrial & Applied Mathematics-American Mathematical Society Symposia-New York, March 1975.
Cottle, Thomas J. Barred from School: Two Million Children. LC 76-20607. 1976. 7.95 o.p. (ISBN 0-915220-12-1); pap. 3.95 o.p. (ISBN 0-915220-40-7, 24165). New Republic.
--Like Fathers, Like Sons: Portraits of Intimacy & Strain. 300p. 1981. price not set (ISBN 0-89391-054-6). Ablex Pub.
Cottle, Thomas J. & Klineberg, Stephen L. The Present of Things Future: Exploring of Time in Human Experience. LC 73-5292. 1974. 9.95 o.s.i. (ISBN 0-02-906820-7). Free Pr.
Cottle, Thomas J., jt. auth. see Greenblat, Cathy.

Cottle, William C. & Downie, N. M. Preparation for Counseling. 2nd ed. 1970. text ed. 17.95 (ISBN 0-13-697227-6). P-H.

Cottler, Susan M., et al. Preliminary Survey of the Mexican Collection: Finding Aids to the Microfilmed Manuscript Collection of the Genealogical Society of Utah. LC 78-71761. (Orig.). 1978. pap. 12.00 (ISBN 0-87480-151-6). U of Utah Pr.

Cotton & Seid. Laryngl Disease in Children. 1981. text ed. write for info. (ISBN 0-443-08054-2). Churchill.

Cotton, Alan & Haddon, Frank. Learning & Teaching Through Art & Crafts. 1979. 15.95 o.p. (ISBN 0-7134-2825-2, Pub. by Batsford England). David & Charles.

Cotton, Albert F. & Wilkinson, Geoffrey. Basic Inorganic Chemistry. LC 75-26832. 579p. (Arabic Translation available). 1976. 23.95 (ISBN 0-471-17557-9). Wiley.

Cotton, C. A. Climatic Accidents in Landscape Making. (Illus.). 1969. Repr. of 1947 ed. 21.75 o.p. (ISBN 0-02-843200-2). Hafner.

--Volcanoes As Landscape Forms. 2nd ed. (Illus.). 1969. Repr. of 1944 ed. 21.75 o.s.i. (ISBN 0-02-843210-X). Hafner.

Cotton, Charles, jt. auth. see Walton, Izaak.

Cotton, E. J. & Mitchell, Ethel. Buffalo Bud: Adventures of an Alberta Cowboy. (Illus.). 130p. (Orig.). 1981. pap. 9.95 (ISBN 0-88839-095-5). Hancock Hse.

Cotton, H. Medical Practice Management. rev. ed. 1977. 23.95 (ISBN 0-87489-098-5). Med Economics.

Cotton, Henry. A History of Golf: Illustrated. LC 75-8530. (Illus.). 240p. 1975. 16.95 o.s.i. (ISBN 0-397-01092-3). Lippincott.

--The Typographical Gazetteer. LC 76-159922. 1975. Repr. of 1825 ed. 18.00 (ISBN 0-8103-4121-2). Gale.

Cotton, Ira W., ed. Office Automation Conference Digest Nineteen-Eighty. LC 80-80155. (Illus.). ix, 373p. 1980. pap. 12.00 (ISBN 0-88283-002-3). AFIPS Pr.

Cotton, Joseph P., ed. The Constitutional Decisions of John Marshall, 2 Vols. LC 67-25445. (Law, Politics & History Ser.). 1969. Repr. of 1905 ed. 55.00 (ISBN 0-306-70947-3). Da Capo.

Cotton, Michael. Porsche 911: Collector's Guide. (Illus.). 128p. 1980. 17.50 (ISBN 0-900549-52-1, Pub. by Motor Racing Pubns. England). Motorbooks Intl.

Cotton, Nancy. Women Playwrights in England: 1363-1750. LC 78-73155. 256p. 1980. 15.00 (ISBN 0-8387-2381-0). Bucknell U Pr.

Cotton, Sir Robert B. The Danger Wherein the Kingdome Now Standeth, & the Remedie. LC 74-28839. (No. 721). 1975. Repr. of 1628 ed. 3.50 (ISBN 90-221-0721-3). Walter J Johnson.

Cotton, S. A. & Hart, E. A. The Heavy Transition Elements. 1975. 28.95 o.p. (ISBN 0-470-17681-4). Halsted Pr.

Cottonwood, Joe. Frank City (Goodbye) 1981. pap. price not set (ISBN 0-440-52906-9, Delta). Dell.

Cottral, George E., ed. Manual of Standardized Methods for Veterinary Microbiology. LC 77-90900. (Illus.). 720p. 1978. 40.00 (ISBN 0-8014-1119-X). Comstock.

Cottrell, A. H. The Mechanical Properties of Matter. LC 80-12439. 340p. 1981. Repr. of 1964 ed. lib. bdg. write for info. (ISBN 0-89874-168-8). Krieger.

Cottrell, Alan. Environmental Economics: An Introduction for Students of the Resource & Environmental Sciences. (Resource & Environmental Science Ser.). 1978. pap. text ed. 6.95 (ISBN 0-470-99395-2). Halsted Pr.

--An Introduction to Metallurgy. LC 75-21731. 1975. pap. 19.50x (ISBN 0-8448-0767-2). Crane-Russak Co.

Cottrell, Alvin, et al. Arms Transfers & U. S. Foreign & Military Policy, Vol. I. LC 80-50062. (Significant Issues Ser.: No. 7). 63p. 1980. 5.95 (ISBN 0-89206-013-1). CSI Studies.

Cottrell, Alvin J. & Dougherty, James E. Iran's Quest for Security: U. S. Arms Transfers & the Nuclear Option. LC 77-80298. (Foreign Policy Reports Ser.). 1977. 5.00 (ISBN 0-89549-004-8). Inst Foreign Policy Anal.

Cottrell, Alvin J. & Hanks, Robert J. The Military Utility of the U. S. Facilities in the Philippines, Vol. II. LC 80-83128. (Significant Issues Ser.: No.11). 34p. 1980. 5.95 (ISBN 0-89206-027-1). CSI Studies.

Cottrell, Alvin J. & Moorer, Thomas H. Overseas Bases: Problems of Projecting American Military Power Abroad. LC 77-88453. (The Washington Papers: No. 47). 1977. 3.50x (ISBN 0-8039-0952-7). Sage.

Cottrell, Alvin J., jt. auth. see Burrell, R. Michael.

Cottrell, Alvin J., ed. The Persian Gulf States. LC 79-19452. 736p. 1980. text ed. 37.50x (ISBN 0-8018-2204-1). Johns Hopkins.

Cottrell, Beekman W., jt. auth. see Slack, Robert C.

Cottrell, Edyth Y. The Oats, Peas, Beans & Barley Cookbook: A Complete Vegetarian Cookbook Using Nature's Most Economical Foods. rev. ed. LC 80-80794. (Illus.). 1980. pap. 4.95 (ISBN 0-912800-85-2). Woodbridge Pr.

--The Oats, Peas, Beans & Barley Cookbook: The Complete Vegetarian Cookbook. LC 73-77411. (Illus.). 272p. 1974. 8.95 o.p. (ISBN 0-912800-08-9); pap. 5.95 o.p. (ISBN 0-912800-07-0). Woodbridge Pr.

--Stretching the Food Dollar Cookbook. LC 80-36894. (Illus., Orig.). 1981. pap. 3.95 (ISBN 0-912800-80-1). Woodbridge Pr.

--Sugar-Coated Teddy. LC 75-37441. (Illus.). 80p. (Orig.). 1976. pap. 4.95 (ISBN 0-912800-25-9). Woodbridge Pr.

Cottrell, Jack. Authority of the Bible. (Direction Bks.). 1979. pap. 1.95 (ISBN 0-8010-2436-6). Baker Bk.

Cottrell, James E. & Turndorf, Herman. Anesthesia & Neurosurgery. LC 79-24676. (Illus.). 1979. text ed. 49.50 (ISBN 0-8016-1036-2). Mosby.

Cottrell, Jane E. Alberto Moravia. LC 73-84599. (Modern Literature Ser.). 174p. 1974. 10.95 (ISBN 0-8044-2131-5). Ungar.

Cottrell, John. Mexico City. (The Great Cities Ser.). (Illus.). 1979. lib. bdg. 14.94 (ISBN 0-8094-3105-X); kivar bdg. 9.93 (ISBN 0-8094-3106-8). Silver.

Cottrell, Leonard. Lost Pharaohs: The Romance of Egyptian Archaeology. LC 72-90140. Repr. of 1951 ed. lib. bdg. 21.75x (ISBN 0-8371-2260-0, COLP). Greenwood.

--Reading the Past. (Illus.). (gr. 7-12). 1971. 5.95 o.s.i. (ISBN 0-02-724820-8, CCPr). Macmillan.

--The Secrets of Tutankhamen. (Illus.). 1978. pap. 3.95 (ISBN 0-8467-0456-0, Pub. by Two Continents). Hippocrene Bks.

--Up in a Balloon. LC 69-17423. (Illus.). (gr. 8 up). 1970. 10.95 (ISBN 0-87599-142-4). S G Phillips.

Cottrell, Robert D. Colette. LC 73-84598. (Modern Literature Ser.). 1974. 10.95 (ISBN 0-8044-2130-7). Ungar.

--Simone De Beauvoir. LC 74-34131. (Modern Literature Ser.). 1975. 10.95 (ISBN 0-8044-2132-3). Ungar.

Cottrell, Sue. Hoof Beats North & South: Horses & Horsemen of the Civil War. 1975. 7.50 o.p. (ISBN 0-682-48280-3, University). Exposition.

Cottrell, T. L. Chemistry. 2nd ed. (Oxford Paperbacks University Ser). 1970. pap. 1.95x o.p. (ISBN 0-19-888047-2). Oxford U Pr.

Cottrill, Phillip K. Automobile Ads List: Life Magazine Nineteen Forty to Nineteen Forty-Nine. 100p. (Orig.). 1980. pap. 9.95 (ISBN 0-937234-40-0). Rigel.

--Automobile Ads List: Life Magazine Nineteen-Fifty to Nineteen Fifty-Nine. 100p. (Orig.). 1980. pap. 9.95 (ISBN 0-937234-50-8). Rigel.

--Automobile Ads List Life Magazine Nineteen Sixty to Nineteen Sixty-Nine. LC 80-52108. 91p. (Orig.). 1980. pap. 9.95 (ISBN 0-937234-60-5). Rigel.

Couch, A. S., jt. auth. see Armor, D. J.

Couch, John D., jt. auth. see Barrett, William A.

Couch, Robert H. Everyday Is Easter in Alabama. LC 76-21358. (Illus.). 1976. 10.00 (ISBN 0-916624-02-1). TSU Pr.

Coudert, Allison. Alchemy: The Philosopher's Stone. LC 79-67688. (Illus.). 1980. pap. 9.95 (ISBN 0-394-73733-4). Shambhala Pubns.

Coudert, Jo. The Alcoholic in Your Life. LC 70-185955. 264p. 1981. pap. 6.95 (ISBN 0-8128-6121-3). Stein & Day.

--The Alcoholic in Your Life. 288p. 1974. pap. 2.25 o.s.i. (ISBN 0-446-92240-4). Warner Bks.

Coudurier, L. & Wilkomirsky, I. Fundamentals of Metallurgical Processes. 1978. text ed. 52.00 (ISBN 0-08-019612-8); pap. text ed. 17.00 (ISBN 0-08-019654-3). Pergamon.

Coues, Elliot, ed. see Lewis, Meriwether & Clark, William.

Coufal, H., jt. ed. see Luscher, E.

Couffignal, Huquette. The People's Cookbook. 1977. 10.00 o.p. (ISBN 0-312-60007-0). St Martin.

Couger, Dan & McFadden, Fred. First Course in Data Processing with BASIC. LC 80-22130. 450p. 1981. pap. text ed. 17.95 (ISBN 0-471-08046-2). Wiley.

--First Course in Data Processing with BASIC, COBOL, FORTRAN, RPG II. 2nd ed. LC 80-22129. 550p. 1981. pap. text ed. 17.50 (ISBN 0-471-05581-6). Wiley.

Couger, Daniel. Computer & the School of Business. 98p. 1967. 4.00 (ISBN 0-89478-006-9). U CO Busn Res Div.

Couger, Daniel & Shannon, Loren E. Plaid for Fortran: A Beginners Approach. 1977. pap. 5.50 (ISBN 0-256-01986-X, 14-0826-02). Learning Syst.

Couger, J. D. & McFadden, F. A First Course in Data Processing. 1977. 21.95 (ISBN 0-471-17738-5). Wiley.

Couger, J. Daniel & McFadden, Fred R. Introduction to Computer-Based Information Systems. LC 74-28437. 655p. 1975. text ed. 25.95 (ISBN 0-471-17736-9). Wiley.

Couger, J. Daniel & Shannon, Loren E. Fortran IV: A Programmed Instruction Approach. 3rd ed. 1976. pap. text ed. 11.50x (ISBN 0-256-01632-1). Irwin.

Couger, J. Daniel & Knapp, Robert W., eds. System Analysis Techniques. LC 73-14818. 509p. 1974. text ed. 25.50 (ISBN 0-471-17735-0). Wiley.

Coughlan, Michael P. Molybdenum & Molybdenum-Containing Enzymes. (Illus.). 1980. 94.00 (ISBN 0-08-024398-3). Pergamon.

Coughlan, Robert. World of Michelangelo. (Library of Art). (Illus.). 1966. 15.95 (ISBN 0-8094-0232-7). Time-Life.

--World of Michelangelo. LC 66-16540. (Library of Art Ser.). (Illus.). (gr. 6 up). 1966. 12.96 (ISBN 0-8094-0261-0, Pub. by Time-Life). Silver.

Coughlan, Rupert. Napper Tandy. (Illus.). 1976. 18.50 (ISBN 0-900068-34-5). Irish Bk Ctr.

Coughlin. Applied Calculus. 2nd ed. 480p. 1980. text ed. 20.95 (ISBN 0-205-06910-X, 5669103). Allyn.

Coughlin, C. E. A Series of Lectures on Social Justice. LC 71-173652. (FDR & the Era of the New Deal). 242p. 1972. Repr. of 1935 ed. lib. bdg. 27.50 (ISBN 0-306-70373-4). Da Capo.

Coughlin, Caroline M., ed. Recurring Library Issues: A Reader. LC 79-14966. 543p. 1979. 19.00 (ISBN 0-8108-1227-4). Scarecrow.

Coughlin, Charles E. Money, Questions & Answers. 1978. pap. 4.00x (ISBN 0-911038-28-0). Noontide.

Coughlin, Edward V. Adelardo Lopez De Ayala. (World Authors Ser.: No. 466). 1977. lib. bdg. 12.50 (ISBN 0-8057-6303-1). Twayne.

Coughlin, George G. Your Introduction to Law. 2nd ed. 1975. pap. 3.95 o.p. (ISBN 0-06-463472-8, 472, EH). Har-Row.

Coughlin, Joseph W. Jack Dawn & the Vanishing Horses. 140p. (Orig.). (gr. 5-8). 1980. pap. 2.25. BMA Pr.

Coughlin, Kevin. Finding God in Everyday Life. 80p. (Orig.). 1981. pap. 3.95 (ISBN 0-8091-2351-7). Paulist Pr.

Coughlin, Mary T., jt. auth. see Brinckloe, William D.

Coughlin, R. & Driscoll, F. Operational Amplifiers & Linear Integrated Circuits. 312p. 1977. text ed. 18.95 (ISBN 0-13-637850-1). P-H.

Coughlin, R. E., et al. Urban Analysis for Branch Library System Planning. LC 71-133496. (Contributions in Librarianship & Information Science: No. 1). 1972. lib. bdg. 15.95 (ISBN 0-8371-5161-9, CLP/). Greenwood.

Coughlin, R. F. & Driscoll, F. F. Semiconductor Fundamentals. (Illus.). 336p. 1976. 18.95 (ISBN 0-13-806406-7). P-H.

Coughlin, Raymond F. Applied Calculus. 384p. 1976. text ed. 15.95x o.p. (ISBN 0-205-04890-0); instr. supplement free o.p. (ISBN 0-205-04891-9). Allyn.

--Elementary Applied Calculus: A Short Course. 2nd ed. 1978. text ed. 19.90 (ISBN 0-205-05965-1); instr's man. avail. (ISBN 0-205-05966-X). Allyn.

Coughlin, Violet L. Larger Units of Public Library Service in Canada. LC 67-12066. 1968. 10.00 (ISBN 0-8108-0079-9). Scarecrow.

Coughlin, William. The Stalking Man. 1979. 8.95 o.s.i. (ISBN 0-440-08334-6). Delacorte.

Couhat, Jean L. Combat Fleets of the World Nineteen Eighty & Eighty-One: Their Ships, Aircraft, & Armament. LC 78-50192. (Illus.). 808p. 1980. 64.95x (ISBN 0-87021-123-4). Naval Inst Pr.

Coulam, Craig M. Physical Basis of Medical Imaging. 416p. 1981. 35.00 (ISBN 0-8385-7844-6). ACC.

Coulbourn, Tyler. Intramural Director's Guide to Program Evaluation. 104p. (Orig.). 1981. pap. price not set (ISBN 0-918438-67-5). Leisure Pr.

Couldrey, Vivienne. The Swans of Brhyadr. 224p. 1981. pap. 1.75 (ISBN 0-449-50166-3, Coventry). Fawcett.

Couldridge, Alan & Dowell, Celia. The Hat Book. 128p. 1981. 16.95 (ISBN 0-13-384222-3, Spec); pap. 8.95 (ISBN 0-13-384214-2). P-H.

Coull, Bruce C., jt. ed. see Tenore, Kenneth R.

Coull, James R. The Fisheries of Europe. (Advanced Economic Geography Ser.). 1972. lib. bdg. 22.00x (ISBN 0-7135-1612-7). Westview.

Coullery, Marie-Therese & Newstead, Martin S. Netsuke: Selected Pieces. (Baur Collection Catalogues Ser.: Vol. 6). (Illus.). 1978. 225.00 (ISBN 0-685-39558-8). Routledge & Kegan.

Coulling, Sidney. Matthew Arnold & His Critics: A Study of Arnold's Controversies. LC 74-82498. xiv, 351p. 1974. 16.00x (ISBN 0-8214-0161-0). Ohio U Pr.

Coulmas, Florian, ed. Conversational Routine. (Janua Linguarum, Ser. Maior-Rasmus Rask Studies in Pragmatic Linguistics: Vol. 2). 1980. text ed. 38.25x (ISBN 90-279-3098-8). Mouton.

Coulot, Maurice, et al. Victor Bourgeois Architect. (Archives d'Architecture Moderne). 150p. (Orig., Fr. & Eng.). 1980. write for info. (ISBN 0-8150-0924-0). Wittenborn.

Couloumbis, Theo. A., jt. auth. see Wolfe, James H.

Coulson, C. A. & Boyd, T. J. Electricity. 2nd ed. (Longman Mathematical Texts Ser.). (Illus.). 1979. pap. text ed. 18.95 (ISBN 0-582-44281-8). Longman.

Coulson, C. A. & Jeffrey, A. Waves: A Mathematical Approach to the Common Types of Wave Motion. 2nd ed. (Illus.). 1978. pap. text ed. 12.95x (ISBN 0-582-44954-5). Longman.

Coulson, Charles A. Coulson's Valence. 3rd ed. McWeeny, Roy, ed. (Illus.). 49.50x (ISBN 0-19-855144-4); pap. 23.00x (ISBN 0-19-855145-2). Oxford U Pr.

Coulson, Herbert H., jt. auth. see Cave, Roy C.

Coulson, J. M., et al. Chemical Engineering S.I. Ed, Vol. 1. 3rd ed. LC 75-42295. (Illus.). 412p. 45.00 (ISBN 0-08-020614-X); pap. 17.50 (ISBN 0-08-021015-5). Pergamon.

--Chemical Engineering, Vol. 5: Solutions to the Problems in Volume Two. 3rd ed. LC 78-40923. (Chemical Engineering Technical Ser.). (Illus.). 1979. 37.00 (ISBN 0-08-022951-4); pap. 16.50 (ISBN 0-08-022952-2). Pergamon.

Coulson, Jessie, tr. see Dostoyevsky, Fedor M.

Coulson, Juanita. Dark Priestess. (Orig.). 1977. pap. 1.95 o.p. (ISBN 0-345-24958-5). Ballantine.

Coulson, Margaret A. & Riddell, C. Approaching Sociology: A Critical Introduction. (Students Library of Sociology). 1970. 12.95 (ISBN 0-7100-6877-8); pap. 5.00 (ISBN 0-7100-6878-6). Routledge & Kegan.

Coulson, N. J. Succession in the Muslim Family. 1971. 44.00 (ISBN 0-521-07852-0). Cambridge U Pr.

Coulson, Zoe, intro. by. Good Housekeeping Illustrated Cookbook. LC 79-92727. 512p. 1980. 19.95 (ISBN 0-87851-037-0). Hearst Bks.

Coulston, F. & Korte, F., eds. Environmental Quality: Global Aspects of Chemistry, Toxicology & Technology As Applied to the Environment, 5 vols. Vol. 1, 1972. 27.50 (ISBN 0-12-227001-0); Vol. 2, 1973. 36.00 (ISBN 0-12-227002-9); Vol. 3, 1974. 32.00 (ISBN 0-12-227003-7); Vol.4, 1975. 27.50 (ISBN 0-12-227004-5); Vol. 5, 1976. 24.00 (ISBN 0-12-227005-3). Acad Pr.

Coult, S. Kye. Solo Kill. 1977. pap. 1.50 o.p. (ISBN 0-425-03560-3, Medallion). Berkley Pub.

Coulter. Principles of Politics & Government. 336p. 1980. text ed. 9.95 (ISBN 0-205-07177-5, 767177-6). Allyn.

Coulter, Catherine. The Generous Earl. (Orig.). 1981. pap. price not set (ISBN 0-451-09899-4, Sig). NAL.

--Lord Harry's Folly. 1980. pap. 1.75 (ISBN 0-451-09531-6, E9531, Sig). NAL.

Coulter, E. Merton. William G. Brownlow: Fighting Parson of the Southern Highlands. LC 71-136309. (Tennesseana Editions Ser.). (Illus.). 458p. 1971. 10.50x o.p. (ISBN 0-87049-118-0). U of Tenn Pr.

Coulter, James. The Literary Microcosm: Theories of Interpretation of the Later Neoplatonists. (Columbia Studies in the Classical Tradition: No. II). 1976. text ed. 27.50x (ISBN 90-04-04489-2). Humanities.

Coulter, Jeff. Approaches to Insanity: A Philosophical & Sociological Study. 170p. 1973. 23.50x (ISBN 0-85520-049-9, Pub. by Martin Robertson, England); pap. 11.50x (ISBN 0-85520-048-0). Biblio Dist.

Coulter, M. O., ed. Modern Chlor-Alkali Technology. 280p. 1980. 89.95x (ISBN 0-470-27005-5). Halsted Pr.

Coulthard, A. R. The Writer's Craft: A Concise Rhetoric & Handbook. 416p. 1980. pap. text ed. 7.95x (ISBN 0-534-00768-6); wkbk. 3.95x (ISBN 0-534-00845-3). Wadsworth Pub.

Coulthard, Malcolm. Introduction to Discourse Analysis. (Applied Linguistics & Language Study). 1978. pap. text ed. 9.00x (ISBN 0-582-55087-4). Longman.

Coulthard, Malcolm, et al. Discourse Intonation & Language Teaching. (Applied Linguistics & Language Study). 1980. pap. text ed. 9.00 (ISBN 0-582-55366-0); cassette 15.00 (ISBN 0-582-55367-9). Longman.

Coulton, G. G., ed. & tr. see Salimbene Di Adam.

Coulton, George G. Life in the Middle Ages. 71.95 (ISBN 0-521-06947-5); pap. 18.50x (ISBN 0-521-09400-3). Cambridge U Pr.

Coulton, Jill. Sports Acrobatics. (Illus.). 112p. 1981. 12.95 (ISBN 0-8069-9184-4, Pub. by EP Publishing England); pap. 6.95 (ISBN 0-8069-9185-2). Sterling.

--Women's Gymnastics. (EP Sport Ser.). (Illus.). 116p. 1979. 12.95 (ISBN 0-8069-9168-2, Pub. by EP Publishing England); pap. 6.95 (ISBN 0-8069-9170-4, Pub. by EP Publishing England). Sterling.
Council for Economic Planning & Development (Republic of China) Taiwan Statistical Data Book, 1980. LC 72-219425. (Illus.). 318p. (Orig.). 1980. pap. 12.50x (ISBN 0-8002-2749-2). Intl Pubns Serv.
Council for Exceptional Children & Martinson, Ruth A. Abilities of Young Children. 1967. 3.50 o.p. (ISBN 0-86586-000-9). Coun Exc Child.
Council of Europe. Yearbook of the European Convention on Human Rights, Vol. 21. (Anruaire de la Convention Europeenne des droits de l'Homme, 1978). 1980. lib. bdg. 155.25 (ISBN 90-247-2215-2, Martinus Nijhoff Pubs). Kluwer Boston.
--Yearbook of the European Convention on Human Rights, 1978, Vol. 21. rev. ed. LC 60-1388. 844p. 1979. 195.00x (ISBN 90-247-2215-2). Intl Pubns Serv.
Council of Europe, ed. Collected Edition of the "Travaux Preparatoires of the European Convention on Human Rights". Vol. V Legal Committee-Ad Hoc Joint Committee-Committee of Ministers-Consultative Assembly 23 June - 28 August 1950. 356p. 1979. lib. bdg. 131.60 (ISBN 90-247-1970-4, Pub. by Martinus Nijhoff). Kluwer Boston.
--Monument Protection in Europe. 1980. lib. bdg. 31.50 (ISBN 90-268-1107-1, Kluwer Law & Taxation Pubs). Kluwer Boston.
--Yearbook of the European Convention on Human Rights. (European Convention on Human Rights: No. 22). 688p. 1980. lib. bdg. 132.00 (ISBN 90-247-2383-3, Pub. by Martinus Nijhoff). Kluwer Boston.
Council on Economic Priorities & Boothe, Joan N. Cleaning Up: The Cost of Refinery Pollution Control. LC 75-10535. (Praeger Special Studies). 1977. 20.95 (ISBN 0-03-040936-5). Praeger.
Council on Economic Priorities & Buchsbaum, Steven. Jobs & Energy: The Employment & Economic Impacts of Nuclear Power, Conservation, & Other Energy Options. Schwartz, Wendy C., ed. LC 79-91065. 1979. 300.00 (ISBN 0-87871-011-6). CEP.
Council on Economic Priorities & Simcich, Tina L. Women & Minorities in Banking: Shortchanged-Update. LC 76-50522. (Praeger Special Studies). 1977. 20.95 (ISBN 0-03-040336-7). Praeger.
Council on Energy Resources. National Energy Policy: A Continuing Assessment. (Illus.). 395p. 1978. 4.00. Bur Econ Geology.
Council on International Educational Exchange. Where to Stay USA. (Illus.). 368p. 1980-81. pap. 4.95 (ISBN 0-671-25496-0). Frommer-Pasmantier.
--The Whole World Handbook: A Guide to Study, Travel, & Work Abroad. 352p. 1981. pap. 5.95 (ISBN 0-525-93171-6). Dutton.
Council on Interracial Books for Children, Inc. Chronicles of American Indian Protest. 2nd, rev. ed. 400p. (gr. 11-12). pap. 5.95 (ISBN 0-930040-30-9). CIBC.
--Guidelines for Selecting Bias-Free Textbooks & Storybooks. LC 80-165903. 105p. 1980. pap. 6.95 (ISBN 0-930040-33-3). CIBC.
--Human (& Anti-Human) Values in Children's Books. LC 76-11665. (A Content Rating Instrument for Educators & Concerned Parents Ser.). 280p. 1976. 14.95 o.s.i. (ISBN 0-930040-00-7); pap. 7.95 (ISBN 0-930040-01-5). CIBC.
Council on Law Related Studies. No-Fault Auto Insurance. 1977. 24.00 (ISBN 0-379-00391-0). Oceana.
Council on Learning, jt. auth. see Educational Testing Service.
Council on Learning's National Task Force. Education for a Global Century: Issues & Some Solutions. LC 80-69769. 112p. (Orig.). Date not set. pap. 7.95 (ISBN 0-915390-29-9). Change Mag.
--What College Students Know About Their World. LC 80-69768. 56p. (Orig.). 1980. pap. 5.95 (ISBN 0-915390-30-2). Change Mag.
Council on Tall Buildings & Urban Habitats of Fritz Engineering Lab., Lehigh Univ. Structural Design of Tall Steel Buildings. LC 79-63736. 1080p. 1979. text ed. 60.00 (ISBN 0-87262-228-2). Am Soc Civil Eng.
Council on Tall Buildings & Urban Habitat. Tall Buildings: Systems & Concepts. LC 80-65692. (Monographs on Planning & Design of Tall Buildings: No. 4). 651p. 1980. text ed. 40.00 (ISBN 0-87262-239-8). Am Soc Civil Eng.
Cound, John L., et al. Civil Procedure, Cases & Materials. 3rd ed. LC 80-14621. (American Casebook Ser.). 1223p. 1980. text ed. 22.95 (ISBN 0-8299-2092-7). West Pub.
Coundakis, Anthony L. Mannerism on Space Communication. 256p. 1981. 12.50 (ISBN 0-682-49734-7). Exposition.
Counsilman, James. Science of Swimming. 1968. ref. ed. 17.95 (ISBN 0-13-795385-2). P-H.
Counsilman, James E. The Complete Book of Swimming. LC 72-82682. (Illus.). 1979. 9.95 (ISBN 0-689-10530-4); pap. 5.95 (ISBN 0-689-70583-2, 246). Atheneum.
Count, Ellen, jt. auth. see August, Bonnie.
Counte, Michael A. & Christman, Luther. Interpersonal Behavior & Health Care. (Behavioral Sciences for the Health Care Professional Ser.). 128p. (Orig.). 1981. lib. bdg. 15.00x (ISBN 0-86531-008-4); pap. text ed. 6.00x (ISBN 0-86531-009-2). Westview.
Counter, R. T. The Yachtsman's Doctor. 148p. 1980. 27.00 (ISBN 0-245-53425-3, Pub. by Nautical England). State Mutual Bk.
Country Beautiful Foundation, ed. America the Beautiful in the Words of Henry David Thoreau. 1966. 7.95 o.p. (ISBN 0-688-01046-6). Morrow.
Country Music Magazine Editors. The Illustrated History of Country Music. Carr, Patrick, ed. LC 77-82936. (Illus.). 1979. 14.95 (ISBN 0-385-11601-2); pap. 8.95 (ISBN 0-385-15385-6). Doubleday.
Countryman, Kathleen M., jt. auth. see Gekas, Alexandra B.
Countryman, L. Wm. The Rich Christian in the Church of the Early Empire: Contradictions & Accomodations. (Texts & Studies in Religion: Vol. 7). 1980. soft cover 24.95x (ISBN 0-88946-970-9). E Mellen.
Countryside Press Editors, ed. The Psalms Around Us. (Illus.). 96p. 1974. deluxe ed. 9.95 (ISBN 0-385-01087-7). Doubleday.
Counts, George S. Dare the School Build a New Social Order? LC 78-18895. (Arcturus Books Paperbacks). 64p. 1978. pap. 4.95 (ISBN 0-8093-0878-9). S Ill U Pr.
Counts, Robert, ed. Independent Living Rehabilitation for Severely Handicapped People: A Preliminary Appraisal. (An Institute Paper). 67p. 1978. pap. 3.50 (ISBN 0-87766-228-2, 22600). Urban Inst.
Count-van Manen, Gloria. Crime & Suicide in the Nation's Capital: Toward Macro-Historical Perspectives. LC 76-24347. (Praeger Special Studies). 1977. text ed. 25.95 (ISBN 0-275-56860-1). Praeger.
Coupe, W. A., ed. see Meyer, Conrad F.
Couper, A. D. The Geography of Sea Transport. 1972. text ed. 8.25x (ISBN 0-09-112850-1, Hutchinson U Lib). Humanities.
Coupland, R. T., ed. Grassland Ecosystems of the World. LC 77-83990. (International Biological Programme Ser.: No. 18). 1979. 75.00 (ISBN 0-521-21867-5). Cambridge U Pr.
Coupland, Reginald. Exploitation of East Africa, 1856-1890: The Slave Trade & the Scramble. LC 67-31335. 1968. 16.75x o.s.i. (ISBN 0-8101-0068-1). Northwestern U Pr.
Courakis, Anthony S., ed. Inflation, Depression & Economic Policy in the West. LC 79-55497. 1980. text ed. 32.50x (ISBN 0-06-491293-0). B&N.
Courant, R. Differential & Integral Calculus, 2 vols. Incl. Vol. 1. 630p. 1937. 26.95 (ISBN 0-471-17820-9); Vol. 2. 692p. 1936. 26.95 (ISBN 0-471-17853-5). Pub. by Wiley-Interscience). Wiley.
Courant, R. & Hilbert, D. Methods of Mathematical Physics, 2 Vols. Set. 60.50 (ISBN 0-471-17990-6, Pub. by Wiley-Interscience); Vol. 1, 1953. 31.95 (ISBN 0-470-17952-X); Vol. 2, 1962. 43.50 (ISBN 0-470-17985-6). Wiley.
Courant, Richard & John, Fritz. Introduction to Calculus & Analysis, 2 vols. LC 65-16403. 912p. 1975. Vol. 1. 33.95 (ISBN 0-470-17860-4); Vol. 2, 1974. 39.50 (ISBN 0-471-17862-4, Pub. by Wiley-Interscience). Wiley.
Courant, Richard & Robbins, Herbert. What Is Mathematics? An Elementary Approach to Ideas & Methods. (Illus.). 1979. pap. 8.95 (ISBN 0-19-502517-2, GB576, GB). Oxford U Pr.
Courcy, G. I. C. Paganini: The Genoese, 2 vols. LC 76-5892. (Music Reprint Series). 1977. Repr. of 1957 ed. lib. bdg. 57.50 (ISBN 0-306-70872-8). Da Capo.
Courjon, Jean, et al, eds. Clinical Applications of Evoked Potentials in Neurology. 1981. text ed. price not set (ISBN 0-89004-619-0). Raven.
Courlander, Harold. The Drum & the Hoe: Life & Lore of the Haitian People. (California Library Reprint Series: No. 31). (Illus.). 1973. 22.95x o.p. (ISBN 0-520-00273-3). U of Cal Pr.
--The Drum & the Hoe: Life & Lore of the Haitian People. (California Library Reprint Ser.: No. 31). (Illus.). 436p. 1981. Repr. of 1973 ed. 25.00x (ISBN 0-520-02364-1). U of Cal Pr.
--Negro Folk Music, U.S.A. LC 63-18019. 1963. 20.00x (ISBN 0-231-02365-0); pap. 7.50x (ISBN 0-231-08634-2). Columbia U Pr.
Cournand, Antoine De see De Cournand, Antoine.
Cournos, John, ed. American Short Stories of the Nineteenth Century. 1955. 11.50x (ISBN 0-460-00840-4, Evman); pap. 3.95 (ISBN 0-460-01840-X). Dutton.
Cournot, Antoine A. An Essay on the Foundations of Our Knowledge. Moore, M. H., tr. 1956. pap. 3.95 (ISBN 0-672-60400-0). Bobbs.
Couro, Ted & Langdon, Margaret. Let's Talk 'Iipay Aa: An Introduction to the Mesa Grande Diegueno Language. 1975. pap. 7.50 (ISBN 0-686-22652-6). Malki Mus Pr.
Couro, Teo. San Diego County Indians As Farmers & Wage Earners. pap. 1.00 (ISBN 0-686-69102-4). Acoma Bks.
Courrier, Kathleen & Munson, Richard, eds. Life After Eighty: Environmental Choices We Can Live with. LC 80-11783. 304p. 1980. pap. 6.95 (ISBN 0-931790-13-1). Brick Hse Pub.
Courrier, Kathleen, jt. ed. see Gunn, Anita.
Course, Edwin. The Railways of Southern England Secondary & Branch Lines. 1974. 22.50 o.p. (ISBN 0-7134-2835-X, Pub. by Batsford England). David & Charles.
--Railways Then & Now. 1979. 24.00 (ISBN 0-7134-0533-3, Pub. by Batsford England). David & Charles.
Coursen, H. R. After the War. (Illus.). 1980. 12.95 (ISBN 0-918606-06-3); pap. 7.95 (ISBN 0-918606-05-5). Heidelberg Graph.
Court, J., jt. auth. see Dierauf, E., Jr.
Court, John H. Pornography. Bockmuehl, Klaus, ed. LC 80-7668. (World Evangelical Fellowship Outreach & Identity Theological Monograph: No. 5). 96p. (Orig.). 1980. pap. 2.95 (ISBN 0-87784-494-1). Inter-Varsity.
Court, John M. Myth & History in Revelation: The Book of Revelation. LC 79-16586. 1980. 16.50 (ISBN 0-8042-0346-6). John Knox.
Court, Margaret & McGann. Court on Court: A Life in Tennis. LC 75-17650. (Illus.). 256p. 1975. 8.95 (ISBN 0-396-07210-0). Dodd.
Court, William H. British Economic History, Eighteen Seventy - Nineteen Fourteen. (Orig.). 1966. 53.95 (ISBN 0-521-04731-5); pap. 19.50x (ISBN 0-521-09362-7). Cambridge U Pr.
--Concise Economic History of Britain. pap. 11.95x (ISBN 0-521-09217-5). Cambridge U Pr.
Courtel, R., jt. auth. see Latanision, R. M.
Courtenay, Ashley. Let's Halt Awhile in Great Britain (Including Ireland) 1979. (Illus.). 1979. pap. 12.95 o.p. (ISBN 0-8038-4310-0). Hastings.
--Lets Halt Awhile in Great Britain 1981. (Illus.). 600p. (Orig.). 1981. pap. 13.95 (ISBN 0-8038-4338-0). Hastings.
Courtenay, Jan Baudouin de see Baudouin de Courtenay, Jan.
Courtenay, P. P. Plantation Agriculture. 2nd rev. ed. 250p. 1980. lib. bdg. 30.00x (ISBN 0-86531-090-4). Westview.
Courtenay, William J., ed. see Weinberg, Julius R.
Courteney, Sally, jt. auth. see Goeldner, C. R.
Courter, Gay. The Midwife. 512p. 1981. 13.95 (ISBN 0-395-29463-0). HM.
Courthion, Pierre. Georges Rouault. (Illus.). 1977. 35.00 (ISBN 0-8109-0459-4). Abrams.
--Manet. (Library of Great Painters Ser.). (Illus.). 1963. 35.00 (ISBN 0-8109-0260-5). Abrams.
--Seurat. LC 68-13066. (Library of Great Painters Ser.). (Illus.). 1968. 35.00 (ISBN 0-8109-0474-8). Abrams.
Courtial, Donald C., jt. auth. see Rantz, Marilyn.
Courtine, Robert. The Hundred Glories of French Cooking. 1973. 15.00 o.p. (ISBN 0-374-17357-5). FS&G.
Courtine, Robert J. Dictionnaire des fromages. 255p. (Fr.). 1972. pap. 8.50 (ISBN 2-03-075473-0, 3792). Larousse.
--Larousse des fromages. new ed. (Illus.). 253p. (Fr.). 1973. 38.95x (ISBN 2-03-019012-8). Larousse.
Courtiour, Roger, jt. auth. see Penrose, Barry.
Courtis, Stuart A. & Watters, Garnette. Courtis-Watters Illustrated Golden Dictionary for Young Readers. rev. ed. (Illus.). 672p. (gr. 2-4). 1972. 6.95 (ISBN 0-307-15544-7, Golden Pr); PLB 13.77 (ISBN 0-307-66544-5). Western Pub.
Courtiss, Eugene H., ed. Aesthetic Surgery: Trouble - How to Avoid It & How to Treat It. LC 78-4958. 1978. text ed. 42.50 (ISBN 0-8016-1060-5). Mosby.
Courtiss, Eugene H., jt. ed. see Goulian, Dicran.
Courtman-Davies, Mary. Your Deaf Child's Speech & Language. 1980. 14.95 (ISBN 0-370-30149-8, Pub. by Chatto Bodley Jonathan). Merrimack Bk Serv.
Courtney, Caroline. Abandoned for Love. 224p. (Orig.). 1981. pap. 1.75 (ISBN 0-446-94298-7). Warner Bks.
--Dangerous Engagement. 1980. lib. bdg. 12.95 (ISBN 0-8161-3094-9, Large Print Bks). G K Hall.
--Forbidden Love. 224p. 1980. pap. 1.75 (ISBN 0-446-94297-9). Warner Bks.
--The Fortunes of Love. 1980. pap. 1.75 (ISBN 0-446-94055-0). Warner Bks.
--The Fortunes of Love. 1981. lib. bdg. 12.95 (ISBN 0-8161-3138-4, Large Print Bks). G K Hall.
--Guardian of the Heart. (Large Print Bks.). 1980. lib. bdg. 11.95 (ISBN 0-8161-3095-7). G K Hall.
--Heart of Honor. 1980. pap. 1.75 (ISBN 0-446-94294-4). Warner Bks.
--Libertine in Love. 1980. pap. 1.75 (ISBN 0-446-94295-2). Warner Bks.
--Love Triumphant. 1980. pap. 1.75 (ISBN 0-446-94293-6). Warner Bks.
--Love's Masquerade. 1980. pap. 1.75 (ISBN 0-446-94292-8). Warner Bks.
--Tempestuous Affair. (Orig.). 1981. pap. 1.75 (ISBN 0-446-94608-7). Warner Bks.
Courtney, E. A Commentary on the Satires of Juvenal. 650p. 1981. text ed. 75.00x (ISBN 0-485-11190-X, Athlone Pr). Humanities.
Courtney, Elise & Celeste, Emily. How to Feenbd Music Easily for Good Times in Harmony. LC 80-51888. (Illus.). 317p. (Orig.). 1980. pap. 6.00 (ISBN 0-686-28899-8). Merk.
Courtney, Geoff. The Power Behind Aston Martin. (Illus.). 1979. 16.95 (ISBN 0-902280-58-9, Pub. by Oxford Ill Pr Ltd. England). Motorbooks Intl.
Courtney, R. G., ed. Energy Conservation in the Built Environment. 1978. text ed. 60.00x (ISBN 0-904406-28-8). Longman.
Courtney, Richard. The Dramatic Curriculum. 130p. 1980. text ed. 10.00x (ISBN 0-89676-061-8); pap. text ed. 6.95x (ISBN 0-89676-063-4). Drama Bk.
Courtney, Richard, jt. ed. see Schattner, Gertrud.
Courtney, Star L. Now Is Too Soon(a Mother's Prayers As Her Daughter Nears Marriage) 64p. 1974. 2.95 o.p. (ISBN 0-8007-0652-8). Revell.
Courtney, William P. Secrets of Our National Literature: Chapters in the History of the Anonymous & Pseudonymous Writings of Our Countrymen. LC 68-21761. 1968. Repr. of 1908 ed. 20.00 (ISBN 0-8103-3140-3). Gale.
Courville, Jacques, et al, eds. The Inferior Olivary Nucleus: Anatomy & Physiology. 407p. 1980. text ed. 49.00 (ISBN 0-89004-414-7). Raven.
Coury, F. F. A Practical Guide to Minicomputer Applications. LC 70-182820. (IEEE Press Selected Reprint Ser). 1972. pap. text ed. 10.50 (ISBN 0-471-18051-3, Pub. by Wiley-Interscience). Wiley.
Cousens, John. An Introduction to Woodland Ecology. (Ecology Ser). (Illus.). 155p. (gr. 1-6). 1974. pap. text ed. 6.00x (ISBN 0-05-002775-1). Longman.
Cousin, Jean. Etudes sur la Poesie Latine: Nature et Mission du Poete. Commager, Steele, ed. LC 77-70760. (Latin Poetry Ser.). 1979. Repr. of 1945 ed. lib. bdg. 28.00 (ISBN 0-8240-2965-8). Garland Pub.
Cousins, Albert N. & Nagpaul, Hans. Urban Life: The Sociology of Cities & Urban Society. LC 78-14427. 1979. text ed. 18.95 (ISBN 0-471-03026-0). Wiley.
Cousins, Frank W. Sundials: The Art & Science of Gnomonics. (Illus.). 248p. 1970. 22.50x o.p. (ISBN 0-87663-704-7, Pica Pr). Universe.
Cousins, M. F. Engineering Drawing from the Beginning. 1964. Vol. 1. 1964. 28.00 (ISBN 0-08-010839-3); pap. 11.25 (ISBN 0-08-010840-7). Pergamon.
Cousins, Margaret. Thomas Alva Edison. (Landmark Ser.: No. 110). (Illus.). (gr. 4-8). 1965. PLB 5.99 (ISBN 0-394-90410-9, BYR). Random.
Cousins, Michael J. & Bridenbaugh, Phillip O. Neural Blockade in Clinical Anesthesia & Management of Pain. (Illus.). 1188p. 1980. text ed. 95.00 (ISBN 0-397-50439-X). Lippincott.
Cousins, Norman. Anatomy of an Illness As Perceived by the Patient. 176p. 1981. pap. 4.95 (ISBN 0-553-01293-2). Bantam.
--The Human Option: An Autobiographical Notebook. (Illus.). 1981. 9.95 (ISBN 0-393-01430-4). Norton.
Cousoneau, Eric & Richardson, Peter R. Gold: The World Industry & Canadian Corporate Strategy. 192p. (Orig.). 1979. pap. text ed. 10.00x (ISBN 0-88757-013-5, Pub. by Ctr Resource Stud Canada). Renouf.
Cousse, Raymond. Death Sty: A Pig's Tale. LC 79-2349. Orig. Title: Strategie Pour Deux Jambons. 1980. 5.95 (ISBN 0-394-17573-5, E747, Ever). Grove.
Coussement, R., jt. ed. see Perez, A.
Cousteau, Jacques Y. & Diole, Philippe. Diving Companions: Sea Lion-Elephant Seal-Walrus. LC 73-20508. (The Undersea Discoveries of Jacques-Yves Cousteau). (Illus.). 1977. pap. 8.95 (ISBN 0-89104-078-1). A & W Pubs.
--Dolphins. LC 74-9481. (The Undersea Discoveries of Jacques-Yves Cousteau). (Illus.). 1977. pap. 8.95 (ISBN 0-89104-076-5). A & W Pubs.
Cousteau, Jacques-Yves. A Bill of Roghts for Future Generations. (Illus.). 33p. (Orig.). 1980. pap. 1.50 (ISBN 0-913098-31-0). Myrin Institute.

--The Cousteau Almanac of the Environment: An Inventory of Life on a Water Planet. 864p. 1981. 24.95 (ISBN 0-385-14875-5). Doubleday.
--Salmon, Beavers & Sea Otters. (Illus.). 1980. 19.95 o.p. (ISBN 0-8227-8031-3). Petersen Pub.
Cousteau, Jacques-Yves & Cousteau, Philippe. The Shark. (The Undersea Discoveries of Jacques-Yves Cousteau). (Illus.). 1978. pap. 8.95 (ISBN 0-89104-112-5). A & W Pubs.
Cousteau, Jacques-Yves & Cousteau Society Staff. The Cousteau Almanac of the Environment: An Inventory of Life on a Water Planet. LC 79-7862. (Illus.). 864p. 1981. pap. 12.95 (ISBN 0-385-14876-3, Dolp). Doubleday.
Cousteau, Jacques-Yves & Diole, Philippe. Diving Companions: Sea-Lion-Elephant Seal-Walrus. LC 73-20508. 304p. 1974. 12.95 o.p. (ISBN 0-385-00031-6). Doubleday.
--Diving for Sunken Treasure. LC 76-158349. 1972. 12.95 o.p. (ISBN 0-385-06894-8). Doubleday.
--Diving for Sunken Treasure. (The Underseas Discoveries of Jacques-Yves Cousteau). (Illus.). 1978. pap. 8.95 (ISBN 0-89104-110-9). A & W Pubs.
--Life & Death in a Coral Sea. 1971. 12.95 o.p. (ISBN 0-385-06893-X). Doubleday.
--Life & Death in a Coral Sea. LC 69-13003. (The Undersea Discoveries of Jacques-Yves Cousteau). (Illus.). 1978. pap. 8.95 (ISBN 0-89104-089-7). A & W Pubs.
--Octopus & Squid: The Soft Intelligence. (The Undersea Discoveries of Jacques-Yves Cousteau). (Illus.). 1978. pap. 8.95 (ISBN 0-89104-111-7). A & W Pubs.
--Three Adventures: Galapagos, Titcaca, the Blue Holes. LC 72-93396. (The Undersea Discoveries of Jacques-Yves Cousteau). (Illus.). 1978. pap. 8.95 (ISBN 0-89104-090-0). A & W Pubs.
--Three Adventures: Galapagos, Titicaca, the Blue Holes. LC 72-93396. 304p. 1973. 12.95 o.p. (ISBN 0-385-06921-9). Doubleday.
--The Whale: Mighty Monarch of the Sea. LC 71-180052. (The Undersea Discoveries of Jacques-Yves Cousteau). (Illus.). 1977. pap. 8.95 (ISBN 0-89104-077-3). A & W Pubs.
Cousteau, Jacques-Yves & Dugan, James. The Living Sea. (Illus.). 320p. 1975. pap. 1.95 (ISBN 0-685-52455-8, 24504-0-195). Ballantine.
Cousteau, Jacques-Yves & Dumas, Frederic. The Silent World. LC 52-5431. 1953. 15.00 o.s.i. (ISBN 0-06-010890-8, HarpT). Har-Row.
Cousteau, Philippe, jt. auth. see Cousteau, Jacques-Yves.
Cousteau, Pierre. Pegmes: The Renaissance & the Gods. Orgel, Stephen, ed. LC 78-68181. (Philosophy of Images Ser.). (Illus.). 1980. lib. bdg. 66.00 (ISBN 0-8240-3677-8). Garland Pub.
Cousteau Society Staff, jt. auth. see Cousteau, Jacques-Yves.
Coustillas, Pierre & Partridge, Colin, eds. Gissing: The Critical Heritage. (Critical Heritage Ser.). 1972. 40.00 (ISBN 0-7100-7367-4). Routledge & Kegan.
Cousy, Robert J. & Power, Frank, Jr. Basketball: Concepts & Techniques. 1970. 19.95 (ISBN 0-205-02749-0, 622749X). Allyn.
Coutarelli, Spiro A. Venture Capital in Europe. LC 76-2902. (Special Studies). 1977. text ed. 23.95 (ISBN 0-275-56680-3). Praeger.
Coutinho, Alfranio. Introduction to Literature in Brazil. Rabassa, Gregory, tr. LC 69-15569. 1969. 20.00x (ISBN 0-231-02993-4). Columbia U Pr.
Coutsouradis, D., et al, eds. High Temperature Alloys for Gas Turbines. (Illus.). 1978. text ed. 91.00x (ISBN 0-85334-815-4, Pub. by Applied Science). Burgess-Intl Ideas.
Coutts, K., et al. Industrial Pricing in the United Kingdom. LC 77-8976. (Applied Economics Monograph: No. 26). (Illus.). 1978. 31.50 (ISBN 0-521-21725-3). Cambridge U Pr.
Coutts-Smith, Kenneth. The Dream of Icarus. LC 74-104700. 1970. 5.95 o.s.i. (ISBN 0-8076-0533-6). Braziller.
Couzens, Gerald S. A Baseball Album. LC 79-25044. (Illus.). 256p. 1980. 14.00 (ISBN 0-690-01864-9). Lippincott & Crowell.
Couzens, Reginald C. Stories of the Months & Days. LC 70-124662. (Illus.). 1971. Repr. of 1923 ed. 22.00 (ISBN 0-8103-3013-X). Gale.
Couzens, Tim, ed. see Plaatje, Solomon T.
Coval, S. C., jt. ed. see Macintosh, J. J.
Covalt, Nila K. Bed Exercises for Convalescent Patients. 244p. 1968. pap. 19.75 photocopy ed. spiral (ISBN 0-398-00352-1). C C Thomas.
Covarrubias, Ana, tr. see Radlauer, Ed.
Cove, D. J. Genetics. LC 75-160089. (Illus.). 1972. 35.50 (ISBN 0-521-08255-2); pap. text ed. 10.95x (ISBN 0-521-09663-4). Cambridge U Pr.
Covell, Jon Carter & Yamada, Abbot S. Unraveling Zen's Red Thread: Ikkyu's Controversial Way. LC 80-81040. (Illus.). 341p. 1980. 18.50 (ISBN 0-930878-19-1). Hollym Intl.
Covelli, Pasquale. Borrowing Time: Growing up with Juvenile Diabetes. LC 79-7083. 1979. 9.95 (ISBN 0-690-01841-X, TYC-T). T Y Crowell.
Coveney, D., jt. auth. see Medlicott, W. N.
Coveney, J., ed. International Organization Documents for Translation from French. 93p. 1972. 16.00 (ISBN 0-08-016287-8); pap. 7.00 o.p. (ISBN 0-08-016286-X). Pergamon.
Coveney, James. Glossary of English & German Management Terms. 1977. pap. text ed. 6.00x (ISBN 0-582-55525-6). Longman.
Coveney, James & Amey, J. Glossary of Spanish & English Management Terms. 1978. pap. text ed. 6.00x (ISBN 0-582-55541-8). Longman.
Coveney, James & Moore, Shelia J., eds. Glossary of French & English Management Terms. 158p. 1972. pap. 6.00x (ISBN 0-582-55502-7). Longman.
Coventry, Camilla, tr. see Shestov, Lev.
Coventry, Francis. The History of Pompey the Little; or, the Life & Adventures of a Lap-Dog, 1751. Shugrue, Michael F., ed. (The Flowering of the Novel, 1740-1775 Ser: Vol. 32). 1974. lib. bdg. 50.00 (ISBN 0-8240-1131-7). Garland Pub.
Cover, Arthur B. Flash Gordon. (Orig.). pap. 2.50 (ISBN 0-515-05848-3). Jove Pubns.
Coverdale, John F. The Political Transformation of Spain After Franco. LC 78-19777. (Praeger Special Studies). 1979. 22.95 (ISBN 0-03-044326-1). Praeger.
Coverdale, M., tr. from Dutch. The Original & Sprynge of All Sectes & Orders by Whome, Wha or Where (Sic) They Beganne. LC 79-84127. (English Experience Ser.: No. 946). 140p. (Eng.). 1979. Repr. of 1537 ed. lib. bdg. 11.50 (ISBN 90-221-0946-1). Walter J Johnson.
Coverdale, Myles. A Confutacion of That Treatise Which One John Standish Made Agaynst the Protestacion of D. Barnes. LC 79-84096. (English Experience Ser.: No. 917). 212p. 1979. Repr. of 1541 ed. lib. bdg. 16.00 (ISBN 90-221-0917-8). Walter J Johnson.
Covert, Alice L. The Distant Drum. 256p. (YA) 1974. 5.95 (ISBN 0-685-49584-1, Avalon). Bouregy.
--The Glass House. 1972. 5.95 (ISBN 0-685-25147-0, Avalon). Bouregy.
Covert, Catherine L., jt. auth. see Christians, Clifford G.
Covey, Alma A. Reviewing Reference Books: An Evaluation of the Efectiveness of Selected Announcement, Review & Index Media in Their Coverage of Reference Books. LC 70-182831. 142p. 1972. lib. bdg. 10.00 (ISBN 0-8108-0456-5). Scarecrow.
Covey, Cyclone, ed. & tr. see De Vaca, Cabeza.
Covey, Richard B. The Marital Deduction & the Use of Formula Provisions. 2nd ed. 1978. with 1980 suppl. 17.50 (ISBN 0-672-83719-6, Bobbs-Merrill Law); 1980 suppl. 7.50 (ISBN 0-672-83718-8). Michie.
Covici, Pascal, Jr., ed. see Steinbeck, John.
Coville, Bruce & Coville, Katherine. The Foolish Giant. LC 77-18522. (I-Like-to-Read Bks). (Illus.). (gr. k-2). 1978. 6.89 (ISBN 0-397-31800-6). Lippincott.
Coville, Katherine, jt. auth. see Coville, Bruce.
Coville, Walter J., et al. Abnormal Psychology. (Orig.). 1960. pap. 3.95 (ISBN 0-06-460094-7, CO 94, COS). Har-Row.
Covina, Gina & Galana, Laurel, eds. Lesbian Reader. 1975. pap. 5.95 (ISBN 0-686-22379-9). Amazon Pr.
Covington, A. K., ed. Ion Selective Electrode Methodology, 2 vols. 1979. Vol. 2, 144p. 59.95 (ISBN 0-8493-5247-9); Vol. 2. 42.95 (ISBN 0-8493-5248-7). CRC Pr.
Covington, H. A. Rose of Honor. 207p. 1980. 8.95 (ISBN 0-8059-2735-2). Dorrance.
Covington, James W. The Billy Bowlegs War. (Illus.). Date not set. write for info (ISBN 0-913122-06-8). Mickler Hse. Postponed.
Covington, James W., ed. see Forbes, James G.
Covington, John P. Motorcycle Racer. LC 78-121950. 144p. (gr. 6-11). 1973. 5.95 o.p. (ISBN 0-385-02325-1). Doubleday.
Covino, Frank. Snowballing. (Orig.). 1975. pap. 1.50 o.p. (ISBN 0-685-54128-2, LB290DK, Leisure Bks). Nordon Pubns.
Covino, Willam A., jt. auth. see Weber, Loraine J.
Covino, William A. & Coda-Messerle, Margaret. GED Reading Skills Test Preparation Guide: High School Equivalency Examination. (Cliffs Test Preparation Ser.). 105p. (Orig.). (gr. 10 up). 1981. pap. 2.95 (ISBN 0-8220-2014-9). Cliffs.
Covino, William A., jt. auth. see Bobrow, Jerry.
Covino, William A., et al. Graduate Record Examination Aptitude Test Preparation Guide. (Cliffs Test Preparation Ser.). (Illus.). 267p. (Orig.). 1980. wkbk. 4.95 (ISBN 0-8220-2008-4). Cliffs.
--GRE (Graduate Record Examination) Date not set. pap. text ed. cancelled. Cliffs.
Covo, Jacqueline. The Blinking Eye: Ralph Waldo Ellison & His American, French, German & Italian Critics, 1952-1971; Bibliographic Essays & a Checklist. LC 74-13042. (Author Bibliographies Ser.: No. 18). 1974. 10.00 (ISBN 0-8108-0736-X). Scarecrow.
Cowan, Daniel A. Language & Negation: The Two-Level Structure That Prevents Paradox. LC 76-21954. 112p. 1980. pap. 6.00 (ISBN 0-915878-03-8). Joseph Pub Co.
Cowan, David. Introduction to Modern Literary Arabic. 1958. pap. 11.95x (ISBN 0-521-09240-X, 240). Cambridge U Pr.
Cowan, Elizabeth, jt. auth. see Cowan, Gregory.
Cowan, Gregory & Cowan, Elizabeth. Writing. LC 79-24989. 1980. text ed. 14.95 (ISBN 0-471-01559-8); tchr's manual (ISBN 0-471-07692-9); wkbk. 7.95 (ISBN 0-471-07691-0). Wiley.
Cowan, H. J., jt. auth. see Gero, John S.
Cowan, H. J., ed. Solar Energy Applications in the Design of Buildings. (Illus.). x, 325p. 1980. 50.00x (ISBN 0-85334-883-9). Burgess-Intl Ideas.
Cowan, Henry J. A Dictionary of Architectural Science. LC 73-15839. (Illus.). 300p. 1973. pap. 14.95 (ISBN 0-470-18070-6). Halsted Pr.
--The Master Builders: A History of Structural & Environmental Design from Ancient Egypt to the Nineteenth Century. LC 77-5125. 1977. 26.50 (ISBN 0-471-02740-5, Pub. by Wiley-Interscience). Wiley.
--Science & Building: Structural & Environmental Design in the Nineteenth & Twentieth Centuries. LC 77-7297. 1978. 30.00 (ISBN 0-471-02738-3, Pub. by Wiley-Interscience). Wiley.
--Structural System. (Illus.). 356p. 1981. price not set (ISBN 0-442-21714-5); pap. price not set (ISBN 0-442-21713-7). Van Nos Reinhold.
Cowan, Henry J. & Dixon, John. Building Science Laboratory Manual. (Illus.). 1978. text ed. 28.50x (ISBN 0-85334-747-6, Pub. by Applied Science). Burgess-Intl Ideas.
Cowan, J. L. Pleasure & Pain. LC 68-13019. 1968. 18.95 (ISBN 0-312-61705-4). St Martin.
Cowan, Kenneth. Implant & Transplant Surgery. 1972. pap. 6.75 (ISBN 0-7195-2249-8). Transatlantic.
Cowan, L. Gray. Cost of Learning: The Policies of Primary Education in Kenya. LC 71-106991. 1970. pap. 5.75x (ISBN 0-8077-1193-4). Tchrs Coll.
Cowan, Lore. Children of the Resistance. (YA) (gr. 7-9). 1971. pap. 1.25 (ISBN 0-671-29834-8). PB.
Cowan, Marvin W. Los Mormones: Sus Doctrinas Refutadas a la Luz De la Biblia. De La Fuente, Tomas, tr. from Eng. 1978. pap. 2.75 (ISBN 0-311-05763-2). Casa Bautista.
Cowan, Michael A., jt. auth. see Egan, Gerard.
Cowan, Peter. The Tins & Other Stories. (Paperback Prose Ser.). 124p. 1973. 7.25x o.s.i. (ISBN 0-7022-0824-8); pap. 3.50x o.s.i. (ISBN 0-7022-0823-X). U of Queensland Pr.
Cowan, Rex. Castaway & Wrecked. (Illus.). 1978. pap. 6.75 o.p. (ISBN 0-7156-1146-1, Pub. by Duckworth England). Biblio Dist.
Cowan, S. D., jt. auth. see Orr, William I.
Cowan, S. T. A Dictionary of Microbial Taxonmix Usage. 1968. 7.50 (ISBN 0-934454-28-0). Lubrecht & Cramer.
--A Dictionary of Microbial Taxonomy. Hill, L. R., ed. LC 77-85705. (Illus.). 1978. 42.50 (ISBN 0-521-21890-X). Cambridge U Pr.
Cowan, Stuart D., jt. auth. see Orr, William I.
Cowan, Susan, ed. We Don't Live in Snow Houses Now. (Illus.). 194p. (Inuktitut, Eng.). 1981. pap. 11.95 (ISBN 0-920234-00-3, 08912-6, Pub. by Canadian Artic Producers Ltd). U of Chicago Pr.
Cowan, W. M., et al, eds. Annual Review of Neuroscience, Vol. 4. (Illus.). 1981. 20.00 (ISBN 0-8243-2404-8). Annual Reviews.
Cowan, William M. Adding Room, Saving Energy--Upstairs, Downstairs, Sideways. (Illus.). 1979. 14.95 (ISBN 0-02-528540-8, Collier); pap. 7.95 (ISBN 0-02-000280-7, Collier). Macmillan.
Cowan, Z. Individual Liberty & the Law. 1977. 10.00 (ISBN 0-379-00597-2). Oceana.
Coward, Barry. The Stuart Age. (A History of England Ser.). (Illus.). 512p. 1980. text ed. 32.00 (ISBN 0-582-48279-8); pap. 18.95 (ISBN 0-582-48833-8). Longman.
Coward, Harold G. Bhartrhari. (World Authors Ser.: India: No. 403). 1976. lib. bdg. 12.50 (ISBN 0-8057-6243-4). Twayne.
Coward, Joan W. Kentucky in the New Republic: The Process of Constitution Making. LC 77-92920. (Illus.). 232p. 1979. 17.00x (ISBN 0-8131-1380-6). U Pr of Ky.
Coward, R. E. & Yelland, M., eds. The Interchange of Bibliographic Information in Machine Readable Form. 1975. 8.95 (ISBN 0-85365-338-0, Pub. by Lib Assn England). Oryx Pr.
Coward, Raymond T. & Smith, William M., eds. The Family in Rural Society. (Special Studies in Contemporary Social Issues). 280p. 1981. lib. bdg. 25.00x (ISBN 0-86531-121-8). Westview.
Coward, Rosalind & Ellis, John. Language & Materialism: Developments in Semiology & the Theory of the Subject. 1977. 15.00x (ISBN 0-7100-8620-2); pap. 7.95 (ISBN 0-7100-8627-X). Routledge & Kegan.
Cowart, Andrew T. & Brofoss, Karl E. Decisions, Politics & Change: A Study of Norwegian Urban Budgeting. 1979. pap. 15.00x (ISBN 82-00-01882-2, Dist. by Columbia U. Pr.). Universitet.
Cowart, David. Thomas Pynchon: The Art of Allusion. LC 79-20157. (Crosscurrents-Modern Critiques-New Ser.). 160p. 1980. 10.95 (ISBN 0-8093-0944-0). S Ill U Pr.
Cowart, David, ed. Twentieth-Century American Science Fiction Writers. (Dictionary of Literary Biography Ser.). 1981. 54.00 (ISBN 0-8103-0918-1, Bruccoli Clark). Gale.
Cowart, Jack. Roy Lichtenstein: 1970-1980. LC 80-28348. (Illus.). 192p. 1981. 35.00 (ISBN 0-933920-14-8); pap. 16.00 (ISBN 0-933920-15-6). Hudson Hills.
Cowasjee, Saros. Stories & Sketches. (Writers Workshop Greenbird Ser.). 85p. 1975. 11.00 (ISBN 0-88253-646-X); pap. text ed. 6.00 (ISBN 0-88253-645-1). Ind-US Inc.
Cowd, M. A. & Miller, P. J. Revision Chemistry. LC 79-41164. 1980. text ed. 8.95 (ISBN 0-408-10607-7). Butterworths.
Cowdray, Rosalind. Lord of Creation. (Harlequin Romances Ser.). 192p. (Orig.). 1981. pap. 1.25 (ISBN 0-373-02381-2, Pub. by Harlequin). PB.
Cowdry, E. V. Aging Better. (Illus.). 500p. 1972. pap. 19.75 spiral, photocopy ed. (ISBN 0-398-02263-1). C C Thomas.
Cowdry, E. V. & Seno, S. Nucleic Acid Metabolism, Cell Differentiation & Cancer Growth. 1968. 75.00 (ISBN 0-08-013252-9). Pergamon.
Cowell & Muller. Jaina Sutras. Muller, F. Max, ed. (Sacred Books of the East Ser.: Vols. 22 & 45). 15.00x ea.; Vol. 22. (ISBN 0-8426-1217-3); Vol. 45. (ISBN 0-8426-1218-1). Verry.
Cowell, Cyril. Your Book of Animal Drawing. (gr. 7 up). 7.50 (ISBN 0-571-05139-1). Transatlantic.
Cowell, D. W., jt. auth. see Blois, K. J.
Cowell, E. B., jt. ed. see Beynon, L. R.
Cowell, E. B., et al. Buddhist Mahayana Texts. Mueller, F. Max, ed. LC 68-9450. (Sacred Books of the East Ser). 1969. pap. 6.50 (ISBN 0-486-22093-1). Dover.
Cowell, F. A. Measuring Inequality: Techniques for the Social Sciences. LC 77-20851. 1978. 11.95 (ISBN 0-470-99349-9). Halsted Pr.
Cowell, Henry & Cowell, Sidney. Charles Ives & His Music. LC 54-10000. (Illus.). 1969. pap. 4.95 o.p. (ISBN 0-19-500780-8, GB). Oxford U Pr.
Cowell, Pattie. Women Poets in Pre-Revolutionary America, 1650-1775. LC 80-50492. (Illus.). 400p. 1981. 25.00x (ISBN 0-87875-192-0). Whitston Pub.
Cowell, Raymond. W. B. Yeats. LC 76-101771. (Literary Critiques Ser). (Illus., Orig.). 1970. PLB 4.95 o.p. (ISBN 0-668-02180-2). Arco.
Cowell, Raymond, ed. Critics on Wordsworth. (Readings in Literary Criticism). 1973. pap. text ed. 6.75x (ISBN 0-04-801015-4). Allen Unwin.
Cowell, Sidney, jt. auth. see Cowell, Henry.
Cowen, Emory L., et al. New Ways in School Mental Health: Early Detection & Prevention of School Maladaptation. LC 74-11815. 396p. 1975. 22.95 (ISBN 0-87705-214-X). Human Sci Pr.
Cowen, Eve. Catch the Sun. (Storytellers Ser.). (Illus.). 64p. (gr. 5 up). 1981. PLB 7.95 (ISBN 0-516-02261-X). Childrens.
--High Escape. (Sportellers Ser.). (Illus.). 64p. (gr. 5 up). 1981. PLB 7.95 (ISBN 0-516-02264-4). Childrens.
--Race to Win. (Sportellers Ser.). (Illus.). 64p. (gr. 5 up). 1981. PLB 7.95 (ISBN 0-516-02266-0). Childrens.
Cowen, Painton. Rose Windows. LC 78-23286. (Illus.). 1979. 22.50 (ISBN 0-87701-121-4, Prism Edition). Chronicle Bks.
Cowen, Roy C. Christian Dietrich Grabbe. (World Authors Ser.: Germany: No. 206). lib. bdg. 10.95 (ISBN 0-8057-2396-X). Twayne.
Cowgill, Joy. Wagon Train Nineteen Fifty-Eight. (Illus.). 78p. 1980. pap. 12.95 (ISBN 0-916552-21-7). Acoma Bks.
Cowherd, Raymond G. The Humanitarians & the Ten Hour Movement in England. (Kress Library of Business & Economics: No. 10). (Illus.). 1956. pap. 5.00x (ISBN 0-678-09905-7, Baker Lib). Kelley.

--Political Economists & the English Poor Laws: A Historical Study of the Influence of Classical Economics on the Formation of Social Welfare Policy. LC 76-8301. xvii, 300p. 1977. 16.95x (ISBN 0-8214-0233-1). Ohio U Pr.

Cowie, Alfred T., jt. ed. see Kon, S. K.

Cowie, Donald. Ireland: The Land & the People. LC 74-9279. (Illus.). 240p. 1976. 12.00 o.p. (ISBN 0-498-01499-1). A S Barnes.

Cowie, J. M. Polymers: Chemistry & Physics of Modern Materials. (Illus.). 1973. pap. text ed. 21.00x (ISBN 0-7002-0222-6). Intl Ideas.

Cowie, James B. & Roebuck, Julian B. An Ethnography of a Chiropractic Clinic: Definitions of a Deviant Situation. LC 75-2811. (Illus.). 1975. 14.95 (ISBN 0-02-906730-8). Free Pr.

Cowie, Leonard W. Sixteenth-Century Europe. (Illus.). 1977. pap. text ed. 10.95x (ISBN 0-05-002828-6). Longman.

Cowie, Peter. Eighty Years of Cinema. LC 75-5175. (Illus.). 1977. 17.50 o.p. (ISBN 0-498-01762-1). A S Barnes.

Cowie, Peter, ed. Fifty Major Film-Makers. LC 73-107. (Illus.). 384p. 1976. 20.00 o.p. (ISBN 0-498-01255-7). A S Barnes.

--International Film Guide, 1977. LC 64-1076. pap. 7.95 (ISBN 0-498-01907-1). A S Barnes.

--International Film Guide 1981. LC 64-1076. (Illus.). 512p. 1981. pap. 9.95 (ISBN 0-498-02530-6). A S Barnes.

Cowin, S. C., ed. Mechanics Applied to the Transport of Bulk Materials, Bk. No. G00146. LC 87-3754. (Applied Mechanics Division Ser.: Vol. 31). 140p. 1979. 20.00 o.p. (ISBN 0-686-62960-4). ASME.

Cowing, Sheila. Our Wild Wetlands. LC 80-17600. (Illus.). 96p. (gr. 4-6). 1980. PLB 7.79 (ISBN 0-671-33089-6). Messner.

Cowing, T. G. & Stevenson, R. E., eds. Productivity Measurement in Regulated Industries. (Economic Theory, Econometrics & Mathematical Economic Ser.). 1981. price not set (ISBN 0-12-194080-2). Acad Pr.

Cowle, Jerry. Discover the Trees. LC 76-51174. (Illus.). (gr. 5 up). 1977. 7.95 (ISBN 0-8069-3734-3); PLB 7.49 (ISBN 0-8069-3735-1). Sterling.

Cowles, Ginny. Nicholas. LC 74-11432. (Illus.). 40p. (ps-3). 1975. 6.95 (ISBN 0-395-28785-5, Clarion). HM.

Cowles, H. Robert. Opening the Old Testament. LC 80-65149. (Illus.). 158p. (Orig.). Date not set. pap. 4.50 (ISBN 0-87509-279-9). Chr Pubns.

Cowles, Julia. The Diaries of Julia Cowles. Mosely, ed. 1931. 24.50x (ISBN 0-685-89746-X). Elliots Bks.

Cowles, Kathleen. The Bugs Bunny Book. (Illus.). 24p. (ps-4). 1977. PLB 5.38 (ISBN 0-307-68913-1, Golden Pr). Western Pub.

--El Conejo de la Suerte. Sanchez, Rene, tr. Orig. Title: Bugs Bunny Book. (Illus.). 24p. (Span.). (ps-3). 1977. PLB 5.92 (ISBN 0-307-68813-5, Golden Pr). Western Pub.

--What Will I Be? (A Young Reader Ser.). (gr. k-3). 1979. PLB 5.00 (ISBN 0-307-60174-9, Golden Pr). Western Pub.

Cowles, Raymond B. Zulu Journal: Field Notes of a Naturalist in South Africa. 1959. 17.50x (ISBN 0-520-00274-1); pap. 1.95 (ISBN 0-520-00276-8, CAL73). U of Cal Pr.

Cowley. The Silent One. LC 80-21853. (Illus.). (gr. 4-6). 1981. 8.95 (ISBN 0-394-84761-X); PLB 7.99 (ISBN 0-394-94761-4). Knopf.

Cowley, F. G. The Monastic Order in South Wales, 1066-1349. (Studies in Welsh History: Vol. 1, History & Law Committee, Univ. of Wales). 1978. text ed. 40.00x (ISBN 0-685-04716-4). Verry.

Cowley, J. Health Education in Schools. 1981. text ed. 21.00 (ISBN 0-06-318178-9, Pub. by Har-Row England Ltd); pap. text ed. 11.90 (ISBN 0-06-318179-7). Har-Row.

Cowley, Joy. The Growing Season. LC 77-81785. 1978. 7.95 o.p. (ISBN 0-385-04449-6). Doubleday.

--The Secret Life of the Underwater Champ. LC 80-15651. (Capers Ser.). (Illus.). 128p. (gr. 5 up). 1981. pap. 4.99 (ISBN 0-686-67782-5); pap. 1.95 (ISBN 0-394-84563-3). Knopf.

Cowley, Malcolm. Many-Windowed House: Collected Essays on American Writers & American Writing. Piper, Henry D., ed. LC 74-112384. 297p. 1970. 14.95x (ISBN 0-8093-0444-9). S Ill U Pr.

--Many-Windowed House: Collected Essays on American Writers & American Writing. Piper, Henry D., ed. LC 72-11923. (Arcturus Books Paperbacks). 297p. 1973. pap. 6.95 (ISBN 0-8093-0626-3). S Ill U Pr.

--Think Back on Us. A Contemporary Chronicle of the 1930s. Piper, Henry D., ed. LC 67-10024. 416p. 1967. 19.95x (ISBN 0-8093-0232-2). S Ill U Pr.

--Think Back on Us. A Contemporary Chronicle of the 1930s: The Literary Record. Piper, Henry D., ed. LC 72-5606. (Arcturus Books Paperbacks). 210p. (Pt. 2 of the hardbound ed. of Think Back On Us). 1972. pap. 7.95 (ISBN 0-8093-0599-2). S Ill U Pr.

--Think Back on Us. A Contemporary Chronicle of the 1930s: The Social Record. Piper, Henry D., ed. LC 72-5606. (Arcturus Books Paperbacks). 213p. (Pt. 1 of the hardbound ed. of Think Back On Us). 1972. pap. 7.95 (ISBN 0-8093-0598-4). S Ill U Pr.

--The View from Eighty. 1981. lib. bdg. 9.95 (ISBN 0-8161-3156-2, Large-Print Bks). G K Hall.

Cowley, Malcolm, ed. After the Genteel Tradition: American Writers 1910-1930. rev. ed. LC 64-11608. (Crosscurrents-Modern Critiques Ser.). 220p. 1964. 11.95 (ISBN 0-8093-0118-0). S Ill U Pr.

Cowley, Malcolm, ed. see Whitman, Walt.

Cowley, R. Adams & Trump, Benjamin F. Pathophysiology of Shock, Anoxia & Ischemia. 600p. 1981. write for info. (2149-4). Williams & Wilkins.

Cowley, Robert. Nineteen-Eighteen: Gamble for Victory. (gr. 6 up). 1964. 7.95 (ISBN 0-02-724830-5). Macmillan.

Cowling, Elizabeth. The Cello. 1977. pap. 4.95 o.p. (ISBN 0-684-14784-X, ScribT). Scribner.

Cowling, Ellis B., jt. ed. see Horsfall, James G.

Cowling, K., et al. Resource Structure of Agriculture: An Economic Analysis. LC 70-114570. 1970. 23.00 (ISBN 0-08-015585-5). Pergamon.

Cowling, Keith, et al. Advertising & Economic Behaviour. 202p. 1975. text ed. 35.00x o.p. (ISBN 0-8419-5006-7). Holmes & Meier.

Cowling, M. The Impact of Hitler: British Politics & British Policy 1933-1940. LC 74-12968. (Studies in the History & Theory of Politics). 448p. 1975. 59.50 (ISBN 0-521-20582-4). Cambridge U Pr.

--Religion & Public Doctrine in Modern England. (Cambridge Studies in the History & Theory of Politics). 498p. 1981. 49.50 (ISBN 0-521-23289-9). Cambridge U Pr.

Cowling, T. G. Magnetohydrodynamics. LC 76-38002. (Monographs on Astronomical Subjects). 1977. 39.50x (ISBN 0-8448-1060-6). Crane-Russak Co.

Cowling, T. G., jt. auth. see Chapman, S.

Cowling, T. M. & Steeley, G. C. Sub-Regional Planning Studies: An Evaluation. LC 73-4476. 1973. text ed. 16.00 (ISBN 0-08-017019-6). Pergamon.

Cowman, Charles E. & Serrano, Antonio. Manantiales En el Desierto. 1980. pap. 3.50 (ISBN 0-311-40028-0, Edit Mundo). Casa Bautista.

Cowman, Mrs. Charles E. Mountain Trailways for Youth: Devotions for Young People. 1979. pap. 4.95 (ISBN 0-310-37641-6). Zondervan.

--Springs in the Valley. 1938. 5.95 o.p. (ISBN 0-310-22510-8, Pub. by Cowman). Zondervan.

--Springs in the Valley. 1977. large-print ed. 6.95 (ISBN 0-310-22517-5). Zondervan.

--Streams in the Desert, Vol. 2. large print ed. 384p. 1976. kivar bdg. 6.95 (ISBN 0-310-22537-X). Zondervan.

--Words of Comfort & Cheer. kivar bdg. o. p. 6.95 (ISBN 0-310-22550-7); pap. 4.95 (ISBN 0-310-22551-5). Zondervan.

Cowper, Denis A., ed. Public Utilities Law Anthology, 1980-1981, Vol. VI. LC 74-77644. (National Law Anthology Ser.). 1981. text ed. 59.95. Intl Lib.

Cowper, Richard. Profundis. 1980. pap. write for info. (ISBN 0-671-83502-5). PB.

Cowper, W. John Gilpin's Ride. (Peter Possum Paperbacks Ser). 1967. pap. 0.95 o.p. (ISBN 0-531-05125-0). Watts.

Cowsik, R., ed. see COSPAR, Twenty-Second Plenary Meeting, Bangalore, India, 1979.

Cox, Albert W. Sonar & Underwater Sound. LC 74-15547. (Illus.). 1975. 17.95 (ISBN 0-669-95935-9). Lexington Bks.

Cox, Allan, ed. Plate Tectonics & Geomagnetic Reversals. LC 73-4323. (Geology Ser.). (Illus.). 1973. text ed. 33.95x (ISBN 0-7167-0259-2); pap. text ed. 21.95x (ISBN 0-7167-0258-4). W H Freeman.

Cox, Alwyn see Milne, John.

Cox, Anthony & Groves, Philip. Design for Health. (Newnes-Butterworth Design Ser.). 1981. text ed. price not set (ISBN 0-408-00389-8, Newnes-Butterworth). Butterworth.

Cox, Archibald. The Role of the Supreme Court in American Government. 128p. 1976. 10.95x (ISBN 0-19-827411-4). Oxford U Pr.

--The Role of the Supreme Court in American Government. x1976 ed. LC 75-29958. 1977. pap. 2.95 (ISBN 0-19-519909-X, 482, GB). Oxford U Pr.

Cox, Arthur M. The Myths of National Security: The Peril of Secret Government. LC 75-5288. 256p. 1975. 9.95 o.p. (ISBN 0-8070-0496-0); pap. 4.50 (ISBN 0-8070-0497-9, BP538). Beacon Pr.

Cox, B., jt. auth. see Vale, J.

Cox, Barbara G., ed. see International Conference On Hyperbaric Medicine - 3rd - Durham - N. C. - 1965.

Cox, Barry, jt. auth. see Foster, R. W.

Cox, Barry C., et al. Biogeography: An Ecological & Evolutionary Approach. 3rd ed. LC 79-22636. 1980. pap. text ed. 19.95x (ISBN 0-470-26893-X). Halsted Pr.

Cox, Benjamin G., Jr. Care & Rehabilitation of the Stroke Patient. (Illus.). 100p. 1973. pap. 14.75 spiral (ISBN 0-398-02890-7). C C Thomas.

Cox, Beverly. Gourmet Minceur: A Week of Gourmet Diet Meals. LC 79-63111. (Illus., Orig.). 1977. pap. 7.95 (ISBN 0-8149-0783-0). Vanguard.

--Minceur Italienne: Slimming Gourmet Menus & Recipes. LC 79-63111. (Gourmet Minceur Ser.). (Illus.). 1979. 8.95 (ISBN 0-8149-0820-9). Vanguard.

Cox, Beverly & Benois, George. Cellulite: Defeat It Through Diet & Exercise. (Illus.). 192p. 1981. 12.50 (ISBN 0-8149-0845-4); pap. 9.95 (ISBN 0-8149-0846-2). Vanguard.

Cox, C. B. & Dyson, A. E., eds. The Twentieth-Century Mind: History, Ideas, & Literature in Britain, Vol. I: Nineteen Hundred to Nineteen Eighteen. 540p. 1972. pap. text ed. 6.95x (ISBN 0-19-281118-5). Oxford U Pr.

--The Twentieth-Century Mind: History, Ideas, & Literature in Britain, Vol. II: Nineteen Eighteen to Nineteen Forty-Five. 526p. 1972. pap. text ed. 16.75x (ISBN 0-19-212192-8). Oxford U Pr.

--The Twentieth Century Mind: History, Ideas, & Literature in Britain, Vol. III: Nineteen Forty-Five to Nineteen Sixty-Five. 522p. 1972. pap. text ed. 16.75x (ISBN 0-19-212193-6). Oxford U Pr.

Cox, C. B. & Hinchliffe, Arnold P., eds. T. S. Eliot: The Wasteland. (Casebook Ser.). 1970. 2.50 o.s.i. (ISBN 0-87695-040-3). Aurora Pubs.

Cox, C. B., ed. see Eliot, T. S.

Cox, C. B., et al. Biogeography: An Ecological & Evolutionary Approach. 2nd ed. LC 75-33270. 1976. text ed. 12.95 o.p. (ISBN 0-470-18131-1). Halsted Pr.

Cox, Charles, jt. auth. see Beck, John.

Cox, Clyde C. Evangelical Precepts of the Revelation. 1972. 4.95 (ISBN 0-87148-278-9). Pathway Pr.

Cox, D. R. Analysis of Binary Data. (Monographs on Applied Probability & Statistics). 142p. 1970. text ed. 14.50x o.p. (ISBN 0-412-15340-8, Pub. by Chapman & Hall). Methuen Inc.

--Analysis of Binary Data. (Moonographs on Applied Probability & Statistics). 1970. 10.95 o.p. (ISBN 0-470-18125-7). Halsted Pr.

Cox, Daniel J. & Daitzman, Reid J., eds. Exhibitionism Description, Assessment, & Treatment. 1980. lib. bdg. 32.50 (ISBN 0-8240-7033-X). Garland Pub.

Cox, David. Modern Psychology: The Teachings of Carl Gustav Jung. 1968. pap. 2.95 (ISBN 0-06-463231-8, EH 231, EH). Har-Row.

Cox, Dennis P. & Cox, Helen R. Geology: Principles & Concepts: a Programmed Text. (Illus.). 1974. pap. text ed. 12.25x o.p. (ISBN 0-7167-0262-2). W H Freeman.

Cox, Don R., jt. auth. see Anderson, W. Steve.

Cox, Don R., jt. auth. see Ralston, Melvin B.

Cox, Dorothy. Modern Upholstery. (Illus.). 152p. 1980. pap. 11.75x (ISBN 0-7135-1599-6, LTB). Soccer.

Cox, E. K. Where Is the Lord God of Elijah? pap. 2.95 o.p. (ISBN 0-686-12926-1). Schmul Pub Co.

Cox, Edwin. Changing Aims in Religious Education. (Students Library of Education Ser.). 1966. pap. text ed. 3.00x (ISBN 0-7100-4207-8). Humanities.

Cox, Edwin, jt. auth. see Boot, John C.

Cox, Edwin B., et al. The Bank Director's Handbook. (Illus.). 200p. 1981. 19.95 (ISBN 0-86569-056-1). Auburn Hse.

Cox, Eli P., 3rd. Marketing Research: Information for Decision Making. 1979. text ed. 20.50 scp (ISBN 0-912212-14-4, HarpC); free instr. manual (ISBN 0-06-361361-1). Har-Row.

Cox, Eunice W., jt. auth. see Winters, Stanley A.

Cox, Frank D. Human Intimacy: Marriage, the Family & Its Meaning. 2nd ed. (Illus.). 475p. 1981. text ed. 13.56 (ISBN 0-8299-0367-4). West Pub.

--Human Intimacy: Marriage, the Family & Its Meaning. (Illus.). 1978. text ed. 16.95 (ISBN 0-8299-0152-3); instrs.' manual avail. (ISBN 0-8299-0473-5). West Pub.

Cox, Fred M., et al, eds. Community-Action, Planning, Development: A Casebook. 250p. 1974. pap. text ed. 8.50 (ISBN 0-87581-158-2). Peacock Pubs.

--Strategies of Community Organizations: A Book of Readings. 3rd ed. LC 77-83396. 1979. pap. text ed. 12.95 (ISBN 0-87581-230-9). Peacock Pubs.

Cox, G. M., jt. auth. see Cochran, W. G.

Cox, George D., tr. see Zola, Emile.

Cox, George W. Introduction to the Science of Comparative Mythology & Folklore. LC 68-20124. 1968. Repr. of 1883 ed. 18.00 (ISBN 0-8103-3425-9). Gale.

Cox, George W. & Atkins, Michael D. Agricultural Ecology: An Analysis of World Food Production Systems. LC 78-25745. (Illus.). 1979. text ed. 29.95x (ISBN 0-7167-1046-3). W H Freeman.

Cox, H. & Morgan, D. City Politics & the Press. LC 72-96678. (Illus.). 200p. 1973. 23.95 (ISBN 0-521-20162-4). Cambridge U Pr.

Cox, Halley & Stasack, Edward. Hawaiian Petroglyphs. LC 78-111491. (Special Publication Ser.: No. 60). (Illus.). 1977. 7.50 (ISBN 0-910240-09-4). Bishop Mus.

Cox, Helen. The Floral Art Book of Reference. LC 70-91462. 1970. text ed. 16.50 (ISBN 0-08-007100-7). Pergamon.

Cox, Helen R., jt. auth. see Cox, Dennis P.

Cox, Hyde, ed. see Frost, Robert.

Cox, J. D. & Pilcher, G. Thermochemistry of Organic & Organometallic Compounds. 1970. 90.50 o.s.i. (ISBN 0-12-194350-X). Acad Pr.

Cox, Jack, ed. see Davey, Gilbert.

Cox, James. Financial Information, Accounting & the Law: Cases & Materials. 1980. text ed. 20.00 (ISBN 0-316-15861-5). Little.

Cox, James A. A Century of Light. LC 78-19104. (Illus.). 1979. 17.50 (ISBN 0-87502-062-3). Larousse.

--Put Your Foot in Your Mouth & Other Silly Sayings. LC 80-12877. (Step-up Book: No. 31). (Illus.). 72p. (gr. 2-5). 1980. bds. 3.95 (ISBN 0-394-84503-X); PLB 3.99 (ISBN 0-394-94503-4). Random.

--Shells: Treasures from the Sea. LC 79-7520. (Illus.). 1979. 19.95 o.p. (ISBN 0-88332-118-1). Larousse.

Cox, James W. & Cox, Patricia P., eds. Twentieth Century Pulpit, Vol. II. 1981. pap. 8.95 (ISBN 0-687-42716-9). Abingdon.

Cox, Jan. Magnus Machina: The Great Machine. 1970. 7.95 (ISBN 0-87707-092-X); pap. 5.95 (ISBN 0-686-65960-0). Chan Shal Imi.

Cox, Jimmie, jt. auth. see Robinson, James.

Cox, John Harrington. Folk-Songs Mainly from West Virginia. Herzog, George & Halpert, Herbert, eds. LC 76-58548. (Music Reprint Series). 1977. Repr. of 1939 ed. lib. bdg. 22.50 (ISBN 0-306-70786-1). Da Capo.

Cox, John J., jt. auth. see Rubinstein, Mark.

Cox, K. G., et al. Interpretation of Igneous Rocks. 1979. text ed. 45.00x (ISBN 0-04-552015-1); pap. text ed. 22.95x (ISBN 0-04-552016-X). Allen Unwin.

Cox, Keith, jt. auth. see Kotler, Philip.

Cox, Keith K., jt. ed. see Enis, Ben M.

Cox, Keith M., jt. auth. see Enis, Ben M.

Cox, Kenneth E. & Williamson, Kenneth D., Jr., eds. Hydrogen: Its Technology & Implications, Vols. 2-5. Incl. Vol. 2. Transmission & Storage of Hydrogen. 144p. 1977. 44.95 (ISBN 0-8493-5122-7); Vol. 3. Hydrogen Properties. 336p. 1975. 67.95 (ISBN 0-8493-5123-5); Vol. 4. Utilization of Hydrogen. 256p. 1979. 59.95 (ISBN 0-8493-5124-3); Vol. 5. Implications of Hydrogen Energy. 144p. 1979. 44.95 (ISBN 0-8493-5125-1). LC 74-29484. (Uniscience Ser.). CRC Pr.

Cox, Klaudia, ed. see Hadden, Wilbur C.

Cox, Klaudia, ed. see Hing, Ester.

Cox, Klaudia, ed. see Hodgson, Thomas A.

Cox, Klaudia, ed. see Jack, Susan S. & Ries, Peter W.

Cox, Klaudia, ed. see Kozak, Lola J.

Cox, Klaudia, ed. see O'Brien, Richard J. & Drizd, Terence A.

Cox, Klaudia, ed. see Sirrocco, Al.

Cox, Klaudia, ed. see Weed, James A.

Cox, Klaudia, ed. see Zappolo, Aurora.

Cox, Louis A., Jr., jt. auth. see Murray, Charles A.

Cox, M. E. Practical Laundrywork. 147p. 1961. 11.50x (ISBN 0-85264-080-3, Pub. by Griffin England). State Mutual Bk.

Cox, M. V., ed. Are Young Children Egocentric? 1980. 20.00 (ISBN 0-312-04839-4). St Martin.

Cox, Margaret. The Challenge of Reading Failure. (Exploring Education Ser.). 1968. pap. text ed. 3.25x (ISBN 0-901225-16-9, NFER). Humanities.

--One School for All. (Exploring Education Ser.). 1969. pap. text ed. 2.50x (ISBN 0-901225-03-7, NFER). Humanities.

Cox, Martha H. see Heasley Cox, Martha & Chatterton, Wayne.

Cox, Michael & Crockett, Dresda. The Subversive Vegetarian. LC 80-635. (Illus.). 129p. (Orig.). 1980. pap. 3.95 (ISBN 0-912800-83-6). Woodbridge Pr.

Cox, Michael & Crockett, Desda. The Subversive Vegetarian. 128p. (Orig.). 1980. pap. 3.95 o.s.i. (ISBN 0-7225-0559-0). Newcastle Pub.

Cox, Millard. Derby: The Life & Times of the 12th Earl of. (Illus.). 31.50 (ISBN 0-85131-199-7, Dist. by Sporting Book Center). J A Allen.

Cox, Murray. Coding the Therapeutic Process: Emblems of Encounter. LC 77-30463. 1978. text ed. 18.00 (ISBN 0-08-021454-1); pap. text ed. 7.50 (ISBN 0-08-021453-3). Pergamon.
--Structuring the Therapeutic Process: Compromise with Chaos - a Therapist's Response to the Individual & the Group. LC 77-4181. 1978. text ed. 37.00 (ISBN 0-08-020403-1); pap. text ed. 12.50 (ISBN 0-08-020402-3). Pergamon.
Cox, P. Brownies. (Peter Possum Paperbacks Ser). 1967. pap. 0.95 o.p. (ISBN 0-531-05105-6). Watts.
Cox, Palmer. The Brownies at Home. LC 68-28403. (Illus.). (ps-3). 1968. pap. 2.00 o.p. (ISBN 0-486-21969-0). Dover.
Cox, Pat M. Deep Freezing. 2nd ed. (Illus.). 1979. 32.00 o.p. (ISBN 0-571-04954-0, Pub. by Faber & Faber). Merrimack Bk Serv.
Cox, Patricia P., jt. ed. see Cox, James W.
Cox, Peter. Dwarf Rhododendrons. (Illus.). 288p. 1973. 14.95 (ISBN 0-02-528560-2). Macmillan.
--The Larger Species of Rhododendron. (Illus.). 352p. 1980. 49.95 (ISBN 0-7134-1747-1, Pub. by Batsford England). David & Charles.
Cox, Peter R., ed. Demography. 5th ed. LC 70-92245. (Illus.). 1976. 49.50 (ISBN 0-521-21003-8); pap. 15.95x (ISBN 0-521-29020-1). Cambridge U Pr.
Cox, Peter R., et al, eds. see Eugenics Society Annual Symposium, 11th, London, 1973.
Cox, R., jt. auth. see Johnson, R.
Cox, R. A. & Hadjiolov, A. A., eds. Functional Units in Protien Biosynthesis. 1972. 57.50 (ISBN 0-12-194550-2). Acad Pr.
Cox, R. H., jt. auth. see Leyden, D. E.
Cox, R. Merritt. Eighteenth Century Spanish Literature. (World Authors Ser.: No. 526). 1979. lib. bdg. 10.95 (ISBN 0-8057-6367-8). Twayne.
--Juan Melendez Valdez. (World Authors Ser.: Spain: No. 302). 1974. lib. bdg. 10.95 (ISBN 0-8057-2918-6). Twayne.
--Tomas de Iriarte. (World Authors Ser.: Spain: No. 228). lib. bdg. 10.95 (ISBN 0-8057-2456-7). Twayne.
Cox, Richard G. Singer's Manual of German & French Diction. 1970. pap. text ed. 6.95 (ISBN 0-02-870650-1). Schirmer Bks.
Cox, Richard H. & Ezua, Truman G. Regressive Therapy: Therapeutic Regression in Schizophrenic Children, Adolescents & Young Adults. LC 73-84135. 1974. 10.00 o.p. (ISBN 0-87630-081-6). Brunner-Mazel.
Cox, Richard H., ed. Religious Systems & Psychotherapy. 520p. 1973. text ed. 29.75 (ISBN 0-398-02753-6). C C Thomas.
Cox, Richard H., jt. ed. see Cole, Richard J.
Cox, Robert G., jt. auth. see Wixon, Rufus.
Cox, S. W. & Filby, D. E. Instrumentation in Agriculture. 1972. 13.75 o.s.i. (ISBN 0-02-843290-8). Hafner.
Cox, Sidney. Indirections for Those Who Want to Write. 1981. pap. 8.95 (ISBN 0-87923-389-3). Godine.
--A Swinger of Birches: A Portrait of Robert Frost. LC 54-6902. 1957. 12.00x (ISBN 0-8147-0105-1). NYU Pr.
Cox, Stafford G., et al. Wellness R. S. V. P. Your Personal Invitation. 1980. pap. 3.95 (ISBN 0-8053-2304-X, 800100). Benjamin Cummings.
Cox, Stephen D. The Stranger Within Thee: Concepts of the Self in Late-Eighteenth-Century Literature. LC 80-5252. (Illus.). 195p. 1980. 14.95x (ISBN 0-8229-3424-8). U of Pittsburgh Pr.
Cox, Steven R., jt. ed. see Brandis, Royall.
Cox, Vivian, tr. see De Montherlant, Henry.
Cox, Warren, jt. auth. see Sullivan, George E.
Cox, William. Amillenialism Today. 1972. pap. 2.75 (ISBN 0-87552-151-7). Presby & Reformed.
Cox, William E. Biblical Studies in Final Things. 1967. 3.95 (ISBN 0-87552-152-5). Presby & Reformed.
Cox, William R. Battery Mates. LC 77-16871. (gr. 5 up). 1978. 5.95 (ISBN 0-396-07525-8). Dodd.
--Game, Set, & Match. LC 76-13140. (gr. 5 up). 1977. 5.95 (ISBN 0-396-07400-6). Dodd.
Cox, Winston B. Socialism & Social Change in the Seventies: A Reader. 1978. pap. text ed. 16.00 (ISBN 0-8191-0375-6). U Pr of Amer.
Coxe, Brinton. An Essay on Judicial Power & Unconstitutional Legislation. LC 79-99476. 1970. Repr. of 1893 ed. 39.50 (ISBN 0-306-71853-7). Da Capo.
Coxe, George H. Murder with Pictures. LC 80-8410. 288p. 1981. pap. 2.25 (ISBN 0-06-080527-7, P 527, PL). Har-Row.
Coxe, Louis. Enabling Acts: Selected Essays in Criticism. LC 76-4485. 1976. 11.00x (ISBN 0-8262-0200-4). U of Mo Pr.
Coxe, Weld. Managing Architectural & Engineering Practice. LC 80-17196. 192p. 1980. 18.95 (ISBN 0-471-08203-1, Pub. by Wiley-Interscience). Wiley.
Coxe, William. Anecdotes of Frederick Handel & John Christopher Smith. (Music Reprint Ser.). 1979. Repr. of 1799 ed. 22.50 (ISBN 0-306-79512-4). Da Capo.
Coxeter, H. S. Introduction to Geometry. 2nd ed. LC 72-93909. 1969. 27.95 (ISBN 0-471-18283-4). Wiley.
--Regular Polytopes. (Illus.). 321p. 1973. pap. 5.50 (ISBN 0-486-61480-8). Dover.
Coxeter, H. S. & Moser, W. O. Generators & Relations for Discrete Groups. 3rd rev. ed. LC 72-79063. (Ergebnisse der Mathematik und Ihrer Grenzgebiete: Vol. 14). (Illus.). 174p. 1972. 17.80 o.p. (ISBN 0-387-05837-0). Springer-Verlag.
Coxeter, H. S., jt. auth. see Ball, Walter W.
Coxhead, Elizabeth. Daughters of Erin. (Orig.). pap. text ed. 7.25x (ISBN 0-901072-60-5). Humanities.
--Lady Gregory: A Literary Portrait. rev. ed. 1976. Repr. of 1961 ed. text ed. 4.75x (ISBN 0-900675-74-8). Humanities.
Coxhead, Nona. The Richest Girl in the World. 1979. pap. 2.50 o.s.i. (ISBN 0-515-05080-6). Jove Pubns.
Coxon, Anthony P. & Jones, Charles L. Class & Hierarchy: The Social Meaning of Occupations. (Illus.). 1979. 21.95 (ISBN 0-312-14256-0). St Martin.
Coxon, Dewayne. Practical Solar Heating Manual Wih Blueprints: For Air & Water Systems. 150p. 1981. text ed. 19.95 (ISBN 0-250-40446-X). Ann Arbor Science.
Coxon, Howard. Australian Official Publications. LC 80-40046. (Guides to Official Publications Ser.: Vol. 5). (Illus.). 227p. 1980. 36.00 (ISBN 0-08-023131-4). Pergamon.
Coxon, J. M. & Halton, B. Organic Photochemistry. LC 73-82447. (Chemistry Texts Ser). (Illus.). 270p. 1974. 35.50 (ISBN 0-521-20322-8); pap. 13.95x (ISBN 0-521-09824-6). Cambridge U Pr.
Cox-Rearick, Janet. The Drawings of Pontormo, 2 vols. rev. ed. LC 79-93167. (Illus.). 880p. 1980. Repr. of 1964 ed. Set. lib. bdg. 90.00 (ISBN 0-87817-272-6). Hacker.
Coy, Genevieve. Counsels of Perfection: A Baha'i Guide to Mature Living. 1979. 7.50 (ISBN 0-85398-079-9, 7-32-33, Pub. by G Ronald England); pap. 2.50 (ISBN 0-85398-080-2, 7-32-34, Pub. by G Ronald England). Baha'i.
Coy, Harold. First Book of Hospitals. LC 74-3075. (First Bks). (Illus.). (gr. 4-6). 1964. PLB 4.90 o.p. (ISBN 0-531-00550-X). Watts.
--First Book of Presidents. rev. ed. LC 66-10157. (First Bks). (Illus.). (gr. 4-6). 1973. PLB 6.45 (ISBN 0-531-00615-8); pap. 1.25 (ISBN 0-531-02316-8). Watts.
--First Book of the Supreme Court. (First Bks). (Illus.). (gr. 7 up). 1958. PLB 4.90 o.p. (ISBN 0-531-00648-4). Watts.
--Presidents. (First Bks.). (Illus.). (gr. 4-6). 1977. PLB 6.45 s&l (ISBN 0-531-02906-9). Watts.
Coy, Kendrick. Multi-Sensory Educational Aids from Scrap. (Illus.). 232p. 1980. text ed. 19.50 spiral bdg. (ISBN 0-398-03934-8). C C Thomas.
Coy, Owen C. California County Boundaries. rev. ed. (Illus.). 1973. Repr. 9.95 (ISBN 0-913548-14-6, Valley Calif). Western Tanager.
Coy, Walter T. My Uncle Sam Don't Like Me. LC 79-56105. 1980. 8.95 (ISBN 0-533-04513-4). Vantage.
Coykendall, Ralf. Duck Decoys & How to Rig Them. (Illus.). 1965. 7.95 o.p. (ISBN 0-03-026910-5). HR&W.
Coykendall, Ralph W., Jr. You & Your Retriever. LC 63-7707. 1963. 5.95 o.p. (ISBN 0-385-02892-X). Doubleday.
Coyle, E. Wallace, jt. auth. see Fowler, William.
Coyle, John J. & Bardi, Edward. The Management of Business Logistics. 2nd ed. 500p. 1980. text ed. 17.95 (ISBN 0-8299-0325-9); instrs.' manual avail. (ISBN 0-8299-0472-7). West Pub.
Coyle, Neva. Living Free. 160p. 1981. pap. 3.95 (ISBN 0-87123-346-0, 210346). Bethany Fell.
Coyle, Terence, jt. auth. see Hale, Robert B.
Coyle, William. Research Papers. 5th ed. LC 79-14110. 1980. pap. 5.95 (ISBN 0-672-61500-2). Bobbs.
Coyle, William, ed. Young Man in American Literature: The Initiation Theme. LC 68-31707. (Perspectives on American Lit. Ser). (Orig.). 1969. pap. 7.95 (ISBN 0-672-63147-4). Odyssey Pr.
Coyne, John. The Searing. 1981. pap. 2.75 (ISBN 0-425-04924-8). Berkley Pub.
Coyne, John, ed. The New Golf for Women. LC 72-94173. 192p. 1973. 4.95 o.p. (ISBN 0-385-00849-X). Doubleday.
Coyne, John R., Jr. Fall in & Cheer. LC 78-7751. 1979. 8.95 o.p. (ISBN 0-385-11119-3). Doubleday.
Coyne, Thomas J., et al. Readings in Managerial Economics. rev. ed. 1977. pap. 9.95x (ISBN 0-256-01904-5). Business Pubns.
Coynik, David. Film: Real to Reel. rev. ed. (Illus., Orig.). 1976. pap. text ed. 10.95 scp (ISBN 0-06-382530-9, HarpC). Har-Row.
Coysh, Victor. Channel Islands: A New Study. 1977. 25.00 (ISBN 0-7153-7333-1). David & Charles.
Cozad, R. L., ed. The Speech Clinician & the Hearing-Impaired Child. (Illus.). 232p. 1974. 17.50 (ISBN 0-398-02983-0). C C Thomas.
Cozby, Paul C. Methods in Behavioral Research. 2nd ed. (Illus.). 300p. 1981. pap. text ed. price not set (ISBN 0-87484-521-1). Mayfield Pub.
Cozen, L. Office Orthopedics. 4th ed. (Illus.). 588p. 1975. 39.75 (ISBN 0-398-03068-5); pap. 29.75 (ISBN 0-398-03069-3). C C Thomas.
Cozen, Lewis. Difficult Orthopedic Diagnosis. (Illus.). 104p. 1972. text ed. 14.75 (ISBN 0-398-02212-7). C C Thomas.
Cozens & Goodslall. Dictionary of Archaeology. 3.75 o.p. (ISBN 0-685-28352-6). Philos Lib.
Cozens, W. H. King-Hunt in Chess. (Illus.). (gr. 9 up). 1971. 6.95 o.p. (ISBN 0-8069-4916-3); PLB 6.69 o.p. (ISBN 0-8069-4917-1). Sterling.
--Lessons in Chess Strategy. 1970. 2.95 o.p. (ISBN 0-87749-052-X). Sterling.
Cozzens, J. H., et al, eds. see International Conference, Kent State U., April 4-5, 1975.
Cozzens, James G. By Love Possessed. 1977. pap. 2.25 o.p. (ISBN 0-449-22954-8, Crest). Fawcett.
--Just Representation: A James Gould Cozzens Reader. Bruccoli, Matthew, ed. & intro. by. LC 78-9357. 1978. pap. 6.95 (ISBN 0-15-646611-2, Harv). HarBraceJ.
--Men & Brethren. LC 36-755. (Illus.). 1958. 4.00 o.p. (ISBN 0-15-159135-0). HarBraceJ.
Cozzolino, John M. Management of Oil & Gas Exploration Risk. LC 77-84169. (Business Risk Analysis Ser.). 1977. 47.50 (ISBN 0-9601408-1-6). Cozzolino Assocs.
Cozzolino, John M., jt. auth. see Gupta, Shiv K.
CPA Study Aids Inc. Bradley CPA Review Auditing. 9th ed. LC 77-93927. 1979. pap. 15.00 (ISBN 0-932788-00-9). Bradley CPA.
--Bradley CPA Review Law. 9th ed. LC 77-94481. 1979. pap. 15.00 (ISBN 0-932788-01-7). Bradley CPA.
--Bradley CPA Review Q & A Auditing. LC 79-83863. pap. 12.00 (ISBN 0-932788-07-6). Bradley CPA.
--Bradley CPA Review Summary of Apb Opinions & Fasb Statements. 12th ed. LC 78-54096. 1974. pap. 7.95 o.p. (ISBN 0-932788-05-X). Bradley CPA.
CPA Study Aids, Inc. CPA Review Summary of APB Opinions & FASB Statements. 13th ed. LC 79-55006. 1979. pap. 8.00 (ISBN 0-932788-12-2). Bradley CPA.
CPUSA. The People vs. Monopoly: Nineteen Eighty Draft Program of the Communist Part, USA. 62p. (Orig.). 1980. pap. 0.50 (ISBN 0-87898-142-X). New Outlook.
Crabb, George. Crabb's English Synonyms. 1966. Repr. of 1916 ed. 22.50 (ISBN 0-7100-1234-9). Routledge & Kegan.
Crabb, Lawrence J., Jr. & Crabb, Lawrence J., Sr. Adventures of Captain Al Scabbard, No. 1. 128p. (Orig.). (gr. 6-8). 1981. pap. 1.95 (ISBN 0-8024-0280-1). Moody.
--The Adventures of Captain Al Scabbard, No. 2. 128p. (Orig.). (gr. 6-8). 1981. pap. 1.95 (ISBN 0-8024-0281-X). Moody.
Crabb, M. C. ZZ-Two-Homotopy Theory. (London Mathematical Lecture Note Ser.: No. 44). 100p. (Orig.). 1980. pap. 15.95 (ISBN 0-521-28051-6). Cambridge U Pr.
Crabbe, George. Tales & Other Selected Poems. Mills, Howard W., ed. 1967. 58.00 (ISBN 0-521-04747-1); pap. 14.95x (ISBN 0-521-09420-8, 420). Cambridge U Pr.
Crabbe, John. Hi-Fi in the Home. (Illus.). 1971. 9.95 (ISBN 0-7137-0589-2). Transatlantic.
Crabbe, Katharyn F. J. R. R. Tolkien. LC 80-53699. (Modern Literature Ser.). 200p. 1981. 9.95 (ISBN 0-8044-2134-X); pap. 4.95 (ISBN 0-8044-6091-4). Ungar.
Crabill, Calvin, jt. auth. see Stein, Sherman.
Crabill, Calvin D., jt. auth. see Stein, Sherman K.
Crable, Richard E. One to Another: A Guidebook for Interpersonal Communication. (Illus.). 300p. 1980. pap. text ed. 12.50 scp (ISBN 0-06-041395-6, HarpC); avail. Har-Row.
Crabtree, Catherine G. A la San Francisco: Restaurant Recipes. (Illus.). 240p. (Orig.). 1980. pap. 6.50 (ISBN 0-937070-01-7). Crabtree.
--A'la Aspen: Restaurant Recipes. rev. ed. pap. 6.50 (ISBN 0-937070-05-X). Crabtree.
--A'la Vail: Restaurant Recipes. LC 80-67564. pap. 6.50 (ISBN 0-937070-03-3). Crabtree.
Crabtree, Derek & Thirlwall, A. P., eds. Keynes & the Bloomsbury Group. 1980. text ed. 30.00x (ISBN 0-8419-5066-0). Holmes & Meier.
Crabtree, Harold. Spinning Tops & Gyroscopic Motion. LC 66-23755. (Illus.). 1977. text ed. 9.95 (ISBN 0-8284-0204-3). Chelsea Pub.
Crabtree, J. Michael & Moyer, Kenneth E., eds. Bibliography of Aggressive Behavior: A Reader's Guide to the Research Literature. LC 77-12900. 442p. 1977. 41.00x (ISBN 0-8451-0200-1). A R Liss.
Crabtree, June. Effective Teaching: Basic Principles & Activities for Individualizing Instruction. rev. ed. 96p. (Orig.). 1981. pap. 5.95 (ISBN 0-87239-454-9, 3653). Standard Pub.
--Learning Center Ideas. (Ideas Ser). (Illus.). 1977. pap. text ed. 1.75 (ISBN 0-87239-120-5, 7960). Standard Pub.
--Teach 'em Like God Made 'em. LC 75-28681. (Illus.). 96p. 1976. pap. 5.50 (ISBN 0-87239-034-9, 3230). Standard Pub.
Crabtree, T. T. The Zondervan Pastor's Annual, 1981. 384p. 1980. kivar 7.95 (ISBN 0-310-22641-4). Zondervan.
Crabtree, Tom. Tom Crabtree on Teenagers. 160p. 1980. pap. 14.95 (ISBN 0-241-10398-3, Pub. by Hamish Hamilton England). David & Charles.
Crackanthorpe, Hubert. Collected Stories, 1893-1897, 4 Vols. in One. LC 74-75379. 1969. 75.00x (ISBN 0-8201-1056-6). Schol Facsimiles.
Cracknell, A. P. Applied Group Theory. 1968. 46.00 (ISBN 0-08-013328-2); pap. 12.75 (ISBN 0-08-012286-8). Pergamon.
--Magnetism in Crystalline Materials (Applications of the Groups of Cambiant Symmetry) 1975. text ed. 37.00 (ISBN 0-08-017935-5). Pergamon.
Cracknell, A. P. & Wong, K. C. Fermi Surface: Its Concept, Determination & Use in the Physics of Metals. (Monographs on the Physics & Chemistry of Materials). (Illus.). 558p. 1973. 65.00x (ISBN 0-19-851330-5). Oxford U Pr.
Cracknell, A. P., jt. auth. see Bradley, C. J.
Cracknell, Basil E. Portrait of London River: The Tidal Thames from Teddington to the Sea. LC 68-115971. (Portrait Bks.). (Illus.). 1968. 7.50x (ISBN 0-7091-0300-X). Intl Pubns Serv.
Cracraft, Joel & Eldredge, Niles, eds. Phylogenetic Analysis & Paleonology. LC 78-31404. (Illus.). 1979. 25.00x (ISBN 0-231-04692-8); pap. 10.00x (ISBN 0-231-04693-6). Columbia U Pr.
Craddock, C., ed. Virgil: Selection from Aeneid Two Handbook. (Cambridge Latin Text Ser.). 80p. 1976. pap. 6.95x (ISBN 0-521-20858-0). Cambridge U Pr.
--Virgil: Selections from Aeneid II. (Latin Texts Ser). 1975. pap. 2.95x (ISBN 0-521-20827-0). Cambridge U Pr.
Craddock, C. H., ed. Virgil Selections from Aeneid VIII. (Latin Texts Ser.). 48p. 1973. pap. 2.95x (ISBN 0-521-20280-9). Cambridge U Pr.
Craddock, Fred & Keck, Leander. Pentecost 3. LC 75-24971. (Proclamation 1: Aids for Interpreting the Lessons of the Church Year, Ser. B). 64p. 1975. pap. 1.95 (ISBN 0-8006-4078-0, 1-4078). Fortress.
Craddock, Fred B. The Gospels. LC 80-26270. 160p. (Orig.). 1981. pap. 6.95 (ISBN 0-687-15655-6). Abingdon.
--Overhearing the Gospel. LC 77-19106. 1978. 6.95 (ISBN 0-687-29938-1). Abingdon.
Craddock, Jerry R. Latin Legacy Versus Substratum Residue: The Unstressed Derivational Suffixes in the Romance Vernaculars of the Western Mediterranean. (U. C. Publ. in Linguistics: Vol. 53). 1969. pap. 8.50x (ISBN 0-520-09248-1). U of Cal Pr.
Craddock, Patricia B., ed. see Gibbon, Edward.
Cradock, Eveline. Musical Appreciation in an Infant School. (Illus.). 50p. (Orig.). 1977. pap. text ed. 6.75 (ISBN 0-19-321055-X). Oxford U Pr.
Cradock, Fanny. War Comes to Castle Rising. 1978. 9.95 o.p. (ISBN 0-525-23009-2). Dutton.
Cradock, S. & Hinchcliffe, A. J. Matrix Isolation. LC 74-31786. (Illus.). 140p. 1975. 29.95 (ISBN 0-521-20759-2). Cambridge U Pr.
Craemer, Willy De see De Craemer, Willy.
Craft, Ann, jt. auth. see Craft, Michael.
Craft, Benjamin C. & Hawkins, M. F. Applied Petroleum Reservoir Engineering. 1959. 31.95 (ISBN 0-13-041285-6). P-H.
Craft, Benjamin C., et al. Well Design: Drilling & Production. 1962. ref. ed. 31.95x (ISBN 0-13-950022-7). P-H.
Craft, Berniece. An Introduction to Legal Typing. LC 78-2421. 1978. pap. 8.55 (ISBN 0-672-97097-X); tchr's manual 3.33 (ISBN 0-672-97313-8). Bobbs.
Craft, Harvey M. Logic, Style, & Arrangement: Literature for Composition. 1971. pap. text ed. 7.95x (ISBN 0-02-474010-1, 47401). Macmillan.
Craft, J. L., jt. ed. see Whelan, A.
Craft, John L., et al. Child Welfare Forecasting: Context & Technique. (Illus.). 216p. 1980. 21.75 (ISBN 0-398-04045-1). C C Thomas.

Craft, M. & Miles, L. Patterns of Care for the Mentally Subnormal. 1967. 22.00 (ISBN 0-08-012265-5); pap. 10.75 (ISBN 0-08-012264-7). Pergamon.
Craft, M., ed. Psychopathic Disorders. 1966. 12.10 o.p. (ISBN 0-08-011618-3); pap. 6.05 o.p. (ISBN 0-08-011617-5). Pergamon.
Craft, Maurice, jt. ed. see Lytton, Hugh.
Craft, Michael & Craft, Ann. Sex & the Mentally Handicapped. 1978. 12.50x (ISBN 0-7100-8847-7). Routledge & Kegan.
Craft, Robert, jt. auth. see Stravinsky, Igor.
Crafts, Alden S. & Crisp, Carl E. Phloem Transport in Plants. LC 71-125130. (Biology Ser.). (Illus.). 1971. text ed. 31.95x (ISBN 0-7167-0683-0). W H Freeman.
Crafts, Alden S., jt. auth. see Ashton, Floyd M.
Crafts, Glenna C. How to Raise & Train a Norwegian Elkhound. (Orig.). pap. 2.00 (ISBN 0-87666-342-0, DS1101). TFH Pubns.
Crafts, R. C. & Binhammer, R. T. A Guide to Regional Dissection: Study of the Human Body. 4th ed. LC 79-14417. 324p. 13.50 (ISBN 0-471-05154-3). Wiley.
Crafts, Roger C. A Textbook of Human Anatomy. 2nd ed. LC 78-11424. 1979. 32.95 (ISBN 0-471-04454-7, Pub. by Wiley Medical). Wiley.
Cragan, John F. & Shields, Donald C. Applied Communication Research: A Dramatistic Approach. 432p. 1981. text ed. 17.95x (ISBN 0-917974-53-0). Waveland Pr.
Cragan, John F. & Wright, David W. Communications Small Group Discussions: A Case Study Approach. (Illus.). 400p. 1980. text ed. 12.95 (ISBN 0-8299-0338-0); instrs.' manual avail. (ISBN 0-8299-0474-3). West Pub.
--Introduction to Speech Communication. 400p. 1980. pap. text ed. 9.95x (ISBN 0-917974-45-X). Waveland Pr.
Cragg, J. B., ed. Advances in Ecological Research. Vol. 1 1963. 29.00 o.s.i. (ISBN 0-12-013901-4); Vol. 2 1965. 35.50 (ISBN 0-12-013902-2); Vol. 3 1966. 45.00 (ISBN 0-12-013903-0); Vol. 4 1967. 43.00 (ISBN 0-12-013904-9); Vol. 6 1969. 32.50 (ISBN 0-12-013906-5); Vol. 7 1971. 34.00 (ISBN 0-12-013907-3); Vol. 8 1974. 57.50 (ISBN 0-12-013908-1); Vol. 9 1975. 55.00 (ISBN 0-12-013909-X); Vol. 10, 1978. 24.50 (ISBN 0-12-013910-3). Acad Pr.
--Advances in Ecological Research, Vol. 11. 1981. 66.50 (ISBN 0-12-013911-1). Acad Pr.
Cragg, Kenneth. The Event of the Qur'an. 1971. text ed. 17.95x o.p. (ISBN 0-04-297024-5). Allen Unwin.
Craggs, J. D., jt. auth. see Meek, J. M.
Cragin, Valerie. Method Modeling. LC 80-81778. (Illus.). 160p. (Orig.). 1980. pap. 13.95 (ISBN 0-8227-4045-1). Petersen Pub.
--Photographic Modeling. LC 75-10066. (Photography How-to Ser.). 1977. pap. 4.50 (ISBN 0-8227-0102-2). Petersen Pub.
Cragin, Wesley E., jt. auth. see Beter, Thais R.
Cragoe, Elizabeth. Buttercups & Daisy. LC 76-62760. 1977. 7.95 o.p. (ISBN 0-312-11007-3). St Martin.
--Yorkshire Relish. 1979. 17.95 (ISBN 0-241-10054-2, Pub by Hamish Hamilton). David & Charles.
Craib, I. Existentialism in Sociology. LC 75-44579. 280p. 1976. 32.50 (ISBN 0-521-21047-X). Cambridge U Pr.
Craig, et al. Hearing Aids & You. 121p. (gr. 4 up). 3.95 (ISBN 0-86575-028-9). Dormac.
Craig, Albert M., jt. auth. see Reischauer, Edwin O.
Craig, Alisa. The Grub & Stakers Move a Mountain. LC 80-2074. (Crime Club Ser.). 192p. 1981. 9.95 (ISBN 0-385-17411-X). Doubleday.
--A Pint of Murder. LC 80-22948. 318p. 1980. Repr. of 1980 ed. large print ed. 9.95 (ISBN 0-89621-255-6). Thorndike Pr.
Craig, Bette & Kornbluh, Joyce. I Just Wanted Someone to Know. 1981. pap. price not set (ISBN 0-918266-16-5). Smyrna.
Craig, Betty, tr. see Machado, Antonio.
Craig, David. The Sandaled Foot. (Cleveland Poets Ser.: No. 27). 60p. (Orig.). 1980. pap. 3.50 (ISBN 0-914946-25-0). Cleveland St Univ Poetry Ctr.
Craig, Donald M., ed. see Garner, William R.
Craig, Dorothy. Hip Pocket Guide to Planning & Evaluation: Manual & Trainers Manual. LC 77-13388. 1978. pap. text ed. write for info. (ISBN 0-89384-024-6). Learning Concepts.
Craig, Edward G. Index to the Story of My Days. 320p. Date not set. price not set (ISBN 0-521-23609-6); pap. price not set (ISBN 0-521-28070-2). Cambridge U Pr.
Craig, G. Child Development. 1979. 18.95 (ISBN 0-13-131250-2); study guide & wkbk. 6.95 (ISBN 0-13-131268-5). P-H.
Craig, George. Mr. Mizzen's Rocket. (Illus.). (ps-5). 1968. 6.95 (ISBN 0-571-08669-1, Pub. by Faber & Faber). Merrimack Bk Serv.
Craig, Gordon. On the Art of the Theatre. (Illus.). 1925. pap. 5.95 (ISBN 0-87830-570-X). Theatre Arts.
Craig, Gordon A. Politics of the Prussian Army Sixteen Forty - Nineteen Forty-Five. 1964. pap. 7.95 (ISBN 0-19-500257-1, GB). Oxford U Pr.
Craig, Gordon A., ed. see Kehr, Eckart.
Craig, Grace J. Human Development. 2nd ed. (Illus.). 1980. text ed. 18.95 (ISBN 0-13-444984-3); study guide 6.95 (ISBN 0-13-445015-9). P-H.
Craig, Hardin. Interpretation of Shakespeare. 1966. Repr. text ed. 5.95x perfect bdg. (ISBN 0-87543-005-8). Lucas.
Craig, Hardin, ed. Literature of the English Renaissance, Vol. 2. rev. ed. (Orig.). 1962. pap. 0.95 o.s.i. (ISBN 0-02-050000-9, Collier). Macmillan.
Craig, Hardin, ed. see Poe, Edgar A.
Craig, Hazel T. Thresholds to Adult Living. rev. ed. (gr. 9-12). 1976. text ed. 18.60 (ISBN 0-87002-175-3); tchr's guide 6.64 (ISBN 0-87002-283-0). Bennett IL.
Craig, James. Designing with Type. Meyer, Susan E., ed. 1971. 15.95 o.p. (ISBN 0-8230-1320-0). Watson-Guptill.
--Designing with Type. rev. ed. Meyer, Susan, ed. (Illus.). 1980. 15.95 (ISBN 0-8230-1321-9). Watson-Guptill.
Craig, James H. & Craig, Marguerite. Synergic Power: Beyond Domination, Beyond Permissiveness. 2nd ed. LC 79-67184. (Illus.). 1979. pap. 4.95x (ISBN 0-914158-28-7). ProActive Pr.
Craig, James R. & Vaughan, David J. Ore Microscopy. 325p. 1981. 32.95 (ISBN 0-471-08596-0, Pub. by Wiley-Interscience). Wiley.
Craig, James R., jt. auth. see Vaughan, David J.
Craig, James V. Domestic Animal Behavior: Causes & Implications for Animal Care & Management. (Illus.). 400p. 1981. text ed. 19.95 (ISBN 0-13-218339-0). P-H.
Craig, John. All G.O.D.'s Children. LC 75-1256. 210p. 1975. 6.95 o.p. (ISBN 0-688-02913-2). Morrow.
--Chappie & Me. LC 79-664. 1979. 8.95 (ISBN 0-396-07660-2). Dodd.
Craig, Julia F., jt. auth. see McVicar, Marjorie.
Craig, M. Jean. Dinosaurs & More Dinosaurs. 2nd ed. LC 68-27276. (Illus.). 96p. (gr. 1-4). 1968. 9.95 (ISBN 0-590-07028-2, Four Winds). Schol Bk Serv.
--Questions & Answers About Weather. (gr. k-3). 1977. pap. 1.50 (ISBN 0-590-10414-4, Schol Pap). Schol Bk Serv.
Craig, M. Jean, rev. by. Puss in Boots. (gr. k-3). 1970. pap. 1.25 (ISBN 0-590-00395-X, Schol Pap); pap. 3.50 bk. & record (ISBN 0-590-04400-1). Schol Bk Serv.
Craig, M. Jean, ed. The Sand, the Sea, & Me. (Illus.). 32p. (gr. k-3). 1972. PLB 4.50 o.s.i. (ISBN 0-8027-6107-0); reinforced bdg. 4.41 o.s.i. (ISBN 0-8027-6108-9). Walker & Co.
Craig, Margaret M. It Could Happen to Anyone. (gr. 7-10). 1970. pap. 0.95 o.p. (ISBN 0-425-02988-3, S2591, Highland). Berkley Pub.
--Marsha. (gr. 7-10). pap. 0.95 o.p. (ISBN 0-425-03512-3, Highland). Berkley Pub.
--Trish. (gr. 7-10). pap. 0.95 o.p. (ISBN 0-425-03180-2, Highland). Berkley Pub.
Craig, Marguerite, jt. auth. see Craig, James H.
Craig, Marjorie. Miss Craig's Face-Saving Exercises. 1970. 7.95 (ISBN 0-394-42412-3). Random.
--Miss Craig's Growing-up Exercises. (Illus.). 1973. 7.95 o.p. (ISBN 0-394-48491-6). Random.
Craig, Mary. Were He a Stranger? LC 78-19073. 1978. 6.95 (ISBN 0-396-07590-8). Dodd.
Craig, Maurice. Dublin Sixteen Sixty - Eighteen Sixty. (Illus.). 1969. pap. 3.00 o.p. (ISBN 0-686-12064-7). Irish Bk Ctr.
Craig, Norman C., et al. Composition, Reaction, & Equilibrium: Experiments in Chemistry. LC 76-104966. 1970. pap. 11.95 (ISBN 0-201-01216-2); instructor's guide 2.50 (ISBN 0-201-01217-0). A-W.
Craig, Oman & Apley, John. Childhood Diabetes. 2nd ed. (Postgraduate Pediatric Ser.). 1981. text ed. price not set (ISBN 0-407-00209-X). Butterworth.
Craig, Paula M. Build Your Own Dreamhouse. (Illus.). 44p. (Orig.). 1974. pap. 1.25 o.p. (ISBN 0-87604-076-8). ARE Pr.
Craig, R., jt. auth. see Jarvis, R. C.
Craig, Robert C., et al. Contemporary Educational Psychology: Concepts, Issues & Applications. LC 74-13462. 558p. 1975. pap. text ed. 23.50 (ISBN 0-471-18351-2). Wiley.
Craig, Robert G. Restorative Dental Materials. 6th ed. LC 80-12105. (Illus.). 1980. pap. text ed. 23.95 (ISBN 0-8016-3866-6). Mosby.
Craig, Robert G., et al. Dental Materials: Properties & Manipulation. 2nd ed. LC 78-16677. (Illus.). 1979. pap. text ed. 12.95 (ISBN 0-8016-1072-9); wkbk. 6.95. Mosby.
Craig, Robert G., et al, eds. Dental Materials: A Problem Oriented Approach. LC 77-18734. (Illus.). 1978. text ed. 15.95 (ISBN 0-8016-1064-8). Mosby.
Craig, Ruth P. Diccionario de 201 Verbos Ingleses. LC 77-184894. 1972. pap. text ed. 7.95 (ISBN 0-8120-0417-5). Barron.
Craig, Susan, compiled by. Bible Quizzes for Everyone. (Fountain Bks). 96p. 1975. pap. 1.95 o.p. (ISBN 0-87239-039-X, 2294). Standard Pub.
Craig, Tom, jt. auth. see Shogan, Robert.
Craig, Warren. Great Songwriters of Hollywood. LC 79-87793. 256p. 1980. 14.95 (ISBN 0-498-02439-3). A S Barnes.
--Sweet & Lowdown: America's Popular Song Writers. LC 77-20223. 1978. 30.00 (ISBN 0-8108-1089-1). Scarecrow.
Craige, Betty Jean. Lorca's "Poet in New York". The Fall into Consciousness. LC 76-4339. (Studies in Romance Languages: No. 15). 112p. 1977. 10.50x (ISBN 0-8131-1349-0). U Pr of Ky.
Craiger-Smith, Alan. Tin-Glaze Pottery. 1973. 58.00 (ISBN 0-571-09349-3, Pub. by Faber & Faber). Merrimack Bk Serv.
Craighead, W. Edward, et al. Behavior Modification. 2nd ed. LC 80-83115. 576p. 1981. text ed. 18.50 (ISBN 0-395-29721-4). HM.
Craighill, Lloyd R., tr. see Hosono, Masanobu.
Craigie, J. S., jt. auth. see Hellebust, J. A.
Craigie, Pearl M. The School for Saints, Repr. Of 1897 Ed. Wolff, Robert L., ed. Bd. with Robert Orange. Repr. of 1900 ed. LC 75-463. (Victorian Fiction Ser.). 1975. lib. bdg. 66.00 (ISBN 0-8240-1541-X). Garland Pub.
Craigie, William A. Scandinavian Folk-Lore. LC 74-78129. 1970. Repr. of 1896 ed. 26.00 (ISBN 0-8103-3587-5). Gale.
Craigie, William A. & Hulbert, James R., eds. Dictionary of American English on Historical Principles, 4 Vols. LC 36-21500. 1938-1944. Set. 200.00 (ISBN 0-226-11741-3); 40.00 o.s.i.; Vol. 1. o.s.i. (ISBN 0-226-11737-5); Vol. 2. o.s.i. (ISBN 0-226-11738-3); Vol. 3. o.s.i. (ISBN 0-226-11739-1); Vol. 4. o.s.i. (ISBN 0-226-11740-5). U of Chicago Pr.
Craigie, Sir William. Dictionary of the Older Scottish Tongue, 4 vols. 29 pts. 1967. Vol. I A-C. 70.00x o.s.i. (ISBN 0-226-11674-3); Vol. II D-G. 60.00x o.s.i. (ISBN 0-226-11675-1); Vol. III H-L. 80.00x o.s.i. (ISBN 0-226-11677-8); Vol. IV M-N. 50.00x o.s.i. (ISBN 0-226-11678-6); Pts. 5-8, 26, 27-29. vols. I-IV 260.00 o.s.i. (ISBN 0-226-11679-4); Pts. 8-29. 16.00 ea. o.s.i. U of Chicago Pr.
Craik, Dinah M. Olive. Wolff, Robert L., ed. LC 75-1521. (Victorian Fiction Ser.). 1975. Repr. of 1850 ed. lib. bdg. 66.00 (ISBN 0-8240-1593-2). Garland Pub.
Craik, Kenneth J. Nature of Explanation. 1943. 19.95 (ISBN 0-521-04755-2); pap. 7.95 (ISBN 0-521-09445-3, 445). Cambridge U Pr.
Craik, T. W. Tudor Interlude. 1958. text ed. 9.75x (ISBN 0-7185-1014-3, Leicester). Humanities.
Crain Books Staff, ed. Advertising Yearbook. 1981. price not set (ISBN 0-87251-056-5). Crain Bks.
Crain, Cynthia D. Movement & Phythmic Activities for the Mentally Retarded. 1981. write for info. (ISBN 0-398-04174-1). C C Thomas.
Crain, Ernest, jt. auth. see Maxwell, William E.
Crain, Jim. Historic Country Inns of California. LC 77-727. 170p. 1980. pap. 5.95 (ISBN 0-87701-208-3). Chronicle Bks.
Crain, Robert L. Southern Schools: An Evaluation of the Emergency School Assistance Program (EASP) & of School Desegregation. (Report Ser: Nos. 124A-124B). 1973. Set. 10.00 (ISBN 0-932132-21-9). NORC.
Crain, Stanley M. Neurophysiologic Studies in Tissue Culture. LC 75-14567. 1976. 29.50 (ISBN 0-89004-048-6). Raven.
Crain, Steve. Bible Fun Book, No. 7. 32p. (Orig.). (gr. k-4). 1981. oversized saddle stitched .89 (ISBN 0-87123-766-0, 220766). Bethany Fell.
Crain, W. Mark. Vehicle Safety Inspection Systems: How Effective? 1980. pap. 4.25 (ISBN 0-8447-3361-X). Am Enterprise.
Crain, William C. Theories of Development: Concepts & Applications. (Illus.). 1980. text ed. 16.95 (ISBN 0-13-913566-9). P-H.
Crakes, Sylvester. Five Years a Captive Among the Black-feet Indians. LC 75-7099. (Indian Captivities Ser.: Vol. 74). 1976. Repr. of 1858 ed. lib. bdg. 44.00 (ISBN 0-8240-1698-X). Garland Pub.
Crall, William H. Poems of Love & War. 112p. 1979. 4.95 (ISBN 0-8059-2505-8). Dorrance.
Cram, Donald J., jt. auth. see Cram, Jane M.
Cram, Jane M. & Cram, Donald J. Essence of Organic Chemistry. LC 77-73957. (Chemistry Ser.). 1978. text ed. 18.95 (ISBN 0-201-01031-3); study guide 5.50 (ISBN 0-201-01032-1). A-W.
Cramblit, Joella & Loebel, JoAnn. Flowers Are for Keeping: How to Dry Flowers & Make Gifts & Decorations. LC 79-12892. (Illus.). 128p. (gr. 5 up). 1979. PLB 8.29 (ISBN 0-671-33007-1). Messner.
Cramblit, Joella, jt. auth. see Belton, John.
Cramer, C. H. Newton D. Baker: A Biography. Freidel, Frank, ed. LC 78-66521. (The History of the United States: Vol. 4). 316p. 1979. lib. bdg. 24.00 (ISBN 0-8240-9708-4). Garland Pub.
Cramer, Carl, ed. see Havighurst, Walter.
Cramer, Edith. Handbook of Early American Decoration. 7.50 o.p. (ISBN 0-8231-7007-1). Branford.
Cramer, Gail L. & Jensen, Clarence W. Agricultural Economics & Agribusiness: An Introduction. LC 78-11713. 1979. text ed. 23.95 (ISBN 0-471-04429-6); tchrs. manual avail. (ISBN 0-471-04430-X). Wiley.
Cramer, Harald. Random Variables & Probability Distribution. 3rd ed. (Cambridge Tracts in Mathematics & Mathematical Physics). 1970. 22.95 (ISBN 0-521-07685-4). Cambridge U Pr.
Cramer, James A., ed. Preventing Crime. LC 78-8400. (Sage Criminal Justice System Annuals: Vol. 10). 1978. 20.00x (ISBN 0-8039-1047-9); pap. 9.95x (ISBN 0-8039-1048-7). Sage.
Cramer, Raymond L. Psicologia de Jesus y la Salud Mental. Vargas, Carlos A., tr. from Eng. LC 76-16438. 191p. (Orig., Span.). 1976. pap. 3.25 (ISBN 0-89922-074-6). Edit Caribe.
Cramer, Stanley, jt. ed. see Hansen, James.
Cramer, Thomas, tr. & notes by see Hartmann von Ave.
Crammond, Joan. Zoo. (Illus.). 74p. (gr. 3-8). 1973. 5.95 (ISBN 0-7153-5660-7). David & Charles.
Cramp, Stanley, et al, eds. Handbook of the Birds of Europe, the Middle East & North Africa: The Birds of Western Palearctic, Vol. 2, Hawks to Buzzards. (Illus.). 704p. 1980. text ed. 85.00x (ISBN 0-19-857505-X). Oxford U Pr.
Crampton, E. W. & Harris, L. E. Applied Animal Nutrition: The Use of Feedstuffs in the Formulation of Livestock Rations. 2nd ed. LC 68-10996. (Animal Science Ser.). (Illus.). 1969. text ed. 26.95x (ISBN 0-7167-0814-0). W H Freeman.
Crampton, Gertrude. The Large & Growly Bear. (Illus.). 24p. (ps-4). 1961. PLB 5.00 (ISBN 0-307-60510-8, Golden Pr). Western Pub.
--Scuffy the Tugboat. (Illus.). 24p. (ps-2). 1973. 1.95 (ISBN 0-307-10490-7, Golden Pr); PLB 7.62 (ISBN 0-307-60490-X); 4.57 (ISBN 0-307-60633-3, Golden Pr). Western Pub.
--Tootle. (Illus.). 24p. (gr. k-1). 1976. PLB 5.38 (ISBN 0-307-68949-2, Golden Pr). Western Pub.
--Your Own Joke Book. (gr. 6-8). pap. 1.25 (ISBN 0-590-08125-X, Schol Pap). Schol Bk Serv.
Crampton, Helen. The Highland Coontess. (Orig.). 1981. pap. 1.95 (ISBN 0-671-83493-2). PB.
Crampton, Patricia, tr. see Bomans, Godfried.
Crampton, Patricia, tr. see Broger, Achim.
Crampton, Patricia, tr. see Koerner, Wolfgang.
Crampton, Patricia, tr. see Valencak, Hannelore.
Crampton, Richard. The Hollow Detente: Anglo-German Relations in the Balkans, 1911-1914. (Illus.). 250p. 1980. text ed. 18.75x (ISBN 0-391-02159-1). Humanities.
Cranch, Christopher P. Collected Poems, 1835-1892. DeFalco, Joseph, ed. LC 70-161930. 1971. 65.00x (ISBN 0-8201-1091-4). Schol Facsimiles.
Crandall, Dorothy & Ambuter, Jeanne. Mrs. Filbert's His & Her Cookbook. 7.95 (ISBN 0-916752-13-5). Green Hill.
Crandall, Hugh. Grand Teton: The Story Behind the Scenery. DenDooven, Gweneth R., ed. LC 78-57539. (Illus.). 1978. lib. bdg. 7.95 (ISBN 0-916122-47-6); pap. 3.00 (ISBN 0-916122-22-0). K C Pubns.
--Shenandoah: The Story Behind the Scenery. DenDooven, Gweneth R., ed. LC 74-30797. (Illus.). 1975. 7.95 (ISBN 0-916122-40-9); pap. 2.50 (ISBN 0-916122-15-8). K C Pubns.
--Yellowstone: The Story Behind the Scenery. DenDooven, Gweneth R., ed. LC 76-57453. (Illus.). 1977. 7.95 (ISBN 0-916122-46-8); pap. 3.00 (ISBN 0-916122-21-2). K C Pubns.
Crandall, Jo Ann. Adult Vocational ESL. (Language in Education Ser.: No. 22). 51p. 1979. pap. 5.95 (ISBN 0-87281-108-5). Ctr Appl Ling.
Crandall, Stephen H. & Mark, W. D. Random Vibration in Mechanical Systems. 1963. 25.00 o.s.i. (ISBN 0-12-196750-6). Acad Pr.
Crane, et al. An Introduction to Linguistics. 320p. (Orig.). 1981. pap. text ed. 11.95 (ISBN 0-316-16015-6). Little.
Crane, Arthur G. Education for the Disabled in War & Industry: Army Hospital Schools. (Columbia University. Teachers College. Contributions to Education: No. 110). Repr. of 1921 ed. 17.50 (ISBN 0-404-55110-6). AMS Pr.

Crane, Barbara. ES 1 Skillbooklet. (Crane Reading System - English Ser.). (Illus.). (gr. k-2). 1977. pap. text ed. 12.20 per 10 (ISBN 0-89075-037-8). Crane Pub Co.
--A Head Start Through Reading. (Crane Reading System-English Ser.). (Illus.). (gr. k-2). 1977. pap. text ed. 20.20 (ISBN 0-89075-135-8). Crane Pub Co.
Crane, Barbara J. Apple & the Ax. (Crane Reading System-English Ser.). (Illus.). (gr. k-2). 1977. pap. text ed. 2.95 (ISBN 0-89075-097-1). Crane Pub Co.
--AS One Skill Booklet. (Crane Reading System - English Ser.). (Illus.). (gr. k-2). 1977. pap. text ed. 12.20 per 10 (ISBN 0-89075-026-2). Crane Pub Co.
--AS Two Skill Booklet. (Crane Reading System - English Ser.). (Illus.). (gr. k-2). 1977. pap. text ed. 12.20 per 10 (ISBN 0-89075-028-9). Crane Pub Co.
--The Bee Book. (Crane Reading System-English Ser.). (Illus.). (gr. k-2). 1977. pap. text ed. 2.80 (ISBN 0-89075-094-7). Crane Pub Co.
--Crane Reading System, Practice Bks, A-J. Incl. Practice Book A (ISBN 0-89075-052-1); Practice Book B (ISBN 0-89075-054-8); Practice Book C (ISBN 0-89075-055-6); Practice Book D (ISBN 0-89075-056-4); Practice Book E (ISBN 0-89075-057-2); Practice Book F (ISBN 0-89075-058-0); Practice Book G (ISBN 0-89075-059-9); Practice Book H (ISBN 0-89075-060-2); Practice Book I (ISBN 0-89075-061-0); Practice Book J (ISBN 0-89075-062-9). (Illus.). (gr. k-2). 1977. pap. text ed. 2.55 ea. A-E; pap. 2.90 ea. F-J. Crane Pub Co.
--Crane Reading System in Spanish, Levels A-e. Wasser, Lyneil L. & Gallegos, Louisa M., eds. Lasarte, Francisco, tr. Incl. Level A. Libro De Lectura. 2.85 (ISBN 0-89075-163-3); Libro De Ejercicios. 2.60 (ISBN 0-89075-158-7); Level B. Libro De Lectura. 2.85 (ISBN 0-89075-164-1); Libro De Ejercicios. 2.60 (ISBN 0-89075-159-5); Level C. Libro De Lectura. 2.85 (ISBN 0-89075-166-8); Libro De Ejercicios. pap. 2.60 (ISBN 0-89075-160-9); Level D. Libro De Lectura. 2.85 (ISBN 0-89075-167-6); Libro De Ejercicios. 2.60 (ISBN 0-89075-161-7); Level E. Libro De Lectura. 2.85 (ISBN 0-89075-168-4); Libro De Ejercicios. pap. 2.60 (ISBN 0-89075-162-5). (Illus.). (gr. k-6). 1978. levels A-E guidebook to system 20.35 (ISBN 0-89075-169-2). Crane Pub Co.
--Crane Reading System in Spanish: Libros de trabajo, Levels A-E. Incl. Level A-1 (ISBN 0-89075-152-8); Level A-2 (ISBN 0-89075-153-6); Level B-1 (ISBN 0-89075-154-4); Level C-1 (ISBN 0-89075-155-2); Level D-1 (ISBN 0-89075-156-0); Level E-1 (ISBN 0-89075-157-9). (Illus.). (gr. k-2). 1978. per 10 12.40 (ISBN 0-686-67205-4). Crane Pub Co.
--CS 1 Skill Booklet. (Crane Reading System - English Ser.). (Illus.). (gr. k-2). 1977. pap. text ed. 12.20 per 10 (ISBN 0-89075-032-7). Crane Pub Co.
--DS 1 Skill booklet. (Crane Reading System - English Ser.). (Illus.). (gr. k-2). 1977. pap. text ed. 12.20 per 10 (ISBN 0-89075-034-3). Crane Pub Co.
--GS 1 Skill booklet. (Crane Reading System - English Ser.). (Illus.). (gr. k-2). 1977. pap. text ed. 12.20 per 10 (ISBN 0-89075-041-6). Crane Pub Co.
--I'm Late. (Crane Reading System-English Ser.). (Illus.). (gr. k-2). 1977. pap. text ed. 2.95 (ISBN 0-89075-099-8). Crane Pub Co.
--Me. (Crane Reading System-English Ser.). (gr. k-2). 1977. pap. text ed. 2.80 (ISBN 0-89075-092-0). Crane Pub Co.
--My New Friends. (Crane Reading System-English Ser.). (gr. k-2). 1977. pap. text ed. 2.95 (ISBN 0-89075-102-1). Crane Pub Co.
--Only for a Day. (Crane Reading System-English Ser.). (Illus.). (gr. k-2). 1977. pap. text ed. 2.95 (ISBN 0-89075-101-3). Crane Pub Co.
--Over the Top. (Crane Reading System - English Ser.). (Illus.). (gr. k-2). 1977. pap. text ed. 2.95 (ISBN 0-89075-100-5). Crane Pub Co.
--Playmates. (Crane Reading System-English Ser.). (Illus.). (gr. k-2). 1977. pap. text ed. 2.80 (ISBN 0-89075-096-3). Crane Pub Co.
--The Queen & I. (Crane Reading System-English Ser.). (Illus.). (gr. k-2). 1977. pap. text ed. 2.80 (ISBN 0-89075-093-9). Crane Pub Co.
Crane, Caroline. Coast of Fear. LC 80-26819. 224p. 1980. 8.95 (ISBN 0-396-07950-4). Dodd.
--The Girls Are Missing. LC 80-14784. 224p. 1980. 8.95 (ISBN 0-396-07877-X). Dodd.
--Summer Girl. 1981. pap. 2.50 (ISBN 0-451-09806-4, E9806, Signet Bks). NAL.
Crane, Dale. A&P Mechanics General Handbook Study Guide. (Aviation Maintenance Training Course Ser.). (Illus.). 172p. 1977. pap. text ed. 6.00 (ISBN 0-89100-072-0, EA-65-9ASG). Aviation Maintenance.
--A&P Mechanics Powerplant Handbook Study Guide. (Aviation Maintenance Training Course Ser.). 161p. 1978. pap. 6.00 (ISBN 0-89100-073-9, EA-65-12ASG). Aviation Maintenance.
--Aircraft Fabric Covering. (Aviation Maintenance Training Course Ser.). (Illus.). 54p. 1978. pap. 4.95 (ISBN 0-89100-077-1, EA-ADF). Aviation Maintenance.
--Aircraft Fuel Metering Systems. (Aviation Maintenance Training Course Ser.). (Illus.). 70p. 1975. pap. 5.95 (ISBN 0-89100-057-7, EA-FMS). Aviation Maintenance.
--Aviation Maintenance Handbook & Standard Hardware Digest. (Illus.). 1976. pap. 4.95 (ISBN 0-89100-060-7). Aviation Maint.
--So You Think You Know...? Quiz Book. (Aviation Training Ser.). (Illus.). 297p. 1980. pap. 6.95 (ISBN 0-89100-071-2, E*A-Q*B). Aviation Maintenance.
--Technical Instruction. 140p. 1980. pap. text ed. write for info. (ISBN 0-89100-183-2). Aviation Maintenance.
Crane, Dale & Carlson, Neal. Aircraft Painting & Finishing. (Aviation Maintenance Training Course Ser.). (Illus.). 67p. 1980. pap. 5.95 (ISBN 0-89100-152-2, E*A-A*P-2). Aviation Maintenance.
Crane, Dale, jt. ed. see Jones, David.
Crane, Dale, et al. Aircraft Technical Dictionary. 2nd ed. (Aviation Maintenance Training Course Ser.). Date not set. pap. price not set (ISBN 0-89100-124-7). Aviation Maintenance.
Crane, Dwight B., jt. auth. see Bradley, Stephen P.
Crane, Dwight D. & Riley, Michael J. NOW Accounts. LC 77-6580. 1978. 18.95 (ISBN 0-669-01612-8). Lexington Bks.
Crane, Edgar. Marketing Communications. 2nd ed. LC 72-4505. (Marketing Ser). 1972. 20.95 o.p. (ISBN 0-471-18401-2). Wiley.
Crane, Edgar G., et al. State Government Productivity: The Environment for Improvement. LC 76-11716. (Illus.). 1976. text ed. 22.95 o.p. (ISBN 0-275-56850-4). Praeger.
Crane, Edgar G., Jr. Legislative Review of Government Programs: Tools for Accountability. LC 76-12846. (Special Studies). 1977. text ed. 29.95 (ISBN 0-275-23720-6). Praeger.
Crane, Eva. Honey: A Comprehensive Survey. LC 74-14447. 1975. 52.50x (ISBN 0-8448-0062-7). Crane-Russak Co.
Crane, Frederick G. Insurance Principles & Practices. LC 79-19510. 1980. text ed. 20.95 (ISBN 0-471-01763-9); tcher's ed. avail. (ISBN 0-471-01768-X). Wiley.
Crane, Hart. Complete Poems & Selected Letters & Prose of Hart Crane. 1966. pap. 2.95 (ISBN 0-385-01531-3, A537, Anch). Doubleday.
Crane, Hewitt D. The New Social Marketplace: Notes on Effecting Social Change in America's Third Century. LC 80-11674. (Communication & Information Science Ser.). (Illus.). 112p. 1980. text ed. 14.95 (ISBN 0-89391-063-5). Ablex Pub.
Crane, Ila H. My First Prayer Book. LC 79-91677. 32p. (gr. k up). 1981. 5.95 (ISBN 0-89896-100-9). Larksdale.
Crane, J. D. El Espiritu Santo en la Experiencia del Cristiano. De Lerin, Olivia, tr. 1979. 3.50 (ISBN 0-311-09093-1). Casa Bautista.
Crane, John K. T. H. White. LC 74-4121. (English Authors Ser.: No. 172). 1974. lib. bdg. 10.95 (ISBN 0-8057-1573-8). Twayne.
Crane, Jules M. Introduction to Marine Biology (a Laboratory Text) LC 73-76466. 1973. pap. text ed. 11.95 (ISBN 0-675-08954-9); instructor's manual 3.95 (ISBN 0-686-66860-X). Merrill.
Crane, Louise. Ms. Africa: Profiles of Modern African Women. LC 72-11767. (gr. 7 up). 1973. 7.95 o.p. (ISBN 0-397-31446-9). Lippincott.
Crane, Lucy. Art & the Formation of Taste. LC 76-17755. (Aesthetic Movement Ser.: Vol. 9). (Illus.). 1977. Repr. of 1882 ed. lib. bdg. 44.00x (ISBN 0-8240-2458-3). Garland Pub.
Crane, Marjorie Boyer, ed. see Institute for Information Studies, et al.
Crane, P. W. Electronics for Technicians. 1971. pap. 9.00 o.p. (ISBN 0-08-016101-4). Pergamon.
--Worked Examples in Basic Electronics. 1967. 18.00 (ISBN 0-08-012217-5); pap. 7.00 (ISBN 0-08-012216-7). Pergamon.
Crane, Philip, jt. auth. see Bush, George.
Crane, Robert. Understanding Today's Economics. (Impact Ser.). (Illus.). (gr. 7 up). 1979. PLB 6.90 s&l (ISBN 0-531-02285-4). Watts.
Crane, Robert D. Planning the Future of Saudi Arabia: A Model for Achieving National Priorities. LC 78-5730. (Praeger Special Studies). 1978. 28.95 (ISBN 0-03-042276-0). Praeger.
Crane, Robert I., ed. Aspects of Political Mobilization in South Asia. LC 76-5434. (Foreign & Comparative Studies-South Asia Ser.: No. 1). 1976. pap. text ed. 4.50x (ISBN 0-915984-75-X). Syracuse U Foreign Comp.
Crane, Stephen. Great Short Works of Stephen Crane: Red Badge of Courage, Monster, Maggie, Open Boat, Blue Hotel, Bride Comes to Yellow Sky & Other Works. rev ed. Colvert, J., ed. pap. 2.50 (ISBN 0-06-083032-8, P3032, PL). Har-Row.
--Maggie, a Girl of the Streets: A Story of New York. LC 66-20867. 1978. Repr. of 1893 ed. 22.00 (ISBN 0-8201-1268-2). Schol Facsimiles.
--Poems of Stephen Crane. McDonald, Gerald D., ed. & compiled by. (Apollo Eds.). (Illus.). 1971. pap. 1.25 o.p. (ISBN 0-8152-0310-1, A310, TYC-T). T Y Crowell.
--The Portable Stephen Crane. Katz, Joseph, ed. (Portable Library: No. 68). 1969. 10.00 o.p. (ISBN 0-670-67041-3). Viking Pr.
--Red Badge of Courage. (Literature Ser). (gr. 7-12). 1969. pap. text ed. 3.42 (ISBN 0-87720-712-7). AMSCO Sch.
--Red Badge of Courage. Bradley, Van A., ed. LC 76-76032. (First Edition American Classics in Fascimile Ser., No. 1). 1969. 8.50 o.p. (ISBN 0-8303-0075-9). Fleet.
--Red Badge of Courage. (gr. 9 up). 1962. 3.95g o.s.i. (ISBN 0-02-724910-7). Macmillan.
--Red Badge of Courage. (Keith Jennison Large Type Bks). (gr. 6 up). PLB 7.95 o.p. (ISBN 0-531-00270-5). Watts.
--Red Badge of Courage. (gr. 7-12). 1972. pap. 1.25 (ISBN 0-590-02117-6, Schol Pap). Schol Bk Serv.
--The Red Badge of Courage. rev. ed. Dixson, Robert J., ed. (American Classics Ser.: Bk. 10). (gr. 9 up). 1974. pap. text ed. 2.75 (ISBN 0-88345-206-5); cassettes 40.00 (ISBN 0-685-38931-6, 18129); tapes 35.00 (ISBN 0-685-38932-4). Regents Pub.
--The Red Badge of Courage. (Childrens Illustrated Classics Ser). (Illus.). 1971. 9.00x o.p. (ISBN 0-460-05090-7, Pub. by J. M. Dent England). Biblio Dist.
--The Red Badge of Courage. LC 69-13318. (Merrill Standard Ser). 1975. 6.00 (ISBN 0-910294-29-1); pap. 4.00 (ISBN 0-910294-30-5). Brown Bk.
--Red Badge of Courage, with Reader's Guide. (AMSCO Literature Program). (gr. 9-12). 1971. pap. text ed. 4.17 (ISBN 0-87720-811-5); tchrs. ed. 2.70 (ISBN 0-87720-911-1). AMSCO Sch.
Crane, Theodore R. The Dimensions of American Education. 1974. pap. text ed. 8.50 (ISBN 0-201-01212-X). A-W.
Crane, Theodore R., ed. Colleges & the Public 1787-1862. LC 63-9583. (Orig.). 1963. text ed. 8.75 (ISBN 0-8077-1200-0); pap. text ed. 4.00x (ISBN 0-8077-1197-7). Tchrs Coll.
Crane, Thomas E. The Message of St. John: The Spiritual Teachings of the Beloved Disciple. LC 80-11779. 184p. (Orig.). 1980. pap. 5.95 (ISBN 0-8189-0402-X). Alba.
Crane, Thomas F. Italian Popular Tales. LC 68-21762. 1968. Repr. of 1885 ed. 20.00 (ISBN 0-8103-3462-3). Gale.
Crane, Verner W. The Southern Frontier 1670-1732. 1980. pap. 5.95 (ISBN 0-393-00948-3). Norton.
Crane, Walter. Artist's Reminiscences. LC 68-21763. (Illus.). 1968. Repr. of 1907 ed. 18.00 (ISBN 0-8103-3522-0). Gale.
--The Bases of Design. Stansky, Peter & Shewan, Rodney, eds. LC 76-17756. (Aesthetic Movement & the Arts & Crafts Movement Ser.: Vol. 10). 1977. Repr. of 1898 ed. lib. bdg. 44.00 (ISBN 0-8240-2459-1). Garland Pub.
--Ideals in Art. Stansky, Peter & Shewan, Rodney, eds. LC 76-17775. (Aesthetic Movement & the Arts & Crafts Movement Ser.). 1978. Repr. of 1905 ed. lib. bdg. 44.00x (ISBN 0-8240-2480-X). Garland Pub.
--Of the Decorative Illustration of Books Old & New. LC 68-30611. 1968. Repr. of 1905 ed. 24.00 (ISBN 0-8103-3299-X). Gale.
Crane, Walter, illus. The Baby's Opera. (Illus.). 56p. (gr. k up). 1981. 4.95 (ISBN 0-671-42551-X, Pub. by Windmill). S&S.
Crane, William. Oom-Pah. LC 80-18404. 204p. (gr. 5-9). 1981. PLB 9.95 (ISBN 0-689-30804-3). Atheneum.
Cranfield, C. E. Romans, Vol.i. (International Critical Commentary Ser.). 480p. Repr. of 1980 ed. text ed. 24.00x (ISBN 0-567-05040-8). Attic Pr.
--Romans, Vol. Ii. (International Critical Commentary Ser.). 448p. Repr. of 1979 ed. text ed. 28.50x (ISBN 0-567-05041-6). Attic Pr.
Cranfield Fluidics Conference, 1st. Proceedings. 1965. 24.00. BHRA Fluid.
Cranfield Fluidics Conference, 6th. Proceedings. 1974. 45.00. BHRA Fluid.
Cranfield Fluidics Conference, 7th. Proceedings. 1977. 58.00 (ISBN 0-900983-50-7). BHRA Fluid.
Cranfield, Geoffrey A. The Press & Society: From Caxton to Northcliffe. LC 77-21904. (Themes in British Social History). 1978. text ed. 22.00x (ISBN 0-582-48983-0); pap. text ed. 11.50x (ISBN 0-582-48984-9). Longman.
Cranford, Carolyn E., ed. see American Automobile Association.
Crang, Richard E. & Ward, Jack A. Electron Microscopy: Principles & Practices. 80p. (Incl. sound filmstrip). 1975. pap. text ed. 150.00 o.p. (ISBN 0-7216-9880-8). Saunders.
Cranin, A. Norman. Oral Implantology. (Illus.). 384p. 1970. text ed. 38.75 (ISBN 0-398-00357-2). C C Thomas.
Crank, J. The Mathematics of Diffusion. 2nd ed. (Illus.). 424p. 1975. 45.00x o.p. (ISBN 0-19-853344-6). Oxford U Pr.
Crankshaw, Edward. Gestapo. 1977. pap. 1.50 o.s.i. (ISBN 0-515-04236-6). Jove Pubns.
Cranor, Phoebe. How Am I Supposed to Love Myself? LC 79-14229. 1979. pap. 3.50 (ISBN 0-87123-236-7, 210236). Bethany Fell.
--Why did God let Grandpa Die? LC 76-17737. 1976. pap. 1.95 (ISBN 0-87123-603-6, 200603). Bethany Fell.
--Why Doesn't God Do Something? LC 78-118. (YA) 1978. pap. 1.95 (ISBN 0-87123-605-2, 200605). Bethany Fell.
Cransten, M. Sartre. 1978. cancelled (ISBN 0-685-54459-1). Chips.
Cranston, Ross. Regulating Business: Law & Consumer Agencies. (Oxford Socio-Legal Studies Ser.). 1979. text ed. 27.50x (ISBN 0-333-23890-7). Humanities.
Cranston, Toller. Ram on the Rampage. 1977. pap. 4.95 o.s.i. (ISBN 0-685-76850-3). Vanguard.
Crapanzano, V. & Garrison, V. Case Studies in Spirit Possession. LC 76-26653. 1977. 29.50 (ISBN 0-471-18460-8). Wiley.
Crapanzano, Vincent. The Hamadsha: A Study in Moroccan Ethnopsychiatry. LC 72-75529. 1973. 21.50x (ISBN 0-520-02241-6). U of Cal Pr.
Crapo, Lawrence M., jt. auth. see Fries, James F.
Crapps, Robert W., et al. Introduction to the New Testament. LC 72-75637. (Illus.). 566p. 1969. 18.95 (ISBN 0-8260-2225-1, Pub. by Wiley Medical). Wiley.
Crary, David T., et al. Personal Finance. 7th ed. LC 79-27578. 1980. text ed. 20.95 (ISBN 0-471-05639-1); tchr's ed. (ISBN 0-471-07802-6); study guide (ISBN 0-471-07919-7). Wiley.
Crary, Elizabeth. Without Spanking or Spoiling: A Practical Approach to Toddler & Preschool Guidance. LC 79-18253. (Illus.). 104p. (Orig.). 1979. pap. 6.95 (ISBN 0-9602862-0-9); write for info leaders' guide (ISBN 0-9602862-1-7). Parenting Pr.
Crase, Douglas. The Revisionist. 96p. 1981. 10.95 (ISBN 0-316-16062-8); pap. 5.95 (ISBN 0-316-16060-1). Little.
Crasemann, B., jt. auth. see Powell, John L.
Crashaw, W., tr. see Balbani, Niccolo.
Craske, Margaret. The Dance of Love: My Life with Meher Baba. LC 80-53859. 180p. 1980. pap. 6.95 (ISBN 0-913078-40-9). Sheriar Pr.
Crass, Hans M. Bibliotheksbauten Des 19 Jahrhunderts in Deutschland. (Illus.). 291p. (Ger.). 1976. text ed. 84.00 (ISBN 3-7940-3177-6, Pub. by K G Saur). Shoe String.
Craton, M. & Walvin, J. Slavery, Abolition & Emancipation. LC 76-18302. 1977. text ed. 21.00x (ISBN 0-582-48092-2); pap. text ed. 11.95x (ISBN 0-582-48093-0). Longman.
Craton, Michael. Roots & Branches: Current Directions in Slave Studies. LC 79-22464. 304p. 1980. 41.00 (ISBN 0-08-025367-9). Pergamon.
Cratty, B. Teaching Motor Skills. (Man in Action Ser.). (Illus.). 1973. pap. text ed. 7.95 (ISBN 0-13-893958-6). P-H.
Cratty, Bryant J. Active Learning: Games to Enhance Academic Abilities. (Physical Education Ser). (Illus.). 1971. pap. text ed. 9.50 (ISBN 0-13-003491-6). P-H.
--Career Potentials in Physical Activity. LC 79-136631. (Physical Education Ser). 1971. ref. ed. 15.95 (ISBN 0-13-114710-2). P-H.
--Intelligence in Action: Physical Activities for Enhancing Intellectual Abilities. (Illus.). 160p. 1973. ref. ed. 10.95 (ISBN 0-13-469049-4). P-H.
--Psycho-Motor Behavior in Education & Sport: Selected Papers. (Illus.). 190p. 1974. text ed. 18.50 (ISBN 0-398-03099-5). C C Thomas.
--Psychology in Contemporary Sport: Guidelines for Coaches & Athletes. (Illus.). 336p. 1973. ref. ed. 16.95 (ISBN 0-13-734079-6). P-H.
--Social Psychology in Athletics. (Illus.). 320p. 1981. text ed. 15.95 (ISBN 0-13-817650-7). P-H.
Cratty, Bryant J., et al. Movement Activities, Motor Ability & the Education of Children. (Illus.). 192p. 1970. pap. 18.75 photocopy ed. spiral (ISBN 0-398-00360-2). C C Thomas.
Cratty, Bryant S. Perceptual & Motor Development in Infants & Young Children. 2nd ed. 1979. 14.95 (ISBN 0-13-657023-2). P-H.

Crauford, Emma, tr. see Marcel, Gabriel.
Craven, John & Cockroft, John. How About Railway Modelling. (How About Paperback Ser.). 96p. 1980. pap. 3.95 (ISBN 0-8069-9092-9, Pub. by EP Publishing England). Sterling.
Craven, Margaret. Again Calls the Owl. 1981. pap. 2.25 (ISBN 0-440-10074-7). Dell.
--The Home Front. 252p. 1981. 11.95 (ISBN 0-686-69591-7). Putnam.
--I Heard the Owl Call My Name. LC 73-10800. 144p. 1973. 6.95 (ISBN 0-385-02586-6). Doubleday.
Craven, Roy C. A Concise History of Indian Art. (World of Art Ser.). (Illus.). 1976. pap. 9.95 (ISBN 0-19-519944-8). Oxford U Pr.
Craven, Sara. Moon of Aphrodite. (Harlequin Presents Ser.). 192p. (Orig.). 1981. pap. 1.50 (ISBN 0-373-10411-1, Pub. by Harlequin). PB.
--Shadow of Desire. (Harlequin Presents Ser.). 192p. 1980. pap. 1.50 (ISBN 0-373-10398-0, Pub. by Harlequin). PB.
Craven, Wesley F. White, Red, & Black: The Seventeenth Century Virginian. LC 79-163980. (Richard Lecture Ser). 1971. 9.95x (ISBN 0-8139-0372-6). U Pr of Va.
Cravens, David W. & Hills, Gerald E. Marketing Decision Making. rev. ed. 1980. 20.95x (ISBN 0-256-02348-4). Irwin.
Cravens, David W., et al. Marketing Decision Making: Concepts & Strategy. 1976. text ed. 16.95x (ISBN 0-256-01799-9). Irwin.
Cravens, Hamilton. Triumph of Evolution: American Scientists & the Heredity-Environment Controversy, 1900-1941. LC 77-20570. (Illus.). 1978. 19.95x (ISBN 0-8122-7744-9). U of Pa Pr.
Cravens, Richard, jt. auth. see Crockett, James U.
Craver, John. Graph Paper From Your Copier. (Illus.). 232p. 1980. pap. 12.95 (ISBN 0-89586-045-7). H P Bks.
Craver, Samuel, jt. auth. see Ozmon, Howard.
Cravis, Howard. Communications Network Analysis. LC 75-39314. 1981. price not set (ISBN 0-669-00443-X). Lexington Bks.
Cravit, Lawrence. The Forty-Year Parallel in Presidential Election. 1980. 10.00 (ISBN 0-533-04611-4). Vantage.
Crawford. Evacuation of Americans from Beirut. (Arab Background Ser.). 1972. pap. 3.95x (ISBN 0-685-77093-1). Intl Bk Ctr.
Crawford, Albert B. & Burnham, Paul S. Forecasting College Achievement: A Survey of Aptitude Tests for Higher Education, Part I., General Considerations in the Measurement of Academic Progress. 1946. 37.50x (ISBN 0-686-51387-8). Elliots Bks.
Crawford, Ann. This Is No Place for a Nervous Person. (Illus., Orig.). 1981. pap. 5.00x (ISBN 0-915494-12-4). Fibonacci Corp.
Crawford, Ann & Wittliff, William D., eds. Eagle: The Autobiography of Santa Anna. LC 68-5896. (Illus.). 12.50 o.p. (ISBN 0-8363-0026-2); limited ed 45.00 o.p. (ISBN 0-685-13271-4). Jenkins.
Crawford, Ann F. & Keever, Jack. John B. Connally: Portrait in Power. (Illus.). 460p. 1974. 9.50 o.p. (ISBN 0-8363-0121-8). Jenkins.
Crawford, Annie L. & Kilander, Virginia C. Psychiatric Nursing: A Basic Manual. 5th ed. LC 80-15880. 140p. 1980. pap. text ed. 7.25 (ISBN 0-8036-2112-4). Davis Co.
Crawford, Arthur A. A Doll Named Moses. 1981. 12.50 (ISBN 0-682-49729-0). Exposition.
Crawford, Arthur W. Monetary Management Under the New Deal. LC 70-173988. (FDR & the Era of the New Deal Ser.). 380p. 1972. Repr. of 1940 ed. lib. bdg. 39.50 (ISBN 0-306-70374-2). Da Capo.
Crawford, C. C. Genesis, Vol. II. (The Bible Study Textbook Ser.). 1968. 15.00 (ISBN 0-89900-003-7). College Pr Pub.
--Passion of Our Lord. 6.95 (ISBN 0-89225-140-9). Gospel Advocate.
Crawford, Carol G. Math Without Fear. (New Viewpoints Vision Bks.). 288p. 1980. 11.95 (ISBN 0-531-06377-1). Watts.
Crawford, Charles, ed. Cal Alley. LC 72-82797. (Illus.). 382p. 1973. 15.00 (ISBN 0-87870-013-7). Memphis St Univ.
Crawford, Charles W., ed. see Broer, Jill S., et al.
Crawford, Charles W., ed. see Holt, Edgar A.
Crawford, Charles W., ed. see Livingood, James W.
Crawford, D. F., jt. auth. see Messel, H.
Crawford, David. The City of London: Its Architectural Heritage. (Illus.). 144p. 1980. 15.00 (ISBN 0-85941-049-8); pap. 9.95 (ISBN 0-85941-043-9). Herman Pub.
Crawford, Donald W. Kant's Aesthetic Theory. LC 73-15259. 1974. 19.50x (ISBN 0-299-06510-3, 651). U of Wis Pr.
Crawford, Dorothy J. Kerkeosiris: An Egyptian Village in the Ptolemaic Period. LC 70-96083. (Classical Studies). (Illus.). 1971. 34.50 (ISBN 0-521-07607-2). Cambridge U Pr.
Crawford, Elisabeth & Rokkan, Stein, eds. Sociological Praxis: Current Roles & Settings. LC 75-31292. (Sage Studies in International Sociology: Vol. 3). 1976. 18.00x (ISBN 0-8039-9956-9); pap. 9.95x (ISBN 0-8039-9973-9). Sage.
Crawford, Elizabeth D., jt. ed. see De Montreville, Doris.
Crawford, Elizabeth D., tr. see Broger, Achim.
Crawford, Elizabeth D., tr. see Brothers Grimm.
Crawford, Elizabeth D., tr. see Fuchshuber, Annegert.
Crawford, Elizabeth D., tr. see Koci, Marta.
Crawford, Elizabeth D., tr. see Rettich, Margaret.
Crawford, Emmanuel J. Oil & the Changed Structure of the World at the Beginning of the 21st Century. 1980. 54.75 (ISBN 0-930008-49-9). Inst Econ Pol.
Crawford, Fred L. Career Planning for the Blind. (Keith Jennison Large Type Bks). 8.95 o.p. (ISBN 0-531-00171-7). Watts.
--Career Planning for the Blind: A Manual for Students & Teachers. 189p. 1966. 3.95 (ISBN 0-374-11905-8). FS&G.
Crawford, Fred R., ed. Exploring Mental Health Parameters, Vol. III. LC 80-67929. (Orig.). 1980. pap. 8.00 (ISBN 0-89937-030-6). Ctr Res Soc Chg.
Crawford, Fred R. The Seventy-First Came...to Gunskirchen Lager. LC 79-51047. (Witness to the Holocaust: No. 1). (Illus.). 1979. pap. 1.00 (ISBN 0-89937-027-6). Ctr Res Soc Chg.
Crawford, H. W. & McDowell, Milton C. Math Workbook for Foodservice-Lodging. 1971. pap. 11.95 (ISBN 0-8436-0519-7); pap. text ed. 11.95 (ISBN 0-8436-0534-0); answer bk. 1.95 (ISBN 0-8436-0538-3). CBI Pub.
Crawford, H. Warren & Rodgers, John F. Maryland Supplement for Modern Real Estate Practice. rev. 2nd ed. 176p. (Orig.). 1978. pap. 9.25 (ISBN 0-88462-303-3). Real Estate Ed Co.
--Maryland Supplement for Modern Real Estate Practice. 3rd ed. 140p. (Orig.). 1981. pap. 7.95 (ISBN 0-88462-267-3). Real Estate Ed Co.
Crawford, Hollie & McDowell, Milton C. Metric Workbook for Food Service & Lodging. LC 76-22181. 224p. 1976. pap. 11.95 (ISBN 0-8436-2103-6); pap. text ed. 8.95 o.p. (ISBN 0-8436-2104-4); answer book 1.95 (ISBN 0-8436-2168-0). CBI Pub.
Crawford, James. The Creation of States in International Law. 1979. 49.95x (ISBN 0-19-825347-8). Oxford U Pr.
Crawford, Jean. Jugtown Pottery: History & Design. LC 64-8376. (Illus.). 1964. 8.00 o.p. (ISBN 0-910244-39-1). Blair.
Crawford, Jeffrey L., et al. Computer Application in Mental Health: A Source Book. 1980. write for info. (ISBN 0-88410-712-4). Ballinger Pub.
Crawford, Jeffrey L., et al, eds. Progress in Mental Health Information Systems: Computer Applications. LC 73-17348. 384p. 1974. text ed. 25.00 o.p. (ISBN 0-88410-109-6). Ballinger Pub.
Crawford, John. Introducing Jewelry Making. LC 69-10796. (Introducing Ser). (Illus.). (gr. 1-4). 1969. 9.95 o.p. (ISBN 0-8230-6200-7). Watson-Guptill.
--Romantic Criticism of Shakespearean Drama. (Salzberg Studies in English Literature: Romantic Reassessment Ser.: No. 79). 1978. pap. text ed. 25.00x (ISBN 0-391-01352-1). Humanities.
Crawford, John & Okita, Saburo, eds. Australia & Japan: Issues in the Economic Relationship. (Australia-Japan Economic Relations Research Project Monograph: No. 2). (Illus.). 140p. 1980. pap. text ed. 5.95 (ISBN 0-9596197-1-2). Bks Australia.
Crawford, John R. How to Be a Consistent Winner in the Most Popular Card Games. pap. 2.95 (ISBN 0-385-09687-9, C180, Dolp). Doubleday.
Crawford, John S. Wolves, Bears & Bighorns: Wilderness Observations & Experiences of a Professional Outdoorsman. (Illus.). 192p. 1980. 19.95 (ISBN 0-88240-146-7); pap. 12.95 (ISBN 0-686-63422-5). Alaska Northwest.
Crawford, John T., III & Hustrulid, William A., eds. Open Pit Planning & Design. LC 79-52269. (Illus.). 367p. 1979. text ed. 27.00x (ISBN 0-89520-253-0). Soc Mining Eng.
Crawford, John W. Discourse: Essay on English & American Literature. (Costerus New Ser.: No. XIV). 1978. pap. text ed. 25.00x (ISBN 90-6203-672-4). Humanities.
--Steps to Success: A Study Skills Handbook. rev. ed. 1978. pap. text ed. 5.50 o.p. (ISBN 0-8403-0975-9). Kendall-Hunt.
Crawford, Kenneth, jt. auth. see Simmons, Paul D.
Crawford, Linda. In a Class by Herself. 1978. pap. 1.95 o.p. (ISBN 0-445-04218-4). Popular Lib.
Crawford, Lloyd V. Pediatric Allergic Diseases - Focus on Clinical Diagnosis. 1977. spiral bdg. 16.50 (ISBN 0-87488-826-3). Med Exam.
Crawford, Lucy C. & Meyer, Warren G. Organization & Administration of Distributive Education. LC 70-187803. 336p. 1972. text ed. 18.95x (ISBN 0-675-09112-8). Merrill.
Crawford, Marshal A., jt. auth. see Grauer, Robert T.
Crawford, Mary C. In the Days of the Pilgrim Fathers. LC 74-129572. 1970. Repr. of 1921 ed. 20.00 (ISBN 0-8103-3470-4). Gale.
--Little Pilgrimages Among Old New England Inns: Being an Account of Little Journeys to Various Quaint Inns & Hostelries of Colonial New England. LC 76-107629. (Illus.). 1970. Repr. of 1907 ed. 18.00 (ISBN 0-8103-3536-0). Gale.
--Social Life in Old New England. LC 71-102645. (Tower Bks). (Illus.). 1971. Repr. of 1914 ed. 30.00 (ISBN 0-8103-3924-2). Gale.
Crawford, Max. The Backslider. 1978. pap. 1.75 o.s.i. (ISBN 0-380-01921-3, 37663). Avon.
--Waltz Across Texas. 1977. pap. 1.95 (ISBN 0-380-01856-X, 36533). Avon.
Crawford, Mel. Bambi. Sanchez, Rene, tr. (Illus.). 24p. (Span.). (ps-3). 1977. PLB 5.92 o.p. (ISBN 0-307-68830-5, Golden Pr). Western Pub.
--The Cowboy Book. (Illus.). 24p. (gr. k-1). 1976. PLB 5.38 (ISBN 0-307-68981-6, Golden Pr). Western Pub.
--The Turtle Book. (Illus.). (ps-4). 1965. PLB 5.38 (ISBN 0-307-68922-0, Golden Pr). Western Pub.
Crawford, Mel, illus. Old MacDonald Had a Farm. (Illus.). (ps-1). 1967. PLB 5.38 (ISBN 0-307-68931-X, Golden Pr). Western Pub.
Crawford, Michael. The Roman Republic. (Fontana History of the Ancient World Ser.). 1978. text ed. 24.75x (ISBN 0-391-00832-3). Humanities.
--Roman Republican Coinage. LC 77-164450. (Illus.). 750p. 1975. 190.00 (ISBN 0-521-07492-4). Cambridge U Pr.
Crawford, Michael, jt. auth. see Kays, William M.
Crawford, Michael H., jt. ed. see Mielke, James H.
Crawford, O. William & Gautot, Henri J., eds. X-Ray Technology Examination Review Book, Vol. 2. 3rd ed. 1973. pap. 9.50 (ISBN 0-87488-442-X). Med Exam.
Crawford, Patricia. Homesteading: A Practical Guide to Living off the Land. LC 74-9826. 224p. 1975. 11.95 (ISBN 0-02-583820-2, 52879). Macmillan.
Crawford, Petrina. Seed of Evil. 1976. pap. 1.25 o.p. (ISBN 0-685-73459-5, LB410, Leisure Bks). Nordon Pubns.
Crawford, R. M. Australia. 3rd. rev. ed. 1970. text ed. 5.00x (ISBN 0-09-105110-X, Hutchinson U Lib). Humanities.
Crawford, Richard. A Historian's Introduction to Early American Music. (Illus.). 1980. pap. 4.00 (ISBN 0-912296-44-5, Dist. by U Pr of Va). Am Antiquarian.
--Men, Women & Bridge: Startling Tales of the Bridge Table. LC 77-93316. (Illus.). 1978. 8.95 (ISBN 0-8069-4934-1); lib. bdg. 8.29 (ISBN 0-8069-4935-X). Sterling.
Crawford, Richard A. Andrew Law: American Psalmodist. LC 68-15331. (Pi Kappa Lambda Studies in American Music). (Illus.). 1968. 16.75x o.s.i. (ISBN 0-8101-0070-3). Northwestern U Pr.
Crawford, Ronald L. Lignin Biodegradation & Transformation. 192p. 1981. 22.50 (ISBN 0-471-05743-6, Pub. by Wiley-Interscience). Wiley.
Crawford, Rudd, et al. Achievement in Mathematics, 2 vols. (Mathematics Program). (gr. 7-8). 1974. Vol. 1. text ed. 14.60 (ISBN 0-205-03976-6, 563976X); Vol. 2. text ed. 14.60 (ISBN 0-205-04225-2, 5642256); tchrs'. guide for vol. 1 10.96 (ISBN 0-205-03977-4, 5639778); tchrs'. guide for vol. 2 10.96 (ISBN 0-205-04226-0, 5642264). Allyn.
Crawford, Samuel D., jt. auth. see Bentley, Robert H.
Crawford, Susan, jt. ed. see Rees, Alan M.
Crawford, T., ed. see Woolf, Neville.
Crawford, Tad. Legal Guide for the Visual Artist. 1980. pap. 5.95 (ISBN 0-8015-4472-6, Hawthorn). Dutton.
--Legal Guide for the Visual Artist. 1977. 10.95 o.p. (ISBN 0-8015-4471-8). Dutton.
--The Visual Artist's Guide to the New Copyright Law. 1978. pap. 5.50 o.s.i. (ISBN 0-8038-7763-3). Hastings.
Crawford, Tad & Kopelman, Arie. Selling Your Graphic Design & Illustration. 272p. 1981. 13.95 (ISBN 0-312-71252-9). St Martin.
Crawford, Tad & Mellon, Susan. The Artist Gallery Partnership: A Practical Guide to Consignment. LC 80-28108. (Orig.). 1981. pap. 4.50 (ISBN 0-915400-26-X). Am Council Arts.
Crawford, Ted. The Writer's Legal Guide. LC 76-56516. 1978. 10.95 (ISBN 0-8015-8937-1, Hawthorn); pap. 5.95 (ISBN 0-8015-8938-X, Hawthorn). Dutton.
Crawford, Teri. The First Wild West Rodeo. LC 78-14549. (Famous Firsts Ser.). (Illus.). 1978. lib. bdg. 7.35 (ISBN 0-686-51109-3). Silver.
--Protectors of the Wilderness: The First Forest Rangers. LC 78-14492. (Famous Firsts Ser.). (Illus.). 1978. lib. bdg. 7.35 (ISBN 0-686-51114-X). Silver.
Crawford, Thomas. Society & the Lyric: A Study of the Song Culture of Eighteenth-Century Scotland. 208p. 1980. text ed. 13.50 (ISBN 0-7073-0227-7, Pub. by Scottish Academic Pr). Columbia U Pr.
Crawford, Thomas, ed. Love, Labour & Liberty: The Eighteenth-Century Scottish Lyric. (Essays, Prose, & Scottish Literature Ser.). 1979. 9.95 (ISBN 0-85635-182-2, Pub. by Carcanet New Pr England); pap. 5.95 (ISBN 0-85635-195-4). Persea Bks.
Crawford, Thomas E. West of the Texas Kid, Eighteen Eighty-One to Nineteen Ten: Recollections of Thomas Edgar Crawford, Cowboy, Gun Fighter, Rancher, Hunter, Miner. Dykes, Jeff C., ed. (Western Frontier Library: No. 20). (Illus.). 1962. bds. 5.95 (ISBN 0-8061-0513-5); pap. 3.95 (ISBN 0-8061-1117-8). U of Okla Pr.
Crawford, Walter B., ed. Reading Coleridge: Approaches & Applications. LC 79-7616. 1979. 17.50x (ISBN 0-8014-1219-6). Cornell U Pr.
Crawford, William R. Bibliography of Chaucer, 1954-1963. LC 66-29836. (Publications in Language & Literature: No. 17). 188p. 1967. 11.50 (ISBN 0-295-74027-2). U of Wash Pr.
Crawhall, Joseph. Chap-Book Chaplets 1883. (Illus.). 1976. Repr. of 1883 ed. 40.00x (ISBN 0-85967-260-3, Pub. by Scolar Pr England). Biblio Dist.
Crawley, C. W. The Question of Greek Independence: A Study of British Policy in the Near East, 1821-1833. LC 74-144130. 272p. 1973. Repr. of 1930 ed. 16.00 (ISBN 0-86527-161-5). Fertig.
Crawley, Derek. Character in Relation to Action in the Tragedies of George Chapman. (Salzburg Studies in English Literature, Jacobean Drama Studies: No. 16). 202p. 1974. pap. text ed. 25.00x (ISBN 0-391-01353-X). Humanities.
Crawley, Eduardo, ed. Latin America Annual Review. rev. ed. (Annual Review Ser.). (Illus.). 1981. pap. 24.95 (ISBN 0-528-84518-7). Rand.
Crawley, Ernest. Mystic Rose: A Study of Primitive Marriage & of Primitive Thought in Its Bearing on Marriage, 2 Vols. rev. & enl. ed. Besterman, Theodore, ed. LC 72-164193. 1971. Repr. of 1927 ed. 28.00 (ISBN 0-8103-3781-9). Gale.
Crawley, Frank, jt. auth. see Bartholomew, Rolland.
Crawley, Lawrence, et al. Reproduction, Sex, & Preparation for Marriage. 2nd ed. (Illus.). 256p. 1973. pap. 10.95 (ISBN 0-13-773937-0). P-H.
Crawley, Stanley M. & Dillion, Robert W. Steel Buildings: Analysis & Design. 2nd ed. LC 76-39934. 1977. text ed. 29.95 (ISBN 0-471-18552-3). Wiley.
Crawley, Tony. The Films of Sophia Loren. (Illus.). pap. 6.95 (ISBN 0-8065-0700-4). Citadel Pr.
Crawshaw, B. H. & Ritchie, J. H. OGrade Questions in Physics. (Orig.). 1979. pap. text ed. 8.25x o.p. (ISBN 0-435-67045-X). Heinemann Ed.
Cray, Ed. Chrome Colossus: General Motors & Its Times. (Illus.). 548p. 1980. 14.95 (ISBN 0-07-013493-6). McGraw.
Crayder, Dorothy. Ishkabibble! LC 75-30862. (Illus.). (gr. 4-6). 1976. 5.95 o.p. (ISBN 0-689-30499-4). Atheneum.
Crayson, Suzanne. Plants from Plants: How to Grow New Houseplants for Next to Nothing. LC 76-12559. (Illus.). 1976. pap. 6.95 (ISBN 0-397-01175-X). Lippincott.
Craytor, Josephine K. & Fass, Margot L. Nurse & the Cancer Patient: A Programmed Textbook. LC 71-124393. (Prog. Bk.). 1970. pap. text ed. 5.95x o.p. (ISBN 0-397-54103-1). Lippincott.
Creagh, Monty. Nobask. 100p. 1980. 7.95 (ISBN 0-533-04510-X). Vantage.
Creamer, Robert H. Machine Design. 2nd ed. LC 75-12093. (Engineering Technology Ser.). (Illus.). 544p. 1976. text ed. 21.95 (ISBN 0-201-01178-6); instr's guide 1.50 (ISBN 0-201-01179-4). A-W.
Crean, John E., et al. Deutsche Sprach und Landeskunde. Incl. Ratyck, Joanna. wkbk. 6.95 (ISBN 0-394-32649-0); Crean, John E. lab manual 6.95 (ISBN 0-394-32650-4). 608p. 1981. text ed. 17.95 (ISBN 0-394-32648-2). Random.
Creasey, John. Department of Death. 1979. pap. 1.75 o.p. (ISBN 0-445-04371-7). Popular Lib.
--Elope to Death. LC 76-43493. 1977. 6.95 o.p. (ISBN 0-03-020621-9). HR&W.
--The Enemy Within. 1977. pap. 1.25 o.p. (ISBN 0-445-00454-1). Popular Lib.

--Go Away Death. 1976. pap. 1.25 o.p. (ISBN 0-445-00427-4). Popular Lib.
--Help from the Baron. 1977. 6.95 o.s.i. (ISBN 0-8027-5368-X). Walker & Co.
--Hide the Baron. LC 77-91362. 1978. 7.95 o.s.i. (ISBN 0-8027-5383-3). Walker & Co.
--The Island of Peril. 1976. pap. 1.25 o.p. (ISBN 0-445-00379-0). Popular Lib.
--The Killers of Innocence. 1980. pap. 1.95 (ISBN 0-441-44275-7). Charter Bks.
--A Kind of Prisoner. 1975. pap. 0.95 o.p. (ISBN 0-445-00675-7). Popular Lib.
--The League of Dark Men. 176p. 1975. pap. 0.95 o.p. (ISBN 0-445-00655-2). Popular Lib.
--A Plague of Demons. 1977. 6.95 o.p. (ISBN 0-03-017541-0). HR&W.
--Prophet of Fire. 1978. 7.95 o.s.i. (ISBN 0-8027-5394-9). Walker & Co.
--A Sharp Rise in Crime. 1979. 7.95 o.p. (ISBN 0-684-14921-4, ScribT). Scribner.
--The Toff at Butlins. 1976. 6.95 o.s.i. (ISBN 0-8027-5358-2). Walker & Co.
--Wings of Peace. 1978. 7.95 o.s.i. (ISBN 0-8027-5388-4). Walker & Co.

Creasey, John S. Victorian & Edwardian Country Life. 1977. 22.50 (ISBN 0-7134-0819-7, Pub. by Batsford England). David & Charles.

Creasey, William A., ed. Clinical Pharmacology: Symposium Proceedings. 248p. 1976. text ed. 30.00 (ISBN 0-08-018949-0). Pergamon.

Creasman, William T., jt. auth. see DiSaia, Philip J.

Creasy, John. Day of Fear. LC 77-73867. 1978. 6.95x o.p. (ISBN 0-03-022396-2). HR&W.
--Let's Kill Uncle Lionel. 1976. 6.95 o.p. (ISBN 0-679-50589-X). McKay.

Creative Editors. How to Have Fun Making Dinner. LC 74-8612. (Creative Craft Bks.). (Illus.). 32p. (gr. 2-6). 1974. PLB 5.25 o.p. (ISBN 0-87191-358-5). Creative Ed.
--How to Have Fun Making Lunch. LC 74-8459. (Creative Craft Bks.). (Illus.). 32p. (gr. 2-6). 1974. PLB 5.95 (ISBN 0-87191-357-7). Creative Ed.
--How to Have Fun with a Flower Garden. LC 74-12442. (Creative Craft Bks.). (Illus.). 32p. (gr. 2-6). 1974. PLB 5.25 o.p. (ISBN 0-87191-364-X). Creative Ed.
--How to Have Fun with a Vegetable Garden. LC 74-12297. (Creative Craft Bks.). (Illus.). 32p. (gr. 2-6). 1974. PLB 5.95 (ISBN 0-87191-363-1). Creative Ed.
--Life in the Sea. LC 70-140638. (Our Changing Environment Ser). (Illus.). (gr. 4-8). 1971. PLB 6.95 o.p. (ISBN 0-87191-073-X). Creative Ed.

Creative Educational Society Editors. How to Have Fun Baking Cookies & Cakes. LC 73-10467. 1974. PLB 5.95 (ISBN 0-87191-260-0). Creative Ed.
--How to Have Fun Building a Sailboat. LC 73-9707. 1974. PLB 5.95 (ISBN 0-87191-250-3). Creative Ed.
--How to Have Fun Knitting. LC 73-12471. (Creative Craft Bks.). (Illus.). 32p. (gr. 2-5). 1973. PLB 5.95 (ISBN 0-87191-274-0). Creative Ed.
--How to Have Fun Making a Kite. LC 73-12514. (Creative Craft Bks.). (Illus.). 32p. (gr. 2-5). 1973. PLB 5.90 (ISBN 0-87191-273-2). Creative Ed.
--How to Have Fun Making Bird Feeders & Bird Houses. LC 73-10463. (Creative Craft Bks.). (Illus.). 32p. (gr. 2-5). 1973. PLB 5.25 o.p. (ISBN 0-87191-271-6). Creative Ed.
--How to Have Fun Making Breakfast. LC 73-18257. (Creative Craft Bks.). (Illus.). 32p. (gr. 2-5). 1973. PLB 5.95 (ISBN 0-87191-291-0). Creative Ed.
--How to Have Fun Making Christmas Decorations. LC 73-20197. (Creative Craft Bks.). (Illus.). 32p. (gr. 2-5). 1973. PLB 5.95 (ISBN 0-87191-292-9). Creative Ed.
--How to Have Fun Making Mobiles. LC 73-18210. (Creative Craft Bks.). (Illus.). 32p. (gr. 2-5). 1973. PLB 5.95 (ISBN 0-87191-293-7). Creative Ed.
--How to Have Fun Making Paper Air Planes. LC 73-19589. (Creative Craft Bks.). (Illus.). 32p. (gr. 2-5). 1973. PLB 5.95 (ISBN 0-87191-294-5). Creative Ed.
--How to Have Fun Making Puppets. LC 73-18225. (Creative Craft Bks.). (Illus.). 32p. (gr. 2-5). 1973. PLB 5.95 (ISBN 0-87191-295-3). Creative Ed.
--How to Have Fun Sewing. LC 73-10066. (Creative Craft Bks.). (Illus.). 32p. 1973. PLB 5.75 o.p. (ISBN 0-87191-252-X). Creative Ed.
--How to Have Fun Weaving. LC 73-12467. (Creative Craft Bks). (Illus.). 32p. (gr. 2-5). 1973. PLB 5.75 o.p. (ISBN 0-87191-272-4). Creative Ed.
--How to Have Fun with an Indoor Garden. LC 73-18258. (Creative Craft Bks.). (Illus.). 32p. (gr. 2-5). 1973. PLB 5.95 (ISBN 0-87191-297-X). Creative Ed.
--How to Have Fun with Macrame. LC 73-19667. (Creative Craft Bks.). (Illus.). 32p. (gr. 2-5). 1973. PLB 5.95 (ISBN 0-87191-290-2). Creative Ed.
--How to Have Fun with Needlepoint. LC 73-18226. (Creative Craft Bks.). (Illus.). 32p. (gr. 2-5). 1973. PLB 5.95 (ISBN 0-87191-296-1). Creative Ed.

Crebillon, Claude see Voltaire, Francois.

Crebillon, Claude P. Letters from the Marchioness De M to the Count De R, Vol. 60. LC 72-170590. (Novel in England, 1700-1775). lib. bdg. 50.00 (ISBN 0-8240-0572-4). Garland Pub.

Credle, Ellis. Down, Down the Mountain. (Illus.). (gr. k-3). 1934. 6.95 (ISBN 0-525-66020-8). Elsevier-Nelson.

Cree, D. Ann, jt. auth. see King, F. W.

Creed, Charles. Jubilee College State Park: Retrospective by Way of Explanation. 20p. 1980. pap. 2.50 (ISBN 0-933180-11-X). Spoon Riv Poetry.

Creed, Lisa, ed. The House Within Me: An Anthology of Poems by Children from Little River School. 64p. (Orig.). (ps). 1981. pap. 4.00 (ISBN 0-932112-10-2). Carolina Wren.

Creed, R. S., et al. Reflex Activity of the Spinal Cord. (Illus.). 210p. 1972. 24.95x (ISBN 0-19-857355-3). Oxford U Pr.

Creed, Virginia. France. rev. ed. LC 77-83911. (World Culture Ser). (Illus.). 168p. (gr. 6 up). 1978. text ed. 9.95 ea. 1-4 copies (ISBN 0-88296-188-8); text ed. 7.96 ea. 5 or more copies; tchrs'. guide 8.94 (ISBN 0-88296-369-4). Fideler.

Creed, Virginia & Douglas Jackson, W. A. France & Soviet Union. rev. ed. LC 77-83892. (World Cultures Ser.). (Illus.). 298p. (gr. 6 up). 1978. text ed. 12.43 ea. 1-4 copies (ISBN 0-88296-154-3); text ed. 9.94 ea. 5 or more copies; tchrs'. guide 8.94 (ISBN 0-88296-369-4). Fideler.

Creedman, Theodore S. Historical Dictionary of Costa Rica. LC 77-6390. (Latin American Historical Dictionaries Ser.: No. 16). 1977. 12.00 (ISBN 0-8108-1040-9). Scarecrow.

Creedy. The Economics of Unemployment in Britain. 1981. text ed. price not set (ISBN 0-408-10703-0). Butterworth.

Creek, F. N. & Rutherford, Don. Rugby. (Teach Yourself Ser.). 1975. pap. 5.50 (ISBN 0-679-10374-0). McKay.

Creel, Herrlee G. Chinese Thought from Confucius to Mao Tse-Tung. LC 53-10054. 1971. pap. 5.95 (ISBN 0-226-12030-9, P394, Phoen). U of Chicago Pr.

Creel, Richard. Religion & Doubt: Toward a Faith of Your Own. 1977. 10.50 o.p. (ISBN 0-13-771949-3); pap. 7.95 (ISBN 0-13-771931-0). P-H.

Creeley, Robert. For Love: Poems Nineteen Fifty to Nineteen Sixty. LC 62-8903. (Orig.). pap. 2.95 o.p. (ISBN 0-684-71738-7, SL178, ScribT). Scribner.
--Quick Graph: Collected Notes & Essays. Allen, Donald, ed. LC 67-30650. (Writing Ser.: No. 22). 150p. (Orig.). 1970. 10.00 (ISBN 0-87704-010-9). Four Seasons Foun.
--Words. LC 67-12213. (Orig.). 1967. 7.95 o.p. (ISBN 0-684-10090-8, ScribT). Scribner.

Creeley, Robert, jt. auth. see Olson, Charles.

Creger, W. P., et al, eds. Annual Review of Medicine: Selected Topics in the Clinical Sciences, Vol. 32. LC 51-1659. (Illus.). 1981. 20.00 (ISBN 0-8243-0532-9). Annual Reviews.

Creigh, Dorothy W. Adams County, 2 vols. Incl. A Study of the Great Plains. 1972. 25.00 (ISBN 0-934858-00-4); The/People. 1971. 25.00 (ISBN 0-934858-01-2). (Illus.). Set. 45.00 (ISBN 0-934858-02-0). Adams County.
--Nebraska: A History. (States & the Nation Ser.). (Illus.). 1977. 12.95 (ISBN 0-393-05598-1, Co-Pub. by Aaslh). Norton.
--Tales from the Prairie, 4 vols. Incl. Vol. 1. 1977. pap. 2.95 (ISBN 0-686-19306-7); Vol. 2. 1973. pap. 2.95 (ISBN 0-686-17269-8); Vol. 3. 1976. pap. 5.95 (ISBN 0-686-17321-X); Vol. 4. 1979. pap. 9.95 (ISBN 0-934858-06-3). LC 74-157038. (Illus.). Set. pap. write for info. Adams County.

Creighton, B., tr. see Junger, Ernst.

Creighton, Donald. Story of Canada. 1971. pap. 3.95 (ISBN 0-571-09070-2, Pub. by Faber & Faber). Merrimack Bk Serv.

Creighton, Helen. Law Every Nurse Should Know. 4th ed. 480p. 1981. text ed. 14.95 (ISBN 0-7216-2573-8). Saunders.
--Songs of Nova Scotia. 1968. pap. 6.00 (ISBN 0-486-21703-5). Dover.

Creighton, J., tr. see Wundt, Wilhelm M.

Creighton, Jane. Ceres in an Open Field. LC 79-26248. (Illus.). 80p. 1980. pap. 3.50 (ISBN 0-918314-12-7). Out & Out.

Creighton, Jo Anne. Dark Side of Paradise. 256p. 1976. pap. 1.25 o.p. (ISBN 0-445-00390-1). Popular Lib.
--Harlan Legacy. 1977. pap. 1.50 o.p. (ISBN 0-445-03206-5). Popular Lib.

Creighton, Joanne V. Joyce Carol Oates. (United States Authors Ser.: No. 321). 1979. lib. bdg. 10.95 (ISBN 0-8057-7212-X). Twayne.

Creighton, Margo N. & Cohen, Patricia F. Nursing Care Planning Guides for Long Term Care. 1980. pap. write for info. (ISBN 0-935236-13-9). Nurseco.

Creighton, Margo N. & Reighley, Joan. Nursing Care Planning Guides, Set 5. 1981. pap. 11.95 (ISBN 0-935236-14-7). Nurseco.

Creighton, Warren S. The Contributions of Mussolini to the Civilization of Mankind. (Illus.). 137p. 1981. 51.55 (ISBN 0-89266-282-4). Am Classical Coll Pr.

Crelinsten, Ronald D. & Szabo, Denis. Hostage-Taking: Theory & Practice. (Illus.). 1979. 16.95 (ISBN 0-669-02841-X). Lexington Bks.

Crelinsten, Ronald D., et al, eds. Terrorism & Criminal Justice. LC 77-887185. (Illus.). 1978. 16.95 (ISBN 0-669-01983-6). Lexington Bks.

Cremer, Hermann. Biblico-Theological Lexicon of New Testament Greek. 4th ed. 960p. Repr. of 1895 ed. text ed. 32.00x (ISBN 0-567-01004-X). Attic Pr.

Cremer, J. E., jt. ed. see Balazs, R.

Cremin, Lawrence A. The Wonderful World of Ellwood Patterson Cubberley: An Essay on the Historiography of American Education. LC 65-20759. (Orig.). 1965. text ed. 4.25x (ISBN 0-8077-1215-9); pap. text ed. 2.25x (ISBN 0-8077-1212-4). Tchrs Coll.

Cremin, Lawrence A., ed. Republic & the School: Horace Mann on the Education of Free Men. 7th ed. LC 57-9102. (Orig.). 1957. pap. text ed. 3.50x (ISBN 0-8077-1206-X). Tchrs Coll.

Cremlyn, R. Pesticides: Preparation & Mode of Action. LC 77-28590. 1978. 35.00 (ISBN 0-471-99631-9, Pub. by Wiley-Interscience); pap. 18.50 (ISBN 0-471-27669-3). Wiley.

Cremlyn, R. J. College Organic Chemistry. 1970. text ed. 15.95x o.p. (ISBN 0-435-66192-2); pap. text ed. 9.95x o.p. (ISBN 0-435-66193-0). Heinemann Ed.

Cremona, J., tr. see Pallottino, Massimo.

Cren, E. D. Le see Le Cren, E. D. & Lowe-McConnell, R. H.

Crenshaw, James L. Hymnic Affirmation of Divine Justice. LC 75-22349. (Society of Biblical Literature. Dissertation Ser.). 180p. 1975. pap. 7.50 (ISBN 0-89130-016-3, 060124). Scholars Pr Ca.
--Old Testament Wisdom: An Introduction. LC 80-82183. 262p. 1981. 16.50 (ISBN 0-8042-0143-9); pap. 9.95 (ISBN 0-8042-0142-0). John Knox.

Crenshaw, Mary A. The End of the Rainbow. 224p. 1981. 12.95 (ISBN 0-02-528810-5). Macmillan.

Crenshaw, Mary A. & Kounovsky, Nicholas. Shape up for Super Sex. 1977. 8.95 o.s.i. (ISBN 0-440-07931-4). Delacorte.

Crenshaw, Roger, jt. auth. see Crenshaw, Theresa.

Crenshaw, Theresa & Crenshaw, Roger. Expressing Your Feelings: The Key to an Intimate Relationship. 240p. (Orig.). (gr. 11-12). 1981. pap. text ed. 9.95x (ISBN 0-8290-0252-9). Irvington.

Creore, JoAnn, jt. auth. see Anderson, James M.

Crepps, John E., jt. ed. see Mason, Robert M.

Creps, David B. Randy Roy Persnazznur. (Orig.). 1980. pap. write for info.; pap. write for info. Great Basin.

Cresap, Bernard. Appomatax Commander. (Illus.). 384p. 1981. 15.00 (ISBN 0-498-02432-6). A S Barnes.

Creson, Betty, jt. auth. see Barsch, Jeffrey.

Crespe, Mary A., ed. Pipeline Rates on Crude Petroleum Oil. 800p. Date not set. 95.00. CSG Pr.

Crespigny, Anthony De see De Crespigny, Anthony & Minogue, Kenneth.

Crespigny, R. de see De Crespigny, R. R.

Cress, P., et al. Fortran IV with Watfor & Watfiv. 1970. ref. ed. 14.95x (ISBN 0-13-329433-1). P-H.
--Strucured FORTRAN with Watfiv-S. 1980. pap. 13.95 (ISBN 0-13-854752-1). P-H.

Cresser, Malcolm S. Solvent Extraction in Flame Spectroscopic Analysis. 1978. 52.95 (ISBN 0-408-71307-0). Butterworths.

Cressey, Donald R. & Ward, David A., eds. Delinquency, Crime & Social Process. 1969. text ed. write for info. o.p. (ISBN 0-06-041414-6, HarpC). Har-Row.

Cressey, William W. & Napoli, Donna J., eds. Linguistic Symposium on Romance Languages, No. 9. (Orig.). 1981. pap. text ed. 8.95x (ISBN 0-87840-081-8). Georgetown U Pr.

Cresson, B. C., jt. auth. see Flanders, H. J.

Cresswell, Anthony M. & Murphy, Michael J., eds. Education & Collective Bargaining. LC 76-46121. xviii, 513p. 1976. 14.00 (ISBN 0-8211-0227-3, Co-Pub. & Co-Distrib. by McCutchan); pap. 13.00 (ISBN 0-87367-769-2, Co-Pub. & Co-Distrib. by McCutchen). Phi Delta Kappa.
--Education & Collective Bargaining: Readings in Policy & Research. LC 76-46121. 1977. 20.50 (ISBN 0-685-78476-2); text ed. 18.50x 10 or more copies (ISBN 0-8211-0227-3). McCutchan.

Cresswell, Anthony M., et al. Teachers, Unions, & Collective Bargaining in Public Education. LC 79-91436. 350p. 1980. text ed. 18.50 10 or more copies (ISBN 0-8211-0229-X). McCutchan.

Cresswell, Helen. Absolute Zero: Being the Second Part of the Bagthorpe Saga. LC 77-12675. (gr. 5 up). 1978. 7.95 (ISBN 0-02-725550-6, 72555). Macmillan.
--Bagthorpes Unlimited. 1980. pap. 1.75 (ISBN 0-380-49296-2, 49296, Camelot). Avon.
--The Bagthorpes vs the World. (Illus.). (gr. 1 up). 1980. pap. 1.95 (ISBN 0-380-51102-9, 51102, Camelot). Avon.
--Bagthorpes vs the World: Being the Fourth Part of the Bagthorpe Saga. LC 79-13260. (gr. 5 up). 1979. 7.95 (ISBN 0-02-725420-8, 72542). Macmillan.
--The Beachcombers. 144p. (gr. 5up). 1972. 7.95 (ISBN 0-02-725470-4). Macmillan.
--The Bongleweed. LC 73-4057. 128p. (gr. 5-9). 1973. 7.95 (ISBN 0-02-725500-X). Macmillan.
--A Game of Catch. LC 76-46991. (Illus.). (gr. 3-6). 1977. 7.95 (ISBN 0-02-725440-2, 72544). Macmillan.
--Ordinary Jack. (gr. 1-4). 1979. pap. 1.50 (ISBN 0-380-43349-4, 43349, Camelot). Avon.
--Ordinary Jack: Being the First Part of the Bagthorpe Saga. LC 77-5146. (gr. 5 up). 1977. 7.95 (ISBN 0-02-725540-9, 72554). Macmillan.
--The Piemakers. LC 80-14433. (Illus.). 128p. (gr. 3-7). 1980. 8.95 (ISBN 0-02-725410-0). Macmillan.
--Up the Pier. LC 79-178598. (Illus.). 128p. (gr. 5-7). 1972. 7.95 (ISBN 0-02-725490-9). Macmillan.
--The Winter of the Birds. LC 75-34278. 192p. (gr. 7 up). 1976. 9.95 (ISBN 0-02-725510-7, 72551). Macmillan.

Cresswell, Henry, jt. auth. see Colles, William M.

Cresswell, Michael, jt. auth. see Vincent, Denis.

Cresswell, Roy. Quality in Urban Planning & Design. 1979. pap. 35.95 (ISBN 0-408-00363-4). Butterworths.

Cresswell, Roy, ed. Passenger Transport & the Environment: The Integration of Public Transport with the Urban Environment. (Illus.). 1977. 37.50x (ISBN 0-249-44153-5). Intl Ideas.

Cressy, David. Literacy & the Social Order. (Illus.). 250p. 1980. 32.95 (ISBN 0-521-22514-0). Cambridge U Pr.

Creswell. Short Account of Early Muslim Architecture. 1968. 15.00x (ISBN 0-685-77130-X). Intl Bk Ctr.

Creswell, John. Sea Warfare, 1939-1945. (Illus.). 1967. 20.00x (ISBN 0-520-00277-6). U of Cal Pr.

Creswell, William H., Jr., jt. auth. see Anderson, C. L.

Creswell, William H., Jr., jt. auth. see Anderson, Carl L.

Creswick, Alice. Red Book of Fruit Jars, No. 3. (Illus.). 1978. pap. 11.95 (ISBN 0-89145-076-9). Collector Bks.

Cretan, Gladys Y. Lobo. (Illus.). (gr. k-3). 1969. PLB 6.96 o.p. (ISBN 0-688-50035-8). Lothrop.
--Lobo & Brewster. LC 73-135295. (Illus.). (gr. k-3). 1971. 7.25 o.p. (ISBN 0-688-41149-5); PLB 6.48 o.p. (ISBN 0-688-51149-X). Lothrop.

Creth, Sheila & Duda, Fred. Personnel Management in Libraries. 300p. 1980. 17.95 (ISBN 0-918212-25-1). Neal-Schuman.

Cretien, Troyes de see De Troyes, Chretien.

Cretzmeyer, Francis X., et al. Track & Field Athletics. 8th ed. LC 74-2486. (Illus.). 1974. 15.00 (ISBN 0-8016-1075-3). Mosby.

Creutzfeldt, W., ed. The Entero-Insular Axis. (Frontiers of Hormone Research: Vol. 7). (Illus.). x, 310p. 1980. 69.00 (ISBN 3-8055-0795-X). S Karger.

Crevecoeur, Michel-Guillanme St. J. De see De Crevecoeur, Michel-Guillanme St. J.

Creveld, Martin L. Van see Van Creveld, Martin L.

Crew, Anna, jt. auth. see Von Haag, Michael.

Crew, Michael A., ed. Issues in Public-Utility Pricing & Regulation. LC 79-6033. 1980. 22.95 (ISBN 0-669-03606-4). Lexington Bks.
--Problems in Public-Utility Economics & Regulation. 192p. 1979. 17.95 (ISBN 0-669-02775-8). Lexington Bks.

Crew, P. Mack. Calvinist Preaching & Iconoclasm in the Netherlands, 1544-1569. LC 77-77013. (Studies in Early Modern History). 1978. 32.95 (ISBN 0-521-21739-3). Cambridge U Pr.

Crews, Donald. Freight Train. LC 78-2303. (Illus.). (gr. k-3). 1978. 7.95 (ISBN 0-688-80165-X); PLB 7.63 (ISBN 0-688-84165-1). Greenwillow.
--Light. LC 80-20273. (Illus.). 32p. (ps-1). 1981. 7.95 (ISBN 0-688-00303-6); lib. bdg. 7.63 (ISBN 0-688-00310-9). Greenwillow.

Crews, Frederick. Random House Handbook. 2nd ed. 1977. pap. text ed. 9.50 o.p. (ISBN 0-394-31211-2). Random.

--The Random House Reader. 432p. 1981. pap. text ed. 8.95 (ISBN 0-394-32268-1). Random.
Crews, Harry. Childhood, the Biography of a Place. 1979. lib. bdg. 12.95 (ISBN 0-8161-6752-4). G K Hall.
Crews, Judson. Nolo Contendere. 6.50 (ISBN 0-930324-08-0). Green Hill.
Crews, Katherine. Music & Perceptual Motor Development. (Classroom Music Enrichment Units Ser.). (Illus.). 1974. pap. text ed. 5.95x (ISBN 0-87628-213-3). Ctr Appl Res.
Cribb, A. B. & Cribb, J. W. Wild Food in Australia. 1980. pap. 5.95x (ISBN 0-00-634436-4, Pub. by W Collins Australia). Intl Schol Bk Serv.
Cribb, J. W., jt. auth. see Cribb, A. B.
Crichlow, Henry B. Modern Reservoir Engineering: A Simulation Approach. (Illus.). 1977. 34.95 (ISBN 0-13-597468-2). P-H.
Crichton, Anne. Health Policy Making: The Fundamental Issues. (Illus.). 432p. 1981. text ed. write for info. (ISBN 0-914904-44-2). Health Admin Pr.
Crichton, George H. Nicola Pisano & the Revival of Sculpture in Italy. LC 78-59011. (Illus.). 1981. Repr. of 1938 ed. 23.50 (ISBN 0-88355-686-3). Hyperion Conn.
Crichton, Ian. The Art of Dying. 166p. 1976. text ed. 17.00x (ISBN 0-7206-0353-6). Humanities.
Crichton, J. M., jt. auth. see Howells, W. W.
Crichton, Tom. Naval Warfare. LC 77-430997. (Pegasus Books: No. 22). (Illus.). 1969. 7.50x (ISBN 0-234-77184-4). Intl Pubns Serv.
--Sailing. LC 68-1556. (Pegasus Books: No. 4). 1965. 7.50x (ISBN 0-234-77848-2). Intl Pubns Serv.
Crichton, Whitcomb. Practical Course in Modern Locksmithing. 1943. 13.95 (ISBN 0-911012-06-0). Nelson-Hall.
Crick, Bernard. The American Science of Politics: Its Origins & Conditions. 1959. 6.75x o.p. (ISBN 0-520-00278-4). U of Cal Pr.
--George Orwell: A Life. 1981. 19.95 (ISBN 0-316-16112-8). Little.
Crick, Francis. Of Molecules & Men. LC 66-26994. (Jesse & John Danz Lecture Ser.). 118p. 1967. pap. 3.95 (ISBN 0-295-97869-4, WP-26). U of Wash Pr.
Crick, Malcolm. Explorations in Language & Meaning: Towards a Semantic Anthropology. LC 76-17290. 1977. text ed. 27.95 (ISBN 0-470-15144-7). Halsted Pr.
Cricket Magazine Editors, jt. auth. see Leonard, Marcia.
Cricket Magazine Editors, jt. auth. see Leverich, Kathleen.
Cricket Magazine Editors, jt. auth. see Watson, Pauline.
Crickmay, Marie C. Helping the Stroke Patient to Talk. (Illus.). 132p. 1977. pap. 11.75 (ISBN 0-398-03593-8). C C Thomas.
Criddle, Byron. Socialists & European Integration: A Study of the French Socialist Party. (Library of Political Studies). 1969. text ed. 7.25x (ISBN 0-7100-6423-3). Humanities.
Criddle, W. J. & Ellis, G. P. Spectral & Chemical Characterization of Organic Compounds: A Laboratory Handbook. 2nd ed. LC 80-40497. 1980. write for info. (ISBN 0-471-27813-0, Pub. by Wiley-Interscience); pap. write for info. (ISBN 0-471-27812-2). Wiley.
--Spectral & Chemical Characterization of Organic Compounds: A Laboratory Handbook. LC 75-23296. 128p. 1976. 19.95 (ISBN 0-471-18767-4, Pub. by Wiley-Interscience); pap. text ed. 8.95 (ISBN 0-471-01499-0, Pub. by Wiley-Interscience). Wiley.
Crifer, Sr. Carmel, jt. auth. see Patricius, Bro.
Crigelionis, B., ed. Stochastic Differential Systems; Filtering & Control: Proceedings. (Lecture Notes in Control & Information Sciences Ser.: Vol. 25). 362p. 1981. pap. 24.20 (ISBN 0-387-10498-4). Springer-Verlag.
Crighton, D. B., et al, eds. Control of Ovulation. new ed. LC 78-40043. 1978. 74.95 (ISBN 0-408-70924-3). Butterworths.
Crighton, Richard. The Million Dollar Lift. 288p. 1981. pap. 2.50 (ISBN 0-380-76604-3, 76604). Avon.
Crigorieff, R. D., jt. ed. see Alefeld, G.
Crile, George, Jr. What Women Should Know About the Breast Cancer Controversy. 128p. 1973. 4.95 o.s.i. (ISBN 0-02-528800-8). Macmillan.
Crilly, Eugene R. Material & Process Applications: Land, Sea, Air, Space. (The Science of Advanced Materials & Process Engineering Ser.). 1981. price not set. Soc Adv Material.
Crilly, Howard M. The Tinted Photograph. 1981. 10.95 (ISBN 0-533-04653-X). Vantage.
Crim, D., jt. auth. see Misner, Gordon E.
Crim, Keith, tr. see Westermann, Claus.
Crimes, T. P. & Harper, J. C. Trace Fossils Two: Geological Journal Special Issue, No. 9. (Liverpool Geological Society & the Manchester Geological Association). 360p. 1980. 64.95 (ISBN 0-471-27756-8, Pub. by Wiley-Interscience). Wiley.
Crinkley, Richmond. Walter Pater: Humanist. LC 70-119811. 200p. 1970. 10.00x (ISBN 0-8131-1221-4). U Pr of Ky.
Crip, H. & Rudduck, L. The Mothering Years: The Story of the Canberra Mothercraft Society 1926-79. (Illus.). 112p. (Orig.). 1980. pap. text ed. 7.95 (ISBN 0-9595400-0-8, 0584). Bks Australia.
Crippen, Lee F. Simon Cameron: Ante Bellum Years. LC 76-168674. (American Scene Ser). 1972. Repr. of 1942 ed. lib. bdg. 32.50 (ISBN 0-306-70362-9). Da Capo.
Crippen, Thomas G. Christmas & Christmas Lore. LC 69-16067. (Illus.). x, 223p. 1972. Repr. of 1923 ed. 24.00 (ISBN 0-8103-3029-6). Gale.
Cripps, T. F. & Tarling, R. J. Growth in Advanced Capitalist Economics: 1950-1970. LC 73-84317. (Dept. of Applied Economics, Occasional Papers: No. 40). (Illus.). 64p. 1973. 6.95x (ISBN 0-521-09828-9). Cambridge U Pr.
Cripps, Thomas. Slow Fade to Black: The Negro in American Film, 1900-1942. LC 76-21818. (Illus.). 1977. 24.95 (ISBN 0-19-501864-8). Oxford U Pr.
--Slow Fade to Black: The Negro in American Film, 1900-1942. (Illus.). 1977. pap. 7.95 (ISBN 0-19-502130-4, 484, GB). Oxford U Pr.
Cripps, Yvonne M. Controlling Technology: Genetic Engineering & the Law. 170p. 1980. 20.95 (ISBN 0-03-056806-4). Praeger.
Cripwell, Kenneth. Language. Yapp, Malcolm, et al, eds. (World History Ser.). (Illus.). (gr. 10). 1980. Repr. of 1977 ed. lib. bdg. 5.95 (ISBN 0-89908-146-0); pap. text ed. 1.95 (ISBN 0-89908-121-5). Greenhaven.
Crisci, Elizabeth. What Do You Do with Joe? Problem Pupils & Tactful Teachers. (Illus.). 64p. (Orig.). 1981. pap. 3.50 (ISBN 0-87239-414-X, 3650). Standard Pub.
Criscuolo, Nicholas. A Tutor's Guidebook for Remedial Reading. LC 72-80433. 1972. pap. 3.00 o.p. (ISBN 0-87812-042-4). Pendell Pub.
Criscuolo, Nicholas P. Supervising the Reading Program. LC 72-98020. 1973. pap. 9.00 o.p. (ISBN 0-87812-049-1). Pendell Pub.
Crisler, Lois. Captive Wild. LC 68-28191. (Illus.). (YA) 1968. 10.00 o.s.i. (ISBN 0-06-010916-5, HarpT). Har-Row.
Crisp, Carl E., jt. auth. see Crafts, Alden S.
Crisp, Clement, jt. auth. see Clarke, Mary.
Crisp, D. J., ed. European Marine Biology Symposium, Fourth. (Illus.). 1971. 97.50 (ISBN 0-521-08101-7). Cambridge U Pr.
Crisp, N. J. The London Deal. 208p. 1981. pap. 1.95 (ISBN 0-380-50740-4, 50740). Avon.
--The Odd Job Man. 208p. 1981. pap. 2.25 (ISBN 0-380-54528-4). Avon.
Crisp, Quentin. The Naked Civil Servant. LC 77-73866. 1977. 7.95 o.p. (ISBN 0-03-022451-9). HR&W.
Crisp, Wynnlee. Development & Use of the Outdoor Classroom: An Annotated Bibliography. LC 75-15537. 145p. 1975. 10.00 (ISBN 0-8108-0831-5). Scarecrow.
Crispen, Margaret. How Any Woman Can Get Rich Fast in Real Estate. 1980. pap. 4.95. Warner Bks.
--How Any Woman Can Get Rich Fast in Real Estate. 1978. 9.95 o.p. (ISBN 0-8362-6402-9). Andrews & McMeel.
Crispens, Charles G., Jr. Handbook on the Laboratory Mouse. 278p. 1975. pap. 14.75 spiral (ISBN 0-398-03403-6). C C Thomas.
Crispin, Edmund. Beware of the Trains. 1981. pap. 2.95 (ISBN 0-14-005834-6). Penguin.
--Buried for Pleasure. 191p. Repr. of 1948 ed. lib. bdg. 9.70x (ISBN 0-89190-691-6). Am Repr-Rivercity Pr.
--The Case of the Gilded Fly. 1980. lib. bdg. 13.95 (ISBN 0-8161-3018-3). G K Hall.
--The Case of the Gilded Fly. LC 79-52173. (Walker Mystery Ser.). 223p. 1979. Repr. 8.95 o.s.i. (ISBN 0-8027-5410-4). Walker & Co.
--Holy Disorders. 240p. (Orig.). 1980. pap. 2.25 (ISBN 0-380-51508-3, 51508). Avon.
--The Long Divorce. (Penguin Crime Monthly Ser.). 256p. 1981. pap. 2.95 (ISBN 0-14-001304-0). Penguin.
--Love Lies Bleeding. 9.95 (ISBN 0-8027-5444-9). Walker & Co.
--The Moving Toyship. LC 80-54479. 1981. 9.95 (ISBN 0-8027-5434-1). Walker & Co.
Crispin, Edmund, ed. Outwards from Earth. (Orig.). 1974. pap. 3.95 (ISBN 0-571-10489-4, Pub. by Faber & Faber). Merrimack Bk Serv.
Crispin, John. Pedro Salinas. (World Authors Ser.: Spain: No. 283). 1974. lib. bdg. 10.95 (ISBN 0-8057-2784-1). Twayne.
Crispin, John, jt. auth. see Crispin, Ruth K.
Crispin, Ruth K. & Crispin, John. Progress in Spanish: Grammar & Practice for the Second Year. 2nd ed. 1978. 13.95x (ISBN 0-673-15147-6). Scott F.
--Workbook & Laboratory Manual for Progress in Spanish. 2nd ed. 1978. pap. 4.95x (ISBN 0-673-15148-4). Scott F.
Crispino, James A. The Assimilation of Ethnic Groups: The Italian Case. 175p. Date not set. 9.95x (ISBN 0-913256-39-0). Ctr Migration.
Criss, Lillian M. That Tent by the Sawdust Pile. LC 76-41462. (Destiny Ser.). 1976. pap. 4.95 (ISBN 0-8163-0267-7, 20249-9). Pacific Pr Pub Assn.
Criss, Wayne E., jt. ed. see Sharma, Rameshwar K.
Criss, Wayne E., et al, eds. Control Mechanisms in Cancer. LC 75-30234. (Progress in Cancer Research & Therapy Ser: Vol.1). 1976. 46.00 (ISBN 0-89004-083-4). Raven.
Crissey, Clair. Layman's Bible Book Commentary: Matthew, Vol. 15. 1981. 4.75 (ISBN 0-8054-1185-2). Broadman.
Crissey, John T., jt. auth. see Shelley, Walter B.
Crissy, W. J., jt. auth. see Cash, Harold C.
Crissy, W. J., et al. Selling: The Personal Force in Marketing. LC 76-45848. (Marketing Ser.). 1977. text ed. 21.95 (ISBN 0-471-18757-7). Wiley.
Crist, jt. auth. see Krause.
Crist, Evamae B. Take This House. (Illus.). 1977. pap. 2.25 (ISBN 0-8361-1817-0). Herald Pr.
Crist, Lyle M. Through the Rain & Rainbow: The Remarkable Life of Richard Kinney. LC 73-22386. 224p. 1974. 5.95 o.p. (ISBN 0-687-42036-9). Abingdon.
Crist, Raymond F., jt. auth. see Burrill, Harry.
Crist, Steven. Off Track: Bets & Pieces. LC 79-6662. 168p. 1981. 9.95 (ISBN 0-385-15215-9). Doubleday.
Cristenson, Larry. The Renewed Mind. LC 74-12770. 144p. (Orig.). 1974. pap. 3.50 (ISBN 0-87123-487-4, 210487). Bethany Fell.
Cristescu, Cornelia & Klepczynski, W. J., eds. Asteroids, Comets, Meteoric Matter: Proceedings. (Illus.). 333p. 1975. text ed. 50.00x (ISBN 0-87936-008-9). Scholium Intl.
Cristiani, Leon. St. Margaret Mary Alacoque. 1976. 5.00 (ISBN 0-8198-0456-8); pap. 4.00 o.s.i. (ISBN 0-8198-0457-6). Dghtrs St Paul.
Cristofer, Michael. The Shadow Box. 1977. pap. 2.25 (ISBN 0-380-01865-9, 46839, Bard). Avon.
Cristoforo, R. J. De see De Cristoforo, R. J.
Criswell, Ann. Dining in Houston, Vol. II. (Dining in Ser.). 200p. 1980. pap. 7.95 (ISBN 0-89716-065-7). Peanut Butter.
Criswell, Carl S. The Still House of Time. 1980. 5.50 (ISBN 0-8233-0325-X). Golden Quill.
Criswell, W. A. Acts: An Exposition, Vol. 3. 320p. 1980. 10.95 (ISBN 0-310-22900-6, 9413). Zondervan.
--Ephesians: An Exposition. 308p. 1981. pap. 6.95 (ISBN 0-310-22781-X). Zondervan.
--Ephesians: An Exposition. 288p. 1974. 11.95 (ISBN 0-310-22780-1). Zondervan.
--Exposition of Galatians. 160p. 1980. pap. 5.95 (ISBN 0-310-22791-7). Zondervan.
--Expository Sermons on the Book of Daniel. 14.95 (ISBN 0-310-22800-X). Zondervan.
--Expository Sermons on the Epistles of Peter. 216p. (Orig.). 1980. pap. 4.95 (ISBN 0-310-22811-5). Zondervan.
--The Holy Spirit in Today's World. 192p. 1976. pap. text ed. 5.95 (ISBN 0-310-22852-2). Zondervan.
Critchfield, Howard J. General Climatology. 3rd ed. (Illus.). 416p. 1974. ref. ed. 18.95 (ISBN 0-13-350264-3). P-H.
Critchfield, Margot, jt. auth. see Dwyer, Thomas.
Critchfield, Richard. Golden Bowl Be Broken: Peasant Life in Four Cultures. LC 73-77855. (Midland Bks.: No. 187). (Illus.). 320p. 1974. 12.50x (ISBN 0-253-13260-6). Ind U Pr.
--Shahhat: An Egyptian. 1978. 12.95 (ISBN 0-8156-2202-3); pap. 6.96 o.p. (ISBN 0-8156-0151-4). Syracuse U Pr.
--Shahhat: An Egyptian. 1979. pap. 3.50 (ISBN 0-380-48405-6, 48405, Discus). Avon.
--Villages. LC 80-1721. (Illus.). 384p. 1981. 17.95 (ISBN 0-385-17212-5). Doubleday.
Critchley, Eileen A., jt. auth. see Critchley, Macdonald.
Critchley, Macdonald. The Divine Banquet of the Brain. LC 78-24621. 1979. text ed. 19.50 (ISBN 0-89004-348-5). Raven.
Critchley, Macdonald & Critchley, Eileen A. Dyslexia Defined. (Illus.). 172p. 1978. 17.00 (ISBN 0-398-03885-6). C C Thomas.
Critchley, Macdonald, ed. Butterworths Medical Dictionary. 2nd ed. LC 77-30154. 1978. 159.95 (ISBN 0-407-00061-5). Butterworths.
Critchley, Macdonald, et al, eds. International Headache Congress, 1980. 1980. write for info. Raven.
Crites, John O. Career Counseling: Models, Methods & Materials. (Illus.). 240p. 1981. text ed. 14.95x (ISBN 0-07-013781-1, C). McGraw.
Crites, Laura, ed. The Female Offender: A Total Look at Women in the Criminal Justice System. 1977. 21.50 (ISBN 0-669-00635-1). Lexington Bks.
Crites, Stephen. In the Twilight of Christendom: Hegel Vs. Kierkegaard on Faith & History. LC 77-188905. (American Academy of Religion. Studies in Religion). 1972. pap. text ed. 7.50 (ISBN 0-89130-154-2, 010002). Scholars Pr Ca.
Critser, James R., Jr. Antioxidants & Stabilizers for Polymers. (Ser. 3-75). 1976. 100.00 (ISBN 0-914428-34-9). Lexington Data.
--Blood Technology. (Series 10BT-79). 101p. 1980. 80.00 (ISBN 0-914428-75-6). Lexington Data.
--Cancer: Diagnosis & Therapy. (Ser. 10CDT - 80). 1981. 60.00 (ISBN 0-914428-77-2). Lexington Data.
--Clinical Assays. (Ser. 10CA 80). 1981. 80.00 (ISBN 0-914428-78-0). Lexington Data.
--Clinical Assays. (Ser. 10CA-79). 122p. 1980. 80.00 (ISBN 0-914428-65-9). Lexington Data.
--Energy Systems: Solar, Wind, Water, Geothermal. (Ser. 11-78). 1979. 125.00 (ISBN 0-914428-58-6). Lexington Data.
--Energy Systems: Solar, Wind, Water, Geothermal. (Ser. 11-79). 1981. 125.00 (ISBN 0-914428-70-5). Lexington Data.
--Energy Systems: Solar, Wind, Water, Geothermal. (Ser. 11-77). 1978. 125.00 (ISBN 0-914428-47-0). Lexington Data.
--Flame Retardants for Plastics, Rubber & Textiles: Including Indexes & Abstracts 1967 to 1971. Incl. 285.00 (ISBN 0-914428-03-9). (Ser. 2-6771b). 1971. Lexington Data.
--Flame Retardants for Plastics, Rubber, Textiles & Paper: Series No. 2-7980, July 1979 - June 1980. 136p. 1981. refer. - ring bdg. 110.00 (ISBN 0-914428-73-X). Lexington Data.
--Herbicides. (Ser. 12-77). 1978. 80.00 (ISBN 0-914428-48-9). Lexington Data.
--Lasers: Equipment & Applications. (Ser. 6-78). Date not set. 300.00 (ISBN 0-914428-62-4). Lexington Data Postponed.
--Medical Diagnostic Apparatus-Systems. (Serie 10DAS-79). 142p. 1980. 80.00 (ISBN 0-914428-66-7). Lexington Data.
--Medical Technology: Advanced Medical Apparatus-Systems. (Ser. 10 AMA-78). 1980. 300.00 (ISBN 0-914428-59-4). Lexington Data.
--Medical Technology: Advanced Medical Apparatus-Systems. (Ser 10AMA-77). 1978. 300.00 (ISBN 0-914428-46-2). Lexington Data.
--Medical Technology: Electrical-Electronic Apparatus 1976. (Ser. 10 - 76). 1977. 200.00 (ISBN 0-914428-41-1). Lexington Data.
--Medical Therapeutic Apparatus-Systems: Series No. 10tas-79. 1981. 60.00 (ISBN 0-914428-69-1). Lexington Data.
--Membrane Separation Processes. (Ser. 5-79). 1980. 110.00 (ISBN 0-914428-72-1). Lexington Data.
--Pesticides. (Ser. 13-78). 1979. 150.00 (ISBN 0-914428-63-2). Lexington Data.
--Prosthetics & Contact Lens: Series 10PC - 79. 1981. refer. - ring bdg. 60.00 (ISBN 0-686-69159-8). Lexington Data.
--Radiology. 99p. 1980. 60.00 (ISBN 0-914428-68-3, 10R-79). Lexington Data.
Crittall, Elizabeth, ed. The Victoria History of the Counties of England: A History of Wiltshire, Vol. 10. (Illus.). 370p. 1975. 75.00x o.p. (ISBN 0-19-722740-6). Oxford U Pr.
Crittenden, Max D., Jr., et al, eds. Cordilleran Metamorphic Core Complexes. Davis, George A. & Coney, Peter J. (Memoir: No. 153). 1980. write for info. (ISBN 0-8137-1153-3). Geol Soc.
Crittenden, Penelope, jt. auth. see North, Barbara.
Crittenden, R. J., jt. auth. see Bishop, Richard L.
Crix, Frederick C. Reprographic Management Handbook. 2nd ed. 332p. 1979. text ed. 30.75x (ISBN 0-220-67010-2, Pub. by Busn Bks England). Renouf.
Croatto, J. Severino. Exodus: A Hermeneutics of Freedom. 112p. (Orig.). 1981. pap. 4.95 (ISBN 0-88344-111-X). Orbis Bks.
Croce, Benedetto. Aesthetic. Ainslie, Douglas, tr. LC 78-58500. 544p. 1979. pap. 7.50 (ISBN 0-87923-255-2, Nonpareil Bk.). Godine.
--Benedetto Croce's Poetry & Literature: An Introduction to the Criticism & History of Poetry & Literature. Gullace, Giovanni, tr. from Ital. & intro. by. LC 80-19511. 1981. 24.95x (ISBN 0-8093-0982-3). S Ill U Pr.
--Historical Materialism & the Economics of Karl Marx. (Social Science Classics). 1981. 19.95 (ISBN 0-87855-313-4); pap. text ed. 6.95 (ISBN 0-87855-695-8). Transaction Bks.
--My Philosophy. 1962. pap. 0.95 o.s.i. (ISBN 0-02-064870-7, Collier). Macmillan.
--Philosophy of the Practical. Ainslie, Douglas, tr. LC 66-30790. 1913. 15.00x (ISBN 0-8196-0192-6). Biblo.
--Philosophy, Poetry, History: An Anthology of Essays. Sprigge, Cecil, tr. 1966. 55.00x (ISBN 0-19-711621-3). Oxford U Pr.
Crochetti, Gino & Stella, Frank. What's for Dinner Tomorrow? Corporate Views of New Food Products. LC 79-93419. 1979. pap. 5.00 (ISBN 0-918780-15-2). Inform.
Crocker, A. C. Predicting Teaching Success. (General Ser.). 230p. 1974. pap. text ed. 17.00x (ISBN 0-85633-037-X, NFER). Humanities.

--Statistics for the Teacher. 144p. 1974. pap. text ed. 7.75x (ISBN 0-85633-042-6, NFER). Humanities.

Crocker, Betty. Betty Crocker's Breads. (Illus.). 1974. PLB 7.62 o.p. (ISBN 0-307-69574-3, Golden Pr); pap. 2.95 (ISBN 0-307-09919-9). Western Pub.

--Betty Crocker's Salads. (Illus.). 1977. PLB 9.15 o.p. (ISBN 0-307-69900-5, Golden Pr); pap. 2.95 (ISBN 0-307-09900-8). Western Pub.

Crocker, Betty, ed. Cookie Book. 96p. 1980. 3.95 (ISBN 0-307-09930-X); lib. bdg. 5.95. Western Pub.

Crocker, Chester A., jt. ed. see Bissel, Richard E.

Crocker, George N. Roosevelt's Road to Russia. LC 74-26540. (Fdr & the Era of the New Deal Ser.). (Illus.). xvii, 312p. 1975. Repr. of 1959 ed. lib. bdg. 32.50 (ISBN 0-306-70714-4). Da Capo.

Crocker, J. Christopher, jt. ed. see Sapir, J. David.

Crocker, Lawrence P. The Army Officer's Guide. 41st, rev. ed. (Illus.). 560p. (Orig.). 1981. pap. 12.95 (ISBN 0-8117-2040-3). Stackpole.

Crocker, Lester G. Jean-Jacques Rousseau: The Prophetic Voice, 1758-78. 384p. 1973. 10.95 o.s.i. (ISBN 0-02-528840-7). Macmillan.

--Jean-Jacques Rousseau: The Quest, 1712-1758. LC 68-22818. 1968. 9.95 o.s.i. (ISBN 0-02-528830-X). Macmillan.

Crocker, Lester G., ed. see Rousseau, Jean-Jacques.

Crocker, Lester G., jt. ed. see Seibert, Louise C.

Crocker, Lionel. Harry Emerson Fosdick's Art of Preaching: An Anthology. (Illus.). 296p. 1971. pap. 19.75 photocopy ed. spiral (ISBN 0-398-00368-8). C C Thomas.

Crocker, Richard L. The Early Medieval Sequence. LC 74-84143. 1977. 38.50x (ISBN 0-520-02847-3). U of Cal Pr.

Crocket, Dresda, jt. auth. see Cox, Michael.

Crockett, Andrew D. Money: Theory, Policy & Institutions. 1973. pap. text ed. 14.95x (ISBN 0-17-712206-4). Intl Ideas.

Crockett, Desda, jt. auth. see Cox, Michael.

Crockett, Dina B., tr. see Apresjan, Ju. D.

Crockett, George W., et al, eds. National Roster of Black Judicial Officers, 1980. 120p. (Orig.). 1980. pap. 2.95 (8562). Am Judicature.

Crockett, James U. Annuals. (Encyclopedia of Gardening Ser). (Illus.). 1971. 11.95 (ISBN 0-8094-1081-8). Time-Life.

--Annuals. LC 78-140420. (Time-Life Encyclopedia of Gardening). (Illus.). (gr. 6 up). 1971. lib. bdg. 11.97 (ISBN 0-8094-1082-6, Pub. by Time-Life). Silver.

--Bulbs. (Encyclopedia of Gardening Ser). (Illus.). 1971. 11.95 (ISBN 0-8094-1101-6). Time-Life.

--Bulbs. LC 78-140420. (Time-Life Encyclopedia of Gardening). (Illus.). (gr. 6 up). 1971. lib. bdg. 11.97 (ISBN 0-8094-1102-4, Pub. by Time-Life). Silver.

--Evergreens. (Encyclopedia of Gardening Ser). (Illus.). 1971. 11.95 (ISBN 0-8094-1105-9); lib. bdg. avail. (ISBN 0-685-02974-3). Time-Life.

--Evergreens. LC 78-140420. (Time-Life Encyclopedia of Gardening). (Illus.). (gr. 6 up). 1971. lib. bdg. 11.97 (ISBN 0-8094-1106-7, Pub. by Time-Life). Silver.

--Flowering House Plants. (Encyclopedia of Gardening Ser). (Illus.). 1971. 11.95 (ISBN 0-8094-1097-4); lib. bdg. avail. (ISBN 0-685-00195-4). Time-Life.

--Flowering House Plants. LC 78-140420. (Time-Life Encyclopedia of Gardening). (Illus.). 1971. lib. bdg. 11.97 (ISBN 0-8094-1098-2, Pub. by Time-Life). Silver.

--Flowering Shrubs. (Encyclopedia of Gardening Ser). (Illus.). 1972. 11.95 (ISBN 0-8094-1113-X); lib. bdg. avail. (ISBN 0-685-24678-7). Dist. by Little. Time-Life.

--Flowering Shrubs. LC 78-140420. (Time-Life Encyclopedia of Gardening). (Illus.). (gr. 6 up). 1972. lib. bdg. 11.97 (ISBN 0-8094-1114-8, Pub. by Time-Life). Silver.

--Foliage House Plants. (Encyclopedia of Gardening Ser). (Illus.). 1972. 11.95 (ISBN 0-8094-1121-0); lib. bdg. avail. (ISBN 0-685-25145-4). Time-Life.

--Landscape Gardening. (Encylopedia of Gardening Ser). (Illus.). 1971. 11.95 (ISBN 0-8094-1089-3); lib. bdg. avail. (ISBN 0-685-04842-X). Time-Life.

--Landscape Gardening. LC 64-140420. (Time-Life Encyclopedia of Gardening). (Illus.). (gr. 6 up), 1971. lib. bdg. 11.97 (ISBN 0-8094-1090-7, Pub. by Time-Life). Silver.

--Lawns & Ground Covers. (Encyclopedia of Gardening Ser). (Illus.). 1971. 11.95 (ISBN 0-8094-1093-1); lib. bdg. avail. (ISBN 0-685-00194-6). Time-Life.

--Perennials. (Encyclopedia of Gardening Ser). (Illus.). 1972. 11.95 (ISBN 0-8094-1109-1). Time-Life.

--Perennials. LC 78-140420. (Time-Life Encyclopedia of Gardening). (Illus.). (gr. 6 up). 1972. lib. bdg. 11.97 (ISBN 0-8094-1110-5, Pub. by Time-Life). Silver.

--Roses. (Encycloedia of Gardening Ser). (Illus.). 1971. 11.95 (ISBN 0-8094-1085-0); lib. bdg. avail. (ISBN 0-685-04844-6). Time-Life.

--Roses. LC 78-140420. (Time-Life Encyclopedia of Gardening). (Illus.). (gr. 6 up). 1971. lib. bdg. 11.97 (ISBN 0-8094-1086-9, Pub. by Time-Life). Silver.

--Trees. (Encyclopedia of Gardening Ser.). (Illus.). 160p. 1972. 11.95 (ISBN 0-8094-1117-2); lib. bdg. avail. (ISBN 0-685-27223-0). Time-Life.

--Trees. LC 78-140420. (The Time-Life Encyclopedia of Gardening Ser.). (Illus.). 1972. lib. bdg. 11.97 (ISBN 0-686-51063-1). Silver.

--Vegetables & Fruits. (The Encyclopedia of Gardening Ser.). (Illus.). 1972. 11.95 (ISBN 0-8094-1069-9); lib. bdg. avail. (ISBN 0-685-27455-1). Time-Life.

--Vegetables & Fruits. LC 78-140420. (Time-Life Encyclopedia of Gardening). (Illus.). 1972. lib. bdg. 11.97 (ISBN 0-8094-1071-0, Pub. by Time-Life). Silver.

--Vegetables & Fruits. LC 78-140420. (The Time-Life Encyclopedia of Gardening Ser.). (Illus.). 1972. lib. bdg. 11.97 (ISBN 0-686-51064-X). Silver.

Crockett, James U. & Allen, Oliver E. Decorating with Plants. LC 77-95146. (The Time-Life Encyclopedia of Gardening Ser.). (Illus.). 1978. lib. bdg. 10.98 (ISBN 0-686-51058-5). Silver.

--Pruning & Grafting. (The Time-Life Encyclopedia of Gardening Ser.). (Illus.). 1978. lib. bdg. 10.98 (ISBN 0-686-50001-6). Silver.

--Shade Gardens. (The Time-Life Encyclopedia of Gardening Ser.). (Illus.). 1979. lib. bdg. 11.97 (ISBN 0-8094-2646-3); kivar bdg. 8.95 (ISBN 0-8094-2647-1). Silver.

Crockett, James U. & Cravens, Richard. Pests & Diseases. (The Time-Life Encyclopedia of Gardening Ser.). (Illus.). 1977. lib. bdg. 11.97 (ISBN 0-686-51062-3). Silver.

--Vines. (The Time-Life Encyclopedia of Gardening Ser.). (Illus.). 1979. lib. bdg. 11.97 (ISBN 0-686-51067-4). Silver.

Crockett, James U. & Murphy, Wendy B. Gardening Under Lights. (The Time-Life Encyclopedia of Gardening Ser.). (Illus.). 1978. lib. bdg. 11.96 (ISBN 0-686-51060-7). Silver.

--Japanese Gardens. (The Time-Life Encyclopedia of Gardening Ser.). (Illus.). 1979. lib. bdg. 11.97 (ISBN 0-686-66220-2); kivar bdg. 8.95 (ISBN 0-686-66221-0). Silver.

Crockett, James U. & Perl, Philip. Cacti & Succulents. (The Time-Life Encyclopedia of Gardening Ser.). (Illus.). 1978. lib. bdg. 11.97 (ISBN 0-686-51057-7). Silver.

--Miniatures & Bonsai. (The Time-Life Encyclopedia of Gardening Ser.). (Illus.). 1979. lib. bdg. 11.96 (ISBN 0-686-51066-6). Silver.

Crockett, James U. & Prendergast, C. Easy Gardens. (The Time-Life Encyclopedia of Gardening Ser.). (Illus.). 1979. lib. bdg. 11.97 (ISBN 0-686-51065-8). Silver.

Crockett, James U. & Skelsy, Alice F. Orchids. (The Time-Life Encyclopedia of Gardening Ser.). (Illus.). 1978. lib. bdg. 11.97 (ISBN 0-686-51061-5). Silver.

Crockett, James U. & Tanner, Ogden. Garden Construction. (The Time-Life Encyclopedia of Gardening Ser.). (Illus.). 1978. lib. bdg. 11.96 (ISBN 0-686-51059-3). Silver.

--Rock & Water Gardens. (The Time-Life Encyclopedia of Gardening Ser.). (Illus.). 1979. lib. bdg. 10.98 (ISBN 0-8094-2626-9); kivar bdg. 8.95 (ISBN 0-8094-2627-7). Silver.

Crockett, James V. Foliage House Plants. LC 78-140420. (Time-Life Encyclopedia of Gardening). (Illus.). (gr. 6 up). 1972. lib. bdg. 11.97 (ISBN 0-8094-1123-7, Pub. by Time-Life). Silver.

--Lawns & Ground Covers. LC 78-140420. (Time-Life Encyclopedia of Gardening). (Illus.). (gr. 6 up). 1971. lib. bdg. 11.97 (ISBN 0-8094-1094-X, Pub. by Time-Life). Silver.

Crockett, James V., et al. Greenhouse Gardening. LC 76-51513. (Time-Life Encyclopedia of Gardening). (Illus.). (gr. 6 up). 1977. PLB 11.97 (ISBN 0-8094-2563-7, Pub by Time-Life). Silver.

Crockett, Jim, ed. The Guitar Player Book. rev. ed. LC 79-2350. (Illus.). 416p. 1979. pap. 9.95 (ISBN 0-394-17169-1, E739, Ever). Grove.

Crockett, Joseph P. Federal Tax System of the United States: A Survey of Law & Administration. LC 72-100154. Repr. of 1955 ed. lib. bdg. 17.50x (ISBN 0-8371-3681-4, CRTS). Greenwood.

Crockett, Lawrence J. Wildly Successful Plants: Handbook of North American Weeds. (Illus.). 1977. 12.95 o.s.i. (ISBN 0-02-528850-4, 52885). Macmillan.

Crockett, Maline C. Stories to See & Share. 80p. 1980. pap. 2.95 (ISBN 0-87747-828-7). Deseret Bk.

Crockett, Norman L. The Woolen Industry of the Midwest. LC 75-111505. (Illus.). 176p. 1970. 10.50x (ISBN 0-8131-1195-1). U Pr of Ky.

Crockford, H. D., et al. Laboratory Manual of Physical Chemistry. 2nd ed. 1976. text ed. 14.95 (ISBN 0-471-18844-1). Wiley.

Crockford, Neil. An Introduction to Risk Management. 112p. 1980. 27.00x (ISBN 0-85941-116-8, Pub. by Woodhead-Faulkner England). State Mutual Bk.

--An Introduction to Risk Management. 112p. 1980. 17.50x. Herman Pub.

Crocombe, Ron, ed. see Ta'unga.

Croft, B. A., jt. auth. see Welch, S. M.

Croft, Barbara Y., jt. auth. see Rhodes, Buck A.

Croft, David. Applied Statistics for Management Studies. 2nd ed. (Illus.). 304p. (Orig.). 1976. pap. text ed. 15.95x (ISBN 0-7121-0136-5, Pub. by Macdonald & Evans England). Intl Ideas.

Croft, David R. & Lilley, David G. Heat Transfer Calculations Using Finite Difference Equations. (Illus.). 1977. 55.90x (ISBN 0-85334-720-4, Pub. by Applied Science). Burgess-Intl Ideas.

Croft, Doreen. Be Honest with Yourself. 1976. pap. text ed. 8.95x (ISBN 0-534-00452-0). Wadsworth Pub.

Croft, Doreen & Hess, Robert D. Activities Handbook for Teachers of Young Children. 3rd ed. LC 79-90365. 1980. pap. text ed. 10.95 (ISBN 0-395-28698-0). HM.

Croft, Doreen J. Parents & Teachers: A Resource Book for Home, School & Community Relations. 1979. pap. text ed. 9.95x (ISBN 0-534-00610-8). Wadsworth Pub.

Croft, Doreen J., jt. auth. see Hess, Robert.

Croft, J. H. Going Metric in Catering. 1969. pap. 4.20 (ISBN 0-08-006512-0). Pergamon.

Croft, Kenneth. A Practice Book on English Stress & Intonation. 81p. 1961. pap. 4.95 (ISBN 0-87789-013-7); cassette tapes 90.00 (ISBN 0-87789-125-7). Eng Language.

--Reading & Word Study: For Students of English As a Second Language. (Illus.). 1969. pap. text ed. 9.50 (ISBN 0-13-756742-1). P-H.

Croft, L. R. Handbook of Protein Sequences: A Compilation of Amino Acid Sequences of Proteins. LC 79-41487. 608p. 1980. 105.00 (ISBN 0-471-27703-7). Wiley.

--Protein Sequence Determination. LC 79-41488. 157p. 1980. 14.00 (ISBN 0-471-27710-X). Wiley.

Croft, Robert J., jt. auth. see Hess, Robert D.

Croft, Terrell, et al. American Electrician's Handbook. 10th ed. 1664p. 1980. 39.50 (ISBN 0-07-013931-8, P&RB). McGraw.

Croft-Cooke, Rupert & Cotes, Peter. Circus. (Illus.). 1977. 6.95 o.s.i. (ISBN 0-02-528860-1, 52886). Macmillan.

Crofton, H. T., jt. auth. see Smart, Bath C.

Crofton, John & Douglas, Andrew. Respiratory Diseases. 3rd ed. (Illus.). 912p. 1980. 85.00 (ISBN 0-632-00577-7, Blackwell). Mosby.

Crofts, Freeman W. The Cask. lib. bdg. 12.95x (ISBN 0-89966-245-5). Buccaneer Bks.

--The Cheyne Mystery. (Crime Ser). 1978. pap. 2.50 (ISBN 0-14-000917-5). Penguin.

Crofts, Muriel, tr. see Hansen, Harold A.

Croghan, Anthony. Manual & Code of Rules for Simple Cataloging. 2nd ed. 1974. pap. 6.95x plus 24 audio cassettes (ISBN 0-9501212-6-6). J Norton Pubs.

Croghan, Martin J. & Croghan, Penelope P. Idealogical Training in Communist Education. LC 79-47986. 209p. 1980. text ed. 17.75 (ISBN 0-8191-0992-4); pap. text ed. 9.50 (ISBN 0-8191-0993-2). U Pr of Amer.

--Role Models & Readers: A Sociological Analysis. LC 79-5430. 1980. pap. 9.00 (ISBN 0-8191-0879-0). U Pr of Amer.

Croghan, Penelope P., jt. auth. see Croghan, Martin J.

Croissant, Kay & Dees, Catherine. The Immortality Principle: Continuum. 1978. pap. 4.75 (ISBN 0-934704-00-7, Pub. by Palm Publications Pr.). Theos U Pr.

Croix, Grethe La see La Croix, Grethe.

Croix, Horst de la see De la Croix, Horst & Tansey, Richard G.

Croker, J. W., jt. auth. see Scott, W.

Croll, E. J., jt. auth. see Eason, T. W.

Croll, Elisabeth. The Politics of Marriage in Contemporary China. LC 80-40586. (Contemporary China Institute Publications Ser.). (Illus.). 224p. Date not set. 36.00 (ISBN 0-521-23345-3). Cambridge U Pr.

Croll, Elisabeth J. Feminism & Socialism in China. 1978. 27.50 (ISBN 0-7100-8816-7). Routledge & Kegan.

Croll, Neil A. & Matthews, B. E. Biology of Nematodes. LC 75-505520. (Tertiary Level Biology Ser.). 1977. 18.95 (ISBN 0-470-99028-7). Halsted Pr.

Crombie, Alistair C. Robert Grosseteste & the Origins of Experimental Science, 1100-1700. 1955. 49.00x (ISBN 0-19-824189-5). Oxford U Pr.

Crombie, I. M. An Examination of Plato's Doctrines, 2 vols. Incl. Vol. 1. Plato on Man & Society. 1962. text ed. 24.75x (ISBN 0-7100-3608-6); Vol. 2. Plato on Knowledge & Reality. 1963. text ed. 40.50x (ISBN 0-391-01053-0). (International Library of Philosophy & Scientific Method). Set. text ed. 40.50x (ISBN 0-686-66629-1). Humanities.

Crome. Wilderness Family Pt. 2. (gr. 3-5). pap. 1.50 (ISBN 0-590-12113-8, Schol Pap). Schol Bk Serv.

Cromie. Steven & the Green Turtle. (Illus.). (gr. 2). Date not set. pap. cancelled (ISBN 0-590-30904-8, Schol Pap). Schol Bk Serv.

Cromie, Alice. Lucky to Be Alive? 1979. pap. 1.95 (ISBN 0-345-28432-1). Ballantine.

Cromie, Alice H. Tour Guide to the Civil War. 1975. 12.95 (ISBN 0-87690-153-4). Dutton.

Crommelin, Jennyfer. Fabric Crafts. LC 79-20121. (Pegasus Books: No. 26). 1970. 7.50x (ISBN 0-234-77275-1). Intl Pubns Serv.

Crompton, Anne. The Untamed. 256p. (Orig.). 1981. pap. 2.50 (ISBN 0-523-41151-0). Pinnacle Bks.

Crompton, Anne E. A Woman's Place. (Illus.). 224p. 1980. pap. 2.25 (ISBN 0-345-28790-8). Ballantine.

Crompton, D. W. & Joyner, S. M. Parasitic Worms. LC 79-20223. (Wykeham Science Ser.: No. 57). 1980. pap. 15.95x (ISBN 0-8448-1342-7). Crane-Russak Co.

Crompton, Louis, ed. see Dickens, Charles.

Crompton, Louis, ed. see Shaw, Bernard.

Crompton, Louis, ed. see Shaw, George B.

Crompton, Margaret. Respecting Children: Social Work with Young People. LC 80-5820. (Illus.). 246p. 1980. 20.00 (ISBN 0-8039-1544-6); pap. 9.95 (ISBN 0-8039-1545-4). Sage.

Crompton, Paul H. Kung Fu Theory & Practice. (Illus.). 136p. 1976. 10.50 o.p. (ISBN 0-7207-0670-X). Transatlantic.

Crompton, Richard. The Mansion of Magnanimitie: Wherein Is Shewed the Acts of Sundrie English Kings. LC 74-28841. (No. 722). 1975. Repr. of 1599 ed. 9.50 (ISBN 90-221-0722-1). Walter J Johnson.

--Star-Chamber Cases, Shewing What Causes Properly Belong to the Cognizance of That Court. LC 74-28842. (English Experience Ser.: No. 723). 1975. Repr. of 1630 ed. 6.00 (ISBN 90-221-0723-X). Walter J Johnson.

Crompton, T. R. Additive Migration from Plastics into Food. 1979. 54.00 (ISBN 0-08-022465-2). Pergamon.

--The Analysis of Organoaluminium & Organozinc Compounds. 1968. text ed. 56.00 (ISBN 0-08-012578-6). Pergamon.

Cromwell, Harvey & Van Dusen, C. R. Oral Approach to Phonetics. LC 72-84441. 1969. pap. text ed. 12.50 (ISBN 0-675-09415-1). Merrill.

Cromwell, Leslie, et al. Biomedical Instrumentation & Measurements. 2nd ed. (Illus.). 1980. text ed. 22.95 (ISBN 0-13-076448-5). P-H.

Cromwell, Liz & Hibner, Dixie. Finger Frolics: Fingerplays for Young Children. 2nd ed. 1976. pap. 7.95 (ISBN 0-933212-09-7, Dist. by Gryphon House). Partner Pr.

Cromwell, Paul F., Jr., ed. Jails & Justice. (Illus.). 336p. 1975. 24.50 (ISBN 0-398-03144-4); pap. 17.50 (ISBN 0-398-03145-2). C C Thomas.

Cromwell, R. & Olson, D. E., eds. Power in Families. LC 75-17648. 264p. 1975. 17.95 (ISBN 0-470-18846-4); pap. 9.95 (ISBN 0-470-18847-2). Halsted Pr.

Cromwell, Rue L., et al. Acute Myocardial Infarction: Reaction and Recovery. LC 76-49883. (Illus.). 1977. text ed. 12.95 o.p. (ISBN 0-8016-1079-6). Mosby.

Cronan, Marion & Atwood, June. First Foods. rev. ed. (gr. 7-9). 1976. text ed. 11.88 (ISBN 0-87002-168-0); tchr's guide avail. Bennett IL.

Cronan, Marion L. & Atwood, June. Foods in Homemaking. rev. ed. (Illus.). (gr. 9-12). 1972. text ed. 18.00 (ISBN 0-87002-121-4); tchr's guide avail. (ISBN 0-685-06847-1). Bennett IL.

Cronbach, Lee J. Essentials of Psychological Testing. 3rd ed. (Murphy-Holtzman Ser). 1970. text ed. 24.50 scp (ISBN 0-06-041421-9, HarpC); test items avail. (ISBN 0-06-361421-9). Har-Row.

Cronbach, Lee J. & Snow, Richard E. Aptitudes & Instructional Methods: A Handbook for Research on Interactions. LC 76-5510. (Illus.). 1981. pap. text ed. 18.50x (ISBN 0-8290-0103-4). Irvington.

Cronbach, Lee J., et al. Toward Reform of Program Evaluation: Aims, Methods, & Institutonal Arrangements. LC 80-8013. (Social & Behavioral Science & Higher Education Ser.). 1980. text ed. 16.95x (ISBN 0-87589-471-2). Jossey-Bass.

Crone, Moira. The Winnebago Mysteries & Other Stories. Date not set. pap. cancelled (ISBN 0-916300-17-X). Gallimaufry.

Crone, Moira, ed. see Linney, et al.

Crone, Patricia. Slaves on Horses. LC 79-50234. 1980. 39.50 (ISBN 0-521-22961-8). Cambridge U Pr.
Crone, Patricia & Cook, M. Hagarism. LC 75-41714. 1980. pap. 11.95 (ISBN 0-521-29754-0). Cambridge U Pr.
--Hagarism: The Making of the Islamic World. LC 75-41714. 268p. 1977. 29.95 (ISBN 0-521-21133-6). Cambridge U Pr.
Crone, Robert & Malone, John. Continuities in Education: The Northern Ireland Schools Curriculum Project. 156p. 1980. pap. text ed. 16.50x (ISBN 0-85633-181-3, NFER). Humanities.
Crone, Ruth, jt. auth. see Brown, Marion.
Croneis, Carey G. & Krumbein, William C. Down to Earth: An Introduction to Geology. LC 36-10420. (Illus.). 1961. pap. 3.50 o.s.i. (ISBN 0-226-12099-6, P501, Phoen). U of Chicago Pr.
Cronen, Vernon E., jt. auth. see Pearce, W. Barnett.
Croner, Helga, tr. see Thoma, Clemens.
Croner, John A. The Basque & the Boy. 1981. 10.95 (ISBN 0-87949-176-0). Ashley Bks.
Cronhjort, B., ed. see IFAC-IFIP Workshop, Mariehamn-Aland, Finland, 1978.
Cronin. Mathematics of Cell Electrophysiology. 144p. 1981. 19.75 (ISBN 0-8247-1157-2). Dekker.
Cronin, Denis. Anxiety, Depression & Phobia. 1979. 9.95x o.s.i. (ISBN 0-8464-0054-5). Beekman Pubs.
Cronin, Gaynell B. Activities for the Christian Family Handbook (Paths of Life) 1980. 2.45 (ISBN 0-8091-2273-1). Paulist Pr.
--Holy Days & Holidays: Prayer Celebrations with Children. 1979. pap. 6.95 (ISBN 0-03-042761-4). Winston Pr.
Cronin, J. Gerald Griffin: A Critical Biography 1803-1840. LC 77-80831. (Illus.). 1978. 24.50 (ISBN 0-521-21800-4). Cambridge U Pr.
Cronin, James E. Industrial Conflict in Modern Britain. 242p. 1979. 25.00x (ISBN 0-8476-6188-1). Rowman.
Cronin, Joseph M. The Control of Urban Schools: Perspective on the Power of Educational Reformers. LC 72-78608. 288p. 1973. 10.95 (ISBN 0-02-906910-6). Free Pr.
Cronin, Richard. Shelley's Poetic Thoughts. 1981. 22.50 (ISBN 0-312-71664-8). St Martin.
Cronin, Vincent. The Companion Guide to Paris. (Illus.). 1977. pap. 6.95 o.p. (ISBN 0-684-14952-4, SL 708, ScribT). Scribner.
Cronin, Vincent, ed. Essays by Divers Hands L: Innovation in Contemporary Literature. (Being the Transactions of a Royal Society of Literature, New Ser.: Vol. XL). 162p. 1979. 21.50x (ISBN 0-8476-3043-9). Rowman.
Cronkhite, Gary. Persuasion: Speech & Behavioral Change. LC 73-75140. (Speech Communication Ser). 1969. pap. 5.50 (ISBN 0-672-61075-2, SC4). Bobbs.
Cronkite, E. P. & Carstens, A. L. Diffusion Chamber Culture: Hemopoiesis, Cloning of Tumors, Cytogenetic & Carinogenic Assays. (Illus.). 270p. 1980. pap. 46.00 (ISBN 0-387-10064-4). Springer-Verlag.
Cronkite, Kathy. On the Edge of the Spotlight: Celebrities' Children Speak Out About Their Lives. LC 80-21255. (Illus.). 320p. 1981. 12.95 (ISBN 0-688-00357-5). Morrow.
Cronley, Jay. Fall Guy. 1979. pap. 1.95 o.p. (ISBN 0-451-08890-5, J8890, Sig). NAL.
--Quick Change. LC 80-5450. (Illus.). 216p. 1981. 11.95 (ISBN 0-385-15180-2). Doubleday.
Cronon, E. David. Black Moses: The Story of Marcus Garvey & the Universal Negro Improvement Association. 2nd ed. (Illus.). 1969. pap. 7.95 (ISBN 0-299-01214-X). U of Wis Pr.
Cronquist, A., et al. Intermountain Flora, Vol. 6. LC 73-134298. 1977. 60.00x (ISBN 0-231-04120-9). Columbia U Pr.
Cronquist, Arthur. The Evolution & Classification of Flowering Plants. pap. 5.00 o.p. (ISBN 0-89327-212-4). NY Botanical.
Cronquist, Arthur, jt. auth. see Gleason, Henry A.
Cronyn, George W., ed. American Indian Poetry: An Anthology of Songs & Chants. new ed. LC 73-133483. 1970. pap. 5.95 (ISBN 0-87140-026-X). Liveright.
Crook, Beverly C. Fair Annie of Old Mule Hollow. (YA) (gr. 7 up). 1979. pap. 1.95 (ISBN 0-380-49007-2, 49007). Avon.
--Invite a Bird to Dinner: Simple Feeders You Can Make. LC 78-8657. (Illus.). (gr. 3-7). 1978. 6.95 (ISBN 0-688-41849-X); PLB 6.67 (ISBN 0-688-51849-4). Lothrop.
Crook, David P. American Democracy in English Politics, 1815-1850. 1965. 7.25x o.p. (ISBN 0-19-821338-7). Oxford U Pr.
Crook, Howard. The Brownstone Cavalry. 1981. 13.95 (ISBN 0-671-44776-9). Summit Bks.
Crook, John H. The Evolution of Human Consciousness. (Illus.). 462p. 1980. 39.00x (ISBN 0-19-857174-7). Oxford U Pr.
Crook, Roger H., ed. Affectionately, Dad. LC 80-67461. 1981. 5.95 (ISBN 0-8054-5641-4). Broadman.
Crook, William G. Can Your Child Read? Is He Hyperactive? rev. ed. 1977. pap. 6.95 (ISBN 0-933478-01-1). Prof Bks.
--Tracking Down Hidden Food Allergy. 2nd ed. (Illus.). 104p. (Orig.). 1980. pap. 5.95 (ISBN 0-933478-05-4). Prof Bks.
Crookall, R. Intimations of Immortality. 157p. 1965. 10.75 (ISBN 0-227-67662-9). Attic Pr.
--Supreme Adventure: Analyses of Psychic. Communications. rev. ed. 288p. 1975. 13.95 (ISBN 0-227-67606-8). Attic Pr.
Crookall, Robert. Case-Book of Astral Projection, 545-746. 160p. 1980. pap. 3.95 (ISBN 0-8065-0730-6). Citadel Pr.
--Psychic Breathing: Cosmic Vitality from the Air. 96p. (Orig.). 1980. pap. 4.95 o.s.i. (ISBN 0-85030-176-9). Newcastle Pub.
--The Study & Practice of Astral Projection. 1977. pap. 3.95 (ISBN 0-8065-0547-8). Lyle Stuart.
Crooke, S. T. & Prestayko, A. W., eds. Cancer & Chemotherapy: Antineoplastic Agents, Vol. 3. 1981. write for info. (ISBN 0-12-197803-6). Acad Pr.
Crooke, Stanley T. & Prestayko, Archie W. Cancer & Chemotherapy: Introduction to Clinical Oncology, Vol. 2. LC 79-8536. 1981. write for info. (ISBN 0-12-197802-8). Acad Pr.
Crooke, Stanley T. & Reich, Steven D., eds. Anthracyclines: Current Status & New Developments. 1980. 27.50 (ISBN 0-12-197780-3). Acad Pr.
Crooke, W. North-Western Provinces of India: Their History, Ethnology & Administration. (Illus.). 365p. 1973. Repr. text ed. 15.00x o.p. (ISBN 0-8426-0506-1). Verry.
Crooke, William, ed. see Sharif, Ja'Far.
Crookenden, Napier. Airborne at War. (Illus.). 1978. 14.95 o.p. (ISBN 0-684-15658-X, ScribT). Scribner.
Crooks, Michael. Growing Flowers. (Practical Gardening Ser.). (Illus.). 112p. (Orig.). 1979. pap. 10.50 (ISBN 0-589-01241-X, Pub. by Reed Bks Australia). C E Tuttle.
Crooks, R. & Baur, K. Our Sexuality. 1980. 16.95 (ISBN 0-8053-1910-7); instrs guide 3.95 (ISBN 0-8053-1911-5); 6.95 (ISBN 0-8053-1912-3). A-W.
Crooks, Robert & Baur, Karla. Our Sexuality. 1980. 16.95 (ISBN 0-8053-1910-7); study guide 6.95 (ISBN 0-8053-1912-3). Benjamin Cummings.
Crookston, Peter. Village London. 190p. 1979. pap. 4.95 (ISBN 0-500-27150-X). Thames Hudson.
Crookston, Peter, ed. Village England. 1980. 16.95 (ISBN 0-686-68275-0). Methuen Inc.
Crools, J. Mordaunt, ed. see Eastlake, Charles.
Croom, George E., Jr. & Van Der Wal, John. Now You Can Profit from Inflation. 264p. 1981. 14.95 (ISBN 0-442-25397-4). Van Nos Reinhold.
Croome, D. Empaytaz de see De Croome, D. Empaytaz.
Croome, D. J. & Roberts, B. M. Air Conditioning & Ventilation of Buildings, Vol. 1. 2nd ed. LC 79-40965. (International Ser. in Heating, Ventilation & Refrigeration: Vol. 14). (Illus.). 1981. 60.00 (ISBN 0-08-024779-2). Pergamon.
Croome, D. J. & Sherratt, A. F., eds. Condensation in Buildings. (Illus.). 1972. text ed. 40.90x (ISBN 0-85334-548-1, Pub. by Applied Science). Burgess-Intl Ideas.
Croome-Gale, Derek J. Noise, Buildings, & People. LC 73-7982. 500p. 1975. text ed. 76.00 (ISBN 0-08-019690-X); pap. text ed. 45.00 (ISBN 0-08-019816-3). Pergamon.
Crooney, John. Anthropometry for Designers. rev. ed. 144p. 1981. pap. 12.00 (ISBN 0-442-22013-8). Van Nos Reinhold.
Cropley, A. J. Lifelong Education: A Psychological Analysis. LC 77-5702. 1977. text ed. 23.00 (ISBN 0-08-021814-8); pap. 8.50 o.p. (ISBN 0-08-021815-6). Pergamon.
--Towards a System of Lifelong Education: Some Practical Considerations. LC 80-40417. (Advances in Lifelong Education: Vol. 7). (Illus.). 234p. 1980. 23.00 (ISBN 0-08-026068-3); pap. 11.50 (ISBN 0-08-026067-5). Pergamon.
Cropley, A. J. & Ravindra, H, eds. Lifelong Education & the Training of Teachers. 1978. text ed. 37.00 (ISBN 0-08-022987-5); pep. text ed. 15.00 (ISBN 0-08-023008-3). Pergamon.
Cropper, William H. Quantum Physicists & an Introduction to Their Physics. 1970. pap. 6.95x (ISBN 0-19-500861-8). Oxford U Pr.
Cropsey, Joseph, jt. auth. see Strauss, Leo.
Crosbie, Robert. Answers to Questions on the Ocean. 249p. 1933. 5.00 (ISBN 0-938998-12-9). Theosophy.
--The Friendly Philosopher. (Illus.). vii, 415p. 1934. Repr. 6.00 (ISBN 0-938998-13-7). Theosophy.
Crosbie, Robert, jt. auth. see Judge, William Q.
Crosby. Art of Holding the Violin & Bow As Exemplified by Ole Bull. Repr. lib. bdg. 19.00 (ISBN 0-403-03869-3). Scholarly.
Crosby & Emery. Building College Spelling Skills. 192p. (Orig.). 1981. pap. text ed. 7.95 (ISBN 0-316-16186-1); tchrs'. manual free (ISBN 0-316-16188-8). Little.
Crosby, Alexander L. Tarantulas. LC 80-7672. (Illus.). 64p. (gr. 3-7). 1981. 8.50 (ISBN 0-8027-6393-6); PLB 8.85 (ISBN 0-8027-6394-4). Walker & Co.
Crosby, Benjamin, jt. auth. see Lindenberg, Marc.
Crosby County Historical Commission. A History of Crosby County, 1876-1977. 1978. write for info. Crosby County.
Crosby, Elizabeth C. & Schnitzlein, H. N., eds. Comparative Correlative Neuroanatomy of the Vertebrate Telencephalon. (Illus.). 1981. text ed. 65.00 (ISBN 0-02-325690-7). Macmillan.
Crosby, Harry. Shadows of the Sun: The Diaries of Harry Crosby. Germain, Edward, ed. 300p. (Orig.). 1977. 14.00 (ISBN 0-87685-304-1); pap. 7.50 (ISBN 0-87685-303-3). Black Sparrow.
Crosby, John. An Affair of Strangers. 272p. 1976. pap. 1.95 o.s.i. (ISBN 0-446-89280-7). Warner Bks.
--Nightfall. 1977. pap. 1.95 o.s.i. (ISBN 0-446-89354-4). Warner Bks.
--Party of the Year. (gr. 7-12). 1980. PLB 13.95 (ISBN 0-8161-3067-1, Large Print Bks). G K Hall.
--Penelope Now. LC 80-6149. 256p. 1981. 12.95 (ISBN 0-8128-2793-7). Stein & Day.
Crosby, John A., tr. see Godfrey, W. Earl.
Crosby, Michael H. The Spirituality of the Beatitudes: Matthew's Challenge for First World Christians. 256p. (Orig.). 1981. pap. 7.95 (ISBN 0-88344-465-8). Orbis Bks.
Crosby, Nina. Tomorrow's Decisions Today: The Corporation. 51p. (Orig.). 1979. pap. text ed. 4.95 (ISBN 0-914634-72-0, 7910). DOK Pubs.
Crosby, Nina E. & Marten, Elizabeth H. Don't Teach Let Me Learn About Aerodynamics, Robots & Computers, Science Fiction & Astronomy. (Illus.). 80p. (Orig.). 1979. pap. 4.95 (ISBN 0-914634-60-7). DOK Pubs.
Crosby, Philip B. The Art of Getting Your Own Sweet Way. 1975. pap. 3.95 o.p. (ISBN 0-8015-0358-2). Dutton.
--The Art of Getting Your Own Sweet Way. 2nd ed. (Illus.). 224p. 1981. 12.95 (ISBN 0-07-014515-6). McGraw.
Crosby, Thelma & Ball, Eve. Bob Crosby: World Champion Cowboy. 6.00 o.p. (ISBN 0-685-48824-1). Nortex Pr.
Crosby, Travis L. English Farmers & the Politics of Protection. 228p. 1977. text ed. 20.75x (ISBN 0-85527-116-7). Humanities.
Crosfield, T., jt. auth. see Austin, D.
Crosher, Judith & Strongman, Harry. The Greeks. LC 77-86190. (Peoples of the Past Ser.). (Illus.). 1977. lib. bdg. 7.95 (ISBN 0-686-51157-3). Silver.
Crosher, Judith, et al. The Aztecs. LC 77-86189. (Peoples of the Past Ser.). (Illus.). 1977. lib. bdg. 7.95 (ISBN 0-686-51154-9). Silver.
Crosier, Barney. Vermont Blood. 128p. 1980. pap. 5.95 (ISBN 0-9603900-6-5). Lanser Pr.
Crosland, Andrew, compiled by. Concordance to F. Scott Fitzgerald's The Great Gatsby. LC 74-11607. (A Bruccoli Clark Book). (Illus.). 425p. 1975. 52.00 (ISBN 0-8103-1005-8). Gale.
--Concordance to the Complete Poetry of Stephen Crane. LC 74-30426. (A Bruccoli Clark Book). 1975. 60.00 (ISBN 0-8103-1006-6). Gale.
Crosland, M., tr. see De Goncourt, Edmond.
Crosland, Margaret, tr. see Cocteau, Jean.
Crosland, Maruice P. & Bugge, Thomas, eds. Science in France in the Revolutionary Era. 1969. 15.00x o.p. (ISBN 0-262-03029-2). MIT Pr.
Crosley, David R., ed. Laser Probes for Combustion Chemistry. LC 80-17137. (ACS Symposium Ser.: No. 134). 1980. 44.50 (ISBN 0-8412-0570-1). Am Chemical.
Crosman, Inge, jt. ed. see Suleiman, Susan.
Cross, Aleene. Home Economics Evaluation. LC 73-75679. 1973. text ed. 20.95x (ISBN 0-675-08933-6). Merrill.
Cross, Amanda. Death in a Tenured Position. 1981. 9.95 (ISBN 0-525-08935-7). Dutton.
--In the Last Analysis. 176p. 1981. pap. 1.95 (ISBN 0-380-54510-1). Avon.
--The Theban Mysteries. 1979. pap. 1.75 (ISBN 0-380-45021-6, 45021). Avon.
Cross, Barbara M., ed. Educated Woman in America: Selected Writings of Catharine Beecher, Margaret Fuller & M. Carey Thomas. LC 65-23578. (Illus.). 1965. text ed. 8.75 (ISBN 0-8077-1221-3); pap. text ed. 4.00x (ISBN 0-8077-1218-3). Tchrs Coll.
Cross, Claire. Church & People, 1450-1600. LC 76-25005. (Fontana Library of English History). 288p. 1976. text ed. 18.25x (ISBN 0-391-00649-5). Humanities.
Cross, Cliff. Central America Guide. LC 72-15593. 1974. pap. 4.95 o.p. (ISBN 0-912656-37-9). H P Bks.
Cross, Colin, ed. Sayings of the Seventies. 1980. 8.95 (ISBN 0-7153-7938-0). David & Charles.
Cross, Crispin P., ed. Interviewing & Communication in Social Work. (Library of Social Work). 192p. 1974. 16.00 (ISBN 0-7100-7879-X); pap. 6.00 (ISBN 0-7100-7880-3). Routledge & Kegan.
Cross, Diana H. Some Birds Have Funny Names. (Illus.). 1980. lib. bdg. 6.95 (ISBN 0-517-54005-3). Crown.
Cross, Dolores E., et al, eds. Teaching in a Multicultural Society: Perspectives & Professional Strategies. LC 76-14291. (Illus.). 1977. 15.95 (ISBN 0-02-906710-3). Free Pr.
Cross, F. L. & Livingstone, Elizabeth A. The Oxford Dictionary of the Christian Church. 1512p. 1974. 49.95x (ISBN 0-19-211545-6). Oxford U Pr.
Cross, Frank L., jt. ed. see Young, Richard A.
Cross, Frank L., Jr. Management Primer on Water Pollution Control. LC 74-76523. 150p. 1974. pap. 25.00 (ISBN 0-87762-136-5). Technomic.
Cross, Frank M., Jr. & Freedman, David N. Early Hebrew Orthography: A Study of the Epigraphic Evidence. (American Oriental Ser.: Vol. 36). 1952. pap. 9.00x (ISBN 0-686-00019-6). Am Orient Soc.
Cross, Frank M., Jr., ed. see Zimmerli, Walther.
Cross, Frank R. Elementary School Career Education: A Humanistic Model. LC 73-92002. (Occupational Education Ser.). 160p. 1974. pap. text ed. 7.95x (ISBN 0-675-08824-0). Merrill.
Cross, George L. Blacks in White Colleges. 1975. 8.95x o.p. (ISBN 0-8061-1266-2); pap. 3.95 (ISBN 0-8061-1267-0). U of Okla Pr.
--The University of Oklahoma & World War II: A Personal Account, 1941-1946. LC 80-16934. (Illus.). 320p. 1980. 15.95 (ISBN 0-8061-1662-5). U of Okla Pr.
Cross, George W. Classroom Teachers' Guide for Elementary Physical Education: Games-Relays-Stunts. (Brighton Series in Health & Physical Education). 1979. pap. text ed. 7.95 (ISBN 0-89832-010-0). Brighton Pub Co.
Cross, Glenda. Friendly Fairways of Michigan. LC 78-54174. (Orig.). 1978. 4.95 (ISBN 0-686-12255-0). Friendly Fairways.
Cross, Gordon R. The Psychology of Learning: An Introduction for Students of Education. 1974. text ed. 29.00 (ISBN 0-08-018136-8); pap. text ed. 17.00 (ISBN 0-08-018135-X). Pergamon.
Cross, Gustav, ed. see Shakespeare, William.
Cross, Hardy. Arches, Continuous Frames, Columns, & Conduits: Selected Papers. LC 63-17046. (Illus.). 1963. 14.00 (ISBN 0-252-72315-5). U of Ill Pr.
Cross, Helen R. The Real Tom Thumb. LC 80-11447. (Illus.). 96p. (gr. 3-7). 1980. 8.95 (ISBN 0-590-07606-X, Four Winds). Schol Bk Serv.
Cross, I., jt. auth. see O'Flaherty, C. A.
Cross, Ira B. A History of the Labor Movement in California. (California Library Reprint Ser.). 1974. Repr. 22.50x (ISBN 0-520-02646-2). U of Cal Pr.
Cross, J. A., jt. auth. see Alderman, R. K.
Cross, James A. Answers from the Word. 1974. pap. 2.25 (ISBN 0-87148-012-3). Pathway Pr.
--Glorious Gospel. 1956. 2.95 (ISBN 0-87148-350-5). Pathway Pr.
Cross, Jeannette W. & Saunders, Blanche. New Standard Book of Dog Care & Training. (Illus.). (gr. 9 up). 1962. 12.95 (ISBN 0-8015-5372-5, Hawthorn). Dutton.
Cross, Jed. All God's Chillun Got Guns. 192p. (Orig.). 1976. pap. 0.95 o.p. (ISBN 0-445-00691-9). Popular Lib.
--Kildeer's Pride. 192p. (Orig.). 1976. pap. 0.95 o.p. (ISBN 0-445-00687-0). Popular Lib.
Cross, Jennifer. Supermarket Trap: The Consumer & the Food Industry. rev. ed. LC 75-10806. (Midland Bks.: No. 199). (Illus.). 320p. 1976. 12.50x (ISBN 0-253-35582-6); pap. 3.50x (ISBN 0-253-20199-3). Ind U Pr.
Cross, John, jt. auth. see Cross, Linda.
Cross, John C., jt. auth. see Harney, Malachi L.
Cross, K. Patricia. Adults As Learners: Increasing Participation & Facilitating Learning. LC 80-26985. (Higher Education Series). 1981. text ed. price not set (ISBN 0-87589-491-7). Jossey-Bass.
Cross, K. W., et al, eds. Foetal & Neonatal Physiology: Proceedings. LC 72-93673. (Illus.). 600p. 1973. 95.00 (ISBN 0-521-20178-0). Cambridge U Pr.
Cross, Lee & Goin, Kenneth, eds. Identifying Handicapped Children. LC 76-52246. (First Chance Ser.). 1977. 8.95 o.s.i. (ISBN 0-8027-9041-0); pap. 7.95 (ISBN 0-8027-7111-4). Walker & Co.
Cross, Linda & Cross, John. Kitchen Crafts. LC 73-8351. (Illus.). 224p. 1974. pap. 3.95 o.s.i. (ISBN 0-02-009430-2, Collier). Macmillan.

Cross, M. Urbanization & Urban Growth in the Caribbean. LC 78-67307. (Urbanization in Developing Countries Ser.). 1979. 23.95 (ISBN 0-521-22426-8); pap. 7.95x (ISBN 0-521-29491-6). Cambridge U Pr.

Cross, M., et al. Modelling & Simulation in Practice. LC 78-31375. 1979. 42.95x (ISBN 0-470-26645-7). Halsted Pr.

Cross, Malcolm. East Indians of Guyana & Trinidad. (Minority Rights Group: No. 13). 1972. 2.50 (ISBN 0-89192-114-1). Interbk Inc.

Cross, Milton & Ewen, David. Milton Cross New Encyclopedia of the Great Composers & Their Music, 2 Vols. LC 70-87097. two-volume, boxed set 24.95 (ISBN 0-385-03635-3). Doubleday.

Cross, Milton & Kohrs, Karl. Milton Cross More Stories of the Great Operas. LC 77-132495. 1971. 10.95 o.p. (ISBN 0-385-08546-X). Doubleday.

--The New Milton Cross More Stories of the Great Operas. LC 79-8023. 816p. 1980. 17.95 (ISBN 0-385-14776-7). Doubleday.

Cross, Neal M., et al. The Search for Personal Freedom, Vol. 1. 6th ed. 500p. 1981. pap. write for info. (ISBN 0-697-03121-7). Vol. 2 (ISBN 0-697-03122-5). Wm C Brown.

Cross, R., et al. Messerschmitt BF 109, Versions B-E. (No. 2). (Illus.). 112p. 1976. 21.95 (ISBN 0-85059-106-6). Aztex.

Cross, Ralph. Denton's Army. 1979. pap. 1.75 (ISBN 0-505-51388-9). Tower Bks.

--Key to Murder. (Orig.). 1980. pap. 1.95 (ISBN 0-505-51488-5). Tower Bks.

Cross, Rupert. The Precedent in English Law. 3rd ed. 252p. 1977. pap. 11.95x (ISBN 0-19-876073-6). Oxford U Pr.

Cross, Wilbur. Kids & Booze: What You Must Know to Help Them. 1979. 10.95 o.p.; pap. 5.95 (ISBN 0-87690-314-6). Dutton.

Cross, Wilbur & Heffernan, John B. Naval Battles & Heroes. LC 60-13854. (American Heritage Junior Library). (Illus.). 153p. (gr. 5 up). 1960. 9.95 (ISBN 0-06-021375-2, Dist. by Har-Row); PLB 12.89 (ISBN 0-06-021376-0, Dist. by Har-Row). Am Heritage.

Crossan, Gregory D. A Relish for Eternity: The Process of Divinization in the Poetry of John Clare. (Salzburg Studies in English Literature, Romantic Reassessment: No. 53). 291p. 1976. pap. text ed. 25.00x (ISBN 0-391-01354-8). Humanities.

Crossan, John D. Cliffs of Fall: Paradox & Polyvalence in the Parables of Jesus. 128p. 1980. 8.95 (ISBN 0-8164-0113-6). Crossroad NY.

--The Dark Interval: Towards a Theology of Story. 1975. pap. 2.75 (ISBN 0-913592-52-8). Argus Comm.

Crossan, R. M. & Harold, W. Master Standard Data. LC 80-11165. 268p. 1980. Repr. of 1962 ed. lib. bdg. 14.50 (ISBN 0-89874-133-5). Krieger.

Crosse, Howard & Hempel, George. Management Policies for Commercial Banks. 3rd ed. (Illus.). 1980. text ed. 18.95 (ISBN 0-13-549030-8). P-H.

Crosser, P. K., et al. East-West Dialogues: Foundations & Problems of Revolutionary Praxis. (Philosophical Currents Ser: No. 5). 180p. 1973. pap. text ed. 20.50x (ISBN 90-6032-008-5). Humanities.

Crosser, Paul F. A Prolegomena to All Future Metaeconomics. LC 72-13845. 240p. 1974. 10.00 (ISBN 0-87527-099-9). Fireside Bks.

Crossette, Barbara. America's Wonderful Little Hotels & Inns. (Illus.). 400p. 1981. 14.95 (ISBN 0-312-92016-4); pap. 8.95 (ISBN 0-312-92016-4). St Martin.

Crossette, Barbara, ed. America's Wonderful Little Hotels & Inns: New, Revised 1981-82 Edition. (Illus.). 400p. 1981. 14.95 (ISBN 0-312-92016-4); pap. 8.95 (ISBN 0-312-92017-2). Congdon & Lattes.

Crossgrove, Hannelore & Crossgrove, William C. Graded German Reader. 2nd ed. 1978. pap. text ed. 6.95x (ISBN 0-669-01533-4). Heath.

Crossgrove, William C., jt. auth. see Crossgrove, Hannelore.

Crosskey, R. W., ed. Catalogue of the Diptera of the Afrotropical Region. 1437p. 1980. 140.50x (ISBN 0-565-00821-8, Pub. by Brit Mus Nat Hist England). Sabbot-Natural Hist Bks.

Crosskey, W. W. & Jeffrey, William, Jr. Politics & Constitution in the History of the United States, 3 vols. 2040p. 1981. lib. bdg. 100.00x (ISBN 0-226-12134-8). U of Chicago Pr.

Crosskey, William W. & Jeffrey, William, Jr. Politics & the Constitution in the History of the United States: Vol. III, The Political Background of the Federal Convention. LC 53-7433. 1981. lib. bdg. 27.00x (ISBN 0-226-12138-0). U of Chicago Pr.

Crossland, James. Lewis's Pharmacology. 5th ed. 960p. 1981. lib. bdg. price not set; pap. text ed. 49.50 (ISBN 0-443-01173-7). Churchill.

Crossley-Holland, Kevin. Pedlar of Swaffham. LC 70-129208. (Illus.). (gr. 1-4). 1971. 6.95 (ISBN 0-395-28786-3, Clarion). HM.

Crossley-Holland, Kevin & Mitchell, Bruce. The Battle of Maldon & Other Old English Poems. LC 65-13048. 138p. 1975. pap. 3.95 o.p. (ISBN 0-312-07000-4). St Martin.

Crossley-Holland, Kevin, ed. The Faber Book of Northern Folk-Tales. (Illus.). 157p. (gr. 3-12). 1981. 11.95 (ISBN 0-571-11519-5, Pub. by Faber & Faber). Merrimack Bk Serv.

Crossley-Holland, Kevin C. Green Blades Rising: The Anglo-Saxons. LC 75-4576. (Illus.). 144p. (gr. 6-12). 1976. 8.95 (ISBN 0-395-28902-5, Clarion). HM.

Crossman, E. J., jt. auth. see McAllister, D. E.

Crossman, Richard, ed. The Diaries of a Cabinet Minister, III. LC 76-30680. (Illus.). 1978. 22.95 o.p. (ISBN 0-03-040871-7). HR&W.

Crosson, Frederick J., ed. Human & Artificial Intelligence. LC 78-131431. (Orig.). 1970. pap. text ed. 6.95x (ISBN 0-89197-220-X). Irvington.

Crosson, Pierre R., jt. auth. see Silvers, Arthur.

Crosswell, C. Legal Aspects of International Business. 1980. 40.00 (ISBN 0-379-20683-8). Oceana.

Crosten, William L. French Grand Opera: An Art & a Business. LC 73-171381. 132p. 1972. Repr. of 1948 ed. lib. bdg. 22.50 (ISBN 0-306-70405-6). Da Capo.

Croteau, Leo H. Generative Rhetoric, a Teaching Guide for English Composition. 300p. 1980. tchrs.' ed. 25.00 (ISBN 0-9602582-0-5). Neechee Assoc.

Crothers, J. Frances. Puppeteer's Library Guide: A Bibliographic Index to the Literature of the World Puppet Theatre, Vol. 1, The Historical Background Of Puppetry & Its Related Fields. LC 71-149991. 1971. 20.50 (ISBN 0-8108-0319-4). Scarecrow.

Crottel, L. & Mendez, M. Lapland. (Illus.). 1968. 17.50x (ISBN 0-686-66879-0, N503). Vanous.

Crotts, Gwen, jt. auth. see Williams, Bill R.

Crotty, William, ed. The Party Symbol: Readings on Political Parties. LC 79-22945. (Illus.). 1980. 18.95x (ISBN 0-7167-1144-3); pap. text ed. 9.95x (ISBN 0-7167-1145-1). W H Freeman.

Crotwell, Helen G., ed. Women & the Word: Sermons. LC 77-78627. 144p. (Orig.). 1978. pap. 4.25 (ISBN 0-8006-1318-X, 1-1318). Fortress.

Crouch. Coordinated Cross Number Puzzle Books, 8 bks. Incl. Bks. A1 & A2. (gr. 1-2). pap. 1.64 ea. worktexts; Bk. A1, Gr. 1. pap. (ISBN 0-8009-0722-1); Bk. A2, Gr. 2. pap. (ISBN 0-8009-0725-6); spirit masters 15.32 ea. Bk. A1 (ISBN 0-8009-0746-9). Bk. A2 (ISBN 0-8009-0748-5). ans. keys. Bk. A1 (ISBN 0-8009-0764-7). Bk. A2 (ISBN 0-8009-0766-3); Bks. A-F. (gr. 3-8). Bk. A, Gr. 3. pap. (ISBN 0-8009-0727-2); Bk. B, Gr. 4. pap. (ISBN 0-8009-0729-9); Bk. C, Gr. 5. pap. (ISBN 0-8009-0735-3); Bk. D, Gr. 6. pap. (ISBN 0-8009-0739-6); Bk. E, Gr. 7. pap. (ISBN 0-8009-0742-6); Bk. F, Gr. 8. pap. (ISBN 0-8009-0744-2). (gr. 1-8). 1979. Bks. A-F. pap. 1.76 ea. worktexts; spiritmasters for Bks. A-F 16.68 ea.; ans. keys for Bks. A1, A2, A-F 3.32 ea. McCormick-Mathers.

Crouch, Austin. Bright Side of Death. (Illus.). 1951. pap. 1.25 o.p. (ISBN 0-8054-9201-1). Broadman.

Crouch, B. M. The Keepers. 368p. 1980. 24.75 (ISBN 0-398-03970-4). C C Thomas.

Crouch, Brodie. The Myth of Mormon Inspiration. 6.50 (ISBN 0-89315-158-0). Lambert Bk.

--Study of Minor Prophets. pap. 2.50 (ISBN 0-89315-291-9). Lambert Bk.

Crouch, Bruce L. & Chamala, Shankarish. Extension Education & Rural Development, Vol. 2: International Experience in Strategies for Planned Change. LC 79-41221. 1981. price not set (ISBN 0-471-27675-8, Pub. by Wiley-Interscience). Wiley.

Crouch, Bruce R. & Chamala, Shankarish. Extension Education & Rural Development, Vol. 1: International Experience in Communication & Innovation. LC 79-41221. 1981. price not set (ISBN 0-471-27829-7, Pub. by Wiley-Interscience). Wiley.

Crouch, Colin & Pizzorno, Alessandro, eds. Resurgence of Class Conflict in Western Europe Since 1968. 349p. 1980. pap. text ed. cancelled (ISBN 0-8419-0647-5). Holmes & Meier.

Crouch, Edmond, jt. auth. see Wilson, Richard.

Crouch, Holmes F. Nuclear Ship Propulsion. LC 59-13449. (Illus.). 1960. 20.00x (ISBN 0-87033-071-3). Cornell Maritime.

Crouch, James & Carr, Micheline. Anatomy & Physiology: A Laboratory Manual. LC 76-56507. (Illus.). 1977. pap. text ed. 11.95 (ISBN 0-87484-356-1). Mayfield Pub.

Crouch, M. & Ellis, A., eds. Chosen for Children. 3rd ed. 1977. 15.50x (ISBN 0-85365-349-6, Pub. by Lib Assn England). Oryx Pr.

Crouch, Marcus. The Ivory City: And Other Stories from India & Pakistan. (Illus.). 192p. (gr. 8-12). 1981. 11.95 (ISBN 0-7207-1188-6). Merrimack Bk Serv.

Crouch, Owen. What the Bible Says About the Bible. (What the Bible Says Ser.). 400p. 1981. 13.50 (ISBN 0-89900-082-7). College Pr Pub.

Crouch, T. Matrix Methods Applied to Engineering Rigid Body Mechanics. LC 80-41186. 385p. 1980. 45.00 (ISBN 0-08-024245-6); pap. 18.00 (ISBN 0-08-024246-4). Pergamon.

Crouch, Tom D. Charles A. Lindbergh: An American Life. LC 77-14537. (Illus.). 128p. 1977. 8.95 (ISBN 0-87474-342-7); pap. 4.95 (ISBN 0-87474-343-5). Smithsonian.

--A Dream of Wings: Americans & the Airplane, Eighteen Seventy-Five to Nineteen Hundred Five. (Illus.). 1981. 15.95 (ISBN 0-393-01385-5). Norton.

Crouch, W. W., et al. California Government & Politics. 6th ed. 1977. pap. text ed. 8.95 (ISBN 0-13-112458-7). P-H.

Crouch, Winston W. Organized Civil Servants: Public Employer-Employee Relations in California. LC 77-91767. 1978. 20.00x (ISBN 0-520-03626-3). U of Cal Pr.

Crouch, Winston W. & Dinerman, Beatrice. Southern California Metropolis: A Study in Development of Government for a Metropolitan Area. (Illus.). 1963. 22.50x (ISBN 0-520-00280-6). U of Cal Pr.

Crouch, Winston W., et al. California Government & Politics. 7th ed. (Illus.). 288p. 1981. pap. 8.95 (ISBN 0-13-112433-1). P-H.

Croucher, John S. Operations Research: A First Course. (Illus.). 320p. 1980. 27.00 (ISBN 0-08-024798-9); pap. 13.50 (ISBN 0-08-024797-0). Pergamon.

Crounse, Robert G., jt. ed. see Brown, A. C.

Crouse, Anna & Crouse, Russell. Alexander Hamilton & Aaron Burr. (Landmark Ser.: No. 85). 1963. PLB 5.99 (ISBN 0-394-90385-4, BYR). Random.

Crouse, Russell, jt. auth. see Crouse, Anna.

Crouse, Timothy. The Boys on the Bus: Riding with the Campaign Press Corps. 1976. pap. 2.95 (ISBN 0-345-29338-X). Ballantine.

Crouse, William H. Automotive Electronics & Electrical Equipment. 9th ed. (Illus.). 1980. pap. text ed. 14.50 (ISBN 0-07-014831-7); instructor's planning guide 2.50 (ISBN 0-07-014833-3); wkbk. 6.95 (ISBN 0-07-014832-5). McGraw.

Crouse, William H. & Anglin, Donald L. Automotive Engines. 6th ed. (Illus.). 96p. 1980. 14.50 (ISBN 0-07-014825-2, G); instructor's planning guide 2.50 (ISBN 0-07-014827-9). McGraw.

--Automotive Fuel, Lubricating & Cooling Systems. 6th ed. Gilmore, D. E., ed. (Illus.). 352p. 1980. pap. text ed. 17.95 (ISBN 0-07-014862-7, G); wkbk. avail. (ISBN 0-07-014863-5). McGraw.

--Workbook for Automotive Engines. 6th ed. (Automotive Technology Ser.). (Illus.). 96p. 1981. pap. 6.95 (ISBN 0-07-014826-0, G). McGraw.

Crout, Robert R., jt. auth. see Heggoy, Alf A.

Crouter, George. Colorado's Highest: The Magestic Fourteeners. (Illus.). 144p. 16.50 (ISBN 0-913582-22-0). Sundance.

Crovello, Theodore J. A Numerical Taxonomic Study of the Genus Salix, Section Sitchenses. (U. C. Publ. Botany: Vol. 44). 1968. pap. 5.00x (ISBN 0-520-09017-9). U of Cal Pr.

Crow, Alice, jt. auth. see Crow, Lester D.

Crow, Christine. Paul Valery: Conciousness & Nature. LC 71-160088. 300p. 1972. 47.50 (ISBN 0-521-08257-9). Cambridge U Pr.

Crow, Duncan. Tanks of World War II. (Illus.). 128p. 1979. 16.50x (ISBN 0-85383-006-1). Intl Pubns Serv.

Crow, Harte C., jt. auth. see Bartrum, Royal J., Jr.

Crow, Jack E., et al, eds. Crystalline Electric Fields & Structural Effects in f-Electron Systems. 650p. 1980. 69.50 (ISBN 0-306-40443-5, Plenum Pr). Plenum Pub.

Crow, James T. New Baja Handbook. rev. ed. LC 73-81325. 1974. enlarged ed. 3.95 (ISBN 0-87880-020-4). Norton.

Crow, James T. & Warren, Cameron A. Four Wheel Drive Handbook. 96p. 1976. Repr. 3.95 (ISBN 0-87880-004-2). Norton.

Crow, John A. The Epic of Latin America. 1000p. 1980. 29.95 (ISBN 0-520-04107-0); pap. 14.95 (ISBN 0-520-03776-6, CAL. NO. 458). U of Cal Pr.

--Mexico Today. rev. ed. LC 71-156517. (Illus.). 1972. 13.95 o.p. (ISBN 0-06-010923-8, HarpT). Har-Row.

--Se Habla Espanol. 1979. text ed. 16.95 scp (ISBN 0-06-041434-0, HarpC); scp tapes 229.00 (ISBN 0-06-047489-0); inst. manual free (ISBN 0-06-361450-2); scp student wkbk. 7.50 (ISBN 0-06-041435-9). Har-Row.

Crow, John A., ed. An Anthology of Spanish Poetry from the Beginnings to the Present Day, Including Both Spain & Spanish America. LC 79-4619. 1979. text ed. 8.95 (ISBN 0-8071-0482-5); pap. text ed. 7.95x (ISBN 0-8071-0483-3). La State U Pr.

Crow, Leonard R., jt. auth. see Baker, Glenn E.

Crow, Lester D. & Crow, Alice. Child Psychology. 1953. pap. 3.75 o.p. (ISBN 0-06-460079-3, CO 79, COS). Har-Row.

--Outline of General Psychology. rev. ed. (Quality Paperback: No. 28). (Orig.). 1976. pap. 3.95 (ISBN 0-8226-0028-5). Littlefield.

Crow, Mark A., jt. auth. see Danskin, David G.

Crow, R., et al, eds. Experiments with Normal & Transformed Cells. 175p. 1979. lab manual 18.00x (ISBN 0-87969-123-9). Cold Spring Harbor.

Crowder, C. M., ed. English Society & Government in the Fifteenth Century. LC 68-79460. (Selections from History Today Ser.,No. 2). (Illus.). 1967. 5.00 (ISBN 0-05-000809-9); pap. 3.95 (ISBN 0-685-09164-3). Dufour.

Crowder, D. F., jt. auth. see Tabor, R. W.

Crowder, M., jt. auth. see Brokensha, D.

Crowder, M., ed. see Tarikh.

Crowder, Michael, jt. ed. see Ajayi, J. F.

Crowder, Richard. Carl Sandburg. (U. S. Author's Ser.: No. 47). 1963. lib. bdg. 9.95 (ISBN 0-8057-0648-8). Twayne.

Crowder, Robert G. Principles of Learning & Memory. (Experimental Psychology Ser.). 1976. 19.95 o.p. (ISBN 0-470-15027-0). Halsted Pr.

Crowdis, David, jt. auth. see Crowdis, Kay.

Crowdis, David G. & Wheeler, Brandon W. Precalculus Mathematics. 1976. text ed. 13.95x (ISBN 0-02-472030-5). Macmillan.

Crowdis, David G., et al. Calculus for Business & the Social Biological Sciences. 2nd ed. 1976. text ed. 14.95x (ISBN 0-02-473030-0). Macmillan.

--Concepts of Calculus with Applications to Business & Economics. 1975. text ed. 14.95x (ISBN 0-02-473010-6); tchrs' manual free (ISBN 0-02-473020-3). Macmillan.

Crowdis, Kay & Crowdis, David. Designing & Building Your Own Home. (Illus.). 240p. 1980. text ed. 14.95 (ISBN 0-8359-1272-8). Reston.

Crowe. Concepts in Climatology. 1979. pap. text ed. 16.95 o.p. (ISBN 0-582-30013-4). Longman.

Crowe, Charles, ed. Age of Civil War & Reconstruction, 1830-1900: A Book of Interpretative Essays. rev. ed. 1975. pap. text ed. 12.50x (ISBN 0-256-01528-7). Dorsey.

Crowe, Clayton T., jt. auth. see Roberson, John A.

Crowe, Clayton T. see Heat Transfer & Fluid Mechanics Institute.

Crowe, Eyre E. Yesterday in Ireland, 3 vols. Wolff, Robert L., ed. (Ireland Nineteenth Century Fiction - Ser. Two: Vol. 15). 984p. 1979. Set. lib. bdg. 96.00 (ISBN 0-8240-3464-3). Garland Pub.

Crowe, Frederick E. The Lonergan Enterprise. LC 80-51569. 120p. (Orig.). 1980. pap. 5.00 (ISBN 0-936384-02-6). Cowley Pubns.

--Theology of the Christian Word: A Study in History. LC 78-51595. 1978. pap. 6.95 (ISBN 0-8091-2106-9). Paulist Pr.

Crowe, J. A. & Cavalcaselle, G. B. The Early Flemish Painters: Notices of Their Lives & Works. Freedberg, Sydney J., ed. LC 77-18679. (Connoisseurship, Criticism, & Art History Ser.: Vol. 6). 383p. 1979. lib. bdg. 38.00 (ISBN 0-8240-3263-2). Garland Pub.

--New History of Painting in Italy from the Second to the Sixteenth Century, 3 vols. Freedberg, Sydney J., ed. LC 77-19372. (Connoisseurship Criticism & Art History Ser.: Vol. 7). (Illus.). 1980. Set. lib. bdg. 132.00 (ISBN 0-8240-3264-0). Garland Pub.

--Titan, His Life & Times: With Some Account of His Family, 2 vols. Freedberg, Sydney J., ed. LC 77-19373. (Connoisseurship Criticism & Art History Ser.: Vol. 8). 1032p. 1979. lib. bdg. 80.00 (ISBN 0-8240-3265-9). Garland Pub.

Crowe, James W., jt. auth. see Brennan, William T.

Crowe, Jerome. The Acts. Harrington, Wilfrid & Senior, Donald, eds. (New Testament Message Ser.: Vol. 8). 204p. 1980. 9.95 (ISBN 0-89453-131-X); pap. 4.95 (ISBN 0-89453-196-4). M Glazier.

Crowe, John. Close to Death: A Buena Costa Country Mystery. LC 79-1213. (Red Badge Novel of Suspense Ser.). 1979. 7.95 (ISBN 0-396-07675-0). Dodd.

Crowe, John H. & Clegg, James S., eds. Anhydrobiosis. LC 73-12354. (Benchmark Papers in Biological Concepts Ser.). 496p. 1973. text ed. 43.50 (ISBN 0-12-786277-3). Acad Pr.

Crowe, Kenneth, et al. Exotic Atoms Nineteen Seventy-Nine: Fundamental Interactions & Structure of Matter. (Ettore Majorana International Science Ser., Physical Science: Vol. 4). 410p. 1980. 45.00 (ISBN 0-306-40322-6, Plenum Pr). Plenum Pub.

Crowe, Patrick H. How to Teach School & Make a Living at the Same Time. 1978. 9.95 o.p. (ISBN 0-8362-2605-4); pap. 5.95 o.p. (ISBN 0-8362-2600-3). Andrews & McMeel.

Crowe, Robert L. Tyler Toad & the Thunder. LC 80-347. (Illus.). 32p. (ps-1). 1980. 9.95 (ISBN 0-525-41795-8). Dutton.

Crowe, Walter C., et al. Laboratory Manual in Adapted Physical Education & Recreation: Experiments, Activities, & Assignments. (Illus.). 1977. pap. text ed. 9.50 (ISBN 0-8016-1099-0). Mosby.

--Priciples & Methods of Adapted Physical Education & Recreation. 4th ed. (Illus.). 602p. 1981. text ed. 20.95 (ISBN 0-8016-0327-7). Mosby.

Crowell, Marnie R. Great Blue. 1980. 9.95 (ISBN 0-8129-0905-4). Times Bks.

Crowell, Muriel B. The Fine Art of Needlepoint. (Illus.). 128p. 1973. 10.95 (ISBN 0-690-29799-8, TYC-T). T Y Crowell.

Crowell, Thomas, Jr., ed. see Bender, James F.

Crowell, W., ed. Portability of Numerical Software: Proceedings. LC 77-13623. (Lecture Notes in Computer Science: Vol. 57). 1977. pap. text ed. 21.90 (ISBN 0-387-08446-0). Springer-Verlag.

Crowest, Frederick J. Musicians' Wit, Humour, & Anecdote. LC 72-78131. (Illus.). 1971. Repr. of 1902 ed. 26.00 (ISBN 0-8103-3729-0). Gale.

Crowhurst, Eric. Precision Bidding for Acol. 1974. 13.95 (ISBN 0-7207-0765-X, Pub. by Michael Joseph). Merrimack Bk Serv.

Crowhurst, Norman. Basic Mathematics, 2 vols. (Illus., Orig.). (gr. 9 up). 1961. Vol. 1 Arithmetic. pap. 7.65 (ISBN 0-8104-0447-8); Vol. 2 Integrated Algebra, Geometry & Calculus. pap. 7.65 (ISBN 0-8104-0448-6); Vol. 1. exam set 0.50 (ISBN 0-8104-0567-9); Vol. 2. exam set 0.50 (ISBN 0-8104-0568-7). Hayden.

Crowhurst, Norman E. Problem Solving Arts: Part Three Syllabus. 1978. pap. text ed. 10.45 (ISBN 0-89420-040-2, 256130); cassette recordings 196.20 (ISBN 0-89420-177-8, 256090). Natl Book.

Crowhurst, Norman H. Basic Electronics Course. LC 75-178692. 1972. 11.95 (ISBN 0-8306-2588-7); pap. 9.95 (ISBN 0-8306-1588-1, 588). TAB Bks.

--English: Syllabus. 138p. 1974. pap. text ed. 7.45 (ISBN 0-89420-073-9, 171050); cassette recordings 130.25 (ISBN 0-89420-145-X, 171000). Natl Book.

--How to Select & Install Your Own Speakers. (Illus.). 1979. 9.95 (ISBN 0-8306-9823-X); pap. 6.95 (ISBN 0-8306-1034-0, 1034). TAB Bks.

--Introductory Physics: Syllabus. 1974. pap. text ed. 9.35 (ISBN 0-89420-084-4, 230330); cassette recordings 164.70 (ISBN 0-89420-158-1, 230000). Natl Book.

--Problem Solving Arts: Part One Syllabus. 1976. pap. text ed. 9.95 (ISBN 0-89420-085-2, 256040); cassette recordings 227.10 (ISBN 0-89420-175-1, 256000). Natl Book.

--Problem Solving Arts: Part Two Syllabus. 1977. pap. text ed. 10.25 (ISBN 0-89420-029-1); cassette recordings 195.80 (ISBN 0-89420-176-X, 256050). Natl Book.

Crowley, Aleister. Book Four. pap. 4.95 (ISBN 0-87728-513-6). Weiser.

--Magical Record of the Beast 666 by Symonds & Grant. 16.00 o.p. (ISBN 0-685-47276-0). Weiser.

--Magick, in Theory & Practice. 10.00 (ISBN 0-8446-5476-0). Peter Smith.

--Vision & the Voice. 7.50 (ISBN 0-685-47278-7). Weiser.

Crowley, Aleister & Motta, Marcelo R. The Equinox Vol. V, No. 2. LC 78-68846. 1979. 31.00 (ISBN 0-933454-00-7); deluxe ed. 93.00 limited (ISBN 0-933454-01-5). Troll Pub.

Crowley, Alister see DeKerval, Alastor, pseud.

Crowley, Charles B. Universal Mathematics in Aristotelian-Thomistic Philosophy: The Hermeneutics of Aristotelian Texts Relative to Universal Mathematics. LC 79-48093. 239p. 1980. text ed. 18.50 (ISBN 0-8191-1009-4); pap. text ed. 9.50 (ISBN 0-8191-1010-8). U Pr of Amer.

Crowley, Ellen T., ed. Acronyms, Initialisms, & Abbreviations Dictionary, Vol. 1. 7th ed. 1500p. 1980. 75.00 (ISBN 0-8103-0504-6). Gale.

--New Trade Names 1980: Supplement to Trade Names Dictionary. 2nd ed. LC 79-12685. (Incl. 1981 supplement). 1980. pap. 95.00 (ISBN 0-8103-0693-X). Gale.

--Reverse Acronyms, Initialisms, & Abbreviations Dictionary. 7th ed. (Acronyms, Initialisms & Abbreviations Dictionary: Vol. 3). 1500p. 1980. 74.00 (ISBN 0-8103-0506-2). Gale.

--Trade Names Dictionary, 2 vols. 2nd ed. LC 79-12685. 907p. 1979. 120.00 (ISBN 0-8103-0694-8). Gale.

--Trade Names Dictionary: Company Index. 2nd ed. LC 79-19239. 1979. 135.00 (ISBN 0-8103-0695-6). Gale.

Crowley, Frances G. Domingo Faustino Sarmiento. (World Authors Ser.: No. 156). lib. bdg. 10.95 (ISBN 0-8057-2798-1). Twayne.

Crowley, J. Donald, ed. Hawthorne: The Critical Heritage. 1971. 36.00 (ISBN 0-7100-6886-7). Routledge & Kegan.

Crowley, J. Donald, ed. see James, Henry.

Crowley, James B. Japan's Quest for Autonomy: National Security & Foreign Policy, 1930-1938. 1966. 22.50x o.p. (ISBN 0-691-03031-6). Princeton U Pr.

Crowley, John W. George Cabot Lodge. LC 75-44429. (U. S. Authors Ser.: No. 264). 1976. lib. bdg. 10.95 (ISBN 0-8057-7165-4). Twayne.

Crowley, Kitty A. First Women of the Skies. LC 78-21907. (Famous Firsts Ser.). (Illus.). 1978. lib. bdg. 7.35 (ISBN 0-686-51112-3). Silver.

Crowley, Maureen, ed. Energy: Sources of Print & Nonprint Materials. LC 79-26574. (Neal-Schuman Sourcebook Ser.). 341p. 1980. 19.95x (ISBN 0-918212-16-2). Neal-Schuman.

Crowley, Richard. The Way to Wealth, Wherein Is Plainly Taught a Remedy for Sedicion. LC 74-28843. (English Experience Ser.: No. 724). 1975. Repr. of 1550 ed. 3.50 (ISBN 90-221-0724-8). Walter J Johnson.

Crown, David A. Forensic Examination of Paints & Pigments. (August Vollmer Criminalistics Ser). 276p. 1968. 24.75 (ISBN 0-398-00372-6). C C Thomas.

Crown, Francis, Jr. Confederate Postmaster Provisionals. 1981. lib. bdg. 60.00 (ISBN 0-88000-124-0). Quarterman.

Crown, J. Conrad & Bittinger, Marvin L. Finite Mathematics: A Modeling Approach. 2nd ed. LC 80-19472. (Mathematics Ser.). (Illus.). 480p. 1981. text ed. 15.95 (ISBN 0-201-03145-0). A-W.

Crown, J. Conrad, jt. auth. see Bittinger, Marvin L.

Crown, James Tracy. The Kennedy Literature: A Bibliographical Essay on John F. Kennedy. LC 68-29428. 1968. 12.00x (ISBN 0-8147-0109-4). NYU Pr.

Crown, S. Essential Principles of Psychiatry. LC 72-128608. 1970. text ed. 13.50 (ISBN 0-911216-16-2). Raven.

Crowne, John. City Politiques. Wilson, John H., ed. LC 67-12641. (Regents Restoration Drama Ser). 1967. 9.75x (ISBN 0-8032-0355-1); pap. 1.65x (ISBN 0-8032-5355-9, BB 262, Bison). U of Nebr Pr.

Crowner, David L. & Marschall, Laurence A., eds. Computers & Human Communication: Problems & Prospects. LC 79-52964. 1979. pap. text ed. 9.75 (ISBN 0-8191-0787-5). U Pr of Amer.

Crownhart-Vaughan, E. A., tr. see Krasheninnikov, Stepan P.

Crowningshield, Gerald & Gorman, Kenneth A. Cost Accounting: Principles & Managerial Applications. 4th ed. LC 78-69551. (Illus.). 1979. text ed. 20.95 (ISBN 0-395-26797-8); inst. manual 4.00 (ISBN 0-395-26798-6). HM.

Crownover, Arthur, Jr. Gibson's Suits in Chancery, 2 vols. 5th ed. 1100p. 1955. text ed. 50.00 (ISBN 0-87215-083-6). Michie.

Crowquill, Alfred, ed. The Laughing Philosopher. 329p. 1980. Repr. of 1899 ed. lib. bdg. 40.00 (ISBN 0-89760-123-8). Telegraph Bks.

Crows, Eyre E. Today in Ireland, 3 vols. Wolff, Robert L., ed. (Ireland Nineteenth Century Fiction - Ser. Two: Vol. 14). 1036p. 1979. lib. bdg. 96.00 (ISBN 0-8240-3463-5). Garland Pub.

Crowson, Lydia. The Esthetic of Jean Cocteau. LC 77-95326. 206p. 1978. text ed. 12.50x (ISBN 0-87451-149-6). U Pr of New Eng.

Crowson, P. C. & Richards, B. A. Economics for Managers. (Illus.). 248p. 1978. pap. 16.95x (ISBN 0-7131-3397-X). Intl Ideas.

Crowther, Bruce. Deadman's Cocktail. 1978. 7.95 o.s.i. (ISBN 0-8027-5385-X). Walker & Co.

--Sleeper. 1977. 6.95 o.s.i. (ISBN 0-8027-5372-8). Walker & Co.

Crowther, Duane S. Family Ancestral Record: Adult Genealogy Starter Kit. LC 78-52113. 1978. 4.50 (ISBN 0-88290-088-9). Horizon Utah.

--God & His Church. LC 76-173392. (Scripture Guide Ser.). 1971. pap. 4.95 (ISBN 0-88290-006-4). Horizon Utah.

--My Family Heritage: Youth Genealogy Starter Kit. LC 78-52120. 1979. 4.50 (ISBN 0-88290-087-0). Horizon Utah.

--Teaching Aids Supplement to Teaching Choral Concepts. 100p. (Orig.). 1981. pap. 5.95 (ISBN 0-88290-162-1, 2022). Horizon Utah.

--Teaching Choral Concepts: Simple Lesson Plans & Teachng Aids for in-Rehearsal Choir Instruction. LC 79-89356. (Illus.). 1979. 14.95 (ISBN 0-88290-119-2). Horizon Utah.

--This Is My Life: Personal History Guide. LC 78-52406. 1979. 4.50 (ISBN 0-88290-089-7). Horizon Utah.

--Thus Saith the Lord. LC 80-83862. 300p. 1981. 7.95 (ISBN 0-88290-168-0, 1061). Horizon Utah.

Crowther, G., jt. auth. see Gilligan, C.

Crowther, J. G. The Cavendish Laboratory: 1874-1974. 349p. 1974. text ed. 50.00x o.p. (ISBN 0-88202-029-3, Sci Hist). N Watson.

--Fifty Years with Science. (Illus.). 1970. text ed. 12.50x (ISBN 0-248-65220-6). Humanities.

Crowther, Jean D. What Do I Do Now, Mom? LC 80-82257. (Illus.). 86p. (gr. 9-12). 1980. 5.50 (ISBN 0-88290-134-6). Horizon Utah.

Crowther, Robert. The Most Amazing Hide & Seek Counting Book. (Illus.). 14p. 1981. 8.95 (ISBN 0-670-48997-2). Viking Pr.

Croxford, Leslie. Solomon's Folly. LC 75-1458. 1978. 7.95 (ISBN 0-8149-0763-6). Vanguard.

Croxton, C. A. Liquid State Physics. LC 72-89803. (Physics Monographs). (Illus.). 400p. 1974. 57.50 (ISBN 0-521-20117-9). Cambridge U Pr.

Croxton, Clive A. Statistical Mechanics of the Liquid Surface. LC 79-40819. 1980. 75.00 (ISBN 0-471-27663-4, Pub. by Wiley-Interscience). Wiley.

Croy, O. R. The Complete Book of Printing & Enlarging. Date not set. cancelled o.p. (ISBN 0-8038-1239-6). Hastings.

--Croy's Camera Trickery. Date not set. cancelled o.p. (ISBN 0-8038-1216-7). Hastings.

--Design by Photography. rev. ed. Date not set. 15.95 o.p. (ISBN 0-8038-1548-4). Hastings.

Croze, Harvey, jt. auth. see Reader, John.

Crozet, Felix. Revue De la Musique Dramatique En France. Bd. with Supplement a la Revue De la Musique Dramatique En France. LC 80-2270. 1981. 48.50 (ISBN 0-404-18833-8). AMS Pr.

Crozey, Alan, tr. see Gorshkov, Sergei.

Crozier, Brian. The Man Who Lost China. LC 76-10246. (Encore Edition). (Illus.). 480p. 1976. 5.95 o.p. (ISBN 0-684-15940-6, ScribT). Scribner.

--The Minimum State: Beyond Party Politics. 1979. 27.00 (ISBN 0-241-10242-1, Pub. by Hamish Hamilton England). David & Charles.

Crozier, Brian, ed. Annual of Power & Conflict, 1978-1979: A Survey of Political Violence & International Influence. 8th ed. 1979. 34.00 (ISBN 0-8103-1035-X, Pub. by Inst Study Conflict). Gale.

--Annual of Power & Conflict, 1979-80: A Survey of Political Violence & International Influence. 9th ed. LC 77-370326. 510p. 1980. 65.00x (ISBN 0-8002-2671-2). Intl Pubns Serv.

Crozier, Michel & Friedberg, Erhard. Actors & Systems: The Politics of Collective Action. Goldhammer, Arthur, tr. LC 80-13803. 272p. 1980. lib. bdg. 25.00x (ISBN 0-226-12183-6). U of Chicago Pr.

Crozier, Michel, et al. The Crisis of Democracy: Report on the Governability of Democracies to the Trilateral Commission. LC 75-27167. 1975. 12.00x (ISBN 0-8147-1364-5); pap. 5.00x (ISBN 0-8147-1365-3). NYU Pr.

Cruden, Alexander. Cruden's Concordance. handy reference ed. 7.50 (ISBN 0-8010-2341-6). Baker Bk.

--Cruden's Unabridged Concordance. 14.95 (ISBN 0-8010-2316-5). Baker Bk.

Cruden, R. War That Never Ended: The American Civil War. 1973. pap. text ed. 9.95 o.p. (ISBN 0-13-944355-X). P-H.

Crue, Benjamin L., Jr. Pain & Suffering: Selected Aspects. (Illus.). 224p. 1970. pap. 19.75 photocopy ed. spiral (ISBN 0-398-00374-2). C C Thomas.

Cruess, William V. Commercial Fruit & Vegetable Products. 4th ed. (Agricultural Sciences Ser). 1958. text ed. 26.00 o.p. (ISBN 0-07-014808-2, C). McGraw.

Cruickshank, Don W., jt. auth. see Wilson, Edward M.

Cruickshank, J. G. Soil Geography. 1972. 14.95 o.p. (ISBN 0-470-18919-3). Halsted Pr.

Cruickshank, John. Benjamin Constant. (World Authors Ser.: France: No. 297). 1974. lib. bdg. 12.50 (ISBN 0-8057-2242-4). Twayne.

Cruickshank, R., et al. Epidemiology & Community Health in Warm Climate Countries. LC 75-5573. (Illus.). 512p. 1976. text ed. 32.00 (ISBN 0-443-01303-9); pap. text ed. 26.50x (ISBN 0-443-01145-1). Churchill.

Cruickshank, W., jt. auth. see Hallahan, D.

Cruickshank, William M. & Johnson, G. Orville. Education of Exceptional Children & Youth. 3rd ed. (Illus.). 736p. 1975. 21.95 (ISBN 0-13-240382-X). P-H.

Cruickshank, William M., ed. Approaches to Learning: The Best of ACLD, Vol. 1. (Illus.). 240p. 1980. pap. 11.95x (ISBN 0-8156-2203-1). Syracuse U Pr.

--Cerebral Palsy: A Developmental Disability. rev. 3rd ed. LC 75-34275. 1976. text ed. 26.00x (ISBN 0-8156-2168-X). Syracuse U Pr.

--Learning Disabilities in Home, School, & Community. 1979. pap. 7.95x (ISBN 0-8156-2208-2). Syracuse U Pr.

Cruickshank, William M. & Hallahan, Daniel P., eds. Perceptual & Learning Disabilities in Children. Incl. Vol. 1. Psychoeducational Practices. LC 74-24303. 496p. 20.50x (ISBN 0-8156-2165-5); Vol. 2. Research & Theory. LC 74-24303. 498p. 25.00x (ISBN 0-8156-2166-3). (Illus.). 1975. Set. 40.00x (ISBN 0-685-51977-5). Syracuse U Pr.

Cruickshank, William M., et al. Learning Disabilities: The Struggle from Adolescence Toward Adulthood. (Illus.). 304p. 1980. 18.00x (ISBN 0-8156-2220-1); pap. 8.95x (ISBN 0-8156-2221-X). Syracuse U Pr.

Cruikshank, Eleanor P. French-English Instant Vocabulary Francais-Anglais. 88p. 1980. pap. 4.00 (ISBN 0-9505284-0-7). Cruikshank.

Cruikshank, George. The Tragical Comedy or Comical Tragedy of Punch & Judy. (Illus.). 1976. pap. 2.25 (ISBN 0-7100-8199-5). Routledge & Kegan.

Cruikshank, George see Lear, Edward.

Cruikshank, Margaret L. Thomas Babington Macaulay. (English Author Ser.: No. 217). 1978. lib. bdg. 10.95 (ISBN 0-8057-6686-3). Twayne.

Cruikshank, W. Psychology of Exceptional Children & Youth. 4th ed. 1980. 20.95 (ISBN 0-13-733808-2). P-H.

Cruise, Boyd. Boyd Cruise. LC 76-24712. (Illus.). 72p. 1976. 20.00x (ISBN 0-917860-01-2). Historic New Orleans.

Cruise, Edwina, tr see Bitsilli, Peter.

Crum, Howard A. & Anderson, Lewis E. Mosses of Eastern North America, 2 Vols. LC 79-24789. (Illus.). 576p. 1981. 60.00x (ISBN 0-231-04516-6). Columbia U Pr.

Crum, J. K. Art of Inner Listning. 1975. pap. 1.25 (ISBN 0-89129-092-3, PV092). Jove Pubns.

Crum, Lawrence L. Time Deposits in Present-Day Commercial Banking. LC 64-63739. (U of Fla. Social Sciences Monographs: No. 20). 1963. pap. 3.25 (ISBN 0-8130-0051-3). U Presses Fla.

Crum, Lawrence L., jt. auth. see Grant, Joseph M.

Crum, Milton, Jr., jt. auth. see Reid, Richard.

Crum, Roy L. & Derkinderen, Frans G., eds. Capital Budgeting Under Conditions of Uncertainty. (Nijenrode Studies in Business: Vol. 5). 240p. 1980. lib. bdg. 20.00 (ISBN 0-89838-045-6, Pub. by Martinus Nijhoff). Kluwer Boston.

Crum, Walter E., ed. Coptic Dictionary. 1939. 89.00x (ISBN 0-19-864404-3). Oxford U Pr.

Crum, William L. The Age Structure of the Corporate System. (Institute of Business & Economic Research, UC Berkeley). (Illus.). 1953. 14.00x (ISBN 0-520-00281-4). U of Cal Pr.

Crumbaker, Marge & Tucker, Gabe. Up & Down with Elvis Presley. (Illus.). 320p. 1981. 12.95 (ISBN 0-399-12571-X). Putnam.

Crumbaugh, James C. Everything to Gain: A Guide to Self-Fulfillment Through Logoanalysis. LC 72-80164. 1973. 10.95 (ISBN 0-91012-14-1). Nelson-Hall.

Crumbaugh, James C., et al. Logotherapy: New Help for Problem Drinkers. LC 79-18635. 176p. 1981. 10.95 (ISBN 0-88229-421-0). Nelson-Hall.

Crumbley, D. Larry. A Practical Guide to Preparing a Federal Estate Tax Return. 7th ed. 1980. pap. 8.50 (ISBN 0-88450-057-8, 1703-B). Lawyers & Judges.

--A Practical Guide to Preparing a Federal Gift Tax Return. 5th ed. 1980. pap. text ed. 8.50 (ISBN 0-88450-058-6, 1705-B). Lawyers & Judges.

Crumbley, D. Larry & Davis, P. Michael. Organizing, Operating & Terminating Subchapter S Corporations, Law, Taxation & Accounting. rev. ed. 1980. text ed. 35.00 (ISBN 0-88450-063-2, 1711-B). Lawyers & Judges.

Crume. Unidentified Flying Oddball. (gr. 3-5). 1980. pap. 1.50 (ISBN 0-590-30061-X, Schol Pap). Schol Bk Serv.

Crume, Vic, adapted by. The Parent Trap. (gr. 4-6). 1969. pap. 1.25 (ISBN 0-590-02961-4, Schol Pap). Schol Bk Serv.

Crumley, James. The Last Good Kiss. 1980. pap. write for info. (ISBN 0-671-82813-4). PB.

Crummey, Robert O. Old Believers & the World of Antichrist: The Vyg Community & the Russian State, 1694-1855. LC 79-98121. 1970. 25.00 (ISBN 0-299-05560-4). U of Wis Pr.

Crummey, Robert O., jt. ed. see Berry, Lloyd E.

Crumne. C.H.O.M.P.S. (gr. 3-5). 1980. pap. 1.50 (ISBN 0-590-30528-X, Schol Pap). Schol Bk Serv.

Crump, C. G. & Jacob, E. F., eds. Legacy of the Middle Ages. (Legacy Ser.). (Illus.). 1926. 29.50x (ISBN 0-19-821907-5). Oxford U Pr.

Crump, J. I., Jr., tr. Chan-Kuo Ts'e. (Oxford Library of East Asian Literature). 1970. 48.00x (ISBN 0-19-815439-9). Oxford U Pr.

Crump, Mary M. The Epyllion from Theocritus to Ovid. Commager, Steele, ed. LC 77-70761. (Latin Poetry Ser.). 1978. lib. bdg. 32.00 (ISBN 0-8240-2966-6). Garland Pub.

Crump, Ralph W., ed. The Design Connection: Energy & Technology in Architecture. Harms, Martin J. (Preston Thomas Memorial Series in Architecture). 144p. 1981. text ed. 19.95 (ISBN 0-442-23125-3). Van Nos Reinhold.

Crump, Spencer. Rail Car, Locomotive & Trolley Builders: An All-Time Directory. 1980. write for info. (ISBN 0-87046-032-3). Trans-Anglo.

Crunkilton, John, jt. auth. see Hillison, John.
Crunkilton, John R., jt. auth. see Finch, Curtis R.
Cruse, Allan & Granberg, Millianne. Lectures on Freshman Calculus. LC 79-136118. (Mathematics Ser). 1971. text ed. 20.95 (ISBN 0-201-01301-0); instructor's manual 1.00 (ISBN 0-201-01302-9). A-W.
Cruse, Julius M. Immunology Examination Review Book, Vol. 1. 2nd ed. 1975. spiral bdg. 12.00 o.p. (ISBN 0-87488-424-1). Med Exam.
Cruseturner, Wayne. Forever & Ever. 240p. (Orig.). 1981. pap. 2.50 (ISBN 0-515-05529-8). Jove Pubns.
Crusius, Vera C. Principles & Applications of Quantity Food Management. (Orig.). 1981. pap. text ed. pns (ISBN 0-8087-2966-7). Burgess.
Crusius, Vera C., jt. auth. see Smith, E. Evelyn.
Crusoe, Robinson. Robinson Crusoe: My Journals & Sketchbooks. LC 74-2240. 80p. (gr. 3-7). 1974. 6.95 (ISBN 0-15-267836-0, HJ). HarBraceJ.
Crutchfield, Marjorie A. Elementary Social Studies: An Inter-Disciplinary Approach. (Elementary Education Ser.). 1978. text ed. 13.95 (ISBN 0-675-08365-6); instructor's manual 3.95 (ISBN 0-685-86835-4). Merrill.
Crutchley, B., ed. see Morison, Stanley.
Crutchley, Brooke. To Be a Printer. 200p. 1980. 19.95 (ISBN 0-521-23663-0). Cambridge U Pr.
Cruttwell, Charles R. History of the Great War, 1914-1918. 2nd ed. (Illus.). 1936. 36.00x o.p. (ISBN 0-19-821416-2). Oxford U Pr.
Cruttwell, Patrick. The Shakespearean Moment & Its Place in the Poetry of the Seventeenth Century. LC 55-541. 262p. 1955. 20.00x (ISBN 0-231-02082-1). Columbia U Pr.
Cruz, Daniel Da see Da Cruz, Daniel.
Cruz, F. De La see De La Cruz, F. & LaVeck, G. D.
Cruz, Felix de la, jt. ed. see Lubs, Herbert.
Cruz, Felix F. De La see Davidson, Richard L. & De La Cruz, Felix F.
Cruz, Jose B. & Van Valkenburg, M. E. Signals in Linear Circuits. 480p. 1974. text ed. 24.95 (ISBN 0-395-16971-2); lab. manual 6.50 (ISBN 0-395-17838-X). HM.
Cruz, Lopez. La Musica Folklorica De Puerto Rico. 1967. 19.95 (ISBN 0-87751-008-3, Pub by Troutman Press). E Torres & Sons.
Cruz, Nicky. Run Baby Run: The Story of a Gang-Lord Turned Crusader. LC 68-23446. 240p. 1968. pap. 2.95 (ISBN 0-912106-58-1). Logos.
Cruz, Nicky & Buckingham, Jamie. Run Baby Run. (gr. 9-12). 1969. pap. 2.25 (ISBN 0-515-05562-X). Jove Pubns.
Cruz, Nicky & Harris, Madalene. Lonely, but Never Alone. 192p. (Orig.). 1981. pap. 5.95 (ISBN 0-310-43361-4). Zondervan.
Cruz, Nicky, tr. Corre, Nicky, Corre. (Spanish Bks.). (Span.). 1978. 1.95 (ISBN 0-8297-0434-5). Life Pubs Intl.
--Os Corruptores. (Portuguese Bks.). 1979. 1.65 (ISBN 0-8297-0792-1). Life Pubs Intl.
--Sata Anda Solto. (Portugese Bks.). (Port.). 1979. 1.30 (ISBN 0-8297-0686-0). Life Pubs Intl.
--Satana Anda Suelto. (Spanish Bks.). (Span.). 1978. 1.90 (ISBN 0-8297-0595-3). Life Pubs Intl.
Cruz, Rosa M., jt. ed. see Sanchez, Rosaura.
Cruz, Rudolfo A. Instrucciones Practicas Para Nuevos Creyentes. LC 77-71308. 78p. (Orig., Span.). 1970. pap. text ed. 1.25 (ISBN 0-89922-002-9). Edit Caribe.
Cruz, Vera Da see Da Cruz, Vera.
Cruz, Victor H. Snaps. LC 69-16456. 1969. 6.95 o.p. (ISBN 0-394-40496-3). Random.
Cruz-Coke, Ricardo. Color Blindness: An Evolutionary Approach. (Amer. Lec. in Living Chemistry Ser.). (Illus.). 172p. 1970. text ed. 19.50 (ISBN 0-398-00375-0). C C Thomas.
Cruz Costa, Joao. A History of Ideas in Brazil: The Development of Philosophy in Brazil & the Evolution of National History. Macedo, Suzette, tr. 1964. 25.00x (ISBN 0-520-00282-2). U of Cal Pr.
Cruz Monclava, Lidio. Historia De Puerto Rico: Siglo XIX, 6 vols. Set. pap. 60.00 (ISBN 0-8477-0801-2). U of PR Pr.
--Historia Del Ano 1887. 3rd ed. 4.35 o.s.i. (ISBN 0-8477-0808-X); pap. 3.10 (ISBN 0-8477-0809-8). U of PR Pr.
Cryderman, Lynx, jt. auth. see Knutzleman, Charles T.
Crystal, D. Prosodic Systems & Intonation in English. LC 69-13792. (Cambridge Studies in Linguistics: No. 1). (Illus.). 1969. 49.50 (ISBN 0-521-07387-1); pap. 15.50x (ISBN 0-521-29058-9). Cambridge U Pr.
Crystal, D. J., jt. auth. see Bolton, W. F.
Crystal, David. Child Language, Learning, & Linguistics: An Overview for the Teaching & Therapeutic Professions. 1976. pap. 9.95x (ISBN 0-7131-5890-5). Intl Ideas.
--A First Dictionary of Linguistics & Phonetics. (Language Library Ser.). 404p. 1980. lib. bdg. 32.50x (ISBN 0-86531-051-3, Pub. by Andre Deutsch); pap. text ed. 12.00 (ISBN 0-86531-050-5). Westview.
Crystal, David, ed. Eric Partridge in His Own Words. 224p. 1981. 12.95 (ISBN 0-02-528960-8). Macmillan.
Crystal, Graef S. Financial Motivation for Executives. LC 77-116716. 1970. 12.95 o.p. (ISBN 0-8144-5230-2). Am Mgmt.
Crystal, John, jt. auth. see Bolles, R. N.
Crystal-Smith. Estimating for Building & Civil Engineering Works. 7th ed. 1981. text ed. write for info. (ISBN 0-408-00515-7). Butterworth.
CSAAT. What to Tell Your Child About Sex. rev. ed. 1974. 4.95 (ISBN 0-686-12277-1). Jewish Bd Family.
Csaky, T. Z., ed. Intestinal Absorption & Malabsorption. LC 74-80532. 1975. 27.00 (ISBN 0-89004-020-6). Raven.
Cshl Banbury Center Report 8 - Hormones & Breast Cancer, et al. Proceedings. Siiteri, Pentti K. & Welsch, Clifford W., eds. (Banbury Report Ser.: Vol. 8). 1981. 60.00 (ISBN 0-87969-207-3). Cold Spring Harbor.
Csida, Joseph. The Magic Ground. 1981. pap. 3.50 (ISBN 0-671-83135-6). PB.
Csikszentmihalyi, Mihaly, jt. auth. see Getzels, Jacob W.
Csizmadia. Socialist Agriculture in Hungary. 1971. 12.50 (ISBN 0-9960000-6-2, Pub. by Kaido Hungary). Heyden.
Csokits, Janos, tr. see Pilinszky, Janos.
CSPI Staff. School Food Action Packet. new ed. (Illus.). 1977. 1.50 o.p. (ISBN 0-89329-009-2). Ctr Sci Public.
Csuti, Blair. Patterns of Adaptation & Variation in the Great Basin Kangaroo Rat. LC 78-54792. (Publications in Zoology Ser.: Vol. III). 1979. 8.00x (ISBN 0-520-09597-9). U of Cal Pr.
Cua, Antonio S. Reason & Virtue: A Study in the Ethics of Richard Price. LC 66-10868. xv, 196p. 1966. 12.00x (ISBN 0-8214-0014-2). Ohio U Pr.
Cuadra, Pablo A. Songs of Cifar & the Sweet Sea. Schulman, Grace & De Zavala, Ann M., trs. from Sp. (A Center for Inter-American Relations Book). 1979. 15.00x (ISBN 0-231-04772-X); pap. 7.50x (ISBN 0-231-04773-8). Columbia U Pr.
Cuadra, Samuel, tr. see Feaver, Douglas.
Cuatrecasas, J. Brunelliaceae. 1970. pap. 12.95 o.s.i. (ISBN 0-02-843320-3). Hafner.
Cuban Economic Research Project, University of Miami. Labor Conditions in Communist Cuba. LC 63-21349. 1963. pap. 2.95x (ISBN 0-87024-303-9). U of Miami Pr.
Cuban, Larry. To Make a Difference: Teaching in the Inner City. LC 74-102197. 1970. pap. text ed. 3.95 (ISBN 0-02-906890-8). Free Pr.
Cubberley, Ellwood P., ed. see Chapman, J. C., et al.
Cube, Hans L. von see Von Cube, Hans L. & Staimle, Fritz.
Cubit, Harry. Electrical Construction Cost Estimating. (Illus.). 320p. 1981. 27.50 (ISBN 0-07-014885-6). McGraw.
Cubitt, J. M., ed. Mathematical Models in the Earth Sciences: Proceedings of the 7th Geochautauqua, Syracuse University, Oct. 1978. 90p. pap. 41.25 (ISBN 0-08-025305-9). Pergamon.
Cucco, Ulisse, jt. auth. see Joseph, Lou.
Cucuel, G. La Poupliniere et la Musique De Chambre Au Xv111 Siecle. LC 70-158961. (Music Ser). 1971. Repr. of 1913 ed. lib. bdg. 49.50 (ISBN 0-306-70186-3). Da Capo.
Cucuel, Georges. Les Createurs de l'Opera-Comique Francais. LC 80-2271. 1981. Repr. of 1914 ed. 29.50 (ISBN 0-404-18834-6). AMS Pr.
Cuddihy, John M. No Offense: Civil Religion & Protestant Taste. 1978. 12.95 (ISBN 0-8164-0385-6). Crossroad NY.
Cuddy, Dennis L. Contemporary Australian-American Relations. LC 80-65615. 155p. 1981. perfect bdg. 12.95 (ISBN 0-86548-027-3). Century Twenty One.
Cuddy, J. D. International Price Indexation. (Illus.). 1977. 17.95 (ISBN 0-347-01140-3, 00684-X, Pub. by Saxon Hse England). Lexington Bks.
Cudjoe, Selwyn R. Resistance & Caribbean Literature. LC 76-25616. xii, 319p. 1981. 16.95x (ISBN 0-8214-0353-2); pap. 8.95x (ISBN 0-8214-0573-X). Ohio U Pr.
Cudlipp, Hugh. The Prerogative of the Harlot: Press Barons & Power. (Illus.). 304p. 1981. 13.50 (ISBN 0-370-30238-9, Pub. by Chatto-Bodley-Jonathan). Merrimack Bk Serv.
Cudworth, Ralph. A Treatise Concerning Eternal & Immutable Morality. Wellek, Rene, ed. LC 75-11214. (British Philosophers & Theologians of the 17th & 18th Centuries: Vol. 17). 1976. Repr. of 1731 ed. lib. bdg. 42.00 (ISBN 0-8240-1768-4). Garland Pub.
--The True Intellectual System of the Universe, 2 vols. Wellek, Rene, ed. LC 75-11213. (British Philosophers & Theologians of the 17th & 18th Centuries Ser.: Vol. 16). 1978. Repr. of 1678 ed. Set. lib. bdg. 76.00 (ISBN 0-8240-1767-6); lib. bdg. 42.00 ea. Garland Pub.
Cuenod, M. A., ed. see IFAC Symposium, Zurich, Switzerland, 29-31 Aug. 1979.
Cuenot, Claude, et al. Evolution, Marxism & Christianity. (Teilhard Study Library). 1967. text ed. 3.50x (ISBN 0-900391-06-5). Humanities.
Cueva, Agustin. The Process of Political Domination in Ecuador. Salti, Danielle, tr. from Span. 190p. 1981. 14.95 (ISBN 0-87855-338-X). Transaction Bks.
Cuff, David J. & Young, William J. The United States Energy Atlas. (Illus.). 1980. 75.00 (ISBN 0-02-691250-3). Free Pr.
Cuff, P. J., tr. see Gabba, Emilio.
Cuisin, Michel. Dictionnaire oiseaux. (Illus., Fr.). pap. 8.50 (ISBN 0-685-13879-8, 3729). Larousse.
Culberson, Chicita F. Chemical & Botanical Guide to Lichen Products. 1979. pap. text ed. 78.00 (ISBN 3-87429-165-0). Lubrecht & Cramer.
Culberson, W. L., ed. see Tuckerman, E.
Culbert, Elizabeth, tr. see Alegria, Ricardo E.
Culbert, T. Patrick, jt. auth. see Schusky, Ernest.
Culbertson, Jack A. & Henson, Curtis. Performance Objectives for School Principals. LC 74-75367. 1974. 16.00x (ISBN 0-8211-0223-0); text ed. 14.50x (ISBN 0-685-42628-9). McCutchan.
Culbertson, Judi & Bard, Patti. Games Christians Play: An Irreverent Guide to Religion Without Tears. 125p. 1973. pap. 1.25 o.p. (ISBN 0-06-087046-X, HW). Har-Row.
Culbertson, Judi, jt. auth. see Chaffee, John.
Culbertson, Robert G. & Tezak, Mark R. Order Under Law-Readings in Criminal Justice. 272p. 1981. pap. text ed. 6.95x (ISBN 0-917974-52-2). Waveland Pr.
Cule, John. A Doctor for the People: 2000 Years of General Practice in Britain. (Illus.). 1981. PLB 38.70 (ISBN 0-906141-29-X, Pub. by Update Books Ltd). Kluwer Boston.
Culi, Yaakov. The Torah Anthology: Mem Lo'ez, 7 vols. Kaplan, Aryeh, tr. Incl. Vol. 1. Beginnings: From Creation Until Abraham. 540p. 13.95 (ISBN 0-686-28206-X); Vol. 2. The Patriarchs: From Abraham Until Jacob. 600p. 14.95 (ISBN 0-686-28207-8); Vol. 3. The Twelve Tribes: From Jacob Until Joseph. 708p. 16.95 (ISBN 0-686-28208-6); Vol. 4. Israel in Egypt: Subjugation & Prelude to the Exodus. 280p. 11.95 (ISBN 0-686-28209-4); Vol. 5. Redemption: The Exodus from Egypt. 436p. 14.95 (ISBN 0-686-28210-8); Vol. 6. The Ten Commandments: Revelation at Sinai. 534p. 15.95 (ISBN 0-686-28211-6); Vol. 7. The Law: The First Codification. 363p. 12.95 (ISBN 0-686-28212-4). (Illus.). 1977-1980. Maznaim.
Culin, Charlotte. Cages of Glass, Flowers of Time. LC 79-14460. (gr. 7 up). 1979. 9.95 (ISBN 0-87888-157-3). Bradbury Pr.
Culinary Arts Inst., jt. auth. see Spitler, Sue.
Culinary Arts Institute, tr. see Goock, Roland.
Culinary Arts Institute Staff. Wok, Fondue, & Chafing Dish. LC 78-54625. (Adventures in Cooking Ser.). (Illus.). 1980. cancelled (ISBN 0-8326-0606-5, 1518); pap. 3.95 (ISBN 0-8326-0605-7, 2518). Delair.
Culinary Arts Institute Staff, jt. auth. see Carter, Linda.
Culinary Arts Institute Staff, jt. auth. see Phillips, Margot.
Culinary Arts Institute Staff, jt. auth. see Stover, Annette A.
Culinary Inst. of America, jt. auth. see Folsom, Le Roi.
Culinary Institute of America. The Professional Chef. 5th ed. Folsom, LeRoj, ed. 608p. Date not set. text ed. 29.95 (ISBN 0-8436-2201-6). CBI Pub. Postponed.
--The Professional Chef's Knife. LC 77-26689. (Illus.). 1978. pap. 8.95 (ISBN 0-8436-2125-7). CBI Pub.
Cull, John C., jt. auth. see Hardy, Richard E.
Cull, John G. & Hardy, Richard E. Counseling Strategies with Special Populations. (American Lectures in Social & Rehabilitation Psychology Ser.). (Illus.). 360p. 1975. 24.75 (ISBN 0-398-03284-X). C C Thomas.
Cull, John G., jt. auth. see Hardy, Richard E.
Cull, John G. & Hardy, Richard, eds. Problems of Disadvantaged & Deprived Youth. (Amer. Lec. Social & Rehabilitation Psychology). 272p. 1975. 22.75 (ISBN 0-398-03171-1). C C Thomas.
Cull, John G. & Hardy, Richard E., eds. Adjustment to Work. (Amer. Lec. Social & Rehabilitation Psychology). 360p. 1973. pap. 32.75 photocopy ed. spiral (ISBN 0-398-02799-4). C C Thomas.
--Alcohol Abuse & Rehabilitation Approaches. (American Lecture in Social & Rehabilitation Psychology Ser.). (Illus.). 220p. 1974. text ed. 18.75 (ISBN 0-398-03017-0). C C Thomas.
--Behavior Modification in Rehabilitation Settings: Applied Principles. (American Lectures in Social & Rehabilitation Psychology Ser.). (Illus.). 272p. 1974. text ed. 19.75 (ISBN 0-398-03131-2). C C Thomas.
--The Big Welfare Mess: Public Assistance and Rehabilitation Approaches. (Amer. Lec. Social & Rehabilitation Psychology). 368p. 1973. 32.50 (ISBN 0-398-02796-X). C C Thomas.
--Counseling & Rehabilitating the Diabetic. (American Lectures in Social & Rehabilitation Psychology Ser.). (Illus.). 164p. 1974. text ed. 12.95 (ISBN 0-398-02997-0). C C Thomas.
--Counseling High School Students: Special Problems & Approaches. (Amer. Lec. Social & Rehabilitation Psychology). (Illus.). 272p. 1974. 19.75 (ISBN 0-398-02913-X). C C Thomas.
--Deciding on Divorce: Personal & Family Considerations. (American Lectures in Social & Rehabilitation Psychology Ser.). 172p. 1974. 12.75 (ISBN 0-398-03035-9). C C Thomas.
--Fundamentals of Criminal Behavior & Correctional Systems. (American Lectures in Social & Rehabilitation Psychology Ser.). (Illus.). 364p. 1973. 24.50 (ISBN 0-398-02637-8). C C Thomas.
--Law Enforcement & Correctional Rehabilitation. (American Lectures in Social & Rehabilitation Psychology Ser.). 280p. 1973. 18.75 (ISBN 0-398-02870-2). C C Thomas.
--The Neglected Older American: Social & Rehabilitation Services. (American Lectures in Social Rehabilitation Psycholology Ser.). (Illus.). 288p. 1973. 24.75 (ISBN 0-398-02835-4). C C Thomas.
--Organization & Administration of Drug Abuse Treatment Programs. (American Lectures in Social & Rehabilitation Psychology Ser.). (Illus.). 360p. 1974. text ed. 27.50 (ISBN 0-398-03113-4). C C Thomas.
--Physical Medicine & Rehabilitation Approaches in Spinal Cord Injury. (American Lectures on Social & Rehabilitation Psychology Ser.). (Illus.). 336p. 1977. 24.75 (ISBN 0-398-03609-8). C C Thomas.
--Problems of Runaway Youth. (American Lectures in Social & Rehabilitation Psychology Ser.). (Illus.). 184p. 1976. pap. 16.75 (ISBN 0-398-03425-7). C C Thomas.
--Rehabilitation Facility Approaches in Severe Disabilities. (American Lectures in Social & Rehabilitation Psychology Ser.). (Illus.). 352p. 1975. 26.75 (ISBN 0-398-03324-2). C C Thomas.
--Rehabilitation of the Urban Disadvantaged. (Amer. Lec. Social & Rehabilitation Psychology Ser.). 232p. 1973. 19.75 (ISBN 0-398-02795-1). C C Thomas.
--Rehabilitation Techniques in Severe Disability: Case Studies. (American Lectures in Social & Rehabilitation Psychology Ser.). 256p. 1974. text ed. 22.75 (ISBN 0-398-02963-6). C C Thomas.
--Types of Drug Abusers & Their Abuses. (American Lectures in Social & Rehabilitation Psychology Ser.). (Illus.). 228p. 1974. 16.75 (ISBN 0-398-02928-8). C C Thomas.
--Understanding Disability for Social & Rehabilitation Services. (American Lectures in Social & Rehabilitation Psychology Ser.). (Illus.). 220p. 1973. 18.75 (ISBN 0-398-02889-3). C C Thomas.
--Vocational Rehabilitation: Profession & Process. (Amer. Lec. in Social & Rehabilitation Psychology Ser.). (Illus.). 576p. 1977. 29.75 (ISBN 0-398-02266-6). C C Thomas.
--Volunteerism: An Emerging Profession. (Amer. Lec. Social & Rehabilitation Psychology Ser.). (Illus.). 220p. 1974. 16.75 (ISBN 0-398-02788-9). C C Thomas.
Cull, John G., jt. ed. see Hardy, Richard E.
Cullen, Catherine, tr. see Favret-Saada, Jeanne.
Cullen, Charles G. Matrices & Linear Transformations. 2nd ed. LC 70-174334. 1972. text ed. 16.95 (ISBN 0-201-01209-X). A-W.
Cullen, Countee, ed. Caroling Dusk: An Anthology of Verse by Negro Poets. LC 73-18651. 256p. (YA) 1974. 10.95 o.s.i. (ISBN 0-06-010926-2, HarpT). Har-Row.
Cullen, D. E., jt. auth. see Chamberlain, Neil W.
Cullen, D. J., jt. auth. see Cook, T. M.
Cullen, J., jt. auth. see Davis, P. H.
Cullen, J., ed. Experimental Behavior: A Basis for the Study of Mental Disturbance. (Illus.). 440p. 1974. 25.00x (ISBN 0-7165-2231-4, Pub by Irish Academic Pr). Biblio Dist.
Cullen, Jean, jt. auth. see Gross, Robin.
Cullen, Jim. How to Be Your Own Power Company: The Low-Voltage Direct-Current, Power-Generating System. 142p. 1980. 16.95 (ISBN 0-442-24340-5); pap. 10.95 (ISBN 0-442-24345-6). Van Nos Reinhold.
Cullen, John B. Structure of Professionalism. (Illus.). 1979. text ed. 17.50 (ISBN 0-89433-084-5). Petrocelli.

Cullen, Joseph, ed. Legacies in the Study of Behavior: The Wisdom & Experience of Many. (American Lectures in Objective Psychiatry Ser.). (Illus.). 288p. 1975. text ed. 24.50 (ISBN 0-398-03147-9). C C Thomas.
Cullen, Joseph W., et al, eds. Cancer: The Behavioral Dimensions. LC 75-43192. 1976. 24.50 (ISBN 0-89004-104-0). Raven.
Cullen, L. M. Life in Ireland. 1979. pap. 14.95 (ISBN 0-7134-1449-9, Pub. by Batsford England). David & Charles.
Cullen, Margaret. Living Today: Decorating Your Home. 1972. pap. text ed. 3.95x o.p. (ISBN 0-435-42205-7). Heinemann Ed.
--Living Today: Feeding the Family. 1971. pap. text ed. 3.95x o.p. (ISBN 0-435-42200-6). Heinemann Ed.
--Living Today: Good Grooming & Clothes Care. 1971. pap. text ed. 3.95x o.p. (ISBN 0-435-42202-2). Heinemann Ed.
--Living Today: Health & Care of the Family. 1971. pap. text ed. 3.95x o.p. (ISBN 0-435-42201-4). Heinemann Ed.
--Living Today: Homemaking. 1972. pap. text ed. 3.95x o.p. (ISBN 0-435-42204-9). Heinemann Ed.
--Living Today: Housing the Family. 1972. pap. text ed. 3.95x o.p. (ISBN 0-435-42203-0). Heinemann Ed.
--Living Today: Managing Your Money. 1974. pap. text ed. 3.95x o.p. (ISBN 0-435-42208-1). Heinemann Ed.
--Living Today: The Family & the Social Services. 1973. pap. text ed. 3.95x o.p. (ISBN 0-435-42206-5). Heinemann Ed.
--Living Today: The Kitchen. 1974. pap. text ed. 3.95x o.p. (ISBN 0-435-42207-3). Heinemann Ed.
--Living Today: Topics & Questions in Home Economics. 1975. pap. text ed. 3.95x o.p. (ISBN 0-435-42209-X). Heinemann Ed.
Cullen, Maurice R., Jr. The Mass Media & the First Amendment: An Introduction to the Issues, Problems, & Practices. 1981. pap. text ed. write for info. (ISBN 0-697-04344-4); write for info. instr's. manual (ISBN 0-697-04346-0). Wm C Brown.
Cullen, Patrick R. Greyhound Racing 's Precision Players. (Orig.). 1980. pap. write for info. Precision Pub Co.
Cullen, William. First Lines for the Practice of Physic. Bd. with Physiology. Peart, E. (Contributions to the History of Psychology Ser., Vol. XII, Pt. A: Orientations). 1980. Repr. of 1822 ed. 30.00 (ISBN 0-89093-314-6). U Pubns Amer.
Cullen-Tanaka, Janet. Fire Mountain. 288p. (Orig.). 1980. pap. 2.50 (ISBN 0-89083-646-9). Zebra.
Culler, Jonathan. Ferdinand De Saussure. (Modern Masters Ser.). 1977. pap. 3.95 (ISBN 0-14-004369-1). Penguin.
--Structuralist Poetics: Structuralism, Linguistics & the Study of Literature. LC 74-11608. 1975. 19.50x (ISBN 0-8014-0928-4); pap. 5.95 (ISBN 0-8014-9155-X). Cornell U Pr.
Culler, R. D. Skiffs & Schooners. LC 74-17905. (Illus.). 406p. 1975. 20.00 (ISBN 0-87742-047-5). Intl Marine.
--The Spray: Building & Sailing a Replica of Joshua Slocum's Famous Vessel. LC 78-55738. (Illus.). 1978. 10.95 (ISBN 0-87742-099-8). Intl Marine.
Culley, Iris. New Life for Your Sunday School. 1979. pap. 3.95 (ISBN 0-8164-2208-7). Crossroad NY.
Culley, M. B. The Pilchard. 1972. 55.000 (ISBN 0-08-016523-0). Pergamon.
Culley, Margaret, ed. see Chopin, Kate.
Culley, Thomas R., jt. auth. see Hansen, David A.
Culligan, Emmett. The Last World War & the End of Time. (Illus.). 1975. pap. 4.50 o.p. (ISBN 0-89555-034-2, 301). TAN Bks Pubs.
Cullinan, Angeline M., jt. auth. see Cullinan, John E.
Cullinan, Douglas & Epstein, Michael. Special Education for Adolescents: Issues & Perspectives. (Special Education Ser.). 1979. text ed. 17.50 (ISBN 0-675-08407-5). Merrill.
Cullinan, John E. & Cullinan, Angeline M. Illustrated Guide to X-Ray Technics. 1980. text ed. write for info. o.p. (ISBN 0-397-50425-X). Lippincott.
Cullinan, Thomas. Besieged. 1970. 6.95 o.p. (ISBN 0-8180-0607-2). Horizon.
Culliney, John L. Forests of the Sea: Life & Death on the Continental Shelf. LC 78-8208. 1979. pap. 5.95 (ISBN 0-385-14417-2, Anch). Doubleday.
Culling, C. F. Handbook of Histopathological & Histochemical Techniques. 3rd ed. 1974. 53.95 (ISBN 0-407-72901-1). Butterworths.
Cullingford, Elizabeth. Yeats, Ireland & Facism. LC 80-12734. (The Gotham Library). 256p. 1980. 25.00x (ISBN 0-8147-1380-7). NYU Pr.
Cullingford, R. A., et al. Timescales in Geomorphology. LC 79-40517. 1980. 77.95 (ISBN 0-471-27600-6, Pub. by Wiley-Interscience). Wiley.
Cullingworth, J. B. Problems of an Urban Society: Vol. 1, the Social Framework of Planning. (Urban & Regional Studies Ser.). 1973. pap. text ed. 8.95x o.p. (ISBN 0-04-352045-6). Allen Unwin.
--Problems of an Urban Society: Vol. 2, Social Content of Planning. (Urban & Regional Studies Ser.). 1973. pap. text ed. 8.95x o.p. (ISBN 0-04-352043-X). Allen Unwin.
--Problems of an Urban Society: Vol. 3, Planning for Social Change. (Urban & Regional Studies Ser.). 1973. pap. text ed. 8.95x o.p. (ISBN 0-04-352047-2). Allen Unwin.
Culliton, J. W., jt. auth. see Lewis, H. T.
Cullity, B. D. Elements of X-Ray Diffraction. 2nd ed. LC 77-73950. (Illus.). 1978. text ed. 26.95 (ISBN 0-201-01174-3). A-W.
Cullity, Berrard D. Introduction to Magnetic Materials. LC 71-159665. 1972. text ed. 27.95 (ISBN 0-201-01218-9). A-W.
Cullity, Maurice. The History of Dairying in Western Australia. 488p. 1980. 35.00x (ISBN 0-85564-177-0, Pub. by U of West Australia Pr Australia). Intl Schol Bk Serv.
Cullman, Elissa, jt. auth. see Brant, Sandra.
Cullmann, Oscar. The Christology of the New Testament. rev. ed. Guthrie, Shirley C. & Hall, Charles A., trs. LC 59-10178. pap. 11.95. Westminster.
Cullmann, Oscar & Leenhardt, Franz J. Essays on the Lord's Supper. LC 58-8979. 1958. pap. 3.95 (ISBN 0-8042-3748-4). John Knox.
Cullom, Shelby. Fifty Years of Public Service: Personal Recollections of Shelby M. Cullom. LC 75-87504. (American Public Figures Ser). Repr. of 1911 ed. lib. bdg. 45.00 (ISBN 0-306-71410-8). Da Capo.
Cullum, Elizabeth. Cottage Herbal. LC 75-10563. (Illus.). 144p. 1976. 11.50 o.p. (ISBN 0-7153-7108-8). David & Charles.
Cully, Iris V. Ways to Teach Children. LC 66-24201. 1966. 1.00x o.p. (ISBN 0-8006-0076-2). Fortress.
Cully, Thomas D. Jesuits & Music. 1970. pap. 14.00 (ISBN 0-8294-0335-3). Jesuit Hist.
Culp, Gordon, et al. Wastewater Reuse & Recycling Technology. LC 80-21778. (Pollution Technology Review Ser.: 72). (Illus.). 838p. 1981. 49.00 (ISBN 0-8155-0829-8). Noyes.
Culp, Mary B., jt. ed. see Spann, Sylvia.
Culp, Robert D., ed. Guidance & Control 1979. LC 57-43769. (Advances in the Astronautical Sciences: Vol. 39). lib. bdg. 45.00x (ISBN 0-87703-100-2); fiche suppl. 5.00 (ISBN 0-87703-128-2). Univelt Inc.
Culpeper, Nicholas. Culpeper's Complete Herbal. (Illus.). 1959. 12.95 (ISBN 0-8069-3900-1); lib. bdg. 10.79 (ISBN 0-8069-3901-X). Sterling.
--Culpeper's Herbal Remedies. pap. 3.00 (ISBN 0-87980-025-9). Wilshire.
Culpepper, Robert H. God's Calling: A Missionary Autobiography. LC 80-68643. 1981. 4.95 (ISBN 0-8054-6323-2). Broadman.
Cultural Assistance Center. Public & Private Support for the Arts in New York City: A Review with Recommendations for Improvement in the 80's. LC 80-65497. 160p. (Orig.). 1980. pap. 6.00 (Pub. by Cultural Assist). Pub Ctr Cult Res.
Culver, John H. & Syer, John C. Power & Politics in California. LC 79-18497. 1980. pap. text ed. 8.95 (ISBN 0-471-04866-6); tchrs' manual (ISBN 0-471-08076-4). Wiley.
Culver, Robert. The Living God. 1978. pap. 3.95 (ISBN 0-88207-765-1). Victor Bks.
Culver, Robert D. The Histories & Prophecies of Daniel. 192p. (Orig.). 1980. pap. 4.95 (ISBN 0-88469-131-4). BMH Bks.
Culver, Roger B. Astronomy. (Illus.). 1979. pap. 4.95 (ISBN 0-06-460158-7, CO 158, COS). Har-Row.
--An Introduction to Experimental Astronomy: Preliminary Edition. (Illus.). 1974. pap. text ed. 8.95x (ISBN 0-7167-0347-5). W H Freeman.
Culver, Timothy. Ex Officio. LC 70-106590. 512p. 1970. 6.95 (ISBN 0-87131-006-6). M Evans.
Culverwel, Nathanael. An Elegant & Learned Discourse on the Light of Nature, 1652: Nathanael Colverwel (1618-1651) Wellek, Rene, ed. LC 75-11215. (British Philosophers & Theologians of the 17th & 18th Centuries Ser.). 1978. lib. bdg. 42.00 (ISBN 0-8240-1769-2). Garland Pub.
Culyer, A. J. The Political Economy of Social Policy. 1980. 27.50 (ISBN 0-312-62242-2). St Martin.
Culyer, A. J. & Wright, K. G. Economic Aspects of Health Services. 190p. 1978. 35.00x (ISBN 0-85520-227-0, Pub. by Martin Robertson England). Biblio Dist.
Culyer, A. J., et al, eds. An Annotated Bibliography of Health Economics. LC 77-79018. 1977. 29.95x (ISBN 0-312-03873-9). St Martin.
Cumberland, Charles C. Mexican Revolution. Incl. Genesis Under Madero. ix, 298p. 1952. 15.00x (ISBN 0-292-75018-8); pap. 7.95 (ISBN 0-292-75017-X); The Constitutionalist Years. LC 74-38506. (Illus.). xx, 450p. 1972. 17.50x (ISBN 0-292-75000-5); pap. 9.95 (ISBN 0-292-75016-1). U of Tex Pr.
Cumberland, K. B. & Whitelaw, J. S. New Zealand. (The World's Landscapes Ser.). (Illus.). 1970. pap. text ed. 10.95x (ISBN 0-582-31157-8). Longman.
Cumberland, Richard. A Treatise of the Laws of Nature, Made English from the Latin by John Maxwell. Wellek, Rene, ed. LC 75-11216. (British Philosophers & Theologians of the 17th & 18th Centuries: Vol. 19). 1977. Repr. of 1727 ed. lib. bdg. 42.00 (ISBN 0-8240-1770-6). Garland Pub.
Cumes, J. W. The Indigent Rich: A Theory of General Equilibrium in a Keynesian System. 224p. 1972. 16.50 (ISBN 0-08-017534-1). Pergamon.
--Inflation: A Study in Stability. 202p. 1976. text ed. 16.75 (ISBN 0-08-018167-8). Pergamon.
Cumine, Earl. Shringar: The Golden Book of Indian Hair Styles. (Illus.). 1975. pap. 2.50 English, Urdu, & Tamil (ISBN 0-88253-454-8). Ind-US Inc.
Cuming, G. J., ed. Mission of the Church & the Propagation of the Faith. LC 77-108105. (Cambridge Studies in Church History: Vol. 6). 1970. 36.00 (ISBN 0-521-07752-4). Cambridge U Pr.
Cuming, G. J. & Baker, D., eds. Councils & Assemblies. LC 70-132384. (Cambridge Studies in Church History: No. 7). 1971. 47.50 (ISBN 0-521-08038-X). Cambridge U Pr.
Cuming, G. J. & Baker, Derek, eds. Popular Belief & Practice. LC 77-155583. (Studies in Church History: Vol. 8). 1972. 47.50 (ISBN 0-521-08220-X). Cambridge U Pr.
Cuming, G. J., ed. see Church of England.
Cuming, Geoffrey. A History of Anglican Liturgy. (Illus.). 450p. 1980. Repr. of 1969 ed. text ed. 39.00x (ISBN 0-333-30661-9). Humanities.
Cuming, Pamela. The Power Handbook: A Strategic Guide to Personal & Organizational Effectiveness. LC 80-14039. 340p. 1980. pap. 12.95 (ISBN 0-8436-0778-5). CBI Pub.
Cumings, Bruce. The Origins of the Korean War: Liberation & the Emergence of Separate Regimes. LC 80-8543. (Illus.). 552p. 1981. 35.00x (ISBN 0-691-09383-0); pap. 14.50x (ISBN 0-691-10113-2). Princeton U Pr.
Cumings, J. N., ed. see Migraine Symposium, 5th, London, 1972.
Cumming, Candy & Newman, Vicky. Eater's Guide: Nutrition Basics for Busy People. (Illus.). 192p. 1981. 11.95 (ISBN 0-13-223057-7); pap. 5.95 (ISBN 0-13-223040-2). P-H.
Cumming, Diane, tr. see Michaelle.
Cumming, E. E., ed. Hospital & Welfare Library Services: An International Bibliography. 1977. 24.50 (ISBN 0-85365-139-6, Pub. by Lib Assn England). Oryx Pr.
Cumming, E. E., jt. ed. see Burnett, D.
Cumming, Elaine & Cumming, John H. Closed Ranks: An Experiment in Mental Health Education. LC 57-9073. (Commonwealth Fund Publications Ser). 1957. 7.50x (ISBN 0-674-13600-4). Harvard U Pr.
Cumming, Elaine, jt. auth. see Cumming, John.
Cumming, Henry H. Franco-British Rivalry in the Post-War Near East: The Decline of French Influence. LC 79-2854. (Illus.). 229p. 1981. Repr. of 1938 ed. 19.75 (ISBN 0-8305-0029-4). Hyperion Conn.
Cumming, John. Runners & Walkers. (Illus.). 196p. 1981. pap. 9.95 (ISBN 0-89526-889-2). Regnery-Gateway.
Cumming, John & Cumming, Elaine. Ego & Milieu: Theory & Practice of Environmental Therapy. LC 62-18829. 1962. pap. 7.95x (ISBN 0-202-26044-5). Aldine Pub.
Cumming, John H., jt. auth. see Cumming, Elaine.
Cumming, Marsue & Epton, Arli, eds. Theatre Profiles-Three: Resource Book of Nonprofit Professional Theatres in the United States. (Illus., Orig.). 1978. pap. 9.95x (ISBN 0-930452-02-X, Pub. by Theatre Comm). Pub Ctr Cult Res.
Cumming, Patricia. Afterwards. LC 73-94068. 64p. 1974. pap. 4.95 (ISBN 0-914086-02-2). Alicejamesbooks.
--Letter from an Outlying Province. LC 76-19884. 80p. 1976. pap. 4.95 (ISBN 0-914086-14-6). Alicejamesbooks.
Cumming, Primrose. Mystery Pony. LC 57-11520. (Illus.). (gr. 7 up). 1957. 8.95 (ISBN 0-87599-024-X). S G Phillips.
Cumming, Valerie. Exploring Costume History. (Illus.). 72p. 1981. 17.95 (ISBN 0-7134-1829-X, Pub. by Batsford England). Doubleday.
Cummings see Bentley, Eric.
Cummings, Abbot L., ed. Architecture in Colonial Massachusetts: A Conference Held by the Colonial Society of Massachusetts, September 19 & 20, 1974. LC 79-51657. 1979. 25.00x (ISBN 0-8139-0855-8). U Pr of Va.
Cummings, Bernice & Schuck, Victoria. Women Organizing: An Anthology. LC 79-18956. 422p. 1979. 21.50 (ISBN 0-8108-1245-2). Scarecrow.
Cummings, Betty S. Turtle. LC 80-24062. (Illus.). (gr. 2-5). 1981. PLB 9.95 (ISBN 0-689-30805-1). Atheneum.
Cummings, Bob. House Warming. pap. 7.95 (ISBN 0-930096-08-8). G Gannett.
Cummings, D., tr. see Makrakis, Apostolos.
Cummings, D., tr. see Philaretos, S. D.
Cummings, D., tr. see Philaretos, Sotirios D.
Cummings, Denver, tr. see Agapius, et al.
Cummings, Denver, tr. see Livadeas, Themistocles & Charitos, Minas.
Cummings, Denver, tr. see Makrakis, Apostolos.
Cummings, Donald W. & Herum, John, eds. Tempo: Life, Work & Leisure. (Illus.). 336p. 1974. pap. text ed. 9.95 (ISBN 0-395-17839-8, 3-12925); instructors' guide 1.50 (ISBN 0-395-17867-3, 3-12926). HM.
Cummings, E. E. Complete Poems Nineteen-Thirteen to Nineteen Sixty-Two. LC 80-14213. 1980. pap. 9.95 (ISBN 0-15-621062-2, Harv). HarBraceJ.
--Enormous Room. new ed. LC 77-114387. 1950. 5.95 (ISBN 0-87140-956-9); pap. 3.25 (ISBN 0-87140-001-4, L-001). Liveright.
--Ninety Five Poems. LC 58-10909. 1971. pap. 1.95 (ISBN 0-15-665950-6, HPL51, HPL). HarBraceJ.
Cummings, E. E. & Firmage, George J., eds. Hist Whist & Other Poems for Children. (Illus.). 1981. 9.95 (ISBN 0-87140-640-3). Liveright.
--Hist Whist & Other Poems for Children. (Illus.). 1981. 9.95 o.p. (ISBN 0-686-67746-3). Liveright.
Cummings, Frederick J. & Elam, Charles H., eds. The Detroit Institute of Arts Illustrated Handbook. LC 76-168631. (Illus.). 1971. 8.95x (ISBN 0-8143-1457-0); pap. 3.95 (ISBN 0-8143-1458-9). Wayne St U Pr.
Cummings, Harold J. Prescription for Tomorrow. LC 80-25723. 112p. 1980. write for info. (ISBN 0-87863-034-1). Farnswth Pub.
Cummings, Homer & McFarland, Carl. Federal Justice. LC 76-109552. (American Constitutional & Legal History Ser). 1970. Repr. of 1937 ed. lib. bdg. 49.50 (ISBN 0-306-71906-1). Da Capo.
Cummings, Jack. Playboy's Guide to Real Estate Investing for the Single Person. LC 80-7790. (Playboy's Lifestyles Library). 288p. 1980. 13.95 (ISBN 0-87223-621-8, Dist. by Har-Row). Playboy.
Cummings, James E. A Handbook on the Holy Spirit. LC 77-79551. 1977. pap. 3.50 (ISBN 0-87123-541-2, 200541). Bethany Fell.
Cummings, Jean. Alias the Buffalo Doctor. LC 80-81714. (Illus.). 266p. 1981. 11.95 (ISBN 0-8040-0815-9). Swallow.
--They Call Him the Buffalo Doctor. LC 73-147172. 320p. 1980. Repr. of 1971 ed. 7.00 (ISBN 0-8187-0035-1). Harlo Pr.
--Why They Call Him The Buffalo Doctor. LC 73-147172. 309p. 1980. Repr. of 1971 ed. 10.95 (ISBN 0-8187-0035-1). Swallow.
Cummings, John T., jt. auth. see Askari, Hossein.
Cummings, Keith. The Technique of Glass Forming. (Illus.). 168p. 1980. 27.00 (ISBN 0-7134-1612-2, Pub. by Batsford England). David & Charles.
Cummings, L. L. & Dunham, Randall B. Introduction to Organizational Behavior: Text & Readings. 1980. pap. 14.95x (ISBN 0-256-02043-4). Irwin.
Cummings, L. L., jt. auth. see Scott, William E.
Cummings, Milton C. Congressmen & the Electorate. LC 66-17692. 1966. 8.95 o.s.i. (ISBN 0-02-906920-3). Free Pr.
Cummings, Milton C., Jr., et al, eds. The National Election of 1964. 1966. 9.95 (ISBN 0-8157-1642-7). Brookings.
Cummings, O. R. Street Cars of Boston, Vol.6: Birneys, Type 5, Semiconvertibles, Parlor, Private, & Mail Cars. (Illus.). 84p. 1980. pap. 9.00 (ISBN 0-911940-34-0). Cox.
Cummings, Oveta, jt. auth. see Reum, Earl.
Cummings, Paul, jt. auth. see Bame, E. Allen.
Cummings, R. D., tr. see Plato.
Cummings, Ray. Insect Invasion. (YA) 4.95 o.p. (ISBN 0-685-07437-4, Avalon). Bouregy.
Cummings, Raymond. Girl in the Golden Atom. 1976. lib. bdg. 12.95x (ISBN 0-89968-175-1). Lightyear.
Cummings, Richard. Make Your Own Comics for Fun & Profit. (gr. 7 up). 1975. 9.95 (ISBN 0-8098-3929-6). Walck.
--Make Your Own Dollhouse. (Illus.). 1978. 8.95 o.p. (ISBN 0-679-20439-3). McKay.
--Proposition Fourteen: A Secessionist Remedy. LC 80-8917. 128p. 1981. pap. 5.95 postponed (ISBN 0-394-17890-4, Ever). Grove.

--Proposition Fourteen: The Secessionist Remedy. LC 80-80357. 112p. 1980. 11.95 (ISBN 0-932966-09-8); pap. 5.95 (ISBN 0-932966-16-0). Permanent Pr.

Cummings, Richard L. & Lemke, Donald A. Educational Innovations in Latin America. LC 73-390. 1973. 13.50 (ISBN 0-8108-0585-5). Scarecrow.

Cummings, Thomas G. & Molloy, Edmond S. Improving Productivity & the Quality of Work Life. LC 76-24348. (Praeger Special Studies). 1977. text ed. 29.95 (ISBN 0-275-56870-9); pap. 10.95 (ISBN 0-03-022601-5). Praeger.

Cummings, Thomas G. & Srivastva, Suresh. Management of Work: A Socio-Technical Systems Approach. LC 76-47659. 1977. 15.00x o.p. (ISBN 0-87338-188-2, Pub. by Comp. Adm. Research Inst.). Kent St U Pr.

Cummings, Thomas G., ed. Systems Theory for Organization Development. LC 79-42906. (Individuals, Groups & Organizations Ser.). 384p. 1980. 49.00 (ISBN 0-471-27691-X, Pub. by Wiley-Interscience). Wiley.

Cummings, Thomas S. Historic Annals of the National Academy of Design. LC 71-87503. (Library of American Art). 1969. Repr. of 1865 ed. 39.50 (ISBN 0-306-71411-6). Da Capo.

Cummings, William K., et al. Changes in the Japanese University: A Comparative Perspective. LC 78-19787. 1979. 25.95 (ISBN 0-03-045546-4). Praeger.

Cummins. An Econometric Model of the Life Insurance Sector of the U. S. Economy. LC 73-11654. 1975. 24.95 (ISBN 0-669-89490-7). Lexington Bks.

Cummins, C. Lyle, Jr. Internal Fire: The Internal Combustion Engine, 1673-1900. LC 75-40701. (Illus.). 1976. 20.00x (ISBN 0-917308-01-8). Carnot Pr.

Cummins, D. Duane & Hohweiler, Daryl, eds. An Enlisted Soldier's View of the Civil War: The Wartime Papers of Joseph R. Ward, Jr. (Illus., Orig.). 1981. pap. price not set (ISBN 0-9605732-0-8). Belle Pubns.

Cummins, J. David. Investment Activities of Life Insurance Companies. 1977. 16.00x (ISBN 0-256-01974-6). Irwin.

Cummins, J. G. The Spanish Traditional Lyric. LC 76-1222. 1977. 18.75 (ISBN 0-08-018117-1); pap. 9.25 (ISBN 0-08-018116-3). Pergamon.

Cummins, Jacqueline. End of Innocence. 1961. 8.95 (ISBN 0-8392-1028-0). Astor-Honor.

Cummins, Kenneth L., ed. see Proceedings of a Workshop, Palo Alto, California, July 1979, et al.

Cummins, Marsha Z. & Slade, Carole. Writing the Research Paper: A Guide & Sourcebook. LC 78-69613. (Illus.). 1978. pap. text ed. 8.75 (ISBN 0-395-27259-9); inst. manual 0.30 (ISBN 0-395-27260-2). HM.

Cummins, Mary Ann, jt. auth. see Burnett, Millie.

Cummins, Thomas J., jt. auth. see Dunphy, Thomas.

Cummins, W. A., jt. ed. see McKClough, T. H.

Cummins, Walter, jt. auth. see Gordon, George G.

Cummins, Walter M., et al. The Other Sides of Reality: Myths, Visions & Fantasies. LC 75-182677. 400p. 1972. pap. 7.95x (ISBN 0-87835-038-1). Boyd & Fraser.

Cundall, R. B., jt. ed. see Jennings, K. R.

Cundiff, Edward, et al. Fundamentals of Modern Marketing. 2nd ed. 480p. 1976. 15.95 o.p. (ISBN 0-13-341248-2); student guide 6.95 o.p. (ISBN 0-13-341255-5). P-H.

Cundiff, Edward W. & Still, Richard R. Basic Marketing: Concepts, Decisions & Strategies. 2nd ed. LC 79-138478. 1971. ref. ed. 18.95 (ISBN 0-13-062638-4); study guide 4.95 (ISBN 0-13-062620-1). P-H.

Cundiff, Edward W., jt. auth. see Still, Richard R.

Cundiff, Edward W., ed. Marketing Doctoral Dissertations Abstracts, 1977. LC 78-13138. (Bibliography Ser.: No. 32). 1979. 10.00 o.p. (ISBN 0-87757-114-7). Am Mktg.

Cundiff, Edward W., et al. Sales Management. (Illus.). 656p. 1981. text ed. 20.95 (ISBN 0-13-788059-6). P-H.

--Fundamentals of Modern Marketing. 3rd ed. 1980. text ed. 18.95 (ISBN 0-13-341388-8). P-H.

Cundiff, Paul A. Robert Browning: A Shelley Promethean. LC 77-77039. 1977. 12.95 o.p. (ISBN 0-912760-49-4); pap. 9.95 o.p. (ISBN 0-685-81416-5). Valkyrie Pr.

Cundiff, W. E. & Reid, Mado. Issues in Canadian-U. S. Transborder Computer Data Flows. 89p. 1979. pap. text ed. 6.50x (ISBN 0-920380-12-3, Pub. by Inst Res Pub Canada). Renouf.

Cuney-Hare, Maud. Negro Musicians & Their Music. LC 74-4108. (Music Reprint Ser.). 1974. Repr. of 1936 ed. 35.00 (ISBN 0-306-70652-0). Da Capo.

Cunff, Madeleine Le. Sur le Vif. (Illus., Fr.). 1977. pap. text ed. 5.75 (ISBN 0-88436-454-2). EMC.

Cunha, Deborah, ed. Public Welfare Directory: 1980-1981. LC 41-4981. 1980. pap. 35.00x (ISBN 0-910106-11-8). Am Pub Welfare.

Cunha, Dorothy G., jt. auth. see Cunha, George M.

Cunha, George M. & Cunha, Dorothy G. Conservation of Library Materials: A Manual & Bibliography on the Care, Repair, & Restoration of Library Materials, 2 vols. 2nd ed. LC 77-163871. Vol. 1, 1971. 15.00 (ISBN 0-8108-0760-2); Vol. 2, 1972. 15.00 (ISBN 0-8108-0525-1); Set. 27.50 (ISBN 0-686-60803-8). Scarecrow.

Cunha, Tony J. Horse Feeding & Nutrition. LC 80-531. (Animal Feeding & Nutrition Ser.). 1980. 26.50 (ISBN 0-12-196560-0). Acad Pr.

Cunha, Tony J., et al, eds. Factors Affecting Calf Crop. LC 66-22000. (Illus.). 1967. 16.00 (ISBN 0-8130-0053-X). U Presses Fla.

Cunha-Vaz, Jose G., ed. The Blood-Retinal Barriers. (NATO Advanced Study Institutes Ser., Ser. A: Life Sciences: Vol. 32). 405p. 1980. 39.50 (ISBN 0-306-40430-3, Plenum Pr). Plenum Pub.

Cuni, Antonio, tr. see Emanuel, W. D.

Cunitz, Jonathan A. Computer Cases in Accounting. (Illus.). 96p. 1972. pap. 6.95 ref. ed. (ISBN 0-13-166140-X). P-H.

Cunliffe, Barry. Iron Age Communities in Britain. 2nd ed. (Archaeology of Britain Ser). (Illus.). 1978. 42.00 (ISBN 0-7100-8725-X). Routledge & Kegan.

--Roman Bath Discovered. (Illus.). 1971. 25.00 (ISBN 0-7100-6826-3). Routledge & Kegan.

Cunliffe, John. The Farmer, the Rooks & the Cherry Tree. LC 80-65671. (Illus.). 32p. (ps-2). 1980. 8.95 (ISBN 0-233-96571-8). Andre Deutsch.

--Giant Kippernose & Other Stories. LC 80-2694. 112p. (gr. k-5). 1981. 8.95 (ISBN 0-233-96386-3). Andre Deutsch.

--The Giant Who Swallowed the Wind. LC 79-64314. (Illus.). (gr. k-2). 1980. 8.95 (ISBN 0-233-96310-3). Andre Deutsch.

--Great Dragon Competition & Other Stories. (Illus.). (gr. k-5). 1980. 6.95 (ISBN 0-233-96472-X). Andre Deutsch.

--King's Birthday Cake. (Illus.). (ps-2). 1979. PLB 8.95 (ISBN 0-233-96453-3). Andre Deutsch.

--Mr. Gosling & the Great Art Robbery. (Illus.). (ps-3). 1979. PLB 8.95 (ISBN 0-233-96956-X). Andre Deutsch.

--Mr. Gosling & the Runaway Chair. LC 80-2696. (Illus.). 32p. (gr. k-3). 1981. 8.95 (ISBN 0-233-96956-X). Andre Deutsch.

--Sara's Giant & the Upside-Down House. (Illus.). (ps-2). 1980. 8.95 (ISBN 0-233-97202-1). Andre Deutsch.

Cunliffe, John W., et al, eds. Century Readings in English Literature. 5th ed. 1955. 35.00x (ISBN 0-89197-068-1); pap. text ed. 14.95x (ISBN 0-89197-694-9). Irvington.

Cunliffe, Marcus. The Right to Property: A Theme in American History. (Sir George Watson Lectures Ser). 1974. pap. text ed. 1.50x (ISBN 0-7185-1129-8, Leicester). Humanities.

--Soldiers & Civilians. LC 68-22898. (Illus.). 1973. pap. text ed. 5.95 o.s.i. (ISBN 0-02-906860-6). Free Pr.

Cunliffe, Marcus & Morris, Richard B. George Washington & the Making of a Nation. LC 66-2290. (American Heritage Junior Library). (Illus.). (gr. 5 up). 1966. PLB 12.89 (ISBN 0-06-021378-7, Dist. by Har-Row). Am Heritage.

Cunliffe, W. Gordon. Gunter Grass. (World Authors Ser.: Germany: No. 65). 1969. lib. bdg. 10.95 (ISBN 0-8057-2400-1). Twayne.

Cunliffe, W. J. & Cotterill, J. A. The Acnes: Clinical Features, Pathogenesis & Treatment. LC 75-21145. (Major Problems in Dermatology Ser.: Vol. 6). (Illus.). 306p. 1975. 30.00 (ISBN 0-7216-2785-4). Saunders.

Cunningham. Cunningham's Manual of Practical Anatomy: Upper & Lower Limbs, Vol. 1. 14th ed. Romanes, G. J., ed. (Illus.). 270p. 1976. pap. text ed. 10.95x (ISBN 0-19-263129-2). Oxford U Pr.

Cunningham, Alastair J., jt. ed. see Sercarz, Eli E.

Cunningham, Aline. The Surprise. (Caterpillar Bk. Ser.). (Illus.). 16p. (ps-k). 0.69 (ISBN 0-570-06906-8, 56Y1271). Concordia.

--Today. (Caterpillar Bk. Ser.). (Illus.). 12p. (ps-k). 0.69 (ISBN 0-570-06907-6, 56Y1272). Concordia.

--The Tree & Four Friends. (Caterpillar Bk. Ser.). (Illus.). 12p. (ps-k). 0.69 (ISBN 0-570-06908-4, 56Y1273). Concordia.

Cunningham, Ben. Green Eyes. 1976. pap. 1.50 o.p. (ISBN 0-345-25465-1). Ballantine.

Cunningham, Beryl M. & Holtrop, Wm. Woodshop Tool Maintenance. rev. ed. (Illus.). 296p. 1974. text ed. 18.40 (ISBN 0-87002-145-1). Bennett IL.

Cunningham, Bruce L., jt. auth. see McKinney, Peter.

Cunningham, Chet. Bloody Gold. 1980. pap. 1.75 (ISBN 0-505-51492-3). Tower Bks.

--Devil's Gold. (Orig.). 1980. pap. 1.95 (ISBN 0-505-51510-5). Tower Bks.

--Die of Gold. 1980. pap. 1.50 (ISBN 0-505-51471-0). Tower Bks.

--The Gold Wagon. 1980. pap. 1.50 (ISBN 0-505-51460-5). Tower Bks.

--Seeds of Rebellion. (Patriots Bicentennial Ser.). 1977. pap. 1.75 (ISBN 0-505-51129-0). Tower Bks.

--Tuscon Temptress. (Agent Brad Spear Ser.: No. 3). (Orig.). 1981. pap. 2.25 (ISBN 0-440-09140-3, Banbury). Dell.

--Two Hundred & Twenty-Two Ways to Save Gas: And Get the Best Possible Mileage. LC 80-26423. (Illus.). 96p. 1981. pap. 3.95 (ISBN 0-13-935213-9). P-H.

Cunningham, Cliff & Sloper, Patricia. Helping Your Exceptional Baby: A Practical & Honest Approach to Raising a Mentally Handicapped Child. (Illus.). 1981. pap. 6.95 (ISBN 0-394-73867-5). Pantheon.

Cunningham, Dixon C., et al. Cases on Financial Institutions. LC 77-90644. (Finance Ser.). 1979. text ed. 18.50 (ISBN 0-88244-120-5). Grid Pub.

Cunningham, Donna. An Astrological Guide to Self-Awareness. LC 78-57820. 1978. pap. 5.95 (ISBN 0-916360-09-1). CRCS Pubns NV.

--Being a Lunar Type in a Solar World. 1981. pap. 6.95 (ISBN 0-87728-521-7). Weiser.

Cunningham, E. V. The Case of the Russian Diplomat. 1979. pap. 1.75 o.s.i. (ISBN 0-515-04881-X, 04881-X). Jove Pubns.

Cunningham, Eileen S. Lower Illinois Valley, Greene County 1821, Containment: Morgan to 1823, Scott to 1823, Macoupin to 1829, Jersey to 1839. 1980. 98.40 (AU00128); pap. 88.40. E S Cunningham.

--Lower Illinois Valley Limestone Houses. 1976. 17.00 (AU00127); pap. 12.00. E S Cunningham.

Cunningham, Eileen S., ed. Old Settlers Association of Greene County, Illinois: Coda of the Deep Snow of 1830. 1976. 17.00 (AU00122); pap. 12.00. E S Cunningham.

Cunningham, Eugene, ed. see Poe, Sophie A.

Cunningham, Frank. Objectivity in Social Science. LC 72-95461. 1973. 10.00x o.p. (ISBN 0-8020-1943-9). U of Toronto Pr.

Cunningham, G. R., et al, eds. Regulation of Male Fertility. (Clinics in Andrology Ser.: No. 5). (Illus.). 245p. 1981. PLB 68.50 (ISBN 90-247-2373-6, Pub. by Martinus Nijhoff). Kluwer Boston.

Cunningham, Gail. The New Woman & the Victorian Novel. LC 78-6179. 1978. text ed. 21.50x (ISBN 0-06-491347-3). B&N.

Cunningham, Gladys, jt. auth. see Hutton, Jessie.

Cunningham, Glen. The Phoenix Man. 1980. write for info. o.p. (ISBN 0-912376-52-X). Chosen Bks Pub.

Cunningham, H. H. Doctors in Gray: The Confederate Medical Service. (Illus.). 8.50 (ISBN 0-8446-0566-2). Peter Smith.

Cunningham, Imogen. After Ninety. LC 77-73306. (Illus.). 112p. 1977. 20.00 (ISBN 0-295-95559-7); pap. 10.95 (ISBN 0-295-95673-9). U of Wash Pr.

--Imogen Cunningham: Photographs. LC 71-117733. (Illus.). 128p. 1970. 20.00 (ISBN 0-295-95080-3); pap. 10.95 (ISBN 0-295-95452-3). U of Wash Pr.

--Imogen! Imogen Cunningham Photographs 1910-1973. LC 74-2490. (Index of Art in the Pacific Northwest Ser.: No. 7). (Illus.). 112p. 1974. 20.00 (ISBN 0-295-95332-2); pap. 10.95 (ISBN 0-295-95333-0). U of Wash Pr.

Cunningham, J. V. Collected Essays of J. V. Cunningham. LC 75-21800. xii, 463p. 1977. o.p 20.00 (ISBN 0-8040-0670-9); pap. 9.95 (ISBN 0-8040-0671-7). Swallow.

--Collected Poems and Epigrams. LC 71-132578. 142p. 1971. pap. 8.95 (ISBN 0-8040-0517-6). Swallow.

--Exclusions of a Rhyme: Poems & Epigrams. LC 60-8072. 120p. (Orig.). 1960. 7.00x (ISBN 0-8040-0763-2); pap. 4.50 (ISBN 0-8040-0102-2). Swallow.

--Journal of John Cardan. LC 64-16116. 56p. 1964. 2.50x (ISBN 0-8040-0173-1). Swallow.

--Woe or Wonder: The Emotional Effect of Shakespearean Tragedy. 134p. 1964. pap. 4.50x (ISBN 0-8040-0323-8, 67). Swallow.

Cunningham, James. Sources of Finance for Higher Education in America. LC 79-6081. 165p. 1980. pap. text ed. 9.00 (ISBN 0-8191-0980-0). U Pr of Amer.

Cunningham, James P. Competition Law of the European Economic Community. LC 73-166765. 397p. 1973. pap. 30.00x (ISBN 0-85038-033-2). Intl Pubns Serv.

Cunningham, Jere. Hunter's Blood. 1977. pap. 1.75 o.p. (ISBN 0-449-13794-5, GM). Fawcett.

Cunningham, John. Handbook of Remote Control & Automation Techniques. 1979. 12.95 o.p. (ISBN 0-8306-9848-5); pap. 8.95 (ISBN 0-8306-1077-4, 1077). TAB Bks.

Cunningham, John M. High Noon: A Screen Adaptation, Directed by Fred Zinneman. Garrett, George P., et al, eds. LC 71-135273. (Film Scripts Ser.). 1971. pap. text ed. 5.95x (ISBN 0-89197-788-0). Irvington.

Cunningham, John R., jt. auth. see Johns, Harold E.

Cunningham, Julia. Burnish Me Bright. (gr. k-6). 1980. pap. 1.25 (ISBN 0-440-40870-9, YB). Dell.

--Dear Rat. (gr. 2-5). 1976. pap. 1.50 (ISBN 0-380-00908-0, 46615, Camelot). Avon.

--Dorp Dead. (Illus.). (gr. 3-7). 1974. pap. 1.95 (ISBN 0-380-00709-6, 51458, Camelot). Avon.

--Flight of the Sparrow. LC 80-12788. 144p. (gr. 5-9). 1980. 6.95 (ISBN 0-394-84501-3); PLB 6.99 (ISBN 0-394-94501-8). Pantheon.

Cunningham, Kitty. Conversations with a Dancer. (Illus.). 192p. 1980. 12.95 (ISBN 0-312-16942-6). St Martin.

Cunningham, Lavern, ed. see Phi Delta Kappa Symposium on Educational Research, 12th.

Cunningham, Lawrence S. Saint Francis of Assisi. LC 76-14219. (World Authors Ser: No. 409). 1976. lib. bdg. 12.50 (ISBN 0-8057-6249-3). Twayne.

Cunningham, Lee N. & Edington, D. W. Biological Awareness: Statements for Self-Discovery. (Illus.). 224p. 1975. 14.95x (ISBN 0-13-077180-5). P-H.

Cunningham, Louis & Peters, Herman J. Counseling Theories: A Selective Examination for School Counselors. LC 72-83704. 1973. text ed. 15.95 (ISBN 0-675-09066-0). Merrill.

Cunningham, Luvern L. Governing Schools: New Approaches to Old Issues. LC 70-137520. 1971. 9.95x (ISBN 0-675-09255-8); pap. text ed. 7.95 (ISBN 0-675-09256-6). Merrill.

Cunningham, Luvern L. & Gephart, William J., eds. Leadership: The Science & the Art Today. LC 60-2874. 1973. text ed. 10.00 (ISBN 0-87581-155-8). Peacock Pubs.

Cunningham, Luverne, et al, eds. Educational Administration: The Developing Decades. LC 76-27956. 1977. 20.00x (ISBN 0-8211-0226-5); text ed. 18.00x (ISBN 0-685-71408-X). McCutchan.

Cunningham, Madelyn. Monique. (Historical Romance Ser.). (Orig.). 1979. pap. 2.50 (ISBN 0-515-05113-6). Jove Pubns.

Cunningham, Noble E., Jr. The Image of Thomas Jefferson in the Public Eye: Portraits for the People, 1800-1809. LC 80-22757. (Illus.). 1981. write for info. (ISBN 0-8139-0821-3). U Pr of Va.

Cunningham, P. J., jt. auth. see Riley, P. A.

Cunningham, Richard, tr. see Bombal, Maria L.

Cunningham, Robert C. Filled with the Spirit. LC 73-190446. 1972. pap. 0.75 (ISBN 0-88243-712-7, 02-0712). Gospel Pub.

Cunningham, Robert, Jr. Governing Hospitals: Trustees & the New Accountabilities. LC 75-44127. 1976. pap. 12.50 (ISBN 0-87258-182-9, 1665). Am Hospital.

Cunningham, Robert L., ed. Liberty & the Rule of Law. LC 78-6372. (Illus.). 496p. 1979. 25.00 (ISBN 0-89096-056-9). Tex A&M Univ Pr.

Cunningham, Robert M., Jr. Asking & Giving: A Report on Hospital Philanthropy. LC 79-28315. 148p. (Orig.). 1980. pap. 12.50 (ISBN 0-87258-300-7, 1030). Am Hospital.

Cunningham, Susanne A. & Reagan, Cora L. Handbook of Visual Perceptual Training. 120p. 1972. text ed. 14.75 (ISBN 0-398-02267-4). C C Thomas.

Cunningham, W. P., ed. see Resource Publications, Inc. Staff.

Cunningham, W. Patrick, ed. Musicatalog: The Recording Locator, 1980 Supplement. LC 79-67309. 130p. 1980. pap. 21.95 (ISBN 0-89390-023-0). Resource Pubns.

Cunningham, William. Alien Immigrants to England. LC 72-94541. (Illus.). Repr. of 1897 ed. lib. bdg. 22.50x (ISBN 0-678-05098-8). Kelley.

--Historical Theology, 2 vols. 1979. Set. 31.95; Vol. 1. (ISBN 0-85151-286-0); Vol. 2. (ISBN 0-85151-287-9). Banner of Truth.

--Reformers & the Theology of Reformation. 1979. 15.95 (ISBN 0-85151-013-2). Banner of Truth.

Cunningham, William & Mahanand, Marilyn. Blacks in the Performing Arts. 1981. 25.00 (ISBN 0-208-01849-2, Lib. Prof Pubns). Shoe String.

Cunningham, William H. & Lopreato, Sally C. Energy Use & Conservation Incentives: A Study of the Southwestern United States. LC 77-7485. (Praeger Special Studies). 1977. text ed. 22.95 (ISBN 0-03-022276-1). Praeger.

Cunningham-Smith, Judy & Herbert, Mollie. Self-Sufficient Pottery. LC 79-53741. (Illus.). 1979. 14.95 (ISBN 0-7153-7674-8). David & Charles.

Cunnington, P. Children's Costume in England. 1972. text ed. 17.00x (ISBN 0-7136-0371-2). Humanities.

--Costume for Births, Marriages & Deaths. 1978. Repr. of 1972 ed. text ed. 22.75x (ISBN 0-7136-1192-8). Humanities.

Cunnington, Phillis. Costumes of the Seventeenth & Eighteenth Century. LC 70-115950. (Illus.). 1971. 5.95 o.p. (ISBN 0-8238-0086-5). Plays.
Cunnington, Phillis & Lucas, Catherine. Charity Costume: Of Children, Scholars, Almsfolk, Pensioners. (Illus.). 331p. 1978. 26.50x (ISBN 0-06-491346-5). B&N.
Cunnington, Phyllis & Mansfield, Alan. English Costume for Sports & Outdoors Recreation: From the Sixteenth to the Nineteenth Centuries. (Illus.). 1978. Repr. of 1969 ed. text ed. 23.50x (ISBN 0-7136-1017-4). Humanities.
Cunnison, Ian G. Luapula Peoples of Northern Rhodesia. 1959. text ed. 18.25 (ISBN 0-7190-1015-2). Humanities.
Cunsolo & Mokanski. Study Guide for Calculus with Analytic Geometry. 5th ed. 5.95x o.p. (ISBN 0-205-04220-1, 5642205). Allyn.
Cunynghame, Henry H. Time & Clocks: A Description of Ancient & Modern Methods of Measuring Time. LC 77-78127. (Illus.). 1970. Repr. of 1906 ed. 15.00 (ISBN 0-8103-3576-X). Gale.
Cunz, Dieter, ed. see Huch, Ricarda.
Cupitt, Don. Taking Leave. 192p. 1981. 9.95 (ISBN 0-8245-0045-8). Crossroad NY.
Cuppleditch, David. The John Hassell Lifestyle: A Biography of an Artist. (Illus.). 140p. 1980. 25.00 o.p. (ISBN 0-8390-0250-5). Allanheld & Schram.
Cupps, Thomas R. & Fauci, Anthony S. The Vasculitides. 1981. pap. price not set. Saunders.
Curatorial Staff, Metropolitan Museum of Art. Metropolitan Museum of Art: Notable Acquisitions, 1965-1975. LC 75-31761. (Illus.). 304p. 1975. pap. 15.95 (ISBN 0-87099-141-8). Metro Mus Art.
Cure, Karen. MiniVacations, U.S.A. (Illus.). 256p. (Orig.). 1976. pap. 6.95 o.p. (ISBN 0-695-80529-0). Follett.
--The Travel Catalogue. 1978. 9.95 o.p. (ISBN 0-03-020711-8); pap. 6.95 o.p. (ISBN 0-03-020706-1). HR&W.
Curelaru, M., jt. auth. see Eisenstadt, S. N.
Curet, Miriam De Anda De see Curet de De Anda, Miriam.
Curet de De Anda, Miriam. Le Poesia De Jose Gautier Benitez. LC 80-17629. (Coleccion Mente y Palabra Ser.). (Illus.). 232p. Date not set. 6.25 (ISBN 0-8477-0570-6); pap. 5.00 (ISBN 0-8477-0571-4). U of PR Pr.
Cureton, Thomas K. Physiological Effects of Exercise Programs on Adults. (American Lectures in Sportsmedicine Ser.). (Illus.). 228p. 1971. 19.75 (ISBN 0-398-00377-7). C C Thomas.
--The Physiological Effects of Wheat Germ Oil on Humans in Exercise: Forty-two Physical Training Programs Utilizing 894 Humans. (Illus.). 552p. 1972. 46.50 (ISBN 0-398-02270-4). C C Thomas.
Cureton, Thomas K., Jr., ed. see Bosco, James S.
Curi, K. Treatment & Disposal of Liquid & Solid Industrial Wastes: Proceedings of the Third Turkish-German Environmental Engineering Symposium, Istanbul, July 1979. LC 80-40993. (Illus.). 515p. 1980. 75.00 (ISBN 0-08-023999-4). Pergamon.
Curie, Jean I., jt. ed. see Whethan, Edith J.
Curl, Donald W. Murat Halstead & the Cincinnati Commercial. LC 80-12046. (Illus.). ix, 186p. 1980. 17.50 (ISBN 0-8130-0669-4). U Presses Fla.
Curl, Elroy, jt. auth. see Johnson, Leander F.
Curl, James S. European Cities & Society. 2nd ed. (Illus.). 1972. pap. 14.95x (ISBN 0-249-44109-8). Intl Ideas.
Curley, Arthur & Varlejs, Jana. Akers' Simple Library Cataloging. 6th, completely rev. ed. LC 76-26897. 1977. 11.00 (ISBN 0-8108-0978-8). Scarecrow.
Curley, Dorothy N., et al, eds. Modern American Literature, 3 Vols. 4th enl. ed. LC 76-76599. (Library of Literary Criticism Ser.). (gr. 9-12). 1969. text ed. 90.00 (ISBN 0-8044-3046-2). Ungar.
Curley, Maureen. The Beatitudes. (Children of the Kingdom Activities Ser.). (gr. 4-7). 1977. 7.95 (ISBN 0-686-13692-6). Pflaum Pr.
--Bible Heroes & Heroines. (Children of the Kingdom Activities Ser.). (gr. 4-7). 1975. 7.95 (ISBN 0-686-13688-8). Pflaum Pr.
--Church Feasts & Seasons. (Children of the Kingdom Activities Ser.). (gr. 1-4). 1974. 7.95 (ISBN 0-686-13684-5). Pflaum Pr.
--Early Helpers of God. (Children of the Kingdom Activities Ser.). (gr. 1-4). 1975. 7.95 (ISBN 0-686-13685-3). Pflaum Pr.
--First Prayers for Young Catholics. (Children of the Kingdom Activities Ser.). (gr. 1-4). 1978. 7.95 (ISBN 0-686-13686-1). Pflaum Pr.
--God Loves Me. (Children of the Kingdom Ser.). (gr. 1-4). 1977. 7.95 (ISBN 0-686-13681-0). Pflaum Pr.
--God's Early Helpers. (gr. 4-7). 1974. 7.95 (ISBN 0-686-13690-X). Pflaum Pr.
--Growing with God. (Children of the Kingdom Activities Ser.). (ps). 1976. 7.95 (ISBN 0-686-13680-2). Pflaum Pr.
--Jesus Miracles. (Children of the Kingdom Acitivities Ser.). (gr. 4-7). 1973. 7.95 (ISBN 0-686-13689-6). Pflaum Pr.
--Jesus of Nazareth. (Children of the Kingdom Activities Ser.). (gr. 5-10). 1977. 7.95 (ISBN 0-686-13695-0). Pflaum Pr.
--Lands of the Bible. (Children of the Kingdom Activities Ser.). (gr. 5-10). 1975. 7.95 (ISBN 0-686-13693-4). Pflaum Pr.
--My Friends & I. (Children of the Kingdom Activities Ser.). (gr. 7-9). 1978. 7.95 (ISBN 0-686-13694-2). Pflaum Pr.
--The Sacraments. (Children of the Kingdom Activities Ser.). (gr. 4-7). 1975. 7.95 (ISBN 0-686-13691-8). Pflaum Pr.
--The Ten Commandments. (Children of the Kingdom Activities Ser.). (gr. 4-7). 1976. 7.95 (ISBN 0-686-13687-X). Pflaum Pr.
--Twenty Centuries of Christianity. (Children of the Kingdom Acitivites Ser.). (gr. 7-12). 1977. 7.95 (ISBN 0-686-13698-5). Pflaum Pr.
--Values Guidance for Teens. (Children of the Kingdom Activities Ser.). (gr. 7-12). 1977. 7.95 (ISBN 0-686-13697-7). Pflaum Pr.
Curley, Richard T. Elders, Shades, & Women: Ceremonial Change in Lango, Uganda. 1973. 17.50x (ISBN 0-520-02149-5). U of Cal Pr.
Curling, Audrey. Enthusiasts in Love. 1978. pap. 1.75 o.p. (ISBN 0-445-04260-5). Popular Lib.
Curling, B. C. The History of the Institute of Marine Engineers. 242p. 1961. 3.00x (ISBN 0-900976-92-6, Pub. by Inst Marine Eng). Intl Schol Bk Serv.
Curling, Bill. Royal Champion: The Story of Steeplechasing's First Lady. (Illus.). 272p. 1981. 29.95 (ISBN 0-7181-1930-4). Merrimack Bk Serv.
Curme, George O. English Grammar. (Orig.). 1947. pap. 3.95 (ISBN 0-06-460061-0, CO 61, COS). Har-Row.
--A Grammar of the English Language. 1978. 40.00 set (ISBN 0-930454-03-0). Verbatim.
--A Grammar of the English Language: Parts of Speech. LC 77-87423. 1978. 20.00 (ISBN 0-930454-02-2). Verbatim.
--A Grammar of the English Language: Syntax. LC 77-87422. 1978. 20.00 (ISBN 0-930454-01-4). Verbatim.
Curno, Paul, ed. Political Issues & Community Work. 1978. 23.00x (ISBN 0-7100-8975-9); pap. 12.50 (ISBN 0-7100-8976-7). Routledge & Kegan.
Curnutt, Joanne, tr. see Andersen, Poul-Gerhard.
Curr, John. Coal Viewer & Engine Builder's Practical Companion. LC 74-96376. (Illus.). Repr. of 1797 ed. lib. bdg. 19.50x (ISBN 0-678-05104-6). Kelley.
Curran, Charles E., ed. Absolutes in Moral Theology? LC 75-3988. 320p. 1976. Repr. of 1968 ed. lib. bdg. 25.00x (ISBN 0-8371-7450-3, CUMT). Greenwood.
Curran, Charles E. & McCormick, Richard A., eds. Readings in Moral Theology, No. 2: The Distinctiveness of Christian Ethics. 360p. 1980. pap. 8.95 (ISBN 0-8091-2303-7). Paulist Pr.
Curran, Desmond, et al. Psychological Medicine. 9th ed. 480p. 1980. pap. text ed. 21.50x (ISBN 0-443-02192-9). Churchill.
Curran, Dolores. Family: A Church Challenge for the 80's. (Orig.). 1980. pap. 3.50 (ISBN 0-03-057549-4). Winston Pr.
--In the Beginning There Were the Parents: Discussion Guide. 1980. pap. 2.95 (ISBN 0-03-056978-8). Winston Pr.
--In the Beginning There Were the Parents. 1978. pap. 4.95 (ISBN 0-03-042766-5). Winston Pr.
Curran, Donald J. Metropolitan Financing: The Milwaukee Experience, 1920-1970. LC 72-7984. 192p. 1973. 20.00x (ISBN 0-299-06290-2). U of Wis Pr.
Curran, Donald J., ed. see Groves, Harold M.
Curran, J., jt. auth. see Stanworth, M. J.
Curran, J. T. Fetal Heart Monitoring. 1975. 21.95 (ISBN 0-407-00014-3). Butterworths.
Curran, James, et al, eds. Mass Communication & Society. LC 78-68700. 1979. pap. 9.95x (ISBN 0-8039-1193-9). Sage.
Curran, John P. Primer of Sports Injuries. (Illus.). 112p. 1968. pap. 11.75 photocopy ed. spiral (ISBN 0-398-00378-5). C C Thomas.
Curran, June. Drawing Home Plans: A Simplified Drafting System for Planning & Design. Giumarra, Nancy & Weine, Ruth, eds. LC 78-72188. (Illus.). 1979. 19.95 (ISBN 0-932370-01-2); pap. 12.95 (ISBN 0-932370-02-0). Brooks Pub Co.
Curran, Michael, jt. auth. see MacKenzie, David.
Curran, Patrick J. Principles & Procedures of Tour Management. LC 77-16399. 1978. 14.95 (ISBN 0-8436-0754-8). CBI Pub.
Curran, Polly. Raggedy Ann & Andy: The Little Grey Kitten. (Illus.). 24p. (ps-3). 1975. PLB 5.00 (ISBN 0-307-60139-0, Golden Pr). Western Pub.
Curran, Stuart, ed. Le Bossu & Voltaire on the Epic: Rene Le Bossu, Treatise of the Epick Poem, 1695 & Voltaire, Essay on Epick Poetry, 1727. LC 73-133363. 1970. 37.00x (ISBN 0-8201-1086-8). Schol Facsimiles.
Curran, Stuart & Wittreich, Joseph A., Jr., eds. Blake's Sublime Allegory: Essays on the Four Zoas, Milton, & Jerusalem. LC 72-1377. (Illus.). 504p. 1973. 29.50 (ISBN 0-299-06180-9). U of Wis Pr.
Curran, Thomas J. Xenophobia & Immigration, 1820-1930. LC 74-10865. (The Immigrant Heritage of American Ser). 1975. lib. bdg. 10.95 (ISBN 0-8057-3294-2). Twayne.
Curran, Thomas J. & Coppa, Frank J. The Immigrant Experience in America. (Immigrant Heritage of America Ser). 1977. lib. bdg. 9.95 (ISBN 0-8057-8406-3). Twayne.
Curran, William. Banking & the Global System. 184p. 1980. 19.95 (ISBN 0-85941-030-7). Herman Pub.
--Beautiful New York. LC 79-90287. 80p. 1979. 14.95 (ISBN 0-89802-004-2); pap. 7.95 (ISBN 0-89802-003-4). Beautiful Am.
--Beautiful Northern California, Vol. II. Shangle, Robert D., ed. LC 78-9901. 72p. 1978. 14.95 (ISBN 0-915796-87-2); pap. 7.95 (ISBN 0-915796-86-4). Beautiful Am.
--Beautiful Wisconsin. Shangle, Robert D., ed. LC 79-777. 80p. 1979. 14.95 (ISBN 0-915796-63-5); pap. 7.95 (ISBN 0-915796-62-7). Beautiful Am.
--Colorful Northern California, Vol. II. Shangle, Robert D., ed. LC 78-9901. (Illus.). 72p. 1978. 12.95 (ISBN 0-915796-32-5); pap. 7.95 (ISBN 0-915796-31-7). Beautiful Am.
Curran, William C. Beautiful Los Angeles. Shangle, Robert D., ed. LC 79-12045. 72p. 1979. 14.95 (ISBN 0-89802-056-5); pap. 7.95 (ISBN 0-89802-055-7). Beautiful Am.
--Beautiful Washington D. C. Shangle, Robert D., ed. LC 79-17658. (Illus.). 80p. 1979. 14.95 (ISBN 0-89802-010-7); pap. 7.95 (ISBN 0-89802-009-3). Beautiful Am.
Curran, William J. & Shapiro, E. Donald. Law, Medicine & Forensic Science. 2nd ed. 1046p. 1970. 24.25 (ISBN 0-316-16512-3). Little.
Currell, David. Learning with Puppets. 208p. 1980. 15.95 (ISBN 0-8238-0250-7). Plays.
Curren, Anna M. Math for Meds: A Programmmed Text. 3rd ed. LC 76-43259. 1979. pap. text ed. 6.95 (ISBN 0-918082-01-3). Wallcur Inc.
Current, Karen, jt. auth. see Current, William R.
Current, Richard N. The Lincoln Nobody Knows. 314p. 1963. pap. 5.25 (ISBN 0-8090-0059-8, AmCen). Hill & Wang.
--The Lincoln Nobody Knows. LC 80-16138. x, 314p. 1980. Repr. of 1958 ed. lib. bdg. 25.00x (ISBN 0-313-22450-1, CULN). Greenwood.
--Old Thad Stevens: A Story of Ambition. LC 80-15189. (Illus.). v, 344p. 1980. Repr. of 1942 ed. lib. bdg. 27.50x (ISBN 0-313-22569-9, CUOT). Greenwood.
--The Political Thought of Abraham Lincoln. LC 67-30069. 1967. pap. 6.95 (ISBN 0-672-60068-4, AHS46). Bobbs.
--Wisconsin: A History. LC 77-2176. (States & the Nation Ser.). (Illus.). 1977. 12.95 (ISBN 0-393-05624-4, Co-Pub by AASLH). Norton.
Current, Richard N., ed. see Randall, J. G.
Current, William R. & Current, Karen. Greene & Greene: Architects in the Residential Style. (Illus.). 1977. pap. 10.95 (ISBN 0-88360-036-6). Amon Carter.
Current-Garcia, Eugene. O. Henry. (U. S. Authors Ser.: No. 77). 1972. lib. bdg. 9.95 (ISBN 0-8057-0368-3). Twayne.
Current-Garcia, Eugene & Patrick, Walton R. American Short Stories. 3rd ed. 1976. pap. 9.95x (ISBN 0-673-15008-9). Scott F.
Currey, H. L., jt. ed. see Mason, Michael.
Currey, J. D., jt. ed. see Vincent, J. F.
Currey, John R., jt. auth. see Mac Duff, J. N.
Currey, L. W. & Reginald, R. Science Fiction & Fantasy Reference Guide: An Annotated History of Critical & Biographical Works. LC 80-22715. (Borgo Reference Library: Vol. 4). 64p. (Orig.). 1981. lib. bdg. 8.95x (ISBN 0-89370-145-9); pap. text ed. 2.95x (ISBN 0-89370-245-5). Borgo Pr.
Currey, L. W., jt. auth. see Reginald, R.
Curriculm Development Unit Dublin Vocation Ed. Comm., jt. ed. see McMahon, Agnes.
Curriculum Adaptation Network for Bilingual Bicultural Education. A Boy Named Manuel, ESL Reader. Quinones, Nathan, ed. LC 76-5999. (Illus.). (gr. 1-3). 1976. pap. text ed. 2.50 o.p. (ISBN 0-8120-0676-3). Barron.
Curriculum Committee of St. Paul Technical Vocational Institute. Arithmetic for Careers. LC 78-52661. (Mathematics Ser.). 1980. pap. text ed. 15.00 (ISBN 0-8273-1676-3); instructor's guide 1.75 (ISBN 0-8273-1677-1). Delmar.
Curriculum Design & Development Course Team. Curriculum Design. LC 75-20255. 1975. pap. 19.95 (ISBN 0-470-99202-6). Halsted Pr.
--Curriculum Innovation. LC 75-22488. 1975. pap. 17.95 (ISBN 0-470-26333-4). Halsted Pr.
Curriculum Development Unit. Dublin Divided City: Portrait of Dublin 1913. 1978. text ed. 10.50x (ISBN 0-905140-50-8). Humanities.
--A World of Stone: Life, Folklore & Legends of the Aran Islands, Bk. 1. text ed. 22.00x (ISBN 0-905140-15-X). Humanities.
Curriculum Information Center Staff. CIC's School Directory Nineteen Seventy-Eight to Nineteen Seventy-Nine, 7 vols. LC 77-88521. 1978. 48.00 ea. o.p. (ISBN 0-89770-023-6); 295.00 set o.p. (ISBN 0-685-58438-0). Curriculum Info Ctr.
Currie, David & Peters, Will, eds. Contemporary Economic Analysis: Vol. 2, Papers Presented at the Conference of the Association of University Teachers of Economics 1978. 490p. 1980. 39.00x (ISBN 0-85664-803-5, Pub. by Croom Helm Ltd England). Biblio Dist.
Currie, Donald J. & Smialowski, Arthur. Photographic Illustration for Medical Writing. (Illus.). 132p. 1962. 14.75 (ISBN 0-398-00379-3). C C Thomas.
Currie, Donald J., jt. auth. see Smialowski, Arthur.
Currie, G., ed. see Lakatos, I.
Currie, G., ed. see Lakatos, Imre.
Currie, Harold W. Eugene V. Debs. LC 76-3780. (U. S. Authors Ser.: No. 267). 1976. lib. bdg. 12.50 (ISBN 0-8057-7167-0). Twayne.
Currie, Ian. You Cannot Die. LC 80-83590. 288p. 1981. pap. 2.50 (ISBN 0-87216-791-7). Playboy Pbks.
Currie, J. M. The Economic Theory of Agricultural Land Tenure. LC 80-41114. (Illus.). Date not set. price not set (ISBN 0-521-23634-7). Cambridge U Pr.
Currie, Janice K., jt. auth. see Heyneman, Stephen P.
Currie, Jean. The Travellers' Guide to Rhodes & the Dodecanese. LC 76-351618. (Travellers' Guide Ser.). (Illus.). 1979. 9.95 (ISBN 0-224-61836-9, Pub. by Chatto Bodley Jonathan). Merrimack Bk Serv.
Currie, Jean I., jt. ed. see Whetham, Edith J.
Currie, John M. & British Columbia Institute of Technology. Unit Operations in Mineral Processing. 1978. Repr. of 1973 ed. 15.00 (ISBN 0-918062-13-6). Colo Sch Mines.
Currie, Robert. Industrial Politics. LC 78-40480. 1979. 37.50x (ISBN 0-19-827419-X). Oxford U Pr.
Currie, Robert, et al. Churches & Churchgoers: Patterns of Church Growth in the British Isles Since 1700. (Illus.). 1978. 45.00x (ISBN 0-19-827218-9). Oxford U Pr.
Currimbhoy, A. Tourist Mecca & the Clock. 4.75x o.p. (ISBN 0-210-33971-3). Asia.
Currimbhoy, Asif. Darjeeling Tea? (Writers Workshop Bluebird Ser.). 64p. 1975. 8.00 (ISBN 0-88253-522-6); pap. text ed. 4.80 (ISBN 0-88253-521-8). Ind-US Inc.
--The Dissident M. L. A. (Bluebird Bk.). 56p. 1975. 8.00 (ISBN 0-88253-841-1); pap. 4.80 (ISBN 0-88253-842-X). Ind-US Inc.
--An Experiment with Truth. (Writers Workshop Bluebird Book Ser.). 62p. 1975. 10.00 (ISBN 0-88253-538-2); pap. text ed. 4.80 (ISBN 0-88253-537-4). Ind-US Inc.
--Goa. (Writers Workshop Bluebird Book Ser.). 82p. 1975. 8.00 (ISBN 0-88253-550-1); pap. text ed. 4.80 (ISBN 0-88253-549-8). Ind-US Inc.
--Inquilab. 1970. 10.00 (ISBN 0-89253-784-1); pap. text ed. 4.80 (ISBN 0-88253-807-1). Ind-US Inc.
--The Miracle Seed. (Writers Workshop Bluebird Ser.). 38p. 1975. 8.00 (ISBN 0-88253-576-5); pap. text ed. 4.80 (ISBN 0-88253-575-7). Ind-US Inc.
--Om Mane Padme Hum! Hail to the Jewel in the Lotus. (Bluebird Ser.). 67p. 1975. 12.00 (ISBN 0-88253-594-3); pap. text ed. 4.80 (ISBN 0-88253-593-5). Ind-US Inc.
--Sonar Bangla. 1972. pap. text ed. 4.80 (ISBN 0-88253-764-4). Ind-US Inc.
--This Alien...Native Land. 12.00 (ISBN 0-89253-796-5); flexible cloth 6.75 (ISBN 0-89253-527-X). Ind-US Inc.
Curry, Alan. Poison Detection in Human Organs. 3rd ed. (American Lectures in Living Chemistry Ser.). (Illus.). 376p. 1976. 34.50 (ISBN 0-398-03433-8). C C Thomas.
Curry, Ann. Teaching About the Other Americans: Minorities in United States History. LC 80-69120. 110p. 1981. perfect bdg. 8.95 (ISBN 0-86548-028-1). Century Twenty One.
Curry, Barbara. Model Aircraft. (First Bks.). (Illus.). (gr. 4 up). 1979. PLB 6.45 s&l (ISBN 0-531-02260-9). Watts.
Curry, Bob, jt. auth. see Louis, Harry.

Curry, Dudley & Frame, Robert. Accounting Principles: A Multimedia Program. LC 72-95544. 1973. Modules 1-15. pap. text ed. 15.95 (ISBN 0-675-08992-1); Modules 16-30. pap. text ed. 16.95x (ISBN 0-675-08924-7); media: audiocassettes & filmstrips for modules 1-15 325.00, 2-7 sets, 280.00 ea., 8-15 sets 247.50 ea., 16 or more sets, 197.50 ea. (ISBN 0-675-08930-1); media: audiocassettes & filmstrips for modules 16-30 325.00, 2-7 sets, 280.00 ea., 8-15 sets 247.50 ea., 16 or more sets, 197.50 ea. (ISBN 0-675-08908-5). test 3.95 (ISBN 0-686-66866-9). Merrill.

Curry, Dudley, jt. auth. see Frame, Robert.

Curry, Dudley W. Introduction to Management Accounting: Student Guide. 4th ed. (Illus.). 1978. pap. text ed. 8.95 ref. (ISBN 0-13-487587-7). P-H.

Curry, E. R. Hoover's Dominican Diplomacy & the Origins of the Good Neighbor Policy. Freidel, Frank, ed. LC 78-62379. (Modern American History Ser.: Vol. 5). 1979. lib. bdg. 30.00 (ISBN 0-8240-3629-8). Garland Pub.

Curry, Estell H., jt. auth. see Silvius, G. Harold.

Curry, Estell H., jt. auth. see Silvius, George H.

Curry, Gene. Colorado Crossing. (Jim Saddler Ser.: No. 3). 1979. pap. 1.75 (ISBN 0-505-51418-4). Tower Bks.

--A Dirty Way to Die. (Saddler Ser.: No. 1). 1979. pap. 1.75 (ISBN 0-505-51398-6). Tower Bks.

Curry, George E. Jake Gaither, America's Most Famous Black Coach. LC 76-50580. (Illus.). 1977. 7.95 (ISBN 0-396-07381-6). Dodd.

Curry, Georgene & Pearson, Larry, eds. The Poets Tree. (Anthology Ser.: Vol. 1). (Illus.). 104p. (Orig.). 1980. pap. 4.50. Pikes Peak.

Curry, Herbert F., jt. ed. see Pollitt, Ronald.

Curry, Jane L. The Bassumtyte Treasure. LC 77-14381. (gr. 4-7). 1978. 8.95 (ISBN 0-689-50100-5, McElderry Bk). Atheneum.

--Ghost Lane. LC 78-73319. 1979. 7.95 (ISBN 0-689-50129-3, Mcelderry Bk). Atheneum.

--The Wolves of Aam. LC 80-24370. 204p. (gr. 7 up). 1981. 9.95 (ISBN 0-689-50173-0, McElderry Book). Atheneum.

Curry, Judith B. & Peppe, Kathryn K., eds. Mental Retardation: Nursing Approaches to Care. LC 77-26307. 1978. pap. text ed. 11.50 (ISBN 0-8016-1196-2). Mosby.

Curry, Kenneth. Southey. (Author Guides). 1975. 18.00 (ISBN 0-7100-8112-X). Routledge & Kegan.

Curry, Martha M. The Writer's Book by Sherwood Anderson: A Critical Edition. LC 74-22088. 1975. 19.50 (ISBN 0-8108-0737-8). Scarecrow.

Curry, O. J. & Pearson, John E. Basic Mathematics for Business Analysis. rev. ed. 1970. text ed. 10.95x o.p. (ISBN 0-256-00087-5). Irwin.

Curry, Peggy S. Creating Fiction from Experience. rev. ed. 1975. 8.95 (ISBN 0-87116-089-7). Writer.

Curry, Richard A. Ramon De Mesonero Romanos. (World Authors Ser.: Spain: No. 385). 1976. lib. bdg. 12.50 (ISBN 0-8057-6226-4). Twayne.

Curry, Robert L., Jr., jt. auth. see Rothchild, Donald.

Curry, Timothy J. & Clarke, Alfred C. Introducing Visual Sociology. (Illus.). 1978. pap. text ed. 6.50 (ISBN 0-8403-2267-4, 40226701). Kendall-Hunt.

Curry, W. H. Sun Rising on the West: The Saga of Henry Clay & Elizabeth Smith. 1979. write for info. Crosby County.

Curry, Walter C. Milton's Ontology, Cosmogony & Physics. LC 57-5833. (Illus.). 226p. 1966. pap. 4.00x (ISBN 0-8131-0102-6). U Pr of Ky.

Curry-Lindahl, Kai. Let Them Live: A Worldwide Survey of Animals Threatened with Extinction. (Illus.). 416p. 1972. 9.95 (ISBN 0-688-00046-0); pap. 3.95 o.p. (ISBN 0-688-05046-8). Morrow.

Curtayne, Alice. St. Catherine of Siena. LC 80-53745. 1980. pap. write for info. (ISBN 0-89555-162-4). Tan Bks Pubs.

Curti, Merle. American Philanthropy Abroad: A History. 1963. 35.00 (ISBN 0-8135-0422-8). Rutgers U Pr.

Curtin, Dennis. Your Automatic Camera. (Your Automatic Camera Ser.). (Illus.). 128p. (Orig.). 1980. lib. bdg. 6.95 (ISBN 0-930764-17-X). Curtin & London.

Curtin, Dennis & London, Barbara. Your Automatic Camera. 144p. 1980. pap. 6.95 (ISBN 0-442-25871-2). Van Nos Reinhold.

Curtin, Philip D. Atlantic Slave Trade: A Census. 1969. 25.00x (ISBN 0-299-05400-4); pap. 8.50x (ISBN 0-299-05404-7). U of Wis Pr.

--Economic Change in Pre-Colonial Africa: Senegambia in the Era of the Slave Trade, 2 vols. LC 74-5899. 1975. Vol. 1. 30.00 (ISBN 0-299-06640-1); Vol. 2. 30.00x (ISBN 0-299-06650-9). U of Wis Pr.

--Image of Africa: British Ideas & Action, 1780-1850, 2 vols. in 1. (Illus.). 1964. 37.50x (ISBN 0-299-03020-2); Vol. 1. pap. 6.95 (ISBN 0-299-83025-X); Vol. 2. pap. 6.95 (ISBN 0-299-83026-8). U of Wis Pr.

--Two Jamaicas: The Role of Ideas in a Tropical Colony, 1830-1865. LC 69-10082. (Illus.). 1968. Repr. of 1955 ed. lib. bdg. 22.75 (ISBN 0-8371-0055-0, CUTJ). Greenwood.

Curtin, Philip D., ed. Africa & the West: Intellectual Responses to European Culture. LC 77-176409. 274p. 1972. 25.00 (ISBN 0-299-06121-3); pap. 7.95x (ISBN 0-299-06124-8). U of Wis Pr.

--Africa Remembered: Narratives by West Africans from the Era of the Slave Trade. (Illus.). 1968. 25.00 (ISBN 0-299-04281-2); pap. 8.95 (ISBN 0-299-04284-7). U of Wis Pr.

--Imperialism. LC 75-142853. (Documentary History of Western Civilization Ser.). 368p. 1972. 15.00x o.s.i. (ISBN 0-8027-2046-3). Walker & Co.

Curtin, Richard T. Income Equity Among U. S. Workers: The Bases & Consequences of Deprivation. LC 76-24349. (Praeger Special Studies). 1977. 22.95 (ISBN 0-275-23780-X). Praeger.

Curtin, Rosalie, et al. R.C.I.A. A Practical Approach to Christian Initiation. 136p. (Orig.). 1981. pap. 6.95. Wm C Brown.

Curtis. Invasion of the Brain Sharpeners. LC 80-21434. (Capers Ser.). (Illus.). 128p. (gr. 3-6). 1981. PLB 4.99 (ISBN 0-394-84676-1); pap. 1.95 (ISBN 0-394-94676-6). Knopf.

Curtis, et al. Soils in the British Isles. LC 75-46527. (Illus.). 1976. text ed. 29.00x (ISBN 0-582-48555-X). Longman.

Curtis, A. & Cooper, J. Mathematics of Accounting. 4th ed. 1961. 21.95 (ISBN 0-13-563908-5); text ed. 25.95 (ISBN 0-686-66514-7). P-H.

Curtis, Audrey & Hill, Sheelagh. My World. (General Ser.). 1978. pap. text ed. 8.25x (ISBN 0-85633-156-2, NFER). Humanities.

Curtis, Benjamin R. A Memoir of Benjamin Robbins Curtis, 2 Vols. LC 77-75298. (The American Scene Ser). 1970. Repr. of 1879 ed. 95.00 (ISBN 0-306-71267-9). Da Capo.

Curtis, Bernard & Mays, Wolfe, eds. Phenomenology & Education: Self-Consciousness & Its Development. 150p. 1978. pap. 9.95 (ISBN 0-416-70960-5, 6368). Methuen Inc.

Curtis, Brian. Life Story of the Fish. 2nd ed. 1949. pap. 4.00 (ISBN 0-486-20929-6). Dover.

Curtis, Charles, et al. Perspectives on God: Sociological, Theological & Philosophical. LC 78-62943. 1978. pap. text ed. 9.25 (ISBN 0-8191-0605-4). U Pr of Amer.

Curtis, Charles P., Jr., jt. auth. see Homans, George C.

Curtis, Charles W. Linear Algebra: An Introductory Approach. 3rd ed. 522p. 1974. text ed. 20.95 (ISBN 0-205-04008-X, 5640083). Allyn.

Curtis, Charles W. & Reiner, Irving. Representation Theory of Finite Groups & Associative Algebras. LC 62-16994. (Pure & Applied Mathematics Ser). 1962. 48.50 (ISBN 0-470-18975-4, Pub. by Wiley-Interscience). Wiley.

Curtis, Charles W., jt. auth. see Reiner, Irving.

Curtis, Charlotte. The Rich & Other Atrocities. LC 76-5121. (Illus.). 1976. 12.95 o.s.i. (ISBN 0-06-010931-9, HarpT). Har-Row.

Curtis, Dan B. & Brewer, Robert S. Speaking As a Farmer: Winning FFA Speeches, Principles of Speech Preparation & Presentation. 256p. 1980. pap. text ed. 8.95 (ISBN 0-8403-2248-8). Kendall-Hunt.

Curtis, E. L. & Madsen, A. A. Chronicles, I & II. LC 10-14958. (International Critical Commentary Ser.). 560p. Repr. of 1910 ed. text ed. 23.00x (ISBN 0-567-05007-6). Attic Pr.

Curtis, Edward S. In the Land of Head-Hunters. (Illus.). Date not set. 7.95 (ISBN 0-913668-48-6); pap. 3.95 (ISBN 0-913668-47-8). Ten Speed Pr.

--Indian Days of Long Ago. (Illus.). Date not set. 8.95 (ISBN 0-913668-46-X); pap. 3.95 (ISBN 0-913668-45-1). Ten Speed Pr.

--Portraits from North American Indian Life. 192p. 1981. pap. 10.95 (ISBN 0-89104-003-X). A & W Pubs.

Curtis, Emily B. Reflected Glory in a Bottle: Chinese Snuff Bottle Portraits. (Illus.). 128p. 1980. 25.00 (ISBN 0-9605096-0-7). Soho Bodhi.

Curtis, Francis D. Digest of Investigations in the Teaching of Sciences in the Elementary & Secondary Schools. LC 74-153694. 1971. Repr. of 1926 ed. text ed. 12.25x (ISBN 0-8077-1223-X). Tchrs Coll.

--Reviews of Research in Science Education Series, 6 vols. 1971. Set. 57.75x (ISBN 0-8077-2433-5). Tchrs Coll.

--Second Digest of Investigations in the Teaching of Science. LC 74-153694. 1971. Repr. of 1931 ed. text ed. 12.75x (ISBN 0-8077-1225-6). Tchrs Coll.

--Third Digest of Investigations in the Teaching of Science. LC 74-153694. 1971. Repr. of 1939 ed. text ed. 12.75x (ISBN 0-8077-1226-4). Tchrs Coll.

Curtis, G. H., jt. auth. see Williams, Howell.

Curtis, George T. Constitutional History of the United States: From Their Declaration of Independence to the Close of Their Civil War, 2 vols. (American Constitution & Legal History Ser.). 1100p. 1974. Repr. of 1896 ed. lib. bdg. 115.00 (ISBN 0-306-70611-3). Da Capo.

Curtis, George W., ed. see Downing, Andrew J.

Curtis, Helena. Biology. 3rd ed. LC 78-68582. (Illus.). 1979. text ed. 21.95x (ISBN 0-87901-100-9); study guide 6.95x (ISBN 0-87901-101-7). Worth.

--Invitation to Biology. 2nd ed. LC 76-50677. (Illus.). 1977. 15.95x o.p. (ISBN 0-87901-072-X); study guide 5.95x o.p. (ISBN 0-87901-073-8). Worth.

Curtis, Helena & Barnes, N. Sue. Invitation to Biology. 3rd ed. 1981. text ed. write for info. (ISBN 0-87901-131-9); write for info. study guide (ISBN 0-87901-139-4). Worth.

Curtis, Henry. Beauties of the Rose. facsimile ed. (Illus.). 120p. 65.00x (ISBN 0-936736-00-3). Sweetbrier.

Curtis, Howard M. Two Thousand Five Hundred Years of European Helmets. LC 76-20423. 346p. 1978. 19.75 (ISBN 0-917714-06-7). Beinfeld Pub.

Curtis, Jack. Eagles Over Big Sur. 144p. (Orig.). 1981. pap. 6.95 (ISBN 0-88496-160-5). Capra Pr.

Curtis, Jack & Detert, Richard. How to Relax: A Holistic Approach to Stress Management. 190p. (Orig.). 1981. pap. text ed. price not set (ISBN 0-87484-527-0). Mayfield Pub.

Curtis, James C. The Fox at Bay: Martin Van Buren & the Presidency, 1837-1841. LC 72-111507. 248p. 1970. 13.00x (ISBN 0-8131-1214-1). U Pr of Ky.

Curtis, Jane & Curtis, Will. Welcome the Birds to Your Home. LC 79-20819. (Illus.). 1980. 9.95 (ISBN 0-8289-0353-0); pap. 5.95 (ISBN 0-8289-0354-9). Greene.

Curtis, John T. Vegetation of Wisconsin: An Ordination of Plant Communities. 1959. 19.50 (ISBN 0-299-01940-3). U of Wis Pr.

Curtis, Joseph E. Recreation: The Profession. LC 78-31266. (Illus.). 1979. pap. text ed. 13.95 (ISBN 0-8016-1183-0). Mosby.

Curtis, Joseph E., jt. auth. see Kraus, Richard G.

Curtis, Joy, jt. auth. see Benjamin, Martin.

Curtis, L. G. Papers Relating to the Application of the Principle of Dyarchy to the Government of India. 667p. 1972. Repr. of 1920 ed. 45.00x (ISBN 0-7165-2117-2, Pub. by Irish Academic Pr Ireland). Biblio Dist.

Curtis, L. P., ed. see Sterne, Laurence.

Curtis, L. P., Jr., ed. see Lecky, W. E.

Curtis, L. Perry, Jr. Apes & Angels: The Irishman in Victorian Caricature. LC 75-607991. (Illus.). 140p. 1971. 8.95x o.p. (ISBN 0-87474-107-6). Smithsonian.

Curtis, Laura. The Elusive Daniel Defoe. 200p. 1981. 19.50x (ISBN 0-389-20063-8). B&N.

Curtis, Michael, ed. Great Political Theories, Vol. 1. 1976. pap. 2.50 (ISBN 0-380-00785-1, 40626, Discus). Avon.

--The Great Political Theories, Vol 1. 464p. 1981. pap. 3.95 (77222, Discus). Avon.

--Great Political Theories, Vol. 2. 1976. pap. 2.50 (ISBN 0-380-01235-9, 49858, Discus). Avon.

--The Great Political Theories, Vol 2. 496p. 1981. pap. 3.95 (77230, Discus). Avon.

--Religion & Politics in the Middle East. 300p. 1981. lib. bdg. 24.00x (ISBN 0-86531-065-3). Westview.

Curtis, Mike. The Savage Women. 1976. pap. 1.50 o.p. (ISBN 0-685-72353-4, LB379DK, Leisure Bks). Nordon Pubns.

Curtis, Nancy. Cockatiels. (Orig.). pap. 2.50 (ISBN 0-87666-420-6, M517). TFH Pubns.

Curtis, Patricia. Animal Doctors: What It's Like to Be a Veterinarian. LC 76-5593. (Illus.). (gr. 5 up). 1977. 7.95 o.s.i. (ISBN 0-440-00140-4). Delacorte.

--Animal Rights: Stories of People Who Defend the Rights of Animals. LC 79-22451. (Illus.). 160p. (gr. 7 up). 1980. 8.95 (ISBN 0-590-07650-7, Four Winds). Schol Bk Serv.

--Cindy, a Hearing Ear Dog. LC 80-24487. (Illus.). (gr. 3-5). 1981. PLB 9.95 (ISBN 0-525-27950-4). Dutton.

--The Indoor Cat: How to Understand, Enjoy & Care for House Cats. (Illus.). 192p. 1981. 10.95 (ISBN 0-385-15368-6). Doubleday.

Curtis, Richard. Genial Idiots: The American Saga As Seen by Our Humorists. LC 68-22815. (America in the Making Ser). (Illus.). (gr. 7 up). 1968. 3.95g o.s.i. (ISBN 0-02-725530-1, CCPr). Macmillan.

--How to Prosper in the Coming Apocalypse. (Illus.). 96p. 1981. pap. 3.95 (ISBN 0-312-39611-2); prepack 39.50 (ISBN 0-312-39612-0). St Martin.

Curtis, Richard & Hogan, Elizabeth. Nuclear Lessons. 288p. 1980. 16.95 (ISBN 0-8117-1851-4). Stackpole.

Curtis, Richard, jt. auth. see Ward, Melanie.

Curtis, Richard F., jt. auth. see Borhek, James T.

Curtis, Rosalee M. John Hemphill: First Chief Justice of Texas. (Illus.). 1971. 9.50 (ISBN 0-8363-0054-8). Jenkins.

Curtis, Seng-gye T. & Hunt, Christopher. The Airbrush Book: Art, History, & Technique. 160p. 1980. 24.95 (ISBN 0-442-21213-5). Van Nos Reinhold.

Curtis, Tony. Kid Andrew Cody & Julie Sparrow. 1977. 8.95 o.p. (ISBN 0-385-12405-8). Doubleday.

Curtis, Tony, compiled by. Lyle Official Antiques Review 1973 to 74. 1973. text ed. 25.00 (ISBN 0-8277-2219-2). British Bk Ctr.

Curtis, Will, jt. auth. see Curtis, Jane.

Curtiss, Ellen T. & Untersee, Philip A. Corporate Responsibilities & Opportunities to 1990. (Arthur D. Little Books). (Illus.). 1979. 25.95 (ISBN 0-669-02848-7). Lexington Bks.

Curtiss, F. H., jt. auth. see Curtiss, H. A.

Curtiss, George B. Protection & Prosperity: An Account of Tariff Legislation & Its Effect in Europe & America, 2 vols. (The Neglected American Economists Ser.). 1974. Set. lib. bdg. 76.00 (ISBN 0-8240-1032-9); lib. bdg. 50.00 ea. Garland Pub.

Curtiss, H. A. & Curtiss, F. H. The Message of Aquaria. 487p. 1981. pap. 17.50 (ISBN 0-89540-065-0). Sun Pub.

Curtiss, H. C., Jr., jt. auth. see Dowell, E. H.

Curtiss, Harriete & Homer, F. Potent Prayers. pap. 1.00 o.p. (ISBN 0-87516-362-9). De Vorss.

Curtiss, John S., ed. Essays in Russian & Soviet History, in Honor of Geroid Tanquary Robinson. LC 62-9706. 1963. 22.00x (ISBN 0-231-02521-1). Columbia U Pr.

Curtiss, Richard A. Taking off. Schriver, Peter, ed. 188p. (Orig.). 1981. pap. 4.95 (ISBN 0-517-53901-2, Harmony). Crown.

Curtiss, Richard D., et al, eds. A Guide for Oral History Programs. 10.00 (ISBN 0-930046-03-X). CSUF Oral Hist.

Curtiss, Thomas Q. Von Stroheim. LC 78-143300. (Illus.). xxii, 357p. 1971. 10.00 o.p. (ISBN 0-374-28520-9). FS&G.

Curtiss, Ursula. Poisoned Orchard. LC 79-25977. 192p. 1980. 7.95 (ISBN 0-396-07807-9). Dodd.

Curtiss, Vienna I. I Should Be Glad to Help You, Madame. LC 78-58850. 6.00 (ISBN 0-9602742-1-9). Collectors Choice.

--Pageant of Art. LC 76-280. (Illus.). 27.50 (ISBN 0-9602742-0-0). Collectors Choice.

Curtius, E. R. European Literature & the Latin Middle Ages. Trask, Willard R., tr. LC 52-10619. (Bollingen Ser., Vol. 36). 682p. 1953. 30.00 (ISBN 0-691-09739-9); pap. 7.50 (ISBN 0-691-01793-X). Princeton U Pr.

Curtler, Hugh M. A Prologue to Philosophy. LC 79-51465. 1979. pap. text ed. 6.40 o.p. (ISBN 0-8191-0750-6). U Pr of Amer.

Curwen, C. A. Taiping Rebel: The Deposition of Li Hsiu-Ch'eng. LC 76-8292. (Cambridge Studies in Chinese History, Literature & Institutions). (Illus.). 1977. 39.95 (ISBN 0-521-21082-8). Cambridge U Pr.

Curwen, C. A., tr. see Chesneaux, Jean.

Curwen, Henry. History of Booksellers, the Old & the New. LC 68-19656. (Illus.). 1968. Repr. of 1873 ed. 20.00 (ISBN 0-8103-3300-7). Gale.

Curwen, Peter J. The UK Publishing Industry. (Illus.). 176p. 1981. 24.00 (ISBN 0-08-024081-X). Pergamon.

Curwen, Samuel. Journal & Letters of Samuel Curwen, an American in England, from 1775-1783. Ward, George A., ed. LC 70-14720. (Era of the American Revolution Ser). 1970. Repr. of 1864 ed. lib. bdg. 65.00 (ISBN 0-306-71923-1). Da Capo.

Curwin, Richard & Fuhrmann, Barbara. Discovering Your Teaching Self: Humanistic Approaches to Effective Teaching. LC 74-11371. (Curriculum & Teaching Ser.). (Illus.). 256p. 1975. pap. text ed. 10.95 (ISBN 0-13-216077-3). P-H.

Curwin, Richard & Mendler, Allen. The Discipline Book: A Complete Guide to School & Classroom Management. (Illus.). 1979. text ed. 13.95 (ISBN 0-8359-1338-4). Reston.

Curzon, Daniel. Human Warmth & Other Stories. LC 80-23270. 144p. 1981. 12.00 (ISBN 0-912516-53-4); pap. 4.95 (ISBN 0-912516-54-2). Grey Fox.

--The Misadventures of Tim McPick: A Gay Comedy. LC 75-32707. 1980. pap. 4.00 (ISBN 0-930650-02-6). D Brown Bks.

--The Revolt of the Perverts: Gay Short Stories. 1978. pap. 4.50 (ISBN 0-930650-01-8). D Brown Bks.

Curzon, G., ed. The Biochemistry of Psychiatric Disturbances. LC 80-40498. 1981. write for info. (ISBN 0-471-27814-9, Pub. by Wiley-Interscience). Wiley.

Curzon, L. B. A Dictionary for Law. 384p. 1979. pap. 14.95x (ISBN 0-7121-0380-5, Pub. by Macdonald & Evans England). Intl Ideas.

--English Legal History. 2nd ed. 352p. 1979. pap. 12.95x (ISBN 0-7121-0578-6, Pub. by Macdonald & Evans England). Intl Ideas.

--Roman Law. 240p. 1974. pap. 9.95x (ISBN 0-7121-1853-5, Pub. by Macdonald & Evans England). Intl Ideas.

Curzon, Lucia. The Chadbourne Luck. (Second Chance at Love, Regency Ser.: No. 3). 192p. (Orig.). 1981. pap. 1.75 (ISBN 0-515-05624-3). Jove Pubns.

Curzon, Martin E. Trace Elements & Dental Disease. 1981. write for info. (ISBN 0-88416-172-2). PSG Pub.

Cusens, Anthony R., jt. auth. see Loo, Yew C.

Cushenbery, Donald C. & Gilreath, Kenneth J. Effective Reading Instruction for Slow Learners. 178p. 1972. 14.75 (ISBN 0-398-02543-6). C C Thomas.

Cushenbery, Donald C. & Howell, Helen. Reading & the Gifted Child: A Guide for Teachers. 186p. 1974. 16.50 (ISBN 0-398-03186-X). C C Thomas.

Cushenbery, Donald C. & Meyer, Ronald E. Reading Comprehension Mastery Kits, 6 bks. Incl. Critiical Reading (ISBN 0-87628-701-1); Drawing Conclusions (ISBN 0-87628-698-8); Following Directions (ISBN 0-87628-699-6); Locating Hidden Meaning (ISBN 0-87628-700-3); Recognizing Main Ideas (ISBN 0-87628-697-X); Understanding Details (ISBN 0-87628-696-1). 1980. pap. 6.95x ea. Ctr Appl Res.

Cushing, Barry E. Accounting Information Systems & Business Organizations. 2nd ed. LC 77-83024. (Illus.). 1978. text ed. 19.95 (ISBN 0-201-01016-X). A-W.

Cushing, Barry E., jt. auth. see Davis, James R.

Cushing, C. E., Jr., ed. see Symposium on Radioecology, Oregon State University, May 12-14, 1975.

Cushing, D. H. Detection of Fish. 220p. 1973. text ed. 42.00 (ISBN 0-08-017123-0). Pergamon.

--Marine Ecology & Fisheries. LC 74-82218. (Illus.). 228p. 1975. 52.50 (ISBN 0-521-20501-8); pap. 17.50x (ISBN 0-521-09911-0). Cambridge U Pr.

Cushing, D. H. see Russell, F. S.

Cushing, David H. Recruitment & Parent Stock in Fishes. (Washington Sea Grant). 197p. 1973. pap. 10.50 (ISBN 0-295-95311-X). U of Wash Pr.

Cushing, Frank H. Zuni Fetishes. LC 66-23329. (Illus.). 1966. 7.95 (ISBN 0-916122-28-X); pap. 3.00 (ISBN 0-916122-03-4). K C Pubns.

Cushing, G. F., ed. Hungarian Prose & Verse. (London East European Ser.). 1956. text ed. 13.25x (ISBN 0-485-17501-0, Athlone Pr). Humanities.

Cushing, Harvey W. Tumors of the Nervous Acustious & the Syndrome of the Cerebellopontile Angle. (Illus.). 1963. Repr. of 1917 ed. 23.00 o.s.i. (ISBN 0-02-843340-8). Hafner.

Cushing, James T. Applied Analytical Mathematics for Physical Scientists. LC 75-9611. 672p. 1975. text ed. 28.95 (ISBN 0-471-18997-9). Wiley.

Cushing, Luther S., ed. see Domat, Jean.

Cushing, Richard J. Mary. 1960. 3.50 o.s.i. (ISBN 0-8198-0087-2); pap. 2.25 o.s.i. (ISBN 0-8198-0088-0). Dghtrs St Paul.

Cushing, Thomas, tr. see Cossery, Albert.

Cushion, J. P. Pocket Book of British Ceramic Marks. new ed. 1976. 19.95 (ISBN 0-571-04869-2, Pub. by Faber & Faber). Merrimack Bk Serv.

Cushion, J. P. & Honey, W. B. Handbook of Pottery & Porcelain Marks. 4th, rev. ed. (Illus.). 272p. 1980. 30.00 (ISBN 0-571-04922-2, Pub. by Faber & Faber). Merrimack Bk Serv.

--Handbook of Pottery & Porcelain Marks. 3rd ed. (Illus.). 1965. 19.95 o.p. (ISBN 0-571-06372-1, Pub. by Faber & Faber). Merrimack Bk Serv.

Cushion, John P. Pottery & Porcelain Tablewares. LC 75-45518. (Illus.). 1976. 22.50 o.p. (ISBN 0-688-03055-6). Morrow.

Cushman, Donald P. & McPhee, Robert D., eds. Message-Attitude-Behavior Relationship: Theory, Methodology & Application. LC 80-529. (Human Communications Research Ser.). 1980. 27.00 (ISBN 0-12-199760-X). Acad Pr.

Cushman, Doug, compiled by. Giants. LC 79-55012. (Deluxe Illustrated Ser.). (Illus.). 48p. (ps-3). 1980. 5.95 (ISBN 0-448-47486-7); PLB 11.85 (ISBN 0-448-13623-6). Platt.

Cushman, Joseph D., Jr., ed. see Eppes, Susan B.

Cushman, M. L. Governance of Teacher Education. LC 76-52063. 1977. 16.00x (ISBN 0-685-78477-0); text ed. 14.50 (ISBN 0-8211-0228-1). McCutchan.

--The Governance of Teacher Education. LC 76-52063. 1977. 12.60 (ISBN 0-8211-0228-1, Co-Pub with McCutchan); pap. 7.00 (ISBN 0-87367-770-6). Phi Delta Kappa.

Cushman, Robert F. Leading Constitutional Decisions. 15th ed. 1977. pap. text ed. 11.95 (ISBN 0-13-527358-7). P-H.

Cushman, Robert F., et al. The Business Insurance Handbook. 600p. 1981. 37.50 (ISBN 0-87094-237-9). Dow Jones-Irwin.

Cushman, Ronald, jt. auth. see Keyes, Ruth.

Cushman, Rudolf E. Peculiar Forms of Ancient Religious Cults. (Illus.). 1980. deluxe ed. 41.50 (ISBN 0-89266-234-4). Am Classical Coll Pr.

Cushner, Nicholas P. Landed Estates in the Colonial Philippines. (Monograph: No. 20). (Illus.). x, 146p. 1976. 10.50 o.p. (ISBN 0-686-63723-2). Yale U Pr.

Cusine, Douglas J. & Grant, John P., eds. The Impact of Marine Pollution. LC 80-670. 336p. 1980. text ed. 32.50 (ISBN 0-916672-54-9). Allanheld.

Cussans, John E. Handbook of Heraldry. LC 76-132520. 1971. Repr. of 1893 ed. 26.00 (ISBN 0-8103-3012-1). Gale.

Cussler, Clive. Raise the Titanic! 384p. 1980. pap. 2.75 (ISBN 0-553-13880-4). Bantam.

--Vixen O-Three. 1978. 9.95 o.p. (ISBN 0-670-74741-6). Viking Pr.

Cust, M. M. Needlework As Art. Stansky, Peter & Shewan, Rodney, eds. LC 76-17770. (Aesthetic Movement & the Arts & Crafts Movement Ser.). 1978. Repr. of 1886 ed. lib. bdg. 44.00x (ISBN 0-8240-2474-5). Garland Pub.

Custer, Elizabeth B. The Kid. (Custer Monograph: No. 2). (Illus.). 47p. 1978. Repr. of 1900 ed. limited ed. 8.00x (ISBN 0-686-28493-3). Monroe County Lib.

Custer, George A. My Life on the Plains. Quaife, Milo M., ed. LC 67-2618. (Illus.). 1966. pap. 6.95 (ISBN 0-8032-5042-8, BB 328, Bison). U of Nebr Pr.

--My Life on the Plains. 1976. pap. 1.25 o.p. (ISBN 0-685-69509-3, LB377ZK, Leisure Bks). Nordon Pubns.

--My Life on the Plains: Personal Experiences with Indians. (Western Frontier Library Ser.: No. 52). 1976. 10.95 (ISBN 0-8061-0523-2); pap. 6.95 (ISBN 0-8061-1357-X). U of Okla Pr.

Custer, R. Philip, ed. Atlas of the Blood & Bone Marrow. 2nd ed. LC 78-165276. (Illus.). 562p. 1974. text ed. 45.00 (ISBN 0-7216-2815-X). Saunders.

Custodio, Maurice, ed. Peace & Pieces: An Anthology of Contemporary American Poetry. 2nd ed. LC 73-83883. (Illus.). 216p. Date not set. pap. cancelled o.p. (ISBN 0-914024-09-4). SF Arts & Letters.

Custodio, Maurice, et al, eds. Piece & Pieces: An Anthology of Contemporary American Poetry. LC 73-83883. 216p. 1973. pap. 5.00 o.p. (ISBN 0-914024-08-6). SF Arts & Letters.

Cusumano, Michele. Just As the Boy Dreams of White Thighs Under Flowered Skirts. (Backstreet Editions Ser.). 24p. (Orig.). 1980. pap. 2.00 (ISBN 0-935252-24-X); signed 5.00 (ISBN 0-686-63441-1). Street Pr.

Cusworth, D. C. Biochemical Screening in Relation to Mental Retardation. LC 73-129632. 1971. pap. 7.00 (ISBN 0-08-016416-1). Pergamon.

Cutchin, Debbie. Guide to Public Administration. LC 80-84211. 130p. 1981. pap. text ed. 4.95 (ISBN 0-87581-272-4). Peacock Pubs.

Cutcliffe, Stephen H., et al, eds. Technology & Values in American Civilization: A Guide to Information Sources. (American Information Guide Ser.: Vol. 9). 680p. 1980. 30.00 (ISBN 0-8103-1475-4). Gale.

Cutforth, Rene. Later Than We Thought: A Portrait of the Thirties. LC 76-46679. 1977. 12.50x (ISBN 0-8448-1041-X). Crane-Russak Co.

--Order to View. 1970. 7.95 (ISBN 0-571-09103-2, Pub. by Faber & Faber). Merrimack Bk Serv.

Cuthbertson, K. Macroeconomic Policy: New Cambridge, Keynesian and Monetarist Controversies. LC 79-12195. (New Studies in Economic Ser.). 209p. 1979. 27.95x (ISBN 0-470-26740-2). Halsted Pr.

Cuthbertson, Tom. Alan Chadwick's Enchanted Garden. (Illus.). 1978. pap. 7.50 o.p. (ISBN 0-525-47509-5). Dutton.

--Anybody's Roller Skating Book. (Illus.). (YA) 1981. 8.95 (ISBN 0-89815-042-6); pap. 4.95 (ISBN 0-89815-040-X). Ten Speed Pr.

--Better Bikes: A Manual for an Alternative Mode of Transportation. LC 80-5101. (Illus.). 1980. 7.95 (ISBN 0-89815-025-6); pap. 4.95 (ISBN 0-89815-024-8). Ten Speed Pr.

--The Bike Bag Book. (Illus.). 128p. (Orig.). 1981. pap. 2.95 (ISBN 0-89815-039-6). Ten Speed Pr.

Cuthbertson, Tom & Cole, Lee. I Can Swim, You Can Swim. (Illus., Orig.). (gr. 4-8). 1978. pap. 4.00 (ISBN 0-913668-79-6). Ten Speed Pr.

Cutie, Anthony J., jt. auth. see Plakogiannis, Fotios M.

Cutland, N. J. Computability. LC 79-51823. (Illus.). 300p. 1980. 49.50 (ISBN 0-521-22384-9); pap. 16.50x (ISBN 0-521-29465-7). Cambridge U Pr.

--Computability: An Introduction to Recursive Function Theory. 1980. 49.50 (ISBN 0-521-22384-9); pap. 16.50 (ISBN 0-521-29465-7). Cambridge U Pr.

Cutler & Davis. Detergency, Pt. III. 384p. Date not set. 47.50 (ISBN 0-8247-6982-1). Dekker.

Cutler, A. J., jt. ed. see Hart, A. B.

Cutler, Abbot. Eighteen Forty-Three Rebecca Eighteen Forty-Seven. (Chapbook Ser.: No. 4). 64p. (Orig.). 1981. pap. 4.95 (ISBN 0-937672-03-3). Rowan Tree.

Cutler, Antony, et al. Marx's Capital & Capitalism Today, Vol. 1. 1977. 22.00x (ISBN 0-7100-8745-4); pap. 10.50 (ISBN 0-7100-8746-2). Routledge & Kegan.

--Marx's Capital & Capitalism Today, Vol. 2. 1978. 22.00x (ISBN 0-7100-8855-8); pap. 10.50 (ISBN 0-7100-8856-6). Routledge & Kegan.

Cutler, Barbara C. Unraveling the Special Education Maze: An Action Guide for Parents. LC 80-54006. 260p. (Orig.). 1981. pap. text ed. 7.95 (ISBN 0-87822-224-3, 2243). Res Press.

Cutler, Carl C. Mystic: The Story of a Small New England Seaport. (Illus.). 56p. 1980. pap. 7.00 (ISBN 0-913372-14-5). Mystic Seaport.

Cutler, D. F. Applied Plant Anatomy. LC 77-3290. (Illus.). 1978. pap. text ed. 14.95x (ISBN 0-582-44128-5). Longman.

Cutler, D. F. see Metcalfe, C. R.

Cutler, Ivor. The Animal House. (Illus.). (gr. k-3). 1977. 8.25 (ISBN 0-688-22110-6); PLB 7.92 (ISBN 0-688-32110-0). Morrow.

--Elephant Girl. (Illus.). 32p. (ps-1). 1976. 6.25 (ISBN 0-688-22065-7); PLB 6.00 (ISBN 0-688-32065-1). Morrow.

Cutler, James E. Lynch Law: An Investigation into the History of Lynching in the United States. LC 77-88428. Repr. of 1905 ed. 17.50x (ISBN 0-8371-1821-2). Negro U Pr.

Cutler, Jervis. A Topographical Description of the State of Ohio, Indiana Territory, & Louisiana. Washburn, Wilcomb E., ed. LC 75-7056. (Narratives of North American Indian Captivities: Vol. 34). 1975. lib. bdg. 44.00 (ISBN 0-8240-1658-0). Garland Pub.

Cutler, Katherine. Flower Arranging for All Occasions. rev. ed. LC 80-2850. (Illus.). 256p. 1981. 12.95 (ISBN 0-385-18508-1). Doubleday.

Cutler, Katherine N. Creative Shellcraft. LC 73-148484. (Illus.). (gr. 3 up). 1971. PLB 7.44 (ISBN 0-688-50988-6); pap. 2.95 (ISBN 0-688-45011-3). Lothrop.

--From Petals to Pinecones: A Nature Art & Craft Book. LC 70-81753. (Illus.). (gr. 4 up). 1969. PLB 7.92 (ISBN 0-688-51594-0); pap. 2.95 o.p. (ISBN 0-688-45003-2). Lothrop.

Cutler, Katherine N. & Bogle, Kate. Crafts for Christmas. LC 74-8750. (Illus.). 128p. (gr. 3 up). 1974. PLB 7.44 (ISBN 0-688-51663-7). Lothrop.

Cutler, Lloyd N. Global Interdependence & the Multinational Firm. LC 78-58094. (Headline Ser.: 239). 1978. pap. 2.00 (ISBN 0-87124-046-7). Foreign Policy.

Cutler, Merritt. Basic Tennis Illustrated. (Illus.). 111p. 1980. pap. 4.95 0 (ISBN 0-486-24006-1). Dover.

Cutler, Roland. Firstborn. 1978. pap. 1.75 o.p. (ISBN 0-449-14002-4, GM). Fawcett.

--The Gates of Sagittarius. 344p. 1980. 10.95 (ISBN 0-8037-3268-6). Dial.

Cutler, Wayne & Harris, Michael H., eds. Justin Winsor: Scholar-Librarian. LC 80-19310. (Heritage of Librarianship Ser.: No. 5). 196p. 1980. lib. bdg. 25.00x (ISBN 0-87287-200-9). Libs Unl.

Cutlip, Ralph. Action Stories of Yesterday & Today. (Orig.). (gr. 7-12). 1971. pap. text ed. 4.58 (ISBN 0-87720-351-2). AMSCO Sch.

--Stories from the Four Corners. (gr. 7-12). 1975. pap. text ed. 4.58 (ISBN 0-87720-354-7). AMSCO Sch.

--Stories That Live. (gr. 7-12). 1973. 4.58 (ISBN 0-87720-352-0). AMSCO Sch.

Cutlip, Scott H., jt. auth. see Center, Allen H.

Cutlip, Scott M. Fund Raising in the United States. LC 64-8261. 1965. 12.50 (ISBN 0-910294-21-6). Brown Bk.

Cutright, Paul R. & Brodhead, Michael J. Elliott Coues: Naturalist & Frontier Historian. LC 80-12424. (Illus.). 510p. 1981. 28.95 (ISBN 0-252-00802-2). U of Ill Pr.

Cutright, Phillips & Jaffe, Fredericks S. Impact of Family Planning Programs on Fertility: The U. S. Experience. LC 76-12847. 1977. text ed. 22.95 (ISBN 0-275-23350-2). Praeger.

Cutt, Nancy & Cutt, W. Towrie. Hogboon of Hell & Other Strange Orkney Tales. (Illus.). (gr. 2-7). 1979. PLB 8.95 (ISBN 0-233-97020-7). Andre Deutsch.

Cutt, Thomas & Nyenhuis, Jacob E., eds. Petronius: Cena Trimalchionis. rev. ed. LC 73-105090. (Classical Text Ser). (Latin). 1970. pap. text ed. 4.95x (ISBN 0-8143-1410-4). Wayne St U Pr.

Cutt, W. Towrie. Seven for the Sea. LC 73-93556. 96p. (gr. 3-6). 1974. 4.95 o.p. (ISBN 0-695-80480-4); lib. bdg. 4.98 o.p. (ISBN 0-695-40480-6). Follett.

Cutt, W. Towrie, jt. auth. see Cutt, Nancy.

Cutten, George B. Speaking with Tongues: Historically & Psychologically Considered. 1927. 27.50x (ISBN 0-685-69805-X). Elliots Bks.

Cutter, Fred. Coming to Terms with Death: How to Face the Inevitable with Wisdom & Dignity. LC 74-8397. 262p. 1974. 14.95 (ISBN 0-911012-29-X); pap. 7.95 (ISBN 0-88229-498-9). Nelson-Hall.

Cuttino, George P. Saddle Bag & Spinning Wheel. LC 80-83663. 330p. 1981. 18.95x (ISBN 0-86554-004-7). Mercer Univ Pr.

Cutts, Edward L. Scenes & Characters of the Middle Ages. LC 67-27866. (Social History Reference Ser.). (Illus.). 1968. Repr. of 1872 ed. 22.00 (ISBN 0-8103-3257-4). Gale.

Cutts, J. Jarry, jt. auth. see Krause, William J.

Cutts, Paddy, jt. auth. see Payne, Christina.

Cutul, Ann-Marie, ed. Twentieth-Century European Painting: A Guide to Information Sources. LC 79-24249. (Art & Architecture Information Guide Ser.: Vol. 9). 1980. 30.00 (ISBN 0-8103-1438-X). Gale.

Cuviella, Patrick & Woosley, Hugh. Basic Medical Laboratory Subjects. LC 74-18675. (Allied Health Ser). 1975. pap. 5.10 (ISBN 0-672-61383-2). Bobbs.

Cuyas, A., ed. New Appleton's Cuyas English-Spanish & Spanish-English Dictionary. 5th ed. 1972. 16.95 (ISBN 0-13-611749-X); thumb-indexed 17.95 (ISBN 0-13-611756-2). P-H.

Cuyler, Margery, ed. see Adkins, Jan.

Cuzin, Jean-Pierre, jt. auth. see Laclotte, Michel.

Cuzner, Bernard. A First Book of Metal-Work. 2nd ed. (Illus.). 162p. 1979. pap. 7.50x (ISBN 0-905418-54-9). Intl Pubns Serv.

CWLA Research Center & Grow, Lucille. Early Childrearing by Young Mothers: A Research Study. LC 79-53504. 1979. pap. text ed. 8.95 o.p. (ISBN 0-87868-138-8). Child Welfare.

Cybulski, Jerome S., jt. ed. see Sigmon, Becky A.

Cyert, Richard M. & March, J. G. Behavioral Theory of the Firm. 1963. ref. ed. 19.95 (ISBN 0-13-073304-0). P-H.

Cyert, Richard M., jt. auth. see Argyris, Chris.

Cyert, Richard M., jt. auth. see Cohen, Kalman J.

Cyprian. De Lapsis & De Ecclesiae Catholicae Unitate. Benevot, Maurice, ed. (Oxford Early Christian Texts Ser). 151p. 1971. 22.50x (ISBN 0-19-826804-1). Oxford U Pr.

Cyprian, St. Selected Treatises. (Fathers of the Church Ser.: Vol. 36). 18.50 (ISBN 0-8132-0036-9). Cath U Pr.

Cypser, R. J. Communications Architecture for Distributed Systems. LC 76-52673. (Illus.). 1978. text ed. 21.95 (ISBN 0-201-14458-1). A-W.

Cyr, Helen W. A Filmography of the Third World: An Annotated List of 16mm Films. LC 76-22584. 1976. 13.50 (ISBN 0-8108-0940-0). Scarecrow.

Cyr, John & Sobeck, Joan M. How to Establish a Successful Real Estate Brokerage. 1981. 21.95 (ISBN 0-88462-359-9). Real Estate Ed Co.

Cyriax, George, ed. World Index of Economic Forecasts. LC 78-56982. (Praeger Special Studies). 1978. 175.00 (ISBN 0-03-046216-9). Praeger.

Cyriax, James. The Slipped Disc: Relieving & Understanding Your Back Troubles. 2nd ed. LC 74-185562. (Illus.). 180p. 1975. 15.00 (ISBN 0-7161-0142-4). Herman Pub.

Cyriax, James, jt. auth. see Schiotz, Eiler H.

Cyril. The Roaring Twenties: An Album of Early Motor Racing. (Illus.). 128p. 1980. 17.50 (ISBN 0-7137-0967-7, Pub. by Blandford Pr England). Sterling.

Cyrus, D. & Robson, N. Bird Atlas of Natal. (Illus.). 320p. 1980. text ed. 37.50 (ISBN 0-86980-215-1). Verry.

Cyrus-Zetterstroem, Ulla. Manual of Swedish Handweaving. new ed. (Illus.). 184p. 1977. 15.75 (ISBN 0-8231-5019-4). Branford.

Cyster, R., et al. Parental Involvement in Primary Schools. 210p. 1981. pap. text ed. 19.25x (ISBN 0-85633-211-9, NFER). Humanities.

Cywinski, Jozef. The Essentials in Pressure Monitoring: Blood & Other Body Fluids. (The Tardieu Ser.: No. 3). (Illus.). 120p. 1980. pap. 20.00 (ISBN 90-247-2385-X). Kluwer Boston.

Cyzevs'Kyj, Dmytro. A History of Ukrainian Literature from the 11th to the End of the 19th Century. Ferguson, D., tr. LC 73-94029. 650p. 1975. lib. bdg. 30.00x (ISBN 0-87287-093-6); pap. text ed. 20.00 (ISBN 0-87287-170-3). Ukrainian Acad.

Czajka, Peter A. & Duffy, James P. Poisoning Emergencies: A Guide for Emergency Medical Personnel. LC 79-20542. 1980. pap. text ed. 8.95 (ISBN 0-8016-1205-5). Mosby.

Czamanski, Stan. Regional & Interregional Social Accounting. LC 73-9857. (Regional Science Monograph Ser.). (Illus.). 192p. 1973. 19.95 (ISBN 0-669-90563-1). Lexington Bks.

Czaplinski, Rosemary, et al. Self-Assessment of Current Knowledge in Orthopedic & Rehabilitative Nursing. 1979. pap. 9.50 (ISBN 0-87488-230-3). Med Exam.

Czarra, Fred R. & Heaps, Joseph F. Censorship & the Media: Mixed Blessing or Dangerous Threat. Fraenkel, Jack R., ed. (Crucial Issues in American Government Ser.). (gr. 9-12). 1977. pap. text ed. 4.96 (ISBN 0-205-04910-9, 764910X). Allyn.

Czaykowski, Bogdan, tr. see Bialoszewski, Miron.

Czech, Danuta, et al. Auschwitz: Nazi Extermination Camp. Taylor, Iain W., tr. from Pol. (Illus.). 192p. (Orig.). 1978. pap. 7.50x (ISBN 0-8002-2294-6). Intl Pubns Serv.

Czempiel, Ernst-Otto & Rustow, Dankwart A., eds. The Euro-American System: Economic & Political Relations Between North America & Western Europe. LC 76-4557. 1976. 31.00x (ISBN 0-89158-601-6). Westview.

Czepiel, John & Backman, Jules. Changing Marketing Strategies in a New Economy. LC 77-11109. (Key Issues Lecture Ser). 1977. pap. 5.50 (ISBN 0-672-97199-2). Bobbs.

Czerni, Sergiusz & Skrzynska, Maria, eds. English-Polish Dictionary of Science & Technology. 5th ed. 1976. 30.00x (ISBN 0-686-23574-6). Intl Learn Syst.

Czerny, Carl. School of Practical Composition, 3 vols. (Music Reprint Ser.). 1979. Repr. of 1848 ed. Set. lib. bdg. 75.00 (ISBN 0-306-79595-7). Da Capo.

Czerwinski, Barara S. A Manual of Patient Education for Cardiopulmonary Dysfunction. LC 79-21435. (Illus.). 1980. pap. text ed. 13.95 (ISBN 0-8016-1197-0). Mosby.

Czerwinski, Frank L., jt. auth. see Samaras, Thomas T.

Czestochowski, Joseph S. John Stewart Curry & Grant Wood: A Portrait of Rural America. 240p. 1981. text ed. 26.00x (ISBN 0-8262-0336-1). U. of Mo Pr.

Czestochowski, Joseph S., ed. see Hassam, Childe.

Czompo, Andor. Hungarian Dances. 2nd rev. ed. LC 74-11041. (Illus.). 1980. pap. text ed. 5.95 (ISBN 0-935496-01-7). AC Pubns.

Czompo, Andor, ed. see Czompo, Ann I.

Czompo, Ann I. Recreational Jazz Dance. 2nd ed. Czompo, Andor, ed. LC 79-26223. (Illus.). 1979. pap. text ed. 9.95 (ISBN 0-935496-00-9). AC Pubns.

Czuczka, George T., ed. see John Paul, Pope.

Czuma, Stanislaw. Indian Art: From the George P. Bickford Collection. LC 74-29377. (Illus.). 136p. 1975. 10.00x o.p. (ISBN 0-910386-21-8, Pub. by Cleveland Mus Art); pap. 5.00x (ISBN 0-910386-50-1). Ind U Pr.

D

D. C. Comics. D C Super Heroes Super Healthy Cookbook. (Illus., Orig.). 1981. pap. 8.95 (ISBN 0-446-51227-3). Warner Bks.

--DC Super Heroes Super Healthy Cookbook. (Illus., Orig.). 1981. 8.95 (ISBN 0-446-51227-3). Warner Bks.

Daalder, Hans. Cabinet Reform in Britain, 1914-1963. 1963. 17.50x (ISBN 0-8047-0139-3). Stanford U Pr.

D'Abadal y Vinyals, Ramon & Taberner, Ferran V., eds. Ustages De Barcelona. LC 80-1999. 1981. Repr. of 1913 ed. 26.00 (ISBN 0-404-18552-5). AMS Pr.

Dabberdt, Walter. Weather for Outdoormen. (Illus.). 224p. 1981. 12.95 (ISBN 0-684-16865-0, ScribT). Scribner.

Dabberdt, Walter F. The Whole Air Weather Guide. (Illus.). 1976. pap. 3.50 (Pub. by Solstice). Aviation.

Dabbs, Jack A. Glossary of Agricultural Terms, English-Bengali. LC 79-626525. 1969. 3.00 (ISBN 0-911494-05-7). Dabbs.

--Short Bengali-English, English-Bengali Dictionary. 3rd ed. LC 78-149931. 1971. 4.00 o.s.i. (ISBN 0-911494-01-4). Dabbs.

--Spoken Bengali: Standard, East Bengal. LC 66-63243. 1966. 3.00 (ISBN 0-911494-03-0). Dabbs.

--Word Frequency in Newspaper Bengali. LC 66-64723. 1966. 3.00 (ISBN 0-911494-04-9). Dabbs.

Dabcovich, Lydia. Follow the River. LC 80-10173. (Illus.). 32p. (ps-2). 1980. PLB 8.95 (ISBN 0-525-30015-5). Dutton.

Dabney, Joseph E. Herk, Hero of the Skies. 12.95 (ISBN 0-932298-07-9). Green Hill.

--Mountain Spirits II. 1981. 4.95 (ISBN 0-932298-05-2). Green Hill.

Dabney, Robert L. On Preaching. 1979. 10.95 (ISBN 0-85151-290-9). Banner of Truth.

Dabney, Virginius. Across the Years. LC 77-15147. 1978. 10.00 o.p. (ISBN 0-385-12247-0). Doubleday.

--The Jefferson Scandals. (Illus.). 156p. 1981. 8.95 (ISBN 0-396-07964-4). Dodd.

--Richmond: The Story of a City. LC 73-9150. 1976. 12.95 (ISBN 0-385-02046-5, Pub. by Doubleday). U Pr of Va.

--Virginia: The New Dominion, a History from 1607 to the Present. LC 78-157580. (Illus.). 629p. 14.95 (ISBN 0-385-07150-7). U Pr of Va.

Dabrowski, Richard A. Advanced Designs for the Woodcarver. LC 77-94903. (Illus.). 1979. spiral bdg. 10.15 (ISBN 0-918036-04-6). Woodcraft Supply.

--Designs for the Woodcarver. LC 76-1141. (Illus.). 1979. Repr. of 1976 ed. spiral bdg. 9.50 (ISBN 0-918036-02-X). Woodcraft Supply.

DaCal, E. G. & Ucelay, M., eds. Literatura Del Siglo XX: Nueva Edicion, Revisada y Aumentada. (Spanish.). 1968. 28.50x o.p. (ISBN 0-03-055170-6); pap. text ed. 16.50x o.p. (ISBN 0-686-57886-4). Irvington.

Dacey, John. Adult Development. 1981. text ed. write for info. (ISBN 0-8302-0114-9). Goodyear.

--Where the World Is, Teaching Basic Skills Outdoors. (Illus.). 192p. (Orig.). 1981. pap. 10.95 (ISBN 0-8302-9605-0). Goodyear.

Dacey, Philip. The Boy Under the Bed. LC 80-8858. (Johns Hopkins Poetry & Fiction). 1981. text ed. 10.95x (ISBN 0-8018-2601-2); pap. text ed. 5.95x (ISBN 0-8018-2602-0). Johns Hopkins.

Dachs. TV Jokes. (gr. 7-12). pap. 1.25 (ISBN 0-590-05402-3, Schol Pap). Schol Bk Serv.

Dachs, David, ed. Pop-Rock Question & Answer Book. (YA) (gr. 7-12). 1977. pap. 1.25 (ISBN 0-590-11893-5, Schol Pap). Schol Bk Serv.

Dack, M. R. Techniques of Chemistry: Vol. 8, Pt. 1, Solutions & Solubilities. 475p. 1975. 48.50 (ISBN 0-471-93266-3). Wiley.

Dackerman, Gerald, jt. auth. see Sohl, Marcia.

Da Costa, Beverley, ed. see American Heritage Editors.

Da Costa, Beverly, ed. see American Heritage Editors.

DaCosta, Frank. How to Build Your Own Working Robot Pet. (Illus.). 1979. 11.95 (ISBN 0-8306-9796-9); pap. 7.95 (ISBN 0-8306-1141-X, 1141). TAB Bks.

Da Costa, Leon see Costa, Leon Da.

Dacre, Charlotte. Hours of Solitude: A Collection of Original Poems by Charlotte Dacre, Better Known by the Name Rosa Matilda, 2 vols. in 1. Reiman, Donald, ed. LC 75-31190. (Romantic Context Ser.: Poetry 1789-1830: Vol. 42). 1979. Repr. of 1805 ed. lib. bdg. 47.00 (ISBN 0-8240-2141-X). Garland Pub.

Da Cruz, Daniel. The Captive City. 224p. (Orig.). 1976. pap. 1.50 o.p. (ISBN 0-345-24769-8). Ballantine.

Da Cruz, Vera. C. M. B. Questions & How to Answer Them. 5th ed. (Illus.). 1977. pap. 3.95 (ISBN 0-571-04919-2, Pub. by Faber & Faber). Merrimack Bk Serv.

Dada. Beyond the Mind: Conversations on the Deeper Significance of Living. LC 77-85723. (Illus.). 1978. pap. 4.95 (ISBN 0-930608-01-1). Dada Ctr.

--Towards the Unknown. LC 81-65123. (Illus.). 128p. (Orig.). 1981. pap. 4.95 (ISBN 0-930608-02-X). Dada Ctr.

Dadant & Sons, ed. The Hive & the Honey Bee. LC 63-15838. (Illus.). 3740p. 1976. 17.50 (ISBN 0-684-14790-4, ScribT). Scribner.

Dadant & Sons, Inc. The Honey Kitchen. LC 80-66361. (Illus.). 208p. 1980. 6.95 (ISBN 0-915698-06-4). Dadant & Sons.

D'Addario, Joseph D. Build It: Out of Sight Sewing Center. 1972. pap. 3.95 (ISBN 0-686-01898-2). Classic Furn Kits.

Dadeklan, A. The Strategy of Puts & Calls. LC 68-57498. 1973. pap. 2.95 o.p. (ISBN 0-684-13310-5, SL430, ScribT). Scribner.

Dadourian, H. M. Introduction to Analytic Geometry & Calculus. (Illus.). 1949. 15.95x o.p. (ISBN 0-8260-2285-5). Wiley.

--Introduction to Analytic Geometry & the Calculus. 256p. 1981. Repr. of 1949 ed. lib. bdg. price not set (ISBN 0-89874-267-6). Krieger.

Daellenbach, Hans G. & George, John A. Introduction to Operations Research Techniques. 1978. text ed. 26.95 (ISBN 0-205-05755-1); answer book (ISBN 0-205-05756-X). Allyn.

Daemmrich, Horst S. Wilhelm Raabe. (World Authors Ser.: No. 594). 1981. lib. bdg. 13.95 (ISBN 0-8057-6436-4). Twayne.

Daems, W. T., jt. ed. see Carr, Ian.

Daems, W. T. see Sbarra, Anthony J. & Strauss, Robert.

Daems, W. T., et al, eds. Cell Biological Aspects of Disease: The Plasma Membrane & Lysosomes. (Boerhaave Series for Postgraduate Medical Education: No. 19). 330p. 1981. PLB 68.50 (ISBN 90-6021-466-8, Pub. by Leiden U Pr). Kluwer Boston.

Daenell, E. Bluetezeit der deutsche Hanse: Hansische Geschichte Von der Zweiten Haelfte des Xiv Bis Zum Letzten Viertel Des Xv Jahrhunderts, 2 vols. 1035p. 1973. Repr. of 1906 ed. Set. 135.30x (ISBN 3-11-004562-1). De Gruyter.

Daenzer, Bernard J. Excess & Surplus Lines Manual. 1981. 186.00 (ISBN 0-930868-01-3). Merritt Co.

D'Aeth, Richard. Education & Development in the Third World. 138p. 1976. 18.95 (ISBN 0-347-01083-0, 99846-X, Pub. by Saxon Hse). Lexington Bks.

Daffner. Case Studies in Radiology. 1975. pap. 15.50 o.p. (ISBN 0-8385-1072-8). ACC.

Daffner, Richard H. Introduction to Diagnostic Radiology: A Correlated Approach to Imaging. LC 78-5680. 1978. pap. text ed. 16.95 (ISBN 0-8016-1203-9). Mosby.

Da Foligno, Angela. Divine Consolation of the Blessed Angela Da Foligno. Steegman, M. G., tr. LC 66-30731. (Medieval Library). (Illus.). 265p. 1966. Repr. of 1926 ed. 22.50x (ISBN 0-8154-0072-1). Cooper Sq.

Da Fonseca, F. Peixoto. Dictionnaire bilingue Larousse, francais-portugais et portugais-francais. (Apollo). (Fr. & Port.). 10.50 (ISBN 2-03-020909-0, 3791). Larousse.

Da Free, John. What to Remember to Be Happy. (Illus.). pap. 4.95 (ISBN 0-913922-36-6). Dawn Horse Pr.

Da Free John. Compulsory Dancing. LC 80-80912. 1980. pap. 2.95 (ISBN 0-913922-50-1). Dawn Horse Pr.

--Conscious Exercise & the Transcendental Sun. 3rd rev. ed. LC 77-83388. (Illus.). 55p. 1977. 10.95 (ISBN 0-913922-30-7); pap. 5.95. Dawn Horse Pr.

--The Four Fundamental Questions. 2nd ed. LC 79-92923. 1980. pap. 1.95 (ISBN 0-913922-49-8). Dawn Horse Pr.

--Scientific Proof of the Existence of God Will Soon Be Announced by the White House. LC 80-81175. 1980. pap. 12.95 (ISBN 0-913922-48-X). Dawn Horse Pr.

--Scientific Proof of the Existence of God Will Soon Be Announced by the White House. 1980. pap. 12.95 (ISBN 0-913922-48-X). Dawn Horse Pr.

D'Agapeyeff, Alexander. Codes & Ciphers. LC 73-19772. (Illus.). 1974. Repr. of 1939 ed. 18.00 (ISBN 0-8103-3716-9). Gale.

Dage, John H. La see La Dage, John H.

Dagg, A. I. & James, A. Running, Walking & Jumping: The Science of Locomotion. LC 77-15301. (Wykeham Science Ser.: No. 42). 1977. 14.95x (ISBN 0-8448-1169-6). Crane-Russak Co.

Dagg, Anne I & Foster, J. Bristol. The Giraffe: Its Biology, Behavior, & Ecology. 210p. 1980. Repr. of 1976 ed. text ed. write for info. (ISBN 0-89874-275-7). Krieger.

Dagg, Anne I., jt. auth. see Gauthier-Pilters, Hilde.

Daggett, Emerson. The Sentinel. 12p. (Orig.). 1981. pap. 2.00 (ISBN 0-932942-01-6). Pacific NW Labor.

Daggett, R. M., ed. & illus. see Kalakaua.

Dagher, Joseph P. Writing a Practical Guide. LC 74-11784. (Illus.). 1975. pap. text ed. 10.50 (ISBN 0-395-18621-8); inst. manual 1.25 (ISBN 0-395-18803-2). HM.

Daglarca, Fazil Husnu. The Bird & I. Barkan, Stanley H., ed. Halman, Talat Sait, tr. (Cross-Cultural Review Chapbook 4). 16p. (Turkish & Eng.). 1980. pap. 2.00 (ISBN 0-89304-803-8). Cross Cult.

Daglio, S. Daniel, tr. see Yates, Kyle M. & Owens, J. J.

Daglish, E. Fitch. The Basset Hound. (Foyle's Handbks). 1973. 3.95 (ISBN 0-685-55818-5). Palmetto Pub.

--Beagles. Foyle, Christina, ed. (Foyle's Handbks). 1973. 3.95 (ISBN 0-685-55802-9). Palmetto Pub.

--Dog Breeding. Foyle, Christina, ed. 1973. 3.95 (ISBN 0-685-55810-X). Palmetto Pub.

Dagmar, et al, trs. see Tichy, M. & Rakosnik, J.

Dagnal, Cynthia. The Supergroups. (Illus.). 192p. (Orig.). (gr. 6 up). 1981. pap. 1.95 (ISBN 0-448-17228-3, Tempo). G&D.

Dagnini, Giorgio. Clinical Laparoscopy. (Illus.). xii, 307p. 1980. 130.00 (ISBN 88-212-0746-3, Pub. by Piccin Italy). J K Burgess.

D'Agostino, Dennis. This Date in New York Mets History. LC 80-6157. (This Date Ser.). 256p. 1981. pap. 9.95 (ISBN 0-8128-6068-3). Stein & Day.

Dagostino, Frank. Materials of Construction. 1981. text ed. 18.95 (ISBN 0-8359-4286-4). Reston.

Dagostino, Frank R. Contemporary Architectural Drawing: Residential & Commercial. 1977. 17.95 (ISBN 0-87909-132-0). Reston.

--Estimating in Building Construction. 2nd ed. (Illus.). 1978. ref. ed. 19.95 (ISBN 0-87909-275-0); text ed. 15.95 (ISBN 0-87909-275-0); solutions manual free (ISBN 0-8359-2749-0). Reston.

--Methods & Materials of Commercial Construction. LC 73-196221. 304p. 1974. text ed. 13.50 (ISBN 0-87909-486-9); ref. ed. 18.00 (ISBN 0-686-66910-X). Reston.

Dagut, Merton, tr. see Sambursky, S.

Dahan, Bonnie, ed. see Kan, Johnny & Leong, Charles L.

Dahiels, Dorothy. The Caldwell Shadow. (Orig.). 1975. pap. 1.50 o.s.i. (ISBN 0-446-88560-6). Warner Bks.

Dahinden, Rene, jt. auth. see Hunter, Don.

Dahl, A. M. & Joseph, Joan E., eds. Directory of Directors in the City of New York & Surburbs, 1980. rev. ed. 680p. 1980. 115.00 (ISBN 0-936612-01-0). DODC.

Dahl, Borghild. Good News. (gr. 7 up). 1966. PLB 5.95 o.p. (ISBN 0-525-30828-8). Dutton.

--I Wanted to See. 1967. 8.95 (ISBN 0-02-529380-X). Macmillan.

Dahl, C. Food & Menu Dictionary. LC 77-123002. 1972. 10.95 (ISBN 0-8436-0556-1). CBI Pub.

Dahl, Cornwall. Consistent Profits in Short Selling Speculation. (Illus.). 267p. 1976. 41.50 (ISBN 0-89266-011-2). Am Classical Coll Pr.

Dahl, Eilif & Krog, Hildur. Macrolichens of Denmark, Finland, Norway, & Sweden. (Scandinavian University Books). (Illus.). 180p. 1973. 17.00x (ISBN 8-200-02262-5, Dist. by Columbia U Pr). Universitet.

Dahl, Fred, jt. auth. see Sippl, Charles J.

Dahl, Gerald. Everybody Needs Somebody Sometime. 190p. 1980. 3.95 (ISBN 0-8407-5751-4). Nelson.

Dahl, Hartvig. Word Frequencies of Spoken American English. LC 80-116646. 1980. 60.00 (ISBN 0-930454-07-3). Verbatim.

Dahl, John I., jt. auth. see Rice, F. Philip.

Dahl, John I., jt. auth. see Rice, F. Phillip.

Dahl, Otto C. Proto-Austronesian. 2nd ed. (Scandinavian Institute of Asian Studies Monograph: No. 15). 146p. (Orig.). 1977. pap. text ed. 11.00x (ISBN 0-7007-0064-1). Humanities.

Dahl, Roald. Charlie & the Chocolate Factory. 176p. (gr. 4-6). 1981. pap. 2.25 (ISBN 0-553-15097-9, Skylark). Bantam.

--James & the Giant Peach. 160p. (gr. 4-6). pap. 2.50 (ISBN 0-553-15113-4, Skylark). Bantam.

--My Uncle Oswald. 208p. 1981. pap. 2.95 (ISBN 0-345-29410-6). Ballantine.

Dahl, Robert A. Modern Political Analysis. 3rd ed. (Foundations of Modern Political Science Ser). (Illus.). 176p. 1976. ref. ed. o.p. 8.95x (ISBN 0-13-596999-9); pap. text ed. 6.95x (ISBN 0-13-596981-6). P-H.

--Preface to Democratic Theory. LC 56-6642. (Walgreen Foundation Lecture Ser). 1963. pap. 3.95 (ISBN 0-226-13426-1, P115, Phoen). U of Chicago Pr.

Dahl, Robert A., et al, eds. Social Science Research on Business: Product & Potential. LC 60-9783. 1959. pap. 10.00 (ISBN 0-231-02407-X). Columbia U Pr.

Dahl, Svend. History of the Book. 2nd ed. LC 68-12627. (Illus.). 1968. 10.00 (ISBN 0-8108-0057-8). Scarecrow.

Dahl, Vladimir I. Dahl's Russian Dictionary, 4 vols. LC 79-40161. (Illus.). 3000p. 1981. Set. 255.00 (ISBN 0-08-023573-5). Pergamon.

Dahlberg, Edwin T. I Pick up Hitchhikers. LC 77-25498. 1978. pap. 2.95 o.p. (ISBN 0-8170-0774-1). Judson.

Dahlberg, Francis, ed. Woman the Gatherer. LC 80-25262. (Illus.). 288p. 1981. text ed. 15.00x (ISBN 0-300-02572-6). Yale U Pr.

Dahlen, Beverly. Out of the Third. 3.00x o.p. (ISBN 0-685-46992-1); signed ed. 15.00x o.p. (ISBN 0-685-46993-X). Momos.

Dahlhaus, Carl. Between Romanticism & Modernism: Four Studies in the Music of the Later Nineteenth Century. Kerman, Joseph, ed. Whittall, Mary, tr. from Ger. LC 78-54793. (California Studies in 19th Century Music). 100p. 1980. 10.00x (ISBN 0-520-03679-4). U of Cal Pr.

--Richard Wagner's Music Dramas. Whittall, Mary, tr. LC 78-68359. 1979. 14.95 (ISBN 0-521-22397-0). Cambridge U Pr.

Dahlhaus, Carl & Eggebrecht, Hans H. Brockhaus Riemann Musiklexikon, Vol. 1, A-K. (Ger.). 1978. 99.50 (ISBN 3-7653-0303-8). Eur-Am Music.

Dahlin, David C. Bone Tumors: General Aspects & Data on 6,221 Cases. 3rd ed. (Illus.). 464p. 1978. 44.75 (ISBN 0-398-03692-6). C C Thomas.

Dahlin, Doris. The Sit-in Game. Tate, Joan, tr. from Swedish. 96p. (gr. 7 up). 1974. 4.95 o.p. (ISBN 0-670-64730-6). Viking Pr.

Dahlin, Therrin C., et al. The Catholic Left in Latin America: A Comprehensive Bibliography. (Reference Bks.). 1981. lib. bdg. 35.00 (ISBN 0-8161-8396-1). G K Hall.

Dahlke, Paul. Buddhism & Its Place in the Mental Life of Mankind. LC 78-72403. Repr. of 1927 ed. 29.00 (ISBN 0-404-17265-2). AMS Pr.
Dahlman, C. J. The Open Field System & Beyond. LC 79-7658. 1980. 27.50 (ISBN 0-521-22881-6). Cambridge U Pr.
Dahlquist, Albert B. Conversation Today. 14.95 (ISBN 0-911012-66-4). Nelson-Hall.
Dahlquist, Allan. Megasthenes & Indian Religion. 1977. 10.00 (ISBN 0-89684-277-0, Pub. by Motilal Banarsidass India). Orient Bk Dist.
Dahlstrom, A. H., ed. see Thoma.
Dahlstrom, J. & Ryel, D. Promises to Keep: Reading & Writing About Values. 1977. pap. text ed. 10.95 (ISBN 0-13-731059-5). P-H.
Dahmer, Sondra & Kahl, Kurt. The Waiter & Waitress Training Manual. LC 73-83574. 1974. pap. 7.95 (ISBN 0-8436-0575-8). CBI Pub.
Dahms, Alan M. Thriving: Beyond Adjustment. LC 79-17954. 1980. pap. text ed. 13.95 (ISBN 0-8185-0358-0). Brooks-Cole.
Dahnsen, Alan. Bicycles. LC 78-7346. (Easy-Read Fact Bks.). (Illus.). (gr. 2-4). 1978. PLB 6.45 s&l (ISBN 0-531-01372-3). Watts.
Dahrendorf, Ralf. Life Changes: Approaches to Social & Political Theory. LC 79-18685. x, 182p. 1981. pap. 5.95 (ISBN 0-226-13443-1). U of Chicago Pr.
Daiche, David. Edinburgh. 1979. 22.50 (ISBN 0-241-89878-1, Pub. by Hamish Hamilton England). David & Charles.
Daiches. Critical Approaches to Literature. 1979. pap. text ed. 11.50x (ISBN 0-582-48411-1). Longman.
Daiches, D. A Critical History of English Literature, 2 vols. 2nd ed. 1970. Set. 30.00 (ISBN 0-471-06962-0). Wiley.
Daiches, David. James Boswell & His World. LC 75-29826. 1976. 8.95 o.p. (ISBN 0-684-14549-9, ScribT). Scribner.
--More Literary Essays. LC 68-16688. 1968. 11.00x o.s.i. (ISBN 0-226-13472-5). U of Chicago Pr.
--A Study of Literature for Readers & Critics. LC 71-152593. 240p. 1972. Repr. of 1948 ed. lib. bdg. 21.00x (ISBN 0-8371-6026-X, DARC). Greenwood.
--Two Worlds. 1971. 12.50x (ISBN 0-85621-001-3, Pub. by Scottish Academic Pr Scotland). Columbia U Pr.
Daiches, David & Flower, John. Literary Landscape of the British Isles: A Narrative Atlas. 288p. 1981. pap. 7.95 (ISBN 0-14-005735-8). Penguin.
Daigneault, Ernest A., jt. auth. see Brown, R. Don.
Daigon, Arthur & Dempsey, Richard A. School: Pass at Your Own Risk. (Illus.). 228p. 1973. pap. text ed. 10.95 (ISBN 0-13-793877-2). P-H.
Dailey, Charles A. Assessment of Lives: Personality Evaluation in a Bureaucratic Society. LC 70-168860. (Behavioral Science Ser.). 1971. 14.95x o.p. (ISBN 0-87589-108-X). Jossey-Bass.
Dailey, D. H. & Popence, W. P. Mollusca from the Upper Cretaceous Jalama Formation, Santa Barbara County, California. (U. C. Publ. in Geological Sciences: Vol. 65). 1966. pap. 6.00x (ISBN 0-520-09166-3). U of Cal Pr.
Dailey, Donald H. Early Cretaceous Forminifera from the Budden Canyon Formation, Northwestern Sacramento Valley, California. (U. C. Publ. in Geological Sciences: Vol. 106). 1975. pap. 12.00x (ISBN 0-520-09486-7). U of Cal Pr.
Dailey, Jane T. Enemy in Camp. (Harlequin Presents Ser.). 192p. 1980. pap. 1.50 (ISBN 0-373-10373-5, Pub. by Harlequin). PB.
Dailey, Janet. Difficult Decision. (Harlequin Presents Ser.). 192p. 1980. pap. 1.50 (ISBN 0-373-10386-7, Pub. by Harlequin). PB.
--Night Way. (Orig.). 1981. pap. 2.75 (ISBN 0-671-83605-6). Pb.
--One of the Boys. (Harlequin Presents Ser.). 192p. 1980. pap. 1.50 (ISBN 0-373-10399-9, Pub. by Harlequin). PB.
--Ride the Thunder. pap. 2.75 (ISBN 0-686-68324-2). PB.
--The Rogue. (Orig.). 1980. pap. 2.75 (ISBN 0-671-82843-6). PB.
--A Tradition of Pride. (Harlequin Presents Ser.). 192p. 1981. pap. 1.50 (ISBN 0-373-10421-9, Pub. by Harlequin). PB.
--The Travelling Kind. (Harlequin Presents Ser.). 192p. 1981. pap. 1.50 (ISBN 0-373-10427-8, Pub. by Harlequin). PB.
--Wild & Wonderful. (Harlequin Presents Ser.). 192p. 1981. pap. 1.50 (ISBN 0-373-10416-2, Pub. by Harlequin). PB.
Daily, Elaine K. & Schroeder, John S. Techniques in Bedside Hemodynamic Monitoring. 2nd ed. LC 80-16594. (Illus.). 198p. 1980. pap. text ed. 11.95 (ISBN 0-8016-4363-5). Mosby.
Daily, Jay E., jt. auth. see Immroth, J. Philip.
Daily Nonpareil Office. Sketches of Springfield in 1856. (Annual Monograph Ser.). 96p. 1973. pap. 3.00 facsimile reprint. Clark County Hist Soc.
Daims, Diva, jt. auth. see Grimes, Janet.
Dain, Norman. Clifford W. Beers: Advocate for the Insane. LC 79-24290. (Contemporary Community Health Ser.). 1980. 19.95 (ISBN 0-8229-3419-1). U of Pittsburgh Pr.
--Concepts of Insanity in the United States, 1789-1865. 1964. 18.50 (ISBN 0-8135-0443-0). Rutgers U Pr.
Daines, David R. & Falconi, Gonazalo. Legislacion de Aguas en los Paises del Grupo Andino. 200p. (Span.). 1974. pap. 10.00 (ISBN 0-87421-067-4). Utah St U Pr.
Daintith, John. Facts on File: Dictionary of Astronomy. (Illus.). 1979. 17.50 (ISBN 0-87196-326-4). Facts on File.
Daintith, John, ed. The Facts on File Dictionary of Biology. 288p. 1981. 14.95 (ISBN 0-87196-510-0). Facts on File.
--The Facts on File Dictionary of Chemistry. 224p. 1981. 14.95 (ISBN 0-87196-513-5). Facts on File.
--The Facts on File Dictionary of Mathematics. 224p. 1981. prepub. 14.95 (ISBN 0-87196-512-7). Facts on File.
--The Facts on File Dictionary of Physics. 248p. 1981. 14.95 (ISBN 0-87196-511-9). Facts on File.
Dainty, J. C., ed. Laser Speckle & Related Phenomena. (Topics in Applied Physics: Vol. 9). (Illus.). 250p. 1976. 49.20 (ISBN 0-387-07498-8). Springer-Verlag.
Daisy, Carol A., jt. ed. see Laliberte, Elizabeth.
Daitch, Paul B. Introduction to College Engineering. LC 72-2651. 1973. pap. text ed. 10.95 (ISBN 0-201-01417-3). A-W.
Daitzman, Reid J. Clinical Behavior Therapy & Behavior Modification, Vol. 2. 304p. 1981. lib. bdg. 32.50 (ISBN 0-8240-7217-0). Garland Pub.
--Clinical Behavior: Therapy & Behavior Modification, Vol. 2. LC 79-14455. 304p. 1980. lib. bdg. 32.50 (ISBN 0-8240-7217-0). Garland Pub.
--Modern Modern Times. 75p. 1981. pap. text ed. 2.95 (ISBN 0-938340-01-8). World Univ Pr.
Daitzman, Reid J., jt. ed. see Cox, Daniel J.
Daix, Pierre & Rosselet, Joan. Picasso, a Catalogue Raisonne of the Paintings & Related Works. LC 78-71109. (Illus.). 1979. 125.00 (ISBN 0-8212-0672-9, 706981). NYGS.
Dajka, B., et al, trs. see Kardos, Lajos.
Dakin, Douglas. The Greek Struggle for Independence, 1821-1833. LC 72-89798. 1973. 22.50x (ISBN 0-520-02342-0). U of Cal Pr.
Dakin, Tony, ed. Sales Promotion Handbook. 450p. 1974. 25.00 o.p. (ISBN 0-7161-0097-5). Herman Pub.
Dakyns, Jannie R. The Middle Ages in French Literature 1851-1900. new ed. (Oxford Modern Languages & Literature Monographs). 364p. 1973. 29.95x (ISBN 0-19-815522-0). Oxford U Pr.
Dalai Lama, see Gyatso, Tenzin.
Dalal, Nergis. The Inner Door. 144p. 1975. pap. 1.85 (ISBN 0-89253-028-6). Ind-US Inc.
Daland, Robert T. Exploring Brazilian Bureaucracy: Performance & Pathology. LC 80-67246. 455p. 1981. lib. bdg. 24.24 (ISBN 0-8191-1468-5); pap. text ed. 15.75 (ISBN 0-8191-1469-3). U Pr of Amer.
D'Albert, Joseph L. & Herbert, Richard A. You & the Psychic Within. 1977. 6.00 o.p. (ISBN 0-682-48879-8). Exposition.
Dalbor, John B. Beginning College Spanish: From Sounds to Structures. 672p. 1972. text ed. 15.95 (ISBN 0-394-31175-2, RanC); wkbk. 5.50 (ISBN 0-394-31182-5); tapes 200.00x (ISBN 0-686-66665-8). Random.
Dalbor, John B. & Sturcken, H. Tracy. Spanish in Review. LC 78-27055. 1979. pap. text ed. 12.95x (ISBN 0-471-03991-8); tchrs. manual (ISBN 0-471-04191-2); wkbk. 3.95 (ISBN 0-471-03992-6); tapes (ISBN 0-471-05673-1). Wiley.
Dalby, Stuart. Making Model Buildings. (Illus.). 96p. 12.95 (ISBN 0-7137-0976-6, Pub. by Blandford Pr England). Sterling.
Dal Co, Francesco, jt. auth. see Tafuri, Manfredo.
Dale, A. M. Collected Papers. Webster, T. B. & Turner, E. G., eds. LC 69-10574. 1969. 48.00 (ISBN 0-521-04763-3). Cambridge U Pr.
Dale, A. M., ed. see Euripides.
Dale, Anthony. The Theatre Royal Brighton. 180p. 1980. 25.00 (ISBN 0-85362-185-3). Routledge & Kegan.
Dale, Arbie M. Change Your Job, Change Your Life. 1978. pap. 1.95 (ISBN 0-87216-721-6). Playboy Pbks.
Dale, Celia. Act of Love. 1977. pap. 1.75 (ISBN 0-505-51211-4). Tower Bks.
Dale, Charles W., jt. auth. see Oliva, Ralph A.
Dale, D. C. Applied Audiology for Children. 2nd 4th pt ed. (Illus.). 176p. 1979. 14.75 (ISBN 0-398-00387-4). C C Thomas.
Dale, D. M. Language Development in Deaf & Partially Hearing Children. (Illus.). 270p. 1975. 24.75 (ISBN 0-398-03164-9). C C Thomas.
Dale, Delbert A. Trumpet Technique. (YA) (gr. 9 up). 1965. 7.75 (ISBN 0-19-318702-7). Oxford U Pr.
Dale, Doris. Career Patterns of Women Librarians with Doctorates. (Occasional Papers: No. 147). 1980. pap. 3.00. U of Ill Lib Sci.
Dale, Doris C., ed. Carl H. Milam & the United Nations Library. LC 76-14866. 149p. 1976. 10.00 (ISBN 0-8108-0941-9). Scarecrow.
Dale, E., jt. auth. see Schachter, G.
Dale, E. E. & Litton, Gaston. Cherokee Cavaliers: Forty Years of Cherokee History As Told in the Correspondence of the Ridge-Watie-Boudinot Family. (Civilization of the American Indian Ser.: No. 19). (Illus.). 1969. Repr. of 1939 ed. 16.95 o.p. (ISBN 0-8061-0085-0). U of Okla Pr.
Dale, Edward E. Cow Country. (Western Frontier Library: Vol. 27). 258p. 1965. pap. 3.95 (ISBN 0-8061-1153-4). U of Okla Pr.
Dale, Edward E., ed. see Canton, Frank M.
Dale, Ernest. Great Organizers: Theory & Practice of Organizations. 1971. pap. 2.95 o.p. (ISBN 0-07-015173-3, SP). McGraw.
Dale, Jean N. The Monkey's Paw. rev. ed. (Reading & Exercise Ser.: No. 5). 1976. pap. 2.50 (ISBN 0-89285-054-X); cassette tapes 29.50 (ISBN 0-89285-072-8). ELS Intl.
--Tale from Tangier. rev. ed. (Reading & Exercise Ser.: No. 6). 1976. pap. 2.50 (ISBN 0-89285-055-8); cassette tapes 29.50 (ISBN 0-89285-073-6). ELS Intl.
Dale, Jean N. & Sheeler, Willard D. The Angry Sea. rev. ed. (Reading & Exercise Ser.: No. 2). 1975. pap. 2.50 (ISBN 0-89285-051-5); cassette tapes 29.50 (ISBN 0-89285-069-8). ELS Intl.
--The Quiet Man. rev. ed. (Reading & Exercise Ser.: No. 4). 1975. pap. 2.50 (ISBN 0-89285-053-1); cassette tapes 29.50 (ISBN 0-89285-071-X). ELS Intl.
--Winds of Virtue. rev. ed. (Reading & Exercise Ser.: No. 3). 1975. pap. 2.50 (ISBN 0-89285-052-3); cassette tapes 29.50 (ISBN 0-89285-070-1). ELS Intl.
Dale, Jean N. & Sheeler, Williard D. The Whistler. rev. ed. (Reading & Excercise Ser.: No. 1). 1976. pap. 2.50 (ISBN 0-89285-050-7); cassette tapes 29.50 (ISBN 0-89285-068-X). ELS Intl.
Dale, Jean N., ed. The Monkey's Paw. (Reading & Exercise Ser.). (Illus.). (gr. k-6). 1974. pap. text ed. 2.50x (ISBN 0-19-433623-9). Oxford U Pr.
--Tale from Tangier. (Reading & Exercise Ser.). (Illus.). (gr. k-6). 1974. pap. text ed. 2.50x (ISBN 0-19-433624-7). Oxford U Pr.
Dale, Jean N. & Sheeler, Willard D., eds. The Angry Sea. (Reading & Exercise Ser.). (Illus.). (gr. k-6). 1973. pap. text ed. 2.50x (ISBN 0-19-433620-4). Oxford U Pr.
--The Quite Man. (Reading & Exercise Ser.). (gr. k-6). 1974. pap. text ed. 2.50x (ISBN 0-19-433622-0). Oxford U Pr.
--The Whistler. (Reading & Exercise Ser.). (gr. k-6). 1973. pap. text ed. 2.50x (ISBN 0-19-433619-0). Oxford U Pr.
--Winds of Virtue. (Reading & Exercise Ser.). (gr. k-6). 1974. pap. text ed. 2.50x (ISBN 0-19-433621-2). Oxford U Pr.
Dale, Kathleen. Nineteenth Century Piano Music: A Handbook for Pianists. LC 70-87500. (Music Ser.). Repr. of 1954 ed. 27.50 (ISBN 0-306-71414-0). Da Capo.
Dale, Laura A., jt. auth. see White, Rhea A.
Dale, Peter. Mortal Fire. LC 74-29409. ix, 181p. 1976. 16.00 (ISBN 0-8214-0185-8); pap. 5.00 (ISBN 0-8214-0187-4). Ohio U Pr.
Dale, Richard. Anti-Dumping Law in a Liberal Trade Order. Date not set. price not set (ISBN 0-312-04373-2). St Martin.
Dale, Richard, jt. ed. see Potholm, Christian.
Dale, Robert D. To Dream Again. 1981. pap. 4.95 (ISBN 0-8054-2541-1). Broadman.
Dale, Stephen F. Islamic Society on the South Asian Frontier: The Mappilas of Malabar, 1498 - 1922. (Illus.). 352p. 1981. 49.00x (ISBN 0-19-821571-1). Oxford U Pr.
Dale, Tom, jt. auth. see Carter, Vernon G.
D'Alembert, jt. ed. see Diderot.
D'Alembert, Family. Strangler's Moon. (E.E. Doc Smith Ser: No. 2). 1976. pap. 1.75 (ISBN 0-515-04731-7). Jove Pubns.
D'Alembert, Jean L. Preliminary Discourse to the Encyclopedia of Diderot. Schwab, Richard & Rex, Walter, trs. LC 63-21831. (Orig.). 1963. 6.50 (ISBN 0-672-51037-5); pap. 5.50 (ISBN 0-672-60276-8, LLA88). Bobbs.
Dalen, James E. & Alpert, Joseph E. Valvular Heart Disease. 1981. text ed. price not set. Little.
Dalen, Linda Van see Van Dalen, Linda.
Dales, D. N., jt. auth. see Thiessen, Frank.
Dales, Davis, jt. auth. see Thiessen, Frank J.
Dales, Richard C. Marius on the Elements. 200p. 1977. 13.50x (ISBN 0-520-02856-2). U of Cal Pr.
--Middle Ages Ser. (Sources of Medieval History Ser.). (Illus.). 1973. text ed. 14.00x (ISBN 0-8122-7673-6); pap. text ed. 5.95x (ISBN 0-8122-1057-3). U of Pa Pr.
Dalesman, compiled by. Yorkshire Legends. 2nd ed. (Illus.). 71p. (Orig.). 1976. pap. 3.00 (ISBN 0-686-64123-X). Legacy Bks.
Dalessio, Donald J., ed. Wolff's Headache & Other Head Pain. 4th ed. (Illus.). 750p. 1980. text ed. 35.00x o.p. (ISBN 0-19-502624-1). Oxford U Pr.
Dalet, Roger. How to Safeguard Your Health & Beauty with the Simple Pressure of a Finger. LC 80-5497. (Illus.). 160p. 1981. 10.95 (ISBN 0-8128-2742-2). Stein & Day.
Daley, Arthur, jt. auth. see Kieran, John.
Daley, Brian. The Doomfarers of Coramonde. (A Del Rey Bk.). (Orig.). 1977. pap. 2.25 (ISBN 0-345-29180-8). Ballantine.
Daley, Ken. Basic Film Technique. (Media Manual Series). (Illus.). 160p. 1980. pap. 9.95 (ISBN 0-240-51016-X). Focal Pr.
Daley, Maxime & Lochner, Barbara. How to Get a Man After You're Forty. 1978. pap. 2.95 (ISBN 0-06-464026-4, BN 4026, BN). Har-Row
Daley, Robert. The Fast One. 1979. pap. 2.25 o.p. (ISBN 0-345-28147-0). Ballantine.
Daley, William J., et al. Ethylene Oxide Control in Hospitals. LC 79-22184. 48p. (Orig.). 1979. pap. 6.25 (ISBN 0-87258-291-4, 1400). Am Hospital.
Dalferes, Clayelle & Young, David. Per Se Award Plays, 1972-1973: Special Issue 29 - the Smith. 44p. pap. 1.00 o.p. (ISBN 0-685-78410-X). The Smith.
Dalgliesh, Alice. America Begins. rev. ed. (Illus.). (gr. 2-5). 1958. reinforced bdg. 6.95 o.p. (ISBN 0-684-13455-1, ScribJ). Scribner.
--Little Wooden Farmer. LC 68-12081. (Illus.). (gr. k-1). 1971. pap. 0.95 o.s.i. (ISBN 0-02-042790-5, Collier). Macmillan.
--Little Wooden Farmer. LC 68-12081. (Illus.). (ps-1). 1968. 4.95g o.s.i. (ISBN 0-02-725920-X). Macmillan.
--Thanksgiving Story. (Illus.). (gr. k-3). 1954. reinforced bdg. 9.95 (ISBN 0-684-12330-4, ScribJ); pap. 2.95 (ISBN 0-684-16005-6, SL823, ScribJ). Scribner.
Dalis, Gus T., jt. auth. see Fodor, John T.
Da Liu. T'ai Chi Ch'uan & I Ching. 1978. pap. 1.95 o.p. (ISBN 0-06-080452-1, P 452, PL). Har-Row.
Dalkey, N. C. Group Decision Theory. 1981. cancelled (ISBN 0-201-01430-0, Adv Bk Prog). A-W.
Dallas, D. M. Sex Education in School & Society. (Exploring Education Ser.). 104p. (Orig.). 1972. pap. text ed. 5.00x (ISBN 0-901225-91-6, NFER). Humanities.
Dallas, Daniel B. Manufacturing Engineering Transactions: 1974, Vol. 3. 1975. 25.00 o.p. (ISBN 0-87263-104-4). SME.
Dallas, Richard J. & Thompson, James M. Clerical & Secretarial Systems for the Office. (Office Occupations Ser.). (Illus.). 448p. 1975. ref. ed. 16.95 (ISBN 0-13-136390-5). P-H.
Dallas, Rita & Ratcliffe, Jeanira. The Kennedy Case. 368p. 1974. pap. 1.75 o.p. (ISBN 0-445-08259-3). Popular Lib.
Dallas, Robert C. Robert Charles Dallas. Reiman, Donald H., ed. LC 75-31192. (Romantic Context Ser.: Poetry 1789-1830). 1977. lib. bdg. 47.00 (ISBN 0-8240-2143-6). Garland Pub.
Dallas, Sandra. No More Than Five in a Bed: Colorado Hotels in the Old Days. (Illus.). 1967. 9.95 (ISBN 0-8061-0742-1). U of Okla Pr.
--Vail. LC 78-94879. (Illus.). 1969. pap. 2.50 o.p. (ISBN 0-87108-005-2). Pruett.
Dallas-Damis, Athena. Windswept. (Orig.). 1981. pap. 2.25 (ISBN 0-451-09666-5, E9666, Sig). NAL.
--Windswept. LC 78-75130. Date not set. write for info. (ISBN 0-89241-087-6). Caratzas Bros. Postponed.
Dallas-Damis, Athena, tr. see Mouzaki, Rozanna.
Dallek, Robert. Franklin D. Roosevelt & American Foreign Policy, 1932-1945. (A Galaxy Book: No. 628). 690p. 1981. pap. 9.95 (ISBN 0-19-502894-5). Oxford U Pr.
Dallen. Piano Study for Beginners. 1981. pap. 14.95 (ISBN 0-13-675603-4). P-H.
Dallimore, Arnold. George Whitefield: The Life & Times of the Great Evangelist of the 18th Century Revival, Vol. II. LC 79-67152. 640p. 1980. 19.95 (ISBN 0-89107-168-7, Cornerstone Bks). Good News.
--George Whitefield: The Life & Times of the Great Evangelist of the 18th Century Revival, Vol. 1. LC 79-67152. 598p. 1980. 19.95 (ISBN 0-89107-167-9, Cornerstone Bks). Good News.

Dallin, Alexander, ed. The Twenty-Fifth Congress of the CPSU: Assessment & Context. LC 77-2445. (Publication Ser: No. 184). (Illus.). 1977. pap. 5.95 (ISBN 0-8179-6842-3). Hoover Inst Pr.

Dallin, Alexander, et al, eds. Diversity in International Communism: A Documentary Record. LC 62-21515. (Orig.). 1963. pap. 15.00x (ISBN 0-231-08611-3). Columbia U Pr.

Dallin, David J. New Soviet Empire. 1951. 27.50x (ISBN 0-685-69806-8). Elliots Bks.

--Real Soviet Russia. 1947. 24.50x (ISBN 0-685-69807-6). Elliots Bks.

--Russia & Postwar Europe. 1943. 24.50x (ISBN 0-685-69808-4). Elliots Bks.

--Soviet Russia's Foreign Policy, 1939-42. 1942. 42.50x (ISBN 0-685-88556-9). Elliots Bks.

Dallin, Leon. Foundations in Music Theory. 2nd ed. 1967. pap. 12.95x (ISBN 0-534-00659-0). Wadsworth Pub.

Dallinger, Jane. Frogs & Toads. (Lerner Natural Science Bks.). (Illus.). (gr. 4-10). 1981. PLB 7.95 (ISBN 0-8225-1454-0). Lerner Pubns.

--Grasshoppers. (Lerner Natural Science Bks.). (Illus.). (gr. 4-10). 1981. PLB 7.95 (ISBN 0-8225-1455-9). Lerner Pubns.

--Spiders. (Lerner Natural Science Bks.). (Illus.). (gr. 4-10). 1981. PLB 7.95 (ISBN 0-8225-1456-7). Lerner Pubns.

Dallington, R., tr. see Colonna, Francesco.

Dallman, Elaine, et al, eds. Woman Poet - the Northeast. (Woman Poet Ser.). 140p. (Orig.). 1981. 12.95 (ISBN 0-935634-03-7); pap. text ed. 6.00 (ISBN 0-935634-02-9). Women-in-Lit.

--Woman Poet - the West. LC 79-55988. (Woman Poet Ser.). 100p. (Orig.). 1980. 12.95 (ISBN 0-935634-01-0); pap. 6.00 (ISBN 0-935634-00-2). Women-in-Lit.

Dallman, John C. Investigation of Separated Flow Model in Annular Gas-Liquid Two-Phase Flows. LC 78-75007. (Outstanding Dissertations on Energy Ser.). 1979. lib. bdg. 20.00 (ISBN 0-8240-3988-2). Garland Pub.

Dallmayr, Fred A. Beyond Dogma & Despair: Toward a Critical Phenomenology of Politics. LC 80-53179. 256p. 1981. text ed. 19.95 (ISBN 0-268-00661-X). U of Notre Dame Pr.

Dallmayr, Fred R. Twilight of Subjectivity: Contributions to a Post-Individualist Theory of Politics. LC 80-23433. 416p. 1981. lib. bdg. 20.00x (ISBN 0-87023-314-9); pap. text ed. 10.00x (ISBN 0-87023-315-7). U of Mass Pr.

Dallmayr, Winfried R., jt. auth. see Rankin, Robert S.

Dally, Ann. Understanding. LC 78-66254. 192p. 1981. pap. 6.95 (ISBN 0-8128-6104-3). Stein & Day.

Dally, James W. & Riley, William F. Experimental Stress Analysis. 2d ed. LC 77-393. (Illus.). 1977. text ed. 27.50x (ISBN 0-07-015204-7, C); solutions manual 9.95 (ISBN 0-07-015205-5). McGraw.

Dally, Peter & Gomez, Joan. Obesity & Anorexia Nervosa: A Question of Shape. 128p. 1980. 17.95 (ISBN 0-571-10542-4, Pub. by Faber & Faber); pap. 6.95 (ISBN 0-571-11472-5). Merrimack Bk Serv.

Dalmais, Anne-Marie. The Adventures of Little Rabbit. (ps-2). 1972. PLB 9.15 o.p. (ISBN 0-307-63633-X, Golden Pr). Western Pub.

D'Alonzo, C. Anthony. Handbook of Heart Disease, Blood Pressure & Strokes. 1962. pap. 0.95 o.s.i. (ISBN 0-02-058670-1, Collier). Macmillan.

D'Alpuget, Lou. Successful Sailing. LC 77-180469. (Illus.). 80p. 1973. pap. 2.95 o.s.i. (ISBN 0-02-028200-1, Collier). Macmillan.

Dalrymple, Bryon. How to Call Wildlife. LC 74-33568. (Funk & W Bk.). (Illus.). 192p. 1975. 8.95 (ISBN 0-308-10208-8, TYC-T); pap. 4.50 o.s.i. (ISBN 0-308-10209-6, TYC-T). T Y Crowell.

Dalrymple, Byron. Fishing for Fun. (Illus.). 192p. 1975. 8.95 o.p. (ISBN 0-87691-164-5). Winchester Pr.

--Survival in the Outdoors. 1972. 6.95 o.p. (ISBN 0-525-21290-6). Dutton.

Dalrymple, Byron W. Complete Book of Deer Hunting. 1973. 12.95 (ISBN 0-87691-108-4). Winchester Pr.

Dalrymple, D. J. Retailing: An Economic View. LC 69-11840. 1969. text ed. 12.95 (ISBN 0-02-906970-X). Free Pr.

Dalrymple, D. J., jt. auth. see Thompson, D. L.

Dalrymple, Dana & Dalrymple, Helen. Guide to the Appalachian Trail from the Susquehanna River to the Shenandoah National Park. 9th ed. 1974. pap. 3.50 o.p. (ISBN 0-915746-06-9). Potomac Appalach.

Dalrymple, Dana & Dalrymple, Helen, eds. Guide to the Appalachian Trail & Side Trails in the Shenandoah National Park. 7th ed. 1973. pap. 3.50 o.p. (ISBN 0-915746-05-0). Potomac Appalach.

Dalrymple, Douglas J. & Parsons, Leonard J. Marketing Mangement: Text & Cases. 2nd ed. LC 79-24833. (Wiley Ser. in Marketing). 1980. text ed. 23.95 (ISBN 0-471-03606-4); tchrs' manual avail. (ISBN 0-471-07767-4). Wiley.

Dalrymple, G. Brent & Lanphere, Marvin A. Potassium-Argon Dating, Principles, Techniques, & Applications to Geochronology. LC 71-84047. (Geology Ser.). (Illus.). 1969. text ed. 22.95x (ISBN 0-7167-0241-X). W H Freeman.

Dalrymple, Glenn V. & Slayden, John E., eds. Radiology in Primary Care. LC 74-28277. (Illus.). 330p. 1975. pap. text ed. 26.50 o.p. (ISBN 0-8016-1198-9). Mosby.

Dalrymple, Glenn V., jt. ed. see Boyd, Charles M.

Dalrymple, Helen, jt. auth. see Dalrymple, Dana.

Dalrymple, Helen, jt. ed. see Dalrymple, Dana.

Dalsass, Diana. Cashews & Lentils, Apples & Oats. (Illus.). 1981. 14.95 (ISBN 0-8092-5935-4); pap. 7.95 (ISBN 0-8092-5934-6). Contemp Bks.

Dalton, G. E., ed. Study of Agricultural Systems. (Illus.). 1975. 63.30x (ISBN 0-85334-640-2, Pub. by Applied Science). Burgess-Intl Ideas.

Dalton, Gene W. & Lawrence, Paul R., eds. Motivation & Control in Organizations. 1971. pap. text ed. 10.95x (ISBN 0-256-00609-1). Irwin.

Dalton, Gene W., et al, eds. Organizational Change & Development. 1970. pap. text ed. 10.95x (ISBN 0-256-00606-7). Irwin.

--Organizational Structure & Design. 1970. pap. text ed. 10.95x (ISBN 0-256-00607-5). Irwin.

Dalton, J. Michael & Kuipers, Katharina. Essentials of Chiropody for Students. 6th ed. 1969. 7.95 o.p. (ISBN 0-571-04623-1, Pub. by Faber & Faber). Merrimack Bk Serv.

Dalton, John. The Professional Cosmetologist. 2nd ed. (Illus.). 1979. text ed. 14.95 (ISBN 0-8299-0186-8); pap. text ed. 11.50 (ISBN 0-8299-0231-7); study guide 8.50 (ISBN 0-8299-0280-5); cancelled (ISBN 0-686-52297-4); state board review questions 4.95 (ISBN 0-8299-0290-2); answer key 1.00 (ISBN 0-8299-0264-3). West Pub.

Dalton, John J. The Cattle Mutilators. (Orig.). 1980. pap. 1.95 (ISBN 0-532-23117-1). Manor Bks.

Dalton, K. C. Geography of Sierra Leone. 1965. text ed. 5.95x (ISBN 0-521-04764-1). Cambridge U Pr.

Dalton, Katharina. Depression After Childbirth: How to Recognize & Treat Postnatal Illness. (Illus.). 192p. 1981. 13.95 (ISBN 0-19-217701-X); pap. 6.95 (ISBN 0-19-286008-9). Oxford U Pr.

--Premenstrual Syndrome & Progesterone Therapy. 1979. 19.95x (ISBN 0-433-07091-9). Intl Ideas.

Dalton, Michael. Countrey Justice, Containing the Practise of the Justices of the Peace Out of Their Sessions. LC 74-28844. (English Experience Ser.: No. 725). 1975. Repr. of 1618 ed. 42.00 (ISBN 90-221-0725-6). Walter J Johnson.

Dalton, T. H., jt. auth. see Archer, J. E.

Dalven, Rae. Anna Comnena. LC 78-169634. (World Authors Ser.: Greece: No. 213). lib. bdg. 10.95 (ISBN 0-8057-2240-8). Twayne.

Dalven, Richard. Introduction to Applied Solid State Physics: Topics on the Applications of Semiconductors, Superconductors, & the Nonlinear Optical Properties of Solids. (Illus.). 345p. 1980. 27.50 (ISBN 0-306-40385-4, Plenum Pr). Plenum Pub.

Dalvi, Quasin, jt. auth. see Hensher, David.

Dalwood, C., jt. auth. see Biggs, P.

Daly. Steve Martin: A Wild & Crazy Guy. 1980. pap. 2.25 o.p. (ISBN 0-451-09060-8, Sig). NAL.

Daly, Barbara J. Intensive Care Nursing. LC 78-78019. (Current Clinical Nursing Ser.). 1979. pap. 13.50 (ISBN 0-87488-575-2). Med Exam.

Daly, Bruce. The Psychological Theory of the Voluptuous Woman. (Illus.). 1978. deluxe ed. 49.75 (ISBN 0-930582-18-7). Gloucester Art.

Daly, D. D., jt. ed. see Penry, J. K.

Daly, David D., jt. ed. see Klass, Donald W.

Daly, Donald F. Aim for a Job in Air Conditioning & Refrigeration. LC 70-114141. (Career Guidance Ser). 1971. pap. 3.50 (ISBN 0-668-02224-8). Arco.

--Aim for a Job in the Building Trades. LC 72-110289. (Aim High Vocational Guidance Ser.). (Illus.). (gr. 7 up). 1970. PLB 5.97 o.p. (ISBN 0-8239-0213-7). Rosen Pr.

--Your Career in Air Conditioning, Refrigeration & Related Engineering Careers. LC 78-701. 1979. lib. bdg. 6.95 (ISBN 0-668-04562-0); pap. 3.50 (ISBN 0-668-04573-6). Arco.

Daly, Dorothy. The Veneto: Padua, Vicenza & Verona. (Batsford Countries Ser.). (Illus.). 192p. 1975. 9.95 o.p. (ISBN 0-8038-7755-2). Hastings.

Daly, Eileen. My Little Book of Dinosaurs. (Tell-a-Tale Readers). (Illus.). (gr. k-3). 1973. PLB 4.77 (ISBN 0-307-68482-2, Whitman). Western Pub.

--Raggedy Ann & Andy & the Five Birthday Parties in a Row. (A Young Reader Ser.). (Illus.). (gr. k-3). 1979. PLB 5.00 (ISBN 0-307-60263-X, Golden Pr). Western Pub.

Daly, Elizabeth. Death & Letters. 1981. pap. 2.25 (ISBN 0-440-11791-7). Dell.

Daly, Gabriel. Transcendence & Immanence: A Study in Catholic Modernism & Integralism. 266p. 1980. 34.95x (ISBN 0-19-826652-9). Oxford U Pr.

Daly, H. V. Skeleto-Muscular Morphogenesis of the Thorax & Wings of the Honey Bee Apis Mellifera (Hymenoptera: Apidea) (U. C. Publ. in Entomology: Vol. 39). 1964. pap. 6.75x (ISBN 0-520-09111-6). U of Cal Pr.

Daly, Herman E. Steady-State Economics: The Economics of Biophysical Equilibrium & Moral Growth. LC 77-8264. (Illus.). 1977. text ed. 15.95x (ISBN 0-7167-0186-3); pap. text ed. 7.95x (ISBN 0-7167-0185-5). W H Freeman.

Daly, Herman E., ed. Economics, Ecology, Ethics: Essays Toward a Steady-State Economy. LC 79-29712. (Illus.). 1980. text ed. 17.95x (ISBN 0-7167-1178-8); pap. text ed. 8.95x (ISBN 0-7167-1179-6). W H Freeman.

Daly, Howell V., Jr. Bees of the Genus Ceratina in America North of Mexico (Hymenoptera: Apidea) (U. C. Publ. in Entomology: Vol. 74). 1973. pap. 11.25x (ISBN 0-520-09484-0). U of Cal Pr.

Daly, Kathleen. The Cat Book. (Illus.). (ps-2). 1974. PLB 7.62 (ISBN 0-307-60837-9, Golden Pr). Western Pub.

--Dinosaurs. (Look-Look Ser.). (Illus.). 1977. PLB 5.38 (ISBN 0-307-61835-8, Golden Pr); pap. 0.95 (ISBN 0-307-11835-5). Western Pub.

--Dinosaurs, Giants of the Past. (gr. 4-7). 1974. 1.95 (ISBN 0-307-10501-6, Golden Pr); PLB 7.62 (ISBN 0-307-60501-9). Western Pub.

--Four Little Kittens. (ps-1). 1957. PLB 5.00 (ISBN 0-307-60322-9, Golden Pr). Western Pub.

--Hide & Defend. (Look-Look Ser.). (Illus.). 1977. PLB 5.38 (ISBN 0-307-61837-4, Golden Pr); pap. 0.95 (ISBN 0-307-11837-1). Western Pub.

--Home Is Best Book. Orig. Title: The Nest Book. (Illus.). 24p. (ps-4). 1977. PLB 5.38 (ISBN 0-307-68919-0, Golden Pr). Western Pub.

--My Doctor Bag Book. (Carry-Me Book). (Illus.). 24p. (ps-3). 1977. PLB 5.38 (ISBN 0-307-68851-8, Golden Pr). Western Pub.

--My Flight Bag Book. (Carry-Me Books). (Illus.). 24p. (ps-3). 1977. PLB 5.38 (ISBN 0-307-68850-X, Golden Pr). Western Pub.

--My Lunch Box Book. (Carry-Me Books). (Illus.). (ps-3). 1977. PLB 5.38 (ISBN 0-307-68855-0, Golden Pr). Western Pub.

--My Picnic Basket Book. (Carry-Me Books). (Illus.). 24p. 1977. PLB 5.38 (ISBN 0-307-68852-6, Golden Pr). Western Pub.

--My Sports Bag Book. (Carry-Me Bks.). (Illus.). 24p. (ps-3). 1977. PLB 5.38 (ISBN 0-307-68854-2, Golden Pr). Western Pub.

--Today's Biggest Animals. (Look-Look Ser.). (Illus.). 1977. PLB 5.38 (ISBN 0-307-61836-6, Golden Pr); pap. 0.95 (ISBN 0-307-11836-3). Western Pub.

--Unusual Animals. (Look-Look Ser.). (Illus.). 1977. PLB 5.38 (ISBN 0-307-61834-X, Golden Pr); pap. 0.95 (ISBN 0-307-11834-7). Western Pub.

--Wild Animal Babies. (Illus.). (ps-1). 1958. PLB 5.00 (ISBN 0-307-60332-6, Golden Pr). Western Pub.

Daly, Leo. James Joyce & the Mullingar Connection. (Dolmen Editions: No. 20). 40p. (Demi quarto size). 1975. text ed. 22.50x (ISBN 0-391-00418-2, Dolmen Pr). Humanities.

Daly, Mary. Gyn-Ecology: The Metaethics of Radical Feminism. LC 78-53790. 1979. 14.95 (ISBN 0-8070-1510-5, BP-601); pap. 7.95 (ISBN 0-8070-1511-3). Beacon Pr.

Daly, Maxine E., jt. auth. see Parker, Robert P., Jr.

Daly, Robert. God's Altar: The World & the Flesh in Puritan Poetry. LC 77-76182. 1978. 14.00x (ISBN 0-520-03480-5). U of Cal Pr.

Daly, Robert W., ed. see Keeler, William F.

Daly, Saralyn. In the Web. 1978. pap. 1.95 o.p. (ISBN 0-449-14043-1, GM). Fawcett.

Daly, Saralyn R. Katherine Mansfield. (English Authors Ser.: No. 23). 1965. lib. bdg. 9.95 (ISBN 0-8057-1372-7). Twayne.

Daly, Sheila J. Blondes Prefer Gentlemen-Brunettes, Too-Redheads Included. LC 49-10484. (Illus.). (gr. 9 up). 1949. 3.95 (ISBN 0-396-03061-0). Dodd.

Daly, Treve, jt. auth. see Thompson, Raymond.

Dalzell, J. Ralph. Simplified Concrete Masonry Planning & Building. 2nd, rev. ed. Merritt, Frederick S., rev. by. LC 81-385. 398p. 1981. Repr. of 1972 ed. lib. bdg. price not set (ISBN 0-89874-278-1). Krieger.

Dalziel, Allan. Evatt the Enigma: Controverial Australian. 9.95x (ISBN 0-392-07809-0, SpS). Soccer.

Dam, Mogens, jt. ed. see Penry, J. Kiffin.

Dam, Nguyen C. & Linh, Tran C. Vietnam, Our Beloved Land. LC 68-21116. (Illus.). (gr. 5 up). 1968. pap. 3.85 o.p. (ISBN 0-8048-0614-4). C E Tuttle.

Damachi, Ukandi G. Leadership Ideology in Africa: Attitudes Toward Socioeconomic Development. LC 75-19772. (Illus.). 128p. 1976. text ed. 17.95 o.p. (ISBN 0-275-56760-5). Praeger.

Damachi, Ukandi G. & Diejomaoh, Victor P. Human Resources & African Development. LC 78-19133. (Praeger Special Studies). 1978. 34.95 (ISBN 0-03-022826-3). Praeger.

Damachi, Ukandi G, et al. Development Paths in Africa & China. LC 75-45447. 1976. 26.25x (ISBN 0-89158-541-9). Westview.

D'Amanda, Christopher & Korcok, Milan, eds. The Women Next Door. 1981. 5.95 (ISBN 0-932194-07-9). Green Hill.

Damane, M. & Sanders, P. B., eds. Lithoko: Sotho Praise Poems. Damane, M. & Sanders, P. B., trs. (Oxford Library of African Literature). 297p. 1974. 21.00x o.p. (ISBN 0-19-815143-8). Oxford U Pr.

Damane, M., tr. see Damane, M. & Sanders, P. B.

Damask, Arthur. Medical Physics: External Senses, Vol. 2. 1981. write for info. (ISBN 0-12-201202-X). Acad Pr.

D'Amato, Alex, jt. auth. see D'Amato, Janet.

D'Amato, Francesco. Nuclear Cytology in Relation to Development. LC 76-46045. (Developmental & Cell Biology Ser.: No. 6). 1977. 54.00 (ISBN 0-521-21508-0). Cambridge U Pr.

D'Amato, Janet & D'Amato, Alex. Cardboard Carpentry. (Activity Bks). (Illus.). (gr. 2-5). PLB 7.21 (ISBN 0-87460-085-5). Lion.

--Handicrafts for Holidays. (Illus.). (gr. 1-4). 1967. PLB 7.21 (ISBN 0-87460-086-3). Lion.

--Indian Crafts. (Illus.). (gr. 1-4). PLB 7.95 (ISBN 0-87460-088-X). Lion.

--More Colonial Crafts for You to Make. LC 77-6333. (Illus.). (gr. 4-6). 1977. PLB 7.79 o.p. (ISBN 0-671-32841-7). Messner.

Damazo, Joseph S. The Pastor Dispenses. (Uplook Ser.). 1976. pap. 0.75 (ISBN 0-8163-0265-0, 16037-4). Pacific Pr Pub Assn.

D'Ambrosio, Bobbe, et al. Spell Well. (Makemaster Bk.). 1980. pap. 7.50 (ISBN 0-8224-6455-1). Pitman Learning.

D'Ambrosio, Charles. Guide to Successful Investing. 1969. pap. text ed. 10.95x (ISBN 0-13-370817-9). P-H.

D'Ambrosio, Charles A. Principles of Modern Investments. LC 75-34094. (Illus.). 512p. 1976. text ed. 19.50 (ISBN 0-574-19210-7, 13-2210); instr's guide avail. (ISBN 0-574-19211-5, 13-2211). SRA.

D'Ambrosio, Richard. No Language but a Cry. LC 75-111154. 1970. 8.95 o.p. (ISBN 0-385-05380-0). Doubleday.

Dambry, Patricia, ed. see Hardy, Judith, et al.

Dame, Enid. Confessions. Barkan, Stanley H., ed. (Cross-Cultural Review Chapbook 12). 16p. 1980. pap. 2.00 (ISBN 0-89304-811-9). Cross Cult.

--On the Road to Damascus, Maryland. 56p. (Orig.). 1980. pap. 2.50 (ISBN 0-917402-15-4). Downtown Poets.

Dame, F. J., et al. Exploratory Business: Selling, Office Occupation, Shorthand. 4th ed. 1965. 5.68 o.p. (ISBN 0-07-015235-7, G). McGraw.

D'Amelio. Severely Retarded Children: Wider Horizons. LC 74-147053. text ed. 9.95x (ISBN 0-675-09220-5). Merrill.

D'Amelio, Dan. Silvababma. (Pacesetters Ser.). (Illus.). 64p. (gr. 4 up). 1978. PLB 7.95 (ISBN 0-516-02158-3). Childrens.

Damer, T. Edward. Attacking Faulty Reasoning. 1979. pap. text ed. 6.95x (ISBN 0-534-00750-3). Wadsworth Pub.

Dameron, J. Lasley. Popular Literature: Poe's Not So Soon Forgotten Lore. Kadis, Averil J., ed. 1980. pap. 2.50 (ISBN 0-910556-16-4). Enoch Pratt.

Dames, Ralph T. The Winning Option. LC 79-23369. 128p. 1981. 14.95 (ISBN 0-88229-527-6). Nelson-Hall.

Damiani, Bruno M. Francisco Lopez De Ubeda. (World Authors Ser.: Spain: No. 431). 1977. lib. bdg. 12.50 (ISBN 0-8057-6271-X). Twayne.

D'Amico, Robert. Marx & Philosophy of Culture. LC 80-24405. (University of Florida Humanities Monograph: No. 50). viii, 108p. (Orig.). 1981. pap. 7.00 (ISBN 0-8130-0689-9). U Presses Fla.

Damien, Yvonne M. & Smith, Margo L., eds. Selected Guide to Anthropological Bibliographies. 1981. write for info. (ISBN 0-913178-63-2). Redgrave Pub Co.

Damisch, Isabel M. Les Images Chez John Webster, Tome 1 & 2. (Salzburg Studies in English Literature: Jacobean Drama Studies: No. 66 & 67). (Fr.). 1977. pap. text ed. 25.00x; Tome 1. pap. text ed. (ISBN 0-391-01355-6); Tome 2. pap. text ed. (ISBN 0-391-01356-4). Humanities.

Damjan, Mischa. Little Green Man. LC 76-166286. (gr. k-3). 1972. 5.95 o.s.i. (ISBN 0-8193-0535-9, Four Winds); PLB 5.41 o.s.i. (ISBN 0-8193-0536-7). Schol Bk Serv.
Damjanov, Ivan. General Pathology. (Medical Outline Ser.). 1976. spiral bdg. 12.00 o.p. (ISBN 0-87488-628-7). Med Exam.
--Ultrastructural Pathology of Human Tumors, Vol. 1. Horrobin, D. F., ed. LC 79-319782. (Annual Research Reviews Ser.). 1979. 24.00 (ISBN 0-88831-045-5). Eden Med Res.
--Ultrastructural Pathology of Human Tumors, Vol. 2. Horrobin, D. F., ed. (Annual Research Reviews). 144p. 1980. 24.00 (ISBN 0-88831-082-X). Eden Med Res.
Damjanovich, S., ed. New Trends in the Description of the General Mechanism & Regulation of Enzymes. (Illus.). 312p. 1978. 30.00x (ISBN 963-05-1881-3). Intl Pubns Serv.
Dammann, Erik. The Future in Our Hands. (Illus.). 1979. 25.00 (ISBN 0-08-024284-7); pap. 11.50 (ISBN 0-08-024283-9). Pergamon.
Damon, Albert. Human Biology & Ecology. LC 77-559. (Illus.). 1977. pap. text ed. 8.95x (ISBN 0-393-09103-1). Norton.
Damon, Dave, ed. see Damon, Valerie H.
Damon, Phillip. Modes of Analogy in Ancient & Medieval Verse. (California Library Reprint Series: No. 33). 1973. 14.00x (ISBN 0-520-02366-8). U of Cal Pr.
Damon, Phillip, ed. Literary Criticism & Historical Understanding. LC 67-24335. 1967. 12.50x (ISBN 0-231-03086-X). Columbia U Pr.
Damon, S. Foster. Blake Dictionary: The Ideas & Symbols of William Blake. LC 65-18187. (Illus.). 460p. 1973. Repr. of 1965 ed. 25.00 (ISBN 0-87057-088-9, Pub. by Brown U Pr). Univ Pr of New England.
--Heaven & Hell. Brown, Catherine, ed. (Illus., Orig.). 1978. pap. 5.50 (ISBN 0-914278-17-7). Copper Beech.
Damon, S. Foster, ed. Series of Old American Songs. 1936. boxed set 6.00 (ISBN 0-87057-014-5, Pub. by Brown U Pr). Univ Pr of New England.
Damon, S. Foster, ed. see Blake, William.
Damon, Valerie H. Grindle Lamfoon & the Procurnious Fleekers. Damon, Dave, ed. LC 78-64526. (Illus.). (gr. 1-12). 1979. 8.95 (ISBN 0-932356-05-2); fleeker ed. 10.95 (ISBN 0-932356-06-0). Star Pubns MO.
Damore, Leo. In His Garden: The Anatomy of a Murderer. LC 79-54008. (Illus.). 1981. 14.95 (ISBN 0-87795-250-7). Arbor Hse.
D'Amour, Fred E. Basic Physiology. LC 61-5603. (Illus.). 1961. text ed. 17.50x (ISBN 0-226-13517-9). U of Chicago Pr.
Damour, Jacques. One Hundred & One Tips & Hints for Your Boat. Howard-Williams, Jeremy, tr. from Fr. (Illus.). 1981. 13.95 (ISBN 0-393-03262-0). Norton.
Dampier, William C. History of Science. 1965. pap. 19.95x (ISBN 0-521-09366-X, 366). Cambridge U Pr.
Damren, Betty R., et al. Training Effective Teachers: A Competency-Based Practicum Model for Teachers of Emotionally Disturbed Children. 53p. 1975. pap. text ed. 4.00x (ISBN 0-89039-134-3). Ann Arbor Pubs.
Damrosch, Leopold, Jr. Symbol & Truth in Blake's Myth. LC 80-7515. (Illus.). 504p. 1980. 25.00x (ISBN 0-691-06433-4); pap. 9.50x (ISBN 0-691-10095-0). Princeton U Pr.
--The Uses of Johnson's Criticism. LC 75-19431. 1976. 13.95x (ISBN 0-8139-0625-3). U Pr of Va.
Damroth, Marion. Country Dogs & City Cousins(the Care & Loving of All Puppies) LC 80-81371. (Illus.). 125p. Date not set. price not set (ISBN 0-937118-01-X). Home Frosted.
Dams, R., jt. auth. see Adams, F.
Dams, T., et al, eds. Food & Population: Priorities in Decision Making. 208p. 1979. text ed. 21.00x (ISBN 0-566-00250-7, Pub. by Gower Pub Co England). Renouf.
Dams, Theodor & Hunt, Kenneth E., eds. Decision-Making & Agriculture. LC 77-93962. 1978. pap. 21.50x o.p. (ISBN 0-8032-7201-4). U of Nebr Pr.
Damste, P. H. & Lerman, J. W. An Introduction to Voice Pathology: Functional & Organic. (Illus.). 120p. 1975. pap. 14.75 photocopy ed. spiral (ISBN 0-398-03289-0). C C Thomas.
Dan, Alice, et al. The Menstrual Cycle: A Synthesis of Interdisciplinary Research, Vol. 1. LC 80-18837. (Illus.). 1980. text ed. 28.00 (ISBN 0-8261-2630-8). Springer Pub.
Dana, Alan S., Jr., jt. auth. see Samitz, M. H.
Dana, Barbara. Crazy Eights. 176p. (gr. 7-9). 1981. pap. 1.75 (ISBN 0-553-14435-9). Bantam.
Dana, E. S. & Ford, W. E. Textbook of Mineralogy. 4th ed. 1932. 34.95 (ISBN 0-471-19305-4). Wiley.
Dana, E. S. & Hurlbut, C. S. Minerals & How to Study Them. 3rd ed. pap. 13.50 (ISBN 0-471-19195-7). Wiley.
Dana, H. E. El Mundo Del Nuevo Testamento. Villarello, Ildefonso, tr. 1977. pap. 4.25 (ISBN 0-311-04342-9). Casa Bautista.
Dana, H. E. & Mantey, J. R. Gramatica Griega Del Nuevo Testamento. Robleto, Adolfo & De Clark, Catalina, trs. 1979. pap. 8.95 (ISBN 0-311-42010-9). Casa Bautista.
Dana, J. D., et al. Systems of Minerology, 3 vols. 7th ed. Incl. Vol. 1. Elements, Sulfides, Sulfosalts, Oxides. 1944. 46.50 (ISBN 0-471-19239-2); Vol. 2. Halides, Nitrates, Borates, Carbonates, Sulfates, Phosphates, Arsenates, Tungstates, Molybdates. 1951. 42.95 (ISBN 0-471-19272-4); Vol. 3. Silica Minerals. 1962. 23.95 (ISBN 0-471-19287-2). Pub. by Wiley-Interscience). Wiley.
Dana, Richard. The Seaman's Friend. LC 79-4623. 1979. Repr. of 1841 ed. lib. bdg. 25.00x (ISBN 0-8201-1330-1). Schol Facsimiles.
Dana, Richard H. Two Years Before the Mast. 1969. 11.50x (ISBN 0-460-00588-X, Evman); pap. 4.95 (ISBN 0-460-01588-5). Dutton.
Dana, Robert. In a Fugitive Season. LC 79-64294. 80p. 1980. 8.95 (ISBN 0-8040-0804-3); pap. 5.95 (ISBN 0-8040-0805-1). Swallow.
--Power of the Visible. LC 79-171877. 71p. 1971. 7.50 (ISBN 0-8040-0551-6); pap. 3.95 (ISBN 0-8040-0646-6). Swallow.
Dana, Robert see Judson, John.
Dana, Samuel T. Forest & Range Policy: Its Development in the U. S. (The American Forestry Ser). 1956. text ed. 18.00 o.p. (ISBN 0-07-015285-3, C). McGraw.
Dana, Samuel T. & Fairfax, Sally K. Forest & Range Policy. 2nd ed. (Illus.). 496p. 1980. text ed. 19.95 (ISBN 0-07-015288-8, P&RB). McGraw.
Danadian, R., ed. NMR in Medicine. (NMR--Basic Principles & Progress Ser.). (Illus.). 230p. 1981. 57.90 (ISBN 0-387-10460-7). Springer-Verlag.
Danaher, Brian G. & Lichtenstein, Edward. Become an Ex-Smoker. LC 78-1679. (Self-Management Psychology Ser.). (Illus.). 1978. 11.95 (ISBN 0-13-072249-9, Spec); pap. 5.95 (ISBN 0-13-072231-6, Spec). P-H.
Danaher, Kate, jt. auth. see Williamson, John D.
Danbom, David B. The Resisted Revolution: Urban America & the Industrialization of Agriculture, 1900-1930. 1979. text ed. 10.95 (ISBN 0-8138-0945-2). Iowa St U Pr.
Danbury, Hazel. Teaching Practical Social Work. 85p. 1979. pap. text ed. 7.40x (ISBN 0-7199-0953-8, Pub. by Bedford England). Renouf.
Danby, H. & Segal, M. Concise Hebrew-English, English-Hebrew Dictionary. 15.00x o.p. (ISBN 0-686-00848-0). Colton Bk.
Danby, Herbert, tr. Mishnah. 1933. 29.95x (ISBN 0-19-815402-X). Oxford U Pr.
Danby, John F. Shakespeare's Doctrine of Nature: A Study of King Lear. (Orig.). 1961. pap. 5.50 (ISBN 0-686-24621-7, Pub. by Faber & Faber). Merrimack Bk Serv.
Dance in Canada Annual Conference, 7th, Waterloo, Ontario, June 27-July 2, 1979. New Directions in Dance: Proceedings. Taplin, ed. (Pergamon International Series on Dance & the Related Arts). (Illus.). 200p. 1979. 35.00 (ISBN 0-08-024773-3). Pergamon.
Dance, J. B. Cold Cathode Tubes. (Illus.). 1969. 10.00x (ISBN 0-685-20566-5). Transatlantic.
Dance, Stanley. The World of Duke Ellington. (Da Capo Quality Paperbacks Ser.). xii, 311p. pap. 7.95 (ISBN 0-306-80136-1). Da Capo.
--The World of Earl Hines. LC 77-2269. (Illus.). 1977. pap. 5.95 encored. o.p. (ISBN 0-684-16351-9, ScribT, ScribT). Scribner.
Dance, Stanley, jt. auth. see Ellington, Mercer.
Dancey, William S. Archaeology: Field Methods. (Modern Physical Anthropology Ser.). 184p. (Orig.). 1981. pap. text ed. write for info. (ISBN 0-8087-0440-0). Burgess.
Danchik, Kathleen M. & Schoenborn, Charlotte A. Highlights: National Survey of Personal Health Practices & Consequences, United States, 1979. Olmsted, Mary, ed. (Ser. 10: No. 137). 50p. 1981. pap. 1.75 (ISBN 0-8406-0218-9). Natl Ctr Health Stats.
Danco, Leon A. Beyond Survival: A Guide for the Business Owner & His Family. LC 74-29583. (Illus.). Date not set. Repr. of 1975 ed. 19.95 (ISBN 0-9603614-0-5). Univ Pr OH.
--Inside the Family Business. (N A). 1980. 19.95x (ISBN 0-9603614-1-3). Univ Pr OH.
Dandekar, Kumudini & Bhate, Vaijayanti. Prospects of Population Control: Evaluation of Contraception Activity. 1951-1964. 12.00 (ISBN 0-8046-8802-8). Kennikat.
Dandekar, M. M. & Sharma, N. K. Water Power Engineering. 1980. pap. text ed. 12.50x (ISBN 0-7069-0700-0, Pub. by Vikas India). Advent Bk.
Dandelowski, Margarete. Women, Health, & Choice. (Illus.). 288p. 1981. pap. text ed. 11.95 (ISBN 0-13-962183-0). P-H.
Dando, J., jt. ed. see Laverack, M. S.
Dando, S. Japanese Law of Criminal Procedure. George, B. J., Jr., tr. (New York University Comparative Criminal Law Project, Pubns: Vol. 4). 1965. 25.00x (ISBN 0-8377-0500-2). Rothman.
Dandrea, Carmine. Heart's Crow. (Redbird Book). 27p. 1975. 8.00 (ISBN 0-88253-714-8); pap. text ed. 4.80 (ISBN 0-685-53424-3). Ind-US Inc.
D'Andrea, Jeanne, ed. see Los Angeles County Museum of Art Curatorial Staff.
D'Andrea, Jeanne, ed. see Museum Staff.
D'Andrea, Vincent J. Psychoactive Drugs. LC 76-24507. 1977. pap. 6.95 (ISBN 0-8465-1290-4). Benjamin-Cummings.
Danelski, David J. A Supreme Court Justice Is Appointed. LC 80-21229. (Studies in Political Science). x, 242p. 1980. Repr. of 1964 ed. lib. bdg. 23.50x (ISBN 0-313-22652-0, DASJ). Greenwood.
Danelski, David J., ed. see Hughes, Charles E.
Daneman, Meredith. A Chance to Sit Down. 176p. 1981. pap. 2.25 (ISBN 0-380-54163-7, 54163). Avon.
Danenshyar, M. One-Dimensional Compressible Flow. 1977. text ed. 30.00 (ISBN 0-08-020414-7); pap. text ed. 10.75 (ISBN 0-08-020413-9). Pergamon.
Danes, B. Shannon, et al, eds. In Vitro Epithelia & Birth Defects: Proceedings. LC 80-7693. (Birth Defects: Original Article Ser.: Vol. XVI, No. 2). 390p. 1980. 46.00x (ISBN 0-8451-1036-5). A R Liss.
Danes, Gibson A. The Sculpture & Drawing of Charles Umlauf. (Illus.). 128p. Date not set. 25.00 (ISBN 0-292-77561-X). U of Tex Pr.
Danford, John W. Wittgenstein & Political Philosophy: A Reexamination of the Foundations of Social Science. LC 78-6716. xiv, 166p. 1981. pap. 6.95 (ISBN 0-226-13594-2). U of Chicago Pr.
Danforth, Brian, jt. auth. see Sullivan, Donald.
Dang, Nghiem. Viet-Nam: Politics & Public Administration. (Illus.). 1966. 15.00x (ISBN 0-8248-0049-4, Eastwest Ctr). U Pr of Hawaii.
Dangeard, P. Le Vacuome de la Cellule Vegetale: Morphologie. Bd. with Le Vacuome Animal. Hovasse, R. (Illus.). 37p; Contractile Vacuoles of Protozoa; Food Vacuoles: Food Vacuoles. Kitching, J. A. (Protoplasmatologia: Vol. 3, Pt. D1, 2, 3a, 3b). (Illus.). iv, 41p. 1956. pap. 57.90 o.p. (ISBN 0-387-80423-4). Springer-Verlag.
D'Angelo, Dorie. Living with Angels. 1980. pap. 7.50 (ISBN 0-912216-22-0). Angel Pr.
D'Angelo, Edward. The Teaching of Critical Thinking. (Philosophical Currents Ser: No. 1). 78p. 1971. text ed. 17.25x (ISBN 90-6032-482-X). Humanities.
D'Angelo, Gary, jt. auth. see Stewart, John.
D'Angelo, Mary R. Moses in the Letter to the Hebrews. LC 78-12917. (Society of Biblical Literature, Dissertation Ser.: No. 42). 1979. 12.00 (ISBN 0-89130-265-4, 060142); pap. 7.50 (ISBN 0-89130-333-2). Scholars Pr Ca.
Dangerfield, George. Era of Good Feelings. LC 51-14815. 1963. pap. 5.50 (ISBN 0-15-629000-6, H034, Hbgr). HarBraceJ.
Dangerfield, Stanley, jt. ed. see Howell, Elsworth S.
Dangott, Lilliam & Kalish, Richard. A Time to Enjoy: The Pleasures of Aging. (Illus.). 1978. 11.95 (ISBN 0-13-921692-8, Spec); pap. 4.95 (ISBN 0-13-921684-7). P-H.
Danhof, Kenneth & Smith, Carol. Computing System Fundamentals: An Approach Based on Microcomputers. LC 79-14933. 1981. text ed. 21.95 (ISBN 0-201-01298-7). A-W.
Daniel, Ana. Bali: Behind the Mask. LC 79-3481. (Illus.). 224p. 1981. 30.00 (ISBN 0-394-50264-7); pap. 15.00 (ISBN 0-394-73844-6). Knopf.
Daniel, Becky, jt. auth. see Daniel, Charlie.
Daniel, Charlie. Teacher Time Savers. (gr. k-3). 1978. 5.95 (ISBN 0-916456-20-X, GA76). Good Apple.
Daniel, Charlie & Daniel, Becky. Freaky Fractions. (gr. 1-5). 1978. 4.95 (ISBN 0-916456-19-6, GA77). Good Apple.
--Going Bananas Over Language Skills. (gr. 2-6). 1978. 5.95 (ISBN 0-916456-22-6, GA83). Good Apple.
--The Great Paper Airplane Factory. (gr. 2-6). 1978. 3.95 (ISBN 0-916456-21-8, GA84). Good Apple.
--My Very Own Dictionary. (gr. 1-4). 1978. 5.50 (ISBN 0-916456-17-X, GA81). Good Apple.
--Super Spelling Fun. (gr. 2-6). 1978. 5.95 (ISBN 0-916456-31-5, GA82). Good Apple.
--Warm Smiles, Happy Faces. (gr. k-4). 1978. 4.95 (ISBN 0-916456-24-2, GA79). Good Apple.
--Writing About My Feelings. (gr. 1-4). 1978. 5.95 (ISBN 0-916456-18-8, GA80). Good Apple.
Daniel, Clarence. Haunted Derbyshire. (Illus.). 80p. (Orig.). (gr. 6 up). 1975. pap. write for info. (ISBN 0-913714-40-2). Legacy Bks.
Daniel, Cletus E. The ACLU & the Wagner Act: An Inquiry into the Depression-Era Crisis of American Liberalism. LC 80-22450. (Cornell Studies in Industrial & Labor Relations: No. 20). 146p. 1981. 13.50 (ISBN 0-87546-082-8); pap. 7.95 (ISBN 0-87546-083-6). NY Sch Indus Rel.
--Bitter Harvest: A History of California Farmworkers, 1879-1941. LC 80-25664. 368p. 1981. 19.50x (ISBN 0-8014-1284-6). Cornell U Pr.
Daniel, Cuthbert. Applications of Statistics to Industrial Experimentation. LC 76-2012. (Applied Probability & Statistics Ser.). 294p. 1976. 25.95 (ISBN 0-471-19469-7, Pub. by Wiley-Interscience). Wiley.
--Fitting Equations to Data: Computer Analysis of Multifactor Data for Scientists & Engineers. LC 79-130429. (Wiley Series in Probability & Mathematical Statistics). 1980. 21.95 o.p. (ISBN 0-471-05370-8, Pub. by Wiley-Interscience). Wiley.
Daniel, Donald C., ed. International Perceptions of the Superpower Military Balance. LC 78-19456. 1978. 23.95 (ISBN 0-03-046471-4). Praeger.
Daniel, Doris T. Pauline & the Peacock. LC 80-50301. (Illus.). 64p. (Orig.). (ps-8). 1980. pap. 4.95 (ISBN 0-936650-00-1). E C Temple.
Daniel, E. J. Any Other Song: A Plea for Holistic Communication. LC 79-24892. 185p. 1980. pap. text ed. 9.95 (ISBN 0-87619-460-9). R J Brady.
Daniel, Eleanor. Vacation Bible School Ideas. (Ideas Ser.). (Illus.). 1977. pap. text ed. 1.75 (ISBN 0-87239-128-0, 7971). Standard Pub.
Daniel, Elton L. The Political & Social History of Khurasan Under Abbasid Rule 747-820. LC 79-53302. 1979. 28.00x (ISBN 0-88297-025-9). Bibliotheca.
Daniel, Glenda. Dune Country: A Guide for Hikers & Naturalists. LC 77-78782. (Illus.). 167p. 1977. pap. 5.95 (ISBN 0-8040-0757-8). Swallow.
Daniel, Glenda & Sullivan, Jerry. A Sierra Club Naturlist's Guide to the North Woods of Michigan, Wisconsin, & Minnesota. (Naturalist's Guide Ser.). (Illus.). 384p. 1981. 24.95 (ISBN 0-87156-248-0); pap. 9.95 (ISBN 0-87156-277-4). Sierra.
Daniel, Glyn. First Civilizations: The Archaeology of Their Origins. LC 68-26868. (Apollo Eds.). (Illus.). 1970. pap. 4.95 o.s.i. (ISBN 0-8152-0262-8, A262G, TYC-T). T Y Crowell.
Daniel, Glyn, ed. The Illustrated Encyclopedia of Archaology. LC 77-4817. (Illus.). 1977. 17.95 o.s.i. (ISBN 0-690-01473-2, TYC-T). T Y Crowell.
--Towards a History of Archaeology. 192p. 1981. 27.50 (ISBN 0-500-05039-2). Thames Hudson.
Daniel, Hawthorne, jt. auth. see Kyner, James H.
Daniel, Howard, ed. see Callot, Jacques.
Daniel, J., jt. auth. see Cohen, D.
Daniel, James W. & Moore, Ramon E. Computation & Theory in Ordinary Differential Equations. LC 71-117611. (Mathematics Ser.). (Illus.). 1970. text ed. 17.95x (ISBN 0-7167-0440-4). W H Freeman.
Daniel, James W., jt. auth. see Noble, Ben.
Daniel, Joseph C., Jr., ed. Methods in Mammalian Embryology. LC 76-116894. (Animal Science Ser.). (Illus.). 1971. text ed. 39.95x (ISBN 0-7167-0819-1). W H Freeman.
Daniel, Katinka S. Kodaly Approach, Method Book One. 2nd ed. LC 79-53162. 204p. 1979. wire 20.00 (ISBN 0-916656-13-6); materials for transparencies 20.00 (ISBN 0-916656-14-4). Mark Foster Mus.
Daniel, Megan. Amelia. 1980. pap. 1.75 (ISBN 0-451-09487-5, E9487, Sig). NAL.
--The Reluctant Suitor. (Orig.). 1981. pap. 1.95 (ISBN 0-451-09671-1, J9671, Sig). NAL.
Daniel, Norman. Islam, Europe, & Empire. 1967. 35.00x (ISBN 0-85224-108-9, Pub. by Edinburgh U Pr Scotland). Columbia U Pr.
Daniel, P. Africanisation, Nationalisation & Inequality. LC 78-31563. (DAE-Industrial Relations & Labour Ser.). 1979. 35.50 (ISBN 0-521-22719-4); pap. 15.50x (ISBN 0-521-29623-4). Cambridge U Pr.
Daniel, Pete. The Shadow of Slavery: Peonage in the South, 1901-1969. LC 70-174779. (Illus.). 222p. 1973. pap. 3.95x (ISBN 0-19-519742-9, GB396). Oxford U Pr.
Daniel, Peter & Hopkinson, Michael. The Geography of Settlement. (Conceptual Frameworks in Geography Ser.). (Illus.). 289p. 1979. pap. text ed. 10.95 (ISBN 0-05-003128-7). Longman.
Daniel, Ralph T. The Anthem in New England Before Eighteen Hundred. (Music Reprint Ser.). 1979. Repr. of 1966 ed. 27.50 (ISBN 0-306-79511-6). Da Capo.
Daniel, Robert L. American Philanthropy in the Near East, 1820-1960. LC 74-81451. xii, 322p. 1970. 15.00x (ISBN 0-8214-0063-0). Ohio U Pr.
Daniel, Sol, jt. ed. see Gilbert, Leopold.

Daniel, Theodore W., et al. Principles of Silviculture. 2nd ed. (Illus.). 1979. text ed. 22.95x (ISBN 0-07-015297-7). McGraw.

Daniel, Wayne W. Applied Nonparametric Statistics. LC 77-74515. (Illus.). 1978. text ed. 21.50 (ISBN 0-395-25795-6); sol. manual 1.15 (ISBN 0-395-25796-4). HM.

--Biostatistics: A Foundation for Analysis in the Health Sciences. 2nd ed. LC 77-28253. (Probability & Mathematical Statistics Ser.). 1978. text ed. 23.95 (ISBN 0-471-02591-7); tchrs. ed. avail. (ISBN 0-471-03364-2). Wiley.

--Introductory Statistics with Applications. LC 76-10897. (Illus.). 1977. text ed. 17.95 (ISBN 0-395-24430-7); inst. guide with solutions 3.00 (ISBN 0-395-24431-5); study guide 7.75 (ISBN 0-395-24843-4). HM.

Daniel, Wayne W. & Terrell, James C. Business Statistics: Basic Concepts & Methodology. 2nd ed. LC 78-69607. (Illus.). 1979. text ed. 19.50 (ISBN 0-395-26762-5); inst. manual 1.95 (ISBN 0-395-26763-3); study guide 7.95 (ISBN 0-395-26764-1). HM.

Daniela. How to Eat, Exercise & Dress Like a Professional Model. (Illus.). 1980. pap. 12.95 o.p. (ISBN 0-930490-19-3). Future Shop.

Daniele, Joseph. Building Masterpiece Miniatures. (Illus.). 352p. 1981. text ed. 24.95 (ISBN 0-8117-0306-1). Stackpole.

Daniele, Joseph W. Building Colonial Furnishings, Miniatures, & Folk Art. LC 76-17006. (Illus.). 256p. 1976. 15.95 (ISBN 0-8117-0451-3). Stackpole.

--Building Early American Furniture. LC 74-10953. (Illus.). 256p. 1974. 19.95 (ISBN 0-685-49912-X). Stackpole.

--Building Miniature Furniture. (Illus.). 256p. 1981. 24.95 (ISBN 0-8117-1000-9). Stackpole.

--Early American Metal Projects. LC 75-130495. 14.00 (ISBN 0-87345-142-2). McKnight.

Daniell, David. Coriolanus in Europe. 192p. 1981. text ed. 26.00x (ISBN 0-485-11192-6). Humanities.

Daniell, Rosemary. A Sexual Tour of the Deep South. LC 74-15473. 112p. 1975. 6.95 o.p. (ISBN 0-03-013726-8); pap. 3.95 o.p. (ISBN 0-685-93059-9). HR&W.

Danielle, T. The Lawyers. 1976. 17.50 (ISBN 0-379-00593-X). Oceana.

Danielli, J. F., jt. auth. see Bourne, G. H.

Danielli, J. F., jt. ed. see Bourne, G. H.

Danielli, J. F., et al, eds. Recent Progress in Surface & Membrane Science. Incl. Vol. 4. 1971. 53.50 (ISBN 0-12-571804-7); Vol. 5. 1972. 53.50 (ISBN 0-12-571805-5); Vol. 6. 1973. 53.50 (ISBN 0-12-571806-3); Vol. 7. 1973. 153.50 (ISBN 0-12-571807-1); Vol. 8. 1974. 53.50 (ISBN 0-12-571808-X); Vol. 9. 1975. 53.50 (ISBN 0-12-571809-8); lib ed 68.00 (ISBN 0-12-571874-8); microfiche 38.50 (ISBN 0-12-571875-6); Vol. 10. 1976. 53.50 (ISBN 0-12-571810-1); Vol. 11. 1976. 53.50 (ISBN 0-12-571811-X); lib. ed 68.00 (ISBN 0-12-571878-0); microfiche 38.50 (ISBN 0-12-571879-9). Orig. Title: Progress in Surface & Membrane Science. Acad Pr.

Danielli, James, jt. ed. see Bourne, Geoffrey.

Danielli, James F., jt. ed. see Bourne, Geoffrey H.

Danielou, Alain. Hindu Polytheism. (Bollingen Ser.: Vol. 73). 1964. 20.00 o.p. (ISBN 0-691-09745-3). Princeton U Pr.

Daniel-Rops, Henri - Daily Life in the Time of Jesus. O'Brian, Patrick, tr. from Fr. (Illus.). 518p. 1981. pap. 7.95 (ISBN 0-89283-085-9). Servant.

Daniels. Performing for Others. write for info. (ISBN 0-87628-215-X). Ctr Appl Res.

Daniels, Alan & Yeates, Donald, eds. Systems Analysis. (Illus.). 1971. text ed. 14.95 (ISBN 0-574-17885-6, 13-0885); instr's guide avail. (ISBN 0-574-17886-4, 13-0886). SRA.

Daniels, Bennet, jt. auth. see Daniels, Else.

Daniels, Bruce C. The Connecticut Town: Growth & Development, Sixteen Thirty-Five to Seventeen Ninety. LC 79-65331. (Illus.). 1979. 17.50x (ISBN 0-8195-5036-1, Pub. by Wesleyan U Pr). Columbia U Pr.

Daniels, Cora L. & Stevans, C. M., eds. Encyclopedia of Superstitions, Folklore & the Occult Sciences of the World, 3 Vols. LC 70-141151. 1971. Repr. of 1903 ed. 72.00 (ISBN 0-8103-3286-8). Gale.

Daniels, David. Orchestral Music: A Source Book. LC 72-6274. 1972. 10.00 (ISBN 0-8108-0537-5). Scarecrow.

Daniels, David, jt. auth. see Lombardy, William.

Daniels, Dorothy. The Apollo Fountain. 224p. 1976. pap. 1.75 o.s.i. (ISBN 0-446-84800-X). Warner Bks.

--The Beaumont Tradition. 192p. (Orig.). 1976. pap. 1.25 o.s.i. (ISBN 0-446-86254-1). Warner Bks.

--Bell. (Orig.). 1971. pap. 1.75 o.s.i. (ISBN 0-446-84964-2). Warner Bks.

--The Carson Inheritance. 160p. (Orig.). 1975. pap. 0.95 o.s.i. (ISBN 0-446-75562-1). Warner Bks.

--Castle Morvant. 1972. pap. 1.75 o.s.i. (ISBN 0-446-84828-X). Warner Bks.

--Dark Island. 272p. (Orig.). 1972. pap. 1.75 (ISBN 0-446-84801-8). Warner Bks.

--The Dark Stage. 160p. 1970. pap. 0.95 (ISBN 0-446-75553-2). Warner Bks.

--Darkhaven. 160p. 1965. pap. 0.95 (ISBN 0-446-75564-8). Warner Bks.

--House of Silence. (Orig.). 1980. pap. 1.75 (ISBN 0-451-09423-9, E9423, Sig). NAL.

--Monte Carlo. 1981. pap. 2.75 (ISBN 0-8439-0900-5, Leisure Bks). Nordon Pubns.

--Shadows from the Past. (Orig.). 1975. pap. 1.75 o.s.i. (ISBN 0-446-84808-5). Warner Bks.

--Silent Halls of Ashenden. (Orig.). 1973. pap. 1.75 o.s.i. (ISBN 0-446-84659-7). Warner Bks.

--The Sisters of Valcour. 416p. (Orig.). 1981. pap. 2.75 (ISBN 0-446-95484-5). Warner Bks.

--The Watcher in the Dark. (Orig.). 1973. pap. 0.95 o.p. (ISBN 0-685-32391-9, 345-26509-2-095). Ballantine.

Daniels, Douglas H. Images of Our Roots: Photographic, Oral, & Written Documents of the San Francisco Bay Area's Black Pioneers, 1850-1930. (National History Ser.). (Illus.). 1981. 22.50 (ISBN 0-89482-054-0); pap. 12.50 (ISBN 0-89482-055-9). Stevenson Pr.

Daniels, Elam J. Como Ser Feliz En el Matrimonio. Orig. Title: How to Be Happily Married. 96p. 1979. pap. 1.65 (ISBN 0-311-46066-6). Casa Bautista.

Daniels, Elizabeth A. Jessie White Mario: Risorgimento Revolutionary. LC 78-158178. (Illus.). vii, 199p. 1972. 12.95 (ISBN 0-8214-0103-3). Ohio U Pr.

Daniels, Else & Daniels, Bennet. Vacation at Sea: A Travel Guide for Cruises. (Illus.). 1979. 12.95 (ISBN 0-671-18438-5); pap. 5.95 (ISBN 0-346-12423-9). Cornerstone.

Daniels, Farrington. Direct Use of the Sun's Energy. 1974. pap. 2.50 (ISBN 0-345-29226-X). Ballantine.

Daniels, Florence M. Why Art? LC 77-28084. (Illus.). 1978. 14.95 (ISBN 0-88229-173-4); pap. 8.95 (ISBN 0-88229-604-3). Nelson-Hall.

Daniels, Frederick H. Mind Stimulative Correlations in Art Education. (Illus.). 110p. 1981. Repr. of 1909 ed. 37.85 (ISBN 0-89901-024-5). Found Class Reprints.

Daniels, George & Markarian, Ohannes. Watchess & Clocks in the Sir David Salomons Collection. (Illus.). 320p. 1981. 80.00x (ISBN 0-85667-074-X, Pub. by Sotheby Parke Bernet England). Biblio Dist.

Daniels, George, jt. auth. see Clutton, Cecil.

Daniels, George, ed. The Complete Home Carpenter. LC 74-17659. (Illus.). 1978. pap. 9.95 (ISBN 0-672-52067-2). Bobbs.

Daniels, George & Clutton, Cecil, eds. Clocks & Watches: The Collection of the Worshipful Company of Clockmakers. (Illus.). 160p. 1975. 52.50x (ISBN 0-85667-019-7, Pub. by Sotheby Park Bernet England). Biblio Dist.

Daniels, George H. American Science in the Age of Jackson. LC 67-28710. 1968. 20.00x (ISBN 0-231-03073-8). Columbia U Pr.

Daniels, Guy, tr. from Rus. Peasants Pea Patch. LC 70-132355. (Illus.). (gr. k-2). 1971. PLB 5.47 o.s.i. (ISBN 0-440-06826-6). Delacorte.

Daniels, Guy, tr. see Bunin, Ivan.

Daniels, Guy, tr. see Casals, Felipe G.

Daniels, Guy, tr. see Turchin, Valentin.

Daniels, Guy Trans. by see Carrera, Liane.

Daniels, Harold R. Press Brake & Shear Handbook. rev. ed. LC 74-13643. 184p. 1974. 17.95 (ISBN 0-8436-0815-3). CBI Pub.

Daniels, Harold R., ed. Mechanical Press Handbook. 3rd ed. LC 71-79187. (Illus.). 1969. 27.50 (ISBN 0-89047-036-7). Herman Pub.

Daniels, Jack, et al. Conditioning for Distance Running: The Scientific Aspects. LC 77-22538. (American College of Sports Medicine Ser.). 1978. text ed. 13.95 (ISBN 0-471-19483-2). Wiley.

Daniels, Jerry C., jt. ed. see Ritzmann, Stephan E.

Daniels, John S. War Party. Bd. with The Crossing. 1979. pap. 1.95 (ISBN 0-451-08761-5, J8761, Sig). Norton.

Daniels, Jonathan. Devil's Backbone: The Story of the Natchez Trace. (American Trails Library Ser). (Illus.). 1962. 9.95 o.p. (ISBN 0-07-015302-7, GB). McGraw.

--The End of Innocence. LC 73-37285. (FDR & the Era of the New Deal Ser.). 351p. 1972. Repr. of 1954 ed. 35.00 (ISBN 0-306-70423-4). Da Capo.

--Frontier on the Potomac. LC 70-37284. (FDR & the Era of the New Deal Ser). 262p. 1972. Repr. of 1946 ed. lib. bdg. 35.00 (ISBN 0-306-70425-0). Da Capo.

--A Southerner Discovers the South. LC 68-16228. (The American Scene Ser.). 1970. Repr. of 1938 ed. lib. bdg. 35.00 (ISBN 0-306-71011-0). Da Capo.

--The Time Between the Wars: Armistice to Pearl Harbor. Freidel, Frank, ed. LC 78-66523. (The History of the United States Ser.: Vol. 5). 382p. 1979. lib. bdg. 24.00 (ISBN 0-8240-9707-6). Garland Pub.

Daniels, Keith W., compiled by. Recycling & Repairing, Nineteen Twelve to Nineteen Forty Eight. (Illus.). 290p. (Orig.). 1978. pap. 7.95 (ISBN 0-937468-00-2). Lost Data.

Daniels, Les. The Black Castle. 1979. pap. 2.25 o.p. (ISBN 0-425-04198-0). Berkley Pub.

--Citizen Vampire. 228p. 1980. cancelled (ISBN 0-684-16827-8, ScribT). Scribner.

--Citizen Vampire. 204p. 1981. 9.95 (ISBN 0-684-16827-8, ScribT). Scribner.

Daniels, Linda M., jt. auth. see Kochar, Mahendra S.

Daniels, Lloyd K., ed. Vocational Rehabilitation of the Mentally Retarded: A Book of Readings. (Illus.). 648p. 1974. text ed. 37.75 (ISBN 0-398-02582-7). C C Thomas.

Daniels, Lucille & Worthingham, Catherine. Muscle Testing: Techniques of Manual Examination. 4th ed. LC 79-67302. (Illus.). 191p. 1980. 11.95 (ISBN 0-7216-2877-X). Saunders.

Daniels, M. E. Fireplaces & Wood Stoves. LC 76-26948. (Illus.). 1977. 13.95 (ISBN 0-672-52175-X). Bobbs.

--Fireplaces & Wood Stoves. LC 76-26948. (Illus.). 1978. pap. 7.95 (ISBN 0-672-52402-3). Bobbs.

--How to Remodel & Enlarge Your Home. LC 77-15443. 1978. pap. 8.95 (ISBN 0-672-52585-2). Bobbs.

Daniels, Marilyn. The Dance in Christianity. (Illus.). 112p. (Orig.). 1981. pap. 4.95 (ISBN 0-8091-2381-9). Paulist Pr.

Daniels, Mary. Cat Astrology. 96p. 1976. 5.95 o.p. (ISBN 0-688-03024-6). Morrow.

Daniels, Michael. Split in Two. 8.00 (ISBN 0-89253-680-2). Ind-US Inc.

--That Damn Romantic Fool. 14.00 (ISBN 0-89253-624-1); flexible cloth 6.75 (ISBN 0-89253-625-X). Ind-US Inc.

Daniels, Michael C. Anything Out of Place Is Dirt. (Writers Workshop Ser.). 106p. 1975. 9.00 (ISBN 0-88253-498-X); pap. text ed. 4.80 (ISBN 0-88253-497-1). Ind-US Inc.

Daniels, Norman. Wyndward Passion. (Orig.). 1978. pap. 2.25 o.s.i. (ISBN 0-446-82669-3). Warner Bks.

Daniels, P. W. Office Location & the Journey to Work: A Comparative Study of Five Urban Centers. 175p. 1980. text ed. 30.00x (ISBN 0-566-00352-X, Pub. by Gower Pub Co England). Renouf.

Daniels, Pamela, jt. ed. see Ruddick, Sara.

Daniels, Patricia. Snow White & the Dwarfs. LC 79-28431. (Raintree Fairy Tales Ser.). (Illus.). 24p. (gr. k-3). 1980. lib. bdg. 8.65 (ISBN 0-8393-0251-7). Raintree Child.

Daniels, Patricia, ed. Let's Discover Series, 16 vols. Incl. Vol. 1. Warm-blooded Animlas. LC 80-22951; Vol. 2. Prehistoric World. LC 80-22949; Vol. 3. People & Customs. LC 80-22960; Vol. 4. Cold-blooded Animals. LC 80-24150; Vol. 5. The Earth. LC 80-22952; Vol. 6. The Sea. LC 80-22953; Vol. 7. People of Long Ago. LC 80-22955; Vol. 8. What People Do. LC 80-22965; Vol. 9. You & Your Body. LC 80-22970; Vol. 10. Sport & Entertainment. LC 80-22975; Vol. 11. The World of Machines. LC 80-22980; Vol. 12. Land Travel. LC 80-22954; Vol. 13. Ships & Boats. LC 80-22959; Vol. 14. Flying. LC 80-22964; Vol. 15. Outer Space. LC 80-22974; Vol. 16. Index. LC 80-22978. (Illus.). (gr. k-3). 1981. Set, 80 Pages Ea. PLB 239.79 (ISBN 0-8172-1782-7). Raintree Pubs.

Daniels, Roger. The Politics of Prejudice: The Anti-Japanese Movement in California & the Struggle for Japanese Exclusion. (California Library Reprint Ser). 1978. 16.00x (ISBN 0-520-03412-0); pap. 3.45 (ISBN 0-520-03411-2). U of Cal Pr.

Daniels, Roger & Kitano, Harry H. American Racism: Exploration of the Nature of Prejudice. 1969. pap. text ed. 7.95 (ISBN 0-13-028993-0). P-H.

Daniels, Shouri. Salt Doll: A Novel on India. 1977. 6.50x o.p. (ISBN 0-8364-0055-0). South Asia Bks.

Daniels, Stuart R. Inelastic Steel Structures. LC 65-25460. (Illus.). 1966. 12.50x (ISBN 0-87049-064-8). U of Tenn Pr.

Daniels, Velma S. Patches of Joy. 1979. 5.95 (ISBN 0-88289-101-4); pap. 3.95 (ISBN 0-88289-101-4). Pelican.

Daniels, Victor & Horowitz, Laurence J. Being & Caring: A Journey to Self. 1976. pap. text ed. 9.95 (ISBN 0-87484-374-X). Mayfield Pub.

Daniels, Winthrop M. Essays. 1943. 17.50x (ISBN 0-685-89750-8). Elliots Bks.

--Recollections of Woodrow Wilson. 1944. 17.50x (ISBN 0-685-89776-1). Elliots Bks.

Danielsen, John. Winter Hiking & Camping. 2nd ed. (Illus.). 1977. 6.95 (ISBN 0-935272-04-6). ADK Mtn Club.

Danielson. Radio Systems for Technicians, No. 2. 1981. text ed. price not set (ISBN 0-408-00561-0). Butterworth.

--Transmission Systems for Technicians, No. 2. 1981. text ed. price not set (ISBN 0-408-00562-9). Butterworth.

Danielson, Dorothy, et al. Reading in English: For Students of ESL. 2nd ed. (Illus.). 1980. pap. text ed. 8.50 (ISBN 0-13-753442-6). P-H.

Danielson, Eva, jt. auth. see Jonsson, Bengt R.

Danielson, Henry. Arthur Machen: A Bibliography. LC 79-149784. 1971. Repr. of 1923 ed. 15.00 (ISBN 0-8103-3682-0). Gale.

Danielson, Michael N. Federal-Metropolitan Politics & the Commuter Crisis. LC 65-16197. (Illus.). 1965. 16.00x (ISBN 0-231-02782-6). Columbia U Pr.

--Politics of Exclusion. LC 76-7609. 384p. 1976. 22.50x (ISBN 0-231-03697-3); pap. 9.00x (ISBN 0-231-08342-4). Columbia U Pr.

Danielson, Michael N., et al. One Nation, So Many Governments: A Ford Foundation Report. LC 76-53868. 1977. 16.95 (ISBN 0-669-01293-9). Lexington Bks.

Danielson, Peter. Children of the Lion. 480p. (Orig.). 1980. pap. 2.95 (ISBN 0-553-14249-6). Bantam.

--The Shepherd Kings. 448p. (Orig.). 1981. pap. 2.95 (ISBN 0-553-14653-X). Bantam.

Danielsson, Bror. Engelsk-Svensk Ordbok (Prisma Modern) 5th ed. 396p. 1979. text ed. 15.00x o.p. (ISBN 91-518-0550-2, SW205); Svensk-engelsk, 3rd Ed. text ed. 17.50x o.p. (ISBN 9-1518-0942-7, SW-204). Vanous.

Daniken, Erich. Unsolved Mysteries of the Past. 189p. 1981. 28.50 (ISBN 0-686-68311-0). Porter.

Daniken, Erich Von see Von Daniken, Erich.

Daniker, Relmond Van see McCullers, Levis D. & Van Daniker, Relmond P.

Danilevskii, J. A. Lappo see Lappo-Danilevskii, J. A.

Daniloff, R. Physiology of Speech & Hearing: An Introduction. 1980. 20.95 (ISBN 0-13-674747-7). P-H.

Daninos, Pierre. Carnets Du Major W. Marmaduke Thompson. (Illus.). 1963. pap. text ed. 5.95x (ISBN 0-521-04767-6). Cambridge U Pr.

Danish, Barbara. Writing As a Second Language. 1981. worktext 6.00 (ISBN 0-915924-10-2). Tchrs & Writers Coll.

Danish Handcraft Guild. Book of Danish Stiitchery. 136p. 1980. pap. 9.95 (ISBN 0-442-20179-6). Van Nos Reinhold.

--Counted Cross-Stitch Designs for Christmas. (Illus.). 1978. pap. 8.95 (ISBN 0-684-15975-9, SL821, ScribT). Scribner.

Danish, Steve, et al. Helping Skills: A Basic Training Program. 2nd ed. 226p. 1980. wkbk softcover 8.95x (ISBN 0-87705-484-3); lab manual softcover 4.95x (ISBN 0-87705-483-5); Set. 10.95x (ISBN 0-87705-474-6). Human Sci Pr.

Dank, Leonard, jt. auth. see Tovell, Harold.

Dank, Milton. The Dangerous Game. (YA) (gr. 7-12). 1980. pap. 1.50 (ISBN 0-440-91765-4, LFL). Dell.

--The Dangerous Game. LC 77-23453. (gr. 5-9). 1977. 8.95 (ISBN 0-397-31753-0). Lippincott.

--The French Against the French. LC 74-10735. 1974. 12.50 o.s.i. (ISBN 0-397-01040-0). Lippincott.

--Game's End. LC 78-12625. 1979. 8.95 (ISBN 0-397-31821-9). Lippincott.

Danker, F. W., tr. see Gingrich, F. Wilbur.

Danker, Frederick W. Invitation to the New Testament Epistles IV: A Commentary on Hebrews, James, 1 & 2 Peter, 1, 2 & 3 John & Jude, with Complete Text from the Jerusalem Bible. LC 79-6743. 256p. (Orig.). 1980. pap. 3.95 (ISBN 0-385-14799-6, Im). Doubleday.

--Jesus & the New Age According to Saint Luke. LC 72-83650. 255p. 1980. pap. 12.00 (ISBN 0-915644-21-5). Clayton Pub Hse.

--Jesus & the New Age: According to St. Luke, A Commentary on the Third Gospel. 3rd rev. ed. LC 72-83650. xxiv, 256p. 1974. pap. text ed. 9.00 o.p. (ISBN 0-915644-03-7). Clayton Pub Hse.

--Luke. Krodel, Gerhard, ed. LC 76-5954. (Proclamation Commentaries: the New Testament Witnesses for Preaching). 128p. 1976. pap. 2.95 (ISBN 0-8006-0583-7, 1-583). Fortress.

Danker, Frederick W., jt. auth. see Gingrich, Wilbur F.

Danks, J. H., jt. auth. see Glucksberg, S.

Danks, Susan M., jt. auth. see Whittaker, P. A.

Danky, James P., jt. auth. see Hady, Maureen E.

Danky, James P., jt. auth. see Strache, Neil E.

Danky, James P., ed. Alternative Acquisitions Handbook. 250p. 1981. pap. text ed. 15.95 (ISBN 0-918212-44-8). Neal-Schuman.

Danky, James P., et al. Women's History: Resources at the State Historical Society of Wisconsin. 4th, rev., enl. ed. LC 79-17522. 1981. pap. 3.00 (ISBN 0-87020-189-1). State Hist Soc Wis.

Danley, Jerry J. Useful Science. (Illus.). 1977. pap. 2.25x (ISBN 0-88323-127-1, 216); tchr's key free (ISBN 0-88323-132-8, 222). Richards Pub.

Danley, William, Jr., jt. auth. see Willis, Jerry.

Danloux-Dumesnils, M. The Metric System: A Critical Study of Its Principles & Practice. 1969. pap. text ed. 4.50x (ISBN 0-485-12013-5, Athlone Pr). Humanities.
Danmole, Mashood B. The Heritage of Imperialism: A Study in Historical & Economic Analysis. c, 600p. 1974. 25.00x (ISBN 0-210-40547-3). Asia.
Dann, Florence. Write to Read, Level C. (MCP Writing Skillbooster Ser.). (gr. 3). 1978. pap. text ed. 2.40 (ISBN 0-87895-340-X). Modern Curr.
--Write to Read, Level D. (MCP Writing Skillbooster Ser.). 1978. pap. text ed. 2.40 (ISBN 0-87895-410-4). Modern Curr.
--Write to Read, Level E. (MCP Writing Skillbooster Ser.). (gr. 5). 1978. pap. text ed. 2.40 (ISBN 0-87895-510-0). Modern Curr.
--Write to Read, Level F. (MCP Writing Skillbooster Ser.). (gr. 6). 1978. pap. text ed. 2.40 (ISBN 0-87895-610-7). Modern Curr.
Dann, Jack. Junction. (Orig.). 1981. pap. 2.50 (ISBN 0-440-14416-7). Dell.
Dann, Jack, ed. Wandering Stars: Anthology of Jewish Fantasy & Science Fiction. LC 73-4146. 252p. 1974. 8.95 o.s.i. (ISBN 0-06-010944-0, HarpT). Har-Row.
Danna, Mark, jt. auth. see Poynter, Dan.
Dannebring, David D. & Starr, Martin K. Management Science: An Introduction. (Quantitative Methods in Management Ser.). 1981. text ed. 22.00 (ISBN 0-07-015352-3, C); write for info study guide (ISBN 0-07-015353-1); write for info instrs.' manual (ISBN 0-07-015354-X). McGraw.
Dannen, Donna & Dannen, Kent. Walks with Nature in Rocky Mountain National Park. LC 80-26665. (Illus.). 64p. 1981. pap. 3.95 (ISBN 0-914788-38-8). East Woods.
Dannen, Donna, jt. auth. see Dannen, Kent.
Dannen, Kent & Dannen, Donna. Rocky Mountain National Park Hiking Trails-Including Indian Peaks. LC 77-25701. (Illus.). 288p. 1978. lib. bdg. 10.25 o.p. (ISBN 0-914788-06-X). East Woods.
Dannen, Kent, jt. auth. see Dannen, Donna.
Dannenberg, William P., et al. Introduction to Wholesale Distribution. (Illus.). 1978. 18.50 (ISBN 0-13-500777-1); stud. ed. 16.95 (ISBN 0-685-85447-7). P-H.
Danner, Douglas. Pattern Deposition Checklists. LC 73-84916. 1973. 47.50 (ISBN 0-686-14525-9, 648A). Lawyers Co-Op.
--Pattern Interrogatories: 1970-73, 5 vols. LC 75-102027. 1970. 236.00 (ISBN 0-686-14526-7). Lawyers Co-Op.
Danner, Horace C. Words from the Romance Languages. LC 80-82095. (Clavis Ser.). (Illus.). 232p. 1980. pap. 7.00 (ISBN 0-937600-00-8). Imprimis.
Danner, Peter L. An Ethics for the Affluent. LC 80-5528. 424p. 1980. lib. bdg. 22.50 (ISBN 0-8191-1163-5); pap. text ed. 14.25 (ISBN 0-8191-1164-3). U Pr of Amer.
Dannett, Sylvia G. & McCabe, Maureen. The Low Blood Sugar Gourmet Cookbook. 176p. 1975. pap. 3.50 (ISBN 0-06-463428-0, EH 428, EH). Har-Row.
D'Annunzio, Gabriele. The Triumph of Death. Harding, G., tr. 315p. 1975. Repr. of 1898 ed. 18.00 (ISBN 0-86527-318-9). Fertig.
Danois, Vivian De see De Danois, Vivian.
Danos, Paul, jt. auth. see Arnett, Harold.
Dansereau, P. Biogeography: An Ecological Perspective. (Illus.). 1957. 22.50 (ISBN 0-8260-2330-4, Pub. by Wiley-Interscience). Wiley.
Dansereau, Pierre. Inscape & Landscape. 132p. 1975. 15.00x (ISBN 0-231-03991-3); pap. 5.00x (ISBN 0-231-03992-1). Columbia U Pr.
Danskin, David G. & Crow, Mark A. Biofeedback: An Introduction & Guide. 150p. (Orig.). 1981. pap. text ed. price not set (ISBN 0-87484-530-0). Mayfield Pub.
Dante. On World Government (De Monarchia) Schneider, H. W., tr. LC 57-1099. 1957. pap. 3.50 (ISBN 0-672-60176-1, LLA 15). Bobbs.
Dante Alighieri. The Ardent Love Poetry by Dante Alighieri. Norton, Elliott, tr. (The Most Meaningful Classics in World Culture Ser.). (Illus.). 117p. 1981. 59.45. Am Classical Coll Pr.
--Dante's Vita Nuova: A Translation & an Essay. new ed. Musa, Mark, tr. from It. LC 72-79905. (Midland Bks.: No. 162). 224p. 1973. 8.50x (ISBN 0-253-31620-0); pap. 4.50x (ISBN 0-253-20162-4). Ind U Pr.
--Divine Comedy. Fletcher, J. B., tr. 1951. 27.50x (ISBN 0-231-01806-1, A51-9849). Columbia U Pr.
--The Divine Comedy. rev. ed. Bickersteth, Geoffrey, tr. from It. 805p. 1972. 22.50x (ISBN 0-87471-295-5). Rowman.
--Literary Criticism of Dante Alighieri. Haller, Robert S., ed. & tr. LC 72-85402. (Regents Critics Ser). xlix, 190p. 1974. 11.00x (ISBN 0-8032-0467-1); pap. 2.75x (ISBN 0-8032-5469-5, BB 417, Bison). U of Nebr Pr.
Dante Aligieri. The Divine Comedy: The Inferno, Vol. 1. Singleton, Charles S., tr. from Italian. LC 68-57090. (Bollingen Ser: Lxxx). (Illus.). 1088p. (Bilingual ed.). 1980. pap. 12.50 (ISBN 0-691-01832-4). Princeton U Pr.
Danto, A. Nietzche As Philosopher. 1965. 9.95 (ISBN 0-02-529490-3); pap. 2.45 (ISBN 0-02-084570-7). Macmillan.
Danto, Arthur. Nietzsche As Philosopher. 250p. 1980. pap. 6.95x (ISBN 0-231-05053-4). Columbia U Pr.
Danto, Arthur C. The Transfiguration of the Commonplace: A Philosophy of Art. 1981. text ed. 17.50x (ISBN 0-674-90345-5). Harvard U Pr.
Danto, Bruce, et al, eds. Homicide & Survivors. (Thanatology Service Ser.). 225p. 1980. pap. 9.95 o.p. (ISBN 0-686-64831-5). Highly Specialized.
Danton, G. L. The Theory & Practice of Seamanship. (Illus., Metric ed). 1972. 45.00 (ISBN 0-7100-7487-5). Routledge & Kegan.
Danton, Graham. Theory & Practice of Seamanship. 8th, rev. ed. 1980. 45.00 (ISBN 0-7100-0502-4). Routledge & Kegan.
Danton, Rebecca. Amethyst Love. (Regency Romance Ser.). 1977. pap. 1.50 o.p. (ISBN 0-449-23400-2, Crest). Fawcett.
Dantzig, Tobias. Number: The Language of Science. 4th ed. (Illus.). 1967. pap. text ed. 8.95 (ISBN 0-02-906990-4). Free Pr.
Danz, Ernst & Manges, Axel. Modern Fireplaces. Date not set. 29.95 (ISBN 0-8038-0165-3). Hastings.
Danzig, Alan & Schor, Edith. Thesis: Rhetoric of the Essay. 2nd ed. 352p. 1979. pap. text ed. 7.95x (ISBN 0-534-00726-0). Wadsworth Pub.
Danziger, Jeff. The Champlain Monster. (Illus.). 64p. 1981. pap. 3.95 (ISBN 0-9603900-7-3). Lanser Pr.
--The Vermont Woodfired Automobile. 80p. 1980. pap. 3.95 (ISBN 0-9603900-2-2). Lanser Pr.
Danziger, Jeff & Davis, Tom. Unofficial Hunting Rules. (Illus.). 64p. (Orig.). 1980. pap. 3.95 (ISBN 0-9603900-5-7). Lanser Pr.
Danziger, Kurt. Interpersonal Communication. 250p. 1976. text ed. 23.00 (ISBN 0-08-018757-9); pap. text ed. 14.00 (ISBN 0-08-018756-0). Pergamon.
--Readings in Child Socialization. 1970. 21.00 (ISBN 0-08-006882-0); pap. 9.75 (ISBN 0-08-006881-2). Pergamon.
Danziger, Marlies K. & Johnson, Wendell S., eds. Poetry Anthology. (Orig.). 1967. pap. text ed. 8.95 (ISBN 0-394-30187-0). Random.
Danziger, Paula. Can You Sue Your Parents for Malpractice? LC 78-72856. 1979. 7.95 (ISBN 0-440-01050-0). Delacorte.
--The Cat Ate My Gymsuit. LC 74-5501. 160p. (gr. 5-9). 1974. 7.95 (ISBN 0-440-01612-6); PLB 6.46 (ISBN 0-440-01696-7). Delacorte.
--The Cat Ate My Gymsuit. (gr. k-6). 1980. pap. 1.50 (ISBN 0-440-41612-4, YB). Dell.
--The Pistachio Prescription. LC 77-86330. (gr. 7 up). 1978. 7.95 (ISBN 0-440-06936-X). Delacorte.
--There's a Bat in Bunk Five. LC 80-64833. 160p. (gr. 5-8). 1980. 7.95 (ISBN 0-440-08605-1); PLB 7.45 (ISBN 0-440-08606-X). Delacorte.
Danziger, Raphael. Abd al-Qadir & the Algerians: Resistance to the French & Internal Consolidation. LC 76-18061. 1977. text ed. 34.50x (ISBN 0-8419-0236-4, Africana). Holmes & Meier.
Danzin, A. Science & the Second Renaissance of Europe. 1978. pap. text ed. 25.00 (ISBN 0-08-022442-3). Pergamon.
Daoust, Yvette. Roger Planchon: Director & Playwright. (Illus.). 200p. Date not set. 44.95 (ISBN 0-521-23414-X). Cambridge U Pr.
Daphne & Nelson, eds. Beauty Unknown Color Lithographs. (New Age Ser.: No. 502). 1976. 12.00 (ISBN 0-89007-502-6). C Stark.
Dapkus, F. Statistics 1: A Text for Beginners. 1979. pap. text ed. 13.95 (ISBN 0-89669-042-3). Collegium Bk Pubs.
Dappagne, A. Trois Aspects du francais contemporain. (Langue vivante). (Fr). pap. 8.25 (ISBN 0-685-14087-3, 3629). Larousse.
Dapunt, Otto, jt. auth. see Wittliff, James L.
D'Aquili, Eugene G., jt. auth. see Laughlin, Charles D.
D'Aquili, Eugene G., et al. The Spectrum of Ritual. 1979. 25.00x (ISBN 0-231-04514-X). Columbia U Pr.
Darabant, E., tr. see Remenyi, Karoly.
Darack, Arthur. Playboy's Book of Sports Car Repair. LC 79-90917. (Playboy's Lifestyles Library). (Illus.). 224p. 1980. 14.95 (ISBN 0-87223-602-1, Dist by Har-Row). Playboy.
Darack, Arthur, et al. The Great Eating, Great Dieting Cookbook. LC 77-4246. 1978. 14.95 o.s.i. (ISBN 0-690-01684-0, TYC-T). T Y Crowell.
Darahan, Iurii. Sahaidak: Virshi, 1922-1924. LC 75-546612. (Ukrai.). 1965. pap. 2.75 (ISBN 0-918884-16-0). Slavia Lib.
Darbee, Harry & Francis, Mac. Catskill Flytier: My Life, Times, & Techniques. LC 77-22503. (Illus.). 1977. 8.95 o.p. (ISBN 0-397-01214-4). Lippincott.
Darbelnet, John. Pensee & Structure. 2nd ed. LC 68-19906. (Fr). 1977. text ed. 9.95x (ISBN 0-684-14882-X, ScribC); wkbk. 6.95x (ISBN 0-684-15932-5, ScribC); wkbk. 5.95 (ISBN 0-684-15091-3, ScribC). Scribner.
Darbishire, Helen, ed. see Milton, John.
Darboux, Gaston. Theorie Generale Des Surfaces, 4 Vols. 2nd ed. LC 67-16997. (Fr). 1968. Set. 75.00 (ISBN 0-8284-0216-7). Chelsea Pub.
Darby, Catharine. The King's Falcon. (Falcon Ser.: No. 2). 1975. pap. 1.25 o.p. (ISBN 0-445-00321-9). Popular Lib.
Darby, Catherine. Cobweb Across the Moon. (The Moon Chalice Quest: No. 5). 1978. pap. 1.50 o.p. (ISBN 0-445-04143-9). Popular Lib.
--A Falcon for a Witch. (Falcon Ser.: No. 1). 1975. pap. 1.25 o.p. (ISBN 0-445-00313-8). Popular Lib.
--Falcon Rising. (Falcon Ser.: No. 8). 1976. pap. 1.25 o.p. (ISBN 0-445-00405-3). Popular Lib.
--Falcon to the Lure. (Falcon Ser: No. 12). 1978. pap. 1.75 o.p. (ISBN 0-445-04322-9). Popular Lib.
--Fortune for a Falcon. (Falcon Ser: No. 3). 256p. (Orig.). 1975. pap. 1.25 o.p. (ISBN 0-445-00329-4). Popular Lib.
--Frost on the Moon. (Moon Chalice Quest Ser.: No. 2). 1977. pap. 1.50 o.p. (ISBN 0-445-04010-6). Popular Lib.
Darby, H. C., jt. auth. see Fullard, Harold.
Darby, H. C., ed. Domesday England. LC 76-11485. (The Domesday Geography of England Ser.). (Illus.). 1977. 77.50 (ISBN 0-521-21307-X). Cambridge U Pr.
--A New Historical Geography of England After 1600. LC 76-26029. 1978. 59.50 (ISBN 0-521-22123-4); pap. 19.50 (ISBN 0-521-29145-3). Cambridge U Pr.
--A New Historical Geography of England Before 1600. LC 76-26141. 1978. 49.50 (ISBN 0-521-22122-6); pap. 17.50 (ISBN 0-521-29144-5). Cambridge U Pr.
Darby, John J. & Hecker, Michael, eds. Speech Evaluation in Psychiatry. 1980. 34.00 (ISBN 0-8089-1315-8). Grune.
Darby, Joseph J., tr. from Ger. Alternative Draft of a Penal Code for the Federal Republic of Germany. LC 76-43177. (American Ser. of Foreign Penal Codes: Vol. 21). 157p. 1977. text ed. 17.50x (ISBN 0-8377-0041-8). Rothman.
Darby, Joseph R., jt. auth. see Sears, J. Kern.
Darby, Michael R. Effects of Social Security on Income & the Capital Stock. 1979. pap. 4.25 (ISBN 0-8447-3329-6). Am Enterprise.
Darby, Michele L. & Bowen, Denise M. Research Methods for Oral Health Professionals: An Introduction. LC 79-18208. 1979. pap. text ed. 13.95 (ISBN 0-8016-1207-1). Mosby.
Darby, Paul H., jt. auth. see Bauer, Royal D.
Darby, W. J., et al, eds. Annual Review of Nutrition, Vol. 1. (Illus.). 1981. text ed. 20.00 (ISBN 0-8243-2801-9). Annual Reviews.
Darby, William O. & Baumer, William H. We Led the Way: Darby's Rangers. LC 80-10431. (Illus.). 1980. 14.95 (ISBN 0-89141-082-1). Presidio Pr.
D'Arcangelo, et al. Mathematics for Plumbers & Pipefitters. LC 73-2166. 199p. 1973. 6.80 (ISBN 0-8273-0291-6); instr's manual 1.60 (ISBN 0-8273-0292-4). Delmar.
D'Arcangelo, B. F., et al. Mathematics for Plumbers & Pipefitters. 3rd rev. ed. (Applied Mathematics Ser.). (Illus.). 210p. 1981. pap. text ed. price not set (ISBN 0-8273-1291-1); price not set instr's guide. Delmar.
D'Arcangelo, Bartholomew, et al. Blueprint Reading for Plumbers: Residential & Commercial. rev. ed. LC 78-24844. (Blueprint Reading Ser.). (gr. 7). 1980. pap. text ed. 9.68 (ISBN 0-8273-1367-5); instr's guide 1.60 (ISBN 0-8273-1368-3). Delmar.
Darcy, Clare. Allegra. LC 74-82400. 1975. 7.95 o.s.i. (ISBN 0-8027-0475-1). Walker & Co.
--Eugenia. 1977. 8.95 o.s.i. (ISBN 0-8027-0556-1). Walker & Co.
--Lady Pamela. LC 75-12192. 1975. 8.95 o.s.i. (ISBN 0-8027-0504-9). Walker & Co.
--Letty. 1981. pap. price not set (ISBN 0-451-09810-2, Signet Bks). NAL.
--Letty. (Large Print Bks.). 1980. lib. bdg. 12.95 (ISBN 0-8161-3127-9). G K Hall.
D'Arcy, Ella. Monochromes. Fletcher, Ian & Stokes, John, eds. LC 76-20056. (Decadent Consciousness Ser.). 1978. lib. bdg. 38.00 (ISBN 0-8240-2754-X). Garland Pub.
D'Arcy, P. F. Latrogenic Diseases. 2nd ed. (Illus.). 1980. text ed. 67.50x (ISBN 0-19-264179-4). Oxford U Pr.
D'Arcy, Pamela. Angel in the House. (Orig.). 1980. pap. 1.75 (ISBN 0-515-05199-3). Jove Pubns.
--Heritage of the Heart. 176p. (Orig.). 1980. pap. 1.75 (ISBN 0-515-05201-9). Jove Pubns.
--The Hired Heart. 1978. pap. 1.75 o.p. (ISBN 0-425-03768-1, Medallion). Berkley Pub.
--Magic Moment. 192p. (Orig.). 1980. pap. 1.75 (ISBN 0-515-05200-0). Jove Pubns.
D'Arcy, Paula. Song for Sarah. 128p. 1981. pap. 2.50 (ISBN 0-553-14728-5). Bantam.
D'Arcy, Susan. The Films of Elizabeth Taylor. Castell, David, ed. (The Films of...Ser.). (Illus.). (gr. 7-12). 1978. Repr. of 1974 ed. PLB 5.95 (ISBN 0-912616-83-0). Greenhaven.
--The Films of Liza Minelli. Castell, David, ed. (The Films of...Ser.). (Illus.). (gr. 7-12). 1978. Repr. of 1973 ed. PLB 5.95 (ISBN 0-912616-82-2). Greenhaven.
Darden, Ellington. The Athlete's Guide to Sports Medicine. (Illus.). 1981. 14.95 (ISBN 0-8092-7160-5); pap. 6.95 (ISBN 0-8092-7159-1). Contemp Bks.
--How Your Muscles Work: Featuring Nautilus Training Equipment. Darden, Ellington, ed. LC 77-75757. (Physical Fitness & Sports Medicine Ser.). (Illus.). 1977. pap. 3.95 (ISBN 0-89305-010-5). Anna Pub.
--Nutrition for Athletics. LC 76-10811. 1975. pap. 5.95 (ISBN 0-87095-058-4). Athletic.
--Power Racquetball Featuring PST. LC 80-84215. (Illus.). 128p. (Orig.). 1981. pap. text ed. 4.95 (ISBN 0-918438-65-9). Leisure Pr.
Darden, Joe T., ed. The Ghetto: Readings with Interpretations. (National University Publications, Interdisciplinary Urban Ser.). 1981. 19.50 (ISBN 0-8046-9277-7); pap. 9.95 (ISBN 0-8046-9279-3). Kennikat.
Dardess, John. Conquerors & Confucians: Aspects of Political Change in Late Yuan China. (Studies in Oriental Culture Ser.). 240p. 1973. 20.00x (ISBN 0-231-03689-2). Columbia U Pr.
Dardess, Margaret B., tr. see Chomin, Nakae.
Dardig, Jill C. & Heward, William L. Sign Here: A Contracting Book for Children & Their Parents. 2nd ed. LC 76-18757. (Illus.). 166p. 1981. pap. 10.00 (ISBN 0-917472-04-7); leader's manual 3.00 (ISBN 0-914474-27-8). F Fournies.
Dardis, Tom. Keaton: The Man Who Wouldn't Lie Down. 1980. pap. 4.95 (ISBN 0-14-005701-3). Penguin.
--Some Time in the Sun. 1981. pap. 4.95 (ISBN 0-14-005831-1). Penguin.
Dare, Dan. Rogue Planet. (Illus.). 112p. 1980. pap. 9.95 (ISBN 0-8256-9553-8, Quick Fox). Music Sales.
Dareff, Hal. Fun with ABC & 1-2-3. LC 65-18659. (Illus.). (ps-2). 1965. 5.95 o.s.i. (ISBN 0-8193-0105-1, Four Winds); PLB 5.41 o.s.i. (ISBN 0-8193-0106-X). Schol Bk Serv.
Darell-Brown, Susan. The Mississippi. LC 78-62982. (Rivers of the World Ser.). (Illus.). 1978. lib. bdg. 7.95 (ISBN 0-686-51135-2). Silver.
Dar El Mashreq. Arabic-English Students Dictionary. 12.00x (ISBN 0-686-53116-7). Intl Bk Ctr.
Dargan, E. Preston & Weinberg, Bernard. The Evolution of Balzac's Comedie Humaine. LC 72-91802. 441p. 1973. Repr. of 1942 ed. lib. bdg. 16.50x (ISBN 0-8154-0452-2). Cooper Sq.
Dargan, James F. My Experiences in Service, or a Nine Months Man. Tanis, Norman E., ed. (American Classics Facsimile Ser.: Pt. I). 416p. 1974. pap. 10.00 (ISBN 0-937048-00-3). CSUN.
Darin-Drabkin, H. Land Policy & Urban Growth. LC 76-39912. 1977. text ed. 23.00 (ISBN 0-08-020401-5). Pergamon.
Darin-Drabkin, Haim, jt. auth. see Lichfield, Nathaniel.
Dario, Ruben. Azul... Otras Poemas. (Span). 3.75x o.s.i. (ISBN 0-686-00843-X). Colton Bk.
Dark, Harris E. Wankel Rotary Engine: Introduction & Guide. LC 73-16676. (Illus.). 160p. 1974. 8.50x (ISBN 0-253-19021-5). Ind U Pr.
Dark, Irene. First Book of Hymns. (Ladybird Ser). 1968. bds. 1.49 (ISBN 0-87508-838-4). Chr Lit.
Dark, Philip J. An Introduction to Benin Art & Technology. (Illus.). 209p. 1973. 36.00x (ISBN 0-19-817191-9). Oxford U Pr.
Dark, Sidney & Grey, Rowland. W. S. Gilbert, His Life & Letters. LC 71-164210. 1971. Repr. of 1923 ed. 18.00 (ISBN 0-8103-3789-4). Gale.
Darke, Marjorie. The First of Midnight. LC 77-13435. (gr. 6 up). 1978. 6.95 (ISBN 0-395-28854-1, Clarion). HM.
Darkes, Anna S. How to Make & Use Overhead Transparancies. (Illus.). 1977. pap. 2.50 (ISBN 0-8024-3652-8). Moody.
Darkow, Michael T. The Sensual Gospel. Date not set. 8.95 (ISBN 0-533-04774-9). Vantage.
Darley, Frederic L., jt. ed. see Keith, Robert L.
Darley, George. George Darley (Seventeen Ninety-Five to Eighteen Forty-Six) Reiman, Donald H., ed. LC 75-31193. (Romantic Context Ser.: Poetry 1789-1830). 1978. lib. bdg. 47.00 (ISBN 0-8240-2144-4). Garland Pub.

Darley, J. Psychology. 1981. 17.95 (ISBN 0-13-733154-1); pap. 5.95 (ISBN 0-13-733188-6). P-H.
Darley, John M., jt. auth. see Latane, Bibb.
Darley, Lionel S. Introduction to Bookbinding. (Illus.). 1977. pap. 7.95 (ISBN 0-571-11082-7, Pub. by Faber & Faber). Merrimack Bk Serv.
Darline, R., jt. auth. see Robinson, James H.
Darling, Edward, jt. auth. see Ashley Montagu.
Darling, F. & Boyd, J. Highlands & the Islands. 1964. pap. 2.25 o.p. (ISBN 0-531-06011-X, Fontana Pap). Watts.
Darling, J. S., ed. Colonial Keyboard Tunes. LC 80-12691. 1980. pap. 1.50 (ISBN 0-87935-055-5). Williamsburg.
Darling, John R., jt. auth. see Lipson, Harry A.
Darling, Lois & Darling, Louis. Sixty Million Years of Horses. (Illus.). (gr. 3-7). 1960. PLB 6.48 (ISBN 0-688-31000-1). Morrow.
--Turtles. (Illus.). (gr. 3-7). 1962. PLB 6.48 (ISBN 0-688-31547-X). Morrow.
--Worms. LC 77-102408. (Illus.). 48p. (gr. 2-5). 1972. pap. 6.48 (ISBN 0-688-31773-1). Morrow.
Darling, Louis. Kangaroos & Other Animals with Pockets. (Illus.). (gr. 3-7). 1958. PLB 6.48 (ISBN 0-688-31501-1). Morrow.
Darling, Louis, jt. auth. see Darling, Lois.
Darling, Renny. The Joy of Eating French Food: Great French Dishes Made Easy. 1980. pap. 8.95 (ISBN 0-930440-05-6). Royal Calif.
Darling, Sharon S. Chicago Ceramics & Glass. LC 79-91566. (Illus.). 240p. 1980. 25.00 (ISBN 0-913820-10-5). Chicago Hist.
--Chicago Ceramics & Glass: An Illustrated History from 1871 to 1933. LC 79-91566. (Illus.). xiv, 222p. 1980. 25.00 o.p. (ISBN 0-913820-10-5). Chicago Hist.
Darlington, Arnold. World of a Tree. 1972. 6.95 (ISBN 0-571-09624-7, Pub. by Faber & Faber). Merrimack Bk Serv.
Darlington, C. D. Chromosome Botany & the Origins of Cultivated Plants. 3rd ed. (Illus.). 1973. text ed. 25.00x (ISBN 0-04-581011-7). Allen Unwin.
Darlington, C. D. & La Cour, F. L. The Handling of Chromosomes. (Illus.). 1942. pap. text ed. 16.50x o.p. (ISBN 0-04-574014-3). Allen Unwin.
Darlington, C. D. & LaCour, L. F. The Handling of Chromosomes. 6th ed. LC 75-20130. 1976. 18.95 (ISBN 0-470-19527-4). Halsted Pr.
Darlington, Joy. Fast Friends. 1980. pap. 2.50 (ISBN 0-425-04742-3). Berkley Pub.
Darlington, Sandy. Buzz: New York in the Fifties. LC 80-69533. 160p. (Orig.). 1981. pap. 4.00 (ISBN 0-9604152-1-1). Arrowhead Bks.
Darlington, William. Reliquiae Baldwinianae. (Classica Botanica Americana Ser: Suppl. 2). 1968. Repr. of 1843 ed. 19.25 o.s.i. (ISBN 0-02-843650-4). Hafner.
Darlison, John L. & Fordyce, M. W. Glass Reinforced Concrete. 1981. text ed. price not set. Butterworth.
Darmady, E. M. & McIver, A. Renal Pathology. LC 79-42838. (Postgraduate Pathology Ser.). 560p. 1980. 99.95 (ISBN 0-407-00119-0). Butterworths.
Darmesteter, tr. see Mueller, F. Max.
Darmody, William R., ed. Current Concepts in Emergency Medicines: Vol. 1, Management of the Unconscious Patient. LC 75-37770. (Illus.). 120p. 1976. 13.50 (ISBN 0-8016-2748-6). Mosby.
D'Arms, John H. Commerce & Social Standing in Ancient Rome. LC 80-25956. (Illus.). 224p. 1981. text ed. 20.00 (ISBN 0-674-14475-9). Harvard U Pr.
Darmstadter, Joel, et al. How Industrial Societies Use Energy: A Comparative Analysis. LC 77-83780. (Illus.). 300p. 1978. text ed. 18.50x (ISBN 0-8018-2041-3). Johns Hopkins.
Darnbrough, Ann & Kinrade, Derek. Directory for the Disabled: A Handbook of Information & Opportunities for Disabled & Handicapped People. 2nd ed. 208p. 1980. 27.00x (ISBN 0-85941-106-0, Pub. by Woodhead-Faulkner England); pap. 12.00x (ISBN 0-85941-108-7). State Mutual Bk.
--Directory of Sexual Advisory Services (in Great Britain) 128p. 1980. 24.00x (ISBN 0-85941-162-1, Pub. by Woodhead-Faulkner England); pap. 9.00. State Mutual Bk.
--Fund-Raising & Grant-Aid: A Practical & Legal Guide for Charities & Voluntary Organisations. 160p. 1980. 24.00x (ISBN 0-85941-075-7, Pub. by Woodhead-Faulkner England). State Mutual Bk.
Darnell, D. K. & Brockriede, W. Persons Communicating. (Speech Communication Ser.). (Illus.). 256p. 1976. pap. text ed. 14.95 (ISBN 0-13-657387-8). P-H.
Darnell, Donald G. William Hickling Prescott. LC 74-26789. (U. S. Authors Ser.: No. 251). 1975. lib. bdg. 10.95 (ISBN 0-8057-0598-8). Twayne.
Darnell, Eula K. Sonny & the Mountain. LC 79-63420. (Illus.). 1979. 4.50 (ISBN 0-533-04262-3). Vantage.
Darr, Jack. How to Test Almost Everything Electronic. LC 66-30560. 1967. 8.95 (ISBN 0-685-24819-4); pap. 4.95 (ISBN 0-8306-6132-8, 132). TAB Bks.
Darracott, J., ed. see Fitzwilliam Museum.
Darrah, John. The Real Camelot: Paganism & the Arthurian Romances. 160p. 1981. 13.95 (ISBN 0-500-01250-4). Thames Hudson.
Darrah, L. B. Food Marketing. rev. ed. 1971. 25.95 (ISBN 0-8260-2345-2). Wiley.
Darras, Jacques. Joseph Conrad & the West: Signs of Empire. 1981. 26.50x (ISBN 0-389-20071-9). B&N.
Darrell, Elizabeth. The Jade Alliance. Date not set. pap. 2.95 (ISBN 0-440-14057-9). Dell.
Darrow, Clarence. The Skeleton in the Closet. 1936. pap. 2.00 (ISBN 0-8283-1438-1). Branden.
Darrow, Gerald F. Four Decades of Choral Training. LC 74-31205. 1975. 10.00 (ISBN 0-8108-0791-2). Scarecrow.
Darrow, Robert A., jt. auth. see Benson, Lyman.
Darst, David H. Juan Boscan. (World Authors Ser.: No. 475). 1978. lib. bdg. 11.95 (ISBN 0-8057-6316-3). Twayne.
Darst, David M. The Handbook of the Bond & Money Markets. (Illus.). 320p. 1981. 29.95 (ISBN 0-07-015401-5, P&RB). McGraw.
Darst, Paul W. & Armstrong, George P. Outdoor Adventure Activities for School & Recreation Programs. (Orig.). pap. text ed. 13.95 (ISBN 0-8087-0489-3). Burgess.
Dart, John O. & Johnson, Daniel M. Oregon: Wet, High, & Dry. 500p. (Orig.). 1981. pap. 18.95x (ISBN 0-913244-53-8). Hapi Pr.
Dart, Thurston. Interpretation of Music. 1975. Repr. of 1967 ed. pap. text ed. 9.25x (ISBN 0-09-031683-5, Hutchinson U Lib). Humanities.
Dartford, Gerald P. The British Constitution. 1978. pap. text ed. 2.75x (ISBN 0-88334-107-7). Ind Sch Pr.
--The French Revolution. (gr. 9-12). 1972. pap. text ed. 3.25x (ISBN 0-88334-046-1). Ind Sch Pr.
Dartnell. Trees & Shrubs of the British Isles. 8.50x (ISBN 0-392-06756-0, LTB). Soccer.
Darton, Harvey. Arnold Bennett. 127p. 1980. Repr. lib. bdg. 17.50 (ISBN 0-89760-131-9). Telegraph Bks.
Darton, Harvey F. From Surtees to Sassoon, Some Eng. Contrasts. (1938-1928) 222p. 1980. Repr. lib. bdg. 25.00 (ISBN 0-8492-4219-3). R West.
Daruwalla, K. N. Apparition in April. 8.00 (ISBN 0-89253-454-0); flexible cloth 4.80 (ISBN 0-89253-455-9). Ind-US Inc.
--Under Orion. (Writers Workshop Redbird Ser.). 93p. 1975. 8.00 (ISBN 0-88253-728-8); flexible bdg. 4.80 (ISBN 0-89253-597-0). Ind-US Inc.
Darvas, F. & Knoll, J., eds. Chemical Structure - Biological Activity Relationships, Quantitative Approaches: Proceedings of the Third Congress of the Hungarian Pharmacological Society, Budapest, 1979. LC 80-41281. (Advances in Pharmacological Research & Practice Ser.: Vol. III). 355p. 1981. 67.00 (ISBN 0-08-026388-7). Pergamon.
Darveniza, M. Electrical Properties of Wood & Line Design. (Illus.). 197p. (Orig.). 1980. pap. text ed. 36.25x (ISBN 0-7022-1523-6). U of Queensland Pr.
Darvill, Fred T., Jr. Stehekin: The Enchanted Valley. LC 80-16628. (Illus.). 96p. (Orig.). 1980. pap. 5.95 (ISBN 0-913140-42-2). Signpost Bk Pub.
Darwen, Hugh. Bridge Magic. (Illus.). 1973. 13.50 (ISBN 0-686-24597-0, Pub. by Faber & Faber). Merrimack Bk Serv.
Darwin, Charles. The Collected Papers of Charles Darwin, 2 vol. set. Barrett, Paul H., ed. 886p. pap. 13.50. U of Chicago Pr.
--Darwin on Humus & the Earthworm: The Formation of Vegetable Mould. 4th ed. 1966. text ed. 5.00x (ISBN 0-571-06778-6). Humanities.
--The Descent of Man & Selection in Relation to Sex. LC 80-8679. (Illus.). 935p. 1981. 30.00x (ISBN 0-691-08278-2); pap. 8.95 (ISBN 0-691-02369-7). Princeton U Pr.
--The Descent of Man & Selection in Relation to Sex. LC 73-20158. (Illus.). 672p. 1974. Repr. of 1874 ed. 35.00 (ISBN 0-8103-3963-3). Gale.
--Metaphysics, Materialism, & the Evolution of the Mind: Early Writings of Charles Darwin. LC 80-15763. 1980. pap. 6.95 (ISBN 0-226-13659-0, P906, Phoen). U of Chicago Pr.
--The Movements & Habits of Climbing Plants. 1979. Repr. of 1897 ed. lib. bdg. 35.00 (ISBN 0-89760-128-9, Telegraph). Dynamic Learn Corp.
--The Origin of Species. abr. ed. Appleman, Philip, ed. 1975. pap. text ed. 2.95x (ISBN 0-393-09219-4). Norton.
--The Power of Movement in Plant. 2nd ed. LC 65-23402. 1966. Repr. of 1881 ed. lib. bdg. 39.50 (ISBN 0-306-70921-X). Da Capo.
--The Structure & Distribution of Coral Reefs. (Library Reprint Ser.). 1976. 19.50x (ISBN 0-520-03282-9). U of Cal Pr.
--Voyage of the Beagle. 1955. 15.00x (ISBN 0-460-00104-3, Evman); pap. 7.95 (ISBN 0-460-01104-9). Dutton.
Darwin, Charles & Huxley, Thomas H. Autobiographies. De Beer, Gavin, ed. (Oxford English Memoirs & Travels Ser.). (Illus.). 190p. 1974. 14.95x o.p. (ISBN 0-19-255410-7). Oxford U Pr.
Darwin, Erasmus. The Botanic Garden; a Poem in Two Parts. Reiman, Donald H., ed. Bd. with Pt. 1. Containing the Economy of Vegetation; Pt. 2. The Loves of the Plants. with Philosopical Notes. LC 75-31194. (Romantic Context Ser.: Poetry 1789-1830). 1979. Repr. of 1791 ed. lib. bdg. 47.00 (ISBN 0-8240-2145-2). Garland Pub.
--The Golden Age, a Poetical Epistle from Erasmus D---N M.D., to Thomas Beddoes, Repr. Of 1794 Ed. Reiman, Donald H., ed. Bd. with The Temple of Nature; or the Origin of Society: A Poem, with Philosophical Notes. Repr. of 1803 ed. LC 75-31195. (Romantic Context Ser.: Poetry 1789-1830: Vol. 47). 1979. lib. bdg. 47.00 (ISBN 0-8240-2146-0). Garland Pub.
Darwin, Joan, et al. Bedside Nursing: An Introduction. 3rd ed. (Illus.). 236p. 1976. pap. 12.95x (ISBN 0-433-07133-8). Intl Ideas.
Darwin, John. Britain, Egypt & the Middle East. LC 80-14718. 1980. write for info. (ISBN 0-312-09736-0). St Martin.
Darwish, Mahmoud. The Music of Human Flesh. Johnson-Davies, Denys, tr. from Arabic. (Modern Arab Writers Ser.). 96p. (Orig.). 1980. 9.00x (ISBN 0-89410-202-8); pap. 6.00x (ISBN 0-89410-203-6). Three Continents.
Darwwin. Darwin's Forgotten World. 9.98 (ISBN 0-517-29559-8). Bonanza.
Dary, David. Cowboy Culture. LC 80-2699. (Illus.). 1981. 17.95 (ISBN 0-394-42605-3). Knopf.
Dary, David D. The Buffalo Book: The Full Saga of the American Animal. LC 73-13211. (Illus.). 374p. 1973. 17.50 (ISBN 0-8040-0653-9, SB); limited ed. o.p. 100.00 (ISBN 0-8040-0717-9). Swallow.
Daryanani, Gobind. Principles of Active Network Synthesis & Design. LC 76-20659. 495p. 1976. text ed. 28.95 (ISBN 0-471-19545-6). Wiley.
Daryanani, Sital. Building Systems Design with Programmable Calculators. 1980. 27.50 (ISBN 0-07-015415-5, P&RB). McGraw.
Daryusl, A. A., et al. Persian Words in English. Commager, Steele, ed. Incl. The German Influence on the English Vocabulary; H.W. Fowler; The Dutch Influence on English Vocabulary; American Variations; Fine Writing; Names, Designations, & Appelations; Linguistic Self-Criticism; The Formation & Use of Compound Epithets in English Poetry; Northern Words in Modern English. (Society for Pure English Ser.: Vol. 5). 1979. lib. bdg. 42.00 (ISBN 0-8240-3669-7). Garland Pub.
Das, A. C., jt. auth. see Halim, A.
Das, B. C. The President of India. 1977. text ed. 22.50x o.p. (ISBN 0-8426-1043-X). Verry.
Das, Deb K. The Eyes of Autumn: An Experiment in Poetry. 13p. 1975. 6.00 (ISBN 0-88253-706-7). Ind-US Inc.
--The Fire Canto. 8.00 (ISBN 0-89253-487-7); flexible cloth 4.00 (ISBN 0-89253-488-5). Ind-US Inc.
--The Labyrinths: A Long Poem. (Bluebird Book). 26p. 1975. 8.00 (ISBN 0-88253-713-X); pap. text ed. 4.00 flexible bdg. (ISBN 0-89253-598-9). Ind-US Inc.
--The Night Before Us. 8.00 (ISBN 0-89253-489-3); flexible cloth 4.00 (ISBN 0-89253-490-7). Ind-US Inc.
--Through a Glass Darkly. (Writers Workshop Redbird Ser.). 53p. 1975. flexible cloth 3.00 (ISBN 0-89253-519-9); pap. 3.00 (ISBN 0-88253-723-7). Ind-US Inc.
Das, Deb K., tr. see Sankaracarya.
Das, Deb K., tr. see Upanisads.
Das, Debesh. Maharajas & Men. 1981. 11.00x o.p. (ISBN 0-685-59379-7). South Asia Bks.
Das, J., jt. auth. see Dutta-Majumdar, D.
Das, J. P. Verbal Conditioning & Behavior. 1970. 25.00 (ISBN 0-08-012818-1). Pergamon.
Das, J. P. & Baine, David. Mental Retardation for Special Educators. (Illus.). 332p. 1978. 27.50 (ISBN 0-398-03665-9); pap. 18.50 (ISBN 0-398-03666-7). C C Thomas.
Das, J. P., jt. auth. see Jarman, Ronald F.
Das, Jatin. Poems. (Redbird Bk.). 1976. 8.00 (ISBN 0-89253-537-7); flexible bdg. 4.00 (ISBN 0-89253-098-7). Ind-US Inc.
Das, Jibanananda. Banalata Sen. Lal, P., tr. from Bengali. 20p. 1975. 8.00 (ISBN 0-88253-512-9); pap. text ed. 4.00 (ISBN 0-88253-511-0). Ind-US Inc.
Das, Kamala. The Descendants. (Writers Workshop Redbird Ser.). 35p. 1975. 8.00 (ISBN 0-88253-526-9); pap. text ed. 4.00 (ISBN 0-88253-525-0). Ind-US Inc.
Das, Manoj. Stories of Light & Delight. (Nehru Library for Children). (Illus.). (gr. 2-8). 1979. pap. 1.50 o.p. (ISBN 0-89744-181-8). Auromere.
Das, Nilima, ed. see Alfassa, Mira.
Das, R. Industrial Chemistry, Pt. 1. pap. 5.00x (ISBN 0-210-22520-3). Asia.
Das, Ram. Appropriate Technology. 1981. 11.95 (ISBN 0-533-04744-7). Vantage.
Das, S. K. Changing Image of India: The Twenty-Point Programme. 1977. 7.50 o.p. (ISBN 0-88386-965-9). South Asia Bks.
Das, S. Sunder. General Psychology. 1964. 6.75x (ISBN 0-210-22575-0). Asia.
--Hypnosis: A Clinical Study. 1968. 5.50x (ISBN 0-210-22697-8). Asia.
Das, Sarat C. Journey to Lhasa & Central Tibet. (Illus.). 1970. Repr. of 1902 ed. 12.00x o.p. (ISBN 0-685-19325-X). Paragon.
DaSanto, J. A., ed. Mathematical Methods & Applications of Scattering Theory: Proceedings. (Lecture Notes in Physics: Vol. 130). 331p. 1980. pap. 22.00 (ISBN 0-387-10023-7). Springer-Verlag.
Dasbach, Fernando L. Blight or Bloom. 198p. 1981. 12.50. Regenbogen-Verlag.
--The Father Has Come. 113p. 1981. 10.00. Regenbogen-Verlag.
D'Ascenzo, Juliann, ed. see Clark, Merrian E.
Dasch. Neotropic Mesochorinae - Hymenoptera, Ichneumonidae. (Memoirs Ser: No. 22). (Illus.). 509p. 1974. 30.00 (ISBN 0-686-17149-7). Am Entom Inst.
Dasch, Clement E. Ichneumonidae of America North of Mexico: Subfamily Diplazontinae. (Memoirs Ser: No. 3). (Illus.). 1964. 20.00 (ISBN 0-686-00422-1). Am Entom Inst.
--Ichneumonidae of America North of Mexico: Subfamily Mesochorinae. (Memoirs Ser: No. 16). (Illus.). 376p. 1971. 30.00 (ISBN 0-686-01269-0). Am Entom Inst.
Dascher, Paul E., jt. auth. see Copeland, Ronald M.
Dasent, George W. Popular Tales from the Norse: With an Introductory Essay on the Origin & Diffusion of Popular Tales. 3rd ed. LC 74-136733. clii, 443p. 1971. Repr. of 1888 ed. 20.00 (ISBN 0-8103-3796-7). Gale.
Dasent, George W., tr. see Rask, Rasmus K.
Dasgupta, A. K., ed. Methodology in Economic Research. 6.50x (ISBN 0-210-27183-3). Asia.
Dasgupta, Biplab. The New Agrarian Technology & India. 1980. 17.50x (ISBN 0-8364-0635-4, Pub. by Macmillan India). South Asia Bks.
Dasgupta, Gautam, jt. auth. see Marranca, Bonnie.
Das Gupta, Jyotirindra. Language Conflict & National Development: Group Politics & National Language Policy in India. LC 75-94992. (Center for South & Southeast Asia Studies, UC Berkeley). 1970. 16.50x (ISBN 0-520-01590-8). U of Cal Pr.
Dasgupta, Mary A. The Circus of Love. 8.00 (ISBN 0-89253-463-X); flexible cloth 4.80 (ISBN 0-89253-464-8). Ind-US Inc.
--The Peacock Smiles. 8.00 (ISBN 0-89253-471-0); flexible cloth 4.00 (ISBN 0-89253-472-9). Ind-US Inc.
Dasgupta, P. S. & Heal, G. M. Economic Theory & Exhaustible Resources. LC 79-51749. (Cambridge Economic Handbooks Ser.). 1980. 42.50 (ISBN 0-521-22991-X); pap. 16.95x (ISBN 0-521-29761-3). Cambridge U Pr.
Dasgupta, S. Yoga As Philosophy & Religion. 1978. Repr. 9.00 (ISBN 0-8426-0488-X). Orient Bk Dist.
Dasgupta, Samir. Bengali Poems on Calcutta. 1973. 15.00 (ISBN 0-88253-324-X); pap. text ed. 6.75 (ISBN 0-88253-795-4). Ind-US Inc.
--Paling Shadows. (Writers Workshop Redbird Ser.). 1975. 8.00 (ISBN 0-88253-606-0); pap. text ed. 4.80 (ISBN 0-88253-605-2). Ind-US Inc.
Dasgupta, Samir, ed. see Dey, Bishnu.
Dasgupta, Sipra. Agriculture: Producers Rationality & Technical Change. 196p. 1972. lib. bdg. 8.25x (ISBN 0-210-22517-3). Asia.
Das Gupta, Sipra. The Home Book of Indian Cookery. 184p. 1979. pap. 6.95 (ISBN 0-571-11508-X, Pub by Faber & Faber). Merrimack Bk Serv.
Dasgupta, Somesh. Come, Solitude, Speak to Me. 8.00 (ISBN 0-89253-683-7); flexible cloth 4.80 (ISBN 0-89253-684-5). Ind-US Inc.
Dasgupta, Subhoranjan. Bodhisattva. 8.00 (ISBN 0-89253-465-6); flexible cloth 4.00 (ISBN 0-89253-466-4). Ind-US Inc.
--Nandini Night. (Writers Workshop Redbird Ser.). 1975. 8.00 (ISBN 0-88253-582-X); pap. text ed. 4.00 (ISBN 0-88253-581-1). Ind-US Inc.
--Pritish Nandy. (Indian Writers Ser.: Vol. XII). 1977. 8.50 (ISBN 0-89253-450-8). Ind-US Inc.
Dasgupta, Surendranath. Indian Idealism. 1962. 26.95 (ISBN 0-521-04783-8); pap. 7.95x (ISBN 0-521-09194-2, 194). Cambridge U Pr.
Dash, Bhagan & Kashyap, Lalitesh. Basic Principles of Ayurveda. 655p. 1980. 37.00x (ISBN 0-391-02208-3). Humanities.

Dash, J. G. Films on Solid Surfaces. 1975. 42.50 (ISBN 0-12-203350-7). Acad Pr.

Dash, J. G. & Ruvalds, J., eds. Phase Transitions in Surface Films. (NATO Advanced Studies Institutes Ser., Series B- Physical Sciences: Vol. 51). 375p. 1980. 42.50 (ISBN 0-306-40348-X). Plenum Pub.

Dash, J. Michael. Literature & Ideology in Haiti: 1915-1961. 1981. 26.50x (ISBN 0-389-20092-1). B&N.

Dash, Samuel, et al. Eavesdroppers. LC 71-136498. (Civil Liberties in American History Ser). (Illus.). 1970. Repr. of 1959 ed. lib. bdg. 25.00 (ISBN 0-306-70074-3). Da Capo.

Dash, V. & Kashyap, L., eds. Materia Medica of Ayurveda. 1980. text ed. 38.00x (ISBN 0-391-01813-2). Humanities.

D'A. Shaw, Robert. Jobs & Agricultural Development. LC 79-145446. (Monographs: No. 3). 84p. 1970. 1.00 (ISBN 0-686-28692-8). Overseas Dev Council.

--Rethinking Economic Development. (Development Papers: No. 8). 58p. 1972. pap. 1.00 (ISBN 0-686-28680-4). Overseas Dev Council.

Dasheff, Bill & Dearborn, L. Good Garb. (Orig.). 1980. pap. 9.95 (ISBN 0-440-52588-8, Delta). Dell.

Dashti, Ali. In Search of Omar Khayyam. Elwell-Sutton, L. P., tr. from Persian. LC 77-168669. (Persian Studies Monographs). 276p. 1972. 20.00x (ISBN 0-231-03188-2). Columbia U Pr.

Da Silva, F. H., jt. auth. see Niedermeyer, Ernest.

Da Silva, F. H. Lopes see Niedermeyer, Ernest & Da Silva, F. H.

DaSilva, Leon. Mercenary-Green Hell. 1976. pap. 1.50 o.p. (ISBN 0-685-73458-7, LB388, Leisure Bks). Nordon Pubns.

Da Silva, Zenia S. Beginning Spanish: A Concept Approach. 4th ed. (Illus.). 1978. text ed. 19.50 scp (ISBN 0-06-047488-2, HarpC); scp tape manual 7.50 (ISBN 0-06-041507-X); scp tapes 275.00 (ISBN 0-686-68024-3). Har-Row.

--Spanish: A Short Course. 2nd ed. (Illus.). 1980. text ed. 16.50 scp (ISBN 0-06-041518-5, HarpC); instr' manual free; scp student wkbk. & tape man. 6.50 (ISBN 0-06-041524-X); scp tapes 250.00 (ISBN 0-06-047492-0). Har-Row.

Dasmann, Raymond F. Destruction of California. 1966. pap. 2.95 (ISBN 0-02-072800-X, Collier). Macmillan.

--Last Horizon. 1971. pap. 2.95 o.s.i. (ISBN 0-02-072790-9, Collier). Macmillan.

--Wildlife Biology. 256p. 1981. text ed. 17.95 (ISBN 0-471-08042-X). Wiley.

Dasmann, William. Deer Range: Management & Improvement. 2nd ed. LC 80-28280. Orig. Title: If Deer Are to Survive. (Illus.). 175p. 1981. lib. bdg. write for info (ISBN 0-89950-027-7). McFarland & Co.

Das Melwani, Murli see Melwani, Murli D.

Dass, Arvind. Agrarian Relations in India. 1980. 18.50x (ISBN 0-8364-0648-6, Pub. by Manohar India). South Asia Bks.

Dass, Baba Hari. A Child's Garden of Yoga. LC 80-80299. (Illus.). 108p. (Orig.). (gr. 3-12). 1980. pap. 5.95 (ISBN 0-918100-02-X). Starmont Hse.

--Sweeper to Saint: Stories of the Holy India. Denu, Ma, ed. (Illus.). 200p. (Orig.). 1980. pap. 6.95 (ISBN 0-918100-03-8). Sri Rama.

Dass, Ram. The Only Dance There Is: Thoughts Along the Spiritual Way. LC 73-14054. 295p. 1974. pap. 4.95 (ISBN 0-385-08413-7, Anch). Doubleday.

D'Assigny, Marius, tr. see Gautruche, Pierre.

Dasso, Jerome, jt. auth. see Ring, Alfred A.

Dasss, Baba Hari, et al. Silence Speaks--from the Chalkboard of Baba Hari Dass. LC 76-53902. (Illus.). 224p. (Orig.). 1977. pap. 4.95 (ISBN 0-918100-01-1). SRI Rama.

Daswani, Chander J., jt. auth. see Southworth, Franklin C.

Datan, Nancy, et al. A Time to Reap: The Middle Age of Women in Five Israeli Subcultures. LC 80-26776. 176p. 1981. text ed. 14.00x (ISBN 0-8018-2516-4). Johns Hopkins.

Datar, Asha L. India's Economic Relations with the USSR & Eastern Europe, 1953-54 to 1969-70. LC 76-178285. (Soviet & East European Studies Ser). (Illus.). 1972. 42.50 (ISBN 0-521-08219-6). Cambridge U Pr.

Date, C. J. Introduction to Database Systems. 3rd ed. LC 80-17603. (IBM Systems Programming Ser.). (Illus.). 704p. 1981. text ed. 20.95 (ISBN 0-201-14471-9). A-W.

--Introduction to Database Systems. 2nd ed. LC 76-55633. (IBM Systems Programming Series). 1977. text ed. price not set (ISBN 0-201-14456-5). A-W.

Date, V. H. Vedanta Explained: Samkara's Commentary on the Brahma-Sutrais, 2 vols. 952p. 1974. text ed. 24.00x o.p. (ISBN 0-8426-0599-1). Verry.

Datel, Robin E. A Selected Annotated Bibliography of Works on Western European Building Conservation, Housing, & Inner Cities. (Architecture Ser.: Bibliography: A-396). 51p. 1980. pap. 7.50. Vance Biblios.

Datesh, John N. The Nightmare Machine. 1979. pap. 1.75 (ISBN 0-505-51372-2). Tower Bks.

Datesman, Susan K., ed. Women, Crime & Justice. Scarpitti, Frank R. (Illus., Orig.). 1980. pap. text ed. 5.95x (ISBN 0-19-502676-4). Oxford U Pr.

Datesman, Susan K., jt. ed. see Scarpitti, Frank R.

Dati, Gregorio, jt. auth. see Pitti, Buonaccorso.

Datta, Amaresh. Captive Moments. (Redbird Bk.). 1976. 8.00 (ISBN 0-89253-528-8); flexible bdg. 4.00 (ISBN 0-89253-082-0). Ind-US Inc.

Datta, Dhirendra M. Philosophy of Mahatma Gandhi. 1953. pap. 5.45 (ISBN 0-299-01014-7). U of Wis Pr.

Datta, Lois-Ellin & Perloff, Robert, eds. Improving Evaluations. LC 79-13627. (Sage Focus Editions: Vol. 12). (Illus.). 1979. 18.95x (ISBN 0-8039-1240-4); pap. 9.95x (ISBN 0-8039-1241-2). Sage.

Datta, Surajit K. De see De Datta, Surajit K.

Datz, I. Mortimer. Power Transmission & Automation for Ships & Submersibles. (Illus.). 190p. 30.00 (ISBN 0-85238-074-7, FN). Unipub.

Dau, Frederick W. Florida Old & New. LC 74-13957. 1975. Repr. of 1934 ed. 22.00 (ISBN 0-8103-4060-7). Gale.

Dau, Peter C. Plasmapheresis & the Immunobiology of Myasthenia Gravis. (Illus.). 1979. 35.00x (ISBN 0-89289-404-0). HM Prof Med Div.

Daub, Edward E. Fire. LC 77-26664. (Read About Ser.). (Illus.). (gr. k-3). 1978. PLB 9.95 (ISBN 0-8393-0080-8). Raintree Child.

Daub, Edward E., et al. Comprehending Technical Japanese. LC 74-5900. 400p. 1975. 32.50x (ISBN 0-299-06680-0). U of Wis Pr.

Daub, Grudo H., jt. auth. see Seese, William S.

Daub, Guido H., jt. auth. see Seese, William S.

Dauben, Joseph W., ed. Mathematical Actives: Essays on Mathematics & Its Historical Development. LC 80-1781. 1981. write for info. (ISBN 0-12-204050-3). Acad Pr.

Dauben, William G., ed. Organic Reactions, Vols. 20-25. LC 42-20265. (Organic Reaction Ser.). Vol. 20, 1973. 37.50 (ISBN 0-471-19621-5); Vol. 21, 1974. 34.95 (ISBN 0-471-19622-3); Vol. 22, 1975. 36.95 (ISBN 0-471-19623-1); Vol. 23, 1975. 37.50 (ISBN 0-471-19624-X); Vol. 24, 1975. 36.95 (ISBN 0-471-19625-8); Vol. 25, 1977. 33.95 (ISBN 0-471-01741-8, Pub. by Wiley-Interscience). Wiley.

Dauber, Roslyn & Cain, Melinda, eds. Women & Technological Change in Developing Countries. (AAAS Selected Symposium: No. 53). 250p. 1980. lib. bdg. 21.50x (ISBN 0-89158-791-8). Westview.

Daubert, Darlene M., jt. auth. see Brownstein, Oscar L.

D'Aubigne, Agrippa. Les Tragiques, a Selection. McFarlane, I. D., ed. 1970. text ed. 10.75x (ISBN 0-485-12803-4, Athlone Pr); pap. text ed. 5.50x (ISBN 0-485-12803-9, Athlone Pr). Humanities.

D'Aubigne, J. H. Life & Times of Martin Luther. pap. 9.95 (ISBN 0-8024-4899-2). Moody.

D'Aubigne, Merle. The Reformation in England, 2 vols. 1977. Vol. 1. 14.95 (ISBN 0-85151-059-0); Vol. 2. 14.95 (ISBN 0-85151-094-9); Set. 27.95. Banner of Truth.

Daudel, P. Radioactive Tracers in Chemistry & Industry. 2nd ed. Eisner, U., tr. from Fr. 210p. 1960. 27.00x (ISBN 0-85264-101-X, Pub. by Griffin England). State Mutual Bk.

Daudel, R. The Fundamentals of Theoretical Chemistry. 1967. 26.00 (ISBN 0-08-012300-7). Pergamon.

Daudel, Raymond, et al, eds. Quantum Theory of Chemical Reactions: Solvent Effect, Reaction Mechanisms, Photochemical Processes, Vol. 11. 340p. 1980. PLB 42.00 (ISBN 90-277-1182-8). Kluwer Boston.

Daudet, Alphonse. Tartarin De Tarascon: Andre Humbert Benedict d'Arlon. Amateau, E. I., et al, eds. 1941. 3.95 (ISBN 0-672-73246-7). Odyssey Pr.

--Tartarin of Tarascon. Incl. Tarin on the Alps. 1954. 12.95x (ISBN 0-460-00423-9, Evman). Dutton.

Dauenhauer, Richard. Glacier Bay Concerto. (Alaska Book Ser.: No. 38). 120p. (Orig.). 1980. 12.95 (ISBN 0-935094-02-4); pap. 4.95 (ISBN 0-935094-04-0). Alaska Pacific.

Dauer, jt. auth. see Pangrazi.

Dauer, Manning J., ed. Florida's Politics & Government. LC 80-20723. (Orig.). 1980. pap. 10.00x (ISBN 0-8130-0671-6). U Presses Fla.

Dauer, Rosamond. My Friend, Jasper Jones. LC 76-2459. (Illus.). 40p. (ps-4). 1977. 5.95 o.s.i. (ISBN 0-8193-0887-0, Four Winds); PLB 5.41 o.s.i. (ISBN 0-8193-0888-9). Schol Bk Serv.

D'Augelli, Anthony, et al. Helping Others. LC 80-17819. 170p. 1980. pap. text ed. 8.95 (ISBN 0-8185-0401-3). Brooks-Cole.

Daugherty, D. H., et al. A Bibliography of Periodical Literature in Musicology & Allied Fields, No. 1 & 2. LC 71-177974. 148p. 1971. Repr. of 1940 ed. lib. bdg. 29.50 (ISBN 0-306-70413-7). Da Capo.

Daugherty, J. S. & Powell, R. E. Sheet-Metal Pattern Drafting & Shop Problems. rev. ed. 196p. 1975. pap. text ed. 11.96 (ISBN 0-87002-155-9). Bennett IL.

Daugherty, James. The Landing of the Pilgrims. LC 80-21430. (Landmark Bks.). (Illus.). 160p. (gr. 5-9). 1981. pap. 2.95 (ISBN 0-394-84697-4). Random.

--Poor Richard. (Illus.). (gr. 9 up). 1941. 6.50 o.p. (ISBN 0-670-56450-8). Viking Pr.

Daugherty, Richard D., jt. auth. see Kirk, Ruth.

Daugherty, Sarah B. The Literary Criticism of Henry James. LC 80-36753. xiv, 232p. 1981. 15.95x (ISBN 0-8214-0440-7). Ohio U Pr.

Daughters of St. Paul. Always with Jesus. rev. ed. (Illus.). 1973. 3.95 o.s.i. (ISBN 0-8198-0265-4). Dghtrs St Paul.

--My Favorite Prayers & Reflections. 1973. plastic bdg. 4.00 o.s.i. (ISBN 0-8198-0276-X). Dghtrs St Paul.

--Sixteen Documents of Vatican Two. 6.95 o.s.i. (ISBN 0-8198-0145-3); pap. 3.25 (ISBN 0-8198-0146-1). Dghtrs St Paul.

--Spiritual Life in the Bible. 1980. price not set. Dghtrs St Paul.

--Teachings & Miracles of Jesus. LC 76-118182. (Illus.). 136p. (gr. 4-8). 1970. pap. 3.00 o.s.i. (ISBN 0-8198-0154-2). Dghtrs St Paul.

Daughters Of St. Paul, ed. Bible Stories for Everyone. 1956. 6.00 o.s.i. (ISBN 0-8198-0008-2); pap. 5.00 o.s.i. (ISBN 0-8198-0009-0). Dghtrs St Paul.

--Church's Amazing Story. LC 68-59043. (Divine Master Ser., Vol. 2). (gr. 10). 1969. 5.00 (ISBN 0-8198-0028-7); pap. 4.00 (ISBN 0-8198-0029-5); discussion questions & projects 0.50 (ISBN 0-8198-0030-9). Dghtrs St Paul.

Daughters of St Paul. Blessed Kateri Takakwitha: Mohawk Maiden. 1980. 3.75 (ISBN 0-8198-1100-9); pap. 2.25 (ISBN 0-8198-1101-7). Dghtrs St Paul.

Daughtry, Dewitt C., ed. Thoracic Trauma. 1980. text ed. 35.00 (ISBN 0-316-17380-0). Little.

D'Aulaire, Edgar P., jt. auth. see D'Aulaire, Ingri.

D'Aulaire, Edgar Parin, jt. auth. see D'Aulaire, Ingri.

D'Aulaire, Ingri & D'Aulaire, Edgar P. D'Aulaires' Trolls. LC 76-158897. 64p. (gr. 1-3). 1972. 6.95a (ISBN 0-385-08255-X); limited ed. 50.00 (ISBN 0-385-04343-0); PLB (ISBN 0-385-01275-6). Doubleday.

D'Aulaire, Ingri & D'Aulaire, Edgar Parin. D'Aulaires' Book of Greek Myths. LC 62-15877. 1962. 10.95a (ISBN 0-385-01583-6); PLB (ISBN 0-385-07108-6). Doubleday.

--Don't Count Your Chicks. (ps-1). 1973. pap. 1.95 (ISBN 0-385-05233-2, Zephyr). Doubleday.

--George Washington. (gr. 1-4). 8.95a (ISBN 0-385-07306-2); PLB (ISBN 0-385-07611-8). Doubleday.

D'Aulnoy, Marie C. Tales of the Fairies in Three Parts, Compleat: As Extracted from the Second Edition in English of Her "Diverting Works". Lurie, Alison & Schiller, Justin G., eds. LC 75-32137. (Classics of Children's Literature Ser.: 1621-1932). PLB 38.00 (ISBN 0-8240-2254-8). Garland Pub.

Dauman, Jan, jt. auth. see Hargreaves, John.

Daumas, Maurice. Scientific Instruments of the Seventeenth & Eighteenth Centuries. Holbrook, Mary, ed. & tr. from Fr. LC 77-112019. (Illus.). 1972. text ed. 39.75x (ISBN 0-7134-0727-1). Humanities.

Daumas, Maurice, ed. A History of Technology & Invention Progress Through the Ages, Vol. 1: The Origins of Technological Civilization to 1450. 520p. 1980. 40.00x (ISBN 0-7195-3730-4, Pub. by Murray Pubs England). State Mutual Bk.

--A History of Technology & Invention Progress Through the Ages, Vol. 3: The Expansion of Mechanization 1725-1860. 700p. 1980. 40.00x (ISBN 0-7195-3732-0, Pub. by Murray Pubs England). State Mutual Bk.

--A History of Technology & Invention Through the Ages, Vol. 2: The First Stages of Mechanization 1450-1725. 694p. 1980. 40.00x (ISBN 0-7195-3731-2, Pub. by Murray Pubs England). State Mutual Bk.

Daumeister, W., ed. Electron Microscopy at Molecular Dimensions. (Proceedings in Life Sciences). (Illus.). 300p. 1980. 57.90 (ISBN 0-387-10131-4). Springer-Verlag.

Daumier, Honore. Daumier & Music. (Music Ser.). 1981. 25.00 (ISBN 0-306-76054-1). Da Capo.

Daun, Lowell G., jt. auth. see Hooley, James R.

Dauncey, Richard, ed. Lab Index 1980. (Annual Ser.). 1980. pap. text ed. 45.00 o.p. (ISBN 0-933916-03-5). Medical Busn.

Daunt, P. E. Comprehensive Values. (Organization in Schools Ser.). 1975. text ed. 15.95x (ISBN 0-435-80270-4). Heinemann Ed.

Daunt, W. J. A Life Spent for Ireland. 440p. 1972. Repr. of 1896 ed. 17.00x (ISBN 0-7165-0025-6, Pub. by Irish Academic Pr Ireland). Biblio Dist.

Daunton, M. J. Coal Metropolis: Cardiff 1870-1914. 1977. text ed. 31.25x (ISBN 0-7185-1139-5, Leicester). Humanities.

Dauphinais, Raymond, tr. see Lubich, Chiara.

Dauphinais, Raymond, tr. see Moran, Hugh.

Daus, Paul H. & Whyburn, William M. Introduction to Mathematical Analysis with Applications to Problems of Economics. 1958. 13.95 (ISBN 0-201-01445-9). A-W.

Dause, Charles A., jt. auth. see Ziegelmueller, George W.

Dauten, Dale A. Quitting: Knowing When to Leave. 216p. 1980. 12.95 (ISBN 0-8027-0660-6). Walker & Co.

D'Auvergne, Martial. Amant Rendu Cordelier a L'observance D'amours. (Societe Des Anciens Textes Francais Ser: Vol. 15). (Fr). 1881. 20.00; pap. 15.50 (ISBN 0-384-56560-3). Johnson Repr.

Dauvillier, Jean. Le Mariage En Droit Canonique Oriental. LC 80-2357. 1981. Repr. of 1936 ed. 35.00 (ISBN 0-404-18905-9). AMS Pr.

Dauw, Dean C. Creativity & Innovation in Organizations. 380p. 1980. pap. text ed. 12.95x (ISBN 0-917974-42-5). Waveland Pr.

--Increasing Your Self Esteem: How to Feel Better About Yourself. (Illus.). 128p. 1980. pap. text ed. 4.95x (ISBN 0-917974-43-3). Waveland Pr.

--Stranger in Your Bed: A Guide to Emotional Intimacy. LC 78-23444. 1979. 10.95 (ISBN 0-88229-472-5). Nelson-Hall.

--Up Your Career. 3rd ed. (Illus.). 256p. 1980. pap. text ed. 8.95 (ISBN 0-917974-40-9). Waveland Pr.

Dauzat, A. Dictionnaire des noms de famille et prenoms de France. (Fr). 23.50 (ISBN 2-03-020260-6, 3615). Larousse.

Dauzat, A., et al. Nouveau Dictionnaire etymologique. (Fr). 27.50 (ISBN 2-03-020210-X, 3612). Larousse.

Dauzat, Joann, jt. auth. see Dauzat, Sam V.

Dauzat, Sam V. & Dauzat, Joann. Reading: The Teacher & the Learner. LC 80-19435. 518p. 1981. pap. text ed. 15.50 (ISBN 0-471-02668-9); tchr's manual 4.50 (ISBN 0-471-08582-0). Wiley.

Davaney, Sheila G. Feminism & Process Thought: The Harvard Divinity School-Claremont Center for Process Studies Symposium Papers. (Symposium Ser.: Vol. 5). 1980. soft cover 9.95x (ISBN 0-88946-903-2). E Mellen.

Davanloo, H., ed. Short-Term Dynamic Therapy. LC 80-67986. 1980. 30.00 (ISBN 0-87668-418-5). Aronson.

D'Avanzo, Mario L. Keats Metaphors for the Poetic Imagination. LC 67-17149. 1967. 12.75 o.p. (ISBN 0-8223-0043-5). Duke.

Dave, Ravindra H., jt. auth. see Skager, R.

D'Avenant, David. What the Sophisticated Man of the World Ought to Know About Women. (Illus.). 1980. 41.45 (ISBN 0-89266-213-1). Am Classical Coll Pr.

Davenant, William. The Shorter Poems & Songs from the Plays & Masques. Gibbs, A. M., ed. 568p. 1972. 39.00x (ISBN 0-19-812434-1). Oxford U Pr.

Davenport, Cyril. The Book: Its History & Development. LC 79-164212. (Tower Bks). (Illus.). viii, 258p. 1971. Repr. of 1930 ed. 20.00 (ISBN 0-8103-3944-7). Gale.

Davenport, Diana. The Desperate Season. 1978. pap. 1.95 o.p. (ISBN 0-449-13981-6, GM). Fawcett.

--One-Parent Families. 1979. 19.95 (ISBN 0-686-63744-5, Pub. by Batsford England). David & Charles.

Davenport, Donald H. Index to Business Indices. LC 70-153015. 1971. Repr. of 1937 ed. 18.00 (ISBN 0-8103-3706-1). Gale.

Davenport, Elaine. Ferns for Modern Living. Wilson, Helen V., ed. (Modern Living Ser.). (Illus.). 80p. (Orig.). 1977. pap. 2.95 (ISBN 0-89484-004-5, 10105). Merchants Pub Co.

Davenport, Elsie G. Your Handspinning. (Illus.). 1964. pap. 5.50 (ISBN 0-910458-01-4). Select Bks.

--Your Handweaving. (Illus.). 1970. pap. 5.50 (ISBN 0-910458-03-0). Select Bks.

--Your Yarn Dyeing. (Illus.). 1970. pap. 5.50 (ISBN 0-910458-02-2). Select Bks.

Davenport, Guy. Da Vinci's Bicycle: Ten Stories by Guy Davenport. LC 78-22513. 1979. 12.95 o.p. (ISBN 0-8018-2208-4); pap. 4.95 (ISBN 0-8018-2220-3). Johns Hopkins.

--The Geography of the Imagination. 384p. 1980. 20.00 (ISBN 0-86547-000-6); pap. 10.00 (ISBN 0-86547-001-4). N Point Pr.

Davenport, Guy, ed. & tr. see Herondas.

Davenport, Guy, tr. see Heraclitus of Ephesius & Diogenes, the Cynic.

Davenport, H. Multiplicative Number Theory. (Graduate Texts in Mathematics Ser.: Vol. 74). 177p. 1981. 19.80 (ISBN 0-387-90533-2). Springer-Verlag.

Davenport, Humphrey. An Abridgement of the Lord Coke's Commentary on Littleton. Berkowitz, David S. & Thorne, Samuel E., eds. LC 77-89239. (Classics of English Legal History in the Modern Era Ser.: Vol. 74). 484p. 1979. lib. bdg. 40.00 (ISBN 0-8240-3173-3). Garland Pub.

Davenport, John. A Just Complaint Against an Unjust Doer, Mr. J. Paget. LC 76-57376. (English Experience Ser.: No. 793). 1977. Repr. of 1634 ed. lib. bdg. 5.00 (ISBN 90-221-0793-0). Walter J Johnson.

--Letters of John Davenport, Puritan Divine. Calder, Isabel M., ed. 1937. 47.50x (ISBN 0-685-69794-0). Elliots Bks.

Davenport, John W. Baseball's Pennant Races: A Graphic View. 1981. 19.95 (ISBN 0-934794-02-2); pap. 12.95 (ISBN 0-934794-03-0). First Impressions.

Davenport, Marcia. The Constant Image. 1979. pap. 2.25 o.p. (ISBN 0-445-00279-4). Popular Lib.

--Mozart. (Illus.). 1956. lib. rep. ed. 20.00 (ISBN 0-684-14504-9, ScribT). Scribner.

--Mozart. 1979. pap. 3.50 (ISBN 0-380-45534-X, 45534, Discus). Avon.

--Too Strong for Fantasy. 1979. pap. 3.50 (ISBN 0-380-45195-6, 45195, Discus). Avon.

Davenport, Marge. Best of the Old Northwest. LC 80-83780. (Illus., Orig.). 1981. pap. 6.95 (ISBN 0-938274-00-7). Paddlewheel.

Davenport, Nicholas. The Honour of St Valery: The Story of an English Manor House. (Illus.). 168p. (Orig.). 1979. pap. 7.95 (ISBN 0-85967-463-0, Pub. by Scolar Pr England). Biblio Dist.

Davenport, Odessa, jt. auth. see Porter, Mae R.

Davenport, Peter, jt. ed. see Thompson, Philip.

Davenport, R. Edward. Person to Person Evangelism. new ed. LC 77-23716. 1978. pap. 2.25 (ISBN 0-87148-691-1). Pathway Pr.

Davenport, Richard. Outline of Animal Development. LC 78-62548. (Life Sciences Ser.). (Illus.). 1979. text ed. 19.95 (ISBN 0-201-01814-4). A-W.

Davenport, Rita. Rita Davenport's Sourdough Cookery. new ed. LC 77-71168. (Illus.). 1977. 6.95 o.p. (ISBN 0-912656-64-6); pap. 4.95 o.p. (ISBN 0-912656-63-8). H P Bks.

Davenport, Robert. The City-Night Cap. Monie, Willis J. & Orgel, Stephen, eds. LC 78-66832. (Renaissance Drama Ser.). 1979. lib. bdg. 22.00 (ISBN 0-8240-9738-6). Garland Pub.

--King John & Matilda: A Critical Edition. Davis, Joyce O., ed. LC 79-54334. (Renaissance Drama Ser.). 200p. 1980. lib. bdg. 22.00 (ISBN 0-8240-4452-5). Garland Pub.

Davenport, Russell W., jt. auth. see Fortune Magazine.

Davenport, T. C., ed. The Rheology of Lubricants. LC 72-13462. (Illus.). 148p. 1973. 15.95 o.p. (ISBN 0-470-19672-6). Halsted Pr.

Davenport, Thomas, jt. auth. see Fundaburk, Emma L.

Davenport, W. Athens. (The Great Cities Ser.). (Illus.). 1978. lib. bdg. 14.94 (ISBN 0-686-51001-1). Silver.

--Modern Data Communication: Concepts, Language & Media. (Illus.). 1971. pap. 10.95 (ISBN 0-8104-5667-2). Hayden.

Davenport, W. A. The Art of the Gawain-Poet. 1978. text ed. 28.50x (ISBN 0-485-11173-X, Athlone Pr). Humanities.

Davenport, W. G., jt. auth. see Peacey, J. G.

Davenport, W. H. The One Culture. LC 70-106054. 1970. 12.75 (ISBN 0-08-016322-X). Pergamon.

Davenport, William. Athens. new ed. Time-Life Books, ed. (The Great Cities Ser.). (Illus.). 1978. 14.95 (ISBN 0-8094-2298-0). Time-Life.

Davenport, William W. Gyro! The Life & Times of Lawrence Sperry. LC 78-17826. (Illus.). 1978. 12.95 o.p. (ISBN 0-684-15793-4, ScribT). Scribner.

Davern, Cedric I., intro. by. Genetics: Readings from Scientific American. LC 80-25208. (Illus.). 1981. text ed. 17.95x (ISBN 0-7167-1200-8); pap. text ed. 8.95x (ISBN 0-7167-1201-6). W H Freeman.

Davern, Jeanne, ed. see Architectural Record Magazine.

Davern, W. A., jt. auth. see Lhuede, E. P.

Daves, Michael. Young Readers Book of Christian Symbolism. (Illus.). (gr. 5 up). 1967. 10.95 (ISBN 0-687-46824-8). Abingdon.

Davey, Cyril. Monk Who Shook the World (Martin Luther) 1960. pap. 1.95 (ISBN 0-87508-614-4). Chr Lit.

Davey, Gilbert. Fun with Short Wave Radio. rev. ed. Cox, Jack, ed. (Learning with Fun Ser.). (Illus.). 64p. 1980. text ed. 11.50x (ISBN 0-7182-1319-X, Sps). Soccer.

Davey, H. & Mercer, H. Real Estate Principles in California. 4th ed. 1981. 19.95. P-H.

Davey, Harold W. Contemporary Collective Bargaining. 3rd ed. LC 74-152315. 1972. ref. ed. 18.95 (ISBN 0-13-169607-6). P-H.

Davey, Henry. History of English Music. 3rd ed. LC 69-15620. (Music Ser). 1969. Repr. of 1921 ed. lib. bdg. 35.00 (ISBN 0-306-71133-8). Da Capo.

Davey, Herbert. The Law Relating to the Mentally Defective. (Historical Foundations of Forensic Psychiatry & Psychology Ser.). 568p. 1980. Repr. of 1914 ed. lib. bdg. 49.50 (ISBN 0-306-76070-3). Da Capo.

Davey, Homer C. & Mercer, H. Glenn. Real Estate Principles in California. 3rd ed. 1976. 18.95 (ISBN 0-13-765693-9). P-H.

Davey, Homer C. & Sharum, Abert. How to Pass Your California Real Estate Exam. 350p. 1975. pap. text ed. 15.50 scp (ISBN 0-06-453608-4, HarpC). Har-Row.

Davey, Homer C. & Sharum, Albert. Financing Real Estate in California. 1976. text ed. 20.50 scp (ISBN 0-06-453607-6, HarpC). Har-Row.

Davey, Homer C., jt. auth. see Driscoll, Donald C.

Davey, Jocelyn. Treasury Alarm. 229p. 1981. 9.95 (ISBN 0-8027-5431-7). Walker & Co.

Davey, John. Mining Coal. (Junior Reference Ser.). (Illus.). 64p. 7.95 (ISBN 0-7136-1596-6). Dufour.

Davey, Keith. Australian Desert Life. 6.50x (ISBN 0-392-07552-0, SpS). Soccer.

Davey, Patrick J. Leasing: Experiences & Expectations, Report No. 791. (Illus.). v, 58p. (Orig.). 1980. pap. 15.00 (ISBN 0-8237-0222-7). Conference Bd.

Davey, R., et al, eds. Electrical Inspection. (Engineering Craftsmen: No. G24). (Illus.). 1969. spiral bdg. 24.95x (ISBN 0-85083-066-4). Intl Ideas.

Davey, William G., ed. Intercultural Theory & Practice: Perspectives on Education, Training & Research. LC 79-91280. (Orig.). 1980. pap. text ed. 6.50 o.p. (ISBN 0-933662-05-X). Intercult Pr.

David, tr. see Mueller, F. Max.

David, Alfred & Meek, Mary E. Twelve Dancing Princesses & Other Fairy Tales. LC 73-16517. (Midland Bks.: No. 173). (Illus.). 320p. (gr. 1-6). 1974. 10.00x (ISBN 0-253-36100-1); pap. 3.95x (ISBN 0-253-20173-X). Ind U Pr.

David, Alfred, jt. ed. see Pace, George B.

David, Andrew. Famous Political Trials. LC 79-16923. (On Trial Ser.). (Illus.). (YA) (gr. 5 up). 1980. PLB 6.95g (ISBN 0-8225-1429-X). Lerner Pubns.

--Rock Stars: People at the Top of the Charts. (Illus.). 96p. 1979. 4.98 (ISBN 0-89196-076-7, Domus Bks). EPWP.

David, Ann. How to Get Out of Debt & Stay Out of Debt. 160p. 1980. 5.95 (ISBN 0-346-12480-8). Cornerstone.

David, Carl. Collecting & Care of Fine Art. Michelman, Herbert, ed. 160p. 1981. 10.00 (ISBN 0-517-54287-0, Michelman Books). Crown.

David, D. J. Gas Chromatographic Detectors. LC 73-4773. 295p. 1974. 29.95 o.p. (ISBN 0-471-19674-6, Pub. by Wiley-Interscience). Wiley.

--Pet Basics. 225p. 1981. pap. 9.95 (ISBN 0-918398-47-9). Dilithium Pr.

David, David S. Calcium Metabolism in Renal Failure & Nephrolithiasis. LC 76-30308. (Perspectives in Nephrology & Hypertension). 1977. 54.50 (ISBN 0-471-19673-8, Pub. by Wiley Medical). Wiley.

David, Deborah S. & Brannon, Robert. Forty-Nine Percent Majority: The Male Sex Role. LC 75-18152. 352p. 1976. text ed. 9.95 (ISBN 0-201-01448-3). A-W.

David, Deirdre. Fictions of Resolution in Three Victorian Novels. LC 80-16262. 304p. 1981. text ed. 20.00x (ISBN 0-231-04980-3). Columbia U Pr.

David, Elizabeth. Elizabeth David Classics: Mediterranean Food, French Country Cooking, Summer Cooking. LC 80-7648. (Illus.). 672p. 1980. 15.95 (ISBN 0-394-49153-X). Knopf.

--French Provincial Cooking. rev. ed. LC 80-8369. (Illus.). 520p. 1981. 16.95 (ISBN 0-06-014827-6, HarpT). Har-Row.

David, F. N., et al. Symmetric Function & Allied Tables. 278p. 1966. 27.00x (ISBN 0-85264-702-6, Pub. by Griffin England). State Mutual Bk.

David, Georges & Price, Wendel S., eds. Human Artificial Insemination & Semen Preservation. 620p. 1980. 65.00 (ISBN 0-306-40547-4, Plenum Pr). Plenum Pub.

David, H. Submicroscopic Ortho- & Patho-Morphology of the Liver. 1964. 195.00 (ISBN 0-08-010903-9). Pergamon.

David, H. A. Order Statistics. LC 78-114915. (Probability & Mathematics Statistics Ser.). 1970. 26.50 o.p. (ISBN 0-471-19675-4, Pub. by Wiley-Interscience). Wiley.

David, H. A., ed. Order Statistics. 2nd ed. LC 80-16928. (Probability & Mathematical Statistics Ser.). 350p. 1981. 24.95 (ISBN 0-471-02723-5, Pub. by Wiley-Interscience). Wiley.

David, Henry W. & Whitwell, R. J., eds. Regesta Regum Anglo-Normannorum, 1066 to 1135, 2 vols. LC 80-2220. 1981. Repr. of 1956 ed. Set. 135.00 (ISBN 0-686-69546-1); 67.50 ea. AMS Pr.

David, Lester. Joan: The Reluctant Kennedy. (Illus.). 256p. 1975. pap. 1.75 o.s.i. (ISBN 0-446-59761-9). Warner Bks.

--The Lonely Lady of San Clemente: The Story of Pat Nixon. LC 78-3299. (Illus.). 1978. 9.95 o.s.i. (ISBN 0-690-01688-3, TYC-T). T Y Crowell.

David, M. H. Environmental Quality & Social Behavior: Strategies for Research. 1973. pap. 6.25 (ISBN 0-309-02048-4). Natl Acad Pr.

David, Martin. Alternative Approaches to Capital Gains Taxation. LC 68-30592. (Studies of Government Finance). 1968. 9.95 (ISBN 0-8157-1742-3); pap. 3.95 (ISBN 0-8157-1741-5). Brookings.

David, Miriam E. Reform, Reaction & Resources: The 3 Rs of Educational Planning. (General Ser.). 1977. pap. text ed. 25.50x (ISBN 0-85633-127-9, NFER). Humanities.

--The State, the Family, & Education. (Radical Social Policy Ser.). 304p. (Orig.). 1980. pap. 17.50 (ISBN 0-7100-0601-2). Routledge & Kegan.

David, P. & Voge, J. Propagation of Waves. 1969. 37.00 (ISBN 0-08-012114-4). Pergamon.

David, P. A. Technical Choice, Innovation & Economic Growth. (Illus.). 320p. 1975. 39.50 (ISBN 0-521-20518-2); pap. 12.50x (ISBN 0-521-09875-0). Cambridge U Pr.

David, Paul A., et al. Reckoning with Slavery: Critical Essays in the Quantitative History of American Negro Slavery. LC 75-38098. 352p. 1976. 19.95 (ISBN 0-19-502034-0); pap. text ed. 5.95x (ISBN 0-19-502033-2). Oxford U Pr.

David, Paul R., jt. auth. see Snyder, Laurence H.

David, Paul T. Party Strength in the United States 1872-1970. LC 77-183897. 1972. 13.95x (ISBN 0-8139-0396-3). U Pr of Va.

David, Paul T., et al, eds. The Presidential Election & Transition of 1960-61: Brookings Lectures & Additional Papers. 1961. 10.95 (ISBN 0-8157-1746-6). Brookings.

David, Percival, ed. Chinese Connoisseurship. 1971. 68.00 (ISBN 0-571-09979-3, Pub. by Faber & Faber). Merrimack Bk Serv.

David, Peter. Julius Caesar. LC 68-10817. (gr. 7 up). 1968. 3.50g o.s.i. (ISBN 0-02-726300-2, CCPr). Macmillan.

David, R. Shakespeare in the Theatre. LC 77-82494. (Illus.). 1978. 22.50 (ISBN 0-521-21833-0). Cambridge U Pr.

David, Rene & Brierly, John E. Major Legal Systems in the World Today: An Introduction to the Comparative Study of Law. 2nd ed. LC 78-67751. 1978. 25.00 (ISBN 0-02-907590-4); pap. text ed. 10.95 (ISBN 0-02-907610-2). Free Pr.

David, Rodolfo. Apartamento de Soltero. new ed. (Pimienta Collection Ser). 160p. (Span.). 1974. pap. 1.00 o.p. (ISBN 0-88473-198-7). Fiesta Pub.

David, Thomas G. & Wright, Benjamin D., eds. Learning Environments. 248p. 1975. 12.00x o.s.i. (ISBN 0-226-13724-4). U of Chicago Pr.

David, Wilfred L., ed. Public Finance, Planning & Economic Development: Essays in Honor of Ursula Hicks. LC 73-77734. (Illus.). 349p. 1980. 28.50x (ISBN 0-8290-0201-4). Irvington.

David, William. The Harmonics of Sound, Color & Vibration. (Illus.). 160p. (Orig.). 1980. pap. 6.95 (ISBN 0-87516-411-0). De Vorss.

David, William & Gibson, Margaret. Reincarnation & the Soul in the Parables of Jesus. 80p. 1980. pap. 3.95 (ISBN 0-87516-412-9). De Vorss.

Davidescu, D. & Davidescu, V. Evaluation of Plant & Soil Fertility. 1980. write for info. (ISBN 0-85626-123-8, Pub. by Abacus Pr). Intl Schol Bk Serv.

Davidescu, V., jt. auth. see Davidescu, D.

Davidge, D. Alyce. The Day After Christmas. (Illus.). 30p. (Orig.). (gr. k-4). 1981. pap. 4.00 (ISBN 0-9604780-1-9). Soup to Nuts.

Davidge, R. W. Mechanical Behaviour of Ceramics. LC 77-90206. (Solid State Science Ser.). (Illus.). 1979. 47.50 (ISBN 0-521-21915-9). Cambridge U Pr.

Davidge, William F. & Hollman, Kenneth W. An Analysis of Mississippi Industrial Location Factors. 1978. 4.00 (ISBN 0-938004-02-6). U MS Bus Econ.

David-Neel, Alexandra. Buddhism. pap. 2.75 (ISBN 0-380-46185-4, 46185, Discus). Avon.

Davidoff, Leonore & Hawthorn, Ruth. A Day in the Life of a Victorian Domestic Servant. (Victorian Day Ser.). 1976. text ed. 10.95x o.p. (ISBN 0-04-942142-5); pap. text ed. 5.95x (ISBN 0-04-942143-3). Allen Unwin.

Davids, tr. see Mueller, F. Max.

Davids, Anthony, ed. Child Personality & Psychopathology: Current Topics, 3 vols. LC 74-7030. 256p. Vol. 1, 1974. 23.95 o.p. (ISBN 0-471-19696-7); Vol. 2, 1975. 25.95 o.p. (ISBN 0-471-19700-9); Vol. 3, 1976. 28.95 o.p. (ISBN 0-471-19702-5, Pub. by Wiley-Interscience). Wiley.

Davids, Jules, ed. American Diplomatic & Public Papers, the United States & China, Ser. 1: The Treaty System & the Taiping Rebellion, 1842-1860, 21 vols. LC 73-77510. 1974. Set. 1095.00 (ISBN 0-8420-1703-8). Scholarly Res Inc.

--The Inquiry Handbooks. LC 74-21632. (41 vols. in 20). 1975. 795.00 (ISBN 0-8420-1798-4). Scholarly Res Inc.

Davids, Kenneth. Coffee: A Guide to Buying, Brewing & Enjoying. LC 76-13003. (Illus.). 192p. 1976. 8.95 (ISBN 0-89286-103-7); pap. 5.95 (ISBN 0-685-66660-3). One Hund One Prods.

Davids, Kenneth & Duniec, M. L. Coffee: A Revised Guide to Buying, Brewing & Enjoying. rev. ed. (Illus.). 192p. 1981. pap. 6.95 (ISBN 0-89286-186-X). One Hurd One Prods.

Davids, Lewis E. Dictionary of Banking & Finance. 229p. 1980. 15.00x (ISBN 0-8476-6132-6). Rowman.

Davids, Lewis E., jt. auth. see Spero, Herbert.

Davids, Rhys, tr. see Mueller, F. Max.

Davids, Richard C. Man Who Moved a Mountain. LC 75-99609. (Illus.). 270p. 1972. pap. 4.25 (ISBN 0-8006-1237-X, 1-1237). Fortress.

Davids, T. Rhys. Lectures on the Origin & Growth of Religion As Illustrated by Some Points in the History of Indian Buddhism. 267p. 1972. Repr. text ed. 12.50x o.p. (ISBN 0-8426-0402-2). Verry.

Davidsen, et al. CPA Exam Intermediate Acct. 1980. 5.95 (ISBN 0-03-058087-0). Dryden Pr.

Davidsohn, A. & Milwidski, B. M. Synthetic Detergents. 6th ed. LC 77-13133. 1978. 29.95 (ISBN 0-470-99312-X). Halsted Pr.

Davidsohn, Israel & Stern, Kurt. Problem Solving in Immunohematology. 2nd ed. LC 77-93058. 1978. pap. text ed. 20.00 (ISBN 0-89189-035-1, 45-6-012-00). Am Soc Clinical.

Davidson, et al. Managerial Accounting. 1978. 20.95 (ISBN 0-03-017416-3). Dryden Pr.

Davidson, A. B. Hebrew Syntax. 3rd ed. 248p. pap. text ed. 12.00x (ISBN 0-567-21007-3). Attic Pr.

--An Introductory Hebrew Grammar, with Progressive Exercises in Reading & Writing. 26th ed. Mauchline, John, ed. 336p. 1966. text ed. 14.50x (ISBN 0-567-01005-8). Attic Pr.

--The Theology of the Old Testament. (International Theological Library Ser.). 567p. Repr. of 1904 ed. text ed. 13.95x (ISBN 0-567-27206-0). Attic Pr.

Davidson, A. E. & Davidson, C. N., eds. The Art of Margaret Atwood: Essays in Criticism. 250p. 1981. 18.95 (ISBN 0-88784-080-9, Pub. by Hse Anansi Pr Canada). U of Toronto Pr.

Davidson, Abraham A. Story of American Painting. LC 74-5116. (Illus.). 164p. 1975. 15.95 o.p. (ISBN 0-8109-0498-5); pap. 6.95 o.p. (ISBN 0-8109-2069-7). Abrams.

Davidson, Alan. Fish and Fish Dishes of Laos. LC 75-29794. (Illus.). 1975. pap. 4.75 o.p. (ISBN 0-8048-1170-9). C E Tuttle.

Davidson, Alastair. Antonio Gramsci: Towards an Intellectual Bibliography. (International Library of Social & Political Thought). 1977. text ed. 19.50x (ISBN 0-391-00671-1). Humanities.

Davidson, Angus, tr. see Moravia, Alberto.

Davidson, Angus, tr. see Praz, Mario.

Davidson, Avram. Peregrine: Primus. 1977. pap. 1.95 (ISBN 0-441-65951-9). Ace Bks.

--Peregrine: Secundus. (Orig.). 1981. pap. 2.25 (ISBN 0-425-04829-2). Berkley Pub.

--The Redward Edward Papers. LC 74-27578. 1978. 7.95 o.p. (ISBN 0-385-02058-9). Doubleday.

Davidson, B. R. The Northern Myth: Limits to Agricultural & Pastoral Development in Tropical Australia. (Illus.). 320p. 1972. o.p. 2nd ed. (ISBN 0-522-83577-5, Pub. by Melbourne U Pr); pap. 11.50x 3rd ed. (ISBN 0-522-84035-3, Pub. by Melbourne U Pr). Intl Schol Bk Serv.

Davidson, Basil. African Kingdoms. LC 66-25647. (Great Ages of Man). (Illus.). (gr. 6 up). 1966. PLB 11.97 (ISBN 0-8094-0371-4, Pub. by Time-Life). Silver.

--African Kingdoms. (Great Ages of Man Ser). (Illus.). 1971. 12.95 (ISBN 0-8094-0349-8). Time-Life.

--The African Slave Trade. rev. enl. ed. 312p. 1981. 12.50 (ISBN 0-686-69142-3, Pub. by Atlantic Monthly Pr); pap. 6.95 (ISBN 0-686-69143-1). Little.

--East & Central Africa to the Late Nineteenth Century. LC 68-104173. 1967. 8.00x (ISBN 0-582-60245-9). Intl Pubns Serv.

--A Guide to African History. LC 70-164025. 3.75 o.p. (ISBN 0-385-04138-1); pap. 1.45 o.p. (ISBN 0-385-04922-6). Doubleday.

--History of East & Central Africa. LC 69-20103. pap. 2.50 (ISBN 0-385-00520-2, A677, Anch). Doubleday.

--A History of West Africa 1000-1800. Buah, F. A. & Ade Ajayi, J. F., eds. (The Growth of African Civilisation Ser.). (Illus.). 1978. pap. text ed. 7.50x (ISBN 0-582-60340-4). Longman.

Davidson, Basil, et al, eds. Behind the War in Eritrea. 150p. 1980. pap. text ed. 8.95. Barber Pr.

Davidson, Benjamin. Analytical Hebrew & Chaldee Lexicon. 16.95 (ISBN 0-310-20290-6, Pub. by Bagster). Zondervan.

Davidson, C. N., jt. ed. see Davidson, A. E.

Davidson, C. W. Transmission Lines for Communications. 1978. 29.95 (ISBN 0-470-99160-7). Halsted Pr.

--Wideband Voltage Amplifiers. 1974. pap. text ed. 12.00x (ISBN 0-7002-0235-8). Intl Ideas.

Davidson, Charles S. Liver Pathophysiology: Its Relevance to Human Disease. 296p. 1970. pap. 11.50 o.p. (ISBN 0-316-17429-7). Little.

Davidson, Clifford. Drama & Art: An Introduction to the Use of Evidence from the Visual Arts for the Study of Early Drama. (Early Drama, Art, & Music Ser.). (Illus.). 1977. pap. 4.95 (ISBN 0-918720-00-1). Medieval Inst.

Davidson, Clifford, ed. A Middle English Treatise on the Playing of Miracles. LC 81-40028. 93p. 1981. lib. bdg. 14.75 (ISBN 0-8191-1514-2); pap. text ed. 6.75 (ISBN 0-8191-1515-0). U Pr of Amer.

Davidson, David & Blot, David. Put It in Writing: Writing Activities for Students of ESL. (Illus.). 96p. (Orig.). 1981. pap. text ed. 3.95 (ISBN 0-88377-175-6). Newbury Hse.

Davidson, David L., jt. ed. see Zusman, Jack.

Davidson, David M. Current Approaches to the Teaching of Grammar in ESL. (Language in Education Ser.: No. 5). 1978. pap. 2.95 (ISBN 0-87281-081-X). Ctr Appl Ling.

Davidson, Delphine. Soft Toys. 1971. 6.50 o.p. (ISBN 0-8231-5028-3). Branford.

Davidson, Donald. Essays on Actions & Events. 320p. 1980. 29.50x (ISBN 0-19-824529-7); pap. 9.95x (ISBN 0-19-824637-4). Oxford U Pr.

--Reference Service. 1980. text ed. 19.00 (ISBN 0-89664-423-5, Pub. by K G Saur). Shoe String.

--Science for Physical Geographers. LC 78-11957. 1978. 16.95 (ISBN 0-470-26556-6). Halsted Pr.

--Tennessee: The Old River, Frontier to Secession. (Rivers of American Ser). (Illus.). 1946. 4.00 o.p. (ISBN 0-03-028870-3). HR&W.

--Tennessee: Vol. 1: the Old River-Frontier to Secession. LC 78-15103. 1979. 12.50 (ISBN 0-87049-265-9). U of Tenn Pr.

Davidson, Donald A. & Shackley, Myra, eds. Geoarchaeology: Earth Science of the Past. rev. ed. LC 76-25224. 1977. lib. bdg. 45.00x (ISBN 0-89158-635-0). Westview.

Davidson, Elizabeth W., ed. Pathogenesis of Invertebrate Microbial Diseases. 500p. 1981. text ed. 40.00 (ISBN 0-86598-014-4). Allanheld.

Davidson, Eugene. The Making of Adolph Hitler. (Illus.). 1977. 22.95 o.s.i. (ISBN 0-02-529700-7). Macmillan.

--Trial of the Germans: An Account of the Twenty-Two Defendants Before the International Tribunal at Nuremburg. 1972. pap. 3.95 o.s.i. (ISBN 0-02-031270-9, Collier). Macmillan.

Davidson, Frank P. & Meador, C. Lawrence, eds. How Big & Still Beautiful? Macro-Engineering Revisited. (AAAS Selected Symposium: No. 30). 383p. 1980. lib. bdg. 28.50x (ISBN 0-89158-792-6). Westview.

Davidson, Frank P., et al. Macroengineering & the Infra-Structure of Tomorrow. 1979. lib. bdg. 27.50x (ISBN 0-89158-294-0). Westview.

Davidson, Fredrick, jt. auth. see Tersine, Richard J.

Davidson, Georgie. Origami. LC 75-44992. (Larousse Craft Ser.). (Illus.). 1978. pap. 5.95 (ISBN 0-88332-027-4, 8036). Larousse.

Davidson, Glen W., ed. The Hospice: Development & Administration. LC 78-3836. 1978. text ed. 19.50 (ISBN 0-89116-103-1). Hemisphere Pub.

Davidson, Gustov. A Dictionary of Angels: Including the Fallen Angels. LC 66-19757. (Illus.). 1967. 17.00 (ISBN 0-02-906940-8); pap. 9.95 (ISBN 0-02-907050-3). Free Pr.

Davidson, H. A. The Philosophy of Abraham Shalom: A Fifteenth-Century Exposition & Defense of Maimonides. (U. C. Publ. in Near Eastern Studies: Vol. 5). 1964. pap. 6.75x (ISBN 0-520-09298-8). U of Cal Pr.

Davidson, H. F., jt. auth. see Certon, M. J.

Davidson, H. W., et al. Manufactured Carbon. 1968. 15.00 (ISBN 0-08-012667-7); pap. 7.00 (ISBN 0-08-012666-9). Pergamon.

Davidson, Harold & Mechlenburg, Roy. Nursery Management: Administration & Culture. (Illus.). 464p. 1981. text ed. 19.95 (ISBN 0-13-627455-2). P-H.

Davidson, Henry. Short History of Chess. 1968. 6.95 o.p. (ISBN 0-679-13035-7). McKay.

Davidson, Herbert A., ed. see Averrois.

Davidson, Hilda, ed. Saxo Grammaticus: The History of the Danes, Vol. 1-Englist Text. Fisher, Peter, tr. 297p. 1979. 36.50x (ISBN 0-8476-6221-7). Rowman.

Davidson, Hilda E., ed. Saxo Grammaticus: History of the Danes, Vol. II. Fisher, Peter, tr. (Illus.). 209p. 1980. 35.00x (ISBN 0-8476-6938-6). Rowman.

Davidson, Hugh M., jt. auth. see Dube, Pierre H.

Davidson, Hugh M. & Dube, Pierre H., eds. A Concordance to the Pascal's Pensees. LC 75-16808. (Cornell Concordances Ser.). 1488p. 1975. 40.00x (ISBN 0-8014-0972-1). Cornell U Pr.

Davidson, I., et al, eds. Electronic Maintenance, Vol. 2. (Engineering Craftsmen: No. J24). (Illus.). 1970. spiral bdg. 18.95x (ISBN 0-685-90140-8). Intl Ideas.

Davidson, Ian D. Britain & the Making of Europe. LC 74-182185. 1972. text ed. 18.95 (ISBN 0-312-09800-6). St Martin.

Davidson, Isobel. Real Stories from Baltimore County History. LC 70-9245. (Illus.). x, 296p. Repr. of 1917 ed. 15.00 (ISBN 0-8103-5033-5). Gale.

Davidson, J. New Mathematics. (Teach Yourself Ser.). 1974. pap. 4.95 (ISBN 0-679-12326-1). McKay.

Davidson, J. F., ed. Fluidization. Keairns, D. L. LC 77-82495. (Illus.). 1978. 52.50 (ISBN 0-521-21943-4). Cambridge U Pr.

Davidson, J. F., jt. ed. see Von Kaulla, K. N.

Davidson, J. M. & Edds, G. T., eds. Sludge: Health Risks of Land Application. (Illus.). 400p. 1980. 37.50 (ISBN 0-250-40374-9). Ann Arbor Science.

Davidson, J. N., et al, eds. Progress in Nucleic Acid Research & Molecular Biology: An International Series. Incl. Vol. 3. 1964. 48.00 (ISBN 0-12-540003-9); Vol. 4. 1965. 48.00 (ISBN 0-12-540004-7); Vol. 5. 1966. 48.00 (ISBN 0-12-540005-5); Vol. 6. 1967. 48.00 (ISBN 0-12-540006-3); Vol. 7. 1967. 48.00 (ISBN 0-12-540007-1); Vol. 8. 1968. 48.00 (ISBN 0-12-540008-X); Vol. 9. 1969. 48.00 (ISBN 0-12-540009-8); Vol. 10. 1970. 41.00 (ISBN 0-12-540010-1); Vol. 11. 1970. 51.00 (ISBN 0-12-540011-X); Vol. 12. 1972. 40.00 (ISBN 0-12-540012-8); Vol. 13. 1973. 44.50 (ISBN 0-12-540013-6); Vol. 20. 1977. 39.00 (ISBN 0-12-540020-9); lib. ed. 55.50 (ISBN 0-12-540084-5); microfiche 27.50 (ISBN 0-12-540085-3); Vol. 21. 1978. 28.00 (ISBN 0-12-540021-7); lib. ed. 35.00 (ISBN 0-12-540086-1); microfiche o. s. i. 21.00 (ISBN 0-12-540087-X); Vol. 22. 1979. 40.00 (ISBN 0-12-540022-5); lib ed. o. s. i. 54.50 (ISBN 0-12-540088-8); microfiche 29.00 (ISBN 0-12-540089-6). Acad Pr.

Davidson, J. P. & Kern, Bernard D., eds. Fifth Symposium on the Structure of Low-Medium Mass Nuclei. LC 73-77254. (Illus.). 312p. 1973. 17.00x (ISBN 0-8131-1293-1). U Pr of Ky.

Davidson, James. Effective Time Management: A Practical Workbook. LC 78-6126. 1978. 9.95 (ISBN 0-87705-332-4). Human Sci Pr.

Davidson, James J. The Vision of an Artist & Writer. 1981. 6.95 (ISBN 0-533-04806-0). Vantage.

Davidson, James M., jt. ed. see Overcash, Michael R.

Davidson, James R. A Dictionary of Protestant Church Music. LC 74-30101. 1975. 15.00 (ISBN 0-8108-0788-2). Scarecrow.

Davidson, Jeffrey L. Political Partnerships: Neighborhood Residents & Their Council Members. LC 79-13107. (The City & Society: Vol. 5). (Illus.). 231p. 1979. 18.00 (ISBN 0-8039-1050-9). Sage.

--Political Partnerships: Neighborhood Residents & Their Council Members. LC 79-13107. (The City & Society: Vol. 5). (Illus.). 231p. 1979. pap. 8.95 (ISBN 0-8039-1051-7). Sage.

--Political Partnerships: Neighborhood Residents & Their Council Members. LC 79-13107. (City & Society Ser.: Vol. 5). (Illus.). 231p. 1979. pap. 8.95 (ISBN 0-8039-1051-7); pap. 8.95 (ISBN 0-8039-1051-7). Sage.

Davidson, Jessica. How to Improve Your Spelling & Vocabulary. (gr. 7 up). 1980. PLB 6.45 (ISBN 0-531-04133-6). Watts.

--Is That Mother in the Bottle? LC 72-1997. (Illus.). 128p. (gr. 9 up). 1972. PLB 4.90 o.p. (ISBN 0-531-02575-6). Watts.

Davidson, Jessica & Martin, William C. Mind-Boggling Brain Benders. (Illus.). (gr. 7-12). pap. 1.95 (ISBN 0-13-583336-1). P-H.

Davidson, John. Diabolus Amans. Fletcher, Ian, ed. Bd. with The North Wall. LC 76-20055. (Decadent Consciousness Ser.: Vol. 6). 1978. Repr. of 1885 ed. lib. bdg. 38.00 (ISBN 0-8240-2755-8). Garland Pub.

--A Full Account of the Wonderful Mission of Earl Lavender. Fletcher, Ian & Stokes, John, eds. LC 76-20049. (Decadent Consciousness Ser.: Vol. 7). 1977. Repr. of 1894 ed. lib. bdg. 38.00 (ISBN 0-8240-2756-6). Garland Pub.

--The Way to End Inflation. 1980. 7.95 (ISBN 0-533-04736-6). Vantage.

Davidson, John & Casady, Cort. The Singing Entertainer. LC 79-17183. 227p. 1979. pap. 9.95 (ISBN 0-88284-095-9). Alfred Pub.

Davidson, John F. & Harrison, David. Fluidised Particles. 1963. 27.50 (ISBN 0-521-04789-7). Cambridge U Pr.

Davidson, John F., ed. Progress in Chemical Fibrinolysis & Thrombolysis, Vol. 2. LC 75-14335. 1976. 19.00 (ISBN 0-89004-136-9). Raven.

Davidson, John F., et al, eds. Progress in Chemical Fibrinolysis & Thrombolysis, Vol. 3. LC 75-14335. 1978. 56.00 (ISBN 0-89004-137-7). Raven.

--Progress in Chemical Fibrinolysis & Thrombolysis, Vol. 1. LC 75-14335. 425p. 1975. 36.00 (ISBN 0-89004-036-2). Raven.

Davidson, Julian M., jt. ed. see Davidson, Richard J.

Davidson, Kerry. Twentieth Century Civilization. 1976. pap. 3.95 o.p. (ISBN 0-06-460146-3, Cos). Har-Row.

Davidson, Leon. Flying Saucers - an Analysis of the Air Force Project Blue Book Special Report No. 14: Including the C. I. A. & the Saucers. 4th ed. (Illus.). 1977. pap. 12.95 o.p. (ISBN 0-685-80881-5). Saucerian.

Davidson, Margaret. The Golda Meir Story. rev. ed. (Illus.). 240p. (gr. 3-7). 1981. 9.95 (ISBN 0-684-16877-4). Scribner.

--Helen Keller. (Illus.). (gr. 2-4). 1970. PLB 5.95 o.p. (ISBN 0-8038-3015-7). Hastings.

--Nine True Dolphin Stories. 72p. (gr. 2-6). 1975. 6.95g (ISBN 0-8038-5037-9). Hastings.

--Seven True Dog Stories. (gr. 2-4). 1977. 6.95 (ISBN 0-8038-6738-7). Hastings.

--Seven True Horse Stories. (Illus.). (gr. 2-5). 1979. 6.95g (ISBN 0-8038-6760-3). Hastings.

--Successful Studios & Work Centers. LC 76-52980. (Illus.). 144p. 1977. 12.00 (ISBN 0-912336-36-6); pap. 5.95 (ISBN 0-912336-37-4). Structures Pub.

Davidson, Marshall B. The American Heritage History of Notable American Houses. LC 75-149724. (Illus.). 384p. 1971. 19.95 (ISBN 0-8281-0258-9, Dist. by Scribner); deluxe ed. 22.50 slipcased (ISBN 0-8281-0259-7, Dist. by Scribner). Am Heritage.

Davidson, Mary R. Buffalo Bill. (gr. k-6). 1980. pap. 1.25 (ISBN 0-440-40748-6, YB). Dell.

Davidson, Michael, tr. see Mehnert, Klaus.

Davidson, Mildred. Link of Three. 192p. (gr. 3-7). 1981. 9.95 (ISBN 0-7011-2486-5, Pub. by Chatto-Bodley-Jonathan). Merrimack Bk Serv.

Davidson, Neil A. & Gulick, Frances F. Abstract Algebra: An Active Learning Approach. LC 75-19537. (Illus.). 1976. text ed. 19.50 (ISBN 0-395-20663-4); inst. manual 1.75 (ISBN 0-395-20664-2). HM.

Davidson, Nicole & UNITAR, eds. Paths to Peace: The UN Security & Its Prsidency. LC 80-20166. (Pergamon Policy Studies on International Politics). 380p. 1981. 42.50 (ISBN 0-08-026322-4). Pergamon.

Davidson, Norman, jt. ed. see Rich, Alexander.

Davidson, Paul. Money & the Real World. 2nd ed. 1978. pap. text ed. 14.95 (ISBN 0-470-99217-4). Halsted Pr.

Davidson, Phyllis. Home Management. 1975. pap. 16.95 (ISBN 0-7134-3047-8, Pub. by Batsford England). David & Charles.

Davidson, R. J. Methods in Nonlinear Plasma Theory. (Pure & Applied Physics Ser.). 1972. 48.00 o.s.i. (ISBN 0-12-205450-4). Acad Pr.

Davidson, Richard, jt. auth. see Goleman, Daniel.

Davidson, Richard J. & Davidson, Julian M., eds. Psychobiology of Consciousness. 465p. 1980. 32.50 (ISBN 0-306-40138-X, Plenum Pr). Plenum Pub.

Davidson, Richard L. & De La Cruz, Felix F. Somatic Cell Hybridization. LC 74-75725. 1974. 31.50 (ISBN 0-911216-75-8). Raven.

Davidson, Robert L., ed. see Volk, William.

Davidson, Robyn. Tracks. (Illus.). 1981. 11.95 (ISBN 0-394-51473-4). Pantheon.

Davidson, Roger H. The Role of the Congressman. LC 68-27986. 1969. 18.50x (ISBN 0-672-53587-4). Irvington.

Davidson, Roger H. & Oleszek, Walter J. Congress against Itself. LC 76-12378. (Midland Bks.: No. 223). 320p. 1977. 15.00x (ISBN 0-253-31405-4); pap. 5.95x (ISBN 0-253-20223-X). Ind U Pr.

Davidson, Roslyn. Rehabilitation Administrative Procedures for Extended Care Facilities. (Illus.). 116p. 1973. pap. 11.75 spiral (ISBN 0-398-02611-4). C C Thomas.

Davidson, Sara. Loose Change. 1981. pap. price not set (ISBN 0-671-43119-6). PB.

--Real Property. 1981. pap. 2.95 (ISBN 0-671-41269-8). PB.

Davidson, Sharon V. PSRO: Utilization & Audit in Patient Care. LC 75-43980. (Illus.). 380p. 1976. 18.95 (ISBN 0-8016-1209-8). Mosby.

Davidson, Sharon V., ed. Alcoholism & Health. LC 80-12354. 216p. 1980. text ed. 24.50 (ISBN 0-89443-292-3). Aspen Systems.

Davidson, Sharon V., et al. Nursing Care Evaluation: Concurrent & Retrospective Review Criteria. LC 77-5069. 1977. 19.95 (ISBN 0-8016-1210-1). Mosby.

Davidson, Sidney, ed. see Ventolo, William L., Jr.

Davidson, Sidney, et al. C.P.A. Exam Booklet. 2nd ed. 1981. pap. text ed. 6.95 (ISBN 0-686-69576-3). Dryden Pr.

--Intermediate Accounting. 2nd ed. LC 80-65795. 1088p. 1981. text ed. 24.95 (ISBN 0-03-058081-1). Dryden Pr.

Davidson, Stephen M. Medicaid Decisions: Systematic Analysis of the Cost Problem. LC 80-10998. 1980. 23.50 (ISBN 0-88410-142-8). Ballinger Pub.

Davidson, Stephen M., et al. The Cost of Living Longer: National Health Insurance & the Elderly. LC 79-2756. 160p. 1980. 19.95 (ISBN 0-669-03242-5). Lexington Bks.

Davidson, W. R., et al. Retailing Management. 4th ed. 1975. 24.50 (ISBN 0-8260-2423-8); instructors' manual avail. (ISBN 0-471-07457-8). Wiley.

Davidson, William, et al. Evaluation Strategies in Criminal Justice. (Pergamon General Psychology Ser.). Date not set. 27.51 (ISBN 0-08-024664-8). Pergamon.

Davidson, William L. Political Thought in England: The Utilitarians, from Bentham to J. S. Mill. LC 79-1624. 1981. Repr. of 1916 ed. 21.50 (ISBN 0-88355-929-3). Hyperion Conn.

Davidson, William S., jt. auth. see Fairweather, George W.

Davidson Pratt, J. & West, T. F. Services for the Chemical Industry. 1968. 21.00 (ISBN 0-08-012665-0); pap. 10.50 (ISBN 0-08-012664-2). Pergamon.

Davidson Pratt, J., jt. auth. see Hardie, D. W.

Davie, Cedric T. Musical Structure & Design. (Illus.). 1966. pap. 3.25 (ISBN 0-486-21629-2). Dover.

Davie, Donald. Articulate Energy. 1976. 17.50x (ISBN 0-7100-8155-3). Routledge & Kegan.

--Events & Wisdoms. LC 65-21077. (Wesleyan Poetry Program: Vol. 27). (Orig.). 1965. 10.00x (ISBN 0-8195-2027-6, Pub. by Wesleyan U Pr); pap. 4.95x (ISBN 0-8195-1027-0). Columbia U Pr.

--New & Selected Poems. LC 61-14214. (Wesleyan Poetry Program: Vol. 12). (Orig.). 1961. 10.00x (ISBN 0-8195-2012-8, Pub. by Wesleyan U Pr); pap. 4.95x (ISBN 0-8195-1012-2). Columbia U Pr.

--Trying to Explain. (Poets on Poetry Ser.). 1979. pap. 5.95 (ISBN 0-472-06310-3). U of Mich Pr.

Davie, Donald, ed. Augustan Lyric. (The Poetry Bookshelf). 1974. pap. text ed. 3.95x (ISBN 0-435-15701-9). Heinemann Ed.

Davie, Elspeth. The Night of the Funny Hats. 192p. 1980. 18.50 o.p. (ISBN 0-241-10377-0, Pub. by Hamish Hamilton England). David & Charles.

Davie, John, ed. see Austen, Jane.

Davie, Maurice R. Constructive Immigration Policy. 1923. pap. 12.50x (ISBN 0-685-69809-2). Elliots Bks.

--Evolution of War: A Study of Its Role in Early Societies. 1929. 12.50x (ISBN 0-686-51382-7). Elliots Bks.

Davies & Goldsmith. Statistical Methods Research. 1976. 19.95 (ISBN 0-582-03040-4). Longman.

Davies, A. F. Skills, Outlooks, Passions: A Psychoanalytic Contribution to Lthe Study of Politics. 2nd ed. LC 78-54575. (Illus.). 456p. Date not set. 55.00 (ISBN 0-521-22081-5); pap. 14.95 (ISBN 0-521-29349-9). Cambridge U Pr.

Davies, A. Mervyn. Presbyterian Heritage. LC 65-10136. (Orig.). 1965. pap. 2.25 (ISBN 0-8042-0972-3). John Knox.

Davies, Alan J. The Finite Element Method: A First Approach. (Oxford Applied Mathematics & Computing Science Ser.). (Illus.). 300p. 1980. 49.50x (ISBN 0-19-859630-8); pap. 27.50x (ISBN 0-19-859631-6). Oxford U Pr.

Davies, Alice I. Allart van Everdingen. LC 77-94692. (Outstanding Dissertations in the Fine Arts Ser.). 1979. lib. bdg. 64.50 (ISBN 0-8240-3223-3). Garland Pub.

Davies, Andrew. Conrad's War. (gr. 5 up). 1980. 7.95 (ISBN 0-517-54007-X). Crown.

--The Fantastic Feats of Doctor Boox. (gr. 4-6). 1977. pap. 1.25 (ISBN 0-590-10335-0, Schol Pap). Schol Bk Serv.

Davies, Aneirin T. Dylan: Druid of the Broken Body. 1977. text ed. 11.25x (ISBN 0-7154-0347-8). Humanities.

Davies, Ann. This Is Truth About the Self. 2nd ed. 1974. 2.25 (ISBN 0-938002-03-1). Builders of Adytum.

Davies, Anthea. White Horse with Wings. (gr. 5-8). 1970. 4.95g o.s.i. (ISBN 0-02-726230-8). Macmillan.

Davies, Arthur C. The Science & Practice of Welding. 7th ed. LC 77-71408. (Illus.). 1977. 23.95x (ISBN 0-521-21557-9). Cambridge U Pr.

Davies, Barbara S. & Davies, J. Clarence, 3rd. The Politics of Pollution. 2nd ed. LC 74-20996. (Studies in Contemporary America Ser.). 256p. 1975. 6.50 (ISBN 0-672-53720-6); pap. 5.95 (ISBN 0-672-63720-0). Pegasus.

Davies, Bettilu D. Really, Marty! 128p. (gr. 6-10). 1981. pap. 1.95 (ISBN 0-8024-9299-1). Moody.

Davies, Bleddyn. Variatons in Childrens Services Among Urban Authorities. 159p. 1972. pap. text ed. 6.25x (ISBN 0-7135-1676-3, Pub. by Bedford England). Renouf.

Davies, Bleddyn & Knapp, Martin. Old People's Homes & the Production of Welfare. (Library of Social Work Ser.). 240p. 1981. 32.50 (ISBN 0-7100-0700-0). Routledge & Kegan.

Davies, Bleddyn P. Variations in Services for the Aged. 164p. 1971. pap. text ed. 6.25x (ISBN 0-7135-1621-6, Pub. by Bedford England). Renouf.

Davies, Brian. Seal Song. (Large Format Ser). (Illus.). 1979. pap. 5.95 o.p. (ISBN 0-14-004740-9). Penguin.

Davies, C., et al. Organization for Program Management. LC 78-27660. 1980. 34.95 (ISBN 0-471-27571-9, Pub. by Wiley-Interscience). Wiley.

Davies, C. N. Health Conditions in the Ceramic Industry. 286p. 1970. 46.00 (ISBN 0-08-013347-9). Pergamon.

Davies, C. W. & James, A. M. Dictionary of Electrochemistry. LC 76-4876. 525p. 1976. 29.95 (ISBN 0-470-15064-5). Halsted Pr.

Davies, Celia, ed. Rewriting Nursing History. 226p. 1981. 23.50x (ISBN 0-389-20153-7). B&N.

Davies, Charles M. Broad Church. Wolff, Robert L., ed. LC 75-1505. (Victorian Fiction Ser.). 1975. Repr. of 1875 ed. lib. bdg. 66.00 (ISBN 0-8240-1579-7). Garland Pub.

--Philip Paternoster: A Tractarian Love Story, 1858. Wolff, Robert L., ed. LC 75-477. (Victorian Fiction Ser.). 1975. lib. bdg. 66.00 (ISBN 0-8240-1555-X). Garland Pub.

--Verts; or, the Three Creeds, 1876. Wolff, Robert L., ed. LC 75-1506. (Victorian Fiction Ser.). 1975. lib. bdg. 66.00 (ISBN 0-8240-1580-0). Garland Pub.

Davies, Charles N., ed. Aerosol Science. 1967. 64.50 o.s.i. (ISBN 0-12-205650-7). Acad Pr.

Davies, Chris, et al, eds. Jesus: One of Us. 148p. 1981. pap. 3.95 (ISBN 0-87784-618-9). Inter Varsity.

Davies, D., ed. Central Action of Drugs in the Regulation of Blood Pressure. (Illus.). 1976. 39.50 (ISBN 0-8391-0800-1). Univ Park.

Davies, D. A. Waves, Atoms, & Solids. LC 77-2192. (Illus.). 1978. pap. text ed. 19.50x (ISBN 0-582-44174-9). Longman.

Davies, D. S., et al. The Humane Technologist. (Science & Engineering Policy Ser.). (Illus.). 1976. 15.95x (ISBN 0-19-858325-7). Oxford U Pr.

Davies, D. W., et al. Computer Networks & Their Protocols. LC 78-21973. (Wiley Series in Computing). 487p. 1979. 53.25 (ISBN 0-471-99750-1, Pub. by Wiley Interscience). Wiley.

Davies, David. The Influence of Teeth, Diet & Habits on the Human Face. 1972. 16.00x (ISBN 0-8448-0743-5). Crane-Russak Co.

Davies, David W. Public Libraries As Culture & Social Centers: The Origin of the Concept. LC 74-8420. 1974. 9.00 (ISBN 0-8108-0738-6). Scarecrow.

Davies, David W. & Wrigley, Elizabeth S., eds. Concordance to the Essays of Francis Bacon. LC 73-8947. 392p. 1973. 48.00 (ISBN 0-8103-1004-X). Gale.

Davies, Don, ed. Communities & Their Schools. (Study of the Schooling in the United States Ser.). 352p. 1981. 16.95 (ISBN 0-07-015503-8, P&RB). McGraw.

--Schools Where Parents Make a Difference. 163p. (Orig.). 1976. pap. text ed. 3.95 (ISBN 0-917754-00-X). Inst Responsive.

Davies, Don & Zerchykov, Ross, eds. Citizen Participation in Education: Annotated Bibliography. 386p. (Orig.). 1978. pap. text ed. 15.00 (ISBN 0-917754-05-0). Inst Responsive.

Davies, Don, et al. Federal & State Impact on Citizen Participation in the Schools. 147p. (Orig.). 1978. pap. text ed. 5.00 (ISBN 0-917754-04-2). Inst Responsive.

Davies, E. L. & Grove, E. J. Dartmouth: The Royal Naval College, Seventy-Five Years in Pictures. (Illus.). 96p. 1980. 14.95 (ISBN 0-85997-462-6). McCartan & Root.

Davies, E. W., ed. see Cicero.

Davies, Edward. Celtic Researches, on the Origin, Traditions & Language, of the Ancient Britons. Feldman, Burton & Richardson, Robert D., eds. LC 78-60902. (Myth & Romanticism Ser.: Vol. 8). (Illus.). 1979. lib. bdg. 66.00 (ISBN 0-8240-3557-7). Garland Pub.

Davies, Eirian. On the Semantics of Syntax: Mood & Condition in English. (Croom Helm Linguistic Ser.). 1979. text ed. 26.00x (ISBN 0-391-00936-2). Humanities.

Davies, Eryl. Prophecy & Ethics: Isaiah & the Ethical Traditions of Israel. (Journal for the Study of the Old Testament, Supplement Ser.: No. 16). 1980. 19.95x (ISBN 0-905774-26-4, Pub. by JSOT Pr England). Eisenbrauns.

Davies, Frederick, tr. see Labiche, Eugene M.

Davies, G. I. The Way of the Wilderness. LC 77-95442. (Society for Old Testament Monographs). (Illus.). 1979. 22.50 (ISBN 0-521-22057-2). Cambridge U Pr.

Davies, Garth W., jt. auth. see Bingham, John E.

Davies, Hilary, tr. see Hoeper, Claus-Juergen, et al.

Davies, Hugh. International Electronic Music Catalog. 1968. 21.00x (ISBN 0-262-04012-3). MIT Pr.

Davies, Hugh S; see Bloomfield, Paul.

Davies, Hunter. William Wordsworth: A Biography. LC 80-66004. (Illus.). 1980. 17.95 (ISBN 0-689-11087-1). Atheneum.

Davies, Ivor K. Instructional Technique. (Illus.). 352p. 1980. text ed. 14.95x (ISBN 0-07-015502-X, TD). McGraw.

Davies, J., ed. Esenin: A Biography in Memoirs, Letters, & Documents. 400p. 1981. 22.50 (ISBN 0-88233-491-3). Ardis Pubs. Postponed.

Davies, J. C. When Men Revolt & Why. LC 74-142361. 1971. 12.95 (ISBN 0-02-907310-3); pap. text ed. 9.95 (ISBN 0-02-907000-7). Free Pr.

Davies, J. Clarence. Neighborhood Groups & Urban Renewal. LC 65-27764. 1966. 17.50x (ISBN 0-231-02792-3). Columbia U Pr.

Davies, J. Clarence, 3rd, jt. auth. see Davies, Barbara S.

Davies, J. H. Musicalia: Sources of Information in Music. 2nd ed. 1969. 12.25 (ISBN 0-08-006357-8); pap. 7.00 (ISBN 0-08-006356-X). Pergamon.

Davies, J. K. Democracy & Classical Greece. (Fontana History of the Ancient World Ser.). 1978. text ed. 22.25x (ISBN 0-391-00766-1). Humanities.

Davies, Jack. Ffolks. 320p. (Orig.). 1980. pap. 2.50 (ISBN 0-515-05430-5). Jove Pubns.

Davies, Jane, jt. auth. see Andrian, Gustave W.

Davies, Jeffrey W., jt. auth. see Hall, Timothy C.

Davies, John. Wittes Pilgrimage, (by Poeticall Essaies) Through a World of Amorous Sonnets, Etc. LC 79-84099. (English Experience Ser.: No. 919). 172p. 1979. Repr. of 1605 ed. lib. bdg. 17.00 (ISBN 90-221-0919-4). Walter J Johnson.

Davies, John, ed. see Douglas, David.

Davies, John, tr. see Scarron, Paul.

Davies, John E., jt. auth. see Beck, J. Walter.

Davies, Julian & Littlewood, Barbara S. Elementary Biochemistry: An Introduction to the Chemistry of Living Cells. (P-H Biology Ser.). (Illus.). 1979. ref. 18.95 (ISBN 0-13-252809-6). P-H.

Davies, K. G. Documents of the American Revolution, 1770-1783, Vols. 8 & 9. Incl. Vol. 8. Transcript 1774. 244p (ISBN 0-7165-2093-1); Vol. 9. Transcript Jan.-June, 1775. 244p (ISBN 0-7165-2094-X). 1976. 50.00x ea. (Pub. by Irish Academic Pr Ireland). Biblio Dist.

--Documents of the American Revolution 1770-1783: Transcripts 1776, Vol. 12. (Colonial Office Ser.). 308p. 1976. 50.00x (ISBN 0-7165-2097-4, Pub. by Irish Academic Pr Ireland). Biblio Dist.

Davies, K. G., ed. Documents of the American Revolution: Calendar 1777-1778, Vol. 13. (Colonial Office Ser.). 1976. 60.00x (ISBN 0-7165-2098-2, Pub. by Irish Academic Pr Ireland). Biblio Dist.

--Documents of the American Revolution 1770-1783: Calender 1781-1783 with Addenda 1770-1780. (Colonial Office Ser: Vol. 19). 550p. 1978. 60.00x (ISBN 0-7165-2104-0, Pub by Irish Academic Pr Ireland). Biblio Dist.

--Documents of the American Revolution 1770-1783: Calendar 1779-1780, Vol. 16. (Colonial Office Ser.). 556p. 1977. 60.00x (ISBN 0-7165-2101-6, Pub. by Irish Academic Pr Ireland). Biblio Dist.

--Documents of the American Revolution, 1770-1783: Transcripts 1781, Vol. 20. (Colonial Office Ser.). 309p. 1980. 50.00x (ISBN 0-7165-2105-9, Pub. by Irish Academic Pr Ireland). Biblio Dist.

--Documents of the American Revolution 1770-1783: Transcripts 1777, Vol. 14. (Colonial Office Ser.). 1977. 50.00x (ISBN 0-7165-2099-0, Pub. by Irish Academic Pr Ireland). Biblio Dist.

--Documents of the American Revolution 1770-1783: Transcripts 1778, Vol. 15. (Colonial Office Ser.). 1977. 50.00x (ISBN 0-7165-2100-8, Pub. by Irish Academic Pr Ireland). Biblio Dist.

--Documents of the American Revolution 1770-1783: Transcripts 1779, Vol. 17. (Colonial Office Ser.). 296p. 1977. 50.00x (ISBN 0-7165-2102-4, Pub. by Irish Academic Pr Ireland). Biblio Dist.

--Documents of the American Revolution 1770-1783, Vol. 21, Transcripts & Addenda: 1782-1783, Vol. 21. (Colonial Offices Ser.). 1981. 50.00x (ISBN 0-7165-2106-7, Pub. by Irish Academic Pr Ireland). Biblio Dist.

Davies, L., jt. auth. see Watts, C. T.

Davies, L., et al. Further Topics in Investigating Chemistry. 1974. text ed. 6.25x o.p. (ISBN 0-435-64162-X). Heinemann Ed.

--Investigating Chemistry. 1973. pap. text ed. 9.95x o.p. (ISBN 0-435-64164-6); tchr's notes 7.50 o.p. (ISBN 0-435-64161-1). Heinemann Ed.

Davies, Laurence. Cesar Franck & His Circle. LC 77-4231. (Music Reprint Ser.). (Illus.). 1977. Repr. of 1970 ed. lib. bdg. 27.50 (ISBN 0-306-77410-0). Da Capo.

Davies, Louise. Easy Cooking for One or Two. (Handbook Ser). 1981. pap. 2.95 (ISBN 0-14-046379-8). Penguin.

Davies, M., ed. see Dzyuba, Ivan.

Davies, M. Benedict, tr. see Boros, Ladislaus.

Davies, M. J. Pathology of Cardiac Valves. LC 80-40487. (Butterworths Postgraduate Pathology Ser.). 192p. 1980. text ed. 52.95 (ISBN 0-407-00179-4). Butterworths.

Davies, M. S., et al. A Directory of Clothing Research. 136p. 1968. 35.00x (ISBN 0-686-63762-3). State Mutual Bk.

Davies, Martin. Prisoners of Society: Attitudes & After-Care. (International Library of Sociology Ser.). 1974. 18.50 (ISBN 0-7100-7989-3). Routledge & Kegan.

--Support Systems in Social Work. (Library of Social Work). 1977. 16.00x (ISBN 0-7100-8616-4); pap. 7.95 (ISBN 0-7100-8617-2). Routledge & Kegan.

Davies, Melissa. The Face of Chalk. 1977. pap. 1.50 o.p. (ISBN 0-445-04008-4). Popular Lib.

Davies, Merton & Murray, Bruce C. View from Space: Photographic Exploration of the Planets. LC 75-16887. 1971. 20.00x (ISBN 0-231-03557-8); pap. 7.50x (ISBN 0-231-08330-0). Columbia U Pr.

Davies, Michael. Archbishop Lefebvre & Religious Liberty. 1980. 1.00. Tan Bks Pubs.

--Communion Under Both Kinds- an Ecumenical Surrender. 1980. pap. 1.00 (ISBN 0-89555-141-1). Tan Bks Pubs.

--Liturgical Revolution, Vol. One: Cranmer's Godly Order. 1977. 7.95 o.p. (ISBN 0-87000-395-X). Arlington Hse.

--Liturgical Revolution: Vol. Three: Pope Paul's New Mass. 1979. 9.95 o.p. (ISBN 0-87000-413-1). Arlington Hse.

--Liturgical Revolution: Vol. Two, Pope John's Council. 1977. 9.95 o.p. (ISBN 0-87000-396-8). Arlington Hse.

--Open Lesson to a Bishop. 1980. pap. 1.00 (ISBN 0-89555-142-X). Tan Bks Pubs.

Davies, Nicholas B., jt. ed. see Krebs, John R.

Davies, Nigel. The Aztecs. LC 80-12141. (Illus.). 419p. 1980. 15.95 (ISBN 0-8061-1686-2); pap. 7.95 (ISBN 0-8061-1691-9). U of Okla Pr.

--Human Sacrifice: In History & Today. LC 80-21981. (Illus.). 320p. 1981. 13.95 (ISBN 0-688-03755-0). Morrow.

Davies, P. C. The Forces of Nature. LC 78-72084. (Illus.). 1979. 32.50 (ISBN 0-521-22523-X); pap. 9.95 (ISBN 0-521-29535-1). Cambridge U Pr.

--The Physics of Time Asymmetry. LC 74-81536. 1974. 20.00x (ISBN 0-520-02825-2); pap. 4.95x (ISBN 0-520-03247-0). U of Cal Pr.

--The Search for Gravity Waves. (Illus.). 160p. 1980. 13.95 (ISBN 0-521-23197-3). Cambridge U Pr.

Davies, P. L. Biochemistry: Level Three. (Illus.). 224p. (Orig.). 1980. pap. text ed. 19.95x (ISBN 0-7121-0276-0). Intl Ideas.

Davies, P. L., jt. auth. see Wedderburn, K. W.

Davies, P. M. Medical Terminology in Hospital Practice. 3rd ed. 1979. pap. 15.95x (ISBN 0-433-07183-4). Intl Ideas.

Davies, P. Spencer & Sunderland, N. Perspectives in Experimental Biology: Zoology & Botany, 2 pts. 1090p. 1976. text ed. 230.00 (ISBN 0-08-019939-9); Pt. 1. text ed. 130.00 (ISBN 0-08-018767-6); Pt. 2. text ed. 130.00 (ISBN 0-08-019868-6). Pergamon.

Davies, P. W. Space & Time in the Modern Universe. LC 76-27902. (Illus.). 1977. 28.95 (ISBN 0-521-21445-9); pap. 9.95 (ISBN 0-521-29151-8). Cambridge U Pr.

Davies, Pamela A., et al. Medical Care of Newborn Babies, Vol. 44-45. (Clinics in Developmental Medicine Ser.). 1972. 32.00 (ISBN 0-685-34616-1). Lippincott.

Davies, Paul. Other Worlds. 1981. 11.95 (ISBN 0-671-42227-8). S&S.

--The Runaway Universe. LC 78-2128. (Illus.). 1978. 11.95 o.s.i. (ISBN 0-06-010971-8, HarpT). Har-Row.

Davies, Paul & Freedland, Mark. Labour Law: Text & Materials. (Law in Context Ser.). xliv, 766p. 1979. 50.00x (ISBN 0-297-77591-X, Pub. by Weidenfield & Nicolson); suppl., 1980 4.00 (ISBN 0-297-77888-9). Rothman.

Davies, Penny. Growing up in the Medieval Times. (Growing Up Ser.). 1979. 14.95 (ISBN 0-7134-0483-3, Pub. by Batsford England). David & Charles.

Davies, Peter. Roots: Family Histories of Familiar Words. (Illus.). 224p. Date not set. 15.95 (ISBN 0-07-015449-X, P&RB). McGraw.

Davies, Peter, ed. The American Heritage Dictionary. Date not set. pap. 2.50 (ISBN 0-440-10207-3). Dell.

Davies, Peter J., jt. auth. see Galston, Arthur W.

Davies, R. & Grant, M. D. Forgotten Railways: Chilterns & Cotswolds. LC 74-83307. (Forgotten Railways Ser). (Illus.). 240p. 1975. 14.95 (ISBN 0-7153-6701-3). David & Charles.

--Railway History in Pictures: Chilterns & Cotswolds. 1977. 11.95 (ISBN 0-7153-7299-8). David & Charles.

Davies, R., et al. Intermediate Moisture Foods. (Illus.). 1976. 63.30x (ISBN 0-85334-702-6). Intl Ideas.

Davies, R. L., jt. auth. see Bennison, D. J.

Davies, R. T., ed. Medieval English Lyrics. 1966. 17.95 (ISBN 0-571-05522-2, Pub. by Faber & Faber); pap. 7.95 (ISBN 0-571-06571-6). Merrimack Bk Serv.

--Sir Thomas Malory: King Arthur & His Knights. 1967. 9.95 o.p. (ISBN 0-571-08030-8, Pub. by Faber & Faber). Merrimack Bk Serv.

--Sir Thomas Malory: King Arthur & His Knights. 1968. pap. 4.95 o.p. (ISBN 0-571-08608-X, Pub. by Faber & Faber). Merrimack Bk Serv.

Davies, R. W. The Socialist Offensive: The Collectivization of Soviet Agriculture, Nineteen Twenty Nine to Nineteen Thirty. (Industrialization of Soviet Russia Ser.: Vol. 1). 576p. 1980. 35.00 (ISBN 0-674-81480-0). Harvard U Pr.

Davies, R. W., ed. The Soviet Union. (Illus.). 1978. text ed. 16.50x (ISBN 0-04-947022-1); pap. text ed. 8.95x (ISBN 0-04-947023-X). Allen Unwin.

Davies, Rhys. The Best of Rhys Davies. 16.95 (ISBN 0-7153-7756-6). David & Charles.

Davies, Robert A. The Story of the Black Beauty. 1981. 10.00 (ISBN 0-8062-1712-X). Carlton.

Davies, Robertson. Leaven of Malice. 1980. pap. 3.50 (ISBN 0-14-005433-2). Penguin.

--The Manticore. 1977. pap. 2.95 (ISBN 0-14-004388-8). Penguin.

Davies, Rupert E., jt. ed. see Flew, Robert N.

Davies, S. The Diffusion of Process Innovations. LC 78-15143. 1979. 32.95 (ISBN 0-521-22193-5). Cambridge U Pr.

Davies, Samuel. Collected Poems. Davis, Richard B., ed. LC 68-17019. 1968. 29.00x (ISBN 0-8201-1011-6). Schol Facsimiles.

Davies, Stanley P. & Ecob, E. G. Mentally Retarded in Society. 2nd ed. LC 58-59911. 1959. 17.50x (ISBN 0-231-02220-4). Columbia U Pr.

Davies, Stevan L. The Revolt of the Widows: The Social World of the Apocryphal Acts. LC 80-11331. 160p. 1980. 10.95x (ISBN 0-8093-0958-0). S Ill U Pr.

Davies, Thomas D. Star Sight Reduction Tables for Forty-Two Stars: Assumed Altitude Method of Celestial Navigation. LC 79-7464. 1980. 28.50x (ISBN 0-87033-250-3). Cornell Maritime.

Davies, Thomas L. Supplementary English Glossary. LC 68-23468. 1968. Repr. of 1881 ed. 28.00 (ISBN 0-8103-3245-0). Gale.

Davies, Thomas M., Jr., jt. ed. see Loveman, Brian.

Davies, W. D. The Gospel & the Land: Early Christianity & Jewish Territorial Doctrine. LC 72-82228. 1974. 22.50x (ISBN 0-520-02278-5). U of Cal Pr.

--Invitation to the New Testament. LC 65-17223. 1969. pap. 4.95 (ISBN 0-385-04767-3, A013, Anch). Doubleday.

--Paul & Rabbinic Judaism: Some Rabbinic Elements in Pauline Theology. LC 80-8049. 448p. 1980. pap. 13.95 (ISBN 0-8006-1438-0, 1-1438). Fortress.

Davies, W. E. Footloose with a Fishing Rod. 6.50x (ISBN 0-392-06479-0, LTB). Soccer.

Davies, W. J. The Romney, Hythe & Dymchurch Railway. (Railway History Ser). (Illus.). 184p. 1975. 14.95 (ISBN 0-7153-6827-3). David & Charles.

Davies, William. Building Plant & Equipment Sheets. (Illus.). 1978. wirebound 13.95x (ISBN 0-7198-2740-X). Intl Ideas.

Davies, William D. Sermon on the Mount. (Orig.). 1966. pap. 6.50x (ISBN 0-521-09384-8, 384). Cambridge U Pr.

--Setting of the Sermon on the Mount. 1964. 64.00 (ISBN 0-521-04797-8); pap. 16.95x (ISBN 0-521-29124-0). Cambridge U Pr.

Davies, William H. Captive Lion & Other Poems. 1921. 17.50x (ISBN 0-685-89738-9). Elliots Bks.

Davies-Spiell, Michael, jt. auth. see Marshall, John.

Davila, Maria D. Castro De see Castro De Davila, Maria D.

Davila, Mario L., tr. see Abrey, Emilo.

Davin, Delia. Woman-Work: Women & the Party in Revolutionary China. (Illus.). 1979. pap. 4.50 (ISBN 0-19-285080-6, GB 566, GB). Oxford U Pr.

Davin, N. F. The Irishman in Canada. 718p. Repr. of 1877 ed. 30.00x (ISBN 0-686-27787-2, Pub. by Irish Academic Pr Ireland). Biblio Dist.

Da Vinci, Leonardo. Codex Atlanticus: A Facsimile of the Restored Manuscript, 12 vols. Set. 12000.00 (ISBN 0-685-32599-7). Johnson Repr.

Davinson, Donald. The Periodicals Collection. 2nd ed. (A Grafton Book). 1978. lib. bdg. 25.50x (ISBN 0-89158-883-3). Westview.

Davis. Short History of South Africa. 1979. pap. 5.95 (ISBN 0-582-60349-8). Longman.

Davis, jt. auth. see Cutler.

Davis, jt. auth. see Hall.

Davis, A., tr. see Graeff, H. & Kuhn, W.

Davis, A. C., jt. ed. see Scott, P. H.

Davis, A. E. & Bolin, T. D. Physical Diagnosis in Medicine. 122p. 1974. pap. 12.00 (ISBN 0-08-017376-4). Pergamon.

Davis, Adelle. Let's Cook It Right. 1970. pap. 2.95 (ISBN 0-451-09427-1, E9427, Sig). NAL.

--Let's Eat Right to Keep Fit. 1970. pap. 2.95 (ISBN 0-451-09644-4, E9644, Sig). NAL.

Davis, Alan. Relationships Between Doctors & Patients. 1978. 17.95 (ISBN 0-566-00200-0, 01896-X, Pub. by Saxon Hse England). Lexington Bks.

Davis, Albert J. & Schubert, Robert P. Alternative Natural Energy Sources in Building Design. 2nd ed. 256p. 1981. 17.95 (ISBN 0-442-23143-1); pap. 9.95 (ISBN 0-442-22008-1). Van Nos Reinhold.

Davis, Alec. Graphics: Design into Production. 1973. 11.95 o.p. (ISBN 0-571-08810-4, Pub. by Faber & Faber). Merrimack Bk Serv.

Davis, Alexandra & Davis, O. B. Exercises in Reading & Writing. (gr. 10-11). 1978. pap. text ed. 5.60x (ISBN 0-8104-5935-3). Hayden.

Davis, Alice V. Timothy Turtle. LC 40-32634. (Illus.). (gr. k-3). 1940. 5.95 o.p. (ISBN 0-15-288368-1, HJ). HarBraceJ.

Davis, Allan F., ed. For Better or Worse: The American Influence in the World. LC 80-1048. (Contributions in American Studies Ser.: No. 51). 240p. 1981. lib. bdg. 29.95 (ISBN 0-313-22342-4, DBO/). Greenwood.

Davis, Allen F. Spearheads for Reform: The Social Settlements & the Progressive Movement, 1890-1914. (Urban Life in America Ser). 15.95 (ISBN 0-19-500527-9); pap. 4.95x (ISBN 0-19-500862-6). Oxford U Pr.

Davis, Allen F., ed. see Bordin, Ruth.

Davis, Allen F., ed. see Marsh, Margaret.

Davis, Angela. Angela Davis: An Autobiography. LC 73-20580. 1974. 8.95 o.p. (ISBN 0-394-48978-0, Co-Pub. with Geis). Random.

Davis, Ann N. & Richardson, Robert A. The Helicopter: Its Importance to Commerce & to the Public. 138p. 1978. 10.00 (ISBN 0-911721-70-3, Pub. by Helicopter Assn). Aviation.

Davis, Anne, jt. auth. see Kalkman, Marion.

Davis, Anthony, jt. auth. see Quanty, Carol.

Davis, Arthur P. & Redding, Saunders, eds. Cavalcade: Negro American Writing from 1760 to the Present. LC 70-20257. 1971. text ed. 19.50 (ISBN 0-395-04345-X); tchrs. manual pap. 2.00 (ISBN 0-395-04346-8). HM.

Davis, Barbara. Learning Science & Metric Through Cooking. LC 64-15112. (Illus.). (gr. 5 up). 1977. 7.95 (ISBN 0-8069-3090-X); PLB 7.49 (ISBN 0-8069-3091-8). Sterling.

Davis, Barbara, jt. auth. see Stuart, Richard B.

Davis, Barbara, et al. The Evaluation of Composition Instruction. LC 80-68774. 160p. (Orig.). 1981. pap. 6.95x (ISBN 0-918528-11-9). Edgepress.

Davis, Barbara S. Forest Hotel. (Illus.). 24p. (gr. k-1). 1976. PLB 5.00 (ISBN 0-307-60350-4, Golden Pr). Western Pub.

Davis, Ben. Rapid Healing Foods. LC 79-22770. 1980. 10.95 (ISBN 0-13-753137-0, Parker). P-H.

Davis, Bernard & Davis, Elizabeth, eds. Poets of the Early Seventeenth Century. (Routledge English Texts). 1967. pap. 3.95 (ISBN 0-7100-4512-3). Routledge & Kegan.

Davis, Bernard D. Microbiology. (Illus.). 1274p. 1980. 39.50 (ISBN 0-06-140691-0, Harper Medical). Har-Row.

Davis, Bernard D., et al. Microbiology. 2nd ed. (Illus.). 1973. text ed. 34.95x o.p. (ISBN 0-06-140683-X, Harper Medical). Har-Row.

Davis, Bertha & Whitfield, Susan. How to Improve Your Comprehension. (gr. 7 up). 1980. PLB 6.45 (ISBN 0-531-04132-8). Watts.

Davis, Bette. Mother Goddam. rev. ed. 1979. pap. 2.75 (ISBN 0-425-04119-0). Berkley Pub.

Davis, Bill C. Mass Appeal. 80p. 1981. pap. 2.50 (ISBN 0-380-77396-1, Bard). Avon.

Davis, Blanche W. As I Remember. 1981. 7.95 (ISBN 0-8062-1660-3). Carlton.

Davis, Bob J., ed. Information Sources in Transportation, Material Management, & Physical Distribution: An Annotated Bibliography & Guide. LC 75-23864. (Orig.). 1976. lib. bdg. 45.00 (ISBN 0-8371-8379-0, DBT/). Greenwood.

Davis, Boyd H. & O'Cain, Raymond K., eds. Toward a History of Twentieth Century American Linguistics: Papers from the First Conference on Oral Linguistics. (Studies in the History of Linguistics Ser.: No. 21). 300p. 1980. text ed. 34.25x (ISBN 90-272-4502-9). Humanities.

Davis, Brian L. U. S. Army Airborne Forces, Europe 1942-45. LC 73-83746. (Key Uniform Guides). 1974. pap. 1.95 o.p. (ISBN 0-668-03366-5). Arco.

Davis, Britton. The Truth About Geronimo. Quaife, M. M., ed. LC 75-37958. (Illus.). xxx, 253p. 1976. 15.50x (ISBN 0-8032-0877-4); pap. 5.25 (ISBN 0-8032-5840-2, BB 622, Bison). U of Nebr Pr.

Davis, Bruce & Davis, Genny W. The Lovers Book: Your Secret Source of Love. (Illus.). 1980. pap. 3.95 (ISBN 0-02-529860-7); write for info. prepack (ISBN 0-02-529890-9). Macmillan.

Davis, Bruce, jt. auth. see Feinblatt, Ebria.

Davis, Burke. The Campaign That Won America: The Story of Yorktown. (Illus.). 319p. (Orig.). 1979. pap. 3.50 (ISBN 0-686-27872-0, Pub. by Eastern Natl Park). Eastern Acorn.

--Williamsburg Galaxy. LC 68-12135. 1968. 4.95 o.p. (ISBN 0-03-068690-3, Pub. by Williamsburg). HR&W.

Davis, Burke, jt. auth. see Davis, Evangeline.

Davis, C. J. Utopia & the Ideal Society. 410p. Date not set. price not set (ISBN 0-521-23396-8). Cambridge U Pr.

Davis, Calvin D. The United States & the First Hague Peace Conference. (Beveridge Award Books Ser.). 248p. 1962. 19.50x (ISBN 0-8014-0099-6). Cornell U Pr.

Davis, Carolyn. Making Every Moment Count. (Illus.). 1980. 7.95 (ISBN 0-87707-225-6). CSA Pr.

Davis, Carroll. Room to Grow: A Study of Parent-Child Relationships. LC 66-6602. 1966. 10.00 o.p. (ISBN 0-8020-5173-1). U of Toronto Pr.

Davis, Charles. Body As Spirit: The Nature of Religious Feeling. 160p. 1976. 8.95 (ISBN 0-8164-0288-4). Crossroad NY.

--Industrial Electronics: Design & Application. LC 72-92570. 1973. text ed. 21.95x (ISBN 0-675-09010-5); instructors manual 3.95 (ISBN 0-686-66861-8). Merrill.

--Theology & Political Society. LC 80-40014. 180p. 1980. 19.95 (ISBN 0-521-22538-8). Cambridge U Pr.

--Why I Left the Roman Catholic Church. 1976. pap. 3.00. Am Atheist.

Davis, Charles G. Shipping & Craft in Silhouette. LC 70-162509. (Tower Bks). (Illus.). 221p. 1972. Repr. of 1929 ed. 18.00 (ISBN 0-8103-3945-5). Gale.

Davis, Charlie, ed. see Membership of the Society.

Davis, Cheri. W. S. Merwin. (United States Authors Ser.: No. 360). 1981. lib. bdg. 11.95 (ISBN 0-8057-7301-0). Twayne.

Davis, Christopher. Plains Indians. (Illus.). (gr. 5-8). 1978. PLB 6.90 s&l (ISBN 0-531-01429-0). Watts.

Davis, Creath, tr. Victoria En la Crisis. (Spanish Bks.). (Span.). 1977. 1.95 (ISBN 0-8297-0785-9). Vida Pub.

Davis, D. D., tr. see Pinel, Philippe.

Davis, D. O. Exporting to China & Japan. cancelled (ISBN 0-932812-04-X). Bradley CPA.

Davis, D. Russell. An Introduction to Psychopathology. 3rd ed. 180p. 1973. pap. text ed. 5.95x o.p. (ISBN 0-19-264417-3). Oxford U Pr.

Davis, D. S., jt. ed. see Mosher, R. H.

Davis, D. W. Elizabethans Errant. LC 67-16462. 1967. 9.50 (ISBN 0-8014-0098-8). Brown Bk.

Davis, Daniel S. Marcus Garvey. LC 72-3992. (Illus.). 192p. (gr. 7-12). 1972. PLB 5.88 o.p. (ISBN 0-531-02577-2). Watts.

Davis, Daphne. The Baby Animal Book. 24p. (ps-1). 1964. PLB 5.38 (ISBN 0-307-68902-6, Golden Pr). Western Pub.

--The Donald Duck Book. (ps-1). 1964. PLB 5.38 (ISBN 0-307-68911-5, Golden Pr). Western Pub.

Davis, David, compiled by. A Single Star: An Anthology of Christmas Poetry. (Illus.). 1978. 7.95 (ISBN 0-370-01269-0, Pub. by Chatto Bodley Jonathan). Merrimack Bk Serv.

Davis, David B. Antebellum American Culture: An Interpretive Anthology. 1979. pap. text ed. 8.95 (ISBN 0-669-01476-1). Heath.

Davis, David E., ed. Behavior As an Ecological Factor. LC 74-3006. (Benchmark Papers in Ecology Ser: Vol. 2). 408p. 1974. text ed. 37.50 (ISBN 0-12-786322-2). Acad Pr.

Davis, David O. Basic Principles of Computerized Tomography. 1981. write for info. (ISBN 0-87527-200-2). Green.

Davis, Deane C. Justice in the Mountains: Stories & Tales by a Vermont Country Lawyer. LC 80-82866. (Illus.). 192p. 1980. 9.95 (ISBN 0-933050-05-4); pap. 6.95 (ISBN 0-933050-06-2). New Eng Pr VT.

Davis, Dee. Decoupage, Step by Step. (Step by Step Craft Ser.). (Illus.). 1976. PLB 9.15 o.p. (ISBN 0-307-62017-4, Golden Pr); pap. 2.95 (ISBN 0-307-42017-5). Western Pub.

Davis, Dennis K. & Baran, Stanley J. Mass Communication & Everyday Life: A Perspective on Theory & Effects. 240p. 1980. pap. text ed. 7.95x (ISBN 0-534-00883-6). Wadsworth Pub.

Davis, Denny C., jt. auth. see Hall, Carl W.

Davis, Devra, jt. ed. see Ng, Lorenz K.

Davis, Don D. Induced Task Competence & Effects on Problem Solving Behavior. (Illus.). 52p. (Orig.). 1980. pap. text ed. 3.00 (ISBN 0-907152-00-7). Prytaneum Pr.

Davis, Donald G., Jr. The Association of American Library Schools, 1915-1968: An Analytical History. LC 73-16014. 1974. 15.00 (ISBN 0-8108-0642-8). Scarecrow.

Davis, Dorothy C. Reading Through the Newspaper. 1980. write for info. (ISBN 0-88252-108-X). Paladin Hse.

Davis, Dwight & Borgen, Joe. Planning, Implementing & Evaluating Career Preparation Programs. 1974. 50.00 (ISBN 0-87345-590-8). McKnight.

Davis, E. H., jt. auth. see Poulos, H. G.

Davis, E. W. & Yeomans, K. A. Company Finance & the Capital Market. LC 74-16990. (Department of Applied Economics, Occasional Papers Ser.: No. 39). (Illus.). 200p. 1975. 25.50 (ISBN 0-521-20144-6); pap. 13.50x (ISBN 0-521-09792-4). Cambridge U Pr.

Davis, E. W., jt. auth. see Nevin, Edward.

Davis, Ed. Teachers As Curriculum Evaluators. (Classroom & Curriculum in Australia Ser.: No. 4). 180p. 1981. text ed. 21.00x (ISBN 0-86861-090-9, 2517); pap. text ed. 9.95x (ISBN 0-86861-098-4, 2518). Allen Unwin.

Davis, Edith, ed. see Walt Disney Productions.

Davis, Edward Z. Translations of German Poetry in American Magazines, 1741-1810. LC 66-27663. 1966. Repr. of 1905 ed. 15.00 (ISBN 0-8103-3209-4). Gale.

Davis, Eleanor H. Abraham Fornander: A Biography. LC 78-31368. 1979. 0.95 (ISBN 0-8248-0459-7). U Pr of Hawaii.

Davis, Elise M. Answer Is God. 1975. pap. 1.25 (ISBN 0-685-84181-2, PV068). Jove Pubns.

Davis, Elizabeth. A Guide to Midwifery: Heart & Hands. (Illus., Orig.). 1981. pap. 9.00 (ISBN 0-912528-22-2). John Muir.

Davis, Elizabeth, jt. ed. see Davis, Bernard.

Davis, Ellen N. The Vapheio Cups & Aegean Gold & Silver Ware. LC 76-23609. (Outstanding Dissertations in the Fine Arts). (Illus.). 1977. Repr. of 1973 ed. lib. bdg. 63.00 (ISBN 0-8240-2681-0). Garland Pub.

Davis, Elsie S. Descendants of Jacob Young of Shelby County, Kentucky: Including President Harry S. Truman. LC 80-70981. (Illus.). 171p. (Orig.). 1980. 16.00 (ISBN 0-9605618-1-1); pap. 9.00 (ISBN 0-9605618-0-3). E S Davis.

Davis, Elwyn. Introductory Modern Algebra. LC 73-87837. 1974. text ed. 16.95x (ISBN 0-675-08872-0). Merrill.

Davis, Emily C. Ancient Americans: The Archaeological Story of Two Continents. LC 74-12555. (Illus.). 311p. 1975. Repr. of 1931 ed. lib. bdg. 15.00x (ISBN 0-8154-0497-2). Cooper Sq.

Davis, Enid. A Comprehensive Guide to Children's Literature with a Jewish Theme. LC 80-54139. 256p. 1981. 18.95x (ISBN 0-8052-3760-7). Schocken.

Davis, Evangeline & Davis, Burke. Rebel Raider: A Biography of Admiral Semmes. (Illus.). (gr. 7-9). 1966. 4.95 o.p. (ISBN 0-397-30910-4). Lippincott.

Davis, F. Nationalism & Socialism. 1979. 24.50 o.p. (ISBN 0-685-67810-5). Porter.

Davis, F. James. Minority-Dominant Relations: A Sociological Analysis. LC 77-90659. 1978. pap. text ed. 11.95x (ISBN 0-88295-209-9). AHM Pub.

--Social Problems. LC 76-111934. 1970. text ed. 11.95 (ISBN 0-02-906980-7). Free Pr.

--Understanding Minority Dominant Relations: Sociological Contributions. LC 77-90671. 1979. 12.95x (ISBN 0-88295-210-2). AHM Pub.

Davis, F. James & Stivers, Richard, eds. The Collective Definition of Deviance. LC 74-10138. 1975. pap. text ed. 9.95 (ISBN 0-02-907260-3). Free Pr.

Davis, Flora. Eloquent Animals. 1979. pap. 2.25 o.p. (ISBN 0-425-04039-9). Berkley Pub.

Davis, Francis W. Horse Packing in Pictures. LC 75-946. 1975. 10.95 (ISBN 0-684-14259-7, ScribT). Scribner.

Davis, Frank. Early Eighteenth Century English Glass. (Country Life Collectors Guides Ser). 1972. 4.95 (ISBN 0-600-43601-2). Transatlantic.

--The Plain Man's Guide to Second-Hand Furniture. 1972. 8.95 (ISBN 0-7181-0936-8). Transatlantic.

--The Plain Man's Guide to Second Hand Furniture. 1971. 6.95 (ISBN 0-7181-0936-8, Pub. by Michael Joseph). Merrimack Bk Serv.

Davis, Frank & Williams, Alise D. One Hundred Years Ago. 1980. pap. 4.95 (ISBN 0-910286-79-5). Boxwood.

Davis, Frank G. The Economics of Black Community Development: An Analysis & Program for Autonomous Growth & Development. 1976. pap. text ed. 9.50x (ISBN 0-8191-0008-0). U Pr of Amer.

Davis, Franklin M. Across the Rhine. Time-Life Books, ed. (World War II Ser.). (Illus.). 208p. 1980. 13.95 (ISBN 0-8094-2542-4). Time-Life.

Davis, Fred. Yearning for Yesterday: A Sociology of Nostalgia. LC 78-19838. 1979. 12.95 (ISBN 0-02-906950-5). Free Pr.

Davis, G. A., jt. ed. see Beasley, Daniel S.

Davis, G. Gordon, jt. auth. see Liroff, Richard A.

Davis, Genny W., jt. auth. see Davis, Bruce.

Davis, George A. see Crittenden, Max D., Jr., et al.

Davis, Georgia. Your Moneyscopes. Incl. Aries (ISBN 0-346-12260-0); Taurus (ISBN 0-346-12261-9); Gemini (ISBN 0-346-12262-7); Cancer (ISBN 0-346-12263-5); Leo (ISBN 0-346-12264-3); Virgo (ISBN 0-346-12265-1); Libra (ISBN 0-346-12266-X); Scorpio (ISBN 0-346-12267-8); Sagittarius (ISBN 0-346-12268-6); Capricorn (ISBN 0-346-12269-4); Aquarius (ISBN 0-346-12270-8); Pisces (ISBN 0-346-12271-6). 1977. Set. pap. 54.00 o.p. (ISBN 0-685-75535-5); pap. 1.50 ea o.p. Cornerstone.

Davis, Geraldine H. The Moving Experience. (Illus.). 150p. (Orig.). 1980. pap. 5.95 (ISBN 0-89865-029-1); moving calendar 2.50 (ISBN 0-89865-098-4). Donning Co.

Davis, Gibbs. Maud Flies Solo. 176p. (gr. 5-7). 1981. 8.95 (ISBN 0-87888-173-5). Bradbury Pr.

Davis, Gordon. Bloody Bush. (Sergeant Ser.: No. 3). 288p. (Orig.). 1980. pap. 2.25 (ISBN 0-89083-647-7). Zebra.

--The Goering Treasure. 288p. (Orig.). 1980. pap. 2.28 (ISBN 0-89083-692-2). Zebra.

--The Sergeant Series, No. 4. 192p. (Orig.). 1981. pap. 2.25 (ISBN 0-553-14708-0). Bantam.

Davis, Grania. The Great Perpendicular Path. 1980. pap. 1.95 (ISBN 0-380-47217-1, 47217). Avon.

--The Rainbow Annals. 1980. pap. 1.95 (ISBN 0-686-69268-3, 76224). Avon.

--The Rainbows Annals. 1980. pap. 1.95 (ISBN 0-380-76224-2, 76224). Avon.

Davis, Grant M. & Dillard, John E., Jr. Increasing Motor Carrier Productivity: An Empirical Analysis. LC 77-7821. (Praeger Special Studies). 1977. text ed. 20.95 (ISBN 0-03-022641-4). Praeger.

Davis, Grant M. & Shephard, Eugene. Motor Carrier Rate Structure: The Need for Basic Revision. LC 78-24194. 1979. 21.95 (ISBN 0-03-049136-3). Praeger.

Davis, Grant M. & Sherwood, Charles S. Rate Bureaus & Antitrust Conflicts in Transportation Public Policy Issues. (Special Studies). (Illus.). 138p. 1975. text ed. 19.95 (ISBN 0-275-09880-X). Praeger.

Davis, Grant M., et al. Management of Transportation Carriers. LC 73-21465. (Special Studies). (Illus.). 308p. 1975. text ed. 32.95 (ISBN 0-275-08680-1). Praeger.

Davis, Guillermo H. Gramatica Elemental Del Griego Del Nuevo Testamento. McKibben, Jorge F., tr. 1980. Repr. of 1978 ed. 3.75 (ISBN 0-311-42008-7). Casa Bautista.

Davis, H. Beginning Gymnastics for College Women. (Illus.). pap. 4.50 wrappers (ISBN 0-8363-0011-4). Jenkins.

Davis, H. S. Culture & Diseases of Game Fishes. (Illus.). 1953. 18.50x (ISBN 0-520-00293-8). U of Cal Pr.

Davis, Harold E. Latin American Thought: A Historical Introduction. LC 78-181564. 1974. pap. text ed. 5.95 (ISBN 0-02-907160-7). Free Pr.

Davis, Harold E. & Durfee, Harold A. Teaching of Philosophy in Universities of the United States. (Philosophy Ser). 1965. pap. 5.00 (ISBN 0-8270-5845-4). OAS.

Davis, Harold Eugene, et al. Latin American Foreign Policies: An Analysis. LC 74-24386. (Illus.). 488p. 1975. 25.00x o.p. (ISBN 0-8018-1694-7); pap. 5.95x (ISBN 0-8018-1695-5). Johns Hopkins.

Davis, Harold T. Introduction to Nonlinear Differential & Integral Equations. 1960. pap. 7.50 (ISBN 0-486-60971-5). Dover.

Davis, Harry F. & Snider, Arthur D. Introduction to Vector Analysis. 4th ed. LC 78-27618. 1979. text ed. 21.55 (ISBN 0-205-06598-8). Allyn.

Davis, Harry L. & Silk, Alvin J. Behavioral & Management Science in Marketing. LC 77-18878. 1978. 29.95 (ISBN 0-471-07179-X). Ronald Pr.

Davis, Henry. Compiler Writing in PASCAL. (Pascal Notebook Ser.: Vol. 3). 150p. 1981. pap. 9.95 (ISBN 0-918398-45-2). Dilithium Pr.

--Introduction to PASCAL. (Pascal Notebook Ser.: Vol. 1). 150p. 1981. pap. 9.95 (ISBN 0-918398-43-6). Dilithium Pr.

--The PASCAL Compiler. (Pascal Notebook Ser.: Vol. 2). 150p. 1981. pap. 9.95 (ISBN 0-918398-44-4). Dilithium Pr.

Davis, Herbert, ed. see Swift, Jonathan.

Davis, Hiram S. Productivity Accounting. 3rd ed. 194p. 1980. pap. 15.00 (ISBN 0-89546-009-2). Indus Res Unit-Wharton.

Davis, Horace B. Toward a Marxist Theory of Nationalism. 1978. 17.50 o.p. (ISBN 0-85345-441-8, CL 441-8). Monthly Rev.

Davis, Horace B., ed. see Luxemburg, Rosa.

Davis, Howard T., jt. auth. see Hayden, Jerome D.

Davis, Hubert J. Christmas in the Mountains: Southwest Virginia Christmas Customs & Their Origins. (Illus.). 144p. 1972. 7.50 (ISBN 0-930230-06-X). Johnson NC.

--Great Dismal Swamp: Its Science, History & Folklore. (Illus.). 1971. 7.50 (ISBN 0-930230-11-6). Johnson NC.

--Pon My Honor Hit's the Truth: Tales from the South Western Virginia Mountains. (Illus.). 1973. 4.95 (ISBN 0-930230-19-1). Johnson NC.

Davis, I., ed. Disasters & the Small Dwelling. 220p. 1981. 30.00 (ISBN 0-08-024753-9). Pergamon.

Davis, J. Land & Family in Pisticci. (London School of Economics Monographs on Social Anthropology Ser: No. 48). 200p. 1973. text ed. 19.50x (ISBN 0-391-00288-0, Athlone Pr). Humanities.

Davis, J., ed. Choice & Change: Essays in Honour of Lucy Mair. (London School of Economics Monographs on Social Anthropology Ser: No. 50). 264p. 1974. text ed. 13.50x (ISBN 0-391-00328-3, Athlone Pr). Humanities.

Davis, J. A. High Cost Oil & Gas Resources. 240p. 1981. 40.00x (ISBN 0-85664-588-5, Pub. by Croom Helm LTD England). Biblio Dist.

Davis, J. Boyce & Knight, E. Leslie. CVR Fitness: A Basic Guide for Cardio-Vascular-Respiratory Exercise. 2nd ed. (Illus.). 1978. pap. text ed. 6.95 (ISBN 0-8403-1442-6). Kendall-Hunt.

Davis, J. Cary, jt. auth. see Canfield, D. Lincoln.

Davis, J. W., Jr. National Executive Branch. LC 72-96834. 1970. 8.95 o.s.i. (ISBN 0-02-907070-8). Free Pr.

Davis, Jack & Loveless, E. E. The Administrator & Educational Facilities. LC 80-1445.*272p. 1981. lib. bdg. 19.00 (ISBN 0-8191-1391-3); pap. text ed. 10.50 (ISBN 0-8191-1392-1). U Pr of Amer.

Davis, Jacquelyn K., jt. auth. see Pfaltzgraff, Robert L., Jr.

Davis, Jacquelyn K., et al. Salt II & U. S.-Soviet Strategic Forces. LC 79-2713. (Special Reports Ser.). 1979. 5.00 (ISBN 0-89549-016-1). Inst Foreign Policy Anal.

--The Soviet Union & Ballistic Missile Defense. LC 79-3298. (Special Reports). 50p. 1980. 6.50 (ISBN 0-89549-021-8). Inst Foreign Policy Anal.

Davis, James A. Do People Like Me Have Any Control Over Politics? A Study of the Locus of Political Control As Perceived by Mexican-American Adolescents of South Texas. LC 80-65614. 140p. 1981. perfect bdg. 11.50 (ISBN 0-86548-029-X). Century Twenty One.

--Education for Positive Mental Health: A Review of Existing Research & Recommendations for Future Studies. LC 64-15607. (Monographs in Social Research: No. 5). 1965. 7.95x (ISBN 0-202-09009-4). NORC.

--Elementary Survey Analysis. (Methods of Social Science Ser). (Illus.). 1971. pap. text ed. 10.95 (ISBN 0-13-260547-3). P-H.

Davis, James A. & Smith, Tom W. General Social Surveys, 1972-1980: Cumulative Codebook. 1980. 8.00 (ISBN 0-932132-25-1). NORC.

Davis, James A., et al. General Social Surveys, 1972-1980: Cumulative Codebook. 1980. pap. 8.00 (ISBN 0-932132-25-1). NORC.

Davis, James H. Group Performance. Kiesler, Charles A., ed. (Psychology-Topics in Social Psychology). 1969. pap. text ed. 6.95 (ISBN 0-201-01476-9). A-W.

Davis, James H., Jr. Fenelon. (World Authors Series: No. 542). 1979. lib. bdg. 14.95 (ISBN 0-8057-6384-8). Twayne.

Davis, James R. & Cushing, Barry E. Accounting Information Systems: A Book of Readings. LC 78-74681. pap. 8.95 (ISBN 0-201-01099-2). A-W.

Davis, James W. & Ruigquist, Delbert. The President & Congress: Toward a New Power Balance. LC 74-26595. (Politics of Government Ser). 224p. 1975. pap. 2.95 o.p. (ISBN 0-8120-0965-7). Barron.

Davis, James W., Jr. & Dolbeare, Kenneth M. Little Groups of Neighbors: The Selective Service System. LC 80-25861. xv, 276p. 1981. Repr. of 1968 ed. lib. bdg. 35.00x (ISBN 0-313-22777-2, DALN). Greenwood.

Davis, Jean, jt. auth. see Kahn, Sandra.

Davis, Jed H. & Evans, Mary J. Theatre, Children & Youth. 1981. text ed. 19.95 (ISBN 0-87602-016-3); pap. 16.25 (ISBN 0-87602-017-1). Anchorage.

Davis, Jefferson. Rise & Fall of the Confederate Government. abr. ed. 11.50 (ISBN 0-8446-0074-1). Peter Smith.

Davis, Jerry C. Rehabbing for Profit. (Illus.). 224p. 1981. 17.50 (ISBN 0-07-015695-6, P&RB). McGraw.

Davis, Jessica H., ed. see Weigle, Marta.

Davis, Jim. Garfield at Large. 1980. pap. 4.95 (ISBN 0-345-28779-7). Ballantine.

--Garfield Gains Weight. 128p. (Orig.). 1981. pap. 4.95 (ISBN 0-345-28844-0). Ballantine.

Davis, Jinnie Y. & Abrera, Joseph B. Monographic Searching on the OCLC Terminal: A Programmed Text with Teacher's Guide. (Illus.). 1980. pap. 14.50x (ISBN 0-208-01843-3, Linnet). Shoe String.

Davis, Joe. Complete Snooker. (Illus.). 286p. 1975. 12.95 o.p. (ISBN 0-491-01521-6). Transatlantic.

Davis, John. Energy, to Use or Abuse? (Illus.). 186p. (Orig.). 1979. pap. 5.00x (ISBN 0-905381-00-9). Intl Pubns Serv.

--The Evasive Peace. 1970. pap. 2.95 (ISBN 0-911026-01-0). New World Press NY.

--People of the Mediterranean: An Essay in Comparative Social Anthropology. (Library of Man). 1976. 17.00x (ISBN 0-7100-8412-9). Routledge & Kegan.

--The Post-Captain: Or, the Wooden Walls Well Manned; Comprehending a View of Naval Society & Manners, Repr. Of 1806 Ed. Bd. with Struggle of Capt. Thomas Keith in America, Including the Manner in Which He, His Wife & Child Were Decoyed by the Indians. Repr. of 1808 ed. LC 75-7048. (Indian Captivities Ser.: Vol. 26). 1977. lib. bdg. 44.00 (ISBN 0-8240-1650-5). Garland Pub.

Davis, John A., jt. ed. see Kitzinger, Sheila.

Davis, John E. An Introduction to Tool Marks, Firearms & the Striagraph. 302p. 1958. pap. 24.50 photocopy ed. spiral (ISBN 0-398-00402-1). C C Thomas.

Davis, John G. Leviathan. 1977. pap. 1.95 o.p. (ISBN 0-449-23339-1, Crest). Fawcett.

Davis, John G. & Newman, Phyllis, eds. California International Trade Register. 750p. 1980. pap. 59.95 (ISBN 0-911510-82-6). Times-M Pr.

--California Manufacturers Register, 1981. 34th rev. ed. LC 48-3418. 880p. 1981. 85.00 (ISBN 0-911510-83-4). Times-M Pr.

--California Services Register, 1981. 2nd ed. 680p. 1981. 60.00 (ISBN 0-911510-84-2). Times-M Pr.

Davis, John J. Abortion & the Evangelical. LC 80-82736. (The Nordland Series in Contemporary American Social Problems). 150p. (Orig.). 1980. pap. 7.95 (ISBN 0-913124-43-5). Nordland Pub.

--The Birth of a Kingdom: Studies in I & II Samuel & I Kings I-II. pap. 4.95 (ISBN 0-88469-053-9). BMH Bks.

--Birth of a Kingdom: Studies in One & Two Samuel & One Kings. 1970. pap. 3.95 o.p. (ISBN 0-8010-2803-5). Baker Bk.

--Mummies, Men & Madness. (Illus.). pap. 3.00 o.p. (ISBN 0-88469-004-0). BMH Bks.

--Paradise to Prison: Studies in Genesis. 10.95 (ISBN 0-88469-050-4). BMH Bks.

--Psalms, Studies in the Hebrew Text. pap. 8.00 o.p. (ISBN 0-88469-117-9). BMH Bks.

--Theology Primer. 128p. (Orig.). 1981. pap. 5.95 (ISBN 0-8010-2912-0). Baker Bk.

Davis, John J. & Whitcomb, John C. History of Israel. 14.95 (ISBN 0-88469-061-X). BMH Bks.

Davis, John L. The Texas Rangers: Their First 150 Years. (Illus.). 114p. 1975. 5.95 (ISBN 0-933164-19-X). U of Tex Inst Tex Culture.

--Treasure, People, Ships & Dreams. (Illus.). 75p. 1977. pap. 5.95 (ISBN 0-933164-20-3). U of Tex Inst Tex Culture.

Davis, John M., et al. An Atlas of Pedodontics. 2nd ed. (Illus.). 425p. 1980. 32.50 (ISBN 0-7216-2977-6). Saunders.

Davis, John T. Walking! 1979. 12.95 o.p. (ISBN 0-8362-2403-5); pap. 5.95 o.p. (ISBN 0-8362-2404-3). Andrews & McMeel.

Davis, John W., ed. Value & Valuation: Axiological Studies in Honor of Robert S. Hartman. LC 72-146661. 1972. 17.50x (ISBN 0-87049-130-X). U of Tenn Pr.

Davis, John W., et al, eds. Infectious Diseases of Wild Mammals. 2nd ed. 436p. 1981. text ed. 35.00 (ISBN 0-8138-0445-0). Iowa St U Pr.

Davis, Joseph A. Samaki: The Story of an Otter in Africa. 1979. 10.95 o.p. (ISBN 0-525-19601-3). Dutton.

Davis, Joseph K., et al. Literature. 1977. 13.95x (ISBN 0-673-15009-7). Scott F.

Davis, Joseph L. Sectionalsim in American Politics, 1774-1787. LC 76-11310. 1977. 22.50 (ISBN 0-299-07020-4). U of Wis Pr.

Davis, Joseph S. Wheat & the AAA. LC 76-172868. (FDR & the Era of the New Deal Ser.). 468p. 1973. Repr. of 1935 ed. 49.50 (ISBN 0-306-70375-0). Da Capo.

Davis, Joyce E. Chrysalis. Bennett, Heather, ed. LC 80-84927. 170p. 1981. write for info. (ISBN 0-913420-91-3). Olympus Pub Co.

Davis, Joyce O., ed. see Davenport, Robert.

Davis, Judith. Amazing Grace. 1981. 12.95 (ISBN 0-453-00399-0, H399). NAL.

Davis, Judy & Spellman, Shirley. Cardiac Rehabilitation for the Patient & Family. (Illus.). 176p. 1980. text ed. 10.95 (ISBN 0-8359-0679-5). Reston.

Davis, Julian C. & Foreyt, John P. Mental Examiner's Source Book. (Illus.). 248p. 1975. 19.75 (ISBN 0-398-03410-9). C C Thomas.

Davis, Karen. National Health Insurance: Benefits, Costs, & Consequences. (Studies in Social Economics). 182p. 1975. 10.95 (ISBN 0-8157-1760-1); pap. 4.95 (ISBN 0-8157-1759-8). Brookings.

Davis, Karen & Schoen, Cathy. Health & the War on Poverty: A Ten-Year Appraisal. (Studies in Social Economics). 1978. 14.95 (ISBN 0-8157-1758-X); pap. 5.95 (ISBN 0-8157-1757-1). Brookings.

Davis, Karl D., et al. Emergency & Disaster Nursing Continuing Education Review. 1976. spiral bdg. 8.00 o.p. (ISBN 0-87488-371-7). Med Exam.

Davis, Katie B. Federico Garcia Lorca & Sean O'Casey: Powerful Voices in the Wilderness. (Salzburg Studies in English Literature: Poetic Drama & Poetic Theory: No. 43). 1978. text ed. 25.00x (ISBN 0-391-01357-2). Humanities.

Davis, Katrina. Charm Course for College Coeds. (Illus.). 80p. (Orig.). 1981. pap. 9.95 (ISBN 0-937242-05-5). Scandia Pubs.

--Toothpick Building Illustrated. (Illus.). 48p. (Orig.). 1980. pap. 3.95 (ISBN 0-937242-04-7). Scandia Pubs.

Davis, Keith. Human Behavior at Work. 6th ed. (Management Ser.). (Illus.). 576p. 1981. text ed. 18.95x (ISBN 0-07-015516-X, C); instrs'. manual & test file avail. (ISBN 0-07-015517-8); study guide avail. (ISBN 0-07-015535-6) (ISBN 0-686-68262-9). McGraw.

Davis, Keith & Blomstrom, Robert. Business & Society: Environment & Responsibility. (Management Ser.). (Illus.). 608p. 1975. text ed. 15.95 o.p. (ISBN 0-07-015524-0, C); instructor's manual 4.95 o.p. (ISBN 0-07-015525-9). McGraw.

Davis, Keith & Newstrom, John. Organizational Behavior: A Book of Readings. 6th ed. (Illus.). 468p. Date not set. text ed. price not set (ISBN 0-07-015500-3, C). McGraw.

--Organizational Behavior: A Book of Readings. 6th ed. (Illus.). 468p. text ed. 11.95 (ISBN 0-07-015500-3). McGraw.

Davis, Keith, jt. auth. see Werther, William.

Davis, Keith A., jt. auth. see Schroeder, W. Widick.

Davis, Ken & Taylor, Tom. The Adventure of Making Money. LC 79-24749. (Illus., Orig.). (gr. 5-10). 1980. pap. 2.95 (ISBN 0-916392-47-3). Oak Tree Pubns.

--Kids & Cash. 320p. 1981. pap. 2.95 (ISBN 0-553-14152-X). Bantam.

--Kids & Cash: Solving a Parent's Dilemma. LC 79-13092. (Illus.). 1979. 8.95 (ISBN 0-916392-26-0). Oak Tree Pubns.

Davis, Ken, et al. Inflation, Taxes & Other Economic Mysteries. LC 79-25124. (Illus., Orig.). (gr. 6-10). 1980. pap. write for info. (ISBN 0-916392-46-5). Oak Tree Pubns.

Davis, Kenneth & Henvey, Thom. Restoring Furniture. LC 77-11401. (Illus.). 1978. 16.95 o.p. (ISBN 0-668-04545-0, 4545). Arco.

Davis, Kenneth C. Administrative Law Treatise. 2nd ed. LC 77-86317. 1977. 47.50 o.p. (ISBN 0-686-22900-2). Lawyers Co-Op.

--Discretionary Justice: A Preliminary Inquiry. LC 80-16898. xii, 233p. 1980. Repr. of 1969 ed. lib. bdg. 21.25x (ISBN 0-313-22503-6, DADC). Greenwood.

Davis, Kenneth L. & Berger, Philip A., eds. Brain Acetylcholine & Neuropsychiatric Disease. LC 79-862. 614p. 1979. 39.50 (ISBN 0-306-40157-6, Plenum Pr). Plenum Pub.

Davis, Kenneth R. Marketing Management. 3rd ed. 1972. pap. text ed. instr's. manual o.p. avail. o.p. (ISBN 0-8260-2510-2); instructors' manual avail. o.p. (ISBN 0-471-07455-1). Wiley.

--Marketing Management. 4th ed. (Marketing Ser.). 800p. 1981. text ed. 20.95 (ISBN 0-471-05948-X). Wiley.

Davis, Kenneth R. & Webster, Frederick E., Jr. Sales Force Management. LC 68-12886. (Illus.). 1968. 24.95 (ISBN 0-8260-2525-0, 22271). Wiley.

Davis, Kenneth S. Kansas: A Bicentennial History. (States & the Nation Ser). (Illus.). 1976. 12.95 (ISBN 0-393-05593-0, Co-Pub by AASLH). Norton.

Davis, Kenneth S. & Leopold, Luna. Water. LC 66-18677. (Life Science Library). (Illus.). (gr. 5 up). 1970. PLB 8.97 o.p. (ISBN 0-8094-0473-7, Pub. by Time-Life). Silver.

Davis, Kenneth S., ed. Arms, Industry & America. (Reference Shelf Ser.). 1971. 5.75 (ISBN 0-8242-0446-8). Wilson.

--Paradox of Poverty in America. (Reference Shelf Ser: Vol. 41, No. 2). 1969. 6.25 (ISBN 0-8242-0107-8). Wilson.

Davis, Kim, jt. auth. see Tollefson, Stephen.

Davis, King E. Fund Raising in the Black Community: History, Feasibility, & Conflict. LC 75-25586. 1975. 10.00 (ISBN 0-8108-0870-6). Scarecrow.

Davis, L. Christian Handbook. 5.00 o.p. (ISBN 0-8062-1218-7). Carlton.

Davis, Lance & North, Douglass. Institutional Change & American Economic Growth. 1971. 27.50 (ISBN 0-521-08111-4). Cambridge U Pr.

Davis, Larry, jt. auth. see Bard, Ray.

Davis, Larry N. Planning, Conducting, Evaluating Workshops. LC 74-82809. 1975. 17.95 (ISBN 0-89384-001-7); pap. 9.95 (ISBN 0-89384-002-5). Learning Concepts.

Davis, Lenwood G. The Black Aged in the United States: An Annotated Bibliography. LC 80-1193. xviii, 200p. 1980. lib. bdg. 22.50 (ISBN 0-313-22560-5, DAB/). Greenwood.

--The Black Family in the United States: A Selected Bibliography of Annotated Books, Articles, & Dissertations on Black Families in America. LC 77-89109. 1978. lib. bdg. 12.95 (ISBN 0-8371-9851-8, DBF/). Greenwood.

Davis, Lenwood G., compiled By. Marcus Garvey: An Annotated Bibliography. LC 80-653. 200p. 1980. lib. bdg. 22.50 (ISBN 0-313-22131-6, DMG/). Greenwood.

Davis, Leo G. Ounce of Prevention Is Worth a Pound of Cure. 1981. 6.50 (ISBN 0-8062-1569-0). Carlton.

Davis, Lily A., jt. auth. see Hanson, Louise G.

Davis, Lloyd & Irwin, Robert. Contemporary American Poetry: A Checklist. LC 75-19028. 1975. 10.00 (ISBN 0-8108-0832-3). Scarecrow.

Davis, Lorin R. see Heat Transfer & Fluid Mechanics Institute.

Davis, Louis E. & Cherns, Albert B., eds. Quality of Working Life: Cases & Commentary. Vol. 2. LC 74-24370. 1975. 19.95 (ISBN 0-02-907330-8); pap. text ed. 9.95 (ISBN 0-02-907340-5). Free Pr.

--The Quality of Working Life: Problems, Prospects & the State of the Art, Vol.1. LC 74-24369. 1975. 19.95 (ISBN 0-02-907390-1); pap. text ed. 9.95 (ISBN 0-02-907380-4). Free Pr.

Davis, Lydia, tr. see Clastres, Pierre.

Davis, Lynn. Na Pa'i Ki'i: The Photographers in the Hawaiian Islands, 1900-1945. LC 80-70100. (Special Publication Ser.: No. 69). (Illus.). 48p. Date not set. pap. 5.50 (ISBN 0-910240-29-9). Bishop Mus.

Davis, M. Visual Design in Dress. 1979. 16.95 (ISBN 0-13-942409-1). P-H.

Davis, M. Edward & Meilach, Dona. Doctor Discusses Menopause & Estrogens. (Illus.). 1980. pap. 2.50 (ISBN 0-910304-26-2). Budlong.

Davis, M. I. IBM Series One Design Decisions: Architecture. (Illus.). 48p. (Orig.). 1979. pap. text ed. 4.40 (ISBN 0-933186-01-0, G360-0066). IBM Armonk.

Davis, M. L., ed. Memoirs of Aaron Burr, 2 Vols. LC 73-152836. (Era of the American Revolution Ser). 1971. Repr. of 1836 ed. Set. lib. bdg. 65.00 (ISBN 0-306-70139-1). Da Capo.

Davis, Madeleine & Wallbridge, David. Boundary & Space: An Introduction to the Work of D. W. Winnicott. 212p. 1981. 17.50 (ISBN 0-87630-251-7). Brunner-Mazel.

Davis, Maggie. Eagles. LC 80-14471. 384p. 1980. 13.95 (ISBN 0-688-03727-5). Morrow.

--The Sheik. 1978. pap. 1.95 o.p. (ISBN 0-449-23554-8, Crest). Fawcett.

Davis, Marcella Z. Living with Multiple Sclerosis: A Social Psychological Analysis. 80p. 1973. 9.50 (ISBN 0-398-02850-8). C C Thomas.

Davis, Marcella Z., et al. Nurses in Practice: A Perspective on Work Environments. LC 74-13232. 1975. 8.95 o.p. (ISBN 0-8016-1208-X). Mosby.

Davis, Margaret D. Piero Della Francesca's Mathematical Treatises: The "Trattato d'Abaco" & "Libellus de Quinque Corporibus Regularibus". (Speculum Artium: No. 1). (Illus.). 165p. (It.). 1977. pap. 17.50x (ISBN 0-8150-0912-7). Wittenborn.

Davis, Marilyn K., jt. auth. see Broido, Arnold.

Davis, Marion M. see Meredith, Grace E.

Davis, Martin. Applied Nonstandard Analysis. LC 76-28484. (Pure & Applied Mathematics Ser.). 1977. text ed. 25.95 (ISBN 0-471-19897-8, Pub. by Wiley-Interscience). Wiley.

Davis, Mary B. James Elroy Flecker: A Critical Study. (Salzburg Studies in English Literature: Poetic Drama & Poetic Theory: No. 33). 1977. text ed. 25.00x (ISBN 0-391-01358-0). Humanities.

Davis, Mel. High Uinta Trails. (Illus.). 132p. 1974. pap. 3.50 (ISBN 0-915272-02-4). Wasatch Pubs.

Davis, Melinda D. Winslow Homer: An Annotated Bibliography of Periodical Literature. LC 75-29243. 1975. 10.00 (ISBN 0-8108-0876-5). Scarecrow.

Davis, Michael. The Image of Lincoln in the South. LC 73-158115. 1971. 11.50x (ISBN 0-87049-133-4). U of Tenn Pr.

Davis, Mildred. Art of Crewel Embroidery. 13.95 o.p. (ISBN 0-87245-074-0). Textile Bk.

Davis, Monte, jt. auth. see Woodcock, Alexander.

Davis, Morton. Mathematically Speaking. 484p. 1980. text ed. 16.95 (ISBN 0-686-68334-X, HC); instr's guide avail. HarBraceJ.

Davis, Moshe, ed. Zionism in Transition. 1980. pap. 8.00 (ISBN 0-930832-61-2). Herzl Pr.

Davis, Muriel, ed. Inscape: Stories, Plays, & Poems. LC 73-130272. 1971. pap. text ed. 5.95x o.p. (ISBN 0-397-47240-4); pap. instructor's manual avail. o.p. (ISBN 0-397-47241-2). Lippincott.

Davis, Murray S. Intimate Relations. LC 73-1859. (Illus.). 1973. 12.95 (ISBN 0-02-907020-1); pap. 3.95 (ISBN 0-02-907200-X). Free Pr.

Davis, Myrna. The Potato Book. LC 73-7890. (Illus.). 1978. pap. 2.95 (ISBN 0-688-05186-3, Quill). Morrow.

Davis, Nancy. Vocabulary Improvement. 3rd ed. 1978. pap. text ed. 10.50x (ISBN 0-07-015543-7, C). McGraw.

Davis, Nancy B. Vocabulary Improvement: A Program for Self-Instruction. rev. 2nd ed. 192p. 1973. pap. text ed. 7.95 (ISBN 0-07-015513-5, C); instructor's manual 5.95 (ISBN 0-07-015543-7). McGraw.

Davis, Norman. Journeys to the Past. 1980. 10.00 (ISBN 0-910286-83-3); pap. 6.95 (ISBN 0-910286-78-7). Boxwood.

Davis, Norman, ed. The Paston Letters: A Selection in Modern Spelling. (World's Classics Ser: No. 591). 1975. 12.95 (ISBN 0-19-250591-2). Oxford U Pr.

--Paston Letters & Papers of the Fifteenth Century, Pt. 1. 760p. 1971. 55.00x (ISBN 0-19-812415-5). Oxford U Pr.

Davis, Norman, et al. A Chaucer Glossary. 1979. 19.95x (ISBN 0-19-811168-1); pap. 9.95x (ISBN 0-19-811171-1). Oxford U Pr.

Davis, O. B. Introduction to Biblical Literature. (Literature Ser.). 1976. pap. text ed. 6.65x (ISBN 0-8104-5834-9). Hayden.

Davis, O. B., jt. auth. see Davis, Alexandra.

Davis, O. B., jt. auth. see Fuller, Edmund.

Davis, O. L., Jr., jt. ed. see Mehlinger, Howard.

Davis, P. Medical Dictation & Transcription. 2nd ed. 400p. 1981. pap. 12.95 (ISBN 0-471-06023-2, Pub. by Wiley Med). Wiley.

Davis, P. E., jt. auth. see Smith, G. L.

Davis, P. H. & Cullen, J. The Identification of Flowering Plant Families. LC 78-8125. (Illus.). 1979. 21.50 (ISBN 0-521-22111-0); pap. 5.95x (ISBN 0-521-29359-6). Cambridge U Pr.

Davis, P. Michael, jt. auth. see Crumbley, D. Larry.

Davis, P. R., ed. Performance Under Sub-Optimal Condition. 1971. pap. text ed. 12.95x (ISBN 0-85066-044-0). Intl Ideas.

Davis, Pat. Badminton Complete. rev. ed. LC 75-5170. (Illus.). 192p. 1976. 7.95 o.p. (ISBN 0-498-01696-X). A S Barnes.

Davis, Patricia T. A Family Tapestry: Five Generations of the Curwens of Walnut Hill & Their Various Relatives. LC 72-14325. (Illus.). 224p. 1972. lib. bdg. 10.00 (ISBN 0-915010-15-1). Sutter House.

Davis, Paul. Paul Davis: Posters & Paintings. 1977. pap. 7.95 o.p. (ISBN 0-525-47484-6). Dutton.

Davis, Pauline C., jt. auth. see Biedenharn, Norma W.

Davis, Pedr & McCarthy, Mike. Ride, & Stay Alive. Robinson, Jeff, ed. (Illus.). 128p. 1973. pap. text ed. 4.95 (ISBN 0-89287-024-9, X910). Clymer Pubns.

Davis, Perry. Chicago: Creating New Traditions. LC 76-45167. (Illus.). 1976. 12.50 (ISBN 0-913820-03-2); pap. 7.95 (ISBN 0-913820-05-9). Chicago Hist.

Davis, Peter. The Social Context of Dentistry. 189p. 1980. 27.50x (ISBN 0-7099-0152-6, Pub. by Croom Helm Ltd England). Biblio Dist.

Davis, Phil. Beyond the Zone System. (Illus.). 256p. 1981. 19.95 (ISBN 0-930764-23-4); wkbk 8.95 (ISBN 0-930764-28-5). Curtin & London.

--The Dancer's Death. 176p. 1981. pap. 2.25 (ISBN 0-380-76612-4, 76612). Avon.

Davis, Philip E. Dialogues of Modern Philosophy. 1977. pap. text ed. 12.95x o.p. (ISBN 0-205-05511-7). Allyn.

Davis, Philip E., ed. Moral Duty & Legal Responsibility: A Philosophical-Legal Casebook. 2nd ed. LC 66-24252. (Century Philosophy Ser). (Orig.). 1981. Repr. of 1966 ed. 14.95x. Irvington.

Davis, Philip J. Circulant Matrices. LC 79-10551. (Pure & Applied Mathematics: Texts, Monographs, & Tracts). 1979. 19.95 (ISBN 0-471-05771-1, Pub. by Wiley-Interscience). Wiley.

Davis, Philip W. Modern Theories of Language. (Illus.). 496p. 1973. 15.95 (ISBN 0-13-598987-6). P-H.

Davis, Philip W., ed. see Bennett, Michael, et al.

Davis, Phyllis. Medical Shorthand. 2nd ed. 275p. 1981. pap. 11.95 (ISBN 0-471-06024-0). Wiley.

Davis, Phyllis E., jt. auth. see Smith, Genevieve L.

Davis, Polly Ann. Alben W. Barkley: Senate Majority Leader & Vice President. Freidel, Frank, ed. LC 78-62380. (Modern American History Ser.: Vol. 6). 1979. lib. bdg. 30.00 (ISBN 0-8240-3630-1). Garland Pub.

Davis, R., et al, eds. Advanced Bacterial Genetics. 150p. (Orig.). 1980. lab manual 24.00x (ISBN 0-87969-130-1). Cold Spring Harbor.

--Experiments in Genetic Engineering: Advanced Bacterial Genetics Manual. 150p. (Orig.). 1980. cancelled lab manual (ISBN 0-87969-130-1). Cold Spring Harbor.

Davis, R. F., et al, eds. Processing of Crystalline Ceramics. (Materials Science Research Ser.: Vol. 11). 664p. 1978. 49.50 (ISBN 0-306-40035-9, Plenum Pr). Plenum Pub.

Davis, R. H. C. A History of Medieval Europe. (Illus.). 1971. pap. text ed. 10.50x (ISBN 0-582-48208-9). Longman.

--King Stephen. LC 77-4291. (Illus.). 1977. pap. text ed. 8.95x (ISBN 0-582-48727-7). Longman.

--King Stephen, 1135-1154. 1967. 17.50x (ISBN 0-520-00298-9). U of Cal Pr.

Davis, Ralph. The Industrial Revolution & British Overseas Trade. (Illus.). 1978. text ed. 20.50x (ISBN 0-391-00925-7, Leicester); pap. text ed. 9.75x (ISBN 0-391-00927-3). Humanities.

--The Rise of the English Shipping Industry in the 17th & 18th Centuries. 427p. 1972. Repr. of 1962 ed. 17.50x (ISBN 0-87471-314-5). Rowman.

Davis, Ralph, ed. see Williams, Judith B.

Davis, Ray J. Ecology & Conservation of Natural Resources. 1978. lib. bdg. 6.65 (ISBN 0-931054-02-8). Clark Pub.

Davis, Ray J. & Grant, Lewis, eds. Weather Modification: Technology & Law. LC 78-55519. (AAAS Selected Symposia Ser.). 1978. lib. bdg. 17.50x (ISBN 0-89158-153-7). Westview.

Davis, Raymond E. & Kelly, J. W. Elementary Plane Surveying. 4th ed. (Illus.). 1967. text ed. 20.50 (ISBN 0-07-015771-5, C); solutions 1.50 (ISBN 0-07-015772-3). McGraw.

Davis, Richard. Space Two: A New Collection of Science Fiction Stories. 140p. 1975. 8.95 (ISBN 0-200-72275-1). Transatlantic.

Davis, Richard A. Principles of Oceanography. 2nd ed. LC 76-10436. (Illus.). 1977. text ed. 18.95 (ISBN 0-201-01464-5). A-W.

Davis, Richard B. A Colonial Southern Bookshelf: Reading in the Eighteenth Century. LC 78-3832. (Lamar Memorial Lectures: No. 21). 152p. 1979. 10.50x (ISBN 0-8203-0450-6). U of Ga Pr.

--Intellectual Life in Jefferson's Virginia, 1790-1830. LC 64-13548. (Illus.). 524p. 1972. Repr. of 1964 ed. 14.50x (ISBN 0-87049-144-X). U of Tenn Pr.

Davis, Richard B., jt. auth. see Steiner, Charles V., Jr.

Davis, Richard B., compiled by. American Literature Through Bryant. LC 76-79172. (Goldentree Bibliographies in Language & Literature Ser.). 160p. (Orig.). 1969. pap. 6.95x (ISBN 0-88295-510-1). AHM Pub.

Davis, Richard B., ed. see Davies, Samuel.

Davis, Richard C. & Miller, Linda A., eds. Duke University Guide to Manuscripts. LC 79-28688. 1005p. 1980. lib. bdg. 32.50 (ISBN 0-87436-299-7). Abc-Clio.

Davis, Richard F. Modern Dairy Cattle Management. 1962. ref. ed. 18.95 (ISBN 0-13-590794-2). P-H.

Davis, Richard H. Soldiers of Fortune. 300p. Repr. lib. bdg. 12.95x (ISBN 0-89966-284-6). Buccaneer Bks.

--Television & the Aging Audience. LC 80-68093. (Illus.). 107p. (Orig.). 1980. 8.50 (ISBN 0-88474-096-X); pap. 6.50 (ISBN 0-686-28656-1). USC Andrus Geron.

Davis, Richard H., ed. Aging: Prospects & Issues. 3rd rev. ed. LC 80-53413. 427p. 1981. pap. 10.00 (ISBN 0-88474-097-8). USC Andrus Geron.

--Aging: Prospects & Issues. rev. ed. 1980. 10.00 (ISBN 0-88474-097-8). USC Andrus Geron.

--Stress & the Organization. Birren, James E. LC 78-66074. 1979. pap. 3.00 (ISBN 0-88474-086-2). USC Andrus Geron.

Davis, Robert B. George Russell. (English Authors Ser.: No. 208). 1977. lib. bdg. 10.95 (ISBN 0-8057-6677-4). Twayne.

Davis, Robert C., ed. The Fictional Father: Lacanian Readings of the Text. LC 80-26222. 240p. 1981. lib. bdg. 15.00x (ISBN 0-87023-111-1). U of Mass Pr.

Davis, Robert D., jt. auth. see Moon, Robert A.

Davis, Robert H., ed. Historical Dictionary of Colombia. LC 76-54245. (Latin American Historical Dictionaries Ser: No. 14). (Illus.). 1977. 13.50 (ISBN 0-8108-0999-0). Scarecrow.

Davis, Robert M. A Catalogue of the Evelyn Waugh Collection at the Humanities Research Center: The Universtiy of Texas at Austin. LC 80-50840. 375p. 1981. 25.00x (ISBN 0-87875-194-7). Whitston Pub.

--Evelyn Waugh, Writer: The Making of a Man of Letters. 270p. 1980. 21.95x (ISBN 0-937664-00-6). Pilgrim Bks OK.

Davis, Robert M., ed. Steinbeck: A Collection of Critical Essays. 1972. 10.95 (ISBN 0-13-846659-9, Spec); pap. 2.95 (ISBN 0-13-846642-4, Spec). P-H.

Davis, Robert P., jt. auth. see Schmidt, J. William.

Davis, Robert T., et al. Marketing Management Casebook. 3rd ed. 1980. 20.95x (ISBN 0-256-02347-6). Irwin.

Davis, Ron. Women & Horses. (Illus., Orig.). 1981. pap. 2.50 (ISBN 0-914140-11-6). Carpenter Pr.

Davis, Ronald F. Pathaway of Life & Other Poems. 1981. 4.75 (ISBN 0-8062-1563-1). Carlton.

Davis, Ronald L. A History of Music in American Life, Vol. 1: The Formative Years, 1620-1865. LC 79-25359. 386p. 1981. lib. bdg. 17.50 (ISBN 0-89874-002-9). Krieger.

--A History of Music in American Life, Vol. 2: The Gilded Years, 1865-1920. LC 79-25359. 314p. 1980. lib. bdg. 14.25 (ISBN 0-89874-003-7). Krieger.

--A History of Music in American Life, Vol. 3: The Modern Era, 1920 to the Present. LC 79-25359. 522p. 1981. lib. bdg. 23.50 (ISBN 0-89874-004-5); lib. bdg. 49.50 (ISBN 0-686-66036-6). Krieger.

--Opera in Chicago. (Illus.). 393p. 1980. Repr. of 1966 ed. text ed. 22.50x (ISBN 0-8290-0225-1). Irvington.

Davis, Ross, jt. ed. see Goldstein, Benjamin.

Davis, Roy E. An Easy Guide to Meditation. 1978. 3.95x (ISBN 0-87707-208-6). CSA Pr.

--Time, Space & Circumstance. rev. ed. LC 73-77614. 1973. 4.95 (ISBN 0-8119-0399-0). Fell.

--With God We Can. 1978. pap. 4.95 (ISBN 0-87707-211-6). CSA Pr.

Davis, Russell G. & Ashabranner, B. Chief Joseph: War Chief of the Nez Perce. (gr. 5-7). 1962. PLB 7.95 o.p. (ISBN 0-07-015926-2, GB). McGraw.

Davis, S. H. Victims of the Miracle. (Illus.). 1977. 29.95 (ISBN 0-521-21738-5); pap. 6.95x (ISBN 0-521-29246-8). Cambridge U Pr.

Davis, S. Rufus. The Federal Principle: A Journey Through Time in Quest of Meaning. 1978. 16.50x (ISBN 0-520-03146-6). U of Cal Pr.

Davis, Sam. The Form of Housing. 320p. 1981. pap. text ed. 14.95 (ISBN 0-442-27218-9). Van Nos Reinhold.

Davis, Sammy, Jr. Hollywood in a Suitcase. LC 80-14792. (Illus.). 1980. 11.95 (ISBN 0-688-03736-4). Morrow.

Davis, Samuel M. Rights of Juvenile: The Juvenile Justice System. 1980. 45.00 (ISBN 0-87632-104-X). Boardman.

Davis, Sandra T. Intellectual Change & Political Development in Early Modern Japan: Ono Azusa, a Case Study. LC 76-14762. 1979. 24.50 (ISBN 0-8386-1953-3). Fairleigh Dickinson.

Davis, Stanley M. & Goodman, Louis W., eds. Workers & Managers in Latin America. LC 72-3745. 192p. 1972. o. p. 12.50 o.p. (ISBN 0-669-74658-4); pap. 6.95 o.p. (ISBN 0-686-66688-7). Heath.

Davis, Stanley M., et al. Matrix. LC 77-81192. (An Organization Development Ser.). 1977. pap. text ed. 7.95 (ISBN 0-201-01115-8). A-W.

Davis, Stephen & Simon, Peter. Reggae Bloodlines. LC 76-42428. 1977. pap. 8.95 (ISBN 0-385-12330-2, Anch). Doubleday.

Davis, Stephen T., ed. Encountering Evil: Live Options in Theodicy. LC 80-84647. 1981. pap. 7.95 (ISBN 0-686-69554-2). John Knox.

Davis, Steven. Philosophy & Language. LC 75-15910. (Traditions in Philosophy Ser.). 1976. pap. 7.95 (ISBN 0-672-63674-3). Pegasus.

Davis, Steven, ed. Causal Theories of Mind. (Foundations of Communications Ser.). 400p. 1980. 81.50x (ISBN 3-11-007730-2). De Gruyter.

Davis, Steven I. The Euro-Bank: Its Origins, Management & Outlook. 2nd ed. LC 80-13337. 154p. 1980. 24.95x (ISBN 0-470-26955-3). Halsted Pr.

--The Euro-Bank: It's Origins, Managements & Outlook. LC 76-15912. 1976. 19.95 (ISBN 0-470-15060-2). Halsted Pr.

Davis, Susan. I Was a Stranger. LC 78-58077. (Destiny Ser.). 1979. pap. 4.95 (ISBN 0-8163-0237-5). Pacific Pr Pub Assn.

--Password to Heaven. (My Church Teaches Ser.). 32p. (gr. k-3). 1980. pap. 1.50 (ISBN 0-8127-0298-0). Southern Pub.

--A Way to Remember. Davis, Tom, ed. 32p. (ps up). 1980. pap. write for info. (ISBN 0-8280-0023-9). Review & Herald.

Davis, Thomas. Experimentation with Microprocessor Applications. (Orig.). 1980. pap. text ed. 9.95 (ISBN 0-8359-1812-2). Reston.

Davis, Thomas M. & Davis, Virginia L. Edward Taylor Vs. Solomon Stoddard: The Nature of the Lord's Supper, Vol. II. (American Literary Manuscripts Ser.). 1981. lib. bdg. 30.00 (ISBN 0-8057-9653-3). Twayne.

--The Unpublished Writings of Edward Taylor, 3 vols. (American Literary Manuscripts Ser.). 1981. Set. lib. bdg. 90.00 (ISBN 0-8057-9655-X). Twayne.

Davis, Thomas M. & Davis, Virginia L., eds. Edward Taylor's "Church Record" & Related Sermons. (American Literary Manuscripts Ser.: Vol. 1). 1981. lib. bdg. 35.00 (ISBN 0-8057-9650-9). Twayne.

--Edward Taylor's Minor Poetry, Vol. 3. (American Literary Manuscripts Ser.). 1981. lib. bdg. 35.00 (ISBN 0-8057-9654-1). Twayne.

Davis, Thomas X., tr. see William Of St. Tierry.

Davis, Tom, jt. auth. see Danziger, Jeff.

Davis, Tom, ed. see Davis, Susan.

Davis, Tom, ed. see Down, Goldie.

Davis, Tom, ed. see Hannum, Harold E.

Davis, Uri. Israel: Utopia Incorporated. 182p. 1977. 10.00 (ISBN 0-905762-12-6, Pub. by Zed Pr); pap. 6.00 (ISBN 0-905762-13-4). Lawrence Hill.

Davis, Vincent, ed. The Post Imperial Presidency. 288p. 1980. 19.95 (ISBN 0-03-055741-0). Praeger.

Davis, Vincent, ed. see Bucknell, Howard.

Davis, Virginia L., jt. auth. see Davis, Thomas M.

Davis, Virginia L., jt. ed. see Davis, Thomas M.

Davis, W. Hints to Philanthropists. 176p. 1971. Repr. of 1821 ed. 20.00x (ISBN 0-7165-1564-4, Pub. by Irish Academic Pr Ireland). Biblio Dist.

Davis, W. N. California Indians Five: Sagebrush Corner - Opening of California's Northeast. (American Indian Ethnohistory Ser: California & Basin - Plateau Indians). (Illus.). lib. bdg. 42.00 (ISBN 0-8240-0775-1). Garland Pub.

Davis, W. T., ed. Bradford's History of Plymouth Plantation 1606-1646. (Original Narratives Ser.). 436p. 1959. Repr. of 1908 ed. 18.50x (ISBN 0-686-63939-1). B&N.

Davis, Wallace. Corduroy Road, Glenn McCarthy: Texas Oil Field Saga. (Illus.). 1951. 15.00 (ISBN 0-685-04999-X). A Jones.

Davis, Wilbur W., jt. auth. see Blake, Maurice C.

Davis, William. Bench & Bar of the Commonwealth of Massachusetts, 2 vols. (American Constitutional & Legal History Ser). 1299p. 1974. Repr. of 1895 ed. Set. lib. bdg. 115.00 (ISBN 0-306-70612-1). Da Capo.

--The Best of Everything. 224p. 1981. 9.95 (ISBN 0-312-07713-0). St Martin.

--History of the Judiciary of Massachusetts. LC 74-8535. (American Constitutional & Legal History Ser). xxiv, 446p. 1974. Repr. of 1900 ed. lib. bdg. 45.00 (ISBN 0-306-70613-X). Da Capo.

--It's No Sin to Be Rich: A Defense of Capitalism. LC 77-9527. 1977. 8.95 o.p. (ISBN 0-525-66560-9). Elsevier-Nelson.

Davis, William C. The Orphan Brigade: The Kentucky Confederates Who Couldn't Go Home. LC 79-7491. (Illus.). 336p. 1980. 12.95 (ISBN 0-385-14893-3). Doubleday.

Davis, William C., jt. auth. see Fickett, Wildon.

Davis, William F. Educator's Resource Guide to Special Education: Terms-Laws-Tests-Organizations. 270p. 1980. text ed. 17.95 (ISBN 0-205-06876-6). Allyn.

Davis, William G. Social Relations in a Philippine Market: Self-Interest & Subjectivity. LC 71-145783. 1973. 22.50x (ISBN 0-520-01904-0). U of Cal Pr.

Davis, William H. Beginner's Grammar of the Greek New Testament. 1923. 8.95x (ISBN 0-06-061710-1, HarpR). Har-Row.

Davis, William S. BASIC: Getting Started. 69p. 1981. pap. text ed. 5.95 (ISBN 0-201-03258-9). A-W.

--Business Data Processing. LC 77-81199. 1978. text ed. 14.95 (ISBN 0-201-01116-6); instr's man. o.p. 2.95 (ISBN 0-201-01001-1); wkbk. o.p. 5.95 (ISBN 0-686-68524-5). A-W.

--Computers & Business Information Processing. LC 80-10946. 448p. 1981. pap. text ed. 14.95 (ISBN 0-201-03161-2). A-W.

--Day in Old Athens. LC 60-16707. (Illus.). (gr. 7 up). 10.00x (ISBN 0-8196-0111-X). Biblo.

--Day in Old Rome. LC 61-24993. (Illus.). (gr. 7 up). 10.00x (ISBN 0-8196-0106-3). Biblo.

--Information Processing Systems. 2nd ed. LC 79-26775. (First Course in Computers: Lo7). (Illus.). 480p. 1981. text ed. price not set (ISBN 0-201-03183-3). A-W.

--Information Processing Systems: An Introduction to Modern Computer-Based Information Systems. LC 77-76115. (Illus.). 1978. text ed. 14.95 o.p. (ISBN 0-201-00999-4); wkbk. 5.95 o.p. (ISBN 0-201-01113-1); instr's man. 2.95 o.p. (ISBN 0-201-01000-3). A-W.

--Operating Systems: A Systematic View. LC 76-10414. (Illus.). 1977. text ed. 17.95 (ISBN 0-201-01118-2). A-W.

--Victor of Salamis. 1925. 5.95 o.s.i. (ISBN 0-02-530040-7). Macmillan.

Davis, William S. & Fisher, Richard H. Cobol: An Introduction to Structured Logic & Modular Program Design. 1979. pap. 13.95 (ISBN 0-201-01431-9); instrs'. manual 2.95 (ISBN 0-686-67461-8). A-W.

Davison. The Splendors of Egypt. pap. 8.98 (ISBN 0-517-28591-6). Bonanza.

Davison, Ann, et al. Great Voyages in Small Boats Solo Transatlantic. 1981. 15.00 (ISBN 0-8286-0085-6). De Graff.

Davison, D. J. The Environmental Factor: An Approach for Managers. LC 77-20123. 1978. 27.95 (ISBN 0-470-99351-0). Halsted Pr.

Davison, Dennis, ed. Restoration Comedies. (Oxford Paperbacks Ser). 1970. pap. 5.95x (ISBN 0-19-281063-4). Oxford U Pr.

Davison, Edward. Some Modern Poets & Other Critical Essays. 255p. 1980. Repr. lib. bdg. 35.00 (ISBN 0-89987-157-7). Century Bookbindery.

--Some Modern Poets & Other Critical Essays. 255p. 1980. Repr. of 1928 ed. lib. bdg. 35.00 (ISBN 0-89760-149-1). Telegraph Bks.

Davison, Frank, tr. see Alain-Fournier, Henri.

Davison, Gerald C. & Neale, John M. Abnormal Psychology: An Experimental Clinical Approach. 2nd ed. LC 77-13940. 1978. text ed. 21.95x (ISBN 0-471-19923-0); tchrs. manual avail. (ISBN 0-471-01731-0); study guide 7.95 (ISBN 0-471-03401-0); tests avail. (ISBN 0-471-03772-9). Wiley.

Davison, Jane, jt. auth. see Vila, Bob.

Davison, Jean. Dreaming Witness. 1978. pap. 1.75 o.p. (ISBN 0-425-03667-7, Medallion). Berkley Pub.

Davison, Juliana. The Golden Locket. 1978. pap. 1.75 o.p. (ISBN 0-425-03769-X, Medallion). Berkley Pub.

--Petals of the Rose. 192p. (Orig.). 1980. pap. 1.75 (ISBN 0-446-94272-3). Warner Bks.

--Pink Phaeton. (Orig.). 1980. pap. 1.75 (ISBN 0-446-94270-7). Warner Bks.

--Velvet Ribbons. (Orig.). 1980. pap. 1.75 (ISBN 0-446-94271-5). Warner Bks.

Davison, Leslie. Pathway to Power: A Concise History of the Modern Pentecost. 104p. 1972. pap. 2.95 o.p. (ISBN 0-901398-22-5). Logos.

Davison, Michael. Ancient Rome. LC 79-57555. (Abbeville Library of Art Ser.: No. 1). (Illus.). 112p. (Orig.). 1980. pap. 4.95 (ISBN 0-89659-124-7). Abbeville Pr.

--The Glory of Greece & World of Alexander. LC 79-92450. (Illus.). 172p. 1980. pap. 14.95 (ISBN 0-89659-104-2). Abbeville Pr.

Davison, Peter. Barn Fever & Other Poems. 64p. 1981. 10.00 (ISBN 0-689-11126-6); pap. 5.95 (ISBN 0-689-11163-0). Atheneum.

--Contemporary Drama & the Popular Dramatic Tradition in England. LC 79-55526. 184p. 1981. text ed. 26.00x (ISBN 0-06-491617-0). B&N.

--Popular Appeal in English Drama to Eighteen Fifty. LC 79-55528. 1981. text ed. 26.00x (ISBN 0-06-491618-9). B&N.

Davison, Peter, et al, eds. Literature & Society. LC 77-90613. (Literary Taste, Culture & Mass Communication Ser.: Vol. 5). 1978. lib. bdg. 32.00x (ISBN 0-914146-48-3). Somerset Hse.

Davison, W. Phillips & Boylan, James. Mass Media: Systems & Effects. LC 74-31000. 245p. 1976. pap. text ed. 10.95x (ISBN 0-03-038896-1). Praeger.

Davison, W. Phillips & Gordenker, Leon, eds. Resolving Nationality Conflicts: The Role of Public Opinion Research. LC 80-15128. 245p. 1980. 23.95 (ISBN 0-03-056229-5). Praeger.

Davison, W. Phillips & Yu, Frederick T. C., eds. Mass Communication Research: Major Issues & Future Directions. LC 74-5576. (Special Studies). 215p. 1974. 20.95 o.p. (ISBN 0-275-09320-4); pap. 9.95 student ed. o.p. (ISBN 0-275-88870-3). Praeger.

Davison, W. Phillips, et al. News from Abroad & the Foreign Policy Public. LC 80-68024. (Headline Ser.: No. 250). (Illus.). 64p. (Orig.). 1980. pap. 2.00 (ISBN 0-87124-063-7). Foreign Policy.

Davisson, Emmett D. Art & Mysteries in Tombs, Mummies & Catacombs. (Illus.). 1980. deluxe ed. 41.50 deluxe binding (ISBN 0-930582-63-2). Gloucester Art.

Davisson, Lee D., jt. ed. see Gray, Robert M.

Davisson, William I. & Harper, James E. European Economic History: The Ancient World. LC 75-172518. (Illus.). 1972. 24.00x (ISBN 0-89197-153-X); pap. text ed. 10.95x (ISBN 0-89197-154-8). Irvington.

Davitz, Joel & Davitz, Lois. Making It: Forty & Beyond, Surviving the Mid-Life Crisis. 1979. pap. 6.95 (ISBN 0-03-051561-0). Winston Pr.

Davitz, Joel R. & Davitz, Lois L. Inferences of Patients' Pain & Psychological Distress: Studies of Nursing Behaviors. (Illus.). 1980. text ed. 25.00 (ISBN 0-8261-3360-6). Springer Pub.

Davitz, Joel R., et al. Terminology & Concepts in Mental Retardation. LC 62-61261. (Orig.). 1964. pap. text ed. 5.00x (ISBN 0-8077-1233-7). Tchrs Coll.

Davitz, Lois, jt. auth. see Davitz, Joel.

Davitz, Lois L., jt. auth. see Davitz, Joel R.

Davrout, L., tr. see Wieger, L.

Davson. The Eye. 1974. Vol. 5. 61.00, by subscription 49.50 (ISBN 0-12-206755-X); Vol. 6. 57.00, by subscription 41.25 (ISBN 0-12-206756-8). Acad Pr.

Davson, Hugh. Physiology of the Eye. 3rd ed. 1972. 36.50 o.p. (ISBN 0-12-206740-1). Acad Pr.

Davson, Hugh, jt. ed. see Zadunaisky, Jose A.

Davy, H. Nitrous Oxide. (Illus.). 606p. 1972. 38.50 (ISBN 0-407-33150-6). Butterworths.

Davy McKee Corp. Plant Conversion Potential to Fuel Alcohol Production. 125p. 1981. pap. 24.50 (ISBN 0-89934-095-4). Solar Energy Info.

Davy, Yvonne. Frau Luther. LC 78-57355. (Destiny Ser.). 1979. pap. 4.95 (ISBN 0-8163-0235-9). Pacific Pr Pub Assn.

--Louis Braille & His Magic Dots. LC 75-36533. (Panda Ser.). 1976. pap. 4.95 (ISBN 0-8163-0226-X, 12680-5). Pacific Pr Pub Assn.

--Mr. Creator's Borrowed Brown Hands. LC 75-46424. (Panda Ser.). 1976. pap. 4.95 (ISBN 0-8163-0263-4, 13698-6). Pacific Pr Pub Assn.

Davye, Arnold, et al. Lagonga: A History of the Marque. 1979. 42.00 (ISBN 0-7153-7695-0). David & Charles.

Davys, Mary. The Reform'd Coquet. Bd. with Familiar Letters Betwixt a Gentleman & a Lady; The Mercenary Lover: or the Unfortunate Heiresses. Haywood, Eliza. LC 72-170558. (Foundations of the Novel Ser.: Vol. 42). lib. bdg. 50.00 (ISBN 0-8240-0553-8). Garland Pub.

Daw, Stephen. The Music of Johann Sebastion Bach. LC 78-68624. (Illus.). 240p. 1981. 19.50 (ISBN 0-8386-1682-8). Fairleigh Dickinson.

Dawber, Thomas R. The Framingham Study: The Epidemiology of Atherosclerotic Disease. LC 80-11189. (Commonwealth Fund Ser.). 1980. text ed. 17.50x (ISBN 0-674-31730-0). Harvard U Pr.

Dawdy, Doris. Artists of the American West: A Biographical Dictionary, Vol. II. LC 72-91919. 300p. 1981. 22.95x (ISBN 0-8040-0352-1). Swallow.

Dawe & Dornan. One-to-One: Resources for Conference-Centered Writing. (Orig.). 1981. pap. text ed. 7.95 (ISBN 0-316-17722-9); tchrs'. manual free (ISBN 0-316-17723-7). Little.

Dawe, R. D. Collation & Investigation of Manuscripts of Aeschylus. 1964. 56.00 (ISBN 0-521-04800-1). Cambridge U Pr.

Da-Wei, Kwo. Chinese Brushwork: Its History, Aesthetics, & Techniques. (Illus.). 220p. 1981. 37.50 (ISBN 0-8390-0267-X). Alanheld & Schram.

Dawes, Benjamin. Trematoda. 1946. 79.00 (ISBN 0-521-07219-0). Cambridge U Pr.

Dawes, E. A. Quantitative Problems in Biochemistry. 6th ed. (Illus.). 340p. 1981. text ed. 32.00 (ISBN 0-582-44402-0). Longman.

Dawes, I. W. & Sutherland, I. W. Microbial Physiology. (Basic Microbiology Ser.: Vol. 4). 1976. pap. text ed. 14.95 (ISBN 0-470-15159-5). Halsted Pr.

Dawes, John. Design & Planning of Swimming Pools. LC 79-40059. 276p. 1979. 52.50 (ISBN 0-8436-0169-8). CBI Pub.

--Rugby Union. (Pelham Pictorial Sports Instruction Ser). (Illus.). 1977. 10.95 (ISBN 0-7207-0792-7). Transatlantic.

Dawes, Walter A. The Ghost of Old Capernaum. (Illus.). 358p. (Orig.). 1980. pap. text ed. 24.95 (ISBN 0-686-28901-3). New Capernaum.

--Impact: The Religion of the Twenty-First Century. (Illus.). 79p. (Orig.). 1980. pap. text ed. 8.95 (ISBN 0-938792-05-9). New Capernaum.

--Light Shines on Mystery Babylon the Great. (Orig.). 1981. pap. price not set (ISBN 0-938792-10-5). New Capernaum.

Dawidoff, Donald J. The Malpractice of Psychiatrists: Malpractice in Psychoanalysis, Psychotherapy & Psychiatry. (American Lecture in Behavioral Science & Law Ser.). 184p. 1973. 16.75 (ISBN 0-398-02711-0). C C Thomas.

Dawisha, A. I. Egypt in the Arab World 1952-1970: The Elements of a Dynamic Foreign Policy. LC 76-7517. 1976. 32.95 (ISBN 0-470-19960-1). Halsted Pr.

Dawisha, Karen & Hanson, Philip, eds. Soviet-East European Dilemmas. LC 80-28573. 226p. 1981. text ed. 31.00x (ISBN 0-8419-0697-1); pap. text ed. 15.00x (ISBN 0-8419-0698-X). Holmes & Meier.

Dawkins, J. V., ed. Developments in Polymer Characterisation - Two. (Illus.). x, 240p. 1980. 55.00x (ISBN 0-85334-909-6). Burgess-Intl Ideas.

Dawkins, Michael & MacGregor, W. G., eds. Gestational Age, Size & Maturity. (Clinics in Developmental Medicine Ser. No. 19). 115p. 1965. 9.00 (ISBN 0-685-24719-8). Lippincott.

Dawkins, Richard. The Selfish Gene. 1976. 12.95 (ISBN 0-19-857519-X). Oxford U Pr.

--The Selfish Gene. LC 76-29168. 1978. pap. 3.95 (ISBN 0-19-520000-4, GB500, GB). Oxford U Pr.

Dawley, Alan. Class & Community: The Industrial Revolution in Lynn. LC 75-29049. (Harvard Studies in Urban History Ser.). (Illus.). 1979. 17.50x (ISBN 0-674-13390-0); pap. 6.95x (ISBN 0-674-13395-1). Harvard U Pr.

Dawley, Powel M. Chapters in Church History. rev. ed. (Orig.). 1963. pap. 3.95 (ISBN 0-8164-2004-1, SP2). Crossroad NY.

--Episcopal Church & Its Work. rev. ed. (Orig.). 1955. 3.50, case o.p. (ISBN 0-8164-0125-X); pap. 2.95 (ISBN 0-8164-2017-3, SP6). Crossroad NY.

Dawood, N. J., tr. Koran. (Classics Ser.). 1964. pap. 3.50 (ISBN 0-14-044052-6). Penguin.

Daws, Gavan. Shoal of Time. (Illus.). 1968. 9.95 o.s.i. (ISBN 0-02-530070-9). Macmillan.

Daws, Ron. Self-Made Olympian. LC 75-20960. (Illus.). 158p. 1977. pap. 3.95 (ISBN 0-89037-103-2); handbk. 5.95 (ISBN 0-89037-104-0). Anderson World.

Dawson, Alan. Fifty Five Days: The Fall of South Vietnam. LC 77-22768. 1978. 12.50 o.p. (ISBN 0-13-314476-3). P-H.

Dawson, Albert C. & Dawson, Laila M. Dicho y Hecho: Beginning Spanish: A Simplified Approach. LC 80-19506. 352p. 1981. text ed. 13.95 (ISBN 0-471-06476-9); tchr's ed. 7.00 (ISBN 0-471-08577-4); wkbk. avail. (ISBN 0-471-06103-4); tapes 1.00 (ISBN 0-471-06475-0). Wiley.

Dawson, Amy. Bobbin Lacemaking for Beginners. (Illus.). 1978. 6.95 (ISBN 0-7137-0817-4, Pub by Blandford Pr England). Sterling.

Dawson, C. A. The New North-West. (Scholarly Reprint Ser.). 1980. 45.00 (ISBN 0-8020-7105-8). U of Toronto Pr.

Dawson, Carl. His Fine Wit: A Study of Thomas Love Peacock. LC 78-97050. 1970. 14.50x (ISBN 0-520-01632-7). U of Cal Pr.

--Victorian Noon: English Literature in 1850. LC 78-13939. 1979. text ed. 16.95x (ISBN 0-8018-2110-X). Johns Hopkins.

Dawson, Carl & Pfordresher, John, eds. Matthew Arnold: Prose Writings. (The Critical Heritage Ser.). 1979. 15.00x (ISBN 0-7100-0244-0). Routledge & Kegan.

Dawson, Christopher. The Age of the Gods. LC 68-9653. (Illus., Maps, Tabs). 1971. Repr. of 1928 ed. 18.50 (ISBN 0-86527-001-5). Fertig.

--Dynamics of World History. 12.95 (ISBN 0-89385-009-8). Green Hill.

--Mission to Asia. (Medieval Academy Reprints for Teaching Ser.). 228p. 1981. pap. 6.00x (ISBN 0-8020-6436-1). U of Toronto Pr.

Dawson, Coningsby W., jt. auth. see Dawson, William J.

Dawson, David. No Fear in His Presence. LC 80-50261. 192p. 1980. text ed. 9.95 (ISBN 0-8307-0753-0, 5108918). Regal.

Dawson, David, jt. ed. see Tyler, H. Richard.

Dawson, Fielding. Three Penny Lane. 150p. (Orig.). 1981. signed ed. 20.00 (ISBN 0-87685-447-1); pap. 5.00 (ISBN 0-87685-446-3). Black Sparrow.

Dawson, Francis W. Reminiscences of Confederate Service. Wiley, Bell I., ed. LC 79-26720. (Library of Southern Civilization). 220p. 1980. 14.95x (ISBN 0-8071-0689-5). La State U Pr.

Dawson, George G., jt. auth. see Gordon, Sanford D.

Dawson, Grace. No Little Plans: Fairfax County's PLUS Program with Managing Growth. 168p. 1977. pap. 3.95 (ISBN 0-87766-185-5, 17100). Urban Inst.

Dawson, Grace, jt. auth. see Muller, Thomas.

Dawson, J. B. Kimberlites & Their Xenoliths. (Minerals & Rocks: Vol. 15). (Illus.). 252p. 1980. 47.25 (ISBN 0-387-10208-6). Springer-Verlag.

Dawson, J. L. & Blowers, G. H., eds. Perspectives in Asian Cross-Cultural Psychology: Selected Papers of the First Asian Regional Conference of the IACCP, March 19-23, 1979. 1981. pap. write for info. (ISBN 90-265-0359-8). Swets North Am.

Dawson, John & Palmer, George. Cases on Restitution. 2nd ed. 1969. 22.00 (ISBN 0-672-81193-6, Bobbs-Merrill Law). Michie.

Dawson, John, jt. auth. see Kirby, David.

Dawson, John A. Retail Geography. 175p. 1980. 29.95 (ISBN 0-470-27014-4, Pub. by Hlasted Pr). Wiley.

Dawson, Laila M., jt. auth. see Dawson, Albert C.

Dawson, Lawrence H. Nicknames & Pseudonyms. LC 73-164216. viii, 312p. 1974. Repr. of 1908 ed. 24.00 (ISBN 0-8103-3177-2). Gale.

Dawson, Linda, jt. auth. see Furchgott, Terry.

Dawson, Mary. Tecwyn, the Last of the Welsh Dragons. LC 67-10354. (Illus.). 72p. (gr. 3-7). 1967. 5.95 o.s.i. (ISBN 0-8193-0189-2, Four Winds); 5.41 o.s.i. (ISBN 0-8193-0190-6). Schol Bk Serv.

--Tinker Tales. LC 73-3496. (A Humpty Dumpty Bk.). (Illus.). 72p. (gr. k-3). 1973. 5.95 o.s.i. (ISBN 0-8193-0698-3, Four Winds); PLB 5.41 o.s.i. (ISBN 0-8193-0699-1). Schol Bk Serv.

Dawson, Mildred A., jt. auth. see Collins, Alberta C.

Dawson, Mildred A., jt. auth. see Newman, Georgiana C.

Dawson, Mildred A., et al. Five Words Long. 3rd ed. Bamman, Henry A., ed. (Kaleidoscope Ser.). 1978. pap. text ed. 6.08 (ISBN 0-201-40875-9, Sch Div); tchr's. ed. 6.64 (ISBN 0-201-40876-7). A-W.

Dawson, Nelson L. Louis D. Brandeis, Felix Frankfurter & the New Deal. 280p. 1980. 19.50 (ISBN 0-208-01817-4, Archon). Shoe String.

Dawson, Nelson L., jt. ed. see Harrison, Lowell H.

Dawson, P. M. The Unacknowledged Legislator: Shelley & Politics. 320p. 1980. 48.00x (ISBN 0-19-812095-8). Oxford U Pr.

Dawson, P. S., ed. Microbial Growth. LC 74-26644. (Benchmark Papers in Microbiology Ser: Vol. 8). 400p. 1975. 43.00 (ISBN 0-12-786330-3). Acad Pr.

Dawson, Peter. Gunsmoke Graze. 224p. 1980. pap. 1.75 (ISBN 0-553-14179-1). Bantam.

--High Country. 144p. 1981. pap. 1.75 (ISBN 0-553-14537-1). Bantam.

--Making a Comprehensive Work: The Road from Bomb Alley. 160p. 1981. 25.00x (ISBN 0-631-12534-5, Pub. by Basil Blackwell England); pap. 12.50x. Biblio Dist.

--Trail Boss. 192p. (Orig.). 1981. pap. 1.95 (ISBN 0-553-12968-6). Bantam.

Dawson, Peter E. Evaluation, Diagnosis, & Treatment of Occlusal Problems. LC 74-12409. 1974. 49.50 (ISBN 0-8016-1216-0). Mosby.

Dawson, Peter P. & Gallegos, Frederick. Case Study II: MEDCO, Inc. (Illus.). 89p. 1973. pap. text ed. 5.95 (ISBN 0-574-17920-8, 13-0920); instr's guide avail. (ISBN 0-574-17921-6, 13-0921). SRA.

Dawson, R. J. Fusion Welding & Brazing of Copper & Copper Alloys. LC 73-7969. 139p. 1973. 15.95 (ISBN 0-470-19981-4). Halsted Pr.

Dawson, Raymond. The Chinese Experience. (Illus.). 1978. 20.00 o.p. (ISBN 0-684-15912-0, ScribT). Scribner.

--An Introduction to Classical Chinese. 1978. pap. 13.95x (ISBN 0-19-815451-8). Oxford U Pr.

Dawson, Robert O. Standards Relating to Adjudication. (Juvenile Justice Standards Project Ser.). 1980. softcover 7.95 (ISBN 0-88410-809-0); casebound 12.50 (ISBN 0-88410-236-X). Ballinger Pub.

--Standards Relating to Adjudication. LC 77-1755. (Juvenile Justice Standards Project Ser.). 1977. softcover 5.95 o.p. (ISBN 0-88410-767-1); 12.50, casebound o.p. Ballinger Pub.

Dawson, Thomas F. The Ute War: A History of the White River Massacre & the Privations & Hardships of the Captive White Women Among the Hostiles on Grand River. Bd. with The Ute Massacre! Brave Miss Meeker's Captivity. Meeker, Josephine. LC 75-7119. (Indian Captivities Ser.: Vol. 93). 1976. Repr. of 1879 ed. lib. bdg. 44.00 (ISBN 0-8240-1717-X). Garland Pub.

Dawson, Townes L. & Mounce, Earl W. Business Law: Text & Cases. 4th ed. 1979. text ed. 21.95x (ISBN 0-669-01690-X); instructor's manual free (ISBN 0-669-01691-8). Heath.

Dawson, W. A. Introductory Guide to Central Labour Legislation. 10.00x (ISBN 0-210-27188-4). Asia.

Dawson, Warren R. Beginnings, Egypt & Assyria. (Illus.). 1964. pap. 8.25 o.s.i. (ISBN 0-02-843800-0). Hafner.

Dawson, Warren R., ed. The Banks Letters: A Calendar of the Manuscript Correspondence of Sir Joseph Banks Preserved in the British Museum, the British Museum (Natural History) & Other Collections in Great Britain. 965p. 1958. 78.00x (ISBN 0-565-00085-3, Pub. by Brit Mus Nat Hist England). Sabbot-Natural Hist Bks.

Dawson, William F. Christmas, Its Origin & Associations, Together with Its Historical Events & Festive Celebrations During Nineteen Centuries. LC 68-54857. 1968. Repr. of 1902 ed. 26.00 (ISBN 0-8103-3351-1). Gale.

Dawson, William H. Bismarck & State Socialism. 8.50 (ISBN 0-86527-009-0). Fertig.

Dawson, William J. & Dawson, Coningsby W. The Great English Letter-Writers, 2 vols. 1980. Set. lib. bdg. 50.00 (ISBN 0-8492-4218-5). R West.

Dawson, William M., jt. auth. see Mokwa, Michael P.

Dawydoff, W. Technical Dictionary of Higher Polymers: English, French, German, Russian. 1969. 120.00 (ISBN 0-08-013112-3). Pergamon.

Day, A. C. Fortran Techniques. LC 72-78891. (Illus.). 104p. 1972. 16.95 (ISBN 0-521-08549-7); pap. 6.95x (ISBN 0-521-09719-3). Cambridge U Pr.

Day, A. Grove. Eleanor Dark. LC 75-23369. (World Authors Ser.: Australia: No. 382). 1976. lib. bdg. 12.50 (ISBN 0-8057-6224-8). Twayne.

--James A. Michener. 2nd ed. (U. S. Authors Ser.: No. 60). 1977. lib. bdg. 10.95 (ISBN 0-8057-7184-0). Twayne.

--Modern Australian Prose, Nineteen One to Nineteen Seventy-Five: A Guide to Information Sources, Vol. 32. Day, A. Grove, ed. LC 74-11536. (American Literature, English Literature & World Literatures in English Information Guide Ser.). 425p. 1980. 30.00 (ISBN 0-8103-1243-3). Gale.

--Robert D. FitzGerald. (World Authors Ser.: Australia: No. 286). 1974. lib. bdg. 10.95 (ISBN 0-8057-2311-0). Twayne.

--Sky Clears: Poetry of the American Indians. LC 65-38538. 1964. pap. 2.45 (ISBN 0-8032-5047-9, BB 142, Bison). U of Nebr Pr.

Day, Alan E. J. B. Priestley: An Annotated Bibliography. LC 78-68251. (Garland Reference Library of the Humanities). 350p. 1980. lib. bdg. 35.00 (ISBN 0-8240-9798-X). Garland Pub.

Day, Albert E. Discipline & Discovery. rev. ed. 1977. pap. 2.95x (ISBN 0-8358-0354-6). Upper Room.

Day, Angell. English Secretary. LC 67-10122. 1967. Repr. of 1599 ed. 35.00 (ISBN 0-8201-1012-4). Schol Facsimiles.

Day, Avenelle, jt. auth. see Fink, Edith.

Day, Beth & Liley, H. M. The Secret World of the Baby. (gr. 5 up). 1968. 3.95 o.p. (ISBN 0-394-81555-6). Random.

Day, Beth, jt. auth. see Schiff, Jacqui L.

Day, Betty, jt. auth. see Schiff, Jacqui L.

Day, Brian H. Orthopedic Appliances. (Illus.). 1972. 7.95 o.p. (ISBN 0-571-09051-6, Pub. by Faber & Faber); pap. 4.95 o.p. (ISBN 0-571-09947-5). Merrimack Bk Serv.

Day, C. J., jt. auth. see Shaw, W. C.

Day, Candra, jt. auth. see Hess, Patricia.

Day, Charles E., ed. Atherosclerosis Drug Discovery. LC 76-5395. (Advances in Experimental Medicine & Biology: Vol. 67). 468p. 1976. 42.50 (ISBN 0-306-39067-1, Plenum Pr). Plenum Pub.

Day, Christopher. Drama for Middle & Upper Schools. 1975. 19.95 o.p. (ISBN 0-7134-2969-0, Pub. by Batsford England); pap. 13.50 (ISBN 0-7134-2980-1). David & Charles.

--Pattern Design. 1979. 24.00 (ISBN 0-7134-3299-3, Pub. by Batsford England). David & Charles.

Day, Clarence B. Philosophers of China. LC 61-12618. 1962. pap. 6.00 (ISBN 0-8022-0366-3). Philos Lib.

Day, D. D., jt. auth. see Hull, T. E.

Day, Dan. But I'm So Afraid. (Uplook Ser.). 1975. pap. 0.75 (ISBN 0-8163-0171-9, 02655-9). Pacific Pr Pub Assn.

--Ever Been Irritated? (Uplook Ser.). 31p. 1972. pap. 0.75 (ISBN 0-8163-0070-4, 05630-9). Pacific Pr Pub Assn.

--Hurting. (Uplook Ser.). 1978. pap. 0.75 (ISBN 0-8163-0088-7, 08889-8). Pacific Pr Pub Assn.

--I've Got This Problem with Sex... (Uplook Ser.). 32p. (YA) 1973. pap. 0.75 (ISBN 0-8163-0012-7, 09790-7). Pacific Pr Pub Assn.

Day, David, jt. auth. see Jackson, Albert.

Day, David A. Construction Equipment Guide. LC 72-10163. (Practical Construction Guides Ser.). 563p. 1973. 47.50 (ISBN 0-471-19985-0, Pub. by Wiley-Interscience). Wiley.

Day, Dawn. The Adoption of Black Children. LC 77-18585. (Illus.). 1979. 17.95 (ISBN 0-669-02107-5). Lexington Bks.

Day, Dick, ed. see Kart Magazine.

Day, Donald, ed. see Houston, Samuel.

Day, Edward. The Catholic Church Story. rev ed. LC 75-27612. (Illus.). 192p. (Orig.). 1975. pap. 3.50 (ISBN 0-89243-105-9, 65300). Liguori Pubns.

Day, Frank. If You Can Walk, You Can Ski. 1966. pap. 1.50 o.s.i. (ISBN 0-02-028320-2, Collier). Macmillan.

Day, Frank P. Rockbound: A Novel. LC 73-81763. (Literature of Canada Ser.). 1973. pap. 6.95 (ISBN 0-8020-6200-8). U of Toronto Pr.

Day, Fraser, jt. auth. see Carriere, Dean.

Day, G. S. Buyer Attitudes and Brand Choice Behavior. LC 74-81374. 1970. 12.95 (ISBN 0-02-907210-7). Free Pr.

Day, George S., jt. auth. see Aaker, David A.

Day, George S., jt. ed. see Aaker, David A.

Day, Glenn R., jt. auth. see Likes, Robert C.

Day, Ingeborg. Ghost Waltz: A Memoir. LC 80-16411. 240p. 1980. 11.95 (ISBN 0-670-29485-3). Viking Pr.

Day, Ivan. Perfumery with Herbs. 1980. 30.00x (ISBN 0-232-51414-3, Pub. by. Darton-Longman-Todd England). State Mutual Bk.

Day, J. H., jt. auth. see Drohan, N. T.

Day, J. S. Subcontracting Policy in the Airframe Industry. 1970. 28.00 (ISBN 0-08-018745-5). Pergamon.

Day, James. Literary Background of Bach's Cantatas. (Student's Music Library-Historical & Critical Studies Ser). (Illus.). 1961. 10.95 (ISBN 0-234-77522-X). Dufour.

Day, James, jt. auth. see Le Huray, Peter.

Day, James M. Captain Clint: Peoples Texas Ranger. 1980. 17.50 (ISBN 0-87244-055-9). Texian.

Day, Janis K. A Working Approach to Human Relations in Organizations. LC 79-24589. 1980. pap. text ed. 15.95 (ISBN 0-8185-0347-5). Brooks-Cole.

Day, Jenifer W. What Is a Bird? (Child's Golden Science Bks). (Illus.). 32p. (gr. k-4). 1975. PLB 6.92 (ISBN 0-307-61805-6, Golden Pr). Western Pub.

--What Is a Flower? (Child's Golden Science Bks). (Illus.). 32p. (gr. k-4). 1975. PLB 6.92 (ISBN 0-307-61800-5, Golden Pr). Western Pub.

--What Is a Fruit? (Child's Golden Science Bks.). (Illus.). (gr. k-4). 1976. PLB 6.92 (ISBN 0-307-61801-3, Golden Pr). Western Pub.

--What Is a Mammal? (Child's Golden Science Bks). (Illus.). 32p. (gr. k-4). 1975. PLB 6.92 (ISBN 0-307-61802-1, Golden Pr). Western Pub.

--What Is a Tree? (Child's Golden Science Bks). (Illus.). 32p. (gr. k-4). 1975. PLB 6.92 (ISBN 0-307-61804-8, Golden Pr). Western Pub.

--What Is an Insect? (Child's Golden Science Bks.). (Illus.). (gr. k-4). 1976. PLB 6.92 (ISBN 0-307-61803-X, Golden Pr). Western Pub.

Day, John. The Bosch Book of the Motor Car: Its Evolution & Engineering Development. LC 75-39516. (Illus.). 256p. 1976. 15.00 o.p. (ISBN 0-312-09310-1). St Martin.

--The Parliament of Bees. Orgel, Stephen & Cocke, William T., III, eds. LC 78-66742. (Renaissance Drama Ser.). 1979. lib. bdg. 16.50 (ISBN 0-8240-9748-3). Garland Pub.

Day, John A., jt. auth. see Schaefer, Vincent J.

Day, John W., Jr., jt. ed. see Hall, Charles A.

Day, Joycelyn. Glitter Girl. (Second Chance at Love, Contemporary Ser.: No. 5). 192p. (Orig.). 1981. pap. 1.75 (ISBN 0-515-05878-5). Jove Pubns.

Day, Kenneth. William Caxton & Charles Knight. (Illus.). 240p. pap. 9.50 (ISBN 0-913720-06-2). Sandstone.

Day, Kenneth F. Eden Phillpots on Dartmoor. (Illus.). 248p. 1981. 19.95 (ISBN 0-7153-8118-0). David & Charles.

Day, Kent C., jt. ed. see Moseley, Micheal E.

Day, L. Automation in the Office. 1981. text ed. price not set (ISBN 0-86103-044-3, Westbury Hse). Butterworth.

Day, Lewis F. Alphabets Old & New for the Use of Craftsmen. 3rd ed. LC 68-23148. 1968. Repr. of 1910 ed. 15.00 (ISBN 0-8103-3301-5). Gale.

--The Anatomy of Pattern. Stansky, Peter & Shewan, Rodney, eds. LC 76-17764. (Aesthetic Movement & the Arts & Crafts Movement Ser.). (Illus.). 1977. Repr. of 1887 ed. lib. bdg. 44.00 (ISBN 0-8240-2469-9). Garland Pub.

--The Application of Ornament. Stansky, Peter & Shewan, Rodney, eds. LC 76-17767. (Aesthetic Movement & the Arts & Crafts Movement Ser.). 1977. Repr. of 1888 ed. lib. bdg. 44.00x (ISBN 0-8240-2471-0). Garland Pub.

--Everyday Art. LC 76-17763. (Aesthetic Movement Ser.: Vol. 19). 1977. Repr. of 1882 ed. lib. bdg. 44.00 (ISBN 0-8240-2468-0). Garland Pub.

--Instances of Accessory Art. Stansky, Peter & Shewan, Rodney, eds. LC 76-17762. (Aesthetic Movement & the Arts & Crafts Movement Ser.: Vol. 18). 1978. Repr. of 1880 ed. lib. bdg. 44.00 (ISBN 0-8240-2467-2). Garland Pub.

--Nature & Ornament: Nature the Raw Material of Design. LC 74-137355. (Illus.). 1971. Repr. of 1930 ed. 18.00 (ISBN 0-8103-3328-7). Gale.

--Nature in Ornament. LC 70-159852. (Illus.). 1971. Repr. of 1898 ed. 18.00 (ISBN 0-8103-3207-8). Gale.

--Nature in Ornament. LC 76-17768. (Aesthetic Movement Ser.: Vol. 23). (Illus.). 1977. Repr. of 1892 ed. lib. bdg. 44.00 (ISBN 0-8240-2472-9). Garland Pub.

--Ornament & Its Application. LC 71-136735. (Illus.). 1971. Repr. of 1904 ed. 18.00 (ISBN 0-8103-3324-4). Gale.

--The Planning of Ornament. Stansky, Peter & Shewan, Rodney, eds. LC 76-17766. (Aesthetic Movement & the Arts & Crafts Movement Ser.). 1977. Repr. of 1887 ed. lib. bdg. 44.00x (ISBN 0-8240-2470-2). Garland Pub.

Day, Lewis F. & Buckle, Mary. Art in Needlework. Stansky, Peter & Shewan, Rodney, eds. LC 76-17769. (Aesthetic Movement & the Arts & Crafts Movement Ser.). 1977. Repr. of 1900 ed. lib. bdg. 44.00x (ISBN 0-8240-2473-7). Garland Pub.

--Art in Needlework: A Book About Embroidery. LC 74-159927. Repr. of 1900 ed. 18.00 (ISBN 0-8103-3062-8). Gale.

Day, M., tr. see Francis De Sales, Saint.

Day, Martin S. History of English Literature Sixteen Sixty-Eighteen Thirty-Seven. LC 63-18042. 1963. pap. 3.95 (ISBN 0-385-01372-8, U12, CCG). Doubleday.

--History of English Literature to Sixteen Sixty. LC 63-7694. 1963. pap. 4.95 o.p. (ISBN 0-385-01371-X, U10, CCG). Doubleday.

Day, Mary C. & Parker, Ronald K. The Preschool in Action: Exploring Early Childhood Programs. 2nd ed. 1977. text ed. 19.95 o.p. (ISBN 0-205-05513-3). Allyn.

Day, Millard F. Basic Bible Doctrine. 1953. pap. 1.50 (ISBN 0-8024-0239-9). Moody.

Day, Peter R. Communication in Social Work. LC 72-8466. 128p. 1973. text ed. 18.75 (ISBN 0-08-017064-1); pap. text ed. 9.25 (ISBN 0-08-017065-X). Pergamon.

--Genetics of Host-Parasite Interaction. LC 73-17054. (Illus.). 1974. text ed. 23.95x (ISBN 0-7167-0844-2). W H Freeman.

--Methods of Learning Communication Skills. 324p. 1977. text ed. 35.00 (ISBN 0-08-018954-7); pap. text ed. 19.50 (ISBN 0-08-018953-9). Pergamon.

Day, R. A., Jr. & Johnson, Ronald C. General Chemistry. (Illus.). 592p. 1974. text ed. 20.95 (ISBN 0-13-349340-7). P-H.

Day, R. A., Jr. & Underwood, Arthur L. Quantitative Analysis. 4th ed. (Illus.). 1980. text ed. 23.95 (ISBN 0-13-746545-9); pap. 3.95 solutions manual (ISBN 0-13-746560-2); lab manual 9.95 (ISBN 0-13-746552-1). P-H.

Day, R. H. & Singh, I. Economic Development As an Adaptive Process. LC 76-9173. (Illus.). 1977. 44.50 (ISBN 0-521-21114-X). Cambridge U Pr.

Day, Ralph L., tr. see Ness, Thomas E.

Day, Richard. Automotive Engine Tuning. 1981. pap. text ed. 14.95 (ISBN 0-8359-0270-6). Reston.

--Automotive Mechanics. (Illus.). 1980. text ed. 15.95 (ISBN 0-8359-0272-2). Reston.

--Easy Things to Make with Concrete & Masonry. LC 72-85574. (Illus.). 112p. 1972. lib. bdg. 4.95 o.p. (ISBN 0-668-02698-7); pap. 2.50 o.p. (ISBN 0-668-04130-7). Arco.

--How to Build Patios & Decks. LC 75-31065. (Popular Science Skill Bk.). 192p. 1976. 6.95 o.p. (ISBN 0-06-011028-7, HarpT); pap. 3.95 o.p. (ISBN 0-06-011056-2, TD-282, HarpT). Har-Row.

--How to Remodel Your Attic or Basement. LC 69-19821. 1977. 4.95 o.p. (ISBN 0-668-01876-3); pap. 2.50 o.p. (ISBN 0-668-04068-8). Arco.

--How to Service & Repair Your Own Car. rev. ed. LC 72-97173. (Popular Science Ser.). (Illus.). 1980. 14.95 (ISBN 0-06-010985-8, HarpT). Har-Row.

--Remodelling Rooms. LC 68-54468. (Illus.). 1977. 4.95 (ISBN 0-668-01814-3); pap. 2.50 o. p. (ISBN 0-668-04073-4). Arco.

Day, Richard B. Crisis & the "Crash". Soviet Studies of the West(1917-1939) 320p. 1981. 22.50 (Pub. by NLB England). Schocken.

Day, Robert. How to Write & Publish a Scientific Paper. 1979. pap. 8.95 (ISBN 0-89495-006-1); 15.00 (ISBN 0-89495-008-8). ISI Pr.

--The Last Cattle Drive. 1977. pap. 1.95 (ISBN 0-380-01832-2, 36228). Avon.

Day, Rosemary, jt. auth. see Riley, Terry.

Day, Satis B. & Day, Stacey B. A Hindu Interpretation of the Hand & Its Portents As Practiced by the Palmists of India. LC 73-85296. 5.50 (ISBN 0-912922-25-7); pap. 2.50 (ISBN 0-912922-25-7). U of Minn Bell.

Day, Stacey. Tuluak & Amaulik. LC 73-93517. (Illus.). 176p. 1973. 6.50 (ISBN 0-912922-07-9); pap. 3.75 (ISBN 0-912922-07-9). U of Minn Bell Mus.

Day, Stacey B. Health Communications. LC 79-87888. (Foundation Publication Ser.). (Illus.). 356p. (Orig.). 1979. pap. 26.50 (ISBN 0-934314-00-4). Intl Found Biosocial Dev.

Day, Stacey B., jt. auth. see Day, Satis B.

Day, Stacey B., et al. Biopsychosocial Health. 225p. 1980. pap. 10.50 (ISBN 0-934314-02-0). Intl Found Biosocial Dev.

--Readings in Oncology. LC 80-80708. (Foundation Publication Ser.). (Illus.). 227p. (Orig.). pap. 12.00 (ISBN 0-934314-01-2). Intl Found Biosocial Dev.

Day, Stacey B., et al, eds. Cancer Invasion & Metastasis: Biologic Mechanisms & Therapy. LC 77-83695. (Progress in Cancer Research & Therapy Ser: Vol. 5). 1977. 43.50 (ISBN 0-89004-184-9). Raven.

Day, Thomas. The History of Little Jack. Bd. with Original Stories from Real Life. Wollstonecraft, Mary. LC 75-32149. (Classics of Children's Literature, 1621-1932: Vol. 15). 1976. Repr. of 1788 ed. PLB 38.00 (ISBN 0-8240-2263-7). Garland Pub.

--The History of Sandford & Merton, 3 vols. in 1. LC 75-32143. (Classics of Children's Literature, 1621-1932: Vol. 11). 1977. Repr. of 1789 ed. PLB 38.00 ea. (ISBN 0-8240-2260-2). Garland Pub.

Day, William D. Introduction to Vector Analysis for Radio & Electronic Engineers. 14.00x (ISBN 0-685-20598-3). Transatlantic.

--Tables of La Place Transforms. 2.50 (ISBN 0-685-20639-4). Transatlantic.

Dayal, Vijay S. Clinical Otolaryngology. (Illus.). 304p. 1981. pap. text ed. write for info (ISBN 0-397-50499-3). Lippincott.

Dayan, Ruth & Dudman, Helga. And Perhaps: The Story of Ruth Dayan. LC 72-79920. 1973. 6.95 o.p. (ISBN 0-15-106845-3). HarBraceJ.

Dayan, Ruth & Feinberg, Willie. Crafts of Israel. LC 73-10787. (Illus.). 160p. 1974. 19.95 o.s.i. (ISBN 0-02-534420-X). Macmillan.

Dayananda, James Y. Manohar Malgonkar. (World Authors Ser.: India: No. 340). 1975. lib. bdg. 12.50 (ISBN 0-8057-2566-0). Twayne.

Dayer, Roberta A. Bankers & Diplomats in China Nineteen Seventeen to Nineteen Twenty-Five: The Anglo-American Relationship. 324p. 1980. 25.00x (ISBN 0-7146-3118-3, F Cass Co). Biblio Dist.

Daykin, Leonard, ed. Loss Prevention: A Management Guide to Improving Retail Security. 1981. 19.50 (ISBN 0-911790-51-9). Prog Grocer.

Daynes, Byron W. & Tatalovich, Raymond. Contemporary Readings in American Government. (Orig.). 1980. pap. text ed. 7.95 (ISBN 0-669-01163-0). Heath.

Dayrell, Elphinstone. Why the Sun & the Moon Live in the Sky. (Illus.). (gr. k-3). 1977. 3.75 (ISBN 0-395-25381-0, Sandpiper); pap. 1.95 (ISBN 0-686-68009-X). HM.

Dayringer, Richard, ed. Pastor & Patient. LC 80-70247. 240p. 1981. 20.00 (ISBN 0-87668-437-1). Aronson.

Days, G. D. Threshold of the McCarthy Era & the McCarthy Era-Beginning of the End: Print Media Guide to the Audio Cassettes. Haldeman, Marian, ed. (Illus.). 56p. 1980. three ring binder 7.00x (ISBN 0-918628-52-0, 52-0). Congeros Pubns.

Days, G. D., ed. McCarthy Era-Beginning of the End: Audio Cassette. LC 80-740530. cassette 9.00 (ISBN 0-918628-08-3). Congeros Pubns.

--Theshold of the McCarthy Era: The Audio Cassette. LC 80-740529. cassette 11.00 (ISBN 0-918628-07-5). Congeros Pubns.

--Threshold of the McCarthy Era & the McCarthy Era - Beginning of the End. 60p. 1980. pap. 19.95 includes cassettes (ISBN 0-918628-54-7, 54/7). Congeros Pubns.

Dayton, D. H., jt. ed. see Bellanti, J. A.

Dayton, Delbert H., jt. ed. see Cooper, Max D.

Dayton, Delbert H., jt. ed. see Ogra, P. L.

Dayton, Edward R. God's Purpose & Man's Plans. 1976. pap. 3.75 (ISBN 0-912552-11-5). MARC.

Dayton, Edward R., jt. auth. see Wagner, C. Peter.

Dayton, Edward R., ed. Mission Handbook: North American Protestant Ministries Overseas. 1977. 15.00 (ISBN 0-912552-06-9). MARC.

--That Everyone May Hear. 1979. pap. 3.75 (ISBN 0-912552-29-8). MARC.

Dayton, Laura. I'd Rather Be Me. LC 78-72137. (Illus.). (gr. k-3). Date not set. price not set (ISBN 0-89799-115-X); pap. price not set (ISBN 0-89799-062-5). Dandelion Pr. Postponed.

--Mommies & Daddies Work. LC 78-73532. (Illus.). (ps-2). Date not set. price not set (ISBN 0-89799-158-3); pap. price not set (ISBN 0-89799-076-5). Dandelion Pr. Postponed.

Dayton, Laura, retold by. More Aesop's Fables. LC 78-73537. (Illus.). (gr. 2-5). Date not set. price not set (ISBN 0-89799-149-4); pap. price not set (ISBN 0-89799-067-6). Dandelion Pr. Postponed.

Dayton, O. W. Athletic Training & Conditioning. rev. ed. (Illus.). 1965. 16.50 (ISBN 0-8260-2555-2). Wiley.

Dazai, Osamu. No Longer Human. Keene, Donald, tr. from Jap. & intro. by. LC 58-9509. 192p. 1973. pap. 4.95 (ISBN 0-8112-0481-2, NDP357). New Directions.

Dazeley, G. H. Organic Chemistry. LC 69-10061. 1969. text ed. 15.95x (ISBN 0-521-07171-2). Cambridge U Pr.

D'Azevedo, Warren L., ed. Traditional Artist in African Societies. LC 79-160126. (Illus.). 480p. 1973. pap. 5.95x (ISBN 0-253-39902-5). Ind U Pr.

D'Azzo, John & Houpis, Constantine. Linear Control System Analysis & Design. 2nd ed. (Electrical Engineering Ser.). (Illus.). 864p. 1981. text ed. write for info (ISBN 0-07-016183-6, C); write for info solutions manual (ISBN 0-07-016184-4). McGraw.

De, Ira. The Hunt & Other Poems. 8.00 (ISBN 0-89253-467-2); flexible cloth 4.00 (ISBN 0-89253-468-0). Ind-US Inc.

De, Monique P. Ladebat see De Ladebat, Monique P.

Dea, Kay, ed. Perspectives for the Future: Social Work Practice in the 80's. LC 80-83988. (Professional Conference Vols. Ser.). 192p. (Orig.). 1980. pap. text ed. 12.50x (ISBN 0-87101-089-5, CBO-089-C). Natl Assn Soc Wkrs.

Deacon, Alan. In Search of the Scrounger. 110p. 1976. pap. text ed. 7.50x (ISBN 0-7135-1992-4, Pub. by Bedford England). Renouf.

Deacon, Eileen. Making Jewelry. LC 77-7942. (Beginning Crafts Ser.). (Illus.). (gr. k-3). 1977. PLB 9.30 (ISBN 0-8393-0116-2). Raintree Child.

Deacon, Margaret B., ed. Oceanography: Concepts & History. (Benchmark Papers in Geology: Vol. 35). 1978. 32.00 (ISBN 0-12-786340-0). Acad Pr.

Deacon, Richard. The Chinese Secret Service. (Illus.). 544p. 1976. pap. 2.25 o.p. (ISBN 0-345-24901-1). Ballantine.

--A History of the British Secret Service: Covers the Development of the Intelligence System from the Days of Henry VII to the Present. 6.50 (ISBN 0-686-28849-1). Academy Chi Ltd.

--Napoleon's Book of Fate. Orig. Title: The Book of Fate: Its Origins & Uses. 1977. 10.00 (ISBN 0-8065-0564-8); pap. 4.95 (ISBN 0-8065-0577-X). Citadel Pr.

--Richard Deacon's Microwave Cookery. LC 73-93782. (Illus.). 160p. 1977. 7.95 o.p. (ISBN 0-912656-74-3); pap. 5.95 (ISBN 0-912656-73-5). H P Bks.

Deacon, Ruth E. & Firebaugh, Francille M. Family Resource Management: Principles & Applications. 280p. 1980. text ed. 16.95 (ISBN 0-205-06994-0, 4569946); tchr's. manual free (ISBN 0-205-07000-0). Allyn.

Deady, Matthew P. Pharisee Among Philistines: The Diary of Judge Matthew P. Deady, 1871-1892, 2 vols. Clark, Malcolm, Jr., intro. by. LC 74-75363. (Illus.). 712p. 1975. 27.95 (ISBN 0-87595-046-9); deluxe ed. 30.00 (ISBN 0-87595-080-9); pap. 21.95 (ISBN 0-87595-080-9). Oreg Hist Soc.

Deagon, Ann. Indian Summer. LC 74-31937. (Illus.). 32p. 1975. 15.00 (ISBN 0-87775-078-5); pap. write for info. (ISBN 0-87775-107-2). Unicorn Pr.

Deak, Francis. American International Law Cases: 1971-1978, Vols. 1-20. 45.00 ea. Oceana.

Deak, Istvan. Everyman in Europe: Essays in Social History, Vol. 1. 224p. 1981. pap. text ed. 9.95 (ISBN 0-13-293621-6). P-H.

--The Lawful Revolution. LC 78-22063. Orig. Title: Reluctant Rebels. (Illus.). 1979. 20.00 (ISBN 0-231-04602-2). Columbia U Pr.

--Weimar Germany's Left-Wing Intellectuals: A Political History of the Weltbuhne & Its Circle. (Illus.). 1968. 23.75x (ISBN 0-520-00309-8). U of Cal Pr.

De'ak, Stephen. David Popper: Violoncello Virtuoso & Composer. (Illus.). 320p. 1980. 14.95 (ISBN 0-87666-621-7, Z-32). Paganiniana Pubns.

Deakin, Edward B., jt. auth. see Neuner, John J.

Deakin, Mary H. The Early Life of George Eliot. 188p. 1980. Repr. of 1913 ed. lib. bdg. 30.00 (ISBN 0-8495-1121-6). Arden Lib.

Deal, Babs H. Goodnight Ladies. LC 77-76229. 1978. 7.95 o.p. (ISBN 0-385-00831-7). Doubleday.

Deal, Borden. Adventure. LC 77-74297. 1978. 8.95 o.p. (ISBN 0-385-05227-8). Doubleday.

Deal, Terrence & Nolan, Robert, eds. Alternative Schools: Ideologies, Realities, Guidelines. LC 78-18505. (Illus.). 1978. 18.95x (ISBN 0-88229-383-4); pap. 10.95x (ISBN 0-88229-613-2). Nelson-Hall.

Deal, William S. John Bunyan: Tinker of Bedford. LC 77-81556. pap. 3.95 (ISBN 0-89107-153-9). Good News.

--Picking a Partner. (Orig.). 1972. pap. 2.25 (ISBN 0-87123-456-4, 200456). Bethany Fell.

De Alcantara, Shimon. The Dog & Cat Owner's & Consumer Handbook. Fox, Lay C., ed. (Pet Owners Ser.). (Orig.). 1980. pap. write for info. North Am Consumer.

De Alencar, Jose M. Iracema, the Honey-Lips: A Legend of Brazil. LC 75-44263. 1977. Repr. of 1886 ed. 12.50 (ISBN 0-86527-263-8). Fertig.

Dealey, J. Q. Growth of American State Constitutions. LC 75-124891. (American Constitutional & Legal History Ser). 308p. 1972. Repr. of 1915 ed. lib. bdg. 32.50 (ISBN 0-306-71985-1). Da Capo.

De Almeida, Hermione. Byron & Joyce Through Homer: Don Juan & Ulysses. 256p. 1981. 20.00x (ISBN 0-231-05092-5). Columbia U Pr.

De Alvarez, Russell R., ed. The Kidney in Pregnancy. LC 76-13184. (Clinical Obstetrics & Gynecology Ser.). 1976. 33.95 (ISBN 0-471-20030-1, Pub. by Wiley Medical). Wiley.

Deamer, D. W., jt. auth. see Branton, D.

Dean, A. C., et al, eds. Continuous Culture: Applications & New Fields. 1976. 42.95x (ISBN 0-470-98984-X). Halsted Pr.

Dean, Andrew. Wages & Earnings. (Reviews of United Kingdom Statistical Sources Ser.: Vol. XIII). 1980. 45.00 (ISBN 0-08-024060-7). Pergamon.

Dean, Bashford. A Bibliography of Fishes, 3 vols. 1973. 169.50 (ISBN 3-87429-036-0). Lubrecht & Cramer.

Dean, Bessie. Let's Learn About Jesus: A Child's Coloring Book of the Life of Christ. (Children's Inspirational Coloring Bk.). (Illus.). (ps-6). 1979. pap. 3.95 (ISBN 0-88290-131-1). Horizon Utah.

--Paul, God's Special Missionary. (Story Books to Color.). 72p. (Orig.). (gr. k-5). 1980. pap. 3.95 (ISBN 0-88290-152-4). Horizon Utah.

--Paul's Letters. (Story Books to Color). (Illus.). 72p. (Orig.). (gr. k-5). 1980. pap. 3.95 (ISBN 0-88290-170-2). Horizon Utah.

Dean, D. H., et al, eds. Gene Structure & Expression. (Ohio State University Biosciences Colloquia: No. 6). (Illus.). 369p. 1980. 22.50 (ISBN 0-8142-0321-3). Ohio St U Pr.

Dean, Frank. Cowboy Fun. LC 79-91384. (Illus.). 160p. 1980. 9.95 (ISBN 0-8069-4608-3); PLB 9.29 (ISBN 0-8069-4609-1). Sterling.

Dean, G. D., jt. auth. see Read, B. E.

Dean, J. & Choppin, B. Educational Provision 16-19. (General Ser.). (Orig.). 1977. pap. text ed. 7.75x (ISBN 0-85633-129-5, NFER). Humanities.

Dean, Joan F. Tom Stoppard: Comedy As Moral Matrix. LC 80-26400. 128p. 1981. text ed. 9.00x (ISBN 0-8262-0332-9). U of Mo Pr.

Dean, Joel. Capital Budgeting. LC 51-11344. (Illus.). 1951. 20.00x (ISBN 0-231-01847-9). Columbia U Pr.

--Managerial Economics. 1951. ref. ed. 19.95 (ISBN 0-13-549972-0). P-H.

Dean, John. Restless Wanderers: Shakespeare & the Pattern of Romance. (Orig.). 1979. text ed. 25.00x (ISBN 0-391-01708-X). Humanities.

Dean, John, jt. auth. see Henke, James T.

Dean, Judy, jt. auth. see Vincent, Denis.

Dean, Judy, et al. The Sixth Form & Its Alternatives. (Orig.). 1979. pap. text ed. 27.50x (ISBN 0-85633-182-1, NFER). Humanities.

Dean, K. J., et al. Physics & Chemistry of Baking. (Illus.). vii, 225p. 1980. pap. 22.50x (ISBN 0-85334-867-7). Intl Ideas.

Dean, Karen S. Maggie Adams, Dancer. 1980. pap. 1.75 (ISBN 0-380-75366-9, 75366, Camelot). Avon.

Dean, Leonard F., ed. Twentieth Century Interpretations of Julius Caesar. LC 69-11355. 1968. 8.95 (ISBN 0-13-512285-6, Spec). P-H.

Dean, Leslie. How to Collect Old & Rare Books & Make a Fortune Out of Them. (Illus.). 1979. 8.95 (ISBN 0-89266-188-7); plastic spiral bdg. 18.95 (ISBN 0-685-92187-5). Am Classical Coll Pr.

Dean, M. R. Basic Anatomy & Physiology for Radiographers. 2nd ed. (Illus.). 1976. 21.00 (ISBN 0-632-00287-5, Blackwell). Mosby.

Dean, Malcolm. The Astrology Game. 256p. 1981. 11.95 (ISBN 0-8253-0002-9). Beaufort Bks NY.

Dean, Margaret C. The Stress Survival Foodbook. 1981. pap. 5.95 (ISBN 0-87491-295-4). Acropolis.

Dean, Martha H., jt. auth. see Stewart, Emily.

Dean, Norman L. Energy Efficiency in Industry. 1980. 30.00 (ISBN 0-88410-056-1). Ballinger Pub.

Dean, Patricia G. Self-Assessment of Current Knowledge in Gynecologic Nursing & Women's Health Care. LC 79-92917. 1980. pap. 9.50 (ISBN 0-87488-268-0). Med Exam.

Dean, Paul J., jt. auth. see Bergh, Arpad A.

Dean, Peter. Teaching & Learning Mathematics. (The Woburn Educational Ser.). 1981. 18.50x (ISBN 0-7130-0168-2, Pub by Woburn Pr England). Biblio Dist.

Dean, R. D., et al. Spatial Economic Theory. LC 79-90899. 1970. pap. text ed. 10.95 (ISBN 0-02-907110-0). Free Pr.

Dean, Roy. The Dean's List. (Illus.). 1980. write for info. Rho-Delta Pr.

Dean, Sandra L. Success As a Consultant: The Complete Guide. 225p. 1981. 14.95 (ISBN 0-913864-61-7). Enterprise Del.

Dean, Stanley R. Psychiatry & Mysticism. LC 75-8771. (Illus.). 446p. 1975. 21.95 (ISBN 0-88229-189-0); pap. 12.95 (ISBN 0-88229-657-4). Nelson-Hall.

Dean, Thomas Scott & Hedden, Jay W. How to Solarize Your House. (Illus.). 192p. 1980. 20.00 (ISBN 0-684-16295-4, ScribT). Scribner.

Dean, W., ed. see Dent, E. J.

Dean, Warren, pref. by see Fernandes, Florestan.

Dean, Winton. Handel & the Opera Seria. (Ernest Bloch Lectures). 1969. 23.75x (ISBN 0-520-01438-3). U of Cal Pr.

DeAndrea, William L. The Hog Murders. 1979. pap. 1.95 (ISBN 0-380-47548-0, 47548). Avon.

Deane, Elisabeth, compiled by. A Gift of Tenderness. 1979. 2.95 (ISBN 0-442-82589-7). Peter Pauper.

Deane, Forbes, et al. Fidelio: Beethoven. Hammond, Tom & Blumer, Rodney, trs. 1981. pap. 4.95 (ISBN 0-7145-3823-X). Riverrun NY.

Deane, Herbert A. Political & Social Ideas of St. Augustine. LC 63-9809. 1963. pap. 7.00x (ISBN 0-231-08569-9). Columbia U Pr.

Deane, Leslie. The Girl with the Golden Hair. (Orig.). 1978. pap. 2.25 (ISBN 0-515-04807-0). Jove Pubns.

--Star Power. 1980. pap. 2.75 (ISBN 0-515-05282-5, Jove). BJ Pub Group.

--Star Power. (Orig.). pap. 2.75 (ISBN 0-515-05282-5). Jove Pubns.

Deane, P., jt. auth. see Mitchell, Brian R.

Deane, Phyllis & Cole, W. A. British Economic Growth, Sixteen Eighty-Eight - Nineteen Fifty-Nine: Trends & Structure. 2nd ed. LC 67-21956. (Cambridge Department of Applied Economics Monographs). (Illus.). 1969. 47.50 (ISBN 0-521-04801-X); pap. 14.95x (ISBN 0-521-09569-7). Cambridge U Pr.

Deane, Seamus. Rumours. 1977. pap. text ed. 6.25x (ISBN 0-85105-320-3, Dolmen Pr). Humanities.

Deane-Drummond, Anthony. Riot Control. LC 75-7555. 158p. 1975. 14.00x (ISBN 0-8448-0711-7). Crane-Russak Co.

De Angeli, Marguerite. Book of Nursery & Mother Goose Rhymes. (Illus.). (gr. k-3). 1954. 9.95a (ISBN 0-385-07232-5); PLB (ISBN 0-385-06246-X). Doubleday.

--Bright April. (gr. 2-5). 1946. 5.95 o.p. (ISBN 0-385-07238-4). Doubleday.

--Butter at the Old Price. LC 77-116199. 1971. 9.95 (ISBN 0-385-06813-1). Doubleday.

--The Door in the Wall: Story of Medieval London. LC 64-7025. (gr. 3-6). 7.95a (ISBN 0-385-07283-X); PLB (ISBN 0-385-05743-1); pap. 1.95 (ISBN 0-385-07909-5). Doubleday.

--Friendship & Other Poems. LC 79-6857. (Illus.). 48p. 1981. 5.95a (ISBN 0-385-15854-8); PLB (ISBN 0-385-15855-6). Doubleday.

--The Lion in the Box. LC 74-33676. 80p. (gr. 3-7). 1975. 5.95 (ISBN 0-385-03317-6). Doubleday.

--Marguerite De Angeli's Book of Nursery & Mother Goose Rhymes. (Illus.). (gr. 1-3). 1979. pap. 4.95 (ISBN 0-385-15291-4, Zephyr). Doubleday.

--Petite Suzanne. (gr. 1-5). 3.50 o.p. (ISBN 0-385-07447-6). Doubleday.

DeAngelis, Anthony M. Surgical Anatomy of Peripheral Nerves. LC 72-96490. (Illus.). 152p. 1973. 16.50 (ISBN 0-87993-019-5). Futura Pub.

Deanin, Rudolph D. Polymer Structure, Properties & Applications. LC 70-156478. 1972. 29.95 o.p. (ISBN 0-8436-1202-9). CBI Pub.

Deans, Alexander S. The Bee Keepers Encyclopedia. LC 75-23248. (Illus.). 1979. Repr. of 1949 ed. 18.00 (ISBN 0-8103-4176-X). Gale.

Dear, Ian. The America's Cup: An Informal History. LC 80-65596. (Illus.). 192p. 1980. 19.95 (ISBN 0-396-07848-6). Dodd.

De Aragon, Maximo. The Pearl. LC 80-83435. (Illus.). 50p. (Orig.). (gr. 7-12). 1981. pap. 2.95 (ISBN 0-932906-08-7). Pan-Am Publishing Co.

De Araujo, Virginia, ed. see Andrade, Carlos D.

De Araujo-Aaugse, Vera L. see Lauerhass, Ludwig & A Raujo-Haugse, Vera L. De.

Dearborn, L., jt. auth. see Dasheff, Bill.

Dearden, Ann, ed. Arab Women. (Minority Rights Reports Ser.: No. 27). 20p. 1976. pap. 2.50 (ISBN 0-89192-037-4). Interbk Inc.

Dearden, C. W. The Stage of Aristophanes. (University of London Classical Ser: No. 7). 224p. 1976. text ed. 23.75x (ISBN 0-485-13707-0, Athlone Pr). Humanities.

Dearden, John. Cost Accounting & Financial Control Systems. LC 73-184160. 1973. text ed. 18.95 (ISBN 0-201-01507-2). A-W.

--Essentials of Cost Accounting. (Orig.). 1969. pap. text ed. 10.95 (ISBN 0-201-01484-X); instructor's guide 0.50 (ISBN 0-201-01496-3). A-W.

Dearden, John, jt. auth. see Anthony, Robert N.

Dearden, Paul F. The Rhode Island Campaign of 1778: Inauspicious Dawn of Alliance. LC 78-68920. (Illus.). 1980. 6.95 (ISBN 0-917012-17-8). RI Pubns Soc.

Dearden, R. F. Philosophy of Primary Education: An Introduction. LC 68-21589. (Students' Library of Education). 1968. text ed. 5.75x (ISBN 0-7100-4223-X); pap. text ed. 3.00x (ISBN 0-7100-6648-1). Humanities.

Dearden, R. F., et al. Educational & the Development of Reason, 3 pts. Incl. Pt. 1. Critique of Current Educational Aims. pap. 7.95 (ISBN 0-7100-8084-0); Pt. 2. Reason. pap. 7.95 (ISBN 0-7100-8101-4); Pt. 3. Education & Reason. pap. 6.95 (ISBN 0-7100-8102-2). 1975. Routledge & Kegan.

Dearden, R. F., et al, eds. Education & the Development of Reason. (International Library of the Philosophy of Education). 1972. 38.00x (ISBN 0-7100-7201-5). Routledge & Kegan.

Dearen, Patrick. The Illegal Man. 1981. pap. 2.25 (ISBN 0-8439-0872-6, Leisure Bks). Nordon Pubns.

Dearholt, Donald W., jt. auth. see Stark, Richard.

Dearing, Brian E., jt. auth. see Hartwig, Frederick.

Dearing, Vinton A. Principles & Practice of Textual Analysis. 1975. 22.50x (ISBN 0-520-02430-3). U of Cal Pr.

Dearing, Vinton A. see Dryden, John.

Dearling, Robert, et al. Music Facts & Feats. rev. ed. (Illus.). 288p. 1981. 19.95 (ISBN 0-8069-9250-6, Pub. by Guinness Superlatives England). Sterling.

Dearlove, John. The Reorganization of British Local Government. LC 78-18092. 1979. 39.95 (ISBN 0-521-22341-5); pap. 10.95 (ISBN 0-521-29456-8). Cambridge U Pr.

De Armand, Frances U. Very, Very Special Day. LC 63-8176. (Illus.). (gr. k-2). 1963. 5.95 o.s.i. (ISBN 0-8193-0042-X, Four Winds). Schol Bk Serv.

De Assis, Joaquim M. Machado see Machado de Assis, Joaquim M.

De Assis, Machado. Dom Casmurro. 1980. pap. 2.95 (ISBN 0-380-49668-2, 49668, Bard). Avon.

--Epitaph of a Small Winner. 1977. pap. 2.25 (ISBN 0-380-01712-1, 33878, Bard). Avon.

Deasy, C. M. Design for Human Affairs. LC 74-5198. 250p. 1974. text ed. 10.95 o.p. (ISBN 0-470-20454-0). Halsted Pr.

Death Education Directory Staff, jt. auth. see Elin, Caren.

Deaton, Angus. Essays in the Theory & Measurement of Consumer Behavior. 300p. Date not set. price not set (ISBN 0-521-22565-5). Cambridge U Pr.

Deaton, David, jt. auth. see Thomas, Barry.

Deaton, John G. & Pascoe, Elizabeth J. Book of Family Medical Questions. Alper, Philip R., ed. LC 79-4804. 1979. 15.95 (ISBN 0-394-41468-3). Random.

Deaux, Kay, jt. auth. see Wrightsman, Lawrence.

De Ayala, Ramon Perez see Perez de Ayala, Ramon.

Deb, K. The Early History & Growth of Calcutta. rev. ed. 1978. 12.00x o.p. (ISBN 0-8364-0252-9). South Asia Bks.

Debaca, Carlos. Vicente Silva: The Terror of Las Vegas. (Wild & Woolly West Ser: No. 35). (Illus.). 1978. 7.00 (ISBN 0-910584-50-8); pap. 2.00 (ISBN 0-910584-93-1). Filter.

De Bacan, Alvaro. Relation of the Expongnable Attempt & Conquest of the Ylande of Tercera. LC 76-57352. (English Experience Ser.: No. 772). 1977. Repr. of 1584 ed. lib. bdg. 6.00 (ISBN 90-221-0772-8). Walter J Johnson.

DeBach, P. Biological Control by Natural Enemies. LC 73-90812. (Illus.). 325p. 1974. 39.50 (ISBN 0-521-20380-5); pap. 11.95x (ISBN 0-521-09835-1). Cambridge U Pr.

De Baeza, Luis, tr. see Nogales, Manuel C.

Debahy, M. Dictionary Hebrew Verbs. 1974. 12.00x (ISBN 0-685-77115-6). Intl Bk Ctr.

DeBakey, Lois. The Scientific Journal: Editorial Policies & Practices. LC 76-6046. 1976. text ed. 12.50 (ISBN 0-8016-1223-3). Mosby.

De Bakker, M. Mathematical Theory of Program Correctness. 1980. 28.00 (ISBN 0-13-562132-1). P-H.

De Balaguer, Josemaria E. Holy Rosary. (Illus.). 49p. 1979. pap. 8.00x (ISBN 0-906127-15-7, Pub. by Irish Academic Pr). Biblio Dist.

De Balaguer, Josemaria E. see Balaguer, Josemaria E. de.

De Balzac, Honore. Eugenie Grandet. (Literature Ser). (gr. 10-12). 1970. pap. text ed. 3.42 (ISBN 0-87720-746-1). AMSCO Sch.

--The Plays of Honore De Balzac. 1976. Repr. 35.00 (ISBN 0-86527-291-3). Fertig.

De Bartolo, Dick & Clarke, Bob. Mad-Vertising. 1979. pap. 1.50. Warner Bks.

De Bartolo, Dick & North, Henry. Mad Guide to Fraud & Deception. 192p. (Orig.). 1981. pap. 1.75 (ISBN 0-446-94154-9). Warner Bks.

DeBartolo, Dick & Torres, Angelo. A Mad Look at TV. (Mad Ser). (Illus.). 192p. (Orig.). 1974. pap. 1.75 (ISBN 0-446-94436-X). Warner Bks.

DeBartolo, Dick & Woodbridge, George. A Mad Guide to Leisure Time. (Illus.). 192p. 1976. pap. 1.75 (ISBN 0-446-94431-9). Warner Bks.

De Bary, W. Theodore, ed. The Unfolding of Neo-Confucianism. LC 74-10929. (Studies in Oriental Culture Ser.: No. 10). 672p. 1975. 25.00x (ISBN 0-231-03828-3); pap. 12.50x (ISBN 0-231-03829-1). Columbia U Pr.

De Bary, William T. & Embree, T. Guide to Oriental Classics. 2nd ed. (Companions to Asian Studies). 1974. 12.50x (ISBN 0-231-03891-7); pap. 7.50x (ISBN 0-231-03892-5). Columbia U Pr.

De Bary, William T., ed. Self & Society in Ming Thought. LC 78-101229. (Studies in Oriental Culture Ser). 1969. 27.50x (ISBN 0-231-03271-4); pap. 12.50x (ISBN 0-231-08313-0). Columbia U Pr.

--Sources of Chinese Tradition, 2 Vols. LC 60-9911. (Records of Civilization, Sources & Studies). 1960. 1 vol. ed. o.p 30.00x (ISBN 0-231-02255-7); Vol. 1. pap. 9.00x (ISBN 0-231-08602-4); Vol. 2. pap. 7.00x (ISBN 0-231-08603-2). Columbia U Pr.

De Bary, William T. & Embree, Ainslie T., eds. Approaches to Asian Civilizations. LC 63-20226. (Companions to Asian Studies). 1964. 17.50x (ISBN 0-231-02648-X). Columbia U Pr.

De Basily, Lascelle. Memoirs of a Lost World: Special Project. LC 75-29793. 308p. 1975. 8.00 (ISBN 0-8179-4151-7, Pub.by Laselle de Basily). Hoover Inst Pr.

De Baye, J. The Industrial Arts of the Anglo-Saxons. 1980. Repr. of 1893 ed. lib. bdg. 40.00 (ISBN 0-89341-380-1). Longwood Pr.

De Bear, Nicol, jt. auth. see Jones, Thora B.

De Beaumarchais, Pierre. The Barber of Seville. Luciani, Vincent, tr. from Fr. Bd. with The Marriage of Figaro. (World Classics in Tr.). (Eng.). 1965. 6.50 (ISBN 0-8120-5007-X); pap. 3.25 (ISBN 0-8120-0029-3). Barron.

De Beaumont, Gustave & De Tocqueville, Alexis. On the Penitentiary System in the United States & Its Application in France. LC 79-431. (Arcturus Bks Paperbacks). 264p. 1979. pap. 7.95 (ISBN 0-8093-0913-0). S Ill U Pr.

De Beaumont, Madame. Beauty & the Beast. LC 76-57884. (Illus.). (ps-2). 1978. 8.95 (ISBN 0-87888-119-0). Bradbury Pr.

De Beaumont, Marguerite. Horses & Ponies: Their Breeding, Feeding & Management. (Illus.). 10.50 o.p. (ISBN 0-85131-220-9, Dist. by Sporting Book Center). J A Allen.

De Beausobre, Louis. Nouvelles Considerations Sur les Annees Climateriques. (Principal French Demographic Works of the 18th Century Ser.). (Fr.). 1976. lib. bdg. 20.00x o.p. (ISBN 0-8287-0068-0); pap. text ed. 10.00x o.p. (ISBN 0-685-71511-6). Clearwater Pub.

De Beauvoir, Simone. All Said & Done. 1975. pap. 2.50 o.s.i. (ISBN 0-446-81191-2). Warner Bks.

--Coming of Age. 880p. 1973. pap. 2.95 o.s.i. (ISBN 0-446-83680-X). Warner Bks.

--Memoirs of a Dutiful Daughter. 1974. pap. 4.95 (ISBN 0-06-090351-1, CN351, CN). Har-Row.

De Becker, Eric V. Survey of Some Japanese Tax Laws. (Studies in Japanese Law & Government). 182p. 1979. Repr. of 1931 ed. 18.50 (ISBN 0-89093-218-2). U Pubns Amer.

De Becker, Joseph E. Elements of Japanese Law: Studies in Japanese Law & Government. 1979. Repr. of 1916 ed. 34.00 (ISBN 0-89093-210-7). U Pubns Amer.

--Principles & Practice of the Civil Code of Japan: A Complete Theoretical & Practical Exposition of the Motifs of the Japanese Civil Code. (Studies in Japanese Law & Government). 852p. 1979. Repr. of 1921 ed. Set. 60.00 (ISBN 0-89093-216-6). U Pubns Amer.

De Becker, Joseph E., tr. from Japanese. Annotated Civil Code of Japan, 4 vols. (Studies in Japanese Law & Government). 1200p. 1979. 95.00 (ISBN 0-89093-215-8). U Pubns Amer.

De Bedts, Ralph F. The New Deal's SEC: The Formative Years. LC 64-14236. 1964. 20.00x (ISBN 0-231-02713-3). Columbia U Pr.

--Recent American History, 2 vols. 1973. Vol. 1. pap. text ed. 11.50x (ISBN 0-686-66959-2); Vol. 2. (ISBN 0-256-01414-0); pap. text ed. (ISBN 0-256-01510-4). Dorsey.

Debee, Rajlukshmee. The Owl & Other Poems. Debee, Rajlukshmee, tr. from Bengali. (Writers Workshop Redbird Ser.). 1975. 12.00 (ISBN 0-88253-604-4); pap. text ed. 4.80 (ISBN 0-88253-603-6). Ind-US Inc.

DeBeer, E. S., ed. see Locke, John.

De Beer, Gavin, ed. see Darwin, Charles & Huxley, Thomas H.

De Bekker, Leander J., jt. auth. see Vizetelly, Frank H.

De Belenoi, Aimeric. Poesies Du Troubadour Aimeric De Belenoi. Dumitrescu, Maria, ed. LC 80-2174. 1981. Repr. of 1935 ed. 33.50 (ISBN 0-404-19000-6). AMS Pr.

DeBell, Garrett. The New Environmental Handbook. LC 79-56911. (Orig.). 1980. pap. 5.95 (ISBN 0-913890-36-7). Friends Earth.

De Bellay, Jaochim. Regrets: Choix de poemes. (Documentation thematique). (Illus., Fr.). 1975. pap. 2.95 (ISBN 0-685-64173-2). Larousse.

DeBenedetti, Charles. Peace Reform in American History. LC 79-2173. 274p. 1980. 18.50x (ISBN 0-253-13095-6). Ind U Pr.

De Benedictis, Daniel J. Complete Real Estate Adviser. 1977. pap. 4.95 (ISBN 0-346-12212-0). Cornerstone.

Debenham, Michael J. Microprocessors: An Introduction to the Principles & Applications. 1979. 21.00 (ISBN 0-08-024206-5); pap. 8.75 (ISBN 0-08-024207-3). Pergamon.

De Benitez, Ana M. Prehispanic Cookbook(Cocina Prehispanica) 1960. pap. 8.50 o.p. (ISBN 0-911268-24-3). Rogers Bk.

--Prehistoric Cooking. 8.50 o.p. (ISBN 0-685-82108-0). Rogers Bk.

De Berker, Paul, ed. Interaction. 1969. 8.95 (ISBN 0-85181-016-0, Pub. by Faber & Faber). Merrimack Bk Serv.

De Bersaques, J., ed. Symposium sur les Tumeurs Cutanees des Enfants. Gent. November 1978. (Journal: Dermatologica: Vol. 161, Suppl. 1, 1980). (Illus.). iv, 160p. 1980. pap. 11.00 (ISBN 3-8055-2238-X). S Karger.

De Bertier De Sauvigny, Guillaume. Bourbon Restoration. Case, Lynn M., tr. LC 67-20654. 1967. 12.50 o.p. (ISBN 0-8122-7552-7). U of Pa Pr.

Debets, G. F. Physical Anthropology of Afghanistan. LC 72-116739. (Russian Translation Ser.: Vol. 5, No. 1). 1970. pap. text ed. 15.00 (ISBN 0-87365-763-2). Peabody Harvard.

Debey, Harold J. Introduction to the Chemistry of Life: Biochemistry. 2nd ed. 272p. 1976. text ed. 8.95 (ISBN 0-201-01474-2). A-W.

Debey, Harold J., jt. auth. see Embree, Harland D.

De Bhaldraithe, Tomas, tr. see O'Sullivan, Humphrey.

De Bie, John. Story of the Old World. 1954. pap. 6.50 (ISBN 0-8028-1781-5). Eerdmans.

De Billon, Francois. Le Fort Inexpugnable De L'honneur Du Sexe Femenin. Repr. of 1555 ed. 43.00 (ISBN 0-384-04270-8). Johnson Repr.

De Blasis, Celeste. The Night Child. 1979. pap. 1.95 o.p. (ISBN 0-449-23927-6, Crest). Fawcett.

De Bliek, Ruth, jt. auth. see Pena, Alberto.

De Blij, H. J. Earth: A Topical Geography. 2nd ed. LC 79-18051. 1980. text ed. 21.95 (ISBN 0-471-05169-1); tchr's manual (ISBN 0-471-06358-4). Wiley.

De Blij, Harm J. Geography: Regions & Concepts. 3rd ed. LC 80-17961. 593p. 1981. text ed. 18.95 (ISBN 0-471-08015-2); tchr's ed. avail. (ISBN 0-471-08106-X); study guide avail. (ISBN 0-471-07882-4). Wiley.

--Geography: Regions & Concepts. 2nd ed. LC 77-17536. 1978. text ed. 20.95x o.p. (ISBN 0-471-20051-4); tchrs. manual avail. o.p. (ISBN 0-471-04040-1); wkbk. 6.95x o.p. (ISBN 0-471-04039-8). Wiley.

--Human Geography: Culture, Society, & Space. LC 76-25994. 1977. text ed. 20.95 (ISBN 0-471-20047-6); study guide 7.95x (ISBN 0-471-01932-1). Wiley.

Deblij, Harm J., jt. auth. see Glassner, Martin I.

Debnam, Betty. The Mini Page Kids' Cookbook. 1978. spiral bd. 5.95 (ISBN 0-8362-4202-5). Andrews & McMeel.

Debnam, Betty & Avery, Lois. The Mini Page & Your Newspaper Activity Book. 128p. (gr. k-6). 1980. pap. 5.95 (ISBN 0-8362-4209-2). Andrews & McMeel.

Debo, Angie. Geronimo: The Man, His Time, His Place. LC 76-13858. (The Civilization of the American Indian Ser: No.142). 1976. 14.95 (ISBN 0-8061-1333-2). U of Okla Pr.

--History of the Indians of the United States. LC 73-108802. (Civilization of the American Indian Ser.: Vol. 106). (Orig.). 1970. 13.50 (ISBN 0-8061-0911-4). U of Okla Pr.

--Rise & Fall of the Choctaw Republic. 2nd ed. LC 69-7973. (Civilization of the American Indian Ser.: No. 6). (Illus.). 1934. pap. 5.95 (ISBN 0-8061-1247-6). U of Okla Pr.

Debo, Harvey V. & Diamant, Leo. Construction Superintendent's Job Guide. LC 79-17979. (Ser. on Practical Construction Guides). 1980. 22.00 (ISBN 0-471-20457-9, Pub. by Wiley-Interscience). Wiley.

De Bock, G., jt. ed. see Vokaer, R.

De Bock, Harold, jt. ed. see Wilhoit, G. Cleveland.

DeBoer, J. B., jt. auth. see Van Bommel, W. J.

De Boer, Jan & Baillie, Thomas W., eds. Disasters: Medical Organization. (Illus.). 112p. 1980. 16.75 (ISBN 0-08-025491-8). Pergamon.

DeBoer, John C. Let's Plan: A Guide to the Planning Process for Voluntary Organizations. LC 72-124329. (Illus., Orig.). 1970. pap. 3.95 (ISBN 0-8298-0177-4). Pilgrim NY.

De Boer, P., jt. ed. see Searle, A. G.

De Bono, E. Lateral Thinking. pap. 4.95 (ISBN 0-06-090325-2, CN325, CN). Har-Row.

De Bono, Edward. Teaching Thinking. 1977. 18.00 (ISBN 0-85117-085-4). Transatlantic.

DeBoodt, M. & Gabriels, D. Assessment of Erosion. 400p. 1981. 67.50 (ISBN 0-471-27899-8, Pub. by Wiley-Interscience). Wiley.

De Boodt, M., ed. Assessment of Erosion. Gabriels, D. 400p. 1981. 79.00 o.p. (ISBN 0-8260-7790-0, Pub. by Wiley-Interscience). Wiley.

De Boor, W. & Kohlmann, G., eds. Obsessionsdelikte. (Schriftenreihe des Instituts Fuer Konfliktforschung: No. 6). 1980. pap. 13.25 (ISBN 3-8055-3015-3). S Karger.

De Borchgrave, Arnaud & Moss, Robert. The Spike. 1981. pap. 2.95. Avon.

De Bougainville, Louis A. see Bougainville, Louis A. De.

De Boyer Argens, Jean Baptiste see Baptiste De Boyer Argens, Jean.

De Brabander, M., et al, eds. Cell Movement & Neoplasia: Proceedings of the Annual Meeting of the Cell Tissue & Organ Culture Study Group, Held at the Janssen Research Foundation, Beerse, Belgium, May 1979. (Illus.). 174p. 1980. 35.00 (ISBN 0-08-025534-5). Pergamon.

De Bray, Reginald G. Guide to the Slavonic Languages, 2 pts. rev., enl., 3rd ed. Incl. Pt. 1. South. 399p. 24.95 (ISBN 0-89357-060-5); Pt. 2. West. 483p. 27.95 (ISBN 0-89357-061-3). 1980. Slavica.

DeBray, Reginald G. Guide to the Slavonic Languages: Part 2. 3rd rev. ed. 483p. 80. 27.95 (ISBN 0-89357-061-3). Slavica.

De Bray, Reginald G. Guide to the Slavonic Languages: Pt. 1, Guide to the South Slavonic Languages. 3rd rev. ed. 399p. 1980. 24.95 (ISBN 0-89357-060-5). Slavica.

--Guide to the Slavonic Languages: Pt. 3, Guide to the East Slavonic Languages. 3rd rev. ed. 254p. 1980. 22.95 (ISBN 0-89357-062-1). Slavica.

Debray, Regis. Strategy for Revolution: Essays on Latin America. Blackburn, Robin, ed. LC 78-105315. (Illus.). 1970. 6.50 (ISBN 0-85345-127-3, CL-1273); pap. 2.95 o.p. (ISBN 0-85345-180-X, PB-180X). Monthly Rev.

--Teachers, Writers, Celebrities: The Intellectuals of Modern France. 300p. 1981. 17.50 (ISBN 0-8052-7086-8, Pub. by NLB England). Schocken.

Debreczeni, Arpad, tr. see Pogany-Balas, Edit.

Debreczeni, L. A., jt. ed. see Hutas, I.

De Breffney, Brian & Folliott, Rosemary. The Houses of Ireland: Domestic Architecture from the Medieval Castle to the Edwardian Villa. (Illus.). 240p. 1981. 19.95 (ISBN 0-500-24091-4). Thames Hudson.

DeBreffny. Heritage of Ireland. Date not set. 12.98 (ISBN 0-517-53809-1). Bonanza.

De Brie, G. A., ed. Bibliographia Philosophica, 1934-45, 2 vols. LC 51-5942. 1569p. 1954. Set. 92.50x (ISBN 0-8002-1231-2). Intl Pubns Serv.

De Brouwer, A. Creating with Flexible Foam. LC 71-167657. (Little Craft Bk.). (Illus.). (gr. 4 up). 1971. 5.95 (ISBN 0-8069-5182-6); PLB 6.69 (ISBN 0-8069-5183-4). Sterling.

De Bruchard, Gisele, jt. auth. see Corbasson, Nadine.

De Bruicker, S., jt. auth. see Ward, S.

DeBruin, Jerry, jt. auth. see Sheperak, Rita.

DeBrunhoff. Babar & the Wully-Wully. (Illus.). (gr. 3). Date not set. pap. cancelled o.p. (ISBN 0-590-30046-6, Schol Pap). Schol Bk Serv.

De Brunhoff, Jean. Babar & Zephir. Haas, Merle, tr. (Illus.). (ps). 1942. 4.95 (ISBN 0-394-80579-8, BYR); PLB 5.99 (ISBN 0-394-90579-2). Random.

De Brunhoff, Laurent. Babar & the Ghost. LC 80-5753. (Illus.). 32p. 1981. PLB 6.99 (ISBN 0-394-94660-X); pap. 4.95 boards (ISBN 0-394-84660-5). Random.

--Babar Comes to America. (Illus.). (gr. k-2). 1965. 4.95 (ISBN 0-394-80588-7, BYR); PLB 5.99 (ISBN 0-394-90588-1). Random.

--Babar Learns to Cook. LC 78-11769. (Picturebacks Ser.). (Illus.). (ps-1). 1979. PLB 4.99 (ISBN 0-394-94108-X, BYR); pap. 1.25 (ISBN 0-394-84108-5). Random.

--Babar's Birthday Surprise. (ps-2). 1970. 4.95 (ISBN 0-394-80591-7, BYR); PLB 5.99 (ISBN 0-394-90591-1). Random.

--Babar's French Lessons. (Illus.). (ps). 1963. 5.95 (ISBN 0-394-80587-9, BYR); PLB 5.99 (ISBN 0-394-90587-3). Random.

--Babar's Mystery. LC 78-55912. (Illus.). (gr. 1-3). 1978. 4.95 (ISBN 0-394-83920-X, BYR); PLB 5.99 (ISBN 0-394-93920-4). Random.

--Babar's Spanish Lessons. (Illus.). (gr. k-3). 1965. 5.95 (ISBN 0-394-80589-5, BYR); PLB 5.99 (ISBN 0-394-90589-X). Random.

--The One Pig with Horns. Howard, Richard, tr. from Fr. LC 78-4917. (Illus.). (gr. k-3). 1979. 5.95 (ISBN 0-394-83673-1); PLB 6.99 (ISBN 0-394-93673-6). Pantheon.

Debrunner, H. U., jt. auth. see Gschwend, N.

De Brunoff, Laurent. Babar Saves the Day. LC 76-11684. (Picturebacks Ser.). (Illus.). (gr. 3-6). 1976. pap. 1.25 (ISBN 0-394-83341-4, BYR). Random.

DeBruyn, Monica. Lauren's Secret Ring. Fay, Ann, ed. LC 79-27261. (Concept Bk.: Level 1). (Illus.). (gr. 1-3). 1980. 6.95g (ISBN 0-8075-4391-8). A Whitman.

De Bruyn, Monica G. The Beaver Who Wouldn't Die. LC 75-2968. (Picture Bk). (Illus.). 32p. (gr. 2-4). 1975. 5.95 o.p. (ISBN 0-695-80586-X); lib. ed. 5.97 o.p. (ISBN 0-695-40586-1). Follett.

DeBruzzi, D. J., jt. auth. see Healy, J. J.

De Bry, Theodor. Conquistadores, Aztecs & Incas: A Facasimile of 16th Century Engravings. (Illus.). 108p. 1981. 60.00 (ISBN 0-8390-0257-2). Allanheld & Schram.

Debuer, Eddy & Debuer, Henriette. Seeing the Real Amsterdam. Date not set. pap. 7.95 (ISBN 0-8120-2243-2). Barron. Postponed.

Debuer, Henriette, jt. auth. see Debuer, Eddy.

Debuigne, Gerard. Dictionnaire vins. (Illus., Fr.). pap. 8.50 (ISBN 0-03-075459-3, 3742). Larousse.

--Larousse des plantes qui guerissent. new ed. (Illus.). 254p. (Fr.). 1974. 38.95x (ISBN 2-03-019013-6). Larousse.

--Larousse des vins. new ed. (Illus.). 271p. (Fr.). 1970. 47.50x (ISBN 2-03-019010-1, 4095). Larousse.

De Bury, Richard. Philobiblon: Of the Advantages of the Love of Books. Maclagan, Michael, ed. Thomas, E. C., tr. Repr. of 1970 ed. 20.00x o.p. (ISBN 0-631-12620-1, Pub. by Basil Blackwell). Biblio Dist.

Debus, A. G. Man & Nature in the Renaissance. LC 77-91085. (Cambridge History of Science Ser.). (Illus.). 1978. 22.95 (ISBN 0-521-21972-8); pap. 7.95x (ISBN 0-521-29328-6). Cambridge U Pr.

Debus, Allen G., ed. A Symposium Held at UCLA in Honor of C. D. O'Malley. (Illus.). 1974. 22.50x (ISBN 0-520-02226-2). U of Cal Pr.

De Busbecq, Ogier G. see Busbecq, Ogier G. De.

Debussy, Claude. Piano Music 1888-1905. 175p. 1972. pap. 5.50 (ISBN 0-486-22771-5). Dover.

--Songs, 1880 to 1904. Benson, Rita, ed. (Orig.). 1981. pap. price not set (ISBN 0-486-24131-9). Dover.

D'Eca, Raul & Greenfield, Eric V. Portuguese Grammar. 1979. pap. 3.95 (ISBN 0-06-460185-4, CO 185, COS). Har-Row.

De Cadenet, J. J., jt. auth. see Castro, R.

De Cadiz, Luis M., tr. see De Cesarea, Eusebio.

Decalo, Samuel. Historical Dictionary of Chad. LC 77-23585. (African Historical Dictionaries Ser.: No. 13). 1977. 19.50 (ISBN 0-8108-1046-8). Scarecrow.

--Historical Dictionary of Dahomey. LC 75-42168. (African Historical Dictionaries Ser.: No. 7). 1976. 11.00 (ISBN 0-8108-0833-1). Scarecrow.

--Historical Dictionary of Niger. LC 79-15704. (African Historical Dictionaries Ser.: No. 20). 376p. 1979. 19.00 (ISBN 0-8108-1229-0). Scarecrow.

--Historical Dictionary of Togo. LC 76-14926. (African Historical Dictionaries Ser.: No. 9). 261p. 1976. 12.00 (ISBN 0-8108-0942-7). Scarecrow.

De Cambrai, Fenelon. Spiritual Letters to Women. LC 80-82324. (Shepherd Classic Ser.). 1980. pap. 5.95 (ISBN 0-87983-233-9). Keats.

De Camoens, Luis. The Lusiad; or the Discovery of India. Feldman, Burton & Richardson, Robert, eds. LC 78-60914. (Myth & Romanticism Ser.: Vol. 6). 1980. lib. bdg. 66.00 (ISBN 0-8240-3555-0). Garland Pub.

De Camp, Catherine C., jt. auth. see De Camp, L. Sprague.

De Camp, L. Sprague. The Ancient Engineers. 1977. pap. 2.25 o.p. (ISBN 0-394-25777-4). Ballantine.

--The Fallible Fiend. 160p. 1981. pap. 1.95 (ISBN 0-345-29367-3, Del Rey). Ballantine.

DeCamp, L. Sprague. The Hostage of Zir. LC 77-10137. (YA) 1977. 7.95 o.p. (ISBN 0-399-12097-1, Dist. by Putnam). Berkley Pub.

De Camp, L. Sprague. Lost Continents: The Atlantis Theme. 384p. 1975. pap. 1.95 (ISBN 0-345-27089-4). Ballantine.
--Lovecraft: A Biography. 480p. 1976. pap. 1.95 o.p. (ISBN 0-345-25115-6). Ballantine.
--The Ragged Edge of Science. LC 79-92640. (Illus.). 254p. 1980. 16.00 (ISBN 0-913896-06-3). Owlswick Pr.
De Camp, L. Sprague & De Camp, Catherine C. Science Fiction Handbook, Revised. LC 75-21796. 1975. 8.50 o.p. (ISBN 0-913896-03-9). Owlswick Pr.
De Camp, L. Sprague & Pratt, Fletcher. The Compleat Enchanter. 416p. (Orig.). 1976. pap. 1.95 o.p. (ISBN 0-345-24638-1). Ballantine.
De Camp, L. Sprague see Sprague De Camp, L.
De Capno, A. Clear & Simple Guide to Business Spelling. (Clear & Simple Guides Ser.). 96p. (Orig.). 1981. pap. 4.95 (ISBN 0-686-68915-1). Monarch Pr.
DeCaprio, Annie. A Modern Approach to Business English. LC 73-90044. 1974. pap. text ed. 10.95 (ISBN 0-672-96102-4); tchr's manual 6.67 (ISBN 0-672-96103-2). Bobbs.
Decareau, Robert V., jt. auth. see Goldblith, Samuel A.
DeCarlo, Tessa, tr. see Luxemburg, Rosa.
DeCarlo, Thomas. Executive's Handbook of Balanced Physical Fitness: A Guide to a Personalized Exercise Program. (Illus.). 1975. pap. 4.95 o.p. (ISBN 0-8096-1900-8, Assn Pr). Follett.
Decarpentry. Academic Equitation. Bartle, Nicole, tr. from Fr. (Illus.). Repr. of 1949 ed. pap. 5.25 (ISBN 0-85131-036-2, Dist. by Sporting Book Center). J A Allen.
--Piaffer & Passage. Galvin, Patricia, tr. (Illus.). 9.75 o.p. (ISBN 0-85131-095-8, Dist. by Sporting Book Center). J A Allen.
DeCarrico, Jeanette S. Anaphoric Options of Indefinite Noun Phrases in English. (Linguistics Research Monograph Ser.: Vol. 3). 1981. text ed. 32.00 (ISBN 0-932998-03-8). Noit Amrofer.
De Castille, Vernon. Health & Physical Well Being: The Essential Knowledge of the Basic Rules on Being Healthy, Staying Healthy & Live a Long & Happy Life Which Everyone, but Absolutely Everyone Ought to Possess for the Benefit & Success of His Existence. (The Essential Knowledge Ser. Books). (Illus.). 1978. plastic spiral bdg. 27.35 (ISBN 0-89266-121-6). Am Classical Coll Pr.
--How to Reconquer Your Lost Youth. (A Science of Man Library Bk). (Illus.). 67p. 1975. 27.95 (ISBN 0-913314-57-9); lib. bdg. 33.35 (ISBN 0-685-52671-2). Am Classical Coll Pr.
--Man's Self-Discovery in the Order of the Universe. 1979. 37.50 (ISBN 0-89266-147-X). Am Classical Coll Pr.
De Castillejo, Irene Claremont see Claremont De Castillejo, Irene.
De Castro, Fernando J., et al. The Pediatric Nurse Practitioner: Guidelines for Practice. 2nd ed. LC 75-42493. (Illus.). 240p. 1976. pap. 9.50 (ISBN 0-8016-1221-7). Mosby.
De Castro, Josue. Of Men & Crabs. LC 79-139980. 1979. 7.95 (ISBN 0-8149-0667-2). Vanguard.
De Catanzaro, C. J. Symeon, the New Theologian: The Discourses. (Classics of Western Spirituality Ser.). 1980. 11.95 (ISBN 0-8091-0292-7); pap. 7.95 (ISBN 0-8091-2230-8). Paulist Pr.
DeCato, Clifford M. & Wicks, Robert J. Case Studies of the Clinical Interpretation of the Bender Gestalt Test: Illustrations of the Interpretive Process for Graduate Training & Continuing Professional Education. (Illus.). 152p. 1976. 14.50 (ISBN 0-398-03554-7). C C Thomas.
Decatur, Stephen. The Private Affairs of George Washington. LC 77-86596. (American Scene Ser). 1969. Repr. of 1933 ed. 37.50 (ISBN 0-306-71416-7). Da Capo.
De Caussade, Jean-Pierre. Abandonment to Divine Providence. LC 74-2827. 120p. 1975. pap. 1.95 (ISBN 0-385-02544-0, Im). Doubleday.
De Cecco, Marcello. Money & Empire: The International Gold Standard 1890-1914. 254p. 1975. 22.50x (ISBN 0-87471-625-X). Rowman.
DeCenzo, John. The Seekers. LC 76-5073. (Destiny Ser.). 1977. pap. 4.95 (ISBN 0-8163-0285-5). Pacific Pr Pub Assn.
De Cerfvol, Chevalier. Memoire Sur la Population. (Principal French Demographic Works of the 18th Century Ser.). (Fr.). 1976. lib. bdg. 25.00x o.p. (ISBN 0-8287-0175-X); pap. text ed. 15.00x o.p. (ISBN 0-685-71505-1). Clearwater Pub.
De Cervantes, Miguel. Don Quijote. (Span). 6.00x (ISBN 0-686-00858-8). Colton Bk.
--Don Quixote. Cohen, John M., tr. (Classics Ser.). (Orig.). (YA) (gr. 9 up). 1951. pap. 4.95 (ISBN 0-14-044010-0). Penguin.
--Don Quixote. Jones, Joseph R. & Douglas, Kenneth, eds. (Critical Editions Ser.). 1980. 29.95x (ISBN 0-393-04514-5); pap. text ed. 8.95x (ISBN 0-393-09018-3). Norton.
--Entremeses. (Span). 4.50x o.s.i. (ISBN 0-686-00862-6). Colton Bk.
--Novelas Ejemplares. (Span). 4.50x o.s.i. (ISBN 0-686-00878-2). Colton Bk.
De Cervantes, Miguel see Cervantes, Miguel de.
De Cervantes, Miguel see Cervantes, Miguel De.
De Cervantes, Miguel see Cervantes, Miguel de.
De Cervantes Saavedra, Miguel. Don Quijote De la Mancha, Pt. 2. (Illus., Span.). (gr. 11-12). 1971. pap. 3.95 (ISBN 0-88345-138-7); manual, filmstrips, & cassettes o.p. 145.00 (ISBN 0-685-69627-8). Regents Pub.
De Cesarea, Eusebio. Historia Eclesiastica De Eusebio. De Cadiz, Luis M., tr. (Biblioteca Mundo Hispano de Obras Clasicas). (Span.). Date not set. pap. price not set (ISBN 0-311-15042-X, Edit Mundo). Casa Bautista.
De Chamblain De Marivaux, Pierre C. Le Paysan Parvenu: Or, the Fortunate Peasant. LC 78-60836. (Novel 1720-1805 Ser.: Vol. 2). 1979. lib. bdg. 45.00 (ISBN 0-8240-3651-4); lib. bdg. 31.00 ea. Garland Pub.
De Chambrun, Adolphe. The Executive Power in the United States: A Study of Constitutional Law. LC 74-75460. 303p. 1974. Repr. 32.00x (ISBN 0-912004-13-4). W W Gaunt.
Dechanet, Jean M. Yoga in Ten Lessons. LC 65-20461. (Illus.). 1966. 7.95 o.p. (ISBN 0-06-001240-4, HarpT). Har-Row.
Dechant, Emarld V. Psychology in Teaching Reading. 2nd ed. 1977. text ed. 18.95 (ISBN 0-13-736686-8). P-H.
Dechant, Emerald. Improving the Teaching of Reading. 2nd ed. 1970. ref. ed. 18.95 (ISBN 0-13-453415-8). P-H.
--Reading Improvement in the Secondary School. (Illus.). 448p. 1973. ref. ed. 18.95x (ISBN 0-13-755017-0). P-H.
De Chardin, Pierre Teilhard see Teilhard De Chardin, Pierre.
De Chasca, Edmund. The Poem of the Cid. LC 75-30597. (World Authors Ser.,: Spain: No.378). 1976. lib. bdg. 12.50 (ISBN 0-8057-6194-2). Twayne.
De Chateaubriand, Francois R. The Genius of Christianity. LC 75-25532. 1975. Repr. of 1856 ed. 35.00 (ISBN 0-86527-254-9). Fertig.
--The Martyrs. Wight, O. W., ed. & tr. from Fr. LC 76-15294. 451p. 1976. Repr. of 1859 ed. 22.50 (ISBN 0-86527-275-1). Fertig.
De Chateaubriand, Francois-Rene. Memoires d'outre-tombe, 2 vols. (Documentation thematique). (Fr). pap. 2.95 ea. Larousse.
De Chazal, Malcolm. Sens-Plastique. 2nd, rev. ed. Weiss, Irving, ed. LC 79-25078. 163p. (Orig.). 1980. pap. 6.00 (ISBN 0-915342-29-4). SUN.
DECHEMA, Deutsche Gesellschaft Fuer Chemisches Apparatewesen E. V., ed. Biotechnology: Proceedings of the First European Congress on Biotechnology. (Dechema Monographs: Vol. 82). 304p. 1979. pap. text ed. 37.50 (ISBN 3-527-10765-7). Verlag Chemie.
--Characterization of Immobilized Biocatalysts. (DECHEMA Monographs: Vol. 84). 400p. (Orig.). 1979. pap. text ed. 46.00 (ISBN 3-527-10767-3). Verlag Chemie.
Dechema: the West German National Scientific Society. Seawater Corrosion Data. (Chemical Engineering Book Ser.). 160p. 1981. 57.50 (ISBN 0-07-016207-7). McGraw.
De Cherney, Alan, ed. Obstetrics & Gynecology: PreTest Self-Assessment & Review. LC 77-78446. (Clinical Sciences: PreTest Self-Assessment & Review Ser.). (Illus.). 1978. pap. 9.95 (ISBN 0-07-051602-2). McGraw-Pretest.
Dechert, Hans & Raupach, Manfred, eds. Pausological Implications of Speech Production: An Interdisciplinary Workshop. (Janua Linguarum, Series Maior: No. 86). 1979. text ed. 47.00x (ISBN 90-279-7946-4). Mouton.
DeChiars, Joseph. Handbook of Architectural Details for Commercial Buildings. 512p. 1980. 32.50 (ISBN 0-07-016215-8, P&RB). McGraw.
DECHMA, Deutsche Gesellschaft Fuer Chemisches Apparatewesen E. V., ed. Microbiology Applied to Technology: Proceedings XIIth International Congress of Microbiology. (DECHEMA Monographs: Vol. 83). 230p. (Orig.). 1979. pap. text ed. 25.80 (ISBN 3-527-10766-5). Verlag Chemie.
DeChristoforo, R. J. Woodworking Techniques: Joints & Their Applications. (Illus.). 1979. ref.ed. 16.95 (ISBN 0-8359-8785-X). Reston.
Deci, Edward L. The Psychology of Self-Determination. LC 80-8373. 1980. 19.95 (ISBN 0-669-04045-2). Lexington Bks.
De Cicco, Alfred. The Handyman's Primer. (Illus.). 192p. 1975. pap. 5.95 (ISBN 0-8473-1123-6). Sterling.
Deck, Allan. Francisco Javier Alagre: A Study in Mexican Literary Criticism. 1976. pap. 9.00 (ISBN 0-8294-0337-X). Jesuit Hist.
Deck, E., jt. auth. see Folta, J.
Decker, Barbara, jt. auth. see Decker, Robert.
Decker, Beatrice & Kooiman, Gladys. After the Flowers Have Gone. 160p. 1973. 5.95 o.p. (ISBN 0-310-23240-6). Zondervan.
Decker, Brian C. Margaret Fuller's Woman in the Nineteenth Century: A Literary Study of Form & Content, of Sources & Influence. LC 79-7475. (Contributions in Women's Studies: No. 13). 1980. lib. bdg. 17.95 (ISBN 0-313-21475-1, UMF/) (ISBN 0-86577). Greenwood.
Decker, Cecil A. & Decker, John R. Planning & Administering Early Childhood Programs. 2nd ed. (Elementary Education Ser.: No. C22). 480p. 1980. pap. text ed. 15.95 (ISBN 0-675-08160-2). Merrill.
Decker, David L. Social Gerontology: An Introduction to the Dynamics of Aging. 304p. 1980. text ed. 14.95 (ISBN 0-316-17918-3); test bank free (ISBN 0-316-17919-1). Little.
Decker, Donald M. Mastering the International Phonetic Alphabet. (gr. 9 up). 1970. pap. text ed. 1.95 (ISBN 0-88345-099-2, 17757). Regents Pub.
Decker, Douglas, jt. auth. see Mackie, Dustin.
Decker, Duane. Third-Base Rookie. (gr. 7 up). 1959. 7.25 (ISBN 0-688-21726-5). Morrow.
Decker, Erwin A. Look Pride. 1981. 7.95 (ISBN 0-8062-1642-5). Carlton.
Decker, Eugene, jt. ed. see Teague, Richard D.
Decker, Harold A. & Herford, Julius, eds. Choral Conducting: A Symposium. LC 72-94347. (Illus.). 320p. 1973. 18.50 (ISBN 0-13-133355-0). P-H.
Decker, John R., jt. auth. see Decker, Cecil A.
Decker, Leslie E. Railroads, Lands & Politics: The Taxation of the Railroad Land Grants, 1864-1897. LC 64-11940. (Illus.). 435p. 1966. Repr. of 1964 ed. 20.00x (ISBN 0-87057-084-6, Pub. by Brown U Pr). Univ Pr of New England.
Decker, Marjorie A. The Christian Mother Goose Treasury: Part II of the Original Christian Mother Goose Book. LC 80-69167. (Three Part Series: Vol. II). (Illus.). 112p. (gr. k-4). 1980. PLB 10.95 (ISBN 0-933724-01-2). CMG Prods.
Decker, Raymond F., ed. Source Book on Maraging Steels. 1979. 38.00 (ISBN 0-87170-079-4). ASM.
Decker, Robert & Decker, Barbara. Volcanoes: A Primer. LC 80-20126. (Geology Ser.). (Illus.). 1981. text ed. 17.95x (ISBN 0-7167-1241-5); pap. text ed. 8.95x (ISBN 0-7167-1242-3). W H Freeman.
Decker, Robert & Marquez, Esther T. The Proud Mexicans. (Illus.). 250p. (gr. 7-12). 1976. pap. 5.25 (ISBN 0-88345-254-5). Regents Pub.
Decker, Robert O. The Whaling City, a History of New London. LC 74-30794. (Illus.). 413p. 1976. 15.00 (ISBN 0-87106-053-1). New London County.
Decker, William. The Holdouts. 1981. pap. price not set (ISBN 0-671-42081-X). PB.
De Clark, Catalina, tr. see Dana, H. E. & Mantey, J. R.
DeClements, Barthe. Nothing's Fair in Fifth Grade. 144p. (gr. 3-7). 1981. 8.95 (ISBN 0-670-51741-0). Viking Pr.
De Clerq, C., jt. auth. see Johl, S. S.
De Cock, Liliane, ed. James Van der Zee. new ed. LC 73-75105. (Morgan & Morgan Monographs). 160p. 1974. 14.00 o.p. (ISBN 0-87100-039-3). Morgan.
De Commynes, Philippe. Memoirs of Philippe De Commynes, Vol. 1, Bks 1-5 & Vol. 2, Bks. 6-8. Kinser, Samuel, ed. Cazeaux, Isabelle, tr. from Fr. LC 68-9363. (Illus.). 1969. Vol. 1. 19.50x (ISBN 0-87249-224-9); Vol. 2. 19.50x (ISBN 0-87249-224-9); Set. 37.50x (ISBN 0-87249-199-4). U of SC Pr.
Deconde, Alexander. This Affair of Louisiana. LC 76-12468. 1976. 12.50 o.p. (ISBN 0-684-14687-8, ScribT). Scribner.
De Coppens, Peter R. Spiritual Man in the Modern World. 1976. pap. text ed. 5.75x o.p. (ISBN 0-8191-0066-8). U Pr of Amer.
--Spiritual Perspective II: The Spiritual Dimension & Implications of Love, Sex, & Marriage. LC 80-6302. 175p. (Orig.). 1981. pap. text ed. 8.75 (ISBN 0-8191-1512-6). U Pr of Amer.
De Coppens Peter, Roche see Roche De Coppens, Peter.
De Cordemoy, Geraud see Cordemoy, Geraud de.
De Cossart, Michael. The Food of Love: Princess Edmond De Polignac (1865-1943) & Her Salon. (Illus.). 1978. 21.95 o.p. (ISBN 0-241-89785-8, Pub. by Hamish Hamilton England). David & Charles.
DeCosta, ed. see Carnegie Commission On Higher Education.
DeCosta, Miriam, ed. Blacks in Hispanic Literature: A Collection of Critical Essays. (Literary Criticism Ser). 1976. 12.00 (ISBN 0-8046-9140-1, Natl U). Kennikat.
DeCosta, Steven E., jt. auth. see Burton, William C.
DeCoster, Cyrus. Juan Valera. LC 74-3058. (World Authors Ser.: Spain: No. 316). 192p. 1974. lib. bdg. 12.50 (ISBN 0-8057-2919-4). Twayne.
DeCoster, Cyrus C. Pedro Antonio de Alarcon. (World Authors Ser.: No. 549). 1979. lib. bdg. 13.50 (ISBN 0-8057-6391-0). Twayne.
Decoster, D. T., et al. Accounting for Managerial Decision Making. 2nd ed. LC 77-15785. (Accounting & Information Systems Ser.). 1978. pap. text ed. 14.50 (ISBN 0-471-02204-7). Wiley.
Decoteau, A. E. The Handbook of Amazon Parrots. (Illus.). 221p. 1980. 12.95 (ISBN 0-87666-892-9, H-1025). TFH Pubns.
DeCourcy, Judith, jt. auth. see DeCourcy, Peter.
DeCourcy, Peter & DeCourcy, Judith. A Silent Tragedy: Child Abuse in the Community. LC 72-95493. 231p. 1973. pap. 14.50 (ISBN 0-88284-005-3). Alfred Pub.
De Cournand, Antoine. De la Propriete Ou la Cause Du Pauvre Plaidee Au Tribunal De la Raison, De la Justice et De la Verite. (Fr.). 1977. lib. bdg. 18.75x o.p. (ISBN 0-8287-0231-4); pap. text ed. 8.75x o.p. (ISBN 0-685-74922-3). Clearwater Pub.
De Courtivron, Isabelle, jt. ed. see Marks, Elaine.
De Craemer, Willy. The Jamaa & the Church: A Bantu Catholic Movement in Zaire. (Oxford Studies in African Affairs). 1977. 45.00x (ISBN 0-19-822708-6). Oxford U Pr.
Decraon, Pierre, jt. auth. see Amauri, Maurice.
De Crespigny, Anthony & Minogue, Kenneth, eds. Contemporary Political Philosophers. LC 74-26158. 320p. (Orig.). 1975. pap. text ed. 11.50 scp (ISBN 0-06-041603-3, HarpC). Har-Row.
Decrespigny, R. C. China: The Land & Its People. 1973. pap. 7.95 (ISBN 0-312-13265-4). St. Martin.
De Crespigny, R. R. China This Century. LC 75-10977. 300p. 1975. text ed. 19.95 (ISBN 0-312-13335-9). St Martin.
De Crevecoeur, J. Hector. Letters from an American Farmer. Repr. of 1782 ed. 8.00 (ISBN 0-8446-1139-5). Peter Smith.
De Crevecoeur, Michel-Guillanme St. J. Journey into Northern Pennsylvania & the State of New York. Bostelmann, Clarissa S., tr. LC 63-14014. (Illus.). 1964. 15.00 o.p. (ISBN 0-472-25100-7). U of Mich Pr.
De Cristoforo, R. J. De Cristoforo's House Building Illustrated. LC 77-6659. (Popular Science Bk.). (Illus.). 1978. 18.95 (ISBN 0-06-010987-4, HarpT). Har-Row.
DeCristoforo, R. J. Handtool Handbook. LC 77-89289. (Illus.). 1977. pap. 5.95 (ISBN 0-912656-53-0). H P Bks.
De Cristoforo, R. J. How to Build Your Own Furniture. (Illus.). 176p. pap. 3.50 (ISBN 0-06-463352-7, EH 352, EH). Har-Row.
DeCristoforo, R. J. The Magic of Your Radial Arm Saw. 1980. text ed. 12.95 (ISBN 0-8359-4183-3). Reston.
Decroly, J. C., et al. Parametric Amplifiers. 1973. 48.95 (ISBN 0-470-20065-0). Halsted Pr.
De Croome, D. Empaytaz. Albor: Mediaeval & Renaissance Dawn-Songs in the Iberian Peninsula. LC 80-23767. (Sponsor Ser.). 106p. (Orig.). 1980. pap. 12.75 (ISBN 0-8357-0531-5, SS-00144). Univ Microfilms.
Decroux, Etienne. Words on Mime. 208p. 1981. 12.00x (ISBN 0-89676-045-6). Drama Bk.
DeCrow, Karen. The Young Woman's Guide to Liberation: Alternatives to a Half-Life While the Choice Is Still Yours. LC 72-141377. 1971. pap. 7.50 (ISBN 0-672-63615-8). Pegasus.
DeCrow, Roger. New Learning for Older Americans. 1975. 5.75 (ISBN 0-685-84004-2). Adult Ed.
DeCrow, Roger, ed. Adult Education Dissertation Abstracts 1963-19. League, Nehume. 1970. write for info. Adult Ed.
Decter, Moshe, ed. Profile of Communism: A Fact-By-Fact Primer. rev. ed. 1961. pap. 0.95 o.s.i. (ISBN 0-02-072820-4, Collier). Macmillan.
De Curet, Miriam De Anda see Curet de De Anda, Miriam.
De Danois, Vivian. Abortion & the Moral Degeneration of the American Medical Profession. (A Science of Man Library Bk). 92p. 1975. 41.50 (ISBN 0-913314-56-0). Am Classical Coll Pr.
De Datta, Surajit K. Principles & Practices of Rice Production. 704p. 1981. 40.00 (ISBN 0-471-08074-8, Pub. by Wiley-Interscience). Wiley.
De Davila, Maria D. Castro see Castro De Davila, Maria D.
De Deguileville, Guillaume see Deguileville, Guillaume de.
De Deiros, Norma H. C. Dramatizaciones Infantiles Para Dias Especiales. 1978. pap. 1.95 (ISBN 0-311-07606-8). Casa Bautista.
Dedekind, R., jt. auth. see Lejeune-Dirichlet, P. G.
De Dienes, Andre. Exotic Nudes. (Illus.). 4.95 (ISBN 0-910550-04-2). Elysium.
--Glory of De Dienes Women. (Illus.). 7.95 (ISBN 0-910550-05-0). Elysium.

--Sun-Warmed Nudes. (Illus.). 10.00 (ISBN 0-910550-15-8, Dist. by Lyle Stuart). Elysium.

Dedmond, Francis B. Sylvester Judd. (United States Authors Ser.). 1980. lib. bdg. 11.95 (ISBN 0-8057-7305-3). Twayne.

Dedo, Herbert H. & Shipp, Thomas. Spastic Dysphonia: A Surgical & Voice Therapy Treatment Program. LC 80-65193. (Illus.). 96p. 1980. pap. text ed. 12.95 (ISBN 0-933014-58-9). College-Hill.

De Dombal, F. T. Diagnosis of Acute Abdominal Pain. (Illus.). 192p. 1981. pap. text ed. 12.50 (ISBN 0-443-01901-0). Churchill.

De Duran, Helen C. Blonde Chicana Bride's Mexican Cookbook. (Wild & Woolly West Ser.: No. 40). (Illus., Orig.). 1980. 7.00 (ISBN 0-910584-95-8); pap. 2.00 (ISBN 0-910584-96-6). Filter.

Deeb, Marius. The Lebanese Civil War. LC 79-19833. (Praeger Special Studies). 176p. 1980. 25.95 (ISBN 0-03-039701-4). Praeger.

Deedy, Jack. Apologies, Good Friends... An Interim Biography of Daniel Berrigan, S. J. 152p. 1981. pap. 6.95 (ISBN 0-8190-0641-6). Fides Claretian.

Deedy, John. First Book of the Vatican. LC 70-102275. (First Bks). (Illus.). (gr. 7 up). 1970. PLB 4.90 o.p. (ISBN 0-531-00697-2). Watts.

--Literary Places: A Guided Pilgrimage; New York & New England. (Illus.). 1978. 12.95 o.p. (ISBN 0-8362-7102-5); pap. 5.95 o.p. (ISBN 0-8362-7101-7). Andrews & McMeel.

Deedy, John & Nobile, Philip, eds. The Complete Ecology Fact Book. LC 73-175364. 408p. 1972. pap. 3.95 o.p. (ISBN 0-385-07803-X). Doubleday.

Deegan, Arthur X., 2nd. Coaching: A Management Skill for Improving Individual Performance. LC 79-619. 1979. pap. text ed. 8.95 (ISBN 0-201-01266-9). A-W.

--Management by Objectives for Hospitals. LC 76-45523. 1977. 24.95 (ISBN 0-912862-33-5). Aspen Systems.

Deegan, Paul. Animals of East Africa. LC 72-140641. (World's People Ser.). (Illus.). (gr. 5-12). 1971. PLB 6.95 (ISBN 0-87191-050-0). Creative Ed.

--Catfish Hunter. (Sports Superstars Ser.). (Illus.). (gr. 3-9). 1979. PLB 5.95 (ISBN 0-87191-720-3); pap. 2.95 (ISBN 0-89812-159-0). Creative Ed.

--Hank Aaron: Superstars. LC 73-20300. 1974. PLB 5.95 (ISBN 0-87191-321-6); pap. 2.95 (ISBN 0-89812-172-8). Creative Ed.

--Mexican Village: Life in a Zapotec Community. LC 76-140642. (World's People Ser.). (Illus.). (gr. 4-8). 1971. PLB 6.95 (ISBN 0-87191-047-0). Creative Ed.

--O. J. Simpson. LC 73-17056. (Creative Superstars Ser.). 1974. PLB 5.95 (ISBN 0-87191-312-7); pap. 2.95 (ISBN 0-89812-166-3). Creative Ed.

Deegan, Paul & Larson, Bruce. Hospital: Life in a Medical Center. LC 76-156064. (gr. 5-9). 1970. PLB 6.95 (ISBN 0-87191-052-7). Creative Ed.

Deegan, Paul, ed. see Coffey, Richard A.

Deegan, Paul J. Almost a Champion. LC 74-14517. (Dan Murphy Sports Ser). 40p. (gr. 3-6). 1975. PLB 5.95 (ISBN 0-87191-402-6); pap. 2.95 (ISBN 0-89812-151-5). Creative Ed.

--The Basic Strokes. LC 75-41383. (Sports Instruction Ser.). (Illus.). (gr. 3-9). 1976. PLB 5.95 (ISBN 0-87191-502-2); pap. 2.95 (ISBN 0-686-67434-0). Creative Ed.

--Bill Russell. LC 73-13749. (Creative Superstars Ser.). 1974. PLB 5.95 o.p. (ISBN 0-87191-281-3). Creative Ed.

--Checking & Defensive Play. LC 76-13849. (Sports Instruction Ser.). (Illus.). (gr. 3-9). 1976. PLB 5.95 (ISBN 0-87191-525-1); pap. 2.95 (ISBN 0-686-67439-1). Creative Ed.

--Close but Not Quite. LC 74-16334. (Dan Murphy Sports Ser.). 40p. (gr. 3-6). 1975. PLB 5.95 (ISBN 0-87191-405-0); pap. 2.95 (ISBN 0-89812-152-3). Creative Ed.

--Dan Moves up. LC 74-17069. (Dan Murphy Sports Ser.). 40p. (gr. 3-6). 1975. PLB 5.95 (ISBN 0-87191-406-9); pap. 2.95 (ISBN 0-89812-153-1). Creative Ed.

--Important Decision. LC 74-14514. (Dan Murphy Sports Ser.). (Illus.). 40p. (gr. 3-6). 1975. PLB 5.95 (ISBN 0-87191-401-8); pap. 2.95 (ISBN 0-89812-154-X). Creative Ed.

--Jerry West: Superstars. LC 73-19525. 1974. PLB 5.95 o.p. (ISBN 0-87191-311-9). Creative Ed.

--Scoring: The Shots. LC 76-12423. (Sports Instruction Ser.). (Illus.). (gr. 3-9). 1976. PLB 5.95 (ISBN 0-87191-526-X); pap. 2.95 (ISBN 0-686-67438-3). Creative Ed.

--Team Manager. LC 74-14515. (Dan Murphy Sports Ser.). (Illus.). 40p. (gr. 3-6). 1974. PLB 5.95 (ISBN 0-87191-403-4); pap. 2.95 (ISBN 0-89812-155-8). Creative Ed.

--Tom Seaver. LC 73-13650. (Creative Superstars Ser.). 1974. PLB 5.50 o.p. (ISBN 0-87191-280-5). Creative Ed.

--Tournaments. LC 74-149436. (Dan Murphy Sports Ser.). 40p. (gr. 3-6). 1975. PLB 5.95 (ISBN 0-87191-404-2); pap. 2.95 (ISBN 0-89812-156-6). Creative Ed.

Deegan, Paul J. & Shazar, Yair. A Kibbutz: Life in an Israeli Commune. LC 72-156063. (Illus.). 80p. (gr. 4-9). 1970. PLB 5.95 o.p. (ISBN 0-87191-053-5). Creative Ed.

Deeley, T. J., ed. The Planning of Radiotherapy Departments. 1980. 50.00x (Pub. by Brit Inst Radiology). State Mutual Bk.

Deeley, Thomas J. Principles of Radiation Therapy. 160p. 1976. 17.95 (ISBN 0-407-00030-5). Butterworths.

Deem, Bill, jt. auth. see Muchow, Kenneth.

Deem, Bill, et al. Digital Computer Circuits & Concepts. 3rd ed. (Illus.). 1980. text ed. 18.95 (ISBN 0-8359-1299-X); free instrs'. manual. Reston.

Deem, Rosemary. Women & Schooling. (Education Bks). 1978. 16.00x (ISBN 0-7100-8957-0); pap. 7.95 (ISBN 0-7100-8958-9). Routledge & Kegan.

Deem, W. Electronics Math. 1980. 19.95 (ISBN 0-13-252304-3). P-H.

Deeming, Sue. Bean Cookery. (Orig.). 1980. pap. 5.95 (ISBN 0-89586-037-6). H P Bks.

Deems, Betty. Easy-to-Make Felt Ornaments for Christmas and Other Occasions. (Dover Needlework Ser). (Illus., Orig.). 1976. pap. 3.00 (ISBN 0-486-23389-8). Dover.

Deems, Edward M., ed. Holy-Days & Holidays: A Treasury of Historical Material, Sermons in Full & in Brief, Suggestive Thoughts & Poetry, Relating to Holy Days & Holidays. LC 68-17940. 1968. Repr. of 1902 ed. 34.00 (ISBN 0-8103-3352-X). Gale.

Deen, Edith. Bible's Legacy for Womanhood. 1976. pap. 1.50 (ISBN 0-89129-100-8). Jove Pubns.

--Family Living in the Bible. (Family Lib Ser.). 1969. pap. 1.25 (ISBN 0-89129-107-5). Jove Pubns.

De Enden, Michel. Rasputin & the Waning of the Russian Monarchy. 300p. (Orig.). 1980. pap. write for info. (ISBN 0-913124-46-X). Nordland Pub.

Deeney, John J., ed. Chinese-Western Comparative Literature & Strategy. 220p. 1981. 17.50 (ISBN 0-295-95810-3, Pub. by Chinese Univ Hong Kong). U of Wash Pr.

Deep, Samuel D. & Brincklow, William D. Introduction to Business: A Systems Approach. (Illus.). 576p. 1974. ref. ed. 18.95 (ISBN 0-13-478529-0); study guide 4.95 (ISBN 0-13-478552-5). P-H.

Deep, Samuel D., jt. auth. see Vaughn, James A.

Deepak, Adarsh, ed. Inversion Methods in Atmospheric Remote Sounding. 1977. 40.00 (ISBN 0-12-208450-0). Acad Pr.

--Remote Sensing of Atmospheres & Oceans. LC 80-18881. 1980. 45.00 (ISBN 0-12-208460-8). Acad Pr.

Deeping, Warwick. Fox Farm. 1976. lib. bdg. 17.75x (ISBN 0-89968-021-6). Lightyear.

--Kitty. 1976. lib. bdg. 16.75x (ISBN 0-89968-020-8). Lightyear.

--The Red Saint. 1976. lib. bdg. 16.75x (ISBN 0-89968-024-0). Lightyear.

Deer, W. A., et al. Rock-Forming Minerals, Vol. 2A. 2nd ed. LC 78-40451. 1979. 59.95x (ISBN 0-470-26455-1). Halsted Pr.

Deerforth, Daniel. Knock Wood! Superstition Through the Ages. LC 79-164220. 200p. 1974. Repr. of 1928 ed. 20.00 (ISBN 0-8103-3964-1). Gale.

Dees, Benjamin. E. A. Baratynsky. (World Authors Ser.: Russia: No. 202). 1972. lib. bdg. 10.95 (ISBN 0-8057-2092-8). Twayne.

Dees, Catherine, jt. auth. see Croissant, Kay.

Dees, Jerome S. Sir Thomas Elyot & Roger Ascham: A Reference Guide. (Reference Books Ser.). 1981. 25.00 (ISBN 0-8161-8353-8). G K Hall.

Deese, David & Nye, Joseph. Energy & Security. 1980. 14.50 (ISBN 0-88410-640-3). Ballinger Pub.

Deese, David A. Nuclear Power & Radioactive Waste. LC 77-18496. (Illus.). 1978. 19.95 (ISBN 0-669-02114-8). Lexington Bks.

Deese, David A. see Williams, Frederick C.

Deetz, James. In Small Things Forgotten: The Archaeology of Early American Life. LC 76-50760. 1977. pap. 2.50 (ISBN 0-385-08031-X, Anch). Doubleday.

De Faire, Ulf & Theorell, Tores. Life Stress & Coronary Heart Disease. 250p. 1981. 18.50 (ISBN 0-87527-201-0). Green.

DeFalco, Joseph, ed. see Cranch, Christopher P.

De Falla, Manue. On Music & Musicians. 136p. 1981. pap. 7.95 (ISBN 0-7145-2735-1, Pub. by M. Boyars). Merrimack Bk Serv.

DeFanti, Charles L., Jr. The Wages of Expectation: A Biography of Edward Dahlberg. LC 77-94390. (Gotham Library). 1978. 15.00x (ISBN 0-8147-1763-2); pap. 7.00x (ISBN 0-8147-1764-0). NYU Pr.

DeFatta, Joseph & Titard, Pierre. Practice Set to Accompany Introduction to Accounting. 1976. pap. 4.95 o.p. (ISBN 0-7216-3014-6). Saunders.

DeFelice, Louis J. Introduction to Membrane Noise. 440p. 1981. 39.50 (ISBN 0-306-40513-X, Plenum Pr). Plenum Pub.

De Felitta, Frank. Audrey Rose. 1977. pap. 3.25 (ISBN 0-446-82472-0). Warner Bks.

--Oktoberfest. 208p. 1980. pap. 2.50 (ISBN 0-380-53546-7, 53546). Avon.

--Sea Trial. 288p. 1980. pap. 4.95 (ISBN 0-380-76042-8, 76042). Avon.

De Fenoyl, Pierre, ed. Photography Album No. One. LC 79-20063. (Illus.). 232p. (Fr. & Eng.). 50.00 (ISBN 0-9601068-3-9). Agrinde Pubns.

Defense Technology Seminar, Yuma, Arizona, 1979. Powder Metallurgy in Defense Technology: Proceedings, Vol. 5. (Orig.). 1980. pap. text ed. 40.00 (ISBN 0-918404-50-9). Metal Powder.

De Ferriere, J. C., tr. Mais Puro Que O Diamante. (Portugese Bks.). (Port.). 1979. 1.10 (ISBN 0-686-28816-5). Life Pubs Intl.

DeFeudis, F. & DeFeudis, P. Elements of the Behavioral Code. 1978. 52.50 (ISBN 0-12-208760-7). Acad Pr.

De Feudis, F. V. Central Cholinergic Systems & Behavior. 1975. 32.50 (ISBN 0-12-208750-X). Acad Pr.

DeFeudis, Francis V. & Mandel, Paul, eds. Amino Acid Neurotransmitters, Vol. 29. (Advances in Biochemical Psychopharmacology). 500p. 1981. 45.00 (ISBN 0-89004-595-X). Raven.

DeFeudis, P., jt. auth. see DeFeudis, F.

Deffner, Don. Bound to Be Free. LC 80-81841. 1980. pap. 6.95 (ISBN 0-933350-38-4). Morse Pr.

--The Real Word for the Real World. (Preacher's Workshop Ser.). 48p. 1977. pap. 2.25 (ISBN 0-570-07402-9, 12-2674). Concordia.

Deffner, Donald. Celebration of Adulthood. LC 80-81839. pap. 4.50 (ISBN 0-933350-41-4). Morse Pr.

--Two Lives to Live. LC 80-81840. 1981. pap. 4.50 (ISBN 0-933350-40-6). Morse Pr.

--You Promised Me God. LC 12-2792. (Illus.). 1981. pap. 4.95 (ISBN 0-570-03827-8). Concordia.

Deffner, Donald L. Bold Ones on Campus. LC 73-78104. 1973. pap. 2.50 o.p. (ISBN 0-570-03162-1, 12-2566). Concordia.

Deffner, Wenonah S. Scripture Word Search. (Quiz & Puzzle Bks.). 1980. pap. 2.45 (ISBN 0-8010-2897-3). Baker Bk.

De Figueiredo, M. P. & Splittstoesser, D. F. Food Microbiology: Public Health & Spoilage Aspects. (Illus.). 1976. lib. bdg. 39.50 (ISBN 0-87055-209-0). AVI.

De Filippi, Joseph see Lacroix, Paul.

DeFilipps, Robert A., jt. auth. see Ayensu, Edward S.

De Fleur, Melvin L. & Ball-Rokeach, Sandra. Theories of Mass Communication. 3rd ed. LC 74-112656. 1975. pap. 9.95x (ISBN 0-582-28017-6). Longman.

DeFleur, Melvin L. & Dennis, Everette E. Understanding Mass Communication. LC 80-82762. (Illus.). 528p. 1981. pap. text ed. 11.95 (ISBN 0-395-29722-2); price not set instr's. manual (ISBN 0-395-29723-0). HM.

DeFleur, Melvin L., et al. Sociology: Human Society. 2nd brief ed. 1977. pap. 12.95x (ISBN 0-673-07928-7). Scott F.

--Sociology: Human Society. 3rd ed. 1981. text ed. 17.95x (ISBN 0-673-15211-1). Scott F.

De Fleury, C. Rohault. La Sainte Vierge: Etudes Archeologiques et Iconographiques, 2 vols. (Illus., Fr.). 1981. Repr. of 1878 ed. Set. 325.00x (ISBN 0-89241-154-6). Caratzas Bros.

Defliese, P. L., et al. Montgomery's Auditing. 9th ed. 869p. 1975. 36.50 (ISBN 0-471-06527-7). Wiley.

--Montgomery's Auditing. 9th ed. 1975. 36.50 (ISBN 0-8260-2562-5). Ronald Pr.

De Flumiani, Carlo M. The Eternal Principles of Managerial Excellence for the Benefit of Businessmen: Corporate Executives, Junior Clerks, Housewives, Students, Politicians, Statesmen & Anyone Genuinely Interested in Improving His Station in Life. (Illus.). 1977. 34.75 (ISBN 0-89266-061-9). Am Classical Coll Pr.

Defoe, Daniel. Colonel Jack: The History & Remarkable Life of the Truly Honorable Colonel Jacque, Commonly Called Colonel Jack. Monk, Samuel H., ed. (Oxford English Novels Ser). 1965. pap. 3.95x (ISBN 0-19-281076-6, OPB). Oxford U Pr.

--Conjugal Lewdness, or Matrimonial Whoredom. LC 67-10178. 1967. Repr. of 1727 ed. 43.00x (ISBN 0-8201-1013-2). Schol Facsimiles.

De Foe, Daniel. The Consolidator or Memoirs of Sundry Transactions from the World in the Moon. LC 75-170513. (Foundations of the Novel Ser.: Vol. 9). lib. bdg. 50.00 (ISBN 0-8240-0521-X). Garland Pub.

Defoe, Daniel. The Four Years Voyages of Captain George Roberts. LC 79-170566. (Foundations of the Novel Ser.: Vol. 47). lib. bdg. 50.00 (ISBN 0-8240-0559-7). Garland Pub.

--Journal of the Plague Year. 1953. 10.50x (ISBN 0-460-00289-9, Evman); pap. 3.95 (ISBN 0-460-01289-4). Dutton.

--The Life, Adventures, & Pyracies of the Famous Captain Singleton... Being Set on Shore in the Island of Madagascar. LC 70-170544. (Foundations of the Novel Ser.: Vol. 33). lib. bdg. 50.00 (ISBN 0-8240-0545-7). Garland Pub.

--Memoirs of a Cavalier. LC 74-170545. (Novel in England, 1700-1775 Ser). lib. bdg. 50.00 (ISBN 0-8240-0546-5). Garland Pub.

--Moll Flanders. (Classics Ser). (gr. 11 up). 1969. pap. 1.95 (ISBN 0-8049-0200-3, CL-200). Airmont.

--Robinson Crusoe. (Literature Ser). (gr. 7-12). 1970. pap. text ed. 3.58 (ISBN 0-87720-736-4). AMSCO Sch.

--Robinson Crusoe. (Illus.). (gr. 7 up). 1962. 3.95 o.s.i. (ISBN 0-02-726460-2); PLB 4.24 o.s.i. (ISBN 0-02-726470-X). Macmillan.

--Robinson Crusoe. (Keith Jennison Large Type Bks). (gr. 4-6). PLB 7.95 o.p. (ISBN 0-531-00273-X). Watts.

--Robinson Crusoe. (gr. 7-12). 1973. pap. 0.95 o.p. (ISBN 0-590-01357-2, Schol Pap). Schol Bk Serv.

--Robinson Crusoe. Shinagel, Michael, ed. (Critical Editions Ser.). 399p. 1975. pap. text ed. 4.95x (ISBN 0-393-09231-3). Norton.

--Robinson Crusoe. (Span.). 7.95 (ISBN 84-241-5636-6). E Torres & Sons.

--Robinson Crusoe. LC 78-3384. (Raintree's Illustrated Classics). (Illus.). (gr. 5-8). 1978. PLB 9.65 (ISBN 0-8393-6212-9). Raintree Child.

--Robinson Crusoe & Other Writings. Sutherland, James, ed. LC 77-77300. (Gotham Library). 416p. 1977. 12.00x (ISBN 0-8147-7784-8); pap. 7.00x (ISBN 0-8147-7785-6). NYU Pr.

--Tour Thro' the Whole Island of Great Britain 1724-26, 2 Vols. LC 68-138261. Repr. of 1927 ed. Set. 30.00x (ISBN 0-678-05165-8). Kelley.

De Fontenelle, Maurice. The Early History of French Painting. (Illus.). 121p. 1981. 39.55 (ISBN 0-930582-93-4). Gloucester Art.

De Ford, Miriam A. & Jackson, Joan S., eds. Who Was When? 3rd ed. 1976. 30.00 (ISBN 0-8242-0532-4). Wilson.

DeFord, Sara & Lott, Clarinda H. Forms of Verse: British & American. LC 77-94257. (Illus., Orig.). 1971. 24.50x (ISBN 0-89197-169-6); pap. text ed. 12.95x (ISBN 0-89197-170-X). Irvington.

--Forms of Verse, British & American. LC 77-94257. 393p. Repr. 12.95 (ISBN 0-390-26000-2). New Poets.

De Ford, Tamara. Like It Is: From Voices of Today's Youth. Faville, Mary & Otero, Ray, eds. (Illus.). 185p. 1980. pap. text ed. 9.95 (ISBN 0-931908-06-X). Sag Scriptory.

De Forest, Grant E. God in the American Schools: Religious Education in a Pluralistic Society. (Illus.). 1979. 39.45 (ISBN 0-89266-181-X). Am Classical Coll Pr.

Deforges, Regine. Confessions of O: Conversations with Pauline Reage. D'Estree, Sabine, tr. from Fr. (A Richard Seaver Bk). 1979. 9.95 o.p. (ISBN 0-670-23720-5). Viking Pr.

De Foulkes, E. Tamez & De Foulkes, I. W. Diccionario Conciso Griego-Espanol Del Nuevo Testamento. 1978. vinyl 3.50 (ISBN 3-438-06005-1, 56530). United Bible.

De Foulkes, I. W., jt. auth. see De Foulkes, E. Tamez.

Defourneaux, Mercelin. Daily Life in Spain in the Golden Age. Branch, Newton, tr. (Illus.). 1971. 12.50x (ISBN 0-8047-1036-8); pap. 4.95 (ISBN 0-8047-1029-5, SP-153). Stanford U Pr.

De France, J. J. Electrical Fundamentals, 2 pts. Incl. Pt. 1. Direct Current; Pt. 2. Indirect Current. 1969. Set. text ed. 21.95 (ISBN 0-13-247197-3). P-H.

De France, Marie. The Lais of Marie De France. Hanning, Robert & Ferrante, Joan, trs. 1978. 14.95 o.p. (ISBN 0-525-14340-8). Dutton.

--Shadow of the Hawk & Other Stories. Reeves, James, ed. LC 76-28949. (gr. 3-9). 1977. 7.95 (ISBN 0-395-28820-7, Clarion). HM.

De France, Marie see France, Marie de.

Defrancesco, Henry F. Quantitative Analysis Methods for Substantive Analysts. LC 80-11355. 448p. 1981. Repr. of 1975 ed. lib. bdg. write for info (ISBN 0-89874-139-4). Krieger.

DeFrancis, John. Annotated Quotations from Chairman Mao. LC 74-20080. (Linguistic Ser). 336p. 1975. text ed. 22.50x (ISBN 0-300-01749-9); pap. text ed. 8.95x (ISBN 0-300-01870-3). Yale U Pr.

--Character Text for Intermediate Chinese. (Illus.). 1965. pap. text ed. 8.95x (ISBN 0-300-00062-6). Yale U Pr.

--Intermediate Chinese. 1964. text ed. 35.00x (ISBN 0-300-00412-5); pap. text ed. 8.95x (ISBN 0-300-00064-2). Yale U Pr.

Defrancis, John, jt. auth. see Choi, Juliet.

DeFrancis, John, et al. Intermediate Chinese Reader, 2 Pts. text ed. 40.00x ea.; Pt. 1 1967. pap. 7.95x (ISBN 0-300-00413-3); Pt. 2 1968. pap. 8.50x (ISBN 0-300-00414-1); Pt. 1. pap. 8.95x (ISBN 0-300-00065-0); Pt. 2. pap. text ed. 8.95x (ISBN 0-300-00066-9). Yale U Pr.

DeFranco, Ellen B. TV on-off: Better Family Use of Television. 1980. pap. text ed. 7.95 (ISBN 0-8302-9128-8). Goodyear.

DeFries, J. C., jt. auth. see McClearn, G. E.

DeFriese, Gordon, et al. Strategies for the Promotion of Health. 1981. price not set (ISBN 0-88410-719-1). Ballinger Pub.

De Froment, Diana. Art at Auction Nineteen Seventy-Eight to Nineteen Seventy-Nine: Two Hundred & Forty-Fifth Season. (Illus.). 496p. 1979. 40.00 (ISBN 0-85667-063-4, Pub. by Sotheby Parke Bernet England). Biblio Dist.

De Funiack, William Q., jt. auth. see Reppy, William A.

De Gaetano, Giovanni & Garattini, Silvio, eds. Platelets: A Multidisciplinary Approach. LC 78-66352. (Monographs of the Mario Negri Institute for Pharmacological Research). 1978. 43.00 (ISBN 0-89004-252-7). Raven.

De Galiana Mingot, Tomas see Mingot, Tomas De Galiana.

De Galvez, Bernardo. Diario. 52p. 1966. pap. 5.00. South Pass Pr.

De Galway, Alberic. Assess Your Chess Fast. 1978. 17.95 (ISBN 0-7134-1055-8, Pub. by Batsford England); pap. 10.95 (ISBN 0-7134-1056-6). David & Charles.

Degani, Meir H. Astronomy Made Simple. rev. ed. LC 76-2836. 224p. 1976. pap. 3.95 (ISBN 0-385-08854-X). Doubleday.

De Garay, Alfonso L., et al, eds. Genetic & Anthropological Studies of Olympic Athletes. 1974. 24.50 (ISBN 0-12-208650-3). Acad Pr.

De Garcia, Carmen I. Raffucci see Raffucci de Garcia, Carmen I.

Degas. Degas' Drawings. (Illus.). 10.00 (ISBN 0-8446-5022-6). Peter Smith.

Degas, Edgar G. Degas Letters. Guerin, Marcel, ed. Kay, Marguerite, tr. (Illus.). 12.95 (ISBN 0-912158-53-0). Hennessey.

Degas, Hilaire G. Drawings. (Illus.). 1974. pap. 4.50 (ISBN 0-486-21233-5). Dover.

De Gasparis, Priscilla, jt. auth. see Bower, Robert T.

De Gelder, Willem. A Dutch Homesteader on the Prairies: Letters of William De Gelder, 1910-1913. Ganzevoort, Herman, tr. LC 73-85658. (Social History of Canada Ser.). (Illus.). 1973. pap. 4.50x (ISBN 0-8020-6192-3). U of Toronto Pr.

Degen, Clara, jt. ed. see Stearns, Betty.

Degenhard, William. The Regulators. 600p. Repr. of 1943 ed. 22.50 (ISBN 0-933256-22-1). Second Chance.

Degenkolb, Oris H. Concrete Box Girder Bridges. (Monograph No. 10). 1977. 19.00 (ISBN 0-685-85763-8) (ISBN 0-685-85764-6). ACI.

De Gennes, P. G. The Physics of Liquid Crystals. (International Series of Monographs on Physics). (Illus.). 367p. 1974. 55.00x (ISBN 0-19-851285-6). Oxford U Pr.

De Gennes, Pierre-Gilles. Scaling Concepts in Polymer Physics. LC 78-21314. 1979. 42.50x (ISBN 0-8014-1203-X). Cornell U Pr.

Degens, T. Friends. 160p. (gr. 7 up). 1981. 9.95 (ISBN 0-670-33051-5). Viking Pr.

De George, Fernande, jt. ed. see De George, Richard T.

De George, Richard T., ed. Semiotic Themes. (University of Kansas Humanistic Studies: No. 53). (Illus.). 284p. 1981. pap. 12.00 (ISBN 0-686-28731-2). U of KS Pubns.

De George, Richard T. & De George, Fernande, eds. The Structuralists: From Marx to Levi-Strauss. LC 76-175409. 3.50 (ISBN 0-385-00930-5, Anchor Pr). Doubleday.

Degerando, Joseph-Marie. The Observation of Savage Peoples: Considerations on Methods. Moore, F. C., tr. (Illus.). 1969. 16.50x (ISBN 0-520-01500-2). U of Cal Pr.

Degering, Etta B. Once Upon a Bible Time. Van Dolson, Bobbie J., ed. LC 76-14118. (Illus.). (gr. k-3). 1976. 4.95 (ISBN 0-8280-0052-2). Review & Herald.

Degering, F., ed. Organic Chemistry. 6th ed. 1965. pap. 4.95 (ISBN 0-06-460006-8, CO 6, COS). Har-Row.

Degge, Rogena M., jt. auth. see McFee, June K.

Degh, Linda, ed. Indiana Folklore: A Reader. LC 79-2970. (Illus.). 320p. 1980. 20.00x (ISBN 0-253-10986-8); pap. 7.95x (ISBN 0-253-20239-6). Ind U Pr.

Deghan, Bijan & Webster, Grady L. Morphology & Infrageneric Relationships of the Genus "Jatropha" (Euphorbiaceae) LC 77-83116. (Publications in Botany Ser.: Vol. 74). 1979. 11.50x (ISBN 0-520-09585-5). U of Cal Pr.

De Ghelderode, Michel see Ghelderode, Michel De.

De Gheyn, Jacob. The Exercise of Arms. LC 77-146168. (Illus.). 1976. Repr. of 1607 ed. 65.00 o.p. (ISBN 0-07-016237-9); Edition Of 10 Copies, Hand Colored & Illuminated In Gold & Silver. 1000.00 o.p. (ISBN 0-686-15687-0). Arma Pr.

DeGiacomo, F. P. Chiropractic Analysis Through Palpation. McDonnell, James, ed. (Illus.). 192p. 1980. 12.00 (ISBN 0-938470-00-0). NY Chiro Coll.

De Giorgio, A., ed. Criteria for Selecting Appropriate Technologies Under Different Cultural, Technical & Social Conditions: IFAC Symposium, Bari, Italy, May 21-22, 1979. (IFAC Proceedings Ser.). (Illus.). 320p. 1980. 66.00 (ISBN 0-08-024455-6). Pergamon.

Degiorgio, V., et al, eds. Light Scattering in Liquids & Macromolecular Solutions. 290p. 1980. pap. 35.00 (ISBN 0-306-40558-X, Plenum Pr). Plenum Pub.

Degler, Carl N. Affluence & Anxiety: America Since Nineteen Forty-Five. 2nd ed. 210p. 1975. pap. 7.95x (ISBN 0-673-07956-2). Scott F.

--The Age of the Economic Revolution: 1876-1900. 2nd ed. 1977. pap. 7.95x (ISBN 0-673-07967-8). Scott F.

--At Odds: Women & the Family in America from the Revolution to the Present. 544p. 1981. pap. 8.95 (ISBN 0-19-502934-8, GB 645, GB). Oxford U Pr.

--The Other South: Southern Dissenters in the Nineteenth Century. 1975. pap. 3.95x o.p. (ISBN 0-06-131856-6, TB1856, Torch). Har-Row.

--Out of Our Past: The Forces That Shaped Modern America. rev. ed. LC 77-88637. 1970. pap. 5.95 (ISBN 0-06-090002-4, CN2, CN). Har-Row.

--Out of Our Past: The Forces That Shaped Modern America. rev. ed. 1970. 12.50 o.s.i. (ISBN 0-06-011012-0, HarpT). Har-Row.

Degler, Carl N., et al. The Democratic Experience, 2 vols. 5th ed. 1981. pap. text ed. 14.95x (ISBN 0-673-15450-5); Vol. 1. pap. text ed. 9.95x (ISBN 0-673-15451-3); Vol. 2. pap. text ed. 9.95x (ISBN 0-673-15452-1). Scott F.

De Gohm, Richard De see Van De Gohm, Richard.

De Golia, Jack. Everglades: The Story Behind the Scenery. DenDooven, Gweneth R., ed. LC 78-71200. (Illus.). 1978. 7.95 (ISBN 0-916122-56-5); pap. 3.50 (ISBN 0-916122-55-7). K C Pubns.

De Gomez, Madeleine Angelique Poisson see Poisson De Gomez, Madeleine Angelique.

De Goncourt, Edmond. Elisa. Crosland, M., tr. from Fr. 190p. 1975. Repr. of 1959 ed. 16.50 (ISBN 0-86527-242-5). Fertig.

--La Faustin. Monkshood, G., tr. from Fr. 1976. Repr. of 1906 ed. 16.00 (ISBN 0-86527-267-0). Fertig.

De Goncourt, Edmond & De Goncourt, Jules. Sister Philomene. Ensor, L., tr. 292p. 1975. Repr. of 1890 ed. 16.50 (ISBN 0-86527-304-9). Fertig.

De Goncourt, Jules, jt. auth. see De Goncourt, Edmond.

De Gourmont, Remy. The Natural Philosophy of Love. Pound, Ezra, tr. 170p. 1972. pap. 1.25 o.s.i. (ISBN 0-02-064950-9, Collier). Macmillan.

De Gouy, Louis P. The Bread Tray: Nearly 600 Recipes for Homemade Breads, Rolls, Muffins, & Biscuits. LC 73-88329. vii, 463p. 1974. pap. 4.50 (ISBN 0-486-23000-7). Dover.

DeGowin, Elmer L. & DeGowin, Richard L. Bedside Diagnostic Examination. 3rd ed. (Illus.). 1976. pap. text ed. 16.95 (ISBN 0-02-328050-6). Macmillan.

DeGowin, Richard L., jt. auth. see DeGowin, Elmer L.

De Goyon De La Plombanie, H. L' Homme En Societe Ou Nouvelles Vues Politiques et Economiques Pour Porter la Population Au Plus Haut Degre En France. (Fr.). 1977. Repr. of 1763 ed. lib. bdg. 47.50x o.p. (ISBN 0-8287-0386-8). Clearwater Pub.

DeGraaff, A., et al. Hope for the Family. 1971. pap. 1.25 o.p. (ISBN 0-686-11978-9). Wedge Pub.

De Graaff, John H. Van see Van De Graaff, John H., et al.

Degras, Jane. Calendar of Soviet Documents on Foreign Policy, 1917-1941. LC 79-4912. 1981. Repr. of 1948 ed. 19.75 (ISBN 0-88355-962-5). Hyperion Conn.

DeGrave, Louise. From This Day Forward: Staying Married When No One Else Is & Other Reckless Acts. 228p. 1981. 10.95 (ISBN 0-316-17930-2). Little.

De Gravelles, William D. & Kelley, John H. Injuries Following Rear-End Automobile Collisions. (Illus.). 256p. 1969. photocopy ed. spiral 22.75 (ISBN 0-398-00414-5). C C Thomas.

Degravelles, William D., Jr. & Kelley, John H. Injuries Following Rear-End Automobile Collisions. 256p. 1969. pap. 16.00 spiral o.p. (ISBN 0-398-00418-8). C C Thomas.

De Grazia, Victoria. The Culture of Consent: Mass Organization of Leisure in Fascist Italy. LC 80-24361. (Illus.). 304p. Date not set. price not set (ISBN 0-521-23705-X). Cambridge U Pr.

De Graziani, Vincenzo G. The Franco-German Coalition & the Emergence of a New International Superpower: Its Effects Upon the Future Course of History. (Illus.). 1979. deluxe ed. 47.75 (ISBN 0-930008-31-6). Inst Econ Pol.

De Greene, Kenyon. Sociotechnical Systems: Factors in Analysis, Design & Management. (Illus.). 416p. 1973. ref. ed. 18.95 (ISBN 0-13-821553-7). P-H.

DeGregorio, George. Joe DiMaggio: An Informal Biography. LC 80-6159. 272p. 1981. 12.95 (ISBN 0-8128-2777-5). Stein & Day.

Degremont. Water Treatment Handbook. 5th ed. LC 79-87503. 1186p. 1979. 73.95x (ISBN 0-470-26749-6). Halsted Pr.

Degrood, David. Dialectics & Revolution. (Philosophical Currents Ser.: No. 25). 1980. pap. text ed. 27.50x (ISBN 9-0603-2154-5). Humanities.

--Radical Currents in Contemporary Philosophy, Vol. II. 1981. write for info. Fireside Bks.

Degrood, David H. Dialectics & Revolution, Vol. 1. (Philosophical Currents Ser.: No. 21). 1978. pap. text ed. 23.00x (ISBN 90-6032-097-2). Humanities.

--Dialectics & Revolution, Vol. 2. (Philosophical Currents Ser.: No. 25). (Orig.). 1978. pap. text ed. 28.50x (ISBN 90-6032-154-5). Humanities.

--Philosophies of Essence: An Examination of the Category of Essence. 2nd ed. (Praxis Ser.: No. 1). 1976. pap. text ed. 17.25x (ISBN 90-6032-076-X). Humanities.

De Groot, J. J. Le Code Du Mahayana En Chine: Amsterdam, 1892. LC 78-74288. (Oriental Religions Ser.: Vol. 15). 281p. 1980. lib. bdg. 33.00 (ISBN 0-8240-3917-3). Garland Pub.

--Sectarianism & Religious Persecution in China: A Page in the History of Religions, 2 vols. 872p. 1972. Repr. of 1903 ed. 55.00x (ISBN 0-7165-2035-4, Pub. by Irish Academic Pr Ireland). Biblio Dist.

DeGroot, Leslie J. & Stanbury, John B. The Thyroid Diseases. 4th ed. LC 75-17916. 823p. 1975. 51.95 (ISBN 0-471-20530-3, Pub. by Wiley-Medimedia Publications). Wiley.

Degroot, Morris. Probability & Statistics. LC 74-19691. (Behavioral Science Quantitative Methods Ser). (Illus.). 624p. 1975. text ed. 20.95 (ISBN 0-201-01503-X); sol. manual 7.95 (ISBN 0-201-01509-9). A-W.

De Groot, Silvia W. Djuka Society & Social Change: History of an Attempt to Develop a Bush Negro Community in Surinam, 1917-1926. 1969. text ed. 19.25x (ISBN 90-232-0108-6). Humanities.

De Gros, J. H. Candy Cookbook. LC 59-13673. (Illus.). 1976. pap. 2.95 o.p. (ISBN 0-668-04003-3). Arco.

De Grouchy, Jean & Turleau, Catherine. Clinical Atlas of Human Chromosomes. LC 77-2282. 1977. 49.95 (ISBN 0-471-01704-3, Pub. by Wiley Medical). Wiley.

De Gubernatis, Angelo see Gubernatis, Angelo De.

Deguileville, Guillaume de. The Pylgremage of the Sowle. Lydgate, J., tr. LC 74-28845. (English Experience Ser.: No. 726). 1975. Repr. of 1483 ed. 24.00 (ISBN 90-221-0740-X). Walter J Johnson.

De Guillebon, Regine P. Porcelain of Paris, 1770-1850. LC 72-80541. (Illus.). 376p. 1972. 35.00 o.s.i. (ISBN 0-8027-0395-X). Walker & Co.

DeGuilmo, Joseph M. Electricity-Electronics: Principles & Applications. LC 79-54909. (Electronics Technology Ser.). (Illus.). 672p. (Orig.). 1981. pap. 19.60 (ISBN 0-8273-1686-0); price not set instr's. guide (ISBN 0-8273-1687-9). Delmar.

De Guinard, Frances. From Brass Hat to Bowler Hat. 1979. 19.95 (ISBN 0-241-10165-4, Pub. by Hamish Hamilton England). David & Charles.

DeHaan, M. R. & Bosch, H. G. Bread for Each Day. large print ed. 1979. 8.95 (ISBN 0-310-23267-8); 7.95 (ISBN 0-310-23260-0). Zondervan.

DeHaan, Martin R. Adventures in Faith: Studies in the Life of Abraham. 1979. pap. 3.95 (ISBN 0-310-23251-1). Zondervan.

De Haan, Martin R. Daniel the Prophet. 1947. 10.95 (ISBN 0-310-23320-8). Zondervan.

DeHaan, Martin R. Five Hundred & Eight Answers to Bible Questions. 1979. pap. 5.95 (ISBN 0-310-23341-0). Zondervan.

De Haan, Martin R. Law or Grace. 1965. pap. 4.95 (ISBN 0-310-23401-8). Zondervan.

--Ruth: Romance of Redemption. 4.95 (ISBN 0-310-23451-4). Zondervan.

--Simon Peter. 1954. 4.95 (ISBN 0-310-23481-6). Zondervan.

De Haan, Martin R. & Bosch, H. G. Our Daily Bread. 7.95 o.p. (ISBN 0-310-23410-7). Zondervan.

DeHaan, Richard. El Culto a Satanas. De la Cerda, Rodolfo, tr. from Eng. 136p. (Orig., Span.). 1975. pap. 2.25 (ISBN 0-89922-059-2). Edit Caribe.

Dehaan, Richard W. How to Tell the Truth. 1977. pap. 2.50 (ISBN 0-88207-750-3). Victor Bks.

De Haan, Richard W. Israel & the Nations in Prophecy. LC 68-22171. 1971. pap. 1.50 o.p. (ISBN 0-310-23512-X). Zondervan.

DeHaan, Richard W. Pray: God Is Listening. 80p. (Orig.). 1980. pap. 1.95 (ISBN 0-310-23542-1). Zondervan.

DeHaan, Robert L., jt. auth. see Nason, Alvin.

DeHaller, Rodolphe, jt. ed. see Junod, Alain F.

De Hartog, Jan. The Flight of the Henny. LC 80-8228. 265p. Date not set. 10.95 (ISBN 0-06-010983-1, HarpT). Har-Row. Postponed.

De Harven, Emile. Caminos Peligrosos. LC 75-38833. (Illus.). 140p. 1976. pap. 4.25 (ISBN 0-88436-259-0). EMC.

--Chemins Dangereux. LC 75-38836. (Illus.). 140p. 1976. pap. 4.25 (ISBN 0-88436-260-4). EMC.

--Suivez la Piste. 1972. pap. 3.50 (ISBN 0-912022-30-2). EMC.

De Havenon, Andre, ed. A Touch of Paris: A Selective Guide to Paris in Plain English. (Illus.). 255p. (Orig.). 1981. pap. 9.95 (ISBN 0-933982-14-3). Bradt Ent.

Dehejia, Harsha V. The Allergy Book. 184p. 1981. 10.95 (ISBN 0-442-21887-7). Van Nos Reinhold.

De Hirsch, Katrine, et al. Predicting Reading Failure. (Illus.). 1966. 8.95 o.s.i. (ISBN 0-06-031630-6, HarpT). Har-Row.

De Hita, Arcipreste see Arcipreste de Hita.

De Hoog, F. R., jt. ed. see Anderson, R. S.

De Hunter, Elena Mellado see Mellado De Hunter, Elena.

Dei-Anang, Michael. The Administration of Ghana's Foreign Relations 1957-65: A Personal Memoir. (Commonwealth Papers Ser: No. 17). 96p. 1975. pap. text ed. 8.75x (ISBN 0-485-17617-3, Athlone Pr). Humanities.

Deighton, Lee. Fight for the Valley. 160p. 1981. pap. 1.75 (ISBN 0-345-29076-3). Ballantine.

--Tomahawk. 156p. 1981. pap. 1.75 (ISBN 0-345-29431-9). Ballantine.

--You'll Never Hang Me. 160p. 1981. pap. 1.75 (ISBN 0-345-29119-0). Ballantine.

Deighton, Lee C. Vocabulary Development in the Classroom. LC 59-8372. 1959. pap. text ed. 3.75 (ISBN 0-8077-1236-1). Tchrs Coll.

Deighton, Len. The Billion Dollar Brain. 1980. pap. 2.25 (ISBN 0-425-04470-X). Berkley Pub.

--An Expensive Place to Die. 1980. pap. 2.25 o.p. (ISBN 0-425-04470-X). Berkley Pub.

--Ipcress File. 1976. pap. 1.95 (ISBN 0-345-28439-9). Ballantine.

--SS-GB. 1980. pap. 2.95 (ISBN 0-345-29317-7). Ballantine.

--XPD. LC 80-7629. 384p. 1981. 12.95 (ISBN 0-394-51258-8). Knopf.

Deihl, David. Quill. 1980. pap. 1.75 (ISBN 0-505-51472-9). Tower Bks.

Deindorfer, Robert G. Positive Fishing. LC 79-67600. 224p. 1981. 10.95 (ISBN 0-87223-660-9). Seaview Bks.

Deiros, P. A. Que Paso Con Estos Pecados? 1979. pap. 1.95 (ISBN 0-311-42063-X). Casa Bautista.

Deiros, Pablo, compiled by. Figuras De Plata. 1978. pap. 3.15 (ISBN 0-311-42053-2, Edit Mundo). Casa Bautista.

Deiros, Pablo A., tr. see Duval, Evelyn M.

D'Eisenberg, Reis. The Classical Riding School. (Illus.). 1979. 9.95 o.p. (ISBN 0-670-22509-6, The Vendome Pr.). Viking Pr.

Deisher, Joe, jt. auth. see Chuang Shu Chi.

Deisher, Joe, jt. auth. see Chuang Shu Chih.

Deiss, Joseph J. The Roman Years of Margaret Fuller. (Illus.). 352p. 1976. pap. 4.95 o.s.i. (ISBN 0-690-01017-6, TYC-T). T Y Crowell.

Deissman, Adolf. Light from the Ancient East. (Twin Brooks Ser). 1978. pap. 10.95 (ISBN 0-8010-2886-8). Baker Bk.

Deissmann, G. Adolf. Bible Studies. 385p. 1979. 14.95 (ISBN 0-88469-146-2). BMH Bks.

Deist, Wilhelm. The Wehrmacht & German Rearmament. 230p. 1981. 30.00x (ISBN 0-8020-2423-8). U of Toronto Pr.

Deitch, Gene. A Visit from a Turtle. LC 74-469. (ps-3). 1974. 2.95 o.p. (ISBN 0-531-02727-9); PLB 4.90 o.p. (ISBN 0-531-02726-0). Watts.

Deitch, Lillian & Weinstein, David. Prepaid Legal Services: Socio-Economic Impacts. LC 76-5582. 1976. 19.50 (ISBN 0-669-00659-9). Lexington Bks.

Deitchman, Seymour J. New Technology & Military Power: General Purpose Military Forces for the 1980's & Beyond. (Special Studies in Military Affairs). 1979. lib. bdg. 28.00x (ISBN 0-89158-358-0). Westview.

Deitel, Harvey, jt. auth. see Lorin, Harold.

Deitel, Mervyn. Nutrition in Clinical Surgery. (Illus.). 284p. 1980. 43.95 (ISBN 0-683-02449-3). Williams & Wilkins.
Deitrick & Bizzell. Plaid for Advanced Accounting. 1981. price not set (ISBN 0-256-02398-0, 01-1435-01). Learning Syst. Postponed.
Deitzer, Bernard & Shilliff, Karl. Incidents in Modern Business. new ed. 200p. 1975. pap. text ed. 10.95x (ISBN 0-675-08785-6). Merrill.
Deitzer, Bernard A. & Shilliff, Karl A. Contemporary Management Incidents. LC 76-44998. (Management Ser.). 1977. pap. text ed. 9.95 (ISBN 0-88244-123-X). Grid Pub.
Deitzer, Bernard A., et al. Contemporary Management Concepts. LC 79-11974. 1979. text ed. 18.50 (ISBN 0-88244-187-6). Grid Pub.
De Jager, C., ed. The Brightest Stars. (Geophysics & Astrophysics Monographs: No. 19). 472p. 1981. PLB 73.50 (ISBN 90-277-1109-7, Pub. by D. Reidel); pap. 1.50 (ISBN 90-277-1109-7). Kluwer Boston.
De Jager, C., ed. see Bilderberg Conference - Arnhem - Holland - 1968.
De Jager, E. J. Contemporary African Art in South Africa. (Illus.). 168p. 1973. text ed. 22.50x o.p. (ISBN 0-86977-025-X). Verry.
DeJ Ellis, Maria see Ellis, Maria deJ.
Dejene, Alemneh. Non-Formal Education As a Strategy in Development: Comparative Analysis of Rural Development Projects. LC 80-5882. 131p. 1980. lib. bdg. 16.25 (ISBN 0-8191-1346-8); pap. text ed. 7.75 (ISBN 0-8191-1347-6). U Pr of Amer.
De Jim, Strange. Visioning. LC 79-66208. (Illus., Orig.). 1979. pap. 5.95 (ISBN 0-9605308-0-0). Ash-Kar Pr.
DeJoia, Alex & Stenton, Adrian. Terms in Systemic Linguistics. LC 80-5089. 1980. 17.95 (ISBN 0-312-79180-1). St Martin.
De Joinville, Jean, jt. auth. see De Villehardouin, Geoffrey.
Dejon, William L. Principles of Management: Text & Cases. LC 77-75123. 1978. 18.95 (ISBN 0-8053-2336-8); instr's man. 8.95 (ISBN 0-8053-2337-6). Benjamin-Cummings.
De Jong, Alexander C. An Introduction to Bible Truths. 1978. pap. 2.45 (ISBN 0-8010-2887-6). Baker Bk.
De Jong, Constance & Glass, Philip. Satyagraha: M. K. Gandhi in South Africa, 1893-1914. (Illus., Orig.). 1980. pap. 5.00 (ISBN 0-918746-04-3). Standard Edns.
De Jong, David C. Squirrel & the Harp. (Illus.). (gr. k-3). 1966. 3.95g o.s.i. (ISBN 0-02-726530-7). Macmillan.
DeJong, Dola. The Field. Perkins, Maxwell, ed. Van Duyn, A. V., tr. from Dutch. LC 79-84437. 1979. 15.95 (ISBN 0-933256-02-7); pap. 7.95 (ISBN 0-933256-05-1). Second Chance.
De Jong, Dola. House on Charlton Street. LC 62-9644. (Illus.). (gr. 3-7). 1962. pap. 0.95 o.p. (ISBN 0-684-12802-0, SBF 20, ScribT). Scribner.
De Jong, Frits J., et al, eds. Quadrilingual Economics Dictionary. 1981. lib. bdg. 48.00 (ISBN 90-247-2243-8, Pub. by Martinus Nijhoff). Kluwer Boston.
De Jong, Gerald F. The Dutch in America, 1609-1974. (The Immigrant Heritage of America Ser). 1975. lib. bdg. 12.50 (ISBN 0-8057-3214-4). Twayne.
De Jong, Gordon F. Appalachian Fertility Decline. LC 68-12966. (Illus.). 154p. 1968. pap. 6.75x (ISBN 0-8131-1160-9). U Pr of Ky.
De Jong, H. G. Bungenberg see Booij, H. L. & Bungenberg De Jong, H. G.
De Jong, Henry W., jt. auth. see Jacquemin, Alex.
De Jong, J. L., jt. auth. see Falb, P. L.
De Jong, Kees A. & Scholten, Robert, eds. Gravity & Tectonics. LC 73-1580. (Illus.). 502p. 1973. 47.50 (ISBN 0-471-20305-X, Pub. by Wiley-Interscience). Wiley.
De Jong, Marvin L. Programming & Interfacing the Sixty-Five-o-Two, with Experiments. LC 79-67130. 1980. pap. 14.95 (ISBN 0-672-21651-5). Bobbs.
DeJong, Meindert. The Almost All-White Rabbity Cat. LC 72-178599. (Illus.). 128p. (gr. 3-6). 1972. 7.95 (ISBN 0-02-726560-9). Macmillan.
--Along Came a Dog. LC 57-9265. (Illus.). 192p. (gr. 4-7). 1980. pap. 1.95 (ISBN 0-06-440114-6, Trophy). Har-Row.
De Jong, Meindert. Easter Cat. LC 78-141933. (Illus.). (gr. 4-6). 1971. 5.95g o.s.i. (ISBN 0-02-726550-1). Macmillan.
DeJong, Meindert. Horse Came Running. LC 71-99119. (Illus.). (gr. 4 up). 1970. 8.95 (ISBN 0-02-726540-4). Macmillan.
--Horse Came Running. LC 71-99119. 192p. (gr. 5-7). 1972. pap. 1.25 o.s.i. (ISBN 0-02-042800-6, Collier). Macmillan.
--Shadrach. LC 53-5250. (Illus.). 192p. (gr. 3-6). 1980. pap. 1.95 (ISBN 0-06-440115-4, Trophy). Har-Row.
DeJong, Peter, ed. Pest Management in Transition. LC 79-53138. (A Westview Replica Edition Ser.). 1979. lib. bdg. 19.00x (ISBN 0-89158-679-2). Westview.
De Jong, Ralph. The Life of Mary Magdalene in the Paintings of the Great Masters, 2 vols. (Illus.). 1979. deluxe ed. 69.75 (ISBN 0-930582-30-6). Gloucester Art.
De Jong, Tine H. Amse see Amse-De Jong, Tine H.
De Jonge, M. The Testaments of the Twelve Patriarchs: A Study of Their Text, Composition & Origin. (Van Gorcum's Theologische Bibliotheek: No. 25). 1975. pap. text ed. 24.50x (ISBN 90-232-1339-4). Humanities.
De Jonge, Marinus. Jesus: Stranger from Heaven & Son of God. Steely, John E., ed. LC 77-9984. (Society of Biblical Literature. Sources for Biblical Studies). 1977. pap. 7.50 (ISBN 0-89130-134-8, 060311). Scholars Pr Ca.
DeJose, Grace. The Hempstead Plan: Sensible Approach to Dieting & Nutrition. (Illus.). 1980. 7.50 (ISBN 0-682-49516-6). Exposition.
De Jourlet, Marie. Legacy of Windhaven. (The Windhaven Saga). 1978. pap. 2.75 (ISBN 0-523-41267-3). Pinnacle Bks.
--Return to Windhaven. (Windhaven). 1978. pap. 2.50 (ISBN 0-523-40348-8). Pinnacle Bks.
--Storm Over Windhaven. 1977. pap. 2.75 (ISBN 0-523-41464-1). Pinnacle Bks.
--Windhaven Plantation. (Orig.). 1977. pap. 2.75 (ISBN 0-523-41472-2). Pinnacle Bks.
--Windhaven's Peril. (Windhaven Ser.). 1979. pap. 2.75 (ISBN 0-523-41258-4). Pinnacle Bks.
De Jouvenel, Bertrand see Jouvenel, Bertrand de.
De Jussieu-Pontcarral, Pierre. Encyclopedie de l'electricite, 2 vols. (Illus.). 1970. 82.50x ea. Larousse.
De Kay, George C., ed. see Nash, Jay R.
De Kay, George C., ed. see Ogle, Jane.
Dekay, Ormonde. N'heures Souris Rames: The Coucy Castle Manuscript. (Clarkson N. Potter Bks.). 1980. 7.95 (ISBN 0-517-54081-9). Crown.
De Kay, Ormonde, Jr. Meet Andrew Jackson. (Step-up Books Ser.). (Illus.). (gr. 2-6). 1967. PLB 4.99 (ISBN 0-394-90066-9, BYR). Random.
--Meet Theodore Roosevelt. (Step-up Books Ser.). (Illus.). (gr. 2-6). 1967. PLB 4.99 (ISBN 0-394-90065-0, BYR). Random.
Dekeijzer, Arne J. & Kaplan, Frederic M. The China Guidebook: 1980-81 Edition. rev. ed. LC 80-7860. (Illus.). 448p. 1980. 14.95 (ISBN 0-690-01953-X); pap. 10.95 (ISBN 0-690-01955-6). Lippincott & Crowell.
DeKerval, Alastor, pseud. Amrita - Liber CCCXLIII. LC 77-8311. 1980. 45.00 (ISBN 0-913576-29-8); deluxe ed. (ISBN 0-913576-19-0). Thelema Pubns.
Dekieffer, Donald. How to Lobby Congress: A Guide for the Citizen Lobbyist. 228p. 1981. 12.95 (ISBN 0-396-07965-2); pap. 7.95 (ISBN 0-396-07969-5). Dodd.
DeKiewiet, C. W. History of South Africa, Social & Economic. 1941. pap. 14.95x (ISBN 0-19-821638-6). Oxford U Pr.
De Kimpe, C. R., tr. see Duchaufour, Philippe.
Dekker, George & McWilliams, John P., eds. Fenimore Cooper: The Critical Heritage. (The Critical Heritage Ser). 318p. 1973. 27.00x (ISBN 0-7100-7635-5). Routledge & Kegan.
Dekker, H. C., et al. Planning in a Dutch & a Yugoslav Steelworks: A Comparative Study. (Illus.). 1976. pap. text ed. 23.00x (ISBN 90-6032-078-6). Humanities.
Dekker, J., ed. see Symposia in Pure Mathematics-New York-1961.
Dekker, Julian. How to Master the Forces of Your Imagination for the Pursuit of Your Scientific Objectives. (Illus.). 1978. deluxe ed. 37.50 (ISBN 0-930582-07-1). Gloucester Art.
Dekker, Thomas. Dramatic Works of Thomas Dekker, 4 vols. Bowers, Fredson, ed. 1953-61. Vol. 1. 72.00 (ISBN 0-521-04808-7); Vol. 2. 72.00 (ISBN 0-521-04809-5); Vol. 3. 72.00 (ISBN 0-521-04810-9); Vol. 4. 72.00 (ISBN 0-521-04811-7). Cambridge U Pr.
De Kock, M. A. Dynamic Bronchoscopy. 1977. 59.60 (ISBN 0-387-08109-7). Springer-Verlag.
DeKock, M. H. Central Banking. 4th ed. LC 74-78896. 318p. 1974. 25.00 (ISBN 0-312-12740-5). St Martin.
DeKornfeld, Thomas J. & Finch, Jay S. Respiratory Care Case Studies, Vol. 1. 2nd ed. 1976. spiral bdg. 12.75 (ISBN 0-87488-019-X). Med Exam.
DeKornfeld, Thomas J., ed. Selected Papers in Inhalation Therapy. 416p. 1971. spiral bdg. 12.00 o.p. (ISBN 0-87488-523-X). Med Exam.
--Selected Papers in Respiratory Therapy. 2nd ed. 1979. pap. 24.00 (ISBN 0-87488-525-6). Med Exam.
DeKornfeld, Thomas J. & Detmar, Michael W., eds. Anesthesiology. 5th ed. LC 61-66847. 1980. pap. 15.00. Med Exam.
Dekornfeld, Thomas J., et al. Respiratory Therapy Examination Review Book, Vol. 2. 2nd ed. Orig. Title: Inhalation Therapy Examination Review Book, Vol. 2. 1974. spiral bdg. 9.50 (ISBN 0-87488-344-X). Med Exam.
DeKorte, Juliann. Finally Home. (Illus.). 1977. 5.95 o.p. (ISBN 0-8007-0934-9). Revell.
DeKosky, Robert K. Knowledge & Cosmos: Development & Decline of the Medieval Perspective. LC 79-66226. 1979. text ed. 18.50 (ISBN 0-8191-0814-6); pap. text ed. 12.00 (ISBN 0-8191-0815-4). U Pr of Amer.
Dekoster, Lester, ed. Locke's Second Treatise of Civil Government. 1978. pap. 2.95 o.p. (ISBN 0-8028-1732-7). Eerdmans.
Dekovic, Gene. Self-Reliance. LC 75-12544. (Funk & W Bk.). (Illus.). 96p. 1975. 9.95 o.s.i. (ISBN 0-308-10203-7, TYC-T); pap. 3.95 o.s.i. (ISBN 0-308-10204-5, TYC-T). T Y Crowell.
Dekoxher, Lester, ed. The Federalist Papers. LC 75-42310. pap. 2.95 o.p. (ISBN 0-8028-1620-7). Eerdmans.
Dekretser, David, jt. ed. see Burger, Henry.
DeKruyter, Arthur H. Complete Candlelight Services for Christmas, No. 2. 48p. 1980. pap. 2.95 (ISBN 0-310-42031-8, 10646P). Zondervan.
de la, Walter Mare see De La Mare, Walter.
Delacato, Carl H. The Elementary School of the Future: A Guide for Parents. 108p. 1969. pap. 11.50 photocopy ed. spiral (ISBN 0-398-00419-6). C C Thomas.
--Neurological Organization & Reading. 200p. 1973. pap. 16.75 photocopy ed. spiral (ISBN 0-398-00420-X). C C Thomas.
--A New Start for the Child with Reading Problems. rev. ed. 1977. 8.95 o.p. (ISBN 0-679-50760-4); pap. 4.95 o.p. (ISBN 0-679-50765-5). McKay.
--The Treatment & Prevention of Reading Problems: The Neuro-Psychological Approach. 136p. 1971. pap. 14.50 photocopy ed. spiral (ISBN 0-398-00421-8). C C Thomas.
Delacato, Carl H., Dr. The Ultimate Stranger: The Autistic Child. LC 73-9019. 240p. 1974. 6.95 o.p. (ISBN 0-385-01074-5). Doubleday.
De la Cerda, Rodolfo, tr. see DeHaan, Richard.
De Lachapelle-Skubly, Jacqueline, jt. auth. see Rassias, John A.
De La Chavignerie, Emile B. & Auvray, Louis. Dictionnaire General, 5 vols. Rosenblum, Robert, ed. LC 78-68412. 1979. Repr. of 1885 ed. lib. bdg. 275.00 (ISBN 0-8240-3539-9). Garland Pub.
De Laclos, Choderlos see Laclos, Choderlos de.
Delacorte, Toni, et al. Free Press. 240p. (Orig.). 1981. pap. 9.95 (ISBN 0-936602-15-5). Harbor Pub CA.
--Free Press: A Do It Yourself Guide to Promote Your Interests, Organization or Business. 240p. 1981. 9.95 (ISBN 0-936602-15-5). Harbor Pub CA.
Delacour, Jean. The Waterfowl of the World, 4 vols. LC 73-76659. (Illus.). 284p. 1974. slipcased 150.00 o.p. (ISBN 0-668-02970-6). Arco.
--Wild Pigeons & Doves. rev. ed. (Illus.). 189p. 1980. 9.95 (ISBN 0-87666-968-2, AP-6810). TFH Pubns.
Delacour, Jean-Baptiste. Glimpses of the Beyond. 214p. 1974. 6.95 o.p. (ISBN 0-440-03287-3). Delacorte.
Delacroix, Eugene. The Journal of Eugene Delacroix. Freedberg, Sydney J., ed. LC 77-19378. (Connoisseurship Criticism & Art History Ser.: Vol. 9). (Illus.). 1980. lib. bdg. 44.00 (ISBN 0-8240-3266-7). Garland Pub.
Delacroix, Eugene & Manet, Edouard. The Complete Illustrations from Delacroix's "Faust" & Manet's "Raven". (Illus.). 64p. (Orig.). 1981. pap. price not set (ISBN 0-486-24127-0). Dover.
De la Croix, Horst & Tansey, Richard G. Art Through the Ages, 2 vol. ed. 7th ed. Incl. Vol. 1. Ancient Medieval & Non-European Art. 481p. pap. text ed. 11.95 (ISBN 0-686-65008-5); Vol. 2. Renaissance & Modern Art. 489p. pap. text ed. 4.95 (ISBN 0-686-65009-3). 1980. write for info. study guide (HC). HarBraceJ.
Delacruz, Chester, jt. auth. see Sewell, George E.
De La Cruz, F. & LaVeck, G. D., eds. Human Sexuality & the Mentally Retarded. LC 72-92057. 1973. 12.50 (ISBN 0-87630-063-8). Brunner-Mazel.
De la Cruz, Felix see Lubs, Herbert & Cruz, Felix de la.
De La Cruz, Felix F., jt. auth. see Davidson, Richard L.
De Laczay, Etelka, tr. see Hajdu, Tibor.
De Ladebat, Monique P. The Village That Slept. (Children's Literature Ser.). 1980. PLB 8.95 (ISBN 0-8398-2610-9). Gregg.
De La Falaise, Maxime. Food in Vogue. LC 79-8920. (Illus.). 336p. 1980. 15.95 (ISBN 0-385-09220-2). Doubleday.
De La Fayette, Marie-Madeleine. La Princesse de Cleves. (Documentation thematique). (Illus., Fr.). pap. 2.95 (ISBN 0-685-14059-8, 143). Larousse.
De La Fontein, Charles B. Conversations with My Soul. (Intimate Life of Man Library). (Illus.). 1979. 37.50 (ISBN 0-89266-185-2). Am Classical Coll Pr.
De La Fronde, Eugene. An Introduction to Psychology. (The Library of Scientific Psychology). (Illus.). 1979. 27.45 (ISBN 0-89266-178-X). Am Classical Coll Pr.
De La Fuente, Tomas. Auxiliares Basicos Para el Estudio Biblico. (Illus.). 424p. (Span.). 1980. pap. 4.80 (ISBN 0-311-42067-2). Casa Bautista.
De La Fuente, Tomas, tr. see Cowan, Marvin W.
De La Fuente, Tomas R. Jesus Nos Habla Por Medio De Sus Parabolas. 1978. 2.40 (ISBN 0-311-04344-5). Casa Bautista.
DeLage. ABC Triplets at the Zoo. PLB 5.49 (ISBN 0-8116-4357-3). Garrard.
DeLage, Ida. The Pilgrim Children on the Mayflower. LC 79-21812. (Ida DeLage Bks.). (Illus.). (gr. 1-5). 1980. PLB 5.58 (ISBN 0-8116-4315-8). Garrard.
Delagi, Edward F. & Perotto, Aldo. Anatomic Guide for Electromyographer: The Limbs. 2nd ed. (Illus.). 224p. 1980. 18.75 (ISBN 0-398-03951-8). C C Thomas.
De Laguna, Asela Rodriguez-Seda see Rodriguez-Seda de Laguna, Asela.
De La Haye, Yves, ed. see Marx, Karl & Frederick, Engels.
Delaisse, L. M. A Century of Dutch Manuscript Illumination. (California Studies in the History of Art: No. VI). (Illus.). 1968. 52.50x (ISBN 0-520-00315-2). U of Cal Pr.
De La Jonchere, E. L. Systeme D'un Nouveau Gouvernment En France, 2 vols. (Fr.). 1977. Repr. of 1720 ed. lib. bdg. 75.00x o.p. (ISBN 0-8287-0492-9). Clearwater Pub.
Delalande, Michel-Richard. De Profundis: Grand Motet for Soloists, Chorus, Woodwinds, Strings, & Continuo. Anthony, James R., ed. LC 79-29740. viii, 173p. 1981. write for info. (ISBN 0-8078-1439-3). U of NC Pr.
De La Luz, Antonio. La Empresa y la Funcion De Personal. 7.50 (ISBN 0-8477-2620-7); pap. 6.25 (ISBN 0-8477-2609-6). U of PR Pr.
De La Mare, Walter. Animal Stories. (Encore Ser.). (Illus.). (gr. 3-7). 1940. 5.95 (ISBN 0-684-20797-4, ScribJ). Scribner.
--Peacock Pie. 1958. 8.95 (ISBN 0-571-04683-5, Pub. by Faber & Faber); pap. 3.50 (ISBN 0-571-05609-1). Merrimack Bk Serv.
--Peacock Pie. (Fanfares Ser.). (gr. 4 up). 1980. pap. 3.25 (ISBN 0-571-18014-0, Pub. by Faber & Faber). Merrimack Bk Serv.
--Selected Poems. 1973. pap. 5.95 (ISBN 0-571-10401-0, Pub. by Faber & Faber). Merrimack Bk Serv.
--Some Stories. (Orig.). 1962. pap. 4.95 (ISBN 0-571-04581-2, Pub. by Faber & Faber). Merrimack Bk Serv.
--Songs of Childhood. LC 75-32200. (Classics of Children's Literature, 1621-1932: Vol. 61). 1976. Repr. of 1902 ed. PLB 38.00 (ISBN 0-8240-2310-2). Garland Pub.
--Tales Told Again. (Faber Fanfares Ser.). (Illus.). 208p. (Orig.). (gr. 4-7). 1980. pap. 3.25 (ISBN 0-571-18013-2, Pub. by Faber & Faber). Merrimack Bk Serv.
--The Warmint. LC 76-454. (Illus.). 32p. (gr. k-2). 1976. 4.95 (ISBN 0-684-14663-0, ScribJ). Scribner.
De Lamartine, Alphonse see Lamartine, Alphonse de.
De Lamater, John, jt. ed. see Fidell, Linda S.
Delamere, C., jt. auth. see Calhoun, G. M.
Delamont, Sara, jt. ed. see Chanan, Gabriel.
Delamont, Victor L. The Ministry of Music in the Church. 1980. pap. 5.95 (ISBN 0-8024-5673-1). Moody.
De la Morandiere, Turmeau. Appel Des Etrangers Dans Nos Colonies. (Principal French Demographic Works of the 18th Century Ser.). (Fr.). 1976. lib. bdg. 27.50x o.p. (ISBN 0-8287-0839-8); pap. text ed. 17.50x o.p. (ISBN 0-685-71507-8). Clearwater Pub.
Delamore, I. W., jt. auth. see Israels, M. G.
De La Mothe, Francois De Salignac see Fenelon & De Salignac De La Mothe, Francois.
DeLamotte, Roy C. The Alien Christ. LC 80-5902. 276p. 1980. lib. bdg. 18.75 (ISBN 0-8191-1304-2); pap. text ed. 10.50 (ISBN 0-8191-1305-0). U Pr of Amer.
--Jalaluddin Rumi: Songbird of Sufism. LC 80-5884. 187p. 1980. lib. bdg. 16.75 (ISBN 0-8191-1286-0); pap. text ed. 8.75 (ISBN 0-8191-1287-9). U Pr of Amer.
DeLancey, Mark W. Bibliography of African International Relations. (Westview Special Studies on Africa). 1980. lib. bdg. 26.50x (ISBN 0-89158-680-6). Westview.
Delaney & Laney. The Osmonds. 32p. (gr. 4-6). 1975. PLB 5.95 (ISBN 0-87191-461-1); pap. 2.95 (ISBN 0-89812-113-2). Creative Ed.
Delaney, A. The Butterfly. LC 77-72651. 32p. (gr. k-1). 1977. 4.95 o.s.i. (ISBN 0-440-00890-5); PLB 4.58 o.s.i. (ISBN 0-440-00891-3). Delacorte.

Delaney, Douglas. How to Overcome Rejection & Become a Better Person. (Illus.). 1980. pap. 12.95 o.p. (ISBN 0-930490-22-3). Future Shop.

Delaney, Edmund T., et al. Greenwich Village: A Photographic Guide. LC 74-78593. (Illus.). 128p. (Orig.). 1976. pap. 4.00 (ISBN 0-486-23114-3). Dover.

Delaney, J. W. & Garratty, G. Handbook of Hematological & Blood Transfusion Technique. 2nd ed. (Illus.). 1969. pap. text ed. 11.95x (ISBN 0-407-72852-X). Butterworths.

Delaney, Janice, et al. The Curse: A Cultural History of Menstruation. 1977. pap. 1.95 o.p. (ISBN 0-451-61560-3, MJ1560, Ment). NAL.

Delaney, John J. Dictionary of Saints. LC 79-7783. (Illus.). 648p. 1980. 22.50 (ISBN 0-385-13594-7). Doubleday.

Delaney, John J., ed. Woman Clothed with the Sun. LC 60-5922. pap. 3.50 (ISBN 0-385-08019-0, D118, Im). Doubleday.

Delaney, John J., tr. The Practice of the Presence of God. LC 77-70896. 1977. pap. 2.25 (ISBN 0-385-12861-4, Im). Doubleday.

Delaney, Laurence. Blood Red Wine. (Orig.). Date not set. pap. 3.25 (ISBN 0-440-10714-8). Dell.

Delaney, Samuel R. & Chayken, Howard. Empire. LC 78-19575. 1978. 19.95 o.p. (ISBN 0-399-12245-1). Berkley Pub.

--Empire. 1978. pap. 9.95 o.p. (ISBN 0-425-03900-5, Medallion). Berkley Pub.

Delaney, Samuel R., et al. The Technical Imagination: Theories & Fictions. LC 80-18718. (Theories of Contemporary Culture Ser.: Vol. 3). 212p. (Orig.). 1980. 12.95 (ISBN 0-930956-10-9); pap. 5.95 (ISBN 0-930956-11-7). Coda Pr.

Delange, F. Endemic Goitre & Thyroid Function in Central Africa. Falkner, F., et al, eds. (Monographs in Pediatrics: Vol. 2). (Illus.). xvi, 160p. 1974. 44.50 (ISBN 3-8055-1687-8). S Karger.

De Lange, N. R. Origin & the Jews. LC 75-36293. (Oriental Publications Ser.: No. 25). 160p. 1977. 36.00 (ISBN 0-521-20542-5). Cambridge U Pr.

De Lange, Nicholas, tr. see Oz, Amos.

De Langre, Jacques. Food Consciousness for Spiritual Development. LC 80-84993. (Illus., Orig.). 1980. pap. 6.00 (ISBN 0-916508-05-6). Happiness Pr.

--Seasalt & Your Life. LC 80-84990. (Illus.). 128p. (Orig.). 1980. 8.00 (ISBN 0-916508-08-0). Happiness Pr.

--Survival First Aid. (Illus.). 164p. 1980. 10.00 (ISBN 0-916508-14-5); pap. 8.00 (ISBN 0-916508-13-7). Happiness Pr.

De Langre, Jacques, ed. see De Langre, Yvette.

De Langre, Jacques, ed. see Kervan, L. C.

De Langre, Yvette. Cooking Good Food with Grains & Vegetables. De Langre, Jacques, ed. LC 80-84991. (Illus.). 128p. (Orig.). 1980. spiral bdg 8.00 (ISBN 0-916508-11-0); pap. 6.00 (ISBN 0-916508-12-9). Happiness Pr.

Delano, Irene, ed. see Andersen, Hans C.

Delano, Jack, ed. see Andersen, Hans C.

Delano, Kenneth J. Many Worlds, One God. 1977. 7.00 o.p. (ISBN 0-682-48644-2). Exposition.

De La Nuez, Manual. Eduardo Marquina. LC 76-5796. (World Authors Ser.: Spain: No. 396). 1976. lib. bdg. 12.50 (ISBN 0-8057-6238-8). Twayne.

De Lanville, Ranulph see Glanville, Ranulph de.

Delany, George & Delany, Sandra. The No. One Home Business Book. LC 80-84427. (Illus.). 176p. 1981. pap. 4.95 (ISBN 0-89709-022-5). Liberty Pub.

Delany, Paul. British Autobiography in the Seventeenth Century. LC 69-19285. 1969. 17.50x (ISBN 0-231-03273-0). Columbia U Pr.

Delany, Samuel R., ed. see Disch, Thomas M.

Delany, Sandra, jt. auth. see Delany, George.

Delany, Veronica, ed. see Cary, Patrick.

De La Pena, Augustin. The Psychobiology of Cancer: Implications for a General Model of Health & Disease. 300p. 1981. 19.95x (ISBN 0-89789-004-3). J F Bergin.

De la Perouse. The Voyages of de la Perouse. Gant, Michael S., ed. Orig. Title: Voyage Round the World. (Illus.). 265p. pap. 6.95 o.s.i. (ISBN 0-934136-02-5). Western Tanager. Postponed.

DeLapp, G. Leslie. In the World. LC 73-75884. 1973. 7.50 o.p. (ISBN 0-8309-0099-3). Herald Hse.

De la Ramee, Pierre see La Ramee, Pierre de.

De La Ramee, Pierre see La Ramee, Pierre De.

De La Ree, Gerry, ed. The Sixth Book of Virgil Finlay. (Illus.). 1980. 15.75 (ISBN 0-938192-06-X). De La Ree.

De Larma, Dominique-Rene. Bibliography of Black Music: Reference Materials, Vol. 1. LC 80-24681. (The Greenwood Encyclopedia of Black Music). 144p. 1981. lib. bdg. 25.00 (ISBN 0-313-21340-2, DBI/01). Greenwood.

De La Roche, Harry, jt. auth. see Roesch, Roberta.

De La Roche, Mazo. Mary Wakefield. 1977. pap. 1.50 o.p. (ISBN 0-449-23057-0, Crest). Fawcett.

--Variable Winds at Jalna. 288p. 1975. pap. 1.50 o.p. (ISBN 0-449-22567-4, Q2567, Crest). Fawcett.

--Whiteoaks of Jalna. (Jaina Ser.). 1977. pap. 2.25 (ISBN 0-449-23510-6, Crest). Fawcett.

De La Rochefoucauld, Francois. The Dynamic Power of Self-Love. (Illus.). 1980. Repr. of 1899 ed. 33.45 (ISBN 0-89901-006-7). Found Class Reprints.

De la Rosa, Denise M., jt. auth. see Kolin, Michael J.

De La Rosa, Denise M., jt. auth. see Kolin, Michael J.

De Larrabeiti, Michael. The Borribles. LC 77-12743. (gr. 5 up). 1978. 8.95 (ISBN 0-02-726700-8, 72670). Macmillan.

De La Ruffiniere Du Prey, Pierre. John Soane's Architectural Education, 1753-1780. LC 76-23615. (Outstanding Dissertations in the Fine Arts Ser.). 1977. lib. bdg. 87.00x (ISBN 0-8240-2686-1). Garland Pub.

De La Salle, Innocent. The Illustrated Guidebook to Japanese Painting. (Illus.). 1978. 49.50 (ISBN 0-89266-138-0). Am Classical Coll Pr.

De las Heras, F. G. & Vega, S. Medicinal Chemistry Advances: Proceedings of the Seventh International Symposium on Medicinal Chemistry, Torremolinos, 2-5 September 1980. (Illus.). 500p. 1981. 80.00 (ISBN 0-08-025297-4); pap. 25.00 (ISBN 0-08-026198-1). Pergamon.

De La Taille, Jean. Dramatic Works. Hall, Kathleen M. & Smith, C. N., eds. 1972. text ed. 15.00x (ISBN 0-485-13804-2, Athlone Pr); pap. text ed. 6.50x (ISBN 0-485-12804-7, Athlone Pr). Humanities.

De La Torre Bueno, Laura, jt. ed. see Graham, Munir.

De La Torriente, Donna D. In the Shadow of a Bell. 112p. 1981. 7.95 (ISBN 0-87881-100-1). Mojave Bks.

Delaunois, A. L., ed. Biostatistics in Pharmacology. new ed. LC 78-40220. (International Encyclopedia of Pharmacology & Therapeutics: Section 7, Vol. 3). (Illus.). 1979. text ed. 75.00 (ISBN 0-08-021514-9). Pergamon.

--Biostatistics in Pharmacology, Vol. 1-2. 1128p. 1973. Set. text ed. 125.00 (ISBN 0-08-016556-7). Pergamon.

DeLaura, David J. Hebrew & Hellene in Victorian England: Newman, Arnold, & Pater. 1969. 16.50x o.p. (ISBN 0-292-78404-X). U of Tex Pr.

DeLaurentis, Teresa & Heath, Stephen, eds. The Cinematic Apparatus. 1980. 18.95 (ISBN 0-312-13907-1). St Martin.

DeLaurier, Nancy, ed. Slide Buyers Guide. rev. ed. LC 80-84877. (Mid-America College Art Association Visual Resources Guides Ser.). 128p. 1980. 8.00 (ISBN 0-938852-07-8). Mid Am Coll.

De La Vega, Garcilasco. Incas. 1964. pap. 3.50 (ISBN 0-380-01269-3, 45542, Discus). Avon.

De La Vega, Sara L. & Parr, Carmen S. Avanzando: Gramatica espanola y lectura. LC 77-18537. 1978. text ed. 12.95 (ISBN 0-471-02731-6); wkbk. a 6.95x (ISBN 0-471-02732-4); wkbk. b 6.95x (ISBN 0-471-02733-2). Wiley.

Delavnay, Charles. Dejango Reinhardt (Jazz) 247p. 22.50 (ISBN 0-306-76057-6). Da Capo.

Delbanco, Nicholas. Stillness. LC 80-14395. 224p. 1980. 9.95 (ISBN 0-688-03708-9). Morrow.

Delbecq, Andre & Filley, Alan. Program & Project Management in a Matrix Organization: A Case Study. (Wisconsin Business Monographs: No. 9). (Orig.). 1974. pap. 5.00 (ISBN 0-86603-001-8). Bureau Busn Res U Wis.

Delbene, Ron & Montgomery, Herb. Breath of Life: A Simple Way to Pray. 128p. (Orig.). 1981. pap. 3.95 (ISBN 0-03-059059-0). Winston Pr.

Delblac, Sven. Castrati. 7.95 (ISBN 0-89720-020-9). Green Hill.

Del Borgo, S. Classical Faces & Figures from the 16th to the 19th Century Fully Illustrated & Described. (Science of Man Library Bks.). (Illus.). 115p. 1981. 47.85 (ISBN 0-89901-028-8). Found Class Reprints.

Delbridge, Pauline N., jt. auth. see Boyle, Elisabeth L.

Delbruck, Hans. Das Mittelalter. LC 80-2677. 1981. Repr. of 1907 ed. 63.50 (ISBN 0-404-18559-2). AMS Pr.

Delbrueck, Berthold, jt. auth. see Brugmann, Karl.

Del Bueno, Dorothy. Money: A Financial Guide for Nurses. (Illus.). 208p. 1981. text ed. 12.50 (ISBN 0-86542-007-6). Blackwell Sci.

Del Carril, Bonifacio, tr. see De Saint-Exupery, Antoine.

Del Castillo, Adelaida, jt. ed. see Mora, Magdalena.

Del Castillo, Ronald. Commodity Futures Trading: The Essential Knowledge Which Everybody, but Absolutely Everybody Ought to Possess About Speculating in Commodity Futures. (Essential Knowledge Ser.). (Illus.). 1978. plastic spiral bdg. 28.95 (ISBN 0-89266-117-8). Am Classical Coll Pr.

Del Chiaro, Mario A. Etruscan Red-Figured Vase-Painting at Caere. 1975. 35.00x (ISBN 0-520-02578-4). U of Cal Pr.

Delclos, Luis, jt. auth. see Van Roosenbeek, Earl.

D'Elden, Karl H. Van see Van D'Elden, Karl H.

Delderfield, Eric R. Inns and Their Signs: Fact and Fiction. LC 75-10564. (Illus.). 96p. 1975. 11.95 (ISBN 0-7153-7112-6). David & Charles.

--West Country Historic Houses & Their Families: The Cotswolds Area, Vol. 3. (Illus.). 1973. 13.50 (ISBN 0-7153-6089-2). David & Charles.

--West Country Historic Houses & Their Families, Vol. 2: Dorset, Wiltshire & N. Somerset. 13.50 (ISBN 0-7153-4910-4). David & Charles.

De Lee, James, et al. Developing Teaching Competencies. LC 79-9910. 72p. 1979. pap. 3.95 (ISBN 0-88289-215-0). Pelican.

De Leener, M. F., jt. auth. see Resibois, P.

De Leeuw, Adele. Barred Road. (gr. 7-10). 1964. 5.95g o.s.i. (ISBN 0-02-726760-1). Macmillan.

De Leeuw, Frank & Tarutis, Eleanor L. Operating Costs in Public Housing: A Financial Crisis. 63p. 1969. pap. 1.50 o.p. (ISBN 0-87766-002-6, 30001). Urban Inst.

De Leeuw, Frank, et al. The Design of a Housing Allowance. 42p. 1970. pap. 2.75 o.p. (ISBN 0-87766-049-2, 30005). Urban Inst.

De Leeuw, Frank see De Leeuw, Frank, et al.

DeLeeuw, Hendrik. Cities of Sin. Winick, Charles, ed. LC 78-60861. (Prostitution Ser.: Vol. 5). 297p. 1979. lib. bdg. 30.00 (ISBN 0-8240-9723-8). Garland Pub.

Delehanty, Randolph. San Francisco: Walks & Tours in the Golden Gate City. (Illus.). 340p. 1980. pap. 9.95 (ISBN 0-8037-7651-9). Dial.

Delehanty, Suzanne. Paul Thek - Processions. LC 77-92423. 1977. pap. 8.00 (ISBN 0-88454-023-5). U of Pa Contemp Art.

Delehanty, Suzanne & Lippard, Lucy. Dwellings. (Illus.). 1978. pap. 4.00 (ISBN 0-88454-050-2). U of Pa Contemp Art.

Delehanty, Suzanne & Pincus-Witten, Robert. Improbable Furniture. (Illus.). 48p. 1977. pap. 7.00 (ISBN 0-88454-022-7). U of Pa Contemp Art.

Delehanty, Suzanne, et al. Agnes Martin. (Illus.). 1976. pap. 8.00 (ISBN 0-88454-010-3). U of Pa Contemp Art.

De Leiris, Alain. The Drawings of Edouard Manet. (Studies in the History of Art: No. 10). 1969. 52.50x (ISBN 0-520-01547-9). U of Cal Pr.

Delellis. Diagnostic Immunohistochemistry of Tumor Markers. 1981. write for info. Masson Pub.

De Lemos, M. see Lemos, M. De.

DeLenc, Marcus F., ed. see Felix, Ervin J.

De Leon, Jose L. Ponce see Ponce De Leon, Jose L.

De Leon, Sherry. The Basketry Book. LC 77-2777. (Illus.). 1978. 12.95 o.p. (ISBN 0-03-017866-5); pap. 7.95 o.p. (ISBN 0-03-042851-3). HR&W.

De Leon, Virgil. The Failure of Modern Art As an Aesthetic Instrument for the Emotional & Moral Uplifting of Mankind. (Illus.). 1978. deluxe bdg. 37.50 (ISBN 0-930582-00-4). Gloucester Art.

De Lerin, Olivia, tr. see Crane, J. D.

De Lerin, Olivia S. Enviame a Mi: Aventuras de los esposos Davis, fundadores de la C. B. P. 64p. 1980. pap. 1.25 (ISBN 0-311-01062-8). Casa Bautista.

De Lerin, Olivia S. D., tr. see Bisagno, Juan.

De Lerma, Dominique-Rene. Black Music in Our Culture: Curricular Ideas on the Subjects, Materials & Problems. LC 70-131429. 1970. 12.00x o.p. (ISBN 0-87338-110-6). Kent St U Pr.

DeLespinasse, Paul. Thinking About Politics: American Government in Associational Perspective. (Orig.). 1980. pap. 14.95 (ISBN 0-442-25409-1). D Van Nostrand.

Delessert, Etienne. The Endless Party. Tabberner, Jeffrey, tr. from Fr. Orig. Title: San Fin la Fete. (Illus.). 32p. (ps-3). 1981. 9.95 (ISBN 0-19-279753-0). Oxford U Pr.

Delestre-Poirson, Charles-Gaspard, jt. auth. see Scribe, Eugene.

Deleuze, Gilles. Masochism, an Interpretation of Coldness & Cruelty. LC 78-148733. Orig. Title: Sacher-Masoch: Une Interpretation. 1971. 6.95 o.p. (ISBN 0-8076-0561-1). Braziller.

Delevoy, Robert. Ensor. (Alpine Fine Arts Collection). (Illus.). 367p. 1981. 135.00 (ISBN 0-686-64750-5, Pub by Alpine Fine Arts). Hippocrene Bks.

Delevoy, Robert L., et al. The Landscape of Industry. (Archives d'Architecture Moderne Ser.). Orig. Title: Le Paysage de l'Industrie Region du Nord-Wallonie-Ruhr. (Illus.). 175p. (Orig., Eng. & Fr.). 1975. pap. 25.00x (ISBN 0-8150-0926-7). Wittenborn.

Delfiore, Clarence T. Purity & the Carnal Element in Love: The Story of a Concrete Case. (Intimate Life of Man Library). (Illus.). 111p. 1981. 39.75 (ISBN 0-89266-298-0). Am Classical Coll Pr.

Delfosse, Edita. How to Raise & Train an Akita. (Orig.). pap. 2.00 (ISBN 0-87666-234-3, DS1041). TFH Pubns.

Delgado, Enrique, jt. ed. see Cline, William R.

Delgado, Jose M. Physical Control of the Mind: Toward a Psychocivilized Society. Anshen, Ruth N., ed. LC 71-89871. (World Perspectives). (Illus.). 1969. 10.00 o.s.i. (ISBN 0-06-011016-3, HarpT). Har-Row.

Delgass, William, et al. Spectroscopy in Heterogeneous Catalysis. LC 78-27885. 1979. 38.00 (ISBN 0-12-210150-2). Acad Pr.

Del Grande, J. J. & Duff, G. F. Introduccion Al Calculo Elemental. 1976. text ed. 7.20x (ISBN 0-06-310070-3, IntlDept). Har-Row.

Delibes, Miguel. U. S. A. y Yo. Gordon, F. L., ed. LC 77-117216. 1970. pap. 4.50 (ISBN 0-672-63133-4). Odyssey Pr.

Deligne, P., ed. see International Summer School, University of Antwerp, 1972.

De Limos, Antonio A. Briquet see Briquet de Limos, Antonio A.

De Limur, Charles, jt. auth. see Highman, Arthur.

Delisle, Fanny. A Study of Shelley's "a Defence of Poetry". A Textual & Critical Evaluation, 2 vols. (Salzburg Studies in English Literature,Romantic Reassessment: Nos.27-28). 633p. 1974. Set. pap. text ed. 50.25x (ISBN 0-391-01359-9). Humanities.

Delitzsch, Franz. Commentary on the Epistle to the Hebrews, 2 vols. 1978. Set. 29.95 (ISBN 0-686-12950-4). Klock & Klock.

--A New Commentary on Genesis, 2 vols. 1978. 27.75 (ISBN 0-686-12963-6). Klock & Klock.

--Old Testament History of Redemption. Date not set. pap. 6.95 (ISBN 0-88469-141-1). BMH Bks.

Delitzsch, Franz, jt. auth. see Keil, Carl F.

Delizio, Evonne. One Step Further. LC 80-52186. 1981. 5.95 (ISBN 0-533-04748-X). Vantage.

Dell, Cecily. A Primer for Movement Description Using Effort Shape & Supplementary Concepts. 2nd rev. ed. LC 78-111086. (Illus.). 1970. pap. text ed. 8.95x (ISBN 0-932582-03-6). Dance Notation.

Dell, Edwin La see La Dell, Edwin.

Dell, Ethel. The Knave of Diamonds. (Barbara Cartland's Library of Love: Vol. 3). 280p. 1979. 12.95x (ISBN 0-7156-1379-0, Pub. by Duckworth England). Biblio Dist.

Dell, Ethel M. The Bars of Iron. (Barbara Cartland's Library of Love: Vol. 9). 278p. 1979. 12.95x (ISBN 0-7156-1384-7, Pub. by Duckworth England). Biblio Dist.

--Charles Rex. (Barbara Cartland's Library of Love: Vol. 18). 216p. 1980. 12.95x (ISBN 0-7156-1478-9, Pub. by Duckworth England). Biblio Dist.

--Greatheart. (Barbara Cartland's Library of Love: Vol. 15). 247p. 1980. 12.95x (ISBN 0-7156-1475-4, Pub. by Duckworth England). Biblio Dist.

--The Hundredth Chance. (Barbara Cartland's Library of Love: Vol. 5). 306p. 1980. 12.95x (ISBN 0-7156-1381-2, Pub. by Duckworth England). Biblio Dist.

--The Knave of Diamonds. 1975. lib. bdg. 21.50x (ISBN 0-89966-069-X). Buccaneer Bks.

--The Obstacle Race. 160p. (Orig.). 1980. pap. 1.50 (ISBN 0-553-13912-6). Bantam.

--The Way of an Eagle. (Barbara Cartland's Library of Love: Vol. 7). 193p. 1979. 12.95x (ISBN 0-7156-1383-9, Pub. by Duckworth England). Biblio Dist.

Dell, F. Generative Phonology. LC 79-14139. (Illus.). 1980. 42.50 (ISBN 0-521-22484-5); pap. 9.95x (ISBN 0-521-29519-X). Cambridge U Pr.

Dell, Penelope. Nettie & Sissie: A Biography of Ethel M. Dell & Her Sister Ella. (Illus.). 1978. 16.95 (ISBN 0-241-89663-0, Pub. by Hamish Hamilton England). David & Charles.

Dell, Sidney. The Inter-American Development Bank: A Study in Development Financing. LC 70-185778. (Special Studies in International Economics & Development). 1972. 26.75x (ISBN 0-275-28606-1). Irvington.

Dell, Sidney & Lawrence, Roger. The Balance of Payments Adjustment Process in Developing Countries. LC 79-22818. (Pergamon Policy Studies Ser.). 120p. 1980. 18.25 (ISBN 0-08-025577-9). Pergamon.

Dell, Susanne. Silent in Court. 64p. 1971. pap. text ed. 5.00x (ISBN 0-7135-1576-7, Pub. by Bedford England). Renouf.

Della Cava, Ralph. Miracle at Joaseiro. LC 76-127364. (Illus.). 1970. 16.00x (ISBN 0-231-03293-5). Columbia U Pr.

Della Chiesa, Carol, tr. see Collodi, C.
Della Corte, Andrea see Corte, Andrea Della.
Della Fazia, Alba see Fazia, Alba della.
Della Mirandola, Giovanni Pico see Pico Della Mirandola, Giovanni.
Della Porta, G., ed. see International Pigment Cell Conference - 6th.
Dellaquila, William. The Metaphysics of History at the End of the Twentieth Century. (Illus.). 1977. 49.45 (ISBN 0-89266-028-7). Am Classical Coll Pr.
Dellenbrant, Jan-Ake. Soviet Regional Policy: A Quantitative Inquiry into the Social & Political Development of the Soviet Republics. 208p. 1980. text ed. 30.00x (ISBN 0-391-01797-7). Humanities.
Deller, Anthony W. Deller's Walker on Patents: 1964-76. 2nd ed. LC 64-6861. 1976. Vols. 1-9. 42.50 ea.; Set. 382.50 (ISBN 0-686-14533-X). Lawyers Co-Op.
--Patent Claims, 3 vols. 2nd ed. LC 76-112643. 1971. 150.00 (ISBN 0-686-14534-8). Lawyers Co-Op.
Delligan, William. Cherry Grove. 1976. pap. 1.75 o.p. (ISBN 0-445-08485-5). Popular Lib.
--Fire Island Pines. 1977. pap. 1.95 o.p. (ISBN 0-445-04020-3). Popular Lib.
Dellmann, Horst-Dieter & Brown, Esther M., eds. Textbook of Veterinary Histology. LC 75-16329. (Illus.). 513p. 1976. text ed. 24.50 o.p. (ISBN 0-8121-0528-1). Lea & Febiger.
Dello Buno, Carmen J. Rare Early Essays on William Shakespeare: Third Series. 206p. 1980. lib. bdg. 17.50 (ISBN 0-8482-3651-3). Norwood Edns.
Dello Buono, Carmen J. Rare Early Essays on Charles Dickens. 207p. 1980. lib. bdg. 22.50 (ISBN 0-8482-0647-9). Norwood Edns.
--Rare Early Essays on George Eliot. 202p. 1980. lib. bdg. 25.00 (ISBN 0-8482-3661-0). Norwood Edns.
--Rare Early Essays on John Keats. 208p. 1980. lib. bdg. 17.50 (ISBN 0-8482-3675-0). Norwood Edns.
--Rare Early Essays on Percy Bysshe Shelley. 220p. 1981. lib. bdg. 22.50 (ISBN 0-8482-3653-X). Norwood Edns.
--Rare Early Essays on Walt Whitman. 202p. 1980. lib. bdg. 17.50 (ISBN 0-8482-3699-8). Norwood Edns.
Delloff, Linda M., ed. see Sittler, Joseph A.
Dellon, A. Lee. Evaluation of Sensibility & Reeducation of Sensation of the Hand. (Illus.). 140p. 1981. write for info. (2427-2). Williams & Wilkins.
Delman, Abner & Stein, Emanuel. Dynamic Cardiac Auscultation & Phonocardiography. LC 77-16990. (Illus.). 1979. text ed. 55.00 o.p. (ISBN 0-7216-3022-7). Saunders.
Delmar, Rosalind, tr. see Aleramo, Sibilla.
Del Mar, W., jt. auth. see Pender, H.
Delmar-Morgan, Edward. Normandy Harbors & Pilotage. 1979. 29.95x (ISBN 0-8464-0073-1). Beekman Pubs.
--North Sea Harbors & Pilotage. 1979. 29.95x (ISBN 0-8464-0070-7). Beekman Pubs.
Del Mastro, M. L., jt. tr. see Meisel, Anthony C.
Delmon, Philip. Ten Types of Table Wine. 1973. pap. 2.50 (ISBN 0-263-51788-8). Transatlantic.
Delmonte, John. Technology of Carbon & Graphite Fiber Composites. 464p. 1981. text ed. 32.00 (ISBN 0-442-22072-3). Van Nos Reinhold.
DeLo, James S. & Green, William A. Multicultural Transactions: A Workbook Focusing on Communication Between Groups. LC 80-69328. 125p. 1981. perfect bdg. 11.50 (ISBN 0-86548-030-3). Century Twenty One.
DeLoach, Charles. The Armstrong Error: A Reporter Exposes Herbert W. Armstrong. 124p. 1971. pap. 1.25 o.p. (ISBN 0-912106-13-1). Logos.
--Seeds of Conflict. LC 73-92247. 1974. 4.95 o.p. (ISBN 0-88270-077-4); pap. 2.95 o.p. (ISBN 0-88270-076-6). Logos.
DeLoach, Jane E. General Surgical Nursing. (Nursing Outline Ser.). 1979. pap. 9.50 (ISBN 0-87488-393-8). Med Exam.
Delobez, A., jt. auth. see Beaujeu-Garnier, J.
De Lobo, Virginia P., tr. see Barrett, Ethel.
De Lollis, Nicholas J. Adhesives: Adherends, Adhesion. 2nd ed. LC 79-1371. 280p. 1980. Repr. of 1970 ed. lib. bdg. 26.50 (ISBN 0-88275-981-7). Krieger.
De Lolme, Jea L. The Rise & Progress of the English Constitution, 2 vols. Berkowitz, David S. & Thorne, Samuel E., eds. LC 77-86589. (Classics of English Legal History in the Modern Era Ser.: Vol. 20). 1322p. 1979. lib. bdg. 80.00 (ISBN 0-8240-3069-9). Garland Pub.
De Lolme, Jean L. The Rise & Progress of the English Constitution, Vol. 82. Berkowitz, David & Thorne, Samuel, eds. LC 77-86589. (Classics of English Legal History in the Modern Era). 1979. Repr. of 1838 ed. lib. bdg. 55.00 (ISBN 0-8240-3069-9). Garland Pub.
DeLone, R. P. Music: Patterns & Style. 1971. 15.95 (ISBN 0-201-01489-0). A-W.
DeLone, R. P. & Winold, A. Music Reading: An Ensemble Approach. 1971. pap. 13.50 o.p. (ISBN 0-201-01501-3). A-W.
Delone, Richard, et al. Aspects of Twentieth-Century Music. (Illus.). 541p. 1974. 20.95x (ISBN 0-13-049346-5). P-H.
Delone, Richard P., jt. auth. see Christ, William.
DeLong, David C., ed. Texas, 2 vols. (Historic American Buildings Ser.). 1980. Set. lib. bdg. 180.00 (ISBN 0-686-52663-5); Vol. 1. (ISBN 0-8240-3198-9); Vol. 2. (ISBN 0-8240-3199-7). Garland Pub.
De Long, David G. The Architecture of Bruce Goff Buildings & Projects, 1916-1974, 2 vols. LC 76-23610. (Outstanding Dissertations in the Fine Arts - 2nd Series - American). (Illus.). 1977. Repr. Set. lib. bdg. 121.00 (ISBN 0-8240-2682-9). Garland Pub.
Delong, David G., ed. California, 4 vols. (Historic American Buildings). (Illus.). 1980. Set. lib. bdg. 360.00. Vol. 1 (ISBN 0-8240-3197-0). Vol. 2 (ISBN 0-8240-3194-6). Vol. 3 (ISBN 0-8240-3195-4). Vol. 4 (ISBN 0-8240-3196-2). Garland Pub.
--New York, 8 vols. Incl. Vol. 1. lib. bdg. 100.00 (ISBN 0-8240-3186-5); Vol. 2. lib. bdg. 100.00 (ISBN 0-8240-3187-3); Vol. 3. lib. bdg. 100.00 (ISBN 0-8240-3188-1); Vol. 4. lib. bdg. 100.00 (ISBN 0-8240-3189-X); Vol. 5. lib. bdg. 100.00 (ISBN 0-8240-3190-3); Vol. 6. lib. bdg. 100.00 (ISBN 0-8240-3191-1); Vol. 7. lib. bdg. 100.00 (ISBN 0-8240-3192-X); Vol. 8. lib. bdg. 100.00 (ISBN 0-8240-3193-8). (Historic American Buildings). 1979. lib. bdg. 600.00 set. Garland Pub.
Delong, Fred J. Aim for a Job in Drafting. LC 68-10505. (Aim High Vocational Guidance Ser.). (gr. 7 up). 1976. PLB 5.97 (ISBN 0-8239-0365-6). Rosen Pr.
DeLong, George M., jt. auth. see Holler, Ronald F.
DeLong, George W. Waterfront Living: How to Buy Real Estate on the Water. LC 79-57321. (Illus., Orig.). 1981. pap. 10.00 (ISBN 0-9603414-0-4). DeLong & Assoc.
DeLong, Howard. Profile of Mathematical Logic. (Intermediate Mathematics Geometry Topology Ser). 1970. text ed. 17.95 (ISBN 0-201-01499-8). A-W.
De Long, Patrick D. Art in the Humanities. 2nd ed. 1970. pap. text ed. 8.50 (ISBN 0-13-046979-3). P-H.
De Longchamps, Joanne. One Creature. (Illus.). 1977. pap. 5.00 o.p. (ISBN 0-915596-19-9). West Coast.
De Longueville, Thomas see Longueville, Thomas de.
DeLora, Joann S. & Warren, Carol A. Understanding Sexual Interaction. LC 76-10902. (Illus.). 1976. pap. text ed. 16.50 (ISBN 0-395-24314-9); inst. manual 1.50 (ISBN 0-395-24316-5). HM.
Delora, Joann S., et al. Understanding Human Sexuality. LC 79-89744. (Illus.). 1980. pap. text ed. 12.50 (ISBN 0-395-28255-1); inst manual 0.75 (ISBN 0-395-28256-X); study guide 4.95 (ISBN 0-395-28981-5). HM.
--Understanding Sexual Interaction. 2nd ed. (Illus.). 672p. 1981. text ed. 16.95 (ISBN 0-395-29724-9); write for info. instr's manual (ISBN 0-395-29725-7). HM.
Deloria, Vine, Jr. Custer Died for Your Sins: An Indian Manifesto. 1969. 12.95 o.s.i. (ISBN 0-02-530650-2). Macmillan.
--Indians of the Pacific Northwest. LC 74-18789. (gr. 6-9). 1977. PLB 6.95 (ISBN 0-385-09791-3). Doubleday.
Deloria, Vine, Jr., jt. auth. see Wise, Jennings C.
DeLorme, David, ed. The Maine Atlas & Gazetteer. 2nd ed. (Illus.). 96p. 1978. pap. 6.95 (ISBN 0-89933-003-7). DeLorme Pub.
Delorme, Robert L. Latin America Nineteen Sixty-Seven to Nineteen Seventy-Eight: A Comprehensive Social Science Bibliography & Research Guide. 288p. 1981. text ed. 26.50 (ISBN 0-87436-292-X). ABC-Clio.
De Lorris, Guillaume & De Meun, Jean. Romance of the Rose. Robbins, Harry W., tr. 1962. pap. 6.50 (ISBN 0-525-47090-5). Dutton.
Deloughery, Grace L. History & Trends of Professional Nursing. 8th ed. LC 77-386. (Illus.). 1977. pap. 14.95 (ISBN 0-8016-1974-2). Mosby.
Deloughery, Grace L. & Gebbie, Kristine M. Political Dynamics: Impact on Nurses & Nursing. LC 74-22120. 1975. text ed. 11.50 o.p. (ISBN 0-8016-1245-4). Mosby.
DeLozier, M. Wayne & Woodside, Arch G. Marketing Management: Strategies & Cases. (Marketing & Management Ser.). 1978. text ed. 19.95 (ISBN 0-675-08417-2); instructors manual 3.95 (ISBN 0-686-67981-4). Merrill.
DeLozier, Wayne. Consumer Behavior Dynamics: A Casebook. (Business Ser.). 1977. text ed. 12.95 (ISBN 0-675-08504-7); instructors manual 3.95 (ISBN 0-686-67643-2). Merrill.
Delp, Frank. Aircraft Governors. (Aviation Technician Training Course Ser.). 96p. (Orig.). 1980. pap. text ed. 4.95 (ISBN 0-89100-119-0). Aviation Maintenance.
Delp, Mahlon H. & Manning, Robert T. Major's Physical Diagnosis: An Introduction to the Clinical Process. 9th ed. (Illus.). 650p. 1981. text ed. write for info. (ISBN 0-7216-3002-2). Saunders.
Delphine, Freda. I Promise You Tomorrow. LC 73-91782. (Illus.). 112p. 1974. 5.95 (ISBN 0-88415-660-5). Pacesetter Pr.
Delpit, George & Johnson, Stephen. Electronics in Action, Bk. 1. new ed. (gr. 10-12). 1975. text ed. 10.60 (ISBN 0-87002-022-6); wkbk & ans. sheet 2.60 (ISBN 0-87002-039-0). Bennett IL.
Delpit, George H. Electronics in Action, Bk. 2. (gr. 9-12). 1972. text ed. 11.44 (ISBN 0-87002-115-X); wkbk & ans. sheet 2.52 (ISBN 0-87002-143-5); tchr's guide avail. (ISBN 0-685-24134-3). Bennett IL.
Del Prado, Carlos, jt. auth. see Calvo, Juan A.
Del Re, G., et al. Electronic States of Molecules & Atom Clusters. (Lecture Notes in Chemistry: Vol. 13). (Illus.). 180p. 1980. pap. 17.50 (ISBN 0-387-09738-4). Springer-Verlag.
Del Regato, Juan A. & Spjut, Harlan J. Ackerman & Del Ragato's Cancer: Diagnosis, Treatment, & Prognosis. 5th ed. LC 76-26170. (Illus.). 1977. pap. 69.50 (ISBN 0-8016-1250-0). Mosby.
Del Rey, Judy Lynn, ed. The Best of Fritz Leiber. 352p. (Orig.). 1974. pap. 2.25 (ISBN 0-345-28351-1). Ballantine.
Del Rey, Judy-Lynn, ed. Stellar Science Fiction Stories. 192p. (Orig.). 1981. pap. 2.25 (ISBN 0-345-28969-2, Del Rey). Ballantine.
--Stellar Science Fiction Stories, No. 2. 1976. pap. 1.50 o.p. (ISBN 0-345-24584-9). Ballantine.
--Stellar Short Novels. 1976. pap. 1.50 o.p. (ISBN 0-345-25501-1). Ballantine.
Del Rey, Lester. Early Del Rey, 2 vols. 352p. 1976. Vol. 1. pap. 1.95 o.p. (ISBN 0-345-25063-X); Vol. 2. pap. 1.95 o.p. (ISBN 0-345-25111-3). Ballantine.
--Eleventh Commandment. 1976. pap. 1.50 (ISBN 0-345-29641-9). Ballantine.
--Police Your Planet. 224p. 1975. pap. 1.50 o.p. (ISBN 0-345-24465-6). Ballantine.
Del Rey, Lester, ed. see LeGuin, Ursula K.
Delrio, Giovanni, ed. Steroids & Their Mechanisms of Action in Non Mammalian Vertebrates. (Progress in Cancer Research & Theory Ser.). 250p. 1980. text ed. 24.50 (ISBN 0-89004-487-2). Raven.
Del Rio, Ignacio. A Guide to the Archivo Franciscano of the National Library of Mexico. (Miscellaneous Ser.). 1975. 20.00 (ISBN 0-88382-257-1). AAFH.
Del Santo, Louise. Mastering Mathematics. LC 75-2049. (High School Equivalency Prog. Ser.). 205p. (Orig.). (gr. 9-12). 1975. pap. text ed. 5.00 (ISBN 0-913310-38-7). Par Inc.
Del Sesto, Steven L. Science, Politics & Controversy: Civilian Nuclear Power in the United States, 1946-1974. LC 79-5227. (Westview Special Studies in Science, Technology & Public Policy). 1979. lib. bdg. 23.00x (ISBN 0-89158-566-4). Westview.
Delsol, Paula. Chinese Astrology. 1976. pap. 2.50 (ISBN 0-446-91800-8). Warner Bks.
Delson, Roberta M. Readings in Caribbean History & Economics: An Introduction to the Region. 300p. 1981. write for info. (ISBN 0-677-05280-4). Gordon.
Delton, Jina. Two Blocks Down. LC 80-8458. (YA) (gr. 7 up). 1981. 8.95 (ISBN 0-06-021590-9, HarpJ); PLB 8.79g (ISBN 0-06-021591-7). Har-Row.
Delton, Judy. Groundhog's Day at the Doctor. (Illus.). 48p. (ps-3). 1981. PLB 5.95 (ISBN 0-8193-1042-5); pap. 4.95 (ISBN 0-8193-1041-7). Parents.
--I Never Win! LC 80-27618. (A Carolrhoda on My Own Bk). (Illus.). 32p. (gr. k-3). 1981. PLB 5.95 (ISBN 0-87614-139-4). Carolrhoda Bks.
--It Happened on Thursday. Pacini, Kathy, ed. LC 77-19086. (Concept Bks.). (Illus.). (gr. 1-3). 1978. 6.50 (ISBN 0-8075-3669-5). A Whitman.
--Lee Henry's Best Friend. Fay, Ann, ed. LC 79-16902. (Concept Bk.: Level I). (Illus.). (gr. k-3). 1980. 6.50g (ISBN 0-8075-4417-5). A Whitman.
--My Mom Hates Me in January. LC 77-5749. (Concept Books). (Illus.). (gr. 1-3). 1977. 6.50g (ISBN 0-685-75662-9). A Whitman.
--My Mother Lost Her Job Today. Fay, Ann, ed. LC 80-19067. (Concept Bks.). (Illus.). 32p. (gr. k-3). 1980. 6.50 (ISBN 0-8075-5359-X). A Whitman.
Delton, Judy & Knox-Wagner, Elaine. The Best Mom in the World. Pacini, Kathy, ed. LC 78-27238. (Concept Bk.: Level I). (Illus.). (gr. k-2). 1979. 6.50g (ISBN 0-8075-0665-6). A Whitman.
Del Toro, V. Electromechanical Devices for Energy Conversion & Control Systems. 1968. ref. ed. 26.95 (ISBN 0-13-250068-X). P-H.
Del Tredici, Robert. The People of Three Mile Island. LC 80-13558. (Illus.). 124p. (Orig.). 1980. pap. 7.95 (ISBN 0-87156-237-5). Sierra.
De Lubicz, Isha S. Her-Bak: Egyptian Initiate, Vol. 2. 1978. pap. 8.95 (ISBN 0-685-62083-2). Weiser.
--Her-Bak: The Living Face of Ancient Egypt, Vol. 1. 1978. pap. 8.95 (ISBN 0-685-62082-4). Weiser.
--The Opening of the Way. Gleaolow, Rupert, tr. 1981. pap. 8.95 (ISBN 0-89281-015-7). Inner Tradit.
DeLuca, A. Michael & Giuliano, William. Selections from Italian Poetry. LC 66-10394. (Illus.). 128p. (gr. 9 up). 1966. PLB 5.29 (ISBN 0-8178-3792-2). Harvey.
Deluca, Anthony R. Great Power Rivalry at the Turkish Straits: The Montreux Conference & Convention of 1936. (East European Monographs: No. 77). 224p. 1981. text ed. 16.00x (ISBN 0-914710-71-0). East Eur Quarterly.
DeLuca, H. F. & Suttie, J. W., eds. Fat-Soluble Vitamins. 1970. 37.50x (ISBN 0-299-05600-7). U of Wis Pr.
DeLuca, J. Practical Problems in Mathematics for Printers. LC 76-3942. 1976. pap. 6.00 (ISBN 0-8273-1285-7); instructor's guide 1.60 (ISBN 0-8273-1286-5). Delmar.
Deluca, Marlene & McElroy, William, eds. Bioluminescience & Chemiluminescence: Basic Chemistry & Analytical Applications. 1981. price not set (ISBN 0-12-208820-4). Acad Pr.
DeLuca, Sam. The Football Playbook. LC 74-188241. (Illus.). 1972. 8.95 o.p. (ISBN 0-8246-0143-2). Jonathan David.
De Luca, Stuart M. Television's Transformation. LC 80-15254. 1980. 9.95 (ISBN 0-498-02474-1). A S Barnes.
Deluca, Stuart M., jt. auth. see Stone, Alfred R.
De Lucchi, Lorna see Lucchi, Lorna De.
De Lucchi, M. R., et al. The Stereotaxic Atlas of the Chimpanzee Brain. 1965. 48.50x (ISBN 0-520-00304-7). U of Cal Pr.
Delucchi, V. L., ed. Studies in Biological Control. LC 75-16867. (International Biological Programme Ser.: No. 9). (Illus.). 380p. 1975. 72.00 (ISBN 0-521-20910-2). Cambridge U Pr.
DeLucia, Alan A., et al. Mineral Atlas: Pacific Northwest. LC 80-52312. (Orig.). 1980. pap. 8.95 (ISBN 0-89301-072-3). U Pr of Idaho.
De Lucio-Meyer, J. Visual Aesthetics. LC 74-120. (Icon Editions). (Illus.). 240p. 1974. pap. 7.95x o.s.i. (ISBN 0-06-430052-8, IN-52, HarpT). Har-Row.
Delupis, Ingrid. Finance & Protection of Investments in Developing Countries. LC 73-12149. 183p. 1973. 27.95 (ISBN 0-470-20637-3). Halsted Pr.
DeLurgio, Stephen A., jt. auth. see Kwak, No Kyoon.
Del-Valle, Gonzalez, jt. auth. see Shaw, Bradley.
Del Valle, Inclan. Divinas Palabras. Faulkner, T., tr. from Span. (National Theatre Plays Ser.). 1977. pap. text ed. 5.75 o.p. (ISBN 0-435-23425-0). Heinemann Ed.
Del Vasto, Lanza. Definitions of Nonviolence. Sidgwick, Jean, tr. Orig. Title: Fr. 27p. (Orig.). 1972. pap. 1.00 (ISBN 0-934676-06-2). Greenlf Bks.
--Make Straight the Way of the Lord. 1974. 7.95 o.p. (ISBN 0-394-49387-7). Knopf.
Delves, L. M. & Walsh, J., eds. Numerical Solution of Integral Equations. (Illus.). 352p. 1974. 28.00 (ISBN 0-19-853342-X). Oxford U Pr.
Delvin, David. The Book of Love. 1977. pap. 1.95 o.s.i. (ISBN 0-515-04305-2). Jove Pubns.
Delwiche, C. C. Denitrification, Nitrification, & Atmospheric Nitrous Oxide. LC 80-22698. 260p. 1981. 27.50 (ISBN 0-471-04896-8, Pub. by Wiley-Interscience). Wiley.
Delworth, Ursula, et al. Student Services: A Handbook for the Profession. LC 80-8008. (Higher Education Ser.). 1980. text ed. 25.00x (ISBN 0-87589-476-3). Jossey-Bass.
Delworth, Ursula, et al, eds. Crisis Center Hotline: A Guidebook to Beginning & Operating. (Illus.). 160p. 1972. photocopy ed. spiral 14.75 (ISBN 0-398-02561-4). C C Thomas.
Delyannis, A. E. & Delyannis, E. E. Seawater & Desalting, Vol. 1. 180p. 1980. 34.90 (ISBN 0-387-10206-X). Springer-Verlag.
Delyannis, E. E., jt. auth. see Delyannis, A. E.
DeLyre, Wolf F. Essentials of Dental Radiography for Dental Assistants & Hygienists. 2nd ed. (Illus.). 1980. text ed. 16.95 (ISBN 0-13-285676-X). P-H.
Delzell, Charles F., ed. Mediterranean Fascism, 1919-1949. (Documentary History of Western Civilization Ser). 1971. 15.00x o.p. (ISBN 0-8027-2051-X). Walker & Co.
De Maar, Harko Gerrit. A History of Modern English Romanticism. 246p. 1980. Repr. of 1924 ed. lib. bdg. 30.00 (ISBN 0-8492-4217-7). R West.

De Madariaga, Isabel. Russia in the Age of Catherine the Great. LC 80-21993. (Illus.). 728p. 1981. 40.00x (ISBN 0-300-02515-7). Yale U Pr.

De Madlener, Judith Cooper see Cooper Madlener, Judith.

De Maestri, Victor. Life, Oneself & the Conquest of the Universe. (Intimate Life of Man Library). (Illus.). 1979. 29.75 (ISBN 0-89266-185-2). Am Classical Coll Pr.

Demaine, Jack. Contemporary Theories in the Sociology of Education. 192p. 1980. text ed. 37.50x (ISBN 0-333-23448-0). Humanities.

De Maio, Gerald, jt. auth. see Kushner, Harvey W.

Demaitre, Edmund. Eyewitness: A Journalist Covers the Twentieth Century. (Illus.). 450p. 1981. 17.50 (ISBN 0-8044-1218-9). Ungar.

De Malherbe, Francois. Poesies choisies de Malherbe, Racan & Mainard. (Nouveaux Classiques Larousse). (Illus., Fr.). pap. 2.95 o.p. (ISBN 0-685-14053-9, 163). Larousse.

DeMallie, Raymond J., ed. see Walker, James R.

De Malynes, Gerard see Malynes, Gerard De.

DeMan, J. M. Principles of Food Chemistry. rev. ed. (Illus.). 1980. lib. bdg. 32.00 o.p. (ISBN 0-87055-216-3); pap. text ed. 19.00 (ISBN 0-87055-287-2). AVI.

DeMan, J. M. & Melnychyn, P. Phosphates in Food Processing: Symposium. (Illus.). 1971. 25.50 o.p. (ISBN 0-87055-105-1). AVI.

DeMan, J. M., et al, eds. Rheology & Texture in Food Quality. (Illus.). 1976. lib. bdg. 48.00 (ISBN 0-87055-197-3); pap. text ed. 26.00 (ISBN 0-87055-295-3). AVI.

De Man, Paul, ed. see Flaubert, Gustave.

Demand, Carlo, jt. auth. see Georgano, G. N.

Demand, Carlo, jt. auth. see Schrader, Halwart.

De Mandiargues, Andre P. Arcimboldo the Marvelous. LC 77-25439. (Illus.). 1978. 28.50 o.p. (ISBN 0-8109-0689-9). Abrams.

--Blaze of Embers. FitzLyon, April, tr. 1980. 10.95 (ISBN 0-7145-0131-X). Riverrun NY.

Demaray, Donald E. Bible Study Sourcebook. (Illus.). kivar 8.95 (ISBN 0-310-23621-5). Zondervan.

--Blow Wind of God: Spirited Messages from the Writings of Billy Graham. 1977. pap. 1.50 o.p. (ISBN 0-451-07380-0, W7380, Sig). NAL.

--Preacher Aflame. 1972. pap. 1.25 o.p. (ISBN 0-8010-2816-7). Baker Bk.

Demaray, Donald E., ed. see Brother Lawrence.

DeMarco, Carl, ed. Pharmacy & the Law. LC 75-34698. 412p. 1975. 27.50 (ISBN 0-912862-16-5). Aspen Systems.

DeMarco, Guy. Third from the Sun. 64p. 1981. 10.00 (ISBN 0-682-49670-7). Exposition.

DeMarco, Tom. Structures Analysis & System Specification. (Software Ser.). 1979. text ed. 25.00 o.p. (ISBN 0-13-854380-1). P-H.

De Mare, Eric. London's River: The Story of a City. (Illus.). 1978. 7.95 (ISBN 0-370-00846-4, Pub. by Chatto Bodley Jonathan). Merrimack Bk Serv.

--Your Book of Bridges. (Year Book Ser.). (Illus.). 1963. 6.95 (ISBN 0-571-05285-1, Pub. by Faber & Faber). Merrimack Bk Serv.

DeMare, George. Communicating at the Top: What You Need to Know About Communicating to Run an Organization. LC 78-31951. 1979. 15.95 (ISBN 0-471-05681-2, Pub. by Wiley-Interscience). Wiley.

Demaree, G. E. Drugs: Action, Reactions. (Clinical Monographs Ser.). (Illus.). 1973. pap. 7.95 (ISBN 0-87618-057-8). R J Brady.

Demarest, Arthur J. Resettlement. 166p. 1970. 6.50x (ISBN 0-911038-75-2, New Voices). Noontide.

Demarest, Bruce A. Jesus Christ: The God-Man. 1978. pap. 3.95 (ISBN 0-88207-760-0). Victor Bks.

Demarest, Gary. Colossians: The Mystery of Christ in Us. 1979. 7.95 (ISBN 0-8499-0120-0). Word Bks.

Demarest, Robert, jt. auth. see Noback, Charles.

Demarest, Rosemary. Accounting Information Sources. LC 70-120908. (Management Information Guide Ser.: No. 18). 1970. 30.00 (ISBN 0-8103-0818-5). Gale.

Demargne, Pierre. The Birth of Greek Art. LC 64-21312. (Arts of Mankind Ser). 30.00 o.s.i. (ISBN 0-8076-0502-6). Braziller.

DeMaria, Robert. Blowout. (Orig.). 1979. pap. 2.25 (ISBN 0-515-04527-6). Jove Pubns.

--The Language of Grammar. LC 63-15677. 1973. 7.95 (ISBN 0-88427-008-4); pap. text ed. 5.95 (ISBN 0-88427-009-2, Dist. by Caroline House Pubs). North River.

De Maria, Robert. Outbreak. (Orig.). 1978. pap. 1.95 o.s.i. (ISBN 0-515-04433-4). Jove Pubns.

DeMaria, Robert. Secret Places. (Orig.). 1980. pap. 2.25 (ISBN 0-515-05160-8). Jove Pubns.

DeMaris, Ovid. The Last Mafioso: The Treacherous World of Jimmy Fratianno. 1981. 15.00 (ISBN 0-686-62159-X). Times Bks.

De Marivaux, Pierre. Seven Comedies by Marivaux. Mandel, Oscar & Mandel, Adrienne, eds. LC 68-16386. 1979. Repr. of 1968 ed. 26.50x (ISBN 0-686-60850-X). Irvington.

De Marivaux, Pierre C. De Chamblain see De Chamblain De Marivaux, Pierre C.

De Marley, Diana. Worth: Father of Haute Couture. (Illus.). 220p. 1980. text ed. 29.50x (ISBN 0-8419-7400-4). Holmes & Meier.

Demarolle, P. Villon: Un Testament ambique. new ed. (Collection themes et textes). (Orig., Fr.). 1973. pap. 6.75 (ISBN 2-03-035019-2, 2648). Larousse.

DeMaroo, Cettie & O'Connor, Del, eds. Aries Press Journal: The New Age Anthology. (Illus.). 1980. pap. 3.00 quarterly (ISBN 0-933646-14-3); annual subscription 10.00. Aries Pr.

De Martin, Elena L., jt. auth. see Marshall, William H.

De Martini, Francesco, jt. ed. see Burstein, Elias.

De Maupassant, Guy. The Complete Novels of Guy De Maupassant. 756p. 1980. Repr. of 1928 ed. lib. bdg. 35.00 (ISBN 0-89987-564-5). Darby Bks.

--Odd Number. 1889. 10.00 o.s.i. (ISBN 0-06-012855-0, HarpT). Har-Row.

--Short Stories. 1956. 6.00x (ISBN 0-460-00907-9, Evman); pap. 8.95 (ISBN 0-460-01907-4). Dutton.

Demaus, A. B. Motoring in the Twenties & Thirties. 1979. 17.95 (ISBN 0-7134-1538-X, Pub. by Batsford England). David & Charles.

--Victorian & Edwardian Cycling & Motoring. 1977. 16.95 o.p. (ISBN 0-7134-0556-2, Pub. by Batsford England). David & Charles.

DeMause, Lloyd, ed. The History of Childhood. 1974. pap. 8.50x (ISBN 0-06-131848-5, TB1848, Torch). Har-Row.

Dember, Sol. Complete Airbrush Techniques for Commercial, Technical, & Industrial Applications. 1980. pap. 15.95 (ISBN 0-672-21783-X). Bobbs.

Dembo, L. S. & Pondrom, Cyrena N., eds. Contemporary Writer: Interviews with Sixteen Novelists & Poets. LC 71-176410. 318p. 1972. 22.50 (ISBN 0-299-06141-8); pap. 7.95 (ISBN 0-299-06144-2). U of Wis Pr.

Dembo, L. S., jt. ed. see Krieger, Murray.

Dembo, Myron. Teaching for Learning. 2nd ed. 1981. pap. text ed. write for info. (ISBN 0-8302-8856-2). Goodyear.

Dembrinski, P., ed. Mathematical Foundation of Computer Science: Proceedings. (Lecture Notes in Computer Science: Vol. 88). 723p. 1980. pap. 37.20 (ISBN 0-387-10027-X). Springer-Verlag.

Deme, Rona. Country Host Cookbook. (Illus.). 288p. 1980. pap. 8.95 (ISBN 0-8256-3172-6, Quick Fox). Music Sales.

De Meis, jt. auth. see Leopoldo.

De Mello, Fernando, ed. The International Geographic Encyclopedia & Atlas. 1024p. 1979. text ed. 55.00x (ISBN 3-11008-137-7). De Gruyter.

De Mello, Walmor C., ed. Electrical Phenomena in the Heart. (Clinical Engineering Ser). 1972. 47.25 (ISBN 0-12-208950-2). Acad Pr.

De Menil, Dominique, intro. by. Constant Companions: An Exhibition of Mythological Animals, Demons, & Monsters. (Illus.). 1964. pap. 6.00 (ISBN 0-914412-19-1). Inst for the Arts.

De Menil, Dominique, ed. Jim Love up to Now. LC 80-82000. (Illus.). 1980. pap. 8.00 (ISBN 0-914412-16-7). Inst for the Arts.

De Menil, Dominique, intro. by. Through the Porthole: Exhibition Catalog. (Illus.). 1965. pap. 2.50 (ISBN 0-913456-89-6). Interbk Inc.

--Unromantic Agony: An Exhibition. (Illus.). 1965. pap. 2.50 (ISBN 0-914412-26-4). Inst for the Arts.

De Menil, Dominique see Lemagny, J. C.

Dement, William C., jt. auth. see Miles, Laughton E.

DeMente, Boye. Bachelor's Japan. LC 67-11428. (Orig.). 1967. pap. 5.95 (ISBN 0-8048-0052-9). C E Tuttle.

De Mente, Boye. Exotic Japan: The Traveler's Wonderland. LC 72-21365. (Illus.). 160p. 1976. pap. 3.95 (ISBN 0-914778-12-9). Phoenix Bks.

--Guide to Arizona's Indian Reservations. 1978. pap. 3.95 (ISBN 0-914778-14-5). Phoenix Bks.

--How to Do Business in Japan. 1974. 12.00 (ISBN 0-914778-15-3). Phoenix Bks.

--Japanese Manners & Ethics in Business. 1980. pap. 9.95 (ISBN 0-914778-00-5). Phoenix Bks.

--Secrets of Graceful Living. 1980. pap. 4.95 (ISBN 0-914778-22-6). Phoenix Bks.

De Mente, Boye, ed. see Longo, Peter.

De Mente, Boye, ed. see Whitlach, John.

Demerath, N. J., et al. Dynamics of Idealism: White Activists in a Black Movement. LC 75-148656. (Social & Behavioral Science Ser.). 1971. 13.95x o.p. (ISBN 0-87589-100-4). Jossey-Bass.

Demerath, N. J., et al, eds. Social Policy & Sociology. (Studies in Quantitative Relations Ser.). 1975. 30.50 (ISBN 0-12-209450-6). Acad Pr.

Demerath, N. S. & Peterson, R. A. System, Change & Conflict. LC 67-12512. 1967. 15.95 (ISBN 0-02-907180-1). Free Pr.

Demerec, M. & Kaufmann, B. P. Drosophila Guide: Introduction to the Genetics & Cytology of Drosophila melanogaster. rev. ed. (Illus.). 47p. 1969. lab manual 2.50 (ISBN 0-87279-950-6). Carnegie Inst.

Demerec, M., ed. Advances in Genetics. Incl. Vol. 1. 1947 (ISBN 0-12-017601-7); Vol. 2. 1948 (ISBN 0-12-017602-5); Vol. 3. 1950 (ISBN 0-12-017603-3); Vol. 4. 1951 (ISBN 0-12-017604-1); Vol. 5. 1953 (ISBN 0-12-017605-X); Vol. 6. 1954 (ISBN 0-12-017606-8); Vol. 7. 1955 (ISBN 0-12-017607-6); Vol. 8. 1956 (ISBN 0-12-017608-4); Vol. 9. 1958 (ISBN 0-12-017609-2); Vol. 10. Caspari, E. W. & Thoday, J. M., eds. 1961 (ISBN 0-12-017610-6); Vol. 11. 1962 (ISBN 0-12-017611-4); Vol. 12. 1964 (ISBN 0-12-017612-2); Vol. 13. 1965 (ISBN 0-12-017613-0); Vol. 14. Caspari, E. W., ed. 1968 (ISBN 0-12-017614-9); Vol. 15. Caspari, E. W., ed. 1970 (ISBN 0-12-017615-7); Vol. 16. Caspari, E. W., ed. 1971 (ISBN 0-12-017616-5); Vol. 17. The Genetics of Tribolium & Related Species. 1973. 48.50 (ISBN 0-12-017617-3); Vol. 18. 1976. 52.50 (ISBN 0-12-017618-1); Vol. 19. 1977. 55.00 (ISBN 0-12-017619-X); Suppl. 1. The Genetics of Tribolium & Related Species. Sokoloff, Alexander. 1966. 33.00 (ISBN 0-12-017661-0). Vols. 1-16. **48.00 ea. Acad Pr.**

Demers, Aline, jt. auth. see Chaplin, James P.

DeMers, Donald O., Jr. & Beilharz, Edwin A. San Jose: California's First City. Blakey, Ellen S. & Silvey, Larry P., eds. LC 80-66340. (The American Portrait Ser.). (Illus.). 223p. 1980. 24.95 (ISBN 0-932986-13-7). Continent Herit.

Demers, Ralph M. The Circuit. 1977. pap. 1.95 o.p. (ISBN 0-345-25722-7). Ballantine.

Demetz, Hana. The House on Prague Street. 1980. lib. bdg. 12.95 (ISBN 0-8161-3143-0, Large Print Bks). G K Hall.

De Meun, Jean, jt. auth. see De Lorris, Guillaume.

De Meza, David & Osborne, Michael. Problems in Price Theory. LC 80-16597. (Illus.). xiv, 302p. 1980. lib. bdg. 25.00 (ISBN 0-226-14293-0). U of Chicago Pr.

Demidoff, Lorna B. How to Raise & Train a Siberian Husky. (Orig.). pap. 2.00 (ISBN 0-87666-391-9, DS1118). TFH Pubns.

DeMile, James W. Power Punch: Bruce Lee's 1 & 3 Power Punch. (Illus.). 1980. pap. 3.95 (ISBN 0-918642-02-7). Tao of Wing.

--Tao of E Wing Chun Do, 2 pts, Vol. 1. 2nd ed. (Illus.). 1980. 6.95 ea.; Pt. 1. Pt. 2. Tao of Wing.

--Tao of Wing Chun Do, Vol 1, Part 2. (Illus.). 1978. 6.95 (ISBN 0-918642-03-5). Tao of Wing.

De Mille, Agnes. America Dances. (Illus.). 1980. 24.95 (ISBN 0-02-530730-4). Macmillan.

De Mille, Richard. Put Your Mother on the Ceiling: Children's Imagination Games. LC 67-23698. 192p. (gr. 1 up). 1981. Repr. of 1967 ed. 9.95 (ISBN 0-915520-39-7). Ross-Erikson.

De Mille, Richard, ed. The Don Juan Papers: Further Castaneda Controversies. LC 80-10158. 520p. 1980. 15.95 (ISBN 0-915520-25-7); pap. 8.95 (ISBN 0-915520-24-9). Ross-Erikson.

Demillo, Richard A., et al, eds. Foundations of Secure Computation. 1978. 25.50 (ISBN 0-12-210350-5). Acad Pr.

Deming, Barbara. Remembering Who We Are. LC 80-66371. 224p. (Orig.). 1980. pap. cancelled (ISBN 0-9603628-1-9). Frog in Well.

Deming, R. H., ed. James Joyce: Critical Heritage, 2 vols. Incl. Vol. 1. 1907-1927; Vol. 2. 1928-1941. 1970. 35.00 ea. Routledge & Kegan.

Deming, Richard. Sleep: Our Unknown Life. 1973. 6.95 o.p. (ISBN 0-525-66230-8). Elsevier-Nelson.

Deming, Robert H., ed. James Joyce: The Critical Heritage, 2 vols. (The Critical Heritage Ser.). 1970. Set. 65.00 (ISBN 0-7100-6747-X). Vol. 1, 1907-1927. Vol. 2, 1928-1941. Routledge & Kegan.

Deming, W. Edwards, ed. see Bayes, Thomas.

Deming, William E. Sample Design in Business Research. LC 60-6451. (Probability & Mathematical Statistics Ser.). 1960. 39.95 (ISBN 0-471-20724-1, Pub. by Wiley-Interscience). Wiley.

Demir, Soliman. Arab Development Funds in the Middle East. LC 79-503. (Pergamon Policy Studies). 1979. 28.00 (ISBN 0-08-022489-X). Pergamon.

--The Kuwait Fund & the Political Economy of Arab Regional Development. LC 75-45305. (Special Studies). (Illus.). 160p. 1976. text ed. 24.95 (ISBN 0-275-22980-7). Praeger.

De Moges, Marquis. Recollections of Baron Gros's Embassy to China & Japan in 1857 to 1858. 1972. Repr. of 1860 ed. 30.00x (ISBN 0-686-28318-X, Pub. by Irish Academic Pr). Biblio Dist.

De Moivre, Abraham. Doctrine of Chances: Including Treatise on Annuities. 3rd ed. LC 66-23756. 1967. 15.95 (ISBN 0-8284-0200-0). Chelsea Pub.

Demolen, Richard, ed. Richard Mulcaster's Positions. LC 77-168389. 1970. text ed. 9.75 (ISBN 0-8077-1238-8). Tchrs Coll.

Demolen, Richard L., et al. Meaning of the Renaissance & Reformation. 440p. 1974. pap. text ed. 9.75 (ISBN 0-395-12632-0). HM.

--One Thousand Years: Western Europe in the Middle Ages. 325p. 1974. pap. text ed. 9.75 (ISBN 0-395-14032-3). HM.

Demone, Harold W., Jr., jt. auth. see Chafetz, Morris E.

De Money, Netta D., tr. Geografia Historica Do Mundo Biblico. (Portuguese Bks.). 1979. 2.25 (ISBN 0-8297-0723-9). Life Pubs Intl.

De Money, Netta K., tr. Geografia Historica Del Mundo Biblico. (Spanish Bks.). (Span.). 1979. 2.95 (ISBN 0-8297-0558-9). Life Pubs Intl.

Demong, Denise, jt. auth. see Embery, Joan.

Demong, Phyllis. Rare & Undone Saints. LC 80-16731. (Illus.). 96p. 1981. 4.95 (ISBN 0-8397-7071-5). Eriksson.

De Montaigne, Michel see Montaigne, Michel De.

De Montault, X. Barbier. Traite d'Iconographie Chretienne. (Illus.). 972p. (Fr.). 1981. Repr. of 1890 ed. lib. bdg. 200.00x (ISBN 0-89241-137-6). Caratzas Bros.

De Montbrial, Thierry. Energy: The Countdown: A Report to the Club of Rome. LC 78-41103. (Illus.). 1979. 45.00 (ISBN 0-08-024225-1); pap. 14.00 (ISBN 0-08-024224-3). Pergamon.

De Montchrestien, Antoine. Two Tragedies: Hector & la Reine D'Escosse, Montchrestien/antoine De. Smith, C. N., ed. 1972. text ed. 13.00x (ISBN 0-485-13805-0, Athlone Pr); pap. text ed. 6.50x (ISBN 0-485-12805-5). Humanities.

De Monte, John R. The King James' Versions of the Games of Golfe. (Illus.). 82p. (Orig.). 1980. pap. 3.50 (ISBN 0-9605176-0-X). Raycol Prods.

De Montfaucon, Bernard. The Supplement to Antiquity Explained. Humphreys, David, tr. LC 75-27882. (Renaissance & the Gods Ser.: Vol. 37). (Illus.). 1976. Repr. of 1725 ed. lib. bdg. 73.00 (ISBN 0-8240-2086-3). Garland Pub.

De Montfort, St. Louis. Love of Eternal Wisdom. pap. 4.95 (ISBN 0-910984-05-0) (ISBN 0-910984-51-4). Montfort Pubns.

De Montherlant, Henry. The Fire That Consumes. Cox, Vivian, tr. from Fr. LC 80-51842. Orig. Title: La Ville Dont le Prince Est un Enfant. 88p. 1980. 24.00 (ISBN 0-9604392-1-8). G F Ritchie.

De Montherlant, Henry see Montherlant, Henry de.

De Montreville, Doris & Crawford, Elizabeth D., eds. Fourth Book of Junior Authors & Illustrators. 1978. 17.00 (ISBN 0-8242-0568-5). Wilson.

Demopoulos, H. B. & Mehlman, M. A., eds. Cancer & the Environment. LC 79-91048. 1980. 33.00 (ISBN 0-930376-13-7). Pathotox Pubs.

Demorest, Steve. Alice Cooper. (Circus Magazine Rock Ser.: No. 1). (Illus.). 192p. 1974. pap. 1.50 o.p. (ISBN 0-445-03046-1). Popular Lib.

De Morgan, Augustus, jt. auth. see Smith, David E.

De Morgan, Mary. On a Pincushion, 2 vols, Repr. Of 1877 Ed. Incl. The Necklace of Princess Fiorimonde, & Other Stories. Repr. of 1880 ed. LC 75-32181. (Classics of Children's Literature, 1621-1932). (Illus.). 1977. Set. PLB 76.00 (ISBN 0-8240-2293-9); PLB 38.00 ea. Garland Pub.

Demos, George D., jt. auth. see Bennett, James C.

Demos, John. Little Commonwealth: Family Life in Plymouth Colony. (Illus.). 1971. pap. 4.95 (ISBN 0-19-501355-7, 344, GB). Oxford U Pr.

Demos, John, ed. Remarkable Providences. LC 74-160130. (American Culture Ser). 1972. 8.95 (ISBN 0-8076-0617-0); pap. 7.95 (ISBN 0-8076-0616-2). Braziller.

Demos, Raphael. Plato: Selections. 1927. pap. text ed. 6.95 (ISBN 0-684-14321-6, ScribC). Scribner.

Demou, Doris B. A Part of Myself I Give to You. 40p. 1976. pap. 2.95x (ISBN 0-9604794-0-6). M Demou & Assocs.

De Mourgues, Odette. Racine: Or, the Triumph of Relevance. (Orig.). 1967. 34.50 (ISBN 0-521-06023-0); pap. 11.95x (ISBN 0-521-09428-3). Cambridge U Pr.

--Two French Moralists. LC 77-82506. (Major European Authors Ser.). 1978. 32.50 (ISBN 0-521-21823-3). Cambridge U Pr.

Demouzon. The First-Born of Egypt. LC 78-54648. 1979. 8.95 o.p. (ISBN 0-85690-077-X). Peebles Pr.

DeMoya, Armando, et al. The Practical Medical Dictionary of Sex. LC 80-5799. 304p. 1981. 16.95 (ISBN 0-8128-2794-5). Stein & Day.

Dempcy, Mary & Tihista, Rene. Your Stress Personalities: A Look at Your Selves. (Illus.). 252p. (Orig.). 1981. pap. 8.95 (ISBN 0-89141-077-5). Presidio Pr.
Dempsey, Al. Dog Kill. LC 75-46552. 1976. 7.95 o.p. (ISBN 0-13-217257-7). P-H.
Dempsey, Arthur, jt. auth. see Dempsey, Particia.
Dempsey, B., jt. ed. see Serjeant, E. P.
Dempsey, Barbara P., jt. auth. see Dempsey, Jack.
Dempsey, David. The Way We Die. Orig. Title: Dying in America. 288p. 1975. 12.95 (ISBN 0-02-530750-9). Macmillan.
Dempsey, David & Zimbardo, Philip G. Psychology & You. 1978. 16.95x (ISBN 0-673-15086-0). Scott F.
Dempsey, Hugh A. Charcoal's World. LC 79-14920. (Illus.). 1979. 11.95 (ISBN 0-8032-1651-3); pap. 3.95 (ISBN 0-8032-6552-2, BB 717, Bison). U of Nebr Pr.
--Red Crow, Warrior Chief. LC 80-51872. (Illus.). viii, 247p. 1980. 16.95 (ISBN 0-8032-1657-2). U of Nebr Pr.
Dempsey, Jack & Dempsey, Barbara P. Dempsey. LC 76-26220. (Illus.). 1977. 12.50 o.s.i. (ISBN 0-06-011054-6, HarpT). Har-Row.
Dempsey, Jerry A. & Reed, Charles E., eds. Exercise & the Lung. 1977. 35.00x (ISBN 0-299-07220-7). U of Wis Pr.
Dempsey, John A. Basic Digital Electronics with MSI Applications. LC 75-9009. 320p. 1976. text ed. 20.95 (ISBN 0-201-01478-5). A-W.
Dempsey, John J. The Family & Public Policy: The Issue of the 1980s. (Illus.). 120p. 1981. text ed. price not set (ISBN 0-933716-15-X). P H Brookes.
Dempsey, Michael & Chinery, Michael. Concise Color Encyclopedia of Nature. LC 73-13688. (Illus.). 254p. 1972. 9.95 o.s.i. (ISBN 0-690-20859-6, TYC-T). T Y Crowell.
Dempsey, Particia & Dempsey, Arthur. The Research Process in Nursing. 1980. 13.95 (ISBN 0-442-20884-7). D Van Nostrand.
Dempsey, Paul. How to Repair Briggs & Stratton Engines. (Illus.). 1978. 8.95 (ISBN 0-8306-9873-6); pap. 4.95 (ISBN 0-8306-1087-1, 1087). TAB Bks.
--How to Repair Small Gasoline Engines. 2nd ed. LC 76-45056. 1976. 12.95 (ISBN 0-8306-6917-5); pap. 9.95 (ISBN 0-8306-5917-X, 917). TAB Bks.
--Motorcycle Repair Handbook. LC 76-24787. (Illus.). 1976. 9.95 o.p. (ISBN 0-8306-6789-X); pap. 9.95 (ISBN 0-8306-5789-4, 789). TAB Bks.
Dempsey, Richard A., jt. auth. see Daigon, Arthur.
Dempster, Al, ed. Walt Disney's Mother Goose. (ps-1). 1952. PLB 5.00 (ISBN 0-307-60079-3, Golden Pr). Western Pub.
Dempster, G. C., jt. ed. see Bryan, William F.
Dempster, Germaine. Dramatic Irony in Chaucer. 1959. text ed. 8.50x (ISBN 0-391-00492-1). Humanities.
Dempster, Lauramay T. The Genus Galium (Rubiaceae) in Mexico & Central America. (Publications in Botany: No. 73). 1978. pap. 7.00x (ISBN 0-520-09578-2). U of Cal Pr.
--The Polygamous Species of the Genus Galium (Rubiaceae), Section Lophogalium, of Mexico & Southwestern United States. (U. C. Publ. in Botany: Vol. 64). 1973. pap. 6.50x (ISBN 0-520-09457-3). U of Cal Pr.
Dempster, M. A., jt. auth. see Adby, P. R.
Dempster, Stuart. The Modern Trombone: A Definition of Its Idioms. (The New Instrumentation Ser.: Vol. III). 1979. 16.50x (ISBN 0-520-03252-7). U of Cal Pr.
Dempsy, Paul. How to Convert Your Car, Van or Pickup to Diesel. (Illus.). 1978. pap. 6.95 (ISBN 0-8306-7968-5, 968). TAB Bks.
Demske, Dick. Home Repairs Made Easy. Wolf, Donald D., ed. LC 79-84283. (Illus.). 1979. pap. 9.95 (ISBN 0-8326-2240-0, 7725). Delair.
Demske, Richard. Year-Round Outdoor Building Projects: An Encyclopedia of Building Techniques & Construction Plans. 304p. 1980. pap. 9.95 (ISBN 0-442-21259-3). Van Nos Reinhold.
Demski. Instant Home Repair Guide. (Career Institute Instant Reference Library). 1973. 2.95 (ISBN 0-531-02086-X). Watts.
Demski, Joel S. Information Analysis. LC 78-184156. 1972. pap. text ed. 4.95 o.p. (ISBN 0-201-01477-7). A-W.
--Information Analysis. 2nd ed. LC 80-15971. (A-W Paperback Series in Accounting). 200p. 1980. pap. text ed. 6.50 (ISBN 0-201-01231-6). A-W.
Demtroeder, W. Laser Spectrosopy: Basic Concepts & Instrumentation. (Springer Series in Chemical Physics: Vol. 5). (Illus.). 700p. 1981. 35.00 (ISBN 0-387-10343-0). Springer-Verlag.
De Mundo Lo, Sara. Index to the Spanish American Biography: The Andean Countries, Vol. 1. (Reference Bks.). 1981. lib. bdg. 60.00 (ISBN 0-8161-8181-0). G K Hall.
Demura, Fumio. Sai Karate Weapon of Self-Defense. LC 74-83597. (Ser. 115). (Illus.). 1974. pap. text ed. 6.95 (ISBN 0-89750-010-5). Ohara Pubns.
--Shito-Ryu Karate. LC 74-169720. (Ser. 110). (Illus.). 1971. pap. text ed. 5.95 (ISBN 0-89750-005-9). Ohara Pubns.
Demura, Funio. Bo Karate Weapon of Self-Defense. Johnson, Gil & Adachi, Geraldine, eds. LC 76-13757. (Ser. 124). (Illus.). 1976. pap. text ed. 6.95 (ISBN 0-89750-019-9). Ohara Pubns.
Demus, Otto. Byzantine Art & the West. LC 78-88132. (Wrightsman Lectures Ser.: Vol. 3). (Illus.). 1970. 22.50, uk (ISBN 0-8147-0116-7). NYU Pr.
De Musset see Bentley, Eric.
De Musset, Alfred. Les Contes d'Espagne et D'italie. Rees, Margaret, ed. (Athlone French Poets Ser.). 1973. text ed. 16.25x (ISBN 0-485-14703-3, Athlone Pr); pap. text ed. 5.50x (ISBN 0-485-12703-2, Athlone Pr). Humanities.
--Poesies. (Documentation thematique). (Fr). pap. 2.95 (ISBN 0-685-14019-9, 226). Larousse.
Demuth, Norman. Musical Trends in the Twentieth Century. LC 73-6258. (Illus.). 359p. 1975. Repr. of 1952 ed. lib. bdg. 30.75x (ISBN 0-8371-6896-1, DEMT). Greenwood.
DeMuth, Vivienne, illus. Ten Little Fingers & Ten Little Toes. (Illus.). (ps-k). 1979. 1.95 (ISBN 0-525-69010-7, Gingerbread Bks); PLB 5.95 o.p. (ISBN 0-525-69011-5). Dutton.
Demyanov, V. & Malozemov, V. N. Introduction to Minimax. Louvish, D., tr. from Rus. LC 74-8156. 1974. 32.95 (ISBN 0-470-20850-3). Halsted Pr.
Denaes, Raymond. General Guide to Paris. 1978. pap. 9.95 (ISBN 0-933982-04-6, Pub by Editions L'indispensable). Bradt Ent.
Denan, Corinne. Dragon & Monster Tales. new ed. LC 79-66329. (Illus.). 48p. (gr. 2-6). 1980. PLB 4.89 (ISBN 0-89375-326-2); pap. 1.50 (ISBN 0-89375-325-4). Troll Assocs.
--Goblin Tales. new ed. LC 79-66326. (Illus.). 48p. (gr. 2-6). 1980. lib. bdg. 4.89 (ISBN 0-89375-320-3); pap. 1.50 (ISBN 0-89375-319-X). Troll Assocs.
--Once Upon a Time Tales. new ed. LC 79-66337. (Illus.). 48p. (gr. 2-6). 1980. lib. bdg. 4.89 (ISBN 0-89375-340-8); pap. 1.50 (ISBN 0-89375-339-4). Troll Assocs.
--Troll Tales. new ed. LC 79-66327. (Illus.). 48p. (gr. 2-6). 1980. lib. bdg. 4.89 (ISBN 0-89375-322-X); pap. 1.50 (ISBN 0-89375-321-1). Troll Assocs.
--Witch's Tales. new ed. LC 79-66328. (Illus.). 48p. (gr. 2-6). 1980. lib. bdg. 4.89 (ISBN 0-89375-324-6); pap. 1.50 (ISBN 0-89375-323-8). Troll Assocs.
--Wizard Tales. new ed. LC 79-66331. (Illus.). 48p. (gr. 2-6). 1980. lib. bdg. 4.89 (ISBN 0-89375-330-0); pap. 1.50 (ISBN 0-89375-329-7). Troll Assocs.
Denan, Jay. Burnout: Funny Car Races. LC 79-64700. (gr. 5-9). 1979. PLB 5.89 (ISBN 0-89375-256-8); pap. 2.50 (ISBN 0-89375-257-6). Troll Assocs.
Denaro, A. R. Elementary Electrochemistry. 2nd ed. 246p. 1971. pap. 9.95 (ISBN 0-408-70071-8). Butterworths.
Denaro, A. R. see Wilson, J. R., et al.
DeNault, Phyllis M., jt. auth. see Jacobs, Erwin M.
De Navarre, Marguerite. Tales from the Heptameron. Clive, H. P., ed. (Athlone Renaissance Library). 1970. text ed. 10.75x (ISBN 0-485-13801-8, Athlone Pr); pap. text ed. 5.50x (ISBN 0-485-12801-2, Athlone Pr). Humanities.
Den Beeg, Peter, tr. see Duras, Marguerita.
Denbigh, K. G. The Principles of Chemical Equilibrium. (Illus.). 506p. Date not set. 59.50 (ISBN 0-521-23682-7); pap. 19.95 (ISBN 0-521-28150-4). Cambridge U Pr.
Denbigh, Kenneth. Chemical Equilibrium. 3rd ed. LC 74-152638. (Illus.). 1971. text ed. 47.50 (ISBN 0-521-08151-3); pap. text ed. 15.95x (ISBN 0-521-09655-3). Cambridge U Pr.
Denbo, Bruce F., ed. see Wharton, Mary E. & Bowen, Edward L.
Denbow, William. Chandler. 1977. pap. 1.50 (ISBN 0-505-51169-X). Tower Bks.
Denby, Cumore B. Mystical Lady. 80p. 1981. 5.95 (ISBN 0-87881-095-1). Mojave Bks.
Denby, David, ed. Film Seventy-Two to Seventy-Three: An Anthology by the National Association of Film Critics. LC 73-1746. 304p. 1973. 7.95 o.p. (ISBN 0-685-32270-X); pap. 3.95 o.p. (ISBN 0-672-51871-6). Bobbs.
Denby, Edwin. Collected Poems. LC 75-23024. 1975. 14.95 (ISBN 0-916190-00-5); pap. 6.00 (ISBN 0-916190-01-3). Full Court NY.
--Looking at the Dance. 1978. pap. 2.50 o.p. (ISBN 0-445-04270-2). Popular Lib.
--Mrs. W's Last Sandwich. 1972. 6.95 o.p. (ISBN 0-685-25558-1). Horizon.
Denby-Wrightson, Kathryn, jt. auth. see Fry, Joan.
D'Encausse, Helene C. Decline of an Empire: The Soviet Socialist Republic in Revolt. LC 80-8402. (Illus.). 304p. 1981. pap. 4.95 (ISBN 0-06-090844-0, CN 844, CN). Har-Row.
Dence, Joseph B. Mathematical Techniques in Chemistry. LC 75-16337. 442p. 1975. text ed. 22.95 (ISBN 0-471-20319-X, Pub. by Wiley-Interscience). Wiley.
Dendel, Esther Warner. Needleweaving-Easy As Embroidery. 1976. pap. 4.95a o.p. (ISBN 0-385-12543-7). Doubleday.
Dendle, Brian J. Galdos: The Mature Thought. LC 80-51013. (Studies in Romance Languages: No. 23). 216p. 1980. 16.50x (ISBN 0-8131-1407-1). U Pr of Ky.
DenDooven, Gweneth R., jt. auth. see Borglum, Lincoln.
DenDooven, Gweneth R., ed. see Beal, Merrill D.
Dendooven, Gweneth R., ed. see Bezy, John.
DenDooven, Gweneth R., ed. see Buskirk, Steve.
DenDooven, Gweneth R., ed. see Cantu, Rita.
Dendooven, Gweneth R., ed. see Clark, William D.
DenDooven, Gweneth R., ed. see Crandall, Hugh.
DenDooven, Gweneth R., ed. see De Golia, Jack.
DenDooven, Gweneth R., ed. see Eardley, A. J., et al.
DenDooven, Gweneth R., ed. see Fiero, G. William.
DenDooven, Gweneth R., jt. ed. see Helms, Christopher L.
DenDooven, Gweneth R., ed. see Hibben, Frank C.
DenDooven, Gweneth R., ed. see Kaye, Glen.
DenDooven, Gweneth R., ed. see Mack, Jim.
DenDooven, Gweneth R., ed. see Maxon, James C.
DenDooven, Gweneth R., ed. see Olson, Virgil J.
DenDooven, Gweneth R., ed. see Pike, Donald & Muench, David.
DenDooven, Gweneth R., ed. see Robinson, Alan H.
DenDooven, Gweneth R., ed. see Rothe, Robert.
DenDooven, Gweneth R., ed. see Schoch, Henry A.
DenDooven, Gweneth R., ed. see Tweed, William C.
DenDooven, Gweneth R., ed. see Weinbaum, Paul.
Deneau, Daniel P. Byron's Narratice Poems of Eighteen Thirteen. (Salzburgstudies in English Literature, Romantic Reassessment Ser.: No. 55). 106p. 1975. pap. text ed. 25.00x (ISBN 0-391-01360-2). Humanities.
Denecke, H. J. & Meyer, R. Corrective & Reconstructive Rhinoplasty. Oxtoby, L., tr. (Plastic Surgery of Head & Neck: Vol. 1). (Illus.). 1967. 289.10 (ISBN 0-387-03757-8). Springer-Verlag.
Deneke, Frederick J., jt. auth. see Grey, Gene W.
Denenberg, Herbert S., et al. Risk & Insurance. 2nd ed. 1974. 18.95 (ISBN 0-13-781294-9). P-H.
Denenberg, R. V., jt. auth. see Stern, Judith.
Denenberg, Victor H., ed. Education of the Infant & Young Child. LC 77-137617. 1970. 16.50 (ISBN 0-12-209150-7). Acad Pr.
De Nerval, Gerard. Les Chimeres. Rinsler, Norma, ed. 1973. text ed. 19.50x (ISBN 0-485-14702-5, Athlone Pr); pap. text ed. 10.50x (ISBN 0-485-12702-4, Athlone Pr). Humanities.
Denes, Peter B. & Pinson, Elliot N. The Speech Chain: The Physics & Biology of Spoken Language. LC 74-180069. 192p. 1973. pap. 2.50 (ISBN 0-385-04238-6, Anch). Doubleday.
Denevan, William N., ed. The Native Population of the Americas in 1492. LC 75-32071. 1976. 22.50x (ISBN 0-299-07050-6). U of Wis Pr.
DeNevers, Noel. Fluid Mechanics. LC 78-91144. (Engineering Ser). 1970. text ed. 24.95 (ISBN 0-201-01497-1). A-W.
De Nevers, Noel, ed. Technology & Society. LC 77-172801. 1972. pap. text ed. 7.95 o.p. (ISBN 0-201-01493-9). A-W.
DeNevi, Don, jt. auth. see Moulin, Tom.
DeNevi, Don, jt. auth. see Saul, Eric.
DeNevi, Donald P., jt. ed. see Stone, James C.
Denfen, Dietrich Von see Von Denffer, Dietrich, et al.
Deng, Francis M. The Dinka & Their Songs. (Oxford Library of African Literature Ser). 308p. 1973. 24.95x (ISBN 0-19-815138-1). Oxford U Pr.
Denger, Louis A. A Few Pieces of Australia, 1979. 1981. 8.95 (ISBN 0-533-04458-8). Vantage.
Dengler, Marianne. Vicki. 135p. (gr. 7 up). 1980. pap. 1.25 (ISBN 0-590-31324-X, Schol Pap). Schol Bk Serv.
Dengler, Sandy. Arizona Longhorn Adventure. 128p. (gr. 5-8). 1980. pap. 1.95 (ISBN 0-8024-0299-2). Moody.
--Beasts of the Field Puzzles. 1979. pap. 1.95 (ISBN 0-8024-0680-7). Moody.
--Birds of the Air. 1979. pap. 1.95 (ISBN 0-8024-0681-5). Moody.
--Summer of the Wild Pig. (gr. 6-8). 1979. pap. 1.95 (ISBN 0-8024-8429-8). Moody.
Dengrove, Edward. Hypnosis & Behavior Therapy. (Illus.). 428p. 1976. 36.75 (ISBN 0-398-03336-6). C C Thomas.
Denham, Robert D. Northrop Frye: An Enumerative Bibliography. LC 73-20345. (Author Bibliographies Ser.: No. 14). 1974. 10.00 (ISBN 0-8108-0693-2). Scarecrow.
Denhardt, D. T., et al, eds. The Single-Stranded DNA Phages. LC 78-60445. (Monograph: No. 8). (Illus.). 720p. 1978. 65.00 (ISBN 0-87969-122-0). Cold Spring Harbor.
Denhardt, Robert B. In the Shadow of Organization. LC 80-23775. 168p. 1981. 17.50x (ISBN 0-7006-0210-0). Regents Pr KS.
Denhardt, Robert M. The Horse of the Americas. LC 74-5955. (Illus.). 343p. 1981. pap. 8.95 (ISBN 0-8061-1724-9). U of Okla Pr.
Den Hartog, Jacob P. Strength of Materials. 1949. pap. 5.00 (ISBN 0-486-60755-0). Dover.
Den Hartog, Jacob P., ed. see Prandtl, Ludwig & Tietjens, O. G.
Denhoff, Eric. Cerebral Palsy-the Preschool Years: Diagnosis, Treatment & Planning. 144p. 1968. pap. 14.75 photocopy ed. spiral (ISBN 0-398-00432-3). C C Thomas.
Denhoff, Eric & Stern, Leo. Minimal Brain Dysfunction. LC 78-61473. (Illus.). 208p. 1979. 26.25 (ISBN 0-89352-038-1). Masson Pub.
Denhoff, Eric, ed. Drugs in Cerebral Palsy. (Clinics in Developmental Medicine Ser. No. 16). 88p. 1964. 4.50 o.p. (ISBN 0-685-24718-X). Lippincott.
Den Hollander, A., ed. Diverging Parallels: A Comparison of American & European Thought & Actions. 222p. 1971. text ed. 28.00x (ISBN 90-0402-635-5). Humanities.
Den Hollander, C. Christian Political Options. 1980. pap. 9.00x o.p. (ISBN 0-686-27478-4). Radix Bks.
De Nicola, P., et al. Nail Diseases in Internal Medicine. (Illus.). 128p. 1974. 14.75 (ISBN 0-398-03178-9). C C Thomas.
Denieffe, Joseph. A Personal Narrative of the Irish Revolutionary Brotherhood. (Illus.). 1969. Repr. of 1906 ed. 17.00x (ISBN 0-686-28341-4, Pub. by Irish Academic Pr). Biblio Dist.
Denig, Edwin T. Five Indian Tribes of the Upper Missouri: Sioux, Arickaras, Assiniboines, Crees & Crows. Ewers, John C., ed. (Civilization of the American Indian Ser.: No. 59). (Illus.). 1961. 12.95 (ISBN 0-8061-0493-7); pap. 6.95 (ISBN 0-8061-1308-1). U of Okla Pr.
Deniker, P., ed. Collegium Internationale Neuro-Psychopharmacologicum, 10th Congress: Proceedings, 2 vols. 1977. Set. text ed. 255.00 (ISBN 0-08-021506-8). Pergamon.
Denikin, Anton I. The Career of a Tsarist Officer: Memoirs, 1872-1916. Patoski, Margaret, tr. from Rus. LC 75-14625. (Illus.). 355p. 1975. 22.50x (ISBN 0-8166-0698-6). U of Minn Pr.
--The White Army. Zvegintzov, Catherine, tr. from Rus. LC 72-97041. (The Russian Ser.: Vol. 45). (Illus.). 368p. 1973. Repr. of 1930 ed. lib. bdg. 15.00 (ISBN 0-87569-052-1). Academic Intl.
Dening, Walter. Japan in Days of Yore. (Illus.). 1978. 18.00 (ISBN 0-87773-748-7). Great Eastern.
Denis, Paul. Daytime TV's Star Directory. 1976. pap. 1.50 o.p. (ISBN 0-445-03161-1). Popular Lib.
Denisoff, R. Serge, jt. ed. see Rush, Gary B.
Denison, Cara D. & Mules, Helen B. European Drawings, 1375-1825. (Fine Art Ser.). (Illus.). 316p. (Orig.). 1981. pap. price not set. Dover.
Denison, Edward F. Accounting for Slower Economic Growth: The United States in the 1970s. LC 79-20341. 212p. 1979. 18.95 (ISBN 0-8157-1802-0); pap. 8.95 (ISBN 0-8157-1801-2). Brookings.
--Accounting for United States Economic Growth: 1929-1969. LC 74-278. 355p. 1974. 18.95 (ISBN 0-8157-1804-7); pap. 7.95 (ISBN 0-8157-1803-9). Brookings.
--Why Growth Rates Differ: Postwar Experience in Nine Western Countries. 1967. 18.95 (ISBN 0-8157-1806-3); pap. 7.95 (ISBN 0-8157-1805-5). Brookings.
Denison, Edward F. & Chung, William K. How Japan's Economy Grew So Fast: The Sources of Postwar Expansion. 1976. 14.95 (ISBN 0-8157-1808-X); pap. 5.95 (ISBN 0-8157-1807-1). Brookings.
Denison, R. A., jt. ed. see Martin, M. J.
Denitch, Bogdan, ed. Democratic Socialism: The Mass Left in Advanced Industrial Societies. 220p. 1981. text ed. 26.00 (ISBN 0-86598-015-2). Allanheld.
--Legitimation of Regimes: International Frameworks for Analysis. LC 78-63117. (Sage Studies in International Sociology: Vol. 17). (Illus.). 305p. 1979. 18.00x (ISBN 0-8039-9898-8); pap. 9.95x (ISBN 0-8039-9899-6). Sage.
Denk, Roland. Sailing. (Illus.). 140p. 1981. 12.95 (ISBN 0-8069-9144-5, Pub. by EP Publishing England). Sterling.

Denker, Arnold S. My Best Games of Chess 1929-75. Orig. Title: If You Must Play Chess. 190p. 1981. pap. price not set (ISBN 0-486-24035-5). Dover.
Denker, Elenor R., jt. auth. see Tittle, Carol K.
Denker, Henry. Error of Judgement. 1980. pap. write for info. (ISBN 0-671-81959-3). PB.
--Horowitz & Mrs. Washington. 1980. pap. 2.50 o.p. (ISBN 0-425-04657-5). Berkley Pub.
--The Warfield Syndrome. 324p. 1981. 12.95 (ISBN 0-399-12612-0). Putnam.
Denker, Joel S. Unions & Universities: The Rise of the New Labor Leader. LC 80-67093. 192p. 1981. text ed. 20.00 (ISBN 0-916672-58-1). Allanheld.
Denlinger, Charles & Denlinger, Elaine. Algebra Review. 116p. 1978. pap. text ed. 2.50 (ISBN 0-12-059568-0). Acad Pr.
Denlinger, Elaine, jt. auth. see Denlinger, Charles.
Denman, D. R. & Prodano, Sylvio. Land Use: An Introduction to Proprietary Land Use Analysis. 1972. text ed. 25.00x (ISBN 0-04-333013-4). Allen Unwin.
Denman, Scott, jt. auth. see Bossong, Ken.
Denmark, Florence, ed. Who Discriminates Against Women. LC 74-78560. (Sage Contemporary Social Science Issues: Vol. 15). 1974. 4.95x (ISBN 0-8039-0440-1). Sage.
Denmark, Florence L., ed. Psychology: The Leading Edge, Vol. 340. new ed. (N.Y. Academy of Sciences Annals: Vol. 340). 114p. 1980. 20.00 (ISBN 0-89766-068-4); pap. write for info. (ISBN 0-89766-069-2). NY Acad Sci.
Denn, M. Process Fluid Mechanics. 1980. 24.95 (ISBN 0-13-723163-6). P-H.
Denne, L. & Johnson, M. Decorating with Stitches. 104p. 1975. 13.95 (ISBN 0-8231-5047-X). Branford.
Dennehy, Henry E. see Sheehan, Patrick A.
Dennenberg, Herb. Herb Denenberg's Smart Shopper's Guide. LC 80-66978. 208p. Date not set. pap. 6.95 (ISBN 0-8019-7003-2). Chilton.
Dennerline, Jerry. The Chia-Ting Loyalists: Confucian Leadership & Social Change in Seventeenth-Century China. LC 80-21417. (Historical Publications Miscellany Ser.: No. 126). (Illus.). 416p. 1981. text ed. 35.00 (ISBN 0-300-02548-3). Yale U Pr.
Dennett, D. C. Content & Consciousness. (International Library of Philosophy & Scientific Method). 1969. text ed. 16.25x (ISBN 0-391-01015-8). Humanities.
Dennett, Daniel C. Brainstorms: Philosophical Essays on Mind & Psychology. LC 78-13723. (Higher Mental Processes Ser.). (Illus.). 384p. 1978. text ed. 21.50 (ISBN 0-89706-001-6); pap. 10.00 (ISBN 0-89706-002-4). Bradford Bks.
Dennett, M. F. Fire Investigation: A Practical Guide for Fire Students & Officers, Insurance Investigators, Loss Adjustors, & Police Officers. (Illus.). 80p. 1980. 17.25 (ISBN 0-08-024741-5); pap. 9.75 (ISBN 0-08-024742-3). Pergamon.
Dennett, M. W. Birth Control Laws. LC 70-119053. (Civil Liberties in American History Ser). 29.50 (ISBN 0-306-71942-8). Da Capo.
Denney, Martyn. London's Waterways. (Illus.). 1978. 11.50 o.s.i. (ISBN 0-7134-0558-9). Hippocrene Bks.
Denney, Reuel. The Astonished Muse. rev. ed. LC 57-6985. (Midway Reprint Ser). xx, 282p. 1975. pap. text ed. 9.00x o.s.i. (ISBN 0-226-14303-1). U of Chicago Pr.
Dennie, Joseph. The Lay Preacher. LC 43-9749. 1979. Repr. of 1796 ed. lib. bdg. 22.00x (ISBN 0-8201-1204-6). Schol Facsimiles.
Denning, Mark. Beyond the Prize. 1978. pap. 1.25 o.s.i. (ISBN 0-515-04473-3). Jove Pubns.
--Shades of Grey. (Orig.). 1976. pap. 1.25 o.s.i. (ISBN 0-515-03891-1). Jove Pubns.
--The Swiss Abduction. 1981. pap. 1.95 (ISBN 0-8439-0858-0, Leisure Bks). Nordon Pubns.
Denning, Peter J., jt. auth. see Coffman, Edward G., Jr.
Denning, Peter J., et al. Machines, Languages & Computation. (Automatic Computation Ser.). (Illus.). 1978. ref. ed. 25.95 (ISBN 0-13-542258-2). P-H.
Dennis, Barbara D., ed. see National Academy of Arbitrators, Annual Meeting.
Dennis, Benjamin G. The Gbandes: A People of the Liberian Hinterland. LC 72-88580. 1973. 20.95 (ISBN 0-911012-50-8). Nelson-Hall.
Dennis, Brad & Rutan, Al. Vaporizing Carburetors: One Hundred Miles per Gallon--the Real Facts. (Illus.). 150p. (Orig.). 1981. pap. 14.95 (ISBN 0-936222-06-9). Rutan Pub.
Dennis, Charles. The Dealmakers. (Orig.). 1981. pap. 2.95 (ISBN 0-440-11852-2). Dell.
Dennis, Deborah E., jt. ed. see Zikmund, Joseph.
Dennis, Ervin A. Lithographic Technology. LC 79-16756. 1980. 19.95 (ISBN 0-672-97164-X); tchr's manual 6.67 (ISBN 0-672-97165-8); student manual 7.95 (ISBN 0-672-97166-6). Bobbs.
Dennis, Erwin A. & Jenkins, John D. Comprehensive Graphic Arts. LC 72-92620. 1974. 20.95 (ISBN 0-672-97607-2); tchrs' manual 6.67 (ISBN 0-686-67512-6); students' manual 9.50 (ISBN 0-672-97608-0). Bobbs.
Dennis, Everette E., jt. auth. see DeFleur, Melvin L.
Dennis, Frank A., ed. Southern Miscellany: Essays in Honor of Glover Moore. LC 80-20373. 202p. 1981. 15.00 (ISBN 0-87805-129-5). U Pr of Miss.
Dennis, Franklin. Antique Firearms. LC 77-86542. (Illus.). 1978. Repr. 14.95 o.p. (ISBN 0-89141-050-3). Presidio Pr.
Dennis, G. E. Monetary Economics. (Modern Economic Ser.). (Illus.). 320p. (Orig.). 1981. pap. text ed. 18.95x (ISBN 0-582-45573-1). Longman.
Dennis, J. Richard. Fractions Are Parts of Things. LC 73-127603. (Illus.). 40p. (gr. 2-5). 1971. 7.95 (ISBN 0-690-31520-1, TYC-J); PLB 7.89 (ISBN 0-690-31521-X); pap. 1.45 (ISBN 0-690-31522-8, TYC-J). T Y Crowell.
Dennis, Jack, ed. Socialization to Politics: A Reader. LC 72-8329. 527p. 1973. pap. text ed. 16.95 (ISBN 0-471-20926-0). Wiley.
Dennis, Jan P., ed. The How-to Book: Loving God, Loving Others. LC 76-17671. pap. 3.95 (ISBN 0-89107-145-8). Good News.
Dennis, John. The Impartial Critick. Bd. with Miscellaneous Letters & Essays. Gildon, Charles. LC 72-170436. (The English Stage Ser.: Vol. 21). lib. bdg. 50.00 (ISBN 0-8240-0604-6). Garland Pub.
--The Usefulness of the Stage: To Government & to Religion. LC 71-170441. (The English Stage Ser.: Vol. 26). lib. bdg. 50.00 (ISBN 0-8240-0609-7). Garland Pub.
Dennis, John see Collier, Jeremy.
Dennis, John, jt. auth. see Knapp, Daniel.
Dennis, John see Law, William.
Dennis, John G. Structural Geology. 532p. 1972. 25.50 (ISBN 0-8260-2615-X). Wiley.
Dennis, Landt. Catch the Wind: A Book of Windmills & Windpower. LC 75-45002. (Illus.). 128p. (gr. 5 up). 1976. 8.95 (ISBN 0-590-07414-8, Four Winds). Schol Bk Serv.
Dennis, Landt & Dennis, Lisl. Collecting Photographs: A Guide to the New Art Boom. 1977. 12.95 (ISBN 0-87690-236-0); pap. 6.95 o.p. Dutton.
Dennis, Lane T. A Reason for Hope. 1976. 5.95 o.p. (ISBN 0-8007-0772-9). Revell.
Dennis, Larry, jt. auth. see Geiberger, Al.
Dennis, Larry, jt. auth. see Nelson, Byron.
Dennis, Lawrence & Martin, James J. The Dynamics of War & Revolution. 2nd ed. 259p. 1941. pap. 10.00 (ISBN 0-911038-91-4, Inst Hist Rev). Noontide.
Dennis, Lisl, jt. auth. see Dennis, Landt.
Dennis, Marshall. Mortgage Lending Fundamentals & Practices. (Illus.). 1981. text ed. 16.95 (ISBN 0-8359-4651-7). Reston.
Dennis, Nigel. Cards of Identity. LC 55-10479. 1955. 9.95 (ISBN 0-8149-0083-6). Vanguard.
--Jonathan Swift. 1965. 3.95 o.s.i. (ISBN 0-685-15394-0). Macmillan.
--Malta. LC 73-83041. (Illus.). 64p. 1974. 6.95 (ISBN 0-8149-0732-6). Vanguard.
Dennis, Norman. People Planning. (Society Today & Tomorrow Ser.). (Illus.). 1970. 12.95 o.p. (ISBN 0-571-09011-7, Pub. by Faber & Faber). Merrimack Bk Serv.
Dennis, P. O., et al, eds. Food Control in Action. (Illus.). xii, 280p. 1980. 45.00x (ISBN 0-85334-894-4). Burgess-Intl Ideas.
Dennis, Patrick. Auntie Mame. LC 54-11512. 1954. 8.95 (ISBN 0-8149-0085-2). Vanguard.
Dennis, Patrick & Hooton, Barbara. Guestward Ho. LC 56-5034. 1955. 8.95 (ISBN 0-8149-0086-0). Vanguard.
Dennis, Ralph. Down Among the Jocks. (Hardman Ser.: No. 5). 176p. 1974. pap. 0.95 o.p. (ISBN 0-445-00605-6). Popular Lib.
--Hump's First Case. (Hardman Ser.: No. 10). 1977. pap. 1.25 o.p. (ISBN 0-685-76989-5). Popular Lib.
--The Last of the Armageddon Wars. (Hardman Ser.: No. 11). 1977. pap. 1.25 o.p. (ISBN 0-445-00450-9). Popular Lib.
Dennis, Richard J., jt. auth. see Clout, Hugh D.
Dennis, Robert. Conversations with a Corpse. 192p. 1976. pap. 1.50 o.p. (ISBN 0-345-25216-0). Ballantine.
Dennis, Robert C. Sweet of Fear. 176p. 1976. pap. 1.50 o.p. (ISBN 0-345-25148-2). Ballantine.
Dennis, Stephen N. Recommended Model Provisions for a Preservation Ordinance. 151p. (Orig.). 1980. pap. text ed. 7.95 (ISBN 0-89133-090-9). Preservation Pr.
Dennison, Darwin. The Dine System: For Better Nutrition & Health. 96p. 1981. pap. text ed. 7.95 (ISBN 0-8403-2371-9). Kendall-Hunt.
Dennison, Darwin, et al. Alcohol & Behavior: An Activated Education Approach, No. 1. LC 79-25741. 1980. pap. text ed. 7.95 (ISBN 0-8016-1252-7). Mosby.
Dennison, Mark A. Preparing for the Greatest Two Years of Your Life. pap. 3.95 (ISBN 0-89036-128-2). Hawkes Pub Inc.
Dennison, S., jt. auth. see Robertson, Dennis.
Denniston, Denise & McWilliams, Peter. The TM Book: How to Enjoy the Rest of Your Life. 1975. pap. 1.95 o.s.i. (ISBN 0-446-89123-1). Warner Bks.
Denniston, Denise, jt. auth. see Goldhaber, Nat.
Denniston, J. D., ed. & intro. by see Cicero.
Denniston, J. D., ed. see Euripides.
Denny, jt. auth. see White.
Denny, Alison. The Mixer & Blender Cookery Book. (Illus.). 1978. 11.95 (ISBN 0-571-09736-7, Pub. by Faber & Faber); pap. 5.95 (ISBN 0-571-11073-8). Merrimack Bk Serv.
Denny, M. Ray. Comparative Psychology: An Evolutionary Analysis of Animal Behavior. LC 79-21123. 1980. text ed. 22.95 (ISBN 0-471-70930-1). Wiley.
Denny, Neville, ed. Medieval Drama. (Stratford-Upon-Avon Studies: No. 16). 254p. 1973. text ed. 27.50x (ISBN 0-8419-5824-6); pap. text ed. 19.50 (ISBN 0-8419-5823-8). Holmes & Meier.
--Pan African Short Stories: An Anthology for Schools. (Illus.). 1965. pap. text ed. 3.50x (ISBN 0-17-511099-9). Humanities.
Denny, Norman, tr. see Hugo, Victor.
Denny, Walter A. Stories from the Old Ones: As Told to Walter A. Denny. (Illus., Orig.). (gr. 4 up). 1979. pap. 4.95 (ISBN 0-686-27639-6). Rising Wolf.
Denny, Walter B. The Ceramics of the Mosque of Rustem Pasha & the Environment of Change. LC 76-23612. (Outstanding Dissertations in the Fine Arts Ser.). 1977. lib. bdg. 67.00x (ISBN 0-8240-2684-5). Garland Pub.
Dennys, Nicholas B. The Folk-Lore of China, & Its Affinities with That of the Aryan & Semitic Races. LC 79-89262. (Illus.). iv, 163p. 1972. Repr. of 1876 ed. 20.00 (ISBN 0-8103-3932-3). Gale.
Deno, Evelyn N., ed. Instructional Alternatives for Exceptional Children. 194p. 1973. pap. 4.50 o.p. (ISBN 0-86586-044-0). Coun Exc Child.
Denoeu, Francois & Hall, Robert A., Jr. Spoken French. Incl. Units 1-12. ix, 182p. pap. 8.00x (ISBN 0-87950-080-8); Records, Six 12-Inch LP (33.3 rpm) o.p. (ISBN 0-87950-083-2); Record Course-Bk. & Records. pap. 45.00x (ISBN 0-87950-084-0); Cassettes, Six Dual Track. 60.00x (ISBN 0-87950-085-9); Cassette Course-Bk. & Cassettes. 65.00x (ISBN 0-87950-086-7). LC 74-152740. (Spoken Language Ser.). (Prog. Bk.). 1974. Spoken Lang Serv.
Denoeu, Francois & Sices, David. Two Thousand & One French & English Idioms: Idiotismes Francais et Anglais 2001. Date not set. pap. text ed. 7.50 (ISBN 0-8120-0435-3). Barron. Postponed.
Denomme, Robert T. Leconte de Lisle. (World Authors Ser.: France: No. 278). 1973. lib. bdg. 10.95 (ISBN 0-8057-2518-0). Twayne.
Denoon, David B., ed. The New International Economic Order: A U. S. Response. LC 79-1997. (A UNA-USA Bk.). 1979. 20.00x (ISBN 0-8147-1769-1); pap. 9.00x (ISBN 0-8147-1770-5). NYU Pr.
Denoon, Donald. Southern Africa Since 1800. 1979. pap. text ed. 9.95x (ISBN 0-582-60321-8). Longman.
De Noriega, L. A. & Leach, F. Broadcasting in Mexico. (Case Studies on Broadcasting Systems). (Orig.). 1979. pap. 12.50 (ISBN 0-7100-0416-8). Routledge & Kegan.
Den Ouden, Bernard see Ouden, Bernard D.
Denslow, Van Buren. Principles of the Economic Philosophy of Society, Government & Industry. (The Neglected American Economists Ser.). 1974. lib. bdg. 50.00 (ISBN 0-8240-1023-X). Garland Pub.
Denslow, William R. Ten Thousand Famous Freemasons, 4 vols. 1979. Repr. Set. pap. 29.95 slip cover (ISBN 0-686-68268-8). Macoy Pub.
Densmore, D., tr. see Tchernia, P.
Densmore, Frances. Chippewa Customs. LC 79-15400. (Illus.). 204p. 1979. pap. 7.50 (ISBN 0-87351-142-5). Minn Hist.
--Chippewa Music, 2 vols. LC 77-164513. (Illus.). 1972. Repr. of 1913 ed. Set. lib. bdg. 45.00 (ISBN 0-306-70459-5). Da Capo.
--Choctaw Music. LC 72-1883. (Music Ser.). (Illus.). 110p. 1972. Repr. of 1943 ed. lib. bdg. 14.00 (ISBN 0-306-70511-7). Da Capo.
--Handbook of the Collection of Musical Instruments in the United States National Museum. LC 79-155231. (Music Ser). 1971. Repr. of 1927 ed. lib. bdg. 25.00 (ISBN 0-306-70167-7). Da Capo.
--How Indians Use Wild Plants for Food, Medicine & Crafts. Orig. Title: Use of Plants by the Chippewa Indians. (Illus.). 7.50 (ISBN 0-8446-5029-3). Peter Smith.
--Mandan & Hidatsa Music. LC 72-1886. (Music Ser.). (Illus.). 236p. 1972. Repr. of 1923 ed. lib. bdg. 19.50 (ISBN 0-306-70514-1). Da Capo.
--Menominee Music. LC 72-1882. (Music Ser.). (Illus.). 286p. 1972. Repr. of 1932 ed. lib. bdg. 19.50 (ISBN 0-306-70510-9). Da Capo.
--Music of Acoma, Isleta, Cochiti, & Zuni Pueblos. LC 72-1877. (Music Ser.). (Illus.). 142p. 1972. Repr. of 1957 ed. lib. bdg. 16.50 (ISBN 0-306-70505-2). Da Capo.
--Music of the Indians of British Columbia. LC 72-1879. (Music Ser.). (Illus.). 118p. 1972. Repr. of 1943 ed. lib. bdg. 14.50 (ISBN 0-306-70507-9). Da Capo.
--The Music of the North American Indian, 14 vols. in 13. (Music Ser.). 1972. Set. 250.00 (ISBN 0-306-70517-6). Da Capo.
--Nootka & Quileute Music. LC 72-1885. (Music Ser.). (Illus.). 416p. 1972. Repr. of 1939 ed. lib. bdg. 29.50 (ISBN 0-306-70513-3). Da Capo.
--Northern Ute Music. LC 72-1887. (Music Ser.). (Illus.). 236p. 1972. Repr. of 1922 ed. lib. bdg. 19.50 (ISBN 0-306-70515-X). Da Capo.
--Papago Music. LC 72-1881. (Music Ser.). (Illus.). 276p. 1972. Repr. of 1929 ed. lib. bdg. 19.50 (ISBN 0-306-70509-5). Da Capo.
--Pawnee Music. LC 72-1880. (Music Ser.). 160p. 1972. Repr. of 1929 ed. lib. bdg. 14.50 (ISBN 0-306-70508-7). Da Capo.
--Seminole Music. LC 72-1878. (Music Ser.). (Illus.). 276p. 1972. Repr. of 1956 ed. lib. bdg. 19.50 (ISBN 0-306-70506-0). Da Capo.
--Teton Sioux Music. LC 72-1889. (Music Ser.). (Illus.). 722p. 1972. Repr. of 1918 ed. lib. bdg. 39.50 (ISBN 0-306-70516-8). Da Capo.
--Yuman & Yaqui Music. LC 72-1884. (Music Ser.). (Illus.). 272p. 1972. Repr. of 1932 ed. lib. bdg. 19.50 (ISBN 0-306-70512-5). Da Capo.
Densmore, Mary J., jt. auth. see Emanuelsen, Kathy L.
Denson, Alan. Letters from A. E. (Collected Edition of the Writings of G. W. Russell VII). 1980. text ed. write for info. (ISBN 0-391-01139-1). Humanities.
Denson, Alan, ed. The Poetry of A. E. (Collected Edition of the Writings of G.W. Russell Ser. V). 1980. text ed. write for info. (ISBN 0-391-01144-8). Humanities.
Dent, A., tr. see Andrist, Friedrich.
Dent, Anthony. Cleveland Bay Horses. (Illus.). 1978. 7.85 (ISBN 0-85131-283-7, Dist. by Sporting Book Center). J A Allen.
Dent, Anthony, tr. see Geurts, Reiner.
Dent, E. J. The Future of Music. 1966. pap. 5.75 (ISBN 0-08-011354-0). Pergamon.
--The Rise of Romantic Opera. Dean, W., ed. LC 76-14029. (Illus.). 1976. 32.95 (ISBN 0-521-21337-1); pap. 8.50x (ISBN 0-521-29659-5). Cambridge U Pr.
Dent, E. J., ed. see Piave, F. M.
Dent, Edward J. Foundations of English Opera. 2nd ed. LC 65-18501. (Music Ser). 1965. Repr. of 1928 ed. lib. bdg. 22.50 (ISBN 0-306-70905-8). Da Capo.
Dent, Edward J., tr. see Gieseke, Carl L. & Schikaneder, Emanuel.
Dent, J. B. & Blackie, M. J. Systems Simulation in Agriculture. (Illus.). 1979. 29.90x (ISBN 0-85334-827-8, Pub. by Applied Science). Burgess-Intl Ideas.
Dent, J. B., jt. ed. see Blackie, M. J.
Dent, R. W. Shakespeare's Proverbial Language: An Index. 378p. 1981. 24.50x (ISBN 0-520-03894-0). U of Cal Pr.
Dent, Roxanne. Streetwater Saga. 1979. pap. cancelled o.p. (Sig). NAL.
Den Tak Richard, Van see Van Den Tak, Richard.
Dentan, Robert C. Apocrypha: Bridge of the Testaments. 1954. pap. 3.00 (ISBN 0-8164-2002-5, SP13). Crossroad NY.
--First Reader in Biblical Theology: The Design of the Scriptures. 1965. pap. 3.95 (ISBN 0-8164-2022-X, SP20). Crossroad NY.
--Holy Scriptures: A Survey. (Orig.). 1949. pap. 3.95 (ISBN 0-8164-2031-9, SP1). Crossroad NY.
Den Tex, Jan. Oldenbarnevelt, 2 vols. Powell, Ralph, tr. from Dutch. LC 73-177937. (Illus.). 368p. 1973. Set. 145.00 (ISBN 0-521-08429-6). Cambridge U Pr.
Denti, Renzo. Dizionario Tecnico Italiano-Inglese--Inglese-Italiano. 9th rev. ed. 1811p. 1979. 44.00x (ISBN 88-203-1052-X). S F Vanni.
Denton, Clive. Susan Hayward & the Movie. 300p. Date not set. cancelled o.p. (ISBN 0-498-02316-8). A S Barnes. Postponed.
Denton, Derek A. & Coghlan, John P., eds. Olfaction & Taste, Vol. 5. 1975. 36.50 (ISBN 0-12-209750-5). Acad Pr.
Denton, E. N., jt. auth. see Glanvill, A. B.
Denton, G. H. & Hughes, T. J. The Last Great Ice Sheets. LC 79-27808. 1980. write for info. (ISBN 0-471-06006-2, Pub. by Wiley-Interscience). Wiley.

Denton, Geoffrey. Economic & Monetary Union in Europe: The Economic Implications of Monetary Integration. LC 74-18622. 118p. 1975. 19.95 (ISBN 0-470-20940-2). Halsted Pr.

Denton, J. H. Robert Winchelsey & the Crown, 1294-1313. (Cambridge Studies in Medieval Life & Thought: No. 14). 1980. 42.50 (ISBN 0-521-22963-4). Cambridge U Pr.

Denton, James. Circuit Hikes in Shenandoah National Park. 11th ed. LC 80-81762. 86p. 1980. pap. write for info. (ISBN 0-915746-15-8). Potomac Appalach.

Denton, James W., ed. Circuit Hikes in the Shenandoah National Park. 10th ed. LC 76-21937. 1976. pap. 2.00 o.p. (ISBN 0-915746-08-5). Potomac Appalach.

Denton, John A. Medical Sociology. LC 77-94098. (Illus.). 1978. text ed. 19.25 (ISBN 0-395-25805-7). HM.

Denton, Molly T., ed. Guide to the Appalachian Trail & Side Trails in the Shenandoah National Park. 8th ed. LC 76-17452. 265p. 1977. pap. 5.00 o.p. (ISBN 0-915746-07-7). Potomac Appalach.

Denton, T. E. Fish Chromosome Methodology. (Illus.). 176p. 1973. 17.50 (ISBN 0-398-02831-1). C C Thomas.

D'Entremont, E., ed. see Ynamuno.

D'Entreves, A. P. Natural Law: An Introduction to Legal Philosophy. 2nd rev. ed. 1964. text ed. 10.25x (ISBN 0-09-102600-8, Hutchinson U Lib); pap. text ed. 8.50x (ISBN 0-09-102601-6, Hutchinson U Lib). Humanities.

D'Entreves, Alexander P. Medieval Contribution to Political Thought: Thomas Aquinas, Marsilius of Padua, Richard Hooker. 1959. Repr. of 1939 ed. text ed. 8.50x (ISBN 0-391-00513-8). Humanities.

Denu, Ma, ed. see Dass, Baba Hari.

Denuziere, Maurice. Bagatelle. LC 78-655. 1978. 9.95 o.p. (ISBN 0-688-03316-4). Morrow.

Denver, Shad & McKinley, Brett. The Sundown Man-Sunday in Choctaw Country. 1980. pap. 2.25 (ISBN 0-8439-0732-0, Leisure Bks). Nordon Pubns.

Denvir, B. Fauvism & Expressionism. LC 77-80181. (Modern Movements in Art Ser.). 1978. pap. 1.95 (ISBN 0-8120-0878-2). Barron.

--Impressionism. LC 77-80177. (Modern Movements in Art Ser.). 1978. pap. 1.95 (ISBN 0-8120-0879-0). Barron.

Denvir, John. The Life Story of an Old Rebel. 306p. 1972. Repr. of 1910 ed. 15.00x (ISBN 0-7165-0012-4, Pub. by Irish Academic Pr Ireland). Biblio Dist.

Denyer, C. P., tr. see Halley, Henry H.

Denyer, Carlos. Concordancia De las Sagradas Escripturas. LC 74-21722. 936p. (Span.). 1969. 24.95 (ISBN 0-89922-004-5); pap. 15.95 (ISBN 0-89922-121-1). Edit Caribe.

Denyer, J. C. Office Management. 5th ed. (Illus.). 528p. 1980. pap. text ed. 17.95x (ISBN 0-7121-1525-0). Intl Ideas.

Denys, Teresa. Flesh & the Devil. 488p. 1981. 12.95 (ISBN 0-312-29583-9). St Martin.

Denzel, Justin F. Hiboy: Young Devil Horse. LC 80-10578. 48p. (gr. 3). 1980. PLB 5.67 (ISBN 0-8116-4866-4). Garrard.

Deo, Narsingh. Graph Theory with Applications to Engineering & Computer Science. 1974. 25.95 (ISBN 0-13-363473-6). P-H.

Deodhar, Sharad & Nakamura, Robert M. Atlas of Autoimmune Diseases. (Atlas Ser.). 1976. 95.00 (ISBN 0-685-78052-X, 15-A-002-00). Am Soc Clinical.

Deodhar, Sharad, jt. auth. see Nakamura, Robert M.

Deodhar, Sharad D., jt. auth. see Valenzuela, Rafael.

Deogaonkar, S. G. Problems of Development in Tribal Areas. 192p. 1980. text ed. 13.50x (ISBN 0-391-02132-X). Humanities.

De Oliveira, Fernandes E., et al. Building Energy Management--Conventional & Solar Approaches: Proceedings of the International Congress, 12-16 May 1980, Povoa de Varzim, Portugal. LC 80-40415. 800p. 1981. 160.00 (ISBN 0-08-026144-2). Pergamon.

De Olivera Marques, Antonia H. History of Portugal. Incl. Vol. 1. From Lusitania to Empire. 507p. 22.50x (ISBN 0-231-03159-9); Vol. 2. From Empire to Corporate State. 303p. 20.00x (ISBN 0-231-08700-4). LC 77-184748. 1972. pap. 15.00x (ISBN 0-686-66878-2) (ISBN 0-231-08353-X). Columbia U Pr.

De Olivieri, Evelyn R., tr. see Blazier, Kenneth D.

De Olivieri, Matilde Vilarino see Vilarino De Olivieri, Matilde.

Deonanan, Carlton R., jt. auth. see Deonanan, Venus E.

Deonanan, Venus E. & Deonanan, Carlton R. Teaching Spanish in the Secondary School in Trinidad, West Indies: A Curriculum Perspective. LC 79-6199. 373p. 1980. pap. text ed. 11.50 (ISBN 0-8191-1005-1). U Pr of Amer.

De Onis, Federico see Seminario De Estudios Hispanicos & Onis, Federico de.

De Onis, Harriet, tr. from Span. Life of Lazarillo De Tormes. (gr. 11 up). 1959. pap. text ed. 2.95 (ISBN 0-8120-0128-1). Barron.

De Onis, Harriet, tr. see Guzman, Martin L.

De Onis, Jose, ed. The Hispanic Contribution to the State of Colorado. LC 76-7014. 1976. 17.50x o.p. (ISBN 0-89158-100-6). Westview.

De Ortiz, Sutti R. Uncertainties in Peasant Farming, Ortiz/sutti R. De. (London School of Economics Monographs on Social Anthropology Ser.). (Illus.). 312p. 1973. text ed. 27.50x (ISBN 0-391-00268-6, Athlone Pr). Humanities.

De Osa, Veronica. Sinan: The Turkish Michelangelo. 1981. 10.95 (ISBN 0-533-04655-6). Vantage.

De Pacheco, Blanca Silvestrini see Silvestrini De Pacheco, Blanca.

Depalma, Anthony F., ed. see Association of Bone & Joint Surgeons.

De Palma, Anthony F., ed. see Association of Bone & Joint Surgeons.

De Palma, D. J. & Foley, J. M. Moral Development: Current Theory & Research. LC 75-14211. 1975. 14.95 o.p. (ISBN 0-470-20950-X). Halsted Pr.

DePaola. The Clown of God. (Illus.). (gr. 2-3). Date not set. pap. cancelled (ISBN 0-590-30068-7, Schol Pap). Schol Bk Serv.

De Paola, T. Andy: That's My Name. (ps-3). 1973. 6.95 (ISBN 0-13-036731-1); pap. 2.50 (ISBN 0-13-036749-4). P-H.

--Charlie Needs a Cloak. 1974. 6.95 (ISBN 0-13-128355-3). P-H.

De Paola, Tomie. Big Anthony & the Magic Ring. LC 78-23631. (gr. k-3). 1979. 7.95 (ISBN 0-15-207124-5, HJ). HarBraceJ.

--The Comic Adventures of Old Mother Hubbard & Her Dog. LC 80-19270. (Illus.). 32p. (ps-3). 1981. pap. 5.95 (ISBN 0-15-219542-4, VoyB). HarBraceJ.

--The Comic Adventures of Old Mother Hubbard & Her Dog. LC 80-19270. (Illus.). 32p. (ps-3). 1981. 11.95 (ISBN 0-15-219541-6, HJ). HarBraceJ.

--The Family Christmas Tree Book. LC 80-12081. (Illus.). 32p. (ps-3). 1980. PLB 8.95 (ISBN 0-8234-0416-1). Holiday.

--The Legend of Old Befana. LC 80-12293. (Illus.). 32p. (gr. k-3). 1980. pap. 3.95 (ISBN 0-15-243817-3, VoyB). HarBraceJ.

--The Legend of Old Befana. LC 80-12293. (Illus.). 32p. (gr. k-3). 1980. 8.95 (ISBN 0-15-243816-5, HJ). HarBraceJ.

--Michael Bird-Boy. (Illus.). (ps-2). 1975. 5.95 (ISBN 0-13-580803-0); pap. 2.50 (ISBN 0-13-580811-1). P-H.

--Now One Foot, Now the Other. (Illus.). 48p. (gr. 3-7). 1981. 7.95 (ISBN 0-399-20774-0); pap. 2.95 (ISBN 0-399-20775-9). Putnam.

--Pancakes for Breakfast. LC 79-18524. (Illus.). 32p. (ps-3). 1978. pap. 2.50 (ISBN 0-15-263528-9, VoyB). HarBraceJ.

--The Popcorn Book. (gr. k-3). 1979. pap. 1.50 (ISBN 0-590-03142-2, Schol Pap). Schol Bk Serv.

--The Prince of the Dolomites. LC 79-18524. (Illus.). 48p. (ps-3). 1980. pap. 4.50 (ISBN 0-15-263529-7, VoyB). HarBraceJ.

--The Prince of the Dolomites. LC 79-18524. (Illus.). (gr. k-3). 1980. 8.95 (ISBN 0-15-263528-9, HJ). HarBraceJ.

--St. Francis of Assisi. (Illus.). 48p. (ps). 1981. PLB 10.95 (ISBN 0-8234-0435-8). Holiday.

--Strega Nona. LC 75-11565. (Illus.). (ps-3). 1975. 8.95 (ISBN 0-13-851600-6); pap. 3.95. P-H.

--Things to Make & Do for Valentine's Day. (Things to Make & Do Ser.). (Illus.). 48p. (gr. k-3). 1976. PLB 7.90 (ISBN 0-531-01187-9). Watts.

--Watch Out for the Chicken Feet in Your Soup. LC 74-8201. (Illus.). (ps-3). 1974. PLB 6.95 (ISBN 0-13-945782-8); pap. 1.95 (ISBN 0-13-945766-6). P-H.

De Paola, Tomie see Paola, Tomie de.

De Paola, Tomie, illus. & retold by. Fin M'Coul: The Giant of Knockmany Hill. LC 80-2254. (Illus.). 32p. (ps-3). 1981. PLB 10.95 (ISBN 0-8234-0384-X); pap. 4.95 (ISBN 0-8234-0385-8). Holiday.

De Papp Severo, Emoke. The Good-Hearted Youngest Brother. (Illus.). 32p. (gr. k-3). 1981. 9.95 (ISBN 0-87888-141-7). Bradbury Pr.

Deparcieux, Antoine. Essai Sur les Probabilites De la Duree De la Vie Humaine. (Principal French Demographic Works of the 18th Century Ser.). (Fr.). 1976. lib. bdg. 60.00x o.p. (ISBN 0-8287-0261-6); pap. text ed. 50.00x o.p. (ISBN 0-685-71513-2). Clearwater Pub.

Department of American Decorative Arts & Sculpture, Museum of Fine Arts, Boston. Paul Revere's Boston: Seventeen Thirty-Five to Eighteen Eighteen. (Illus.). 1975. 16.00 (ISBN 0-87846-088-8). Mus Fine Arts Boston.

Department of Classical Art. Art of Ancient Cyprus. 1972. pap. 2.95 (ISBN 0-87846-068-3). Mus Fine Arts Boston.

--Romans & Barbarians. 1977. 35.00 o.p. (ISBN 0-87846-110-8); pap. 12.00 o.p. (ISBN 0-87846-178-7). Mus Fine Arts Boston.

Department of Energy. National Program for Solar Heating & Cooling of Buildings: Annual Report. 1979. pap. cancelled (ISBN 0-930978-22-6). Solar Energy Info.

--National Program Plan for Research & Development in Solar Heating & Cooling for Buildings, Agricultural, & Industrial Applications. 1979. pap. cancelled (ISBN 0-930978-23-4). Solar Energy Info.

--Solar Thermal Power Systems: Annual Technical Progress Report. 134p. 1980. pap. 14.95 (ISBN 0-89934-028-8). Solar Energy Info.

Department of Textiles, Museum of Fine Arts, Boston. Nancy Graves Cabot, in Memoriam, Sources of Design for Textiles & Decorative Arts. 1973. pap. 2.50 (ISBN 0-87846-175-2). Mus Fine Arts Boston.

Department of the Interior, U. S. Geologicaal Survey, Monograph & Osborn, Henry F. The Titanotheres of Ancient Wyoming, Dakota, & Nebraska. Gould, Stephen J., ed. LC 79-83341. (The History of Paleontology Ser.: 55 2vols.). (Illus.). 1980. Repr. of 1929 ed. Set. lib. bdg. 195.00x (ISBN 0-405-12729-4); lib. bdg. 97.50 ea. Vol. 1 (ISBN 0-405-12730-8). Vol. 2 (ISBN 0-405-12731-6). Arno.

DePasquale, Nicholas P. & Bruno, Michael S. Cardiology Case Studies. 2nd ed. LC 79-91847. 1980. pap. 15.00 (ISBN 0-87488-001-7). Med Exam.

DePasquale, Nicholas P. & Bruno, Michael S., eds. Cardiology Case Studies. 1973. spiral bdg. 12.00 o.p. (ISBN 0-87488-001-7). Med Exam.

DePaula, jt. auth. see Smith, Kussel.

De Paula, F. Clive. Management Accounting in Practice. 4th ed. 1972. 13.95x (ISBN 0-8464-0587-3); pap. 9.50x. Beekman Pubs.

DePaula, H. & Mueller, C. Marketing Today's Fashion. 1980. 15.95 (ISBN 0-13-558155-9). P-H.

De Pauw, John W. Soviet-American Trade Negotiations. LC 78-25883. (Praeger Special Studies). 1979. 22.95 (ISBN 0-03-048446-4). Praeger.

Depel, Jim. The Baseball Handbook for Coaches & Players. LC 75-19308. (Illus.). 96p. 1976. 7.95 o.p. (ISBN 0-684-14264-3, ScribT); pap. 4.95 (ISBN 0-684-14265-1, SL 593, ScribT). Scribner.

De Perro, Anthony. The Mosque of Omyad. 23p. 1980. 4.95 (ISBN 0-533-04410-3). Vantage.

De Peters, Amalia B., jt. auth. see Lombardi, Ronald P.

Depew, Creighton A. see Heat Transfer & Fluid Mechanics Institute.

De Pisan, Christine. Book of the Duke of True Lovers. Kemp-Welch, Alice, et al, trs. LC 66-23313. (Illus.). Repr. of 1926 ed. 7.50x (ISBN 0-8154-0177-9). Cooper Sq.

DePlatt, Lyman, ed. Genealogical Historical Guide to Latin America. LC 78-75146. (Genealogy & Local History Ser.: Vol. 4). 1978. 30.00 (ISBN 0-8103-1389-8). Gale.

De Plou, Dafne C., tr. see Drakeford, John W.

DePoe, Charles, et al. Laboratory Manual for General Botany. 4th ed. 1976. pap. text ed. 6.95 (ISBN 0-8403-1448-5). Kendall-Hunt.

De Poix, Carol. Jo, Flo & Yolanda. 35p. (ps-1). 1973. pap. 2.50 (ISBN 0-914996-04-5). Lollipop Power.

De Polnay, Peter. Blood & Water. LC 75-40784. 199p. 1976. 7.95 o.p. (ISBN 0-312-08435-8). St Martin.

De Pomiane, Edouard. Cooking in Ten Minutes. (Illus.). 1967. pap. 4.95 (ISBN 0-571-08160-6, Pub by Faber & Faber). Merrimack Bk Serv.

De Poor, Betty M., tr. Dios, Tu y Tu Familia. (Dios, Tu y la Vida). Orig. Title: Deus, Voce E Sua Familia. 1978. 0.75 (ISBN 0-311-46202-2). Casa Bautista.

DePorte, A. W. Europe & the Superpower Balance. LC 79-92257. (Headline Ser.: No. 247). (Illus.). 80p. (gr. 11-12). 1979. pap. 2.00 (ISBN 0-87124-058-0). Foreign Policy.

Depp, Roberta J., jt. ed. see Wynar, Bohdan S.

Deppe, Phillip, et al. The High Risk Child: A Guide for Concerned Parents. 224p. 1981. 12.95 (ISBN 0-02-531010-0). Macmillan.

DePree, Gladis & DePree, Gordon. Catch a Red Leaf. (Illus.). 128p. (Orig.). 1980. pap. 3.95 (ISBN 0-310-23671-1, 9485P). Zondervan.

--A Time to Grow. 112p. (Orig.). 1981. pap. 3.95 (ISBN 0-310-23681-9). Zondervan.

De Pree, Gladis, jt. auth. see De Pree, Gordon.

DePree, Gladis, jt. auth. see DePree, Gordon.

Depree, Gladis L. The Self-Anointed: Love & Terror in My Father's House. LC 77-3746. 1978. 9.95 o.s.i. (ISBN 0-06-011058-9, HarpT). Har-Row.

De Pree, Gordon & De Pree, Gladis. Blade of Grass. LC 65-19504. 1971. pap. 3.95 (ISBN 0-310-23641-X). Zondervan.

DePree, Gordon & DePree, Gladis. The Gift. (Illus.). 128p. 1976. padded cover & boxed 10.95 (ISBN 0-310-23650-9). Zondervan.

--The Gift. (Illus.). 1979. pap. 7.95 (ISBN 0-310-23651-7). Zondervan.

DePree, Gordon, jt. auth. see DePree, Gladis.

DePree, Mildred. A Child's World of Stamps: Stories, Poems, Fun & Facts from Many Lands. LC 72-10178. (Illus.). 128p. (gr. 3 up). 1973. 5.95 o.s.i. (ISBN 0-8193-0661-4, Four Winds); PLB 5.41 o.s.i. (ISBN 0-8193-0662-2). Schol Bk Serv.

De Prez, Caroline S. & De Prez, Richard J. Resume Manual for the Military: A Complete Job-Hunting Guide for Present & Future Veterans. LC 80-68132. (Illus.). 177p. (Orig.). 1980. pap. 10.95 (ISBN 0-9604728-0-0). Alfa Sierra.

De Prez, Richard J., jt. auth. see De Prez, Caroline S.

DePrist, jt. auth. see Wegman.

Dept. of Defense-Defense Supply Agency. Defense in-Plant Quality Assurance Program. 1976. 9.50x (ISBN 0-912702-08-7). Global Eng.

Dept. of the Army, Washington D. C. Counterguerilla Operations: FM 1-16. (Illus.). 163p. 1967. pap. 8.00 (ISBN 0-87364-038-1). Paladin Ent.

Depta, Victor. The Creek. LC 72-85541. 1973. 7.95 (ISBN 0-8214-0121-1). Ohio U Pr.

Depue, Richard A., ed. The Psychobiology of the Depressive Disorders: Implications for the Effects of Stress. LC 79-51676. (Personality & Psychopathology Ser.). 1979. 32.00 (ISBN 0-12-211650-X). Acad Pr.

De Purucker, G. Dialogues of G. De Purucker, 3 vols. Conger, Arthur L., ed. LC 79-65630. 1948. Set. 20.00 (ISBN 0-911500-59-6). Theos U Pr.

--The Four Sacred Seasons. LC 79-63565. 1979. 4.50 (ISBN 0-911500-83-9); pap. 2.75 softcover (ISBN 0-911500-84-7). Theos U Pr.

--Fundamentals of the Esoteric Philosophy. 2nd, rev. ed. Knoche, Grace F., ed. LC 78-74258. 1979. 13.50 (ISBN 0-911500-63-4); softcover 8.95 (ISBN 0-911500-64-2). Theos U Pr.

--Golden Precepts of Esotericism. 3rd, rev. ed. LC 78-74257. 1979. 5.00 (ISBN 0-911500-85-5); pap. 3.00 (ISBN 0-911500-86-3). Theos U Pr.

--Man in Evolution. 2nd rev. ed. Knoche, Grace F., ed. LC 76-45503. 1977. softcover 5.00 (ISBN 0-911500-55-3). Theos U Pr.

--Occult Glossary. LC 53-37086. 1972. Repr. of 1933 ed. 6.00 (ISBN 0-911500-50-2); softcover 3.50 (ISBN 0-911500-51-0). Theos U Pr.

DePuy, Charles H. & Rinehart, Kenneth L. Introduction to Organic Chemistry. 2nd ed. LC 74-19442. 323p. 1975. text ed. 22.95 (ISBN 0-471-20350-5). Wiley.

De Quehen, Hugh, ed. see Butler, Samuel.

De Quericize, F., jt. auth. see Chaffurin, L.

De Quevedo y Villegas, Francisco G. see Quevedo y Villegas, Francisco G. de.

DeQuincey, Thomas. The Caesars. (Illus.). 300p. 1981. 12.95 (ISBN 0-8180-0824-5). Horizon.

De Quincey, Thomas. Selected Essays on Rhetoric. Burwick, Frederick, ed. LC 67-21038. (Landmarks in Rhetoric & Public Address Ser.). 329p. 1967. 11.95x (ISBN 0-8093-0262-4). S Ill U Pr.

De Quincy, A. C. History of the Life & Works of Rafaello. Freedberg, Sydney J., ed. LC 77-25764. (Connoisseurship Criticism & Art History Ser.: Vol. 19). (Illus.). 1980. lib. bdg. 52.00 (ISBN 0-8240-3277-2). Garland Pub.

De Quiros, J. & Schrager, O. Neuropsychological Fundamentals. 2nd ed. (Illus.). 292p. 1980. 20.00 (ISBN 0-87879-240-6). Acad Therapy.

Der, Mehden, Fred R. Von see Von Der Mehden, Fred R., pseud.

Derache, R., ed. see Commission of the European Communities.

De Rachewiltz, Boris. Black Eros. Longanesi & Co., tr. 1964. 10.50 o.p. (ISBN 0-04-390001-1). Allen Unwin.

De Rachewiltz, Mary. Discretions. (Illus.). 1971. 9.95 o.p. (ISBN 0-571-09623-9, Pub. by Faber & Faber). Merrimack Bk Serv.

De Rachwiltz, I. & Wang, M. Index to Biographical Material in Chin & Yuan Literary Works - Third Series. LC 78-52594. (Faculty of Asian Studies Oriental Monograph: No. 20). 341p. 1980. pap. text ed. 19.95 (ISBN 0-7081-0179-8, 0556). Bks Australia.

Derber, M. & Young, E., eds. Labor & the New Deal. LC 70-169656. (Fdr & the Era of the New Deal Ser.). 394p. 1972. Repr. of 1957 ed. lib. bdg. 29.50 (ISBN 0-306-70364-5). Da Capo.

Derby, Pat & Beagle, Peter S. The Lady & Her Tiger. 1977. pap. 1.95 o.p. (ISBN 0-345-25711-1). Ballantine.

Derbyshire, A. Leslie. Mastering Management. LC 80-83028. 300p. 1981. 9.95 (ISBN 0-88290-159-1, 2046). Horizon Utah.

Derbyshire, E., et al. Geomorphological Processes. LC 79-5285. (Studies in Physical Geography Ser.). 312p. 1980. lib. bdg. 27.50x (ISBN 0-89158-695-4, Pub. by Dawson Pub); pap. text ed. 13.50x (ISBN 0-89158-864-7). Westview.

Derbyshire, Edward, ed. Geomorphology & Climate. LC 75-4523. 514p. 1976. 81.50 (ISBN 0-471-20954-6, Pub. by Wiley-Interscience). Wiley.
Derbyshore, Caroline. The New Woman's Guide to Health & Medicine. (Appleton Consumer Health Guides). (Illus.). 316p. 1980. 12.95 (ISBN 0-8385-6759-2); pap. 5.95 (ISBN 0-8385-6758-4). ACC.
De Reamer, Russell. Modern Safety Practices. LC 58-12708. 372p. 1958. 11.50 (ISBN 0-471-20361-0). Krieger.
De Reedy, Ginette D., tr. see Wallace, Lew.
De Regniers. Abraham Lincoln Joke Book. (gr. 3-5). 1980. pap. 1.25 (ISBN 0-590-30968-4, Schol Pap). Schol Bk Serv.
De Regnier, Beatrice S. Catch a Little Fox. LC 75-97036. (Illus.). (ps-2). 1970. 6.50 (ISBN 0-395-28821-5, Clarion). HM.
De Regniers, Beatrice & Gilman, Esther. Little Girl & Her Mother. LC 63-13794. (gr. 4 up). 6.95 (ISBN 0-8149-0295-2). Vanguard.
De Regniers, Beatrice S. A Bunch of Poems & Verses. LC 76-28324. (Illus.). (gr. 1-5). 1977. 6.95 (ISBN 0-395-28881-9, Clarion). HM.
--It Does Not Say Meow. LC 72-75704. (Illus.). 40p. (ps-1). 1972. 5.95 (ISBN 0-395-28822-3, Clarion). HM.
--Laura's Story. LC 78-12623. (Illus.). (ps-1). 1979. 8.95 (ISBN 0-689-30677-6). Atheneum.
--May I Bring a Friend. LC 64-19562. (Illus.). (ps-2). 1964. PLB 8.95 (ISBN 0-689-20615-1). Atheneum.
De Regniers, Beatrice S. & Gordon, Isabel. Shadow Book. LC 60-10244. (Illus.). (gr. k-3). 1960. 5.95 o.p. (ISBN 0-15-272991-7, HJ). HarBraceJ.
De Regniers, Beatrice S. & Pierce, Leona. Who Likes the Sun. LC 61-6112. (Illus.). (gr. k-2). 1961. 3.95 o.p. (ISBN 0-15-296065-1, HJ). HarBraceJ.
Derenski, Arlene & Landsburg, Sally. Older Women - Younger Men. 272p. 1981. 11.95 (ISBN 0-316-51366-0). Little.
De Renty, Ivan. The Businessman's Everyday English to Spanish Dictionary: El Mundo De Negocios. 1978. pap. 9.95 (ISBN 0-88332-100-9, 8138). Larousse.
--Lexique de l'anglais des affaires. new ed. 320p. 1973. pap. 7.95 (ISBN 0-88332-247-1, 4100). Larousse.
De Renzo, D. J., ed. Biodegradation Techniques for Industrial Organic Wastes. LC 80-12834. (Pollution Technology Review Ser. 65; Chemical Technology Review Ser. 158). (Illus.). 358p. 1980. 28.00 (ISBN 0-8155-0800-X). Noyes.
--European Technology for Obtaining Energy from Solid Waste. LC 78-61896. (Energy Technology Review No. 74: Pollution Technology Review No. 54). (Illus.). 1978. 39.00 (ISBN 0-8155-0730-5). Noyes.
Dereshinsky, Ralph M. & Berkowitz, Alan D. The NLRB & Secondary Boycotts. rev. ed. 1980. pap. 15.00 (ISBN 0-89546-027-0). Indus Res Unit-Wharton.
De Reyna, Rudy. Painting in Opaque Watercolor. LC 69-12492. (Illus.). 1969. 15.95 o.p. (ISBN 0-8230-3775-4). Watson-Guptill.
Deri, Susan. Transitional Phenomena, Vicissitudes of Symbolization, & Creativity. 1981. write for info. (ISBN 0-8236-6641-7). Intl Univs Pr.
Derian, Jean-Claude, jt. auth. see Bupp, Irvin C.
DeRidder, Richard R., jt. auth. see Brink, William P.
De Riencourt, Amaury. The Eye of Shiva: Eastern Mysticism & Science. LC 80-22032. 221p. 1981. 8.95 (ISBN 0-688-00038-X); pap. 4.95 (ISBN 0-686-63396-2). Morrow.
Derigs, U., jt. auth. see Burkhard, R. E.
De Rijk, L. M., ed. Petrus Abaelardus Dialectica. 2nd ed. 1970. text ed. 82.75x (ISBN 0-685-12392-8). Humanities.
De Rijk, Lambertus M. Logica Modernorum, Vol. 2. (Philos. Texts & Studies: Vol. 16). 1967. text ed. 116.50x (ISBN 90-232-0440-9). Humanities.
Dering, Edward. Parliamentary Diary of Sir Edward Dering, 1670-73. Henning, Basil D., ed. (Yale Historical Pubs. Miscellany Ser.: No. XVI). 1940. 42.50x (ISBN 0-685-69825-4). Elliots Bks.
Dering, Edward H. Sherborne; or, the House at the Four Ways, 1875. Wolff, Robert L., ed. LC 75-457. (Victorian Fiction Ser.). 1975. lib. bdg. 66.00 (ISBN 0-8240-1536-3). Garland Pub.
De River, J. Paul. Crime & the Sexual Psychopath. (Illus.). 384p. 1958. 27.50 (ISBN 0-398-00436-6). C C Thomas.
De Rivero, Oswaldo. New Economic Order & International Development Law. LC 79-41222. 132p. 1980. 18.50 (ISBN 0-08-024706-7). Pergamon.
Derk, Francis H. Names of Christ: A Pocket Guide. LC 75-44928. 1976. pap. 2.50 (ISBN 0-87123-390-8, 200390). Bethany Fell.
Derkinderen, Frans G., jt. ed. see Crum, Roy L.
Der Klip, Rita Van see Van Der Klip, Rita.
Der Kulk, W. Van see Schouten, Jan A. & Van Der Kulk, W.
Derlega, Valerian & Janda, Louis H. Personal Adjustment: Selected Readings. 1979. pap. text ed. 8.95x (ISBN 0-673-15288-X). Scott F.
Derlega, Valerian J. & Janda, Louis. Personal Adjustment: The Psychology of Everyday Life. 2nd ed. 1981. text ed. 16.95x (ISBN 0-673-15470-X). Scott F.
Derlega, Valerian J., jt. auth. see Chaikin, Alan L.
Derleth, August. The Mask of Cthulhu. 1976. pap. 1.50 o.p. (ISBN 0-345-25095-8). Ballantine.
--Someone in the Dark. 1978. pap. 1.75 o.s.i. (ISBN 0-685-54634-9, 04738-4). Jove Pubns.
--Someone in the Dark. 335p. 1980. Repr. of 1941 ed. lib. bdg. 15.50x (ISBN 0-89968-213-8). Lightyear.
--The Trail of Cthuthu. 1976. pap. 1.50 o.p. (ISBN 0-345-25017-6). Ballantine.
Derleth, August W. Some Notes on H. P. Lovecraft. 50p. 1980. Repr. of 1959 ed. lib. bdg. 10.00 (ISBN 0-8495-1059-7). Arden Lib.
--Three Literary Men. 56p. 1980. Repr. of 1963 ed. lib. bdg. 15.00 (ISBN 0-8482-0645-2). Norwood Edns.
Derlon, Pierre. Secrets of the Gypsies. 1977. pap. 1.75 o.p. (ISBN 0-345-25405-8). Ballantine.
Derman, Cyrus. Finite State Markovian Decision Processes. (Mathematics in Science & Engineering Ser.: Vol. 67). 1970. 25.50 (ISBN 0-12-209250-3). Acad Pr.
Derman, Martha. The Friendstone. 160p. (gr. 4-7). 1981. 8.95 (ISBN 0-8037-2472-1); PLB 8.44 (ISBN 0-8037-2480-2). Dial.
Derman, Sylvia, ed. see Tarthang Tulku.
Derman, William. Serfs, Peasants, & Socialists: A Former Serf Village in the Republic of Guinea. LC 78-117148. 1973. 21.50x (ISBN 0-520-01728-5). U of Cal Pr.
Der Meer, Wybe J. van see Van Der Meer, Wybe J.
Der Mehden, Fred R. Von see Von Der Mehden, Fred R.
Der Meid, Louise B. Van see Van Der Meid, Louise B.
Dermer, Jerry. Management Planning & Control Systems: Advanced Concepts & Cases. 1977. 18.95x (ISBN 0-256-01874-X). Irwin.
Dermer, Joseph, ed. America's Most Successful Fund Raising Letters. 14.75 (ISBN 0-686-24210-6). Public Serv Materials.
Dermer, O. C. & Ham, G. E. Ethylenimine & Other Aziridines: Chemistry - Applications. 1969. 67.00 (ISBN 0-12-209650-9). Acad Pr.
Der Merwe, Henrik van see Van der Merwe, Henrik.
Der Meulen, Jan van see Van der Meulen, Jan & Price, Nancy W.
D'Ermo, Dominique. The Chef's Dessert Cookbook. LC 75-13679. 1976. pap. 5.95 (ISBN 0-689-70571-9, 239). Atheneum.
--Dominique's Famous Fish, Game & Meat Recipes. 1981. 12.95 (ISBN 0-87491-083-8); pap. 6.95 (ISBN 0-87491-080-3); ltd. edition hidebound 50.00 (ISBN 0-87491-082-X). Acropolis.
Dermody, Thomas. Poems, Repr. Of 1789. Reiman, Donald H., ed. Bd. with Poems, Consisting of Essays, Lyric, Elegiac, Etc. Repr. of 1792 ed; Poems, Moral & Descriptive. Repr. of 1800 ed; The Histroniade: or, Theatric Tribunal; a Poem...by Marmaduke Myrtle (Pseud.) Repr. of 1802 ed; Poems on Various Subjects. Repr. of 1802 ed. LC 75-31196. (Romantic Context Ser.: Poetry 1789-1830). 1979. lib. bdg. 47.00 (ISBN 0-8240-2147-9). Garland Pub.
Dernberger, Robert, ed. China's Development Experience in Comparative Perspective: A Social Science Research Council Study. LC 80-418. (East Asian Ser.: No. 93). 1980. text ed. 30.00x (ISBN 0-674-11890-1). Harvard U Pr.
Dernburg, Thomas F., et al. Studies in Household Economic Behavior. 1958. 32.50x (ISBN 0-686-51317-7). Elliots Bks.
Dernoncourt, Wayne L., jt. auth. see Robinson, James W.
DeRobertis, Eduardo & Schacht, Jochen, eds. Neurochemistry of Cholinergic Receptors. LC 73-91105. 156p. 1974. 18.00 (ISBN 0-911216-66-9). Raven.
De Robigne, Bennel. Trial of D. M. Bennett: Upon the Charge of Depositing Prohibited Matter in the Mail. LC 72-8110. (Civil Liberties in American History Ser). 202p. 1973. Repr. of 1879 ed. lib. bdg. 22.50 (ISBN 0-306-70525-7). Da Capo.
De Roche, A. C., et al. Principles of Auto-Body Repairing & Repainting. 2nd ed. (Illus.). 1976. 18.95x (ISBN 0-13-705699-0). P-H.
Deroche, Andre & Huldebrand, Nicholas. The Principles of Autobody Repairing & Repainting. 3rd ed. (Illus.). 672p. 1981. text ed. 18.95 (ISBN 0-686-63447-0). P-H.
De Rochement, Richard, jt. auth. see Root, Waverley.
De Rocher, F., jt. auth. see Hagiwara, M. P.
DeRocher, Francoise & DeRocher, Gregory. Options: Apercus de la France. LC 79-27245. 1980. pap. text ed. 7.95 (ISBN 0-471-04260-9). Wiley.
De Rocher, Francoise, jt. auth. see Hagiwara, Michio P.
DeRocher, Gregory, jt. auth. see DeRocher, Francoise.
De Rockville, Alphonse, ed. The Fibonacci Method of Trading in Stocks & Commodities, 2 vols. in 1. (Illus.). 1979. deluxe ed. 64.75 (ISBN 0-918968-39-9). Inst Econ Finan.
De Rodriquez, Judy Z. & Ziek, Nona M. Weaving on a Backstrap Loom: Pattern Design from Guatemala. (Illus.). 1978. 14.95 o.p. (ISBN 0-8015-3187-X). Dutton.
De Ronsard, Pierre. Selected Poems. Scollen, Christine M., ed. 192p. 1974. text ed. 13.00x (ISBN 0-485-13807-7, Athlone Pr); pap. text ed. 6.25x (ISBN 0-485-12807-1, Athlone Pr). Humanities.
De Roo, Ann. Scrub Fire. LC 80-12267. 120p. (gr. 4-7). 1980. 7.95 (ISBN 0-689-30775-6). Atheneum.
De Roover, Raymond. Money, Banking & Credit in Mediaeval Bruges. 1966. Repr. of 1948 ed. 15.00 o.p. (ISBN 0-910956-25-1). Medieval Acad.
--San Bernardino of Siena & Sant Antonino of Florence. (Kress Library of Business & Economics: No. 9). (Illus.). 1967. pap. 5.00x (ISBN 0-678-09913-8, Baker Lib). Kelley.
De Ropp, Robert S. Church of the Earth: The Ecology of a Creative Community. (Illus.). 288p. 1974. 8.95 o.p. (ISBN 0-440-01232-5, Sey Lawr). Delacorte.
--Eco-Tech: The Whole-Earther's Guide to the Alternate Society. 352p. 1975. 10.00 o.p. (ISBN 0-440-02233-9, Sey Lawr). Delacorte.
--Master Game. 1968. 5.95 o.s.i. (ISBN 0-440-05481-8, Sey Lawr). Delacorte.
--Sex Energy: The Sexual Force in Man & Animals. 1969. 6.95 o.p. (ISBN 0-440-07818-0, Sey Lawr). Delacorte.
DeRosa, Paul & Stern, Gary H. In the Name of Money: A Professional's Guide to the Federal Reserve, Interest Rates & Money. (Illus.). 192p. 1980. 16.95 (ISBN 0-07-016521-1, P&RB). McGraw.
De Rosario. Vocabulario Puertorriqueno. 1966. 10.95 (ISBN 0-87751-010-5, Pub by Troutman Press). E Torres & Sons.
De Rose, Peter L. Jane Austen & Samuel Johnson. LC 78-7813. 133p. 1980. lib. bdg. 16.25 (ISBN 0-8191-1073-6); pap. text ed. 7.50 (ISBN 0-8191-1074-4). U Pr of Amer.
DeRosier, Arthur H., Jr. Removal of the Choctaw Indians. LC 70-111044. (Illus.). 1970. 12.50 (ISBN 0-87049-113-X). U of Tenn Pr.
De Rosier, John. Chuck Foreman. (Sports Superstars Ser.). (Illus.). (gr. 3-9). 1976. o. p. 5.95 (ISBN 0-87191-543-X); pap. 2.95 (ISBN 0-89812-168-X). Creative Ed.
DeRosis, Helen & Pellegrino, Victoria Y. The Book of Hope: How Women Can Overcome Depression. 1976. 9.95 o.s.i. (ISBN 0-02-531040-2). Macmillan.
DeRossi, C. Learning COBOL Fast: A Structured Approach. 1976. pap. text ed. 11.95 (ISBN 0-87909-447-8). Reston.
DeRossi, Claude. Making BASIC Work for You: Reward Edition. (Illus.). 224p. 1980. pap. text ed. 6.95 (ISBN 0-8359-4185-X). Reston.
DeRossi, Claude J. Exploring the World of Data Processing. LC 74-28054. (Illus.). 272p. 1975. 14.95 (ISBN 0-87909-259-9); instr's. manual free. Reston.
De Rossi, Claude J. Learning BASIC Fast. rev. ed. LC 74-3355. (Illus.). 1979. pap. text ed. 12.95 (ISBN 0-8359-3977-4). Reston.
De Rothwell, Helene F. see Rothwell, Helene F. de.
De Rougemont, Denis, ed. The State of the Union of Europe: Report of the CADMOS Group to the European People. 1979. 14.50 (ISBN 0-08-024483-1); pap. 8.75 (ISBN 0-08-024476-9). Pergamon.
DeRoy, Benjamin E. Automatic Control Theory. (Electronic Technology Ser.). (Illus.). 1966. pap. 11.95 (ISBN 0-471-20371-8). Wiley.
Derozio, Henry. Henry Derozio: Poems. Lal, P., ed. 67p. 1975. 14.00 (ISBN 0-88253-716-4); pap. 6.75 (ISBN 0-88253-848-9). Ind-US Inc.
Der Porten, Ronald P. Von see Von Der Porten, Ronald P.
Der Post, Laurens Van see Van Der Post, Laurens.
Derr, C. Brooklyn, ed. Organizational Development in Urban School Systems. LC 74-78559. (Sage Contempory Social Science Issues: Vol. 14). 1974. 4.95x (ISBN 0-8039-0439-8). Sage.
--Work, Family & the Career: New Frontiers in Theory & Research. LC 80-13598. 320p. 1980. 25.95 (ISBN 0-03-056717-3). Praeger.
Derrett, D. R. Ship Stability for Masters & Mates. 3rd ed. 1977. 20.00 o.p. (ISBN 0-540-01403-6). Heinman.
Derrett, J. Duncan, tr. see Lingat, Robert.
Derrick, Christopher. Church Authority & Intellectual Freedom. LC 81-80129. 95p. (Orig.). 1981. pap. price not set (ISBN 0-89870-011-6). Ignatius Pr.
--C.S. Lewis & the Church of Rome. LC 80-83049. (Orig.). 1981. pap. price not set (ISBN 0-89870-009-4). Ignatius Pr.
--Escape from Scepticism: Liberal Education As If Truth Mattered. 2.45 (ISBN 0-89385-002-0). Green Hill.
--Joy Without a Cause: Selected Essays. 9.95 (ISBN 0-89385-007-1). Green Hill.
Derrick, Judith L., jt. auth. see Derrick, William R.
Derrick, June. The Child's Acquisition of Language. (Orig.). 1977. pap. text ed. 5.75x (ISBN 0-85633-110-4, NFER). Humanities.
--Language Needs of Minority Group Children. (Orig.). 1977. pap. text ed. 6.25x (ISBN 0-85633-118-X, NFER). Humanities.
Derrick, Lionel. Penetrator: Hell's Hostages, No. 41. 192p. (Orig.). 1981. pap. 1.75 (ISBN 0-523-41116-2). Pinnacle Bks.
Derrick, William R. & Derrick, Judith L. Finite Mathematics with Calculus for the Management, Life & Social Sciences. LC 78-18639. (Illus.). 1979. text ed. 18.95 (ISBN 0-201-01400-9). A-W.
Derrick, William R. & Grossman, Stanley I. Elementary Differential Equations with Applications. LC 75-12094. 1976. text ed. 18.95 o.p. (ISBN 0-201-01470-X). A-W.
--Elementary Differential Equations with Applications. 2nd ed. (Mathematics Ser.). (Illus.). 576p. 1981. text ed. price not set (ISBN 0-201-03162-0). A-W.
--Elementary Differential Equations with Applications: A Short Course. (Illus.). 448p. 1976. text ed. 16.95 o.p. (ISBN 0-201-01472-6); ans. bk. avail. o.p. (ISBN 0-201-01471-8). A-W.
--Elementary Differential Equations with Applications: A Short Course. 2nd ed. (Mathenatics Ser.). (Illus.). 384p. 1981. text ed. 18.95 (ISBN 0-201-03164-7). A-W.
Derricott, R., jt. auth. see Blyth, W. A.
Derricott, R., jt. auth. see Chissick, S. S.
Derrida, Jacques. The Archaeology of the Frivolous: Reading Condillac. Leavey, John P., Jr., tr. from Fr. (Duquesne Studies - Philosophical Ser.: Vol. 37). 130p. 1980. text ed. 10.95x (ISBN 0-391-01636-9). Duquesne.
--Positions. Bass, Alan, tr. from Fr. LC 80-17620. 1981. 11.95 (ISBN 0-226-14332-5). U of Chicago Pr.
--Spurs: Nietzsche's Styles. Harlow, Barbara, tr. from Fr. LC 79-31. vi, 166p. 1981. pap. 4.50 (ISBN 0-226-14333-3). U of Chicago Pr.
--Writing & Difference. Bass, Alan, tr. from Fr. LC 77-25933. 1980. pap. 6.95 (ISBN 0-226-14329-5, P865, Phoen). U of Chicago Pr.
Derriere, Pierre. Up Yours! 1976. pap. 0.95 o.p. (ISBN 0-8439-0325-2, Leisure Bks). Nordon Pubns.
Derry, Duncan. Concise World Atlas of Geology & Mineral Deposits: Non-Metallic Minerals, Metallic Minerals & Energy Minerals. LC 80-675233. 110p. 1980. 61.95 (ISBN 0-470-26996-0). Halsted Pr.
Derry, John W. Castlereagh. LC 75-29820. (British Political Biography Ser.). 250p. 1976. 18.95 (ISBN 0-312-12355-8). St Martin.
--Charles James Fox. 1972. 42.00 (ISBN 0-7134-1118-X, Pub. by Batsford England). David & Charles.
Derry, T. K. A History of Modern Norway, 1814-1972. (Illus.). 1973. 45.00x (ISBN 0-19-822503-2). Oxford U Pr.
Dersch, Lou. Beer, Bubbles & Bucks. 225p. 1981. 9.95 (ISBN 0-86629-008-7). Sunrise MO.
Dershimer, Richard A. The Federal Government & Educational R&D. LC 74-293. (Politics of Educations Ser.). (Illus.). 1976. 18.95 (ISBN 0-669-92700-7). Lexington Bks.
Der Tak, Herman G. van see Squire, Lyn & Van der Tak, Herman G.
Derthick, Martha. New Towns in-Town: Why a Federal Program Failed. 102p. 1972. pap. 4.00 (ISBN 0-87766-022-0, 70006). Urban Inst.
--Policymaking for Social Security. LC 78-24811. 1979. 19.95 (ISBN 0-8157-1816-0); pap. 8.95 (ISBN 0-8157-1815-2). Brookings.
--Uncontrollable Spending for Social Services Grants. 80p. 1975. pap. 4.95 (ISBN 0-8157-1813-6). Brookings.
Derthick, Martha A. National Guard in Politics. LC 65-11588. (Political Studies Ser). 1965. 10.00x (ISBN 0-674-60200-5). Harvard U Pr.
DeRusso, P. M., et al. State Variables for Engineers. LC 65-21443. 1965. 39.95 (ISBN 0-471-20380-7). Wiley.
Derveer, Paul D. Van see Van Derveer, Paul D. & Haas, Leonard E.
Derven, Ronald & Nichols, Carol. Book of Successful Swimming Pools. LC 75-40520. (Illus.). 1976. 13.95 (ISBN 0-912336-20-X); pap. 6.95 (ISBN 0-912336-21-8). Structures Pub.

--How to Cut Your Energy Bills. 2nd rev. ed. Horowitz, Shirley & Frohn, Peggy, eds. LC 80-13162. (Successful Series). (Illus.). 1980. 13.95 (ISBN 0-89999-004-5); pap. 6.95 (ISBN 0-89999-005-3). Structures Pub.

--Sucessful Swimming Pools. 2nd ed. Case, Virginia A., ed. (Successful Ser.). (Illus.). 128p. 1981. 18.95 (ISBN 0-89999-025-8); pap. 8.95 (ISBN 0-89999-026-6). Structures Pub.

Derven, Ronald & Rand, Ellen. Successful Vacation Homes. LC 78-31270. 1979. 13.95 (ISBN 0-912336-79-X); pap. 6.95 (ISBN 0-912336-80-3). Structures Pub.

Derven, Ronald, jt. auth. see Nichols, Carol.

Dervin, Brenda, jt. ed. see Voigt, Melvin J.

Dervitsiotis, Kostas. Operations Management. (Industrial Engineering & Management Science). (Illus.). 784p. 1980. text ed. 21.95x (ISBN 0-07-016537-8, C); solutions manual 9.50 (ISBN 0-07-016538-6). McGraw.

Der Wal, John Van see Croom, George E., Jr. & Van Der Wal, John.

Derwing, Bruce L., jt. auth. see Schutz, Noel W., Jr.

Der Zee, Karen Van see Van Der Zee, Karen.

Desa, Joe V., jt. auth. see Claussen, Claus F.

De Sackerville, Wellington. Beautiful Women in Art & Poetry. (Illus.). 1979. deluxe ed. 31.75 (ISBN 0-930582-39-X). Gloucester Art.

De Sade, Marquis Adelaide of Brunswick. x1954 ed. Ryland, Hobart, tr. LC 72-11856. 1973. 10.00 (ISBN 0-8108-0574-X). Scarecrow.

De Sahagun, Bernardino. Florentine Codex, General History of the Things of New Spain, 12 bks. Anderson, Arthur J. & Dibble, Charles E., trs. Incl. Bk. 1. Gods. 15.00x (ISBN 0-87480-000-5); Bk. 2. Ceremonies. 20.00 o.p. (ISBN 0-87480-001-3); Bk. 3. Origin of the Gods. 15.00x (ISBN 0-87480-002-1); Bks. 4 & 5. The Soothsayers, the Omens. 20.00x (ISBN 0-87480-003-X); Bk. 6. Rhetoric & Moral Philosophy. 20.00x (ISBN 0-87480-010-2); Bk. 7. Sun, Moon & Stars, & the Binding of the Years. 15.00x (ISBN 0-87480-004-8); Bk. 8. Kings & Lords. 20.00x (ISBN 0-87480-005-6); Bk. 9. Merchants. 15.00x (ISBN 0-87480-006-4); Bk. 10. People. 20.00x (ISBN 0-87480-007-2); Bk. 11. Earthly Things. 25.00x (ISBN 0-87480-008-0); Bk. 12. Conquest of Mexico. 20.00x (ISBN 0-87480-096-X). U of Utah Pr.

Desai, Anita. Bye-Bye Blackbird. 266p. 1971. pap. 3.50 (ISBN 0-88253-033-X). Ind-US Inc.

--Clear Light of Day. LC 80-7603. 224p. 1980. 11.95 (ISBN 0-06-010984-X, HarpT). Har-Row.

--Games at Twilight. LC 79-4943. 1980. 9.95 (ISBN 0-06-011079-1, HarpT). Har-Row.

Desai, C. S. Elementary Finite Element Method. (Civil Engineering & Engineering Mechanics Ser.). (Illus.). 1979. ref. ed. 26.95 (ISBN 0-13-256636-2). P-H.

Desai, C. S., jt. ed. see American Society of Civil Engineers.

Desai, Meghnad. Marxian Economic Theory. 1974. 13.50x o.p. (ISBN 0-85641-012-8, Pub. by Basil Blackwell England). Biblio Dist.

--Marxian Economics. 265p. 1979. 27.50x (ISBN 0-8476-6204-7). Rowman.

Desai, Morarji. The Story of My Life. LC 78-40613. 1979. text ed. 41.00 (ISBN 0-08-023566-2). Pergamon.

Desai, Narayan. Handbook for Satyagrahis. 1980. pap. 3.00 perfect bdg. (ISBN 0-86571-002-3). Movement New Soc.

Desai, R. W., ed. Johnson on Shakespeare. 1979. text ed. 12.50x (ISBN 0-86131-120-5). Humanities.

Desai, S. K. Santha Rama Rau. (Indian Writers Ser.: Vol. Xiil). 1977. 8.50 (ISBN 0-89253-451-6). Ind-US Inc.

Desai, Tripta. Indo-American Relations Between 1940-1974. 1977. pap. text ed. 9.00x (ISBN 0-8191-0155-9). U Pr of Amer.

Desai, V. G., tr. see Gandhi, M. K.

De Saint-Didier, Guillem. Poesies Du Troubadour Guillem de Saint-Didier. LC 80-2179. 1981. Repr. of 1956 ed. 31.00 (ISBN 0-404-19007-3). AMS Pr.

De Sainte Colombe, Paul. Grapho-Therapeutics. 352p. 1973. pap. 1.25 o.p. (ISBN 0-445-00175-5). Popular Lib.

--Grapho-Therapeutics: Pen & Pencil Therapy. 1966. pap. 8.95 (ISBN 0-87516-297-5). De Vorss.

De Saint-Exupery, Antoine. Flight to Arras. Galantiere, Lewis, tr. LC 43-12440. 1969. pap. 3.50 (ISBN 0-15-631880-6, HPL45, HPL). HarBraceJ.

--Little Prince. Woods, Katherine, tr. LC 67-1144. (Illus.). (gr. 3-7). 1968. pap. 1.95 (ISBN 0-15-652820-7, HPL30, HPL). HarBraceJ.

--Night Flight. Gilbert, Stuart, tr. from Fr. LC 73-16016. Orig. Title: Vol De Nuit. 87p. 1974. pap. 1.95 (ISBN 0-15-665605-1, HPL63, HPL). HarBraceJ.

--El Principito. Del Carril, Bonifacio, tr. from Fr. LC 73-5511. (Illus.). 113p. (Span.). 1973. pap. 1.75 (ISBN 0-15-628450-2, HPL61, HPL). HarBraceJ.

--Southern Mail. Cate, Curtis, tr. LC 79-182749. 1972. pap. 2.50 (ISBN 0-15-683901-6, HPL55, HPL). HarBraceJ.

--Wind, Sand & Stars. LC 65-35872. 1967. pap. 2.75 (ISBN 0-15-697090-2, HPL14, HPL). HarBraceJ.

De Saint-Exupery, Antoine see Saint-Exupery, Antoine de.

De Saint-Germain, C. Practical Astrology. LC 80-19738. 257p. 1980. Repr. of 1973 ed. lib. bdg. 10.95x (ISBN 0-89370-618-3). Borgo Pr.

--The Practice of Palmistry for Professional Purposes. LC 80-23774. 416p. 1980. Repr. of 1973 ed. lib. bdg. 11.95x (ISBN 0-89370-619-1). Borgo Pr.

De Saint-Phalle, Therese see Saint-Phalle, Therese de.

De Saint Phalle, Thibaut. U. S. Productivity & Competitiveness in International Trade, Vol. II. LC 80-68434. (Significant Issues Ser.: No. 12). 115p. 1980. 5.95 (ISBN 0-89206-028-X). CSI Studies.

De Saint-Pierre, Jacques H. Bernardin see Bernardin De Saint-Pierre, Jacques H.

De Saint-Pierre, Leland. Love Within & Outside the Cloister. (An Intimate Life of Man Library Bk). (Illus.). 1979. 29.45 (ISBN 0-89266-168-2). Am Classical Coll Pr.

De Saix, Guillot. Les Songes Merveilleux Du Dormeur Eveille: Le Chant Du Dvgne: Contes Parles D'Oscar Wilde. LC 76-25932. (Decadent Consciousness Ser.). lib. bdg. 38.00 (ISBN 0-8240-2785-X). Garland Pub.

De Salignac De La Mothe, Francois, jt. auth. see Fenelon.

De Salincourt, Ernest, ed. see Wordsworth, William.

De Saluste, Guillaume & Du Bartas, Sieur. The Divine Weeks & Works of Guillaume de Saluste, Sieur du Bartas, 2 vols. Synder, Susan, ed. Sylvester, Joshua, tr. (Oxford English Texts Ser.). (Illus.). 964p. 1979. text ed. 98.00x (ISBN 0-19-812717-0). Oxford U Pr.

De Salvo, Louis J. Consumer Finance. LC 76-46450. 1977. pap. text ed. 15.95 (ISBN 0-471-04391-5); tchr's manual avail. (ISBN 0-471-02418-X). Wiley.

De Salvo, Louise. Virginia Woolf's "First Voyage". A Novel in the Making. 202p. 1980. 19.50x (ISBN 0-8476-6199-7). Rowman.

DeSalvo, Louise A., ed. see Woolf, Virginia.

Desani, G. V. All About H. Hatterr. rev. ed. LC 77-97137. 1970. 5.95 o.p. (ISBN 0-374-10280-5). FS&G.

De Santa Ana, Julio. Towards a Church of the Poor. LC 80-25667. (Orig.). 1981. pap. 8.95 (ISBN 0-88344-502-6). Orbis Bks.

De Santillana, Giorgio. Origins of Scientific Thought. pap. 2.95 o.p. (ISBN 0-452-25006-4, Z5006, Plume). NAL.

De Santis, Vincent, compiled by. Gilded Age, Eighteen Seventy-Seven to Eighteen Ninety-Six. LC 72-96558. (Goldentree Bibliographies in American History Ser.). 168p. (Orig.). 1973. pap. 6.95x (ISBN 0-88295-536-5). AHM Pub.

De Sapio, Rodolfo. Calculus for the Life Sciences. LC 77-21312. (Illus.). 1978. text ed. 21.95x (ISBN 0-7167-0371-8). W H Freeman.

De Saussure, Eric see Saussure, Eric De.

De Saussure, Ferdinand. Course in General Linguistics. Baskin, Wade, tr. 1966. pap. 4.95 (ISBN 0-07-016524-6, SP). McGraw.

Desautels, Paul. The Gem Kingdom. 1971. 25.00 (ISBN 0-394-46533-4); pap. 7.95 (ISBN 0-394-73373-8). Random.

De Sauvigny, Guillaume. Metternich & His Times. 1962. text ed. 12.50x (ISBN 0-232-48202-0). Humanities.

De Sauvigny Guillaume De, Bertier see De Bertier De Sauvigny, Guillaume.

Descargues, Pierre. Perspective. (Illus.). 1977. 15.00 o.p. (ISBN 0-8109-1454-9); pap. 6.95 o.p. (ISBN 0-8109-2075-1). Abrams.

Descartes. Discourse on Method & Meditations. Lafleur, Laurence J., tr. LC 60-13395. 1960. pap. 3.95 (ISBN 0-672-60278-4, LLA 89). Bobbs.

Descartes, Rene. Discourse on Method. 2nd ed. Lafleur, Laurence J., tr. LC 60-13395. (Orig.). 1956. pap. 2.50 (ISBN 0-672-60180-X, LLA19). Bobbs.

--Meditations on First Philosophy. Lafleur, Laurence J., tr. 1960. pap. 2.95 (ISBN 0-672-60191-5, LLA29). Bobbs.

--Philosophical Essays: Discourse on Method; Meditations; Rules for the Direction of the Mind. Lafleur, Laurence J., tr. LC 63-16951. (Orig.). 1964. 5.50 (ISBN 0-672-60292-X, LLA99). Bobbs.

--Philosophical Works, 2 Vols. Haldane, E. S. & Ross, G. R., eds. 1967. Vol. 1. 47.50 (ISBN 0-521-06943-2); Vol. 2. 47.50 (ISBN 0-521-06944-0); Vol. 1. pap. 8.95x (ISBN 0-521-09416-X); Vol. 2. pap. 9.95x (ISBN 0-521-09417-8). Cambridge U Pr.

--Philosophical Writings. Anscombe, Elizabeth & Geach, Peter T., eds. Anscombe, Elizabeth & Geach, Peter T., trs. LC 79-171798. 1971. pap. 4.95 (ISBN 0-672-61274-7, LLA198). Bobbs.

Descartes, Rinaldo. El Discurso Del Metodo. billingual ed. (Biblioteca De Cultura Basica). pap. 2.50 o.p. (ISBN 0-8477-0704-0); pap. 2.50 (ISBN 0-8477-0705-9). U of PR Pr.

Desch, H. E. Structural Surveying. 269p. 1970. 33.95 (ISBN 0-85264-167-2, Pub. by Griffin England). State Mutual Bk.

--Timber: Its Structure, Properties, & Utilization. 6th ed. 416p. (Orig.). 1980. pap. text ed. 24.95x (ISBN 0-917304-62-4, Pub. by Timber Press). Intl Schol Bk Serv.

Deschamps, Paul. French Sculpture of the Romanesque Period. LC 78-143343. (Illus.). 1972. Repr. of 1930 ed. 40.00 o.p. (ISBN 0-87817-063-4). Hacker.

Deschampsneufs, H. Marketing Overseas. 1967. 25.00 (ISBN 0-08-012523-9); pap. 13.25 (ISBN 0-08-012522-0). Pergamon.

Descharnes, Robert. Dali. LC 74-4257. (Library of Great Painters Ser.). (Illus.). 176p. 1976. 35.00 (ISBN 0-8109-0222-2). Abrams.

Deschner, Gunther. Reinhard Heydrich. LC 80-6263. 376p. 1981. 16.95 (ISBN 0-8128-2809-7). Stein & Day.

Deschner, Whit. Does the Wet Suit You? The Confessions of a Kayak Bum. LC 80-70510. (Illus.). 96p. 1981. pap. 6.45 (ISBN 0-9605388-0-1). Tern Pr.

De Schweinitz, Karl. Growing Up. 4th ed. (Illus.). (gr. 2-5). 1968. 4.50g o.s.i. (ISBN 0-02-729170-7). Macmillan.

Descloux, J., ed. see Proceedings of the Colloquium on Numerical Analysis, Lausanne, Oct. 11-13, 1976.

Descombes, Vincent. Modern French Philosophy. Scott-Fox, L. & Harding, J. M., trs. 240p. Date not set. 32.50 (ISBN 0-521-22837-9); pap. 11.50 (ISBN 0-521-29672-2). Cambridge U Pr.

De Segonzac, Catherine. Jewish Yoga: A System of Visualization & Movement Rooted in Genesis. 208p. 1981. pap. 7.95 (ISBN 0-87728-529-2). Weiser.

De Segur, Comtesse. The Angel Inn. Aiken, Joan, tr. from Fr. LC 78-12784. (Illus.). (gr. 3 up). 1978. 9.95 (ISBN 0-916144-28-3); pap. 6.95 (ISBN 0-916144-29-1). Stemmer Hse.

De Selincourt, Aubrey. Six Great Englishmen. 221p. 1980. lib. bdg. 20.00 (ISBN 0-8482-3652-1). Norwood Edns.

De Selincourt, Aubrey, tr. see Livy.

DeSelincourt, Aubrey, tr. see Livy.

De Selincourt, Ernest. English Poets & the National Ideal. 119p. 1980. Repr. of 1916 ed. text ed. 20.00 (ISBN 0-8492-4226-6). R West.

De Selincourt, Ernest, ed. see Spenser, Edmund.

De Selincourt, Ernest, ed. see Wordsworth, William.

Deser, Stanley, et al, eds. Lectures on Elementary Particles & Quantum Field Theory, 2 Vols. 1971. Vol. 1. pap. 8.95x (ISBN 0-262-54013-4); Vol. 2. pap. 7.95x o.p. (ISBN 0-262-54015-0). MIT Pr.

Deserrano, Irma G. Manual Para la Preparacion De Informes y Tesis. LC 76-11003. 1980. 6.25 (ISBN 0-8477-2311-9); pap. 5.00 (ISBN 0-8477-2312-7). U of PR Pr.

De Serrano, Irma Garcia see Garcia de Serrano, Irma.

De Serville, Paul see Serville, Paul De.

De Sestero, Albertet. Les Poesies Du Troubadour Albertet. Boutiere, Jean, ed. LC 80-2173. 1981. Repr. of 1937 ed. 24.50 (ISBN 0-404-19001-4). AMS Pr.

Desfosses, Helen, ed. Soviet Population Policy: Conflicts & Constraints. (Pergamon Policy Studies). 150p. Date not set. 19.51 (ISBN 0-08-025976-6). Pergamon.

Desfosses, Helen & Levesque, Jacques, eds. Socialism in the Third World. LC 75-19774. (Special Studies). (Illus.). 340p. 1975. text ed. 23.95 (ISBN 0-275-55560-7); pap. text ed. 10.95 (ISBN 0-275-89460-6). Praeger.

De Sherbinin, Michael see Sherbinin, Michael de.

Deshler, Betty, intro. by. School Social Work & the Law. LC 80-83075. (Conference Proceedings Ser.). 192p. (Orig.). pap. text ed. 7.50 (ISBN 0-87101-088-7, CBP-088-C). Natl Assn Soc Wkrs.

Deshmukh, D. G. Thoreau and Indian Thought: A Study of the Impact of Indian Thought on the Life of Henry David Thoreau. LC 80-2505. 1981. Repr. of 1974 ed. price not set (ISBN 0-404-19053-7). AMS Pr.

DeShong, Barbara. The Special Educator: Stress & Survival. 350p. 1981. text ed. price not set (ISBN 0-89443-358-X). Aspen Systems.

Deshpande, C. D., et al. Impact of a Metropolitan City on the Surrounding Region. (Illus.). 167p. 1980. pap. text ed. 8.00x (ISBN 0-391-02206-7). Humanities.

Deshpande, Gauri. An Anthology of Indo-English Poetry. 162p. 1975. pap. text ed. 2.50 (ISBN 0-88253-455-6). Ind-US Inc.

--Between Births. 1975. 8.00 (ISBN 0-88253-508-0); pap. text ed. 4.00 (ISBN 0-88253-507-2). Ind-US Inc.

--Lost Love. 8.00 (ISBN 0-89253-685-3). Ind-US Inc.

Deshpande, Madhav. Critical Studies in Indian Grammarians I, Theory of Homogeneity: Savarnya. LC 75-36896. (The Michigan Series in South & Southeast Asian Languages & Linguistics: No. 2). 223p. 1975. pap. 6.00x (ISBN 0-89148-052-8). Ctr S&SE Asian.

--Evolution of Syntactic Theory in Sanskrit Grammar: Syntax of the Sanskrit Infinitive Ser. (Linguista Extranea: Studia: No. 10). 164p. 1980. 10.50 (ISBN 0-89720-029-2); pap. 7.50 (ISBN 0-89720-030-6). Karoma.

Deshpande, Madhav M. Sociolinguistic Attitudes in India: An Historical Reconstruction. (Linguistica Extranea Ser.: Studia 5). 178p. 1979. lib. bdg. 10.50 (ISBN 0-89720-007-1); pap. 5.50 (ISBN 0-89720-008-X). Karoma.

Deshpande, Madhav M. & Hook, Peter E., eds. Aryan & Non-Aryan in India. LC 78-60016. (Michigan Papers on South & Southeast Asia: No. 14). 350p. 1979. 16.50x (ISBN 0-89720-012-8); pap. 12.50x (ISBN 0-89148-014-5). Ctr S&SE Asian.

Desiderato, Otello, et al. Investigating Behavior: Principles of Psychology. (Illus.). 672p. 1976. text ed. 19.50 scp o.p. (ISBN 0-06-041614-9, HarpC); instructor's manual free o.p. (ISBN 0-06-361630-0); scp wkbk. & study guide 6.50 o.p. (ISBN 0-06-041618-1); pamphlet of test items free o.p. (ISBN 0-685-66557-7). Har-Row.

Design Bulletins. Housing the Family. 1974. 19.95 (ISBN 0-8436-0129-9). CBI Pub.

Design Concept Associates. Homes in the Earth. (Illus.). 112p. 1980. pap. 7.95 (ISBN 0-87701-212-1). Chronicle Bks.

Desika Char, S. V. Centralised Legislation-Legislative System of British India 1834-1861. 9.00x o.p. (ISBN 0-210-34010-X). Asia.

Desikachar, T. K. Religiousness in Yoga: Lectures on Theory & Practice. Skelton, Mary L. & Carter, J. R., eds. LC 79-9643. (Illus.). 314p. 1980. text ed. 19.00 (ISBN 0-8191-0966-5); pap. text ed. 10.50 (ISBN 0-8191-0967-3). U Pr of Amer.

Desiles, Clara. Japan Today. (Illus.). 1979. bds. 14.95 (ISBN 2-8525-8110-8, Pub. by Two Continents). Hippocrene Bks.

De Silva, D. M. Pemato Jayati Soko (Love Is the Bringer of Sorrow) De Silva, D. M., tr. from Singhalese. (Salzburg Studies in English Literature: Poetic Drama & Poetic Theory: No. 25). 55p. 1976. pap. text ed. 25.00x (ISBN 0-391-01524-9). Humanities.

De Simone, Donald. A Kiss on Each Cheek. 448p. (Orig.). 1981. pap. 2.95 (ISBN 0-523-40469-7). Pinnacle Bks.

De Simoni, Felix. Mary Magdalene & the Theory of Sin, 2 vols. LC 72-84832. (Illus.). 35p. 1972. 77.50 (ISBN 0-913314-04-8). Am Classical Coll Pr.

Desirant, M., ed. Solid State Physics in Electronics & Telecommunications: Magnetic & Optical Properties. 1960. 76.00 (ISBN 0-12-211503-1); Vol. 4. Part 2. 56.00 (ISBN 0-12-211504-X). Acad Pr.

Desirant, M. & Michiels, J. L., eds. Electromagnetic Wave Propagation: Proceedings. 1960. 94.50 (ISBN 0-12-211550-3). Acad Pr.

Desmarest, Marie A. Torrents. Bair, Lowell, tr. 1977. pap. 1.75 o.p. (ISBN 0-451-07614-1, E7614, Sig). NAL.

Desmedt, J. E., ed. Motor Unit Types, Recruitment Patterns & Plasticity with Usage in Health & Disease. (Progress in Clinical Neurophysiology Ser.: Vol. 9). (Illus.). x, 350p. 1981. 82.75 (ISBN 3-8055-1929-X). S Karger.

De Smith, Josie. El Hogar Que Dios Me Dio. 1979. pap. 1.65 (ISBN 0-311-46082-8). Casa Bautista.

Desmond, Adrian J. The Hot-Blooded Dinosaurs. (Illus.). 336p. 1977. pap. 2.50 o.s.i. (ISBN 0-446-81359-1). Warner Bks.

Desmond, Alice C. Titus of Rome. LC 75-38353. (Illus.). (gr. 7). 1976. 5.95 (ISBN 0-396-07299-2). Dodd.

Desmond, Glenn M. & Kelley, Richard E. Business Valuation Handbook. rev ed. LC 80-51554. 1980. 42.50 (ISBN 0-930458-02-8). Valuation.

--Business Valuation Handbook. LC 77-365976. 1977. 42.50 o.s.i. (ISBN 0-685-83502-2). Valuation.

Desmond, Hilary. Linton Park, Number One: Charlotte. 176p. (Orig.). 1981. pap. 1.75 (ISBN 0-523-41062-X). Pinnacle Bks.

Desmond, John F., ed. A Still Moment: Essays on the Art of Eudora Welty. LC 78-3719. 1978. 10.00 (ISBN 0-8108-1129-4). Scarecrow.

Desmond, Kevin. The Man with Two Shadows. (Illus.). 160p. 1981. 10.95 (ISBN 0-906071-09-7). Proteus Pub NY.

--Motorboating Facts & Feats. (Illus.). 256p. 1980. 17.95 (ISBN 0-8069-9204-2, Pub by Guinness Superlatives England). Sterling.

Desmond, Ray, jt. auth. see Satow, Michael.

Desmond, Robert. Windows on the World: World News Reporting Nineteen Hundred to Nineteen Twenty. LC 80-19397. 565p. 1980. text ed. 28.50 (ISBN 0-87745-104-4). U of Iowa Pr.

Desmond, Robert M., jt. auth. see Karlekar, Bhalchandra V.

Desnick, Robert J., ed. Enzyme Therapy in Genetic Diseases: Part 2. LC 79-48026. (Alan R. Liss Ser.: Vol. 16, No. 1). 1980. 64.00. March of Dimes.

--Enzyme Therapy in Genetic Diseases: Proceedings, No. 2. 2nd ed. LC 79-48026. (Birth Defects: Original Article Ser.: Vol. XVI, No. 1). 568p. 1980. 26.00 (ISBN 0-8451-1035-7). A R Liss.

Desnick, Shirley G. Geriatric Contentment: A Guide to Its Achievement in Your Home. 76p. 1971. text ed. 9.75 (ISBN 0-398-00440-4). C C Thomas.

Desoer, C. A. & Vidyasagar, M. Feedback Systems: Input-Output Properties. (Electrical Science Ser.). 1975. 43.50 (ISBN 0-12-212050-7). Acad Pr.

De Sounin, Leonie. Magic in Herbs. 1972. pap. 1.25 (ISBN 0-515-02855-X, N2855). Jove Pubns.

DeSourdis, Ron, jt. auth. see Henry, Marilyn.

De Sousa, Maria. Lymphocyte Circulation: Experimental & Clinical Aspects. 316p. 1981. 57.00 (ISBN 0-471-27854-8, Pub. by Wiley-Interscience). Wiley.

Desoutter, D. M. Your Book of Sound. Jenkins, D. L., tr. (Illus.). (gr. 7 up). 1971. 5.95 (ISBN 0-571-09530-5). Transatlantic.

Desoutter, Denis M. Your Book of Space Travel. (gr. 7 up). 6.50 (ISBN 0-571-04720-3). Transatlantic.

Desoutter, Denny. The Boat-Owner's Practical Dictionary. (Practical Handbooks for the Yachtsman Ser.). (Illus.). 1978. 13.50 (ISBN 0-370-30041-6); pap. 7.95 (ISBN 0-370-30042-4). Transatlantic.

--The Small-Boat Skipper's Safety Book. 224p. 1972. pap. 8.50 (ISBN 0-370-30010-6). Transatlantic.

Desoutter, Denny, ed. see Greenfield, Pete.

DeSouza, A. R. & Porter, P. W. The Underdevelopment & Modernization of the Third World. LC 74-20053. (CCG Resource Papers Ser.: No. 28). (Illus.). 1974. pap. text ed. 4.00 (ISBN 0-89291-075-5). Assn Am Geographers.

Desouza, Amaury, jt. auth. see McDonough, Peter.

De Souza, Anthony, jt. ed. see Vogeler, Ingolf.

DeSouza, Glenn R. Energy Policy & Forecasting: Economic, Financial, & Technological Dimensions. LC 79-9671. (Arthur D. Little Bk.). 1980. write for info. (ISBN 0-669-03614-5). Lexington Bks.

--System Methods for Socio-Economic & Environmental Impact Analysis. LC 79-7183. (Arthur D. Little Bk.). 176p. 1979. 19.95 (ISBN 0-669-02953-X). Lexington Bks.

De Souza, Luis A. & Ribeiro, Lucia. Youth Participation in the Development Process: A Case Study in Panama. (International Bureau of Education Experiments & Innovations in Education Ser: No. 18). 1976. pap. 4.75 (ISBN 92-3-101308-4, U735, UNESCO). Unipub.

Desowitz, Robert S. Ova & Parasites. (Illus.). 224p. 1980. pap. text ed. 22.50 (ISBN 0-06-140688-0, Harper Medical). Har-Row.

D'Espagnat, B., ed. Foundations of Quantum Mechanics. (Italian Physical Society: Course 49). 1972. 54.50 (ISBN 0-12-368849-3). Acad Pr.

Despain, Goldie B. Tiny Ant Who Scared a Horned Toad. (Illus.). (ps-3). 1970. 4.25 o.p. (ISBN 0-8313-0029-9); PLB 6.19 o.p. (ISBN 0-685-13787-2). Lantern.

D'Espanha, Guiraut. Die Lieder Des Trobadors Guiraut d'Espanha: Inaugural-Dissertation. Hoby, Otto, ed. LC 80-2178. 1981. Repr. of 1915 ed. 24.50 (ISBN 0-404-19008-1). AMS Pr.

Despert, J. Louis. Emotionally Disturbed Child. LC 79-97700. 1970. pap. 2.95 (ISBN 0-385-07035-7, A720, Anch). Doubleday.

De Spinoza, Benedictus. The Principles of Descartes' Philosophy. Britan, Halbert H., tr. from Lat. LC 74-3096. 1974. pap. 3.95 (ISBN 0-87548-053-5). Open Court.

Des Pommelles, Chevaliers. Tableau De la Population De Toutes les Provinces De France. (Principal French Demographic Works of the 18th Century Ser.). (Fr.). 1976. lib. bdg. 32.00x o.p. (ISBN 0-8287-0270-5); pap. text ed. 22.00x o.p. (ISBN 0-685-71499-3). Clearwater Pub.

DesPortes, Elisa. Congregations in Change. (Project Test Pattern Ser.). (Orig.). 1973. pap. 3.95 (ISBN 0-8164-2085-8). Crossroad NY.

Desposito, Franklin, jt. auth. see Walters, Thomas R.

D'Espouy, Hector. Fragments from Greek & Roman Architecture: The Classical America Edition of Hector D'Espouy's Plates. (Illus.). 1981. 19.95 (ISBN 0-393-01427-4); pap. 9.95 (ISBN 0-393-00052-4). Norton.

Desramaut, Francis. Don Bosco & the Spiritual Life. Luna, Roger M., tr. from Fr. LC 79-52674. (Orig.). 1979. pap. text ed. 8.95 (ISBN 0-89944-022-3). D Bosco Pubns.

DesRoches, Diane. San Diego Disco & Dance Guide: Guide to San Diego's Dance Spots. LC 80-51178. (Disco & Dance Directories Ser.). 60p. (Orig.). 1981. pap. 2.50 (ISBN 0-936854-00-6). Word Factory.

Desroches-Noblecourt, Christiane. Tutankhamen. LC 63-15145. (Illus.). 1963. 19.95 (ISBN 0-8212-0151-4, 857009). NYGS.

Desrosier, John N., jt. auth. see Desrosier, Norman W.

Desrosier, Norman W. Rietz Master Food Guide. (Illus.). 1978. pap. text ed. 19.00 (ISBN 0-87055-246-5). AVI.

Desrosier, Norman W. & Desrosier, John N. Economics of New Food Product Development. (Illus.). 1971. 28.50 (ISBN 0-87055-102-7). AVI.

--Technology of Food Preservation. 4th ed. (Illus.). 1977. text ed. 22.50 o.p. (ISBN 0-87055-232-5); pap. text ed. 17.00 (ISBN 0-87055-286-4). AVI.

Desrosier, Norman W. & Tressler, Donald K. Fundamentals of Food Freezing. (Illus.). 1977. 27.50 o.p. (ISBN 0-87055-233-3); pap. text ed. 18.00 (ISBN 0-87055-290-2). AVI.

Desrosier, Norman W., jt. auth. see Sivetz, Michael.

Desrosier, Norman W., ed. Elements of Food Technology. (Illus.). 1977. pap. 19.50 (ISBN 0-87055-284-8). AVI.

Dessain, Charles S., ed. see Newman, John H.

Dessaint, Alain Y. Minorities of Southwest China: An Introduction to the Yi - Lolo; & Related Peoples & an Annotated Bibliography. LC 80-80017. (Bibliography Ser.). viii, 373p. 1980. 18.00 (ISBN 0-87536-250-8). HRAFP.

Dessaix, tr. see Svirski, Grigory.

Dessau, Joanna. The Red-Haired Brat. 1979. 7.95 o.p. (ISBN 0-312-66720-5). St Martin.

Dessaur, C. I. Science Between Culture & Counter Culture. 128p. 1975. pap. text ed. 12.25x (ISBN 90-255-9813-7). Humanities.

Dessel, Sabine Van see Van Dessel, Sabine.

Dessler, G. Organization Theory: Integrating Structure & Behavior. 1980. 19.95 (ISBN 0-13-641886-4). P-H.

Dessler, Gary. Personnel Management. 2nd ed. 500p. 1981. text ed. 18.95 (ISBN 0-8359-5518-4); study guide 7.95 (ISBN 0-8359-5521-4); instr's. manual free. Reston.

Dessner, Lawrence J. How to Write a Poem. LC 78-65447. 1979. 11.00x (ISBN 0-8147-1766-7); pap. 5.95 (ISBN 0-8147-1767-5). NYU Pr.

DeStefano, Johanna S. Language, the Learner & the School. LC 77-13511. 1978. pap. text ed. 10.95 (ISBN 0-471-02378-7). Wiley.

De St-Exupery, Antoine. Petit Prince. (Illus., Fr.). pap. 1.95 (ISBN 0-685-20246-1). Schoenhof.

Desti, Mary. The Untold Story: The Life of Isadora Duncan 1921-1927. (Dance Ser.). (Illus.). 281p. 1981. Repr. of 1929 ed. lib. bdg. 25.00 (ISBN 0-306-76044-4). Da Capo.

Destiny, Warner, jt. auth. see Butler, William.

Destiny, Warner, jt. auth. see Coddington, Mary.

Destler, I. M. Making Foreign Economic Policy. LC 79-5119. 256p. 1980. 14.95 (ISBN 0-8157-1822-5); pap. 5.95 (ISBN 0-8157-1821-7). Brookings.

De Stoeckl, Agnes. Mistress of Versailles, the Life of Madame Du Barry. 1967. 8.95 (ISBN 0-685-20605-X). Transatlantic.

D'Estree, Sabine, tr. see Deforges, Regine.

D'Estree, Sabine, tr. see Reage, Pauline.

De Stroumillo, Elisabeth. Greece. (Thornton Cox's Traveller's Guide Ser.). (Illus.). 1974. pap. 5.95 (ISBN 0-8038-2665-6). Hastings.

De Summers, Jessica. Gozo Al Crecer, Summer/jessica De. Date not set. pap. price not set (ISBN 0-311-38550-8, Edit Mundo). Casa Bautista.

Deszoe, Laslo. Studies on Syntactic Topology & Contrastive Grammar. (Janua Linguarum, Series Practica). 1979. pap. text ed. 27.75x (ISBN 90-279-3108-9). Mouton.

DeTar, Delos F., ed. Molecular Mechanics: A Symposium. LC 77-14614. 1978. pap. text ed. 33.00 (ISBN 0-08-022070-3). Pergamon.

De Terra, Helmut. Humboldt: The Life & Times of Alexander Humboldt. LC 78-27653. 386p. 1979. Repr. of 1955 ed. lib. bdg. 24.00x (ISBN 0-374-92134-2). Octagon.

Detert, Richard, jt. auth. see Curtis, Jack.

De Tevis, Rose, et al, eds. El Oro y el Futuro del Pueblo. (Illus.). 155p. 1979. pap. 5.00 (ISBN 0-918358-11-6). Pajarito Pubns.

Dethier. Life & Times of a Maine Clam. 1981. 5.95 (ISBN 0-89272-085-9). Down East.

Dethier, V. G. The World of the Tent-Makers: A Natural History of the Eastern Tent Caterpillar. LC 80-11361. (Illus.). 160p. 1980. lib. bdg. 12.50x (ISBN 0-87023-300-9); pap. 5.95 (ISBN 0-87023-301-7). U of Mass Pr.

Dethier, Vincent G. & Stellar, Eliot. Animal Behavior. 3rd ed. 1970. pap. 9.95 ref ed. (ISBN 0-13-037440-7). P-H.

Dethlefson, Ronald, ed. Edison Blue Amberol Recordings: 1912-1914. (American Popular Series Live Recordings). (Illus.). 1980. 19.95 (ISBN 0-937612-00-6). A P M Pr.

Dethloff, Henry C. Americans & Free Enterprise. LC 78-15515. (Illus.). 1979. ref. ed. 16.95 (ISBN 0-13-032490-6). P-H.

Detienne, Marcel. The Gardens of Adonis. (European Philoaophy & the Human Sciences). (Illus.). 1977. text ed. 26.75x (ISBN 0-391-00611-8). Humanities.

Detienne, Marcel & Vernant, Jean-Pierre. Cunning Intelligence in Greek Culture & Society. Lloyd, J., tr. from Greek. (European Philosophy & the Human Sciences Ser.). 1978. text ed. 33.75x (ISBN 0-391-00740-8). Humanities.

Detmar, Michael W., jt. ed. see DeKornfeld, Thomas J.

Detmer, Josephine & Pancoast, Patricia. Portland. Dibner, Martin, ed. LC 72-172820. (Illus.). 1973. collector's 25.00x (ISBN 0-9600612-0-7). Greater Portland.

De Tocqueville, Alexis. Democracy in America. abr. ed. Heffner, Richard D., ed. pap. 2.75 (ISBN 0-451-61620-0, ME1888, Ment). NAL.

De Tocqueville, Alexis, jt. auth. see De Beaumont, Gustave.

De Tocqueville, Alexis see Tocqueville, Alexis de.

De Tocqueville, Alexis C. Journey to America. rev. ed. Mayer, J. P., ed. Lawrence, George, tr. from Fr. LC 80-22556. xvi, 424p. 1981. Repr. of 1971 ed. lib. bdg. 35.00x (ISBN 0-313-22712-8, TOJA). Greenwood.

De Toledano, Ralph. The Greatest Plot in History. 2nd ed. 1977. 8.95 o.p. (ISBN 0-87000-371-2). Arlington Hse.

De Tolnay, Charles Q. Michelangelo, 6 vols. Incl. Vol. 1. The Youth of Michelangelo. 1969. 55.00 (ISBN 0-691-03858-9); Vol. 2. The Sistine Ceiling. 1969. 55.00 (ISBN 0-691-03856-2); Vol. 3. The Medeci Chapel. 1970. 55.00 (ISBN 0-691-03854-6); Vol. 4. The Tomb of Julius Two. 1970. 55.00 (ISBN 0-691-03857-0); Vol. 5. The Final Period. 1970. 55.00 (ISBN 0-691-03855-4); Vol. 6. Michelangelo, Architect. 40.00 (ISBN 0-691-03853-8); Michelangelo: Sculpter-Painter-Architect. (One vol. condensation). 27.50 (ISBN 0-691-03876-7). Princeton U. Pr.

DeTornyay, Rheba. Strategies of Teaching Nursing. LC 73-134038. (Paperback Nursing Ser.). 1971. pap. 9.50 (ISBN 0-471-20395-5, Pub. by Wiley Medical). Wiley.

De Toro, M. & Gisbert. Dictionnaire bilingue Larousse, francais-espagnol, espanol-frances. (Apollo). (Fr. & Span.). 10.50 (ISBN 0-685-13857-7, 3774). Larousse.

DeTreville, Stan, jt. auth. see DeTreville, Susan.

DeTreville, Susan & DeTreville, Stan. Butterflies & Moths. (Illus.). 32p. (Orig.). 1981. pap. 3.50 (ISBN 0-89844-026-2). Troubador Pr.

--Reptiles & Amphibians. (Illus.). 32p. (Orig.). 1981. pap. 3.50 (ISBN 0-89844-025-4). Troubador Pr.

De Trevino, Elizabeth B. Among the Innocent. 360p. 1981. 13.95 (ISBN 0-385-13397-9). Doubleday.

De Trevino, Elizabeth B. see Trevino, Elizabeth B. De.

De Trevino, Elizabeth Borton. The Heart Possessed. LC 77-26523. 1978. 7.95 o.p. (ISBN 0-385-03536-5). Doubleday.

Detroit Institute of Arts. The Legend of John Brown: Twenty-Two Gouaches by Jacob Lawrence. (Illus.). 1979. 6.00x (ISBN 0-8143-1633-6, Pub. by Detroit Inst Arts). Wayne St U Pr.

Detroit Institute of Arts, Grand Palais, Paris, jt. auth. see Philadelphia Museum of Art.

Detroit Public Library. Catalog of the E. Azalia Hackley Memorial Collection of Negro Music, Dance & Drama. 1979. lib. bdg. 100.00 (ISBN 0-8161-0299-6). G K Hall.

De Troyes, Chretien. Yvain Ou le Chevalier Au Lion. Nelson, Jan, et al, eds. LC 68-22800. (Medieval French Literature Ser). (Orig., Fr). 1968. pap. text ed. 5.95x (ISBN 0-89197-477-6). Irvington.

Detterman, Douglas K., jt. ed. see Sternberg, Robert J.

DeTure, L., jt. auth. see Rowe, M. B.

Detweiler, Robert. John Updike. (U. S. Authors Ser.: No. 214). lib. bdg. 9.95 (ISBN 0-8057-0752-2). Twayne.

--Story, Sign, & Self: Phenomenology & Structuralism As Literary-Critical Methods. Beardslee, William A., ed. LC 76-9713. (Semeia Studies). 240p. 1978. pap. 5.95 (ISBN 0-8006-1505-0, 1-1505). Fortress.

Detweiler, Robert, ed. John Updike. LC 74-187611. (Twayne's U. S. Authors Ser.). 183p. 1972. pap. text ed. 4.95 (ISBN 0-672-61506-1). Bobbs.

Detwiler, Donald S. Germany: A Short History. LC 76-4563. 288p. 1976. 14.95x (ISBN 0-8093-0491-0); pap. 7.95 (ISBN 0-8093-0768-5). S Ill U Pr.

Detwiler, Donald S., ed. World War Two German Military Studies, 10 pts. in 23 vols. Incl. Pt. 1. Introduction & Guide (ISBN 0-8240-4300-6); Pt. 2. The Extinct Series (European Theatre Interrogations, 2 pts. Pt. A (ISBN 0-8240-4301-4). Pt. B (ISBN 0-8240-4302-2); Pt. 3. Command Structure, 3 pts. Pt. A (ISBN 0-8240-4303-0). Pt. B (ISBN 0-8240-4304-9). Pt. C (ISBN 0-8240-4305-7); Pt. 4. The OKW (Oberkommando der Wehrmacht) War Diary Series, 5 pts. Pt. A (ISBN 0-8240-4306-5). Pt. B (ISBN 0-8240-4307-3). Pt. C (ISBN 0-8240-4308-1). Pt. D (ISBN 0-8240-4309-X). Pt. E (ISBN 0-8240-4310-3); Pt. 5. The Western Theatre (ISBN 0-8240-4311-1); Pt. 6. The Mediterranean Theatre, 2 pts. Pt. A (ISBN 0-8240-4312-X). Pt. B (ISBN 0-8240-4313-8); Pt. 7. The Eastern Theatre, 5 pts. Pt. A (ISBN 0-8240-4314-6). Pt. B (ISBN 0-8240-4315-4). Pt. C (ISBN 0-8240-4316-2). Pt. D (ISBN 0-8240-4317-0). Pt. E (ISBN 0-8240-4318-9); Pt. 8. Diplomacy, Strategy & Military Theory, 2 pts. Pt. A (ISBN 0-8240-4319-7). Pt. B (ISBN 0-8240-4320-0); **Pt. 9. German Military Government (ISBN 0-8240-4321-9); Pt. 10. Special Topics, 2 pts. Pt. A (ISBN 0-8240-4322-7). Pt. B (ISBN 0-8240-4323-5). 1979. lib. bdg. 60.50 ea., vol. Garland Pub.**

Detwiler, Donald S. & Burdick, Charles B., eds. Defense of the Homeland & the End of the War: Japanese Military Studies 1937-1949. (War in Asia & the Pacific Ser., 1937 to 1949: Vol. 12). 1980. lib. bdg. 60.50 (ISBN 0-8240-3296-9); lib. bdg. 650.00 set of 15 vols. (ISBN 0-686-60101-7). Garland Pub.

--Introduction & Guide: Japanese & Chinese Studies & Documents, Vol. 1. (War in Asia & the Pacific Ser., 1937 to 1949). 460p. 1980. lib. bdg. 60.50 (ISBN 0-8240-3285-3). Garland Pub.

--Japan & the Soviet Union, Pt. 1. (War in Asia & the Pacific Ser., 1937 to 1949: Vol. 10). 670p. 1980. lib. bdg. 50.60 ea. (ISBN 0-8240-3294-2). Garland Pub.

--Japanese Military Studies Nineteen Thirty-Seven to Nineteen Forty-Nine, Naval Armament Program & Naval Operations: Japanese & Chinese Studies & Documents, Vol. 4. (War in Asia & the Pacific Ser., 1937 to 1949). 550p. 1980. Part I. lib. bdg. 60.50 (ISBN 0-8240-3288-8); lib. bdg. 650.00 set of 15 vols. (ISBN 0-686-60107-6). Garland Pub.

--Japanese Military Studies Nineteen Thirty-Seven to Nineteen Forty-Nine, Naval Armament Program & Naval Operations: Japanese & Chinese Studies & Documents, Vol. 5. (War in Asia & the Pacific Ser., 1937 to 1949). 520p. 1980. Part II. lib. bdg. 60.50 (ISBN 0-8240-3289-6); lib. bdg. 650.00 set 15 vols. (ISBN 0-686-60108-4). Garland Pub.

--Japanese Military Studies: The Southern Area: Japanese & Chinese Studies & Documents, Vol. 7. (War in Asia & the Pacific Ser., 1937 to 1949). 420p. 1980. Part II. lib. bdg. 60.50 (ISBN 0-8240-3291-8); lib. bdg. 650.00 set of 15 vols. (ISBN 0-686-60114-9). Garland Pub.

--Japanese Military Studies 1937-1949: Command, Administration, & Special Operations; Japanese & Chinese Studies & Documents. (War in Asia & the Pacific Ser., 1937 to 1949: Vol. 3). 660p. 1980. lib. bdg. 60.50 (ISBN 0-8240-3287-X); lib. bdg. 650.00 set of 15 vols. Garland Pub.

--Japanese Military Studies 1937-1949: China, Manchuria, & Korea, Pt. 1. (War in Asia & the Pacific Ser., 1937 to 1949: Vol. 8). 630p. 1980. lib. bdg. 55.00 (ISBN 0-8240-3292-6); lib. bdg. 650.00 set of 15 vols. (ISBN 0-686-60097-5). Garland Pub.

--Japanese Military Studies 1937-1949: China, Manchuria, & Korea, Pt. 2. (War in Asia & the Pacific Ser., 1937 to 1949: Vol. 9). 650p. 1980. lib. bdg. 55.00 (ISBN 0-8240-3293-4); lib. bdg. 60.50 set of 15 vols. Garland Pub.

--Japanese Military Studies, 1937-1949: Political Background of the War: Japanese & Chinese Studies & Documents, Vol. 2. (War in Asia & the Pacific Ser., 1937 to 1949). 500p. 1980. lib. bdg. 60.50 (ISBN 0-8240-3286-1); lib. bdg. 650.00 set of 15 vols. Garland Pub.

--Japanese Military Studies, 1937-1949: The Southern Area: Japanese & Chinese Studies & Documents, Vol. 6. (War in Asia & the Pacific Ser., 1937 to 1949). 530p. 1980. Part I. lib. bdg. 60.50 (ISBN 0-8240-3290-X); lib. bdg. 650.00 set of 15 vols. (ISBN 0-686-60113-0). Garland Pub.

--Japanese Military Studies, 1937-1949: The Sino-Japanese & the Chinese Civil Wars, Pt. 1. (War in Asia & the Pacific Ser., 1937 to 1949: Vol. 13). 460p. 1980. lib. bdg. 60.50 (ISBN 0-8240-3297-7); lib. bdg. 650.00 set of 15 vols. (ISBN 0-686-60110-6). Garland Pub.
--Japanese Military Studies, 1937-1949: The Sino-Japanese & the Chinese Civil Wars, Pt. 2. (War in Asia & the Pacific Ser., 1937 to 1949: Vol. 14). 610p. 1980. lib. bdg. 60.50 (ISBN 0-8240-3298-5); lib. bdg. 650.00 set of 15 vols. (ISBN 0-686-60111-4). Garland Pub.
--Japanese Military Studies, 1939-1949: The Sino-Japanese & the Chinese Civil Wars, Pt. 3. (War in Asia & the Pacific Ser., 1937 to 1949: Vol. 15). 570p. 1980. lib. bdg. 60.50 (ISBN 0-8240-3299-3); lib. bdg. 650.00 set of 15 vols. (ISBN 0-686-60112-2). Garland Pub.
Detwyler, T. R. Man's Impact on Environment. 1970. text ed. 13.95 o.p. (ISBN 0-07-016592-0, C). McGraw.
Detzer, David. The Brink: The Cuban Missile Crisis, 1962. LC 78-4758. (Illus.). 1979. 11.95 o.s.i. (ISBN 0-690-01682-4, TYC-T). T Y Crowell.
--Thunder of the Captains: The Short Summer in 1950. LC 76-25472. (Illus.). 1977. 10.00 o.s.i. (ISBN 0-690-01202-0, TYC-T). T Y Crowell.
Detzer, Diane. Planet of Fear. (YA) 4.95 o.p. (ISBN 0-685-07454-4, Avalon). Bouregy.
Deubofsky, T. J., ed. see Ruckdeschel, Fred.
Deuel, Leo, ed. The Memoirs of Heinrich Schliemann. LC 74-15820. (Illus.). 320p. 1977. 25.00 o.s.i. (ISBN 0-06-011106-2, HarpT). Har-Row.
Deukmejian, jt. auth. see California Dept. of Justice.
Deumlich, Fritz. Surveying Instruments. 336p. 1979. text ed. 47.00x (ISBN 3-11-007765-5). De Gruyter.
De Unamuno, Miguel. Tragic Sense of Life. 8.50 (ISBN 0-8446-3100-0). Peter Smith.
De Unamuno, Miguel see Unamuno, Miguel De.
Deusen, Glyndon G. Van see Van Deusen, Glyndon G.
Deussen, Paul. Sixty Upanishads, 2 vols. Bedekar, V. M. & Palsule, G. B., trs. 1030p. 1980. text ed. 45.00x (ISBN 0-8426-1645-4). Verry.
--The System of the Vedanta. 544p. 1973. pap. 4.00 o.p. (ISBN 0-486-22958-0). Dover.
Deutch, Sinai. Unfair Contracts: The Doctrine of Unconscionability. LC 76-20048. 1977. 24.95 (ISBN 0-669-00875-3). Lexington Bks.
Deutch, Yvonne, ed. The Sew-It-Yourself Decorating Book: Manual Making Home Furnishings. LC 77-7456. (Illus.). 1978. 14.95 o.s.i. (ISBN 0-690-01660-3, TYC-T). T Y Crowell.
Deutermann, P. T. OPS Officer's Manual. LC 79-89179. (Illus.). 216p. 1980. 14.95x (ISBN 0-87021-505-1). Naval Inst Pr.
Deutsch, Albert. Mentally Ill in America. LC 49-7527. 1949. 23.50x (ISBN 0-231-01556-5). Columbia U Pr.
Deutsch, Albert, ed. Encyclopedia of Mental Health. LC 63-7150. 1970. Repr. of 1963 ed. 45.00 (ISBN 0-8108-0357-7). Scarecrow.
Deutsch, Arnold R. The Complete Job Book. 228p. (Orig.). 1980. pap. 6.95 (ISBN 0-346-12481-6). Cornerstone.
Deutsch, Babette. Poetry Handbook: A Dictionary of Terms. 4th ed. (Funk & W Bk.). 1976. pap. 4.95 (ISBN 0-308-10248-7, M8, TYC-T). T Y Crowell.
--Poetry Handbook: Dictionary of Terms. 4th ed. (Funk & W Bk.). 224p. 1974. 10.95 (ISBN 0-308-10088-3, TYC-T). T Y Crowell.
Deutsch, David J. & Chemical Engineering Magazine, eds. Process Piping Systems. LC 80-13774. (Chemical Engineering Ser.). 484p. 1980. 32.50 (ISBN 0-07-010706-8); pap. 27.50 (ISBN 0-07-606675-4). McGraw.
Deutsch, Diana, jt. auth. see Deutsch, J. Anthony.
Deutsch, Eliot & Van Buitenen, J. A. Source Book of Advaita Vedanta. 1971. 15.00x o.p. (ISBN 0-87022-189-2). U Pr of Hawaii.
Deutsch, Francine, jt. auth. see Hultsch, David F.
Deutsch, Georg, jt. auth. see Springer, Sally P.
Deutsch, Helga, jt. auth. see Franks, E. Don.
Deutsch, Henri & Bustow, Sheldon M. Developmental Disabilities: A Training Guide. (American Health Care Association Ser.). 192p. 1981. 15.95 (ISBN 0-8436-0851-X). CBI Pub.
Deutsch, Herbert. Synthesis: An Introduction to the History, Theory, & Practice of Electronic Music. LC 76-20709. (Illus.). 250p. 1976. pap. text ed. 7.95x (ISBN 0-88284-043-6). Alfred Pub.
Deutsch, J. Anthony & Deutsch, Diana. Physiological Psychology. rev. ed. 1973. text ed. 18.95x (ISBN 0-256-01081-1). Dorsey.
Deutsch, Jan G. Selling the People's Cadillac: The Edsel & Corporate Responsibility. LC 75-37292. 300p. 1976. 25.00x (ISBN 0-300-01950-5); pap. 9.95x (ISBN 0-300-02014-7). Yale U Pr.
Deutsch, K. Analysis of International Relations. 2nd ed. (Foundations of Modern Political Science Ser.). 1978. pap. 9.95 (ISBN 0-13-033217-8). P-H.
Deutsch, Karl W. Politics & Government: How People Decide Their Fate. 2nd ed. 650p. 1974. text ed. 17.95 o.p. (ISBN 0-395-17840-1); instructor's manual .90 o.p. (ISBN 0-395-17866-5, 3-13707). HM.
--Politics & Government: How People Decide Their Fate. 3rd ed. LC 79-90262. (Illus.). 1980. text ed. 18.95 (ISBN 0-395-28486-4); instrs'. manual 0.90 (ISBN 0-395-28487-2). HM.
--Tides Among Nations. LC 78-57053. 1979. 19.95 (ISBN 0-02-907300-6). Free Pr.
Deutsch, Karl W., et al. Nerves of Government. LC 67-4864. 1963. 12.95 (ISBN 0-02-907280-8). Free Pr.
--Comparative Government: Politics of Industrialized & Developing Nations. (Illus.). 496p. 1981. text ed. 16.25 (ISBN 0-395-29759-1). HM.
Deutsch, Keith. Space Travel in Fact & Fiction. (gr. 5 up). 1980. PLB 7.90 (ISBN 0-686-65170-7). Watts.
Deutsch, Leonhard. Piano: Guided Sight-Reading: A New Approach to Piano Study. (Illus.). 1978. 10.95 (ISBN 0-88229-555-1); pap. 7.95 (ISBN 0-88229-556-X). Nelson-Hall.
Deutsch, Marilyn W., jt. ed. see Leland, Henry.
Deutsch, Otto. Handel: A Documentary Biography. LC 74-3118. (Music Ser.). 942p. 1974. Repr. of 1954 ed. lib. bdg. 55.00 (ISBN 0-306-70624-5). Da Capo.
Deutsch, Otto E. Schubert: A Documentary Biography. Blom, Eric, tr. LC 77-5499. (Music Reprint Ser.). (Illus.). 1977. Repr. of 1946 ed. lib. bdg. 57.50 (ISBN 0-306-77420-8). Da Capo.
Deutsch, Ronald. Realities of Nutrition. LC 76-23508. (Berkeley Series in Nutrition). (Illus.). 1976. 13.95 (ISBN 0-915950-07-3); pap. 9.95 (ISBN 0-915950-19-7). Bull Pub.
Deutsch, Ronald M., jt. auth. see Bach, George R.
Deutsch, Rosamund E. The Pattern of Sound in Lucretius. Commager, Steele, ed. LC 77-70763. (Latin Poetry Ser.). 1979. Repr. of 1939 ed. lib. bdg. 21.00 (ISBN 0-8240-2967-4). Garland Pub.
Deutsche Gesellschaft Fur Luft und Raumfahrt. Utilization of Space Shuttle & Spacelab: Proceedings of an International Meeting Held in Bonn, 1976. (Illus.). 1976. pap. 30.00x (ISBN 3-88135-034-9). Univelt Inc.
Deutscher, Isaac. The Prophet Armed: Trotsky, 1879-1921. 1980. pap. 8.95 (ISBN 0-19-281064-2, GB 605, GB). Oxford U Pr.
--The Prophet Outcast: Trotsky, 1929-1940. 1980. pap. 8.95 (ISBN 0-19-281066-9, GB 607, GB). Oxford U Pr.
--The Prophet Unarmed: Trotsky, 1921-1929. 1980. pap. 8.95 (ISBN 0-19-281065-0, GB 606, GB). Oxford U Pr.
--Stalin: A Political Biography. 2nd ed. pap. 9.95 (ISBN 0-19-500273-3, GB). Oxford U Pr.
--Unfinished Revolution: Russia,1917-1967. LC 67-23012. 1969. pap. 3.95 (ISBN 0-19-500786-7, GB). Oxford U Pr.
Deutsches Kommitee Fur Reprographie, ed. Dictionary of Reprography: Terms & Definitions. 273p. (Ger. & Fr.). 1976. pap. text ed. 34.00 (ISBN 3-7940-3186-5, Pub. by K G Saur). Gale.
De Vaca, Cabeza. Adventures in the Unknown Interior of America. Covey, Cyclone, ed. & tr. 152p. 1972. pap. 1.25 o.s.i. (ISBN 0-02-031580-5, Collier). Macmillan.
Devadhar, C. R., tr. Abhijnana Sakuntalam of Kalidasa. 4th ed. 1972. pap. 4.95 (ISBN 0-89684-164-2). Orient Bk Dist.
Devahuti. Bias in Indian Historiography. 1980. text ed. write for info. (ISBN 0-391-02174-5). Humanities.
--Problems of Indian Historiography. 1979. text ed. 11.50x (ISBN 0-391-01862-0). Humanities.
De Vall, Mark Van see Van De Vall, Mark.
Devall, William B., jt. auth. see Harry, Joseph.
Devall, William S., Jr. Junior High School Art Curriculum. LC 79-6770. 79p. 1980. pap. text ed. 6.50 (ISBN 0-8191-0951-7). U Pr of Amer.
Devambez, Pierre. Great Sculpture of Ancient Greece. LC 78-55511. (Reynal's World History of Great Sculpture Ser.). (Illus.). 1978. 25.00 o.p. (ISBN 0-688-61205-9). Reynal.
Devaney, John. The Bobby Orr Story. (Pro Hockey Library: No. 6). (Illus.). (gr. 5 up). 1973. 2.50 o.p. (ISBN 0-394-82612-4, BYR); PLB 3.69 (ISBN 0-394-92612-9). Random.
--The Pocket Book of Pro Basketball 1980. 1980. pap. 2.75 (ISBN 0-671-41863-7). PB.
--Star Pass Receivers of the NFL. (NFL Punt, Pass & Kick Library: No. 17). (Illus.). (gr. 5 up). 1972. 2.50 o.p. (ISBN 0-394-82439-3, BYR); PLB 3.69 (ISBN 0-394-92439-8). Random.
Devaney, John & Goldblatt, Burt. The World Series: A Complete Pictoral History. rev. ed. (Illus.). 416p. 1981. pap. 10.95 (ISBN 0-528-88044-6). Rand.
Devaney, John, jt. auth. see Lorimer, Lawrence T.
Devaney, Kathleen, ed. Building a Teachers' Center. 1979. pap. 9.75x (ISBN 0-8077-2566-8, Pub. by Teach Ctr Exchange). Tchrs Coll.
DeVany, A. S. Master Optical Techniques. LC 80-24442. (Pure & Applied Optics Ser.). 625p. 1981. 45.00 (ISBN 0-471-07720-8, Pub. by Wiley-Interscience). Wiley.
De Vany, Arthur S., et al. A Property System Approach to the Electromagnetic Spectrum: A Legal-Economic-Engineering Study. (Cato Paper Ser.: No. 10). 112p. 1980. pap. 4.00 (ISBN 0-932790-11-9). Cato Inst.
Devaraja, N. K. The Mind & Spirit of India. 1967. 5.00 (ISBN 0-89684-281-9). Orient Bk Dist.
De Varigny, Charles. Fourteen Years in the Sandwich Islands. Korn, Alfons L., tr. LC 80-26141. (Illus.). 320p. (Fr.). 1981. 24.95 (ISBN 0-8248-0709-X). U Pr of Hawaii.
DeVault, M. Vere, jt. auth. see Cooper, James M.
Devavrata Basu Ray, tr. see Swami Vishwashrayananda.
De Vazquez, Margot Arce see Pales Matos, Luis.
De Veen, J. J. The Rural Access Roads Programme: Apropriate Technology in Kenya. International Labour Office, Geneva, ed. (Illus.). 175p. (Orig.). 1980. pap. 11.40 (ISBN 92-2-102204-8). Intl Labour Office.
De Vega, Lope. The Pilgrim: or the Stranger in His Own Country, Vol. 69. LC 71-170598. (Novel in England, 1700-1775 Ser). lib. bdg. 50.00 (ISBN 0-8240-0581-3). Garland Pub.
--Stupid Lady. 3.00 (ISBN 0-8283-1426-8). Branden.
Deventer, Marylon Van see Friends of the Earth Staff.
Dever, William G. Gezer Two. 1974. 35.00x (ISBN 0-685-56198-4). Ktav.
Deverall, B. J. Defence Mechanisms of Plants. LC 76-12917. (Monographs in Experimental Biology Ser.: No. 19). (Illus.). 1977. 21.50 (ISBN 0-521-21335-5). Cambridge U Pr.
Deveraux, Jude. The Black Lyon. 1980. pap. 2.50 (ISBN 0-686-69258-6, 75911). Avon.
--The Enchanted Land. 1980. pap. 2.50 (ISBN 0-686-69270-5, 76422). Avon.
Devere. Black Genesis. (Illus.). 120p. 1980. 13.95 (ISBN 0-312-08313-0). St Martin.
DeVere, S., tr. see Spielhagen, Friedrich.
Deverell, William. Needles. 288p. 1981. pap. 2.75 (ISBN 0-553-13974-6). Bantam.
Devereux, Frederick L., Jr. Backyard Pony: Selecting & Owning a Horse. LC 75-5544. 96p. (gr. 6 up). 1975. 5.88 o.p. (ISBN 0-531-02833-X). Watts.
--Horseback Riding. LC 75-34189. (First Bks.). (Illus.). 72p. (gr. 4-6). 1976. PLB 6.45 (ISBN 0-531-00844-4). Watts.
--Horses. LC 75-4897. (Illus.). 72p. (gr. 4-6). 1975. PLB 3.90 o.p. (ISBN 0-531-00836-3). Watts.
--Jump Your Horse Right. LC 78-7734. (Illus.). (gr. 5 up). 1978. 6.50 (ISBN 0-396-07611-4). Dodd.
Devereux, George. Dreams in Greek Tragedy: An Ethno-Psycho-Analytic Study. 400p. 1976. 25.00x (ISBN 0-520-02921-6). U. of Cal Pr.
--Ethnopsychoanalysis: Psychoanalysis & Anthropology As Complementary Frames of Reference. LC 74-16708. 1978. 27.50x (ISBN 0-520-02864-3). U. of Cal Pr.
Devereux, Hugo B. The Small State As the Major Troublemaker in History & the Need to Eliminate Its Existence for the Peace of the World. (Illus.). 1979. deluxe ed. 49.75 (ISBN 0-930008-34-0). Inst Econ Pol.
Devereux, Robert & Wingfield, Anthony. True Copie of a Discourse Written by a Gentleman, Employed in the Late Voyage of Spaine & Portingale. LC 78-38172. (English Experience Ser.: No. 449). 1972. Repr. of 1589 ed. 9.50 (ISBN 90-221-0449-4). Walter J Johnson.
Devers, Dorothy. Faithful Friendship. 1980. 2.00 (ISBN 0-686-28777-0). Forward Movement.
De Vet, Charles & MacLean, Katherine. Second Game. (Science Fiction Ser.). 1981. pap. 2.25 (ISBN 0-87997-620-9, UE1620). DAW Bks.
De Vet, Therese, jt. auth. see Shaw, Peter.
De Veubeke, B. F. Advanced Problems & Methods for Space Flight Optimization. 1969. 46.00 (ISBN 0-08-013290-1). Pergamon.
De Veubeke, B. F., et al, eds. see CISM (International Center for Mechanical Sciences).
De Vezins, Elie. Hounds for a Pack. Woolner, Lionel R., tr. (Illus.). 7.00 (ISBN 0-85131-210-1, Dist. by Sporting Book Center). J A Allen.
Devi, Gayatri & Rau, Santha Rama. A Princess Remembers: The Memoirs of the Maharani of Jaipur. LC 75-33293. (Illus.). 1977. 12.50 o.p. (ISBN 0-397-01103-2). Lippincott.
Devi, Indira, jt. auth. see Roy, Dilip K.
Devi, Indra. Renew Your Life Through Yoga. (Illus.). 256p. 1972. pap. 1.95 o.s.i. (ISBN 0-446-89515-6). Warner Bks.
Devi, Maitreyi. It Does Not Die. (Translated from Bengali). 15.00 (ISBN 0-89253-644-6); flexible cloth 11.00 (ISBN 0-89253-645-4). Ind-US Inc.
Devi, Sahkuntala. Figuring. 160p. 1981. pap. 3.95 (ISBN 0-06-463530-9, EH). Har-Row.
Devi, Savitrix. The Lightning & the Sun. (Illus.). 440p. (Orig.). 1960. pap. 12.00 (ISBN 0-911038-84-1, Samisdat). Noontide.
Devi, Shree. The Purple-Braided People. 8.00 (ISBN 0-89253-652-7); flexible cloth 4.80 (ISBN 0-89253-653-5). Ind-US Inc.
--Shades of Green. (Writers Workshop Redbird Ser). 1975. 8.00 (ISBN 0-88253-632-X); pap. text ed. 4.00 (ISBN 0-88253-631-1). Ind-US Inc.
Devi, Shyamashree, tr. see Tagore, Rabindranath.
Devi, Shyamasree, tr. see Roy, Tarapada.
Devieux, Violet S. The One Stringed Harp. 1980. 6.50 (ISBN 0-8233-0311-X). Golden Quill.
De Vigenere, Blaise, tr. see Philostratus.
De Vila, Maria Arsuaga see Arsuaga De Vila, Maria.
DeVille, Jard, jt. auth. see DeVille, Roberta.
Deville, Lawrence. American Foreign Policy & American Business, 2 vols. new ed. (Illus.). 1979. Set. 77.50 (ISBN 0-89266-143-7). Am Classical Coll Pr.
--American Foreign Policy & American Business: The Two Worlds in Conflict. (Illus.). 85p. 1975. 51.75 (ISBN 0-913314-46-3). Am Classical Coll Pr.
DeVille, Roberta & DeVille, Jard. Lovers for Life: The Key to a Loving & Lasting Marriage. LC 80-10652. 224p. 1980. 8.95 (ISBN 0-688-03618-X). Morrow.
De Villehardouin, Geoffrey & De Joinville, Jean. Chronicles of the Crusades. Shaw, Margaret R., tr. (Classics Ser.). (Orig.). 1963. pap. 3.95 (ISBN 0-14-044124-7). Penguin.
De Ville Leyda, Seraphia see Leyda, Seraphia De Ville.
De Villeneuve, Joachim F. L' Econome Politique. (Principal French Demographic Works of the 18th Century Ser.). (Fr.). 1976. lib. bdg. 35.00x o.p. (ISBN 0-8287-1366-9); pap. text ed. 25.00x o.p. (ISBN 0-685-71509-4). Clearwater Pub.
De Villiers, Gerard. The Man from Kabul. (Malko Ser., No. 3). 192p. 1973. pap. 0.95 o.p. (ISBN 0-523-00253-X). Pinnacle Bks.
Devin-Adair Staff. Dogmatic Canons & Decrees of the Council of Trent, Vatican Council I, Plus the Decree on the Immaculate Conception & the Syllabus of Errors. LC 79-112469. (Eng.). 1977. pap. 4.00 (ISBN 0-89555-018-0, 197). TAN Bks Pubs.
Devin, Flanna. Alien Encounter. 1981. pap. 1.95 (ISBN 0-8439-0898-X, Leisure Bks). Nordon Pubns.
De Vinck, Catherine. A Book of Eve. 1979. text ed. 6.00 (ISBN 0-911726-40-3); stero record incl. Alleluia Pr.
De Vinck, Jose, jt. auth. see Raya, Joseph.
Devine, Donald F. & Kaufman, Jerome E. Mathematics for Elementary Education. LC 73-14692. 609p. 1973. 19.95 (ISBN 0-471-20969-4). Wiley.
Devine, Donald F. & Kaufmann, Jerome E. Elementary Mathematics. LC 76-24805. 1977. text ed. 20.95 (ISBN 0-471-20970-8); instructor's manual avail. (ISBN 0-471-02394-9). Wiley.
Devine, George. American Catholicism: Where Do We Go from Here? 144p. (Orig.). 1974. pap. 9.95 (ISBN 0-13-023986-0). P-H.
Devine, George F., jt. ed. see Starr, William J.
Devine, Mary, ed. The Cartulary of Cirencester Abbey, Gloucestershire, Vol. 3. 1977. 45.00x (ISBN 0-19-711637-X). Oxford U Pr.
Devine, Michael J. John W. Foster: Politics & Diplomacy in the Imperial Era-1873-1917. LC 80-17387. (Illus.). 200p. 1981. 14.95x (ISBN 0-8214-0437-7). Ohio U Pr.
Devine, Peter, ed. see Gafney, Leo & Beers, John C.
DeVinne, Theodore L. Invention of Printing. LC 68-17971. 1969. Repr. of 1876 ed. 24.00 (ISBN 0-8103-3302-3). Gale.
De Vinne, Theodore L. Manual of Printing Office Practice. Lew, Irving, ed. (Bibliographical Reprint Ser.). 1980. Repr. of 1926 ed. text ed. 25.00 ltd. ed. (ISBN 0-89782-003-7). Battery Pk.
--The Printers' Price List, a Manual for the Use of Clerks & Book-Keepers in Job Printing Offices. Bidwell, John, ed. LC 78-74396. (Nineteenth-Century Book Arts & Printing History Ser.: Vol. 10). 1980. lib. bdg. 38.00 (ISBN 0-8240-3884-3). Garland Pub.
Devinney, Edward J., Jr., et al. Contemporary Astronomy. (Physical Science Ser). 288p. 1975. text ed. 19.95x (ISBN 0-675-08727-9). Merrill.
De Visscher, Michel, ed. The Thyroid Gland. (Comprehensive Endocrinology Ser.). 1980. 53.50 (ISBN 0-89004-342-6, 396). Raven.

DeVitis, A. A. Anthony Burgess. (English Authors Ser.: No. 132). lib. bdg. 10.95 (ISBN 0-8057-1068-X). Twayne.
DeVito, Albert. Chord Dictionary. LC 75-40685. 1980. 3.95 (ISBN 0-934286-01-9). Kenyon.
--Chord Encyclopedia. LC 75-43441. 1980. 4.95 (ISBN 0-934286-02-7). Kenyon.
Devito, Alfred, jt. auth. see Krockover, Gerald.
DeVito, Joseph. Elements of Public Speaking. (Illus.). 480p. 1980. pap. text ed. 14.50 scp (ISBN 0-06-041653-X, HarpC); avail. Har-Row.
De Vito, Joseph A. Communication: Concepts & Processes. rev. ed. (Speech Communications Ser.). (Illus.). 352p. 1976. pap. text ed. 10.95x (ISBN 0-13-153023-2). P-H.
DeVito, Joseph A. Communication: Concepts & Processes. 3rd ed. (Illus.). 320p. 1981. pap. text ed. 10.95 (ISBN 0-13-153411-4). P-H.
De Vito, Joseph A. Language: Concepts & Processes. (Speech Communication Ser). (Illus.). 288p. 1973. pap. 10.95 ref. ed. o.p. (ISBN 0-13-522904-9). P-H.
DeVito, Joseph A. Psycholinguistics. LC 73-183112. (Studies in Communicative Disorders Ser). 36p. 1971. pap. 1.95 (ISBN 0-672-61277-1). Bobbs.
DeVito, Joseph A., et al. Articulation & Voice: Effective Communication. LC 74-14615. (No. 20). 127p. 1975. 3.95 (ISBN 0-672-61350-6, SC20). Bobbs.
De Vito, Robert A. & Tapley, Richard P., eds. A View into a Modern, State-Operated Mental Health Facility: The Madden Zone Center. 308p. 1975. 27.50 (ISBN 0-398-03207-6). C C Thomas.
DeVitt, Joan Q., jt. auth. see Benson, Evelyn P.
Devitt, Michael. Designation. LC 80-26471. 304p. 1981. 22.50x (ISBN 0-231-05126-3). Columbia U Pr.
Devivre, Joe, jt. auth. see Devivre, O.
Devivre, O. & Devivre, Joe. Perfection Perception. (Illus.). 128p. 1981. pap. 5.00 (ISBN 0-933280-08-4). Island CA.
De Vleeschauwer, H. J. La Deduction Transcendentale Dans L'oueuvre De Kant, 3 vols. Beck, Lewis W., ed. LC 75-32049. (Philosophy of Immanuel Kant Ser.). 1976. Set. lib. bdg. 100.00 (ISBN 0-8240-2326-9). Garland Pub.
De Vlieger, M. Brain Edema. 185p. 1981. 27.50 (ISBN 0-471-04477-6, Pub. by Wiley-Med). Wiley.
DeVlieger, M., et al. Handbook of Clinical Ultrasound. LC 78-14458. 1978. 122.00 (ISBN 0-471-02744-8, Pub. by Wiley Medical). Wiley.
Devlin, jt. auth. see Wende.
Devlin, D. D. The Author of Waverley. LC 71-146129. 142p. 1971. 12.00 (ISBN 0-8387-7925-5). Bucknell U Pr.
--Wordworth & the Poetry of Epitaphs. 143p. 1980. 26.00x (ISBN 0-389-20040-9). B&N.
Devlin, George A., et al. The Dimensions of Parking. LC 79-64130. (Illus.). 120p. 1979. pap. text ed. 18.00 (ISBN 0-87420-585-9). Urban Land.
Devlin, Harry. Tales of Thunder & Lightning. LC 74-41057. 48p. (gr. 1-4). 1975. 5.95 o.s.i. (ISBN 0-8193-0805-6, Four Winds); PLB 5.41 o.s.i. (ISBN 0-8193-0806-4). Schol Bk Serv.
--To Grandfather's House We Go: A Roadside Tour of American Homes. LC 80-15294. (Illus.). 48p. (gr. 5 up). 1980. Repr. of 1967 ed. 9.95 (ISBN 0-590-07764-3, Four Winds). Schol Bk Serv.
--What Kind of a House Is That? LC 78-77792. (Illus.). (gr. 5 up). 1969. 5.95 o.s.i. (ISBN 0-8193-0315-1, Four Winds); PLB 5.41 o.s.i. (ISBN 0-8193-0316-X). Schol Bk Serv.
Devlin, Harry, jt. auth. see Devlin, Wende.
Devlin, J. Frank, et al. Sports Illustrated Badminton. rev. ed. LC 72-10556. 1973. 4.95 o.s.i. (ISBN 0-397-00967-4); pap. 2.95 (ISBN 0-397-00968-2, LP80). Lippincott.
Devlin, John F. The Ba'th Party: A History from Its Origins to 1966. LC 75-41903. (Publications Ser.: No. 156). 372p. 1976. 11.95 (ISBN 0-8179-6561-0). Hoover Inst Pr.
Devlin, Laura K. Looking Inward: Studies in James Joyce, E.M. Forster, & the Twentieth Century Novel. 1980. lib. bdg. 59.95 (ISBN 0-87700-269-X). Revisionist Pr.
Devlin, Patrick. Criminal Prosecution in England. 1958. 24.50x (ISBN 0-685-69811-4). Elliots Bks.
--Enforcement of Morals. 1970. pap. 4.95 (ISBN 0-19-500305-5, GB). Oxford U Pr.
Devlin, Wende & Devlin, Harry. Cranberry Christmas. LC 80-16971. (Illus.). 40p. (ps-3). 1980. Repr. of 1976 ed. 8.95 (ISBN 0-590-07760-0, Four Winds). Schol Bk Serv.
--Cranberry Mystery. LC 78-6219. (Illus.). 40p. (ps-3). 1978. 7.95 (ISBN 0-8193-0972-9, Four Winds); PLB 5.41 o.p. (ISBN 0-8193-0973-7). Schol Bk Serv.
--Cranberry Thanksgiving. LC 80-17070. (Illus.). 48p. (ps-3). 1980. Repr. of 1971 ed. 8.95 (ISBN 0-590-07761-9, Four Winds). Schol Bk Serv.
--How Fletcher Was Hatched. LC 69-12614. (Illus.). (gr. k-3). 1969. 5.95 o.s.i. (ISBN 0-8193-0247-3, Four Winds); PLB 5.41 o.s.i. (ISBN 0-8193-0248-1). Schol Bk Serv.
--Old Black Witch! LC 80-17064. (Illus.). 32p. (ps-3). 1980. Repr. of 1966 ed. 8.95 (ISBN 0-590-07785-6, Four Winds). Schol Bk Serv.
--Old Witch & the Polka-Dot Ribbon. LC 80-15284. (Illus.). 40p. (ps-3). 1980. Repr. of 1970 ed. 8.95 (ISBN 0-590-07787-2, Four Winds). Schol Bk Serv.
--Old Witch Rescues Halloween. LC 80-17071. (Illus.). 48p. (ps-3). 1980. Repr. of 1972 ed. 8.95 (ISBN 0-590-07786-4, Four Winds). Schol Bk Serv.
Devoe, Shirleys S. The Tinsmiths of Connecticut. (Illus.). 1968. 15.00x (ISBN 0-686-26749-4). Conn Hist Soc.
De Voe, Thomas F. The Market Assistant. LC 72-174033. (Illus.). 455p. 1975. Repr. of 1867 ed. 32.00 (ISBN 0-8103-4117-4). Gale.
De Vogel, C. J. Greek Philosophy, 3 Vols. 1960-1964. Vol. 1. text ed. 24.00x (ISBN 90-04-02356-9). Vol. 2. text ed. 24.00x (ISBN 90-04-02357-7). Vol. 3. text ed. 42.25x (ISBN 90-040374-3-8). Humanities.
--Philosophia: Studies in Greek Philosophy, Pt. 1. (Philosophical Texts & Studies: No. 19). 1970. text ed. 40.50x (ISBN 90-232-0733-5). Humanities.
De Volpi, A., et al. Governmental Secrecy & National Security: The Progressive Case. (Pergamon Policy Studies on International Politics). (Illus.). 400p. 1980. 30.00 (ISBN 0-08-025995-2); pap. 15.00 (ISBN 0-08-027529-X). Pergamon.
De Volpi, Alexander. Proliferation, Plutonium & Policy: Institutional & Technological Impediments to Nuclear Weapons Propogation. (Pergamon Policy Studies). (Illus.). 1979. 39.50 (ISBN 0-08-023872-6). Pergamon.
De Voltaire, Framcois M. Candide. Taylor, O. R., ed. (French Texts Ser.). 1978. pap. text ed. 9.95x (ISBN 0-631-00400-9, Pub. by Basil Blackwell). Biblio Dist.
De Voltaire, Francois M. Candide. LC 62-19952. 1963. pap. text ed. 2.95 (ISBN 0-8120-0038-2). Barron.
--Candide. Bd. with Zadig. (Classics Ser). pap. 1.25 (ISBN 0-8049-0117-1, CL-117). Airmont.
--Candide. Brumfitt, J. H., ed. 1968. pap. 6.95x (ISBN 0-19-832372-7). Oxford U Pr.
--Candide. Adams, Robert M., ed. (Critical Edition Ser). 1966. pap. 3.95x (ISBN 0-393-09649-1). Norton.
--Oeuvres philosophiques. (Documentation thematique). (Fr). pap. 2.95 (ISBN 0-685-14012-1, 351). Larousse.
--Philosophical Letters. Dilworth, Ernest N., tr. LC 60-53370. 1961. pap. 4.50 (ISBN 0-672-60326-8, LLA124). Bobbs.
Devon, Lynn. Jade. 1978. pap. 1.75 o.p. (ISBN 0-449-13941-7, GM). Fawcett.
Devon, T. K. & Scott, A. I. Handbook of Naturally Occurring Compounds, 2 vols. Incl. Vol. 1. Acetogenins, Shikimates & Carbohydrates. 1975. 51.50 (ISBN 0-12-213601-2); Vol. 2. Terpenes. 1972. 42.00 (ISBN 0-12-213602-0). Acad Pr.
Devon Trust for Nature Conservation, ed. School Projects in Natural History. 1972. pap. text ed. 6.50x o.p. (ISBN 0-435-59920-8). Heinemann Ed.
Devons, Samuel, ed. Biology & the Physical Sciences. LC 78-80272. 1969. 23.50x (ISBN 0-231-03134-3). Columbia U Pr.
Devor, Barbara. Aunt Maude & the Faisan D'or. 1980. 6.00 (ISBN 0-682-49563-8). Exposition.
De Vore, Irven & Eimerl, Sarel. Primates. LC 65-17071. (Life Nature Library). (Illus.). (gr. 5 up). 1965. PLB 8.97 o.p. (ISBN 0-8094-0635-7, Pub. by Time-Life). Silver.
DeVore, Irven, jt. auth. see Eimerl, Sarel.
De Vore, Irven, jt. ed. see Lee, Richard B.
DeVore, Paul W. Technology: An Introduction. LC 79-53782. (Technology Ser.). (Illus.). 397p. 1980. text ed. 16.95 (ISBN 0-87192-115-4, 000-5). Davis Pubns.
DeVore, R. A. & Scherer, K., eds. Quantitative Approximation. LC 80-17554. 1980. 22.00 (ISBN 0-12-213650-0). Acad Pr.
De Vore, R. W., jt. ed. see Rose, J. G.
De Vore, R. William, ed. Annual Report: A Kentucky Energy Resource Utilization Program. (Illus., Orig.). 1979. pap. 4.50 (ISBN 0-89779-026-X, IMMR45-PR8-79); microfiche 3.50 (ISBN 0-89779-027-8). OES Pubns.
--Carnahan Conference on Crime Countermeasures: Proceedings Nineteen Seventy-Nine. Jackson, J. S. LC 79-64890. (Illus., Orig.). 1979. pap. 22.50 (ISBN 0-89779-018-9, UKY BU117); microfiche 3.50 (ISBN 0-89779-019-7). OES Pubns.
--Semiannual Report: A Kentucky Energy Resource Utilization Program. 1978. pap. text ed. 5.00 (ISBN 0-89779-004-9); microfiche 1.50 (ISBN 0-89779-005-7). OES Pubns.
De Vore, R. William & Carpenter, Stanley B., eds. Symposium on Surface Mining Hydrology, Sedimentology, & Reclamation. LC 79-91553. (Illus.). 353p. (Orig.). 1979. pap. 33.50 (ISBN 0-89779-024-3, UKY BU119); microfiche 4.50 (ISBN 0-89779-025-1). OEA Pubns.
De Vore, R. William & Graves, Donald H., eds. Symposium on Surface Mining Hydrology, Sedimentology, & Reclamation 1980: Proceedings. (Illus., Orig.). 1980. pap. 33.50 (ISBN 0-89779-044-8, UKYBU123); microfiche 5.50 (ISBN 0-89779-045-6). OES Pubns.
De Vore, R. William & Haan, Charles T., eds. International Symposium on Urban Storm Water Management: Proceedings. 1978. pap. text ed. 33.50 (ISBN 0-89779-002-2); microfiche 4.50 (ISBN 0-89779-003-0). OES Pubns.
De Vore, R. William & Huffsey, R. R., eds. International Symposium on Urban Storm Runoff: Proceedings. LC 79-66289. (Illus., Orig.). 1979. pap. 33.50 (ISBN 0-89779-020-0, UKY BU118); microfiche 4.50 (ISBN 0-89779-023-5). OES Pubns.
De Vore, R. William & Jackson, J. S., eds. Carnahan Conference on Crime Countermeasures: Proceedings, 1980. LC 79-644630. (Illus.). 160p. (Orig.). 1980. pap. 22.50 (ISBN 0-89779-030-8, UKY BU120); microfiche 2.50 (ISBN 0-89779-031-6). OES Pubns.
De Vore, R. William & Jackson, John S., eds. Carnahan Conference on Crime Countermeasures, 1978: Proceedings. 1978. pap. text ed. 22.50 (ISBN 0-89779-000-6); microfiche 3.50 (ISBN 0-89779-001-4). OES Pubns.
DeVore, R. William, ed. see Hayes, J., et al.
De Vore, R. William, ed. see Reucroft, P. J., et al.
De Vore, R. William, ed. see Third International Conference.
De Vore, R. William, et al, eds. Fifth Energy Resource Conference: Proceedings. (Illus.). 1978. pap. text ed. 7.50 (ISBN 0-89779-006-5); microfiche 2.50 (ISBN 0-89779-007-3). OES Pubns.
DeVore, Ronald M. The Arab-Israeli Conflict: A Historical, Political, Social, & Military Bibliography. LC 76-17575. (War-Peace Bibliography Ser.: No. 4). 273p. 1976. text ed. 9.65 (ISBN 0-87436-229-6). ABC-Clio.
DeVore, Russell B. Practical Problems in Mathematics for Heating & Cooling Technicians. LC 79-57141. (Practical Problems in Mathematics Ser.). 175p. 1981. pap. text ed. 6.60 (ISBN 0-8273-1682-8); instr's. guide 2.10 (ISBN 0-8273-1683-6). Delmar.
DeVore, Sally & White, Thelma. The Appetites of Man: An Invitation to Better Nutrition from Nine Healthier Societies. LC 77-11231. 1978. pap. 4.95 o.p. (ISBN 0-385-13512-2, Anch). Doubleday.
DeVore, Steven, et al, Sybervision: Muscle Memory Programming for Any Sport. (Illus.). 250p. 1981. 12.95 (ISBN 0-914090-98-4). Chicago Review.
DeVos, George, jt. auth. see Lee, Changsoo.
DeVos, George A. Socialization for Achievement: Essays on the Cultural Psychology of the Japanese. LC 78-132420. 613p. 1973. 23.75 o.p. (ISBN 0-520-01827-3); pap. 11.95x (ISBN 0-520-02893-7). U of Cal Pr.
De Vos, George A. & Witherall, William O. Japan's Minorities: Burakumin, Koreans, Ainu. (Minority Rights Group: No. 3). 1974. pap. 2.50 (ISBN 0-89192-093-5). Interbk Inc.
De Vos, Richard. Believe! 1981. pap. price not set (ISBN 0-671-41757-6). PB.
DeVos, Richard M. & Conn, Charles P. Believe! 1975. 5.95 (ISBN 0-8007-0732-X); pap. 2.50 (ISBN 0-8007-8267-4, Spire Bks). Revell.
DeVos, Ton. U. S. Multinationals & Worker Participation in Management: The American Experience in the European Community. LC 80-23597. 1981. lib. bdg. 29.95 (ISBN 0-89930-004-9, DUM/, Quorum Bks). Greenwood.
Devoto, Giacimo. Linguistics & Literary Criticism. Edgerton, M. F., Jr., tr. 1963. 6.00 (ISBN 0-913298-08-5). S F Vanni.
Devoy, J. Recollections of an Irish Rebel. 508p. 1969. Repr. of 1929 ed. 25.00x (ISBN 0-7165-0045-0, Pub. by Irish Academic Pr Ireland). Biblio Dist.
DeVoy, Robert, jt. auth. see Costonis, John.
Devreese, J. T., ed. Theoretical Aspects & the New Developments in Megneto-Optics. (NATO Advanced Study Institutes Ser.: B Physics: Vol. 60). 635p. 1981. 69.50 (ISBN 0-306-40555-5, Plenum Pr). Plenum Pub.
Devreese, J. T., jt. ed. see Papadoupoulos, G.
De Vries, J. Economy of Europe in an Age of Crisis: 1600 to 1750. LC 75-30438. (Illus.). 240p. 1976. 29.50 (ISBN 0-521-21123-9); pap. 7.95x (ISBN 0-521-29050-3). Cambridge U Pr.
DeVries, J. J. & Appelo, C. A. J. Aqua-Vu: Some Calculation Method for Determination of the Travel Time of Groundwater. (Communications of the Inst. of Earth Sciences, Ser. A: No. 5). pap. text ed. 8.75x (ISBN 0-685-78791-5). Humanities.
De Vries, J. J. see Vries, J. J. De.
De Vries, Leonard. Book of Experiments. (Illus.). (gr. 4-6). 1959. 4.95g o.s.i. (ISBN 0-02-730000-5). Macmillan.
De Vries, Peter. Forever Panting. 1974. pap. 1.25 o.p. (ISBN 0-445-00191-7). Popular Lib.
--Let Me Count the Ways. 1977. pap. 1.50 o.p. (ISBN 0-445-08531-2). Popular Lib.
DeVries, Rheta, jt. auth. see Kamli, Constance.
DeVries, Robert A., frwd. by. Future Agenda. (Education for Health Administration: Vol. 3). (Illus.). 1977. pap. text ed. 7.50 (ISBN 0-914904-23-X). Health Admin Pr.
DeVries, Simon J. Prophet Against Prophet. pap. 7.95x (ISBN 0-8028-1743-2). Eerdmans.
Dew, Donald & Jensen, Alfred D. Phonetic Transcription. 2nd ed. 1979. text ed. 7.95 (ISBN 0-675-08309-5); instructors manual 3.95 (ISBN 0-686-67278-X). Merrill.
Dew, Donald & Jensen, Paul J. Phonetic Processing: The Dynamics of Speech. 1977. text ed. 14.95 (ISBN 0-675-08594-2). Merrill.
Dew, James F., jt. auth. see Wilhite, J. Portert.
Dew, Robb F. Dale Loves Sophie to Death. 1981. 12.95 (ISBN 0-374-13450-2). FS&G.
De Waal, M. Medicinal Herbs in the Bible. Meijlink, Jane, ed. 96p. 1981. pap. 4.95 (ISBN 0-87728-527-6). Weiser.
De Waal, Victor. What Is the Church? LC 70-121057. (Orig.). 1970. pap. 1.95 o.p. (ISBN 0-8170-0492-0). Judson.
De Waard, J. & Nida, E. A. Translators Handbook on the Book of Ruth. (Helps for Translators Ser.). 1976. Repr. of 1973 ed. softcover 2.00 (ISBN 0-8267-0107-8, 08518). United Bible.
De Waard, J. & Smalley, W. A. Translators Handbook on the Book of Amos. (Helps for Translators Ser.). 1979. softcover 2.50 (ISBN 0-8267-0128-0, 08577). United Bible.
De Walt, B. R. Modernization in a Mexican Ejido. LC 78-3412. (Latin American Studies: No. 33). (Illus.). 1979. 29.95 (ISBN 0-521-22064-5). Cambridge U Pr.
Dewar, A. J., jt. auth. see Russell, W. Ritchie.
Dewar, David & Ellis, George. Low Income Housing Policies in South Africa. (Illus.). 256p. 1980. pap. 15.00x (ISBN 0-8476-3285-7). Rowman.
Dewar, Diana. Orphans of the Living: A Study of Bastardy. 1968. text ed. 6.00x (ISBN 0-09-089120-1, Hutchinson U Lib). Humanities.
Dewar, Donald L. The Quality Circle Handbook. (Quality Circle Leader Manual & Instructional Guide, Quality Circle Member Manual). 640p. 1980. pap. 60.00 (ISBN 0-937670-03-0). Quality Circle.
--Quality Circle Leader Manual & Instructional Guide. (Quality Circle Member Manual: Quality Circle Handbook). 248p. 1980. pap. 15.00 (ISBN 0-937670-02-2). Quality Circle.
--Quality Circle Member Manual. (Quality Circle Handbook & Quality Circle Leader Manual & Instructional Guide Ser.). (Orig.). 1980. pap. 8.00 (ISBN 0-937670-01-4). Quality Circle.
--Quality Circles: Questions & Answers to 100 Frequently Asked Questions. rev. ed. (Illus.). 1980. pap. 3.25 (ISBN 0-937670-00-6). Quality Circle.
Dewar, M. J. & Jones, R. Computer Compilation of Molecular Weights & Percentage Compositions for Organic Compounds. 1969. 79.00 (ISBN 0-08-012707-X). Pergamon.
De Warsenburg, Hans van see Van de Warsenburg, Hans.
De Water, John W. Van see Van De Water, J. W.
Dewdney, John C. A Geography of the Soviet Union. 3rd ed. LC 78-40992. (Pergamon Oxford Geography Ser.). (Illus.). 1979. text ed. 29.00 (ISBN 0-08-023739-8); pap. text ed. 13.25 (ISBN 0-08-023738-X). Pergamon.
--The USSR. LC 76-16744. (Westview Special Studies in Industrial Geography). (Illus.). 1976. lib. bdg. 26.50x (ISBN 0-89158-616-4). Westview.
De Weck, A. L., ed. Differentiated Lymphocyte Functions & Their Ontogeny. (Progress in Allergy Ser.: Vol. 28). (Illus.). 250p. 1981. 90.00 (ISBN 3-8055-1834-X). S Karger.
De Weck, Alain L., et al, eds. Biochemical Characterization of Lymphokines: Proceedings of the Second International Lymphokine Workshop. LC 80-289. 1980. 39.50 (ISBN 0-12-213950-X). Acad Pr.
DeWeerd, H. A., ed. see Marshall, George C.
Dewees, Donald N. Economics & Public Policy: The Automobile Pollution Case. 208p. 1974. 21.00x (ISBN 0-262-04043-3). MIT Pr.
Deweese, David D. & Saunders, William H. Textbook of Otolaryngology. LC 76-30466. (Illus.). 1977. 29.50 (ISBN 0-8016-1272-1). Mosby.

DeWeese, Jean. The Backhoe Gothic. LC 80-1670. (Romantic Suspense Ser.). 192p. 1981. 9.95 (ISBN 0-385-12099-0). Doubleday.
--Cave of the Moaning Winds. 1976. pap. 1.25 o.p. (ISBN 0-345-25160-1). Ballantine.
De Weese, Jean. Doll with the Opal Eyes. 1977. pap. 1.95 o.p. (ISBN 0-445-04197-8). Popular Lib.
--Nightmare in Pewter. LC 78-3257. 1978. 7.95 o.p. (ISBN 0-385-12097-4). Doubleday.
DeWelt, Don. The Acts of the Apostles. LC 79-53712. (The Pictorial New Testament Ser.). (Illus.). 1979. 7.95 (ISBN 0-89900-200-5). College Pr Pub.
--The Church in the Bible. (The Bible Study Textbook Ser.). (Illus.). 1958. 13.00 (ISBN 0-89900-049-5). College Pr Pub.
--Power of the Holy Spirit, Vol. II. (Orig.). 1971. pap. 3.95 (ISBN 0-89900-124-6). College Pr Pub.
--Romans Realized. LC 72-1068. (The Bible Study Textbook Ser.). (Illus.). 1959. 11.50 (ISBN 0-89900-037-1). College Pr Pub.
--What the Bible Says About Fasting & Prayer. LC 79-57087. (What the Bible Says Ser.). 1981. 13.50 (ISBN 0-89900-077-0). College Pr Pub. Postponed.
DeWelt, Don, jt. auth. see Kidwell, R. J.
DeWelt, Don, ed. see Rotherham, Joseph B.
De Wesselow, M. R. Donkeys: Their Care & Management. 5.00 (ISBN 0-8283-1369-5). Branden.
Dewett, Don, jt. auth. see Van Buren, James.
Dewey, Ariane. The Thunder God's Son. LC 80-16325. (Illus.). 32p. (gr. k-4). 1981. 7.95 (ISBN 0-688-80295-8); PLB 7.63 (ISBN 0-688-84295-X). Greenwillow.
Dewey, Ariane, jt. auth. see Aruego, Jose.
Dewey, Arthur J., jt. tr. see Cameron, Ron.
Dewey, Clive & Hopkins, A. G. The Imperial Impact: Studies in the Economic History of Africa & India. (Commonwealth Papers Ser.: No.21). 1978. text ed. 41.75x (ISBN 0-485-17621-1, Athlone Pr). Humanities.
Dewey, Donald. Modern Capital Theory. LC 65-22157. (Illus.). 1965. 16.00x (ISBN 0-231-02831-8). Columbia U Pr.
--Theory of Imperfect Competition: A Radical Reconstruction. LC 73-79190. (Illus.). 1969. 16.00x (ISBN 0-231-03164-5). Columbia U Pr.
Dewey, Edward R. & Mandino, Og. Cycles: The Mysterious Forces That Trigger Events. 1976. pap. 4.95 o.p. (ISBN 0-8015-1880-6). Dutton.
Dewey, Godfrey. English Spelling: Roadblock to Reading. LC 77-141240. 1971. text ed. 15.75x (ISBN 0-8077-1242-6). Tchrs Coll.
Dewey, Jane, jt. auth. see Henderson, Nancy.
Dewey, Joanna. Markan Public Debate: Literary Technique, Concentric Structure & Theology in Mark 2: 1-3: 6. LC 79-17443. (Society of Biblical Literature Ser.: No. 48). 12.00x (ISBN 0-89130-337-5); pap. 7.50x (ISBN 0-89130-338-3). Scholars Pr CA.
Dewey, John. The Early Works of John Dewey, 1882-1898, 5 vols. MLA-CEAA textual ed. Boydston, Jo Ann, ed. Incl. Vol. 1 (1882-1888): Collected Essays & Leibniz's New Essays Concerning the Human Understanding. Hahn, Lewis E., intro. by. 493p. 1969 (ISBN 0-8093-0349-3). pap. (ISBN 0-8093-0722-7); Vol. 2 (1887): Psychology. Schneider, Herbert W., intro. by. 420p. 1967 (ISBN 0-8093-0282-9). pap. (ISBN 0-8093-0723-5); Vol. 3 (1889-1892): Collected Essays & Outline of a Critical Theory of Ethics. Eames, S. Morris, intro. by. 495p. 1969 (ISBN 0-8093-0402-3). pap. (ISBN 0-8093-0724-3); Vol. 4 (1893-1894): Collected Essays & the Study of Ethics. Leys, Wayne A., intro. by. 463p. 1971 (ISBN 0-8093-0496-1). pap. (ISBN 0-8093-0725-1); Vol. 5 (1895-1898): Collected Essays. McKenzie, William R., intro. by. 670p. 1972. (ISBN 0-8093-0540-2); pap. (ISBN 0-8093-0726-X). LC 67-13938. Vols. 1,3,4. 17.50x (ISBN 0-686-57468-0); Vol. 5. 18.95x (ISBN 0-686-57469-9); Vol. 2. 19.95x; pap. 7.95; pap. 6.95; Vol. 5. **pap. 8.95. S Ill U Pr.**
--Interest & Effort in Education. LC 74-18471. (Arcturus Books Paperbacks). 120p. 1975. pap. 6.95 (ISBN 0-8093-0716-2). S Ill U Pr.
--The Later Works of John Dewey, Nineteen Twenty-Five to Nineteen Fifty-Three: Volume 1, Nineteen Twenty-Five. Boydston, Jo Ann, et al, eds. 1981. price not set (ISBN 0-8093-0986-6). S Ill U Pr.
--Logic: Theory of Inquiry. 1981. Repr. of 1938 ed. 24.50x (ISBN 0-89197-831-3). Irvington.
--The Middle Works of John Dewey, 1899-1924, Vols. 1-8, Vols. 1-8. MLA-CEAA textual ed. Boydston, Jo Ann, ed. Incl. Vol. 1 (1899-1901): Collected Articles & "The School & Society" & "The Educational Situation". Burnett, Joe R., intro. by. 1976. 19.95x (ISBN 0-8093-0753-7); Vol. 2 (1902-1903): Collected Articles & "Studies in Logical Theory" & "The Child & the Curiculum". Hook, Sidney, intro. by. 1976. 19.95x (ISBN 0-8093-0754-5); Vol. 3 (1903-1906): Collected Articles. Baysinger, Patricia R., ed. 1977. 19.95x (ISBN 0-8093-0775-8); Vol. 4 (1907-1909): Collected Articles & "The Pragmatic Movement of Contemporary Thought" & "Moral Principles in Education". Levine, Barbara, ed. 1977. 19.95x (ISBN 0-8093-0775-8); Vol. 5 (1908): "Ethics". Stevenson, Charles L. 1978. 18.95x (ISBN 0-8093-0834-7); Vol. 6 (1910-1911): Collected Essays & "The Problem of Truth". Thayer, H. S. 1978. 24.95x (ISBN 0-8093-0835-5); Vol. 9 (1916) Boydston, Jo Ann, ed. 480p. 1980. 19.95x (ISBN 0-8093-0933-5); Vol. 10 (1916-7) Boydston, Jo Ann, ed. 564p. 22.50x (ISBN 0-686-66317-9); Vol. 7. Boydston, Jo Ann, ed. 1979. 24.95x (ISBN 0-8093-0881-9); Vol. 8. Boydston, Jo Ann, ed. 1979. 24.95x (ISBN 0-8093-0882-7). LC 76-7231. S Ill U Pr.
--Moral Principles in Education. LC 74-18472. (Arcturus Books Paperbacks). 80p. 1975. pap. 2.95 (ISBN 0-8093-0715-4). S Ill U Pr.
--Philosophy of Education. (Quality Paperback: No. 126). 1971. pap. 3.50 (ISBN 0-8226-0126-5). Littlefield.
--Public & Its Problems. LC 76-178242. 236p. 1954. pap. 4.95x (ISBN 0-8040-0254-1, 11). Swallow.
--Theory of the Moral Life. LC 60-9060. 1980. pap. text ed. 6.95x (ISBN 0-8290-0263-4). Irvington.
Dewey, John & Bentley, Arthur F. Knowing & the Known. LC 75-31432. 334p. 1976. Repr. of 1949 ed. lib. bdg. 25.00x (ISBN 0-8371-8498-3, DEKK). Greenwood.
Dewey, John & Kallen, Horace M. The Bertrand Russell Case. LC 78-37289. (Civil Liberties in American History Ser). 228p. 1972. Repr. of 1941 ed. lib. bdg. 25.00 (ISBN 0-306-70426-9). Da Capo.
Dewey, Melvil. Clasificacion Decimal de Dewey Para Pequenas Bibliotecas Publicas y Escolares. (Span). 1967. pap. 2.00x, public & school lib. ed (ISBN 0-910608-08-3). Forest Pr.
--Classification Decimale de Dewey et Index, 2 vols. Incl. Vol. 1. Tables Generales (ISBN 0-910608-14-8); Vol. 2. Index (ISBN 0-910608-15-6). (Fr.). 1974. Set. 60.00x (ISBN 0-685-47821-1); 30.00x ea. Forest Pr.
--Dewey Decimal Classification & Relative Index. 11th abridged ed. LC 78-12514. 1979. 24.00x (ISBN 0-910608-22-9). Forest Pr.
--Dewey Decimal Classification & Subject Index for Arranging the Books & Pamphlets of a Library (1876) facsimile ed. 1975. 5.00x (ISBN 0-910608-16-4). Forest Pr.
--Dewey Decimal Classification: Proposed Revision of 780 Music. Sweeney, Russell, et al, eds. LC 80-16730. 1980. pap. text ed. 5.00x (ISBN 0-910608-25-3). Forest Pr.
--Sistema de Clasificacion Decimal, con adaptaciones para los paises de habla espanola, basado en la 18a edicion con adiciones de la 19a edicion, 3 vols. Aguayo, Jorge, tr. LC 80-24527. (Span.). 1980. Set. 75.00x (ISBN 0-910608-26-1); Vol. 1, Introduccion, Tablas Auxiliares. 25.00x (ISBN 0-910608-27-X); Vol. 2, Esquemas. 25.00x (ISBN 0-910608-28-8); Vol. 3, Indice. 25.00x (ISBN 0-910608-29-6). Forest Pr.
De Weydenthal, Jan B. The Communists of Poland: An Historical Outline. Staar, Richard F., ed. LC 78-59465. (Publications Ser.: No. 202). (Illus.). 236p. 1979. pap. 7.95 (ISBN 0-8179-7022-3). Hoover Inst Pr.
--Poland: Communism Adrift. LC 79-67732. (The Washington Papers: Vol. 72). 88p. 1979. pap. 3.50 (ISBN 0-8039-1430-X). Sage.
Dewhirst, Martin & Farrell, Robert, eds. The Soviet Censorship. LC 73-9844. 1973. 10.00 (ISBN 0-8108-0674-6). Scarecrow.
Dew-Hughes, D., jt. auth. see Wyatt, Oliver H.
Dewhurst. Practical Pediatric & Adolescent Gynaclogy. 344p. 1980. 35.00 (ISBN 0-8247-6978-3). Dekker.
Dewhurst, D. J. An Introduction to Biomedical Instrumentation. 2nd ed. 288p. 1975. text ed. 50.00 (ISBN 0-08-018755-2); pap. text ed. 31.00 (ISBN 0-08-018884-2). Pergamon.
Dewhurst, Eileen. Drink This. LC 80-2320. 192p. 1981. 9.95 (ISBN 0-385-17457-8). Doubleday.
Dewhurst, Jack. Royal Confinements. 198p. 1981. 12.95 (ISBN 0-312-69466-0). St Martin.
Dewhurst, Kenneth. Dr. Thomas Sydenham (1624-1689) His Life & Original Writings. (Wellcome Institute of the History of Medicine). 1966. 18.50x (ISBN 0-520-00320-9). U of Cal Pr.
Dewhurst, Kenneth & Reeves, Nigel. Friedrich Schiller--Medicine, Psychology, & Literature: With the First English Edition of His Complete Medical & Psychological Writings. 1978. 29.50x (ISBN 0-520-03250-0). U of Cal Pr.
De Wiest, Roger J. Night Flight to Brussels. LC 80-84739. 1981. 15.00 (ISBN 0-686-68869-4). Philos Lib.
De Wildemann, E. see Wildemann, E. De.
DeWindt, Gaye. Poems of Reality. 1981. 6.00 (ISBN 0-8062-1615-8). Carlton.
Dewine, Sue, jt. auth. see Phelps, Lynn.
De Winter, F., ed. Sun: Mankind's Future Source of Energy, 3 vols. 1979. text ed. 320.00 (ISBN 0-08-022725-2). Pergamon.
De Winter, Francis. How to Design & Build a Solar Swimming Pool Heater: With Sample Calculations, 2 vols. (Illus.). 1978. pap. 8.65 set (ISBN 0-930978-07-2). Solar Energy Info.
De Winter, Francis, ed. see Bereny, Justin A.
De Winter, Michelle. Janine. 1979. pap. 1.95 o.p. (ISBN 0-449-14215-9, GM). Fawcett.
De Winton, Dorothy. Sunrise Cookbook. 1976. 3.00 (ISBN 0-686-27657-4). Cole-Outreach.
Dewire, Robert, jt. auth. see Russo, Monica.
DeWit, C. T. & Houdriaan, J. Simulation of Ecological Processes. 2nd ed. 1978. pap. 20.95 (ISBN 0-470-26357-1). Halsted Pr.
DeWit, C. T., et al. Simulation of Assimilation, Respiration & Transpiration of Crops. 1978. pap. 18.95 (ISBN 0-470-26494-2). Halsted Pr.
De Wit, Dorothy. The Talking Stone. LC 79-13798. (gr. 5 up). 1979. 8.95 (ISBN 0-688-80204-4); PLB 8.59 (ISBN 0-688-84204-6). Greenwillow.
De Wit, H. C. Plants of the World, 3 vols. Pomerans, A. J., tr. LC 66-25815. 1966-69. Vol. 1. o.p.; Vol. 2. 19.95 o.p. (ISBN 0-525-18040-0); Vol. 3. o.p. Dutton.
De Wit, Joost & Barkan, Stanley H., eds. Fifty Dutch & Flemish Novelists. 220p. 25.00 (ISBN 0-89304-031-2); pap. 15.00 (ISBN 0-89304-032-0). Cross Cult.
De Witt, Charles G. see Diffenderffer, Henry.
Dewitt, David. Answering the Tough Ones. 160p. 1980. pap. 3.95 (ISBN 0-8024-8971-0). Moody.
DeWitt, David P., ed. see Incropera, Frank P.
Dewitt, Howard A. Chuck Berry: Rock'n'roll Music. (Illus.). 120p. (Orig.). 1981. 12.95 (ISBN 0-938840-01-0); pap. 5.95 (ISBN 0-938840-00-2). Horizon Bks CA.
--Readings in California Civilization: Interpretative Issues. LC 80-83492. 240p. 1981. pap. text ed. 12.95 (ISBN 0-8403-2311-5). Kendall-Hunt.
De Witt, Johanna. The Littlest Reindeer. (Pacesetters). (Illus.). 32p. (gr. k-3). 1979. PLB 7.95 (ISBN 0-516-03534-7). Childrens.
Dewitt, Norman J., et al. College Latin. 1954. 16.95x (ISBN 0-673-05105-6). Scott F.
DeWitt, R. Peter, Jr. The Inter-American Development Bank & Political Influence: With Special Reference to Costa Rica. LC 77-2929. (Special Studies). 1977. text ed. 24.95 (ISBN 0-275-24460-1). Praeger.
Dewitt, Sherri. Worker Participation & the Crisis of Liberal Democracy. (Westview Replica Edition Ser.). 150p. 1980. lib. bdg. 18.00x (ISBN 0-89158-922-8). Westview.
DeWolf, L. Harold. What Americans Should to Do About Crime. LC 75-36728. (Illus.). 160p. (Orig.). 1976. pap. 4.95 (ISBN 0-06-061912-0, RD138, HarpR). Har-Row.
DeWolf, Rose, jt. auth. see Moldovsky, Joel.
De Wolfe, Ivor. Italian Townscape. LC 66-10392. (Illus.). 1966. 12.50 o.p. (ISBN 0-8076-0350-3). Braziller.
Dews, Peter B., jt. ed. see Thompson, Travis.
Dexter, Beverly L. Special Education & the Classroom Teacher: Concepts, Perspectives & Strategies. (Illus.). 272p. 1977. 22.50 (ISBN 0-398-03607-1). C C Thomas.
Dexter, Collin. Service of All the Dead. 1980. 9.95 (ISBN 0-312-71316-9). St Martin.
Dexter, Dave, Jr. Jazz Cavalcade. LC 77-8035. (Roots of Jazz). (Illus.). 1977. Repr. of 1946 ed. lib. bdg. 22.50 (ISBN 0-306-77431-3). Da Capo.
Dexter, Franklin B. Biographical Sketches of the Graduates of Yale College, with Annals of the College History, Seventeen Hundred One to Eighteen Fifteen, 6 vols. (Two vols. are unbound). 1912. Set. 350.00x (ISBN 0-686-51346-0). Elliots Bks.
Dexter, Lewis A. & White, David M., eds. People, Society & Mass Communications. LC 64-11222. 1964. text ed. 15.95 (ISBN 0-02-907400-2). Free Pr.
Dexter, Lewis Anthony. How Organizations Are Represented in Washington. LC 69-15729. 1969. pap. 5.95 (ISBN 0-672-60748-4). Bobbs.
Dexter, N. C. & Rayner, E. G. Liberal Studies: An Outline Course, 2 Vols. 1963. Vol. 1. pap. 7.00 (ISBN 0-08-010451-7); Vol. 2. pap. 6.25 (ISBN 0-08-010453-3). Pergamon.
Dexter, Pat E. The Boy Who Snuck in. (Apple Bks.). (Illus.). (gr. 5 up). 1981. pap. 3.50 (ISBN 0-570-07902-0, 56-1602). Concordia.
--The Emancipation of Joe Tepper. LC 76-26594. (gr. 4-12). 1976. 6.50 o.p. (ISBN 0-525-66519-6). Elsevier-Nelson.
Dexter, Stephen C. Handbook of Oceanographic Engineering Materials. LC 78-26196. (Ocean Engineering Ser.). 1979. 28.95 (ISBN 0-471-04950-6, Pub. by Wiley-Interscience). Wiley.
Dexter, W. A. Field Guide to Astronomy Without a Telescope. (Earth Science Curriculum Project Pamphlet Ser.). (gr. 11-12). 1971. pap. text ed. 3.20 (ISBN 0-395-02623-7). HM.
Dey, Bishnu. Selected Poems. Dasgupta, Samir, ed. (Writers Workshop Saffronbird Ser). 1975. 12.00 (ISBN 0-88253-626-5); pap. text ed. 4.80 (ISBN 0-88253-625-7). Ind-US Inc.
Dey, Mukul K. Methods of Experimental Psychology. LC 79-66485. 1979. pap. text ed. 8.25 (ISBN 0-8191-0818-9). U Pr of Amer.
Deyneka, Anita. Alexi's Secret Mission. LC 74-29466. (Illus.). 128p. (Orig.). (gr. 3-7). 1975. pap. 1.95 (ISBN 0-912692-58-8). Cook.
Deyneka, Anita & Deyneka, Peter, Jr. Christians in the Shadow of the Kremlin. LC 74-17730. (Illus.). 112p. 1975. pap. 1.95 (ISBN 0-912692-48-0). Cook.
Deyneka, Peter, Jr., jt. auth. see Deyneka, Anita.
Deyo, Fredric C. Dependent Development & Industrial Order. (Fraeger Special Studies). 1980. 19.95 (ISBN 0-03-047386-1). Praeger.
DeYoung, Gordon. Dial-a-Word from the Bible. (Quiz & Puzzle Bks). 1977. pap. 0.95 (ISBN 0-8010-2862-0). Baker Bk.
Deyrup, Astrith. Tie Dyeing & Batik. LC 73-9020. 64p. (gr. 4-7). 1974. 6.95 o.p. (ISBN 0-385-03626-4). Doubleday.
Dezamy, Alexandre-Theodore. Code de la Communaute. (Fr.). 1977. lib. bdg. 31.25x o.p. (ISBN 0-8287-0274-8); pap. text ed. 21.25x o.p. (ISBN 0-685-75740-4). Clearwater Pub.
De Zavala, Ann M., tr. see Cuadra, Pablo A.
DeZayas, Alfred M. Nemesis at Potsdam. rev. ed. (Illus.). 1979. pap. 9.50 (ISBN 0-7100-0170-3). Routledge & Kegan.
De Zayas, Zoila. Desarrollando Destrezas En Preparacion Para el Examen Equivalencia De Escuela Superior En Espanol: Mathematicas: Developing Skills in Math for High School Equivalency Test in Spanish. (gr. 10-12). Date not set. pap. text ed. 3.75 (ISBN 0-8120-0560-0). Barron.
DeZayas, Zoila E. Developing Skills in Mathematics for the High School Equivalency Exam (GED) in Spanish. Date not set. pap. 3.75 (ISBN 0-8120-0560-0). Barron.
DeZeng, R. P. The Fur Rendezvous or Rendezvous on the Green. 1981. 5.95 (ISBN 0-533-04700-5). Vantage.
Dezettel, Louis M. Masons & Builders Library, 2 vols. 2nd ed. LC 78-186134. (Illus.). 1972. 9.95 ea. Vol. 1 (ISBN 0-672-23182-4, 23182). Vol. 2 (ISBN 0-672-23183-2, 23183). Set. 17.95 (ISBN 0-672-23185-9, 23185). Audel.
De Zirkoff, Boris, ed. see Blavatsky, Helena P.
De Zoete, Beryl. Dance & Magic Drama in Ceylon. (Illus.). 1957. 4.95 (ISBN 0-87830-032-5). Theatre Arts.
De Zorita, Alonso. Life & Labor in Ancient Mexico: The Brief & Summary Relation of the Lords of New Spain. Keen, Benjamin, tr. 1964. 20.00 (ISBN 0-8135-0442-2). Rutgers U Pr.
Dezso, L. & Hajdu, P., eds. Theoretical Problems of Typology & the Northern Eurasian Languages. 184p. 1970. text ed. 34.25x (ISBN 0-685-75720-X). Humanities.
Dhake, Arvind M. Television Engineering. (Illus.). 1980. 14.50 (ISBN 0-07-096389-4, P&RB). McGraw.
Dhaky, M. A. The Indian Temple Forms. 1977. 28.00x (ISBN 0-8364-0060-7). South Asia Bks.
Dhamija, Jasleen. Living Tradition of Iran's Crafts. 1979. 40.00x (ISBN 0-7069-0728-0, Pub. by Croom Helm Ltd England). Biblio Dist.
Dhande, S. G., jt. auth. see Chakraborty, J.
Dhar, D. N. The Chemistry of Chalcones & Related Compounds. 300p. 1981. 29.50 (ISBN 0-471-08007-1, Pub. by Wiley-Interscience). Wiley.
Dhar, Prithvi N. & Sastry, D. U. Demand for Energy in North-West India. 1967. 5.50 o.p. (ISBN 0-210-22506-8). Asia.
Dhar, Sheila. Children's History of India. 7th rev. ed. (Illus.). 178p. (gr. 5-7). pap. text ed. 1.50x (ISBN 0-88253-919-1). Ind-US Inc.
Dhar, T. N., et al. Education & Employment in India: The Policy Nexus. LC 76-52202. 1976. 12.50x o.p. (ISBN 0-88386-802-4). South Asia Bks.
Dharan, Murali. Total Quality Control in the Clinical Laboratory. LC 76-30688. (Illus.). 1977. pap. 16.95 (ISBN 0-8016-1290-X). Mosby.
Dharmaraj, Leela. Slum Silouette. 8.00 (ISBN 0-89253-551-2); flexible cloth 4.00 (ISBN 0-89253-552-0). Ind-US Inc.
D'Harnoncourt, Anne & Celant, Germano. Futurism & the International Avant-Garde. LC 80-83095. (Illus.). 144p. (Orig.). 1980. pap. 10.95 (ISBN 0-87633-037-5). Phila Mus Art.

Dhasmana, M. M. The Ramos of Arunachal. 1980. text ed. 16.50x (ISBN 0-391-01827-2). Humanities.
Dhavamony, M., ed. Buddhism & Christianity. (Concilium Ser.: Vol. 116). pap. 4.95 (ISBN 0-8164-2612-0). Crossroad NY.
Dhavamony, Mariasusai. Love of God According to Saiva Siddhanta: A Study in the Mysticism & Theology of Saivism. 1971. 23.00x o.p. (ISBN 0-19-826523-9). Oxford U Pr.
Dhillon, B. S., jt. auth. see Singh, Chanan.
Dhir, R. K. & Munday, J. G. Advances in Concrete Slab Technology: Materials Design, Construction & Finishing. 1980. 115.00 (ISBN 0-08-023256-6). Pergamon.
Dhondt, Jan. Etudes Sur la Naissance Des Principautes Territoriales En France, IXe-IXe Siecle. LC 80-2033. 1981. Repr. of 1948 ed. 38.50 (ISBN 0-404-18560-6). AMS Pr.
Dhonte, Pierre. Clockwork Debt: Trade & the External Debt of Developing Countries. LC 79-1753. 144p. 1979. 16.95 (ISBN 0-669-02925-4). Lexington Bks.
Diagram Group. The Body Manual: A Complete Family Guide. LC 79-21673. (Illus.). 1980. 16.95 (ISBN 0-448-22214-0). Paddington.
--Comparisons. (Illus.). 240p. 1980. 15.00 (ISBN 0-312-15484-4). St Martin.
--The Complete Encyclopedia of Exercises. 336p. 1981. pap. 9.95 (ISBN 0-442-23148-2). Van Nos Reinhold.
--The Diagram Group. Date not set. 19.95 (ISBN 0-686-69378-7). Facts on File.
--Musical Instruments of the World: An Illustrated Encyclopedia. (Illus.). 320p. 1978. 29.95 (ISBN 0-87196-320-5). Facts on File.
--Sex: A User's Manual. (Illus.). 196p. 1981. 14.95 (ISBN 0-399-12574-4, Perigee); pap. 6.95 (ISBN 0-399-50517-2). Putnam.
--Weapons. (Illus.). 320p. 1980. 25.00 (ISBN 0-312-85946-5). St Martin.
Diakonoff, Iger M. Pre-History of the Armenian People. 1980. write for info. o.p. (ISBN 0-88206-039-2). Caravan Bks.
Dial, Joan. Susanna. 1978. pap. 1.75 o.p. (ISBN 0-449-13961-1, GM). Fawcett.
Dial, O. E. & Goldberg, Edward M. Privacy, Security, & Computers: Guidelines for Municipal & Other Public Information Systems. LC 74-13617. (Special Sutdies). (Illus.). 186p. 1975. text ed. 23.95 (ISBN 0-275-09890-7). Praeger.
Diamant, Leo, jt. auth. see Debo, Harvey V.
Diamant, R. M. The Chemistry of Building Materials. (Illus.). 258p. 1970. 19.50x o.p. (ISBN 0-8464-0240-8). Beekman Pubs.
--Total Energy. 1970. 37.00 (ISBN 0-08-006918-5). Pergamon.
Diament, Bert, jt. auth. see Losen, Stuart.
Diamond, Bernard & Oderman, Stuart. Per-Se Award Plays, 1970: Special Issue 14. pap. 1.00 o.p. (ISBN 0-685-78408-8). The Smith.
Diamond, Cora & Teichman, Jenny, eds. Intention & Intentionality: Essays in Honour of G. E. M. Anscombe. LC 79-2478. (Illus.). 1980. 32.50x (ISBN 0-8014-1275-7). Cornell U Pr.
Diamond, D. R. & McLoughlin, J. B., eds. Progress in Planning, Vol. 7. (Illus.). 1979. 50.00 (ISBN 0-08-020333-7). Pergamon.
--Progress in Planning, Vol. 9. 300p. 1979. 50.00 (ISBN 0-08-025221-4). Pergamon.
--Progress in Planning, Vol. 10. (Illus.). 247p. 42.00 (ISBN 0-08-025788-7). Pergamon.
--Progress in Planning, Vol. 11. (Illus.). 280p. 1980. 50.00 (ISBN 0-08-025802-6). Pergamon.
--Progress in Planning, Vol. 12. 224p. 1980. 47.00 (ISBN 0-08-026100-0). Pergamon.
Diamond, Donna, adapted by. & illus. The Bremen Town Musicians: A Grimms' Fairytale. LC 80-36838. (Illus.). 32p. (gr. k-2). 1981. 8.95 (ISBN 0-440-00826-3); PLB 8.44 (ISBN 0-440-00827-1). Delacorte.
Diamond, Dorothy. Aerial Models. LC 77-82978. (Teaching Primary Science Ser.). 1978. pap. text ed. 6.95 (ISBN 0-356-05074-2). Raintree Child.
--Mirrors & Magnifiers. LC 77-82982. (Teaching Primary Science Ser.). (Illus.). 1977. pap. text ed. 6.95 (ISBN 0-356-05078-5). Raintree Child.
--Science from Wood. LC 77-82981. (Teaching Primary Science Ser.). (Illus.). 1977. pap. text ed. 6.95 (ISBN 0-356-05073-4). Raintree Child.
--Seeds & Seedlings. LC 77-82986. (Teaching Primary Science Ser.). (Illus.). 1977. pap. text ed. 6.95 (ISBN 0-356-05072-6). Raintree Child.
--Teacher's Guide to Primary Science. LC 77-82977. (Teaching Primary Science Ser.). (Illus.). 1978. 15.95 (ISBN 0-356-05082-3). Raintree Child.
Diamond, Dorothy & Tiffin, Robert. Musical Instruments. LC 77-82979. (Teaching Primary Science Ser.). (Illus.). 1977. pap. text ed. 6.95 (ISBN 0-356-05077-7). Raintree Child.
Diamond, Dorothy, jt. auth. see Bird, John.
Diamond, E. Nervous System: Disease, Diagnosis, Treatment. (Clinical Monographs Ser.). (Illus.). 1976. pap. 7.95 (ISBN 0-87618-065-9). R J Brady.
Diamond, Edwin. Good News, Bad News. 288p. (Orig.). 1980. 14.00; pap. 5.95. MIT Pr.
--Good News, Bad News. 1978. 14.00 (ISBN 0-262-04057-3); pap. 5.95 (ISBN 0-262-54035-5). MIT Pr.
Diamond, Elliot, jt. auth. see Le Bendig, Michael.
Diamond, Graham. The Beasts of Hades. LC 80-84370. (Adventures of the Empire Princess Ser: No. 4). 256p. (Orig.). 1981. pap. 2.25 (ISBN 0-87216-821-2). Playboy Pbks.
--Lady of the Haven. LC 78-55733. 384p. (Orig.). 1981. pap. 1.95 (ISBN 0-87216-477-2). Playboy Pbks.
--Samarkand Dawn. LC 80-82850. 256p. (Orig.). 1981. pap. 2.25 (ISBN 0-87216-781-X). Playboy Pbks.
Diamond, Harold J. Music Criticism: An Annotated Guide to the Literature. LC 79-22279. 326p. 1979. 17.50 (ISBN 0-8108-1268-1). Scarecrow.
Diamond, J. & Pintel, G. Introduction to Contemporary Business. 1975. 15.95 (ISBN 0-13-487991-0); study guide 5.95 (ISBN 0-13-488015-3). P-H.
Diamond, Jared M., jt. ed. see Cody, Martin L.
Diamond, Jay & Pintel, Gerald. Principles of Marketing. 2nd ed. (Illus.). 1980. 15.95 (ISBN 0-13-701417-1); pap. text ed. 6.95 study guide (ISBN 0-13-701425-2). P-H.
--Successful Selling. (Illus.). 384p. 1980. text ed. 14.95 (ISBN 0-8359-7246-1). Reston.
Diamond, Lucy. Child of the Temple. (Ladybird Ser). (Illus.). 1955. bds. 1.49 (ISBN 0-87508-836-8). Chr Lit.
--Jesus by the Sea of Galilee. (Ladybird Ser). (Illus.). 1958. bds. 1.49 (ISBN 0-87508-840-6). Chr Lit.
--Jesus Calls His Disciples. (Ladybird Ser). (Illus.). 1959. bds. 1.49 (ISBN 0-87508-842-2). Chr Lit.
--Little Lord Jesus. (Ladybird Ser). (Illus.). 1954. bds. 1.49 (ISBN 0-87508-846-5). Chr Lit.
--Moses, Prince & Shepherd. (Ladybird Ser). (Illus.). 1954. bds. 1.49 (ISBN 0-87508-850-3). Chr Lit.
--Naaman & the Little Maid. (Ladybird Ser). (Illus.). 1959. bds. 1.49 (ISBN 0-87508-852-X). Chr Lit.
--Shepherd Boy of Bethlehem. (Ladybird Ser). (Illus.). 1954. bds. 1.49 (ISBN 0-87508-858-9). Chr Lit.
--Story of Daniel. (Ladybird Ser). (Illus.). 1958. bds. 1.49 (ISBN 0-87508-866-X). Chr Lit.
--Story of Joseph. (Ladybird Ser). (Illus.). 1954. bds. 1.49 (ISBN 0-87508-868-6). Chr Lit.
--Two Stories Jesus Told. (Ladybird Ser). (Illus.). 1959. bds. 1.49 (ISBN 0-87508-870-8). Chr Lit.
Diamond, Malcolm L. & Litzenburg, Thomas V., Jr. The Logic of God: Theology & Verification. LC 74-32235. 562p. 1975. 17.95 (ISBN 0-672-60792-1). Bobbs.
Diamond, Marie J. Flaubert: The Problem of Aesthetic Discontinuity. 1975. 12.50 (ISBN 0-8046-9075-8, Natl U). Kennikat.
Diamond, Martin. The Founding of the Democratic Republic. LC 80-84210. 192p. 1981. pap. text ed. 5.50 (ISBN 0-87581-271-6). Peacock Pubs.
Diamond, Norman. Acute Ambulatory Care for the House Officer. (House Officer Ser.). (Illus.). 200p. 1981. price not set softcover (ISBN 0-683-02504-X). Williams & Wilkins.
Diamond, Robert M. & Woodward, John C. The Amateur Psychologist's Dictionary. LC 66-17176. (Illus.). 1966. 4.50 o.p. (ISBN 0-668-01454-7). Arco.
Diamond, Sander A. The Nazi Movement in the United States, Nineteen Twenty-Four to Nineteen Forty-One. LC 73-16654. 380p. 1973. 22.50x (ISBN 0-8014-0788-5). Cornell U Pr.
Diamond, Seymour & Furlong, William B. More Than Two Aspirin: Help for Your Headache Problem. 372p. 1976. 8.95 o.p. (ISBN 0-695-80612-2). Follett.
Diamond, Seymour, et al, eds. Vasoactive Substances Relevant to Migraine. (Illus.). 112p. 1975. 14.50 (ISBN 0-398-03348-X). C C Thomas.
Diamond, Sheldon. Fundamental Concepts of Modern Physics. (gr. 11-12). 1970. pap. text ed. 6.58 (ISBN 0-87720-178-1). AMSCO Sch.
Diamond, Sheldon R., jt. auth. see Ahner, Walter L.
Diamond, Sidney A. Trademark Problems & How to Avoid Them. 2nd ed. 1981. 19.95 (ISBN 0-87251-059-X). Crain Bks.
Diamond, Sigmund. In Quest. LC 79-26717. (Illus.). 1980. 14.95 (ISBN 0-231-04842-4). Columbia U Pr.
--The Reputation of the American Businessman. 6.75 (ISBN 0-8446-0581-6). Peter Smith.
Diamond, Stanley. Culture in History: Essays in Honor of Paul Radin. 1980. Repr. of 1960 ed. lib. bdg. 70.00x (ISBN 0-374-92155-5). Octagon.
--In Search of the Primitive. 387p. 1981. pap. 9.95 (ISBN 0-87855-582-X). Transaction Bks.
Diamond, Stanley, ed. Primitive Views of the World. Orig. Title: Culture in History. 1964. pap. 6.00x (ISBN 0-231-08552-4). Columbia U Pr.
--Theory & Practice: Essays Presented to Gene Weltfish. (Studies in Anthropology). 1979. text ed. 49.50 (ISBN 90-279-7958-8). Mouton.
Diamond, Stuart. No-Cost Low Cost Energy Tips: Fifty-Two Ways to Save One Thousand Dollars a Year in Energy Cost Without Sacrifice. 112p. 1980. pap. 1.95 (ISBN 0-553-14239-9). Bantam.
Diamond, Susan Z. Preparing Administrative Manuals. 199p. 1981. 17.95 (ISBN 0-8144-5631-6). Am Mgmt.
Diamond, William J. Practical Experiment Designs for Engineers & Scientists. 400p. 1981. text ed. 28.00x (ISBN 0-534-97992-0). Lifetime Learn.
Diamonstein, Barbaralee. Collaboration: Artists & Architects. 176p. (Orig.). 1981. 32.50 (Whitney Lib). Watson-Guptill.
Dianin, Sergei A. Borodin. Lord, Robert, tr. from Rus. (Illus.). xi, 356p. 1980. Repr. of 1963 ed. lib. bdg. 29.75x (ISBN 0-313-22529-X, DIBO). Greenwood.
Di Antonio. Plaid for CPA Review Package. 1981. price not set (ISBN 0-256-02400-6, 01-1436-01). Learning Syst. Postponed.
Dian Wen K. Chinn. Practical Chinese Letter Writing. xii, 124p. (Orig.). 1980. pap. text ed. 9.50x (ISBN 0-89644-642-5). Chinese Materials.
Diara, Agadem L. Love Poem to an African Violet. 1981. pap. 2.50 (ISBN 0-913358-13-4). Shabazz Pr. Postponed.
Dias, Robert M. Franchised & Independent Business: How to Evaluate, Start & Run It. cancelled (ISBN 0-932812-05-8). Bradley CPA.
Dias, Robert M., jt. auth. see Gurnick, Stanley.
Dias, Robert Vas see Vas Dias, Robert.
Diaz, Janet. Miguel Delibes. (World Authors Ser.: Spain: No. 186). lib. bdg. 10.95 (ISBN 0-8057-2264-5). Twayne.
Diaz, Jose Luis Martinez see Thomas, I. D., et al.
Diaz, Olimpia, tr. see Norquist, Marilyn.
Diaz, Olimpia, Sr., tr. see Gonzalez-Balado, Jose.
Diaz, Olimpia, Sr., tr. see Tickle, John.
Diaz Del Castillo & Bernal. Discovery & Conquest of Mexico. 478p. 1956. pap. 8.95 (ISBN 0-374-50384-2). FS&G.
Dib, Albert. Forms & Agreements for Architects, Engineers & Contractors. 1976. with 1979 suppl. 110.00 (ISBN 0-87632-215-1). Boardman.
Dibacco, Thomas V., ed. Presidential Power in Latin American Politics. LC 77-4727. (Special Studies). 1977. text ed. 21.95 (ISBN 0-03-021816-0). Praeger.
Di Bartolo, Baldassare see Bartolo, Baldassare De.
DiBattista, William J., jt. ed. see Kaldor, George.
Dibble, Charles E., tr. see De Sahagun, Bernardino.
Dibble, Ernest F. Young Prophet Niebuhr: Reinhold Niebuhr's Early Search for Social Justice. 1978. pap. text ed. 11.50x (ISBN 0-8191-0377-2). U Pr of Amer.
Dibden, Kenneth, jt. auth. see Tomlinson, James.
Dibdin, Charles. The Professional Life of Mr. Dibdin, Written by Himself, 4 vols. in 2. LC 80-2272. 1981. Repr. of 1803 ed. Set. 150.00 (ISBN 0-404-18835-4). Vol. 1 (ISBN 0-404-18836-2). Vol. 2 (ISBN 0-404-18837-0). AMS Pr.
Dibelius, Martin. James. Koester, Helmut, ed. Willims, Michael A., tr. LC 74-80428. (Hermeneia: a Critical & Historical Commentary on the Bible). 252p. 1975. 16.95 (ISBN 0-8006-6006-4, 20-6006). Fortress.
Dibelius, Martin & Conzelmann, Hans. The Pastoral Epistles. Koester, Helmut, ed. Buttolph, Philip & Yarbro, Adela, trs. from Ger. LC 71-157549. (Hermeneia: a Critical & Historical Commentary on the Bible). 1972. 15.00 (ISBN 0-8006-6002-1, 20-6002). Fortress.
Dibell, Ansen. Circle, Crescent, Star. (Science Fiction Ser.). 1981. pap. 2.25 (ISBN 0-87997-603-9, UE1603). Daw Bks.
Di Bella, Geoffrey A., et al. Day Treatment & Other Partial Hospitals: A Comprehensive Guide. 450p. 1981. 30.00 (ISBN 0-87630-270-3). Brunner-Mazel.
DiBiaggio, John A., jt. auth. see Cooper, Thomas M.
Dible, Don M., ed. Build a Better You-Starting Now, Vol. 7. LC 79-63064. 1980. 12.95 (ISBN 0-88205-206-3). Showcase Fairfield.
--Build a Better You-Starting Now, Vol. 8. LC 79-63064. 1980. 12.95 (ISBN 0-88205-207-1). Showcase Fairfield.
Dibner, A. S., jt. auth. see Dibner, S. S.
Dibner, Martin. Ransom Run. 1978. pap. 1.95 o.p. (ISBN 0-345-27172-6). Ballantine.
Dibner, Martin, ed. see Detmer, Josephine & Pancoast, Patricia.
Dibner, S. S. & Dibner, A. S. Integration or Segregation for the Physically Handicapped Child? 228p. 1973. 14.75 (ISBN 0-398-02817-6). C C Thomas.
DiCaprio, Nicholas S. Adjustment: Fulfilling Human Potentials. (Illus.). 1980. text ed. 14.95 (ISBN 0-13-004101-7). P-H.
DiCara, L. V., et al, eds. Biofeedback & Self-Control, 1974: An Aldine Annual on the Regulation of Bodily Processes & Consciousness. LC 74-151109. 530p. 1975. 34.95x (ISBN 0-202-25109-8). Aldine Pub.
DiCerto, Joseph. Star Voyage. Orig. Title: One Hundred Two Questions & Answers About Outer Space. (Illus.). 96p. (gr. 4-7). 1981. PLB price not set (ISBN 0-671-33034-9). Messner.
DiCerto, Joseph J. The Electric Wishing Well. 1976. 14.95 (ISBN 0-02-531320-7). Macmillan.
--From Earth to Infinity: A Guide to Space Travel. LC 80-12812. (Illus.). 320p. (gr. 7 up). 1980. PLB 9.29 (ISBN 0-671-33017-9). Messner.
Di Cesare, Mario. The Altar & the City. 240p. 1974. 17.50x (ISBN 0-231-03830-5); pap. 7.50x (ISBN 0-231-03831-3). Columbia U Pr.
Di Cesare, Marion, ed. The Game of Chess: Marco Girolamo Vido's Scacchia Ludus. (Bibliotheca, Humanistica & Reformatorica: No. 13). 1975. text ed. 27.50x (ISBN 90-6004-335-9). Humanities.
Dicey, Albert V. The Privy Council. LC 79-1625. 1981. Repr. of 1887 ed. 16.00 (ISBN 0-88355-930-7). Hyperion Conn.
Di Chiro, Giovanni. Atlas of Detailed Normal Pneumoencephalographic Anatomy. 2nd ed. (Illus.). 360p. 1971. 35.50 (ISBN 0-398-00447-1). C C Thomas.
Di Chiro, Giovanni, et al. Atlas of Pathologic Pneumoencephalographic Anatomy. (Illus.). 594p. 1967. 74.50 (ISBN 0-398-00448-X). C C Thomas.
Dichter, Ernest. Getting Motivated: The Secret Behind Individual Motivations by the Man Who Was Not Afraid to Ask "Why?". LC 78-21168. (Illus.). 1979. 14.50 (ISBN 0-08-023687-1). Pergamon.
--Packaging: The Sixth Sense. LC 73-76439. 192p. 1975. 21.50 (ISBN 0-8436-1103-0). CBI Pub.
DiCicco, Philip P., jt. auth. see Krutza, William J.
Dicicco, Philip P., jt. auth. see Krutza, William J.
DiCicco, Philip P., jt. auth. see Krutza, William J.
Dick, A. Emmy Noether: 1882-1935. (Supplement Ser.: No. 13). 72p. (Ger.). 1970. pap. 12.00 (ISBN 3-7643-0519-3). Birkhauser.
Dick, A. J., jt. auth. see Fowler, R. S.
Dick, Alexandra, tr. see Lagerkvist, Par.
Dick, Bernard F. The Anatomy of Film. LC 76-28140. 1978. pap. text ed. 7.95 (ISBN 0-312-03395-8). St Martin.
--Billy Wilder. (Theater Arts Ser.). 1980. lib. bdg. 10.95 (ISBN 0-8057-9274-0). Twayne.
--William Golding. (English Authors Ser.: No. 57). 1968. lib. bdg. 10.95 (ISBN 0-8057-1224-0). Twayne.
Dick, Carson W., jt. auth. see Buchanan, Watson W.
Dick, E., et al. GUIDE: Gathering up Information for Developmental Education for the TMR. 1979. spiral bound 16.95 (ISBN 0-87804-358-6). Mafex.
Dick, Everett. The Sod-House Frontier: A Social History of the Northern Plains from the Creation of Kansas & Nebraska to the Admission of the Dakotas. LC 78-24204. (Illus.). 1979. pap. 7.95 (ISBN 0-8032-6551-4, BB 700, Bison). U of Nebr Pr.
--Tales of the Frontier: From Lewis & Clark to the Last Roundup. LC 62-14664. (Illus.). 1963. 14.95x (ISBN 0-8032-0038-2); pap. 4.25 (ISBN 0-8032-5744-9, BB 539, Bison). U of Nebr Pr.
--Vanguards of the Frontier: A Social History of the Northern Plains & Rocky Mountains from the Fur Traders to the Sod Busters. LC 41-6157. (Illus.). 1965. pap. 9.95 (ISBN 0-8032-5048-7, BB 189, Bison). U of Nebr Pr.
Dick, George. Immunisation. (Illus.). 1978. text ed. 12.50x (ISBN 0-906141-10-9, Pub. by Update Pubns England). Kluwer Boston.
Dick, James C. Violence & Oppression. LC 78-2235. 224p. 1979. 12.00x (ISBN 0-8203-0446-8). U of Ga Pr.

Dick, Jane. Volunteers & the Making of Presidents. LC 79-27734. (Illus.). 250p. 1980. 10.95 (ISBN 0-396-07839-7); pap. 6.95 (ISBN 0-396-07840-0). Dodd.

Dick, Lenox. Art & Science of Fly Fishing. 2nd ed. (Illus.). 1972. 7.95 o.p. (ISBN 0-87691-053-3). Winchester Pr.

--The Art & Science of Fly Fishing. 1977. pap. 3.95 (ISBN 0-8065-0587-7). Citadel Pr.

Dick, Manfred, ed. see Wentzlaff-Eggebert, Friedrich-Wilhelm.

Dick, Philip K. Confessions of a Crap Artist. 184p. 1978. pap. 5.95 (ISBN 0-9601428-2-7). Entwhistle Bks.

--Martian Time-Slip. 4th ed. 224p. 1981. pap. 2.25 (ISBN 0-345-29560-9). Ballantine.

--Valis. 240p. (Orig.). 1981. pap. 2.25 (ISBN 0-553-14156-2). Bantam.

Dick, Trevor J. Economic History of Canada: A Guide to Information Sources. LC 73-17571. (Economics Information Guide Ser.: Vol. 9). 1978. 30.00 (ISBN 0-8103-1292-1). Gale.

Dick, W. F., jt. auth. see Brookes, B. C.

Dick, Walter & Carey, Lou. The Systematic Design of Instruction. 1978. pap. 8.95x (ISBN 0-673-15122-0). Scott F.

Dick, Walter, jt. auth. see Singer, Robert N.

Dick, William M. Labor & Socialism in America: The Gompers Era. LC 71-189555. (National University Publications). 1972. 15.00 (ISBN 0-8046-9005-7). Kennikat.

Dicke, Karen & Goeldner, C. R. Bibliography of Tourism & Travel Research Studies, Reports, & Articles, 9 vols. 1980. Set. 60.00 (ISBN 0-89478-052-2). U CO Busn Res Div.

--Colorado Ski Industry Characteristics & Financial Analysis. 1981. 25.00 (ISBN 0-686-69386-8). U CO Busn Res Div.

Dicke, Karen, jt. auth. see Goeldner, C. R.

Dicke, Robert H. & Wittke, J. P. Introduction to Quantum Mechanics. 1960. 22.95 (ISBN 0-201-01510-2). A-W.

Dicken, Peter & Lloyd, Peter. Geography of Industrial Society. 1981. text ed. 25.85 (ISBN 0-06-318030-8, IntlDept); pap. text ed. 13.10 (ISBN 0-06-318048-0). Har-Row.

Dicken, Peter, jt. auth. see Lloyd, Peter.

Dicken, Samuel N. & Pitts, Forrest R. Introduction to Cultural Geography. 2nd ed. 1970. text ed. 19.50x o.p. (ISBN 0-471-00117-1). Wiley.

Dickens, Charles. Adventures of Oliver Twist. (World's Classics Ser: No. 8). 12.95 (ISBN 0-19-250008-2). Oxford U Pr.

--American Notes. 7.50 (ISBN 0-8446-1154-9). Peter Smith.

--Barnaby Rudge. 1966. 17.95x (ISBN 0-460-00076-4, Evman); pap. 2.95 o.p. (ISBN 0-460-01076-X, Evman). Dutton.

--Bleak House. Dyson, A. E., ed. LC 73-127567. (Casebook Ser). 1970. pap. text ed. 2.50 o.s.i. (ISBN 0-87695-038-1). Aurora Pubs.

--Bleak House. (Critical Edition Ser.). 1978 17.50 (ISBN 0-393-04374-6); pap. 6.95x 1977 (ISBN 0-393-09332-8). Norton.

--Child's History of England. (gr. 4-6). 1970. 12.95x (ISBN 0-460-00291-0, Evman). Dutton.

--Christmas Carol. (Illus.). (gr. 7-9). 1952. 8.95 o.s.i. (ISBN 0-397-00033-2). Lippincott.

--Christmas Carol. (gr. 4 up). 1963. 3.95g o.s.i. (ISBN 0-02-730300-4). Macmillan.

--A Christmas Carol. 150p. 1980. Repr. PLB 11.95x (ISBN 0-89967-017-2). Harmony & Co.

--A Christmas Carol. 1976. deluxe ed. 9.95 o.p. (ISBN 0-385-12816-9). Doubleday.

--A Christmas Carol. (Illus.). 1979. 9.95 (ISBN 0-312-13403-7). St Martin.

--A Christmas Carol: And Other Christmas Books. 1979. 10.00x (ISBN 0-460-00239-2, Evman). Dutton.

--A Christmas Carol: Retold by A. Sweaney. (Oxford Progressive English Readers Ser.). (gr. k-6). 1975. pap. text ed. 2.95x (ISBN 0-19-580724-3). Oxford U Pr.

--A Christmas Carol: The Original Manuscript. 8.50 (ISBN 0-8446-0078-4). Peter Smith.

--Christmas Stories. 1979. 6.00x (ISBN 0-460-00414-X, Evman); pap. 2.75 (ISBN 0-460-01414-5). Dutton.

--David Copperfield. (Macmillan Classics). (gr. 7 up). 1962. 5.95g o.s.i. (ISBN 0-02-730440-X). Macmillan.

--David Copperfield. Burgis, Nina, ed. (The Clarendon Dickens Ser.). (Illus.). 948p. 1981. 115.00 (ISBN 0-19-812492-9). Oxford U Pr.

--Dombey & Son. Horsman, Alan, ed. (Illus.). 931p. 1974. 74.00x (ISBN 0-19-812491-0). Oxford U Pr.

--Great Expectations. pap. 1.95. Bantam.

--Great Expectations. Crompton, Louis, ed. LC 62-21261. 1964. pap. 6.50 (ISBN 0-672-60967-3, LL2). Bobbs.

--Great Expectations. 1979. 12.95x (ISBN 0-460-00234-1, Evman); pap. 2.95 (ISBN 0-460-01234-7). Dutton.

--Great Expectations. 1962. pap. 0.95 o.s.i. (ISBN 0-02-050320-2, Collier). Macmillan.

--Great Expectations. McMaster, R. D., ed. LC 65-2026. (College Classics in English Ser). 1965. pap. 4.95 (ISBN 0-672-63042-7). Odyssey Pr.

--Great Expectations. (World's Classics Ser.). 7.50 o.p. (ISBN 0-19-250128-3). Oxford U Pr.

--Great Expectations. Calder, Angus, ed. (English Lib.). (Orig.). (YA) (gr. 9 up). 1965. pap. 2.25 (ISBN 0-14-043003-2). Penguin.

--Great Expectations. (Keith Jennison Large Type Bks). (gr. 5 up). PLB 9.95 o.p. (ISBN 0-531-00194-6). Watts.

--Great Expectations. (Literature Ser). (gr. 9-12). 1970. pap. text ed. 4.17 (ISBN 0-87720-725-9). AMSCO Sch.

--Great Expectations. Clay, N. L., ed. (The Guide Novel Ser.). pap. text ed. 5.50x (ISBN 0-435-16234-9). Heinemann Ed.

--Great Expectations with Reader's Guide. (gr. 10-12). 1975. pap. text ed. 7.00 (ISBN 0-87720-800-X); tchrs ed. 4.40 (ISBN 0-87720-900-6). AMSCO Sch.

--Hard Times. pap. 1.95. Bantam.

--Hard Times. 1954. 8.95x o.p. (ISBN 0-460-00292-9, Evman); pap. 2.50 o.p. (ISBN 0-460-01292-4). Dutton.

--The Letters of Charles Dickens: The Pilgrim Edition, Vol. 3, 1842-1843. House, Madeline, et al, eds. 657p. 1974. text ed. 55.00x (ISBN 0-19-812474-0). Oxford U Pr.

--The Life of Our Lord. LC 80-22131. (Illus.). 1981. Repr. of 1934 ed. price not set (ISBN 0-664-21382-0). Westminster.

--Little Dorrit. Holloway, John, ed. (English Library Ser.). 1968. pap. 3.95 (ISBN 0-14-043025-3). Penguin.

--Little Dorrit. Sucksmith, Harvey P., ed. (The Claredon Dickens Ser.). (Illus.). 1979. 74.00x (ISBN 0-19-812513-5). Oxford U Pr.

--Magic Fishbone. LC 53-10806. (Illus.). (gr. 3 up). 1953. 5.95 (ISBN 0-8149-0296-0). Vanguard.

--The New Oxford Illustrated Dickens, 21 vols. Incl. The Old Curiosity Shop. Cattermole, George & Phiz, illus. (Illus.). 1951. 19.50x (ISBN 0-19-254506-X); Our Mutual Friend. Stone, Marcus, illus. (Illus.). 1952. 22.50x (ISBN 0-19-254510-8); The Personal History of David Copperfield. (Illus.). 17.95x (ISBN 0-19-254502-7); The Posthumous Papers of the Pickwick Club. (Illus.). 1947. 22.50x (ISBN 0-19-254501-9); Sketches by Boz: Illustrative of Every-Day Life & Every-Day People. Cruickshank, George, illus. (Illus.). 1957. 22.50x (ISBN 0-19-254518-3); A Tale of Two Cities. (Illus.). 1949. 17.95x (ISBN 0-19-254504-3); The Uncommercial Traveller, & Reprinted Pieces, Etc. Pinwell, G. J., et al, illus. (Illus.). 1958. 22.50x (ISBN 0-19-254521-3); The Adventures of Oliver Twist. Cruickshank, George, illus. 1949. 17.95x (ISBN 0-19-254505-1); American Notes & Pictures from Italy. Stone, Marcus, et al, illus. 1957. 17.95x (ISBN 0-19-254519-1); Barnaby Rudge: A Tale of the Riots of 'eighty. Cattermole, George & Browne, H. K., illus. 1954. 21.00x (ISBN 0-19-254513-2); Bleak House. Phiz, illus. 1948. 22.50x (ISBN 0-19-254503-5); Christmas Books. Farjeon, Eleanor, intro. by. (Illus.). 1954. 17.95x (ISBN 0-19-254514-0); Christmas Stories. Dalziel, E. G., et al, illus. 1956. 21.00x (ISBN 0-19-254517-5); Dealings with the Firm of Dombey, & Son, Wholesale, Retail, & for Exploration. Phiz, illus. 1950. 22.50x (ISBN 0-19-254507-8); Great Expectations. Pailthorpe, F. W., illus. 1953. 12.50x (ISBN 0-19-254511-6); Hard Times for These Times. Walker, F. & Greiffenhagen, Maurice, illus. 1955. 17.95x (ISBN 0-19-254515-9); The Life & Adventures of Martin Chuzzlewit. Phiz, illus. 1951. 22.50x (ISBN 0-19-254509-4); The Life & Adventures of Nicholas Nickleby. Phiz, illus. 1950. 22.50x (ISBN 0-19-254508-6); Little Dorrit. Phiz, illus. 1953. 22.50x (ISBN 0-19-254512-4); Master Humphrey's Clock & a Child's History of England. Hudson, Derek, intro. by. 1958. 17.95x (ISBN 0-19-254520-5); The Mystery of Edwin Drood. Fildes, Luke & Collins, Charles, illus. 1956. 17.95x (ISBN 0-19-254516-7). (Illus.). (gr. 7 up). Set. 365.00x (ISBN 0-19-254522-1); Boxed Set Ecrase. 595.00x (ISBN 0-19-195252-4). Oxford U Pr

--Nicholas Nickelby. 1957. 15.50x (ISBN 0-460-00238-4, Evman); pap. 4.95 o.p. (ISBN 0-460-01238-X). Dutton.

--Nicholas Nickelby. Slater, Michael, ed. (English Library). 1978. pap. 4.95 (ISBN 0-14-043113-6). Penguin.

--Oliver Twist. (Literature Ser). (gr. 10-12). 1970. pap. text ed. 3.83 (ISBN 0-87720-747-X). AMSCO Sch.

--Oliver Twist. Shefter, Harry, et al, eds. (YA) pap. 2.50 (ISBN 0-671-42073-9, Re). WSP.

--Oliver Twist. 1957. 12.95x (ISBN 0-460-00233-3, Evman); pap. 2.95 (ISBN 0-460-01233-9). Dutton.

--Oliver Twist. (Arabic.). pap. 8.95x (ISBN 0-686-63548-5). Intl Bk Ctr.

--Quilp: The Old Curiosity Shop: Movie Edition. (Movie Edition Ser.). 320p. (RL 9). Date not set. pap. 1.25 (ISBN 0-451-06420-8, Y6420, Sig). NAL.

--The Strange Gentleman & Other Plays. Tillett, Jeffrey, ed. 1972. pap. text ed. 2.50x o.p. (ISBN 0-435-23225-8). Heinemann Ed.

--A Tale of Two Cities. pap. 1.50. Bantam.

--Tale of Two Cities. (Literature Ser). (gr. 7-12). 1969. pap. text ed. 4.00 (ISBN 0-87720-716-X). AMSCO Sch.

--Tale of Two Cities. Shefter, Harry, et al, eds. (YA) pap. 2.50 (ISBN 0-671-48931-3, Re). WSP.

--Tale of Two Cities with Reader's Guide. (Amsco Literature Program). (gr. 10-12). 1971. pap. text ed. 4.67 (ISBN 0-87720-813-1); tchrs. ed. s.p. 3.00 (ISBN 0-87720-913-8). AMSCO Sch.

--Three Novels. Incl. Oliver Twist; A Tale of Two Cities; Great Expectations. 1978. 14.00 (ISBN 0-600-32930-5). Transatlantic.

Dickens, Charles & Clare, Andrea M. Tale of Two Cities. abr. ed. LC 73-80400. (Pacemaker Classics Ser). (Adapted to grade 2 reading level). 1973. pap. 3.80 (ISBN 0-8224-9228-8); tchrs' manual free (ISBN 0-8224-5200-6). Pitman Learning.

Dickens, Charles & Garfield, Leon. The Mystery of Edwin Drood. (Illus.). 1981. 12.95 (ISBN 0-394-51918-3). Pantheon.

Dickens, Charles see Ruskin, John.

Dickens, E. Larry & Bertone, Pamela S. Fundamentals of Texas Government. LC 76-2572. (Illus.). 149p. (Orig.). 1976. lib. bdg. 7.95 (ISBN 0-88408-046-3); pap. text ed. 5.95 (ISBN 0-88408-127-3). Sterling Swift.

Dickens, E. Larry, et al. Texas: Lone Star State Government. (Illus.). 152p. (Orig.). 1980. pap. text ed. 6.95 (ISBN 0-88408-135-4). Sterling Swift.

Dickens, Frank. Boffo: The Great Motorcycle Race. LC 77-22087. (Illus.). 40p. (ps-3). 1978. 6.95 (ISBN 0-590-07715-5, Four Winds); PLB 5.41 o.p. (ISBN 0-8193-0957-5). Schol Bk Serv.

Dickens, Frank, et al, eds. Carbohydrate Metabolism & Its Disorders, 2 Vols. 1968. Vol. 1. o. s. i. 74.00 (ISBN 0-12-214901-7); Vol. 2. 54.50 (ISBN 0-12-214902-5). Acad Pr.

Dickens, Michael & Storey, Eric. The World of Butterflies. (Illus.). 128p. 1973. 5.95 o.s.i. (ISBN 0-02-531400-9). Macmillan.

--The World of Moths. (Illus.). 128p. 1974. 6.95 o.s.i. (ISBN 0-02-531390-8). Macmillan.

Dickens, Norman. Jack Nicholson: The Search for a Superstar. (Film Ser.). (Illus., Orig.). 1975. pap. 1.50 o.p. (ISBN 0-451-06726-6, W6726, Sig). NAL.

Dickens, Peter. Night Action. 256p. 1981. pap. 2.50 (ISBN 0-553-14764-1). Bantam.

Dickens, Roy S. & Hill, Carole E. Cultural Resources: Planning & Management. 1978. lib. bdg. 21.50x (ISBN 0-89158-254-1). Westview.

Dickens, Roy S., Jr. Cherokee Prehistory: The Pisgah Phase in the Appalachian Summit Region. LC 76-1972. 1976. 16.50x (ISBN 0-87049-193-8). U of Tenn Pr.

Dickenson, A. F. see Trotman-Dickenson, A. F. & Parfitt, G. D.

Dickenson, D. I. Trotman see Trotman-Dickenson, D. I.

Dickenson, John P. Brazil. (Westview Special Studies in Industrial Geography). 1978. lib. bdg. 24.50x (ISBN 0-89158-832-9, Dawson). Westview.

Dicker, Herman. Piety & Perservance: The Hassidic Jewish Communities of Hungary & Their Descendants in the United States. (Illus.). 208p. 1981. 12.95 (ISBN 0-87203-094-6). Hermon.

Dicker, Ralph L. & Syracuse, Victor R. A Consultation with a Plastic Surgeon. LC 74-30176. (Illus.). 384p. 1975. 14.95 (ISBN 0-88229-201-3). Nelson-Hall.

Dickerman, Don. Protected by Angels. 1977. pap. 1.95 (ISBN 0-89728-054-7, 677228). Omega Pubns OR.

Dickerman, Edmund H. Bellievre & Villeroy: Power in France Under Henry Third & Henry Fourth. LC 70-127365. (Illus.). 200p. 1971. 10.00x (ISBN 0-87057-131-1, Pub. by Brown U Pr). Univ Pr of New England.

Dickerman, Pat. Adventure Travel, North America. LC 77-25745. (Illus.). 1978. 9.95 o.p. (ISBN 0-690-01750-2, TYC-T); pap. 5.95 (ISBN 0-690-01751-0, TYC-T). T Y Crowell.

--Farm, Ranch & Country Vacations. LC 60-2113. (Illus.). 1979. pap. 5.95 o.p. (ISBN 0-913214-02-7). Berkshire Traveller.

--Farm, Ranch, & Country Vacations. (Illus.). 1981. pap. 7.95 (ISBN 0-913214-03-5). Farm & Ranch.

Dickerman, Patricia. Adventure Travel. LC 79-57153. 256p. 1980. 7.95 (ISBN 0-913216-03-8). Berkshire Traveller.

--Farm, Ranch, Countryside Guide. LC 60-2113. 256p. 1981. 7.95 (ISBN 0-913214-03-5). Berkshire Traveller.

Dickerson, Albert I. Albert Inskip Dickerson: Selected Writings. LC 74-84230. (Illus.). 232p. 1974. text ed. 10.00x (ISBN 0-87451-107-0). U Pr of New Eng.

Dickerson, Beverly, jt. auth. see Short, J. Rodney.

Dickerson, F. Reed. Materials on Legal Drafting. (American Casebook Ser.). 407p. 1981. text ed. 14.95. West Pub.

Dickerson, Grace. Jesus. 1981. 5.50 (ISBN 0-533-03936-3). Vantage.

Dickerson, Gregory W., tr. see Sophocles.

Dickerson, Martha U. Our Four Boys: Foster Parenting Retarded Teenagers. 1978. 11.95x o.p. (ISBN 0-8156-0146-8); pap. 6.95 (ISBN 0-8156-0155-7). Syracuse U Pr.

--Social Work Practice with the Mentally Retarded. Turner, Francis J. & Strean, Herbert S., eds. LC 80-2316. (Fields of Practice Ser.). 1981. text ed. 14.95 (ISBN 0-02-907430-4). Free Pr.

Dickerson, Mary C. Frog Book. (Illus.). 1969. pap. 6.50 (ISBN 0-486-21973-9). Dover.

Dickerson, Oliver M., ed. Boston Under Military Rule 1768-1769. LC 70-118029. (Era of the American Revolution Ser). 1970. Repr. of 1936 ed. 17.50 (ISBN 0-306-71943-6). Da Capo.

Dickerson, Reed. Products Liability & the Food Consumer. LC 77-139130. 339p. 1972. Repr. of 1951 ed. lib. bdg. 27.50x (ISBN 0-8371-5746-3, DIPL). Greenwood.

Dickerson, Richard E. & Geis, Irving. Chemistry, Matter, & the Universe. 1976. 21.95 (ISBN 0-8053-2369-4); study guide 5.25 (ISBN 0-8053-5260-0); instr's guide 3.95 (ISBN 0-8053-2380-5). Benjamin-Cummings.

Dickerson, Richard E., et al. Chemical Principles. 3rd ed. LC 77-87336. 1979. pap. text ed. 22.95 (ISBN 0-8053-2398-8); instr's guide 3.95 (ISBN 0-8053-2410-0); programmed reviews 99.95 (ISBN 0-8053-6027-1); problems 10.95 (ISBN 0-8053-1587-X); study guide 7.95 (ISBN 0-8053-2399-6); transparency masters 50.00 (ISBN 0-8053-2396-1). Benjamin-Cummings.

Dickerson, Steven L. & Robertshaw, Joseph E. Planning Design: The Systems Approach. LC 74-23977. (Illus.). 1975. 24.95 (ISBN 0-669-96602-9). Lexington Bks.

Dickerson, W. & Cheremisinoff, P., eds. Solar Energy Technology Handbook: Part B, Applications. (Energy, Power & Environment Ser.). 1980. 85.00 (ISBN 0-8247-6927-9). Dekker.

Dickes, E. W., tr. see Charles-Roux, Francois.

Dickes, E. W., tr. see Doberer, Kurt K.

Dickey, Charley. Charley Dickey's Bobwhite Quail Hunting. LC 74-79232. (Illus.). 200p. 1975. 9.95 o.p. (ISBN 0-8487-0397-9). Oxmoor Hse.

Dickey, Dan W. The Kennedy Corridos: A Study of the Ballads of a Mexican American Hero. (Mexican American Monographs: No. 4). (Illus.). 125p. 1978. pap. 4.25 (ISBN 0-292-74305-3, Pub by Ctr Mex Am Stud). U of Tex Pr.

Dickey, Glenn. The History of National League Baseball: Since 1876. LC 80-6261. 336p. 1981. 13.95 (ISBN 0-8128-2818-6); pap. 9.95 (ISBN 0-8128-6101-9). Stein & Day.

Dickey, Imogene B., jt. auth. see Bindseil, Kenneth R.

Dickey, James. Buckdancer's Choice. LC 65-21079. (Wesleyan Poetry Program: Vol. 28). (Orig.). 1965. 7.50x o.p. (ISBN 0-8195-2028-4, Pub. by Wesleyan U Pr); pap. 4.95 (ISBN 0-8195-1028-9). Columbia U Pr.

--Drowning with Others. LC 62-10570. (Wesleyan Poetry Program: Vol. 14). (Orig.). 1962. 10.00x (ISBN 0-8195-2014-4, Pub. by Wesleyan U Pr); pap. 3.95 o.p. (ISBN 0-8195-1014-9). Columbia U Pr.

--God's Images: A New Vision. LC 78-17465. (Illus., Orig.). 1978. pap. 7.95 (ISBN 0-8164-2194-3). Crossroad NY.

--Helmets. LC 64-13610. (Wesleyan Poetry Program: Vol. 21). (Orig.). 1964. 10.00x (ISBN 0-8195-2021-7, Pub. by Wesleyan U Pr). Columbia U Pr.

--Poems, Nineteen Fifty-Seven to Nineteen Sixty-Seven. LC 67-15230. 1978. pap. 7.95 (ISBN 0-8195-6055-3, Pub. by Wesleyan U Pr). Columbia U Pr.

Dickey, John S. The Dartmouth Experience: Convocation Addresses..., Valedictories..., & Honorary-Degree Citations. Lathem, Edward C., ed. (Illus.). 322p. 1977. text ed. 15.00x (ISBN 0-87451-154-2). U Pr of New Eng.

Dickey, John Sloan. Canada & the American Presence: The United States Interest in an Independent Canada. LC 75-10905. (A Council on Foreign Relations Book). 202p. 1975. 14.00x (ISBN 0-8147-1758-6). NYU Pr.

Dickey, R. I. Accountants Cost Handbook. 2nd ed. 1050p. 1960. 39.50 (ISBN 0-471-06519-6). Wiley.

Dickey, Richard P. Managing Contraceptive Pill Patients. 2nd rev. ed. (Illus.). 116p. 1980. vinyl 7.95 (ISBN 0-917634-08-X). Creative Infomatics.

Dickey, Ronald W. & Klachko, Wolodymyr. Investing in New Jersey. LC 79-93331. 1980. 14.95 (ISBN 0-686-64291-0). W H Wise.

Dickey, W., jt. auth. see Schneider, R.

Dickey, William. More Under Saturn. LC 70-153102. (Wesleyan Poetry Program: Vol. 58). 1971. 10.00 (ISBN 0-8195-2058-6, Pub. by Wesleyan U Pr); pap. 4.95 (ISBN 0-8195-1058-0). Columbia U Pr.

Dickhut, Harold W. The Professional Resume & Job Search Guide. 272p. 1981. 5.95 (ISBN 0-13-725713-9, Spec); pap. 6.95 (ISBN 0-13-725705-8). P-H.

Dickie, D. E. & Short, Douglas. Crane Handbook. 1981. text ed. price not set (ISBN 0-408-00445-2, Newnes-Butterworth). Butterworths.

--Lifting Tackle Manual. 1981. text ed. price not set (ISBN 0-408-00446-0, Fnewnes-Butterworth). Butterworth.

Dickie, George. Aesthetics: An Introduction. (Traditions in Philosophy Ser). 1971. pap. 4.95 (ISBN 0-672-63500-3). Pegasus.

Dickie, George & Sclafani, R. J. Aesthetics: A Critical Anthology. LC 76-28127. (Illus.). 1977. text ed. 15.95 (ISBN 0-312-00910-0). St Martin.

Dickie, James. Draw Your Own Zoo & Color It Too. 1973. pap. 4.95 (ISBN 0-8224-2400-2). Pitman Learning.

Dickie, Kenneth J., jt. auth. see Lang, Gerald S.

Dickie, R. S. Diet in Health & Disease: Rationale & Practice. 296p. 1975. 24.75 (ISBN 0-398-02899-0); pap. 18.50 (ISBN 0-398-02919-9). C C Thomas.

Dickinson, jt. auth. see Taylor, Robert B.

Dickinson, A. Contemporary Animal Learning Theory. (Problems in the Behavioral Sciences Ser.). (Illus.). 180p. 1981. 27.50 (ISBN 0-521-23469-7); pap. 9.95 (ISBN 0-521-29962-4). Cambridge U Pr.

Dickinson, A. K., ed. History Teaching & Historical Understanding. Lee, P. J. LC 79-300044. 1978. pap. text ed. 10.95x (ISBN 0-435-80291-7). Heinemann Ed.

Dickinson, A. T., Jr. American Historical Fiction. 3rd ed. LC 78-146503. 1971. 12.50 o.p. (ISBN 0-8108-0370-4). Scarecrow.

Dickinson, Alice. Charles Darwin & Natural Selection. LC 64-11921. (Biography Ser). (gr. 7 up). 1964. PLB 5.90 o.p. (ISBN 0-531-00865-7). Watts.

--The Colony of Massachusetts. rev ed. LC 74-8744. (First Bks). (Illus.). 96p. (gr. 5-8). 1975. PLB 4.90 o.p. (ISBN 0-531-02775-9). Watts.

--First Book of Prehistoric Animals. (First Bks). (Illus.). (gr. 4-6). 1954. PLB 4.90 o.p. (ISBN 0-531-00613-1). Watts.

--The Salem Witchcraft Trials: Have You Made No Contract with the Devil? LC 73-12085. (Focus Bks). (Illus.). 72p. (gr. 7 up). 1974. PLB 4.90 o.p. (ISBN 0-531-01049-X). Watts.

--Stamp Act: Taxation Without Representation Is Tyranny. LC 75-104187. (Focus Bks). (Illus.). (gr. 7 up). 1970. PLB 4.90 o.p. (ISBN 0-531-01012-0). Watts.

--Taken by the Indians: True Tales of Captivity. LC 75-22307. (Illus.). 192p. (gr. 7 up). 1976. PLB 6.90 o.p. (ISBN 0-531-01107-0). Watts.

Dickinson, Alice, ed. see Lang, Andrew.

Dickinson, Alice B. Differential Equations: Theory & Use in Time & Motion. LC 77-136120. (Mathematics Ser). 1972. text ed. 18.95 (ISBN 0-201-01515-3). A-W.

Dickinson, Arthur L. Accounting Practice & Procedure. LC 73-13487. 1975. Repr. of 1918 ed. text ed. 13.00 (ISBN 0-914348-17-5). Scholars Bk.

Dickinson, Brian. Developing Structured Systems: A Methodology Using Structured Techniques. LC 80-54609. (Illus.). 392p. 1981. 45.00 (ISBN 0-917072-23-5). Yourdon.

Dickinson, C. H. & Lucas, J. A. Plant Pathology & Plant Pathogens. LC 77-8689. (Basic Microbiology Ser.: Vol. 6). 1977. pap. 11.95 (ISBN 0-470-99212-3). Halsted Pr.

Dickinson, Emily. Acts of Light: Emily Dickinson. Langton, Jane, ed. 188p. 1980. 24.95 (ISBN 0-8212-1098-X, 006505); deluxe ed. 50.00 (ISBN 0-8212-1118-8, 006513DXLE). NYGS.

--Bolts of Melody: New Poems of Emily Dickinson. Bingham, Millicent T. & Todd, Mabel L., eds. (Illus.). 1945. 8.95 o.s.i. (ISBN 0-06-011035-X, HarpT). Har-Row.

--I'm Nobody! Who Are You? Poems of Emily Dickinson for Children. LC 78-6828. (Illus.). (gr. 1 up). 1978. 11.95 (ISBN 0-916144-21-6); pap. 5.95 (ISBN 0-916144-22-4). Stemmer Hse.

--Letter to the World. Godden, Rumer, ed. LC 78-78083. (Illus.). (gr. 7 up). 1969. 3.95 o.p. (ISBN 0-02-730550-3). Macmillan.

--The Manuscript Books of Emily Dickinson: 1883-1895. Franklin, Ralph W., ed. LC 80-17861. 1980. pre-Apr. 85.00x (ISBN 0-674-54828-0, Belknap Pr); text ed. 100.00 (ISBN 0-686-63335-0). Harvard U Pr.

--Poems, Eighteen Ninety to Eighteen Ninety-Six, 3 Vols. in 1. LC 67-25640. 1967. 55.00x (ISBN 0-8201-1014-0). Schol Facsimiles.

--Two Poems. (Illus.). 1968. 4.95 o.p. (ISBN 0-8027-0291-0); boxed ed. 10.00 o.p. (ISBN 0-8027-0292-9). Walker & Co.

Dickinson, Fidelia, jt. auth. see Kehler, Dorothea.

Dickinson, Francis & Monteith, Lesley. Handbook for Weight Reduction. (Creative Arts Communications Ser.). (Illus.). cancelled o.s.i. (ISBN 0-916870-20-0). Creative Arts Bk.

Dickinson, G. C. Maps & Air Photographs: Images of Earth. 2nd ed. LC 78-31287. 348p. 1979. 39.95x o.p. (ISBN 0-470-26640-6); pap. 17.95 o.p. (ISBN 0-470-26641-4). Halsted Pr.

Dickinson, G. M., jt. auth. see Cockerell, H. A.

Dickinson, George. The Dynamic Principle of Historical Growth. (Illus.). 1978. 39.95 (ISBN 0-89266-089-9). Am Classical Coll Pr.

Dickinson, George S. A Handbook of Style in Music. 2nd ed. LC 72-90211. (Music Reprint Ser). 1969. Repr. of 1965 ed. 18.50 (ISBN 0-306-71820-0). Da Capo.

Dickinson, J. P. Statistics for Business, Finance, & Accounting. (Illus.). 328p. 1976. text ed. 21.00x (ISBN 0-7121-1939-6, Pub. by Macdonald & Evans England); pap. text ed. 14.95x (ISBN 0-7121-1948-5). Intl Ideas.

Dickinson, John. Political Writings of John Dickinson, 1764-1774. Ford, P. L., ed. LC 70-119061. (Era of the American Revolution Ser). 1970. Repr. of 1895 ed. lib. bdg. 35.00 (ISBN 0-306-71950-9). Da Capo.

Dickinson, John P., ed. Risk & Uncertainty in Accounting & Finance. LC 74-3917. 239p. 1975. 21.95x o.p. (ISBN 0-347-01042-3, 93468-2, Pub. by Saxon Hse). Lexington Bks.

Dickinson, Jonathan. Gods Protecting Providence Man's Surest Help & Defense...Remarkable Deliverance of Divers Person, from the Devouring Waves of the Sea...& Also...the Inhumane Canibals of Florida, Repr. Of 1699 Ed. Bd. with Good Fetch'd Out of Evil. Mather, Cotten. Repr. of 1706 ed; A Memorial of the Present Deplorable State of New England. Mather, Cotten. Repr. of 1707 ed. LC 75-7023. (Indian Captivities Ser.: Vol. 4). 1977. lib. bdg. 44.00 (ISBN 0-8240-1628-9). Garland Pub.

Dickinson, Joycelyne G. Congress of Arras, Fourteen Thirty-Five. 1973. Repr. of 1955 ed. 15.00x (ISBN 0-8196-0281-7). Biblo.

Dickinson, L., et al. The Immigrant School Learner: A Study of Pakistani Pupils in Glasgow. (General Ser.). 161p. 1975. pap. text ed. 18.25x (ISBN 0-85633-062-0, NFER). Humanities.

Dickinson, Louise R. Summer at High Kingdom. 128p. (gr. 5-9). 1975. 5.90 (ISBN 0-531-02809-7). Watts.

Dickinson, Mary. Alex's Bed. (Illus.). (ps-1). 1980. 7.95 (ISBN 0-233-97207-2). Andre Deutsch.

Dickinson, Pamela I. Music with ESN Children. (General Ser.). 144p. 1976. pap. text ed. 13.75x (ISBN 0-85633-085-X, NFER). Humanities.

Dickinson, Patric, tr. see Aristophanes.

Dickinson, Peter. The Blue Hawk. 1977. pap. 1.95 o.p. (ISBN 0-345-25759-6). Ballantine.

--City of Gold & Other Stories from the Old Testament. (Illus.). 1980. 13.95 (ISBN 0-394-51385-1). Pantheon.

--The Gift. 192p. (gr. 7-12). 1974. 8.95 (ISBN 0-316-18427-6, Pub. by Atlantic Monthly Pr.). Little.

--Thhe Glass-Sided Ant's Nest. 1981. pap. 2.95 (ISBN 0-14-005864-8). Penguin.

--Hepzibah. LC 80-65425. (Illus.). 32p. 1980. 8.95 (ISBN 0-87923-334-6). Godine.

--The Iron Lion. 48p. 1973. pap. 4.50 o.p. (ISBN 0-04-823108-8). Allen Unwin.

--King & Joker. 1977. pap. 1.50 (ISBN 0-380-01767-9, 35006). Avon.

--One Foot in the Grave. 224p. 1981. pap. 2.95 (ISBN 0-14-005779-X). Penguin.

--Retirement Edens. 1981. 14.95 (ISBN 0-525-93173-2); pap. 8.95 (ISBN 0-525-93174-0). Dutton.

--A Summer in the Twenties. 1981. 10.95 (ISBN 0-394-51330-4). Pantheon.

--Sunbelt Retirement: The Complete State-By-State Guide to Retiring in the South & West of the United States. 2nd ed. (Illus.). 1980. 14.95 (ISBN 0-525-93123-6); pap. 8.95 (ISBN 0-525-93107-4). Dutton.

--The Walking Dead. LC 77-5299. 1978. 6.95 o.p. (ISBN 0-394-42010-1). Pantheon.

Dickinson, Roger A. Retail Management: A Marketing Channels Approach. 1974. 16.95x o.p. (ISBN 0-534-00318-4). Wadsworth Pub.

Dickinson, Thomas H. Outline of Contemporary Drama. LC 70-88059. 1969. Repr. of 1927 ed. 12.00x (ISBN 0-8196-0249-3). Biblo.

Dickinson, W. C. & Brown, K. C. Economic Analysis of Solar Industrial Process Heat Systems: A Methodology to Determine Annual Required Revenue & Internal Rate of Return. 1980. pap. 6.95 (ISBN 0-89934-012-1). Solar Energy Info.

Dickinson, W. Croft. Scotland from the Earliest Times to 1603. 3rd ed. Duncan, Archibald A., ed. (Illus.). 1977. text ed. 36.00x (ISBN 0-19-822453-2). Oxford U Pr.

Dickman, A. I., ed. see Sisk, B. F.

Dickmeyer, Lowell A. Hockey Is for Me. LC 78-54362. (The Sports for Me Bks). (Illus.). (gr. 2-5). 1978. PLB 5.95 (ISBN 0-8225-1080-4). Lerner Pubns.

--Swimming Is for Me. LC 80-15366. (Sports for Me Bks.). (Illus.). (gr. 2-5). 1980. PLB 5.95g (ISBN 0-8225-1084-7). Lerner Pubns.

Dickmeyer, Nathan & Hughes, K. Scott. Financial Self-Assessment: A Workbook for Colleges. 72p. 1980. pap. text ed. 15.00 (ISBN 0-915164-11-6). Natl Assn Coll.

Dickneider, William C., Jr. & Kaplan, David. Choice & Change: An Introduction to Economics. (Illus.). 1978. pap. text ed. 12.50 (ISBN 0-8299-0165-5); test bank avail. (ISBN 0-8299-0475-1). West Pub.

Dickoff, James, tr. see Arnauld, Antoine.

Dick-Read, Grantly. Childbirth Without Fear: The Original Approach to Natural Childbirth. new, 4th ed. Wessel, Helen & Ellis, Harlan F., eds. LC 77-181616. (Illus.). 352p. 1972. 13.95 o.s.i. (ISBN 0-06-011034-1, HarpT). Har-Row.

--Natural Childbirth Primer. (Illus.). 1956. 6.95 o.s.i. (ISBN 0-06-001320-6, HarpT). Har-Row.

Dicks, Brian. The Ancient Persians: How They Lived & Worked. 1979. 14.95 (ISBN 0-7153-7711-6). David & Charles.

--Corfu. LC 76-48823. (Islands Ser.). (Illus.). 1977. 14.95 (ISBN 0-7153-7311-0). David & Charles.

--Greece: The Traveller's Guide to History & Mythology. LC 79-91497. (Illus.). 1980. 17.95 (ISBN 0-7153-7797-3). David & Charles.

--The Isle of Wight. LC 78-74082. 1979. 14.95 (ISBN 0-7153-7657-8). David & Charles.

--The Israelis: How They Live & Work. LC 74-30350. 156p. 1975. text ed. 8.95 (ISBN 0-03-029706-0, HoltC). HR&W.

--Rhodes. (Islands Ser.). 1974. 14.95 (ISBN 0-7153-6571-1). David & Charles.

Dicks, G. R., ed. Sources of World Financial & Banking Information. LC 80-28654. 720p. 1981. lib. bdg. 125.00 (ISBN 0-313-22966-X, DSW/). Greenwood.

Dicks, Terrance. The Baker Street Irregulars in the Case of the Cinema Swindle. 128p. (gr. 4 up). 1981. 8.95 (ISBN 0-525-66728-8). Elsevier-Nelson.

--The Baker Street Irregulars in the Case of the Ghost Grabbers. 128p. (gr. 4 up). 1981. 8.95 (ISBN 0-525-66729-6). Elsevier-Nelson.

--Case of the Blackmail Boys. (gr. 4 up). 1981. 7.95 (ISBN 0-525-66710-5). Elsevier-Nelson.

--The Case of the Crooked Kids. (gr. 4 up). 1980. 7.95 (ISBN 0-525-66702-4). Elsevier-Nelson.

Dickson. Scottish Capitalism. 1980. text ed. 24.75x (ISBN 0-85315-482-1). Humanities.

Dickson, Billy, jt. auth. see McAleer, John.

Dickson, Carter. Death in Five Boxes. 1977. pap. 1.50 (ISBN 0-505-51203-3). Tower Bks.

--A Graveyard to Let. 1978. pap. 1.50 (ISBN 0-505-51222-X). Tower Bks.

Dickson, D. Bruce. Prehistoric Pueblo Settlement Patterns: The Arroy Hondo, New Mexico, Site Survey. (Arroyo Hondo Archaeological Ser.: Vol. 2). (Illus.). 1979. pap. 6.25 (ISBN 0-686-65919-8). Schol Am Res.

Dickson, David. The Politics of Alternative Technology. LC 75-7919. 224p. 1975. 8.00x o.s.i. (ISBN 0-87663-224-X). Universe.

Dickson, David, jt. auth. see Hargie, Owen.

Dickson, David R. & Maue, Wilma M. Human Vocal Anatomy. (Illus.). 172p. 1977. 18.75 (ISBN 0-398-00449-8). C C Thomas.

Dickson, Edward M., et al. The Hydrogen Energy Economy: A Realistic Appraisal of Prospects & Impacts. LC 76-56807. (Special Studies). 1977. text ed. 31.95 (ISBN 0-275-24290-0). Praeger.

Dickson, George E. & Saxe, Richard W. Partners for Educational Reform & Renewal. LC 73-7241. 1973. 17.00x (ISBN 0-8211-1825-0); text ed. 15.75x (ISBN 0-685-42629-7). McCutchan.

Dickson, Gordon. The Alien Way. 1977. pap. 1.75 o.s.i. (ISBN 0-446-84552-3). Warner Bks.

Dickson, Gordon R. The Dragon & the George. 1978. pap. 2.25 (ISBN 0-345-29514-5). Ballantine.

--The Far Call. 1978. pap. 2.25 o.s.i. (ISBN 0-440-12284-8). Dell.

--Home from the Shore. Baen, James P., ed. 1979. pap. 2.25 (ISBN 0-441-34256-6). Ace Bks.

--In Iron Years. LC 73-20509. (Doubleday Science Fiction Ser.). 256p. 1980. 9.95 (ISBN 0-385-01555-0). Doubleday.

--The R-Master. LC 73-13837. 1973. 6.95 o.p. (ISBN 0-397-00920-8). Lippincott.

--Tactics of Mistake. (Science Fiction Ser.). 256p. 1972. pap. 1.95 (ISBN 0-87997-521-0, U51534). DAW Bks.

Dickson, Gordon R. & Harrison, Harry. The Lifeship. LC 75-25079. 192p. (YA) 1976. 9.95 o.s.i. (ISBN 0-06-011764-8, HarpT). Har-Row.

Dickson, Gordon R., jt. auth. see Anderson, Poul.

Dickson, H., et al, eds. Thin Plate Working, Vol. 1. 2nd ed. (Illus.). 1977. 15.95x (ISBN 0-686-65561-3). Vol. 1 (ISBN 0-85083-387-6). Vol. 2 (ISBN 0-85083-047-8). Intl Ideas.

--Thin Plate Working, Vol. 2. (Engineering Craftsmen: No. D22). (Illus.). 1969. spiral bdg. 13.95x (ISBN 0-85083-033-8). Intl Ideas.

Dickson, H. R. The Arab of the Desert: A Glimpse into Badawin Life in Kuwait & Saudi Arabia. 1952. 47.50 o.p. (ISBN 0-04-953001-1). Allen Unwin.

--Kuwait & Her Neighbors. 1956. 21.00 o.p. (ISBN 0-04-953002-X). Allen Unwin.

Dickson, Harry E. Arthur Fiedler & the Boston Pops. 276p. 1981. 12.95 (ISBN 0-686-69044-3). HM.

Dickson, J. H. Bryophytes of the Pleistocene: The British Record & Its Chorological & Ecological Implications. 1973. 79.00 (ISBN 0-521-08576-4). Cambridge U Pr.

Dickson, J. H. see Bowen, D. Q.

Dickson, James F., 3rd see Kenedi, R. M.

Dickson, K., jt. ed. see Cairns, John, Jr.

Dickson, Keith A. Towards Utopia: A Study of Brecht. 1978. 36.00x (ISBN 0-19-815750-9). Oxford U Pr.

Dickson, L. E. Researches on Waring's Problem. 257p. 1935. 13.75 o.p. (ISBN 0-87279-474-1, 464). Carnegie Inst.

Dickson, Leonard E. History of the Theory of Numbers, 3 Vols. LC 66-26932. 49.50 (ISBN 0-8284-0086-5). Chelsea Pub.

--On Varients & Theory of Numbers. 1967. pap. 2.00 (ISBN 0-486-61667-3). Dover.

--Studies in the Theory of Numbers. LC 61-13494. 9.95 (ISBN 0-8284-0151-9). Chelsea Pub.

Dickson, Leonard E; see Sierpinski, Waclaw, et al.

Dickson, Naida. The Littlest Helper. (Early Childhood Bk.). (Illus.). (ps-2). PLB 4.95 o.p. (ISBN 0-513-00511-0). Denison.

Dickson, P. Kissinger & the Meaning of History. LC 78-5633. 1978. 19.95 (ISBN 0-521-22113-7). Cambridge U Pr.

Dickson, Paul. The Future File. 1978. pap. 1.95 (ISBN 0-380-42242-5, 42242). Avon.

--The Official Explanations. (Illus.). 225p. 1980. 9.95 (ISBN 0-440-06513-5). Delacorte.

Dickson, Robert. Robert's Dinner for Six. LC 78-64486. 1978. 5.00 (ISBN 0-937684-05-8). Tradd St Pr.

Dickson, Roy W. The Greatest Quiz Book Ever. LC 73-14252. (Illus.). 216p. (YA) 1974. 7.95 o.s.i. (ISBN 0-06-011032-5, HarpT). Har-Row.

Dickson, Stanley, et al. Communication Disorders: Remedial Principles & Practices. 520p. 1974. 17.95x (ISBN 0-673-07742-X). Scott F.

Dickson, T. R. The Computer & Chemistry: An Introduction to Programming & Numerical Methods. LC 68-16758. (Illus.). 1968. text ed. 17.95x (ISBN 0-7167-0141-3). W H Freeman.

--Introduction to Chemistry. 3rd ed. LC 78-17406. 1979. text ed. 18.95x (ISBN 0-471-02223-3); tchrs. manual avail. (ISBN 0-471-04750-3); experiments 7.95x (ISBN 0-471-04747-3); transparencies avail. (ISBN 0-471-04757-0); study guide 7.50x (ISBN 0-471-04748-1). Wiley.

Dickson, W. Patrick, ed. Children's Oral Communication Skills. (Developmental Psychology Ser.). 1981. write for info. (ISBN 0-12-215450-9). Acad Pr.

Di Clemente, F. F. Soccer Illustrated for Coach & Player. 2nd ed. 260p. 1968. 14.95 (ISBN 0-471-07138-2). Wiley.

DiClemente, Frank F. Soccer Illustrated: For Coach & Player. 2nd ed. LC 68-8624. (Illus.). 260p. 1968. 14.95 (ISBN 0-8260-2690-7). Ronald Pr.

DiClerico, Robert. The American President. (Illus.). 1979. pap. 10.50 ref. ed. (ISBN 0-13-028555-2). P-H.

DiCyan, Erwin. Vitamin E & Aging. pap. 1.95 o.s.i. (ISBN 0-685-30713-1, V2761). Jove Pubns.

DiCyan, Irwin. Creativity: Road to Self Discovery. 1978. pap. 1.95 o.s.i. (ISBN 0-515-04234-X). Jove Pubns.

Diczfalusy, E., ed. Pharmacology of Reproduction, Vol. 2. LC 67-19416. 1968. 32.00 (ISBN 0-08-012368-6). Pergamon.

Didactic Systems Staff. Effective Delegation. Euro-Training & Garcia De Leon, Luis, trs. (Simulation Game Ser.). 1971. pap. 24.90 (ISBN 0-89401-145-6); pap. 21.50 two or more; pap. 24.90 french ed. (ISBN 0-89401-017-4); pap. 21.50 ea. two or more; pap. 24.90 spanish ed. (ISBN 0-89401-018-2); pap. 21.50 ea. two or more spanish eds. Didactic Syst.

Didday, Rich. Home Computers: Two to the Tenth Questions & Answers, 2 vols. 1977. Vol. I. 9.95 (ISBN 0-918398-00-2); Vol. II. 9.95 (ISBN 0-918398-01-0). Dilithium Pr.

Didday, Richard & Page, Rex. Fortran for Humans. 3rd ed. (Illus.). 450p. 1981. pap. text ed. 10.36 (ISBN 0-8299-0356-9). West Pub.
--Using BASIC. 450p. 1980. pap. text ed. 10.36 (ISBN 0-8299-0357-7). West Pub.

Didday, Richard, jt. auth. see Page, Rex.

Didear, Hedwig K., compiled by. History of Karnes County & Old Helena. LC 78-15120. (Illus.). 9.50 o.p. (ISBN 0-685-13274-9). Jenkins.

Didelot, J., ed. Interavia ABC: World Dictionary of Aviation & Astronautics, 1980. 28th ed. 1126p. 1980. 107.50x (ISBN 0-8002-2697-6). Intl Pubns Serv.

Diderot & D'Alembert, eds. Encyclopedie, 18 vols. (Fr., 12 vols. of plates & 6 texts). 1971-1979. 190.00 ea. (ISBN 0-8277-3025-X). Maxwell Sci Intl.
--Encyclopedie; Ou, Dictionnaire Raisonne Des Sciences, Des Arts et Des Metiers, 35 Vols. 1751. Repr. 4750.00 (ISBN 0-8277-3054-3). Maxwell Sci Intl.

Diderot, Denis. De la poesie dramatique. new ed. (Nouveaux Classiques Larousse). (Illus.). 1976. pap. 2.95 (ISBN 0-685-66282-9, 86). Larousse.
--Diderot, Interpreter of Nature: Selected Writings. Kemp, Jonathon, ed. Stewart, Jean & Kemp, Jonathon, trs. from Fr. LC 78-65607. 1981. Repr. of 1937 ed. 26.50 (ISBN 0-88355-841-6). Hyperion Conn.
--Encyclopedia: Selections. Cassirer, Thomas & Hoyt, Nelly S., trs. LC 65-26535. 1965. pap. 8.80 o.p. (ISBN 0-672-60479-5). Bobbs.
--Neveu de rameau. (Documentation thematique). (Fr). pap. 2.95 (ISBN 0-685-13999-9, 85). Larousse.
--The Nun. Tancock, Leonard, tr. (Classics Ser). 1977. pap. 2.75 (ISBN 0-14-044300-2). Penguin.
--Rameau's Nephew & Other Works. Barzun, Jacques & Bowen, Ralph, trs. LC 55-9755. 1964. pap. 6.50 (ISBN 0-672-60440-X, LLA200). Bobbs.

Didi, Dolli, tr. see Rajneesh, Bhagwan S.

Didier, Noel. Le Droit Des Fiefs Dans la Coutume De Hainaut Au Moyen Age. LC 80-2032. 1981. Repr. of 1945 ed. 29.50 (ISBN 0-404-18561-4). AMS Pr.

Didinger, Ray. The Professionals: Portraits of NFL Stars by America's Most Prominent Illustrators. 1980. 16.95 (ISBN 0-453-00391-5, H-391). NAL.

Didion, Joan. Run River. 1961. 9.95 (ISBN 0-8392-1094-9). Astor-Honor.

Di Donato, Georgia. Woman of Justice. (Large Print Bks.). 1980. lib. bdg. 15.95 (ISBN 0-8161-3132-5). G K Hall.

Di Donato, Pietro see Donato, Pietro di.

Diebel, Don. How to Pick up Women in Discos. LC 80-67924. (Illus.). 128p. 1981. pap. 6.95 (ISBN 0-937164-00-3). Gemini Pub Co.

Dieckmann, Edward A. Practical Homicide Investigation. 96p. 1961. 10.50 (ISBN 0-398-00450-1). C C Thomas.

Dieckmann, H., et al, eds. Kreativitaet des Unbewussten. (Journal: Analytische Psychologie: Vol. 11, No. 3). (Illus.). 216p. 1980. soft cover 17.50 (ISBN 3-8055-1543-X). S Karger.

Dieckmann, Liselotte. Johann Wolfgang Goethe. (World Authors Ser.: Germany: No. 292). 1974. lib. bdg. 10.95 (ISBN 0-8057-2378-1). Twayne.

Diederich, Bernard. Somoza. 1981. 16.95 (ISBN 0-525-20670-1). Dutton.

Diedrich, Richard C. & Dye, H. Allan. Group Procedures: Purposes, Processes, & Outcomes. 1972. pap. text ed. 14.95 (ISBN 0-395-04364-6). HM.

Diedrich, William M. & Bangert, Jeff. Articulation Learning. 416p. 1980. text ed. 24.50 (ISBN 0-933014-59-7). College-Hill.

Diedrich, William M. & Youngstrom, Karl A. Alaryngeal Speech. (Illus.). 232p. 1977. 18.75 (ISBN 0-398-00451-X). C C Thomas.

Diefenderfer, Hope, ed. see Scharff, Robert.

Diehl, Bernhard, jt. auth. see Schwinn, Monika.

Diehl, Charles F. Introduction to the Anatomy & Physiology of the Speech Mechanisms. (Illus.). 192p. 1968. pap. 14.75 photocopy ed. spiral (ISBN 0-398-00452-8). C C Thomas.

Diehl, Edith. Bookbinding: Its Background & Technique. (Illus.). 748p. 1980. pap. 12.00 (ISBN 0-486-24020-7). Dover.

Diehl, Katharine S. Hymns & Tunes: An Index. LC 66-13743. 1242p. 1979. lib. bdg. 45.00 (ISBN 0-8108-0062-4). Scarecrow.

Diehl, Kathryn & Hodenfield, G. K. Johnny Still Can't Read...but You Can Teach Him at Home. 5th ed. (Illus.). 75p. 1979. pap. 2.50 (ISBN 0-9603552-0-0). K Diehl.

Diehl, Richard, jt. ed. see Feldman, Lawrence H.

Diehl, William. Sharky's Machine. 1979. pap. 2.50 o.s.i. (ISBN 0-440-18292-1). Dell.

Diehl, William E. Christianity & Real Life. LC 76-7860. 128p. 1976. pap. 3.95 (ISBN 0-8006-1231-0, 1-1231). Fortress.

Diehr, George. Business Programming with BASIC. LC 76-39639. 366p. 1972. 16.95 (ISBN 0-471-21370-5). Wiley.

Diejomack, Victor P., jt. auth. see Sheffield, James R.

Diejomaoh, V. P., jt. ed. see Bienen, Henry.

Diejomaoh, Victor P., jt. auth. see Damachi, Ukandi G.

Diekelmann, Nancy & Broadwell, Martin M. The New Hospital Supervisor. (Illus.). 1977. pap. text ed. 8.95 (ISBN 0-201-00773-8). A-W.

Diekhoff, John S. Milton's Paradise Lost: A Commentary on the Argument. 1963. Repr. of 1946 ed. text ed. 10.00x (ISBN 0-391-00447-6). Humanities.

Dielman, Louis H., ed. see Marine, William M.

Dielman, Terry E. Pooled Data for Financial Markets. Dufey, Gunter, ed. (Research for Business Decisions). 148p. 1980. 24.95 (ISBN 0-8357-1130-7, Pub. by UMI Res Pr). Univ Microfilms.

Diem, Aubrey. Western Europe: Geographical Analysis. LC 77-24617. 1979. text ed. 27.95 (ISBN 0-471-21400-0). Wiley.

Diemer, Ferdinand, et al, eds. Advanced Concepts in Ocean Measurements for Marine Biology. LC 79-24801. (Belle Baruch Library Ser.: Vol. 10). (Illus.). 572p. 1980. text ed. 27.50x (ISBN 0-87249-388-1). U of SC Pr.

Diener, Royce. How to Finance Your Growing Business. 416p. 1981. pap. 8.95 (ISBN 0-13-406546-8, Spec). P-H.

Diener, T. O. & Romberger, J. A., eds. Virology in Agriculture. (Landmark Studies Ser). 1977. 23.50x o.p. (ISBN 0-87663-805-1). Universe.

Dienes, Andre De see De Dienes, Andre.

Dienes, Andre de see De Dienes, Andre.

Dienes, C. Thomas, jt. auth. see Barron, Jerome A.

Dienes, Z. P. Mathematics Through the Senses: Games, Dance & Art. (General Ser). 160p. (Orig.). 1973. pap. text ed. 13.75x (ISBN 0-901225-87-8, NFER). Humanities.
--The Six Stages in the Process of Learning Mathematics. Seabourne, P. L., tr. (NFER General Ser). 64p. 1973. pap. text ed. 5.75x (ISBN 0-85633-022-1, NFER). Humanities.

Dienes, Zoltan P. Concept Formation & Personality. 1959. text ed. 3.50x (ISBN 0-7185-1019-4, Leicester). Humanities.

Dienhart. Football Scouting Workbook. write for info. (ISBN 0-392-07843-0). Soccer.

Dienhart, Charlotte M. Basic Human Anatomy & Physiology. 3rd ed. LC 78-64706. (Illus.). 1979. pap. text ed. 11.95 (ISBN 0-7216-3082-0). Saunders.

Dienstbier, Richard & Cole, James K., eds. Nebraska Symposium on Motivation, 1973: Human Sexuality. LC 53-11655. (Nebraska Symposia on Motivation Ser: Vol. 21). (Illus.). xvi, 323p. 1974. 13.50x (ISBN 0-8032-0615-1); pap. 5.95x (ISBN 0-8032-5621-3). U of Nebr Pr.

Dienstein, William. How to Write a Narrative Investigation Report. (Police Science Ser.). 128p. 1975. 11.75 (ISBN 0-398-00454-4). C C Thomas.
--Technics for the Crime Investigator. 2nd ed. 272p. 1974. 16.50 (ISBN 0-398-03112-6). C C Thomas.

Dienstfrey. Protides of the Biological Fluids: Proceedings, Colloquium on Protides of the Biological Fluids, 25th. LC 58-5908. 1978. text ed. 150.00 (ISBN 0-08-021524-6). Pergamon.

Dierauf, E., Jr. & Court, J. Unified Concepts in Applied Physics. 1979. 20.95 (ISBN 0-13-938753-6). P-H.

Dieren, W. V. & Hummelinck, M. W. Nature Is Price: The Economics of Mother Earth. (Ideas in Progress Ser). 1979. 15.00 (ISBN 0-7145-2663-0, Pub. by M Boyars); pap. 6.95 (ISBN 0-7145-2664-9). Merrimack Bk Serv.

Dierenfield, Richard B. Learning to Teach. LC 80-69119. 135p. 1981. perfect bdg. 10.95 (ISBN 0-86548-031-1). Century Twenty One.

Dieringer, Beverly. The Paper Bead Book. LC 76-13251. (Illus.). (gr. 7 up). 1977. 9.95 o.p. (ISBN 0-679-20319-2); pap. 4.95 o.p. (ISBN 0-679-20378-8). McKay.

Dierker, E. Topological Methods in Walrasian Economics. (Lecture Notes in Economics & Mathematical Systems: Vol. 92). 130p. 1974. pap. 8.30 o.p. (ISBN 0-387-06622-5). Springer-Verlag.

Diesendorf, Mark. Energy & People. LC 80-670075. 1980. pap. 11.95x (ISBN 0-909509-12-3, Pub. by Soc Res Sci). Intl Schol Bk Serv.

Diesing, Paul R. Patterns of Discovery in the Social Sciences. LC 72-106978. 1971. 20.50x (ISBN 0-202-30101-X). Aldine Pub.

Diessenhaus, H. I., jt. auth. see Millon, T.

Dietary Allowances Comm. & Food & Nutrition Board. Recommended Dietary Allowances. 9th ed. (Illus.). 1980. pap. 6.00 (ISBN 0-686-64858-7). Natl Acad Pr.

Dietary Allowances Committee & Food & Nutrition Board. Recommended Dietary Allowances. 8th ed. LC 74-5170. (Illus.). 136p. 1974. pap. 4.25 o.p. (ISBN 0-309-02216-9). Natl Acad Pr.

Dietel, Werner. Seefahrts-Worterbuch: Dictionary of Nautical Terms. 2nd ed. LC 66-56741. (Ger. Eng.). 1964. 32.00x (ISBN 3-7637-0028-5). Intl Pubns Serv.

Dieter, Melvin E. The Holiness Revival of the Nineteenth Century. LC 80-17259. (Studies in Evangelicalism: No. 1). 366p. 1980. 17.50 (ISBN 0-8108-1328-9). Scarecrow.

Dieterich, T., et al. Assessing Comprehension in a School Setting. Griffin, Peg, ed. LC 78-59785. (Linguistics & Reading Ser.: No. 3). 1978. pap. text ed. 6.95x (ISBN 0-87281-072-0). Ctr Appl Ling.

Dieterich, Thomas G. & Freeman, Cecilia. A Linguistic Guide to English Proficiency Testing in Schools. (Language in Education Ser.: No. 23). 53p. 1979. pap. text ed. 5.95 (ISBN 0-87281-110-7). Ctr Appl Ling.

Dieterle, Gwendolyn. M'lady Gets a Beastie. 32p. (gr. 3-5). 1981. 5.95 (ISBN 0-89962-203-8). Todd & Honeywell.

Diethrich, Edward R. Advances in Cardiovascular Nursing. LC 79-9375. 150p. 1979. pap. text ed. 19.95 (ISBN 0-87619-457-9). R J Brady.

Dietiker, Simone R. Franc-Parler. 2nd ed. 1980. text ed. 16.95x (ISBN 0-669-02491-0); instrs.' guide avail. (ISBN 0-669-02494-5); wkbk. 5.95 (ISBN 0-669-02492-9); tapes-reels 45.00 (ISBN 0-669-02496-1); cassettes 45.00 (ISBN 0-669-02497-X); demo tape (ISBN 0-669-02498-8); tapescript (ISBN 0-669-02495-3). Heath.

Dietl, Clara-Erika. Dictionary of Commercial, Economic, & Legal Terms; Woerterbuch der Wirschafts-, Rechts-, und Handelssprache: Including the Terminology of the European Community, 2 vols. Incl. Vol. 1. English-German. 1971 (ISBN 0-8002-1256-8); Vol. 2. German-English. 1974. LC 72-326078. 25.00x ea. Intl Pubns Serv.

Dietl, Walter. Standortgemasse Verbesserung und Bewirtschaftung von Alpenweiden-Okologie, Ethologie, Gesundheit. Grob, Regula, et al, trs. (Tierhaltung: No. 7). (Illus., Ger.). 1979. pap. 13.00 (ISBN 3-7643-1028-6). Birkhauser.

Dietmeyer. Logic Design of Digital Systems. 2nd ed. 1978. text ed. 28.95 (ISBN 0-205-05960-0). Allyn.

Dietrich, B. C. Death, Fate & the Gods: The Development of a Religious Idea in Greek Popular Belief & in Homer. 1967. text ed. 21.50x (ISBN 0-485-13703-8, Athlone Pr). Humanities.

Dietrich, E. B. & Fried, J. J. Code Arrest: A Heart Stops. 1975. pap. 1.50 o.s.i. (ISBN 0-515-03797-4). Jove Pubns.

Dietrich, Gunther, et al. General Oceanography: An Introduction. 2nd ed. LC 80-12919. 1980. 50.00 (ISBN 0-471-02102-4, Pub. by Wiley-Interscience). Wiley.

Dietrich, J. W. & Lonsdale, J. T. Mineral Resources of the Colorado River Industrial Development Association Area. (Illus.). 84p. 1958. 1.50 (RI 37). Bur Econ Geology.

Dietrich, Martin O. & Lehmann, Helmut T., eds. Luther's Works: Devotional Writings I, Vol. 42. LC 55-9893. (Prog. Bk.). 1969. 15.95 (ISBN 0-8006-0342-7, 1-342). Fortress.

Dietrich, R. F. Portrait of the Artist As a Young Superman: A Study of Shaw's Novels. LC 75-77613. 7.50 (ISBN 0-8130-0277-X). Brown Bk.

Dietrich, R. V. Stones: Their Collection, Identification, & Uses. LC 79-24760. (Geology Ser.). (Illus.). 1980. text ed. 13.95x (ISBN 0-7167-1138-9); pap. text ed. 7.95x (ISBN 0-7167-1139-7). W H Freeman.

Dietrich, Richard, ed. Realities of Literature. LC 70-136507. 1971. text ed. 16.50x long ed. (ISBN 0-471-00122-8); pap. text ed. 11.95 short ed. (ISBN 0-471-00123-6). Wiley.

Dietrich, Richard V. Geology & Virginia. LC 76-110752. (Illus.). 1971. 13.95x (ISBN 0-8139-0289-4). U Pr of Va.

Dietrich, Richard V. & Skinner, Brian J. Rocks & Rock Minerals. LC 79-1211. 1979. text ed. 14.95 (ISBN 0-471-02934-3). Wiley.

Dietrich, T. Stanton. Florida's Older Population Revisited. (Illus.). vi, 78p. (Orig.). 1978. pap. 6.00 (ISBN 0-8130-0686-4). U Presses Fla.

Dietrich, Wendell, ed. see Kane, John F.

Dietrich, Wendell, ed. see Orr, Robert P.

Dietrich, Wilfred O. The Blazing Story of Washington County. 10.95 (ISBN 0-685-48809-8). Nortex Pr.

Dietrichson, J. & Overland, O. Norwegian Pocket Dictionary: English-Norwegian, Norwegian-English. 7th ed. 1980. 8.00x (ISBN 8-2573-0054-3, N-407). Vanous.

Dietsche, Doreen, jt. auth. see Gerrick, David J.

Dietschy, John M., ed. see American Physiological Society.

Diettert, Gerald A., jt. auth. see Braun, Harold A.

Dietz. Andre. 1979. pap. 6.95 (ISBN 0-89272-052-2). Down East.

Dietz, A. A. & Grannis, G. F., eds. Aging-Its Chemistry: Proceedings of the Third Arnold O. Beckman Conference in Clinical Chemistry. LC 80-65825. 448p. 1980. 31.95 (ISBN 0-915274-10-8). Am Assn Clinical Chem.

Dietz, J. Rehabiltation Oncology. LC 80-22911. 1981. write for info. (ISBN 0-471-08414-X). Wiley.

Dietz, J. Herbert. Rehabilitation Oncology. 224p. 1981. 24.50 (ISBN 0-471-08414-X, Pub. by Wiley Med). Wiley.

Dietz, Lew. The Allagash. LC 78-8326. 1978. 11.50x o.p. (ISBN 0-89621-001-4); pap. 5.95x (ISBN 0-89621-000-6). Thorndike Pr.
--Jeff White: Young Woodsman. LC 79-22669. (Illus.). 224p. (gr. 6-10). 1979. pap. 4.95 (ISBN 0-89621-042-1). Thorndike Pr.

Dietz, Marjorie J., ed. Ten Thousand Garden Questions Answered by Twenty Experts. LC 73-17596. (Illus.). 1400p. 1974. 12.95 (ISBN 0-385-08743-8). Doubleday.

Dietz, Norman D. Fables & Vaudevilles & Plays: Theatre More-or-Less at Random. LC 68-16685. 176p. (Orig.). 1968. pap. 4.25 (ISBN 0-936520-00-0). Norman & Sandra.

Dietz, Susan. The Correct Waitress. 2nd ed. 1978. pap. 3.55 (ISBN 0-8104-9468-X). Hayden.

Dietz, Thomas, jt. ed. see McEvoy, James, III.

Dietze, Charles E. God's Trustees. new ed. 112p. (Orig.). 1976. pap. 1.25 (ISBN 0-8272-1216-X). Bethany Pr.

Dieudonne, J. A. Treatise on Analysis, 6 vols. Incl. Vol. 1. 1960. 22.95 (ISBN 0-12-215550-5); Vol. 2. rev. ed. 1970. 44.50 (ISBN 0-12-215502-5); Vol. 3. 1972. 48.50 (ISBN 0-12-215503-3); Vol. 4. 1974. 49.00 (ISBN 0-12-215504-1); Vol. 5. 1977. 34.50 (ISBN 0-12-215505-X); Vol. 6. 1978. 32.00 (ISBN 0-12-215506-8). (Pure & Applied Mathematics Ser.). Acad Pr.

Dieudonne, Jean. A Panorama of Pure Mathematics: As Seen by N. Bourbaki. Macdonald, I., tr. LC 80-2330. (Pure & Applied Mathematics Ser.). 1981. write for info. (ISBN 0-12-215560-2). Acad Pr.
--Special Functions & Linear Representations of Lie Groups. (CBMS Regional Conference Ser. in Mathematics: No. 42). 1980. 8.40 (ISBN 0-8218-1692-6). Am Math.

Dieudonne, Jean & Hua, L. K. On the Automorphisms of the Classical Groups. LC 52-42839. (Memoirs: No. 2). 1980. pap. 9.60 (ISBN 0-8218-1202-5, MEMO-2). Am Math.

Dieulesaint, E. & Royer, D. Elastic Waves in Solids: Applications to Signal Processing. LC 80-49980. 1981. write for info. (ISBN 0-471-27836-X, Pub. by Wiley-Interscience). Wiley.

Diez, E. Die Kunst der Islamischen Volker. (Handbuch der Kunstwissenschaft Ser.). (Illus.). xxii, 218p. (Ger.). 1981. Repr. of 1917 ed. lib. bdg. 150.00x (ISBN 0-89241-144-9). Caratzas Bros.

Diez, Roy L. & Maloney, Lawrence D. Builders' Estimating Fact Book. 132p. 1974. 13.95 (ISBN 0-8436-0115-9). CBI Pub.

DiFederico, Frank. The Mosaics of the National Shrine of the Immaculate Conception. (Illus.). 96p. 1981. 16.95 (ISBN 0-916276-09-0). Decatur Hse.

Di Ferrante, R. K. Trace Metals: Exposure & Health Effects. 1979. text ed. 41.00 (ISBN 0-08-022446-6). Pergamon.

Diffenderffer, Henry. The Young Merchant & the Indian Captive, a Tale Founded on Fact, Repr. Of 1851 Ed. Bd. with Revolutionary Incident, the Captivity of Capt. Jeremiah Snyder & Elias Snyder of Saugerties: In: Saugerties Telegraph, V. 5, No. 13-14, Jan. 25 & Feb. 1, 1851. De Witt, Charles G. Repr. of 1851 ed; Historical Traditions of Tennessee. the Captivity of Jane Brown & Her Family. Extract from American Whig Review, v.15, p.233-349. Repr. of 1852 ed; Scenes in Texas, Being a Recital of the Sufferings of a Lady in Her Escape from the Indians... by I. Call, Who Saw the Lady Before Her Recovery from the Affects of Her Sufferings. Call, I. Repr. of 1852 ed; The Lost Child: Or the Child Claimed by Two Mothers: a Narrative of the Loss & Discovery of Casper A. Partridge Among the Menomonee Indians, with a Concise Abstract of Court Testimony, & a Review of Commissioner Buttrick's Decision. Plimpton, Florus B. Repr. of 1852 ed; Indian Battles, Murders, Sieges & Forays in the Southwest. Containing the **Narratives of Gen. Hall, Col. Brown, Capt. Carr, John Davis, John Bosley, Samuel Blair, John Rains, Dr. Shelby, Thomas Everett. Repr. of 1853 ed. LC 75-7088. (Indian Captivities Ser.: Vol. 64). 1976. lib. bdg. 44.00 (ISBN 0-8240-1688-2). Garland Pub.**

Diffie, Bailey W. Prelude to Empire: Portugal Overseas Before Henry the Navigator. LC 60-14301. (Illus., Orig.). 1960. pap. 2.25x (ISBN 0-8032-5049-5, BB 108, Bison). U of Nebr Pr.

Diffrient, Niels. Humanscale, Vols. 4-9. 1981. Vols. 4-6. 37.50 (ISBN 0-686-69225-X); Vols. 7-9. 50.00 (ISBN 0-262-04061-1). MIT Pr.
--Humanscale Four-Five-Six. Date not set. price not set. MIT Pr.
--Humanscale Seven-Eight-Nine. Date not set. price not set. MIT Pr.
DiFiore. Toys. 121p. Date not set. 2.95 (ISBN 0-07-016921-7). McGraw.
Difloe, D. How to Buy Furniture. 1972. pap. 2.95 o.s.i. (ISBN 0-02-079750-8, Collier). Macmillan.
Digby, Anne & Searby, Peter. Children, School & Society in Nineteenth Century England. (Illus.). 282p. 1980. text ed. 24.00x (ISBN 0-333-24678-0). Humanities.
Digby, K. H. Lawyer in the Wilderness, Data Paper No. 114. 150p. 1980. 5.75 (ISBN 0-87727-114-3). Cornell SE Asia.
Digby, Sir Kenelm. Two Treatises: The Nature of Bodies; the Nature of Man's Soule, 1644. Wellek, Rene, ed. LC 75-11217. (British Philosophers & Theologians of the 17th & 18th Centuries Ser.). 1978. lib. bdg. 42.00 (ISBN 0-8240-1771-4). Garland Pub.
Digerness, David S. The Mineral Belt: Old South Park-Across the Great Divide, Vol. 2. (Illus.). 416p. 49.00 (ISBN 0-913582-21-2). Sundance.
--The Mineral Belt: Old South Park-Denver to Leadville, Vol. 1. (Illus.). 416p. 49.00 (ISBN 0-913582-20-4). Sundance.
--The Mineral Belt: Old South Park Railroads, 2 vols. new ed. Collman, Russ, ed. (Illus.). 1977. Vol. 1. 49.00 (ISBN 0-913582-20-4); Vol. 2. 49.00 (ISBN 0-913582-21-2). Sundance.
Digges, Leonard. A Prognostication Everlastinge of Righte Good Effecte: Lately Corrected & Augmented by Thomas Digges, His Sonne. LC 74-28846. (English Experience Ser.: No. 727). 1975. Repr. of 1576 ed. 9.50 (ISBN 90-221-0727-2). Walter J Johnson.
Digges, Leonard, tr. see Gonzalo, Cespedes & Gonzalo, Meneses.
Diggins, John P. Up from Communism: Conservative Odysseys in American Intellectual History. LC 74-24505. (Illus.). 544p. 1975. 20.00 o.p. (ISBN 0-06-011042-2, HarpT). Har-Row.
Diggle, J. & Goodyear, F. R., eds. Flavii Cresconii Corippi Iohannidos Libri 8. LC 78-85717. 1970. 39.00 (ISBN 0-521-07626-9). Cambridge U Pr.
Diggle, James, ed. Euripides. Bd. with Phaeton. LC 73-96084. (Classical Texts & Commentaries: No. 12). (Illus.). 1970. 42.50 (ISBN 0-521-07700-1). Cambridge U Pr.
Diggory, Peter & McEwan, John. Planning or Prevention: The New Face of Family Planning. (Ideas in Progress Ser.). 1978. 11.95 (ISBN 0-7145-2552-9, Pub. by M Boyars); pap. 5.95 (ISBN 0-7145-2553-7). Merrimack Bk Serv.
Diggs, Bernard J. Love & Being: An Investigation into the Metaphysics of St. Thomas Aquinas. 180p. 1947. 6.75 (ISBN 0-913298-45-X). S F Vanni.
DiGiacomo, James, jt. auth. see Shannon, Thomas A.
DiGiovanni. Flat & Corrugated Diapharm Design Handbook. Date not set. price not set. Dekker.
Di Giovanni, Norman T., tr. see Borges, Jorge L.
Di Giovanni, Norman T., et al, eds. see Borges, Jorge L.
Di Girolamo, Costanzo. A Critical Theory of Literature. 1981. 15.00 (ISBN 0-299-08120-6). U of Wis Pr.
Digital Signal Processing Committee, ed. Programs for Digital Signal Processing. LC 79-89028. 1979. 35.95; tape version 50.00. Inst Electrical.
Digital Signal Processing Committee (IEEE) Selected Papers in Digital Signal Processing II. (IEEE Press Selected Reprint Ser.). 582p. 1976. 21.95 (ISBN 0-471-01519-9). Wiley.
Digital Signal Processing Committee, ed. Selected Papers in Digital Signal Processing, II. LC 75-22925. 1976. 21.95 (ISBN 0-87942-059-6). Inst Electrical.
Di Giuseppe, Raymond, ed. see National Conference on Rational Psychotherapy, 2nd, June 1977.
D'Ignazio, Fred. Super Games & Projects to Do with Your Home Computer. LC 79-6860. (Illus.). 144p. (gr. 6). 1981. 9.95a (ISBN 0-385-15313-9); PLB (ISBN 0-385-15314-7). Doubleday.
Di Grazia, jt. auth. see Clifton.
DiIorio, Gino J. Direct Physical Measurement of Mass Yields in Thermal Fission of Uranium. LC 78-75005. (Outstanding Disserations on Energy Ser.). 1979. lib. bdg. 11.00 (ISBN 0-8240-3985-8). Garland Pub.
Dijen, F. S. van see Van Dijen, F. S.
Dijkhuizen, N. Van see Van Dijkhuizen, N.
Dijksman, E. A. Motion Geometry of Mechanism. LC 75-3977. (Illus.). 250p. 1976. 35.50 (ISBN 0-521-20841-6). Cambridge U Pr.
Dijkstra, Edward W. A Discipline of Programming. (Illus.). 240p. 1976. 22.95x (ISBN 0-13-215871-X). P-H.
Dikshit, D. P. Political History of the Chalukyas of Badami. 1980. 26.00x (ISBN 0-8364-0645-1, Pub. by Abhinav India). South Asia Bks.
Dikstein, S., ed. Fundamentals of Cell Pharmacology. (Illus.). 572p. 1973. 54.75 (ISBN 0-398-02504-5). C C Thomas.
Dil, A. S., ed. see Haugen, Einar.
Dil, Anwar S., ed. see Frake, Charles O.
Dil, Anwar S., ed. see Lieberson, Stanley.
Diles, Dave L. & Bradshaw, Terry. Terry Bradshaw: Man of Steel. 224p. 1980. pap. 4.95 (ISBN 0-310-39461-9, 12025P). Zondervan.
Diles, Dave L., jt. auth. see Bradshaw, Terry.
Diles, David, jt. auth. see Bradshaw, Terry.
Dilham, Ilham. Induction & Deduction: A Study in Wittgenstein. 1973. 29.75x (ISBN 0-631-14640-7, Pub. by Basil Blackwell England). Biblio Dist.
DiLiello, Leo R. Clinical Microbiology. (Illus.). 1979. pap. text ed. 12.00 (ISBN 0-87055-325-9). AVI.
Dilke, Christopher, tr. see Poma, Huaman.
Dilke, O. A. W. The Ancient Romans: How They Lived & Worked. 1975. 11.95 (ISBN 0-7153-6553-3). Dufour.
Dilker, Barbara. Stage Management Forms & Formats. LC 79-16689. (Illus.). 192p. (Orig.). 1981. pap. text ed. 15.00x (ISBN 0-910482-85-3). Drama Bk.
Dill, Forrest, jt. auth. see Lemert, Edwin M.
Dill, John R. Child Psychology in Contemporary Society. 1978. text ed. 18.95 (ISBN 0-205-05775-6, 795775-0). Allyn.
Dillard, Annie. Pilgrim at Tinker Creek. LC 73-18655. 232p. 1974. 10.00 (ISBN 0-06-121980-0). Har-Row.
Dillard, Dudley. Economic Development of the North Atlantic Community: Historical Introduction to Modern Economics. 1967. text ed. 21.95 (ISBN 0-13-223305-3). P-H.
Dillard, J. L. Lexicon of Black English. LC 76-30389. 1977. pap. 6.95 (ISBN 0-8164-9320-0); 12.95 o.p. (ISBN 0-8164-9309-X, Continuum). Continuum.
--Perspectives on American English. (Contributions to the Sociology of Language Ser.). 1980. 40.50x (ISBN 90-279-3367-7). Mouton.
Dillard, John E., Jr., jt. auth. see Davis, Grant M.
Dillaway, Newton. Prophet of America: Emerson & the Problems of Today. LC 80-2530. 1981. Repr. of 1936 ed. 44.50 (ISBN 0-404-19254-8). AMS Pr.
Dille, Robert C., ed. see Calkins, Dick & Nowlan, Phil.
Dillenberger, John, ed. John Calvin: Selections from His Writings. LC 75-26875. (American Academy of Religion. Aids for the Study of Religion). 590p. 1975. pap. 10.50 (ISBN 0-89130-025-2, 010302). Scholars Pr Ca.
Diller, Angela. Keyboard Harmony Course, 2 bks. 1937. pap. 2.95 ea. Bk. I (ISBN 0-02-870730-3). Bk. II (ISBN 0-02-870740-0). Schirmer Bks.
Diller, Karl C. Individual Differences & Universals in Language Learning Aptitude. (Orig.). 1981. pap. text ed. 15.95 (ISBN 0-88377-164-0). Newbury Hse.
Diller, Phyllis. The Joys of Aging & How to Avoid Them. LC 79-7863. (Illus.). 192p. 1981. 8.95 (ISBN 0-385-14555-1). Doubleday.
Dilley, Authur U. Oriental Rugs & Carpets. rev. enl. ed. Dimand, M. S., ed. LC 59-13247. (Illus.). 1959. 18.25 o.s.i. (ISBN 0-397-00110-X). Lippincott.
Dilley, Roy. Model Soldiers in Color. (Illus.). 1979. 12.95 (ISBN 0-7137-0907-3, Pub by Blandford Pr England). Sterling.
Dilligan, Robert J., jt. ed. see Bedford, Emmett G.
Dilling, Elizabeth. The Plot Against Christianity. 1978. pap. 10.00x (ISBN 0-911038-35-3). Noontide.
Dillingham, Beth, jt. auth. see White, Leslie A.
Dillingham, William B. Melville's Short Fiction, 1853-1856. LC 76-28922. 390p. 1977. 20.00x (ISBN 0-8203-0411-5). U of Ga Pr.
Dillingham, William B., jt. auth. see Watkins, Floyd C.
Dillingham, William B., jt. ed. see Cohen, Hennig.
Dillion, Robert W., jt. auth. see Crawley, Stanley M.
Dillman, Don. A. Mail & Telephone Surveys: The Total Design Method. LC 78-581. 1978. 29.50 (ISBN 0-471-21555-4, Pub. by Wiley-Interscience). Wiley.
Dillman, Peter, jt. auth. see Barber, Janet.
Dillon, Ann, jt. auth. see Bix, Cynthia.
Dillon, Barbara. The Beast in the Bed. LC 80-15069. (Illus.). 32p. (gr. k-3). 1981. 7.95 (ISBN 0-688-22254-4); PLB 7.63 (ISBN 0-688-32254-9). Morrow.
Dillon, Catherine. Constantine Cay. 1976. pap. 1.95 o.p. (ISBN 0-451-08307-5, J8307, Sig). NAL.
--White Fires Burning. 1977. pap. 1.95 o.p. (ISBN 0-451-08281-8, J8281, Sig). NAL.
Dillon, Eilis. The Wild Geese. 1981. 12.95 (ISBN 0-671-22852-8). S&S.
Dillon, Elizabeth & Dillon, Lawrence. A Manual of Common Beetles of Eastern North America, 2 vols. (Illus.). 1972. pap. 7.00 ea. Vol. 1 (ISBN 0-486-61180-9). Vol. 2 (ISBN 0-486-61190-6). Dover.
Dillon, J. F. The Law & Jurisprudence of England & America. LC 75-99475. (American Constitutional & Legal History Ser). 1970. Repr. of 1894 ed. lib. bdg. 42.50 (ISBN 0-306-71854-5). Da Capo.
Dillon, Janette. Shakespeare & the Solitary Man. 191p. 1981. 23.50x (ISBN 0-8476-6254-3). Rowman.
Dillon, John B., jt. auth. see Cohen, David D.
Dillon, John M., jt. auth. see O'Hehir, Brendan.
Dillon, Karen & Brown, Gail. Sew a Beautiful Wedding. 1980. pap. 4.95 (ISBN 0-935278-05-2). Palmer-Pletsch.
Dillon, Lawrence, jt. auth. see Dillon, Elizabeth.
Dillon, Lawrence S. Evolution: Concepts & Consequences. 2nd ed. LC 77-9033. (Illus.). 1978. pap. text ed. 17.50 (ISBN 0-8016-1299-3). Mosby.
--Ultrastructure,Macromolecules, & Evolution. 750p. 1981. 69.50 (ISBN 0-306-40528-8, Plenum Pr). Plenum Pub.
Dillon, Mary E., ed. see Benson, George C.
Dillon, Mary E., jt. ed. see Hamil, Ralph E.
Dillon, Mary E., ed. see Metz, Joseph G.
Dillon, Mary E., ed. & intro. by see Withers, William.
Dillon, Mary Earhart. Wendell Wilkie, Eighteen Ninety Two to Nineteen Fourty Four. LC 71-39040. (FDR & the Era of the New Deal Ser). 378p. 1972. Repr. of 1952 ed. lib. bdg. 35.00 (ISBN 0-306-70456-0). Da Capo.
Dillon, Mary T. Magazine Article Writing. 1977. 9.95 (ISBN 0-87116-107-9). Writer.
Dillon, Merton L. The Abolitionists: The Growth of a Dissenting Minority. Rischin, Moses, ed. LC 73-15096. (American Minorities Ser). (Illus.). 300p. (gr. 12). 1974. 10.00 (ISBN 0-87580-044-0); pap. 4.00 (ISBN 0-87580-513-2). N Ill U Pr.
--The Abolitionists: The Growth of a Dissenting Minority. 1979. pap. 4.95 (ISBN 0-393-00957-2). Norton.
--Elijah P. Lovejoy, Abolitionist Editor. LC 80-11000. ix, 190p. 1980. Repr. of 1961 ed. lib. bdg. 18.75x (ISBN 0-313-22352-1, DIEJ). Greenwood.
Dillon, Michael. China Profiles. 1981. 25.00x (ISBN 0-7146-3152-3, F Cass Co). Biblio Dist.
--The Chinese Porcelain Industry. 1981. 27.50x (ISBN 0-7146-3148-5, F Cass Co). Biblio Dist.
Dillon, Ray. Zero Base Budgeting for Health Care Institutions. LC 79-15046. 1979. text ed. 30.00 (ISBN 0-89443-150-1). Aspen Systems.
Dillon, Richard. The Legend of Grizzly Adams. 1977. pap. 1.50 o.p. (ISBN 0-425-03646-4, Medallion). Berkley Pub.
Dillon, Richard, et al. High Steel. LC 78-72833. (Illus.). 1978. pap. 25.00 o.p. (ISBN 0-89087-239-2). Celestial Arts.
Dillon, Richard S. Handbook of Endocrinology: Diagnosis & Management of Endocrine & Metabolic Disorders. 2nd ed. LC 79-10531. (Illus.). 760p. 1980. text ed. 52.00 (ISBN 0-8121-0642-3). Lea & Febiger.
Dillow, Jeffery. Adventures in High Fantasy. 1981. 15.95 (ISBN 0-8359-0165-3); pap. 13.95 (ISBN 0-8359-0164-5). Reston.
--High Fantasy. 1981. 14.95 (ISBN 0-8359-2827-6). Reston.
Dillow, Joseph. The Waters Above. 1980. 12.95 (ISBN 0-8024-9198-7). Moody.
Dillow, Linda & Arp, Claudia. Sanity in the Summertime. 224p. 1981. 8.95 (ISBN 0-8407-5237-7); pap. 4.95 (ISBN 0-8407-5754-9). Nelson.
Dillow, Louise B. & Carver, Deenie B. Mrs. Blackwell's Heart-of-Texas Cookbook. (Illus.). 130p. 1980. pap. 6.95 (ISBN 0-931722-06-3). Corona Pub.
Dills, Lanie. Official CB Slanguage Language Dictionary: Including Cross Reference. 4th ed. pap. 2.95 o.p. (ISBN 0-685-52921-5). L J Martin.
Dilman, Ilham. Studies in Language & Reason. LC 79-55527. 230p. 1981. text ed. 27.50x (ISBN 0-06-491691-X). B&N.
Dilman, Vladimir M. Law of Deviation of Homeostasis & Diseases of Aging. LC 79-21456. (Illus.). 346p. 1981. 35.00 (ISBN 0-88416-250-8). PSG Pub.
Dilson, J. Electronics. (Quick & Easy Series). 1966. pap. 2.95 o.s.i. (ISBN 0-02-079800-8, Collier). Macmillan.
Dilson, Jesse. Abacus. (Illus.). (gr. 5-8). 1969. 6.95 (ISBN 0-312-00105-3); pap. 4.95 (ISBN 0-312-00140-1). St Martin.
Dilson, Jesse, tr. see Baudot, Marcel, et al.
Dilts, James D., jt. auth. see Dorsey, John.
Dilts, P. V., Jr., et al. Core Studies in Obstetrics & Gynecology. 3rd ed. (Illus.). 248p. 1981. write for info. softcover (2572-4). Williams & Wilkins.
Dilts, R., et al. Neuro-Linguistic Programming, Vol. 1. LC 80-50147. 1980. limited boxed ed. 24.00x (ISBN 0-916990-07-9). Meta Pubns.
Dilworth, Ernest N., tr. see De Voltaire, Francois M.
Dima-Dragan, Cornelius. Studia Bibliologica. 1980. 15.00 (ISBN 0-917944-02-X). Am Inst Writing Res.
Dimand, M. S. & Mailey, Jean. Oriental Rugs in the Metropolitan Museum of Art. LC 73-2846. (Illus.). 1973. 65.00 (ISBN 0-87099-124-8). Metro Mus Art.
Dimand, M. S., ed. see Dilley, Authur U.
Dimarco, A., jt. ed. see Iacobelli, Stefano.
Dimarco, Vincent & Perelman, Leslie. The Middle English Letter of Alexander to Aristotle. (Costerus New Ser.: No. XIII). 1978. pap. text ed. 17.75x (ISBN 90-6203-662-7). Humanities.
Di Marzo, Luigi. Component Units of Federal States & International Agreement. LC 80-83265. 272p. 1980. 45.00x (ISBN 90-286-0330-1). Sijthoff & Noordhoff.
DiMascio, A. & Goldberg, H. Emotional Disorders: Diagnosis & Pharmacological Treatment. 3rd ed. 1980. 15.95 (ISBN 0-87489-255-4). Med Economics.
DiMascio, Alberto & Shader, Richard, eds. Clinical Handbook of Psychopharmacology. LC 75-118581. 1970. 30.00x (ISBN 0-87668-033-3). Aronson.
Dimbleby, Geoffrey W. Plants & Archeology. 2nd ed. LC 67-23020. (Illus.). 1978. 15.00x (ISBN 0-391-00926-5). Humanities.
Dimendberg, David C., jt. auth. see Bowers, Warner F.
Diment, Judith & Harvey, Anthony. Animals of Long Ago. LC 78-64663. (Fact Finders Ser.). (Illus.). 1979. lib. bdg. 3.96 (ISBN 0-686-51123-9). Silver.
Dimento, Joseph F. Managing Environmental Change: A Legal & Behavioral Perspective. LC 75-19776. (Special Studies). (Illus.). 1976. text ed. 19.95 o.p. (ISBN 0-275-56640-4). Praeger.
Dimick, Kenneth & Krause, Frank. Practicum Manual for Counseling & Psychotherapy. 4th rev. ed. 1980. pap. 9.95 (ISBN 0-915202-26-3). Accel Devel.
Dimitriev, P. P., jt. auth. see Gusev, N. G.
Dimitrijevic, Dimitrije & Macesich, George. Money & Finance in Contemporary Yugoslavia. LC 72-92889. (Special Studies in International Economics & Development). 1973. 28.50x (ISBN 0-275-28725-4); pap. text ed. 16.50x (ISBN 0-89197-857-7). Irvington.
Dimitriou, B. Politics & Planning. 1977. text ed. 12.50 o.p. (ISBN 0-08-016867-1). Pergamon.
Dimmitt, Richard B. Actor Guide to the Talkies, 1949-1964, 2 vols. LC 67-12057. 1967. Set. 45.00 (ISBN 0-8108-0000-4). Scarecrow.
--Title Guide to the Talkies, 2 Vols. LC 65-13556. 1965. Set. 60.00 (ISBN 0-8108-0171-X). Scarecrow.
Dimmock, N. J., jt. auth. see Primrose, S. B.
D'Immperio, Dan. Antique Valentines. LC 80-23002. (Illus.). 160p. 1981. write for info. (ISBN 0-498-02505-5). A S Barnes.
Dimock, Anthony Weston & Dimock, Julian A. Florida Enchantments. LC 74-13789. (Illus.). 318p. 1975. Repr. of 1908 ed. 20.00 (ISBN 0-8103-4061-5). Gale.
Dimock, George E., Jr., tr. see Euripides.
Dimock, Julian A., jt. auth. see Dimock, Anthony Weston.
Dimock, Marshall E. Law & Dynamic Administration. 176p. 1980. 19.95 (ISBN 0-03-057367-X); text ed. 8.95 (ISBN 0-03-057396-3). Praeger.
Dimond, Paul R. Dilemma of Local Government: Discrimination in the Provision of Public Services. LC 78-57187. (Illus.). 1978. 21.95 (ISBN 0-669-02372-8). Lexington Bks.
Dimond, S. J. Neuropsychology: A Textbook of Systems & Psychological Functions of the Human Brain. LC 79-40087. 1980. text ed. 72.95 (ISBN 0-407-00152-2). Butterworths.
--The Social Behavior of Animals. 1970. 32.00 (ISBN 0-7134-0957-6, Pub. by Batsford England). David & Charles.
Dimont, Max I. Jews, God & History. 1972. pap. 2.50 (ISBN 0-451-07870-5, E8995, Sig). NAL.
Dimsdale, Parks B., jt. auth. see Wright, John S.
Dimsdale, Thomas J. Vigilantes of Montana. (Western Frontier Library: No. 1). 1978. Repr. of 1953 ed. 8.95 o.p. (ISBN 0-8061-0274-8, WFL 1); pap. 4.95 (ISBN 0-8061-1379-0). U of Okla Pr.
Dinaburg & Akel. Nutrition Survival Kit. (Orig.). pap. 1.75 (ISBN 0-515-04654-X). Jove Pubns.
Dinardo, C. T., ed. Computers & Security, Vol. III. (The Information Technology Ser.). (Illus.). 247p. 1977. pap. 20.00 (ISBN 0-88283-016-3). AFIPS Pr.
Dincauze, Dena F. Cremation Cemeteries in Eastern Massachusetts. LC 68-2247. (Peabody Museum Papers Ser.: Vol. 59, No.1). 1968. pap. text ed. 10.00 (ISBN 0-87365-171-5). Peabody Harvard.

Dincauze, Dina F. The Neville Site: 8,000 Years at Amoskeag. Flint, Emily, ed. LC 75-40771. (Peabody Museum Monographs Ser.: No. 4). (Illus.). 1976. pap. 12.00 (ISBN 0-87365-903-1). Peabody Harvard.

Dincher, Judy, jt. auth. see Hood, Gail H.

Dinculeanu, N. Vector Measures. LC 68-6701. 1967. 36.30 o.p. (ISBN 0-08-012192-6). Pergamon.

D'Indy, Vincent. Beethoven: A Critical Biography. LC 72-125054. (Music Ser). (Illus.). 1970. Repr. of 1913 ed. lib. bdg. 14.50 (ISBN 0-306-70019-0). Da Capo.

Diner, Hasia R., ed. Women & Urban Society: A Guide to Information Sources. LC 78-13109. (Urban Studies Information Guide Ser.: Vol. 7). 1979. 30.00 (ISBN 0-8103-1425-8). Gale.

Diner, Helen. Mothers & Amazons. 280p. 1973. pap. 2.50 o.p. (ISBN 0-385-00733-7, Anch). Doubleday.

Diner, Jeff. Physical & Mental Suffering of Experimental Animals. Animal Welfare Institute, ed. 195p. (Orig.). 1979. pap. text ed. 4.00 (ISBN 0-938414-03-8). Animal Welfare.

Diner, Steven J., jt. ed. see Breul, Frank R.

Dinerman, Beatrice, jt. auth. see Crouch, Winston W.

Dines, Glen. Bull Wagon. (gr. 4-6). 1963. 4.25g o.s.i. (ISBN 0-02-730870-7). Macmillan.

--Overland Stage. (gr. 4-6). 1967. 3.95g o.s.i. (ISBN 0-02-731730-7). Macmillan.

--Sir Cecil & the Bad Blue Beast. LC 70-125868. (Illus.). (gr. k-2). 1970. 8.95 (ISBN 0-87599-175-0). S G Phillips.

Dinesen, Isak. Anecdotes of Destiny. 1958. 8.95 o.p. (ISBN 0-394-41528-0). Random.

--Ehrengard. LC 74-17033. 1975. pap. 1.95 (ISBN 0-394-71431-8, Vin). Random.

--Letters from Africa, 1914 to 1931. Lasson, Frans, ed. Born, Anne, tr. LC 80-25856. 1981. 25.00 (ISBN 0-226-15309-6). U of Chicago Pr.

--Shadows on the Grass. 160p. 1961. pap. 1.95 (ISBN 0-394-71062-2, Vin). Random.

Dinet, Pierre. Cinq Livres Des Hieroglyphiques. Orgel, Stephen, ed. LC 78-68199. (Philosophy of Images Ser.: Vol. 11). 1980. lib. bdg. 66.00 (ISBN 0-8240-3685-9). Garland Pub.

Dinges, John & Landau, Saul. Assassination on Embassy Row. 432p. 1981. pap. 5.95 (ISBN 0-07-016998-5). McGraw.

Dingle, A. E. The Campaign for Prohibition in Victorian England: The United Kingdom Alliance Eighteen Seventy-Two to Eighteen Ninety-Five. 240p. 1980. 21.00 (ISBN 0-8135-0909-2). Rutgers U Pr.

Dingle, J. T., et al, eds. Lyposomes in Applied Biology & Therapeutics. (Lyposomes in Biology & Pathology Ser.: Vol. 6). 714p. 1979. 109.50 (ISBN 0-686-63105-6, North Holland). Elsevier.

Dingledine, Raymond C., Jr. Our Home, Virginia, & the World. 1962. pap. text ed. 1.41 o.p. (ISBN 0-684-51514-8, ScribC). Scribner.

Dings, John G. The Mind in Its Place: Wordsworth, "Michael" & the Poetry of 1800. (Salzburg Studies in English Literature, Romantic Reassessment: No.8). 1973. pap. text ed. 25.00x (ISBN 0-391-01361-0). Humanities.

Ding Shu De, et al. The Chinese Book of Table Tennis. LC 80-65996. 1981. 10.95 (ISBN 0-689-11082-0). Atheneum.

Dingwall, James, tr. see Menger, Carl.

Dingwall, John. Sunday Too Far Away! (Australian Theatre Workshop Ser.). pap. text ed. 6.50x (ISBN 0-686-65422-6, 00532). Heinemann Ed.

Dingwall, Robert. The Social Organisation of Health Visitor Training. 1977. 30.00x (ISBN 0-85664-487-0, Pub. by Croom Helm Ltd England). Biblio Dist.

Dingwell, Joyce. Come Back to Love. (Harlequin Romances). 192p. 1981. pap. 1.25 (ISBN 0-373-02402-9, Pub. by Harlequin). PB.

Dinitz, Simon, jt. auth. see Conrad, John P.

Dinitz, Simon, jt. ed. see Scott, Joseph E.

Dinkel, John. The Road & Track Illustrated Auto Dictionary. (Illus.). 96p. 1981. pap. 3.95 (ISBN 0-393-00028-1). Norton.

Dinkel, John J., et al. Management Science: Text & Applications. 1978. text ed. 20.95x (ISBN 0-256-02037-X). Irwin.

Dinkelspiel, John R. & Selesnick, Herbert. Condominiums: The Effects of Conversion on a Community. 160p. 1981. 19.95 (ISBN 0-86569-059-6). Auburn Hse.

Dinkin, Eleanor & Urbont, Rosalind. Parallel Play for Parents: A Guide to Playground Exercise. LC 78-23450. (Illus.). 1978. 11.95 (ISBN 0-88229-424-5); pap. 6.95 (ISBN 0-88229-600-0). Nelson-Hall.

Dinkin, Robert J. Voting in Provincial America: A Study of Elections in the Thirteen Colonies, 1689-1776. LC 77-71861. (Contributions in American History: No. 64). (Illus.). 1977. lib. bdg. 18.95 (ISBN 0-8371-9543-8, DIV/). Greenwood.

Dinkler, Erich. Kunst und Geschichte Nubiens in Christlicher Zeit: Ergebnisse und Probleme Auf Grund der Jungsten Ausgrabungen. (Illus.). 379p. 1970. text ed. 92.00x (ISBN 0-685-23524-6). Humanities.

Dinkmeyer, D. & Caldwell, E. Developmental Counseling & Guidance in the Elementary School. (Guidance Counseling & Student Personnel in Education). 1970. 16.95 o.p. (ISBN 0-07-017003-7, C). McGraw.

Dinkmeyer, Don & Carlson, Jon. Consulting: Facilitating Human Potential & Change Processes. LC 72-97006. 1973. text ed. 18.50 (ISBN 0-675-08958-1). Merrill.

Dinkmeyer, Don & McKay, Gary D. Systematic Training for Effective Parenting (STEP) Parent's Handbook. (Illus.). 117p. 1976. pap. text ed. 4.85 (ISBN 0-913476-77-3). Am Guidance.

Dinkmeyer, Don, et al. Systematic Training for Effective Teaching: Teacher's Handbook. (Illus.). 291p. (Orig.). 1980. pap. text ed. 12.00 (ISBN 0-913476-75-7). Am Guidance.

--Systematic Training for Effective Teaching (STET) Teacher's Resource Book: Special Ctivities for Teachers & Students. (Illus.). 161p. (Orig.). 1980. pap. 7.00 (ISBN 0-913476-76-5). Am Guidance.

Dinkmeyer, Don C. & Carlson, Jon. Consultation: A Book of Readings. LC 74-34048. 295p. 1975. text ed. 19.95 (ISBN 0-471-21562-7). Wiley.

Dinkmeyer, Don C. & Muro, James J. Group Counseling: Theory & Practice. 2nd ed. LC 77-83357. 1979. text ed. 14.95 (ISBN 0-87581-206-6). Peacock Pubs.

Dinman, Bertram D. The Nature of Occupational Cancer: A Critical Review of Present Problems. 112p. 1974. 14.75 (ISBN 0-398-02907-5). C C Thomas.

Dinn, Freda. The Observer's Book of Music. rev. ed. (Illus.). 1979. 3.95 (ISBN 0-684-16590-2, ScribT). Scribner.

Dinnage, Rosemary. The Handicapped Child: Research Review, Visual Impairment, Hearing Impairment, Vol. 2. (Studies in Child Development). (Illus.). 447p. 1972. text ed. 12.00x (ISBN 0-582-32452-1). Humanities.

Dinneen, Betty. The Family Howl. LC 80-25385. (Illus.). 96p. (gr. 4-6). 1981. PLB 8.95 (ISBN 0-02-732150-9). Macmillan.

Dinner, Joan, jt. auth. see Riddle, Janet T.

Dinnerstein, Dorothy. The Mermaid & the Minotaur: Sexual Arrangements & Human Malaise. LC 75-23879. 352p. 1976. 10.95 o.s.i. (ISBN 0-06-011047-3, HarpT). Har-Row.

Dinnerstein, L. Leo Frank Case. LC 68-99750. 16.00x (ISBN 0-231-03067-3). Columbia U Pr.

DiNoto, Andrea. Collector's Guide to U.S. Auctions & Flea Markets. 320p. (Orig.). 1981. pap. 7.95 (ISBN 0-14-046481-6). Penguin.

Dinsdale, Tim. Loch Ness Monster. 3rd ed. (Illus.). 1976. pap. 7.95 (ISBN 0-7100-8394-7). Routledge & Kegan.

--Project Water Horse. (Illus.). 1975. 16.95 (ISBN 0-7100-8029-8); pap. 7.95 (ISBN 0-7100-8030-1). Routledge & Kegan.

Dinsmoor, W. Bell. The Architecture of Ancient Greece. LC 73-12401. 1973. 21.00x (ISBN 0-8196-0283-3). Biblo.

Dintiman, George B. How to Run Faster: A Do-It-Yourself Book for Athletes in All Sports. LC 76-54436. (Illus.). 60p. 1979. text ed. 3.25. Champion Athle.

Dintiman, George B. & Barrow, Loyd M. Comprehensive Manual of Physical Education Activities for Men. (Illus., Orig.). 1970. pap. text ed. 11.00 (ISBN 0-13-165548-5). P-H.

Dintiman, George B. & Greenberg, Jerrold S. Health Through Discovery. LC 79-20714. (Illus.). 1980. pap. text ed. 14.95 (ISBN 0-201-01256-1). A-W.

Dintiman, George B., et al. Doctor Tennis: A Complete Guide to Conditioning & Injury Prevention for All Ages. LC 80-65623. (Illus.). 106p. (Orig.). 1980. text ed. 4.95 (ISBN 0-938074-00-8). Champion Athlete.

Diocese of Cleveland & Torrence, Rosemary. Mending Our Nets. 160p. (Orig.). 1980. pap. 7.95 (ISBN 0-697-01757-5). Wm C Brown.

Diogenes. The April Game. 224p. 1981. pap. 2.50 (ISBN 0-87216-784-4). Playboy Pbks.

Diogenes, the Cynic, jt. auth. see Heraclitus of Ephesius.

Dioguardi, Nicola, ed. see European Symposium On Medical Enzymology - 1st - Milan - 1960.

Diole, Philippe, jt. auth. see Cousteau, Jacques Y.

Diole, Philippe, jt. auth. see Cousteau, Jacques-Yves.

Dion, Paula. Wings of Desire. 1978. pap. 2.25 o.p. (ISBN 0-685-66223-3). Ballantine.

Dionisotti, C., jt. ed. see Lucas, St. John.

DiOrio, Al, Jr. Borrowed Time: The Thirty-Seven Years of Bobby Darin. (Illus.). 1980. 9.95 (ISBN 0-89471-111-3); lib. bdg. 12.90 (ISBN 0-89471-110-5). Running Pr.

DiOrio, Ralph A. & Gropman, Donald. The Man Beneath the Gift: The Story of My Life. LC 80-17619. (Illus.). 224p. 1980. 9.95 (ISBN 0-688-03740-2). Morrow.

Diosdado, Ana. Olvida los Tambores. new ed. Maroto, Angel R., ed. 112p. (Orig.). (gr. 11-12). 1974. pap. text ed. 3.25x (ISBN 0-88334-063-1). Ind Sch Pr.

Diot, Alain. Quality Educators, Ltd. LC 77-73532. (gr. 1 up). 1977. pap. 1.95 (ISBN 0-8252-0478-X). Quist.

DiPalma, Giuseppe. Apathy & Participation. LC 70-120924. 1970. 9.95 o.s.i. (ISBN 0-02-907470-3). Free Pr.

DiPalma, Guiseppe. Surviving Without Governing: The Italian Parties in Parliament. LC 75-46035. 1977. 21.00x (ISBN 0-520-03195-4). U of Cal Pr.

DiPalma, J. & Rodman, M. Basic Readings in Drug Therapy. 1972. pap. 6.95 (ISBN 0-87489-084-5). Med Economics.

DiPalma, Joseph R. Basic Pharmacology in Medicine. 2nd ed. (Illus.). 640p. 1981. text ed. 25.00 (ISBN 0-07-017011-8, HP). McGraw.

--Drug Interactions. 1976. pap. text ed. 4.95 o.p. (ISBN 0-8273-1313-6). Delmar.

Di Palma, Vera. Your Fringe Benefits. 1978. 11.95 (ISBN 0-7153-7517-2). David & Charles.

DiPaul, H. Bert. Focusing Industrial Arts on Career Education. LC 79-53500. (Illus.). 143p. (Orig.). (gr. 9-12). 1979. pap. 3.95 (ISBN 0-9605418-0-2). DiPaul.

Dipchand, C., jt. auth. see Hanrahan, J.

Dipego, jt. auth. see Hurwood.

Di Pietro, Robert J., ed. see Linguistic Association of Canada & the U.S.

Dippie, Brian W., ed. Nomad: George A. Custer in Turf, Field & Farm, Vol 3. (John Fielding & Lois Lasater Maher Ser: No. 3). (Illus.). 176p. Date not set. 22.50 (ISBN 0-292-75519-8). U of Tex Pr.

Di Prampero, P. E. & Poortsmans, J., eds. Physiological Chemistry of Exercise & Training. (Medicine & Sport Ser.: Vol. 13). (Illus.). xii, 200p. 1981. 76.75 (ISBN 3-8055-2028-X). S Karger.

Di Prete, John. TV Ad Trivia Quiz Book. LC 80-15375. (Illus.). 96p. 1980. pap. 3.95 (ISBN 0-498-02464-4). A S Barnes.

Diprima, Richard. Headline History of the Sixties. LC 80-71081. 73p. (Orig.). (gr. 6-12). pap. text ed. write for info. (ISBN 0-86652-011-2). Educ Indus.

DiPrima, Richard C., jt. auth. see Boyce, William E.

Di Prima, Richard C., jt. auth. see Boyce, William E.

Dirac, Pam, et al. Directions in Physics: Lectures Delivered During a Visit to Australia & New Zealand, August & September, 1975. LC 77-24892. 1978. 17.50 (ISBN 0-471-02997-1, Pub. by Wiley-Interscience). Wiley.

Dirac, Paul A. General Theory of Relativity. LC 75-8690. 71p. 1975. 15.95 (ISBN 0-471-21575-9, Pub. by Wiley-Interscience). Wiley.

--Principles of Quantum Mechanics. 4th ed. (Int'l Series of Monographs on Physics). 1958. 29.95x (ISBN 0-19-851208-2). Oxford U Pr.

Dircks, Richard. Richard Cumberland. LC 76-28361. (English Authors Ser.: No. 196). 1976. lib. bdg. 12.50 (ISBN 0-8057-6654-5). Twayne.

Dirckx, John H. Dr. Thorndyke's Dilemma. (Illus.). 95p. (Orig.). 1974. pap. 5.00 o.p. (ISBN 0-915230-04-6). Rue Morgue.

Director, S. W. Circuit Theory: The Computational Approach. LC 75-2016. 679p. 1975. text ed. 31.95 (ISBN 0-471-21580-5); tchrs manual avail. (ISBN 0-471-21582-1). Wiley.

Director, S. W., ed. Computer-Aided Circuit Design: Simulation & Optimization. LC 73-16060. (Benchmark Papers in Electrical Engineering). 400p. 1974. 37.50 (ISBN 0-12-786350-8). Acad Pr.

Directory of Private Presses & Letterpress Printers & Publishers. Second International Directory of Private Presses (Letterpresses) Westreich, Budd, ed. (Illus.). 132p. (Orig.). 1980. 18.00 (ISBN 0-686-27375-3); pap. 10.00 (ISBN 0-936300-01-9). Pr Arden Park.

DiRenzo, Gordon J., ed. We, the People: American Character & Social Change. LC 76-51926. (Contributions in Sociology: No. 24). (Illus.). 1977. lib. bdg. 25.00 (ISBN 0-8371-9481-4, DWP/). Greenwood.

Dirkes, M. Ann. Learning to Think--to Learn. LC 80-65613. 145p. 1981. perfect bdg. 11.50 (ISBN 0-86548-032-X). Century Twenty One.

Dirks, Ray. Heads You Win, Tales You Win. 192p. 1980. pap. 2.75 (ISBN 0-553-13223-7). Bantam.

Dirksen, Charles J. & Kroeger, Arthur. Advertising Principles & Problems. 5th ed. 1977. text ed. 17.95x (ISBN 0-256-01925-8). Irwin.

Dirlam, Joel B. Fair Competition: The Law & Economics of Antitrust Policy. LC 73-100157. Repr. of 1954 ed. lib. bdg. 18.75x (ISBN 0-8371-2971-0, DIFC). Greenwood.

Dirlik, Arif. Revolution & History: Origins of Marxist Historiography in China, 1919-1937. LC 77-80469. 1978. 23.75x (ISBN 0-520-03541-0). U of Cal Pr.

Dirst, Richard D. Sign Language Evaluation Manual for Evaluators. 51p. 1980. pap. text ed. 3.50 (ISBN 0-9602220-3-0). RIFD.

Dirsztay, Patricia. Church Furnishings: The Nadfas Guide. (Illus.). 1978. 16.00 (ISBN 0-7100-8820-5); pap. 7.95 (ISBN 0-7100-8897-3). Routledge & Kegan.

DiSaia, Philip J. & Creasman, William T. Clinical Gynecologic Oncology. LC 80-18687. (Illus.). 478p. 1980. text ed. 29.50 (ISBN 0-8016-1314-0). Mosby.

DiSaia, Philip J., et al. Synopsis of Gynecologic Oncology. LC 74-34307. (Clinical Monographs in Obstetrics & Gynecology Ser). 344p. 1975. 32.50 (ISBN 0-471-21590-2, Pub. by Wiley-Med). Wiley.

Disalvo, Vincent. Business and Professional Communication: Basic Skills and Principles. (Speech and Drama Ser.). 1977. text ed. 14.95 (ISBN 0-675-08486-5); instrs' manual 3.95 (ISBN 0-675-08486-5). Merrill.

DiSanto, Mario, tr. see Ferrarotti, Franco.

Disbrow, Mildred A., et al. Maternity Nursing Case Studies. 1976. spiral bdg. 9.50 (ISBN 0-87488-036-X). Med Exam.

Disch, Thomas M. Fundamental Disch. Delany, Samuel R., ed. 416p. (Orig.). 1980. pap. 2.50 (ISBN 0-553-13670-4). Bantam.

Disch, Thomas M., ed. The New Improved Sun: An Anthology of Utopian S-F. LC 74-15866. (Illus.). 216p. (YA) 1975. 8.95 o.s.i. (ISBN 0-06-011052-X, HarpT). Har-Row.

Discovery Magazine Editors. Traveler's Choice: A Treasury of America's Regional Restaurants & Their Favorite Recipes. LC 80-53813. (Illus.). 256p. (Orig.). 1981. pap. 4.95 (ISBN 0-528-88042-X). Rand.

DiSessa, Andrea, jt. auth. see Abelson, Harold.

Diska, Pat & Jenkyns, Chris. Andy Says Bonjour. LC 54-11522. (Illus.). (gr. 1-3). 1954. 5.95 (ISBN 0-8149-0297-9). Vanguard.

Diskin, Eve. Yoga for Children. LC 76-28685. (Illus.). (gr. 7-11). 1977. 8.95 o.p. (ISBN 0-668-04075-0). Arco.

Diskin, Eve, jt. auth. see Rawls, Eugene S.

Diskin, Lahna. Theodore Sturgeon. (Starmont Reader's Guide Ser.: No. 7). 80p. 1981. Repr. lib. bdg. 9.95x (ISBN 0-89370-038-X). Borgo Pr.

Diskin, Lana. Reader's Guide to Theodore Sturgeon. Schlobin, Roger C., ed. LC 80-21423. (Reader's Guides to Contemporary Science Fiction & Fantasy Author Ser.: Vol. 7). (Illus., Orig.). 1980. pap. text ed. 3.95 (ISBN 0-916732-09-6). Starmont Hse.

Disley, John. Orienteering. rev. 2nd ed. LC 67-22990. (Illus.). 176p. 1979. lib. bdg. 6.95 (ISBN 0-8117-2023-3). Stackpole.

Dismukes, Newton B., Jr. & McConnall, James M. Soviet Naval Diplomacy. rev. ed. (Pergamon Policy Studies). (Illus.). 450p. 1979. 39.00 (ISBN 0-08-023906-4); pap. 11.25 (ISBN 0-08-023905-6). Pergamon.

Disney, Doris M. Only Couples Need Apply. 160p. 1974. pap. 0.95 o.p. (ISBN 0-451-05953-0, Q5953, Sig). NAL.

Disney, R. L., jt. auth. see Clarke, A. B.

Disney, Walt. Alice in Wonderland Meets White Rabbit. (Illus.). (ps-3). 1977. PLB 5.00 (ISBN 0-307-60019-X, Golden Pr). Western Pub.

--The Bambi Book. (ps-1). 1966. PLB 5.38 (ISBN 0-307-68930-1, Golden Pr). Western Pub.

--Donald Duck & the One Bear. (Illus.). (ps-3). 1977. PLB 5.00 (ISBN 0-307-60039-4, Golden Pr). Western Pub.

--Favorite Nursery Tales. (Illus.). (ps-3). 1977. PLB 5.00 (ISBN 0-307-12068-6, Golden Pr). Western Pub.

--Mickey Mouse & the Mouseketeers: Ghost Town Adventures. (Illus.). (gr. k-3). 1977. PLB 5.00 (ISBN 0-307-60135-8, Golden Pr). Western Pub.

--Mickey Mouse & the Second Wish. (Tell-a-Tale Readers). (Illus.). (gr. k-3). 1973. PLB 4.77 (ISBN 0-307-68418-0, Whitman). Western Pub.

--Mickey Mouse & the World's Friendliest Monster. (Tell-a-Tale Readers). (Illus.). (gr. k-3). 1976. PLB 4.77 (ISBN 0-307-68605-1, Whitman). Western Pub.

--Mickey Mouse: Best Neighbor Contest. (Illus.). (gr. k-3). 1977. PLB 5.00 (ISBN 0-307-60134-X, Golden Pr). Western Pub.

--Mickey Mouse Club. (Illus.). 24p. (ps-2). 1977. Repr. of 1975 ed. PLB 5.38 (ISBN 0-307-68997-2, Golden Pr). Western Pub.

--Mickey Mouse: Missing Mouseketeers. (Illus.). (gr. k-3). 1977. PLB 5.00 (ISBN 0-307-60057-2, Golden Pr). Western Pub.

--Mickey Mouse: The Kitten Sitters. (Young Reader Ser.). (Illus.). (gr. k-3). 1976. PLB 5.00 (ISBN 0-307-60133-1, Golden Pr); pap. 1.95 (ISBN 0-307-10823-6). Western Pub.

--The Mouseketeer's Train Ride. (Illus.). (gr. k-2). 1977. PLB 5.38 (ISBN 0-307-68894-1, Golden Pr). Western Pub.

--Walt Disney's Winnie-the-Pooh's Blanket Book. (Illus.). (ps). 1980. 5.95 (ISBN 0-525-69517-6, Gingerbread). Dutton.

--Winnie Puh. Sanchez, Rene, tr. from Eng. Orig. Title: Winnie-the-Pooh Book. (Illus.). 24p. (Span.). (ps-3). 1977. PLB 5.92 o.p. (ISBN 0-307-68827-5, Golden Pr). Western Pub.

--Winnie-the-Pooh & His Friends. (Illus.). (ps-3). 1976. PLB 5.38 (ISBN 0-307-68957-3, Golden Pr). Western Pub.

Dison, Norma. Clinical Nursing Techniques. 3rd ed. LC 74-28411. 1975. pap. text ed. 10.50 o.p. (ISBN 0-8016-1307-8). Mosby.

--Clinical Nursing Techniques. 4th ed. LC 78-31262. (Illus.). 1979. pap. text ed. 14.95 (ISBN 0-8016-1308-6). Mosby.

--Simplified Drugs & Solutions for Nurses, Including Arithmetic. 7th ed. LC 79-28198. (Illus.). 1980. pap. text ed. 8.50 (ISBN 0-8016-1311-6). Mosby.

Disraeli, Benjamin. The Complete Letters of Benjamin Disraeli, 1815 to 1834. Matthews, John, et al, eds. 640p. 1981. 45.00x (ISBN 0-8020-5523-0). U of Toronto Pr.

--Lothair. Bogdanor, Vernon, ed. (Oxford English Novels Ser). 414p. 1975. 16.95x (ISBN 0-19-255356-9). Oxford U Pr.

--Lothair, Repr. Of 1870 Ed. Wolff, Robert L., ed. Bd. with Lothaw; or, the Adventures of a Young Gentleman in Search of a Religion. Harte, Bret. (Victorian Fiction Ser). 1975. lib. bdg. 66.00 (ISBN 0-8240-1556-8). Garland Pub.

Dissemination Center-Bilingual-Bicultural Education. Mundo Fisico: Physical Science Worktext. 1976. pap. text ed. 1.95 o.p. (ISBN 0-8120-0681-X); tchr's manual avail. o.p. (ISBN 0-8120-0739-5). Barron.

Dissemination Center for Bilingual-Bicultural Education. Guide to Title VII ESEA Bilingual Bicultural Projects: 1973-1974. Cordasco, Francesco, ed. LC 77-90544. (Bilingual Bicultural Education in the U. S. Ser.). 1978. Repr. of 1974 ed. lib. bdg. 18.00x (ISBN 0-405-11084-7). Arno.

Dissinger, Katherine. Old, Poor, Alone, & Happy: How to Live Nicely on Nearly Nothing. 1980. 17.95 (ISBN 0-88229-629-9). Nelson-Hall.

Disston, Harry. Beginning the Rest of Your Life: A Guide to an Active Retirement. LC 78-75301. Date not set. cancelled (ISBN 0-498-02356-7). A S Barnes.

--Beginning the Rest of Your Life: A Guide to an Active Retirement. 160p. (Orig.). 1981. pap. 4.95 (ISBN 0-87000-518-9). Arlington Hse.

Distelhorst, David F. How to Prepare for the Texas Real Estate Exam. 2nd ed. 248p. (Orig.). 1980. pap. 14.95 (ISBN 0-88462-270-3). Real Estate Ed Co.

Distler, A., jt. ed. see Philip, T.

Ditchburn, R. W. Eye-Movements & Visual Perception. (Illus.). 420p. 1973. 49.00x (ISBN 0-19-857371-5). Oxford U Pr.

Ditchfield, P. H. Old English Customs Extant at the Present Time. LC 68-21765. 1968. Repr. of 1896 ed. 18.00 (ISBN 0-8103-3427-5). Gale.

--The Old-Time Parson. 342p. 1980. Repr. of 1908 ed. lib. bdg. 35.00 (ISBN 0-89760-130-0). Telegraph Bks.

--Vanishing Old Castles in England. (A Philosophy of History Library Book). (Illus.). 109p. 1981. 49.75 (ISBN 0-86650-003-0). Gloucester Art.

Ditchfield, P. H. & Jones, Sydney. The Charm of the English Village. 1977. 24.00 (ISBN 0-7134-1068-X, Pub. by Batsford England). David & Charles.

Ditlea. Rock Stars. (gr. 7-12). 1980. pap. 1.25 (ISBN 0-590-31206-5, Schol Pap). Schol Bk Serv.

Ditlevsen, Ove. Uncertainty Modeling: With Applications to Multidimensional Civil Engineering. (Illus.). 448p. 1980. text ed. 69.50 (C). McGraw.

Ditmars, Raymond. Strange Animals I Have Known. (Illus.). 1966. 6.95 o.p. (ISBN 0-15-185631-1). HarBraceJ.

Ditmars, Raymond L. Snakes of the World. (Illus.). 1966. 8.50 o.s.i. (ISBN 0-02-531730-X). Macmillan.

--Strange Animals I Have Known. 1966. pap. 0.60 o.p. (ISBN 0-15-685632-8, HPL3, HPL). HarBraceJ.

Dito, William R., jt. ed. see Baer, Daniel M.

D'Itri, Frank M., ed. Renovation & Re-Use of Waste Waters. 1978. text ed. 33.21 o.p. (ISBN 0-08-021774-5). Pergamon.

Ditsky, John. Friend & Lover: Poems. LC 80-84832. (Ontario Review Press Poetry Ser.). 80p. 1981. 9.95 (ISBN 0-86538-011-2); pap. 4.95 (ISBN 0-86538-012-0). Ontario Rev NJ.

--The Onstage Christ: Studies in the Persistence of a Theme. (Critical Studies Ser.). 188p. 1980. 25.00x (ISBN 0-389-20059-X). B&N.

Ditter, Francis J., Jr., tr. see Halbwachs, Maurice.

Ditter, Vida Y., tr. see Halbwachs, Maurice.

Dittersdorf, Karl D. Von see Von Dittersdorf, Karl D.

Dittert, Alfred E., Jr. & Plog, Fred. Generations in Clay: Pueblo Pottery of the American Southwest. LC 80-81831. (Illus.). 168p. 1980. 27.50 (ISBN 0-87358-271-3); pap. 14.95 (ISBN 0-87358-270-5). Northland.

Dittman, Richard, jt. auth. see Zemansky, Mark.

Dittmer, Bernice. Aunt Blanche's Memory Book. LC 79-92334. 1980. 50.00 o.p. (ISBN 0-930208-08-0). Mangan Bks.

Dittmer, John. Black Georgia in the Progressive Era, 1900-1920. LC 77-24249. (Blacks in the New World Ser.). 251p. 1980. pap. 5.95 (ISBN 0-252-00813-8). U of Ill Pr.

Dittmer, Lowell. Liu Shao-Ch'i & the Chinese Cultural Revolution: The Politics of Mass Criticism. (Center for Chinese Studies). 1975. 20.00x (ISBN 0-520-02574-1); pap. 4.95 (ISBN 0-520-02957-7). U of Cal Pr.

Dittmer, Paul. Accounting Practices for Hotels, Motels, & Restaurants. LC 79-142507. 1971. text ed. 17.95 (ISBN 0-672-96062-1); tchr's manual 5.00 (ISBN 0-672-26064-6); wkbk., 1972 9.95 (ISBN 0-672-96063-X). Bobbs.

Dittmer, Paul R. & Griffin, Gerald C. Principles of Food, Beverage & Labor Cost Control for Hotels & Restaurants. 2nd ed. LC 79-20301. 1979. text ed. 15.95 (ISBN 0-8436-2177-X). CBI Pub.

Dittmorc, Ray H. Double Leverage: The Whole Truth. 1979. 5.95 (ISBN 0-685-66731-6). Vantage.

Ditto, Tanya. The Longest Street: A History of Lafourche Parish & GrandIsle. Woolfolk, Doug, ed. (Illus.). 136p. 1980. 13.00 (ISBN 0-86518-013-X). Moran Pub Corp.

Ditton, Jason. Contrology: Beyond the New Criminology. (Illus.). 1979. text ed. 23.25x (ISBN 0-333-25965-3). Humanities.

--Part-Time Crime: An Ethnography of Fiddling & Pilferage. 1977. text ed. 35.00x o.p. (ISBN 0-333-21466-8). Verry.

Ditton, Pam, jt. auth. see Bell, Diane.

Ditton, Robert B., et al. Coastal Resources Management: Beyond Bureaucracy & the Market. (Lexington Books Studies in Marine Affairs). 1977. 21.00 (ISBN 0-669-00970-9). Lexington Bks.

Dittrick, Mark, ed. Design Crochet. LC 78-53411. 1979. 14.95 (ISBN 0-8015-2019-3, Hawthorn). Dutton.

--Design Knitting. LC 78-53411. 1979. 14.95 (ISBN 0-8015-2021-5, Hawthorn). Dutton.

Di Tullio, Benigno. Horizons in Clinical Criminology. (New York University Criminal Law Education & Research Center Monograph: No. 3). 232p. (Orig.). 1969. pap. 20.00x (ISBN 0-8377-0501-0). Rothman.

Div. of Earth Sciences. Geographical Perspectives & Urban Problems. (Illus.). 120p. 1973. pap. 8.00 (ISBN 0-309-02106-5). Natl Acad Pr.

Divac, Ivan, et al, eds. The Neostriatum: Proceedings of a Workshop Sponsored by the European Brain & Behaviour Society, Denmark, 17-19 April 1978. (Illus.). 1979. 55.00 (ISBN 0-08-023174-8). Pergamon.

Divale, William T. Warfare in Primitive Societies: A Bibliography. rev. ed. LC 73-81978. (War-Peace Bibliography Ser.: No. 2). 123p. 1973. pap. text ed. 2.50 (ISBN 0-87436-122-2). ABC-Clio.

Di Valentin, Louis, jt. auth. see Di Valentin, Maria.

Di Valentin, Maria & Di Valentin, Louis. Getting Started in Leathercraft. 104p. 1972. pap. 2.95 o.s.i. (ISBN 0-02-011300-5, Collier). Macmillan.

Diven, Anne, ed. The Scribner Anthology for Young People. LC 76-48217. 192p. (gr. 2 up). 1976. reinforced bdg. 8.95 (ISBN 0-684-14757-2, ScribT). Scribner.

DiVenuti, Biaggio. Money & Banking in Puerto Rico. 2.50 o.p. (ISBN 0-8477-2605-3). U of PR Pr.

Diver, Bradford B. Van see Van Diver, Bradford B.

Divien, Emmanuel, jt. auth. see Scholberg, Henry.

Divilbiss, J. L., ed. see Clinic on Library Applications of Data Processing, 1980.

Divine, Robert A. American Immigration Policy Nineteen Twenty Four to Nineteen Fifty Two. LC 70-166323. (Civil Liberties in American History Ser). 200p. 1972. Repr. of 1957 ed. lib. bdg. 22.50 (ISBN 0-306-70244-4). Da Capo.

--Blowing on the Wind: The Nuclear Test Ban Debate, 1954-1960. LC 77-25057. 1978. 15.95x (ISBN 0-19-502390-0). Oxford U Pr.

--Eisenhower & the Cold War. (Illus.). 160p. 1981. 14.95 (ISBN 0-19-502823-6). Oxford U Pr.

--Eisenhower & the Cold War. 160p. 1981. pap. 3.95 (ISBN 0-19-502824-4, 621, GB). Oxford U Pr.

--Since Nineteen Forty-Five: Politics & Diplomacy in Recent American History. 2nd ed. LC 79-12157. 1979. pap. text ed. 8.95 (ISBN 0-471-04908-5). Wiley.

Division Of Behavioral Sciences. Behavioral Science Research in New Guinea. 1967. pap. 8.75 (ISBN 0-309-01493-X). Natl Acad Pr.

Division of Biology & Agriculture. Alternative Sources of Protein for Animal Production. (Illus.). 184p. 1973. pap. 8.25 o.p. (ISBN 0-309-02114-6). Natl Acad Pr.

--Degradation of Synthetic Organic Molecules in the Biosphere. (Illus.). 352p. pap. 19.50 (ISBN 0-309-02046-8). Natl Acad Pr.

Division Of Biology And Agriculture. Eutrophication: Causes, Consequences, Correctives. LC 68-62704. 1969. text ed. 14.75 (ISBN 0-309-01700-9). Natl Acad Pr.

Division of Biology and Agriculture - Agricultural Board. Principles of Plant & Animal Pest Control, Vol. 4, Control Of Plant Parasitic Nematodes. 1968. pap. 10.00 (ISBN 0-309-01696-7). Natl Acad Pr.

Division Of Biology And Agriculture Of The Agricultural Board. U. S. - Canadian Tables of Feed Composition. 1969. pap. 4.50 (ISBN 0-309-01684-3). Natl Acad Pr.

Division of Chemistry and Chemical Technology. Characterization of Macromolecular Structure. (Illus.). 1968. 16.00 (ISBN 0-309-01573-1). Natl Acad Pr.

--Chemical Structure Information Handling: A Review of the Literature, 1962-1968. LC 70-602073. (Orig.). 1969. pap. 6.95 (ISBN 0-309-01733-5). Natl Acad Pr.

Division of Chemistry & Chemical Technology. Critical Evaluation of Chemical & Physical Structural Information. LC 74-4164. (Illus.). 624p. 1974. pap. 36.50 (ISBN 0-309-02146-4). Natl Acad Pr.

--Principles for Evaluating Chemicals in the Environment. 1975. pap. 16.00 (ISBN 0-309-02248-7). Natl Acad Pr.

--Specifications & Criteria for Biochemical Compounds. 3rd ed. 224p. 1972. 21.25 (ISBN 0-309-01917-6). Natl Acad Pr.

Division Of Chemistry And Chemical Technology. Survey of Chemical Notation Systems. 1964. pap. 8.00 o.p. (ISBN 0-309-01150-7). Natl Acad Pr.

Division Of Earth Sciences. Japanese Colonization in Eastern Paraguay. 1967. pap. 9.00 o.p. (ISBN 0-309-01490-5). Natl Acad Pr.

--Rock-Mechanics Research in the U. S. (Illus.). 1966. pap. 4.25 (ISBN 0-309-01466-2). Natl Acad Pr.

Division Of Earth Sciences, jt. auth. see Geophysics Research Board.

Division Of Engineering. Rapid Excavation: Significance, Needs Opportunities. (Orig.). 1968. pap. 3.75 (ISBN 0-309-01690-8). Natl Acad Pr.

Division of Mathematics - Committee on Support of Research in Mathematical Sciences. Mathematical Sciences: A Report. 1968. pap. 7.25 (ISBN 0-309-01681-9). Natl Acad Pr.

Division of Medical Sciences. Contraception: Science, Technology & Application. 1979. pap. 16.00 (ISBN 0-309-02892-2). Natl Acad Pr.

--Phototherapy in the Newborn: An Overview. LC 74-31207. 1975. pap. 12.50 (ISBN 0-309-02313-0). Natl Acad Pr.

Division of Medical Sciences, Assembly of Life Sciences, National Research Council. Chlorine & Hydrogen Chloride. LC 76-39940. (Medical & Biological Effects of Environmental Pollutants Ser.). 1976. pap. 10.00 (ISBN 0-309-02519-2). Natl Acad Pr.

Division of Medical Sciences, National Research Council. Copper. LC 76-57888. (Medical & Biologic Effects of Environmental Pollutants Ser.). 1977. pap. 7.00 (ISBN 0-309-02536-2). Natl Acad Pr.

--Genetic Screening: Programs, Principles & Research. LC 75-5790. xv, 388p. 1975. pap. 10.50 (ISBN 0-309-02403-X). Natl Acad Pr.

Division of Medical Sciences, NRC. Preservation of Red Blood Cells. (Illus.). 384p. 1973. pap. 9.75 (ISBN 0-685-31902-4). Natl Acad Pr.

Division of Physical Sciences. Physics in Perspective, Vol. 1. (Illus.). 1024p. 1972. pap. 28.00 (ISBN 0-309-02037-9). Natl Acad Pr.

--Research in Optical Spectroscopy: Present Status & Prospects. (Orig.). 1968. pap. 3.25 o.p. (ISBN 0-309-01699-1). Natl Acad Pr.

--Research in Solid State Sciences: Opportunities & Relevance to National Needs. LC 8-61848. 1968. pap. 4.75 (ISBN 0-309-01600-2). Natl Acad Pr.

DIVO Institut fuer Wirtschaftsforschung, Sozialforschung und angewandte Mathematik. German Election Study, October 1965. 1975. codebk. 10.00 (ISBN 0-89138-109-0). ICPSR.

Divry, D. C. Divry's Greek-English Dialogues. 1947. pocket ed. 5.00 (ISBN 0-685-09028-0). Divry.

Divry, George C. Divry's English-To-Greek Phrase & Conversation Pronouncing Manual. 1966. flexible bdg. 5.00 (ISBN 0-685-09027-2). Divry.

--Divry's New Self Taught English Method for Greeks. 1956. 5.00 (ISBN 0-685-09032-9). Divry.

--Greek Made Easy. 3rd ed. 1953. 5.00 (ISBN 0-685-09037-X). Divry.

Diwan, Romesh K. & Livingston, Dennis. Alternative Development Strategies & Appropriate Technology: Science Policy for an Equitable World Order. (Pergamon Policy Studies). 1979. 28.00 (ISBN 0-08-023891-2). Pergamon.

Dix, George E. & Sharlot, M. Michael. Basic Criminal Law, Cases & Materials. 2nd ed. 650p. 1980. text ed. 17.95 (ISBN 0-8299-0318-6); instrs.' manual avail. (ISBN 0-8299-0588-X). West Pub.

--Cases & Materials on Criminal Law. 2nd ed. LC 79-16929. (American Casebook Ser.). 764p. 1979. text ed. 19.95 (ISBN 0-8299-2056-0). West Pub.

Dix, H. M. Environmental Pollution Atmosphere, Land, Water & Noise. LC 80-40287. (Institution of Environmental Sciences Ser.). 300p. 1981. 38.50 (ISBN 0-471-27797-5, Pub. by Wiley-Interscience); pap. write for info. (ISBN 0-471-27905-6). Wiley.

Dix, Samuel M. Energy Economics. Date not set. 25.00 (ISBN 0-918998-05-0). Energy Educ. Postponed.

Dixhoorn, Jan J. Van see Karnopp, Dean, et al.

Dixit, A. & Norman, V. D. Theory of International Trade. (Cambridge Economic Handbooks). 250p. 1980. 34.50 (ISBN 0-521-23481-6); pap. 13.95 (ISBN 0-521-29969-1). Cambridge U Pr.

Dixit, A. K. Optimization in Economic Theory. (Illus.). 1977. pap. 8.95x (ISBN 0-19-877103-7). Oxford U Pr.

Dixit, Avinash. The Theory of Equilibrium Growth. (Illus.). 1976. text ed. 14.50x (ISBN 0-19-877080-4); pap. text ed. 9.95x (ISBN 0-19-877081-2). Oxford U Pr.

Dixon, A. E., ed. see Solar Energy Conversion Course, 5th, University of Waterloo, Ontario, August 6-19, 1978.

Dixon, Alan C. Network Analysis. LC 72-90475. 1973. text ed. 21.95 (ISBN 0-675-09024-5). Merrill.

Dixon, C. W. Society, Schools & Progress in Scandinavia. 1965. 25.00 (ISBN 0-08-011405-9); pap. 13.75 (ISBN 0-08-011404-0). Pergamon.

Dixon, Charles. Advanced Calculus. 192p. 1981. 36.00 (ISBN 0-471-27913-7, Pub. by Wiley-Interscience); pap. 17.95 (ISBN 0-471-27914-5). Wiley.

Dixon, Conrad. Basic Astronavigation. (Illus.). 1979. 8.95 (ISBN 0-229-98579-3, ScribT). Scribner.

--Start to Navigate. (Illus.). 1979. 6.95 (ISBN 0-229-11573-X, ScribT). Scribner.

Dixon, Conrad & Sevious, Edward. Sailing with Children. 1969. text ed. 3.00x o.p. (ISBN 0-685-09503-7). Humanities.

Dixon, D. Can You Retire? 1968. 8.50 (ISBN 0-08-012725-8). Pergamon.

Dixon, Daphne, jt. auth. see Francis, Dorothy.

Dixon, Diana. Return Engagement. 192p. (Orig.). 1980. pap. 1.50 (ISBN 0-671-57030-7). S&S.

Dixon, Dwight R. & Dixon, Paul B. Photography: Experiments & Projects. (Illus.). 1976. pap. text ed. 9.95 (ISBN 0-02-329840-5). Macmillan.

Dixon, E. J. see Taliaferro, W. H. & Humphrey, J. H.

Dixon, F. J., jt. ed. see Kunkel, H. G.

Dixon, F. J., Jr. see Taliaferro, W. H. & Humphrey, J. H.

Dixon, Frank J., jt. ed. see Kunkel, Henry G.

Dixon, Franklin W. The Hardy Boys: Mystery of Smugglers Cove. (The Hardy Boys Ser.). 192p. (gr. 3-7). 1980. PLB 7.95 (ISBN 0-671-41117-9); pap. 1.95 (ISBN 0-671-41112-8). Wanderer Bks.

--The Hardy Boys: The Mummy Case. (The Hardy Boys Ser.). 192p. (gr. 3-7). 1980. PLB 7.95 (ISBN 0-671-41116-0); pap. 1.95 (ISBN 0-671-41111-X). Wanderer Bks.

--Hardy Boys Who-Dunnit Mystery Book. 64p. (gr. 3-7). 1980. pap. 3.95 (ISBN 0-671-95721-X). Wanderer Bks.

--The Stone Idol. Barish, Wendy, ed. (Hardy Boys Ser.). (Illus.). 192p. (gr. 3-5). 1981. price not set (ISBN 0-671-42289-8); pap. price not set (ISBN 0-671-42290-1). Wanderer Bks.

--The Vanishing Thieves. Barish, Wendy, ed. (Hardy Boys Ser.). (Illus.). 192p. (Orig.). (gr. 2-7). 7.95 (ISBN 0-671-42292-8); pap. 1.95 (ISBN 0-671-42291-X). Wanderer Bks.

Dixon, James M. English Idioms. LC 73-163172. vi, 288p. 1975. Repr. of 1927 ed. 24.00 (ISBN 0-8103-3986-2). Gale.

Dixon, John, jt. auth. see Cowan, Henry J.

Dixon, John R. Thermodynamics One: An Introduction to Energy. (P-H Ser. in Mechanical Engineering). (Illus.). 512p. 1975. 24.95 (ISBN 0-13-914887-6). P-H.

Dixon, John W., Jr. Art & Theological Imagination. (Illus.). 1978. 12.95 (ISBN 0-8164-0397-X). Crossroad NY.

Dixon, Keith. Sociological Theory: Pretence & Possibility. (Monographs in Social Theory). 142p. 1973. 14.95 (ISBN 0-7100-7601-0); pap. 6.95 (ISBN 0-7100-7698-3). Routledge & Kegan.

Dixon, Lawrence W. Wills, Death & Taxes: Basic Principles for Protecting Estates. (Quality Paperback: No. 228). (Orig.). 1977. pap. 2.95 (ISBN 0-8226-0228-8). Littlefield.

Dixon, Linda K. & Johnson, Ronald C. The Roots of Individuality: A Survey of Human Behavior Genetics. LC 79-26601. 1980. pap. text ed. 9.95 (ISBN 0-8185-0376-9). Brooks-Cole.

Dixon, Marlene. Women in Class Struggle. 2nd ed. LC 79-67272. (Orig.). 1980. pap. 4.00 (ISBN 0-89935-005-4). Synthesis Pubns.

Dixon, Marlene & Jonas, Susanne, eds. Contradictions of Socialist Construction. 100p. (Orig.). 1979. pap. 4.00 (ISBN 0-89935-008-9). Synthesis Pubns.

--Strategies for the Class Struggle in Latin America. (Contemporary Marxism Ser.). (Illus.). 104p. (Orig.). 1980. pap. 5.00 (ISBN 0-89935-010-0). Synthesis Pubns.

Dixon, Mim. What Happened to Fairbanks? The Effects of the Trans-Alaska Oil Pipeline on the Community of Fairbanks, Alaska. (Social Impact Assessment Ser.: No. 1). (Illus.). 337p. 1980. pap. text ed. 9.50x (ISBN 0-89158-961-9). Westview.

Dixon, Nancy, et al. Quality, Trending, & Management for the Eighties (QTM-80) 236p. 1980. pap. 40.00 (ISBN 0-87258-345-7, 1377). Am Hospital.

Dixon, Nancy P. Children of Poverty with Handicapping Conditions: How Teachers Can Cope Humanistically. write for info. (ISBN 0-398-04478-3). C C Thomas.

Dixon, Paige. Skipper. LC 79-10420. (gr. 5-10). 1979. 8.95 (ISBN 0-689-30706-3). Atheneum.

Dixon, Paul B., jt. auth. see Dixon, Dwight R.

Dixon, Peter. Creative Expression in the Primary School. (Practical Guides for Teachers Ser.). (Illus.). 1974. pap. 5.95x (ISBN 0-631-94120-7, Pub. by Basil Blackwell). Biblio Dist.

Dixon, Peter, jt. auth. see Dixon, Sarah.

Dixon, Peter, ed. Writers & Their Background: Alexander Pope. LC 72-85534. (Writers & Their Background Ser.). xx, 324p. 1972. 15.00x (ISBN 0-8214-0113-0); pap. 6.00 (ISBN 0-8214-0114-9). Ohio U Pr.

Dixon, Peter, ed. see Swift, Jonathan.

Dixon, Peter L. Young Adventurers' Series, 6 vols. Incl. Deep Dive. LC 79-178208 (ISBN 0-8372-1867-5); Fast Snow. LC 70-178211 (ISBN 0-8372-1870-5); Fire Guard. LC 71-178206 (ISBN 0-8372-1869-1); Silent Flight. LC 75-178207 (ISBN 0-8372-1868-3); Test Run. LC 72-178209 (ISBN 0-8372-1866-7); Wipe Out. LC 77-178210 (ISBN 0-8372-1865-9). (gr. 3 up). 1971. 6 bks. of 1 title with tchr's guide 16.77 o.p. (ISBN 0-685-56188-7); text ed. 115.83 complete series o.p. (ISBN 0-8372-0469-0); tchr's guide 3.21, free with 10 or more books o.p. (ISBN 0-8372-0729-0); posters avail. o.p. (ISBN 0-8372-0742-8); 12.00 set o.p. (ISBN 0-686-67218-6). Bowmar-Noble.

Dixon, R. Dynamic Astronomy. 2nd ed. 1975. pap. 13.95 o.p. (ISBN 0-13-221234-X). P-H.

Dixon, R., tr. see Pisarev, Dimitri I.

Dixon, R. C. Spread Spectrum Systems. LC 75-31707. 1976. text ed. 29.50 (ISBN 0-471-21629-1, Pub. by Wiley-Interscience). Wiley.

Dixon, R. G., et al. Right of Privacy: A Symposium. LC 75-147833. (Symposia on Law & Society Ser). 1971. Repr. of 1965 ed. lib. bdg. 17.50 (ISBN 0-306-70114-6). Da Capo.

Dixon, R. J. & Thirlwall, A. P. Regional Growth & Unemployment in the United Kingdom. 1975. text ed. 35.00x (ISBN 0-8419-5010-5). Holmes & Meier.

Dixon, R. M. The Dyirbal Language of North Queensland: Studies in Linguistics. LC 78-190415. (No. 9). (Illus.). 448p. 1973. 57.50 (ISBN 0-521-08510-1); pap. 15.95x (ISBN 0-521-09748-7). Cambridge U Pr.

--A Grammar of Yidin. LC 76-27912. (Cambridge Studies in Linguistics: No. 19). (Illus.). 1977. 75.00 (ISBN 0-521-21462-9). Cambridge U Pr.

--The Languages of Australia. LC 79-21353. (Cambridge Language Surveys Ser.). (Illus.). 400p. 1980. 69.50 (ISBN 0-521-22329-6); pap. 19.95 (ISBN 0-521-29450-9). Cambridge U Pr.

Dixon, R. M. & Blake, B. J. Handbook of Australian Languages, Vol. 1. 1200p. 1980. text ed. 49.50x (ISBN 9-0272-0512-4). Humanities.

Dixon, R. M. & Blake, B. J., eds. Handbook of Australian Languages, Vol. 1. (Handbook of Australian Languages Ser.). 390p. (Orig.). 1980. pap. text ed. 23.95 (ISBN 0-7081-1201-3, 0435). Bks Australia.

Dixon, R. W. Christs' Company. Fletcher, Ian & Stokes, John, eds. LC 76-20033. (Decadent Consciousness Ser.). 1978. lib. bdg. 38.00 (ISBN 0-8240-2776-0). Garland Pub.

Dixon, Richard E., ed. Nosocomial Infections. (Illus.). 500p. 1981. text ed. price not set (ISBN 0-914316-24-9). Yorke Med.

Dixon, Robert. Dynamic Astronomy. 3rd ed. (Illus.). 1980. pap. text ed. 16.95 (ISBN 0-13-221267-6). P-H.

--El Ingles En Accion: See It& Say It in English. pap. 1.75 (ISBN 0-451-08060-2, E8060, Sig). NAL.

Dixon, Robert G. Benchwork. 2nd ed. LC 80-66607. (Machine Trades - Machine Shop Ser.). (Illus.). 208p. 1981. pap. text ed. 7.40 (ISBN 0-8273-1743-3); instr's. guide 1.10 (ISBN 0-8273-1744-1). Delmar.

Dixon, Roger & Muthesius, Stefan. Victorian Architecture. (World of Art Ser.). (Illus.). 1978. 17.95 (ISBN 0-19-520048-9); pap. 9.95 (ISBN 0-19-520049-7). Oxford U Pr.

Dixon, S. L. Fluid Mechanics, Thermodynamics of Turbomachinery. 2nd ed. 1974. text ed. 19.25 o.p. (ISBN 0-08-018072-8); pap. text ed. 11.00 o.p. (ISBN 0-08-018071-X). Pergamon.

--Worked Examples in Turbomachinery: Fluid Mechanics & Thermodynamics. LC 75-9757. 116p. 1975. text ed. 18.75 (ISBN 0-08-019797-3); pap. text ed. 9.00 (ISBN 0-08-019700-0). Pergamon.

Dixon, Samuel, jt. auth. see Trojanowicz, Robert.

Dixon, Samuel L. Working with People in Crisis: Theory & Practice. LC 78-31227. (Illus.). 1979. pap. text ed. 9.95 (ISBN 0-8016-1320-5). Mosby.

Dixon, Sarah & Dixon, Peter. West Coast Beaches: A Complete Guide from Baha to Canada. 1979. pap. 8.95 o.p. (ISBN 0-87690-285-9). Dutton.

Dixon, Stephen. Fourteen Stories. LC 80-14911. (Johns Hopkins Poetry & Fiction Program). 145p. 1980. 9.95 (ISBN 0-8018-2445-1). Johns Hopkins.

--Quite Contrary: The Mary & Newt Stories. LC 78-20202. 1979. 9.95 o.s.i. (ISBN 0-06-011072-4, HarpT). Har-Row.

Dixon, Thomas, Jr. The Clansman: An Historical Romance of the Ku Klux Klan. LC 71-104761. (Novel As American Social History Ser.). 392p. 1970. pap. 7.00x (ISBN 0-8131-0126-3). U Pr of Ky.

Dixon, Trudy, ed. see Suzuki, Shunryu.

Dixon, W. G. Special Relativity. LC 77-83991. (Illus.). 1978. 49.50 (ISBN 0-521-21871-3). Cambridge U Pr.

Dixon, W. J. & Nicholson, W. L. Exploring Data Analysis: The Computer Revolution in Statistics. 1974. 20.00x (ISBN 0-520-02470-2). U of Cal Pr.

Dixon, W. J., ed. BMD: Biomedical Computer Programs. new ed. Orig. Title: BMD & BMD: X-Series Supplement (2 Books) (Orig.). 1973. pap. 12.95x (ISBN 0-520-02426-5). U of Cal Pr.

Dixon, W. J. & Brown, M. B., eds. BMDP 1981. (Orig.). 1981. pap. 20.00x (ISBN 0-520-04408-8). U of Cal Pr.

Dixson & Fox. Mi Primer Diccionario Illustrado De Ingles. rev. ed. 67p. (gr. 3-6). 1974. 5.75 (ISBN 0-88345-253-7); pap. 3.75 (ISBN 0-88345-232-4). Regents Pub.

Dixson, jt. auth. see Boggs.

Dixson, Robert J. Easy Reading Selections in English. rev. ed. (Illus., Orig., Sequel to Elementary Reader in English). (gr. 7-9). 1971. pap. text ed. 2.75 (ISBN 0-88345-043-7, 17976); cassettes 40.00 (ISBN 0-685-19788-3); tapes o.p. 40.00 (ISBN 0-685-19789-1). Regents Pub.

--Elementary Reader in English. rev. ed. (Illus., Orig.). (gr. 9-12). 1971. pap. text ed. 2.75 (ISBN 0-88345-044-5, 17977); cassettes 40.00 (ISBN 0-685-19790-5); tapes o.p. 40.00 (ISBN 0-685-19791-3). Regents Pub.

--Graded Exercises in English. rev. ed. (Orig.). (gr. 8-10). 1971. pap. text ed. 2.95 (ISBN 0-88345-058-5, 18009); answer key 1.00 (ISBN 0-685-19797-2). Regents Pub.

--El Ingles En Accion. (Illus.). 1977. pap. text ed. 3.50 (ISBN 0-88345-295-2); records 60.00 (ISBN 0-685-77024-9); cassettes 60.00 (ISBN 0-685-77025-7). Regents Pub.

--Ingles Practico Sin Maestro, 2 vols. (gr. 9 up). 1972. One-vol. Ed. pap. text ed. 5.95 (ISBN 0-88345-068-2, 17382); Vol. 1. pap. text ed. 3.50 (ISBN 0-88345-069-0); Vol. 2. pap. text ed. 3.50 (ISBN 0-88345-070-4); records ea. level 18.00 (ISBN 0-685-04774-1); 60.00 ea.tapes o.p.; ea cassettes 60.00. Regents Pub.

--Modern American English, 2 bks. (gr. 7-12). 1977. pap. text ed. 3.45 ea.; Bk. 1. pap. text ed. (ISBN 0-88345-308-8); wkbk. 2.25 (ISBN 0-88345-314-2); Bk. 2. pap. text ed. (ISBN 0-88345-309-6); wkbk. 2.25 (ISBN 0-88345-315-0); cassette 80.00 ea. Regents Pub.

--Modern American English, Bk. 3. (Illus.). (gr. 7-12). 1977. pap. text ed. 3.45 (ISBN 0-88345-310-X); wkbk. 2.25 (ISBN 0-88345-316-9); cassettes 80.00 (ISBN 0-686-68052-9). Regents Pub.

--Modern American English, Bk. 4. 1978. pap. text ed. 3.45 (ISBN 0-88345-311-8); tchr's manual 1 4.95 (ISBN 0-88345-319-3); tchr's manual 2 4.95 (ISBN 0-88345-321-5); wkbk. 4 2.25 (ISBN 0-88345-317-7). Regents Pub.

--Modern American English, Bk. 5. (Illus.). 167p. (gr. 7-12). 1980. pap. text ed. 3.75 (ISBN 0-88345-312-6, 18724); tchr's manual 4.95 (ISBN 0-88345-324-X); wkbk. 2.25 (ISBN 0-88345-318-5). Regents Pub.

--Modern American English, Bk. 6. (Illus.). 1980. pap. text ed. 3.75 (ISBN 0-88345-313-4); tchr's manual 4.95 (ISBN 0-88345-325-8); wkbk 2.25 (ISBN 0-88345-320-7). Regents Pub.

--Modern American English: Teacher's Manual 3. (Modern American English Ser.). (Illus.). 187p. 1978. pap. text ed. 4.95 (ISBN 0-88345-322-3). Regents Pub.

--Modern Short Stories in English. rev. ed. (Illus., Orig., Sequel to Easy Reading Selections in English). (gr. 9-11). 1971. pap. text ed. 2.75 (ISBN 0-88345-117-4, 17986); tapes o.p. 35.00 (ISBN 0-685-19799-9); cassettes 40.00 (ISBN 0-685-19800-6). Regents Pub.

--Oral Pattern Drills in Fundamental English. (gr. 9 up). 1963. pap. text ed. 3.50 (ISBN 0-88345-124-7, 17410); with cassettes 70.00 (ISBN 0-685-04777-6). Regents Pub.

--Practical Guide to the Teaching of English As a Foreign Language. 1975. pap. text ed. 3.25 (ISBN 0-88345-244-8, 18132). Regents Pub.

--Practice Exercises in Everyday English. (Orig.). (gr. 9 up). 1957. pap. text ed. 2.95 (ISBN 0-88345-131-X, 17414); answer key 1.00 (ISBN 0-685-19801-4). Regents Pub.

--Regents English Workbooks, 3 Bks. (gr. 6 up). 1956-1969. pap. text ed. 2.95 ea.; Bk. 1. pap. text ed. (ISBN 0-88345-139-5, 17420); Bk. 2. pap. text ed. (ISBN 0-88345-140-9, 17421); Bk. 3. pap. text ed. (ISBN 0-88345-141-7, 17742); answer key 1.25 (ISBN 0-685-19803-0). Regents Pub.

Dixson, Robert J. & Boggs, Ralph S. English Step by Step with Pictures. rev. ed. (Illus., Orig.). (gr. 4 up). 1971. pap. text ed. 2.45 o.p. (ISBN 0-88345-046-1, 17978). Regents Pub.

Dixson, Robert J., jt. auth. see Angel, Juvenal L.

Dixson, Robert J., jt. auth. see Clarey, Elizabeth M.

Dixson, Robert J., jt. auth. see Clarey, M. Elizabeth.

Dixson, Robert J., ed. see Cooper, James F.

Dixson, Robert J., ed. see Crane, Stephen.

Dixson, Robert J., ed. see Eggleston, Edward.

Dixson, Robert J., ed. see Harte, Bret.

Dixson, Robert J., ed. see Hawthorne, Nathaniel.

Dixson, Robert J., ed. see Howells, William D.

Dixson, Robert J., ed. see James, Henry.

Dixson, Robert J., ed. see Poe, Edgar A.

Dixson, Robert J., ed. see Twain, Mark.

Dizenfeld, Bruce, et al, eds. see UCLA Moot Court Honors Program.

Dizeno, Patricia. Why Me? The Story of Jenny. (gr. 7 up). 1976. pap. 1.50 (ISBN 0-380-00563-8, 41269). Avon.

Dizikes, John. Britain, Roosevelt & the New Deal: British Opinion, 1932-1938. Freidel, Frank, ed. LC 78-63282. (Modern American History Ser.: Vol. 7). 200p. 1979. lib. bdg. 30.00 (ISBN 0-8240-3631-X). Garland Pub.

Djamour, Judith. Malay Kinship & Marriage in Singapore. (Monographs on Social Anthropology: No. 21). (Orig.). 1959. pap. text ed. 10.50x (ISBN 0-485-19621-2, Athlone Pr). Humanities.

--Muslim Matrimonial Court in Singapore. (Monographs on Social Anthropology: No. 31). 1966. text ed. 20.75x (ISBN 0-485-19531-3, Athlone Pr). Humanities.

Djerassi, Norma L. Glimpses of China from a Galloping Horse (a Woman's Journal). LC 74-19098. 1975. 9.00 (ISBN 0-08-018215-1). Pergamon.

Djilas, Milovan. Tito: The Story from Inside. 1980. 9.95 (ISBN 0-686-68552-0). HarBraceJ.

--Under the Colors. LC 76-134576. 1971. 9.75 o.p. (ISBN 0-15-153470-5). HarBraceJ.

--Wartime. LC 80-16174. 1980. 7.95 (ISBN 0-15-694712-9, Harv). HarBraceJ.

Djordjevic, Dimitrije, ed. The Creation of Yugoslavia, Nineteen Fourteen to Nineteen Eighteen. LC 79-22331. 256p. 1980. text ed. 19.50 (ISBN 0-87436-253-9). ABC-Clio.

Djordjevic, Dmitrije & Fischer-Galati, Stephen. The Balkan Revolutionary Tradition. LC 80-24039. 272p. 1981. 17.50x (ISBN 0-231-05098-4). Columbia U Pr.

Djung, Lu-Dzai. History of Democratic Education in Modern China. (Studies in Chinese History & Civilization). 258p. 1977. Repr. of 1934 ed. 19.00 (ISBN 0-89093-080-5). U Pubns Amer.

Dlab, V. & Gabriel, P., eds. Representation Theory I. (Lecture Notes in Mathematics Ser.: Vol. 831). 373p. 1981. pap. 22.00 (ISBN 0-387-10263-9). Springer-Verlag.

--Representation Theory II. (Lecture Notes in Mathematics: Vol. 832). 673p. 1981. pap. 40.20 (ISBN 0-387-10264-7). Springer-Verlag.

Dlugacz, Dorothy H., jt. auth. see Carter, Mildred C.

Dlugatch, Irving. Dynamic Cost Reduction. LC 78-21078. (Systems & Controls for Financial Management Ser.). 1979. 29.50 (ISBN 0-471-03565-3, Pub. by Wiley-Interscience). Wiley.

Dlugosch, Sharon. Table Setting Teachers Manual. 1980. 7.00 (ISBN 0-918420-02-4). Brighton Pubns.

Dlugosch, Sharon & Battcher, Joyce. Food Processor Recipes for Conventional & Microwave Cooking. LC 78-74899. 1979. pap. 3.50 (ISBN 0-918420-03-2); pap. 12.00 tchrs' manual (ISBN 0-918420-04-0). Brighton Pubns.

Dluhy, Robert. Maritime Dictionary: Covering Shipbuilding, Shipping, Marine Engineering & Related Fields, 2 vols. 3rd enl. ed. Incl. Vol. 1. (Ger. -Eng.). 1967. 60.00x (ISBN 0-8002-1299-1); Vol. 2. (Eng. -Ger.). 1968. LC 74-357050. 60.00x (ISBN 0-8002-1300-9). Intl Pubns Serv.

Dmytryshyn, Basil. A History of Russia. (Illus.). 1977. 19.95 (ISBN 0-13-392134-4). P-H.

--U.S.S.R. A Concise History. 3rd ed. LC 77-17636. (Illus.). 1978. 12.95x (ISBN 0-684-15277-0, ScribC); pap. text ed. 10.95x (ISBN 0-684-15278-9, ScribC). Scribner.

Doan, Eleanor. Bible Word Search Puzzles, No. 2. (Fun-to-Learn Ser.). 96p. (Orig.). 1980. pap. 1.75 (ISBN 0-310-23812-9). Zondervan.

--A Mother's Sourcebook of Inspiration. Orig. Title: A Sourcebook for Mothers. 192p. 1972. padded cover, gift-boxed 11.95 (ISBN 0-310-23740-8). Zondervan.

Doan, Eleanor, ed. Bible Story Picture Book. LC 73-152801. (ps-3). 1972. 5.95 o.s.i. (ISBN 0-8307-0093-5, 5103509). Regal.

Doan, Eleanor, compiled by. Your Treasury of Inspiration. rev. ed. 216p. 1980. gift ed. 9.95 (ISBN 0-310-23790-4, 9525). Zondervan.

Doan, Robert L. Early Childhood Achievement Units. Incl. Language Development Achievement Activities: Bk. 1. (ISBN 0-87628-281-8); Arts & Crafts Achievement Activities: Bk. 2. (ISBN 0-87628-282-6); Number Readiness Achievement Activities: Bk. 3. (ISBN 0-87628-283-4); Body Management Achievement Activities: Bk. 4. (ISBN 0-87628-284-2); Science Discovery Achievement Activities: Bk. 5. (ISBN 0-87628-285-0); Social Development Achievement Activities: Bk. 6. (ISBN 0-87628-286-9). 1979. 5.95x ea. Ctr Appl Res.

Doane, Alger N. Genesis A. LC 77-77437. 1978. 40.00 (ISBN 0-299-07430-7). U of Wis Pr.

Doane, D. Howard. Vertical Farm Diversification. (Illus.). 184p. 1950. 6.95 o.p. (ISBN 0-8061-0218-7). U of Okla Pr.

Doane, Doris C., et al. How to Read Tarot Cards. LC 67-19976. (Funk & W Bk.). (Illus.). 1968. pap. 2.95 o.p. (ISBN 0-308-90086-3, F57, TYC-T). T Y Crowell.

Doane, Gilbert H. & Bell, James B. Searching for Your Ancestors: The How & Why of Geneaology. 5th ed. 1980. 10.95 (ISBN 0-8166-0934-9). U of Minn Pr.

Doane, Jim. Great Smoky Mountains Picture Book. Castaldo, George, ed. (Color Pictorial of Great Smoky Mountains Ser.: No. 1). (Illus.). 72p. (Orig.). 1981. price not set (ISBN 0-936672-13-7); pap. price not set (ISBN 0-936672-14-5). Aerial Photo.

--North Carolina: From the Mountains to the Sea. LC 80-80955. 72p. 1980. 10.95 (ISBN 0-936672-01-3); pap. text ed. 7.50 (ISBN 0-936672-00-5). Aerial Photo.

Dobb, Maurice. On Economic Theory & Socialism: Collected Papers. 1965. Repr. of 1955 ed. 26.00x (ISBN 0-7100-1283-7). Routledge & Kegan.

--Soviet Economic Development Since 1917. 6th ed. 1966. pap. 16.00 (ISBN 0-7100-4658-8). Routledge & Kegan.

--Studies in the Development of Capitalism. rev. ed. LC 74-13744. (Orig.). 1964. 7.50 o.p. (ISBN 0-7178-0198-5); pap. 3.95 (ISBN 0-7178-0197-7). Intl Pub Co.

--Theories of Value & Distribution Since Adam Smith. LC 72-88619. (Illus.). 264p. 1973. 35.50 (ISBN 0-521-20100-4); pap. 13.95 (ISBN 0-521-09936-6). Cambridge U Pr.

--Welfare Economics & the Elements of Socialism. LC 69-16280. (Illus.). 1969. 41.50 (ISBN 0-521-07462-2); pap. 13.95x (ISBN 0-521-09937-4). Cambridge U Pr.

Dobb, Maurice, ed. see Marx, Karl.

Dobb, Maurice H. Capitalist Enterprise & Social Progress. LC 79-1577. 1981. Repr. of 1925 ed. 27.50 (ISBN 0-88355-883-1). Hyperion Conn.

Dobbert, John A. If Being a Christian Is So Great, Why Do I Have the Blahs? LC 79-65420. 160p. 1980. pap. 3.95 (ISBN 0-8307-0729-8, 5413206). Regal.

Dobbins, G. S. Aprenda a Ser Lider. Molina, S. P., tr. from Eng. Orig. Title: Learning to Lead. 126p. (Span.). Date not set. pap. price not set (ISBN 0-311-17013-7). Casa Bautista.

Dobbins, Gaines. Zest for Living. LC 76-48526. 1977. 5.95 o.p. (ISBN 0-87680-511-X, 80511). Word Bks.

Dobbins, Gaines S. Ministering Church. LC 60-9530. 1960. 7.50 (ISBN 0-8054-2505-5). Broadman.

Dobbins, Richard A. Atmospheric Motion & Air Pollution: An Introduction for Students of Engineering & Science. LC 79-952. (Environmental Science & Technology: Texts & Monographs). 1979. 32.50 (ISBN 0-471-21675-5, Pub. by Wiley-Interscience). Wiley.

Dobbs, Betty J. The Foundation of Newton's Alchemy; or, "the Hunting of the Greene Lyon". LC 74-31795. (Illus.). 320p. 1976. 47.50 (ISBN 0-521-20786-X). Cambridge U Pr.

Dobbs, Brian & Dobbs, Judy. Dante Gabriel Rossetti: An Alien Victorian. 1977. text ed. 20.75x (ISBN 0-685-02497-0). Humanities.

Dobbs, Frank W. Age of the Molecule: Chemistry in the World & Society. 337p. 1976. text ed. write for info. (ISBN 0-06-041659-9, HarpC); instructor's manual free (ISBN 0-06-361640-8). Har-Row.

Dobbs, J. B., jt. auth. see Fiske, Roger.

Dobbs, Jeannine, et al. Three Some Poems. LC 75-23819. 88p. 1976. pap. 4.95 (ISBN 0-914086-11-1). Alicejamesbooks.

Dobbs, Judy, jt. auth. see Dobbs, Brian.

Dobbs, Rose, ed. see Grimm Brothers.

Dobelis, M. C. Anonymous & Pseudononymous Publications of Twentieth Century Authors. Date not set. 16.95x (ISBN 0-918230-06-3). Barnstable.

Dobell, Bertram. Catalogue of Books Printed for Private Circulation. LC 66-25693. 1966. Repr. of 1906 ed. 15.00 (ISBN 0-8103-3303-1). Gale.

Dobelstein, A. Politics, Economics, & the Public Welfare. 1980. 15.95 (ISBN 0-13-683979-7). P-H.

Dobereiner, Peter. The Game with the Hole in It. (Illus.). 1970. 4.95 o.p. (ISBN 0-571-08923-2, Pub. by Faber & Faber); pap. 3.95 (ISBN 0-571-10421-5). Merrimack Bk Serv.

--Golf Explained: How to Take Advantage of the Rules. LC 76-51177. 9.95 (ISBN 0-8069-4110-3); lib. bdg. 9.29 (ISBN 0-8069-4111-1); PLB write for info. Sterling.

Doberer, Kurt K. The Goldmakers: Ten Thousand Years of Alchemy. Dickes, E. W., tr. LC 79-8605. Repr. of 1948 ed. 29.50 (ISBN 0-404-18465-0). AMS Pr.

Doberstein, John W., jt. ed. see Lehmann, Helmut T.

Doberstein, John W., tr. see Girgensohn, Herbert.

Doberstein, John W., tr. see Lehmann, Helmut T. & Doberstein, John W.

Doberstein, Richard. Regulations Made Easy for Commercial Pilots. (Illus.). Date not set. pap. 4.95x (Pub. by Simplified). Aviation.

--Regulations Made Easy for Instrument Pilots. (Illus.). Date not set. pap. 4.95x (Pub. by Simplified). Aviation.

--Regulations Made Easy for Private Pilots. (Illus.). Date not set. pap. 4.95x (Pub. by Simplified). Aviation.

Dobie, Elliott V., jt. ed. see Krapp, George P.

Dobie, J. F. The Flavor of Texas. 176p. (YA) 1975. 12.50 (ISBN 0-8363-0130-7). Jenkins.

Dobie, J. Frank. The Ben Lilly Legend. (Illus.). 253p. 1981. pap. 6.95x (ISBN 0-292-70728-2). U of Tex Pr.

--Coronado's Children: Tales of Lost Mines & Buried Treasures of the Southwest. (Barker Texas History Center Ser.: No. 3). (Illus.). 1978. 9.95 (ISBN 0-292-71050-X). pap. 5.95 (ISBN 0-292-71052-6). U of Tex Pr.

--Cow People. (Illus.). 317p. 1981. pap. 6.95 (ISBN 0-292-71060-7). U of Tex Pr.

--The Longhorns. LC 79-67706. (Illus.). 405p. 1980. pap. 7.95 (ISBN 0-292-74627-X). U of Tex Pr.

--Up the Trail from Texas. (Landmark Ser, No. 60). (Illus.). (gr. 7-9). 1955. PLB 4.39 o.p. (ISBN 0-394-90360-9). Random.

--Voice of the Coyote. LC 49-8879. (Illus.). 1961. pap. 3.95 (ISBN 0-8032-5050-9, BB 109, Bison). U of Nebr Pr.

Dobie, J. Frank, jt. auth. see Goddard, Ruth.

Dobie, J. Frank, ed. Puro Mexicano. LC 35-1517. (Texas Folklore Society Publication Ser.: No. 12). 272p. 1980. Repr. of 1935 ed. 7.95 (ISBN 0-87074-041-5). SMU Press.

Dobie, J. Frank, et al, eds. In the Shadow of History. (Texas Folklore Society Publication Ser.: No. 25). 192p. 1980. Repr. of 1939 ed. 6.95 (ISBN 0-87074-173-X). SMU Press.

Dobie, M. R., tr. see Grenier, Albert.

Dobin, Abraham. Fertile Fields: Recollections & Reflections of a Busy Life. LC 74-290. (Illus.). 480p. 1975. 8.95 o.p. (ISBN 0-498-01545-9). A S Barnes.

Dobinson, B., et al. The Determination of Epoxide Groups. 1969. 19.50 (ISBN 0-08-012788-6). Pergamon.

Dobkin, Alexander. Principles of Figure Drawing. LC 74-16373. (Funk & W Bk.). (Illus.). 272p. 1975. 10.00 o.s.i. (ISBN 0-308-10084-0, TYC-T). T Y Crowell.

Dobkins, David H. & Kneller, Richard. Workbook for Speech Fundamentals. 128p. 1980. pap. text ed. 5.25 (ISBN 0-8403-2257-7). Kendall-Hunt.

Doble, Henry P., Jr. Medical Office Design, Territory & Conflict. 320p. 1981. 36.50 (ISBN 0-87527-243-6). Green.

Dobler, Lavinia & Brown, William A. Great Rulers of the African Past. LC 65-17230. pap. 2.50 (ISBN 0-385-03845-3, 27, Zenith). Doubleday.

Dobler, Lavinia G. & Toppin, Edgar A. Pioneers & Patroits: The Lives of Six Negroes of the Revolutionary Era. LC 65-17241. (gr. 6-12). pap. 2.50 o.p. (ISBN 0-385-04191-8, Z6, Zenith). Doubleday.

Dobler, Max. Ionophores & Their Structure. 350p. 1981. 35.00 (ISBN 0-471-05270-1, Pub. by Wiley-Interscience). Wiley.

Doblhofer, W. Voices in Stone. 1971. pap. 2.95 o.s.i. (ISBN 0-02-046150-X, Collier). Macmillan.

Doblin, Alfred. Men Without Mercy. Blewitt, Trevor & Blewitt, Phyllis, trs. from Ger. LC 75-31978. 446p. 1976. Repr. of 1937 ed. 19.75 (ISBN 0-86527-277-8). Fertig.

Dobos, et al. Family Portrait. 1977. pap. text ed. 6.95x o.p. (ISBN 0-534-00560-8). Wadsworth Pub.

--Family Portrait. alternate ed. 1978. pap. text ed. 6.95x o.p. (ISBN 0-534-00691-4). Wadsworth Pub.

Dobos, David E., et al. Family Portrait: A Study of Contemporary Life Styles. 2nd alt. ed. 192p. 1980. pap. text ed. 6.95x (ISBN 0-534-00876-3). Wadsworth Pub.

--Family Portrait: A Study of Contemporary Life Styles. 2nd ed. 264p. 1980. pap. text ed. 6.95x (ISBN 0-534-00874-7). Wadsworth Pub.

Dobree, Alfred. Japanese Sword Blades. 3rd ed. LC 72-161471. (Illus.). 71p. 1971. softbound 6.00 o.p. (ISBN 0-87387-034-4). Shumway.

Dobree, Bonamy. English Literature in the Early Eighteenth Century, 1700-1740. (Oxford History of English Literature Ser.). 1959. 37.50x (ISBN 0-19-812205-5). Oxford U Pr.

--Three Eighteenth Century Figures: Sarah Churchill, John Wesley, Giacomo Casanova. LC 80-19398. xi, 248p. 1981. Repr. of 1962 ed. lib. bdg. 25.00x (ISBN 0-313-22682-2, DOTF). Greenwood.

Dobree, Bonamy, jt. auth. see Manwaring, George E.

Dobree, Bonamy, ed. see Pope, Alexander.

Dobree, Bonamy, ed. see Radcliffe, Ann.

Dobree, Bonamy, et al, eds. see Blackstone, Bernard.

Dobree, Bonamy, et al, eds. see Bloomfield, Paul.

Dobree, Bonamy, et al, eds. see Bradbrook, M. C.

Dobree, Bonamy, et al, eds. see Coghill, Nevill.

Dobree, Bonamy, et al, eds. see Doughty, Oswald.

Dobree, Bonamy, et al, eds. see Henderson, Philip.

Dobree, Bonamy, et al, eds. see Muir, Kenneth.

Dobree, Bonamy, et al, eds. see Swan, Michael.

Dobretsov, L. N. & Gomoyunova, M. V. Emission Electronics. 44.95 (ISBN 0-470-21680-8). Halsted Pr.

Dobrian, Walter A. & Jeffers, Coleman R., eds. Spanish Readings for Conversation. (Orig., Prog. Bk., Span). 1970. pap. text ed. 8.80 (ISBN 0-395-04367-0). HM.

Dobrin, Arnold. Irish. LC 75-10053. (Illus.). 64p. (gr. 2-5). 1976. 6.95 o.s.i. (ISBN 0-8027-6225-5); PLB 6.85 o.s.i. (ISBN 0-8027-6230-1). Walker & Co.

--Jillions of Gerbils. LC 72-11502. (Fun-To-Read Bk.). (Illus.). (gr. 1-4). 1973. 6.95 o.p. (ISBN 0-688-40051-5); PLB 6.67 (ISBN 0-688-50051-X). Lothrop.

--Make a Witch, Make a Goblin: A Book of Halloween Crafts. LC 77-177. (Illus.). 128p. (gr. 2-5). 1977. 7.95 (ISBN 0-590-07450-4, Four Winds). Schol Bk Serv.

Dobrin, Arthur. Gentle Spears. Barkan, Stanley H., ed. (Cross-Cultural Review Chapbook 3). 16p. 1980. pap. 2.00 (ISBN 0-89304-802-X). Cross Cult.

--Little Heroes. (Ethical Humanist Society Monograph: No. 1). (Illus.). 1977. pap. 2.50x (ISBN 0-89304-200-5, CCC111). Cross Cult.

--Sunbird. 64p. signed ed. 15.00 (ISBN 0-89304-046-0); pap. 3.95 (ISBN 0-89304-012-6). Cross Cult.

Dobrin, Arthur, ed. Lace: Poetry from the Poor, the Homeless, the Aged, the Physically & Emotionally Disabled. 96p. 15.00 (ISBN 0-89304-036-3); pap. 7.95 (ISBN 0-89304-037-1). Cross Cult.

Dobroliubov, Nikolai A. Selected Philosophical Essays. Finberg, J., tr. LC 79-2899. 659p. 1981. Repr. of 1956 ed. 42.50 (ISBN 0-8305-0070-7). Hyperion Conn.

Dobrovol'Skii, Andreevich. Prepodobny Feodor, Igumen Studiisky, 2 vols. in 1. LC 80-2355. 1981. Repr. of 1913 ed. 115.00 (ISBN 0-404-18907-5). AMS Pr.

Dobry, Ricardo, jt. ed. see O'Neill, Michael W.

Dobrzynski, Judith H. Fasting. LC 78-26063. 1979. 7.95 (ISBN 0-671-18408-3); pap. 3.95 (ISBN 0-671-18355-9). Sovereign Bks.

Dobschiner, Johanna R., tr. Destinada a Viver. (Portugese Bks.). (Port.). 1979. 1.60 (ISBN 0-8297-0655-0). Life Pubs Intl.

Dobschutz, E. Von see Von Dobschutz, E.

Dobson, Austin. Collected Poems. 567p. 1980. Repr. of 1907 ed. lib. bdg. 25.00 (ISBN 0-89984-151-1). Century Bookbindery.

--Samuel Richardson. LC 67-23877. 1968. Repr. of 1902 ed. 15.00 (ISBN 0-8103-3055-5). Gale.

--Thomas Bewick & His Pupils. LC 69-17340. 1968. Repr. of 1884 ed. 15.00 (ISBN 0-8103-3523-9). Gale.

Dobson, Christopher. Black September: Its Short, Violent History. Griffin, H. W., ed. (Illus.). 160p. 1974. 11.95 (ISBN 0-02-531900-0). Macmillan.

Dobson, Danae. Woof! 1979. 4.95 (ISBN 0-8499-0142-1). Word Bks.

Dobson, Edward D. Commodities: A Chart Anthology. rev. ed. LC 79-112544. (Illus.). 1979. 3 ring looseleaf bdg 26.50 (ISBN 0-934380-00-7). Traders Pr.

--Commodity Spreads: A Historical Chart Perspective, 2 vols. LC 79-112547. (Illus.). 1979. Set. 3 ring looseleaf bdg. 22.50 (ISBN 0-934380-00-7). Traders Pr.

Dobson, Eileen. New Zealand Ways with Flowers. 84p. 1980. pap. 4.50 (ISBN 0-85467-012-2, Pub. by Viking Sevenseas New Zealand). Intl Schol Bk Serv.

Dobson, James. Emotions: Can You Trust Them? LC 79-91703. 144p. 1980. text ed. 6.95 (ISBN 0-8307-0730-1, 5109108). Regal.

Dobson, James, tr. Atrevete a Disciplinar. (Spanish Bks.). (Span.). 1978. 1.90 (ISBN 0-8297-0499-X). Life Pubs Intl.

--Dr. Dobson Fala Sobre Amor, Ira. (Portugese Bks.). (Port.). 1979. write for info. (ISBN 0-8297-0674-7). Life Pubs Intl.

--La Felicidad Del Nino. (Spanish Bks.). (Span.). 1978. 1.90 (ISBN 0-8297-0893-6). Life Pubs Intl.

--Ouse Disciplinar. (Portuguese Bks.). 1979. 1.45 (ISBN 0-8297-0768-9). Life Pubs Intl.

Dobson, Julia M. & Hawkins, Gerald S. Conversation in English: Professional Careers. (Illus.). 108p. (gr. 9-12). 1978. pap. text ed. 3.96 (ISBN 0-278-46440-8). Litton Educ Pub.

Dobson, Julia M. & Sedwick, Frank. Conversation in English: Points of Departure. 2nd ed. (Illus.). 112p. 1981. pap. text ed. 3.80 (ISBN 0-278-46430-0). Litton Educ Pub.

Dobson, R. B. Durham Priory, Fourteen Hundred to Fourteen Fifty. LC 72-89809. (Studies in Medieval Life & Thought). 390p. 1973. 53.95 (ISBN 0-521-20140-3). Cambridge U Pr.

Dobson, William. The Child Player. (Orig.). 1981. pap. 1.95 (ISBN 0-451-09604-5, J9604, Sig). NAL.

--Fangs. (Orig.). 1980. pap. 1.95 (ISBN 0-451-09346-1, J9346, Sig). NAL.

Dobyns, Henry F. From Fire to Flood: Historic Human Destruction of Sonoran Desert Riverine Oases. (Anthropological Papers Ser.: No. 20). (Illus.). 222p. (Orig.). 1981. pap. 11.95 (ISBN 0-87919-092-2). Ballena Pr.

--Hualapai Indians, Vol. 1: Prehistoric Indian Occupation Within the Eastern Area of the Yuman Complex: a Study in Applied Archaeology. (American Indian Ethnohistory Ser: Indians of the Southwest). (Illus.). lib. bdg. 42.00 (ISBN 0-8240-0722-0). Garland Pub.

--Indians of the Southwest: A Critical Bibliography. LC 80-8036. (The Newberry Library Center for the History of the American Indian Bibliographical Ser.). 176p. 1980. pap. 4.95x (ISBN 0-253-35110-3). Ind U Pr.

Dobyns, Henry F. & Doughty, Paul L. Peru: A Cultural History. LC 76-9224. (Latin American Histories). (Illus.). 1976. 15.95x (ISBN 0-19-502089-8); pap. 5.95x (ISBN 0-19-502091-X). Oxford U Pr.

Dobyns, Henry F., et al, eds. Peasants, Power, & Applied Social Change: Vicos As a Model. LC 76-162437. 1971. 17.50x (ISBN 0-8039-0049-X). Sage.

Dobyns, Stephen. Heat Death. LC 79-55592. 1980. 10.00 (ISBN 0-689-11034-0); pap. 5.95 (ISBN 0-689-11063-4). Atheneum.

Dobzhansky, Theodosius. Dobzhansky's Genetics of Natural Populations: I-XLIII. Lewontin, R. C., et al, eds. 1024p. 1981. 42.50x (ISBN 0-231-05132-8). Columbia U Pr.

--Genetics & the Origin of Species. 3rd ed. 1951. pap. 7.50x (ISBN 0-231-08551-6). Columbia U Pr.

--Genetics of the Evolutionary Process. LC 72-127363. 1971. 22.50x (ISBN 0-231-02837-7); pap. 10.00x (ISBN 0-231-08306-8). Columbia U Pr.

Dobzhansky, Theodosius, jt. ed. see Ayala, Francisco.

Dobzhansky, Theodosius, et al. Evolution. LC 77-23284. (Illus.). 1977. text ed. 25.95x (ISBN 0-7167-0572-9). W H Freeman.

Do Carmo, Pamela B. & Patterson, Angelo T. First Aid Principles & Procedures. (Illus.). 256p. 1976. pap. text ed. 8.95 (ISBN 0-13-317933-8). P-H.

Dock, V. Thomas & Essick, Edward. Principles of Business Data Processing. 4th ed. 512p. 1980. text ed. 15.95 (ISBN 0-574-21295-7, 13-4295); instr's guide avail. (ISBN 0-574-21296-5, 13-4296); transparency masters 30.00 (ISBN 0-574-21303-1, 13-4303); study guide 5.95 (ISBN 0-574-21297-3). SRA.

--Principles of Business Data Processing: (with MIS Including BASIC) 4th ed. 1980. text ed. 16.95 (ISBN 0-574-21305-8, 13-4305); instructor's guide avail. (ISBN 0-574-21301-5); study guide 5.95 (ISBN 0-574-21302-3, 13-4303). SRA.

Dock, William. Prevention of Obstruction of Coronary & Vital Arteries. new ed. 316p. 1981. 38.50 (ISBN 0-87527-202-9). Green.

Dockar-Drysdale, Barbara. Therapy in Child Care: Collected Papers. (Papers on Residential Work Ser.: No. 3). (Orig.). 1974. pap. text ed. 4.00x (ISBN 0-582-42854-8). Humanities.

Dockeray, James C., jt. auth. see Husband, William H.

Dockery, F. A., jt. auth. see Whittle, Elizabeth.

Dockhorn, Robert J., jt. auth. see Speer, Frederic.

Docking, Jim. Controlling Discipline in Schools. 1980. text ed. 18.35 (ISBN 0-06-318152-5, IntlDept); pap. text ed. 10.45 (ISBN 0-06-318153-3). Har-Row.

Dockrell, W. B., et al. School & After: A European Symposium. (General Ser.). 1978. pap. text ed. 27.00x (ISBN 0-85633-169-4, NFER). Humanities.

Dockrill, M. L., jt. auth. see Lowe, C. J.

Dockrill, Michael & Gould, Douglas. Peace Without Promise: Britain & the Peace Conferences 1919-1923. 320p. 1981. 25.00 (ISBN 0-208-01909-X, Archon). Shoe String.

Dockstader, Fred J. The American Indian in Graduate Studies: A Bibliolgrapy of Theses & Dissertations, 2 vols, Vol. 25. 1973. Set. pap. 18.00 (ISBN 0-934490-06-6); Vol. 1. pap. 10.00 (ISBN 0-934490-07-4); Vol. 2. pap. 10.00 (ISBN 0-934490-08-2). Mus Am Ind.

Dockstader, Frederick J. Weaving Arts of the North American Indian. LC 78-381. (Illus.). 1978. 25.00 (ISBN 0-690-01739-1, TYC-T). T Y Crowell.

Docs, Diane L. Visual Defects. (Illus.). 1978. 20.00 (ISBN 0-685-89697-8). Dayton Labs.

Doctor, Adi H. Sarvodaya: A Political & Economic Study. 1968. 7.25x (ISBN 0-210-22653-6). Asia.

Doctorow, E. L. Loon Lake. LC 79-5526. 1980. 12.95 (ISBN 0-394-50691-X); limited ed. 35.00 (ISBN 0-394-51176-X). Random.

--Ragtime. 384p. 1980. pap. 2.95 (ISBN 0-553-14128-7). Bantam.

--Welcome to Hard Times. 224p. 1975. 8.95 (ISBN 0-394-49833-X); pap. 3.95 (ISBN 0-394-73107-7). Random.

Doctors, Samuel, et al. Curriculum Development for Public Management Innovation. LC 80-39481. 160p. 1981. text ed. 20.00 (ISBN 0-89946-079-8). Oelgeschlager.

Doczi, Gyorgy. The Power of Limits: Proportional Harmony in Art, Architecture, Nature, & Man. LC 77-90883. (Illus.). 224p. 1981. 19.95 (ISBN 0-394-51352-5); pap. 9.95 (ISBN 0-394-73580-3). Shambhala Pubns.

Dod, Charles. Electoral Facts from 1832-1853, Impartially Stated. A Complete Political Gazetteer. Hanham, H. J., ed. 388p. 1972. Repr. of 1853 ed. 25.00x (ISBN 0-8476-6051-6). Rowman.

Dodd & White. Cognition: Mental Structures & Processes. 500p. 1980. text ed. 17.95 (ISBN 0-205-06930-4, 7969309). Allyn.

Dodd, A. H. Life in Wales. 1972. 19.95 (ISBN 0-7134-1463-4, Pub. by Batsford England). David & Charles.

--A Short History of Wales: Welsh Life & Customs. 1977. pap. 11.95 (ISBN 0-7134-1466-9, Pub. by Batsford England). David & Charles.

Dodd, C. H. The Apolistic Preaching & Its Developments: Three Lectures with an Appendix on Eschatology & History. (Twin Brooks Ser.). 96p. 1980. pap. 4.95 (ISBN 0-8101-2404-1). Baker Bk.
--Democracy & Development in Turkey. 1980. text ed. 27.50 (ISBN 0-906719-01-1); pap. text ed. 13.75x (ISBN 0-906719-00-3). Humanities.
--Politics & Government in Turkey. LC 78-85453. 1969. 20.00x (ISBN 0-520-01430-8). U of Cal Pr.
Dodd, Charles H. Bible Today. 1946-1960. 19.95 (ISBN 0-521-04844-3); pap. 7.50 (ISBN 0-521-09118-7, 118). Cambridge U Pr.
--Founder of Christianity. LC 73-90222. 1970. pap. 3.95 (ISBN 0-02-084640-1). Macmillan.
--Historical Tradition in the Fourth Gospel. 1975. 64.00 (ISBN 0-521-04847-8); pap. 14.95x (ISBN 0-521-29123-2). Cambridge U Pr.
--Interpretation of the Fourth Gospel. 59.50 (ISBN 0-521-04848-6); pap. text ed. 13.95x (ISBN 0-521-09517-4, 517). Cambridge U Pr.
--The Parables of the Kingdom. LC 80-8420. 160p. 1981. pap. cancelled o.p. (ISBN 0-06-061932-5, HarpR). Har-Row.
Dodd, Edward. Polynesia's Sacred Isle. LC 75-26513. (The Ring of Fire Ser.: Vol. 3). (Illus.). 1976. 10.00 (ISBN 0-396-07227-5). Dodd.
Dodd, Edward, ed. see Martin, Henry B.
Dodd, Erica Cruikshank. Byzantine Silver Stamps. LC 61-16953. (Dumbarton Oaks Studies: Vol. 7). (Illus.). 238p. 1961. 15.00 o.p. (ISBN 0-88402-007-X, Ctr Byzantine). Dumbarton Oaks.
Dodd, K. N. Teach Yourself Data Processing. 1976. pap. 2.95 o.p. (ISBN 0-679-10379-1). McKay.
Dodd, Lawrence C., ed. Texas Monthly's Political Reader. 2nd ed. 264p. 1980. pap. 8.00 (ISBN 0-932012-09-4). Texas Month Pr.
Dodd, Lynley. The Nickle Nackle Tree. LC 77-12493. (Illus.). (gr. k-3). 1978. 8.95 (ISBN 0-02-732610-1, 73261). Macmillan.
Dodd, Marjorie L. Heavenly Bits of Specialness. Van Dolson, Bobbie J., ed. (Illus.). (gr. k-3). 1976. pap. 1.50 (ISBN 0-8280-0048-4). Review & Herald.
Dodd, Marylin J. Oncology Nursing Case Studies. 1978. spiral bdg. 10.50 (ISBN 0-87488-044-0). Med Exam.
Dodd, Robert J. & Stanton, Robert J., Jr. Paleoecology, Concepts &Applications. LC 80-19623. 500p. 1981. 32.95 (ISBN 0-471-04171-8, Pub. by Wiley-Interscience). Wiley.
Dodd, W. A., jt. auth. see Cameron, J.
Dodd, W. F. Revision & Amendment of State Constitutions. LC 73-120854. (American Constitutional & Legal History Ser). 1970. Repr. of 1910 ed. lib. bdg. 35.00 (ISBN 0-306-71959-2). Da Capo.
Dodd, Wayne. A Time of Hunting. LC 75-4779. 128p. (gr. 6 up). 1975. 6.95 (ISBN 0-395-28903-3, Clarion). HM.
Dodd, William. Factory System Illustrated. LC 67-28260. (Illus.). Repr. of 1842 ed. 24.00x (ISBN 0-678-05043-0). Kelley.
Doddridge, Joseph. Notes, on the Settlement & Indian Wars, of the Western Parts of Virginia & Pennsylvania, from the Year 1763 Until the Year 1783 Inclusive. LC 75-7062. (Indian Captivities Ser.: Vol. 40). 1977. Repr. of 1824 ed. lib. bdg. 44.00 (ISBN 0-8240-1664-5). Garland Pub.
Doddridge, Philip. The Rise & Progress of Religion in the Soul. (Summit Bks). 1977. pap. 2.95 (ISBN 0-8010-2875-2). Baker Bk.
--Some Remarkable Passages in the Life of the Honourable Col. James Gardiner, 1747. Shugrue, Michael F., ed. (The Flowering of the Novel, 1740-1775 Ser: Vol. 19). 1974. lib. bdg. 50.00 (ISBN 0-8240-1118-X). Garland Pub.
Dodds, E. R., jt. ed. see MacNeice, Louis.
Dodds, E. R., ed. see Plato.
Dodds, E. R., tr. see Proclus.
Dodds, Gordan B. Hiram Martin Chittenden: His Public Career. LC 72-91664. 232p. 1973. 14.00x (ISBN 0-8131-1283-4). U Pr of Ky.
Dodds, Gordon B. Oregon: A History. (States & the Nation Ser.). (Illus.). 1977. 12.95 (ISBN 0-393-05632-5, Co-Pub. by AASLH). Norton.
Dodds, J. C., jt. auth. see Bridge, J.
Dodds, Robert H. Writing for Technical & Business Magazines. LC 70-93486. (Human Communications Ser). 1969. 14.95 o.p. (ISBN 0-471-21725-5, Pub. by Wiley-Interscience). Wiley.
Doderidge, Esme. The New Gulliver. LC 79-63120. 220p. 1980. pap. 3.95 (ISBN 0-8008-5507-8, Pivot). Taplinger.
Dodge & Safonov. Eye of the Peacock. (YA) 5.95 (ISBN 0-685-07432-3, Avalon). Bouregy.
Dodge, Alice M. Girl in Exile. (YA) 1969. 5.95 (ISBN 0-685-07435-8, Avalon). Bouregy.
Dodge, B. F. Industrial Marketing. 1970. text ed. 18.95 o.p. (ISBN 0-07-017301-X, C). McGraw.
Dodge, Bertha S. The Road West: Saga of the Thirty Fifth Parallel. LC 79-21051. (Illus.). 222p. 1980. 15.95 (ISBN 0-8263-0526-1). U of NM Pr.
Dodge, C. W. Some Lichens of Tropical Africa V: Lecanoraceae to Physiaceae. 1971. pap. 50.00 (ISBN 3-7682-5438-0). Lubrecht & Cramer.
Dodge, Calvert R., ed. A Nation Without Prisons. LC 74-16928. (Illus.). 1976. 21.95 (ISBN 0-669-96438-7). Lexington Bks.
Dodge Cost Information Systems Division. Dodge Construction Systems Costs, 1980. 262p. 1979. pap. 39.80 (ISBN 0-07-017331-1, P&RB). McGraw.
--Dodge Guide to Public Works & Heavy Construction Costs, 1980. 232p. 1979. pap. 28.80 o.p. (ISBN 0-07-017332-X, P&RB). McGraw.
--Dodge Guide to Public Works & Heavy Construction Costs, 1981. 232p. 1981. 31.80 (ISBN 0-07-017326-5). McGraw.
--Dodge Manual for Building Construction Pricing & Scheduling, 1980. 292p. 1979. pap. 39.80 (ISBN 0-07-017330-3, P&RB). McGraw.
--Dodge Manual for Building Construction Pricing & Scheduling, 1981. 292p. 1981. 29.80 (ISBN 0-07-017328-1). McGraw.
Dodge, D. & Baird, D. H., eds. Continuities & Discontinuities in Political Thought. LC 74-16197. 1975. text ed. 14.95 (ISBN 0-470-21744-8); pap. text ed. 9.95x (ISBN 0-470-21745-6). Halsted Pr.
Dodge, D. O., jt. auth. see Kyriss, S. E.
Dodge, Daniel, jt. auth. see Griffen, Edmund.
Dodge, Ernest S. Morning Was Starlight: My Maine Boyhood. LC 80-82791. (Illus.). 224p. 1981. price not set (ISBN 0-87106-049-3); pap. 8.95 (ISBN 0-87106-047-7). Globe Pequot.
--The Polar Rosses. (Great Travellers Ser.). (Illus.). 1973. 6.95 o.p. (ISBN 0-571-08914-3, Pub. by Faber & Faber). Merrimack Bk Serv.
Dodge, Guy H., ed. Jean-Jacques Rousseau: Authoritarian Libertarian? LC 77-158944. (Problems in Political Science Ser.). 1971. pap. text ed. 2.95x o.p. (ISBN 0-669-74534-0). Heath.
Dodge, Harold F. & Romig, Harry G. Sampling Inspection Tables: Single & Double Sampling. 2nd ed. LC 59-6763. (Ser. in Probability & Mathematical Statistics). (Illus.). 1959. 32.95 (ISBN 0-471-21747-6, Pub. by Wiley-Interscience). Wiley.
Dodge, James W., ed. The Case for Foreign Language Study: A Collection of Readings. 52p. 1971. pap. 2.00x o.p. (ISBN 0-915432-01-3). NE Conf Teach Foreign.
--Other Words, Other Worlds: Language in Culture. 1972. pap. 7.95x (ISBN 0-915432-72-2). NE Conf Teach.
--Sensitivity in the Foreign Language Classroom. Incl. Individualization of Instruction. Gougher, Ronald L; Interaction in the Foreign Language Class. Moskowitz, Gertrude; Teaching Spanish to the Native Spanish Speaker. LaFontaine, Herman. 142p. 1973. pap. 7.95x (ISBN 0-915432-73-0). NE Conf Teach Foreign.
Dodge, Jane. New Macreme. (Step by Step Craft Ser.). Date not set. pap. 2.95 (ISBN 0-307-42023-X, Golden Pr). Western Pub.
Dodge, Mary L. Sticks & Stones. (Orig.). 1979. pap. 1.75 (ISBN 0-532-23279-8). Manor Bks.
Dodge, Philip R., et al. Nutrition & the Developing Nervous System. (Illus.). 538p. 1975. 60.00 o.p. (ISBN 0-8016-1392-2). Mosby.
Dodge, Plunkett, tr. see Kravette, Steve.
Dodge, R. & Lindblom, P. Of Time & Experience: Literary Themes. 1972. pap. 11.95 (ISBN 0-87626-630-8, 630). P-H.
Dodge, R. V. Rails of the Silver Gate. LC 75-97231. (Illus.). 144p. 1975. 15.95 (ISBN 0-87095-019-3). Golden West.
Dodge, Raymond. Conditions & Consequences of Human Variability. 1931. 32.50x (ISBN 0-685-69812-2). Elliots Bks.
Dodge, Raymond & Kahn, Eugen. The Craving for Superiority. 1931. 24.50 (ISBN 0-686-51366-5). Elliots Bks.
Dodge, Richard H. How to Read & Write in College: A Complete Course, 5 forms. (Orig.). pap. text ed. 10.95 scp ea. (ISBN 0-686-66443-4, HarpC); Form 2. pap. text ed. (ISBN 0-06-041661-0); Form 3. pap. text ed. (ISBN 0-06-041662-9); Form 4. pap. text ed. (ISBN 0-06-041663-7); Form 5. pap. text ed. (ISBN 0-06-041664-5). Form 6 (ISBN 0-06-041657-2). Part 1. achievement tests & short quizzes avail. (ISBN 0-06-361687-4). Part 2 (ISBN 0-06-361688-2). Har-Row.
Dodge, Tom. A Literature of Sports. 1980. pap. text ed. 9.95 (ISBN 0-669-02744-8). Heath.
Dodge, Yadolah, jt. auth. see Arthanari, Subramanvam.
Dodgson, Charles L. The Diaries of Lewis Carroll, 2 vols. Green, Roger L., ed. & suppl. by. LC 74-110268. (Illus.). Repr. of 1954 ed. lib. bdg. 33.00x (ISBN 0-8371-4494-9, DOLC). Greenwood.
--Lewis Carroll Picture Book: A Selection from the Unpublished Writings & Drawings of Lewis Carroll, Together with Reprints from Scare & Unacknowledged Work. LC 70-159931. (Tower Bks). (Illus.). 1971. Repr. of 1899 ed. 18.00 (ISBN 0-8103-3915-3). Gale.
Dodgson, Charles L. see Carroll, Lewis, pseud.
Dodgson, John, jt. auth. see Pryke, Richard.
Dods, M. Genesis. (Handbooks for Bible Classes Ser.). 224p. Repr. of 1956 ed. 3.50 (ISBN 0-567-08101-X). Attic Pr.
--Haggai, Zachariah, Malachi. (Handbooks for Bible Classes Ser.). 153p. Repr. of 1956 ed. 3.50 (ISBN 0-567-08109-5). Attic Pr.
Dods, Marcus. The Prayer That Teaches Us to Pray. LC 80-82323. (Shepherd Classic Ser.). 1980. pap. 5.95 (ISBN 0-87983-232-0). Keats.
Dodson. How to Grandparent. 1981. 8.95 (ISBN 0-686-69161-X). Lippincott & Crowell.
Dodson, Carolyn, ed. see Meketa, Charles & Meketa, Jacqueline.
Dodson, Daniel B. Looking for Zoe. LC 80-16930. 340p. 1981. 12.95 (ISBN 0-396-07878-8). Dodd.
--Malcolm Lowry. LC 70-126542. (Columbia Essays on Modern Writers Ser.: No. 51). (Orig.). 1970. pap. 2.00 (ISBN 0-231-03244-7, MW51). Columbia U Pr.
Dodson, Fitzhugh. How to Grandparent. 1981. 10.95 (ISBN 0-690-01874-6, H&R). Lippincott.
--How to Parent. 444p. 1973. pap. 2.95 (ISBN 0-451-09401-8, E9401, Sig). NAL.
Dodson, Fitzhugh & Reuben, Paula. The Carnival Kidnap Caper. LC 79-20260. (gr. 5-9). 1979. 7.95 (ISBN 0-916392-40-6). Oak Tree Pubns.
Dodson, Fitzhugh & Ruben, Paula. How to Grandparent. LC 80-7849. 304p. 1981. 12.95 (ISBN 0-690-01874-6, HarpT). Har-Row.
Dodson, Guy, et al, eds. Structural Studies on Molecules of Biological Interest: A Volume in Honour of Professor Dorothy Hodgkin. (Illus.). 400p. 1981. 115.00 (ISBN 0-19-855362-5). Oxford U Pr.
Dodson, Norman E. Math Poetry & Stuff. 1981. 5.95 (ISBN 0-8062-1618-2). Carlton.
Dodson, Owen. Powerful Long Ladder. 103p. 1970. 4.95 (ISBN 0-374-23668-2); pap. 1.95 o.p. (ISBN 0-374-50880-1, N395). Fs&G.
Dodson, Reynolds, jt. auth. see Baginski, Frank.
Dodson, Reynolds, jt. auth. see Rosenblatt, Seymour.
Dodson, Rita. Life, Love & God. Date not set. 4.95 (ISBN 0-533-04647-5). Vantage.
Dodson, Sam. I, Victoria. 1979. pap. 1.95 o.p. (ISBN 0-449-14152-7, GM). Fawcett.
--Sausalito. 1978. pap. 1.95 o.p. (ISBN 0-449-13940-9, GM). Fawcett.
Dodson, Susan. The Creep. LC 79-1102. 224p. (gr. 7 up). 1979. 7.95 (ISBN 0-590-07599-3, Four Winds). Schol Bk Serv.
Dodsworth, T. L. Beef Production. 100p. 1972. text ed. 18.75 (ISBN 0-08-017016-1); pap. text ed. 7.75 (ISBN 0-08-017017-X). Pergamon.
Dodwell, Peter C. Perceptual Processing: Stimulus, Equivalence & Pattern Recognition. (Century Psychology Ser.). (Illus.). 1981. Repr. of 1971 ed. text ed. 24.50x (ISBN 0-8290-0063-1). Irvington.
Dody, Sandford, jt. auth. see Hayes, Helen.
Doe, Jane. Alcoholism - One Family's Story. 1978. pap. 2.50 (ISBN 0-8309-0231-7). Herald Hse.
Doe, Paul. Tallis. 2nd ed. (Oxford Studies of Composers). (Illus.). 1976. pap. 7.95x (ISBN 0-19-314122-1). Oxford U Pr.
Doebele-Fluegel, Verena. Motivgeschichtliche Untersuchung Zur Deutschen Literatur, Insbesondere Zur Deutschen Lyrik. 1977. 57.65x (ISBN 3-11-005909-6). De Gruyter.
Doebelin, E. O. System Dynamics: Modeling & Response. LC 77-187802. 448p. 1972. 26.95x (ISBN 0-675-09120-9). Merrill.
Doebelin, Ernest O. System Modeling & Response: Theoretical & Experimental Approaches. LC 79-27609. 587p. 1980. text ed. 26.95 (ISBN 0-471-03211-5). Wiley.
Doebler, John, ed. see Beaumont, Francis.
Doeff, Annick M., jt. auth. see Barker, William F.
Doehring, Donald O., ed. Geomorphology in Arid Regions. (Binghamton Symposia in Geomorphology: International Ser.: No. 8). (Illus.). 276p. 1980. text ed. 20.00x (ISBN 0-04-551041-5, 2508). Allen Unwin.
Doel, Van Den H. see Van Den Doel, H.
Doelp, Alan, jt. auth. see Franklin, Jon.
Doenecke, Justus D. The Presidencies of James A. Garfield & Chester A. Arthur. LC 80-18957. (The American Presidency Ser.). 232p. 1981. 15.00x (ISBN 0-7006-0208-9). Regents Pr KS.
Doenecke, Justus D., compiled by. The Diplomacy of Frustration: The Manchurian Crisis of 1931-1933 As Revealed in the Paper of Stanley K. Hornbeck. (Publication Ser.: No. 231). 1981. 22.95 (ISBN 0-8179-7311-7). Hoover Inst Pr.
Doerffler, Alfred. The Burden Made Light. abr. ed. LC 74-34213. 128p. 1981. pap. 4.95 (ISBN 0-570-03026-9, 6-1154). Concordia.
--Open the Meeting with Prayer. LC 55-7442. 1955. 3.25 (ISBN 0-570-03147-8, 12-2531). Concordia.
--Treasures of Hope. 1945. pap. 6.95 (ISBN 0-570-03763-8, 12-2697). Concordia.
--The Yoke Made Easy. LC 75-2344. 128p. 1974. pap. 4.95 (ISBN 0-570-03027-7, 6-1155). Concordia.
Doerflinger, William. Magic Catalogue: A Guide to the World of Magic. 1977. 19.95 (ISBN 0-87690-272-7); pap. 9.95 o.p. Dutton.
Doerflinger, William, ed. see Dunham, Terry B., et al.
Doerig, J. A. Marx Vs. Russia. LC 62-12958. 1962. pap. 1.95 (ISBN 0-8044-6123-6). Ungar.
Doering, Charles, tr. see Karlson, P.
Doering, David & Doering, Susan. California Fractional Gold. (Illus.). 1980. lib. bdg. 60.00 (ISBN 0-686-64452-2). S J Durst.
Doering, George G. & Jensen, Harlan E. Clinical Dermatology of Small Animals: A Stereoscopic Presentation. LC 73-14545. 1973. 61.50 o.p. (ISBN 0-8016-1404-X). Mosby.
Doering, Henry, ed. The World Almanac Book of Buffs, Masters, Mavens & Uncommon Experts. LC 80-81179. 352p. (Orig.). 1980. pap. 6.95 (ISBN 0-911818-13-8). World Almanac.
Doering, Susan, jt. auth. see Doering, David.
Doering, Susan G., jt. auth. see Entwisle, Doris B.
Doeringer, Peter B. & Piore, Michael J. Internal Labor Markets & Manpower Analysis. 1971. 13.95 (ISBN 0-669-63529-4). Lexington Bks.
Doeringer, Peter B., ed. Workplace Perspectives on Education & Training. (Boston Studies in Applied Economics). 184p. 1981. lib. bdg. 17.50 (ISBN 0-89838-054-5, Pub. by Martinus Nijhoff). Kluwer Boston.
Doeringer, Suzannah, et al, eds. Art & Technology: A Symposium on Classical Bronzes. 1970. 15.00 (ISBN 0-262-04030-1). MIT Pr.
Doerksen, Vernon C., rev. by see Thiessen, Henry C.
Doerkson, Margaret. Jazzy. 272p. 1981. 11.95 (ISBN 0-8253-0039-8). Beaufort Bks NY.
Doermann, Humphrey. Crosscurrents in College Admissions. LC 68-54672. 1970. text ed. 10.25x (ISBN 0-8077-1249-3). Tchrs Coll.
Doern, G. Bruce. Canadian Nuclear Policies. 1980. pap. text ed. 14.95x (ISBN 0-920380-25-5, Pub. by Inst Res Pub Canada). Renouf.
--Government Intervention in the Canadian Nuclear Industry. 1980. pap. text ed. 8.95x (ISBN 0-920380-46-8, Pub. by Inst Res Pub Canada). Renouf.
Doern, G. Bruce & Maslove, Allan M. Public Evaluation of Government Spending. 192p. 1979. pap. text ed. 10.95x (ISBN 0-920380-19-0, Pub. by Inst Res Pub Canada). Renouf.
Doerner, Klaus. Madness & Modern Society. Steinberg, Jean, tr. 1981. 17.50 (ISBN 0-916354-42-3); pap. 8.95 (ISBN 0-916354-54-7). Urizen Bks.
Doerr, Carol. Microcomputers & the Three R's. 1979. pap. 8.85x (ISBN 0-8104-5113-1). Hayden.
Doerr, Jerry, jt. auth. see Lewis, Theodore.
Doerries, Hermann. Constantine & Religious Liberty. 1960. 29.50x (ISBN 0-686-51363-0). Elliots Bks.
Doerter, Jim. All the Times (The East-West Chronicles) (Illus.). 1980. pap. 7.00 (ISBN 0-913232-69-6). W Kaufmann.
Doesschate, G. Ten. Perspective: Fundamentals, Controversials, History. 1964. text ed. 25.75x (ISBN 90-6004-042-2). Humanities.
Doessel, D. P., jt. auth. see Bulter, J. R.
Doetsch, Raymond N. Journey to the Green & Golden Lands: The Epic of Survival on the Wagon Trail. 1976. 11.50 (ISBN 0-8046-9142-8, Natl U). Kennikat.
Doezema, Linda P., ed. Dutch Americans: A Guide to Information Sources. LC 79-13030. (Ethnic Studies Information Guide Ser.: Vol. 3). 1979. 30.00 (ISBN 0-8103-1407-X). Gale.
Doezema, Marianne & Hargrove, June. Public Monument & Its Audience. LC 77-25428. (Themes in Art Ser.). (Illus.). 76p. 1977. pap. 4.95x (ISBN 0-910386-38-2, Pub. by Cleveland Mus Art). Ind U Pr.
Doggett, G. The Electronic Structure of Molecules: Theory & Application to Inorganic Molecules. 1972. 49.00 (ISBN 0-08-016588-5). Pergamon.
Dogin, Yvette. Help Yourself to a Job, 3 pts. (Illus.). (gr. 7 up). Set. text ed. 6.75 (ISBN 0-912486-00-7); Pt. 1, 1977. text ed. 2.25 (ISBN 0-912486-32-5); Pt. 2, 1976. text ed. 2.25 (ISBN 0-912486-02-3); Pt. 3, 1978. text ed. 2.25 (ISBN 0-912486-03-1). Finney Co.
--Lots of Things, 2 Vols. (Illus.). (gr. 4 up). Set. wkbk 4.50 (ISBN 0-912486-04-X); Bk. 1, 1978. wkbk 2.25 (ISBN 0-912486-37-6); Bk. 2, 1972. wkbk. 2.25 (ISBN 0-912486-06-6). Finney Co.

Dogramaci, Ali & Adam, Nabil R. Aggregate & Industry-Level Productivity Analysis. (Productivity Analysis Studies: Vol. 2). 204p. 1981. lib. bdg. 25.00 (ISBN 0-89838-037-5, Pub. by Martinus Nijhoff). Kluwer Boston.

Dohanian, Diran D. The Mahayana Buddhist Sculpture of Ceylon. LC 76-23613. (Outstanding Dissertations in the Fine Arts). (Illus.). 1977. Repr. of 1964 ed. lib. bdg. 48.00 (ISBN 0-8240-2685-3). Garland Pub.

Doherty, Cecelia & Ilyin, Donna. Technical Manual for ELSA: English Language Skills Assessment in a Reading Context. (ELSA Tests Ser.). 1981. pap. text ed. 3.95 (ISBN 0-686-69474-0). Newbury Hse.

Doherty, Donna M. The Boatcook. (Illus.). 1979. pap. 4.50 o.p. (ISBN 0-915160-05-6). McKay.

Doherty, G. D., ed. Aspects of Science Fiction. (gr. 9 up). 1959. pap. 4.95 (ISBN 0-7195-2215-3). Transatlantic.

Doherty, Grace, jt. auth. see Abraham, Henry J.

Doherty, J. K. Track & Field Omnibook. 3rd ed. (Illus.). 1980. 16.95x (ISBN 0-911520-99-6). Tafnews.

Doherty, James, jt. auth. see Hickey, Denis.

Doherty, Linda. Tempo Word Finds, No. 4. 128p. (gr. 4 up). 1981. pap. 1.25 (ISBN 0-448-05572-4, Tempo). G&D.

--Tempo Word Finds: No. 5. (No. 5). 128p. (gr. 6 up). 1981. pap. 1.50 (ISBN 0-448-05567-8, Tempo). G&D.

Doherty, Michael E. & Shemberg, Kenneth M. Asking Questions About Behavior: An Introduction to What Psychologists Do. 2nd ed. 1978. pap. 6.95x (ISBN 0-673-15043-7). Scott F.

Doherty, Neil. Insurance Pricing & Loss Prevention. 1976. 17.95 (ISBN 0-347-01097-0, 00308-5, Pub. by Saxon Hse). Lexington Bks.

Doherty, P. D., jt. auth. see Martin, J. W.

Doherty, Paul. Atlas of the Planets. LC 80-12347. (Illus.). 144p. 1980. 16.95 (ISBN 0-07-017341-9, GB). McGraw.

Doherty, R. D., jt. auth. see Martin, J. W.

Doherty, Robert E., jt. auth. see Aboud, Grace S.

Doherty, Robert E., jt. ed. see Adler, Joseph.

Doi, Mary L., et al. Pacific-Asian American Research: An Annotated Bibliography. (Orig.). 1981. pap. write for info. (ISBN 0-934584-11-7). Pacific-Asian.

Doi, Teruo & Shattuck, Warren L., eds. Patent & Know-How Licensing in Japan & the United States. LC 76-7785. (Asian Law Ser.: No.5). 444p. 1977. 30.00 (ISBN 0-295-95513-9). U of Wash Pr.

Doig, Carol, jt. auth. see Doig, Ivan.

Doig, Desmond. Mother Teresa: Her Work & Her People. LC 75-39857. (Illus.). 176p. 1980. pap. 9.95 (ISBN 0-06-061941-4, HarpR). Har-Row.

Doig, Ivan & Doig, Carol. News: A Consumer's Guide. (Illus.). 256p. 1972. pap. text ed. 6.95 o.p. (ISBN 0-13-615617-7). P-H.

Doig, Jameson W. Metropolitan Transportation Politics & the New York Region. LC 66-16768. (Metropolitan Politics Ser.). (Illus.). 1966. 22.50x (ISBN 0-231-02791-5). Columbia U Pr.

Doig, Jameson W., jt. auth. see Mann, Dean E.

Doig, William B. & Montford, Alison. Medical Paediatrics. (Modern Practical Nursing Ser: No. 1). (Illus.). 1972. pap. text ed. 9.95x (ISBN 0-433-07694-1). Intl Ideas.

Doiron, Claude J. Laboratory Exercises in Earth Science. 1978. pap. text ed. 7.50 (ISBN 0-8403-1132-X). Kendall-Hunt.

Doiron, Joyce. It's About Love. 1981. 4.95 (ISBN 0-8062-1610-7). Carlton.

Doise, W. & Douglas, G. Groups & Individuals. LC 77-84800. (Illus.). 1978. 29.95 (ISBN 0-521-21953-1); pap. 8.95x (ISBN 0-521-29320-0). Cambridge U Pr.

Doj, A. R. Hadith: An Introduction. 1980. pap. 4.95 (ISBN 0-686-64661-4). Kazi Pubns.

Dokey, Richard. The Crazy Woman of Wales Hotel. (Short Story Discovery Ser.). pap. 5.00 (ISBN 0-933906-12-9). Gusto Pr.

--Sanchez & Other Stories. (Regional Ser.). 125p. (Orig.). 1981. pap. 4.75 (ISBN 0-933906-14-5). Gusto Pr.

Doksum, K. A., jt. auth. see Bickel, P. J.

Doktor, Robert H. & Moses, Michael A. Managerial Insights: Analysis, Decisions, & Implementation. (Illus.). 432p. 1973. pap. text ed. 11.95 (ISBN 0-13-550103-2). P-H.

Dokulil, M., et al, eds. Shallow Lakes: Contributions to Their Limnology. (Developmrnts in Hydrobiology Ser.: No. 3). 218p. 1981. PLB 59.50 (ISBN 0-686-28842-4, Pub. by W. Junk). Kluwer Boston.

Dolan. The Bermuda Triangle & Other Mysteries of Nature. (Triumph Bks.). 1980. PLB 6.90 (ISBN 0-531-04113-1, A23). Watts.

Dolan, C. Terrence, ed. Subcutaneous Mycoses. (Atlases of Clinical Mycology: 5). 1976. text & slides 78.00 (ISBN 0-89189-043-2, 15-7-009-00); microfiche ed. 22.00 (ISBN 0-89189-091-2, 17-7-009-00). Am Soc Clinical.

--Superficial Mycoses. (Atlases of Clinical Mycology: 4). 1975. text & slides 78.00 (ISBN 0-89189-042-4, 15-7-005-00); microfiche ed. 22.00 (ISBN 0-89189-090-4, 17-7-005-00). Am Soc Clinical.

--Systemic Mycoses: Deep Seated. (Atlases of Clinical Mycology: 2). (Illus.). 1975. text & slides 78.00 (ISBN 0-89189-040-8, 15-7-003-00); microfiche ed. 22.00 (ISBN 0-89189-089-0, 17-7-003-00). Am Soc Clinical.

--Systemic Mycoses: Opportunistic Pathogens. (Atlases of Clinical Mycology: 3). 1975. text & slides 78.00 (ISBN 0-89189-041-6, 15-7-004-00); microfiche ed. 22.00 (ISBN 0-89189-089-0, 17-7-004-00). Am Soc Clinical.

--Systemic Mycoses: Saprobic Fungi. (Atlases of Clinical Mycology: 6). (Illus.). 1976. text & slides 78.00 (ISBN 0-89189-044-0, 15-7-010-00); microfiche ed. 22.00 (ISBN 0-89189-092-0, 17-7-010-00). Am Soc Clinical.

--Systemic Mycoses: Yeasts. (Atlases of Clinical Mycology: 1). (Illus.). 1975. text & slides 78.00 (ISBN 0-89189-039-4, 15-7-002-00); microfiche ed. 22.00 (ISBN 0-89189-087-4, 17-7-002-00). Am Soc Clinical.

Dolan, Edward F. Let's Make Magic. LC 79-8014. (Illus.). 96p. (gr. 2-6). 1981. 7.95a (ISBN 0-385-15192-6); PLB (ISBN 0-385-15193-4). Doubleday.

Dolan, Edward F., Jr. Basic Football Strategy: An Introduction for Young Players. LC 76-3438. 144p. (gr. 5-9). 1976. 7.95a (ISBN 0-385-03998-0); PLB (ISBN 0-385-04184-5). Doubleday.

--The Complete Beginners Guide to Ice Skating. LC 73-10803. 192p. (gr. 5-9). 1974. 5.95 o.p. (ISBN 0-385-03779-1). Doubleday.

--The Complete Beginner's Guide to Magic. LC 76-56281. (gr. 4-7). 1977. PLB 6.95 (ISBN 0-385-11555-5). Doubleday.

--The Complete Beginnger's Guide to Making & Flying Kites. LC 75-36585. (gr. 4-7). 1977. PLB 6.95 (ISBN 0-385-04937-4). Doubleday.

--Explorers of the Arctic & Antarctic. (World in the Making Series). (Illus.). (gr. 7 up). 1968. 3.95g o.s.i. (ISBN 0-02-732630-6, CCPr). Macmillan.

--Gun Control: A Decision for Americans. LC 78-5576. (Impact Bks). (Illus.). (gr. 7 up). 1978. PLB 6.90 s&l (ISBN 0-531-02202-1). Watts.

--It Sounds Like Fun: How to Use & Enjoy Your Tape Recorder & Stereo. (Illus.). 192p. 1981. PLB price not set (ISBN 0-671-34053-0). Messner.

Dolan, Edward F., Jr. & Lyttle, Richard B. Archie Griffen. (Illus.). (gr. 4 up). 1978. pap. 1.25 (ISBN 0-671-78694-6). PB.

Dolan, Edward F., Jr. & Silver, H. T. William Crawford Gorgas: Warrior in White. LC 68-14243. (Illus.). (gr. 8 up). 1968. 4.50 (ISBN 0-396-05708-X). Dodd.

Dolan, Edwin, intro. by. The Foundations of Modern Austrian Economics. LC 76-5894. (Studies in Economic Theory). 238p. 1976. 12.00; pap. 4.95. NYU Pr.

Dolan, Edwin G. Basic Economics. 2nd ed. 736p. 1980. text ed. 20.95 (ISBN 0-03-050356-6). Dryden Pr.

--Basic Macroeconomics: Understanding National Income, Inflation & Unemployment. 400p. 1980. pap. text ed. 12.95 (ISBN 0-03-051276-X). Dryden Pr.

--Basic Microeconomics: Understanding Prices & Markets. 2nd ed. 400p. 1980. pap. text ed. 12.95 (ISBN 0-03-051281-6). Dryden Pr.

Dolan, Edwin G., jt. auth. see Goodman, John C.

Dolan, John P. Catholicism. LC 67-28536. (Orig.). 1968. text ed. 10.00 (ISBN 0-8120-6013-X); pap. text ed. 3.75 (ISBN 0-8120-0273-3). Barron.

Dolan, John P., jt. ed. see Jedin, Hubert.

Dolan, John P., tr. see Erasmus, Desiderius.

Dolan, Jonni. Two Crows Came. LC 80-18252. 156p. 1980. pap. 5.95 (ISBN 0-914718-53-3). Pacific Search.

Dolan, Josephine A. Nursing in Society: A Historical Perspective. 14th ed. LC 77-88313. (Illus.). 380p. 1978. 22.00 (ISBN 0-7216-3133-9). Saunders.

Dolan, Mike. Ziggy & His Friends. (Illus.). 1980. 7.95g (ISBN 0-516-09203-0). Childrens.

Dolan, Paul J., jt. auth. see Quinn, Edward G.

Dolan, Robert, jt. ed. see Fisher, John S.

Dolan, T. P., jt. ed. see Dunning, Thomas.

Dolan, Thomas J. Fusion Research, 2 vols. LC 80-18383. 1000p. Set. 100.01 (ISBN 0-08-025565-5); Vol. I. pap. 25.01 (ISBN 0-08-025566-3); Vol. II. pap. 25.01 (ISBN 0-08-025567-1). Pergamon.

Dolbeare. American Political Thought. 300p. 1981. text ed. price not set (ISBN 0-87872-276-9). Duxbury Pr.

Dolbeare, Kenneth M. & Edelman, Murray J. American Politics: Policies, Power, & Change. 3rd rev ed. 1979. pap. text ed. 12.95x o.p. (ISBN 0-669-01724-8); instr's manual o.p. (ISBN 0-669-00149-X). Heath.

--American Politics: Policies, Power, & Change. 4th ed. 592p. 1981. pap. text ed. 12.95 (ISBN 0-669-03348-0); student guide 5.95 (ISBN 0-669-03957-8); instructor's guide (ISBN 0-669-03701-X). Heath.

Dolbeare, Kenneth M., jt. auth. see Davis, James W., Jr.

Dolbeare, Kenneth M., ed. Public Policy Evaluation. LC 75-14631. (Sage Yearbooks in Politics & Public Policy: Vol. 2). 1975. 20.00x (ISBN 0-8039-0268-9); pap. 9.95x (ISBN 0-8039-0312-X). Sage.

Dolby, James R. Dare to Be You. Orig. Title: I, Too, Am Man. 1977. pap. 1.50 (ISBN 0-89129-207-1). Jove Pubns.

Dolby, William, tr. Eight Chinese Plays. 1978. 13.00x (ISBN 0-231-04488-7). Columbia U Pr.

Dolce, Ludovico. Transformationi. Orgel, Stephen, ed. LC 78-68191. (Philosophy of Images Ser.: Vol. 4). (Illus.). 1980. lib. bdg. 66.00 (ISBN 0-8240-3678-6). Garland Pub.

Dolce, Philip C., jt. ed. see Coppa, Frank J.

Dolce, Phillip C., ed. Suburbia: The American Dream & Dilemma. LC 76-2838. pap. 2.95 o.p. (ISBN 0-385-01336-1). Doubleday.

Dolci, Danilo. Creature of Creatures: Selected Poems. Vitiello, Justin, ed. (Stanford French & Italian Studies: Col. 22). Orig. Title: Creatura Di Creature, Poseie, 1949-1978. 136p. 1980. pap. 20.00 (ISBN 0-915838-17-6). Anma Libri.

Dolciani, Mary P. & Sorgenfrey, Robert H. Elementary Algebra for College Students. LC 78-146720. 1971. text ed. 14.95 o.p. (ISBN 0-395-12069-1); tchrs. guide. pap. 4.00 o.p. (ISBN 0-395-12071-3); answers to even-numbered problems 1.65 o.p. (ISBN 0-395-12070-5). HM.

Dolciani, Mary P., et al. Intermediate Algebra for College Students. LC 71-146721. 1971. text ed. 15.70 (ISBN 0-395-12072-1); tchrs. ed. & key 5.80 (ISBN 0-395-12074-8). HM.

--Modern Introductory Analysis. 2nd ed. (gr. 11-12). 1977. text ed. 16.28 (ISBN 0-395-25157-5); tchr's ed. 17.20 (ISBN 0-395-25158-3). HM.

Dold, A. Lectures on Algebraic Topology. (Grundlehren der Mathematischen Wissenschaften Ser.: Vol. 200). (Illus.). 377p. 1981. 38.00 (ISBN 0-387-10369-4). Springer-Verlag.

Dolder, Eugene J. & Durrer, Gustav T. The Bar Joint Denture. (Illus.). 150p. 1978. 42.00 (ISBN 0-931386-02-0). Quint Pub Co.

Dolejs, Ladislaw, jt. auth. see Sorm, Frantisek.

Dolejsi, Robert. Modern Viola Technique. LC 72-8343. (Music Ser). (Illus.). viii, 133p. 1973. Repr. of 1939 ed. lib. bdg. 21.50 (ISBN 0-306-70552-4). Da Capo.

Dolensek, Emil P. & Burn, Barbara. The Penguin Books of Pets: A Practical Guide to Animal Keeping. (Handbooks Ser). (Illus.). 1978. pap. 4.95 o.p. (ISBN 0-14-046318-6). Penguin.

Dolezal, Ivan. Asian & African Studies, Vol. 12. 1977. text ed. 11.75x (ISBN 0-7007-0101-X). Humanities.

Dolezal, Ivan, ed. Asian & African Studies, Vol. 15. 1980. text ed. 13.00x (ISBN 0-7007-0130-3). Humanities.

--Asian & African Studies, Vol. 16. 360p. 1980. text ed. 13.00x (ISBN 0-7007-0137-0). Humanities.

--Asian & African Studies, Vol. 14, No. 14. 1978. text ed. 13.00x (ISBN 0-7007-0121-4). Humanities.

--Asian & African Studies: 1972, Vol. 8. 360p. 1972. text ed. 9.00x (ISBN 0-7007-0040-4). Humanities.

Dolezal, R. & Varcop, L. Process Dynamics: Automatic Control of Steam Generation Plant. (Illus.). 1970. 70.80x (ISBN 0-444-20042-8). Intl Ideas.

Dolezelova-Velingerova, Milena, ed. The Chinese Novel at the Turn of the Century. (Modern East Asian Studies). 1980. 30.00x (ISBN 0-8020-5473-0). U of Toronto Pr.

Dolge, Alfred. Pianos & Their Makers. (Illus.). 581p. 1972. pap. 6.00 (ISBN 0-486-22856-8). Dover.

--Pianos & Their Makers: A Comprehensive History of the Development of the Piano from the Monochord to the Concert Grand Player Piano. (Illus.). 10.00 (ISBN 0-8446-4540-0). Peter Smith.

Dolgin, Janet L., et al, eds. Symbolic Anthropology, a Reader in the Study of Symbols & Meanings. LC 77-3176. 1977. text ed. 32.50x (ISBN 0-231-04032-6); pap. 13.50x (ISBN 0-231-04033-4). Columbia U Pr.

Dolgoff, Ralph, jt. ed. see Loewenberg, Frank.

Dolgoff, Sam, ed. The Anarchist Collectives: Workers' Self-Management in the Spanish Revolution (1936 to 1939) LC 73-88239. (Illus.). 160p. (Orig.). 1974. 10.00 (ISBN 0-914156-03-9); pap. 4.95 o.p. (ISBN 0-914156-02-0). Free Life.

Doling, J. F., jt. auth. see Hobbs, F. D.

Dolinsky, Mike. A Corporate Affair. (Orig.). 1981. pap. 2.95 (ISBN 0-440-11435-7). Dell.

Dolive, Linda L. Electoral Politics at the Local Level in the German Federal Republic. LC 76-26473. (U of Fla. Social Science Monographs: No. 56). (Illus.). 1976. pap. 4.00 (ISBN 0-8130-0554-X). U Presses Fla.

D'Olivier, Abbe Pierre. Essai Sur la Justice Primitive, Pour Servir de Principe Generateur au Seul Ordre Social Qui Peut Assurer a l'Homme Tous Ses Droits et Tous Sesmoyens de Bonheur. (Fr.). 1977. lib. bdg. 15.00x o.p. (ISBN 0-8287-0245-4); pap. text ed. 5.00x o.p. (ISBN 0-685-75748-X). Clearwater Pub.

Dolkart, Ronald, jt. ed. see Falcoff, Mark.

Doll, Edgar A. Measurement of Social Competence. (Illus.). 1953. 15.00 (ISBN 0-913476-09-9). Am Guidance.

Doll, John & George, Terry, eds. The On-Your-Own Guide to Asia: Budget Handbook to East & Southeast Asia, 1981-82. rev. ed. LC 77-90889. (Illus.). 1981. pap. 4.95 (ISBN 0-8048-1353-1). C E Tuttle.

Doll, John P. & Orazem, Frank. Production Economics: Theory with Applications. LC 76-41478. (Agricultural Economics Ser.). 1978. text ed. 21.50 (ISBN 0-88244-118-3). Grid Pub.

Doll, R., et al, eds. Cancer Incidence in Five Continents Vol. 1. 1966. 42.50 (ISBN 0-387-03475-7). Springer-Verlag.

Doll, Richard, ed. see Royal Society of London.

Doll, Ronald C. Curriculum Improvement: Decision Making & Process. 4th ed. 1978. text ed. 18.95 (ISBN 0-205-06046-3). Allyn.

Dollar, Alta, jt. auth. see Burnett, Mary J.

Dollar, C. M. America Changing Time: A Brief History. LC 80-10684. 729p. 1980. 12.95 (ISBN 0-471-06087-9). Wiley.

Dollar, Charles M. America, 2 vols. Incl. Vol. 1. Changing Times to 1877. 13.95 (ISBN 0-471-21767-0); study guide avail. (ISBN 0-471-05908-0); Vol. 2. Changing Times Since 1865. 13.95 (ISBN 0-471-04769-4); study guide avail. (ISBN 0-471-05907-2). LC 78-12242. 1979. Combined Ed. 19.95 (ISBN 0-471-05029-6); tchr's manual avail. (ISBN 0-471-04906-9). Wiley.

Dollarhide, Louis. Of Art & Artists. LC 80-52629. (Illus.). 168p. 1981. 24.95. Yoknapatawpha.

Dollberg, Donald D. & Verstuyft, Allen W., eds. Analytical Techniques in Occupational Health Chemistry. LC 79-28460. (ACS Symposium Ser.: No. 120). 1980. 28.00 (ISBN 0-8412-0539-6). Am Chemical.

Dollen, Charles J. Abortion in Context: A Select Bibliography. 1970. 10.00 (ISBN 0-8108-0337-2). Scarecrow.

Dollerup, Cay. Denmark, Hamlet & Shakespeare, 2 vols. (Salzburg Studies in English Literature, Elizabethan & Renaissance Studies Ser.: No. 47). 347p. (Orig.). 1975. Set. pap. text ed. 50.25x (ISBN 0-391-01363-7). Humanities.

Dollinger, Alfred. Six Language Dictionary of Welding Technique. LC 75-591161. 1974. 45.00x (ISBN 0-8002-0400-X). Intl Pubns Serv.

Dollinger, Johann J. Von. see Von Dollinger, Johann J.

Dolloff, Francis W. & Perkinson, Roy L. How to Care for Works of Art on Paper. (Illus.). 1971. pap. 2.00 (ISBN 0-87846-136-1). Mus Fine Arts Boston.

Dolman, Anthony J. & Ettinger, Jan Van, eds. Partners in Tomorrow: Strategies for a New International Order. 1978. 9.95 (ISBN 0-87690-294-8). Dutton.

Dolmetsch, Mabel. Personal Recollections of Arnold Dolmetsch. (Music Reprint Ser.). (Illus.). 1980. Repr. of 1957 ed. lib. bdg. 19.50 (ISBN 0-306-76022-3). Da Capo.

Dolney, Pam C., jt. auth. see Ito, Robert.

Dolphin, David. Vitamin B-Twelve, Vols. 1 & 2. 1070p. 1981. Set. 95.00 (ISBN 0-471-03655-2, Pub. by Wiley-Interscience). Wiley.

Dolphin, David, ed. The Porphyrins. Incl. Vol. 1, Pt. A. 59.00 (ISBN 0-12-220101-9); Physical Chemistry. Vol. 3, Pt. A. 71.00 (ISBN 0-12-220103-5); Vol. 4, Pt. B. 50.00 (ISBN 0-12-220104-3); Vol. 5, Pt. C. 57.50 (ISBN 0-12-220105-1). LC 77-14197. 1978-79. Acad Pr.

--The Porphyrins Vol. 6: Biochemistry Part A. 1979. 93.00 (ISBN 0-12-220106-X); 79.50 set (ISBN 0-12-220106-X). Acad Pr.

Dolphin, Lambert T. Que De las Drogas, el Ocultismo y la Astrologia? Swenson, Ana Maria, tr. 1977. Repr. of 1972 ed. 1.45 (ISBN 0-311-46034-8). Casa Bautista.

Dolson, Bobbie J. Van see Aaen, Bernhard.

Dolson, Bobbie J. Van see Degering, Etta B.

Dolson, Bobbie J. Van see Dodd, Marjorie L.

Dolson, Bobbie J. Van see Hills, Desmond B.

Dolson, Bobbie J. Van see Johnston, Madeline.

Dolson, Bobbie J. Van see Jones, Lucile.

Dolson, Bobbie J. Van see Loller, Sherry G.

Dolson, Bobbie J. Van see Osman, Jack & Van Dolson, Bobbie J.

Dolson, Bobbie J. Van see Parker, Lois M.

Dolson, Bobbie J. Van see Todd, Sharon.

Dolson, Bobbie J. Van see Willis, Mary.

Dolson, Frank. Always Young: A Biography. new ed. LC 75-20961. (Illus.). 206p. (Orig.). 1975. pap. 3.95 (ISBN 0-89037-072-9); handbk. 4.95 (ISBN 0-89037-073-7). Anderson World.

Doman, Bruce K. Goodbye Mommy. (The Gentle Revolution Ser.). (Illus.). 86p. 1977. 4.95 (ISBN 0-936676-00-0). Better Baby.

Doman, Glenn. How to Teach Your Baby How to Read. 160p. 1975. pap. 3.50 (ISBN 0-385-11161-4, Dolp). Doubleday.

--How to Teach Your Baby to Read. rev. ed. (The Gentle Revolution Ser.). 166p. 1979. Repr. of 1964 ed. 9.50 (ISBN 0-936676-01-9). Better Baby.

--Teach Your Baby to Read. 160p. 1980. 9.95 (ISBN 0-224-60064-8, Pub. by Chatto Bodley Jonathan); instruction kit 7.95 (ISBN 0-224-60081-8, Pub. by Chatto Bodley Jonathan). Merrimack Bk Serv.

--What to Do About Your Brain Injured Child. LC 72-92202. 312p. 1974. 9.95 (ISBN 0-385-02139-9). Doubleday.

Doman, Glenn & Armentrout, J. Michael. The Universal Multiplication of Intelligence. (The Gentle Revolution Ser.). 223p. 1980. 12.50 (ISBN 0-936676-02-7). Better Baby.

Doman, Glenn, et al. In a Word: --Answers to 1001 Questions Parents Ask About Their Brain-Injured Children. LC 75-36620. 8.95 o.p. (ISBN 0-385-09401-9). Doubleday.

Domandi, Mario, tr. see Cassirer, Ernst.

Domanska, Janina. The Best of the Bargain. LC 76-13010. (Illus.). (gr. k-3). 1977. 8.95 (ISBN 0-688-80062-9); PLB 8.59 (ISBN 0-688-84062-0). Greenwillow.

--Din Dan Don It's Christmas. LC 75-8509. (Illus.). 32p. (ps-3). 1975. 8.25 (ISBN 0-688-80003-3); PLB 7.92 (ISBN 0-688-84003-5). Greenwillow.

--I Saw a Ship A-Sailing. LC 75-185147. (Illus.). (ps-3). 1972. 8.95 (ISBN 0-02-732940-2). Macmillan.

--If All the Seas Were One Sea. (Illus.). (gr. k-3). 1971. 8.95 (ISBN 0-02-732930-5). Macmillan.

--King Krakus & the Dragon. LC 78-12934. (Illus.). (gr. k-3). 1979. 8.95 (ISBN 0-688-80189-7); PLB 8.59 (ISBN 0-688-84189-9). Greenwillow.

--Marilka. (Illus.). (gr. k-3). 1970. 4.95g o.s.i. (ISBN 0-02-732880-5). Macmillan.

--Spring Is. LC 75-25953. (Illus.). 32p. (gr. k-3). 1976. 8.25 (ISBN 0-688-80026-2); PLB 7.92 (ISBN 0-688-84026-4). Greenwillow.

--The Tortoise & the Tree. LC 77-14572. (Illus.). (gr. k-3). 1978. 8.95 (ISBN 0-688-80132-3); PLB 8.59 (ISBN 0-688-84132-5). Greenwillow.

--Turnip. LC 69-18235. (Illus.). (gr. k-3). 1969. 5.95g o.s.i. (ISBN 0-02-732810-4). Macmillan.

--What Do You See? LC 73-6052. (Illus.). 32p. (gr. k-2). 1974. 8.95 (ISBN 0-02-732830-9, 73283). Macmillan.

Domanska, Janina, adapted by. & illus. Little Red Hen. LC 72-92436. (Illus.). 32p. (ps-2). 1973. 8.95 (ISBN 0-02-732820-1). Macmillan.

Domany, Clara. Sweet Love, Bitter Honey. LC 78-66061. 1980. 7.95 (ISBN 0-533-04139-2). Vantage.

Domat, Jean. The Civil Law in Its Natural Order, 2 vols. Cushing, Luther S., ed. Strahan, William, tr. from Fr. 1763p. 1981. Repr. of 1850 ed. Set. lib. bdg. 97.50x (ISBN 0-8377-0511-8). Rothman.

Domatilla, John. The Last Crime. LC 80-20650. 1981. 8.95 (ISBN 0-689-11121-5). Atheneum.

Domb, C. & Green, M., eds. Phase Transitions & Critical Phenomena. Vol. 1. 1973. 72.00 (ISBN 0-12-220301-1); Vol. 2. 1972. 74.00 (ISBN 0-12-220302-X); Vol. 5a. 1976. 59.00 (ISBN 0-12-220305-4); Vol. 5B. 1976. 56.00 (ISBN 0-12-220351-8); Vol. 6. 1977. 79.50 (ISBN 0-12-220306-2). Acad Pr.

Dombal, F. T. De see De Dombal, F. T.

Dombal, Robert W. Residential Condominiums: A Guide to Analysis & Appraisal. 1976. pap. 10.00 (ISBN 0-911780-37-8). Am Inst Real Estate Appraisers.

Dombrosk, Stephen J., jt. auth. see Phillip, P. Joseph.

Dombroski, Robert S., ed. Critical Perspectives on the "Decameron". LC 76-24068. 1977. text ed. 16.50x o.p. (ISBN 0-06-491735-5). B&N.

Dombrowski, Daniel A. Plato's Philosophy of History. LC 80-5853. 225p. 1981. lib. bdg. 17.75 (ISBN 0-8191-1356-5); pap. text ed. 9.50 (ISBN 0-8191-1357-3). U Pr of Amer.

Domenet, J. G., jt. ed. see Mitchell, J. R.

Domer, Larry R., et al. Dental Practice Management: Concepts & Application. LC 80-15309. (Illus.). 376p. 1980. text ed. 32.50 (ISBN 0-8016-1422-8). Mosby.

Domes, Jurgen. China After the Cultural Revolution. Goodman, David, tr. from Ger. 1977. 21.50x (ISBN 0-520-03064-8). U of Cal Pr.

Domhoff, G. William, ed. Power Structure Research. (Sage Focus Editons: No. 17). (Illus.). 270p. 1980. 18.95x (ISBN 0-8039-1431-8); pap. 9.95x (ISBN 0-8039-1432-6). Sage.

Domingo, Xavier. The Dreams of Reason. Kemp, L., tr. LC 65-10198. 1966. 5.00 o.s.i. (ISBN 0-8076-0344-9). Braziller.

Domingos, J. J., et al, eds. Foundations of Continuum Thermodynamics. LC 74-23460. 337p. 1975. 42.95 (ISBN 0-470-21777-4). Halsted Pr.

Dominguez & Lemus. El Hijo Prodigo y Otros Dramas. 1977. pap. 0.75 (ISBN 0-311-07602-5). Casa Bautista.

Dominguez, G. S. Marketing in Regulated Environment. (Marketing Management Ser.). 341p. 1978. 26.95 (ISBN 0-471-02402-3). Wiley.

Dominguez, George S. Marketing in a Regulated Environment. LC 77-22099. (Marketing Management Ser.). 1978. 26.95 (ISBN 0-471-02402-3). Ronald Pr.

Dominguez, John R. Venture Capital. LC 73-11667. (Illus.). 224p. 1974. 18.95 (ISBN 0-669-86918-X). Lexington Bks.

Dominguez, Jorge I., et al. Enhancing Global Human Rights. (Illus.). 1979. text ed. 9.95 o.p. (ISBN 0-07-017397-4, P&RB); pap. text ed. 6.95 o.p. (ISBN 0-07-017398-2). McGraw.

Dominguez, Richard H. The Complete Book of Sports Medicine. (Encore Editions). (Illus.). 1979. 4.95 (ISBN 0-684-16896-0, ScribT). Scribner.

--Complete Book of Sports Medicine. 1980. pap. 4.95 (ISBN 0-446-97213-4). Warner Bks.

Dominian. Depression. 1976. pap. 2.95 o.p. (ISBN 0-531-06071-3, Fontana Pap). Watts.

Dominicis, jt. auth. see Sallese.

Domino, E. F., ed. PCP Phencyclidine: Historical & Current Perspectives. LC 80-81498. (Illus.). 300p. 1980. 30.00x (ISBN 0-916182-03-7). NPP Bks.

Dominowski, R. Research Methods. 1980. 18.95 (ISBN 0-13-774315-7). P-H.

Dominy, Eric. Judo: Self-Taught. (Everyday Handbook Ser.). (Illus.). 208p. 1976. pap. 1.95 o.p. (ISBN 0-06-463440-X). B&N.

--Karate: Self-Taught. (Everyday Handbook Ser.). (Illus.). 192p. 1976. pap. 1.95 o.p. (ISBN 0-06-463441-8). B&N.

Domjan, Evelyn A. Edge of Paradise: A Collection of Color Woodcuts. Emig, Jane, ed. LC 78-73442. (Illus.). 1979. 20.00x (ISBN 0-933652-14-3). Domjan Studio.

--Eternal Wool. Brogan, Peggy, ed. (Illus.). 160p. 1980. 25.00 (ISBN 0-933652-15-1). Domjan Studio.

Domjan, Evelyn A., jt. auth. see Domjan, Joseph.

Domjan, Joseph & Domjan, Evelyn A. Pacatus, a Trade-Mark from Antiquity. Emig, Jane, ed. LC 78-73444. (Illus.). 1979. 15.00 (ISBN 0-933652-13-5). Domjan Studio.

Domke, Martin, ed. International Trade Arbitration. LC 73-11852. 320p. 1974. Repr. of 1958 ed. lib. bdg. 25.00x (ISBN 0-8371-7075-3, DOTA). Greenwood.

Domning, Daryl. Sirenian Evolution in the North Pacific Ocean. (Publications in Geological Science Ser.: Vol. 118). 1978. 11.00x (ISBN 0-520-09581-2). U of Cal Pr.

Domsch, K. H. & Gams, W. Fungi in Agricultural Soils. Hudson, P. S., tr. from Ger. LC 72-3604. 1972. 24.50 o.p. (ISBN 0-470-21776-6). Halsted Pr.

Domstead, Mary M. From an Oilfield Brat to a Child of the King. 1981. 5.95 (ISBN 0-533-04913-X). Vantage.

Domville, Eric, ed. Editing British & American Literature: 1880-1920. LC 76-7323. (Conference on Editorial Problems Ser.). 1976. lib. bdg. 16.50 (ISBN 0-8240-2409-5). Garland Pub.

Don, Marvin, et al, eds. Self-Assessment of Current Knowledge in Family Practice. 2nd ed. 1976. pap. 14.50 (ISBN 0-87488-261-3). Med Exam.

Donabedian, Avedis. The Criteria & Standards of Quality, Vol. II. (Explorations in Quality Assessment & Monitoring Ser.). (Illus.). 420p. 1981. text ed. price not set (ISBN 0-914904-67-1); pap. text ed. price not set. Health Admin Pr.

--The Definition of Quality & Approaches to Its Assessment, Vol. 1. (Explorations in Quality Assessment & Monitoring Ser.). (Illus.). 180p. 1980. text ed. 17.95 (ISBN 0-914904-47-7); pap. text ed. 12.95 (ISBN 0-914904-48-5). Health Admin Pr.

Donabedian, Avedis, et al. Medical Care Chartbook. 7th ed. (Illus.). 420p. 1980. text ed. 42.50 (ISBN 0-914904-61-2); pap. 22.50 (ISBN 0-914904-62-0). Health Admin Pr.

Donagan, Alan. Theory of Morality. LC 76-25634. 1979. pap. 5.95 (ISBN 0-226-15567-6, P838, Phoen). U of Chicago Pr.

Donaghey, John. An Architect: The First Ten Years. LC 80-66726. (Illus.). 96p. (Orig.). (gr. 12). 1980. pap. text ed. 7.50 (ISBN 0-9604298-0-8). J Donaghey.

Donaghue, Carroll & Enger, Janice. The PET-CBM Personal Computer Guide. (Orig.). 1980. pap. 15.99 (ISBN 0-931988-30-6). Osborne-McGraw.

Donaghy, Henry J. James Clarence Mangan. (English Authors Ser.: No. 171). 1974. lib. bdg. 10.95 (ISBN 0-8057-1370-0). Twayne.

Donaghy, William, jt. auth. see Emmert, Philip.

Donahoe, John W. & Wessells, Michael G. Learning, Language, & Memory. (Illus.). 1979. text ed. 18.95 scp (ISBN 0-06-041685-8, HarpC); instructors manual free (ISBN 0-06-361699-8). Har-Row.

Donahue, Benedict. The Cultural Arts of Africa. LC 79-66646. (Illus.). 1979. pap. text ed. 9.50 (ISBN 0-8191-0845-6). U Pr of Amer.

Donahue, Bud. The Language of Layout. LC 78-6949. (Art & Design Ser.). 1978. 19.95 (ISBN 0-13-522953-7, Spec); pap. 9.95 (ISBN 0-13-522961-8). P-H.

Donahue, John R., jt. auth. see Sleeth, Ronald E.

Donahue, John R., ed. see Hamerton-Kelly, Robert.

Donahue, John R., ed. see Harrelson, Walter.

Donahue, John R., ed. see Harrington, Daniel J.

Donahue, John R., ed. see Johnson, Luke T.

Donahue, John R., ed. see Patrick, Dale.

Donahue, John R., ed. see Westermann, Claus.

Donahue, Leo O. Encyclopedia of Batik Designs. LC 80-67121. 520p. 1981. 60.00 (ISBN 0-87982-035-7). Art Alliance.

Donahue, Marilyn C. The Pearl Is in the Oyster. 1980. pap. text ed. 3.95 (ISBN 0-8423-4808-5). Tyndale.

Donahue, Phil, et al. Donahue: My Own Story. 288p. 1981. pap. 2.95 (ISBN 0-449-24358-3, Crest). Fawcett.

Donahue, Roy L., et al. Soils: An Introduction to Soils & Plant Growth. 4th ed. (Illus.). 1977. 20.95 (ISBN 0-13-821918-4). P-H.

Donahue, Thomas J. The Theater of Fernando Arrabal: A Garden of Earthly Delights. LC 79-2598. (The Gotham Library). 1980. 15.00x (ISBN 0-8147-1771-3); pap. 7.00x (ISBN 0-8147-1772-1). NYU Pr.

Donahue, Warren. Foundations of Technical Mathematics. LC 75-96962. 1970. 19.95 (ISBN 0-471-21774-3). Wiley.

Donald, David, compiled by. The Nation in Crisis, 1861-1877. LC 74-79169. (Goldentree Bibliographies in American History Ser.). 112p. 1969. pap. 6.95x (ISBN 0-88295-511-X). AHM Pub.

Donald, David H. Lincoln Reconsidered: Essays on the Civil War Era. LC 80-22804. (Illus.). xiii, 200p. 1981. Repr. of 1956 ed. lib. bdg. 23.50x (ISBN 0-313-22575-3, DOLR). Greenwood.

Donald, David H., ed. see Mowry, George E. & Brownell, Blaine E.

Donald, Leroy. Trail to Lometa. 192p. (YA) 1976. 5.95 (ISBN 0-685-62630-X, Avalon). Bouregy.

Donald, Robert B., et al. Writing Clear Paragraphs. (Illus.). 1978. pap. text ed. 8.95 (ISBN 0-13-970350-0). P-H.

Donald, Robyn. Bay of Stars. (Harlequin Romances). 192p. 1981. pap. 1.25 (ISBN 0-373-02391-X, Pub. by Harlequin). PB.

Donald, Vivian. For Love or Money. pap. 1.25 (ISBN 0-451-07756-3, Y7756, Sig). NAL.

Donaldson, Betty, jt. auth. see Donaldson, Norman.

Donaldson, David D. Atlas of External Disease of the Eye: The Crystalline Lens, Vol. 5. LC 66-26959. (Illus.). 1976. 58.50 o.p. (ISBN 0-8016-1428-7). Mosby.

--Atlas of External Diseases of the Eye: The Cornea & Sclera, Vol. 3. 2nd ed. LC 79-20605. 1979. text ed. 89.50 (ISBN 0-8016-1434-1). Mosby.

Donaldson, Dwight M. The Shi'ite Religion: A History of Islam in Persia & Irak. LC 80-1933. 45.00 (ISBN 0-404-18959-8). AMS Pr.

Donaldson, E. F., et al. Personal Finance. 6th ed. LC 77-71238. 1977. 18.95 o.p. (ISBN 0-8260-2766-0); instructors' manual avail. o.p. (ISBN 0-471-07561-2). Wiley.

Donaldson, E. T., ed. Chaucer's Poetry: An Anthology for the Modern Reader. 2nd ed. LC 74-22536. 1975. 21.95 (ISBN 0-8260-2781-4). Wiley.

Donaldson, E. Talbot, jt. ed. see Kane, George.

Donaldson, E. Talbot, tr. see Tuso, Joseph F.

Donaldson, Elaine. Scrooge. LC 71-127561. (Illus.). (gr. 3-10). 1970. pap. 1.95 o.s.i. (ISBN 0-87695-118-3). Aurora Pubs.

Donaldson, Elvin F., et al. Corporate Finance. 4th ed. 1975. 24.50 (ISBN 0-8260-2751-2); instrs'. manual avail. (ISBN 0-471-07459-4). Wiley.

Donaldson, Frances. Edward the Eighth. LC 74-31274. (Illus.). 1975. 17.50 (ISBN 0-397-00765-5). Lippincott.

--King George VI & Queen Elizabeth. LC 77-5122. (Illus.). 1977. 12.95 o.p. (ISBN 0-397-01229-2). Lippincott.

Donaldson, Francis. Trees. (Easy-Read Fact Bks.). (Illus.). 48p. (gr. 2-4). 1976. PLB 3.90 o.p. (ISBN 0-531-00360-4). Watts.

Donaldson, G. The Scottish Reformation. 42.00 (ISBN 0-521-08675-2). Cambridge U Pr.

Donaldson, Gerald. Frogs. 127p. 1980. 14.95 (ISBN 0-442-22650-0). Van Nos Reinhold.

--The Walking Book. LC 78-14161. (Illus.). 1979. 8.95 o.p. (ISBN 0-03-049361-7); pap. 5.95 o.p. (ISBN 0-03-049356-0). HR&W.

Donaldson, Gerald, jt. auth. see Michener, Leslie.

Donaldson, Gordon. Scotland: Shaping of a Nation. rev. ed. 272p. 1980. 25.00 (ISBN 0-7153-7975-5). David & Charles.

Donaldson, Gordon & Morpeth, Robert S. Who's Who in Scottish History. (Comparative Literature Ser.). (Illus.). 254p. 1973. 18.00x o.p. (ISBN 0-686-63951-0). B&N.

Donaldson, H., et al. Computer by the Tail: A User's Guide to Computer Management. 1976. text ed. 25.00x (ISBN 0-04-658220-7). Allen Unwin.

Donaldson, Hamish. Designing a Distributed Processing System. LC 79-22523. 233p. 1980. 34.95x (ISBN 0-470-26889-1). Halsted Pr.

Donaldson, James A., jt. auth. see Anson, Barry.

Donaldson, James H. Casualty Claim Practice. 3rd ed. 1976. text ed. 23.50x (ISBN 0-256-00116-2). Irwin.

Donaldson, Les & Scannell, Edward. Human Resource Development: The New Trainer's Guide. 1978. pap. text ed. 8.95 (ISBN 0-201-03081-0). A-W.

Donaldson, Margaret. Children's Minds. (Illus.). 1979. 10.95 (ISBN 0-393-01185-2); pap. 3.95x (ISBN 0-393-95101-4). Norton.

--The Moon's on Fire. LC 80-65664. (Illus.). 152p. (gr. 2-7). 1980. 9.95 (ISBN 0-233-97249-8). Andre Deutsch.

Donaldson, Norman & Donaldson, Betty. How Did They Die? 1980. 12.95 (ISBN 0-312-39488-8). St Martin.

Donaldson, Robert H., jt. auth. see Nogee, Joseph L.

Donaldson, Robert H., ed. The Soviet Union in the Third World: Success & Failures. (Westview Special Studies in International Relations). 350p. 1980. lib. bdg. 25.00x (ISBN 0-89158-974-0); pap. text ed. 12.00 (ISBN 0-86531-147-1). Westview.

Donaldson, Scott. Suburban Myth. LC 77-79191. 1969. 17.00x (ISBN 0-231-03192-0); pap. 5.00x (ISBN 0-231-08659-8). Columbia U Pr.

Donaldson, Stephen R. The Wounded Land: Book One of the Second Chronicles of Thomas Covenant. 512p. 1981. 12.95 (ISBN 0-345-28647-2); pap. 2.95 (ISBN 0-345-27831-3); 36 copy floor display. Ballantine.

Donaldson, T. Ngiyambaa: The Language of the Wangaaybuwan. LC 79-7646. (Cambridge Studies in Linguistics: No. 29). (Illus.). 320p. 1980. 59.50 (ISBN 0-521-22524-8). Cambridge U Pr.

Donaldson, T. & Werhare, P. Ethical Issues in Business: A Philosophical Approach. 1979. pap. 11.50 (ISBN 0-13-290064-5). P-H.

Donaldson, William. The Life & Adventures of Sir Bartholomew Sapskull Baronet, 1768, 2 vols. in 1. LC 74-26834. (Novel in England, 1700-1775 Ser). 1974. lib. bdg. 44.00 (ISBN 0-8240-1183-X). Garland Pub.

Donaldson-Evans, Lancelot K. Love's Fatal Glance: A Study of Eye Imagery in the Poets of the Ecole lyonnaise. LC 80-10415. (Romance Monographs: No. 39). 155p. 1980. 14.50 (ISBN 84-499-3694-2). Romance.

Donaruma, L. Guy & Vogl, Otto, eds. Polymeric Drugs. 1978. 25.50 (ISBN 0-12-220750-5). Acad Pr.

Donaruma, L. Guy, et al. Anionic Polymeric Drugs. LC 80-11364. (Polymers in Biology & Medicine Ser.: Vol. 1). 1980. 39.50 (ISBN 0-471-05530-1, Pub. by Wiley-Interscience). Wiley.

Donat, Hans. Practical Points on Boat Engines. 204p. 1980. 8.00x (ISBN 0-245-53333-8, Pub. by Nautical England). State Mutual Bk.

Donath, A. & Righetti, A., eds. Cardiovascular Nuclear Medicine. (Progress in Nuclear Medicine: Vol. 6). (Illus.). viii, 228p. 1980. 88.75 (ISBN 3-8055-0618-X). S Karger.

Donath, A., jt. ed. see Juge, O.

Donath, Ferenc. Reform & Revolution: Transformation of Hungary's Agriculture 1945-1970. Vizmathy-Susits, Gisela, tr. (Illus.). 489p. (Orig.). 1980. pap. 10.00x (ISBN 963-13-0911-8). Intl Pubns Serv.

Donati, Maria B., et al, eds. Malignancy & the Hemostatic System. (Monographs of the Mario Negri Institute for Pharmacological Research). 148p. 1981. text ed. 17.00 (ISBN 0-89004-463-5). Raven.

Donati, Robert M., jt. auth. see Newton, William T.

Donato, Georgia di see Di Donato, Georgia.

Donato, Joseph. Tell It to the Mafia. 1975. pap. 2.50 o.p. (ISBN 0-88270-322-6). Logos.

Donato, Pietro di. Christ in Concrete. LC 39-10762. 320p. 1975. 8.95 (ISBN 0-672-52161-X); pap. 5.95 (ISBN 0-672-52187-3). Bobbs.

Donatus, Cornelius. How to Anticipate the Business Future Without the Need of Computers: The Laws of Inevitabilities in Economics, Sociology & History. new ed. (Illus.). 1977. 39.50 (ISBN 0-89266-060-0). Am Classical Coll Pr.

--How to Anticipate the Business Future Without the Use of Computers. (Illus.). 47p. 1974. 39.50 (ISBN 0-913314-27-7). Am Classical Coll Pr.

Donauer, Friedrich. Swords Against Carthage. Cooper, F. T., tr. LC 61-12878. (Illus.). (gr. 7-11). 1932. 8.50x (ISBN 0-8196-0112-8). Biblo.

Donavan, Marilee. Cancer Care: A Guide for Patient Education. 288p. 1981. pap. 11.50 (ISBN 0-8385-1028-0). ACC.

Doncaster, Islay. Traditional China. Killingray, Margaret & O'Connor, Edmund, eds. (World History Ser.). (Illus.). (gr. 10). 1980. Repr. of 1977 ed. lib. bdg. 5.95 (ISBN 0-89908-032-4); pap. text ed. 1.95 (ISBN 0-89908-007-3). Greenhaven.

Dondi, Beda, jt. auth. see Ray, Mary F.

Dondo, Muthurin & Le Vois, Camille. Modern French Course. 3rd ed. 1966. text ed. 10.95x o.p. (ISBN 0-669-27144-6). Heath.

Donfried, Karl P. The Dynamic Word: New Testament Insights for Contemporary Christians. LC 80-8905. 244p. 1981. 12.95 (ISBN 0-06-061945-7). Har-Row.

Dong, Collin H. & Banks, Jane. New Hope for the Arthritic. LC 75-16388. 184p. 1975. 7.95 (ISBN 0-690-00964-X, TYC-T). T Y Crowell.

Dongier, Maurice & Wittkower, Eric D. Divergent Views in Psychiatry. (Illus.). Date not set. text ed. price not set (ISBN 0-06-140695-3, Harper Medical). Har-Row.

Donhauser, Paul S. History of American Ceramics: The Studio Potter. (Illus.). 1978. text ed. 17.95 (ISBN 0-8403-1864-2). Kendall-Hunt.

Donhoffer, Sz. Homeothermia of the Brain. (Illus.). 140p. (Orig.). 1980. pap. 13.50x (ISBN 963-05-2405-8). Intl Pubns Serv.

Donia, Robert J. Islam Under the Double Eagle: The Muslims of Bosnia & Hercegovina, 1878-1914. (East European Monographs: No. 78). 256p. 1981. text ed. 17.50x (ISBN 0-914710-72-9). East Eur Quarterly.

Doniach, N. S., ed. Oxford English-Arabic Dictionary of Current Usage. 1972. 48.00x (ISBN 0-19-864312-8). Oxford U Pr.

Doniach, Seb, jt. ed. see Winick, Herman.

Doniger, David D. Law & Policy of Toxic Substances Control: A Case Study of Vinyl Chloride. LC 78-24624. 1979. 12.50x (ISBN 0-8018-2234-3); pap. 4.95 (ISBN 0-8018-2235-1). Johns Hopkins.

Doniger, Joan, jt. auth. see Rothwell, Naomi.

Donin, Hayim H. To Pray As a Jew. LC 80-50554. 384p. 1980. 15.00 (ISBN 0-465-08628-4). Basic.

Donini, I., jt. auth. see Battezzati, M.

Donizetti, Gaetano. Dom Sebastien, Gaetano Donizetti, 2 vols. Rosen, Charles & Gossett, Philip, eds. LC 76-49210. (Early Romantic Opera Ser.: Vol. 29). 1980. lib. bdg. 82.00 (ISBN 0-8240-2928-3). Garland Pub.

Donizetti, P. Shadow & Substance. 1967. 15.00 (ISBN 0-08-012182-9); pap. 11.25 (ISBN 0-08-012181-0). Pergamon.

Donkin, R. A. Manna: An Historical Geography. (Biogeographica Ser.: No. 17). (Illus.). vii, 160p. 1980. lib. bdg. 47.40 (ISBN 90-6193-218-1, Dr W Junk Pub). Kluwer Boston.

Donlan, Dan, jt. auth. see Singer, Harry.

Donlan, Walter, intro. by. Classical World Bibliography of Greek & Roman History. LC 76-52511. (Library of Humanities Reference Bks.: No. 94). lib. bdg. 27.00 (ISBN 0-8240-9879-X). Garland Pub.

Donleavy, J. P. A Fairy Tale of New York. 352p. 1973. 7.95 o.s.i. (ISBN 0-440-02624-5, Sey Lawr). Delacorte.

--Schulz. 1980. pap. 6.95 o.p. (ISBN 0-440-58378-0, Delta). Dell.

--The Unexpurgated Code: A Complete Manual of Survival & Manners. (Illus.). 304p. 1975. 10.00 o.s.i. (ISBN 0-440-07794-X, Sey Lawr). Delacorte.

Donley, R. Tucker. Law of Coal, Oil & Gas in Virginia & West Virginia. 1951. with 1972 supplement. 25.00 (ISBN 0-87215-084-4). Michie.

Donlon, T. A. & Echternacht, G. A Feasibility Study of the SAT Performance of High-Ability Students from 1960 to 1974(Valedictorian Study) 1977. 3.00 (ISBN 0-87447-044-7, 251712). College Bd.

Donn, William. The Earth: Our Physical Environment. LC 79-37431. 621p. 1972. 26.95 (ISBN 0-471-21785-9). Wiley.

Donnachie, Ian & MacLeod, Innes. Victorian & Edwardian Scottish Lowlands from Historic Photographs. (Illus.). 120p. 1980. 17.95 (ISBN 0-7134-1297-6, Pub. by Batsford England). David & Charles.

Donnan, Christopher B. The Moche Occupation of the Santa Valley, Peru. (U. C. Publ. in Anthropology: Vol. 8). 1973. pap. 10.50x o.p. (ISBN 0-520-09410-7). U of Cal Pr.

Don Nanjira, Daniel D. The Status of Aliens in East Africa: Asians & Europeans in Tanzania, Uganda, & Kenya. LC 75-19804. (Special Studies). 1976. text ed. 23.95 o.p. (ISBN 0-275-55570-4). Praeger.

Donnay, jt. auth. see Heinz.

Donne, John. The Anniversaries, Epithalamions & Epicedes. Milgate, W., ed. (Elglish Texts Ser.). (Illus.). 1978. 45.00x (ISBN 0-19-812729-4). Oxford U Pr.

--Complete Poems. Bennett, Roger, ed. 1969. pap. 3.45 (ISBN 0-87532-103-8). Hendricks House.

--The Divine Poems. 2nd ed. Gardner, Helen, ed. (Oxford English Texts). 1979. 37.50x (ISBN 0-19-812745-6). Oxford U Pr.

--John Donne's Sermons on the Psalms & Gospels: With a Selection of Prayers & Meditations. Simpson, Evelyn M., ed. & intro. by. 1963. 14.00x (ISBN 0-520-00338-1); pap. 2.65 (ISBN 0-520-00340-3, CAL84). U of Cal Pr.

--Paradoxes & Problems: Oxford English Texts Ser. Peters, Helen, ed. (Illus.). 242p. 37.50x (ISBN 0-19-812753-7). Oxford U Pr.

--Poems. Grierson, Herbert J., ed. (Oxford Standard Authors Ser.). 1933. 23.00 (ISBN 0-19-254123-4); pap. 7.50x (ISBN 0-19-281113-4). Oxford U Pr.

Donne, Sr. John. Devotions Upon Emergent Occasions: A Critical Edition with an Introduction & Commentary, 2 vols. Savage, Elizabeth, ed. (Salzburg Studies in English Literature, Elizabethan & Renaissance Studies Ser.: No. 21). 392p. (Orig.). 1975. Set. pap. text ed. 50.25 (ISBN 0-391-01364-5). Humanities.

Donne, W. B., ed. Correspondence of King George the Third with Lord North, 1768-1783. LC 76-154697. (Era of the American Revolution Ser). 1971. Repr. of 1867 ed. lib. bdg. 75.00 (ISBN 0-306-70155-3). Da Capo.

Donnell, John D., et al. Law for Business. 18.95x (ISBN 0-256-02316-6). Irwin.

Donnell, Marianne, ed. Toponyms of Florida: An Alphabetical Listing of Names Approved by the United States Board on Geographic Names Through 1976, with 1977 Addendum. LC 78-23662. 1978. pap. 6.50x o.p. (ISBN 0-8130-0622-8). U Presses Fla.

Donnellan, T. Lattice Theory. LC 67-28661. 1968. 35.00 (ISBN 0-08-012563-8); pap. 9.75 (ISBN 0-08-012562-X). Pergamon.

Donnelly, Dorothy. Kudzu & Other Poems. (Pourboire Ser.). 1979. pap. 3.50 (ISBN 0-930900-57-X). Burning Deck.

Donnelly, E. L. Electrical Installation Theory & Practice. 2nd ed. (Illus.). 1972. pap. text ed. 14.95x (ISBN 0-245-51007-9). Intl Ideas.

Donnelly, G. F., et al. The Nursing System: Issues, Ethics & Politics. LC 80-12402. 224p. 1980. 10.95 (ISBN 0-471-04441-5). Wiley.

Donnelly, Ignatius. Atlantis: Antediluvidan World. LC 80-8340. (Harper's Library of Spiritual Wisdom). (Illus.). 512p. 1981. pap. 6.95 (ISBN 0-06-061960-0, HarpR). Har-Row.

Donnelly, James, et al. Fundamentals of Management: Functions, Behavior, Models. 3rd ed. 1978. 18.50x (ISBN 0-256-02073-6). Business Pubns.

--Fundamentals of Management: Selected Readings. 3rd ed. 1978. pap. 9.95x (ISBN 0-256-02075-2). Business Pubns.

Donnelly, James H., et al. Analysis for Marketing Decisions. 1970. text ed. 14.95x o.p. (ISBN 0-256-00139-1). Irwin.

Donnelly, James S. Land & People of Nineteenth-Century Cork. 1975. 42.50 (ISBN 0-7100-7986-9). Routledge & Kegan.

Donnelly, Jane. A Man to Watch. (Harlequin Romance Ser.). (Orig.). 1980. pap. 1.25 o.p. (ISBN 0-373-02325-1, Pub. by Harlequin). PB.

--No Way Out. (Harlequin Romances Ser.). 192p. 1980. pap. 1.25 (ISBN 0-373-02373-1, Pub. by Harlequin). PB.

Donnelly, K., ed. see Mecking, P. R.

Donnelly, Kenneth, ed. Interpreting Hearing Aid Technology. (Illus.). 320p. 1974. text ed. 21.50 (ISBN 0-398-03087-1). C C Thomas.

Donnelly, Linda, jt. auth. see Lee, Kaiman.

Donnelly, Sr. Mary Louise. Imprints Sixteen Hundred Eight to Nineteen Eighty, Hamilton, Allied Families. LC 80-84574. (Illus.). 660p. 1980. 38.00. Donnelly.

Donnelly, R. H., et al. Active Games & Contests. 2nd ed. 672p. 1958. 17.50 (ISBN 0-471-07088-2). Wiley.

Donnelly, R. J., et al. Active Games & Contests. 2nd ed. (Illus.). (gr. 7 up). 1958. 17.50 (ISBN 0-8260-2795-4). Ronald Pr.

Donnelly, Thomas C., jt. auth. see Peel, Roy V.

Donner, Andre M. Role of the Lawyer in the European Communities. LC 68-17735. (Julius Rosenthal Memorial Lectures Ser.: 1968). 1968. 7.95x o.s.i. (ISBN 0-8101-0032-0). Northwestern U Pr.

Donner, Martin W., jt. auth. see Ramsey, Elizabeth M.

Donner, Michael. How to Beat the SAT's. (gr. 11-12). 1981. pap. 3.95 (ISBN 0-89480-154-6). Workman Pub.

Donnersberger, Anne, et al. A Manual of Anatomy & Physiology: Lab Animal: the Cat. 2nd ed. 1979. pap. text ed. 11.95 (ISBN 0-669-02481-3); answer key (ISBN 0-669-03168-2). Heath.

Donnersberger, Anne B., et al. A Manual of Anatomy & Physiology. fetal pig ed. 1978. pap. text ed. 10.95x (ISBN 0-669-01490-7); instr's manual (ISBN 0-669-01632-2). Heath.

Donnison, David & Eversley, David, eds. London: Urban Patterns, Problems, & Policies. LC 73-80440. (Centre for Environmental Studies Ser.: Vol. 2). 1973. 32.50x (ISBN 0-8039-0270-0). Sage.

Donno, Daniel J., ed. see Campanella, Tommaso.

Donno, Elizabeth S., ed. Elizabethan Minor Epics. LC 63-20343. 1963. 22.50x o.p. (ISBN 0-231-02530-0). Columbia U Pr.

D'Onofrio-Flores, Pamela, jt. ed. see Nicol, Davidson.

Donoghue, D. Jonathan Swift. LC 77-79053. 1969. 42.00 (ISBN 0-521-07564-5). Cambridge U Pr.

Donoghue, Denis. The Sovereign Ghost: Studies in Imagination. 1977. 14.50 (ISBN 0-520-03134-2). U of Cal Pr.

Donoghue, John D. Pariah Persistence in Changing Japan: A Case Study. 1977. pap. text ed. 7.75x (ISBN 0-8191-0170-2). U Pr of Amer.

Donoghue, William E. & Tilling, Thomas. William E. Donoghue's Complete Money Market Guide. LC 80-8200. (Illus.). 256p. 1981. 12.95 (ISBN 0-690-02008-2, HarpT). Har-Row.

Donohue, Jerry. The Structures of the Elements. 448p. 1981. Repr. of 1974 ed. lib. bdg. price not set (ISBN 0-89874-230-7). Krieger.

Donohue, John W. Jesuit Education: An Essay on the Foundations of Its Ideas. LC 63-11902. 1963. 17.50 o.p. (ISBN 0-8232-0490-1). Fordham.

Donohue, Joseph W., Jr., ed. Theatrical Manager in Britain & America: Players of a Perilous Game. LC 72-154992. (Illus.). 1971. 14.50x (ISBN 0-691-06188-2). Princeton U Pr.

Donoso, Ephraim, ed. Advances & Controversies in Cardiology. (Current Cardiovascular Topics: Vol. VI). (Illus.). 350p. 1981. text ed. 35.00 (ISBN 0-86577-024-7). Thieme-Stratton.

Donoso, Jose. The Obscene Bird of Night. St. Martin, Hardie & Mades, Leonard, trs. from Span. LC 79-88419. 1979. pap. 7.50 (ISBN 0-87923-191-2, Nonpareil Bks.). Godine.

--Personal History of the "Boom". LC 76-53747. 1977. pap. 5.00x (ISBN 0-231-04164-0); pap. 4.95 (ISBN 0-231-04165-9). Columbia U Pr.

Donoughue, Carol. Development of Writing. (Jackdaw Ser: No. 47). (Illus.). 1969. 5.95 o.s.i. (ISBN 0-670-27074-1, Grossman). Viking Pr.

Donovan, Barry J. Revision of North American Bees of the Subgenus Cnemidandrena. (Publ. in Entomolgy Ser: Vol. 81). pap. 7.75x (ISBN 0-520-09566-9). U of Cal Pr.

Donovan, Frank R. & Bell, Whitfield J. Many Worlds of Benjamin Franklin. LC 63-21834. (American Heritage Junior Library). (Illus.). 153p. (gr. 5 up). 1963. 9.95 (ISBN 0-8281-0390-9, J013-0). Am Heritage.

Donovan, Helen M. Nursing Service Administration: Managing the Enterprise. LC 75-26845. (Illus.). 272p. 1975. pap. 12.95 (ISBN 0-8016-1423-6). Mosby.

Donovan, J. Creative Retirement. 1977. 110.00 o.p. (ISBN 0-201-01059-3); 5 pack wkbks. 55.00 o.p. (ISBN 0-201-01060-7). A-W.

Donovan, John A. Dogs in Shakespeare. 9.95 (ISBN 0-87714-074-X). Green Hill.

Donovan, John C. The Nineteen Sixties: Politics & Public Policy. LC 80-5757. 142p. 1980. lib. bdg. 15.50 (ISBN 0-8191-1189-9); pap. text ed. 6.75 (ISBN 0-8191-1190-2). U Pr of Amer.

--The Politics of Poverty. 3rd ed. LC 80-5046. 201p. 1980. text ed. 17.50 (ISBN 0-8191-1025-6); pap. text ed. 7.25 (ISBN 0-8191-1026-4). U Pr of Amer.

--The Politics of Poverty. 2nd ed. LC 72-10008. (Studies in Contemporary American Politics Ser). 1973. pap. 2.95 (ISBN 0-672-63715-4). Pegasus.

Donovan, John C., et al. People, Power & Politics: An Introduction to Political Science. (Illus.). 384p. 1981. pap. text ed. 11.95 (ISBN 0-201-03246-5). A-W.

Donovan, Josephine, ed. Feminist Literary Criticism: Explorations in Theory. LC 75-12081. 96p. 1975. pap. 4.50x (ISBN 0-8131-1334-2). U Pr of Ky.

Donovan, Josephine L. Sarah Orne Jewett. LC 80-5334. (Modern Literature Ser.). 160p. 1980. 10.95 (ISBN 0-8044-2137-4). Ungar.

Donovan, Kathryn N. General Surgical Nursing Continuing Review. LC 80-81906. 1980. pap. 9.75 (ISBN 0-87488-318-0). Med Exam.

Donovan, Peter. Interpretating Religious Experience. 1979. pap. 3.95 (ISBN 0-8164-2209-5). Crossroad NY.

--Interpreting Religious Experience. (Orig.). 1979. pap. 3.95 (ISBN 0-8164-2209-5). Crossroad NY.

Donovan, Robert K., ed. Current Research in British Studies. 8th ed. 1980. pap. write for info. (ISBN 0-89126-084-6). Military Aff Aero.

Donovan, Timothy P. & Gatewood, Willard B., Jr., eds. The Governors of Arkansas: Essays in Political Biography. 1981. text ed. 24.00x (ISBN 0-938626-00-0). U of Mo Pr.

Donovan, Timothy R. & McClelland, Ben W. Eight Approaches to Teaching Composition. 160p. 1980. pap. 6.50 (ISBN 0-8141-1303-6). NCTE.

Donow, Herbert S. Concordance to the Sonnet Sequences of Daniel, Drayton, Shakespeare, Sidney & Spenser. LC 72-76188. 1969. 17.50x o.p. (ISBN 0-8093-0400-7). S Ill U Pr.

Donsbach, Kurt W., ed. see Goeltz, Judith.

Donze, Marie-Ange & Sauvageot, Claude. China Today. (Illus.). 255p. 1980. 14.95 (ISBN 0-686-64605-3, Pub. by Two Continents). Hippocrene Bks.

Doob, Joseph L. Stochastic Processes. LC 52-11857. (Wiley Series in Probability & Mathematical Statistics). 1953. 36.95 (ISBN 0-471-21813-8, Pub. by Wiley-Interscience). Wiley.

Doob, Leonard W. Panorama of Evil: Insights from the Behavioral Sciences. LC 77-87964. (Contributions in Philosophy: No. 10). 1978. lib. bdg. 16.95 (ISBN 0-313-20030-0, DPE/). Greenwood.

--The Pursuit of Peace. LC 80-1201. 376p. 1981. lib. bdg. 29.95 (ISBN 0-313-22630-X, DPO/). Greenwood.

Doody, Margaret. Aristotle Detective. (Penguin Crime Monthly Ser.). 1981. pap. 2.95 (ISBN 0-14-005753-6). Penguin.

Dooley, A. R., et al. Basic Problems, Concepts & Techniques. rev. ed. 738p. 1968. 28.95 (ISBN 0-471-21829-4). Wiley.

Dooley, Anne. Every Wall a Door. 1974. pap. 2.95 o.p. (ISBN 0-525-47380-7). Dutton.

Dooley, Anne M. A Quest for Religious Maturity: The Obsessive-Compulsive Personality--Implications for Pastoral Counseling. LC 80-67255. 124p. (Orig.). 1981. lib. bdg. 16.00 (ISBN 0-8191-1442-1); pap. text ed. 7.50 (ISBN 0-8191-1443-X). U Pr of Amer.

Dooley, Catherine. The Saints Book. 64p. (Orig.). (gr. k-3). 1981. pap. 2.95 (ISBN 0-8091-6547-3). Paulist Pr.

Dooley, D. J. Art of Sinclair Lewis. LC 65-17173. 1967. pap. 4.25x (ISBN 0-8032-5051-7, BB 199, Bison). U of Nebr Pr.

--Compton Mackenzie. (English Authors Ser.: No. 173). 176p. 1974. lib. bdg. 9.95 (ISBN 0-8057-1361-1). Twayne.

Dooley, D. J., ed. Conversion Integrated Circuits. LC 80-10541. 1980. 26.95 (ISBN 0-87942-131-2). Inst Electrical.

Dooley, Daniel J. Data-Conversion Integrated Circuits. (IEEE Press Selected Reprint Ser.). 298p. 1980. 26.95 (ISBN 0-471-08154-X, Pub. by Wiley-Interscience); pap. 17.50 (ISBN 0-471-08155-8). Wiley.

Dooley, H. H. Last Rights. 224p. 1981. pap. 2.50 (ISBN 0-449-24392-3, Crest). Fawcett.

Dooley, Mary T. & Goff, James F. Physical Geography Manual. 1969. spiral bdg. 9.95 (ISBN 0-8087-0420-6). Burgess.

Dooley, Patrick K. Pragmatism As Humanism: The Philosophy of William James. LC 73-86935. 200p. 1974. 15.95 (ISBN 0-88229-125-4); pap. 7.95x (ISBN 0-88229-582-9). Nelson-Hall.

Dooley, Peter C. Elementary Price Theory. 2nd ed. (Illus., Orig.). 1973. pap. text ed. 9.95x (ISBN 0-13-259531-1). P-H.

Dooley, Roger. From Scarface to Scarlett: American Films in the 1930s. (Illus.). 700p. 1981. 25.00 (ISBN 0-15-133789-6). HarBraceJ.

Dooley, Thomas W. Real Estate Brokerage in the Eighties: Survival Among the Giants. 1980. 10.95 (ISBN 0-88462-364-5). Real Estate Ed Co.

Dooling, D. M., ed. A Way of Working. LC 78-68366. 1979. pap. 3.50 (ISBN 0-385-14163-7, Anch). Doubleday.

Doolitle, Jerry. The Southern Appalachians. (The American Wilderness Ser.). (Illus.). 1976. 12.95 (ISBN 0-8094-1346-9). Time-Life.

Doolittle, Hilda see H. D., pseud.

Doolittle, Jerome. Canyons & Mesas. LC 74-77772. (American Wilderness). (Illus.). (gr. 6 up). 1974. PLB 11.97 (ISBN 0-8094-1238-1, Pub. by Time-Life). Silver.

--The Southern Appalachians. LC 75-27179. (American Wilderness). (Illus.). (gr. 6 up). 1976. PLB 11.97 (ISBN 0-8094-1347-7, Pub. by Time-Life). Silver.

Doolittle, Jerry. Canyons & Mesas. (The American Wilderness Ser). (Illus.). 184p. 1974. 12.95 (ISBN 0-8094-1237-3). Time-Life.

Doonican, Val. The Special Years: An Autobiography. (Illus.). 192p. 1981. 17.95 (ISBN 0-241-10499-8, Pub. by Hamish Hamilton England). David & Charles.

Doorn, J. Van see Van Doorn, J.

Doorn, Jacques Van see Van Doorn, Jacques.

Doorn, Willem V. Theory & Practice of English Narrative Verse Since Eighteen Thirty-Three. 253p. 1980. Repr. of 1833 ed. lib. bdg. 25.00 (ISBN 0-8492-4220-7). R West.

Doornkamp, John C., jt. auth. see Cooke, Ronald U.

Dooyeweerd, H., et al. The Idea of a Christian Philosophy. 1973. pap. 6.95x (ISBN 0-686-11979-7). Wedge Pub.

Dooyeweerd, Herman. Roots of Western Cultures: Pagan, Secular & Christian Options. 1979. 12.95 (ISBN 0-88906-104-1). Radix Bks.

Dopagne, Jacques. Magritte. (Masters of Art Ser.). (Illus.). 1979. pap. 3.95 (ISBN 0-8120-2154-1). Barron.

Dopfer, Kurt C., ed. Economics in the Future: Toward a New Paradigm. LC 76-2600. 1976. 21.00x (ISBN 0-89158-548-6). Westview.

Dopsch, Alfons. The Economic & Social Foundations of European Civilization. LC 68-9591. 1969. Repr. of 1937 ed. 16.50 o.p. (ISBN 0-86527-050-3). Fertig.

Dopyera, John E., jt. auth. see Lay, Margaret Z.

Doraiswamy, T. K. Words for the Wind. (Greenbird Book). 76p. 1975. 14.00 (ISBN 0-88253-676-1); pap. 6.75 (ISBN 0-88253-675-3). Ind-US Inc.

Doran, Adelaide L. Pieces of Eight Channel Islands: A Bibliographical Guide & Source Book. LC 80-66447. (Illus.). 341p. 1981. 26.50 (ISBN 0-87062-132-7). A H Clark.

Doran, Charles F. Myth, Oil, & Politics: Introduction to the Political Economy of Petroleum. LC 77-4571. (Illus.). 1979. pap. text ed. 7.95 (ISBN 0-02-907710-9). Free Pr.

Doran, Jeffry W. Search on Mount St. Helens. Pica, George, ed. (Illus.). 96p. (Orig.). pap. 7.95 (ISBN 0-938700-00-6). Imagesmith.

Doran, Madeleine. Endeavors of Art: A Study of Form in Elizabethan Drama. (Illus.). 1954. pap. text ed. 8.50x (ISBN 0-299-01084-8). U of Wis Pr.

--Shakespeare's Dramatic Language. LC 75-32072. 240p. 1976. 19.50 (ISBN 0-299-07010-7). U of Wis Pr.

--Something About Swans: Essays by Madeleine Doran. 100p. 1973. 5.00 (ISBN 0-299-06170-1). U of Wis Pr.

Doran, Robert M. Subject & Psyche: Ricoeur, Jung, & the Search for Foundations. 1977. 10.75 (ISBN 0-8191-0257-1). U Pr of Amer.

Doran, Rodney L. Basic Measurement & Evaluation of Science Instruction. (Illus.). 144p. (Orig.). 1980. pap. 3.00 (ISBN 0-87355-016-1). Natl Sci Tchrs.

Dor Bahadur Bista. People of Nepal. (Illus.). 1976. 8.95x (ISBN 0-685-89509-2). Himalaya Hse.

Dordick, B. F., jt. ed. see Babb, Janice B.

Dordick, Herbert S., et al. The Emerging Network Marketplace. (Communication & Information Science Ser.). 288p. 1980. 24.95 (ISBN 0-89391-036-8). Ablex Pub.

D'Ordonez, Carlo. Seven Symphonies. Brown, Peter & Brook, Barry S., eds. LC 79-12057. (The Symphony 1720-1840, Ser. B: Vol. IV). 255p. 1980. lib. bdg. 60.00 (ISBN 0-8240-3800-2). Garland Pub.

Dore, Gustave. Dore Bible Illustrations. (Illus.). 256p. 1974. pap. 6.00 (ISBN 0-486-23004-X). Dover.

--Dore Gallery. LC 73-91686. 15.00 o.p. (ISBN 0-668-03444-0). Arco.

Dore, Henri. Les Lecture Des Talismans Chinois: Shanghai, 1913. LC 78-74290. (Oriental Religions Ser.: Vol. 17). 190p. 1981. lib. bdg. 20.00 postponed (ISBN 0-8240-3919-X). Garland Pub.

Dore, Ronald P. British Factory - Japanese Factory: The Origins of National Diversity in Employment Relations. LC 72-78948. 1973. 18.50x (ISBN 0-520-02268-8); pap. 7.95x (ISBN 0-520-02495-8, CAMPUS96). U of Cal Pr.

--City Life in Japan: A Study of a Tokyo Ward. (Illus.). 1958. pap. 4.85x (ISBN 0-520-00343-8, CAMPUS49). U of Cal Pr.

--The Diploma Disease: Education, Qualification, & Development. 1976. 20.00x (ISBN 0-520-03107-5); CAMPUS 181. pap. 6.95x (ISBN 0-520-03270-5). U of Cal Pr.

Doreian, Patrick. Mathematics & the Study of Social Relations. LC 75-163328. (Illus.). 1971. 8.00x (ISBN 0-8052-3415-2). Schocken.

Doren, A., ed. see Salimbene Ognibene Di Guido Di Adamo.

Doren, Carl C. Van see Van Doren, Carl C.

Doren, Carl Van see Lazarillo de Tormes.

Doren, Carl Van see Van Doren, Carl.

Doren, Mark Van see Bartram, William.

Doren, W. H. Van see Van Doren, W. H.

Dorer, Frances, jt. auth. see Dorer, Nancy.

Dorer, Nancy & Dorer, Frances. Journey at Dawn. (Orig.). 1980. pap. 1.95 (ISBN 0-532-23179-1). Manor Bks.

--Return of the Eagle. (Orig.). 1979. pap. 1.95 (ISBN 0-532-23267-4). Manor Bks.

--Terra Incognita. (Orig.). 1980. pap. 1.95 (ISBN 0-532-23178-3). Manor Bks.

--Two Came Calling. (Orig.). 1980. pap. 1.95 (ISBN 0-532-23226-7). Manor Bks.

--The Wings of the Eagle. (Orig.). 1979. pap. 1.95 (ISBN 0-532-23287-9). Manor Bks.

Dorey, T. A., ed. Latin Historians. (Studies in Latin Literature). 1966. 19.50x (ISBN 0-7100-1293-4). Routledge & Kegan.

Dorf, Barbara. Introduction to Still Life & Flower Painting. (Illus.). 184p. 1976. 15.95 (ISBN 0-7207-0885-0). Transatlantic.

Dorf, Martin E. The Role of the Major Histocompatibility Complex in Immunobiology. LC 80-772. 525p. 1981. lib. bdg. 47.50 (ISBN 0-8240-7129-8). Garland Pub.

Dorf, R. C. Technology, Society & Man. LC 74-76445. (Illus.). 1974. text ed. 16.00x (ISBN 0-87835-047-0); pap. 10.95x (ISBN 0-87835-052-7). Boyd & Fraser.

Dorf, Richard. Introduction to Computers & Computer Science. 2nd ed. LC 77-81994. (Illus.). 1977. text ed. 15.95x (ISBN 0-87835-061-6). Boyd & Fraser.

Dorf, Richard C. Computers & Man. 2nd ed. 1978. pap. text ed. 11.95x (ISBN 0-87835-064-0). Boyd & Fraser.

--The Energy Factbook 1980-1981. 1980. 16.95 (ISBN 0-07-017623-X); pap. 7.95 (ISBN 0-07-017629-9). McGraw.

--Energy, Resources & Policy. LC 76-45151. 1978. text ed. 18.95 (ISBN 0-201-01673-7); instr's guide 2.50 (ISBN 0-201-01674-5). A-W.

--Matrix Algebra: A Programmed Introduction. 1969. pap. 14.95 (ISBN 0-471-21909-6). Wiley.

--Modern Control Systems. 3rd ed. LC 79-16320. (Electrical Engineering Ser.). (Illus.). 1980. text ed. 23.95 (ISBN 0-201-01258-8). A-W.

Dorfman, Ariel & Mattelart, Armand. How to Read Donald Duck: Imperialist Ideology in the Disney Comic. Kunzle, David, tr. from Span. Orig. Title: Para Leer Al Pato Donald. (Illus.). 112p. (Orig.). 1975. pap. 4.25 (ISBN 0-88477-003-6). Intl General.

Dorfman, Bruce, jt. auth. see Cobleigh, Ira.

Dorfman, Gerald A. Government Versus Trade Unionism in British Politics Since 1968. LC 78-70886. (Publication 224 Ser.). 187p. 1979. 12.95 (ISBN 0-8179-7241-2). Hoover Inst Pr.

Dorfman, John. Consumer Tactics Manual: How to Get Action on Your Complaints. LC 80-65987. 1980. 9.95 (ISBN 0-689-11105-3); pap. 6.95 (ISBN 0-689-11115-0). Atheneum.

Dorfman, Leslie J., ed. see Proceedings of a Workshop, Palo Alto, California, July 1979, et al.

Dorfman, Mark S. Introduction to Insurance. LC 77-22029. (Illus.). 1978. ref. 18.95 (ISBN 0-13-485359-8). P-H.

Dorfman, Robert, et al, eds. Measuring Benefits of Government Investments. (Studies of Government Finance). 429p. 1965. pap. 6.95 (ISBN 0-8157-1901-9). Brookings.

Dorfmeister, Margery, jt. auth. see Schwebke, Phyllis.

Doria, Charles, ed. The Tenth Muse: Classical Drama in Translation. LC 77-88695. vi, 587p. 1980. 19.95 (ISBN 0-8040-0781-0). Swallow.

Doria, Charles & Lenowitz, Harris, eds. Origins: Creation Texts from the Ancient Mediterranean. LC 74-18844. 384p. 1976. pap. 4.95 (ISBN 0-385-01922-X, Anch). Doubleday.

Dorian, Marguerite. The Year of the Waterbearer. 180p. 1976. 7.95 o.s.i. (ISBN 0-02-532180-3). Macmillan.

Dorian, Nancy. Language Death: A Case of Study at a Gaelic-Speaking Community. 1980. text ed. 25.00x (ISBN 0-8122-7785-6); pap. text ed. 11.95x (ISBN 0-8122-1111-1). U of Pa Pr.

Dorill, J. F. & Harwell, C. W. Models & Methods: Guide to Effective Composition. (Illus.). 352p. 1976. pap. 9.95 (ISBN 0-13-586040-7). P-H.

Dorin, Patrick C. The Milwaukee Road East. LC 78-3834. (Illus.). 1977. 15.95 o.s.i. (ISBN 0-87564-528-3). Superior Pub.

--Yesterday's Trains. (Superwheels & Thrill Sports Bks.). (Illus.). (gr. 4 up). 1981. PLB 6.95 (ISBN 0-8225-0448-0). Lerner Pubns.

Doring, P. F. Colloquial German. (Trubners Colloquial Manuals). 1975. 9.50 (ISBN 0-7100-8031-X); pap. 4.95 (ISBN 0-7100-8032-8). Routledge & Kegan.

--Learn German for English Speakers. pap. 7.00 (ISBN 0-87557-027-5). Saphrograph.

Dorington-Ward, Carol. Fans from the East. (Illus.). 1979. 18.95 o.p. (ISBN 0-670-30705-X, Debrett's Peerage, Ltd.). Viking Pr.

Dorkin, C. M., jt. auth. see Munden, D. L.

Dorling. Use of Mathematical Literature. 1977. 34.95 (ISBN 0-408-70913-8). Butterworths.

Dorman, Lynn, ed. see Forman, George E. & Sigel, Irving E.

Dorman, Michael. Confrontation: Politics & Protest. LC 72-7962. 256p. (gr. 7 up). 1974. 5.95 o.s.i. (ISBN 0-440-01628-2). Delacorte.

--Detectives of the Sky: Investigating Aviation Tragedies. LC 74-858. (Illus.). 128p. (gr. 6 up). 1976. PLB 6.90 (ISBN 0-531-00342-6). Watts.

Dorman, N. B. Laughter in the Background. (gr. 9-12). 1980. 8.95 (ISBN 0-525-66714-8). Elsevier-Nelson.

Dorman, Sonya. Stretching Fence. LC 75-14550. 61p. 1975. 8.95 (ISBN 0-8214-0188-2); pap. 4.95 (ISBN 0-8214-0209-9). Ohio U Pr.

Dormann, Genevieve. The Seasons of Love. 1960. 4.50 o.s.i. (ISBN 0-8076-0120-9). Braziller.

--The Way Life Is. LC 66-12903. 1966. 5.00 o.s.i. (ISBN 0-8076-0345-7). Braziller.

Dormer, Albert, jt. auth. see Reese, Terence.

Dormer, K. J. Fundamental Tissue Geometry. LC 79-50235. (Illus.). 1980. 32.50 (ISBN 0-521-22326-1). Cambridge U Pr.

Dorn, Charles H. Van see Van Dorn, Charles H.

Dorn, Edward. Interviews. Allen, Donald, ed. LC 78-6100. (Writing: 38). 126p. 1980. pap. 5.00 (ISBN 0-87704-038-9). Four Seasons Foun.

--Views. Allen, Donald, ed. LC 79-25498. (Writing 40 Ser.). 144p. 12.00 (ISBN 0-87704-050-8); pap. 5.95 (ISBN 0-87704-051-6). Four Seasons Foun.

--Yellow Lola. Clark, Tom & Miller, Jeffrey, eds. LC 80-68260. Orig. Title: Japanese Neon. 132p. 1981. signed limited ed. 20.00 (ISBN 0-932274-14-5); pap. 6.00 (ISBN 0-932274-13-7). Cadmus Eds.

Dorn, Frank. The Sino-Japanese War, 1937-41: From Marco Polo Bridge to Pearl Harbor. LC 74-10828. (Illus.). 416p. 1974. 17.50 o.s.i. (ISBN 0-02-532200-1). Macmillan.

--Sunwatch. (Orig.). 1980. pap. 1.95 (ISBN 0-532-23239-9). Manor Bks.

Dorn, Raymond. Twenty Problems--Twenty Solutions: The Basic Design Workbook. (Illus.). 88p. 1980. pap. 9.95 (ISBN 0-931368-03-0). Ragan Comm.

Dorn, William G. Van see Van Dorn, William G.

Dorn, William S. & Greenberg, Herbert J. Mathematics & Computing: With FORTRAN Programming. LC 67-19940. 1967. 24.95x o.p. (ISBN 0-471-21915-0). Wiley.

Dorn, William S. & McCracken, Daniel D. Introductory Finite Mathematics with Computing. LC 75-30647. 449p. 1976. text ed. 19.95 (ISBN 0-471-21917-7); instructor's manual (ISBN 0-471-01539-3). Wiley.

Dornan, jt. auth. see Dawe.

Dornan, James E., et al, eds. Rhodesia Alone. 1977. pap. 10.00 (ISBN 0-685-85741-7). Coun Am Affairs.

Dornan, Robert K. & Vedlik, Csaba. Judicial Supremacy: The Supreme Court on Trial. LC 80-82300. (The Nordland Series in Contemporary American Social Problems). 145p. (Orig.). 1980. pap. 5.95 (ISBN 0-913124-38-9). Nordland Pub.

Dornberg, John. The New Germans: Thirty Years After. 320p. 1976. 11.95 o.s.i. (ISBN 0-02-532170-6). Macmillan.

Dornbusch, Rudiger. Open Economy Macroeconomics. LC 80-66308. (Illus.). 293p. 1980. text ed. 17.95x (ISBN 0-465-05286-X). Basic.

Dornbusch, Rudiger & Fischer, Stanley. Macroeconomics. 2nd ed. (Illus.). 736p. 1980. text ed. 18.95 (ISBN 0-07-017754-6, C); instructor's manual 6.95 (ISBN 0-07-017755-4); study guide 6.95 (ISBN 0-07-017756-2). McGraw.

Dorner, Peter, ed. Cooperative & Commune: Group Farming in the Economic Development of Agriculture. LC 76-53651. 1977. 25.00 (ISBN 0-299-07380-7). U of Wis Pr.

Dorner, Peter & El-Shafie, Mahmoud A., eds. Resources & Development: Natural Resource Policies & Economic Development in an Interdependent World. 516p. 1980. 20.00 (ISBN 0-299-08250-4). U of Wis Pr.

Dornfeld, Ernst. Butterflies of Oregon. 275p. 1980. pap. 24.95x (ISBN 0-917304-58-6, Pub. by Timber Pr). Intl Schol Bk Serv.

Dornfield, Ernst. Butterflies of Oregon. 275p. 1980. 25.00 (ISBN 0-917304-58-6, Pub. by Timber Pr). Intl Schol Bk Serv.

Dornier, Ann, ed. Mercian Studies. 250p. 1977. pap. text ed. 18.25x (ISBN 0-7185-1148-4, Leicester). Humanities.

Dornin, May, jt. auth. see Pickerell, Albert G.

Doron, Gideon. The Smoking Paradox: Public Regulation in the Cigarette Industry. LC 79-50400. 1979. text ed. 22.50 (ISBN 0-89011-531-1). Abt Assoc.

Dorp, Rolf Von see Myrdal, Jan.

Dorr, B. F. The Surveyor's Guide. 1978. pap. 8.50 (ISBN 0-686-25542-9, 514). CARBEN Survey.

Dorr, Dave, jt. auth. see Heidenreich, Steve.

Dorr, E. L. General Methodology Manual for Occupational Manuals & Projects in Marketing Series. 1969. 6.50 o.p. (ISBN 0-07-017647-7, G); general methodology manual 3.95 o.p. (ISBN 0-07-017648-5). McGraw.

Dorr, Rheta C. A Woman of Fifty. Baxter, Annette K., ed. LC 79-8787. (Signal Lives Ser.). 1980. Repr. of 1924 ed. lib. bdg. 40.00x (ISBN 0-405-12835-5). Arno.

Dorre, Pamela. Wind Over Stonehenge. (Pacesetters Ser.). (Illus.). 64p. (gr. 4 up). 1978. PLB 7.95 (ISBN 0-516-02175-3). Childrens.

Dorsen, Norman, et al. Emerson, Haber & Dorsen's Political & Civil Rights in the United States, Vol. I. 4th ed. 1976. lawyers ed. 48.00 (ISBN 0-316-23624-1); students ed 28.00 (ISBN 0-316-19046-2); pap. 8.95 1980 suppl (ISBN 0-316-19105-1); Vol. II. lawyers ed (ISBN 0-316-23627-6). Little.

Dorsett, Joseph L. College Algebra. 2nd ed. 1977. pap. text ed. 11.95 o.p. (ISBN 0-8403-1690-9). Kendall-Hunt.

Dorsett, Lyle W. Franklin D. Roosevelt & the City Bosses. (National University Publications Interdisciplinary Urban Ser.). 1977. 12.50 (ISBN 0-8046-9186-X); pap. 4.95 o.p. (ISBN 0-8046-9203-3). Kennikat.

--The Pendergast Machine. LC 80-11581. (Illus.). xvi, 163p. 1980. 13.50x (ISBN 0-8032-1655-6); pap. 3.95 (ISBN 0-8032-6554-9, BB 744, Bison). U of Nebr Pr.

Dorsett, Lyle W., jt. auth. see Brown, A. Theodore.

Dorsett, Lyle W., jt. auth. see Brown, A. Theodore.

Dorsey, Anne G., jt. auth. see Sciarra, Dorothy J.

Dorsey, John & Dilts, James D. A Guide to Baltimore Architecture. 2nd ed. 1981. 3.95x (ISBN 0-87033-272-4, Pub by Tidewater). Cornell Maritime.

Dorsey, John M. American Government: Conscious Self Sovereignty. 1969. 4.95x (ISBN 0-8143-1637-9). Wayne St U Pr.

--University Professor John M. Dorsey. (Illus.). 224p. 1980. 12.00 (ISBN 0-8143-1645-X). Wayne St U Pr.

Dorson, Richard M. America Rebels: Personal Narratives of the American Revoulution. 354p. Date not set. pap. 3.95 (ISBN 0-394-73277-4). Pantheon.

--American Folklore & the Historian. pap. write for info. (ISBN 0-226-15869-1). U of Chicago Pr.

Dorson, Richard M., ed. American Negro Folktales. 1976. pap. 1.50 o.p. (ISBN 0-449-30791-3, Prem). Fawcett.

Dorson, Ron. The Indy Five Hundred. 1974. 9.95 (ISBN 0-87880-025-5). Norton.

Dorst, Jean. The Life of Birds, 2 vols. (Illus.). 700p. 1974. 50.00x (ISBN 0-231-03909-3). Columbia U Pr.

D'Ortigue, M. J. Dictionnaire De Plain-Chant et De Musique D'eglise. LC 79-155353. (Music Ser). 1971. Repr. of 1854 ed. lib. bdg. 65.00 (ISBN 0-306-70165-0). Da Capo.

Dorward, Douglas. Wild Australia. (Illus.). 128p. 1980. 20.95x (ISBN 0-00-211446-1, Pub. by W Collins Australia). Intl Schol Bk Serv.

Dosa, Marta L., tr. Libraries in the Political Scene: Georg Leyh & German Librarianship, 1933-53. LC 72-5218. (Contributions in Librarianship & Information Science: No. 7). 256p. 1973. lib. bdg. 16.95 (ISBN 0-8371-6443-5, DGL/). Greenwood.

Dosch, Hans-Michael, jt. ed. see Gelfand, Erwin W.

Doscher, Paul, et al. Intensive Gardening Round the Year. (Illus.). 224p. 1981. pap. 15.00 (ISBN 0-8289-0399-9). Greene.

Doshi, Malvi. A Surti Touch: Adventures in Indian Cooking. LC 80-21847. (Illus.). 1980. pap. 7.95 (ISBN 0-89407-042-8). Strawberry Hill.

Doskey, John S., jt. auth. see Rosenberg, Kenyon C.

Dos Passos, John. Big Money. 1969. pap. 2.50 (ISBN 0-451-51353-3, CE1353, Sig Classics). NAL.

--Facing the Chair: Story of the Americanization of Two Foreign-Born Workmen. LC 72-104066. (Civil Liberties in American History Ser). 1970. Repr. of 1927 ed. 14.95 (ISBN 0-306-71871-5). Da Capo.

--Manhattan Transfer. LC 79-10459. 1980. Repr. of 1953 ed. lib. bdg. 15.00x (ISBN 0-8376-0433-8). Bentley.

--One Man's Initiation: Nineteen Seventeen. LC 69-15945. (Illus.). 180p. 1970. pap. 2.95 (ISBN 0-8014-9082-0, CP82). Cornell U Pr.

Doss, Calvin L. School & Community Relations: A Book of Readings. 1976. pap. text ed. 6.75x (ISBN 0-8191-0030-7). U Pr of Amer.

Doss, Helen. The Air Force: From Balloons to Space Ships. (Illus.). 64p. (gr. 4-6). 1981. PLB 6.97 (ISBN 0-686-69305-1). Messner.

Doss, Margot P. The Bay Area at Your Feet: Walks with San Francisco's Margot Patterson Doss. rev. ed. (Illus.). 288p. (Orig.). 1981. pap. 7.95 (ISBN 0-89141-097-X). Presidio Pr.

--Paths of Gold: A Walker's Guide to the Golden Gate National Recreation Area. (Illus.). 176p. 1974. pap. 3.50 o.p. (ISBN 0-87701-053-6). Chronicle Bks.

Dossat, R. J. ARA Principles of Refrigeration: SI Version. 2nd ed. 1980. 14.95 (ISBN 0-471-06326-6). Wiley.

Dossat, Roy J. Principles of Refrigeration. 2nd ed. LC 78-2938. 1978. text ed. 25.95 (ISBN 0-471-03550-5); solutions manual 4.00 (ISBN 0-471-03771-0). Wiley.

Doster, James F. Creek Indians. Horr, David A., ed. (American Indian Ethnohistory Ser.). 1978. lib. bdg. 42.00 (ISBN 0-8240-0788-3). Garland Pub.

Doster, W., ed. Barron's How to Prepare for the CLEP Examinations - General Examination. rev. ed. LC 78-32129. 1979. pap. 6.50 (ISBN 0-8120-2011-1). Barron.

Doster, W. C., et al. How to Prepare for the College-Level Examination Program (CLEP) rev. ed. LC 78-32129. (gr. 9-12). 1979. pap. text ed. 6.50 (ISBN 0-8120-2011-1). Barron.

Doster, William C. Differing Eye: An Introduction to Literature. LC 74-85767. 350p. (Orig.). 1970. pap. 6.95x (ISBN 0-02-473980-4, 47398); teachers' manual free (ISBN 0-685-11740-5, 47397). Macmillan.

Dostoevsky, Fyodor. The Gambler. MacAndrew, Andrew R., tr. 192p. 1981. pap. 4.95 (ISBN 0-393-00044-3). Norton.

--The Idiot. pap. 2.25. Bantam.

Dostoyevsky, Fedor. Crime & Punishment. Garnett, Constance, tr. 1955. 12.95x (ISBN 0-460-00501-4, Evman); pap. 4.50 (ISBN 0-460-01501-X). Dutton.

--Crime & Punishment. Magarshack, David, tr. (Classics Ser.). (Orig.). 1952. pap. 3.95 (ISBN 0-14-044023-2). Penguin.

--Grand Inquisitor on the Nature of Man. Garnett, Constance, tr. 1948. pap. 2.50 (ISBN 0-672-60237-7, LLA63). Bobbs.

--Poor Folk. Hogarth, C. J., tr. Incl. The Gambler. 1956. 6.00x (ISBN 0-460-00711-4, Evman); pap. 5.95 (ISBN 0-460-01711-X, Evman). Dutton.

Dostoyevsky, Fedor M. Crime & Punishment: A Novel in 6 Pts. & Epilogue. Coulson, Jessie, tr. (World Classics Ser). Set. 9.95 (ISBN 0-19-250619-6). Oxford U Pr.

Dostoyevsky, Feodor. Crime & Punishment. (Literature Ser). (gr. 9-12). 1969. pap. text ed. 3.83 (ISBN 0-87720-705-4). AMSCO Sch.

--Crime & Punishment with Reader's Guide. (Amsco Literature Program). (gr. 10-12). 1970. pap. text ed. 4.50 (ISBN 0-87720-805-0); tchr's ed. 2.95 (ISBN 0-87720-905-7). AMSCO Sch.

Dostoyevsky, Fodor. The Grand Inquisitor. LC 56-7503. (Milestones of Thought Ser.). pap. 1.45 (ISBN 0-8044-6125-2). Ungar.

Dostoyevsky, Fyodor. Crime & Punishment. (Now Age Illustrated V Ser.). (Illus.). 64p. (gr. 4-12). 1979. text ed. 4.50 (ISBN 0-686-26918-7); pap. text ed. 1.45 (ISBN 0-88301-386-X); student activity bk. 0.95 (ISBN 0-88301-410-6). Pendulum Pr.

--Idiot. (Classic Ser.). 1969. pap. 2.25 (ISBN 0-451-51374-6, CE1374, Sig Classics). NAL.

Dostoyevsky, Fyodor M. Letters from the Underworld: The Gentle Maiden & the Landlady. 1979. pap. 2.95 (Evman). Dutton.

Dotan, Aron. Ben Asher's Creed. LC 76-27649. (Society of Biblical Literature. Masoretic Studies). 1977. pap. 7.50 (ISBN 0-89130-084-8, 060503). Scholars Pr Ca.

Dotson, Marlice, tr. see Kane, Wanden M.

Dott, Robert H. & Batten, Roger L. Evolution of the Earth. 3rd ed. (Illus.). 576p. 1980. text ed. 22.95 (ISBN 0-07-017625-6, C); write for info. McGraw.

Dotts, Maryann. I Am Happy. (Illus.). (gr. k-2). 1971. 3.50 o.p. (ISBN 0-687-18203-4). Abingdon.

Dotts, Maryann J. When Jesus Was Born. LC 79-3958. (Illus.). (ps-3). 1979. 5.95g (ISBN 0-687-45020-9). Abingdon.

Dotts, Maryann J., jt. auth. see Franklin, M.

Doty, Betty. Marriage Insurance. 8.95 (ISBN 0-930822-01-3). Green Hill.

--Publish Your Own Handbound Books. LC 80-67947. (Illus.). 127p. 1980. 8.95 (ISBN-0-930822-02-1); lib. bdg. 7.95 (ISBN 0-930822-03-X). Bookery.

--Publish Your Own Hardbound Books. 1981. 7.95. Green Hill.

Doty, C. Stewart. From Cultural Rebellion to Counterrevolution: The Politics of Maurice Barres. LC 75-15337. 294p. 1976. 16.00 (ISBN 0-8214-0191-2). Ohio U Pr.

Doty, Gladys G. & Ross, Janet. Language & Life in the USA: Communicating in English, Vol. I. 4th ed. (Illus.). 1981. pap. text ed. 9.50 scp (ISBN 0-06-041693-9, HarpC); avail. Har-Row.

--Language & Life in the USA: Reading English, Vol. II. (Illus.). 1981. pap. text ed. 8.50 scp (ISBN 0-06-041694-7, HarpC). Har-Row.

Doty, Jean & Doty, Roy. Macmillan Children's Calendar, 1981. Larkin, Phyllis, ed. 15p. (gr. 3 up). 1980. spiral bdg 4.95 (ISBN 0-02-732980-1). Macmillan.

Doty, Jean S. The Crumb. LC 75-33648. 128p. (gr. 5-9). 1976. PLB 6.96 (ISBN 0-688-84035-3). Greenwillow.

--Gabriel. LC 73-6045. (Illus.). 128p. (gr. 3-5). 1974. 4.95g o.s.i. (ISBN 0-02-732740-X). Macmillan.

--The Monday Horses. LC 77-13310. (gr. 5-9). 1978. 7.95 (ISBN 0-688-80134-X); PLB 7.63 (ISBN 0-688-84134-1). Greenwillow.

--Monday Horses. (gr. 5-7). 1979. pap. 1.75 (ISBN 0-671-41856-4). Archway.

--Summer Pony. 128p. (gr. 3-7). 1973. 8.95 (ISBN 0-02-732750-7). Macmillan.

--Winter Pony. (Illus.). 112p. (gr. 4-6). 1975. 7.95 (ISBN 0-02-732760-4). Macmillan.

Doty, Mark A. Tell Me Who I Am: James Agee's Search for Selfhood. LC 80-22440. 176p. 1981. 15.95x (ISBN 0-8071-0758-1). La State U Pr.

Doty, Richard L., ed. Mammalian Olfaction: Reproducive Processes, & Behavior. 1976. 38.50 (ISBN 0-12-221250-9). Acad Pr.

Doty, Roy. Gunga Your Din Din Is Ready & Pinocchio Was Nosey. (gr. 3-5). 1978. pap. 1.50 (ISBN 0-671-29856-9). Archway.

--Gunga, Your Din-Din Is Ready: Son of Puns, Gags, Quips & Riddles. LC 75-24624. 64p. (gr. 4-7). 1976. PLB 4.95 (ISBN 0-385-11522-9). Doubleday.

--Pinocchio Was Nosy: Grandson of Puns, Gags, Quips & Riddles. LC 76-57873. (gr. 4-7). 1977. PLB 4.95 (ISBN 0-385-12920-3). Doubleday.

--Puns, Gags, Quips, & Riddles & Q's Are Weird O's. (Illus.). (gr. 3-5). 1976. pap. 1.50 (ISBN 0-671-29909-3). PB.

--Tinkerbell Is a Ding-a-Ling. LC 79-6973. (Illus.). (gr. 4-6). 1980. 4.95a (ISBN 0-385-13490-8); PLB 4.95 (ISBN 0-385-13491-6). Doubleday.

Doty, Roy & Maar, Len. Where Are You Going with That Coal? LC 75-36586. (gr. 4-7). 1978. 5.95a (ISBN 0-385-11515-6); PLB (ISBN 0-385-11516-4). Doubleday.

--Where Are You Going with That Energy? LC 75-36587. (gr. 2-5). 1978. 5.95a (ISBN 0-385-11519-9); PLB (ISBN 0-385-11520-2). Doubleday.

Doty, Roy, jt. auth. see Doty, Jean.

Doty, T. K. Lessons in Holiness. pap. 2.00 o.p. (ISBN 0-686-12889-3). Schmul Pub Co.

Doty, Walter, jt. auth. see Burke, Ken.

Doty, William G. Letters in Primitive Christianity. Via, Dan O., Jr., ed. LC 72-87058. (Guides to Biblical Scholarship: New Testament Ser.). 96p. 1973. pap. 3.25 (ISBN 0-8006-0170-X, 1-170). Fortress.

Doty, William G., ed. see Eliade, Mircea.

Douarin, N. Le see Le Douarin, N.

Douassot, Jean. La Gana. Trocchi, Alexander, tr. 1980. 15.95 (ISBN 0-7145-0327-4). Riverrun NY.

Double, Don. Life in a New Dimension. 1979. pap. 1.95 o.p. (ISBN 0-88368-083-1). Whitaker Hse.

Doubleday, Neal F. Writing the Research Paper. rev. ed. 1971. pap. text ed. 5.95x (ISBN 0-669-81224-2). Heath.

Doubleday, Richard. Readings, 3 vols. 1970. Vol. 1. pap. text ed. 3.95x ea. o.p. (ISBN 0-435-11235-X); Vol. 2. pap. text ed. (ISBN 0-435-11236-8); Vol. 3. pap. text ed. (ISBN 0-435-11237-6). Heinemann Ed.

Doubtfire. Girl Called Rosemary. (gr. 7-12). pap. 1.25 (ISBN 0-590-09243-X, Schol Pap). Schol Bk Serv.

--Girl with Wings. (gr. 7-12). pap. 1.25 o.p. (ISBN 0-590-05370-1, Schol Pap). Schol Bk Serv.

Doubtfire, Dianne. The Craft of Novel Writing. 1981. pap. 5.95 (ISBN 0-8052-8087-1, Pub. by Allison & Busby England). Schocken.

Doucette, John & Freedman, Ruth. Progress Tests for the Developmentally Disabled: An Evaluation. LC 79-55773. 1979. text ed. 27.50 (ISBN 0-89011-539-7). Abt Assoc.

Doudna, Martin K. Concerned About the Planet: The Reporter Magazine & American Liberalism, 1949-1968. LC 77-10048. (Contributions in American Studies: No. 32). 1977. lib. bdg. 16.95 (ISBN 0-8371-9698-1, DCA/). Greenwood.

Doudoroff, Peter. A Critical Review of Recent Literature on Toxicity of Cyanides to Fish. LC 80-68588. 71p. (Orig.). 1980. pap. 3.60 (ISBN 0-89364-039-5, API 847-87000). Am Petroleum.

Dougall, Herbert E. & Gaumnitz, Jack E. Capital Markets & Institutions. 4th ed. (Foundations of Finance Ser.). (Illus.). 1980. pap. text ed. 10.95 (ISBN 0-13-113670-4). P-H.

Dougall, Herbert E. & Graumnitz, Jack E. Capital Markets & Institutions. 3rd ed. (Foundations of Finance Ser.). 240p. 1975. pap. text ed. 9.95 o.p. (ISBN 0-13-113654-2). P-H.

Dougall, Neil. Horses & Ponies on Small Areas. (Illus.). pap. 2.65 (ISBN 0-85131-273-X, Dist. by Sporting Book Center). J A Allen.

Dougan, R. O. W. B. Yeats, Manuscripts & Printed Books, Exhibited in the Library of Trinity College, Dublin. 50p. 1980. Repr. of 1956 ed. lib. bdg. 10.00 (ISBN 0-8492-4216-9). R West.

Dougherty, Ching-yi, et al. Chinese Character Indexes: Vol. 1: Telegraphic Code Index. Vol. 2: Romanization Index. Vol. 3: Radical Index. Vol. 4: Total Stroke Count Index. Vol. 5: Four Corner System Index. 1963. 82.50x (ISBN 0-520-00346-2). U of Cal Pr.

Dougherty, James E. & Pfaltzgraff, Diane K. Eurocommunism & the Atlantic Alliance. LC 76-53142. (Special Reports Ser.). 1977. 3.00 (ISBN 0-89549-003-X). Inst Foreign Policy Anal.

Dougherty, James E., jt. auth. see Cottrell, Alvin J.

Dougherty, James J. The Politics of Wartime Aid: American Economic Assistance to France & French Northwest Africa, 1940-1946. LC 77-84770. (Contributions in American History: No. 71). 1978. lib. bdg. 18.95 (ISBN 0-8371-9882-8, DPW/). Greenwood.

Dougherty, R. W. Experimental Surgery in Farm Animals. (Illus.). 1981. write for info. (ISBN 0-8138-1540-1). Iowa St U Pr.

Dougherty, Richard M. & Blomquist, Laura L. Improving Access to Library Resources. LC 73-20482. (Illus.). 1974. 10.00 (ISBN 0-8108-0637-1). Scarecrow.

Dougherty, Richard M. & Heinritz, Fred. J. Scientific Management of Library Operations. LC 66-13741. 1966. 10.00 (ISBN 0-8108-0132-9). Scarecrow.

Dougherty, Richard M. & Maier, Joan M. Centralized Processing for Academic Libraries. LC 73-155716. 1971. 16.50 (ISBN 0-8108-0381-X). Scarecrow.

Dougherty, Thomas A. The Enigma of the Eighties: Environment, Economic, Energy. (The Science of Advanced Materials Process Engineering Ser). (Illus.). 1979. 55.00 o.p. (ISBN 0-686-15770-2). Soc Adv Material.

Doughtie, Venton L. & Vallance, A. Design of Machine Members. 4th ed. 1964. text ed. 22.50 o.p (ISBN 0-07-017635-3, C). McGraw.

Doughty, O., ed. see Rossetti, Dante G.

Doughty, Oswald. Dante Gabriel Rossetti. Dobree, Bonamy, et al, eds. Bd. with William Morris. Henderson, Philip; Algernon Charles Swinburne. Grierson, H. J. LC 63-63096. (British Writers & Their Work Ser: Vol. 7). 1965. pap. 1.60x (ISBN 0-8032-5657-4, BB 456, Bison). U of Nebr Pr.

--Perturbed Spirit: The Life & Personality of Samuel Taylor Coleridge. LC 78-66792. 450p. Date not set. price not set (ISBN 0-8386-2353-0). Fairleigh Dickinson. Postponed.

Doughty, Paul L., jt. auth. see Dobyns, Henry F.

Doughty, Robin W. Feather Fashions & Bird Preservation. LC 72-619678. 1975. 16.50x (ISBN 0-520-02588-1). U of Cal Pr.

Douglas & Waksler. Deviance. 1981. text ed. 16.95 (ISBN 0-316-19111-6); tchrs'. manual free (ISBN 0-316-19112-4). Little.

--The Sociology of Deviance: An Introduction. 512p. 1981. text ed. 16.95 (ISBN 0-316-19111-6); tchr's ed free (ISBN 0-316-19112-4). Little.

Douglas, et al. Introduction to the Sociologies of Everyday Life. 1980. text ed. 12.95 (ISBN 0-205-06813-8, 816813X). Allyn.

Douglas, A G. & Maxwell, J. R., eds. Advances in Organic Geochemistry 1979: Proceedings of the 9th International Meeting on Organic Geochemistry Held at Newcastle-Upon-Tyne, England, Sept. 1979. LC 80-41078. (International Ser. in Earth Sciences: Vol. 36). (Illus.). 750p. 1980. 150.00 (ISBN 0-08-024017-8). Pergamon.

Douglas, A. G., et al. New Product Development: A Systematic Approach to Diversification. LC 78-2398. 1978. 24.95 (ISBN 0-470-26328-8). Halsted Pr.

Douglas, A. H. An Approach to Engineering Mathematics. 1971. pap. 10.75 (ISBN 0-08-016016-6). Pergamon.

Douglas, Adrian P. & Kerr, David. Short Textbook of Kidney Disease. (Illus.). 1968. 12.00 o.p. (ISBN 0-397-58081-9). Lippincott.

Douglas, Alan. Electronic Music Production. LC 74-75216. (Illus.). 156p. 1974. 7.95 o.p. (ISBN 0-8306-4718-X); pap. 3.95 (ISBN 0-8306-3718-4, 718). TAB Bks.

Douglas, Alfred. Tails with a Twist: Animal Nonsense Verse. (Illus.). 64p. 1980. 14.95 (ISBN 0-7134-1870-2, Pub. by Batsford England). David & Charles.

Douglas, Althea see Burney, Fanny.

Douglas, Andrew, jt. auth. see Crofton, John.

Douglas, Ann. The Feminization of American Culture. 1978. pap. 3.95 (ISBN 0-380-01968-X, 51870, Discus). Avon.

--Industrial Peacemaking. LC 62-14463. (Illus.). viii, 675p. 1962. 27.50x (ISBN 0-231-02487-8). Columbia U Pr.

Douglas, Auriel. The Ghost of Staghorn. 192p. (Orig.). 1981. pap. 1.95 (ISBN 0-523-41323-8). Pinnacle Bks.

Douglas, Bob. Wrestling: The Making of a Champion. (Illus.). 1979. 9.95 (ISBN 0-8014-9177-0). Cornell U Pr.

Douglas, Bodie E. & McDaniel, D. H. Concepts & Models of Inorganic Chemistry. 1965. text ed. 26.95 (ISBN 0-471-00129-5). Wiley.

Douglas, Carole N. Amberleigh. 352p. (Orig.). 1980. pap. 2.50 (ISBN 0-515-05715-0). Jove Pubns.

Douglas, Charles. Natural History Notebook, 2 bks. (Illus.). 1977. No. 1. pap. 2.00 (ISBN 0-660-00092-X, 56440-1, Pub. by Natl Mus Canada); No. 2. pap. 2.00 (ISBN 0-660-00094-6, 56442-8). U of Chicago Pr.

--Natural History Notebook, No. 3. (Illus.). iv, 54p. Date not set. pap. 2.00 (ISBN 0-660-10341-9, 56444-4, Pub. by Natl Mus Canada). U of Chicago Pr. Postponed.

Douglas, Charles N., jt. auth. see John, Robert W.

Douglas, Charlotte C. Swans of Other Worlds: Kazimir Malevich & the Origins of Abstraction in Russia. (Studies in Fine Arts: The Avant-Garde, No. 2). 1980. 23.95 (ISBN 0-8357-1058-0). Univ Microfilms.

Douglas, Colin. Sickness & Health: A Novel. LC 80-28316. 200p. 1981. 8.95 (ISBN 0-8008-7178-2). Taplinger.

Douglas, David. Douglas of the Forests: The North American Journals of David Douglas. Davies, John, ed. LC 80-12535. (Illus.). 194p. 1980. 14.95 (ISBN 0-295-95707-7). U of Wash Pr.

Douglas, David C. The Norman Achievement: 1050-1100. LC 74-88028. 1969. 20.00x (ISBN 0-520-01383-2). U of Cal Pr.

--The Norman Fate, 1100-1154. LC 75-13155. 350p. 1976. 29.50x (ISBN 0-520-03027-3). U of Cal Pr.

--William the Conqueror: The Norman Impact Upon England. (English Monarchs Ser.). 1964. 20.00x (ISBN 0-520-00348-9); pap. 5.95 (ISBN 0-520-00350-0, CAL131). U of Cal Pr.

Douglas, Evan J. Managerial Economics: Theory, Practice & Problems. (Illus.). 1979. ref. 20.95 (ISBN 0-13-550236-5). P-H.

Douglas, Frederick. My Bondage & My Freedom. 10.00 (ISBN 0-8446-0588-3). Peter Smith.

Douglas, G., jt. auth. see Doise, W.

Douglas, G. R., ed. see Carnegie Commission on Higher Education.

Douglas, George A. Writing for Public Relations. (Marketing & Management Ser.). 192p. 1980. pap. text ed. 8.95 (ISBN 0-675-08171-8). Merrill.

Douglas, Gertrude. Linked Lives. Wolff, Robert L., ed. (Victorian Fiction Ser.). 1975. Repr. of 1876 ed. lib. bdg. 66.00 (ISBN 0-8240-1537-1). Garland Pub.

Douglas, Gina. The Ganges. LC 78-62983. (Rivers of the World Ser.). (Illus.). 1978. lib. bdg. 7.95 (ISBN 0-686-51134-4). Silver.

Douglas, Gregory A. The Nest. 1980. 2.75 (ISBN 0-89083-662-0). Zebra.

Douglas, Herman. Are You Paying Too Much for Your Car? Sweitzer, Peggy, ed. 1979. write for info. Web Pub Hse.

Douglas, Hugh. Portrait of the Burns Country. LC 68-117106. (Portrait Bks.). (Illus.). 1968. 10.50x (ISBN 0-7091-5368-6). Intl Pubns Serv.

Douglas, J. Defining America's Social Problems. 1974. pap. 11.95 (ISBN 0-13-197624-9). P-H.

Douglas, J., et al. Units in Woodworking. (Construction-Industrial Arts Ser.). 208p. pap. text ed. 7.80 o.p. (ISBN 0-8273-0112-X); instr's guide 0.50 o.p. (ISBN 0-8273-0115-4); extra test bks free o.p. (ISBN 0-8273-0114-6). Delmar.

Douglas, J. Andrew. The Amazing Lost Money-Secret of the U. S. Government. 228p. 1981. 9.95 (ISBN 0-8119-0417-2, Pegasus Rex). Fell.

Douglas, J. D. American Social Order. LC 70-142360. 1971. 8.95 (ISBN 0-02-907510-6); pap. text ed. 8.95 (ISBN 0-02-907530-0). Free Pr.

Douglas, J. D., ed. New Bible Dictionary. 1962. 24.95 (ISBN 0-8028-2282-7). Eerdmans.

Douglas, J. D. & Johnson, J. M., eds. Existential Sociology. LC 76-47198. 1977. 34.50 (ISBN 0-521-21515-3); pap. 10.95x (ISBN 0-521-29225-5). Cambridge U Pr.

Douglas, Jack D. Research on Deviance. 320p. 1972. pap. text ed. 4.95x o.p. (ISBN 0-394-31154-X, RanC). Random.

Douglas, Jack D., ed. Introduction to Sociology: Situations & Structures. LC 75-163608. 1973. text ed. 14.95 (ISBN 0-02-907540-8). Free Pr.

--Observations of Deviance: Deviant Situations, Styles, & Ways of Life. (Orig.). 1970. pap. text ed. 5.95x (ISBN 0-394-30130-7, RanC). Random.

--Relevance of Sociology. (Orig.). 1970. 10.95 (ISBN 0-13-773093-4). P-H.

Douglas, James S. Beginner's Guide to Hydroponics (Soilless Gardening) 1972. 8.50 (ISBN 0-7207-0572-X, Pub. by Michael Joseph). Merrimack Bk Serv.

Douglas, Janet, jt. auth. see Hanson, A. H.

Douglas, John. Parent Power. 1979. pap. 2.50 (ISBN 0-915106-11-6, Pub. by Two Continents). Hippocrene Bks.

Douglas, John, jt. auth. see Massie, J. L.

Douglas, John, jt. auth. see Massie, Joseph L.

Douglas, John S. Secret of the Undersea Bell. LC 51-13649. (gr. 9 up). 1951. 5.95 (ISBN 0-396-03322-9). Dodd.

Douglas, Kathryn. Cavendish Square. 224p. (Orig.). 1976. pap. 1.50 o.p. (ISBN 0-345-24910-0). Ballantine.

Douglas, Kenneth, ed. see De Cervantes, Miguel.

Douglas, Kenneth, tr. see Tsogyal, Yeshe.

Douglas, Lewis W. The Liberal Tradition. LC 77-171382. (FDR & the Era of the New Deal Ser). 136p. 1972. Repr. of 1935 ed. lib. bdg. 15.00 (ISBN 0-306-70376-9). Da Capo.

Douglas, Lloyd V., et al. Teaching Business Subjects. 3rd ed. (Illus.). 1973. ref. ed. 18.95 (ISBN 0-13-891457-5). P-H.

Douglas McHenry International Symposium in Concrete & Concrete Structures. Proceedings. 1978. 28.95 (SP-55); 21.25. ACI.

Douglas, Mark, jt. auth. see Moore, Marcia.

Douglas, Martin, jt. auth. see Brandes, Joseph.

Douglas, Mary. Implicit Meanings: Essays in Anthropology. (Illus.). 1978. pap. 8.95 (ISBN 0-7100-0047-2). Routledge & Kegan.

--Implicit Meanings: Essays in Anthropology. (Illus.). 220p. 1975. 17.95x o.s.i. (ISBN 0-7100-8226-6). Routledge & Kegan.

--Purity & Danger: An Analysis of Concepts of Pollution & Taboo. 1978. pap. 7.95 (ISBN 0-7100-8827-2). Routledge & Kegan.

Douglas, Mary A. The Secretarial Dental Assistant. LC 75-19522. 1976. pap. 9.20 (ISBN 0-8273-0349-1); instructor's guide 1.60 (ISBN 0-8273-0350-5). Delmar.

--Secretarial Dental Assistant. 304p. 1981. text ed. 14.95 (ISBN 0-442-21860-5). Van Nos Reinhold.

Douglas, Nathan, et al. The Defiant Ones: A Screen Adaptation of the Story of "The Long Road". Garrett, George, et al, eds. LC 71-135273. (Film Scripts Ser.). 1971. pap. text ed. 5.95x (ISBN 0-89197-725-2). Irvington.

Douglas, Nik & Slinger, Penny. The Pillow Book. (Illus.). 1981. 24.95 (ISBN 0-686-69423-6, Destiny Bks). Inner Tradit.

Douglas, Norman. London Street Games. 2nd ed. LC 68-31089. 1968. Repr. of 1931 ed. 15.000 (ISBN 0-8103-3477-1). Gale.

Douglas, Paul H. Social Security in the United States: An Analysis & Appraisal of the Federal Social Security Act. 2nd ed. LC 70-167847. (FDR & the Era of the New Deal). 1971. Repr. of 1939 ed. lib. bdg. 42.50 (ISBN 0-306-70323-8). Da Capo.

Douglas, Peter. Kitchen Planning & Design. (Case Studies Ser.: Vol. 2). (Illus.). 128p. 1980. 19.95 (ISBN 0-7137-0982-0, Pub. by Blandford Pr England); pap. 14.95 (ISBN 0-7137-1034-9). Sterling.

Douglas, Peter, jt. auth. see Walsh, Barry.

Douglas, R. Alan. John Prince, Seventeen Ninety-Six to Eighteen Seventy: A Collection of Documents. (Champlain Society Ontario Ser.). 350p. 1980. 20.00 (ISBN 0-8020-2378-9). U of Toronto Pr.

Douglas, R. G. Banach Algebra Techniques in the Theory of Toeplitz Operators. LC 73-1021. (CBMS Regional Conference Ser. in Mathematics: No. 15). 1980. Repr. of 1973 ed. 11.20 (ISBN 0-8218-1665-9, CBMS-15). Am Math.

--C-Algebra Extensions & K-Homology. 1980. 12.50 (ISBN 0-691-08265-0); pap. 4.50 (ISBN 0-691-08266-9). Princeton U Pr.

Douglas, R. G., ed. see Kurpel, N. S.

Douglas, Robert K. Li-Hung-Chang. (Studies in Chinese History & Civilization). 1977. Repr. of 1895 ed. 19.75 (ISBN 0-89093-110-0). U Pubns Amer.

Douglas, Ronald G. C-Algebra Extensions & K-Homology. LC 80-424. (Annals of Mathematics Studies: No. 95). (Illus.). 87p. 1980. 12.50x (ISBN 0-691-08265-0); pap. 4.50x (ISBN 0-691-08266-9). Princeton U Pr.

Douglas, Ronald M. The Irish Book: A Miscellany of Facts & Figures, Folklore & Fragments, Poems & Prose to Do with Ireland & Her People. LC 74-164227. xxvi, 393p. 1972. Repr. of 1936 ed. 20.00 (ISBN 0-8103-3166-7). Gale.

Douglas, Roy. Advent of War, Nineteen Thirty-Nine to Nineteen Forty. LC 78-12266. 1979. 21.95 (ISBN 0-312-00650-0). St Martin.

--From War to Cold War: 1942-48. 1980. 19.95 (ISBN 0-312-30862-0). St Martin.

Douglas, S. W. & Williamson, H. D. Principles of Veterinary Radiography. 3rd ed. 296p. 1980. text ed. write for info. (ISBN 0-8121-0737-3). Lea & Febiger.

Douglas, Shawhan. Physics with the Computer: Teacher's Edition. 288p. (Orig.). 1980. 19.95 (ISBN 0-87567-037-7). Entelek.

Douglas, Sheila. The Girl Between. (Harlequin Romances). 192p. 1981. pap. 1.25 (ISBN 0-373-02392-8, Pub. by Harlequin). PB.

--Return to Lanmore. (Harlequin Presents Ser.). (Orig.). 1980. pap. text ed. 1.25 o.p. (ISBN 0-373-02336-7, Pub. by Harlequin). PB.

Douglas, Thorne. Mustang Men. 1977. pap. 1.25 o.p. (ISBN 0-449-13918-2, GM). Fawcett.

Douglas, W. M. Andrew Murray & His Message. (Christian Biography Ser.). 336p. 1981. pap. 3.95 (ISBN 0-8010-2908-2). Baker Bk.

Douglas, William O. The Court Years: Nineteen Thirty-Nine to Nineteen Seventy-Five. (Illus.). 434p. 16.95 (ISBN 0-394-49240-4). Random.

Douglas Jackson, W. A., jt. auth. see Creed, Virginia.

Douglass, et al. Units in Woodworking. 208p. 1973. 7.80 o.p. (ISBN 0-8273-0112-X); pap. 6.20 o.p. (ISBN 0-8273-0113-8); tests & ans. avail. o.p. Delmar.

Douglass, A. E. Climatic Cycle & Tree Growth, 3 vols. in one. (Vols. 1 & 2, A Study of the Annual Rings of Trees in Relation to Climate & Solar Activity; Vol. 3, A Study of Cycles). 1971. 75.00 (ISBN 3-7682-0720-X). Lubrecht & Cramer.

Douglass, Amanda H. Charlotte. 1978. pap. 1.95 (ISBN 0-505-51271-8). Tower Bks.

--Christabel. 1978. pap. 2.25 (ISBN 0-505-51310-2). Tower Bks.

--The Heavens Blaze Forth. 1978. pap. 1.75 (ISBN 0-505-51252-1). Tower Bks.

--Jamaica. 1977. pap. 1.75 (ISBN 0-8439-0492-5, Leisure Bks). Nordon Pubns.

Douglass, Barbara. Sizzle Wheels. LC 80-39750. (Illus.). (gr. 3-6). 1981. 9.95 (ISBN 0-664-32680-3). Westminster.

Douglass, D. L. The Metallurgy of Zirconium. (Illus.). 470p. (Orig.). 1972. pap. 26.75 (ISBN 92-0-159071-7, IAEA). Unipub.

Douglass, David R. How to Solve Conflicts: Leader's Guide. (Leader's Guide Ser.). (Illus.). 1978. pap. 4.95 (ISBN 0-8024-3657-9). Moody.

Douglass, E. P. Rebels & Democrats. LC 77-160853. (Era of the American Revolution Ser.). 368p. 1971. Repr. of 1955 ed. 35.00 (ISBN 0-306-70402-1). Da Capo.

Douglass, Elisha P. Coming of Age of American Business. LC 78-132254. 1971. 24.00x (ISBN 0-8078-1170-X). U of NC Pr.

Douglass, Fenner. Cavaille-Coll & the Musicians. (Illus.). 48p. 78.00 (ISBN 0-915548-09-7). Sunbury Pr.

Douglass, Frederick. Life & Times of Frederick Douglass. Ritchie, Barbara, ed. LC 66-10063. (gr. 7 up). 1966. 7.95 (ISBN 0-690-50088-2, TYC-J). T Y Crowell.

--Mind & Heart of Frederick Douglass: Excerpts from Speeches of the Great Negro Orator. Ritchie, Barbara, ed. LC 68-13587. (gr. 7 up). 1968. 7.95 (ISBN 0-690-54206-2, TYC-J). T Y Crowell.

--Narrative of the Life of Frederick Douglass. pap. 2.95 (ISBN 0-385-00705-1, C419, Anch). Doubleday.

Douglass, Gordon K. The New Interdependence: The European Community & the United States. LC 79-5121. 160p. 1979. 17.95 (ISBN 0-669-03203-4). Lexington Bks.

Douglass, Harl R. Modern Methods in High School Teaching. 544p. 1981. Repr. lib. bdg. 25.00 (ISBN 0-8495-1061-9). Arden Lib.

Douglass, Harl R., jt. auth. see Gruhn, William T.

Douglass, Herbert. The End. LC 79-88435. (Dimension Ser.). 1979. 7.95 (ISBN 0-8163-0341-X); pap. 5.95 (ISBN 0-8163-0328-2, 20251-5). Pacific Pr Pub Assn.

Douglass, J. H. Woodworking Basics. 320p. 1980. 14.95 (ISBN 0-442-23152-0). Van Nos Reinhold.

Douglass, J. H., et al. Units in Woodworking. LC 79-8737. (Industrial Arts Ser.). 320p. 1981. text ed. 12.00 (ISBN 0-8273-1332-2); pap. text ed. 9.00 (ISBN 0-8273-1333-0); comprehensive tests 0.60 (ISBN 0-8273-1334-9); instr's guide 1.30. Delmar.

Douglass, J. Harvey. Projects in Wood Furniture. rev. ed. LC 67-21721. (Illus.). (gr. 7 up). 1967. text ed. 14.00 (ISBN 0-87345-027-2). McKnight.

Douglass, Joseph D., Jr. Soviet Military Strategy in Europe. LC 79-19320. (Pergamon Policy Studies. An Institute for Foreign Policy Analysis Bk.). 270p. 1980. 33.00 (ISBN 0-08-023702-9). Pergamon.

Douglass, Joseph D., Jr. & Hoeber, Amoretta M. Soviet Strategy for Nuclear War. Staar, Richard F., ed. LC 79-1787. (Publications 208 Ser.). 1979. pap. 5.95 (ISBN 0-8179-7082-7). Hoover Inst Pr.

Douglass, Laura M. The Effective Nurse: Leader & Manager. LC 80-10860. (Illus.). 1980. pap. text ed. 9.95 (ISBN 0-8016-1448-1). Mosby.

--Review of Leadership in Nursing. 2nd ed. LC 76-41258. 1977. pap. text ed. 9.95 (ISBN 0-8016-1442-2). Mosby.

Douglass, Laura M. & Bevis, Em O. Nursing Management & Leadership in Action: Principles & Applications to Staff Situations. 3rd ed. LC 78-31960. (Illus.). 1979. pap. text ed. 12.75 (ISBN 0-8016-1441-4). Mosby.

Douglass, Leslie S. Women in Business: How to Make Yourself Marketable. (Illus.). 192p. 1980. 10.95 (ISBN 0-13-962019-2, Spec); pap. 4.95 (ISBN 0-13-962001-X). P-H.

--Women in Business: How to Make Yourself Marketable. (Illus.). 192p. 1980. 9.95 (Spec); pap. 4.95. P-H.

Douglass, Robert W. Forest Recreation. 2nd ed. 1975. text ed. 19.50 (ISBN 0-08-018008-6). Pergamon.

Douglass, Steve. Managing Yourself Leaders Guide. 150p. (Orig.). 1980. pap. 2.95 (ISBN 0-918956-69-2). Campus Crusade.

Douglass, W. A., jt. ed. see Aceves, J. B.

Douglass, William A., as told to see Paris, Beltran.

Douglass, Winsome. Toys for Your Delight. (Illus.). 208p. 1973. 9.95 o.p. (ISBN 0-263-70035-6). Transatlantic.

Douie, James M. The Panjab, North-West Frontier Province, & Kashmir. LC 74-903982. 1974. Repr. 16.00x o.p. (ISBN 0-8364-0443-2). South Asia Bks.

Doukhobor Research Committee. The Doukhobors of British Columbia. Hawthorn, Harry B., ed. LC 79-8711. (Illus.). xii, 288p. 1980. Repr. of 1955 ed. lib. bdg. 28.50x (ISBN 0-313-20652-X, DOBC). Greenwood.

Doulis, Thomas. Disaster & Fiction: The Impact of the Asia Minor Disaster of 1922 on Modern Greek Fiction. 1977. 17.50x (ISBN 0-520-03112-1). U of Cal Pr.

--George Theotokas. (World Authors Ser.: Greece: No. 339). 1975. lib. bdg. 12.50 (ISBN 0-8057-2881-3). Twayne.

Doulton, Joan & Hay, David. Managerial & Professional Staff Grading. (Studies in Management). 1962. pap. text ed. 4.95x (ISBN 0-04-658028-X). Allen Unwin.

Doumato, Lamia, ed. American Drawing: A Guide to Information Sources. LC 79-63743. (Art & Architecture Information Guide Ser.: Vol. 11). 1979. 30.00 (ISBN 0-8103-1441-X). Gale.

Doupnik, Joseph, jt. auth. see Banks, Peter M.

Douros, John D., jt. ed. see Cassady, John M.

Douty, H. M. The Wage Bargain & the Labor Market. 160p. 1980. 12.00 (ISBN 0-8018-2393-5); pap. 4.95 (ISBN 0-8018-2394-3). Johns Hopkins.

Dove, Rita. The Yellow House on the Corner. LC 80-65700. (Poetry Ser.). 1980. 9.95 (ISBN 0-915604-39-6); pap. 4.95 (ISBN 0-915604-40-X). Carnegie-Mellon.

Dove, W. F. & Rusch, H. P., eds. Growth & Differentiation in Physarum Polycephalum. LC 79-3202. (Illus.). 240p. 1980. 25.00x (ISBN 0-691-08254-5). Princeton U Pr.

Dover, A. T. Theory & Practice of Alternating Currents. 35.00x o.p. (ISBN 0-392-04926-0, SpS). Soccer.

Dover, K. J. Aristophanic Comedy. 1972. 14.00 o.p. (ISBN 0-520-01976-8); pap. 7.95x (ISBN 0-520-02211-4, CAMPUS77). U of Cal Pr.

--Greek Popular Morality in the Time of Plato & Aristotle. 1975. 23.75x (ISBN 0-520-02721-3). U of Cal Pr.

--Lysias & the Corpus Lysiacum. LC 68-63337. (Sather Classical Lectures: No. 39). 1968. 19.50x (ISBN 0-520-00351-9). U of Cal Pr.

Dover, K. J., ed. see Thucydides.

Dover, Kenneth. Ancient Greek Literature. 196p. 1980. 15.50 (ISBN 0-19-219137-3); pap. 6.95 (ISBN 0-19-289124-3). Oxford U Pr.

Dover, S. D., jt. auth. see Richards, E. G.

Dovring, Karin. Frontiers of Communication: The Americas in Search of Political Culture. 176p. 1975. 6.95 (ISBN 0-8158-0328-1). Chris Mass.

Dow, Allen. The Official Guide to Ballroom Dancing. (Illus.). 96p. 1980. 5.98 (ISBN 0-89196-065-1, Domus Bks). Quality Bks IL.

--The Official Guide to Jazz Dancing. (Illus.). 96p. 1980. 5.98 (ISBN 0-89196-064-3, Domus Bks). Quality Bks IL.

--The Official Guide to Latin Dancing. (Illus.). 96p. 1980. 5.98 (ISBN 0-89196-067-8, Domus Bks). Quality Bks IL.

Dow, Bea & Tabatch, Jack. Zany Word Search & Find Puzzles, No. 4. (Orig.). 1974. pap. 0.95 o.p. (ISBN 0-345-23893-1). Ballantine.

Dow, Clista & Smith, Linda H. Lunchroom Waste: A Study of "How Much & How Come". 1978. pap. 3.95 (ISBN 0-936386-04-5). Creative Learning.

Dow, G. Steven. Your Aquarium - Your Vacation - Your Relocation. (Illus.). 64p. (Orig.). 1976. pap. 2.50 (ISBN 0-87666-456-7, M528). TFH Pubns.

Dow, George F. Arts & Crafts in New England. 1704-1775. LC 67-2035. (Architecture & Decorative Art Ser). (Illus.). 1967. Repr. of 1927 ed. 29.50 (ISBN 0-306-70955-4). Da Capo.

--Slave Ships & Slaving. LC 68-57116. (Illus.). 1927. 10.00 (ISBN 0-87033-112-4). Cornell Maritime.

Dow, Gwyneth. Learning to Teach: Teaching to Learn. (Education Bks.). 1979. 22.00x (ISBN 0-7100-0093-6). Routledge & Kegan.

Dow, J. B., jt. auth. see Campbell, R. H.

Dow, J. C. Management of the British Economy, Nineteen Forty- Five-Sixty. LC 64-21542. (National Institute of Economic & Social Research Economic & Social Studies: No. 22). 1970. pap. 14.95x (ISBN 0-521-09467-4). Cambridge U Pr.

Dow, Miroslava W., ed. A Variorum Edition of Elizabeth Barrett Browning's Sonnets from the Portuguese. 201p. 1980. 12.50 (ISBN 0-87875-179-3). Whitston Pub.

Dow, Paul E. Discretionary Justice. 1981. price not set reference (ISBN 0-88410-835-X). Ballinger Pub.

Dow, Paul E., ed. Criminology in Literature. (Longman English & Humanities Ser.). 1980. pap. text ed. 8.95 (ISBN 0-582-28164-4). Longman.

Dow, R. Changing Societal Roles & Teaching. LC 76-39645. 1977. pap. 2.50 (ISBN 0-686-21734-9, 261-08428). Home Econ Educ.

--Marketing & Work Study. 1969. 27.00 (ISBN 0-08-006430-2); pap. 14.00 (ISBN 0-08-006429-9). Pergamon.

Dow, Roger W. Business English. LC 78-18253. 1979. 14.95 (ISBN 0-471-36661-7); wkbk. 7.95 (ISBN 0-471-04959-X); tchrs' manual avail. (ISBN 0-471-05251-5). Wiley.

Dow, Sterling. Fifty Years of Sathers: The Sather Professorship of Classical Literature in the University of California, Berkeley, 1913-14-1963-64. 1965. 14.50x (ISBN 0-520-00353-5). U of Cal Pr.

Dowaliby, Margaret. Practical Aspects of Ophthalmic Optics. 222p. 1980. 27.00, leatherette (ISBN 0-87873-010-9). Prof Press.

Dowall, David E. & Mingilton, Jesse. Effects of Environmental Regulations on Housing Costs. (CPL Bibliographies: No. 6). 67p. 1979. pap. 7.00 (ISBN 0-86602-006-3). CPL Biblios.

Doward, Jan. Seventh Escape. LC 68-54399. (Destiny Ser.). 1979. pap. 4.95 (ISBN 0-8163-0385-1, 19295-5). Pacific Pr Pub Assn.

Dowd, D. W., et al, eds. Medical, Moral & Legal Implications of Recent Medical Advances: A Symposium. LC 71-152124. (Symposia on Law & Society Ser). 1971. Repr. of 1968 ed. lib. bdg. 14.50 (ISBN 0-306-70128-6). Da Capo.

Dowd, Douglas F. Modern Economic Problems in Historical Perspective. 2nd ed. (Orig.). 1965. pap. text ed. 6.95x o.p. (ISBN 0-669-25536-X). Heath.

Dowd, James J. Stratification Among the Aged. LC 79-25143. (Social Gerontology Ser.). (Orig.). 1980. pap. text ed. 6.95 (ISBN 0-8185-0386-6). Brooks-Cole.

Dowd, John. Sea Kayaking: A Manual for Long-Distance Touring. (Illus.). 300p. 1981. 10.00 (ISBN 0-295-95807-3). U of Wash Pr.

Dowd, Merle E., jt. auth. see Garrison, William E.

Dowdell, Dorothy. Glory Land. 384p. (Orig.). 1981. pap. 2.75 (ISBN 0-449-14404-6, GM). Fawcett.

--Hibiscus Lagoon. (Orig.). 1981. pap. 1.50 (ISBN 0-440-14494-9). Dell.

--Tahoe. LC 77-76126. 1977. pap. 1.95 o.p. (ISBN 0-87216-408-X). Playboy Pbks.

Dowden, Ann O. Look at a Flower. LC 63-12650. (Illus.). (gr. 5 up). 1963. 10.95 (ISBN 0-690-50656-2, TYC-J). T Y Crowell.

Dowden, Anne O. The Blossom on the Bough: A Book of Trees. LC 74-6192. (Illus.). (gr. 5 up). 1975. 10.95 (ISBN 0-690-00384-6, TYC-J). T Y Crowell.

--State Flowers. LC 78-51927. (Illus.). (gr. 5 up). 1978. 8.95 (ISBN 0-690-01339-6, TYC-J); PLB 9.89 (ISBN 0-690-03884-4). T Y Crowell.

--This Noble Harvest: A Chronicle of Herbs. LC 79-12021. (Illus.). 1979. 12.95 (ISBN 0-529-05548-1). Philomel.

--Wild Green Things in the City: A Book of Weeds. LC 72-158687. (Illus.). (gr. 5-8). 1972. 8.95 o.p. (ISBN 0-690-89067-2, TYC-J). T Y Crowell.

Dowden, C. James. Community Associations: A Guide for Public Officials. LC 79-57077. (Community Association Ser.). (Illus.). 88p. 1980. pap. text ed. 13.50 (ISBN 0-87420-590-5, C18). Urban Land.

Dowden, R. Rosemary, ed. Fluid Flow Measurement Bibliography. 1972. microfiche 25.00 (ISBN 0-900983-21-3, Dist. by Air Science Co.). BHRA Fluid.

Dowdeswell, W. H. Mechanisms of Evolution. (Scholarship Series in Biology). 1975. text ed. 11.95x o.p. (ISBN 0-435-61251-4). Heinemann Ed.

Dowding, Howard & Boyce, Sheila. Getting the Job You Want. (Orig.). 1980. pap. 5.95x (ISBN 0-8464-1012-5). Beekman Pubs.

Dowdy, Andrew. Films of the Fifties. LC 75-2132. 242p. 1975. 6.95 o.p. (ISBN 0-688-00198-X); pap. 3.50 o.p. (ISBN 0-688-05198-7). Morrow.

Dowdy, Homer E., jt. auth. see Brandt, Henry R.

Dowell, Arlene Taylor. Cataloging with Copy: A Decision-Makers Handbook. LC 76-1844. (Illus.). 295p. 1976. lib. bdg. 22.50x (ISBN 0-87287-153-3). Libs Unl.

Dowell, Celia, jt. auth. see Couldridge, Alan.

Dowell, E. H. Aeroelasticity of Plates & Shells. (Mechanics: Dynamical System Ser.: No. 1). 154p. 1978. 25.00x (ISBN 90-286-0404-9). Sijthoff & Noordhoff.

Dowell, E. H. & Curtiss, H. C., Jr. A Modern Course in Aeroelasticity. (Mechanics: Dynamical Systems Ser.: No. 4). 479p. 1978. 85.00x (ISBN 90-286-0057-4); pap. 25.00x (ISBN 90-286-0737-4). Sijthoff & Noordhoff.

Dowell, Eldridge F. History of Criminal Syndicalism Legislation in the United States. LC 73-87517. (American History, Politics & Law Ser). 1969. Repr. of 1939 ed. 19.50 (ISBN 0-306-71426-4). Da Capo.

Dowell, J., jt. auth. see Greenwood, B.

Dowell, J. Linus, jt. auth. see Corbin, Charles B.

Dowell, L. Handbook of Teaching & Coaching Points for Basic Physical Education Skills. 288p. 1974. pap. 14.50 (ISBN 0-398-03194-0). C C Thomas.

Dowell, Stephen. History of Taxation & Taxes in England, 4 Vols. 2nd ed. LC 67-5737. Repr. of 1884 ed. 85.00x (ISBN 0-678-05167-4). Kelley.

Dowell, Susan S. & Kitching, Frances. Mrs. Kitching's Smith Island Cookbook. 1981. 9.50x (ISBN 0-686-69483-X, Pub by Tidewater). Cornell Maritime.

Dower, W. Barrett, tr. see Lacaze, Andre.

Dowers, Patrick. One Day Scene Through a Leaf. (Illus.). 40p. 1981. 10.95 (ISBN 0-914676-56-3); pap. 6.95 (ISBN 0-914676-55-5). Green Tiger.

Dowis, Edward. How to Install Your Own Home or Mobile Electric Power Plant. (Illus.). 1979. 8.95 o.p. (ISBN 0-8306-9861-2); pap. 5.95 o.p. (ISBN 0-8306-1063-4, 1063). TAB Bks.

Dowland, Robert. Varietie of Lute-Lessons. LC 79-84102. (English Experience Ser.: No. 921). 76p. 1979. Repr. of 1610 ed. lib. bdg. 14.00 (ISBN 90-221-0921-6). Walter J Johnson.

Dowlatshahi, Ali. Persian Designs & Motifs for Artists & Craftsmen. (Illus.). 1979. pap. 4.00 (ISBN 0-486-23815-6). Dover.

Dowler, Bryan, jt. auth. see Arneil, Steve.

Dowling, Allen see King, Jack, pseud.

Dowling, Christopher, ed. see Bond, Brian.

Dowling, Christopher, ed. see Jackson, William.

Dowling, Colette. The Cinderella Complex: Women's Hidden Fear of Independence. 288p. 1981. 13.95 (ISBN 0-671-40052-5). Summit Bks.

Dowling, Jerry L. Teaching Materials on Criminal Procedure. (Criminal Justice Ser.). 1976. text ed. 17.95 (ISBN 0-685-99576-3); pap. text ed. write for info. (ISBN 0-8299-0616-9); instrs.' manual avail. (ISBN 0-8299-0617-7). West Pub.

Dowling, John. Diego De Saavedra Fajardo. (World Authors Ser.: No. 437). 1977. lib. bdg. 12.50 (ISBN 0-8057-6200-0). Twayne.

--Leandro Fernandez de Moratin. (World Authors Ser.: Spain: No. 149). lib. bdg. 10.95 (ISBN 0-8057-2630-6). Twayne.

Dowling, John E., jt. ed. see Cone, Richard A.

Dowling, John R., jt. auth. see Drolet, Robert P.

Dowling, William C. Language & Logos in Boswell's Life of Johnson. LC 80-8545. (Essays in Literature Ser.). 232p. 1981. 15.00x (ISBN 0-691-06455-5). Princeton U Pr.

Dowling, William L. Hospital Production: A Linear Programming Approach. LC 74-14408. (Illus.). 1976. 17.95 (ISBN 0-669-93187-X). Lexington Bks.

--Prospective Rate Setting. LC 77-18700. 1977. text ed. 28.95 (ISBN 0-89443-028-9). Aspen Systems.

Down, C. G. & Stocks, J. Environmental Impact of Mining. LC 77-23129. 1977. 59.95 (ISBN 0-470-99086-4). Halsted Pr.

Down, Edith. What's to Eat. 1981. text ed. 11.96 (ISBN 0-87002-333-0). Bennett Co.

Down, Goldie. More Lives Than a Cat. LC 79-17814. (Crown Ser.). 1979. pap. 4.50 (ISBN 0-8127-0243-3). Southern Pub.

--You Never Can Tell When You May Meet a Leopard. Davis, Tom, ed. 128p. 1980. pap. write for info. (ISBN 0-8280-0026-3). Review & Herald.

Down, Goldie M. No Forty-Hour Week. LC 77-19223. (Crown Ser.). (gr. 8-12). 1978. pap. 4.50 (ISBN 0-8127-0167-4). Southern Pub.

Down, P. G. Heating & Cooling Load Calculations. 1969. 26.00 (ISBN 0-08-013001-1). Pergamon.

Down, P. J. & Taylor, F. E. Why Distributed Computing? An NCC Review of Potential & Experience in UK. LC 77-363488. 168p. 1976. pap. 25.00x (ISBN 0-85012-170-1). Intl Pubns Serv.

Downard, William L. Dictionary of the History of the American Brewing & Distilling Industries. LC 79-6826. (Illus.). xxv, 268p. 1980. lib. bdg. 35.00 (ISBN 0-313-21330-5, DOD/). Greenwood.

Downen, Robert. The Taiwan Pawn in the China Game: Congress to the Rescue, Vol. I. LC 79-88334. (Significant Issues Ser.: No. 1). 80p. 1979. 5.95 (ISBN 0-89206-007-7). CSI Studies.

Downer, Alan S. British Drama: A Handbook & Brief Chronicle. (Illus.). 1950. 29.50x (ISBN 0-89197-047-9); pap. text ed. 16.95x (ISBN 0-89197-048-7). Irvington.

Downer, Ann H. Physical Therapy for Animals: Selected Techniques. (Illus.). 196p. 1978. 14.75- (ISBN 0-398-03702-7). C C Thomas.

Downer, Craig C. Spiritual Evolution. Date not set. 10.00 (ISBN 0-533-04704-8). Vantage.

Downer, L. J., ed. Leges Henrici Primi. 464p. 1972. 48.00x (ISBN 0-19-825301-X). Oxford U Pr.

Downer, Marion. Kites: How to Make & Fly Them. LC 58-14497. (Illus.). (gr. 4-6). 1959. PLB 7.44 (ISBN 0-688-51227-5). Lothrop.

--Long Ago in Florence: The Story of Della Robbia Sculpture. LC 68-27707. (Illus.). (gr. 3-6). 1968. 6.50 o.p. (ISBN 0-688-41205-X); PLB 6.24 (ISBN 0-688-51205-4). Lothrop.

Downer, Richard C. Dancer's Dream. 1981. 9.95 (ISBN 0-8062-1620-4). Carlton.

Downes, David A. Temper of Victorian Belief: Studies in the Religious Novels of Pater, Kingsley, & Newman. LC 76-147189. 159p. 1972. text ed. 16.50x (ISBN 0-8290-0209-X). Irvington.

Downes, Edward. The Guide to Symphonic Music. LC 76-13813. Orig. Title: The New York Philharmonic Guide to the Symphony. (Illus.). 1058p. pap. 14.95 (ISBN 0-8027-7178-5). Walker & Co.

Downes, John see Wright, James.

Downes, Randolph C. Council Fires on the Upper Ohio. LC 40-34394. (Illus.). 1940. pap. 4.95 (ISBN 0-8229-5201-7). U of Pittsburgh Pr.

Downey, Bill. Black Viking. 320p. (Orig.). 1981. pap. 2.50 (ISBN 0-449-14393-7, GM). Fawcett.

Downey, Douglas W., ed. see Standard Education Corporation.

Downey, Fritz K. Jack Parsley. 1981. 6.95 (ISBN 0-8062-1682-4). Carlton.

Downey, Glanville. Constantinople in the Age of Justinian. (Centers of Civilization Ser.: No. 3). 1980. Repr. of 1960 ed. 5.95 (ISBN 0-8061-0465-1). U of Okla Pr.

--Constantinople in the Age of Justinian. LC 60-13473. (The Centers of Civilization Ser.: Vol. 3). (Illus.). 181p. 1981. pap. 3.95 (ISBN 0-8061-1708-7). U of Okla Pr.

--The Late Roman Empire. LC 76-15145. (Berkshire Studies). 158p. 1976. pap. 5.50 (ISBN 0-88275-441-6). Krieger.

Downey, Harold. Handbook of Hematology, 4 Vols. (Illus.). 1965. Repr. of 1938 ed. Set. 192.50 o.s.i. (ISBN 0-02-843980-5). Hafner.

Downey, J. A. U. S. Federal Official Publications: The International Dimension. 1978. text ed. 60.00 (ISBN 0-08-021839-3). Pergamon.

Downey, Jack. Doomstar. LC 79-66398. 97p. 1980. 6.95 (ISBN 0-533-04388-3). Vantage.

Downey, M. E. & Kelly, A. V. Theory & Practice of Education. 2nd ed. 1979. text ed. 16.95 (ISBN 0-06-318113-4, IntlDept); pap. text ed. 10.45 (ISBN 0-06-318114-2). Har-Row.

Downey, Meriel. Interpersonal Judgments in Education. 1977. text ed. 15.70 (ISBN 0-06-318051-0, IntlDept); pap. text ed. 7.80 (ISBN 0-06-318052-9, IntlDept). Har-Row.

Downey, Meriel, jt. auth. see Kelly, A. V.

Downey, Robert J. Weapon Retention Techniques for Officer Survival. (Illus.). 128p. 1980. write for info. o.p. (ISBN 0-398-04108-3). C C Thomas.

Downey, Robert J. & Roth, Jordon T. Weapon Retention Techniques for Officer Survival. (Illus.). 128p. 1980. text ed. 14.75 (ISBN 0-398-04108-3). C C Thomas.

Downey, W. David & Trocke, John K. Agribusiness Management. (Illus.). 480p. 1980. text ed. 17.95 (ISBN 0-07-017645-0, C); study guide 5.95 (ISBN 0-07-017646-9); study guide 7.95 (ISBN 0-07-017649-3). McGraw.

Downey, W. K., ed. Food Quality & Nutrition: Research Priorities for Thermal Processing. (Illus.). 1978. text ed. 71.30x (ISBN 0-85334-803-0, Pub. by Applied Science). Burgess-Intl Ideas.

Downie, Don & Downie, Julia L. Ins & Outs of Ferry Flying. (Modern Aviation Ser.). (Illus.). 288p. (Orig.). 1980. cancelled (ISBN 0-8306-9936-8, 2280); pap. 7.95 (ISBN 0-8306-2280-2). Tab Bks.

Downie, J. A. Robert Harley & the Press. LC 78-67810. 1979. 33.50 (ISBN 0-521-22187-0). Cambridge U Pr.

Downie, Julia L., jt. auth. see Downie, Don.

Downie, N. M. & Heath, Robert W. Metodos Estadisticos Aplicados. (Sp.). 1971. pap. 8.00 (ISBN 0-06-310074-6, IntlDept). Har-Row.

Downie, N. M., jt. auth. see Cottle, William C.

Downie, Patricia A. & Kennedy, Pat. Lifting, Handling & Helping Patients. (Illus.). 160p. 1981. 19.95 (ISBN 0-571-11630-2, Pub. by Faber & Faber); pap. 8.95 (ISBN 0-571-11631-0). Merrimack Bk Serv.

Downie, R. S. & Telfer, Elizabeth. Caring & Curing: A Philosophy of Medicine & Social Work. LC 80-40246. 180p. 1980. 19.95 (ISBN 0-416-71800-0, 2063). Methuen Inc.

Downing, A. B., ed. Euthanasia & the Right to Death: The Case for Voluntary Euthanasia. (Contemporary Issues Ser.: No. 2). 1970. text ed. 17.25x (ISBN 0-391-00022-5). Humanities.

Downing, Andrew J. Architecture of Country Houses. LC 68-16230. (Architecture & Decorative Art Ser). (Illus.). 1968. Repr. of 1850 ed. 39.50 (ISBN 0-306-71034-X). Da Capo.

--Rural Essays. Curtis, George W., ed. LC 69-13713. (Architecture & Decorative Art Ser). 640p. 1974. Repr. of 1854 ed. lib. bdg. 39.50 (ISBN 0-306-71035-8). Da Capo.

--Victorian Cottage Residences. Harney, George E., ed. (Illus.). 352p. 1981. pap. price not set (ISBN 0-486-24078-9). Dover.

Downing, C. T. The Fan-Qui in China in 1836-7, 3 vols. (Illus.). 980p. 1972. Repr. of 1838 ed. 84.00x (ISBN 0-7165-2026-5, Pub. by Irish Academic Pr Ireland). Biblio Dist.

Downing, Chris, jt. auth. see Clanton, Gordon.

Downing, Donald O. & Mackenzie, Brian W. Public Policy Aspects of Information Exchange in Canadian Mineral Exploration. 60p. (Orig.). 1979. pap. text ed. 3.00x (ISBN 0-686-63138-2, Pub. by Ctr Resource Stud Canada). Renouf.

Downing, Douglas. Calculus by Discovery. 224p. (gr. 10-12). 1981. pap. text ed. 4.50 (ISBN 0-8120-2380-3). Barron.

Downing, Elizabeth. Keeping Goats. (Pelham Ser.). (Illus.). 1976. 8.95 (ISBN 0-7207-0883-4, Pub. by Michael Joseph). Merrimack Bk Serv.

Downing, Frank & Bardoff, O. The Hollywood Emergency Diet. 192p. 1981. 9.95 (ISBN 0-8119-0419-9, Pegasus Rex). Fell.

Downing, George. Massage & Meditation. 1974. 7.95 o.p. (ISBN 0-394-49237-4); pap. 1.65 (ISBN 0-394-70648-X). Random.

Downing, George D. Basic Marketing. LC 79-142984. 448p. 1971. 17.95x (ISBN 0-675-09233-7); instructor's manual 3.95 (ISBN 0-686-66708-5). Merrill.

Downing, J. C. & Yelland, M., eds. Dewey International: Papers Given at the European Centenary Seminar, Banbury, 1976. 1977. pap. 9.95x (ISBN 0-85365-469-7, Pub. by Lib Assn England). Oryx Pr.

Downing, Lester N. Counseling Theories & Techniques: Summarized & Critiqued. LC 74-23725. 240p. 1975. 16.95 (ISBN 0-88229-203-X); pap. 9.95 (ISBN 0-88229-502-0). Nelson-Hall.

Downing, Mildred H. Introduction to Cataloging & Classification. 5th ed. LC 80-20299. (Illus.). 240p. 1981. lib. bdg. 14.95x (ISBN 0-89950-017-X). McFarland & Co.

Downing, Robert E., jt. auth. see Beall, James R.

Downing, Sybil & Barker, Jane V. Florence Rena Sabin. (Illus.). 80p. (Orig.). (gr. 5-6). 1981. pap. 5.50 (ISBN 0-87108-237-3). Pruett.

Downing, Sybil, jt. auth. see Barker, Jane V.

Downs, A. J. & Adams, C. J. The Chemistry of Chlorine, Bromine, Iodine & Astatine. (Pergamon Texts in Inorganic Chemistry: Vol. 7). 488p. 1975. text ed. 64.00 (ISBN 0-08-018788-9); pap. text ed. 35.00 (ISBN 0-08-018787-0). Pergamon.

Downs, A. M., jt. auth. see Burghes, David N.

Downs, Barry. Sacred Places: Religious Architecture of the 18th & 19th Centuries in British Columbia. (Illus.). 160p. 1980. 29.95 (ISBN 0-295-95774-3, Pub. by Douglas & McIntyre Canada). U of Wash Pr.

Downs, Brian W. Modern Norwegian Literature, Eighteen Eighty-Nineteen Eighteen. 1966. 47.50 (ISBN 0-521-04854-0). Cambridge U Pr.

Downs, Carolyn. Dirt. (Illus.). 1980. pap. 9.95 o.p. (ISBN 0-930490-31-2). Future Shop.

Downs, Florence S. & Fleming, Juanita W., eds. Issues in Nursing Research. LC 78-21914. 1979. 10.95 (ISBN 0-8385-4436-3). ACC.

Downs, George W., Jr. Bureaucracy, Innovation & Public Policy. (Illus.). 1976. 16.95x o.p. (ISBN 0-669-00872-9). Lexington Bks.

Downs, Hugh & Roll, Richard J. Hugh Downs' The Best Years Book: How to Plan for Fulfillment, Security, & Happiness in the Retirement Years. 1981. 14.95 (ISBN 0-440-04064-7, E Friede). Delacorte.

Downs, Hugh R. Rhythms of a Himalayan Village. LC 79-2983. (Illus.). 240p. (Orig.). 1980. pap. 9.95 (ISBN 0-06-250240-9). Har-Row.

Downs, James F. Cultures in Crisis. 2nd ed. 1975. pap. text ed. 5.95x (ISBN 0-02-472300-2, 47230). Macmillan.

--Human Nature: An Introduction to Cultural Anthropology. LC 72-86791. 350p. 1973. text ed. 10.95x (ISBN 0-02-474090-X). Macmillan.

Downs, James F. & Bleibtreu, Hermann. Human Variation: An Introduction to Physical Anthropology. 2nd ed. 1972. text ed. 10.95x (ISBN 0-02-474490-5, 47449). Macmillan.

Downs, James F., jt. auth. see Bleibtreu, Hermann K.

Downs, Kathy see Stortz, Diane, et al.

Downs, Michael. James Harrington. (English Authors Ser.: No. 188). 1977. lib. bdg. 12.50 (ISBN 0-8057-6693-6). Twayne.

Downs, Robert B. Friedrich Froebel. (World Leaders Ser.: No. 74). 1978. lib. bdg. 10.95 (ISBN 0-8057-7668-0). Twayne.

--Heinrich Pestalozzi. (World Leaders Ser.). 1975. lib. bdg. 9.95 (ISBN 0-8057-3560-7). Twayne.

--Henry Barnard. LC 77-1775. (World Leaders Ser.: No. 59). 1977. 9.95 (ISBN 0-8057-7710-5). Twayne.

--Horace Mann. (World Leaders Ser: No. 29). 1974. lib. bdg. 9.95 (ISBN 0-8057-3544-5). Twayne.

Downs, Robert B., ed. Bear Went Over the Mountain: Tall Tales of American Animals. LC 73-148835. 1971. Repr. of 1964 ed. 18.00 (ISBN 0-8103-3279-5). Gale.

Downs, Robert J. Controlled Environments for Plant Growth. (Illus.). 200p. 1975. 17.50x (ISBN 0-231-03561-6). Columbia U Pr.

Downs, Robert M. & Stea, David, eds. Image & Environment: Cognitive Mapping & Spatial Behavior. LC 72-78215. 438p. 1973. 23.95x (ISBN 0-202-10058-8). Aldine Pub.

Downs, T. Nelson. The Art of Magic. Hilliard, John N., ed. 352p. 1980. pap. 4.50 (ISBN 0-486-24005-3). Dover.

Downton, James V., Jr. Rebel Leadership: Commitment & Charisma in the Revolutionary Process. LC 72-77283. 1973. 19.95 (ISBN 0-02-907560-2). Free Pr.

--Sacred Journeys: Conversion & Commitment to Divine Light Mission. LC 79-546. (Illus.). 1979. 15.00 (ISBN 0-231-04198-5). Columbia U Pr.

Dowrick, F. E. Human Rights. 1979. text ed. 23.00x (ISBN 0-566-00281-7, Pub. by Gower Pub Co England). Renouf.

Dowse, R. E., ed. see Hardie, James K.

Dowse, Robert E. Modernization in Ghana & the USSR. (Library of Political Studies). 1969. text ed. 7.00x (ISBN 0-7100-6171-4). Humanities.

Dowsett, Norman C. Psychology for Future Education. LC 80-51427. 1980. 11.95 (ISBN 0-533-04679-3). Vantage.

Dowsett, Rosemary. Let's Look at the Phillipines. 1974. pap. 0.90 (ISBN 0-85363-103-4). OMF Bks.

Dowson, Ernest. Poems of Ernest Dowson. Longaker, Mark, ed. LC 62-14213. 1963. 9.00x o.p. (ISBN 0-8122-7331-1). U of Pa Pr.

Dowson, Ernest & Moore, Arthur. A Comedy of Masks. Fletcher, Ian & Stokes, John, eds. LC 76-20066. (Decadent Consciousness Ser.: Vol. 8). 1977. Repr. of 1896 ed. lib. bdg. 38.00 (ISBN 0-8240-2757-4). Garland Pub.

Dowson, John. A Classical Dictionary of Hindu Mythology. 10th ed. 1968. Repr. of 1961 ed. 27.00 (ISBN 0-7100-1302-7). Routledge & Kegan.

Dowst, Somerby R. Basics for Buyers: A Practical Guide to Better Purchasing. LC 74-156479. (Illus.). 1971. 15.95 (ISBN 0-8436-1301-7). CBI Pub.

--More Basics for Buyers. LC 79-11755. 1979. 15.95 (ISBN 0-8436-0780-7). CBI Pub.

Dowty, Stuart, jt. auth. see Goldwasser, Janet.

Doxey, William. Dead Wrong. 1980. pap. 1.75 (ISBN 0-505-51455-9). Tower Bks.

Doxey, William S. E.S.P.Ionage. 1979. pap. 1.95 (ISBN 0-505-51363-3). Tower Bks.

Doxford, Kay. The Cocker Spaniel: It's Care & Training. (Illus.). 100p. 1980. 3.95 (ISBN 0-903264-29-3, 4946-4, Pub. by K & R Bks England). Arco.

Doxiadis, Constantino. Ecology & Ekistics. LC 76-20459. (Illus.). 1978. lib. bdg. 17.50x (ISBN 0-89158-624-5). Westview.

Doxiadis, Constantinos A. Emergence & Growth of an Urban Region: The Developing Urban Detroit Area Vol. 3-A Concept for Future Development. LC 66-29622. 1969. 20.00x (ISBN 0-8143-1506-2). Wayne St U Pr.

--Emergence & Growth of an Urban Region: The Developing Urban Detroit Area, Vol. 2, Future Alternatives. LC 66-29622. 1969. 20.00x (ISBN 0-8143-1505-4). Wayne St U Pr.

Doxiadis, Spyros, ed. see Institute of Child Health Athens International Symposium 2-8, July 1978 Athens, Greece.

Doyen, John T. Systematics of the Genus Coelocnemis (Coleoptera: Tenebrionidae: A Quantitative Study of Variation. (U. C. Publ. in Entomology: Vol. 73). 1973. pap. 7.50x (ISBN 0-520-09481-6). U of Cal Pr.

Doyle, A. Conan. Beyond the City. LC 80-67703. (Conan Doyle Centennial Ser.). (Illus.). 150p. 1981. 11.95 (ISBN 0-934468-44-3). Gaslight.

--The Doings of Raffles Haw. LC 80-67702. (Conan Doyle Centennial Ser.). (Illus.). 147p. 1981. 11.95 (ISBN 0-934468-43-5). Gaslight.

--A Duet with an Occasional Chorus. LC 80-67707. (Conan Doyle Centennial Ser.). (Illus.). 1982. price not set (ISBN 0-934468-48-6). Gaslight.

--The Parasite. LC 80-67704. (Conan Doyle Centennial Ser.). (Illus.). 100p. Date not set. price not set (ISBN 0-934468-45-1). Gaslight.

--The Stark Munro Letters. LC 80-67705. (Conan Doyle Centennial Ser.). (Illus.). 250p. 1981. price not set (ISBN 0-934468-46-X). Gaslight.

--The Tragedy of the Korosko. LC 80-67706. (Conan Doyle Centennial Ser.). (Illus.). 250p. 1981. price not set (ISBN 0-934468-47-8). Gaslight.

Doyle, A. Conan, et al. Tales of Mystery & Suspense. (gr. 9 up). 1980. Boxed Set. pap. text ed. 3.75 (ISBN 0-307-13622-1, Golden Pr). Western Pub.

Doyle, Arthur C. Brigadier Gerard. 192p. (Orig.). 1981. pap. 1.95 (ISBN 0-515-05530-1). Jove Pubns.

--Hound of the Baskervilles. lib. bdg. 13.95x (ISBN 0-89966-229-3). Buccaneer Bks.

--The Lost World. lib. bdg. 13.95x (ISBN 0-89966-233-1). Buccaneer Bks.

--Sign of the Four. lib. bdg. 13.95x (ISBN 0-89966-230-7). Buccaneer Bks.

--A Study in Scarlet. 160p. 1975. pap. 1.25 o.p. (ISBN 0-345-24714-0). Ballantine.

--A Study in Scarlet. lib. bdg. 13.95x (ISBN 0-89966-231-5). Buccaneer Bks.

--Valley of Fear. lib. bdg. 13.95x (ISBN 0-89966-232-3). Buccaneer Bks.

Doyle, Sir Arthur C. Sherlock Holmes. (Young Fiction & Classics). pap. 1.25 (ISBN 0-307-12215-8, Golden Pr). Western Pub.

--Tales of Terror & Mystery. (Illus.). 1979. pap. 3.50 (ISBN 0-14-004878-2). Penguin.

Doyle, Arthur Conan. Sherlock Holmes: Selected Stories. 12.95 (ISBN 0-19-250528-9, WC528). Oxford U Pr.

--The Valley of Fear. pap. 1.95 (ISBN 0-425-04911-6). Berkley Pub.

Doyle, Arthur Conan see Conan Doyle, Arthur.

Doyle, Arthur Conan, Sir. Complete Sherlock Holmes. LC 65-6074. 11.95 (ISBN 0-385-00689-6); Two-volume edition 15.95 (ISBN 0-385-04591-3). Doubleday.

--The Hound of the Baskervilles. LC 76-27103. 1977. 7.95 o.p. (ISBN 0-385-12282-9). Doubleday.

Doyle, Austin E. Pharmacological & Therapeutic Aspects of Hypertension. LC 78-27898. 1980. Vol. 1, 224p. 64.95 (ISBN 0-8493-5385-8); Vol. 2, 256p. 66.95 (ISBN 0-8493-5386-6). CRC Pr.

Doyle, Charles. James K. Baxter. LC 75-33781. (World Authors Ser.: New Zealand: No. 384). 1976. lib. bdg. 12.50 (ISBN 0-8057-6227-2). Twayne.

Doyle, Dennis. The Complete Series 6 Study Book. (Illus.). 350p. (Orig.). 1980. pap. text ed. 23.50 (ISBN 0-914234-14-5). Human Res Dev Pr.

Doyle, Dennis M. Efficient Accounting & Record Keeping. Brownstone, David, ed. LC 78-2474. (The Small Business Profit Program Ser.). 1978. pap. text ed. 4.95 (ISBN 0-471-05044-X). Wiley.

--Efficient Accounting & Record Keeping, 5 vol. set. LC 78-2474. (Wiley Small Business Ser.). 1977. 19.95 o.p. (ISBN 0-471-04295-1). Wiley.

Doyle, Derek. Terminal Care: Symposium. (Illus.). 1979. pap. text ed. 12.50 o.p. (ISBN 0-443-01920-7). Churchill.

Doyle, Edwin S. & Mittler, Abe, eds. Control of Critical Points in Food Processing: A Systems Approach. (Illus.). 270p. 1977. text ed. 25.00 (ISBN 0-937774-04-9). Food Processors.

Doyle, H. C. & Kliment, C. K. Czechoslovak Armoured Fighting Vehicles, 1918-1945. (Illus.). 139p. (Orig.). pap. 11.25x (ISBN 0-85242-628-3). Intl Pubns Serv.

Doyle, Hortense A., jt. auth. see Cantwell, Zita M.

Doyle, J. G. Louis Moreau Gottschalk. (Bibliographies in American Music). 1981. write for info. (ISBN 0-911772-66-9). Info Coord.

Doyle, Jack. The American Indian from Beginning to End. 6.95 o.p. (ISBN 0-685-58603-0). Vantage.

Doyle, James F., ed. Educational Judgments. (International Library of the Philosophy of Education). 1973. 25.00 (ISBN 0-7100-7458-1); pap. 9.50 (ISBN 0-7100-8082-4). Routledge & Kegan.

Doyle, James M. & Grimes, George H. Reference Resources: A Systematic Approach. LC 76-7080. 1976. 12.00 (ISBN 0-8108-0928-1). Scarecrow.

Doyle, John. The Auto Repair Book. 1977. 9.95 (ISBN 0-385-12193-8); school & library ed. 12.95 (ISBN 0-385-13306-5). Doubleday.

Doyle, John R., Jr. Arthur Shearly Cripps. (World Authors Ser.: No. 365). 1975. lib. bdg. 12.50 (ISBN 0-8057-6216-7). Twayne.

--Francis Carey Slater. (World Authors Ser.: South Africa: No. 173). lib. bdg. 10.95 (ISBN 0-8057-2834-1). Twayne.

--Thomas Pringle. (World Authors Ser.: South Africa: No. 238). lib. bdg. 10.95 (ISBN 0-8057-2718-3). Twayne.

--William Charles Scully. (World Authors Ser.: No. 490). 1978. lib. bdg. 13.50 (ISBN 0-8057-6331-7). Twayne.

Doyle, Kenneth O., Jr. Student Evaluation of Instruction. LC 74-7859. (Illus.). 1975. 17.95 (ISBN 0-669-93328-7). Lexington Bks.

Doyle, Kenneth O., Jr., jt. auth. see Arnold, Darlene B.

Doyle, L. B. Information Retrieval & Processing. LC 75-1179. (Information Science Ser.). 1975. 29.95 (ISBN 0-471-22151-1, Pub. by Wiley-Interscience). Wiley.

Doyle, L. E., et al. Manufacturing Processes & Materials for Engineers. 2nd ed. 1969. text ed. 26.95 (ISBN 0-13-555862-X). P-H.

Doyle, Leonard A. Inter-Economy Comparisons: A Case Study. (Institute of Business & Economic Research, UC Berkeley). 1965. 18.00x (ISBN 0-520-00355-1). U of Cal Pr.

Doyle, Marvyl & Mittwer, Marie. Basic Reading Patterns: Words & Sentences. (gr. 10 up). 1969. pap. text ed. 8.95 (ISBN 0-13-068031-1). P-H.

Doyle, Michael, et al, eds. see Anderson-Sannes, Barbara.

Doyle, Michael E. Color Drawing: A Marker-Colored-Pencil Approach. 320p. 1981. 35.00 (ISBN 0-442-22184-3). Van Nos Reinhold.

Doyle, Michael P. & Mungall, William S. Experimental Organic Chemistry. LC 79-18392. 1980. text ed. 18.95 (ISBN 0-471-03383-9); tchrs' manual 2.50 (ISBN 0-471-08053-5). Wiley.

Doyle, Micheal & Straus, Davis. How to Make Meetings Work. 240p. 1981. pap. 2.50 (ISBN 0-87216-614-7). Playboy Pbks.

Doyle, Owen, et al. Analysis Manual for Hospital Information Systems. (Illus.). 463p. (Orig.). 1980. pap. text ed. 42.50 (ISBN 0-914904-41-8). Health Admin Pr.

Doyle, Paul A. Liam O'Flaherty. (English Authors Ser.: No. 108). lib. bdg. 10.95 (ISBN 0-8057-1424-3). Twayne.

--Pearl Buck. (U. S. Authors Ser.: No. 85). 1965. lib. bdg. 8.50 o.p. (ISBN 0-8057-0112-5). Twayne.

Doyle, Phyllis B., et al. Helping the Severely Handicapped Child: A Guide for Parents & Teachers. LC 78-3300. (John Day Bk. in Special Education). (Illus.). 1979. 10.95 (ISBN 0-381-90063-0, TYC-T). T Y Crowell.

Doyle, Polly. Grief Counseling & Sudden Death: A Manual & Guide. (Illus.). 352p. 1980. 26.50 (ISBN 0-398-04060-5). C C Thomas.

Doyle, Robert V. Careers for a Small World: Working & Living with Appropriate Technology. (Illus.). 190p. (gr. 9-12). 1981. PLB price not set. Messner.

--Your Career in Interior Design. rev ed. LC 75-12634. (Messner Career Bks). (Illus.). 208p. (gr. 7 up). 1975. PLB 7.79 o.p. (ISBN 0-671-32755-0). Messner.

Doyle, Tim. Born Loser. Mooney, Thomas J., ed. (Beginning Pal Paperbacks Ser.). (Illus., Orig.). (gr. 7-12). 1977. pap. text ed. 1.25 (ISBN 0-8374-3465-3). Xerox Ed Pubns.

Doyle, William. Old European Order Sixteen Sixty to Eighteen Hundred. (Short Oxford History of the Modern World Ser.). (Illus.). 1978. 36.00x (ISBN 0-19-913073-6); pap. 12.95 (ISBN 0-19-913131-7). Oxford U Pr.

--Origins of the French Revolution. 272p. 1981. 37.50 (ISBN 0-19-873020-9); pap. 14.95 (ISBN 0-19-873021-7). Oxford U Pr.

Doz, Yves L. Government Control & Multinational Strategic Management: Power Systems & Telecommunication Equipment. LC 79-11793. (Praeger Special Studies Ser.). 298p. 1979. 24.95 (ISBN 0-03-049476-1). Praeger.

Dozer, Donald M. Portrait of the Free State. LC 76-47023. (Illus.). 1976. 17.50 (ISBN 0-87033-226-0, Pub. by Tidewater). Cornell Maritime.

Dozier, Edward P. The Kalinga of Northern Luzon, Philippines. Spindler, George & Spindler, Louise, eds. (Case Studies in Cultural Anthropology). (Illus.). 112p. pap. text ed. 4.95x (ISBN 0-8290-0279-0). Irvington.

Dozier, Jeffrey, jt. auth. see Marsh, William.

Dozier, Zoe. Home Again, My Love. (YA) 1978. 5.95 (ISBN 0-685-86408-1, Avalon). Bouregy.

Dozois, Gardner. Best Science Fiction Stories of the Year: Tenth Annual Collection. 256p. 1981. 11.95 (ISBN 0-525-06499-0). Dutton.

--Strangers. 1978. pap. 1.75 o.p. (ISBN 0-425-03924-2, Dist. by Putnam). Berkley Pub.

--Strangers. (YA) 1978. 7.95 o.p. (ISBN 0-399-12095-5, Dist. by Putnam). Berkley Pub.

Dozois, Gardner & Effinger, George A. Nightmare Blue. (Orig.). 1975. pap. 0.95 o.p. (ISBN 0-425-02819-4, Medallion). Berkley Pub.

Dozois, Gardner, ed. Another World: Adventures in Otherness. (gr. 7 up). 1977. 7.95 o.s.i. (ISBN 0-695-80695-5); lib. ed. 7.98 o.s.i. (ISBN 0-695-40695-7). Follett.

--A Day in the Life. LC 78-160655. 1972. 7.95 o.s.i. (ISBN 0-06-011076-7, HarpT). Har-Row.

Dozy. Dictionary Noms de Vetements Chez Arabes. 16.00x (ISBN 0-685-85422-1). Intl Bk Ctr.

Dozy, R. Glossaire Des Mots Espagnols et Portugais Derives De L'arabe. 1974. 20.00x (ISBN 0-685-72045-4). Intl Bk Ctr.

--Supplement Aux Dictionnaire Arabe (Arabic-French, 2 vols. 1969. 70.00x (ISBN 0-685-72061-6). Intl Bk Ctr.

Dr. A., pseud. The Sensuous Dirty Old Man. pap. 1.50 (ISBN 0-451-07199-9, W7199, Sig). NAL.

Drabble, Margaret. The Waterfall. 1977. pap. 2.50 (ISBN 0-445-04118-8). Popular Lib.

Drabble, Phil. Phil Drabble's Country Scene. 1974. 8.95 (ISBN 0-7207-0779-X, Pub. by Michael Joseph). Merrimack Bk Serv.

Drabeck, Bernard A., et al. Structures for Composition. 2nd ed. LC 77-77675. (Illus.). 1978. pap. text ed. 10.50 (ISBN 0-395-25567-8); inst. manual 0.25 (ISBN 0-395-25568-6). HM.

Drabek, Gordon, jt. ed. see Sinha, Radha.

Drabek, Jan. The Lister Legacy. 384p. 1980. 13.95 (ISBN 0-8253-0015-0). Beaufort Bks NY.

Drabik, Harry. The Spirit of Canoe Camping. (Illus.). 126p. 1981. pap. 5.95 (ISBN 0-931714-11-7). Nodin Pr.

Drabkin, Israel E., jt. ed. see Drabkin, Miriam F.

Drabkin, Miriam F. & Drabkin, Israel E., eds. Caelius Aurelianus, Gynaecia: Fragments of a Latin version of Soranus' Gynaecia from a thirteenth century manuscript. (Supplements Bulletin of the History of Medicine Ser: No.13). 136p. 1951. pap. 6.00x o.p. (ISBN 0-8018-0175-3). Johns Hopkins.

Drachkovitch, Milorad M., ed. Marxism in the Modern World. 1965. 12.50x (ISBN 0-8047-0254-3); pap. 3.25 o.p. (ISBN 0-8047-0255-1). Stanford U Pr.

Drachler, Jacob, ed. Black Homeland - Black Diaspora: Cross Currents of the African Relationship. LC 74-80066. 1975. 15.00 (ISBN 0-8046-9077-4, Natl U). Kennikat.

Drachman, Virginia & Harvey-Felder, Zena, eds. Women's History: A Literature of Struggle Program Guide. (MicroSources: Social Science Skills Development Program Ser.). 67p. (gr. 9-12). 1980. pap. text ed. 7.95 (ISBN 0-667-00618-4). Microfilming Corp.

Drackett, Phil. Vintage Cars. 4.50x (ISBN 0-392-06952-0, SpS). Soccer.

Draeger, Donn. Ninjutsu: The Art of Invisibility. 2nd ed. (Illus.). 1980. pap. 4.95 (ISBN 0-914778-19-6). Phoenix Bks.

Draeger, Donn F. Japanese Swordsmanship. (Illus.). 1981. 19.95 (ISBN 0-8348-0146-9). Weatherhill.

Draeger, Donn F. & Chambers, Quintin. Javanese Silat: The Fighting Art of Perisai Diri. LC 78-60969. (Illus.). 128p. 1979. pap. 7.95 (ISBN 0-87011-353-4). Kodansha.

Draeger, Donn F. & Otaki, Tadao. Kodokan Judo. (Illus.). Date not set. cancelled (ISBN 0-8048-1187-3). C E Tuttle.

Draeger, Donn F. & Smith, Robert W. Asian Fighting Arts. 1974. pap. 1.95 o.p. (ISBN 0-425-02501-2, Medallion). Berkley Pub.

Draeger, Donn F. & Warner, Gordon. Japanese Swordsmanship: Technique & Practice. (Illus.). 224p. Date not set. 19.95 (ISBN 0-8348-0146-9, Pub. by John Weatherhill Inc Japan). C E Tuttle.

Draeger, Donn F., jt. auth. see Nakayama, Masatoshi.

Draeger, Donn F., jt. auth. see Smith, Robert W.

Draeger, Donn F., et al. Pentjak-Silat: The Indonesian Fighting Art. LC 73-82659. (Illus.). 150p. 1970. 8.95 o.p. (ISBN 0-87011-104-3). Kodansha.

Draffan, I. W. & Poole, F., eds. Distributed Data Bases. LC 80-40399. 400p. Date not set. 29.95 (ISBN 0-521-23091-8). Cambridge U Pr.

Draghi, Paul A., ed. see Permanent International Altaistic Conference, 18th Meeting, Bloomington, June 29-July 5, 1975.

Draghi, Suzanne C., jt. auth. see Flach, Frederic F.

Dragnich, Alex N. Serbia, Nikola Pasic & Yugoslavia. 1974. 19.00 (ISBN 0-8135-0773-1). Rutgers U Pr.

Dragnich, Alex N. & Rasmussen, Jorgen S. Major European Governments. 5th ed. 1978. text ed. 18.50x (ISBN 0-256-02054-X). Dorsey.

Drago, Russell S. Principles of Chemistry with Practical Perspectives. 2nd ed. 1977. text ed. 21.95 (ISBN 0-205-05568-0, 6855687); student guide 7.95 (ISBN 0-205-05570-2, 6855709); tchr's manual 1.50x (ISBN 0-205-05569-9, 6855695). Allyn.

Drago, Russell S. & Brown, Theodore L. Experiments in General Chemistry. 4th ed. 1977. text ed. 12.95 (ISBN 0-205-05702-0); instr's manual avail. (ISBN 0-205-05703-9). Allyn.

Dragomir, V., jt. ed. see Gheorghiu, A.

Dragonetti, Roger. La Technique Poetique Des Trouveres Dans la Chanson Courtoise: Contribution a l'etude De la Rhetorique Medievale. LC 80-2163. 1981. Repr. of 1960 ed. 76.00 (ISBN 0-404-19029-4). AMS Pr.

Dragoo, Alva W. General Shop Metalwork. rev. ed. (gr. 8-9). 1964. pap. text ed. 5.00 (ISBN 0-87345-109-0). McKnight.

Dragsted, Ove. Gems & Jewelry in Color. LC 75-2391. (Illus.). 240p. 1975. 10.95 (ISBN 0-02-533500-6, 53350). Macmillan.

Draguns, jt. auth. see Triandis.

Drain, L. E. The Laser Doppler Technique. LC 79-40638. 1980. text ed. 50.25 (ISBN 0-471-27627-8, Pub. by Wiley-Interscience). Wiley.

Drakakis, John. British Radio Drama. 300p. Date not set. 47.50 (ISBN 0-521-22183-8); pap. 15.95 (ISBN 0-521-29383-9). Cambridge U Pr.

Drakakis-Smith, David. Urbanization, Housing & the Development Process. 256p. 1980. write for info. (ISBN 0-312-83519-1). St Martin.

Drake, et al. Study Guide to Principles of Management. 176p. 1980. wkbk. 7.95 (ISBN 0-8359-5597-4). Reston.

Drake, Alvin W., et al, eds. Analysis of Public Systems. 480p. 1972. 24.00x (ISBN 0-262-04038-7). MIT Pr.

Drake, Asa. Crimson Kisses. 304p. 1981. pap. 2.50 (ISBN 0-380-77131-4, 77131). Avon.

Drake, Barbara. Field Poems. (Illus.). 1975. 1.00 o.p. (ISBN 0-686-23606-8). Stone Pr MI.

--Life in a Gothic Novel. (WEP Poetry Ser: No. 4). 24p. (Orig.). 1981. pap. 2.50 (ISBN 0-917976-09-6). White Ewe.

--Narcissa Notebook. (Illus.). 1973. 1.00 o.p. (ISBN 0-686-23603-3). Stone Pr MI.

Drake, Bonnie. The Passionate Touch. 1981. pap. 1.50 (ISBN 0-440-16776-0). Dell.

--Surrender by Moonlight. (Orig.). 1981. pap. 1.50 (ISBN 0-440-18426-6). Dell.

--Sweet Ember. (Candlelight Romance Ser.). (Orig.). Date not set. pap. 1.50 (ISBN 0-440-18459-2). Dell.

Drake, Charles, jt. ed. see Burk, Creighton A.

Drake, Dana B. Cervantes' Novelas Ejemplares: A Selective, Annotated Bibliography. 2nd,rev. ed. LC 80-8492. 250p. 1981. lib. bdg. 35.00 (ISBN 0-8240-9473-5). Garland Pub.

Drake, Daniel. Physician to the West: Selected Writings of Daniel Drake on Science & Society. Shapiro, Henry D. & Miller, Zane L., eds. LC 73-94071. (Illus.). 464p. 1970. 18.00x (ISBN 0-8131-1197-8). U Pr of Ky.

Drake, David. The Dragon Lord. 1979. 8.95 o.p. (ISBN 0-399-12380-6). Berkley Pub.

Drake, F. R., ed. see Logic Colloquim '79 Leeds, August 1979, et al.

Drake, Francis S. Dictionary of American Biography Including Men of the Time. LC 73-11061. 1974. Repr. of 1872 ed. 56.00 (ISBN 0-8103-3731-2). Gale.

--Tea Leaves: Being a Collection of Letters & Documents Relating to the Shipment of Tea to the American Colonies in the Year 1773, by the East India Tea Company. LC 77-95778. (Illus.). 1970. Repr. of 1884 ed. 18.00 (ISBN 0-8103-3577-8). Gale.

Drake, George. Small Gas Engines: Maintenance, Troubleshooting & Repair. 500p. 1981. text ed. 16.95 (ISBN 0-8359-7014-0); pap. text ed. 7.95 (ISBN 0-8359-7013-2); soln. manual avail. (ISBN 0-8359-7015-9). Reston.

Drake, George R. Weatherizing Your Home. (Illus.). 1978. ref. ed 13.95 (ISBN 0-8359-8592-X). Reston.

Drake, Glendon F. The Role of Prescriptivism in American Linguistics, 1820-1970. (Studies in the History of Linguistics: No. 13). 1977. text ed. 23.00x (ISBN 90-27209-54-5). Humanities.

Drake, H. A. In Praise of Constantine: A Historical Study of Eusebius' Tricennial Orations. (Library Reprint Ser.: No. 93). 1978. 14.50x (ISBN 0-520-03694-8). U of Cal Pr.

Drake, James. The Antient & Modern Stages Survey'd. LC 70-170446. (The English Stage Ser.: Vol. 32). lib. bdg. 50.00 (ISBN 0-8240-0615-1). Garland Pub.

Drake, Kirsten, et al. Women's Work & Women's Studies 1971. (Annual). 1972. pap. 4.50x o.p. (ISBN 0-912786-18-3). Know Inc.

Drake, M., tr. see Sundt, Eilert.

Drake, Maurice & Drake, Wilfred. Saints & Their Emblems. LC 68-18021. xiv, 235p. 1972. Repr. of 1916 ed. 25.00 (ISBN 0-8103-3032-6). Gale.

Drake, Michael. Population & Society in Norway, 1735-1865. LC 69-14393. (Cambridge Studies in Economic History). (Illus.). 1969. 35.50 (ISBN 0-521-07319-7). Cambridge U Pr.

Drake, Milton. Almanacs of the United States, 2 Vols. LC 62-10127. 1962. Set. 45.00 (ISBN 0-8108-0001-2). Scarecrow.

Drake, Miriam A. User Fees: A Practical Perspective. 120p. 1981. lib. bdg. 15.00x (ISBN 0-87287-244-0). Libs Unl.

Drake, Peter J. Money, Finance & Development. 244p. 1980. 27.95x (ISBN 0-470-26992-8). Halsted Pr.

Drake, Richard. Byzantium for Rome: The Politics of Nostalgia in Umbertian Italy, 1878-1900. LC 79-16578. 335p. 1980. 20.00x (ISBN 0-8078-1405-9). U of NC Pr.

Drake, Robert. The Home Place: A Memory & a Celebration. LC 80-24110. (Illus.). 192p. 1980. 14.95 (ISBN 0-87870-198-2). Memphis St Univ.

Drake, Samuel A. Book of New England Legends & Folk Lore. LC 69-19881. 1969. Repr. of 1901 ed. 20.00 (ISBN 0-8103-3829-7). Gale.

--Nooks & Corners of the New England Coast. LC 69-19883. 1969. Repr. of 1875 ed. 20.00 (ISBN 0-8103-3827-0). Gale.

--Old Boston Taverns & Tavern Clubs. LC 78-162511. 132p. 1971. Repr. of 1917 ed. 18.00 (ISBN 0-8103-3293-0). Gale.

--Old Landmarks & Historic Personages of Boston. LC 76-99068. (Illus.). 1970. Repr. of 1900 ed. 20.00 (ISBN 0-8103-3582-4). Gale.

Drake, Samuel G. Indian Captivities: Being a Collection of the Most Remarkable Narratives of Persons Taken Captives by the North American Indians. LC 75-7077. (Indian Captivities Ser.: Vol. 55). 1976. Repr. of 1839 ed. lib. bdg. 44.00 (ISBN 0-8240-1679-3). Garland Pub.

Drake, Stanley. Though You Die. 2nd ed. 1974. pap. 4.50 (ISBN 0-900285-09-5, Pub. by Floris Books). St George Bk Serv.

Drake, Stillman. Galileo. (Pastmasters Ser.). 1981. 7.95 (ISBN 0-8090-4850-7); pap. 2.95 (ISBN 0-8090-1416-5). Hill & Wang.

--Galileo at Work: His Scientific Biography. LC 78-5239. xxiv, 536p. 1981. pap. 9.95 (ISBN 0-226-16227-3). U of Chicago Pr.

Drake, Stillman, tr. from Italian. Galileo Galilei: Operations of the Geometric & Military Compass. LC 78-606002. (Illus.). 95p. 1978. text ed. 5.95x (ISBN 0-87474-383-4). Smithsonian.

Drake, Stillman, tr. see Galilei, Galileo.

Drake, Stillman, tr. & intro. by see Galilei, Galileo.

Drake, W. Raymond. Gods & Spacemen in the Ancient West. pap. 1.50 (ISBN 0-451-06055-5, W6055, Sig). NAL.

Drake, Wilfred, jt. auth. see Drake, Maurice.

Drakeford, J. W. Psicologia y Religion. 1980. pap. 8.95 (ISBN 0-311-46035-6, Edit Mundo). Casa Bautista.

Drakeford, John W. Hechos el Uno Para el Otro. De Plou, Dafne C., tr. (Sexo en la Vida Cristiana Ser.). 1977. pap. 2.75 (ISBN 0-311-46256-1). Casa Bautista.

--People to People Therapy. LC 77-20447. 1978. 7.95 o.p. (ISBN 0-06-062062-5, HarpR). Har-Row.

Drakeford, John W., jt. auth. see Drakeford, Robina.

Drakeford, Robina & Drakeford, John W. In Praise of Women: A Christian Approach to Love, Marriage, & Equality. LC 79-3000. 160p. 1980. 8.95 (ISBN 0-06-062063-3). Har-Row.

Dranov, Paula, et al. Video in the Eighties: Emerging Uses for Television in Business, Education & Government. LC 80-15745. (Video Bookshelf Ser.). 186p. 1980. text ed. 34.95 (ISBN 0-914236-58-X). Knowledge Indus.

Dransfield, P. & Haber, D. F. Introducing Root Locus. (Illus.). 150p. 1973. 12.95x (ISBN 0-521-20118-7). Cambridge U Pr.

Drant, Thomas H., tr. see Horatius Flaccus, Quintus.

Drapela, Victor J. Guidance & Counseling Around the World. LC 79-64966. 344p. 1981. lib. bdg. 20.50 (ISBN 0-8191-1384-0); pap. text ed. 11.50 (ISBN 0-8191-0777-8). U Pr of Amer.

Draper. Analylitic Methods in Communicative Algebra. Date not set. price not set (ISBN 0-8247-1282-X). Dekker.

--Caring for Children. 1979. text ed. 13.60 (ISBN 0-87002-281-4); tchr's guide 8.56 (ISBN 0-87002-286-5); student's guide 3.16 (ISBN 0-87002-291-1). Bennett IL.

--Studying Children: Observing & Participating. 1977. pap. text ed. 9.28 (ISBN 0-87002-291-1). Bennett IL.

Draper & Bailey. Steps in Clothing Skills. (gr. 7-9). 1978. text ed. 13.28 (ISBN 0-87002-265-2); avail. tchr's guide. Bennett IL.

Draper, C. G. The Gift of the Magi & Other Stories. (Hewbury House Reader Ser.: Stage 2 - Beginner). (Illus., Orig.). 1981. pap. text ed. 1.95 (ISBN 0-88377-169-1). Newbury Hse.

Draper, Cena C. Dandy & the Mystery of the Locked Room. (Illus.). (gr. 6 up). 1974. 7.50 o.p. (ISBN 0-8309-0114-0, 15-0118-6). Independence Pr.

Draper, Delores. The Doll Book. (Illus.). (gr. k-2). 1977. PLB 5.38 (ISBN 0-307-68917-4, Golden Pr). Western Pub.

Draper, Hal. Karl Marx's Theory of Revolution, Part One: The State & Bureaucracy, 2 vols. LC 76-26319. 1977. 28.50 set o.p. (ISBN 0-85345-387-X, CL-387-X). Monthly Rev.

Draper, Harold H., ed. Advances in Nutritional Research, Vols. 1-3. Incl. Vol. 1. 362p. 1977. 27.50 (ISBN 0-306-34321-5); Vol. 2. 264p. 1979. 27.50 (ISBN 0-306-40213-0); Vol. 3. 300p. 1980. 32.50 (ISBN 0-306-40415-X). Plenum Pub. (Illus., Plenum Pr). Plenum Pub.

Draper, Hilary. Private Police. 1978. text ed. 19.50x (ISBN 0-391-00852-8). Humanities.

Draper, James D., ed. see Bode, Wilhelm.

Draper, Jean. Mathematics Para Administration y Economia. new ed. 1976. text ed. 12.00x (ISBN 0-06-310100-9, IntlDept). Har-Row.

Draper, John E., ed. Napoleon's Thoughts on History, Politics & the Management of Men. (Illus.). 1980. deluxe ed. 39.75 (ISBN 0-89266-232-8). Am Classical Coll Pr.

Draper, John W. Thoughts on the Future Civil Policy of America. Incl. Memoir of John William Draper, 1811-1882. Barker, George F. (The Neglected American Economists Ser.). 1974. lib. bdg. 50.00 (ISBN 0-8240-1017-5). Garland Pub.

Draper, Maurice L., ed. Restoration Studies, Nineteen Eighty. 1980. pap. 12.00 (ISBN 0-8309-0292-9). Herald Hse.

Draper, N. R. & Smith, H. Applied Regression Analysis. 2nd ed. LC 80-17951. (Wiley Ser. in Probability & Mathematical Statics - Applied Probability & Statistics). 720p. 1981. 22.50 (ISBN 0-471-02995-5, Pub. by Wiley-Interscience). Wiley.

Draper, Norman R., jt. auth. see Box, George E.

Draper, R. P., ed. D. H. Lawrence: The Critical Heritage. (Critical Heritage Ser.). 1970. 35.00x (ISBN 0-7100-6591-4). Routledge & Kegan.

Draper, Ronald P. D. H. Lawrence. (English Authors Ser.: No. 7). 1964. lib. bdg. 9.95 (ISBN 0-8057-1320-4). Twayne.

Draper, Simon R. Biochemical Analysis in Crop Service. (Illus.). 1976. 22.50x (ISBN 0-19-854128-7). Oxford U Pr.

Draper, Thomas, ed. Emerging China. (Reference Shelf Ser.). 1980. 6.25 (ISBN 0-8242-0644-4). Wilson.

Draper, Verden R., jt. auth. see Irving, Robert H., Jr.

Drastrup, A., jt. auth. see Riberholt, K.

Draves, Pamela, ed. Citizens Media Directory. 1977. pap. 3.50 (ISBN 0-9603466-3-5); 1980 update avail. NCCB.

Draves, William A. The Free University: A Model for Lifelong Learning. 324p. 1980. 17.95 (ISBN 0-695-81443-5, Assn Pr). Follett.

Drawbaugh, Susan M. What Pet Will I Get? LC 77-83881. 1977. 5.95 (ISBN 0-89430-017-2). Morgan-Pacific.

Drawbell, Marjorie. Making Pottery Figures. (gr. 9 up). 6.95 (ISBN 0-85458-080-8); pap. 7.50 (ISBN 0-85458-081-6). Transatlantic.

Drawson. Do Something Special on Your Birthday. (ps-3). pap. 1.25 (ISBN 0-590-05799-5, Schol Pap). Schol Bk Serv.

--I Like Hats. (ps-3). pap. 1.50 (ISBN 0-590-05800-2, Schol Pap). Schol Bk Serv.

Dray, William H. Philosophy of History. (Orig.). 1964. pap. 7.95x ref. ed. (ISBN 0-13-663849-X). P-H.

Draycott, A. P. Sugar-Beet Nutrition. 1972. 28.95 (ISBN 0-470-22160-7). Halsted Pr.

Drayer, Adam M. Problems in Middle & High School Teaching: A Handbook for Student Teachers & Beginning Teachers. new ed. 1980. text ed. 16.95 (ISBN 0-205-06146-X, 2361310); pap. text ed. 10.95 (ISBN 0-205-06131-1). Allyn.

Drayton, Mary. All Our Secrets. 384p. (Orig.). 1981. pap. 2.95 (ISBN 0-449-14391-0, GM). Fawcett.

Drazan, Joseph G. The Pacific Northwest: An Index to People & Places in Books. LC 79-16683. 176p. 1979. 10.00 (ISBN 0-8108-1234-7). Scarecrow.

--The Unknown Eric: A Selection of Documents for the General Library. LC 80-25975. 239p. 1981. lib. bdg. 12.50 (ISBN 0-8108-1402-1). Scarecrow.

Draze, Dianne. Creative Coloring I. (Illus.). (gr. 1-6). 1978. wkbk 1.50 o.p. (ISBN 0-931724-05-8). Dandy Lion.

--Creative Coloring II. (Illus.). (gr. 1-6). 1978. wkbk 1.50 o.p. (ISBN 0-931724-06-6). Dandy Lion.

--Patchwork (Activities in Flexible Thinking) (Illus., Orig.). 1980. pap. text ed. 7.00 (ISBN 0-931724-13-9); tchr's ed. avail. Dandy Lion.

Drazin, P. & Reid, W. Hydrodynamic Stability. LC 80-40273. (Cambridge Monographs on Mechanics & Applied Mathematics). (Illus.). 600p. Date not set. 77.00 (ISBN 0-521-22798-4). Cambridge U Pr.

Draznin, Yaffa. The Family Historian's Handbook. 1978. pap. 2.50 o.s.i. (ISBN 0-515-04516-0). Jove Pubns.

Drazniowsky, Roman. Map Librarianship: Readings. LC 74-19244. (Illus.). 1975. 22.00 (ISBN 0-8108-0739-4). Scarecrow.

Dreadstone, Carl. The Mummy. (Universal Horror Library). 1977. pap. 1.25 o.p. (ISBN 0-425-03445-3, Medallion). Berkley Pub.

--The Werewolf of London. (Orig.). 1977. pap. 1.25 o.p. (ISBN 0-425-03413-5, Medallion). Berkley Pub.

--The Wolfman. (Universal Horror Library). 1977. pap. 1.25 o.p. (ISBN 0-425-03446-1, Medallion). Berkley Pub.

Drebin. Managerial Accounting. 3rd ed. 1978. 20.95 (ISBN 0-7216-3188-6). Dryden Pr.

Dreeben, Robert. On What Is Learned in School. LC 68-25923. (Education Ser). (Orig.). 1968. pap. 6.95 (ISBN 0-201-01610-9). A-W.

Dreeben, Robert & Thomas, J. Alan, eds. Issues in Microanalysis, Vol. 1. LC 79-62118. (Analysis of Educational Productivity Ser.: Vol. 1). 320p. 1980. reference 25.00 (ISBN 0-88410-191-6). Ballinger Pub.

Drees, Jack & Mullen, James C. Where Is He Now? Sports Heroes of Yesterday Revisited. LC 71-188243. (Illus.). 1973. 7.95 o.p. (ISBN 0-8246-0145-9). Jonathan David.

Dreesman, Cecile. Embroidery. (Illus.). 1969. 9.95 (ISBN 0-02-533470-0). Macmillan.

Drefus, M. Bertrand, ed. International Codata Conference on Generation, Compilation, Evaluation & Dissemination of Data for Science & Technology, 4th: Proceedings. 160p. 1975. pap. 21.00 (ISBN 0-08-019850-3). Pergamon.

Dreghorn, William. Geology Explained: In the Forest of Dean & the Wye Valley. 1968. pap. 4.95 (ISBN 0-7153-4263-0). David & Charles.

--Geology Explained in the Severn Vale & Cotswolds. (Illus.). 192p. 1974. 14.95 (ISBN 0-7153-4102-2). David & Charles.

Dreher, E., ed. Schweizerische Gesellschaft fuer Gynaekologie, Bericht ueber die Jahresversammlung, Montreux, Juni 1979. (Journal: Gynaekologische Rundschau: Vol. 19, Suppl. 2). 1980. pap. 19.75 (ISBN 3-8055-0456-X). S Karger.

--Schweizerische Gesellschaft Fuer Gynaekologie Bericht Ueber Die Jahresversammlung, St. Gallen. June 1980. (Journal: Gynaekologische Rundschau: Vol. 20, No. 1). (Illus.). iv, 144p. 1980. pap. write for info. (ISBN 3-8055-2126-X). S Karger.

Dreikurs, Rudolf. The Challenge of Child Training. 1972. pap. 4.50 (ISBN 0-8015-1146-1, Hawthorn). Dutton.

--Challenge of Marriage. 1978. 9.95 o.p. (ISBN 0-8015-1176-3, Hawthorn); pap. 4.95 (ISBN 0-8015-1177-1, Hawthorn). Dutton.

--Coping with Children's Misbehavior. 1972. pap. 4.50 (ISBN 0-8015-1764-8, Hawthorn). Dutton.

--Psychology in the Classroom. rev., enl. ed. 1968. pap. text ed. 14.95 scp (ISBN 0-06-041756-0, HarpC). Har-Row.

--Psychology in the Classroom: A Manual for Teachers. rev. & enl. ed. 1968. 8.95x o.p. (ISBN 0-06-031801-5, HarpT). Har-Row.

Dreikurs, Rudolf & Grey, Loren. Logical Consequences: A New Approach to Discipline. LC 68-28720. 1968. 9.95 (ISBN 0-8015-4638-9, Hawthorn); pap. 4.50 (ISBN 0-8015-4632-X, Hawthorn). Dutton.

--Parent's Guide to Child Discipline. 1970. pap. 3.95 (ISBN 0-8015-5736-4, Hawthorn). Dutton.

Dreikurs, Rudolf & Soltz, Vicki. Children: The Challenge. 1964. 9.95 (ISBN 0-8015-1248-4, Hawthorn); pap. 5.95 (ISBN 0-8015-1249-2). Dutton.

Dreikurs, Rudolf, et al. Maintaining Sanity in the Classroom: Illustrated Teaching Techniques. 1971. pap. 14.95 scp (ISBN 0-06-041758-7, HarpC). Har-Row.

Dreikurs, Rudolph. Discipline Without Tears. 1974. pap. 3.95 (ISBN 0-8015-2132-7, Hawthorn). Dutton.

Dreisbach. Balsa Wood & Its Properties. 3.00 o.p. (ISBN 0-686-00166-4). Columbia Graphs.

Dreiser, Theodore. An American Tragedy. LC 78-55741. 1978. Repr. of 1948 ed. lib. bdg. 16.50x (ISBN 0-8376-0424-9). Bentley.

--Selected Poems from Moods. Saalbach, Robert Palmer, ed. 1969. 7.50 o.p. (ISBN 0-682-46914-9, University). Exposition.

--Sister Carrie. (Literature Ser). (gr. 10-12). 1970. pap. text ed. 3.75 (ISBN 0-87720-739-9). AMSCO Sch.

--Sister Carrie. LC 78-183140. 472p. 1971. Repr. lib. bdg. 12.50x (ISBN 0-8376-0401-X). Bentley.

--Sister Carrie. LC 69-13798. (Merrill Standard Ser). 6.00 (ISBN 0-675-09527-1); pap. 4.00 (ISBN 0-675-09528-X). Brown Bk.

--Sister Carrie. 557p. 1980. Repr. of 1907 ed. lib. bdg. 17.95x (ISBN 0-89968-207-3). Lightyear.

--Sister Carrie. Salzman, Jack, ed. LC 69-16530. 1970. 6.95 (ISBN 0-685-91574-3); pap. 4.50 (ISBN 0-672-61014-0). Bobbs.

--Sister Carrie: The Pennsylvania Edition. West, James L., III, et al, eds. 1981. text ed. 29.95x (ISBN 0-8122-7784-8); pap. text ed. 14.95x (ISBN 0-8122-1110-3). U of Pa Pr.

Dreiser, Theodore, et al. Harlan Miners Speak Report on Terrorism in the Kentucky Coal Fields. LC 70-107410. (Civil Liberties in American History Ser.). 1970. Repr. of 1932 ed. lib. bdg. 22.50 (ISBN 0-306-71889-8). Da Capo.

Dreiser, Theordore. The Genius. 463p. 1980. Repr. of 1917 ed. lib. bdg. 17.25x (ISBN 0-89968-206-5). Lightyear.

Dreizen, LaVerne & Audet, Thelma. Medical Assistant's Examination Review Book, Vol. 1. 2nd. ed. 1979. 9.50 (ISBN 0-87488-490-X). Med Exam.

Dreman, David N. Psychology & the Stock Market. 1979. pap. 6.95 o.s.i. (ISBN 0-446-97071-9). Warner Bks.

--Psychology & the Stock Market. new ed. LC 76-49986. 1977. 13.95 (ISBN 0-8144-5429-1). Am Mgmt.

Drendel, Lou. Aircraft of the Vietnam War. LC 79-113405. (Famous Aircraft Ser.). (Illus.). 64p. 1980. pap. 4.95 (ISBN 0-8168-5651-6). Aero.

--And Kill MIGs. pap. 6.95 (ISBN 0-89747-056-7). Squad Sig Pubns.

Dresch, Stephen P. An Economic Perspective on the Evolution of Graduate Education: A Technical Report Presented to the National Board on Graduate Education. 88p. 1974. pap. text ed. 2.00 (ISBN 0-309-02221-5). Natl Acad Pr.

Drescher, Horst. Let Us Die Fighting: Nambia Under the Germans. 1981. 18.95 (ISBN 0-905762-77-0); pap. 8.95 (ISBN 0-905762-37-1). Lawrence Hill.

Drescher, John M. Siete Necesidades Basicas Del Nino. 160p. (Span.). 1981. pap. write for info. (ISBN 0-311-46085-2). Casa Bautista.

--Testimony of Triumph. 1980. pap. 4.95 (ISBN 0-310-23920-6). Zondervan.

Dresden, Donald. Marquis De Mores: Emperor of the Badlands. LC 69-16720. (Illus.). 1970. 13.95 (ISBN 0-8061-0869-X); pap. 6.95 o.p. (ISBN 0-8061-1196-8). U of Okla Pr.

Dresher, Seymour, jt. auth. see Bolt, Christine.

Dresnack, R. & Golub, E. Environmental Impact Assessment: An Interdisciplinary Approach. (Theoretical & Applied Environmental Reviews Ser.). 200p. 1980. cancelled (ISBN 0-686-61666-9). Harwood Academic.

Dresner, Joanne, ed. It's Up to You. (Illus.). 1979. pap. text ed. 3.95x (ISBN 0-582-79727-6); cassette 8.95x (ISBN 0-582-79728-4); plastic tote (book & cassette) 10.95 (ISBN 0-582-79771-3). Longman.

Dresnick, Stephen J., jt. auth. see Meislin, Harvey W.

Dressel, Paul L. Improving Degree Programs: A Guide to Curriculum Development, Administration, & Review. LC 80-82376. (Higher Education Ser.). 1980. text ed. 15.95x (ISBN 0-87589-486-0). Jossey-Bass.

Dressel, Paul L. & Thompson, Mary M. Independent Study: A New Interpretation of Concepts, Practices, & Problems. LC 73-50. (Higher Education Ser.). 1973. 11.95x o.p. (ISBN 0-87589-169-1). Jossey-Bass.

Dresser, Christopher. The Art of Decorative Design. LC 76-17751. (Aesthetic Movement Ser.: Vol. 4). (Illus.). 1977. Repr. of 1862 ed. lib. bdg. 44.00x (ISBN 0-8240-2453-2). Garland Pub.

--The Development of Ornamental Art in the International Exhibition. Stansky, Peter & Shewan, Rodney, eds. LC 76-17750. (Aesthetic Movement & the Arts & Crafts Movement Ser.). 1978. Repr. of 1862 ed. lib. bdg. 44.00x (ISBN 0-8240-2452-4). Garland Pub.

--Japan: Its Art, Architecture, & Art Manufacture. LC 76-17752. (Aesthetic Movement & the Arts & Crafts Movement Ser.: Vol. 5). 1977. Repr. of 1882 ed. lib. bdg. 44.00 (ISBN 0-8240-2454-0). Garland Pub.

--Modern Ornamentation. Stansky, Peter & Shewan, Rodney, eds. LC 76-17771. (Aesthetic Movement & the Arts & Crafts Movements Ser.: Vol. 26). 1978. Repr. of 1886 ed. lib. bdg. 44.00 (ISBN 0-8240-2475-3). Garland Pub.

--Unity in Variety. Stansky, Peter & Shewan, Rodney, eds. LC 76-17748. (Aesthetic Movement & the Arts & Crafts Movement Ser.). 1978. Repr. of 1859 ed. lib. bdg. 44.00x (ISBN 0-8240-2451-6). Garland Pub.

Dresser, William, jt. ed. see Hayakawa, S. I.

Dressler, David. Practice & Theory of Probation & Parole. 1969. 15.00x (ISBN 0-231-02956-X). Columbia U Pr.

--Readings in Criminology & Penology. 2nd ed. LC 75-181783. 700p. 1972. 25.00x (ISBN 0-231-03429-6); pap. 12.00x (ISBN 0-231-08672-5). Columbia U Pr.

Dressler, David, jt. auth. see Greenblat, Cathy.

Dressler, Isidore. Current Mathematics: A Work-Text. (gr. 7 up). 1977. Bk. I. wkbk 8.67 (ISBN 0-87720-239-7). AMSCO Sch.

Dressler, Isidore. Algebra I. (gr. 9). 1966. text ed. 10.67 (ISBN 0-87720-208-7). AMSCO Sch.

--Algebra One Review Guide. (Illus., Orig.). (gr. 9). 1966. pap. text ed. 5.00 (ISBN 0-87720-207-9). AMSCO Sch.

--Geometry. (Orig.). (gr. 10-12). 1973. text ed. 12.58 (ISBN 0-87720-235-4); pap. text ed. 8.33 (ISBN 0-87720-234-6). AMSCO Sch.

--Geometry Review Guide. (gr. 10-12). 1973. pap. text ed. 5.42 (ISBN 0-87720-215-X). AMSCO Sch.

--Preliminary Mathematics. (gr. 8). 1981. text ed. 17.92 (ISBN 0-87720-243-5). AMSCO Sch.

--Preliminary Mathematics. (Orig.). 1980. pap. text ed. 10.83 (ISBN 0-87720-242-7). AMSCO Sch.

--Preliminary Mathematics Review Guide. (Illus.). (gr. 8-10). 1965. pap. text ed. 5.00 (ISBN 0-87720-205-2). AMSCO Sch.

--Review Text in Preliminary Mathematics. (Illus.). (gr. 7-9). 1962. text ed. 9.83 (ISBN 0-87720-203-6); pap. text ed. 6.25 (ISBN 0-87720-202-8). AMSCO Sch.

Dressler, Isidore & Dressler, Robert. Introductory Algebra for College Students. (Orig.). 1976. pap. text ed. 10.00 (ISBN 0-87720-975-8). AMSCO Sch.

Dressler, Isidore & Keenan, Edward P. Integrated Mathematics: Course I. (Orig.). (gr. 9). 1980. text ed. 19.17 (ISBN 0-87720-249-4); pap. text ed. 12.09 (ISBN 0-87720-248-6). AMSCO Sch.

Dressler, Isidore & Rich, Barnett. Algebra Two & Trigonometry: A Modern Integrated Course. (gr. 11-12). 1972. text ed. 12.50 (ISBN 0-87720-221-4); pap. text ed. 7.53 (ISBN 0-87720-220-6). AMSCO Sch.

--Modern Algebra Two. (Orig.). (gr. 11-12). 1973. text ed. 12.17 (ISBN 0-87720-233-8); pap. text ed. 6.50 (ISBN 0-87720-232-X). AMSCO Sch.

--Trigonometry. (gr. 10-12). 1975. pap. text ed. 5.83 (ISBN 0-87720-219-2). AMSCO Sch.

Dressler, Isidore, et al. Intermediate Algebra for College Students. 1977. pap. text ed. 10.00 (ISBN 0-87720-977-4). AMSCO Sch.

Dressler, Robert, jt. auth. see Dressler, Isidore.

Dressler, Wolfgang U. Morphonology: The Dynamics of Derivation. (Linguistica Extranea: Studia: No. 12). 250p. 13.50 (ISBN 0-89720-034-9); pap. 10.50 (ISBN 0-89720-035-7). Karoma.

Dressner, Howard R., jt. auth. see Janis, J. Harold.

Dretske, Fred I. Knowledge & the Flow of Information. LC 81-21633. (Illus.). 288p. 1981. text ed. 18.50 (ISBN 0-89706-009-1). Bradford Bks.

--Seeing & Knowing. pap. write for info. (ISBN 0-226-16245-1). U of Chicago Pr.

Drevdahl, Elmer R. Profitable Use of Excavation Equipment. 14.95 (ISBN 0-89741-009-2); pap. 11.25 (ISBN 0-89741-009-2). Roadrunner Tech.

Drew, Clifford J. Introduction to Designing & Conducting Research. 2nd. ed. LC 79-25403. (Illus.). 1980. 14.95 (ISBN 0-8016-1460-0). Mosby.

--Introduction to Designing Research & Evaluation. LC 75-20115. (Illus.). 224p. 1976. text ed. 13.95 o.p. (ISBN 0-8016-1464-3). Mosby.

Drew, Clifford J. & Hardman, Michael L. Mental Retardation: Social & Education Perspectives. LC 73-26680. (Illus.). 1977. pap. 12.00 (ISBN 0-8016-1462-7). Mosby.

Drew, D. P., jt. ed. see Smith, D. I.

Drew, Donald. Images of Man: A Critique of the Contemporary Cinema. LC 74-20099. (Illus.). 144p. 1974. pap. 2.95 o.p. (ISBN 0-87784-482-8). Inter-Varsity.

Drew, Jane, jt. auth. see Fry, Maxwell.

Drew, Jon S. Doing Business in the European Community. (Illus.). 1979. text ed. 28.95 (ISBN 0-408-10631-X). Butterworths.

Drew, Katherine F. The Lombard Laws. (Middle Ages Ser). 240p. 1973. 15.00x (ISBN 0-8122-7661-2); pap. 5.95x (ISBN 0-8122-1055-7, Pa Paperbacks). U of Pa Pr.

Drew, Katherine F., tr. Burgundian Code: Book of Constitutions or Law of Gundobad & Additional Enactments. LC 70-182499. (Middle Ages Ser). (Orig.). 1972. 10.00x (ISBN 0-8122-7654-X); pap. 4.95x (ISBN 0-8122-1035-2, Pa Paperbks). U of Pa Pr.

Drew, Leslie & Wilson, Douglas. Argillite: Art of the Haida. (Illus.). 350p. 1980. 40.00x (ISBN 0-87663-609-1). Universe.

Drew, Philip. Frei Otto: Form & Structure. LC 76-178. (Illus.). 1976. 42.50 o.p. (ISBN 0-89158-535-4). Westview.

--Tensile Architecture: From the Tent to the Bubble Dome. (Illus.). 1979. 45.00 (ISBN 0-89158-550-8). Westview.

Drew, Thomas B. & Hoopes, John W. Advances in Chemical Engineering, Vol. 10. (Serial Publication). 1978. 43.50 (ISBN 0-12-008510-0). Acad Pr.

Drew, Thomas B. & Hoopes, John W., Jr., eds. Advances in Chemical Engineering. Incl. Vol. 1. 1956. 52.50 (ISBN 0-12-008501-1); Vol. 2. 1958. 52.50 (ISBN 0-12-008502-X); Vol. 3. Drew, Thomas B., et al, eds. 1962. 52.50 (ISBN 0-12-008503-8); Vol. 4. 1963. 52.50 (ISBN 0-12-008504-6); Vol. 5. 1964. 52.50 (ISBN 0-12-008505-4); Vol. 6. 1966. 52.50 (ISBN 0-12-008506-2); Vol. 7. 1968. 52.50 (ISBN 0-12-008507-0); Vol. 8. 1970. 52.50 (ISBN 0-12-008508-9); Vol. 9. 1974. 52.50 (ISBN 0-12-008509-7). Acad Pr.

Drew, Wayland. Dragonslayer. (Orig.). 1981. pap. 2.75 (ISBN 0-345-29694-X, Del Rey). Ballantine.

Dreway, Gavin, ed. see Blom-Cooper, L.

Drew-Bear, Marie. Le Nome Hermopolite. LC 78-13005. (American Studies in Papyrology: No. 21). 45.00x (ISBN 0-89130-258-1, 310021). Scholars Pr CA.

Drewett, P. L., ed. The Archaeology in Sussex to AD1500. 110p. 1980. pap. 20.95x (ISBN 0-900312-67-X, Pub. by Council Brit Arch England). Intl Schol Bk Serv.

Drewett, R., jt. auth. see Drewitt, M.

Drewitt, M. & Drewett, R. Nature of Settle Structure & Change: A European View. Date not set. 48.01 (ISBN 0-08-023157-8). Pergamon.

Drewry, Cecelia H., jt. ed. see Drewry, Henry N.

Drewry, Henry N. & Drewry, Cecelia H., eds. Afro-American History, Past to Present. LC 74-136591. 585p. (gr. 9-12). 1971. pap. text ed. 8.95x o.p. (ISBN 0-684-41232-2, ScribC). Scribner.

Drewry, William S. Southampton Insurrection. (Illus.). 1968. Repr. of 1900 ed. 12.00 (ISBN 0-930230-21-3). Johnson NC.

Drexel, Henry W., tr. see Raeder, Erich.

Drexler, Arthur. Ludwig Mies Van Der Rohe. LC 60-6077. (Masters of World Architecture Ser). 1960. 7.95 o.s.i. (ISBN 0-8076-0108-X); pap. 3.95 o.s.i. (ISBN 0-8076-0222-1). Braziller.

Drexler, Charles H. The Authority to Teach: A Study in the Ecclesiology of Henry Edward Manning. LC 77-18567. 1978. pap. text ed. 9.00 (ISBN 0-8191-0410-8). U Pr of Amer.

Drexler, Rosalyn. The Cosmopolitan Girl. 208p. 1976. pap. 1.75 o.s.i. (ISBN 0-446-59057-6). Warner Bks.

Drey, Rudolf E. Apothecary Jars: Pharmaceutical Pottery & Porcelain in Europe & the East 1150-1850. (Illus.). 1978. 48.00 (ISBN 0-571-09965-3, Pub. by Faber & Faber). Merrimack Bk Serv.

Dreyer, Jacob S., ed. Breadth & Depth in Economics. LC 77-238. 1978. 18.95 (ISBN 0-669-01430-3). Lexington Bks.

Dreyer, Julie, jt. auth. see Olshan, Neil.

Dreyer, Peter & Stackpole, Edouard. Nantucket in Color. (Profiles of America Ser). (Illus.). 1974. 6.95 (ISBN 0-8038-5030-1). Hastings.

Dreyer, Sharon, et al. A Guide to Nursing Management of Psychiatric Patients. 2nd ed. LC 78-31432. 1979. pap. text ed. 10.95 (ISBN 0-8016-0832-5). Mosby.

Dreyer, Sharon S. The Bookfinder: A Guide to Children's Literature About the Needs & Problems of Youth Aged 2 to 15, 2 vols. 1981. Set. text ed. 69.50 (ISBN 0-913476-44-7); Vol. 1. text ed. 32.00 (ISBN 0-686-69405-8); Vol. 2. text ed. 37.50 (ISBN 0-913476-46-3). Am Guidance.

--The Bookfinder: A Guide to Children's Literature About the Needs & Problems of Youth, Vol. 1. (ps up). 1977. text ed. 37.50 (ISBN 0-913476-45-5). Am Guidance.

Dreyers, F. Traveller Discovering Norway. 1968. 25.00x (N499). Vanous.

Dreyfack, Raymond. The Complete Book of Walking. LC 80-26185. (Illus.). 288p. 1981. pap. 5.95 (ISBN 0-668-05167-1, 5167). Arco.

--Making It in Management. 156p. 1980. cancelled (ISBN 0-87863-006-6). Farnswth Pub.

Dreyfus, B., jt. auth. see Dreyfus, J. C.

Dreyfus, Bertrand, ed. see International Codata Conference, 6th Biennial, Santa Flavia, Italy, May 22-25, 1978.

Dreyfus, Edward A. Adolescence: Theory & Experience. new ed. 256p. 1976. pap. text ed. 11.95 (ISBN 0-675-08679-5). Merrill.

Dreyfus, Hubert L. What Computers Can't Do: A Critique of Artificial Reason. LC 67-22524. (Illus.). 1972. 12.95 o.p. (ISBN 0-06-011082-1, HarpT). Har-Row.

Dreyfus, Hubert L. & Hall, Harrison, eds. Husserl, Intentionality & Cognitive Science. 1981. text ed. write for info. (ISBN 0-89706-010-5). Bradford Bks.

Dreyfus, J. C. & Dreyfus, B. Hematopoietic Agents. 1971. 55.00 (ISBN 0-08-016211-8). Pergamon.

Dreyfus, S., jt. auth. see Bellman, Richard E.

Dreyfuss, P. Poly (Tetrahydrofuran) (Polymer Monographs Ser.). Date not set. price not set (ISBN 0-677-03330-3). Gordon.

Dreyfuss, Robert. Hostage to Khomeini. LC 80-24288. (Illus.). 260p. (Orig.). 1981. pap. 3.95 (ISBN 0-933488-11-4). New Benjamin.

Dreze, Jacques H. Allocation Under Uncertainty: Equilibrium & Optimality Proceedings. (IEA Ser.). 1974. 29.95 (ISBN 0-470-22166-6). Halsted Pr.

Drickamer, H. G. & Frank, C. W. Electronic Transitions & the High Pressure Chemistry & Physics of Solids. LC 72-12341. (Studies in Chemical Physics). 220p. 1973. text ed. 29.50x o.p. (ISBN 0-412-11650-2, Pub. by Chapman & Hall). Methuen Inc.

--Electronic Transitions & the High Pressure Chemistry & Physics of Solids. LC 72-12341. (Studies in Chemical Physics). 330p. 1973. 29.50 o.p. (ISBN 0-470-22180-1). Halsted Pr.

Driel, G. Van see Van Driel, G.

Drieu La Rochelle, Pierre. Secret Journal & Other Writings. Hamilton, Alastair, tr. from Fr. 1974. 13.25 (ISBN 0-86527-300-6). Fertig.

Driggs, Don W., jt. auth. see Bushnell, Eleanore.

Drijkoningen, F., ed. Recherches Sur le Surreslisme, No. 2. 1978. 19.25x (ISBN 0-391-02035-8). Humanities.

Drijvers, H. J. Cults & Beliefs at Edessa. 1980. text ed. 54.75x (ISBN 90-04-06050-2). Humanities.

Drijvers, H. J. W. Cults & Beliefs at Edessa. (Illus.). 204p. 1980. text ed. 54.75 (ISBN 90-04-06050-2). Humanities.

Drilon, J. D., ed. Agribusiness Management Resource Materials. Incl. Vol. I. Introduction to Agribusiness Management. LC 72-170364. 236p. 1973. 13.50 (ISBN 0-685-56587-4, APO1); Vol. II. Agribusiness (Asian Case Studies) 748p. 1971. Pt. 2. 13.50 (ISBN 0-685-56589-0, APO8); Vol. III. 1975. 29.00 (ISBN 0-685-56590-4, APO10). APO). Unipub.

Drimmer, Melvin, ed. Black History: A Reappraisal. LC 67-19105. 1969. pap. 5.95 o.p. (ISBN 0-385-08869-8, A08, Anch). Doubleday.

Drinker, Henry S., jt. auth. see Thorp, Willard.

Drinker, Henry S., jt. auth. see Thorp, William.

Drinker, Henry S., tr. see Schubert, Franz.

Dripps, Robert D., et al. Introduction to Anesthesia: The Principles of Safe Practice. 5th ed. LC 76-51011. (Illus.). 1977. text ed. 19.95 (ISBN 0-7216-3193-2). Saunders.

Driscole, Dee & Ross, Dorothy. Materials & Techniques of 20th Century Artists. LC 76-29167. (Illus.). 48p. 1976. pap. 4.95x (ISBN 0-910386-37-4, Pub. by Cleveland Mus Art). Ind U Pr.

Driscoll, Charles B. The Life of O. O. McIntyre. (American Newspapermen 1790-1933 Ser.). (Illus.). 344p. 1974. Repr. of 1938 ed. 17.50x (ISBN 0-8464-0022-7). Beekman Pubs.

Driscoll, Dennis M., jt. auth. see Griffiths, John F.

Driscoll, Donald C. & Davey, Homer C. The Practice of Real Estate in California. (Illus.). 304p. 1981. 18.95 (ISBN 0-13-693606-7). P-H.

Driscoll, Dorothy L., et al. The Nursing Process in Later Maturity. (Illus.). 1980. text ed. 18.95 (ISBN 0-13-627570-2). P-H.

Driscoll, Edward J. Minnesota Supplement for Modern Real Estate Practice. 3rd ed. 184p. (Orig.). 1980. pap. 10.95 (ISBN 0-88462-324-6). Real Estate Ed Co.

Driscoll, F., jt. auth. see Coughlin, R.

Driscoll, F. F., jt. auth. see Coughlin, R. F.

Driscoll, Frederick, Jr. Analysis of Electric Circuits. LC 72-3691. (Illus.). 544p. 1973. text ed. 19.95 (ISBN 0-13-032912-6). P-H.

Driscoll, P., et al. Decimals. West, K. & Johnston, D., eds. (Math Skills for Daily Living Ser.). (Illus.). 32p. (gr. 7-12). 1979. pap. text ed. 3.95x (ISBN 0-87453-093-8, 82093). Denoyer.

--Fractions. West, K. & Johnston, D., eds. (Math Skills for Daily Living Ser.). (Illus.). 40p. (gr. 7-12). 1979. pap. text ed. 3.95x (ISBN 0-87453-092-X, 82092). Denoyer.

--Ratio, Proporation & Percent. West, K. & Johnston, D., eds. (Math Skills for Daily Living Ser.). (Illus.). 32p. (gr. 7-12). 1979. pap. text ed. 3.95x (ISBN 0-87453-094-6). Denoyer.

--Whole Numbers. West, K. & Johnston, D., eds. (Math Skills for Daily Living Ser.). (Illus.). 32p. (gr. 7-12). 1979. pap. text ed. 3.95x (ISBN 0-87453-091-1, 82091). Denoyer.

Driscoll, Peter. The Barboza Credentials. LC 76-10483. 1976. 8.95 o.p. (ISBN 0-397-01145-8). Lippincott.

--In Connection with Kilshaw. LC 90-20288. 1974. 7.95 o.s.i. (ISBN 0-397-00985-2). Lippincott.

--In Connection with Kilshaw. 288p. 1975. pap. 1.75 o.p. (ISBN 0-445-08366-2). Popular Lib.

--The White Lie Assignment. LC 72-688. 216p. 1975. 7.50 o.p. (ISBN 0-397-00904-6). Lippincott.

Driscoll, Robert G., intro. by. R & R Catolog & Guide to First Day Cover Collecting: 1980-1981 Edition. (Illus.). 112p. (Orig.). 1980. pap. 1.95 (ISBN 0-937458-05-8). Harris & Co.

Driscoll, Tim, jt. auth. see Murphy, Gene.

Driskell, David C. Two Centuries of Black American Art. LC 76-13691. 1976. pap. text ed. 7.95 o.p. (ISBN 0-87587-070-8). LA Co Art Mus.

Driskill, Linda & Simpson, Margaret. Decisive Writing: An Improvement Program. (Illus.). 1977. pap. text ed. 6.95x (ISBN 0-19-502121-5). Oxford U Pr.

Driskoll, David, compiled by. Two Centuries of Black American Art. 1976. 15.00 o.p. (ISBN 0-394-40887-X). Knopf.

Driver, B. L. Elements of Outdoor Recreation Planning. 316p. 1974. pap. text ed. 5.95x (ISBN 0-472-08284-1). U of Mich Pr.

Driver, Clive E. The Art of Claud Lovat Fraser. 1971. pap. 6.50 (ISBN 0-686-28309-0). Rosenbach Mus and Lib.

Driver, G. R. Aramaic Documents of the Fifth Century B. C. abr. & rev. ed. 1957. 7.00x o.p. (ISBN 0-19-815404-6). Oxford U Pr.

Driver, Godfrey. Semitic Writing: From Pictograph to Alphabet. 3rd ed. (Schweich Lectures). (Illus.). 1976. 47.50x (ISBN 0-19-725917-0). Oxford U Pr.

Driver, Harold, et al. California Indians One: Indians Land Use & Occupancy in California, 3 vols. Beals, Ralph L., ed. (American Indian Ethnohistory Ser: California & Basin-Plateau Indians). (Illus.). lib. bdg. 42.00 (ISBN 0-8240-0771-9). Garland Pub.

Driver, Harold E., ed. Culture Groups & Language Groups in Native North America. 1975. pap. text ed. 1.00x (ISBN 90-316-0065-2). Humanities.

Driver, Harold E., et al. California Indians Four. Horr, David A., ed. (American Indian Ethnohistory Ser.). 1978. lib. bdg. 42.00 (ISBN 0-8240-0774-3). Garland Pub.

Driver, S. R. Deuteronomy. 3rd ed. LC 2-25926. (International Critical Commentary Ser.). 556p. 20.00x (ISBN 0-567-05003-3). Attic Pr.

--An Introduction to the Literature of the Old Testament. 9th ed. (International Theological Library). 640p. Repr. of 1913 ed. 13.95x (ISBN 0-567-07205-3). Attic Pr.

Driver, S. R. & Gray, G. Buchanan. Job. LC 21-15647. (International Critical Commentary Ser.). 816p. Repr. of 1921 ed. 23.00x (ISBN 0-567-05010-6). Attic Pr.

Driver, Tom F. Jean Genet. LC 66-26003. (Essays on Modern American Writers Ser.: No. 20). (Orig.). 1966. pap. 2.00 (ISBN 0-231-02942-X, MW20). Columbia U Pr.

--Romantic Quest and Modern Query: A History of the Modern Theater. LC 80-5756. 510p. 1980. lib. bdg. 18.50 (ISBN 0-8191-1217-8); pap. text ed. 10.00 (ISBN 0-8191-1218-6). U Pr of Amer.

--Sense of History in Greek & Shakespearean Drama. LC 59-15146. 1960. pap. 6.00x (ISBN 0-231-08576-1). Columbia U Pr.

Drivers License Guide Co. Drivers License Guide Nineteen Eighty-One. (Illus.). 96p. 1981. pap. 9.45. Drivers License.

--U. S. Identification Manual. rev. ed. (Illus.). 700p. 1981. text ed. 90.00. Drivers License.

Drizd, Terence A., jt. auth. see O'Brien, Richard J.

Drobert, Belinda. Political Economy of the Northern Ireland Crisis. 1979. 24.50 o.p. (ISBN 0-685-65705-1). Porter.

Drogin, Marc. Yours Truly, King Arthur. LC 79-66643. 1981. 8.95 (ISBN 0-8008-8765-4, Pentalic). Taplinger.

Drohan, N. T. & Day, J. H. Australian Economic Framework. 4th ed. (Illus.). 1975. 12.50x (ISBN 0-686-60736-8). Intl Pubns Serv.

Drolet, Robert P. & Dowling, John R. Developing & Administering an Industrial Training Program. LC 79-10713. (Illus.). 1979. pap. 11.95 (ISBN 0-8436-0777-7). CBI Pub.

--Operator's Training Program for Powered Industrial Trucks. 2nd ed. 96p. 1980. pap. 13.50 (ISBN 0-8436-0797-1); of 10 79.50 set. CBI Pub.

Drollinger, William C. & Drollinger, William C. Jr. Tax Shelters & Tax-Free Income for Everyone, Vol II. 4th ed. 1981. write for info. (ISBN 0-914244-06-X). Epic Pubns.

Drollinger, William C. & Drollinger, William C., Sr. You Are a Money Brain. 1981. write for info. (ISBN 0-914244-07-8). Epic Pubns.

Drollinger, William C. Jr., jt. auth. see Drollinger, William C.

Drone, Eaton S. A Treatise on the Law of Property in Intellectual Productions in Great Britain & the United States. LC 70-189788. liv, 774p. 1972. Repr. of 1879 ed. lib. bdg. 45.00x (ISBN 0-8377-2027-3). Rothman.

Drone, Jeanette M. Index to Opera, Operetta & Musical Comedy Synopses in Collections & Periodicals. LC 77-25822. 1978. 10.00 (ISBN 0-8108-1100-6). Scarecrow.

Dronke, P. The Medieval Lyric. 1978. 28.50 (ISBN 0-521-21944-2); pap. 8.95x (ISBN 0-521-29319-7). Cambridge U Pr.
Dronke, Peter. Medieval Latin & the Rise of the European Love Lyric, 2 Vols. 2nd ed. (Latin). 1969. Set. 59.00x (ISBN 0-19-814346-X). Oxford U Pr.
Dronke, Ursula, ed. Poetic Edda Vol. 1: Heroic Poems. 1969. 27.00x (ISBN 0-19-811497-4). Oxford U Pr.
Droogers, Andre. The Dangerous Journey: Symbolic Aspects of Boys' Initiation Among the Wagenia of Kisangani, Zaire. (Change & Continuity in Africa Ser.). 1979. pap. text ed. 34.75x (ISBN 90-279-3357-X). Mouton.
Drooyan, Irving & Wooten, William. Intermediate Mathematics. 1971. 17.95x (ISBN 0-534-00095-9). Wadsworth Pub.
Drooyan, Irving & Wooton, William. Beginning Algebra: An Individualized Approach. LC 78-625. 1978. 18.50 (ISBN 0-471-03877-6). Wiley.
--Elementary Algebra for College Students. 5th ed. LC 78-31666. 1980. text ed. 18.50 (ISBN 0-471-03607-2); solutions manual 7.95 (ISBN 0-471-05868-8); test (ISBN 0-471-05911-0). Wiley.
--Elementary Algebra with Geometry. LC 75-35736. 334p. 1976. text ed. 18.50 (ISBN 0-471-22245-3). Wiley.
Drooyan, Irving, jt. auth. see Beckenbach, Edwin F.
Drooyan, Irving, jt. auth. see Carico, Charles C.
Drooyan, Irving, jt. auth. see Wooton, William.
Drooyan, Irving, et al. Elementary Algebra: Structure & Skills. 4th ed. LC 76-15018. 390p. 1977. text ed. 18.50 (ISBN 0-471-22249-6); 5.95x (ISBN 0-471-01825-2). Wiley.
Dropkin, Victor H. Introduction to Plant Nematology. LC 80-13556. 336p. 1980. 36.00 (ISBN 0-471-05578-6, Pub. by Wiley Interscience). Wiley.
Dror, Yehezkel. Crazy States: A Counterconventional Strategic Problem. LC 80-81613. 1980. Repr. lib. bdg. 18.00 (ISBN 0-527-25140-2). Kraus Repr.
Drosdowski, Bohdan, ed. Twentieth Century Polish Theatre. Itzin, Cathy, tr. 1980. 16.95 (ISBN 0-7145-3738-1). Riverrun NY.
Droske, Susan C. Pediatric Diagnostic Procedures. 272p. 1981. pap. 11.95 (ISBN 0-471-04928-X, Pub. by Wiley Med). Wiley.
Drost, Walter H. David Snedden & Education for Social Efficiency. (Illus.). 1967. 22.50x (ISBN 0-299-04460-2). U of Wis Pr.
Drotar, David L., jt. auth. see Madison, Arnold.
Drotning, Phillip T. Black Heroes in Our Nation's History. 1970. pap. 0.95 o.s.i. (ISBN 0-671-47834-6). WSP.
Drotter, Stephen J. Steps to High-School Education: Students Plus Teachers Plus Parents Equal Success. 94p. 1980. 5.95 (ISBN 0-8059-2755-7). Dorrance.
Drouet, F. Revision of the Stigonematacaea: With a Summary of the Classification of Blue-Green Algae. (Nova Hedwigia Beiheft: No. 66). (Illus.). 300p. 1981. lib. bdg. 60.00x (ISBN 3-7682-5466-6). Lubrecht & Cramer.
Drouillard, Anne & Keefe, William F. How to Earn Twenty-Five Thousand Dollars a Year or More Typing at Home. rev. ed. 176p. 1980. 9.95 (ISBN 0-8119-0222-6). Fell.
Drover, Glenn, jt. ed. see Moscovitch, Allan.
Drowatzky, John N. Motor Learning: Principles & Practices. 2nd ed. 1981. text ed. write for info. (ISBN 0-8087-0495-8). Burgess.
Droz, Eugenie, et al, eds. Trois Chansonniers Francais Du XV Siecle. (Music Reprint Ser., 1978). 1978. lib. bdg. 27.50 (ISBN 0-306-77561-1). Da Capo.
Droz, Jacques. Europe Between Revolutions, Eighteen Fifteen to Eighteen Forty-Eight. LC 80-66909. (History of Europe Ser.; Cornell Paperbacks Ser.). 228p. 1980. pap. 4.95 (ISBN 0-8014-9206-8). Cornell U Pr.
Drozd, Ann M. Living Monsters. McCarthy, Patricia, ed. (Pal Paperbacks Kit A Ser.). (Illus., Orig.). (gr. 7-12). 1974. pap. text ed. 1.25 (ISBN 0-8374-3471-8). Xerox Ed Pubns.
Drozdova, T. V., jt. auth. see Manskaya, S. M.
Dr. Seuss. And to Think That I Saw It on Mulberry Street. LC 37-38873. (gr. k-3). 5.95 (ISBN 0-8149-0387-8). Vanguard.
--Five Hundred Hats of Bartholomew Cubbins. LC 38-30610. (Illus.). (gr. k-3). 5.95 (ISBN 0-8149-0388-6). Vanguard.
--I Can Lick Thirty Tigers Today! & Other Stories. LC 71-86940. (Dr. Seuss Paperback Classics Ser.). (Illus.). 64p. (gr. k-3). 1980. pap. 2.95 (ISBN 0-394-84543-9). Random.
--I Had Trouble in Getting to Solla Sollew. LC 65-23994. (Dr. Seuss Paperback Classics Ser.). (Illus.). 64p. (gr. k-3). 1980. pap. 2.95 (ISBN 0-394-84542-0). Random.
--If I Ran the Circus. LC 56-9469. (Dr. Seuss Paperback Classics Ser.). (Illus.). 64p. (gr. k-3). 1980. pap. 2.95 (ISBN 0-394-84546-3). Random.
--If I Ran the Zoo. LC 50-10185. (Illus.). 64p. (gr. k-3). 1980. pap. 2.95 (ISBN 0-394-84545-5). Random.
--On Beyond Zebra! LC 55-9321. (Dr. Seuss Paperback Classics Ser.). (Illus.). 64p. (gr. k-3). 1980. pap. 2.95 (ISBN 0-686-64846-3). Random.
--Scrambled Eggs Super! LC 53-5013. (Dr. Seuss Paperback Classics Ser.). (Illus.). 64p. (gr. k-3). 1980. pap. 2.95 (ISBN 0-394-84544-7). Random.
--Thidwick, the Big-Hearted Moose. LC 48-8129. (Dr. Seuss Paperback Classics Ser.). (Illus.). 48p. (gr. k-3). 1980. pap. 2.95 (ISBN 0-394-84540-4). Random.
Dru, Alexander, ed. & tr. see Kierkegaard, Soren.
Dru, Ricki. The First Blue Jeans. LC 78-14398. (Famous Firsts Ser.). (Illus.). 1978. lib. bdg. 7.35 (ISBN 0-686-51100-X). Silver.
Druck, Kitty, jt. ed. see Groth, Patricia C.
Drucker, D. B. Microbiological Applications of Gas Chromatography. LC 80-40447. 300p. Date not set. price not set (ISBN 0-521-22365-2). Cambridge U Pr.
Drucker, H. M., ed. Multi-Party Britain. LC 79-52940. (Praeger Special Studies). 256p. 1979. 25.95 (ISBN 0-03-053446-1). Praeger.
Drucker, Henry M. & Clarke, Michael G., eds. The Scottish Government Year Book, 1978. 208p. 1978. 22.50x (ISBN 0-87471-878-3). Rowman.
Drucker, Howard. The Organization & Management of the Resource Room: A Cookbook Approach. (Illus.). 184p. 1976. 18.75 (ISBN 0-398-03538-5). C C Thomas.
Drucker, Malka. Hanukkah: Eight Nights, Eight Lights. LC 80-15852. (A Jewish Holidays Book). (Illus.). 96p. (gr. 5 up). 1980. PLB 8.95 (ISBN 0-8234-0377-7). Holiday.
--Passover: A Season of Freedom. LC 80-8810. (A Jewish Holidays Book). (Illus.). 96p. (gr. 5 up). 1981. PLB 8.95 (ISBN 0-8234-0389-0). Holiday.
Drucker, Malka & Seaver, Tom. Tom Seaver: Portrait of a Pitcher. LC 77-17519. (Illus.). (gr. 5 up). 1978. 7.95 o.p. (ISBN 0-8234-0322-X). Holiday.
Drucker, Mark, ed. Urban Decision Making...a Guide to Information Sources. LC 80-19252. (Urban Studies Information Guide Ser. Part of the Gale Information Guide Library: Vol. 13). 200p. 1981. 30.00 (ISBN 0-8103-1481-9). Gale.
Drucker, Peter. People & Performance: The Best of Peter Drucker on Management. 1977. pap. text ed. 9.50 scp (ISBN 0-06-166400-6, HarpC). Har-Row.
Drucker, Peter F. Adventures of a Bystander. LC 78-2120. 344p. 1980. pap. 5.95 (ISBN 0-06-090774-6, CN 774, CN). Har-Row.
--The Concept of the Corporation. LC 72-74. (John Day Bk.). 352p. 1972. 11.95 (ISBN 0-381-98093-6, A16190, TYC-T). T Y Crowell.
--An Introductory View of Management. 1978. text ed. 19.50 scp (ISBN 0-06-166402-2, HarpC); scp casebk 9.50 (ISBN 0-06-166403-0); inst. manual avail. (ISBN 0-685-88069-9). Har-Row.
--Toward the Next Economics & Other Essays. LC 80-8370. 256p. 1981. 11.95 (ISBN 0-06-014828-4, HarpT). Har-Row.
Drucker, Philip. Cultures of the North Pacific Coast. (Culture Area Studies Ser.). (Illus., Orig.). 1965. pap. text ed. 10.95 scp (HarpC). Har-Row.
Drucker, Trudy & Backscheider, Paula R., eds. The Plays of George Lillo. LC 78-66658. (Eighteenth-Century English Drama Ser.: Vol. 27). 1980. lib. bdg. 50.00 (ISBN 0-8240-3601-8). Garland Pub.
Dructor, Robert M. Guide to Geneological Sources at the Pennsylvania State Archives. (Illus.). 129p. (Orig.). pap. 5.00 (ISBN 0-89271-011-X). Pa Hist & Mus.
Drudy, P. J. Irish Studies, Vol. 1. LC 80-40084. 192p. Date not set. 27.50 (ISBN 0-521-23336-4). Cambridge U Pr.
--Regional & Rural Development: Essays in Theory & Practice. (Illus.). 1976. text ed. 11.00x (ISBN 0-905193-02-4). Humanities.
Druffel, Ann & Rogo, D. Scott. The Tujunga Canyon Contacts: A Continuing "Chain Reaction" of UFO Encounters & Abductions. (Illus.). 264p. 1980. 9.95 (ISBN 0-13-932541-7). P-H.
Drug Abuse Council. The Facts About "Drug Abuse". LC 79-54668. (Illus.). 1980. 14.95 (ISBN 0-02-907720-6). Free Pr.
Druger, M. Individualized Biology, 13 units. Incl. Unit 1. The Microscope & Measurement. pap. 1.25 (ISBN 0-201-01371-1); Unit 2. A Visit to the Great Barrier Reef. pap. 1.50 (ISBN 0-201-01372-X); Unit 3. How to Make Sense Out of the Diversity of Life. pap. 1.25 (ISBN 0-201-01373-8); Unit 4. Evolution & the Past Diversity of Life. pap. 1.50 (ISBN 0-201-01374-6); Unit 5. Unity of Life & Adaptation. pap. 1.50 (ISBN 0-201-01375-4); Unit 6. Microscopy & the Electron Microscope. pap. 1.25 (ISBN 0-201-01377-0); Unit 7. The Architecture of Cells. pap. 1.50 (ISBN 0-201-01378-9); Unit 8. How Substances Get in & Out of Cells. pap. 1.50 (ISBN 0-201-01379-7); Unit 9. Chemicals of Life. pap. 1.95 (ISBN 0-201-01381-9); Unit 10. Proteins & Enzymes. pap. 1.25 (ISBN 0-201-01382-7); Unit 11. Origin of Life. pap. 1.25 (ISBN 0-201-01383-5); Unit 12. Cell Reproduction. pap. 1.75 (ISBN 0-201-01384-3); Unit 13. Animal Development. pap. 1.50 (ISBN 0-201-01444-0). 1971-74. A-W.
Druger, Marvin. Individualized Biology, Unit XV: Energy & Life. 1978. pap. text ed. 1.95 (ISBN 0-201-01388-6). A-W.
--Individualized Biology, Vol.14: Genetics - Script. (Life Sciences Ser.). 74p. 1976. pap. 1.95 (ISBN 0-201-01387-8). A-W.
Drukier, Boleslaw, jt. auth. see Polonsky, A.
Drum, David J. & Figler, Howard E. Outreach in Counseling: Applying the Growth & Prevention Model in Schools & Colleges. LC 77-8091. 1973. pap. 7.50 (ISBN 0-910328-11-0). Carroll Pr.
Drum, David J. & Knott, J. Eugene. Structured Groups for Facilitating Development: Acquiring Life Skills, Resolving Life Themes, & Making Life Transitions. LC 77-1947. (New Vistas in Counseling Ser.: Vol. 1). 1977. 16.95 (ISBN 0-87705-308-1). Human Sci Pr.
Drumm, Stella M., ed. see Magoffin, Susan S.
Drummond. The Western Hemisphere. (Our World Today Ser.). (gr. 5-8). 1978. text ed. 15.80 (ISBN 0-205-05856-6, 7758561); tchr's guide 9.60 (ISBN 0-205-05857-4, 77857X). Allyn.
Drummond, A. H., Jr. The Complete Beginner's Guide to Sailing. new ed. LC 70-103742. 192p. (YA) (gr. 7 up). 1975. 6.95 o.p. (ISBN 0-385-09356-X). Doubleday.
--Sailboarding: A Beginner's Guide to Boardboat Sailing. LC 73-83627. 160p. (gr. 5-9). 1974. 4.95 o.p. (ISBN 0-385-08670-9). Doubleday.
Drummond, Andrew H. American Opera Librettos. LC 72-8111. 1973. 10.00 (ISBN 0-8108-0553-7). Scarecrow.
Drummond, David A. & Perkins, G. Dictionary of Russian Obscenities. (Orig., Eng. & Rus.). 1979. pap. 2.95 o.p. (ISBN 0-933884-06-0). Berkeley Slavic.
--Dictionary of Russian Obscenities. rev. ed. 79p. (Rus. & Eng.). 1980. pap. text ed. 3.50 (ISBN 0-933884-17-6). Berkeley Slavic.
Drummond, G. I., et al, eds. see International Conference on Cyclic Amp, 2nd, July, 1974.
Drummond, George I., jt. auth. see Baer, Hans P.
Drummond, H. J., compiled by. A Short-Title Catalogue of Books Printed on the Continent of Europe, Fifteen Hundred to Sixteen Hundred, in Aberdeen University Library. 326p. 1979. text ed. 65.00x (ISBN 0-19-714106-4). Oxford U Pr.
Drummond, Harold D. & Hughes, James W. The Eastern Hemisphere. (Our World Today Ser.). (gr. 7-12). 1980. text ed. 16.20 (ISBN 0-205-06627-5, 7766270); 18.00 (ISBN 0-205-06628-3); wkbk 5.12 (ISBN 0-205-06629-1). Allyn.
Drummond, Helga, tr. see Spuler, Bertold.
Drummond, Henry. Greatest Thing in the World. (Inspirational Classic Ser). 1968. 4.95 (ISBN 0-8007-1078-9); pap. 1.25 (ISBN 0-8007-8018-3, Spire Bks). Revell.
Drummond, Hugh. Dr. Drummond's Spirited Guide to Health Care in a Dying Empire. LC 80-994. 288p. 1980. pap. 2.95 (ISBN 0-394-17674-X, BC-447, BC). Grove.
Drummond, Ian. Economics: Principles & Policies in an Open Economy. 1976. text ed. 17.50 (ISBN 0-256-01776-X); wkbk 4.50 (ISBN 0-256-01870-7). Irwin.
--The Floating Pound & the Sterling Area, 1931-1939. LC 80-14539. 352p. Date not set. 37.50 (ISBN 0-521-23165-5). Cambridge U Pr.
Drummond, Ian M. The Canadian Economy. rev ed. 1972. pap. text ed. 8.25 (ISBN 0-256-00243-6). Irwin.
Drummond, June. Funeral Urn. 1977. 6.95 o.s.i. (ISBN 0-8027-5363-9). Walker & Co.
Drummond, M., tr. see Haberlandt, G.
Drummond, M. F. Principles of Economic Appraisal in Health Care. (Illus.). 130p. 1980. pap. 12.95 (ISBN 0-19-261273-5). Oxford U Pr.
Drummond, Maldwin. Salt-water Palaces. 1980. 16.95 (ISBN 0-670-61636-2). Viking Pr.
Drummond, Mansford E., Jr. Evaluation & Measurement Techniques for Digital Computer Systems. (Illus.). 352p. 1973. ref. ed. 24.00x (ISBN 0-13-292102-2). P-H.
Drummond, Robert R. Early German Music in Philadelphia. LC 74-125068. (Music Ser). 1970. Repr. of 1910 ed. lib. bdg. 14.50 (ISBN 0-306-70005-0). Da Capo.
Drummond, V. H. Mrs. Easter's Parasol. (Illus.). (ps-5). 1977. pap. 6.95 (ISBN 0-571-11134-3, Pub. by Faber & Faber). Merrimack Bk Serv.
Drury, Allen. Advise & Consent. LC 59-9137. 1959. 12.95 (ISBN 0-385-05419-X). Doubleday.
--Advise & Consent. 1972. pap. 2.50 (ISBN 0-380-01007-0, 35543). Avon.
--Anna Hastings: The Story of a Washington Newspaperperson. LC 77-4151. 1977. 8.95 o.p. (ISBN 0-688-03221-4). Morrow.
--Come Nineveh, Come Tyre. LC 73-9347. 480p. 1973. 8.95 o.p. (ISBN 0-385-04392-9). Doubleday.
--The Hill of Summer. LC 80-1849. 504p. 1981. 14.95 (ISBN 0-385-00234-3). Doubleday.
--Mark Coffin, U. S. S. 1980. pap. 2.75 (ISBN 0-441-51965-2). Ace Bks.
--A Senate Journal, 1943-1945. LC 76-38824. (FDR & the Era of the New Deal Ser.). 1972. Repr. of 1963 ed. lib. bdg. 45.00 (ISBN 0-306-70448-X). Da Capo.
--The Throne of Saturn. 736p. 1977. pap. 1.95 (ISBN 0-380-00792-4, 22996). Avon.
Drury, Blanche J. & Schmid, Andrea B. Introduction to Women's Gymnastics. 1976. pap. 3.50 (ISBN 0-8015-4084-4, Hawthorn). Dutton.
Drury, Elizabeth. Lamps & Lights. 1979. 17.95x (ISBN 0-8464-0056-1). Beekman Pubs.
Drury, Elizabeth, jt. auth. see Bridgeman, Harriet.
Drury, G. H. Perspectives on Geomorphic Processes. LC 78-80970. (CCG Resource Papers Ser.: No. 3). (Illus.). 1969. pap. text ed. 3.50 o.p. (ISBN 0-89291-050-X). Assn Am Geographers.
Drury, Horace B., jt. auth. see Nourse, Edwin G.
Drury, John, tr. see Dussel, Enrique.
Drury, John, tr. see Flugaur, Florence.
Drury, John, tr. see Flugaur, Florence & Brokering, Mark.
Drury, John, tr. see Mesters, Carlos.
Drury, John, tr. see Thielcke, Gerhard.
Drury, John, tr. see Torres, Sergio & Eagleson, John.
Drury, Jolyon, jt. auth. see Falconer, Peter.
Drury, Kitty & Lynn, Bill. How to Raise & Train a Newfoundland. (Orig.). pap. 2.00 (ISBN 0-87666-341-2, DS1100). TFH Pubns.
Drury, Michael. Every Whit Whole. LC 78-18389. 1978. 5.95 (ISBN 0-396-07578-9). Dodd.
Drury, Nevill. Don Juan, Mescalito & Modern Magic: The Mythology of Inner Space. 1978. pap. 7.95 (ISBN 0-7100-8582-6). Routledge & Kegan.
Drury, R. A., ed. see Carleton, H. M.
Drury, R. A., jt. ed. see Carleton, H. M.
Drury, Richard S. My Secret War. LC 79-50359. (Illus.). 1979. 10.95 (ISBN 0-8168-6841-7). Aero.
Drury, Robert L. & Ray, Kenneth C. Principles of School Law: With Cases. 1965. 18.95 (ISBN 0-13-709949-5). P-H.
Drury, T. F., jt. ed. see Biderman, A. D.
Druxman, Michael B. Basil Rathbone: His Life & His Films. LC 74-3611. (Illus.). 256p. 1975. 12.00 o.p. (ISBN 0-498-01471-1). A S Barnes.
--Make It Again, Sam. LC 74-19810. (Illus.). 320p. 1975. 17.50 o.p. (ISBN 0-498-01470-3). A S Barnes.
Dryden, Cecil P. Give All to Oregon. (Illus.). 1968. 8.95 (ISBN 0-8038-2606-0). Hastings.
Dryden, Deborah. Fabric Painting & Dyeing for the Theatre. 1981. 27.50x (ISBN 0-89676-056-1). Drama Bk.
Dryden, H. L., et al see Von Mises, Richard & Von Karman, Theodore.
Dryden, John. All for Love. Vieth, David, ed. LC 72-128912. (Regents Restoration Drama Ser). 1972. 9.75x (ISBN 0-8032-0380-2); pap. 2.95x (ISBN 0-8032-5379-6, BB 276, Bison). U of Nebr Pr.
--Aureng-Zebe. Link, Frederick M., ed. LC 78-123119. (Regents Restoration Drama Series). 1971. 8.75x (ISBN 0-8032-0377-2); pap. 2.35x (ISBN 0-8032-5376-1, BB 275, Bison). U of Nebr Pr.
--A Choice of Dryden's Verse. Auden, W. H., ed. 1973. 8.95 (ISBN 0-571-10238-7, Pub. by Faber & Faber); pap. 3.95 (ISBN 0-571-10255-7). Merrimack Bk Serv.
--Essay of Dramatic Poesy, A Defence of Dramatic Poesy, & Preface to the Fables. Mahoney, John L., ed. LC 65-26522. 1965. pap. text ed. 4.95x (ISBN 0-672-60298-9). Irvington.
--Literary Criticism of John Dryden. Kirsch, Arthur C., ed. LC 66-23019. (Regents Critics Ser). 1967. 9.95x o.p. (ISBN 0-8032-0453-1). U of Nebr Pr.

--Poems & Fables of John Dryden. Kinsley, James, ed. (Oxford Paperbacks Ser). 1970. pap. 12.95x (ISBN 0-19-281073-1). Oxford U Pr.
--Poems & Fables of John Dryden. Kinsley, James, ed. (Oxford Standard Authors Ser.). 1962. 27.50 (ISBN 0-19-254124-2). Oxford U Pr.
--The Works of John Dryden. Incl. Vol. I, Poems, 1649-1680. Hooker, Edward N. & Swedenberg, H. T., eds. 1956. 34.00x (ISBN 0-686-60761-9); Vol. II, Poems, 1681-1684. Swedenberg, H. T., ed. 1973. 34.00x (ISBN 0-686-60762-7); Vol. III, Poems, 1684-1692. Miner, Earl & Dearing, Vinton A., eds. 1970. 34.00 (ISBN 0-520-01625-4); Vol. IV, Poems, 1693-1699. Chambers, A. B., et al, eds. 1974. 39.50x (ISBN 0-686-60763-5); Vol. VIII, Plays, The Wild Gallant, The Rival Ladies, The Indian Ladies. Smith, John H., et al, eds. 1962. 34.00x (ISBN 0-520-00359-4); Vol. IX, Plays; The Indian Emporour, Secret Love, Sir Martin Mar-All. Loftis, John & Dearing, Vinton A., eds. 1966. 34.00x (ISBN 0-520-00360-8); Vol. X, Plays; The Tempest, Tyrannick Love, An Evenings Love. Novak, Maximillan E. & Giuffey, George R., eds. 1970. 34.00x (ISBN 0-520-01589-4); Vol. XI, Plays; The Conquest of Granada, Part I & II, Marriage-a-la Mode, & The Assignation-or, Love in a Nunnery. Loftis, John, et al, eds. 1978. 40.00x (ISBN 0-520-02125-8); Vol. XV, Plays; Albion & Albanios, Don Sebastion, Anphitryon. Miner, Earl, ed. 1976. 42.50x (ISBN 0-520-02129-0); Vol. XVII, Prose, 1668-1691, an Essay of Dramatic Poesie & Shorter Works. Monk, Samuel A. & Maurer, A. E., eds. 1972. 35.00x (ISBN 0-520-01814-1); Vol. XVIII, The History of the League, 1684. Roper, Alan & Vinton, Dearing, eds. 1974. 36.50x (ISBN 0-686-60764-3); Vol. XIX, Prose, The Life of St. Francis Xavier. Roper, Alan & Vinton, Dearing A., eds. 1979. 42.00x (ISBN 0-520-02132-0). U of Cal Pr.

Dryer, Murray & Tandberg-Hanssen, Einar, eds. Solar & Interplanetary Dynamics. (International Astronomical Union Symposia: No. 91). 570p. 1980. lib. bdg. 66.00 (ISBN 90-277-1162-3, Pub. by D. Reidel); pap. 28.95 (ISBN 90-277-1163-1). Kluwer Boston.

Dryhurst, G. Periodate Oxidation of Diol & Other Functional Groups. LC 72-101490. 1970. 25.00 (ISBN 0-08-006877-4). Pergamon.

Dryjanski, Deborah A. Conquering Word Problems in Mathematics. (gr. 6-8). 1979. incl. manual & cassettes 149.95 (ISBN 0-917792-02-5). Math Hse.

Drysdale, Rosemary. Miniature Crocheting & Knitting for Dollhouses. (Illus.). 50p. 1981. pap. 2.00 (ISBN 0-486-23964-0). Dover.

Drzewiecki, T. M. & Franke, M. E., eds. Twentieth Anniversary of Fluidics Symposium. 232p. 1980. 30.00 (G00177). ASME.

D'Souza, Neela. Karna. 105p. (gr. 6-8). 1969. 1.00 (ISBN 0-88253-328-2). Ind-US Inc.

Du, Gard, Robert Martin see Martin Du Gard, Roger, pseud.

Du, Gerard & Lecherbonnier, Bernard. Le Surrealisme: Theories, themes, techniques. new ed. (Collection themes et textes). 288p. (Orig., Fr.). 1972. pap. 6.75 (ISBN 2-03-035004-4, 2691). Larousse.

Duane, James E. Media About Media: An Annotated Listing of Media Software. LC 80-21339. (The Instructional Media Library: Vol. 6). 232p. 1981. 18.95 (ISBN 0-87778-166-4). Educ Tech Pubns.

Duane, James E., ed. see Baker, Dan & Weisgerber, Bill.

Duane, James E., ed. see Beatty, LaMond F.

Duane, James E., ed. see Bullough, Sr. Robert V.

Duane, James E., ed. see Cluff, E. Dale.

Duane, James E., jt. ed. see Flanagan, Cathleen C.

Duane, James E., ed. see Kueter, Roger A. & Miller, Janeen.

Duane, James E., ed. see Schneider, Edward W. & Bennion, Junius.

Duane, James E., ed. see Soulier, J. Steven.

Duane, James E., ed. see Sparks, Jerry D.

Duane, James E., ed. see Wood, Rulon K.

Duane, Thomas, ed. see Loose Leaf Reference Service.

Duarte, Cristobal G. Renal Function Tests. (Laboratory Medicine Ser.). 1980. text ed. 27.50 (ISBN 0-316-19398-4). Little.

Du'Arte, Jack, jt. auth. see Joynes, St. Leger M.

Dua-Sharma, Shushil & Sharma, K. N. Human Physiology: Mechanism of Functions & Clinical Co-Relates. 560p. Date not set. text ed. 50.00x (ISBN 0-7069-1232-2, Pub. by Vikas India). Advent Bk.

Duba, Arlo D., jt. auth. see Carson, Mary F.

Dubach, Harold W., jt. auth. see Taber, Robert W.

Dubane, Janet & Friend, Diane. Kid Crafts. (Illus.). 64p. (Orig.). 1980. pap. 2.00 (ISBN 0-918178-23-1). Simplicity.
--Knit & Crochet. (Illus.). 64p. (Orig.). 1980. pap. 2.00 (ISBN 0-918178-21-5). Simplicity.

DuBane, Janet & Friend, Diane, eds. Needlework Plus. new ed. (Illus.). 96p. 1980. pap. 2.00 (ISBN 0-918178-18-5). Simplicity.

DuBane, Janet & Kuman, Alexandra, eds. Pillow Ideas. (Illus.). 64p. (Orig.). 1980. pap. 1.75 (ISBN 0-918178-19-3). Simplicity.

Dubard, Etoile. Teaching Aphasics & Other Language Deficient Children: Theory & Application of the Association Method. rev. ed. LC 73-93329. (Illus.). 1976. 15.00 (ISBN 0-87805-134-1); pap. 12.50 (ISBN 0-87805-053-1). U Pr of Miss.

DuBarry, Michele. Into Passion's Dawn. (The Loves of Angela Carlyle Ser.: No. 1). 1981. pap. 2.50 (ISBN 0-8439-0902-1, Leisure Bks). Nordon Pubns.

Du Bartas, Sieur, jt. auth. see De Saluste, Guillaume.

Dubasov, Yu V., jt. auth. see Vdovenko, V. M.

Dubay, Elaine C. & Grubb, Reba D. Infection: Prevention & Control. 2nd ed. LC 77-9512. (Illus.). 1978. 11.50 (ISBN 0-8016-1463-5). Mosby.

DuBay, Sandra. Mistress of the Sun King. (Orig.). 1980. pap. 2.25 (ISBN 0-505-51495-8). Tower Bks.

Dubbel, S. Earl. Daughter of the Plain Folk. 192p. 1975. pap. 2.25 (ISBN 0-8024-1762-0). Moody.

Dubbert, Joe L. A Man's Place: Masculinity in Transition. 1979. text ed. 11.95 (ISBN 0-13-552059-2, Spec); pap. text ed. 5.95 (ISBN 0-13-552042-8). P-H.

Dubbey, J. M. Development of Modern Mathematics. LC 72-88125. 153p. 1975. pap. 9.50x (ISBN 0-8448-0656-0). Crane-Russak Co.
--The Mathematical Work of Charles Babbage. LC 77-71409. (Illus.). 1978. 47.50 (ISBN 0-521-21649-4). Cambridge U Pr.

Dubbs & Whitney. Cultural Contexts: An Introduction to the Anthropological Perspective. 320p. 1980. pap. text ed. 10.45 (ISBN 0-205-06871-5, 6668712). Allyn.

Dubbs, Chris & Heberle, Dave. The Easy Art of Smoking Food. 1978. pap. 7.95 (ISBN 0-87691-264-1). Winchester Pr.

Dube, Anthony, et al. Structure & Meaning: An Introduction to Literature. LC 75-31038. (Illus.). 1152p. 1976. text ed. 15.95 (ISBN 0-395-21967-1); inst. manual 1.00 (ISBN 0-395-21968-X). HM.

Dube, H. C. An Introduction to Fungi. 400p. 1980. 24.00x (Pub. by Croom Helm England). State Mutual Bk.
--A Textbook of Fungi, Bacteria & Viruses. 1978. 12.50 (ISBN 0-7069-0587-3, Pub. by Vikas India). Advent Bk.

Dube, H. C., jt. auth. see Bilgrami, K. S.

Dube, Pierre H. & Davidson, Hugh M. A Concordance to Pascal's "Les Provinciales". LC 79-54323. (Garland Reference Library of the Humanities). 1000p. 1980. lib. bdg. 100.00 (ISBN 0-8240-9536-7). Garland Pub.

Dube, Pierre H., jt. ed. see Davidson, Hugh M.

Dube, Shiv K. & Pierog, Sophie H., eds. Immediate Care of the Sick & Injured Child. LC 78-763. 1978. pap. 24.50 (ISBN 0-8016-1459-7). Mosby.

Dube, Wolf-Dieter. Expressionism. (World of Art Ser.). (Illus.). 1977. pap. 9.95 (ISBN 0-19-519933-2). Oxford U Pr.

Dubeck, Paula J & Miller, Zane L., eds. Urban Professionals & the Future of the Metropolis. (National University Publications, Interdisciplinary Urban Ser.). 134p. 1980. 12.50 (ISBN 0-8046-9261-0). Kennikat.

Duberman, Lucile. Reconstituted Family: A Study of Remarried Couples & Their Children. LC 75-8840. 185p. 1975. 16.95 (ISBN 0-88229-168-8). Nelson-Hall.
--Social Inequality: Classes & Caste in America. LC 75-40327. 314p. 1976. pap. text ed. 9.50 scp (ISBN 0-397-47345-1, HarpC). Har-Row.

Duberman, Lucile & Hartjen, Clayton. Sociology: Focus on Society. 1979. text ed. 17.95x (ISBN 0-673-15287-1); study guide 4.95x (ISBN 0-673-15294-4). Scott F.

Dubey, Deepak. Praise to the Morning Koel. 8.00 (ISBN 0-89253-477-X); flexible cloth 4.00 (ISBN 0-89253-478-8). Ind-US Inc.
--Stories for Ramu. 10.00 (ISBN 0-89253-794-9); flexible cloth 5.00 (ISBN 0-89253-795-7). Ind-US Inc.

Dubey, Leon B., Jr. No Need to Count. LC 79-23884. 176p. 1980. pap. 4.95 (ISBN 0-498-02465-2). A S Barnes.

Dubie, Norman. Comes Winter, the Sea Hunting. (The Maguey Press Poetry Chapbook Ser.). (Orig.). Date not set. pap. 3.50 (ISBN 0-930778-08-1). Maguey Pr. Postponed.

Dubiel, Helmut, jt. auth. see Loewenthal, Leo.

Dubin, Beverly, jt. auth. see Pallidini, Jody R.

Dubin, Harry N. Collegefields: From Delinquency to Freedom. 176p. (Orig.). 1980. text ed. 16.95x (ISBN 0-8290-0273-1); pap. text ed. 8.95x (ISBN 0-8290-0274-X). Irvington.
--Coping Successfully: A How-To Manual for Operational Improvement. 138p. (Orig.). 1980. text ed. 16.95x (ISBN 0-8290-0262-6); pap. text ed. 9.95x (ISBN 0-8290-0270-7). Irvington.

Dubin, Robert. Human Relations in Administration. 4th ed. (Illus.). 640p. 1974. ref. ed. 19.95 (ISBN 0-13-446435-4). P-H.
--Theory Building. rev. ed. LC 77-90010. (Illus.). 1978. text ed. 15.95 (ISBN 0-02-907620-X). Free Pr.

Dubinin, N. P. & Gol'dfarb, D. M., eds. Molecular Mechanisms of Genetic Processes. Mercado, A., tr. from Rus. LC 74-30205. 373p. 1975. 58.95 (ISBN 0-470-22330-8). Halsted Pr.

Dubisch, Roy. Basic Concepts of Mathematics for Elementary Teachers. 2nd ed. LC 80-19446. (Mathematics Ser.). (Illus.). 483p. 1981. write for info. (ISBN 0-201-03170-1). A-W.
--Basic Concepts of Mathematics for Elementary Teachers. LC 76-1742. 1977. text ed. 16.95 o.p. (ISBN 0-201-01167-0); instr's manual 2.50 o.p. (ISBN 0-201-01168-9). A-W.

Dubisch, Roy & Hood, Vernon. Elementary Algebra. LC 76-3846. 1977. text ed. 18.95 (ISBN 0-8053-2338-4); instr's guide 3.95 (ISBN 0-8053-2339-2). Benjamin-Cummings.

Duble, Richard & Kell, J. Carroll. Southern Lawns & Groundcovers. LC 77-73533. (Illus.). 1977. pap. 3.95 (ISBN 0-88415-426-2). Pacesetter Pr.

Dublin, Arthur B., jt. auth. see Dublin, William B.

Dublin, Stanley W., jt. auth. see Lyons, John S.

Dublin, Thomas. Farm & Factory: The Mill Experience & Women's Lives in New England, Eighteen Thirty to Eighteen Sixty. LC 80-28034. 220p. 1981. 15.00x (ISBN 0-231-05118-2). Columbia U Pr.
--Women at Work: The Transformation of Work & Community in Lowell, Massachusetts, 1826-1860. 360p. 1981. pap. 7.50x (ISBN 0-231-04167-5). Columbia U Pr.

Dublin University. John Millington Synge, Eighteen Seventy-One to Nineteen Hundred & Nine: A Catalogue of an Exhibition Held at Trinity College Library, Dublin on the Occasion of the 50th Anniversary of His Death. 53p. 1980. Repr. of 1959 ed. lib. bdg. 8.50 (ISBN 0-8492-8117-2). R West.

Dublin, William B. Fundamentals of Vestibular Pathology. 380p. 1981. 32.50 (ISBN 0-87527-203-7). Green. Postponed.

Dublin, William B. & Dublin, Arthur B. Atlas of Neuroanatomy for Radiologists: Surface & Sectional-with CT Scanning Correlation. (Illus.). 320p. 1981. 37.50 (ISBN 0-87527-204-5). Green.

Dubner, et al, eds. The Neural Basis of Oral & Facial Function. LC 78-4048. (Illus.). 495p. 1978. 37.50 (ISBN 0-306-31094-5, Plenum Pr). Plenum Pub.

Dubofsky, Melvyn, et al. United States in the Twentieth Century. LC 77-13246. (Illus.). 1978. pap. 16.95 ref. ed. (ISBN 0-13-938712-9). P-H.

Dubois, C. Pluri Dictionnaire. new ed. (Illus.). 1974. 31.50x (ISBN 2-03-020124-3, 3677). Larousse.

Dubois, Daniel, jt. auth. see Fronval, George.

Dubois, Didier & Prade, Henri. Fuzzy Sets & Systems: Theory & Applications. LC 79-6952. (Mathematics in Science & Engineering Ser.). 1980. 65.60 (ISBN 0-12-222750-6). Acad Pr.

Du Bois, Edward. St. Godwin: A Tale of the Sixteenth, Seventeenth, & Eighteenth Centuries, by Count Reginald De St. Leon. Luria, Gina, ed. (The Feminist Controversy in England, 1788-1810 Ser.). 1974. lib. bdg. 50.00 (ISBN 0-8240-0853-7). Garland Pub.

Dubois, Edward N. Essential Methods in Business Statistics. 1964. text ed. 16.95 (ISBN 0-07-017875-5, C); solutions manual 4.95 (ISBN 0-07-017874-7). McGraw.

Dubois, Ellen, ed. Elizabeth Cady Stanton-Susan B. Anthony: Correspondence, Writings, Speeches. LC 80-6190. (Studies in the Life of Women Ser.). 1981. 17.95x (ISBN 0-8052-3759-3); pap. 6.95 (ISBN 0-8052-0672-8). Schocken.

DuBois, Ellen C. Feminism & Suffrage: The Emergence of an Independent Women's Movement in America Eighteen Forty-Eight to Eighteen Sixty-Nine. 1978. 17.50 (ISBN 0-8014-1043-6); pap. 4.95 1980 ed. (ISBN 0-8014-9182-7). Cornell U Pr.
--Feminism & Suffrage: The Emergence of an Independent Women's Movement in America, 1848-1869. LC 77-90902. 1978. 17.50x o.p. (ISBN 0-8014-1043-6). Cornell U Pr.

Dubois, J. L' Assommoir De Zola. (La Collection Themes & Textes Ser.). 224p. (Orig., Fr.). 1973. pap. 6.50 (ISBN 2-03-035018-4, 2647). Larousse.

Dubois, J. & Giacomo, M. Dictionnaire de linguistique. 516p. (Fr.). 1974. 27.50 (ISBN 2-03-020299-1, 1002). Larousse.

Dubois, J. B., ed. Immunopharmacologic Effects of Radiation Therapy. (European Organization for Research on Treatment of Cancer (EORTC) Monographs: Vol. 8). 475p. 1981. 45.00 (ISBN 0-89004-531-3). Raven.

Dubois, J. Harry. Plastics. 6th ed. 480p. 1981. text ed. 32.00 (ISBN 0-442-26263-9). Van Nos Reinhold.
--Plastics History, U. S. A. LC 79-156480. (Illus.). 1972. 23.95 (ISBN 0-8436-1203-7). CBI Pub.

Dubois, Jacques, et al. Rhetorique generale. (Langue et langage). (Fr). 1970. pap. 12.25 (ISBN 0-685-14067-9, 3638). Larousse.
--A General Rhetoric. Burrell, Paul B. & Slotkin, Edgar M., trs. from Fr. LC 80-24495. (Illus.). 288p. 1981. text ed. 18.95x (ISBN 0-8018-2326-9). Johns Hopkins.

Dubois, Jean. Grammaire de base. new ed. (Orig., Fr.). 1976. pap. 7.25 (ISBN 2-03-040166-8). Larousse.
--Grammaire structurale du francais, 3 vols. Incl. Vol. 1. Nom et pronom. 192p (3630); Vol. 2. Verbe. 192p (3631); Vol. 3. Phrase et transformations. 180p (3632). (Fr.). pap. 14.50 ea. Larousse.
--Vocabulaire politique et social en France de 1869 a 1872. (Fr). pap. 11.95x (ISBN 0-685-14095-4). Larousse.

Dubois, Jean & Lagane, Rene. La Nouvelle Grammaire du francais. 272p. (Orig., Fr.). 1973. pap. 10.95 (ISBN 2-03-040165-X, 3772). Larousse.

Dubois, Jean, ed. Lexis-Dictionnaire de la Largue francaise. 1979. 56.25 (ISBN 0-686-60644-2, 2427). Larousse.

Dubois, Jean, et al. Dictionnaire du francais contemporain. 940p. (Fr.). 1975. pap. 16.50 (ISBN 2-03-029325-3, 3935). Larousse.

DuBois, Nelson, et al. Educational Psychology & Instructional Decisions. 1979. pap. text ed. 16.95x (ISBN 0-256-02056-6). Dorsey.

Dubois, Paul. The Hospice Way of Death. LC 79-12326. 1979. text ed. 17.95 (ISBN 0-87705-415-0). Human Sci Pr.

Dubois, Paul M. Modern Administrative Practices in Human Services. 1981. write for info. (ISBN 0-398-04164-4). C C Thomas.

Dubois, Rochelle H. A Legend in His Time. (Illus., Orig.). (gr. 8-10). 1979. pap. 3.00 (ISBN 0-934536-01-5). Merging Media.
--Living Memories. 1979. 2.50 o.p. (ISBN 0-686-23747-1). Merging Media.

Dubois, Rochelle H., ed. Valhalla Seven: Women's Fiction. (Illus.). 55p. (Orig.). 1981. pap. 2.50 (ISBN 0-934536-05-8). Merging Media. Postponed.

Dubois, Sally. The Marriage Season. (Candlelight Romance Ser.). (Orig.). 1981. pap. 1.50 (ISBN 0-440-16058-8). Dell.

DuBois, Shirley G. His Day Is Marching on: Memoirs of W. E. B. DuBois. LC 71-14693. 1971. 10.00 (ISBN 0-89388-156-2); pap. 5.95 (ISBN 0-89388-157-0). Okpaku Communications.
--Zulu Heart: A Novel. LC 73-92801. 1973. 8.95 (ISBN 0-89388-132-5). Okpaku Communications.

Du Bois, W. E. Prayers for Dark People. Aptheker, Herbert, ed. LC 80-12234. 88p. 1980. lib. bdg. 10.00x (ISBN 0-87023-302-5); pap. 4.50 (ISBN 0-87023-303-3). U of Mass Pr.

Du Bois, William E. Autobiography of W. E. Burghardt Du Bois: A Soliloquy on Viewing My Life from the Last Decade of Its First Century. Aptheker, Herbert, ed. LC 68-14103. (Illus.). 1968. 15.00 (ISBN 0-7178-0235-3); pap. 3.95 (ISBN 0-7178-0234-5). Intl Pub Co.
--John Brown. rev. ed. LC 62-21668. (Orig.). 1962. pap. 2.25 (ISBN 0-7178-0112-8). Intl Pub Co.
--Souls of Black Folk. 1977. pap. 1.75 o.p. (ISBN 0-449-30823-5, Prem). Fawcett.
--Suppression of the African Slave Trade to the United States of America, Sixteen Thirty-Eight to Eighteen Seventy. reprint, orig. pub. 1970 ed. Foner, Philip S., ed. LC 70-110748. (Rediscovery Ser). 1970. pap. 2.50 o.p. (ISBN 0-486-22463-5). Dover.
--World & Africa: Inquiry into the Part Which Africa Has Played in World History. rev. ed. LC 65-16392. (Illus., Orig.). 1965. 8.95 (ISBN 0-7178-0222-1); pap. 4.25 (ISBN 0-7178-0221-3). Intl Pub Co.

Du Bois, William Pene see Pene Du Bois, William.

Du Bois, William Pene see Pene du Bois, William.

Dubois-Charlier, F., et al. Dictionnaire d'anglais. 868p. (Fr.). 1975. pap. text ed. 11.50 (ISBN 2-03-040531-0). Larousse.

DuBois-Reymond, E; see Brodie, Benjamin.

DuBois-Reymond, E. see Whytt, Robert.

Dubos, Rene. A God Within. LC 76-37224. 1972. text ed. 22.50x (ISBN 0-684-12768-7). Irvington.

--Louis Pasteur: Free Lance of Science. LC 75-21919. (Encore Edition). (Illus.). 1976. Repr. of 1950 ed. 4.95 o.p. (ISBN 0-684-15691-1, ScribT). Scribner.
--Man Adapting. enl. ed. LC 80-16492. (Silliman Lectures Ser.). (Illus.). 527p. 1980. pap. 7.95x (ISBN 0-300-02581-5). Yale U Pr.
Dubos, Rene J. Dreams of Reason: Science & Utopias. (George B. Pegram Lecture Ser.). 1961. 12.00x (ISBN 0-231-02493-2); pap. 3.00 (ISBN 0-231-08544-3). Columbia U Pr.
--Reason Awake: Science for Man. LC 70-111327. 1970. 16.00x (ISBN 0-231-03181-5); pap. 5.00 (ISBN 0-231-08629-6). Columbia U Pr.
Duboscq, Genevieve. My Longest Night. Woodward, Richard S., tr. from Fr. LC 80-23169. (Illus.). 288p. 1981. 12.95 (ISBN 0-394-51590-0). Seaver Bks.
Du Bose, J. W. The Life & Times of William Lowndes Yancey, 2 vols. Set. 18.00 (ISBN 0-8446-1161-1). Peter Smith.
Dubose, Joel C., ed. Notable Men of Alabama: Personal & Genealogical with Portraits, 2 vols. LC 75-45385. (Illus.). 1976. Repr. of 1904 ed. 25.00 ea.; Vol. 1. (ISBN 0-87152-225-X). Vol. 2 (ISBN 0-87152-226-8). Set. 50.00 (ISBN 0-87152-310-8). Reprint.
Du Boulay, G. H. Principles of X-Ray Diagnosis of the Skull. 2nd ed. (Illus.). 384p. 1979. text ed. 115.00x. Butterworths.
DuBoulay, G. H., ed. Considerations About the Use of Computers in Radiodiagnostic Departments. 1980. 45.00x (Pub. by Brit Inst Radiology England). State Mutual Bk.
Du Boulay, George. Cranial Arteries of Mammals. (Illus.). 1973. 45.00x (ISBN 0-433-07850-2). Intl Ideas.
Dubov, Irving, ed. Contemporary Agricultural Marketing. LC 67-29414. 1968. 13.50x (ISBN 0-87049-082-6). U of Tenn Pr.
Dubov, Paul, jt. auth. see Bagni, Gwen.
Dubovik, A. S. Photographic Recording of High-Speed Processes. 1968. 60.00 (ISBN 0-08-012017-2). Pergamon.
Dubovik, Alexander. The Photographic Recording of High-Speed Processes. 2nd ed. Aksenov, Arthur, tr. LC 80-17318. 624p. 1981. 35.00 (ISBN 0-471-04204-8, Pub. by Wiley-Interscience). Wiley.
Dubovsky, E. V., et al. Nuclear Medicine Technology Continuing Education Review. 1976. sprial bdg. 13.50 (ISBN 0-87488-331-8). Med Exam.
Dubovsky, Steven L. Clinical Psychiatry in Primary Care. 1978. pap. 12.95 (ISBN 0-683-02671-2); package set o.p. 49.50 (ISBN 0-686-67997-0). Williams & Wilkins.
--Psychotherapeutics in Primary Care. 1981. price not set (ISBN 0-8089-1337-9). Grune.
Dubowitz, Lilly M. & Dubowitz, Victor. Gestational Age of the Newborn: A Clinical Manual. LC 76-62906. 1977. text ed. 19.95 (ISBN 0-201-01171-9, M&N Div). A-W.
Dubowitz, Victor. Developing & Diseased Muscle: A Histochemical Study, Vol. 2. (Clinics in Developmental Medicine Research Monographs). 1968. 7.50 o.p. (ISBN 0-685-34619-6). Lippincott.
Dubowitz, Victor & Brooke, Michael H. Muscle Biopsy: A Modern Approach. LC 72-88846. (Major Problems in Neurology Ser.: No.2). (Illus.). 490p. 1973. 30.00 o.p. (ISBN 0-7216-3220-3). Saunders.
Dubowitz, Victor, jt. auth. see Dubowitz, Lilly M.
Dubowitz, Victor, ed. The Floppy Infant. 2nd ed. (Clinics in Developmental Medicine Ser.: No. 76). 109p. 1980. 25.00 (ISBN 0-685-24726-0). Lippincott.
Dubpernell, George. Electrodeposition of Chromium from Chromic Acid Solutions. LC 77-549. 1977. text ed. 16.00 (ISBN 0-08-021925-X). Pergamon.
DuBreiul, Linda. Housewife Hustlers. (Orig.). 1976. pap. 1.50 o.p. (ISBN 0-685-64009-4, LB334DK, Leisure Bks). Nordon Pubns.
DuBreuil, Linda. Crooked Letter. 1979. pap. 1.75 (ISBN 0-505-51385-4). Tower Bks.
--Deadly Party. 1979. pap. 1.50 (ISBN 0-505-51374-9). Tower Bks.
--Follow the Leader. 1979. pap. 1.95 (ISBN 0-505-51433-8). Tower Bks.
--The Girl Who Writes Dirty Books. 1975. pap. 1.50 o.p. (ISBN 0-685-51413-7, LB225KK, Leisure Bks). Nordon Pubns.
--Kept Men. (Orig.). 1976. pap. 1.50 o.p. (ISBN 0-685-64010-8, LB341DK, Leisure Bks). Nordon Pubns.
--Mirror Image. 1979. pap. 1.75 (ISBN 0-505-51393-5). Tower Bks.
--Poppy. 1976. pap. 1.50 o.p. (ISBN 0-685-69146-2, LB357ZK, Leisure Bks). Nordon Pubns.
--Sex Clinic. 1975. pap. 1.50 o.p. (ISBN 0-685-59193-X, LB307DK, Leisure Bks). Nordon Pubns.
--The Sunday Seducer. 1975. pap. 1.50 o.p. (ISBN 0-685-52173-7, LB246DK, Leisure Bks). Nordon Pubns.
--The Trial. 1975. pap. 1.50 o.p. (ISBN 0-685-52172-9, LB245DK, Leisure Bks). Nordon Pubns.
Du Breuil, Linda. Ultimate Sex. 1976. pap. 1.50 o.p. (ISBN 0-8439-0347-3, Leisure Bks). Nordon Pubns.
Dubreuil, Linda. Without a Man of Her Own. (Orig.). 1975. pap. 1.50 o.p. (ISBN 0-685-53906-7, LB282DK, Leisure Bks). Nordon Pubns.
DuBrin, Andrew. Human Relations: A Job-Oriented Approach. 2nd ed. 300p. 1981. text ed. 16.95 (ISBN 0-8359-3002-5); cancelled (ISBN 0-8359-3006-8); instr's. manual avail. (ISBN 0-8359-3003-3). Reston.
--Personnel & Human Resource Management. 1980. text ed. 18.95 (ISBN 0-442-25407-5); instr's. manual 2.00 (ISBN 0-442-25406-7). D Van Nostrand.
Du Brin, Andrew J. Fundamentals of Organizational Behavior: An Applied Perspective. LC 72-12998. 1974. text ed. 19.25 o.p. (ISBN 0-08-017110-9); pap. text ed. 11.00 o.p. (ISBN 0-08-017111-7); 0.55 o.p. (ISBN 0-08-017112-5). Pergamon.
--Fundamentals of Organizational Behavior: An Applied Perspective. 2nd ed. LC 77-12720. 1978. text ed. 44.00 (ISBN 0-08-022252-8); pap. text ed. 15.00 (ISBN 0-08-022251-X). Pergamon.
DuBrin, Andrew J. Human Relations: A Job Oriented Approach. (Illus.). 1978. text ed. 15.95 (ISBN 0-87909-371-4); instrs'. manual avail. Reston.
--The New Husbands & How to Become One. LC 76-15359. 1976. 12.95 (ISBN 0-88229-358-3). Nelson-Hall.
Du Brin, Andrew J. The Practice of Managerial Psychology. 1972. 23.00 (ISBN 0-08-016764-0); pap. 14.50 (ISBN 0-08-018126-0). Pergamon.
Dubrin, Andrew J. The Practice of Supervision: Achieving Results Through People. 1980. 16.95x (ISBN 0-256-02272-0). Business Pubns.
--Winning at Office Politics. Date not set. pap. 2.95 (ISBN 0-345-29532-3). Ballantine.
--Women in Transition. (Illus.). 196p. 1972. 13.75 o.p. (ISBN 0-398-02273-9). C C Thomas.
Dubrov, A. P. The Geomagnetic Field & Life: Geomagnetobiology. (Illus.). 318p. 1978. 25.00 (ISBN 0-306-31072-4, Plenum Pr). Plenum Pub.
Dubrovin, M. I. A Book of Russian Idioms Illustrated. LC 79-40433. (Illus.). 328p. 1981. 8.00 (ISBN 0-08-023594-8). Pergamon.
DuBrul, E. Lloyd. Sicher's Oral Anatomy. 7th ed. LC 80-15943. (Illus.). 578p. 1980. text ed. 27.95 (ISBN 0-8016-4605-7). Mosby.
Dubs, H. H., tr. see Pan Ku.
Dubus, Andre. Finding a Girl in America. 1981. pap. 6.95 (ISBN 0-87923-393-1). Godine.
Duby, G. Histoire de la France. 1978. pap. text ed. 33.95 (ISBN 2-03-079951-3, 3916). Larousse.
Duby, Georges. The Age of the Cathedrals: Art & Society, 980-1420. Levieux, Eleanor & Thompson, Barbara, trs. LC 80-22769. (Illus.). 1981. price not set (ISBN 0-226-16769-0). U of Chicago Pr.
--The Chivalrous Society. Postan, Cynthia, tr. from Fr. LC 74-81431. 1978. 29.50x (ISBN 0-520-02813-9); pap. 4.95 (ISBN 0-520-04271-9). U of Cal Pr.
Duc, William G. Le see Le Duc, William G.
Ducanis, Alex J. & Golin, Anne K. The Interdisciplinary Team: A Handbook for the Education of Exceptional Children. 200p. 1981. text ed. price not set. Aspen Systems.
Ducasse, C. J. Critical Examination of the Belief in a Life After Death. (American Lecture Philosophy Ser). 336p. 1974. pap. 12.75 (ISBN 0-398-03037-5). C C Thomas.
--A Critical Examination of the Belief in a Life After Death. (American Lectures of Philosophy). 336p. 1974. pap. text ed. 9.75 o.p. (ISBN 0-398-02772-2). C C Thomas.
--Paranormal Phenomena, Science, & Life After Death. LC 79-76282. (Parapsychological Monographs No. 8). 1969. pap. 2.25 (ISBN 0-912328-12-6). Parapsych Foun.
Ducasse, Isidore. Lautreamont's Maldoror. Lykiard, Alexis, tr. from Fr. (Apollo Eds.). (Illus.). 218p. 1973. pap. 2.45 o.s.i. (ISBN 0-8152-0343-8, A343, TYC-T). T Y Crowell.
Du Castel, Christine. Here Begynneth the Boke of the Fayt of Armes & of Chyualrye. Caxton, William, tr. LC 78-6332. (English Experience Ser.: No. 13). 1968. Repr. of 1489 ed. 49.00 (ISBN 90-221-0013-8). Walter J Johnson.
Ducceschi, Frank, ed. see Campbell, Patricia.
Duce, R. A., jt. auth. see Windom, H. L.
Ducey, Agnes C. A Family Lifeline. LC 80-820. (Ducey Bks.). (Illus.). 160p. 1981. 9.95x (ISBN 0-9605110-0-8); pap. 7.50x (ISBN 0-9605110-1-6). World Issues.
Duchacek, Ivo D. Power Maps: Comparative Politics of Constitutions. LC 72-95265. (Studies in International & Comparative Politics: No. 2). (Illus.). 252p. 1973. pap. text ed. 2.85 (ISBN 0-87436-115-X). ABC-Clio.
Du Chaillu, Paul. Land of the Long Night. LC 75-159938. (Tower Bks). (Illus.). (gr. 5 up). 1971. Repr. of 1899 ed. 18.00 (ISBN 0-8103-3905-6). Gale.
--Lost in the Jungle. LC 79-159939. 1971. Repr. of 1872 ed. 18.00 (ISBN 0-8103-3766-5). Gale.
Duchane, Emma, ed. User's Manual, Advanced Fortran IV Utilities for Data General Computers. (Illus.). viii, 223p. 1980. pap. 20.00 (ISBN 0-938876-03-1). Entropy Ltd.
DuCharme, Diane, et al. The Cigarette Papers: Snip the Strings to Your Habit. LC 79-54085. (Illus., Orig.). 1981. pap. 5.95 (ISBN 0-89638-039-4). CompCare.
Ducharme, Raymond A., et al. Bibliography for Teachers of Social Studies. LC 68-18106. 1968. pap. text ed. 3.50x (ISBN 0-8077-1255-8). Tchrs Coll.
Duchaufour, Philippe. Ecological Atlas of Soils of the World. De Kimpe, C. R., tr. from Fr. LC 77-94822. (Illus.). 178p. 1978. 35.75 (ISBN 0-89352-012-8). Masson Pub.
Duchein, Michael. Archive Buildings & Equipment. (ICA Handbook Ser.: Vol. 1). 201p. 1977. pap. text ed. 25.00 (ISBN 3-7940-3780-4, Pub. by K G Saur). Gale.
Duchein, Michel, compiled by. Basic International Bibliography of Archive Administration. (Archivum Ser.: Vol. 25). 1978. pap. 35.00 (ISBN 0-89664-005-1, Pub. by K G Saur). Gale.
Duchene, A. & Jammet, H., eds. Recommendations de la Comision Internationale de Protection Radiologique. (ICRP Publicaton Ser.: No. 26). 63p. 1980. pap. 15.75 (ISBN 0-08-025529-9). Pergamon.
Du Choul, Guillaume. Discours De la Religion Des Anciens Romains Illustre. LC 75-27851. (Renaissance & the Gods Ser.: Vol. 9). (Illus.). 1976. Repr. of 1556 ed. lib. bdg. 73.00 (ISBN 0-8240-2058-8). Garland Pub.
Duck. Teaching with Charisma. 364p. 1980. text ed. 12.95 (ISBN 0-205-07256-9, 2372568). Allyn.
Duck, Leonard. Amateur Orchestra. (Student's Music Library Ser). 1949. 6.95 (ISBN 0-234-77312-X). Dufour.
Duck, Ruth, jt. auth. see Bausch, Michael.
Duck, Ruth C. Bread for the Journey. 96p. 1981. pap. 3.95 (ISBN 0-8298-0423-4). Pilgrim NY.
Duck, Steve, jt. auth. see Baggaley, J. P.
Duck, Steven. The Study of Acquaintance. 1977. 24.95 (ISBN 0-566-00160-8, 01085-5, Pub. by Saxon Hse England). Lexington Bks.
Duckert, Audrey, jt. ed. see Roseler, Robert.
Duckett, Eleanor S. Death & Life in the Tenth Century. (Illus.). 1971. pap. 3.45 o.p. (ISBN 0-472-06172-0, 172, AA). U of Mich Pr.
--Gateway to the Middle Ages: France & Britain. 1961. pap. 1.75 o.p. (ISBN 0-472-06050-3, 50, AA). U of Mich Pr.
Duckett, George, jt. auth. see Burnet, Sir Thomas.
Duckett, Margaret. Mark Twain & Bret Harte. (Illus.). 1964. 17.50 o.p. (ISBN 0-8061-0634-4). U of Okla Pr.
Duckitt, M. & Wragg, H. Selected English Letters: Fifteenth to Nineteenth Centuries. 599p. 1981. Repr. of 1941 ed. lib. bdg. 20.00 (ISBN 0-89987-158-5). Darby Bks.
Duckles, Vincent. Music Reference & Research Materials: An Annotated Bibliography. 3rd ed. LC 73-10697. 1974. text ed. 14.95 (ISBN 0-02-907700-1). Free Pr.
Duckles, Vincent & Elmer, Minnie. Thematic Catalog of a Manuscript Collection of Eighteenth-Century Italian Instrumental Music in the University of California, Berkeley, Music Library. 1963. 25.00x (ISBN 0-520-00361-6). U of Cal Pr.
Duckworth, Alistair M. The Improvement of the Estate: A Study of Jane Austen's Novels. LC 75-161839. 264p. 1972. 16.50x o.p. (ISBN 0-8018-1269-0). Johns Hopkins.
Duckworth, D. The Experimental Certificate of Extended Education: Summer 1974. (General Ser.). 99p. 1975. pap. text ed. 12.50x (ISBN 0-85633-082-5, NFER). Humanities.
Duckworth, D., jt. auth. see Ormerod, M. B.
Duckworth, Derek. The Continuing Swing? Pupils' Reluctance to Study Science. (General Ser.). (Illus.). 1979. pap. text ed. 7.00x (ISBN 0-85633-174-0, NFER). Humanities.
Duckworth, John, et al. Muhammad & the Arab Empire. Yapp, Malcolm & Killingray, Margaret, eds. (World History Ser.). (Illus.). (gr. 10). 1980. lib. bdg. 5.95 (ISBN 0-89908-036-7); pap. text ed. 1.95 (ISBN 0-89908-011-1). Greenhaven.
Duckworth, Marion. The Greening of Mrs. Duckworth. 1980. pap. 3.95 (ISBN 0-8423-1187-4). Tyndale.
Duckwotth, Rita L. see Lucy, Reda, pseud.
DuCoffe, Jean & Cohen, Sherry S. Making It Big: A Guide to Beauty, Health & Style for the Large Woman. 1980. 14.95 (ISBN 0-671-25097-3). S&S.
Ducrot, Nicolas, ed. see Kertesz, Andre.
Duczman, Linda. The Baby-Sitter. LC 76-44229. (Moods & Emotions Ser.). (Illus.). (gr. k-3). 1977. PLB 8.95 (ISBN 0-8172-0065-7, Raintree Editions). Raintree Pubs.
Duda, Deborah. Dying at Home with Dignity. (Illus., Orig.). 1981. pap. 7.00 (ISBN 0-686-69339-6). John Muir.
Duda, Fred, jt. auth. see Creth, Sheila.
Dudbridge, Glen. Hsi-Yu Chi. LC 71-85718. (Studies in Chinese History, Literature & Institutions). (Illus.). 1970. 42.00 (ISBN 0-521-07632-3). Cambridge U Pr.
Dudding, Burton, jt. auth. see Cho, Cheng.
Duddington, C. L. Beginner's Guide to Botany. 1970. 6.95 (ISBN 0-7207-0365-4, Pub. by Michael Joseph). Merrimack Bk Serv.
--Beginner's Guide to the Fungi. 1972. 6.95 (ISBN 0-7207-0448-0, Pub. by Michael Joseph). Merrimack Bk Serv.
Duddington, D. L. Evolution in Plant Design. (Illus.). 1969. 7.95 o.p. (ISBN 0-571-09065-6, Pub. by Faber & Faber). Merrimack Bk Serv.
Duddy, Neil T. & Spiritual Counterfeits Project. The God-Men: An Inquiry into Witness Lee & the Local Church. rev. ed. (Orig.). Date not set. pap. 4.95 (ISBN 0-87784-833-5). Inter-Varsity.
Dudeck, C. V. Hegel's Phenomenology of Mind: Analysis & Commentary. LC 80-67258. 292p. 1981. lib. bdg. 19.75 (ISBN 0-8191-1406-5); pap. text ed. 10.25 (ISBN 0-8191-1407-3). U Pr of Amer.
Dudeney, Henry E. Canterbury Puzzles. 1919. pap. 3.50 (ISBN 0-486-20474-X). Dover.
--Three Hundred Best Word Puzzles. Gardner, Martin, ed. LC 68-12499. (Illus.). 1972. pap. 2.25 o.p. (ISBN 0-684-13068-8, SL370, ScribT). Scribner.
Duderstadt, James & Kikuchi, Chihiro. Nuclear Power: Technology on Trial. 1979. 16.00 (ISBN 0-472-09311-8); pap. 8.50 (ISBN 0-472-06312-X). U of Mich Pr.
Duderstadt, James J. & Hamilton, Louis J. Nuclear Reactor Analysis. LC 75-20389. 650p. 1976. text ed. 34.95 (ISBN 0-471-22363-8). Wiley.
Dudewicz, Edward J. Introduction to Statistics & Probability. LC 75-26827. 1976. text ed. 22.95 (ISBN 0-03-086688-X); solns. manual o.p. 20.00 (ISBN 0-03-089629-0). Am Sciences Pr.
--Solutions in Statistics & Probability. LC 80-68285. (The American Sciences Press Ser. in Mathematical & Management Sciences: Vol. 3). 1980. pap. text ed. 24.95 (ISBN 0-935950-00-1). Am Sciences Pr.
Dudewicz, Edward J. & Koo, Joo Ok. The Complete Categorized Guide to Statistical Selection & Ranking Procedures. LC 80-68288. (The American Sciences Press Ser. in Mathematical & Management Sciences: Vol. 6). 1981. text ed. write for info. (ISBN 0-935950-03-6). Am Sciences Pr.
Dudewicz, Edward J. & Ralley, Thomas G. The Handbook of Random Number Generation & Testing with TESTRAND Computer Code. LC 80-68286. (The American Sciences Press Ser. in Mathematical & Management Sciences: Vol. 4). 1981. text ed. write for info. (ISBN 0-935950-01-X). Am Sciences Pr.
Dudick, Thomas S. Profile for Profitability: Using Cost Control & Profitability Analysis. LC 72-4353. (Systems & Controls for Financial Management Ser.). 253p. 1972. 30.50 (ISBN 0-471-22362-X, Pub. by Wiley-Interscience). Wiley.
Dudick, Thomas S. & Cornell, Ross. Inventory Control for the Financial Executive. LC 79-10699. (Systems & Controls for Financial Management Ser.). 1979. 28.95 (ISBN 0-471-01503-2). Ronald Pr.
Dudley, B. J. Parties & Politics in Northern Nigeria. 1968. text ed. 11.50 (ISBN 0-7146-1658-3). Humanities.
--Parties & Politics in Northern Nigeria. 352p. 1968. 27.50x (ISBN 0-7146-1658-3, F Cass Co). Biblio Dist.
Dudley, Billy J. Murtala Muhammed. 1981. 27.50x (ISBN 0-7146-3130-2, F Cass Co). Biblio Dist.
Dudley, Cliff, ed. see Bakker, Jim.
Dudley, Cliff, ed. see Miles, Austin.
Dudley, Dean, jt. auth. see Jones, Ray G.
Dudley, Donald L. & Welke, Elton. How to Survive Being Alive. LC 76-50763. 1977. 6.95 o.p. (ISBN 0-385-12107-5). Doubleday.
Dudley, E., ed. S. R. Ranganathan: Papers Given at Memorial Meeting in January, 1973. 1974. pap. 5.50x (ISBN 0-85365-197-3, Pub. by Lib Assn England). Oryx Pr.
Dudley, Gordon H., jt. auth. see Sumich, James L.
Dudley, H. C. The Morality of Nuclear Planning?? LC 76-11464. 1976. pap. 7.00 (ISBN 0-917994-00-0). Kronos Pr.

Dudley, Jim. Promoting the Organization: A Guide to Low Budget Publicity. 1975. 16.95x (ISBN 0-7002-0259-5). Intl Ideas.

Dudley, Joseph B. Self-Assessment of Current Knowledge in Blood Banking. 1974. spiral bdg. 8.50 o.s.i. (ISBN 0-87488-289-3). Med Exam.

Dudley, L. Architectural Illustration. 1976. 29.95 (ISBN 0-13-044610-6). P-H.

Dudley, Robert J. Think Like a Lawyer: How to Get What You Want by Using Advocacy Skills. LC 79-26488. 234p. 1980. 15.95 (ISBN 0-88229-571-3); pap. 8.95 (ISBN 0-88229-749-X). Nelson-Hall.

Dudley, Ruth H. Our American Trees. LC 56-9800. (Illus.). (gr. 3-7). 1956. 7.95 (ISBN 0-690-60383-5, TYC-J). T Y Crowell.

Dudley, Underwood. Elementary Number Theory. 2nd ed. LC 78-5661. (Mathematical Sciences Ser.). (Illus.). 1978. text ed. 17.95x (ISBN 0-7167-0076-X); ans. book avail. W H Freeman.

Dudman, Helga, jt. auth. see Dayan, Ruth.

Dudrick, Stanley J. & Miller, Thomas A., eds. The Management of Difficult Surgical Problems. (Seminars in Surgery Ser.: No. 1). (Illus.). Date not set. text ed. 35.00x (ISBN 0-292-75049-8). U of Tex Pr.

Dudycha, George J. Psychology for Law Enforcement Officers. (Police Science Ser). (Illus.). 416p. 1976. 16.75 (ISBN 0-398-00482-X). C C Thomas.

Due, Jean M. Costs, Returns & Repayment Experience of Ujamaa Villages in Tanzania, Nineteen Seventy-Three to Ninteen Seventy-Six. LC 80-490. 167p. 1980. text ed. 17.25 (ISBN 0-8191-1019-1); pap. text ed. 8.75 (ISBN 0-8191-1020-5). U Pr of Amer.

Due, John F. & Friedlaender, Ann F. Government Finance: Economics of the Public Sector. 6th ed. 1977. text ed. 19.95x (ISBN 0-256-01399-3). Irwin.

Due, John F., jt. auth. see Clower, Robert W.

Dueker, Marilynn, jt. auth. see Spirer, Herbert F.

Duellman, William E., et al. The South American Herpetofauna: Its Origin, Evolution, & Dispersal. (U of KS Museum of Nat. Hist. Monograph: No. 7). (Illus.). 485p. Date not set. 30.00 (ISBN 0-89338-009-1); pap. 25.00 (ISBN 0-89338-008-3). U of KS Mus Nat Hist.

Duenk, Lester G., et al. Autobody Repair. 1977. 15.84 (ISBN 0-87002-164-8); student's guide 3.96 (ISBN 0-685-73828-0); student's guide 3.24 (ISBN 0-87002-243-1). Bennett IL.

Duerden, Dennis. The Invisible Present: African Art & Literature. LC 74-25153. (Icon Editions). (Illus.). 184p. 1975. 10.00x o.s.i. (ISBN 0-06-432000-6, HarpT). Har-Row.

Duerksen, Roland A., ed. see Shelley, Percy B.

Duerr, William A. Fundamentals of Forestry Economics. (The American Forestry Ser). 1960. text ed. 20.00 o.p. (ISBN 0-07-017978-6, C). McGraw.

Duesen, Nancy Van see Van Duesen, Nancy.

Duewer, Lawrence A., jt. ed. see Schneidau.

Duey, Phillip A. Bel Canto & Its Golden Age. (Music Reprint Ser.: 1980). 1980. Repr. of 1951 ed. lib. bdg. 22.50 (ISBN 0-306-76021-5). Da Capo.

Dufau, Micheline see Bishop, G. Reginald, Jr.

Dufault, Joan. Vintage: The Bold Survivors. (Illus.). 256p. 1978. 12.95 (ISBN 0-8298-0356-4). Pilgrim NY.

Dufek, George J., jt. auth. see Andrist, Ralph K.

Dufey, Gunter & Giddy, Ian H. International Money Market. LC 78-1298. (Foundations of Finance Ser.). (Illus.). 1978. ref. ed. o.p. 13.95 (ISBN 0-13-470914-4). P-H.

Dufey, Gunter, ed. see Butler, David H.

Dufey, Gunter, ed. see Dielman, Terry E.

Dufey, Gunter, ed. see Goehle, Donna G.

Dufey, Gunter, ed. see Kennedy, William F.

Dufey, Gunter, ed. see Morsicato, Helen G.

Dufey, Gunter, ed. see Olson, Margrethe H.

Dufey, Gunter, ed. see Smith, Francis G.

Dufey, Gunter, ed. see Swary, Itzhak.

Dufey, Gunter, ed. see Vinh Quang Tran.

Dufey, Gunter, ed. see Wakabayashi, Mitsuru.

Dufey, Gunter, ed. see Wilson, Brent D.

Duff, Alan. The Third Language: Recurrent Problems of Translation into English. LC 80-41116. (Language Teaching Methodology Ser.). 160p. 1981. 23.65 (ISBN 0-08-027248-7); pap. 11.95 (ISBN 0-08-025334-2). Pergamon.

Duff, Alan & Chesterton, D. W. Your Book of Cricket. (Your Book Ser.). (Illus.). 1970. 6.95 (ISBN 0-571-10237-9, Pub. by Faber & Faber). Merrimack Bk Serv.

Duff, Alan, tr. see Touraine, Alain.

Duff, Alan, tr. see Varady, Tibor.

Duff, Bill. Getting Married. LC 73-331250. (New Citizen Books). (Illus.). 80p. 1973. 7.50x (ISBN 0-85340-238-8). Intl Pubns Serv.

Duff, Charles. French for Beginners. 1955. pap. 3.95 (ISBN 0-06-463252-0, EH 252, EH). Har-Row.

--Italian for Beginners. 2nd rev ed. 1959. pap. 3.95 (ISBN 0-06-463214-8, EH 214, EH). Har-Row.

--Spanish for Beginners. (Orig.). 1958. pap. 3.95 (ISBN 0-06-463271-7, EH 271, EH). Har-Row.

Duff, Charles & Makaroff, Dmitri. Russian for Beginners. 1962. pap. 3.95 (ISBN 0-06-463287-3, EH 287, EH). Har-Row.

Duff, Charles & Stamford, Paul. German for Beginners. 2nd rev. ed. 1960. pap. 3.95 (ISBN 0-06-463217-2, EH 217, EH). Har-Row.

Duff, Charles L., jt. auth. see Hackert, Adelbert F.

Duff, Clarence W. Cards of Love. 1980. pap. 6.95 (ISBN 0-87552-248-3). Presby & Reformed.

Duff, David. Eugenie & Napoleon III. LC 78-57058. (Illus.). 1978. 12.95 o.p. (ISBN 0-688-03338-5). Morrow.

--Hessian Tapestry: The Hesse Family & British Royalty. (Illus.). 1979. 28.00 (ISBN 0-7153-7838-4). David & Charles.

Duff, Ernest A. & McCamant, John F. Violence & Repression in Latin America: A Quantitative & Historical Analysis. LC 75-16645. (Illus.). 1976. 19.95 (ISBN 0-02-907690-0). Free Pr.

Duff, G. F., jt. auth. see Del Grande, J. J.

Duff, Gail. Pick of the Crop: The Best of Vegetable Cooking. 1979. 19.95 (ISBN 0-241-10175-1, Pub. by Hamish Hamilton England). David & Charles.

Duff, George F. & Naylor, D. Differential Equations of Applied Mathematics. 1966. 27.95 o.p. (ISBN 0-471-22367-0). Wiley.

Duff, Gerald. William Cobbett & the Politics of Earth. (Salzburg Studies in English Literature, Romantic Reassessment: No. 24). 143p. 1972. pap. text ed. 25.00x (ISBN 0-391-01366-1). Humanities.

Duff, J. D., tr. see Rostovtzeff, Mikhail I.

Duff, James D., ed. see Juvenal.

Duff, James D., ed. see Lucretius.

Duff, Jim. Whiz, the Elf Who Made Christmas Special. (Story Book Ser.). (Illus.). (ps-5). 1980. 5.95 (ISBN 0-89305-030-X); pap. 0.89 coloring book (ISBN 0-89305-031-8). Anna Pub.

Duff, John R. & Kaufman, Milton. Alternating Current Fundamentals. (Electrical Trades Ser.). (gr. 9-10). 1980. 16.00 (ISBN 0-8273-1133-8); pap. 14.20 (ISBN 0-8273-1142-7); instr's guide 1.75 (ISBN 0-8273-1142-7). Delmar.

Duff, Maggie. Dancing Turtle. LC 80-24683. (Illus.). 32p. (gr. k-3). 1981. PLB 7.95 (ISBN 0-02-733010-9). Macmillan.

--Rum Pum Pum. LC 77-12389. (ps-3). 1978. 8.95 (ISBN 0-02-732950-X, 73295). Macmillan.

Duff, Mary K., jt. auth. see Gilmore, John S.

Duff, William. The History of Rhedi, the Hermit of Mount Ararat: An Oriental Tale, 1773. (The Flowering of the Novel, 1740-1775 Ser: Vol. 101). 1974. lib. bdg. 50.00 (ISBN 0-8240-1200-3). Garland Pub.

--Letters on the Intellectual & Moral Character of Women. (The Feminist Controversy in England, 1788-1810 Ser.). 1974. lib. bdg. 50.00 (ISBN 0-8240-0854-5). Garland Pub.

Duff, Wilson. Arts of the Raven: Masterworks by the Northwest Coast Indian. (Illus.). 112p. 1967. pap. 11.50 (ISBN 0-295-95583-X, Pub. by Vancouver Art Canada). U of Wash Pr.

Duffee, David, et al. Criminal Justice: Organization, Structure & Analysis. (Criminal Justice Ser.). 1978. ref. 17.95 (ISBN 0-13-193490-2). P-H.

Duffee, David E. Correctional Management: Change & Control in Correctional Organizations. (Criminal Justice Ser.). (Illus.). 1980. text ed. 17.95 (ISBN 0-13-178400-5). P-H.

Duffendack, Stanley D. Effective Management Through Work Planning. 1971. 28.95 (ISBN 0-932078-00-1). GE Tech Prom & Train.

Duffer, H. F., Jr., tr. see Maston, T. B.

Duffer, Hiram F., Jr., tr. see Bunyan, Juan & Leavell, L. P.

Duffett-Smith, Peter. Practical Astronomy with Your Calculator. LC 79-4632. (Illus.). 1980. 26.95 (ISBN 0-521-22761-5); pap. 7.50 (ISBN 0-521-29636-6). Cambridge U Pr.

Duffey, Dave. Hunting Dog Know-How. (Illus.). 1972. 9.95 (ISBN 0-87691-081-9). Winchester Pr.

--Hunting Hounds: How to Choose, Train & Handle America's Trail & Tree Hounds. (Illus.). 1972. 8.95 (ISBN 0-87691-062-2). Winchester Pr.

Duffey, Eric. The Forest World. LC 79-91274. (Illus.). 224p. 1980. 18.95 (ISBN 0-89479-060-9). A & W Pubs.

--Nature Reserves & Wildlife. 1974. pap. text ed. 9.95x o.p. (ISBN 0-435-61256-5). Heinemann Ed.

Duffey, George H. Theoretical Physics: Classical & Modern Views. LC 79-23794. 704p. 1980. Repr. of 1973 ed. lib. bdg. 27.50 (ISBN 0-89874-062-2). Krieger.

Duffie, J. A. & Beckman, W. A. Solar Energy Thermal Processes. LC 74-12390. 1974. 27.50 (ISBN 0-471-22371-9, Pub. by Wiley-Interscience). Wiley.

--Solar Engineering in Thermal Processes. LC 80-13297. 1980. 25.95 (ISBN 0-471-05066-0, Pub. by Wiley-Interscience). Wiley.

Duffield, Anne. Come Back, Miranda. 1974. pap. 1.25 o.p. (ISBN 0-425-02971-9, Medallion). Berkley Pub.

--Dusty Dawn. 1975. pap. 1.25 o.p. (ISBN 0-425-02714-7, Medallion). Berkley Pub.

--Forever Tomorrow. 1974. pap. 1.25 o.p. (ISBN 0-425-02672-8, Medallion). Berkley Pub.

--The Grand Duchess. 1973. pap. 1.25 o.p. (ISBN 0-425-02726-0, 22726, Medallion). Berkley Pub.

--Harbor Lights. 1973. pap. 1.25 o.p. (ISBN 0-425-02727-9, 22727, Medallion). Berkley Pub.

--Tomorrow Is Theirs. large type ed. 1974. pap. 1.25 o.p. (ISBN 0-425-02713-9, Medallion). Berkley Pub.

Duffield, Guy P. Handbook of Bible Lands. LC 77-80446. 1969. pap. 2.75 (ISBN 0-8307-0073-0, 5001854). Regal.

Duffield, Mary R. & Jones, Warren. Plants for Dry Climates. (Orig.). 1981. pap. 7.95 (ISBN 0-89586-042-2). H P Bks.

Duffield, Robert. Rogue Bull. 320p. 1980. 20.95x (ISBN 0-00-216423-X, Pub. by W Collins Australia); pap. 8.95x (ISBN 0-00-634515-8). Intl Schol Bk Serv.

Duffield, William. The Art of Flower Painting. (The Library of the Arts). (Illus.). 1977. 37.50 (ISBN 0-89266-070-8). Am Classical Coll Pr.

Duffus, C. M. & Slaughter, J. C. Seeds & Their Uses. LC 80-40283. 176p. 1980. 34.00 (ISBN 0-471-27799-1, Pub. by Wiley-Interscience); pap. write for info. (ISBN 0-471-27798-3). Wiley.

Duffus, John H. Environmental Toxicology. (An Environmental Science Ser.). 132p. 1981. 15.95 (ISBN 0-470-27051-9). Halsted Pr.

Duffus, Robert L. The Santa Fe Trail. LC 30-26894. (Zia Bks). (Illus.). 283p. 1972. pap. 7.95 (ISBN 0-8263-0235-1). U of NM Pr.

Duffy, Charles G. Young Ireland. LC 71-127257. (Europe 1815-1945 Ser.). 796p. 1973. Repr. of 1881 ed. lib. bdg. 59.50 (ISBN 0-306-71119-2). Da Capo.

Duffy, Christopher. Siege Warfare: The Fortress in the Early Modern World, 1494-1660. (Illus.). 1979. 30.00x (ISBN 0-7100-8871-X). Routledge & Kegan.

Duffy, Edward. Rousseau in England: The Context for Shelley's Critique of the Enlightenment. 1979. 14.00x (ISBN 0-520-03695-6). U of Cal Pr.

Duffy, Gerald G. & Sherman, George B. Systematic Reading Instruction. 2nd ed. 1977. pap. text ed. 13.50 scp (ISBN 0-06-041794-3, HarpC). Har-Row.

Duffy, J. I. Printing Inks: Developments Since 1975. LC 79-16231. (Chemical Technology Review Ser.: No. 139). (Illus.). 1980. 42.00 (ISBN 0-8155-0772-0). Noyes.

Duffy, J. I., ed. Electroless & Other Nonelectrolytic Plating Techniques: Recent Developments. LC 80-19494. (Chemical Tech. Rev. 171). (Illus.). 366p. 1981. 45.00 (ISBN 0-8155-0818-2). Noyes.

--Glass Technology: Developments Since 1978. LC 80-26045. (Chmical Tech. Rev. Ser.: 184). (Illus.). 323p. 1981. 48.00 (ISBN 0-8155-0838-7). Noyes.

--Refractory Materials: Developments Since 1977. LC 80-21945. (Chemical Technology Review: No. 178). (Illus.). 367p. 1981. 42.00 (ISBN 0-8155-0827-1). Noyes.

--Vaccine Preparation Techniques. LC 80-10174. 403p. 1980. 48.00 (ISBN 0-8155-0796-8). Noyes.

Duffy, James P., jt. auth. see Czajka, Peter A.

Duffy, John. The Songs & Motets of Alfonso Ferrabosco, the Younger (1575-1628) Buelow, George, ed. (Studies in Musicology). 435p. 1981. 39.95 (ISBN 0-8357-1110-2, Pub. by UMI Res Pr). Univ Microfilms.

Duffy, John, ed. Synodicon Vetus. Parker, John, tr. LC 79-52935. (Dumbarton Oaks Texts: Vol. 5). 209p. 1979. 35.00 (ISBN 0-88402-088-6, Ctr Byzantine). Dumbarton Oaks.

Duffy, John C. Child Psychiatry. 3rd ed. (Medical Examination Review Bks.: Vol. 23). 1977. spiral bdg. 16.50 (ISBN 0-87488-126-9). Med Exam.

Duffy, John C., ed. Child Psychiatry. 2nd ed. (Medical Outline Ser.). 1977. spiral bdg 13.50 (ISBN 0-87488-613-9). Med Exam.

Duffy, John C. & Gerber, Lane A., eds. Psychiatry Continuing Education Review. 2nd. ed. LC 79-91844. 1980. text ed. 13.75 (ISBN 0-87488-352-0). Med Exam.

Duffy, Joseph. Power: Prime Mover of Technology. rev. ed. (gr. 11-12). 1972. text ed. 17.16 (ISBN 0-87345-420-0). McKnight.

Duffy, Maureen. The Erotic World of Faery. 1980. pap. 3.50 (ISBN 0-686-69241-1, 48108, Discus). Avon.

--Inherit the Earth. (Illus.). 192p. 1980. 19.95 (ISBN 0-241-10205-7, Pub. by Hamish Hamilton England). David & Charles.

--Memorials of the Quick & the Dead. 1979. 14.95 (ISBN 0-241-10316-9, Pub. by Hamish Hamilton England). David & Charles.

Duffy, Neil & Assad, Mike. Information Management: An Executive Approach. (Illus.). 224p. 1981. 34.50 (ISBN 0-19-570190-9). Oxford U Pr.

Duffy, Patrick Gavin. Official Mixer's Manual. rev. ed. LC 74-25119. 1956. 6.95 (ISBN 0-385-02328-6). Doubleday.

Duffy, Thomas. Let's Write a Feature, 1969 Edition. (Lucas Text Ser). text ed. 4.00x perfect bdg. (ISBN 0-87543-056-2). Lucas.

Duffy, William J., jt. auth. see Neuberger, Egon.

Dufourcq, N., ed. Musique, 2 Vols. (Illus., Fr.). 62.50x ea. Vol. 1 (ISBN 2-03-014110-0). Vol. 2 (ISBN 2-03-014120-8). Larousse.

Dufournyde Villiers, Pierre. Cahiers du Quatrieme Ordre. (Fr.). 1977. lib. bdg. 13.75x o.p. (ISBN 0-8287-0290-X); pap. text ed. 3.75x o.p. (ISBN 0-685-75738-2). Clearwater Pub.

Dufrenoy, Marie-Louise. L' Orient Romanesque en Frances: 1704-1789, Tomes I & II. 1978. pap. text ed. 40.00x (ISBN 0-685-59420-3). Humanities.

DuFresne, Eugene, ed. see Heide, Fritz.

Dufresne, Francine. Cooking Fish & Wild Game. LC 75-25760. (Illus.). 144p. 1975. 4.95 (ISBN 0-912238-75-5). One Hund One Prods.

Dufty, J. H., jt. auth. see Sloss, V.

Dufty, N. F. Industrial Relations in the Public Sector: The Firemen. (Illus.). 1980. 24.25x (ISBN 0-7022-1408-6). U of Queensland Pr.

Dufty, William. Sugar Blues. 256p. 1976. pap. 2.95 (ISBN 0-446-93786-X). Warner Bks.

Dufty, William, jt. auth. see Holiday, Billie.

Duga, Jules J., ed. Technology & Productivity in Urban Government: The 1980's. (Illus.). 288p. 1981. 24.50 (ISBN 0-935470-06-9). Battelle.

Dugan, Bill. All About Houses. 72p. (gr. 4-8). 1975. 3.95 o.p. (ISBN 0-307-15789-X, Golden Pr); PLB 10.69 o.p. (ISBN 0-307-65789-2). Western Pub.

Dugan, J. Magee, ed. see Magee, David S.

Dugan, James, jt. auth. see Cousteau, Jacques-Yves.

Dugan, LeRoy. How to Live the Jesus Life. Orig. Title: Youth's Exciting Possibilities. 128p. (YA) 1973. pap. 1.50 (ISBN 0-87123-660-5, 200660). Bethany Fell.

--Old Testament Heroes, No. 1. 80p. (Orig.). (ps-4). 1981. pap. 1.49 oversized, saddle stitched (ISBN 0-87123-705-9, 220705). Bethany Fell.

--The Uncomplicated Christian. LC 78-66886. 1978. pap. 1.95 (ISBN 0-87123-572-2, 200572). Bethany Fell.

Dugan, Richard. How to Know You Are Born Again. 1978. pap. 1.95 (ISBN 0-89728-037-7, 679385). Omega Pubns OR.

Dugan, William. The Bug Book. (Illus.). 24p. (ps-4). 1965. PLB 5.38 (ISBN 0-307-68903-4, Golden Pr). Western Pub.

--The Sign Book. (Illus.). 24p. (gr. k-1). 1976. PLB 5.38 (ISBN 0-307-68974-3, Golden Pr). Western Pub.

Dugan, William, jt. auth. see Sukus, Jan.

Duganne, Augustine J. Parnassus in Pillory. LC 76-122648. 1971. Repr. of 1851 ed. 10.00 (ISBN 0-8046-1296-X). Kennikat.

Duganne, Mary Ann, jt. auth. see Olney, Ross R.

Dugard, John, ed. The South West Africa-Namibia Dispute: Documents & Scholarly Writings on the Controversy Between South Africa & the United Nations. LC 76-142052. (Perspectives on Southern Africa: No. 9). 1973. 33.75 o.p. (ISBN 0-520-01886-9); pap. 18.50x (ISBN 0-520-02614-4). U of Cal Pr.

Du Gard, Roger. Jean Barois. Weber, Eugen, ed. 1969. pap. 7.95 (ISBN 0-672-60306-3). Bobbs.

Du Gas, Beverly W. Introduction to Patient Care. 3rd ed. LC 76-58601. (Illus.). 1977. text ed. 16.95 (ISBN 0-7216-3226-2). Saunders.

Dugas, H. & Penney, C. Bioorganic Chemistry: A Chemical Approach to Enzyme Action. (Springer Advanced Texts in Chemistry Ser.). (Illus.). 416p. 1981. 29.80 (ISBN 0-387-90491-3). Springer-Verlag.

Dugdale, D. S. Elements of Elasticity. 1968. 23.00 (ISBN 0-08-012634-0); pap. 11.25 (ISBN 0-08-012633-2). Pergamon.

Dugdale, John S. Entropy & Low Temperature Physics. (Orig.). pap. text ed. 3.50x (ISBN 0-09-078251-8, Hutchinson U Lib). Humanities.

Dugdale, R. H. Surveying. 3rd ed. (Illus.). 224p. 1980. pap. text ed. 14.95x (ISBN 0-7114-5641-0). Intl Ideas.

Duggal, Kartar S. Death of a Song & Other Stories. (Indian Short Stories Ser.). 186p. 1974. 4.95 (ISBN 0-88253-458-0). Ind-US Inc.

Duggan, Alfred. The Story of the Crusades: 1097-1291. (Illus., Orig.). 1969. pap. 1.95 o.p. (ISBN 0-571-08990-9, Pub. by Faber & Faber). Merrimack Bk Serv.

Duggan, Anne. Thomas Becket: A Textual History of His Letters. 384p. 1980. 49.50 (ISBN 0-19-822486-9). Oxford U Pr.
Duggan, Anne S. The Complete Tap Dance Book. 1977. pap. text ed. 7.50x (ISBN 0-8191-0137-0). U Pr of Amer.
Duggan, Hayden A. A Second Chance. LC 77-15814. (Illus.). 1978. 18.95 (ISBN 0-669-02060-5). Lexington Bks.
Duggan, Joseph J. The Song of Roland: Formulaic Style & Poetic Craft. LC 75-186101. 1973. 16.00x (ISBN 0-520-02201-7). U of Cal Pr.
Duggan, Joseph J., ed. Oral Literature: Seven Essays. LC 74-33851. 107p. 1975. text ed. 10.00x o.p. (ISBN 0-06-491819-X). B&N.
Duggan, Lawrence G. Bishop & Chapter: The Governance of the Bishopric of Speyer to 1552. 1978. 22.00 (ISBN 0-8135-0857-6). Rutgers U Pr.
Duggan, Maurice. Falter Tom & the Water Boy. LC 59-12200. (Illus.). (gr. 3-6). 1959. 6.95 (ISBN 0-87599-027-4). S G Phillips.
Duggan, Michael A., et al, eds. The Computer Utility: Implications for Higher Education. LC 75-12104. 1969. 28.00x (ISBN 0-89197-708-2); pap. text ed. 14.95x (ISBN 0-89197-709-0). Irvington.
Duggan, William R. Our Neighbors Upstairs: The Canadians. LC 79-1308. 1979. 17.95 (ISBN 0-88229-530-6); pap. 9.95 (ISBN 0-88229-667-1). Nelson-Hall.
Duggar, John W. Ministerial Ethics. 1979. pap. 1.00 o.p. (ISBN 0-89114-002-6). Baptist Pub Hse.
Dugger, James G. The New Professional: An Introduction for the Human Service Worker. 2nd ed. LC 80-13324. 200p. 1980. text ed. 8.95 (ISBN 0-8185-0393-9). Brooks-Cole.
Dugger, W., Jr., jt. auth. see Gerrish, H.
Dugger, William & Patrick, Dale R. Electricity & Electronics Laboratory Manual. (Illus.). 1980. 4.96 (ISBN 0-87006-310-3). Goodheart.
Dugger, William E., Jr., jt. auth. see Gerrish, Howard H.
Dugger, William E., Jr., jt. auth. see Patrick, Dale.
Duguid, J. P., et al, eds. Medical Microbiology, Vol. 1. 13th ed. (Illus.). 1979. text ed. 35.00 (ISBN 0-443-01787-5); pap. text ed. 25.00 (ISBN 0-443-01788-3). Churchill.
Duguit, Leon. Law in the Modern State. LC 68-9647. 1970. Repr. 16.50 (ISBN 0-86527-115-1). Fertig.
Dugundji, James. Topology. 1966. text ed. 26.20 (ISBN 0-205-00271-4, 5602718). Allyn.
Duguy, R., ed. see International Conference on the Mediterranean Monk Seal, 1st, Rhodes, Greece, 1978.
Du Halde. Cotton & Silk Making in Manchu China. LC 79-93005. (Illus.). 112p. 1980. pap. 12.50 (ISBN 0-8478-0306-6). Rizzoli Intl.
Duhamel, P. A., jt. auth. see Hughes, Richard E.
Duhamel, P. Albert. After Strange Fruit: Changing Literary Tastes in Post-World-War II Boston. write for info. Boston Public Lib.
Duhem, Pierre M. The Evolution of Mechanics. Oravas, G. A., ed. (Genesis & Method Ser.: No. 1). Orig. Title: L'evolution De la Mecanique. 234p. 1980. Repr. 47.50x (ISBN 90-286-0688-2). Sijthoff & Noordhoff.
Duic, Walter, ed. Europa Administration: Directory of Administration & Justice for the European Community. 1161p. 1976. text ed. 110.00 (ISBN 3-7940-3017-6, Pub. by K G Saur). Gale.
Duic, Walter Z. Africa Administration, 1 vol. 1978. 95.00 set (ISBN 0-89664-017-5, Pub. by K G Saur). Gale.
Duigan, Peter, jt. auth. see Gann, L. H.
Duignan, Peter & Conover, Helen F. Guide to Research & Reference Works on Sub-Saharan Africa. LC 76-152424. (Bibliographical Ser.: No. 46). 1972. 19.50 (ISBN 0-8179-2461-2); pap. 8.95 (ISBN 0-8179-2462-0). Hoover Inst Pr.
Duignan, Peter & Gann, L. H. North Africa & the Middle East: The Challenge to Western Security. (Publication Ser.: No.239). 180p. 1981. pap. 9.95 (ISBN 0-8179-7392-3). Hoover Inst Pr.
Duignan, Peter, jt. auth. see Gann, L. H.
Duignan, Peter & Rabushka, Alvin, eds. The United States in the 1980's. LC 79-5475. (Publication Ser.: No. 228). 1980. 20.00 (ISBN 0-8179-7281-1). Hoover Inst Pr.
Duiker, William. The Communist Road to Power in Vietnam. (Westview Special Studies on South & Southeast Asia). 375p. 1981. lib. bdg. 32.50x (ISBN 0-89158-794-2). Westview.
Duiker, William J. Vietnam Since the Fall of Saigon. LC 80-21166. (Southeast Asia Ser., Ohio University Papers in International Studies). (Illus.). 78p. (Orig.). 1981. pap. 9.00 (ISBN 0-89680-106-3). Ohio U Ctr Intl.
Du Jardin, Rosamond. Double Date. (gr. 4-9). 1952. 9.89 (ISBN 0-397-30208-8). Lippincott.
--Double Feature. LC 53-8910. (gr. 4-9). 1953. 8.95 o.p. (ISBN 0-397-31599-6). Lippincott.
--Double Feature. (gr. 7-10). pap. 0.75 o.p. (ISBN 0-425-02666-3, Highland). Berkley Pub.
--One of the Crowd. LC 61-15257. (gr. 4-9). 1961. 9.89 (ISBN 0-397-30582-6). Lippincott.
--Practically Seventeen. (gr. 4-9). 1949. 9.89 (ISBN 0-397-30153-7). Lippincott.
--Senior Prom. (gr. 7-10). pap. 0.95 o.p. (ISBN 0-425-03534-4, Highland). Berkley Pub.
--Senior Prom. (gr. 4-9). 1957. 9.89 (ISBN 0-397-30388-2). Lippincott.
--Wedding in the Family. LC 58-10145. (gr. 4-9). 1958. 7.95 o.p. (ISBN 0-397-30441-2). Lippincott.
Du Jardin, Rosamond see Du Jardin, Rosamond.
Du Jonchay, Yvan. Handbook of World Transport. 221p. 1980. 20.00 (ISBN 0-87196-393-0). Facts on File.
Dukahz, Casimir. Vice Versa. LC 76-27586. 1976. 12.00 (ISBN 0-917372-01-8). Coltsfoot.
Dukas, Helen & Hoffman, Banesh. Albert Einstein, the Human Side: New Glimpses from His Archives. LC 78-70289. 168p. 1981. pap. 3.95 (ISBN 0-691-02368-9). Princeton U Pr.
Dukas, Peter. How to Plan & Operate a Restaurant. rev., 2nd ed. 1972. text ed. 15.45x (ISBN 0-8104-9461-2). Hayden.
--Planning Profits in the Food and Lodging Industry. 180p. 1976. 12.95 (ISBN 0-8436-2080-3). CBI Pub.
Duke, Bill, jt. auth. see Lyon, William.
Duke, Daniel. Managing Student Behavior Problems. LC 80-10443. 1980. pap. 11.95x (ISBN 0-8077-2583-8). Tchrs Coll.
Duke, Daniel L. The Retransformation of the School: The Emergence of Contemporary Alternative Schools in the United States. LC 77-25257. 1978. 16.95 (ISBN 0-88229-294-3); pap. 8.95 (ISBN 0-88229-606-X). Nelson-Hall.
Duke, David A. Christ's Coming--Satan's Kingdom. 220p. (Orig.). 1981. pap. 2.95 (ISBN 0-9605056-0-1). D A Duke.
Duke, Donald. Southern Pacific Steam Locomotives. LC 62-6982. (Illus.). 12.95 (ISBN 0-87095-012-6). Golden West.
Duke, Donald & Kistler, Stan. Santa Fe: Steel Rails Through California. LC 63-23869. (Illus.). 1963. 18.95 (ISBN 0-87095-009-6). Golden West.
Duke, Dulcie. Lincoln: The Growth of a Medieval City. LC 73-80476. (Introduction to the History of Mankind Ser). (Illus.). 48p. (gr. 9-12). 1974. pap. text ed. 3.95 (ISBN 0-521-08712-0). Cambridge U Pr.
Duke, Gaylon. Potboilers. 64p. 1980. pap. text ed. 15.00 (ISBN 0-87879-275-9). Acad Therapy.
Duke, James, tr. see Schleiermacher, Friedrich.
Duke, James A. Handbook of Legumes of World Economic Importance. (Illus.). 350p. 1981. 45.00 (ISBN 0-306-40406-0, Plenum Pr). Plenum Pub.
Duke, Judith S. Religious Publishing & Communications. (Communications Library). 235p. 1980. 24.95x (ISBN 0-914236-61-X). Knowledge Indus.
Duke, Kenneth L., jt. auth. see Mossman, Harland W.
Duke, Maurice. James Branch Cabell: A Reference Guide. (Reference Bks.). 1979. lib. bdg. 14.00 (ISBN 0-8161-7838-0). G K Hall.
Duke, Michael S. Lu You. (World Author Ser.: No. 427). 1977. lib. bdg. 12.50 (ISBN 0-8057-6267-1). Twayne.
Duke, Richard D. & Greenblat, Cathy S. Game-Generating-Games: A Trilogy of Games for Community & Classroom. LC 79-15721. (Illus.). 1979. pap. 9.95x (ISBN 0-8039-1282-X). Sage.
Duke, Robert W. The Sermon As God's Word: Theologies for Preaching. LC 80-18094. (Abingdon Preacher's Library). 128p. (Orig.). 1980. pap. 4.95 (ISBN 0-687-37520-7). Abingdon.
Duke-Elder, Stewart. Clinical Surgery: Eye. (Illus.). 1964. 18.75 o.p. (ISBN 0-397-58001-0). Lippincott.
Duke-Elder, Stewart & Ellis, Maxwell. Eyes, Ears, Nose & Throat: Operative Surgery Ser. Vol. 10. (Illus.). 350p. 1970. 26.00 o.p. (ISBN 0-397-58032-0). Lippincott.
Duke-Elder, Stewart, ed. System of Ophthalmology Series. Incl. Vol. 1. The Eye in Evolution. (Illus.). 843p. 1958. 61.50 (ISBN 0-8016-8282-7); Vol. 2. The Anatomy of the Visual System. (Illus.). 901p. 1961. 63.50 (ISBN 0-8016-8283-5); Vol. 3, Pt. 1. Normal & Abnormal Development: Embryology. (Illus.). 330p. 1963. 49.00 (ISBN 0-8016-8285-1); Vol. 3, Pt. 2. Normal & Abnormal Development: Congenital Deformities. (Illus.). 1190p. 1964. 69.00 (ISBN 0-8016-8286-X); Vol. 4. The Physiology of the Eye & of Vision. (Illus.). xx, 734p. 1968. 75.50 o.p. (ISBN 0-8016-8296-7); Vol. 5. Ophthalmic Optics & Refraction. (Illus.). xix, 879p. 1970. 65.50 o.p. (ISBN 0-8016-8298-3); Vol. 7. The Foundations of Ophthalmology: Heredity, Pathology, Diagnosis & Therapeutics. (Illus.). 829p. 1962. 65.50 (ISBN 0-8016-8284-3); Vol. 8. Diseases of the Outer Eye: Conjunctiva, Cornea & Sclera, 2 vols. (Illus.). 1339p. 1965. 100.00 (ISBN 0-8016-8287-8); Vol. 9. Diseases of Uveal Tract. (Illus.). xvi, 978p. 1966. 80.00 (ISBN 0-8016-**8290-8); Vol. 10. Diseases of the Retina. (Illus.). xv, 878p. 1967. 80.00 (ISBN 0-8016-8295-9); Vol. 11. Diseases of the Lens & Vitreous: Glaucoma & Hypotony. (Illus.). xx, 779p. 1969. 80.00 (ISBN 0-8016-8297-5); Vol. 12. Neuro-Ophthalmology. (Illus.). xxi, 994p. 1971. 83.50 (ISBN 0-8016-8299-1); Vol. 14. Injuries, 2 vols. 1357p. 1972. Set. 117.00 (ISBN 0-8016-8300-9). Mosby.**
Dukelow, W. Richard. Graduate Student Survival. (Illus.). 88p. 1980. 6.75 (ISBN 0-398-04068-0). C C Thomas.
Dukeminier, Jesse, Jr. Perpetuities Law in Action: Kentucky Case Law & the 1960 Reform Act. LC 62-13459. (Illus.). 180p. 1962. 8.50x (ISBN 0-8131-1070-X). U Pr of Ky.
Duke Of Beaufort. Fox Hunting. LC 79-56043. (Illus.). 236p. 1980. 29.95x (ISBN 0-7153-7896-1). David & Charles.
Duker, Sam. Individualized Instruction in Mathematics. LC 72-5739. 1972. 13.50 (ISBN 0-8108-0533-2). Scarecrow.
--Individualized Reading. 288p. 1971. pap. 22.50 photocopy ed. spiral (ISBN 0-398-02274-7). C C Thomas.
--Time-Compressed Speech, 3 vols. Incl. Vols 1 & 2. An Anthology & Bibliography. 50.00 (ISBN 0-8108-0643-6); Vol. 3. Annotated Bibliography. 10.00 (ISBN 0-8108-0644-4). LC 73-8756. 1974. Set. 50.00 (ISBN 0-685-34676-5). Scarecrow.
Duker, William F. A Constitutional History of Habeas Corpus. LC 79-6834. (Contributions in Legal Studies: No. 13). 349p. 1980. lib. bdg. 29.95 (ISBN 0-313-22264-9, DHC/). Greenwood.
Dukes, Ona B. & Johnston, Beverly. Lord, What Are You Doing Next Tuesday? 1978. pap. 2.95 (ISBN 0-8272-2114-2). Bethany Pr.
Dukes, P. Catherine the Great & the Russian Nobility. 1968. 38.50 (ISBN 0-521-04858-3). Cambridge U Pr.
Dukes, Paul. Russia Under Catherine the Great, 2 vols. 1978. 24.00 set (ISBN 0-89250-104-9); Vol. 1. 12.00 ea. (ISBN 0-89250-106-5). Vol. 2 (ISBN 0-89250-105-7). pap. 0.00 set o. p. (ISBN 0-89250-107-3). Orient Res Partners.
Dukes, Richard L. & Seidner, Constance J., eds. Learning with Simulations & Games. LC 78-51496. (Sage Contemporary Social Science Anthologies: No. 2). 1978. pap. 5.50x (ISBN 0-8039-1036-3). Sage.
Dukhin, S. S. & Shilov, V. N. Dielectric Phenomena & the Double Layer in Disperse Systems & Polyelectrolytes. Greenberg, P., ed. Lederman, D., tr. from Rus. LC 74-13579. 200p. 1974. 34.95 (ISBN 0-470-22415-0). Halsted Pr.
Dukor, P., et al, eds. Cell Mediated Reactions: Vol. 3, PAR. Pseudo-Allergic Reactions. Involvement of Drugs & Chemicals. (Illus.). 250p. 1981. 72.00 (ISBN 3-8055-0960-X). S Karger.
--Cytotoxic & Complement Mediated Reactions. (Par Pseudo-Allergic Reactions. Involvement of Drugs & Chemicals: Vol. 2). (Illus.). viii, 144p. 1980. 39.00 (ISBN 3-8055-0666-X). S Karger.
--Genetic Aspects Anaphylactoid Reactions. (Par Pseudo-Allergic Reactions. Involvement of Drugs & Chemicals Ser.: Vol. 1). (Illus.). 250p. 1980. 78.00 (ISBN 3-8055-0537-X). S Karger.
Dukore, Bernard, jt. ed. see Cohn, Ruby.
Dukore, Bernard, ed. see Shaw, George B.
Dukore, Bernard F. Bernard Shaw, Director. LC 79-11727. (Illus.). 199p. 1971. 9.50 o.p. (ISBN 0-295-95083-8). U of Wash Pr.
--Seventeen Plays: Sophocles to Baraka. 1976. scp 10.95 (ISBN 0-690-00846-5, HarpC). Har-Row.
Dukore, Bernard F. & Gerould, Daniel C. Avant-Garde Drama: A Casebook. 1976. scp 7.50 (ISBN 0-690-00848-1, HarpC). Har-Row.
Dukore, Bernard F., ed. Drama & Revolution. LC 71-130652. 1971. pap. text ed. 10.95x (ISBN 0-03-083569-0). Irvington.
Dukore, Bernard F., ed. see Shaw, Bernard.
Dukore, Bernard F., ed. see Shaw, G. B.
DuKore, Lawrence, jt. auth. see Vose, Kenneth.
Dula, Lucile N. The Pelican Guide to Hillsborough: Historic Orange County, North Carolina. LC 78-26081. (The Pelican Guide Ser). (Illus.). 1979. pap. 4.95 (ISBN 0-88289-208-8). Pelican.
Dulac, Colette, jt. auth. see Madrigal, Margarita.
Dulac, Collette, jt. auth. see Madrigal, Margarita.
Dulack, Tom, jt. auth. see Patrick, Ted.
Dulbecco, Renato & Ginsberg, Harold. Virology. (Illus.). 408p. 1980. 20.00 (ISBN 0-06-140725-9, Harper Medical). Har-Row.
Duleba, Wladyslaw & Sokolowska, Zofia. Ignacy Paderewski. Litwinski, Wiktor, tr. from Polish. (Library of Polish Studies: Vol. VII). (Illus.). text ed. 8.95 (ISBN 0-917004-14-0). Kosciuszko.
Dulfano, Mauricio J., ed. Sputum: Fundamentals & Clinical Pathology. (Illus.). 648p. 1973. 48.50 (ISBN 0-398-02737-4). C C Thomas.
Du Liban, Librarie. Spoken Arabic of the Arabian Gulf. 1976. pap. 2.95x. Intl Bk Ctr.
Dulin, Mark. Fish Diseases. 1979. 2.95 (ISBN 0-87666-524-5, KW-066). TFH Pubns.
Dulin, Robert O., Jr. & Garzke, William H., Jr. Battleships: Allied Battleships of World War Two. LC 79-90551. (Battleships Ser.: Vol. 2). (Illus.). 352p. 1980. 38.95 (ISBN 0-87021-100-5). Naval Inst Pr.
Dull, Elaine & Sekowsky, Jo Anne. Ensenanos a Orar. Fast, Todd H., tr. (Estudio Biblico De Aglow: No. E-2(S)). 64p. (Span.). 1980. pap. 1.95 (ISBN 0-930756-55-X, 4220-E2). Women's Aglow.
Dull, Jack, ed. see Hsu, Cho-yun.
Dull, Lloyd W. Educational Supervision: A Handbook. (Illus.). 504p. 1981. text ed. 18.95 (ISBN 0-675-08060-6). Merrill.
Dulles, Avery. Models of the Church. LC 77-11246. 1978. pap. 3.50 (ISBN 0-385-13368-5, Im). Doubleday.
--Revelation Theology. 1969. 6.95 (ISBN 0-8164-1112-3). Crossroad NY.
Dulles, Foster R. America in the Pacific. LC 73-86595. (American Scene Ser). 1969. Repr. of 1932 ed. 29.50 (ISBN 0-306-71431-0). Da Capo.
--American Policy Toward Communist China, 1949-1969. LC 70-184974. 1972. pap. 8.95x (ISBN 0-88295-728-7). AHM Pub.
--History of Recreation: America Learns to Play. 2nd ed. (Illus., Orig.). 1965. pap. text ed. 15.95 (ISBN 0-13-391953-6). P-H.
--Labor in America: A History. LC 66-19224. 1968. pap. 8.95x (ISBN 0-88295-729-5). AHM Pub.
--Prelude to World Power: American Diplomatic History, 1860-1900. 1971. pap. 2.95 o.s.i. (ISBN 0-02-031780-8, Collier). Macmillan.
Dulles, John W. President Castello Branco: Brazilian Reformer. LC 79-5281. (Illus.). 536p. 1980. 27.50x (ISBN 0-89096-092-5). Tex A&M Univ Pr.
Dulsey, Bernard M., tr. see Icaza, Jorge.
Dumas, Alexander. Three Musketeers. (Illus.). (gr. 7 up). 1962. 4.95 o.s.i. (ISBN 0-02-732840-6). Macmillan.
Dumas, Alexandre. Count of Monte Cristo. 1976. lib. bdg. 15.95x (ISBN 0-89968-147-6). Lightyear.
--Man in the Iron Mask. (Classics Ser). (gr. 9 up). 1967. pap. 1.95 (ISBN 0-8049-0150-3, CL-150). Airmont.
--Man in the Iron Mask. 1976. lib. bdg. 11.95x (ISBN 0-89968-146-8). Lightyear.
--The Three Musketeers. abr. ed. 168p. (RL 7). 1974. pap. 1.50 o.p. (ISBN 0-451-08107-2, W8107, Sig). NAL.
--Three Musketeers. 1974. pap. 1.75 o.s.i. (ISBN 0-515-03492-4, V3492). Jove Pubns.
--The Three Musketeers. 1976. lib. bdg. 15.95x (ISBN 0-89968-148-4). Lightyear.
Dumas, Alexandre, fils see Stanton, Stephen S.
Dumas, Enoch & Schminke, C. W. Math Activities for Child Involvement. 3rd ed. 1977. pap. 17.95 (ISBN 0-685-71779-8); pap. text ed. 10.95 (ISBN 0-205-05577-X). Allyn.
Dumas, F. M. Gunfighter's Choice. 192p. (YA) 1976. 4.95 o.p. (ISBN 0-685-61053-5, Avalon). Bouregy.
Dumas, Frederic, jt. auth. see Cousteau, Jacques-Yves.
Dumas, Henry. Ark of Bones: And Other Stories. Redmond, Eugene, ed. LC 74-4143. 1974. pap. 2.95 o.p. (ISBN 0-394-70947-0). Random.
--Play Ebony Play Ivory. LC 74-4126. 1974. 5.95 o.p. (ISBN 0-394-48970-5); pap. 2.95 o.p. (ISBN 0-394-70948-9). Random.
Dumas, Jean-Louis R., jt. auth. see Poirier, Jacques.

Dumas, Philippe. The Story of Edward. LC 76-28720. (Illus.). 48p. (gr. k-4). 1977. 5.95 o.s.i. (ISBN 0-8193-0868-4, Four Winds); PLB 5.41 o.s.i. (ISBN 0-8193-0869-2); pap. 1.95 o.s.i. (ISBN 0-8193-0905-2). Schol Bk Serv.

Dumas, Phillipe. Lucie: A Tale of a Donkey. (Illus.). (ps-2). 1979. 7.95 (ISBN 0-13-541169-6). P-H.

Dumas, T. & Bulani, W. Oxidation of Petrochemicals: Chemistry & Technology. LC 74-11232. 186p. 1974. 27.95 (ISBN 0-470-22480-0). Halsted Pr.

DuMaurier, Daphne. Don't Look Now. 1977. pap. 2.50 (ISBN 0-380-01144-1, 45252). Avon.

Du Maurier, Daphne. Frenchman's Creek. LC 70-184730. 320p. 1971. Repr. lib. bdg. 12.50x (ISBN 0-8376-0412-5). Bentley.

--Hungry Hill. LC 78-184732. 416p. 1971. Repr. of 1945 ed. lib. bdg. 12.50x (ISBN 0-8376-0414-1). Bentley.

--The Loving Spirit. LC 71-184733. 384p. 1971. Repr. lib. bdg. 12.50x (ISBN 0-8376-0415-X). Bentley.

--Mary Anne. LC 76-184729. 352p. 1971. Repr. of 1954 ed. lib. bdg. 12.50x (ISBN 0-8376-0411-7). Bentley.

--My Cousin Rachel. LC 74-184731. 352p. 1971. Repr. lib. bdg. 12.50x (ISBN 0-8376-0413-3). Bentley.

--The Parasites. LC 72-184728. 320p. 1971. Repr. of 1950 ed. lib. bdg. 12.50x (ISBN 0-8376-0410-9). Bentley.

--Rebecca. 1948. 9.95 (ISBN 0-385-04380-5). Doubleday.

--Rebecca. 1971. pap. 2.50 (ISBN 0-380-00917-X, 48603). Avon.

--The Rebecca Notebook & Other Memories. LC 80-652. 288p. 1980. 12.50 (ISBN 0-385-15885-8). Doubleday.

--The Winding Stair. 1972. pap. 2.25 (ISBN 0-380-01848-9, 36459). Avon.

Dumaurier, Daphne, jt. auth. see Quiller-Couch, Arthur.

Du Maurier, George. Trilby. 1956. 7.50x (ISBN 0-460-00863-3, Evman); pap. 5.95 (ISBN 0-460-01863-9). Dutton.

Dumbleton, John, jt. auth. see Black, Jonathan.

Dumbleton, Susanne & Older, Anne. In & Around Albany: A Guide for Residents, Students & Visitors. (Illus.). 183p. (Orig.). 1980. pap. 4.50 (ISBN 0-9605460-0-6). Wash Park.

Dumery, Henry. Phenomenology & Religion: Structures of the Christian Institution. Barrett, Paul, tr. (Hermeneutics Series: Studies in the History of Religion). 1975. 14.00x (ISBN 0-520-02714-0). U of Cal Pr.

Dumezil, Georges. Camillus: A Study of Indo-European Religion As Roman History. Strutynski, Udo, ed. Aronowicz, Annette, et al, trs. from Fr. 250p. 1980. 16.95x (ISBN 0-520-02841-4). U of Cal Pr.

--Gods of the Ancient Northmen. Haugen, Einar, ed. & tr. (Study of Comparative Folklore & Mythology, No. 3). 1974. 18.50x (ISBN 0-520-02044-8); CAL 371. pap. 3.95 (ISBN 0-520-03507-0). U of Cal Pr.

Dumitrescu, Maria, ed. see De Belenoi, Aimeric.

Dummelow, John R. Commentary on the Holy Bible. 1909. 12.95 (ISBN 0-02-533770-X). Macmillan.

Dummer, Geoffrey W. Electronic Inventions & Discoveries. 2nd rev. & exp. ed. 1978. text ed. 45.00 (ISBN 0-08-022730-9); pap. text ed. 16.50 (ISBN 0-08-023223-X). Pergamon.

--Electronic Reliability. Griffin, N. B., ed. 1966. 16.00 (ISBN 0-08-011448-2); pap. 7.75 (ISBN 0-08-011447-4). Pergamon.

Dummer, Geoffrey W. & Winton, R. C. An Elementary Guide to Reliability. 2nd ed. LC 73-16199. 66p. 1974. pap. text ed. 7.00 (ISBN 0-08-017821-9). Pergamon.

Dummer, Geoffrey W. & Robertson, J. M., eds. Fluidic Components & Equipment, 1968-69. 1969. 105.00 (ISBN 0-08-013446-7). Pergamon.

Dummer, Geoffrey W., et al, eds. Banking Automation, 1970-71, 2 Vols. 1971. 300.00 set (ISBN 0-08-016120-0). Pergamon.

Dummett, Clifton O. Community Dentistry: Contributions to New Directions. (American Lectures in Dentistry). (Illus.). 232p. 1974. 18.75- (ISBN 0-398-02882-6). C C Thomas.

Dummett, Michael. The Game of Tarot. (Illus.). 600p. 1980. 95.00 (ISBN 0-7156-1014-7, Pub. by Duckworth England). Biblio Dist.

Dummett, Michael & Minio, Robert. Elements of Intuitionism. (Oxford Logic Guides Ser.). 1977. text ed. 37.50x (ISBN 0-19-853158-3). Oxford U Pr.

Dumond, Dwight L., jt. ed. see Barnes, Gilbert H.

Dumonde, D. C. & Path, M. R. Infection & Immunology in the Rheumatic Diseases. (Blackwell Scientific Pubns.). (Illus.). 1976. 95.00 (ISBN 0-397-60361-4). Mosby.

Dumonde, D. C. & Maini, R. N., eds. Research into Rheumatoid Arthritis & Allied Diseases. Date not set. 34.50 o.p. (ISBN 0-8391-1180-0). Univ Park.

Dumont, Bernard. Functional Literacy in Mali: Training for Development. LC 73-77353. (Educational Studies & Documents, No. 10). (Illus.). 67p. (Orig.). 1973. pap. 2.50 (ISBN 92-3-101113-8, U257, UNESCO). Unipub.

Dumont, Francis M. French Grammar. 2nd ed. 1969. pap. 3.95 (ISBN 0-06-460035-1, CO 35, COS). Har-Row.

Dumont, H. J. & Green, J., eds. Rotatoria. (Developments in Hydrobiology Ser.: No. 1). 268p. 1980. lib. bdg. 79.00 (ISBN 90-6193-754-X, Pub. by Dr. W. Junk). Kluwer Boston.

Dumont, Lora L. Consonant Articulation Drills. 2nd ed. 268p. 1980. pap. text ed. 5.95x (ISBN 0-8134-2129-2, 2129). Interstate.

--Consonant Articulation Drills. LC 71-187778. 268p. 1972. pap. text ed. 5.95x o.p. (ISBN 0-8134-1463-6, 1463). Interstate.

Dumont, Louis. From Mandeville to Marx: Genesis & Triumph of Economic Ideology. LC 76-8087. 1977. lib. bdg. 16.50x o.s.i. (ISBN 0-226-16981-2). U of Chicago Pr.

--Homo Hierarchicus: The Caste System & Its Implications. rev. ed. Gulati, Basia, tr. LC 80-16480. 1981. 27.50x (ISBN 0-226-16962-6); pap. 9.95 (ISBN 0-226-16963-4, P601, Phoen). U of Chicago Pr.

Dumont, M., ed. see Bentham, Jeremy.

Dumont, Pierre. Citroen, the Great Marque of France: 1961-1976. Ellaway, Tom, tr. from Fr. LC 80-22034. Orig. Title: Quai De Javel Quai Andre Citroen. (Illus.). 1976. 35.00 (ISBN 0-903192-72-1, EPA France). Motorbooks Int.

Dumoulin, Heinrich & Maraldo, John C., eds. Buddhism in the Modern World. LC 75-42342. 400p. 1976. 12.95 o.s.i. (ISBN 0-02-533790-4). Macmillan.

Dumpleton, John. Make Your Own Booklet. LC 79-3815. 1980. pap. 2.95 (ISBN 0-8008-5058-0, Pentalic). Taplinger.

Dumville, David, ed. see Hughes, Kathleen.

Dun, Philip. The Cabal. (Orig.). 1981. pap. 2.25 (ISBN 0-425-04845-4). Berkley Pub.

Dun, Smith. Memoirs of the Four-Foot Colonel, Data Paper No. 113. 125p. 1980. 6.00 (ISBN 0-87727-113-5). Cornell SE Asia.

Dunaway, et al. Bragon the Dragon Calendar Capers. (gr. 1-5). 1978. 9.95 (ISBN 0-916456-36-6, GA93). Good Apple.

--Bragon the Dragon Tells Time. 1978. 9.95 (ISBN 0-916456-37-4, GA94). Good Apple.

Dunaway, James O. & Sports Illustrated Editors. Sports Illustrated Track: Running Events. rev. ed. LC 76-8268. (Illus.). 96p. 1972. 5.95 (ISBN 0-397-01172-5); pap. 2.95 (ISBN 0-397-01171-7, LP-64). Lippincott.

Dunaway, James O., jt. auth. see Sports Illustrated Editors.

Dunaway, John M. Jacques Maritain. (World Authors Ser.). 1978. lib. bdg. 12.50 (ISBN 0-8057-6315-5). Twayne.

--The Metamorphoses of the Self: The Mystic, the Sensualist, & the Artist in the Works of Julien Green. LC 78-88007. (Studies in Romance Languages: No. 19). 128p. 1978. 11.50x (ISBN 0-8131-1364-4). U Pr of Ky.

Dunaway, Vic. Modern Saltwater Fishing. 288p. 1975. 11.95 (ISBN 0-87691-168-8). Winchester Pr.

Du Nay, Andre. The Early History of the Rumanian Language. LC 79-115770. (Edward Sapir Monograph Series in Language, Culture, & Cognition: No. 3). (Illus.). xii, 275p. 1977. pap. 7.00x (ISBN 0-933104-03-0). Jupiter Pr.

Dunayevskaya, Raya. Philosophy & Revolution. 320p. 1973. 8.95 o.s.i. (ISBN 0-440-07253-0). Delacorte.

Dunbabin, Katherine M. The Mosaics of Roman North Africa: Studies in Iconography & Patronage. (Monographs on Classical Archaeology). (Illus.). 1979. 85.00x (ISBN 0-19-813217-4). Oxford U Pr.

Dunbar, Carl O. & Rodgers, John. Principles of Stratigraphy. LC 57-8883. 1957. 21.50 o.p. (ISBN 0-471-22539-8). Wiley.

Dunbar, Carl O. & Waage, Karl M. Historical Geology. 3rd ed. LC 72-89681. (Illus.). 1969. text ed. 23.95 (ISBN 0-471-22507-X). Wiley.

Dunbar, Ernest. Nigeria. LC 74-913. (First Bks). (Illus.). 96p. (gr. 6 up). 1974. PLB 4.90 o.p. (ISBN 0-531-02720-1). Watts.

Dunbar, J. G. The Architecture of Scotland. 1978. 30.00 (ISBN 0-7134-1142-2, Pub. by Batsford England). David & Charles.

Dunbar, M. J., ed. Marine Production Mechanisms. LC 77-88675. (International Biological Programme Ser: No. 20). (Illus.). 1979. 72.00 (ISBN 0-521-21937-X). Cambridge U Pr.

Dunbar, Paul L. The Complete Poems of Paul Laurence Dunbar. LC 80-16651. 1980. pap. 4.95 (ISBN 0-396-07895-8). Dodd.

--Little Brown Baby: Paul Laurence Dunbar Poems for Young People. LC 40-4721. (Illus.). (gr. 4-6). 1940. 4.95 (ISBN 0-396-01993-5). Dodd.

Dunbar, Robert E. A Doctor Discusses a Man's Sexual Health. (Illus.). 1979. pap. 2.50 (ISBN 0-685-64313-1). Budlong.

--Heredity. (First Bks.). (Illus.). (gr. 4 up). 1978. PLB 6.45 s&l (ISBN 0-531-01408-8). Watts.

--Mental Retardation. (First Bks). (Illus.). (gr. 4-6). 1978. PLB 6.45 (ISBN 0-531-01491-6). Watts.

--Zoology Careers. (Illus.). (YA) (gr. 7 up). 1977. lib. bdg. 6.45 (ISBN 0-531-01312-X). Watts.

Dunbar, Robert E. & Segall, Harold F. A Doctor Discusses Learning to Cope with Arthritis Rheumatism & Govt. (Illus., Orig.). 1973. pap. 2.50 (ISBN 0-685-35675-2). Budlong.

Dunbar, Telfer. History of Highland Dress. (Illus.). 248p. 1980. 50.00 (ISBN 0-7134-1894-X, Pub. by Batsford England). David & Charles.

Dunbar, William. Poems. Kinsley, James, ed. (Clarendon Medieval & Tudor Ser.). 1958. pap. 9.95x (ISBN 0-19-871017-8). Oxford U Pr.

--The Poems of William Dunbar. Mackenzie, W. Mackay, ed. 1933. 8.95 (ISBN 0-571-06896-0, Pub. by Faber & Faber). Merrimack Bk Serv.

--The Poems of William Dunbar. Mackenzie, W. Mackay, ed. 1970. pap. 3.95 o.p. (ISBN 0-571-09239-X, Pub. by Faber & Faber). Merrimack Bk Serv.

Dunbaugh, Edwin. World History. (Quick & Easy Ser). (Orig.). 1963. pap. 1.95 o.s.i. (ISBN 0-02-079950-0, Collier). Macmillan.

Duncan & Hollander. Plaid for Retailing. 3rd ed. 1979. 6.95 (ISBN 0-256-02245-3, 09-0838-03). Learning Syst.

Duncan, A. S., et al, eds. Dictionary of Medical Ethics. 496p. 1981. 24.50 (ISBN 0-8245-0038-5). Crossroad NY.

--Dictionary of Medical Ethics. 1977. pap. text ed. 15.50x (ISBN 0-232-51302-3). Humanities.

Duncan, Acheson J. Quality Control & Industrial Statistics. 4th ed. 1974. text ed. 22.95 (ISBN 0-256-01558-9). Irwin.

Duncan, Alistair. The Noble Heritage: Jerusalem & Christianity - a Portrait of the Church of the Resurrection. 1974. 10.00x (ISBN 0-685-61499-9). Intl Bk Ctr.

Duncan, Alistair M., ed. see Copernicus, Nicholas.

Duncan, Archibald A., ed. see Dickinson, W. Croft.

Duncan, Bowie. Critical Reception of Howard Nemerov: A Selection of Essays & a Bibliography. LC 70-154299. 1971. 10.00 (ISBN 0-8108-0400-X). Scarecrow.

Duncan, Carol. The Pursuit of Pleasure: the Rococo Revival in French Romantic Art. LC 75-23789. (Outstanding Dissertations in the Fine Arts - 19th Century). (Illus.). 1976. lib. bdg. 31.00 (ISBN 0-8240-1985-7). Garland Pub.

Duncan, D. Ben Jonson & the Lucianic Tradition. LC 78-18093. 1979. 29.95 (ISBN 0-521-22359-8). Cambridge U Pr.

Duncan, David. Strange but True: Twenty-Two Amazing Stories. (gr. 4-6). 1974. pap. 1.25 (ISBN 0-590-03528-2, Schol Pap). Schol Bk Serv.

Duncan, David, jt. auth. see Litwiller, Bonnie.

Duncan, David D. The Fragile Miracle of Martin Gray. LC 79-88367. (Illus.). 96p. 7.95 (ISBN 0-89659-073-9). Abbeville Pr.

Duncan, Delbert J., et al. Modern Retailing Management. 9th ed. 1977. text ed. 18.95 (ISBN 0-256-01926-6). Irwin.

Duncan, Dougal. My Sons, My England. 1980. 11.95 (ISBN 0-684-16603-8). Scribner.

Duncan, Edmondstoune. Story of Minstrelsy. LC 69-16802. (Music Story Ser). 1968. Repr. of 1907 ed. 18.00 (ISBN 0-8103-4240-5). Gale.

--Story of the Carol. LC 69-16805. 1968. Repr. of 1911 ed. 18.00 (ISBN 0-8103-3547-6). Gale.

Duncan, Elmer H., ed. see Reid, Thomas.

Duncan, Erika. A Wreath of Pale White Roses. LC 76-53373. 1977. 7.95 o.s.i. (ISBN 0-8027-0570-7); pap. 4.95 o.s.i. (ISBN 0-8027-7107-6). Walker & Co.

Duncan, F. Microprocessor Programming & Software Development. 1979. 29.95 (ISBN 0-13-581405-7). P-H.

Duncan, George. Physics for Biologists. LC 74-18621. 1975. pap. 12.95 (ISBN 0-470-22568-8). Halsted Pr.

Duncan, Horace G., jt. auth. see Club Managers Association.

Duncan, I. M., jt. auth. see Johnstone, A. H.

Duncan, Irma. Duncan Dancer. LC 79-7759. (Dance Ser.). 1980. Repr. of 1966 ed. lib. bdg. 33.00x (ISBN 0-8369-9288-1). Arno.

Duncan, Isadora. Art of the Dance. LC 71-85671. (Illus.). 14.95 (ISBN 0-87830-005-8); pap. 8.95 (ISBN 0-87830-555-6). Theatre Arts.

--My Life. (Black & Gold Lib). (Illus.). 1955. 10.00 (ISBN 0-87140-942-9); pap. 5.95 (ISBN 0-87140-074-X). Liveright.

Duncan, J., jt. auth. see Bonsall, F. F.

Duncan, J. A. & Gumaer, J. Developmental Groups for Children. (Illus.). 440p. 1980. 29.75 (ISBN 0-398-04025-7). C C Thomas.

Duncan, James K., jt. auth. see Hough, John B.

Duncan, Jane. Janet Reachfar & Chickabird. LC 77-12709. (gr. 1-5). 1978. 7.95 (ISBN 0-395-28788-X, Clarion). HM.

--Janet Reachfar & the Kelpie. LC 75-44166. (Illus.). 32p. (gr. 1-4). 1976. 7.50 (ISBN 0-395-28789-8, Clarion). HM.

Duncan, Jeffrey L. The Power & Form of Emerson's Thought. LC 73-85043. 150p. 1974. 7.95x (ISBN 0-8139-0510-9). U Pr of Va.

Duncan, John, jt. auth. see Webb, Brian.

Duncan, John, jt. ed. see McCarthy, Paul.

Duncan, K. & Rutledge, I., eds. Land & Labour in Latin America. LC 76-11076. (Cambridge Latin American Studies: No. 26). (Illus.). 1978. 49.95 (ISBN 0-521-21206-5). Cambridge U Pr.

Duncan, K. D., et al, eds. Changes in Working Life. LC 80-40129. 1981. 68.75 (ISBN 0-471-27777-0, Fpub. by Wiley-Interscience). Wiley.

Duncan, Karen, ed. Information Technology & Health Care: The Critical Issues. 200p. 1980. write for info. (ISBN 0-88283-031-7). AFIPS Pr.

Duncan, Kathleen M. Crispin's Castle. (Pathfinder Ser.). (Illus.). (gr. 2-6). 1979. pap. 2.95 (ISBN 0-310-37821-4). Zondervan.

Duncan, Lois. Daughters of Eve. (YA) (gr. 7-12). 1980. pap. 1.75 (ISBN 0-440-91864-2, LFL). Dell.

--Five Were Missing ("Ransom") (RL 7). 1972. pap. 1.50 (ISBN 0-451-08678-3, W8678, Sig). NAL.

--Gift of Magic. (Illus.). (gr. 5-7). 1972. pap. 1.75 (ISBN 0-671-56096-4). PB.

--I Know What You Did Last Summer. (gr. 7-9). 1975. pap. 1.95 (ISBN 0-671-41676-6). Archway.

--I Know What You Did Last Summer. (gr. 7-9). 1975. pap. 1.75 (ISBN 0-671-56080-8). PB.

--Killing Mr. Griffin. (YA) 1980. pap. 1.75 (ISBN 0-440-94515-1, LFL). Dell.

Duncan, Louise, jt. auth. see Coen, Luciano.

Duncan, Marti. Being & Breakfast. 1975. 1.00. Windless Orchard.

Duncan, Molly. Spin Your Own Wool & Dye It & Weave It. rev. ed. (Illus.). 52p. 1978. 7.50 (ISBN 0-589-00334-8, Pub by Reed Books Australia). C E Tuttle.

Duncan, Otis D., jt. auth. see Blau, Peter M.

Duncan, Otis D., et al. Introduction to Structural Equation Models. (Studies in Population Ser.). 1975. 20.00 (ISBN 0-12-224150-9). Acad Pr.

Duncan, Patricia D. Tallgrass Prairie: The Inland Sea. LC 78-60177. (Illus.). 1979. 20.00 (ISBN 0-913504-44-0); pap. 12.95 (ISBN 0-913504-56-4). Lowell Pr.

Duncan, R. F. The Practical Sailor. (Illus.). 224p. 1981. 14.95 (ISBN 0-684-16621-6, ScribT). Scribner.

Duncan, R. S. A History of the Baptists in Missouri. Date not set. Repr. of 1882 ed. price not set. Church History.

Duncan, Riana. A Nutcracker in a Tree: A Book of Riddles. LC 80-67492. (Illus.). 32p. (gr. k-2). 1981. 8.95 (ISBN 0-440-06426-0); PLB 8.44 (ISBN 0-440-06429-5). Delacorte.

Duncan, Robert. Kiss. 1978. pap. 1.95 (ISBN 0-445-04112-9). Popular Lib.

--Opening of the Field. rev. ed. LC 72-93976. 96p. 1973. pap. 4.95 (ISBN 0-8112-0480-4, NDP356). New Directions.

--Peiping Municipality & the Diplomatic Quarter. LC 78-74355. (Modern Chinese Economy Ser.). 146p. 1980. lib. bdg. 16.50 (ISBN 0-8240-4271-9). Garland Pub.

--The Truth & Life of Myth. 1968. pap. 2.45 o.s.i. (ISBN 0-912090-18-9). Sumac Mich.

Duncan, Robert, jt. auth. see Zaltman, Gerald.

Duncan, Robert L. The Day the Sun Fell. 1979. pap. 2.25 o.p. (ISBN 0-345-27167-X). Ballantine.

--Temple Dogs. LC 76-51781. 1977. 8.95 o.p. (ISBN 0-688-03181-1). Morrow.

Duncan, Roger F. & Ware, John P. A Cruising Guide to the New England Coast. rev. ed. LC 78-22734. (Illus.). 1979. 19.95 (ISBN 0-396-07629-7). Dodd.

Duncan, Ronald J., ed. Investigacion Social En Puerto Rico. LC 80-23445. 350p. 1980. text ed. 13.00 (ISBN 0-913480-45-2); pap. 8.00 (ISBN 0-913480-44-4). Inter Am U Pr.

Duncan, Ronald J., et al. Manual De Tecnicas De Investigacion Social. LC 80-23411. (Illus.). 78p. 1980. 5.00 (ISBN 0-913480-46-0). Inter Am U Pr.

Duncan, S. & Fiske, D. W. Face-to-Face Interaction: Research, Methods, & Theory. LC 77-1841. 1977. 18.50 o.p. (ISBN 0-470-99113-5). Halsted Pr.

Duncan, S. Blackwell. The Build-It Book of Cabinets & Built-Ins. (Illus.). 1979. 12.95 o.p. (ISBN 0-8306-9854-X); pap. 7.95 (ISBN 0-8306-1002-2, 1002). TAB Bks.

--The Complete Handbook of Electrical & House Wiring. LC 77-1770. (Illus.). 1977. 10.95 o.p. (ISBN 0-8306-7913-8); pap. 6.95 (ISBN 0-8306-6913-2, 913). TAB Bks.

--Plumbing with Plastic. (Illus., Orig.). 1980. 15.95 (ISBN 0-8306-9958-9); pap. 9.95 (ISBN 0-8306-1214-9, 1214). TAB Bks.

Duncan, S. S., ed. Qualitative Change in Human Geography. (Illus.). 127p. 1981. 29.00 (ISBN 0-08-025222-2). Pergamon.

Duncan, Theodore G., ed. Over Fifty-Five: A Handbook on Aging. 1981. write for info. Franklin Inst Pr.

Duncan, Thomas. Electronics & Nuclear Physics. (gr. 9-12). text ed. 14.95 (ISBN 0-7195-2003-7). Transatlantic.

--A Taxonomic Study of the Ranunculus hispidus. (U. C. Publications in Botany V Ser.: Vol. 77). 1980. 7.00 (ISBN 0-520-09617-7). U of Cal Pr.

Duncan, Thomas, ed. see Ward-Jackson, Annis.

Duncan, W., et al. Thyroid Cancer. (Recent Results in Cancer Research Ser.: Vol. 73). (Illus.). 190p. 1980. 35.40 (ISBN 0-387-09328-1). Springer-Verlag.

Duncan, W. Jack. Essentials of Management. LC 77-81236. 1978. text ed. 19.95 (ISBN 0-03-039826-6). Dryden Pr.

--Organizational Behavior. 2nd ed. LC 80-82460. (Illus.). 464p. 1981. text ed. 18.95 (ISBN 0-395-29640-4); write for info. instr's manual (ISBN 0-395-29641-2). HM.

--Organizational Behavior. LC 77-76344. (Illus.). 1978. text ed. 17.95 (ISBN 0-395-25744-1); inst. manual 0.50 (ISBN 0-395-25745-X). HM.

Duncan, W. Raymond. Soviet Policy in the Third World. (Policy Studies). 1980. 35.00 (ISBN 0-08-025125-0). Pergamon.

Duncan, W. Raymond, ed. Soviet Policy in Developing Countries. LC 78-20847. 368p. 1981. Repr. of 1970 ed. lib. bdg. 12.50 (ISBN 0-88275-846-2). Krieger.

Duncan, Wilbur H. & Kartesz, John T. Vascular Flora of Georgia: An Annotated Checklist. 149p. 1981. pap. 5.00 (ISBN 0-8203-0538-3). U of Ga Pr.

Duncan, William. Doing Business with Japan. 1976. 27.50 o.s.i. (ISBN 0-7161-0303-6). Herman Pub.

Duncan, William R. Thailand: A Complete Guide. LC 75-28719. (Illus.). 1976. 15.00 (ISBN 0-8048-1158-X); pap. 7.50 (ISBN 0-8048-1158-X). C E Tuttle.

Duncan-Jones, Katherine, ed. see Sidney, Phillip.

Duncan-Jones, R. The Economy of the Roman Empire Quantitative Studies. LC 72-93146. (Illus.). 320p. 1974. 51.00 (ISBN 0-521-20165-9). Cambridge U Pr.

Dundes, Alan. Analytic Essays in Folklore. (Studies in Folklore Ser.: No. 2). 1975. pap. text ed. 28.25x (ISBN 90-279-3231-X). Mouton.

--Interpreting Folklore. LC 79-2969. 304p. 1980. 25.00x (ISBN 0-253-14307-1); pap. 9.95x (ISBN 0-253-20240-X). Ind U Pr.

--Study of Folklore. (Illus.). 1965. text ed. 14.95 (ISBN 0-13-858944-5). P-H.

Dundes, Alan & Falassi, Allesandro. La Terra in Piazza: An Interpretation of the Palio in Siena. LC 73-91675. (Illus.). 1975. 24.50 (ISBN 0-520-02681-0). U of Cal Pr.

Dundes, Alan, ed. Mother Wit from the Laughing Barrel: Readings in the Interpretation of Afro-American Folklore. LC 80-8528. 688p. 1981. lib. bdg. 38.00 (ISBN 0-8240-9456-5). Garland Pub.

Dundon, H. Dwyer, jt. ed. see Jackson, Elinor.

Duner, Anders, ed. Research into Personal Development: Educational & Vocational Choice. 192p. 1978. pap. text ed. 16.00 (ISBN 90-265-0284-2, Pub. by Swets Serv Pub Holland). Swets North Am.

Dunes of Dare Garden Club. Wildflowers of the Outer Banks: Kitty Hawk to Hatteras. LC 79-18927. (Illus.). 1980. pap. 6.95 (ISBN 0-8078-4061-0, 4061). U of NC Pr.

Dunetz, Martin. How to Finance Your Retirement. (Illus.). 1979. 17.95 (ISBN 0-8359-2950-7). Reston.

Dunfee, Maxine. Social Studies for the Real World. 1978. pap. text ed. 15.95 (ISBN 0-675-08366-4); instructor's manual 3.95 (ISBN 0-686-67992-X). Merrill.

Dunfee, Thomas W. & Gibson, Frank F. Modern Business Law: An Introduction to Government & Business. 2nd ed. LC 76-44997. 1977. pap. text ed. 10.50 (ISBN 0-88244-146-9). Grid Pub.

Dunfee, Thomas W. & Reitzel, J. David. Business Law: Key Issues & Concepts. LC 78-17091. (Law Ser.). 1978. pap. text ed. 6.95 o.p. (ISBN 0-88244-177-9). Grid Pub.

Dunfee, Thomas W., et al. Modern Business Law: An Introduction to the Legal Environment of Business. LC 77-71017. (Law Ser.). 1978. pap. text ed. 9.95 (ISBN 0-88244-117-5). Grid Pub.

--Modern Business Law. LC 78-13129. (Law Ser.). 1979. text ed. 20.95 o.p. (ISBN 0-88244-179-5). Grid Pub.

--Modern Business Law: Contracts. LC 77-91087. (Law Ser.). 1978. pap. text ed. 14.95 (ISBN 0-88244-166-3). Grid Pub.

Dunford, Brian. Elements of Diatomic Molecular Spectra. LC 68-13548. (Chemistry Ser). (Illus., Orig.). 1968. pap. 10.95 (ISBN 0-201-01615-X). A-W.

Dunford, Nelson & Schwartz, Jacob T. Linear Operators, 3 pts. Incl. Pt. 1. General Theory. 1958. 54.50 (ISBN 0-470-22605-6); Pt. 2. Spectral Theory, Self Adjoint Operators in Hilbert Space. 69.95 (ISBN 0-470-22638-2); Pt. 3. Spectral Operators. 1971. 59.50 (ISBN 0-471-22639-4). LC 57-10545. (Pure & Applied Mathematics Ser, Pub. by Wiley-Interscience). Wiley.

Dungan, David L., jt. auth. see Cartlidge, David R.

Dunham, Dows. The Barkal Temples. 1970. 40.00 (ISBN 0-87846-108-6). Mus Fine Arts Boston.

--Recollections of an Egyptologist. (Illus.). 1972. pap. 3.25 (ISBN 0-87846-082-9). Mus Fine Arts Boston.

--Royal Cemeteries of Kush, 5 vols. Incl. Vol. 1. El Kurru. 1950. 25.00 (ISBN 0-685-72186-8); Vol. 2. Nuri. 1955. 35.00 (ISBN 0-87846-040-3); Vol. 3. Decorated Chapels of the Meroitic Pyramids at Meroe & Barkal. Chapman, Suzanne E. 1952. 30.00 (ISBN 0-87846-041-1); Vol. 4. Royal Tombs at Meroe & Barkal. 1957. 35.00 (ISBN 0-87846-043-8); Vol. 5. The West & South Cemeteries of Meroe. 1963. 35.00 (ISBN 0-87846-043-8). (Illus.). Mus Fine Arts Boston.

--The Tomb of Queen Hetep-heres. (Illus.). 1972. pap. 1.00 (ISBN 0-87846-181-7). Mus Fine Arts Boston.

Dunham, Dows, et al. The Mastaba of Queen Mersyankh III, Vol. 1. (Illus.). 1974. 35.00 (ISBN 0-87846-174-4). Mus Fine Arts Boston.

Dunham, H. Warren. Social Realities & Community Psychiatry. LC 74-10967. 252p. 1976. 22.95 (ISBN 0-87705-215-8). Human Sci Pr.

--Social Systems & Schizophrenia: Selected Papers. LC 80-14193. 332p. 1980. 28.95 (ISBN 0-03-056134-5). Praeger.

Dunham, Harold H. Government Handout: A Study in the Administration of the Public Lands 1875-1891. LC 79-87564. (American Scene Ser). 1970. Repr. of 1941 ed. lib. bdg. 35.00 (ISBN 0-306-71433-7). Da Capo.

Dunham, Lowell & Ivask, Ivar. Cardinal Points of Borges. LC 76-163635. (Illus.). 1971. 9.95 (ISBN 0-8061-0983-1); pap. 4.95 (ISBN 0-8061-0984-X). U of Okla Pr.

Dunham, Lowell, tr. see Caso, Alfonso.

Dunham, Lowell, tr. see Zea, Leopoldo.

Dunham, Philip J. Experimental Psychology: Theory & Practice. LC 77-5688. (Harper's Experimental Psychology Ser.). (Illus.). 1977. text ed. 19.50 scp (ISBN 0-06-041805-2, HarpC); tchr's manual free (ISBN 0-06-361783-8). Har-Row.

Dunham, Randall B., jt. auth. see Cummings, L. L.

Dunham, Terry B. & Gustin, Lawrence R. The Buick: A Complete History. (Illus.). 444p. 1980. 59.95 (ISBN 0-915038-19-6); leather ed. 79.95 (ISBN 0-915038-27-7). Princeton Pub.

Dunham, Terry B., et al. Buick: The Complete History. Doerflinger, William, ed. (Automobile Quarterly Library Ser.). 444p. 1981. 59.95 (ISBN 0-525-07230-6). Dutton.

Dunham, Vera S. In Stalin's Time. LC 75-10238. 368p. 1976. 36.00 (ISBN 0-521-20949-8); pap. 9.95 (ISBN 0-521-29650-1). Cambridge U Pr.

Dunham, Wm. H. Fane Fragment of the 1461 Lord's Journal. (Yale Historical Pubs., Manuscripts & Edited Texts: No. XIV). 1935. 34.50x (ISBN 0-685-69813-0). Elliots Bks.

Dunhill, Thomas F. Sullivan's Comic Operas: A Critical Appreciation. (Music Ser.). 256p. 1981. Repr. of 1928 ed. lib. bdg. 25.00 (ISBN 0-306-76080-0). Da Capo.

Duniec, M. L., jt. auth. see Davids, Kenneth.

Dunitz, J. D., et al. Bonding Problems. (Structure & Bonding Ser.: Vol.43). (Illus.). 240p. 1981. 58.00 (ISBN 0-387-10407-0). Springer-Verlag.

Dunitz, J. D., et al, eds. Luminescence & Energy Transfer. (Structure & Bonding Ser.: Vol. 42). (Illus.). 133p. 1981. 40.00 (ISBN 0-387-10395-3). Springer-Verlag.

Dunitz, Jack D. X-Ray Analysis & the Structure of Organic Molecules. LC 78-15588. (George Fisher Baker Non-Resident Lectureship Ser.). 1979. 60.00x (ISBN 0-8014-1115-7). Cornell U Pr.

Dunkelberg, William C., jt. auth. see Shay, Robert P.

Dunkelberg, William C., jt. auth. see Sonquist, John A.

Dunkelman, Mark H. & Winey, Michael J. The Hardtack Regiment: An Illustrated History of the 154th Regiment, New York State Infantry Volunteers. LC 79-64502. (Illus.). 220p. 1981. 20.00 (ISBN 0-8386-3007-3). Fairleigh Dickinson.

Dunkels, Marjorie. Donkey Wrinkles & Tales. (Illus.). pap. 4.35 (ISBN 0-85131-274-8). J A Allen.

Dunkerley, Joy. Trends in Energy Use in Industrial Countries. LC 80-8022. (Resources for the Future Research Ser.: Paper R-19). (Illus., Orig.). 1980. pap. text ed. 8.00x (ISBN 0-8018-2487-7). Johns Hopkins.

Dunkerley, Joy, ed. International Energy Strategies: Proceedings of the 1979 IAEE-RFF Conference. LC 80-16503. 384p. 1980. text ed. 27.50 (ISBN 0-89946-039-9). Oelgeschlager.

Dunlap, Alice. Hospital Literature Subject Headings. 2nd ed. LC 77-519. 200p. 1977. pap. 20.00 (ISBN 0-87258-202-7, 1371). Am Hospital.

Dunlap, Alice, et al, eds. Hospital Literature Index: 1980 Cumulative Annual, Vol. 36. 704p. 1981. 72.00 (ISBN 0-87258-348-1). Am Hospital.

Dunlap, Edward A., ed. Gordon's Medical Management of Ocular Disease. 2nd ed. (Illus.). 1976. 39.50x o.p. (ISBN 0-06-140730-5, Harper Medical). Har-Row.

Dunlap, G. Dale. Successful Celestial Navigation with H.O. 229. LC 76-8771. (Illus.). 1977. 19.95 (ISBN 0-87742-075-0). Intl Marine.

Dunlap, George A. Black, White & Red: The Problem of Shawnee College. 64p. 1979. 3.95 (ISBN 0-8059-2622-4). Dorrance.

--One Hectic Summer. 64p. 1981. 4.95 (ISBN 0-8059-2784-0). Dorrance.

Dunlap, L. C. Mental Health Concepts Applied to Nursing. 256p. 1978. 15.95 (ISBN 0-471-04360-5). Wiley.

Dunlap, Leslie W. American Historical Societies: 1790-1860. LC 73-16331. (Perspectives in American History Ser.: No. 7). 238p. Repr. of 1944 ed. lib. bdg. 15.00x (ISBN 0-87991-343-6). Porcupine Pr.

Dunlap, Rhodes, ed. see Carew, Thomas.

Dunlap, Roy F. Gunsmithing. LC 63-21755. (Illus.). 748p. 1963. 19.95 (ISBN 0-8117-0770-9). Stackpole.

Dunlap, Thomas R. DDT: Scientists, Citizens, & Public Policy. LC 80-8546. 304p. 1981. 18.50x (ISBN 0-691-04680-8). Princeton U Pr.

Dunlap, W. Crawford, ed. see International Conference on Hot Electrons in Semiconductors, Denton, TX, 6-8 Jul. 1977.

Dunlap, William. Four Plays, 1789-1812. LC 76-46978. 300p. 1976. lib. bdg. 25.00x (ISBN 0-8201-1283-6). Schol Facsimiles.

Dunleavy, Patrick. Urban Political Analysis: The Politics of Collective Consumption. 176p. 1980. text ed. 22.50x (ISBN 0-333-23948-2). Humanities.

Dunleavy, Steve. The Very First Lady. 1980. 13.95 (ISBN 0-671-24691-7). S&S.

Dunlop, Burton D. The Growth of Nursing Home Care. LC 78-14715. 1979. 18.95 (ISBN 0-669-02704-9). Lexington Bks.

Dunlop, D., jt. ed. see Bossert, T.

Dunlop, David W., jt. ed. see Mushkin, Selma J.

Dunlop, Douglas. Arab Civilization to A.D. 1500. (Arab Background Ser.). 1971. 25.00x (ISBN 0-685-77094-X). Intl Bk Ctr.

Dunlop, Eileen. Elizabeth, Elizabeth. LC 76-46758. (gr. 5 up). 1977. 6.95 o.p. (ISBN 0-03-019311-7). HR&W.

Dunlop, Ian & Schrand, Heinrich. In & About English: Authentic Texts for Developing Reading Skills. LC 80-40438. 96p. 1980. pap. 4.91 (ISBN 0-08-024570-6). Pergamon.

Dunlop, John B., et al. Alexsandr Solzhenitsyn. 1975. pap. 5.95 o.s.i. (ISBN 0-02-050550-7, Collier). Macmillan.

Dunlop, John T. Industrial Relations Systems. LC 77-24354. (Arcturus Books Paperbacks). 412p. 1977. pap. 8.95x (ISBN 0-8093-0850-9). S Ill U Pr.

Dunlop, Richard S. Helping the Bereaved. LC 78-13534. 188p. 1978. pap. 9.95 (ISBN 0-913486-91-4). Charles.

Dunman, Jack. Agriculture: Capitalist & Socialist. 1975. text ed. 13.00x (ISBN 0-85315-330-2). Humanities.

Dunmore. The Stalinist Command Economy. LC 79-26712. 224p. 1980. write for info. St Martin.

Dunmore, John. French Explorers in the Pacific Vol. 2: The Nineteenth Century. 1969. 22.00x o.p. (ISBN 0-19-821540-1). Oxford U Pr.

Dunn. Advertising. 4th ed. 1978. 21.95 (ISBN 0-03-014341-1). Dryden Pr.

Dunn, Alan, jt. auth. see Thorpe, Denis.

Dunn, Albert H. & Johnson, Eugene M. Managing Your Sales Team. (Illus.). 224p. 1980. 13.95 (ISBN 0-13-550905-X, Spec); pap. 6.95 (ISBN 0-13-550897-5). P-H.

Dunn, Charles. The Upstream Christian in a Downstream World. 1979. pap. 3.50 (ISBN 0-88207-789-9). Victor Bks.

Dunn, Charles W. Highland Settler: A Portrait of the Scottish Gael in Nova Scotia. LC 53-7025. 1953. pap. 5.95 (ISBN 0-8020-6094-3). U of Toronto Pr.

Dunn, Charles W., ed. Actors' Analects. (Studies in Oriental Culture Ser). (Illus.). 1970. 17.00x (ISBN 0-231-03391-5). Columbia U Pr.

Dunn, Christine & McMahon, Eileen. Desire. (Orig.). 1980. pap. 2.50 (ISBN 0-446-91174-7). Warner Bks.

Dunn, David. Sky Drift. LC 80-80806. (Illus.). 90p. 1979. soft wrap-around cover 15.95. Lingua Pr.

Dunn, Delmer D. Financing Presidential Campaigns. (Studies in Presidential Selection). 1972. pap. 4.95 (ISBN 0-8157-1961-2). Brookings.

--Public Officials & the Press. (Political Science Ser). 1969. pap. 6.95 (ISBN 0-201-01565-X). A-W.

Dunn, Dennis J. Detente & Papal-Communist Relations, 1962-1978. (Westview Replica Edition). 1979. lib. bdg. 23.50x (ISBN 0-89158-197-9). Westview.

--Religion & Modernization in the Soviet Union. LC 77-86372. 1978. lib. bdg. 28.50x (ISBN 0-89158-241-X). Westview.

Dunn, Deryl. The Unsuccessful Do-It-Yourselfer. LC 80-51917. (Successful Ser.). (Illus.). 112p. 1980. pap. 3.95 (ISBN 0-89999-011-8). Structures Pub.

Dunn, Diana R., jt. auth. see Hatry, Harry P.

Dunn, Donald J., jt. auth. see Reams, Bernard D., Jr.

Dunn, Douglas. Terry Street. 1971. pap. 3.95 (ISBN 0-571-09713-8, Pub. by Faber & Faber). Merrimack Bk Serv.

Dunn, Douglas, ed. The Poetry of Scotland. (Illus.). 127p. 1980. 17.95 (ISBN 0-7134-1414-6, Pub. by Batsford England). David & Charles.

Dunn, Douglas, ed. see Byron, Lord.

Dunn, Edgar S., Jr. Social Information Processing & Statistical Systems: Change & Reform. LC 74-5289. 246p. 1974. 22.95 (ISBN 0-471-22747-1, Pub. by Wiley-Interscience). Wiley.

Dunn, Eleanor, ed. Let's Cook Today. (gr. k-3). 1974. 3.95x (ISBN 0-933892-03-9). Child Focus Co.

--Lexikits. (gr. k-3). 1973. 6.95x (ISBN 0-933892-04-7). Child Focus Co.

--Lexilogs. (gr. k-3). 1973. 6.95x (ISBN 0-933892-05-5). Child Focus Co.

Dunn, Esther C. Ben Jonson's Art. 159p. 1980. Repr. of 1925 ed. lib. bdg. 30.00 (ISBN 0-8495-1122-4). Arden Lib.

Dunn, F. & O'Brien, W. D., Jr., eds. Ultrasonic Biophysics. LC 75-30715. (Benchmark Papers in Acoustics: Vol. 7). 400p. 1976. 44.50 (ISBN 0-12-786395-8). Acad Pr.

Dunn, Finlay. American Farming & Food. 1980. lib. bdg. 75.00 (ISBN 0-8490-3185-0). Gordon Pr.

Dunn, George E., ed. Gilbert & Sullivan Dictionary. LC 72-125070. (Music Ser). 1971. Repr. of 1936 ed. lib. bdg. 14.50 (ISBN 0-306-70007-7). Da Capo.

Dunn, Ginette. The Fellowship of Song: Popualr Singing Traditions in East Suffolk. (Illus.). 254p. 1980. 30.00x (ISBN 0-7099-0044-9, Pub. by Croom Helm Ltd England). Biblio Dist.

Dunn, Harold. Our Hysterical Heritage: The American Presidential Election Process, Out of the Mouths of Babes. LC 79-22777. (Illus.). 1980. 7.95 (ISBN 0-916144-50-X); pap. 3.95 (ISBN 0-916144-51-8). Stemmer Hse.

Dunn, Henry. Guatimala, or the Republic of Central America, in 1827-8: Being Sketches & Memorandums Made During a Twelve-Months Residence. LC 80-25556. 1981. Repr. of 1829 ed. 25.00 (ISBN 0-87917-073-5). Blaine Ethridge.

Dunn, I. S., et al. Fundamentals of Geotechnical Analysis. LC 79-13583. 1980. text ed. 20.95 o.p. (ISBN 0-471-03698-6); solutions manual avail. o.p. (ISBN 0-471-04997-2). Wiley.

Dunn, J. Political Obligation in Its Historical Context. LC 80-40037. (Illus.). 360p. 1980. 34.50 (ISBN 0-521-22890-5). Cambridge U Pr.

--Western Political Theory in the Face of the Future. LC 78-25625. (Themes in the Social Sciences Ser.). 1979. 24.95 (ISBN 0-521-22619-8); pap. 5.95x (ISBN 0-521-29578-5). Cambridge U Pr.

Dunn, J. & Robertson, A. F. Independence & Opportunity: Political Change in Ahafo. LC 73-79303. (African Studies, No. 8). (Illus.). 420p. 1974. 36.00 (ISBN 0-521-20270-1). Cambridge U Pr.

Dunn, J. F. & Wakefield, G. L. Exposure Manual. 3rd ed. 1978. 21.95 o.p. (ISBN 0-85242-361-6, Pub. by Fountain). Morgan.

Dunn, James A., jt. auth. see Bergan, John R.

Dunn, James A., Jr. Transportation Policy in Comparative Perspective. (Transportation Ser.). 288p. 1981. text ed. 25.00x (ISBN 0-262-04062-X). MIT Pr.

Dunn, James D. Christology in the Making: A New Testament Inquiry into the Origins of the Doctrine of the Incarnation. LC 80-16968. 1980. pap. 24.50 (ISBN 0-664-24356-8). Westminster.

Dunn, Jane. Moon in Eclipse: A Life of Mary Shelley. LC 78-850. 1978. 16.95 (ISBN 0-312-54692-0). St Martin.

Dunn, Jerry G. Alcoholics Victorious. pap. 3.00 (ISBN 0-8024-0200-3). Moody.

Dunn, Jimmy, jt. auth. see Manocchio, Anthony J.

Dunn, John. Modern Revolutions: An Introduction to the Analysis of a Political Phenomenon. LC 72-177942. 352p. 1972. 34.95 (ISBN 0-521-08441-5); pap. 9.95xx (ISBN 0-521-09698-7). Cambridge U Pr.
--Ornamentation in the Works of Frederick Chopin. LC 78-125069. (Music Ser). (Illus.). 1970. Repr. of 1921 ed. lib. bdg. 12.50 (ISBN 0-306-70006-9). Da Capo.
--Political Thought of John Locke. 1969. 34.95 (ISBN 0-521-07408-8). Cambridge U Pr.
Dunn, Joseph, jt. auth. see Wilkins, Alfred T., Jr.
Dunn, Joseph, ed. see Kyle, Louisa V.
Dunn, Joy B., ed. see Holt, Edgar A.
Dunn, Joy B., ed. see Livingood, James W.
Dunn, Judy. Animal Friends. LC 73-125913. (Illus.). (gr. k-3). 1970. PLB 6.75 (ISBN 0-87191-044-6). Creative Ed.
--Feelings. LC 70-125915. (Illus.). (gr. k-3). 1970. PLB 6.75 (ISBN 0-87191-045-4). Creative Ed.
--Friends. LC 77-125914. (Illus.). (gr. k-3). 1970. PLB 6.75 (ISBN 0-87191-046-2). Creative Ed.
--Having Fun. LC 70-128851. (Illus.). (gr. k-3). 1970. PLB 6.75 (ISBN 0-87191-067-5). Creative Ed.
--The Little Goat. LC 77-91658. (Picturebacks Ser.). (Illus.). (ps-1). 1979. PLB 4.99 (ISBN 0-394-93872-0, BYR); pap. 1.25 (ISBN 0-394-83872-6). Random.
--The Little Lamb. LC 76-24167. (Picturebacks Ser). (Illus.). (ps-1). 1977. pap. 1.25 (ISBN 0-394-83455-0, BYR). Random.
--The Little Rabbit. LC 79-5241. (Picturebacks Ser.). (Illus.). 32p. (ps). 1980. PLB 4.99 o.p. (ISBN 0-394-94377-5, BYR); pap. 1.25 (ISBN 0-394-84377-0). Random
Dunn, Judy, jt. auth. see Shaffer, David.
Dunn, Kenneth & Dunn, Rita. Teaching Students Through Their Individual Learning Styles: A Practical Approach. (Illus.). 1978. ref. ed. 15.95 (ISBN 0-87909-808-2). Reston.
Dunn, Laurence. Merchant Ships of the World in Color, 1910-1929. LC 74-23925. (Illus.). 215p. 1975. 6.95 o.s.i. (ISBN 0-02-533920-6). Macmillan.
Dunn, Lesoie C. Race & Biology. 1965. pap. 2.50 (ISBN 92-3-100436-0, U505, UNESCO). Unipub.
Dunn, M. & Tranter, P. The Structure of British Industry. (Studies in the British Economy). 1979. pap. text ed. write for info. (ISBN 0-435-84544-6). Heinemann Ed.
Dunn, Martin J. Dental Auxiliary Practice. Incl. Module 2. Dentofacial Growth & Development - Orthodontics. pap. 8.95 (ISBN 0-683-02688-7); Module 3. Oral Pathology. pap. 8.95 (ISBN 0-685-59330-4); Module 4. Internal Med. pap. 8.95 (ISBN 0-683-02690-9); Module 5. Pharmacology, Pain Control, Sterile Technique, & Oral Surgery. pap. 10.95 (ISBN 0-683-02691-7); Module 6. Periodontics. pap. 10.95 (ISBN 0-683-02692-5). 1975. Williams & Wilkins.
Dunn, Miriam. Let's Look at Malaysia. pap. 1.25 (ISBN 0-85363-096-8). OMF Bks.
Dunn, Olive J. Basic Statistics: A Primer for the Biomedical Sciences. 2nd ed. LC 77-9328. (Probability & Mathematical Statistics: Applied Probability & Statistics Section). 1977. 19.95 (ISBN 0-471-22744-7, Pub. by Wiley-Interscience). Wiley.
Dunn, Olive J. & Clark, Virginia A. Applied Statistics: Analysis of Variance & Regression. LC 73-13683. (Probability & Mathematical Statistics Ser.). 387p. 1974. 25.95 (ISBN 0-471-22700-5, Pub. by Wiley-Interscience). Wiley.
Dunn, P. D. & Reay, D. A. Heat Pipes. 1975. text ed. 24.20 o.p. (ISBN 0-08-019854-6); pap. text ed. 16.50 o.p. (ISBN 0-08-021240-9). Pergamon.
--Heat Pipes. 2nd ed. 1977. text ed. 45.00 (ISBN 0-08-022127-0); pap. text ed. 17.00 (ISBN 0-08-022128-9). Pergamon.
Dunn, P. N., ed. Calderon de la Barca: El Lcade de Zalemea. 1965. 6.00 (ISBN 0-08-011549-7); pap. 5.40 (ISBN 0-08-011548-9). Pergamon.
Dunn, Peter N. Spanish Picaresque Novel. (World Authors Ser.: No. 557). 1979. lib. bdg. 14.50 (ISBN 0-8057-6399-6). Twayne.
Dunn, Richard, tr. see Zampaglione, Gerardo.
Dunn, Richard J., ed. see Bronte, Charlotte.
Dunn, Richard S. Age of Religious Wars, Fifteen Fifty-Nine to Seventeen Fifteen. 2nd ed. (Illus.). 1979. 18.95 (ISBN 0-393-05694-5); pap. text ed. 5.95x (ISBN 0-393-09021-3). Norton.
Dunn, Rita, jt. auth. see Dunn, Kenneth.
Dunn, Robert. Green Leaf, Green Bough: Collected Poems. 25p. 1973. pap. 1.50 (ISBN 0-934676-02-X). Greenlf Bks.
Dunn, Robert & Ullman, Richard. Quality Assurance for Computer Software. (Illus.). 1981. 19.50 (ISBN 0-07-018312-0, P&R&B). McGraw.
Dunn, S. Watson & Lorimor, E. S. International Advertising & Marketing. LC 78-6802. 1979. text ed. 22.50 (ISBN 0-88244-174-4). Grid Pub.
Dunn, Stephen P., ed. Sociology in the USSR: A Collection of Readings from Soviet Sources. LC 66-23895. 1969. 17.50 o.p. (ISBN 0-87332-029-8). M E Sharpe.
Dunn, Stephen P., tr. see Yanov, Alexander.
Dunn, Thomas, ed. Renaissance Singer. LC 75-20077. 1976. 7.00 (ISBN 0-911318-10-0). E C Schirmer.
Dunn, W. Public Policy Analysis: An Introduction. 1981. pap. 18.50 (ISBN 0-13-737957-9). P-H.
Dunn, William, ed. Social Values & Public Policy. (Illus., Orig.). 1981. pap. 5.00 (ISBN 0-918592-44-5). Policy Studies.
Dunn, William J. Enjoy Europe by Train. LC 73-19289. 1974. pap. 5.95 o.p. (ISBN 0-684-13789-5, SL514, ScribT). Scribner.
Dunnam, Laura. One Hundred Fifty Fantastic Fund Raisers. LC 77-94856. 1979. 10.00 o.p. (ISBN 0-89430-018-0). Morgan-Pacific.
Dunnam, Maxie D. Barefoot Days of the Soul. LC 75-19910. 1976. 4.95 o.p. (ISBN 0-87680-432-6, 80432). Word Bks.
--Dancing at My Funeral. (Illus.). 1973. pap. 2.95x (ISBN 0-8358-0297-3). Upper Room.
--The Sanctuary for Lent, Nineteen Eighty. (Creative Leadership Ser.). 1980. per 100 20.00 o.p. (ISBN 0-687-36842-1). Abingdon.
--Sanctuary for Lent, Nineteen Eighty-One. (Orig.). 1981. pap. 20.00 per 100 (ISBN 0-687-36843-X). Abingdon.
Dunne, Carrin. Buddha & Jesus: Conversations. 1975. pap. 3.95 (ISBN 0-87243-057-X). Templegate.
Dunne, Gerald T. Hugo Black & the Judicial Revolution. 1977. text ed. 22.50x (ISBN 0-8290-0344-4). Irvington.
Dunne, Jim, jt. auth. see Norbye, Jan P.
Dunne, John G. The Studio. 255p. 1969. 5.95 (ISBN 0-374-27112-7). FS&G.
--Vegas: A Memoir of a Dark Season. 1975. pap. 2.25 o.s.i. (ISBN 0-446-82931-5). Warner Bks.
Dunne, John S. The Reasons of the Heart. 1978. 7.95 o.s.i. (ISBN 0-02-533950-8). Macmillan.
--Time & Myth. LC 74-32289. 128p. 1975. pap. 3.45 (ISBN 0-268-01828-6). U of Notre Dame Pr.
Dunne, Mary C. Hoby & Stub. LC 80-18449. 168p. (gr. 5-9). 1981. PLB 9.95 (ISBN 0-689-30806-X). Atheneum.
Dunne, Mary Collins. Nurse of the Crystalline Valley. (YA) 1977. 4.95 o.p. (ISBN 0-685-74273-3, Avalon). Bouregy.
Dunne, P. M. Engineering Drawing for Advanced Students. 1967. pap. 4.20 (ISBN 0-08-012135-7). Pergamon.
Dunne, Patrick M., ed. see Theory Conference, Phoenix, Arizona, February, 1980.
Dunne, Peter M. Black Robes in Lower California. (California Library Reprint Series: No. 3). (Illus.). 1968. Repr. 22.50x (ISBN 0-520-00362-4). U of Cal Pr.
Dunne, Thomas & Leopold, Luna B. Water in Environmental Planning. LC 78-8013. (Illus.). 1978. text ed. 33.95x (ISBN 0-7167-0079-4). W H Freeman.
Dunne, Thomas L. The Scourge. 1979. pap. 2.50 o.p. (ISBN 0-345-28063-6). Ballantine.
Dunnett, Alastair. No Thanks to the Duke. LC 80-1984. (Crime Club Ser.). 192p. 1981. 9.95 (ISBN 0-385-17389-X). Doubleday.
Dunnett, Alastair I. Scotland in Colour. 1977. 13.50 (ISBN 0-7134-0019-6, Pub. by Batsford England). David & Charles.
Dunnett, Dorothy. Checkmate. 1976. pap. 2.50 o.p. (ISBN 0-445-08483-9). Popular Lib.
--Checkmate. 736p. 1981. pap. 2.95 (ISBN 0-445-08483-9). Popular Lib.
--The Disorderly Knights. 576p. 1980. pap. 2.75 (ISBN 0-445-08497-9). Popular Lib.
--Pawn in Frankincense. 576p. 1981. pap. 2.75 (ISBN 0-445-08472-3). Popular Lib.
--Queen's Play. 1974. pap. 2.75 (ISBN 0-445-08496-0). Popular Lib.
--The Ringed Castle. 640p. 1981. pap. 2.75 (ISBN 0-445-08495-2). Popular Lib.
Dunnett, Margaret. No Pets Allowed & Other Animal Stories. LC 80-2692. 144p. (gr. 2-7). 1981. 8.95 (ISBN 0-233-97103-3). Andre Deutsch.
--No Pets Allowed & Other Animal Stories. LC 80-2692. (Illus.). 144p. (gr. 2-7). 1981. 8.95 (ISBN 0-233-97103-3). Andre Deutsch.
Dunnett, W. M. Sintesis Del Nuevo Testamento. Blanch, Jose M., tr. from Eng. (Curso Para Maestros Cristianos: No. 3). Orig. Title: New Testament Survey. 128p. (Span.). 1972. pap. 2.50 (ISBN 0-89922-012-6); instructor's manual 1.50 (ISBN 0-89922-013-4). Edit Caribe.
Dunnette, Marvin D. Work & Non-Work in the Year 2001. LC 72-94643. 1973. pap. text ed. 7.95 o.p. (ISBN 0-8185-0080-8). Brooks-Cole.
Dunnette, Marvin D. & Kirchner, Wayne K. Psychology Applied to Industry. (Orig.). 1965. pap. 10.95 (ISBN 0-13-733253-X). P-H.
Dunnette, Marvin D. & Fleishman, Edwin A., eds. Human Capability Assessment. (Human Performance & Productivity Ser.: Vol. 3). 336p. 1981. professional ref. text 19.95 (ISBN 0-89859-085-X). L Erlbaum Assocs.
Dunnigan, Ann, tr. see Ferrucci, Franco.
Dunnigan, James F., ed. see Strategy & Tactics Staff.
Dunnill, Michael. Pathological Basis of Renal Disease. LC 76-26775. (Illus.). 1976. text ed. 40.00 (ISBN 0-7216-3230-0). Saunders.
Dunning, H. R. The Story of Samuel Chadwick. pap. 1.50 o.p. (ISBN 0-686-12918-0). Schmul Pub Co.
Dunning, J., jt. auth. see Meltzer, E.
Dunning, James B. Ministries: Sharing God's Gifts. LC 80-52058. (Illus.). 136p. (Orig.). 1980. pap. 5.95 (ISBN 0-88489-123-2). St Marys.
--New Wine: New Wineskins. 128p. (Orig.). 1981. pap. 6.80 (ISBN 0-8215-9807-4). Sadlier.
Dunning, John. Deadline. 224p. (Orig.). 1981. pap. 2.50 (ISBN 0-449-14398-8, GM). Fawcett.
Dunning, John & Stepford, John. World Directory of Multinational Enterprises, 2 vols. 1500p. 1980. 195.00 set (ISBN 0-686-65762-4); Vol. 1. (ISBN 0-87196-440-6); Vol. 2. (ISBN 0-87196-441-4). Facts on File.
Dunning, John H., ed. The Multinational Enterprise. 1971. text ed. 36.00x (ISBN 0-04-330189-4). Allen Unwin.
Dunning, Kenneth A. Getting Started in General Purpose Simulation System. LC 80-28281. 117p. (Orig.). 1981. pap. 5.95x (ISBN 0-910554-34-X). Eng Pr.
Dunning, Lawrence. Neutron Two Is Critical. 1977. pap. 1.75 (ISBN 0-380-01775-X, 35089). Avon.
--Taking Liberty. 496p. (Orig.). 1981. pap. 2.95 (ISBN 0-380-77297-3, 77297). Avon.
Dunning, R. W. Social & Economic Change Among the Northern Ojibwa. LC 60-50269. 1959. 12.50x o.p. (ISBN 0-8020-5073-5); pap. 5.00 (ISBN 0-8020-6131-1). U of Toronto Pr.
Dunning, Stephen. Walking Home Dead. (Poetry Ser.: No. 12). 40p. (Orig.). 1981. pap. 4.50 (ISBN 0-930020-11-1). Stone Country.
Dunning, Stephen & Howes, Alan B. Literature for Adolescents: Teaching Poems, Stories, Novels, & Plays. 491p. 1975. 9.95x (ISBN 0-673-05841-7). Scott F.
Dunning, Stephen N. The Tongues of Men. LC 79-10729. (American Academy of Religion, Dissertation Ser.: No. 27). 1979. 12.00 (ISBN 0-89130-283-2, 010127); pap. 7.50 (ISBN 0-89130-302-2). Scholars Pr Ca.
Dunning, Thomas & Dolan, T. P., eds. Piers Plowman: An Interpretation of the A Text. 2nd ed. 192p. 1980. 34.95x (ISBN 0-19-812446-5). Oxford U Pr.
Dunninger. One Hundred Classic Houdini Tricks You Can Do. LC 74-14200. (Illus.). 144p. 1975. pap. 3.50 (ISBN 0-668-03617-6). Arco.
Dunninger, J. Monument to Magic. 1974. 14.95 (ISBN 0-8184-0160-5). Lyle Stuart.
Dunninger, Joseph. Dunninger's Monument to Magic. LC 73-76824. 224p. 1974. 14.95 (ISBN 0-8184-0160-5). Lyle Stuart.
Dunphy, J. Englebert & Way, Lawrence W., eds. Current Surgical Diagnosis & Treatment. 4th ed. LC 79-88082. (Illus.). 1162p. 1979. lexotone cover 19.00 (ISBN 0-87041-193-4). Lange.
Dunphy, Philip W., ed. Career Development for the College Student. LC 76-8405. (gr. 9-12). 1976. pap. 4.75 o.p. (ISBN 0-910328-02-1). Carroll Pr.
--Career Development for the College Student. 5th ed. 128p. 1981. pap. 6.50 (ISBN 0-910328-02-1). Carroll Pr.
Dunphy, Thomas & Cummins, Thomas J. Remarkable Trials of All Countries; Particularly of the United States, Great Britain, Ireland & France: With Notes & Speeches of Counsel. Containing Thrilling Narratives of Fact from the Court-Room, Also Historical Reminiscences of Wonderful Events. 464p. 1981. Repr. of 1867 ed. lib. bdg. 35.00x (ISBN 0-8377-0512-6). Rothman.
Dunsany, Lord Edward. The Food of Death: Fifty-One Tales. Reginald, R. & Menville, Douglas, eds. LC 80-19151. (Newcastle Forgotten Fantasy Library: Vol. 3). Orig. Title: Fifty-One Tales. 138p. 1980. Repr. of 1974 ed. lib. bdg. 9.95x (ISBN 0-89370-502-0). Borgo Pr.
Dunsire, A. Administration: The Word & the Science. LC 73-7176. 262p. 1973. text ed. 13.95 (ISBN 0-470-22752-4). Halsted Pr.
Dunsire, A., jt. ed. see Chapman, Richard A.
Dunsker, Stewart, ed. Cervical Spondylosis. (Seminars in Neurological Surgery). 229p. 1980. text ed. 25.00 (ISBN 0-89004-421-X). Raven.
Dunsmore, I. R., jt. auth. see Aitchinson, J.
Dunsmore, I. R., jt. auth. see Aitchison, J.
Dunsmuir, Tom. The Continuing Story of Love of Chair. (Electric Company Ser.). (Illus.). (gr. 1-5). 1973. PLB 5.38 (ISBN 0-307-64822-2, Golden Pr). Western Pub.
--Fargo North Decoder, His Coat & Hat. (Electric Company Ser). (gr. 1-5). 1973. PLB 5.38 (ISBN 0-307-64820-6, Golden Pr). Western Pub.
Duns Scotus, John. Philosophical Writings of John Duns Scotus. Wolter, Allan, tr. 1964. pap. 4.95 (ISBN 0-672-60432-9, LLA194). Bobbs.
Dunstan, G. R., ed. see Kirk, Kenneth E.
Dunstan, John. Paths to Excellence & the Soviet School. (General Ser.). 1978. pap. text ed. 29.50x (ISBN 0-85633-150-3, NFER). Humanities.
Dunstan, Ralph. A Cyclopaedic Dictionary of Music. LC 72-14060. 642p. 1973. Repr. of 1925 ed. lib. bdg. 52.50 (ISBN 0-306-70559-1). Da Capo.
Dunster, Mark. Corky: Kel, Pt. 2. (Rin: Pt. 29). 82p. (Orig.). 1981. pap. 5.00 (ISBN 0-89642-072-8). Linden Pubs.
--Hoop, 2 vols. 140p. (Orig.). 1980. Set. pap. 8.00 (ISBN 0-89642-070-1). Linden Pubs.
--Jiggs. (Rin Ser.: Pt. 49). 82p. (Orig.). 1981. pap. 5.00 (ISBN 0-89642-076-0). Linden Pubs.
--Kel, Part 1: Les. (Rin Ser.: Pt. 28). (Illus.). 60p. 1981. pap. 4.00 (ISBN 0-89642-075-2). Linden Pubs.
--Octavian: Prolog to Actium, Antony, Pt. 10. 50p. (Orig.). 1981. pap. 4.00 (ISBN 0-89642-074-4). Linden Pubs.
--Sumner: John Brown, Second Prolog. 1980. pap. 4.00 (ISBN 0-89642-065-5). Linden Pubs.
--Tib. (The Holiday Ser.: Pt. 6: Easter). 77p. (Orig.). 1981. pap. 5.00 (ISBN 0-89642-077-9). Linden Pubs.
--Tiger. (Holiday Ser.: New Years Eve: Pt. 4). 79p. (Orig.). 1980. pap. 4.00 (ISBN 0-89642-068-X). Linden Pubs.
--Tuck. (Holiday Series, Thanksgiving: Pt. 2). 55p. (Orig.). 1981. pap. 4.00 (ISBN 0-89642-073-6). Linden Pubs.
Dunsworth, Charles E. A Treasury of Old & Historical American & British Furniture. (Illus.). 1979. deluxe ed. 37.85 (ISBN 0-930582-33-0). Gloucester Art.
Dunton, John. Teague Land or a Journey Among the Wilde Irish. 80p. 1981. Repr. 10.00x (ISBN 0-906127-25-4, Pub. by Irish Academic Pr Ireland). Biblio Dist.
Duong, Quyen Van see Van Duong, Quyen & Coburn, Jewell R.
Duong Thanh Binh, jt. auth. see Gage, William.
Du Pan, Jacques Mallet see Mallet Du Pan, Jacques.
Dupee, F. W. Henry James. LC 73-16722. 280p. 1974. pap. 2.95 (ISBN 0-688-06776-X). Morrow.
Dupee, F. W. see Trotsky, Leon.
Duplaix, Georges. The Big Brown Bear. (Illus.). (gr. k-3). 1946. PLB 5.00 (ISBN 0-307-60335-0, Golden Pr). Western Pub.
Duplaix, Michael. The Adventures of Captain William Walrus. (ps-3). 1972. PLB 7.62 o.p. (ISBN 0-307-64545-2, Golden Pr). Western Pub.
Du Plessis, N. Introduction to Potential Theory. (University Mathematical Monographs Ser.: No. 7). 1970. 13.75 o.s.i. (ISBN 0-02-844130-3). Hafner.
Duplessis, Yvonne. The Paranormal Perception of Colors. LC 75-19563. (Parapsychological Monograph: No. 16). 1975. pap. 5.50 (ISBN 0-912328-27-4). Parapsych Foun.
Duplissey, Claude, jt. auth. see Khailany, Asad.
Du Ponceau, Peter S. A Brief View of the Constitution of the United States. LC 72-124893. (American Constitutional & Legal History Ser.). 1974. Repr. of 1834 ed. lib. bdg. 14.95 (ISBN 0-306-71986-X). Da Capo.
Dupont, Betty, jt. ed. see Schlaich, Joan.
Du Pont, Diane. The French Passion. 1977. pap. 1.95 o.p. (ISBN 0-449-13888-7, GM). Fawcett.
DuPont, Elizabeth N. Landscaping with Native Plants in the Middle-Atlantic Region. Williams, Wick, ed. LC 78-21194. (Illus.). 1978. 6.95. Brandywine Conserv.
Dupont, Etienne. La Participation De la Bretagne a la Conquete De l'Angleterre Par les Normands. LC 80-2229. 1981. Repr. of 1911 ed. 17.50 (ISBN 0-404-18758-7). AMS Pr.
Dupont, Herbert & Dupont, Margaret. Travel with Health. (Appleton Consumer Health Guides). 195p. 1981. 13.95 (ISBN 0-8385-9009-8); pap. 7.95 (ISBN 0-8385-9008-X). ACC.
DuPont, Herbert L. Practical Antimicrobial Therapy. (Illus.). 1978. 8.75 (ISBN 0-8385-7869-1). ACC.
Dupont, Herbert L. & Pickering, Larry K. Infections of the Gastrointestinal Tract: Microbiology, Pathophysiology & Clinical Features. (Current Topics in Infectious Disease Ser.). (Illus.). 266p. 1980. 24.50 (ISBN 0-306-40409-5, Plenum Med Bk). Plenum Pub.

Dupont, J. L. & Madsen, J. H., eds. Algebraic Topology: Aarhus Nineteen Seventy-Eight. (Lecture Notes in Mathematics: Vol. 763). 695p. 1980. pap. 33.60 (ISBN 0-387-09721-X). Springer-Verlag.

DuPont, Marcella M. Definitions & Criteria. LC 65-16526. 1965. 3.50 (ISBN 0-8040-0065-4). Swallow.

Dupont, Margaret, jt. auth. see Dupont, Herbert.

Du Pontet, R. L., ed. see Caesar.

Dupre, Catherine. Kelston Knoll. 1981. pap. 2.75 (ISBN 0-451-09895-1, E9895, Sig). NAL.

--Kelston Knoll. 364p. 1980. 11.95 (ISBN 0-312-45137-7). St Martin.

DuPre, Flint O. Your Career in Federal Civil Service. 288p. 1981. pap. 4.95 (ISBN 0-06-463529-5, EH529, EH). Har-Row.

Dupre, Louis. The Deeper Self: A Meditation on Christian Mysticism. 128p. (Orig.). 1981. pap. 4.50 (ISBN 0-8245-0007-5). Crossroad NY.

--Transcendent Selfhood: The Loss & Rediscovery of the Inner Life. 1976. 8.95 (ISBN 0-8164-0306-6). Crossroad NY.

Dupre, N. J. The Classification & Structure of C-Algebra Bundles. LC 79-17975. (Memoirs Ser.: No. 222). 1979. 6.40 (ISBN 0-8218-2222-5). Am Math.

Dupree, Herbert & Dupree, Sherry. Busy Bookworm: Good Conduct Book. (Illus.). 1980. pap. 1.10. Displays Sch.

Dupree, Louis. Afghanistan: 1980 Edition. LC 76-154993. (Illus.). 784p. 1980. 35.00 (ISBN 0-691-00023-9); pap. 9.95. Princeton U Pr.

Dupree, Sherry, jt. auth. see Dupree, Herbert.

Dupreez, Peter. The Politics of Identity. 1980. 25.00 (ISBN 0-312-62697-5). St Martin.

Dupry, Renee J. The University Teaching of Social Sciences: International Law. 1967. pap. 6.00 (ISBN 92-3-100653-3, U707, UNESCO). Unipub.

Dupuch, S. P., ed. Bahamas Handbook & Businessman's Annual 1980-81. 18th ed. LC 61-45647. (Illus.). 1980. pap. 15.00x (ISBN 0-8002-2694-1). Intl Pubns Serv.

--Bahamas Handbook & Businessman's Annual, 1980 to 1981. 18th ed. (Illus.). 478p. (Orig.). 1980. pap. 15.00x (ISBN 0-8002-2694-1). Intl Pubns Serv.

Dupuy, R. J., ed. The Right to Health As a Human Right: Colloquim 1978 of the Hague Academy of International Law. 513p. 1980. 40.00x (ISBN 90-286-1028-6). Sijthoff & Noordhoff.

Dupuy, T. N. The Evolution of Weapons & Warfare. LC 80-781. 350p. 1980. 14.95 (ISBN 0-672-52050-8). Bobbs.

Dupuy, Trevor N. Military Life of Abraham Lincoln, Commander in Chief. LC 69-19688. (Military Lives Ser). (gr. 7 up). 1969. PLB 6.45 (ISBN 0-531-01874-1). Watts.

--Military Life of Adolph Hitler Fuhrer of Germany. LC 69-14500. (Military Lives Ser). (gr. 7 up). 1969. PLB 4.90 o.p. (ISBN 0-531-01873-3). Watts.

--Military Life of Alexander the Great of Macedon. LC 69-11604. (Military Lives Ser). (gr. 7 up). 1969. PLB 4.90 o.p. (ISBN 0-531-01875-X). Watts.

--Military Life of Frederick the Great of Prussia. LC 69-17460. (Military Lives Ser). (gr. 7 up). 1969. PLB 4.90 o.p. (ISBN 0-531-01876-8). Watts.

--The Military Life of Genghis Khan, Khan of Khans. LC 79-80894. (Military Lives Ser). 160p. 1969. PLB 4.90 o.p. (ISBN 0-531-01877-6). Watts.

--Military Life of George Washington, American Soldier. LC 69-15881. (Military Lives Ser). (gr. 7 up). 1969. PLB 4.90 o.p. (ISBN 0-531-01871-7). Watts.

--Military Life of Gustavus Adolphus: Father of Modern War. LC 79-77239. (Military Lives Ser). (gr. 7 up). 1969. PLB 6.45 (ISBN 0-531-01878-4). Watts.

--Military Life of Hannibal, Father of Strategy. LC 69-11602. (Military Lives Ser). (gr. 7 up). 1969. PLB 4.90 o.p. (ISBN 0-531-01879-2). Watts.

--Military Life of Napoleon, Emperor of the French. LC 73-87927. (Military Lives Ser). (gr. 7 up). 1969. PLB 4.90 o.p. (ISBN 0-531-01870-9). Watts.

--Military Life of Winston Churchill of Britain. LC 69-17459. (Military Lives Ser). (gr. 7 up). 1969. PLB 6.45 (ISBN 0-531-01881-4). Watts.

--Military Lives of Hindenburg & Ludendorff of Imperial Germany. LC 72-80895. (Military Lives Ser). (gr. 7 up). 1969. PLB 4.90 o.p. (ISBN 0-531-01882-2). Watts.

Dupuy, Trevor N., ed. Holidays: Days of Significance for All Americans. LC 65-21633. (gr. 9 up). 1965. PLB 6.90 (ISBN 0-531-01687-0). Watts.

Duquoc, Christian. Concrete Christian Life. LC 78-168653. (Concilium Ser.: Religion in the Seventies: Vol. 69). 1971. pap. 4.95 (ISBN 0-8164-2525-6). Crossroad NY.

--Gift of Joy. (Concilium Ser.: Vol. 39). pap. 6.95 (ISBN 0-8091-1578-6). Paulist Pr.

Duquoc, Christian, ed. Dimensions of Spirituality. (Concilium Ser.: Religion in the Seventies: Vol. 59). 1970. pap. 4.95 (ISBN 0-8164-2515-9). Crossroad NY.

Duquoc, Christian & Floristan, Casiano, eds. Discernment of the Spirit & the Spirits. (Concilium Ser.: Vol. 119). (Orig.). 1978. pap. 4.95 (ISBN 0-8164-2199-4). Crossroad NY.

--Models of Holiness. (The New Concilium: Vol. 129). 120p. (Orig.). 1980. pap. 4.95 (ISBN 0-8164-2037-8). Crossroad NY.

--Spiritual Revivals. LC 73-6432. (Concilium Ser.: Religion in the Seventies: Vol. 89). 156p. (Orig.). 1973. pap. 4.95 (ISBN 0-8164-2573-6). Crossroad NY.

Duquoc, Christian & Geffre, Claude, eds. The Prayer Life. LC 72-3944. (Concilium Ser.: Religion in the Seventies: Vol. 79). 156p. 1972. pap. 4.95 (ISBN 0-8164-2535-3). Crossroad NY.

Duquoc, Christian, jt. ed. see Floristan, Casiano.

Durack, Elizabeth, jt. auth. see Durack, Mary.

Durack, Mary & Durack, Elizabeth. Kookanoo & the Kangaroo. LC 66-15844. (Foreign Lands Bks). (gr. 2-7). 1966. PLB 3.95 o.p. (ISBN 0-8225-0356-5). Lerner Pubns.

Duram, James C. Norman Thomas. (U. S. Authors Ser.: No. 234). 1974. lib. bdg. 12.50 (ISBN 0-8057-0727-1). Twayne.

Duran, Cheli. Kindling. LC 78-23629. (gr. 7 up). 1979. 7.50 (ISBN 0-688-80199-4); PLB 7.20 (ISBN 0-688-84199-6). Greenwillow.

Duran, Cheli, ed. The Yellow Canary Whose Eye Is So Black: Poems from Spanish-Speaking Latin Amercica. LC 77-6354. (Eng. & Span.). (gr. 6 up). 1977. 14.95 (ISBN 0-02-732910-0, 732910). Macmillan.

Duran, Fr. Diego. Book of the Gods & Rites & the Ancient Calendar. Horcasitas, Fernando & Heyden, Doris, trs. LC 73-88147. (Civilization of the American Indian Ser.: No. 102). (Illus.). 1971. 19.95 (ISBN 0-8061-0889-4); pap. 9.95 (ISBN 0-8061-1201-8). U of Okla Pr.

Duran, Gloria. The Archetypes of Carlos Fuentes: From Witch to Androgne. 240p. 1980. 22.50 (ISBN 0-208-01775-5, Archon). Shoe String.

Duran, Helen C. de see De Duran, Helen C.

Duran, Manuel. Cervantes. LC 74-7006. (World Author's Ser.: Spain: No. 329). 1974. lib. bdg. 9.95 (ISBN 0-8057-2206-8). Twayne.

Duran, Manuel, ed. Graded Spanish Reader. 3rd ed. 1978. pap. text ed. 6.95x (ISBN 0-669-00880-X). Heath.

Duran, Richard P., ed. Latino Language & Communicative Behavior, Vol. 6. 384p. 1981. 29.50 (ISBN 0-89391-038-4). Ablex Pub.

Durand, Angelique. Mandarin Orange Sunday. 384p. (Orig.). 1981. pap. 2.75 (ISBN 0-553-14709-9). Bantam.

Durand, Douglas E., jt. auth. see Schoen, Sterling H.

Durand, John. Life & Times of Asher Brown Durand. LC 68-8688. (Library of American Art Ser). 1970. Repr. of 1894 ed. lib. bdg. 27.50 (ISBN 0-306-71167-2). Da Capo.

Durand, John & Miller, A. T. The Business of Trading in Stocks. Repr. of 1967 ed. flexible cover 5.00 (ISBN 0-87034-019-0). Fraser Pub Co.

Durand, Pauline & Languirand, Yolande. Brunch: Great Ideas for Planning, Cooking & Serving. LC 77-21616. 1978. pap. text ed. 2.95 (ISBN 0-8120-0726-3). Barron.

Durand, T. see Jackson, B. D., et al.

Durand, W. Fredrick, ed. Aerodynamic Theory: A General View of Progress, 6 vols. Incl. Vol. 1. Mathematical Aids, Fluid Mechanics, Historical Sketch. 12.00 (ISBN 0-8446-0603-0); Vol. 2. General Aerodynamic Theory, Perfect Fluids. 12.00 (ISBN 0-8446-0604-9); Vol. 3. Theory of Single Burbling, Mechanics of Viscous Fluids, Etc. 12.00 (ISBN 0-8446-0605-7); Vol. 4. Applied Airfoil Theory, Airplane Body Drag & Influence, Etc. 12.00 (ISBN 0-8446-0606-5); Vol. 5. Dynamics of the Airplane, Airplane Performance. 12.00 (ISBN 0-8446-0607-3); Vol. 6. Airplanes As a Whole, Aerodynamics of Airships, Etc. 12.00 (ISBN 0-8446-0739-8). Set. 72.00 (ISBN 0-8446-0602-2). Peter Smith.

Durand-Drouhin, Jean-Louis & Szwengrub, Lili-Marie, eds. Rural Community Studies in Europe: Trends, Selected & Annotated Bibliographies, Analyses, Vol. I. LC 80-41523. (Publications of the Vienna Centre Ser.). (Illus.). 342p. 1981. 70.50 (ISBN 0-08-021384-7). Pergamon.

Durant, David. Ralegh's Lost Colony. LC 80-65992. (Illus.). 320p. 1981. 12.95 (ISBN 0-689-11098-7). Atheneum.

Durant, David S. Ann Radcliffe's Novels: Experiments in Setting. Varma, Devendra P., ed. LC 79-8450. (Gothic Studies & Dissertations Ser.). 1980. lib. bdg. 21.00x (ISBN 0-405-12665-4). Arno.

Durant, Helen, jt. auth. see Durant, Kenneth.

Durant, Jack D. Richard Brinsley Sheridan. LC 75-1094. (English Authors Ser.: No. 183). 1975. lib. bdg. 12.50 (ISBN 0-8057-6650-2). Twayne.

--Richard Brinsley Sheridan: A Reference Guide. (Reference Books Ser.). 1981. lib. bdg. 30.00 (ISBN 0-8161-8146-2). G K Hall.

Durant, John. Highlights of the World Series. rev. 3rd ed. (Illus.). 208p. (gr. 6 up). 1973. 6.95g o.s.i. (ISBN 0-8038-3028-9). Hastings.

--The Story of Baseball. rev. 3rd ed. (Illus.). 302p. (gr. 6 up). 1973. 9.95 (ISBN 0-8038-6715-8). Hastings.

Durant, John & Etter, Les. Highlights of College Football. (gr. 7 up). 1970. 8.95 (ISBN 0-8038-3013-0). Hastings.

Durant, John R. & Smalley, Richard V. The Chronic Leukemias: Chemistry, Pathophysiology & Treatment. (Amer. Lec. Living Chemistry Ser). (Illus.). 240p. 1972. 19.75 (ISBN 0-398-02275-5). C C Thomas.

Durant, Kenneth & Durant, Helen. The Adirondack Guide-Boat. LC 80-80778. (Illus.). 224p. 1980. 30.00 (ISBN 0-87742-125-0). Intl Marine.

Durant, Mary. Who Named the Daisy? Who Named the Rose? LC 76-22513. (Illus.). 1977. 7.95 (ISBN 0-396-07332-8). Dodd.

Durant, Mary & Harwood, Michael. On the Road with John James Audubon. LC 79-22734. (Illus.). 576p. 1980. 19.95 (ISBN 0-396-07740-4). Dodd.

Durante, F. Western Europe & the Development of the Law of the Sea. 1980. 75.00 (ISBN 0-379-20288-3). Oceana.

Duras, Marguerita. The Little Horses of Tarquinia. Den Beeg, Peter, tr. 1980. pap. 4.95 (ISBN 0-7145-0348-7). Riverrun NY.

Duras, Marguerite. The Sailor from Gibraltar. 1980. pap. 6.95 (ISBN 0-7145-0511-0). Riverrun NY.

--Whole Days in the Trees. Barrows, Anita, tr. 1981. 10.95 (ISBN 0-7145-3820-5); pap. 5.95 (ISBN 0-7145-3854-X). Riverrun NY.

Durasoff, Steve. Bright Wind of the Spirit. LC 72-6536. 1976. pap. 2.95 o.p. (ISBN 0-88270-168-1). Logos.

--Pentecost Behind the Iron Curtain. LC 72-93080. 170p. (Orig.). 1973. pap. 2.95 o.p. (ISBN 0-88270-018-9). Logos.

Durbach, Errol. Ibsen the Romantic: Analogues of Paradise in the Later Plays. 192p. 1981. lib. bdg. 19.00x (ISBN 0-8203-0554-5). U of Ga Pr.

Durbach, Errol, ed. Ibsen & the Theatre: The Dramatist in Production. LC 79-47995. 1980. 25.00x (ISBN 0-8147-1773-X). NYU Pr.

Durbin, Harold C. Printing & Computer Technology. LC 80-65655. 206p. (Orig.). 1980. pap. 9.50 (ISBN 0-936786-00-0); pap. text ed. 8.50 (ISBN 0-936786-01-9). Durbin Assoc.

Durbin, John R. Modern Algebra: An Introduction. LC 78-15778. 1979. text ed. 19.50 (ISBN 0-471-02158-X); tchrs. manual avail. (ISBN 0-471-03753-2). Wiley.

Durbin, Mary L. Teaching Techniques: For Retarded & Pre-Reading Students. (Illus.). 276p. 1973. pap. 14.50 (ISBN 0-398-00487-0). C C Thomas.

Durbin, Richard L. & Springall, W. Herbert. Organization & Administration of Health Care: Theory, Practice, Environment. 2nd ed. LC 74-1114. 1974. 16.95 o.p. (ISBN 0-8016-1472-4). Mosby.

Durckheim, Karlfried. The Grace of Zen: Zen Texts for Meditation. 1977. pap. 3.95 (ISBN 0-8164-2151-X). Crossroad NY.

Durden, Robert F. The Climax of Populism: The Election of 1896. LC 65-11824. 208p. 1965. pap. 3.00x (ISBN 0-8131-0103-4). U Pr of Ky.

Durden-Smith, Jo. Who Killed George Jackson? Fantasies, Paranoia, & the Revolution. 1976. 10.00 o.p. (ISBN 0-394-48291-3). Knopf.

Durel, Marie. Speak English: A Practical Course for Foreign Students. (Orig.). 1972. pap. 3.95 (ISBN 0-06-463320-9, EH 320, EH). Har-Row.

Durer, Albert. Drawings of Albrecht Durer: Selected. (Illus.). 8.75 (ISBN 0-8446-0593-X). Peter Smith.

Durer, Albrecht. Of the Just Shaping of Letters. Nichol, tr. 7.50 (ISBN 0-8446-2016-5). Peter Smith.

--Of the Just Shaping of Letters: From the Applied Geometry of Albrecht Durer, Book 3. Nichol, R. T., tr. (Illus.). 1917. pap. 3.00 (ISBN 0-486-21306-4). Dover.

Dures, Alan & Dures, Katherine. Mao Tse-Tung. (Leaders Ser.). (Illus.). 96p. (gr. 9-12). 1980. 16.95 (ISBN 0-7134-1923-7, Pub. by Batsford England). David & Charles.

Dures, Katherine, jt. auth. see Dures, Alan.

Durey, Michael. The Return of the Plague: British Society & the Cholera 1831-32. 1979. text ed. 39.00x (ISBN 0-391-01038-7). Humanities.

Durey, Peter. Staff Management in University & College Libraries. Chandler, C., ed. 144p. 1976. text ed. 16.00 (ISBN 0-08-019718-3). Pergamon.

Durey De Noinville, Jacques B. Histoire Du Theatre De l'Academie Royale De Musique En France, Depuis Son Etablissement Jusqu' a Present, 2 vols. in 1. 2nd ed. 1981. Repr. of 1757 ed. 47.50 (ISBN 0-404-18838-9). AMS Pr.

Durfee, David A. Power in American Society: Burden or Blessing. Fraenkel, Jack R., ed. (Crucial Issues in American Government Ser.). (gr. 9-12). 1976. pap. text ed. 4.96 (ISBN 0-205-04907-9, 764907X). Allyn.

Durfee, Harold A., jt. auth. see Davis, Harold E.

Durfort, Claire de. Ourika. Fowles, John, tr. 1977. signed ed. 110.00 (ISBN 0-935072-01-2). W Thomas Taylor.

Durgin, J., jt. auth. see Bartilucci, A.

Durgin, Jane M., et al. Manual for Pharmacy Technicians. 2nd ed. LC 77-20007. (Illus.). 1978. pap. 15.50 (ISBN 0-8016-1479-1). Mosby.

Durgnat, Raymond. Durgnat on Film. (Illus.). 1976. pap. 7.95 (ISBN 0-571-10656-0, Pub. by Faber & Faber). Merrimack Bk Serv.

--Franju. movie ed. LC 68-31139. 1967. 7.95 (ISBN 0-520-00366-7); pap. 1.95 (ISBN 0-520-00367-5, CAL171). U of Cal Pr.

--Jean Renoir. LC 72-82221. (Illus.). 1975. 22.50 (ISBN 0-520-02283-1); pap. 4.95 (ISBN 0-520-02743-4). U of Cal Pr.

Durham. One Hundred Careers: How to Pick the One That's Best for You. 1977. 10.95 (ISBN 0-13-634717-7, Spec); pap. 4.95 (ISBN 0-13-634709-6). P-H.

Durham, Bill, ed. Steamboats & Modern Steam Launches. (Illus.). 631p. 1981. Repr. of 1963 ed. 25.00. A S Barnes.

--Steamboats & Modern Steam Launches. (Illus.). 631p. 1981. Repr. of 1963 ed. 25.00. Howell-North.

--Steamboats & Modern Steam Launches, 3 vols. LC 64-5849. (Illus.). 631p. 1980. Boxed Set. 27.50 (ISBN 0-8310-7126-5); 9.95 ea. Vol. 1, 206 Pp (ISBN 0-8310-7130-3). Vol. 2, 217 Pp (ISBN 0-8310-7131-1). Vol. 3, 208 Pp (ISBN 0-8310-7132-X). Howell-North.

Durham, Deanna. Life Among the Moonies: Three Years in the Unification Church. (Orig.). 1981. pap. 2.95 (ISBN 0-88270-496-6). Logos.

Durham, Jackie, jt. ed. see Joyner, Nelson T., Jr.

Durham, Philip & Jones, Everett, eds. Frontier in American Literature. LC 68-31708. 1969. pap. 8.95 (ISBN 0-672-63040-0). Odyssey Pr.

Durham, Quentin. Minigroup Science. (Illus.). 232p. (gr. 7-10). 1980. pap. 25.00 (ISBN 0-87879-244-9). Acad Therapy.

Durham, T. R. Introduction to Benefit-Cost Analysis for Evaluating Public Programs. (Learning Packages in the Policy Sciences: No. 14). (Illus.). 70p. (Orig.). 1979. pap. text ed. 3.50 (ISBN 0-936826-03-7). Pol Stud Assocs.

Durie, Alastair. The Scottish Linen Industry in the Eighteenth Century. (Illus.). 1979. text ed. 31.25x (ISBN 0-685-94719-X). Humanities.

Durie, G. M., jt. auth. see Russell, D. H.

During, Ingemar. Aristotle's De Partibus Animalium: Critical & Literary Commentaries. LC 78-66548. (Ancient Philosophy Ser.). 223p. 1980. lib. bdg. 22.00 (ISBN 0-8240-9602-9). Garland Pub.

--Ptolemaios und Porphyrios Uber Die Musik. LC 78-20290. (Ancient Philosophy Ser.). 293p. 1980. lib. bdg. 28.50 (ISBN 0-8240-9599-5). Garland Pub.

Durio, Alice. Cajun Columbus. LC 75-20484. (Illus.). 40p. (gr. 2 up). 1975. 7.95 (ISBN 0-88289-074-3). Pelican.

Durkheim, Emile. Division of Labor in Society. 1947. 14.95 (ISBN 0-02-907840-7); pap. text ed. 7.95 (ISBN 0-02-907850-4). Free Pr.

--Education & Sociology. LC 55-11002. 1956. 10.95 (ISBN 0-02-907920-9). Free Pr.

--Elementary Forms of the Religious Life. Swain, Joseph W., tr. 1965. 12.95 (ISBN 0-02-908000-2); pap. text ed. 7.95 (ISBN 0-02-908010-X). Free Pr.

--Evolution of Educational Thought: Lectures on the Formation & Development of Secondary Education in France. Collins, Peter, tr. from Fr. 1977. 25.00x (ISBN 0-7100-8446-3). Routledge & Kegan.

--Montesquieu & Rousseau: Forerunners of Sociology. 1960. pap. 3.95x (ISBN 0-472-08291-4, AA). U of Mich Pr.

--Moral Education. LC 59-6815. 1961. 12.95 (ISBN 0-02-908330-3); pap. text ed. 4.95 (ISBN 0-02-908320-6). Free Pr.

--Rules of Sociological Method. 8th ed. 1950. 10.95 (ISBN 0-02-908490-3); pap. text ed. 5.95 (ISBN 0-02-908500-4). Free Pr.

--Sociology & Philosophy. 1953. 12.95 (ISBN 0-02-908570-5). Free Pr.

--Sociology & Philosophy. Pocock, D. F., tr. LC 54-2835. 1974. pap. text ed. 1.95 (ISBN 0-02-908580-2). Free Pr.

--Suicide. 1951. 14.95 (ISBN 0-02-908650-7); pap. text ed. 4.95 (ISBN 0-02-908660-4). Free Pr.

Durkin. Teaching Young Children to Read. 3rd ed. 544p. 1980. text ed. 17.50 (ISBN 0-205-06903-7, 2369036). Allyn.

Durkin, Dolores. Children Who Read Early. LC 66-25980. 1966. text ed. 8.75x (ISBN 0-8077-1260-4). Tchrs Coll.

--Strategies for Identifying Words: A Workbook for Teachers & Those Preparing to Teach. 2nd ed. 1980. pap. 9.50 (ISBN 0-205-07229-1, 2372290). Allyn.

--Teaching Young Children to Read. 2nd ed. 448p. 1976. text ed. 13.95x o.s.i. (ISBN 0-205-05020-4). Allyn.

Durkin, Henry P. Forty-Four Hours to Change Your Life: Marriage Encounter. (Orig.). pap. 1.25 (ISBN 0-89129-139-3). Jove Pubns.

Durkin, James E., ed. Living Groups: Group Psychotherapy & General Systems Theory. 400p. 1981. 25.00 (ISBN 0-87630-253-3). Brunner-Mazel.

Durkin, Mary G. The Suburban Woman: Her Changing Role in the Church. 180p. 1975. 6.95 (ISBN 0-8164-1200-6). Crossroad NY.

Durkin, Mary G. & Anzia, Joan M. Marital Intimacy. 92p. 1980. pap. 6.95 (ISBN 0-8362-3601-7). Andrews & McMeel.

Durlacher, Jennifer, jt. ed. see Blauvelt, Euan.

Durland, William R. No King but Caesar? LC 74-30093. 184p. 1975. 6.95 (ISBN 0-8361-1757-3). Herald Pr.

Durnbaugh, Donald F. The Brethren in Colonial America. (Illus.). 659p. (YA) 1967. 13.95 (ISBN 0-87178-110-7). Brethren.

--European Origins of the Brethren. 463p. 1958. 8.95 (ISBN 0-87178-256-1). Brethren.

Durnell, Jane B. & Stevens, Norman D., eds. The Librarian: Selections from the Column of That Name by Edmund L. Pearson. LC 75-35725. 1976. 27.50 (ISBN 0-8108-0851-X). Scarecrow.

Durocher, Joseph F. Practical Ice Carving. 112p. 1981. pap. text ed. 9.95 (ISBN 0-8436-2206-7). CBI Pub.

Durodola, James I. Scientific Insights into Yoruba Traditional Medicine. (Traditional Healing Ser.). 1981. 27.50 (ISBN 0-932426-17-4). Trado-Medic.

Duron, J. Langue francaise, langue humaine. (Langue Vivante Ser). (Fr). pap. 8.25 (ISBN 0-685-13956-5, 3626). Larousse.

Durozoi, Gerard & Lecherbonnier, Bernard. Andre Breton: L'Ecriture surrealiste. (Collection themes et textes). 255p. (Orig., Fr.). 1974. pap. 6.50 (ISBN 2-03-035025-7, 2664). Larousse.

Durran, C. P. Dublin Decorative Plasterwork. 1967. 25.00 (ISBN 0-693-01112-2). Transatlantic.

Durran, I. M., jt. auth. see Cashell, G. T.

Durran, J. H. Statistics & Probability. LC 70-96086. (School Mathematics Project Handbks). 1970. text ed. 24.95 (ISBN 0-521-06933-5). Cambridge U Pr.

Durrant, Geoffrey H. William Wordsworth. (British Authors Ser). 28.50 (ISBN 0-521-07608-0); pap. 7.95 (ISBN 0-521-09584-0). Cambridge U Pr.

--Wordsworth & the Great System: A Study of Wordsworth's Poetic Universe. LC 78-92247. 1970. 34.00 (ISBN 0-521-07704-4). Cambridge U Pr.

Durrant, W. R., et al. Machine Printing. (Library of Printing Technology). Date not set. 17.95 (ISBN 0-8038-4671-1). Hastings.

Durrell, Gerald. Catch Me a Colobus. 1977. pap. 1.95 o.s.i. (ISBN 0-14-004337-3). Penguin.

Durrell, Julie & Rosner, Ruth. The Storytime Tiny Library, 4 bks. (Illus.). (ps-2). 1980. slipcased 5.95 (ISBN 0-525-69481-1, Gingerbread). Dutton.

Durrell, L. W., jt. auth. see Harrington, H. D.

Durrell, Lawrence. Alexandria Quartet. Incl. Justine; Balthazar; Mountolive; Clea. 1961. Set. pap. 15.95 (ISBN 0-525-47795-0). Dutton.

--Balthazar. 1961. pap. 2.50 o.p. (ISBN 0-525-47081-6). Dutton.

--Clea. 1961. pap. 2.50 o.p. (ISBN 0-525-47083-2). Dutton.

--Collected Poems Nineteen Thirty-One to Nineteen Seventy-Four. Brigham, James A., ed. 352p. 1980. 22.95 (ISBN 0-670-22792-7). Viking Pr.

--The Greek Islands. (Illus.). 1978. 25.00 o.p. (ISBN 0-670-35296-9, Studio). Viking Pr.

--The Ikons, & Other Poems. 2nd ed. LC 80-17105. (Mediterranean Culture Ser.). (Illus.). 64p. 1981. 15.00x (ISBN 0-933806-01-9). Black Swan CT.

--Justine. 1957. 5.95 o.p. (ISBN 0-525-13807-2); pap. 3.75 (ISBN 0-525-47080-8). Dutton.

--Key to Modern British Poetry. 1952. pap. 5.95 (ISBN 0-8061-0919-X). U of Okla Pr.

--Mountolive. 1961. pap. 2.50 o.p. (ISBN 0-525-47082-4). Dutton.

--Sappho: A Play in Verse. 1967. pap. 4.95 (ISBN 0-571-08161-4, Pub. by Faber & Faber). Merrimack Bk Serv.

--Sauve Qui Peut. (Illus.). 82p. 1980. 4.95 (ISBN 0-571-09224-1, Pub by Faber & Faber). Merrimack Bk Serv.

--Spirit of Place. Thomas, Alan G., ed. 1971. Repr. of 1969 ed. 10.00 o.p. (ISBN 0-525-20828-3). Dutton.

--Vega & Other Poems. LC 73-75122. 58p. 1973. 10.00 (ISBN 0-87951-009-9). Overlook Pr.

--White Eagles Over Serbia. LC 58-7779. 1958. 9.95 (ISBN 0-87599-030-4). S G Phillips.

Durrenmatt, Friedrich. Der Besuch der Alten Dame. Ackermann, Paul K., ed. LC 60-3863. (Ger). (gr. 11-12). 1960. pap. text ed. 7.20 (ISBN 0-395-04089-2). HM.

--Drei Horspiele. Regensteiner, Henry, ed. LC 79-22768. (Ger.). 1980. pap. text ed. 7.95x (ISBN 0-8290-0116-6). Irvington.

--Play Strindberg. Kirkup, James, tr. 1973. pap. 1.95 (ISBN 0-394-17798-3, E-612, Ever). Grove.

--The Quarry. 1979. pap. 1.95 (ISBN 0-446-79909-2). Warner Bks.

--Der Richter und Sein Henker. Gillis, William & Neumaier, J. J., eds. 1964. pap. text ed. 6.95 (ISBN 0-395-04499-5). HM.

--Der Verdacht. Gillis, William, ed. (gr. 9-12). 1964. pap. text ed. 7.20 (ISBN 0-395-04500-2). HM.

Durrenmatt, Friedrich see Otten, Anna.

Durrer, Gustav T., jt. auth. see Dolder, Eugene J.

Durry, Jean. Bicycling. Wadley, J. B., ed. (Illus.). 220p. 1980. 19.95 (ISBN 0-8069-9226-3, Pub by Guinness Superlatives England). Sterling.

Durso, Joseph, jt. auth. see Gehrig, Eleanor.

D'Urso, S. & Smith, R. A., eds. Changes, Issues & Prospects in Australian Education. 2nd ed. (Illus.). 333p. 1981. pap. text ed. 19.95x (ISBN 0-7022-1582-1). U of Queensland Pr.

Durst, Franz, et al, eds. Two-Phase Momentum, Heat & Mass Transfer in Chemical, Process, & Energy Engineering Systems, 2 vols. LC 79-12405. (Thermal & Fluid Engineering & Proceedings of the International Centre for Heat & Mass Transfer Ser.). (Illus.). 1079p. 1979. text ed. 105.00 set (ISBN 0-89116-154-6, Co-Pub by McGraw International). Hemisphere Pub.

Durst, Gary M. Management by Responsibility. (Illus.). 100p. 1980. pap. write for info. (ISBN 0-9602552-1-4). Ctr Art Living.

--Napkin Notes: On the Art of Living. LC 79-50554. (Illus.). 1979. pap. text ed. 4.95 o.p. (ISBN 0-9602552-0-6). Ctr Art Living.

--Napkin Notes: On the Art of Living. LC 79-50554. (Illus.). 200p. 1980. pap. 6.95 (ISBN 0-9602552-2-2). Ctr Art Living.

Durst, Lorraine S. & Durst, Sanford J. World Gold Coin Value Guide. LC 80-51832. 1980. softcover 9.00 (ISBN 0-686-64442-5); lib. bdg. 12.00 (ISBN 0-915262-54-1). S J Durst.

--World Silver Coin Value Guide. LC 80-51831. 1980. softcover 9.00 (ISBN 0-686-64441-7); lib. bdg. 12.00 (ISBN 0-915262-46-0). S J Durst.

Durst, Sanford J., jt. auth. see Durst, Lorraine S.

Durst, Sanford J., jt. auth. see Reisman, Daniel.

Dury, G. H. Map Interpretation. 19.50x (SpS). Soccer.

Dusek, Dorothy & Girdano, Daniel. Drugs: A Factual Account. 3rd ed. LC 79-21381. 1980. text ed. 8.95 (ISBN 0-201-02962-6). A-W.

Dusek, Dorothy, jt. auth. see Girdano, Daniel A.

Dusek, Jerome B., jt. auth. see Meyer, William J.

Dusen, C. R. Van see Cromwell, Harvey & Van Dusen, C. R.

Dusen Pysh, Margaret Van see Van Dusen Pysh, Margaret & Chalfant, James C.

Dusik, Dennis. Electricity Planning & the Environment: Toward a New Role for Government in the Decision Process. Date not set. price not set (ISBN 0-88410-638-1). Ballinger Pub.

Dusinberre, Juliet. Shakespeare & the Nature of Women. LC 75-3514. 1979. Repr. of 1975 ed. 23.50x (ISBN 0-06-491842-4). B&N.

Dussault, Gilles. Theory of Supervision in Teacher Education. LC 76-121817. (Illus.). 1970. pap. text ed. 6.50x (ISBN 0-8077-1261-2). Tchrs Coll.

Dussel, Enrique. History & the Theology of Liberation. Drury, John, tr. from Span. LC 75-21773. 205p. 1976. 8.95x o.p. (ISBN 0-88344-179-9). Orbis Bks.

Dussere, Carolyn, jt. tr. see Thomas, J. W.

Dust, Phillip, ed. Carmen Gratulans Adventu Serenissimi Principis Federici Comitis Palatini Ad Academian Cantalrig En Sem: An Edition with Introduction, Translation & Commentary, 2 vols. (Salzburg Studies in English Literature, Elizabethan & Renaissance Studies Ser.: No. 8). 1975. pap. text ed. 50.25x (ISBN 0-391-01367-X). Humanities.

Duster, Troy. The Legislation of Morality: Laws, Drugs & Moral Judgement. LC 72-80469. (Illus.). 1972. pap. text ed. 7.95 (ISBN 0-02-908680-9). Free Pr.

Dustoor, P. E. World of Words. 1968. 10.00x (ISBN 0-210-34050-9). Asia.

Duthie, Enid L. The Themes of Elizabeth Gaskell. 217p. 1980. 29.50x (ISBN 0-8476-6224-1). Rowman.

Duthrie, H. Gastrointestinal Motility. 1978. 39.50 (ISBN 0-8391-1268-8). Univ Park.

Dutka, JoAnna. Music in the English Mystery Plays. (Early Drama, Art, & Music Ser.). (Illus.). 171p. 1980. 18.80 (ISBN 0-918720-10-9); 11.801321. Medieval Inst.

Du Toit, Bettie. Ukubamba Amadolo. 155p. 1980. text ed. 15.75x (ISBN 0-906383-00-5). Humanities.

Du Toit, Brian M., ed. Ethnicity in Modern Africa. LC 78-58295. (Special Studies on Africa Ser.). 1978. lib. bdg. 27.50x (ISBN 0-89158-314-9). Westview.

Du Toit, Darcy. Capital & Labour in South Africa. (Monographs from the African Studies Centre, Leiden). 480p. 1981. price not set (ISBN 0-7103-0001-8). Routledge & Kegan.

Dutra, Francis A. A Guide to the History of Brazil: 1500 to 1822. LC 80-10933. 625p. 1980. lib. bdg. 52.50 (ISBN 0-87436-263-6). ABC Clio.

Dutt, Ashok K., ed. Contemporary Perspectives on the Medical Geography of South & Southeast Asia. (Illus.). 78p. 1980. pap. 20.00 (ISBN 0-08-026762-9). Pergamon.

Dutt, Gargi. Rural Communes in China - Organizational Problems. (Indian School of International Studies Series). 1968. 5.25x o.p. (ISBN 0-210-22704-4). Asia.

Dutt, Gargi & Dutt, V. P. China's Cultural Revolution. 1970. 10.00x (ISBN 0-210-98192-X). Asia.

Dutt, Indu, tr. see Tagore, Rabindranath.

Dutt, Toru. Ancient Ballads & Legends of Hindustan. 1975. 15.00 (ISBN 0-88253-496-3); pap. text ed. 6.75 (ISBN 0-88253-495-5). Ind-US Inc.

Dutt, V. P., jt. auth. see Dutt, Gargi.

Dutta, Reginald. Beginner's Guide to Tropical Fish: Fish Tanks, Aquarium Fish, Pond Fish, Ponds & Marines. 1977. 14.00 (ISBN 0-7207-0832-X). Transatlantic.

--Fell's Beginner's Guide to Tropical Fish & Fish Tanks. LC 75-4357. 1975. 7.95 (ISBN 0-8119-0254-4). Fell.

Dutta, S. & Kanunga, R. N. Affect & Memory: A Reformulation. LC 75-8628. 148p. 1975. text ed. 25.00 (ISBN 0-08-018270-4). Pergamon.

Dutta-Majumdar, D. & Das, J. Digital Computers' Memory Technology. 424p. 1980. 19.95x (ISBN 0-470-26932-4). Halsted Pr.

Duttarer, Janet & Edberg, E. Quadriplegia After Spinal Cord Injury: A Treatment Guide for Physical Therapists. LC 72-84793. 50p. 7.00x o.p. (ISBN 0-913590-03-7). C B Slack.

Dutton, Bertha P. Indians of the American Southwest. 336p. 1981. 17.50 (ISBN 0-8263-0551-2); pap. 8.95 (ISBN 0-8263-0552-0). U of NM Pr.

--The Pueblos. (Illus.). 112p. 1976. pap. text ed. 3.25 o.p. (ISBN 0-13-740159-0, Spec). P-H.

Dutton, G. J. Glucuronidation of Drugs & Other Compounds. 304p. 1980. 69.95 (ISBN 0-8493-5295-9). CRC Pr.

Dutton, Geoffrey. Australia's Last Explorer: Ernest Giles. (The Great Travellers Ser.). (Illus.). 1970. 7.50 (ISBN 0-571-09325-6, Pub. by Faber & Faber). Merrimack Bk Serv.

Dutton, June. The Adventures of the S. S. Happiness Crew: Cap'n Joshua's Dangerous Dilemma. (Illus.). 1980. 4.95 (ISBN 0-915696-36-3). Determined Prods.

Dutton, Robert R. Saul Bellow. (U. S. Authors Ser.: No. 181). lib. bdg. 12.50 (ISBN 0-8057-0044-7). Twayne.

Dutton, S. P., et al. Geology & Geohydrology of the Palo Duro Basin, Texas Panhandle: A Report on the Progress of Nuclear Waste Isolation Feasibility Studies. (Illus.). 99p. 1979. 2.50 (GC 79-1). Bur Econ Geology.

Duty, Guy. Divorce & Remarriage. LC 96-2485. 1967. 6.95 (ISBN 0-87123-097-6, 230097). Bethany Fell.

--Escape from the Coming Tribulation. LC 75-17979. 160p. (Orig.). 1975. pap. 2.95 (ISBN 0-87123-131-X, 210131). Bethany Fell.

--God's Covenants & Our Time. LC 73-8587. 1964. pap. 2.45 (ISBN 0-87123-180-8, 210180). Bethany Fell.

--If Ye Continue. LC 82-2314. 1966. pap. 4.95 (ISBN 0-87123-243-X, 210243). Bethany Fell.

Duty, Lenna P. Collected Poems. Date not set. 4.95 (ISBN 0-533-04771-4). Vantage.

Duus, Peter. The Rise of Modern Japan. LC 75-33416. (Illus.). 304p. 1976. text ed. 13.50 (ISBN 0-395-20665-0). HM.

Duval, Evelyn M. Por Que Esperar Hasta el Matrimonio? Deiros, Pablo A., tr. from Eng. Orig. Title: Why Wait till Marriage? 1979. pap. 2.25 (ISBN 0-311-46044-5, Edit Mundo). Casa Bautista.

DuVal, F. Alan, et al. Moderne Deutsche Sprachlehre. 3rd ed. 672p. 1980. text ed. 15.95 (ISBN 0-394-32345-9); wkbk. 6.95 (ISBN 0-394-32406-4); tapes 200.00 (ISBN 0-394-32407-2); individualized instruction program 5.95 (ISBN 0-394-32434-X). Random.

Duval, Godfrey R. British Flying Boats & Amphibians, 1909-1952. LC 66-19522. (Illus.). 1966. 8.75 o.p. (ISBN 0-370-00031-5). Aero.

Duval, Jean-Jacques. Working with Stained Glass: Fundamental Techniques & Applications. LC 74-184975. (Illus.). 1972. 10.95 o.s.i. (ISBN 0-690-89706-5, TYC-T). T Y Crowell.

--Working with Stained Glass: Fundamental Techniques & Applications. LC 74-184975. (Funk & W Bk.). (Illus.). 144p. 1975. pap. 5.95 (ISBN 0-308-10153-7, F112, TYC-T). T Y Crowell.

Duval, Jeanne. The Ravishers. (Orig.). 1980. pap. 2.50 (ISBN 0-451-09523-5, E9523, Sig). NAL.

Duval, John C. The Adventures of Big-Foot Wallace. Major, Mabel & Lee, Rebecca S., eds. LC 36-334. 1966. pap. 4.50 (ISBN 0-8032-5053-3, BB 343, Bison). U of Nebr Pr.

Du Val, P. Elliptic Functions & Elliptic Curves. (Condon Mathematical Society Lecture Notes Ser.: No. 9). (Illus.). 200p. 1972. 26.50 (ISBN 0-521-20036-9). Cambridge U Pr.

Duval, William & Monahan, Valerie. Collecting Postcards in Color 1894-1914. (Illus.). 1978. 10.95 (ISBN 0-7137-0823-9, Pub. by Blandford Pr England). Sterling.

Duvall, Charles R., jt. auth. see Krepel, Wayne J.

Duvall, Evelyn M. Marriage & Family Development. 5th ed. LC 76-30744. 1977. scp 19.50 (ISBN 0-397-47362-1, HarpC). Har-Row.

Duvall, Evelyn M. & Hill, Reuben L. Being Married. 1960. text ed. 9.95x o.p. (ISBN 0-669-22780-3). Heath.

DuVall, J. Barry, et al. Getting the Message. LC 79-57016. (Technology Ser.). 384p. 1981. text ed. 15.50 (ISBN 0-87192-123-5, 000-6); tchr's guide 18.60 (ISBN 0-87192-125-1, 00-6A); activity manual 5.95 (ISBN 0-87192-124-3, 00-6B). Davis Mass.

Du Vall, Stephen. The Song of Hero. 1977. 4.00 o.p. (ISBN 0-682-48860-7). Exposition.

Duvall, W. L., jt. auth. see Obert, Leonard.

Duveen, Anneta, jt. auth. see Motz, Lloyd.

Duvillard, A. & Toussaint, J. P. Ski Waxing for High Performance. LC 77-21481. 1977. pap. 2.50 (ISBN 0-8120-0865-0). Barron.

Duvoisin, Roger. Donkey-Donkey. LC 68-11655. (Illus.). (gr. k-3). 1968. 5.95 o.s.i. (ISBN 0-8193-0209-0, Four Winds); PLB 5.41 o.s.i. (ISBN 0-8193-0210-4). Schol Bk Serv.

Duvoisin, Roger C. Parkinson's Disease: A Guide for Patient & Family. LC 76-19845. 1978. 19.00 (ISBN 0-89004-205-5); pap. 12.00 (ISBN 0-685-87129-0). Raven.

Duxbury, A. The Earth & Its Oceans. LC 73-131202. (Earth Science Ser.). 1971. 19.95 (ISBN 0-201-01616-8). A-W.

Duxler, Margot, jt. auth. see Sala, Andre.

Duyckaerts, Francois. The Sexual Bond. 1970. 6.95 o.p. (ISBN 0-440-07847-4). Delacorte.

Duyckinck, Evert A. & Duyckinck, George L. Cyclopaedia of American Literature, 2 vols. Simons, M. Laird, ed. LC 66-31801. 1965. Repr. of 1875 ed. Set. 68.00 (ISBN 0-8103-3021-0). Gale.

Duyckinck, George L., jt. auth. see Duyckinck, Evert A.

Duyn, John Van see Van Duyn, John & Southworth.

Duyne, Carl Van see Van Duyne, Carl.

Duyvendak, Jan J., tr. see Ching-Shan.

Dvinov, Boris. Ot Legal 'nostik Podpol'-Iu (From Legality to the Underground) LC 67-19592. (Foreign Language Ser.: No. 2). (Rus). 1968. 8.00 (ISBN 0-8179-4021-9). Hoover Inst Pr.

Dvorin, Eugene P. & Misner, Arthur J. Governments Within the States. LC 70-136121. (Political Science Ser). 1971. pap. 5.95 (ISBN 0-201-01620-6). A-W.

Dvorin, Eugene P. & Simmons, Robert H. From Amoral to Humane Bureaucracy: The Coming Journey of Public Administration. (Orig.). 1972. pap. text ed. 6.50 scp (ISBN 0-06-382585-6, HarpC). Har-Row.

Dvorkin, Elizabeth & Himmelstein, Jack. Becoming a Lawyer: A Humanistic Perspective on Legal Education, Professionalism. 200p. 1981. pap. text ed. 17.95 (ISBN 0-8299-2126-5). West Pub.

Dvornik, F. Photian Schism. 1970. 70.00 (ISBN 0-521-07770-2). Cambridge U Pr.

Dvornik, Francis. Byzantine Missions Among the Slavs. (Byzantine Ser). (Illus.). 1970. 32.50 (ISBN 0-8135-0613-1). Rutgers U Pr.

--The Slavs in European History & Civilization. 726p. 1975. pap. 12.50x (ISBN 0-8135-0799-5). Rutgers U Pr.

Dvos, H. J. & Dyos, H. J., eds. Urban History Yearbook, 1978. 255p. 1978. pap. 18.75x (ISBN 0-8476-3164-8). Rowman.

Dwarakanath, T. Guide to Practicals in Electronics. 1968. pap. 4.50x (ISBN 0-210-26932-4). Asia.

Dward, Jeannette W. I Have a Question, God. (gr. 3-7). 4.95 (ISBN 0-8054-4265-0). Broadman.

Dwarkadas, K. Forty-Five Years with Labour. 6.95x o.p. (ISBN 0-210-33983-7). Asia.

Dweck, Carol S., jt. auth. see Langer, Ellen J.

Dwek, Raymond, jt. auth. see Price, Nicholas.

Dwek, Raymond A. Nuclear Magnetic Resonance (Nmr) in Biochemistry: Applications to Enzyme Systems. (Monographs on Physical Biochemistry Ser.). 387p. 1974. 42.00x (ISBN 0-19-854614-9). Oxford U Pr.

Dwelley. Spring Wildflowers of N. E. 1980. pap. 6.95 (ISBN 0-89272-008-5). Down East.

--Summer & Fall Wildflowers of N. E. 1980. pap. 8.95 (ISBN 0-89272-020-4). Down East.

--Trees & Shrubs of New England. 425p. 1980. 12.95 (ISBN 0-89272-064-6). Down East.

Dwelly. Illustrated Gaelic-English Dictionary. 8th ed. (Illus.). 35.00x (ISBN 0-686-00868-5). Colton Bk.

Dwiggins, B. Automotive Air Conditioning. LC 76-14093. (gr. 9-12). 1978. pap. 11.00 (ISBN 0-8273-1007-2); instructor's guide 3.00 (ISBN 0-8273-1008-0). Delmar.

Dwiggins, Boyce. Automobile Repair Guide. 4th ed. LC 78-50206. 1978. 14.95 (ISBN 0-672-23291-X). Audel.

Dwiggins, Boyce H. Automotive Electricity. (Illus.). 352p. 1981. text ed. 18.95 (ISBN 0-8359-0268-4); pap. text ed. 12.95 (ISBN 0-8359-0267-6). Reston.

Dwiggins, Don. Bailout: The Story of Parachuting & Skydiving. LC 69-10892. (America in the Making Ser). (Illus.). (gr. 5 up). 1969. 5.95g o.s.i. (ISBN 0-02-732890-2, CCPr). Macmillan.

--Build Your Own Sport Plane. 1979. pap. 6.95 (ISBN 0-8015-0971-8, Hawthorn). Dutton.

Dwight, Allan. Drums in the Forest. (Illus.). (gr. 7 up). 1936. 8.95 (ISBN 0-02-732960-7). Macmillan.

--To the Walls of Cartagena. LC 67-21645. (Young Readers Ser.). (Illus., Orig.). (gr. 4-7). 1967. 3.95 o.p. (ISBN 0-910412-59-6). Williamsburg.

Dwight, Henry Otis, et al, eds. Encyclopedia of Missions: Descriptive, Historical, Biographical, Statistical. 2nd ed. LC 74-31438. 851p. 1975. Repr. of 1904 ed. 44.00 (ISBN 0-8103-3325-2). Gale.

Dwight, John A. & Peel, William J. Video Reading Technics, Bk. 1. 1976. pap. text ed. 4.80 (ISBN 0-934902-00-3); tchr's ed. 10.00 (ISBN 0-934902-04-6). Learn Concepts OH.

Dwight, John A. & Speer, Dana C. How to Write a Research Paper. LC 79-3012. (gr. 11-12). 1979. pap. text ed. 6.95 (ISBN 0-934902-01-1); tchr's ed. 30.00 (ISBN 0-934902-02-X); work pad 1.50 (ISBN 0-934902-03-8). Learn Concepts OH.

Dwight, Ravena. Buck Rogers & the Children of Hopetown. (A Young Reader Ser.). (Illus.). (gr. k-3). 1979. PLB 5.00 (ISBN 0-307-60500-0, Golden Pr). Western Pub.

Dwight, Revena. Bert's Hall of Great Inventions. (Sesame Street Bks.). (Illus.). 1972. PLB 5.00 (ISBN 0-307-60321-0, Golden Pr). Western Pub.

Dwight, Theodore. History of the Hartford Convention. LC 77-99474. (American Constitutional & Legal History Ser). 1970. Repr. of 1833 ed. 45.00 (ISBN 0-306-71855-3). Da Capo.

Dwight, Timothy. Major Poems: 5 Vols. in 1. LC 68-24207. 1969. 52.00x (ISBN 0-8201-1059-0). Schol Facsimiles.

Dwivedi, A. N. Indian Poetry in English: A Literary History & Anthology. 159p. 1980. text ed. 9.50x (ISBN 0-391-01789-6). Humanities.

Dwivedi, D. N. Managerial Economics. 1980. text ed. 20.00x (ISBN 0-7069-0794-9, Pub. by Vikas India). Advent Bk.

Dwivedi, S. Hindi on Trial. 250p. 1980. text ed. 25.00x (ISBN 0-7069-1210-1, Pub by Vikas India). Advent Bk.

Dworak, Robert J. Taxpayers, Taxes, & Government Spending: Perspectives on the Taxpayers Revolt. 272p. 1980. 24.95 (ISBN 0-03-056111-6); pap. 9.95 (ISBN 0-03-056109-4). Praeger.

Dworetzky, John. Developmental Psychology. (Illus.). 550p. 1981. pap. text ed. 12.76 (ISBN 0-8299-0368-2). West Pub.

Dwork, Martin, ed. Dewey on Education: Selections, with an Introduction & Notes. LC 59-15893. (Illus.). 1959. text ed. 8.50 (ISBN 0-8077-1266-3); pap. text ed. 3.95x (ISBN 0-8077-1263-9). Tchrs Coll.

Dworkin, Andrea. Pornography: Men's Graphic Depiction of Whores. 288p. 1981. 12.95 (ISBN 0-399-12619-8, Perigee); pap. 5.95 (ISBN 0-399-50532-6). Putnam.

Dworkin, Daniel, jt. auth. see Baumann, Duane.

Dworkin, Florence, jt. auth. see Dworkin, Stanley.

Dworkin, Floss & Dworkin, Stan. Floss & Stan's "Why Are My Leaves Turning Yellow & Falling Off" Answer Book. 1978. 9.95 o.p. (ISBN 0-87690-267-0). Dutton.

Dworkin, Floss, jt. auth. see Dworkin, Stan.

Dworkin, Rita, jt. auth. see Adelman, Irving.

Dworkin, Samuel F., et al. Behavioral Science & Dental Practice. new ed. LC 77-26634. (Illus.). 1978. text ed. 16.95 (ISBN 0-8016-1484-8). Mosby.

Dworkin, Stan & Dworkin, Floss. The Good Goodies. 1979. pap. 2.50 (ISBN 0-449-23964-0, Crest). Fawcett.

Dworkin, Stan, jt. auth. see Dworkin, Floss.

Dworkin, Stanley & Dworkin, Florence. Bake Your Own Bread. (Illus.). 224p. 1973. pap. 1.95 (ISBN 0-451-09424-7, J9424, Sig). NAL.

Dworkin, Susan, jt. auth. see Cooke, Cynthia W.

Dworsky, Lawrence N. Modern Transmission Line Theory & Applications. LC 79-9082. 1979. 21.50 (ISBN 0-471-04086-X, Pub. by Wiley-Interscience). Wiley.

Dwyer, D. J. People & Housing in Third World Cities. LC 74-84346. (Illus.). 30p. 1979. pap. text ed. 13.95x (ISBN 0-582-49017-0). Longman.

Dwyer, Daisy H. Images & Self-Images. (Illus.). 1978. 13.00x (ISBN 0-231-04302-3); pap. 5.50x (ISBN 0-231-04303-1). Columbia U Pr.

Dwyer, Fred. Georgian People. 1978. 16.95 (ISBN 0-7134-0045-5, Pub. by Batsford England). David & Charles.

Dwyer, John, ed. Medicine: PreTest Self-Assessment & Review. LC 77-86707. (Clinical Sciences: PreTest Self-Assessment & Review Ser.). (Illus.). 1978. pap. 9.95 (ISBN 0-07-051601-4). McGraw-Pretest.

Dwyer, John N. Summer Gold: A Camper's Guide to Amateur Prospecting. LC 73-19267. 1974. 5.95 o.p. (ISBN 0-684-13706-2, ScribT). Scribner.

Dwyer, Joseph D. Russia, the Soviet Union & Eastern Europe: A Survey of Holdings at the Hoover Institution on War, Revolution & Peace. LC 78-70888. (Survey Ser.: No. 6). 245p. 1980. 18.95 (ISBN 0-8179-5011-7). Hoover Inst Pr.

Dwyer, Richard E. Labor Education in the U. S. An Annotated Bibliography. LC 77-21572. 1977. 14.50 (ISBN 0-8108-1058-1). Scarecrow.

Dwyer, Thomas & Critchfield, Margot. You Paid One Thousand Dollars for a Personal What? (Orig.). 1980. pap. 11.95 (ISBN 0-07-018492-5, BYTE Bks). McGraw.

Dwyer, William W. A Study of John Webster's Use of Renaissance Natural & Moral Philosophy. (Salzburg Studies in English Literature, Jacobean Drama Studies: No. 18). 206p. 1973. pap. text ed. 25.00x (ISBN 0-391-01368-8). Humanities.

Dwyer-Joyce, Alice. The Glitter-Dust. LC 77-25771. 1978. 7.95 o.p. (ISBN 0-312-32947-4). St Martin.

--Lachlan's Woman. LC 78-19863. 1979. 7.95 o.p. (ISBN 0-312-46359-6). St Martin.

--The Penny-Box. 192p. 1981. 8.95 (ISBN 0-312-60002-X). St Martin.

--The Storm of Wrath. LC 77-6153. 1978. 7.95 o.p. (ISBN 0-312-76248-8). St Martin.

Dyak, Miriam. Dying. LC 78-70873. 1978. pap. 3.00 (ISBN 0-934678-00-6). New Victoria Pubs.

Dyboski, Roman. Seven Years in Russia & Siberia, 1914-1921. Coleman, Marion M., tr. from Polish. LC 79-137001. (Illus., Orig.). 1971. pap. 5.00 (ISBN 0-910366-09-8). Alliance Coll.

Dybwad, Gunnar. Challenges in Mental Retardation. 1964. 15.00 o.p. (ISBN 0-231-02702-8). Columbia U Pr.

Dyce, James M. Stress & Decision Making in the Dental Practice. (Illus.). 165p. 1973. 24.00. Quint Pub Co.

Dychtwald, Ken. Bodymind. 1978. pap. 2.25 (ISBN 0-515-05561-1). Jove Pubns.

Dychtwald, Kenneth, jt. ed. see Villoldo, Alberto.

Dyck, et al. Computing: An Introduction to Structured Problem Solving Using Pascal. 1981. text ed. 18.95 (ISBN 0-8359-0902-6); instr's. manual free (ISBN 0-8359-0903-4). Reston.

Dyck, C. J. An Introduction to Mennonite History. 400p. 1981. pap. 9.95 (ISBN 0-8361-1955-X). Herald Pr.

Dyck, J. W. Boris Pasternak. (World Authors Ser.: Russia: No. 225). lib. bdg. 10.95 (ISBN 0-8057-2678-0). Twayne.

Dyckman, Katharine M., jt. auth. see Carroll, L. Patrick.

Dyckman, Thomas & Thomas, L. Joseph. Algebra & Calculus for Business. (Illus.). 464p. 1974. text ed. 18.95 (ISBN 0-13-021758-1). P-H.

Dyckman, Thomas, et al. Efficient Capital Markets & Accounting: A Critical Analysis. (Contemporary Topics in Accounting Ser.). (Illus.). 144p. 1975. pap. 9.95 (ISBN 0-13-246967-7). P-H.

Dyckman, Thomas R. & Thomas, L. Joseph. Fundamental Statistics for Business & Economics. 1977. 19.95 (ISBN 0-13-344523-2). P-H.

D'Ydewalle, Gery & Lens, Willy, eds. Cognition in Human Motivation & Learning. LC 80-23715. 380p. 1981. text ed. 15.00 (ISBN 0-89859-067-1). L Erlbaum Assocs.

Dye & Zeigler. The Irony of Democracy. 420p. 1981. pap. text ed. 12.95 (ISBN 0-87872-278-5). Duxbury Pr.

Dye, Daniel S. The New Book of Chinese Lattice Designs. (Pictorial Archive Ser.). (Illus.). 128p. (Orig.). 1981. pap. price not set (ISBN 0-486-24128-9). Dover.

Dye, Frank & Dye, Margaret. Ocean Crossing Wayfarer. 1977. 14.95 (ISBN 0-7153-7371-4). David & Charles.

Dye, Gerald. Acts. (Double Trouble Puzzles Ser.). (Illus.). 1977. pap. 1.25 (ISBN 0-87239-151-5, 2822). Standard Pub.

--Growing in Christ. (Double Trouble Puzzles Ser.). 48p. (Orig.). (gr. 6 up). 1981. pap. 1.25 (ISBN 0-87239-447-6, 2837). Standard Pub.

--Hebrews. (Double Trouble Puzzles Ser.). (Illus.). 1977. pap. 1.25 (ISBN 0-87239-154-X, 2825). Standard Pub.

--Matthew. (Double Trouble Puzzles Ser.). (Illus.). 1977. pap. 1.25 (ISBN 0-87239-149-3, 2820). Standard Pub.

--Paul's Letters to Churches. (Double Trouble Puzzles Ser). (Illus.). 1977. pap. 1.25 (ISBN 0-87239-152-3, 2823). Standard Pub.

--Paul's Letters to His Friends. (Double Trouble Puzzles Ser). (Illus.). 1977. pap. 1.25 (ISBN 0-87239-153-1, 2824). Standard Pub.

--Writings of John. (Double Trouble Puzzles Ser.). (Illus.). 1977. pap. 1.25 (ISBN 0-87239-150-7, 2821). Standard Pub.

Dye, H. Allan, jt. auth. see Diedrich, Richard C.

Dye, Harold E. No Rocking Chair for Me. 1980. pap. 3.95 (ISBN 0-8054-5286-9). Broadman.

Dye, Joseph M. Ways to Shiva: Life & Ritual in Hindu India. LC 80-25113. (Illus.). 94p. (Orig.). 1980. pap. 4.95 (ISBN 0-87633-038-3). Phila Mus Art.

Dye, Margaret, jt. auth. see Dye, Frank.

Dye, O. David & Baxter, Gerald D. Speech Communication Laboratory Manual. 1977. pap. text ed. 4.95 (ISBN 0-8403-1765-4). Kendall-Hunt.

Dye, Thomas R. Politics in States & Communities. 4th ed. (Illus.). 512p. 1981. text ed. 16.95 (ISBN 0-13-685131-2). P-H.

--Understanding Public Policy. 4th ed. (Illus.). 464p. 1981. text ed. 16.95 (ISBN 0-13-936260-6). P-H.

--Understanding Public Policy. 3rd ed. (Illus.). 1978. text ed. 16.95 (ISBN 0-13-936195-2). P-H.

Dyen, D. & Aberle, D. F. Lexical Reconstruction. LC 73-92780. (Illus.). 484p. 1974. 59.50 (ISBN 0-521-20369-4). Cambridge U Pr.

Dyer, Alan D. The City of Worcester in the Sixteenth Century. 320p. 1971. text ed. 15.00x (ISBN 0-7185-1102-6, Leicester). Humanities.

Dyer, Anne. Design Your Own Stuffed Toys. LC 75-105680. (Illus.). 1970. 8.50 (ISBN 0-8231-5021-6). Branford.

--Dyes from Natural Sources. 88p. 1976. 7.50 (ISBN 0-8231-5049-6). Branford.

Dyer, Carole, jt. ed. see Marsh, Judy.

Dyer, Ceil. Coffee Cookery. LC 78-6188. (Illus.). 1978. 7.95 o.p. (ISBN 0-89586-010-4); pap. 4.95 (ISBN 0-89586-009-0). H P Bks.

--Plan-Ahead Cookbook. 1970. pap. 1.50 o.s.i. (ISBN 0-02-009440-X, Collier). Macmillan.

--Wok Cookery. LC 77-83279. (Illus.). 1977. pap. 5.95 (ISBN 0-912656-75-1). H P Bks.

Dyer, Christopher. Lords & Peasants in a Changing Society: The Estates of the Bishopric of Worcester, 680-1540. LC 79-51225. (Past & Present Publications Ser.). (Illus.). 466p. 1980. 49.50 (ISBN 0-521-22618-X). Cambridge U Pr.

Dyer, D. G., tr. see Bidermann, Jacob.

Dyer, Dewey A. So You Want to Start a Restaurant? LC 71-168741. 1971. 12.95 (ISBN 0-8436-0535-9). CBI Pub.

--So You Want to Start a Restaurant? rev. 2nd ed. 192p. 1981. 12.95 (ISBN 0-8436-2199-0). CBI Pub.

Dyer, Esther & Berger, Pam, eds. Public School & Academic Media Centers: A Guide to Information Sources. LC 74-11554. (Books, Publishing & Libraries Information Guide Ser.: Vol. 3). 350p. 1980. 30.00 (ISBN 0-8103-1286-7). Gale.

Dyer, Esther R. Cooperation in Library Service to Children. LC 77-28190. 1978. 10.00 (ISBN 0-8108-1111-1). Scarecrow.

Dyer, George. Odes by George Dyer, M. Robinson, Anna Laetitia Barbauld, Repr. Of 1800 Ed. Reiman, Donald H., ed. Bd. with The Poet's Fate, a Poetical Dialogue. Repr. of 1797 ed. LC 75-31197. (Romantic Context Ser.: Poetry 1789-1830). 1979. lib. bdg. 47.00 (ISBN 0-8240-2148-7). Garland Pub.

--Poems, 2 vols. in 1. LC 75-31198. (Romantic Context Ser.: Poetry 1789-1830: Vol. 50). 1978. Repr. of 1802 ed. lib. bdg. 47.00 (ISBN 0-8240-2149-5). Garland Pub.

Dyer, George, ed. An American Catholic Catechism. LC 75-7786. 320p. 1975. 10.00 o.p. (ISBN 0-8164-1196-4); pap. 4.95 (ISBN 0-8164-2588-4). Crossroad NY.

Dyer, Henry. Parents Can Understand Testing. LC 80-80939. 1980. pap. 3.50 (ISBN 0-934460-08-6). NCCE.

Dyer, J. Applications of Absorption Spectroscopy of Organic Compounds. 1965. pap. 10.95 (ISBN 0-13-038802-5). P-H.

Dyer, James. Southern England: An Arcaeological Guide. (Illus., Orig.). 1973. pap. 10.95 (ISBN 0-571-10334-0, Pub. by Faber & Faber). Merrimack Bk Serv.

--Your Book of Prehistoric Britain. (Your Book Ser.). (Illus.). (gr. 5 up). 1974. 7.95 (ISBN 0-571-09883-5, Pub. by Faber & Faber). Merrimack Bk Serv.

Dyer, James A., jt. auth. see Bernstein, Robert A.

Dyer, James S., jt. auth. see Buffa, Elwood S.

Dyer, Jean R. Understanding & Evaluating Educational Research. LC 78-67952. (Education Ser.). (Illus.). 1979. text ed. 17.95 (ISBN 0-201-01184-0). A-W.

Dyer, Jon C. Handbook of Industrial Wastes Pretreatment. LC 79-25702. 300p. 1981. lib. bdg. 32.50 (ISBN 0-8240-7066-6). Garland Pub.

Dyer, K. R., ed. Estuarine Hydrography & Sedimentation. LC 78-67308. (Illus.). 1980. 47.50 (ISBN 0-521-22435-7); pap. 15.95 (ISBN 0-521-29496-7). Cambridge U Pr.

Dyer, Lee, ed. A & P: Past, Present & Future. (Illus.). 4.95 o.p. (ISBN 0-911790-06-3). Prog Grocer.

Dyer, Louise, tr. see Cossa, Luigi.

Dyer, Mike. Getting into Pro Baseball. (Getting into the Pros Ser.). (Illus.). (gr. 6 up). 1979. PLB 6.45 s&l (ISBN 0-531-01319-7). Watts.

Dyer, P. & McReynolds, S. R. Computation & Theory of Optimal Control. (Mathematics in Science & Engineering Ser., Vol. 65). 1970. 36.50 o.s.i. (ISBN 0-12-226250-6). Acad Pr.

Dyer, Philip, jt. auth. see Spencer, Charles.

Dyer, Richard. Light Entertainment. (BFI Television Monographs: No. 2). (Orig.). 1977. pap. 3.25 o.p. (ISBN 0-85170-036-5). NY Zoetrope.

Dyer, Richard, et al. Gays & Film. 2nd ed. (BFI Ser.). (Illus., Orig.). 1981. pap. 6.25 (ISBN 0-85170-106-X). NY Zoetrope.

--Gays & Film. (BFI Ser.). 1977. pap. 5.00 o.p. (ISBN 0-85170-065-9). NY Zoetrope.

Dyer, T. A. A Way of His Own. (gr. 5-8). 1981. 7.95 (ISBN 0-395-30443-1). HM.

Dyer, Thomas G. Theodore Roosevelt & the Idea of Race. 198p. 1980. 14.95 (ISBN 0-8071-0658-5). La State U Pr.

Dyer, Wayne. The Sky's the Limit. 1980. 12.95 (ISBN 0-671-24989-4, 24989). S&S.

Dyer, Wayne W. Your Erroneous Zones. LC 75-35621. (Funk & W Bk.). 256p. 1976. 10.95 (ISBN 0-308-10228-2, TYC-T). T Y Crowell.

--Your Erroneous Zones. 1977. pap. 2.75 (ISBN 0-380-01669-9, 46243). Avon.

Dyer, William G. Modern Theory & Method in Group Training. 256p. 1981. Repr. of 1972 ed. text ed. write for info. (ISBN 0-89874-280-3). Krieger.

--Team Building: Issues & Alternatives. LC 77-76115. 1977. pap. text ed. 6.50 (ISBN 0-201-01191-3). A-W.

Dygaard, Thomas. Outside Shooter. LC 78-24002. (gr. 7-9). 1979. 7.50 (ISBN 0-688-22177-7); PLB 7.20 (ISBN 0-688-32177-1). Morrow.

Dygard, Thomas. Running Scared. LC 76-56862. (gr. 7 up). 1977. 7.25 (ISBN 0-688-22103-3); PLB 6.96 (ISBN 0-688-32103-8). Morrow.

Dygard, Thomas J. Soccer Duel. 192p. (gr. 7-9). 1981. 7.95 (ISBN 0-688-00366-4); PLB 7.63 (ISBN 0-688-00367-2). Morrow.

--Winning Kicker. LC 77-17727. (gr. 7 up). 1978. PLB 7.20 (ISBN 0-688-32140-2). Morrow.

Dyk, Carol, jt. auth. see Taylor, Mary.

Dyk, Ruth B., jt. auth. see Dyk, Walter.

Dyk, Walter & Dyk, Ruth B. Left-Handed Mariage & Adult Life. (Illus.). 624p. 1980. 25.00 (ISBN 0-231-04946-3). Columbia U Pr.

Dyk, Walter, ed. Son of Old Man Hat: A Navaho Autobiography. LC 44-2654. 1967. pap. 4.95 (ISBN 0-8032-5054-1, BB 355, Bison). U of Nebr Pr.

Dyke, B. & Morrill, W. T., eds. Genealogical Demography. LC 80-17683. (Population & Social Structure: Advances in Historical Demography Ser.). 1980. 19.50 (ISBN 0-12-226380-4). Acad Pr.

Dyke, Frank E. How to Raise & Train a Belgian Sheepdog. (Orig.). pap. 2.00 (ISBN 0-87666-246-7, DS1054). TFH Pubns.

Dyke, Henry Van see Van Dyke, Henry.

Dyke, M. Van see Van Dyke, M., et al.

Dyke, S. F., et al. Organic Spectroscopy: An Introduction. 2nd ed. (Illus.). 1979. pap. text ed. 11.95 (ISBN 0-582-45076-4). Longman.

Dyken, A. R. Van see Silverman, Joseph & Van Dyken, A. R.

Dyken, Paul D. & Miller, Max D. Facial Features in Neurologic Syndromes. LC 79-17012. (Illus.). 1979. text ed. 56.50 (ISBN 0-8016-1485-6). Mosby.

Dykes, J. C., jt. auth. see Fisher, Ovie C.

Dykes, J. C., jt. auth. see Ward, Don.

Dykes, Jeff C., ed. see Crawford, Thomas E.

Dykhuizen, George. Life & Mind of John Dewey. LC 73-4602. (Illus.). 472p. 1973. 19.95x (ISBN 0-8093-0616-6). S Ill U Pr.

Dykstra, Andrew. The Kanji ABC. LC 76-58964. (Illus.). 185p. 1977. pap. 7.95 (ISBN 0-913232-37-8). W Kaufmann.

Dykstra, Gerald, et al. Ananse Tales: A Course in Controlled Composition. (Prog. Bk.). (gr. 9-12). 1966. pap. text ed. 2.95x (ISBN 0-8077-1269-8); tchr's. manual 1.15 (ISBN 0-8077-1272-8); wkbk. 3.95x (ISBN 0-8077-1273-6). Tchrs Coll.

--Composition: Guided - Free Kit Prog. 5-8. 1978. pap. text ed. 12.25x (ISBN 0-8077-2515-3). Tchrs Coll.

--Composition: Guided Free Manual. 1978. pap. text ed. 2.50 (ISBN 0-8077-2388-6). Tchrs Coll.

--Composition: Guided Free Program 5. 1978. pap. text ed. 2.95x (ISBN 0-8077-2389-4). Tchrs Coll.

--Composition: Guided Free Program 6. 1978. pap. text ed. 2.95x (ISBN 0-8077-2390-8). Tchrs Coll.

--Composition: Guided Free Program 7. 1978. pap. text ed. 2.95x (ISBN 0-8077-2391-6). Tchrs Coll.

--Composition: Guided Free Program 8. 1978. pap. text ed. 2.95x (ISBN 0-8077-2392-4). Tchrs Coll.

Dykstra, Gerald, et al, eds. Composition: Guided-Free. LC 73-76064. (gr. 1-6). 1974. Program 1. pap. text ed. 2.50x (ISBN 0-8077-2384-3); Program 2. pap. text ed. 2.50x (ISBN 0-8077-2385-1); Program 3. pap. text ed. 2.50x (ISBN 0-8077-2386-X); Program 4. pap. text ed. 2.50x (ISBN 0-8077-2387-8); tchrs. manual 2.50x (ISBN 0-8077-2383-5). Tchrs Coll.

Dyller, Fran, jt. auth. see Mason, David.

Dym, C. L. Stability Theory & Its Applications to Structural Mechanics. (Mechanics of Elastic Stability Ser.: No. 3). 200p. 1974. 22.50x (ISBN 90-286-0094-9). Sijthoff & Noordhoff.

Dym, Clive L. Introduction to the Theory of Shells. LC 73-13563. 172p. 1974. text ed. 27.00 o.p. (ISBN 0-08-017784-0); pap. text ed. 17.50 o.p. (ISBN 0-08-017785-9). Pergamon.

Dym, Clive L. & Ivey, Elizabeth. Principles of Mathematical Modeling. LC 79-65441. (Computer Science & Applied Mathematics Ser.). 261p. 1980. tchrs' ed. 18.95 (ISBN 0-12-226550-5); solutions manual 3.00 (ISBN 0-12-226560-2). Acad Pr.

Dym, H. & McKean, H. P. Fourier Series & Integrals. (Probability & Mathematical Statistics Ser). 1972. 39.00 (ISBN 0-12-226450-9). Acad Pr.

Dyment, John. Meet the Men Who Sailed the Seven Seas. (Step-up Bk). (gr. 2-6). 1966. PLB 4.69 (ISBN 0-394-90064-2, BYR). Random.

Dymond, J. H. & Smith, E. B. The Second Virial Coefficients of Pure Gases & Mixtures: A Critical Compilation. (Oxford Science Research Papers Ser.). (Illus.). 534p. 1980. pap. text ed. 69.00x (ISBN 0-19-855361-7). Oxford U Pr.

--Virial Coefficients of Gases: A Critical Compilation. (Oxford Science Research Papers Ser). 1969. pap. 18.95x o.p. (ISBN 0-19-855345-5). Oxford U Pr.

Dymond, Jonathan. War, An Essay. LC 72-147433. (Library of War & Peace; Proposals for Peace: a History). lib. bdg. 38.00 (ISBN 0-8240-0480-9). Garland Pub.

Dymond, Rosalind F., jt. ed. see Rogers, Carl R.

Dymov, A. M. & Savostin, A. P. Analytical Chemistry of Gallium. (Analytical Chemistry of the Elements Ser.). 1971. 31.95 (ISBN 0-470-22932-2). Halsted Pr.

Dynes, Wayne. The Illuminations of the Stavelot Bible. LC 77-94693. (Outstanding Dissertations in the Fine Arts Ser.). (Illus.). 1979. lib. bdg. 36.00 (ISBN 0-8240-3225-X). Garland Pub.

Dyos, H. J. & Wolff, Michael. The Victorian City-Images & Realities, Vol. 1: Past & Present & Numbers of People. (Illus.). 1978. pap. 12.00 (ISBN 0-7100-8458-7). Routledge & Kegan.

Dyos, H. J., jt. ed. see Dvos, H. J.

Dyrness, W. A. Christian Art in Asia. 1979. pap. text ed. 11.50x (ISBN 0-391-01157-X). Humanities.

Dyrvik, Stale, et al, eds. The Satellite State: Problems in the History of the 17th & 18th Centuries. 1979. pap. 18.00x (ISBN 8-2000-5283-4, Dist. by Columbia U. Pr.). Universitet.

Dyson, A. E., ed. The English Novel: Select Bibliographical Guides. 384p. 1974. text ed. 19.50x (ISBN 0-19-871033-X); pap. 7.95x o.p. (ISBN 0-19-871027-5). Oxford U Pr.

Dyson, A. E., jt. ed. see Cox, C. B.

Dyson, A. E., ed. see Dickens, Charles.

Dyson, Freeman. Disturbing the Universe. LC 78-20665. 304p. 1981. pap. 4.95 (ISBN 0-06-090771-1, CN 771, CN). Har-Row.

Dyson, J. E. & Williams, D. A. Physics of the Interstellar Medium. LC 80-13713. 194p. 1980. 24.95x (ISBN 0-470-26983-9). Halsted Pr.

Dyson, James, jt. auth. see Gore, William J.

Dyson, Ketaki K. A Various Universe: A Study of the Journals & Memoirs of British Men & Women in the Indian Subcontinent Seventeen Sixty Five to Eighteen Fifty Six. 1979. 22.00x (ISBN 0-19-561074-1). Oxford U Pr.

Dyson, N. A. X-Rays in Atomic & Nuclear Physics. (Illus.). 256p. 1973. text ed. 26.00 o.p. (ISBN 0-582-46218-5). Longman.

Dyson, Robert D. Cell Biology: A Molecular Approach. 2nd ed. 1978. text ed. 20.95 (ISBN 0-205-05942-2). Allyn.

--Essentials of Cell Biology. 2nd ed. 1978. text ed. 18.95 (ISBN 0-205-06117-6). Allyn.

Dyson, S. L. The Stories of the Trees. LC 78-175735. (Illus.). 272p. 1974. Repr. of 1890 ed. 18.00 (ISBN 0-8103-3033-4). Gale.

Dzacab, Bolon & Truck, Fred. The Left Ear of the Machine. 25.00 (ISBN 0-938236-00-8). Cookie Pr.

Dzaman, Fern L., et al, eds. Who's Who in Chiropractic, International 1976-78. LC 77-79754. (Illus.). 1977. 49.50 (ISBN 0-918336-01-5); (ISBN 0-685-93606-6). Chiropractic.

Dzidzienyo, Anani. Position of Blacks in Brazilian Society. (Minority Rights Group: No. 7). 1971. pap. 2.50 (ISBN 0-89192-096-X). Interbk Inc.

Dziewanowski, M. K. A History of Soviet Russia. LC 78-133392. (Illus.). 1979. pap. text ed. 15.95 (ISBN 0-13-392159-X). P-H.

--Poland in the Twentieth Century. (Illus.). 309p. 1980. pap. 9.00x (ISBN 0-231-08372-6). Columbia U Pr.

--Poland in the 20th Century. LC 76-51216. (Illus.). 1977. 20.00x (ISBN 0-231-03577-2). Columbia U Pr.

Dzyuba, Ivan. Internationalism or Russification? A Study in the Soviet Nationalities Problem. 2nd ed. Davies, M., ed. 1970. text ed. 9.50x (ISBN 0-297-17613-7). Humanities.

E

E R C Editorial Staff. E R C's President's Guide. 1970. 97.50 (ISBN 0-13-925438-2). P-H.

Eachus, Irv. Raid on the Bremerton. 252p. 1980. 12.95 (ISBN 0-670-58912-8). Viking Pr.

Eacker, Jay. Problems of Philosophy & Psychology. LC 75-17548. 160p. 1975. 14.95 (ISBN 0-88229-202-1); pap. 8.95 (ISBN 0-88229-489-X). Nelson-Hall.

Eade, Alfred T. Expanded Panorama Bible Study Course. (Illus.). 8.95 (ISBN 0-8007-0086-4). Revell.

--Panorama De la Biblia. 1979. Repr. of 1977 ed. 3.00 (ISBN 0-311-03657-0). Casa Bautista.

Eadie, M. J. & Tyrer, J. H. Anticonvulsant Therapy. 2nd ed. (Illus.). 1980. text ed. 42.50 (ISBN 0-443-01917-7). Churchill.

Eadie, Mervyn, jt. auth. see Sutherland, John M.

Eadie, Mervyn J. & Tyrer, John H. Neurological Clinical Pharmacology. 470p. 1980. text ed. 47.50 (ISBN 0-909337-07-1). ADIS Pr.

Eadington, William R. Gambling & Society: Interdisciplinary Studies on the Subject of Gambling. (Illus.). 488p. 1976. 45.75 (ISBN 0-398-03459-1). C C Thomas.

Eadmer. The Life of St. Anselm, Archbishop of Canterbury. Southern, R. W., ed. & tr. from Latin. (Oxford Medieval Texts Ser.). 386p. 1972. 31.00x (ISBN 0-19-822225-4). Oxford U Pr.

Eads, Buryl. Let the Evidence Speak. Reynolds, Amy, ed. LC 79-17377. (Illus., Orig.). 1979. pap. 4.95 (ISBN 0-931948-02-9). Peachtree Pubs.

Eads, Douglas H. The Care & Handling of the 1000 LB. Dog. (Illus.). 96p. (Orig.). 1980. pap. 4.95 (ISBN 0-89769-019-2). Pine Mntn.

Eads, George C. The Local Service Airline Experiment. (Studies in the Regulation of Economic Activity: No. 6). 225p. 1972. 11.95 (ISBN 0-8157-2022-X). Brookings.

Eagan, Andrea B. Why Am I So Miserable If These Are the Best Years of My Life? LC 75-43726. (gr. 8 up). 1976. 8.95 (ISBN 0-397-31655-0). Lippincott.

--Why Am I So Miserable If These Are the Best Years of My Life? 1979. pap. 2.25 (ISBN 0-380-46136-6, 46136). Avon.

Eager, Alan R. A Guide to Irish Bibliographical Material: A Bibliography of Irish Bibliographies and Sources of Information. LC 80-12368. xv, 502p. 1980. lib. bdg. 65.00 (ISBN 0-313-22343-2, EIB/). Greenwood.

Eagers, R. Y. Toxic Properties of Inorganic Flourine Compounds. 1969. 26.00x (ISBN 0-444-20044-4, Pub. by Applied Science). Burgess-Intl Ideas.

Eagle, Arnold. Beginner's Guide to Super Eight Film Making. (Illus.). 1980. cancelled (ISBN 0-679-50925-9); pap. cancelled (ISBN 0-679-50926-7). McKay.

Eagle, Audrey. Eagle's Trees & Shrubs of New Zealand in Colour. LC 76-361038. (Illus.). 311p. 1975. 75.00x (ISBN 0-685-61095-0). Intl Pubns Serv.

Eagle, Dorothy & Carnell, Hilary. The Oxford Literary Guide to the British Iles. (Illus.). 464p. 1980. pap. 8.95 (ISBN 0-19-285098-9, GB 617). Oxford U Pr.

Eagle, Dorothy & Carnell, Hilary, eds. The Oxford Illustrated Literary Guide to Great Britain & Ireland. (Illus.). 352p. 1981. 19.95 (ISBN 0-19-869125-4). Oxford U Pr.

Eagle, M. R. Introduction to Basic. 1977. pap. 11.95 o.p. (ISBN 0-7135-1928-2). Transatlantic.

Eagle, Robert. Eating & Allergy. LC 80-1860. 216p. 1981. pap. 5.95 (ISBN 0-385-17361-X, Dolp). Doubleday.

Eaglefield-Hull, A., ed. Dictionary of Modern Music & Musicians. LC 78-139192. (Music Ser). 1971. Repr. of 1924 ed. lib. bdg. 27.00 (ISBN 0-306-70086-7). Da Capo.

Eaglefort, Alexander. The New Fully Illustrated Family Book on the Life of Christ. (The Most Meaningful Classics in World Culture Ser.). (Illus.). 1979. 37.50 (ISBN 0-89266-190-9). Am Classical Coll Pr.

Eagleman, Joe R. Visualization of Climate. LC 75-36988. (Illus.). 1976. 19.95 (ISBN 0-669-00408-1). Lexington Bks.

Eagleman, Joe R., et al. Thunderstorms, Tornadoes & Building Damage. LC 74-30674. 320p. 1975. 25.95 (ISBN 0-669-98137-0). Lexington Bks.

Eaglesham, Eric J. Foundations of Twentieth Century Education in England. (Students Library of Education Ser.). (Orig.). 1967. text ed. 3.00x (ISBN 0-7100-4221-3). Humanities.

Eagleson, John, jt. ed. see Torres, Sergio.

Eagleton Institute Of Politics. Contemporary Issues in American Democracy. 2nd ed. (gr. 11-12). 1969. text ed. 8.96 o.p. (ISBN 0-07-018717-7,*W). McGraw.

Eagleton, Terry. Marxism & Literary Criticism. 1976. 10.95x (ISBN 0-520-03237-3); pap. 2.65 (ISBN 0-520-03243-8, CAL 337). U of Cal Pr.

--Walter Benjamin: Or Toward a Revolutionary Criticism. 224p. 1981. 19.50 (ISBN 0-8052-7100-7, Pub. by NLB England); pap. 8.50 (ISBN 0-8052-7099-X). Schocken.

Eagon, Angelo. Catalog of Published Concert Music by American Composers. LC 68-9327. (Suppl. to 2nd ed.). 1971. 10.00 (ISBN 0-8108-0387-9). Scarecrow.

--Catalog of Published Concert Music by American Composers. LC 68-9327. (2nd suppl. to 2nd ed.). 1974. 10.00 (ISBN 0-8108-0728-9). Scarecrow.

Eakin, Ed. Moods of the Prairie. (Illus.). 4.95 (ISBN 0-685-48785-7). Nortex Pr.

Eakin, Frank E. Religion & Culture of Israel: Selected Issues. 1977. pap. 10.50 (ISBN 0-8191-0208-3). U Pr of Amer.

--Religion & Western Culture: Selected Issues. 1977. 10.75 (ISBN 0-8191-0256-3). U Pr of Amer.

Eakin, Sue, ed. see Northup, Solomon.

Eakins, Barbara & Eakins, R. Gene. Sex Differences in Human Communication. LC 77-77660. (Illus.). 1978. pap. text ed. 7.75 (ISBN 0-395-25510-4). HM.

Eakins, R. Gene, jt. auth. see Eakins, Barbara.

Eakle, Arlene H. & Gunn, L. Ray. Descriptive Inventory of the New York Collection. (Finding Aids to the Microfilmed Manuscript Collection of the Genealogical Society of Utah). (Orig.). 1980. pap. 15.00x (ISBN 0-87480-170-2). U of Utah Pr.

Eakle, Arlene H., et al. Descriptive Inventory of the English Collection. (Finding Aids to the Microfilmed Manuscript Collection of the Genealogical Society of Utah). 1979. pap. 12.00x (ISBN 0-87480-154-0). U of Utah Pr.

Eales, R. G. & Williams, A. H. Alekhine's Defence. 1973. 15.95 (ISBN 0-7134-0366-7, Pub. by Batsford England). David & Charles.

Eames, Alexandra. Windows & Walls: Designs-Patterns-Projects. LC 80-80753. 160p. 1980. 17.95 (ISBN 0-8487-0507-6). Oxmoor Hse.

Eames, Edwin & Goode, Judith G. Anthropology of the City: An Introduction to Urban Anthropology. LC 76-57696. 1977. pap. text ed. 11.95 (ISBN 0-13-038414-3). P-H.

--Urban Poverty in a Cross-Cultural Context. LC 72-90545. 1973. 14.95 (ISBN 0-02-908720-1). Free Pr.

Eames, Edwin, jt. ed. see Saran, Parmatma.

Eames, S. Morris. Pragmatic Naturalism: An Introduction. LC 76-58441. 256p. 1977. pap. 7.95x (ISBN 0-8093-0803-7). S Ill U Pr.

Eames, Steward, tr. see Piaget, Jean.

Eames, Wilberforce. Early New England Catechisms. LC 68-31081. 1969. Repr. of 1898 ed. 15.00 (ISBN 0-8103-3478-X). Gale.

Eardley, A. J., et al. Zion: The Story Behind the Scenery. rev. ed. DenDooven, Gweneth R., ed. LC 77-157458. (Illus.). 1979. 7.95 (ISBN 0-916122-32-8); pap. 3.00 (ISBN 0-916122-07-7). K C Pubns.

Eareckson, Joni & Estes, Stephen. Un Paso Mas. Mercado, Ben, ed. Flores, Rhode, tr. (Span.). 1979. 1.90. Vida Pubs.

Eareckson, Joni & Musser, Joe. Joni. (Illus.). 256p. 1980. pap. 2.95 (ISBN 0-310-23982-6). Zondervan.

--Joni. 1976. o. p. 6.95 (ISBN 0-310-23960-5); kivar, large print 4.95 (ISBN 0-310-23967-2); pap. 3.95 (ISBN 0-310-23961-3); pap. 2.95 (ISBN 0-310-23962-1). Zondervan.

Eareckson, Joni, tr. Joni. (Portuguese Bks.). 1979. 1.40 (ISBN 0-8297-0800-6). Life Pubs Intl.

--Joni. (Spanish Bks.). (Span.). 1977. 1.90 (ISBN 0-8297-0774-3). Life Pubs Intl.

Eargle, D. H., et al. Uranium Geology & Mines, South Texas. (Illus.). 59p. 1971. 1.75 (GB 12). Bur Econ Geology.

Eargle, John. The Microphone Handbook. 1980. write for info. Elar Pub Co.

Earhart, Amelia. The Fun of It: Random Records of My Own Flying & of Women in Aviation. LC 71-159945. 1975. Repr. of 1932 ed. 18.00 (ISBN 0-8103-4078-X). Gale.

Earhart, H. Bryon. Japanese Religion: Unity & Diversity. 2nd ed. 1974. pap. text ed. 7.95x (ISBN 0-8221-0123-8). Dickenson.

Earl, D. E. Forest Energy & Economic Development. (Illus.). 140p. 1975. 22.50x (ISBN 0-19-854521-5). Oxford U Pr.

Earl, Donald. The Age of Augustus. 1968. 19.95 o.p. (ISBN 0-236-40026-6, Pub. by Paul Elek); pap. 7.95 o.p. (ISBN 0-236-31130-1). Merrimack Bk Serv.

Earl, Donald A. The Moral & Political Tradition of Rome. (Aspects of Greek & Roman Life Ser.). 1967. 18.50x (ISBN 0-8014-0110-0). Cornell U Pr.

Earl, Gloria. The Book. 1981. 6.75 (ISBN 0-8062-1572-0). Carlton.

Earl, Guy C. Indian Songs & Legends. LC 80-67271. 80p. (gr. 4-12). 1980. 10.00g (ISBN 0-87062-135-1). A H Clark.

Earl, John. John Muir's Longest Walk. 1975. 7.95 o.p. (ISBN 0-385-09216-4). Doubleday.

Earle, Alice M. China Collecting in America. LC 77-99044. 1970. Repr. of 1892 ed. 18.00 (ISBN 0-8103-3579-4). Gale.

--Colonial Days in Old New York. LC 68-21767. 1968. Repr. of 1896 ed. 15.00 (ISBN 0-8103-3428-3). Gale.

--Costume of Colonial Times. LC 75-159946. xiv, 264p. 1975. Repr. of 1924 ed. 20.00 (ISBN 0-8103-3965-X). Gale.

--Curious Punishments of Bygone Days. LC 68-31516. (Illus.). 1968. Repr. of 1896 ed. 15.00 (ISBN 0-8103-3504-2). Gale.

--Customs & Fashions in Old New England. LC 68-17959. 1968. Repr. of 1893 ed. 15.00 (ISBN 0-8103-0155-5). Gale.

--Home & Child Life in Colonial Days. abr. ed. Glubok, Shirley, ed. LC 69-11295. (Illus.). (gr. 5 up). 1969. 9.95 (ISBN 0-02-733250-0). Macmillan.

--Home Life in Colonial Days. LC 74-11507. 470p. 1974. lib. bdg. 9.95 o.p. (ISBN 0-912944-23-4); pap. 5.95 (ISBN 0-912944-23-4). Berkshire Traveller.

--Old Time Gardens, Newly Set Forth. LC 68-31219. (Illus.). 1968. Repr. of 1901 ed. 18.00 (ISBN 0-8103-3429-1). Gale.

--Sabbath in Puritan New England. LC 68-17961. 1968. Repr. of 1891 ed. 15.00 (ISBN 0-8103-3430-5). Gale.

--Stage-Coach & Tavern Days. LC 68-17962. (Illus.). 1968. Repr. of 1900 ed. 20.00 (ISBN 0-8103-3431-3). Gale.

--Sun Dials & Roses of Yesterday. LC 79-75790. 1969. Repr. of 1902 ed. 20.00 (ISBN 0-8103-3830-0). Gale.

Earle, Allic M., ed. see Winslow, Anna G.

Earle, Alvin M. & Metcalf, William K. Neuroanatomy Review. (Basic Science Review Bks.). 1977. spiral bdg. 8.00 o.p. (ISBN 0-87488-218-4). Med Exam.

Earle, Ann M., et al, eds. The Nurse As Caregiver for the Terminal Patient & His Family. LC 76-14441. 1976. 20.00x (ISBN 0-231-04020-2). Columbia U Pr.

Earle, Edward M., ed. Makers of Modern Strategy: Military Thought from Machiavelli to Hitler. 1943. 35.00 (ISBN 0-691-06907-7); pap. 6.95 (ISBN 0-691-01853-7). Princeton U Pr.

Earle, H. H. Police-Community Relations. 3rd ed. 116p. 1980. pap. 5.75 spiral (ISBN 0-398-04468-6); instrs' guide avail. (ISBN 0-398-03900-3). C C Thomas.

Earle, J. H. Design Drafting. (gr. 7-12). 1972. text ed. 16.95 o.p. (ISBN 0-201-01677-X, Sch Div). A-W.

--Engineering Design Graphics Problems-One. 1976. pap. text ed. 8.50 o.p. (ISBN 0-201-01719-9). A-W.

Earle, James H. Descriptive Geometry. 2nd ed. LC 76-55640. (Illus.). 384p. 1978. text ed. 17.95 (ISBN 0-201-01776-8). A-W.

--Engineering Design Graphics. 3rd ed. LC 76-2931. 1977. text ed. 22.95 (ISBN 0-201-01774-1). A-W.

Earle, Joe, tr. see Tanaka, Ikko.

Earle, John. Gloucester Fragments. 116p. 1980. Repr. of 1861 ed. lib. bdg. 65.00 (ISBN 0-8482-0717-3). Norwood Edns.

Earle, John R., et al. Spindles & Spires. LC 75-13461. 400p. 1976. 15.95 (ISBN 0-8042-0854-9). John Knox.

Earle, Kenneth M. & Rubinstein, Lucien J. Central Nervous System. (Anatomic Pathology Seminars). (Illus.). 1976. atlas slides 55.00 (ISBN 0-89189-052-1, 15-1-015-00); proceedings 5.00 (ISBN 0-89189-003-3, 50-1-040-00). Am Soc Clinical.

Earle, Olive L. Birds & Their Nests. (Illus.). (gr. 5 up). 1952. PLB 6.00 o.p. (ISBN 0-688-31098-2). Morrow.

--Camels & Llamas. (Illus.). (gr. 3-7). 1961. PLB 6.48 (ISBN 0-688-31138-5). Morrow.

--Peas, Beans, & Licorice. LC 77-126737. (Illus.). (gr. 3-7). 1971. 6.25 o.p. (ISBN 0-688-21570-X). Morrow.

--Scavengers. LC 72-3799. (Illus.). 64p. (gr. 3-7). 1973. PLB 6.00 o.p. (ISBN 0-688-31933-5). Morrow.

--State Birds & Flowers. (Illus.). (gr. 3-7). 1961. Repr. of 1951 ed. PLB 6.48 (ISBN 0-688-31536-4). Morrow.

--State Trees. rev. ed. LC 73-4932. (Illus.). 64p. (gr. 3-7). 1973. PLB 6.48 (ISBN 0-688-31956-4). Morrow.

Earle, Olive L. & Kantor, Michael. Animals & Their Ears. LC 73-13047. (Illus.). 64p. (gr. 3-7). 1974. PLB 6.48 (ISBN 0-688-30106-1). Morrow.

--Nuts. LC 74-26800. (Illus.). 64p. (gr. 3-7). 1975. 6.75 (ISBN 0-688-22025-8); PLB 6.48 (ISBN 0-688-32025-2). Morrow.

Earle, Peter, ed. Essays in European Economic History 1500-1800. 282p. 1974. 22.50x (ISBN 0-19-877054-5). Oxford U Pr.

Earle, Peter G. Prophet in the Wilderness: The Works of Ezequiel Martinez Estrada. (Texas Pan American Ser). 1971. 12.00 (ISBN 0-292-70107-1). U of Tex Pr.

Earle, Ralph. Peloubet's Notes 1980-81. 1980. pap. 4.95 (ISBN 0-8010-3361-6). Baker Bk.

--Peloubet's Notes 1981-82. 408p. (Orig.). 1981. pap. 4.95 (ISBN 0-8010-3363-2). Baker Bk.

--What the Bible Says About the Second Coming. (Direction Bks). 1973. pap. 1.95 (ISBN 0-8010-3307-1). Baker Bk.

Earle, Ralph, ed. Adam Clarke's Commentary on the Entire Bible. 22.95 (ISBN 0-8010-2321-1). Baker Bk.

Earle, Vana. Numbers Workbook Four (with the Scarecrow from Oz) (Funny Face Activity Bks.). (Illus.). 48p. (ps-1). 1981. pap. 1.95 saddle-stitched (ISBN 0-394-84670-2). Random.

Earle, William. Mystical Reason. LC 79-92079. 164p. 1980. pap. 6.95 (ISBN 0-89526-677-6). Regnery-Gateway.

Earley, Michael, ed. Information for Playwrights. 54p. 1979. pap. 4.00 (ISBN 0-930452-09-7, Pub. by Theatre Comm). Pub Ctr Cult Res.

Earlley, Elsie C., jt. auth. see Cook, J. E.

Earl Of Dunraven. Great Divide: Travels in the Upper Yellowstone in the Summer of 1874. LC 67-26059. (Illus.). 1967. pap. 3.95 o.p. (ISBN 0-8032-5052-5, 369, Bison). U of Nebr Pr.

Earls, William. The Gladiator. (Orig.). Date not set. pap. 2.50 (ISBN 0-440-12995-8). Dell.

Early, Eileen. Joy in Exile. LC 79-5429. 1980. pap. text ed. 7.50 (ISBN 0-8191-0878-2). U Pr of Amer.

Early, Els, tr. see Mulisch, Harry.

Early, J. & Marshall, M. Biology: Functional Man. (Illus.). 1978. text ed. 15.00x o.p. (ISBN 0-8464-0196-7). Beekman Pubs.

Early, Paul J., jt. auth. see Sodee, D. Bruce.

Early, Paul J., et al. Textbook of Nuclear Medicine Technology. 2nd ed. LC 74-28229. (Illus.). 464p. 1975. pap. text ed. 21.95 o.p. (ISBN 0-8016-1487-2). Mosby.

--Textbook of Nuclear Medicine Technology. 3rd ed. LC 78-31659. (Illus.). 1979. text ed. 32.95 (ISBN 0-8016-1488-0). Mosby.

Earnest, Ernest. A Forward to Literature. 332p. 1980. Repr. of 1945 ed. lib. bdg. 25.00 (ISBN 0-89987-205-0). Century Bookbindery.

--The Single Vision: The Alienation of American Intellectuals. LC 78-116132. 1970. 10.00x (ISBN 0-8147-0459-X); pap. 5.00x (ISBN 0-8147-0460-3). NYU Pr.

--The Volunteer Fire Company. LC 78-8785. (Illus.). 224p. 1980. pap. 6.95 (ISBN 0-8128-6094-2). Stein & Day.

Earnest, Rebecca, jt. ed. see Brewster, David.

Earnest, Rebecca, ed. see Prater, Yvonne.

Earney, Fillmore C. Petroleum & Hard Minerals from the Sea. LC 80-17653. (Scripta Series in Geography). 1438p. 1980. 29.95 (ISBN 0-470-27009-8, Pub. by Halsted Pr). Wiley.

--Researcher's Guide to Iron Ore: An Annotated Bibliography on the Economic Geography of Iron Ore. LC 74-76986. 1974. lib. bdg. 50.00 (ISBN 0-87287-095-2). Libs Unl.

Earnshaw, A. & Harrington, T. J. The Chemistry of the Transition Elements. (Oxford Chemistry Ser.). (Illus.). 112p. 1973. pap. 8.95x (ISBN 0-19-855425-7). Oxford U Pr.

Earnshaw, Judith, ed. Sprouts on Helicon. (gr. 9 up). 5.95 (ISBN 0-233-95784-7). Transatlantic.

Earthday X Colloquium, University of Denver, April 21-24, 1980. Ecological Consciousness: Essays from the Earthday X Colloquium. Schultz, Robert C. & Hughes, J. Donald, eds. LC 80-6084. 510p. 1981. lib. bdg. 26.50 (ISBN 0-8191-1496-0); pap. text ed. 16.75 (ISBN 0-8191-1497-9). U Pr of Amer.

Earthquake Problems Related to the Siting of Critical Facilities, Committee on Seismology. Earthquake Research for the Safer Siting of Critical Facilities. LC 80-82030. 1980. pap. text ed. 5.50 (ISBN 0-309-03082-X). Natl Acad Pr.

Eary, Donald F. & Reed, Edward A. Techniques of Pressworking Sheet Metal: An Engineering Approach to Die Design. 2nd ed. 1974. ref. ed. 25.95 (ISBN 0-13-900696-6). P-H.

Eash, Nancy Greene see West, Betty M.

Easlea, Brian. Witch Hunting, Magic & the New Philosophy. (Harvester Studies in Philosophy Ser.: No. 14). 280p. 1980. text ed. 42.50x (ISBN 0-391-01807-8); pap. text ed. 16.50x (ISBN 0-391-01808-6). Humanities.

Easley, Eddie, et al. Contemporary Business: Challenges & Opportunities. (Illus.). 1978. pap. text ed. 13.95 (ISBN 0-8299-0166-3); study guide 6.50 (ISBN 0-8299-0218-X); instrs.' manual avail. (ISBN 0-8299-0476-X); transparency masters avail. (ISBN 0-8299-0477-8). West Pub.

Easlick, Kenneth A., et al, eds. Communicating in Dentistry: Sources & Evaluation of Information & Preparation of Manuscripts, Oral Reports, & Proposals for Research. (Illus.). 240p. 1974. pap. 24.50 photocopy ed. spiral (ISBN 0-398-02856-7). C C Thomas.

Eason, G., et al. Mathematics & Statistics for the Bio-Sciences. LC 79-41815. (Ellis Horwood Series: Mathematics & Its Applications). 578p. 1980. 78.95x (ISBN 0-470-26963-4). Halsted Pr.

Eason, J. Lawrence. New Bible Survey. 16.95 (ISBN 0-310-24000-X). Zondervan.

Eason, T. W. Colleges of Education: Academic or Professional? (Higher Education Monograph: No. 2). 1970. pap. text ed. 6.25x (ISBN 0-685-23326-X, NFER). Humanities.

Eason, T. W. & Croll, E. J. Staff & Student Attitudes in Colleges of Education. (Higher Education Monograph: No. 3). 1971. pap. text ed. 7.00x (ISBN 0-901225-72-X, NFER). Humanities.

Easson, Angus. Elizabeth Gaskell. 1979. 22.00x (ISBN 0-7100-0099-5). Routledge & Kegan.

Easson, William M. Dying Child: The Management of the Child or Adolescent Who Is Dying. (Illus.). 112p. 1977. pap. 8.50 (ISBN 0-398-03676-4). C C Thomas.

East, Ben & Nentl, Jerolyn. Forty Days Lost. Schroeder, Howard, ed. LC 79-5185. (Survival Ser.). (Illus., Orig.). (gr. 3 up). 1979. PLB 5.95 (ISBN 0-89686-042-6); pap. 2.95 (ISBN 0-89686-050-7). Crestwood Hse.

East, Ben, jt. auth. see Fredrickson, Olive A.

East, D. J., jt. auth. see Garnell, P.

East, Edward M., ed. Biology in Human Affairs. 399p. 1980. Repr. of 1931 ed. lib. bdg. 30.00 (ISBN 0-8495-1348-0). Arden Lib.

East, Frank Reynolds. The Entity Process: The Accumulation of a Physical Property As a Function of Mortality & Magnitude of Rank. 1977. 10.00 o.p. (ISBN 0-682-48630-2, University). Exposition.

East, G. C., jt. auth. see Margerison, D.

East India Company. The Petition & Remonstrance of the Governor & Company, Etc. LC 78-25744. (English Experience Ser.: No. 305). 38p. Repr. of 1628 ed. 8.00 (ISBN 90-221-0305-6). Walter J Johnson.

East, Maurice A., et al, eds. Why Nations Act: Theoretical Perspectives for Comparative Foreign Policy Studies. Salmore, Stephen A. & Hermann, Charles F. LC 77-22119. (Sage Focus Editions: Vol. 2). 1978. 18.95x (ISBN 0-8039-0718-4); pap. 9.95x (ISBN 0-8039-0719-2). Sage.

East, Reginald. Heal the Sick. LC 77-80678. (Orig.). 1977. pap. 1.95 (ISBN 0-87123-232-4, 200232). Bethany Fell.

East, Robert. John Adams. (World Leaders Ser.). 1979. lib. bdg. 13.50 (ISBN 0-8057-7723-7). Twayne.

Eastaugh, Kenneth. The Carry-on Book. 1978. 10.95 (ISBN 0-7153-7403-6). David & Charles.

Eastcott, John, jt. auth. see Momatiuk, Yva.

Eastcott, Michal J. I: The Story of the Self. LC 80-51552. (Illus.). 201p. (Orig.). 1980. pap. 5.50 (ISBN 0-8356-0541-8, Quest). Theos Pub Hse.

Eastcott, R. Sketches of the Origin, Process & Effects of Music. LC 70-159680. (Music Ser). 1971. Repr. of 1793 ed. lib. bdg. 27.50 (ISBN 0-306-70184-7). Da Capo.

Easter, Jade. The Healing Handbook. (Illus.). 128p. (Orig.). 1981. pap. 6.95 (ISBN 0-913300-15-2). Unity Pr.

Easterbrook, David L. & Lohrentz, Kenneth P. African Microfilms at the E. S. Bird Library, Syracuse University: An Annotated Guide. (Foreign & Comparative Studies-African Special Publications Ser.: No.7). 72p. 1975. pap. 3.50x. Syracuse U Foreign Comp.

Easterbrook, David L., jt. auth. see Myrick, Bismarck.

Easterbrook, Frank H., jt. auth. see Posner, Richard A.

Easterday, Kate C. Peaceable Kitchen Cookbook: Cooking for Personal & Global Well-Being. LC 79-92912. (Orig.). 1980. pap. 8.95 (ISBN 0-8091-2225-1). Paulist Pr.

Easterlin, Richard A. Birth & Fortune: The Impact of Numbers on Personal Welfare. LC 79-56369. 205p. 1980. 11.95 (ISBN 0-465-00688-4). Basic.

Easterling, Jack & Pasanen, Jack. Confront, Construct, Complete: A Comprehensive Approach to Writing, 2 bks. (gr. 9-12). 1978. pap. text ed. 5.95x ea.; Bk. 1. pap. text ed. (ISBN 0-8104-6031-9); Bk. 2. pap. text ed. (ISBN 0-8104-6032-7); tchr's guide 1.50 (ISBN 0-8104-6029-7). Hayden.

Easterling, K., ed. Mechanisms of Deformation & Fracture: Proceedings of the Interdisciplinary Conference, Held at the University of Lulea-Sweden, 20-22, September 1978. (Strength & Fracture of Materials & Structures). 1979. 89.00 (ISBN 0-08-024258-8). Pergamon.

Easterly, Lane, ed. Great Bible Stories for Children. 5.95 o.p. (ISBN 0-8407-4988-0). Nelson.

Eastern & Western Disciples of Vivekananda. The Life of Swami Vivekananda, Vol. 1. rev. ed. 629p. 1980. 16.00x (ISBN 0-87481-196-1). Vedanta Pr.

Eastern Kentucky University, Dept. of Geology. Principles of Physical Geology Laboratory Manual. 80p. 1980. pap. text ed. 5.50 (ISBN 0-8403-2285-2). Kendall-Hunt.

Eastham, R. C. Interpretation Klinisch-Chemischer Laborresultate. 2nd ed. Peheim, E., tr. Colombo, J. P., ed. xii, 248p. 1981. pap. 17.00 (ISBN 3-8055-1879-X). S Karger.

Eastlake, Charles. History of the Gothic Revival. 2nd ed. Crools, J. Mordaunt, ed. (Victorian Library). 1978. Repr. of 1872 ed. text ed. 44.25x (ISBN 0-7185-5033-1, Leicester). Humanities.

Eastlake, F. Warrington, jt. auth. see Yamada, Yosi-Aki.

Eastlake, William, ed. Portrait of an Artist with Twenty-Six Horses. (Zia Bks.). 224p. 1980. pap. 5.95 (ISBN 0-8263-0558-X). U of NM Pr.

Eastlick, John T., jt. auth. see Stueart, Robert D.

Eastman, Carol M. Aspects of Language & Culture. LC 74-28741. (Publications in Anthropology Ser.). (Illus.). 168p. 1975. pap. text ed. 5.95x (ISBN 0-88316-514-7). Chandler & Sharp.

Eastman, Charles. The All-American Boy. (Illus.). 1973. pap. 2.75 o.p. (ISBN 0-374-50922-0, N406). FS&G.

--Indian Boyhood. LC 76-46274. (Beautiful Rio Grande Classics Ser). 1976. lib. bdg. 10.00 o.p. (ISBN 0-87380-139-3). Rio Grande.

Eastman, Charles A. From the Deep Woods to Civilization: Chapters in the Autobiography of an Indian. LC 77-7226. (Illus.). 1977. 11.95x (ISBN 0-8032-0936-3); pap. 3.75 (ISBN 0-8032-5873-9, BB 651, Bison). U of Nebr Pr.

--Indian Boyhood. (Illus.). 7.25 (ISBN 0-8446-0085-7). Peter Smith.

Eastman, Charles M., ed. Spatial Synthesis in Computer-Aided Building Design. LC 75-7416. 333p. 1975. 49.95 (ISBN 0-470-22946-2). Halsted Pr.

Eastman, Dick. Up with Jesus. 1971. pap. 0.95 (ISBN 0-8010-3327-6). Baker Bk.

Eastman, Ediwn. Seven & Nine Years Among the Camanches & Apaches: An Autobiography. LC 75-7115. (Indian Captivities Ser.: Vol. 88). 1977. Repr. of 1873 ed. lib. bdg. 44.00 (ISBN 0-8240-1712-9). Garland Pub.

Eastman, George D. & Chapman, Samuel G. Short of Merger: Countywide Police Resource Pooling. LC 75-36013. (Illus.). 1976. 17.95 (ISBN 0-669-00373-5). Lexington Bks.

Eastman, Jerry R. Radiographic Fundamentals & Technique Guide. (Illus.). 1979. pap. text ed. 12.50 (ISBN 0-8016-1493-7). Mosby.

Eastman Kodak. Kodak Microelectronics Seminar - Interface '79, G-102: Proceedings. (Illus.). 180p. 1980. pap. 4.50 (ISBN 0-87985-246-1). Eastman Kodak.

Eastman Kodak, ed. Cinematographer's Field Guide, (H-2) 3rd rev. ed. (Illus.). 100p. Date not set. text ed. 6.95 (ISBN 0-87985-276-3). Eastman Kodak.

Eastman Kodak Co. A Guide for Processing Black-&-White Motion Picture Films (H-7) LC 79-55036. (Illus.). 1979. pap. 5.95 (ISBN 0-87985-229-1, CAT 143 9892). Eastman Kodak.

Eastman Kodak Co., jt. auth. see American Photographic Book Publishing Co.

Eastman Kodak Co., ed. Guidelines for Better Platemaking. (Illus., Orig.). 1976. pap. 3.95 o.s.i. (ISBN 0-87985-065-5, Q213). Eastman Kodak.

Eastman Kodak Company. Analysis, Treatment & Disposal of Ferricyanide in Photographic Effluents. 65p. 1979. pap. 5.75 (ISBN 0-87985-244-5, J-54). Eastman Kodak.

--The Eleventh Here's How. LC 79-55802. (Here's How Ser.). (Illus.). 1979. pap. 4.25 (ISBN 0-87985-230-5). Eastman Kodak.

--Images, Images, Images: The Book of Programmed Multi-Image Production. rev. ed. (Illus.). 264p. (Orig.). 1980. pap. 19.95 (ISBN 0-87985-285-2, S-12). Eastman Kodak.

--Kodak Guide to Thirty-Five MM Photography. LC 79-54310. (Illus.). 288p. (Orig.). 1980. text ed. 16.50 (ISBN 0-87985-242-9, AC-95H); pap. text ed. 9.95 (ISBN 0-87985-236-4, AC-95S). Eastman Kodak.

--Photocomposition with Kodak Phototypesetting Products. LC 75-36853. (Illus.). 40p. 1978. 4.00 o.p. (ISBN 0-87985-168-6, Q-5). Eastman Kodak.

Eastman Kodak Company, ed. Basic Production Techniques for Motion Pictures. 2nd ed. LC 76-16716. (Illus.). 64p. (Orig.). 1976. pap. 5.00 (ISBN 0-87985-004-3, P18). Eastman Kodak.

--Cinematographer's Field Guide. 3rd ed. (Illus.). 1980. 6.95 (ISBN 0-87985-276-3, H-2). Eastman Kodak.

--Copy Preparation & Platemaking Using Kodak PMT Materials. (Illus.). 1980. pap. 4.50 (ISBN 0-87985-261-5, Q-71). Eastman Kodak.

--Filming Sports: The How-to Book for Coaches, Sports Information Directors, Motion Picture - Still Sports Photographers (S-65) (Illus.). 288p. (Orig.). 1981. pap. 19.95 (ISBN 0-87985-268-2). Eastman Kodak.

--Fundamental Techniques of Direct-Screen Color Reproduction. (Illus.). 44p. 1980. pap. 5.50 (ISBN 0-87985-260-7, Q-10). Eastman Kodak.

--Kodak Black & White Darkroom Dataguide. rev. ed. 1979. pap. 9.95 (ISBN 0-87985-157-0, R-20). Eastman Kodak.

--Kodak Color Darkroom Dataguide. rev. ed. (Illus.). 1980. pap. 9.95 (ISBN 0-87985-086-8, R-19). Eastman Kodak.

--Kodak Sourcebook: Kodak Ektagraphic Slide Projectors. LC 77-90640. (Illus.). 1977. pap. 4.75 o.p. (ISBN 0-87985-201-1, S-74). Eastman Kodak.

--Photofabrication Methods with Kodak Photo Resists. 1979. pap. 3.75 (ISBN 0-87985-013-2, P246). Eastman Kodak.

--Photography Through the Microscope. (Illus.). 96p. 1980. pap. 9.95 (ISBN 0-87985-248-8, P-2). Eastman Kodak.

--Practical Processing in Black & White Photography: P-229. 1978. pap. 2.50 (ISBN 0-87985-014-0). Eastman Kodak.

--Visual Marketing: A Program for the Design Profession. (Illus.). 92p. (Orig.). 1978. pap. 6.25 (ISBN 0-87985-249-6, V1-36). Eastman Kodak.

Eastman, Max. Enjoyment of Poetry. 1951. lib. rep. ed. 20.00x (ISBN 0-684-15162-6, ScribT). Scribner.

--Reflections on the Failure of Socialism. LC 55-7352. 128p. 1981. pap. 4.95 (ISBN 0-8159-6707-1). Devin.

Eastman, Moira & Poussard, Wendy. The Christmas Book. LC 80-68368. (Illus.). 40p. 1980. 5.95 (ISBN 0-87793-214-X). Ave Maria.

Eastman, P. D., jt. tr. see Rivera, Carlos.

Eastman, Peter F. Advanced First Aid Afloat. 2nd ed. LC 72-78241. (Illus.). 1974. pap. 6.00 (ISBN 0-87033-169-8). Cornell Maritime.

--Advanced First Aid for All Outdoors. LC 76-44658. (Illus.). 1976. pap. 6.00 (ISBN 0-87033-223-6). Cornell Maritime.

Eastman, Philip D. The Cat in the Hat Beginner Book Dictionary in French. (ps-2). 1965. 7.95 (ISBN 0-394-81063-5, BYR); PLB 8.99 (ISBN 0-394-91063-X). Random.

Eastman, Richard M. Style: Writing & Reading As the Discovery of Outlook. 2nd ed. (Illus.). 1978. pap. 7.95x (ISBN 0-19-502277-7). Oxford U Pr.

Eastman, Susan T. & Head, Sidney W. Broadcast Programming: Strategies for Winning Television & Radio Audiences. 400p. 1980. text ed. 15.95x (ISBN 0-534-00882-8). Wadsworth Pub.

Eastmann, C. R., ed. see Von Zittel, K. A.

Easton, Allen, jt. auth. see Brearley, Joan M.

Easton, Brian. Social Policy & the Welfare State in New Zealand. 200p. 1980. text ed. 21.00x (ISBN 0-86861-393-2, 2390); pap. text ed. 11.50x (ISBN 0-86861-002-X, 2391). Allen Unwin.

Easton, K. C. Rescue Emergency Care. (Illus.). 1977. 29.95x (ISBN 0-433-08000-0). Intl Ideas.
Easton, Lloyd & Guddat, Kurt H., eds. Writings of the Young Marx on Philosophy & Society. LC 67-12896. pap. 3.50 (ISBN 0-385-07171-X, A563, Anch). Doubleday.
Easton, Loyd D. Hegel's First American Followers: The Ohio Hegelians. LC 66-20062. ix, 353p. 1966. 15.00 (ISBN 0-8214-0026-6). Ohio U Pr.
Easton, Richard J. & Graham, George P. Intermediate Algebra. LC 72-4744. (Illus.). 305p. 1973. text ed. 17.95x (ISBN 0-471-22939-3); student wkbk. 9.95 (ISBN 0-471-22943-1). Wiley.
Easton, Robert. Black Tide: The Santa Barbara Oil Spill & Its Consequences. 1972. 10.00 o.s.i. (ISBN 0-440-00858-1). Delacorte.
--Max Brand the Big "Westerner". LC 68-16732. (Illus.). 1970. 17.90 (ISBN 0-8061-0870-3); pap. 8.95 (ISBN 0-8061-1233-6). U of Okla Pr.
Easton, Robert & Brown, MacKenzie. Lord of Beasts: The Saga of Buffalo Jones. LC 61-14501. (Illus.). 1970. pap. 2.95 (ISBN 0-8032-5727-9, BB 522, Bison). U of Nebr Pr.
Easton, Stewart C. Rudolf Steiner: Herald of a New Epoch. LC 80-67026. (Illus.). 1980. pap. 9.95 (ISBN 0-910142-93-9). Anthroposophic.
Easton Kupsinel, Penelope. Occupational Home Economics Notebook. (gr. 9-12). text ed. 2.90 o.p. (ISBN 0-686-66739-5, 1109-1110). Interstate.
Eastop, T. D. & McConkey, A. Applied Thermodynamics for Engineering Technologists. 3rd ed. (Illus.). 1978. pap. text ed. 18.50x (ISBN 0-582-44197-8). Longman.
Eastwick, Ivy O. In & Out the Windows: Happy Poems for Children. LC 73-90841. (Illus.). (ps-3). 1969. 6.25 (ISBN 0-87486-007-5). Plough.
Eastwood, D. G., jt. auth. see Harre, R.
Eastwood, Eric, ed. Wireless Telegraphy. LC 73-22705. 391p. 1974. 42.95 (ISBN 0-470-22950-0). Halsted Pr.
Eastwood, F. W., et al. Organic Chemistry: A First University Course in Twelve Programs. 2nd ed. 1970. text ed. 13.95x (ISBN 0-521-07951-9). Cambridge U Pr.
Eastwood, Susan. Prisling. 1977. pap. 1.00 o.p. (ISBN 0-931832-07-1). No Dead Lines.
Eastwood, W. A Book of Science Verse. 279p. 1980. Repr. of 1961 ed. lib. bdg. 30.00 (ISBN 0-89984-177-5). Century Bookbindery.
Easty, Dorothy M., jt. auth. see Ambrose, E. J.
Easwaran, Eknath. Dialogue with Death: The Spiritual Psychology of the Katha Upanishad. 288p. (Orig.). 1981. pap. 6.00 (ISBN 0-915132-24-9). Nilgiri Pr.
Eather, Robert. Majestic Lights. 1980. write for info (ISBN 0-87590-215-4). Am Geophysical.
Eathorne, Richard H. The Analysis of Outdoor Recreation Demand: A Review & Annotated Bibliography of the Current State-of-the-Art. (Public Administration Ser.: Bibliography P-563). 93p. 1980. pap. 10.00. Vance Biblios.
Eaton, Charles, intro. by. Karl Knaths: Five Decades of Painting. LC 73-82318. (Illus.). 160p. 1973. pap. 8.00 (ISBN 0-88397-056-2). Intl Exhibit Foun.
Eaton, Clement. The Civilization of the Old South: Writings of Clement Eaton. Kirwan, Albert D., ed. LC 68-29638. 328p. 1968. 11.00x (ISBN 0-8131-1162-5). U Pr of Ky.
--Growth of Southern Civilization, 1790-1860. (New American Nation Ser). (Illus.). pap. 6.95x (ISBN 0-06-133040-X, TB3040, Torch). Har-Row.
--History of the Southern Confederacy. 1954. pap. text ed. 3.95 (ISBN 0-02-908710-4). Free Pr.
--A History of the Southern Confederacy. 1954. 7.95 o.s.i. (ISBN 0-02-534730-6). Macmillan.
--Jefferson Davis. LC 77-2512. 1979. pap. text ed. 7.95 (ISBN 0-02-908740-6). Free Pr.
--Jefferson Davis: The Sphinx of the Confederacy. LC 77-2512. 1977. 14.95 (ISBN 0-02-908700-7). Free Pr.
--Mind of the Old South. rev. ed. LC 67-11648. (Walter Lynwood Fleming Lectures). (Illus.). 1967. 20.00x (ISBN 0-8071-0443-4); pap. text ed. 8.95 (ISBN 0-8071-0120-6). La State U Pr.
Eaton, Clement, ed. Leaven of Democracy: The Growth of the Democratic Spirit in the Time of Jackson. LC 63-17877. (American Epochs Ser). pap. 7.95 (ISBN 0-8076-0394-5). Braziller.
Eaton, Faith. Dolls in Color. LC 75-17668. (Illus.). 176p. 1976. 6.95 o.s.i. (ISBN 0-02-534710-1, 53471). Macmillan.
Eaton, Howard O. Happinism: A Goal for All Humanity. 1976. 4.00 o.p. (ISBN 0-682-48540-3). Exposition.
--Happinism Revisited. 2nd rev. & enlarged ed. 1978. 4.50 o.p. (ISBN 0-682-49012-1). Exposition.
Eaton, J., jt. auth. see Hatter, D.
Eaton, J. D., jt. auth. see Adriani, John.
Eaton, Jeffrey C. The Logic of Theism: An Analysis of the Thought of Austin Farrer. LC 80-67260. 288p. 1980. lib. bdg. 19.25 (ISBN 0-8191-1337-9); pap. text ed. 10.50 (ISBN 0-8191-1338-7). U Pr of Amer.
Eaton, Jonathan. Four Essays in the Theory of Uncertainty & Portfolio Choice. LC 78-75071. (Outstanding Dissertations in Economics). 1980. lib. bdg. 24.00 (ISBN 0-8240-4145-3). Garland Pub.
Eaton, K. J. & Eaton, K. J., eds. Proceedings of International Conference on Wind Effects on Buildings & Structures: Heathrow Nineteen Seventy-Five. LC 75-2730. 650p. 1976. 97.50 (ISBN 0-521-20801-7). Cambridge U Pr.
Eaton, Leonard K. Landscape Artist in America: The Life & Work of Jens Jensen. LC 64-23422. (Illus.). 1964. 15.00x o.s.i. (ISBN 0-226-18053-0). U of Chicago Pr.
Eaton, Margaret E; see Levy, Harold L.
Eaton, Margaret H. & Amey, Vera E. Diary of a Sea Captain's Wife: Tales of Santa Cruz Island. Timbrook, Janice, ed. (Illus.). 272p. 1980. 16.50 (ISBN 0-87461-032-X); pap. 9.50 (ISBN 0-87461-033-8). McNally.
Eaton, Merrill T., et al. Psychiatry. 4th ed. (Medical Outline Ser). 1981. 12.00 (ISBN 0-87488-621-X). Med Exam.
Eaton, Peggy & Eiring, Leslie. Joy of Learning. (Illus.). 10.50 (ISBN 0-86575-027-0, 106). Dormac.
Eaton, Quaintance. The Boston Opera Company. (Music Reprint Ser.). 1980. Repr. of 1965 ed. 25.00 (ISBN 0-306-79619-8). Da Capo.
--Opera Caravan. LC 78-9128. (Music Reprint 1978 Ser.). (Illus.). 1978. lib. bdg. 29.50 (ISBN 0-306-77596-4); pap. 6.95 (ISBN 0-306-80089-6). Da Capo.
--Opera Production One: A Handbook. LC 73-20232. (Music Ser.). 266p. 1974. Repr. of 1961 ed. lib. bdg. 22.50 (ISBN 0-306-70635-0). Da Capo.
Eaton, Randall L. The Cheetah: The Biology, Ecology, & Behavior of an Endangered Species. 178p. 1974. 13.95 (ISBN 0-442-22229-7). Krieger.
Eaton, Roy. Trout & Salmon Fishing. LC 80-68897. (Illus.). 192p. 1981. 22.50 (ISBN 0-7153-8117-2). David & Charles.
Eaton, S. Boyd, Jr. & Ferrucci, Joseph T. Radiology of the Pancreas & Duodenum. LC 72-97909. (Monographs in Clinical Radiology: No. 3). (Illus.). 385p. 1973. text ed. 29.00 (ISBN 0-7216-3310-2). Saunders.
Eaton, Sally L. What's Worrying You, Timothy Joe. 1979. 4.50 o.p. (ISBN 0-8062-1209-8). Carlton.
Eaton, Samuel D. The Forces of Freedom in Spain 1974-1979, P-245. LC 80-8383. (Illus.). 216p. 1981. pap. 11.95 (ISBN 0-8179-7452-0). Hoover Inst Pr.
Eaton, Tom. The Organized Week. (YA) (gr. 7-12). 1977. pap. 1.25 (ISBN 0-590-09858-6, Schol Pap). Schol Bk Serv.
Eaton, William. The Sociology of Mental Disorders. 1979. 19.95 (ISBN 0-03-046466-8). Praeger.
Eaton, Winifred K. Contrasts in the Representation of Death by Sophocles, Webster, & Strindberg. (Salzburg Studies in English Literature, Jacobean Drama Ser.: No. 17). 1975. pap. text ed. 25.00x (ISBN 0-391-01369-6). Humanities.
Eatwell, David & Cooper-Smith, John H. Live Steam: Locomotives & Lines Today. (Illus.). 120p. 1980. 19.95 (ISBN 0-7134-2079-0, Pub. by Batsford England). David & Charles.
--Return to Steam: Steam Tours on British Rail from Nineteen Sixty-Nine. 1978. 19.95 (ISBN 0-7134-0864-2, Pub. by Batsford England). David & Charles.
Eatwell, Roger. The Labour Governments Nineteen Forty-Five to Nineteen Fifty-One. 1979. 40.00 (ISBN 0-7134-0262-8, Pub. by Batsford England); pap. 14.95 (ISBN 0-7134-0263-6). David & Charles.
Eaves, Edgar D. & Carruth, J. H. Introductory Mathematical Analysis. 5th ed. 1978. text ed. 22.00 (ISBN 0-205-05991-0, 5659914); instr's man. avail. (ISBN 0-205-05992-9); student study guide avail. (ISBN 0-205-05993-7). Allyn.
Eaves, Howard. Survey of Geometry. rev. ed. 1972. text ed. 25.15x (ISBN 0-205-03226-5, 5632269). Allyn.
Eaves, L. J., jt. auth. see Eysenck, H. J.
Eavey, C. B. Chapel Talks. (Pocket Pulpit Library). 120p. 1981. pap. 2.95 (ISBN 0-8010-3365-9). Baker Bk.
Eavey, Charles B. History of Christian Education: Study Guide. 1.50 (ISBN 0-8024-3580-7). Moody.
--Principles of Teaching for Christian Teachers. 1940. 11.95 (ISBN 0-310-24030-1). Zondervan.
Eayrs, James. Diplomacy & Its Discontents. LC 73-163811. 198p. 1971. pap. 3.50 (ISBN 0-8020-6121-4). U of Toronto Pr.
--In Defence of Canada, Vol. I: From the Great War to the Great Depression. LC 66-3834. (Studies in the Structure of Power). 1964. pap. 5.00 (ISBN 0-8020-6072-2). U of Toronto Pr.
--In Defence of Canada, Vol. II: Appeasement & Rearmament. LC 66-3834. (Studies in the Structure of Power). 1965. 12.50x (ISBN 0-8020-1485-2); pap. 5.00 (ISBN 0-8020-6076-5). U of Toronto Pr.
Ebadi, M. & Costa, E., eds. Role of Vitamin B-Six in Neurobiology. LC 73-84113. (Advances in Biochemical Psychopharmacology Ser.: Vol. 4). (Illus.). 1972. 24.50 (ISBN 0-911216-18-9). Raven.
Eban, Abba. Abba Eban: An Autobiography. 1977. 15.00 (ISBN 0-394-49302-8); lmtd. ed. 25.00 (ISBN 0-394-42644-4). Random.
--Promised Land. LC 78-6241. (Illus.). 1978. 49.50 o.p. (ISBN 0-8407-4061-1). Nelson.
Ebashi, S., et al, eds. Muscle Contraction: Its Regulatory Mechanism. 549p. 1981. 64.00 (ISBN 0-387-10411-9). Springer-Verlag.
Ebbatson, Roger. Lawrence & the Nature Tradition: A Theme in English Fiction, 1859-1914. 1980. text ed. 40.00x (ISBN 0-391-01884-1). Humanities.
Ebbels, R. N. The Australian Labor Movement: Eighteen Fifty to Nineteen Seven. 15.00x (ISBN 0-392-07633-0, SpS). Soccer.
Ebbighausen, E. G. Introductory Astronomy. LC 73-89492. 1974. pap. 14.95x (ISBN 0-675-08843-7). Merrill.
Ebbitt, David, jt. auth. see Ebbitt, Wilma R.
Ebbitt, David R., jt. auth. see Ebbitt, Wilma R.
Ebbitt, Wilma R. & Ebbitt, David. Writer's Guide. 6th ed. 1979. pap. text ed. 8.95x (ISBN 0-673-15329-0). Scott F.
Ebbitt, Wilma R. & Ebbitt, David R. Writer's Guide & Index to English. 6th ed. 1978. 12.95x (ISBN 0-673-15109-3). Scott F.
Ebbs, John D. The Principle of Poetic Justice Illustrated in Restoration Tragedy. (Salzburg Studies in English Literature, Poetic Drama & Poetic Theory Ser.: No. 4). 211p. 1973. pap. text ed. 25.00x (ISBN 0-391-01370-X). Humanities.
Ebdon, David. Statistics in Geography: A Practical Approach. 1977. 9.95x (ISBN 0-631-16880-X, Pub. by Basil Blackwell); pap. 12.95x (ISBN 0-631-10131-4). Biblio Dist.
Ebel, Jurgen. Banking in Canada. Blythe, L. N., ed. 80p. (Orig.). 1978. pap. text ed. 10.95x (ISBN 0-7121-0259-0, Pub. by Macdonald & Evans England). Intl Ideas.
Ebel, Robert L. Essentials of Educational Measurement. 3rd ed. LC 78-13392. 1979. ref. ed. 18.95 (ISBN 0-13-286013-9). P-H.
Ebeling, Gerhard. Introduction to a Theological Theory of Language. Wilson, R. A., tr. from Ger. LC 72-87057. 224p. 1973. 6.50 (ISBN 0-8006-0256-0, 1-256). Fortress.
--The Nature of Faith. Smith, Ronald G., tr. from Ger. LC 62-7194. 192p. 1967. pap. 5.95 (ISBN 0-8006-1914-5, 1-1914). Fortress.
Ebeling, Walter. The Fruited Plain: The Story of American Agriculture. 1980. 24.50 (ISBN 0-520-03751-0). U of Cal Pr.
Ebenstein, W. & Fogelman, E. Today's Isms. 8th ed. 1980. 14.95 (ISBN 0-13-924399-2); pap. 9.95 (ISBN 0-13-924381-X). P-H.
Eber, Christine E. Just Momma & Me. LC 75-30308. (Illus.). 40p. (Orig.). (ps-3). 1975. pap. 3.00 (ISBN 0-914996-09-6). Lollipop Power.
Eber, Dorothy, ed. see Pitseolak, Peter.
Eberhard, Mary J., jt. auth. see Evans, Howard E.
Eberhard, Wolfram. A History of China. rev.,4th ed. 1977. 20.00x (ISBN 0-520-03227-6); pap. 5.95x (ISBN 0-520-03268-3). U of Cal Pr.
Eberhardt, Jo. Good Beginnings with Dairy Goats. Date not set. 6.00 (ISBN 0-686-26687-0). Dairy Goat.
Eberhardt, Louise. A Woman's Journey, Vol. I. 1976. pap. 6.50 (ISBN 0-686-15678-1). New Comm Pr.
--A Woman's Journey, Vol. II. 1978. pap. 6.50 (ISBN 0-686-15679-X). New Comm Pr.
Eberhart, David G. Upa Gurus. 10.00 (ISBN 0-89253-679-9). Ind-US Inc.
Eberhart, Dikkon. On the Verge. LC 79-9810. 1979. 9.95 (ISBN 0-916144-40-2). Stemmer Hse.
Eberhart, E. T. Burnt Offerings: Parables for Twentieth Century Christians. LC 77-23158. 1977. pap. 3.95 o.p. (ISBN 0-687-04375-1). Abingdon.
Eberhart, George M., compiled By. A Geo-Bibliography of Anomalies: Primary Access to Observations of UFOs, Ghosts, & Other Mysterious Phenomena. LC 79-6183. xl, 1114p. 1980. lib. bdg. 59.95 (ISBN 0-313-21337-2, EBA/). Greenwood.
Eberhart, Mignon E. Five Passengers from Lisbon. 160p. 1976. pap. 1.25 o.p. (ISBN 0-685-68756-2). Popular Lib.
Eberhart, Mignon G. Another Woman's House. 192p. 1973. pap. 0.95 o.p. (ISBN 0-445-00507-6). Popular Lib.
--Casa Madrone. 256p. 1981. pap. 2.25 (ISBN 0-445-04645-7). Popular Lib.
--The Chiffon Scarf. 1975. pap. 0.95 o.p. (ISBN 0-445-00679-X). Popular Lib.
--Danger Money. 192p. 1976. pap. 1.25 o.p. (ISBN 0-445-00343-X). Popular Lib.
--Dead Men's Plans. 176p. 1974. pap. 0.95 o.p. (ISBN 0-445-00549-1). Popular Lib.
--Fair Warning. 176p. 1975. pap. 0.95 o.p. (ISBN 0-445-00648-X). Popular Lib.
--Family Fortune. 1978. pap. 1.75 o.p. (ISBN 0-445-04203-6). Popular Lib.
--From This Dark Stairway. 1976. Repr. of 1931 ed. lib. bdg. 13.20 (ISBN 0-88411-760-X). Amereon Ltd.
--Hunt with the Hounds. 192p. 1974. pap. 0.95 o.p. (ISBN 0-445-00527-0). Popular Lib.
--Jury of One. 144p. 1974. pap. 0.95 o.p. (ISBN 0-445-00544-0). Popular Lib.
Eberhart, Perry. Treasure Tales of the Rockies. 3rd ed. (Illus.). 315p. 1969. 12.95 (ISBN 0-8040-0295-9, SB). Swallow.
Eberhart, Perry & Schmuck, Philip. Fourteeners: Colorado's Great Mountains. LC 72-75740. (Illus.). 128p. 1970. 12.00 (ISBN 0-8040-0122-7, SB); pap. 6.95 (ISBN 0-8040-0123-5). Swallow.
Eberhart, Philip. Guide to the Colorado Ghost Towns & Mining Camps. 4th ed. LC 59-11061. (Illus.). 496p. 1969. pap. 11.95 (ISBN 0-8040-0140-5, SB). Swallow.
Eberhart, Richard. Quarry: New Poems. 1964. 9.95 (ISBN 0-19-500536-8). Oxford U Pr.
Eberle, Bob & Standish, Bob. C. P. S. for Kids: A Resource Book for Teaching Creative Problem-Solving to Children. (Illus.). 128p. (Orig.). 1980. tchr's ed 7.95 (ISBN 0-914634-79-8, 8005). DOK Pubs.
Eberle, Irmengarde. Modern Medical Discoveries. 3rd ed. LC 68-17084. (gr. 5-9). 1968. 7.95 (ISBN 0-690-55271-8, TYC-J). T Y Crowell.
--Penguins Live Here. LC 74-1383. (gr. 1-5). 1975. 4.95 o.p. (ISBN 0-385-05715-6). Doubleday.
--Prairie Dogs in Prairie Dog Town. LC 73-9921. (Illus.). 64p. (gr. 3-6). 1974. 7.95 (ISBN 0-690-00069-3, TYC-J). T Y Crowell.
Eberle, Sarah, rev. by see Grogg, Evelyn.
Eberly, Carole. More Michigan Cooking.... & Other Things, Vol. 2. (Illus.). 112p. (Orig.). 1981. pap. 4.95 (ISBN 0-932296-07-6). Eberly Pr.
--Wild Mushroom Recipes. (Illus.). 64p. (Orig.). 1979. pap. 1.50 (ISBN 0-932296-05-X). Eberly Pr.
Eberly, J. H., jt. auth. see Allen, A.
Eberly, Joyce E., jt. ed. see Masterton, James R.
Ebersohn, Wessel. Store up the Anger. LC 80-2076. 288p. 1981. 12.95 (ISBN 0-385-17406-3). Doubleday.
Ebersole, Frank B. Language & Perception: Essays in the Philosophy of Language. LC 79-88305. 1979. pap. text ed. 11.00 (ISBN 0-8191-0776-X). U Pr of Amer.
--Meaning & Saying: Essays in the Philosophy of Language. LC 79-88304. 1979. pap. text ed. 10.00 (ISBN 0-8191-0775-1). U Pr of Amer.
Ebersole, Priscilla & Hess, Patricia. Toward Healthy Aging: Human Needs & Nursing Response. LC 80-26668. (Illus.). 600p. 1981. text ed. 18.95 (ISBN 0-8016-1491-0). Mosby.
Eberson, Frederick. Early Physicians of the West. LC 79-63659. 1979. 6.95 (ISBN 0-912760-92-3). Valkyrie Pr.
--Profiles: Giants in Medicine. (Illus.). 120p. (Orig.). 1980. pap. 5.95 (ISBN 0-934616-11-6). Valkyrie Pr.
Eberson, L. Organic Electrochemistry. LC 70-31906. (Topics in Current Chemistry: Vol. 21). (Illus.). 1971. pap. 48.40 o.p. (ISBN 0-387-05463-4). Springer-Verlag.
Ebert, Alan. Intimacies: Stars Share Their Confidences & Feelings. (Orig.). 1980. pap. 2.95 o.s.i. (ISBN 0-440-13653-9). Dell.
Ebert, Alan, jt. auth. see Fletcher, Ron.
Ebert, Friedrich A. General Bibliographical Dictionary, 4 Vols. LC 68-19956. 1968. Repr. of 1837 ed. 130.00 (ISBN 0-8103-3304-X). Gale.
Ebert, H., et al, eds. Radiation Protection Optimization--Present Experience & Methods: Proceedings of the European Scientific Seminar, Luxembourg, Oct. 1979. LC 80-41671. (Illus.). 330p. 1980. pap. 50.00 (ISBN 0-08-027291-6). Pergamon.
Ebert, H. G., ed. Seventh Symposium on Microdosimetry. 550p. 1980. 82.50 (ISBN 3-7186-0049-8). Harwood Academic.
Ebert, H. G., ed. see Symposium on Microdosimetry, Sixth, Brussels, Belgium, May 1978.
Ebert, J. D. & Okada, T. S. Mechanisms of Cell Change. LC 78-24040. 343p. 1979. 46.50 (ISBN 0-471-03097-X). Wiley.
Ebert, John & Ebert, Katherine. American Folk Painters. LC 75-11914. (Encore Edition). (Illus.). 1975. 7.95 o.p. (ISBN 0-684-14966-4, ScribT). Scribner.
Ebert, Katherine, jt. auth. see Ebert, John.

Ebert, R. J. & Mitchell, T. R. Organizational Decision Processes. LC 74-13324. (Illus.). 320p. 1975. 29.50x (ISBN 0-8448-0619-6); pap. 8.75x (ISBN 0-8448-0620-X). Crane-Russak Co.

Ebert, Richard. Lawrence of Arabia. LC 78-31450. (Raintree Great Adventures). (Illus.). (gr. 3-6). 1979. PLB 8.95 (ISBN 0-8393-0150-2). Raintree Child.

Eberto, Roger see Walsh, Gene.

Eberwein, Jane D. Early American Poetry: Bradstreet, Taylor, Dwight, Freneau & Bryant. LC 77-91051. 1978. 25.00 (ISBN 0-299-07440-4); pap. 7.95 (ISBN 0-299-07444-7). U of Wis Pr.

Eberwein, Robert T. A Viewer's Guide to Film Theory & Criticism. LC 79-9380. 243p. 1979. 13.50 (ISBN 0-8108-1237-1). Scarecrow.

Ebestin, Reinheld. The Annual Diagram. 160p. 1980. pap. 9.95 (ISBN 0-88231-122-0). ASI Pub Inc.

Ebison, Maurice, ed. see Mackay, Alan L.

Eble, Kenneth. F. Scott Fitzgerald. rev ed. (U.S. Authors Ser.: No. 36). 1977. lib. bdg. 9.95 (ISBN 0-8057-7183-2). Twayne.

--F. Scott Fitzgerald. LC 77-429. (Twayne's U. S. Authors Ser.). 187p. 1977. pap. text ed. 4.95 (ISBN 0-672-61503-7). Bobbs.

Ebling, F. J., ed. Population Control by Social Behavior. Stoddart, D. M. LC 78-70352. 1978. 27.95 (ISBN 0-03-048981-4). Praeger.

Ebling, F. J., ed. see Royal Geographical Society, Symposium, London, 1974.

Ebner, Michael H. & Tobin, Eugene M., eds. The Age of Urban Reform: New Perspectives on the Progressive Era. LC 77-4959. (National University Pubns., Interdisciplinary Urban Ser.). 1977. 15.00 (ISBN 0-8046-9192-4); pap. text ed. 8.95 (ISBN 0-8046-9204-1). Kennikat.

Ebner, Ronald J. Martian Odyssey. 1981. 4.95 (ISBN 0-8062-1624-7). Carlton.

Ebon, Martin, ed. Exorcism: Fact Not Fiction. pap. 1.25 (ISBN 0-451-05701-5, Y5701, Sig). NAL.

--The Satan Trap: Dangers of the Occult. LC 75-14816. 288p. 1976. 7.95 o.p. (ISBN 0-385-07941-9). Doubleday.

--World's Greatest Unsolved Mysteries. (Orig.). 1981. pap. 2.25 (ISBN 0-451-09684-3, E9684, Sig). NAL.

Ebon, Martin, ed. see Von Hassler, Gerd.

Ebrey, Patricia B., ed. Chinese Civilization & Society: A Sourcebook. LC 80-639. 1981. 19.95 (ISBN 0-02-908750-3); pap. text ed. 10.95 (ISBN 0-02-908760-0). Free Pr.

Ebsworth, E. A., et al. The Chemistry of Oxygen. (Pergamon Texts in Inorganic Chemistry: Vol. 16). 110p. 1975. text ed. 23.00 (ISBN 0-08-018858-3); pap. text ed. 13.25 (ISBN 0-08-018857-5). Pergamon.

Ebsworth, E. A., et al, eds. New Pathways in Inorganic Chemistry. (Illus.). 1969. 46.00 (ISBN 0-521-07254-9, 68-26984). Cambridge U Pr.

Eby, Frank H. & O'Neill, William J. The Management of Sales Forecasting. 1977. 23.95 (ISBN 0-669-00046-9). Lexington Bks.

Eby, J. Brian. My Two Roads. 2nd ed. LC 75-30380. (Illus.). 1976. 7.95 (ISBN 0-88415-570-6). Pacesetter Pr.

Eca de Queiroz. The Illustrious House of Ramires. Stevens, Ann, tr. from Port. LC 68-29766. 310p. (Port). 1969. 12.00x (ISBN 0-8214-0044-4). Ohio U Pr.

--The Mandarin & Other Stories. Goldman, R. F., tr. from Port. LC 65-13907. 176p. 1965. 10.95x (ISBN 0-8214-0008-8). Ohio U Pr.

Eccles, J. The Human Psyche. (Illus.). 300p. 1980. 25.00 (ISBN 0-387-09954-9). Springer-Verlag.

Eccles, Mark, ed. see Shakespeare, William.

Eccles, Marriner S. Economic Balance & a Balanced Budget. LC 72-2367. (FDR & the Era of the New Deal Ser). 328p. 1973. Repr. of 1940 ed. lib. bdg. 35.00 (ISBN 0-306-70479-X). Da Capo.

Eccles, W. J. Canadian Frontier, 1534-1760. LC 70-81783. (Histories of the American Frontier Ser.). (Illus.). 234p. 1974. pap. 6.50x (ISBN 0-8263-0311-0). U of NM Pr.

Eccleshall, Robert. Order & Reason in Politics: Theories of Absolute & Limited Monarchy in Early Modern England. 1978. text ed. 24.95x (ISBN 0-19-713431-9). Oxford U Pr.

Eccleshare, Elizabeth & St. Johnston, Valerie. British History Nineteen Two - Nineteen Fifty-Five. 1974. pap. text ed. 3.95x o.p. (ISBN 0-435-31170-0). Heinemann Ed.

--European History, Nineteen Four to Nineteen Sixty-Eight. 1975. pap. text ed. 3.95x o.p. (ISBN 0-435-31171-9). Heinemann Ed.

Eccli, Eugene, ed. Low-Cost, Energy-Efficient Shelter for the Owner & Builder. LC 75-38886. 1976. 12.95 (ISBN 0-87857-116-7); pap. 8.95 (ISBN 0-87857-114-0). Rodale Pr Inc.

Echlin, Edward P. Deacon in the Church. LC 75-158571. 1971. 4.95 (ISBN 0-8189-0213-2). Alba.

Echols, Barbara E. Vegetarian Feast. 1981. pap. text ed. 6.95 (ISBN 0-8120-2163-0). Barron.

Echols, Edvardus C. Freddus Elephantus et Horatius Porcus Saltans Cincinnatis. 129p. (Orig., Latin.). (gr. 10-11). 1980. pap. text ed. 3.50x (ISBN 0-88334-139-5). Ind Sch Pr.

Echols, Evaline. Climb up Through Your Valleys. 1980. 6.95; pap. 5.95. Pathway Pr.

Echols, John M. & Shadily, Hassan. An Indonesian-English Dictionary. 2nd ed. 431p. 1963. 25.00x (ISBN 0-8014-0112-7). Cornell U Pr.

Echternacht, G., jt. auth. see Donlon, T. A.

Eck, B. Fans: Design & Operation of Centrifugal, Axial Flow & Cross Flow Fans. LC 72-137613. 612p. 1974. 105.00 (ISBN 0-08-015872-2). Pergamon.

Eck, Ellen, tr. from Eng. Himnos de la Vida Cristiana. 1980. write for info. (ISBN 0-87509-277-2); pap. write for info. (ISBN 0-87509-275-6). Chr Pubns.

Eck, Margaret. Lest We Forget. 72p. pap. 0.75; pap. 2.00 3 copies. Faith Pub Hse.

Eck, Paul & Childers, N. F., eds. Blueberry Culture. 1967. 25.00 (ISBN 0-8135-0535-6). Rutgers U Pr.

Eck, Roger D. Operations Research for Business. 1976. text ed. 24.95x (ISBN 0-534-00424-5). Wadsworth Pub.

--Q M: An Introduction to Quantitative Methods for Business Applications. 1979. text ed. 21.95x (ISBN 0-534-00625-6). Wadsworth Pub.

Eckardt, Alice & Eckardt, Roy. Encounter with Israel: A Challenge to Conscience. 1970. 7.95 o.p. (ISBN 0-8096-1783-8, Assn Pr). Follett.

Eckardt, Roy, jt. auth. see Eckardt, Alice.

Eckardt, Wolf Von see Von Eckardt, Wolf.

Eckartsberg, Rolf Von, jt. ed. see Valle, Ronald S.

Eckberg, Douglas L. Intelligence & Race: The Origins & Dimensions of the IQ Controversy. LC 79-19795. (Illus.). 298p. 1979. 27.95 (ISBN 0-03-052556-X). Praeger.

Ecke, Gustav. Chinese Domestic Furniture. LC 62-21540. (Illus.). 1962. boxed 59.50 (ISBN 0-8048-0098-7). C E Tuttle.

Ecke, Wolfgang. Flight Toward Home. Knight, Anthony, tr. LC 78-89582. (gr. 5 up). 1970. 4.50 o.s.i. (ISBN 0-02-733260-8). Macmillan.

Eckel, jt. auth. see Wang Chu-Kia.

Eckenfelder, W. W. & Ford, D. Water Pollution Control. (Illus.). 17.50 (ISBN 0-8363-0099-8). Jenkins.

Eckenfelder, W. W., Jr., et al. Control, Operation & Management of Activated Sludge Plants. (Series I,Book 3). text ed. 40.00 (ISBN 0-937976-01-6). Enviro Pr.

Eckenfelder, Walter W. Principles of Water Quality Management. LC 79-20509. (Illus.). 1980. 29.95 (ISBN 0-8436-0338-0). CBI Pub.

Eckenfielder, W. W., jt. ed. see Thackston, Edward L.

Eckenhoff, James E., et al, eds. Year Book of Anesthesia, 1980. 400p. 1980. 27.50 (ISBN 0-8151-3040-6). Year Bk Med.

Eckenrod, James S. Who Controls the Controllers? A Case Study of Political Behavior. Fraenkel, Jack R., ed. (Crucial Issues in American Government Ser.). (gr. 9-12). 1976. pap. text ed. 4.96 (ISBN 0-205-04908-7, 7649088). Allyn.

Eckenrode, Hamilton J. Separation of Church & State in Virginia. LC 75-122164. (Civil Liberties in American History Ser). 1971. Repr. of 1910 ed. lib. bdg. 17.50 (ISBN 0-306-71969-X). Da Capo.

Eckensberger, Lutz H., et al, eds. Cross-Cultural Contributions to Psychology: Selected Papers from the 4th International Conference of the International Association for Cross-Cultural Psychology, Munich, July 28-August 5, 1978. 442p. 1979. pap. text ed. 31.75 (ISBN 90-265-0300-8, Pub. by Swets Pub Serv Holland). Swets North Am.

Eckenstein, Lina. Comparative Studies in Nursery Rhymes. LC 68-23469. 1968. Repr. of 1906 ed. 15.00 (ISBN 0-8103-3479-8). Gale.

--Spell of Words: Studies in Language Bearing on Custom. LC 68-23153. 1969. Repr. of 1932 ed. 15.00 (ISBN 0-8103-3892-0). Gale.

Eckermann, R., ed. see Gmehling, J., et al.

Eckert, Allen W. Savage Journey. LC 79-13646. 1979. 9.95 (ISBN 0-316-20876-0). Little.

Eckert, Charles. Emergency-Room Care. 4th ed. 1981. text ed. price not set; pap. text ed. price not set. Little.

Eckert, Charles, ed. Emergency-Room Care. 3rd ed. 1976. 22.50 (ISBN 0-316-20873-6); pap. 15.95 (ISBN 0-316-20874-4). Little.

Eckert, E. R. Heat & Mass Transfer. 2nd ed. LC 81-359. 344p. 1981. Repr. lib. bdg. price not set (ISBN 0-89874-332-X). Krieger.

Eckert, John E. & Shaw, Frank R. Beekeeping. (Illus.). 1960. 15.95 (ISBN 0-02-534910-4). Macmillan.

Eckert, Roger. Animal Physiology. LC 77-6648. (Biology Ser.). (Illus.). 1978. text ed. 26.95x (ISBN 0-7167-0570-2). W H Freeman.

Eckert, Ross D. The Enclosure of Ocean Resources: Economics & the Law of the Sea. LC 78-70388. (Publications Ser.: No. 210). (Illus.). 1979. 16.95 (ISBN 0-8179-7101-7). Hoover Inst Pr.

Eckert, Thomas B. The Young Apostle: A Story of Torment & Revelation. LC 79-67515. 122p. 1980. 6.50 (ISBN 0-533-04471-5). Vantage.

Eckert, William G. Introduction to Forensic Sciences. LC 80-10864. (Illus.). 1980. pap. text ed. 9.95 (ISBN 0-8016-1489-9). Mosby.

Eckes, Alfred E. The United States & the Global Struggle for Minerals. LC 78-11082. 1979. text ed. 19.95 (ISBN 0-292-78506-2). U of Tex Pr.

Eckes, Alfred E., Jr., jt. auth. see Roseboom, Eugene H.

Eckhard, Frederic & Linden, Ronald H., eds. Issues Before the Thirty-Third General Assembly of the United Nations. LC 76-640166. 1978. 10.00x (ISBN 0-8147-2155-9); pap. 5.00x (ISBN 0-8147-2156-7). NYU Pr.

Eckhard, Frederic & Puchala, Donald J., eds. Issues Before the Thirty-Fifth General Assembly of the United Nations. 150p. 1980. text ed. 12.50x (ISBN 0-8147-2159-1). NYU Pr.

Eckhard, Frederick & Puchala, Donald J., eds. Issues Before the Thirty-Fourth U.N. General Assembly. LC 76-43509. (A UNA-USA Book). 132p. 1979. 11.00x (ISBN 0-8147-2158-3). NYU Pr.

Eckhardt, Bob & Black, Charles. The Tides of Power: Conversations on the American Constitution. LC 75-32630. 250p. 1976. 15.00x (ISBN 0-300-01974-2); pap. 3.95x (ISBN 0-300-02118-6). Yale U Pr.

Eckhardt, Caroline D. & Stewart, David H. The Wiley Reader: Designs for Writing. brief ed. LC 78-15326. 1979. pap. 8.95 (ISBN 0-471-03499-1); tchrs. manual avail. (ISBN 0-471-04877-1). Wiley.

Eckhardt, Caroline D., et al. The Wiley Reader: Designs for Writing. LC 75-29499. 592p. 1976. 9.95 (ISBN 0-471-22970-9); instructor's manual avail. (ISBN 0-471-01458-3). Wiley.

Eckholm, E. P. Losing Ground: Environmental Stress & World Food Prospects. 1978. text ed. 27.00 (ISBN 0-08-021496-7); pap. text ed. 11.25 (ISBN 0-08-021495-9). Pergamon.

Eckhouse, Richard H. & Levy, Henry M. Computer Programming & Architecture: The VAX-11. (Illus.). 432p. 1980. 26.00 (ISBN 0-932376-07-X). Digital Pr.

Eckhouse, Richard H., Jr. & Morrison, L. Robert. Minicomputer Systems: Organization, Programming & Applications (PDP-11) 2nd ed. (Illus.). 1979. text ed. 25.00 (ISBN 0-13-583914-9). P-H.

Eckles, Robert B. Purdue Pharmacy: The First Century. LC 78-58099. (Illus.). 116p. 1979. 10.00 (ISBN 0-931682-01-0). Purdue Univ Bks.

Eckles, Robert W. & Carmichael, Ronald L. Supervisory Management. (Management Ser.). 550p. 1981. text ed. 22.95 (ISBN 0-471-05947-1); tchrs.' ed. avail. (ISBN 0-471-08941-9). Wiley.

Eckles, Robert W., et al. Essentials of Management for First-Line Supervision. LC 73-17037. 642p. 1974. text ed. 23.95 (ISBN 0-471-23000-6, Pub. by Wiley Hamilton). Wiley.

Eckley, Grace. Benedict Kiely. LC 72-187616. (English Authors Ser.: No. 145). lib. bdg. 10.95 (ISBN 0-8057-1304-2). Twayne.

--Finley Peter Dunne. (United States Authors Ser.: No. 402). 1981. lib. bdg. 11.95 (ISBN 0-8057-7295-2). Twayne.

Eckley, Mary, ed. McCall's Superb Dessert Cookbook. 1978. 9.95 (ISBN 0-394-41279-6). Random.

Eckley, Wilton. Harriette Arnow. (U. S. Authors Ser.: No. 245). 1974. lib. bdg. 10.95 (ISBN 0-8057-0023-4). Twayne.

--Herbert Hoover. (United States Author Ser.). 1980. lib. bdg. 10.95 (ISBN 0-8057-7285-5). Twayne.

--T. S. Stribling. LC 75-1096. (U. S. Authors Ser.: No. 255). 1975. lib. bdg. 10.95 (ISBN 0-8057-7151-4). Twayne.

Eckroate, Norma, jt. auth. see Frazier, Anitra.

Eckstaedt, A. & Kluwer, R., eds. Zeit Allein Heilt Keine Wunden Psychoanalytische Erstgespraeche Mit Kindern und Eltern. (Edition Taschenbuecher Wissenschaft). (Orig.). 1980. pap. text ed. 7.15 (ISBN 3-518-07908-5, Pub. by Insel Verlag Germany). Suhrkamp.

Eckstein, A. China's Economic Revolution. LC 76-9176. (Illus.). 1977. 41.95 (ISBN 0-521-21283-9); pap. 9.95x (ISBN 0-521-29189-5). Cambridge U Pr.

Eckstein, Alexander. China's Economic Development: The Interplay of Scarcity & Ideology. LC 74-25951. (Michigan Studies on China Ser.). (Illus.). 1975. 16.50 o.p. (ISBN 0-472-29872-0); pap. 7.95x (ISBN 0-472-08310-4). U of Mich Pr.

Eckstein, Alexander, ed. Comparison of Economic Systems: Theoretical & Methodological Approaches. LC 79-118085. 1971. 25.00x (ISBN 0-520-01729-3); pap. 5.50x (ISBN 0-520-02489-3). U of Cal Pr.

Eckstein, Eleanor. Menu Planning. 2nd ed. (Illus.). text ed. 21.50 (ISBN 0-87055-260-0). AVI.

Eckstein, Eleanor F. Food, People & Nutrition. (Illus.). 1980. pap. text ed. 19.50 (ISBN 0-87055-355-0). AVI.

Eckstein, Everett E. South of Dusk. LC 79-90667. 53p. 1980. 4.95 (ISBN 0-533-04460-X). Vantage.

Eckstein, Gustav. The Body Has a Head. LC 62-14529. 1970. 15.95 o.s.i. (ISBN 0-06-011153-4, HarpT). Har-Row.

Eckstein, Harry & Gurr, Ted R. Patterns of Authority: A Structural Basis for Political Inquiry. LC 75-19003. (Comparative Studies in Behavioral Science Ser). 488p. 1975. 28.95 (ISBN 0-471-23076-6, Pub. by Wiley-Interscience). Wiley.

Eckstein, Harry, ed. Internal War: Problems & Approaches. LC 80-23162. x, 339p. 1980. Repr. of 1964 ed. lib. bdg. 27.50x (ISBN 0-313-22451-X, ECIW). Greenwood.

Eckstein, J. & Gleit, J. The Best Joke Book for Kids. (Illus.). (gr. 7-12). 1977. pap. 1.50 (ISBN 0-380-01734-2, 43385, Camelot). Avon.

Eckstein, Jerome. The Death of Socrates: Living, Dying & Immortality--the Theater of Ideas in Plato's Phaedo. 288p. 1981. 18.00 (ISBN 0-914366-19-X). Columbia Pub.

Eckstein, Joan & Gleit, Joyce. Fun with Growing Things. (Illus.). 1975. pap. 2.95 o.p. (ISBN 0-380-00344-9, 23861). Avon.

Eckstein, Otto. Water-Resource Development: The Economics of Project Evaluation. LC 58-7501. (Economic Studies: No. 104). (Illus.). 1958. 16.50x (ISBN 0-674-94785-1). Harvard U Pr.

Eckstein, P. & Knowles, F., eds. Techniques in Endocrine Research. 1963. 43.50 (ISBN 0-12-230150-1). Acad Pr.

Eckstorm, Fanny. Minstrelsy of Maine. LC 79-152248. 1971. Repr. of 1927 ed. 20.00 (ISBN 0-8103-3707-X). Gale.

Eckstrom, Jack D. Time of the Hedrons. (YA) 5.95 (ISBN 0-685-07461-7, Avalon). Bouregy.

Eckstrom, Lawrence J. & Goldscheider, Robert. Licensing in Foreign & Domestic Operations, 4 vols. rev. ed. 1979. looseleaf in post binders pages 210.00 (ISBN 0-87632-075-2). Boardman.

ECMT, jt. auth. see Organization for Economic Cooperation & Development.

ECMT for OCED. Scope for Railway Transport in Urban Areas: Scope for Railway Transport in Urban Areas. (ECMT Round Table Ser.: No. 47). (Illus.). 375p. (Orig.). 1980. pap. 20.00x (ISBN 92-821-1063-X, 75-80-06-1). OECD.

Eco, Umberto. Theory of Semiotics. LC 74-22833. (Advances in Semiotics Ser.). 368p. 1976. 15.00x (ISBN 0-253-35955-4); pap. 5.95x (ISBN 0-253-20217-5). Ind U Pr.

Ecob, E. G., jt. auth. see Davies, Stanley P.

Economic & Foreign Affairs Research Association. Statistical Survey of Japan's Economy 1979. LC 54-43626. (Illus.). 83p. (Orig.). 1980. pap. 15.00x (ISBN 0-8002-2022-6). Intl Pubns Serv.

Economic & Social Committee of the European Communities - General Secretariat, ed. Community Advisory Committees for the Representation of Socio-Economic Interest. 240p. 1980. text ed. 24.75x (ISBN 0-566-00328-7, Pub. by Gower Pub Co England). Renouf.

Economic Commission for Latin America. Development Problems in Latin America: An Analysis by the United Nations Economic Commission for Latin America: (ECLA). 318p. 1970. 15.00x (ISBN 0-292-70042-3). U of Tex Pr.

Economic Planning Agency (Govt. of Japan) Economic Survey of Japan, 1978-1979. 28th ed. LC 51-61351. (Illus.). 204p. (Orig.). 1979. pap. 35.00x (ISBN 0-8002-2757-3). Intl Pubns Serv.

Economou, George. Ameriki: Book One, & Selected Earlier Poems. LC 77-3612. 1977. pap. 4.00 (ISBN 0-915342-20-0). SUN.

Economou, George D., jt. ed. see Ferrante, Joan M.

Economy, James, ed. New & Specialty Fibers. (Applied Polymer Symposia: No. 29). 1976. 22.50 (ISBN 0-471-02302-7, Pub. by Wiley-Interscience). Wiley.

Ecorcheville, Jules A. Catalogue Du Fonds De Musique Ancienne De la Bibliotheque Nationale, 4 vols. LC 79-166103. (Music Ser). (Illus.). 1973. Repr. of 1914 ed. Set. lib. bdg. 165.00 (ISBN 0-306-70280-0). Da Capo.

Edberg, E., jt. auth. see Duttarer, Janet.

Eddington, Arthur S. The Mathematical Theory of Relativity. 3rd ed. LC 74-1458. ix, 270p. 1975. text ed. 11.95 (ISBN 0-8284-0278-7). Chelsea Pub.

--Space, Time & Gravitation. 26.50 (ISBN 0-521-04865-6). Cambridge U Pr.

Eddington, Neil A., jt. ed. see Helmer, John.

Eddison, E. R. A Fish Dinner in Memison. (A Del Rey Bk.). 1978. pap. 2.25 o.p. (ISBN 0-345-27222-6). Ballantine.

Eddleman, H. Leo. Commentary on Philippians. 176p. (Orig.). 1981. pap. 4.75 (ISBN 0-682-49700-2). Exposition.

Eddowes, Maurice. Crop Production in Europe. (Illus.). 1977. 36.00x (ISBN 0-19-859444-5). Oxford U Pr.

Eddowes, Maurice, jt. auth. see Park, R. D.

Edds, G. T., jt. ed. see Davidson, J. M.

Edds, John A. Management Auditing: Concepts & Practice. 432p. 1980. text ed. 20.95 (ISBN 0-8403-2209-7). Kendall-Hunt.

Eddy, Beverley D. Abbeys, Ghosts & Castles: A Guide to the Folk History of the Middle Rhine. 1979. 8.95 o.p. (ISBN 0-8062-1205-5). Carlton.

Eddy, Donald D. Samuel Johnson - Book Reviewer in the Literary Magazine: Or Universal Review 1756-1758. LC 78-53000. 170p. 1979. lib. bdg. 17.00 (ISBN 0-8240-3425-2). Garland Pub.

Eddy, Donald D., ed. see Johnson, Samuel.

Eddy, Elizabeth M. Becoming a Teacher: The Passage to Professional Status. LC 71-90069. 1969. pap. 6.00x (ISBN 0-8077-1274-4). Tchrs Coll.

Eddy, Elizabeth M. & Partridge, William L., eds. Applied Anthropology in America. 1978. 25.00x (ISBN 0-231-04466-9); pap. 10.00x (ISBN 0-231-04467-4). Columbia U Pr.

Eddy, Frederick D., ed. The Language Learner. Incl. Definition of Language Competences Through Testing. Brooks, Nelson; Elementary & Junior High School Curricula. Peloro, Filomena C; Modern Foreign Language Learning: Assumptions & Implications. Starr, Wilmarth H; A Six-Year Sequence. Silber, Gordon R; Teaching Aids & Techniques: The Secondary School Language Laboratory. Eddy, Frederick D; The Teaching of Classical & Modern Foreign Languages: Common Areas & Problems. Bree, Josephine P. 70p. 1959. pap. 7.95x (ISBN 0-915432-59-5). NE Conf Teach Foreign.

Eddy, Henry H. & Simonetti, Martha L. Guide to the Published Archives of Pennsylvania. LC 49-9973. 1976. 3.50 (ISBN 0-911124-09-8). Pa Hist & Mus.

Eddy, John, et al. Counseling Methods: Developing Counselors. LC 80-6315. 285p. 1981. lib. bdg. 19.25 (ISBN 0-8191-1474-X); pap. text ed. 10.25 (ISBN 0-8191-1475-8). U Pr of Amer.

--Counseling Theories: Developing Counselors. LC 80-6316. 138p. 1981. lib. bdg. 16.50 (ISBN 0-8191-1476-6); pap. text ed. 7.50 (ISBN 0-8191-1477-4). U Pr of Amer.

Eddy, John A., ed. The New Solar Physics. LC 78-66338. (AAAS Selected Symposium Ser.: No. 17). 1978. lib. bdg. 20.00x (ISBN 0-89158-444-7). Westview.

Eddy, Mary B. Christ & Christmas, Poem. (Illus.). 12.50 (ISBN 0-686-00511-2). First Church.

--The First Church of Christ, Scientist, & Miscellany. German Ed. pap. 7.00 (ISBN 0-686-00513-9). First Church.

--Prose Works. new type ed. 35.00 (ISBN 0-686-00519-8); garnet new type ed. o.p. 60.00 (ISBN 0-686-00520-1); standard ed. 22.00 (ISBN 0-686-00521-X); new type bonded lea. ed. 47.00 (ISBN 0-686-00522-8). First Church.

Eddy, Peter, et al. Chinese Language Study in American Higher Education: State of the Art. (Language in Education Ser.: No. 30). 1980. pap. text ed. 7.95 (ISBN 0-87281-129-8). Ctr Appl Ling.

Eddy, Samuel & Hodson, Alexander C. Taxonomic Keys to the Common Animals of the North Central States. 3rd. ed. LC 61-11811. 1961. spiral bdg. 8.95 (ISBN 0-8087-0501-6). Burgess.

Eddy, William B. & Burke, W. Warner, eds. Behavioral Science & the Manager's Role. rev. & enl. 2nd ed. LC 79-67692. 375p. 1980. pap. 18.50 (ISBN 0-88390-123-4). Univ Assocs.

Ede, D. A., et al, eds. Vertebrate Limb & Somite Morphogenesis: The Third Symposium of the British Society for Developmental Biology. LC 76-50312. (British Society for Developmenal Biology Symposium: No. 3). 1978. 75.00 (ISBN 0-521-21552-8). Cambridge U Pr.

Ede, Donald A. An Introduction to Developmental Biology. LC 78-16359. (Tertiary Level Biology Ser.). 1978. text ed. 19.95 (ISBN 0-470-26469-1). Halsted Pr.

Ede, H. S. Savage Messiah. 1972. 6.95 (ISBN 0-87690-081-3). Dutton.

Ede, Mary. Arts & Society in England Under William & Mary. (Illus.). 218p. 1979. 23.50x (ISBN 0-8476-6261-6). Rowman.

Edebo, L., ed. Endocytosis & Exocytosis in Host Defence, Vol. 17. (Monographs in Allergy). (Illus.). 240p. 1981. pap. 78.00 (ISBN 3-8055-1865-X). S Karger.

Edeiken, Jack. Roentgen Diagnosis of Diseases of the Bone. (Golden's Diagnostic Radiology Ser.: Section No. 6). (Illus.). 1752p. 1981. price not set (2744-1). Williams & Wilkins.

Edel, Abraham. Ethical Judgment: The Use of Science in Ethics. LC 55-7339. 1964. pap. text ed. 3.00 o.s.i. (ISBN 0-02-908900-X). Free Pr.

Edel, Leon. Bloomsbury: A House of Lions. 1979. pap. 2.75 (ISBN 0-380-50005-1, 50005). Avon.

--Henry James, 4 vols. Incl. Vol. 2. The Conquest of London, 1870-1881. (Illus.). 350p. 1962; Vol. 3. The Middle Years: 1882-1895. (Illus.). 400p. 1962 (ISBN 0-397-00216-5); Vol. 4. The Treacherous Years: 1895-1901. (Illus.). 384p. 1969 (ISBN 0-397-00583-0). 10.00 ea. o.s.i. Lippincott.

--Modern Psychological Novel. 8.50 (ISBN 0-8446-2020-3). Peter Smith.

Edel, Leon, jt. auth. see Brown, E. K.

Edel, Leon, jt. auth. see Brown, Edward K.

Edel, Leon, ed. The Bodley Head Henry James, 11 vols. Incl. Vol. 1. The Europeans, Washington Square. 392p (ISBN 0-370-00616-X); Vol. 2. The Awkward Age. 430p (ISBN 0-370-00617-8); Vol. 3. The Bostonians. 448p (ISBN 0-370-00625-9); Vol. 4. The Spoils of Poynton. 208p (ISBN 0-370-00626-7); Vol. 5. The Portrait of a Lady. 626p (ISBN 0-370-00640-2); Vol. 6. What Maisie Knew. 284p (ISBN 0-370-00586-4); Vol. 7. The Wings of the Dove. 540p (ISBN 0-370-01423-5); Vol. 8. The Ambassadors. 468p (ISBN 0-370-01432-4); Vol. 9. The Golden Bowl. 604p (ISBN 0-370-01456-1); Vol. 10. The Princess Casamassima. 618p (ISBN 0-370-10237-1); Vol. 11. Daisy Miller, the Turn of the Screw. 198p (ISBN 0-370-10532-X). 1980. 12.95 ea. (Pub. by Chatto Bodley Jonathan); 130.00 set. Merrimack Bk Serv.

Edel, Leon, ed. see Wilson, Edmund.

Edel, Leon, et al. Telling Lives: The Biographer's Art. Pachter, Marc, ed. LC 79-698. 1979. 9.95 o.p. (ISBN 0-915220-54-7). New Republic.

Edel, Matthew. Economies & the Environment. (Foundations of Modern Economics Ser). (Illus.). 160p. 1973. pap. 6.95 ref. ed. o.p. (ISBN 0-13-231308-1). P-H.

Edelen, D. G. Lagrangian Mechanics of Nonconservative Nonholding Systems. (Mechanics: Dynamical Systems Ser.: No. 2). 250p. 1977. 30.00x (ISBN 90-286-0077-9). Sijthoff & Noordhoff.

Edelen, Dominic G. The Structure of Field Space: An Axiomatic Formulation of Field Physics. 1962. 27.50x (ISBN 0-520-00372-1). U of Cal Pr.

Edelhart, Michael. Breaking in Book Two: Real Life Stories on the Career Trail. LC 80-2047. 240p. 1981. pap. 6.95 (ISBN 0-385-15581-6, Anch). Doubleday.

Edelhart, Mike. Living on a Shoestring. LC 79-6535. (Illus.). 216p. 1980. pap. 5.95 (ISBN 0-385-15580-8, Anch). Doubleday.

Edelhertz, Herbert & Walsh, Marilyn. The White-Collar Challenge to Nuclear Safeguards. LC 77-15816. (Human Affairs Research Center Ser.). (Illus.). 1978. 13.95 (ISBN 0-669-02058-3). Lexington Bks.

Edelhertz, Herbert & Rogovin, Charles, eds. A National Strategy for Continuing White-Collar Crime. LC 79-2373. (Human Affairs Research Center Ser.). 160p. 1980. 15.95x (ISBN 0-669-03166-6). Lexington Bks.

Edelman, Alice & Stuzin, Roz. How to Survive a Second Marriage. 1980. 11.95 (ISBN 0-8184-0307-1). Lyle Stuart.

Edelman, Elaine. Boom-De-Boom. (Illus.). (ps-2). 1980. 4.95 (ISBN 0-394-84341-X); PLB 5.99 (ISBN 0-394-94341-4). Pantheon.

Edelman, Gerald M., ed. Cellular Selection & Regulation in the Immune Response. LC 73-93857. (Society of General Physiologists Ser.: Vol. 29). 1974. 34.50 (ISBN 0-911216-71-5). Raven.

Edelman, I. S., et al, eds. Annual Review of Physiology, Vol. 42. LC 39-15404. (Illus.). 1980. text ed. 17.00 (ISBN 0-8243-0342-3). Annual Reviews.

--Annual Review of Physiology, Vol. 43. LC 39-15404. (Illus.). 1981. text ed. 20.00 (ISBN 0-8243-0343-1). Annual Reviews.

Edelman, Lily. Japan in Story & Pictures. LC 53-9027. (Illus.). (gr. 4-6). 1953. 4.95 o.p. (ISBN 0-15-239701-9, HJ). HarBraceJ.

Edelman, Marian W. Portrait of Inequality: Black & White Children in America. LC 80-68585. 144p. (Orig.). 1980. pap. 5.00 (ISBN 0-938008-00-5). Childrens Defense.

Edelman, Murray J., jt. auth. see Dolbeare, Kenneth M.

Edelson, et al. Federal Income Tax: Nineteen Eighty-One Edition. 250p. (Orig.). 1981. pap. text ed. 10.95 (ISBN 0-8359-1873-4); instrs. manual avail. (ISBN 0-8359-1874-2). Reston.

Edelson, Charles B., et al, eds. Federal Income Tax: Nineteen Eighty Edition. (Illus.). 1980. pap. text ed. 10.95 o.p. (ISBN 0-8359-1871-8); free instrs' manual o.p. Reston.

Edelson, Edward. The Funny Men of the Movies. LC 75-14817. 128p. (gr. 4-7). 1976. PLB 5.95 (ISBN 0-385-09693-3). Doubleday.

--Great Monsters of the Movies. (gr. 4-6). 1974. pap. 1.75 (ISBN 0-671-56108-1). Archway.

--Great Movie Spectaculars. LC 76-56. 144p. (gr. 4-7). 1976. PLB 6.95 (ISBN 0-385-11180-0). Doubleday.

--Great Movies Spectaculars. (Illus.). (YA) (gr. 7-9). 1977. pap. 1.50 (ISBN 0-671-29994-8). PB.

--Tough Guys & Gals of the Movies. LC 77-17002. (gr. 4-7). 1978. PLB 5.95 (ISBN 0-385-12789-8). Doubleday.

Edelson, Edward, jt. auth. see Boikess, Robert S.

Edelson, Mary B. Seven Cycles: Public Rituals. (Illus.). 64p. (Orig.). 1980. pap. 10.00x (ISBN 0-9604650-0-6). Ede son.

Edelstein, Alex S., et al. Information Societies: Comparing the Japanese & American Experiences. LC 78-71366. 314p. (Orig.). 1979. pap. 10.95 (ISBN 0-295-95667-4, Pub. by Intl Communication Ctr). U of Wash Pr.

Edelstein, Arthur, ed. Images & Ideas in American Culture: The Functions of Criticism - Essays in Memory of Philip Rahv. LC 78-63584. 232p. 1979. text ed. 12.50x (ISBN 0-87451-164-X). U Pr of New Eng.

Edelstein, Barbara. The Woman Doctor's Diet for Teenage Girls. 288p. 1981. pap. 2.50 (ISBN 0-345-28879-3). Ballantine.

--The Woman Doctor's Diet for Women. 199p. 1981. pap. 2.50 (ISBN 0-345-29488-2). Ballantine.

--The Woman Doctor's Diet for Women. Date not set. pap. 2.50 (ISBN 0-345-28015-6). Ballantine.

Edelstein, L. & Kidd, I. G., eds. Posidonius: Vol. 1, The Fragments. LC 77-145609. (Classical Texts & Commentaries Ser, No. 13). 352p. 1972. 59.00 (ISBN 0-521-08046-0). Cambridge U Pr.

Edelstein, Norman, ed. Lanthanide & Actinide Chemistry & Spectroscopy. LC 80-17468. (ACS Symposium Ser.: No. 131). 1980. 40.00 (ISBN 0-8412-0568-X). Am Chemical.

Edelstein, Stuart J., jt. auth. see Widom, Joanne M.

Eden, tr. see Marx, Karl.

Eden, Alvin. Handbook for New Parents. 1979. pap. 2.50 (ISBN 0-425-04285-5). Berkley Pub.

Eden, Alvin N. & Heilman, Joan. Dr. Eden's Diet & Nutrition Program for Children. 1980. 9.95 (ISBN 0-8015-3180-2, Hawthorn); pap. 6.95 (ISBN 0-8015-3181-0). Dutton.

Eden, Alvin N. & Heilman, Joan R. Growing up Thin. pap. 1.50 o.p. (ISBN 0-425-03169-1). Berkley Pub.

Eden, Anthony, Earl of Avon, K.G., P.C., M.C. Another World. LC 77-74298. 1977. 7.95 o.p. (ISBN 0-385-12719-7). Doubleday.

Eden, D. J. Mental Handicap. 128p. 1976. pap. 11.25x (ISBN 0-04-371042-5). Intl Pubns Serv.

--Mental Handicap: An Introduction. (Unwin Education Bks.). 1976. pap. text ed. 7.95x (ISBN 0-04-371042-5). Allen Unwin.

Eden, David. Mental Handicap: An Introduction. LC 75-34375. 128p. 1976. 13.95 (ISBN 0-470-01373-7). Halsted Pr.

Eden, Dorothy. Darkwater. 1978. pap. 2.25 (ISBN 0-449-23544-0, Crest). Fawcett.

--Lady of Mallow. 1978. pap. 1.95 (ISBN 0-449-23167-4, Crest). Fawcett.

--Listen to Danger. 208p. 1976. pap. 1.95 (ISBN 0-441-48481-6). Ace Bks.

--The Marriage Chest. 60p. 1978. pap. 1.50 o.p. (ISBN 0-449-23032-5, Crest). Fawcett.

--The Millionaire's Daughter. 1978. pap. 2.25 (ISBN 0-449-23186-0, Crest). Fawcett.

--Ravenscroft. 1978. pap. 1.95 (ISBN 0-449-23760-5, Crest). Fawcett.

--Shadow Wife. 1978. pap. 1.95 (ISBN 0-449-23699-4, Crest). Fawcett.

--Siege in the Sun. 1979. pap. 2.25 (ISBN 0-449-23884-9, Crest). Fawcett.

--Sleep in the Woods. 1978. pap. 1.95 o.p. (ISBN 0-449-23706-0, Crest). Fawcett.

--Waiting for Willa. 1977. pap. 1.95 (ISBN 0-449-23187-9, Crest). Fawcett.

Eden, Emily. Up the Country. 1980. Repr. 18.00x (ISBN 0-8364-0660-5, Pub. by Curzon Pr). South Asia Bks.

Eden, Horatia K. Juliana Horatia Ewing & Her Books. LC 71-77001. (Library of Lives & Letters). (Illus.). 1969. Repr. of 1896 ed. 18.00 (ISBN 0-8103-3897-1). Gale.

Eden, Jerome. Planet in Trouble: The UFO Assault on Earth. 1973. 8.50 (ISBN 0-682-47822-9). Exposition.

Eden, Matthew. The Murder of Lawrence of Arabia. LC 78-69528. 1979. 9.95 o.s.i. (ISBN 0-690-01790-1, TYC-T). T Y Crowell.

Eden, R. J. High Energy Collisions of Elementary Particles. LC 75-22560. (Illus.). 312p. 1975. pap. 16.95 (ISBN 0-521-29030-9). Cambridge U Pr.

Eden, R. J., et al. Energy Economics: Growth, Resources & Policies. (Illus.). 445p. Date not set. 34.95 (ISBN 0-521-23685-1). Cambridge U Pr.

Eden, Richard J., et al. Analytic S-Matrix. 1966. 44.50 (ISBN 0-521-04869-9). Cambridge U Pr.

Eden, Sydney. The Intelligent Understanding of Stained & Painted Glass. (Illus.). 131p. 1980. 49.85 (ISBN 0-930582-81-0). Gloucester Art.

Eden, T. Tea. 3rd ed. (Tropical Agriculture Ser.). (Illus.). 1976. text ed. 36.00x (ISBN 0-582-46806-X). Longman.

Edens, Cooper. Caretakers of Wonder. (Illus.). 40p. (Orig.). 1980. pap. 6.95 (ISBN 0-914676-76-8). Green Tiger.

--Caretakers of Wonder. (Illus.). 40p. 1981. 10.95 (ISBN 0-914676-78-4). Green Tiger.

--If You're Afraid of the Dark Remember the Night Rainbow. (Illus.). 1981. 10.95 (ISBN 0-914676-26-1, Star & Elephant Bk); pap. 6.95 (ISBN 0-914676-27-X). Green Tiger.

--Starleaner Reunion. (Illus.). 1979. 16.95 (ISBN 0-914676-31-8, Star & Elephant Bk). Green Tiger.

--With Secret Friends. (Illus.). 44p. (Orig.). 1981. pap. 8.95 (ISBN 0-914676-57-1). Green Tiger.

Edens, David G. Oil & Development in the Middle East. LC 79-848. 1979. 22.95 (ISBN 0-03-049141-X). Praeger.

Eder, Gernot. Nuclear Forces: Introduction to Theoretical Nuclear Physics. 2nd ed. 1974. pap. 6.95x (ISBN 0-262-55004-0). MIT Pr.

Edera, Bruno, ed. Full Length Animated Feature Films. (Library of Animation Technology). Date not set. 37.50 (ISBN 0-8038-2317-7). Hastings.

Ederer, Grace M., jt. ed. see Blazevic, Donna J.

Edersheim, Alfred. Old Testament Bible History. 1972. 18.95 (ISBN 0-8028-8028-2). Eerdmans.

Edet, Edna S., ed. The Griot Sings: Songs from the Black World. 96p. (Orig.). 1978. pap. 6.95 (ISBN 0-89062-064-4, Pub. by Medgar Evers Coll). Pub Ctr Cult Res.

--The Griot Sings: Songs from the Black World. LC 78-10713. Date not set. pap. 6.95 (ISBN 0-89062-064-4, Pub. by Medgar Evers Coll). Pub Ctr Cult Res.

Edey, Harold C. Business Budgets & Accounts. 3rd ed. 1966. pap. text ed. 2.75x (ISBN 0-09-022422-1, Hutchinson U Lib). Humanities.

Edey, Harold C. & Peacock, Alan. National Income & Social Accounting. 1966. text ed. 5.50x (ISBN 0-09-036763-4, Hutchinson U Lib); pap. text ed. 3.00x (ISBN 0-09-036764-2, Hutchinson U Lib). Humanities.

Edey, Maitland. Lost World of the Aegean. LC 74-21774. (Emergence of Man Ser.). (Illus.). 160p. (gr. 6 up). 1975. PLB 9.63 o.p. (ISBN 0-8094-1289-6). Silver.

--The Missing Link. LC 72-89569. (Emergence of Man Ser). (Illus.). 1972. lib. bdg. 9.63 o.p. (ISBN 0-8094-1256-X, Pub. by Time-Life). Silver.

--The Northeast Coast. LC 70-187925. (American Wilderness Ser). (Illus.). (gr. 6 up). 1972. lib. bdg. 11.97 (ISBN 0-8094-1149-0, Pub. by Time-Life). Silver.

--The Sea Traders. LC 73-92665. (Emergence of Man Ser.). (gr. 6 up). 1974. PLB 9.63 o.p. (ISBN 0-8094-1317-5, Pub. by Time-Life). Silver.

Edey, Maitland A. The Missing Link. (The Emergence of Man Ser.). (Illus.). 160p. 1972. 9.95 (ISBN 0-8094-1255-1); lib. bdg. avail. (ISBN 0-685-28517-0). Time-Life.

--The Northeast Coast. (The American Wilderness Ser.). (Illus.). 184p. 1972. 12.95 (ISBN 0-8094-1148-2). Time-Life.

--The Sea Traders. (The Emergence of Man Ser.). (Illus.). 1974. 9.95 (ISBN 0-8094-1316-7); lib. bdg. avail. (ISBN 0-685-48125-5). Time-Life.

Edey, Maitland A., jt. auth. see Johanson, Donald C.

Edgar, A. H. John Bull & the Papists; or, Passages in the Life of an Anglican Rector, 1846. Wolff, Robert L., ed. (Victorian Fiction Ser.). 1975. lib. bdg. 66.00 (ISBN 0-8240-1527-4). Garland Pub.

Edgar, Alan D. Experimental Petrology: Basic Principles & Techniques. 221p. 1973. 34.95x (ISBN 0-19-854402-2). Oxford U Pr.

Edgar, E. Ware. Report on a Visit to Sikhim & the Thibetan Border. (Illus.). 1970. Repr. of 1874 ed. 8.50x o.p. (ISBN 0-685-19340-3). Paragon.

Edgar, Eugene, jt. auth. see Rutherford, Robert B.

Edgar, Eugene, jt. auth. see Rutherford, Robert B., Jr.

Edgar, Matilda R. Ten Years of Upper Canada in Peace & War, 1805-1815, Being the Ridout Letters with Annotations by Matilda Edgar: Also an Appendix of the Narrative of the Captivity Among the Shawanese Indians in 1788 of Thos. Ridout. LC 75-7125. (Indian Captivities Ser.: Vol. 98). 1977. Repr. of 1890 ed. lib. bdg. 44.00 (ISBN 0-8240-1722-6). Garland Pub.

Edgar, Neal L. A History & Bibliography of American Magazines: 1810-1820. LC 75-11882. 384p. 1975. 18.00 (ISBN 0-8108-0821-8). Scarecrow.

Edgar, William J. Evidence. LC 80-67262. 471p. 1980. lib. bdg. 22.75 (ISBN 0-8191-1292-5); pap. text ed. 13.75 (ISBN 0-8191-1293-3). U Pr of Amer.
Edgcumbe, Richard. Musical Reminiscences of the Earl of Mount Edgcumbe. LC 76-125071. 294p. 1973. Repr. of 1834 ed. lib. bdg. 27.50 (ISBN 0-306-70008-5). Da Capo.
Edge, Alfred G., et al. The Multinational Management Game. 1980. pap. 7.95x (ISBN 0-256-02362-X). Business Pubns.
Edge, Billy L., ed. Coastal Zone '80, 3 vols. LC 80-69152. 2470p. 1980. pap. text ed. 110.00 (ISBN 0-87262-258-4). Am Soc Civil Eng.
Edge, Brian, compiled by. Coins & All About Them: A Numismatic Quiz. 1973. 6.95 o.p. (ISBN 0-571-09984-X). Transatlantic.
Edge, Findley B. Pedagogia Fructifera. Lopez, Alberto, tr. 1977. pap. 2.95 (ISBN 0-311-11025-8). Casa Bautista.
Edge, Graham & Walmsley, Keith. Rothmans Book of Sporting Records 1979. 1979. 17.95 o.s.i. (ISBN 0-8464-0801-5). Beekman Pubs.
Edge, Henry T. Design & Purpose: A Study in the Drama of Evolution. (Study Ser.: No. 4). 1980. 1.25 (ISBN 0-686-59832-6, 913004-37). Point Loma Pub.
Edge, Hoyt L., jt. auth. see Wheatley, James.
Edge, L. L. Run the Cat Roads: A True Story of Bank Robbers in the Thirties. LC 80-25930. 1981: 12.50 (ISBN 0-934878-01-3). Dembner Bks.
Edge, Nellie. Kindergarten Cooks. LC 76-48558. (Illus.). (gr. k-6). 1976. pap. write for info. o.p. (ISBN 0-918146-00-3). Peninsula Pub WA.
Edge, Nellie & Leitz, Pierr M. Kids in the Kitchen. Orig. Title: Kindergarten Cooks. (Illus.). 165p. (gr. k-6). 1979. pap. 6.95 (ISBN 0-918146-18-6). Peninsula WA.
Edgecombe, Rodney. Sweetness Readie Penn'd Imagery, Syntax & Metric in the Poetry of George Herbert. (Elizabethan Studies). 1980. pap. text ed. 25.00x (ISBN 0-391-02185-0). Humanities.
Edgell, Stephen. Middle Class Couples: A Study of Segregation, Domination & Inequality in Marriage. 160p. 1980. text ed. 18.50x (ISBN 0-04-301109-8, 2381). Allen Unwin.
Edgerton, Eleanor, tr. see Kalidasa.
Edgerton, F. Mills see Bird, Thomas E.
Edgerton, Franklin, ed. Buddhist Hybrid Sanscrit Reader. 1953. 37.50x (ISBN 0-685-69814-9). Elliots Bks.
Edgerton, Franklin, ed. see Nilakantha.
Edgerton, Franklin, tr. see Apadeva.
Edgerton, Franklin, tr. see Kalidasa.
Edgerton, M. F., Jr., tr. see Devoto, Giacimo.
Edgerton, Mills F., Jr., ed. Sight & Sound: The Sensible & Sensitive Use of Audio-Visual Aids. 1969. pap. 7.95x (ISBN 0-915432-69-2). NE Conf Teach.
Edgerton, Milton T., jt. ed. see Tanzer, Radford C.
Edgerton, R. N., ed. see Langness, L. L. & Frank, Gelya F.
Edgerton, Robert B. Deviance: A Cross-Cultural Perspective. new ed. LC 75-28641. (Cummings Modular Program in Anthropology). 1976. pap. text ed. 6.95 (ISBN 0-8465-1301-3). Benjamin-Cummings.
--The Individual in Cultural Adaptation: A Study of Four East African Peoples. LC 73-117948. 1971. 21.50 (ISBN 0-520-01730-7). U of Cal Pr.
Edgerton, Robert B., jt. auth. see MacAndrew, Craig.
Edgerton, V. Reggie, jt. auth. see Edington, Dee.
Edgerton, William H. How to Renovate Townhouses & Brownstones. 2nd ed. 156p. 1980. text ed. 14.95 (ISBN 0-442-24841-5). Van Nos Reinhold.
Edgerton, William H. & Hlibok, Albert J. Real Estate Valuation Cost File, 1980: Square Foot & Cubic Foot Prices. 169p. 1980. pap. text ed. 29.95 (ISBN 0-442-25740-6). Van Nos Reinhold.
Edgeworth, Maria. The Absentee. Wolff, Robert L., ed. (Ireland: Nineteenth Century Fiction Ser.). 1979. lib. bdg. 46.00 (ISBN 0-8240-3453-8). Garland Pub.
--Castle Rackrent. Wolff, Robert L., ed. (Ireland Nineteenth Century Fiction - Ser. 2). 1979. Repr. of 1800 ed. lib. bdg. 46.00 (ISBN 0-8240-3450-3). Garland Pub.
--Ennui. Wolff, Robert L., ed. (Ireland Nineteenth Century Fiction Ser. Two: Vol. 3). 428p. 1979. lib. bdg. 32.00 (ISBN 0-8240-3452-X). Garland Pub.
--An Essay on Irish Bulls. Wolff, Robert L., ed. (Ireland Nineteenth Century Fiction, Ser. Two: Vol. 2). 1979. lib. bdg. 46.00 (ISBN 0-8240-3451-1). Garland Pub.
--Letters for Literary Ladies. (The Feminist Controversy in England, 1788-1810 Ser.). 1974. lib. bdg. 50.00 (ISBN 0-8240-0855-3). Garland Pub.
--Moral Tales for Young People, 3 vols. (The Feminist Controversy in England, 1788-1810 Ser.). 1974. lib. bdg. 50.00 ea. (ISBN 0-8240-0856-1). Garland Pub.
--Ormond. 1972. Repr. of 1900 ed. 13.00x (ISBN 0-7165-1799-X, Pub. by Irish Academic Pr Ireland). Biblio Dist.
--The Parent's Assistant, 6 vols. in 2. 3rd, rev. ed. LC 75-32150. (Classics of Children's Literature, 1621-1932: Vol. 16). 1977. Repr. of 1800 ed. Set. PLB 60.00 (ISBN 0-8240-2264-5); PLB 38.00 ea. Garland Pub.
Edgeworth, Maria & Edgeworth, Richard L. Practical Education, 2 vols. Luria, Gina, ed. (The Feminist Controversy in England, 1788-1810 Ser.). 1974. Set. lib. bdg. 100.00 (ISBN 0-685-40809-4); lib. bdg. 50.00 ea. Garland Pub.
Edgeworth, Marie. Ormond, 2 vols. Wolff, Robert L., ed. (Ireland Nineteenth Century Fiction - Ser. Two). 786p. 1979. lib. bdg. 64.00 (ISBN 0-8240-3454-6). Garland Pub.
Edgeworth, Richard L., jt. auth. see Edgeworth, Maria.
Edgeworth, Stanley. The Three Major Social, Economic, Political Tragedies in Contemporary United States History, 2 vols. in one. (Illus.). 243p. 1976. lib. bdg. 54.75 (ISBN 0-89266-006-6). Am Classical Coll Pr.
Edgington, Dorothy. The Physically Handicapped Child in Your Classroom: A Handbook for Teachers. (Illus.). 92p. 1976. pap. 10.75 (ISBN 0-398-03496-6). C C Thomas.
Edgington, E., ed. Randomization Texts. (Statistics, Textbooks & Monographs). 1980. 29.50 (ISBN 0-8247-6878-7). Dekker.
Edginton, J. K. & Sherman, H. J. Physical Science for Biologists. 1971. text ed. 6.25x (ISBN 0-09-107860-1, Hutchinson U Lib); pap. text ed. 3.50x (ISBN 0-09-107861-X, Hutchinson U Lib). Humanities.
Edgley, Charles, jt. auth. see Brissett, Dennis.
Edgren, Gosta, et al. Wage Formation & the Economy. Eklof, Margareta, tr. (Illus.). 1973. text ed. 32.50x (ISBN 0-04-330232-7). Allen Unwin.
Edholm, Felicity, tr. see Meillassoux, C.
Edie, Carolyn A. Irish Cattle Bills: A Study in Restoration Politics. LC 76-111461. (Transactions Ser.: Vol. 60, Pt. 2). 1970. pap. 1.00 o.p. (ISBN 0-87169-602-9). Am Philos.
Edie, Harry H. Ferns of Hongkong. (Illus.). 285p. (Orig.). 1977. pap. 14.00x o.p. (ISBN 962-209-002-8, Pub. by Hong Kong U Pr). Paragon.
Edinburgh Festival. Douglas Sirk. (EIFF Ser.). 1978. pap. 3.50 o.p. (ISBN 0-918432-14-6). NY Zoetrope.
--Jacques Tourneur. (EIFF Ser). 1978. pap. 4.00 (ISBN 0-918432-15-4). NY Zoetrope.
Edinburgh University Library. First Supplement to Manuscripts, Edinburgh University Library. (Library Catalogs-Supplements). lib. bdg. 115.00 (ISBN 0-8161-0319-4). G K Hall.
Edinger, Edward F. Ego & Archetype. 1973. pap. 6.95 (ISBN 0-14-021728-2, Pelican). Penguin.
--Melville's Moby-Dick: A Jungian Commentary. LC 78-6146. 1978. pap. 3.95 (ISBN 0-8112-0691-2). New Directions.
Edington, D. W., jt. auth. see Cunningham, Lee N.
Edington, Dee & Edgerton, V. Reggie. Biology of Physical Activity. LC 75-26095. (Illus.). 352p. 1976. text ed. 16.75 (ISBN 0-395-18579-3); inst. manual 1.75 (ISBN 0-395-18801-6). HM.
Edinin, M. & Johnson, M. H., eds. Immunobiology of Gametes. LC 76-49952. (Clinical & Experimental Immunoreproduction Ser.: No. 4). (Illus.). 1977. 57.50 (ISBN 0-521-21441-6). Cambridge U Pr.
Edison, Michael & Heimann, Susan. Public Opinion Polls. LC 79-18542. (First Bks). (Illus.). 72p. (gr. 5-9). 1972. PLB 4.90 o.p. (ISBN 0-531-00764-2). Watts.
Edison, Nancy, jt. ed. see Ciesielski, Stephen D.
Edite, Kroll, tr. see Fuchs, Erich.
Editions des Belles Images Staff, tr. from Fr. The Butterfly Book of Birds. (Butterfly Bks). (Illus.). 16p. (Orig.). (ps-2). 1976. pap. 1.50 (ISBN 0-8467-0226-6, Pub. by Two Continents). Hippocrene Bks.
--Hidden in the Meadow. (Butterfly Bks). (Illus.). 16p. (Orig.). (ps-2). 1976. pap. 1.50 o.p. (ISBN 0-8467-0223-1, Pub. by Two Continents). Hippocrene Bks.
Editions les Belle Images Staff, tr. from Fr. Hidden by the Pond. (Butterfly Bks). (Illus.). 16p. (Orig.). (ps-2). 1976. 1.50 o.p. (ISBN 0-8467-0224-X, Pub. by Two Continents). Hippocrene Bks.
Editions les Belles Images Staff, ed. Hidden in the Woods. (Butterfly Bks). (Illus., Orig.). (gr. 2-6). 1977. pap. 1.50 (ISBN 0-8467-0332-7, Pub. by Two Continents). Hippocrene Bks.
Editions les Belles Images Staff, tr. Butterfly Book of Mammals. (Butterfly Bks). (Orig.). (ps-2). 1976. pap. 1.50 (ISBN 0-8467-0225-8, Pub. by Two Continents). Hippocrene Bks.
Editions les Belles Images Staff, tr. from Fr. Butterfly Books - Little Red Riding Hood. 16p. (Orig.). (ps-2). 1976. pap. 1.50 (ISBN 0-8467-0222-3, Pub. by Two Continents). Hippocrene Bks.
--Butterfly Books: The Catnip Family. (Illus., Orig.). (gr. 1-2). 1977. pap. 1.50 (ISBN 0-8467-0330-0, Pub. by Two Continents). Hippocrene Bks.
--In My Garden: Learning to Count. (Butterfly Bks). (Illus.). 16p. (Orig.). (ps-2). 1976. pap. 1.50 (ISBN 0-8467-0219-3, Pub. by Two Continents). Hippocrene Bks.
Editions les Belles Images Staff, tr. Mother Goose Rhymes. (Butterfly Bks). (Illus., Orig.). (gr. 1-2). 1977. pap. 1.50 (ISBN 0-8467-0331-9, Pub. by Two Continents). Hippocrene Bks.
Editiors of The National Notary Magazine of the National Notary Assn. Journal of Notarial Acts & Recordkeeping Practices. 2nd ed. LC 73-75903. 1979. 11.65 (ISBN 0-933134-01-0). Natl Notary.
Editorial & Technical Staff of Radio Shack. All About CB Two-Way Radio. (RL 9). 1976. pap. 1.25 o.p. (ISBN 0-451-82043-6, XY2043, Sig). NAL.
Editorial Board. Civil Service Handbook. 7th ed. 128p. (Orig.). 1981. pap. 4.00 (ISBN 0-668-05166-3, 5166). Arco.
Editorial Research Reports. America in the 1980's. Editorial Research Reports, ed. (Editorial Research Reports Ser.). 220p. Date not set. pap. 6.95 (ISBN 0-87187-194-7). Congr Quarterly.
Editorial Staff. California Corporations Code & Corporate Securities Rules. 1981. pap. 14.50 (ISBN 0-911110-14-3). Parker & Son.
Editorial Staff, ed. Beautiful Crafts Book. LC 76-21846. (Illus.). (YA) 1976. 16.95 (ISBN 0-8069-5366-7); PLB 14.99 (ISBN 0-8069-5367-5). Sterling.
Editorial Turabo, Inc., ed. see Sharp, Richard M. & Mitzner, Seymour.
Editors, Change Magazine, ed. Guide to Effective Teaching. LC 78-64963. 1978. pap. 6.95 o.p. (ISBN 0-915390-18-3). Change Mag.
--In the Public Interest: The Governmental Role in Academic Institutions. LC 78-64964. 1980. cancelled (ISBN 0-915390-19-1). Change Mag.
Editors of Bicycling. Best Bicycle Tours, Vol. 2. Fones, Kathy, ed. (Bicycling Magazine Book Ser.). (Illus.). 96p. (Orig.). 1981. pap. 2.95 (ISBN 0-87857-324-0). Rodale Pr Inc.
Editors of Farm Journal & Larson, Kathryn. Listen to the Land. LC 76-56946. (Illus.). 1977. 8.95 o.p. (ISBN 0-13-537084-1). P-H.
Editors of Fine Woodworking Magazine. Design, Bk. 2. LC 78-68950. (Illus.). 1979. 15.95 (ISBN 0-918804-08-6, Dist. by Van Nostrand Reinhold); pap. 11.95 (ISBN 0-918804-07-8). Taunton.
Editors of Flying Magazine, ed. I Learned About Flying from That! 1976. 10.95 (ISBN 0-440-04041-8, E Friede). Delacorte.
Editors of Guitar Player Magazine, ed. Rock Guitarists, Vol II. LC 77-87210. (Illus.). 222p. 1977. 6.95 (ISBN 0-8256-9506-6). Guitar Player.
Editors of Gun Digest. Gun Digest's Book of Gun Accessories. Schroeder, Joseph J., ed. (Illus.). 288p. 1979. pap. 8.95 (ISBN 0-695-81313-7). Follett.
Editors of Hamlyn Publishing Group. Instant Metric Conversion Tables. LC 75-24712. 144p. 1979. 2.50 (ISBN 0-89196-001-5, Domus Bks). Quality Bks IL.
Editors of Hot Rod Magazine. Chevrolet High Performance. LC 80-80176. (Illus.). 256p. (gr. 9-12). 1980. pap. 7.95 (ISBN 0-8227-6005-3). Petersen Pub.
Editors of Hudson Home Magazine. Practical Guide to Home Restoration. 144p. 1980. 12.95 (ISBN 0-442-25400-8). Van Nos Reinhold.
Editors of Ideals. The Book of Comfort & Joy. LC 80-1192. 96p. 1981. 9.95 (ISBN 0-385-17289-3, Galilee). Doubleday.
Editors of NCTE Committee & Stanford, Gene, eds. Classroom Practices in Teaching English, 1980-1981: Dealing with Differences. (Classroom Practices in Teaching English Ser.). 144p. 1980. 5.00 (ISBN 0-8141-0690-0, 06900). NCTE.
Editors of Organic Gardening Magazine. Organic Farming Yesterday's & Tomorrow's Agriculture. (Illus.). 352p. 1977. pap. 5.95 (ISBN 0-87857-175-2). Rodale Pr Inc.
Editors of Runner's World, ed. Complete Diet Guide: For Runners & Other Athletes. LC 77-84521. (Illus.). 232p. 1978. pap. 4.95 (ISBN 0-89037-090-7); handbk. 7.95 (ISBN 0-89037-089-3). Anderson World.
Editors of the Fire Casualty & Surety Bulletins. Agent's & Buyer's Guide: Annual Edition 1980. rev ed. 540p. 1980. pap. 10.50 (ISBN 0-87218-305-X). Natl Underwriter.
--Non-Resident & Surplus Line Laws: Annual Edition 1980. rev. ed. 60p. 1980. pap. 5.00 (ISBN 0-87218-306-8). Natl Underwriter.
Editors of The National Notary Magazine of the National Notary Assn. The California Notary Law Primer. 3rd ed. 1980. pap. 5.95 (ISBN 0-933134-00-2). Natl Notary.
--Journal of Notarial Acts & Recordkeeping Practices. 8th ed. LC 73-75903. 1979. sewn bdg. semi hard cover 6.85 (ISBN 0-933134-02-9). Natl Notary.
--The Missouri Notary Law Primer. 1981. pap. 5.95 (ISBN 0-933134-04-5). Natl Notary.
--The Pennsylvania Notary Law Primer. 1981. pap. 5.95 (ISBN 0-933134-07-X). Natl Notary.
--The Texas Notary Law Primer. 1981. pap. 5.95 (ISBN 0-933134-06-1). Natl Notary.
Editors of the Novosti Press. USSR - 1981. LC 80-7938. (Illus.). 288p. 1981. 15.95 (ISBN 0-15-184601-4); pap. 8.95 (ISBN 0-15-683923-7). HarBraceJ.
Editors of the Overseas Assignment Directory. Business with China. LC 79-11413. 1979. pap. 19.95 (ISBN 0-914236-39-3). Knowledge Indus.
Editors of Time-Life Books. Boutique Attire. LC 75-7826. (The Art of Sewing). (Illus.). (gr. 6 up). 1975. PLB 11.97 (ISBN 0-8094-1751-0, Pub. by Time Life). Silver.
--Classic Desserts. (The Good Cook Ser.). (Illus.). 1980. 12.95 (ISBN 0-8094-2870-9). Time-Life.
--The Custom Look. LC 73-87766. (The Art of Sewing). (Illus.). (gr. 6 up). 1973. PLB 11.97 (ISBN 0-8094-1707-3, Pub. by Time-Life). Silver.
--Eggs & Cheese. (The Good Cook Ser.). (Illus.). 176p. 1981. 12.95 (ISBN 0-8094-2887-3). Time-Life.
--Life Goes to the Movies. LC 75-13606. (Illus.). 1975. kivar 19.92 o.p. (ISBN 0-8094-1645-X, Pub. by Time-Life). Silver.
--Making Home Furnishings. LC 75-15877. (The Art of Sewing). (Illus.). (gr. 6 up). 1975. PLB 11.97 (ISBN 0-8094-1755-3, Pub. by Time-Life). Silver.
--Novel Materials. LC 74-16950. (The Art of Sewing). (Illus.). (gr. 6 up). 1974. PLB 11.97 (ISBN 0-8094-1723-5, Pub. by Time-Life). Silver.
--Repairing Furniture. (Home Repair & Improvement). (Illus.). 128p. 1981. 10.95 (ISBN 0-8094-2438-X). Time-Life.
--Separates That Travel. LC 75-21824. (The Art of Sewing). (Illus.). (gr. 6 up). 1975. PLB 11.97 (ISBN 0-8094-1759-6, Pub. by Time-Life). Silver.
--Shortcuts to Elegance. LC 73-91757. (The Art of Sewing). (Illus.). (gr. 6 up). 1974. PLB 11.97 (ISBN 0-8094-1711-1, Pub. by Time-Life). Silver.
--Traditional Favorites. LC 73-94381. (The Art of Sewing). (Illus.). (gr. 6 up). 1974. PLB 11.97 (ISBN 0-8094-1715-4, Pub. by Time-Life). Silver.
Editors of Time-Life Books, ed. see Rigge, Simon.
Editors of Traffic World. Traffic World's Question & Answer Book, Vol. 27. 1979. text ed. 16.00 (ISBN 0-87408-015-0). Traffic Serv.
Edito T. De La Cruz, jt. tr. see Fuentes, Milma M.
Edkins, Diana, jt. auth. see Newhall, Beaumont.
Edkins, Joseph. The Revenue & Taxation of the Chinese Empire. LC 78-74331. (The Modern Chinese Economy Ser.). 240p. 1980. lib. bdg. 26.00 (ISBN 0-8240-4252-2). Garland Pub.
Edland, H. The Pocket Encyclopedia of Roses in Color. (Illus.). 1963. 9.95 (ISBN 0-7137-0632-5, Pub by Blandford Pr England). Sterling.
Edler, Howard, jt. ed. see Lett, J. T.
Edler, Timothy. The Adventures of Crawfish-Man. (Tim Edler's Tales from the Atchafalaya Ser.). (Illus.). 40p. (gr. k-8). 1979. 5.00x (ISBN 0-931108-04-7). Little Cajun.
--Crawfish-Man Rescues Ron Guidry. (Tim Edler's Tales from the Atchafalaya). (Illus.). (gr. k-8). 1980. lea. 5.00 (ISBN 0-931108-05-5). Little Cajun.
--Dark Gator. (Tim Edler's New Swamp Wars Ser.). (Illus.). (gr. k-8). 1980. lea. 5.00 (ISBN 0-931108-06-3). Little Cajun.
--Maurice the Snake & Gaston the Near-Sighted Turtle. (Tim Edler's Tales from the Atchafalaya). (Illus.). (gr. k-8). 1977. lea. 5.00 (ISBN 0-931108-00-4). Little Cajun.
--T-Boy in Mossland. (Tim Edler's Tales from the Atchafalaya). (Illus.). (gr. k-8). 1978. leather 5.00 (ISBN 0-931108-03-9). Little Cajun.
--T-Boy the Little Cajun. (Tim Edler's Tales from the Atchafalaya). (Illus.). (gr. k-8). 1978. leather 5.00 (ISBN 0-931108-01-2). Little Cajun.
Edlin, Herbert L. The Observer's Book of Trees. (The Observer Bks). (Illus.). 1979. 4.95 (ISBN 0-684-16037-4, ScribT). Scribner.
--Trees & Man. 1976. 27.50x (ISBN 0-231-04158-6). Columbia U Pr.
--Woodland Crafts in Britain: An Account of the Traditional Uses of Trees & Timbers in the British Countryside. new ed. (Illus.). 182p. 1973. 14.95 (ISBN 0-7153-5852-9). David & Charles.

Edlin, Herbert L. & Huxley, Anthony. Atlas of Plant Life. LC 73-734361. (John Day Bk.). (Illus.). 128p. 1973. 11.95 (ISBN 0-381-98245-9, TYC-T). T Y Crowell.

Edlow, R. B. Galen on Language & Ambiguity "De Captionibus" (on Fallacies) An English Translation of Galen's. (Philosophia Antiqua: No. 31). 1977. pap. text ed. 25.25x (ISBN 90-04-04869-3). Humanities.

Edlund, Mary, jt. auth. see Edlund, Sidney.

Edlund, Sidney & Edlund, Mary. Pick Your Job & Land It. 1973. 5.00 (ISBN 0-686-17213-2). Sandollar Pr.

Edman, David. A Bit of Christmas Whimsy. LC 74-6474. (Illus.). 160p. 1971. 6.95 (ISBN 0-570-03234-2, 15-2128). Concordia.

Edman, David, jt. auth. see Castle, Wendell.

Edman, V. Raymond. But God! 1980. 5.95 (ISBN 0-310-24047-6). Zondervan.

--Crisis Experiences in the Lives of Noted Christians. 1970. pap. 1.95 (ISBN 0-87123-065-8, 200065). Bethany Fell.

--Finney Lives On. 1970. pap. 3.95 (ISBN 0-87123-150-6, 210150). Bethany Fell.

Edmands, Allen, jt. auth. see Edmands, Dodie.

Edmands, Dodie & Edmands, Allen. The Children's Astrologer. LC 78-53406. (Illus.). 1978. 7.95 o.p. (ISBN 0-8015-1227-1). Dutton.

Edmond, Carolyn E., jt. auth. see Washington, Allyn J.

Edmond, Joseph B. & Ammerman, C. R. Sweet Potatoes: Production, Processing, Marketing. LC 73-165213. (Illus.). 1971. 31.00 o.p. (ISBN 0-87055-103-5). AVI.

Edmonds, Cecil J. Kurds, Turks, & Arabs: Politics, Travel, & Research in North-Eastern Iraq, 1919-1925. LC 80-1930. 1981. Repr. of 1957 ed. 49.50 (ISBN 0-404-18960-1). AMS Pr.

Edmonds, David C. Yankee Autumn in Acadiana: A Narrative of the Great Texas Overland Expedition Through Southwestern Louisiana. 2nd ed. LC 79-67333. (Illus.). 512p. 1980. Repr. 15.95 (ISBN 0-937614-01-7). Acadiana Pr.

Edmonds, I. G. Buddhism. (First Books Ser.). (Illus.). (gr. 5-8). 1978. PLB 6.45 s&l (ISBN 0-531-01349-9). Watts.

--Hinduism. (First Bks.). (Illus.). (gr. 4 up). 1979. PLB 6.45 s&l (ISBN 0-531-02943-3). Watts.

--Islam. LC 77-2664. (First Bks.). (gr. 5-8). 1977. PLB 6.45 s&l (ISBN 0-531-01288-3). Watts.

--Minibikes & Minicycles for Beginners. (gr. 5-7). 1975. pap. 1.25 (ISBN 0-671-29783-X). Archway.

--Minibikes & Minicycles for Beginners. (Illus.). (gr. 5-7). pap. 1.25 (ISBN 0-671-29783-X). PB.

--The Mysteries of Homer's Greeks. (Illus.). 1981. 10.95 (ISBN 0-525-66692-3). Elsevier-Nelson.

--Oscar Directors. 1980. 17.95 (ISBN 0-498-02533-0); pap. write for info. (ISBN 0-498-02444-X). A S Barnes.

Edmonds, I. G. & Gonzales, Ronald F. Introduction to Welding. 1975. pap. text ed. 14.95 scp (ISBN 0-06-453303-4, HarpC); tchr's ed. avail. (ISBN 0-685-66883-5). Har-Row.

Edmonds, Irene, jt. tr. see Walsh, Kilian.

Edmonds, J. M., tr. Lyra Graeca, 3 Vols. (Loeb Classical Library: No. 142-144). 9.50x ea. Vol. 1 (ISBN 0-674-99157-5). Vol. 2 (ISBN 0-674-99158-3). Vol. 3 (ISBN 0-674-99159-1). Harvard U Pr.

Edmonds, Martin, jt. ed. see Beaumont, Roger A.

Edmonds, Peggy, ed. Harris Michigan Industrial Directory. rev. ed. (Illus., Annual). 1981. 58.75 (ISBN 0-916512-15-0). Harris Pub.

Edmonds, Ronald R., jt. ed. see Willie, Charles V.

Edmonds, Rosemary, tr. see Tolstoy, Leo.

Edmonds, Rosemary, tr. see Turgenev, Ivan.

Edmonds, S. J., jt. auth. see Stephen, A. C.

Edmonds, Simeon. ESP, Extrasensory Perception. pap. 2.00 o.p. (ISBN 0-87980-207-3). Wilshire.

Edmonds, Walter D. Matchlock Gun. LC 41-17547. (Illus.). (gr. 4-6). 1941. PLB 5.95 (ISBN 0-396-06369-1). Dodd.

--The Night Raider & Other Stories. 96p. (gr. 7 up). 1980. 6.95g (ISBN 0-316-21141-9). Little.

--Two Logs Crossing. LC 43-17980. (Illus.). (gr. 7-9). 1943. 4.50 (ISBN 0-396-02505-6). Dodd.

Edmondson, C. Earl. The Heimwehr & Austrian Politics. LC 77-21924. 384p. 1978. 25.00x (ISBN 0-8203-0437-9). U of Ga Pr.

Edmondson, E. B. Chess Scandals: The Nineteen Seventy-Eight World Championship Match. (Pergamon Chess Ser.). (Illus.). 260p. 1981. 24.00 (ISBN 0-08-024145-X); pap. 14.40 (ISBN 0-08-024144-1). Pergamon.

Edmondson, Jolee. The Woman Golfer's Catalogue. LC 79-65116. (Illus.). 1980. 18.95 (ISBN 0-8128-2685-X); pap. 10.95 (ISBN 0-8128-6041-1). Stein & Day.

Edmondson, Madeleine. The Witch's Egg. LC 72-97769. (Illus.). (gr. 1-4). 1974. 5.95 (ISBN 0-395-28790-1, Clarion). HM.

Edmondson, Madeleine, jt. auth. see Cole, Joanna.

Edmonson, A. S. Campbell's Operative Orthopaedics, 2 Vols. 6 ed. LC 80-14731. 1980. Set. 189.50 (ISBN 0-8016-1071-0). Mosby.

Edmonson, Madeleine & Rounds, David. From Mary Noble to Mary Hartman. 1977. pap. 1.75 o.s.i. (ISBN 0-515-04423-7). Jove Pubns.

Edmonston, Phil. Lemon-Aid. 1977. 9.95 o.p. (ISBN 0-679-50764-7); pap. 4.95 o.p. (ISBN 0-679-50730-2). McKay.

--Lemon Aid: Everything You Need to Know About American & Foreign Cars, Trucks, & Vans: Rating, Buying, Maintaining, Repairing, & Selling, & How to Turn a Bad Trip into a Good Buy. LC 80-25807. (Illus.). 600p. 1981. pap. 8.95 (ISBN 0-8253-0014-2). Beaufort Bks NY.

--The Used Car Guide. (Illus.). 254p. 1981. pap. 8.95 (ISBN 0-8253-0051-7). Beaufort Bks NY.

Edmonston, William E. Hypnosis & Relaxation: Modern Verification of an Old Equation. LC 80-22506. (Personality Processes Ser.). 280p. 1981. 21.00 (ISBN 0-471-05903-X, Pub. by Wiley Interscience). Wiley.

Edmunds, Edward W. Chaucer & His Poetry. 218p. 1980. Repr. of 1920 ed. lib. bdg. 8.00 (ISBN 0-8495-1349-9). Arden Lib.

Edmunds, G. & Kendrick, D. G. The Measurement of Human Aggressiveness. LC 79-40970. 223p. 1980. 29.95x (ISBN 0-470-26871-9). Halsted Pr.

Edmunds, Lowell. The Silver Bullet: The Martini in American Civilization. LC 80-1196. (Contributions in American Studies: No. 52). (Illus.). 160p. 1981. lib. bdg. 19.95 (ISBN 0-313-22225-8, ESB/). Greenwood.

Edmunds, M. G., jt. auth. see Solomon, P. M.

Edmunds, Malcolm. Defence in Animals. LC 73-92246. (Illus.). 288p. 1975. pap. text ed. 16.95x (ISBN 0-582-44132-3). Longman.

Edmunds, R. David, ed. American Indian Leaders: Studies in Diversity. LC 80-431. (Illus.). xiv, 260p. 1980. 19.50x (ISBN 0-8032-1800-1); pap. 5.95 (ISBN 0-8032-6705-3, BB 746, Bison). U of Nebr Pr.

Edmunds, Stahrl & Rose, Adam. Geothermal Energy & Regional Development. 1979. 31.95 (ISBN 0-03-053316-3). Praeger.

Edmunds, Stahrl W. Basics of Private & Public Management. LC 77-9147. 1978. 22.95 (ISBN 0-669-01679-9). Lexington Bks.

Edmunds, Stahrl W. & Rose, Adam Z., eds. Geothermal Energy & Regional Development: The Case of Imperial County, California. LC 79-19219. (Illus.). 398p. 1979. 31.95 (ISBN 0-03-053316-3). Praeger.

Edney, Margon & Grimm, Ede. The Elegant Hors d'Oeuvre. Rand, Elizabeth & Polster, Diane, eds. LC 77-86167. (Illus.). 1977. plastic comb 5.95 (ISBN 0-914488-13-9). Rand-Tofua.

Edsall, John T. & Wyman, Jeffries. Biophysical Chemistry, Vol. 1: Thermodynamics, Electrostatics & the Biological Significance of the Properties of Matter. 1958. 49.50 (ISBN 0-12-232201-0). Acad Pr.

Edson, Doris, jt. auth. see Barton, Lucy.

Edson, J. T. Bloody Border. (J.T. Edson Ser.). 1978. pap. 1.50 o.p. (ISBN 0-425-03844-0, Medallion). Berkley Pub.

--Comanche. (J. T. Edson Ser.). 1978. pap. 1.50 o.p. (ISBN 0-425-03843-2, Medallion). Berkley Pub.

--Cuchilo. (Orig.). 1981. pap. 1.95 (ISBN 0-425-04836-5). Berkley Pub.

--The Fast Gun. (Orig.). 1981. pap. 1.95 (ISBN 0-425-04802-0). Berkley Pub.

--The Half Breed. (Orig.). 1981. pap. 1.95 (ISBN 0-425-04736-9). Berkley Pub.

--Renegade. (J. T. Edson Ser.). 1978. pap. 1.50 o.p. (ISBN 0-425-03845-9, Medallion). Berkley Pub.

--Sidewinder. 1979. pap. 1.75 o.p. (ISBN 0-425-04416-5). Berkley Pub.

--Viridian's Trail. (J. T. Edson Ser.). 1978. pap. 1.50 o.p. (ISBN 0-425-03847-5, Medallion). Berkley Pub.

--The Wildcats. 192p. (Orig.). 1981. pap. 1.95 (ISBN 0-425-04755-5). Berkley Pub.

--The Ysabel Kid. (J. T. Edson Ser.). 1978. pap. 1.50 o.p. (ISBN 0-685-54608-X, Medallion). Berkley Pub.

Edson, Jean S. Organ Preludes: An Index to Compositions on Hymn Tunes, Chorales, Plainsong Melodies, Gregorian Tunes & Carols, 2 Vols. LC 73-8960. 1970. Set. 40.00 (ISBN 0-8108-0287-2). Scarecrow.

--Organ Preludes: Supplement. 1974. 12.00 (ISBN 0-8108-0663-0). Scarecrow.

Edson, Lee. How We Learn. (Human Behavior Ser). 176p. 1975. 9.95 (ISBN 0-8094-1916-5); lib. bdg. avail. (ISBN 0-685-52491-4). Time-Life.

--How We Learn. LC 74-33050. (Human Behavior Ser.). (Illus.). 1975. lib. bdg. 9.99 o.p. (ISBN 0-686-51076-3). Silver.

Edson, Russell. The Clam Theater. LC 72-11052. (Wesleyan Poetry Program: Vol. 64). 1973. 10.00x (ISBN 0-8195-2064-0, Pub. by Wesleyan U Pr). Columbia U Pr.

--The Intuitive Journey & Other Works. LC 75-30331. 188p. 1976. 10.00 o.p. (ISBN 0-06-011118-6, HarpT); pap. 4.95 o.p. (ISBN 0-06-011121-6, TD-254, HarpT). Har-Row.

--The Reason Why the Closet-Man Is Never Sad. LC 76-55942. (Wesleyan Poetry Program: Vol. 84). 1977. 10.00x (ISBN 0-8195-2084-5, Pub. by Wesleyan U Pr); pap. 4.95 (ISBN 0-8195-1084-X). Columbia U Pr.

Education Development Center Introductory Physical Science Group. College Introductory Physical Science. 1969. pap. text ed. 13.95 (ISBN 0-13-145524-9); achievement tests 12.00 (ISBN 0-13-145540-0); ans. sheets (40 per pkg) 2.00 (ISBN 0-13-145557-5). P-H.

Educational Challenges, Inc. Map Skills. Hayes, Heidi, ed. Incl. Book C (ISBN 0-8372-3505-7). tchr's ed.; Book D (ISBN 0-8372-3506-5). tchr's ed. (ISBN 0-8372-9196-8); Book E (ISBN 0-8372-3507-3). tchr's ed (ISBN 0-8372-9197-6); Book F (ISBN 0-8372-3508-1). tchr's ed (ISBN 0-8372-9198-4). (Elementary Skills Ser). 1977. 1.35 ea. Bowmar-Noble.

Educational Development Corporation. Spell-Write, 8 bks. (Illus.). (gr. 1-8). 1975. Bks. 2-8. text ed. 4.98 ea.; Bk. 1. text ed. 4.98 ea. (ISBN 0-8107-1350-0); Bks. 2-8. pap. text ed. 3.93 ea.; Bks. 2-8. tchrs'. ed. 4.98 ea.; Bk. 1. tchrs' pap. ed. 3.42 (ISBN 0-685-04625-7); Bks. 2-8. tchrs' pap. eds. 4.80 ea.; Bks. 3-6. activity duplicating masters 9.00 ea. Bowmar-Noble.

Educational Materials Sector Committee of the American National Metric Council. Metric Guide for Educational Materials: A Handbook for Teachers, Writers & Publishers. 1977. pap. text ed. 3.00 (ISBN 0-916148-09-2). Am Natl.

Educational Research Council. Agriculture: People & the Land. (Concepts & Inquiry Ser). (gr. 4). 1975. pap. text ed. 7.24 (ISBN 0-205-04436-0, 8044368); tchrs'. guide 7.24 (ISBN 0-205-04437-9, 8044376). Allyn.

--The American Adventure, 2 vols. (Concepts & Inquiry Ser). (Orig.). (gr. 8). 1975. Vol. 1. text ed. 16.92 (ISBN 0-205-04623-1, 8046239); 12.00 (ISBN 0-205-04624-X, 8046247); Vol. 2. text ed. 16.92 (ISBN 0-205-04625-8, 8046255); 12.00 (ISBN 0-205-04626-6, 8046263). Allyn.

--Early Years: Twenty Thousand B.C. to Seventeen Sixty-Three A. D. (The American Adventure Concepts & Inquiry Ser.). (gr. 8). 1975. pap. text ed. 8.96 (ISBN 0-205-04628-2, 804628X). Allyn.

--Expansion, Conflict, & Reconstruction 1825-1880. (The American Adventure Concepts & Inquiry Ser). (Orig.). (gr. 8). 1975. pap. text ed. 8.96 (ISBN 0-205-04629-0, 8046298). Allyn.

--The Forming of the Republic (1763-1825) (The American Adventure Concept & Inquiry Ser). (gr. 8). 1975. pap. text ed. 8.96 (ISBN 0-205-04630-4, 8046301). Allyn.

--Greek & Roman Civilization. (The Human Adventure, Concepts & Inquiry Ser). (gr. 5). 1975. pap. text ed. 6.20 (ISBN 0-205-04446-8, 8044465); tchrs.' guide 5.20 (ISBN 0-205-04447-6, 8044473). Allyn.

--Into the Twentieth Century (1880-1939) (American Adventure Concepts & Inquiry Ser.). (Orig.). (gr. 8). 1977. pap. 9.40 (ISBN 0-205-04631-2, 804631X). Allyn.

--The Making of Tomorrow (1940-Present) (The American Adventure Concepts & Inquiry Ser). (gr. 8). 1977. pap. text ed. 9.40 (ISBN 0-205-04627-4, 8046271). Allyn.

--Medieval Civilization. (The Human Adventure, Concepts & Inquiry Ser). (gr. 5). 1975. pap. text ed. 6.20 (ISBN 0-205-04448-4, 8044481); tchrs'. guide 5.20 (ISBN 0-205-04449-2, 804449X). Allyn.

--New World & Eurasian Cultures. (The Human Adventure Concepts and Inquiry Ser). (gr. 6). 1975. pap. text ed. 7.20 (ISBN 0-205-04454-9, 8044546); tchrs'. guide 5.20 (ISBN 0-205-04455-7, 8044554). Allyn.

Educational Research Council of America. Choices & Decisions: Economics & Society. new ed. (Challenges of Our Time Ser.). (Orig.). (gr. 7). 1972. pap. text ed. 9.32 (ISBN 0-205-05035-2, 805035X); tchrs'. guide 6.60 (ISBN 0-205-05036-0, 8050368). Allyn.

--Nations in Action: International Tensions. (Challenges of Our Time Ser.). (gr. 7). 1972. pap. text ed. 9.32 (ISBN 0-205-05033-6, 8050333); tchrs'. guide 6.60 (ISBN 0-205-05034-4, 8050341). Allyn.

--Prejudice & Discrimination. (Challenges of Our Time Ser.). (gr. 7). 1973. pap. text ed. 9.32 (ISBN 0-205-05031-X, 8050317); tchrs'. guide 6.60 (ISBN 0-205-05032-8, 8050325). Allyn.

--Technology: Promises & Problems. new ed. (Challenges of Our Time Ser.). (Orig.). (gr. 7). 1972. pap. text ed. 9.32 (ISBN 0-205-05029-8, 8050295); tchrs'. guide 6.60 (ISBN 0-205-05030-1, 8050309). Allyn.

Educational Research Symposium Organised by the Council of Europe & the Research & Development Unit of the Chancellor of the Swedish Universities, Goteborg, Sweden, September 7-12, 1975. Strategies for Research & Development in Higher Education: Proceedings. Entwistle, Noel, ed. 282p. 1976. pap. text ed. 25.50 (ISBN 90-265-0242-7, Pub. by Swets Pub Serv Holland). Swets North Am.

Educational Resources Center. Social Science Skills: Activities for the Secondary Classroom, 7 vols. Incl. American Government Issues (ISBN 0-8077-2649-4); American Lifestyle Issues (ISBN 0-8077-2648-6); Consumer Issues (ISBN 0-8077-2647-8); Economic Issues (ISBN 0-8077-2645-1); Energy Issues (ISBN 0-8077-2646-X); Global Issues (ISBN 0-8077-2643-5); Population Issues (ISBN 0-8077-2644-3); Basic Skills (ISBN 0-8077-2650-8). (Orig.). 1981. price not set. Tchrs Coll.

Educational Resources Information Center. Current Index to Journals in Education, Annual Cumulation 1970. 1971. 75.00 o.s.i. (ISBN 0-02-469880-6). Macmillan Info.

--Current Index to Journals in Education, Annual Cumulation 1969. 1970. 75.00 o.s.i. (ISBN 0-02-469870-9). Macmillan Info.

--Current Index to Journals in Education: Annual Cumulation 1971. 1972. 75.00 o.s.i. (ISBN 0-02-469890-3). Macmillan Info.

Educational Resources Information Center (ERIC) Educational Documents Abstracts, 1978. LC 72-75009. 1979. 90.00 (ISBN 0-02-692870-1). Macmillan Info.

--Educational Documents Index, 1978. LC 71-130348. 1979. 60.00 (ISBN 0-02-692880-9). Macmillan Info.

Educational Resources Information Center. Educational Finance: An ERIC Bibliography. 1972. pap. 9.95 o.s.i. (ISBN 0-02-468880-0). Macmillan Info.

--Information Analysis Products: 1967-1972. 1973. 14.95 o.s.i. (ISBN 0-02-468820-7). Macmillan Info.

--Reading: An ERIC Bibliography, 1970-1972. rev. ed. LC 73-6203. 1973. 11.50 o.s.i. (ISBN 0-02-469340-5). Macmillan Info.

--Social Studies & Social Science Education 1970-1972: An ERIC Bibliography. LC 72-82740. 1973. 11.50 o.s.i. (ISBN 0-02-469840-7). Macmillan Info.

Educational Testing Service & Council on Learning. What College Students Know. LC 80-69767. 200p. (Orig.). 1980. pap. 10,95 (ISBN 0-915390-31-0). Change Mag.

EDUCOM Fall Conference, Oct. 1977. Closing the Gap Between Technology & Application: Proceedings. Emery, James C., ed. 1978. lib. bdg. 26.75x (ISBN 0-89158-167-7). Westview.

Edvarsen, Aril, tr. Les Dons Spirituels. (French Bks.). (Fr.). 1979. 2.10 (ISBN 0-686-28819-X). Life Pubs Intl.

Edvinsson, Lars, jt. ed. see Owman, Christer.

Edward, Derek, jt. auth. see Tilbury, Fred.

Edward, Joyce, et al. Separation-Individuation Theory & Clinical Practice. 324p. 1981. text ed. 22.95 (ISBN 0-89876-018-6). Gardner Pr.

Edward, W. Visually & Transfer Skill Mastery, 2 levels. Incl. Level 1. Addition & Multiplication (ISBN 0-89039-948-4); Level 2. Subtraction & Division (ISBN 0-89039-850-X). pap. 7.00 ea. Ann Arbor FL.

Edwardes, Michael. Ralph Fitch: Elizabethan in the Indies. (Great Travellers Ser.). (Illus.). 1973. 6.95 o.p. (ISBN 0-571-10133-X, Pub. by Faber & Faber). Merrimack Bk Serv.

Edwardine, Mary. Dialogue for Christmas Eve. 2.00 (ISBN 0-8283-1569-8). Branden.

Edwards, jt. auth. see Keene.

Edwards, jt. auth. see Logan.

Edwards, frwd. by see Nutt, Grady.

Edwards, et al. Plaid for The Basic Accounting Cycle. 1975. pap. 6.95 (ISBN 0-256-01707-7, 01-1137-00). Learning Syst.

--Advances in the Management of Cleft Palate. (Illus.). 1981. text ed. 30.00 (ISBN 0-443-01601-1). Churchill.

Edwards, A. & Wohl, G. The Picture Life of Muhammad Ali. 1977. pap. 1.75 (ISBN 0-380-01904-3, 51623, Camelot). Avon.

--The Picture Life of Stevie Wonder. 1977. pap. 1.75 (ISBN 0-380-01907-8, 51656, Camelot). Avon.

Edwards, A. D. Changing Sixth-Form in the Twentieth Century. (Students Library of Education Ser.). 1970. text ed. 5.50x (ISBN 0-7100-6742-9); pap. text ed. 2.75x (ISBN 0-7100-6743-7). Humanities.

--Language in Culture & Class. 1976. 19.50x (ISBN 0-8448-1063-0). Crane-Russak Co.

Edwards, A. S. & Pearsall, Derek, eds. Middle English Prose: Essays on Bibliographical Problems. LC 80-8595. 150p. 1981. lib. bdg. 25.00 (ISBN 0-8240-9453-0). Garland Pub.

Edwards, A. S., ed. see Renaissance English Text Society & Cavendish, George.

Edwards, A. W. Foundations of Mathematical Genetics. LC 76-9168. (Illus.). 1977. 23.95 (ISBN 0-521-21325-8). Cambridge U Pr.

Edwards, Alfred L., ed. see International Association for the Advancement of Appropriate Technology for Developing Countries, 1979 Symposium.

Edwards, Allen L. An Introduction to Linear Regression & Correlation. LC 75-38811. (Illus.). 1976. pap. text ed. 9.95x (ISBN 0-7167-0561-3). W H Freeman.
--Multiple Regression & the Analysis of Variance & Covariance. LC 79-12873. (Psychology Ser.). (Illus.). 1979. pap. text ed. 8.95x (ISBN 0-7167-1081-1). W H Freeman.

Edwards, Anne. Child of Night. 1978. pap. 1.75 o.p. (ISBN 0-445-04156-0). Popular Lib.
--Sonya: The Life of Countess Tolstoy. 1981. 13.95 (ISBN 0-671-24040-4). S&S.

Edwards, Anthony S. John Skelton. (The Critical Heritage Ser.). 300p. 1981. price not set (ISBN 0-7100-0724-8). Routledge & Kegan.

Edwards, Anthony S., ed. see Cavendish, George.

Edwards, Archie L., Sr. Expository Outlines from Paul's Epistles. (Sermon Outline Ser.). 1978. pap. 1.95 (ISBN 0-8010-3333-0). Baker Bk.

Edwards, Audrey & Wohl, Gary. The Picture Life of Bobby Orr. (Picture Lives Ser.). (Illus.). 48p. (gr. k-3). 1976. PLB 4.90 o.p. (ISBN 0-531-01208-5). Watts.
--The Picture Life of Muhammad Ali. LC 76-10999. (Picture Lives Ser.). (Illus.). 48p. (gr. k-3). 1976. PLB 4.90 o.p. (ISBN 0-531-00327-2). Watts.
--The Picture Life of Stevie Wonder. (Picture Life Bks.). (Illus.). (gr. k-3). 1977. PLB 6.45 s&l (ISBN 0-531-01271-9). Watts.

Edwards, B. Quantitative & Accounting Methods. 192p. 1980. pap. text ed. 14.95x (ISBN 0-7121-1704-0). Intl Ideas.

Edwards, Barba J. & Brilhart, John K. Communications in Nursing Practice. (Illus.). 240p. 1981. pap. text ed. 9.95 (ISBN 0-8016-0786-8). Mosby.

Edwards, Barry. The Readable Maths & Statistics Book. (Illus.). 336p. (Orig.). 1980. text ed. 34.95x (ISBN 0-04-310007-4, 2550); pap. text ed. 13.50x (ISBN 0-04-310008-2, 2551). Allen Unwin.

Edwards, Betty. Drawing on the Right Side of the Brain. LC 78-62794. (Illus.). 1979. 12.50 o.p. (ISBN 0-312-90491-6); pap. 7.50 o.p. (ISBN 0-312-90492-4). St Martin.
--Drawing on the Right Side of the Brain. 1980. cloth. 13.95 (ISBN 0-87477-087-4); pap. 8.95 (ISBN 0-87477-088-2). HM.

Edwards, Bill. Imperial Carnival Glass. (Illus.). 1980. pap. 9.95 (ISBN 0-89145-138-2). Collector Bks.

Edwards, C. H. Advanced Calculus of Several Variables. 1973. 22.95 (ISBN 0-12-232550-8). Acad Pr.

Edwards, C. H., Jr. The Historical Development of the Calculus. (Illus.). 351p. 1980. 28.00 (ISBN 0-387-90436-0). Springer-Verlag.

Edwards, Charles. John Knox, Bold One for God. LC 78-61733. (Destiny Ser.). 1979. pap. 4.95 (ISBN 0-8163-0238-3). Pacific Pr Pub Assn.
--Perfecting Your Card Memory. (Gambler's Book Shelf). 64p. 1974. pap. 2.95 (ISBN 0-89650-545-6). Gamblers.

Edwards, Charles L. Understanding Biblical Symbols. 96p. 1981. 6.00 (ISBN 0-682-49704-5). Exposition.

Edwards, Charles M., Jr. & Lebowitz, Carl R. Retail Advertising & Sales Promotion. (Illus.). 576p. 1981. text ed. 19.95 (ISBN 0-13-775098-6); pap. 17.95 (ISBN 0-13-775080-3). P-H.

Edwards, Clark. Broadcast News Deskbook. 1972. text ed. 2.00x spiral bdg. (ISBN 0-87543-082-1). Lucas.

Edwards, Clifford H., et al. Planning, Teaching & Evaluating: A Competency Approach. LC 76-41903. 1977. 18.95 (ISBN 0-88229-204-8). Nelson-Hall.

Edwards, Clifford Q. Summer at Sea. LC 73-84576. 1976. pap. 2.25 o.p. (ISBN 0-87680-836-4, 98093). Word Bks.

Edwards, D. J. Growing Food. LC 69-18748. (Finding Out About Science Ser). (Illus.). (gr. 3-6). 1969. PLB 7.89 (ISBN 0-381-99835-5, A31710, JD-J). John Day.

Edwards, David L. Christian England: Its Story to the Reformation. (Illus.). 356p. 1981. 19.95 (ISBN 0-19-520229-5). Oxford U Pr.
--The Last Things Now. LC 76-121056. (Orig.). 1970. pap. 1.95 o.p. (ISBN 0-8170-0493-9). Judson.
--What Anglican (Episcopalians) Believe. 1975. 1.00 (ISBN 0-686-28799-1). Forward Movement.

Edwards, David L., adapted by. The Children's Bible: Selections from the Good News Bible. (Illus.). 1978. 8.95 (ISBN 0-529-05623-2, Pub. by Collins Pubs). World Bible.

Edwards, David V. The American Political Experience: An Introduction to Government. 1979. 17.95 (ISBN 0-13-028373-8); pap. 4.95 learning guide (ISBN 0-13-028340-1). P-H.

Edwards, Dudley. Daniel O'Connell & His World. LC 77-77380. (Illus.). 1977. 9.95 o.p. (ISBN 0-684-15302-5, ScribT). Scribner.

Edwards, E. H. Saddlery. (Illus.). Date not set. 12.25 (ISBN 0-85131-151-2, Dist. by Sporting Book Center). J A Allen.

Edwards, E. Hartley. All About Horses & Ponies. 1976. 7.95 (ISBN 0-491-01726-X). Transatlantic.

Edwards, Edgar O., et al. Accounting for Economic Events. LC 79-22971. 1979. text ed. 26.00 (ISBN 0-914348-28-0). Scholars Bk.

Edwards, Edward O., ed. Employment in Developing Nations. LC 74-16724. 1974. 22.50x (ISBN 0-231-03873-9); pap. 11.00x (ISBN 0-231-03874-7). Columbia U Pr.

Edwards, Eleanor M., compiled by. Great Mystery Stories. LC 60-6578. (The Lion Classics Ser). (Illus.). 160p. (YA) 1981. lib. bdg. 6.98 (ISBN 0-87460-194-0); pap. 1.95 (ISBN 0-87460-195-9). Lion.

Edwards, Eliezer E. Words, Facts & Phrases: A Dictionary of Curious, Quaint, & Out-of-the-Way Matters. LC 68-21768. 1968. Repr. of 1881 ed. 24.00 (ISBN 0-8103-3087-3). Gale.

Edwards, Elmer E. A Handicappers Guide to Dogtrack Astrology. (Illus.). 104p. 1980. pap. 10.00 (ISBN 0-9604834-0-3). Elmer Edwards.

Edwards, Elwyn H., ed. A Standard Guide to Horse & Pony Breeds. LC 79-23921. (Illus.). 352p. 1980. 24.95 (ISBN 0-07-019035-6). McGraw.

Edwards, Ernest P. A Field Guide to the Birds of Mexico. LC 78-185930. (Illus., With 1978 appendix bound in plastic ring binding). 1972. pap. 12.00 set (ISBN 0-911882-03-0). E P Edwards.
--Finding Birds in Mexico. 2nd ed. LC 68-58738. (Illus., Incl. 1976 Supplement to Finding Birds in Mexico). 1968. pap. 12.00 set (ISBN 0-911882-05-7). E P Edwards.

Edwards, Ernest P. & Loftin, Horace. Finding Birds in Panama. 2nd ed. LC 73-21847. (Illus.). 1971. softcover 5.00 (ISBN 0-911882-02-2). E P Edwards.

Edwards, Everett E. Bibliography of the History of Agriculture in the U. S. LC 66-27834. 1967. Repr. of 1930 ed. 18.00 (ISBN 0-8103-3102-0). Gale.

Edwards, F. Henry. History of the Reorganized Church of Jesus Christ of Latter Day Saints Vol. 5: 1890-1902. 1969. 15.00 (ISBN 0-8309-0019-5). Herald Hse.
--The History of the Reorganized Church of Jesus Christ of Latter Day Saints, Vols. 6 & 7. Incl. Vol. 6. 1903-1914. 1970 (ISBN 0-8309-0030-6); Vol. 7. 1915-1925. 1973 (ISBN 0-8309-0075-6). 15.00 ea. Herald Hse.
--History of the Reorganized Church of Jesus Christ of the Latter Day Saints, Vol. 8: 1926-1946. 1976. 15.00 (ISBN 0-8309-0157-4). Herald Hse.

Edwards, Francis. Ritual & Drama: The Mediaeval Theater. (Illus.). 1976. pap. text ed. 11.00x (ISBN 0-7188-2180-7). Intl Ideas.

Edwards, G. & Grant, M. Alcoholism: New Knowledge & New Responses. 368p. 1980. 35.00x (Pub. by Croom Helm England). State Mutual Bk.

Edwards, G., jt. ed. see Edwards, R. A.

Edwards, G. B. The Book of Ebenezer le Page. LC 80-2719. 416p. 1981. 13.95 (ISBN 0-394-51651-6). Knopf.

Edwards, Gabrielle & Bleifeld, Maurice. Biology. LC 58-19074. (High School Regents Exams & Answer Ser.). 1977. pap. 3.50 (ISBN 0-8120-0191-5). Barron.

Edwards, Gabrielle I. & Cimmino, Marion. Laboratory Techniques for High Schools: A Worktext of Biomedical Methods. rev. ed. LC 75-23111. (gr. 10-12). 1975. pap. text ed. 5.95 (ISBN 0-8120-0649-6). Barron.

Edwards, George C., III. Presidential Influence in Congress. LC 79-21975. (Illus.). 1980. text ed. 14.95x (ISBN 0-7167-1161-3); pap. text ed. 7.95x (ISBN 0-7167-1162-1). W H Freeman.

Edwards, George C., 3rd & Sharkansky, Ira. The Policy Predicament: Making & Implementing Public Policy. LC 77-28212. (Illus.). 1978. text ed. 15.95x (ISBN 0-7167-0019-0). W H Freeman.

Edwards, George T., jt. auth. see Carrington, John C.

Edwards, Gerald M., ed. see Homer.

Edwards, Goronwy. The Second Century of the English Parliament. 1978. 22.50x (ISBN 0-19-822479-6). Oxford U Pr.

Edwards, Griffith, ed. Alcoholism Treatment in Transition. 336p. 1980. 35.00x (Pub. by Croom Helm England). State Mutual Bk.

Edwards, Griffith, et al. Alcohol Dependence & Smoking Behavior. LC 75-30137. 280p. 1976. 23.95 (ISBN 0-347-01127-6, 00368-9, Pub. by Saxon Hse). Lexington Bks.
--Drugs & Drug Dependence. LC 75-30136. 264p. 1976. 23.95 (ISBN 0-347-01126-8, 00369-7, Pub. by Saxon Hse). Lexington Bks.

Edwards, Gwynne. Lorca: The Theatre Beneath the Sand. LC 79-56839. 320p. 1980. 20.00 (ISBN 0-7145-2698-3, Pub. by M Boyars). Merrimack Bk Serv.

Edwards, H., jt. auth. see Katzeff, I. E.

Edwards, H. Sutherland. The Prima Donna: Her History & Surroundings from the 17th to the 19th Century, 2 vols, Vol. 1. LC 77-17875. (Music Reprint Ser.). 1978. Repr. of 1888 ed. Set. lib. bdg. 45.00 (ISBN 0-306-77558-1). Da Capo.

Edwards, Hardy M., jt. auth. see Lassiter, J. W.

Edwards, Harry. The Struggle That Must Be: An Autobiography. 304p. 1980. 13.95 (ISBN 0-02-535040-4). Macmillan.

Edwards, Harry T. Higher Education & the Unholy Crusade Against Governmental Regulation. LC 80-26334. 62p. (Orig.). 1980. pap. text ed. 5.95x (ISBN 0-934222-04-5). Inst Ed Management.

Edwards, Harry T. & Nordin, Virginia D. Higher Education & the Law. LC 79-88195. 844p. 1979. 25.00x (ISBN 0-934222-00-2). Inst Ed Management.
--An Introduction to the American Legal System: A Supplement to Higher Education & the Law. LC 80-82033. 76p. (Orig.). 1980. pap. text ed. 5.95 (ISBN 0-934222-02-9). Inst Ed Manage.
--Nineteen Eighty Cumulative Supplement Higher Education & the Law. LC 80-82432. 136p. (Orig.). 1980. pap. text ed. 4.95 (ISBN 0-934222-03-7). Inst Ed Manage.

Edwards, Henry S. The Lyrical Drama, 2 vols. LC 80-2274. 1981. Repr. of 1881 ed. 67.50 (ISBN 0-404-18840-0). AMS Pr.

Edwards, Herbert W., jt. auth. see Horton, Rod W.

Edwards, I. E., et al, eds. Cambridge Ancient History. Incl. Vol. 1, Pt. 1. Prolegomena & Prehistory. pap. 29.50 (ISBN 0-521-29821-0); Vol. 1, Pts. 2A & 2B. Early History of the Middle East. pap. 34.50 (ISBN 0-521-29822-9); Vol. 2, Pt. 1. The Middle East & the Aegean Region, c 1800-1380 B.C. pap. 29.50 (ISBN 0-521-29823-7); Vol. 2, Pts. 2A & 2B. The Middle East & the Aegean Region, c 1380-1000 B.C. pap. 34.50 (ISBN 0-521-29824-5). LC 75-85719. (Illus.). Date not set. Cambridge U Pr.

Edwards, I. G. Roller Skating: A Beginner'sguide. (Illus.). (gr. 5-7). 1979. pap. 1.95 (ISBN 0-671-43292-3). PB.

Edwards, J. D. Electrical Machines: An Introduction to Principles & Characteristics. 1973. text ed. 14.95x (ISBN 0-7002-0267-6). Intl Ideas.

Edwards, J. Don, jt. auth. see Lemke, Bernhard C.

Edwards, J. R. Language & Disadvantage. (Studies in Language Disability & Remediation: Vol. 5). 172p. 1979. 22.50 (ISBN 0-444-19471-1); pap. 11.95 (ISBN 0-444-19470-3). Elsevier.

Edwards, James & MacDonald, Douglass. Occasions for Philosophy. 1979. pap. text ed. 13.95 (ISBN 0-13-629287-9). P-H.

Edwards, James D. College Accounting Fundamentals: Principles & Procedures. rev. ed. 1981. 16.95x (ISBN 0-256-02460-X); study guides wkbks. 6.95x ea. Vol. 1 (ISBN 0-256-01961-4). Vol. 2 (ISBN 0-256-01962-2). practice sets 4.50x ea. Irwin.
--History of Public Accounting in the United States. Previts, Gary J., ed. LC 66-63369. 1978. pap. 11.95 (ISBN 0-8173-8903-2). U of Ala Pr.

Edwards, James D. & Salmonson, Roland F. Contributions of Four Accounting Pioneers: Kohler, Littleton, May, Paton. LC 60-64043. 1961. 7.50 o.p. (ISBN 0-87744-016-6). Mich St U Busn.

Edwards, James D., et al. Financial Accounting: A Programmed Text. 4th ed. 1978. Vol. 1. text ed. 17.95x (ISBN 0-256-02010-8); Vol. 2. text ed. 14.50x (ISBN 0-256-02008-6); work papers 6.50x (ISBN 0-256-02013-2); Vol. 2. work papers 6.50x (ISBN 0-256-02015-9); Vol. 1. study guide & review manual 5.50x (ISBN 0-256-02011-6); Vol. 2. study guide & review manual 5.50x (ISBN 0-256-02009-4); mini-practice set 4.00x (ISBN 0-256-02014-0). Irwin.

Edwards, Jaroldeen. A Woman Between. 1980. 2.25 (ISBN 0-380-75846-6, 75846). Avon.

Edwards, Jennifer M., jt. auth. see Roberts, Keith D.

Edwards, John, jt. auth. see Weiss, Ulrich.

Edwards, John & Robbins, Peter, eds. Guide to Non-Ferrous Metals & Their Markets. 2nd ed. 250p. 1980. 43.50x (ISBN 0-89397-096-4). Nichols Pub.

Edwards, John F. How to Quit the Rat Race - Successfully! LC 80-82676. (Illus.). 159p. (Orig.). 1981. 9.95 (ISBN 0-937590-00-2, Dist. by Caroline Hse.); pap. 5.95 (ISBN 0-937590-01-0). New Era.
--How to Quit the Rat Race-Successfully. 1981. 9.95 (ISBN 0-937590-00-2); pap. 5.95 (ISBN 0-937590-01-0). Green Hill.
--How to Quit the Rat Race-Successfully! LC 80-82676. (Illus.). 110p. (Orig.). 1980. write for info. (ISBN 0-937590-00-2, New Era); pap. write for info. (ISBN 0-937590-01-0). World Merch Import.

Edwards, John H. & Vasse, William W. Annotated Index to the Cantos of Ezra Pound. 1980. 20.00x (ISBN 0-520-01923-7). U of Cal Pr.

Edwards, John O., ed. Inorganic Reaction Mechanisms, Vol. 1, Pt. 2. LC 72-105386. (Progress in Inorganic Chemistry Ser.). 1972. 52.50 o.p. (ISBN 0-471-23317-X, Pub. by Wiley Interscience). Wiley.

Edwards, Jon. The Social Psychology of Reading. (Language & Literacy Monograph). 256p. 1981. pap. text ed. 14.95 (ISBN 0-88499-603-4). Inst Mod Lang.

Edwards, Jonathan. Charity & Its Fruits. 1978. 9.95 (ISBN 0-85151-009-4). Banner of Truth.
--Freedom of the Will. Kaufman, Arnold S. & Frankena, William K., eds. LC 68-22308. 1969. 24.50x (ISBN 0-672-51063-4); pap. text ed. 12.95x (ISBN 0-672-60360-8). Irvington.
--Life & Diary of David Brainerd. 384p. 1980. pap. 7.95 (ISBN 0-8024-4772-4). Moody.
--Nature of True Virtue. 1960. pap. 3.95 (ISBN 0-472-06037-6, 37, AA). U of Mich Pr.
--Selected Writings of Jonathan Edwards. Simonson, Harold P., ed. LC 78-115064. (Milestones of Thought Ser.). 1970. pap. 3.75 (ISBN 0-8044-6132-5). Ungar.
--The Works of Jonathan Edwards, 2 vols. 1979. Set. 56.95 (ISBN 0-686-12492-8); Vol. 1. 29.95 (ISBN 0-85151-216-X); Vol. 2. 29.95 (ISBN 0-85151-217-8). Banner of Truth.

Edwards, Joseph W. Integral Calculus, 2 Vols. LC 55-234. 35.00 ea. Vol. 1 (ISBN 0-8284-0102-0). Vol. 2 (ISBN 0-8284-0105-5). Chelsea Pub.

Edwards, Josephine C. Malinki of Malawi. LC 78-55903. (Destiny Ser.). 1978. pap. 4.95 (ISBN 0-8163-0089-5, 13054-2). Pacific Pr Pub Assn.
--Swift Arrow. LC 67-17867. 116p. 1967. pap. 4.95 (ISBN 0-8163-0049-6, 19795-4). Pacific Pr Pub Assn.
--With an Holy Calling. LC 78-5367. (Destiny Ser.). 1979. pap. 4.95 (ISBN 0-8163-0250-2). Pacific Pr Pub Assn.

Edwards, Lauton. Industrial Arts Plastics. rev. ed. (gr. 10-12). 1974. 11.28 (ISBN 0-87002-146-X). Bennett IL.

Edwards, Leonard E. PL-One for Business Applications. LC 72-97178. (Illus.). 320p. 1973. ref. ed. 15.95 o.p. (ISBN 0-87909-631-4). Reston.

Edwards, Lisa A. & Krebs, Margie M. Netsuke: The Collection of the Peabody Museum of Salem. (Illus.). 160p. 1980. 30.00 (ISBN 0-87577-059-2); pap. 17.50 (ISBN 0-87577-062-2). Peabody Mus Salem.

Edwards, Loren E. Shoplifting & Shrinkage Protection for Stores. (Illus.). 272p. 1976. 15.75 (ISBN 0-398-00498-6). C C Thomas.

Edwards, Lovett F., ed. see Nenadovic, Proto M.

Edwards, Lowell E., ed. Buying a Swimming Pool - Without Getting Drained. LC 79-57083. 95p. (Orig.). 1980. pap. 4.95 (ISBN 0-936024-00-3). L E Edwards.

Edwards, Lynne. Dead As the Dodo. LC 72-6957. (Illus.). 40p. (ps-3). 1973. 5.95 o.s.i. (ISBN 0-8193-0640-1, Four Winds); PLB 5.41 o.s.i. (ISBN 0-8193-0641-X). Schol Bk Serv.

Edwards, Malcolm, jt. auth. see Holdstock, Robert.

Edwards, N. A. & Hassall, K. A. Cellular Biochemistry & Physiology. 1972. text ed. 19.95 o.p. (ISBN 0-07-094136-X, C). McGraw.

Edwards, O. C. How It All Began. (Orig.). 1973. 5.95 (ISBN 0-8164-2082-3). Crossroad NY.
--How It All Began: Origins of the Christian Church New Edition with Study Guide. 1978. pap. 3.95 (ISBN 0-8164-2164-1). Crossroad NY.
--The Living & Active Word: A Way to Preach from the Bible Today. 166p. 1975. 7.95 (ISBN 0-8164-0265-5). Crossroad NY.

Edwards, O. C., jt. auth. see Abbey, Merrill R.

Edwards, O. C., jt. auth. see Bennett, Robert A.

Edwards, O. C., Jr. & Taylor, Gardner C. Pentecost 3. Achtemeier, Elizabeth, et al, eds. LC 79-7377. (Proclamation 2: Aids for Interpreting the Lessons of the Church Year, Ser. C). 64p. (Orig.). 1980. pap. 2.50 (ISBN 0-8006-4084-5, 1-4084). Fortress.

Edwards, P., jt. ed. see Muir, K.

Edwards, P. D. Anthony Trollope: His Art & Scope. LC 77-27915. 1978. 21.95x (ISBN 0-312-04271-X). St Martin.

Edwards, Paul & Pap, A. Modern Introduction to Philosophy. 3rd ed. LC 65-18470. 1973. text ed. 17.95 (ISBN 0-02-909200-0). Free Pr.

Edwards, Paul, ed. The Encyclopedia of Philosophy, 4 vols. LC 67-10059. 1973. Set. 150.00 (ISBN 0-02-894950-1). Free Pr.

Edwards, Paul, jt. tr. see Palsson, Hermann.

Edwards, Perry & Broadwell, Bruce. Data Processing: Computers in Action. 1979. pap. text ed. 18.95x (ISBN 0-534-00615-9); wkbk. 7.95x (ISBN 0-534-00723-6). Wadsworth Pub.

--Data Processing: Computers in Action with Fortran. 496p. 1980. text ed. 18.95x (ISBN 0-534-00805-4); wkbk. 7.95x (ISBN 0-534-00879-8). Wadsworth Pub.
Edwards, R. A Formal Background to Mathematics: Pt. II, A & B. (Universitext). 1170p. 1980. pap. 39.80 (ISBN 0-387-90513-8). Springer-Verlag.
Edwards, R. A., jt. auth. see McDonald, P.
Edwards, R. A. & Edwards, G., eds. Pedro Calderon De la Barca: Los Cabellos de Absalon. LC 73-4292. 168p. 1973. text ed. 19.50 (ISBN 0-08-017161-3); pap. text ed. 7.00 (ISBN 0-08-017162-1). Pergamon.
Edwards, R. E., ed. Integration & Harmonic Analysis on Compact Groups. LC 77-190412. (London Mathematical Society Lecture Notes Ser.: No. 8). 228p. 1972. 20.50 (ISBN 0-521-09717-7). Cambridge U Pr.
Edwards, R. G. & Johnson, M. H., eds. Physiological Effects of Immunity Against Reproductive Hormones. LC 75-12470. (Clinical & Experimental Immunoreproduction Ser.: No. 3). (Illus.). 300p. 1976. 42.50 (ISBN 0-521-20914-5). Cambridge U Pr.
Edwards, R. G., et al, eds. Immunobiology of Trophoblast. LC 74-31800. (Clinical & Experimental Immunoreproduction Ser.: No. 1). (Illus.). 300p. 1975. 39.50 (ISBN 0-521-20636-7). Cambridge U Pr.
Edwards, R. W., ed. see Zoological Society of London - 29th Symposium.
Edwards, Rachelle. Reckless Masquerade. 1977. pap. 1.50 o.p. (ISBN 0-449-23302-2, Crest). Fawcett.
--The Silken Net. (A Regency Love Story Ser.). 1979. pap. 1.75 o.p. (ISBN 0-449-24233-1, Crest). Fawcett.
--The Thief of Hearts. 1977. pap. 1.50 o.p. (ISBN 0-449-23401-0, Crest). Fawcett.
Edwards, Ralph. Sheraton Furniture Design. (Illus.). 1974. pap. 6.95 (ISBN 0-85458-909-0). Transatlantic.
--Hepplewhite Furniture Designs. 1972. 16.50 (ISBN 0-685-52079-X). Transatlantic.
Edwards, Ray. Choosing & Caring for Garden Shrubs. pap. 4.50 (ISBN 0-7153-7902-X). David & Charles.
--Growing Soft Fruits. 1980. pap. 4.50 (ISBN 0-7153-7903-8). David & Charles.
Edwards, Raymond. Basic Chess Openings. rev. ed. (Routledge Chess Handbooks Ser.: No. 4). (Illus., Orig.). 1981. pap. price not set (ISBN 0-7100-0853-8). Routledge & Kegan.
--Basic Chess Openings. (Chess Handbooks). 144p. 1976. pap. 4.95 (ISBN 0-7100-8296-7). Routledge & Kegan.
--Chess Tactics & Attacking Techniques. (Chess Handbooks: Vol. 5). 1978. pap. 4.95 (ISBN 0-7100-8821-3). Routledge & Kegan.
Edwards, Rem B. Reason & Religion: An Introduction to the Philosophy of Religion. LC 78-66278. 1979. pap. text ed. 11.25 (ISBN 0-8191-0690-9). U Pr of Amer.
Edwards, Rex. Every Believer a Minister. LC 78-59308. (Dimension Ser.). 1979. pap. 5.95 (ISBN 0-8163-0234-0). Pacific Pr Pub Assn.
Edwards, Rhoda. Fortune's Wheel. LC 78-7752. 1979. 8.95 o.p. (ISBN 0-385-11582-2). Doubleday.
Edwards, Richard. Field of Stones: A Study of the Art of Shen Chou (1427-1509) (Illus.). 131p. 1962. 15.00x (ISBN 0-87474-398-2). Smithsonian.
Edwards, Richard A. A Concordance to Q. LC 75-6768. (Society of Biblical Literature. Sources for Biblical Study). iv, 186p. 1975. pap. 7.50 (ISBN 0-89130-056-2, 060307). Scholars Pr Ca.
--A Theology of Q: Eschatology, Prophecy & Wisdom. LC 75-13042. 192p. 1975. 11.95 (ISBN 0-8006-0432-6, 1-432). Fortress.
Edwards, Richard C. Contested Terrain: The Transformation of the Workplace in America. LC 78-19942. 256p. 1980. pap. 4.95 (ISBN 0-465-01413-5). Basic.
Edwards, Robert. The Montecassino Passion & the Poetics of Medieval Drama. LC 75-22655. 1977. 19.50x (ISBN 0-520-03102-4). U of Cal Pr.
Edwards, Robert & Steptoe, Patrick. A Matter of Life. LC 80-17293. (Illus.). 208p. 1980. Repr. 9.95 (ISBN 0-688-03698-8). Morrow.
Edwards, Romaine V. Crisis Intervention & How It Works. (Illus.). 88p. 1979. 11.50 (ISBN 0-398-03580-6). C C Thomas.
Edwards, Ross. Fiddledust. LC 65-25807. 102p. 1965. 4.95 (ISBN 0-8040-0109-X). Swallow.
Edwards, S., jt. auth. see Edwards, W.
Edwards, S., jt. ed. see Edwards, W.
Edwards, Sutherland. History of the Opera: From Monteverdi to Donizetti, 2 vols. in one. LC 77-5587. 1977. Repr. of 1862 ed. lib. bdg. 49.50 (ISBN 0-306-77416-X). Da Capo.
Edwards, T. A., jt. auth. see Halliwell, J. D.
Edwards, Tilden. Spiritual Friend: Reclaiming the Gift of Spiritual Direction. LC 79-91408. 264p. 1980. pap. 7.95 (ISBN 0-8091-2288-X). Paulist Pr.
Edwards, Tryon, ed. New Dictionary of Thoughts. rev. ed. 1955. 12.95 (ISBN 0-335-00127-4). Doubleday.
Edwards, Tudor. Yorkshire. (Illus.). 1978. 8.95 o.p. (ISBN 0-571-11165-3, Pub by Faber & Faber). Merrimack Bk Serv.
Edwards, Una, ed. see Morningstar, Ramon S.
Edwards, Una, et al. So Fine Bovine: The Cow Book. 350p. (Orig.). 1980. pap. write for info. Family Pub CA.
Edwards, W. & Edwards, S. Symbol Discrimination & Sequencing. (Ann Arbor Tracking Program Ser.). 1976. wkbk. 5.00 (ISBN 0-89039-154-8). Ann Arbor Pubs.
Edwards, W. & Edwards, S., eds. Cursive Tracking: Reusable Edition. (gr 3). 1972. wkbk. 5.00 (ISBN 0-89039-021-5). Ann Arbor Pubs.
--Cursive Writing: Words: Reusable Edition, Book 1. (gr. 1-3). 1975. wkbk. 5.00 (ISBN 0-89039-135-1). Ann Arbor Pubs.
--Cursive Writing: Words: Reusable Edition, Book 2. (gr. 3-6). 1975. wkbk. 5.00 (ISBN 0-89039-136-X). Ann Arbor Pubs.
--Cursive Writing 2: Reusable Edition. (gr. 1). 1972. wkbk. 5.00 (ISBN 0-89039-051-7). Ann Arbor Pubs.
--Letter Tracking: Reusable Edition. (Large Type Tracking Ser.). (gr. k-1). 1973. wkbk. 4.00 (ISBN 0-89039-019-3). Ann Arbor Pubs.
--Letter Tracking: Reusable Edition. (Ann Arbor Tracking Program Ser.). (gr. 3-8). 1975. wkbk. 5.00 (ISBN 0-89039-153-X). Ann Arbor Pubs.
--Manuscript Tracking: Reusable Edition. (Large Type Tracking Ser.). (gr. k-1). 1975. 4.00 (ISBN 0-89039-017-7). Ann Arbor Pubs.
Edwards, William, et al. The Renaissance Cookbook, Vol. 1. (Illus.). 184p. 1980. 5.95 (ISBN 0-938054-01-5); pap. 3.25 (ISBN 0-938054-00-7). Tri-B Pubns.
Edwars, Paula. Bewitching Grace. 192p. (Orig.). 1980. pap. 1.50 (ISBN 0-671-57023-4). S&S.
Edwin, B. Psycho-Yoga: The Practice of Mind Control. 128p. (Orig.). 1980. pap. 4.95 o.s.i. (ISBN 0-7225-0543-4). Newcastle Pub.
Edwin Gould Foundation For Children. Our Troubled Children: Our Community's Challenge. Wight, Russell B., ed. LC 67-16461. 1967. 17.50x o.p. (ISBN 0-231-02841-5). Columbia U Pr.
Edwing, Don. Mad's Bizarre Bazaar. 192p. (Orig.). 1980. pap. 1.75 (ISBN 0-446-94285-5). Warner Bks.
Edwinn, Gloria. Just for Starters. LC 80-51771. 272p. 1981. 14.95 (ISBN 0-670-41093-4). Viking Pr.
Eeden, Frederik Van see Van Eeden, Frederik.
Eekman, Thomas, jt. auth. see Birnbaum, Henrik.
Eells, Elsie S. Tales from the Amazon. LC 20-18503. (Illus.). (gr. 4-6). 1938. 4.95 (ISBN 0-396-01809-2). Dodd.
Eells, George, jt. auth. see O'Day, Anita.
Eells, Richard. Government of Corporations. LC 62-15339. 1962. 9.95 o.s.i. (ISBN 0-02-909290-6). Free Pr.
Eells, Richard & Walton, Clarence. Conceptual Foundations of Business. 3rd ed. 1974. 16.50x o.p. (ISBN 0-256-01559-7). Irwin.
Eells, Walter C. & Haswell, Harold A. Academic Degrees. LC 70-128397. Repr. of 1960 ed. 15.00 (ISBN 0-8103-3015-6). Gale.
Een, Jo Ann D. & Rosenberg-Dishman, Marie B., eds. Women & Society: Citations 3601 to 6000, an Annotated Bibliography. LC 77-18985. 1978. 20.00x (ISBN 0-8039-0856-3). Sage.
Eesley, G. L. Coherent Raman Spectroscopy. (Illus.). 150p. 1981. 41.00 (ISBN 0-08-025058-0). Pergamon.
Effendi, Shoghi. The Advent of Divine Justice. LC 63-21643. 9.00 (ISBN 0-87743-044-6, 7-08-01); pap. 4.00 (ISBN 0-87743-045-4, 7-08-02). Baha'i.
--Call to the Nations: Extracts from the Writings of Shoghi Effendi. LC 79-670140. 1978. 5.00 (ISBN 0-85398-068-3, 7-08-50); pap. 2.50 (ISBN 0-85398-069-1, 7-08-51). Baha'i.
--The Dispensation of Baha'u'llah. 1934. pap. 3.00 (ISBN 0-87743-050-0, 7-08-08). Baha'i.
--The Goal of a New World Order. 1971. pap. 1.00 (ISBN 0-87743-100-0, 7-08-28). Baha'i.
--God Passes By. rev. ed. LC 44-51036. 1974. 11.00 (ISBN 0-87743-020-9, 7-08-10); pap. 6.00 (ISBN 0-87743-034-9, 7-08-11). Baha'i.
--Guidance for Today & Tomorrow: A Selection from the Writings of Shoghi Effendi. 1953. pap. 5.00 (ISBN 0-900125-14-4, 7-08-27). Baha'i.
--The Promised Day Is Come. rev. ed. 1980. 10.00 (ISBN 0-87743-132-9, 7-08-17); pap. 5.00 (ISBN 0-87743-138-8, 7-08-18). Baha'i.
--Selected Writings of Shoghi Effendi. rev. ed. 1975. pap. 1.50 (ISBN 0-87743-079-9, 7-08-43). Baha'i.
--The World Order of Baha'u'llah. 2nd rev. ed. LC 56-17685. 1974. 10.00 (ISBN 0-87743-031-4, 7-08-20); pap. 5.00 (ISBN 0-87743-004-7, 7-08-21). Baha'i.
Effendi, Shoghi, ed. & tr. see Nabil-i-A'zam.
Effendi, Shoghi, tr. see Abdu'l-Baha.
Effendi, Shoghi, tr. see Baha'u'llah.
Effinger, George A. Mixed Feelings. LC 74-4858. 1974. 7.95 o.s.i. (ISBN 0-06-011146-1, HarpT). Har-Row.
--Those Gentle Voices. 1976. pap. 1.75 o.s.i. (ISBN 0-446-94017-8). Warner Bks.
Effinger, George A., jt. auth. see Dozois, Gardner.
Effinger, George Alec. Death in Florence. LC 77-80883. 1978. 6.95 o.p. (ISBN 0-385-11190-8). Doubleday.
Effle, Mark, ed. see Swett, Ira L.
Effler, Donald B., ed. Blades' Surgical Diseases of the Chest. 4th ed. LC 78-7047. 1978. 67.50 (ISBN 0-8016-0697-7). Mosby.
Effrat, Andrew. Perspectives in Political Sociology. LC 73-4329. 1973. 24.50x (ISBN 0-672-51746-9). Irvington.
Effrat, Andrew, ed. Perspectives in Political Sociology. LC 73-4329. 320p. 1973. pap. text ed. 6.50 (ISBN 0-672-61322-0). Bobbs.
Effrat, Marcia P., ed. The Community: Approaches & Applications. LC 73-16604. (Illus.). 1974. pap. text ed. 8.95 (ISBN 0-02-909300-7). Free Pr.
Effros, Richard, et al, eds. The Microcirculation: Current Concepts. 1981. write for info. (ISBN 0-12-232560-5). Acad Pr.
Effross, Harris I. County Governing Bodies in New Jersey: Reorganization & Reform on Boards of Chosen Freeholders, 1798-1974. 1976. 25.00x (ISBN 0-8135-0765-0). Rutgers U Pr.
Efrein, Joel. Cablecasting Production Handbook. LC 74-33617. (Illus.). 210p. 1975. 12.95 o.p. (ISBN 0-8306-5768-1, 768). TAB Bks.
Efron, Alexander. Exploring Heat. (Modern Physics Ser.). (Illus.). 1969. pap. 3.15 o.p. (ISBN 0-8104-5656-7). Hayden.
--Exploring Matter & Nuclear Energy. (Modern Physics Ser.). (Illus.). 1969. pap. 3.75 o.p. (ISBN 0-8104-5658-3). Hayden.
Efron, Benjamin & Rubin, Alvan D. Coming of Age: Your Bar or Bat Mitzvah. LC 77-78031. (Illus.). 1977. 5.00 (ISBN 0-8074-0084-X, 142530). UAHC.
Efron, Daniel, et al, eds. Ethnopharmacologic Search for Psychoactive Drugs: Proceedings. LC 79-3955. 1979. Repr. of 1967 ed. text ed. 26.00 softcover (ISBN 0-89004-047-8). Raven.
Efron, Daniel H., jt. auth. see Usdin, Earl.
Efron, Daniel H., ed. Psychotomimetic Drugs. LC 73-89388. (Illus.). 1970. 26.00 (ISBN 0-911216-07-3). Raven.
Efron, Vera see Keller, Mark.
Efros, Israel I. Studies in Medieval Jewish Philosophy. LC 73-12512. 300p. 1974. 20.00x (ISBN 0-231-03194-7). Columbia U Pr.
Efros, Susan. Moving in. 1981. price not set. Waterfall Pr.
Eftekhar, Nas S. Principles of Total Hip Arthroplasty. new ed. LC 78-18471. (Illus.). 1978. text ed. 67.50 (ISBN 0-8016-1496-1). Mosby.
Efvergren, Carl J. Names of Places in a Transferred Sense in English: A Sematological Study. LC 68-17922. 1969. Repr. of 1909 ed. 15.00 (ISBN 0-8103-3233-7). Gale.
Egami, Shigeru. The Way of Karate: Beyond Technique. LC 75-12069. (Illus.). 190p. 1976. 12.95 o.p. (ISBN 0-87011-254-6). Kodansha.
Egan, Ann L. Anxiety Free Statistics. 1977. pap. text ed. 4.95 o.p. (ISBN 0-8403-0928-7). Kendall-Hunt.
Egan, D. F., et al, eds. Developmental Screening 0-5 Years. (Clinics in Developmental Medicine Ser. No. 30). 64p. 1969. 17.00 (ISBN 0-685-24738-4). Lippincott.
Egan, David R. & Egan, Melinda A. Leo Tolstoy: An Annotated Bibliography of English-Language Sources to 1978. LC 79-16536. (The Scarecrow Author Bibliographies Ser.: No. 44). 303p. 1979. 16.50 (ISBN 0-8108-1232-0). Scarecrow.
Egan, E. W., tr. see Fronval, George & Dubois, Daniel.
Egan, E. W., tr. see Riviere, Marie-Claude.
Egan, Gerard & Cowan, Michael A. Moving into Adulthood: Themes & Variations in Self--Directed Development for Effective Living. LC 80-15876. 288p. (Orig.). 1980. pap. text ed. 8.95 (ISBN 0-8185-0406-4). Brooks-Cole.
Egan, John, et al. Housing & Public Policy: A Role for Mediating Structures. 160p. 1981. 16.50 (ISBN 0-88410-827-9). Ballinger Pub.
Egan, Judith. Elena: A Love Story of the Russian Revolution. LC 80-39613. 320p. 1981. 11.95 (ISBN 0-89919-028-6). Ticknor & Fields.
Egan, Kieran. Structural Communication. LC 74-83215. 1976. pap. text ed. 5.95 (ISBN 0-8224-6550-7). Pitman Learning.
Egan, Kieran, jt. ed. see Strike, Kenneth A.
Egan, Lesley. A Choice of Crimes. LC 80-1121. (Crime Club Ser.). 1980. 8.95 (ISBN 0-385-17269-9). Doubleday.
--A Dream Apart. LC 77-82756. 1978. 6.95 o.p. (ISBN 0-385-13412-6). Doubleday.
--Look Back on Death. new large print ed. LC 80-28019. 1981. Repr. of 1978 ed. 9.95 (ISBN 0-89621-267-X). Thorndike Pr.
--Look Back on Death. LC 77-27725. 1978. 7.95 o.p. (ISBN 0-385-14303-6). Doubleday.
Egan, M. David. Concepts in Thermal Comfort. (Illus.). 224p. 1975. 15.95 (ISBN 0-13-166447-6). P-H.
Egan, M. Winston, jt. auth. see Landau, Elliott D.
Egan, Melinda A., jt. auth. see Egan, David R.
Egan, Michael. Mark Twain's Huckleberry Finn: Race, Class & Society. (Text & Context Ser.). 1977. text ed. 9.25x (ISBN 0-391-00930-3); pap. text ed. 4.75x (ISBN 0-85621-061-7). Humanities.
Egan, Michael, ed. Henry James: The Ibsen Years. 154p. 1972. text ed. 8.00x (ISBN 0-85478-242-7). Humanities.
--Ibsen: The Critical Heritage. (Critical Heritage Ser). 1972. 38.50 (ISBN 0-7100-7255-4). Routledge & Kegan.
Egan, Patricia B. & Maran, Marie Y. This Way to Wall Street. LC 80-82137. (Illus.). 200p. 1980. pap. 9.95 (ISBN 0-937470-00-7); instructor's manual 5.95 (ISBN 0-937470-01-5). Market Ed.
Egan, Robert L. Mammography. 2nd ed. (Amer. Lec. Roentgen Diagnosis Ser.). (Illus.). 526p. 1972. text ed. 52.50 (ISBN 0-398-02195-3). C C Thomas.
Egan, William F. Frequency Synthesis by Phase-Lock. LC 80-16917. 304p. 1980. text ed. 20.00 (ISBN 0-471-08202-3, Pub. by Wiley-Interscience). Wiley.
Egbert, jt. auth. see Schuurman.
Egbert, Barbara. Cheerleading & Songleading. LC 80-52322. (Illus.). 128p. (gr. 8 up). 1980. 12.95 (ISBN 0-8069-4626-1); PLB 11.69 (ISBN 0-8069-4627-X); pap. 7.95 (ISBN 0-8069-8950-5). Sterling.
Egbert, Donald D. The Beaux-Arts Tradition in French Architecture. Van Zanten, David, ed. LC 79-23798. (Illus.). 220p. 1980. 22.50x (ISBN 0-691-03943-7); pap. 12.50 (ISBN 0-691-10106-X). Princeton U Pr.
Egbert, Donald D. & Persons, S. Socialism & American Life, 2 vols. Incl. Vol. 1. Text (ISBN 0-691-07521-2); Vol. 2. Bibliography (ISBN 0-691-07522-0). (American Civilization). 1952. 35.00x ea.; Set. 59.50x (ISBN 0-685-23098-8). Princeton U Pr.
Egbuna, Obi B. The Anthill: A Play. (Three Crowns Book). 1965. pap. 1.95x o.p. (ISBN 0-19-911067-0). Oxford U Pr.
Egdahl, R. H., jt. ed. see Walsh, D. C.
Egdahl, Richard H. & Gertman, Paul M. Technology & the Quality of Health Care. LC 78-7307. (Illus.). 1978. text ed. 31.00 (ISBN 0-89443-025-4). Aspen Systems.
Egdahl, Richard H. & Gertman, Paul M., eds. Quality Assurance in Health Care. LC 76-15770. 1976. 28.95 (ISBN 0-912862-23-8). Aspen Systems.
--Quality Health Care: The Role of Continuing Medical Education. LC 77-70434. 1977. 30.00 (ISBN 0-912862-37-8). Aspen Systems.
Ege, Lennart. Balloons & Airships. LC 73-18513. (Color Ser.). (Illus.). 230p. 1974. 9.95 (ISBN 0-02-535050-1). Macmillan.
Egejuru, Phanuel. Origin & Survival of African Folktales in the New World. Date not set. 8.95 (ISBN 0-933184-23-9); pap. 4.95 (ISBN 0-933184-24-7). Flame Intl. Postponed.
Egejuru, Phanuel A. Towards African Literary Independence: A Dialogue with Contemporary African Writers. LC 79-6188. (Contributions in Afro-American & African Studies: No. 53). vii, 173p. 1980. lib. bdg. 23.95 (ISBN 0-313-22310-6, EAL/). Greenwood.
Egeland, Alv, et al, eds. Cosmical Geophysics. (Illus.). 360p. 1973. 33.50x (ISBN 8-200-02256-0, Dist. by Columbia U Pr). Universitet.
Egelstaff, P. A. & Poole, M. J. Experimental Neutron Thermalization. LC 79-86201. 1970. 60.00 (ISBN 0-08-006533-3). Pergamon.
Egelstaff, P. A., ed. Thermal Neutron Scattering. 1966. 72.50 (ISBN 0-12-232950-3). Acad Pr.
Eger, Edith E. Coping & Growth: A Theoretical & Empirical Study for Groups Under Moderate to Severe Stress. (Holocaust Studies Ser.). 1980. text ed. 22.50x (ISBN 0-8290-0292-8). Irvington.
Egermeirer, Elsie G. Egermeier's Bible Story Book. 1975. pap. 1.95 (ISBN 0-89129-010-9). Jove Pubns.
Egert, Stella, jt. auth. see Gillis, Lynn.
Egerton, Clement, tr. from Chinese. The Golden Lotus: A Translation of the Chinese Novel, Chin P'ing Mei, 4 vols. 1572p. 1972. Set. 80.00 (ISBN 0-7100-7349-6); 22.00 ea. Routledge & Kegan.
Egerton, F. N., ed. see Greene, E. L.
Egerton, George. Keynotes. Fletcher, Ian & Stokes, John, eds. LC 76-24384. (Decadent Consciousness Ser.). 1978. lib. bdg. 38.00 (ISBN 0-8240-2758-2). Garland Pub.
Egerton, John, jt. auth. see Center for Equal Education.

Egerton, Judy & Snelgrove, Dudley. British Sporting & Animal Drawings & Paintings. (From the Paul Mellon Collection Ser.). 1980. combined ed. 225.00 (ISBN 0-8120-5390-7). Barron.
Egg, Maria. Educating the Child Who Is Different. LC 68-11293. (John Day Bk.). 1968. 6.95 o.s.i. (ISBN 0-381-98095-2, A22260, TYC-T). T Y Crowell.
Eggan, Fred. The American Indian: Perspectives for the Study of Social Change. LC 80-67926. (Lewis Henry Morgan Lectures). 192p. 1981. 22.50 (ISBN 0-521-23752-1); pap. 6.95 (ISBN 0-521-28210-1). Cambridge U Pr.
Eggan, Lawrence C. & Vanden Eynden, Charles. Mathematics: Models & Applications. 1979. text ed. 16.95x (ISBN 0-669-01051-0); inst. manual free (ISBN 0-669-01052-9). Heath.
Egge, Marion F., jt. auth. see Beidler, Peter G.
Eggebrecht, Hans H., jt. auth. see Dahlhaus, Carl.
Eggeling, tr. see Mueller, F. Max.
Eggeling, H. F. Dictionary of Modern German Prose Usage. 1961. 26.00x (ISBN 0-19-864110-9). Oxford U Pr.
Eggen, Paul, jt. auth. see Kauchak, Donald P.
Eggen, Paul, et al. Strategies for Teachers: Information Processing Models in the Classroom. (Curriculum & Teaching Ser.). (Illus.). 1979. ref. ed. 17.95 (ISBN 0-13-851162-4). P-H.
Eggenberger, David. Dictionary of Battles. (Illus.). 1967. 16.95 o.s.i. (ISBN 0-690-23744-8, TYC-T). T Y Crowell.
--Flags of the U.S.A. enl. ed. 1964. 9.95 (ISBN 0-690-30491-9, TYC-T). T Y Crowell.
Eggenschwiler, David. The Christian Humanism of Flannery O'Connor. LC 79-179560. 156p. 1972. 9.95x (ISBN 0-8143-1463-5). Wayne St U Pr.
Eggerichs, Fred & Palmer, Bernard. A Bag Without Holes: How to Prepare for Your Family, Your Finances, Your Future. LC 74-23435. 96p. 1975. pap. 2.25 o.p. (ISBN 0-87123-028-3). Bethany Fell.
Eggert, Jim. What Is Economics? 2nd ed. LC 77-5781. (Illus.). 176p. 1977. 8.95 (ISBN 0-913232-49-1); pap. 4.95 (ISBN 0-913232-48-3). W Kaufmann.
Eggleston, Edward. The Circuit Rider. LC 77-104768. (Novel As American Social History Ser.). 344p. 1970. 10.00x (ISBN 0-8131-1209-5); pap. 4.50 (ISBN 0-8131-0133-6). U Pr of Ky.
--The Hoosier Schoolmaster. rev. ed. Dixson, Robert J., ed. (American Classics Ser.: Bk. 6). (gr. 9 up). 1974. pap. text ed. 2.75 (ISBN 0-88345-202-2, 18125); cassettes 40.00 (ISBN 0-685-38929-4); tapes 40.00 (ISBN 0-685-38930-8). Regents Pub.
Eggleston, H. G. Convexity. (Cambridge Tracts in Mathematics & Mathematical Physics: No. 47). 1958. 21.50 (ISBN 0-521-07734-6). Cambridge U Pr.
Eggleston, John. Developments in Design Education. (Changing Classroom). (Illus.). 1976. text ed. 10.25x (ISBN 0-7291-0097-9); pap. text ed. 4.75x (ISBN 0-7291-0092-8). Humanities.
--The Sociology of the School Curriculum. 1977. 12.00x (ISBN 0-7100-8565-6); pap. 7.95 (ISBN 0-7100-8566-4). Routledge & Kegan.
Eggleston, John, ed. see European Research in Curriculum & Evaluation, a Report of the European Contact Workshop Held in Austria in December 1976 by the Committee for the Educational Research of the Council of Europe Council for Cultural Cooperation.
Eggleston, S. John. Social Context of the School. (Student's Lib. of Ed.). 1967. text ed. 3.75x (ISBN 0-7100-4217-5); pap. text ed. 2.75x (ISBN 0-7100-4210-8). Humanities.
Eggleton, John E. Discovering the Old Testament. 306p. 1980. Repr. pap. text ed. 7.95 (ISBN 0-933656-07-6). Trinity Pub Hse.
Eghihse. Vasn Vardanay Ew Hayots Paterazmin: On Vardan & the Armenian War. Sanjian, Avedis K., ed. 1981. write for info. (ISBN 0-88206-034-1). Caravan Bks.
Eglamour. Sir Eglamour. Cook, Albert S., ed. 1911. 17.50x (ISBN 0-685-69803-3). Elliots Bks.
Eglash, Albert. The Case Against Assertion Training. (Beyond Assertion Training Ser.: No. 5). 180p. (Orig.). 1981. pap. 20.00 (ISBN 0-935320-12-1). Quest Pr.
--Died on the Fourth of July: A Jewish Unitarian Psychologist Flees a Fascist Fellowship. LC 80-53581. (Illus.). 100p. (Orig.). 1981. pap. 20.00 (ISBN 0-935320-22-9). Quest Pr.
Eglash, Albert, ed. Psychogenesis of Coronary Heart Disease: A Syllabus for Medical Researchers. (Bibliographies in Psychosomatic Medicine Ser.: No. 1, Myocardial Infraction). (Illus.). 110p. (Orig.). 1980. lib. bdg. 20.00 (ISBN 0-935320-20-2). Quest Pr.
Eglesfield, Rbt, tr. see Simenon, Georges.
Egleson, Janet F. Design for Writing Workbook. 1970. pap. text ed. 4.95x (ISBN 0-02-474140-X, 47414). Macmillan.
Egleton, Clive. The Eisenhower Deception. LC 80-69372. 1981. 10.95 (ISBN 0-689-11127-4). Atheneum.
Egli, Glenn. Prayer That Releases Power. (Orig.). 1981. pap. 4.95 (ISBN 0-88270-506-7). Logos.
Egmond, Dorothy Van see Van Egmond, Dorothy.
Egmond-Pannell, Dorothy Van see Van Egmond-Pannell, Dorothy.
Egoff, Sheila, et al, eds. Only Connect: Readings on Children's Literature. 1969. pap. 7.50x o.p. (ISBN 0-19-540161-1). Oxford U Pr.
--Only Connect: Readings on Children's Literature. 2nd ed. (Illus.). 496p. 1980. pap. text ed. 8.95x (ISBN 0-19-540309-6). Oxford U Pr.
--Only Connect: Readings on Children's Literature. 2nd ed. (Illus.). 482p. 1980. pap. 8.95 (ISBN 0-19-540309-6). Oxford U Pr.
Egoff, Sheila A., ed. One Ocean Touching: Papers from the First Pacific Rim Conference on Children's Literature. LC 78-31308. 260p. 1979. lib. bdg. 13.00 (ISBN 0-8108-1199-5). Scarecrow.
Egypt, Ophelia S. James Weldon Johnson. LC 73-9521. (Biographies Ser). (Illus.). 40p. (gr. 2-5). 1974. PLB 7.89 (ISBN 0-690-00215-7, TYC-J). T Y Crowell.
Ehle, John. The Cheeses & Wines of England & France with Notes on Irish Whiskey. LC 72-79659. (Illus.). 320p. 1972. 10.95 o.s.i. (ISBN 0-06-011167-4, HarpT). Har-Row.
Ehler, Stanley W., jt. auth. see Waldren, Richard P.
Ehlers, Ernest G. The Interpretation of Geological Phase Diagrams. LC 75-182129. (Illus.). 1972. text ed. 32.95x (ISBN 0-7167-0254-1). W H Freeman.
Ehlers, F. Edward, et al see Heat Transfer & Fluid Mechanics Institute.
Ehlers, J., ed. Relativity Theory & Astrophysics: Relativity & Cosmology. LC 62-21481. (Lectures in Applied Mathematics Ser.: Vol. 8). 1979. Repr. of 1972 ed. 17.60 (ISBN 0-8218-1108-8, LAM-8). Am Math.
Ehlers, Walter H. & Krishef, Curtis H. An Introduction to Mental Retardation - a Programmed Text. 2nd ed. (Special Education Ser.). 1977. pap. text ed. 14.95 (ISBN 0-675-08526-8). Merrill.
Ehling, Bill. Twenty-Five Ski Tours in Central New York. (Illus.). 128p. 1980. pap. 5.95 (ISBN 0-89725-019-2). NH Pub Co.
Ehlis, Joan. Enigma. 1981. 4.95 (ISBN 0-8062-1673-5). Carlton.
Ehly, Stewart W. & Larsen, Stephen C. Peer Tutoring for Individual Instruction. 247p. 1980. text ed. 16.95 (ISBN 0-205-06878-2). Allyn.
Ehman, Lee, et al, eds. Toward Effective Instruction in Secondary Social Studies. 448p. 1974. text ed. 19.50 (ISBN 0-395-17625-5); instructors' manual 1.85 (ISBN 0-395-17857-6). HM.
Ehninger, Douglas, ed. see Whately, Richard.
Ehrenberg, Miriam & Ehrenberg, Otto. The Psychotherapy Maze. LC 77-71350. 1977. 8.95 o.p. (ISBN 0-03-016886-4); pap. 3.95 o.p. (ISBN 0-03-022881-6). HR&W.
Ehrenberg, Otto, jt. auth. see Ehrenberg, Miriam.
Ehrenberg, Ralph E., jt. auth. see Schwartz, Seymour I.
Ehrenberg, Victor. Alexander & the Greeks. Fraenkel Von Velson, Ruth, tr. from Ger. LC 79-4913. 1981. Repr. of 1938 ed. 12.50 (ISBN 0-88355-963-3). Hyperion Conn.
--Commendation und Huldigung Nach Frankischem Recht. LC 80-2031. 1981. Repr. of 1877 ed. 22.00 (ISBN 0-404-18562-2). AMS Pr.
Ehrenburg, A., jt. auth. see Akeson, A.
Ehrenfeld, Alfred, et al, trs. see Hussein, Mahmoud.
Ehrenfeld, David. The Arrogance of Humanism. (A Galaxy Bk.: No. 637). 304p. 1981. pap. 5.95 (ISBN 0-19-502890-2). Oxford U Pr.
Ehrenfels, U. R. Light Continent: A Study of East African Society. 7.50x (ISBN 0-210-33696-X). Asia.
Ehrenkrantz Group & Mueller Associates Inc. Active Solar Energy System Design Practice Manual: Preliminary Field Experience. 230p. 1981. pap. 24.50 (ISBN 0-89934-091-1). Solar Energy Info.
Ehrenpreis, Anne H., ed. see Smith, Charlotte.
Ehrenpreis, Irvin. Literary Meaning & Augustan Values. LC 73-94275. 120p. 1974. 7.95x (ISBN 0-8139-0564-8). U Pr of Va.
Ehrenpreis, Leon. Fourier Analysis in Several Complex Variables. (Pure & Applied Mathematics Ser.). 1970. 43.50 (ISBN 0-471-23400-1, Pub. by Wiley-Interscience). Wiley.
--Theory of Distributions for Locally Compact Spaces. LC 52-42839. (Memoirs: No. 21). 1978. pap. 5.20 (ISBN 0-8218-1221-1, MEMO-21). Am Math.
Ehrenpreis, Seymour & Kopin, Irwin J., eds. Reviews of Neuroscience, Vol. 1. LC 74-80538. 1974. 34.50 (ISBN 0-911216-84-7). Raven.
--Reviews of Neuroscience, Vol. 2. LC 74-80538. 1976. 27.00 (ISBN 0-89004-105-9). Raven.
--Reviews of Neuroscience, Vol. 3. LC 74-80538. 1978. 24.50 (ISBN 0-89004-168-7). Raven.
Ehrenzweig, Albert A., et al. Jurisdiction in a Nutshell, State & Federal. 4th ed. LC 80-312. (Nutshell Ser.). 298p. 1980. pap. 6.95 (ISBN 0-8299-2086-2). West Pub.
Ehrenzweig, Anton. The Hidden Order of Art: A Study in the Psychology of Artistic Imagination. (California Library Reprint Ser). 1976. 20.00x (ISBN 0-520-03181-4, CAL 418); pap. 6.95 (ISBN 0-520-03845-2). U of Cal Pr.
Ehresmann, Donald L. Applied & Decorative Arts: A Bibliographic Guide to Basic Reference Works, Histories, & Handbooks. LC 76-55416. 1977. lib. bdg. 22.50x (ISBN 0-87287-136-3). Libs Unl.
--Fine Arts: A Bibliographic Guide to Basic Reference Works, Histories & Handbooks. 2nd ed. LC 79-9051. 1979. lib. bdg. 25.00x (ISBN 0-87287-201-7). Libs Unl.
Ehresmann, Julia M., ed. Pocket Dictionary of Art Terms. LC 74-143464. (Illus.). 1971. pap. 2.95 (ISBN 0-8212-0748-2, 712019). NYGS.
Ehret, Arnold. Instructions for Fasting & Dieting. 1980. pap. 2.95 (ISBN 0-87904-003-3). Lust.
Ehret, Walter & Evans, George K. International Book of Christmas Carols. LC 80-13105. (Illus.). 352p. 1980. pap. 12.95 (ISBN 0-8289-0378-6). Greene.
Ehret, Walter, jt. auth. see Trusler, Ivan.
Ehrhardt, Roy. American Pocket Watch Production Totals & Dates, Plus Inventory Pages. 56p. 1979. 3.00 (ISBN 0-913902-30-6). Heart Am Pr.
--Clock Price Up-Date & Index to Clock Identification & Price Guide, 1979, Bk. 1. 1979. 4.00 (ISBN 0-913902-28-4). Heart Am Pr.
--Nineteen Seventy Nine Pocket Watch Price Indicator. (Illus.). 1979. plastic ring bdg. 10.00 (ISBN 0-913902-29-2). Heart Am Pr.
--Pocket Watch Price Indicator. (Illus.). 1980. plastic ring bdg. 12.00 (ISBN 0-913902-32-2). Heart Am Pr.
Ehrhart, W. D. Matters of the Heart. (Orig.). pap. write for info. (ISBN 0-938566-04-0). Adasta Pr.
Ehrich, Robert W. & Pleslova-Stikova, Emilie. Homolka: An Eneolithic Site in Bohemia. LC 79-16861. (American School of Prehistoric Research Ser.). (Orig.). 1968. pap. text ed. 15.00 (ISBN 0-87365-525-7). Peabody Harvard.
Ehrig, H. Universal Theory of Automata. (Illus.). 1976. pap. 18.75 (ISBN 3-5190-2054-8). Adler.
Ehrlich, Anne H., jt. auth. see Ehrlich, Paul R.
Ehrlich, Collis. Attack. 160p. (Orig.). 1981. pap. 2.25 (ISBN 0-345-28476-3). Ballantine.
Ehrlich, David & Wolf, George. The Bowel Book: A Practical Guide to Good Health. LC 80-54140. 192p. 1981. 12.95x (ISBN 0-8052-3763-1); pap. 5.95 (ISBN 0-8052-0673-6). Schocken.
Ehrlich, Eugene. How to Study Better & Get Higher Marks. 2nd, rev. ed. LC 76-41684. (Illus.). 1976. 10.95 (ISBN 0-690-01181-4, TYC-T). T Y Crowell.
Ehrlich, Eugene H. How to Study Better & Get Higher Marks. LC 61-14527. (Apollo Eds.). 1969. pap. 3.25 o.s.i. (ISBN 0-8152-0225-3, A225, TYC-T). T Y Crowell.
Ehrlich, Eugene H. & Murphy, Daniel. Art of Technical Writing: A Manual for Scientists, Engineers, & Students. LC 64-12081. (Apollo Eds.). 1969. pap. 3.95 o.s.i. (ISBN 0-8152-0226-1, A226, TYC-T). T Y Crowell.
Ehrlich, George E. Rehabilitation Management of Rheumatic Conditions. (Rehabilitation Medicine Library Ser.). (Illus.). 336p. 1980. 34.95 (ISBN 0-683-02791-3). Williams & Wilkins.
Ehrlich, George E., jt. auth. see Fries, James F.
Ehrlich, Gretel. To Touch the Water. Trusky, Tom, ed. LC 80-69276. (Modern & Contemporary Poets of the West Ser.). 60p. (Orig.). 1981. pap. 2.50 (ISBN 0-916272-16-8). Ahsahta Pr.
Ehrlich, Howard J., et al. Reinventing Anarchy: What Are Anarchists Thinking These Days? (Illus.). 1979. pap. 15.00 (ISBN 0-7100-0128-2). Routledge & Kegan.
Ehrlich, Ida L. Instant Vocabulary. pap. 2.95 (ISBN 0-671-42415-7). PB.
Ehrlich, Jeffrey & Mannheimer, Marc. The Carpenter's Manifesto. LC 77-73865. 1977. 12.95 o.p. (ISBN 0-03-016756-6); pap. 7.95 (ISBN 0-03-016761-2). HR&W.
Ehrlich, Max. The Big Boys. 288p. 1981. 11.95 (ISBN 0-395-30525-X). HM.
--Shaitan. LC 80-66498. 320p. Date not set. 12.95 (ISBN 0-87795-273-6). Arbor Hse.
Ehrlich, Paul R. & Ehrlich, Anne H. The End of Affluence: A Blueprint for Your Future. 320p. 1974. pap. 2.50 (ISBN 0-345-29049-6). Ballantine.
Ehrlich, Paul R., jt. auth. see Pirages, Dennis C.
Ehrlich, Paul R., et al. Ecoscience: Population, Resources, Environment. LC 77-6824. (Illus.). 1977. text ed. 47.95x (ISBN 0-7167-0567-2); pap. text ed. 23.95x (ISBN 0-7167-0029-8). W H Freeman.
--Human Ecology: Problems & Solutions. LC 72-12828. (Illus.). 1973. pap. 10.95x (ISBN 0-7167-0595-8). W H Freeman.
Ehrlich, Robert. Norman Mailer: The Radical As Hipster. LC 78-14849. 1978. lib. bdg. 12.00 (ISBN 0-8108-1160-X). Scarecrow.
--Physics & Computers: Problems, Simulations, & Data Analysis. LC 72-5640. 125p. (Orig.). 1973. pap. text ed. 10.50 (ISBN 0-395-18010-4). HM.
Ehrlich, Ruth A. & Givens, Ellen D. Patient Care in Radiography. (Illus.). 230p. 1981. pap. text ed. 12.95 (ISBN 0-8016-1507-0). Mosby.
Ehrlich, Stanislaw & Wooton, Graham, eds. Three Faces of Pluralism: Political, Ethnic, & Religious. 232p. 1980. 18.95x (ISBN 0-566-00313-9, 03274-3, Pub. by Gower Pub Co England). Lexington Bks.
Ehrlich, Thomas. Cyprus, Nineteen Fifty-Eight to Nineteen Sixty-Seven. (International Crises & the Role of Law Ser.). 160p. 1974. pap. text ed. 3.95x (ISBN 0-19-825321-4). Oxford U Pr.
Ehrlich, Thomas & Hazard, Geoffrey C., Jr. Going to Law School? Readings on a Legal Career. 252p. 1975. 8.95 (ISBN 0-316-22287-9); pap. 7.95 (ISBN 0-316-22288-7). Little.
Ehrlich, Thomas, ed. see Carnegie Commission on Higher Education.
Ehrman, Kenneth & Flavin, Sean. Taxing California Property. 2nd ed. 1979. 55.00 (ISBN 0-915950-31-6). Bull Pub.
Ehrman, Lee & Parsons, Peter. Behavior Genetics & Evolution. (Illus.). 448p. 1981. text ed. 22.95 (ISBN 0-07-019276-6, C). McGraw.
Ehrmann, Bertha K., ed. see Ehrmann, Max.
Ehrmann, Henry W. Comparative Legal Cultures. 176p. 1976. pap. text ed. 7.95 (ISBN 0-13-153858-6). P-H.
Ehrmann, Jacques. Un Paradis Desespere: L'Amour, L'Illusion. (Yale Romantic Studies). 1963. pap. 29.50x (ISBN 0-685-69816-5). Elliots Bks.
Ehrmann, Max. The Poems of Max Ehrmann. Ehrmann, Bertha K., ed. 1948. 6.50 (ISBN 0-9602450-1-4). R L Bell.
Ehrmantraut, Harry C. Headaches: The Lasting Way to Drugless Relief. LC 80-66697. (Illus.). 144p. 1980. 8.95 (ISBN 0-394-51393-2). Autumn Pr.
Eiby, G. A. Earthquakes. 209p. 1980. 14.95 (ISBN 0-442-25191-2). Van Nos Reinhold.
Eich, Gunter see Otten, Anna.
Eich, Gunter, et al. Four German Poets: Gunter Eich, Hilde Domin, Erich Fried, & Gunter Kunert. Stein, Agnes, ed. & tr. from Ger. LC 78-59474. (Contemporary Poets Ser.). 1980. 12.95 (ISBN 0-87376-034-4). Red Dust.
Eich, J. J., ed. Organometallic Syntheses: Non-Transitional Compounds, Vol. 2. 1981. write for info. (ISBN 0-12-234950-4). Acad Pr.
Eich, Robert H. Introduction to Cardiology. (Illus.). 304p. 1980. pap. text ed. 22.50 (ISBN 0-06-140770-4, Harper Medical). Har-Row.
Eichelberger, Clark M. Organizing for Peace: A Personal History of the Founding of the United Nations. LC 76-5127. 1977. 17.95 o.s.i. (ISBN 0-06-011114-3, HarpT). Har-Row.
Eichelberger, Clayton L. Guide to Critical Reviews of United States Fiction, 1870-1910. LC 77-149998. 1971. 13.50 (ISBN 0-8108-0380-1). Scarecrow.
--A Guide to Critical Reviews of U.S. Fiction, 1870-1910, Vol. 2. LC 77-14998. 1974. 12.00 (ISBN 0-8108-0701-7). Scarecrow.
Eichelberger, Rosa K. Big Fire in Baltimore. LC 78-31311. (gr. 3 up). 1979. 10.95 (ISBN 0-916144-36-4); pap. 6.95 (ISBN 0-916144-37-2). Stemmer Hse.
Eichenberg, Fritz. Endangered Species & Other Fables with a Twist. LC 79-15247. (Illus.). 1979. 27.50 (ISBN 0-916144-42-9); pap. 14.95 (ISBN 0-916144-43-7). Stemmer Hse.
Eicher, Don & McAlester, Lee. History of the Earth. (Illus.). 1980. text ed. 21.95 (ISBN 0-13-390047-9). P-H.
Eicher, Don L. Geologic Time. 2nd ed. (Foundations of Earth Sciences Ser.). (Illus.). 160p. 1976. pap. 7.95 (ISBN 0-13-352484-1). P-H.
Eicher, Joanne B., jt. ed. see Roach, Mary Ellen.
Eichholz, Alice, jt. ed. see Rose, James M.
Eichhorn, S., jt. auth. see Evert, Ray.
Eichinger, H., et al. German Once a Week, 2 bks. 1976. pap. 5.25x ea. (Pub. by Basil Blackwell). Bk. 1, 1977 (ISBN 0-631-96270-0). Bk. 2 (ISBN 0-631-96280-8). Biblio Dist.

Eichler, Edward P. & Kaplan, Marshall. The Community Builders. (California Studies in Urbanization & Environmental Design). 1967. 14.50x (ISBN 0-520-00380-2). U of Cal Pr.

Eichler, Margrit. Martin's Father. 2nd ed. LC 77-81779. 31p. (ps-1). 1977. pap. 2.75 (ISBN 0-914996-16-9); 6.50 o.p. (ISBN 0-914996-17-7). Lollipop Power.

Eichler, Victor B. Atlas of Comparative Embryology: A Laboratory Guide to Invertebrate & Vertebrate Embryos. LC 77-16023. (Illus.). 1978. pap. text ed. 11.50 (ISBN 0-8016-1492-9). Mosby.

Eichner, A. S. The Megacorp & Oligopoly. LC 75-17115. (Illus.). 450p. 1976. 35.50 (ISBN 0-521-20885-8). Cambridge U Pr.

Eichner, James. First Book of the Cabinet of the President of the U. S. LC 69-11536. (First Bks). (gr. 4-6). PLB 6.45 (ISBN 0-531-00491-0). Watts.

--Thomas Jefferson: The Complete Man. LC 65-21647. (Biography Ser). (gr. 7 up). 1966. PLB 4.90 o.p. (ISBN 0-531-00886-X). Watts.

Eichner, James A. The First Book of Local Government. rev. ed. (First Bks.). (Illus.). 72p. (gr. 6-9). 1976. PLB 6.45 (ISBN 0-531-00571-2). Watts.

Eicholz, R. E., ed. Skillseekers, 3 kits. (gr. 3-12). 1977. 185.00 ea. (Sch Div). Kit I (ISBN 0-201-23026-7). tchr's. ed. 5.48 (ISBN 0-201-23027-5); dup. masters 5.48 (ISBN 0-201-23030-5); ans. bk. 8.44 (ISBN 0-201-23028-3). A-W.

Eicholz, Robert, et al. Mathematics in Our World Primer. (Mathematics in Our World Ser.). 1978. pap. text ed. 3.92 (ISBN 0-201-09800-8, Sch Div); tchr's ed. 11.76 (ISBN 0-201-09801-6). A-W.

Eicholz, Robert E. & O'Daffer, Phares G. Success with Mathematics I. (Low Track Ser). (gr. 7-9). 1972. pap. text ed. 10.52 o.p. (ISBN 0-201-01580-3, Sch Div). A-W.

--Success with Mathematics I: Diagnostic Tests. 2nd ed. (Low Track Ser). (gr. 7-9). 1972. 8.72 o.p. (ISBN 0-201-01585-4, Sch Div). A-W.

--Success with Mathematics II: Achievement & Diagnostic Tests. 2nd ed. (Low Track Ser). (gr. 7-9). 1972. Achievement Tests. 8.72 o.p. (ISBN 0-201-01594-3, Sch Div); Diagnostic Tests. 8.72 o.p. (ISBN 0-201-01595-1). A-W.

Eicholz, Robert E., jt. auth. see Forbes, Jack E.

Eicholz, Robert E., et al. Investigating School Mathematics Primer. (Investigating School Math Ser.). (gr. 1-6). 1973. pap. text ed. 3.92 (ISBN 0-201-01290-1, Sch Div); tchr's. ed. 11.84 (ISBN 0-201-01291-X). A-W.

--Mathematics in Our World. Incl. Bk. 1. (gr. 1). text ed. 3.92 kindergarten (ISBN 0-201-09800-8); text ed. 6.08 (ISBN 0-201-09810-5); tchr's. ed. 14.12 (ISBN 0-201-09811-3); wkbk. 2.76 (ISBN 0-201-09813-X); wkbk. tchr's. ed. 3.00 (ISBN 0-201-09814-8); duplicator masters 38.88 (ISBN 0-201-09812-1); enrichment wkbk. 2.76 (ISBN 0-201-09815-6); tchr's. enrichment wkbk. 3.00 (ISBN 0-201-09816-4); Bk. 2. (gr. 2). text ed. 6.08 (ISBN 0-201-09820-2); tchr's ed. 14.12 (ISBN 0-201-09821-0); wkbk. 2.76 (ISBN 0-201-09823-7); wkbk. tchr's ed. 3.00 (ISBN 0-201-09824-5); duplicator masters 38.88 (ISBN 0-201-09822-9); enrichment wkbk. 2.76 (ISBN 0-201-09825-3); tchr's enrichment wkbk 3.00 (ISBN 0-201-09826-1); Bk. 3. (gr. 3). text ed. 10.24 (ISBN 0-201-09830-X); tchr's ed. 16.00 (ISBN 0-201-09831-8); duplicator masters 38.88 (ISBN 0-201-09832-6); wkbk 3.52 (ISBN 0-201-09833-4); wkbk 3.68 (ISBN 0-201-09835-0); wkbk tchr's ed. 3.80 (ISBN 0-201-09836-9); Bk. 4. (gr. 4). text ed. 10.24 (ISBN 0-201-09840-7); tchr's ed. 16.00 (ISBN 0-201-09841-5); duplicator masters 38.88 (ISBN 0-201-09842-3); wkbk 3.52 (ISBN 0-201-09843-1); wkbk tchr's ed. 4.16 (ISBN 0-201-09844-X); Bk. 5. (gr. 5). text ed. 10.24 (ISBN 0-201-09850-4); tchr's ed. 16.00 (ISBN 0-201-09851-2); duplicator masters 38.88 (ISBN 0-201-09852-0); wkbk 3.52 (ISBN 0-201-09853-9); wkbk tchr's ed. 4.16 (ISBN 0-201-09854-7); Bk. 6. (gr. 6). text ed. 10.24 (ISBN 0-201-09860-1); tchr's ed. 16.00 (ISBN 0-201-09861-X); duplicator masters 38.88 (ISBN 0-201-09862-8); wkbk 3.52 (ISBN 0-201-09863-6); wkbk. tchr's ed. 4.16 (ISBN 0-201-09864-4); Bk. 7. (gr. 7). 1980. text ed. 12.32 (ISBN 0-201-09870-9); tchr's ed. 16.00 (ISBN 0-201-09871-7); Bk. 8. (gr. 8). 1978. text ed. 12.32 (ISBN 0-201-09880-6); tchr's ed. 16.00 (ISBN 0-201-09881-4); wkbk 3.52 (ISBN 0-201-09883-0); tchr's ed. wkbk 3.52 (ISBN 0-201-09884-9). (gr. 1-6). 1978. duplicator masters 43.40 ea. (ISBN 0-201-09882-2, Sch Div). A-W.

--Mathematics in Our World: Test Duplicator Masters. (Mathematics in Our World Ser.). (gr. 7-8). 1979. Gr. 7. 34.48 (ISBN 0-201-09875-X, Sch Div); Gr. 8. 43.40 (ISBN 0-201-09882-2). A-W.

--Mathematics in Our World. 2nd ed. Incl. Bk. 1. (gr. k). student ed. 3.92 (ISBN 0-201-16000-5); tchr's ed. 11.76 (ISBN 0-201-16001-3); (gr. 1). pap. 6.08 student ed. (ISBN 0-201-16010-2); tchr's ed. 16.00 (ISBN 0-201-16011-0); wkbk. 2.76 (ISBN 0-201-16013-7); tchr's ed. wkbk. 3.00 (ISBN 0-201-16014-5); (gr. 2). student ed. 6.08 (ISBN 0-201-16020-X); tchr's ed. 16.00 (ISBN 0-201-16021-8); wkbk. 2.76 (ISBN 0-201-16023-4); tchr's ed. wkbk. 3.00 (ISBN 0-201-16024-2); (gr. 3). student ed. 10.24 (ISBN 0-201-16030-7); tchr's ed. 16.00 (ISBN 0-201-16031-5); wkbk. 3.52 (ISBN 0-201-16033-1); tchr's ed. wkbk. 4.16 (ISBN 0-201-16034-X); consumable ed. 7.20 (ISBN 0-201-16009-9); (gr. 4). student ed. 10.24 (ISBN 0-201-16040-4); tchr's ed. 16.00 (ISBN 0-201-16041-2); wkbk. 3.52 (ISBN 0-201-16043-9); tchr's ed. wkbk. 4.16 (ISBN 0-201-16044-7); (gr. 5). student ed. 10.24 (ISBN 0-201-16050-1); tchr's ed. 16.00 (ISBN 0-201-16051-X); wkbk. 3.52 (ISBN 0-201-16053-6); tchr's ed. wkbk. 4.16 (ISBN 0-201-16054-4); (gr. 6). student ed. 10.24 (ISBN 0-201-16060-9); tchr's ed. 16.00 (ISBN 0-201-16064-1); wkbk. 3.52 (ISBN 0-201-16063-3); tchr's ed. wkbk. 4.16 (ISBN 0-201-16064-1); (gr. 7). student ed. 12.32 (ISBN 0-201-16070-6); tchr's ed. 16.00 (ISBN 0-201-16071-4); wkbk. 3.52 (ISBN 0-201-16073-0); tchr's ed. wkbk. 4.16 (ISBN 0-201-16074-9); (gr. 8). student ed. 12.32 (ISBN 0-201-16080-3); tchr's ed. 16.00 (ISBN 0-201-16081-1); wkbk. 3.52 (ISBN 0-201-16083-8); tchr's ed. wkbk. 4.16 (ISBN 0-201-16084-6). (gr. 1-8). 1981 (Sch Div). A-W.

--Mathematics in Our World: Spanish Edition. (gr. 1-6). 1981. Bk. 1. text ed. 6.08 (ISBN 0-201-09700-1, Sch Div); Bk. 2. text ed. 6.08 (ISBN 0-201-09701-X); Bk. 3. text ed. 6.76 (ISBN 0-201-09702-8). A-W.

--Mathematics in Our World. Incl. Enrichment Workbook Grade 3. 1979. tchr's ed 3.40 o.p. (ISBN 0-201-09836-9); wkbk 3.12 o.p. (ISBN 0-201-09835-0); Enrichment Workbook Grade 4. 1979. tchrs' ed 3.40 o.p. (ISBN 0-201-09846-6); wkbk 3.12 o.p. (ISBN 0-201-09845-8); Enrichment Workbook Grade 5. 1979. tchrs' ed 3.40 o.p. (ISBN 0-201-09856-3); wkbk 3.12 o.p. (ISBN 0-201-09855-5); Enrichment Workbook Grade 6. 1979. tchrs' ed 3.40 o.p. (ISBN 0-201-09866-0); wkbk 3.12 o.p. (ISBN 0-686-60616-7); Enrichment Workbook Grade 7. 1979. tchrs' ed 3.40 o.p. (ISBN 0-201-09874-1); wkbk 3.04 o.p. (ISBN 0-686-60617-5); Enrichment Workbook Grade 8. 1979. tchrs' ed 3.40 o.p. (ISBN 0-686-68528-8); wkbk 3.04 o.p. (ISBN 0-686-60618-3). (gr. 3-8). A-W.

--Investigating School Mathematics, 6 bks. (ISM Ser.). (gr. 1-6). 1973. Bk. 1. pap. text ed. 5.44 o.p. (ISBN 0-201-01310-X, Sch Div); tchrs' manual o.p. 12.60 o.p. (ISBN 0-201-01311-8); wkbk. 2.52 o.p. (ISBN 0-201-01317-7); dittomasters o.p. 33.80 o.p. (ISBN 0-201-01318-5). A-W.

--Investigating School Mathematics. pap. text ed. 5.16 o.p. (ISBN 0-201-01303-7); Bk. 2, Gr. K-2. pap. text ed. 5.16 o.p. (ISBN 0-201-01304-5). A-W.

--Investigating School Mathematics, 6 bks. 2nd ed. (ISM Ser.). (ps-6). 1976. text ed. 3.52 primary ext o.p. (ISBN 0-201-01290-1, Sch Div); text ed. 6.08 grade 1 (ISBN 0-201-09510-6); text ed. 6.08 grade 2 (ISBN 0-201-09520-3); text ed. 10.24 grade 3 (ISBN 0-201-09530-0); text ed. 10.24 grade 4 (ISBN 0-201-09540-8); text ed. 10.24 grade 5 (ISBN 0-201-09550-5); text ed. 10.24 grade 6 (ISBN 0-201-09560-2). A-W.

--Investigating School Mathematics, Bk. 8. (ISM Ser.). (gr. 8). 1974. text ed. 12.32 (ISBN 0-201-01280-4, Sch Div); tchr's ed. 16.00 (ISBN 0-201-01281-2); wkbk. 3.52 (ISBN 0-201-01282-0). A-W.

Eicholz, Robert E., et al, eds. Investigating School Mathematics. O'Daffer, Phares G. & Fleenor, Charles R. Incl. Unit P (ISBN 0-201-01293-6); Unit R (ISBN 0-201-01294-4). (Investigating School Mathematics Ser). (gr. k). pap. text ed. 8.04 ea. o.p. (Sch Div). A-W.

Eichorn, Dorothy, et al, eds. Present & Past in Middle Life. 1981. price not set (ISBN 0-12-233680-1). Acad Pr.

Eickmann, Paul E. Wonderful Works of God. (Orig.). 1970. pap. 3.25 (ISBN 0-8100-0015-6, 7-N38); pap. wkbk. avail. (ISBN 0-685-04632-X). Northwest Pub.

Eid, Nimr. Legal Aspects of Marketing Behavior in Lebanon & Kuwait. 7.50x (ISBN 0-685-77095-8). Intl Bk Ctr.

Eide, Asbjorn. Human Rights in the World Society: The Commitments, the Reality, the Future. 300p. 1981. text ed. 25.00 (ISBN 0-930576-39-X). E M Coleman Ent.

Eide, Ashborn, jt. auth. see Kaldor, Mary.

Eidelberg, Lawrence, ed. The Health Sciences Video Directory. LC 76-29480. 1977. pap. 30.00 (ISBN 0-917226-00-3). Nord Media.

--The Health Sciences Video Directory: 1978 Supplement, 4 vols. LC 76-29480. 1978. pap. 30.00 set (ISBN 0-917226-05-4); Vol. 1. (ISBN 0-917226-01-1); Vol. 2. (ISBN 0-917226-02-X); Vol. 3. (ISBN 0-917226-03-8); Vol. 4. (ISBN 0-917226-04-6). Nord Media.

--The Videolog: Programs for Business & Industry. LC 78-74186. 1979. pap. 35.00 (ISBN 0-917226-07-0). Nord Media.

--The Videolog: Programs for General Interest & Entertainment. LC 78-74187. 1979. pap. 20.00 (ISBN 0-917226-08-9). Nord Media.

--The Videolog: Programs for the Health Sciences. LC 78-74188. 1979. pap. 35.00 (ISBN 0-917226-09-7). Nord Media.

Eidelberg, Ludwig, ed. Encyclopedia of Psychoanalysis. LC 67-28974. 1968. 35.00 (ISBN 0-02-909340-6). Free Pr.

Eidelberg, Martin. Watteau's Drawings: Their Use & Significance. LC 76-23616. (Outstanding Dissertations in the Fine Arts - 18th Century). (Illus.). 1977. Repr. of 1965 ed. lib. bdg. 56.00 (ISBN 0-8240-2687-X). Garland Pub.

Eidelberg, Paul. Beyond Detente: Toward an American Foreign Policy. 12.95 (ISBN 0-89385-000-4). Green Hill.

--On the Silence of the Declaration of Independence. LC 76-8759. 148p. 1980. pap. text ed. 5.95x (ISBN 0-87023-313-0). U of Mass Pr.

--The Philosophy of the American Constitution: A Reinterpretation of the Intentions of the Founding Fathers. 1968. 8.50 o.s.i. (ISBN 0-02-909360-0). Free Pr.

Eidelberg, Shlomo, ed. Jews & the Crusaders: The Hebrew Chronicles of the First & Second Crusades. 1977. 17.50 (ISBN 0-299-07060-3). U of Wis Pr.

Eidem, Rolf & Viotti, Staffan. Economic Systems: How Resources Are Allocated. LC 78-19199. 1978. text ed. 18.95 (ISBN 0-470-26364-4). Halsted Pr.

Eidheim, Harald. Aspects of the Lappish Minority Situation. 86p. 1971. 10.50x (ISBN 8-200-02328-1, Dist. by Columbia U Pr). Universitet.

Eidlin, Fred. The Logic of "Normalization". (East European Monograph: No. 74). 256p. 1980. 20.00x (ISBN 0-914710-68-0). East Eur Quarterly.

Eidt, Robert C. Pioneer Settlement in Northeast Argentina. LC 71-138058. 1971. 22.50x (ISBN 0-299-05920-0). U of Wis Pr.

Eidus, J., et al. Atlas of Electronic Spectra of Five-Nitrofuran Compounds. 1972. 22.95 (ISBN 0-470-23430-X). Halsted Pr.

Eiffeis & Schuyt. Tangram: The Ancient Chinese Puzzle. 12.95 (ISBN 0-8109-2174-X). Abrams.

Eigel, Christine, jt. ed. see Zimmermann, Ulrich.

Eigen, Manfred & Winkler, Ruthild. Laws of the Game: How the Principles of Nature Govern Chance. LC 79-3494. (Illus.). 384p. 1981. cancelled o.p. (ISBN 0-394-41806-9). Knopf.

--Laws of the Game: How the Principles of Nature Govern Chance. LC 79-3494. (Illus.). 384p. 1981. 17.95 (ISBN 0-394-41806-9). Knopf.

Eighme, Lloyd. Insects You Have Seen. LC 79-24141. (Crown Ser.). (gr. 6 up). 1980. pap. 4.50 (ISBN 0-8127-0259-X). Southern Pub.

Eighmy, John L. Churches in Cultural Captivity: A History of the Social Attitudes of Southern Baptists. LC 70-111047. 1972. 14.50x (ISBN 0-87049-115-6). U of Tenn Pr.

Eighth International Biometeorological Congress 9-15 September 1979. Biometeorology Seven: Proceedings, Supplement to Volume 24, of the International Journal of Biometeorology, Pts. 1 & 2. Zemel, Z. & Hyslop, N., eds. 1981. pap. text ed. 78.95 (ISBN 90-265-0354-7). Swets North Am.

--Biometeorology Seven: Proceedings, Supplement to Volume 24 of the International Journal of Biometeorology, Pt. 2. Zemel, Z. & Hyslop, N., eds. 1981. pap. text ed. 44.75 (ISBN 90-265-0350-4). Swets North Am.

Eighth International Conference on Fluid Sealing. Proceedings, 2 vols. Stephens, H. S. & Guy, N. G., eds. (Illus.). 1979. pap. text ed. 70.00 (ISBN 0-900983-93-0, Dist. by Air Science Co.). BHRA Fluid.

Eighty-Fifth Symposium of the International Astronomical Union, Victoria, B. C., Canada, August 27-30, 1979. Star Clusters: Proceedings. Hesser, James E., ed. (International Astronomical Union Symposium Ser.: No. 85). 540p. 1980. lib. bdg. 63.00 (ISBN 90-277-1087-2); pap. 31.50 (ISBN 90-277-1088-0). Kluwer Boston.

Eigner, Edwin M. The Metaphysical Novel in England & America: Dickens, Bulwer, Hawthorne, Melville. LC 76-50246. 1978. 16.50x (ISBN 0-520-03382-5). U of Cal Pr.

Eigner, Larry. The World & Its Streets, Places. 180p. (Orig.). 1977. ltd. signed o.p. 15.00 (ISBN 0-87685-269-X); pap. 5.00 (ISBN 0-87685-268-1). Black Sparrow.

Eigsti, jt. auth. see Clemen.

Eijndhoven, J. van see Van Eijndhoven, J.

Eikhenbaum, Boris. Lermontov: An Essay in Literary Historical Evaluation. Parrott, Ray & Weber, Harry, trs. 1981. 16.50. Ardis Pubs.

--Tolstoi in the Seventies. Kaspin, A., tr. 1981. 15.00 (ISBN 0-88233-472-7). Ardis Pubs.

--Tolstoi in the Sixties. White, tr. from Rus. 1981. 15.00 (ISBN 0-88233-470-0). Ardis Pubs.

Eilenberg, S. & Steenrod, N. Foundations of Algebraic Topology. (Mathematical Ser.: Vol. 15). 1952. 22.00 o.p. (ISBN 0-691-07965-X). Princeton U Pr.

Eilenberg, Samuel. Automata, Languages, & Machines. (Pure & Applied Mathematics: A Series of Monographs & Textbooks, Vol. 58). Vol. A 1974. 44.50 (ISBN 0-12-234001-9); Vol. B 1976. 40.00 (ISBN 0-12-234002-7). Acad Pr.

Eilers, Robert. The Hermes Stone. (Orig.). 1980. pap. 1.95 (ISBN 0-532-23264-X). Manor Bks.

Eilers, Robert D. & Jones, Robert C. The Attitudes & Anticipated Behavior of Dentists Under Various Reimbursement Arrangements. 1972. pap. text ed. 2.75x o.p. (ISBN 0-256-00265-7). Irwin.

Eilon, Samuel. Aspects of Management. 2nd ed. 1979. text ed. 26.00 (ISBN 0-08-022480-6); pap. text ed. 11.25 (ISBN 0-08-022479-2). Pergamon.

--Management Control. 2nd ed. 1979. text ed. 19.00 (ISBN 0-08-022482-2); pap. text ed. 9.75 (ISBN 0-08-022481-4). Pergamon.

EIMAC Division of Varian Laboratory Staff, jt. auth. see Sutherland, Robert I.

Eimas, Peter D. & Miller, Joanne L., eds. Perspectives on the Study of Speech. 464p. 1981. text ed. 29.95 (ISBN 0-89859-052-3). L Erlbaum Assocs.

Eimbinder, J., ed. Semiconductor Memories. LC 72-148501. 1971. 20.95 o.p. (ISBN 0-471-23460-5, Pub. by Wiley-Interscience). Wiley.

Eimerl, Sarel. World of Giotto. (Library of Art). (Illus.). 1967. 15.95 (ISBN 0-8094-0239-4). Time-Life.

--World of Giotto. LC 67-23024. (Library of Art Ser.). (Illus.). (gr. 6 up). 1967. 12.96 (ISBN 0-8094-0268-8, Pub. by Time-Life). Silver.

Eimerl, Sarel & DeVore, Irven. The Primates. (Young Readers Library). (Illus.). 1977. lib. bdg. 7.98 (ISBN 0-686-51092-5). Silver.

Eimerl, Sarel & Lee, Russell V. Physician. LC 67-20331. (Life Science Library). (Illus.). (gr. 5 up). 1967. PLB 8.97 o.p. (ISBN 0-8094-0480-X, Pub. by Time-Life). Silver.

Eimerl, Sarel, jt. auth. see De Vore, Irven.

Eims, Leroy. Be a Motivation Leader. 144p. 1981. pap. 3.95 (ISBN 0-89693-008-4). Victor Bks.

--Be the Leader You Were Meant to Be. 132p. 1975. pap. 2.95 (ISBN 0-88207-723-6). Victor Bks.

--Disciples in Action. 324p. 1981. pap. 5.95 (ISBN 0-88207-343-5). Victor Bks.

--Disciples in Action. (Orig.). 1981. pap. price not set (ISBN 0-89109-477-6). NavPress.

--What Every Christian Should Know About Growing. 168p. 1976. pap. 3.95 (ISBN 0-88207-727-9). Victor Bks.

--Winning Ways. LC 74-77319. 160p. 1974. pap. 2.95 (ISBN 0-88207-707-4). Victor Bks.

--Wisdom from Above. 1978. pap. 3.50 (ISBN 0-88207-761-9). Victor Bks.

Ein, Claudia. How to Make Your Own Wedding Gown. LC 77-74299. 1978. pap. 8.95 o.p. (ISBN 0-385-11105-3). Doubleday.

Einarsson, Stefan. History of Icelandic Literature. 1957. 20.00x (ISBN 0-89067-033-1). Am Scandinavian.

Einaudi, Luigi R., ed. Beyond Cuba: Latin America Takes Charge of Its Future. LC 73-8644. 250p. 1973. pap. 14.00x (ISBN 0-8448-0266-2). Crane-Russak Co.

Einaudi, Paula F. A Grammar of Biloxi. LC 75-25114. (American Indian Linguistics Ser.). 1976. lib. bdg. 42.00 (ISBN 0-8240-1965-2). Garland Pub.

Einbinder, Harvey. Myth of the Britannica. LC 63-16997. Repr. of 1964 ed. 15.50 (ISBN 0-384-14050-5). Johnson Repr.

Ein-Dor, Phillip & Segev, Eli. A Paradigm for Management Information Systems. 232p. 1980. 22.95 (ISBN 0-03-058017-X). Praeger.

Einhard & Nofker The Stammerer. Two Lives of Charlemagne. Thorpe, Lewis, tr. & intro. by. (Classics Ser.). 240p. 1969. pap. 2.95 (ISBN 0-14-044213-8). Penguin.

Einhorn, E. C. Old French: A Concise Handbook. 210p. 1975. 29.50 (ISBN 0-521-20343-0); pap. 12.50x (ISBN 0-521-09838-6). Cambridge U Pr.

Einhorn, Henry, jt. auth. see Nutter, G. Warren.

Einhorn, Lawrence H., ed. Testicular Tumors: Management & Treatment, Vol. 3. LC 79-89999. (Cancer Management Series). (Illus.). 224p. 1980. 38.00 (ISBN 0-89352-078-0). Masson Pub.

Einspruch, Norman G., ed. Microstructure Science & Engineering, 2 vols. 1981. Vol. 1. write for info. (ISBN 0-12-234101-5); Vol. 2. write info. (ISBN 0-12-234102-3). Acad Pr.

Einstein. Willie's Time: A Memoir. pap. 2.50 (ISBN 0-425-04658-3). Berkley Pub.
Einstein, Albert. Meaning of Relativity. 5th ed. 1956. 11.00 (ISBN 0-691-08007-0); pap. 3.95 (ISBN 0-691-02352-2). Princeton U Pr.
Einstein, Alfred. Greatness in Music. LC 70-87527. 1972. Repr. of 1941 ed. lib. bdg. 25.00 (ISBN 0-306-71441-8). Da Capo.
--Greatness in Music. LC 76-6984. 1976. pap. 6.95 (ISBN 0-306-80046-2). Da Capo.
--Mozart: His Character, His Work. (Orig.). 1945. 29.95x (ISBN 0-19-500538-4). Oxford U Pr.
--Mozart: His Character, His Work. 1965. pap. 7.95 (ISBN 0-19-500732-8, GB). Oxford U Pr.
--Shubert: A Musical Portrait. (Music Ser.). ix, 343p. 1981. Repr. of 1951 ed. lib. bdg. 27.50 (ISBN 0-306-76083-5). Da Capo.
Einstein Centennial Celebration, Memphis State University, March 14-16, 1979. After Einstein: Proceedings. Barker, Peter & Shugart, Cecil G., eds. LC 80-27347. (Illus.). 1981. 24.95x (ISBN 0-87870-095-1). Memphis St Univ. Postponed.
Einstein, Charles. Basic Blackjack Betting. (Gambler's Book Shelf). (Orig.). 1980. pap. 2.95 (ISBN 0-89650-619-3). Gamblers.
--The Blackjack Hijack. 1976. 6.95 o.p. (ISBN 0-394-49459-8). Random.
--How to Win at Blackjack. (Gambler's Book Shelf). 64p. 1979. pap. 2.95 (ISBN 0-89650-552-9). Gamblers.
--Willie's Time. 1979. 12.95 (ISBN 0-397-01329-9). Lippincott.
Einstein, Charles, ed. The Baseball Reader: Favorites from the Fireside Books of Baseball. 1980. 12.95 (ISBN 0-690-01898-3). Lippincott.
Einstein, Stanley. Beyond Drugs. LC 73-7940. 1974. text ed. 21.00 (ISBN 0-08-017767-0); pap. text ed. 12.00 (ISBN 0-08-017768-9). Pergamon.
Einzig, Paul. Case Against Joining the Common Market. 144p. 1971. 21.95 (ISBN 0-312-12320-5). St Martin.
Eirich, Frederick R., ed. Rheology: Theory & Applications, 5 Vols. 1956-1969. Vol. 1. 1956. 68.50 (ISBN 0-12-234301-8); Vol. 2. 1958. 61.75 (ISBN 0-12-234302-6); Vol. 3. 1959. 61.75 (ISBN 0-12-234303-4); Vol. 4. 1967. 68.50 (ISBN 0-12-234304-2); Vol. 5. 1970. 68.50 (ISBN 0-12-234305-0). Acad Pr.
Eirinberg, Estelle, tr. see Thomas, Edith.
Eiring, Leslie, jt. auth. see Eaton, Peggy.
Eisberg, Robert & Hyde, Wendell. Countdown: Skydiver, Rocket & Satellite Motion on Programmable Calculators. LC 78-24836. 107p. 1979. pap. 7.95 (ISBN 0-918398-26-6). Dilithium Pr.
Eisberg, Robert & Resnick, Robert. Quantum Physics of Atoms, Molecules, Solids, Nuclei, & Particles. LC 74-1195. 816p. 1974. text ed. 29.95 (ISBN 0-471-23464-8). Wiley.
Eisberg, Robert M. Fundamentals of Modern Physics. LC 61-6770. (Illus.). 1961. 28.50 (ISBN 0-471-23463-X). Wiley.
Eisberg, Robert M. & Lerner, Lawrence S. Physics, Foundations & Applications, Vol. I. 720p. 1981. text ed. 21.95x (ISBN 0-07-019091-7, C); write for info study guide (ISBN 0-07-019111-5). McGraw.
--Physics: Foundations & Applications, Vol. II. (Illus.). 864p. 1981. text ed. 21.95 (ISBN 0-07-019092-5, C); solutions maual avail. (ISBN 0-07-019119-0); numerical calculations, suppl. avail. (ISBN 0-07-019120-4). McGraw.
--Physics: Foundations & Applications, Combined Vol. (Illus.). 1552p. 1981. text ed. 28.95x (ISBN 0-07-019110-7, C); price not set instrs'. manual (ISBN 0-07-019110-7); price not set numerical calculation supplement (ISBN 0-07-019120-4). McGraw.
EISCAT School. Radar Probing of the Auroral Plasma: Proceedings. Brekke, Asgeir, ed. 1977. pap. 36.00x (ISBN 82-00-02421-0, Dist. by Columbia U Pr). Universitet.
Eisdorfer, C. & Faun, W. E., eds. Psychopharmacology of Aging. (Illus.). 327p. 1980. text ed. 40.00 (ISBN 0-89335-117-2). Spectrum Pub.
Eisdorfer, C., et al. Conceptual Models for Psychopathology. 1981. text ed. write for info. (ISBN 0-89335-123-7). Spectrum Pub.
Eisdorfer, Carl & Starr, Bernard, eds. Annual Review of Gerontology & Geriatrics. (Illus.). 416p. 1980. text ed. 25.50 (ISBN 0-8261-3080-1). Springer Pub.
Eisele, Carolyn & Martin, Richard M., eds. Studies in the Scientific & Mathematical Philosophy of Charles S. Pierce: Essays by Carolyn Eisele. (Studies in Philosophy). 1979. text ed. 57.00x (ISBN 90-279-7808-5). Mouton.
Eisele, John. Modern Quantum Mechanics with Applications to Elementary Particle Physics: An Introduction to Contemporary Physical Thinking. LC 69-19102. 1969. 38.95 (ISBN 0-471-23466-4, Pub. by Wiley-Interscience). Wiley.
Eiselen, Malcolm R. The Rise of Pennsylvania Protectionsim. (The Neglected American Economists Ser.). 1974. lib. bdg. 50.00 (ISBN 0-8240-1035-3). Garland Pub.
Eiseley, Loren. Another Kind of Autumn. LC 77-8130. (Encore Edition). (Illus.). 1977. 4.95 (ISBN 0-684-16352-7, ScribT). Scribner.
--Darwin's Century: Evolution & the Men Who Discovered It. LC 58-6638. 1958. pap. 3.50 (ISBN 0-385-08141-3, A244, Anch). Doubleday.
--Firmament of Time. rev. ed. LC 60-11032. 1960. pap. 4.95 (ISBN 0-689-70068-7, 95). Atheneum.
Eiseman, Alberta. Candido. (Illus.). (gr. k-2). 1967. 8.95 (ISBN 0-02-733300-0). Macmillan.
Eiseman, Ben. What Are My Chances? LC 79-67118. (Illus.). 1980. text ed. 14.95 (ISBN 0-7216-3344-7). Saunders.
Eisen, Carole, jt. auth. see Eisen, Martin.
Eisen, Gail, jt. auth. see Friedman, Philip.
Eisen, Martin & Eisen, Carole. Finite Mathematics. 1978. text ed. 15.95x (ISBN 0-02-472450-5). Macmillan.
Eisenbach, G. M. & Brod, J., eds. Kidney & Pregnancy. (Contributions to Nephrology Ser.: Vol. 25). (Illus.). vi, 144p. 1981. pap. 54.00 (ISBN 3-8055-1798-X). S Karger.
Eisenbach, S. & Sadler, C. PASCAL for Programmers. (Illus.). 225p. 1981. pap. 8.80 (ISBN 0-387-10473-9). Springer-Verlag.
Eisenberg, ed. Radiation Protection--a Systematic Approach to Safety: Proceedings of the 5th Congress of the International Radiation Protection Society, March 1980, Jerusalem, 2 vols. (Illus.). 1055p. 1980. 215.00 (ISBN 0-08-025912-X). Pergamon.
Eisenberg, et al. Sex Education & the New Morality. 1967. pap. 1.95 (ISBN 0-686-12286-0). Jewish Bd Family.
Eisenberg, Abne M. Living Communication. (Speech Communications Ser.). (Illus.). 336p. 1975. pap. text ed. 13.95 (ISBN 0-13-538900-3). P-H.
Eisenberg, Abne M. & Ilardo, Joseph A. Argument: A Guide to Formal & Informal Debate. 2nd ed. (Speech Communication Ser.). (Illus.). 1980. pap. 11.95 (ISBN 0-13-045989-5). P-H.
Eisenberg, Abne M. & Smith, Ralph R. Nonverbal Communication. LC 77-160790. (Speech Communication Ser.: No. 9). 1971. pap. 4.50 (ISBN 0-672-61155-4). Bobbs.
Eisenberg, Azriel. Witness to the Holocaust. 649p. 1981. 17.95 (ISBN 0-8298-0432-3). Pilgrim NY.
Eisenberg, Azriel, et al, eds. Eyewitnesses to American Jewish History: East European Immigration 1881-1920, Pt. 3. (Illus.). 1978. pap. 5.00 (ISBN 0-8074-0017-3, 144061); tchrs'. guide 5.00 (ISBN 0-8074-0021-1, 204063). UAHC.
--Eyewitnesses to American Jewish History: The German Immigration 1800-1875, Pt. 2. (Illus.). 1977. pap. 5.00 (ISBN 0-8074-0016-5; 144059); tchrs'. guide 5.00 (ISBN 0-8074-0020-3, 204062). UAHC.
--Eyewitnesses to American Jewish History: 1492 - 1793, Pt. 1. 1976. pap. 5.00 (144060); tchrs'. guide 5.00 (ISBN 0-8074-0019-X, 204061). UAHC.
--Eyewitnesses to Jewish History: From Five Eighty-Six B. C. E. to Nineteen Sixty-Seven. (gr. 9-12). 1972. text ed. 12.50 (ISBN 0-8074-0076-9, 144066); tchrs'. guide 5.00 (ISBN 0-8074-0057-2, 204067). UAHC.
Eisenberg, Barry, tr. see Perez de Ayala, Ramon.
Eisenberg, David & Kauzmann, Walter. Structure & Properties of Water. 1969. 13.95x (ISBN 0-19-500320-9); pap. 6.95x (ISBN 0-19-500321-7). Oxford U Pr.
Eisenberg, Helen & Eisenberg, Larry. Fun & Fellowship Resource Book. (Game & Party Bks.). 160p. 1981. pap. 3.95 (ISBN 0-8010-3364-0). Baker Bk.
--Handbook of Skits & Stunts. 1953. 5.95 o.p. (ISBN 0-8096-1086-8, Assn Pr). Follett.
Eisenberg, Henryk. Biological Macromolecules & Polyelectrolytes in Solution. (Monographs on Physical Biochemistry). (Illus.). 1976. 39.95x (ISBN 0-19-854612-2). Oxford U Pr.
Eisenberg, James & Kafka, Francis J. Silk Screen Printing. rev. ed. (Illus.). (gr. 9 up). 1957. pap. 5.00 (ISBN 0-87345-205-4). McKnight.
Eisenberg, John F., ed. Vertebrate Ecology in the Northern Neotropics. LC 79-9436. (Symposia of the National Zoologial Park Ser.: No. 4). (Illus.). 271p. 1980. text ed. 25.00x (ISBN 0-87474-410-5); pap. text ed. 12.50x (ISBN 0-87474-409-1). Smithsonian.
Eisenberg, John M. & Williams, Sarkey V. The Physicians Practice. LC 80-13691. 274p. 1980. 18.50 (ISBN 0-471-05469-0, Pub. by Wiley Med). Wiley.
Eisenberg, Larry, jt. auth. see Eisenberg, Helen.
Eisenberg, Lisa. Falling Star. LC 79-52653. (Laura Brewster Mysteries Ser.). (Illus.). 64p. (gr. 4 up). 1980. PLB 7.95 (ISBN 0-516-02205-9). Childrens.
--Fast-Food King. LC 79-52564. (Laura Brewster Mysteries Ser.). (Illus.). 64p. (gr. 4 up). 1980. PLB 7.95 (ISBN 0-516-02206-7). Childrens.
--Golden Idol. LC 79-52655. (Laura Brewster Mysteries Ser.). (Illus.). 64p. (gr. 4 up). Date not set. PLB 7.95 (ISBN 0-516-02207-5). Childrens.
--House of Laughs. LC 79-52656. (Laura Brewster Mysteries Ser.). (Illus.). 64p. (gr. 4 up). 1980. PLB 7.95 (ISBN 0-516-02208-3). Childrens.
--Killer Music. LC 79-52657. (Laura Brewster Mysteries Ser.). (Illus.). 64p. (gr. 4 up). 1980. PLB 7.95 (ISBN 0-516-02209-1). Childrens.
--Tiger Rose. LC 79-52658. (Laura Brewster Mysteries Ser.). (Illus.). 64p. (gr. 4 up). 1980. PLB 7.95 (ISBN 0-516-02210-5). Childrens.
Eisenberg, Lisa, jt. auth. see Hall, Katy.
Eisenberg, Martin A. Introduction to the Mechanics of Solids. LC 78-74682. (Illus.). 1980. text ed. 24.95 (ISBN 0-201-01934-5). A-W.
Eisenberg, Melvin A., jt. auth. see Cary, William.
Eisenberg, Melvin A., jt. auth. see Cary, William L.
Eisenberg, Mickey, jt. auth. see Copass, Michael K.
Eisenberg, Mickey S. & Copass, Michael. Manual of Emergency Medical Therapeutics. new ed. (Illus.). 1978. pap. text ed. 12.95 (ISBN 0-7216-5048-1). Saunders.
Eisenberg, Peter L. The Sugar Industry in Pernambuco, 1840-1910: Modernization Without Change. 1974. 22.50x (ISBN 0-520-01731-5). U of Cal Pr.
Eisenberg-Berg, Nancy, jt. auth. see Mussen, Paul.
Eisenberger, K. The Expert Consumer: A Complete Handbook. 1977. 13.95 (ISBN 0-13-295402-8, Spec); pap. 5.95 (ISBN 0-13-295394-3). P-H.
Eisenhart, E. J., jt. ed. see Hills, M. T.
Eisenhart, Elizabeth J., ed. Scriptures of the World; a Compilation of 1,659 Languages in Which at Least One Book of the Bible Has Been Published. 7th ed. (Illus.). 1978. pap. 2.00 o.p. (ISBN 0-686-24936-4). United Bible.
Eisenhauer, Laurel A., jt. auth. see Asperheim, Mary K.
Eisenhower, Dwight D. Peace with Justice. 20.00x (ISBN 0-231-02472-X). Columbia U Pr.
Eisenhower, John. Strictly Personal. LC 73-20510. (Illus.). 10.95 o.p. (ISBN 0-385-07071-3). Doubleday.
Eisenhower, Julie Nixon. Julie Eisenhower's Cookbook for Children. 96p. (gr. 5-7). 1975. 6.95 o.p. (ISBN 0-385-11432-X). Doubleday.
Eisenman, Peter & Hejduk, John. John Hejduk: Seven Houses. Frampton, Kenneth, ed. (IAUS Exhibition Catalogues Ser.). (Illus.). 112p. 1979. pap. 12.00 (ISBN 0-932628-03-6). IAUS.
Eisenman, Peter D. & Rossi, Aldo. Aldo Rossi in America: Nineteen Seventy-Six to Nineteen Seventy-Nine. Frampton, Kenneth, ed. Ghirardo, Diane, tr. from Ital. (IAUS Exhibition Catalogues Ser.). (Illus.). 64p. 1979. pap. 10.00 (ISBN 0-932628-02-8). IAUS.
Eisenreich, Steven J. Atmospheric Pollutants in Natural Waters. 1981. text ed. 40.00 (ISBN 0-250-40369-2, Dist. by Butterworths). Ann Arbor Science.
Eisenschmitt, Joachim. Die Szenische Darstellung der Opern G. F. Haendels Auf der Londoner Buhne Seiner Zeit, 2 vols. in 1. LC 80-2275. 1981. Repr. of 1940 ed. 29.50 (ISBN 0-404-18843-5). AMS Pr.
Eisenson, Jon, jt. auth. see Berry, Mildred F.
Eisenstadt, Abraham S., et al, eds. Before Watergate. (Brooklyn College Studies on Society in Change Ser.: No. 4). 1979. 17.50x (ISBN 0-930888-01-4). Brooklyn Coll Pr.
Eisenstadt, S. N. Revolution & the Transformation of Societies: A Comparative Study of Civilizations. LC 77-5203. 1978. 17.95 (ISBN 0-02-909390-2). Free Pr.
--Tradition, Change, & Modernity. LC 73-7560. 367p. 1973. 25.95 (ISBN 0-471-23471-0, Pub. by Wiley-Interscience). Wiley.
Eisenstadt, S. N. & Curelaru, M. The Form of Sociology: Paradigms & Crises. LC 76-7602. 386p. 1976. 25.95 (ISBN 0-471-23472-9, Pub. by Wiley-Interscience). Wiley.
Eisenstadt, S. N., ed. Readings in Social Evolution & Development. LC 78-96463. 1970. 25.00 (ISBN 0-08-006813-8); pap. 13.25 (ISBN 0-08-006812-X). Pergamon.
Eisenstadt, Samuel N. From Generation to Generation: Age Groups & Social Structure. LC 55-10998. 1964. pap. text ed. 6.95 (ISBN 0-02-909380-5). Free Pr.
Eisenstaedt, Alfred. Eisenstaedt's Guide to Photography. (Illus.). 176p. 1981. pap. 11.95 (ISBN 0-14-046483-2). Penguin.
--Witness to Our Time. rev. ed. 352p. 1980. 25.00 (ISBN 0-670-77702-1, Studio). Viking Pr.
Eisenstein, Elizabeth. The Printing Press As an Agent of Change, 2 vols. LC 77-91083. 1979. Vol. 1. 43.50 (ISBN 0-521-21967-1); Vol. 2. 37.50 (ISBN 0-521-21969-8); Set. 69.00 (ISBN 0-521-22044-0). Cambridge U Pr.
--The Printing Press As an Agent of Change, 2 vols. in 1. LC 77-91083. 852p. 1980. pap. 16.95 (ISBN 0-521-29955-1). Cambridge U Pr.
Eisenstein, Gotthold F. Mathematische Werke, 2 vols. LC 75-17855. 926p. 1975. 60.00 set o.p. (ISBN 0-8284-0280-9). Chelsea Pub.
Eisenstein, Judith K. Heritage of Music: The Music of the Jewish People. (Illus.). (YA) (gr. 7-11). 1972. 10.00 o.p. (ISBN 0-685-04887-X, 164043). UAHC.
Eisenstein, L., ed. Capitalist Patriarchy & Socialist Feminism. 1979. 24.50 o.p. (ISBN 0-685-67804-0). Porter.
Eisenstein, Sergei. Film Form. LC 49-8349. 1969. pap. 3.95 (ISBN 0-15-630920-3, HB153, Harv). HarBraceJ.
--Film Sense. LC 47-6064. 1969. pap. 4.95 (ISBN 0-15-630935-1, HB154, Harv). HarBraceJ.
Eisenstein, Zillah R. The Radical Future of Liberal Feminism. (Feminist Theory Ser.). (Illus.). 400p. 1980. text ed. 17.95 (ISBN 0-582-28205-5). Longman.
Eisenstein, Zillah R., ed. Capitalist Patriarchy & the Case for Socialist Feminism. LC 77-76162. 1978. 16.50 o.p. (ISBN 0-85345-419-1, CL4191). Monthly Rev.
Eiser, J. R. & Strobe, Wolfgang, eds. Categorization & Social Judgment. (European Monographs in Social Psychology Ser.: No. 3). 1973. 24.50 (ISBN 0-12-235350-1). Acad Pr.
Eiserer, Len. The American Robin. LC 76-25438. (Illus.). 1976. 16.95 (ISBN 0-88229-228-5). Nelson-Hall.
Eisl, Maria E. Lyrische und Satirische Elemente in Roy Campbell's Dichtung, 2 vols. (Salzburg Studies in England Literature, Poetic Drama & Poetic Theory: No. 46). (Illus.). 1979. Set. pap. text ed. 50.25x (ISBN 0-391-01165-0). Humanities.
Eisler, Benita, ed. The Lowell Offering: Writings by New England Mill Women, 1840-1845. LC 77-24986. 223p. 1980. pap. 4.95 (ISBN 0-06-090796-7, CN 796, CN). Har-Row.
--The Lowell Offering: Writings by New England Mill Women 1840-1845. LC 77-24986. (Illus.). 1978. 12.50 o.p. (ISBN 0-397-01225-X). Lippincott.
Eisler, Colin. The Seeing Hand: A Treasury of Great Master Drawings. LC 74-1804. (Illus.). 264p. 1975. 37.50 o.s.i. (ISBN 0-06-011143-7, HarpT). Har-Row.
Eisler, Colin, ed. Drawings into Sculpture. (Illus.). 108p. (Orig.). 1981. pap. 12.50 (ISBN 0-9601068-7-1). Agrinde Bks.
Eisler, Georg. From Naked to Nude: Life Drawing in the Twentieth Century. LC 76-47085. (Illus.). 1977. pap. 5.95 o.p. (ISBN 0-688-08167-3). Morrow.
Eisler, Paul. California Uninsured Motorist Law Handbook. 3rd ed. 1979. 1980 suppl. incl. 60.00 (ISBN 0-911110-27-5). Parker & Son.
Eisler, Richard M. & Frederiksen, Lee W. Perfecting Social Skills: A/Guide to Interpersonal Behavior Development. (Applied Clinical Psycholgy Ser.). 225p. 1981. 18.95 (ISBN 0-306-40592-X, Plenum Pr). Plenum Pub.
Eisler, Robert. Man into Wolf: An Anthropological Study of Sadism, Masochism, & Lycanthropy. LC 77-2497. 264p. 1978. text ed. 11.95 (ISBN 0-915520-16-8); pap. text ed. 5.95 (ISBN 0-915520-06-0). Ross-Erikson.
Eisman, Greg, jt. auth. see Shaw, Dave.
Eisman, Philip, jt. auth. see Gehlmann, John.
Eisner. Dating & Hanging Out. (gr. 7-12). Date not set. pap. cancelled (ISBN 0-590-30031-8, Schol Pap). Schol Bk Serv.
Eisner, Elliot W. & Vallance, Elizabeth. Conflicting Conceptions of Curriculum. LC 73-17616. 1974. 15.50x (ISBN 0-8211-0411-X); text ed. 14.00x (ISBN 0-685-42630-0). McCutchan.
Eisner, Jack. The Survivor. LC 80-14184. (Illus.). 288p. 1980. 11.95 (ISBN 0-688-03741-0). Morrow.
Eisner, Lotte. Murnau. 1973. 18.50x (ISBN 0-520-02285-8). U of Cal Pr.
Eisner, Sigmund, ed. The Kalendarium of Nicholas of Lynn. MacEoin, Gary, tr. from Lat. LC 78-3532. (The Chaucer Library Ser.: No. 2). 260p. 1979. 30.00x (ISBN 0-8203-0449-2). U of Ga Pr.
Eisner, T., jt. auth. see Wilson, E. O.
Eisner, Thomas & Wilson, Edward O.intro. by. Animal Behavior: Readings from Scientific American. LC 75-2383. (Illus.). 1975. text ed. 19.95x (ISBN 0-7167-0511-7); pap. text ed. 9.95x (ISBN 0-7167-0510-9). W H Freeman.
--The Insects: Readings from Scientific American. LC 77-23843. (Illus.). 1977. text ed. 19.95x (ISBN 0-7167-0047-6); pap. text ed. 9.95x (ISBN 0-7167-0046-8). W H Freeman.
Eisner, U., tr. see Daudel, P.

Eisner, Victor & Callan, Laurence B. Dimensions of School Health. 192p. 1974. 14.75 (ISBN 0-398-02948-2). C C Thomas.

Eisner, Vivien & Shisler, William. Crafting with Newspapers. LC 76-19771. (Little Craft Bk.). (gr. 5up). 1976. 5.95 (ISBN 0-8069-5368-3); PLB 6.69 (ISBN 0-8069-5369-1). Sterling.

Eisold, Kenneth. Loneliness & Communion: A Study of Wordsworth's Thought & Experience. (Salzburg Studies in English Literature, Romantic Reassessment: No. 13). 1973. pap. text ed. 25.00x (ISBN 0-391-01371-8). Humanities.

Eissenstat, Bernard W. Lenin & Leninism: State, Law & Society. LC 71-145909. 1971. 29.50x (ISBN 0-89197-983-2). Irvington.

Eissfeldt, Otto. Old Testament, an Introduction. LC 65-15399. 1965. 12.95x (ISBN 0-06-062171-0, RD162, HarpR). Har-Row.

Eissmann, Harold F., et al. Dental Laboratory Procedures: Fixed Partial Dentures, Vol. 2. LC 79-16785. (Illus.). 367p. 1980. text ed. 37.50 (ISBN 0-8016-3517-9). Mosby.

Eitel, Wilhelm, ed. Silicate Science: A Treatise, 5 vols. Incl. Vol. 1. Silicate Structures. 1964 (ISBN 0-12-236301-9); Vol. 2. Glasses, Enamels, Slags. 1965 (ISBN 0-12-236302-7); Vol. 3. Dry Silicate Systems. 1965 (ISBN 0-12-236303-5); Vol. 4. Hydrothermal Silical Systems. 1966 (ISBN 0-12-236304-3); Vol. 5. Ceramics & Hydraulic Binders. 1966 (ISBN 0-12-236305-1). 67.25 ea.; by subscription 57.50 ea. Acad Pr.

Eiteman, David K., jt. auth. see Smith, Keith V.

Eitinger, Leo & Strom, Axel. Mortality & Morbidity After Excessive Stress. 1973. text ed. 27.00x (ISBN 8-200-04738-5, Dist. by Columbia U Pr). Universitet.

Eitner, Lorenz. Neoclassicism & Romanticism: 1750-1850, 2 vols. Incl. Vol. 1. Enlightenment-Revolution. 1970 (ISBN 0-13-610907-1); Vol. 2. Restoration-the Twilight of Humanism. (Illus.). 1970 (ISBN 0-13-610915-2). pap. 10.95 ea. ref. ed. P-H.

Eitner, Walter H. Walt Whitman's Western Jaunt. LC 80-29336. (Illus.). 144p. 1981. text ed. 18.00 (ISBN 0-7006-0212-7). Regents Pr KS.

Eitzen. Social Problems. 1980. text ed. 17.95 (ISBN 0-205-06816-2, 8168164); instr's manual o.p. avail. Allyn.

Eitzen, D. Stanley. In Conflict & Order: Understanding Society. 1978. pap. text ed. 15.95 (ISBN 0-205-06063-3); instr's man. avail. (ISBN 0-205-06064-1); tests avail. (ISBN 0-205-06065-X). Allyn.

Eitzen, D. Stanley, ed. Sport in Contemporary Society: An Anthology. LC 78-65246. Date not set. pap. text ed. 7.95x (ISBN 0-312-75327-6). St Martin.

Eitzen, Ruth. Ti Jacques: A Story of Haiti. LC 76-158688. (Stories from Many Lands Ser). (Illus.). (gr. k-4). 1972. 7.95 (ISBN 0-690-82429-7, TYC-J). T Y Crowell.

Ek, J. A. Van see Van Ek, J. A.

Ek, J. van see Van Ek, J.

Ek, J. Van see Van Ek, J.

Ekdahl, Janis K., ed. American Sculpture: A Guide to Information Sources. LC 74-11544. (Art & Architecture Information Guide Ser.: Vol. 5). 1977. 30.00 (ISBN 0-8103-1271-9). Gale.

Ekelof, Gunnar. Guide to the Underworld. Lesser, Rika, tr. from Swedish. LC 80-13181. 96p. 1980. cloth. 10.00 (ISBN 0-87023-306-8). U of Mass Pr.

--I Do Best Alone at Night. Bly, Robert, tr. 1977. 7.50 (ISBN 0-685-88901-7). Charioteer.

Ekern, Doris. Slacks Cut-to-Fit. Leppert, Mary, ed. LC 77-70233. 1977. 3.80 (ISBN 0-933956-00-2); tchrs ed. 3.04. Sew-Fit.

--Suit to Fit Your Man. LC 80-50504. (Illus.). 56p. 1980. pap. 3.80 (ISBN 0-933956-05-3); 3.04. Sew-Fit.

Ekert, H., ed. Seminar on Haematology & Oncology. (Journal: Paediatrician: Vol. 9, No. 2). (Illus.). 88p. 1980. softcover 19.75 (ISBN 3-8055-1302-X). S Karger.

Ekin, M. Tagalong. 4.00 o.p. (ISBN 0-8062-1170-9). Carlton.

Ekirch, Arthur A., Jr. Ideologies & Utopias. pap. text ed. 2.95x (ISBN 0-8290-0342-8). Irvington.

Ekland, Britt. True Britt. (Illus.). 242p. 1981. 9.95 (ISBN 0-13-931089-4). P-H.

Eklof, Margareta, tr. see Edgren, Gosta, et al.

Eklund, C. E., jt. auth. see Wyss, Orville.

Eklund, Gordon & Anderson, Poul. Inheritors of Earth. 1979. pap. 1.75 (ISBN 0-515-04496-2). Jove Pubns.

Eklund, Gordon, jt. auth. see Benford, Gregory.

Eklund, Sigvard, ed. see International Atomic Energy Agency.

Ekman, Paul. The Face of Man: Expressions of Unirersal Emotion in a New Guinea Village. LC 79-12934. 154p. 1980. lib. bdg. 25.00 (ISBN 0-8240-7130-1). Garland Pub.

Eknath, Easwaran. Instrucciones En la Meditacion. 1980. pap. 1.00 (ISBN 0-915132-23-0). Nilgiri Pr.

Ekpo, Monday U., ed. Bureaucratic Corruption in Sub-Saharan Africa: Toward a Search for Causes & Consequences. LC 79-66150. 1979. pap. text ed. 14.50 (ISBN 0-8191-0796-4). U Pr of Amer.

Ekrutt, Joachim W. Star Gazer. Kellner, Hugo M., tr. from Ger. (gr. 9-12). 1981. pap. 2.25 (ISBN 0-8120-2043-X). Barron.

Eksell, Olle, jt. auth. see Rand, Ann.

Eksteins, Modris. The Limits of Reason: The German Democratic Press & the Collapse of Weimar Democracy. (Oxford Historical Monographs). 362p. 1975. 42.00x (ISBN 0-19-821862-1). Oxford U Pr.

Ekvall, Robert B. The Lama Knows: A Tibetan Legend Is Born. (Illus.). 144p. 1981. pap. 5.95 (ISBN 0-88316-541-4). Chandler & Sharp.

--Religious Observances in Tibet: Patterns & Functions. LC 64-23423. 1964. 12.50x o.s.i. (ISBN 0-226-20078-7). U of Chicago Pr.

Ekvall, Shirley, jt. auth. see Palmer, Sushma.

Ekwall. Ekwall Reading Inventory. 1979. pap. text ed. 6.95 (ISBN 0-205-06674-7); dupl. masters avail. (ISBN 0-205-06676-3). Allyn.

Ekwall, Eilert. Concise Oxford Dictionary of English Place-Names. 4th ed. 1960. 29.00x (ISBN 0-19-869103-3). Oxford U Pr.

Ekwall, Eldon. Locating & Correcting Reading Difficulties. 2nd ed. (Elementary Education Ser.). 1977. pap. text ed. 7.95 (ISBN 0-675-08560-8). Merrill.

--Psychological Factors in Teaching Reading. LC 72-96688. 1973. text ed. 19.95 (ISBN 0-675-08965-4). Merrill.

Ekwall, Eldon E. Diagnosis & Remediation of the Disabled Reader. 512p. 1976. text ed. 17.95x (ISBN 0-205-05416-1). Allyn.

--Locating & Correcting Reading Difficulties. 3rd ed. (Illus.). 192p. 1981. pap. text ed. 6.95 (ISBN 0-675-08062-2). Merrill.

Ekwensi, Cyprian O. Drummer Boy. 1960. text ed. 2.95x (ISBN 0-521-04882-6). Cambridge U Pr.

--Passport of Mallam Ilia. 1960. text ed. 2.95x (ISBN 0-521-04883-4). Cambridge U Pr.

--Trouble in Form Six. 1966. text ed. 2.95x (ISBN 0-521-04884-2). Cambridge U Pr.

Elaezer Of Worms. Three Tracts. Hirschman, Jack & Altmann, Alexander, trs. pap. 3.00 o.p. (ISBN 0-686-22381-0). Tree Bks.

El-Agra, A. M. & Jones, A. J. Theory of Customs Unions. 1981. 25.00 (ISBN 0-312-79737-0). St Martin.

El-Agraa, A. M. The Economics of the European Community. 1980. 37.50 (ISBN 0-312-23285-3). St Martin.

Elaine, Jonah. Come Love with Me. 1981. 4.95 (ISBN 0-8062-1646-8). Carlton.

Elam, Charles H., jt. ed. see Cummings, Frederick J.

Elam, Yizchak. Social & Sexual Roles of Hima Women: A Study of Nomadic Cattle Breeders in Nyabushozi County, Ankole. (Illus.). 215p. 1973. text ed. 13.50x (ISBN 0-7190-0534-5). Humanities.

Eland, J. H. Photoelectron Spectroscopy. LC 73-17763. 1974. 28.95 (ISBN 0-470-23485-7). Halsted Pr.

Elandt-Johnson, Regina C. & Johnson, Norman L. Survival Models & Data Analysis. LC 79-22836. (Wiley Series in Probability & Mathematical Statistics: Applied Probability & Statistics). 1980. 34.95 (ISBN 0-471-03174-7, Pub. by Wiley-Interscience). Wiley.

El-Ansary, Adel I., jt. auth. see Stern, Louis W.

Elarson, Georgina. Little Workers in the Kitchen. 1979. pap. 5.95 (ISBN 0-8163-0240-5). Pacific Pr Pub Assn.

El-Ashry, Mohamed T., ed. Air Photography & Coastal Problems. (Benchmark Papers in Geology: Vol. 38). 1977. 43.50 (ISBN 0-12-786410-5). Acad Pr.

Elaster, Kenneth see Born, Warren C.

El Badri, Nassan, et al. Ramadan War. 1978. 14.75 (ISBN 0-88254-460-8); pap. 6.95. Hippocrene Bks.

El-Badry, Hamed M. Micromanipulators & Micromanipulation. (Illus.). 1963. 34.90 o.p. (ISBN 0-387-80648-2). Springer-Verlag.

Elbaz, Jean S. & Flageul, G. Plastic Surgery of the Abdomen. Keavy, William T., tr. LC 79-84907. (Illus.). 120p. 1979. 31.75 (ISBN 0-89352-036-5). Masson Pub.

Elberfeld, Katie. Jordan to Jerusalem: A Lenten Pilgrimage. 1979. 1.20 (ISBN 0-686-28783-5). Forward Movement.

Elbert, Donna D., jt. auth. see Chandrasekhar, S.

Elbert, Virginie Fowler. Grow a Plant Pet. LC 76-56284. (gr. 7 up). 1977. PLB 6.95 (ISBN 0-385-11699-3). Doubleday.

Elbing, Alvar. Behavioral Decisions in Organizations. 2nd ed. 1978. 18.95x (ISBN 0-673-15025-9). Scott F.

Elborn, Geoffrey. Edith Sitwell: A Biography. LC 80-1985. 312p. 1981. 14.95 (ISBN 0-385-13467-3). Doubleday.

Elbow, Peter. Oppositions in Chaucer. LC 75-16216. 192p. 1975. 15.00x (ISBN 0-8195-4087-0, Pub. by Wesleyan U Pr). Columbia U Pr.

--Writing with Power: Techniques for Mastering the Writing Process. 356p. 1981. 15.00 (ISBN 0-19-502912-7). Oxford U Pr.

--Writing with Power: Techniques for Mastering the Writing Process. 356p. 1981. pap. 5.95 (ISBN 0-19-502913-5, GB 642, GB). Oxford U Pr.

--Writing Without Teachers. LC 72-96608. 208p. 1975. pap. 3.95 (ISBN 0-19-501679-3, GB435, GB). Oxford U Pr.

Elchaninov, Alexander. The Diary of a Russian Priest. Iswolsky, tr. (Illus.). 1967. 12.95 (ISBN 0-571-08029-4, Pub. by Faber & Faber). Merrimack Bk Serv.

Elcock, E. W. & Michie, D., eds. Machine Intelligence 8: Machine Representations of Knowledge. 1977. 95.95 (ISBN 0-470-99059-7). Halsted Pr.

Elcock, W. D. The Romance Languages. (Great Language Ser.). 1975. text ed. 45.50x (ISBN 0-571-06152-4). Humanities.

Eldad, Israel. The Jewish Revolution: Jewish Statehood. Schmorak, Hannah, tr. LC 79-163739. 184p. 1971. 7.95 (ISBN 0-88400-037-0). Shengold.

Eldefonso, E. & Hartinger, W. Control Treatment & Rehabilitation of Juvenile Offenders. 1976. 14.95x (ISBN 0-02-474160-4, 47416). Macmillan.

Eldefonso, Edward. Issues in Corrections: A Book of Readings. LC 73-7365. (Criminal Justice Ser). 320p. 1974. pap. text ed. 7.95x (ISBN 0-02-474110-8). Macmillan.

--Readings in Criminal Justice. LC 72-85758. (Criminal Justice Ser.). 512p. 1973. text ed. 7.95x (ISBN 0-02-474670-3). Macmillan.

Eldefonso, Edward & Coffey, Alan. Process & Impact of the Juvenile Justice System. 1976. pap. 9.95x (ISBN 0-02-472490-4). Macmillan.

Eldefonso, Edward & Coffey, Alan R. Criminal Law: History, Philosophy, & Enforcement. (Illus.). 304p. 1980. text ed. 17.50 scp (ISBN 0-06-041879-6, HarpC); avail. Har-Row.

Eldefonso, Edward, jt. auth. see Coffey, Alan R.

Elder, Charles D., jt. auth. see Cobb, Roger W.

Elder, Crawford. Appropriating Hegel. Brennan, Andrew & Lyons, William, eds. (Scots Philosophical Monographs: Vol. 3). 116p. 1980. 12.00 (ISBN 0-08-025729-1). Pergamon.

Elder, E. R., ed. see William Of St. Tierry.

Elder, E. Rozanne, ed. Cistercians in the Late Middle Ages. (Cistercian Studies: No. 64). (Illus., Orig.). 1980. pap. 8.95 (ISBN 0-87907-865-0). Cistercian Pubns.

Elder, E. Rozanne & Sommerfeldt, John R., eds. The Chimaera of His Age: Studies in Medieval Cistercian History V. (Cistercian Studies Ser.: No. 63). 146p. 1980. pap. 8.95 (ISBN 0-87907-863-4). Cistercian Pubns.

Elder, E. Rozanne, jt. ed. see Sommerfeldt, John R.

Elder, E. Rozanne, et al, eds. Cistercians in the Late Middle Ages: Studies in Medievel Cistercian History VI. (Cistercian Studies: No. VI). 161p. (Orig.). 1981. pap. 8.97 (ISBN 0-87907-864-2). Cistercian Pubns.

Elder, Gary. Eyes on the Land. 32p. 1980. pap. 3.00 (ISBN 0-88235-043-9). San Marcos.

--Hold Fire: Selected Poems. 96p. (Orig.). 1981. pap. 4.75 (ISBN 0-931896-02-9). Cove View.

--Making Touch. (Illus.). 40p. 1981. pap. 4.00 (ISBN 0-914974-28-9). Holmgangers.

Elder, Glen H., Jr., ed. Linking Social Structure & Personality. LC 73-94131. (Sage Contemporary Social Science Issues: Vol. 12). 1974. 4.95x (ISBN 0-8039-0396-0). Sage.

Elder, H. Y. & Trueman, E. R., eds. Aspects of Animal Movement. LC 79-8520. (Society for Experimental Biology Seminar Ser.: No. 5). (Illus.). 250p. 1980. 44.50 (ISBN 0-521-23086-1); pap. 16.50 (ISBN 0-521-29795-8). Cambridge U Pr.

Elder, H. Y., jt. ed. see Meek, G. A.

Elder, J., jt. auth. see Welsh, J.

Elder, James L., ed. see Stearns, Arthur A.

Elder, Jean. Transactional Analysis in Health Care. LC 78-57376. 1978. 9.95 (ISBN 0-201-01512-9, M&N Div). A-W.

Elder, Jerry O. & Magrab, Phyllis R., eds. Coordinating Services to Handicapped Children: A Handbook for Interagency Collaboration. LC 80-16033. (Illus.). 264p. (Orig.). 1980. pap. text ed. 13.95 (ISBN 0-933716-11-7). P H Brookes.

--Coordinating Services to Handicapped Children: A Handbook for Interagency Collaboration. 272p. 1980. pap. 13.95 (ISBN 0-933716-11-7). P H Brookes.

Elder, Jerry O., jt. ed. see Magrab, Phyllis R.

Elder, Joseph, ed. see Stanbury, David.

Elder, Lauren & Streshinsky, Shirley. And I Alone Survived. 1979. pap. 1.95 o.p. (ISBN 0-449-23864-4, Crest). Fawcett.

--And I Alone Survived. 1978. 7.95 o.p. (ISBN 0-525-05481-2, Thomas Congdon Book). Dutton.

Elder, Lonne, 3rd. Ceremonies in Dark Old Men. LC 70-87212. (Orig.). 1969. pap. 4.95 (ISBN 0-374-50792-9, N372). FS&G.

Elder, M. G. & Hawkins, D. F. Human Fertility Control: The Theory & Practice. 1979. text ed. 61.95 (ISBN 0-407-00127-1). Butterworths.

Elder, M. G. & Hendricks, C. H. Obstetrics & Gynecology: Preterm Labor, Vol. 1. (Butterworths International Medical Reviews Ser.). 1981. text ed. price not set (ISBN 0-407-02300-3). Butterworths.

Elder, Marjorie J. Nathaniel Hawthorne: Transcendental Symbolist. LC 69-18476. vi, 215p. 1969. 12.95x (ISBN 0-8214-0051-7). Ohio U Pr.

Elder, Mark. The Prometheus Operation. LC 80-14577. 312p. 1980. 11.95 (ISBN 0-07-019191-3, GB). McGraw.

--Wolf Hunt. (Orig.). 1976. pap. 1.50 o.p. (ISBN 0-345-25264-0). Ballantine.

Elder, N. C. Government in Sweden: The Executive at Work. 1970. 22.00 (ISBN 0-08-015534-0); pap. text ed. 10.75 (ISBN 0-08-015533-2). Pergamon.

Elder, Robert L., ed. Cosmetic Ingredient: Their Safety Assessment. (Illus.). 1980. pap. text ed. 19.00 (ISBN 0-930376-19-6). Pathotox Pubs.

Elder, Rozanne E., jt. ed. see Sommerfeldt, John R.

Elder, William. Conversations on the Principal Subjects of Political Economy. (The Neglected American Economists Ser.). 1974. lib. bdg. 50.00 (ISBN 0-8240-1021-3). Garland Pub.

Elderfield, John. New Work on Paper. (Illus.). 56p. 1980. pap. 6.95 (ISBN 0-87070-496-6). Museum Mod Art.

Elders, L. Aristotle's Theology: A Commentary on the Book of Metaphysics. (Philosophical Texts & Studies). 336p. 1972. text ed. 43.50x (ISBN 90-232-0978-8). Humanities.

Eldersvels, Samuel J., et al. Elite Images of Dutch Politics: Accommodation & Conflict. 296p. 1981. text ed. 15.00x (ISBN 0-472-10009-2). U of Mich Pr.

Elderton, W. P. & Johnson, N. L. Systems of Frequency Curves. LC 69-10571. Orig. Title: Frequency Curves & Correlation. (Illus.). 1969. 32.95 (ISBN 0-521-07369-3). Cambridge U Pr.

Eldred, Michael, jt. auth. see Roth, Mike.

Eldred, O. John. Women Pastors. 128p. 1981. pap. 4.95 (ISBN 0-8170-0901-9). Judson.

Eldred, Partricia M. Donny & Marie. (Rock 'n Pop Stars Ser.). (Illus.). (gr. 4-12). 1978. PLB 5.95 (ISBN 0-87191-618-5); pap. 2.75 o. p. (ISBN 0-89812-121-3). Creative Ed.

Eldred, Patricia M. Barbra Streisand. (Rock 'n Pop Stars Ser.). (Illus.). (gr. 4-12). 1975. PLB 5.95 o. p. (ISBN 0-87191-459-X); pap. 2.95 (ISBN 0-89812-118-3). Creative Ed.

--Debby Boone. (gr. 4-12). 1979. PLB 5.95 (ISBN 0-87191-696-7); pap. 2.95 (ISBN 0-89812-096-9). Creative Ed.

--Diana Ross. (Rock 'n Pop Stars Ser.). (Illus.). (gr. 4-12). 1975. PLB 5.95 (ISBN 0-87191-462-X); pap. 2.75 o. p. (ISBN 0-89812-112-4). Creative Ed.

--Football's Great Quarterback: Joe Namath. (The Allstars Ser.). (Illus.). (gr. 2-6). 1977. PLB 5.95 o.p. (ISBN 0-87191-580-4). Creative Ed.

--Kathy Whitworth. LC 75-1358. (New Creative Education Superstar Bks.). (Illus.). 32p. (gr. 3-6). 1975. PLB 5.50 o.p. (ISBN 0-87191-436-0). Creative Ed.

--Rose Kennedy. LC 75-1119. (Creative Education Closeup Bks.). (Illus.). 32p. (gr. 3-6). 1975. PLB 5.95 (ISBN 0-87191-423-9). Creative Ed.

--What Do We Do When We're Asleep? (Creative's Questions & Answers Ser.). (Illus.). 32p. (gr. 3-4). Date not set. lib. bdg. 5.65 (ISBN 0-87191-752-1); pap. 2.75 (ISBN 0-89812-221-X). Creative Ed. Postponed.

Eldredge, Niles, jt. ed. see Cracraft, Joel.

Eldridge, Evelyn & Meredith, Nancy. Environmental Issues: Family Impact. 1976. pap. text ed. 10.95 o.p. (ISBN 0-8087-0518-0). Burgess.

Eldridge, F. P. Wind Machines. 1975. pap. 7.50 (ISBN 0-930978-98-6). Solar Energy Info.

Eldridge, James, pseud. Twinkle. (Illus.). 64p. (Orig.). 1980. pap. 3.25 (ISBN 0-938900-00-5). Creations Unltd.

Eldridge, Roswell & Fahn, Stanley, eds. Dystonia. LC 75-25112. (Advances in Neurology Ser: Vol. 14). 1976. 48.00 (ISBN 0-89004-070-2). Raven.

Eldridge, Winfield H., jt. auth. see Brown, Curtis M.

Electric Company. Tickle Yourself with Puzzles. LC 78-68684. (Illus.). (gr. 1-5). 1979. pap. 1.50 (ISBN 0-394-84226-X). Random.

Electric Power Research Institute. Electricity: Today's Technologies, Tomorrow's Alternatives. (Illus.). 128p. (Orig.). 1981. pap. 7.95 (ISBN 0-86576-003-9). Pub Serv Ctr.

--The Kaiparowits Coal Project & the Environment. 1980. text ed. 14.95 (ISBN 0-250-40399-4). Ann Arbor Science.

Electro-Craft Corp. DC Motors, Speed Controls, Servo Systems: An Engineering Handbook. 3rd, expanded ed. LC 76-56647. 1977. text ed. 38.00 (ISBN 0-08-021714-1); pap. text ed. 16.50 (ISBN 0-08-021715-X). Pergamon.

Electronic Design. Four Hundred Ideas for Design, Vol. 3. Grossman, Morris, ed. (Illus.). 1976. 16.60 (ISBN 0-8104-5111-5). Hayden.

Electronic Industries Association & Zbar, Paul B. Industrial Electronics: Atext-Lab Manual. 3rd ed. (Illus.). 320p. Date not set. 12.95x (ISBN 0-07-072793-7, G). McGraw.

Electronics Illustrated Editors. Best Electronics Projects. (Illus.). 112p. (YA) 1973. lib. bdg. 3.95 o.p. (ISBN 0-668-01724-4). Arco.

Electronics Magazine. Active Filters. LC 79-17479. (Illus.). 133p. 1980. pap. text ed. 5.95 (ISBN 0-07-606622-3, R-003). McGraw.

--Applying Microprocessors. Scrupski, Stephen E. & Altman, Laurence, eds. LC 76-30685. (Illus.). 191p. 1977. pap. text ed. 9.95 (ISBN 0-07-099705-5, R-701). McGraw.

--Basics of Data Communications. Karp, Harry R., ed. LC 76-16475. (Illus.). 303p. 1976. pap. text ed. 12.95 (ISBN 0-07-019159-X, R-603). McGraw.

--Circuits for Electronics Engineers. Weber, Samuel, ed. LC 76-57777. (Illus.). 1977. pap. text ed. 15.95 (ISBN 0-07-099706-3, R-711). McGraw.

--Design Techniques for Electronics Engineers. LC 77-8323. (Illus.). 370p. pap. text ed. 15.95 (ISBN 0-07-099711-X, R-726). McGraw.

--Large Scale Integration. Altman, Laurence, ed. LC 76-3298. (Illus.). 208p. 1976. pap. text ed. 9.95 (ISBN 0-07-099701-2, R-602). McGraw.

--Memory Design: Microcomputers to Mainframes. Altman, Laurence, ed. LC 77-26332. (Illus.). 180p. 1978. pap. text ed. 12.95 (ISBN 0-07-099718-7, R-732). McGraw.

--Microelectronics Interconnection & Packaging. Lyman, Jerry, ed. LC 79-21990. (Illus.). 320p. 1979. pap. 12.95 (ISBN 0-07-606600-2, R-927). McGraw.

--Microelectronics Interconnection & Packaging. (Electronics Book Ser.). (Illus.). 1980. 19.95 (ISBN 0-07-019184-0). McGraw.

--Microprocessors. Altman, Laurence, ed. (Illus.). 1975. pap. text ed. 8.95 (ISBN 0-07-019171-9, R-520). McGraw.

--Microprocessors. Aitman, L., ed. 1975. 23.50x (ISBN 0-07-019171-9, P&RB). McGraw.

--Microprocessors & Microcomputers: One-Chip Controllers to High-End Systems. Capece, Raymond P. & Posa, John G., eds. LC 80-11816. (Illus.). 484p. 1980. 24.50 (ISBN 0-07-019141-7, R-011); pap. text ed. 14.95 (ISBN 0-07-606670-3). McGraw.

--Practical Applications of Data Communications: A User's Guide. Karp, Harry R., ed. LC 79-27239. (Illus.). 418p. 1980. pap. text ed. 13.95 (ISBN 0-07-606653-3, R-005). McGraw.

Electronics Magazine Editors. An Age of Innovation: The World of Electronics, 1930-2000. LC 80-14816. (Illus.). 274p. 1980. text ed. 18.50 (ISBN 0-07-606688-6, R-013). McGraw.

Elefteriades, Olga. Modern Greek Reference Grammar. (Orig.). 1981. pap. text ed. 10.00x (ISBN 0-87840-173-3). Georgetown U Pr.

Elegant, Robert. Hong Kong. (The Great Cities Ser.). (Illus.). 1977. lib. bdg. 14.94 (ISBN 0-686-51003-8). Silver.

--Hong Kong. Time-Life Books, ed. (The Great Cities Ser.). (Illus.). 1977. 14.95 (ISBN 0-8094-2286-7). Time-Life.

--Manchu. 592p. 1980. 12.95 (ISBN 0-07-019163-8, GB). McGraw.

Elementary Science Study. Butterflies. 1970. tchr's. guide 8.28 o.p. (ISBN 0-07-017682-5, W). McGraw.

Elena, Tony S., Jr. Good Food. LC 80-65651. 128p. (Orig.). 1981. pap. 6.95 (ISBN 0-89087-265-1). Celestial Arts.

Elenbaas, W. Light Sources. LC 72-79283. (Philips Technical Library). 320p. 1972. 32.50x (ISBN 0-8448-0057-0). Crane-Russak Co.

Elert, Werner. Law & Gospel. Sherman, Franklin, ed. Schroeder, Edward H., tr. from Ger. LC 66-25263. (Facet Bks). 64p. (Orig.). 1967. pap. 1.50 (ISBN 0-8006-3035-1, 1-3035). Fortress.

--Structure of Lutheranism: The Theology & Philosophy of Life of Lutheranism, 16th & 17th Centuries, Vol. 1. Hansen, Walter A., tr. LC 62-19955. 1974. pap. 12.95 (ISBN 0-570-03192-3, 12-2588). Concordia.

Eleventh Gustave Stern Symposium on Perspectives in Virology, New York, February 1980. Perspectives in Virology, Vol. 11: Proceedings. Pollard, Morris, ed. 324p. 1981. 40.00x (ISBN 0-8451-0800-X). A R Liss.

Elevitch, Franklin R. Fluorometric Techniques in Clinical Chemistry. LC 73-155034. (Illus.). 300p. 1973. 16.50 o.p. (ISBN 0-316-23250-5). Little.

Elevitch, M. D. Grips or, Efforts to Revive the Host. LC 73-170613. 111p. 1972. 6.95 (ISBN 0-916452-02-6). First Person.

Elevitch, M. D., ed. First Person, Vol. 1. 1978. pap. 7.50 (ISBN 0-916452-03-4). First Person.

Eley, D. D., et al, eds. Advances in Catalysis, Vol. 27. 1979. 47.00 (ISBN 0-12-007827-9); lib ed. 60.00 (ISBN 0-12-007880-5); microfiche 35.50 (ISBN 0-12-007881-3). Acad Pr.

--Advances in Catalysis, Vol. 29. LC 49-7755. 1980. 45.00 (ISBN 0-12-007829-5); lib. bdg. 58.50 (ISBN 0-12-007884-8); microfiche ed. 31.50 (ISBN 0-12-007885-6). Acad Pr.

Eley, J. T., jt. auth. see **Cooper, J. E.**

Elfenbein, Julien, ed. Editor's Manual. (Illus.). 1970. 15.00 o.p. (ISBN 0-686-08528-0, SP1). Am Journal Nurse.

Elfman, Blossom. The Butterfly Girl. 160p. 1981. pap. 1.95 (ISBN 0-553-14262-3). Bantam.

--The Return of the Whistler. 160p. 1981. 8.95 (ISBN 0-686-69060-5). HM.

Elfrieda, illus. The Gingerbread Man. (Illus.). (ps-2). 1972. PLB 7.15 o.p. (ISBN 0-307-69054-7, Golden Pr). Western Pub.

Elgar, Frank, jt. auth. see **Cognia, Raymond.**

Elgar, Frank, jt. auth. see **Muller, Joseph E.**

Elgart, Denise B., jt. auth. see **Piper, Terrence J.**

Elgerd, Olle I. Basic Electric Power Engineering. LC 76-1751. (Electrical Engineering Ser.). 1977. text ed. 24.95 (ISBN 0-201-01717-2); sol. man. avail. (ISBN 0-201-01918-3). A-W.

Elgers, Pieter T. & Clark, John J. The Lease-Buy Decision: A Simplified Guide to Maximizing Financial & Tax Advantages in the 1980's. LC 80-66131. (Illus.). 1980. 16.95 (ISBN 0-02-909470-4). Free Pr.

Elgin, Kathleen. The Digestive System. LC 73-4417. (Human Body Ser). (gr. 4 up). 1973. PLB 6.90 (ISBN 0-531-01183-6). Watts.

--The Ear. LC 67-10136. (Human Body Ser). (Illus.). (gr. 4-6). 1967. PLB 6.90 (ISBN 0-531-01171-2). Watts.

--The Eye. LC 67-10136. (Human Body Ser). (Illus.). (gr. 4-6). 1967. PLB 4.90 o.p. (ISBN 0-531-01172-0). Watts.

--First Book of Mythology. (First Bks). (Illus.). (gr. 4-6). 1955. PLB 4.90 o.p. (ISBN 0-531-00589-5). Watts.

--The Hand. LC 68-11205. (Human Body Ser). (gr. 4-6). PLB 4.90 o.p. (ISBN 0-531-01173-9). Watts.

--The Heart. (Human Body Ser). (Illus.). (gr. 4-6). 1968. PLB 6.90 (ISBN 0-531-01174-7). Watts.

--The Skeleton. LC 74-152741. (Human Body Ser). (Illus.). (gr. 4 up). 1971. PLB 6.90 (ISBN 0-531-01180-1). Watts.

--The Skin. LC 72-101746. (Human Body Ser). (Illus.). (gr. 4-6). 1970. PLB 4.90 o.p. (ISBN 0-531-01177-1). Watts.

Elgin, Suzette E. Twelve Fair Kingdoms: Book One of the Ozark Fantasy Trilogy. LC 80-2837. 192p. 1981. 9.95 (ISBN 0-385-15876-9). Doubleday.

Elgin, Suzette H. Grand Jubilee. 192p. 1981. 9.95 (ISBN 0-385-15877-7). Doubleday.

--Pouring Down Words. 256p. 1975. pap. 7.95 (ISBN 0-13-686352-3). P-H.

Elgood, John H. Birds of the West African Town & Garden. Savory, H., ed. LC 62-4439. (West African Nature Handbooks Ser). (Illus.). 1968. 5.00x (ISBN 0-582-60850-3). Intl Pubns Serv.

Elgood, Robert, ed. Islamic Arms & Armour. (Illus.). 252p. 1979. 175.00x (ISBN 0-85967-470-3, Pub. by Scolar Pr England). Biblio Dist.

Elgorriaga, Jose A., tr. see **Alberti, Rafael.**

Elgueta, Bernardo, et al. Five Years of Military Government in Chile (1973-1978; 300p. 1981. text ed. 25.00 (ISBN 0-930576-40-3). E M Coleman Ent.

Elhart, Dorothy, et al. Scientific Principles in Nursing. 8th ed. LC 77-23961. (Illus.). 1978. pap. text ed. 15.95 (ISBN 0-8016-1953-X). Mosby.

El-Hifnawi, M., jt. auth. see **Fareed, A.**

El-Hinnawi, Essam E., ed. Nuclear Energy & the Environment. LC 80-40365. (Illus.). 310p. 1980. 52.00 (ISBN 0-08-024472-6). Pergamon.

Eliade, Mircea. Autobiography: Volume I, Journey East, Journey West 1907-1937. LC 80-8357. 352p. 1981. 17.50 (ISBN 0-06-065227-6, HarpR). Har-Row.

--A History of Religious Ideas: From the Stone Age to the Eleusinian Mysteries, Vol. 1. Trask, Willard R., tr. from Fr. LC 77-16784. 1979. Repr. 20.00 (ISBN 0-226-20400-6); pap. 12.50 (ISBN 0-226-20401-4). U of Chicago Pr.

--A History of Religious Ideas, Vol. I: From the Stone Age to the Eleusinian Mysteries. Trask, Willard R., tr. from Fr. LC 77-16784. xviii, 490p. 1981. pap. 8.95 (ISBN 0-226-20401-4). U of Chicago Pr.

--Myths, Rites, Symbols: A Mircea Eliade Reader, 2 vols. Beane, Wendell C. & Doty, William G., eds. 1976. Vol. 1. pap. 5.95x (ISBN 0-06-131955-4, TB 1955, CN); Vol. 2. pap. 4.95 (ISBN 0-06-090511-5, CN511). Har-Row.

--Rites & Symbols of Initiation: The Mysteries of Birth & Rebirth. 8.50 (ISBN 0-8446-2027-0). Peter Smith.

Eliade, Mircea & Tracy, David, eds. What Is Religion? An Inquiry for Christian Theology, Concilium 136. (New Concilium 1980). 128p. 1980. pap. 5.95 (ISBN 0-8245-4769-1). Crossroad NY.

Eliakim, M., ed. International Symposium on Hepatotoxicity. 1974. 25.00 (ISBN 0-12-237850-4). Acad Pr.

Elial, Ernest L., jt. auth. see **Geoffroy, Gregory.**

Elias. English-Arabic Collegiate Dictionary. 9.50 (ISBN 0-686-27677-9). Colton Bk.

Elias, E. A. English-Arabic; Arabic-English Dictionary. pap. 12.00x. Intl Bk Ctr.

Elias, H. & Sherrick, Joseph C. Morphology of the Liver. 1969. 59.75 (ISBN 0-12-237950-0). Acad Pr.

Elias, Hans, et al. Histology & Human Microanatomy. 4th ed. LC 78-9108. 1978. 27.50 (ISBN 0-471-04929-8, Pub. by Wiley Medical). Wiley.

Elias, James, jt. ed. see **Elias, Veronica.**

Elias, Merrill F. & Streeten, David H., eds. Hypertension & Cognitive Processes. LC 80-22618. 165p. 1980. pap. text ed. 10.00 (ISBN 0-933786-04-2); 20.00 (ISBN 0-933786-04-2). Beech Hill.

Elias, Merrill F., et al, eds. Special Review of Experimental Aging Research: Progress in Biology. LC 77-23262. 1976. 24.00 (ISBN 0-933786-00-X); professional individual discount 10.00 (ISBN 0-686-67622-X). Beech Hill.

Elias, N., ed. see **Haidar, Mirza M.**

Elias, Norbert. The Civilizing Process: The/Development of Manners, Vol. 1. Jephcott, Edmund, tr. from Ger. 1977. 20.00 (ISBN 0-916354-32-6). Urizen Bks.

--What Is Sociology? 1978. 15.00x (ISBN 0-231-04550-6). Columbia U Pr.

Elias, Veronica & Elias, James, eds. Sex & the Media. (Pergamon Policy Studies). 200p. Date not set. 20.01 (ISBN 0-08-025984-7). Pergamon.

Elias, Z. M. Cylindrical Shell Roof Design. 1972. pap. 11.95x (ISBN 0-8156-6036-7, Am U Beirut). Syracuse U Pr.

Eliason, Alan. Business Information Processing. 496p. 1979. text ed. 16.95 (ISBN 0-574-21235-3, 13-4235); instr's guide avail. (ISBN 0-574-21236-1, 13-4236). SRA.

Eliason, Alan & Kitts, Kent D. Business Computer Systems & Applications. 2nd ed. LC 78-18447. 384p. 1979. instr's guide avail. (ISBN 0-574-21215-9, 13-4215); instructor's guide 2.25 (ISBN 0-574-21216-7, 13-4216). SRA.

Eliason, Alan L. Mason Oaks: An Online Case Study in Business Systems Design. 128p. 1981. pap. text ed. 5.95 (ISBN 0-574-21310-4, 13-4310); instr's guide avail. (ISBN 0-574-21311-2, 13-4311). SRA.

Eliason, Claudia & Jenkins, Loa T. A Practical Guide to Early Childhood Curriculum. 2nd ed. (Illus.). 330p. 1981. pap. text ed. 12.95 (ISBN 0-8016-1511-9). Mosby.

Eliason, Karine, et al. Make-A-Mix Cookery. LC 78-50687. (Illus.). 1978. pap. 5.95 (ISBN 0-89586-008-2). H P Bks.

--More Make-A-Mix Cookery. (Orig.). 1980. pap. 5.95 (ISBN 0-89586-055-4). H P Bks.

Eliassen, Arnt. Meteorology: An Introductory Course, 2 vols. 1977. Vol. I. pap. 22.00x (ISBN 82-00-02392-3, Dist. by Columbia U Pr); Vol. II. pap. 15.00 (ISBN 82-00-02411-3). Universitet.

Eliasson, Gunnar. Business Economic Planning: Theory, Practice & Comparison. LC 76-5895. 1977. 25.50 (ISBN 0-471-01813-9, Pub. by Wiley-Interscience). Wiley.

Eliel, E. L. & Basolo, F. Elements of Stereochemistry: With a Section on Coordination Compounds. 1969. 6.95 (ISBN 0-471-23745-0). Wiley.

Eliel, Ernest L. & Allinger, Norman L. Topics in Stereochemistry. LC 67-13943. (Topics in Stereochemistry Ser.). 27.50 (ISBN 0-470-23747-3, Pub. by Wiley-Interscience); Vol. 10, 1978. 51.95 (ISBN 0-471-04344-3). Wiley.

Eliel, Ernest L., jt. auth. see **Allinger, Norman L.**

Elimelech, Baruch. A Tonal Grammar of Etsako. (Publications in Linguistics Ser.: Vol. 87). 1979. 10.50x (ISBN 0-520-09576-6). U of Cal Pr.

Elin, Caren & Death Education Directory Staff. Death Educators Directory. 70p. 1981. pap. 7.95 (ISBN 0-930194-06-3). Highly Specialized.

Elinson. Analytical Chemistry of Zirconium & Hafnium. (Analytical Chemistry of the Elements Ser.). 1972. 32.95 (ISBN 0-470-23780-5). Halsted Pr.

Elinson, Jack & Siegman, Athilia E., eds. Sociomedical Health Indicators. 224p. (Orig.). 1979. pap. 9.00x (ISBN 0-89503-013-6). Baywood Pub.

Elinson, Jack, et al, eds. Health Goals & Health Indicators: Policy, Planning & Evaluation. LC 77-14044. (AAAS Selected Symposium Ser.: No. 2). 1978. lib. bdg. 18.50x (ISBN 0-89158-429-3). Westview.

Eliopoulos, Nicholas. Oneness of Politics & Religion. 126p. (Orig.). 1970. pap. 3.00x (ISBN 0-9605396-1-1). Phystiklakis & Eliopoulos.

Eliopoulos, Nicholas C. Golden Arithmetization. 403p. (Orig.). 1980. pap. text ed. 30.00x (ISBN 0-9605396-0-3). Phystiklakis & Eliopoulos.

--Thine Health. Phistiklakis, Nicholas G., ed. (Orig.). 1980. pap. text ed. 12.00 (ISBN 0-9605396-2-X). Phystiklakis & Eliopoulos.

Eliot see **Bentley, Eric.**

Eliot, Charles W., ed. Scientific Papers: Physiology-Medicine-Surgery. LC 75-95626. (Illus.). Repr. of 1910 ed. 15.00x (ISBN 0-678-03757-4). Kelley.

Eliot, Elizabeth A. The Crowned Knot of Tree. LC 79-67045. 1980. 8.95 (ISBN 0-533-04425-1). Vantage.

Eliot, George. Adam Bede. 1960. 12.95x (ISBN 0-460-00027-6, Evman); pap. 4.95 (ISBN 0-460-01027-1). Dutton.

--Felix Holt, the Radical. 1964. 17.95x (ISBN 0-460-00353-4, Evman); pap. 8.95 (ISBN 0-460-01353-X, Evman). Dutton.

--Middlemarch. (The Zodiac Press Ser.). 1979. 15.95 (ISBN 0-7011-1245-X, Pub. by Chatto Bodley Jonathan). Merrimack Bk Serv.

--The Mill on the Floss. (Clarendon Edition of the Novels of George Eliot Ser.). (Illus.). 516p. text ed. 55.00x (ISBN 0-19-812560-7). Oxford U Pr.

--Scenes of Clerical Life. Wolff, Robert L., ed. LC 75-491. (Victorian Fiction Ser.). 1975. Repr. of 1858 ed. lib. bdg. 66.00 (ISBN 0-8240-1567-3). Garland Pub.

--Silas Marner. (Literature Ser). (gr. 9-12). 1969. pap. text ed. 3.42 (ISBN 0-87720-715-1). AMSCO Sch.

--Silas Marner. (The Zodiac Press Ser.). 1979. 9.95 (ISBN 0-7011-1247-6, Pub. by Chatto Bodley Jonathan). Merrimack Bk Serv.

--Silas Marner (with Reader's Guide) (Amsco Literature Program). (gr. 10-12). 1971. pap. text ed. 4.17 (ISBN 0-87720-814-X); tchr's ed. 2.70 (ISBN 0-87720-914-6). AMSCO Sch.

Eliot, J. & Salkind, N. Children's Spatial Development. (Illus.). 312p. 1975. 32.50 (ISBN 0-398-03210-6). C C Thomas.

Eliot, John. The Survey, or Topographical Description of France. with a New Mappe. LC 79-84104. (English Experience Ser.: No. 923). (Illus.). 116p. 1979. Repr. of 1592 ed. lib. bdg. 11.50 (ISBN 90-221-0923-2). Walter J Johnson.

Eliot, John, ed. see **Bowden, Henry W. & Ronda, James P.**

Eliot, Marc. Death of a Rebel: Phil Ochs & a Small Circle of Friends. LC 77-25586. 1979. pap. 4.95 (ISBN 0-385-13610-2, Anch). Doubleday.

Eliot, Simon & Stern, Beverly, eds. The Age of Enlightenment: An Anthology of Eighteenth Century Texts, 2 vols. 1980. Vol. 1. 23.50x; Vol. 2. 23.50x. B&N.

Eliot, Susan B., jt. auth. see **May, Frank B.**

Eliot, T. S. Collected Poems, 1909-1962. LC 63-21424. 1963. 9.95 (ISBN 0-15-118978-1). HarBraceJ.

--Complete Plays of T. S. Eliot. LC 50-14646. 1969. 12.95 (ISBN 0-15-120755-0). HarBraceJ.

--Four Quartets. Bergonzi, Bernard, ed. LC 77-127568. (Casebook Ser). 1970. pap. text ed. 2.50 o.s.i. (ISBN 0-87695-039-X). Aurora Pubs.

--Old Possum's Book of Practical Cats. LC 39-33125. 1968. pap. 1.95 (ISBN 0-15-668570-1, HPL31, HPL). HarBraceJ.

--Selected Poems. LC 67-23064. (gr. 7-12). 1967. pap. 1.75 (ISBN 0-15-680647-9, HPL21, HPL). HarBraceJ.

--Use of Poetry & the Use of Criticism: Studies in the Relation of Criticism to Poetry in England. 2nd ed. 1975. pap. 5.75x (ISBN 0-06-491961-7). B&N.

--Waste Land. Cox, C. B. & Hinchiffe, A. P., eds. LC 70-127569. (Casebook Ser). 1970. pap. text ed. 2.50 o.s.i. (ISBN 0-87695-040-3). Aurora Pubs.

Eliot, T. S; see **Watson, E. Bradlee & Pressey, Benfield.**

Eliot, Thomas H., jt. auth. see **Bragdon, Henry W.**

Eliot Hurst, Michael. I Came to the City: Essays & Comments on the Urban Scene. 1975. pap. text ed. 10.95 (ISBN 0-395-17016-8). HM.

Eliott, P. D. Probabilistic Number Theory Two: Central Limit Theorems. (Grundlehren der Mathematischen Wissenschaften: Vol. 240). 1980. 35.00 (ISBN 0-387-90438-7). Springer-Verlag.

Elisofon, Eliot. Week in Agata's World: Poland. (Face to Face Bks). (Illus.). (gr. k-3). 1970. 4.50 o.p. (ISBN 0-02-733370-1, CCPr); text ed. 1.36 (ISBN 0-02-733380-9, CCPr). Macmillan.

--Week in Leonora's World: Puerto Rico. LC 72-146610. (Face to Face Ser). (Illus.). (gr. k-2). 1971. 4.50g o.s.i. (ISBN 0-02-733350-7, CCPr); pap. text ed. 1.36 o.s.i. (ISBN 0-02-733420-1, CCPr). Macmillan.

--Zaire a Week in Joseph's World. LC 72-81069. (Face to Face Books Ser.). (Illus.). 40p. (gr. k-2). 1973. 8.95 (ISBN 0-02-733400-7, CCPr). Macmillan.

Elison, Craig, ed. Modifying Man: Implications & Ethics. 11.25 (ISBN 0-8191-0302-0). U Pr of Amer.

Elison, George. Deus Destroyed: The Image of Christianity in Early Modern Japan. LC 72-97833. (East Asian Ser: No. 72). 704p. 1974. 30.00x (ISBN 0-674-19961-8). Harvard U Pr.

Elison, George & Smith, Bardwell Z., eds. Warlords, Artists, & Commoners: Japan in the Sixteenth Century. LC 80-24128. (Illus.). 372p. 1981. 20.00x (ISBN 0-8248-0692-1). U Pr of Hawaii.

Elizabeth First. Poems of Queen Elizabeth First. Bradner, Leicester, ed. LC 64-17778. 91p. 1964. 8.00x (ISBN 0-87057-082-X, Pub. by Brown U Pr). Univ Pr of New England.

Elizabeth I. A Book of Devotions. new ed. 1977. pap. text ed. 4.00x (ISBN 0-901072-57-5). Humanities.

Elizondo, Virgil & Greinacher, Norbert, eds. Women in a Man's Church, Concilium 134. (New Concilium 1980: Vol. 134). 128p. 1980. pap. 5.95 (ISBN 0-8164-4767-5). Crossroad NY.

Elizur, Dov. Job Evaluation: A Systematic Approach. 188p. 1980. text ed. 37.25 (ISBN 0-566-02120-X, Pub. by Gower Pub Co England). Renouf.

Elkan, E. & Reichenbach-Klinke, H. Color Atlas of the Diseases of Fishes, Amphibians, & Reptiles. (Illus.). 256p. 1974. 20.00 (ISBN 0-87666-028-6, H-948). TFH Pubns.

Elkanah, Settle. The Compleat Memoirs of the Life of That Notorious Imposter Will Morrell, Alias Bowyer, Alias Wickham,Etc, LC 80-2498. 1981. Repr. of 1694 ed. 47.50 (ISBN 0-404-19134-7). AMS Pr.

El-Kareh, A. B. & El-Kareh, J. C. Electron Beams, Lenses & Optics, Vols. 1 & 2. 1970. Vol. 1. 48.50 (ISBN 0-12-238001-0); Vol. 2. 48.00 (ISBN 0-12-238002-9). Acad Pr.

El-Kareh, J. C., jt. auth. see El-Kareh, A. B.

El-Khawas, Mohamed A., jt. auth. see Serapiao, Luis B.

Elkin, A. P. Aboriginal Men of High Degree. 2nd ed. LC 77-87170. (Illus.). 1978. 15.95x (ISBN 0-312-00167-3). St Martin.

Elkin, Benjamin. How the Tsar Drinks Tea. LC 79-136989. (Illus.). (gr. k-3). 1971. 5.95 o.s.i. (ISBN 0-8193-0455-7, Four Winds); PLB 5.41 o.s.i. (ISBN 0-8193-0456-5). Schol Bk Serv.

--The King Who Could Not Sleep. LC 74-12444. (Illus.). 40p. (gr. k-3). 1975. 5.95 o.s.i. (ISBN 0-8193-0775-0, Four Winds); PLB 5.41 o.s.i. (ISBN 0-8193-0776-9). Schol Bk Serv.

--Such Is the Way of the World. LC 68-11662. (Illus.). (gr. k-3). 1968. 5.95 o.s.i. (ISBN 0-8193-0347-X, Four Winds); PLB 5.41 o.s.i. (ISBN 0-8193-0348-8). Schol Bk Serv.

Elkin, H. V. Cutler No. 4: Yellowstone. (Orig.). 1980. pap. 1.75 (ISBN 0-505-51512-1). Tower Bks.

--Eagle Man. (Cutler Ser.: No. 1). 1978. pap. 1.50 (ISBN 0-505-51295-5). Tower Bks.

--Playground. 1979. pap. 2.25 (ISBN 0-505-51423-0). Tower Bks.

Elkin, Milton, ed. Radiology of the Urinary System, 2 vols. 1980. Set. text ed. 95.00 (ISBN 0-316-23275-0). Little.

Elkin, Stanley. Stanley Elkin's Greatest Hits. 288p. 1980. 10.95 (ISBN 0-525-20940-9). Dutton.

Elkin, Stanley & Ravenel, Shannon, eds. The Best American Short Stories Nineteen Eighty. 496p. 1980. 12.95 (ISBN 0-395-29446-0). HM.

Elkind, Arnold B., jt. auth. see Cotchett, Joseph W.

Elkind, David. Children & Adolescents. 3rd ed. 272p. 1981. text ed. 15.95x (ISBN 0-19-502820-1); pap. text ed. 5.95x (ISBN 0-19-502821-X). Oxford U Pr.

--Sympathetic Understanding of the Child: Birth to Sixteen. 2nd ed. text ed. 15.95 (ISBN 0-205-06016-1). Allyn.

Elkind, David & Weiner, Irving B. Development of the Child. LC 77-14214. 1978. text ed. 21.95 (ISBN 0-471-23785-X); tchrs. manual avail. (ISBN 0-471-04049-5); study guide 7.50 (ISBN 0-471-03435-5). Wiley.

Elkind, David & Flavell, John H., eds. Studies in Cognitive Development: Essays in Honor of Jean Piaget. 1969. 13.95 (ISBN 0-19-500877-4); pap. 8.95x (ISBN 0-19-500878-2). Oxford U Pr.

Elkington, Helen. Swimming. LC 76-53514. (Illus.). 1978. pap. 9.95x (ISBN 0-521-29027-9). Cambridge U Pr.

Elkins, A. Management: Structures, Functions, & Practices. 1980. 17.95 (ISBN 0-201-01517-X). A-W.

Elkins, Arthur. Managing Organizations: Structure, Functions & Practices. LC 79-5371. 1980. text ed. cancelled (ISBN 0-201-01517-X). A-W.

Elkins, Arthur & Callaghan, Dennis W. Managerial Odyssey: Problems in Business & Its Enviroment. 600p. 1981. text ed. 17.50 (ISBN 0-201-03962-1). A-W.

Elkins, Chris. Heavenly Deception. 1980. pap. 3.95 (ISBN 0-8423-1402-4). Tyndale.

Elkins, Dov P. Shepherd of Jerusalem. LC 75-39436. (Illus.). (gr. 8-12). 1976. 6.95 (ISBN 0-88400-045-1). Shengold.

Elkins, Dov P., ed. Being Jewish, Being Human: A Gift Book of Poems & Readings. LC 79-88298. Date not set. softbound 16.50 (ISBN 0-918834-07-4). Growth Assoc. Postponed.

Elkins, Elizabeth A., jt. auth. see Morris, Jacquelyn M.

Elkins, Garland, jt. ed. see Warren, Thomas B.

Elkins, T. H. The Urban Explosion. (Studies in Contemporary Europe). 80p. (Orig.). 1973. pap. text ed. 2.75x (ISBN 0-333-12151-1). Humanities.

Elkins, Wilson H. & Callcott, George H. Forty Years As a College President. 130p. 1981. cancelled o.p. (ISBN 0-686-64814-5). Carrollton Pr.

Elkoff, Marvin. You Can Kiss This Boy Goodbye. 1981. 11.95 (ISBN 0-671-41145-4, Wyndham Bks). S&S.

Elkon, Juliette & Ross, Elaine. Menus for Entertaining. 1960. 8.95 (ISBN 0-8038-4617-7). Hastings.

Elkow, J. D., jt. auth. see Stack, Herbert.

Elkowitz, Edward B. Geriatric Medicine for the Primary Care Practitioner. 1981. text ed. price not set (ISBN 0-8261-3230-8); pap. text ed. price not set (ISBN 0-8261-3231-6). Springer Pub.

Ell Ell Diversified, Inc. Staff. How to Get a Job - with "No Experience" or "Not Enough". rev. ed. LC 80-67678. (Illus.). 56p. 1980. pap. 7.95 (ISBN 0-937428-00-0). Ell Ell Diversified.

Ell, Peter J., et al. Atlas of Computerized Emission Tomography. (Illus.). 288p. 1980. text ed. 115.00x (ISBN 0-443-02228-3). Churchill.

Ellam, June, jt. auth. see Ellam, Patrick.

Ellam, Patrick & Ellam, June. Wind Song: Our Ten Years in the Yacht Delivery Business. LC 75-37353. (Illus.). 256p. 1976. 10.95 (ISBN 0-87742-061-0). Intl Marine.

Ellan, S. E. see Ovennell, Marjorie & Ovennell, C. H.

Ellaway, Tom, tr. see Dumont, Pierre.

Elledge, Jim. James Dickey: A Bibliography, Nineteen Forty-Seven to Nineteen Seventy-Four. LC 79-10405. (Author Bibliographies Ser.: No. 40). 1979. 13.00 (ISBN 0-8108-1218-5). Scarecrow.

Elledge, Scott, ed. see Hardy, Thomas.

Elledge, Scott, ed. see Milton, John.

Ellefson, Ashley C. The Higher Schooling in the United States. LC 77-94531. (Orig.). 1978. pap. 4.95 (ISBN 0-8467-0455-2, Pub. by Two Continents). Hippocrene Bks.

Elleinstein, Jean. The Stalin Phenomenon. 1976. text ed. 13.00x (ISBN 0-85315-375-2). Humanities.

Ellen, Rose, Jr., jt. auth. see Weiner, Robert T.

Ellenberg, H., ed. Progress in Botany, Vol. 42. 430p. 1981. 56.00 (ISBN 0-387-10430-5). Springer-Verlag.

Ellenberg, H., et al, eds. Progress in Botany, Vol. 41. (Illus.). 1980. 70.30 o.p. (ISBN 0-387-09769-4). Springer-Verlag.

--Progress in Botany: Vol. 40. (Illus.). 1979. 77.70 o.p. (ISBN 0-387-09074-6). Springer-Verlag.

Ellenberg, Heinz, jt. auth. see Mueller-Dombois, Dieter.

Ellenberger, Carl, Jr. Perimetry: Principles, Techniques, & Interpretations. 128p. 1980. text ed. 12.00 (ISBN 0-89004-504-6). Raven.

Ellenberger, W., et al. Atlas of Animal Anatomy for Artists. rev. ed. Brown, Lewis S., ed. Weinbaum, Helen, tr. (Illus.). 192p. (YA) (gr. 9-12). 1956. pap. 6.00 (ISBN 0-486-20082-5). Dover.

Ellenbogen, Eileen, ed. see Simenon, Georges.

Ellenbogen, Leon. Controversies in Nutrition. (Contemporary Issues in Clinical Nutrition Ser.). (Illus.). 224p. 1981. lib. bdg. 20.00 (ISBN 0-443-08127-1). Churchill.

Ellenboger, Eileen, tr. see Weintraub, Stanley.

Ellenboren, Leon. Controversies in Nutrition. (Contemporary Issues in Clinical Nutrition Ser.). 1981. text ed. price not set (ISBN 0-443-08127-1). Churchill.

Ellenson, Ann. Human Relations. (Illus.). 304p. 1973. ref. ed. 16.95 (ISBN 0-13-445643-2). P-H.

Ellentuck, Shan. Yankel the Fool. LC 71-175369. 112p. (gr. 3-7). 1973. PLB 4.95 o.p. (ISBN 0-385-07524-3). Doubleday.

Ellenwood, F. O. & Mackay, Charles O. Thermodynamic Charts. 2nd ed. 1944. 11.95 o.p. (ISBN 0-471-23793-0, Pub. by Wiley-Interscience). Wiley.

Eller, Vernard. The Most Revealing Book of the Bible: Making Sense Out of Revelation. 1974. pap. 4.95 (ISBN 0-8028-1572-3). Eerdmans.

--Thy Kingdom Come: A Blumhardt Reader. 160p. (Orig.). 1980. pap. 9.95 (ISBN 0-8028-3544-9). Eerdmans.

--War & Peace from Genesis to Revelation. 232p. 1981. pap. 8.95 (ISBN 0-8361-1947-9). Herald Pr.

Ellerbe, Suellyn. Fluid & Blood Component Therapy in the Critically Ill. (Contemporary Issues in Critical Care Nursing). (Illus.). 224p. 1981. lib. bdg. 20.00 (ISBN 0-443-08129-8). Churchill.

Ellert & Ellert. German A, 5 bks. (gr. 8-12). 1972. pap. text ed. 7.00 each (ISBN 0-686-57754-X). Learning Line.

--German B, 3 bks. (gr. 8-12). 1972. pap. text ed. 7.00 each (ISBN 0-8449-1423-1). Learning Line.

Ellery, John B. John Stuart Mill. (English Authors Ser.: No. 5). 1964. lib. bdg. 10.95 (ISBN 0-8057-1392-1). Twayne.

Ellestad, Myrin H. Stress Testing: Principles & Testing. 1980. 35.00 (ISBN 0-8036-3111-1). Davis Co.

Ellett, Marcella H. Textiles for Teens. 3rd ed. LC 67-26196. 1967. pap. text ed. 4.95 o.p. (ISBN 0-8087-0506-7). Burgess.

Elley, Derek, ed. International Music Guide, 1981. (Illus.). 1981. pap. 8.95 (ISBN 0-686-69099-0). A S Barnes.

Ellfeldt, Lois & Lowman, Charles L. Exercises for the Mature Adult. (Illus.). 120p. 1973. pap. 9.75 spiral (ISBN 0-398-02750-1). C C Thomas.

Ellfeldt, Lois & Morton, Virgil L. This Is Ballroom Dance. LC 73-84770. (Illus.). 1974. pap. text ed. 4.50 (ISBN 0-87484-244-1). Mayfield Pub.

Ellickson, Robert C. & Tarlock, A. Dan. Land Use Controls. 1239p. 1981. price not set (ISBN 0-316-23299-8). Little.

Ellicott, Charles J. Ellicott's Four Volume Bible Commentary (Unabridged) 4580p. 1981. Repr. 119.95 (ISBN 0-310-43878-0). Zondervan.

Elliger, Winfried. Die Darstellung der Landschaft in der griechischen Dichtung: Untersuchungen Zur Antiken Literatur und Geschicht, Vol.15. LC 73-93160. (Ger.). 1975. 103.00x (ISBN 3-11-004794-2). De Gruyter.

Ellin, Stanley. Dreadful Summit. (Foul Play Press Ser.). 192p. pap. 4.95 (ISBN 0-914378-66-X). Countryman.

--The Eighth Circle. (Foul Play Press Ser.). 224p. 1981. pap. 4.95 (ISBN 0-914378-67-8). Countryman.

--Kindly Dig Your Grave & Other Wicked Stories. Queen, Ellery, ed. LC 78-82628. 1977. pap. 1.50 o.p. (ISBN 0-89559-008-5). Davis Pubns.

--Mirror, Mirror on the Wall. 144p. 1975. pap. 1.25 o.s.i. (ISBN 0-440-15599-1). Dell.

--Mirror, Mirror on the Wall. LC 72-2709. 1972. 5.95 o.p. (ISBN 0-394-47168-7). Random.

--The Specialty of the House & Other Stories: The Complete Mystery Tales, 1948-1978. LC 79-67149. 557p. 1979. limited ed. 35.00 (ISBN 0-686-68286-6); 15.00 (ISBN 0-89296-049-3). Mysterious Pr.

--Valentine Estate. LC 68-28541. 1968. 8.95 o.p. (ISBN 0-394-45033-7). Random.

Elling, Ray H., ed. Cross National Study of Health Systems by Countries & World Region, & Special Problems: A Guide to Information Sources. LC 79-26099. (Health Affairs Information Guide Ser.: Vol. 3). 1980. 30.00 (ISBN 0-8103-1453-3). Gale.

--Cross National Study of Health Systems: Concepts, Methods, & Data Sources: a Guide to Information Sources. LC 79-24028. (Health Affairs Information Guide Ser.: Vol. 2). 1980. 30.00 (ISBN 0-8103-1449-5). Gale.

Ellinger, A. G. & Stewart, T. H. A Post-War History of the Stock Market. 80p. 1980. 30.00x (ISBN 0-85941-153-2, Pub. by Woodhead-Faulkner England). State Mutual Bk.

Ellinger, K. Biblia Hebraica Stuttgartensia. 1977. 19.25 (ISBN 3-438-05218-0, 60555). United Bible.

Ellinger, Richard G. Color Structure & Design. 144p. 1980. pap. 9.95 (ISBN 0-442-23941-6). Van Nos Reinhold.

Ellington, Edward Kennedy "Duke". Music Is My Mistress. LC 73-83189. 544p. 1973. 12.95 (ISBN 0-385-02235-2). Doubleday.

Ellington, H. I., et al. Games & Simulations in Science Education. 180p. 1980. 25.00x (ISBN 0-89397-093-X). Nichols Pub.

Ellington, James W., tr. see Kant, Immanuel.

Ellington, Marnie. Unwilling Bride. (Orig.). 1980. pap. 1.50 (ISBN 0-440-19743-0). Dell.

Ellington, Mercer & Dance, Stanley. Duke Ellington in Person. 236p. pap. 5.95 (ISBN 0-306-80104-3). Da Capo.

Ellingworth, P. & Nida, E. A. Translators Handbook on Paul's Letter to the Thessalonians. (Helps for Translators Ser.). 1975. soft cover 2.10 (ISBN 0-8267-0146-9, 08526). United Bible.

Ellinwood, L. & Porter, K. Bio-Biographical Index of Musicians in the United States of America Since Colonial Times. LC 76-159677. (Music Ser). 1971. Repr. of 1956 ed. lib. bdg. 35.00 (ISBN 0-306-70183-9). Da Capo.

Elliot. All About Brook Trout. 1980. Repr. 8.95 (ISBN 0-89272-090-5). Down East.

Elliot, jt. auth. see Tansik.

Elliot, Alfred & Outka, Darryl E. Zoology. 5th ed. (Illus.). 1976. 19.95 (ISBN 0-13-984021-4). P-H.

Elliot, Alison J. Child Language. (Cambridge Textbooks in Linguistics). 180p. Date not set. text ed. price not set (ISBN 0-521-22518-3); pap. text ed. price not set (ISBN 0-521-29556-4). Cambridge U Pr.

Elliot, Aubrey. Magic World of Xhosa. (Encore Edition). 1970. 2.95 o.p. (ISBN 0-684-15241-X, ScribT). Scribner.

Elliot, Bruce. Classic Secrets of Magic. (Illus., Orig.). 1969. pap. 4.95 (ISBN 0-571-09019-2, Pub. by Faber & Faber). Merrimack Bk Serv.

Elliot, C. Orville & Wasley, Robert S. Business Information Processing System. 4th ed. 1975. text ed. 18.95 (ISBN 0-256-01579-1). Irwin.

Elliot, Curtis M., jt. auth. see Vaughan, Emmett J.

Elliot, D. & Elliot, R. The Control of Technology. (Wykeham Science Ser.: Vol. 39). 1976. pap. 9.60 o.p. (ISBN 0-387-91130-8). Springer-Verlag.

Elliot, Daniel G. A Review of the Primates, 3 vols. LC 78-72714. Repr. of 1913 ed. Set. 225.00 (ISBN 0-404-18284-4). Vol. 1 (ISBN 0-404-18285-2). Vol. 2 (ISBN 0-404-18286-0). Vol. 3 (ISBN 0-404-18287-9). AMS Pr.

Elliot, Dave. Imperialism & Underdevelopment. 1978. 24.50 o.p. (ISBN 0-685-85434-5). Porter.

Elliot, Douglass. The New Breed. 1981. pap. 2.95 (ISBN 0-345-29483-1). Ballantine.

Elliot, Elisabeth. The Liberty of Obedience. (Festival Bks). 1981. pap. 1.50 (ISBN 0-687-21730-X). Abingdon.

--Love Has a Price Tag. LC 79-50944. 148p. 1981. pap. 5.95 (ISBN 0-915684-87-X). Christian Herald.

--The Mark of a Man. 1981. 7.95 (ISBN 0-8007-1178-5). Revell.

--These Strange Ashes. LC 74-25684. 144p. 1975. pap. 3.95 (ISBN 0-06-062233-4, RD 306). Har-Row.

Elliot, Elizabeth. Shadow of the Almighty: The Life & Testament of Jim Elliot. LC 58-10365. 1979. pap. 4.95 (ISBN 0-06-062211-3, RD 305, HarpR). Har-Row.

Elliot, Elizabeth, tr. Doce Cestas De Mendrugos. (Spanish Bks.). (Span.). 1977. 1.90 (ISBN 0-8297-0804-9). Life Pubs Intl.

Elliot, Errol T. Quaker Profiles from the American West. LC 72-5126. 1972. pap. 2.95 (ISBN 0-913408-05-0). Friends United.

Elliot, George P. Reaching: Poems by George P. Elliott. (Santa Susana Press Ser.). 1979. numbered 35.00 (ISBN 0-937048-21-6); lettered 60.00 (ISBN 0-937048-28-3). CSUN.

Elliot, Gordon R. Barkerville, Quesnel, & the Cariboo Gold Rush. LC 79-301801. (Illus.). 216p. 1980. pap. 7.95 (ISBN 0-295-95775-1, Pub. by Douglas & McIntyre Canada). U of Wash Pr.

Elliot, Jeffrey M. Fantasy Voices, No. 1: Interviews with Fantasy Authors. LC 80-22575. (Milford Series: Popular Writers of Today: Vol. 31). 64p. (Orig.). 1981. lib. bdg. 8.95x (ISBN 0-89370-146-7); pap. text ed. 2.95x (ISBN 0-89370-246-3). Borgo Pr.

--The Future of the Space Program--Large Corporations & Society: Discussions with 22 Science-Fiction Writers. LC 80-19754. (Great Issues of the Day Ser.: Vol. 1). 64p. (Orig.). 1981. lib. bdg. 8.95x (ISBN 0-89370-140-8); pap. text ed. 2.95x (ISBN 0-89370-240-4). Borgo Pr.

--Science-Fiction Voices, No. 4: Interviews with Science-Fiction Authors. LC 80-22580. (Milford Series: Popular Writers of Today: Vol. 33). 64p. (Orig.). 1981. lib. bdg. 8.95x (ISBN 0-89370-148-3); pap. text ed. 2.95x (ISBN 0-89370-248-X). Borgo Pr.

Elliot, Jeffrey M. & Reginald, R. The Analytical Congressional Directory. (Borgo Reference Library: Vol. 12). 256p. (Orig.). 1981. lib. bdg. 19.95 (ISBN 0-89370-141-6); pap. text ed. 9.95 (ISBN 0-89370-241-2). Borgo Pr.

Elliot, Jeffrey M. & Shieh, Francis. Keys to Economic Understanding. LC 76-13795. 1976. pap. text ed. 8.95 (ISBN 0-8403-1483-3). Kendall-Hunt.

Elliot, Jonathan. The American Diplomatic Code, Embracing a Collection of Treaties & Conventions Between U.S. & Foreign Powers from 1778 to 1834, 2 Vols. LC 74-129032. (Research & Source Works Ser.: No. 605). 1971. Repr. lib. bdg. 63.00 (ISBN 0-8337-1036-2). B Franklin.

Elliot, M., jt. auth. see Lasor, B.

Elliot, Mary, jt. auth. see Elliott, Gordon.

Elliot, P. D. Probabilistic Number Theory One: Mean-Value Theorems. (Grundlehren der Mathematischen Wissenschaften: Vol. 239). 1980. 35.00 (ISBN 0-387-90437-9). Springer-Verlag.

Elliot, R., jt. auth. see Elliot, D.

Elliot, R. F., jt. ed. see Fallick, J. L.

Elliot, R. S. & Ickie, John. Ulster: A Case Study in Conflict Theory. LC 78-182186. 180p. 1971. text ed. 14.95x (ISBN 0-8290-0213-8). Irvington.

Elliot, Ralph. Chaucer's English. (Andre Deutsch Language Library). 1977. lib. bdg. 20.50x (ISBN 0-233-96539-4). Westview.

Elliot, Sharon A. Dinner Can Be a Picnic All Year Round. LC 80-70050. 1981. pap. 5.95 (ISBN 0-9601398-4-2). Fresh Pr.

Elliot, Stewart. Timber Frame Raising. LC 79-84581. 129p. (Orig.). 1979. pap. 9.95 (ISBN 0-932302-01-7). Brick Hse Pub.

Elliot, Sumner L. Water Under the Bridge. 1978. pap. 1.95 o.p. (ISBN 0-685-54639-X, 04722-8). Jove Pubns.

Elliotson, John. Numerous Cases of Surgical Operations Without Pain in the Mesmeric State. Bd. with Mesmerism in India; Philosophy of Sleep. (Contributions to the History of Psychology Ser., Vol. X, Pt. A: Orientations). 1978. Repr. of 1843 ed. 30.00 (ISBN 0-89093-159-3). U Pubns Amer.

Elliott. Plaid for Introduction to Data Processing. 3rd ed. 1979. 5.50 (ISBN 0-256-02128-7, 14-0841-03). Learning Syst.

--Thailand: Origins of Military Rule. 190p. 1978. 11.95 (ISBN 0-905762-10-X); pap. 5.95 (ISBN 0-905762-11-8). Lawrence Hill.

Elliott & Moore. History of Monterey County, Eighteen Eighty One: With Illustrations, Descriptions of Its Scenery, Farms, Residences, Public Buildings, Etc. (Illus.). 1979. Repr. of 1881 ed. 24.95 (ISBN 0-913548-69-3, Valley Calif). Western Tanager.

Elliott, jt. auth. see Smith.

Elliott, Brad. Good Vibrations: The Beach Boys on Records, 1961-1980. 1981. 14.95 (ISBN 0-87650-118-8). Pierian.

Elliott, Charles. The Outdoor Eye: A Sportsman's Guide. 2nd ed. LC 73-100358. (Funk & W Bk.). (Illus.). 1978. 9.95 o.s.i. (ISBN 0-308-10343-2, TYC-T); pap. 4.50 o.s.i. (ISBN 0-308-10344-0, TYC-T). T Y Crowell.

Elliott, Cheri. Backpacker's Digest. 3rd ed. (Illus.). 1981. pap. 8.95 (ISBN 0-910676-21-6, 6536). DBI.

Elliott, David W., ed. The Third Indochina Conflict. (Westview Replica Edition Ser.). 250p. 1981. lib. bdg. 18.50x (ISBN 0-89158-739-X). Westview.

Elliott, Donald & Arrowood, Clinton. Lamb's Tales from the Great Operas. 1981. 9.95 (ISBN 0-87645-110-5). Gambit.

Elliott, Douglas F. & Rao, K. Ramamohan. Fast Transforms: Algorithms, Analyses, Applications. LC 79-8852. (Computer Science & Applied Mathematical Ser.). 1981. write for info. (ISBN 0-12-237080-5). Acad Pr.

Elliott, Ebenezer. Night, a Descriptive Poem, Pt. 1, 4 Bks., Repr. Of 1813. Bd. with Love, a Poem in Three Parts. To Which Is Added, the Giaour, a Satirical Poem. Repr. of 1823 ed. LC 75-31200. (Romantic Context Ser.: Poetry 1789-1830: Vol. 52). 1978. lib. bdg. 47.00 (ISBN 0-8240-2151-7). Garland Pub.

--The Vernal Walk; a Poem, Repr. Of 1801 Ed. Bd. with Peter Faultless to His Brother Simon, Tales of Night, in Rhyme, & Other Poems. Repr. of 1820 ed. LC 75-31199. (Romantic Context Ser.: Poetry 1789-1830: Vol. 51). 1978. lib. bdg. 47.00 (ISBN 0-8240-2150-9). Garland Pub.

--The Village Patriarch; a Poem, Repr. Of 1829 Ed. Reiman, Donald H., ed. Bd. with The Corn-Law Rhymes. Repr. of 1831 ed. LC 75-31202. (Romantic Context Ser.: Poetry 1789-1830). 1979. lib. bdg. 47.00 (ISBN 0-8240-2152-5). Garland Pub.

Elliott, Edwin B. Algebra of Quantics. 2nd ed. LC 63-11320. 11.95 (ISBN 0-8284-0184-5). Chelsea Pub.

Elliott, Errol T. Sing the Faith-Poems of the Spirit. 1975. 3.00 o.p. (ISBN 0-913408-21-2); pap. 2.00 o.p. (ISBN 0-913408-60-3). Friends United.

Elliott, Gordon & Elliot, Mary. The Ideal Life: Fifty & Over. (Illus., Orig.). 1980. pap. 5.95 (ISBN 0-89542-081-3). Ideals.

Elliott, Harley. Darkness at Each Elbow. 1981. pap. 4.00 (ISBN 0-914610-21-X). Hanging Loose.

--Sky Heart. LC 75-14965. (Illus.). 60p. 1975. pap. 3.00x (ISBN 0-915316-13-7); pap. 7.50 limited signed ed (ISBN 0-915316-14-5). Pentagram.

Elliott, J. F. Interception Patrol: An Examination of the Theory of Random Patrol As a Municipal Police Tactic. (Illus.). 88p. 1973. text ed. 11.75 (ISBN 0-398-02721-8). C C Thomas.

--The New Police. 88p. 1973. 9.75 (ISBN 0-398-02680-7). C C Thomas.

Elliott, J. H. Botany. (Teach Yourself Ser.). 1973. pap. 3.50 o.p. (ISBN 0-679-10390-2). McKay.

Elliott, J. H., jt. auth. see Briggs, S. R.

Elliott, J. H., jt. auth. see McKendrick, Melveena.

Elliott, John. Blood on the Snow. LC 76-29859. 1977. 8.95 o.p. (ISBN 0-312-08452-8). St Martin.

--Monarch Notes on Coleridge's the Rime of the Ancient Mariner & Other Poems. (Orig.). pap. 1.95 (ISBN 0-671-00778-5). Monarch Pr.

Elliott, John E. & Grey, Arthur. Economic Issues & Policies: Readings in Introductory Economics. 3rd ed. 1975. pap. text ed. 10.50 (ISBN 0-395-19824-0). HM.

Elliott, John H. Old World & the New, Fourteen Ninety-Two - Sixteen Fifty. LC 73-121362. (Studies in Early Modern History). (Illus.). 1970. 19.95 (ISBN 0-521-07937-3); pap. 5.95x (ISBN 0-521-09621-9). Cambridge U Pr.

Elliott, John H., jt. auth. see Brown, Jonathan.

Elliott, John H., jt. auth. see Vawter, Bruce.

Elliott, K. Benin. (Cambridge Introduction to the History of Mankind Ser.). 1973. 3.95 (ISBN 0-521-08028-2). Cambridge U Pr.

Elliott, Kenneth W., jt. auth. see King, Roy D.

Elliott, Kitt. African School. LC 78-111128. 1970. 22.50x (ISBN 0-521-07722-2). Cambridge U Pr.

Elliott, Lawrence. I Will Be Called John. 1974. pap. 1.75 o.p. (ISBN 0-425-02735-X, Medallion). Berkley Pub.

Elliott, Martin A., ed. Chemistry of Coal Utilization: Supplementary Volume 2. LC 80-13296. 1981. 150.00 (ISBN 0-471-07726-7, Pub. by Wiley-Interscience). Wiley.

Elliott, Neil. The Gods of Life. LC 73-8491. 192p. 1974. 7.95 o.s.i. (ISBN 0-02-535200-8). Macmillan.

Elliott, Norman F., ed. Patterson's American Education, Vol. 76. 1979. 37.50x o.s.i. (ISBN 0-910536-25-2). Ed Direct.

Elliott, Norman F. & Kustra, Mary E., eds. Patterson's American Education, Vol. 77. 1980. 40.00x (ISBN 0-910536-27-9). Ed Direct.

Elliott, Norman W., et al. Typing Power -- Spelling Power, Vol. I. LC 75-8458. pap. 6.50 (ISBN 0-672-96415-5); tchr's manual 2.50 (ISBN 0-672-96791-X). Bobbs.

Elliott, Patricia L. see Lind, Carolyn P., pseud.

Elliott, Peter R. Allied Escort Ships of World War II. LC 77-85752. 1978. 19.50 (ISBN 0-87021-801-8). Naval Inst Pr.

--The Cross & the Ensign: A Naval History of Malta 1798-1978. LC 79-93365. (Illus.). 192p. 1980. 16.95 (ISBN 0-87021-926-X). Naval Inst Pr.

Elliott, Philip. The Making of a Television Series: A Case Study in the Sociology of Culture. LC 79-89075. (Communication & Society: Vol. 2). (Illus.). 1979. 18.50x (ISBN 0-8039-1355-9); pap. 8.95x (ISBN 0-8039-1356-7). Sage.

Elliott, R. N. Nature's Law & the Secret of the Universe. (Illus.). 1980. Repr. 94.75 (ISBN 0-89901-008-3). Found Class Reprints.

--The Reconstruction of the Elliott Wave Principle, 2 vols. rev. & enl. ed. (Institute for Economic & Financial Research Ser). (Illus.). 97p. 1975. Set. 145.00 (ISBN 0-913314-63-3). Am Classical Coll Pr.

Elliott, Ralph H. Reconciliation & the New Age. LC 72-9568. 128p. (Orig.). 1973. pap. 2.95 o.p. (ISBN 0-8170-0586-2). Judson.

Elliott, Ralph N. An Elementary Introduction into the Elliott's Wave Theory. (The New Stock Market Reference Library). (Illus.). 91p. 1981. 27.55 (ISBN 0-918968-92-5). Inst Econ Fina.

--The Wave Principle. (Illus.). 1979. deluxe ed. 79.75 (ISBN 0-918968-33-X). Inst Econ Pol.

Elliott, Ralph W. Runes: An Introduction. LC 80-26090. (Illus.). xvi, 124p. 1981. Repr. of 1959 ed. lib. bdg. 21.00x (ISBN 0-313-22870-1, ELRU). Greenwood.

Elliott, Raymond. Fundamentals of Music. 3rd ed. LC 76-139599. (Illus.). 1971. pap. text ed. 12.50 (ISBN 0-13-341305-5). P-H.

Elliott, Robert C., ed. Twentieth Century Interpretations of Moll Flanders. (Twentieth Century Interpretations Ser). 1970. pap. 1.25 (ISBN 0-13-322230-6, Spec). P-H.

Elliott, Robert M. The Most Significant Stock Market Chart Patterns & the Amazing Anticipatory Meaning They Contain. (Illus.). 151p. 1981. 49.75 (ISBN 0-918968-89-5). Inst Econ Finan.

Elliott, Russell R. History of Nevada. LC 72-187809. (Illus.). 1973. 13.95x (ISBN 0-8032-0781-6). U of Nebr Pr.

Elliott, Sue, ed. On-Shore Britain, 1976-77. (Illus.). 1976. pap. 40.00 o.p. (ISBN 0-7161-0322-2, Gower). Unipub.

Elliott, Sumner L. Signs of Life. LC 80-21914. 288p. 1981. 11.95 (ISBN 0-89919-022-7). Ticknor & Fields.

Elliott, William D. Henry Handel Richardson. LC 75-12692. (World Authors Ser.: Australia: No. 366). 1975. lib. bdg. 12.50 (ISBN 0-8057-6217-5). Twayne.

Ellis, jt. auth. see Thompson, Harwood.

Ellis, et al. BASE. (gr. 4 up). 1974. pap. text ed. 2.58 (ISBN 0-87892-840-5); tchr's handbook 2.58 (ISBN 0-87892-844-8); tapes 129.15 (ISBN 0-87892-845-6). Economy Co.

Ellis, A. Books in the Victorian Elementary School. 1971. pap. 5.50x (ISBN 0-85365-025-X, Pub. by Lib Assn England). Oryx Pr.

Ellis, A., jt. ed. see Crouch, M.

Ellis, Albert. The Case Against Religion: A Psychotherapist's View. 1976. pap. 3.00. Am Atheist.

Ellis, Albert & Knaus, William J. Overcoming Procrastination. LC 76-26333. 1977. pap. 4.95 (ISBN 0-917476-04-2). Rational Living.

--Overcoming Procrastination. LC 76-26333. 1977. pap. 4.95 (ISBN 0-917476-04-2). Inst Rational-Emotive.

Ellis, Albert C. & Slaten, Jeff. Death Jag. (Orig.). 1980. pap. 1.95 (ISBN 0-532-23312-3). Manor Bks.

Ellis, Alec. A History of Children's Reading & Literature. 1968. pap. 9.75 (ISBN 0-08-012586-7). Pergamon.

--How to Find Out About Children's Literature. 3rd ed. 1973. 23.00 (ISBN 0-08-016970-8); pap. text ed. 8.50 (ISBN 0-08-018230-5). Pergamon.

--Library Services for Young People in England & Wales, 1830-1970. 1971. 26.00 (ISBN 0-08-016586-9). Pergamon.

Ellis, Alexander J. & Mendel, Arthur. Studies in the History of Musical Pitch. (Music Ser.). 238p. 1981. lib. bdg. 22.50 (ISBN 0-306-76020-7). Da Capo.

Ellis, Alexandra. The Last Carnival. (Orig.). 1980. pap. 2.50 (ISBN 0-515-04816-X). Jove Pubns.

--Romany Passions. 1978. pap. 1.95 o.p. (ISBN 0-425-03672-3, Medallion). Berkley Pub.

Ellis, Allen R. & Ellis, Phyllis T. Discovering Mayaland. (Illus.). 1965. 8.00 o.p. (ISBN 0-87062-013-4). A H Clark.

Ellis, Anne. The Life of an Ordinary Woman. LC 80-138. (Illus.). xxiv, 301p. 1980. pap. 6.25 (ISBN 0-8032-6704-5, BB 736, Bison). U of Nebr Pr.

Ellis, Arthur, et al. Interdisciplinary Methods: A Thematic Approach. 1980. pap. text ed. write for info. (ISBN 0-8302-4387-9). Goodyear.

Ellis, Arthur K. Teaching & Learning Elementary Social Studies. 2nd ed. 1981. text ed. 17.50 (ISBN 0-205-07221-6). Allyn.

Ellis, Audrey. All About Home Freezing. 1971. pap. 2.95 (ISBN 0-600-31644-0). Transatlantic.

--Cooking for Your Freezer. (Leisure Plan Bks). pap. 2.95 (ISBN 0-600-01360-X). Transatlantic.

Ellis, Bettie H. Word Processing. (Concepts & Applications). (Illus.). 48p. 1980. 7.48 (ISBN 0-07-019242-1, G). McGraw.

Ellis, Brian D. Basic Concepts of Measurement. LC 65-19150. 1968. 42.50 (ISBN 0-521-04889-3); pap. 14.95x (ISBN 0-521-09556-5). Cambridge U Pr.

Ellis, C. H. The British "Intervention" in Transcaspia, 1918-1919. 1963. 18.50x (ISBN 0-520-00381-0). U of Cal Pr.

Ellis, Charles & Ellis, Norma. Heirs Together of Life. pap. 4.95. Banner of Truth.

Ellis, Christopher. Military Transport of World War Two. Bartholomew, Alick, ed. LC 70-152283. (Mechanical Warfare Ser). 1971. 9.95 (ISBN 0-02-535230-X). Macmillan.

Ellis, Christopher, jt. auth. see Bishop, Dennis.

Ellis, Clarence. The Pebbles on the Beach. 2nd ed. (Illus.). 1954. 8.95 (ISBN 0-571-06543-0, Pub. by Faber & Faber); pap. 3.95 (ISBN 0-571-06814-6). Merrimack Bk Serv.

Ellis, D., et al. New York: the Empire State. 4th ed. 1975. 10.40 o.p. (ISBN 0-13-620385-X). P-H.

Ellis, Darryl J. & Pekar, Peter P. Planning for Non-Planners. 1981. 12.95 (ISBN 0-8144-5593-X). Am Mgmt.

Ellis, David. Let's Look at Indonesia. 1973. pap. 1.00 (ISBN 0-85363-077-1). OMF Bks.

Ellis, David, tr. see Stendhal.

Ellis, David M., ed. The Frontier in American Development: Essays in Honor of Paul Wallace Gates. (Illus.). 425p. 1969. 22.50x (ISBN 0-8014-0489-4). Cornell U Pr.

Ellis, Diane & Billings, Diane. Cardiopulmonary Resusitation: Procedures for Basic & Advanced Life Support. LC 79-19356. 1979. pap. text ed. 10.50 (ISBN 0-8016-1557-7). Mosby.

Ellis, E. E. & Wilcox, M. Neotestamentica et Semitica: Studies in Honor of Matthew Black. 320p. Repr. of 1969 ed. 10.50x (ISBN 0-567-02305-2). Attic Pr.

Ellis, Elizabeth A. The Least of My Sisters. LC 79-66928. 229p. 8.95 (ISBN 0-533-04426-X). Vantage.

Ellis, Errington. The Physical Management of Developmental Disorders. (Clinics in Developmental Medicine Ser. No. 26). 50p. 1967. 3.50 o.p. (ISBN 0-685-24740-6). Lippincott.

Ellis, Florence H. Navajo Indians, Vol. 1: Anthropological Study of the Navajo Indians. (American Indian Ethnohistory Ser: Indians of the Southwest). (Illus.). lib. bdg. 42.00 (ISBN 0-8240-0703-4). Garland Pub.

--Pueblo Indians, Vol. Two: Archaeologic & Ethnologic Data: Acoma-Laguna Land Claims. (American Indian Ethnohistory Ser: Indians of the Southwest). (Illus.). lib. bdg. 42.00 (ISBN 0-8240-0726-3). Garland Pub.

Ellis, Forrest D., jt. auth. see Helveston, Eugene M.

Ellis, Frances H. Early Meisterlieder of Hans Sachs. LC 73-81163. (Illus.). 340p. 1974. 20.00x (ISBN 0-253-31853-X). Ind U Pr.

Ellis, Frank H. Canada's Flying Heritage. 1980. pap. 15.00 (ISBN 0-8020-6417-5). U of Toronto Pr.

Ellis, Frank H., ed. Twentieth Century Interpretations of Robinson Crusoe. (Interpretations Ser). 1969. 8.95 (ISBN 0-13-781997-8, Spec); pap. 1.25 (ISBN 0-13-781989-7). P-H.

Ellis, Frederick S. History of St. Tammany Parish. (Illus.). Date not set. 19.95 (ISBN 0-88289-252-5). Pelican.

Ellis, G. P. Chromenes, Chromanones, & Chromones: Chemistry of Heterocyclic Compounds-A Series of Monographs. (Vol. 31). 1977. 155.00 (ISBN 0-471-38212-4). Wiley.

Ellis, G. P., jt. auth. see Criddle, W. J.

Ellis, Geoffrey. Napoleon's Continental Blockade: The Case of Alsace. (Oxford Historical Monographs). (Illus.). 368p. 1981. 49.95 (ISBN 0-19-821881-8). Oxford U Pr.

Ellis, George, jt. auth. see Dewar, David.

Ellis, George A. Inside Folsom Prison: The TM-Sidhi Program. 1979. 13.95 o.p. (ISBN 0-88280-058-2); pap. 8.95 (ISBN 0-88280-059-0). ETC Pubns.

--Inside Folsom Prison: Transcendental Meditation & the TM-Sidhi Program. LC 78-16774. 1979. 13.95 (ISBN 0-88280-059-0); pap. 7.95 (ISBN 0-685-94945-1). Chicago Review.

Ellis, Gerald C. Blood, Sweat, Toil & Tears. (Orig.). 1980. pap. 2.95 (ISBN 0-89260-171-X). Hwong Pub.

Ellis, Harlan F., ed. see Dick-Read, Grantly.

Ellis, Harry B. Ideals & Ideologies: Communism, Socialism & Capitalism. rev. ed. (Illus.). 326p. (RL 7). 1972. pap. 1.25 o.p. (ISBN 0-451-61124-1, MY1124, Ment). NAL.

--Israel: One Land, Two Peoples. LC 73-175104. (Illus.). 210p. 1972. 8.95 (ISBN 0-690-45028-1, TYC-T). T Y Crowell.

Ellis, Havelock. The World of Dreams. LC 75-43879. (Illus.). 1976. Repr. of 1922 ed. 24.00 (ISBN 0-8103-3780-0). Gale.

Ellis, Havelock see Horne, Herbert P., et al.

Ellis, Havelock, ed. see Ford, John.

Ellis, Havelock, ed. see Marlowe, Christopher.

Ellis, Havelock, tr. see Zola, Emile.

Ellis, Henry, illus. Original Letters of Eminent Literary Men of the 16th, 17th, & 18th Centuries. 460p. 1980. Repr. lib. bdg. 85.00 (ISBN 0-89984-199-6). Century Bookbindery.

Ellis, Henry C., et al. Psychology of Learning & Memory. LC 78-16292. (Illus.). 1979. text ed. 17.95 (ISBN 0-8185-0267-3). Brooks-Cole.

Ellis, Howard S. Notes on Stagflation. 1978. pap. 2.25 (ISBN 0-8447-3323-7). Am Enterprise.

Ellis, Howard S., ed. The Economy of Brazil. 1969. 21.50x (ISBN 0-520-01520-7). U of Cal Pr.

Ellis, J. Introduction to the Realestate Profession: Guide to Real Estatelicense Examination. 1981. pap. 8.24 (ISBN 0-13-494005-9). P-H.

Ellis, J. & Harwood, B. Real Estate Practicum. 1978. pap. 7.50 o.p. (ISBN 0-87909-750-7, 750). Reston.

Ellis, J. M. Narration in the German Novelle. LC 73-82460. (Anglica Germanica Ser.: No. 2). 232p. 1974. 45.00 (ISBN 0-521-20330-9). Cambridge U Pr.

--Narration in the German Novelle. LC 78-73602. (Anglica Germanica Ser.: No. 2). 1979. pap. 10.95x (ISBN 0-521-29592-0). Cambridge U Pr.

Ellis, Jack. Guide to Real Estate License Examinations. 2nd ed. LC 78-14423. (Illus.). 1979. pap. 15.95 (ISBN 0-13-371070-X). P-H.

Ellis, Jack, et al. The Film Book Bibliography: 1940-1975. LC 78-4055. 1979. 31.00 (ISBN 0-8108-1127-8). Scarecrow.

Ellis, Jack C. A History of Film. (Illus.). 1979. pap. 14.95 ref. ed. (ISBN 0-13-389460-6). P-H.
Ellis, James, ed. see Gilbert, W. S.
Ellis, Jane, tr. see Vins, Georgi.
Ellis, Janice & Nowlis, Elizabeth. Nursing: A Human Needs Approach. LC 76-12023. (Illus.). 416p. 1977. text ed. 16.75 (ISBN 0-395-24067-0); instructor's manual 1.25 (ISBN 0-395-24068-9). HM.
Ellis, Janice R. & Nowlis, Elizabeth A. Nursing: A Human Needs Approach. 2nd ed. LC 80-82841. (Illus.). 528p. 1981. text ed. 17.95 (ISBN 0-395-29642-0); price not set instr's. manual (ISBN 0-395-29643-9). HM.
Ellis, Janice R., et al. Modules for Basic Nursing Skills, 2 vols. 2nd ed. LC 79-89521. (Illus.). 1980. Vol. 1. pap. text ed. 10.00 (ISBN 0-395-28654-9); Vol. 2. pap. text ed. 9.50 (ISBN 0-395-28655-7). HM.
Ellis, John. The Sharp End. 1980. 17.95 (ISBN 0-684-16728-X, ScribT). Scribner.
Ellis, John, jt. auth. see Coward, Rosalind.
Ellis, John, intro. by. Screen Reader One: Cinema, Ideology, Politics. (Screen Ser.). 1977. pap. 15.00 (ISBN 0-900676-07-8). NY Zoetrope.
Ellis, Joseph & Moore, Robert. School for Soldiers: West Point & the Profession of Arms. LC 74-79638. (Illus.). 303p. 1976. pap. 5.95 (ISBN 0-19-502022-7, 454, GB). Oxford U Pr.
Ellis, Joseph A. Latin America: Its Peoples & Institutions. 2nd ed. 1975. pap. text ed. 8.25x (ISBN 0-02-474200-7, 47420). Macmillan.
Ellis, Joyce K., compiled by. Saved by a Broken Pole & Other Stories. 75p. (Orig.). (gr. 2-6). 1980. pap. 1.75 (ISBN 0-89323-007-3). BMA Pr.
Ellis, Julie. The Hampton Heritage. 1979. pap. 2.25 o.p. (ISBN 0-449-24131-9, Crest). Fawcett.
--The Magnolias. 272p. 1977. pap. 1.75 o.p. (ISBN 0-449-23131-3, Crest). Fawcett.
Ellis, Keith. Number Power. 1980. pap. 4.95 (ISBN 0-312-57989-6). St Martin.
Ellis, L. Ethan. Forty Million Schoolbooks Can't Be Wrong. LC 75-14227. (Illus.). 112p. (gr. 6 up). 1975. 8.95 (ISBN 0-02-733450-3, 73345). Macmillan.
--Republican Foreign Policy, 1921-1933. LC 68-20886. (Illus.). 1968. 25.00 (ISBN 0-8135-0574-7). Rutgers U Pr.
Ellis, Leigh. Tessa of Destiny. 1979. pap. 2.50 (ISBN 0-380-75028-7, 75028). Avon.
Ellis, Loudell, jt. auth. see Thacker, Ronald.
Ellis, Loudell, jt. auth. see Thacker, Ronald J.
Ellis, M. Casualty Officer's Handbook. 3rd ed. 1970. 13.95 o.p. (ISBN 0-407-13052-7). Butterworths.
Ellis, M. Leroy, ed. Prose Classique. LC 65-14565. 1966. pap. text ed. 10.95 (ISBN 0-471-00151-1). Wiley.
Ellis, Marc. A Year at the Catholic Worker. LC 78-61722. 1978. pap. 2.45 (ISBN 0-8091-2140-9). Paulist Pr.
Ellis, Maria deJ. Agriculture & the State in Ancient Mesopotamia: An Introduction to Problems of Land Tenure. (Occasional Publications of the Babylonian Fund: Vol. 1). 1976. 20.00 (ISBN 0-934718-28-8). Univ Mus of U PA.
Ellis, Maxwell, jt. auth. see Duke-Elder, Stewart.
Ellis, Mel. Ironhead. pap. 0.75 (ISBN 0-671-29540-3). PB.
Ellis, Michael D., ed. Dangerous Plants Snakes Anthropods & Marine Life-Toxicity & Treatment. LC 78-50198. 1978. 18.00 (ISBN 0-914768-32-8). Drug Intl Pubns.
Ellis, Norma, jt. auth. see Ellis, Charles.
Ellis, Norman R., ed. Aberrant Development in Infancy: Human & Animal Studies. LC 75-9657. 287p. 1975. 16.50 (ISBN 0-470-23859-3, Pub. by Wiley). Krieger.
Ellis, P. Berresford, ed. James Connolly: Selected Writings. LC 73-90071. 320p. 1974. 11.50 o.p. (ISBN 0-85345-326-8, CL-3628). Monthly Rev.
Ellis, Peter B. The Boyne Water: The Battle of the Boyne, 1690. LC 76-6753. 175p. 1976. text ed. 18.95x (ISBN 0-312-09415-9). St Martin.
Ellis, Phyllis T., jt. auth. see Ellis, Allen R.
Ellis, Richard. The Book of Whales. LC 80-7640. (Illus.). 224p. 1980. 25.00 (ISBN 0-394-50966-8). Knopf.
Ellis, Richard B. Statistical Inference: Basic Concepts. (Illus.). 272p. 1975. text ed. 15.95 (ISBN 0-13-844621-0). P-H.
Ellis, Richard N., ed. Western American Indian: Case Studies in Tribal History. LC 70-181597. xiv, 203p. 1972. 11.95x (ISBN 0-8032-0804-9); pap. 3.95x (ISBN 0-8032-5754-6, BB 548, Bison). U of Nebr Pr.
Ellis, Robert S. The Psychology of Individual Differences. 533p. 1980. Repr. of 1930 ed. lib. bdg. 45.00 (ISBN 0-89760-204-8). Telegraph Bks.
Ellis, Roland, ed. Inborn Errors of Metabolism. 112p. 1980. 30.00x (Pub. by Croom Helm England). State Mutual Bk.
Ellis, Rosemary. Motherhood: An up-to-Date Guide to Pregnancy & the Baby's First Nine Months. 1978. 6.50 o.p. (ISBN 0-214-20296-8, 8036, Dist. by Arco). Barrie & Jenkins.
Ellis, Viola. Teach Yourself Serbo-Croat Phrase Book. (Teach Yourself Ser). pap. 2.95 o.p. (ISBN 0-679-10196-9). McKay.
Ellis, William A. & Glasenapp, C. F. Life of Richard Wagner: Being an Authorized English Version of Das Leben Richard Wagner, Vol. 2. LC 77-2022. (Music Reprint Ser., 1977). 1977. Repr. of 1902 ed. lib. bdg. 37.50 (ISBN 0-306-70882-5). Da Capo.
--Life of Richard Wagner: Being an Authorized English Version of Das Leben Richard Wagner, Vol. 3. LC 77-2022. (Music Reprint Ser., 1977). 1977. Repr. of 1903 ed. lib. bdg. 37.50 (ISBN 0-306-70883-3). Da Capo.
--Life of Richard Wagner: Being an Authorized English Version of Das Leben Richard Wagner, Vol. 5. LC 77-2022. (Music Reprint Ser., 1977). 1977. Repr. of 1906 ed. lib. bdg. 37.50 (ISBN 0-306-70885-X). Da Capo.
Ellis, William A. & Glasenapp, C. P. Life of Richard Wagner: Being an Authorized English Version of Das Leben Richard Wagner, Vol. 6. LC 77-2022. (Music Reprint Ser). Repr. of 1908 ed. lib. bdg. 37.50 (ISBN 0-306-70886-8). Da Capo.
Ellis, William A. & Glassenapp, C. F. Being an Authorized English Version of Das Leben Richard Wagner, 6 vols. LC 77-2022. (Music Reprint Ser., 1977). 1977. Repr. of 1902 ed. lib. bdg. 37.50 ea.; 195.00 (ISBN 0-306-70887-6). Da Capo.
--Life of Richard Wagner: Being an Authorized English Version of das Leben Richard Wagner, Vol. 1. (Music Reprint Ser.: 1977). 1977. Repr. of 1902 ed. lib. bdg. 37.50 (ISBN 0-306-70881-7). Da Capo.
Ellis, William R., Jr., jt. ed. see Orleans, Peter.
Ellis, Willis D., ed. Source Book of Gestalt Psychology. 1967. text ed. 28.75x (ISBN 0-7100-6115-3). Humanities.
Ellison, A. P. & Stafford, E. M. The Dynamics of the Civil Aviation Industry. 1974. 23.95 (ISBN 0-347-01019-9, 91249-2, Pub. by Saxon Hse England). Lexington Bks.
Ellison, Craig W. Loneliness. LC 79-55681. 1980. 8.95 (ISBN 0-915684-57-8). Christian Herald.
Ellison, Glenn R. More Tales from Slim Ellison. 1981. 17.50 (ISBN 0-8165-0715-5); pap. 9.50 (ISBN 0-8165-0681-7). U of Ariz Pr.
Ellison, H. J. The Mystery of Israel: Has God Cast Away His People? 3rd ed. 1976. pap. 3.50 (ISBN 0-85364-169-2). Attic Pr.
Ellison, Harlan. Approaching Oblivion: Road Signs on the Treadmill Toward Tomorrow. LC 73-147791. 1974. 8.95 o.s.i. (ISBN 0-8027-5541-0). Walker & Co.
--Deathbird Stories. LC 73-18663. 352p. (YA) 1975. 12.50 o.s.i. (ISBN 0-06-011176-3, HarpT). Har-Row.
--The Glass Teat. 1975. pap. 1.50 o.s.i. (ISBN 0-515-03701-X, V3701). Jove Pubns.
--Memos from Purgatory. 1975. pap. 1.50 o.s.i. (ISBN 0-515-03706-0, V3706). Jove Pubns.
--Paingod & Other Delusions. 1975. pap. 1.50 o.s.i. (ISBN 0-515-03646-3, V3646). Jove Pubns.
--Spider Kiss. 1975. pap. 1.50 o.s.i. (ISBN 0-515-03883-0). Jove Pubns.
--Strange Wine. 1979. pap. 2.50 (ISBN 0-446-91946-2). Warner Bks.
--Strange Wine: Fifteen New Stories from the Nightside of the World. LC 77-89060. 1978. 9.95 o.s.i. (ISBN 0-06-011113-5, HarpT). Har-Row.
Ellison, Jerome. The Club of Life. LC 80-18444. 1980. pap. 7.95 (ISBN 0-8298-0410-2). Pilgrim NY.
Ellison, Joseph. California & the Nation, Eighteen Fifty to Eighteen Sixty-Nine. LC 78-87529. (American Scene Ser.). 1969. Repr. of 1927 ed. lib. bdg. 25.00 (ISBN 0-306-71443-4). Da Capo.
Ellison, Lucille W. Northwestern Univ., Transportation Center. (Illus.). 144p. (gr. 4-6). 1981. 8.95 (ISBN 0-684-16875-8). Scribner.
Ellison, Lynne. Green Bronze Mirror. LC 75-89663. Date not set. 4.95 (ISBN 0-8149-0709-1). Vanguard. Postponed.
Ellison, Neil M., jt. ed. see Newell, Guy R.
Ellison, S. P., Jr Sulfur in Texas. (Illus.). 1971. 2.00 (HB 2). Bur Econ Geology.
Ellison, Slim. Cowboys Under the Mogollon Rim. LC 68-9337. (Illus.). 240p. 1968. pap. 9.50 (ISBN 0-8165-0642-6). U of Ariz Pr.
Ellison, Stanley A. Divorce & Remarriage in the Church. 160p. 1980. pap. 3.95 (ISBN 0-310-35561-3). Zondervan.
Ellison, Thomas. Cotton Trade of Great Britain. LC 68-20034. Repr. of 1886 ed. 16.50x (ISBN 0-678-05044-9). Kelley.
Ellison, William H. A Self-Governing Dominion: California, 1849-1860. (Library Reprint Ser.: Vol. 95). 1978. 18.50x (ISBN 0-520-03713-8). U of Cal Pr.
Elliston, Frederick, jt. ed. see Baker, Robert.
Elliston, Frederick A., jt. ed. see McCormick, Peter.
Elliston, Frederick A., jt. ed. see Silverman, Hugh J.
Elliston, P., ed. Photography. (Fundamentals of Senior Physics Ser.). 1979. pap. text ed. 7.95x (ISBN 0-686-65410-2). Heinemann Ed.
Ellman, M. Planning Problems in the USSR: The Contribution of Mathematical Economics to Their Solution, 1960-1971. LC 73-75861. (Department of Applied Economics Monographs: No. 24). (Illus.). 240p. 1973. 35.50 (ISBN 0-521-20249-3). Cambridge U Pr.
--Socialist Planning. LC 78-57757. (Modern Cambridge Economics Ser.). 1979. 44.50 (ISBN 0-521-22229-X); pap. 11.95x (ISBN 0-521-29409-6). Cambridge U Pr.
Ellman, Michael. Soviet Planning Today, Proposals for an Optimally Functioning Economic System. LC 72-145613. (Department of Applied Economics, Occasional Papers: No. 25). (Illus.). 1971. 23.95 (ISBN 0-521-08156-4); pap. 10.95x (ISBN 0-521-09648-0). Cambridge U Pr.
Ellman, Richard, ed. Edwardians & Late Victorians. LC 60-13103. 1960. 15.00x (ISBN 0-231-02418-5). Columbia U Pr.
Ellmann, Richard. The Consciousness of Joyce. 160p. 1981. pap. 3.95 (ISBN 0-19-502898-8, GB 636, OPB). Oxford U Pr.
--Golden Codgers: Biographical Speculations. LC 73-86067. 208p. 1976. pap. 4.95 (ISBN 0-19-519845-X, 465, GB). Oxford U Pr.
Ellmann, Richard, ed. Artist As Critic: Critical Writings of Oscar Wilde. LC 69-16431. 1969. 10.00 o.p. (ISBN 0-394-41553-1). Random.
--The New Oxford Book of American Verse. LC 75-46354. 1976. 19.95 (ISBN 0-19-502058-8); deluxe ed. 65.00 leatherbound (ISBN 0-19-502194-0). Oxford U Pr.
Ellmer, R. E. Mechanism of Consolidated Accounts: Accounting for Holding Companies. 1974. 17.95x (ISBN 0-434-90530-5). Intl Ideas.
Ellner, Carolyn L. & Barnes, B. J. Schoolmaking: An Alternative in Teacher Education. LC 77-2679. 1977. 19.95 (ISBN 0-669-01626-8). Lexington Bks.
Ells, M., jt. auth. see Hart, A. W.
Ellsworth, Daisy. What Did You Bring? (Sesame Street Early Bird Bk). (Illus.). 32p. (ps). 1981. 3.50 (ISBN 0-307-11603-4, Golden Pr). Western Pub.
Ellsworth, J. W. & Stahnke, A. A. Politics & Political Systems. 1976. text ed. 14.95x (ISBN 0-07-019250-2, C); instructor's manual 3.95 (ISBN 0-07-019251-0). McGraw.
Ellsworth, Leon W., jt. auth. see Burrill, Claude W.
Ellsworth, Liz. Frederick Wiseman: A Guide to References & Resources. (Reference Bks.). 1979. lib. bdg. 24.95 (ISBN 0-8161-8066-0). G K Hall.
Ellsworth, Ralph E. Ellsworth on Ellsworth. LC 80-12656. 171p. 1980. 10.00 (ISBN 0-8108-1311-4). Scarecrow.
--Planning Manual for Academic Library Buildings. LC 73-14896. (Illus.). 1973. 8.00 o.p. (ISBN 0-8108-0680-0). Scarecrow.
Ellsworth, Richard G., jt. auth. see Ellsworth, Sterling G.
Ellsworth, S. George. Dear Ellen: Two Mormon Women & Their Letters. (Utah, the Mormons, & the West: No. 3). 1974. 12.00 (ISBN 0-87480-159-1, Tanner). U of Utah Pr.
--Utah's Heritage. LC 72-85712. (Illus.). 350p. (gr. 7-12). 1977. text ed. 15.00 (ISBN 0-87905-006-3). Peregrine Smith.
Ellsworth, Sterling G. & Ellsworth, Richard G. Getting to Know the Real You. LC 80-69724. 162p. 1980. 6.95 (ISBN 0-87747-840-6). Deseret Bk.
Ellul, Jacques. Apocalypse: The Book of Revelation. 1977. 10.95 (ISBN 0-8164-0330-9). Crossroad NY.
--False Presence of the Kingdom. 4.95 (ISBN 0-8164-0235-3). Crossroad NY.
--Hope in Time of Abandonment. 1978. pap. 4.95 (ISBN 0-8164-2138-2). Crossroad NY.
--The New Demons. 320p. (Eng.). 1975. 9.95 (ISBN 0-8164-0266-3). Crossroad NY.
--Prayer & Modern Man. Hopkins, C. Edward, tr. from Fr. 192p. 1973. pap. 3.95 (ISBN 0-8164-2081-5). Crossroad NY.
--Presence of the Kingdom. 1967. pap. 3.95 (ISBN 0-8164-2058-0, SP41). Crossroad NY.
--Technological Society. 1967. pap. 3.95 (ISBN 0-394-70390-1, V390, Vin). Random.
--The Technological System. 384p. 1980. 19.50 (ISBN 0-8164-9007-4). Continuum.
Ellul, Jacques, et al. Jacques Ellul: Interpretive Essays. Christians, Clifford G. & Van Hook, Jay M., eds. LC 80-12342. 340p. 1981. 24.95 (ISBN 0-252-00812-X). U of Ill Pr.
Ellwanger, George. Pleasures of the Table. LC 70-82031. 1969. Repr. of 1902 ed. 20.00 (ISBN 0-8103-3560-3). Gale.
Ellwanger, Rico. Tennis: Up to Tournament Standard. (Sports Library). (Illus.). 1979. 12.95 (ISBN 0-8069-9152-6); pap. 6.95 (ISBN 0-8069-9154-2). Sterling.
Ellwood, Caroline. Adult Learning Today: A New Role for the Universities. LC 75-38420. (Sage Studies in Social & Educational Change: Vol. 4). 1977. 18.00x (ISBN 0-8039-9979-8); pap. 9.95x (ISBN 0-8039-9853-8). Sage.
Ellwood, Robert S., Jr. Alternative Altars: Unconventional & Eastern Spirituality in America. LC 78-15089. xvi, 192p. 1981. pap. 5.50 (ISBN 0-226-20620-3). U of Chicago Pr.
--An Invitation to Japanese Civilization. (Illus.). 1980. pap. text ed. 6.95 (ISBN 0-87872-237-8). Duxbury Pr.
--Many People, Many Faiths: An Introduction to the Religious Life of Mankind. (Illus.). 400p. 1976. ref. ed. 16.95x (ISBN 0-13-555995-2). P-H.
--Religious & Spiritual Groups in Modern America. 352p. 1973. pap. 10.95 (ISBN 0-13-773309-7). P-H.
--Words of the World's Religion. 1977. pap. text ed. 11.95x (ISBN 0-13-965004-0). P-H.
Ellwood, Robert S., Jr. & Bashford, James W. Mysticism & Religion. 1980. text ed. 10.95 (ISBN 0-13-608810-4); pap. text ed. 7.95 (ISBN 0-13-608802-3). P-H.
Ellwood, Robert S., Jr., ed. Readings on Religion: From Inside & Outside. 1978. pap. text ed. 12.95 (ISBN 0-13-760942-6). P-H.
Elmaghraby, F. E. Activity Networks: Project Planning & Control by Network Models. LC 77-9501. 443p. 1977. 37.95 (ISBN 0-471-23869-4, Pub. by Wiley-Interscience). Wiley.
Elmaghraby, Salah E., jt. ed. see Moder, Joseph J.
El Mallakh, Kamal & Bianchi, Robert S. Treasures of the Nile. LaFarge, Henry A., ed. LC 80-80044. (Illus.). 176p. 1980. 19.95 (ISBN 0-88225-293-3). Newsweek.
El Mallakh, Ragaei. Kuwait: Trade & Investment. (Special Studies in International Economics & Business). 1979. lib. bdg. 32.50x (ISBN 0-89158-375-0). Westview.
El-Mallakh, Ragaei, et al. Capital Investment in the Middle East: The Use of Surplus Funds for Regional Development. LC 77-7806. (Praeger Special Studies). 1977. text ed. 25.95 (ISBN 0-03-021986-8). Praeger.
Elman, Richard. Cocktails at Somoza's: A Reporter's Sketchbook of Events in Revolutionary Nicaragua. 196p. 1981. 10.95 (ISBN 0-918222-28-1). Apple Wood.
Elman, Robert. The Atlantic Flyway. (Illus.). 280p. 1980. 24.95 (ISBN 0-87691-329-X). Winchester Pr.
--The Hiker's Bible. LC 74-175411. 160p. 1973. pap. 2.50 o.p. (ISBN 0-385-04551-4). Doubleday.
--Hunting America's Game Animals & Birds. (Illus.). 384p. 1980. 12.95 (ISBN 0-87691-172-6). Winchester Pr.
Elman, Robert, ed. The Complete Book of Hunting. (Illus.). 320p. 1981. 49.95 (ISBN 0-89659-174-3); pap. 16.95 (ISBN 0-89659-150-6). Abbeville Pr.
Elmer, June A. Scout of Santa Fe. (Illus.). 1981. 8.95 (ISBN 0-8062-1677-8). Carlton.
Elmer, Lucille A., jt. auth. see Strand, Marcella M.
Elmer, Minnie, jt. auth. see Duckles, Vincent.
Elmer, William B. The Optical Design of Reflectors. 2nd ed. LC 79-14206. (Wiley Ser. in Pure & Applied Optics). 1980. 27.95 (ISBN 0-471-05310-4, Pub. by Wiley-Interscience). Wiley.
--The Optical Design of Reflectors: Condensed Extracts of Book for Engineer's Manuals & Technical Classrooms. (Illus.). 1977. pap. 3.30x (ISBN 0-9601028-2-5). Elmer.
Elmhurst, Ernest F. The World Hoax. 233p. 1976. pap. 4.50x (ISBN 0-911038-81-7). Noontide.
Elmont, Nancy. The Four Seasons Cookbook. 1981. 11.95 (ISBN 0-916752-47-X). Green Hill.
--The Four Seasons Cookbook. LC 80-70101. (Illus.). 144p. 1981. 8.95 (ISBN 0-916752-47-X). Dorison Hse.
--A Knife for All Seasons. (Illus.). 160p. 1980. 8.95 (ISBN 0-916752-48-8). Dorison Hse.
Elmore, D. T. Peptides & Proteins. LC 68-21392. (Cambridge Chemistry Texts Ser). (Illus.). 1968. 27.95 (ISBN 0-521-07107-0); pap. 8.95x (ISBN 0-521-09535-2). Cambridge U Pr.
Elmore, Patricia. Susannah & the Blue House Mystery. LC 79-20491. (Illus.). 176p. (gr. 4-7). 1980. PLB 9.95 (ISBN 0-525-40525-9). Dutton.
Elmsley, Kenneth, jt. auth. see Fraser, Maxwell.
Elmslie, Kenward. Motor Disturbance: "The Frank O'Hara Award Series". (A Full Court Rebound Bk.). 1978. 14.95 (ISBN 0-231-03612-4); pap. 6.00 (ISBN 0-231-03613-2). Full Court NY.

El-Najjar, Mahmoud Y. & McWilliams, K. Richard. Forensic Anthropology: The Structure, Morphology, & Variation of Human Bone & Dentition. (Illus.). 208p. 1978. 17.50 (ISBN 0-398-03648-9). C C Thomas.

Elon, Amos. Flight into Egypt. LC 79-6165. (Illus.). 264p. 1980. 10.95 (ISBN 0-385-15796-7). Doubleday.

Elonka, Stephen M. Standard Plant Operators' Manual. 2nd ed. (Illus.). 384p. 1975. 22.50 o.p. (ISBN 0-07-019296-0, P&RB). McGraw.

Elrod, J. W. Being & Existence in Kierkegaard's Pseudonymous Works. 1975. 16.50 (ISBN 0-691-07204-3). Princeton U Pr.

Elrod, John W. Kierkegaard & Christendom. LC 80-8547. 384p. 1981. 22.50x (ISBN 0-691-07261-2). Princeton U Pr.

Els, T. J. Van see Van Els, T. J.

Elsasser, Nan, et al. Las Mujeres: Conversations from an Hispanic Community. (Women's Lives - Women's Work Ser.). (Illus.). 192p. (gr. 11-12). 1981. 14.95 (ISBN 0-912670-84-3); pap. 4.95 (ISBN 0-912670-70-3). Feminist Pr.

Elsberg, John. The Price of Reindeer. (WEP Poetry Ser.: No. 2). 1979. pap. 1.50 (ISBN 0-917976-05-3). White Ewe.

Elsberg, Ted. Career Exploration: You & Your Future. LC 75-10352. (Illus.). 1975. 6.95 (ISBN 0-87005-145-8); wkbk. 3.50 (ISBN 0-87005-152-0). Fairchild.

Elsbree, Langdon, et al. The Heath Handbook of Composition. 10th ed. 448p. 1981. text ed. 8.95 (ISBN 0-669-03352-9); pap. text ed. 7.95 (ISBN 0-669-03353-7); instr's guide with tests avail. (ISBN 0-669-03356-1); wkbk. 4.95 (ISBN 0-669-03456-8). Heath.

Elsby, F. H. Marketing & the Sales Manager. 1969. 25.00 (ISBN 0-08-006537-6); pap. 13.25 (ISBN 0-08-006536-8). Pergamon.

--Marketing Cases. LC 70-122006. 1970. 25.00 (ISBN 0-08-015784-X); pap. text ed. 13.25 (ISBN 0-08-015783-1). Pergamon.

Elsdon, Ronald. Bent World. 200p. (Orig.). 1981. pap. 5.95 (ISBN 0-87784-834-3). Inter-Varsity.

Elsen, Albert E. Purposes of Art: An Introduction to the History & Appreciation of Art. 3rd ed. LC 77-171524. (Illus.). 488p. 1975. pap. text ed. 15.95x (ISBN 0-03-089708-4, HoltC). HR&W.

Elsgolc, L. E. Calculus of Variations. 1962. text ed. 6.90 o.p. (ISBN 0-08-009554-2). Pergamon.

El'sgol'c, L. E. Qualitative Methods in Mathematical Analysis. LC 64-16170. (Translations of Mathematical Monographs: Vol. 12). 1980. Repr. of 1968 ed. 27.60 (ISBN 0-8218-1562-8, MMONO-12). Am Math.

Elsgolts, L. E. & Norkin, S. B. Introduction to the Theory & Application of Differential Equations with Deviating Arguments. 1973. 31.50 (ISBN 0-12-237750-8). Acad Pr.

El'Shafie, M. & Klippel, C. H. Associated Congenital Anomalies. (Illus.). 200p. 1980. 35.00 (ISBN 0-683-02800-6). Williams & Wilkins.

El-Shafie, Mahmoud A., jt. ed. see Dorner, Peter.

El-Shakhs, Salah S., jt. ed. see Obudho, R. A.

El Shater, Safaa. The Novels of Mary Shelley. (Salzburg Studies in English Literature: Romantic Reassessment Ser.: No. 59). (Orig.). 1977. pap. text ed. 25.00x (ISBN 0-391-01372-6). Humanities.

El Shazly, Saad. The Crossing of the Suez. Benson, Susan, ed. (Illus.). 333p. 1980. 14.00 (ISBN 0-9604562-0-1, 80-67107). Am Mideast.

Elsheikh, Farouk, jt. auth. see Bain, G. S.

El-Sherbini, A A. Food Security Issues in the Arab Near East: A Report of the United Nations Economic Commission for Western Asia. LC 79-40254. (Illus.). 1979. 39.50 (ISBN 0-08-023447-X). Pergamon.

Elskamp, Karen E. & Munzert, Alfred W. Test Your Sex Appeal. LC 80-85277. (Test Yourself Ser.). 64p. 1981. pap. 3.95 (ISBN 0-671-42627-3). Monarch Pr.

Elskus, Albinas. Art of Painting on Glass. (Illus.). 152p. 1980. 17.95 (ISBN 0-684-16465-5, ScribT). Scribner.

Elsmere, Jane S. Justice Samuel Chase. (Illus.). 1981. 14.95 (ISBN 0-937174-00-9). Janevar Pub.

Elsom, J. Post-War British Theater. 1976. 18.00 (ISBN 0-7100-8350-5). Routledge & Kegan.

Elsom, John, ed. Postwar British Theatre Criticism. 224p. 1980. 25.00 (ISBN 0-7100-0535-0); pap. 14.95 (ISBN 0-7100-0536-9). Routledge & Kegan.

Elson, Louis C. Elson's Music Dictionary. LC 70-173097. xii, 306p. 1972. Repr. of 1905 ed. 20.00 (ISBN 0-8103-3268-X). Gale.

--European Reminiscences Musical & Otherwise. LC 72-125046. (Music Ser). (Illus.). 301p. 1972. Repr. of 1896 ed. lib. bdg. 29.50 (ISBN 0-306-70011-5). Da Capo.

--The National Music of America & Its Sources. LC 70-159950. (Illus.). 1975. Repr. of 1911 ed. 20.00 (ISBN 0-8103-4039-9). Gale.

Elson, Mark. Concepts of Programming Languages. LC 72-94972. (Illus.). 333p. 1973. text ed. 19.95 (ISBN 0-574-17922-4, 13-0922); instr's guide avail. (ISBN 0-574-17923-2, 13-0923). SRA.

Elson, Milton, jt. auth. see Fletcher, Paul F.

Elson, Robert. Prelude to War. (World War II Ser.). (Illus.). 1976. 12.95 (ISBN 0-8094-2450-9). Time-Life.

Elson, Robert, et al. Prelude to War. LC 76-10024. (World War II). (Illus.). (gr. 6 up). 1976. PLB 14.94 (ISBN 0-8094-2451-7, Pub by Time-Life). Silver.

Elson, Ruth M. Guardians of Tradition: American Schoolbooks of the Nineteenth Century. LC 64-17219. (Illus.). 1972. pap. 3.25x (ISBN 0-8032-5755-4, BB 553, Bison). U of Nebr Pr.

Elspass, Margy L. Tips & Notes for the Artist, Bk. 1. Elspass, Ralph W., ed. LC 79-93059. (Illus.). 100p. 1980. pap. 10.00 (ISBN 0-935798-00-5). RaMar.

Elspass, Ralph W., ed. see Elspass, Margy L.

Elstein, Max & Sparks, Richard. Intrauterine Contraception, Vol 1. Briggs, Michael, ed. (Annual Research Reviews Ser.). 1978. 12.00 (ISBN 0-88831-021-8). Eden Med Res.

Elster, H., ed. see Sladecek, Vladimir.

Elster, J. Ulysses & the Sirens. LC 78-15444. 1979. 26.95 (ISBN 0-521-22388-1). Cambridge U Pr.

Elstob, Eric. Sweden: A Political & Cultural History. (Illus.). 209p. 1979. 18.50x (ISBN 0-8476-6220-9). Rowman.

Elston, Arnold. String Quartet. (U. C. Publ. in Contemporary Music: Vol. 1.). (Illus.). 1967. pap. 12.50x (ISBN 0-520-00383-7). U of Cal Pr.

Eltherington, L. G., jt. auth. see Barnes, C. D.

Elting, Mary. Aircraft at Work. LC 64-14511. (Illus.). (gr. 4-6). 1964. PLB 5.49 (ISBN 0-8178-3522-9). Harvey.

--Spacecraft at Work. LC 66-10936. (At Work Ser). (Illus.). (gr. 3-6). 1966. PLB 5.39 (ISBN 0-8178-3632-2). Harvey.

--Trains at Work. LC 62-17252. (Illus.). (gr. 3-6). 1962. 5.35 o.p. (ISBN 0-8178-3391-9); PLB 5.39 (ISBN 0-8178-3392-7). Harvey.

Elting, Mary & Folsom, Michael. Q Is for Duck. (Illus.). 64p. (ps-1). 1980. 8.95 (ISBN 0-395-29437-1, Clarion); pap. 3.95 (ISBN 0-395-30062-2). HM.

Elting, Mary & Goodman, Ann. Dinosaur Mysteries. LC 79-55035. (Bronto Bks). (Illus.). 64p. (gr. 3-8). 1980. 4.95 (ISBN 0-448-13617-1); PLB 9.30 (ISBN 0-686-64320-8). Platt.

Eltis, W. A. Economic Growth: Analysis & Policy. (Orig.). 1966. text ed. 5.50x (ISBN 0-09-079462-1, Hutchinson U Lib); pap. text ed. 2.75x (ISBN 0-09-079463-X, Hutchinson U Lib). Humanities.

Elton, E. J. & Gruber, M. J. Portfolio Analysis a Practical Approach. LC 80-19517. 450p. 1981. text ed. 20.95 o.p. (ISBN 0-471-04690-6). Wiley.

Elton, Edwain J. & Gruber, Martin J. Finance As a Dynamic Process. (Foundations of Finance Ser.). (Illus.). 176p. 1975. ref. ed. 14.95 (ISBN 0-13-314690-1); pap. text ed. 10.95 (ISBN 0-13-314682-0). P-H.

Elton, G., ed. Annual Bibliography of British & Irish History: Publications of 1979, Vol. 5. 1981. text ed. 30.00x (ISBN 0-391-01774-8). Humanities.

Elton, G. R. Modern Historians on British History, 1584-1945: A Critical Bibliography, 1945-1969. LC 77-137677. 248p. 1971. 17.50x (ISBN 0-8014-0611-0). Cornell U Pr.

--Reform & Reformation: England, 1509-1558. LC 77-6464. (Harvard Paperback Ser.: No. 146, The New History of England). 1979. 18.50x (ISBN 0-674-75245-7); pap. 7.95x (ISBN 0-674-75248-1). Harvard U Pr.

--Studies in Tudor & Stuart Politics & Government: Papers & Reviews, 1946-1972, 2 vols. LC 73-79305. 700p. 1974. 60.00 set (ISBN 0-521-20388-0); Vol. 1. 41.95 (ISBN 0-521-20282-5); Vol. 2. 29.95 (ISBN 0-521-20288-4). Cambridge U Pr.

Elton, Geoffrey R. Policy & Police: The Enforcement of the Reformation in the Age of Cromwell. LC 79-172831. 400p. 1972. 41.95 (ISBN 0-521-08383-4). Cambridge U Pr.

--Reform & Renewal, Thomas Cromwell & the Common Weal. (Wiles Lectures, 1972). 230p. 1973. 29.50 (ISBN 0-521-20054-7); pap. 7.95x (ISBN 0-521-09809-2). Cambridge U Pr.

--Tudor Constitution: Documents & Commentary. (Orig.). 1960. 47.00 (ISBN 0-521-04891-5); pap. 15.95x (ISBN 0-521-09120-9, 120). Cambridge U Pr.

--Tudor Revolution in Government. 1959. 54.00 (ISBN 0-521-04892-3); pap. 15.95x (ISBN 0-521-09235-3, 235). Cambridge U Pr.

Elton, Geoffrey R., ed. Annual Bibliography of British & Irish History, 1975. 1976. text ed. 31.25x (ISBN 0-391-00619-3). Humanities.

Elton, Lord, ed. General Charles G. (Chinese) Gordan's Khartoum Journal. LC 63-13658. (Illus.). 1963. 6.00 (ISBN 0-8149-0110-7). Vanguard.

Elton, Oliver. A Survey of English Literature: Eighteen Thirty to Eighteen Eighty, 2 vols. (Vol. I 434 pp., Vol. II 432 pp.). 1980. Repr. of 1932 ed. Set. lib. bdg. 85.00 (ISBN 0-8492-0786-X). R West.

--Tennyson & Matthew Arnold. 96p. 1980. Repr. of 1924 ed. lib. bdg. 12.50 (ISBN 0-8492-4411-0). R West.

--Wordsworth. 96p. 1980. Repr. of 1924 ed. 15.00 (ISBN 0-8492-0788-6). R West.

Elton, William, ed. Aesthetics & Language. 1970. 24.00x (ISBN 0-631-04610-0, Pub. by Basil Blackwell). Biblio Dist.

Elton, Y. R., ed. see Loades, D. M.

Eltzbacher. Anarchism. 1970. 15.00 (ISBN 0-686-62261-8). Chips.

Elvander, Nile, jt. ed. see Heidenheimer, Arnold J.

Elvin, Charles N. Hand-Book of Mottoes: Borne by the Nobility, Gentry, Cities, Public Companies. LC 79-122638. (Illus.). 1971. Repr. of 1860 ed. 15.00 (ISBN 0-8103-3387-2). Gale.

Elvin, Lionel. The Place of Commonsense in Educational Thought. (Unwin Educational Books). 1977. text ed. 19.95x (ISBN 0-04-370078-0); pap. text ed. 8.95x (ISBN 0-04-370079-9). Allen Unwin.

Elvin, Mark. Pattern of the Chinese Past: A Social & Economic Interpretation. LC 72-78869. (Illus.). 346p. 1973. 15.00x (ISBN 0-8047-0826-6); pap. 5.95 (ISBN 0-8047-0876-2). Stanford U Pr.

Elving, P. J., jt. auth. see Kolthoff, I. M.

Elvstrom, Paul. Paul Elvstrom Explains the Yacht Racing Rules. rev. ed. 1981. 7.95 (ISBN 0-8286-0088-0). De Graff.

Elward, Margaret & Whiteway, Catherine E. Encyclopedia of Guinea Pigs. (Illus.). 224p. 1980. 9.95 (ISBN 0-87666-916-X, H-975). TFH Pubns.

Elwell. Two-Color New Phonics Workbooks. Incl. Bk. A. (gr. 1). pap. text ed. 3.96 (ISBN 0-87895-136-9); tchr's ed. 2.00 (ISBN 0-87895-135-0); Bk. B. (gr. 2). pap. text ed. 3.88 (ISBN 0-87895-223-3); teacher's ed 2.00 (ISBN 0-87895-228-4); Bk. C. (gr. 3). pap. text ed. 3.80 (ISBN 0-87895-320-5); teacher's ed 2.00 (ISBN 0-87895-322-1). (MCP Basic Program Ser.). 1976. Modern Curr.

Elwell, D. Man-Made Gemstones. LC 78-41291. 1979. 49.95 (ISBN 0-470-26606-6). Halsted Pr.

Elwell, D. & Pointen, A. J. Physics for Engineers & Scientists. 2nd ed. 1978. 52.95 o.p. (ISBN 0-470-99335-9). Halsted Pr.

Elwell, D. & Pointon, A. J. Physics for Engineers & Scientists. 2nd ed. LC 77-16193. 356p. 1979. pap. 19.95x (ISBN 0-470-26872-7). Halsted Pr.

Elwell, Dennis & Pamplin, Brian, eds. Progress in Crystal Growth & Characterization, Vol. 1. (Illus.). 248p. 1980. 112.50 (ISBN 0-08-026013-6). Pergamon.

Elwell, Edward H. Portland & Vicinity. (Illus.). 138p. 1975. pap. 4.95 (ISBN 0-9600612-3-1). Greater Portland.

Elwell, W. T. & Gidley, J. A. Atomic Absorption Spectrophotometry. 2nd ed. 1966. 18.00 (ISBN 0-08-012063-6). Pergamon.

Elwell, W. T. & Wood, D. F. Analytical Chemistry of Molybdenum & Tungsten. 292p. 1971. text ed. 55.00 (ISBN 0-08-016673-3). Pergamon.

Elwell-Sutton, L. P. Colloquial Persian. (Trubner's Colloquial Manuals). 1975. pap. 6.95 (ISBN 0-7100-8083-2). Routledge & Kegan.

--The Persian Metres. 200p. 1976. 44.50 (ISBN 0-521-21089-5). Cambridge U Pr.

Elwell-Sutton, L. P., tr. see Dashti, Ali.

Elwell-Sutton, Lawrence P. Elementary Persian Grammar. pap. 19.95 (ISBN 0-521-09206-X). Cambridge U Pr.

Elwes, R. H., tr. see Spinoza, Benedict.

Elwin, Malcolm. Lord Byron's Wife. (Illus.). 1974. Repr. of 1962 ed. text ed. 20.75x (ISBN 0-7195-3010-5). Humanities.

Elwood, Ann & Raht, John. Walking Out. Becker, Mark, ed. 176p. (gr. 7 up). 1979. pap. 1.50 (ISBN 0-448-17080-9, Tempo). G&D.

Elwood, Douglas J., ed. Asian Christian Theology: Emerging Themes. rev. ed. 1980. pap. write for info. (ISBN 0-664-24354-1). Westminster.

Elwood, J. Harold, jt. auth. see Elwood, J. Mark.

Elwood, J. Mark & Elwood, J. Harold. Epidemiology of Anencephalus & Spina Bifida. (Illus.). 424p. 1980. text ed. 69.50x (ISBN 0-19-261220-4). Oxford U Pr.

Elwood, Maren. Characters Make Your Story. 1973. text ed. 11.95 (ISBN 0-87116-080-3). Writer.

Elwood, Ralph C. see McNeal, Robert H.

Elwood, Roger. Continuum Four. 1976. pap. 0.95 o.p. (ISBN 0-425-03077-6, Medallion). Berkley Pub.

--Golden Paths. 1978. pap. 1.50 o.s.i. (ISBN 0-515-04499-7). Jove Pubns.

--Historias Extranas de Brujeria. Lockward, George, tr. from Eng. Orig. Title: Strange Things Are Happening. 112p. (Orig., Span.). 1974. pap. 1.50 (ISBN 0-89922-028-2). Edit Caribe.

--New Mind. 1973. 5.95 o.s.i. (ISBN 0-686-66933-9). Macmillan.

--New Mind, Vol. 2. 1973. pap. 1.50 o.s.i. (ISBN 0-02-019810-8, Collier). Macmillan.

--Salvation Behind Bars. 1977. pap. 1.50 (ISBN 0-505-51142-8). Tower Bks.

Elwood, Roger & Floren, Myron. Believing: Myron Floren & His Friends' Scrapbook. LC 80-50525. (Illus.). 208p. 1981. 14.95 (ISBN 0-87239-420-4, 5003). Standard Pub.

Elwood, Roger, ed. Children of Infinity: Original Science Fiction Stories for Young Readers. LC 72-8930. (Illus.). 192p. (gr. 6 up). 1973. PLB 5.88 o.p. (ISBN 0-531-02599-3). Watts.

--Continuum One. LC 73-87184. 192p. (YA) 1974. 5.95 o.p. (ISBN 0-399-11283-9, Dist. by Putnam). Berkley Pub.

--Continuum Three. LC 73-87184. 160p. (YA) 1974. 5.95 o.p. (ISBN 0-399-11322-3, Dist. by Putnam). Berkley Pub.

--Continuum Two. 1975. pap. 1.25 o.p. (ISBN 0-425-03127-6, Medallion). Berkley Pub.

--Crisis: Ten Original Stories of Science Fiction. LC 73-19901. 224p. (gr. 6 up). 1974. 7.95 o.p. (ISBN 0-525-66374-6). Elsevier-Nelson.

--The Other Side of Tomorrow. 1975. pap. 1.25 o.s.i. (ISBN 0-515-03937-3). Jove Pubns.

--Science Fiction Tales: Invaders, Creatures, & Alien Worlds. (Illus.). (gr. 5-9). 1973. pap. 2.50 (ISBN 0-528-87028-9). Rand.

--Survival from Infinity: Original Science Fiction Stories for Young Readers. LC 73-14696. (Illus.). 192p. (gr. 7 up). 1974. PLB 6.90 (ISBN 0-531-02666-3). Watts.

--Tomorrow's Alternatives. 192p. 1973. 5.95 o.s.i. (ISBN 0-686-66803-0). Macmillan.

--Tomorrow's Alternatives, Vol. 1. 192p. 1973. pap. 1.50 o.s.i. (ISBN 0-02-019800-0, Collier). Macmillan.

Elwood, Roger & Ghidalia, Vic, eds. Androids, Time Machines, & Blue Giraffes. 384p. 1973. 6.95 o.s.i. (ISBN 0-695-80369-7). Follett.

Elwood, Roger & Goldsmith, Howard, eds. Spine Chillers: Unforgettable Tales of Terror. LC 77-16887. (gr. 7 up). 1978. PLB 8.95 (ISBN 0-385-09722-0). Doubleday.

Elwood, Roger, jt. ed. see Silverberg, Robert.

Elworthy, Frederick. Evil Eye: The Origins & Practices of Superstition. (188 Ils). 1970. pap. 2.95 o.s.i. (ISBN 0-02-075980-0, Collier). Macmillan.

Ely, Alexandre. Erich's Sunrise. 176p. 1981. 7.50 (ISBN 0-682-49709-6). Exposition.

Ely, Carolanne. Love Wounds & Multiple Fractures: Poems. 1975. pap. 3.00 (ISBN 0-915342-02-2). SUN.

Ely, D. P., jt. auth. see Chisolm, M.

Ely, Donald P., jt. auth. see Gerlach, Vernon S.

Ely, Owen. Cat. 320p. 1980. cancelled 9.95 (ISBN 0-906071-50-X). Proteus Pub NY.

Elyot, Thomas. Four Political Treatises, 1533-1541. LC 67-10273. 1967. 44.00x (ISBN 0-8201-1015-9). Schol Facsimiles.

Elytis, Odysseus. The Axion Esti. Keeley, Edmund & Savidis, George, trs. from Gr. LC 79-49274. (Pitt Poetry Ser.). 1979. pap. 4.95 (ISBN 0-8229-5318-8). U of Pittsburgh Pr.

El-Zein, Abdul H. The Sacred Meadows: A Structural Analysis of Religious Symbolism in an East African Town. LC 73-91310. (Studies in African Religion). 1974. text ed. 19.95x o.s.i. (ISBN 0-8101-0443-1). Northwestern U Pr.

Elzinga, Paul. On a Research Program in Early Modern Physics. (Studies in the Theory of Science). 1972. text ed. 12.00x (ISBN 0-391-00245-7). Humanities.

Elzinga, Richard J. Fundamentals of Entomology. 2nd ed. (Illus.). 464p. 1981. text ed. 19.95 (ISBN 0-13-338194-3). P-H.

--Fundamentals of Entomology. (Illus.). 1978. ref. ed. 21.95x (ISBN 0-13-338186-2). P-H.

Emanuel, Elizabeth, jt. auth. see Thayer, Marjorie.

Emanuel, James A. Langston Hughes. (U. S. Authors Ser.: No. 123). 1967. lib. bdg. 9.95 (ISBN 0-8057-0388-8). Twayne.

Emanuel, James A. & Gross, Theodore L., eds. Dark Symphony: Negro Literature in America. LC 68-54984. 1968. 15.95 o.s.i. (ISBN 0-02-909550-6); pap. text ed. 9.95 (ISBN 0-02-909540-9). Free Pr.

Emanuel, N. M. & Evseenko, D. S. Clinical Oncology: A Quantitative Approach. Abramson, J. H., ed. Kaner, N., tr. from Rus. LC 73-16436. 272p. 1974. 45.95 (ISBN 0-470-23891-7). Halsted Pr.

Emanuel, N. M. & Knorre, D. G. Chemical Kinetics (Homogenous Reactions) Slutzkin, D., ed. Kondor, R., tr. from Rus. LC 73-12689. 413p. 1973. text ed. 34.95 (ISBN 0-470-23890-9). Halsted Pr.

Emanuel, N. M., et al. Oxidation of Organic Compounds: Solvent Effects in Radical Reactions. 350p. 1980. 58.01 (ISBN 0-08-022067-3). Pergamon.

Emanuel, W. D. Toda la Fotografia En un Solo Libro. Cuni, Antonio, tr. from Eng. 228p. (Span.). 1975. 7.95 (ISBN 0-240-51098-4, Pub. by Ediciones Spain). Focal Pr.

Emanuelsen, Kathy L. & Densmore, Mary J. Acute Respiratory Care. Percy, R. Craig, ed. (The Fleschner Series in Critical Care Nursing). (Illus.). 190p. (Orig.). 1981. pap. text ed. 9.95 (ISBN 0-937878-01-4). Fleschner.

Ember, C., jt. auth. see Ember, M.

Ember, Carol R. & Ember, Melvin. Anthropology. 3rd ed. (Illus.). 592p. 1981. text ed. 17.95 (ISBN 0-13-037002-9). P-H.

--Cultural Anthropology. 3rd ed. (Illus.). 416p. 1981. pap. text ed. 13.95 (ISBN 0-13-195230-7). P-H.

Ember, M. & Ember, C. Anthropology. 2nd ed. 1977. 17.95 (ISBN 0-13-036962-4); study guide & wkbk. 4.95 (ISBN 0-13-036970-5). P-H.

--Cultural Anthropology. 2nd ed. 1977. pap. text ed. 13.95 (ISBN 0-13-195198-X). P-H.

Ember, Melvin, jt. auth. see Ember, Carol R.

Emberley, Barbara. Drummer Hoff. (Illus.). (ps-1). 1967. PLB 8.95 (ISBN 0-13-220822-9); pap. 2.95 (ISBN 0-13-220855-5). P-H.

--Story of Paul Bunyan. (Illus.). (ps-3). 1963. PLB 4.95 o.p. (ISBN 0-13-850792-9); pap. 2.50 (ISBN 0-13-850784-8). P-H.

Emberley, Ed. Ed Emberley's Big Green Drawing Book. LC 79-16247. (Illus.). (gr. k up). 1979. 6.95 (ISBN 0-316-23595-4); pap. 4.95 (ISBN 0-316-23596-2). Little.

--Ed Emberley's Crazy Mixed-up Face Game. (Illus.). 32p. (gr. 1 up). 1981. 8.95 (ISBN 0-316-23420-6); pap. 4.95 (ISBN 0-316-23421-4). Little.

Emberlin, Diane D. Contributions of Women: Science. LC 76-30621. (Contributions of Women Ser.). (Illus.). (gr. 6 up). 1977. PLB 8.95 (ISBN 0-87518-136-8). Dillon.

Emberly, Ed. Ed Emberly's Big Orange Drawing Book. (Illus.). 96p. 1980. 8.95 (ISBN 0-316-23418-4); pap. 4.95 (ISBN 0-316-23419-2). Little.

Emberson, Frances G. Mark Twain's Vocabulary. 53p. 1980. Repr. of 1935 ed. lib. bdg. 12.50 (ISBN 0-89987-206-9). Darby Bks.

Emberton, Sybil. Garden Foliage for Flower Arrangement. (Illus.). 1968. 12.95 (ISBN 0-571-08512-1, Pub. by Faber & Faber). Merrimack Bk Serv.

Emberton, Sybil C. Multi-Season Shrubs & Trees. (Illus.). 1971. 9.95 o.p. (ISBN 0-571-08748-5, Pub. by Faber & Faber). Merrimack Bk Serv.

Embertson, Jane. Pods: Wildflowers & Weeds in Their Final Beauty. (Illus.). 1979. pap. 9.95 (ISBN 0-684-15543-5, SL 752, ScribT). Scribner.

Embery, Joan & Demong, Denise. My Wild World. 1980. 14.95 (ISBN 0-440-05742-6). Delacorte.

Embleston, C. & King, C. A. Glacial & Periglacial Morphology, 2 vols. 2nd ed. Incl. Vol. 1. Glacial Geomorphology. LC 75-14188. pap. 19.95 (ISBN 0-470-23893-3); Vol. 2. Periglacial Geomorphology. LC 75-14187. pap. 13.95 (ISBN 0-470-23895-X). 1975. Halsted Pr.

Embleton, Clifford & Thornes, John, eds. Process in Geomorphology. LC 79-18747. 436p. 1979. 47.95x (ISBN 0-470-26807-7); pap. 19.95x (ISBN 0-470-26808-5). Halsted Pr.

Embleton, Clifford, et al, eds. Geomorphology: Present Problems & Future Prospects. (Illus.). 1978. text ed. 29.95x (ISBN 0-19-874078-6). Oxford U Pr.

EMBO Workshop, Weizmann Institute of Science, Rehovot, Israel, 1980, et al. Platelets: Cellular Response Mechanisms & Their Biological Significance: Proceedings. 340p. 1980. 52.50 (ISBN 0-471-27896-3, Pub. by Wiley-Interscience). Wiley.

Emboden, William. Sarah Bernhardt. (Illus.). 176p. 1975. 12.95 o.s.i. (ISBN 0-02-535470-1). Macmillan.

Emboden, William A. Bizarre Plants: Magical, Monstrous, Mythical. LC 73-2749. (Illus.). 160p. 1974. 10.95 o.s.i. (ISBN 0-02-535460-4). Macmillan.

Embree, A. T., ed. see Ikram, S. M.

Embree, Ainslie T., jt. ed. see De Bary, William T.

Embree, Harland D. Introduction to the Chemistry of Life: Organic Chemistry. 1968. 9.50 (ISBN 0-201-01868-3). A-W.

Embree, Harland D. & Debey, Harold J. Introduction to the Chemistry of Life. 2nd ed. 1975. text ed. 16.95 (ISBN 0-201-01886-1). A-W.

Embree, T., jt. auth. see De Bary, William T.

Embry, J., tr. see Tournier, Paul.

Embse, Thomas J. Van Der see Murray, John V. & Van Der Embse, Thomas J.

Embury, David A. Fine Art of Mixing Drinks. rev. ed. LC 58-5572. 1948. pap. 3.50 (ISBN 0-385-09683-6, C177, Dolp). Doubleday.

Emcon Associates. Methane Generation & Recovery from Landfills. LC 80-67725. 139p. 1980. 14.95 (ISBN 0-250-40360-9). Ann Arbor Science.

Emde, Fritz, jt. auth. see Jahnke, Eugene.

Emden, Paul H. Regency Pageant. 295p. 1980. Repr. of 1936 ed. lib. bdg. 35.00 (ISBN 0-89987-204-2). Darby Bks.

Emecheta, Buchi. Nowhere to Play. (gr. 4-8). 1981. 6.95 (ISBN 0-8052-8058-8, Pub. by Allison & Busby England). Schocken.

Emeleus, H. J. & Sharpe, A. G. Modern Aspects of Inorganic Chemistry. 4th ed. LC 73-2577. 677p. 1973. text ed. 22.95 (ISBN 0-470-23902-6). Halsted Pr.

Emeleus, H. J. & Sharpe, A. G., eds. Advances in Inorganic Chemistry & Radiochemistry. Incl. Vol. 1. 1959. 52.50 (ISBN 0-12-023601-X); Vol. 2. 1960. 52.50 (ISBN 0-12-023602-8); Vol. 3. 1961. 52.50 (ISBN 0-12-023603-6); Vol. 4. 1962. 52.50 (ISBN 0-12-023604-4); Vol. 5. 1963. 52.50 (ISBN 0-12-023605-2); Vol. 6. 1964. 52.50 (ISBN 0-12-023606-0); Vol. 7. 1965. 52.50 (ISBN 0-12-023607-9); Vol. 8. 1966. 52.50 (ISBN 0-12-023608-7); Vol. 9. 1966. 52.50 (ISBN 0-12-023609-5); Vol. 10. 1968. 52.50 (ISBN 0-12-023610-9); Vol. 11. 1968. 52.50 (ISBN 0-12-023611-7); Vol. 12. 1970. 49.25 (ISBN 0-12-023612-5); Vol. 13. 1970. 49.25 (ISBN 0-12-023613-3); Vol. 14. 1972. 49.25 (ISBN 0-12-023614-1); Vol. 15. 1972. 49.25 (ISBN 0-12-023615-X); Vol. 16. 1974. 47.00 (ISBN 0-12-023616-8); Vol. 20. 1977. 47.00 (ISBN 0-12-023620-6); lib ed. 60.25 (ISBN 0-12-023680-X); microfiche 34.00 (ISBN 0-12-023681-8); Vol. 21. 1978. 37.00 (ISBN 0-12-023621-4); lib ed. 47.50 (ISBN 0-12-023682-6); microfiche 27.00 (ISBN 0-12-023683-4); Vol. 22. 1979. **51.50 (ISBN 0-12-023622-2); lib. ed. 65.50 (ISBN 0-12-023684-2); microfiche 36.50 (ISBN 0-12-023685-0). Acad Pr.**

--Advances in Inorganic Chemistry & Radiochemistry, Vol. 23. 1980. 51.00 (ISBN 0-12-023623-0); lib. ed. 66.50 (ISBN 0-12-023686-9); microfilm ed. 35.75 (ISBN 0-12-023687-7). Acad Pr.

--Advances in Inorganic Chemistry & Radiochemistry, Vol. 24. (Serial Publication Ser.). 1981. write for info. (ISBN 0-12-023624-9). Acad Pr.

Emelity, L. A. Operation & Control of Ion-Exchange Processes for Treatment of Radioactive Wastes. 1967. pap. 6.50 (ISBN 92-0-125067-3, IAEA). Unipub.

Emeljanow, Victor, ed. Chekhov: The Critical Heritage. (The Critical Heritage Ser.). 496p. 1981. 50.00 (ISBN 0-7100-0374-9). Routledge & Kegan.

Emeneau, Murray B., jt. auth. see Burrow, Thomas.

Emeneau, Murray Barnson. Toda Songs. 1052p. 1971. 39.50x (ISBN 0-19-815129-2). Oxford U Pr.

Emenegger, Robert. UFO's Past, Present & Future. Date not set. pap. 2.50 (ISBN 0-345-29047-X). Ballantine.

Emenheiser, Daniel A. Professional Discotheque Management. LC 80-20910. 256p. 1980. text ed. 16.95 (ISBN 0-8436-0768-8). CBI Pub.

--Professional Discotheque Management. 1980. 15.95 o.p. (ISBN 0-8436-0768-8). CBI Pub.

Emerick, Lon. ALD - a New Test for Aphasia. 27.00 (ISBN 0-686-69371-X). Northern Mich.

Emerick, Lon L. A Casebook of Diagnosis & Evaluation in Speech Pathology. (Illus.). 224p. 1981. pap. text ed. 11.95 (ISBN 0-13-117358-8). P-H.

Emerick, Lon L. & Hood, Stephen B., eds. The Client-Clinician Relationship: Essays on Interpersonal Sensitivity in the Therapeutic Transaction. (Illus.). 128p. 1974. 12.75 (ISBN 0-398-03016-2). C C Thomas.

Emerson, Caryl, tr. see Bakhtin, M. M.

Emerson, Dorothy. Among the Mescalero Apaches: The Story of Father Albert Braun, O. F. M. LC 73-76302. 1980. pap. 8.50 (ISBN 0-8165-0714-7). U of Ariz Pr.

Emerson, Edward W. Emerson in Concord. LC 79-78149. (Library of Lives & Letters). (Illus.). 1970. Repr. of 1889 ed. 18.00 (ISBN 0-8103-3601-4). Gale.

Emerson, Everett. Puritanism in America. (World Leaders Ser.: No. 71). 1977. lib. bdg. 9.95 (ISBN 0-8057-7692-3). Twayne.

Emerson, Everett, ed. American Literature, Seventeen Sixty-Four to Seventeen Eighty-Nine: The Revolutionary Years. 1977. 20.00 (ISBN 0-299-07270-3). U of Wis Pr.

Emerson, Everett H. Captain John Smith. (U. S. Authors Ser.: No. 177). lib. bdg. 10.95 (ISBN 0-8057-0676-3). Twayne.

Emerson, Everett H., ed. Major Writers of Early American Literature: Introductions to Nine Major Writers. LC 72-1378. 312p. 1972. 25.00x (ISBN 0-299-06190-6); pap. 8.50 (ISBN 0-299-06194-9). U of Wis Pr.

Emerson, Lloyd & Paquette, Laurence. Fundamental Mathematics for the Management & Social Sciences. alt. ed. 688p. 1981. text ed. 22.00 (ISBN 0-205-07166-X, 567166-3); tchrs. ed. avail. (ISBN 0-205-07169-4). Allyn.

Emerson, Lloyd & Paquette, Lawrence. Fundamental Mathematics for the Management & Social Sciences. 2nd ed. 1978. text ed. 22.00 (ISBN 0-205-06000-5); instr's man. avail. (ISBN 0-205-06001-3); student study guide 7.50 (ISBN 0-205-06002-1). Allyn.

Emerson, M. Jarvin & Lamphear, F. Charles. Urban & Regional Economics: Structure & Change. 375p. 1975. text ed. 15.95x o.p. (ISBN 0-205-04694-0). Allyn.

Emerson, Oliver F. History of the English Language. LC 70-145520. 1971. Repr. of 1909 ed. 26.00 (ISBN 0-8103-3666-9). Gale.

Emerson, Peter, ed. Thoracic Medicine. 1981. text ed. price not set (ISBN 0-407-00210-3). Butterworth.

Emerson, Ralph W. Emerson's Essays: First & Second Series Complete. (Apollo Eds.). (YA) (gr. 9-12). pap. 4.95 (ISBN 0-8152-0001-3, A1, TYC-T). T Y Crowell.

--Essays of Emerson. Spiller, Robert E., ed. pap. 2.50 (ISBN 0-671-44900-1). WSP.

Emerson, Ralph W. & Carlyle, Thomas. Correspondence of Emerson & Carlyle. Slater, Joseph, ed. LC 63-17539. 1964. 22.50x (ISBN 0-231-02462-2). Columbia U Pr.

Emerson, Robert, jt. auth. see Grumbach, Jane.

Emerson, Robert M. Judging Delinquents: Context & Process in Juvenile Court. LC 70-75047. (Law in Action Ser). 1969. 17.95x (ISBN 0-202-23001-5). Aldine Pub.

Emerson, Rupert. State & Sovereignty in Modern Germany. LC 79-1626. 1981. Repr. of 1928 ed. 22.50 (ISBN 0-88355-931-5). Hyperion Conn.

Emerson, Sally. Second Sight of Jennifer Hamilton. LC 80-1722. 312p. 1981. 11.95 (ISBN 0-385-15815-7). Doubleday.

Emerson, W. A., jt. auth. see Irwin, James B., Jr.

Emerson, William M. Tennessee Supplement for Modern Real Estate Practice. 130p. (Orig.). 1981. pap. 7.95 (ISBN 0-88462-338-6). Real Estate Ed Co.

Emerton, J. A., ed. Prophecy: Essays Presented to Georg Fohrer on His Sixty-Fifth Birthday. (Beihefte zur Zeitschrift fur Die Alttest Amentliche Wissenschaft: No. 155). 240p. 1980. text ed. 61.50x (ISBN 3-11-007761-2). De Gruyter.

Emery. Modern Trends in Human Genetics, Vol. 2. 1975. 54.95 (ISBN 0-407-00028-3). Butterworths.

Emery, jt. auth. see Crosby.

Emery, Anne. Dinny Gordon: Sophomore. (gr. 7-10). pap. 0.95 o.p. (ISBN 0-425-03028-8, Highland). Berkley Pub.

Emery, Ashley F. see Heat Transfer & Fluid Mechanics Institute.

Emery, David, jt. auth. see Seaton, Paul.

Emery, Edwin & Emery, Michael. The Press & America. 4th ed. (Illus.). 1978. ref. 19.95 (ISBN 0-13-697979-3). P-H.

Emery, Frederic B. Violin Concerto. LC 75-93979. (Music Ser). 1969. Repr. of 1928 ed. lib. bdg. 45.00 (ISBN 0-306-71822-7). Da Capo.

Emery, Gary. Defeating Depression. 12.95 (ISBN 0-671-24866-9). S&S.

Emery, James C. Planning for Computing in Higher Education. (EDUCOM Ser. in Computing & Telecommunications in Higher Education: No. 5). 218p. 1980. lib. bdg. 25.00x (ISBN 0-86531-025-4). Westview.

Emery, James C. see Bernard, Dan, et al.

Emery, James C., ed. see EDUCOM Fall Conference, Oct. 1977.

Emery, Jared M. & Jacobson, Adrienne C. Current Concepts in Cataract Surgery: Selected Proceedings of the Sixth Biennial Cataract Surgical & Intraocular Lens Congress. LC 80-24694. (Illus.). 466p. 1980. text ed. 64.50 (ISBN 0-8016-1527-5). Mosby.

Emery, Jared M. & Little, James H. Phacoemulsification & Aspiration of Cataracts: Surgical Techniques, Complications & Results. LC 79-13047. 1979. text ed. 45.00 (ISBN 0-8016-3028-2). Mosby.

Emery, Jared M., ed. Current Concepts in Cataract Surgery: Selected Proceedings of the Fifth Biennial Cataract Surgical Congress. 5th ed. LC 78-23408. (Illus.). 1978. text ed. 66.50 (ISBN 0-8016-1524-0). Mosby.

Emery, Joy S. Stage Costume Techniques. (Ser. in Theatre & Drama). (Illus.). 368p. 1981. 18.95 (ISBN 0-13-840330-9). P-H.

Emery, K. O. & Skinner, Brian J. Mineral Deposits of the Deep-Ocean Floor. LC 78-59181. 1978. pap. 4.95x (ISBN 0-8448-1363-X). Crane-Russak Co.

Emery, Laura. George Eliot's Creative Conflict: The Other Side of Silence. LC 75-3768. 1976. 15.75x (ISBN 0-520-02979-8). U of Cal Pr.

Emery, Lucilius A. Concerning Justice. 1914. 22.50x (ISBN 0-685-69818-1). Elliots Bks.

Emery, Michael, jt. auth. see Emery, Edwin.

Emery, Richard D., jt. auth. see Ennis, Bruce J.

Emery, S. I. Bible Answers. 1.95 o.p. (ISBN 0-686-12850-8). Schmul Pub Co.

Emery, Stewart. Actualizations: You Don't Have to Rehearse to Be Yourself. Rogin, Neal, ed. 222p. 1980. Repr. of 1978 ed. 14.95 (ISBN 0-8290-0222-7). Irvington.

--Actualizations: You Don't Have to Rehearse to Be Yourself. LC 77-76276. 1978. pap. 5.95 (ISBN 0-385-13122-4, Dolp). Doubleday.

Emery, William. Culinary Design & Decoration. 135p. 1980. 26.95 (ISBN 0-8436-2187-7). CBI Pub.

Emig, Jane, ed. see Domjan, Evelyn A.

Emig, Jane, ed. see Domjan, Joseph & Domjan, Evelyn A.

Emiliani, Cesare. The Oceanic Lithosphere. LC 62-18366. (The Sea: Ideas & Observations on Progress in the Study of the Seas: Vol. 7). 1712p. 1981. 55.00 (ISBN 0-471-02870-3, Pub. by Wiley-Interscience). Wiley.

Emlen, J. Merritt. Ecology: An Evolutionary Approach. LC 71-172805. 1973. text ed. 19.95 (ISBN 0-201-01894-2). A-W.

Emley, E. F. Principles of Magnesium Technology. 1966. 110.00 o.p. (ISBN 0-08-010673-0). Pergamon.

Emlyn-Jones, C. J. The Ionians & Hellenism: A Study of the Cultural Achievement of the Early Greek Inhabitants of Asia Minor. (States & Cities of Ancient Greece Ser.). (Illus.). 256p. 1980. 30.00 (ISBN 0-7100-0470-2). Routledge & Kegan.

Emmanuel, Arghiri. Unequal Exchange: A Study of the Imperialism of Trade. Pearce, Brian, tr. from Fr. LC 78-158920. (Illus.). 1972. 16.50 o.p. (ISBN 0-85345-152-4, CL-1524); pap. 6.95 (ISBN 0-85345-188-5, PB-1885). Monthly Rev.

Emme, Eugene M., ed. Twenty-Five Years of the American Astronautical Society, Historical Reflections & Projections. (AAS History Ser.: Vol. 2). (Illus.). 248p. 1980. lib. bdg. 25.00x (ISBN 0-87703-117-7); pap. 15.00x (ISBN 0-87703-118-5). Univelt Inc.

--Two Hundred Years of Flight in America. (AAS History Ser.: Vol. 1). (Illus.). 1979. softcover 20.00 (ISBN 0-87703-101-0); lib. bdg. 30.00 (ISBN 0-87703-091-X). Am Astronaut.

--Two Hundred Years of Flight in America. 2nd ed. (AAS History Ser.: Vol. 1). (Illus.). 1977. lib. bdg. 30.00x (ISBN 0-87703-091-X); soft cover 20.00 (ISBN 0-87703-101-0). Univelt Inc.

Emmelin, N. & Zotterman, Yngve. Oral Physiology. 311p. 1972. text ed. 75.00 (ISBN 0-08-016972-4). Pergamon.

Emmelin, N., jt. ed. see Holton, Pamela.

Emmelot, P., ed. see International Conference on Environmental Carcinogensis, Amsterdam, May 1979.

Emmens, C. W. & Axelrod, Herbert. Catfishes for the Advanced Hobbyist. pap. 4.95 (ISBN 0-87666-758-2, PS650). TFH Pubns.

Emmens, Carol A. Famous People on Film. LC 77-3449. 1977. 16.50 (ISBN 0-8108-1051-4). Scarecrow.

--Short Stories on Film. LC 78-13488. 1978. lib. bdg. 25.00x (ISBN 0-87287-146-0). Libs Unl.

Emmens, Carol A. & Maglione, Harry, eds. An Audio-Visual Guide to American Holidays. LC 78-6230. 1978. lib. bdg. 13.50 (ISBN 0-8108-1140-5). Scarecrow.

Emmens, Clifford W. Keep Tropical Fish. (Illus.). (YA) (gr. 7-10). 6.95 (ISBN 0-87666-091-X, H910). TFH Pubns.

Emmer, Rae. Using a Dictionary. Hasinbiller, Dolly, ed. Incl. Book C. Purcell, Darryle & Moore, Madeleine, illus. tchr's ed (ISBN 0-8372-3510-3); Book D. Christianson, David, illus. tchr's ed. (ISBN 0-8372-9201-8) (ISBN 0-8372-3511-1); Book E. Purcell, Darryle, illus. (ISBN 0-8372-3512-X); tchr's ed. (ISBN 0-8372-9202-6); Book F. Christianson, David, illus. (ISBN 0-8372-3513-8); tchr's ed. (ISBN 0-8372-9203-4). (Elementary Skills Ser.). (Illus.). (gr. 3-6). pap. text ed. 1.35 (ISBN 0-8372-3510-3); tchr's ed. 1.35 (ISBN 0-685-81574-9). Bowmar-Noble.

Emmerich, Andre. Sweat of the Sun & Tears of the Moon: Gold & Silver in Pre-Columbian Art. LC 77-72685. (Illus.). 1977. Repr. of 1965 ed. 25.00 (ISBN 0-87817-208-4). Hacker.

Emmerich, Anne C. The Life of the Blessed Virgin Mary. Palairet, Michael, tr. from Ger. 1970. pap. 6.00 (ISBN 0-89555-048-2, 107). TAN Bks Pubs.

Emmerich, Janet. Anthony Trollope: His Perception of Character & the Traumatic Experience. LC 79-3734. 1980. text ed. 13.00 (ISBN 0-8191-0918-5); pap. text ed. 6.00 (ISBN 0-8191-0919-3). U Pr of Amer.

Emmers, Amy P. After the Lesson Plan: Realities of High School Teaching. 1981. pap. 7.95 (ISBN 0-8077-2605-2). Tchrs Coll.

Emmers, Carol A. Album of Television. (gr. 5 up): 1980. PLB 7.90 (ISBN 0-531-01503-3, A15). Watts.
Emmers, Raimond. Pain: A Spike-Interval Coded Message in the Brain. 1981. text ed. price not set (ISBN 0-89004-650-6). Raven.
Emmers, Raimond & Akert, Konrad. Stereotaxic Atlas of the Brain of the Squirrel Monkey. (Illus.). 1963. 100.00x (ISBN 0-299-02690-6). U of Wis Pr.
Emmers, Raimond & Tasker, Ronald R. The Human Somesthetic Thalamus: With Maps for Physiological Target Localization During Stereotactic Neurosurgery. LC 74-80534. 1975. 70.00 (ISBN 0-911216-72-3). Raven.
Emmerson, George S. SS Great Eastern: The Greatest Iron Ship. LC 80-69345. (Illus.). 216p. 1981. 25.50 (ISBN 0-7153-8054-0). David & Charles.
Emmerson, Richard K. Antichrist in the Middle Ages: A Study of Medieval Apocalypticism, Art, & Literature. LC 79-3874. (Illus.). 320p. 1981. 19.50 (ISBN 0-295-95716-6). U of Wash Pr.
Emmert, Philip & Brooks, William D. Methods of Research in Communication. 517p. 1970. text ed. 14.95 (ISBN 0-395-04396-4). HM.
Emmert, Philip & Donaghy, William. Human Communication: Elements & Contexts. LC 80-17595. (Speech Ser.). (Illus.). 46p. 1981. text ed. 12.95 (ISBN 0-201-03597-9). A-W.
Emmert, Philip, jt. auth. see Brooks, William D.
Emmery, Lena & Taylor, Sally. Grape Expeditions: Bicycle Tours of the California Wine Country, Vol. 2. (Illus.). 48p. 1980. pap. text ed. 2.40 (ISBN 0-9604904-0-X). Taylor & Friends.
Emmet, Bob, ed. see Seiden, O. J.
Emmet, Eric R. Handbook of Logic. (Quality Paperback: No. 178). 1974. pap. 4.95 (ISBN 0-8226-0178-8). Littlefield.
Emmett, Chris. Shanghai Pierce: A Fair Likeness. (Illus.). 326p. 1953. 14.95 o.p. (ISBN 0-8061-1125-9); pap. 6.95 (ISBN 0-8061-1151-8). U of Okla Pr.
Emmett, John & Ridley, Gordon. Underwater Swimming. 120p. 1980. 12.95 (ISBN 0-8069-9158-5, Pub. by EP Publishing England). Sterling.
Emmichoven, J. E. Von see Von Emmichoven, J. E.
Emmison, F. G. Archives & Local History. 2nd ed. (Illus.). 111p. 1974. bds. 15.00x (ISBN 0-8476-1283-X). Rowman.
Emmitt, Robert. Actaeon Homeward: A Novel. LC 78-60621. (A Writers West Book). 1979. 8.95 o.p. (ISBN 0-8040-9014-9); pap. 4.50 o.p. (ISBN 0-8040-9010-6). Swallow.
--The Last War Trail: The Utes & the Settlement of Colorado. (Civilization of the American Indian Ser.: Vol. 40). (Illus.). 352p. 1954. 14.95 (ISBN 0-685-25209-4); pap. 5.95 (ISBN 0-8061-1043-0). U of Okla Pr.
--The Legend of Ogden Jenks. 203p. 1980. pap. 5.95 (ISBN 0-8263-0559-8). U of NM Pr.
Emmons, Arthur B., 3rd, jt. auth. see Burdsall, Richard L.
Emmons, G. T. The Tahltan Indians. (Illus.). 1979. Repr. of 1911 ed. text ed. 17.25x (ISBN 0-391-00957-5). Humanities.
Emmons, Michael. Inner Source. 1978. pap. cancelled (ISBN 0-8431-0472-4). Impact Tenn.
Emmons, Michael & Richardson, David. The Assertive Christian. Frost, Miriam, ed. 156p. (Orig.). 1981. pap. 5.95 (ISBN 0-03-059057-4). Winston Pr.
Emmons, Terence. Russian Landed Gentry & the Peasant Emancipation of 1861. LC 68-29654. 1968. 41.95 (ISBN 0-521-07340-5). Cambridge U Pr.
Emory, C. William. Business Research Methods. rev. ed. 1980. 18.95x (ISBN 0-256-02260-7). Irwin.
--Business Research Methods. 1976. text ed. 17.50x o.p. (ISBN 0-256-01851-0). Irwin.
Empedocles. The Fragments of Empedocles. Leonard, William E., tr. from Gr. & intro. by. LC 73-85282. 92p. 1973. 9.95 (ISBN 0-87548-300-3); pap. 3.95 (ISBN 0-87548-301-1). Open Court.
Empey, LaMar T. American Delinquency: Its Meaning & Construction. 1978. 17.95x (ISBN 0-256-01985-1). Dorsey.
Empie, Paul C. Lutherans & Catholics in Dialogue: Personal Notes for a Study. LC 80-69754. (Orig.). 1981. pap. 3.95 (ISBN 0-8006-1449-6, 1-1449). Fortress.
Empie, Paul C., et al, eds. Teaching Authority & Infallibility in the Church, No. 6. LC 79-54109. (Lutherans & Catholics in Dialogue). 352p. (Orig.). 1979. pap. 4.95 (ISBN 0-8066-1733-0, 10-6222). Augsburg.
Empringham, Toni, ed. Chicano Poetry Anthology. 128p. (Orig.). 1981. pap. 6.50 (ISBN 0-88496-164-8). Capra Pr.
Empson, W. Milton's God. LC 80-40109. 320p. Date not set. pap. 15.95 (ISBN 0-521-29910-1). Cambridge U Pr.
Empson, William. Structure of Complex Words. 3rd. ed. 450p. 1979. Repr. of 1951 ed. 22.50x (ISBN 0-8476-6207-1). Rowman.
Emrich, Duncan. The Hodgepodge Book: An Almanac of American Folklore. LC 72-77811. (Illus.). 368p. (gr. 1 up). 1972. 14.95 (ISBN 0-590-07250-1, Four Winds). Schol Bk Serv.
--Riddles & Jokes & Foolish Facts. (gr. 4-6). 1976. pap. 1.25 (ISBN 0-590-04281-5, Schol Pap). Schol Bk Serv.
--The Whim-Wham Book. LC 75-9872. (Illus.). 352p. 1975. 8.95 (ISBN 0-590-07315-X, Four Winds). Schol Bk Serv.
Emrich, Duncan, ed. Nonsense Book. LC 77-105339. (Illus.). 272p. (gr. 1 up). 1970. 8.95 (ISBN 0-590-07157-2, Four Winds). Schol Bk Serv.
Emshoff, James R. Breakthroughs: Action Techniques for Strategic Change. (Illus.). 1980. 15.95 (ISBN 0-8144-5612-X). Am Mgmt.
Emsley. Visual Optics, 2 vols. 5th ed. (Illus.). 1976. Vol. 1. 34.95 (ISBN 0-407-93415-4); Vol. 2. 34.95 (ISBN 0-407-93414-6). Butterworths.
Emsley, J. W. Progress in NMR Spectroscopy, Vol. 12. 288p. 1980. 87.50 (ISBN 0-08-024874-8). Pergamon.
Emsley, J. W. & Lindon, J. C. NMR Spectroscopy Using Liquid Crystal Solvents. 367p. 1975. text ed. 55.00 (ISBN 0-08-019919-4). Pergamon.
Emsley, J. W. & Sutcliffe, L. H., eds. Progress in NMR Spectroscopy: Vol. 11 Complete. LC 66-17931. 282p. 1978. 87.50 (ISBN 0-08-020325-6). Pergamon.
Emsley, J. W., et al. High Resolution Nuclear Magnetic Resonance Spectroscopy, 2 Vols. 1966. 46.00 (ISBN 0-08-011824-0). Pergamon.
Emsley, John & Hall, Dennis. The Chemistry of Phosphorus. LC 75-17432. 1976. 54.95 (ISBN 0-470-23869-0). Halsted Pr.
Encarnacao, J. Computer Aided Design Modelling, Systems Engineering, CAD Systems. (Lecture Notes in Computer Science Ser.: Vol. 89). 459p. 1981. pap. 27.00 (ISBN 0-387-10242-6). Springer-Verlag.
Encel, Sol, jt. ed. see Bell, Colin.
Enchi, Fumiko. The Waiting Years. Bester, John, tr. from Jap. LC 72-15864. 203p. 1980. pap. 4.95 (ISBN 0-87011-424-7). Kodansha.
Encinas, Lydia P. A Beginner's Book of Sewing. LC 76-53438. (gr. 7 up). 1977. 5.95 (ISBN 0-396-07424-3). Dodd.
Enck, John J., et al, eds. Comic in Theory & Practice. (Orig.). 1960. pap. text ed. 10.50 (ISBN 0-13-152561-1). P-H.
Encyclopedia Britannica. The Britannica Book of Music. Hadley, Benjamin, et al, eds. LC 79-7195. (Illus.). 1980. 24.95 (ISBN 0-385-14191-2). Doubleday.
Endacott, G. B. A History of Hong Kong. (Illus.). 351p. 1974. pap. 14.50x (ISBN 0-19-519776-3). Oxford U Pr.
Endacott, G. W. Woodworking & Furniture Making. (Drake Home Craftman Ser.). (Illus.). 1976. pap. 5.95 (ISBN 0-8069-8804-5). Sterling.
Ende, Richard C. von see Von Ende, Richard C.
Endean, R., jt. ed. see Jones, O. A.
Endell, Fritz A. Old Tavern Signs: An Excursion into the History of Hospitality. LC 68-26572. (Illus.). 1968. Repr. of 1916 ed. 18.00 (ISBN 0-8103-3505-0). Gale.
Enden, Michel De see De Enden, Michel.
Ender, K. L., jt. auth. see Newton, F. B.
Enderle, Judith A. Good Junk. (Illus.). 32p. (ps-3). 1981. 5.95 (ISBN 0-525-66720-2). Elsevier-Nelson.
--Let's Be Friends Again. LC 78-73536. (Illus.). (gr. k-3). Date not set. price not set (ISBN 0-89799-156-7); pap. price not set (ISBN 0-89799-074-9). Dandelion Pr. Postponed.
Enderton, Herbert B. A Mathematical Introduction to Logic. 1972. 20.95 (ISBN 0-12-238450-4). Acad Pr.
Endicott, John E. & Heaton, William P. The Politics of East Asia: China, Japan, Korea. LC 77-1346. 1978. lib. bdg. 26.50x (ISBN 0-89158-127-8); pap. text ed. 10.75x (ISBN 0-89158-128-6). Westview.
Endicott, John E., Jr. & Stafford, Roy W., Jr. American Defense Policy. 4th ed. LC 77-23161. (Illus.). 1977. 25.00x o.p. (ISBN 0-8018-1960-1); pap. 9.50x (ISBN 0-8018-1961-X). Johns Hopkins.
Endicott, Kirk. Batek Negrito Religion: The World-View & Rituals of a Hunting & Gathering People of Peninsular Malaysia. (Illus.). 1979. 34.95x (ISBN 0-19-823197-0). Oxford U Pr.
Endicott, Lane D. Beyond the Rainbow Mists: A Journey That Takes You Out of This World. 1981. 6.50 (ISBN 0-8062-1614-X). Carlton.
Endicott, Stephen. James G. Endicott: Rebel Out of China. 1980. 18.95 (ISBN 0-8020-2377-0). U of Toronto Pr.
Endo, Shusaku. A Life of Jesus. Schuchert, Richard, tr. from Japanese. LC 78-61721. 192p. 1980. pap. 2.95 (ISBN 0-8091-2319-3). Paulist Pr.
Endres, Clifford W. Joannes Secundus: The Latin Love Elegy in the Renaissance. 1981. 25.00 (ISBN 0-208-01832-8, Archon). Shoe String.
Endres, H., et al see Von Wiesner, J. & Von Regel, C.
Endres, Jeannette & Rockwell, Robert E. Food, Nutrition, & the Young Child. LC 80-10848. (Illus.). 1980. pap. text ed. 10.95 (ISBN 0-8016-4139-X). Mosby.
Endroczi. Cellular & Molecular Bases of Neuroendocrine Processes. 1976. 41.50 (ISBN 0-9960007-1-2, Pub. by Kaido Hungary). Heyden.
Endroczi, E, jt. auth. see Symposium of the International Society of Psychoneuroendocrinology Visgrad, Hungary, Dec. 1975.
Endsley, Richard & Bradbard, Marilyn. Quality Day Care: A Handbook of Choices for Parents & Caregivers. (Illus.). 256p. 1981. 13.95 (Spectrum); pap. 5.95. P-H.
Enehjelm, Curt A. Australian Finches. Friese, U. Erich, tr. from Ger. Orig. Title: Australische Prachtfinken. (Illus.). 1979. 2.95 (ISBN 0-87666-987-9, KW-O27). TFH Pubns.
Enelow, Allen J. & Swisher, Scott N. Interviewing & Patient Care. 2nd ed. 1979. text ed. 11.95x (ISBN 0-19-502545-8); pap. text ed. 5.95x (ISBN 0-19-502546-6). Oxford U Pr.
Enelow, Allen J. & Wexler, Murray. Psychiatry in the Practice of Medicine. 1966. 9.95x o.p. (ISBN 0-19-501127-9). Oxford U Pr.
Energy Engineering Board, Assembly of Engineering, National Research Council. Criteria for Energy Storage R&D. LC 76-47080. 1976. pap. 6.25 (ISBN 0-309-02530-3). Natl Acad Pr.
Energy Information Administration. Solar Collector Manufacturing Activity. Bereny, J. A., ed. 46p. 1980. pap. 9.95 (ISBN 0-930978-12-9). Solar Energy Info.
Energy Policy Project Staff. A Time to Choose: America's Energy Future. LC 74-14787. (Ford's Foundation's Energy Policy Project Ser.). 1974. 17.50 (ISBN 0-88410-023-5); pap. text ed. 9.95 (ISBN 0-88410-024-3). Ballinger Pub.
Enet, Daniel. Exporting for Small & Medium Sized Firms. 150p. 1977. text ed. 22.00x (ISBN 0-220-66329-7, Pub. by Busn Bks England). Renouf.
Eng, Helga. The Psychology of Children's Drawings: From the First Stroke to the Coloured Drawing. 2nd ed. (International Library of Philosophy, Psychology & Scientific Method Ser). 1964. 22.50 (ISBN 0-7100-3096-7). Routledge & Kegan.
Eng, Maximo, jt. auth. see Lees, Francis A.
Engar, Keith. Merlin's Tale of King Arthur's Magic Sword. (Orig.). 1981. playscript 2.00 (ISBN 0-87602-228-X). Anchorage.
Engberg, Robert & Wesling, Donald. John Muir-to Yosemite & Beyond: Writings from the Years 1863-1875. (Illus.). 192p. 1981. 17.50 (ISBN 0-299-08270-9); pap. 5.95 (ISBN 0-299-08274-1). U of Wis Pr.
Engdahl, Sylvia. Doors of the Universe. LC 80-18804. 276p. (gr. 7 up). 1981. PLB 11.95 (ISBN 0-689-30807-8, Argo). Atheneum.
Engdahl, Sylvia L. Enchantress from the Stars. LC 74-98609. 1970. sparton bdg. 8.69 (ISBN 0-689-20508-2). Atheneum.
Engdahl, Sylvia L. & Roberson, Rick. Tool for Tomorrow: New Knowledge About Genes. LC 78-13777. (Illus.). (gr. 5 up). 1979. 6.95 (ISBN 0-689-30679-2). Atheneum.
Enge, Harald A. Introduction to Nuclear Physics. 1966. 24.95 (ISBN 0-201-01870-5). A-W.
Enge, Harald A., et al. Introduction to Atomic Physics. LC 77-162464. 1972. text ed. 20.95 (ISBN 0-201-01871-3). A-W.
Engel, et al. Consumer Behavior. 3rd ed. 1978. 20.95 (ISBN 0-03-089673-8). Dryden Pr.
Engel, A., et al. Justice Game. 1974. pap. 5.95 (ISBN 0-02-472590-0, 47259). Macmillan.
Engel, C. W., jt. auth. see Engel Enterprises.
Engel, David M. Law & Kingship in Thailand During the Reign of King Chulalongkorn. LC 74-20343. (Michigan Papers on South & Southeast Asia: No. 9). 130p. 1975. pap. 4.50x (ISBN 0-89148-009-9). Ctr S&SE Asian.
Engel, Dolores. Voyage of the Kon-Tiki. LC 78-26766. (Raintree Great Adventures). (Illus.). (gr. 3-6). 1979. PLB 8.95 (ISBN 0-8393-0151-0). Raintree Child.
Engel Enterprises & Engel, C. W. Stimulating Simulations. 2nd ed. 112p. 1979. pap. 5.50 (ISBN 0-8104-5170-0); atari version 5.50 (ISBN 0-8104-5197-2). Hayden.
Engel, Frederic-Andre, ed. Prehistoric Andean Ecologys, Vol. 1. 1980. text ed. 45.00x (ISBN 0-391-01873-6). Humanities.
Engel, George L. Psychological Development in Health & Disease. LC 62-13582. 1962. 11.50 o.p. (ISBN 0-7216-3390-0). Saunders.
Engel, George L. & Morgan, W. L., Jr. Interviewing the Patient. LC 73-81834. 1973. pap. 9.50 (ISBN 0-7216-3393-5). Saunders.
Engel, Jackie, ed. A Survival Kit for School Publications Advisers. 274p. (Orig.). 1980. pap. 9.50 (ISBN 0-936352-04-3, B355). U of KS Ind Stud Div.
Engel, James F. & Norton, Wilbert H. What's Gone Wrong with the Harvest? 192p. 1975. pap. 4.95 kivar (ISBN 0-310-24161-8). Zondervan.
Engel, James F., et al. Cases in Promotional Strategy. 1971. pap. text ed. 10.50 (ISBN 0-256-00611-3). Irwin.
--Promotional Strategy. 4th ed. 1979. text ed. 19.95 (ISBN 0-256-02156-2). Irwin.
Engel, Joel. Handwriting Analysis Self-Taught. (Illus.). 1980. 10.95 (ISBN 0-525-66687-7); pap. 6.95 (ISBN 0-525-66697-4). Elsevier-Nelson.
Engel, Lehman. The American Musical Theater. rev. ed. 388p. 1975. 9.95 o.s.i. (ISBN 0-02-536080-9). Macmillan.
--The Critics. 1976. 14.95 o.s.i. (ISBN 0-02-536060-4). Macmillan.
--The Musical Theater Workshop. (Sound Seminars Ser.). bk., tapes, listening guide 350.00x (ISBN 0-88432-065-0, 11500). J Norton Pubs.
--This Bright Day. LC 73-8352. (Illus.). 352p. 1974. 10.95 o.s.i. (ISBN 0-02-536130-9). Macmillan.
--Words with Music: The Broadway Musical Libretto. LC 80-15412. 1981. pap. 6.95 (ISBN 0-02-870370-7). Schirmer Bks.
Engel, Leonard. Sea. LC 61-15324. (Life Nature Library). (Illus.). (gr. 5 up). 1969. 8.97 o.p. (ISBN 0-8094-0613-6, Pub. by Time-Life). Silver.
--The Sea. (Young Readers Library). (Illus.). 1977. lib. bdg. 7.95 (ISBN 0-686-51094-1). Silver.
Engel, Lyle K. Complete Book of Minibikes & Minicycles. LC 72-88606. (Illus.). 160p. 1975. lib. bdg. 7.95 o.p. (ISBN 0-668-02733-9); pap. 3.95 o.p. (ISBN 0-668-03785-7). Arco.
--The Complete Book of Mobile Home Living. LC 73-85274. (Illus.). 160p. 1974. lib. bdg. 5.95 o.p. (ISBN 0-668-02896-3). Arco.
--The Complete Book of Trailering. LC 72-85679. (Illus.). 160p. 1974. lib. bdg. 5.95 o. p. o.p. (ISBN 0-668-02716-9); pap. 2.95 o.p. (ISBN 0-668-02715-0). Arco.
--The Complete Motorcycle Book. LC 73-88085. (Illus.). 208p. (YA) 1974. 8.95 o.s.i. (ISBN 0-590-17268-9, Four Winds). Schol Bk Serv.
--Racing to Win - Wood Brothers Style. LC 72-91065. (Illus.). 192p. (Orig.). 1974. 5.95 o.p. (ISBN 0-668-02886-6). Arco.
Engel, Lyle K. & Auto Racing Magazine Staff. One Hundred Thirty-Two of the Most Unusual Cars That Ever Ran at Indianapolis. LC 72-103077. 1970. lib. bdg. 4.95 o.p. (ISBN 0-668-02194-2). Arco.
Engel, M., jt. ed. see Hodson, H. V.
Engel, Madeline H., jt. auth. see Tomasi, Silvano M.
Engel, Marian. Inside the Easter Egg. (Anansi Fiction Ser.: No. 33). 172p. 1975. 14.95 (ISBN 0-88784-436-7, Pub. by Hse Anansi Pr Canada). U of Toronto Pr.
--Monodromos. LC 73-85572. (Anansi Fiction Ser.: No. 27). 250p. 1973. 11.95 (ISBN 0-88784-436-7, Pub. by Hse Anansi Pr Canada). U of Toronto Pr.
--The Year of the Child. 192p. 1981. 9.95 (ISBN 0-312-89627-1). St Martin.
Engel, Peter. A Controlling Interest. 384p. 1981. 13.95 (ISBN 0-312-16919-1). St Martin.
Engel, Robert, jt. auth. see Baker, Arthur D.
Engel, S. Analyzing Informal Fallacies. 1980. pap. 7.50 (ISBN 0-13-032854-5). P-H.
Engel, Salo & Metall, R. A., eds. Law, State & International Legal Order: Essays in Honor of Hans Kelsen. LC 64-16881. 1964. 19.50x (ISBN 0-87049-052-4). U of Tenn Pr.
Engel, W. King. Current Concepts of Myopathies. (Clinical Orthopaedics & Related Research Ser, Vol. 39). (Illus.). 4.00 o.p. (ISBN 0-685-14227-2). Lippincott.
Engel, Wilson F., ed. see Shirley, James.
Engelbarts, Rudolf. Books in Stir: A Bibliographic Essay About Prison Libraries & About Books Written by Prisoners & Prison Employees. LC 70-180625. 1972. 10.00 (ISBN 0-8108-0450-6). Scarecrow.
--Librarian Authors. LC 80-28035. 123p. 1981. lib. bdg. write for info. (ISBN 0-89950-007-2). McFarland & Co.
Engelberger, Joseph F. Robotics in Practice. 1981. 39.95 (ISBN 0-8144-5645-6). Am Mgmt.
Engelbrecht, Ted D., et al. Federal Taxation of Estates, Gifts, & Trusts. (Illus.). 528p. 1981. 32.95. P-H.
Engeldinger, Eugene A., jt. auth. see Fairbanks, Carol.

Engelen, G. B. Aqua-Vu: A Limnological Reconnaissance Study of Lago Di Braies ("Prager Wildsee) Dolomites, N. Italy. (Communications of the Inst. of Earth Sciences, Ser. A.: No. 1). (Illus.). 63p. (Orig.). 1976. pap. text ed. 8.75x (ISBN 9-0620-3317-2). Humanities.
--Aqua-Vua: A Catalogue of Hydrological Research Projects Over the Period 1966-1972 in the Hydrology Program of the Inst. of Earth Sciences, Amsterdam, No. 2. (Communication of the Institute of Earth Sciences, Ser. A: No. 2). 35p. 1976. pap. text ed. 4.75x (ISBN 0-685-66839-8). Humanities.
Engeler, Erwin. Introduction to the Theory of Computation. (Computer Science & Applied Mathematics Ser). 1973. text ed. 21.95 (ISBN 0-12-239250-7). Acad Pr.
Engelhardt, W. V., et al. Sedimentary Petrology: The Origin of Sediments & Sedimentary Rocks, Part III. Johns, William D., tr. LC 67-28575. 1977. 64.95 (ISBN 0-470-99142-9). Halsted Pr.
Engell, James. The Creative Imagination: Enlightenment to Romanticism. 1981. write for info. Harvard U Pr.
Engelman, Edmund. Berggasse Nineteen: Sigmund Freud's Home & Offices, Vienna, 1938; the Photographs of Edmund Engelman. LC 80-23056. 1981. pap. 15.00 (ISBN 0-226-20847-8). U of Chicago Pr.
Engelmann, F. The Physiology of Insect Reproduction. LC 70-114850. 1970. 59.00 (ISBN 0-08-015559-6). Pergamon.
Engelmann, Seigfried & Engelmann, Therese. Give Your Child a Superior Mind. 320p. 1981. 5.95 (ISBN 0-346-12532-4). Cornerstone.
Engelmann, Therese, jt. auth. see Engelmann, Seigfried.
Engelmayer, Sheldon D. & Wagman, Robert J. Tax Revolt Nineteen Eighty. 1980. 12.95 (ISBN 0-87000-469-7). Arlington Hse.
Engelmeier, Darlette, ed. see Engelmeier, Philip A.
Engelmeier, Philip A. Auctioneering. Paulaha, Richard & Engelmeier, Darlette, eds. Orig. Title: Be a Journeyman Auctioneer. (Illus.). 70p. (Orig.). 1980. pap. 10.00. Engelmeier.
Engeln, Oscar Dedrich Von & Urquhart, Jane M. The Story Key to Geographic Names. LC 74-13855. 279p. 1976. Repr. of 1924 ed. 20.00 (ISBN 0-8103-4062-3). Gale.
Engels, Donald W. Alexander the Great & the Logistics of the Macedonian Army. LC 76-52025. 1978. 18.00x (ISBN 0-520-03433-3); pap. 4.95 (ISBN 0-520-04272-7, CAL 472). U of Cal Pr.
Engels, F., jt. auth. see Marx, K.
Engels, Frederick. Anti-Duhring. 1976. 4.95 (ISBN 0-8351-0473-7); pap. 3.25 (ISBN 0-8351-0010-3). China Bks.
--Engels on Capital. new ed. LC 73-94192. 132p. 1974. 6.00 o.p. (ISBN 0-7178-0408-9); pap. 1.75 (ISBN 0-7178-0409-7). Intl Pub Co.
--Ludwig Feuerbach. 1976. 3.50 (ISBN 0-8351-0141-X); pap. 1.95 (ISBN 0-8351-0142-8). China Bks.
--Socialism: Utopian & Scientific. 1975. pap. 1.50 (ISBN 0-8351-0357-9). China Bks.
Engels, Frederick, jt. auth. see Marx, Karl.
Engels, Frederick, ed. see Marx, Karl.
Engels, Friedrich & Marx, Karl. Basic Writings on Politics & Philosophy. LC 59-12053. pap. 4.95 (ISBN 0-385-09420-5, A185, Anch). Doubleday.
Engels, Friedrich, jt. auth. see Marx, Karl.
Engels, John. Vivaldi in Early Fall. LC 80-24571. (Contemporary Poetry Ser.). 88p. 1981. 8.50 (ISBN 0-8203-0543-X); pap. 4.50 (ISBN 0-8203-0552-9). U of Ga Pr.
Engelsma, David. Marriage: The Mystery of Christ & the Church. LC 74-31902. 1975. pap. 2.95 (ISBN 0-8254-2520-4). Kregel.
Engelsman, Coert. Engelsman's General Construction Cost File 1981. 409p. 1980. pap. text ed. 29.95 (ISBN 0-442-12222-5). Van Nos Reinhold.
--Engelsman's General Construction Cost Guide, 1980. 1980. pap. text ed. 28.50 (ISBN 0-442-12218-7). Van Nos Reinhold.
--Heavy Construction Cost File, 1980: Unit Prices. 286p. 1980. pap. text ed. 24.50 (ISBN 0-686-63073-4). Van Nos Reinhold.
--Nineteen Hundred Eighty-One Heavy Construction Cost File: Unit Prices. 256p. 1980. pap. text ed. 24.50 (ISBN 0-442-12223-3). Van Nos Reinhold.
--Residential Cost Manual 1981: New Construction, Remodeling, & Valuation. 347p. 1980. pap. text ed. 29.95 (ISBN 0-442-12224-1). Van Nos Reinhold.
Engelsohn, H. S., jt. auth. see Willerding, Margaret F.
Engelsohn, Harold S. Basic Mathematics: Algebra with Arithmetic. LC 79-21287. 1980. text ed. 18.95 (ISBN 0-471-24145-8). Wiley.
--Programming Programmable Calculators. (Computer Programming Ser.). 1978. pap. 11.95 (ISBN 0-8104-5105-0). Hayden.
--Trigonometry: A Complete & Concrete Approach. (Illus.). 1980. text ed. 14.95 (ISBN 0-07-019419-X); instructor's manual avail. (ISBN 0-07-019420-3). McGraw.
Engen, Rodney K. Randolph Caldecott: Lord of the Nursery. (Illus.). 1977. 15.95 (ISBN 0-8467-0244-4, Oresko Bks); pap. 9.95 (ISBN 0-8467-0243-6). Hippocrene Bks.
Engen, Sadie O., et al. Living & Learning. 1980. 6.95 (ISBN 0-8280-0051-4, 12510-4). Review & Herald.
Enger, Janice, jt. auth. see Donaghue, Carroll.
Enger, Norman. Management Standards for Developing Information Systems. 1980. pap. 5.95 (ISBN 0-8144-7527-2). Am Mgmt.
Enger, Norman L. Management Standards for Developing Information Systems. new ed. LC 76-41827. (Illus.). 1977. 13.95 (ISBN 0-8144-5425-9). Am Mgmt.
Enger, Norman L. & Howerton, Paul W. Computer Security: A Management Audit Approach. 272p. 1980. 17.95 (ISBN 0-8144-5582-4). Am Mgmt.
Enggass, Catherine, tr. see Melvasia, Carlo C.
Enggass, Robert & Brown, Jonathan. Italy & Spain: 1600-1750. (Sources & Documents in the History of Art Ser). 1970. pap. 10.95 ref. ed. (ISBN 0-13-508101-7). P-H.
Enggass, Robert, tr. see Melvasia, Carlo C.
Engineering Concepts Curriculum Project. Man-Made World. 1971. text ed. 15.52 o.p. (ISBN 0-07-019502-1, W); teachers' set 29.88 o.p. (ISBN 0-07-019503-X); teachers' manual 10.08 o.p. (ISBN 0-685-14421-6); transparency masters 19.80 o.p. (ISBN 0-07-019504-8). McGraw.
Engineering Foundation Conference, Aug. 1975. Civil & Environmental Aspects of Energy Complexes: Proceedings. American Society of Civil Engineers, compiled By. 456p. 1976. pap. text ed. 14.00 (ISBN 0-87262-153-7). Am Soc Civil Eng.
Engineering Foundation Conference, Jan. 1978. Evaluation & Prediction of Subsidence: Proceedings. American Society of Civil Engineers, compiled By. 600p. 1978. pap. text ed. 36.00 (ISBN 0-87262-137-5). Am Soc Civil Eng.
Engineering Foundation Conference, Mar. 1974. Foundations for Dams: Proceedings. American Society of Civil Engineers, compiled By. 480p. 1974. pap. text ed. 27.50 (ISBN 0-87262-100-6). Am Soc Civil Eng.
Engineering Foundation Conference, Nov. 1976. Evaluation of Dam Safety: Proceedings. American Society of Civil Engineers, compiled By. 532p. 1977. pap. text ed. 16.00 (ISBN 0-87262-088-3). Am Soc Civil Eng.
Engineering Foundation Conference on Shotcrete, 1976. Shotcrete for Ground Support: Proceedings, SP-54. 1977. 29.00 (ISBN 0-685-87992-5) (ISBN 0-685-87993-3). ACI.
Engineering Industry Training Board, ed. First Year Training for Craftsmen & Technicians: An Introduction to General & Special Skills, 16 vols. (Illus.). 1975-1976. Set. spiral bdg. 77.00x (ISBN 0-685-90143-2). Intl Ideas.
--Model Schemes for the Training of Adult Operators in Technical Trades, 40 vols. (Illus.). 1968-1972. Set. 132.50x (ISBN 0-685-90166-1). Intl Ideas.
Engineering Industry Training Board, London, ed. Static Electrical Equipment Winding & Building, 2 vols. (Engineering Craftsmen: No. G1). (Illus.). 1968. Set. spiral bdg. 43.95x (ISBN 0-685-90175-0). Vol. 2 (ISBN 0-85083-128-8). Intl Ideas.
Engineering Industry Training Board, ed. Training for Capstan, Turret, & Sequence Controlled Lathe Setters & Operators, 21 vols. (Illus.). 1973. Set. 39.95x (ISBN 0-685-90180-7). Intl Ideas.
--Training for Drilling Machine Operators, 17 vols. (Illus.). 1978. Set. 36.50x (ISBN 0-685-90182-3). Intl Ideas.
--Training for Industrial Site Radiography, 14 vols. Incl. Vol. 1. Introduction to Radiography; Vol. 2. Ionizing Radiations; Vol. 4. Image Formation; Vol. 5. Safety; Vol. 6. X-Ray Equipment; Vol. 7. Gamma-Ray Equipment; Vol. 8. Exposure; Vol. 9. Operations; Vol. 10. Pipe-Crawler Equipment. (Illus.). 1977. Set. 28.95x (ISBN 0-685-91100-4). Intl Ideas.
--Training for Manual Metal-Arc Welders, 14 vols. Incl. Vol. 1. Metal-Arc Welding; Vol. 2. Welding Electrodes; Vol. 3. Joints & Weld Symbols; Vol. 4. Limiting Distortion; Vol. 5. Basic Welding; Vol. 6. Plate Surfaces; Vol. 7. Fillet Joints; Vol. 8. Single Vee Butt Joints; Vol. 9. Pipe Welding; Vol. 10. Fault Diagnosis; Vol. 11. Branch Connections. (Illus.). 1974. Set. 28.95x (ISBN 0-685-91101-2). Intl Ideas.
--Training for Milling Machine Operators & Setters, 22 vols. (Illus.). 1977. Set. 38.95x (ISBN 0-685-90183-1). Intl Ideas.
--Training for Operators of Numerically Controlled Machines, 17 vols. Incl. Vol. 1. Introduction to NC Machine Tool; Vol. 2. Rotating Tool; Vol. 3. Rotating Work; Vol. 4. Milling Cutters; Vol. 5. Tape NC Machines; Vol. 6. Automatic Tool & Work Exchanging; Vol. 7. X, Y, & Z Axes; Vol. 8. Positioning of the Tool & Workpiece; Vol. 9. Emergency Stop & Switching Operations; Vol. 10. Operation. 1973. Set. 37.50x (ISBN 0-685-91102-0). Intl Ideas.
Engineering Industry Training Board. Training for Pipe Fitters, 23 vols. 1976. 41.95x. Intl Ideas.
Engineering Industry Training Board, ed. Training for Riggers-Erectors, 15 vols. (Illus.). 1976. Set. 31.50x (ISBN 0-685-90181-5). Intl Ideas.
--Training in Safe Working Practice for Power Press Tool Setters & Operators, 9 vols. Incl. Vol. 1. Introduction to Power Press; Vol. 3. Press Brakes; Vol. 4. Safety Tool Setting; Vol. 5. Guards; Vol. 6. Testing Press Guards; Vol. 7. Accident Prevention. 1973. Set. 21.00x (ISBN 0-685-91103-9). Intl Ideas.
--Training Recommendations for Training Officers, 14 vols. Incl. Vol. 1. The Training of Supervisors; Vol. 2. Adult Operators; Vol. 3. Juvenile Operators; Vol. 4. Professional Engineers; Vol. 5. Managers; Vol. 6. Systems Analysts; Vol. 7. Clerks; Vol. 8. Technicians; Vol. 9. Supervisors; Vol. 10. Computer Operators; Vol. 11. Computer Programmers; Vol. 12. Secretaries; Vol. 13. Typists; Vol. 14. Machine Operators. (Illus.). 1973. Set. pap. text ed. 72.50x (ISBN 0-685-91104-7). Intl Ideas.
Engineering Staff of Texas Instruments. The M O S Memory Data Book for Design Engineers, 1980. LC 79-93268. 192p. pap. 3.75 (ISBN 0-89512-105-0, LCC4782). Tex Instr Inc.
Engineers Joint Council Editors. Directory of Engineering Societies & Related Organizations. 1976. pap. 18.00 o.p. (ISBN 0-685-47812-2). AAES.
--Theasurus of Engineering & Scientific Terms. rev. ed. LC 68-6569. 1967. flexible cover 50.00 (ISBN 0-685-09289-5). AAES.
--Who's Who in Engineering. 1976. 50.00 o.p. (ISBN 0-685-41717-4, 107-76). AAES.
Enginger, Bernard, jt. auth. see Alfassa, Mirra.
England, A. Scripted Drama. 260p. Date not set. price not set (ISBN 0-521-23235-X). Cambridge U Pr.
England, A. B. Energy & Order in the Poetry of Swift. LC 78-75200. 1980. 12.00 (ISBN 0-8387-2367-5). Bucknell U Pr.
England, Alma, jt. auth. see Collings, Ellsworth.
England, Ernest J., jt. auth. see Pearman, John W.
England, F. E. Kant's Conception of God. Bd. with Nova Dilucidatio. 1968. Repr. of 1929 ed. text ed. 12.50x (ISBN 0-391-00636-3). Humanities.
England, G. A. Out of the Abyss. (YA) 5.95 (ISBN 0-685-07451-X, Avalon). Bouregy.
England, George, et al. Functioning of Complex Organizations. LC 80-21966. 352p. 1981. lib. bdg. 25.00 (ISBN 0-89946-067-4). Oelgeschlager.
England, George A. Elixir of Hate. 1976. lib. bdg. 12.95x (ISBN 0-89968-176-X). Lighthouse Pr NY.
--Flying Legion. 1976. lib. bdg. 12.95 (ISBN 0-89968-177-8). Lightyear.
England, J. B. Techniques in Nuclear Structure Physics, 2 vols. LC 74-8171. 697p. 1974. 54.95 (ISBN 0-470-24161-6). Halsted Pr.
England, Wilbur B., et al. Purchasing & Materials Management: Principles & Cases. 6th ed. 1975. text ed. 18.95x o.p. (ISBN 0-256-01635-6). Irwin.
Englander, A. Arthur & Petzold, Paul. Filming for Television. (Library of Film & Television Practice). Date not set. 21.50 (ISBN 0-8038-2320-7). Hastings.
Englander, W., jt. auth. see Saxon, J.
Engle, jt. auth. see Hyde, Sarah.
Engle, Eloise & Lott, Arnold. Man in Flight: Biomedical Achievements in Aerospace. LC 79-63780. (A Supplement to the American Astronautical Society History Ser.). (Illus.). 414p. 1979. 20.00x (ISBN 0-915268-24-8). Univelt Inc.
Engle, Eloise & Paananen, Lauri A. The Winter War: The Russo-Finnish Conflict, 1939-1940. LC 72-1217. (Illus.). 250p. 1973. 7.95 o.p. (ISBN 0-684-13047-5, ScribT). Scribner.
Engle, Eloise K., jt. auth. see Ransom, M. A.
Engle, Fannie & Blair, Gertrude. The Jewish Festival Cookbook. 1966. pap. 2.25 o.s.i. (ISBN 0-446-82514-X). Warner Bks.
Engle, Mary A., ed. Pediatric Cardiovascular Disease. LC 80-15616. (Cardiovascular Clinics Ser.: Vol. 11, No. 2). (Illus.). 475p. 1980. text ed. 48.00 (ISBN 0-8036-3204-5). Davis Co.
Englebert, J., jt. ed. see Hunt, Thomas K.
Englebrecht, Ted D., jt. auth. see Kramer, John L.
Englehardt, H. Tristram, jt. auth. see Brody, Baruch A.
Englekirk, John E., et al. Outline History of Spanish American Literature. 4th ed. 1981. 24.50x (ISBN 0-89197-874-7); pap. text ed. 12.95x (ISBN 0-89197-326-5). Irvington.
Englekirk, John E., et al, eds. Anthology of Spanish-American Literature, 2 vols. 2nd ed. (Span.). 1968. Vol. 1. pap. text ed. 11.50 (ISBN 0-13-038786-X); Vol. 2. pap. text ed. 12.50 (ISBN 0-13-038794-0). P-H.
Englemann, S., jt. auth. see Bereiter, Carl.
Engler, A. Hochgebirgsflora Des Tropischen Afrikas. (Akad. D. Wissenschaften, Berlin Ser.). 461p. (Ger.). 1975. pap. text ed. 91.50x (ISBN 3-87429-088-3). Lubrecht & Cramer.
--Syllabus der Pflanzenfamilien, 2 vols. 12th ed. Incl. Vol. 1. Allegmeiner Teil: Bakterien Bis Gymnospermen. 1954. 42.20 (ISBN 3-4433-9015-3); Vol. 2. Angiospermen Vebersicht Ueber Die Florengebiete der Erde. 1964. 75.85 (ISBN 3-4433-9016-1). (Illus.). Lubrecht & Cramer.
Engler, Barbara O. Personality Theories: An Introduction. LC 78-69596. (Illus.). 1979. text ed. 17.50 (ISBN 0-395-26772-2); inst. manual 0.65 (ISBN 0-395-26773-0). HM.
Engler, Calvin. Basic Accounting. 2nd ed. 1969. 8.25 o.p. (ISBN 0-672-96016-8); pap. text ed. 8.95 (ISBN 0-672-96017-6); tchr's manual 5.00 (ISBN 0-672-96018-4); wkbk. 6.60 (ISBN 0-672-96019-2); practice set 6.95 (ISBN 0-672-96020-6). Bobbs.
--Practice Set-Basic Accounting. 2nd ed. 1969. pap. 6.00 o.p. (ISBN 0-672-26020-4). Bobbs.
Engler, Larry & Fijan, Carol. Making Puppets Come Alive: A Method of Learning & Teaching Hand Puppetry. LC 72-6623. (Illus.). 192p. 1980. pap. 7.95 (ISBN 0-8008-5073-4). Taplinger.
Engler, Robert. Brotherhood of Oil: Energy Policy & the Public Interest. 1978. pap. 2.95 (ISBN 0-451-61892-0, ME1892, Ment). NAL.
Engler, Robert, ed. America's Energy: Reports from "the Nation" on 100 Years of Struggles for the Democratic Control of Our Resources. 1981. 17.95 (ISBN 0-394-51142-5); pap. 7.95 (ISBN 0-394-73909-4). Pantheon.
English, Ava C., jt. auth. see English, Horace B.
English, Barbara. The Lord of Holderness, Ten Eighty-Six to Twelve Sixty: A Study in Feudal Society. (Illus.). 288p. 1979. 49.50x (ISBN 0-19-713437-8). Oxford U Pr.
English Benedictine Congregation Members & Rees, Daniel. Consider Your Call. (Cistercian Studies Ser.: No. 20). 447p. 1980. 17.95 (ISBN 0-87907-820-0). Cistercian Pubns.
English, Burt H. Liberacion Nacional En Costa Rica: The Development of a Political Party in a Transitional Society. LC 73-107880. (Latin American Monographs: Ser. 2, No. 8). (Illus.). 1971. 8.25 (ISBN 0-8130-0296-6). U Presses Fla.
English, Dori, jt. auth. see Wiggins, James D.
English, E. Schuyler. Re-Thinking the Rapture. 1954. pap. 2.25 (ISBN 0-87213-144-0). Loizeaux.
English, Fenwick W. & Sharpes, Donald K. Strategies for Differentiated Staffing. LC 75-190058. 1972. 19.00x (ISBN 0-8211-0409-8); text ed. 17.00x (ISBN 0-685-24962-X). McCutchan.
English, Fenwick W., jt. auth. see Steeves, Frank L.
English, Frank P. & Keats, Warren A. Reconstructive & Plastic Surgery of the Eyelids. (Illus.). 112p. 1975. 16.75 (ISBN 0-398-03386-2). C C Thomas.
English, H. Edward, ed. Canada-U. S. Relations. LC 76-38067. (Special Studies). 1976. text ed. 22.95 (ISBN 0-275-23300-6). Praeger.
English, Horace B. & English, Ava C. A Comprehensive Dictionary of Psychological & Psychoanalytical Terms. LC 57-10524. 1958. pap. text ed. 17.95 (ISBN 0-679-30033-3, Pub. by MacKay). Longman.
English, J. M. Cost Effectiveness: Economic Evaluation of Engineered Systems. LC 68-28500. 1968. 38.95 (ISBN 0-471-24170-9, Pub. by Wiley-Interscience). Wiley.
English, Jane, jt. auth. see Bolinger, Judith.
English, John. How to Organise & Operate a Small Business in Australia. 270p. 1981. text ed. 22.50x (ISBN 0-86861-282-0, 2648). Allen Unwin.
English, John W. Criticizing the Critics. (Humanistic Studies in the Communication Arts). Date not set. 14.95 (ISBN 0-8038-1270-1); pap. text ed. 7.95 (ISBN 0-8038-1272-8). Hastings.
English, John W., jt. auth. see Cardiff, Gray E.
English Language Services. Readings & Conversations: About the United States, Its People, Its History & Its Customs, 2 vols. rev. ed. 1976. text ed. 3.95 ea.; Vol. 1. (ISBN 0-87789-195-8); Vol. 2. (ISBN 0-87789-196-6); Set. cassette tapes 85.00 (ISBN 0-686-28557-3). Cassettes 1 (ISBN 0-87789-201-6). Cassettes 2 (ISBN 0-87789-202-4). Eng Language.

English, Maurice. Midnight in the Century. LC 64-20847. 69p. 1964. 4.00 (ISBN 0-8040-0204-5). Swallow.

English, Paul W. & Mayfield, Robert C., eds. Man, Space & Environment: Concepts in Contemporary Human Geography. (Orig.). 1972. text ed. 9.95x (ISBN 0-19-501441-3). Oxford U Pr.

English, Peter. Made in Britain: A Unique Contribution to World Industrial Archaeology, Vol. 1. Faulds, I. C., ed. 1980. text ed. 15.50x (ISBN 0-904980-28-6). Humanities.

English, Peter C. Shock, Physiological Surgery & George Washington Crile: Medical Innovation in the Progressive Era. LC 79-8579. (Contributions in Medical History: No. 5). xi, 271p. 1980. lib. bdg. 25.00 (ISBN 0-313-21490-5, EMI/). Greenwood.

English, Richard A., jt. ed. see Hasenfeld, Yeheskel.

Englund, Harold M., ed. see International Clean Air Congress, 2nd.

Englund, Sergia, tr. see Muggeridge, Malcolm, et al.

Englund, Sr. Sergia, tr. see Balthasar, Hans Urs Von.

Englund, Violet V. The Strand. LC 77-76176. (Illus.). 1977. pap. 6.95 (ISBN 0-9601258-0-9). Golden Owl Pub.

Engrand, Bernard. L' Industrie Photographique en France. Bunnell, Peter C. & Sobieszek, Robert A., eds. LC 78-67656. (Sources of Modern Photography Ser.). (Fr.). 1979. Repr. of 1934 ed. lib. bdg. 15.00x (ISBN 0-405-09897-9). Arno.

Engren, Edith. Marcy Tarrant. 1978. pap. 1.95 o.p. (ISBN 0-449-13974-3, GM). Fawcett.

Engs, Robert F. Freedom's First Generation: Black Hampton, Virginia, Eighteen Sixty-One to Eighteen Ninety. LC 79-5046. (Illus.). 1980. 15.00x (ISBN 0-8122-7768-6). U of Pa Pr.

Engs, Ruth & Wantz, Molly. Teaching Health Education in the Elementary School. (Illus., LC 77-079371). 1978. text ed. 17.75 (ISBN 0-395-25483-3); inst. manual 0.75 (ISBN 0-395-25484-1). HM.

Engs, Ruth C., et al. Health Games Students Play: Creative Strategies for Health Education. 1976. perfect bdg. 7.50 (ISBN 0-8403-1238-5). Kendall-Hunt.

Engstrand, Iris W. San Diego: California's Cornerstone. Blakey, Ellen S. & Silvey, Larry P., eds. LC 80-66336. (The American Portrait Ser.). (Illus.). 224p. 1980. 24.95 (ISBN 0-932986-09-9). Continent Herit.

--Spanish Scientists in the New World: The Eighteenth-Century Expeditions. LC 80-50863. (Illus.). 304p. 1981. 25.00 (ISBN 0-295-95764-6). U of Wash Pr.

Engstrom, jt. auth. see Hay.

Engstrom, Barbie. India, Nepal & Sri Lanka. (Engstrom's Travel Experience Guides Ser.). (Illus., Orig.). 1981. pap. 14.50 (ISBN 0-916588-06-8). Kurios Pr.

Engstrom, Karen M. Consent Manual: Policies, Laws, Procedures. 100p. 1981. pap. 10.00 (ISBN 0-87125-062-4). Cath Health.

Engstrom, Robert E. & Putman, Marc. Planning & Design of Townhouses & Condominiums. LC 79-64813. (Illus.). 256p. 1979. pap. text ed. 26.75 (ISBN 0-87420-587-5). Urban Land.

Engstrom, Ted W. & MacKenzie, Alex. Managing Your Time. LC 67-17239. (Orig.). (YA) 1968. pap. 2.95 (ISBN 0-310-24262-2). Zondervan.

Engstrom, Ted W. & McKenzie, R. A., trs. Administracao Do Tempo. (Portugese Bks.). (Port.). 1979. 1.40 (ISBN 0-8297-0637-2). Life Pubs Intl.

--Como Aprovechar el Tiempo. (Spanish Bks.). (Span.). 1978. 1.50 (ISBN 0-8297-0518-X). Vida Pub.

Engwall, Lars. Newspapers As Organisations. 1979. text ed. 29.00x (ISBN 0-566-00262-0, Pub. by Gower Pub Co England). Renouf.

Enis, Ben M. & Cox, Keith M. Marketing Classics: A Selection of Influential Articles. 4th ed. 528p. 1981. text ed. 13.95 (ISBN 0-205-05715-2); free (ISBN 0-205-07326-3). Allyn.

Enis, Ben M. & Cox, Keith K., eds. Marketing Classics. 3rd ed. 1977. pap. text ed. 13.95 (ISBN 0-205-05715-2, 0857157). Allyn.

Enk, Gordon A. & Hornick, William F. Value Issues in Technology Assessment. (Special Studies in Science, Technology, & Public Policy). 180p. 1981. lib. bdg. 20.00x (ISBN 0-89158-973-2). Westview.

Enk, Gordon A., jt. auth. see Hart, Stuart L.

Enk, P. J. Ad Propertii Carmina Commentarius Criticus, Zutpen. Commager, Steele, ed. LC 77-70813. (Latin Poetry Ser.). 1978. Repr. of 1911 ed. lib. bdg. 48.50 (ISBN 0-8240-2954-2). Garland Pub.

Enke, C. G., jt. auth. see Malmstadt, H. V.

Enlander, Derek. Computers in Medicine: An Introduction. LC 80-12221. (Illus.). 124p. 1980. pap. text ed. 12.95 (ISBN 0-8016-1525-9). Mosby.

Enloe, Cynthia. Ethnic Soldiers: State Security in a Divided Society. LC 79-5418. 269p. 1980. 19.00x (ISBN 0-8203-0507-3). U of Ga Pr.

Enlow, David R. Church Usher: Servant of God. LC 80-66769. 64p. (Orig.). 1980. pap. 1.95 (ISBN 0-87509-284-5). Chr Pubns.

Enna, Carl D., jt. auth. see McDowell, Frank.

Enna, S. J., et al, eds. Brain Neurotransmitters & Receptors in Aging & Age-Related Disorders. (Aging Ser.). 1981. text ed. price not set (ISBN 0-89004-643-3). Raven.

Enna, Salvatore J., et al, eds. Antidepressants: Neurochemical, Behavioral, & Clinical Perspectives. 275p. 1981. 27.00 (ISBN 0-89004-534-8). Raven.

Ennever, Len & Harlen, Wynne. With Objectives in Mind. LC 77-82993. (Science 5-13 Ser.). (Illus.). 1977. pap. text ed. 9.30 (ISBN 0-356-04009-7). Raintree Child.

Ennis, Bruce. Prisoners of Psychiatry. LC 72-79923. 252p. 1972. 7.95 o.p. (ISBN 0-15-173084-9). HarBraceJ.

Ennis, Bruce J. & Emery, Richard D. The Rights of Mental Patients. 1972. pap. 2.50 (ISBN 0-380-01859-4, 36574, Discus). Avon.

Eno, William P. The Story of Highway Traffic Control, Eighteen Ninety-Nine-Nineteen Thirty-Nine. 1939. 34.50x o.p. (ISBN 0-685-89784-2). Elliots Bks.

Enoch, Jay M., et al. Quantitative Layer-by-Layer Perimetry: An Extented Analysis. (Current Ophthalmology Monographs). 1980. 29.50 (ISBN 0-8089-1282-8). Grune.

Enochson, Loren, jt. auth. see Otnes, Robert K.

Enos, L. Reed, jt. auth. see Spinelli, Joseph S.

Enquist, Per O. The Legionnaires. new ed. 468p. 1973. 10.00 o.p. (ISBN 0-440-04725-0, Sey Lawr). Delacorte.

Enquist, Per Olov. The Night of the Tribades: A Play from 1889. Shideler, Ross, tr. from Swedish. 81p. 1977. 9.95 (ISBN 0-8090-7365-X); pap. 3.95 o.p. (ISBN 0-8090-1237-5). Hill & Wang.

Enrick, N. L. Quality Control & Reliability. 1969. 25.95 (ISBN 0-87245-098-8). Textile Bk.

--Quality Control & Reliability. 7th ed. LC 76-54908. (Illus.). 1977. 16.00 (ISBN 0-8311-1115-1). Indus Pr.

--Time Study Manual for the Textile Industry. rev. ed. 1981. write for info. (ISBN 0-89874-044-4). Krieger.

Enrick, Norbert L., jt. auth. see Myers, Buddy L.

Enrick, Norbert Lloyd, jt. auth. see Lester, Ronald H.

Enright, D. J. Shakespeare & the Students. 1979. pap. 6.95 (ISBN 0-7011-1568-8, Pub. by Chatto Bodley Jonathan). Merrimack Bk Serv.

--The Terrible Shears. LC 74-5966. (Wesleyan Poetry Program: Vol. 73). 72p. 1974. 10.00x (ISBN 0-8195-2073-X, Pub. by Wesleyan U Pr); pap. 4.95x (ISBN 0-8195-1073-4). Columbia U Pr.

Enright, Dennis J. Commentary on Goethe's Faust. 158p. 1980. Repr. of 1949 ed. lib. bdg. 20.00 (ISBN 0-8414-1916-7). Folcroft.

Enriquez, Evangelina, jt. auth. see Mirande, Alfredo.

Enriquez, Pablo & Neiman, Richard S. The Pathology of the Spleen: A Functional Approach. LC 76-43298. (Illus.). 1976. text ed. 26.50 perfect bdg (ISBN 0-89189-029-7, 16-1-016-00); slide atlas 131.50 (ISBN 0-89189-058-0, 15-1-016-00). Am Soc Clinical.

Enroth, Ronald M. Youth, Brainwashing & the Extremist Cults. 1977. 7.95 o.p. (ISBN 0-310-24270-3); pap. 4.95 (ISBN 0-310-24271-1). Zondervan.

Enroth, Ronald M., et al. The Story of the Jesus People. 1972. pap. 4.95 (ISBN 0-85364-131-5). Attic Pr.

Enselme, J. Unsaturated Fatty Acids in Atherosclerosis. 2nd ed. 1969. 36.00 (ISBN 0-08-013060-7). Pergamon.

Enser, A. G. S., compiled by. A Subject Bibliography of the Second World War: Books in English 1929-1974. LC 76-54230. (Grafton Books on Library Science). 1977. lib. bdg. 36.00x (ISBN 0-89158-722-5). Westview.

Ensign, Georgianne. Hunt for the Mastodon. LC 78-157749. (gr. 4 up). 1971. PLB 4.90 o.p. (ISBN 0-531-01994-2). Watts.

Ensign, Grayson H. You Can Understand the Bible. (The Bible Study Textbook Ser.). 1978. 13.50 (ISBN 0-89900-057-6). College Pr Pub.

Ensign, John & Ensign, Ruth S. Camping Together As Christians. LC 58-6252. 1958. pap. 1.50 (ISBN 0-8042-1176-0). John Knox.

Ensign, Ruth S. Make That Story Live! (Orig.). (gr. 7-9). 1965. pap. 1.50 (ISBN 0-8042-9317-1). John Knox.

Ensign, Ruth S., jt. auth. see Ensign, John.

Ensingel, Mark, et al. When a Lady: Prose-1981. 70p. 1981. 8.95 (ISBN 0-87376-038-7). Red Dust.

Ensko, Stephen G. & Wenham, Edward. English Silver 1675-1825. rev. ed. (Illus.). 144p. 1980. 24.95x (ISBN 0-938186-00-0). Arcadia Pr.

Enslein, Kurt, et al. Statistical Methods for Digital Computers. LC 60-6509. (Mathematical Methods for Digital Computers Ser.: Vol. 3). 1977. 37.95 (ISBN 0-471-70690-6, Pub. by Wiley-Interscience). Wiley.

Enslin, Theodore. The Fifth Direction. (Orig.). 1980. limited signed ed. 20.00x (ISBN 0-915316-81-1); pap. 5.00x (ISBN 0-915316-80-3). Pentagram.

--Opus Thirty-One, No. 3. 1979. pap. 2.50x (ISBN 0-915316-71-4). Pentagram.

--Ranger, Vol. I. 2nd rev. ed. 432p. 1980. 30.00 (ISBN 0-913028-79-7); pap. 12.95 (ISBN 0-913028-78-9). North Atlantic.

--Ranger Volume II. 256p. (Orig.). 1980. 25.00 (ISBN 0-913028-75-4); pap. 9.95 (ISBN 0-913028-74-6). North Atlantic.

--Two Geese. 1980. pap. 3.00 (ISBN 0-915316-86-2). Pentagram.

Enslin, Theodore, et al. Knee Deep in the Atlantic. 1981. pap. 15.00 (ISBN 0-915316-89-7). Pentagram.

Ensminger, Doris, jt. auth. see Benham, Amy.

Ensminger, M. E. Beef Cattle Science. 5th ed. LC 74-29763. (Illus.). 1976. 29.95 (ISBN 0-8134-1752-X, 1752); text ed. 22.95x (ISBN 0-685-76907-0). Interstate.

--Dairy Cattle Science. 2nd ed. LC 78-78193. (Illus.). 640p. 1980. 29.95 (ISBN 0-8134-2079-2, 2079); text ed. 22.95x (ISBN 0-685-25894-7). Interstate.

--Horses & Horsemanship. 5th ed. LC 76-45238. (Illus.). 1977. 23.35 (ISBN 0-8134-1888-7); text ed. 17.50x (ISBN 0-685-85664-X). Interstate.

--Poultry Science. 2nd ed. (Illus.). (gr. 9-12). 1980. 26.00 (ISBN 0-8134-2087-3, 2087); text ed. 19.50x (ISBN 0-686-60698-1). Interstate.

--The Stockman's Handbook. 5th ed. LC 76-58206. 1978. 29.95 (ISBN 0-8134-1943-3, 1943); text ed. 22.95x (ISBN 0-686-52293-1). Interstate.

Ensminger, M. Eugene. Animal Science. 7th ed. LC 76-1512. (Illus.). 1977. 29.95 (ISBN 0-8134-1798-8, 1798); text ed. 29.95x (ISBN 0-685-03860-2). Interstate.

--Sheep & Wool Science. 4th ed. LC 73-79612. (gr. 9-12). 1970. text ed. 23.35 (ISBN 0-8134-1113-0); pap. text ed. 17.50x (ISBN 0-685-03921-8). Interstate.

--Swine Science. 4th ed. LC 68-21886. (Illus.). (gr. 9-12). 1970. 23.35 (ISBN 0-8134-1026-6); text ed. 17.50x (ISBN 0-685-03929-3). Interstate.

Ensor, Allison. Mark Twain & the Bible. LC 76-80092. 144p. 1969. 7.50x (ISBN 0-8131-1181-1). U Pr of Ky.

Ensor, James. The Prints of James Ensor. LC 76-184012. 1972. Repr. of 1952 ed. lib. bdg. 25.00 (ISBN 0-306-70439-0). Da Capo.

Ensor, L., tr. see De Goncourt, Edmond & De Goncourt, Jules.

Ensor, Phyllis G., et al. Personal Health: Confronting Your Health Behavior. 1977. pap. text ed. 14.95x (ISBN 0-205-05737-3, 6257372); instr's manual avail. (ISBN 0-205-05738-1, 6257380). Allyn.

Ensrud, Barbara. The Pocket Guide to Cheese. 144p. 1981. pap. 4.95 (ISBN 0-399-50518-0, Perigee). Putnam.

Enteen, Shellie & Jacobs, Judy. Passion Planets: The Astrology of Relationships. 288p. (Orig.). 1980. pap. 2.50 (ISBN 0-515-05269-8). Jove Pubns.

Entelis, John P. Comparative Politics of North Africa: Algeria, Morocco, & Tunisia. (Illus.). 240p. 1980. pap. 8.95x (ISBN 0-8156-2214-7). Syracuse U Pr.

Entelis, S. G. & Tiger, R. P. Reaction Kinetics in the Liquid Phase. Kondor, R., tr. from Rus. LC 75-17857. 1976. 54.95 (ISBN 0-470-24330-9). Halsted Pr.

Enterkin, Hugh & Reynolds, Gerald. Estimating for Builders & Surveyors. 2nd ed. 1978. pap. 18.50x (ISBN 0-434-90542-9). Intl Ideas.

Enters, Angna. On Mime. LC 65-21130. 1978. pap. 5.95 (ISBN 0-8195-6056-1, Pub. by Wesleyan U Pr). Columbia U Pr.

Enthoven, Alain C. & Freeman, A. Myrick, 3rd, eds. Pollution, Resources & the Environment. new ed. 1973. pap. 5.95x (ISBN 0-393-09933-4). Norton.

Entin, Elliot E., jt. auth. see Raynor, Joel O.

Entman, Robert M., jt. auth. see Paletz, David L.

Entomological Society of America. Annual Meeting Programs. 5.00 ea. Entomol Soc.

Entrekin, Charles. Casting for the Cutthroat & Other Poems. 46p. (Orig.). 1980. pap. 3.95 (ISBN 0-917658-13-2). Berkeley Poets.

Entrekin, Dee. Make Your Own Silk Flowers. LC 74-31705. (Illus.). 80p. 1981. pap. 6.95 (ISBN 0-8069-8994-7). Sterling.

--Make Your Own Silk Flowers. LC 74-31705. (Illus.). 80p. 1975. 12.95 (ISBN 0-8069-5318-7); PLB 11.69 (ISBN 0-8069-5319-5). Sterling.

Entwisle, Doris B. & Doering, Susan G. The First Birth: A Family Turning Point. LC 80-22741. (Illus.). 304p. 1981. text ed. 25.00x (ISBN 0-8018-2408-7). Johns Hopkins.

Entwistle, Harold. Antonio Gramsci: Conservative Schooling for Radical Politics. (Routledge Education Bks.). 1979. 21.00 (ISBN 0-7100-0333-1); pap. 9.50 (ISBN 0-7100-0334-X). Routledge & Kegan.

Entwistle, Noel. Styles of Learning & Teaching: An Integrated Outline of Educational Psychology for Students, Teachers, & Lecturers. 1981. price not set (ISBN 0-471-27901-3, Pub. by Wiley-Interscience). Wiley.

Entwistle, Noel, ed. see Educational Research Symposium Organised by the Council of Europe & the Research & Development Unit of the Chancellor of the Swedish Universities, Goteborg, Sweden, September 7-12, 1975.

Entwistle, William J. The Spanish Language. 2nd ed. (Great Language Ser.). 1962. text ed. 13.75 (ISBN 0-571-06404-3). Humanities.

Environment Training Programme, Dakar, jt. auth. see United Nations Environment Programme, Nairobi.

Environmental Communications. Musical Houses: Homes & Secret Retreats of Music Stars. (Illus., Orig.). 1980. lib. bdg. 19.80 (ISBN 0-89471-112-1); pap. 7.95 (ISBN 0-89471-138-5). Running Pr.

Environmental Defense Fund & Boyle, Robert H. Malignant Neglect. LC 79-22826. (Illus.). 1980. pap. 3.95 (ISBN 0-686-59861-X, Vin). Random.

Environmental Impact Analysis Research Council at the Chicago National Convention, Oct. 1978. Appropriate Technology in Water Supply & Waste Disposal: Proceedings. American Society of Civil Engineers, ed. 288p. 1979. pap. text ed. 17.00 (ISBN 0-87262-148-0). Am Soc Civil Eng.

Environmental Law Institute. Legal Barriers to Solar Heating & Cooling of Buildings. 368p. 1980. 35.00 (ISBN 0-89499-006-3). Bks Business.

Environmental Resources Ltd, ed. see Commission of the European Communities.

Environmental Studies Board. An Assessment of Mercury in the Environment. 1978. pap. 8.00 (ISBN 0-309-02736-5). Natl Acad Pr.

--Chloroform, Carbon Tetrachloride & Other Halomethanes. 1978. pap. 8.75 (ISBN 0-309-02763-2). Natl Acad Pr.

--The International Mussel Watch. vi, 248p. 1980. pap. text ed. 11.50 (ISBN 0-309-03040-4). Natl Acad Pr.

--Kepone, Mirex, Hexachlorocyclopentadiene. 1978. pap. 5.75 (ISBN 0-309-02766-7). Natl Acad Pr.

--Long-Range Environmental Outlook. x, 198p. 1980. pap. text ed. 10.50 (ISBN 0-309-03038-2). Natl Acad Pr.

--O C S Oil & Gas: An Assessment. 1978. pap. 7.25 (ISBN 0-309-02739-X). Natl Acad Pr.

--Polychlorinated Biphenyls. 1979. pap. 7.25 (ISBN 0-309-02885-X). Natl Acad Pr.

--Underground Disposal of Coal Mine Wastes. 1975. pap. 8.50 (ISBN 0-309-02324-6). Natl Acad Pr.

Environmental Studies Board Commission on Natural Resources, National Research Council. Decision Making for Regulating Chemicals in the Environment. 288p. 1975. pap. 12.75 (ISBN 0-309-02401-3). Natl Acad Pr.

Environmental Studies Board, National Research Council. Contemporary Pest Control Practices & Prospects: Report of the Executive Committee, 5 vols. LC 75-43468. (Pest Control Ser.: An Assessment of Present & Alternative Technologies, Vol. 1). 506p. 1975. pap. 11.75 (ISBN 0-309-02410-2). Natl Acad Pr.

Environmental Studies Board, Natl Research Council. Corn-Soybeans Pest Control, 5 vols. (Pest Control Ser.: An Assessment of Present & Alternative Technologies, Vol. 2). 169p. 1975. pap. 5.50 (ISBN 0-309-02411-0). Natl Acad Pr.

--Cotton Pest Control, 5 vols. LC 75-37180. (Pest Control Ser.: An Assessment of Present & Alternative Technologies, Vol. 3). 139p. 1975. pap. 5.00 (ISBN 0-309-02412-9). Natl Acad Pr.

--Pest Control: An Assesssment of Present & Alternative Technologies, Vols. 1-5. 1976. pap. 26.00 set o.p. (ISBN 0-309-02409-9). Natl Acad Pr.

--Pest Control & Public Health. LC 75-45777. (Pest Control Ser.: Vol.5). 282p. 1976. pap. 8.00 (ISBN 0-309-02414-5). Natl Acad Pr.

Enyeart, James L., ed. & pref. by see Heinecken, Robert F.

Enyedi, Gyoergy, ed. Urban Development in the USA & Hungary. (Illus.). 311p. 1978. 30.00x (ISBN 963-05-1514-8). Intl Pubns Serv.

Enyedi, Gyorgy. Hungary: An Economic Geography. Fischer-Galati, Stephen, ed. LC 76-3742. (Special Studies on Contemporary Eastern Europe Ser). 1976. 31.50x (ISBN 0-89158-030-1). Westview.

Enyedi, Gyorgy & Meszaros, Julia, eds. Development of Settlement Systems. (Studies in Geography in Hungary: 15). (Illus.). 265p. 1980. 27.50x (ISBN 963-05-1898-8). Intl Pubns Serv.

Enyedi, Gyorgy & Volgyes, Ivan, eds. The Effect of Modern Agriculture on Rural Developement. LC 80-25232. (Pergamon Policy Studies on International Developement Comparative Rural Transformations Ser.). (Illus.). 280p. 1981. 32.50 (ISBN 0-08-027179-0). Pergamon.

Enz, C. P., ed. see Pauli, Wolfgang.

Enzer, Selwyn, et al. Neither Feast nor Famine. LC 78-3128. (Illus.). 1978. 15.95 (ISBN 0-669-02317-5). Lexington Bks.

Enzinger, Franz M. & Lattes, Raffaele. Soft Tissue Tumors. (Anatomic Pathology Seminars). (Illus.). 1975. atlas 78.50 o.p. (ISBN 0-89189-059-9, 15-014-00); pap. text ed. 9.00 o.p. (ISBN 0-89189-060-2, 50-1-039-00); slides 22.50 o.p. (ISBN 0-685-78073-2, 01-1-073-01). Am Soc Clinical.

Eogan, George, jt. auth. see Herity, Michael.

Epaulic. Freedom Through Knowledge. 1981. 5.50 (ISBN 0-8062-1602-6). Carlton.

Eperen, Jeannine D. Van see Van Eperen, Jeannine D.

Eperen, Jeannine Van see Tyrack, Mildred & Van Eperen, Jeannine.

Epes, Mary, et al. The Comp-Lab Exercises: Self-Teaching Exercises for Basic Writing. 1980. pap. text ed. 11.95 (ISBN 0-13-153601-X). P-H.

Ephremides, A. Random Processes, Pt. 1: Poisson & Jump Point Processes. LC 75-1287. (Benchmark Papers in Electrical Engineering & Computer Science Ser: No. 11). 352p. 1973. Vol. 1. 42.00 (ISBN 0-12-786431-8); Pt. 2,1975. 42.50 (ISBN 0-12-786432-6). Acad Pr.

Ephron, Delia. How to Eat Like a Child. 2.25 (ISBN 0-345-28504-2). Ballantine.

Ephron, Delia, jt. auth. see Bodger, Lorraine.

Epictetus. Enchiridion. Higginson, T. W., tr. 1955. pap. 2.50 (ISBN 0-672-60170-2, LLA8). Bobbs.

Epicurus. Letters, Principal Doctrines & Vatican Sayings. Geer, Russell, tr. LC 61-18059. (Orig.). 5.50 o.p. (ISBN 0-672-51060-X); pap. 3.95 (ISBN 0-672-60353-5, LLA141). Bobbs.

Epigraphic Survey. The Tomb of Kheruef: Theban Tomb No. 192. LC 79-88739. (Oriental Institute Publications Ser.: Vol. 102). 1980. 90.00x (ISBN 0-918986-23-0). Oriental Inst.

Epilepsy International Symposium, 10th. Advances in Epileptology: Proceedings. Wade, Juhn & Penry, J. Kiffin, eds. 594p. 1980. text ed. 52.00 (ISBN 0-89004-511-9). Raven.

Epinal. Antique Paper Dolls: The Edwardian Era. LC 75-2935. (Illus.). 1975. pap. 2.95 (ISBN 0-486-23175-5). Dover.

Epker, Bruce N. Dentofacial Deformities: Surgical-Orthodontic Correction. LC 80-12405. (Illus.). 400p. 1980. text ed. 59.50 (ISBN 0-8016-1606-9). Mosby.

Epley, Donald R. Arkansas Supplement for Modern Real Estate Practice. nd ed. 160p. (Orig.). 1980. pap. 7.95 (ISBN 0-88462-344-0). Real Estate Ed Co.

--Arkansas Supplement for Modern Real Estate Practice. 1978. pap. 7.95 o.p. (ISBN 0-88462-345-9). Real Estate Ed Co.

Epley, Donald R. & Rabianski, Joseph. Principles of Real Estate Decisions. LC 80-21354. 1981. text ed. 18.95 (ISBN 0-201-03188-4). A-W.

Eply, Donald R. & Millar, James A. Basic Real Estate Finance & Investments. LC 79-19530. 1980. text ed. 21.95 (ISBN 0-471-03635-8); tchrs'. manual avail. (ISBN 0-471-03878-4). Wiley.

Epp, C. D., jt. auth. see Bernard, C. H.

Epp, Margaret. Great Frederick & Other Stories. 128p. (gr. 7 up). 1971. pap. 1.50 (ISBN 0-8024-1325-0). Moody.

--Sarah & the Darnley Boys. 120p. (gr. 6-12). 1981. pap. 2.25 (ISBN 0-88207-490-3). Victor Bks.

Epp, Margret. Sarah & the Magic Twenty-Fifth. (gr. 3-7). 1977. pap. 1.95 (ISBN 0-88207-477-6). Victor Bks.

Eppel, Emanuel M. & Eppel, M. Adolescents & Morality: A Study of Some Moral Values & Dilemmas of Working Adolescents in the Context of a Changing Climate of Opinion. (International Library of Sociology & Social Reconstruction Ser.). (Illus.). 1966. text ed. 8.50x (ISBN 0-7100-3455-5). Humanities.

Eppel, M., jt. auth. see Eppel, Emanuel M.

Eppen, Gary D. & Gould, F. J. Quantitative Concepts for Management Decision Making Without Algorithms. 1979. 21.95 (ISBN 0-13-746602-1). P-H.

Eppendorfer, Hans. Der Ledermann Spricht Mit Hubert Fichte. (Suhrkamp Taschenbuecher: No. 580). (Orig., Ger.). 1980. pap. text ed. 4.55 (ISBN 3-518-37080-4, Pub. by Insel Verlag Germany). Suhrkamp.

Eppens-Van Veen, J. H. Colorful Glass Crafting. (Illus.). 112p. (gr. 9 up). 1973. 9.95 o.p. (ISBN 0-8069-5226-1); PLB 9.29 o.p. (ISBN 0-8069-5227-X). Sterling.

Eppes, Susan B. Through Some Eventful Years. Cushman, Joseph D., Jr., ed. LC 68-21660. (Floridiana Facsimile & Reprint Ser). 1968. Repr. of 1926 ed. 12.75 (ISBN 0-8130-0074-2). U Presses Fla.

Eppink, Norman R. One Hundred & One Prints: The History & Techniques of Printmaking. (Illus.). 272p. 1972. 25.00 (ISBN 0-8061-0915-7); pap. 9.95 (ISBN 0-8061-1181-X). U of Okla Pr.

Epple, A., jt. auth. see Pang, P. K.

Epple, August & Stetson, Milton. Avian Endocrinology. 1980. lib ed 34.00 (ISBN 0-12-240250-2). Acad Pr.

Eppler, Elizabeth E., ed. International Bibliograpy on Jewish Affairs: A Selected Annotated List of Books & Articles Published in the Diaspora, 1976-1977. 450p. 1981. lib. bdg. 35.00x (ISBN 0-86531-164-1). Westview.

Eppler, Klaus, jt. auth. see Robinson, Gerald J.

Eppler, Klaus & Gilroy, Thomas, eds. Representing Publicly Traded Corporations, 1980, 2 vols. LC 80-83000. (Nineteen-Eighty to Nineteen Eighty-One Corporate Law & Practice Course Handbook Ser.). 1925p. 1980. pap. text ed. 40.00 (ISBN 0-686-69171-7, B6-6555). PLI.

Epprights, E., et al. Teaching Nutrition. 2nd ed. 1963. 7.95 (ISBN 0-8138-1660-2). Iowa St U Pr.

Epps, Edgar G. Cultural Pluralism. LC 73-17617. 1974. 15.50x (ISBN 0-8211-0412-8); text ed. 14.00x (ISBN 0-685-42631-9). McCutchan.

Epps, Edgar G., jt. auth. see Gurin, Patricia.

Epstein, A. L. Matupit: Land, Politics & Change Among the Tolai of New Britain. LC 70-92679. 1969. 20.00x (ISBN 0-520-01556-8). U of Cal Pr.

Epstein, A. L., ed. The Craft of Social Anthropology. 1979. 23.00 (ISBN 0-08-023693-6). Pergamon.

Epstein, Alan, jt. ed. see Sprague, James.

Epstein, Alan N., jt. ed. see Sprague, James M.

Epstein, Barbara, jt. auth. see Burn, Duncan.

Epstein, Barbara L. The Politics of Domesticity: Women, Evangelism, & Temperance in Nineteenth-Century America. 224p. 1981. 17.95x (ISBN 0-8195-5050-7). Wesleyan U Pr.

Epstein, Benjamin. Principals: An Organized Force for Leadership. 48p. 1974. pap. text ed. 2.00 o.p. (ISBN 0-88210-052-1). Natl Assn Principals.

Epstein, Beryl, jt. auth. see Epstein, Sam.

Epstein, Beryl, jt. auth. see Epstein, Samuel.

Epstein, Carol. Declining Enrollments. 1976. pap. 8.00 (ISBN 0-87545-005-9). Natl Sch Pr.

--The Gifted & Talented. 1979. pap. 11.95 (ISBN 0-87545-017-2). Natl Sch Pr.

Epstein, Charles J., ed. Risk, Communication, & Decision Making in Genetic Counseling. LC 79-5120. (Alan R. Liss Ser.: Vol. 15, No. 5c). 1979. 36.00 (ISBN 0-8451-1030-6). March of Dimes.

Epstein, Charles J., et al, eds. see Birth Defects Converence, 1978, San Francisco.

Epstein, Charlotte. Classroom Management & Teaching: Persistent Problems & Rational Solutions. 1979. text ed. 13.95 (ISBN 0-8359-0824-0). Reston.

--An Introduction to the Human Services: Developing Knowledge, Skills, & Sensitivity. (Illus.). 368p. 1981. text ed. 15.95 (ISBN 0-686-69277-2). P-H.

--Leadership in Nursing. 225p. 1981. text ed. 14.95 (ISBN 0-8359-3970-7); pap. text ed. 12.95 (ISBN 0-8359-3969-3). Reston.

Epstein, Cynthia F. Woman's Place: Options & Limits in Professional Careers. 1970. 14.00x (ISBN 0-520-01581-9); pap. 3.95 (ISBN 0-520-01870-2, CAL227). U of Cal Pr.

Epstein, Cynthia F. & Coser, Rose L., eds. Access to Power: Cross-National Studies of Women & Elites. (Illus.). 280p. 1980. text ed. 27.50x (ISBN 0-04-301118-7, 2523). Allen Unwin.

Epstein, Daniel M. The Follies. 1979. pap. 5.95 (ISBN 0-87951-075-7). Overlook Pr.

--The Follies. LC 76-8059. 60p. 1977. 10.00 (ISBN 0-87951-048-X). Overlook Pr.

--Young Men's Gold. LC 77-20739. 1978. 10.00 (ISBN 0-87951-071-4); pap. 5.95 (ISBN 0-87951-076-5). Overlook Pr.

Epstein, David G. Brasilia-Plan & Reality: A Study of Planned & Spontaneous Urban Settlement. LC 72-186103. 1973. 20.00x (ISBN 0-520-02203-3). U of Cal Pr.

--Debtor-Creditor Law in a Nutshell. 2nd ed. LC 79-25091. (Nutshell Ser.). 324p. 1980. pap. 6.95 (ISBN 0-8299-2072-2). West Pub.

Epstein, Dena J. Sinful Tunes & Spirituals: Black Folk Music to the Civil War. LC 77-6315. (Music in American Life Ser.). (Illus.). 1977. 17.95 (ISBN 0-252-00520-1); pap. 10.95 (ISBN 0-252-00875-8). U of Ill Pr.

Epstein, Edna. The United Nations. rev ed. LC 73-5965. (First Bks). (Illus.). (gr. 3-7). 1973. PLB 4.90 o.p. (ISBN 0-531-00657-3). Watts.

Epstein, Edward & Morella, Joseph. The Ince Affair. (Orig.). 1978. pap. 1.75 o.p. (ISBN 0-451-08177-3, E8177, Sig). NAL.

Epstein, Elliot, et al. Barron's Guide to Law Schools. LC 77-13268. 1978. pap. 5.50 o.p. (ISBN 0-8120-0737-9). Barron.

Epstein, Erwin H. Politics & Education in Puerto Rico: A Documentary Survey of the Language Issue. LC 73-15379. 1970. 9.50 o.p. (ISBN 0-8108-0309-7). Scarecrow.

Epstein, Irwin & Tripodi, Tony. Research Techniques for Program Planning, Monitoring & Evaluation. LC 76-51825. 1977. 15.00x (ISBN 0-231-03944-1). Columbia U Pr.

Epstein, Israel. Notes on Labor Problems in Nationalist China. LC 78-74341. (The Modern Chinese Economy Ser.). 159p. 1980. lib. bdg. 16.50 (ISBN 0-8240-4281-6). Garland Pub.

Epstein, Jacob. Wild Oats. 1980. pap. 2.75 (ISBN 0-671-83393-6). PB.

Epstein, Jason, ed. see Pritchett, V. S.

Epstein, Joel J. Francis Bacon: A Political Biography. LC 76-25617. 1977. 13.50x (ISBN 0-8214-0232-3). Ohio U Pr.

Epstein, Joseph. Ambition: The Secret Passion. 320p. 1980. 13.95 (ISBN 0-525-05280-1). Dutton.

--Familiar Territory: Observations on American Life. 1979. 13.95 (ISBN 0-19-502604-7). Oxford U Pr.

Epstein, Joseph, ed. Masters: Portraits of Great Teachers. LC 80-68180. 224p. 1981. 14.95 (ISBN 0-465-04420-4). Basic.

--Masters: Portraits of Sixteen Great Teachers. LC 80-68180. 224p. 1980. 13.95 (ISBN 0-465-04420-4). Basic.

Epstein, Joyce L., ed. The Quality of School Life. LC 80-5350. 1980. write for info. (ISBN 0-669-03869-5). Lexington Bks.

Epstein, June, et al. Big Dipper. (Illus.). 112p. (Orig.). (ps-3). 1981. pap. 9.95 (ISBN 0-19-554289-4). Oxford U Pr.

Epstein, Klaus. Matthias Erzberger & the Dilemma of German Democracy. LC 75-80546. 1971. Repr. of 1959 ed. 25.00 (ISBN 0-86527-123-2). Fertig.

Epstein, Laura. Helping People: The Task-Centered Approach. LC 79-21084. (Illus.). 1980. pap. text ed. 9.50 (ISBN 0-8016-1509-7). Mosby.

Epstein, Laura, jt. auth. see Reid, William J.

Epstein, Laurily K. Women in the Professions. LC 75-18051. (Illus.). 160p. 1975. 18.95 (ISBN 0-669-00130-9). Lexington Bks.

Epstein, Leon J., jt. ed. see Simon, Alexander.

Epstein, Leonard H., jt. auth. see Blanchard, Edward B.

Epstein, Leslie. King of the Jews. 1979. pap. 2.50 (ISBN 0-380-48074-3, 48074). Avon.

Epstein, Lewis C. & Hewitt, Paul G. Thinking Physics. (Illus.). 262p. 1979. pap. 5.95x (ISBN 0-935218-00-9). Insight Pr CA.

Epstein, M. A., jt. ed. see Richter, G. W.

Epstein, Michael, jt. auth. see Cullinan, Douglas.

Epstein, Natalie, jt. auth. see Oppenheimer, Lillian.

Epstein, Nathan B., jt. auth. see Westley, William A.

Epstein, Perle. Monsters: Their Histories, Homes & Habits. LC 72-97496. 128p. (gr. 6-9). 1973. 6.95 o.p. (ISBN 0-385-04874-2). Doubleday.

Epstein, Richard A. Modern Products Liability Law. LC 80-11486. (Quorum Bk.). 210p. 1980. lib. bdg. 25.00 (ISBN 0-89930-002-2, EPL/, Quorum). Greenwood.

--The Theory of Gambling & Statistical Logic. rev. ed. 1977. 29.00 (ISBN 0-12-240760-1). Acad Pr.

--A Theory of Strict Liability: Toward a Reformulation of Tort Law. (The Cato Papers Ser.: No. 8). 158p. 1979. pap. 4.00 (ISBN 0-932790-08-9). Cato Inst.

Epstein, Robert, ed. see Skinner, B. F.

Epstein, Sam & Epstein, Beryl. First Book of Codes & Ciphers. (First Bks). (Illus.). (gr. 4-6). 1956. PLB 5.90 (ISBN 0-531-00502-X). Watts.

--The First Book of Electricity. (First Bks.). (Illus.). 72p. (gr. 4-6). 1977. PLB 6.45 (ISBN 0-531-00522-4). Watts.

--The First Book of Italy. rev. ed. LC 72-257. (First Bks). (Illus.). 72p. (gr. 4-6). 1972. PLB 4.90 o.p. (ISBN 0-531-00562-3). Watts.

--First Book of Maps & Globes. (First Bks). (Illus.). (gr. 4-6). 1959. PLB 4.90 o.p. (ISBN 0-531-00577-1). Watts.

--First Book of Mexico. LC 67-10078. (First Bks). (Illus.). (gr. 4-6). 1967. PLB 4.90 o.p. (ISBN 0-531-00583-6). Watts.

--The First Book of Printing. LC 72-2294. (First Bks.). (Illus.). (gr. 4-7). 1974. PLB 6.45 (ISBN 0-531-00616-6). Watts.

--First Book of Switzerland. LC 64-11911. (First Bks). (Illus.). (gr. 4-6). 1964. PLB 4.90 o.p. (ISBN 0-531-00651-4). Watts.

Epstein, Samuel & Epstein, Beryl. First Book of Words. (First Bks). (Illus.). (gr. 4-6). 1954. PLB 4.90 o.p. (ISBN 0-531-00673-5). Watts.

Epstein, Seymour. The Dream Museum. 1973. pap. 1.25 o.p. (ISBN 0-380-01150-6, 15222). Avon.

--Looking for Fred Schmidt. 320p. 1976. pap. 1.75 o.p. (ISBN 0-445-08423-5). Popular Lib.

Epstein, T. Scarlett & Jackson, Darrell, eds. The Feasibility of Fertility Planning: Micro Perspectives. 1977. text ed. 37.00 (ISBN 0-08-021452-5); pap. text ed. 12.25 (ISBN 0-08-021837-7). Pergamon.

Epstein, Vivian S. The ABC's of What a Girl Can Be. (Illus.). 32p. (ps-3). 1980. pap. 3.95 (ISBN 0-9601002-2-9). V S Epstein.

--History of Colorado for Children. (Illus.). 32p. (ps-4). 1977. pap. 2.95 (ISBN 0-9601002-1-0). V S Epstein.

Epstein, W. Stability & Constancy in Visual Perception: Mechanisms & Processes. 1977. 31.50 (ISBN 0-471-24355-8). Wiley.

Epstein, William. John Cleland: A Biography. 1974. 17.50x (ISBN 0-231-03725-2). Columbia U Pr.

--The Last Chance: Nuclear Proliferation & Arms Control. LC 75-22765. 1976. 17.95 (ISBN 0-02-909660-X). Free Pr.

Epstein, William & Toyoda, Toshiyuka, eds. A New Design for Nuclear Disarmament: Pugwash Symposium, Kyoto, Japan. (Illus.). 1977. 30.00x o.p. (ISBN 0-8476-2322-X). Rowman.

Epstein, Yakov M., jt. ed. see Baum, Andrew.

Epstin, David G. & Nickles, Steve H. Consumer Law in a Nutshell. 2nd ed. (Nutshell Ser.). 400p. 1981. pap. text ed. 6.95 (ISBN 0-8299-2130-3). West Pub.

Epton, Arli, ed. Theatre Directory, 1977-1978. 5th ed. LC 77-89021. 1977. pap. 2.00 o.p. (ISBN 0-930452-05-4, Pub by Theatre Comm). Pub Ctr Cult Res.

Epton, Arli, jt. ed. see Cumming, Marsue.

Epton, Nina. Cat Manners & Mysteries. 1973. 8.95 o.p. (ISBN 0-7181-1148-6, Pub. by Michael Joseph). Merrimack Bk Serv.

Epton, Roger, ed. Chromatography of Synthetic & Biological Polymers: Hydrophobic, Ion-Exchange & Affinity Methods, Vol. II. LC 77-40142. 1978. 59.95 (ISBN 0-470-26366-0). Halsted Pr.

Equal Rights Amendment Project, compiled by. The Equal Rights Amendment: A Bibliographic Study. Miller, Anita & Greenberg, Hazel, eds. LC 76-24999. 400p. 1976. lib. bdg. 22.50 (ISBN 0-8371-9058-4, ERA/). Greenwood.

Equipment Guide-Book Co. Machine Tool Value Guide: Grinding Machines, Vol. III. Husek, Jiri, ed. 600p. 1981. pap. 50.00 (ISBN 0-89692-104-2). Equipment Guide.

Erades, P. A. Points of Modern English Syntax. Robat, N. J., ed. (Contributions to English Studies). 260p. 1975. pap. text ed. 17.75 (ISBN 90-265-0184-6, Pub. by Swets Pub Serv Holland). Swets North Am.

Eranko, Olavi, et al, eds. Histochemistry & Cell Biology of Autonomic Neurons: Sif Cells, & Paraneurons. (Advances in Biochemical Psychopharmacology: Vol. 25). 410p. 1980. text ed. 45.00 (ISBN 0-89004-495-3). Raven.

Erasmus. Adages (One to Five Hundred, Vol. 31. Phillips, Margaret M. & Mynors, R. A., trs. (Collected Works of Erasmus). 1981. 35.00x (ISBN 0-8020-2373-8). U of Toronto Pr.

Erasmus, Desiderius. Comparation of a Vyrgin & a Martyr, 1537. Paynell, Thomas, tr. from Latin. LC 70-101148. 1970. Repr. of 1537 ed. 20.00x (ISBN 0-8201-1072-8). Schol Facsimiles.

--Complaint of Peace. Incl. The Adages of Erasmus. Phillips, Margaret M. LC 71-147414. (Library of War & Peace; Proposals for Peace: a History). lib. bdg. 38.00 (ISBN 0-8240-0483-3). Garland Pub.

--The Correspondence of Erasmus, Vol. 6: Letters 842-992 (May 1518 - June 1519) Mynors, R. A. & Thomson, D. F., trs. (Collected Works of Erasmus). 1981. 30.00x (ISBN 0-8020-5500-1). U of Toronto Pr.

--Essential Erasmus. Dolan, John P., tr. (Orig.). 1964. pap. 2.50 (ISBN 0-451-61877-7, ME1877, Ment). NAL.

--One Dialogue or Colloquy Entitled Diversoria. LC 71-26509. (English Experience Ser.: No. 244). 20p. 1970. Repr. of 1566 ed. 7.00 (ISBN 90-221-0244-0). Walter J Johnson.

--Preparation to Deathe: A Boke As Devout As Eloquent. LC 74-28852. (English Experience Ser.: No. 733). 1975. Repr. of 1538 ed. 6.00 (ISBN 90-221-0762-0). Walter J Johnson.

--Ten Colloquies. Thompson, Craig R., tr. 1957. pap. 4.95 (ISBN 0-672-60216-4). Bobbs.

Erath, Thalia, jt. auth. see Heriteau, Jacqueline.

Eraut, M. R., jt. auth. see Tribe, M. A.

Erazmus, Edward T. & Cargas, Harry J. English As a Second Language: A Reader. 3rd ed. 1980. pap. text ed. 9.95 (ISBN 0-697-03958-7). Wm C Brown.

Erb, Glenora L., jt. auth. see Kozier, Barbara B.

Erb, Guy F. Negotiations on Two Fronts: Manufactures & Commodities. LC 78-57199. (Development Papers: No. 25). 80p. 1978. pap. 1.50 (ISBN 0-686-28674-X). Overseas Dev Council.

Erb, Guy F. & Kallab, Valeriana, eds. Beyond Dependency: The Developing World Speaks Out. LC 75-23960. (Special Studies). 254p. 1975. text ed. 19.95 o.p. (ISBN 0-275-55580-1). Praeger.

--Beyond Dependency: The Developing World Speaks Out. LC 75-23960. 268p. 1975. pap. 3.95 (ISBN 0-686-28707-X). Overseas Dev Council.

Erb, Paul, jt. auth. see Bender, Harold S.

Erb, Richard D. & Ross, Stanley R., eds. U. S. Policies Toward Mexico: Perceptions & Perspectives. 1979. pap. 4.25 (ISBN 0-8447-2166-2). Am Enterprise.

Erbse, Hartmut. Beitraege zum Verstaendnis der Odyssee. (Untersuchungen zur Antiken Literatur und Geschichte 13). 1972. 48.25x (ISBN 3-11-004045-X). De Gruyter.

Erbsen, Wayne. A Manual on How to Play the Five String Banjo for the Complete Ignoramus. (Illus.). 52p. 1973. pap. 4.95 (ISBN 0-686-64083-7, PCB 103). Fischer Inc NY.

Erdahl, Carol, jt. auth. see Erdahl, Lowell.

Erdahl, Jeanne, ed. see Reynoldson, George.

Erdahl, Lowell & Erdahl, Carol. Be Good to Each Other-An Open Letter on Marriage. 1976. 3.95 (ISBN 0-8015-0584-4, Hawthorn). Dutton.

--Be Good to Each Other: An Open Letter on Marriage. LC 80-8893. 96p. 1981. pap. 3.95 (ISBN 0-06-062248-2, HarpR). Har-Row.

Erdall, Lowell. Better Preaching. (Preacher's Workshop Ser.). 1981. pap. text ed. 1.95 (ISBN 0-570-07408-8, 12-2680). Concordia.

Erdelyi, A. Higher Transcendental Functions, Vol. 2. 1980. Repr. of 1953 ed. lib. bdg. write for info. (ISBN 0-89874-069-X). Krieger.

Erdey-Gruz, Tibor. Transport Phenomena in Aqueous Solutions. LC 74-13613. 512p. 1974. 54.95 (ISBN 0-470-24371-6). Halsted Pr.

Erdlen, John A., ed. Job Hunting Guide. 2nd ed. LC 75-3824. (Career Guide Management Ser.). 160p. 1981. 12.95 (ISBN 0-89047-044-8); pap. 5.95 (ISBN 0-89047-043-X). Herman Pub.

Erdlen, John D., ed. Job Hunting Guide. LC 75-3824. (Career Management Guides Ser.). 160p. 1975. 11.95 o.p. (ISBN 0-89047-004-9); pap. 5.95 o.p. (ISBN 0-89047-005-7). Herman Pub.

--Job Hunting Guide. condensed ed. 65p. 1981. pap. 2.95 (ISBN 0-89047-026-X). Herman Pub.

Erdman, David V., ed. The Illuminated Blake. LC 74-3702. 416p. 1974. pap. 8.95 (ISBN 0-385-06053-X, Anch). Doubleday.

--Selected Poetry of William Blake. pap. 2.95 (ISBN 0-451-51373-8, CE1373, Sig Classics). NAL.

Erdman, David V., et al, eds. The Romantic Movement: A Selective & Critical Bibliography for Nineteen Seventy-Nine. LC 80-8494. 350p. 1980. lib. bdg. 35.00 (ISBN 0-8240-9512-X). Garland Pub.

Erdman, Donnelley & Holstein, Philip M., eds. Enduring Visions: One Thousand Years of Southwestern Indian Art. LC 79-52784. (Illus.). 1979. pap. 12.95 (ISBN 0-934324-00-X, Pub. by Aspen Ctr Visual Arts). Pub Ctr Cult Res.

Erdoes, Richard. Picture History of Ancient Rome. (gr. 4-6). 1967. 4.95 o.s.i. (ISBN 0-02-733550-X). Macmillan.

--The Sun Dance People. (Illus.). 241p. Date not set. pap. 1.95 (ISBN 0-394-70803-2, Vin). Random.

--The Woman Who Dared. 1978. pap. 1.95 o.p. (ISBN 0-449-13975-1, GM). Fawcett.

Erdozain, Placido. Archbishop Romero: Martyr of Salvador. McFadden, John & Warner, Ruth, trs. (Illus.). 128p. (Orig.). 1981. pap. 4.95 (ISBN 0-88344-019-9). Orbis Bks.

Erdsneker, Barbara & Haller, Margaret. Civil Service Arithmetic & Vocabulary. 320p. 1981. lib. bdg. 9.00 (ISBN 0-668-05116-7, 4872-7); pap. 6.00 (ISBN 0-668-04872-7). Arco.

Erdstein, Erich & Bean, Barbara. Inside the Fourth Reich. pap. 1.95 (ISBN 0-515-04897-6). Jove Pubns.

Erdt, Terrence. Jonathan Edwards: Art & the Sense of the Heart. LC 80-5380. (New England Writers Ser.). 144p. 1980. lib. bdg. 13.50x (ISBN 0-87023-304-1). U of Mass Pr.

Ereira, Alan. The People's England. (Illus.). 288p. 1981. 24.95 (ISBN 0-7100-0596-2). Routledge & Kegan.

Erenberg, Lewis A. Steppin' Out: New York Nightlife & the Transformation of American Culture, 1890-1930. LC 80-930. (Contributions in American Studies Ser.: No. 50). 296p. 1981. lib. bdg. 23.95 (ISBN 0-313-21342-9, EUN/). Greenwood.

Erens, Patricia. The Films of Shirley MacLaine. LC 76-50188. (Illus.). 1978. 17.50 (ISBN 0-498-01993-4); pap. 7.95 o.p. (ISBN 0-498-02302-8). A S Barnes.

Erenwein, Leslie. Mystery Raider. 1975. pap. 0.95 o.p. (ISBN 0-685-54124-X, LB297NK, Leisure Bks). Nordon Pubns.

--Rio Renegade. 1975. pap. 0.95 o.p. (ISBN 0-685-54125-8, LB296NK, Leisure Bks). Nordon Pubns.

Eres, Beth K. Legal & Legislative Information Processing. LC 79-7063. (Illus.). xvi, 299p. 1980. lib. bdg. 29.95 (ISBN 0-313-21343-7, ERL/). Greenwood.

Erfurt, John C. A Compendium of Information Relevant to Manpower Agencies. 1973. pap. 7.00x (ISBN 0-87736-330-7). U of Mich Inst Labor.

Erfurt, John C., jt. auth. see Ferman, Louis A.

Erfurt, John C., jt. auth. see Foote, Andrea.

Erfurth, Waldemar. Last Finnish War. 1979. 22.00 (ISBN 0-89093-205-0). U Pubns Amer.

Ergang, Robert. Europe from the Renaissance to Waterloo. 3rd ed. 1967. text ed. 19.95x (ISBN 0-669-22814-1). Heath.

Ergang, Robert & Rohr, Donald G. Europe Since Waterloo. 3rd ed. 1967. text ed. 19.95x (ISBN 0-669-22830-3). Heath.

Erhart, K. Patricia, et al. Roman Portraits: Aspects of Self & Society. (Illus.). 108p. (Orig.). 1980. pap. 7.75. J P Getty Mus.

Erhart, Katherine P. The Development of the Facing Head Motif on Greek Coins & Its Relation to Classical Art. Freedberg, Sydney J., ed. LC 78-74366. (Outstanding Disserations in the Fine Arts Ser.). (Illus.). 1979. lib. bdg. 50.00 (ISBN 0-8240-3954-8). Garland Pub.

Eriandson, Keith. Gundog Training. (Illus.). 1978. 22.00 (ISBN 0-214-20167-8). Transatlantic.

ERIC & Adult Education Association of the U. S. A. Register of Research: Investigation in Adult Education. 1968 2.30 (ISBN 0-685-85633-X); 1970 6.90 (ISBN 0-685-85634-8). Adult Ed.

ERIC (Educational Information Center) Current Index to Journals in Education: Semi-Annual Cumulation, January-June, 1977. LC 75-7532. 1977. 37.50 (ISBN 0-02-693050-1). Macmillan Info.

ERIC (Educational Resources Information Center) Current Index to Journals in Education: Semi-Annual Cumulation, July-December, 1977. LC 75-7532. 1978. 37.50 (ISBN 0-02-693060-9). Macmillan Info.

--Current Index to Journals in Education: Semi-Annual Cumulation, January-June, 1978. LC 75-7532. 1978. 37.50 (ISBN 0-02-693120-6). Macmillan Info.

--Current Index to Journals in Education: Semi-Annual Cumulation, July-December, 1978. LC 75-7532. 1979. 37.50 (ISBN 0-02-693130-3). Macmillan Info.

Erichsen, Heino R., jt. auth. see Nelson-Erichsen, Jean.

Ericksen, Edsel L., jt. auth. see Brookover, Wilbur.

Ericksen, Kenneth J., ed. see Shirley, James, et al.

Erickson, Alan. Bar Games, Bets & Challenges. (Orig.). 1981. pap. 1.95 (ISBN 0-446-90648-4). Warner Bks.

Erickson, C. L. The Perils of Probation. (Illus.). 238p. 1980. pap. 10.75 (ISBN 0-398-04013-3). C C Thomas.

Erickson, Carlton K., jt. ed. see Goodwin, Donald W.

Erickson, Carolly. Civilization & Society in the West. 1978. pap. 13.95x (ISBN 0-673-15123-9). Scott F.

--Great Harry. LC 79-21868. 1980. 14.95 (ISBN 0-671-40017-7). Summit Bks.

--The Medieval Vision: Essays in History & Perception. LC 75-10179. 256p. 1976. text ed. 14.95 (ISBN 0-19-501964-4); pap. text ed. 5.95x (ISBN 0-19-501963-6). Oxford U Pr.

Erickson, Charlotte. The Freezer Cookbook. (Illus.). 1981. pap. 8.95 (ISBN 0-8092-5888-9). Contemp Bks.

--Shortcut Cooking. rev. ed. (Illus.). 1981. pap. 6.95 (ISBN 0-8092-5887-0). Contemp Bks.

Erickson, Charlotte, ed. Emigration from Europe 1815-1914: Select Documents. (Documents in Economic History). 1976. text ed. 17.00x (ISBN 0-7136-1616-4). Humanities.

Erickson, Donald A., ed. Educational Organization & Administration. LC 76-18037. (Readings in Educational Research Ser.). 1977. 25.00 (ISBN 0-8211-0415-2); text ed. 22.50 10 or more copies (ISBN 0-685-71413-6). McCutchan.

Erickson, Donald A. & Reller, Theodore L., eds. The Principal in Metropolitan Schools. new ed. LC 78-62641. (Contemporary Educational Issues Ser.). 1978. 17.50 (ISBN 0-8211-0417-9); text ed. 15.75 ten or more copies (ISBN 0-686-52389-X). McCutchan.

Erickson, Dorie A. Canyon Christian Academy: An Alternate Education K-12. LC 80-51386. (Illus.). 55p. (Orig.). 1980. pap. 9.95 (ISBN 0-937242-01-2). Scandia Pubs.

--How to Firm Flabby Flesh. (Illus.). 35p. (Orig.). 1981. pap. 3.95 (ISBN 0-937242-02-0). Scandia Pubs.

--Increase Your Child's Learning Capacity: Through Hobbies, Exercise & Nutrition. 200p. 1981. pap. 5.95 (ISBN 0-937242-06-3). Scandia Pubs.

--Start Your Own Private School-Legally! LC 80-51385. 65p. (Orig.). 1980. pap. 16.00 (ISBN 0-937242-00-4). Scandia Pubs.

Erickson, Gerald D. & Hogan, Terrence P. Family Therapy: An Introduction to Theory & Technique. 2nd ed. 448p. (Orig.). 1980. pap. text ed. 12.95 (ISBN 0-8185-0437-4). Brooks-Cole.

Erickson, Gregg K., jt. auth. see Tussing, Arlon R.

Erickson, Janet. Block Printing on Textiles. (Illus.). 168p. 1974. 12.95 o.p. (ISBN 0-8230-0501-1); pap. 9.95 o.p. (ISBN 0-8230-0502-X). Watson-Guptill.

Erickson, John. The Road to Stalingrad. LC 74-24657. (Illus.). 604p. 1975. 25.00 o.p. (ISBN 0-06-011141-0, HarpT). Har-Row.

Erickson, John & Pages, Irene, eds. Proust et le Texte Producteur. vi, 147p. (Orig., Fr & Eng.). 1980. pap. 7.95 (ISBN 0-88955-000-X). U of Guelph.

Erickson, Keith. Aristotle: The Classical Heritage of Rhetoric. LC 74-10775. 1974. 14.00 (ISBN 0-8108-0740-8). Scarecrow.

Erickson, Kenneth P. The Brazilian Corporative State & Working-Class Politics. 1978. 19.50x (ISBN 0-520-03162-8). U of Cal Pr.

Erickson, Lonni R. The Teaching of Evolution in Public Schools: A Comparison of Evolution & Special Creation. (Illus.). 40p. (Orig.). 1980. pap. 3.95 (ISBN 0-937242-03-9). Scandia Pubs.

Erickson, Marcene L., jt. auth. see Barnard, Kathryn E.

Erickson, Marilyn T. Child Psychopathology: Assessment, Etiology & Treatment. 1978. ref. ed. 19.95 (ISBN 0-13-131102-6). P-H.

Erickson, Marilyn T., jt. auth. see Gabel, Stewart.

Erickson, Millard J. Relativism in Contemporary Christian Ethics. 1974. pap. 3.95 (ISBN 0-8010-3315-2). Baker Bk.

--Salvation: God's Amazing Plan. 1978. pap. 3.95 (ISBN 0-88207-772-4). Victor Bks.

Erickson, Millard J., ed. Living God: Readings in Christian Theology. 1973. pap. 9.95 (ISBN 0-8010-3305-5). Baker Bk.

Erickson, Milton & Rossi, Ernest L. Hypnotherapy: An Exploratory Casebook. LC 78-23839. 1979. 34.50 o.p. (ISBN 0-470-26595-7). Halsted Pr.

Erickson, Milton H. A Teaching Seminar with Milton H. Erickson, M.D. Zeig, Jeffrey K., ed. LC 80-23804. 340p. 1980. 20.00 (ISBN 0-87630-247-9). Brunner-Mazel.

Erickson, Milton H. & Rossi, Ernest L. Experiencing Hypnosis: Theraputic Aproaches to Altered States. 300p. 1979. text ed. 34.50x incl. audio cassette (ISBN 0-8290-0246-4). Irvington.

Erickson, Milton H., jt. auth. see Cooper, Linn F.

Erickson, Milton H., et al. Hypnotic Realities: The Induction of Clinical Hypnosis & Forms of Indirect Suggestion. LC 76-20636. 1976. 24.95x (ISBN 0-8290-0112-3); two audio cassetes avail. Irvington.

Erickson, Paul A. Ecological Impact Assessment: Principles & Applications. 1979. 29.00 (ISBN 0-12-241550-7). Acad Pr.

Erickson, Rica, et al. Flowers & Plants of Western Australia. rev. ed. 232p. 1979. 39.95 (ISBN 0-589-50116-X, Pub. by Reed Books Australia). C E Tuttle.

Erickson, Robert. Ricercar A 3 for 3 Contrabasses. (U. C. Publ. in Contemporary Music: Vol. 5). 1975. pap. 10.00x (ISBN 0-520-09357-7). U of Cal Pr.

--Sound Structure in Music. (Illus.). 1975. 16.50x (ISBN 0-520-02376-5). U of Cal Pr.

Erickson, Russell E. Warton & Morton. 1977. pap. 1.25 (ISBN 0-440-49522-9, YB). Dell.

Erickson, Steve M. Management Tools for Everyone. (Illus.). 160p. 1981. 17.50 (ISBN 0-89433-131-0). Petrocelli.

Erickson, V. L. & Julien, H. L., eds. Gas Turbine Heat Transfer: 1978. 1978. 18.00 (ISBN 0-685-66801-0, H00125). ASME.

Ericksson, C. Maillard Reactions in Food: Proceedings of the International Symposium, Uddevalla, Sweden, September 1979. (Progress in Food & Nutrition Science Ser.: Vol. 5). (Illus.). 500p. 1981. 156.00 (ISBN 0-08-025496-9). Pergamon.

Ericson, David. The Money Game. (Pacesetters Ser.). (Illus.). 64p. (gr. 4 up). 1978. PLB 7.95 (ISBN 0-516-02156-7). Childrens.

Ericson, E. E., jt. auth. see Andrews, Robert.

Ericson, Edward E., Jr. Solzhenitsyn: The Moral Vision. 1980. 12.95 (ISBN 0-8028-3527-9). Eerdmans.

Ericson, Eric. The Sorcerer. LC 78-19530. 1979. 8.95 o.p. (ISBN 0-312-74506-0). St Martin.

Ericson, Georgia. Aunt Hack's Rock House Kitchen: A Cookbook with a Story. 1977. write for info. Crosby County.

Ericson, Jon M., jt. auth. see Murphy, James J.

Ericson, Kay. The Solar Jobs Book. LC 80-17886. 220p. 1980. pap. 7.95 (ISBN 0-931790-12-3). Brick Hse Pub.

Ericson, Mary J. Backyard Birddom. LC 66-19146. (Illus.). 1974. 2.95 (ISBN 0-87208-079-X); pap. 1.50 (ISBN 0-87208-010-2). Island Pr.

Ericson, R. F., ed. Improving the Human Condition - Quality & Stability in Social Systems: Proceedings, Silver Anniversary International Meeting, London, England, August 20-24, 1979. LC 79-66355. 1979. 68.20 (ISBN 0-387-90442-5). Springer-Verlag.

Ericson, Virginia, jt. auth. see Townsend, Sallie.

Eriksen. Human Services Today. 1977. text ed. 12.95 (ISBN 0-87909-336-6). Reston.

Eriksen, Donald. Oscar Wilde. (English Authors Ser.: No. 211). 1977. lib. bdg. 9.95 (ISBN 0-8057-6680-4). Twayne.

Eriksen, K. Communication Skills for the Human Services. 1978. 13.95 (ISBN 0-87909-100-2); pap. 7.95 (ISBN 0-87909-101-0). Reston.

Eriksen, Karin. Human Services Today. 2nd ed. 192p. 1981. text ed. 12.95 (ISBN 0-8359-3004-1). Reston.

Eriksen, Svend. Early Neo-Classicism in France. 1974. 98.00 (ISBN 0-571-08717-5, Pub. by Faber & Faber). Merrimack Bk Serv.

Eriksen, Trona. Bios Theoretikos. 1977. pap. 19.00x (ISBN 82-00-05031-9, Dist. by Columbia U Pr). Universitet.

Erikson, Alvar, ed. Letters from Erik Benzelius the Younger from Learned Foreigners, 2 vols. Orig. Title: Acta Regiae Societatis Scientarium et Literarum. (Orig.). 1980. 31.00. Vol. 1, 1697-1722. Vol. 2, 1723-1743 (ISBN 91-85252-22-0). Humanities.

Erikson, Dorie. Increase Your Knowledge Thru Fun. 100p. 1981. pap. 5.95 (ISBN 0-937242-00-4). Scandia Pubs.

Erikson, Erik H. Dimensions of the New Identity: Jefferson Lectures 1973. LC 73-22289. 125p. 1974. 10.95 (ISBN 0-393-05515-9). Norton.

Erikson, Paul. The Dynast. LC 78-12194. 1979. 8.95 (ISBN 0-688-03418-7). Morrow.

Eriksson, B. Sweden Sings. pap. 12.50x o.p. (ISBN 0-89918-120-1, SW120). Vanous.

Eriksson, Brigitte, jt. ed. see Faderman, Lillian.

Eriksson, Goran. The Growth & Financing of the Firm: Models of Firm Behavior Tested with Data from Swedish Industrial Firms. LC 77-26840. 1978. 29.95 (ISBN 0-470-99230-1). Halsted Pr.

Eringen, A. Cemal. Mechanics of Continua. 2nd ed. LC 78-2334. 520p. 1981. Repr. of 1967 ed. lib. bdg. 39.50 (ISBN 0-88275-663-X). Krieger.

Erixon, S. The Possibilities of Charting Modern Life. 1970. 27.00 (ISBN 0-08-013308-8). Pergamon.

Erkkila, Barbara H. Hammers on Stone: The History of Cape Ann Granite. (Illus.). 208p. 1980. 18.95 (ISBN 0-931474-19-1). TBW Bks.

Erkkila, Besty. Walt Whitman Among the French: Poet & Myth. LC 79-3204. 1980. 16.50x (ISBN 0-691-06426-1). Princeton U Pr.

Erlandson. Diagnostic Transmission Electron Miscroscopy. 1981. write for info. Masson Pub.

Erlandson, Becker. Church Fellowship. 1980. 0.80 (ISBN 0-8100-0113-6). Northwest Pub.

Erlandson, Keith. Gundog Training. 1978. 11.95 o.p. (8028, Dist. by Arco). Barrie & Jenkins.

--Home Smoking & Curing: How You Can Smoke-Cure, Salt, & Preserve Fish, Meat, Poultry & Game. 1978. 9.95 o.p. (ISBN 0-214-20322-0, 8048, Dist. by Arco). Barrie & Jenkins.

Erlanger, Ellen. Dan Rather. (The Achievers Ser.). (Illus.). (gr. 4-9). 1981. PLB 5.95 (ISBN 0-8225-0487-1). Lerner Pubns.

--Hubert H. Humphrey: The Happy Warrior. LC 79-1367. (Achievers Ser.). (Illus.). (gr. 4 up). Date not set. PLB 5.95g (ISBN 0-8225-0476-6). Lerner Pubns. Postponed.

--Jane Fonda. (The Achievers Ser.). (Illus.). (gr. 4-9). 1981. PLB 5.95 (ISBN 0-8225-0485-5). Lerner Pubns.

Erlanger, George C. The International Monetary Chaos & a Positive Plan for the Monetary Reconstruction of the World. (Illus.). 127p. 1981. 67.85 (ISBN 0-918968-90-9). Inst Econ Finan.

Erlanger, Rachel. Lucretia Borgia: A Biography. LC 75-39117. (Illus.). 1978. 13.95 (ISBN 0-8015-4725-3, Hawthorn); pap. 7.95 (ISBN 0-8015-4724-5, Hawthorn). Dutton.

Erlewein, David L., et al. Instructions for Veterinary Clients. LC 74-12908. (Illus.). 380p. 1975. pap. 42.00 (ISBN 0-7216-3400-1). Saunders.

Erlich. Geomicrobiology. Date not set. price not set (ISBN 0-8247-1183-1). Dekker.

Erlich, Victor. Russian Formalism: History-Doctrine. 2nd ed. (Slavistic Printings & Reprintings Ser: No. 4). 1965. text ed. 34.75x (ISBN 90-2790-450-2). Mouton.

Ermakov, I. D. Etiudy Po Psikhologii Tvorchestva. (Rus.). 1981. 15.00 (ISBN 0-88233-500-6); pap. 5.00 (ISBN 0-88233-501-4). Ardis Pubs.

Ermans, A. M., jt. auth. see Bastenie, Paul A.

Ermarth, Michael. Wilhelm Dilthey: The Critique of Historical Reason. write for info. (ISBN 0-226-21743-4). U of Chicago Pr.

Ermler, W. C. see Mulliken, Robert S.

Ernenwein, Leslie. Ambush at Jubilo Junction. 1976. pap. 0.95 o.p. (ISBN 0-685-69142-X, LB361, Leisure Bks). Nordon Pubns.

--Boss of Panamint. 1975. pap. 0.95 o.p. (ISBN 0-685-59189-1, LB313, Leisure Bks). Nordon Pubns.

--Bullet Barricade. 1975. pap. 0.95 o.p. (ISBN 0-685-59190-5, LB312, Leisure Bks). Nordon Pubns.

--Give a Man a Gun. 1975. pap. 0.95 o.p. (ISBN 0-685-52175-3, LB239NK, Leisure Bks). Nordon Pubns.

--Rebel Yell. 1979. pap. 1.25 (ISBN 0-505-51358-7). Tower Bks.

--Renegade Ramrod. 1976. pap. 0.95 o.p. (ISBN 0-685-64016-7, LB345, Leisure Bks). Nordon Pubns.

Ernest, Charlotte, jt. auth. see Ernest, John.

Ernest, John & Ashmun, Richard. Selling Principles & Practices. 5th ed. LC 79-17748. (Illus.). 1980. text ed. 11.84 (ISBN 0-07-019620-6); student activity guide 5.32 (ISBN 0-07-019621-4); tchrs. manual & key 3.95 (ISBN 0-07-019622-2). McGraw.

Ernest, John & Ernest, Charlotte. Basic Business Mathematics. 1977. text ed. 13.95 (ISBN 0-02-472610-9). Macmillan.

Ernest, John & Stein, Herbert M. Introduction to Business Mathematics. LC 79-86252. 384p. 1969. pap. text ed. 11.95x (ISBN 0-02-474100-0, 47410); tests 13.95x (ISBN 0-02-474590-1, 47459). Macmillan.

Ernest, John, jt. auth. see Haas, Kenneth B.

Ernest, Verleigh. Typing. college ed. LC 72-142516. 1971. 12.95 (ISBN 0-672-96001-X); pap. 10.50 (ISBN 0-672-96002-8); tchrs' manual 5.00 (ISBN 0-672-96003-6); wkbk. 9.50 (ISBN 0-672-96004-4). Bobbs.

Ernsberger, George. The Mountain King. 1979. pap. 2.25 o.p. (ISBN 0-425-04223-5). Berkley Pub.

Ernst, Bernard D., jt. auth. see Waite, M. O.

Ernst, Bruno. The Magic Mirror of M. C. Escher. (Illus.). 1976. 15.00 o.p. (ISBN 0-394-49217-X). Random.

--The Magic Mirror of M. C. Escher. (Illus.). 1977. pap. 10.95 (ISBN 0-345-24243-2). Ballantine.

Ernst, David. The Evolution of Electronic Music. LC 76-41624. (Illus.). 1977. pap. text ed. 10.95 (ISBN 0-02-870880-6). Schirmer Bks.

Ernst, Eldon. Moment of Truth for Protestant America: Interchurch Campaigns Following World War I. LC 74-16567. (American Academy of Religion. Dissertation Ser.). 1974. pap. 7.50 (ISBN 0-88420-120-1, 010103). Scholars Pr Ca.

Ernst, Franklin H., Jr. The Game Diagram. 1972. softbd 2.50x (ISBN 0-916944-19-0). Addresso'set.

Ernst, John. Jesse James. LC 76-10206. (Illus.). (gr. 4-7). 1976. PLB 6.95 (ISBN 0-13-509695-2); pap. 1.95 (ISBN 0-13-509661-8). P-H.

Ernst, K. F. The Complete Calorie Counter for Dining Out. (Orig.). 1981. pap. 2.95 (ISBN 0-515-05500-X). Jove Pubns.

--The Complete Carbohydrate Counter for Dining Out. 1981. pap. 2.95 (ISBN 0-515-05698-7). Jove Pubns.

Ernst, Kathryn F. Indians: The First Americans. LC 78-13742. (Easy-Read Fact Bk.). (Illus.). (gr. 2-4). 1979. PLB 6.45 s&l (ISBN 0-531-02273-0). Watts.

Ernst, Ken. Pre-Scription: A TA Look at Child Development. LC 75-28755. 1976. pap. 4.95 o.p. (ISBN 0-89087-158-2). Celestial Arts.

--TA Stories for Kids. LC 77-79880. (Illus.). (gr. k-8). 1977. pap. 3.95 o.p. (ISBN 0-89087-208-2). Celestial Arts.

Ernst, M. L. The First Freedom. LC 73-166324. (Civil Liberties in American History Ser.). 316p. 1971. Repr. of 1946 ed. lib. bdg. 29.50 (ISBN 0-306-70242-8). Da Capo.

Ernst, M. L. & Lindey, A. The Censor Marches on. LC 73-164512. (Civil Liberties in American History Ser.). 346p. 1971. Repr. of 1940 ed. lib. bdg. 32.50 (ISBN 0-306-70295-9). Da Capo.

Ernst, Sandra B. The Creative Package: A Working Text for Advertising Copy & Layout. 1979. pap. text ed. 10.50 (ISBN 0-88244-185-X). Grid Pub.

Ernst, W. G. Petrologic Phase Equilibria. LC 76-3699. (Illus.). 1976. text ed. 31.95x (ISBN 0-7167-0279-7). W H Freeman.

Ernst, W. G., ed. The Geotectonic Development of California, Vol. 1. (Illus.). 720p. 1981. text ed. 31.95 (ISBN 0-13-353938-5). P-H.

Ernster, L., jt. auth. see Lindberg, O.

Ernster, L. & Ernster, L., eds. Mitochondria, Structure & Function. 1970. 54.00 (ISBN 0-12-241250-8). Acad Pr.

Ernstine, Bill I. & Mack, Jack A. Profitability Through Loss Control: Manual for Financial Institutions. 1977. pap. text ed. 8.95 o.p. (ISBN 0-87084-719-8). Anderson Pub Co.

Eron, Carol. The Virus That Ate Cannibals: And Other True Stories. 256p. 1981. 12.95 (ISBN 0-02-536250-X). Macmillan.

Eron, Judy & Morgan, Geoffrey. Charlie Rich. (Rock 'n Pop Stars Ser.). (Illus.). (gr. 4-12). 1975. PLB 5.95 (ISBN 0-87191-463-8); pap. 2.95 (ISBN 0-89812-116-7). Creative Ed.

Eron, Leonard D. & Callahan, Robert, eds. Relation of Theory to Practice in Psychotherapy. LC 69-13705. 1969. 29.50x (ISBN 0-202-26017-8). Irvington.

Errera, Maurice & Forssberg, Arne, eds. Mechanisms in Radiobiology, 2 vols. Incl. Vol. 1. General Principles. 1961. 48.50 (ISBN 0-12-241101-3); Vol. 2. Multicellular Organisms. 1960. 48.00 (ISBN 0-12-241102-1). Acad Pr.

Erricker, B. C. Advanced General Statistics. 358p. 1971. 19.50x (ISBN 0-8448-0078-3). Crane-Russak Co.

Errington, Paul L. Muskrats & Marsh Management. LC 77-14177. (Illus.). 1978. 10.95x (ISBN 0-8032-0975-4); pap. 3.25 (ISBN 0-8032-5892-5, BB 664, Bison). U of Nebr Pr.

Errington, R. M. The Dawn of Empire: Rome's Rise to World Power. LC 75-176296. (Illus.). 330p. 1972. 20.00x (ISBN 0-8014-0689-7); pap. 5.95 452p., 1973 (ISBN 0-8014-9128-2, CP128). Cornell U Pr.

Ersek, Robert A. Pain Control with Transcutaneous Electrical Neuro Stimulation (Tens) LC 78-50175. 1980. 23.75 (ISBN 0-87527-168-5). Green.

--Transcutaneous Neuro Stimulation: Principles & Practice. LC 78-50175. 1981. 23.75 (ISBN 0-87527-168-5). Green.

Erskine, Irene. Laboratory Guide for Anatomy & Physiology. 176p. 1980. pap. text ed. 8.95 (ISBN 0-8403-2350-6). Kendall-Hunt.

Erskine, Jim. Fold a Banana: & 146 Other Things to Do When You're Bored. (Illus.). 1978. pap. 5.95 (ISBN 0-517-53503-3, Dist. by Crown). Potter.

--Throw a Tomato. (Illus.). 1979. 5.95 (ISBN 0-517-53865-2); ten copy prepack 59.50 (ISBN 0-517-53971-3). Potter.

Erskine, Jim & Moran, Goerge. Hug a Teddy: And One Hundred & Seventy-One Other Ways to Keep Safe & Secure. 1980. 5.95 (ISBN 0-517-54215-3, 542153); 10 copy prepack 59.50 (ISBN 0-517-54239-0). Potter.

Erskine, John T. Millionaire for God (C. T. Studd) 1968. pap. 1.95 (ISBN 0-87508-611-X). Chr Lit.

Erskine, Kathryn A. What You Always Wanted to Know About Operating a Small Business but Didn't Know Who to Ask. (Illus.). 69p. (Orig.). 1980. pap. 9.95 (ISBN 0-9605058-0-6). Erskine.

Erskine, Noel L. Decolonizing Theology: A Caribbean Perspective. LC 80-21784. 160p. (Orig.). 1981. pap. 6.95 (ISBN 0-88344-087-3). Orbis Bks.

Erskine, William. A History of India Under the Two First Sovereigns of the House of Taimur, Baber & Humayun, 2 vols. 1162p. 1980. Repr. 70.00x (ISBN 0-686-28827-0, Pub. by Irish Academic Pr). Biblio Dist.

--A History of India Under the Two First Sovereigns of the House of Taimur: Baber & Humayun, 2 vols. 1162p. 1972. Repr. of 1854 ed. 70.00x (ISBN 0-7165-2118-0, Pub. by Irish Academic Pr Ireland). Biblio Dist.

Erskine-Hill, Howard. The Social Milieu of Alexander Pope: Lives, Examples, & the Poetic Response. LC 74-29719. 352p. 1975. 27.50x (ISBN 0-300-01837-1). Yale U Pr.

Erskine-Hill, Howard, ed. The Art of Alexander Pope. LC 78-62593. (Critical Studies Ser.). 1979. text ed. 19.75x (ISBN 0-685-62564-8). B&N.

Ersley, Allan J. & Gabuzda, Thomas G. Pathophysiology of Blood. 2nd ed. LC 78-24813. (Illus.). 1979. pap. text ed. 15.00 (ISBN 0-7216-3403-6). Saunders.

Erte. Designs by Erte: Fashion Drawings & Illustrations from Harper's Bazaar. Blum, S., ed. (Illus.). 13.50 (ISBN 0-8446-5571-6). Peter Smith.

--Erte's Costumes & Sets for "Der Rosenkavalier" in Full Color. (Illus.). 48p. 1980. pap. 6.95 (ISBN 0-486-23998-5). Dover.

Ertl, John, jt. auth. see Konrad, Patricia.

Eruch, et al. Tales for the New Life Meher Baba. 191p. 1976. 8.95 (ISBN 0-686-17265-5); pap. 3.95 (ISBN 0-686-17266-3). Meher Baba Info.

Erulkar, Mary, pseud. Mandala Two to the Fifth Power. (Writers Workshop Redbird Ser.). 48p. 1975. 12.00 (ISBN 0-88253-574-9); pap. text ed. 4.80 (ISBN 0-88253-573-0). Ind-US Inc.

Erven, Bernard L., jt. auth. see Forster, D. Lynn.

Erven, Lawrence. First Aid & Emergency Rescue. Gruber, Harvey, ed. LC 71-110984. (Fire Science Ser). (Illus.). 215p. 1970. pap. text ed. 9.95x (ISBN 0-02-474370-4, 47437). Macmillan.

--Techniques of Fire Hydraulics. (Fire Science Ser). 1972. text ed. 11.95x (ISBN 0-02-473000-9, 47300). Macmillan.

Erven, Lawrence W. Fire Company Apparatus & Procedure. 2nd ed. (Fire Science Ser). (Illus.). 360p. 1974. text ed. 14.95x (ISBN 0-02-474150-7, 47415). Macmillan.

--Handbook of Emergency Care & Rescue. rev. ed. 1976. text ed. 14.95x (ISBN 0-02-472630-3). Macmillan.

Ervin, Jane. Phonics Workbook, Level D. (MCP Basic Phonics Program). (gr. 4). 1977. 3.40 (ISBN 0-87895-441-4). Modern Curr.

--Two-Color New Phonics Workbook, Level D. (gr. 4). 1977. 3.76 (ISBN 0-87895-442-2). Modern Curr.

Ervin, Judy, jt. auth. see Andrews, Bart.

Ervin, Thomas. Real Estate Revolution! Who Will Survive. 1980. 10.95 (ISBN 0-88462-387-4). Real Estate Ed Co.

Erwe, F. Differential & Integral Calculus. Fishel, B., tr. (Illus.). 1967. 14.25 o.s.i. (ISBN 0-02-844300-4). Hafner.

Erwin, Annabel. Liliane. 400p. (Orig.). 1976. pap. 2.50 o.s.i. (ISBN 0-446-91219-0). Warner Bks.

Erwin, Betty K. Who Is Victoria? (Illus.). (gr. 4-6). 1976. pap. 1.25 (ISBN 0-671-29752-X). PB.

Erwin, Dell & Erwin, John. The Man Who Keeps Going to Jail. (Illus.). 1980. pap. 1.95 (ISBN 0-89191-200-2). Cook.

Erwin, E. Behavior Therapy: Scientific, Philosophical & Moral Foundations. 1978. 29.95 (ISBN 0-521-22293-1); pap. 8.95x (ISBN 0-521-29439-8). Cambridge U Pr.

Erwin, Edward. Behavior Therapy: Philosophical & Empirical Foundations. 1981. price not set (ISBN 0-12-242150-7). Acad Pr.

Erwin, Jean & Erwin, Jim. How to Choose & Use the Right Therapist for You. 1978. pap. 3.95 o.p. (ISBN 0-8362-2601-1). Andrews & McMeel.

Erwin, Jim, jt. auth. see Erwin, Jean.

Erwin, John, jt. auth. see Erwin, Dell.

Erwin, Wallace M. A Short Reference Grammar of Iraqi Arabic. (Richard Slade Harrell Arabic Ser). 392p. 1963. pap. 8.50 (ISBN 0-87840-002-8); Set. 2 cassettes 10.50 (ISBN 0-87840-013-3); write for info. five-inch reel set (ISBN 0-87840-018-4). Georgetown U Pr.

Esalen, Wilner W. Too Small to Die. LC 79-57586. 114p. 1981. 7.95 (ISBN 0-533-04575-4). Vantage.

Esar, Evan. Twenty Thousand Quips & Quotes. LC 68-18096. 1968. 12.95 (ISBN 0-385-00047-2). Doubleday.

Esarey, Logan. Indiana Home. LC 76-12384. (Illus.). 136p. 1976. 10.00x (ISBN 0-253-32989-2); pap. 3.95x (ISBN 0-253-28325-6). Ind U Pr.

Esau, Helmut, et al. Language & Communication. 1980. pap. 8.75. Hornbeam Pr.

Esau, Katherine. The Phloem. LC 75-566979. (Encyclopedia of Plant Anatomy Ser.). (Illus.). 1969. 126.00x (ISBN 0-8002-0226-0). Intl Pubns Serv.

--Viruses in Plant Hosts: Form, Distribution, & Pathologic Effects. LC 68-9831. (Illus.). 1968. 25.00x (ISBN 0-299-05110-2). U of Wis Pr.

Esau, P. see Mrak, E. M. & Stewart, G. F.

Esau, Theodore. Complete Real Estate Listings Handbook. 265p. 18.95 (ISBN 0-13-162404-0, Busn). P-H.

Esbensen, Thorwald & Richards, Philip. Family Designed Learning. LC 74-83216. 1976. pap. 4.95 (ISBN 0-8224-2825-3). Pitman Learning.

Esbery, Joy E. Knight of the Holy Spirit: A Study of William Lyon Mackenzie King. 336p. 1980. 20.00 (ISBN 0-8020-5502-8). U of Toronto Pr.

Escher, M. C. Graphic Work of M. C. Escher. rev. ed. 1967. 13.95 o.p. (ISBN 0-8015-3102-0). Dutton.

Eschholz, Paul A., jt. ed. see Biddle, Arthur W.

Eschholz, Paul A., jt. ed. see Rosa, Alfred F.

Eschlach, Achim & Rader, Wendelin, eds. Semiotics of Films. 203p. 1978. 26.00 (ISBN 0-89664-080-9, Pub. by K G Saur). Gale.

Eschman, Karl. Changing Forms in Modern Music. 2nd ed. LC 67-26898. (Illus.). 213p. 1967. 5.00 (ISBN 0-911318-01-1). E C Schirmer.

Escobar, Helga, jt. ed. see Wallace, Don, Jr.

Escobar, M. R. & Friedman, H., eds. Macrophages & Lymphocytes: Nature, Functions, & Interaction, Pt. A. LC 79-9566. (Advances in Experimental Medicine & Biology Ser.: Vol. 121A). 660p. 1980. 59.50 (ISBN 0-306-40285-8, Plenum Pr). Plenum Pub.

--Macrophages & Lymphocytes: Nature, Functions & Interaction, Pt. B. (Advances in Experimental Medicine & Biology: Vol. 121B). 625p. 1980. 59.50 (ISBN 0-306-40286-6, Plenum Pr). Plenum Pub.

Escobar, Samuel. Irrupcion Juvenil. LC 77-17648. 96p. (Orig., Span.). 1978. pap. 1.95 (ISBN 0-89922-106-8). Edit Caribe.

Escoffier, Francis & Higginbotham, Jay, eds. A Voyage to Dauphin Island in 1720: The Journal of Bertet De la Clue. Escoffier, Francis & Higginbotham, Jay, trs. LC 73-91909. (Illus., Fr.). 1974. 7.95 (ISBN 0-914224-02-6). Museum Mobile.

Escoffier, Francis, tr. see Escoffier, Francis & Higginbotham, Jay.

Escot, Pozzi, jt. auth. see Cogan, Robert.

Escott, Colin & Hawkins, Martin. Sun Records. (Illus.). 1980. pap. 8.95 (ISBN 0-8256-3161-0). Music Sales.

Escoula, Yvonne. Six Blue Horses. LC 70-103044. (gr. 5-9). 1970. 8.95 (ISBN 0-87599-162-9). S G Phillips.

Escourolle, Raymond & Poirier, Jacques. Manual of Basic Neuropathology. 2nd ed. Rubinstein, Lucien J., tr. LC 77-80748. (Illus.). 1978. pap. text ed. 13.50 (ISBN 0-7216-3406-0). Saunders.

Esdaile, James. Mesmerism in India. Bd. with Numerous Cases of Surgical Operations; The Philosophy of Sleep. (Contributions to the History of Psychology Ser., Vol. X, Pt. A: Orientations). 1978. Repr. of 1846 ed. 30.00 (ISBN 0-89093-159-3). U Pubns Amer.

ESE California. John Lennon. (Front Page News Book Ser.). 1981. lib. bdg. 12.95 (ISBN 0-912076-46-1); pap. 5.95 (ISBN 0-912076-45-3). ESE Calif.

Esenin, Sergei. Izbrannye Stikhi. (Rus.). 1979. 11.00 o.p. (ISBN 0-88233-590-1); pap. 3.95 (ISBN 0-88233-574-X). Ardis Pubs.

Esenwein, J. Berg & Leeds, Arthur. Writing the Photoplay. 425p. 1980. Repr. of 1913 ed. lib. bdg. 35.00 (ISBN 0-8495-1350-2). Arden Lib.

Eser, Albin, jt. ed. see Wallace, Samuel E.

Esfandiary, Fereidoun M. Beggar. 1965. 7.95 (ISBN 0-8392-1154-6). Astor-Honor.

Eshbach, Charles E. Food Service Management. 3rd ed. LC 79-20378. 1979. pap. text ed. 11.95 (ISBN 0-8436-2176-1). CBI Pub.

Eshbach, Charles E., ed. Food Service Trends. LC 74-220. 330p. 1974. 15.95 (ISBN 0-8436-0581-2). CBI Pub.

Eshelman, Ruthe & Winston, Mary. The American Heart Association Cookbook. 1977. pap. 6.95 (ISBN 0-345-28827-0). Ballantine.

Esherick, Joseph W. Reform & Revolution in China: The 1911 Revolution in Hunan & Hubei. 1976. 20.00x (ISBN 0-520-03084-2). U of Cal Pr.

Eshleman, Clayton. Hades in Manganese. 150p. (Orig.). 1981. pap. 5.00 (ISBN 0-87685-472-2); signed cloth ed. 20.00 (ISBN 0-87685-473-0). Black Sparrow.

--Nights We Put the Rock Together. LC 79-55418. 1979. signed numbered ed. 9.00 (ISBN 0-686-59689-7); signed numbered ed. 20.00 (ISBN 0-686-59690-0); signed lettered ed. o.p. (ISBN 0-686-59691-9). Cadmus Eds.

Eshleman, Clayton, tr. see Artaud, Antonin.

Eshleman, Clayton, tr. see Vallejo, Cesar.

Eshleman, J. Ross. The Family: An Introduction. 3rd ed. 640p. 1981. text ed. 19.90 (ISBN 0-205-07241-0, 817241-2); tchrs'. ed. free (ISBN 0-205-07242-9). Allyn.

--The Family: An Introduction. 2nd ed. 1978. text ed. 18.95 (ISBN 0-205-05949-X); instr's man. avail. (ISBN 0-205-05950-3). Allyn.

Eshleman, J. Ross & Clarke, Juanne N. Intimacy, Commitments & Marriage: Development of Relationships. 1978. pap. text ed. 12.55 (ISBN 0-205-05932-5); instr's manual (ISBN 0-205-05934-1). Allyn.

Esho, F. O. African (Yoruba) Case Studies in the Application of Metaphysical, Herbal, & Occult Therapies. (Traditional Healing Ser.: Vol. 4). (Illus.). 1981. 22.50x (ISBN 0-932426-03-4); pap. text ed. 12.50x (ISBN 0-932426-07-7). Trado-Medic.

Esin, Emel. Mecca the Blessed, Madinah the Radiant. 1963. 21.95 (ISBN 0-236-31090-9, Pub. by Paul Elek). Merrimack Bk Serv.

Eskelin, Neil. Yes Yes Living in a No No World. (Orig.). 1980. pap. 2.95 (ISBN 0-88270-417-6). Logos.

Eskew, Harry & McElrath, Hugh T. Sing with Understanding. LC 79-55293. 1980. 12.95 (ISBN 0-8054-6809-9). Broadman.

Eskin, Bernard A., ed. The Menopause: Comprehensive Management. LC 80-80302. (Illus.). 224p. 1980. 27.50 (ISBN 0-89352-085-3). Masson Pub.

Eskin, G. I. Boundary Value Problems for Elliptic Pseudodifferential Equations. (Mathematical Monographs: Vol. 52). 1981. price not set o.p. (ISBN 0-8218-4503-9). Am Math.

Eskinazi, Salamon, ed. Modern Developments in the Mechanics of Continua: Proceedings. 1967. 31.50 (ISBN 0-12-242550-2). Acad Pr.

Esko, Edward & Esko, Wendy. Macrobiotic Cooking for Everyone. LC 79-89344. (Illus., Orig.). 1980. pap. 12.95 (ISBN 0-87040-469-5). Japan Pubns.

Esko, Wendy. Introducing Macrobiotic Cooking. LC 79-1957. (Illus.). 1979. pap. 8.95 (ISBN 0-87040-458-X). Japan Pubns.

Esko, Wendy, jt. auth. see Esko, Edward.

Eskow, John. Smokestack Lightning. 1980. 10.95 (ISBN 0-440-07688-9); pap. 4.95 (ISBN 0-440-07689-7). Delacorte.

Esland, Geoff & Salaman, Graeme, eds. The Politics of Work & Occupations. 416p. 1981. pap. 11.00x (ISBN 0-8020-6429-9). U of Toronto Pr.

Esler, Anthony. Babylon. 320p. 1981. pap. 2.75 (ISBN 0-449-24375-3, Crest). Fawcett.

--For Love of a Pirate. LC 78-17287. 1978. 9.95 o.p. (ISBN 0-688-03375-X). Morrow.

--Forbidden City. 1979. pap. 1.95 o.p. (ISBN 0-449-23836-9, Crest). Fawcett.

--Forbidden City. LC 77-6743. 1977. 9.95 o.p. (ISBN 0-688-03219-2). Morrow.

--Lord Libertine. 1977. pap. 1.75 o.p. (ISBN 0-449-23170-4, Crest). Fawcett.

Esler, Mary K., jt. auth. see Esler, William K.

Esler, William K. The Day the Sparrow Died. (Orig.). 1980. pap. 2.25 (ISBN 0-532-23313-1). Manor Bks.

--Teaching Elementary Science. 2nd ed. 1976. 17.95x (ISBN 0-534-00489-X). Wadsworth Pub.

Esler, William K. & Esler, Mary K. Teaching Elementary Science. 2nd ed. 512p. 1980. text ed. 18.95x (ISBN 0-534-00913-1). Wadsworth Pub.

Esmay, Judith. Collective Bargaining & Teacher Strikes. 1978. pap. text ed. 3.50 (ISBN 0-934460-07-8). NCCE.

Esmay, Merle L. Principles of Animal Environment. 1978. text ed. 22.50 (ISBN 0-87055-263-5). AVI.

Espeland, Pamela. How to Play Word Games. (Creative Activities, Games, Projects Ser.). (Illus.). 32p. (gr. 4-8). 1981. PLB 5.95 (ISBN 0-87191-797-1); pap. 2.75 (ISBN 0-89812-249-X). Creative Ed.

--The Story of Arachne. LC 80-66796. (Myths for Modern Children Ser.). (Illus.). 32p. (gr. 1-4). 1980. PLB 5.95g (ISBN 0-87614-130-0). Carolrhoda Bks.

--The Story of Baucis & Philemon. LC 80-27674. (A Myth for Modern Children Ser.). (Illus.). 32p. (gr. 1-4). 1981. PLB 5.95 (ISBN 0-87614-140-8). Carolrhoda Bks.

--The Story of Cadmus. LC 80-66795. (Myths for Modern Children Ser.). (Illus.). 32p. (gr. 1-4). 1980. PLB 5.95g (ISBN 0-87614-128-9). Carolrhoda Bks.

--The Story of King Midas. LC 80-66794. (Myths for Modern Children Ser.). (Illus.). 32p. (gr. 1-4). 1980. PLB 5.95g (ISBN 0-87614-129-7). Carolrhoda Bks.

--The Story of Pygmalion. LC 80-15792. (Myths for Modern Children Ser.). (Illus.). 32p. (gr. 1-4). 1981. PLB 6.95 (ISBN 0-87614-127-0). Carolrhoda Bks.

--Theseus & the Road to Athens. LC 80-27713. (Myths for Modern Children Ser.). (Illus.). 32p. (gr. 1-4). 1981. PLB 6.95 (ISBN 0-87614-141-6). Carolrhoda Bks.

--Why Do We Eat? (Creative's Questions & Answers Library). (Illus.). 32p. (gr. 3-4). Date not set. PLB 5.75 (ISBN 0-87191-747-5); pap. 2.75 (ISBN 0-89812-216-3). Creative Ed. Postponed.

Espenak, Liljan. Dance Therapy: Theory & Application. (Illus.). 210p. 1981. text ed. 19.75 (ISBN 0-398-04110-5). C C Thomas.

Espenshade, Abraham H. Pennsylvania Place Names. LC 68-30591. 1969. Repr. of 1925 ed. 18.00 (ISBN 0-8103-3234-5). Gale.

Espenshade, Edward B., Jr., ed. Goode's World Atlas. 15th ed. Morrison, Joel. LC 73-21108. 1978. text ed. 16.95 (ISBN 0-528-83061-9); pap. text ed. 10.95 (ISBN 0-528-63004-0). Rand.

Espenshade, Edward B., Jr. & Morrison, Joel L., eds. The World Book Atlas. LC 76-57897. (Illus.). 1977. text ed. 15.95 o.p. (ISBN 0-7166-2026-X). World Bk-Chilcraft.

Espenshade, Jean E. Staff Manual for Teaching Patients About Diabetes Mellitus. LC 78-27479. (Illus.). 396p. 1979. pap. 37.75 (ISBN 0-87258-250-7, 1318). Am Hospital.

Espey, John. Empty Box Haiku. 24p. (Orig.). 1980. s & l wrappers 30.00 (ISBN 0-936576-02-2). Symposium Pr.

Espie, Ian, jt. ed. see Ajayi, J. F.

Espiell, Hector G., ed. The Right to Self-Determination: Implementation of United Nations Resolutions. 1980. 8.00 (E.79.XIV5). UN.

Espien, Mike see Milne, John.

Espina, Noni. Repertoire for the Solo Voice: A Fully Annotated Guide to Works for the Solo Voice Published in Modern Editions and Covering Material from the 13th Century to the Present, Vols. 1&2. LC 76-30441. 1977. 50.00 (ISBN 0-8108-0943-5). Scarecrow.

Espinasse, Francis. Life of Ernest Renan. 242p. 1980. Repr. of 1895 ed. lib. bdg. 15.00 (ISBN 0-89760-205-6). Telegraph Bks.

Espinel, Vincente. The History of the Life of the Squire Marcos de Obregon, 2 vols. in 1. Langton, Algernon, tr. LC 80-2578. 1981. Repr. of 1816 ed. 76.50 (ISBN 0-404-19110-X). AMS Pr.

Espinosa, Aurelio M. & Wonder, John P. Gramatica Analitica. 400p. 1975. text ed. 17.95x (ISBN 0-669-82941-2). Heath.

Espinosa, Aurelio M., jt. auth. see Turk, Laurel H.

Esposito, Anthony. Kinematics for Technology. LC 72-96341. 1973. text ed. 19.95x (ISBN 0-675-09005-9); instructor's manual 3.95 (ISBN 0-686-66863-4). Merrill.

Esposito, James P., jt. auth. see Glickman, Carl D.

Esposito, John L., ed. Islam & Development: Religion & Sociopolitical Change. LC 80-25119. (Contemporary Issues in the Middle East Ser.). 292p. 1980. text ed. 22.00x (ISBN 0-8156-2229-5); pap. text ed. 9.95x (ISBN 0-8156-2230-9). Syracuse U Pr.

--Islam & Development: Religion and Sociopolitical Change. 1980. 18.00x (ISBN 0-8156-2229-5); pap. 9.95 (ISBN 0-8156-2230-9). Syracuse U Pr.

Esposito, Joseph L. Evolutionary Metaphysics: The Development of Peirce's Theory of Catagories. LC 80-15736. (Illus.). x, 152p. 1980. 15.00x (ISBN 0-8214-0551-9). Ohio U Pr.

Esposito, Tony, jt. ed. see King, Jean C.

Espy, Willard. Say It My Way. 220p. 1981. pap. 4.95 (ISBN 0-14-005733-1). Penguin.

Espy, Willard R. An Almanac of Words at Play. (Illus.). 352p. 1975. 12.95 (ISBN 0-517-52090-7); pap. 7.95 (ISBN 0-517-52463-5). Potter.

--Another Almanac of Words at Play. (Illus.). 1980. 14.95 (ISBN 0-517-53187-9); pap. 8.95 (ISBN 0-517-53188-7). Potter.

Essame, H. The Battle for Europe: Nineteen Eighteen. 1972. 22.50 o.p. (ISBN 0-7134-1173-2, Pub. by Batsford England). David & Charles.

--Patton: A Study in Command. LC 73-15498. 1976. 12.95 (ISBN 0-684-13671-6, ScribT); pap. 3.95 (ISBN 0-684-14692-4, SL660, ScribT). Scribner.

Essary, Loris, jt. auth. see Clark, Carl D.

Esse, John. The Story of Jesus: An Interpretation. (Illus.). 96p. (Orig.). 1980. pap. 4.95. Pundarika.

Essen, A. J. Van see Van Essen, A. J. & Menting, J. P.

Esser, Helen M. Flexibility & Health Through Yoga. (Illus.). 1978. pap. text ed. 8.95 (ISBN 0-8403-2236-4). Kendall-Hunt.

Esser, Josef. Why Am I...? A New Thought on Genetics. 122p. 1980. 5.95 (ISBN 0-8059-2716-6). Dorrance.

Esser, K., ed. see International Congress of Botany, Edinburgh, 1964.

Esser, Karl. Cryptograms: Cyanobacteria, Algae, Fungi, Lichens, Textbook & Practical Guide. Hackston, Michael G. & Webster, John, trs. LC 80-41070. 624p. Date not set. text ed. price not set (ISBN 0-521-23621-5); pap. text ed. price not set (ISBN 0-521-28080-X). Cambridge U Pr.

Essery, R. J. & Morgan, K. LMS Wagon. 1977. 14.95 (ISBN 0-7153-7357-9). David & Charles.

Esses, Betty L. If I Can, You Can. 128p. 1974. pap. 2.75 o.p. (ISBN 0-88368-040-8). Whitaker Hse.

Esses, Michael. Jesus in Exodus. 1977. pap. 4.95 (ISBN 0-88270-196-7). Logos.

--Jesus in Genesis. LC 74-82565. 1975. pap. 4.95 (ISBN 0-88270-100-2). Logos.

--Phenomenon of Obedience. LC 73-92248. 1974. pap. 4.95 (ISBN 0-88270-085-5). Logos.

Esses, Michael, tr. Miguel, Miguel, Por Que Me Odeias? (Portugese Bks.). (Port.). 1979. 1.60 (ISBN 0-8297-0826-X). Life Pubs Intl.

--Miguel, Miguel, Por Que Me Odias? (Spanish Bks.). (Span.). 1977. 1.90 (ISBN 0-8297-0724-7). Life Pubs Intl.

Essex, B. J. Diagnostic Pathways in Clinical Medicine. (Medicine in the Tropics Ser.). (Illus.). 208p. 1981. pap. text ed. 17.00 (ISBN 0-443-02050-9). Churchill.

Essex, Benjamin J. Diagnostic Pathways in Clinical Medicine. 2nd ed. (Medicine in the Tropics Ser.). (Illus.). Date not set. pap. text ed. 19.00 (ISBN 0-443-02059-0). Churchill.

Essex, Harry. Marina. LC 81-80082. 288p. (Orig.). 1981. pap. 2.95 (ISBN 0-87216-850-6). Playboy Pbks.

Essex, Myron, et al, eds. Viruses in Naturally Occurring Cancers. LC 80-67166. (Cold Spring Harbor Conferences on Cell Proliferation Ser.: Vol. 7). (Illus.). 1284p. 1980. 2 book set 125.00 (ISBN 0-87969-131-X). Cold Spring Harbor.

Essick, Edward. RPG-Two Programming. 304p. 1981. pap. text ed. 14.95 (ISBN 0-574-21315-5, 13-4315); instr's. guide avail. (ISBN 0-574-21316-3, 13-4316). SRA.

Essick, Edward, jt. auth. see Dock, V. Thomas.

Essien-Udom, E. U. Black Nationalism. LC 62-12632. 368p. 1972. pap. 4.95 o.s.i. (ISBN 0-226-21853-8, P451, Phoen). U of Chicago Pr.

Essig, Edward O. History of Entomology. (Illus.). 1965. Repr. of 1931 ed. 29.00 o.s.i. (ISBN 0-02-844340-3). Hafner.

Esslemont, J. E. Baha'u'llah & the New Era: An Introduction to the Baha'i Faith. 5th rev. ed. 1980. pap. 1.50 (ISBN 0-87743-160-4, 7-31-05). Baha'i.

Esslin, Martin. Bertolt Brecht. LC 74-76246. (Columbia Essays on Modern Writers Ser.: No. 42). 48p. 1969. pap. 2.00 (ISBN 0-231-02962-4, MW42). Columbia U Pr.

--Theatre of the Absurd. LC 61-13814. 1969. pap. 2.95 (ISBN 0-385-08969-4, A279, Anch). Doubleday.

--The Theatre of the Absurd. rev. ed. LC 72-94410. 1973. Repr. of 1961 ed. 12.95 (ISBN 0-87951-005-6). Overlook Pr.

Esslin, Martin, ed. Illustrated Encyclopedia of World Theater. (Illus.). 320p. 1981. pap. 12.95 (ISBN 0-500-27207-7). Thames Hudson.

Essman, W. & Valzelli, L., eds. Current Developments in Psychopharmacology, Vol. VI. (Illus.). 339p. 1981. text ed. 50.00 (ISBN 0-89335-090-7). Spectrum Pub.

Essman, Walter B., ed. Perspectives in Clinical Endocrinology. (Illus.). 390p. 1980. text ed. 45.00 (ISBN 0-89335-077-X). Spectrum Pub.

Essoe, Gabe. The Offical Book of Movie Lists. (Illus.). 256p. 1981. 12.95 (ISBN 0-87000-496-4). Arlington Hse.

--The Offical Book of TV Lists. (Illus.). 256p. 1981. 12.95 (ISBN 0-87000-497-2). Arlington Hse.

Essoka, Gloria C., et al. Pediatric Nursing Continuing Education Review. 1975. spiral bdg. 9.50 (ISBN 0-87488-361-X). Med Exam.

Essrig, Harry & Segal, Abraham. Israel Today. rev. ed. LC 77-7536. (Illus.). (YA) (gr. 8-10). 1977. text ed. 8.50 (ISBN 0-8074-0007-6, 142601); tchrs'. guide 5.00 (ISBN 0-8074-0050-5, 202601). UAHC.

Estabrook, G. F., ed. Proceedings of the Eighth International Conference on Numerical Taxonomy. LC 75-31878. (Illus.). 1976. 31.95x (ISBN 0-7167-0555-9). W H Freeman.

Estabrook, Ronald, jt. ed. see Horecker, Bernard.

Estabrooks, George H. Hypnotism. rev. ed. 1959. pap. 3.95 (ISBN 0-525-47038-7). Dutton.

Estall, R. C. & Buchanan, R. Olgilvie. Industrial Activity & Economic Geography: A Study of the Forces Behind the Geographical Location of Productive Activity in Manufacturing Industry. 3rd rev. ed. 1973. text ed. 13.50x (ISBN 0-09-117310-8, Hutchinson U Lib); pap. text ed. 11.25x (ISBN 0-09-117311-6, Hutchinson U Lib). Humanities.

Estarellas, Juan. Spanish One Two-One: From Sound to Letter. (gr. 9-12). 1975. pap. 6.95 (ISBN 0-88345-239-1); cassettes 75.00 (ISBN 0-685-65048-0); tapes 110.00. Regents Pub.

Esteban, Claude. Transparent God. Cloutier, David, tr. from Fr. LC 80-84603. (Modern Poets in Translation Ser.). 200p. 1981. price not set (ISBN 0-916426-07-6). Kosmos.

--White Road. Cloutier, David, tr. LC 78-64433. 1979. 7.50 (ISBN 0-685-39466-2). Charioteer.

Esterer, Arnulf & Esterer, Louise. The Occult World. LC 78-18267. (gr. 7 up). 1978. PLB 8.29 (ISBN 0-671-32876-X). Messner.

Esterer, Louise, jt. auth. see Esterer, Arnulf.

Esterman, Carlos. Ethnography of Southwestern Angola: The Herero People, Vol. 3. LC 75-8794. (Illus.). 1981. text ed. 39.50x (ISBN 0-8419-0206-2, Africana). Holmes & Meier.

Estermann, Immanuel see Marton, L.

Estes, Eleanor. Miranda the Great. LC 66-10422. (Illus.). 80p. 1967. 4.95 o.p. (ISBN 0-15-254600-6, HJ). HarBraceJ.

--Sleeping Giant & Other Stories. LC 48-9223. (Illus.). (gr. 1-5). 4.50 o.p. (ISBN 0-15-275851-8, HJ). HarBraceJ.

--Witch Family. LC 60-11250. (Illus.). (gr. 3-7). 1960. 7.50 o.p. (ISBN 0-15-298571-9, HJ). HarBraceJ.

Estes, Helen E. Anagraphs: A Slew of Sight Puzzles. LC 80-54813. 1981. pap. 2.95. Walker & Co.

Estes, Hiawatha T. Distinctive Homes. (Illus.). 1981. 2.00 (ISBN 0-911008-18-7). H Estes.

--Hallmark Homes. (Illus.). 1981. 2.00 (ISBN 0-911008-20-9). H Estes.

--Homes by Hiawatha. (Illus.). 1981. 2.00 (ISBN 0-911008-21-7). H Estes.

--Prize Homes. (Illus.). 1981. 2.00 (ISBN 0-911008-22-5). H Estes.

--Ranch & Modern Homes. (Illus.). 1981. 3.00 (ISBN 0-911008-19-5). H Estes.

--Town & Country Homes. (Illus.). 1981. 2.00 (ISBN 0-911008-23-3). H Estes.

Estes, J. Worth. Hall Jackson & the Purple Foxglove: Medical Practice & Research in Revolutionary America, 1760-1820. LC 79-63083. (Illus.). 309p. 1980. text ed. 20.00x (ISBN 0-87451-173-9). U Pr of New Eng.

Estes, Jack C. Interest Amortization Tables. (McGraw-Hill Paperbacks). 224p. (Orig.). 1976. pap. 4.95 (ISBN 0-07-019680-X, SP). McGraw.

Estes, Nada J. & Heinemaann, M. Edith. Alcholism: Development, Consequences & Interventions. LC 77-1676. (Illus.). 1977. pap. text ed. 12.95 (ISBN 0-8016-1529-1). Mosby.

Estes, Nada J., et al. Nursing Diagnosis of the Alcoholic Person. LC 80-11057. (Illus.). 1980. pap. text ed. 9.95 (ISBN 0-8016-1558-5). Mosby.

Estes, R. W. Corporate Social Accounting. 166p. 1976. 18.95 (ISBN 0-471-24592-5, Pub. by Wiley-Interscience). Wiley.

Estes, Ralph W. A Dictionary of Accounting. 300p. 1981. text ed. 15.00x (ISBN 0-262-05024-2); pap. text ed. 4.95x (ISBN 0-262-55009-1). MIT Pr.

Estes, Richard, jt. auth. see Welles, S. P.

Estes, Stephen, jt. auth. see Eareckson, Joni.

Estes, Thomas H. & Vaughan, Joseph L., Jr. Reading & Learning in the Content Classroom: Diagnostic & Instructional Strategies. abr. ed. 1978. pap. text ed. 11.50 (ISBN 0-205-05986-4, 2359863). Allyn.

Estes, W. K., ed. Handbook of Learning & Cognitive Processes, 6 vols. Incl. Vol. 1. Introduction to Concepts & Issues. LC 75-20113. 303p. 1975. o.p. (ISBN 0-470-24585-9); Vol. 2. Conditioning & Behavior Therapy. LC 75-20113. 350p. 1975. 18.50 (ISBN 0-470-24586-7); Vol. 3. Approaches to Human Learning & Motivation. LC 76-15010. 1976. 18.50 (ISBN 0-470-15121-8); Vol. 4. Attention & Memory. LC 76-26002. 1976. o.p. (ISBN 0-470-98908-4); Vol. 5. Human Information Processing. LC 78-3847. 1978. 26.50 (ISBN 0-470-26310-5); Vol. 6. Linguistic Functions in Cognitive Theory. 1978. 18.00 (ISBN 0-470-26311-3). Halsted Pr.

Estes, Winston. Another Part of the House. 1978. pap. 1.75 o.s.i. (ISBN 0-380-01959-0, 38406). Avon.

Estes, Winston M. Andy Jessup. 1977. pap. 1.75 o.s.i. (ISBN 0-380-01852-7, 36491). Avon.

--Homefront. LC 76-17579. 1976. 10.00 o.p. (ISBN 0-397-01147-4). Lippincott.

--A Streetful of People. 1978. pap. 1.75 o.p. (ISBN 0-380-01917-5, 37614). Avon.

Estess, Ted L. Elie Wiesel. LC 80-5337. (Modern Literature Ser.). 160p. 1980. 10.95 (ISBN 0-8044-2184-6). Ungar.

Estevez, Jaime, jt. ed. see Lozoya, Jorge.

Estevez, O., ed. see International Cancer Congress, 12th, Buenos Aires, 5-11 October 1978.

Estleman, Loren D. Aces & Eights. LC 80-2447. (Double D Western Ser.). 192p. 1981. 9.95 (ISBN 0-385-17469-1). Doubleday.

--The Hider. LC 77-81786. 1978. 6.95 o.p. (ISBN 0-385-13627-7). Doubleday.

--Stamping Ground. 1981. pap. write for info. (ISBN 0-671-41861-0). PB.

Estoril, Jean. Ballet for Drina. LC 58-9223. (gr. 5-10). 5.95 (ISBN 0-8149-0299-5). Vanguard.

--Drina Dances in Italy. LC 61-15484. (gr. 3-6). 1961. 5.95 (ISBN 0-8149-0300-2). Vanguard.

Estrada, Alvaro. Maria Sabina: Her Life & Chants. Rothenberg, Jerome, ed. Munn, Henry, tr. from Span. LC 80-20866. (New Wilderness Ser.). 220p. 1981. 16.95 (ISBN 0-915520-33-8); pap. 8.95 (ISBN 0-915520-32-X). Ross-Erikson.

Estrada, Ezequiel Martinez see Martinez Estrada, Ezequiel.

Estrada, Jose R. Dias Sin Gloria. 64p. (Span.). 1980. pap. 1.45 (ISBN 0-311-08213-0, Edit Mundo). Casa Bautista.

Estrello, Francisco E., tr. see White, D. M.

Estrin, Herman A. & Lloyd-Jones, Esther. How Many Roads: The Seventies. 416p. 1970. pap. text ed. 7.95x (ISBN 0-02-474380-1, 47438). Macmillan.

Estrin, Jack C. American History Made Simple. rev. ed. 1956. pap. 3.50 (ISBN 0-385-01214-4, Made). Doubleday.

--World History Made Simple. rev. ed. 1957. pap. 3.50 (ISBN 0-385-01220-9, Made). Doubleday.

Estrin, Marc see Hoffmann, William M.

Estrin, Y. & Panov, V. A Course in the Openings, Vol. 1. (Pergamon Chess Series). 1980. 20.00 (ISBN 0-08-023103-9); pap. 12.95 (ISBN 0-08-023102-0). Pergamon.

Estroff, Sue E. Making It Crazy: An Ethnography of Psychiatric Clients in an American Community. 338p. 1981. 19.95 (ISBN 0-520-03963-7). U of Cal Pr.

Estuarine Study Group. An Atlas of the Biologic Resources of the Hudson Estuary. (Illus.). 104p. (Orig.). 1977. pap. 5.50 (ISBN 0-89062-096-2, Pub. by Boyce Thompson Inst Plant Res). Pub Ctr Cult Res.

Eszenyi, Sandor, et al, trs. see Portisch, Lajos & Sarkozy, Balazs.

ETA Offshore Seminars, Inc. Technology of Offshore Drilling: Completion & Production 1976. LC 75-21903. 31.00 (ISBN 0-87814-066-2). Pennwell Pub.

Etchemendy, Nancy. The Watchers of Space. (Illus.). (gr. 3-7). 1980. pap. 1.50 (ISBN 0-380-75374-X, 75347, Camelot). Avon.
Eterovic, Ivo. Tito's Private Life. (Illus.). 1978. 19.95 (ISBN 0-8467-0472-2, Pub. by Two Continents). Hippocrene Bks.
Eterovich, Francis H. Aristotle's Nicomachean Ethics: Commentary & Analysis. LC 80-5202. 331p. 1980. text ed. 19.75 (ISBN 0-8191-1056-6); pap. text ed. 11.50 (ISBN 0-8191-1057-4). U Pr of Amer.
Etgen, William M. & Reaves, Paul M. Dairy Cattle Feeding & Management. 6th ed. LC 63-20646. 1978. text ed. 28.50 (ISBN 0-471-71199-3). Wiley.
Ethe, Jane. Easy-to-Make Felt Bean Bag Toys. (Illus., Orig.). Date not set. pap. 2.50 (ISBN 0-486-23884-9). Dover. Postponed.
Etherege, George. The Man of Mode. Carnochan, W. B., ed. LC 66-17766. (Regents Restoration Drama Ser). xxii, 158p. 1966. 9.75x (ISBN 0-8032-0357-8); pap. 3.75x (ISBN 0-8032-5356-7, BB 256, Bison). U of Nebr Pr.
--She Would If She Could. Taylor, Charlene M., ed. LC 76-128913. (Regents Restoration Drama Ser). xxx, 132p. 1971. pap. 3.50x (ISBN 0-8032-6700-2, BB 281, Bison). U of Nebr Pr.
Etheridge, Christina. The Cranshaw Inheritance. 1979. pap. 1.95 (ISBN 0-515-05148-9). Jove Pubns.
Etherington, J. R. & Armstrong, W. Environment & Plant Ecology. LC 74-3725. 347p. 1975. 31.75 o.p. (ISBN 0-471-24615-8); pap. 19.95 (ISBN 0-471-99737-4). Wiley.
Ethridge, James M., ed. Directory of Directories: An Annotated Guide to Business & Industrial Directories, Professional & Scientific Rosters, & Other Lists & Guides of All Kinds. 1980. 60.00 (ISBN 0-8103-0270-5, Pub. by Information Ent). Gale.
Ethridge, Willie S. Mark Ethridge: The Life & Times of a Great Newspaperman. (Illus.). 484p. 1981. 20.00 (ISBN 0-8149-0852-7). Vanguard.
--Side by Each. LC 73-83034. 192p. 1973. 7.95 (ISBN 0-8149-0733-4). Vanguard.
--Strange Fires: The True Story of John Wesley's Love Affair in Georgia. LC 77-170902. 7.95 (ISBN 0-8149-0693-1). Vanguard.
--There's Yeast in the Middle East. LC 62-19853. 1962. 7.95 (ISBN 0-8149-0091-7). Vanguard.
--You Can't Hardly Get There from Here. LC 65-28523. 1965. 7.95 (ISBN 0-8149-0089-5). Vanguard.
Etienne, Gilbert. Studies in Indian Agriculture: The Art of the Possible. Mothersole, Megan, tr. (Illus.). 1968. 20.00x (ISBN 0-520-00393-4). U of Cal Pr.
Etienne, Mona, ed. Women & Colonization. Leacock, Eleanor. 1979. 26.95 (ISBN 0-03-052586-1); pap. 9.95 (ISBN 0-03-052581-0). Praeger.
Etienne, Mona & Leacock, Eleanor, eds. Woman & Colonization: Anthropological Perspectives. LC 79-15318. 352p. 1980. 26.95 (ISBN 0-03-052586-1); pap. 9.95 (ISBN 0-03-052581-0). Praeger.
Etkin, Ruth. Playing & Composing on the Recorder. LC 74-31711. (Illus.). 64p. (gr. 2 up). 1975. 7.95 (ISBN 0-8069-4528-1); PLB 7.49 (ISBN 0-8069-4529-X). Sterling.
--The Rhythm Band Book. LC 78-57886. (Illus.). (gr. 2 up). 1978. 8.95 (ISBN 0-8069-4570-2); PLB 8.29 (ISBN 0-8069-4571-0). Sterling.
Etkin, William & Gilbert, Lawrence I., eds. Metamorphosis: A Problem in Developmental Biology. LC 67-29170. 459p. 1968. 32.50 (ISBN 0-306-50019-1, Plenum Pr). Plenum Pub.
Ets, Marie H. & Labastida, Aurora. Nine Days to Christmas. (Illus.). (ps-2). 1959. PLB 9.95 (ISBN 0-670-51350-4). Viking Pr.
Etteldorf, Raymond. The End & the Beginning. 1979. pap. text ed. 5.25x (ISBN 0-86140-012-7). Humanities.
Etter, Don. Curtis Park. LC 78-73982. 1980. 15.00 (ISBN 0-87081-077-4). Colo Assoc.
Etter, Don D. Auraria: Where Denver Began. LC 72-85656. (Illus.). 100p. 1980. pap. 8.95 (ISBN 0-87081-093-6). Colo Assoc.
Etter, Les, jt. auth. see Durant, John.
Etter, Lewis E. Glossary of Words & Phrases Used in Radiology, Nuclear Medicine & Ultrasound. 2nd ed. 384p. 1970. pap. 32.50 photocopy ed. spiral (ISBN 0-398-00526-5). C C Thomas.
Ettinger, Blanche. A Secretary's Reference Guide. 1978. 5.00 o.p. (ISBN 0-89529-030-8). Avery Pub.
Ettinger, Cecil. Congregational Readings. LC 75-8596. 1975. 4.00 o.p. (ISBN 0-8309-0145-0). Herald Hse.
Ettinger, Jan Van, jt. ed. see Dolman, Anthony J.
Ettinger, Karl E. Management Primer. Hook, Ralph C., Jr. & Overton, John R., eds. LC 72-86485. 353p. 1973. 18.25 (ISBN 92-833-1023-3, APO48, APO). Unipub.
Ettinger, Richard P. & Golieb, D. E. Credits & Collections. 5th ed. 1962. text ed. 18.95 (ISBN 0-13-192641-1). P-H.
Ettinghausen, Henry. Francisco de Quevedo & the Neostoic Movement. (Oxford Modern Languages & Literature Monographs). 190p. 1972. 29.95x (ISBN 0-19-815521-2). Oxford U Pr.
Ettlinger, Helen, jt. auth. see Ettlinger, Leopold.
Ettlinger, Leopold & Ettlinger, Helen. Botticelli. LC 76-26747. (World of Art Ser.). (Illus.). 1977. 17.95 (ISBN 0-19-519900-6); pap. 9.95 (ISBN 0-19-519907-3). Oxford U Pr.
Ettlinger, Lester A., et al. High-Temperature Plasma Technology Applications. LC 80-65507. (Electrotechnology Ser.: Vol. 6). (Illus.). 163p. 1980. 29.95 (ISBN 0-250-40376-5). Ann Arbor Science.
Etulain, Richard W., ed. see Paul, Rodman W.
Etzioni, Amitai. Active Society. LC 61-14107. 1971. 13.25 o.s.i. (ISBN 0-02-909590-5); pap. text ed. 10.95 (ISBN 0-02-909580-8). Free Pr.
--Comparative Analysis of Complex Organizations. rev. ed. LC 74-21488. 1975. 19.95 (ISBN 0-02-909650-2); pap. text ed. 10.95 (ISBN 0-02-909620-0). Free Pr.
--Genetic Fix: New Opportunities & Dangers for You, Your Child & the Nation. LC 73-7350. 224p. 1973. 7.95 o.s.i. (ISBN 0-02-536410-3). Macmillan.
--Semi-Professions and Their Organization. LC 69-10481. 1969. 13.95 o.s.i. (ISBN 0-02-909600-6). Free Pr.
Etzioni-Halevy, Eva. Political Manipulation & Administrative Power: A Comparative Study. (International Library of Sociology). 1980. 30.00x (ISBN 0-7100-0352-8). Routledge & Kegan.
--Social Change: Moderization & Post-Modernization. 280p. 1981. price not set (ISBN 0-7100-0767-1); pap. price not set (ISBN 0-7100-0768-X). Routledge & Kegan.
Etzioni-Halevy, Eva & Shapira, Rina. Political Culture in Israel: Cleavage & Integration Among Israeli Jews. LC 76-24350. (Special Studies). 1977. text ed. 26.95 (ISBN 0-275-23790-7). Praeger.
Etzkorn, K. Peter. Georg Simmel: The Conflict in Modern Culture & Other Essays. LC 67-25064. 1968. text ed. 11.25x (ISBN 0-8077-1296-5). Tchrs Coll.
Etzold, Thomas & Gaddis, John L. Containment: Documents on American Policy & Strategy 1945-1950. LC 77-20024. 1978. 27.50x (ISBN 0-231-04398-8); pap. 10.00x (ISBN 0-231-04399-6). Columbia U Pr.
Eubank, H. & Sindoni, E., eds. Course on Plasma Diagnostics & Data Acquisition Systems. new ed. (Commission of the European Communities). (Illus.). 1979. pap. text ed. 65.00 o.p. (ISBN 0-08-024462-9). Pergamon.
Eubank, Keith. Origins of World War Two. LC 73-77338. (AHM Europe Since 1500 Ser.). 1969. pap. 5.95x (ISBN 0-88295-733-3). AHM Pub.
Eubank, Keith, ed. The Road to World War II: A Documentary History. LC 74-179768. 1973. pap. 9.95x (ISBN 0-88295-734-1). AHM Pub.
Eubank, Nancy. A Living Past: Fifteen Historic Places in Minnesota. rev. ed. (Minnesota Historic Sites Pamphlet Ser.: No. 7). (Illus.). 1978. pap. 2.75 (ISBN 0-87351-077-1). Minn Hist.
--Russians in America. LC 72-3598. (In America Bks.). (Illus.). 96p. (gr. 5-11). 1979. PLB 5.95. Lerner Pubns.
--Russians in America. LC 72-3589. (In America Bks.). (Illus.). 96p. (gr. 5-11). 1973. PLB 5.95 o.p. (ISBN 0-8225-0226-7). Lerner Pubns.
Eubanks, David, jt. auth. see Wasserberger, Jonathan.
Eudaly, Maria S. De. El Cuidado De Dios. Villasenor, Emma Z., tr. (gr. 1-3). Date not set. pap. 0.80 (ISBN 0-311-03662-7). Casa Bautista.
Eudes, Dominique. The Kapetanios: Partisans & Civil War in Greece, 1943-1949. Howe, John, tr. from Fr. LC 72-92032. (Illus.). 400p. 1973. 11.50 o.p. (ISBN 0-85345-275-X, CL-275X). Monthly Rev.
Eugenia, De B., tr. see Hugo, Victor.
Eugenics Society Annual Symposium, 11th, London, 1973. Equalities & Inequalities in Education: Proceedings. Cox, Peter R., et al, eds. 1976. 19.50 (ISBN 0-12-194240-6). Acad Pr.
Eulalie, illus. Mother Goose Rhymes. LC 80-83934. (Illus.). 48p. (ps-1). 1981. Repr. of 1953 ed. 2.95 (ISBN 0-448-40114-2); PLB write for info. (ISBN 0-448-13946-4). Platt.
--The True Mother Goose. LC 79-1948. (Illus.). (ps-2). 1979. 1.95 (ISBN 0-525-69004-2, Gingerbread Bks); PLB 5.95 (ISBN 0-525-69005-0, Gingerbread Bks.). Dutton.
Eulau, Heinz. Technology & Civility: The Skill Revolution in Politics. LC 76-48483. (Publications Ser.: No. 167). 1977. pap. 4.95 (ISBN 0-8179-6672-2). Hoover Inst Pr.
Eulenburg, Milton D., et al. Introductory Algebra. 3rd ed. LC 74-24338. 384p. 1975. text ed. 18.50 (ISBN 0-471-24686-7). Wiley.
Euler, C. Von see Von Euler, C. & Lagercrantz, H.
Euler, U. S. Von see Von Euler, U. S., et al.
Eulo, Ken. The Brownstone. (Orig.). 1980. pap. write for info. PB.
Eunson, Roby. The Soong Sisters. LC 75-5952. 192p. (gr. 7 up). 1975. PLB 6.90 (ISBN 0-531-02835-6). Watts.
--When France Was De Gaulle. LC 71-161838. (Illus.). (gr. 7 up). 1971. PLB 6.90 (ISBN 0-531-02005-3). Watts.
Eure, James Bruce. Joey & DeVon. 1976. 8.00 o.p. (ISBN 0-682-48414-8). Exposition.
Eurich, Alvin C., ed. Campus Nineteen Eighty: The Shape of the Future in American Higher Education. 1968. 6.95 o.s.i. (ISBN 0-440-01026-8). Delacorte.
Euripides. Alcestis. Dale, A. M., ed. (Plays of Euripides Ser.). 1954. pap. 11.50x (ISBN 0-19-872097-1). Oxford U Pr.
--Alcestis. Arrowsmith, William, tr. (Greek Tragedy in New Translations Ser). 1973. 10.95 (ISBN 0-19-501861-3). Oxford U Pr.
--Alcestis. Murray, Gilbert, tr. 1915. pap. text ed. 3.95x (ISBN 0-04-882025-3). Allen Unwin.
--Andromache. Stevens, P. T., ed. (Plays of Euripides Ser.). 264p. 1971. 14.95x (ISBN 0-19-814183-1). Oxford U Pr.
--Bacchae of Euripides: A New Translation with a Critical Essay. Sutherland, Donald, tr. LC 68-11566. 1968. pap. 3.50x (ISBN 0-8032-5194-7, BB 377, Bison). U of Nebr Pr.
--Collected Plays of Euripides. Murray, Gilbert, tr. 1976. text ed. 14.95x o.p. (ISBN 0-04-882028-8); pap. text ed. 7.95x o.p. (ISBN 0-04-882056-3). Allen Unwin.
--Cyclops. Simmonds, D. M. & Timberlake, R. R., eds. text ed. 5.75x (ISBN 0-521-04946-6). Cambridge U Pr.
--Electra. Hadas, Moses, tr. LC 63-23331. pap. 2.95 (ISBN 0-672-60186-9, LLA26). Bobbs.
--The Electra. Murray, Gilbert, tr. 1905. pap. text ed. 3.95x (ISBN 0-04-882030-X). Allen Unwin.
--Euripides' Electra. Denniston, J. D., ed. 1979. pap. 14.95x (ISBN 0-19-872094-7). Oxford U Pr.
--Euripides Five: Three Tragedies. Grene, David & Lattimore, Richard, eds. Incl. Electra. Vermeule, Emily T., tr; The Phoenician Women. Wyckoff, Elizabeth, tr; The Bacchae. Arrowsmith, William, tr. LC 55-5787. 228p. 1959. pap. 3.95 (ISBN 0-226-30784-0, P312, Phoen). U of Chicago Pr.
--Hippolytus. Bagg, Robert, tr. (Greek Tragedy in New Translation Ser). 96p. 1973. 10.95 (ISBN 0-19-501740-4). Oxford U Pr.
--Hippolytus. Murray, Gilbert, tr. 1902. pap. text ed. 3.95x (ISBN 0-04-882032-6). Allen Unwin.
--Hippolytus in Drama & Myth. Sutherland, Donald, tr. LC 60-13112. 1960. pap. 3.50x (ISBN 0-8032-5195-5, BB 103, Bison). U of Nebr Pr.
--Ion. Murray, Gilbert, tr. 1954. pap. text ed. 3.95x (ISBN 0-04-882034-2). Allen Unwin.
--Iphigeneia at Aulis. Merwin, W. S. & Dimock, George E., Jr., trs. from Greek. (Greek Tragedy in New Translations). 1978. 10.95 (ISBN 0-19-502272-6). Oxford U Pr.
--Iphigeneia at Tauris. Lattimore, Richmond, tr. (Greek Tragedy in New Translation Ser). 112p. 1973. 10.95 (ISBN 0-19-501736-6). Oxford U Pr.
--Iphigenia in Tauris. Murray, Gilbert, tr. 1910. pap. text ed. 3.95x (ISBN 0-04-882036-9). Allen Unwin.
--The Medea. Murray, Gilbert, tr. 1910. pap. text ed. 3.95x (ISBN 0-04-882038-5). Allen Unwin.
--Medea. Page, Denys, ed. (Plays of Euripides Ser.). 1976. pap. text ed. 12.95 (ISBN 0-19-872092-0). Oxford U Pr.
--Rhesos. Braun, Richard E., tr. from Greek. (Greek Tragedy in New Translations). 1978. 10.95 (ISBN 0-19-502049-9). Oxford U Pr.
--The Rhesus. Murray, Gilbert, tr. 1913. pap. text ed. 3.95x (ISBN 0-04-882040-7). Allen Unwin.
--The Trojan Women. Murray, Gilbert, tr. 1905. pap. text ed. 3.95x (ISBN 0-04-882042-3). Allen Unwin.
European Chemoreception Research Organisation, Symposium, Netherlands, 1979. Preference Behaviour & Chemoreception: Proceedings. (ECRO Minisymposium Ser.). 350p. 1979. 26.00 (ISBN 0-904147-12-6). Info Retrieval.
European Chemoreception Research Organisation, 2nd Interdisciplinary Symposium, Switzerland, 1975. Structure-Activity Relationships in Chemoreception: Proceedings. 197p. 20.00 (ISBN 0-904147-03-7). Info Retrieval.
European Computing Congress. Eurocomp Seventy-Eight: Proceedings. Online Conferences Ltd., ed. 1978. text ed. 108.00x (ISBN 0-903796-23-6, Pub. by Online Conferences England). Renouf.
European Conference of Ministers of Transport, 46th Round Table. Tariff Policies for Urban Transport. 107p. (Fr. & Eng.). 1980. 4.50 (ISBN 9-2821-1060-5). OECD.
European Conference on Mixing, 3rd. Proceedings, 2 vols. Stephens, H. S. & Stapleton, C. A., eds. (European Conferences on Mixing Ser.). 500p. 1979. Set. PLB 73.00 (ISBN 0-906085-31-4, Dist. by Air Science Co.). BHRA Fluid.
European Conference on Psychosomatic Research, 12th July 1978. Proceedings. Freyberger, H., ed. (Psychotherapy & Psychosomatics: Vol. 32, No. 1-4). (Illus.). 324p. 1980. pap. 78.00 (ISBN 3-8055-3044-7). S Karger.
European Congress of Allergology & Clinical Immunology, 9th. Allergy. Frankland, A. W. & Ganderton, M. A., eds. (Illus.). 400p. (Orig.). 1975. pap. text ed. 32.00x o.p. (ISBN 0-8464-0125-8). Beekman Pubs.
European Congress on Sleep Research, 4th, Tirgu-Mures, September 1978. Sleep Nineteen Seventy-Eight. Popoviciu, L., et al, eds. 1980. 118.00 (ISBN 3-8055-0778-X). S Karger.
European Federation of Chemical Engineering, European Symposium, Amsterdam, Holland, June 3-5, 1980. Particle Technology Nineteen Eighty: Proceedings, Vols. A & B. Schonert, K., et al, eds. (E FCE Publication Ser.: No. 7). 1232p. 1980. text ed. 79.00x (ISBN 3-921567-27-0, Pub. by Dechema Germany). Scholium Intl.
European Federation of Chemical Engineering, 2nd Intl. Conference on Phase Equilibria & Fluid Properties in the Chemical Industry, Berlin, 1980. Phase Equilibria & Fluid Properties in the Chemical Industry: Proceedings, Pts. 1 & 2. (EFCE Publication Ser.: No. 11). 1012p. 1980. text ed. 82.50x (ISBN 3-921567-35-1, Pub. by Dechema Germany). Scholium Intl.
European Institute & Johnstad, Trygve, eds. Group Dynamics & Society: A Multinational Approach. LC 80-24932. 352p. 1980. text ed. 27.50 (ISBN 0-89946-070-4). Oelgeschlager.
European Research in Curriculum & Evaluation, a Report of the European Contact Workshop Held in Austria in December 1976 by the Committee for the Educational Research of the Council of Europe Council for Cultural Cooperation. Experimental Education for Pupils Aged Ten to Fourteen. Eggleston, John, ed. 218p. 1977. pap. text ed. 22.50 (ISBN 0-686-27810-0, Pub. by Swets Pub Serv Holland). Swets North Am.
European Symposium on Marine Biology, 12th. Physiology & Behaviour of Marine Organisms: Proceedings. McLusky, D. S. & Berry, A. J., eds. LC 77-30559. 1978. text ed. 60.00 (ISBN 0-08-021548-3). Pergamon.
European Symposium On Medical Enzymology - 1st - Milan - 1960. Proceedings. Dioguardi, Nicola, ed. 1962. 53.50 (ISBN 0-12-216950-6). Acad Pr.
Euro-Training, tr. see Didactic Systems Staff.
Eusebius. Ecclesiastical History. (Twin Brooks Ser). pap. 7.95 (ISBN 0-8010-3306-3). Baker Bk.
--The Proof of the Gospel, 2 vols. in one. Ferrar, W. J., ed. (Twin Brooks Ser.). 568p. 1981. pap. 12.95 (ISBN 0-8010-3366-7). Baker Bk.
Eustace, May. One Hundred Years of Siamese Cats. (Illus.). 1978. 8.95 o.p. (ISBN 0-684-15783-7, ScribT). Scribner.
Eustace, P. J., jt. auth. see Wilcox, B.
Eustis, Alvin, tr. see Chevalier, Francois.
Euw, Eric Von see Von Euw, Eric.
Euwe, Max. Bobby Fischer - the Greatest? LC 78-66270. (Illus.). 1979. 9.95 (ISBN 0-8069-4950-3); lib. bdg. 9.29 (ISBN 0-8069-4951-1). Sterling.
Evan, Paul. Gunsmoke Over Sabado. 256p. (YA) 1974. 5.95 (ISBN 0-685-49199-4, Avalon). Bouregy.
Evan, W. Anatomy & Physiology. 2nd ed. (Illus.). 480p. 1976. pap. 21.95 ref. ed. (ISBN 0-13-035196-2); lab. manual 8.95 (ISBN 0-13-035170-9). P-H.
Evan, W. M. Organization Theory: Structures, Systems, & Environments. LC 76-22742. 1976. 24.95 (ISBN 0-471-01512-1). Wiley.
Evan, William M. Frontiers in Organization & Management. LC 79-20512. (Praeger Special Studies). 192p. 1980. 19.95 (ISBN 0-03-048441-3). Praeger.
Evan, William M., ed. Interorganizational Relations. LC 77-25062. 1978. pap. 7.50x (ISBN 0-8122-7745-7). U of Pa Pr.
Evang, Karl. Health Services in Norway. 1976. pap. 17.00x (ISBN 8-200-02373-7, Dist. by Columbia U Pr). Universitet.

Evangelakis, Miltiades G. A Manual for Residential & Day Treatment of Children. (Illus.). 392p. 1974. text ed. 22.75 (ISBN 0-398-03118-5). C C Thomas.

Evanoff, Vlad. Another One Thousand & One Fishing Tips & Tricks. 1975. pap. 3.95 o.p. (ISBN 0-8015-0308-6). Dutton.

--The Fisherman's Catalog. LC 76-23806. 1977. 6.95 o.p. (ISBN 0-385-12196-2). Doubleday.

--Fishing Rigs for Fresh & Salt Water. LC 76-26221. (Illus.). 1977. 9.95 o.p. (ISBN 0-06-011257-3, HarpT). Har-Row.

--Five Hundred Fishing Experts & How They Catch Fish. LC 77-80884. (Illus.). 1978. 10.95 o.p. (ISBN 0-385-07940-0). Doubleday.

--Fresh-Water Fisherman's Bible. rev. ed. LC 79-7684. (Outdoor Bible Ser.). (Illus.). 1980. pap. 3.95 (ISBN 0-385-14405-9). Doubleday.

--How to Fish in Salt Water. (Illus.). 1962. 7.95 o.p. (ISBN 0-498-08918-5). A S Barnes.

Evans & Matthews. Systematics & Nesting Behavior of Australian Bembix Sand Wasps - Hymenoptera, Sphecidae. (Memoirs Ser: No. 20). (Illus.). 1973. 25.00 (ISBN 0-686-17148-9). Am Entom Inst.

Evans & Novak. Lyndon B. Johnson: The Exercise of Power. pap. 1.95 o.p. (ISBN 0-451-07250-2, J7250, Sig). NAL.

Evans, A. J. Reading & Thinking, 2 vols. 1979. pap. text ed. 8.25x set (ISBN 0-8077-2576-5). Tchrs Coll.

Evans, A. R., ed. see Sheeler, W. D., et al.

Evans, Alan L. Personality Characteristics & Disciplinary Attitudes of Child-Abusing Mothers. LC 80-69240. 145p. 1981. perfect bdg. 11.95 (ISBN 0-86548-033-8). Century Twenty One.

Evans, Alona E. & Murphy, John F., eds. Legal Aspects of International Terrorism. new ed. LC 78-404. 1978. 36.95 (ISBN 0-669-02185-7). Lexington Bks.

Evans, Ambrose see Manley, Mary D.

Evans, Anthony. Aquariums. (Foyle's Handbks). 1973. 3.95 (ISBN 0-685-55811-8). Palmetto Pub.

--Glossary of Molecular Biology. LC 74-26571. 1975. 13.95 (ISBN 0-470-24740-1). Halsted Pr.

--Goldfish. Foyle, Christina, ed. (Foyle's Handbks). 1973. 3.95 (ISBN 0-685-55819-3). Palmetto Pub.

Evans, Audrey E., ed. Advances in Neuroblastoma Research. (Progress in Cancer Research & Therapy Ser.: Vol. 12). 360p. 1980. 38.00 (ISBN 0-89004-459-7, 516). Raven.

Evans, Augusta. St. Elmo. 440p. 1980. Repr. of 1896 ed. lib. bdg. 17.25x (ISBN 0-89968-210-3). Lightyear.

Evans, B. H. & Waites, B. A. IQ & Mental Testing. 1980. text ed. 30.00x (ISBN 0-391-01911-2); pap. text ed. 13.00x (ISBN 0-391-01912-0). Humanities.

Evans, Barbara. Change of Life. LC 79-89935. (Illus.). 1980. pap. cancelled (ISBN 0-89793-012-6). Hunter Hse.

Evans, Barry. Housing Rehabilitation Handbook. (Illus.). 1980. 52.50 (ISBN 0-85139-293-8, Pub. by Architectural Pr). Nichols Pub.

Evans, Barry, ed. Prayer Book Renewal: Worship & the New Book of Common Prayer. 1978. pap. 3.95 (ISBN 0-8164-2157-9). Crossroad NY.

Evans, Bertrand. Shakespeare's Tragic Practice. 1980. 29.95x (ISBN 0-19-812094-X). Oxford U Pr.

Evans, Charles. American Bibliography, 14 vols. Incl. Vols 1-12. 200.00 (ISBN 0-8446-1173-5); Vol. 13. 1799-1800. 25.00 (ISBN 0-8446-1174-3); Vol. 14. Index. Bristol, R. P., compiled by. 25.00 (ISBN 0-8446-1175-1). Peter Smith.

Evans, Charles H. Electronic Amplifiers: Theory, Design, & Use. LC 76-3950. 1979. pap. text ed. 13.20 (ISBN 0-8273-1626-7); instr's manual 2.25 (ISBN 0-8273-1627-5). Delmar.

Evans, Charles M. & Pliner, Roberta L. The Terrarium Book. LC 72-11388. (Illus.). 1973. 7.95 (ISBN 0-394-48364-2); pap. 3.95 (ISBN 0-394-70968-3). Random.

Evans, Christopher, intro. by. Understanding Yourself. 1980. pap. 2.95 (ISBN 0-451-09303-8, E9303, Sig). NAL.

Evans, Colin W., ed. Developments in Rubber & Rubber Composites - One. (Illus.). ix, 184p. 1980. 35.00x (ISBN 0-85334-892-8). Burgess-Intl Ideas.

Evans, Colleen T. Give Us This Day Our Daily Bread: Asking for & Sharing Life's Necessities. LC 78-20070. 168p. 1981. 9.95 (ISBN 0-385-14091-6, Galilee). Doubleday.

--Love Is an Everyday Thing. (Orig.). pap. 1.50 (ISBN 0-89129-243-8). Jove Pubns.

--A New Joy. (Orig.). pap. 1.50 (ISBN 0-89129-015-X). Jove Pubns.

Evans, Craig. On Foot Through Europe: A Trail Guide to Scandinavia. Whitney, Stephen, ed. (Illus.). 480p. 1980. lib. bdg. 13.95 (ISBN 0-933710-12-7); pap. 7.95 (ISBN 0-686-26899-7). Foot Trails.

Evans, D., jt. auth. see Neagley, Ross L.

Evans, D. A., jt. auth. see Landsberg, P. R.

Evans, D. MacLean & Bowen Jones, John. Introduction to Medical Chemistry. 288p. 1976. text ed. 20.50 o.p. (ISBN 0-06-041921-0, HarpC). Har-Row.

Evans, D. S., ed. see International Astronomical Union Symposium, 44th, Uppsala, Sweden, 1970.

Evans, Dale, jt. auth. see Rogers, Roy.

Evans, David. Gravel Springs Fife & Drum: An Essay. 1981. cancelled (ISBN 0-89267-006-1). Ctr South Folklore.

--Jet Propulsion. 9.75x (ISBN 0-392-07180-0, LTB). Soccer.

--Tommy Johnson. (The Paul Oliver Blues Ser.). pap. 2.95 (ISBN 0-913714-46-1). Legacy Bks.

Evans, David, jt. auth. see Landsberg, Peter T.

Evans, David, tr. see Karolak, Tadeusz.

Evans, David A. Train Windows. LC 75-36977. 56p. 1976. 6.95 (ISBN 0-8214-0204-8); pap. 2.50 o.s.i. (ISBN 0-8214-0213-7). Ohio U Pr.

Evans, David J. Geographical Perspectives in Juvenile Delinquency. 144p. 1980. text ed. 27.75x (ISBN 0-566-00351-1, Pub. by Gower Pub Co England). Renouf.

Evans, Don. Texas Business Law. LC 80-17836. 852p. 1980. text ed. 19.95x (ISBN 0-88289-251-7). Pelican.

Evans, Donald. Struggle & Fulfillment: The Inner Dynamics of Religion & Morality. LC 80-8050. 256p. 1981. pap. 7.95 (ISBN 0-8006-1426-7, 1-1426). Fortress.

Evans, Donald P. & Pikelny, Philip S. Rambling Willie: The Horse That God Loved. LC 80-26884. (Illus.). 240p. 1981. 8.95 (ISBN 0-498-02542-X). A S Barnes.

Evans, Dorothy. Mathematics: Friend or Foe? (Classroom Close-Ups Ser.). 1977. text ed. 14.95x o.p. (ISBN 0-04-372022-6); pap. text ed. 8.95x (ISBN 0-04-372023-4). Allen Unwin.

Evans, Dorothy, jt. auth. see Vercoe, Bernice.

Evans, Dorothy & Claiborn, William, eds. Mental Health Issues & the Urban Poor. LC 73-19708. 1974. text ed. 21.00 (ISBN 0-08-017831-6); pap. text ed. 10.75 (ISBN 0-08-017830-8). Pergamon.

Evans, E. E. The Personality of Ireland. LC 72-83667. (Wiles Lectures, 1971). (Illus.). 176p. 1973. 18.95 (ISBN 0-521-08684-1). Cambridge U Pr.

Evans, E. Estyn. Irish Folkways. (Illus.). 1966. 20.00 (ISBN 0-7100-1344-2); pap. 11.95 (ISBN 0-7100-2888-1). Routledge & Kegan.

Evans, E. Everett. Alien Minds. 1976. Repr. of 1955 ed. lib. bdg. 11.95 (ISBN 0-88411-981-5). Amereon Ltd.

Evans, E. F., ed. Psychophysics and Physiology of Hearing. 1978. 45.00 (ISBN 0-12-244050-1). Acad Pr.

Evans, E. G. Modern Educational Psychology: An Historical Introduction. (Students Library of Education Ser.). 1969. pap. text ed. 2.50x (ISBN 0-7100-6515-9). Humanities.

Evans, Earlene G. I Love You, Ugly Old Hag! 1981. 4.50 (ISBN 0-533-04488-X). Vantage.

Evans, Edmund. My Diary: Engravings by Edmund Evans. (Illus.). 1978. 6.95 (ISBN 0-374-35106-6). FS&G.

Evans, Edward, jt. auth. see Reimer, Bennett.

Evans, Eli. The Provincials. LC 73-80747. 1976. pap. 7.95 (ISBN 0-689-70532-8, 221). Atheneum.

Evans, Elizabeth. Eudora Welty. LC 80-53702. (Modern Literature Ser.). 180p. 1981. 9.95 (ISBN 0-8044-2187-0). Ungar.

--Ring Lardner. LC 79-4829. (Modern Literature Ser.). 1980. 10.95 (ISBN 0-8044-2185-4). Ungar.

--Weathering the Storm: Women of the American Revolution. LC 74-10524. (Encore Edition). 1975. 4.95 o.p. (ISBN 0-684-15673-3, ScribT). Scribner.

Evans, Elizabeth C. Physiognomics in the Ancient World. LC 73-85468. (Transactions Ser.: Vol. 59, Pt. 5). 1969. pap. 2.00 o.p. (ISBN 0-87169-595-2). Am Philos.

Evans, Elizabeth M. see Lefebvre, Georges.

Evans, Eric J. & Richards, Jeffrey. A Social History of Britain in Postcards, 1870 to 1930. 151p. (Orig.). 1981. 23.00 (ISBN 0-582-50292-6). Longman.

Evans, Eric J., ed. Social Policy 1830-1914: Individualism, Collectivism & the Origins of the Welfare State. (Birth of Modern Britain Ser). 1978. 23.00x (ISBN 0-7100-8613-X); pap. 10.00 (ISBN 0-7100-8626-1). Routledge & Kegan.

Evans, Eva K. All About Us. (gr. 4-7). 1957. PLB 6.08 o.p. (ISBN 0-307-60180-3, Golden Pr). Western Pub.

--Beginning of Life. LC 69-10462. (Illus.). (gr. k-4). 1969. 3.95g o.s.i. (ISBN 0-02-733710-3, CCPr). Macmillan.

Evans, F. C. A First Geography of Jamaica. 2nd ed. (Illus.). 48p. (gr. 5-8). 1973. 4.75x (ISBN 0-521-20252-3). Cambridge U Pr.

--A First Geography of the Eastern Caribbean. (Illus.). 48p. (gr. 5 up). 1972. text ed. 4.75x (ISBN 0-521-08312-5). Cambridge U Pr.

--A First Geography of the West Indies. (gr. 5 up). 1974. 5.95x (ISBN 0-521-20112-8). Cambridge U Pr.

--A First Geography of Trinidad & Tobago. 2nd ed. LC 67-21957. (Illus.). text ed. 4.75x (ISBN 0-521-20180-2). Cambridge U Pr.

Evans, F. C. & Young, N. The Bahamas. LC 76-16133. (Illus.). 1977. 4.75x (ISBN 0-521-21292-8). Cambridge U Pr.

Evans, F. Gaynor. Biomechanical Studies of the Musculo-Skeletal System. 232p. 1961. pap. 22.50 photocopy ed. spiral (ISBN 0-398-04102-4). C C Thomas.

Evans, F. J., jt. ed. see Van Dixhoorn, J. J.

Evans, Frank L. Equipment Design Handbook for Refineries & Chemical Plants, Vol. 2. 2nd ed. (Illus.). 400p. 1980. 32.95 (ISBN 0-87201-255-7). Gulf Pub.

Evans, G., ed. War on Want. 1962. pap. 4.20 (ISBN 0-08-009667-0). Pergamon.

Evans, G. Blakemore, ed. Shakespearean Prompt-Books of the Seventeenth Century. Incl. Vol. 3, Pt. 1. The Comedy of Errors; Vol. 3, Pt. 2. A Midsummer Night's Dream; Vol. 4. Hamlet. o.p.; Vol. 5, Pt. 1 & 2. Smock Alley Macbeth. LC 60-2680. vol. 1 & 2 o.p. (ISBN 0-685-26270-7); pap. 15.00x boxed set vol. 3 pt. 1 & 2 (ISBN 0-8139-0216-9); Vol. 4. pap. o.p.; Vol. 5. pap. 25.00x boxed set pt. 1 & 2 (ISBN 0-8139-0301-7). U Pr of Va.

Evans, G. Blakemore, et al, eds. see Shakespeare, William.

Evans, G. C., et al, eds. Light As an Ecological Factor 2: Proceedings. LC 76-921. 1976. 54.95 (ISBN 0-470-15043-2). Halsted Pr.

Evans, G. E. Management Techniques for Librarians. (Library & Information Science Ser.). 276p. 1976. 17.00 (ISBN 0-12-243850-7). Acad Pr.

Evans, G. Edward. Developing Library Collections. LC 78-27303. (Library Science Text Ser.). 1979. lib. bdg. 19.50x (ISBN 0-87287-145-2); pap. text ed. 13.50x. Libs Unl.

Evans, G. Edward, jt. auth. see Bloomberg, Marty.

Evans, G. R. Anselm & Talking About God. 1978. 28.50x (ISBN 0-19-826647-2). Oxford U Pr.

Evans, George Bird. Troubles with Bird Dogs & What to Do About Them: Training Experiences with Actual Dogs Under the Gun. (Illus.). 1975. 12.95 (ISBN 0-87691-204-8). Winchester Pr.

Evans, George E. Ask the Fellows Who Cut the Hay. (Illus., Orig.). 1965. pap. 6.95 (ISBN 0-571-06353-5, Pub. by Faber & Faber). Merrimack Bk Serv.

--Days That We Have Seen. 1975. 12.95 (ISBN 0-571-10726-5, Pub. by Faber & Faber). Merrimack Bk Serv.

--The Farm & the Village. (Illus.). (gr. 5 up). 1969. 8.95 (ISBN 0-571-08804-X, Pub. by Faber & Faber); pap. 4.95 (ISBN 0-571-10551-3). Merrimack Bk Serv.

--Horse Power & Magic. (Illus.). 1979. 17.95 (ISBN 0-686-25059-1, Pub. by Faber & Faber). Merrimack Bk Serv.

--The Pattern Under the Plough. (Illus.). 1966. 9.95 (ISBN 0-571-06886-3, Pub. by Faber & Faber); pap. 4.95 (ISBN 0-571-08977-1). Merrimack Bk Serv.

Evans, George E., jt. auth. see Thomson, David.

Evans, George K., jt. auth. see Ehret, Walter.

Evans, Gillian R., tr. see Alan Of Lille.

Evans, Glen. The Family Circle Guide to Self-Help. 1979. pap. 2.25 o.p. (ISBN 0-345-27394-X). Ballantine.

Evans, Griffith C. Logarithmic Potential, 2 vols. in 1. 2nd ed. Incl. Fundamental Existence Theorems. Bliss, Gilbert A. Repr. of 1927 ed. write for info. o.p. (ISBN 0-685-22943-2). Chelsea Pub.

Evans, H. J., et al, eds. Edinburgh Conference, 1979: International Workshop on Human Gene Mapping, 5th, July 1979. (Human Gene Mapping Ser.: No. 5). (Illus.). vi, 236p. 1980. pap. 39.00 (ISBN 3-8055-0649-X). S Karger.

Evans, H. Meurig & Thomas, W. O. The Complete Welsh-English English-Welsh Dictionary: Y Geiriadur Mawr. 8th ed. 1979. text ed. 27.50x (ISBN 0-391-01734-9). Humanities.

Evans, Harold & Taylor, Edwin. Pictures on a Page: Photojournalism & Picture Editing. 320p. 1979. text ed. 14.95x (ISBN 0-534-00812-7). Wadsworth Pub.

Evans, Hazel & Kumm, Alan. Woman's Own Pot Plant Doctor - a Guide to Coping with Pot Plant Ailments. (Illus.). 1978. pap. 4.95 (ISBN 0-600-37150-6). Transatlantic.

Evans, Henry. Botanical Prints: With Excerpts from the Artist's Notebooks. LC 77-24323. (Illus.). 1977. pap. 14.95x (ISBN 0-7167-1118-4). W H Freeman.

Evans, Herndon J. The Newspaper Press in Kentucky. LC 76-24340. (Kentucky Bicentennial Bookshelf Ser.). (Illus.). 138p. 1976. 5.95 (ISBN 0-8131-0221-9). U Pr of Ky.

Evans, Hilary. The Art of Picture Research: A Guide to Current Practice, Procedure, Techniques & Resources. (Illus.). 33.00 (ISBN 0-7153-7763-9). David & Charles.

--Picture Librarianship. (Outlines of Modern Librarianship Ser.). 1980. text ed. 12.00 (ISBN 0-89664-428-6, Pub. by K G Saur). Shoe String.

Evans, Hope H., jt. auth. see Harshaw, Ruth.

Evans, Howard. Sir Randal Cremer: His Life & Work. LC 74-147455. (Garland Library of War & Peace: Peace Leaders: Biographies & Memoirs). xviii, 356p. 1973. Repr. of 1909 ed. lib. bdg. 38.00 (ISBN 0-8240-0250-4). Garland Pub.

Evans, Howard E. & Eberhard, Mary J. Wasps. LC 78-12448. (Ann Arbor Science Library). 1970. pap. 3.45 o.p. (ISBN 0-472-05018-4, 518, AA). U of Mich Pr.

--The Wasps. LC 71-124448. (Ann Arbor Science Library Ser.). 272p. 1970. 7.95 (ISBN 0-472-00118-3); pap. 3.45 (ISBN 0-472-05018-4). U of Mich Pr.

Evans, I. O. Jules Verne & His Work. 188p. 1980. Repr. of 1965 ed. lib. bdg. 35.00 (ISBN 0-89760-224-2). Telegraph Bks.

--The Observer's Book of Flags. (Illus.). 1977. 4.95 (ISBN 0-684-14941-9, ScribT). Scribner.

--Observer's Book of Sea & Seashore. (Observer Bks.). (Illus.). 1977. 4.95 (ISBN 0-684-15218-5, ScribT). Scribner.

Evans, Idella M. & Murdoff, Ron. Psychology for a Changing World. 2nd ed. LC 77-13677. 1978. text ed. 18.95 (ISBN 0-471-24872-X); tchrs. manual avail. (ISBN 0-471-03754-0). Wiley.

Evans, Irene & Paradise, Paul. All About Canaries. rev ed. (Illus.). 96p. 1976. pap. 2.50 (ISBN 0-87666-953-4, PS315). TFH Pubns.

Evans, J. A. Procopius. (World Authors Ser.: Greece: No. 170). lib. bdg. 10.95 (ISBN 0-8057-2722-1). Twayne.

Evans, J. D. Aristotle's Concept of Dialectic. LC 76-22982. 1977. 22.95 (ISBN 0-521-21425-4). Cambridge U Pr.

--The Prehistoric Antiquities of the Maltese Island: A Survey. 1971. 80.00x (ISBN 0-485-11093-8, Athlone Pr). Humanities.

Evans, J. G., jt. ed. see Limbrey, Susan.

Evans, J. Robert. Blowing the Whistle on Intercollegiate Sports. LC 74-78842. 1974. 11.95 (ISBN 0-911012-94-X). Nelson-Hall.

Evans, J. Warren. Horses: A Guide to Their Care & Enjoyment. LC 80-29070. (Illus.). 1981. text ed. price not set (ISBN 0-7167-1253-9). W H Freeman.

Evans, J. Warren, et al. The Horse. LC 76-22686. (Animal Science Ser.). (Illus.). 1977. 27.95x (ISBN 0-7167-0491-9). W H Freeman.

Evans, Jack M., jt. auth. see Cain, Sandra G.

Evans, Jacque, jt. auth. see Leptich, Anne.

Evans, James R. America's Choice. 150p. (Orig.). 1981. lib. bdg. 11.95 (ISBN 0-933028-17-2); pap. 6.95 (ISBN 0-933028-16-4). Fisher Inst.

Evans, Jim. Man of the Southern. (Steam Past Ser.). (Illus.). 96p. 1980. 17.50 (ISBN 0-04-385078-2, 2406). Allen Unwin.

Evans, Joan. English Art Thirteen Hundred Seven to Fourteen Sixty-One. LC 79-91817. (Illus.). 272p. 1980. Repr. of 1949 ed. lib. bdg. 40.00 (ISBN 0-87817-261-0). Hacker.

--Magical Jewels of the Middle Ages & the Renaissance. 7.50 (ISBN 0-8446-5572-4). Peter Smith.

--Monastic Architecture in France from the Renaissance to the Revolution. LC 79-91816. (Illus.). 822p. 1980. Repr. of 1964 ed. lib. bdg. 75.00 (ISBN 0-87817-260-2). Hacker.

--Monastic Iconography in France from the Renaissance to the Revolution. LC 67-12317. (Illus.). 1969. 78.00 (ISBN 0-521-06960-2). Cambridge U Pr.

Evans, Joel R., ed. Consumerism in the United States: An Inter-Industry Analysis. 31.95 (ISBN 0-03-056846-3). Praeger.

Evans, John C. The Environment of Early Man in the British Isles. LC 74-29803. 256p. 1975. 20.00x (ISBN 0-520-02973-9). U of Cal Pr.

--Shorthand. 1963. pap. 2.95 (ISBN 0-06-463225-3, EH 225, EH). Har-Row.

--Touch Typewriting. (Illus., Orig.). 1963. pap. 2.95 (ISBN 0-06-463229-6, EH 229, EH). Har-Row.

Evans, John M. An Introduction to Clinical Scotometry. 1938. 47.50x (ISBN 0-685-89759-1). Elliots Bks.

Evans, Joseph W., tr. see Maritain, Jacques.

Evans, Joyce. Trabajando Con los Padres De Ninos Con Impedimentos. LC 76-11644. 1976. pap. text ed. 3.50 o.p. (ISBN 0-86586-087-4). Coun Exc Child.

Evans, K. M. Attitudes & Interests in Education. 1965. pap. 6.50 (ISBN 0-7100-7166-3). Routledge & Kegan.

--Planning Small-Scale Research: A Practical Guide for Teachers & Students. rev. ed. (Exploring Education Ser.). 1978. pap. text ed. 5.00x (ISBN 0-85633-149-X, NFER). Humanities.

Evans, Kenneth L. A Feast for Spiders. 1980. pap. 1.95 (ISBN 0-451-09484-0, J9484, Sig). NAL.
Evans, L. S. Chemical & Process Plant: A Guide to the Selection of Engineering Materials. 2nd ed. LC 80-20355. 190p. 1981. 34.95 (ISBN 0-470-27064-0). Halsted Pr.
Evans, L. T., ed. Crop Physiology. LC 73-91816. (Illus.). 384p. 1975. 47.50 (ISBN 0-521-20422-4); pap. 17.50x (ISBN 0-521-29390-1). Cambridge U Pr.
Evans, Larry. Chess Questions Answered. (Illus.). 1971. 7.95 o.p. (ISBN 0-571-09707-3, Pub. by Faber & Faber). Merrimack Bk Serv.
--Gnomes Games. (Illus.). 64p. 1980. pap. 4.50 (ISBN 0-89844-020-3). Troubador Pr.
--Invisibles, Two. (Illus.). 40p. (Orig.). 1981. pap. 2.50 (ISBN 0-89844-028-9). Troubador Pr.
--Three-Dimensional Maze Art. (Illus.). 64p. 1980. pap. 4.95 (ISBN 0-89844-012-2). Troubador Pr.
Evans, Laurie, jt. auth. see Colgate, Craig, Jr.
Evans, Leo, ed. see Association for Educational & Training Technology.
Evans, Louis H., Jr. Creative Love. 1979. pap. 1.75 o.p. (ISBN 0-449-14021-0, GM). Fawcett.
Evans, Louis H., Sr. The People Vs. Jesus. 128p. 1980. pap. 5.95 (ISBN 0-8499-2909-1). Word Bks.
Evans, M. E. The Life of Beetles. 1977. pap. text ed. 9.95x (ISBN 0-04-595012-1). Allen Unwin.
Evans, M. L. & Hansen, B. D. Guide to Pediatric Nursing: A Clinical Reference. 284p. 1980. pap. 14.95 (ISBN 0-8385-3533-X). ACC.
Evans, Marcia, jt. auth. see Mackin, Ronald.
Evans, Margiad. Country Dance. 1980. 11.50 (ISBN 0-7145-3593-1); pap. 4.95 (ISBN 0-7145-3728-4). Riverrun NY.
--Ray of Darkness. 1980. 11.50 (ISBN 0-7145-3727-6); pap. 4.95 (ISBN 0-7145-3607-5). Riverrun NY.
Evans, Mari. J. D. LC 72-89129. 64p. (gr. 4 up). 1973. PLB 6.95 o.p. (ISBN 0-385-00429-X). Doubleday.
Evans, Mark. Scott Joplin & the Ragtime Years. LC 75-38362. 1976. 5.95 (ISBN 0-396-07308-5). Dodd.
Evans, Mark, jt. auth. see Stack, Robert.
Evans, Martin. Evening Star. (Illus.). 224p. (Orig.). 1980. pap. 16.50x (ISBN 0-85242-634-8). Intl Pubns Serv.
--LBSC's Shop, Shed & Road. 2nd ed. 192p. (Orig.). 1979. pap. 12.50x (ISBN 0-85242-708-5). Intl Pubns Serv.
--Model Locomotive Construction. 2nd ed. (Illus.). 163p. 1978. pap. 9.50x (ISBN 0-85242-602-X). Intl Pubns Serv.
Evans, Mary. Garden Books, Old & New. LC 71-162512. 1971. Repr. of 1926 ed. 15.00 (ISBN 0-8103-3743-6). Gale.
--How to Make Historic American Costumes. LC 78-159952. (Illus.). xii, 178p. 1976. Repr. of 1942 ed. 24.00 (ISBN 0-8103-4141-7). Gale.
Evans, Mary J., jt. auth. see Davis, Jed H.
Evans, Max. The Hi Lo Country. (Western Fiction Ser.). 1980. lib. bdg. 10.95 (ISBN 0-8398-2685-0). Gregg.
--The Rounders. (Western Fiction Ser.). 1980. lib. bdg. 10.95 (ISBN 0-8398-2686-9). Gregg.
--Shadow of Thunder. LC 69-20469. 78p. 1969. 6.50 (ISBN 0-8040-0274-6). Swallow.
Evans, Michael. Karl Marx. (Political Thinkers). 1975. text ed. 17.95x (ISBN 0-04-921020-3); pap. text ed. 7.50x o.p. (ISBN 0-04-921021-1). Allen Unwin.
Evans, Michele. American Cuisine Minceur Cookbook. (Orig.). 1977. pap. 2.25 o.s.i. (ISBN 0-446-92167-X). Warner Bks.
--Fearless Cooking for One. 1980. 13.95 (ISBN 0-671-24416-7). S&S.
--The Slowcrock Cookbook. 160p. (Orig.). 1975. pap. 1.95 o.s.i. (ISBN 0-446-89033-2). Warner Bks.
Evans, Mike & Summers, Bob. Young Lions of Judah. 116p. 1974. pap. 1.95 o.p. (ISBN 0-88270-059-6). Logos.
Evans, N. Dean, jt. auth. see Neagley, Ross L.
Evans, Nancy, jt. auth. see Appelbaum, Judith.
Evans, Norma P., compiled by. Grandpa with a Stick: Joseph Theolin Landry - His Ancestors & Descendants. LC 80-67365. (Illus.). 100p. (Orig.). 1980. pap. 15.00 (ISBN 0-937418-02-1); special family ed. 15.00 (ISBN 0-937418-03-X). N P Evans.
Evans, Norman. Beginning Teaching in Professional Partnership. LC 78-13675. 1978. pap. text ed. 6.50x (ISBN 0-8419-6215-4). Holmes & Meier.
Evans, Patrick. Janet Frame. (World Authors Ser.). 1977. 9.95 (ISBN 0-8057-6254-X). Twayne.
Evans, Paul. Outlaws of Lost River. 256p. (YA) 1974. 5.95 (ISBN 0-685-39180-9, Avalon). Bouregy.
Evans, Paul & Bartolome, Fernando. Must Success Cost So Much? The Human Toll of Corporate Life. LC 81-68964. 256p. 1981. 13.95 (ISBN 0-465-04746-7). Basic.
Evans, Peter. Cystitis. 1979. 9.95x (ISBN 0-8464-0053-7). Beekman Pubs.
--Mastering Your Migraine. 1979. 8.95 (ISBN 0-87690-331-6); pap. 3.95 (ISBN 0-87690-332-4). Dutton.
--Peter Sellers: The Mask Behind the Mask. 1980. pap. 2.50 (ISBN 0-451-09758-0, E9758, Sig). NAL.
--The Police Revolution. 1974. text ed. 16.95x (ISBN 0-04-350048-X). Allen Unwin.
--Prison Crisis. 192p. (Orig.). 1980. text ed. 18.95 (ISBN 0-04-365003-1, 2549); pap. text ed. 8.95x (ISBN 0-04-365004-X, 2562). Allen Unwin.
Evans, Philip H., jt. auth. see Lovins, Amory.
Evans, Philip R., jt. auth. see Sudhalter, Richard M.
Evans, Pritchard E. The Position of Women in Primitive Societies. (Illus.). 1965. 10.95 (ISBN 0-571-06196-6, Pub. by Faber & Faber). Merrimack Bk Serv.
Evans, R. C. Forty Years in the Mormon Church: Why I Left It. 1976. Repr. of 1920 ed. 6.50 (ISBN 0-89315-054-1). Lambert Bk.
Evans, R. E. The War of American Independence. (Cambridge Introduction to the History of Mankind Ser.). (Illus.). 48p. (gr. 6-9). 1976. pap. 3.95 (ISBN 0-521-20903-X). Cambridge U Pr.
Evans, R. G. & Williamson, M. F. Extending Canadian Health Insurance: Options for Pharmacare & Denticare. (Ontario Economic Council Research Studies). 1978. pap. 12.00 (ISBN 0-8020-3353-9). U of Toronto Pr.
Evans, R. H., jt. auth. see Kong, F. K.
Evans, R. J. The Making of the Habsburg Monarchy: Fifteen Fifty to Seventeen Hundred. 1979. 59.00x (ISBN 0-19-822560-1). Oxford U Pr.
Evans, Rand B., ed. see Watson, Robert I.
Evans, Richard. The Making of Psychology. 1976. text ed. 6.95x o.p. (ISBN 0-394-31153-1). Random.
Evans, Richard, jt. auth. see Fox, Allen.
Evans, Richard & Lee, W. R., eds. The German Family. 224p. 1981. 27.50x (ISBN 0-389-20101-4). B&N.
Evans, Richard J. The Feminists: Women's Emancipation Movements in Europe, America & Australasia 1840-1920. LC 77-77490. 1977. text ed. 20.00x (ISBN 0-06-492037-2); pap. text ed. 8.50x (ISBN 0-06-492044-5). B&N.
Evans, Richard J., ed. Society & Politics in Wilhelmine Germany. LC 77-14746. 1978. text ed. 19.50x (ISBN 0-06-492036-4). B&N.
Evans, Richard T. The Feminist Movement in Germany 1894-1933. LC 75-31571. (Sage Studies in Twentieth Century History: Vol. 6). (Illus.). 1976. 17.50x (ISBN 0-8039-9951-8); pap. 8.95x (ISBN 0-8039-9996-8). Sage.
Evans, Robert, tr. see Polisensky, J. V.
Evans, Robert A. & Parker, Thomas D., eds. Christian Theology: A Case Method Approach. LC 76-9963. 1976. 10.00 o.p. (ISBN 0-06-062251-2, HarpR); pap. 5.95x (ISBN 0-06-062252-0, RD 176, HarpR). Harrow.
Evans, Robert C. Introduction to Crystal Chemistry. 2nd ed. (Illus.). 1964. pap. text ed. 19.95x (ISBN 0-521-09367-8, 367). Cambridge U Pr.
Evans, Robert O. The Osier Cage: Rhetorical Devices in Romeo & Juliet. LC 66-16233. 120p. 1966. 6.00x (ISBN 0-8131-1123-4). U Pr of Ky.
Evans, Robert O., ed. Graham Greene: Some Critical Considerations. LC 63-22005. 304p. 1967. pap. 5.00x (ISBN 0-8131-0114-X). U Pr of Ky.
Evans, Robert O., jt. ed. see Biles, Jack I.
Evans, Robert O., ed. see Borges, Jorge L.
Evans, Robert O., tr. see Borges, Jorge L.
Evans, Roberta. Alcohol & Alcoholism. LC 76-13228. (First Bks. Ser.). (Illus.). 96p. (gr. 4-6). 1976. PLB 6.45 (ISBN 0-531-00334-5). Watts.
Evans, Rosemary G. Anselm & a New Generation. 230p. 1980. 34.50x (ISBN 0-19-826651-0). Oxford U Pr.
Evans, Ruby. Embroidery from Traditional English Patterns. (Illus.). 1971. 8.25 o.p. (ISBN 0-8231-4026-1). Branford.
Evans, Rupert & Herr, Edward. Foundations of Vocational Education. 3rd ed. Taylor, Robert E., ed. (Merrill Series in Career Programs). 1978. text ed. 18.95 (ISBN 0-675-08442-3). Merrill.
Evans, Sabastian, ed. High History of the Holy Grail. (Illus.). 395p. 1969. 12.95 (ISBN 0-227-67727-7). Attic Pr.
Evans, Silvan D., ed. see Rowlands, W.
Evans, T. The Challenge of Change. LC 71-104788. 1970. 16.00 (ISBN 0-08-015825-0); pap. 7.75 (ISBN 0-08-015824-2). Pergamon.
Evans, T. F., ed. Shaw: The Critical Heritage. (Critical Heritage Ser.). 1976. 36.00x (ISBN 0-7100-8280-0). Routledge & Kegan.
Evans, T. J. Bituminous Coal in Texas. (Illus.). 65p. 1974. 2.00 (HB 4). Bur Econ Geology.
Evans, Tabor. Longarm. (Orig.). 1978. pap. 1.95 (ISBN 0-515-05983-8). Jove Pubns.
--Longarm & the Avenging Angels, No. 3. 1978. pap. 1.95 (ISBN 0-515-05899-8, 04791-0). Jove Pubns.
--Longarm & the Bandit Queen. (The Longarm Ser.: No. 17). 256p. (Orig.). 1981. pap. 1.75 (ISBN 0-515-05309-0). Jove Pubns.
--Longarm & the Boot Hillers. (Longarm Ser.: No. 34). (Orig.). 1981. pap. 1.95 (ISBN 0-515-05590-5). Jove Pubns.
--Longarm & the Dragon Hunters. (Longarm Ser.: No. 26). 255p. (Orig.). 1980. pap. 1.75 (ISBN 0-515-05582-4). Jove Pubns.
--Longarm & the Ghost Dancers. (Longarm Ser.: No. 22). 223p. (Orig.). 1980. pap. 1.75 (ISBN 0-515-05314-7). Jove Pubns.
--Longarm & the Golden Lady. (Longarm Ser.: No. 32). (Orig.). 1981. pap. 1.95 (ISBN 0-515-05588-3). Jove Pubns.
--Longarm & the Hatchet Men, No. 9. 1979. pap. 1.95 (ISBN 0-515-05973-0). Jove Pubns.
--Longarm & the Highgraders: No. 7. (Orig.). 1979. pap. 1.95 (ISBN 0-515-05901-3). Jove Pubns.
--Longarm & the Laredo Loop. (Longarm Ser.: No. 33). (Orig.). 1981. pap. 1.95 (ISBN 0-515-05589-1). Jove Pubns.
--Longarm & the Loggers, No. 6. (Orig.). 1979. pap. 1.95 (ISBN 0-515-05900-5). Jove Pubns.
--Longarm & the Molly Maguires. (Longarm Ser.: No. 10). 1979. pap. 1.75 (ISBN 0-515-04753-8). Jove Pubns.
--Longarm & the Mounties. (The Longarm Ser.: No. 16). 252p. (Orig.). 1980. pap. 1.75 (ISBN 0-515-05308-2). Jove Pubns.
--Longarm & the Nesters: No. 8. (Orig.). 1979. pap. 1.95 (ISBN 0-515-05985-4). Jove Pubns.
--Longarm & the Railroaders. (Longarm Ser.: No. 24). 252p. (Orig.). 1980. pap. 1.75 (ISBN 0-515-05316-3). Jove Pubns.
--Longarm & the Rurales. (The Longarm Ser.: No. 27). (Orig.). pap. 1.75 (ISBN 0-515-05583-2). Jove Pubns.
--Longarm & the Sheepherders. (Longarm Ser.: No. 21). 256p. (Orig.). 1980. pap. 1.95 (ISBN 0-515-05906-4). Jove Pubns.
--Longarm & the Texas Rangers. (Longarm Ser.: No. 11). (Orig.). 1979. pap. 1.95 (ISBN 0-515-05902-1). Jove Pubns.
--Longarm & the Town Tamer. (Longarm Ser.: No. 23). 269p. (Orig.). 1980. pap. 1.75 (ISBN 0-515-05315-5). Jove Pubns.
--Longarm & the Wendigo. (The Longarm Ser.: No. 4). 256p. (Orig.). 1979. pap. 1.95 (ISBN 0-515-05972-2). Jove Pubns.
--Longarm at Robber's Roost. (Longarm Ser.: No. 20). 256p. (Orig.). 1980. pap. 1.95 (ISBN 0-515-05931-5). Jove Pubns.
--Longarm in Leadville. (Longarm Ser.: No. 14). (Orig.). 1979. pap. 1.75 (ISBN 0-515-05306-6). Jove Pubns.
--Longarm in Lincoln County. (The Longarm Ser.: No. 12). 254p. (Orig.). 1979. pap. 1.95 (ISBN 0-515-05903-X). Jove Pubns.
--Longarm in Northfield. (Longarm Ser.: No. 31). (Orig.). 1981. pap. 1.95 (ISBN 0-515-05586-7). Jove Pubns.
--Longarm in the Four Corners. (Longarm Ser.: No. 19). 224p. (Orig.). 1980. pap. 1.95 (ISBN 0-515-05905-6). Jove Pubns.
--Longarm in the Indian Nation. (The Longarm Ser.: NO. 5). 272p. (Orig.). 1979. pap. 1.75 (ISBN 0-515-04796-1). Jove Pubns.
--Longarm in the Sand Hills. (Longarm Ser.: No. 13). (Orig.). 1979. pap. 1.75 (ISBN 0-515-05305-8). Jove Pubns.
--Longarm on the Big Muddy. (Longarm Ser.: No. 29). 224p. (Orig.). 1981. pap. 1.95 (ISBN 0-515-05585-9). Jove Pubns.
--Longarm on the Border: No. 2. (Orig.). 1978. pap. 1.95 (ISBN 0-515-05378-3). Jove Pubns.
--Longarm on the Devil's Trail. (The Longarm Ser.: No. 15). 224p. (Orig.). 1979. pap. 1.95 (ISBN 0-515-05904-8). Jove Pubns.
--Longarm on the Humboldt. (Longarm Ser.: No. 28). 256p. (Orig.). 1981. pap. 1.95 (ISBN 0-515-05584-0). Jove Pubns.
--Longarm on the Old Mission Trail. (Longarm Ser.: No. 25). 253p. (Orig.). 1980. pap. 1.95 (ISBN 0-515-05974-9). Jove Pubns.
--Longarm on the Yellowstone. (Longarm Ser.: No. 18). 256p. (Orig.). 1980. pap. 1.75 (ISBN 0-515-05310-4). Jove Pubns.
--Longarm South of the Gila. (Longarm Ser.; Men's Western Ser.: No. 30). 256p. (Orig.). 1981. pap. 1.95 (ISBN 0-515-05587-5). Jove Pubns.
Evans, W. E. The Chemistry of Death. 120p. 1963. pap. 14.75 photocopy ed. spiral (ISBN 0-398-00530-3). C C Thomas.
Evans, W. Glyn. Daily with the King. 1979. pap. 4.50 (ISBN 0-8024-1739-6). Moody.
Evans, W. McKee. To Die Game: The Story of the Lowry Band, Indian Guerrillas of Reconstruction. LC 77-142335. 1971. 17.50x (ISBN 0-8071-0816-2); pap. 5.95 (ISBN 0-8071-0379-9). La State U Pr.
Evans, Walt, jt. auth. see Fernandez, Linda.
Evans, Wayne O. & Kline, Nathan S., eds. Psychotropic Drugs in the Year 2000: Use by Normal Humans. 192p. 1971. text ed. 14.50 (ISBN 0-398-02191-0). C C Thomas.
Evans, Willa M. Ben Jonson & Elizabethan Music. 2nd ed. LC 65-18503. (Music Ser). 1965. Repr. of 1929 ed. 14.50 (ISBN 0-306-70907-4). Da Capo.
Evans, William J. The Scott, Foresman Robert's Rules of Order. rev. ed. 1980. 17.95x (ISBN 0-673-15472-6). Scott F.
Evans, William R. Robert Frost & Sidney Cox: Forty Years of Friendship. 310p. 1981. 15.00 (ISBN 0-87451-195-X). U Pr of New Eng.
Evansen, Virginia. The Flea Market Mystery. LC 77-16863. (gr. 5 up). 1978. 5.95 (ISBN 0-396-07521-5). Dodd.
Evansen, Virginia B., jt. auth. see Wolfers, Elsie E.
Evanson, John M., jt. auth. see Woolley, David E.
Evans-Pritchard, E. E. Sociology of Comte: An Appreciation. (Orig.). 1970. pap. text ed. 2.00x (ISBN 0-7190-0425-X). Humanities.
Evans-Pritchard, Edward. A History of Anthropological Thought. Singer, Andre, ed. LC 80-68955. 256p. 1981. 15.00 (ISBN 0-465-02998-1). Basic.
Evans-Pritchard, Edward E. Anthropology & History. 1961. pap. text ed. 1.25x o.p. (ISBN 0-7190-0254-0). Humanities.
--The Azande: History & Political Institutions. 1971. 36.00x (ISBN 0-19-823170-9). Oxford U Pr.
--Kinship & Marriage Among the Nuer. (Illus.). 1951. 24.00x (ISBN 0-19-823104-0). Oxford U Pr.
--Nuer: A Description of the Modes of Livelihood & Political Institutions of a Nilotic People. (Illus.). 1968. 24.00x (ISBN 0-19-823105-9); pap. 4.95x (ISBN 0-19-500322-5). Oxford U Pr.
--Sanusi of Cyrenaica. 1949. 27.00x (ISBN 0-19-823107-5). Oxford U Pr.
--Theories of Primitive Religion. pap. 6.95x (ISBN 0-19-823131-8). Oxford U Pr.
--Witchcraft, Oracles & Magic Among the Azande. 1937. 45.00x (ISBN 0-19-823103-2). Oxford U Pr.
Evans-Pritchard, Edward E., ed. Zande Trickster. (Oxford Library of African Literature). 1967. 14.95x (ISBN 0-19-815123-3). Oxford U Pr.
Evans-Wentz, W. Y., ed. Tibet's Great Yogi, Milarepa. 2nd ed. (Illus.). 1969. pap. 6.95 (ISBN 0-19-500301-2, 294, GB). Oxford U Pr.
Eva Of Friedenshort, Sr. The Working of the Holy Spirit in Daily Life. 1974. pap. 1.25 (ISBN 0-87123-647-8, 200647). Bethany Fell.
Evarts, C. M. see Hip Society.
Evarts, Hal G. Bigfoot. 190p. (gr. k-3). pap. 2.95 (ISBN 0-689-70487-9, A-114, Aladdin). Atheneum.
--The Purple Eagle Mystery. LC 75-27704. 218p. (gr. 7-10). 1976. 6.95 (ISBN 0-684-16569-4, ScribJ). Scribner.
Eve, Esme & Mamlock, Gwyneth, illus. Three Hundred Sixty-Six Goodnight Stories. (Illus.). 1969. 5.95 o.p. (ISBN 0-307-15568-4, Golden Pr). Western Pub.
Eve, Paul. Cooking with Rice. LC 74-4321. (Orig.). 1974. pap. 3.50 (ISBN 0-374-51132-2). FS&G.
Eveland, H. E. & Tennissen, A. C. Physical Geology Laboratory Manual. 3rd ed. 96p. 1979. pap. text ed. 7.95 (ISBN 0-8403-2061-2). Kendall-Hunt.
Eveleth, P. B. & Tanner, J. M. World-Wide Variation in Human Growth. LC 75-10042. (International Biological Programme Ser.: No. 8). (Illus.). 544p. 1977. 86.50 (ISBN 0-521-20806-8). Cambridge U Pr.
Evely, Louis. In the Christian Spirit. 120p. 1975. pap. 1.45 (ISBN 0-385-06266-4, Im). Doubleday.
--Love Your Neighbor. 120p. 1975. pap. 1.45 (ISBN 0-385-06256-7, Im). Doubleday.
--Suffering. 120p. 1974. pap. 1.45 (ISBN 0-385-02996-9, Im). Doubleday.
--We Are All Brothers. 120p. 1975. pap. 1.45 (ISBN 0-385-04830-0, Im). Doubleday.
--We Dare to Say Our Father. 120p. 1975. pap. 1.45 (ISBN 0-385-06274-5, Im). Doubleday.
Evenhuis, Francis D. Massinger's Imagery. (Salzburg Studies in English Literature, Jacobean Drama Studies: No. 14). 176p. 1973. pap. text ed. 25.00x (ISBN 0-391-01373-4). Humanities.
Evenson. Paris: A Century of Change, Eighteen Seventy-Eight to Nineteen Seventy-Eight. LC 78-10257. 1979. 35.00 (ISBN 0-300-02210-7). Yale U Pr.
Evenson, Norma. Paris, a Century Change Eighteen-Seventy Eight to Nineteen Seventeen Eight. LC 78-10257. (Illus.). 399p. 1981. pap. 12.95 (ISBN 0-300-02667-6). Yale U Pr.
Everage, Edna. The Sound of Edna: Dame Edna's Family Songbook. (Illus.). 96p. 1980. pap. 11.95 (ISBN 0-903443-34-1, Pub. by Hamish Hamilton England). David & Charles.

Everard, Kenneth, jt. auth. see McCullough, Robert J.

Everden, Sue, jt. auth. see Shrader, Robert D.

Evered, David. Diseases of the Thyroid. LC 76-20230. 1976. 15.95 o.p. (ISBN 0-471-02216-0, Pub. by Wiley Medical). Wiley.

Evered, James F. Shirt-Sleeves Management. 273p. 1981. 12.95 (ISBN 0-8144-5636-7). Am Mgmt.

Everest, A. S., jt. auth. see Barlow, B. V.

Everest, A. S., jt. auth. see Tayler, R. J.

Everest, Allan S. Morgenthau, the New Deal & Silver. LC 72-2368. (FDR & the Era of the New Deal Ser.). 209p. 1973. Repr. of 1950 ed. lib. bdg. 25.00 (ISBN 0-306-70469-2). Da Capo.

Everest, Alton. Handbook of Multichannel Recording. LC 75-20842. 322p. 1975. 10.95 (ISBN 0-8306-5781-9); pap. 9.95 (ISBN 0-8306-4781-3, 781). TAB Bks.

Everest, F. A. How to Build a Small Budget Recording Studio from Scratch: With 12 Tested Designs. (Illus.). 1979. 12.95 (ISBN 0-8306-9787-X); pap. 9.95 (ISBN 0-8306-1166-5, 1166). TAB Bks.

Everest, Quinton J. Prescription for Today. pap. 4.95 (ISBN 0-686-12669-6, BE-173). Evangel Indiana.

Everett, Alan. Materials. (Mitchell's Building Construction Ser.). 1978. pap. 14.95 (ISBN 0-470-26353-9). Halsted Pr.

Everett, Alan, jt. auth. see King, Harold.

Everett, Alexander. America; or, a General Survey of the Political Situation of the Several Powers of the Western Continent. Hudson, Michael, ed. (The Neglected American Economists Ser.). 1974. lib. bdg. 50.00 (ISBN 0-8240-1002-7). Garland Pub.

--Journal of the Proceedings of the Friends of Domestic Industry: In General Convention Met at the City of New York, October 26, 1831. Hudson, Michael, ed. Bd. with British Opinions on the Protecting System. (The Neglected American Economists Ser.). 1974. lib. bdg. 50.00 (ISBN 0-8240-1003-5). Garland Pub.

Everett, B. Auden. 1980. 17.50 (ISBN 0-685-99622-0). Chips.

Everett, Eileen. The Hamster, Bk. 1. (gr. 3-7). 1976. pap. 1.00 o.p. (ISBN 0-08-016235-5). Pergamon.

--Mice. 1976. pap. 1.00 o.p. (ISBN 0-08-016241-X). Pergamon.

Everett, Lorne G. Groundwater Monitoring. LC 80-82885. (Illus.). 480p. 1980. 150.00x (ISBN 0-931690-14-5). GE Tech Market.

Everett, Peter. Memorials of Ancient Wrongs. 1980. 10.95 (ISBN 0-316-25837-7). Little.

Everett, T. H. How to Grow Beautiful House Plants. 1978. pap. 1.95 o.p. (ISBN 0-449-13967-0, GM). Fawcett.

--The New York Botanical Garden Illustrated Encyclopedia of Horticulture, 10 vols. 1980. Set. lib. bdg. 525.00 (ISBN 0-8240-7222-7). Garland Pub.

--One Hundred & One Flowering House Plants Anyone Can Grow. 144p. 1975. pap. 2.25 o.p. (ISBN 0-449-13271-4, 3271, GM). Fawcett.

--One Hundred & One More Houseplants. 1976. pap. 1.95 o.p. (ISBN 0-449-13500-4, Gm). Fawcett.

Everett, Thomas H. How to Grow Beautiful Houseplants. LC 76-21286. 1976. pap. 2.50 o.p. (ISBN 0-668-04015-7). Arco.

Everett, W. N., ed. Ordinary & Partial Differential Equations. (Lecture Notes in Mathematics Ser.: Vol. 827). (Illus.). 271p. 1981. pap. 16.80 (ISBN 0-387-10252-3). Springer-Verlag.

Everett, Wade. The Big Drive. 128p. 1981. pap. 1.75 (ISBN 0-345-29142-5). Ballantine.

--Shotgun Marshal. 1981. pap. 1.75 (ISBN 0-345-29434-3). Ballantine.

--Temporary Duty. 1975. pap. 0.95 o.p. (ISBN 0-345-23911-3). Ballantine.

--The Warrior. 160p. 1981. pap. 1.75 (ISBN 0-345-29432-7). Ballantine.

Everett, William W. & Bachmeyer, T. J. Disciplines in Transformation: A Guide to Theology & the Behavioral Sciences. LC 78-68570. 1979. pap. text ed. 9.75 (ISBN 0-8191-0692-5). U Pr of Amer.

Everette, Mable L. Life's Joys. 1981. 4.50 (ISBN 0-8062-1667-0). Carlton.

Everhart, Robert, ed. The Public School Monopoly: Education & State in American Society. (Pacific Institute for Public Policy Research Ser.). 1981. price not set professional reference (ISBN 0-88410-383-8). Ballinger Pub.

Everhart, W. Harry, et al. Principles of Fishery Science. (Illus.). 1975. 14.50x o.p. (ISBN 0-8014-0918-7). Cornell U Pr.

Everitt, A. Abstract Expressionism. LC 77-80188. (Modern Movements in Art Ser.). 1978. pap. 1.95 (ISBN 0-8120-0880-4). Barron.

Everitt, Arthur V. & Burgess, John A. Hypothalamus, Pituitary & Aging. (Illus.). 808p. 1976. 67.50 (ISBN 0-398-03346-3). C C Thomas.

Everitt, Brian. Cluster Analysis. 2nd ed. 136p. 1980. pap. 16.95x (ISBN 0-470-26991-X). Halsted Pr.

Everly, George & Girdano, Daniel. The Stress Mess Solution. LC 79-14652. 174p. 1980. text ed. 11.95 (ISBN 0-87619-666-0); pap. 9.95 (ISBN 0-87619-434-X). R J Brady.

Everly, George S., Jr., jt. auth. see Girdano, Daniel A.

Evers, Hans-Dieter, ed. The Sociology of Southeast Asia: Readings on Social Change & Development. (Illus.). 350p. 1980. 32.50 (ISBN 0-19-580408-2). Oxford U Pr.

Evers, Larry, ed. The South Corner of Time. 250p. 1981. 35.00x (ISBN 0-8165-0732-5); pap. 14.95 (ISBN 0-8165-0731-7). U of Ariz Pr.

Eversley, David. The Planner in Society. 1973. 14.50 o.p. (ISBN 0-686-24620-9, Pub. by Faber & Faber). Merrimack Bk Serv.

Eversley, David, jt. ed. see Donnison, David.

Eversley, George J. & Chirol, Valentine. The Turkish Empire. LC 68-9623. (Illus.). 1969. Repr. of 1892 ed. 22.50 (ISBN 0-86527-198-4). Fertig.

Everson, Mary, jt. auth. see Everson, Ralph.

Everson, Ralph & Everson, Mary. Everson's Best Farm Manual & Helpful Hints. LC 80-68664. (Illus.). 300p. (Orig.). 1980. pap. 9.95 (ISBN 0-89708-027-0). And Bks.

Everson, William. The Veritable Years: 1949-1966. 350p. 1978. 14.00 (ISBN 0-87685-379-3); pap. 7.50 (ISBN 0-87685-378-5). Black Sparrow.

Everson, William, ed. see Jeffers, Robinson.

Evert, Judi. Introduction to Hospitality - Recreation Careers. (gr. 7-10). 1975. pap. text ed. 5.00 activity ed. (ISBN 0-87345-185-6). McKnight.

Evert, Ray & Eichhorn, S. Laboratory Topics in Botany. 1976. 8.95 o.p. (ISBN 0-87901-060-6). Worth.

Evert, Ray, jt. auth. see Raven, Peter.

Evert, Ray, et al. Laboratory Topics in Biology. 1979. text ed. 9.95x (ISBN 0-87901-103-3). Worth.

Everton, Clive. Better Billiards & Snooker. new ed. (Better Sports Ser.). (Illus.). 90p. (gr. 7 up). 1976. text ed. 14.50x (ISBN 0-7182-1441-2, SpS). Soccer.

Evertson, Carolyn M., jt. auth. see Brophy, Jere E.

Evertts, Eldonna & VanRoekel, Byron. Coming to Crossroads, Level 15. (Design for Reading Ser). (Illus.). (gr. 5). 1972. text ed. 11.04 (ISBN 0-06-516008-8, SchDept); tchr's ed. 14.28 (ISBN 0-06-516206-4); wkbk. 3.20 (ISBN 0-06-516307-9); tchr's wkbk. 6.36 (ISBN 0-06-516407-5); dupl. masters 17.68 (ISBN 0-06-516838-0); mastery test pkg. 14.48 (ISBN 0-06-516616-7). Har-Row.

--Spanning the Seven Seas, Level 17. (Design for Reading Ser). (Illus.). (gr. 6). 1972. text ed. 11.16 (ISBN 0-06-516009-6, SchDept); tchr's ed. 14.28 (ISBN 0-06-516207-2); wkbk. 3.20 (ISBN 0-06-516308-7); tchr's ed. wkbk. 5.36 (ISBN 0-06-516408-3); dupl. masters 17.68 (ISBN 0-06-516839-9); mastery test pkg. 14.48 (ISBN 0-06-516617-5). Har-Row.

--Traveling the Trade Winds. 2nd ed. (Design for Reading Ser). (Illus.). (gr. 4). 1972. text ed. 10.68 (ISBN 0-06-516007-X, SchDept); tchr's ed. 14.28 (ISBN 0-06-516205-6); wkbk. 3.20 (ISBN 0-06-516306-0); tchr's wkbk. 6.36 (ISBN 0-06-516406-7); masterly tests pkg. 14.48 (ISBN 0-06-516615-9); dupl.masters with ans. key 17.68 (ISBN 0-06-516837-2). Har-Row.

Every, Dale Van see Van Every, Dale.

Every, Edward Van see Van Every, Edward.

Eves, Howard. Elementary Matrix Theory. 1980. pap. 5.50 (ISBN 0-486-63946-0). Dover.

Evett, Jack & Pinckney, Richard P. Fortran Programming with Applications to Engineering: An Introductory Fortran Manual. 212p. 1981. pap. 5.95 (ISBN 0-910554-32-3). Eng Pr.

Evett, Marianne B., ed. see Porter, Henry.

Evetts, Echo. China Mending: A Guide to Repairing & Restoration. (Illus.). 1978. 15.95 (ISBN 0-571-10822-9, Pub. by Faber & Faber). Merrimack Bk Serv.

Evetts, Julia. The Sociology of Educational Ideas. (Students Library of Education). 176p. 1973. 14.00x (ISBN 0-7100-7609-6); pap. 7.00 (ISBN 0-7100-7619-3). Routledge & Kegan.

Evian, Jasper. Father Daughter. 256p. 1980. 10.95 (ISBN 0-02-536700-5). Macmillan.

Evola, Julius. Metaphysics of Sex. Ormrod, J. A., tr. from Ital. (Illus.). 1981. pap. 8.95 (ISBN 0-89281-025-4). Inner Tradit.

Evory, Ann. Contemporary Authors. (New Revision Ser.: Vol. 2). 500p. 1981. 58.00 (ISBN 0-8103-1931-4). Gale.

Evory, Ann, ed. Contemporary Authors. (New Revisions Ser.: No. 3). 500p. 1981. 58.00 (ISBN 0-8103-1932-2). Gale.

Evory, Ann, jt. ed. see Locher, Frances C.

Evrard, Franklin H. Successful Parole. 140p. 1971. 12.75 (ISBN 0-398-00532-X). C C Thomas.

Evreinov, Nikolai. Samoe Glavnoe. (Rus.). 1980. 13.00 (ISBN 0-88233-700-9); pap. 4.50 (ISBN 0-88233-701-7). Ardis Pubs.

Evseenko, D. S., jt. auth. see Emanuel, N. M.

Evslin, Bernard. Greeks Bearing Gifts: The Epics of Achilles & Ulysses. LC 76-16039. (Illus.). 336p. (YA) 1976. 9.95 (ISBN 0-590-17431-2, Four Winds). Schol Bk Serv.

--Heraclea: A Legend of Warrior Women. LC 77-17967. (Illus.). 272p. 1978. 9.95 (ISBN 0-590-07405-9, Four Winds). Schol Bk Serv.

Evual, Thomas, jt. auth. see Cheffers, John T.

Evyatar, A. & Rosenbloom, P. Motivated Mathematics. LC 80-40491. (Illus.). 250p. Date not set. price not set (ISBN 0-521-23308-9). Cambridge U Pr.

Ewald, Ellen B., jt. auth. see Lappe, Frances M.

Ewald, Ellen B., jt. auth. see Lappe, Francis M.

Ewald, William B., Jr. Eisenhower the President: Crucial Days, 1951-1960. LC 80-22929. 420p. 1981. 12.95 (ISBN 0-13-246868-9). P-H.

Ewald, William R., Jr., ed. Environment & Policy: The Next Fifty Years. LC 68-27344. 476p. 1968. pap. 4.95x (ISBN 0-253-12265-1). Ind U Pr.

Ewalt, Patricia L., ed. Toward a Definition of Clinical Social Work. LC 80-81821. (NASW Conference Proceedings Ser.). 108p. 1980. pap. 5.00x (ISBN 0-87101-086-0, CBP-086-C). Natl Assn Soc Wkrs.

Ewan, D. Mainstreams of Music, 4 vols. (gr. 7-12). 1975. Set. 43.80 o.p. (ISBN 0-531-01102-X). Watts.

Ewan, J. Introduction to the Reprint of Pursh's Flora Americae Septentrionalis. 118p. 1980. pap. text ed. 18.00 (ISBN 3-7682-1272-6). Lubrecht & Cramer.

Ewan, Joseph. William Lobb, Plant Hunter for Veitch & Messenger of the Big Tree. (Publications in Botany, Vol. 67). 1974. pap. 6.75x (ISBN 0-520-09501-4). U of Cal Pr.

Ewan, Joseph, ed. A Short History of Botany in the United States. 1969. 8.95 (ISBN 0-02-844360-8). Hafner.

Ewart, Gavin, ed. The Batsford Book of Light Verse for Children. 1978. 17.95 (ISBN 0-7134-0916-9). David & Charles.

Ewart, Nei. Unsafe As Houses: A Guide to Home Safety. (Illus.). 160p. 1981. 12.50 (ISBN 0-7137-1090-X, Pub. by Blandford Pr England). Sterling.

Ewart, Park J., et al. Probability for Statistical Decision Making. (Illus.). 400p. 1974. ref. ed. 19.95 (ISBN 0-13-711614-4). P-H.

Ewart, W., jt. auth. see Norris, G.

Ewbank, Inga-Stina. Essays & Studies Nineteen Eighty, Vol.33. (Essays & Studies). 158p. 1980. pap. text ed. 22.00x (ISBN 0-391-01766-7). Humanities.

Ewbank, Inga-Stina & Hall, Peter. Henrik Ibsen: John Gabriel Borkman, an English Version. 96p. 1975. pap. text ed. 4.50x (ISBN 0-485-12100-X, Athlone Pr). Humanities.

Ewbank, Weeb, jt. auth. see Broeg, R.

Ewbank, William W. The Poems of Cicero. Commager, Steele, ed. LC 77-70814. (Latin Poetry Ser.). 1978. lib. bdg. 28.00 (ISBN 0-8240-2955-0). Garland Pub.

Ewel, Katherine C., jt. auth. see Vogel, Steven.

Ewell, George W. Microwave Radar Transmitters: Systems, Modulators & Devices. (Illus.). 300p. 1981. 21.50 (ISBN 0-07-019843-8, C&RB). McGraw.

Ewell, Peter T. & Poleman, Thomas T. Uxpanapa: Agricultural Development in the Mexican Tropics. LC 80-12208. (Pergamon Policy Studies). 220p. 1980. 25.00 (ISBN 0-08-025967-7). Pergamon.

Ewen, Alfred. Bell's Miniature Series of Great Writers: Shakespeare. 128p. 1980. Repr. of 1904 ed. lib. bdg. 20.00 (ISBN 0-89984-178-3). Century Bookbindery.

Ewen, Cecil H. Guide to the Origin of British Surnames. LC 68-30596. 1969. Repr. of 1938 ed. 18.00 (ISBN 0-8103-3123-3). Gale.

--History of Surnames of the British Isles: A Concise Account of Their Origin, Evolution, Etymology & Legal Status. LC 68-30597. 1968. Repr. of 1931 ed. 20.00 (ISBN 0-8103-3124-1). Gale.

Ewen, Dale & Topper, Michael A. Mathematics for Technical Education. (Technical Mathematics Ser.). (Illus.). 384p. 1976. 17.95x (ISBN 0-13-565150-6); study guide 2.95 (ISBN 0-13-565143-3). P-H.

--Technical Calculus. (Illus.). 1977. 17.95 (ISBN 0-13-898122-1). P-H.

Ewen, David. George Gershwin: His Journey to Greatness. LC 77-6821. (Illus.). 1977. Repr. of 1970 ed. lib. bdg. 25.00x (ISBN 0-8371-9663-9, EWGG). Greenwood.

--Great Men of American Popular Song. rev. ed. LC 71-37961. 432p. 1972. 14.95 o.p. (ISBN 0-13-364182-1). P-H.

--Vocal Music. LC 74-34115. (Illus.). 272p. (YA) (gr. 7-12). 1975. 10.95 o.p. (ISBN 0-531-02829-1). Watts.

Ewen, David, jt. auth. see Cross, Milton.

Ewen, David, ed. Popular American Composers. (Illus.). 1962. 9.00 (ISBN 0-8242-0040-3). Wilson.

Ewen, David A. Complete Book of the American Musical Theater. rev. ed. (Illus.). 1970. 15.00 o.p. (ISBN 0-03-085060-6). HR&W.

Ewen, Doris & Ewen, Mary. An ABC of Children's Names. (Illus.). 30p. (ps-4). Date not set. pap. cancelled (ISBN 0-914676-41-5). Green Tiger.

Ewen, Mary, jt. auth. see Ewen, Doris.

Ewen, Robert. Contract Bridge. LC 74-9620. (Illus.). 72p. 1975. PLB 4.47 o.p. (ISBN 0-531-02787-2). Watts.

Ewen, Robert B. Choosing the College for You. LC 75-25794. (Career Concise Guides Ser.). (Illus.). 72p. (gr. 8 up). 1976. PLB 6.45 (ISBN 0-531-00290-X). Watts.

--An Introduction to Theories of Personality. 1980. 17.95 (ISBN 0-12-245150-3). Acad Pr.

Ewen, Sol J. & Glickstein, Cyrus. Ultrasonic Therapy in Periodontics. (Illus.). 144p. 1968. pap. 19.75 photocopy ed. spiral (ISBN 0-398-00535-4). C C Thomas.

Ewens, James M. Pass It on. (Orig.). pap. 1.50 (ISBN 0-89129-051-6). Jove Pubns.

Ewer, J. R. & Latorre, G. A Course in Basic Scientific English. 1975. pap. text ed. 5.25x (ISBN 0-582-52009-6); teacher's bk. 2.75x (ISBN 0-582-52059-2). Longman.

Ewerbeck, H. Differential Diagnosis in Pediatrics. 470p. 1980. spiral bdg. 19.00 (ISBN 0-387-90474-3). Springer-Verlag.

Ewers, Hanns H. Edgar Allan Poe. 55p. 1980. Repr. of 1917 ed. lib. bdg. 10.00 (ISBN 0-8495-1347-2). Arden Lib.

Ewers, John C. Artists of the Old West. LC 73-79662. 240p. 1973. 14.95 o.p. (ISBN 0-385-04474-7). Doubleday.

--Chippewa Indians VI. Horr, David A., ed. (American Indian Ethnohistory Ser.). 1978. lib. bdg. 42.00 (ISBN 0-8240-0813-8). Garland Pub.

--The Horse in Blackfoot Indian Culture. x ed. LC 55-60591. (Classics in Smithsonian Anthropology Ser.: No. 3). (Illus.). 374p. 1980. pap. text ed. 9.95x (ISBN 0-87474-419-9). Smithsonian.

Ewers, John C., jt. auth. see Rachlis, Eugene.

Ewers, John C., ed. see Catlin, George.

Ewers, John C., ed. see Denig, Edwin T.

Ewers, William L. Solar Energy: A Biased Guide. LC 76-55551. (International Library of Ecology Ser.). (Illus.). 1977. pap. 4.95 (ISBN 0-89196-013-9, Domus Bks); pap. 4.95 (ISBN 0-89196-013-9). Quality Bks IL.

Ewert, A., ed. see France, Marie de.

Ewert, Alfred, ed. see Beroul.

Ewert, J. P. Neuroethology. (Illus.). 1980. pap. 24.80 (ISBN 0-387-09790-2). Springer-Verlag.

Ewing, Alfred C. Ethics. 1965. pap. text ed. 6.95 (ISBN 0-02-910030-5). Free Pr.

Ewing, Charles P. Crisis Intervention As Psychotherapy. 1978. pap. 4.95x (ISBN 0-19-502271-8). Oxford U Pr.

Ewing, Cortez A. Primary Elections in the South: A Study in Uniparty Politics. LC 80-12616. (Illus.). xii, 112p. 1980. Repr. of 1953 ed. lib. bdg. 14.75x (ISBN 0-313-22452-8, EWPR). Greenwood.

Ewing, David. Freedom Inside the Organization: Bringing Civil Liberties to the Workplace. 1977. 10.00 (ISBN 0-87690-249-2). Dutton.

Ewing, David W. Managerial Mind. LC 64-16957. 1968. pap. text ed. 2.95 (ISBN 0-02-910050-X). Free Pr.

--Writing for Results in Business, Government, the Sciences & the Professions. 2nd ed. LC 79-11756. 1979. 19.95 (ISBN 0-471-05036-9). Wiley.

Ewing, Elizabeth. Underwear: A History. (Illus.). 1972. 6.75 (ISBN 0-87830-145-3). Theatre Arts.

Ewing, John A. Drinking: Everything You Want to Know. 130p. 1981. 10.95 (ISBN 0-8359-1474-7); pap. 6.95 (ISBN 0-8359-1473-9). Reston.

Ewing, Juliana H. Lob-Lie-by-the-Fire, Repr. Of 1874 Ed. Bd. with Jackanapes. Repr. of 1884 ed; Daddy Darwin's Dovecot. Repr. of 1884 ed. LC 75-32178. (Classics of Children's Literature, 1621-1932: Vol. 41). (Illus.). 1976. PLB 38.00 (ISBN 0-8240-2290-4). Garland Pub.

--Mrs. Overtheway's Remembrances. LC 75-32171. (Classics of Children's Literature, 1621-1932: Vol. 34). (Illus.). 1976. Repr. of 1869 ed. PLB 38.00 (ISBN 0-8240-2283-1). Garland Pub.

--Six to Sixteen. LC 75-32179. (Classics of Children's Literature, 1621-1932: Vol. 42). (Illus.). 1977. Repr. of 1875 ed. PLB 38.00 (ISBN 0-8240-2291-2). Garland Pub.

Ewing, Thomas E. Between the Hammer & the Anvil? Chinese & Russian Policies in Outer Mongolia, 1911-1921. (Indiana University Uralic & Altaic Ser.). iv, 300p. 1980. text ed. 19.50 (ISBN 0-933070-06-3). Ind U Res Inst.

--Between the Hammer & the Anvil? Chinese & Russian Policies in Outer Mongolia, 1911-1921. (Indiana University Uralic & Altaic Ser.: Vol. 138). 300p. 1980. 20.00 (ISBN 0-933070-06-3). Ind U Res Inst.
Ewing, Ward B. Job: A Vision of God. 1976. 8.95 (ISBN 0-8164-0285-X). Crossroad NY.
Ewusie, J. Yanney. Elements of Tropical Ecology. (Orig.). 1980. pap. text ed. 16.50 (ISBN 0-435-93700-6). Heinemann Ed.
Ewy, Donna & Ewy, Rodger. The Cycle of Life. (Illus.). 384p. 1981. 17.95 (ISBN 0-525-93181-3). Dutton.
Ewy, Donna, jt. auth. see Ewy, Rodger.
Ewy, Rodger & Ewy, Donna. Preparation for Breastfeeding. LC 74-33606. 144p. 1975. pap. 4.50 (ISBN 0-385-08962-7, Dolp). Doubleday.
Ewy, Rodger, jt. auth. see Ewy, Donna.
Executive Offices Of The National Academy Of Sciences - National Academy Of Engineering. Impact of Science & Technology on Regional Economic Development. LC 74-601605. (Orig.). 1969. pap. 5.00 (ISBN 0-309-01731-9). Natl Acad Pr.
Exell, T. S., jt. auth. see Spence, H. D.
Exner. Fondues. 1981. 8.95 (ISBN 0-8120-5404-0). Barron.
Exner, John E. The Rorschach: A Comprehensive System. (Personality Processes Ser.: Current Research & Advanced Interpretation: Vol 2). 1978. 41.00 (ISBN 0-471-04166-1, Pub. by Wiley-Interscience). Wiley.
Exner, John E., Jr., jt. auth. see London, Harvey.
Exner, John, Jr. The Rorschach: A Comprehensive System. LC 74-8888. (Personality Processes Ser: Vol. 1). 512p. 1974. 41.00 (ISBN 0-471-24964-5, Pub. by Wiley-Interscience). Wiley.
Expilly, Abbe Jean-Joseph. Tableau de la Population de la France, 8 Janvier 1780. (Principal French Demographic Works of the 18th Century Ser.). (Fr.). 1977. lib. bdg. 32.50x o.p. (ISBN 0-8287-0322-1); pap. text ed. 22.50x o.p. (ISBN 0-685-75757-9). Clearwater Pub.
Explorers Ltd., compiled by. Explorers Ltd. Source Book. rev. & enl. ed. LC 76-26224. (Illus.). 1977. 15.00 o.s.i. (ISBN 0-06-011259-X, HarpT); pap. 7.95 (ISBN 0-06-011252-2, TD-257, HarpT). Har-Row.
Exquemelin, Alexandre O. Buccaneers & Marooners of America. Pyle, Howard, ed. LC 78-142007. 1971. Repr. of 1891 ed. 21.00 (ISBN 0-8103-3620-0). Gale.
Extavour, W. C. The Exclusive Economic Zone. 384p. 1979. 30.00x o.p. (ISBN 90-286-0838-9). Sijthoff & Noordhoff.
Exton, Harold. Handbook of Hypergeometric Integrals: Theory Applications, Tables, Computer Programs. (Mathematics & Its Applications Ser.). 1978. 54.95 (ISBN 0-470-26342-3). Halsted Pr.
--Multiple Hypergeometric Functions & Applications. LC 76-20720. 1976. 37.95 (ISBN 0-470-15190-0). Halsted Pr.
Exton, William, Jr. Cost-Effective Error Reduction in Data Processing. 275p. 1981. 20.95 (ISBN 0-471-04682-5, Pub. by Wiley-Interscience). Wiley.
Extraordinario De Sesiones, Primer Periodo, Washington, D. C., 1970. Proceedings: Textos Certificados De las Resoluciones y Otros Documentos, Vol. 1. (General Assembly Ser.). (Fr., Span., Port.). pap. 2.00 (ISBN 0-8270-0880-5). OAS.
Extraordinario De Sesiones, Segundo Periodo, Washington, D. C., Del 24 Al 25 De Agosto De 1970. Actas y Documentos: Textos Certificados De las Resoluciones, Vol. 2. (General Assembly Ser.). (Span., Eng., Fr., & Port.). pap. 2.00 o.p. (ISBN 0-8270-0895-3). OAS.
Exum, Jack. How to Win Souls Today. 3.95 o.p. (ISBN 0-89315-106-8). Lambert Bk.
Exum, Patricia C., ed. Keeping the Faith: Writings by Contemporary Black American Women. 288p. (Orig.). 1974. pap. 1.75 o.p. (ISBN 0-449-30714-X, X714, Prem). Fawcett.
Exum, Wallace L. Battlewagon. 1981. pap. write for info. (ISBN 0-89865-093-3). Donning Co.
Eyck, Erich. Gladstone. Miall, Bernard, tr. LC 68-56055. Repr. of 1938 ed. 25.00x (ISBN 0-678-05045-7). Kelley.
Eyden, Joan L. Social Policy in Action. (Library of Social Policy & Administration). 1969. text ed. 5.50x (ISBN 0-7100-6402-0); pap. text ed. 3.25x (ISBN 0-7100-6404-7). Humanities.
Eyer, Dianne W., jt. auth. see Gonzalez-Mena, Janet.
Eyerly, Jeanette. He's My Baby, Now. (gr. 7-9). 1980. pap. 1.95 (ISBN 0-671-41675-8). Archway.
Eyerly, Jeannette. Drop-Out. (gr. 7-10). 1969. pap. 1.95 (ISBN 0-425-04420-3). Berkley Pub.
--Escape from Nowhere. LC 69-11995. (gr. 7 up). 1969. 9.95 (ISBN 0-397-31070-6). Lippincott.
--The Girl Inside. 1980. pap. 1.75 (ISBN 0-425-04522-6). Berkley Pub.
--Girl Like Me. LC 66-10022. (gr. 7 up). 1966. 9.95 (ISBN 0-397-30869-8). Lippincott.
--The Leonardo Touch. LC 76-18968. (gr. 5-12). 1976. 9.95 (ISBN 0-397-31684-4). Lippincott.
--Phaedra Complex. (YA) (gr. 3-6). 1979. pap. 1.50 (ISBN 0-671-29915-8). PB.
--Radigan Cares. LC 71-11722. (gr. 7-9). 1970. 6.50 (ISBN 0-397-31151-6); PLB 8.79 (ISBN 0-397-31152-4). Lippincott.
--Radigan Cares. (YA) 1978. pap. 1.50 (ISBN 0-671-29914-X). PB.
--See Dave Run. (YA) (gr. 7-9). 1979. pap. 1.75 (ISBN 0-671-56031-X). PB.
--World of Ellen March. LC 64-19039. (gr. 7-9). 1964. 9.95 (ISBN 0-397-30793-4). Lippincott.
Eyers, A. S. Practical Woodwork for Laboratory Technicians. LC 79-117463. 1970. 12.25 (ISBN 0-08-015962-1). Pergamon.
Eyestone, Robert. From Social Issues to Public Policy. LC 78-13334. (Viewpoints on American Politics Ser.). 1978. pap. text ed. 8.95 (ISBN 0-471-24978-5). Wiley.
--Threads of Public Policy: A Study in Policy Leadership. LC 79-106638. (Urban Governor Ser). 1971. pap. 5.95 (ISBN 0-672-61142-2). Bobbs.
--The Threads of Public Policy: A Study in Political Leadership. 216p. pap. text ed. 7.95x (ISBN 0-8290-0325-8). Irvington.
Eyges, Leonard. The Classical Electromagnetic Field. (Illus.). 432p. 1980. pap. text ed. 7.00 (ISBN 0-486-63947-9). Dover.
Eyken, W. Van Der see Van Der Eyken, W.
Eyles, Allen. John Wayne & the Movies. LC 73-13191. (Illus.). 320p. 1976. 17.50 o.p. (ISBN 0-498-01449-5). A S Barnes.
Eyles, John, jt. auth. see Jones, Emrys.
Eyman, Joy S. Prisons for Women: A Practical Guide to Administration Problems. 200p. 1971. 14.50 (ISBN 0-398-00537-0). C C Thomas.
Eyman, William, jt. auth. see Gerald, Mark.
Eynden, Charles Vanden see Eggan, Lawrence C. & Vanden Eynden, Charles.
Eynon, Dana. Adventures Through the Bible. rev. ed. 176p. (gr. 3-6). 1980. pap. 6.95 (ISBN 0-87239-378-X, 3234). Standard Pub.
--Bible One, Two, Three's. (gr. k-1). 1977. pap. 1.00 o.p. (ISBN 0-87239-264-3, 2011). Standard Pub.
--Through the Bible in a Year: Pupil Workbook. 64p. (gr. 3-7). 1975. wkbk. 1.95 (ISBN 0-87239-011-X, 3239). Standard Pub.
--Through the Bible in a Year: Teacher. LC 74-27239. 176p. 1975. tchr's manual 6.95 (ISBN 0-87239-028-4, 3237). Standard Pub.
Eyongetah, Tambi & Brian, Robert. A History of the Cameroon. (Illus.). 192p. 1975. pap. text ed. 5.50x (ISBN 0-582-60254-8). Longman.
Eyre, Katherine W. Monk's Court. pap. 0.95 o.p. (ISBN 0-451-06081-4, Q6081, Sig). NAL.
Eyre, Linda & Eyre, Richard. Teaching Children Joy. (Illus.). 194p. 1980. 6.95 (ISBN 0-87747-816-3). Deseret Bk.
Eyre, Richard, jt. auth. see Eyre, Linda.
Eyre, S. R., ed. World Vegetation Types. LC 78-147779. 1971. 20.00x (ISBN 0-231-03503-9). Columbia U Pr.
Eyring, H., jt. auth. see Krausz, A. S.
Eyring, H., et al, eds. Physical Chemistry: An Advanced Treatise in Eleven Volumes. Incl. Vol. 1. Thermodynamics. Jost, W., ed. 1971. 68.75, by subscription 55.50 (ISBN 0-12-245601-7); Vol. 2. Statistical Mechanics. Eyring, H., ed. 55.50, by subscription 45.50 (ISBN 0-12-245602-5); Vol. 3. Electronic Structure of Atoms & Molecules. Henderson, D., ed. 68.75, by subscription 55.50 (ISBN 0-12-245603-3); Vol. 4. Molecular Properties. Henderson, D., ed. 77.50, by subscription 62.50 (ISBN 0-12-245604-1); Vol. 5. Valency. Eyring, H., ed. 68.75, by subscription 55.50 (ISBN 0-12-245605-X); Vol. 6A. General Introduction & Gas Reactions. Jost, W., ed. Pt. A. 64.75, subscription 52.50 (ISBN 0-12-245606-8); Pt. B. 68.75, by subscription 55.50; Vol. 7. Reactions in Condensed Phases. Eyring, H., ed. 79.50, subscription 64.25 (ISBN 0-12-245607-6); Vol. 8. Liquid State. Henderson, D., ed. Pt. A. 51.50, by subscription 41.75 (ISBN 0-12-245608-4); Pt. B. 55.50, by subscription 45.00 (ISBN 0-12-245658-0); Vol. 9. **Electrochemistry. Eyring, H., ed. Pt. A. 55.50, by subscription 45.00 (ISBN 0-12-245609-2); Pt. B. 55.50, by subscription 45.00 (ISBN 0-12-245659-9). Pt. B; Vol. 10. Solid State Chemistry. Jost, W., ed. 68.75, by subscription 55.50 (ISBN 0-12-245610-6); Vol. 11 Pt. A. Mathematical Applications. Henderson, D., ed. 68.75, by subscription 55.50 (ISBN 0-12-245611-4); Pt. B. 64.75 (ISBN 0-12-245661-0). Acad Pr.**
Eyring, Henry, et al. Quantum Chemistry. 1944. 22.95 (ISBN 0-471-24981-5). Wiley.
Eys, Jan Van see Van Eys, Jan.
Eys, Jan Van see Van Eys, Jan & Sullivan, Margaret P.
Eysenck, H. J. Biological Basis of Personality. (Amer. Lec. in Living Chemistry Ser). (Illus.). 420p. 1977. 27.75 (ISBN 0-398-00538-9). C C Thomas.
--The Dynamics of Anxiety & Hysteria: An Experimental Application of Modern Learning Theory to Psychiatry. (Illus.). 1967. Repr. of 1957 ed. 22.00x (ISBN 0-7100-1354-X). Routledge & Kegan.
--The Inequality of Man. 1975. 10.95 (ISBN 0-912736-16-X). EDITS Pubs.
--You & Neurosis. (Illus.). 224p. 1979. 14.95 (ISBN 0-8039-1287-0). Sage.
Eysenck, H. J. & Eaves, L. J. The Causes & Effects of Smoking. LC 79-48085. (Illus.). 400p. 1980. 39.95 (ISBN 0-8039-1454-7). Sage.
Eysenck, H. J. & Eysenck, Sybil B. G. Personality Structure & Measurement. LC 68-15875. 1968. text ed. 11.95 (ISBN 0-912736-08-9). EDITS Pubs.
Eysenck, H. J., ed. Case Studies in Behaviour Therapy. 400p. 1976. 30.00x (ISBN 0-7100-8164-2). Routledge & Kegan.
Eysenck, Hans J. Know Your Own I.Q. (Orig.). 1962. pap. 2.50 (ISBN 0-14-020516-0, Pelican). Penguin.
Eysenck, Hans J., ed. Experiments in Personality, 2 vols. Incl. Vol. 1. Psychogenetics & Psychopharmacology (ISBN 0-7100-1356-6); Vol. 2. Psychodynamics & Psychodiagnostics (ISBN 0-7100-1357-4). 1960. pap. text ed. 19.00x (ISBN 0-685-23320-0). Humanities.
Eysenck, Michael W. Human Memory: Theory, Research & Individual Differences. 1977. text ed. 18.25 (ISBN 0-08-020405-8). Pergamon.
Eysenck, Sybil B. G., jt. auth. see Eysenck, H. J.
Eysman, Harvey A. Courier's Fist. LC 80-27338. 256p. 1981. 10.95 (ISBN 0-8253-0034-7). Beaufort Bks NY.
Eyster, James J. The Negotiation & Administration of Hotel Management Contracts. 2nd, rev. ed. (Illus.). 209p. 1980. text ed. 22.95 (ISBN 0-937056-04-9). Cornell U Sch Hotel.
Eytan, Walter. The First Ten Years: A Diplomatic History of Israel. (Return to Zion Ser.). (Illus.). x, 239p. 1980. Repr. of 1958 ed. lib. bdg. 17.50x (ISBN 0-87991-140-9). Porcupine Pr.
Ezawa, K., ed. see Zwirner, E. & Zwirner, K.
Ezekiel, Mordecai. Twenty-Five Hundred Dollars a Year. LC 72-2369. (FDR & the Era of the New Deal Ser). 348p. 1973. Repr. of 1936 ed. lib. bdg. 32.50 (ISBN 0-306-70468-4). Da Capo.
Ezekiel, Mordecai & Fox, Karl A. Methods of Correlation & Regression Analysis: Linear & Curvilinear. 3rd ed. LC 59-11993. (Illus.). 1959. 36.95 (ISBN 0-471-25014-7, Pub. by Wiley-Interscience). Wiley.
Ezekiel, Nissim. Three Plays. (Writers Workshop Bluebird Ser.). 95p. 1975. 6.75 (ISBN 0-88253-660-5); pap. text ed. 4.00 (ISBN 0-88253-659-1). Ind-US Inc.
--The Unfinished Man. 6.75 (ISBN 0-89253-686-1); flexible cloth 4.00 (ISBN 0-89253-687-X). Ind-US Inc.
Ezell, John S. The South Since Eighteen Sixty-Five. 2nd ed. LC 74-15132. 1978. 14.95 (ISBN 0-8061-1480-0). U of Okla Pr.
Ezell, Macel D. Unequivocal Americanism: Right-Wing Novels in the Cold War Era. LC 77-3725. 1977. 10.00 (ISBN 0-8108-1033-6). Scarecrow.
Ezersky, Eugene & Theibert, Richard. Facilities in Sports & Physical Education. LC 75-46556. (Illus.). 1976. text ed. 11.95 (ISBN 0-8016-1534-8). Mosby.
Ezra, Derek. Coal & Energy: The Need to Exploit the World's Most Abundant Fossil Fuel. LC 78-5785. 1978. 19.95 (ISBN 0-470-26339-3). Halsted Pr.
Ezrin. Clinical Endocrinology: A Survey of Current Practice. 1977. 24.50 o.p. (ISBN 0-8385-1137-6). ACC.
Ezrin, Calvin, et al. Systematic Endocrinology. 2nd ed. (Illus.). 1979. text ed. 42.00 (ISBN 0-06-140797-6, Harper Medical). Har-Row.
Ezua, Truman G., jt. auth. see Cox, Richard H.
Ezzati, Ali. World Energy Markets & OPEC Stability. LC 77-14615. 1978. 21.00 (ISBN 0-669-01950-X). Lexington Bks.

F

F., G. B. A. A Discovery of the Great Subtiltie & Wonderful Wisdom of the Italians. LC 74-80221. (English Experience Ser.: No. 656). 1974. Repr. of 1591 ed. 10.50 (ISBN 90-221-0656-X). Walter J Johnson.
F., T. The Copie of a Letter Sent from Sea by a Gentleman. LC 72-5984. (English Experience Ser.: No. 511). 1973. Repr. of 1589 ed. 6.00 (ISBN 90-221-0511-3). Walter J Johnson.
Faaland, Just & Parkinson, John R. Bangladesh: The Test Case for Development. LC 76-851. 1976. 26.50x (ISBN 0-89158-546-X). Westview.
Faaland, Just, ed. Aid & Influence: The Case of Bangladesh. LC 80-13481. 1980. 25.00 (ISBN 0-312-01492-9). St Martin.
Faas, Ekbert. Ted Hughes: The Unaccommodated Universe (with Selected Critical Writings by Ted Hughes & Two Interviews) 250p. 1980. 14.00 (ISBN 0-87685-460-9); pap. 7.50 (ISBN 0-87685-459-5); signed ed. 30.00 (ISBN 0-87685-461-7). Black Sparrow.
--Towards a New American Poetics: Essays & Interviews: Olson, Duncan, Snyder, Creeley, Bly, Ginsberg. 300p. 1979. 14.00 (ISBN 0-87685-389-0); pap. 6.00 (ISBN 0-87685-388-2). Black Sparrow.
Faas, Larry A. Children with Learning Problems: A Handbook for Teachers. LC 79-89741. (Illus.). 1980. text ed. 14.95 (ISBN 0-395-28352-3); inst. manual 0.65 (ISBN 0-395-28353-1). HM.
--Emotionally Disturbed Child: A Book of Readings. (Illus.). 400p. 1975. 22.75 (ISBN 0-398-00539-7). C C Thomas.
--Learning Disabilities: A Competency Based Approach. LC 75-31010. (Illus.). 512p. 1976. pap. text ed. 15.25 (ISBN 0-395-20586-7); inst. resource guide 1.25 (ISBN 0-395-20585-9). HM.
--Learning Disabilities: A Competency-Based Approach. 2nd ed. (Illus.). 480p. 1981. pap. text ed. 15.95; instr's. manual 0.75 (ISBN 0-395-29700-1). HM.
Faas, Larry A., ed. Learning Disabilities: A Book of Readings. (Illus.). 272p. 1972. 13.75 (ISBN 0-398-02276-3). C C Thomas.
Fabb, John. Flying & Ballooning from Old Photographs. LC 79-56467. (Illus.). 120p. 1980. 19.95 (ISBN 0-7134-2015-4, Pub. by Batsford England). David & Charles.
--Victorian & Edwardian Army from Old Photographs. 1975. 24.00 (ISBN 0-7134-2973-9). David & Charles.
Fabb, John & McGowan, A. C. Victorian & Edwardian Navy. 1976. 17.95 (ISBN 0-7134-3122-9). David & Charles.
Fabbricante, Thomas. Training Manual for Meat Cutting & Merchandising. (Illus.). 1977. pap. text ed. 10.50 (ISBN 0-87055-243-0). AVI.
Fabbricante, Thomas & Sultan, William J. Practical Meat Cutting & Merchandising: Beef, Vol. 1. 2nd ed. (Illus.). 1978. pap. text ed. 14.50 (ISBN 0-87055-273-2). AVI.
--Practical Meat Cutting & Merchandising, Vol. 2: Pork, Lamb & Veal. (Illus.). 242p. 1975. pap. text ed. 14.50 (ISBN 0-87055-177-9). AVI.
Fabe, Marilyn & Wikler, Norma. Up Against the Clock: Career Women Speak on the Choice to Have Children. 1980. pap. 2.75 (ISBN 0-446-95536-1). Warner Bks.
Faber, Adele & Mazlish, Elaine. How to Talk So Kids Will Listen & Listen So Kids Will Talk. LC 80-51248. (Illus.). 256p. 1980. 11.95 (ISBN 0-89256-140-8). Rawson Wade.
Faber, Bernard L., ed. The Social Structure of Eastern Europe: Transition & Process in Czechoslovakia, Hungary, Poland, Romania & Yugoslavia. LC 75-23961. (Special Studies). (Illus.). 1976. text ed. 35.95 (ISBN 0-275-55590-9). Praeger.
Faber, Donald & Korn, Henri, eds. Neurobiology of the Mauthner Cell. LC 78-66351. 1978. 31.50 (ISBN 0-89004-233-0). Raven.
Faber, Doris. Enough! The Revolt of the American Consumer. LC 72-81486. 192p. (gr. 7 up). 1972. 4.95 (ISBN 0-374-32193-0). FS&G.
Faber, Doris & Faber, Howard. The Assassination of Martin Luther King, Jr. LC 78-1726. (Focus Bks.). (Illus.). 1978. lib. bdg. 6.45 s&l (ISBN 0-531-02465-2). Watts.
Faber, Harold. From Sea to Sea: The Growth of the United States. LC 67-10351. (gr. 7 up). 1967. 5.95 o.p. (ISBN 0-374-32475-1). FS&G.
Faber, Howard, jt. auth. see Faber, Doris.
Faber, Marion, tr. see Hildesheimer, Wolfgang.
Faber, Richard. French & English. 1975. 13.95 (ISBN 0-571-10727-3, Pub. by Faber & Faber). Merrimack Bk Serv.
--Proper Stations. 1971. 6.95 o.p. (ISBN 0-571-09566-6, Pub. by Faber & Faber). Merrimack Bk Serv.
--The Vision & the Need. (Illus.). 1966. 5.95 (ISBN 0-571-06595-3, Pub. by Faber & Faber). Merrimack Bk Serv.
Faber, T. E. Introduction to the Theory of Liquid Metals. LC 76-184903. (Cambridge Monographs in Physics). (Illus.). 600p. 1972. 71.50 (ISBN 0-521-08477-6). Cambridge U Pr.
Fabian, Derek J., ed. Soft X-Ray Band Spectra & the Electronic Structures of Metals & Materials. 1969. 52.00 (ISBN 0-12-247450-3). Acad Pr.

Fabian, Dietrich. Aquatic Buildings - Baederbauten: Vol. 2, Reference Book on Aquatic Buildings, Establishments & Facilities, Construction-Plant-Equipment-Operation-Economy. LC 72-595812. (Illus.). 560p. 1970. 62.50x (ISBN 3-7667-0185-1). Intl Pubns Serv.

Fabian, Dorothy R., jt. auth. see Somers, Anne R.

Fabian, Erica, jt. auth. see Moldvay, Al.

Fabian, Erika, jt. auth. see Moldvay, Albert.

Fabian, Gerald. Odissea Finita. 1969. signed ed. 5.00 (ISBN 0-686-28710-X); pap. 2.00 (ISBN 0-686-28711-8). Man-Root.

Fabian, J. & Hartmann, H. Light Absorption of Organic Colorants: Theoretical Treatment & Empirical Rules. (Reactivity & Structure Ser.: Vol. 12). (Illus.). 280p. 1980. 79.00 (ISBN 0-387-09914-X). Springer-Verlag.

Fabian, John. Fishing for Beginners. 1980. pap. 2.95 (ISBN 0-689-70468-2, Aladdin). Atheneum.

Fabian, Larry L. Soldiers Without Enemies: Preparing the United Nations for Peacekeeping. 1971. 14.95 (ISBN 0-8157-2726-7); pap. 5.95 (ISBN 0-8157-2725-9). Brookings.

Fabian, P., tr. see Breuer, Georg.

Fabiola, Cabeza De Baca see Cabeza De Baca, Fabiola.

Fable, Edmund. The True Life of Billy the Kid. LC 80-18408. 75p. (Orig.). 1980. Repr. 19.95 (ISBN 0-932702-11-2); collector's edition 75.00. Creative Texas.

Fabos, Julius G. Planning the Total Landscape: A Guide to Intelligent Land Use. (Illus.). 1979. lib. bdg. 20.00x (ISBN 0-89158-172-3). Westview.

Fabos, Julius G., et al. Frederick Law Olmsted Sr: Founder of Landscape Architecture in America. LC 68-19670. (Illus.). 1968. 12.00x (ISBN 0-87023-035-2); pap. 6.00x (ISBN 0-87023-052-2). U of Mass Pr.

Fabozzi, Frank J. & Zarb, Frank G. The Handbook of Financial Markets: Securities, Options and Futures. 920p. 1981. 37.50 (ISBN 0-87094-216-6). Dow Jones-Irwin.

Fabre, Genevieve E., et al, eds. Afro-American Poetry & Drama, Seventeen Sixty to Nineteen Seventy-Five: A Guide to Information Sources. LC 74-11518. (American Literature, English Literature, & World Literature in English Information Guide Ser.: Vol. 17). 1979. 30.00 (ISBN 0-8103-1208-5). Gale.

Fabre, J. Henri. The Insect World of J. Henri Fabre. Teale, Edwin W., ed. (Nature Library Ser.). 352p. (Orig.). 1981. pap. 5.95 (ISBN 0-06-090806-8, CN 806, CN). Har-Row.

Fabre, Jean H. Jean Henri Fabre's Insects. Black, David, ed. (Encore Edition). (Illus.). 1979. 4.95 (ISBN 0-684-16820-0, ScribT). Scribner.

Fabre, Michel, ed. see Wright, Richard.

Fabrega, Horatio, Jr. Disease & Social Behavior: An Elementary Exposition. 1974. pap. 9.95x (ISBN 0-262-56020-8). MIT Pr.

Fabri, Charles. Discovering Indian Sculpture. (Illus.). 84p. 1970. 10.00 (ISBN 0-88253-798-9); pap. 5.00 (ISBN 0-88253-037-2). Ind-US Inc.

Fabri, Ralph. Color: A Complete Guide for Artists. (Illus.). 1967. 19.50 (ISBN 0-8230-0700-6); pap. 9.95 o.p. (ISBN 0-8230-0651-4). Watson-Guptill.

--Sculpture in Paper. rev. ed. (Illus.). 1976. pap. 6.95 o.p. (ISBN 0-8230-4699-0). Watson-Guptill.

Fabriant, Benjamin, et al. To Enjoy Is to Live: Psychotherapy Explained. LC 76-40141. 1977. 14.95 (ISBN 0-88229-148-3). Nelson-Hall.

Fabrizio, Al & Fabrizio, Mrs. Al. Why Daddy Loves to Come Home. 0.50 (ISBN 0-89985-108-8). Christ Nations.

Fabrizio, Mrs. Al, jt. auth. see Fabrizio, Al.

Fabroni, Al G. Miracle of Natural Self-Cure. 1981. 6.00 (ISBN 0-8062-1581-X). Carlton.

Fabrycky, W. J. & Thuesen, G. J. Engineering Economy. 5th ed. (Illus.). 1977. text ed. 21.95 (ISBN 0-13-277491-7). P-H.

Fabrycky, Walter J. & Thuesen, G. J. Economic Decision Analysis. 2nd ed. 1980. text ed. 22.95 (ISBN 0-13-223248-0). P-H.

Fabun, Don. Children of Change. (Illus.). 1970. pap. text ed. 2.50 (ISBN 0-02-475230-4, 47523). Macmillan.

--Communications: The Transfer of Meaning. 1968. pap. 2.95x (ISBN 0-02-477490-1, 47749). Macmillan.

--Corporation As a Creative Environment. 1972. pap. text ed. 2.50x (ISBN 0-02-475240-1, 47524). Macmillan.

--Dimensions of Change. 1971. text ed. 6.95x (ISBN 0-02-475500-1, 47550). Macmillan.

--Ecology: The Man-Made Planet. 1971. pap. text ed. 2.50x (ISBN 0-02-475350-5, 47535). Macmillan.

--Energy: Transactions in Time. 1971. pap. text ed. 1.95x (ISBN 0-685-03674-X, 47536). Macmillan.

--Food: An Energy Exchange System. 1971. pap. text ed. 2.50x (ISBN 0-02-475370-X, 47537). Macmillan.

--Mobility: From There to Here. 1971. pap. text ed. 2.50x (ISBN 0-02-475380-7, 47538). Macmillan.

--Shelter: The Cave Re-Examined. 1971. pap. text ed. 2.50x (ISBN 0-02-475390-4, 47539). Macmillan.

--Telecommunication: One World, One Mind. 1971. pap. text ed. 2.50x (ISBN 0-02-475400-5, 47540). Macmillan.

Fachinger, B., jt. auth. see Hundsalz, A.

Fackenheim, Emil L. God's Presence in History: Jewish Affirmations & Philosophical Reflections. LC 79-88135. (Deems Lectureship in Philosophy Ser). 1970. 8.00x (ISBN 0-8147-0142-6). NYU Pr.

Fackler, Herbert V. That Tragic Queen: The Deidre Legend in Anglo-Irish Literature. (Salzburg Studies in English Literature, Poetic Drama & Poetic Theory Ser.: No. 39). 1978. pap. text ed. 25.00x (ISBN 0-391-01374-2). Humanities.

Fackler, John P., Jr. Symmetry in Coordination Chemistry. 1971. text ed. 9.00 (ISBN 0-12-247540-2); pap. 7.95 (ISBN 0-12-247550-X). Acad Pr.

Fackler, John P., Jr., ed. Symmetry in Chemical Theory: The Application of Group Theoretical Techniques to the Solution of Chemical Problems. LC 73-12620. (Benchmark Papers in Inorganic Chemistry Ser.). 528p. 1974. text ed. 44.50 (ISBN 0-12-786453-9). Acad Pr.

Facts on File Digest Staff. Yearbook, 1979. 1980. lib. bdg. 65.00 (ISBN 0-87196-038-9). Facts on File.

Facts on File Staff. FOF Yearbook, 1980. 1200p. 1981. lib. bdg. 65.00 (ISBN 0-87196-039-7). Facts on File.

Faculty of Comparative Literature, Livingston College. A Syllabus of Comparative Literature. 2nd ed. McCormick, John O., ed. LC 72-8502. 1972. 10.00 (ISBN 0-8108-0555-3). Scarecrow.

Fadala, Sam. Black Powder Handgun. LC 81-65102. 288p. (Orig.). 1981. pap. 8.95 (ISBN 0-910676-22-4, 9266). DBI.

Faddeev, D. K. & Sominskii, I. S. Problems in Higher Algebra. Brenner, Joel L., tr. LC 65-18946. 1965. pap. 7.95x (ISBN 0-7167-0426-9). W H Freeman.

Faddeev, L. D. & Slavnov, A. A. Gauge Fields: Introduction to Quantumm Theory. 1981. 28.95 (ISBN 0-8053-9016-2). A-W.

Faddick, R. R., ed. see Pokrovskaya, Vera N.

Faddick, R. R., ed. see Traynis, V. V.

Fadely, Jack L. & Hosler, Virginia. Confrontation in Adolescence. LC 78-6709. (Illus.). 1979. pap. text ed. 10.50 (ISBN 0-8016-1553-4). Mosby.

Fadely, Jack L. & Hosler, Virginia N. Developmental Psychometrics: A Resource Book for Mental Health Workers & Educators. (Illus.). 168p. 1980. 13.75 (ISBN 0-398-04056-7); pap. 9.75 (ISBN 0-398-04057-5). C C Thomas.

Fader, Bruce. Industrial Noise Control. 320p. 1981. 29.95 (ISBN 0-471-06007-0, Pub. by Wiley Interscience). Wiley.

Fader, Daniel. Naked Children. 1971. 10.95 (ISBN 0-02-536900-8). Macmillan.

--The New Hooked on Books. pap. 2.50 (ISBN 0-425-04359-2). Berkley Pub.

--The New Hooked on Books. 1977. 8.95 o.p. (ISBN 0-399-11954-X). Berkley Pub.

Fader, Daniel N. & McNeil, Elton B. Hooked on Books: Program & Proof. new ed. (Orig.). 1977. pap. 1.95 o.p. (ISBN 0-425-04328-2, S1508, Medallion). Berkley Pub.

Fader, Wendy. Qualifying Procedures for Health Visitors. (General Ser.). (Orig.). 1977. pap. text ed. 13.75x (ISBN 0-85633-111-2, NFER). Humanities.

Faderman, Lillian. Surpassing the Love of Men: Love Between Women from the Renaissance to the Present. Guarnaschelli, Maria, ed. LC 80-24482. (Illus.). 488p. 1981. 15.95 (ISBN 0-688-03733-X) (ISBN 0-688-00396-6). Morrow.

--Surpassing the Love of Men: Love Between Women from the Renaissance to the Present. Guarnaschelli, Maria, ed. (Illus.). 488p. 1981. pap. 10.95 (ISBN 0-688-00396-6, Quill). Morrow.

Faderman, Lillian & Eriksson, Brigitte, eds. Lesbian-Feminism in Turn-of-the-Century Germany. LC 79-92799. 125p. (Orig.). 1980. pap. 5.95 (ISBN 0-930044-13-4). Naiad Pr.

Fadia, Babulal. Pressure Groups in Indian Politics. (Illus.). 295p. 1980. text ed. 21.50x (ISBN 0-391-01795-0). Humanities.

Fadiman, Clifton & Aaron, Sam. Wine Buyers Guide. LC 76-47678. (Illus.). 1977. 17.50 o.p. (ISBN 0-8109-1754-8); pap. 8.95 (ISBN 0-8109-2063-8). Abrams.

Fadiman, James, jt. auth. see Hendricks, C. Gaylord.

Fadiman, Regina K. Faulkner's Intruder in the Dust: Novel into Film. LC 77-8417. (Illus.). 1978. 14.50x (ISBN 0-87049-214-4). U of Tenn Pr.

Fadner, Donald E. The Responsible God: A Study of the Christian Philosophy of H. Richard Niebuhr. LC 75-29373. (American Academy of Religion. Dissertation Ser.). 1975. pap. 7.50 (ISBN 0-89130-041-4, 010113). Scholars Pr Ca.

Faegre, Torvald. Tents: Architecture of the Nomads. LC 77-25588. 1979. pap. 5.95 (ISBN 0-385-11656-X, Anch). Doubleday.

Faegri, Knut & Iversen, J. Textbook of Pollen Analysis. 3rd ed. LC 74-12235. 1975. 23.50 o.s.i. (ISBN 0-02-844470-1). Hafner.

Faessler, Shirley. Everything in the Window. 1980. 10.95 (ISBN 0-316-25986-1, Pub. by Atlantic-Little Brown). Little.

Fagan, B. M., jt. auth. see Oliver, R. A.

Fagan, Brian. Elusive Treasure. LC 77-8478. (Encore Edition). (Illus.). 1977. 7.95 o.p. (ISBN 0-684-16212-1, ScribT). Scribner.

--Passagemakers Guide from San Francisco to Ensenada. (Illus.). 120p. (Orig.). 1981. pap. 12.95 (ISBN 0-88496-161-3). Capra Pr.

--The Rape of the Nile: Tomb Robbers, Tourists, and Archaeologists in Egypt. LC 75-11857. (Illus.). 416p. 1975. 14.95 o.p. (ISBN 0-684-14235-X, ScribT). Scribner.

Fagan, Brian M. In the Beginning. 4th ed. 1981. text ed. 16.95 (ISBN 0-686-68258-0). Little.

--Iron Age Cultures in Zambia, Vol. 2: Dambwa, Ingombe Illede & the Tonga. (The Robins Ser.: No. 6). 1969. text ed. 17.00x (ISBN 0-391-01993-7). Humanities.

Fagan, Brian M. & Pomeroy, Graham. Cruising Guide to the Channel Islands. (Illus.). 276p. pap. 16.95 (ISBN 0-88496-093-5). Western Marine Ent.

Fagan, Brian M., intro. by. Avenues to Antiquity: Readings from Scientific American. LC 75-42293. (Illus.). 1976. text ed. 19.95x (ISBN 0-7167-0542-7); pap. text ed. 9.95x (ISBN 0-7167-0541-9). W H Freeman.

--Civilization: Readings from Scientific American. LC 78-15780. (Illus.). 1979. text ed. 17.95x (ISBN 0-7167-1024-2); pap. text ed. 8.95x (ISBN 0-7167-1023-4). W H Freeman.

Fagan, Joen & Shepherd, Irma L., eds. Life Techniques in Gestalt Therapy. 224p. 1973. pap. 1.50 o.p. (ISBN 0-06-080281-2, P281, PL). Har-Row.

Fagan, John J., Jr. Earth Environment. (Illus.). 288p. 1974. pap. 8.95 ref. ed. o.p. (ISBN 0-13-222752-5). P-H.

Fagan, John M. Beautiful North Carolina. Shangle, Robert D., ed. LC 79-18081. (Illus.). 72p. 1980. 14.95 (ISBN 0-89802-075-1); pap. 7.95 (ISBN 0-89802-074-3). Beautiful Am.

Fagan, Kevin. Drabble. 132p. (Orig.). 1981. pap. 3.95 (ISBN 0-449-90052-5, Columbine). Fawcett.

Fagan, Michael. Beautiful Delaware. Shangle, Robert D., ed. LC 80-21494. (Illus.). 72p. 1980. 14.95 (ISBN 0-89802-207-X); pap. 7.95 (ISBN 0-89802-208-8). Beautiful Am.

--Beautiful Vermont. LC 80-14775. (Illus.). 72p. 1980. 14.95 (ISBN 0-89802-105-7); pap. 7.95 (ISBN 0-89802-104-9). Beautiful Am.

Fage, J. D. History of West Africa. 4th ed. LC 71-85742. (Illus.). 1969. 27.50 (ISBN 0-521-07406-1); pap. 8.95x (ISBN 0-521-09579-4). Cambridge U Pr.

Fage, J. D. & Oliver, Roland A. Papers in African Prehistory. LC 74-77286. (Illus.). 1970. 32.50 (ISBN 0-521-07470-3); pap. 9.95x (ISBN 0-521-09566-2, 566). Cambridge U Pr.

Fage, J. D., jt. auth. see Oliver, Roland.

Fagen, Patricia W. Exiles & Citizens: Spanish Republicans in Mexico. LC 72-3781. (Latin American Monographs: No. 29). 272p. 1973. 12.95x (ISBN 0-292-72002-5). U of Tex Pr.

Fagen, Richard R. The Transformation of Political Culture in Cuba. LC 77-83117. (Illus.). xii, 270p. 1969. 10.00x (ISBN 0-8047-0702-2); pap. 5.95 (ISBN 0-8047-0814-2). Stanford U Pr.

Fagen, Robert M. Animal Play Behavior. (Illus.). 688p. 1981. text ed. 29.95x (ISBN 0-19-502760-4); pap. text ed. 12.95x (ISBN 0-19-502761-2). Oxford U Pr.

Fagen, Stanly, et al. Teaching Children Self-Control: Preventing Emotional & Learning Problems in the Elementary School. new ed. (Special Education Ser.). 288p. 1975. pap. text ed. 10.95 (ISBN 0-675-08783-X). Merrill.

Fagence, Michael. Citizen Participation in Planning. 1977. text ed. 26.00 (ISBN 0-08-020397-3); pap. text ed. 14.50 (ISBN 0-08-020398-1). Pergamon.

Fagerberg, Holsten. A New Look at the Lutheran Confession. Lund, Gene J., tr. 336p. 1981. 14.50 (ISBN 0-570-03223-7, 15-2121). Concordia.

Fagerhaugh, Shizuko & Strauss, Anselm. Politics of Pain Management: Staff-Patient Interaction. LC 77-75114. 1977. pap. text ed. 14.95 (ISBN 0-201-06909-1, M&N Div). A-W.

Fagg, Christine. All About Caravan Holidays. 1975. 7.95 (ISBN 0-236-30931-5, Pub. by Paul Elek). Merrimack Bk Serv.

--Raise Cash-Have Fun. 1969. 5.95 o.p. (ISBN 0-236-31121-2, Pub. by Paul Elek). Merrimack Bk Serv.

Fagg, William & Foreman, Michael. The Living Art of Nigeria. LC 72-77278. (Illus.). 160p. 1972. 12.95 o.s.i. (ISBN 0-02-536950-4). Macmillan.

Fagin, Claire M., ed. Readings in Child & Adolescent Psychiatric Nursing. LC 73-12565. 190p. 1974. pap. text ed. 8.95 o.p. (ISBN 0-8016-1536-4). Mosby.

Fagin, Larry. I'll Be Seeing You. LC 77-28219. 1978. 14.95 (ISBN 0-916190-10-2); pap. 6.00 (ISBN 0-916190-11-0). Full Court NY.

Fagnan, E. Additions Aux Dictionnaires Arabes (Arabic-French) 1969. 17.00x (ISBN 0-685-72024-1). Intl Bk Ctr.

Fago, John N. & Farr, Naunerle C. Jim Thorpe - Althea Gibson. (Pendulum Illustrated Biography Ser.). (Illus.). (gr. 4-12). 1979. text ed. 4.50 (ISBN 0-88301-372-X); pap. text ed. 1.45 (ISBN 0-88301-360-6); wkbk. 0.95 (ISBN 0-88301-384-3). Pendulum Pr.

Fago, John N., jt. auth. see Farr, Naunerle C.

Fagrell, B., ed. see Advances in Diagnosis & Therapy, Muenchen, November 1980.

Faherty, Robert, ed. see Marquis, Thomas B.

Fahey, James C. Ships & Aircraft of the U. S. Fleet: 1950, 1958, & 1965 Editions, 3 vols. LC 76-15840. (Illus.). 192p. 1980. soft bdg. slipcased 11.95 (ISBN 0-87021-647-3). Naval Inst Pr.

Fahey, James J. Pacific War Diary, 1942-1945. LC 73-21341. (Illus.). 404p. 1974. Repr. of 1963 ed. lib. bdg. 31.25x (ISBN 0-8371-6176-2, FAWD). Greenwood.

Fahey, James T. Pacific War Diary: 1942-1945. 432p. 1980. pap. 2.50 (ISBN 0-89083-673-6). Zebra.

Fahey, John. The Best of John Fahey. Lescroat, John, ed. LC 77-82830. (Illus.). 176p. 1978. pap. 7.95 (ISBN 0-8256-9515-5). Guitar Player.

--Charley Patton. (The Paul Oliver Blues Ser.). pap. 2.95 (ISBN 0-913714-29-1). Legacy Bks.

Fahey, William A. F. Scott Fitzgerald & the American Dream. LC 73-4523. (Twentieth-Century American Writers Ser). (gr. 6 up). 1973. 8.95 (ISBN 0-690-00078-2, TYC-J). T Y Crowell.

Fahey, William A., jt. auth. see Richardson, Ben.

Fahim, Hussein. Indigenous Anthropology in Non-Western Countries. 276p. 1980. lib. bdg. write for info. (ISBN 0-89089-197-4); pap. text ed. write for info (ISBN 0-89089-198-2). Carolina Acad Pr.

Fahm, L. A. The Waste of Nations: The Economic Utilization of Human Waste in Agriculture. LC 79-88260. (LandMark Studies). (Illus.). 188p. 1980. text ed. 24.50 (ISBN 0-916672-28-X). Allanheld.

Fahn, Abraham. Plant Anatomy. 2nd ed. LC 73-5808. 616p. 1974. text ed. 45.00 o.p. (ISBN 0-08-017241-5); pap. text ed. 18.00 (ISBN 0-08-017242-3). Pergamon.

Fahn, Stanley, jt. ed. see Eldridge, Roswell.

Fahn, Stanley, et al, eds. Cerebral Hypoxia & Its Consequences. LC 78-57236. (Advances in Neurology Ser.: Vol. 26). 1979. text ed. 36.50 (ISBN 0-89004-296-9). Raven.

Fahrney, Ralph R. Horace Greeley & the Tribune in the Civil War. LC 77-135663. (American Scene Ser). 1970. Repr. of 1936 ed. lib. bdg. 25.00 (ISBN 0-306-71120-6). Da Capo.

Fahs, Ned C., jt. ed. see Hamilton, D. Lee.

Fahs, Sophia L. & Cobb, Alice. Old Tales for a New Day: Early Answers to Life's Eternal Questions. LC 80-84076. (Library of Liberal Religion). (gr. 3-9). 1981. 9.95 (ISBN 0-87975-138-X); tchr's manual 7.95 (ISBN 0-87975-132-0). Prometheus Bks.

Fahy, Christopher. Home Remedies: Fixing up Houses and Apartments, Mostly Old but Also Otherwise. LC 74-32200. 1976. pap. 2.95 o.p. (ISBN 0-684-14695-9, SL663, ScribT). Scribner.

Fahy, Everett. Some Followers of Domenico Ghirlandajo. LC 75-23790. (Outstanding Dissertations in the Fine Arts - 15th Century). (Illus.). 1976. lib. bdg. 41.00 (ISBN 0-8240-1986-5). Garland Pub.

Fails Management Institute. Financial Management for Contractors. Jackson, I. J. & Kennihan, Marita, eds. (Illus.). 224p. 1981. 22.50 (ISBN 0-07-019887-X). McGraw.

Fain, B. Theory of Rate Processesin Condensed Media. (Lecture Notes in Chemistry Ser.: Vol. 20). (Illus.). 166p. 1981. 17.50 (ISBN 0-387-10249-3). Springer Verlag.

Fain, Jeff. The Burning. 1981. pap. 2.25 (ISBN 0-8439-0839-4, Leisure Bks). Nordon Pubns.

Fain, Stephen M., et al. Teaching in America. 1979. pap. text ed. 10.95x (ISBN 0-673-15056-9). Scott F.

Fain, V. M. & Khanin, Ya. Quantum Electronics-Vol. 2: Maser Amplifiers & Oscillators. 1969. 32.00 (ISBN 0-08-012238-8). Pergamon.

Fainhaus, David. Lithuanians in Multi-Ethnic Chicago Until World War II. LC 76-5693. 1977. 20.00 (ISBN 0-8294-0370-1). Loyola.

Fainsod, Merle, et al. Government & the American Economy. 3rd ed. 1959. 13.95x (ISBN 0-393-09553-3, NortonC). Norton.
Fainstein, Norman I. & Fainstein, Susan S. Urban Political Movements: The Search for Power by Minority Groups in American Cities. LC 73-21876. 352p. 1974. ref. ed. 11.95 (ISBN 0-13-939330-7); pap. 9.95 ref. ed. (ISBN 0-13-939322-6). P-H.
Fainstein, Susan S., jt. auth. see Fainstein, Norman I.
Fair, Charles M. The Dying Self. LC 77-82538. 1969. 15.00x (ISBN 0-8195-4004-8, Pub. by Wesleyan U Pr). Columbia U Pr.
--Physical Foundations of the Psyche. LC 63-8861. 1963. 20.00x (ISBN 0-8195-3037-9, Pub. by Wesleyan U Pr). Columbia U Pr.
Fair, Gordon M., et al. Elements of Water Supply & Waste Water Disposal. 2nd ed. LC 72-151032. (Illus.). 1971. 35.95 (ISBN 0-471-25115-1). Wiley.
Fair, Harold L. Class Devotions: For Use with the 1981-82 International Lessons. 1981. pap. 3.95 (ISBN 0-687-08621-3). Abingdon.
Fair, John D. British Interparty Conferences: A Study of the Procedure of Conciliation in British Politics, Eighteen Sixty-Seven to Nineteen Twenty-One. 366p. 1980. text ed. 49.00x (ISBN 0-19-822601-2). Oxford U Pr.
Fair, Marvin L. & Williams, Ernest W., Jr. Economics of Transportation & Logistics. 1975. 17.50x (ISBN 0-256-01628-3). Business Pubns.
Fair, Talitha D. The Liberation of Lily. (Orig.). 1981. pap. 4.95 (ISBN 0-89636-059-8). Accent Bks.
Fairbairn, A. N., ed. The Leicestershire Plan. (Organization in Schools Ser.). 1980. text ed. 30.95x (ISBN 0-435-80298-4). Heinemann Ed.
Fairbairn, J. W., ed. see Anthraquinone Symposium, Buergenstock-Luzern, September, 1978.
Fairbairn, Patrick. Jonah: His Life, Character, & Mission. (Summit Bks.). 248p. 1980. pap. 3.95 (ISBN 0-8010-3498-1). Baker Bk.
--The Pastoral Epistles. Date not set. 14.95 (ISBN 0-86524-053-1). Klock & Klock.
--Revelation of Law in Scripture. Date not set. 15.95 (ISBN 0-88469-135-7). BMH Bks.
Fairbairn, W. Ronald. Psychoanalytic Studies of the Personality. 1966. Repr. of 1952 ed. 23.50x (ISBN 0-7100-1361-2). Routledge & Kegan.
Fairbank, Alfred. A Book of Scripts. 2nd ed. (Illus.). 1977. 9.95 o.p. (ISBN 0-571-10876-8, Pub. by Faber & Faber); pap. 6.50 (ISBN 0-571-11080-0). Merrimack Bk Serv.
Fairbank, John K. & Liu, Kwang-Ching. Cambridge History of China, Vol. II, Pt. 2. LC 76-29852. (Cambridge History of China). (Illus.). 1980. 69.00 (ISBN 0-521-22029-7). Cambridge U Pr.
Fairbank, John K. & Reischauer, Edwin O. China: Tradition & Transformation. LC 77-77980. (Illus.). 1977. text ed. 14.25 (ISBN 0-395-25813-8). HM.
Fairbank, John K., et al. East Asia: Tradition & Transformation. 2nd ed. LC 77-77994. (Illus.). 1977. text ed. 19.95 (ISBN 0-395-25812-X). HM.
Fairbank, T. J., jt. auth. see Carter, C. O.
Fairbanks, Carol. More Women in Literature: Criticism of the Seventies. LC 78-26405. 1979. 19.00 (ISBN 0-8108-1193-6). Scarecrow.
Fairbanks, Carol & Engeldinger, Eugene A. Black American Fiction: A Bibliography. LC 78-1351. 1978. 18.00 (ISBN 0-8108-1120-0). Scarecrow.
Fairbanks, Charles H. Florida Indians III. Horr, David A., ed. (American Indian Ethnohistory Ser.). 1978. lib. bdg. 42.00 (ISBN 0-8240-0759-X). Garland Pub.
Fairbanks, G. H., et al. Spoken Sinhalese. (Spoken Languages Ser.). (Prog. Bk.). 1979. Bk. 1, Lessons 1-24. pap. 10.00x (ISBN 0-87950-440-4); Bk. 2, Lessons 25-36. pap. 9.00x (ISBN 0-87950-442-0); cassettes 1 for bk. 1 (21 dual track) 100.00 (ISBN 0-87950-441-2); cassettes 11 for bk. 2 (13 dual track) 65.00x (ISBN 0-87950-443-9). Spoken Lang Serv.
Fairbanks, Gordon H., et al. Russian Readings in Popular Science. LC 63-8805. (gr. 9 up). 1963. 15.00x (ISBN 0-231-02566-1). Columbia U Pr.
Fairbanks, Henry G. Louise Imogen Guiney. (U. S. Authors Ser.: No. 224). 1973. lib. bdg. 10.95 (ISBN 0-8057-0342-X). Twayne.
Fairbanks, Jesse R. Observable Materials Testing Text & Workbook. 1978. pap. text ed. 7.50x (ISBN 0-8191-0386-1). U Pr of Amer.
Fairbanks, Virgil. Hemoglobinopathies & Thalassemias. 1980. 32.50. Thieme Stratton.
Fairbridge, R., ed. Encyclopedia of Atmospheric Sciences & Astrogeology. (Encyclopedia of Earth Sciences Ser: Vol. II). 1967. 58.00 (ISBN 0-12-786458-X). Acad Pr.
--Encyclopedia of Geomorphology. LC 68-58342. (Encyclopedia of Earth Sciences Ser: Vol. III). 1968. 78.00x (ISBN 0-12-786459-8). Acad Pr.
Fairbridge, R, ed. Encyclopedia of Oceanography. LC 66-26059. (Encyclopedia of Earth Sciences Ser: Vol. I). 1966. 90.00 (ISBN 0-12-786457-1). Acad Pr.
Fairbridge, Rhodes W., jt. auth. see Michel, Jean-Pierre.
Fairbrook, Paul. College & University Food Sevice Manual. LC 79-50956. (Illus.). 1979. pap. 17.50 (ISBN 0-9602456-0-X). Colman Pubs.
Fairchild, Arthur H. Shakespeare & the Tragic Theme. 145p. 1980. Repr. of 1944 ed. lib. bdg. 25.00 (ISBN 0-89987-258-1). Darby Bks.
Fairchild, B. H., Jr. Such Holy Song: Music As Idea, Form, & Image in the Poetry of William Blake. LC 79-92809. 1980. 11.00x (ISBN 0-87338-238-2). Kent St U Pr.
Fairchild, Daniel, et al. Everything You Always Wanted to Know About Drinking Problems & Then a Few Things You Didn't Want to Know. 7.50 (ISBN 0-932194-04-4). Green Hill.
Fairchild, David. Prolegomena to a Methodology: Reflections on Merleau-Ponty & Austin. LC 78-58597. 1978. pap. text ed. 7.25 o.p. (ISBN 0-8191-0542-2). U Pr of Amer.
Fairchild, Edward J., ed. Suspected Carcinogens. 1978. pap. 45.00x o.p. (ISBN 0-7194-0000-7). Intl Ideas.
Fairchild, Hoxie N. Religious Trends in English Poetry, 6 vols. Incl. Vol. 1. Protestantism & the Cult of Sentiment: 1700-1740 (ISBN 0-231-08821-3); Vol. 2. Religious Sentimentalism in the Age of Johnson: 1740-1780. 1942 (ISBN 0-231-08822-1); Vol. 3. Romantic Faith: 1780-1830. 1949 (ISBN 0-231-08823-X); Vol. 4. Christianity & Romanticism in the Victorian Era: 1830-1880. 1957 (ISBN 0-231-08824-8); Vol. 5. Gods of a Changing Poetry: 1880-1920. 1962 (ISBN 0-231-08825-6); Vol. 6. Valley of Dry Bones: 1920-1965. 1968 (ISBN 0-231-08826-4). LC 39-12839. 25.00x ea. Columbia U Pr.
Fairchild Market Research Div. Soft Surface Floor Coverings. (Fact Files Ser.). (Illus.). 75p. 1980. pap. 10.00 (ISBN 0-87005-354-X). Fairchild.
Fairchild Market Research Division. Consumer Market Developments. (Fact File Ser.). (Illus.). 100p. 1980. pap. 10.00 (ISBN 0-87005-350-7). Fairchild.
--Consumer Market Developments. (Fact File Ser). (Orig.). 1978. pap. 9.50 o.p. (ISBN 0-87005-250-0). Fairchild.
--Department Store Sales. (Fairchild Fact File Ser.). 1979. pap. 10.00 (ISBN 0-87005-327-2). Fairchild.
--Department Store Sales, Pt. 1. (Fact File Ser). 1978. pap. 10.00 (ISBN 0-87005-220-9). Fairchild.
--Department Store Sales, Pt. 2. (Fact File Ser). 1978. pap. 10.00 (ISBN 0-87005-254-3). Fairchild.
--Department Store Sales, 1980. (Fairchild Fact Files Ser.). (Illus.). 80p. 1980. pap. 10.00 (ISBN 0-87005-355-8). Fairchild.
--Fashion Accessories. (Fact File Ser). (Orig.). 1979. pap. 10.00 (ISBN 0-87005-319-1). Fairchild.
--Floor Coverings. (Fact File Ser). 1978. pap. 10.00 (ISBN 0-87005-255-1). Fairchild.
--Home Electronics. (Fairchild Fact File Ser.). 1979. pap. 10.00 (ISBN 0-87005-320-5). Fairchild.
--Home Textiles. (Fairchild Fact Files Ser.). 90p. 1980. pap. 10.00 (ISBN 0-87005-353-1). Fairchild.
--Household Furniture & Bedding. (Fact File Ser.). (Illus.). 60p. 1980. pap. 10.00 (ISBN 0-87005-346-9). Fairchild.
--Household Furniture & Bedding. (Fact Files Ser). 1978. pap. 10.00 (ISBN 0-87005-222-5). Fairchild.
--Infants', Girls', & Boys' Wear. (Fairchild Fact File Ser.). 1979. pap. 10.00 (ISBN 0-87005-326-4). Fairchild.
--Major Appliances & Electric Housewares. (Fairchild Fact File Ser.). 1979. pap. 10.00 (ISBN 0-87005-324-8). Fairchild.
--Men's & Women's Hosiery & Legwear. (Fact File Ser). 1978. pap. 10.00 (ISBN 0-87005-223-3). Fairchild.
--Men's Clothing, Tailored Sportswear, Rainwear. (Fairchild Fact File Ser.). 1979. pap. 10.00 (ISBN 0-87005-325-6). Fairchild.
--Men's Furnishings, Career - Work Wear. (Fairchilds Fact File Ser.). 1979. pap. 10.00 (ISBN 0-87005-318-3). Fairchild.
--Men's Sportswear & Casual Wear. (Fact File Ser). 1978. pap. 10.00 (ISBN 0-87005-251-9). Fairchild.
--Men's Sportswear, Casual Wear, Jeans & Active Wear. (Fact File Ser.). (Illus.). 100p. 1980. pap. 10.00 (ISBN 0-87005-351-5). Fairchild.
--Men's, Women's & Children's Bodywear, Legwear-Hosiery. (Fact File Ser.). (Illus.). 100p. 1980. pap. 10.00 (ISBN 0-87005-348-5). Fairchild.
--Men's, Women's & Children's Footwear. (Fairchild Fact File Ser.). 1979. pap. 10.00 (ISBN 0-87005-322-1). Fairchild.
--Men's, Women's & Children's Footwear, 1980. (Fact File Ser.). (Illus.). 100p. 1980. pap. 10.00 (ISBN 0-87005-349-3). Fairchild.
--Textile - Apparel Industries. (Fairchild Fact File Ser.). 1979. pap. 9.50 (ISBN 0-87005-321-3). Fairchild.
--Toiletries, Beauty Aids & Cosmetics. (Fact File Ser). 35p. 1978. pap. 10.00 (ISBN 0-87005-221-7). Fairchild.
--Toiletries, Beauty Aids, Cosmetics, Fragrances. (Fact File Ser.). (Illus.). 100p. 1980. pap. 10.00 (ISBN 0-87005-347-7). Fairchild.
--Women's Coats, Suits, Rainwear, Furs. (Fairchild Fact File Ser.). 1980. pap. 10.00 (ISBN 0-87005-328-0). Fairchild.
--Women's Dresses. (Fact File Ser). 1978. pap. 10.00 (ISBN 0-87005-256-X). Fairchild.
--Women's Dresses. (Fairchild Fact Files). (Illus.). 50p. 1981. pap. 10.00 (ISBN 0-87005-356-6). Fairchild.
--Women's Inner Fashions: Nightwear & Daywear. (Fairchild Fact File Ser.). 1979. pap. 10.00 (ISBN 0-87005-323-X). Fairchild.
--Women's Sportswear, Seperates, Jeans & Active Wear. (Fact File Ser.). (Illus.). 100p. 1980. pap. 10.00 (ISBN 0-87005-352-3). Fairchild.
--Women's Sportwear & Casual Wear. (Fact File Ser). 1978. pap. 10.00 (ISBN 0-87005-252-7). Fairchild.
Fairchild, Thomas N. Accountability for School Psychologists: Selected Readings. 1978. pap. text ed. 9.75 (ISBN 0-8191-0371-3). U Pr of Amer.
Fairchild, W. W., et al. Eocene & Oligocene Foraminifera from the Santa Cruz Mountains, California. (U. C. Publ. in Geological Sciences: Vol. 81). 1969. pap. 7.50x (ISBN 0-520-09184-1). U of Cal Pr.
Fairchild, William. Astrology for Dogs (& Owners) (Illus.). 95p. 1981. 8.95 (ISBN 0-241-10380-0, Pub. by Hamish Hamilton England). David & Charles.
Faircloth, Marjorie A., jt. auth. see Faircloth, Samuel R.
Faircloth, Samuel R. & Faircloth, Marjorie A. Phonetic Science: A Program of Instruction. (Illus.). 144p. 1973. pap. text ed. 11.95 (ISBN 0-13-664565-8). P-H.
Fairclough, G. Thomas, ed. see Fitzpatrick, Lilian L.
Faire, Ulf De see De Faire, Ulf & Theorell, Tores.
Faire, Zabrina. Athena's Airs. (Orig.). 1980. pap. 1.75 (ISBN 0-446-94463-7). Warner Bks.
--Bold Pursuit. 192p. (Orig.). 1980. pap. 1.75 (ISBN 0-446-94464-5). Warner Bks.
--Enchanting Jenny. (Orig.). 1979. pap. 1.75 (ISBN 0-446-94103-4). Warner Bks.
--Pretty Kitty. 192p. (Orig.). 1981. pap. 1.75 (ISBN 0-446-94465-3). Warner Bks.
--Wicked Cousin. (Orig.). 1980. pap. 1.75 (ISBN 0-446-94104-2). Warner Bks.
Faires, R. A. & Boswell, G. G. Radioisotope Lab Techniques. 4th ed. LC 80-41045. 272p. 1980. text ed. 39.95 (ISBN 0-408-70940-5). Butterworths.
Faires, V. & Richardson, J. E.I.T Review. 1961. 19.95 (ISBN 0-13-279604-X). P-H.
Fairfax, Ann. Annabelle. 176p. (Orig.). 1980. pap. 1.75 (ISBN 0-515-05399-6). Jove Pubns.
--Henrietta. (Orig.). 1979. pap. 1.75 (ISBN 0-515-05128-4). Jove Pubns.
Fairfax, Geoffrey W. Architecture of Honolulu. (Illus.). 1972. 6.95 (ISBN 0-89610-037-5); pap. 4.95 o.p. (ISBN 0-89610-036-7). Island Her.
Fairfax, Sally K., jt. auth. see Dana, Samuel T.
Fairfax-Blakeborough, Noel, ed. Jack Fairfax-Blakeborough: Memoirs. 1978. 17.35 (ISBN 0-85131-269-1, Dist. by Sporting Book Center). J A Allen.
Fairfield, Pierce A. Michelangelo's Life & His Magnetic Art. (Illus.). 1979. deluxe ed. 39.75 (ISBN 0-930582-43-8). Gloucester Art.
Fairfield, Roy P., ed. The Federalist Papers. 2nd ed. LC 80-8862. 368p. 1981. pap. text ed. 5.95x (ISBN 0-8018-2607-1). Johns Hopkins.
--Federalist Papers: Essays by Hamilton, Madison & Jay. 2nd ed. LC 66-24210. pap. 2.95 o.p. (ISBN 0-385-07146-9, A239, Anch). Doubleday.
Fairfield, Sheila, jt. auth. see Paxton, John.
Fairhall, David & Jordan, Philip. The Wreck of the Amoco Cadiz. LC 80-17512. (Illus.). 256p. 1980. 12.95 (ISBN 0-8128-2743-0). Stein & Day.
Fairholt, Frederick W. Costume in England. 4th ed. LC 68-21769. 1968. Repr. of 1885 ed. 24.00 (ISBN 0-8103-3506-9). Gale.
--Tobacco: Its History & Associations. LC 68-21770. 1968. Repr. of 1859 ed. 15.00 (ISBN 0-8103-3507-7). Gale.
Fairholt, Frederick W., ed. Dictionary of Terms in Art. LC 68-30630. (Illus.). 1969. Repr. of 1854 ed. 20.00 (ISBN 0-8103-3071-7). Gale.
Fairley, Barker. Goethe As Revealed in His Poetry. 2nd ed. LC 63-21991. 9.50 (ISBN 0-8044-2186-2). Ungar.
Fairley, M. C. Safety, Health & Welfare in the Printing Industry. 1969. pap. 5.75 (ISBN 0-08-013033-X). Pergamon.
Fairley, Michael. With Friends Like That. 1981. 12.95 (ISBN 0-87949-194-9). Ashley Bks.
Fairley, Peter. The A-Z of Space. (Illus.). 58p. (gr. 7-12). 1975. 6.95 (ISBN 0-298-12044-5). Transatlantic.
Fairley, R. E., jt. auth. see Riddle, W. E.
Fairley, William B. & Mosteller, Frederick. Statistics & Public Policy. LC 76-10415. (Behavioral Science-Quantitative Methods Ser.). 1977. text ed. 20.95 (ISBN 0-201-02185-4). A-W.
Fairlie, Alison. Imagination & Language. LC 80-40307. (Illus.). 400p. Date not set. 72.00 (ISBN 0-521-23291-0). Cambridge U Pr.
Fairlie, Henry. The Seven Deadly Sins Today. LC 78-3646. (Illus.). 1978. 10.00 o.p. (ISBN 0-915220-41-5). New Republic.
Fairman, Charles & Morrison, Stanley. Fourteenth Amendment & the Bill of Rights: The Incorporation Theory. LC 71-25622. (American Constitutional & Legal History Ser). 1970. Repr. of 1949 ed. lib. bdg. 29.50 (ISBN 0-306-70029-8). Da Capo.
Fairman, H. W., ed. & tr. The Triumph of Horus: An Ancient Egyptian Sacred Drama. 1974. 16.50x (ISBN 0-520-02550-4). U of Cal Pr.
Fairmont Park Associates. Philadelphia Treasures in Bronze & Stone. LC 75-36536. (Illus.). 192p. 1976. pap. 4.95 o.s.i. (ISBN 0-8027-7100-9). Walker & Co.
Fairmount Park Art Association. Sculpture of a City: Philadelphia's Treasures in Bronze & Stone. LC 74-79214. (Illus.). 1974. 25.00 o.s.i. (ISBN 0-8027-0459-X). Walker & Co.
Fairs, Nabih A., tr. see Al-Hamdani & Al-Hasan Ibn Ahmad.
Fairweather, George W. & Davidson, William S. Experimental Community Psychology: A Psychology for the 21th Century. Date not set. write for info. (ISBN 0-88410-363-3). Ballinger Pub. Postponed.
Fairweather, George W., et al. Creating Change in Mental Health Organizations. 200p. 1974. text ed. 19.75 (ISBN 0-08-017833-2); pap. text ed. 10.75 (ISBN 0-08-017832-4). Pergamon.
Fairweather, Nancy. Shadows on the Moon. 1978. pap. 1.50 (ISBN 0-505-51234-3). Tower Bks.
Fairweather, W. From Exile to Advent. 5th ed. (Handbooks for Bible Classes Ser.). 210p. pap. text ed. 3.50 (ISBN 0-567-28128-0). Attic Pr.
Fairweather, W. L. Investment. (Teach Yourself Ser.). 1973. pap. 2.95 o.p. (ISBN 0-679-10473-9). McKay.
Fairweather, William. Among the Mystics: The Development of Mysticism from Its Rise in the East. 161p. Repr. of 1936 ed. 3.50 (ISBN 0-567-02104-1). Attic Pr.
--Background of the Epistles. 1977. 14.50 (ISBN 0-686-12966-0). Klock & Klock.
--Background of the Gospels. 1977. 15.00 (ISBN 0-686-12965-2). Klock & Klock.
Faison, Edmund W. Advertising: A Behavioral Approach for Managers. LC 79-21379. (Wiley Series in Marketing). 1980. text ed. 21.95 (ISBN 0-471-04956-5); tchrs.' manual avail. (ISBN 0-471-07768-2). Wiley.
Faison, S. Lane, Jr. Art Museums of New England. 548p. 1981. 20.00 (ISBN 0-87923-372-9); pap. 10.00 (ISBN 0-87923-373-7). Godine.
Faiss, Fritz. Concerning the Way of Color. 12.50. Green Hut.
Faiss, Fritz W. Concerning the Way of Color: An Artist's Approach. 2nd ed. LC 76-23022. (Illus.). 120p. 1977. Wkbk. Incl. pap. text ed. 15.00 (ISBN 0-916678-02-4). Green Hut.
--Hackney Jade & the War Horse. LC 76-15322. (Illus.). 60p. 1977. ltd. ed. signed 18.50x (ISBN 0-916678-00-8); hand-colored 125.00x (ISBN 0-916678-01-6). Green Hut.
--Modern Art & Man's Search for the Self. (Illus.). 30p. 1974. pap. 6.00 ltd. ed. signed (ISBN 0-916678-12-1); pap. 48.00x hand-colored, signed ltd. ed. (ISBN 0-916678-13-X). Green Hut.
--Out of Loneliness. (Illus.). 81p. 1972. pap. 8.00x ltd ed, signed (ISBN 0-916678-05-9); pap. 4.00 ltd ed (ISBN 0-916678-06-7). Green Hut.
Faiss, Fritz W., ed. Lenticle: Two Radio Interviews with Fritz Faiss. (Illus.). 63p. 1972. deluxe ed. 50.00x ltd ed., signed (ISBN 0-916678-07-5); pap. 8.00x ltd ed., signed (ISBN 0-916678-08-3); pap. 5.00 single interview, ltd. ed., signed (ISBN 0-916678-09-1). Green Hut.
Fait, Hollis F., jt. auth. see Shivers, Jay S.
Faith, Barbara. Matadora. (Orig.). 1981. pap. write for info. (ISBN 0-671-41784-3). PB.
Faith, C. Algebra I: Rings, Modules & Categories. (Grundlehren der Mathematischen Wissenschaften Ser.: Vol. 190). 610p. 1981. 48.00 (ISBN 0-387-05551-7). Springer-Verlag.

--Algebra Two, Ring Theory. LC 72-96724. (Grundlehren der Mathematischen Wissenschaften: Vol. 191). 1976. 49.80 o.p. (ISBN 0-387-05705-6). Springer-Verlag.

Faith, Nicholas. The Winemasters: The Story Behind the Glory & the Scandal of Bordeaux. LC 77-11812. (Illus.). 1978. 12.95 o.p. (ISBN 0-06-011264-6, HarpT). Har-Row.

Faithful, Denise, jt. auth. see Knapp, Elsie M.

Faithorn, Peri E., jt. auth. see Bellak, Leopold.

Faivre, Milton I. How to Raise Rabbits for Fun & Profit. LC 73-81277. 1973. 14.95 (ISBN 0-911012-47-8); pap. 8.95 (ISBN 0-88229-493-8). Nelson-Hall.

Faizi, A. Q. The Prince of Martyrs: A Brief Account of Imam Husayn. 1977. pap. 2.25 (ISBN 0-85398-073-X, 7-39-03, Pub. by G Ronald England). Baha'i.

--Stories from the Delight of Hearts: The Memoirs of Haji Mirza Haydar-'Ali. LC 79-91219. (Illus.). 176p. 1980. 8.95 (ISBN 0-933770-11-1). Kalimat.

Faizi, Gloria. Fire on the Mountain Top. 1973. pap. 1.25 (ISBN 0-685-55705-7, 7-31-68). Baha'i.

Fajana, A. & Biggs, J. Nigeria in History. (Illus., Orig.). 1967. pap. text ed. 2.50x (ISBN 0-582-60242-4). Humanities.

Fakkema, Robert, jt. auth. see Bannerman, Glenn.

Fakoury, Hana. Arabic Dialogue, 4 vols. pap. text ed. 25.00 (ISBN 0-686-63574-4). Intl Bk Ctr.

Falace, jt. auth. see Little, James W.

Falaise, Maxime De La see De La Falaise, Maxime.

Falassi, Allesandro, jt. auth. see Dundes, Alan.

Falb, P. L. & De Jong, J. L. Some Successive Approximation Methods in Control & Oscillation Theory. (Mathematics in Science & Engineering Ser.: Vol. 59). 1969. 36.50 (ISBN 0-12-247950-5). Acad Pr.

Falbe, J. Carbon Monoxide in Organic Synthesis. Adams, C. R., tr. LC 77-108917. (Illus.). 1970. 37.10 (ISBN 0-387-04814-6). Springer-Verlag.

Falbe, Jurgen. Chemical Feedstocks from Coal. 730p. 1981. 50.00 (ISBN 0-471-05291-4, Pub. by Wiley-Interscience). Wiley.

Falcaro, Joe & Goodman, M. Bowling for All. 3rd ed. (Illus.). 1966. 11.50 (ISBN 0-8260-2975-2). Wiley.

Falcione, Raymond L. & Greenbaum, Howard H. Organizational Communication: Abstracts, Analysis, & Overview, Vol. 5. (Illus.). 288p. 1980. 30.00x (ISBN 0-8039-1384-2); pap. 15.00 (ISBN 0-8039-1385-0). Sage.

--Organizational Communication Nineteen Seventy-Six: Abstracts, Analysis, & Overview. 1977. pap. 8.00 o.p. (ISBN 0-931874-03-3). Am Busn Comm Assn.

Falcione, Raymond L., jt. auth. see Greenbaum, Howard H.

Falck, Frank J. Stuttering: Learned & Unlearned. (Illus.). 172p. 1969. 16.75 (ISBN 0-398-00541-9). C C Thomas.

Falco, Giorgio. The Holy Roman Republic: A Historic Profile of the Middle Ages. Kent, K. V., tr. from Italian. LC 80-19696. Orig. Title: La Santa Romana Republica. 336p. 1980. Repr. of 1965 ed. lib. bdg. 35.00x (ISBN 0-313-22395-5, FAHR). Greenwood.

Falco, Maria J. Truth & Meaning in Political Science: An Introduction to Political Inquiry. LC 73-75328. 1973. pap. text ed. 7.50 (ISBN 0-675-08934-4). Merrill.

Falco, Maria J., ed. Through the Looking Glass: Epistemology & the Conduct of Inquiry, an Anthology. LC 79-66471. 1979. pap. text ed. 14.00 (ISBN 0-8191-0841-3). U Pr of Amer.

Falcoff, Mark & Dolkart, Ronald, eds. Prologue to Peron: Argentina in Depression & War, 1930-1943. LC 74-22961. 250p. 1976. 17.50x (ISBN 0-520-02874-0). U of Cal Pr.

Falcon, Guillermo N., jt. auth. see Bonner, Thomas, Jr.

Falcon, William, jt. auth. see Cannavale, Frank J., Jr.

Falcone, Joseph D. How to Design, Build, Remodel & Maintain Your Home. 1980. pap. write for info. (Fireside). S&S.

--How to Design, Build, Remodel & Maintain Your Home. LC 76-42014. 1978. text ed. 24.95 (ISBN 0-471-05042-3). Wiley.

Falconer, D. S. Introduction to Qualitative Genetics. 2nd ed. (Illus.). 1981. pap. text ed. 25.00x (ISBN 0-582-44195-1). Longman.

Falconer, Keith. Guide to England's Industrial Heritage. LC 80-8027. (Illus.). 270p. 1980. text ed. 29.50x (ISBN 0-8419-0646-7). Holmes & Meier.

Falconer, Lee. Gazeteer of the Hyborian World of Conan. LC 80-19671. 160p. 1980. Repr. of 1977 ed. lib. bdg. 10.95x (ISBN 0-89370-031-2). Borgo Pr.

Falconer, Mary W. Patient Studies in Pharmacology: A Guidebook. LC 75-44608. 160p. 1976. pap. text ed. 7.00 (ISBN 0-7216-3545-8). Saunders.

Falconer, Peter & Drury, Jolyon. Building & Planning for Industrial Storage & Distribution. LC 75-28387. 1975. 44.95 (ISBN 0-470-25355-X). Halsted Pr.

Falconer, R. H. The Kilt Beneath My Cassock. 1978. pap. 15.00x (ISBN 0-905312-02-3, Pub. by Scottish Academic Pr Scotland). Columbia U Pr.

Falconi, Gonazalo, jt. auth. see Daines, David R.

Falen, James E. Isaac Babel, Russian Master of the Short Story. LC 74-7169. 1974. 14.50x (ISBN 0-87049-156-3). U of Tenn Pr.

Fales, James, et al. Manufacturing: A Basic Text for Industrial Arts. (Illus.). 1980. 15.96 (ISBN 0-87345-586-X, B82088); instr's guide 5.28 (ISBN 0-87345-587-8). McKnight.

Fales, John T. Functional Housekeeping in Hotels & Motels. LC 72-142508. 1971. text ed. 14.50 (ISBN 0-672-96080-X); tchr's manual 5.00 (ISBN 0-672-96082-6); wkbk. 6.50 (ISBN 0-672-96081-8). Bobbs.

Fales, Martha G. Joseph Richardson & Family: Philadelphia Silversmiths. LC 74-5911. (Illus.). 372p. 1974. 20.00 (ISBN 0-8195-4076-5, Pub. by Wesleyan U Pr). Columbia U Pr.

Faletto, Enzo, jt. auth. see Cardoso, Fernando E.

Falger, P., jt. ed. see Appels, A.

Falk, Doris V. Lillian Hellman. LC 78-4299. (Modern Literature Ser.). 1978. 10.95 (ISBN 0-8044-2194-3); pap. 3.45 (ISBN 0-8044-6144-9). Ungar.

Falk, Eugene H. The Poetics of Roman Ingarden. LC 79-29655. 272p. 1980. 20.00x (ISBN 0-8078-1436-9); pap. 11.00x (ISBN 0-8078-4068-8). U of NC Pr.

Falk, Gerhard, et al. Aging in America & Other Cultures. LC 80-83627. 135p. 1981. perfect bdg. 11.50 (ISBN 0-86548-034-6). Century Twenty One.

Falk, H. S. & Torp, Alf. Norwegisch Daenisches Etymologisches Woerterbuch: Mit Literatur-Nachweisen Strittiger Etymologien Sowie Deutschem und Altnordischen Woerterverzeichnis. 2nd ed. 1722p. 1960. 80.00x (ISBN 8-200-00085-0, Dist. by Columbia U Pr). Universitet.

Falk, Isidore Sydney. Security Against Sickness. LC 79-38822. (FDR & the Era of the New Deal Ser). 424p. 1972. Repr. of 1936 ed. lib. bdg. 37.50 (ISBN 0-306-70447-1). Da Capo.

Falk, John R. Practical Hunter's Dog Book. (Illus.). 1971. 10.95 (ISBN 0-87691-037-1). Winchester Pr.

Falk, Julia S. Language & Linguistics: Bases for a Curriculum. (Language in Education Ser.: No. 10). 1978. pap. text ed. 2.95 (ISBN 0-87281-088-7). Ctr Appl Ling.

--Linguistics & Language: A Survey of Basic Concepts & Implications. 2nd ed. LC 77-22927. 1978. pap. text ed. 13.95x (ISBN 0-471-02529-1). Wiley.

Falk, Mervyn L., jt. auth. see Wicka, Donna K.

Falk, Mervyn L., ed. Cleft Palate Team Addresses the Speech Clinician. 248p. 1971. 22.50 (ISBN 0-398-00542-7). C C Thomas.

Falk, Nicholas & Lee, James. Planning the Social Services. 1978. 17.95 (ISBN 0-347-01135-7, 00559-2, Pub. by Saxon Hse England). Lexington Bks.

Falk, Richard A. Future Worlds. LC 75-43478. (Headline Ser.: 229). (Illus.). 1976. pap. 2.00 (ISBN 0-87124-034-3). Foreign Policy.

--Human Rights & State Sovereignty. 180p. 1981. text ed. 24.00x (ISBN 0-8419-0619-X); pap. text ed. 9.75x (ISBN 0-8419-0620-3). Holmes & Meier.

--A Study of Future Worlds. LC 74-10139. (Preferred Worlds for the 1990's Ser.). (Illus.). 1975. pap. text ed. 10.95 (ISBN 0-02-910080-1). Free Pr.

Falk, Richard A. & Kim, Samuel S., eds. The War System: An Interdisciplinary Approach. LC 79-19566. (Westview Special Studies in Peace, Conflict, & Conflict Resolution). 500p. 1980. lib. bdg. 35.00x (ISBN 0-89158-569-9); pap. text ed. 15.00x (ISBN 0-86531-042-4). Westview.

Falk, Richard A., jt. ed. see Black, C. E.

Falk, Robert, ed. Literature & Ideas in America: Essays in Memory of Harry Hayden Clark. LC 74-27708. xi, 243p. 1975. 13.95x (ISBN 0-8214-0180-7). Ohio U Pr.

Falk, S. Uno & Salkind, A. J. Alkaline Storage Batteries. LC 77-82980. (Electrochemical Society Ser.). 1969. 60.00 (ISBN 0-471-25362-6, Pub. by Wiley-Interscience). Wiley.

Falk, Signi L. Tennessee Williams. 2nd ed. (United States Authors Ser.). 1978. lib. bdg. 10.95 (ISBN 0-8057-7202-2). Twayne.

Falkenberg, Aslaug, jt. auth. see Falkenberg, Johannes.

Falkenberg, Johannes & Falkenberg, Aslaug. The Affinal Relationship System of the Australian Aborigines in the Port Keats District. 224p. 1981. pap. 23.00x. Universitet.

Falkenheim, Jacqueline V. Roger Fry & the Beginnings of Formalist Art Criticism. Kuspit, Donald B., ed. (Studies in Fine Arts: Criticism). 186p. 1980. 23.95 (ISBN 0-8357-1086-6, Pub. by UMI Res Pr). Univ Microfilms.

Falkenmark, Malin & Lindh, Gunnar. Water for a Starving World. LC 76-45475. 1977. 19.75 o.p. (ISBN 0-89158-211-8); pap. text ed. 6.95x o.p. (ISBN 0-89158-212-6). Westview.

Falkin, Gregory R. Reducing Delinquency. (Illus.). 240p. 1979. 21.95 (ISBN 0-669-02318-3). Lexington Bks.

Falkmer, S., et al. Structure & Metabolism of the Pancreatic Islets - a Centennial of Paul Langerhan's Discovery. 1970. 105.00 (ISBN 0-08-015844-7). Pergamon.

Falkner, F., et al, eds. see Delange, F.

Falkner, Frank & Macy, Christopher. Pregnancy & Birth: Pleasure & Problems. (Life Cycle Ser.). 1980. pap. text ed. write for info. (ISBN 0-06-384741-8, HarpC). Har-Row.

Falkowski, Lawrence. Presidents, Secretaries of State & Crisis Management in U.S. Foreign Relations: A Model & Predictive Analysis. LC 77-27049. (Westview Special Studies in International Relations & U.S. Foreign Policy Ser.). (Illus.). 1978. lib. bdg. 22.50x (ISBN 0-89158-072-7); pap. text ed. 9.50x (ISBN 0-89158-073-5). Westview.

Falkowski, Lawrence S., ed. Psychological Models in International Politics. (Special Studies in International Relations). 1979. lib. bdg. 26.50x (ISBN 0-89158-377-7); pap. text ed. 12.50x (ISBN 0-86531-043-2). Westview.

Falkowski, Paul G., ed. Primary Productivity in the Sea: Environmental Science Research Ser. (Vol. 19). 335p. 1980. 49.50 (ISBN 0-306-40623-3). Plenum Pub.

Falkson, Joseph L. HMOs & the Politics of Health System Reform. LC 79-21932. 224p. (Orig.). 1980. casebound 12.75 (ISBN 0-87258-288-4, 1183); pap. 9.75 (ISBN 0-87258-276-0, 1182). Am Hospital.

Falkus, Hugh. Wildtrack, Reminiscences of a Nature Detective. LC 78-16537. 1979. 14.95 o.p. (ISBN 0-03-046506-0). HR&W.

Fall, Thomas. Jim Thorpe. LC 72-94793. (Crocodile Paperback Ser.). (Illus.). (gr. 2-5). 1970. pap. 2.95 (ISBN 0-690-46219-0, TYC-J). T Y Crowell.

Falla, Molly. A Sketchbook of New Zealand Birds. (Illus.). 1966. 6.75 o.p. (ISBN 0-589-00327-5, Dist. by C E Tuttle). Reed.

Falla, P. S., tr. see Mommsen, Wolfgang J.

Fallaci, Oriana. A Man: A Novel. 1980. 15.95 (ISBN 0-671-25241-0). S&S.

Fallen, Nancy & McGovern, Jill. Young Children with Special Needs. (Special Education Ser.). 1978. text ed. 13.95 (ISBN 0-675-08382-6). study guide 3.95 (ISBN 0-675-08383-4). Merrill.

Fallenbuchl, Zbigniew M. & McMillan, Charles H., eds. Partners in East-West Economic Relations: The Determinants of Choice. (Pergamon Policy Studies). (Illus.). 1980. 47.50 (ISBN 0-08-022497-0). Pergamon.

Fallers, Margaret C. Eastern Lacustrine Bantu. LC 70-407857. 1968. 8.50x (ISBN 0-8002-0567-7). Intl Pubns Serv.

Fallick, J. L. & Elliot, R. F., eds. Incomes Policies, Inflation & Relative Pay. (Illus.). 304p. 1981. text ed. 29.95x (ISBN 0-04-331077-X, 2578); pap. text ed. 12.95x (ISBN 0-04-331078-8, 2579). Allen Unwin.

Fallis, George. Housing Programs & Income Distribution in Canada. (Ontario Economic Council Research Studies). 184p. 1980. pap. 8.50x. U of Toronto Pr.

Fallis, W. J. Points for Emphasis, Nineteen Eighty to Eighty-One. LC 35-3640. 1980. kivar 1.75 (ISBN 0-8054-1453-3). Broadman.

Fallis, William J. Points for Emphasis, Nineteen Eighty-One to Eighty Two. 1981. pap. 1.95 (ISBN 0-8054-1467-3). Broadman.

--Points for Emphasis, Nineteen Eighty-One T0 Eighty-Two. larger type ed. 1981. pap. 2.75 (ISBN 0-8054-1466-5). Broadman.

--Points for Emphasis, Nineteen Eighty to Eighty-One. large type ed. LC 35-3640. 1980. pap. 2.50 (ISBN 0-8054-1454-1). Broadman.

--Studies in Acts. pap. 2.25 o.p. (ISBN 0-8054-1346-4). Broadman.

Fallon, Ann C. Katharine Tynan. (English Authors Ser.: No. 272). 1979. 13.50 (ISBN 0-8057-6754-1). Twayne.

Fallon, Berlie J. The Art of Followership (What Happened to the Indians?) LC 73-90397. (Fastback Ser.: No. 33). (Illus., Orig.). 1974. pap. 0.75 (ISBN 0-87367-033-7). Phi Delta Kappa.

Fallon, Berlie J., compiled by. Forty Innovative Programs in Early Childhood Education. LC 72-95010. (Orig.). 1973. pap. 6.75 (ISBN 0-8224-3075-4). Pitman Learning.

Fallon, Carlos. Value Analysis, Vol. 1. rev., 2nd ed. LC 80-16194. (Illus.). 277p. 1980. text ed. 18.75 (ISBN 0-937144-00-2); pap. 10.75 (ISBN 0-937144-01-0). Triangle Pr.

Fallon, Edward B. How to Enjoy a Better Life. LC 79-92719. 125p. 1980. 8.95 (ISBN 0-935976-01-9); pap. 8.95 (ISBN 0-686-28454-2). Midland Pub Co.

Fallon, Francis T. Second Corinthians. (New Testament Message Ser.). 9.95 (ISBN 0-89453-134-4); pap. 4.95 (ISBN 0-89453-199-9). M Glazier.

Fallon, Jack. All About Surf Fishing. (Illus.). 1975. 11.95 (ISBN 0-87691-201-3). Winchester Pr.

Fallon, Norman. Shortwave Listener's Handbook. rev., 2nd ed. (Illus., Orig.). 1976. pap. 5.95 (ISBN 0-8104-5044-5). Hayden.

Fallon, Padraic. Collected Poems. 176p. 1974. text ed. 9.00x (ISBN 0-85105-232-0, Dolmen Pr). Humanities.

Fallon, Padraic, ed. see Lawless, Emily.

Fallon, Patricia, jt. auth. see Rozendal, Nancy.

Fallon, Virginia. Let's Kiss the Pussy-Cats. 28p. 1980. pap. 2.00 (ISBN 0-934616-19-1). Valkyrie Pr.

Fallon, William K., ed. Effective Communication on the Job. 3rd ed. 273p. 1981. 15.95 (ISBN 0-8144-5698-7). Am Mgmt.

Falls, Harold B., et al, eds. Foundations of Conditioning. 1970. text ed. 7.95 (ISBN 0-12-248055-4). Acad Pr.

Falls, Joe. The Boston Marathon. 1977. 12.95 (ISBN 0-02-537100-2). Macmillan.

Falls, William R., jt. auth. see Payne, Charles A.

Fals-Borda, Orlando. Subversion & Social Change in Colombia. Quayle, Jacqueline, tr. LC 69-19458. 1969. 20.00x (ISBN 0-231-03148-3). Columbia U Pr.

Falstein, Louis. Laughter on a Weekday. 1965. 8.95 (ISBN 0-8392-1147-3). Astor-Honor.

Faltermayer, Edmund. Redoing America. 1969. pap. 1.95 o.s.i. (ISBN 0-02-073170-1, Collier). Macmillan.

Faludi, Andreas. Planning Theory. LC 73-11236. 312p. 1973. 28.00 (ISBN 0-08-017741-7); pap. 12.75 (ISBN 0-08-017756-5). Pergamon.

Faludi, Andreas, ed. A Reader in Planning Theory. 416p. 1973. text ed. 27.00 (ISBN 0-08-017066-8); pap. text ed. 10.75 (ISBN 0-08-017067-6). Pergamon.

Falwell, Jerry. Fasting. 1981. pap. 2.25 (ISBN 0-8423-0849-0). Tyndale.

--Listen America. LC 79-6279. 288p. 1980. 8.95 (ISBN 0-385-15897-1, Galilee). Doubleday.

Famera, Karen, jt. ed. see Zaimont, Judith L.

Family Circle, ed. Family Circle Creative Needlecrafts. LC 77-9240. (Illus.). 1979. 14.95 o.p. (ISBN 0-13-301853-9). P-H.

Family Handyman Editors. Outdoor Projects for Home & Garden. (Illus.). 1979. 12.95 o.p. (ISBN 0-8306-9832-9); pap. 8.95 (ISBN 0-8306-1116-9, 1116). TAB Bks.

Family Handyman Editors, ed. The Family Handyman Handbook of Carpentry Plans Projects. 1980. 15.95 (ISBN 0-8306-9728-4); pap. 9.95 (ISBN 0-8306-1110-X, 1110). TAB Bks.

Family Handyman Magazine, ed. Complete Book of Furniture Repair & Refinishing. (Illus.). 288p. 1981. 14.95 (ISBN 0-684-16839-1, ScribT). Scribner.

Family Handyman Magazine Editors. The Family Handyman Handbook of Home Improvement & Remodeling. (Illus.). 1979. 14.95 o.p. (ISBN 0-8306-9863-9); pap. 9.95 (ISBN 0-8306-1084-7, 1084). TAB Bks.

--The Family Handyman Home Improvement Book. (Encore Edition). (Illus.). 1979. pap. 4.95 (ISBN 0-684-16319-5, ScribT). Scribner.

Family Handyman Magazine Staff. The Furniture Maker's Handbook. LC 75-38972. 1977. 17.95 o.p. (ISBN 0-684-14499-9, ScribT). Scribner.

Family Welfare Assn. Guide to the Social Services 1978. 66th ed. 1978. pap. 8.50x o.p. (ISBN 0-7121-0728-2). Intl Pubns Serv.

Fan, Ts'Un-Chung. Dr. Johnson & Chinese Culture. 50p. 1980. Repr. of 1945 ed. lib. bdg. 8.50 (ISBN 0-8495-1714-1). Arden Lib.

Fance, W. J., ed. The New International Confectioner. 3rd rev. ed. (Illus.). 1976. 75.00 (ISBN 0-685-90333-8, Virtue & Co.). CBI Pub.

Fanchiotti, Margherita & Micklem, Nathaniel, eds. Beginner's Bible. (Illus.). 1958. 9.75x o.p. (ISBN 0-19-234104-9). Oxford U Pr.

Fan Dianian, jt. auth. see Xu Liangying.

Fane, Julian. Gentleman's Gentleman. 148p. 1981. 14.95 (ISBN 0-241-10434-3, Pub. by Hamish Hamilton England). David & Chalres.

--Revolution Island. 352p. 1980. 17.95 (ISBN 0-241-10319-3, Pub. by Hamish Hamilton England). David & Charles.

Fane, X., jt. auth. see Baker, K.

Fanelli, Maresa. Histoires et Idees. 1978. pap. text ed. 7.95x (ISBN 0-669-01532-6). Heath.

Fang, Chaoying. The Asami Library: A Descriptive Catalogue. Huff, Elizabeth, ed. LC 69-16505. (Illus.). 1969. 34.50x (ISBN 0-520-01521-5). U of Cal Pr.

Fang, Fu-An. Chinese Labour: An Economic & Statistical Survey of the Labour Conditions & Labour Movements in China. LC 78-22780. (The Modern Chinese Economy Ser.: Vol. 34). 185p. 1980. lib. bdg. 20.00 (ISBN 0-8240-4282-4). Garland Pub.
Fang, Irving E. Television News, Radio News. 3rd, rev. ed. LC 80-50847. Orig. Title: Television News. (Illus.). 414p. 1980. text ed. 16.95x (ISBN 0-9604212-0-3). Rada Pr.
--Television News: Writing, Filming, Editing, Broadcasting. 2nd rev. & enl. ed. (Communication Arts Bks.). (Illus.). 384p. 1972. 12.50 o.s.i. (ISBN 0-8038-7117-1); pap. text ed. 7.50x o.s.i. (ISBN 0-8038-7125-2). Hastings.
Fang, Jen-Ho & Bloss, F. Donald. X-Ray Diffraction Tables. LC 66-21919. 1966. 15.00x o.p. (ISBN 0-8093-0211-X). S Ill U Pr.
Fang, Josephine R. & Songe, Alice H. International Guide to Library, Archival, & Information Science Associations. 2nd ed. 400p. 1980. 32.50 (ISBN 0-8352-1285-8). Bowker.
Fanin, Ferne, ed. Cumulative Index to Nursing & Allied Health Literature, Vol. 24. LC 78-643434. 1979. 50.00 (ISBN 0-910478-15-5). Glendale Advent Med.
Faniran, A. Man's Physical Environment. (Orig.). 1980. pap. text ed. 22.50x (ISBN 0-435-95042-8). Heinemann Ed.
Fann, K. T. Wittgenstein's Conception of Philosophy. 1969. 14.50x (ISBN 0-520-01615-7); pap. 4.75x (ISBN 0-520-01837-0, CAMPUS 171). U of Cal Pr.
Fann, William, et al, eds. Tardive Dyskinesia. new ed. LC 79-4468. (Illus.). 1980. text ed. 55.00 (ISBN 0-89335-076-1). Spectrum Pub.
Fann, William E. & Maddox, George L. Drug Issues in Geropsychiatry. 122p. 1974. pap. 9.50 (ISBN 0-683-03002-7). Krieger.
Fannin, Alice, et al. Woman: An Affirmation. 1978. pap. text ed. 9.95x (ISBN 0-669-01991-7); instructor's manual free (ISBN 0-669-01992-5). Heath.
Fannin, D. R., jt. auth. see Ferry, David K.
Fanning, Buckner. Christ in Your Shoes. LC 74-117305. 1970. 3.50 o.p. (ISBN 0-8054-1913-6). Broadman.
Fanning, Charles. Finley Peter Dunne & Mr. Dooley: The Chicago Years. LC 77-75483. (Illus.). 304p. 1978. 16.00x (ISBN 0-8131-1365-2). U Pr of Ky.
Fanning, John. Working When You Want to Work. 1969. pap. 1.25 o.s.i. (ISBN 0-02-008200-2, Collier). Macmillan.
Fanning, John W. A Common Sense Approach to Community Living Arrangements for the Mentally Retarded. (Illus.). 112p. 1975. 12.50 (ISBN 0-398-03300-5). C C Thomas.
Fanning, Kent A. & Manheim, Frank T. The Dynamic Environment of the Ocean Floor. LC 78-24651. 1981. write for info. (ISBN 0-669-02809-6). Lexington Bks.
Fanning, Louis. Betrayal in Vietnam. 1976. 8.95 o.s.i. (ISBN 0-87000-341-0). Arlington Hse.
Fanning, Robbie & Fanning, Tony. The Complete Book of Machine Quilting. (Illus.). 224p. 1980. 15.95 (ISBN 0-8019-6802-X); pap. 9.95 (ISBN 0-8019-6803-8). Chilton.
Fanning, Tony, jt. auth. see Fanning, Robbie.
Fanshel, David. Far from the Reservation: The Transracial Adoption of American Indian Children. LC 70-181701. 1972. 12.50 o.p. (ISBN 0-8108-0454-9). Scarecrow.
Fanshel, David & Shinn, Eugene. Children in Foster Care: A Longitudinal Investigation. LC 77-3176. 1978. 27.50x (ISBN 0-231-03576-4). Columbia U Pr.
Fanshel, David, jt. auth. see Jaffee, Benson.
Fanshel, David, ed. Future of Social Work Research. LC 79-92733. 246p. 1980. pap. 12.50 (ISBN 0-87101-084-4, CBQ-084-C). Natl Assn Soc Wkrs.
Fant, Clyde E. Bonhoeffer: Worldly Preaching. LC 74-26806. 192p. 1975. 6.95 o.p. (ISBN 0-8407-5087-0); pap. 3.50 o.p. (ISBN 0-8407-5586-4). Nelson.
--Preaching for Today. LC 74-4640. 1977. pap. 4.95 o.p. (ISBN 0-06-062332-2, RD 204, HarpR). Har-Row.
Fant, Louie J., Jr. Intermediate Sign Language. (Illus.). 225p. (gr. 7 up). 1980. text ed. 17.95 (ISBN 0-917002-54-7). Joyce Media.
--Noah. new ed. (Illus.). 14p. 1973. pap. text ed. 2.50 (ISBN 0-917002-70-9). Joyce Media.
--Say It with Hands. (Illus.). 1964. 5.50 (ISBN 0-913072-02-8). Natl Assn Deaf.
Fanthorpe, Lionel, jt. auth. see Fanthorpe, Patricia.
Fanthorpe, Patricia & Fanthorpe, Lionel. The Black Lion. 1980. pap. 1.95 o.s.i. (ISBN 0-906901-00-6). Newcastle Pub.
--The Black Lion. LC 80-19214. 160p. 1980. Repr. of 1979 ed. lib. bdg. 8.95 (ISBN 0-89370-094-0). Borgo Pr.
Fantini, Mario D., ed. Alternative Education: A Sourcebook for Parents, Teachers, Students & Administrators. LC 73-13104. 400p. 1976. pap. 4.50 o.p. (ISBN 0-385-06389-X, Anch). Doubleday.
Fantin-Latour, Victoria. Catalogue De L'qeuve Comblet De Fantin Latour. (Graphic Art Ser.). 320p. (Fr.). 1970. Repr. of 1911 ed. 47.50 (ISBN 0-306-71924-X). Da Capo.
Fantino, Edmund J. & Reynolds, George S. Introduction to Contemporary Psychology. LC 74-23201. (Illus.). 1975. text ed. 21.95x (ISBN 0-7167-0761-6); 4.00 o.p.study guide (ISBN 0-686-67086-8); test items avail. W H Freeman.
Fantom, I., ed. see Second International Symposium on Wind Energy Systems.
Fantoni, Barry. Mike Dime. 208p. 1981. 9.95 (ISBN 0-531-09948-2). Watts.
Far Eastern Economic Review, ed. Asia Yearbook 1980. (Illus.). 320p. 1980. 12.50x (ISBN 962-7010-06-5). Intl Pubns Serv.
Far West Press Editors. Material for Thought, No. 8. LC 79-56899. 88p. 1979. pap. 2.95 (ISBN 0-914480-05-7). Far West Pr.
Fara, Patricia, jt. ed. see Choppin, Bruce.
Farach, H. A., jt. auth. see Poole, C. P., Jr.
Faraday, Ann. Dream Power. 1981. pap. 2.50 (ISBN 0-425-04863-2). Berkley Pub.
Farag, Fahmy. The Opposing Virtues: Two Essays. (New Yeats Papers: No. 15). 1978. pap. text ed. 9.25x (ISBN 0-85105-323-8, Dolmen Pr). Humanities.
Farag, M. M. Materials & Process Selection in Engineering. (Illus.). 1979. 57.00x (ISBN 0-85334-824-3). Intl Ideas.
Farago, Francis T. Abrasive Methods Engineering, Vol. 2. LC 76-14970. (Illus.). 508p. 1980. 55.00 (ISBN 0-8311-1134-8). Indus Pr.
--Handbook of Dimensional Measurement. (Illus.). 1968. 36.00 (ISBN 0-8311-1025-2). Indus Pr.
Farago, Ladislas. The Last Days of Patton. 352p. 1981. 12.95 (ISBN 0-07-019940-X, GB). McGraw.
Farago, Peter. Science & the Media. (Science & Engineering Policy Ser.). 1976. 17.95x (ISBN 0-19-858324-9). Oxford U Pr.
Farah, Caesar E. Islam: Beliefs & Observances. rev. ed. LC 72-135505. (Orig.). (YA) 1970. text ed. op (ISBN 0-8120-6022-9); pap. 3.95 (ISBN 0-8120-0277-6). Barron.
Farah, Charles, Jr. From the Pinnacle of the Temple: Faith or Presumption. 1979. 7.95 o.p. (ISBN 0-88270-361-7); pap. 4.95 (ISBN 0-88270-462-1). Logos.
Farah, Madelain. Lebanese Cuisine. 1979. 8.00 (ISBN 0-89955-011-8, Pub. by Madelain Farah); pap. 6.50 (ISBN 0-89955-202-1). Intl Schol Bk Serv.
Farah, Mark G., jt. auth. see Mikesell, Raymond F.
Faraham, Moulton M. Sailing for Beginners. rev. ed. (Illus.). 272p. 1981. 14.95 (ISBN 0-02-537140-1). Macmillan.
Farazdag, jt. auth. see Jarir.
Farb, P., jt. auth. see Hay, John.
Farb, Peter. Ecology. LC 63-22074. (Life Nature Library Ser.). (Illus.). (gr. 5 up). 1970. PLB 8.97 o.p. (ISBN 0-8094-0627-6, Pub. by Time-Life). Silver.
--Face of North America: The Natural History of a Continent. (YA) 1963. 12.50 o.s.i. (ISBN 0-06-070746-1, HarpT). Har-Row.
--Insects. LC 62-21531. (Life Nature Library). (Illus.). (gr. 5 up). 1962. PLB 8.97 o.p. (ISBN 0-8094-0621-7, Pub. by Time-Life). Silver.
--Land & Wildlife of North America. LC 64-8304. (Life Nature Library). (Illus.). (gr. 5 up). 1964. PLB 8.97 o.p. (ISBN 0-8094-0633-0, Pub. by Time-Life). Silver.
--Story of Butterflies & Other Insects. LC 59-14884. (Story of Science Ser). (Illus.). (gr. 3-6). 1959. PLB 7.29 (ISBN 0-8178-3232-7). Harvey.
--Story of Dams: Hydrology for the Young Scientist. LC 61-15658. (Story of Science Ser). (Illus.). (gr. 5-8). 1961. PLB 7.29 (ISBN 0-8178-3252-1). Harvey.
--The Story of Life: Plants & Animals Through the Ages. LC 62-17247. (Story of Science Ser.). (Illus.). (gr. 5 up). 1962. PLB 7.29 (ISBN 0-8178-3292-0). Harvey.
Farb, Peter, ed. Forest. rev. ed. LC 61-17488. (Life Nature Library). (Illus.). (gr. 5 up). 1969. PLB 8.97 o.p. (ISBN 0-8094-0614-4, Pub. by Time-Life). Silver.
Farb, Stanley N. The Ear, Nose, & Throat Book: A Doctor's Guide to Better Health. (Appleton Consumer Health Guides). (Illus.). 158p. 1980. 12.95 (ISBN 0-8385-2021-9); pap. 5.95 (ISBN 0-8385-2020-0). ACC.
--Otolaryngology. 4th ed. LC 70-94388. (Medical Examination Review Bk.: Vol. 16). 1977. spiral bdg. 16.50 (ISBN 0-87488-116-1). Med Exam.
--Otorhinolaryngology. 2nd. ed. (Medical Outline Ser). 1980. pap. 16.00 (ISBN 0-87488-661-9). Med Exam.
Farber, Carol R., jt. auth. see Levy, Wilbert J.
Farber, Daniel A., jt. auth. see Findley, Roger W.
Farber, Donald C. Producing Theatre: A Comprehensive Legal & Business Guide. 384p. 1981. 17.95 (ISBN 0-89676-051-0). Drama Bk.
Farber, Donald C. & Baumgarten, Paul. Producing, Financing, & Distributing Film. LC 72-87054. 1973. 16.95 (ISBN 0-910482-31-4). Drama Bk.
Farber, Evan I. Combined Retrospective Index to Book Reviews in Scholarly Journals, 1886-1974, 15 vols. LC 79-89137. 1979. lib. bdg. 1232.00 (ISBN 0-8408-0157-2). Carrollton Pr.
Farber, Evan I. & Walling, Ruth. The Academic Library: Essays in Honor of Guy R. Lyle. LC 74-2098. 1974. 10.00 (ISBN 0-8108-0712-2). Scarecrow.
Farber, Evan I., ed. Combined Retrospective Index to Book Reviews in Scholarly Humanities Journals, 1802-1974, 10 vols. 1981. 932.00 set (ISBN 0-8408-0238-2). Carrollton Pr.
Farber, Joseph & Hope, Henry. Palladio's Architecture & Its Influences: A Photographic Guide. (Illus.). 1980. pap. 6.95 (ISBN 0-486-23922-5). Dover.
Farber, Norma. Never Say Ugh! to a Bug. LC 78-13948. (Illus.). (gr. k-3). 1979. 7.50 (ISBN 0-688-80140-4); PLB 7.20 (ISBN 0-688-84140-6). Greenwillow.
--A Ship in a Storm on the Way to Tarsish. LC 77-23288. (Illus.). (ps-3). 1977. 8.25 (ISBN 0-688-80096-3); PLB 7.92 (ISBN 0-688-84096-5). Greenwillow.
--Six Impossible Things Before Breakfast. LC 76-40264. (Illus.). (gr. 5-6). 1977. lib. bdg. 6.95x (ISBN 0-201-01969-8, 1969, A-W Childrens). A-W.
--Something Further: Poems. 1979. 6.95 (ISBN 0-914408-10-0); pap. 3.95. Kylix Pr.
--Up the Down Elevator. LC 79-13199. (Illus.). (ps-3). 1979. 7.95 (ISBN 0-201-01924-8, 1924, A-W Childrens). A-W.
Farber, Raymond C., jt. auth. see Green, Gion.
Farber, Samuel. Revolution & Reaction in Cuba, 1933-1960: A Political Sociology from Machado to Castro. LC 76-7190. 1976. 20.00x (ISBN 0-8195-4099-4, Pub. by Wesleyan U Pr). Columbia U Pr.
Farber, Thomas. The Material Plane. 1980. 9.95 o.p. (ISBN 0-525-15424-8). Dutton.
Farberman, Harvey A., jt. auth. see Stone, Gregory P.
Farberman, Harvey A., jt. ed. see Stone, Gregory P.
Farberow, Norman L. & Shneidman, Edwin S. Cry for Help. 1961. pap. 4.95 o.p. (ISBN 0-07-019943-4, SP). McGraw.
Farberow, Norman L., jt. auth. see Reynolds, David K.
Farberow, Norman L., jt. ed. see Shneidman, Edwin S.
Farbstein, Abraham, tr. see Baumer, Franz.
Fardan, Dorothy B. Understanding Self & Society. LC 80-81696. 1980. 13.95 (ISBN 0-8022-2370-2). Philos Lib.
Fardo, Stephen W., jt. auth. see Patrick, Dale R.
Fardon, G. E., ed. see Young, A. P. & Griffiths, L.
Fardy, Paul S., et al. Cardiac Rehabilitation: Implications for the Nurse & Other Allied Health Professionals. LC 80-16296. (Illus.). 283p. 1980. pap. text ed. 14.95 (ISBN 0-8016-1610-7). Mosby.
Fareed, A. & El-Hifnawi, M. Industrial Housing Systems, an Evaluation: Proceedings of the IAHS Cairo Workshop, 1976. (Illus.). 1979. text ed. 60.00 (ISBN 0-08-024236-7). Pergamon.
Fareed, Jawed, ed. Perspectives in Hemostasis: Proceedings of a Symposium Held 11 May 1979 at Loyola University, Maywood, Ill., U. S. A. (Illus.). 400p. 1981. 50.00 (ISBN 0-08-025092-0). Pergamon.
Farer, Tom J. The Future of the Inter-American System. LC 78-31153. (Praeger Special Studies). 1979. 24.95 (ISBN 0-03-047391-8). Praeger.
--Toward a Humanitarian Diplomacy: A Primer for Policy. LC 79-3514. 1981. 15.00x (ISBN 0-8147-2565-1). NYU Pr.
Farge, John La see La Farge, John.
Farge, Oliver La see La Farge, Oliver & Morgan, Arthur N.
Farge, Phyllis La see La Farge, Phyllis.
Farge, Sheila La see Bodker, Cecil.
Farge, Sheila La see Gripe, Maria.
Farge, W. E. La see La Farge, W. E.
Fargher, Douglas C. Fargher's English Manx Dictionary. 1979. text ed. 6.75x (ISBN 0-904980-23-5). Humanities.
Farguhar, Judith, jt. ed. see Murata, Alice K.
Faria, Anthony J., et al. Compete: A Dynamic Marketing Simulation. rev. ed. 1979. pap. 8.50x (ISBN 0-256-02077-9). Business Pubns.
Faria, I. E. & Cavanagh, P. R. The Psychology & Biomechanics of Cycling. 179p. 1978. 14.95 (ISBN 0-471-25490-8). Wiley.
Faricy, Robert. Praying for Inner Healing. LC 79-92857. (Orig.). 1980. pap. 3.50 (ISBN 0-8091-2250-2). Paulist Pr.
Faries, Clyde J. Concepts in Public Speaking: Consumer Responsibility. 112p. 1980. pap. text ed. 5.95 (ISBN 0-8403-2239-9). Kendall-Hunt.
Faries, David. Advice from the Soccer Pros. LC 79-64730. (Illus.). 166p. 1980. pap. 4.95 (ISBN 0-89037-219-5). Anderson World.
Farina, A. M. Developmental Games Rhythms for Children. (Illus.). 800p. 1980. 48.75 (ISBN 0-398-04022-2). C C Thomas.
Farina, John E. Quantum Theory of Scattering Processes, Pt. 2. LC 72-10162. 164p. 1973. text ed. 42.00 (ISBN 0-08-017047-1); pap. text ed. 19.50 (ISBN 0-08-018985-7). Pergamon.
--Quantum Theory of Scattering Processes, Pt. 1: General Principles & Advanced Topics. McWeeny, R., ed. LC 74-22357. 144p. 1976. text ed. 34.00 (ISBN 0-08-018130-9). Pergamon.
Farina, Mario V. Fortran IV Self-Taught. 1966. pap. 14.95 (ISBN 0-13-329722-5). P-H.
Farina, Richard. Been Down So Long It Looks Like Up to Me. 1966. 8.95 o.p. (ISBN 0-394-41683-X). Random.
Farinas, Maurice E. see O'Neal, William B.
Fariq, K. A. A History of Arbaic Literature: Umayyad Period. 1978. 15.00 (ISBN 0-7069-0661-6, Pub. by Vikas India). Advent Bk.
Fariq, Khurshid A., ed. Tarikh Al-Ridda: Gleaned from Al-Iktifaq of Al-Balansi. 1972. 8.00x o.p. (ISBN 0-210-22334-0). Asia.
Fariqi, Khwaja A. Dastanbuy: A Diary of the Indian Revolt of 1857 by Mirza Asadullah Ghalib. 1971. 7.95x (ISBN 0-210-22338-3). Asia.
Faris, E. Accounting for Lawyers. 3rd ed. LC 75-12479. (Illus.). 1975. 23.00 (ISBN 0-672-82026-9, Bobbs-Merrill Law). Michie.
Faris, Nabih A., ed. The Arab Heritage. LC 79-2856. 279p. 1981. Repr. of 1944 ed. 23.50 (ISBN 0-8305-0030-8). Hyperion Conn.
Faris, Ralph, ed. Crisis & Consciousness. (Philosophical Currents Ser.: 20). 1977. pap. text ed. 23.00x (ISBN 90-6032-093-X). Humanities.
Faris, W. G. Self-Adjoint Operators. (Lecture Notes in Mathematics Ser.: Vol. 433). vii, 115p. 1975. pap. 9.50 (ISBN 0-387-07030-3). Springer-Verlag.
Farish, Donald J. Biology: The Human Perspective. (Illus.). 1978. text ed. 19.50 scp (ISBN 0-06-041995-4, HarpC); inst. manual avail. (ISBN 0-685-86375-1); scp study guide 7.50 (ISBN 0-06-041992-X). Har-Row.
Farish, Hunter D. Circuit Rider Dismounts, a Social History of Southern Methodism 1865-1900. LC 77-87534. (American Scene Ser). 1969. Repr. of 1938 ed. 35.00 (ISBN 0-306-71450-7). Da Capo.
Farish, Margaret K., ed. String Music in Print. 2nd ed. LC 80-18425. (Music in Print Ser.: Vol. 6). 464p. 1980. Repr. lib. bdg. 60.00 (ISBN 0-88478-011-2). Musicdata.
Farish, Starr, ed. see Gittner, Louis.
Farjeon, Eleanor. Eleanor Farjeon's Poems for Children. (Illus.). (gr. 4-6). 1951. 4.95 o.p. (ISBN 0-397-30193-6). Lippincott.
Farkas, Emil & Leeds, Margaret. Fight Back: A Woman's Guide to Self-Defense. LC 78-2536. (Illus.). 1978. 10.95 o.p. (ISBN 0-03-021051-8); pap. 6.95 o.p. (ISBN 0-03-021056-9). HR&W.
Farkas, Emil, ed. see Urquidez, Benny.
Farkas, Janos, ed. Sociology of Science & Research. (Illus.). 503p. 1979. 47.50x (ISBN 963-05-2204-7). Intl Pubns Serv.
Farkas, Sandor B. Journey in North America, 1831. Kadarkay, Arpad, tr. from Hung. LC 77-19145. 230p. 1978. text ed. 7.95 (ISBN 0-87436-270-9). ABC-Clio.
Farks, G. L., ed. see International Protoplast Symposium, 5th, July 1979, Szeged, Hungary.
Farley. How to Prepare for the High School Equivalency Examination: The Science Test. 1981. pap. 4.25 (ISBN 0-8120-2055-3). Barron.
--Son of the Black Stallion. (gr. 4-6). Date not set. pap. cancelled (ISBN 0-686-68471-0, Schol Pap). Schol Bk Serv.
Farley, Alice R., jt. auth. see Farley, Eugene J.
Farley, Benjamin W., ed. see Calvin, John.
Farley, Carol. Bunch on McKellahan Street. LC 75-152736. (Illus.). (gr. 4-6). 1971. PLB 5.88 o.p. (ISBN 0-531-01992-6). Watts.
--The Most Important Thing in the World. LC 73-9675. 256p. (gr. 5-8). 1974. PLB 4.90 o.p. (ISBN 0-531-02663-9). Watts.
--Mystery in the Ravine. 1976. pap. 1.25 (ISBN 0-380-00745-2, 30171, Camelot). Avon.
--Mystery of the Fog Man. 1974. pap. 1.75 (ISBN 0-380-00102-0, 53280, Camelot). Avon.
--Sergeant Finney's Family. LC 78-79667. (Illus.). (gr. 4-6). 1969. PLB 4.90 o.p. (ISBN 0-531-01915-2). Watts.

Farley, Eugene J. Barron's How to Prepare for the High School Equivalency Examination: The Social Studies Test. 1980. pap. text ed. 3.95 (ISBN 0-8120-2056-1). Barron.
--Barron's How to Prepare for the High School Equivalency Examination: The Reading Skills Test. 1980. pap. text ed. 3.95 (ISBN 0-8120-2057-X). Barron.
--Barron's Preview Examination to Prepare for High School Equivalency Tests. 2nd, rev. ed. 1979. pap. text ed. 18.00 (ISBN 0-8120-0992-4). Barron.
--How to Prepare for the High School Equivalency Examination: Vol. III the Reading Skills Test. LC 79-28101. (gr. 11-12). 1980. pap. text ed. 3.95 (ISBN 0-8120-2057-X). Barron.
--How to Prepare for the High School Equivalency Examination, Vol. II: The Social Studies Test. (gr. 11-12). 1980. pap. text ed. 3.95 (ISBN 0-8120-2056-1). Barron.
Farley, Eugene J. & Farley, Alice R. Barron's How to Prepare for the High School Equavalency Examination(GED) Science. (gr. 11-12). 1981. pap. text ed. 4.25 (ISBN 0-8120-2055-3). Barron.
--Developing Reading Skills for the High School Equivalency Examination (Ged) in Social Studies, Science, & Literature: In 26 Lessons. LC 72-84413. 1972. pap. text ed. 5.75 (ISBN 0-8120-0487-6). Barron.
Farley, Frank & Gordon, Neal J., eds. Education & Psychology: The State of the Union. LC 80-82902. 300p. 1981. write for info (ISBN 0-8211-0506-X); text ed. write for info. McCutchan.
Farley, Gordon K., et al. Handbook of Child & Adolescent Psychiatric Emergencies. 1979. pap. 12.50 (ISBN 0-87488-656-2). Med Exam.
Farley, James A. Behind the Ballots. LC 72-2370. (FDR & the Era of the New Deal Ser). (Illus.). 402p. 1973. Repr. of 1938 ed. lib. bdg. 35.00 (ISBN 0-306-70475-7). Da Capo.
Farley, James H., tr. see Simon, Marcel.
Farley, Leonard, jt. auth. see Hubbard, Freeman.
Farley, M. Foster. An Account of the History of Stranger's Fever in Charleston, 1699-1876. LC 78-66421. 1978. pap. text ed. 9.00 (ISBN 0-8191-0320-9). U Pr of Amer.
Farley, Philip J., et al. Arms Across the Sea. LC 77-91804. 1978. 9.95 (ISBN 0-8157-2746-1); pap. 3.95 (ISBN 0-8157-2745-3). Brookings.
Farley, Ralph M. The Radio Beasts. 1976. lib. bdg. 10.95x (ISBN 0-89968-030-5). Lightyear.
Farley, Reuben W., et al. Trigonometry: A Unitized Approach. (Illus.). 1975. pap. text ed. 15.95 (ISBN 0-13-930909-8). P-H.
Farley, Venner. Second Level Nursing: Study Modules. LC 80-70482. (Associate Degree Nursing Ser.). (Illus.). 272p. (Orig.). 1981. pap. text ed. price not set (ISBN 0-8273-1876-6); price not set instr's. guide (ISBN 0-8273-1877-4). Delmar.
Farley, Venner M. First Level Nursing-Study Modules. (Nursing-Registered Ser.). 1981. pap. 10.00 (ISBN 0-8273-1873-1); write for info. instrs'. guide (ISBN 0-8273-1875-8). Delmar.
Farley, Walter. Black Stallion. LC 41-21882. (Illus.). (gr. 3-7). 1944. 3.95 (ISBN 0-394-80601-8, BYR); PLB 5.99 (ISBN 0-394-90601-2); pap. 1.95 (ISBN 0-394-83609-X). Random.
--Black Stallion & Flame. (Illus.). (gr. 5 up). 1960. 3.95 (ISBN 0-394-80615-8, BYR); PLB 5.99 (ISBN 0-394-90615-2); pap. 1.95 (ISBN 0-394-84372-X). Random.
--The Black Stallion & the Girl. (gr. 4 up). 1971. 3.95 (ISBN 0-394-82145-9, BYR); PLB 5.99 (ISBN 0-394-92145-3); pap. 1.95 (ISBN 0-394-83614-6). Random.
--Black Stallion Challenged. (Illus.). (gr. 5-9). 1964. 3.95 (ISBN 0-394-80617-4, BYR); PLB 5.99 (ISBN 0-394-90617-9); pap. 1.95 (ISBN 0-394-84371-1). Random.
--The Black Stallion Mystery. (gr. 4-6). 1957. 3.95 (ISBN 0-394-80613-1, BYR); PLB 5.99 (ISBN 0-394-90613-6); pap. 1.95 (ISBN 0-394-83611-1). Random.
--The Black Stallion Returns. LC 45-8763. (gr. 4-9). 1977. 3.95 (ISBN 0-394-80602-6, BYR); PLB 5.99 (ISBN 0-394-90602-0); pap. 1.95 (ISBN 0-394-83610-3). Random.
--The Black Stallion Revolts. LC 49-6117. (gr. 4-9). 1977. 3.95 (ISBN 0-394-80609-3, BYR); PLB 5.99 (ISBN 0-394-90609-8); pap. 1.95 (ISBN 0-394-83613-8). Random.
--Black Stallion's Courage. (Illus.). (gr. 4-6). 1956. 3.95 (ISBN 0-394-80612-3, BYR); PLB 5.99 (ISBN 0-394-90612-8); pap. 1.95 (ISBN 0-394-83918-8). Random.
--Black Stallion's Filly. (Illus.). (gr. 4-6). 1952. 3.95 (ISBN 0-394-80608-5, BYR); PLB 5.99 (ISBN 0-394-90608-X); pap. 1.95 (ISBN 0-394-83916-1). Random.
--Black Stallion's Ghost. (Illus.). (gr. 5-9). 1969. 3.95 (ISBN 0-394-80618-2, BYR); PLB 5.99 (ISBN 0-394-90618-7); pap. 1.95 (ISBN 0-394-83919-6). Random.
--Black Stallion's Sulky Colt. (Illus.). (gr. 4-6). 1954. 3.95 (ISBN 0-394-80610-7, BYR); PLB 5.99 (ISBN 0-394-90610-1); pap. 1.95 (ISBN 0-394-83917-X). Random.
--Blood Bay Colt. (Illus.). (gr. 4-6). 1950. 3.95 (ISBN 0-394-80606-9, BYR); PLB 5.99 (ISBN 0-394-90606-3); pap. 1.95 (ISBN 0-394-83915-3). Random.
--Great Dane Thor. (Illus.). (gr. 5-9). 1966. 4.95 (ISBN 0-394-81582-3, BYR). Random.
--The Horse-Tamer. LC 58-9030. (Black Stallion Bks.). 160p. 1980. 3.95 (ISBN 0-394-80614-X, BYR); PLB 5.99 (ISBN 0-394-90614-4); pap. 1.95 (ISBN 0-394-84374-6). Random.
--Island Stallion. (Illus.). (gr. 5-6). 1948. 3.95 (ISBN 0-394-80604-2, BYR); PLB 5.99 (ISBN 0-394-90604-7); pap. 1.95 (ISBN 0-394-84376-2). Random.
--Island Stallion Races. (Illus.). (gr. 4-6). 1965. 3.95 (ISBN 0-394-80611-5, BYR); PLB 5.99 (ISBN 0-394-90611-X); pap. 1.95 (ISBN 0-394-84375-4). Random.
--Island Stallion's Fury. (Illus.). (gr. 5-6). 1951. 3.95 (ISBN 0-394-80607-1, BYR); PLB 5.99 (ISBN 0-394-90607-1); pap. 1.95 (ISBN 0-394-84373-8). Random.
--Little Black Pony Races. (Illus.). (ps-1). 1968. 2.95 (ISBN 0-394-81349-9, BYR); PLB 3.69 (ISBN 0-394-91349-3). Random.
--Son of the Black Stallion. (Illus.). (gr. 4-6). 1947. 3.95 (ISBN 0-394-80603-4, BYR); PLB 5.99 (ISBN 0-394-90603-9); pap. 1.95 (ISBN 0-394-83612-X). Random.
--Walter Farley's Black Stallion Books, 4 bks. Incl. The Black Stallion. LC 41-21882; The Black Stallion Returns. LC 45-8763; The Black Stallion & Satan. LC 49-6117; The Black Stallion Mystery. LC 57-7527. (gr. 4-9). 1979. Boxed Set. pap. 7.75 (ISBN 0-394-84176-X, BYR). Random.
--Walter Farley's How to Stay Out of Trouble with Your Horse: Some Basic Safety Rules to Help You Enjoy Riding. LC 79-8922. (Illus.). 80p. (gr. 4-8). 1981. 7.95a (ISBN 0-385-15480-1); lib. bdg. (ISBN 0-385-15481-X). Doubleday.
Farley, William E. Practical Public Relations for the Businessman. 7.95 o.s.i. (ISBN 0-8119-0144-0). Fell.
Farley-Hills, David. The Comic in Renaissance Comedy. 1981. 26.50x (ISBN 0-389-20013-1). B&N.
Farley-Hills, David, ed. Rochester: The Critical Heritage. 1972. 34.00x (ISBN 0-7100-7157-4). Routledge & Kegan.
Farlie, Barbara L. & Clarke, Charlotte L. All About Doll Houses. LC 75-513. (Illus.). 272p. 1975. 16.95 (ISBN 0-672-51976-3). Bobbs.
--All About Doll Houses. LC 75-513. (Illus.). 1977. pap. 18.95 (ISBN 0-672-52367-1). Bobbs.
Farlow, W. C. The Marine Algae of New England & Adjacent Coast. (Illus.). 1969. Repr. of 1881 ed. 50.00 (ISBN 3-7682-0582-7). Lubrecht & Cramer.
Farm Journal Editors. America's Best Vegetable Recipes. LC 74-89068. (Illus.). 1970. 8.95 (ISBN 0-385-03155-6). Doubleday.
Farm Journal Food Editors. Farm Journal's Country-Style Microwave Cookbook. 128p. (Orig.). 1980. pap. 3.50x. Farm Journal.
--Farm Journal's Everyday Favorite Recipes. 128p. (Orig.). 1980. pap. 3.50x (ISBN 0-89795-011-9). Farm Journal.
Farmer & Anderson. Business Transcription. 192p. 1973. text ed. 10.60 (ISBN 0-7715-0740-2). Section A, Units 1-10 (6 Cassettes (ISBN 0-7715-0742-9). Section B, Units 11-20 (6 Cassettes (ISBN 0-7715-0743-7). Section C, Units 21-30 (6 Cassettes (ISBN 0-7715-0744-5). Forkner.
Farmer & Brown. Dicta-Typing: A Short Course. 72p. 1974. text ed. 4.60 wkbk. (ISBN 0-7715-0861-1); tchr's. manual, 136p. 28.33 (ISBN 0-7715-0862-X). Forkner.
Farmer, et al. Business Applications in Typewriting. 368p. 1976. text ed. 15.27 (ISBN 0-7715-0878-6); tchr's. manual 7.93 (ISBN 0-7715-0879-4); stationery & business forms 6.60 (ISBN 0-7715-0880-8); Set Of 26 Cassettes. 269.50 (ISBN 0-7715-0882-4). Forkner.
--Personal Applications in Typewriting. 272p. 1976. text ed. 13.27 (ISBN 0-7715-0875-1); Set Of 26 =cassettes. tchr's. manual 6.67 (ISBN 0-7715-0876-X); 269.50 (ISBN 0-7715-0882-4); book of resource materials 39.93 (ISBN 0-7715-0831-X); typing facts & tips 3.00 ea. (ISBN 0-7715-0889-1); typing facts & tips, package of 10 21.33 (ISBN 0-7715-0896-4); certificate of proficiency (personal, 1 per student) free (ISBN 0-7715-0865-4); roll of honor for production efficiency (1 per classroom) free (ISBN 0-7715-0864-6). Forkner.
--Professional Applications in Typewriting. 260p. 1977. text ed. 15.27 (ISBN 0-7715-0886-7); tchr's. manual 7.67 (ISBN 0-7715-0887-5); stationery & business forms 6.60 (ISBN 0-7715-0888-3); book of resource materials 44.60 (ISBN 0-7715-0833-6); typing facts & tips 3.00 ea. (ISBN 0-7715-0889-1); typing facts & tips, package of 10 21.33 (ISBN 0-7715-0896-4); certificate of proficiency (professional, 1 per student) free (ISBN 0-7715-0867-0); roll of honor for production efficiency (1 per classroom) free (ISBN 0-7715-0864-6). Forkner.
Farmer, B. H. Green Revolution. LC 76-51278. (Cambridge Commonwealth Ser.). (Illus.). 1977. lib. bdg. 32.00x (ISBN 0-89158-709-8). Westview.
Farmer, Charles & Farmer, Kathleen. Family Book of Camping Lists. (Illus.). 224p. (Orig.). 1981. pap. 6.95 (ISBN 0-8117-2136-1). Stackpole.
Farmer, David & Taylor, Bernard, eds. Corporate Planning & Procurement. LC 74-19369. 1975. 27.95 (ISBN 0-470-25499-8). Halsted Pr.
Farmer, Edward L., et al. Comparative History of Civilization in Asia, Vols. 1 & 2. LC 75-12095. (History Ser). (Illus.). 1977. Vol. 1. text ed. 17.95 (ISBN 0-201-01998-1); Vol. 2. text ed. 15.95 (ISBN 0-201-01999-X). A-W.
Farmer, Geraldine M. & Lore, Mary S. Forkner Shorthand Outlines for the Business Vocabulary. 123p. 1972. pap. 6.60x (ISBN 0-912036-23-0). Forkner.
Farmer, Henry G. History of Music in Scotland. LC 70-100613. (Music Ser). (Illus.). 1970. Repr. of 1947 ed. lib. bdg. 29.50 (ISBN 0-306-71865-0). Da Capo.
Farmer, John N. The Protozoa: Introduction to Protozoology. LC 80-10817. (Illus.). 1980. pap. text ed. 26.95 (ISBN 0-8016-1550-X). Mosby.
Farmer, John S. Americanisms: Old & New. LC 75-44079. 1976. Repr. of 1889 ed. 38.00 (ISBN 0-8103-3746-0). Gale.
--Merry Songs & Ballads: Musa Pedestris, 6 vols. Set. 61.50x (ISBN 0-8154-0066-7). Cooper Sq.
--Public School Word-Book. LC 68-17988. 1968. Repr. of 1900 ed. 15.00 (ISBN 0-8103-3280-9). Gale.
Farmer, John S. & Henley, W. E. Dictionary of Slang & Its Analogues, 2 Vols. 1965. Vol. 1. (ISBN 0-8216-0068-0); 15.00 o.p. (ISBN 0-685-20856-7); Vol. 8. 10.00 o.p. (ISBN 0-685-20857-5). Univ Bks.
Farmer, Kathleen. Woman in the Woods. LC 80-22021. (Illus.). 1980. pap. 5.95 (ISBN 0-934802-08-4). Ind Camp Supply.
Farmer, Kathleen, jt. auth. see Farmer, Charles.
Farmer, Kenneth C. Ukrainian Nationalism in the Post-Stalin Era: Myth, Symbols & Ideology in Soviet Nationalities Policy. (Studies in Contemporary History: Vol. 4). 253p. 1980. lib. bdg. 36.50 (ISBN 90-247-2401-5, Pub. by Martinus Nijhoff). Kluwer Boston.
Farmer Magazine. Country Kitchen Cookbook: Eighteen Ninety-Four to Nineteen Seventy-Nine. (Illus.). 1979. pap. 5.95 (ISBN 0-8015-1786-9, Hawthorn). Dutton.
Farmer, Penelope. The Story of Persephone. LC 73-4923. (Illus.). 48p. 1973. 7.75 (ISBN 0-688-20084-2); PLB 7.44 (ISBN 0-688-30084-7). Morrow.
Farmer, Philip J. The Adventure of the Peerless Peer. 112p. 1974. 5.50 o.p. (ISBN 0-915230-06-2). Rue Morgue.
--Dare. (Science Fiction Ser.). 1980. lib. bdg. 11.95 (ISBN 0-8398-2621-4). Gregg.
--The Dark Design. LC 77-5138. (Riverworld Ser.). (YA) 1977. pap. 2.25 (ISBN 0-425-03831-9, Dist. by Putnam). Berkley Pub.
--Doc Savage. LC 81-80083. 288p. 1981. pap. 2.50 (ISBN 0-87216-854-9). Playboy Pbks.
--The Fabulous Riverboat. 256p. 1973. pap. 2.25 (ISBN 0-425-04817-9, Medallion). Berkley Pub.
--Flesh. Bd. with Lord Tyger. 1981. pap. 2.50 (ISBN 0-451-09787-4, E9787, Sig). NAL.
--The Gates of Creation. 1977. pap. 2.25 (ISBN 0-441-27389-0). Ace Bks.
--Inside Outside. (Science Fiction Ser.). 1980. lib. bdg. 11.95 (ISBN 0-8398-2622-2). Gregg.
--The Magic Labyrinth. 1981. pap. 2.75 (ISBN 0-425-04854-3). Berkley Pub.
--The Maker of Universes. rev. ed. (The World of Tiers Ser.). 224p. 1980. Repr. of 1962 ed. 15.00 (ISBN 0-932096-07-7). Phantasia Pr.
--The Maker of Universes. 1977. pap. 2.25 (ISBN 0-441-51624-6). Ace Bks.
--Mother Was a Lovely Beast. 1976. pap. 1.25 o.s.i. (ISBN 0-515-04071-1). Jove Pubns.
--Riverworld & Other Stories. (Science Fiction Ser.). 1981. lib. bdg. 15.95 (ISBN 0-8398-2618-4). Gregg.
--Riverworld War: The Suppressed Fiction of Philip Jose Farmer. 112p. 1980. pap. 6.95 o.p. (ISBN 0-933180-13-6). Ellis Pr.
--The Stone God Awakens. 192p. 1975. pap. 2.25 (ISBN 0-441-78654-5). Ace Bks.
--Strange Relations. 1978. pap. 1.75 (ISBN 0-380-00095-4, 41418). Avon.
--To Your Scattered Bodies Go. 1973. pap. 2.25 (ISBN 0-425-04816-0, Medallion). Berkley Pub.
--Tongues of the Moon. 1978. pap. 1.50 (ISBN 0-515-04595-0). Jove Pubns.
--Wind Whales of Ishmael. (Orig.). 1977. pap. 1.95 (ISBN 0-441-89240-X). Ace Bks.
Farmer, R. D. & Miller, D. L. Lecture Notes on Community Medicine. (Blackwell Scientific Pubns.). (Illus.). 1977. 12.25 (ISBN 0-632-00108-9). Mosby.
Farmer, R. D. & Hirsch, S. R., eds. The Suicide Syndrome. 272p. 1980. 40.00x (ISBN 0-85664-868-X, Pub. by Croom Helm England). State Mutual Bk.
Farmer, Richard & Hirsch, Steven, eds. The Suicide Syndrome. 268p. 1980. 37.50x (ISBN 0-85664-868-X, Pub. by Croom Helm Ltd England). Biblio Dist.
Farmer, Richard E., jt. auth. see Monahan, Lynn H.
Farmer, Richard N. & Hogue, W. Dickerson. Corporate Social Responsibility. LC 72-96061. (Illus.). 223p. 1973. pap. text ed. 9.95 (ISBN 0-574-17930-5, 13-0930); instr's guide avail. (ISBN 0-574-17931-3, 13-0931). SRA.
Farmer, Richard N., jt. auth. see Richman, Barry M.
Farmer, Robert A. One Thousand Ideas for Term Papers in American History. LC 74-77566. (One Thousand Ideas for Term Papers Ser). 160p. 1969. pap. 1.95 o.p. (ISBN 0-668-01925-5). Arc Bks.
--What You Should Know About Contracts. LC 69-11145. (Know Your Law Ser). (Illus.). 1969. lib. bdg. 4.95 o.p. (ISBN 0-668-01826-7). Arco.
Farmer, Silas. History of Detroit & Wayne County & Early Michigan: A Chronological Cyclopedia of the Past & Present. LC 68-26178. 1969. Repr. of 1890 ed. 38.00 (ISBN 0-8103-3326-0). Gale.
Farmer, Silas, jt. auth. see Hall, Theodore P.
Farmer, W. D. Homes for Pleasant Living. 28th ed. (Illus.). 1977. pap. 2.50 o.p. (ISBN 0-931518-05-9). W D Farmer.
--Homes for Pleasant Living. 35th ed. (Illus., Orig.). 1980. pap. 2.50 (ISBN 0-931518-12-1). W D Farmer.
--Homes for Pleasant Living. 36th ed. (Illus.). 72p. (Orig.). 1980. pap. 3.50 (ISBN 0-931518-13-X). W D Farmer.
--Small Homes for Pleasant Living. 35th ed. (Illus.). 1980. pap. 2.50 (ISBN 0-931518-12-1). W D Farmer.
Farmer, W. Paul, jt. ed. see Catanese, Anthony J.
Farmer, W. R. The Last Twelve Verses of Mark. LC 73-89003. (Society for New Testament Studies: Monograph Ser. No. Twenty-Five). 128p. 1974. 21.95 (ISBN 0-521-20414-3). Cambridge U Pr.
Farmer, Wesley M. Sea-Slug Gastropods. (Illus.). 177p. (Orig.). 1980. pap. 10.00 (ISBN 0-937772-00-3). Farmer Ent.
Farmer, Weston. From My Old Boat Shop: One-Lung Engines, Fantail Launches, & Other Marine Delights. LC 78-64786. (Illus.). 1979. 20.00 (ISBN 0-87742-107-2). Intl Marine.
Farmer, William R., ed. Synopticon. 1969. 80.00 (ISBN 0-521-07464-9). Cambridge U Pr.
Farmer, William R., et al. Christian History & Interpretation. 1967. 42.50 (ISBN 0-521-04981-4). Cambridge U Pr.
Farmers Weekly, ed. Farm Workshop & Maintenance. (Illus.). 192p. 1972. text ed. 15.95x (ISBN 0-8464-0404-4). Beekman Pubs.
Farmigier, André. Bonnard. Schlanoff, Althea, tr. LC 69-12442. (Library of Great Painters). (Illus.). 1969. 35.00 (ISBN 0-8109-0041-6). Abrams.
Farmilant, Eunice. The Natural Foods Sweet Tooth Cookbook. 1978. pap. 2.50 (ISBN 0-515-05826-2). Jove Pubns.
Farm Journal, Editors Of. Busy Woman's Cookbook: Containing Short-Cut Cooking & Make-Ahead Cooking. LC 71-143616. 1971. 8.95 o.p. (ISBN 0-385-02407-X). Doubleday.
Farm Journal, Editors Of & Nichols, Nell B. Farm Journal's Complete Pie Cookbook. LC 65-16174. 6.95 o.p. (ISBN 0-385-01843-6). Doubleday.
--Farm Journal's Country Cookbook. rev. & enl. ed. LC 73-175372. 480p. 1972. 10.95 (ISBN 0-385-03036-3). Doubleday.
Farm Journal, Editors Of, et al. Farm Journal's Freezing & Canning Cookbook. rev. ed. LC 77-81787. 1978. 10.95 (ISBN 0-385-13444-4). Doubleday.
Farnam, Anne, ed. see Guren, Pamela, et al.
Farnam, Anne, et al. Furniture Collections of the Essex Institute. (E. I. Museum Booklet Ser.). (Illus.). 64p. (Orig.). 1981. 4.95 (ISBN 0-88389-102-6). Essex Inst.
Farnay, Josie & Soleillant, Claude. Egypt: Activities & Projects in Color. LC 78-66309. (Illus.). 1979. 9.95 (ISBN 0-8069-4554-0); PLB 9.29 (ISBN 0-8069-4555-9). Sterling.
Farndale, W. A., jt. ed. see Leicester, J. H.

Farnell, Lewis R. The Cults of the Greek States, 5 vols. Incl. Vol. 1. Cronos, Zeus, Hera, Athena. 45.00 (ISBN 0-89241-029-9); Vol. 2. Artemis, Aphrodite. 45.00 (ISBN 0-89241-030-2); Vol. 3. Cults of the Mother of the Gods, Reah, Cybele. 45.00 (ISBN 0-89241-031-0); Vol. 4. Poseidon, Apollo. 55.00 (ISBN 0-89241-032-9); Vol. 5. Hermes, Dionysos, Hestia Hephaistos, Ares, the Minor Cults. 55.00 (ISBN 0-89241-033-7). (Illus.). 1977. Repr. 200.00 set (ISBN 0-89241-049-3). Caratzas Bros.

Farner, Donald S. & King, James R. Avian Biology, 5 vols. Vol. 1, 1971. 62.50, by subscription 52.50 (ISBN 0-12-249401-6); Vol. 2, 1972. 55.50, by subscription 47.75 (ISBN 0-12-249402-4); Vol. 3, 1973. 61.25, by subscription 52.50 (ISBN 0-12-249403-2); Vol. 4, 1974. 53.75 (ISBN 0-12-249040-1); Vol. 5, 1975. 68.50, subscription 58.50 (ISBN 0-12-249405-9). Acad Pr.

Farnette, Cherrie, et al. Kids' Stuff: Reading & Writing Readiness. LC 75-5347. (Illus.). (gr. 1-2). 1975. 10.95 (ISBN 0-913916-13-7). Incentive Pubns.

Farneworth, Ellis, tr. see Machiavelli, Niccolo.

Farnham, Emily. Charles Demuth: Behind a Laughing Mask. LC 70-108804. (Illus.). 1971. 13.95 (ISBN 0-8061-0913-0). U of Okla Pr.

Farnham, Rebecca & Link, Irene. Effects of the Works Program on Rural Relief. LC 73-165682. (FDR & the Era of the New Deal Ser). 1971. Repr. of 1938 ed. lib. bdg. 15.00 (ISBN 0-306-70345-9). Da Capo.

Farnham, Stanley E. Guide to Thermoformed Plastic Packaging: Sales Builder-Cost Cutter. LC 72-156481. 1972. 19.95 (ISBN 0-8436-1206-1). CBI Pub.

Farnham, Thomas J. Travels in the Great Western Prairies, 2 vols. in 1. LC 68-16231. (The American Scene Ser.). 612p. 1973. Repr. of 1843 ed. lib. bdg. 35.00 (ISBN 0-306-71012-9). Da Capo.

Farnie, D. A. The English Cotton Industry & the World Market 1815-1896. (Illus.). 1979. 49.50x (ISBN 0-19-822478-8). Oxford U Pr.

Farnol, Jeffrey. The Broad Highway. (Barbara Cartland's Library of Love: Vol. 16). 213p. 1980. 12.95x (ISBN 0-7156-1476-2, Pub. by Duckworth England). Biblio Dist.

Farnsworth, B. A. & Young, Larry C. Nautical Rules of the Road. 1981. 15.00x (ISBN 0-87033-275-9). Cornell Maritime.

Farnsworth, Beatrice. Aleksandra Kollontai: Socialism, Feminism, & the Bolshevik Revolution. LC 79-67775. (Illus.). xii, 448p. 1980. 28.50x (ISBN 0-8047-1073-2). Stanford U Pr.

Farnsworth, E. Allan & Young, William F. Cases & Materials on Contracts. 3rd ed. LC 80-15040. (University Casebook Ser.). 1203p. write for info. (ISBN 0-88277-009-8). Foundation Pr.

Farnsworth, Kirk E. & Lawhead, Wendell H. Life Planning. 96p. (Orig.). 1981. pap. 6.95 (ISBN 0-87784-840-8). Inter-Varsity.

Farnsworth, M. W. Harbinger Press Library. (Illus.). 1978. text ed. 24.50 scp (ISBN 0-06-042003-0, HarpC). Har-Row.

Farnworth, E. G. & Golley, F. B., eds. Fragile Ecosystems: Evaluation of Research & Applications in the Neotropics. LC 74-8290. (Illus.). 280p. 1974. pap. 12.40 (ISBN 0-387-06695-0). Springer-Verlag.

Farnworth, Warren. Clay in the Primary School. 1973. 17.95 (ISBN 0-7134-2323-4, Pub. by Batsford England). David & Charles.

Farquhar, Francis P., ed. see Brewer, William H.

Farquhar, George. Beaux' Stratagem. Hopper, Vincent F. & Lahey, Gerald B., eds. LC 62-1307. (Illus.). 1964. pap. text ed. 1.95 (ISBN 0-8120-0031-5). Barron.

--The Beaux' Stratagem. Fifer, Charles N., ed. LC 77-89834. (Regents Restoration Drama Ser.). 1977. 9.95x (ISBN 0-8032-0384-5); pap. 2.75x (ISBN 0-8032-5384-2, BB 279, Bison). U of Nebr Pr.

--Recruiting Officer. Shugrue, Michael, ed. LC 65-15341. (Regents Restoration Drama Ser). 1965. 8.95x (ISBN 0-8032-0358-6); pap. 2.35x (ISBN 0-8032-5357-5, BB 253, Bison). U of Nebr Pr.

Farquhar, J. D. The National Economy. 184p. 1975. 18.00x (ISBN 0-86003-008-3, Pub. by Allan Pubs England); pap. 9.00x (ISBN 0-86003-109-8). State Mutual Bk.

Farquhar, J. D. & Heidensohn, K. The Market Economy. 160p. 18.00x (ISBN 0-86003-004-0, Pub. by Allan Pubs England); pap. 9.00x (ISBN 0-86003-103-9). State Mutual Bk.

Farquhar, J. N. Modern Religious Movements in India: New York, 1919. LC 78-74274. (Oriental Religions Ser.: Vol. 3). 497p. 1980. lib. bdg. 55.00 (ISBN 0-8240-3909-2). Garland Pub.

--An Outline of Religious Literature of India. 1967. Repr. 6.00 (ISBN 0-89684-287-8). Orient Bk Dist.

Farquhar, James W. The Diabetic Child. (Patient Handbook Ser.). (Illus.). 96p. 1981. pap. 2.95 (ISBN 0-443-02193-7). Churchill.

Farquhar, Judith & Gajdusek, D. Carleton, eds. Kuru: Early Letters & Field Notes from the Collection of D. Carleton Gajdusek. 400p. 1980. text ed. 32.00 (ISBN 0-89004-359-0). Raven.

Farquhar, R. M., jt. auth. see York, D.

Farquharson, Arthur. Marcus Aurelius, His Life & His World. Rees, D. A., ed. & pref. by. LC 75-11854. (Illus.). 154p. 1975. Repr. of 1951 ed. lib. bdg. 13.75x (ISBN 0-8371-8139-9, FAMAU). Greenwood.

Farquharson, Charlie, pseud. Old Charlie Farquharson's Testymint. 1978. 9.95 o.s.i. (ISBN 0-685-52805-7). Vanguard.

Farquharson, R., tr. see Ibsen, Henrik.

Farr, F. A. Live to One Hundred. 200p. 1981. 28.50 o.p. (ISBN 0-686-68305-6). Porter.

Farr, Finis. Chicago. LC 72-78486. (Illus.). 1973. 12.95 o.s.i. (ISBN 0-87000-179-5). Arlington Hse.

Farr, Judith, ed. Twentieth Century Interpretations of Sons & Lovers. 1970. 7.95 o.p. (ISBN 0-13-822700-4, Spec); pap. 1.95 o.p. (ISBN 0-13-822692-X, Spec). P-H.

Farr, Kenneth R. Historical Dictionary of Puerto Rico & the U.S. Virgin Islands. LC 73-7603. (Latin American Historical Dictionaries Ser.: No. 9). 1973. 10.00 (ISBN 0-8108-0670-3). Scarecrow.

Farr, M. L. How to Know the True Slime Molds. 200p. 1981. write for info. wire coil (ISBN 0-697-04779-2). Wm C Brown.

Farr, Naunerle. Madame Curie - Albert Einstein. (Pendulum Illustrated Biography Ser.). (Illus.). (gr. 4-12). 1979. text ed. 4.50 (ISBN 0-88301-368-1); pap. text ed. 1.45 (ISBN 0-88301-356-8); wkbk. 0.95 (ISBN 0-88301-380-0). Pendulum Pr.

Farr, Naunerle C. & Fago, John N. Amelia Earhart - Charles Lindbergh. (Pendulum Illustrated Biography Ser.). (Illus.). (gr. 4-12). 1979. text ed. 4.50 (ISBN 0-88301-361-4); pap. text ed. 1.45 (ISBN 0-88301-349-5); wkbk. 0.95 (ISBN 0-88301-373-8). Pendulum Pr.

Farr, Naunerle C., jt. auth. see Fago, John N.

Farr, Roger & Roser, Nancy. Teaching a Child to Read. 514p. 1979. text ed. 16.95 (ISBN 0-15-586650-8, HC). HarBraceJ.

Farr, Sidney S. Appalachian Women: An Annotated Bibliography. LC 80-5174. 224p. 1981. price not set (ISBN 0-8131-1431-4). U Pr of Ky.

Farr, Stanley. Physics Laboratory Manual. 1977. wire coil bdg. 4.95 o.p. (ISBN 0-685-99415-5). Paladin Hse.

Farragut, Jones J. Forty Fathoms Down (The Silent Service No. 2) (Orig.). 1981. pap. 2.75 (ISBN 0-440-12655-X). Dell.

Farrall, A. W. Food Engineering Systems: Operations, Vol. No. 1. (Illus.). 1976. lib. bdg. 37.50 (ISBN 0-87055-190-6); pap. text ed. 23.50 (ISBN 0-87055-297-X). AVI.

Farrall, Arthur W. Engineering for Dairy & Food Products. 2nd ed. LC 79-1171. (Illus.). 1980. lib. bdg. 28.50 (ISBN 0-88275-859-4). Krieger.

--Food Engineering System, Vol. 2: Utilities. (Illus.). 1979. pap. text ed. 23.50 (ISBN 0-87055-283-X). AVI.

Farrand, Max. Framing of the Constitution of the United States. 1913. 20.00 (ISBN 0-300-00445-1); pap. 6.45x 1962 (ISBN 0-300-00079-0, Y53). Yale U Pr.

Farrands, Barry J. Everything You Always Wanted to Know About Solar Energy: But Didn't Know Who to Ask. Sinclair, Dale, ed. LC 80-81372. (Illus.). 425p. (Orig.). 1980. pap. 39.95x (ISBN 0-936982-00-4). Promise Corp.

Farrant, Don W., Jr. Haunted Houses of Grand Rapids. LC 79-55532. (Illus.). 72p. 1980. pap. 2.95 (ISBN 0-935604-00-6). Ivystone.

Farrar, Austin. Rebirth of Images: The Making of Saint John's Apocalypse. 7.50 (ISBN 0-8446-0617-0). Peter Smith.

Farrar, Clyde. We Need a Creed. 100p. 1981. 7.95 (ISBN 0-9605588-0-2). Farrar Pub.

Farrar, F. W. The First Book of Kings. Date not set. 16.75 (ISBN 0-86524-035-3). Klock & Klock.

--The Life & Work of St. Paul. Date not set. 2 vol. set 43.95 (ISBN 0-86524-055-8). Klock & Klock.

--The Second Book of Kings. Date not set. 16.75 (ISBN 0-86524-036-1). Klock & Klock.

Farrar, Frederick W. Eric, or Little by Little. LC 75-32199. (Classics of Children's Literature, 1621-1932: Vol. 60). (Illus.). 1976. Repr. of 1892 ed. PLB 38.00 (ISBN 0-8240-2309-9). Garland Pub.

Farrar, Frederick W; see Tayler, Charles B.

Farrar, Geraldine. Such Sweet Compulsion, the Autobiography of Geraldine Farrar. LC 70-100656. (Music Ser). 1970. Repr. of 1938 ed. lib. bdg. 25.00 (ISBN 0-306-71863-4). Da Capo.

Farrar, Harry, jt. auth. see Kelly, George V.

Farrar, Kenneth. Hurry Gringo. Ashton, Sylvia, ed. LC 78-31374. Date not set. 12.95 (ISBN 0-87949-143-4). Ashley Bks.

Farrar, Lancelot L., Jr. The Short-War Illusion: German Policy, Strategy & Domestic Affairs, August-December 1914. LC 72-95267. (Twentieth Century Ser.: No. 7). (Illus.). 207p. 1973. text ed. 5.95 (ISBN 0-87436-118-4); pap. text ed. 2.50 (ISBN 0-87436-119-2). ABC-Clio.

Farrar, Margaret. The Funk & Wagnalls-Los Angeles Crossword Treasury, 3 vols. (Funk & W Bk.). 1978. pap. 3.95 ea. o.s.i. (TYC-T); Vol. 1. (ISBN 0-308-10311-4); Vol. 2. (ISBN 0-308-10312-2); Vol. 3. (ISBN 0-308-10313-0). T Y Crowell.

Farrar, Margaret, ed. The Pocket Book of Crossword Puzzles, No. 22. (Orig.). 1980. pap. write for info. (ISBN 0-671-82919-X). PB.

Farrar, Sara. Basic Double Weave Theory. 1980. 4.95 (ISBN 0-686-27271-4). Robin & Russ.

Farre, Henry. Sky Fighters of France: Aerial Warfare, Nineteen Fourteen to Nineteen Eighteen. Gilbert, James, ed. Rush, Catharine, tr. LC 79-7252. (Flight: Its First Seventy-Five Years Ser.). (Illus.). 1979. Repr. of 1919 ed. lib. bdg. 16.00x (ISBN 0-405-12164-4). Arno.

Farre, Rowena. Gypsy Idyll: A Personal Experience Among the Romanies. LC 64-16254. (Illus.). 8.95 (ISBN 0-8149-0092-5). Vanguard.

--Seal Morning. (gr. 7-9). 1972. pap. 0.95 o.p. (ISBN 0-590-02215-6, Schol Pap). Schol Bk Serv.

Farrell, B. A. see Smith, B. Babington.

Farrell, Barry. Pat & Roald. (Illus.). 1969. 8.95 o.p. (ISBN 0-394-43997-X). Random.

Farrell, Charles. Fell's Guide to Small Boat Navigation. rev. ed. LC 61-17228. (Illus.). 1974. 8.95 (ISBN 0-8119-0049-5). Fell.

Farrell, Edward, jt. auth. see Ghani, Noordin.

Farrell, George E. Actinomycosis of the Thorax. (Illus.). 144p. 1981. 16.50- (ISBN 0-87527-205-3). Green.

Farrell, H. Clyde & Kens, Paul. Buying, Renting & Borrowing in Texas: The Rules of the Game. LC 80-52895. (Illus.). 278p. 1980. 10.95 (ISBN 0-937606-00-6); pap. 6.95 (ISBN 0-937606-01-4). Tex Consumer.

Farrell, J. G. The Siege of Krishnapur. LC 74-1228. 352p. 1974. 7.95 o.p. (ISBN 0-15-182323-5). HarBraceJ.

Farrell, Jack, jt. auth. see Grossman, William.

Farrell, Jack, et al, eds. Physical Distribution Forum. LC 72-91981. 1973. 14.95 (ISBN 0-8436-1403-X). CBI Pub.

Farrell, Jack W. Physical Distribution Case Studies. LC 72-91987. 1973. 14.95 (ISBN 0-8436-1404-8). CBI Pub.

Farrell, James T. Eight Short, Short Stories & Sketches. 1981. write for info. (ISBN 0-933292-08-2); pap. price not set (ISBN 0-933292-07-4). Arts End.

--New Year's Eve - 1929. 4.50 (ISBN 0-912292-02-4). The Smith.

--Studs Lonigan. LC 78-56426. 1979. 17.50 (ISBN 0-8149-0791-1). Vanguard.

--Studs Lonigan. 1976. pap. 2.75 (ISBN 0-380-00934-X, 31955, Bard). Avon.

--When Time Was Born. 1966. 3.50 (ISBN 0-912292-04-0); signed ltd. ed. 25.00 (ISBN 0-912292-05-9). The Smith.

Farrell, John, jt. auth. see Wright, Sean.

Farrell, John C. & Smith, Asa P., eds. Image & Reality in World Politics. LC 68-18994. (Orig.). 1968. pap. 5.00x (ISBN 0-231-08588-5). Columbia U Pr.

--Theory & Reality in International Relations. LC 68-18993. 1967. pap. 5.00x (ISBN 0-231-08587-7). Columbia U Pr.

Farrell, Kathy & Sweeney, Mary. What Can We Do Today, Mommy. (Illus.). 127p. (Orig.). 1980. 6.95 (ISBN 0-9604118-0-1). Growing Together.

Farrell, Patricia & Lundegren, Herberta M. The Process of Recreation Programming: Theory & Technique. LC 78-17100. 1978. text ed. 17.50 (ISBN 0-471-01709-4). Wiley.

Farrell, Paul V., jt. auth. see Heinritz, Stuart F.

Farrell, Paul V., ed. see National Association of Purchasing Management.

Farrell, R. B. Dictionary of German Synonyms. 3rd ed. LC 75-36175. 1977. 45.00 (ISBN 0-521-21189-1); pap. 12.95 (ISBN 0-521-29068-6). Cambridge U Pr.

Farrell, R. H. Techniques of Multivariate Calculation. (Lecture Notes in Mathematics: Vol. 520). 1976. pap. 15.60 (ISBN 0-387-07695-6). Springer-Verlag.

Farrell, Robert, jt. ed. see Dewhirst, Martin.

Farrell, Ronald A., jt. auth. see Swigert, Victoria.

Farrell, Ronald A., jt. auth. see Swigert, Victoria L.

Farrell, Susan C. Directory of Contemporary Musical Instrument Makers. LC 80-24924. 320p. 1981. text ed. 24.00x (ISBN 0-8262-0322-1). U of Mo Pr.

Farrelly, D. L. Goethe & Inner Harmony: A Study of 'Schoene Seele' in the Apprenticeship of William Meister. 220p. 1973. 10.00x (ISBN 0-7165-2157-1, Pub. by Irish Academic Pr Ireland). Biblio Dist.

Farren, Mick & Marchbank, Pearce. Elvis Presley. 1978. pap. 4.95 (ISBN 0-8256-3921-2, Omnibus). Music Sales.

Farrenc, Louise. Trio in E Minor: Opus Forty Five for Piano, Flute, (Violin) & Cello. (Women Composers Ser.). 1979. Repr. of 1862 ed. 16.95 (ISBN 0-306-79553-1). Da Capo.

Farrer, James A. Literary Forgeries. LC 68-23156. 1969. Repr. of 1907 ed. 15.00 (ISBN 0-8103-3305-8). Gale.

--Military Manners & Customs. LC 68-21771. 1968. Repr. of 1885 ed. 15.00 (ISBN 0-8103-3510-7). Gale.

Farrington, D. P., jt. auth. see West, D. J.

Farrington, G. H., jt. auth. see Scorer, C. G.

Farrior, Louise H. Una Dedicacion Valiente. Gonzalez, Justo L., tr. from Eng. 123p. (Orig., Span.). 1979. pap. 2.25 (ISBN 0-89922-134-3). Edit Caribe.

Farris, John. When Michael Calls. 1981. pap. price not set (ISBN 0-671-43118-8). PB.

Farris, Martin T. Passenger Transportation. (Illus.). 256p. 1976. ref. ed. 19.95x (ISBN 0-13-652750-7). P-H.

Farris, Martin T. & Sampson, Roy J. Public Utilities: Regulation, Management, & Ownership. LC 72-85908. 420p. 1973. text ed. 20.95 (ISBN 0-395-13884-1). HM.

Farris, Martin T., jt. auth. see Sampson, Roy.

Farris, Paul, jt. auth. see Albion, Mark S.

Farrow, Anthony. George Moore. (English Authors Ser.: No. 244). 1978. 12.50 (ISBN 0-8057-6685-5). Twayne.

Farrow, John. Damien the Leper. 1954. pap. 2.95 (ISBN 0-385-02918-7, D3, Im). Doubleday.

Farrow, Rachi. Charlie's Dream. LC 77-4320. (gr. 1-5). 1978. PLB 5.99 (ISBN 0-394-83595-6); 5.99g (ISBN 0-394-93595-0). Pantheon.

Farson, Dave, jt. auth. see Cinnamon, Kenneth.

Farson, Richard. Birthrights. LC 73-6487. 228p. 1974. 6.95 o.s.i. (ISBN 0-02-537170-3). Macmillan.

Farthing, Alison. The Mystical Beast. (Illus.). (gr. 2-5). 1978. 6.95 (ISBN 0-8038-4707-6). Hastings.

Farthing, Bill. Odiyan Country Cookbook. (Illus.). 1977. pap. 5.95 (ISBN 0-913546-19-4). Dharma Pub.

Farthing, Geoffrey. Theosophy: What's It All About. 1967. 4.95 (ISBN 0-7229-5075-6). Theos Pub Hse.

Farukhi, N. M., jt. ed. see Saha, P.

Faruqi, Harith. Law Dictionary (English-Arabic) rev. ed. 1972. 35.00x (ISBN 0-685-72049-7). Intl Bk Ctr.

Faruqi, Ziya-Ul-Hasan. Deoband School & the Demand for Pakistan. 7.00x (ISBN 0-210-33835-0). Asia.

Farwell, Edith F. A Book of Herbs. 1980. 5.95 (ISBN 0-935720-01-4). Green Hill.

Farwell, George. The House That Jack Built. (Australian Theatre Workshop Ser.). 1970. pap. text ed. 4.25x o.p. (ISBN 0-686-65319-X). Heinemann Ed.

Farwell, L. C., jt. auth. see Leffler, G. L.

Farwell, Ted, jt. auth. see Goeldner, C. R.

Farzan, Massud. Another Way of Laughter: An Anthology of Sufi Humor. 1973. pap. 1.95 o.p. (ISBN 0-525-47357-2). Dutton.

--The Tale of the Reed Pipe: Teaching of the Sufis. 1974. pap. 1.95 o.p. (ISBN 0-525-47362-9). Dutton.

Farzan, Satter, et al. A Concise Handbook of Respiratory Diseases. (Illus.). 1978. text ed. 21.95 (ISBN 0-87909-180-0). Reston.

Fasal, Paul, jt. auth. see Arnold, Harry L., Jr.

Faschingbauer, Thomas R. & Newmark, Charles S. Short Forms of the MMPI. LC 77-6934. 1978. 18.95 (ISBN 0-669-01641-1). Lexington Bks.

Faschlicht, Samuel. Tooth Mutilations & Dentistry in Pre-Columbian Mexico. (Illus.). 152p. 1976. 46.00. Quint Pub Co.

Fashoyin, Tayo. Industrial Relations in Nigeria: Development & Practice. (Illus.). 208p. 1981. pap. text ed. 11.95 (ISBN 0-582-64250-7). Longman.

Fasman, Gerald D. Handbook of Biochemistry & Molecular Biology, CRC: Proteins Section, 3 vols. 3rd ed. LC 75-29514. (Handbook Ser.). 1976. (ISBN 0-685-61396-8); Vol. 2, 790p. 59.95 (ISBN 0-87819-504-1); Vol. 3, 633p. 74.95 (ISBN 0-87819-505-X); Vol. 3. 69.95 (ISBN 0-87819-510-6). CRC Pr.

Fasman, Gerald D, ed. Handbook of Biochemistry & Molecular Biology, CRC: Nucleic Acids Section, 2 vols. 3rd ed. LC 75-29514. (Handbook Ser.). 1976. Vol. 1. 69.95 (ISBN 0-87819-506-8); Vol. 2, 923p. 74.95 (ISBN 0-87819-507-6). CRC Pr.

Faso La, see Flynn, Elizabeth & La Faso, John.

Fasold, Ralph. Tense Marking in Black English: A Linguistic and Social Analysis. (Urban Language Ser.). 1972. pap. text ed. 8.00 (ISBN 0-87281-031-3). Ctr Appl Ling.

Fasold, Ralph W., jt. auth. see Walfman, Walt.
Fasold, Ralph W. & Shuy, Roger W., eds. Studies in Language Variation: Semantics, Syntax, Phonology, Pragmatics, Social Situations. LC 77-20689. 311p. 1977. pap. text ed. 6.95 o.p. (ISBN 0-87840-209-8). Georgetown U Pr.
Fass, Arnold L. & Newman, Claire M. Unified Mathematics: Content, Methods, Materials for Elementary School Teachers. 448p. 1975. text ed. 14.95x o.p. (ISBN 0-669-89359-5). Heath.
Fass, Margot L., jt. auth. see Craytor, Josephine K.
Fass, Paula S. The Damned & the Beautiful: American Youth in the 1920's. LC 76-42644. 1979. pap. 6.95 (ISBN 0-19-502492-3, GB567, GB). Oxford U Pr.
Fass, Peter M., jt. auth. see Augustine, Don.
Fassbender, H. G. Pathology of Rheumatic Diseases. Loewi, G., tr. from Ger. (Illus.). 360p. 1975. 54.20 (ISBN 0-387-07289-6). Springer-Verlag.
Fassett, Linda, jt. auth. see Murdoch, Nancy.
Fassett, Norman C. Manual of Aquatic Plants. rev. ed. 1957. 15.00x (ISBN 0-299-01450-9). U of Wis Pr.
--Spring Flora of Wisconsin. 4th ed. LC 74-27307. 200p. 1976. 15.00 (ISBN 0-299-06750-5); pap. 5.95 (ISBN 0-299-06754-8). U of Wis Pr.
Fassler, D. & Lay, N. Encounter with a New World: A Reading-Writing Text for Speakers of English As a Second Language. 1979. pap. 7.95 (ISBN 0-13-274910-6). P-H.
Fassler, Joan. Howie Helps Himself. LC 74-12284. (Concept Bks). (Illus.). 32p. (gr. 1-3). 1975. 6.95g (ISBN 0-8075-3422-6). A Whitman.
Fast, Barbara. Risking Intimacy: Daring to Be Close, Loving, Committed. (YA) 1978. 8.95 o.p. (ISBN 0-399-11978-7, Dist. by Putnam). Berkley Pub.
Fast, Howard. Departure & Other Stories. LC 80-23584. 197p. 1980. pap. 7.95 (ISBN 0-915238-37-3). Peace Pr.
--The Establishment. 1980. pap. 3.25 o.s.i. (ISBN 0-440-12296-1). Dell.
--Freedom Road. (Literature Ser). (gr. 10-12). 1970. pap. text ed. 3.92 (ISBN 0-87720-752-6). AMSCO Sch.
--The Hessian. 1980. pap. 2.25 (ISBN 0-440-13536-2). Dell.
--The Magic Door. (Illus.). (gr. 3-7). 1980. pap. 1.95 (ISBN 0-380-51193-2, 51193, Camelot). Avon.
--Proud & the Free. 1977. pap. 1.75 o.p. (ISBN 0-449-30777-8, X777, Prem). Fawcett.
--Second Generation. 1979. pap. 3.25 (ISBN 0-440-17915-7). Dell.
Fast, Jonathan. Mortal Gods. LC 77-15901. 1978. 8.95 o.p. (ISBN 0-06-011266-2, HarpT). Har-Row.
Fast, Julius. Body Language. LC 72-106592. (Illus.). 192p. 1970. 8.95 (ISBN 0-87131-039-2). M Evans.
--The Body Language of Sex, Power & Aggression. 1978. pap. 2.25 o.p. (ISBN 0-515-05670-7). Jove Pubns.
--Body Politics. (Orig.). 1980. pap. 2.25 (ISBN 0-505-51513-X). Tower Bks.
Fast, Todd H., tr. see Dull, Elaine & Sekowsky, Jo Anne.
Fast, Todd H., tr. see Goodboy, Eadie.
Fastenrath, Fritz, ed. Railroad Track; Theory & Practice: Material Properties, Cross Sections, Welding & Treatment. Grant, Walter, tr. from Ger. LC 80-5340. (Illus.). 1980. 65.00 (ISBN 0-8044-4231-2). Ungar.
Fastnedge, R. Shearer Furniture Designs. 1966. 8.95 (ISBN 0-685-52092-7). Transatlantic.
Fata, Frank J., tr. see Ilardi, Vincent.
Fatemi, Nasrollah S., et al. Sufism: Message of Brotherhood, Harmony, & Hope. LC 75-29692. 256p. 1976. 12.00 o.p. (ISBN 0-498-01869-5). A S Barnes.
Fath, Gerald. Health Care Ministries. 2nd ed. 1980. pap. 7.50 (ISBN 0-87125-061-6). Cath Health.
Fathaly, Omar I. & Palmer, Monte. Political Development & Social Change in Libya. LC 77-712. 240p. 1980. 22.95 (ISBN 0-669-01127-3). Lexington Bks.
Fathaly, Omar I., et al. Political Development & Bureaucracy in Libya. LC 77-713. 1977. 15.95 (ISBN 0-669-01426-5). Lexington Bks.
Father of Candor. An Enquiry into the Doctrine, Lately Propagated, Concerning Libels, Warrants, & the Seizure of Papers. facsimile ed. LC 76-121100. (Civil Liberties in American History Ser.). 136p. Repr. of 1764 ed. 17.50 (ISBN 0-306-71970-3). Da Capo.
Fatio. The Happy Lioness. 113p. Date not set. lib. bdg. 7.95 (ISBN 0-07-020069-6). McGraw.
Fatio, Louise. Hector & Christina. (Illus.). (ps-3). 1977. 7.95 o.p. (ISBN 0-07-020072-6, GB); PLB 7.95 o.p. (ISBN 0-07-020073-4). McGraw.
Fatout, Paul. Meadow Lake: Gold Town. LC 69-15995. (Illus.). xiv, 178p. 1974. pap. 1.95 (ISBN 0-8032-5788-0, BB 576, Bison). U of Nebr Pr.
Fatt, Irving. Physiology of the Eye: An Introduction to the Vegetative Functions. new ed. 1978. 21.95 (ISBN 0-409-95080-7). Butterworths.
Fau, Margaret E., compiled by. Gabriel Garcia Marquez: An Annotated Bibliography, 1947-1979. LC 80-784. x, 198p. 1980. lib. bdg. 27.50 (ISBN 0-313-22224-X, FGM/). Greenwood.
Faubus, Orval E. Down from the Hills. (Illus.). 528p. 1980. text ed. 25.00. Faubus.
Fauci, Anthony S., jt. auth. see Cupps, Thomas R.
Faudel-Phillips, H. Breaking & Schooling. pap. 6.85 (ISBN 0-85131-185-7, Dist. by Sporting Book Center). J A Allen.
--The Driving Book. pap. 5.25 (ISBN 0-85131-032-X, Dist. by Sporting Book Center). J A Allen.
Faughnan, Victor R. The National Shark-O-Pedia. LC 80-81115. (Illus.). 84p. 1980. pap. 5.95 (ISBN 0-9605532-0-7). Undersea Res.
Faulder, Carolyn, jt. auth. see Brown, Paul.
Faulds, I. C., ed. see English, Peter.
Faules, Don F. & Alexander, Dennis C. Communication & Social Behavior: A Symbolic Interaction Perspective. LC 76-46610. (Speech Communication Ser.). (Illus.). 1978. pap. text ed. 9.95 (ISBN 0-201-01982-5); instr's manual 3.00 (ISBN 0-201-01979-5). A-W.
Faulhaber, Charles. Latin Rhetorical Theory in Thirteenth & Fourteenth Century Castile. (U. C. Publ. in Modern Philology: Vol. 103). 1972. pap. 9.50x (ISBN 0-520-09403-4). U of Cal Pr.
Faulhaber, Martha & Underhill, Janet. Music: Invent Your Own. LC 74-13315. (Music Involvement Ser). (Illus.). 48p. (gr. 3 up). 1974. 6.50g (ISBN 0-8075-5355-7). A Whitman.
Faulhaber, Martha, jt. auth. see Hawkinson, John.
Faulk, Odie B. Arizona: A Short History. (Illus.). 1970. 7.95 (ISBN 0-8061-0917-3); pap. 4.95 (ISBN 0-8061-1222-0). U of Okla Pr.
Faulk, Odie B. & Von Kuehneli, Erik M. Great Issues 75: A Forum on Important Questions Facing the American Public, Vol. 7. LC 76-26349. (Illus.). 1976. 10.95 (ISBN 0-916624-03-X). TSU Pr.
Faulk, Odie B. & Stout, Joseph A., Jr., eds. The Mexican War: Changing Interpretations. LC 72-94389. 243p. 1973. 10.95x (ISBN 0-8040-0642-3, SB); pap. 4.95x (ISBN 0-8040-0643-1). Swallow.
Faulkner, Charles H. & McCollough, Major C. Introductory Report of the Normandy Reservoir Salvage Project: Environmental Setting, Typology & Survey. (Illus.). 1973. pap. 11.00x o.p. (ISBN 0-87049-174-1). U of Tenn Pr.
Faulkner, Claude W. Writing Good Sentences. rev. ed. 1973. pap. text ed. 9.95x (ISBN 0-684-41242-X, ScribC). Scribner.
Faulkner, Dewey R., ed. Twentieth Century Interpretations of The Pardoner's Tale. LC 73-9998. (Twentieth Century Interpretations Ser.). 128p. 1973. pap. 1.45 (ISBN 0-13-648741-6, Spec). P-H.
Faulkner, Edward H. Plowman's Folly. 154p. 1943. 7.95 (ISBN 0-8061-0124-5); pap. 3.95 (ISBN 0-8061-1169-0). U of Okla Pr.
Faulkner, Florence. Clue to Romance. 192p. (YA) 1976. 4.95 o.p. (ISBN 0-685-59252-9, Avalon). Bouregy.
--Three Little Words. 192p. (YA) 1976. 4.95 o.p. (ISBN 0-685-66573-9, Avalon). Bouregy.
Faulkner, Georgene & Becker, John. Melindy's Medal. (Illus.). (gr. 3-6). 1945. 3.50 o.p. (ISBN 0-671-32327-X); PLB 4.79 o.p. (ISBN 0-671-32057-2). Messner.
Faulkner, Harold U see Johnson, Allen & Nevins, Allan.
Faulkner, Kenneth K., jt. auth. see Lachman, Ernest.
Faulkner, Larry R., jt. auth. see Bard, Allen J.
Faulkner, Paul, jt. auth. see Brecheen, Carl.
Faulkner, Peter. Against the Age: An Introduction to William Morris. (Illus.). 192p. 1980. text ed. 28.50 (ISBN 0-04-809012-3, 2524). Allen Unwin.
--Robert Bage. (English Authors Ser.: No. 249). 1979. lib. bdg. 11.95 (ISBN 0-8057-6739-8). Twayne.
Faulkner, Peter, ed. William Morris: The Critical Heritage. (The Critical Heritage Ser.). 480p. 1973. 38.50 (ISBN 0-7100-7520-0). Routledge & Kegan.
Faulkner, Robert K. The Jurisprudence of John Marshall. LC 80-14281. xii, 307p. 1980. Repr. of 1968 ed. lib. bdg. 25.50x (ISBN 0-313-22508-7, FAJU). Greenwood.
Faulkner, T., tr. see Del Valle, Inclan.
Faulkner, Virginia, ed. Roundup: A Nebraska Reader. LC 57-8597. (Illus.). 1975. pap. 4.95 (ISBN 0-8032-5807-0, BB 593, Bison). U of Nebr Pr.
Faulkner, Virginia, ed. see Cather, Willa.
Faulkner, Waldron. Architecture & Color. 142p. 1981. Repr. of 1972 ed. text ed. price not set. Krieger.
Faulkner, Willard R. & Meites, Samuel, eds. Selected Methods for the Small Clinical Chemistry Laboratory. LC 80-66528. (Selected Methods of Clinical Chemistry Ser.: Vol. 9). 450p. 1981. 31.95 (ISBN 0-915274-13-2). Am Assn Clinical Chem.
Faulkner, William. Helen: A Courtship & Mississippi Poems--Early Poetru. 75p. 1981. 89.95. Yoknapatawpha.
--Intruder in the Dust. 1948. 8.95 (ISBN 0-394-43074-3). Random.
--Knight's Gambit. Blotner, Joseph, ed. 256p. Date not set. pap. 1.95 (ISBN 0-394-72729-0, Vin). Random.
--The Mansion. 436p. Date not set. pap. 3.95 (ISBN 0-394-70282-4, Vin). Random.
--Pylon. reissue ed. 1965. 11.95 o.p. (ISBN 0-394-44156-7). Random.
--Three Famous Short Novels. Incl. Spotted Horses; Old Man; Bear. 1958. pap. 1.95 (ISBN 0-394-70149-6, V-149, Vin). Random.
Faulkner, William, jt. auth. see Sayre, Joel.
Fauman, Beverly J & Fauman, Michael. Emergency Psychiatry. (Illus.). 150p. 1981. write for info. softcover (3046-9). Williams & Wilkins.
Fauman, Michael, jt. auth. see Fauman, Beverly J.
Faun, W. E., jt. ed. see Eisdorfer, C.
Faunce, Hilda. Desert Wife. LC 80-22163. (Illus.). xiv, 305p. 1981. 17.95x (ISBN 0-8032-1957-1); pap. 5.95 (ISBN 0-8032-6853-X, BB 761, Bison). U of Nebr Pr.
Faunce, Patricia S. Women & Ambition: A Bibliography. LC 79-18347. 724p. 1980. lib. bdg. 32.50 (ISBN 0-8108-1242-8). Scarecrow.
Faunce, William. Problems of an Industrial Society. 2nd ed. Munson, Eric M., ed. 256p. 1981. pap. text ed. 8.95 (ISBN 0-07-020105-6, C). McGraw.
Faunce, William A., ed. Readings in Industrial Sociology. (Illus., Orig.). 1967. pap. text ed. 15.95 (ISBN 0-13-756577-1). P-H.
Faupel, Charles E., jt. ed. see Inciardi, James A.
Faupel, J. H. & Fisher, F. E. Engineering Design: A Synthesis of Stress Analysis & Materials Engineering. 2nd ed. LC 80-16727. 1980. 40.00 (ISBN 0-471-03381-2, Pub. by Wiley-Interscience). Wiley.
Fauques, Marianne A. Oriental Anecdotes; or, the History of Hardun Alrachid, 1764, 2 vols. in 1. (Novel in England, 1700-1775 Ser). 1974. lib. bdg. 50.00 (ISBN 0-8240-1166-X). Garland Pub.
Faure, G. & Powell, J. L. Strontium Isotope Geology. LC 72-75720. (Minerals, Rocks & Inorganic Materials Ser.: Vol. 5). (Illus.). 200p. 1972. 17.80 (ISBN 0-387-05784-6). Springer-Verlag.
Faure, Gunter. Principles of Isotope Geology. LC 77-4479. (Intermediate Geology Ser.). 1977. text ed. 30.95 (ISBN 0-471-25665-X). Wiley.
Faurot, Albert. Concert Piano Repertoire: A Manual of Solo Literature for Artists & Performers. LC 73-15567. 1974. 12.00 (ISBN 0-8108-0685-1). Scarecrow.
Faurot, Albert, jt. auth. see Chang, Frederic Ming.
Faurot, Ruth M. Jerome K. Jerome. LC 73-15938. (English Authors Ser.: No. 164). 1974. lib. bdg. 10.95 (ISBN 0-8057-1291-7). Twayne.
Fausboll, tr. see Mueller, F. Max.
Fause, Irvin. Foreign Devils. 288p. 1976. pap. 1.75 o.p. (ISBN 0-445-08422-7). Popular Lib.
Fauset, Arthur H. Black Gods of the Metropolis: Negro Religious Cults of the Urban North. LC 75-133446. 1971. pap. 4.50x (ISBN 0-8122-1001-8, Pa Paperbks). U of Pa Pr.
Faussig, F. W. Psychology of Inventors & Money-Makers. (Illus.). 103p. 1981. 43.25 (ISBN 0-89920-020-6). Am Inst Psych.
Faust, Aly. Chemistry of Natural Waters. 450p. 1981. text ed. 40.00 (ISBN 0-250-40387-0). Ann Arbor Science.
Faust, Beatrice. Women, Sex & Pornography: A Controversial Study. (Illus.). 256p. 1981. 11.95 (ISBN 0-02-537050-2). Macmillan.
Faust, Clarence H. & Feingold, Jessica, eds. Approaches to Education for Character: Strategies for Change in Higher Education. LC 70-83386. 1969. 22.50x (ISBN 0-231-03262-5). Columbia U Pr.
Faust, David, jt. auth. see Arbuthnot, Jack.
Faust, Ernest C., et al. Craig & Faust's Clinical Parasitology. 8th ed. LC 76-85841. (Illus.). 1970. text ed. 25.50 o.p. (ISBN 0-8121-0291-6). Lea & Febiger.
Faust, Verne. Five Ways of Parenting: One That Works! LC 79-65211. 1980. 13.95 (ISBN 0-934162-01-8). Thomas Paine Pr.
--I Know More About You Than You Ever Dreamed Possible. LC 79-88004. 1980. 13.95 (ISBN 0-934162-00-X). Thomas Paine Pr.
--Self Esteem in the Classroom. LC 79-65212. 1980. 13.95 (ISBN 0-934162-02-6). Thomas Paine Pr.
Fausten, Dietrich K. The Consistency of British Balance of Payments Policies. 1975. text ed. 32.50x (ISBN 0-8419-5008-3). Holmes & Meier.
Fautsko, Timothy, jt. auth. see Jorgensen, James.
Fauvel, John, jt. auth. see Chant, Colin.
Fauver, William & Birch, Robert L. Memory Dynamics: A Complete Memory System. 1981. 49.95; spiral binding 39.95. Knowledge Bank.
Faux, I. D. & Pratt, M. J. Computational Geometry for Designing & Manufacture. LC 78-40637. 329p. 1980. pap. 22.95 (ISBN 0-470-27069-1). Halsted Pr.
Faux, Ian. Modern Lithography. 2nd ed. (Illus.). 1979. pap. 20.00 (ISBN 0-7121-1294-4). Transatlantic.
--Modern Lithography. (Illus.). 352p. 1978. pap. 15.95x (ISBN 0-7121-1294-4, Pub. by Macdonald & Evans England). Intl Ideas.
Faux, Ronald. Everest: Goddess of the Wind. (Illus.). 1978. 13.95 (ISBN 0-550-20361-3, Pub. by Two Continents); pap. 7.95 (ISBN 0-550-20351-6). Hippocrene Bks.
Favage, Paula. The Winds of Kabul. LC 80-83562. 288p. (Orig.). 1981. pap. 2.75 (ISBN 0-87216-807-7). Playboy Pbks.
Favenc, E. The History of Australian Exploration from 1788-1888: Compiled from State Documents, Private Papers & the Most Authentic Sources of Information. (Illus.). 1967. Repr. of 1888 ed. text ed. 42.75x (ISBN 90-6041-095-5). Humanities.
Favez, G. & Soliman, O. Radiological Examination of the Lung & Mediastinum with the Aid of Posterior Oblique Tomography at an Angle of 55 Degrees. (Illus., Eng., Fr. & Ger.). 1966. 16.25 o.s.i. (ISBN 0-02-844560-0). Hafner.
Favier, Jean. Guide Des Sources De l'Histoire Des Etats-Unis Dans les Archives Francaises. (Orig., Fr.). 1977. pap. text ed. 35.00x o.p. (ISBN 0-8287-1378-2). Clearwater Pub.
Faville, Mary, ed. see De Ford, Tamara.
Favre, Abbe de. Les Droits de l'Homme et du Citoyen ou la Cause des Journaliers, Ouvriers et Artisans. (Fr.). 1977. lib. bdg. 16.25x o.p. (ISBN 0-8287-0334-5); pap. text ed. 6.25x o.p. (ISBN 0-685-75744-7). Clearwater Pub.
Favret-Saada, Jeanne. Deadly Words. Cullen, Catherine, tr. from Fr. LC 79-41607. (Illus.). 1981. 45.00 (ISBN 0-521-22317-2); pap. text ed. 12.95 (ISBN 0-521-29787-7). Cambridge U Pr.
Faw, Chalmer, ed. Lardin Gabas: A Land, a People, a Church. new ed. (Illus.). 128p. 1973. 2.50 (ISBN 0-87178-511-0). Brethren.
Fawcett, Anthony. John Lennon: One Day at a Time. A Personal Biography. 2nd ed. LC 76-14557. (Illus.). 192p. 1980. pap. 8.95 (ISBN 0-394-17754-1, E772, Ever). Grove.
Fawcett, Carolyn, tr. see Chiara, M. L.
Fawcett, Chris. The New Japanese House: Ritual & Anti-Ritual Patterns of Dwelling. LC 80-8224. (Illus.). 192p. 1981. 25.00 (ISBN 0-06-433010-9, HarpT). Har-Row.
Fawcett, Clara H. Dolls: A New Guide for Collectors. 282p. 1964. 15.50 (ISBN 0-8231-3021-5). Branford.
Fawcett, Claude W. School Personnel Systems. LC 78-57240. (Illus.). write for info. (ISBN 0-669-02375-2). Lexington Bks.
Fawcett, Don. The Cell. 2nd ed. (Illus.). 928p. 1981. text ed. write for info. (ISBN 0-7216-3584-9). Saunders.
Fawcett, J. R. Applied Hydraulics & Pneumatics in Industry. (Illus.). 1968. 35.00x (ISBN 0-85461-077-4). Intl Ideas.
--Hydraulic Circuits & Control Systems. (Illus.). 32.500x o.p. (ISBN 0-685-90201-3). Intl Ideas.
--Hydraulic Servo Mechanisms & Their Applications. (Illus.). 1970. 24.95x (ISBN 0-85461-026-X). Intl Ideas.
--Pneumatic Circuits & Low Cost Automation. (Illus.). 1968. 27.50x (ISBN 0-85461-029-4). Intl Ideas.
Fawcett, Ken. High Sierra Hiking Guide to Tower Peak. Winnett, Thomas, ed. LC 74-27687. (High Sierra Hiking Guide Ser: Vol. 16). (Illus., Orig.). 1975. pap. 3.95 (ISBN 0-911824-37-5). Wilderness.
Fawcett, Stephen B., jt. auth. see Borck, Leslie E.
Fawcett, Susan & Sandberg, Alvin. Grassroots: The Writer's Workbook, Form B. LC 80-68139. 272p. 1981. pap. text ed. 9.75 (ISBN 0-395-29726-5); instr's. manual 0.50 (ISBN 0-395-29727-3). HM.
Fawcett, Susan C. & Sandberg, Alvin. Evergreen: A Guide to Basic Writing. LC 79-89001. 1980. pap. text ed. 9.95 (ISBN 0-395-28694-8); instrs' manual 0.35 (ISBN 0-395-28695-6). HM.
--Grassroots: The Writer's Workbook, Form a. LC 75-37475. 30p. 1976. pap. text ed. 9.75 (ISBN 0-395-24063-8); inst. manual 0.75 (ISBN 0-395-24274-6). HM.
Fawdry, Marguerite & Brown, Deborah. The Book of Samplers. (Illus.). 160p. 1980. 20.00 (ISBN 0-312-09006-4). St Martin.

Fawkes, Richard. Dion Boucicault: A Biography. 274p. 1980. 21.95 (ISBN 0-7043-2221-8, Pub. by Quartet England). Horizon.

Fawkes, Wally. The World of Trog. (Illus.). 96p. 1977. bds. 8.75x (ISBN 0-8476-3128-1). Rowman.

Fawtier, Robert. Capetian Kings of France: Monarchy & Nation, 987-1328. (Illus.). 1960. pap. 7.95 (ISBN 0-312-11900-3). St Martin.

Fax, Elton C. Black Artists of the New Generation. LC 77-7053. (Illus.). 1977. 9.95 (ISBN 0-396-07434-0). Dodd.

--Through Black Eyes. LC 73-9270. (Illus.). 250p. 1974. 6.95 o.p. (ISBN 0-396-06842-1). Dodd.

Fay, Allen. Making Things Better by Making Them Worse. LC 77-81960. 1978. 7.95 o.p. (ISBN 0-8015-4807-1). Dutton.

Fay, Amy. Music Study in Germany. (Music Reprint Ser.: 1979). 1979. Repr. of 1880 ed. lib. bdg. 29.50 (ISBN 0-306-79541-8). Da Capo.

Fay, Ann, jt. auth. see Nixon, Joan L.

Fay, Ann, ed. see Aylesworth, Jim.

Fay, Ann, ed. see Christian, Mary B.

Fay, Ann, ed. see Corey, Dorothy.

Fay, Ann, ed. see DeBruyn, Monica.

Fay, Ann, ed. see Delton, Judy.

Fay, Ann, ed. see Green, Phyllis.

Fay, Ann, ed. see Heide, Florence P. & Heide, Roxanne.

Fay, Ann, ed. see Nixon, Joan L.

Fay, Ann, ed. see Stanek, Muriel.

Fay, Ann, ed. see Van Steenwyk, Elizabeth.

Fay, Ann, ed. see Vigna, Judith.

Fay, Brian. Social Theory & Political Practice. (Controversies in Sociology). 1975. pap. text ed. 8.95x (ISBN 0-04-300048-7). Allen Unwin.

Fay, C. E. see Marton, L.

Fay, F. H., et al, eds. A Field Manual of Procedures for Postmortem Examination of Alaskan Marine Mammals. write for info. (ISBN 0-914500-09-0). U of AK Inst Marine.

Fay, Gordon. Rockhound's Manual. (Illus.). 300p. (Orig.). 1973. pap. 4.95 (ISBN 0-06-463323-3, EH 323, EH). Har-Row.

Fay, Gordon S. The Rockhound's Manual. LC 72-79661. (Illus.). 278p. (YA) 1972. 10.95 o.p. (ISBN 0-06-011218-2, HarpT). Har-Row.

Fay, J. D. Theta Functions of Riemann Surfaces. (Lecture Notes in Mathematics: Vol. 352). 137p. 1973. pap. 8.70 (ISBN 0-387-06517-2). Springer-Verlag.

Fay, Jennifer & Adams, Caren. What Do I Say? Protecting Your Child from Sexual Assault. (Illus.). 96p. (Orig.). 1981. pap. 3.95 (ISBN 0-915166-24-0). Impact Pubs Cal.

Fay, John. The Helicopter: History, Piloting & How It Flies. LC 76-54073. (Illus.). 1977. 15.95 (ISBN 0-7153-7249-1). David & Charles.

Fay, Leo, jt. auth. see Smith, Carl.

Fay, Thomas A. And Smoking Flax Shall He Not Quench: Reflections on New Testament Themes. LC 79-57202. 170p. 1979. 8.95 (ISBN 0-936100-00-1). Paraclete Bks.

Faye, Eleanor E. & Hood, Clare M. Low Vision: A Symposium Marking the 20th Anniversary of the Lighthouse Low Vision Service. (Illus.). 320p. 1975. 27.50 (ISBN 0-398-03372-2). C C Thomas.

Fayen, E. G., jt. auth. see Lancaster, F. W.

Fayerweather Street School. The Kids' Book of Divorce. Rofes, Eric, ed. 112p. 1981. 7.95 (ISBN 0-86616-003-5). Lewis Pub Co.

Fayette, Marie-Madeleine De La see De La Fayette, Marie-Madeleine.

Fayle, H. & Newham, A. T. The Waterford & Tramore Railway. (Illus.). 56p. 1972. 5.95 (ISBN 0-7153-5518-X). David & Charles.

Fazal, M. A. Judicial Control of Administrative Action in India & Pakistan: A Comparative Study of Principles & Remedies. 1961. 18.95x o.p. (ISBN 0-19-825186-6). Oxford U Pr.

Fazia, Alba della. Jean Anouilh. (World Authors Ser.: France: No. 76). lib. bdg. 10.95 (ISBN 0-8057-2048-0). Twayne.

Fazio, Frank, et al. Physical Science with Consumer & Environmental Applications: Laboratory Investigations. 1978. pap. text ed. 7.25 (ISBN 0-8403-1075-7). Kendall-Hunt.

Fazio, Michael W. & Prenshaw, Peggy W., eds. Order & Image in the American Small Town. LC 80-24300. (Southern Quarterly Ser.). 1981. price not set (ISBN 0-87805-130-9). U Pr of Miss.

Fazio, Rebecca S. The Do-Anything Wagon. 32p. (gr. 3-5). 1978. 2.95 (ISBN 0-8059-2593-7). Dorrance.

Fazzini, Eugene, et al. A Manual for Surgical Pathologists. (Illus.). 112p. 1972. pap. 12.75 photocopy ed., spiral bdg. (ISBN 0-398-02277-1). C C Thomas.

Fazzolare, Rocco A. & Smith, Craig B. Changing Energy Use Futures: Second International Conference on Energy Use Management, October 1979, L. A., Ca. (Illus.). 1979. 440.00 (ISBN 0-08-025099-8); pap. 350.00 (ISBN 0-08-025100-5). Pergamon.

Fbursk, Dale A., ed. see Konizeski, Dick.

Fea, Allan. Secret Chambers & Hiding-Places. rev. ed. 3rd ed. LC 79-155739. 1971. Repr. of 1901 ed. 20.00 (ISBN 0-8103-3385-6). Gale.

Feachem, Richard. Guide to Prehistoric Scotland. 1977. 19.95 (ISBN 0-7134-3264-0, Pub. by Batsford England). David & Charles.

Feagans, Raymond J. The Railroad That Ran by the Tide. (Illus.). 146p. Date not set. Repr. of 1972 ed. 15.00 (ISBN 0-8310-7042-0). Howell-North.

Feagin, Joe R. Racial & Ethnic Relations. LC 77-27306. (P-H Ser. in Sociology). (Illus.). 1978. ref. 17.95 (ISBN 0-13-749887-X). P-H.

--The Urban Scene: Myths & Realities. 1973. pap. text ed. 4.95 o.p. (ISBN 0-394-31647-9). Random.

Feagin, Joe R., jt. ed. see Stephan, Walter G.

Feagles, Anita M. The Year the Dreams Came Back. (gr. 7-9). 1978. pap. 1.25 (ISBN 0-671-29875-5). Archway.

Fear, David E. Technical Communication. 1977. pap. 9.95x (ISBN 0-673-15017-8). Scott F.

--Technical Communication. 2nd ed. 1981. pap. text ed. 9.95x (ISBN 0-673-15401-7). Scott F.

Fear, David E. & Schiffhorst, Gerald J. Short English Workbook. 1979. pap. text ed. 4.95x (ISBN 0-673-15161-1). Scott F.

Fear, W. H. Warriors with Wings. pap. 2.00x (ISBN 0-392-07289-0, SpS). Soccer.

Feare, Ronald E. Practice with Idioms. 192p. 1980. pap. text ed. 5.95x (ISBN 0-19-502782-5). Oxford U Pr.

Fearn, David A. Food & Beverage Management. 320p. 1973. 29.95 (ISBN 0-408-70158-7). Transatlantic.

Fearn, Leif, et al. Human Development Program Supplementary Idea Guide. rev. ed. 1975. 7.95 (ISBN 0-86584-008-3). Human Dev Train.

Fearn, Robert M. Labor Economics: The Emerging Synthesis. 288p. 1981. text ed. 18.95 (ISBN 0-87626-473-9). Winthrop.

Fearne, Charles. An Essay on the Learning of Contingent Remainders & Executory Devises, 2 vols. 10th ed. Butler, Charles & Smith, Josiah W., eds. 1980. Repr. of 1844 ed. Set. PLB 95.00x (ISBN 0-8377-0539-8). Rothman.

Fearnside, W. Ward. About Thinking. 1980. pap. text ed. 10.30 (ISBN 0-13-000844-3). P-H.

Fearon, et al. Fundamentals of Production Operations Management. 171p. 1979. pap. text ed. 6.95 (ISBN 0-8299-0269-4); instrs.' manual avail. (ISBN 0-8299-0478-6). West Pub.

Fearon, Peter, jt. auth. see Aldcroft, Derek.

Fearon, Peter, jt. ed. see Aldcroft, Derek H.

Fears, J. Wayne. Trout Fishing the Southern Appalachians. LC 79-1277. (Illus.). 192p. 1979. lib. bdg. 10.25 o.p. (ISBN 0-914788-10-8). East Woods.

Feather, Frank, ed. Through the Eighties: Thinking Globally, Acting Locally. 1980. 12.50 (ISBN 0-686-64296-1). World Future.

Feather, L. Inside Jazz. LC 77-23411. (Roots of Jazz Ser.). (Illus.). 1977. lib. bdg. 17.50 (ISBN 0-306-77437-2); pap. 5.95 (ISBN 0-306-80076-4). Da Capo.

Feather, Leonard. The Book of Jazz. 1976. pap. 1.95 (ISBN 0-440-30680-9, LE). Dell.

Feather, Leonard G., tr. see Goffin, Robert.

Feather, Norman T., ed. Expectations & Actions: Expectancy-Value Models in Psychology. 400p. 1981. professional reference text 24.95 (ISBN 0-89859-080-9). L Erlbaum Assocs.

Featherly, Henry I. Taxonomic Terminology of the Higher Plants. 1965. Repr. of 1954 ed. 10.50 o.s.i. (ISBN 0-02-844590-2). Hafner.

Featherman, Buzz. The Fun & Fantasy Book. LC 80-54612. (Illus.). 144p. (Orig.). 1981. pap. text ed. 6.95 (ISBN 0-932238-04-1). Word Shop.

--The Fun & Fantasy Book. new ed. (Illus.). 1980. 6.95 (ISBN 0-932238-03-3). Word Shop.

Featherstone, David. The Diana Show, Pictures Through a Plastic Lens. LC 80-80296. (Untitled 21 Ser.). (Illus., Orig.). 1980. pap. 7.95 (ISBN 0-933286-17-1). Friends Photography.

Featherstone, Donald. Weapons & Equipment of the Victorian Soldier. (Illus.). 1978. 19.95 (ISBN 0-7137-0847-6, Pub. by Blandford Pr England). Sterling.

Featherstone, Donald & Robinson, Keith. Battles with Model Tanks. (Illus.). 160p. 1980. pap. 8.95 (ISBN 0-88254-541-8, Pub. by MacDonald & Jane's England). Hippocrene Bks.

Featherstone, Donald F. Skirmish Wargaming. Reach, D., ed. (Illus.). 1979. pap. 11.75 o.p. (ISBN 0-85059-392-1). Aztex.

Featherstone, Helen. A Difference in the Family: Life with a Disabled Child. LC 79-56668. 262p. 1980. 13.95 (ISBN 0-465-01654-5). Basic.

Feaver, Douglas. El Mundo En Que Vivio Jesus. Cuadra, Samuel, tr. from Eng. Orig. Title: The World to Which Jesus Came. 128p. (Orig., Span.). 1973. pap. write for info o.p. (ISBN 0-89922-023-1). Edit Caribe.

Feaver, William. The Art of John Martin. (Illus.). 360p. 1975. 36.00x (ISBN 0-19-817334-2). Oxford U Pr.

Feazel, Charles E., ed. see Membrane Processes for Industry, Symposium, May 19-20,1966.

Feber, Walter La see La Feber, Walter.

February, V. A. The Coloured Image. (Monographs from the African Studies Center,Leiden). 256p. 1981. price not set (ISBN 0-7103-0002-6). Routledge & Kegan.

FEBS Meeting, 12th, Dresden, 1978. Gene Function: Proceedings. Rosenthal, S., et al, eds. (Federation of European Biochemical Society Ser.: Vol. 51). (Illus.). 1979. 60.00 (ISBN 0-08-023175-6). Pergamon.

--Regulation of Secondary Product & Plant Hormone Metabolism: Proceedings. Luckner, M. & Schreiber, K., eds. (Federation of European Biochemical Society Ser.: Vol. 55). (Illus.). 1979. 60.00 (ISBN 0-08-023179-9). Pergamon.

FEBS Symposium on DNA, Liblice, 24-29 September, 1979. DNA: Recombination, Interactions & Repair. Zadrazil, S. & Sponar, J., eds. (Vol. 63). (Illus.). 600p. 1980. 92.00 (ISBN 0-08-025494-2). Pergamon.

Fecher, Constance. The Lovely Wanton. 1977. pap. 1.75 o.s.i. (ISBN 0-440-16982-8). Dell.

Fechter, Alan. Forecasting the Impact of Technological Change on Manpower Utilization & Displacement: An Analytic Summary. 1975. pap. 2.50 o.p. (ISBN 0-87766-138-3, 99000). Urban Inst.

Fedden, Robin, ed. Treasures of the National Trust. (Illus.). 1976. 24.00 (ISBN 0-224-01241-X). Transatlantic.

Fedder, Edwin H., ed. Defense Politics of the Atlantic Alliance. 180p. 1980. 21.95 (ISBN 0-03-058018-8). Praeger.

Fedder, Norman, ed. Wrestling with God: An Anthology of Contemporary Religious Drama. 1981. pap. 15.00 (ISBN 0-87602-018-X). Anchorage.

Fedder, Ruth. Guidance in the Homeroom. LC 67-24642. 1967. pap. text ed. 5.00x (ISBN 0-8077-1308-2). Tchrs Coll.

Fedder, Ruth & Gabaldon, Jacqueline. No Longer Deprived: Using Minority Cultures & Languages in Educating Disadvantaged Children & Their Teachers. LC 78-76318. 1970. pap. text ed. 6.50x (ISBN 0-8077-1312-0). Tchrs Coll.

Feder, Bernard. Process of American Government: Cases & Problems. (Illus.). (gr. 9-12). 1972. text ed. 9.99 (ISBN 0-8107-2025-6, 9915); tchrs' guide 2.70 (ISBN 0-8107-2026-4, 9916); objectives, teaching techniques & evaluation procedures 2.70 (ISBN 0-8107-2041-8, 9917); tests 1.02 (ISBN 0-8107-2042-6, 9918). Bowmar-Noble.

Feder, J., et al, eds. National Health Insurance: Conflicting Goals & Policy Choices. LC 80-80045. 721p. 1980. text ed. 25.00x; pap. 12.50 (ISBN 0-87766-271-1). Urban Inst.

Feder, Judith. Medicare: The Politics of Federal Hospital Insurance. LC 77-4611. (Illus.). 1977. 19.95 (ISBN 0-669-01447-8). Lexington Bks.

Feder, Judith & Holahan, John. Financing Health Care for the Elderly: Medicare, Medicaid & Private Health Insurance. (Health Policy & the Elderly Ser.). 106p. 1979. pap. 5.50 (ISBN 0-87766-244-4, 24900). Urban Inst.

Feder, Lillian. Crowell's Handbook of Classical Literature: A Modern Guide to the Drama, Poetry, & Prose of Greece & Rome, with Biographies of Their Authors. LC 64-18162. 1980. pap. 7.95 (ISBN 0-06-090802-5, CN 802, CN). Har-Row.

--Crowell's Handbook of Classical Literature. 1964. 12.95 o.p. (ISBN 0-690-22537-7, TYC-T). T Y Crowell.

Feder, William A., jt. auth. see Manning, William J.

Federal Aviation Administration. A&P Mechanics Airframe Written Examination Questions. (Aviation Maintenance Training Course Ser.). (Illus.). 113p. 1979. pap. 3.75 (ISBN 0-89100-158-1, EA-AC65-20). Aviation Maintenance.

--A&P Mechanic's Certification Guide. 4th ed. (Aviation Maintenance Training Course Ser.). 64p. 1976. pap. 2.50 (ISBN 0-89100-082-8, EA-AC65-2D). Aviation Maintenance.

--A&P Mechanics General Written Examination Questions. (Aviation Maintenance Training Course Ser.). 88p. 1979. pap. 3.75 (ISBN 0-89100-157-3, EA-AC65-20). Aviation Maintenance.

--A&P Mechanics Powerplant Written Examination Questions. (Aviation Maintenance Training Course Ser.). (Illus.). 99p. 1979. pap. 3.75 (ISBN 0-89100-159-X, EA-AC65-22). Aviation Maintenance.

--Airframe & Powerplant Mechanics Certification Guide: Ac 65-2d. pap. 2.50 (ISBN 0-685-46348-6). Aviation.

--Airframe & Powerplant Mechanics Powerplant Handbook: Ac 65-12a. pap. 8.75x (ISBN 0-89100-079-8). Aviation Maint.

--Airline Transport Pilot: Airplane (Air Carrier) Written Test Guide. (Pilot Training Ser.). (Illus.). 189p. 1979. pap. 5.95 (ISBN 0-89100-199-9, EA-AC-61-87). Aviation Maintenance.

--Airman's Information Manual. (Pilot Training Ser.). (Illus.). 327p. 1980. pap. 4.95 (ISBN 0-89100-149-2, EA-149-2). Aviation Maintenance.

--Aviation Instructor's Handbook. (Pilot Training Ser.). 170p. 1977. pap. 3.75 (ISBN 0-89100-170-0, E*A-A*C60-14). Aviation Maintenance.

--Aviation Weather. 2nd ed. (Pilot Training Ser.). (Illus.). 219p. 1975. pap. 7.00 (ISBN 0-89100-160-3, E*A-A*C61-006A). Aviation Maintenance.

--Aviation Weather: Ac 00-6A. pap. 7.00 (ISBN 0-685-46352-4, Pub. by Cooper). Aviation.

--Aviation Weather Services. 3rd ed. (Pilot Training Ser.). (Illus.). 123p. 1979. pap. 4.50 (ISBN 0-89100-161-1, E*A-A*C61-0045B). Aviation Maintenance.

--Basic Helicopter Handbook. 3rd ed. (Pilot Training Ser.). (Illus.). 111p. 1978. pap. 3.75 (ISBN 0-89100-162-X, E*A-A*C61-13B). Aviation Maintenance.

--Commercial Pilot Flight Test Guide. 2nd ed. (Pilot Training Ser.: Pilot Training Ser.). 70p. 1975. pap. 1.75 (ISBN 0-89100-172-7, E*A-A*C61-55A). Aviation Maintenance.

--Commercial Pilot Written Test Guide. 3rd ed. (Pilot Training Ser.). (Illus.). 141p. 1979. pap. 4.75 (ISBN 0-89100-110-7, E*A-A*C61-71B). Aviation Maintenance.

--Federal Aviation Regulations for Aviation Mechanics. 6th ed. (Aviation Maintenance Training Course Ser.). 442p. 1980. pap. 10.00 (ISBN 0-89100-177-8, E*A-F*A*R-1E). Aviation Maintenance.

--Federal Aviation Regulations for Pilots, Nineteen Eighty. Aviation Book Company, ed. 128p. 1980. pap. 3.50 (ISBN 0-911721-66-5). Aviation.

--Federal Aviation Regulations Handbook for Pilots. 2nd ed. (Pilot Training Ser.). (Illus.). 448p. 1980. pap. 6.95 (ISBN 0-89100-185-9, E*A-R*P-1A). Aviation Maintenance.

--Flight Instructor Airplane Written Test Guide: Ac 61-72b. 1980. pap. 6.00 (ISBN 0-685-55081-8, Pub. by Flightshop). Aviation.

--Flight Instructor Written Test Guide. 3rd ed. (Pilot Training Ser.). (Illus.). 138p. 1979. pap. 6.00 (ISBN 0-89100-137-9, E*A-A*C61-72B). Aviation Maintenance.

--Flight Training Handbook. LC 80-70552. (Illus.). 352p. 1981. 12.95 (ISBN 0-385-17599-X). Doubleday.

--Flight Training Handbook. 2nd ed. (Pilot Training Ser.). (Illus.). 325p. 1980. pap. 7.40 (ISBN 0-89100-165-4, EA-AC61-21A). Aviation Maintenance.

--Instrument Flying Handbook. 3rd ed. (Pilot Training Ser.). (Illus.). 274p. 1971. pap. 6.00 (ISBN 0-89100-164-6, E*A-A*C61-27B). Aviation Maintenance.

--Instrument Flying Handbook: AC 61-27b. pap. 6.00 (ISBN 0-685-46357-5, Pub. by Cooper). Aviation.

--Instrument Rating Written Test Guide. 5th ed. (Pilot Bks.). (Illus.). 200p. 1977. pap. 3.75 (ISBN 0-89100-169-7, E*A-A*C61-8D). Aviation Maintenance.

--Pilot's Handbook of Aeronautical Knowledge: Ac 61-23b. pap. 11.00 (ISBN 0-685-46359-1, Pub. by Cooper). Aviation.

--Pilot's Handbook of Aeronautical Knowledge. 2nd ed. (Pilot Training Ser.). (Illus.). 207p. 1971. pap. 7.50 (ISBN 0-89100-100-X, E*A-A*C61-23A). Aviation Maintenance.

--Pilots Weight & Balance Handbook: FAA AC 91-23A. (Illus.). 1977. pap. 3.25 (ISBN 0-685-53322-0, Pub. by Cooper). Aviation.

--Private Pilot-Airplane Written Test Guide. 4th ed. (Pilot Training Ser.). (Illus.). 148p. 1979. pap. 3.00 (ISBN 0-89100-166-2, E*A-A*C61-32C). Aviation Maintenance.

--Private Pilot Flight Test Guide. 2nd ed. (Pilot Training Ser.). 92p. 1975. pap. 1.35 (ISBN 0-89100-171-9, E*A-A*C61-54A). Aviation Maintenance.

Federal Aviation Administration & Aviation Book Company Editors. IFR Pilot Exam-O-Grams. (Illus.). 96p. 1980. pap. 2.95 (ISBN 0-911721-79-7). Aviation.

--VFR Pilot Exam-O-Grams. (Illus.). 144p. 1980. pap. 3.50 (ISBN 0-911721-78-9). Aviation.

Federal Aviation Agency. Pilot Instruction Manual. 7.95 (ISBN 0-385-01046-X). Doubleday.

Federal Communications Commission Planning Conference November 8 & 9, 1976 & Hopewell, Lynn. Computers & Communications: Proceedings. (Illus.). 197p. 1976. pap. 10.00 (ISBN 0-88283-022-8). AFIPS Pr.

Federal Construction Council - Building Research Advisory Board. Crack Control in Concrete Masonry Unit Construction. 1964. pap. 3.00 (ISBN 0-309-01198-1). Natl Acad Pr.

--Evaluation of Components for Underground Heat Distribution Systems. 1964. pap. 2.75 (ISBN 0-309-01196-5). Natl Acad Pr.

--Supplementary Field Investigation of Underground Heat Distribution Systems. 1966. pap. 3.25 (ISBN 0-309-01481-6). Natl Acad Pr.

Federal Electric Corporation. A Programmed Introduction to PERT: Program Evaluation & Review Technique. 1963. pap. 15.95 (ISBN 0-471-25680-3, Pub. by Wiley-Interscience). Wiley.

--Special Purpose Transistors: A Self-Instructional Programed Manual. (Illus.). 1966. pap. 11.95 (ISBN 0-13-826537-2). P-H.

Federal Energy Administration. Guide to Energy Conservation in Agriculture, 6 vols. (Reprint Ser.: No. 1). 1980. pap. 29.50 (ISBN 0-89934-039-3). Solar Energy Info.

--Project Independence Blueprint: Final Task Force Report, Solar Energy. 564p. Repr. of 1974 ed. 49.50 (ISBN 0-89934-062-8, V954-PP). Solar Energy Info.

Federal Housing Administration - Building Research Advisory Board. Apartment House Incinerators: Flue-Fed. 1965. pap. 3.00 (ISBN 0-309-01280-5). Natl Acad Pr.

--Criteria for Hydraulic Fills. 1962. pap. 3.75 (ISBN 0-309-01076-4). Natl Acad Pr.

--Heating & Air-Conditioning Ducts Encased in & Under Concrete Slabs-On-Ground. 1961. pap. 3.00 (ISBN 0-309-00838-7). Natl Acad Pr.

--Protection for Wells & Suction Lines for Individual Water Supply Systems. 1962. pap. 3.00 o.p. (ISBN 0-309-00826-3). Natl Acad Pr.

Federal Reserve Bank of Kansas City. Western Water Resources: Coming Problems & the Policy Alternatives. LC 80-14142. 376p. 1980. lib. bdg. 25.00x (ISBN 0-86531-036-X). Westview.

Federal Writer's Project. American Stuff. (FDR & the Era of the New Deal Ser.). 1976. Repr. of 1937 ed. lib. bdg. 29.50 (ISBN 0-306-70806-X). Da Capo.

Federal Writers' Project. Here's New England: A Guide to Vacationland. 1939. Repr. 29.00 (ISBN 0-403-02207-X). Somerset Pub.

--Idaho: A Guide in Word & Picture. 1937. Repr. 45.00 (ISBN 0-403-02163-4). Somerset Pub.

Federal Writers Project. Illinois: A Descriptive & Historical Guide. LC 72-145010. (Illus.). 1971. Repr. of 1947 ed. 59.00 (ISBN 0-403-01292-9). Somerset Pub.

Federal Writers' Project. Indiana: A Guide to the Hoosier State. 564p. 1941. Repr. 49.00 (ISBN 0-403-02165-0). Somerset Pub.

--Iowa: A Guide to the Hawkeye State. 583p. 1938. Repr. 48.00 (ISBN 0-403-02166-9). Somerset Pub.

--Kansas: A Guide to the Sunflower State. 538p. 1939. Repr. 49.00 (ISBN 0-403-02167-7). Somerset Pub.

--Kentucky: A Guide to the Bluegrass State. 492p. 1939. Repr. 45.00 (ISBN 0-403-02168-5). Somerset Pub.

--Lay My Burden Down: A Folk History of Slavery. 285p. 1945. Repr. 39.00 (ISBN 0-403-02212-6). Somerset Pub.

--Los Angeles: A Guide to the City & Its Environs. 1941. Repr. 39.00 (ISBN 0-403-02202-9). Somerset Pub.

--Louisiana: A Guide to the State. 711p. 1941. Repr. 69.00 (ISBN 0-403-02169-3). Somerset Pub.

--Maine: A Guide Down East. 476p. 1936. Repr. 49.00 (ISBN 0-403-02170-7). Somerset Pub.

--Maryland: A Guide to the Old Line State. 1940. Repr. 49.00 (ISBN 0-403-02171-5). Somerset Pub.

--Massachusetts: A Guide to Its Places & People. 675p. 1937. Repr. 49.00 (ISBN 0-403-02150-2). Somerset Pub.

--Minnesota: A State Guide. 545p. 1938. Repr. 49.00 (ISBN 0-403-02173-1). Somerset Pub.

--Mississippi: A Guide to the Magnolia State. 545p. 1938. Repr. 49.00 (ISBN 0-403-02174-X). Somerset Pub.

--Montana: A State Guide Book. 430p. 1939. Repr. 45.00 (ISBN 0-403-02176-6). Somerset Pub.

--Nebraska: A Guide to the Cornhusker State. 424p. 1939. Repr. 39.00 (ISBN 0-403-02177-4). Somerset Pub.

--Nevada: A Guide to the Silver State. 1940. Repr. 45.00 (ISBN 0-403-02178-2). Somerset Pub.

--New Mexico: A Guide to the Colorful State. 1940. Repr. 49.00 (ISBN 0-403-02181-2). Somerset Pub.

--New Orleans: A City Guide. 416p. 1938. Repr. 45.00 (ISBN 0-403-02203-7). Somerset Pub.

--New York: A City Guide. LC 39-27593. (Illus.). 708p. 1939. Repr. 59.00 (ISBN 0-403-02921-X). Somerset Pub.

--New York State: A Guide to the Empire State. 782p. 1940. Repr. 59.00 (ISBN 0-403-02151-0). Somerset Pub.

--North Carolina: A Guide to the Old North State. 649p. 1939. Repr. 54.00 (ISBN 0-403-02182-0). Somerset Pub.

--The Ohio Guide. 634p. 1940. Repr. 49.00 (ISBN 0-403-02184-7). Somerset Pub.

--Oklahoma: A Guide to the Sooner State. 532p. Repr. 49.00 (ISBN 0-403-02185-5). Somerset Pub.

--Oregon: End of the Trail. 548p. 1941. Repr. 49.00 (ISBN 0-403-02186-3). Somerset Pub.

Federal Writers Project. Oregon Trail: The Missouri River to the Pacific Ocean. LC 70-145012. (Illus.). 1971. Repr. of 1939 ed. 35.00 (ISBN 0-403-01290-2). Somerset Pub.

Federal Writers' Project. Rhode Island: A Guide to the Smallest State. 500p. 1937. Repr. 45.00 (ISBN 0-403-02188-X). Somerset Pub.

--San Francisco. 538p. 1940. Repr. 45.00 (ISBN 0-403-02205-3). Somerset Pub.

Federal Writers Project. South Carolina: A Guide to the Palmetto State. 514p. 1941. Repr. 45.00 (ISBN 0-403-02189-8). Somerset Pub.

Federal Writers' Project. South Dakota: A Guide to the State. 421p. 1938. Repr. 45.00 (ISBN 0-403-02190-1). Somerset Pub.

--Tennessee: A Guide to the State. 558p. 1939. Repr. 49.00 (ISBN 0-403-02191-X). Somerset Pub.

--Texas: A Guide to the Lone Star State. LC 40-10658. 717p. 59.00 (ISBN 0-403-02192-8). Somerset Pub.

--Utah: A State Guide. 1941. Repr. 49.00 (ISBN 0-403-02193-6). Somerset Pub.

--Vermont: A Guide to the Green Mountain State. 1937. Repr. 45.00 (ISBN 0-403-02194-4). Somerset Pub.

--Washington: A Guide to the Evergreen State. 688p. 1941. Repr. 49.00 (ISBN 0-403-02196-0). Somerset Pub.

--Washington: City & Capital. 528p. 1942. Repr. 54.00 (ISBN 0-403-02237-1). Somerset Pub.

--Wisconsin: A State Guide. 49.00 (ISBN 0-403-02198-7). Somerset Pub.

Federal Writer's Project see Hansen, Harry.

Federal Writers' Project, jt. ed. see Truett, Randle B.

Federal Writer's Project of the Works Progress Administration. Nebraska: A Guide to the Cornhusker State. LC 78-26756. (Illus.). 1979. 15.95x (ISBN 0-8032-1953-9); pap. 5.50 (ISBN 0-8032-6851-3, BB690, Bison). U of Nebr Pr.

Federal Writers' Project of the Works Projects Administration. Wyoming: A Guide to Its History, Highways, & People. LC 80-23038. (Illus.). xxxviii, 490p. 1981. 24.50x (ISBN 0-8032-1958-X); pap. 9.75 (ISBN 0-8032-6854-8, BB 757, Bison). U of Nebr Pr.

Federal Writers' Projects. U.S. One: Maine to Florida. 344p. 1938. Repr. 39.00 (ISBN 0-403-02208-8). Somerset Pub.

Federation of Feminist Women's Health Centers. A New View of a Woman's Body: A Totally Illustrated Guide. 1981. 14.95 (ISBN 0-671-41214-0); pap. 6.95 (ISBN 0-671-41215-9). S&S.

Federbush, Marcia. An Action Proposal. rev. ed. 1974. pap. 1.20 o.p. (ISBN 0-685-56767-2). Know Inc.

Federer, H. Geometric Measure Theory. LC 69-16846. (Die Grundlehren der Mathematischen Wissenschaften: Vol. 153). 1969. 62.10 (ISBN 0-387-04505-8). Springer-Verlag.

Federico, Pat A., et al. Management Information Systems & Organizational Behavior. Brun, Kim & McCalla, Douglas B., eds. LC 80-15174. 204p. 1980. 20.95 (ISBN 0-03-057021-2). Praeger.

Federico, Ronald C. Sociology. 2nd ed. LC 78-18637. (Illus.). 1979. text ed. 17.95 (ISBN 0-201-03092-6); instr's man. avail. (ISBN 0-201-03093-4). A-W.

Federighi, Francis & Reilly, Edward D. Weighting for Baudot & Other Problems for You & Your Computer. (Illus.). 1978. 9.95 (ISBN 0-89529-061-8). Avery Pub.

Federlin, Anne C. Play in Preschool Mainstreamed & Handicapped Settings. LC 80-65612. 135p. 1981. perfect bdg. 10.50 (ISBN 0-86548-035-4). Century Twenty One.

Federlin, K. Immunopathology of Insulin: Clinical & Experimental Studies. LC 71-154799. (Monographs on Endocrinology: Vol. 6). (Illus.). 1971. 31.10 (ISBN 0-387-05408-1). Springer-Verlag.

Federlin, Tom. A Comprehensive Bibliography on American Sign Language: A Resource Manual. LC 79-54021. 1979. pap. 6.95 (ISBN 0-9603136-0-5). Federlin.

Federman, Raymond. Journey to Chaos: Samuel Beckett's Early Fiction. 1965. 18.00x (ISBN 0-520-00398-5). U of Cal Pr.

Federman, Raymond, ed. Cinq Nouvelles Nouvelles. LC 70-115011. (Illus., Orig., Fr.). 1970. pap. text ed. 5.95x (ISBN 0-89197-079-7). Irvington.

--Surfiction: Fiction Now & Tomorrow. rev. ed. 1981. pap. 7.95. Swallow.

Federman, Raymond, jt. ed. see Graver, Lawrence.

Federoff, S. & Hertz, L., eds. Advances in Cellular Neurobiology, Vol. 2. 1981. write for info. (ISBN 0-12-008302-7). Acad Pr.

Fedida, Sam & Malik, Rex. The Viewdata Revolution. LC 79-23869. 186p. 1980. 34.95 (ISBN 0-470-26879-4). Wiley.

Fedigan, Linda M. The Female Primate. (Illus.). 1981. write for info. (ISBN 0-920792-03-0); pap. write for info. EPWP.

Fedoroff, S. & Hertz, L., eds. Advances in Cellular Neurobiology, Vol. 1. 1980. 39.50 (ISBN 0-12-008301-9). Acad Pr.

Fedoroff, S. & Hertz, Leif, eds. Cell, Tissue & Organ Cultures in Neurobiology. 1978. 40.50 (ISBN 0-12-250450-X). Acad Pr.

Fedorov, A., ed. Chromosome Numbers of Flowering Plants. 926p. 1969. Repr. of 1974 ed. lib. bdg. 121.00x (ISBN 3-87429-067-0). Lubrecht & Cramer.

Fedorov, Evgenii K. Man & Nature: The Ecological Crisis & Social Progress. (Orig.). 1981. 8.00 (ISBN 0-7178-0573-5); pap. 2.75 (ISBN 0-7178-0567-0). Intl Pub Co.

Fedorov, K. N., ed. The Thermohaline Finestructure of the Ocean. Brown, D. A. & Turner, J. S., trs. 1978. text ed. 45.00 (ISBN 0-08-021673-0). Pergamon.

Fedorowicz, J. K. England's Baltic Trade in the Early Seventeenth Century. LC 78-67629. (Cambridge Studies in the Economic History). (Illus.). 1980. 42.50 (ISBN 0-521-22425-X). Cambridge U Pr.

Feduccia, Alan. Structure & Evolution of Vertebrates: A Laboratory Text for Comparative Vertebrate Anatomy. hew ed. 275p. 1974. pap. 7.95x (ISBN 0-393-09291-7). Norton.

Feduccia, Alan, jt. auth. see Torrey, Theodore W.

Fee, Roger D. Basic Ideas About Singing: The Teaching of Theodore Harrison, an American Maestro. LC 78-63254. pap. text ed. 5.75 (ISBN 0-8191-0614-3). U Pr of Amer.

Feegel, John. The Dance Card. 352p. 1981. 11.95 (ISBN 0-8037-1593-5). Dial.

Feeley, Pat, jt. auth. see Archer, Kathy.

Feeley-Harnick, Gillian. The Lord's Table: Eucharist & Passover in Early Christianity. 1980. text ed. 19.95x (ISBN 0-8122-7786-4). U of Pa Pr.

Feelings, Muriel L. Zamani Goes to Market. LC 70-97032. (Illus.). (gr. 1-4). 1970. 6.95 (ISBN 0-395-28791-X, Clarion). HM.

Feely, Malcolm & Sarat, Austin. The Policy Dilemma: Federal Crime Policy & the Law Enforcement Assistance Administration. 1981. 17.50x (ISBN 0-8166-0901-2); pap. 7.95x (ISBN 0-8166-0904-7). U of Minn Pr.

Feenberg, Andrew. Lukacs, Marx & the Sources of Critical Theory. (Philosophy & Society Ser.). 1981. 22.50x (ISBN 0-8476-6272-1). Rowman.

Feeney, Agnes & Leckel, John. The Great Chicago Melting Pot Cookbook. (Illus., Orig.). 1980. pap. 6.95 (ISBN 0-89865-028-3). Donning Co.

Feeney, Mary, tr. see Follain, Jean.

Feeney, Mary, tr. see Graziano, Frank & Follain, Jean.

Feeney, Mary K., jt. auth. see Phillips, Raymond E.

Feeney, Stephanie. A Is for Aloha. (Illus.). 64p. (ps-k). 1980. 7.95 (ISBN 0-8248-0722-7). U Pr of Hawaii.

Feeney, Stephanie & Christensen, Doris. Who Am I in the Lives of Children? An Introduction to Early Childhood Education. (Early Childhood Education Ser.). 1978. text ed. 14.95 (ISBN 0-675-08391-5); instructor's manual 3.95 (ISBN 0-685-86845-1). Merrill.

Feeney, William, ed. Lost Plays of the Irish Renaissance, Vol. 2. 10.00 (ISBN 0-912262-70-2). Proscenium.

Feerer, Virgil C. Christmas in Context. 1980. 4.95 (ISBN 0-533-04785-4). Vantage.

Feerick, Amalie P., jt. auth. see Feerick, John D.

Feerick, John D. & Feerick, Amalie P. The Vice-Presidents of the United States. (First Books). (Illus.). (gr. 4-6). 1977. PLB 6.45 s&l (ISBN 0-531-02907-7). Watts.

Feest, Christian. The Art of War. (Tribal Art Ser.). (Illus.). 96p. 1980. pap. 9.95 (ISBN 0-500-06010-X). Thames Hudson.

Feest, Christian F. Native Arts of North America. (World of Art Ser.). (Illus.). 300p. 1980. 17.95 (ISBN 0-19-520215-5); pap. 9.95 (ISBN 0-19-520216-3). Oxford U Pr.

Fegan, Richard C. & Brosche, Susan L. Fortran Computer Programming for Statistics: A Manual. 1979. pap. 6.95 (ISBN 0-13-329326-2). P-H.

Fegan, Richard G. & Brosche, Susan L. Basic Computer Programming for Statistics: A Manual. 1979. pap. 5.95 o.p. (ISBN 0-13-057950-5). P-H.

Fegely, Thomas D. Wonders of Geese & Swans. LC 75-38360. (Wonder Ser.). 1976. 5.95 (ISBN 0-396-07307-0). Dodd.

--Wonders of Wild Ducks. LC 75-11443. (Wonders Ser.). (Illus.). 80p. (gr. 3-7). 1975. PLB 5.95 (ISBN 0-396-07226-7). Dodd.

--The World of Freshwater Fish. LC 77-16879. (Illus.). (gr. 5 up). 1978. 6.95 (ISBN 0-396-07562-2). Dodd.

Feher, Elizabeth. The Psychology of Birth: Roots of Human Personality. 224p. 1981. 12.95 (ISBN 0-8264-0039-6). Continuum.

Feher, O. & Joo, F., eds. Cellular Analogues of Conditioning & Neural Plasticity: Proceedings of a Satellite Symposium of the 28th International Congress of Physiological Sciences, Szeged, Hungary, 1980. LC 80-41992. (Advances in Physiological Sciences: Vol. 36). (Illus.). 300p. 1981. 40.00 (ISBN 0-08-027372-6). Pergamon.

Fehervari, Geza. Islamic Metalwork of the Eighth to the Fifteenth Century. 1976. 92.00 (ISBN 0-571-09740-5, Pub. by Faber & Faber). Merrimack Bk Serv.

--Islamic Pottery. 1973. 45.00 o.p. (ISBN 0-571-09401-5, Pub. by Faber & Faber). Merrimack Bk Serv.

Fehl, James I., ed. Standard Lesson Commentary, 1981-1982: Twenty-Ninth Annual Edition. (Illus.). 456p. 1981. 6.95 (ISBN 0-87239-436-0, 74008); pap. 5.95 (ISBN 0-87239-435-2, 1982). Standard Pub.

Fehling, Detlef. Quellenangaben bei Herodot: Studien zur Erzaehlkunst Herodots. (Untersuchungen zur Antiken Literatur und Geschichte, 9). 198p. 1971. 25.90x (ISBN 3-11-003634-7). De Gruyter.

Fehr, Terry, jt. auth. see Mangan, Doreen.

Fehr, Terry, jt. auth. see Petersen, W. P.

Fehrenbach, T. R. Crossroads in Korea. (gr. 9-12). 1968. 8.95 (ISBN 0-02-734380-4). Macmillan.

Fehrenbacher, Don E. Chicago Giant: A Biography of Long John Wentworth. (Illus.). 278p. 1957. 10.00 (ISBN 0-87057-042-0, Pub. by Brown U Pr). Univ Pr of New England.

--The Era of Expansion: 1800-1848. LC 68-8713. (American Republic Ser.). 1969. pap. text ed. 8.95x (ISBN 0-471-25691-9). Wiley.

--The Leadership of Abraham Lincoln. LC 77-114013. (Problems in American History Ser.). 194p. 1970. pap. text ed. 8.95 (ISBN 0-471-25689-7). Wiley.

--Manifest Destiny & the Coming of the Civil War, 1840-1861. LC 72-118950. (Goldentree Bibliographies in American History Ser). (Orig.). 1970. pap. 6.95x (ISBN 0-88295-512-8). AHM Pub.

--Slavery, Law, & Politics: The Dred Scott Case in Historical Perspective. (Illus.). 288p. 1981. 16.95 (ISBN 0-19-502882-1). Oxford U Pr.

--Slavery, Law & Politics: The Dred Scott Case in Historical Perspective. (Illus.). 288p. 1981. pap. 6.95 (ISBN 0-19-502883-X, GB639, GB). Oxford U Pr.

Fehrenbacher, Don E., ed. see Potter, David.

Fei, Hsiao-Tung. Peasant Life in China: A Field Study of Country Life in the Yangtze Valley. (Studies in Chinese History & Civilization). (Illus.). 296p. 1977. Repr. of 1939 ed. 21.00 (ISBN 0-89093-081-3). U Pubns Amer.

Fei, Hsiao-Tung & Redfield, Margaret, eds. China's Gentry: Essays in Rural-Urban Relations with Six Life-Histories of Chinese Gentry Families. LC 53-11440. (Midway Reprint Ser.). 296p. 1980. pap. 9.00x (ISBN 0-226-23957-8). U. of Chicago Pr.

Fei, John, et al. Growth with Equity: The Taiwan Case. 1980. 14.95x (ISBN 0-19-520115-9); pap. 5.95x (ISBN 0-19-520116-7). Oxford U Pr.

Feibleman, James K. The New Cosmology. LC 77-81794. 224p. 1981. 14.50 (ISBN 0-87527-171-5). Green.

--Theory of Human Culture. 1968. Repr. of 1946 ed. text ed. 15.00x (ISBN 0-391-00448-4). Humanities.

Feibleman, Peter. The Bayous. LC 73-84544. (American Wilderness Ser). (Illus.). (gr. 6 up). 1973. lib. bdg. 11.97 (ISBN 0-8094-1189-X, Pub. by Time-Life). Silver.

Feibleman, Peter S. American Cooking: Creole & Acadian. (Foods of the World Ser). (Illus.). 1971. 14.95 (ISBN 0-8094-0054-5). Time-Life.

--American Cooking: Creole & Acadian. LC 78-16778. (Foods of the World Ser.). (Illus.). (gr. 6 up). 1971. PLB 14.94 (ISBN 0-8094-0081-2, Pub. by Time-Life). Silver.

--The Bayous. (The American Wilderness Ser.). (Illus.). 240p. 1973. 12.95 (ISBN 0-8094-1188-1). Time-Life.

--Cooking of Spain & Portugal. LC 70-82142. (Foods of the World Ser). (Illus.). (gr. 6 up). 1969. PLB 14.94 (ISBN 0-8094-0066-9, Pub. by Time-Life). Silver.

--Cooking of Spain & Portugal. (Foods of the World Ser). (Illus.). 1969. 14.95 (ISBN 0-8094-0039-1). Time-Life.

Feichtner, Rudy, tr. see Alfven, Hannes.

Feidelson, Charles, Jr., ed. see Melville, Herman.

Feiden, Doug. The Ten Million Dollar Getaway: The Inside Story of the Lufthansa Heist. (Orig.). pap. 2.50 (ISBN 0-515-05452-6). Jove Pubns.

Feider, Helga, tr. see Pinard, Adrien.

Feierman, Steven. The Shambaa Kingdom: A History. LC 72-7985. 224p. 1974. 20.00x (ISBN 0-299-06360-7). U of Wis Pr.

Feifer, George. Moscow Farewell. 1977. pap. 1.95 o.p. (ISBN 0-425-03385-6, Medallion). Berkley Pub.

Feiffer, Jules. Knock, Knock. 1976. pap. 3.45 o.p. (ISBN 0-8090-1234-0, Mermaid). Hill & Wang.

Feig, B. K. The Parents Guide to Weight Control for Children Ages 5 to 13 Years. (Illus.). 200p. 1980. 11.75 (ISBN 0-398-03972-0); pap. 6.95 (ISBN 0-398-04016-8). C C Thomas.

Feig, Konnilyn G. Hitler's Death Camps. (Illus.). 400p. 1981. 29.50x (ISBN 0-8419-0675-0); pap. 12.50x (ISBN 0-8419-0676-9). Holmes & Meier.

Feigenbaum, Edward, jt. ed. see Barr, Avron.

Feigenbaum, Edward A. Computers & Thought. LC 80-29508. 540p. 1981. Repr. of 1963 ed. lib. bdg. write for info. (ISBN 0-89874-199-8). Krieger.

Feigenbaum, Harvey. Echocardiography. 3rd. ed. LC 80-20682. (Illus.). 580p. 1981. text ed. 35.00 (ISBN 0-8121-0758-6). Lea & Febiger.

Feiger, George & Jacquillat, Bertrand. International Finance: Text & Cases. new ed. 496p. 1980. text ed. 19.95 (ISBN 0-205-07137-6, 1071378); tchr's ed. avail. (ISBN 0-205-07138-4). Allyn.

Feigert, Frank B., jt. auth. see Conway, Margaret M.

Feighner, John P., ed. see Schuckit, Marc A.

Feigl, Herbert. New Readings in Philosophical Analysis. Lehrer, Keith & Sellars, Wilfred, eds. LC 72-89406. (Century Philosophy Ser.). 784p. 1972. 22.95 (ISBN 0-13-615526-X). P-H.

Feigl, Herbert & Sellars, Wilfrid, eds. Readings in Philosophical Analysis. x, 593p. 1981. lib. bdg. 25.00 (ISBN 0-917930-29-0); pap. text ed. 12.50x (ISBN 0-917930-09-6). Ridgeview.

Feild, Hubert S. & Bienen, Leigh B. Jurors & Rape: A Study in Psychology & Law. LC 76-48473. (Illus.). 1980. 34.95x (ISBN 0-669-01148-7). Lexington Bks.

Feild, John see Ames, William.

Feild, Lance. Exploring Nova Scotia. LC 79-4903. (Illus.). 192p. 1978. lib. bdg. 10.25 o.p. (ISBN 0-914788-16-7). East Woods.

Feild, Reshad. The Last Barrier. LC 75-9345. 1977. pap. 5.95 (ISBN 0-06-062586-4, RD 202, HarpR). Har-Row.

Feiler, Eva, jt. ed. see Barkan, Stanley H.

Feiler, Eve, tr. see Cassian, Nina.

Feiling, Keith. British Foreign Policy: Sixteen Sixty to Sixteen Seventy-Two. 1968. Repr. of 1930 ed. text ed. 11.50x (ISBN 0-7146-1473-4). Humanities.

Feiman, Sharon, ed. Teacher Centers: What Place in Education. (Orig.). 1980. pap. 1.50. U Chi Ctr Policy.

Fein, Albert. Frederick Law Olmsted & the American Environmental Tradition. LC 72-75831. (Planning & Cities Ser). (Illus.). 160p. 1972. 10.00 (ISBN 0-8076-0650-2); pap. 7.95 (ISBN 0-8076-0649-9). Braziller.

Fein, Bruce E. Significant Decisions of the Supreme Court: 1978-1979 Term. 1980. pap. 6.25 (ISBN 0-8447-3387-3). Am Enterprise.

Fein, Greta. Child Development. (Illus.). 1978. text ed. 18.95 (ISBN 0-13-132571-X); study guide & wkbk. 6.95 (ISBN 0-13-132555-8). P-H.

Fein, Greta G. & Clarke-Stewart, K. Alison. Day Care in Context. LC 72-8588. 359p. 1973. 28.95 (ISBN 0-471-25695-1, Pub. by Wiley - Interscience). Wiley.

Fein, Irving A. Jack Benny: An Intimate Biography. LC 75-30975. (Illus.). 320p. (YA) 1976. 8.95 o.p. (ISBN 0-399-11640-0). Berkley Pub.

Fein, J. M. & Reichman, O. H., eds. Microvascular Anastomoses for Cerebral Ischemia. (Illus.). 1978. 44.60 (ISBN 0-387-90240-6). Springer-Verlag.

Fein, Leonard J. Ecology of the Public Schools: An Inquiry into Community Control. LC 70-128661. 1971. pap. 5.50 (ISBN 0-672-63526-7). Pegasus.

Fein, Richard J. Robert Lowell. 2nd ed. (United States Authors Ser.: No. 176). 1979. lib. bdg. 9.95 (ISBN 0-8057-7279-0). Twayne.

Fein, Sherman E. & Maskell, Arthur M. Selected Cases on the Law of Shoplifting. 92p. 1975. 11.50 (ISBN 0-398-03354-4); pap. 8.50 (ISBN 0-398-03355-2). C C Thomas.

Fein, Sylvia. Heidi's Horse. LC 74-76077. (Illus.). 1976. 10.00 (ISBN 0-917388-01-1). Exelrod Pr.

Feinberg. Applied Business Communications. 1981. 15.95 (ISBN 0-88284-125-4). Alfred Pub.

Feinberg, Barbara S. Franklin D. Roosevelt, Gallant President. LC 80-22307. (Illus.). 96p. (gr. 2-6). 1981. 7.50 (ISBN 0-688-00433-4); PLB 7.20 (ISBN 0-688-00434-2). Morrow.

Feinberg, Barry N., ed. Handbook of Clinical Engineering, Vol. 1. 304p. 1980. 59.95 (ISBN 0-8493-0244-7). CRC Pr.

Feinberg, Barry N., jt. ed. see Fleming, David G.

Feinberg, Charles L. Daniel: The Man & His Visions. LC 80-70117. 212p. 1981. 8.95 (ISBN 0-915684-86-1). Christian Herald.

--Millenialism: The Two Major Views. 1980. 9.95 (ISBN 0-8024-6815-2). Moody.

--The Minor Prophets. rev ed. 384p. 1976. 9.95 (ISBN 0-8024-5306-6). Moody.

Feinberg, Gerald & Schapiro, Robert. Life Beyond Earth: The Intelligent Earthling's Guide to Extraterrestrial Life. LC 80-14009. (Illus.). 480p. 1980. 14.95 (ISBN 0-688-03642-2, Quill); pap. 9.95 (ISBN 0-688-08642-X, Quill). Morrow.

Feinberg, Harold. Simon & Schuster Guide to Shells. (Illus.). 1980. 22.50 (ISBN 0-686-60938-7, 25319); pap. 9.95 (ISBN 0-686-60939-5, 25320). S&S.

Feinberg, Hilda. Title Derivative Indexing Techniques: A Comparative Study. LC 73-2671. 1973. 20.50 (ISBN 0-8108-0602-9). Scarecrow.

Feinberg, Joel. Problems of Abortion. 1973. pap. 7.95x (ISBN 0-534-00334-6). Wadsworth Pub.

--Reason & Responsibility. 4th ed. 1978. text ed. 17.95x (ISBN 0-8221-0209-9). Dickenson.

--Reason & Responsibility. 5th ed. 640p. 1980. text ed. 17.95x (ISBN 0-534-00924-7). Wadsworth Pub.

--Rights, Justice & the Bounds of Liberty: Essays in Social Philosophy. LC 79-48024. (Princeton Series of Collected Essays). 1980. 20.00x (ISBN 0-691-07254-X); pap. 4.95 (ISBN 0-691-02012-4). Princeton U Pr.

--Social Philosophy. 1973. pap. 7.95 ref. ed. (ISBN 0-13-817254-4). P-H.

Feinberg, Joel & Gross, Hyman. Justice: Selected Readings. (The Philosophy of Law Ser.). 1977. pap. text ed. 9.95x (ISBN 0-8221-0201-3). Dickenson.

--Law in Philosophical Perspective: Selected Readings. 1977. pap. text ed. 9.95x (ISBN 0-8221-0203-X). Dickenson.

--Liberty: Selected Readings. 1977. pap. text ed. 9.95x (ISBN 0-8221-0202-1). Dickenson.

--Philosophy of Law. 2nd ed. 656p. 1980. text ed. 20.95x (ISBN 0-534-00835-6). Wadsworth Pub.

--Responsibility: Selected Readings. 1975. pap. text ed. 9.95x (ISBN 0-8221-0171-8). Dickenson.

Feinberg, Joel & West, Henry. Moral Philosophy: Classic Texts & Contemporary Problems. 1977. pap. text ed. 16.95x (ISBN 0-8221-0196-3). Dickenson.

Feinberg, John S. Theologies & Evil. LC 79-66474. 1979. text ed. 14.50 (ISBN 0-8191-0838-3); pap. text ed. 9.00 (ISBN 0-8191-0839-1). U Pr of Amer.

Feinberg, Leonard. Introduction to Satire. facsimile ed. 293p. (gr. 11 up). 1967. pap. 7.50x o.p. (ISBN 0-8138-2410-9). Iowa St U Pr.

--The Secret of Humor. 1978. pap. text ed. 23.00 (ISBN 90-6203-370-9). Humanities.

Feinberg, Milton. Techniques of Photojournalism: Available Light & the 35 mm Camera. LC 73-96959. 1970. 29.95 (ISBN 0-471-25692-7, Pub. by Wiley-Interscience). Wiley.

Feinberg, R., jt. auth. see Jackson, K. G.

Feinberg, R., ed. Modern Power Transformer Practice. LC 78-5608. 1979. 54.95 (ISBN 0-470-26344-X). Halsted Pr.

Feinberg, Richard, et al. Tempest in a Tea House: American Attitudes Toward Breast-Feeding. 50p. (Orig.). 1980. pap. 2.95 (ISBN 0-933522-06-1). Kent Popular.

Feinberg, Walter. Reason & Rhetoric: The Intellectual Foundations of Twentieth Century Liberal Educational Policy. LC 74-16009. 304p. 1975. text ed. 21.95 (ISBN 0-471-25697-8). Wiley.

Feinberg, William H. Ken Stabler. (Sports Superstars Ser). (Illus.). (gr. 3-9). 1978. PLB 5.95 (ISBN 0-87191-670-3); pap. 2.95 (ISBN 0-89812-170-1). Creative Ed.

Feinberg, Willie, jt. auth. see Dayan, Ruth.

Feinblatt, Ebria & Davis, Bruce. Los Angeles Prints: Eighteen Eighty-Three to Nineteen Eighty. (Illus.). 112p. (Orig.). 1980. pap. 10.00 (ISBN 0-87587-097-X). La Co Art Mus.

Feinblatt, Ebria, et al. Los Angeles County Museum of Art Bulletin, 1979, Vol. 25. LC 58-35949. (Illus.). 80p. (Orig.). 1980. pap. 6.00 (ISBN 0-87587-092-9). La Co Art Mus.

Feinbloom, Deborah H. Transvestites & Transsexuals: Mixed Views. 1976. 12.50 o.s.i. (ISBN 0-440-08513-6, Sey Lawr). Delacorte.

Feineman, Neil. Nicolas Roeg. (Theatrical Art Ser.). 1978. 12.50 (ISBN 0-8057-9258-9). Twayne.

Feiner, Harriet, ed. The Uprooted: The Appelberg Collection. LC 77-85136. 1977. pap. text ed. 3.50 o.p. (ISBN 0-87868-169-8). Child Welfare.

Feiner, Johannes & Vischer, Lukas, eds. The Common Catechism: A Book of Christian Faith. LC 75-1070. 690p. 1975. 10.95 (ISBN 0-8164-0283-3). Crossroad NY.

Feingold, Carl. Introduction to Data Processing. 3rd ed. 1980. pap. text ed. 17.95x (ISBN 0-697-08136-2); pap. wkbk. 7.95x (ISBN 0-697-08143-5); pap. instr's man. 6.00x (ISBN 0-686-60814-3). Wm C Brown.

Feingold, Henry L. The Politics of Rescue: The Roosevelt Administration & the Holocaust, 1938-1945. LC 75-127049. 1970. 25.00 (ISBN 0-8135-0664-6). Rutgers U Pr.

--Zion in America. (Immigrant Heritage of America Ser). 1974. lib. bdg. 14.50 (ISBN 0-8057-3298-5). Twayne.

Feingold, Jessica, jt. ed. see Faust, Clarence H.

Feingold, Richard. Monarch Notes on Swift's Gulliver's Travels. (Orig.). pap. 1.95 (ISBN 0-671-00648-7). Monarch Pr.

--Nature & Society: Later Eighteenth Century Uses of the Pastoral & Georgic. 1978. 17.00 (ISBN 0-8135-0847-9). Rutgers U Pr.

Feingold, S. Norman. A Counselor's Handbook: Readings in Counseling, Student Aid & Rehabilitation. LC 79-190226. 288p. (gr. 9-12). 1972. text ed. 12.00x (ISBN 0-910328-05-6). Carroll Pr.

Feingold, S. Norman & Levin, Shirley. What to Do Until the Counselor Comes. (Careers in Depth Ser.). 128p. 1980. lib. bdg. 7.97 (ISBN 0-8239-0506-3). Rosen Pr.

Feininger, Andreas. Color Photo Book. LC 69-12820. (Illus.). 1969. 12.95 o.p. (ISBN 0-13-152181-0). P-H.

--Darkroom Techniques, Vol. 2: Enlarging & Contact Printing. LC 73-82108. (Illus.). 304p. 1973. 8.95 (ISBN 0-13-197533-1). P-H.

--Feininger's Chicago: 1941. (Illus.). 80p. 1980. 12.50 (ISBN 0-486-24007-X); pap. 5.00 (ISBN 0-486-23991-8). Dover.

--Nature Close Up: A Fantastic Journey into Reality. rev. ed. (Illus.). 160p. 1981. pap. price not set (ISBN 0-486-24102-5). Dover.

--Photographic Seeing. LC 73-7567. (Illus.). 200p. 1973. 9.95 o.p. (ISBN 0-13-665372-3). P-H.

Feininger, Lyonel. The Kin-der-Kids: All Thirty-One Strips in Full Color. (Illus.). 32p. (Orig.). 1980. pap. 6.00 (ISBN 0-486-23918-7). Dover.

Feinland, Alexander & Iotti, Oscar R. Violin & Violoncello in Duo Without Accompaniment. LC 77-187707. (Detroit Studies in Music Bibliography Ser.: No. 25). (Based on the work of Alexander Feinland). 1973. 5.75 (ISBN 0-685-30615-1); pap. 4.25 (ISBN 0-911772-48-0). Info Coord.

Feinman, Clarice. Women in the Criminal Justice System. LC 80-12539. (Illus.). 1980. 19.95 (ISBN 0-03-052561-6); pap. 8.95 (ISBN 0-03-052566-7). Praeger.

Feinman, Jeffrey. Advertising for a Small Business. Date not set. cancelled (ISBN 0-671-96123-3); pap. 2.95 (ISBN 0-346-12416-6). Cornerstone.

--Casino Gambling. 128p. (Orig.). 1981. pap. 2.95 (ISBN 0-668-05172-8, 5172). Arco.

--The Money Book of Lists. LC 79-6590. 432p. 1981. pap. 7.95 (ISBN 0-385-15444-5, Dolp). Doubleday.

--The Purple Pages. 1979. pap. 6.95 (ISBN 0-8015-6132-9, Hawthorn). Dutton.

Feinman, Jeffrey, jt. auth. see Adler, Bill.

Feinman, Jeffrey, jt. auth. see Maller, Dick.

Feinman, Max L. & Wilson, Josleen. Live Longer. 1978. pap. 2.50 (ISBN 0-515-05722-3). Jove Pubns.

Feinman, Ronald L. Twilight of Progressivism: The Western Republican Senators & the New Deal. LC 80-20124. (Johns Hopkins Studies in Historical & Political Science). (Illus.). 288p. 1981. text ed. 18.50x (ISBN 0-8018-2373-0). Johns Hopkins.

Feinsilber, Mike & Mead, William B. American Averages. LC 79-8567. pap. 7.95 (Dolp). Doubleday.

--American Averages: Amazing Facts of Everyday Life. LC 79-8567. 432p. 1980. 14.95 (ISBN 0-385-15175-6). Doubleday.

Feinsilver, Alexander, ed. The Talmud Today. 320p. 1980. 14.95 (ISBN 0-312-78479-1). St Martin.

Feinsmith, Leslie S. & Kleid, Jack J., eds. Textbook Study Guide of Internal Medicine. 3rd ed. (Medical Examination Review Book: Vol. 2B). 1977. pap. 8.50 o.s.i. (ISBN 0-87488-130-7). Med Exam.

Feinsod, Ethan. Awake in a Nightmare. 1981. 14.95 (ISBN 0-393-01431-2). Norton.

Feinstein, C. H. Domestic Capital Formation in the United Kingdom. (Publications of the National Institute of Economic & Social Research & Cambridge Department of Applied Economics: No. 4). 45.00 (ISBN 0-521-04986-5, Q). Cambridge U Pr.

--National Income, Expenditure & Output of the United Kingdom, 1855-1965. LC 71-163055. (Studies in the National Income & Expenditure of the United Kingdom: Vol. 6). (Illus.). 1972. 71.50 (ISBN 0-521-07230-1). Cambridge U Pr.

--Statistical Tables of National Income Expenditure & Output of the UK 1855-1965. LC 76-19627. 1976. limp bdg. 21.50x (ISBN 0-521-21396-7). Cambridge U Pr.

Feinstein, Elaine, tr. see Aliger, Margarita, et al.

Feinstein, G. Programmed Writing Skills. 1976. pap. 9.50 (ISBN 0-13-730523-0); instr. manual of tests 1.95 (ISBN 0-13-730515-X). P-H.

Feinstein, George W. Programed Spelling Demons. 240p. 1973. pap. text ed. 8.50 o.p. (ISBN 0-13-730135-9). P-H.

--Programmed College Vocabulary Three Thousand Six Hundred. 1979. pap. text ed. 9.50 (ISBN 0-13-729806-4). P-H.

Feinstein, Irwin K. & Murphy, Kenneth H. College Algebra. (Quality Paperback: No. 39). (Orig.). 1974. pap. 4.95 (ISBN 0-8226-0039-0). Littlefield.

Feinstein, Marnin. Basic Hebrew: A Textbook of Contemporary Hebrew. LC 73-77286. 1973. 6.75x (ISBN 0-8197-0287-0). Bloch.

Feinstein, Maurice B. & Levine, Harriet. Pharmacology. 3rd ed. (Nursing Examination Review Bk.: Vol. 6). 1974. spiral bdg. 6.00 (ISBN 0-87488-506-X). Med Exam.

Feinstein, R. Dermatology. (Illus.). 1975. pap. 7.95 (ISBN 0-87618-066-7). R J Brady.

Feinstein, Sherman C. & Giovacchini, Peter L. Adolescent Psychiatry, Vol. 8. LC 70-147017. 544p. 1981. lib. bdg. 25.00x (ISBN 0-226-24053-3). U of Chicago Pr.

Feirer. Basic Woodworking. (gr. 9-12). 1978. 6.00 (ISBN 0-87002-290-3); pap. 4.32 (ISBN 0-87002-274-1). Bennett IL.

--Bench Woodwork. (gr. 7-9). 1978. text ed. 11.16 (ISBN 0-87002-201-6); student guide 3.00 (ISBN 0-87002-203-2). Bennett IL.

--SI Metric Handbook. 1977. text ed. 25.00 (ISBN 0-87002-908-8). Bennett IL.

--Woodworking for Industry. 1979. text ed. 19.28 (ISBN 0-87002-242-3); wkbk. 5.28 (ISBN 0-87002-300-4). Bennett IL.

Feirer & Hutchings. Advanced Woodwork & Furniture Making. 1978. text ed. 15.36 (ISBN 0-87002-205-9); student guide 3.96 (ISBN 0-87002-269-5); visual masters 14.40 (ISBN 0-87002-148-6). Bennett IL.

--Carpentry Construction & Building. rev. ed. 1981. text ed. 24.60 (ISBN 0-87002-327-6). Bennett IL.

Feirer & Lindbeck. Basic Drafting. (gr. 9-12). 1978. 6.00 (ISBN 0-87002-287-3); pap. 4.32 (ISBN 0-87002-273-3); activities for basic drafting 2.64 (ISBN 0-87002-306-3). Bennett IL.

--Basic Metalwork. (gr. 9-12). 1978. 6.00 (ISBN 0-87002-289-X); pap. 4.32 (ISBN 0-87002-240-7). Bennett IL.

--Metalwork: S.I. Metric Edition. 1979. text ed. 13.28 (ISBN 0-87002-292-X); student guide 5.28 (ISBN 0-87002-316-0). Bennett IL.

Feirer, John. Cabinetmaking & Millwork. 1977. text ed. 21.28 (ISBN 0-87002-238-5); student guide 4.20 (ISBN 0-87002-176-1). Bennett IL.

--Cabinetmaking & Millwork. rev ed. (Illus.). 1977. 37.50 (ISBN 0-684-14914-1, ScribT). Scribner.

--SI Metric Handbook. (Illus.). 1977. 27.50 (ISBN 0-87002-908-8, ScribT). Scribner.

Feirer, John & Hutchings, Gilbert. Carpentry Building & Construction. (gr. 10-12). 1976. text ed. 22.60 (ISBN 0-87002-004-8); student guide 3.92 (ISBN 0-87002-277-6). Bennett IL.

Feirer, John & Hutchings, Gilbert R. Carpentry & Building Constructions. rev. ed. (Illus.). 1981. 37.50 (ISBN 0-684-16981-9, ScribT). Scribner.

Feirer, John L. General Metals. rev, 5th ed. (Industrial Education Ser.). (Illus.). 480p. (gr. 9-10). 1980. text ed. 17.32 (ISBN 0-07-020380-6, W); study guide 4.20 (ISBN 0-07-020382-2); tchrs. resource guide 3.96 (ISBN 0-07-020381-4). McGraw.

--Industrial Arts Woodworking. (gr. 9-12). 1977. text ed. 13.28 (ISBN 0-87002-195-8); wkbk 2.88 (ISBN 0-87002-284-9). Bennett IL.

--Wood: Materials & Processes. 587p. (gr. 7-12). 1975. text ed. 15.96 o.p. (ISBN 0-87002-126-5); wkbk. 4.44 o.p. (ISBN 0-87002-179-6). Bennett IL.

--Wood Materials & Processes. (Illus.). 592p. 1976. 27.50 (ISBN 0-684-14803-X, ScribT). Scribner.

--Wood: Materials & Processes. rev. ed. (gr. 7-12). 1980. text ed. 17.28 (ISBN 0-87002-307-1); student guide 4.44 (ISBN 0-87002-179-6). Bennett IL.

Feirer, John L. & Lindbeck. Drawing & Planning for the Industrial Arts. new ed. (Illus.). (gr. 7-12). 1975. text ed. 11.64 (ISBN 0-87002-159-1); tchr's guide, charts & worksheets 5.60 (ISBN 0-87002-162-1). Bennett IL.

Feirer, John L. & Lindbeck, John R. Metalwork. rev. ed. (gr. 7-9). 1970. 10.60 (ISBN 0-87002-017-X); student guide 3.00 (ISBN 0-87002-048-X). Bennett IL.

Feiring, Evolyn B. Concatenation: Enoch's Prophecy Fulfilling! Hebrew-Christian Metaphysics Supported by Modern Science. LC 72-96989. 3.00x (ISBN 0-9603386-0-8); pap. 2.00x (ISBN 0-9603386-1-6). Rocky Mtn Pr.

Feirstein, Frederick. Manhattan Carnival. 60p. 1981. 9.95 (ISBN 0-914378-68-6); pap. 5.95 (ISBN 0-914378-69-4). Countryman.

Feis, Herbert. The China Tangle: The American Effort in China from Pearl Harbor to the Marshall Mission. 456p. 1953. 20.00x (ISBN 0-691-05606-4); pap. 6.95 o.p. (ISBN 0-691-01064-1). Princeton U Pr.

--Churchill, Roosevelt, Stalin: The War They Waged & the Peace They Sought. 2nd ed. 1967. 23.50x (ISBN 0-691-05607-2); pap. 5.95 (ISBN 0-691-01050-1). Princeton U Pr.

--Ninety-Thirty-Three Characters in Crisis. (FDR & the Era of the New Deal Ser.). 1976. Repr. of 1966 ed. lib. bdg. 32.50 (ISBN 0-306-70807-8). Da Capo.

--Road to Pearl Harbor: The Coming of the War Between the United States & Japan. 1950. 20.00x (ISBN 0-691-05632-3); pap. 5.95 (ISBN 0-691-01061-7). Princeton U Pr.

Feist, Uwe. Aero Armor Series, Vol. 11. LC 79-91946. (Illus.). 1979. pap. 3.95 (ISBN 0-8168-2040-6). Aero.

--Aero-Armor Series, Vol. 12. LC 80-66353. 52p. 1980. pap. 3.95 (ISBN 0-8168-2044-9). Aero.

--Aero Armor Series, Vol. 13. 52p. 1981. pap. 3.95 (ISBN 0-8168-2046-5). Aero.

--Aero Armor Series, Vol. 14. LC 80-66353. (Orig.). 1981. pap. 3.95 (ISBN 0-8168-2048-1). Aero.

--Aero Pictorial, No. 6. 100p. 1980. 6.95 (ISBN 0-8168-0320-X). Aero.

--Aero Pictorial, Vol. 5: Luftwaffe in WW II - Pt. 2. LC 68-28679. 100p. 1980. pap. 6.95 (ISBN 0-8168-0316-1). Aero.

--Military Panorama, No. 1. (Illus.). 1969. pap. 4.95 (ISBN 0-8168-6801-8). Aero.

Feist, Uwe, jt. auth. see Spielberger, Walter J.

Feist, Uwe, et al. The Fighting One O Nine: A Pictorial History of the Messerschmitt BF 109 in Action. LC 77-76232. 1978. 10.50 o.p. (ISBN 0-385-05679-6). Doubleday.

Feit, Edward. Governments & Leaders: An Approach to Comparative Politics. LC 77-77977. (Illus.). 1978. text ed. 18.75 (ISBN 0-395-25367-5). HM.

Feitis, Rosemary, ed. Ida Rolf Talks About Rolfing & Physical Reality. LC 78-2126. (Illus.). 1978. 8.95 o.s.i. (ISBN 0-06-011258-1, HarpT). Har-Row.

Feitz, Leland, jt. auth. see Love, Frank.

Feiwel, George R. Growth & Reform in Centrally Planned Economics: The Lessons of the Bulgarian Experience. LC 76-12849. 1977. text ed. 31.95 (ISBN 0-275-23330-8). Praeger.

--The Intellectual Capital of Michal Kalecki: A Study in Economic Theory & Policy. LC 74-22487. 1975. 25.00x (ISBN 0-87049-161-X). U of Tenn Pr.

--The Soviet Quest for Economic Efficiency: Issues, Controversies, & Reforms. LC 72-145952. (Special Studies in International Economics & Development). 1972. 39.50x (ISBN 0-89197-944-1); pap. text ed. 12.95x (ISBN 0-89197-945-X). Irvington.

Fejfar, James L., jt. auth. see Larsen, Max D.

Fekete, Francois, jt. auth. see Nahum, Henri.

Fekete, John. The Critical Twilight: Explorations in the Ideology of Anglo-American Literary Theory from Eliot to McLuhan. (The International Library of Phenomenology & Moral Sciences). 1978. 22.50x (ISBN 0-7100-8618-0). Routledge & Kegan.

Fel, E., jt. auth. see Hofer, T.

Felber, Helmut, compiled by. International Bibliography of Standardized Vocabularies. (International Bibliography of Infoterm Ser., Vol. 2). 1978. 95.00 (ISBN 0-89664-075-2, Pub. by K G Saur). Gale.

Felber, John E. American's Tourist Manual for Peoples Republic of China. LC 73-93210. 224p. 1980. pap. 7.95 (ISBN 0-686-64369-0). Intl Intertrade.

--American's Tourist Manual for the U.S.S.R. LC 72-78512. (Illus.). 1979. pap. 7.95 (ISBN 0-910794-02-2). Intl Intertrade.

Feld, Barry & Levy, Robert J. Standards Relating to Rights of Minors. (Juvenile Justice Standards Project Ser.). 1980. softcover 7.95 (ISBN 0-88410-810-4); casebound 16.50 (ISBN 0-88410-243-2). Ballinger Pub.

--Standards Relating to Rights of Minors. LC 77-1684. (Juvenile Justice Standards Project Ser.). 1977. 6.95 o.p. (ISBN 0-88410-768-X); 14.00, casebound o.p. Ballinger Pub.

Feld, Bernard T. A Voice Crying in the Wilderness: Essays on the Problem of Science & World Affairs. (Illus.). 1979. 35.00 (ISBN 0-08-023106-3). Pergamon.

Feld, Bernard T., et al, eds. Impact of New Technologies on the Arms Race. 1971. 16.00x o.p. (ISBN 0-262-06042-6); pap. 4.95x (ISBN 0-262-56010-0). MIT Pr.

Feld, Friedrich. Engine Fourteen-Fourteen. LC 65-23882. (Illus.). (gr. 3-5). 1963. 3.95g o.p. (ISBN 0-8075-2057-8). A Whitman.

--Marvellous Matches. LC 66-10787. (Illus.). (gr. 4-7). 1961. 3.95 o.p. (ISBN 0-8075-4978-9). A Whitman.

Feld, Friedrick. Mystery of the Musical Umbrella. (Illus.). (gr. 2-4). 1962. PLB 3.99 o.p. (ISBN 0-394-90124-X, BYR). Random.

Feld, J. Construction Failure. LC 68-30908. (Wiley Series of Practical Construction Guides). 1968. 29.95 (ISBN 0-471-25700-1, Pub. by Wiley-Interscience). Wiley.

Feld, M. S. & Letokhov, V. S., eds. Coherent Nonlinear Optics: Recent Advances. (Topics in Current Physics: Vol. 21). (Illus.). 377p. 1980. 44.50 (ISBN 0-387-10172-1). Springer-Verlag.

Feld, Robyn, illus. Color the ABC's of What Should I Be When I Grow up? 1980. pap. 1.35 (ISBN 0-931868-04-1). Beninda.

Feld, Ross. Philip Couston. LC 79-27425. (Illus.). 152p. 1980. 25.00 (ISBN 0-8076-0962-5); pap. 11.95 (ISBN 0-8076-0962-5). Braziller.

Feld, Werner. The European Community in World Affairs: Political Influence & Economic Reality. LC 75-44209. (Illus.). 250p. 1976. 12.50 (ISBN 0-88284-040-1); pap. text ed. 7.95x (ISBN 0-88284-037-1). Alfred Pub.

--International Relations: A Transnational Policy Approach. LC 77-25959. (Illus.). 1979. text ed. 14.50x (ISBN 0-88284-058-4). Alfred Pub.

Feld, Werner & Boyd, Gavin, eds. Comparative Regional Systems: West & East Europe, North America, the Middle East & Developing Countries. (Pergamon Policy Studies). 1980. 47.00 (ISBN 0-08-023358-9); pap. 13.50 (ISBN 0-08-023357-0). Pergamon.

Feld, Werner J. Multinational Enterprises & U. N. Politics: The Quest for Codes of Conduct. (Pergamon Policy Studies). (Illus.). 1980. 28.00 (ISBN 0-08-022488-1). Pergamon.

Feld, Werner J. & Wilgen, John K. Domestic Political Realities of European Unification: A Study of Mass Public & Elites in the European Community Countries. new ed. LC 76-28703. (Westview Replica Editions). 1977. PLB 21.00x (ISBN 0-89158-149-9). Westview.

Feld, Werner J., ed. The Foreign Policies of West European Socialist Parties. LC 77-83485. (Praeger Special Studies). 1978. 20.95 (ISBN 0-03-039381-7). Praeger.

--Western Europe's Global Reach: Regional Cooperation & Worldwide Aspirations. (Policy Studies). 1980. 30.00 (ISBN 0-08-025130-7). Pergamon.

Feld, Werner J., jt. ed. see Link, Werner.

Feldacker, Bruce S. Labor Guide to Labor Law. (Illus.). 1980. ref. ed. 24.95; text ed. 16.95 (ISBN 0-8359-3921-9). Reston.

Feldbaum, A. A. Optimal Control Systems. (Mathematics in Science & Engineering Ser.: Vol. 22). 1966. 51.50 (ISBN 0-12-251950-7). Acad Pr.

Feldbaum, Eleanor G., jt. auth. see Levitt, Morris J.

Feldbausch, Friedrich K. Finance Dictionary, German-English, English-German. 205p. 1972. 18.75x o.p. (ISBN 0-900537-02-7, Dist. by Hippocrene Books Inc.). Leviathan Hse.

Felde, Nathan & Friedman, Julius. Public Works: The Posters of Nathan Felde & Julius Friedman. (Illus.). 64p. pap. 14.95 (ISBN 0-937246-00-X). Chicago Review.

Feldenkrais, Moshe. The Case of Nora: Body Awareness As Healing Therapy. LC 76-62935. 1977. 6.95 o.p. (ISBN 0-06-062346-2, HarpR). Har-Row.

Felder, Dell. The Challenge of American Democracy 1974. new rev. ed. (gr. 9-12). 1974. text ed. 13.20 (ISBN 0-205-04371-2, 7643713); tchrs'. guide 3.40 (ISBN 0-205-04372-0, 7643721). Allyn.

Felder, Eleanor. Careers in Publishing & Printing. LC 76-5903. (Whole Works Ser). (Illus.). 48p. (gr. 3-7). 1976. PLB 9.65 (ISBN 0-8172-0701-5). Raintree Pubs.

Felder, Emma G. Beginning Phonics for Parents. new ed. LC 77-135316. (Illus.). 1974. pap. 1.55 (ISBN 0-910812-05-5). Johnny Reads.

Felder, Frederick E., jt. auth. see Wishard, William R.

Feldheim, Harold. Negative & Responsive Doubles in Bridge. 64p. (Orig.). 1980. pap. 2.95 (ISBN 0-87643-031-0). Barclay Bridge.

Feldherr, C. M., et al. Nuclear Membrane & Nucleocytoplastic Interchange. (Protoplasmatologia: Vol. 5, Pt. 2). (Illus.). 1964. pap. 16.60 (ISBN 0-387-80690-3). Springer-Verlag.

Feldheym, Len. Pole House Construction. 224p. (Orig.). 1981. pap. 15.75 (ISBN 0-910460-85-X). Craftsman.

Feldman, Abraham J. A Companion to the Bible. LC 64-20096. 3.00x (ISBN 0-8197-0078-9). Bloch.

Feldman, Alan. Frank O'Hara. (United States Authors Ser.: No. 347). 1979. 10.95 (ISBN 0-8057-7277-4). Twayne.

--The Happy Genius. LC 78-15577. 1978. pap. 4.00 (ISBN 0-915342-27-8). SUN.

Feldman, Annette. Fun with Felt. 184p. 1980. 15.95 (ISBN 0-442-25774-0). Van Nos Reinhold.

Feldman, Anthony. Space. 336p. 1980. 19.95 (ISBN 0-87196-416-3). Facts on File.

Feldman, Arnold S., jt. auth. see Tumin, Melvin M.

Feldman, B. Best of Ben, 5 vols. 1981. Set. 8.95 (ISBN 0-87863-205-0). Farnswth Pub.

Feldman, Ben. Creative Selling. LC 79-88528. (Illus.). 1979. 9.95 (ISBN 0-87863-054-6). Farnswth Pub.

Feldman, Burton & Richardson, Robert D. Rise of Modern Mythology, Sixteen Eighty to Eighteen Sixty. LC 71-135005. (Midland Bks.: No. 188). 592p. 1972. 15.00x (ISBN 0-253-35012-3); pap. 5.95x (ISBN 0-253-20188-8). Ind U Pr.

Feldman, Burton, ed. see Bell, John.

Feldman, Burton, ed. see Bryant, Jacob.

Feldman, Burton, ed. see Clavigero, Francesco S.

Feldman, Burton, ed. see Davies, Edward.

Feldman, Burton, ed. see De Camoens, Luis.

Feldman, Burton, ed. see Mallet, Paul H.

Feldman, Burton, ed. see Owen, William.

Feldman, Burton, ed. see Potter, John.

Feldman, Burton, ed. see Rowlands, Henry.

Feldman, Burton, ed. see Volney, C. F.

Feldman, Carol F., et al. The Development of Adaptive Intelligence: A Cross-Cultural Study. LC 73-22557. (Social & Behavioral Science Ser.). 1974. 13.95x o.p. (ISBN 0-87589-224-8). Jossey-Bass.

Feldman, Charles, jt. auth. see Feldman, Sari.

Feldman, Clarice & Silber, Bettina, eds. Alaskan Energy Potential & Constraints to Development. LC 79-91022. (Americans for Energy Independence Energy Policy Ser.). (Orig.). 1979. pap. 5.00 (ISBN 0-934458-01-4). Americans Energy Ind.

Feldman, Clarice R., jt. ed. see Silber, Bettina.

Feldman, Daniel L. Reforming Government: Winning Strategies Against Waste, Corruption, & Mismanagement. LC 80-24963. 225p. 1981. 11.95 (ISBN 0-688-03729-1). Morrow.

Feldman, E., ed. Varieties of Visual Experience. 3rd ed. 1981. pap. 15.95. P-H.

Feldman, Edmund B. Becoming Human Through Art: Aesthetic Experience in the School. 1970. ref. ed. 19.95 (ISBN 0-13-072363-0). P-H.

--Varieties of Visual Experience. 2nd ed. 536p. text ed. 17.95 (ISBN 0-13-940585-2). P-H.

Feldman, Edwin B. How to Use Your Time to Get Things Done. LC 68-18138. 1968. 9.95 (ISBN 0-8119-0110-6). Fell.

--One Thousand Ways to Save Energy & Money: Energy Saving Handbook for Homes, Businesses & Institutions. 1979. 9.95 (ISBN 0-8119-0321-4). Fell.

Feldman, Elliot J. A Practical Guide to the Conduct of Field Research in the Social Sciences. 120p. 1981. lib. bdg. 13.75x (ISBN 0-89158-980-5); pap. text ed. 6.95x (ISBN 0-89158-981-3). Westview.

Feldman, Elliot J. & Nevitte, Neil. The Future of North America: Canada, the United States, & Quebec Nationalism. 378p. 1979. pap. text ed. 9.50x (ISBN 0-87674-045-X, Pub. by Inst Res Pub Canada). Renouf.

Feldman, Frances L. & Scherz, Frances H. Family Social Welfare: Helping Troubled Families. LC 67-18276. 1967. 18.95x (ISBN 0-202-36001-6). Aldine Pub.

Feldman, George. Faint Spirits. (Illus.). 1981. pap. 6.95 (ISBN 0-89407-036-3). Strawberry Hill.

Feldman, Gerald D., jt. ed. see Barnes, Thomas G.

Feldman, Harold & Hindle, John H. Mathematics of Business Affairs. rev. ed. LC 73-94292. 378p. 1980. pap. text ed. 11.25 (ISBN 0-913310-09-3). PAR Inc.

Feldman, Herbert. Land & People of Pakistan. (gr. 5-9). 1958. 3.95g o.s.i. (ISBN 0-02-734370-7). Macmillan.

Feldman, Howard, jt. auth. see Strang, William A.

Feldman, Kenneth A., ed. College & Student: Selected Readings in the Social Psychology of Higher Education. 502p. 1972. text ed. 27.00 (ISBN 0-08-016785-3); pap. text ed. 12.75 (ISBN 0-08-016788-8). Pergamon.

Feldman, L. Mathematical Learning. 224p. 1969. 23.00 (ISBN 0-677-13250-6). Gordon.

Feldman, Lawrence, ed. Annual Report of the Museum of Anthropology, University of Missouri, Columbia, Mo., 1977-1978. (Annual Report Ser.). (Illus.). 1978. pap. 6.30 o.p. (ISBN 0-913134-86-4). Mus Anthro Mo.

Feldman, Lawrence, ed. see Bruhns, Karen O.

Feldman, Lawrence H. & Rowlett, Elsebet S. The Museum of Anthropology 1978-79 Annual Report. (Annual Report Ser.: No. 6). (Illus.). v, 73p. 1979. pap. 3.60 (ISBN 0-913134-84-8). Mus Anthro MO.

Feldman, Lawrence H. & Diehl, Richard, eds. The Annual Report of the Museum of Anthropology, University of Missouri, Columbia, Missouri, 1976-1977. (Annual Report Ser.). (Illus.). 1977. pap. 6.75x o.p. (ISBN 0-913134-92-9). Mus Anthro Mo.

Feldman, Lawrence H. & Walters, Gary H., eds. Excavations in Southeastern Guatemala: 1976-1978. (Miscellaneous Publications in Anthropology Ser.: No. 9, Reports 1 & 2). (Illus.). 1980. pap. 5.00x (ISBN 0-913134-80-5). Mus Anthro Mo.

Feldman, Leon. R. Abraham B. Isaac Ha-Levi Tamakh Commentary on the Song of Songs. 1970. text ed. 14.75x (ISBN 90-232-0367-4). Humanities.

Feldman, Leonard. F M from Antenna to Audio. LC 73-82884. (Illus., Orig.). 1969. pap. 4.95 o.p. (ISBN 0-672-20723-0, 20723). Sams.

Feldman, Lionel D. & Graham, Katherine A. Bargaining for Cities, Municipalities & Intergovernmental Relations: An Assessment. 143p. 1979. pap. text ed. 10.95x (ISBN 0-920380-21-2, Pub. by Inst Res Pub Canada). Renouf.

Feldman, M., jt. ed. see Markl, H.

Feldman, M. P. & Broadhurst, A. Theoretical & Experimental Bases of the Behavior Therapies. 459p. 1975. 63.50 (ISBN 0-471-25705-2). Wiley.

Feldman, M. P. & Macculloch, M. J. Homosexual Behaviour: Therapy & Assessment. 1971. 55.00 (ISBN 0-08-016244-4). Pergamon.

Feldman, M. Philip. Criminal Behaviour: A Psychological Analysis. LC 76-13229. 1977. 36.50 (ISBN 0-471-99401-4, Pub. by Wiley-Interscience). Wiley.

Feldman, M. W., jt. auth. see Cavalli-Sforza, L. L.

Feldman, Michael & Globerson, Amiela, eds. Immune Reactivity of Lymphocytes: Development, Expression, & Control. LC 75-42123. (Advances in Experimental Medicine & Biology Ser.: Vol. 66). 732p. 1976. 49.50 (ISBN 0-306-39066-3, Plenum Pr). Plenum Pub.

Feldman, Morton, jt. auth. see Hess, Thomas B.

Feldman, P. & MacCulloch, M. Human Sexual Behavior. LC 79-41220. 226p. 1980. 34.50 (ISBN 0-471-27676-6, Pub. by Wiley-Interscience). Wiley.

Feldman, Phil, jt. auth. see Rugg, Tom.

Feldman, Philip & Orford, Jim, eds. Psychological Problems: The Social Context. 360p. 1980. write for info. (ISBN 0-471-27741-X, Pub. by Wiley-Interscience). Wiley.

Feldman, Richard S., jt. auth. see Salzinger, Kurt.

Feldman, Ruth & Swann, Brian, trs. from Ital. The Dawn Is Always New: Selected Poetry of Rocco Scotellaro. LC 79-3229. (Lockert Libary of Poetry in Translation). (Ital. & Eng.). 1980. 14.50x (ISBN 0-691-06423-7); pap. 6.95 (ISBN 0-691-01370-5). Princeton U Pr.

Feldman, Ruth, tr. see Bodini, Vittorio.

Feldman, Ruth, tr. see Cattafi, Bartolo.

Feldman, S. Shirley, jt. ed. see Sears, Robert R.

Feldman, Sari & Feldman, Charles. Drugs: A Multimedia Sourcebook for Young Adults. (Selection Guide Ser.: No. 4). 256p. 1980. 14.95 (ISBN 0-87436-281-4, Co-Pub. by Neal-Schuman). ABC-Clio.

Feldman, Saul. The Administration of Mental Health Services. 2nd ed. (Illus.). 544p. 1980. 49.75 (ISBN 0-398-03942-9). C C Thomas.

Feldman, Seth R. Dziga Vertov: A Guide to References & Resources. 1979. lib. bdg. 30.00 (ISBN 0-8161-8085-7). G K Hall.

Feldman, Shirley C. & Merrill, Kathleen K. Learning Ways to Read Words, 4 bks. Incl. Bk. 1. Ways to Read Words (ISBN 0-8077-2509-9); Bk. 2. More Ways to Read Words (ISBN 0-8077-2516-1); Bk. 3. Learning About Words (ISBN 0-8077-2517-X); Bk. 4. Learning More About Words (ISBN 0-8077-2518-8). 1978. pap. 12.50 set (ISBN 0-8077-2505-6); wkbk. 8.10. Tchrs Coll.

Feldman, Stanley, jt. auth. see Sullivan, John L.

Feldman, Stanley A. Muscle Relaxants. 2nd. ed. LC 79-88002. (Major Problems in Anesthesia Ser.: Vol. I). (Illus.). 1979. text ed. 24.00 (ISBN 0-7216-3592-X). Saunders.

Feldmann, Rodney M. & Heimlich, Richard A. Geology Field Guide: The Black Hills. 208p. (Orig.). 1980. pap. 8.95 (ISBN 0-8403-2193-7). Kendall-Hunt.

Feldmann-Mazoyer, Genevieve. Recherches sur les Ceramiaceae de la Mediterranee. 1977. pap. text ed. 88.00x (ISBN 3-87429-120-0). Lubrecht & Cramer.

Feldstein, Martin S. The Rising Cost of Hospital Care. LC 72-171922. (Illus.). 88p. 1971. pap. text ed. 7.50 (ISBN 0-87815-004-8). Info Resources.

Feldstein, Paul J. Health Care Economics. LC 79-14268. (Health Services Ser.). 1979. 21.95 (ISBN 0-471-05361-9, Pub. by Wiley Medical). Wiley.

Feldstein, Sandy, ed. see Zorn, Jay & Hanshumaker, James.
Feldstein, Stanley. Once a Slave: The Slaves' View of Slavery. LC 70-130535. 329p. 1971. pap. 3.50 (ISBN 0-688-07227-5). Morrow.
Feldt, Allan. CLUG: Community Land Use Game. LC 78-190151. Orig. Title: Clug Players Manual. 1972. pap. text ed. 8.95 (ISBN 0-02-910090-9). Free Pr.
Feldvebel, Thomas P. The Ambrotype: Old & New. LC 80-65216. (Illus.). 51p. 1980. pap. 9.95 (ISBN 0-89938-001-8). Graph Arts Res RIT.
Feldweg, Wilhelm B. Metal: Design & Technique. 1975. 70.95 o.p. (ISBN 0-7134-3070-2, Pub. by Batsford England). David & Charles.
Felheim, Marvin & Traci, Philip. Realism in Shakespeare's Romantic Comedies: "O Heavenly Mingle". LC 80-5580. 239p. 1980. lib. bdg. 17.55 (ISBN 0-8191-1282-8); pap. text ed. 9.75 (ISBN 0-8191-1283-6). U Pr of Amer.
Felice, Cynthia. The Sunbound. (Orig.). 1981. pap. 2.50 (ISBN 0-440-18373-1). Dell.
Felice, Raymond. Successful Landscaping. LC 77-16624. (Illus.). 1978. 13.95 (ISBN 0-912336-55-2); pap. 6.95 (ISBN 0-912336-56-0). Structures Pub.
Felicetti, Daniel A. Mental Health & Retardation Politics: The Mind Lobbies in Congress. LC 74-14042. (Illus.). 218p. 1975. text ed. 22.95 (ISBN 0-275-09930-X). Praeger.
Feliciano Mendoza, Ester. Nanas. 3.10 o.s.i. (ISBN 0-8477-3200-2). U. of PR Pr.
Feliciano-Mendoza, Ester & Rodriquez-Baez, Felix. Ala y Trino: Pajaros De Puerto Rico Libro De Ninos Para Colorear. LC 79-24763. (Orig., Span.). 1980. pap. write for info. (ISBN 0-8477-3600-8). U. of PR Pr.
Felitta, Frank De see De Felitta, Frank.
Felix, Ervin J. Banknote Collector's Guide & Companion. DeLenc, Marcus F., ed. (Illus.). 144p. (Orig.). pap. 1.50 (ISBN 0-937458-03-1). Harris & Co.
Felix, Joseph. You Can Buy Your Way into Heaven: But It'll Take Every Cent You Have. 1981. pap. 3.95 (ISBN 0-8407-5766-2). Nelson.
Felix, Lucienne. Modern Mathematics & the Teacher. (Orig.). 1966. 17.95 (ISBN 0-521-04989-X); pap. 6.95x (ISBN 0-521-09385-6). Cambridge U Pr.
Felix, Robert H. Mental Illness: Progress & Prospects. LC 67-20278. 1967. 12.50x (ISBN 0-231-03055-X). Columbia U Pr.
Felkenes, George. Constitutional Law for Criminal Justice. (Criminal Justice Ser.). 1978. ref. 17.95 (ISBN 0-13-167833-7). P-H.
Felkenes, George T. Rules of Evidence. LC 73-11824. 224p. 1974. pap. 9.20 (ISBN 0-8273-1425-6); instructor's guide 1.60 (ISBN 0-8273-0426-9). Delmar.
Felkenes, George T. & Becker, Harold K. Law Enforcement: A Selected Bibliography. 2nd ed. LC 76-50010. 1977. 15.00 (ISBN 0-8108-0995-8). Scarecrow.
Felker, Evelyn. Raising Other People's Kids: Successful Child-Rearing in the Restructured Family. 160p. (Orig.). 1981. pap. 4.95 (ISBN 0-8028-1868-4). Eerdmans.
Felker, Evelyn H. Foster Parenting Young Children: Guidelines from a Foster Parent. LC 73-93885. 1974. pap. 3.95 (ISBN 0-87868-119-1). Child Welfare.
Felker, Rex. Haskell County Texas. (Illus.). 350p. 1975. 17.95 (ISBN 0-89015-097-4). Nortex Pr.
Fell, Albert, ed. Histories & Historians. (History Today Ser). 1968. 5.00 (ISBN 0-05-001654-7); pap. 3.95 (ISBN 0-685-00927-0). Dufour.
Fell, Derek. How to Photograph Flowers, Plants & Landscapes. (Photography Ser.). (Orig.). 1980. pap. 7.95 (ISBN 0-89586-068-6). H P Bks.
Fell, James E., Jr. Ores to Metals: The Rocky Mountain Smelting Industry. LC 79-9093. (Illus.). xvi, 341p. 1979. 21.50x (ISBN 0-8032-1951-2). U. of Nebr Pr.
Fell, John. Delegate from New Jersey: The Journal of John Fell. Whisenhunt, Donald W., ed. LC 73-83264. 222p. 1974. 13.50 (ISBN 0-8046-9041-3). Kennikat.
Fell, John L. Film: An Introduction. LC 73-18865. (Illus.). 274p. 1975. pap. 10.95 (ISBN 0-02-758911-0). Praeger.
Fellegy, Joe, Jr. Walleyes & Walleye Fishing. LC 72-89440. (Illus.). 210p. 1973. 8.95 (ISBN 0-87518-054-X). Dillon.
Felleman, Hazel, ed. Best Loved Poems of the American People. 1936. 8.95 (ISBN 0-385-00019-7). Doubleday.
--Poems That Live Forever. LC 65-13987. 1965. 7.95 (ISBN 0-385-00358-7). Doubleday.
Fellendorf, George W., ed. Supplement to Bibliography on Deafness: 1977 to 1979. 1980. pap. text ed. 4.95 (ISBN 0-88200-139-6, L9435). Alexander Graham.
Feller, I. International Bibliography on Burns, 1981 Supplement. 1981. pap. 12.00 (ISBN 0-917478-12-6). Natl Inst Burn.
Feller, I., jt. ed. see Bowden, M. L.
Feller, I., ed. see National Institute for Burn Medicine.
Feller, I., et al. Planning & Designing a Burn Care Facility. LC 80-83418. (Illus.). 350p. 1981. 75.00 (ISBN 0-917478-21-5). Natl Inst Burn.
Feller, Irving & Grabb, William C., eds. Reconstruction & Rehabilitation of the Burned Patient. LC 78-61362. (Illus.). 1979. text ed. 98.00 (ISBN 0-917478-50-9); text ed. 208.00 genuine leather bdg. (ISBN 0-917478-51-7). Natl Inst Burn.
Feller, William. Introduction to Probability Theory & Its Applications, Vol. 1. 3rd ed. LC 68-11708. (Probability & Mathematical Statistics Ser.). 1968. 26.95 (ISBN 0-471-25708-7). Wiley.
Fellhauer, Cheryl, jt. auth. see Goeldner, C. R.
Fellini, Frederico. Fellini on Fellini. 1976. 7.95 o.p. (ISBN 0-440-02528-1, Sey Lawr). Delacorte.
Fellman, David. The Defendant's Rights Today. 1977. 25.00 (ISBN 0-299-07200-2); pap. 8.95 (ISBN 0-299-07204-5). U. of Wis Pr.
--Religion in American Public Law. LC 65-17006. 1965. 9.50x (ISBN 0-8419-8714-9, Pub. by Boston U Pr). Holmes & Meier.
Fellman, David, ed. Supreme Court & Education. 3rd ed. LC 76-14495. 1976. pap. text ed. 7.00x (ISBN 0-8077-2511-0). Tchrs Coll.
Fellmann, Jerome D., jt. auth. see Harris, Chauncy D.
Fellmeth, Robert C. Politics of Land: The Report on Land Use in California. LC 79-184471. (Ralph Nader Study Group Reports). 1973. pap. 5.95 o.p. (ISBN 0-670-56327-7, N10, Grossman). Penguin.
Fellner, William, ed. Contemporary Economic Problems, 1980. 1980. pap. 8.25 (ISBN 0-8447-3386-5). Am Enterprise.
Fellner, William J., ed. Contemporary Economic Problems, 1979. 1979. pap. 9.25 (ISBN 0-8447-1334-1). Am Enterprise.
Fellowes, Edmund H. English Cathedral Music. 5th, rev. ed. Westrup, J. A., ed. LC 80-24400. (Illus.). xi, 283p. 1981. Repr. of 1973 ed. lib. bdg. 27.50x (ISBN 0-313-22643-1, FEEC). Greenwood.
--English Madrigal Composers. 2nd ed. 1948. pap. 9.95x (ISBN 0-19-315144-8). Oxford U Pr.
--William Byrd. 2nd ed. 1948. 11.25x o.p. (ISBN 0-19-315204-5). Oxford U Pr.
Fellowes, Edmund H., ed. English Madrigal Verse: 1588-1632. 3rd ed. 1967. 59.00x (ISBN 0-19-811474-5). Oxford U Pr.
Fellows. Puzzle Blast. (gr. 3-5). pap. 0.95 (ISBN 0-590-11894-3, Schol Pap). Schol Bk Serv.
Fellows, B. J. The Discrimination Process & Development. 1968. 32.00 (ISBN 0-08-012521-2). Pergamon.
Fellows, Catherine. Entanglement. (A Regency Romance Ser.). 1979. pap. 1.75 o.p. (ISBN 0-449-24079-7, Crest). Fawcett.
Fellows, Donald K. Our Environment: An Introduction to Physical Geography. 2nd ed. LC 79-18159. 1980. text ed. 18.95 (ISBN 0-471-05755-X); tchrs'. manual avail. (ISBN 0-471-06363-0). Wiley.
Fellows, Julian R., jt. auth. see Severns, William H.
Fellows, Lawrence. East Africa. LC 76-165108. (Nations Today Bks). (gr. 7 up). 1972. 7.95 (ISBN 0-02-734450-9). Macmillan.
--A Gentle War: The Story of the Salvation Army. LC 79-14622. (Illus.). (gr. 5 up). 1979. 8.95 (ISBN 0-02-734430-4, 73443). Macmillan.
Fellows, Leonard F. Puzzle Power. (gr. 4-6). 1976. pap. 1.25 (ISBN 0-590-10230-3, Schol Pap). Schol Bk Serv.
Fellows, Otis. Diderot. (World Authors Ser.: France: No. 425). 1977. lib. bdg. 10.95 (ISBN 0-8057-6265-5). Twayne.
Fellows, Otis E. & Milliken, Stephen F. Buffon. LC 76-39777. (World Authors Ser.: France: No. 243). lib. bdg. 10.95 (ISBN 0-8057-2184-3). Twayne.
Fellows, Otis E. & Torrey, Norman L. Age of Enlightenment. 2nd ed. LC 73-147121. 1971. text ed. 17.95 (ISBN 0-13-018465-9). P-H.
Fellowship Church, Baton Rouge, La, Members. Quickies for Singles. McKee, Gwen, ed. (Illus.). 80p. 1980. pap. 4.95 (ISBN 0-937552-03-8). Quail Ridge.
Fellucci, Mario. The Masterpieces of the Vatican. (A Science of Man Library Bk). (Illus.). 40p. 1975. 60.00 (ISBN 0-913314-54-4). Am Classical Coll Pr.
Felmy, Bradford K. & Grady, John C., Jr. Suffering to Silence. (Illus.). 200p. 1975. 9.95 (ISBN 0-89015-098-2). Nortex Pr.
Fels, et al. Casebook of Economic, Microeconomic Problems & Policies: Practice in Thinking. 4th ed. 112p. 1978. 5.95 (ISBN 0-8299-0479-4); staff notes avail. West Pub.
Fels, George. Pool Simplified--Somewhat. LC 77-23697. 1978. 7.95 (ISBN 0-8092-7771-9); pap. 4.95 o.p. (ISBN 0-8092-7770-0). Contemp Bks.
Fels, Gerhard, jt. ed. see Corden, W. M.
Felsen, Henry G. Can You Do It Until You Need Glasses. LC 77-6498. (gr. 7 up). 1977. 5.95g (ISBN 0-396-07483-9). Dodd.
--Cub Scout at Last. (Illus.). (gr. 2-5). 1952. pap. 0.95 o.p. (ISBN 0-684-12785-7, ScribT, SBF14). Scribner.
--Hot Rod. (Literature Ser). (gr. 9-12). 1950. pap. text ed. 3.50 (ISBN 0-87720-754-2). AMSCO Sch.
Felsen, L. B., jt. auth. see Marcuvitz, Nathan.
Felsenfeld, Naomi, jt. auth. see Maclennan, Beryce W.
Felsenstein, Frank, ed. see Smollett, Tobias.
Felsenthal, Carol. The Sweetheart of the Silent Majority. LC 79-6090. (Illus.). 360p. 1981. 13.95 (ISBN 0-385-14912-3). Doubleday.
Felsenthal, Norman. Orientations to Mass Communication. rev. ed. Applbaum, Ronald & Hart, Roderick, eds. (Modcom, Modules in Speech Communication Ser.). 1980. pap. text ed. 2.25 (ISBN 0-574-22569-2, 13-5569). SRA.
Felson, Benjamin, et al. Principles of Chest Roentgenology: A Programed Text. LC 65-23091. (Illus.). 1965. 11.95 (ISBN 0-7216-3605-5). Saunders.
Felstiner, John. Translating Neruda: The Way to Macchu Picchu. LC 79-67773. (Illus.). 240p. 1980. 18.50x (ISBN 0-8047-1079-1). Stanford U Pr.
Feltham, Owen. Resolves, a Duple Century. 3rd ed. LC 74-28853. (English Experience Ser.: No. 734). 1975. Repr. of 1628 ed. 35.00 (ISBN 90-221-0734-5). Walter J Johnson.
Feltner, C. E., Jr. Winning Is Everything--Losing Is Nothing! LC 80-68579. 200p. 1981. 9.95 (ISBN 0-87754-066-7). Chelsea Hse.
Felton, Bruce & Fowler, Mark. Felton & Fowler's Best, Worst & Most Unusual. LC 75-9895. 288p. (YA) 1975. 10.95 (ISBN 0-690-00569-5, TYC-T). T Y Crowell.
Felton, Gary S. & Biggs, Barbara E. Up from Underachievement. (Illus.). 208p. 1977. 14.75 (ISBN 0-398-03627-6); pap. 9.50 (ISBN 0-398-03639-X). C C Thomas.
Felton, Harold W. Deborah Sampson, Soldier of the Revolution. LC 76-13438. (gr. 4 up). 1976. 5.95 (ISBN 0-396-07343-3). Dodd.
--Edward Rose, Negro Trail Blazer. (Illus.). (gr. 5-9). 1967. 5.95 o.p. (ISBN 0-396-05597-4). Dodd.
--Uriah Phillips Levy. LC 78-7726. (Illus.): (gr. 5 up). 1979. 5.95 (ISBN 0-396-07604-1). Dodd.
Felton, J. S., jt. auth. see Katz, Alfred H.
Felton, James. Business Mathematics: A Better Course. 640p. 1981. pap. 15.95 (ISBN 0-205-07323-9, 1073230); tchr's ed. free (ISBN 0-205-07324-7, 1073249). Allyn.
Felton, W. Sidney. Masters of Equitation. (Illus.). 7.35 (ISBN 0-85131-091-5, Dist. by Sporting Book Center). J A Allen.
Felts, Frances I., jt. auth. see Neal, Richard G.
Felts, William J. & Harrison, Richard J., eds. International Review of General & Experimental Zoology, 4 vols. 1964-70. Vol. 1. 48.50, by subscription 40.00 (ISBN 0-12-368101-4); Vol. 2. 48.50, by subscription 40.00 (ISBN 0-12-368102-2); Vol. 3. 48.50, by subscription 40.00 (ISBN 0-12-368103-0); Vol. 4. 48.50, by subscription 40.00 (ISBN 0-12-368104-9); 160.00 (ISBN 0-686-66612-7). Set. Acad Pr.
Feltskog, E. N., ed. see Parkman, Frances.
Feltus, Peter R. Catalogue of Egyptian Revenue Stamps. (Illus.). 240p. 1981. 30.00 (ISBN 0-9605286-0-1). P R Feltus.
Felzer, Ron. High Sierra Hiking Guide to Hetch Hetchy. Winnett, Thomas, ed. LC 72-89914. (High Sierra Hiking Guide Ser: Vol. 12). (Illus., Orig.). 1973. pap. 3.95 (ISBN 0-911824-24-3). Wilderness.
--High Sierra Hiking Guide to Mineral King. Winnett, Thomas, ed. LC 70-186759. (High Sierra Hiking Guide Ser: Vol. 8). (Illus., Orig.). 1972. pap. 2.95 o.p. (ISBN 0-911824-19-7). Wilderness.
Feminist Press. Black Foremothers: Three Lives. (Women's Lives-Women's Work). (Illus.). (gr. 10-12). 1979. pap. text ed. 4.92 (ISBN 0-07-020433-0, W); tchr's. ed. 4.56 (ISBN 0-07-020434-9). McGraw.
Fenady, Andrew J. The Secret Sam Marlow: The Further Adventures of the Man with Bogart's Face. 1979. 9.95 (ISBN 0-8092-5989-3). Contemp Bks.
Fenchel, W., jt. auth. see Bonnesen, T.
Fencl, Shirley & Jager, Susan G. The Two R's: Paragraph to Essay. LC 78-16026. 1979. pap. text ed. 10.95 (ISBN 0-471-01947-X). Wiley.
Fendell, Bob. How to Make Your Car Last a Lifetime. LC 80-19759. (Illus.). 216p. 1981. 12.95 (ISBN 0-03-053661-8); pap. 6.95 (ISBN 0-03-053656-1). HR&W.
--The New Era Car Book & Auto Survival Guide. LC 75-5466. (Illus.). 320p. 1976. 9.95 o.p. (ISBN 0-03-014031-5); pap. 5.95 o.p. (ISBN 0-03-014036-6). HR&W.
Fendelman, Helaine. Tramp Art. 96p. 1975. pap. 6.95 o.p. (ISBN 0-525-47407-2). Dutton.
Fendler, Dolores T., jt. auth. see Becker, Betty G.
Feneday, Andrew J. The Man with Bogart's Face. 184p. 1979. pap. 1.95 (ISBN 0-380-01849-7, 49015). Avon.
Fenelon. Let Go! 1973. pap. 2.25 (ISBN 0-88368-010-6). Whitaker Hse.
Fenelon & De Salignac De La Mothe, Francois. The Adventures of Telemachus, 2 vols. Paulson, Ronald, ed. LC 78-60835. (Novel 1720-1805 Ser.: Vol. 1). 1979. lib. bdg. 31.00 (ISBN 0-8240-3650-6). Garland Pub.
Fenelon, Francois. Christian Perfection. Whiston, Charles F., ed. Stillman, Mildred W., tr. from Fr. LC 75-22545. 224p. 1976. pap. 2.95 (ISBN 0-87123-083-6, 200083). Bethany Fell.
Fenelon, K. G. The United Arab Emirates. 2nd ed. LC 75-42139. (Illus.). 1977. text ed. 15.00x (ISBN 0-582-78066-7). Longman.
Feng, Doreen Y. The Joy of Chinese Cooking. (Illus., Orig.). 1964. pap. 3.95 o.p. (ISBN 0-571-05865-5, Pub. by Faber & Faber). Merrimack Bk Serv.
Feng, G. & Wilkerson, H. Tai-Chi, a Way of Centering. 1969. 6.95 o.s.i. (ISBN 0-02-537290-4). Macmillan.
--Tai-Chi: A Way of Centering. 1970. pap. 4.95 o.s.i. (ISBN 0-02-076130-9, Collier). Macmillan.
Fenger, Frederic A. Alone in the Caribbean. (Illus.). 1958. 6.95 o.p. (ISBN 0-686-00951-7). Wellington.
Fenhagen, James. Mutual Ministry: New Vitality for the Local Church. 1977. 7.95 (ISBN 0-8164-0332-5). Crossroad NY.
Fenhagen, James C. More Than Wanderers: Spiritual Disciplines for Christian Ministry. LC 77-17974. 1978. 6.95 (ISBN 0-8164-0386-4). Crossroad NY.
Fenhagen, James C. & Hahn, Celia A. Study Guide to "Congregations in Change". LC 73-17894. 1974. 1.45 (ISBN 0-8164-2093-9). Crossroad NY.
Fenichel, Carol & Hogan, Thomas. Online Searching: A Primer. 130p. 1981. text ed. 12.95x (ISBN 0-938734-01-6). Learned Info.
Fenlon, D. Heresy & Obedience in Tridentine Italy: Cardinal Pole & the Counter-Reformation. LC 72-87177. 336p. 1973. 47.50 (ISBN 0-521-20005-9). Cambridge U Pr.
Fenlon, Iain. Music & Patronage in Sixteenth Century Mantua. LC 79-41377. (Cambridge Studies in Music). (Illus.). 350p. Date not set. 57.50 (ISBN 0-521-22905-7). Cambridge U Pr.
--Music in Medieval & Early Modern Europe: Patronage, Sources & Texts. LC 80-40490. (Illus.). 290p. Date not set. price not set (ISBN 0-521-23328-3). Cambridge U Pr.
Fenn, Forrest. The African Animals of William R. Leigh. (Illus.). 32p. (Orig.). 1980. pap. 10.00 (ISBN 0-937634-01-8). Fenn Gall Pub.
Fenn, Margaret. Making It in Management: A Behavioral Approach for Women Executives. LC 78-17005. (Illus.). 1978. 10.95 (ISBN 0-13-547638-0, Spec); pap. 5.95 (ISBN 0-13-547620-8). P-H.
Fenn, Wallace O., ed. see American Physiological Society.
Fenn, William. Christian Higher Education in Changing China. 256p. 1976. 5.95 o.p. (ISBN 0-8028-1662-2). Eerdmans.
Fennel, T. G. & Gelsen, H. A Grammar of Modern Latvian, 3 vols. (Slavistic Printings & Reprintings: No. 303). 1980. text ed. 176.50x (ISBN 0-686-26963-2). Mouton.
Fennell, F. A., Jr. Orchids for Home & Garden. rev. ed. 1959. 6.95 o.p. (ISBN 0-03-029060-0, HR&W). HR&W.
Fennell, Francis. Writing Now: A College Handbook. 1980. pap. text ed. 7.95 (ISBN 0-574-22050-X, 13-5050); instr's guide avail. (ISBN 0-574-22051-8, 13-5051). SRA.
Fennell, Francis M. Elementary Mathematics Diagnosis & Correction Kit. 1980. pap. 17.95x comb-bound (ISBN 0-87628-295-8). Ctr Appl Res.
Fennell, Frederick. Basic Band Repertory: British Band Classics from the Conductor's Point of View. 1980. pap. 6.00. Instrumental Co.
Fennell, J. L., tr. Correspondence Between Prince A. M. Kurbsky & Tsar Ivan Fourth of Russia, 1564-1579. 1956. 48.00 (ISBN 0-521-05501-6). Cambridge U Pr.
Fennell, J. L., et al, eds. Oxford Slavonic Papers, Vol. 13. (Illus.). 128p. 1981. 45.00 (ISBN 0-19-815656-1). Oxford U Pr.
Fennell, John & Stokes, Antony. Early Russian Literature. 1974. 26.75x (ISBN 0-520-02343-9). U. of Cal Pr.
Fennell, John, ed. Nineteenth-Century Russian Literature: Studies of Ten Russian Writers. (Library Reprint Ser.). 1976. 22.75x (ISBN 0-520-03203-9). U of Cal Pr.
Fennell, Rosemary. The Common Agricultural Policy of the European Community. LC 79-2961. 255p. 1980. text ed. 21.95 (ISBN 0-916672-29-8). Allanheld.
Fennelly. Handbook of Loss Prevention & Crime Prevention. 1981. text ed. price not set. Butterworth.

Fenner, Carol. The Skates of Uncle Richard. LC 78-55910. (Illus.). (gr. 2-5). 1978. 4.95 (ISBN 0-394-83553-0, BYR); PLB 5.99 (ISBN 0-394-93553-5). Random.

Fenner, Dudley. A Counter-Poyson..., to the Objections & Reproches, Wherewith the Aunswerer to the Abstract, Would Disgrace the Holy Discipline of Christ. LC 74-28854. (English Experience Ser.: No. 735). 1975. Repr. of 1584 ed. 10.50 (ISBN 90-221-0735-3). Walter J Johnson.

Fenner, F., et al. The Biology of Animal Viruses. 2nd ed. 1974. 62.50 (ISBN 0-12-253040-3). Acad Pr.

Fenner, Frank & Ratcliffe, F. N. Myxomatosis. 1966. 65.00 (ISBN 0-521-04991-1). Cambridge U Pr.

Fenner, Peter. Researching Science Information. 250p. (Orig.). 1981. pap. 7.95 (ISBN 0-86576-010-1). W Kaufmann.

Fenner, Phyllis R., compiled by. Consider the Evidence, Stories of Mystery & Suspense. LC 73-792. (Illus.). 192p. (gr. 7 up). 1973. 7.75 (ISBN 0-688-20080-X). Morrow.

--A Dog's Life: Stories of Champions, Hunters, & Faithful Friends. (Illus.). (gr. 7-9). 1978. 7.95 (ISBN 0-688-22156-4); PLB 7.63 (ISBN 0-688-32156-9). Morrow.

--The Endless Dark: Stories of Underground Adventure. LC 77-5494. (Illus.). (gr. 7 up). 1977. 8.25 (ISBN 0-688-22122-X); PLB 7.92 (ISBN 0-688-32122-4). Morrow.

--Gentle Like a Cyclone: Stories of Horses & Their Riders. LC 74-2499. (Illus.). 192p. (gr. 7 up). 1974. 7.25 o.p. (ISBN 0-688-21821-0); PLB 7.92 (ISBN 0-688-31821-5). Morrow.

Fenner, Phyllis R., ed. Ghosts, Ghosts, Ghosts. (Terrific Triple Titles Ser). (Illus.). (gr. 4-6). 1952. PLB 6.90 o.p. (ISBN 0-531-01676-5). Watts.

Fenner, Phyllis R., compiled by. Perilous Ascent, Stories of Mountain Climbing. (Illus.). (gr. 7 up). 1970. 7.75 (ISBN 0-688-21734-6). Morrow.

Fenner, Phyllis R., ed. Wide-Angle Lens: Stories of Time & Space. LC 80-16992. (Illus.). 224p. (gr. 7-9). 1980. 7.95 (ISBN 0-688-22241-2); PLB 7.63 (ISBN 0-688-32241-7). Morrow.

Fenner, R. T. Principles of Polymer Processing. 1980. 35.00 (ISBN 0-8206-0285-X). Chem Pub.

Fenner, Roger T. Finite Element Methods for Engineers. (Illus.). 1976. 23.50 o.p. (ISBN 0-333-18340-1); pap. text ed. 16.95x (ISBN 0-333-18656-7). Scholium Intl.

Fennimore, Keith J. Booth Tarkington. (U. S. Authors Ser.: No. 238). 1974. lib. bdg. 10.95 (ISBN 0-8057-0715-8). Twayne.

Fennow, Karin, tr. see Birket-Smith, Kaj.

Fenoglio. Progress in Surgical Pathology, Vol. III. 1981. 54.50 (ISBN 0-89352-122-1). Masson Pub.

Fenoglio, Cecilia M. & Wolff, Marianne, eds. Progress in Surgical Pathology, Vol. 1. LC 80-80334. (Illus.). 296p. 1980. 54.50 (ISBN 0-89352-087-X). Masson Pub.

--Progress in Surgical Pathology, Vol. 2. LC 80-80334. (Illus.). 304p. 1980. 54.50 (ISBN 0-89352-090-X). Masson Pub.

Fenoyl, Pierre de see De Fenoyl, Pierre.

Fensch. The Superintendency Team. 1964. text ed. 12.50 (ISBN 0-675-09926-9). Merrill.

Fensch, Thomas. The Lions & the Lambs. 1977. 7.95 o.p. (ISBN 0-498-07388-2). A S Barnes.

--Smokey's, Truckers, CB Radios & You: Complete Guide to Citizen's Band Radio. 1976. pap. 1.75 o.p. (ISBN 0-449-22972-6, Crest). Fawcett.

Fenske, S H. My Life in Christ: A Momento of My Confirmation. LC 76-5729. (gr. 8 up). 1976. pap. 1.95 (ISBN 0-8100-0056-3, 16*N0514). Northwest Pub.

Fenson, Harry & Kritzer, Hildreth. Reading, Understanding & Writing About Short Stories. LC 66-15498. (Orig.). 1966. pap. text ed. 8.95 (ISBN 0-02-910120-4). Free Pr.

Fenten. Greenhousing for Purple Thumbs. LC 76-26055. (Illus.). 192p. (Orig.). 1976. 4.95 (ISBN 0-89286-105-3); pap. 4.95 (ISBN 0-89286-104-5). One Hund One Prods.

Fenten, Barbara & Fenten, D. X. Careers in the Sports Industry. LC 76-44506. (Career Concise Guides Ser.). (Illus.). (gr. 7 up). 1977. PLB 6.45 (ISBN 0-531-00372-8). Watts.

--Natural Foods. LC 73-10381. (Concise Guide Ser). (Illus.). 72p. (gr. 5 up). 1974. PLB 5.45 o.p. (ISBN 0-531-02675-2). Watts.

Fenten, D. X. Gardening...Naturally. LC 72-13790. (Illus.). 128p. (gr. 4 up). 1973. PLB 5.88 o.p. (ISBN 0-531-02625-6); pap. 2.95 (ISBN 0-531-02338-9). Watts.

--Indoor Gardening. LC 74-3278. (First Bks). (Illus.). 72p. (gr. 4-10). 1974. PLB 4.90 o.p. (ISBN 0-531-02731-7). Watts.

--Ins & Outs of Gardening. (Illus.). 128p. (YA) 1979. 8.95 o.p. (ISBN 0-87460-263-7). Lion.

--TV & Radio Careers. (Career Concise Guides Ser.). (Illus.). 72p. (gr. 7 up). 1976. PLB 6.45 (ISBN 0-531-01131-3). Watts.

Fenten, D. X., jt. auth. see Fenten, Barbara.

Fenton, Alexander. The Northern Isles: Orkney & Shetland. (Illus.). 1978. text ed. 39.00x (ISBN 0-85976-019-7). Humanities.

Fenton, Alexander & Owen, Trefor. Food in Perspective: Third International Conference of Ethnological Food Research. 1980. text ed. 34.50x (ISBN 0-85976-044-8). Humanities.

Fenton, Alexander & Walker, Bruce. The Rural Architecture of Scotland. (Illus.). 1980. text ed. 34.50x (ISBN 0-85976-020-0). Humanities.

Fenton, Barb, jt. auth. see Fenton, Don.

Fenton, Don & Fenton, Barb. Behind the Circus Scene. Schroeder, Howard, ed. LC 80-14521. (Behind the Scenes Ser.). (Illus.). (gr. 4). 1980. PLB 5.95 (ISBN 0-89686-059-0); pap. 2.95 (ISBN 0-89686-064-7). Crestwood Hse.

--Behind the Newspaper Scene. Schroeder, Howard, ed. LC 80-14593. (Behind the Scenes Ser.). (Illus.). (gr. 4). 1980. PLB 5.95 (ISBN 0-89686-058-2); pap. 2.95 (ISBN 0-89686-063-9). Crestwood Hse.

--Behind the Radio Scene. Schroeder, Howard, ed. LC 80-14594. (Behind the Scenes Ser.). (Illus.). (gr. 4). 1980. PLB 5.95 (ISBN 0-89686-061-2); pap. 2.95 (ISBN 0-89686-066-3). Crestwood Hse.

--Behind the Sports Scene. Schroeder, Howard, ed. LC 80-14070. (Behind the Scenes Ser.). (Illus.). (gr. 4). 1980. PLB 5.95 (ISBN 0-89686-060-4); pap. 2.95 (ISBN 0-89686-065-5). Crestwood Hse.

--Behind the Television Scene. Schroeder, Howard, ed. LC 80-14151. (Behind the Scenes Ser.). (Illus.). (gr. 4). 1980. PLB 5.95 (ISBN 0-89686-062-0); pap. 2.95 (ISBN 0-89686-067-1). Crestwood Hse.

Fenton, Geoffrey, tr. A Discourse of the Civile Warres in Fraunce, Drawn into Englishe by G. Fenton. LC 76-26510. (English Experience Ser.: No. 248). 1970. Repr. of 1570 ed. 20.00 (ISBN 90-221-0248-3). Walter J Johnson.

Fenton, J. C., intro. by. Gospel According to John in the Revised Standard Version. (New Clarendon Bible Ser). 1970. 6.95x (ISBN 0-19-836908-5). Oxford U Pr.

Fenton, John. The A to Z of Sales Management. 168p. 1981. 14.95 (ISBN 0-8144-5655-3). Am Mgmt.

--A-Z Industrial Salesmanship. 1975. text ed. 16.95x (ISBN 0-434-90559-3); pap. text ed. 9.95x (ISBN 0-434-90560-7). Intl Ideas.

Fenton, Judith A. & Lifchez, Aaron S. The Fertility Handbook. (Orig.). 1980. 12.95 (ISBN 0-517-53991-8); pap. 5.95 (ISBN 0-517-54125-4). Potter.

Fenton, Loren L. Thirteen Weeks to Riches (Which Could Be Glory!) (Orig.). 1978. pap. 6.00 (ISBN 0-934178-00-3). Christian Success.

--Whoa! I Yelled Whoa! LC 78-50460. (Destiny Ser.). 1979. pap. 4.95 (ISBN 0-8163-0249-9). Pacific Pr Pub Assn.

Fenton, Norman. Human Relations in Adult Corrections. 224p. 1973. 14.75 (ISBN 0-398-02837-0). C C Thomas.

--Self-Direction & Adjustment. 121p. 1980. Repr. of 1926 ed. lib. bdg. 22.50 (ISBN 0-89760-225-0). Telegraph Bks.

Fenton, Robert S., ed. see Leeming, Joseph.

Fenton, Ruth M. Adventures in Food, Natural Cooking Made Easy: How to Cook Better for Less Without Adding Oil or Sugar. (Orig.). 1980. pap. 6.95 (ISBN 0-934178-01-1). Christian Success.

Fenton, Thomas, ed. Education for Justice (Participant Handbook) LC 74-83519. 120p. 1975. pap. 3.95x o.p. (ISBN 0-88344-120-9). Orbis Bks.

Fenwick, Eliza. Secrecy, or the Ruin on the Rock, 3 vols. Luria, Gina, ed. (The Feminist Controversy in England 1788-1810 Ser.). 1974. Set. lib. bdg. 50.00 ea. (ISBN 0-8240-0859-6); lib. bdg. 45.00 ea. Garland Pub.

--Visits to the Juvenile Library, Repr. Of 1805 Ed. Bd. with The Adventures of Ulysses. Lamb, Charles. Repr. of 1808 ed. LC 75-32152. (Classics of Children's Literature, 1621-1932: Vol. 18). 1976. PLB 38.00 (ISBN 0-8240-2266-1). Garland Pub.

Fenwick, Keith & McBride, Peter. The Government of Education: The Politics & Administration of Education in Britain. 256p. 1981. 20.00x (ISBN 0-85520-255-6, Pub. by Martin Robertson England); pap. 9.95x (ISBN 0-85520-254-8). Biblio Dist.

Fenwick, R. D. The Advocate Guide to Gay Health. (Illus.). 1978. 10.95 o.p. (ISBN 0-525-05050-7). Dutton.

Fenwick, S. A., ed. Library Services for Children in New Zealand Schools & Public Libraries: Statistical Appendix to the Report. (New Zealand Council for Educational Research, Studies in Education: No. 24, Pt. 2). 1977. pap. text ed. 6.00x o.p. (ISBN 0-8426-1052-9). Verry.

Fenwick, Sara I., jt. ed. see Asheim, Lester.

Fenwick, Sheridan. Getting It: The Psychology of EST. LC 76-20617. 1976. 7.95 o.p. (ISBN 0-397-01170-9). Lippincott.

Fenyo, P., tr. see Szobor, A.

Fenyvesi, Charles. Splendor in Exile: The Ex-Majesties of Europe. LC 79-20707. (Illus.). 1979. 12.95 o.p. (ISBN 0-915220-55-5). New Republic.

Fenzi, Jewell. Netherlands Antilles Cookbook. 1972. 5.00 o.p. (ISBN 0-911268-23-5). Rogers Bk.

Feodoroff, Nicholas V. The Truth: Cossacks, the Glory of Russia. 1981. 6.75 (ISBN 0-8062-1704-9). Carlton.

Feray, D. E. & Starnes, J. L. Index to Well Samples. rev. ed. 148p. 1950. 1.65 (PUB 5015). Bur Econ Geology.

Ferber, Edna. Cimarron. LC 30-8609. 1951. 11.95 (ISBN 0-385-04069-5). Doubleday.

--Saratoga Trunk. LC 41-24504. 1951. 5.95 o.p. (ISBN 0-385-04902-1). Doubleday.

Ferber, Ellen, jt. ed. see Fulton, Len.

Ferber, Helen, jt. auth. see Scotten, R. B.

Ferber, Linda S. William Trost Richards (Eighteen Thirty-Three to Nineteen Hundred Five: American Landscape & Marine Painter. LC 78-74367. (Outstanding Dissertations in the Fine Arts Ser.). (Illus.). 525p. 1979. lib. bdg. 50.00 (ISBN 0-8240-3955-6). Garland Pub.

Ferber, Peggy, ed. see Beckey, Fred.

Ferber, Steve, ed. All About Rifle Hunting & Shooting in America. 1977. 12.95 (ISBN 0-87691-244-7). Winchester Pr.

Ferdinand, W. The Enzyme Molecule. LC 76-7530. 1976. 17.25 (ISBN 0-471-01822-8, Pub by Wiley-Interscience); pap. 14.95 (ISBN 0-471-01821-X). Wiley.

Ferdon, Edwin N. Early Tahiti As the Explorers Saw It. LC 80-26469. 1981. text ed. 19.50x (ISBN 0-8165-0708-2); pap. 12.50 (ISBN 0-8165-0720-1). U of Ariz Pr.

Ferdowsi. The Epic of the Kings: Shah- nama. (Persian Heritage Ser). 1973. 27.00 (ISBN 0-7100-1367-1). Routledge & Kegan.

Ferebee, Ann. A History of Design from the Victorian Era to the Present. 128p. 1980. pap. 7.95 (ISBN 0-442-23115-6). Van Nos Reinhold.

Ferencz, Benjamin. An International Criminal Court: A Step Toward World Peace, 2 vols. LC 80-10688. 1212p. 1980. Vol. 1. lib. bdg. 37.50 ea. (ISBN 0-379-20389-8). Vol. 2 (ISBN 0-379-20390-1). Oceana.

Ferenczi, Sandor. Final Contributions to the Problems & Methods of Psycho-Analysis. Balint, Michael, ed. Mosbacher, Eric, tr. from Ger. LC 80-19817. (Brunner-Mazel Classics in Psychoanalysis Ser.: No. 8). 450p. 1980. Repr. of 1955 ed. 20.00 (ISBN 0-87630-256-8). Brunner-Mazel.

--First Contributions to Psycho-Analysis. Jones, Ernest, tr. from Ger. LC 80-19815. (Brunner-Mazel Classics in Psycholoanalysis Ser.: No. 6). Orig. Title: Sex in Psychoanalysis. 340p. 1980. Repr. 20.00 (ISBN 0-87630-254-1). Brunner-Mazel.

--Further Contributions to the Theory & Technique of Psycho-Analysis. Rickman, John, ed. Suttie, Jane I., tr. from Ger. LC 80-19811. (Brunner-Mazel Classics in Psychoanalysis Ser.: No. 7). 480p. 1980. Repr. of 1926 ed. 20.00 (ISBN 0-87630-255-X). Brunner-Mazel.

Ferenczy, Alex & Richart, Ralph M. Female Reproductive System: Dynamics of Scanning & Transmission Electron Microscopy. LC 73-17486. 401p. 1974. 64.95 (ISBN 0-471-25730-3, Pub. by Wiley-Medical). Wiley.

Ferenczy, L., ed. see International Protoplast Symposium, 5th, July 1979, Szeged, Hungary.

Feret, Barbara L. Gastronomical & Culinary Literature: A Survey & Analysis of Historically-Oriented Collections in the U. S. A. LC 78-32098. 1979. lib. bdg. 10.00 (ISBN 0-8108-1204-5). Scarecrow.

Ferguson. Readings on Concepts of Criminal Law. (Criminal Justice Ser.). 1975. pap. text ed. 12.95 (ISBN 0-8299-0619-3). West Pub.

Ferguson, Adam. Institutes of Moral Philosophy. 2nd rev. ed. LC 75-11219. (British Philosophers & Theologians of the 17th & 18th Centuries Ser.: Vol. 22). 1978. Repr. of 1773 ed. lib. bdg. 42.00 (ISBN 0-8240-1773-0). Garland Pub.

--Principles of Moral & Political Science, 2 vols. Wellek, Rene, ed. LC 75-11218. (British Philosophers & Theologians of the 17th & 18th Centuries Ser.: Vol. 21). 1978. Repr. of 1792 ed. Set. lib. bdg. 66.00 (ISBN 0-8240-1772-2); lib. bdg. 42.00 ea. Garland Pub.

Ferguson, Albert. Orthopaedic Surgery in Infancy & Childhood. 5th ed. (Illus.). 654p. 1981. write for info. (3167-8). Williams & Wilkins.

Ferguson, Alfred R., jt. ed. see Sealts, Merton M., Jr.

Ferguson, Allen R., ed. see Public Interest Economics Foundation.

Ferguson, Andrew. Biochemical Systematics & Evolution. LC 79-20298. 1980. 44.95x (ISBN 0-470-26856-5). Halsted Pr.

Ferguson, Anthony, ed. Annual Review of English Books on Asia 1978-79. LC 74-4918. 256p. (Orig.). 1980. pap. 10.00 (ISBN 0-8425-1840-1). Brigham.

Ferguson, Ben E. The Shaping of a Man of Faith. 1979. pap. 1.95 (ISBN 0-88207-516-0). Victor Bks.

Ferguson, Bruce. Canada Video. (Illus.). 112p. 1980. 9.95 (ISBN 0-88884-442-5, 56311-1, Pub. by Natl Mus Canada). U of Chicago Pr.

Ferguson, Bruce K. Landscape Literature of the Twentieth Century Books Reviewed in "Landscape Architecture" Magazine, 1910-1979. (Architecture Ser.: Bibliography A-259). 84p. 1980. pap. 9.00. Vance Biblios.

Ferguson, C., jt. auth. see Snow, Catherine.

Ferguson, C. A., et al, eds. Language in the U. S. A. 650p. Date not set. price not set (ISBN 0-521-23140-X); pap. price not set (ISBN 0-521-29834-2). Cambridge U Pr.

Ferguson, C. E. Neoclassical Theory of Production & Distribution. (Illus.). 1969. 27.50x (ISBN 0-521-07453-3). Cambridge U Pr.

Ferguson, C. E. & Maurice, Charles. Economic Analysis. 3rd ed. 1978. text ed. 18.50x (ISBN 0-256-02027-2). Irwin.

Ferguson, C. E., jt. auth. see Gould, J. P.

Ferguson, Charles E. & Gould, John P. Microeconomic Theory. 4th ed. (Economics Ser.). (Illus.). 450p. 1975. text ed. 16.50x o.p. (ISBN 0-256-01637-2). Irwin.

Ferguson, Charles W. Say It with Words. LC 59-8085. 1969. pap. 3.25x (ISBN 0-8032-5058-4, BB 395, Bison). U of Nebr Pr.

Ferguson, D., tr. see Cyzevs'Kyj, Dmytro.

Ferguson, Dale V., jt. auth. see Buffaloe, Neal D.

Ferguson, Donald N. Image & Structure in Chamber Music. LC 77-5586. (Music Reprint Ser.). 1977. Repr. of 1964 ed. lib. bdg. 25.00 (ISBN 0-306-77415-1). Da Capo.

Ferguson, E. James. The American Revolution: A General History, 1763-1790. rev. ed. 1979. pap. text ed. 10.50x (ISBN 0-256-02195-3). Dorsey.

Ferguson, E. James & Catanzariti, John, eds. The Papers of Robert Morris, 1781-1784: Vol. 5; April 16-July 20, 1782. LC 72-91107. 1981. 27.50x (ISBN 0-8229-3420-5). U of Pittsburgh Pr.

Ferguson, Estelle & Barbaresi, Sara M. How to Raise & Train a Chihuahua. pap. 2.00 (ISBN 0-87666-266-1, DS1008). TFH Pubns.

Ferguson, Everett. A Capella Music in the Public Workshop of the Church. LC 72-76963. (Way of Life Ser: No. 125). 1972. pap. text ed. 2.95 (ISBN 0-89112-125-0). Bibl Res Pr.

Ferguson, Everett, ed. World of the New Testament. (Living Word New Testament Commentary, Vol. 1). 1967. 7.95 (ISBN 0-8344-0023-5). Sweet.

Ferguson, Everett, ed. see Ash, Anthony L.

Ferguson, Everett, ed. see Kelcy, Raymond C.

Ferguson, Everett, ed. see Lewis, Jack.

Ferguson, Everett, ed. see Lewis, Jack P.

Ferguson, Everett, ed. see McMillan, Earle.

Ferguson, Everett, ed. see Pack, Frank.

Ferguson, Everett, ed. see Roberts, J. W.

Ferguson, Everett, ed. see Spain, Carl.

Ferguson, Everett, ed. see Thompson, James.

Ferguson, Everett, ed. see Weed, Michael.

Ferguson, Everett, et al, eds. see Batey, Richard.

Ferguson, Everett, et al, eds. see Harrell, Pat E.

Ferguson, Everett, et al, eds. see Johnson, Robert L.

Ferguson, Everett, et al, eds. see Kelcy, Raymond C.

Ferguson, Francis. Dante. 1966. 4.95 o.s.i. (ISBN 0-02-537300-5). Macmillan.

--Dante. Kronenberger, Louis, ed. LC 75-14006. (Masters of World Literature Ser.). (Illus.). 224p. 1975. pap. 3.95 o.s.i. (ISBN 0-02-069350-8, 06935, Collier). Macmillan.

Ferguson, Franklin C. A Pilgrimage in Faith: An Introduction to the Episcopal Church. rev. ed. LC 75-5220. 180p. (Orig.). 1979. pap. 5.95 (ISBN 0-8192-1277-6). Morehouse.

Ferguson, George. Signs & Symbols in Christian Art. (Illus.). 1959. 18.95 (ISBN 0-19-501168-6). Oxford U Pr.

--Statistical Analysis in Psychology & Education. 4th ed. 1975. text ed. 22.50x (ISBN 0-07-020480-2, C); instructors' manual 4.95 (ISBN 0-07-020481-0). McGraw.

Ferguson, George A. Statistical Analysis in Psychology & Education. 5th, rev. ed. (Psychology Ser.). (Illus.). 560p. 1981. text ed. 21.00x (ISBN 0-07-020482-9, C); instructor's manual 4.95 (ISBN 0-07-020483-7). McGraw.

Ferguson, H. F., ed. Engineering Geology Case Histories: Geologic Mapping for Environmental Purposes, No. 10. LC 73-90839. (Illus., Orig.). 1974. pap. 5.50x o.p. (ISBN 0-8137-4010-X). Geol Soc.

Ferguson, Howard, jt. ed. see Lassimonne, Denise.

Ferguson, James & Taylor, Craig, eds. The Comprehensive Handbook of Behavioral Medicine, 3 vols. Incl. Vol. 1. Systems Intervention. 364p. 1980 (ISBN 0-89335-078-8); Vol. 2. Syndromes & Special Areas. 308p. 1981 (ISBN 0-89335-111-3); Vol. 3. Extended Applications & Issues. 361p. 1980 (ISBN 0-89335-112-1). LC 79-24021. (Illus.). text ed. 30.00 ea. Spectrum Pub.
Ferguson, James M. & Taylor, C. Barr. A Change for Heart: Your Family & the Food You Eat. 1978. pap. 5.95 (ISBN 0-915950-22-7). Bull Pub.
Ferguson, Jeanne & Miller, Maria B. You're Speaking-Who's Listening? 1980. pap. text ed. 8.95 (ISBN 0-574-22560-9, 13-5560); instr's guide avail. (ISBN 0-574-22561-7, 13-5561). SRA.
Ferguson, John. Aristotle. (World Authors Ser.: Greece: No. 211). lib. bdg. 10.95 (ISBN 0-8057-2064-2). Twayne.
--The Arts in Britain in World War One. (Illus.). 131p. 1980. 26.50x (ISBN 0-8476-6262-4). Rowman.
--Bibliotheca Chemica: A Catalogue of the Alchemical, Chemical & Pharmaceutical Books in the Collection of the Late James Young of Kelly & Furris, 2 vols. LC 79-8610. Repr. of 1906 ed. 98.50 set (ISBN 0-404-18472-3). AMS Pr.
--Clement of Alexandria. (World Authors Ser.: Greece: No. 289). 1974. lib. bdg. 10.95 (ISBN 0-8057-2231-9). Twayne.
--Encyclopedia of Mysticism: & the Mystery Religions. (Illus.). 14.95 (ISBN 0-8164-9310-3). Crossroad NY.
--An Illustrated Encyclopedia of Mysticism & the Mystery Religions. LC 76-55812. (Illus.). 1976. 14.95 (ISBN 0-8164-9310-3). Continuum.
--Jesus in the Tide of Time: An Historical Study. 224p. 1980. 35.00 (ISBN 0-7100-0561-X). Routledge & Kegan.
--The Religions of the Roman Empire. LC 71-110992. (Aspects of Greek & Roman Life Ser). (Illus.). 1970. 19.50x (ISBN 0-8014-0567-X). Cornell U Pr.
--War & Peace in the World's Religions. 1978. 10.95 (ISBN 0-19-520073-X); pap. 3.95 (ISBN 0-19-520074-8). Oxford U Pr.
Ferguson, John, jt. auth. see Lawrence, Joy.
Ferguson, John, et al. The American Federal Government. 14th ed. 592p. 1981. text ed. 17.95 (ISBN 0-07-020527-2, C); instr's manual 4.95 (ISBN 0-07-020529-9). McGraw.
Ferguson, John H. & McHenry, Dean E. The American System of Government. 14th ed. Munson, Eric M., ed. (Illus.). 688p. Date not set. text ed. price not set (ISBN 0-07-020528-0, C); instr's manual 4.95 (ISBN 0-07-020529-9). McGraw. Postponed.
Ferguson, Kathy E. Self, Society, & Womankind: The Dialectic of Liberation. LC 79-6831. (Contributions in Women's Studies: No. 17). xii, 200p. 1980. lib. bdg. 22.95 (ISBN 0-313-22245-2, FSS/). Greenwood.
Ferguson, LeBaren O. Approximation by Polynomials with Integral Coefficients. LC 79-20331. (Mathematical Surveys: Vol. 17). 1980. 25.60 (ISBN 0-8218-1517-2). Am Math.
Ferguson, Linda. Canada. LC 79-15871. (Illus.). (gr. 7 up). 1979. 9.95 (ISBN 0-684-16080-3). Scribner.
Ferguson, M. Carr, et al. Federal Income Taxation of Estates & Beneficiaries. 749p. (Orig.). 1970. text ed. 40.00 (ISBN 0-316-27889-0); text ed. 12.50 1979 supplement (ISBN 0-316-27899-8). 1980 supplement (ISBN 0-316-27900-5). Little.
Ferguson, Mary A., compiled by. Bibliography of English Translations from Medieval Sources, Nineteen Forty-Four to Nineteen Sixty-Eight. (Records of Civilization, Sources & Studies: No. 88). 256p. 1974. 20.00x (ISBN 0-231-03435-0). Columbia U Pr.
Ferguson, Mary Ann. Images of Women in Literature. 2nd ed. LC 76-13098. (Illus.). 1976. pap. text ed. 9.95 (ISBN 0-395-24481-1). HM.
Ferguson, Mary Anne. Images of Women in Literature. 3rd ed. LC 80-82761. (Illus.). 528p. 1981. pap. text ed. 10.50 (ISBN 0-395-29113-5). HM.
Ferguson, Pamela. The Sacrifice. 1981. 13.95 (ISBN 0-689-11035-9). Atheneum.
Ferguson, Phil M. Reinforced Concrete Fundamentals. 4th ed. LC 78-21555. 1979. text ed. 29.95 (ISBN 0-471-01459-1); solutions manual (ISBN 0-471-05000-8). Wiley.
--Reinforced Concrete Fundamentals: SI Version. 4th ed. 736p. 1981. text ed. 28.95 (ISBN 0-471-05897-1). Wiley.
Ferguson, R. Fred, jt. auth. see Whisenand, Paul M.
Ferguson, Robert J., Jr. The Polygraph in Private Industry. (Illus.). 352p. 1966. pap. 27.75 photocopy ed. spiral (ISBN 0-398-00557-5). C C Thomas.
--Scientific Informer. (Illus.). 248p. 1971. 16.50 (ISBN 0-398-00558-3). C C Thomas.
Ferguson, Robert J., Jr. & Miller, Allan L. Polygraph for the Defense. 312p. 1974. 24.50 (ISBN 0-398-02877-X). C C Thomas.
Ferguson, Robert T., Jr. & Miller, Allan L. The Polygraph in Court. (Illus.). 372p. 1973. pap. 28.75 photocopy ed. spiral (ISBN 0-398-02679-3). C C Thomas.
Ferguson, Robert W. Concepts of Criminal Law: Selected Readings. (Criminal Justice Ser.). 1975. pap. text ed. 10.95 (ISBN 0-8299-0619-3). West Pub.
Ferguson, Rowena. Church's Ministry with Senior Highs. 1963. 1.50 o.p. (ISBN 0-687-08533-0). Abingdon.
--Editing the Small Magazine. 2nd ed. 208p. 1976. 15.00x (ISBN 0-231-03866-6); pap. 6.00x (ISBN 0-231-03970-0). Columbia U Pr.
Ferguson, Sheila. Growing up in Ancient Egypt. LC 79-56471. (Growing up Ser.). (Illus.). 72p. (gr. 7 up). 1980. text ed. 14.95 (ISBN 0-7134-2683-7, Pub. by Batsford England). David & Charles.
--Growing up in Victorian Britain. (Growing Up Ser.). 1977. 16.95 (ISBN 0-7134-0281-4, Pub. by Batsford England). David & Charles.
--Growing up in Viking Times. (Growing up Ser.). (Illus.). 72p. (gr. 6 up). 1981. 14.95 (ISBN 0-7134-2730-2, Pub. by Batsford England). David & Charles.
--Projects in History. 1970. 16.95 (ISBN 0-7134-2154-1, Pub. by Batsford England). David & Charles.
Ferguson, Sherry D., jt. auth. see Ferguson, Stewart.
Ferguson, Sibyl. The Crystal Ball. 1980. pap. 1.00 (ISBN 0-87728-483-0). Weiser.
Ferguson, Sinclair B. Taking the Christian Life Seriously: Biblical Teaching on Christian Maturity. Orig. Title: Add to Your Life. 192p. 1981. pap. 5.95 (ISBN 0-310-43891-8). Zondervan.
Ferguson, Stewart & Ferguson, Sherry D. Interrcom: Readings in Organizational Communication. 432p. 1980. 12.95x (ISBN 0-8104-5127-1). Hayden.
Ferguson, Susan L., jt. auth. see Hallock, Virginia L.
Ferguson, Ted. Desperate Siege. LC 78-20071. (Illus.). 240p. 1980. 11.95 (ISBN 0-385-14694-9). Doubleday.
Ferguson, Thomas S. Mathematical Statistics: A Decision Theoretic Approach. (Probability and Mathematical Statistics: Vol. 1). 1967. text ed. 22.95 (ISBN 0-12-253750-5). Acad Pr.
Ferguson, Tom. Medical Self-Care: Access to Health Tools. LC 80-14678. 320p. 1980. 19.95 (ISBN 0-671-40033-9); pap. 8.95 (ISBN 0-671-44816-1). Summit Bks.
Ferguson, Valerie, ed. Sayings of the Week. 1978. 8.95 (ISBN 0-7153-7600-4). David & Charles.
Ferguson, W. J. I Saw Booth Shoot Lincoln. LC 70-20379. (Illus.). 8.50 (ISBN 0-8363-0052-1). Jenkins.
Ferguson, Wallace K. & Bruun, Geoffrey. A Survey of European Civilization. 4th ed. Incl. Pt. 1. To 1660. text ed. 17.50 (ISBN 0-395-04427-8); Pt. 2. Since 1660. text ed. o.p. (ISBN 0-395-04428-6); Since 1500. text ed. o.p. (ISBN 0-395-04426-X). 1969. 1 vol. ed. 21.95 (ISBN 0-395-04425-1); instr's manual 4.00 (ISBN 0-395-04432-4). HM.
Ferguson, William D. Statutes of Limitation Saving Statutes. 1978. 35.00 (ISBN 0-87215-214-6). Michie.
Ferguson, William S. Greek Imperialism. LC 63-18045. 1941. 10.50x (ISBN 0-8196-0127-6). Biblo.
Fergusson see Bentley, Eric.
Fergusson, Francis. Literary Landmarks: Essays on the Theory & Practice of Literature. 1975. 11.00 (ISBN 0-8135-0815-0). Rutgers U Pr.
Ferkiss, Victor. Future of Technological Civilization. LC 73-90926. 384p. 1974. 12.50 o.s.i. (ISBN 0-8076-0738-X). Braziller.
Ferkiss, Victor C. Futurology: Promise, Performance, Prospects. LC 77-88625. (Policy Papers Ser.: The Washington Papers, No. 50). 1977. 3.50x (ISBN 0-8039-0977-2). Sage.
--Technological Man. LC 69-13114. 1969. 7.95 o.p. (ISBN 0-8076-0489-5). Braziller.
Ferlatte, William J. A Flora of the Trinity Alps. (Illus.). 1974. 16.50x (ISBN 0-520-02089-8). U of Cal Pr.
Ferlazzo, Paul J. Emily Dickinson. (U.S. Authors Ser.: No. 280). 1976. lib. bdg. 12.50 (ISBN 0-8057-7180-8). Twayne.
Ferlazzo, Paul J., ed. Emily Dickinson. (Twayne's U. S. Authors Ser.). 168p. 1976. pap. text ed. 4.95 (ISBN 0-672-61511-8). Bobbs.
Ferling, John E. A Wilderness of Miseries: War & Warriors in Early America. LC 79-8951. (Contributions in Military History: No. 22). (Illus.). xiv, 227p. 1980. lib. bdg. 25.00 (ISBN 0-313-22093-X, FWW/). Greenwood.
Ferlinghetti, Lawrence. Endless Life: The Selected Poems. 224p. 1981. 14.95 (ISBN 0-8112-0796-X, NDP516); pap. 4.95 (ISBN 0-8112-0797-8). New Directions.
--The Populist Manifestos. LC 80-22105. 56p. 1981. pap. 3.95 (ISBN 0-912516-52-6). Grey Fox.
--A Trip to Italy & France. LC 80-36778. 64p. 1981. signed limited ed. 50.00 (ISBN 0-8112-0782-X). New Directions.
Ferlinghetti, Lawrence & Peters, Nancy J. Literary San Francisco: A Pictorial History from the Beginnings to the Present. LC 79-3598. (Illus.). 224p. 1980. 15.95 (ISBN 0-06-250325-1, HarpR). Har-Row.
Ferlinghetti, Lawrence, jt. ed. see Lettau, Reinhard.
Ferlinghetti, Lawrence, tr. see Prevert, Jacques.
Ferlita, Ernest. The Way of the River: A Book of Scriptural Meditations. LC 76-45675. 1977. pap. 1.95 (ISBN 0-8091-2009-7). Paulist Pr.
Ferm, Vergilius. An Encyclopedia of Religion. LC 75-36508. 844p. 1976. Repr. of 1945 ed. lib. bdg. 55.00x (ISBN 0-8371-8638-2, FEEOR). Greenwood.
--Spoken Arts, Inc. 1952. 3.00 (ISBN 0-8022-0497-X). Philos Lib.
Ferman, Edward L. & Greenberg, Martin H., eds. Fantasy & Science Fiction, April Nineteen Sixty-Five. (Alternatives Ser.). 160p. Date not set. price not set (ISBN 0-8093-1007-4). S Ill U Pr.
Ferman, Louis A. & Erfurt, John C. Overview of the Experiences of the ILIR Manpower Laboratory: The Development of a Model Approach to the Retrieval, Dissemination, & Utilization of Information on Manpower Operations. 1973. looseleaf 3.00x (ISBN 0-87736-332-3). U of Mich Inst Labor.
Ferman, Louis A. & Manela, Roger. Agency Company Relationships in Manpower Operations for the Hard to Employ. 1973. pap. 6.50x (ISBN 0-87736-329-3). U of Mich Inst Labor.
Fermi, Enrico. Thermodynamics. 1937. pap. 3.00 (ISBN 0-486-60361-X). Dover.
Fermi, G. & Perutz, M. F. Haemoglobin & Myoglobin. (Atlas of Molecular Structures in Biology Ser.: No. 2). (Illus.). 100p. 1981. text ed. 45.00x (ISBN 0-19-854706-4). Oxford U Pr.
Fermor, Patrick L. The Violins of Saint-Jacques. LC 76-29863. 1977. 7.95 o.p. (ISBN 0-312-84700-9). St Martin.
Fermor, Patrick L., tr. see Psychoudakis, George.
Fern, R. One Hundred One Ways to Make Money at Home. 1978. 12.50 o.p. (ISBN 0-685-05013-0, 0-911156-28-2). Porter.
Fernald, L. Dodge & Fernald, Peter S. Basic Psychology. 4th ed. LC 77-78910. (Illus.). 1979. pap. text ed. 15.75 (ISBN 0-395-25826-X); inst. manual 0.95 (ISBN 0-395-25827-8); student guidebk. 6.95 (ISBN 0-395-25828-6); test bank 2.95 (ISBN 0-395-25829-4). HM.
--Introduction to Psychology. 4th ed. LC 77-78911. (Illus.). 1978. text ed. 18.95 (ISBN 0-395-25815-4); inst. manual 1.15 (ISBN 0-395-25816-2); student guidebk. 6.95 (ISBN 0-395-25817-0); test item manual 2.00 (ISBN 0-395-25818-9). HM.
Fernald, Mary & Shenton, Eileen. Costume Design & Making. 2nd ed. LC 67-14505. (Illus.). 1967. 13.25 (ISBN 0-87830-021-X). Theatre Arts.
Fernald, Merritt L., et al. Edible Wild Plants: Of Eastern North America. rev. ed. LC 58-7977. (Illus.). 1958. 15.00 o.p. (ISBN 0-06-070810-7, HarpT). Har-Row.
Fernald, Peter S., jt. auth. see Fernald, L. Dodge.
Fernandes, Florestan. Negro in Brazilian Society. LC 78-76247. (Institute of Latin American Studies). 1969. 25.00x (ISBN 0-231-02979-9). Columbia U Pr.
--Reflections on the Brazilian Counterrevolution. Dean, Warren, pref. by. Vale, Michel, tr. from Portuguese. LC 80-5456. 200p. 1981. 25.00 (ISBN 0-87332-177-4). M E Sharpe.
Fernandez, Domingo. El Mormonismo Revelacion Divina O Invencion Humana. 1978. 0.80 (ISBN 0-311-05762-4). Casa Bautista.
Fernandez, Domingo S. Una Interpretacion Del Apocalipsis. 234p. (Span.). 1980. pap. 2.85 (ISBN 0-311-04312-7). Casa Bautista.
Fernandez, Eduardo B., et al. Database Security & Integrity. LC 80-15153. (IBM Systems Programming Ser.). (Illus.). 288p. 1981. text ed. 18.95 (ISBN 0-201-14467-0). A-W.
Fernandez, Enrique F. Las Biblias Castellanas del Exilio. LC 76-5154. (Illus.). 190p. (Span.). 1976. pap. 3.50 (ISBN 0-89922-067-3). Edit Caribe.
Fernandez, Happy. The Child Advocacy Handbook. LC 80-24053. 1981. pap. 6.95 (ISBN 0-8298-0403-X). Pilgrim NY.
--Los Padres se organizan para mejorar las escuelas. NCCE, ed. ASPIRA of New York, tr. (Spanish.). 1976. 3.50 (ISBN 0-934460-03-5). NCCE.
Fernandez, Happy & NCCE. Parents Organizing to Improve Schools. NCCE, ed. ASPIRA of New York, tr. 1976. 3.50 (ISBN 0-934460-01-9). NCCE.
Fernandez, Jack E. Organic Chemistry: An Introduction. (Illus.). 528p. 1981. text ed. 19.95 (ISBN 0-686-68299-8). P-H.
Fernandez, John P. Black Managers in White Corporations. LC 75-6820. 308p. 1975. 29.95 (ISBN 0-471-25764-8, Pub. by Wiley-Interscience). Wiley.
Fernandez, Jose A. Architecture in Puerto Rico. Date not set. 16.95 (ISBN 0-8038-0009-6). Hastings.
Fernandez, Judi & Ashley, Ruth. Introduction to Eighty-Eighty, Eighty Eighty-Five Assembly Language Programming. 300p. 1981. pap. text ed. 8.95 (ISBN 0-471-08009-8). Wiley.
Fernandez, Judi N. Using CPM: A Self Teaching Guide. Ashley, Ruth, ed. (Self-Teaching Guide Ser.). 240p. 1981. pap. text ed. 8.95 (ISBN 0-471-08011-X). Wiley.
Fernandez, Linda & Evans, Walt. Volleyball. (Burns Sports Ser.). 156p. Date not set. pap. cancelled (ISBN 0-695-81570-9). Follett.
Fernandez, Mendez. Viaje Historico De un Pueblo. 24.95 (ISBN 0-87751-003-2, Pub by Troutman Press). E Torres & Sons.
Fernandez, Oscar, jt. auth. see Starnes, George E.
Fernandez, S. D. El Espiritismo. (Coleccion Doctrinas Modernas: No. 1). 1980. pap. 0.55 (ISBN 0-311-05025-5, Edit Mundo). Casa Bautista.
Fernandez De Lizardi, Jose J. The Itching Parrot. Porter, Katherine A., tr. & intro. by. LC 80-2479. (Span.). 1981. Repr. of 1942 ed. 39.50 (ISBN 0-404-19113-4). AMS Pr.
Fernandez-Marcane, Leonardo. Twenty Cuentistas Cubanos. LC 77-89099. 1978. pap. 4.95 (ISBN 0-89729-164-6). Ediciones.
Fernandez-Santamaria, J. A. The State, War & Peace. LC 76-27903. (Studies in Early Modern History). 1977. 42.50 (ISBN 0-521-21438-6). Cambridge U Pr.
Fernandez-Vazquez, Antonio. La Novelistica Cubana De la Revolucion. LC 79-52159. (Coleccion Polymita Ser.). 157p. (Span.). 1980. pap. 9.95 (ISBN 0-89729-228-6). Ediciones.
Fernando, Chitra, jt. ed. see Obeyesekere, Ranjini.
Fernando, H. E. Formulae & Theorems in Mathematics. 1967. pap. text ed. 2.95x o.p. (ISBN 0-435-71060-5). Heinemann Ed.
Fernando, Tissa & Kearney, Robert N., eds. Modern Sri Lanka: A Society in Transition. LC 79-13077. (Foreign & Comparative Studies: South Asian Ser.: No. 4). (Illus.). 297p. 1979. pap. text ed. 7.50x (ISBN 0-915984-80-6). Syracuse U Foreign Comp.
Fernbach, David, tr. see Buci-Glucksmann, Christine.
Fernbach, David, tr. see Heger, Heinz.
Fernea, Elizabeth W. & Bezirgan, Basima Q., eds. Middle Eastern Muslim Women Speak. (Illus.). 1977. 16.95x (ISBN 0-292-75033-1); pap. 8.95x (ISBN 0-292-75041-2). U of Tex Pr.
Fernea, Elizabeth Warnock. A Street in Marrakech. LC 74-12686. 1976. pap. 3.50 (ISBN 0-385-12045-1, Anch). Doubleday.
Ferner, Helmut, ed. see Pernkopf, Eduard.
Ferner, Helmut, ed. see Pernkoph, Eduard.
Fernie, William T. The Occult & Curative Powers of Precious Stones. LC 80-8894. (The Harper Library of Spiritual Wisdom Ser.). 496p. 1981. pap. 7.95 (ISBN 0-06-062360-8). Har-Row.
Ferns, C. S. Aldous Huxley: Novelist. 1980. text ed. 35.00x (ISBN 0-485-11194-2, Athlone Pr). Humanities.
Ferns, G. K. Australian Wheat Varieties. 1980. 25.00x (ISBN 0-643-00143-3, Pub. by CSJRO Australia). State Mutual Bk.
Ferntheil, Carol. Bible Adventures. (Basic Bible Readers Ser.). (Illus.). (gr. 3). 1963. pap. 4.50 (ISBN 0-87239-260-0, 2757). Standard Pub.
--I Read About God's Gifts. (Basic Bible Readers Ser.). (Illus.). (gr. 2). 1962. kivar 4.50 (ISBN 0-87239-259-7, 2756). Standard Pub.
--I Read About God's Love. (Basic Bible Readers Ser.). (Illus.). (gr. 1). 1962. pap. 4.50 (ISBN 0-87239-258-9, 2755). Standard Pub.
--If You Had Been in Bethlehem: Diorama Book. (gr. k-3). 1977. 3.25 (ISBN 0-87239-166-3, 3605). Standard Pub.
--Noah's Ark Diorama Book. (gr. k-3). 1977. 3.25 (ISBN 0-87239-167-1, 3606). Standard Pub.
Ferraby, John. All Things Made New: A Comprehensive Outline of the Baha'i Faith. rev. ed. 1975. 14.00 (ISBN 0-900125-23-3, 7-32-16); pap. 7.50 (ISBN 0-900125-24-1, 7-32-17). Baha'i.
Ferrando, Jose, jt. auth. see Carenas, F.
Ferrante, A. J., jt. auth. see Brebbia, C. A.
Ferrante, Joan, tr. see De France, Marie.
Ferrante, Joan M. & Economou, George D., eds. In Pursuit of Perfection: Courtly Love in Medieval Literature. LC 74-80596. 1975. 15.00 (ISBN 0-8046-9092-8, Natl U). Kennikat.

Ferrante, Joan M., tr. from Fr. Guillaume D'Orange: Four Twelfth-Century Epics. LC 74-4421. (Records of Civilization Ser). 312p. 1974. 18.50x (ISBN 0-231-03809-7). Columbia U Pr.

Ferrar, H. John Osborne. (Columbia Essays on Modern Writers Ser.: No. 67). pap. 2.00 (ISBN 0-231-03361-3, MW67). Columbia U Pr.

Ferrar, H., et al, eds. The Concise Oxford French Dictionary. 912p. 1980. 22.50 (ISBN 0-19-864126-5). Oxford U Pr.

Ferrar, Harold. Denis Johnston's Irish Theatre. (The Irish Theatre Ser.: No.5). 144p. (Orig.). 1973. pap. text ed. 5.25x (ISBN 0-85105-208-8, Dolmen Pr). Humanities.

Ferrar, Harold & Clarke, Brenna K. The Dublin Drama League. (Irish Theatre Ser.: No. 9). 1979. pap. text ed. 5.25x (ISBN 0-85105-316-5, Dolmen Pr). Humanities.

Ferrar, Terry A., ed. The Urban Costs of Climate Modification. LC 76-23288. (Environmental Science & Technology: a Wiley-Interscience Ser. of Texts & Monographs). 1976. 32.95 (ISBN 0-471-25767-2, Pub by Wiley-Interscience). Wiley.

Ferrar, W. J., ed. see Eusebius.

Ferrara, Angelo & Harin, Anantham. Emergency Transfer of the High Risk Neonate: A Working Manual for Medical, Nursing & Administrative Personnel. LC 79-17689. (Illus.). 1979. pap. text ed. 25.00 (ISBN 0-8016-1565-8). Mosby.

Ferrara, Peter J. The Future of Social Security. abr. ed. (Cato Public Policy Research Monograph: No. 4). 100p. (Orig.). 1981. pap. 5.00 (ISBN 0-932790-26-7). Cato Inst.

--Social Security: The Inherent Contradiction. LC 80-18949. (Policy Bks.: No. 1). 496p. 1980. 20.00 (ISBN 0-932790-24-0). Cato Inst.

Ferrari, A. see Rossini, F. P.

Ferrari, T. J. Elements of System-Dynamic Simulation: A Textbook with Exercises. LC 78-10505. 1978. pap. text ed. 16.95 (ISBN 0-470-26548-5). Halsted Pr.

Ferrario, Carlos, jt. ed. see Buckley, Joseph P.

Ferraris, Luigi V., ed. Report on a Negotiation: Helsinki-Geneva-Helsinki Nineteen Seventy-Two to Nineteen Seventy-Five. Barber, Marie-Claire, tr. from Italian. (Collections De Relations Internationales Ser.). 439p. 1980. 46.00x (ISBN 9-0286-0779-X). Sijthoff & Noordhoff.

Ferraro, Douglas P., jt. auth. see Logan, Frank A.

Ferraro, J. R., jt. auth. see Rao, C. N.

Ferrarone, Stephen F., jt. auth. see Schwartz, Steven J.

Ferrarotti, Franco. Max Weber & the Destiny of Reason. DiSanto, Mario, tr. from Ital. LC 80-5457. Orig. Title: Max Weber e il destino ragione. 150p. 1981. 17.50 (ISBN 0-87332-170-7). M E Sharpe.

Ferrars, E. X. Experiment with Death. LC 80-2739. (Crime Club Ser.). 192p. 1981. 9.95 (ISBN 0-385-17523-X). Doubleday.

--Witness Before the Fact. (Large Print Bks.). 1980. lib. bdg. 11.95 (ISBN 0-8161-3126-0). G K Hall.

Ferrater Mora, Jose. Being & Death: An Outline of Integrationist Philosophy. 1965. 18.00x (ISBN 0-520-00402-7). U of Cal Pr.

Ferre, Duane. How to Make Wire Jewelry. (Illus.). 192p. 1980. 13.95 (ISBN 0-8019-6859-3); pap. 7.95 (ISBN 0-8019-6860-7). Chilton.

Ferre, Frederick. Language, Logic, & God: With a New Preface. viii, 184p. 1981. pap. text ed. 6.50x (ISBN 0-226-24456-3). U of Chicago Pr.

--Shaping the Future: Resources for the Post-Modern World. LC 75-36755. 192p. 1976. 7.95 o.p. (ISBN 0-06-062371-3, HarpR). Har-Row.

Ferre, Frederick, ed. see Comte, August.

Ferre, John P. & Pauley, Steven E. Rhetorical Patterns: An Anthology of Contemporary Essays. (Illus.). 208p. 1981. pap. text ed. 6.95 (ISBN 0-675-08023-1). Merrill.

Ferre, Luis A. The Plea of Puerto Rico. (Studies in Puerto Rican History, Literature & Culture). 1980. lib. bdg. 59.95 (ISBN 0-8490-3087-0). Gordon Pr.

Ferreira, E. Fifth Brazilian Symposium on Theoretical Physics. 1975. pap. 35.00 (ISBN 0-470-98956-4). Halsted Pr.

Ferreira, Linda. Notion by Notion. 96p. (Orig.). 1981. pap. text ed. 3.95 (ISBN 0-88377-199-3). Newbury Hse.

Ferrell, Mallory H. The Colorado & Southern Narrow Gauge. (Illus.). 1981. 34.95 (ISBN 0-87108-534-8). Pruett.

--Rails, Sagebrush & Pine. LC 67-28315. (Illus.). 1967. 15.95 (ISBN 0-87095-007-X). Golden West.

Ferrell, O. C., jt. auth. see Luck, David J.

Ferrell, O. C., jt. auth. see Pride, William M.

Ferrell, R. W. Managing Opportunity. LC 77-168772. 1972. 14.50 o.p. (ISBN 0-8144-5281-7, 49189). Am Mgmt.

Ferrell, Robert H. American Diplomacy in the Great Depression: Hoover-Stimson Foreign Policy, 1929-1933. (Illus.). 1969. Repr. of 1957 ed. 16.50 o.p. (ISBN 0-208-00749-0, Archon). Shoe String.

Ferrell, Robert H., ed. & intro. by. The Eisenhower Diaries. (Illus.). 1981. 1.95 (ISBN 0-393-01432-0). Norton.

Ferrell, Robert H., ed. Off the Record: The Private Papers of Harry S. Truman. LC 79-3390. (Illus.). 448p. 1980. 15.00 (ISBN 0-06-011281-6, HarpT). Har-Row.

Ferrell, Robert H., et al. The Talkative President: The off-the-Record Press Conferences of Calvin Coolidge. Freidel, Frank, ed. LC 78-66526. (The History of the United States Ser.: Vol. 6). 287p. 1979. lib. bdg. 23.00 (ISBN 0-8240-9706-8). Garland Pub.

Ferrer, Aldo. The Argentine Economy. 1967. 18.00x (ISBN 0-520-00404-3). U of Cal Pr.

Ferrer, M. Irene, ed. Current Cardiology, Vol. 1. (Current Ser.). 1979. 30.00x (ISBN 0-89289-104-1). HM Prof Med Div.

Ferrer, Rafael & Prokopoff, Stephen. Rafael Ferrer: Enclosures. (Illus.). 1971. 4.00 o.p. (ISBN 0-88454-008-1). U of Pa Contemp Art.

Ferrero, Guglielmo. The Women of the Caesars. (Illus.). 1977. 47.15 (ISBN 0-930582-05-5). Am Classical Coll Pr.

Ferres, John H. & Tucker, Martin, eds. Modern Commonwealth Literature. LC 75-35425. (Library of Literary Criticism). 1977. 35.00 (ISBN 0-8044-3080-2). Ungar.

Ferretti, Paolo A. Estetica Gregoriana. LC 77-5498. (Music Reprint Ser.). 1977. Repr. of 1934 ed. lib. bdg. 35.00 (ISBN 0-306-77414-3). Da Capo.

Ferrez, Gilberto & Naef, Weston J. Poineer Photographers of Brazil, 1840-1920. LC 76-25710. (Center for Inter-American Relations &The American Federation of Arts). (Illus.). 144p. 1980. 16.95 (ISBN 0-295-95737-9). U of Wash Pr.

Ferri, Elsa. Growing up in a One Parent Family. 144p. 1976. pap. text ed. 13.75x (ISBN 0-85633-087-6, NFER). Humanities.

--Streaming: Two Years Later. (Research Reports Ser.). 1971. text ed. 12.50x (ISBN 0-901225-55-X, NFER). Humanities.

Ferri, Elsa & Niblett, Rosalind. Disadvantaged Families & Playgroups. 1977. pap. text ed. 9.75x (ISBN 0-85633-133-3, NFER). Humanities.

Ferri, Elsa & Robinson, Hilary. Coping Alone. (Illus.). 80p. 1976. pap. text ed. 6.25x (ISBN 0-85633-086-8, NFER). Humanities.

Ferrie, Carmen, jt. auth. see Perez, Roman.

Ferrier, D; see Monro, Alexander.

Ferrier, David. Functions of the Brain. (Contributions to the History of Psychology E, III, Physiological Psychology Ser.). 1978. Repr. of 1886 ed. 30.00 (ISBN 0-89093-176-3). U Pubns Amer.

Ferrier, J. M. French Prose Writers of the Fourteenth & Fifteenth Centuries. 1966. pap. 11.75 o.p. (ISBN 0-08-011301-X). Pergamon.

Ferrier, J. P. Caravan Journeys & Wanderings in Persia, Afghanistan, Turkistan & Beloochistan. (Oxford in Asia Historical Reprints Ser.). (Illus.). 1977. 26.00x (ISBN 0-19-577214-8). Oxford U Pr.

Ferrier, Janet M., jt. ed. see Brereton, Georgine E.

Ferriere, J. C. de see De Ferriere, J. C.

Ferries, George. The Growth of Christian Faith. 385p. Repr. of 1905 ed. 3.50 (ISBN 0-567-02106-8). Attic Pr.

Ferriman, David. Human Hair Growth in Health & Disease. (American Lectures in Living Chemistry Ser.). (Illus.). 76p. 1971. 11.75 (ISBN 0-398-00560-5). C C Thomas.

Ferris, Byron, jt. auth. see Nelson, Roy P.

Ferris, Clifford D. Guide to Medical Laboratory Instruments. LC 80-80585. 260p. 1980. text ed. 14.95 (ISBN 0-316-28127-1). Little.

Ferris, Clifford D. & Brown, F. Martin, eds. Butterflies of the Rocky Mountain States. LC 80-22274. (Illus.). 500p. 1981. 35.00 (ISBN 0-8061-1552-1); pap. 15.95 (ISBN 0-8061-1733-8). U of Okla Pr.

Ferris, E. B. Microbiology for Health Careers. (Illus.). 147p. 1974. pap. 7.00 (ISBN 0-8273-1326-8); instructor's guide 1.60 (ISBN 0-8273-1327-6). Delmar.

Ferris, Elvira & Skelley, Esther G. Body Structures & Functions. LC 77-83347. 160p. 1979. pap. 7.20 (ISBN 0-8273-1322-5); instructor's guide 1.60 (ISBN 0-8273-1323-3); slide pocket 29.50 (ISBN 0-8273-1821-9). Delmar.

Ferris, Ernest J. & Seibert, J. J. Urinary Tract & Adrenal Glands: Imaging & Diagnosis. (Multiple Imaging Procedures Ser.). 1980. 59.50 (ISBN 0-8089-1296-8). Grune.

Ferris, Helen, ed. Favorite Poems Old & New. (gr. 3-7). 1957. 11.95a (ISBN 0-385-07696-7); PLB (ISBN 0-385-06249-4). Doubleday.

Ferris, John. Participation in Urban Planning. 95p. 1972. pap. text ed. 6.25x (ISBN 0-7135-1714-X, Pub. by Bedford England). Renouf.

Ferris, Norman B. Desperate Diplomacy: William H. Seward's Foreign Policy, 1861. LC 75-5509. 1976. 14.50x (ISBN 0-87049-170-9). U of Tenn Pr.

Ferris, Rose Marie. The Heart's Awakening. (Candelight Romance Ser.). (Orig.). 1981. pap. 1.50 (ISBN 0-440-13519-2). Dell.

Ferris, Theodore P. This Is the Day: Selected Sermons. 2nd ed. LC 76-39640. 384p. 1980. pap. 10.00 (ISBN 0-911658-16-5, 3077). Yankee Bks.

Ferris, Timothy. Galaxies. LC 80-13139. (Illus.). 200p. 1980. 75.00 (ISBN 0-87156-273-1). Sierra.

Ferriss, G., ed. Treatment of Epilepsy Today. 1978. 15.95 o.p. (ISBN 0-87489-201-5); pap. 12.95 o.p. (ISBN 0-87489-202-3). Med Economics.

Ferriz, David. I Realized God Via Mathematics. Norris, Patrick, tr. from Span. 300p. (Orig.). 1980. pap. 5.95 (ISBN 0-89260-191-4). Hwong Pub.

Ferro, Beatriz. Caught in the Rain. LC 79-2513. (gr. 2). 1980. 6.95a (ISBN 0-385-15624-3); PLB (ISBN 0-385-15625-1). Doubleday.

Ferro, Marc. Great War, Nineteen Fourteen to Nineteen Eighteen. 1973. 16.00x (ISBN 0-7100-7574-X); pap. 8.95 (ISBN 0-7100-7575-8). Routledge & Kegan.

Ferro, Robert. The Others. LC 77-8702. 1977. 6.95 o.p. (ISBN 0-684-15137-5, ScribT). Scribner.

Ferron, Jacques. Tales from the Uncertain Country. Bednarski, Betty, tr. from Fr. LC 71-190704. (Anansi Fiction Ser.: No. 19). 102p. 1972. pap. 3.95 (ISBN 0-88784-320-4, Pub. by Hse Anansi Pr Canada); study guide by Mary Ziroff 1.00x (ISBN 0-88784-053-1). U of Toronto Pr.

Ferrone, J., ed. see Calvino, Italo.

Ferrone, Soldano, jt. ed. see Reisfeld, Ralph A.

Ferrone, Soldano, et al, eds. Current Trends in Immunology. LC 78-31911. (Illus.). 400p. 1979. lib. bdg. 42.50 (ISBN 0-8240-7065-8). Garland Pub.

Ferrucci, Franco. The Poetics of Disguise: The Autobiography of the Work in Homer, Dante, & Shakespeare. Dunnigan, Ann, tr. from It. LC 80-11242. 178p. 1980. 12.50x (ISBN 0-8014-1262-5). Cornell U Pr.

Ferrucci, Joseph T., jt. auth. see Eaton, S. Boyd, Jr.

Ferry, D. K., et al, eds. Physics of Nonlinear Transport in Semiconductors. (NATO Advanced Study Institutes Ser.: Series B: Physics, Volume 52). 634p. 1980. 65.00 (ISBN 0-306-40356-0, Plenum Pr). Plenum Pub.

Ferry, David. On the Way to the Island. LC 60-13156. (Wesleyan Poetry Program: Vol. 7). (Orig.). 1960. 10.00x (ISBN 0-8195-2007-1, Pub. by Wesleyan U Pr); pap. 4.95 (ISBN 0-8195-1007-6). Columbia U Pr.

Ferry, David K. & Fannin, D. R. Physical Electronics. LC 73-128907. (Engineering Science Ser). 1971. text ed. 20.95 (ISBN 0-201-02105-6); ans. bk 2.00 (ISBN 0-201-02106-4). A-W.

Ferry, Diane L., jt. auth. see Van de Ven, Andrew H.

Ferry, John D. Viscoelastic Properties of Polymers. 3rd ed. LC 79-2866. 1980. 48.00 (ISBN 0-471-04894-1, Pub. by Wiley Interscience). Wiley.

Ferry, Ted S. Elements of Accident Investigation. 72p. 1978. pap. 10.75 spiral (ISBN 0-398-03752-3). C C Thomas.

--Modern Accident Investigation & Analysis: An Executive Guide to Accident Investigation. 350p. 1981. 30.00 (ISBN 0-471-07776-3, Pub. by Wiley-Interscience). Wiley.

Ferry, Ted S. & Weaver, D. A. Directions in Safety: A Selection of Safety Readings. (Illus.). 498p. 1976. 34.75 (ISBN 0-398-03365-X). C C Thomas.

Ferry, W. Hawkins. Building of Detroit: A History. rev. ed. (Illus.). 1980. 40.00 (ISBN 0-8143-1665-4). Wayne St U Pr.

--The Buildings of Detroit: A History. LC 68-20167. (Illus.). 1968. deluxe ed. 100.00 o.p. (ISBN 0-8143-1332-9). Wayne St U Pr.

Fersch, Ellsworth A. Psychology & Psychiatry in Courts & Corrections: Controversy & Change. LC 80-11726. (Wiley Series on Personality Processes). 370p. 1980. 24.95 (ISBN 0-471-05604-9, Pub. by Wiley Interscience). Wiley.

Fersch, Ellsworth A., Jr. Law, Psychology, & the Courts: Rethinking Treatment of the Young & the Disturbed. 184p. 1979. 17.50 (ISBN 0-398-03874-0). C C Thomas.

Fersh, Seymour. Asia: Teaching About, Learning From. LC 77-16458. (Illus.). 1978. pap. text ed. 8.25x (ISBN 0-8077-2539-0). Tchrs Coll.

Fersht, Alan. Enzyme Structure & Mechanism. LC 77-6441. (Illus.). 1977. pap. text ed. 14.95x (ISBN 0-7167-0188-X). W H Freeman.

Ferster, C. & Skinner, B. Schedules of Reinforcement. 1957. 23.00 (ISBN 0-13-792309-0). P-H.

Ferster, Charles B., et al. Behavior Principles. 2nd ed. LC 74-19287. (Illus.). 674p. 1975. Repr. text ed. 20.95 (ISBN 0-13-072611-7). P-H.

Ferstle, Jim. Contemporary Jogging. LC 77-91153. 1978. 6.95 o.p. (ISBN 0-8092-7554-6); pap. 3.95 (ISBN 0-8092-7575-9). Contemp Bks.

Ferullo, Dan, jt. auth. see Russell, Harold.

Ferziger, J. H. Numerical Methods for Engineering Applications. 400p. 1981. 36.00 (ISBN 0-471-06336-3, Pub. by Wiley-Interscience). Wiley.

Fesharaki, Fereidun. Development of the Iranian Oil Industry: International & Domestic Aspects. LC 75-19782. (Special Studies). (Illus.). 300p. 1976. text ed. 31.95 (ISBN 0-275-55600-X). Praeger.

Feshbach, Seymour & Fraczek, Adam, eds. Aggression & Behavior Change: Biological & Social Processes. LC 79-17934. (Praeger Special Studies Ser.). (Illus.). 316p. 1979. 26.95 (ISBN 0-03-052446-6). Praeger.

Fesperman, John. Organs in Mexico. (Illus.). 1981. 18.50 (ISBN 0-915548-07-0). Sunbury Pr.

Fess, Elaine, et al. Hand Splinting: Principles & Methods. LC 80-17398. (Illus.). 318p. 1980. text ed. 27.50 (ISBN 0-8016-1569-0). Mosby.

Fessenden, Francis, ed. see Fessenden, William P.

Fessenden, Joan S., jt. auth. see Fessenden, Ralph J.

Fessenden, Ralph J. & Fessenden, Joan S. The Basis of Organic Chemistry. 2nd ed. 1978. text ed. 17.95 (ISBN 0-205-05740-3); ans. bk. avail. (ISBN 0-205-05741-1). Allyn.

--Chemical Principles for the Life Sciences. 2nd ed. 1979. text ed. 20.95x (ISBN 0-205-06506-6); instr's manual (ISBN 0-205-06533-3). Allyn.

Fessenden, William P. Life & Public Services of William Pitt Fessenden, 2 Vols. Fessenden, Francis, ed. LC 70-87532. (American Public Figures Ser). (Illus.). 1970. Repr. of 1907 ed. lib. bdg. 69.50 (ISBN 0-306-71446-9). Da Capo.

Fessler, Daniel W. Alternatives to Incorporation for Persons in Quest of Profit: Cases & Materials on Partnerships, Joint Ventures & Related Agency Concepts. LC 80-18481. (American Casebook Ser.). 284p. 1980. pap. text ed. 8.95 (ISBN 0-8299-2102-8). West Pub.

Fessler, Diane M., ed. see Lehman, Charles A.

Fessler, Donald R. Facilitating Community Change: A Basic Guide. LC 76-12768. 146p. 1976. pap. 11.50 (ISBN 0-88390-121-8). Univ Assocs.

Fessler, Edward A. Directed-Energy Weapons: A Juridical Analysis. LC 79-65950. (Praeger Special Studies). 204p. 1979. 20.95 (ISBN 0-03-053511-5). Praeger.

Fessler, George R. & Westcott, Ray D. The Advanced Real Estate Primer. 20th ed. 336p. pap. 7.95 (ISBN 0-935810-04-8). Primer Pubs.

--The Real Estate Primer. 35th ed. 298p. pap. 8.95 (ISBN 0-935810-00-5). Primer Pubs.

Fessler, Stella L. Chinese Seafood Cooking. 1981. pap. price not set (ISBN 0-452-25265-2, Z5265, Plume). NAL.

Festa-McCormick, Diane. Honore De Balzac. (World Authors Ser.: No. 541). 1979. lib. bdg. 12.50 (ISBN 0-8057-6383-X). Twayne.

Festing, Sally. Fishermen. 1977. 11.95 (ISBN 0-7153-7448-6). David & Charles.

Festinger, Leon, et al. When Prophecy Fails: A Social & Psychological Study of a Modern Group That Predicted the Destruction of the World. pap. 4.95x (ISBN 0-06-131132-4, TB1132, Torch). Har-Row.

Fetherling, Dale. Mother Jones, the Miners' Angel: A Portrait. LC 78-16328. (Arcturus Books Paperbacks). (Illus.). 280p. 1979. pap. 8.95 (ISBN 0-8093-0896-7). S Ill U Pr.

Fethke, Gary C., et al. Investigation of the Conceptual & Qualitative Impact of Employment Tax Credits. LC 78-14292. 1978. pap. 2.50 (ISBN 0-911558-00-4). Upjohn Inst.

Fetler, James. Impossible Appetites. LC 80-17200. (The Iowa School of Letters Award for Short Fiction Ser.: No. 11). 176p. 1980. 9.95 (ISBN 0-87745-101-X); pap. 5.95 (ISBN 0-87745-102-8). U of Iowa Pr.

Fetridge, Clark & Minor, Robert. Office Administration Handbook. 1981. 48.50 (ISBN 0-85013-123-5). Dartnell Corp.

Fetsko, J. M., ed. see Walker, W. C., et al.

Fetter, Bruce, et al. Explorations in Quantitative African History. Smaldone, Joseph P., ed. LC 77-17537. (Foreign & Comparative Studies-African Ser.: No. 27). 1978. pap. 7.00x (ISBN 0-915984-24-5). Syracuse U Foreign Comp.

Fetter, F. W. & Gregory, D. Monetary & Financial Policy in Nineteenth Century Britain. (Government & Society in 19th Century Britain Ser.). 106p. 1973. 15.00x (ISBN 0-7165-2217-9, Pub. by Irish Academic Pr Ireland); pap. 6.00x (ISBN 0-7165-2218-7). Biblio Dist.

Fetter, Frank A. Capital, Interest, & Rent: Essays in the Theory of Distribution. Rothbard, Murray N., ed. & intro. by. 1977. write for info. NYU Pr.
--Capital, Interest & Rent: Essays in the Theory of Distribution. Rothbard, Murray N., ed. LC 76-25587. (Studies in Economic Theory). 400p. 1976. 12.00; pap. 4.95. NYU Pr.
Fetter, Richard L., et al. Front Range Restaurants: The One Hundred Best. 1980. pap. 7.95 (ISBN 0-933472-46-3). Johnson Colo.
Fetterley, Judith. Resisting Reader: A Feminist Approach to American Fiction. LC 78-3242. 224p. 1978. 12.50x (ISBN 0-253-31078-4). Ind U Pr.
Fetterman, Elsie. Buying Food. (Consumer Casebook Ser.). (Illus.). 80p. (gr. 10-12). 1981. pap. text ed. 5.00 (ISBN 0-87005-268-3). Fairchild.
Fetterman, Elsie & Jordan. Consumer Credit. (gr. 10-12). 1976. text ed. 10.60 (ISBN 0-87002-084-6); student guide 3.00 (ISBN 0-87002-183-4); tchr's guide 3.96 (ISBN 0-87002-191-5). Bennett IL.
Fetterman, Elsie & Jordon. Consumer Credit. 1977. pap. 7.68 tchr's guide o.p. (ISBN 0-685-81853-5). Bennett IL.
Fetterman, Elsie & Klamkin, Charles. Consumer Education in Practice. LC 75-38976. 1976. text ed. 12.00 o.p. (ISBN 0-471-25780-X); pap. text ed. 10.95 (ISBN 0-471-25781-8). Wiley.
Fetters, Thomas T. & Swanson, Peter W. The Piedmont & Northern Railway. LC 74-14801. (Illus.). 170p. 18.95 (ISBN 0-87095-051-7). Golden West.
Fettes, E. M. Chemical Reactions of Polymers, Vol. 19. 1304p. 1964. 90.00 (ISBN 0-470-39305-X). Wiley.
Fettig, Art. How to Hold an Audience in the Hollow of Your Hand: Seven Techniques for Starting Your Speech, Eleven Techniques for Keeping It Rolling. LC 79-14145. 1979. 9.95 (ISBN 0-8119-0322-2). Fell.
--Mentor: Secrets Ot the Ages. (Illus.). 112p. 1981. 9.95 (ISBN 0-8119-0333-8). Fell.
--Selling Lucky. LC 77-89820. (Illus.). 1977. 7.95 (ISBN 0-9601334-1-0). Growth Unltd.
--The Three Robots. LC 81-801016. 1981. 5.95 (ISBN 0-9601334-0-2). Growth Unltd.
Fettweis, G. B. World Coal Resources. (Developments in Economic Geology Ser.). 425p. 1979. 80.50 (ISBN 0-444-99779-2). Elsevier.
Fetyko, David F. Financial Accounting: Concepts & Principles. 768p. 1980. text ed. 17.95x (ISBN 0-534-00753-8, Kent Pub.); guide 6.95xstudy (ISBN 0-534-00851-8); papers 6.95xworking (ISBN 0-534-00846-1). Kent Pub Co.
Fetzer, John F. Romantic Orpheus: Profiles of Clemens Brentano. 1974. 21.50x (ISBN 0-520-02312-9). U of Cal Pr.
Feucht, Oscar E. Guidelines for Women's Groups in the Congregation. 1981. pap. 3.95 (ISBN 0-570-03828-6, 12-2793). Concordia.
Feucht, Oscar E., ed. see Norden, Rudolph F.
Feuchtinger, Eugene. Your Voice: Methods for Strengthening & Developing the Voice. Orig. Title: Voice Development Hints. 5.95 (ISBN 0-911012-28-1). Nelson-Hall.
Feuchtwanger, E. J. & Mason, R. A. Air Power in the Next Generation. 1979. text ed. 26.00x (ISBN 0-333-23609-2). Humanities.
Feuchtwanger, E. J., jt. ed. see Bessel, Richard.
Feuchtwanger, Lion. The House of Desdemona or the Laurels & Limitations of Historical Fiction. Basilius, Harold A., tr. LC 63-8063. (Waynebooks Ser: No. 12). (Orig.). 1963. pap. 3.95x o.p. (ISBN 0-8143-1218-7). Wayne St U Pr.
Feuer, H., ed. Chemistry of the Nitro & Nitroso Groups. LC 68-29395. (Chemistry of Functional Groups Ser: Pt. 2). 1970. 37.95 o.p. (ISBN 0-471-25791-5, Pub. by Wiley-Interscience). Wiley.
Feuer, Henry, ed. The Chemistry of the Nitro & Nitroso Groups: Part 1. LC 80-21491. 996p. 1981. Repr. of 1969 ed. text ed. write for info. (ISBN 0-89874-271-4). Krieger.
--The Chemistry of the Nitro & Nitroso Groups: Part 2. LC 80-21491. 450p. 1981. Repr. text ed. write for info. (ISBN 0-89874-272-2). Krieger.
Feuer, Janice. Sweets for Saints & Sinners. LC 80-21934. (Illus.). 144p. 1980. pap. 5.95 (ISBN 0-89286-180-0). One Hund One Prods.
Feuer, Morton & Johnston, Joseph E. Personal Liabilities of Corporate Officers & Directors. 2nd ed. 1974. 24.95 o.p. (ISBN 0-13-657593-5). P-H.
Feuerbach, Ludwig. Thoughts on Death & Immortality. Massey, James A., tr. from Ger. 263p. 1981. 12.95x (ISBN 0-520-04051-1); pap. 5.95 (ISBN 0-520-04062-7, CAL 486). U of Cal Pr.
Feuerbacher, B., et al. Photoemission & the Electronic Properties of Surfaces. 540p. 1978. 61.95 (ISBN 0-471-99555-X). Wiley.
Feuerlicht, Ignace. Thomas Mann. LC 68-24312. (World Authors Ser.: Germany: No. 47). 1969. lib. bdg. 12.50 (ISBN 0-8057-2584-9). Twayne.
Feuerstein, G., tr. Bhagavad Gita: A Critical Rendering. 170p. 1980. text ed. cancelled (ISBN 0-8426-1666-7). Verry.
Feuerstein, Phillis & Roberts, Carol. The Not So Empty Nest: How to Live with Your Kids After They've Lived Someplace Else. 256p. 1981. 10.95 (ISBN 0-695-81441-9). Follett.
Feuerwerker, Albert. Chinese Economy, Ca. Eighteen Seventy to Nineteen Eleven. (Michigan Papers in Chinese Studies Ser.: No. 5). (Illus.). 77p. 1969. pap. 4.00 (ISBN 0-89264-005-7). U of Mich Ctr Chinese.
Feuerwerker, Albert, ed. History in Communist China. 1968. 15.00x o.p. (ISBN 0-262-06021-3); pap. 3.95 o.p. (ISBN 0-262-56006-2). MIT Pr.
Feuille, Peter, jt. auth. see Juris, Hervey A.
Feuillerat, A., ed. see Sidney, Philip.
Feuillerat, Albert. French Life & Ideals. 1925. 34.50x (ISBN 0-685-89753-2). Elliots Bks.
Feuillet, Andre. The Priesthood of Christ & His Ministers. LC 74-9446. 312p. 1975. 8.95 o.p. (ISBN 0-385-06009-2). Doubleday.
Feulner, Edwin J., Jr., ed. China: The Turning Point. 1976. pap. 10.00 (ISBN 0-685-79961-1). Coun Am Affairs.
Feurstein, G. Bhagavad Gita: A Critical Rendering. 1981. text ed. write for info. (ISBN 0-391-02191-5). Humanities.
Feuser, Willfried F., tr. see Zahar, Renate.
Feutry, Michel, et al, eds. Dictionary of Industrial Techniques: English-French-German-Portuguese-Spanish. 1312p. 1979. 80.00 (ISBN 2-85608-000-6). Heinman.
Fevre, P. G. Le see Le Fevre, P. G.
Fewkes, Jesse W. Hopi Katcinas Drawn by Native Artists. LC 62-20282. (Beautiful Rio Grande Classics Ser). lib. bdg. 20.00 o.s.i. (ISBN 0-87380-023-0). Rio Grande.
Fey, James T. Patterns of Verbal Communication in Mathematics Classes. Bellack, Arno A., ed. LC 74-103135. (Illus.). 1970. text ed. 7.50x (ISBN 0-8077-1342-2). Tchrs Coll.
Fey, Marshall. The Slot Machine Story. (Illus.). 1981. 25.00 (ISBN 0-913814-33-4). Nevada Pubns.
Feyerabend, Cessa. Budgerigar Diseases. pap. 4.95 (ISBN 0-87666-413-3, PS671). TFH Pubns.
Feyerabend, Paul. Erkenntnis Fuer Freie Menschen. rev. ed. (Edition Suhrkamp. Neue Folge: es.NF 11). 270p. (Ger.). 1980. pap. text ed. 6.50 (ISBN 3-518-11011-X, Pub. by Insel Verlag Germany). Suhrkamp.
Feynman, R. P., et al. Feynman Lectures on Physics, 3 Vols. Vol. 1. text ed. 18.95 (ISBN 0-201-02010-6); Vol. 2. text ed. 18.95 (ISBN 0-201-02011-4); Vol. 3. text ed. 18.95 (ISBN 0-201-02014-9); Set. pap. 29.95 (ISBN 0-201-02115-3); exercises for vols 2 & 3 2.95 (ISBN 0-685-03072-5). Vol. 2 Excercises (ISBN 0-201-02017-3). Vol. 3 Excercises (ISBN 0-201-02019-X). excercises for vol. 1 2.50 (ISBN 0-686-66303-9). A-W.
Feyrer, Gayle. Demon Letting. 1976. 30.00x o.p. (ISBN 0-931460-05-0). Bieler.
Fezandie, Clement. Through the Earth. LC 80-23960. 48p. 1980. Repr. lib. bdg. 8.95x (ISBN 0-89370-028-2). Borgo Pr.
--Through the Earth. 2.50 (ISBN 0-913960-00-4). Fax Collect.
Fezler, William. Just Imagine: A Guide to Materialization Using Imagery. new ed. 144p. 1980. 9.95 (ISBN 0-934810-00-1). Laurida.
Fezler, William & Shapiro, Jack. Ninety Ways to Leave Your Lover & Survive. 198p. 1980. 9.95 (ISBN 0-934810-01-X). Laurida.
Fflokes, Michael. Fflokes' Cartoon Companion to Classic Mythology. LC 78-15270. (Illus.). 1978. 10.50 (ISBN 0-7153-7585-7). David & Charles.
Ffrench, Florence F. Music & Musicians in Chicago. (Music Reprint Ser.). 1979. Repr. of 1899 ed. lib. bdg. 27.50 (ISBN 0-306-79542-6). Da Capo.
Ffrench, Yvonne. Mrs. Siddons: Tragic Actress. LC 78-13858. (Illus.). 1981. Repr. of 1954 ed. 23.50 (ISBN 0-88355-791-6). Hyperion Conn.
Fiacco, A. V. & McCormick, G. P. Nonlinear Programming: Unconstrained Minimization Techniques. LC 68-30909. 1968. 20.50 o.p. (ISBN 0-471-25810-5, Pub. by Wiley-Interscience). Wiley.
Fiacco, A. V., et al, eds. Extremal Methods & Systems Analysis. (Lecture Notes in Economics & Mathematical Systems Ser.: Vol. 174). 545p. 1980. pap. 39.30 (ISBN 3-540-09730-9). Springer-Verlag.
Fiarotta, Phyllis. Snips & Snails & Walnut Whales. LC 75-9574. (Parents & Children Together). (Illus.). 288p. (ps up). 1975. 9.95 (ISBN 0-911104-75-5); pap. 5.95 (ISBN 0-911104-49-6). Workman Pub.
--Sticks & Stones & Ice Cream Cones. LC 74-160843. (Parents & Children Together Ser.). (Illus.). 316p. (ps up). 1973. 9.95 (ISBN 0-911104-29-1); pap. 5.95 (ISBN 0-911104-30-5). Workman Pub.
Fiberarts Magazine, ed. The Fiberarts Design Book. (Illus.). 176p. 1980. 24.95 (ISBN 0-8038-2394-0, Visual Communications); pap. 15.95 (ISBN 0-8038-2395-9). Hastings.
Fibonacci, Leonardo & Flumiani, Carlo M. The Fibonacci Rhythm Theory As It Applies to Life, History, & the Future of the Stock Market. (Illus.). 1976. 77.50 (ISBN 0-89266-041-4). Am Classical Coll Pr.
Ficat. Contrast Arthography of the Synovial Joints. 1981. price not set. Masson Pub.
Ficchi, Rocco F. Electrical Interference. (Illus.). 1964. 11.45 o.p. (ISBN 0-8104-5512-9). Hayden.
Ficek. Real Estate Principles & Practices. new ed. 1976. text ed. 18.95 (ISBN 0-675-08585-3); instructor's manual 3.95 (ISBN 0-686-67318-2); transparencies 3.95 (ISBN 0-686-67319-0). Merrill.
Fich, S., jt. auth. see Potter, James L.
Fichte, J. G. Fichte's Critique of All Revelation. Green, G. D., tr. LC 77-77756. 1978. 26.95 (ISBN 0-521-21707-5). Cambridge U Pr.
Fichte, Johann G. Characteristics of the Present Age. Smith, W., tr. Bd. with Way Towards the Blessed Life. (Contributions to the History of Psychology Ser., Pt. A: Orientations). 1978. Repr. of 1889 ed. 30.00 (ISBN 0-89093-151-8). U Pubns Amer.
--The Vocation of Man. Smith, William, tr. LC 56-44104. 1956. pap. 3.95 (ISBN 0-672-60220-2, LLA50). Bobbs.
Fichter, George. Bicycles & Bicycling. (First Books Ser.). (Illus.). (gr. 4-6). 1978. PLB 6.45 s&l (ISBN 0-531-01403-7). Watts.
--Iraq. (First Bks). (Illus.). (gr. 4-6). 1978. PLB 6.45 s&l (ISBN 0-531-02236-6). Watts.
Fichter, George S. Animals. 1973. PLB 7.62 o.p. (ISBN 0-307-61453-0, Golden Pr). Western Pub.
--The Future Sea. LC 78-57790. (Illus.). 1978. 14.95 (ISBN 0-8069-3106-X); lib. bdg. 13.29 (ISBN 0-8069-3107-8). Sterling.
--Keeping Amphibians & Reptiles As Pets. (First Bks.). (Illus.). (gr. 4-6). 1979. PLB 6.45 s&l (ISBN 0-531-02257-9). Watts.
--Racquetball. (First Bks.). (Illus.). (gr. 4 up). 1979. PLB 6.45 s&l (ISBN 0-531-04078-X). Watts.
--Snakes Around the World. LC 78-9774. (Easy Read Fact Bks.). (Illus.). (gr. 2-4). 1980. PLB 6.45 s&l (ISBN 0-531-02275-7). Watts.
--Working Dogs. (First Bks.). (Illus.). (gr. 4-6). 1979. PLB 6.45 s&l (ISBN 0-531-02887-9). Watts.
Fichter, George S. & Kingbay, Keith. Bicycling. (Golden Leisure Library). (Illus.). 120p. 1972. PLB 9.15 (ISBN 0-307-64351-4, Golden Pr). Western Pub.
Fichter, George S., ed. see Hoffmeister, Donald F.
Fichter, Harold. The Master Lawnmower Repair Book. (Illus.). 1978. pap. 7.95 (ISBN 0-8306-1067-7, 1067). TAB Bks.
Fichter, Harold O. Wood Heat Is Yours for the Axing. (Illus.). 1980. pap. 4.00 (ISBN 0-918424-02-X). Menaid.
Ficino, Marsilio. The Book of Life. Boer, Charles, tr. from Latin. 217p. 1980. pap. 12.50 (ISBN 0-88214-212-7). Spring Pubns.
--The Letters of Marsilio Ficino, Vol. 3, Bk. 4. 160p. 1980. 39.00x (ISBN 0-85683-045-3, Pub. by Shepheard-Walwyn England). State Mutual Bk.
Fick, G. & Sprague, R. H., Jr., eds. Decision Support Systems--Issues & Challenges: Proceedings of an International Task Foce Meeting, June 23-25, 1980. (IIASA Proceedings: Vol. 11). (Illus.). 190p. 1980. pap. 29.50 (ISBN 0-08-027321-1). Pergamon.
Ficker, Victor & Graves, Herbert S. Deprivation in America. (Studies in Contemporary Issues). 1971. pap. text ed. 4.95x (ISBN 0-02-474680-0, 47468). Macmillan.
Ficker, Victor B. & Rigterink, James M. Values in Conflict: A Text Reader in Social Problems. 512p. 1972. pap. text ed. 8.95x o.p. (ISBN 0-669-63487-5); instructor's manual free o.p. (ISBN 0-669-81067-3). Heath.
Fickett, E. D. Meteorology. Repr. of 1900 ed. pap. 1.50 (ISBN 0-8466-0029-3, SJS29). Shorey.
Fickett, Harold L., Jr. James: Faith That Works. LC 76-169604. (Orig.). 1972. pap. 2.25 (ISBN 0-8307-0130-3, S254123). Regal.
--Keep on Keeping on. LC 75-23517. 160p. (Orig.). 1977. pap. 2.25 (ISBN 0-8307-0371-3, S311-1-00). Regal.
--Peter's Principles, from I & II Peter. LC 73-90620. 1977. pap. 2.95 (ISBN 0-8307-0455-8, S281-1-20). Regal.
Fickett, Lewis P., Jr. The Major Socialist Parties of India: A Study in Leftist Fragmentation. LC 76-20536. (Foreign & Comparative Studies-South Asian Ser.: No. 2). 1976. pap. text ed. 4.50x (ISBN 0-915984-76-8). Syracuse U Foreign Comp.
Fickett, Wildon & Davis, William C. Detonation. LC 77-85760. (Los Alamos Ser. in Basic & Applied Sciences). 1979. 30.00x (ISBN 0-520-03587-9). U of Cal Pr.
Fickle, James E. The New South & the "New Competition". A Case Study of Trade Association Development in the Southern Pine Industry. LC 80-12420. 300p. 1980. 17.50 (ISBN 0-252-00788-3). U of Ill Pr.
Fickling, David, ed. see Townsend, John R.
Fiddle, Seymour. Portraits from a Shooting Gallery: Life Styles from the Drug Addict World. LC 67-13711. 1967. 10.00 o.p. (ISBN 0-06-032065-6, HarpT). Har-Row.
Fiddle, Seymour, ed. Uncertainty: Behavioral & Social Dimensions. LC 80-82073. 410p. 1980. 26.95 (ISBN 0-03-057022-0). Praeger.
Fidell, Linda S. & De Lamater, John, eds. Women in the Professions: What's All the Fuss About? LC 73-89940. (Sage Contemporary Social Science Issues Ser.: Vol. 8). 1974. 4.95x (ISBN 0-8039-0337-5). Sage.
Fidler, John. The British Business Elite: Its Attitudes to Class, Status & Power. 384p. 1981. price not set (ISBN 0-7100-0770-1). Routledge & Kegan.
Fido, Martin, ed. & tr. see Cazamian, Louis.
Fiechter, A., ed. Reactors & Reactions. (Advances in Biochemical Engineering Ser.: Vol. 19). (Illus.). 250p. 1981. 57.90 (ISBN 0-387-10464-X). Springer-Verlag.
Fiechter, Georges-Andre. Brazil Since Nineteen Sixty Four: Modernization Under a Military Regime. LC 75-16325. 296p. 1975. 36.95 o.p. (ISBN 0-470-26332-6). Halsted Pr.
Fiederer, S. M. Easy Money. LC 80-54016. 1981. pap. 14.95 (ISBN 0-938584-00-6, 123058). United Pub NY.
Fiedler, Conrad. On Judging Works of Visual Art. Schaefer-Simmern, Henry, tr. from Ger. (Library Reprint Ser.: Vol. 88). 1978. 12.95x (ISBN 0-520-03597-6). U of Cal Pr.
Fiedler, Fred E. & Chemers, Martin M. Leadership & Effective Management. 1974. pap. 8.95x o.p. (ISBN 0-673-07768-3). Scott F.
Fiedler, Fred E., et al. Improving Leadership Effectiveness: The Leader Match Concept. LC 76-20632. (Self-Teaching Guides). 1976. pap. text ed. 8.95 (ISBN 0-471-25811-3). Wiley.
Fiedler, Judith. Field Research: A Manual for Logistics & Management of Scientific Studies in Natural Settings. LC 78-62562. (Social & Behavioral Science Ser.). (Illus.). 1978. text ed. 13.95x (ISBN 0-87589-381-3). Jossey-Bass.
Fiedler, Kurt, tr. see Goebbels, Joseph.
Fieg, John. InterAct: Thailand-U.S. Renwick, George W., ed. LC 80-83909. (Country Orientation Ser.). 1980. pap. text ed. 10.00 (ISBN 0-933662-14-9). Intercult Pr.
Fiegehen, Guy, et al. Poverty & Progress in Britain, 1953-1973: A Statistical Study of Low Income Households. LC 77-2143. (NIESR, Occasional Paper: No. 29). (Illus.). 1977. 29.95 (ISBN 0-521-21683-4). Cambridge U Pr.
Field, Andrew. Nabokov: His Life in Part. 1978. pap. 3.95 o.p. (ISBN 0-14-004784-0). Penguin.
Field, Annita T. Fingerprint Handbook. (Police Science Ser). (Illus.). 196p. 1976. 14.75 (ISBN 0-398-00562-1). C C Thomas.
Field, Barry C. & Willis, Cleve E., eds. Environmental Economics: A Guide to Information Sources. (Man & the Environment Information Guide Ser.: Vol. 8). 1979. 30.00 (ISBN 0-8103-1433-9). Gale.
Field, C. & Hamley, D. C. Fiction in the Middle School. 1975. 14.95 o.p. (ISBN 0-686-63991-X, Pub. by Batsford England). David & Charles.
Field, Claud H. Dictionary of Oriental Quotations. LC 68-23157. 1969. Repr. of 1911 ed. 21.00 (ISBN 0-8103-3183-7). Gale.
Field, D., ed. Social Psychology for Sociologists. LC 74-952. 1974. text ed. 16.95 (ISBN 0-470-25813-6). Halsted Pr.
Field, David A., jt. auth. see Baley, James A.
Field, Dawn S. Luise. 1978. pap. 1.95 o.p. (ISBN 0-425-03767-3, Medallion). Berkley Pub.
Field, Dick. Change in Art Education. (Students Library of Education). 1970. text ed. 4.75x (ISBN 0-7100-6675-9). Humanities.
Field, Edward. Variety Photoplays. 1980. 3.50 (ISBN 0-917554-02-7). Maelstrom.
Field, Edwin M. Oil Burners. 3rd ed. LC 76-45884. (Illus.). 1977. 9.95 (ISBN 0-672-23277-4, 23277). Audel.
Field, Elinor W., ed. Horn Book Reflections on Children's Books & Reading. LC 75-89793. 1969. pap. 6.50 (ISBN 0-87675-033-1). Horn Bk.
Field, Elinor W., jt. ed. see Miller, Bertha M.
Field, Eugene. Wynken, Blynken & Nod. (Illus.). (gr. k-2). 1980. 6.95 (ISBN 0-8038-8046-4). Hastings.
Field, F. Three French Writers & the Great War. LC 35-22982. 1975. 23.50 (ISBN 0-521-20916-1). Cambridge U Pr.
Field, Frances, jt. auth. see Field, Michael.
Field, Frank. Take It off with Frank. 1979. pap. 1.95 (ISBN 0-345-27921-2). Ballantine.

Field, G. W. The Legal Relations of Infants, Parent & Child, & Guardian & Ward: And a Particular Consideration of Guardianship in the State of New York. xx, 376p. 1981. Repr. of 1888 ed. lib. bdg. 28.50x (ISBN 0-8377-0537-1). Rothman.
Field, George, et al. Cosmic Evolution: An Indroduction to Astronomy. LC 77-76420. (Illus.). 1978. text ed. 19.50 (ISBN 0-395-25321-7). HM.
Field, George W. Hermann Hesse. (World Authors Ser.: Germany: No. 93). lib. bdg. 9.95 (ISBN 0-8057-2424-9). Twayne.
Field, Hazel E. The Fetal Pig. (Illus.). 1939. pap. 0.75x o.p. (ISBN 0-8047-0359-0). Stanford U Pr.
Field, John. Place-Names of Great Britain & Ireland. (Illus.). 208p. 1980. 15.00x (ISBN 0-389-20154-5). B&N.
--Place-Names of Greater London. LC 79-56447. (Illus.). 168p. 1980. 19.95 (ISBN 0-7134-2538-5, Pub. by Batsford England). David & Charles.
Field, John W. Group Practice Development: A Practical Handbook. LC 76-56948. 1976. 32.00 (ISBN 0-912862-26-2). Aspen Systems.
Field, Leslie A., ed. Thomas Wolfe: Three Decades of Criticism. LC 68-13024. (Gotham Library). 304p. (Orig.). 1968. 15.00x (ISBN 0-8147-0147-7); pap. 4.95x (ISBN 0-8147-0148-5). NYU Pr.
Field, Mark G. Soviet Socialized Medicine. LC 67-10148. 1967. 9.95 o.s.i. (ISBN 0-02-910130-1). Free Pr.
Field, Michael & Field, Frances. Quintet of Cuisines. (Foods of the World Ser). (Illus.). 1970. 14.95 (ISBN 0-8094-0048-0). Time-Life.
--Quintet of Cuisines. LC 72-130359. (Foods of the World Ser.). (Illus.). (gr. 6 up). 1970. PLB 14.94 (ISBN 0-8094-0075-8, Pub. by Time-Life). Silver.
Field, Michael, ed. Middle East Annual Review, 1981. 7th ed. Date not set. pap. 24.95 (ISBN 0-528-84519-5). Rand.
Field, Minna. The Aged, the Family, & the Community. LC 79-164500. 304p. 1972. 17.50x (ISBN 0-231-03348-6). Columbia U Pr.
--Patients Are People. 3rd ed. LC 67-31049. xiv, 294p. 1967. 17.50x (ISBN 0-231-03108-4). Columbia U Pr.
Field, O. P. Effect of an Unconstitutional Statute. LC 74-146273. (American Constitutional & Legal History Ser). 1971. Repr. of 1935 ed. lib. bdg. 35.00 (ISBN 0-306-70118-9). Da Capo.
Field, Oliver, tr. see Bukharin, Nikolai I.
Field, P. J., ed. see Malory, Sir Thomas.
Field, Peter. Coyote Gulch. 1976. lib. bdg. 13.50x (ISBN 0-89968-033-X). Lightyear.
Field, Rachel. And Now Tomorrow. 1942. 10.95 (ISBN 0-02-537740-X). Macmillan.
--Calico Bush. (gr. 7-9). 1966. 9.95 (ISBN 0-02-734620-X). Macmillan.
--Hepatica Hawks. (gr. 4-6). 1964. 4.95 o.s.i. (ISBN 0-02-734740-0). Macmillan.
--Hitty: Her First Hundred Years. (gr. 4-6). 1937. 8.95 (ISBN 0-02-734840-7). Macmillan.
--Poems. (gr. k-3). 1957. 3.95g o.s.i. (ISBN 0-02-735060-6). Macmillan.
Field, Richard S. Jasper Johns: Prints 1970-1977. LC 77-93988. (Illus.). 1978. pap. 10.95 (ISBN 0-931266-00-9, Pub. by Wesleyan U Pr). Columbia U Pr.
--Paul Gauguin: The Paintings of the First Voyage to Tahiti. LC 76-23617. (Outstanding Dissertations in the Fine Arts Ser.). 1977. lib. bdg. 63.00 (ISBN 0-8240-2688-8). Garland Pub.
Field, Sandra. The Winds of Winter. (Harlequin Romances). 192p. 1981. pap. 1.25 (ISBN 0-373-02398-7, Pub. by Harlequin). PB.
Field, Stephen J. Personal Reminiscences of Early Days in California. LC 68-29601. (American Scene Ser). 1968. Repr. of 1893 ed. lib. bdg. 35.00 (ISBN 0-306-71157-5). Da Capo.
Field, Thomas W. Essay Towards an Indian Bibliography. LC 67-14026. 1967. Repr. of 1873 ed. 18.00 (ISBN 0-8103-3327-9). Gale.
Field, Tiffany, ed. Culture & Early Interactions. 300p. 1981. ref. ed. 19.95 (ISBN 0-89859-097-3). L Erlbaum Assocs.
Field, William T., jt. auth. see Martinello, Marian.
Field, Xenia. Window Box Gardening. (Illus.). 139p. 1975. 8.95 (ISBN 0-7137-0656-2). Transatlantic.
Fielden, John. Curse of the Factory System. 2nd rev. ed. 74p. 1969. 25.00x (ISBN 0-7146-1394-0, F Cass Co). Biblio Dist.
--Curse of the Factory System. LC 68-23399. Repr. of 1836 ed. 15.00x (ISBN 0-678-05010-4). Kelley.
Fielden, P. S., jt. auth. see Richards, S. A.
Fielder, Mildred. Plant Medicine & Folklore. 1977. pap. 4.95 (ISBN 0-87691-228-5). Winchester Pr.
Fieldhouse, David K. Unilever Overseas: The Anatomy of a Multinational. LC 78-20358. (Publications Ser.: No. 205). 1979. pap. 22.00 (ISBN 0-8179-7051-7). Hoover Inst Pr.
Fielding, Dodge. Fielding's Favorites: Hotels & Inns, Europe 1980. 9th ed. LC 79-642516. 1981. Fieldingflex 5.95 (ISBN 0-688-00293-5). Fielding.
Fielding, Gordon J. Geography As Social Science. 1974. text ed. 20.50 scp (ISBN 0-06-042051-0, HarpC); inst. manual avail. (ISBN 0-06-362080-4). Har-Row.
--Programmed Case Studies in Geography. 299p. 1974. pap. text ed. 8.50 scp (ISBN 0-06-042052-9, HarpC). Har-Row.
Fielding, Henry. An Apology for the Life of Mrs. Shamela Andrews. 80p. 1980. Repr. of 1926 ed. lib. bdg. 12.50 (ISBN 0-8492-4616-4). R West.
--Author's Farce. Woods, Charles, ed. LC 65-27454. (Regents Restoration Drama Ser). 1966. 9.50x (ISBN 0-8032-0359-4); pap. 1.65x (ISBN 0-8032-5358-3, BB 255, Bison). U of Nebr Pr.
--Grub-Street Opera. Roberts, Edgar V., ed. LC 67-12642. (Regents Restoration Drama Ser). 1968. 9.95x (ISBN 0-8032-0360-8); pap. 2.95x (ISBN 0-8032-5359-1, BB 264, Bison). U of Nebr Pr.
--The Historical Register for the Year 1736. Appleton, William W., ed. Bd. with Eurydyce Hissed. LC 67-12643. (Regents Restoration Dramas Ser). 1967. 6.50x (ISBN 0-8032-0361-6); pap. 1.65x (ISBN 0-8032-5360-5, BB 265). U of Nebr Pr.
--The History of Tom Jones, a Foundling, 2 vols. Bowers, Fredson, ed. LC 73-15009. (Wesleyan Edition of the Works of Henry Fielding Ser.). (Illus.). 1250p. 1974. Set. 50.00x (ISBN 0-8195-4068-4, Pub. by Wesleyan U Pr); pap. 7.50x (ISBN 0-8195-6048-0). Columbia U Pr.
--The Jacobite's Journal & Related Writings. Coley, William, ed. LC 73-17020. (Wesleyan Edition of the Works of Henry Fielding Ser.). 1975. 27.50x (ISBN 0-8195-4072-2, Pub. by Wesleyan U Pr). Columbia U Pr.
--Jonathan Wild. Incl. Journal of a Voyage to Lisbon. 1958. 6.00x (ISBN 0-460-00877-3, Evman); pap. 5.95 (ISBN 0-460-01877-9, Evman). Dutton.
--Joseph Andrews. Battestin, Martin, ed. LC 66-23917. (Works of Henry Fielding). 1967. 27.50x (ISBN 0-8195-3070-0, Pub. by Wesleyan U Pr). Columbia U Pr.
--Journey from This World to the Next. 1976. pap. 2.50 o.p. (ISBN 0-460-01112-X, Evman). Dutton.
--The Life of Mr. Jonathan Wild. LC 74-17291. (Novel in England, 1700-1775 Ser). 1974. Repr. of 1754 ed. lib. bdg. 50.00 (ISBN 0-8240-1108-2). Garland Pub.
--Miscellanies, Vol. 1. Miller, Henry K., ed. LC 71-184366. (Wesleyan Edition of the Works of Henry Fielding Ser). 306p. (Textual intro. by Fredson Bowers). 1973. Repr. of 1743 ed. 27.50x (ISBN 0-8195-4046-3, Pub. by Wesleyan U Pr). Columbia U Pr.
Fielding, Henry, jt. auth. see Richardson, Samuel.
Fielding, Henry see Shugrue, Michael F.
Fielding, Joy. Kiss Mommy Goodbye. LC 80-1692. 312p. 1981. 11.95 (ISBN 0-385-17291-5). Doubleday.
--Trance. 1978. pap. 1.95 o.s.i. (ISBN 0-515-04702-3). Jove Pubns.
Fielding, K. J; see Bloomfield, Paul.
Fielding, Kathy. The Total Experiance of Having Your Baby at Home. 2.95 (ISBN 0-912216-23-9). Green Hill.
Fielding, Kenneth J., jt. ed. see Sanders, Charles R.
Fielding, Meral, et al. Fundamentals of College Accounting. LC 72-186146. 1972. text ed. 12.75 (ISBN 0-89702-027-8); wkbk. 6.20 (ISBN 0-89702-028-6); 7.40 (ISBN 0-89702-026-X). PAR Inc.
Fielding, Morton D., ed. see Politz, Murray J.
Fielding, Nancy & Fielding, Temple. Fielding's Low-Cost Europe 1981. 15th ed. LC 75-640820. (Illus.). 1981. pap. 5.95 (ISBN 0-688-61215-6). Fielding.
--Fielding's Selective Shopping Guide to Europe 1981. 25th ed. LC 57-9112. 1981. pap. 4.95 spiral bdg. (ISBN 0-688-61213-X). Fielding.
Fielding, Nancy, jt. auth. see Fielding, Temple.
Fielding, Newton. How to Sketch from Nature. (Illus.). 1980. deluxe ed. 36.45 (ISBN 0-930582-66-7). Gloucester Art.
Fielding, Nigel. The National Front. (International Library of Sociology). 228p. 1980. 38.50 (ISBN 0-7100-0559-8). Routledge & Kegan.
Fielding, P. M., ed. A National Directory of Four Year Colleges, Two Year Colleges & Post High School Training Programs for Young People with Learning Disabilities. 4th ed. 1981. 14.95 (ISBN 0-686-19675-9). PIP.
Fielding, Ray. The Technique of Special Effects Cinematography. 3rd, rev., enl. ed. (Library of Communication Techniques). 24.95 (ISBN 0-8038-7115-5). Hastings.
Fielding, Raymond. The American Newsreel, 1911-1967. LC 73-177334. (Illus.). 392p. 1981. pap. 7.95 (ISBN 0-8061-1717-6). U of Okla Pr.
Fielding, Raymond, compiled by. A Technological History of Motion Pictures & Television. 1967. 27.50x (ISBN 0-520-00411-6). U of Cal Pr.
Fielding, Samuel B. A Double Bed Was Not for Two. 1981. 8.95 (ISBN 0-533-04848-6). Vantage.
Fielding, Sarah. The Adventures of David Simple, 1744, 2 vols. in 1. 2nd ed. Shugrue, Michael F., ed. (The Flowering of the Novel, 1740-1775 Ser: Vol. 14). 1974. lib. bdg. 50.00 (ISBN 0-8240-1113-9). Garland Pub.
--The History of Ophelia. Shugrue, Michael F., ed. (Flowering of the Novel Ser.: 1740-1775). Repr. of 1760 ed. lib. bdg. 50.00 (ISBN 0-8240-1154-6). Garland Pub.
--The History of the Countess of Dellwyn, 1759, 2 vols. in 1. (The Flowering of the Novel, 1740-1775 Ser: Vol. 53). 1974. lib. bdg. 50.00 (ISBN 0-8240-1152-X). Garland Pub.
--The Lives of Cleopatra & Octavia, 1757. LC 74-17294. (Novel in England, 1700-1775 Ser). 1974. lib. bdg. 50.00 (ISBN 0-8240-1147-3). Garland Pub.
Fielding, Temple. Fielding's Europe, 1981. 34th, rev. ed. 1030p. 1980. Fieldingflex bdg. 10.95 (ISBN 0-688-03776-3). Morrow.
Fielding, Temple & Fielding, Nancy. Fielding's Low-Cost Europe, 1981. 15th, rev. ed. (Illus.). 872p. 1980. Fieldingflex bdg. 5.95 (ISBN 0-688-03777-1). Morrow.
Fielding, Temple, jt. auth. see Fielding, Nancy.
Fielding, William J. Strange Customs of Courtship & Marriage. 315p. 1980. Repr. of 1942 ed. lib. bdg. 25.00 (ISBN 0-89987-259-X). Darby Bks.
Fielding, Xan, tr. see Boulle, Pierre.
Fields. The Sun. (gr. 2-4). 1980. PLB 6.45 (ISBN 0-531-03243-4, G23). Watts.
Fields, Alice. Insects. (gr. 2-4). 1980. PLB 7.90 (ISBN 0-531-03244-2). Watts.
--Seals. (gr. 2-4). 1980. PLB 6.45 (ISBN 0-531-03242-6). Watts.
Fields, Annie. Life & Letters of Harriet Beecher Stowe. LC 77-102057. (Library of Lives & Letters). (Illus.). 1970. Repr. of 1897 ed. 20.00 (ISBN 0-8103-3602-2). Gale.
Fields, Gary S. Poverty, Inequality, & Development. LC 79-21017. (Illus.). 256p. 1980. 29.50 (ISBN 0-521-22572-8); pap. 7.95 (ISBN 0-521-29852-0). Cambridge U Pr.
Fields, Harvey J. With All Your Heart: Bechol Levavcha, 2 vols. (Illus.). (gr. 7-9). 1977. 8.00 (ISBN 0-8074-0197-8, 142611). UAHC.
Fields, Joanne & Otto, Lois. Church Banquets Made Easy. LC 76-19480. (Illus.). 1976. pap. 2.25 (ISBN 0-87239-115-9, 2766). Standard Pub.
Fields, Kenneth, jt. ed. see Winters, Yvor.
Fields, Louis W. Bookkeeping Made Simple. 1956. pap. 3.50 (ISBN 0-385-01205-5, Made). Doubleday.
Fields, Marion. Fundamentals of Food Microbiology. (Illus.). 1979. text ed. 19.00 (ISBN 0-87055-250-3). AVI.
Fields, Marion L. Laboratory Manual in Food Preservation. 1977. 11.00 (ISBN 0-87055-241-4). AVI.
Fields, Mary E. Foundations in Truth. LC 80-67931. 275p. 1980. 10.00 (ISBN 0-87516-423-4). De Vorss.
Fields, Phyllis, tr. see Oliveira, Nuno.
Fields, Rona M. Northern Ireland: Society Under Siege. (Orig.). 1981. pap. 5.95 (ISBN 0-87855-806-3). Transaction Bks.
Fields, Sylvia K., jt. ed. see Sherman, Jacques L., Jr.
Fields, Uriah J. The Magic Power of Positive Ideas. 100p. 1981. pap. 4.50 (ISBN 0-938844-00-8). Am Mutuality.
Fields, Victor A. Training the Singing Voice: An Analysis of the Working Concepts Contained Contained in Recent Contributions to Vocal Pedagogy. (Music Reprint Ser.). 1979. Repr. of 1966 ed. lib. bdg. 27.50 (ISBN 0-306-79510-8). Da Capo.
Fields, Wilbert J. Unity in Marriage. LC 61-18222. 1962. 4.95 (ISBN 0-570-03191-5, 12-2593). Concordia.
Fields, Willa, jt. auth. see Berger, Karen.
Fielo, Claud. Dictionary of Arabic-Persian Quotes. 16.00x (ISBN 0-686-53121-3). Intl Bk Ctr.
Fiely, Douglas, jt. auth. see Grabill, James.
Fienberg, S. E. & Hinkley, D. H., eds. R. A. Fisher: An Appreciation. (Lecture Notes in Statistics: Vol. 1). 208p. 1980. pap. 14.00 (ISBN 0-387-90476-X). Springer-Verlag.
Fienberg, Stephen. The Analysis of Cross-Classified Categorical Data. 2nd ed. 1980. text ed. 14.00x (ISBN 0-262-06071-X). MIT Pr.
Fiene, Donald, tr. see Osorgin, Mikhail.
Fiennes, G. F. I Tried to Run a Railway. pap. text ed. 14.95x (ISBN 0-392-07972-0, SpS). Soccer.
Fiennes, R. N. Ecology & Earth History. 250p. 1980. 40.00x (Pub. by Croom Helm England). State Mutual Bk.
Fiennes, R. N., ed. Biology of Nutrition, Pts. 1-2. Incl. Pt. 1. The Evolution & Nature of Living Systems; Pt. 2. The Organizations & Nutritional Methods of Life Forms. 688p. 1972. Set. text ed. 125.00 (ISBN 0-08-016470-6). Pergamon.
Fienup-Riordan, Ann. Shape Up with Baby: Exercise Games for the New Parent & Child. LC 80-82128. (Illus., Orig.). 1980. pap. 5.95 (ISBN 0-937604-04-6). Pennypress.
Fiering, Norman. Moral Philosophy at Seventeenth-Century Harvard: A Discipline in Transition. LC 80-18282. 368p. 1981. 24.00x (ISBN 0-8078-1459-8). U of NC Pr.
Fierman, L. B., ed. Effective Psychotherapy. LC 65-2314. 1965. 15.95 (ISBN 0-02-910140-9). Free Pr.
Fiero, G. William. Nevada's Valley of Fire. DenDooven, Gweneth R., ed. LC 75-18136. (Illus.). 1975. 7.95 (ISBN 0-916122-42-5); pap. 2.50 (ISBN 0-916122-17-4). K C Pubns.
Fierro, Robert D. Tax Shelters in Plain English: New Strategies for the 1980's. 180p. 1981. 11.95 (ISBN 0-87863-023-6). Farnswth Pub.
Fierstein, Harvey. The Torch Song Trilogy. 250p. (Orig.). 1981. pap. 5.95 (ISBN 0-9604724-0-1). Gay Pr NY.
Fieser, Louis F. & Williamson, Kenneth L. Organic Experiments. 4th ed. 1979. text ed. 16.95x (ISBN 0-669-01688-8); instructor's manual free (ISBN 0-669-01689-6). Heath.
Fieser, Mary, et al. Reagents for Organic Synthesis, Vol. 9. (Reagents for Organic Synthesis Ser.). 688p. 1981. 35.00 (ISBN 0-471-05631-6, Pub. by Wiley-Interscience). Wiley.
Fifadara, Haresh, jt. auth. see Hollo, Reuven.
Fife, Alta, jt. auth. see Fife, Austin.
Fife, Austin & Fife, Alta. Saints of Sage & Saddle: Folklore Among the Mormons. 375p. 1981. pap. 15.00 (ISBN 0-87480-180-X). U of Utah Pr.
Fife, Dale. Follow That Ghost! LC 79-11370. (Illus.). (gr. 1-5). 1979. PLB 7.95 (ISBN 0-525-30010-4, Unicorn Bk.). Dutton.
--The Little Park. LC 73-7322. (Self Starter Ser.). (Illus.). 32p. (gr. k-2). 1973. 6.50g (ISBN 0-8075-4634-8). A Whitman.
--North of Danger. (gr. 5 up). 1978. PLB 8.95 (ISBN 0-525-36035-2). Dutton.
Fife, Eric S. Against the Clock: The Story of Ray Buker, Sr., Olympic Runner & Missionary Statesman. (Illus.). 224p. (Orig.). 1981. pap. 5.95 (ISBN 0-310-24351-3). Zondervan.
--The Holy Spirit: Common Sense & the Bible. (Orig.). 1979. pap. 4.95 (ISBN 0-310-24341-6). Zondervan.
--Prayer, Common Sense & the Bible. 1977. pap. 1.50 o.p. (ISBN 0-310-24332-7). Zondervan.
Fifer, Charles N., ed. see Farquhar, George.
Fifield, L. W. Navigation for Watchkeepers. (Illus.). 413p. 1980. 32.50 o.p. (ISBN 0-434-90564-X). Sheridan.
--Navigation for Watchkeepers. (Illus.). 416p. 1980. text ed. 32.50x. Sheridan.
Fifield, Russell H. Woodrow Wilson & the Far East: The Diplomacy of the Shantung Question. (Illus.). 1965. Repr. of 1952 ed. 17.50 (ISBN 0-208-00601-X, Archon). Shoe String.
Fifield, William. Jean Cocteau. (Columbia Essays on Modern Writers Ser.: No. 70). 1974. pap. 2.00 (ISBN 0-231-03369-9). Columbia U Pr.
Fifth Cranfield Fluidics Conference. Proceedings. 1972. text ed. 60.00 (ISBN 0-900983-24-8, Dist. by Air Science Co.). BHRA Fluid.
Fifth European Congress on Sleep Research, Amsterdam, September 1980. Sleep Nineteen Eighty. Koella, W. P., ed. (Illus.). 1981. 108.00 (ISBN 3-8055-2045-X). S Karger.
Fifth Fluid Power Symposium. Proceedings, 2 vols. Stephens, H. S. & Stapleton, C. A., eds. (Illus.). 1979. Set. lib. bdg. 78.00 (ISBN 0-900983-96-5, Dist by Air Science Co.). BHRA Fluid.
Fifth International Conference on Fluid Sealing. Proceedings. 1971. text ed. 50.00 (ISBN 0-900983-12-4, Dist. by Air Science Co.). BHRA Fluid.
Fifth International Conference on the Hydraulic Transport of Solids in Pipes. Proceedings, 2 vols. Stephens, H. S. & Gittins, L., eds. (Illus.). 1979. Set. pap. text ed. 86.00 (ISBN 0-900983-82-5, Dist by Air Science Co.). BHRA Fluid.
Figerot, Henry. The Potential Collapse of Western Civilization & Solutions for One of the Major Crises in World History. (An Institute for Economic & Political World Strategic Studies Bk). (Illus.). 87p. 1975. 49.40 (ISBN 0-913314-55-2). Am Classical Coll Pr.
Figes, Eva. Tragedy & Social Evolution. 1976. 10.95 (ISBN 0-7145-3516-8). Riverrun NY.
Figes, Eva, tr. see Grzimek, Bernhard.

Figg, Keith & Hayward, John. G R P Boat Construction. (Questions & Answers Ser.). (Illus.). 86p. (Orig.). 1979. pap. 7.50 (ISBN 0-408-00317-0). Transatlantic.

Figge, Frank H. Programmed Guide to the Dissection and Study of the Human Body. 2nd rev. ed. (Prog. Bk.). 1968. 12.00 o.s.i. (ISBN 0-02-844630-5). Hafner.

Figge, Frank H., ed. see Sobotta, Johannes.

Figgins, S. The Job Game. 1980. 12.95 o.p. (ISBN 0-13-510099-2); pap. 6.95 o.p. (ISBN 0-13-510081-X). P-H.

Figgis, B. N. Introduction to Ligand Fields. 351p. 1966. 33.95 (ISBN 0-470-25880-2). Wiley.

Figiel, Richard, jt. auth. see Myers, Stanley.

Figler, Howard E., jt. auth. see Drum, David J.

Figley, Charles R. & Leventman, Seymour. Strangers at Home: The Vietnam Veteran Since the War. LC 79-24398. (Praeger Spcial Studies). 1980. student edition 9.95 (ISBN 0-03-049776-0); 24.95 (ISBN 0-03-049771-X). Praeger.

Figueiredo, M. P. De see De Figueiredo, M. P. & Splittstoesser, D. F.

Figueredo, Luis E. Basic Electricity. 1980. pap. text ed. 14.95 (ISBN 0-89669-053-9). Collegium Bk Pubs.

Figueroa, Jose. A Manifesto to the Mexican Republic. Hutchinson, C. Alan, tr. 1978. 19.95 (ISBN 0-520-03347-7). U of Cal Pr.

Figueroa, William G. Hematology: UCLA Postgraduate Medicine for the Internist. (Illus.). 1981. price not set (ISBN 0-89289-377-X). HM.

Figurski, Leszek. Finality & Intelligence. LC 78-62252. 1978. pap. text ed. 9.00 (ISBN 0-8191-0565-1). U Pr of Amer.

Fijan, Carol, jt. auth. see Engler, Larry.

Fike, C. T. PL One for Scientific Programmers. 1970. ref. ed. 17.95x (ISBN 0-13-676502-5). P-H.

Fikentscher, Wolfgang. Draft International Code of Conduct on the Transfer of Technology. (IIC Studies: Vol. 4). 211p. (Orig.). 1980. pap. text ed. 23.80 (ISBN 0-89573-030-8). Verlag Chemie.

Fikhtengol'ts, G. M. Fundamentals of Mathematical Analysis, 2 Vols. 1965. Vol. 1. 25.00 (ISBN 0-08-010059-7); Vol. 2. 25.00 (ISBN 0-08-010060-0); Vol. 1. pap. 18.75 (ISBN 0-08-013473-4); Vol. 2. pap. 21.00 (ISBN 0-08-013474-2). Pergamon.

Filarete. Filarete's Treatise on Architecture: Being the Treatise by Antonio Di Piero Averlino, Known As Filarete, 2 Vols. Spencer, John R., tr. (Publications in the History of Art Ser.: No. 16). (Illus.). 1965. Set. 70.00x o.p. (ISBN 0-300-00970-4). Yale U Pr.

Filas, Joseph. Joseph: The Man Closest to Jesus. 1962. 7.75 (ISBN 0-8198-0070-8); pap. 6.50 o.s.i. (ISBN 0-8198-0071-6). Dghtrs St Paul.

Filbeck, David. The First Fifty Years. LC 80-65966. 400p. 1980. pap. 5.95 (ISBN 0-89900-060-6). College Pr Pub.

Filby, D. E., jt. auth. see Cox, S. W.

Filby, P. W. & Howard, Edward G. Star Spangled Books: Books, Sheet Music, Newspapers, Manuscripts, & Persons Associated with the Star-Spangled Banner. LC 70-187215. (Illus.). 200p. 1972. 15.00 (ISBN 0-938420-17-8). Md Hist.

Filby, P. William, ed. Bibliography of Ship Passenger Lists (1538-1900) Being a Guide to Published Lists of Immigrants to the United States & Canada. 160p. 1981. 44.00 (ISBN 0-8103-1098-8). Gale.

--Passenger & Immigration Lists Index: A Reference Guide to Published Lists of Passengers Who Arrived in America in the Seventeenth, Eighteenth, & Nineteenth Centuries, 3 vols. 1980. 225.00 (ISBN 0-8103-1099-6). Gale.

Filek, Werner Von see Von Filek, Werner.

Filer, L. J., Jr., et al, eds. Glutamic Acid: Advances in Biochemistry & Physiology. LC 78-56782. (Mario Negri Institute for Pharmacological Research Monographs). 1979. text ed. 38.00 (ISBN 0-89004-356-6). Raven.

Filesi, Teobaldo & Morrison, D. L., trs. China & Africa in the Middle Ages. (Illus.). 104p. 1972. 24.00x (ISBN 0-7146-2604-X, F Cass Co). Biblio Dist.

Filgate, Macartney. Runway to Death. Orig. Title: Bravo Charley. 154p. 1980. 9.95 (ISBN 0-8027-5428-7). Walker & Co.

Filing Committee of the Resources & Technical Services Division American Library Association. ALA Filing Rules. LC 80-22186. 62p. 1980. pap. 3.50 (ISBN 0-8389-3255-X). ALA.

Filipovic, R. Croatian-English, English-Croatian Pocket Dictionary. 1977. pap. 7.50 o.p. (ISBN 0-686-22677-1, Y-726). Vanous.

Filipovitch, Anthony & Reeves, Earl, eds. Urban Community: A Guide to Information Sources. LC 78-13171. (The Urban Studies Information Guide Ser.: Vol. 4). 1978. 30.00 (ISBN 0-8103-1429-0). Gale.

Filippone, Samuel R. & Williams, Michael Z. Elementary Mathematics: A Fundamentals & Techniques Approach. LC 75-19539. (Illus.). 448p. 1976. text ed. 17.50 (ISBN 0-395-20028-8); inst. manual 3.25 (ISBN 0-395-20029-6). HM.

Fillenbaum, Samuel & Rapoport, Amnon. Structures in the Subjective Lexicon: An Experimental Approach to the Study of Semantic Fields. 1971. 33.00 (ISBN 0-12-256250-X). Acad Pr.

Filler, Louis. The Rise & Fall of Slavery in America. ix, 165p. 1980. lib. bdg. 9.95x (ISBN 0-89198-122-5); pap. text ed. 5.95x (ISBN 0-89198-123-3). Ozer.

--Seasoned Authors for a New Season: The Search for Standards in Popular Writing. LC 79-90128. 1980. 15.95 (ISBN 0-87972-143-X). Bowling Green.

--Vanguards & Followers: Youth in the American Tradition. LC 78-5893. 1978. 12.95 (ISBN 0-88229-459-8); pap. 7.95 (ISBN 0-88229-608-6). Nelson-Hall.

Filler, Louis, ed. & intro. by. Late Nineteenth-Century American Liberalism: Representative Selections, 1880-1900. LC 61-18060. 250p. 1980. Repr. of 1962 ed. text ed. 21.50x o.p. (ISBN 0-8290-0180-8). Irvington.

Filler, Louis, ed. see Hardy, Irene.

Filley, Alan, jt. auth. see Delbecq, Andre.

Filley, Alan C., et al. Managerial Process & Organizational Behavior. 2nd ed. 1976. text ed. 18.95x (ISBN 0-673-07857-4). Scott F.

Fillian, Barbie & Livingston, Lida. Eat Yourself Thin: Secrets of the Harbor Island Spas. LC 77-84426. 1977. 9.95 (ISBN 0-8119-0284-6). Fell.

Fillingham, Paul. The Balloon Book: How to Launch, Navigate, & Land a Balloon. (Illus.). 1979. pap. 8.95 o.p. (ISBN 0-679-50928-3). McKay.

--Basic Guide to Flying. 1977. pap. 5.95 (ISBN 0-8015-0526-7, Hawthorn). Dutton.

Fillis, James. Breaking & Riding. Hayes, M. H., tr. (Illus.). 15.75 (ISBN 0-85131-044-3, Dist. by Sporting Book Center). J A Allen.

Fillmore, Clyde. Prisoner of War: History of the "Lost Battalion". 5.95 o.p. (ISBN 0-685-48815-2). Nortex Pr.

Filmer, Edward. A Defence of Plays: The Stage Vindicated from...Mr. Collier's Short View. LC 70-170449. (The English Stage Ser.: Vol. 36). lib. bdg. 50.00 (ISBN 0-8240-0619-4). Garland Pub.

Filmer, Sir Robert. A Disclosure Whether It May Be Lawful to Take Use for Money. Berkowitz, David S. & Thorne, Samuel E., eds. LC 77-89250. (Classics of English Legal History in the Modern Era Ser.: Vol. 79). 166p. 1979. lib. bdg. 40.00 (ISBN 0-8240-3179-2). Garland Pub.

Filon, S. P. The National Central Library: An Experiment in Library Cooperation 1916 - 1974. 300p. 1977. lib. bdg. 22.00x (ISBN 0-85365-249-X, Pub. by Lib Assn England). Oryx Pr.

Filonidov, A. M., jt. auth. see Tret'yakov, A. K.

Filoromo, Tina, jt. auth. see Ziff, Dolores.

Fils, David H. The Developmental Disabilities Handbook. LC 79-57296. (Professional Handbook Ser.). 50p. 1980. pap. 7.50x (ISBN 0-87424-139-1). Western Psych.

Filskov, Susan B. & Boll, Thomas J. Handbook of Clinical Neuropsychology. LC 80-15392. (Wiley Ser. on Personality Processes). 768p. 1980. 29.95 (ISBN 0-471-04802-X, Pub. by Wiley-Interscience). Wiley.

Filson, Brent. Smoke Jumpers. LC 76-56289. (gr. 7 up). 1978. pap. 5.95 (ISBN 0-385-12790-1). Doubleday.

Filson, Floyd V. John. LC 59-10454. (Layman's Bible Commentary Ser: Vol. 19). 1963. 4.25 (ISBN 0-8042-3019-6). John Knox.

Filson, Henry J. Little Hands with First Drawing Practice. (Draw-Sketch Practice Ser.). (Illus.). 28p. (gr. 5 up). 1978. bdg. 2.75plastic (ISBN 0-918554-01-2). Old Violin.

--Senior Hi Artist. (Draw-Sketch Practice Ser.). (Illus.). 44p. 1978. plastic bdg. 3.75 (ISBN 0-918554-02-0). Old Violin.

--Sketch & Draw Today. (Draw-Sketch Practice Ser.). (Illus.). 122p. 1976. plastic bdg. 12.00 (ISBN 0-918554-00-4). Old Violin.

Filson, Sidney. Shaping up: How to Reduce Your Sags & Bulges & Reshape Any Area of Your Body in One Month. 1980. 9.95 (ISBN 0-316-28215-4). Little.

Filtzer, Don, tr. see Rubin, Isaac I.

Finacchiaro, Mary & Bonomo, Michael. The Foreign Language Learner: A Guide for Teachers. 1973. text ed. 8.95 (ISBN 0-88345-087-9, 18071); pap. text ed. 5.95 (ISBN 0-88345-088-7, 18072). Regents Pub.

Finance, Charles. Buffet Catering. (Illus.). 1958. 19.95 (ISBN 0-8104-9401-9). Hayden.

Financial Pub Editors, ed. Financial Pass-Through Yield & Value Tables for GNMA Mortgage-Backed Securities No. 715. rev. 5th ed. 25.00 (ISBN 0-685-47818-1). Finan Pub.

Financial Publications. Financial Capitalization Rate Tables No. 73. 25.00 o.p. (ISBN 0-685-47819-X). Finan Pub.

--Financial Monthly Mortgage Handbook: 6 per Cent to 15 per Cent No. 158. 3rd ed. 17.50 (ISBN 0-685-47820-3). Finan Pub.

Financial Publishing Co. Bond Yield Tables, Four Percent to Fourteen Percent Nos. 154, 254, 2 vols. 6.00 ea. Finan Pub.

--Continuous Compounding Savings Factor Tables No. 534. 15.00 (ISBN 0-685-02537-3). Finan Pub.

--Coupon Interest Calendar - 360-Day Basis No. 360. 20.00 (ISBN 0-685-02539-X). Finan Pub.

--Coupon Interest Calendar - 365-Day Basis No. 365. 25.00 (ISBN 0-685-02538-1). Finan Pub.

--Discount & Equivalent Interest Tables No. 948. 42.50 (ISBN 0-685-02540-3). Finan Pub.

--Eight Rate & Prepayment Mortgage Yield Table No. 56. 12.50 o.p. (ISBN 0-685-02556-X). Finan Pub.

--Expanded Bond Values Tables. No. 63. pocket ed. 27.50 (ISBN 0-685-02541-1); No. 83. desk ed. 36.00 (ISBN 0-685-02542-X). Finan Pub.

--Financial Compound Interest & Annuity Tables No. 376. 6th ed. 40.00 (ISBN 0-685-02543-8). Finan Pub.

--Financial Monthly Refun Table, 78's Method No. 227. 20.00 (ISBN 0-685-02545-4). Finan Pub.

--Financial Mortgage Guide No. 149. 2nd ed. 5.00 o.p. (ISBN 0-685-02546-2). Finan Pub.

--High Coupon Callable Bond Values Tables No. 74. 35.00 o.p. (ISBN 0-685-02549-7). Finan Pub.

--Monthly Payment Direct Reduction Loan Amortization Schedules No.185. 12th ed. 40.00 (ISBN 0-685-02550-0). Finan Pub.

--Mortgage Payment Table No. 291. rev ed. 5.00 o.p. (ISBN 0-685-41731-X). Finan Pub.

--Mortgage Values Tables No. 207. 12.50 (ISBN 0-685-02552-7). Finan Pub.

--Net Yield After Capital Gains Tax 25 Percent No. 344, 30 Percent No. 444, 48 Percent No. 544, 3 Vols. 7.50 ea. Finan Pub.

--Net Yield Table for GNMA Mortgage Backed Securities, No. 710. rev ed. 5.00 o.p. (ISBN 0-685-02554-3). Finan Pub.

--U. S. Treasury Bills Table No. 66. 30.00 (ISBN 0-685-02560-8). Finan Pub.

Financial Publishing Company Staff. The Cost of Personal Borrowing in the United States. 9th ed. Gushee, Charles H., ed. (Illus.). 1980. perfect bound 27.50 (ISBN 0-685-87665-9, 830). Finan Pub.

Finar, I. L. Organic Chemistry, Vol. 1. 6th rev. ed. (Illus.). 960p. 1973. text ed. 23.00x (ISBN 0-582-44221-4). Longman.

--Organic Chemistry, Vol. 2. 5th rev. ed. LC 73-157839. (Illus.). 942p. 1975. text ed. 27.00x (ISBN 0-582-44312-1). Longman.

--Stereochemistry & the Chemistry of Natural Products. 2nd ed. (Organic Chemistry Ser.: Vol. 2). 1959. 13.95 (ISBN 0-471-25888-1). Halsted Pr.

Finberg, H. P., ed. Gloucestershire Studies. 1957. text ed. 13.00x (ISBN 0-7185-1013-5, Leicester). Humanities.

Finberg, H. P., ed. see Wainwright, Frederick T.

Finberg, J., tr. see Dobroliubov, Nikolai A.

Finch, Alton V., jt. auth. see Calhoun, Calfrey C.

Finch, Bernard, ed. Multilingual Guide for Medical Personnel. 1967. spiral bdg. 4.50 (ISBN 0-87488-961-8). Med Exam.

Finch, Christofer. Rainbow: The Stormy Life of Judy Garland. 1978. pap. 1.95 o.p. (ISBN 0-345-28113-6). Ballantine.

Finch, Christopher. Norman Rockwell. LC 79-57405. (Abbeville Library of Art: No. 5). (Illus.). 112p. 1980. pap. 4.95 (ISBN 0-89659-090-9). Abbeville Pr.

Finch, Curtis R. & Crunkilton, John R. Curriculum Development in Vocational & Technical Education: Planning Content & Implementation. new ed. 1978. text ed. 17.95 (ISBN 0-205-06148-6). Allyn.

Finch, Frank. A Concise Encyclopedia of Management Techniques. LC 76-5913. 1976. 24.50x (ISBN 0-8448-0963-2). Crane-Russak Co.

Finch, Henry L. Wittgenstein, the Early Philosophy: An Exposition of the Tractatus. LC 73-135985. 1971. text ed. 10.00x o.p. (ISBN 0-391-00123-X). Humanities.

Finch, Sir Henry. Law, or a Discourse Thereof Done into English. Berkowitz, David & Thorne, Samuel, eds. LC 77-86560. (Classics of English Legal History in the Modern Era Ser.: Vol. 65). 1979. Repr. of 1759 ed. lib. bdg. 55.00 (ISBN 0-8240-3052-4). Garland Pub.

Finch, I. J. General Studies: First Handbook for Technical Students. 1965. 15.00 (ISBN 0-08-011106-8); pap. 7.00 (ISBN 0-08-011105-X). Pergamon.

Finch, Jay S., jt. auth. see DeKornfeld, Thomas J.

Finch, Margaret. Style in Art History: An Introduction to Theories of Style & Sequence. LC 73-14705. 178p. 1974. lib. bdg. 10.00 (ISBN 0-8108-0679-7). Scarecrow.

Finch, Philip. Haulin' 1977. pap. 1.75 o.p. (ISBN 0-345-25102-4). Ballantine.

Finch, Phillip. Birthright. 1981. pap. 2.75 (ISBN 0-425-04590-0). Berkley Pub.

--Texas Dawn. LC 80-52414. 512p. 1981. 12.95 (ISBN 0-87223-656-0). Seaview Bks.

Finch, Richard. How to Keep Your Corvair Alive. LC 77-16221. (Illus.). 1977. pap. 5.95 o.p. (ISBN 0-912656-58-1). H P Bks.

Finch, Robert. Common Ground: A Naturalist's Cape Cod. (Illus.). 1981. 12.50 (ISBN 0-87923-383-4); ltd. ed. 40.00 (ISBN 0-87923-384-2). Godine.

Finch, Steven, tr. see Genet, Jean.

Finch, T; see Bowen, D. Q.

Finch, Yolande. Finchy: A Memoir of Peter Finch by His Former Wife. (Illus.). 1981. 12.95 (ISBN 0-671-61008-2, Wyndham Bks). S&S.

Fincham, J. R. Microbial & Molecular Genetics. 2nd ed. LC 75-21729. 155p. 1976. pap. 9.95x (ISBN 0-8448-0769-9). Crane-Russak Co.

Fincham, J. R., et al. Fungal Genetics. 4th ed. (Botanical Monographs). 1979. 62.50x (ISBN 0-520-03818-5). U of Cal Pr.

Fincham, W. H. & Freeman, M. H. Optics. 9th rev. ed. LC 80-40274. (Illus.). 1980. 34.95 (ISBN 0-407-93422-7). Butterworths.

Fincher, E. B. The Bill of Rights. (First Books Ser.). (Illus.). (gr. 4-6). 1978. PLB 6.45 s&l (ISBN 0-531-01347-2). Watts.

--The Vietnam War. (gr. 7 up). 1980. PLB 6.90 (ISBN 0-531-04112-3, C07). Watts.

Fincher, Ernest B. Government of the United States. 3rd ed. (Illus.). 384p. 1976. pap. 12.50 (ISBN 0-13-361881-1). P-H.

Finck, H. T. My Adventures in the Golden Age of Music. LC 70-87496. (Music Ser.). 462p. 1971. Repr. of 1926 ed. lib. bdg. 39.50 (ISBN 0-306-71448-5). Da Capo.

Finck, Henry T. Musical Laughs: Jokes, Tittle-Tattle, & Anecdotes, Mostly Humorous, About Musical Celebrities. LC 79-159955. 1971. Repr. of 1924 ed. 18.00 (ISBN 0-8103-3397-X). Gale.

Findeisen, W., et al. Control & Coordination in Hierarchical Systems. (IIASA International Ser. on Applied Systems Analysis: No. 9). 480p. 1980. 67.50 (ISBN 0-471-27742-8). Wiley.

Findeiss, J. Clifford, ed. Emergency Management of the Critical Patient. LC 74-81651. (Emergency Medical Care Ser.: Vol. 2). (Illus.). 288p. 1975. text ed. 22.95 (ISBN 0-8151-3223-9, Pub. by Symposia Special). Year Bk Med.

Finder, Jan H., ed. Alien Encounters. 256p. 1981. 11.95 (ISBN 0-8008-0168-7). Taplinger.

Findhorn Community, ed. Faces of Findhorn: Images of a Planetary Family. LC 78-20160. (Illus.). 192p. 1980. 12.95 (ISBN 0-06-011268-9, HarpT). Har-Row.

Findlater, R. Joe Grimaldi: His Life & Theatre. LC 78-7465. 1979. 42.00 (ISBN 0-521-22221-4); pap. 12.95x (ISBN 0-521-29407-X). Cambridge U Pr.

Findlay, David A. The Electronic Experimenter's Manual. (Illus.). 1959. 7.95 o.p. (ISBN 0-498-09369-7). A S Barnes.

Findlay, J. N. Axiological Ethics. LC 79-115982. (New Studies in Ethics). 1970. pap. 4.95 (ISBN 0-312-06335-0). St Martin.

--Plato: The Written & Unwritten Doctrines. (International Library of Philosophy & Scientific Method). 350p. 1974. text ed. 30.00x (ISBN 0-391-00334-8). Humanities.

Findlay, J. N., tr. see Hegel, G. W.

Findlay, J. N., tr. see Husserl, Edmund.

Findlay, Jessie Patrick. Footprints of Robert Burns. 174p. 1980. Repr. of 1923 ed. lib. bdg. 22.50 (ISBN 0-8492-4725-X). R West.

Findlay, John N. Discipline of the Cave. (Muirhead Library of Philosophy Ser.). 1966. text ed. 9.00x o.p. (ISBN 0-04-111001-3). Humanities.

--Transcendence of the Cave: Sequel to the Discipline of the Cave. LC 67-16869. (Muirhead Library of Philosophy Ser.). 1978. text ed. 15.00x (ISBN 0-04-111002-1). Humanities.

Findlay, M. C., jt. ed. see Whitmore, G. A.

Findlay, R., jt. auth. see Brockett, O.

Findlay, Ronald E. International Trade & Development Theory. LC 73-8623. 208p. 1973. 17.50x (ISBN 0-231-03546-2). Columbia U Pr.

Findlay, William & Watt, David A. Pascal: An Introduction to Methodical Programming. 2nd ed. (Illus.). Date not set. pap. text ed. price not set (ISBN 0-914894-73-0). Computer Sci.

Findley, Roger W. & Farber, Daniel A. Environmental Law: Cases & Materials. (American Casebook Ser.). 639p. 1981. text ed. 19.95. West Pub.

Findley, Timothy. The Wars. 1977. 8.95 o.s.i. (ISBN 0-440-09397-X, Sey Lawr). Delacorte.

Fine, Ben & Harris, Lawrence. Reading Capital. 1979. 17.50x (ISBN 0-231-04792-4). Columbia U Pr.

Fine, Bernard D., jt. ed. see Orgel, Shelly.

Fine, Carla. Married to Medicine. LC 80-69372. 1981. 11.95 (ISBN 0-689-11128-2). Atheneum.
Fine, David, jt. auth. see Peck, David.
Fine, David M. The City, the Immigrant, & American Fiction, 1880-1920. LC 77-6297. 1977. 10.00 (ISBN 0-8108-1038-7). Scarecrow.
Fine, George. Sex Jokes & Male Chauvinism. (Illus.). 192p. 1981. 9.95 (ISBN 0-8065-0753-5). Citadel Pr.
Fine, Helen. At Camp Kee Tov: Ethics for Jewish Juniors. (Illus.). text ed. 5.00 (ISBN 0-8074-0128-5, 121711). UAHC.
--Behold, the Land: Ayin Letzion. rev. ed. LC 67-21069. (gr. 5-8). 1977. text ed. 6.50 (ISBN 0-8074-0129-3, 127270); teachers guide 1971 o.p. 5.00 (ISBN 0-685-20726-9, 207271). UAHC.
--G'Dee. (Illus.). (gr. 4-5). 1958. text ed. 4.50 (ISBN 0-8074-0137-4, 123702). UAHC.
--G'Dee's Book of Holiday Fun. (Illus.). (gr. 4-6). 1961. pap. 3.00 o.p. (ISBN 0-685-20737-4, 121701). UAHC.
Fine, Jerome, jt. auth. see Botwin, Carol.
Fine, Joan. I Carve Stone. LC 79-63798. (Illus.). (gr. 4-7). 1979. 7.95 (ISBN 0-690-03985-9, TYC-J); PLB 7.89 (ISBN 0-690-03986-7). T Y Crowell.
Fine, Linda. How to Make the Most of the New You. 224p. 1981. 10.95 (ISBN 0-668-04919-7); pap. 6.95 (ISBN 0-668-04923-5). Arco.
Fine, Marvin J. Principles & Techniques of Intervention with Hyperactive Children. (Illus.). 328p. 1977. 29.50 (ISBN 0-398-03570-9). C C Thomas.
Fine, Morris, et al, eds. American Jewish Yearbook, Vol. 80. 650p. 1980. 15.00 (ISBN 0-8276-0173-5, 454). Jewish Pubn.
Fine, Peter H. Troubled Waters. 192p. (Orig.). 1981. pap. 1.95 (ISBN 0-523-41213-4). Pinnacle Bks.
Fine, Peter J., ed. Deafness in Infancy & Early Childhood. LC 73-17327. 250p. 1974. 13.95 o.p. (ISBN 0-683-03208-9). Williams & Wilkins.
Fine, Reuben. Fifty Chess Masterpieces: 1941-1944. Orig. Title: Chess Marches on. 1977. pap. 3.50 o.p. (ISBN 0-486-23450-9). Dover.
--A History of Psychoanalysis. LC 78-31425. 1979. 25.00 (ISBN 0-231-04208-6). Columbia U Pr.
--The Psychoanalytic Vision. LC 80-2154. 1981. 19.95 (ISBN 0-02-910270-7). Free Pr.
--The World's Great Chess Games. rev. ed. (Illus.). 1976. 14.95 o.p. (ISBN 0-679-13046-2). McKay.
Fine, Sara. Developing Career Information Centers in Libraries: A Guide to Collection Building & Counseling. LC 80-11634. 175p. 1980. pap. 17.95x (ISBN 0-918212-19-7). Neal-Schuman.
Fine Woodworking Magazine. Fine Woodworking Biennial Design Book. (Illus.). 1978. pap. 7.95 o.p. (ISBN 0-918804-00-0, ScribT). Scribner.
--Fine Woodworking Techniques One. (Illus.). 1978. 9.95 o.p. (ISBN 0-918804-02-7, ScribT). Scribner.
Fine Woodworking magazine Editors. Fine Woodworking Biennial Design Book. LC 77-79327. (Illus.). 1977. pap. 9.95 (ISBN 0-918804-00-0, Dist. by Van Nostrand Nostrand Reinhold). Taunton.
--Fine Woodworking Techniques, No. 1. LC 78-58221. (Illus.). 1978. 14.95 (ISBN 0-918804-02-7, Dist. by Nostrand Reinhold). Taunton.
--Fine Woodworking Techniques, No. 2. LC 80-52056. (Illus.). 208p. 1980. 14.95 (ISBN 0-918804-09-4, Dist. by Van Nostrand Reinhold). Taunton.
Finean, J. B., et al. Membranes & Their Cellular Functions. 2nd ed. LC 78-9016. 1978. pap. text ed. 12.95 (ISBN 0-470-26389-X). Halsted Pr.
Fineberg, Harvey V., jt. auth. see Weinstein, Milton C.
Fineberg, Marjorie. Everyday Math: Tables, Graphs, & Scale. LC 79-730692. (Illus.). 1979. pap. text ed. 99.00 (ISBN 0-89290-129-2, A514-SATC). Soc for Visual.
Fineberg, Marjorie & Shaw, John. Decimals. LC 79-730043. (Illus.). 1978. pap. text ed. 99.00 (ISBN 0-89290-095-4, A511-SATC). Soc for Visual.
Finegan, Edward. Attitudes Toward English Usage: A History of the War of Words. 1980. pap. 9.95x (ISBN 0-8077-2581-1). Tchrs Coll.
Finegan, Jack. Archaeological History of the Ancient Middle East. (Illus.). 1979. lib. bdg. 35.00 (ISBN 0-89158-164-2, Dawson). Westview.
--The Archaeology of the New Testament: The Mediterranean World of the Early Christian Apostles. (Illus.). 400p. 1981. 35.00x (ISBN 0-86531-064-5). Westview.
--Discovering Israel: A Popular Guide to the Holy Land. LC 80-26952. (Illus.). 176p. 1981. pap. 7.95 (ISBN 0-8028-1869-2). Eerdmans.
--Encountering New Testament Manuscripts. pap. 7.95 (ISBN 0-8028-1836-6). Eerdmans.
--Light from the Ancient Past, 2 vols. 2nd ed. (Illus.). 1959. Vol. 1 2nd Ed. 25.00 (ISBN 0-691-03550-4); Vol. 1 2nd Edition. pap. 8.95 (ISBN 0-691-00207-X); 25.00 (ISBN 0-691-03551-2); Vol. 2. pap. 8.95 (ISBN 0-691-00208-8). Princeton U Pr.
Finegold, Julius J. & Thetford, William N., eds. Choose Once Again. LC 76-20363. (Illus.). 112p. 1981. 8.95 (ISBN 0-89087-285-6). Celestial Arts.
Finegold, Sydney M., et al. Diagnostic Microbiology: A Textbook for the Isolation & Identification of Pathogenic Microorganisms. 5th ed. LC 77-28251. (Illus.). 1978. text ed. 24.95 (ISBN 0-8016-0421-4). Mosby.
Finegold, Wilfred J. Artificial Insemination with Husband Sperm. 112p. 1980. 14.75 (ISBN 0-398-04094-X). C C Thomas.
Fineman, Mark. The Inquisitive Eye. (Illus.). 224p. 1981. pap. text ed. 7.95x (ISBN 0-19-502773-6). Oxford U Pr.
Finer, Herman. The T. V. A. Lessons for International Application. LC 77-172008. (FDR & the Era of the New Deal Ser.). (Illus.). 1972. Repr. of 1944 ed. lib. bdg. 29.50 (ISBN 0-306-70378-5). Da Capo.
Finer, S. E. Changing British Party System 1945-1979. 1980. pap. 7.25 (ISBN 0-8447-3368-7). Am Enterprise.
Finer, S. E., ed. Five Constitutions. 1980. text ed. 30.00x (ISBN 0-391-00967-2). Humanities.
Finerty, James P. The Population Ecology of Cycles in Small Mammals: Mathematical Theory & Biological Fact. LC 79-23774. (Illus.). 1981. text ed. 18.50x (ISBN 0-300-02382-0). Yale U Pr.
Finerty, John F. War-Path & Bivouac: The Big Horn & Yellowstone Expedition. Quaife, Milo M., ed. LC 67-89221. (Illus.). 1966. pap. 7.50 (ISBN 0-8032-5059-2, BB 329, Bison). U of Nebr Pr.
Fines, John. Domesday Book in the Classroom. 48p. 1981. pap. 7.50x (ISBN 0-8476-3165-6). Rowman.
--Tudor People. 1977. 16.95 (ISBN 0-7134-0283-0, Pub. by Batsford England). David & Charles.
Finestone, Harold. Victims of Change: Juvenile Delinquents in American Society. LC 76-5327. (Contributions in Sociology: No. 20). (Illus.). 256p. 1976. lib. bdg. 17.95 (ISBN 0-8371-8897-0, FTD/). Greenwood.
Fingado, Gail, et al. The English Connection: A Text for Speakers of Englisn As a Second Language. (English Ser.). 416p. 1981. text ed. 12.95 (ISBN 0-87626-236-1). Winthrop.
Fingar, Elmer L., et al. New York Wills & Trusts: Laws, Forms & Taxes, 2 vols. rev. 2nd ed. LC 61-9883. 1971. looseleaf with 1979 suppl. 90.00 (ISBN 0-87632-062-0). Boardman.
Fingar, Thomas, ed. China's Quest for Independence: Policy Evolution in the Nineteen Seventy's. (Westview Special Studies on China & East Asia). 245p. 1980. 22.00x (ISBN 0-89158-570-2). Westview.
Fingarette, Herbert. The Meaning of Criminal Insanity. LC 70-165223. 300p. 1972. 21.50x (ISBN 0-520-02082-0); pap. 4.25x (ISBN 0-520-02631-4). U of Cal Pr.
--The Self in Transformation: Psychoanalysis, Philosophy & the Life of the Spirit. LC 63-12846. 1977. pap. text ed. 6.95x (ISBN 0-06-131177-4, TB1177, Torch). Har-Row.
Fingarette, Herbert & Hasse, Ann F. Mental Disabilities & Criminal Responsibilities. LC 77-91756. 1979. 21.50x (ISBN 0-520-03630-1). U of Cal Pr.
Finger, Ellis, jt. auth. see Bergethon, K. Roald.
Finger, Seymour M. Your Man at the UN: People, Politics & Bueaucracy in the Making of Foreign Policy. LC 79-3657. 368p. 1980. 26.50x (ISBN 0-8147-2566-X). NYU Pr.
Finger, Seymour M. & Harbert, Joseph R., eds. U. S. Policy in International Institutions: Defining Reasonable Options in an Unreasonable World. rev. & updated ed. (Special Studies in International Relations). 200p. (Orig.). 1981. lib. bdg. 20.00x (ISBN 0-86531-105-6); pap. 8.50x (ISBN 0-86531-106-4). Westview.
Finger, Seymour M., jt. ed. see Alexander, Yonah.
Fingland, Randy & Schneider, Andrea. Dinosaur Cooler. (Illus.). 1980. pap. 2.25 (ISBN 0-931020-13-1). Crosscut Saw.
Finholt, Richard. American Visionary Fiction: Mad Metaphysics As Salvation Psychology. (National University Publications Literary Criticism Ser.). 1977. 12.00 (ISBN 0-8046-9191-6). Kennikat.
Finigan, Robert. Robert Finigan's Guide to Discriminating Dining in San Francisco. (Illus.). 192p. (Orig.). 1981. pap. 6.95 (ISBN 0-89141-123-2). Presidio Pr.
Finizio, Norman & Ladas, Gerasimos. Ordinary Differential Equations with Modern Applications. 1978. text ed. 20.95x (ISBN 0-534-00552-7); solution manual 6.95x (ISBN 0-534-00586-1). Wadsworth Pub.
Fink, Albert H. International Perspectives on Future Special Education. LC 78-74018. 1979. text ed. 15.00 o.p. (ISBN 0-86586-046-7). Coun Exc Child.
Fink, Albert H., ed. see World Congress on Special Education, 1st.
Fink, Arlene & Kosecoff, Jacqueline. An Evaluation Primer Workbook: Practical Exercises for Educators. LC 77-88462. (Illus.). 57p. 1980. pap. 7.95 (ISBN 0-8039-1481-4). Sage.
--An Evaluation Primer Workbook: Practical Exercises for Health Professionals. LC 77-88463. (Illus.). 89p. 1980. pap. 8.95 (ISBN 0-8039-1482-2). Sage.
Fink, B. Raymond. The Human Larynx: A Functional Study. LC 74-80536. 1975. 19.00 (ISBN 0-911216-86-3). Raven.
Fink, B. Raymond, ed. Molecular Mechanisms of Anesthesia. (Progress in Anesthesiology Ser.: Vol. 2). 528p. 1980. text ed. 48.50 (ISBN 0-89004-456-2). Raven.
--Molecular Mechanisms of Anesthesia. LC 74-14474. (Progress in Anesthesiology Ser: Vol. 1). 1975. 48.00 (ISBN 0-911216-94-4). Raven.
Fink, Candy. Feelings: A Collection of Poems & Potpourri. 1981. 4.95 (ISBN 0-533-04838-9). Vantage.
Fink, Carole, tr. see Bloch, Marc.
Fink, Dale B. Mr. Silver & Mr. Gold. 32p. (gr. 4-8). 8.95 (ISBN 0-87705-447-9). Human Sci Pr.
Fink, Donald G. & Christiansen, Donald. Electronics Engineer's Handbook. 2nd ed. 2496p. Date not set. 46.50 (ISBN 0-07-020981-2). McGraw.
Fink, Edith & Day, Avenelle. Hot Birds & Cold Bottles. 320p. 1972. 10.00 o.s.i. (ISBN 0-440-03750-6). Delacorte.
Fink, Gary M. Labor Unions. LC 76-8734. (Greenwood Encyclopedia of American Institutions). 544p. 1977. lib. bdg. 29.95 (ISBN 0-8371-8938-1, FLU/). Greenwood.
Fink, Greta. Great Jewish Women. LC 77-99193. 1978. 8.95 (ISBN 0-8197-0458-X). Bloch.
Fink, Harold S., ed. see Fulcher Of Chartres.
Fink, Henry S., ed. A History of the Expedition to Jerusalem, 1095-1127. Ryan, Sr. Frances R., tr. 1972. pap. text ed. 6.95x (ISBN 0-393-09423-5). Norton.
Fink, Joseph & Sealy, Lloyd G. The Community & the Police: Conflict or Cooperation? LC 74-1144. 216p. 1974. 18.95 (ISBN 0-471-25894-6, Pub. by Wiley-Interscience). Wiley.
Fink, Karl J. & Marchand, James W., eds. The Quest for the New Science: Language & Thought in Eighteenth-Century Science. LC 79-889. 110p. 1979. 7.95x (ISBN 0-8093-0917-3). S Ill U Pr.
Fink, Lawrence A. Honors Teaching in American History. LC 68-54673. 1969. text ed. 5.25x (ISBN 0-8077-1350-3). Tchrs Coll.
Fink, Manfred, jt. auth. see Bonham, Russell A.
Fink, Max. Convulsive Therapy: Theory & Practice. LC 77-74618. 1979. text ed. 26.00 (ISBN 0-89004-221-7). Raven.
Fink, Paul. Moral Philosophy: An Introduction. 2nd ed. 1977. pap. text ed. 14.95x (ISBN 0-8221-0207-2). Dickenson.
Fink, Reginald. Introducing the Alto Clef for Trombone. 1969. pap. 3.95 (ISBN 0-918194-04-0). Accura.
Fink, Reginald H. From Treble Clef to Bass Clef Baritone. 1972. pap. 3.95 (ISBN 0-918194-05-9). Accura.
--Introducing the Tenor Clef for Trombone. 1968. pap. 3.95 (ISBN 0-918194-03-2). Accura.
Fink, Robert R. & Ricci, Robert. The Language of Twentieth-Century Music. LC 74-13308. 1975. 12.95 (ISBN 0-02-870600-5). Schirmer Bks.
Finkbeiner, Daniel T., 2nd. Introduction to Matrices & Linear Transformations. 3rd ed. LC 78-18257. (Mathematical Sciences Ser.). (Illus.). 1978. text ed. 21.95x (ISBN 0-7167-0084-0). W H Freeman.
Finke, Hubert R. Understanding: How It Grows on You & How You Grow on It. 1977. 4.50 o.p. (ISBN 0-682-48914-X). Exposition.
Finkel, L. & Brown, J. Data Files in BASIC. (Wiley Self-Teaching Guides). 320p. 1981. write for info. (ISBN 0-471-08333-X). Wiley.
--Data Files in Basic. (Wiley Self Teaching Guide Ser.). 320p. 1981. write for info. (ISBN 0-471-08333-X). Wiley.
Finkel, Leroy & Brown, Jerald R. Data File Programming in Basic. (Self-Teaching Guide Ser.). 320p. 1981. pap. text ed. 9.95 (ISBN 0-471-08333-X). Wiley.
Finkel, Leslie G., jt. auth. see Finkel, Norma Y.
Finkel, Maurice. Fresh Hope in Cancer. 128p. 1981. pap. 6.95 (ISBN 0-914794-41-8). Wisdom Garden.
Finkel, Norma Y. & Finkel, Leslie G. Kaleidoscopic Designs & How to Create Them. 1980. pap. 2.00 (ISBN 0-486-23935-7). Dover.
Finkelhor, David. Sexually Victimized Children. LC 79-7104. 1981. pap. text ed. 7.95 (ISBN 0-02-910400-9). Free Pr.
Finkelstein, Bonnie B. Forster's Women: Eternal Differences. LC 74-18418. 192p. 1975. 12.50x (ISBN 0-231-03893-3). Columbia U Pr.
Finkelstein, J. J. The Ox That Gored. LC 80-65852. (Transactions Ser.: Vol. 71, Pt. 1). 1981. 12.00 (ISBN 0-87169-711-4). Am Philos.
Finkelstein, Robert J. Thermodynamics & Statistical Physics: A Short Introduction. LC 78-94103. (Illus.). 1970. text ed. 26.95x (ISBN 0-7167-0325-4). W H Freeman.
Finkelstein, Sidney. Jazz: A People's Music. LC 74-23386. (Roots of Jazz Ser). ix, 278p. 1975. Repr. of 1948 ed. lib. bdg. 22.50 (ISBN 0-306-70659-8). Da Capo.
Finkle, Bernard J. & Runeckles, Victor C., eds. Phenolic Compounds & Metabolic Regulation. LC 66-29065. 157p. 1967. 19.50 (ISBN 0-306-50023-X, Plenum Pr). Plenum Pub.
Finkle, J. L. & Gable, R. W. Political Development & Social Change. 2nd ed. LC 72-149769. 1971. pap. 16.50 o.p. (ISBN 0-471-25891-1). Wiley.
Finkle, Robert B. & Jones, William S. Assessing Corporate Talent: A Key to Managerial Manpower Planning. LC 71-120702. 1970. 23.95 (ISBN 0-471-25896-2, Pub. by Wiley-Interscience). Wiley.
Finkler, Earl, et al. Urban Nongrowth: City Planning for People. LC 75-23962. (Special Studies). 220p. 1976. text ed. 23.95 (ISBN 0-275-02230-7). Praeger.
Finland, M., jt. ed. see Sabath, L. D.
Finland, Maxwell. Drugs Useful Vs Infectious Diseases. LC 74-21394. (Principles & Techniques of Human Research & Therapeutics Ser: Vol. 7). (Illus.). 132p. 1975. 13.50 (ISBN 0-87993-051-9). Futura Pub.
Finlason, W. F. Commentaries Upon Martial Law, with Special Reference to Its Regulation & Restraint: With an Introduction, Containing Comments Upon the Charge of the Lord Chief Justice in the Jamaica Case. 287p. 1980. Repr. of 1867 ed. lib. bdg. 28.50x (ISBN 0-8377-0536-3). Rothman.
Finlay, Iain & Sheppard, Trish. South America Overland. (Illus.). 1981. 19.95 (ISBN 0-207-14122-3, Pub. by Angus England). Hippocrene Bks.
Finlay, Ian. Priceless Heritage: The Future of Museums. 1977. 12.95 o.p. (ISBN 0-571-09107-5, Pub. by Faber & Faber). Merrimack Bk Serv.
Finlay, Ian F. Language Services in Industry. 120p. 1973. 12.50x o.p. (ISBN 0-8464-0546-6). Beekman Pubs.
Finlay, Ian H. Honey by the Water. 60p. (Orig.). 1972. pap. 3.00 o.p. (ISBN 0-87685-142-1). Black Sparrow.
--Poems to Hear & See. LC 71-133557. (Illus.). (gr. 5 up). 1971. 3.95 o.s.i. (ISBN 0-02-735210-2). Macmillan.
Finlay, Patrick, ed. Jane's Freight Containers 1976-77. 1977. 72.50 o.p. (ISBN 0-531-03904-8). Watts.
Finlay, Winifred. Danger at Black Dyke. LC 68-31174. (Illus.). (gr. 7-10). 1968. 9.95 (ISBN 0-87599-150-5). S G Phillips.
Finlayson, Ann. Greenhorn on the Frontier. LC 73-93587. (Illus.). 196p. (gr. 7-12). 1974. 5.95 o.p. (ISBN 0-7232-6104-0). Warne.
--Redcoat in Boston. LC 75-150364. (gr. 7-12). 1971. 5.95 o.p. (ISBN 0-7232-6089-3). Warne.
Finlayson, Brian, jt. auth. see Statham, Ian.
Finlayson, Bruce A. Nonlinear Analysis in Chemical Engineering. (M-H Chemical Engineering Ser.). (Illus.). 384p. 1980. text ed. 44.50 (ISBN 0-07-020915-4). McGraw.
Finlayson, Roderick. D'Arcy Cresswell. (World Authors Ser.: New Zealand: No. 205). lib. bdg. 10.95 (ISBN 0-8057-2248-3). Twayne.
Finletter, Eileen, tr. see Ciano, Edda M.
Finley, Claudette. The Dissector's Guide: A Detailed Investigation of Musculoskeletal Anatomy. (Illus.). 176p. 1975. vinyl cover 16.50 (ISBN 0-398-03084-7). C C Thomas.
Finley, Diane E. End of the Rainbow. 192p. (YA) 1975. 5.95 (ISBN 0-685-50845-5, Avalon). Bouregy.
Finley, George, ed. see Industrial Design Magazine.
Finley, Glenna. Affairs of Love. 1980. pap. 1.75 (ISBN 0-451-09409-3, E909, Sig). NAL.
--Love Lies North. Date not set. pap. 1.75 o.p. (ISBN 0-451-08740-2, E8740, Sig). NAL.
--Midnight Encounter. (Orig.). 1981. pap. 1.75 (ISBN 0-451-09680-0, E9680, Sig). NAL.
Finley, James. Your Future & You. (Illus.). 176p. (Orig.). (gr. 10-12). 1981. pap. 3.50 (ISBN 0-87793-223-9); tchrs. ed. 2.25 (ISBN 0-87793-224-7). Ave Maria.
Finley, K. T. Triazoles. (Chemistry of Heterocyclic Compounds, Series of Monographs: Vol. 39). 368p. 1980. write for info (ISBN 0-471-07827-1). Wiley.
Finley, Lewis M. The Complete Guide to Getting Yourself Out of Debt. LC 75-12716. 1975. 9.95 (ISBN 0-8119-0251-X). Fell.
Finley, Lorraine N. Forever in Eden. 1971. 5.00 o.p. (ISBN 0-685-02641-8). Golden Quill.

Finley, M. I. The Ancestral Constitution. 1971. text ed. 3.25x (ISBN 0-521-08352-4). Cambridge U Pr.
--The Ancient Economy. (Sather Classical Lectures: Vol. 43). 1973. 16.50x (ISBN 0-520-02436-2); pap. 3.95 (ISBN 0-520-02564-4). U of Cal Pr.
--Democracy: Ancient & Modern. 112p. 1973. 8.00 o.p. (ISBN 0-8135-0751-0). Rutgers U Pr.
Finley, M. I. & Pleket, H. W. The Olympic Games: The First Thousand Years. new ed. LC 75-44456. (Illus.). 168p. 1976. 14.95 o.p. (ISBN 0-670-52406-9). Viking Pr.
Finley, M. I., ed. The Legacy of Greece: A New Appraisal. (Illus.). 480p. 1981. 16.95 (ISBN 0-19-821915-6). Oxford U Pr.
--Studies in Roman Property. (Classical Studies). (Illus.). 192p. 1976. 15.95 (ISBN 0-521-21115-8). Cambridge U Pr.
Finley, Martha. Elsie Dinsmore. Lurie, Alison & Schiller, Justin G., eds. LC 75-32168. (Classics of Children's Literature Ser.: 1621-1932). PLB 38.00 (ISBN 0-8240-2281-5). Garland Pub.
Finley, Richard, jt. auth. see Skinner, Bob.
Finn, Chester E., Jr. Education & the Presidency. LC 75-32871. (Politics of Education Ser.). 1977. 18.95 (ISBN 0-669-00365-4). Lexington Bks.
--Scholars, Dollars, & Bureaucrats. LC 78-13363. (Studies in Higher Education Policy). 1978. 14.95 (ISBN 0-8157-2828-X); pap. 5.95 (ISBN 0-8157-2827-1). Brookings.
Finn, D., et al. Teaching Manual for Tutor Librarians. 1978. 10.50 (ISBN 0-85365-830-7, Pub. by Lib Assn England). Oryx Pr.
Finn, D. Chester E., jt. ed. see Breneman, David W.
Finn, Edward E. These Are My Rites: A Brief History of the Eastern Rites of Christianity. (Illus.). 1980. pap. 4.95 (ISBN 0-8146-1058-7). Liturgical Pr.
Finn, F. C. History of Chelsea. 10.00x (ISBN 0-392-07888-0, SpS). Soccer.
Finn, F. E. S., compiled by. Poets of Our Time: An Anthology. 160p. 1976. pap. 7.95 (ISBN 0-7195-3243-4). Transatlantic.
Finn, Fes, compiled by. Here and Human: An Anthology of Contemporary Verse. 1977. pap. 7.50 (ISBN 0-7195-3306-6). Transatlantic.
Finn, Reginald A. Domesday Studies: The Eastern Countries. LC 80-2231. (Illus.). 1981. Repr. of 1967 ed. 34.50 (ISBN 0-404-18759-5). AMS Pr.
--Domesday Studies: The Liber Exoniensis. LC 80-2239. 1981. Repr. of 1964 ed. 29.50 (ISBN 0-404-18760-9). AMS Pr.
Finn, Rex W. Domesday Book: A Guide. 109p. 1973. 12.50x (ISBN 0-87471-640-3). Rowman.
Finnegan, Edward G. Children's Bible Stories. LC 75-18758. (Treasure House Bks). (Illus.). (ps-12). 1978. 8.95 (ISBN 0-8326-1803-9, 3602); deluxe ed. 7.95 (ISBN 0-686-66397-7). Delair.
Finnegan, Edward G., ed. New Webster's Medical Dictionary: Vest Pocket Edition. 1980. pap. 1.95 (ISBN 0-8326-0048-2, 6453). Delair.
Finnegan, Edward G., ed. see Carter, Linda & Culinary Arts Institute Staff.
Finnegan, Edward G., ed. see Magida, Phylis & Staff of the Culinary Arts Institute.
Finnegan, Edward G., ed. see Phillips, Margot & Culinary Arts Institute Staff.
Finnegan, Edward G., ed. see Spitler, Sue & Culinary Arts Inst.
Finnegan, Edward G., ed. see Stover, Annette A. & Culinary Arts Institute Staff.
Finnegan, Frances. Poverty & Prostitution. LC 78-68123. (Illus.). 1979. 29.95 (ISBN 0-521-22447-0). Cambridge U Pr.
Finnegan, Marcus B. & Goldscheider, Robert. The Law & Business of Licensing, 4 vols. LC 75-22337. 1977. Set. looseleaf with 1979 suppl. 210.00 (ISBN 0-87632-136-8). Boardman.
Finnegan, Michael, ed. Theatre Directory: 1980-81. 50p. 1980. pap. 3.50x (ISBN 0-930452-13-5, Pub. by Theatre Comm). Pub Ctr Cult Res.
Finnegan, Michael, jt. ed. see Skal, David J.
Finnegan, Patrick & Matthews, Rose. The Ten Thousand-Point Television Trivia Test. 1979. 5.75 o.p. (ISBN 0-8062-1219-5). Carlton.
Finnegan, Richard B., et al. Law & Politics in the International System: Case Studies in Conflict Resolution. LC 79-66153. (Illus.). 1979. pap. text ed. 9.00 (ISBN 0-8191-0793-X). U Pr of Amer.
Finnegan, Ruth. Oral Poetry: Its Nature, Significance Social Context. LC 76-11077. (Illus.). 1977. 32.00 (ISBN 0-521-21316-9). Cambridge U Pr.
Finnegan, Ruth, ed. World Treasury of Oral Poetry. LC 77-88784. 576p. 1978. 15.00x (ISBN 0-253-36665-8). Ind U Pr.
Finnegan, Ruth H. Limba Stories & Story-Telling. LC 80-25904. (Oxford Library of African Literature). xii, 352p. 1981. Repr. of 1967 ed. lib. bdg. 28.75x (ISBN 0-313-22723-3, FILS). Greenwood.
Finnegan, T. A. Sligo: Sinbad's Yellow Shore. 1979. pap. text ed. 5.25x (ISBN 0-85105-332-7, Dolmen Pr). Humanities.
Finneran, Eugene. Security Supervision: A Handbook for Supervisors & Managers. 300p. 1981. text ed. 19.95 (ISBN 0-409-95025-4). Butterworths.
Finneran, Richard. The Olympian & the Leprachaun: W.B. Yeats & James Stephens. (New Yeats Papers Ser.: No. 16). (Illus.). 1978. pap. text ed. 9.25x (ISBN 0-85105-338-6, Dolmen Pr). Humanities.
Finneran, Richard J. The Prose Fiction of W. B. Yeats: The Search for Those Simple Forms. (New Yeats Papers Ser.: Vol. 4). 1973. pap. text ed. 3.75x (ISBN 0-85105-217-7, Dolmen Pr). Humanities.
Finneran, Richard J., et al, eds. Letters to W. B. Yeats, 2 vols. LC 77-5645. 1977. 50.00x set (ISBN 0-685-81542-0). Vol. 1 (ISBN 0-231-04424-0). Vol. 2 (ISBN 0-231-04425-9). Columbia U Pr.
Finnerty, W. Patrick, et al. Community Structure & Trade at Isthmus Cove: A Salvage Excavation on Catalina Island (Calif.) (Pacific Coast Archaeological Society Occasional Papers: No. 1). 81p. 1981. pap. 2.95. Acoma Bks.
Finneson, Bernard E. Low Back Pain. 2nd ed. (Illus.). 640p. 1981. text ed. 42.00 (ISBN 0-397-50493-4). Lippincott.
Finney & Jepson. It All Adds Up to Love. pap. 2.95 (ISBN 0-89728-040-7, 669881). Omega Pubns OR.
Finney, Ben R. Big-Men & Business: Entrepreneurship & Economic Growth in the New Guinea Highlands. LC 72-93151. (Illus.). 250p. 1973. 12.00x (ISBN 0-8248-0262-4, Eastwest Ctr). U Pr of Hawaii.
Finney, Charles. Reflections on Revival. LC 78-26527. 1979. pap. 3.95 (ISBN 0-87123-157-3, 210157). Bethany Fell.
Finney, Charles G. Finney on Revival. Shelhamer, E. E., ed. 128p. 1974. pap. 1.95 (ISBN 0-87123-151-4, 200151). Bethany Fell.
--Finney's Systematic Theology. LC 76-3500. Orig. Title: Finney's Lectures on Systematic Theology. 1976. pap. 5.95 (ISBN 0-87123-153-0, 210153). Bethany Fell.
--Heart of Truth: Finney's Outlines of Theology. LC 75-46128. Orig. Title: Skeletons of a Course of Theological Lectures. 1976. pap. 4.50 (ISBN 0-87123-226-X, 210226). Bethany Fell.
--Love Is Not a Special Way of Feeling. Orig. Title: Attributes of Love. 1963. pap. 1.95 (ISBN 0-87123-005-4, 200005). Bethany Fell.
--Principles of Prayer. Parkhurst, L. G., ed. 112p. (Orig.). 1980. pap. 2.95 (ISBN 0-87123-468-8, 210468). Bethany Fell.
Finney, D. J. An Introduction to Statistical Science in Agriculture. 4th ed. 1972. 27.95 (ISBN 0-470-25900-0). Halsted Pr.
--Probit Analysis. 3rd ed. LC 78-134618. (Illus.). 1971. 57.50 (ISBN 0-521-08041-X). Cambridge U Pr.
Finney, David. The Power Thyristor & Its Applications. (Illus.). 320p. 1980. 22.50 (ISBN 0-07-084533-6, P&RB). McGraw.
Finney, Edwin A. Better Concrete Pavement Serviceability. (Monograph: No. 7). 1973. 16.75 (ISBN 0-685-85140-0, M-7). ACI.
Finney, Essex E., Jr., ed. Handbook of Transportation & Marketing in Agriculture: Volume 1: Food Commodities. 317p. 1981. 59.95 (ISBN 0-8493-3851-4). CRC Pr.
Finney, Humphrey S. A Stud Farm Diary. 5.25 (ISBN 0-85131-194-6, Dist. by Sporting Book Center). J A Allen.
Finney, Jack. The Body Snatchers. (Science Fiction Ser.). (Illus.). 224p. 1976. Repr. of 1955 ed. lib. bdg. 12.50 (ISBN 0-8398-2332-0). Gregg.
Finney, Ross L. & Ostberg, Donald E. Elementary Differential Equations with Linear Algebra. 2nd ed. LC 75-12096. (Mathematics Ser.). 704p. 1976. text ed. 20.95 (ISBN 0-201-05515-5). A-W.
Finney, Ross L., jt. auth. see Thomas, George B., Jr.
Finnigan, John. Right People in the Right Jobs. 1973. 14.00x o.p. (ISBN 0-8464-0797-3). Beekman Pubs.
Finniston, H. M., ed. Structural Characteristics of Materials. (Illus.). 1971. 48.50x (ISBN 0-444-20045-2, Pub. by Applied Science). Burgess-Intl Ideas.
Finocchiaro, Mary. English As a Second Language from Theory to Practice. rev. ed. 230p. 1974. text ed. 4.95 (ISBN 0-88345-222-7). Regents Pub.
--Hablemos Espanol. 180p. (gr. 9 up). 1976. pap. text ed. 3.50 (ISBN 0-88345-261-8, 18425). Regents Pub.
--Learning to Use English, 2 Bks. (Illus.). (gr. 7 up). 1966. Bk. 1. pap. text ed. 3.95 (ISBN 0-88345-089-5, 17400); Bk. 2. pap. text ed. 3.95 (ISBN 0-88345-090-9, 17401); tchr's manual 4.25 (ISBN 0-88345-091-7, 17402). Regents Pub.
--Let's Talk. (gr. 9 up). 1970. pap. text ed. 3.50 (ISBN 0-88345-094-1, 17743). Regents Pub.
Finocchiaro, Mary & Lavanda, Violet. Growing in English Language Skills. 1977. pap. text ed. 4.75 (ISBN 0-685-79304-4); cassettes 25.00 (ISBN 0-88345-299-5); answer key 1.00 (ISBN 0-685-79305-2). Regents Pub.
Finocchiaro, Mary & Lavanda, Violet H. Selections for Developing English Language Skills. rev. ed. 230p. (gr. 6 up). 1973. pap. 4.75 (ISBN 0-88345-195-6, 18078); cassettes 25.00 (ISBN 0-685-38987-1); ans. key 1.00 (ISBN 0-686-66893-6). Regents Pub.
Finocchiaro, Mary & Sako, Sydney. Foreign Language Testing: A Practical Approach. 1981. pap. text ed. 9.95 (ISBN 0-88345-362-2). Regents Pub.
Finocchiaro, Maurice A. Galileo & the Art of Reasoning: Rhetorical Foundations of Logic & Scientific Method. (Philosophy of Science Studies: No. 61). 463p. 1980. lib. bdg. 42.00 (ISBN 90-277-1094-5, Pub. by D. Reidel); pap. 21.00 (ISBN 90-277-1095-3). Kluwer Boston.
Finsand, Mary J. Caring & Cooking for the Hyperactive Child. LC 80-54335. 192p. 1981. 12.95 (ISBN 0-8069-5560-0); lib. bdg. 11.69 (ISBN 0-8069-5561-9); pap. 6.95 (ISBN 0-8069-8980-7). Sterling.
Finsand, Mary Jane. Complete Diabetic Cookbook. LC 79-91382. (Illus.). 160p. 1980. 12.95 (ISBN 0-8069-5554-6); lib. bdg. 11.69 (ISBN 0-8069-5555-4); pap. 5.95 (ISBN 0-8069-8908-4). Sterling.
Finsterbusch, Gail W. Man & Earth: Their Changing Relationship. LC 76-26914. (Studies in Sociology). (gr. 12). 1976. pap. 3.50 (ISBN 0-672-61325-5). Bobbs.
Finsterbusch, Kurt. Understanding Social Impacts: Assessing the Effects of Public Projects. LC 80-17586. (Sage Library of Social Research: Vol. 110). (Illus.). 311p. 1980. 18.00 (ISBN 0-8039-1015-0); pap. 8.95 (ISBN 0-8039-1016-9). Sage.
Finsterbusch, Kurt & Motz, Annabelle B. Social Research for Policy Decisions. 208p. 1980. pap. text ed. 7.95x (ISBN 0-534-00780-5). Wadsworth Pub.
Fiore, jt. auth. see Streitmatter.
Fiore, Peter A. Milton & Augustine: Patterns of Augustinian Thought in Milton's Paradise Lost. LC 80-17854. 144p. 1981. 14.50x (ISBN 0-271-00269-7). Pa St U Pr.
Fiore, Vito, et al. Sixty-Eight Hundred Family Book. 1982. text ed. 14.95 (ISBN 0-8359-7005-1). Reston.
Fiorentino, Mary R. A Basis for Sensorimotor Development-Normal & Abnormal: The Influence of Primitive, Postural Reflexes on the Development & Distribution of Tone. (Illus.). 184p. 1981. text ed. 14.75 (ISBN 0-398-04179-2). C C Thomas.
--Normal & Abnormal Development: The Influence of Primitive Reflexes on Motor Development. (Illus.). 80p. 1980. 10.75 (ISBN 0-398-02278-X). C C Thomas.
--Reflex Testing Methods for Evaluating C. N. S. Development. 2nd ed. (American Lecture Orthopaedic Surgery). (Illus.). 72p. 1979. 11.75 (ISBN 0-398-02584-3). C C Thomas.
Fiorenza, Elizabeth S. Invitation to the Book of Revelation: A Commentary on the Apocalypse with Complete Text from the Jerusalem Bible. LC 79-6744. 224p. 1981. pap. 3.95 (ISBN 0-385-14800-3, Im). Doubleday.
Fiorenza, Francis S., tr. see Schleiermacher, Friedrich.
Fiorenza, Joseph, jt. auth. see Perry, Glenn.
Fiorina, Morris P. Retrospective Voting in American National Electiona. LC 80-24454. (Illus.). 288p. 1981. text ed. 35.00x (ISBN 0-300-02557-2); pap. 9.95 (ISBN 0-300-02703-6). Yale U Pr.
Fiorito, Len, jt. auth. see Marazzi, Rich.
Firbank, Ronald. Five Novels. Incl. Valmouth: Valmonth; Artifical Princess; Flower Beneath the Foot; Prancing Nigger; Cardinal Pirelli. 1981. pap. 7.95 (ISBN 0-8112-0799-4, NDP518). New Directions.
--Five Novels. Incl. Valmouth; Artificial Princess; Flower Beneath the Foot; Prancing Nigger; Cardinal Pirelli. LC 49-48966. 1969. 8.50 o.p. (ISBN 0-8112-0276-3). New Directions.
--Five Novels. 384p. 1981. pap. 7.95 (ISBN 0-8112-0799-4, NDP518). New Directions.
Fire, Casualty & Surety Bulletins Editors. Agent's & Buyer's Guide, Nineteen Seventy-Nine. 32nd ed. LC 77-92759. 1979. spiral bdg 9.50 o.p. (ISBN 0-87218-300-9). Natl Underwriter.
Fire Casualty &Surety Bulletins Editors. Non-Resident & Surplus Line Laws, Nineteen Seventy-Nine. 1979 rev. ed. pap. 4.00 o.p. (ISBN 0-87218-302-5). Natl Underwriter.
Firebaugh, Francille M., jt. auth. see Deacon, Ruth E.
Fireman, Bert M., jt. auth. see Pare, Madeline F.
Fireman, Bert M., ed. see Theobald, John & Theobald, Lillian.
Fireman, Judy, ed. The Cat Catalog. LC 76-25473. (Illus.). 1976. 12.50 (ISBN 0-911104-81-X); pap. 7.95 (ISBN 0-911104-82-8). Workman Pub.
Firestein, Gary S. & Harrell, Robert A. The Effective Scutboy. LC 80-25057. (Illus.). 96p. 1981. pap. text ed. 6.00 (ISBN 0-668-05159-0, 5159). Arco.
Firestine, Robert E., jt. auth. see Weinstein, Bernard L.
Firestone, Eve & Blackwell, Jim. Las Vegas Guide for New Arrivals: How to Survive in the Fun Capital of the World. (Illus.). 64p. (Orig.). 1980. pap. 2.95 (ISBN 0-89650-790-4). Gamblers.
Firestone, Linda & Morse, Whit. Florida's Enchanting Islands: Sanibel & Captiva. 3rd ed. LC 80-67778. (Illus., Orig.). 1980. pap. 4.95 (ISBN 0-917374-08-8). Good Life VA.
Firestone, Robert & Catlett, Joyce. The Truth. 320p. 1981. 12.95 (ISBN 0-02-538380-9). Macmillan.
Firestone, Ross, ed. The Big Radio Comedy Program. 1978. 14.95 o.p. (ISBN 0-8092-7909-6); pap. 8.95 o.p. (ISBN 0-8092-7908-8). Contemp Bks.
Firestone, William A. Great Expectations for Small Schools: The Limitations of Federal Programs. 215p. 1980. 23.95 (ISBN 0-03-057397-1). Praeger.
--Great Expectations for Small Schools: The Perils of Federal Programs. (Praeger Special Studies). 215p. 1980. 20.95 o.p. (ISBN 0-686-63287-7). Praeger.
Firkens, Peter, ed. A History of Commerce & Industry in Western Australia. 223p. 1980. 17.95x (ISBN 0-85564-150-9, Pub. by U of West Australia Pr Australia). Intl Schol Bk Serv.
Firkins, Oscar W. Ralph Waldo Emerson. LC 80-2532. 1981. Repr. of 1915 ed. 44.50 (ISBN 0-404-19258-0). AMS Pr.
--Two Passengers for Chelsea & Other Plays. LC 77-94340. (One-Act Plays in Reprint Ser.). 1978. Repr. of 1928 ed. 23.75x (ISBN 0-8486-2038-0). Core Collection.
Firmage, George J., jt. ed. see Cummings, E. E.
Firmage, Robert, tr. see Rilke, Rainer M.
Firmin, jt. auth. see Postgate.
Firmin, Peter. Basil Brush Goes Flying. 1977. 4.95 (ISBN 0-13-066639-4). P-H.
Firsoff, V. Axel. At the Crossroads of Knowledge. 146p. 8.95 (ISBN 0-86025-812-2). Ross-Erikson.
First All-European Conference for Directors of National Research Institutions in Education, Hamburg 26-29 April 1976. Educational Research in Europe: Proceedings. Carelli, M. Dino & Sachsenmeier, Peter, eds. 142p. 1977. pap. text ed. 19.50 (ISBN 90-265-0250-8, Pub. by Swets Pub Serv Holland). Swets North Am.
First Conference of the European Society for Comparative Physiology & Biochemistry, 27-31 August, 1979, Liege, Belgium. Animals & Environment Fitness; Physiological & Biochemical Aspects of Adaptations & Ecology: Proceedings, Vol. 1. Gilles, R., ed. (Illus.). 638p. 1980. 105.00 (ISBN 0-686-63496-9). Pergamon.
First Conference, 1961 see Conferences on Brain & Behavior, los Angeles.
First European Conference on Mixing & Centrifugal Separation. Proceedings. 1975. text ed. 56.00 (ISBN 0-900983-39-6, Dist. by Air Science Co.). BHRA Fluid.
First Fluid Power Symposium. Proceedings. 1969. text ed. 29.00 (ISBN 0-900983-03-5, Dist. by Air Science Co.). BHRA Fluid.
First International Conference on Drag Reduction. Proceedings. 1974. text ed. 52.00 (ISBN 0-900983-40-X, Dist. by Air Science Co.). BHRA Fluid.
First International Conference on Pressure Surges. Proceedings. 1973. text ed. 52.00 (ISBN 0-900983-25-6, Dist. by Air Science Co.). BHRA Fluid.
First International Symposium on Dredging Technology. Proceedings. 1976. text ed. 65.00 (ISBN 0-900983-47-7, Dist. by Air Science Co.). BHRA Fluid.
First International Symposium on the Aerodynamics & Ventilation of Vehicle Tunnels. Proceedings. 1973. text ed. 52.00 (ISBN 0-900983-28-0, Dist. by Air Science Co.). BHRA Fluid.
First International Symposium on Wave & Tidal Energy. Proceedings, 2 vols. Stephens, H. S., ed. (Illus.). 1979. Set. pap. 78.00 (ISBN 0-906085-00-4, Dist. by Air Science Co.). BHRA Fluid.
First International Working Conference on Violence & Non-Violent Action in Industrialized Societies, Brussels, March 13-15th, 1974, Part II & Galtung, J. A Structural Theory of Revolutions: Proceedings, Vol. 5. (Publications of the Polemological Centre of the Free University of Brussels). 78p. 1974. pap. text ed. 9.95 (ISBN 90-237-6252-5, Pub. by Swets Pub Serv Holland). Swets North Am.

First, Julia. Flat on My Face. (gr. 4-6). 1975. pap. 1.25 (ISBN 0-380-00204-3, 52324, Camelot). Avon.
--Look Who's Beautiful. (gr. 5 up). 1980. PLB 7.90 (ISBN 0-531-04109-3, B21). Watts.
--Move Over, Beethoven. (gr. 5 up). 1978. PLB 7.90 s&l (ISBN 0-531-01472-X). Watts.
First, Ruth. Libya: The Elusive Revolution. LC 75-9944. 294p. 1975. text ed. 23.50x (ISBN 0-8419-0211-9, Africana). Holmes & Meier.
First World Filtration Congress, May 14-17, 1974. Papers Presented at the First World Filtration Congress, Paris. 1974. 45.95 (ISBN 0-470-25965-5). Halsted Pr.
Firth, C. H., ed. see Clarke, William.
Firth, Charles. Sir Walter Raleigh's History of the World. 49p. 1980. Repr. write for info. (ISBN 0-8492-4707-1). R West.
Firth, Charles H. American Garland, Being a Collection of Ballads Relating to America, 1536-1759. LC 68-20123. 1969. Repr. of 1915 ed. 15.00 (ISBN 0-8103-3411-9). Gale.
Firth, D. C. Elementary Chemical Thermodynamics. 1969. pap. 4.50x o.p. (ISBN 0-19-914001-4). Oxford U Pr.
Firth, Katherine R. The Apocalyptic Tradition in Reformation Britain 1530-1645. (Historical Monographs). (Illus.). 1979. 37.50x (ISBN 0-19-821868-0). Oxford U Pr.
Firth, Michael A. Investment Analysis: The Techniques of Appraising the British Stock Market. 1975. 23.65 (ISBN 0-06-318028-6, IntlDept). Har-Row.
Firth, Raymond. Essays on Social Organization & Values. (Social Anthropology Monographs: No. 28). 1969. pap. text ed. 9.50x (ISBN 0-485-19628-X, Athlone Pr). Humanities.
--Human Types. (Illus.). pap. 1.25 o.p. (ISBN 0-451-61121-7, MY1121, Ment). NAL.
--Rank & Religion in Tikopia. 1970. text ed. 35.00x (ISBN 0-04-200018-1). Allen Unwin.
--Work of the Gods in Tikopia, 2 vols. in 1. 2nd ed. (Monographs on Social Anthropology 1 & 2). 1967. text ed. 25.00x (ISBN 0-485-19501-1, Athlone Pr). Humanities.
Firth, Raymond, ed. Man & Culture: An Evaluation of the Work of Bronislaw Malinouski. 292p. 1980. 27.50x (ISBN 0-7100-1376-0, Pub. by Routledge England). Humanities.
--Man & Culture: An Evaluation of the Work of Bronislaw Malinowski. 1957. pap. 20.00 o.p. (ISBN 0-7100-6892-1). Routledge & Kegan.
Firth, Raymond W. Elements of Social Organization. 3rd ed. LC 80-24763. (Josiah Mason Lectures Ser., 1947). (Illus.). xi, 260p. 1981. Repr. of 1961 ed. lib. bdg. 28.50x (ISBN 0-313-22745-4, FIES). Greenwood.
Firth, Robert H. A Matter of Time. rev. ed. LC 80-68365. 143p. 1981. pap. write for info. (ISBN 0-9605060-0-4). Firth.
Firth, Rosemary. Housekeeping Among Malay Peasants. 2nd ed. (Monographs on Social Anthropology: No. 7). 1966. text ed. 18.75x (ISBN 0-485-19507-0, Athlone Pr). Humanities.
Fisch, Harold. S. Y. Agnon. LC 74-76126. (Modern Literature Ser.). 124p. 1975. 10.95 (ISBN 0-8044-2197-8). Ungar.
Fisch, Max H., ed. Classic American Philosophers. (Orig.). 1966. pap. text ed. 13.95 (ISBN 0-13-135186-9). P-H.
Fischbach, David P. & Fogdall, Richard P. Coagulation: The Essentials. (Illus.). 200p. 1981. write for info. softcover (ISBN 0-683-03312-3). Williams & Wilkins.
Fischel, Walter J. Ibn Khaldun in Egypt: His Public Functions & His Historical Research, (1382-1406); A Study in Islamic Historiography. 1967. 17.50x (ISBN 0-520-00414-0). U of Cal Pr.
Fischer. A Collection of International Concessions & Related Instruments, Vols. 9-10. 1980. 45.00 ea. Vol. 9 (ISBN 0-379-10084-3). Vol. 10 (ISBN 0-379-10085-1). Oceana.
Fischer, jt. auth. see Schimmel.
Fischer, Al, jt. auth. see Fischer, Mildred.
Fischer, Alan M., jt. auth. see Reyes-Guerra, David R.
Fischer, Alfred G. & Judson, Sheldon, eds. Petroleum & Global Tectonics. LC 72-9946. 280p. 1975. 30.00x (ISBN 0-691-08124-7); pap. 9.95 (ISBN 0-691-08128-X). Princeton U Pr.
Fischer, Bill, et al. Growers Weed Identification Handbook. (Illus.). 183p. 1978. 40.00x (ISBN 0-931876-43-5, 4030). Ag Sci Pubns.
Fischer, Carl. What About Me. (Dimensions of Personality Ser.). (gr. 3). 2.65x (ISBN 0-8278-0124-6); tchr's ed. 5.95x (ISBN 0-8278-0106-8); group activity sheets 5.95x (ISBN 0-8278-0195-5, 01955). Pflaum-Standard.
Fischer, Charlotte F. The Hartree-Fock Method for Atoms: A Numerical Approach. LC 76-50115. 1977. 35.00 (ISBN 0-471-25990-X, Pub. by Wiley-Interscience). Wiley.
Fischer, Claude S., et al. Human Aggression & Conflict: Interdisciplinary Perspectives. (Illus.). 352p. 1975. pap. 11.95 ref. ed. (ISBN 0-13-444620-8). P-H.
--Networks & Places: Social Relations in the Urban Setting. LC 76-55101. (Illus.). 1977. 19.95 (ISBN 0-02-910240-5). Free Pr.
Fischer, Cree J. Piano Tuning: A Simple & Accurate Method for Amateurs. 7.25 (ISBN 0-8446-5477-9). Peter Smith.
Fischer, David. Historian's Fallacies. LC 69-15583. 1970. 10.00 o.s.i. (ISBN 0-06-050041-7, HarpT). Har-Row.
Fischer, David H. Growing Old in America: The Bland-Lee Lectures Delivered at Clark University, Expanded Edition. 1978. pap. 4.95 (ISBN 0-19-502366-8, GB532, GB). Oxford U Pr.
Fischer, E. & Shah, H. Rural-Craftsmen & Their Work. 20.00 (ISBN 0-88253-403-3). Ind-US Inc.
Fischer, Eberhard, jt. auth. see Brinker, Helmut.
Fischer, Edward. Light in the Far East: Archbishop Harold Henry's Forty-Two Years in Korea. 1976. 8.95 (ISBN 0-8164-0307-4). Crossroad NY.
--Mindanao Mission: Archbishop Patrick Cronin's Forty Years in the Phillipines. 1979. 8.95 (ISBN 0-8164-0412-7). Crossroad NY.
--Mission in Burma: The Columban Fathers' Forty-Three Years in Kachin Country. 192p. 1980. 9.95 (ISBN 0-8164-0464-X). Crossroad NY.
Fischer, Ernst. Art Against Ideology. LC 70-77506. Orig. Title: Kunst und Koexistence. (Ger). 1969. 6.95 o.s.i. (ISBN 0-8076-0510-7). Braziller.
Fischer, Frank. Politics, Values, & Public Policy. (Westview Special Study Ser.). 275p. 1980. lib. bdg. 23.50x (ISBN 0-89158-799-3). Westview.
Fischer, Frederic E. Fundamental Statistical Concepts. LC 72-3309. 1973. text ed. 18.50 scp (ISBN 0-06-382662-3, HarpC). Har-Row.
Fischer, George, ed. Revival of American Socialism: Selected Papers of the Socialist Scholars Conference. 1971. 17.95 (ISBN 0-19-501412-X). Oxford U Pr.
Fischer, Georges. The Non-Proliferation of Nuclear Weapons. Willey, David, tr. LC 72-189811. 270p. 1971. text ed. 21.50x (ISBN 0-8290-0190-5). Irvington.
Fischer, Georges, jt. ed. see Morris-Jones, W. H.
Fischer, Gerald C., jt. auth. see Hoffman, Margaret A.
Fischer, H. & Hellwege, K. H., eds. Magnetic Properties of Free Radicals: Organic Cation Radicals & Polyradicals. (Landolt-Bernstein Ser. Group II: Vol. 9, Pt. 2). 380p. 1980. 270.30 (ISBN 0-387-09666-3). Springer-Verlag.
Fischer, Hans C. & Kock, Eric. Ludwig Van Beethoven. LC 78-145443. (Illus.). 1971. 12.50 o.p. (ISBN 0-312-50015-7, L77200). St Martin.
Fischer, Helmut, tr. see Mehnert, Klaus.
Fischer, Helmut, tr. see Meinecke, Friedrich.
Fischer, Helmut A. & Werner, Gottfried. Autoradiography. Ashworth, M. R., tr. from Ger. LC 70-164842. (Working Methods in Modern Science Ser). 1971. 39.50x (ISBN 3-1100-3523-5). De Gruyter.
Fischer, I., jt. auth. see Roberts, S.
Fischer, Joel & Gochros, Harvey L. Planned Behavior Change: Behavior Modification in Social Work. LC 74-34554. (Illus.). 1979. pap. text ed. 9.95 (ISBN 0-02-910230-8). Free Pr.
Fischer, Joel, jt. auth. see Gochros, Harvey L.
Fischer, Joel, ed. Interpersonal Helping: Emerging Approaches for Social Work Practice. (Illus.). 704p. 1973. pap. 13.75 (ISBN 0-398-02565-7). C C Thomas.
Fischer, John, jt. ed. see Greenspan, Kalman.
Fischer, Kuno. A Commentary on Kant's Critick of Pure Reason. Beck, Lewis W., ed. LC 75-32039. (The Philosophy of Immanuel Kant Ser.: Vol. 3). 1977. Repr. of 1866 ed. lib. bdg. 26.00 (ISBN 0-8240-2327-7). Garland Pub.
Fischer, Louis. Life of Mahatma Gandhi. 1962. pap. 1.95 o.s.i. (ISBN 0-02-002830-X, Collier). Macmillan.
Fischer, Louis, jt. auth. see Schimmel, David.
Fischer, Mildred. London Theatre Today: A Guide for Travelers. (Illus.). 144p. (Orig.). 1981. pap. 4.50 (ISBN 0-914846-09-4). Golden West Pub.
Fischer, Mildred & Fischer, Al. Chili-Lovers' Cook Book. 1978. pap. 3.00 plastic (ISBN 0-914846-06-X). Golden West Pub.
Fischer, Pauline & Lasker, Anabel. Bargello Magic: How to Design Your Own. LC 79-182757. 1972. 12.95 o.p. (ISBN 0-03-088259-1). HR&W.
Fischer, Pauline & Smith, Mary L. Egyptian Designs in Modern Stitchery. LC 78-11162. (Illus.). 1979. 14.95 o.p. (ISBN 0-87690-316-2). Dutton.
Fischer, Pieter. Music in Paintings of the Low Countries in the 16th & 17th Centuries. 112p. pap. text ed. 15.50 (ISBN 90-265-0185-4, Pub. by Swets Pub Serv Holland). Swets North Am.
Fischer, Raymond L., et al. Speaking to Communicate: An Introduction to Speech. 1972. pap. text ed. 7.95x (ISBN 0-8221-0076-2). Dickenson.
Fischer, Robert. Hot Dog! LC 80-201. (Illus.). 64p. (gr. 3-6). 1980. PLB 6.97g (ISBN 0-671-33045-4). Messner.
--Trick Photography: Crazy Things You Can Do with Cameras. (Illus.). 160p. (gr. 8 up). 1980. 8.95 (ISBN 0-87131-335-9); pap. 4.95 (ISBN 0-87131-335-9). M Evans.
Fischer, Robert H. & Lehmann, Helmut T., eds. Luther's Works, Vol. 37: Word & Sacrament III. LC 55-9893. 1961. 12.95x (ISBN 0-8006-0337-0, 1-337). Fortress.
Fischer, Robert H., tr. see Luther, Martin.
Fischer, Rudolph, tr. see Hajdu, Tibor.
Fischer, Sally. The Tale of the Shining Princess. Keene, Donald, tr. LC 80-1943. (Illus.). 72p. 1981. 10.95 (ISBN 0-670-63971-0). Viking Pr.
Fischer, Stanley, jt. auth. see Dornbusch, Rudiger.
Fischer, Susan K., jt. auth. see Siegel, Carole.
Fischer, Vardis. Mountain Man. 1980. pap. write for info. PB.
Fischer-Galati, Stephen, jt. auth. see Djordjevic, Dmitrije.
Fischer-Galati, Stephen, ed. Eastern Europe in the Nineteen Eighties. 384p. (Orig.). 1981. lib. bdg. 25.00x (ISBN 0-89158-198-7); pap. 11.50x (ISBN 0-686-69586-0). Westview.
Fischer-Galati, Stephen, ed. see Enyedi, Gyorgy.
Fischer-Jorgensen, ed. International Congress of Phonetic Sciences, 9th Special Lectures. Copenhagen, August 1979. (Journal: Phonetica Ser.: Vol. 37, No 1-2). (Illus.). 108p. 1980. pap. 19.75 (ISBN 3-8055-1414-X). S Karger.
Fischer-Jorgensen, ed. see International Congress of Phonetic Sciences, 9th, Copenhagen, 1979.
Fischer-Munstermann, Uta. Jazz Dance & Jazz Gymnastics. Williamson, Liz, ed. LC 78-57794. (Illus.). 1978. 12.95 (ISBN 0-8069-4618-0); lib. bdg. 11.69 (ISBN 0-8069-4619-9); pap. 6.95 (ISBN 0-8069-4620-2). Sterling.
Fischer-Williams, M., ed. see Werner, Percy.
Fischler. Uptown & Downtown. pap. 6.50 (ISBN 0-8015-8196-6, Hawthorn). Dutton.
Fischler, Shirley, jt. auth. see Fischler, Stan.
Fischler, Stan. Garry Unger & the Battling Blues. LC 76-49993. 1977. 7.95 (ISBN 0-396-07388-3). Dodd.
--Heroes of Pro Hockey. (Pro Hockey Library: No. 2). (Illus.). (gr. 5-9). 1971. PLB 3.69 (ISBN 0-394-92146-1, BYR). Random.
--Hockey's Great Rivalries. LC 74-4930. (Pro Hockey Library). (Illus.). 160p. (gr. 5 up). 1974. PLB 3.69 (ISBN 0-394-92830-X, BYR). Random.
--Kings of the Rink. LC 78-7727. (Illus.). (gr. 5 up). 1978. 6.50 (ISBN 0-396-07609-2). Dodd.
--Those Were the Days. LC 75-28233. (Illus.). 1976. 12.50 (ISBN 0-396-07015-9). Dodd.
Fischler, Stan & Fischler, Shirley. The Best, Worst & Most Unusual in Sports. LC 77-4099. (Illus.). 1977. 10.95 (ISBN 0-690-01457-0, TYC-T). T Y Crowell.
--The Best, Worst, & Most Unusual in Sports. 1979. pap. 2.25 (ISBN 0-449-23816-4, Crest). Fawcett.
Fischler, Stan & Friedman, Richard. Getting into Pro Soccer. (Getting into the Pros Ser.). (Illus.). (gr. 6 up). 1979. PLB 6.45 s&l (ISBN 0-531-02280-3). Watts.
Fischler, Stan, jt. auth. see Mazer, Bill.
Fischler, Stan, jt. auth. see Park, Brad.
Fischman, Burton L. Business Report Writing. college ed. LC 75-20317. 200p. (Orig.). 1975. pap. text ed. 10.15 (ISBN 0-913310-40-9). Par Inc.
--Developing Leadership. new ed. LC 76-25925. (Illus.). 1976. pap. text ed. 7.90 o.p. (ISBN 0-913310-43-3). Par Inc.
Fischman, Joyce. Holiday Work & Play. 1961. pap. 2.00 o.p. (ISBN 0-685-02011-8, 101960). UAHC.
--Let's Learn About Jewish Symbols. LC 68-9347. (Illus.). (ps-k). 1969. pap. text ed. 3.50 (ISBN 0-8074-0144-7, 101035); tchrs'. guide o.p. 3.00. UAHC.
Fischman, Leonard L. World Mineral Trends & U. S. Supply Problems. LC 80-8025. (Resources for the Future, Inc. Research Paper R-20). (Illus.). 576p. (Orig.). 1981. pap. text ed. 15.00x (ISBN 0-8018-2491-5). Johns Hopkins.
Fischman, Sheila, tr. see Carrier, Roch.
Fischman, Sheila, tr. see Poulin, Jacques.
Fischman, Sheila, tr. see Tardivel, Jules-Paul.
Fischman, Walter I., jt. auth. see Warren, Frank Z.
Fiscus, Edward D., jt. auth. see Mandell, Colleen J.
Fiser, Robert H., Jr., ed. see Nat'l Foundation-March of Dimes Symposium, April, 1976, New York City.
Fiser, Webb S. Mastery of the Metropolis. LC 80-23244. x, 168p. 1981. Repr. of 1962 ed. lib. bdg. 17.50x (ISBN 0-313-22732-2, FIMAM). Greenwood.
Fish. Dartmoor: A New Study. 1978. 25.00 (ISBN 0-7153-5041-2). David & Charles.
Fish, Byron, et al. Eskimo Boy Today. LC 79-174339. (Illus.). (gr. 7 up). 1971. 6.95 o.p. (ISBN 0-88240-005-3). Alaska Northwest.
Fish, Carl R see Johnson, Allen & Nevins, Allan.
Fish, Chet, ed. McKay's Big Book of Magic. (gr. 4-12). Date not set. cancelled (ISBN 0-679-20542-X). McKay.
--McKay's Big Book of Police Work. (gr. 4 up). Date not set. cancelled (ISBN 0-679-20537-3). McKay.
--McKay's Big Book of Space Travel. (gr. 4 up). Date not set. cancelled (ISBN 0-679-20541-1). McKay.
Fish, Hamilton. F D R: The Other Side of the Coin. 255p. 1976. pap. 8.00 (ISBN 0-911038-64-7, Inst Hist Rev). Noontide.
Fish, Harriet U. Creative Lace-Making with Thread & Yarn. LC 72-81039. (Little Craft Book Ser.). (Illus.). 50p. 1972. 5.95 (ISBN 0-8069-5216-4); lib. bdg. 6.69 (ISBN 0-8069-5217-2). Sterling.
--Whats Down That Road? (Illus.). 100p. (Orig.). 1979. pap. 6.95 (ISBN 0-918146-41-0). Peninsula WA.
Fish, Helen D. Boy's Book of Verse: An Anthology. rev. ed. (gr. 7-9). 1951. 8.95 o.p. (ISBN 0-397-30183-9). Lippincott.
Fish, Jefferson. Placebo Therapy: A Practical Guide to Social Influence in Psychotherapy. LC 73-9068. (Social & Behavioral Science Ser.). 176p. 1973. 13.95x o.p. (ISBN 0-87589-190-X). Jossey-Bass.
Fish, Margery. Cottage Garden Flowers. 1980. pap. 7.95 (ISBN 0-571-11462-8, Pub. by Faber& Faber). Merrimack Bk Serv.
--A Flower for Every Day. 208p. 1981. pap. 9.95 (ISBN 0-571-11738-4, Pub. by Faber & Faber). Merrimack Bk Serv.
--We Made a Garden. (Illus.). 120p. 1970. 10.50 (ISBN 0-7153-4876-0). David & Charles.
Fish, R. J. A Study Guide to the Master Plan of Evangelism. 64p. 1972. pap. 1.25 (ISBN 0-8007-0479-7). Revell.
Fish, Roy J. Every Member Evangelism for Today. rev. ed. LC 75-12289. 128p. 1976. pap. 4.95 (ISBN 0-06-061551-6, RD125, HarpR). Har-Row.
Fish, Sidney M. Reshith Binah: A Hebrew Primer. 1976. pap. 2.50x (ISBN 0-8197-0035-5). Bloch.
--Weekly Torah Reader: Book of Genesis. rev. ed. 1977. pap. 3.45x (ISBN 0-8197-0036-3). Bloch.
Fish, Stanley E. The Living Temple: George Herbert & Catechizing. LC 73-90664. (Quantum Bks.). 1978. 16.50x (ISBN 0-520-02657-8). U of Cal Pr.
Fishbach, Julius. The Children's Moment. (gr. 3-7). 1966. bds. 3.95 o.p. (ISBN 0-8170-0355-X). Judson.
Fishbein, Justin, jt. ed. see Fishbein, Morris.
Fishbein, Martin & Ajzen, Icek. Belief, Attitude, Intention, & Behavior: An Introduction to Theory & Research. 544p. 1975. 20.95 (ISBN 0-201-02089-0). A-W.
--Understanding Attitudes & Predicting Social Behavior. (Illus.). 1980. text ed. 14.95 (ISBN 0-13-936443-9); pap. text ed. 8.95 (ISBN 0-13-936435-8). P-H.
Fishbein, Morris. Medical Writing: The Technic & the Art. 4th ed. (Illus.). 216p. 1978. 13.75 (ISBN 0-398-02279-8). C C Thomas.
Fishbein, Morris & Fishbein, Justin, eds. Fishbein's Illustrated Medical & Health Encyclopedia: Family Health Guide Edition. LC 78-53643. 1978. 24.95 (ISBN 0-87475-250-7). Stuttman.
Fishbein, Morris, M.D. Modern Home Dictionary of Medical Words: With Descriptions, Uses & Standards of Commonly Used Tests. LC 74-18845. 240p. 1976. pap. 1.95 (ISBN 0-385-01105-9, Dolp). Doubleday.
Fishbein, William, ed. Sleep, Dreams & Memory: Advances in Sleep Research. LC 79-23861. (Illus.). 270p. 1981. text ed. 30.00 (ISBN 0-89335-054-0). Spectrum Pub.
Fishburn, Angela. Making Lampshades. LC 77-7729. (Illus.). 1977. pap. 5.95 (ISBN 0-8069-8494-5). Sterling.
Fishburn, Katherine. Richard Wright's Hero: The Faces of a Rebel-Victim. LC 76-51787. 1977. 11.00 (ISBN 0-8108-1013-1). Scarecrow.
Fishel, Andrew & Pottker, Janice. National Politics & Sex Discrimination in Education. LC 75-31291. (Politics of Education Ser.). 1977. 17.95 (ISBN 0-669-00336-0). Lexington Bks.
Fishel, B., tr. see Erwe, F.
Fisher. An Introduction to Epidemiology: A Programmed Text. (Illus.). 1975. pap. 15.50 o.p. (ISBN 0-8385-0091-9). ACC.
Fisher, A. S., jt. auth. see Russell, J. G. B.
Fisher, Aileen. Animal Disguises. (Nature Ser.). (gr. k-6). 1973. PLB 6.96 (ISBN 0-8372-0860-2); filmstrip & 7 records 18.00 (ISBN 0-8372-0205-1); filmstrip & cassette 18.00 (ISBN 0-8372-0871-8). Bowmar-Noble.
--Animal Houses. (Nature Ser.). (gr. k-6). 1973. PLB 6.96 (ISBN 0-8372-0859-9); filmstrip & record 18.00 (ISBN 0-8372-0204-3); filmstrip & cassette 18.00 (ISBN 0-685-27357-1). Bowmar-Noble.

--Animal Jackets. (Nature Ser.). (gr. k-6). 1973. PLB 6.96 (ISBN 0-8372-0861-0); filmstrip & record 18.00 (ISBN 0-685-27352-0); filmstrip & cassette 18.00 (ISBN 0-8372-0872-6). Bowmar-Noble.

--Anybody Home? LC 78-22508. (Illus.). 32p. (ps-2). 1980. 6.95 (ISBN 0-690-04054-7, TYC-J); PLB 6.89 (ISBN 0-690-04055-5). T Y Crowell.

--Cricket in a Thicket. (Illus.). (gr. k-3). 1963. reinforced bdg. 4.95 o.p. (ISBN 0-684-13456-X); pap. 0.95 o.p. (ISBN 0-684-12784-9, SBF15, ScribJ). Scribner.

--Easter. LC 67-23666. (Holiday Ser.). (Illus.). (gr. k-3). 1968. PLB 7.89 (ISBN 0-690-25236-6, TYC-J). T Y Crowell.

--Filling the Bill. (Nature Ser). (gr. k-6). 1973. PLB 6.96 (ISBN 0-8372-0864-5); filmstrip & record 18.00 (ISBN 0-8372-0209-4); cassette & filmstrip avail. (ISBN 0-8372-0875-0). Bowmar-Noble.

--Going Places. (Nature Ser). (gr. k-6). 1973. PLB 6.96 (ISBN 0-8372-0865-3); filmstrip & record 18.00 (ISBN 0-8372-0210-8); filmstrip & cassette 18.00 (ISBN 0-8372-0876-9). Bowmar-Noble.

--Holiday Programs for Boys & Girls. rev. ed. LC 52-11997. (gr. 2-7). 1980. 10.95 (ISBN 0-8238-0244-2). Plays.

--Holiday Programs for Boys & Girls. rev. ed. LC 52-11997. (gr. 2-7). 1980. 12.00 (ISBN 0-8238-0244-2). Plays.

--In One Door & Out the Other: A Book of Poems. LC 70-81949. (Illus.). (gr. 1-4). 1969. 7.89 o.p. (ISBN 0-690-43555-X, TYC-J). T Y Crowell.

--Like Nothing at All. LC 60-9159. (Illus.). (ps-3). 1979. PLB 8.79 (ISBN 0-690-49379-7, TYC-J). T Y Crowell.

--My Cat Has Eyes of Sapphire Blue. LC 72-13925. (Illus.). (ps-3). 1973. 8.95 (ISBN 0-690-56637-9, TYC-J); PLB 7.49 o.p. (ISBN 0-690-56638-7). T Y Crowell.

--My Mother & I. LC 67-10473. (Illus.). (ps-3). 1967. PLB 8.79 o.p. (ISBN 0-690-56976-9, TYC-J). T Y Crowell.

--Now That Days Are Colder. (Natue Ser). (gr. k-6). 1973. PLB 6.96 (ISBN 0-8372-0862-9); filmstrip & record 18.00 (ISBN 0-8372-0207-8); filmstrip & cassette 18.00 (ISBN 0-8372-0873-4). Bowmar-Noble.

--Once We Went on a Picnic. LC 75-9836. (Illus.). 32p. (gr. k-3). 1975. 8.95 (ISBN 0-690-00955-0, TYC-J); PLB 8.79 (ISBN 0-690-00956-9). T Y Crowell.

--Sleepy Heads. (Nature Ser). (gr. k-6). 1973. PLB 6.96 (ISBN 0-8372-0866-1); filmstrip & record 18.00 (ISBN 0-8372-0211-6); filmstrip & cassette 18.00 (ISBN 0-8372-0877-7). Bowmar-Noble.

--Tail Twisters. (Nature Ser). (gr. k-6). 1973. PLB 6.96 (ISBN 0-8372-0863-7); filmstrip & record 18.00 (ISBN 0-8372-0208-6); filmstrip & cassette 18.00 (ISBN 0-8372-0874-2). Bowmar-Noble.

--Ways of Animals, 10 bks. (Nature Ser). (ps-6). 1973. Set. 69.60 (ISBN 0-8372-0880-7); 252.24 set, tchrs. guide, 10 filmstrips, record ed. (ISBN 0-8372-0883-1, 883); 252.24 set, tchrs. guide, 10 filmstrips, cassette ed (ISBN 0-8372-2884-0); tchrs. guide by sue beauregard 3.00 (ISBN 0-8372-0869-6). Bowmar-Noble.

--The Ways of Plants. Incl. Plant Magic (ISBN 0-8372-2391-1); Mysteries in the Garden; Swords & Daggers (ISBN 0-8372-2393-8); And a Sunflower Grew (ISBN 0-8372-2394-6); Petals Yellow & Petals Red (ISBN 0-8372-2395-4); Now That Spring Is Here (ISBN 0-8372-2396-2); As the Leaves Fall Down (ISBN 0-8372-2397-0); Prize Performances (ISBN 0-8372-2398-9); A Tree with a Thousand Uses (ISBN 0-8372-2399-7); Seeds on the Go (ISBN 0-8372-2400-4). (Illus.). 1977. 6.96 ea.; tchr's. guide 3.00 (ISBN 0-685-80031-8); 10 bks., 10 filmstrips, tchr's guide record ed. 252.24 (ISBN 0-8372-3318-6); cassette ed. 252.24 (ISBN 0-8372-3317-8). Bowmar-Noble.

--We Went Looking. LC 68-13568. (Illus.). (gr. k-3). 1968. 7.95 o.p. (ISBN 0-690-87150-3, TYC-J). T Y Crowell.

--You Don't Look Like Your Mother Said the Robin to the Fawn. (Nature Ser). (gr. k-6). 1973. PLB 6.96 (ISBN 0-8372-0867-X); filmstrip & record 18.00 (ISBN 0-8372-0212-4); filmstrip & cassette 18.00 (ISBN 0-8372-0878-5). Bowmar-Noble.

Fisher, Aileen & Rabe, Olive. Human Rights Day. LC 65-25907. (Holiday Ser.). (Illus.). (gr. k-3). 1966. PLB 6.89 o.p. (ISBN 0-690-42349-7, TYC-J). T Y Crowell.

Fisher, Alden L. & Murray, George B., eds. Philosophy & Science As Modes of Knowing: Selected Essays. LC 69-18680. (Orig.). 1969. pap. text ed. 6.95 (ISBN 0-89197-340-0). Irvington.

Fisher, Allan G., tr. see Nachtigal, Gustav.

Fisher, Arthur. The Healthy Heart. Time-Life Bks. Eds., ed. (Library of Health). (Illus.). 176p. 1981. 11.95 (ISBN 0-8094-3750-3). Time-Life.

Fisher, B. Aubrey. Small Group Decision Making: Communication & the Group Process. (Illus.). 288p. 1974. text ed. 12.95 o.p. (ISBN 0-07-021090-X, C). McGraw.

Fisher, Barbara. Big Harold & Tiny Enid. (Illus.). 26p. (Orig.). (gr. 1-3). 1975. pap. 2.00 (ISBN 0-934830-01-0). Ten Penny.

--Dan. (Illus.). 20p. (Orig.). (gr. k-5). 1981. pap. 2.00 (ISBN 0-934830-19-3). Ten Penny.

--Joyce Cary: The Writer & His Theme. 1980. text ed. 25.50x (ISBN 0-391-01763-2). Humanities.

--Max St. Peter McBride & Theodora. (Illus.). 58p. (Orig.). (gr. k-3). 1981. pap. 2.00 (ISBN 0-934830-20-7). Ten Penny.

Fisher, Bill. How to Hotrod Volkswagen Engines. LC 72-28084. (Illus.). 1970. pap. 5.95 o.p. (ISBN 0-912656-03-4). H P Bks.

Fisher, Bill & Waar, Bob. How to Hotrod Small-Block Chevys. rev. ed. LC 73-173702. (Illus.). 192p. 1976. pap. 7.95 (ISBN 0-912656-06-9). H P Bks.

Fisher, Bill, jt. auth. see Urich, Mike.

Fisher, Bruce. Rebuilding: When Your Relationship Ends. LC 79-24440. 1981. pap. 5.95 (ISBN 0-915166-30-5). Impact Pubs Cal.

Fisher, Clay. The Crossing. 288p. (Orig.). 1980. pap. 1.75 (ISBN 0-553-14178-3). Bantam.

--Santa Fe Passage. 176p. 1981. pap. 1.95 (ISBN 0-553-14540-1). Bantam.

--War Bonnet. 1979. pap. 1.50 o.p. (ISBN 0-685-94372-0, 12978-3). Bantam.

Fisher, Clay C. Navarre: A Littel Town & Its People. 2nd ed. LC 74-27622. 1976. 8.00 o.p. (ISBN 0-686-14560-7). C C Fisher.

Fisher, D. A. & Burrow, G. N., eds. Perinatal Thyroid Physiology & Disease. LC 75-14333. 291p. 1975. 27.00 (ISBN 0-89004-044-3). Raven.

Fisher, D. J. The Anglo-Saxon Age. LC 74-159804. (A History of England Ser.). 350p. 1974. text ed. 22.00x (ISBN 0-582-48277-1); pap. text ed. 10.95x (ISBN 0-582-48084-1). Longman.

Fisher, Dalmar. Communication in Organizations. (Illus.). 480p. 1981. text ed. 16.95 (ISBN 0-8299-0374-7). West Pub.

Fisher, Danial, jt. auth. see Smith, Donald E.

Fisher, David E. The Ideas of Einstein. LC 80-10423. (Illus.). 64p. (gr. 3-5). 1980. 8.95 (ISBN 0-03-046516-8). HR&W.

Fisher, David L. Requiem for Heurtebise: Homage to Jean Cocteau. 1974. pap. 1.00 (ISBN 0-686-18853-5); signed ed. 2.00 (ISBN 0-686-18854-3). Man-Root.

Fisher, Dennis, jt. ed. see Nodine, Calvin F.

Fisher, Dennis F., et al, eds. Eye Movements: Cognition & Visual Perception. (Eye Movements Ser.). 368p. 1981. ref. 19.95 (ISBN 0-89859-084-1). L Erlbaum Assocs.

Fisher, Dexter. The Third Woman: Minority Woman Writers of the United States. LC 79-87863. 1979. pap. text ed. 9.95 (ISBN 0-395-27707-8). HM.

Fisher, Douglas. Monetary Policy. LC 75-20330. 91p. 1976. pap. text ed. 7.95x (ISBN 0-470-25996-5). Halsted Pr.

--Monetary Theory & the Demand for Money. LC 77-15504. 278p. 1980. pap. 19.95 (ISBN 0-470-27023-3, Pub. by Halsted Pr). Wiley.

--Money & Banking. (Irwin Ser. in Economics). 1971. text ed. 15.95x o.p. (ISBN 0-256-00152-9). Irwin.

--Money, Banking & Monetary Policy. 1980. 18.95x (ISBN 0-256-02365-4). Irwin.

Fisher, E. G. Extrusion of Plastics. 3rd ed. LC 75-4359. 1976. 28.95 (ISBN 0-470-15012-2). Halsted Pr.

Fisher, Ernest M., jt. auth. see Stokes, Charles J.

Fisher, Eugene & Jensen, C. William. PET & the IEEE 488 Bus (GPIB) 1980. pap. 15.99 (ISBN 0-931988-31-4). Osborne-McGraw.

Fisher, Eugene, jt. auth. see Jensen, C. W.

Fisher, F. E., jt. auth. see Faupel, J. H.

Fisher, Florence. The Search for Anna Fisher. 224p. 1981. pap. 2.50 (ISBN 0-449-23473-8, Crest). Fawcett.

Fisher, Franklin M. & Shell, Karl. The Economic Theory of Price Indices: Two Essays on the Effects of Taste, Quality & Technological Change. (Economic Theory & Mathematical Economics Ser). 1972. 15.00 (ISBN 0-12-257750-7). Acad Pr.

Fisher, Fred. Brokers Beware: Selling Real Estate Within the Law. 220p. 1981. text ed. 15.95 (ISBN 0-8359-0569-1). Reston.

Fisher, Gene. The Fear of Crime: In Public Housing. 1981. 8.50 (ISBN 0-8062-1573-9). Carlton.

Fisher, George H. Stud Poker Blue Book. (Gamblers Book Shelf). 1968. pap. 2.95 (ISBN 0-89650-508-1). Gamblers.

Fisher, Harold W., jt. auth. see Williams, Robley C.

Fisher, Hilda B. Improving Voice & Articulation. 2nd ed. 1975. text ed. 17.50 (ISBN 0-395-19232-3). HM.

Fisher, Humphrey J., tr. see Nachtigal, Gustav.

Fisher, Ida & Lane, Byron. The Widow's Guide to Life: How to Adjust-How to Grow. 224p. 1981. 13.95 (ISBN 0-13-959452-3, Spec); pap. 6.95 (ISBN 0-13-959445-0). P-H.

Fisher, Irving. The Effect of Diet on Endurance. 1918. 14.50x o.p. (ISBN 0-686-51377-0). Elliots Bks.

Fisher, J. R. Government & Society in Colonial Peru: The Intendant System 1784-1814. (Univ. of London Historical Studies: No. 29). 1970. text ed. 26.25x (ISBN 0-485-13129-3, Athlone Pr). Humanities.

Fisher, Jack & Gatland, Bruce. Electronics: From Theory into Practice, 2 vols. 2nd ed. 538p. 1975. Combined Ed. 34.00 (ISBN 0-08-019857-0); Vol. 1. pap. text ed. 15.50 (ISBN 0-08-019855-4); Vol. 2. pap. text ed. 15.50 (ISBN 0-08-019856-2). Pergamon.

Fisher, Jack C. Clinical Procedures: A Concise Guide for Students of Medicine. (Illus.). 1970. pap. 6.95 o.p. (ISBN 0-683-03239-9). Williams & Wilkins.

Fisher, Jack C. & Wachtel, Thomas. Clinical Procedures: A Concise Guide for Students of Medicine. 2nd ed. (Illus.). 251p. 1980. 13.50 (ISBN 0-683-03240-2). Williams & Wilkins.

Fisher, Jakob, tr. see Kawase, Kozyun.

Fisher, Jamer E., jt. auth. see Christensen, James E.

Fisher, James L. Application-Oriented Algebra: An Introduction to Discrete Mathematics. 1977. text ed. 21.50 scp (ISBN 0-7002-2504-8, HarpC). Har-Row.

Fisher, Jeffrey. The Fish Book: How to Buy, Clean, Catch, Cook & Preserve Them. (Illus.). 128p. 1981. 8.95 (ISBN 0-87523-196-9). Emerson.

Fisher, John. Body Magic. LC 78-6387. (Illus.). 158p. 1980. pap. 6.95 (ISBN 0-8128-6088-8). Stein & Day.

--How to Manage a Non-Profit Organization. 1978. 16.50 (ISBN 0-920432-00-X, Pub by Management & Fund Raising Ctr. Canada). Public Serv Materials.

--This Treatise Concernynge the Fruytfull Saynges of Davyd..Was Made & Compyled by..John Fyssher..Bysshop of Rochester. LC 79-84106. (English Experience Ser.: No. 925). 296p. 1979. Repr. of 1509 ed. lib. bdg. 28.00 (ISBN 90-221-0925-9). Walter J Johnson.

Fisher, John, ed. Perceiving Artworks. (Philosophical Monographs: 3rd Ser.). 1980. 17.50x (ISBN 0-87722-164-2). Temple U Pr.

Fisher, John, jt. ed. see Wiener, Philip P.

Fisher, John S. & Dolan, Robert, eds. Beach Processes & Coastal Hydrodynamics. (Benchmark Papers in Geology Ser.: Vol. 39). 1977. 37.50 (ISBN 0-12-786471-7). Acad Pr.

Fisher, Jon. Escape! Strange Places Where You Can Live Free: Antarctica, Blimps, Treehouses, Etc. 1979. pap. cancelled o.p. (ISBN 0-686-23958-X). Loompanics.

Fisher, K. D. & Nixon, A. U., eds. The Science of Life: Contributions of Biology to Human Welfare. LC 77-957. 358p. 1977. softcover 7.50 (ISBN 0-306-20025-2, Rosetta). Plenum Pub.

Fisher, Katherine & Kay, Elizabeth. Quilting in Squares. LC 77-16137. (Illus.). 1978. 14.95 (ISBN 0-684-15501-X, ScribT). Scribner.

Fisher, Lawrence. Industrial Marketing: An Analytical Approach to Planning & Execution. 2nd ed. 270p. 1976. text ed. 29.50x (ISBN 0-220-66292-4, Pub. by Busn Bks England). Renouf.

Fisher, Leonard E. Across the Sea from Galway. LC 75-9513. (Illus.). 112p. (gr. 3-7). 1975. 6.95g o.s.i. (ISBN 0-590-07345-1, Four Winds). Schol Bk Serv.

--Architects. LC 70-101748. (Colonial Americans Ser). (Illus.). (gr. 4-6). 1970. PLB 4.90 o.p. (ISBN 0-531-01041-4). Watts.

--The Art Experience: Oil Painting. LC 72-5406. (Illus.). 64p. 1973. PLB 6.90 (ISBN 0-531-02609-4). Watts.

--The Blacksmiths. LC 75-26684. (Colonial Americans Ser). (Illus.). 49p. (gr. 4-6). 1976. PLB 6.45 (ISBN 0-531-02901-8). Watts.

--Cabinetmakers. LC 66-10580. (Colonial Americans Ser). (Illus.). (gr. 4-6). 1966. PLB 4.90 o.p. (ISBN 0-531-01026-0). Watts.

--Doctors. LC 68-24610. (Colonial Americans Ser). (Illus.). (gr. 4-6). 1968. PLB 4.90 o.p. (ISBN 0-531-01027-9). Watts.

--Glassmakers. LC 64-16320. (Colonial Americans Ser). (Illus.). (gr. 4-6). 1964. PLB 4.90 o.p. (ISBN 0-531-01028-7). Watts.

--The Homemakers. LC 73-5692. (Colonial American Ser). (gr. 4-6). 1973. PLB 4.90 o.p. (ISBN 0-531-01047-3). Watts.

--The Newspapers. LC 80-8812. (A Nineteenth Century America Book). (Illus.). 64p. (gr. 5 up). 1981. PLB 7.95 (ISBN 0-8234-0387-4). Holiday.

--Papermakers. LC 65-13683. (Colonial Americans Ser). (Illus.). (gr. 4-6). 1965. PLB 4.90 o.p. (ISBN 0-531-01030-9). Watts.

--Peddlers. LC 68-10335. (Colonial Americans Ser). (Illus.). (gr. 4-6). 1968. PLB 4.90 o.p. (ISBN 0-531-01031-7). Watts.

--Potters. LC 69-14499. (Colonial Americans Ser). (Illus.). (gr. 4-6). 1969. PLB 4.90 o.p. (ISBN 0-531-01032-5). Watts.

--Printers. (Colonial Americans Ser). (Illus.). (gr. 4-6). 1965. PLB 6.45 (ISBN 0-531-01033-3). Watts.

--A Russian Farewell. LC 80-342. (Illus.). 144p. (gr. 5 up). 1980. 9.95 (ISBN 0-590-07525-X, Four Winds). Schol Bk Serv.

--Schoolmasters. LC 67-18896. (Colonial Americans Ser). (Illus.). (gr. 4-6). 1967. PLB 4.47 o.p. (ISBN 0-531-01034-1). Watts.

--Shipbuilders. LC 72-150733. (Colonial Americans Ser). (Illus.). (gr. 5 up). 1971. PLB 4.90 o.p. (ISBN 0-531-01043-0). Watts.

--Shoemakers. LC 67-10296. (Colonial Americans Ser). (Illus.). (gr. 4-6). 1967. PLB 5.90 o.p. (ISBN 0-531-01035-X). Watts.

--Silversmiths. LC 64-17792. (Colonial Americans Ser). (Illus.). (gr. 4-6). 1965. PLB 4.90 o.p. (ISBN 0-531-01036-8). Watts.

--Storm at the Jetty. (Illus.). 32p. (gr. k up). 1981. 9.95 (ISBN 0-670-67214-9). Viking Pr.

--Tanners. LC 66-10136. (Colonial Americans Ser). (Illus.). (gr. 4-6). 1966. PLB 4.90 o.p. (ISBN 0-531-01038-4). Watts.

--Weavers. LC 66-10581. (Colonial Americans Ser). (Illus.). (gr. 4-6). 1966. PLB 4.90 o.p. (ISBN 0-531-01037-6). Watts.

--Wigmakers. LC 65-21628. (Colonial Americans Ser). (Illus.). (gr. 4-6). 1965. PLB 4.90 o.p. (ISBN 0-531-01039-2). Watts.

Fisher, Leonard Everett. Leonard Everett Fisher's Liberty Book. LC 75-9672. 48p. (gr. 4 up). 1976. 5.95 o.p. (ISBN 0-385-04894-7). Doubleday.

Fisher, Lois I. Sarah Dunes, Weird Person. LC 80-2780. 176p. (gr. 5 up). 1981. PLB 7.95 (ISBN 0-396-07929-6). Dodd.

Fisher, Louis. President & Congress. LC 78-142362. 1972. 14.95 (ISBN 0-02-910320-7); pap. text ed. 4.95 (ISBN 0-02-910340-1). Free Pr.

Fisher, Lucretia. The Butterfly & the Stone. (Illus.). 48p. (Orig.). (ps up). 1981. pap. 2.95 (ISBN 0-916144-69-0). Stemmer Hse.

--Two Monsters. LC 76-21684. (Illus.). 48p. (ps up). 1976. pap. 2.95 (ISBN 0-916144-08-9). Stemmer Hse.

Fisher, Lynn & Fisher, Wesley. The Moscow Gourmet: A Guide to Eating Out in the Soviet Capital. 100p. 1974. pap. 3.95 o.p. (ISBN 0-88233-066-7). Ardis Pubs.

Fisher, M. F. Cooking of Provincial France. (Foods of the World Ser). (Illus.). (gr. 6 up). 1968. PLB 14.94 (ISBN 0-8094-0056-1, Pub. by Time-Life). Silver.

--Cooking of Provincial France. (Foods of the World Ser). (Illus.). 1968. 14.95 (ISBN 0-8094-0029-4). Time-Life.

Fisher, M. Roy. Titian's Assistants During the Later Years. LC 76-23618. (Outstanding Dissertations in the Fine Arts Ser.). 1977. lib. bdg. 56.00x (ISBN 0-8240-2689-6). Garland Pub.

Fisher, Margaret, jt. ed. see Withington, W. A.

Fisher, Margaret B., jt. auth. see Cooper, Russell M.

Fisher, Margaret E., jt. auth. see O'Brien, Edward L.

Fisher, Margery, ed. see Horne, Richard H.

Fisher, Marianne & Roper, Gayle. Time of Storm. LC 80-69310. 160p. 1981. pap. 5.95 (ISBN 0-915684-82-9). Christian Herald.

Fisher, Morris. Provinces & Provincial Capitals of the World. 1967. 10.00 (ISBN 0-8108-0121-3). Scarecrow.

Fisher, O. F. Collector's Guide to Model Aero Engines. (Illus.). 1977. 10.00x (ISBN 0-85242-492-2). Intl Pubns Serv.

Fisher, Ovie C. & Dykes, J. C. King Fisher: His Life & Times. (Western Frontier Library: No. 32). 1967. Repr. of 1966 ed. 4.95 o.p. (ISBN 0-8061-0711-1). U of Okla Pr.

Fisher, Patrick J. Basic Medical Terminology. LC 74-77820. (Allied Health Ser). 1975. pap. text ed. 12.20 (ISBN 0-672-61385-9); tchr's manual 5.00 (ISBN 0-672-61386-7); tape cassette 96.45 (ISBN 0-672-61387-5). Bobbs.

Fisher, Paul. Mont Cant Gold. LC 80-23851. 264p. (gr. 5-9). 1981. PLB 10.95 (ISBN 0-689-30808-6, Argo). Atheneum.

--The Princess & the Thorn. LC 80-12309. 256p. (gr. 4-8). 1980. 9.95 (ISBN 0-689-30776-4). Atheneum.

Fisher, Paul, jt. auth. see Berston, Hyman M.

Fisher, Peter, tr. see Davidson, Hilda.

Fisher, Peter, tr. see Davidson, Hilda E.

Fisher, Philip A. Conservative Investors Sleep Well. LC 74-20401. 188p. 1975. 10.00 o.s.i. (ISBN 0-06-011256-5, HarpT). Har-Row.

Fisher, R. K. Libraries of University Departments of Adult Education & Extra-Mural Studies. 1974. pap. 8.75x (ISBN 0-85365-377-1, Pub. by Lib Assn England). Oryx Pr.

Fisher, R. S., jt. auth. see Spitz, W. U.

Fisher, R. V. Pyrogenic Mineral Stability, Lower Member of the John Day Formation, Eastern Oregon. (U. C. Publ. in Geological Sciences: Vol. 75). 1968. pap. 6.00x (ISBN 0-520-09178-7). U of Cal Pr.

Fisher, Rhoda L., jt. auth. see Fisher, Seymour.

Fisher, Richard H., jt. auth. see Davis, William S.

Fisher, Richard V. & Rensberger, John M. Physical Stratigraphy of the John Day Formation, Central Oregon. (U. C. Publ. in Geological Sciences: Vol. 101). 1972. pap. 6.50x (ISBN 0-520-09460-3). U of Cal Pr.

Fisher, Rick, jt. auth. see Yanda, Bill.

Fisher, Robert, ed. Fodor's Australia, New Zealand & the South Pacific 1980. (Fodor Travel Guide Ser.). (Illus.). 1980. 13.95 o.p. (ISBN 0-679-00562-5); pap. 10.95 o.p. (ISBN 0-679-00563-3). McKay.

--Fodor's Austria 1980. (Fodor Travel Guide Ser.). (Illus.). 1980. 12.95 o.p. (ISBN 0-679-00500-5). McKay.

--Fodor's Canada 1980. (Fodor Travel Guides Ser.). (Illus.). 1977. 13.95 o.p. (ISBN 0-679-00501-3); pap. 10.95 o.p. (ISBN 0-679-00502-1). McKay.

--Fodor's Europe 1980. (Fodor Travel Guides Ser.). 1979. 13.95 o.p. (ISBN 0-679-00506-4); pap. 10.95 o.p. (ISBN 0-679-00507-2). McKay.

--Fodor's Germany 1980. (Fodor Travel Guide Ser.). 1980. 12.95 o.p. (ISBN 0-679-00508-0); pap. 9.95 o.p. (ISBN 0-679-00509-9). McKay.

--Fodor's Hawaii 1980. (Fodor Travel Guides Ser.). (Illus.). 1979. 12.95 o.p. (ISBN 0-679-00450-5); pap. 9.95 o.p. (ISBN 0-679-00469-6). McKay.

--Fodor's Ireland 1980. (Fodor Travel Guide Ser.). (Illus.). 1980. 12.95 o.p. (ISBN 0-679-00515-3); pap. 9.95 o.p. (ISBN 0-679-00516-1). McKay.

--Fodor's Mexico 1980. (Fodor Travel Guides Ser.). (Illus.). 1979. 13.95 o.p. (ISBN 0-679-00525-0); pap. 10.95 o.p. (ISBN 0-679-00526-9). McKay.

--Fodor's New England 1980. (Fodor Travel Guides Ser.). (Illus.). 1980. 10.95 o.p. (ISBN 0-679-00457-2); pap. 7.95 o.p. (ISBN 0-679-00458-0). McKay.

--Fodor's Scandinavia 1980. (Fodor Travel Guide Ser.). 1979. 13.95 o.p. (ISBN 0-679-00530-7); pap. 10.95 o.p. (ISBN 0-679-00531-5). McKay.

--Fodor's South America 1980. (Fodor Travel Guides Ser.). (Illus.). 1979. 13.95 o.p. (ISBN 0-679-00532-3); pap. 10.95 o.p. (ISBN 0-679-00533-1). McKay.

--Fodor's Southeast Asia 1980. (Fodor Travel Guide Ser.). (Illus.). 1979. 13.95 o.p. (ISBN 0-679-00534-X); pap. 10.95 o.p. (ISBN 0-679-00535-8). McKay.

--Fodor's Soviet Union 1980. (Fodor Travel Guide Ser.). (Illus.). 1979. 13.95 o.p. (ISBN 0-679-00536-6). McKay.

--Fodor's U. S. A. 1980. (Fodor Travel Guide Ser.). (Illus.). 1979. 14.95 o.p. (ISBN 0-679-00467-X); pap. 10.95 o.p. (ISBN 0-679-00468-8). McKay.

Fisher, Robert A. An Introduction to RPG: RPG II Programming. LC 74-9537. 393p. 1975. pap. 21.95 (ISBN 0-471-26001-0). Wiley.

Fisher, Robert C. & Ziebur, Allen D. Calculus & Analytic Geometry. 3rd ed. (Illus.). 784p. 1975. text ed. 25.95 (ISBN 0-13-112227-4). P-H.

Fisher, Roger. Improving Compliance with International Law. LC 80-14616. (Procedural Aspects of International Law Ser.: Vol. 14). 1981. 20.00x (ISBN 0-8139-0859-0). U Pr of Va.

Fisher, Russell S., jt. ed. see Spitz, Werner U.

Fisher, Seymour. Body Consciousness. LC 74-9264. 176p. 1974. Repr. 17.50x (ISBN 0-87668-181-X). Aronson.

--Body Consciousness: You Are What You Feel. 192p. 1973. 12.95 (ISBN 0-13-078527-X, Spec). P-H.

--Body Experience in Fantasy & Behavior. LC 71-111878. (Century Psychology Ser). 1970. 29.50x (ISBN 0-89197-046-0); pap. text ed. 10.95x (ISBN 0-89197-683-3). Irvington.

Fisher, Seymour & Fisher, Rhoda L. Pretend the World Is Funny & Forever: A Psychological Analysis of Comedians, Clowns, & Actors. LC 80-7777. 288p. 1981. profess. & reference 19.95 (ISBN 0-89859-073-6). L Erlbaum Assocs.

Fisher, Sidney G. Trial of the Constitution. LC 70-164511. (American Constitutional & Legal History Ser.). Repr. of 1864 ed. lib. bdg. 39.50 (ISBN 0-306-70281-9). Da Capo.

Fisher, Steve. Whatever Happened to...? The Great Pop & Rock Music Nostalgia Book. (Illus.). 192p. 1981. pap. 8.95 (ISBN 0-906071-40-2). Proteus Pub NY. Postponed.

Fisher, Sydney G. Men, Women & Manners in Colonial Times, 2 Vols. LC 70-95776. 1969. Repr. of 1897 ed. Set. 26.00 (ISBN 0-8103-3567-0). Gale.

Fisher, Terry. A Class Act. (Orig.). 1976. pap. 1.75 o.s.i. (ISBN 0-446-84242-7). Warner Bks.

Fisher, W. B. The Oil States. (Illus.). 72p. (gr. 9-12). 1980. 16.95 (ISBN 0-7134-2477-X, Pub. by Batsford England). David & Charles.

Fisher, W. L. Rock & Mineral Resources of East Texas. (Illus.). 439p. 1965. 5.00 (RI 54). Bur Econ Geology.

Fisher, W. L. & McGowen, J. H. Depostional Systems in the Wilcox Group of Texas & Their Relationship to Occurrence of Oil & Gas. 125p. 1967. Repr. 1.00 (GC 67-4). Bur Econ Geology.

Fisher, W. L. & Rodda, P. U. Lower Cretaceous Sands of Texas: Stratigraphy & Resources. (Illus.). 116p. 1967. 1.75 (RI 59). Bur Econ Geology.

Fisher, Wallace E. Because We Have Good News: A Layman's Guide for Person-to-Person Evangelism in Community. LC 73-12233. 128p. (Orig.). 1973. pap. 2.95 (ISBN 0-687-02532-X). Abingdon.

Fisher, Walter, et al. Human Services: The Third Revolution in Mental Health. LC 74-75481. (Illus.). 1974. 14.50x (ISBN 0-88284-013-4). Alfred Pub.

Fisher, Walter R., ed. Rhetoric: a Tradition in Transition. 315p. 1974. 12.50x (ISBN 0-87013-188-5). Mich St U Pr.

Fisher, Wesley, jt. auth. see Fisher, Lynn.

Fisher, William H. Free at Last: A Bibliography of Martin Luther King, Jr. LC 77-22202. 1977. 10.00 (ISBN 0-8108-1081-6). Scarecrow.

Fishkin, Howard. Taxpayers Survival Manual. 1979. pap. 2.95 (ISBN 0-933586-06-X). Book Promo Unltd.

Fishlock, David. The Business of Science. LC 74-4882. 1975. text ed. 20.95 (ISBN 0-470-26154-4). Halsted Pr.

Fishman, Clifford. Wiretapping & Eavesdropping, Vol. 1. LC 78-18629. 1978. 47.50. Lawyers Co-Op.

Fishman, Hertzel. American Protestantism & a Jewish State. LC 72-3746. (Schaver Publication Fund for Jewish Studies Ser). 254p. 1973. 12.95x (ISBN 0-8143-1481-3). Wayne St U Pr.

Fishman, Joshua A. Sociology of Language. 1972. pap. 9.95 (ISBN 0-912066-16-4). Newbury Hse.

Fishman, Joshua A., ed. Never Say Die! A Thousand Years of Jewish Life & Letters. (Contributions to the Sociology of Language Ser.). 1980. 53.00x (ISBN 9-0279-7978-2). Mouton.

--Sociology of Yiddish: International Journal of the Sociology of Language, No. 24. 1980. pap. text ed. 21.00x (ISBN 90-279-3058-9). Mouton.

Fishman, Joshua A. & Keller, Gary D., eds. Bilingual Education for Hispanic Students in the United States. (Orig.). 1981. pap. 17.95 (ISBN 0-8077-2603-6). Tchrs Coll.

Fishman, Judith, jt. auth. see Schor, Sandra.

Fishman, M. E., jt. auth. see Glasscote, R. M.

Fishman, M. E., jt. auth. see Glasscote, Raymond M.

Fishman, Robert. Criminal Recidivism in New York City: An Evaluation of the Impact of Rehabilitation & Diversion Services. LC 76-12850. (Special Studies). 1977. text ed. 24.95 (ISBN 0-275-23580-7). Praeger.

Fishman, William J. Jewish Radicals 1875-1914: From Czarist Stetl to London Ghetto. LC 74-26194. 384p. 1975. Repr. 12.95 o.p. (ISBN 0-394-49764-3). Pantheon.

Fishwick, H. P., et al. Paper Machine Steam & Condensate Systems. 2nd ed. (TAPPI PRESS Reports). (Illus.). 1979. pap. 14.95 (ISBN 0-89852-370-2, 01-01-R070). TAPPI.

Fishwick, J. H. Applications of Lithium in Ceramics. (Illus.). 176p. 1974. 22.50 (ISBN 0-8436-0611-8). CBI Pub.

Fishwick, Marshall. Popular Architecture. 1975. pap. 2.50 (ISBN 0-87972-164-2). Bowling Green Univ.

Fishwick, Marshall W., ed. American Studies in Transition. rev. ed. LC 57-11986. 1968. Repr. of 1964 ed. 9.00x o.p. (ISBN 0-8122-7478-4). U of Pa Pr.

Fisiak, Jacek, ed. Historical Morphology: Papers Prepared for the Conference, Held at Boszkovo, Poland, March 1978. (Trends in Linguistics, Studies & Monographs: No. 17). 1980. text ed. 79.50 (ISBN 90-279-3038-4). Mouton.

--Theoretical Issues in Contrastive Linguistics. (Current Issues in Linguistic Theory: Vol. 12). 1979. text ed. 54.25x (ISBN 0-391-01670-9, Pub. by Benjamins Holland). Humanities.

Fisk, Albert. A New Look at Senility. write for info (ISBN 0-398-04436-8). C C Thomas.

Fisk, Donald, et al. Private Provision of Public Services: An Overview. (An Institute Paper). 105p. 1978. pap. 6.00 (ISBN 0-87766-221-5, 18300). Urban Inst.

Fisk, Donald M. & Lancer, Cynthia A. Equality of Distribution of Recreation Services: A Case Study of Washington, D.C. 46p. 1974. pap. 3.00 o.p. (ISBN 0-87766-129-4, 88000). Urban Inst.

Fisk, E. K., ed. see Howie-Willis, Ian.

Fisk, E. K., ed. see Robinson, Neville K.

Fisk, Edward R. Construction Engineer's Form Book. 256p. 1981. text ed. 40.00 (ISBN 0-471-06307-X). Wiley.

Fisk, George & Nason, Robert W., eds. Macromarketing, Vol. III: New Steps on the Learning Curve. 421p. 1979. 12.00 (ISBN 0-686-69387-6). U CO Busn Res Div.

Fisk, James W. A Practical Guide to Management of the Painful Neck & Back: Diagnosis, Manipulation, Exercises, Prevention. (Illus.). 248p. 1977. 22.50 (ISBN 0-398-03640-3). C C Thomas.

Fisk, Leonard W., Jr., jt. auth. see Lindgren, Henry C.

Fisk, Milton. Ethics & Society: A Marxist Interpretation of Value. LC 79-3513. 1980. 28.00x (ISBN 0-8147-2564-3). NYU Pr.

Fisk, Nicholas. Escape from Splatterbang. LC 79-11494. (Illus.). (gr. 5-9). 1979. 8.95 (ISBN 0-02-735260-9, 73526). Macmillan.

--Grinny: A Novel of Science Fiction. LC 74-10274. 96p. (gr. 5-8). 1974. 6.95 o.p. (ISBN 0-525-66697-4). Elsevier-Nelson.

--Space Hostages. LC 69-12743. (gr. 5-8). 1969. 3.95g o.s.i. (ISBN 0-02-735280-3). Macmillan.

Fisk, Samuel. Letters to Teresa. 91p. 1973. pap. 1.95 (ISBN 0-87398-516-8, Pub. by Bibl Evang Pr). Sword of Lord.

Fiske, D. W., jt. auth. see Duncan, S.

Fiske, Majorie. Book Selection & Censorship: A Study of School & Public Libraries in California. (California Library Reprint Series: No. 1). 1968. 15.75x (ISBN 0-520-00418-3). U of Cal Pr.

Fiske, Marjorie. Middle Age: The Prime of Life. (Life Cycle Ser.). 1980. pap. text ed. write for info. (ISBN 0-06-384749-3, HarpC). Har-Row.

Fiske, Roger & Dobbs, J. B. Oxford School Music Books: Level 3. - Junior Series, 4 Bks. (Oxford School Music Books Ser.). (gr. 4-8). 1954. text ed. 1.00 ea.; Vol. 1. (ISBN 0-19-321141-6); Vol. 2. (ISBN 0-19-321142-4); Vol. 3. (ISBN 0-19-321143-2); Vol. 4. (ISBN 0-19-321144-0); tchrs'. manual for bk. 1 5.00 (ISBN 0-19-321121-1); tchrs'. manual for bk. 2 5.00 (ISBN 0-19-321122-X); tchrs'. manual for bks. 3 & 4 5.00 (ISBN 0-19-321122-X). Oxford U Pr.

Fiskin, A. M., jt. auth. see McGlone, James P.

Fison, Lorimer & Howitt, Alfred W. Kamilaroi & Kurnai: Group Marriage & Relationship, & Marriage by Elopement, the Kurnai Tribe: Their Customs in Peace & War. (Maps). 1967. pap. text ed. 15.50x (ISBN 90-6234-053-9). Humanities.

Fiss, Owen M. Civil Rights Injunction. LC 78-2052. 128p. 1978. 10.95x (ISBN 0-253-31356-2). Ind U Pr.

Fiszel, H. Investment Efficiency in a Socialist Economy. 1966. 13.75 (ISBN 0-08-011760-0). Pergamon.

Fitch, A. A., ed. Developments in Geophysical Exploration Methods, Vol. 1. (Illus.). 1979. 51.80x (ISBN 0-85334-835-9, Pub. by Applied Science). Burgess-Intl Ideas.

Fitch, B. L' Etranger de Camus: Un Texte, ses lecteurs, leurs lectures. new ed. (Collection L). 176p. (Orig., Fr.). 1972. pap. 13.95 (ISBN 2-03-036005-8). Larousse.

Fitch, Bob & Fitch, Lynne. Grandfather's Land. LC 75-190188. (gr. 5-9). 1970. PLB 6.95 (ISBN 0-87191-049-7). Creative Ed.

--Mark Will Ward - a Black Family in the City. LC 74-190185. (gr. 5-9). 1970. PLB 6.95 (ISBN 0-87191-051-9). Creative Ed.

Fitch, Charles M. The Complete Book of Houseplants. 1972. 10.95 o.p. (ISBN 0-8015-1650-1). Dutton.

--The Complete Book of Houseplants. (Illus.). 320p. 1980. pap. 7.95 (ISBN 0-8015-1660-9, Hawthorn). Dutton.

--The Complete Book of Miniature Roses. (Illus.). 352p. 1980. pap. 10.95 (ISBN 0-8015-1507-6, Hawthorn). Dutton.

Fitch, E. C. & Surjaatmadja, J. B. Introduction to Fluid Logic. (McGraw-Hill-Hemisphere in Fluids & Thermal Engineering Ser.). (Illus.). 1978. text ed. 26.50 (ISBN 0-07-021126-4, C). McGraw.

Fitch, Florence M. Their Search for God: Ways of Worship in the Orient. LC 47-11705. (Illus.). (gr. 7-12). 1947. PLB 7.92 o.p. (ISBN 0-688-51599-1). Lothrop.

Fitch, Frederic B. Elements of Combinatory Logic. LC 73-86892. 176p. 1974. 10.50x o.p. (ISBN 0-300-01523-2). Yale U Pr.

Fitch, Helen F., ed. see Chapuis, Alfred.

Fitch, Howard M., ed. see Chapuis, Alfred.

Fitch, James M. Historic Preservation. (Illus.). 448p. 1981. 24.95 (ISBN 0-07-021121-3, P&RB). McGraw.

--Walter Gropius. LC 60-13308. (Masters of World Architecture Ser). (Illus.). 1960. 7.95 o.s.i. (ISBN 0-8076-0130-6); pap. 3.95 o.s.i. (ISBN 0-8076-0228-0). Braziller.

Fitch, John E. & Lavenberg, Robert J. Deep-Water Fishes of California. LC 68-64172. (California-Natural History Guides: No. 25). (Illus.). 1968. pap. 2.25 o.p. (ISBN 0-520-00421-3). U of Cal Pr.

--Tidepool & Nearshore Fishes of California. (Illus.). 1976. 12.95x (ISBN 0-520-02844-9); pap. 5.95 (ISBN 0-520-02845-7). U of Cal Pr.

Fitch, Lynne, jt. auth. see Fitch, Bob.

Fitch, Raymond E. The Poison Sky: Myth & Apocalypse in Ruskin. LC 70-122097. (Illus.). 500p. 1981. 25.00x (ISBN 0-8214-0090-8). Ohio U Pr.

Fitch, Richard D. & Porter, Edward A. Accidental or Incendiary. 224p. 1975. 14.75 (ISBN 0-398-00582-6). C C Thomas.

Fitch, Robert. Right on Dellums. LC 70-161311. (Illus.). (gr. 4-8). 1972. PLB 6.95 (ISBN 0-87191-079-9). Creative Ed.

Fitch, Robert M., ed. Polymer Colloids. LC 70-153721. 187p. 1971. 24.50 (ISBN 0-306-30536-4, Plenum Pr). Plenum Pub.

--Polymer Colloids, II. 695p. 1980. 69.50 (ISBN 0-306-40350-1, Plenum Pr). Plenum Pub.

Fitch, Stanley K. Insights into Human Behavior. 2nd ed. 1974. pap. text ed. 14.95 o.p. (ISBN 0-205-06096-X, 7960964). Allyn.

Fitch, W. H., illus. Refugium Botanicum or Figures & Descriptions from Living Specimens of Little Known or New Plants of Botanical Interest, Vol. II. (Orchid Ser.). (Illus.). 1980. Repr. text ed. 27.50 (ISBN 0-930576-19-5). E M Coleman Ent.

Fitchen, Janet M. Poverty in Rural America: A Cast Study. (Special Studies in Contemporary Social Issues). 266p. (Orig.). 1981. lib. bdg. 20.00x (ISBN 0-89158-868-X); pap. text ed. 9.50x (ISBN 0-89158-901-5). Westview.

Fitchen, John. The Construction of Gothic Cathedrals: A Study of Medieval Vault Erection. (Illus.). xxii, 344p. 1981. pap. 9.95 (ISBN 0-226-25203-5). U of Chicago Pr.

--The Construction of Gothic Cathedrals: A Study of Medieval Vault Erection. (Midway Reprint Ser.). (Illus.). 1977. pap. text ed. 12.00x (ISBN 0-226-25202-7); pap. 9.95 (ISBN 0-226-25203-5). U of Chicago Pr.

Fite, Gilbert C. George N. Peek & the Fight for Farm Parity. (Illus.). 1954. 13.95x o.p. (ISBN 0-8061-0285-3). U of Okla Pr.

--Mount Rushmore. (Illus.). pap. 5.95 (ISBN 0-8061-0959-9). U of Okla Pr.

Fite, Gilbert C., jt. auth. see Peterson, H. C.

Fite, R., jt. auth. see Blair, T.

Fite, W. see Marton, L.

Fitouss, Jean-Paul, jt. ed. see Malinvaud, Edmond.

Fitt, William C., ed. Steam Locomotive Study Course, 4 vols. LC 79-65782. (Illus.). 1500p. 1980. Set. 100.00 (ISBN 0-914104-05-5). Wildwood Pubns MI.

--Union Pacific FEF-3 Class 4-8-4 Locomotive Drawings. LC 75-27822. (Illus.). 54p. 1975. pap. 15.50 (ISBN 0-914104-02-0). Wildwood Pubns MI.

Fitter, Alastair, jt. auth. see Fitter, Richard.

Fitter, Richard & Fitter, Alastair. Wild Flowers of Britain & Northern Europe. LC 74-3756. (Encore Edition). (Illus.). 1974. 3.95 o.p. (ISBN 0-684-15246-0, ScribT). Scribner.

Fitton, Mary, tr. Bravo Maurice. 10.00x o.p. (ISBN 0-8464-0206-8). Beekman Pubs.

Fitts, Dudley, tr. see Sophocles.

Fitzegerald, Robert, jt. tr. see Fitzgerald, Robert.

Fitzell, Lincoln. Selected Poems. 88p. 1955. 4.95 (ISBN 0-8040-0269-X). Swallow.

Fitzer, Joseph. Moehler & Baur in Controversy Eighteen Thirty-Two to Thirty-Eight: Reformation & Counter-Reformation in the Age of Romantic Idealism. LC 74-77619. (American Academy of Religion. Studies in Religion). 1974. 7.50 (ISBN 0-88420-111-2, 010007). Scholars Pr Ca.

Fitzgerald, A. E., et al. Basic Electrical Engineering. 5th ed. (Electrical Engineering Ser.). (Illus.). 832p. 1981. text ed. 28.95x (ISBN 0-07-021154-X); write for info solutions manual (ISBN 0-07-021155-8). McGraw.

Fitzgerald, Anne & Lane, Saunders M., eds. Pure & Applied Math in People's Republic of China. LC 77-79329. (CSCPRC Report: No. 3). 1977. pap. 8.25 (ISBN 0-309-02609-1). Natl Acad Pr.

Fitzgerald, Anne & Slichter, Charles, eds. Solid State Physics in the People's Republic of China: A Trip Report of the American Solid State Physics Delegation. LC 76-49402. (People's Republic of China Ser.: No. 1). 1976. pap. 10.25 (ISBN 0-309-02523-0). Natl Acad Pr.

Fitzgerald, Arlene. The Devil's Gate. 1977. pap. 1.50 o.p. (ISBN 0-445-03178-6). Popular Lib.

Fitzgerald, Barbara, jt. auth. see Aronson, Virginia.

Fitzgerald, Betty, tr. see Kammer, Reinhard.

Fitzgerald, C. P. Birth of Communist China. 1978. pap. 2.95 o.p. (ISBN 0-14-020694-9, Pelican). Penguin.

--China: A Short Cultural History. 1978. 19.95 o.p. (ISBN 0-248-98299-0, 8018, Dist. by Arco). Barrie & Jenkins.

Fitzgerald, C. P., jt. auth. see Heren, Louis.

Fitzgerald, Cathleen. Let's Find Out About Bees. LC 78-186938. (Let's Find Out Bks). (Illus.). 48p. (gr. 3-4). 1973. PLB 4.47 o.p. (ISBN 0-531-00079-6). Watts.

--Let's Find Out About Words. LC 78-134370. (Let's Find Out Bks). (Illus.). (gr. k-3). 1971. PLB 4.47 o.p. (ISBN 0-531-00070-2). Watts.

FitzGerald, E. V. The Political Economy of Peru Nineteen Fifty-Six to Seventy-Seven. LC 78-72086. (Illus.). 1980. 42.50 (ISBN 0-521-22289-3). Cambridge U Pr.

--Public Sector Investment Planning for Developing Countries. 1978. text ed. 28.50x (ISBN 0-8419-5027-X). Holmes & Meier.

--The State & Economic Development: Peru Since 1968. LC 75-30443. (Department of Applied Economics, Occasional Papers Ser.: No. 49). (Illus.). 140p. 1976. pap. 11.95x (ISBN 0-521-29054-6). Cambridge U Pr.

Fitzgerald, Edward. Letters of Edward Fitzgerald. Cohen, J. M., ed. LC 60-9249. (Centaur Classics Ser.). 1960. 7.95x o.p. (ISBN 0-8093-0028-1). S Ill U Pr.

Fitzgerald, Edward, tr. Rubaiyat of Omar Khayaam. (Illus.). 7.95 (ISBN 0-385-00146-0); pap. 2.50 (ISBN 0-385-09499-X). Doubleday.

Fitzgerald, Edward, tr. see Khayyam, Omar.

Fitzgerald, Edward, tr. see Omar Khayyam.

Fitzgerald, Ernest A. God Writes Straight with Crooked Lines. LC 80-65997. 144p. 1981. 7.95 (ISBN 0-689-11073-1). Atheneum.

Fitzgerald, F. Scott. Afternoon of an Author. (Hudson River Edition Ser.). 1981. write for info. (ISBN 0-684-16469-8, ScribT). Scribner.

--Babylon Revisited & Other Stories. 1960. pap. 4.95 (ISBN 0-684-71757-3, ScribT). Scribner.

--Beautiful & Damned. 1920. lib. rep. ed. 17.50x (ISBN 0-684-15153-7, ScribT); pap. 4.95 (ISBN 0-684-71758-1, SL90, ScribT). Scribner.

--Great Gatsby. (Hudson River Edition Ser.). 1981. write for info. (ISBN 0-684-16498-1, ScribT). Scribner.

--Great Gatsby. (gr. 9-12). 1920. 6.95 o.p. (ISBN 0-684-10154-8, ScribT); text ed. 6.95 (ISBN 0-684-51515-6, ScribC); pap. 3.95 (ISBN 0-684-71760-3, SL1, ScribT); pap. text ed. 3.24 (ISBN 0-684-51516-4, SSP2, ScribC); ScribT. pap. 2.25 (ISBN 0-684-16325-X). Scribner.

--Last Tycoon. 1941. lib. rep. ed. 12.50 (ISBN 0-684-15311-4, ScribT); pap. 3.95 (ISBN 0-684-71764-6, SL242, ScribT). Scribner.

--The Letters of F. Scott Fitzgerald. (Hudson River Edition Ser.). 1981. write for info. (ISBN 0-684-16476-0, ScribT). Scribner.

--The Letters of F. Scott Fitzgerald. 1975. 12.50 o.p. (ISBN 0-684-10157-2, ScribT). Scribner.

--Pat Hobby Stories. 1962. pap. 2.95 o.s.i. (ISBN 0-684-71761-1, SL216, ScribT). Scribner.

--The Romantic Egoists: A Pictorial Autobiography from the Albums of Scott & Zelda Fitzgerald. Smith, Scottie F., et al, eds. (Illus.). 1977. Encore Edition. 14.95 (ISBN 0-684-14973-7, ScribT). Scribner.

--Screenplay for "Three Comrades" by Erich Maria Remarque. Bruccoli, Matthew J., ed. LC 77-28077. (Screenplay Library). (Illus.). 303p. 1978. 10.00 (ISBN 0-8093-0854-1); pap. 7.95 (ISBN 0-8093-0853-3). S Ill U Pr.

--Stories of F. Scott Fitzgerald. 1951. pap. 5.95 o.p. (ISBN 0-684-71737-9, SL135, ScribT); lib. rep. ed. 17.50x o.p. (ISBN 0-684-15366-1). Scribner.

--Taps at Reveille. 1935. lib. rep. ed. 15.50x (ISBN 0-684-14742-4, SL274, ScribT); pap. 2.95 (ISBN 0-684-12464-5, SL 274, ScribT). Scribner.

--Tender Is the Night. 1960. lib. rep. ed. 17.50x (ISBN 0-684-15151-0, ScribT); pap. 3.95 (ISBN 0-684-71763-8, SL2, ScribT). Scribner.

--This Side of Paradise. 1920. lib. rep. ed. 17.50x (ISBN 0-684-15601-6, ScribT); pap. 3.95 (ISBN 0-684-71765-4, SL60, ScribT). Scribner.

Fitzgerald, George. A Practical Guide to Preaching. LC 79-67742. (Orig.). 1980. pap. 4.95 (ISBN 0-8091-2281-2). Paulist Pr.

FitzGerald, Gerald F., jt. auth. see Bloomfield, Louis M.

Fitzgerald, Gregory. Hunting the Yahoos. (Illus.). 100p. (Orig.). 1981. pap. 4.50 (ISBN 0-934996-14-8). Am Stud Pr.

Fitzgerald, Hiram E. & Strommen, Ellen. Plaid for Developmental Psychology. 1972. pap. 5.50 (ISBN 0-256-01258-X, 11-0165-00). Learning Syst.

Fitzgerald, Hiram E. & McKinney, John P., eds. Developmental Psychology: Studies in Human Development. rev. ed. 1977. pap. 10.95x (ISBN 0-256-01937-1). Dorsey.

Fitzgerald, Hiram E., et al. Developmental Psychology: The Infant & Young Child. 1977. pap. 8.95x (ISBN 0-256-01888-X). Dorsey.

Fitzgerald, James, jt. auth. see Weil, Robert.

Fitzgerald, James A. Don Carlos & Other Stories. 168p. 1981. 9.95. Bond Pub Co.

Fitzgerald, Janet A. Alfred North Whitehead's Early Philosophy of Space & Time. LC 79-63849. (Illus.). 1979. 9.50 (ISBN 0-8191-0747-6). U Pr of Amer.

FitzGerald, Jerry. Internal Controls for Computerized Systems. LC 78-69677. (Illus.). 93p. 1978. pap. text ed. 11.15 (ISBN 0-932410-04-9). FitzGerald & Assocs.

Fitzgerald, Jerry, et al. Fundamentals of Systems Analysis. 2nd ed. LC 80-11769. 500p. 1980. text ed. 22.95 (ISBN 0-471-04968-9, Pub by Wiley College); write for info. (ISBN 0-471-08117-5). Wiley.

Fitzgerald, Jim, jt. auth. see Jonland, Einar.

Fitzgerald, John D. Brave Buffalo Fighter (Waditaka Tatahka Kisisohitika) LC 73-80213. (Illus.). 192p. (gr. 5-7). 1973. PLB 7.50 o.p. (ISBN 0-8309-0100-0). Independence Pr.

--Great Brain. (Illus.). (gr. 7 up). 1971. pap. 1.50 (ISBN 0-440-40307-3, YB). Dell.

--Great Brain at the Academy. 176p. (gr. 3-7). 1973. pap. 1.50 (ISBN 0-440-43113-1, YB). Dell.

--Great Brain Reforms. 176p. 1975. pap. 1.50 (ISBN 0-440-44841-7, YB). Dell.

--Me & My Little Brain. (gr. 4-7). 1972. pap. 1.50 (ISBN 0-440-45533-2, YB). Dell.

--More Adventures of the Great Brain. 1971. pap. 1.50 (ISBN 0-440-45822-6, YB). Dell.

--The Return of the Great Brain. (gr. 3-5). 1975. pap. 1.50 (ISBN 0-440-45941-9, YB). Dell.

Fitzgerald, John D., jt. auth. see Meredith, Robert C.

FitzGerald, Kathleen W. Brass: Jane Byrne & the Pursuit of Power. 1981. 11.95 (ISBN 0-8092-7006-4). Contemp Bks.

Fitzgerald, Maurice. Embriologia. (Span.). 1980. pap. text ed. 16.50 (ISBN 0-06-313120-X, Pub. by HarLA Mexico). Har-Row.

Fitzgerald, Michael R., jt. auth. see Watson, Richard A.

Fitzgerald, Mike & Sim, Joe. British Prisons. 1979. 16.00x o.p. (ISBN 0-631-11211-1, Pub. by Basil Blackwell England); pap. 6.95x o.p. (ISBN 0-631-11221-9, Pub. by Basil Blackwell England). Biblio Dist.

Fitzgerald, Penelope. The Golden Child. LC 77-93900. 1978. 7.95 o.p. (ISBN 0-684-15645-8, ScribT). Scribner.

Fitzgerald, Percy. Bozland: Dickens' Places & People. LC 70-141754. 1971. Repr. of 1895 ed. 20.00 (ISBN 0-8103-3616-2). Gale.

Fitzgerald, Percy H. The History of Pickwick. 1980. Repr. of 1891 ed. lib. bdg. 45.00 (ISBN 0-8492-4631-8). R West.

Fitzgerald, Peter J. The Basis of Sex Education. 1981. 7.95 (ISBN 0-533-04636-X). Vantage.

Fitzgerald, R. T., et al. Participation in Schools? Five Case Studies. (Australian Council for Educational Research). 1976. pap. text ed. 20.00x o.p. (ISBN 0-85563-138-4). Verry.

Fitzgerald, R. V. Conjoint Marital Therapy. LC 73-81208. 256p. 1973. 25.00x (ISBN 0-87668-091-0). Aronson.

Fitzgerald, R. W. Strength of Materials. 1967. text ed. 20.95 (ISBN 0-201-02050-5); instructor's guide 2.95 (ISBN 0-201-02051-3). A-W.

Fitzgerald, Robert see Homer.

Fitzgerald, Robert & Fitzegerald, Robert, trs. The Iliad & the Odyssey, 2 vols. 1080p. 1975. boxed set 27.50 o.p. (ISBN 0-385-11066-9, Anchor Pr). Doubleday.

Fitzgerald, Robert, tr. see Sophocles.

Fitzgerald, Ross, ed. Comparing Political Thinkers. 320p. 1980. 29.00 (ISBN 0-08-024800-4); pap. 15.75 (ISBN 0-08-024799-7). Pergamon.

--Human Needs & Politics. 1977. text ed. 26.00 (ISBN 0-08-021402-9); pap. text ed. 14.50 (ISBN 0-08-021401-0). Pergamon.

Fitzgerald, Ruth C. A Different Story: A Black History of Fredericksburg, Stafford & Spotsylvania, Virginia. LC 79-67534. (Illus.). 336p. 1980. 9.95 (ISBN 0-9604564-2-2); pap. 4.95 (ISBN 0-9604564-3-0). Unicorn VA.

Fitzgerald, S. China & the Overseas Chinese: A Study of Peking's Changing Policy, 1949-1970. LC 77-177938. (Cambridge Studies in Chinese History, Literature & Institutions). (Illus.). 250p. 1972. 41.00 (ISBN 0-521-08410-5); pap. 13.95 (ISBN 0-521-29810-5). Cambridge U Pr.

Fitzgerald, S. J. The Story of the Savoy Opera in Gilbert & Sullivan Days. (Music Reprint Ser.). 1979. Repr. of 1925 ed. lib. bdg. 25.00 (ISBN 0-306-79543-4). Da Capo.

Fitzgerald, Walter. The New Europe: An Introduction to Its Political Geography. LC 80-24065. (Illus.). xiii, 298p. 1980. Repr. of 1946 ed. lib. bdg. 29.75x (ISBN 0-313-21006-3, FINE). Greenwood.

Fitz-Gerald, William. The Harness Maker's Illustrated Manual. 15.00. Green Hill.

--The Harness Makers' Illustrated Manual. (Illus.). 1977. Repr. of 1875 ed. 15.00x (ISBN 0-88427-014-9, Dist. by Caroline House Pubs). North River.

Fitzgerald, Zelda. Save Me the Waltz. LC 32-30021. (Arcturus Books Paperbacks). 224p. 1967. pap. 6.95 (ISBN 0-8093-0255-1). S Ill U Pr.

Fitz-Gibbon, Carol T. & Morris, Lynn L. How to Calculate Statistics. LC 78-58659. (Program Evaluation Kit: Vol. 7). 1978. pap. 8.50x (ISBN 0-8039-1072-X). Sage.

--How to Design a Program Evaluation. LC 78-57011. (Program Evaluation Kit: Vol. 3). 1978. pap. 7.50x (ISBN 0-8039-1068-1). Sage.

Fitz-Gibbon, Carol T., jt. auth. see Morris, Lynn L.

Fitz-Gibbon, Carol T., jt. auth. see Morrris, Lynn L.

Fitzgibbon, Constantine. Man in Aspic. 1979. 14.95x (ISBN 0-8464-0084-7). Beekman Pubs.

Fitzgibbon, Constantine & Morrison, George. The Life & Times of Eamon De Valera. LC 73-7353. (Illus.). 156p. 1974. 8.95 o.s.i. (ISBN 0-02-538500-3). Macmillan.

Fitzgibbon, Louis. Katyn. (Illus.). 1979. Repr. of 1971 ed. 12.00 (ISBN 0-911038-25-6, Inst Hist Rev); pap. 8.00 (ISBN 0-911038-60-4). Noontide.

Fitzgibbon, Russell H. The Selected Writings of Russell H. Fitzgibbon. Date not set. text ed. price not set (ISBN 0-87918-039-0). ASU Lat Am St.

Fitzharris, Timothy L. The Desirability of a Correctional Ombudsman. LC 72-13057. 114p. (Orig.). 1973. pap. 4.00x (ISBN 0-87772-155-6). Inst Gov Stud Berk.

Fitzherbert, John. Fitxharbets Booke of Husbandrie: Newlie Corrected. LC 79-84107. (English Experience Ser.: No. 926). 220p. 1979. Repr. of 1598 ed. lib. bdg. 21.00 (ISBN 90-221-0926-7). Walter J Johnson.

Fitzhugh, Lester N., ed. Cannon Smoke: The Letters of Captain John J.Good, Good-Douglas Texas Battery, CSA. new ed. LC 73-177902. (Illus.). 1973. 7.50 o.p. (ISBN 0-912172-16-9). Hill Jr Coll.

Fitzhugh, Louise. Sport. (gr. 7-12). 1980. pap. 1.75 (ISBN 0-440-98350-9, LFL). Dell.

Fitzlyon, April, tr. see Bokov, Nikolai.

FitzLyon, April, tr. see De Mandiargues, Andre P.

Fitzmaurice, Eugene. Circumstantial Evidence. 1978. pap. 1.95 o.s.i. (ISBN 0-515-04265-X). Jove Pubns.

Fitzmaurice, George. The Plays of George Fitzmaurice. Incl. Realistic Plays. Slaughter, Howard, intro. by. 164p. (Fitzmaurice plays 3). 1970. text ed. 4.50x (ISBN 0-85105-174-X); Folk Plays. Slaughter, Howard, intro. by. 153p. (Fitzmaurice plays 2). 1969. text ed. 4.50x (ISBN 0-85105-013-1). Dolmen Pr). Humanities.

Fitzmaurice, John. The European Parliament. LC 78-67229. (Praeger Special Studies). 1979. 20.95 (ISBN 0-03-046221-5). Praeger.

Fitzmaurice, Victor. Bel-Heirs. 1981. 9.95 (ISBN 0-533-04875-3). Vantage.

Fitzmyer, J. A. To Advance the Gospel: New Testament Essays. 320p. 1981. 19.50 (ISBN 0-8245-0008-3). Crossroad NY.

Fitzmyer, Joseph A. The Dead Sea Scrolls: Major Publications & Tools for Study. LC 75-5987. (Society of Biblical Literature. Sources for Biblical Study). xiv, 171p. 1975. pap. 7.50 (ISBN 0-88414-053-9, 060308). Scholars Pr Ca.

--Essays on the Semitic Background of the New Testament. LC 74-83874. (Society of Biblical Literature. Sources for Biblical Study). 1974. pap. 10.50 (ISBN 0-89130-309-X, 060305). Scholars Pr Ca.

--A Wandering Aramean: Collected Aramaic Essays. LC 77-21379. (Society of Biblical Literature. Monograph: No. 25). 1979. 15.00 (ISBN 0-89130-150-X); pap. 12.00 (ISBN 0-89130-152-6, 060025). Scholars Pr Ca.

Fitzmyer, Joseph F. Pauline Theology: A Brief Sketch. (Orig.). 1967. pap. text ed. 7.25 (ISBN 0-13-654525-4). P-H.

Fitzpatrick, Anthony. English for International Conferences: A Language Course for Those Working in the Field of Science, Economics, Politics & Administration. (MFLP Ser.). 64p. 1980. pap. 60.00 includes 4 cassettes (ISBN 0-08-027225-8). Pergamon.

FitzPatrick, E. A. An Introduction to Soil Science. (Ecology Ser). (Illus.). 176p. 1974. pap. text ed. 7.50x (ISBN 0-05-002777-8). Longman.

Fitzpatrick, Eva & Stubbs, Joanna. Kirsty at the Lodge. (Illus.). (ps-5). 1972. 6.95 (ISBN 0-571-09769-3, Pub. by Faber & Faber). Merrimack Bk Serv.

Fitzpatrick, James K. How to Survive in Your Liberal School. (Illus.). 1975. 7.95 o.p. (ISBN 0-87000-323-2). Arlington Hse.

--To Form a More Perfect Union: America's Struggle for a National Identity. 1979. 9.95 o.p. (ISBN 0-87000-446-8). Arlington Hse.

Fitzpatrick, Jim. The Book of Conquests. 1978. pap. 8.95 o.p. (ISBN 0-525-47511-7). Dutton.

Fitzpatrick, John, ed. see Van Buren, Martin.

Fitzpatrick, Lilian L. Nebraska Place-Names. Fairclough, G. Thomas, ed. LC 60-15471. 1960. pap. 3.50 (ISBN 0-8032-5060-6, BB 107, Bison). U of Nebr Pr.

Fitzpatrick, M. Louise, ed. Historical Studies in Nursing. LC 78-12192. 1978. text ed. 9.25x (ISBN 0-8077-2527-7). Tchrs Coll.

--Present Realities: Future Imperatives in Nursing Education. LC 76-55404. 1977. pap. text ed. 5.25x (ISBN 0-8077-2513-7). Tchrs Coll.

Fitzpatrick, Philip M. Principles of Celestial Mechanics. 1970. text ed. 18.95 (ISBN 0-12-257950-X). Acad Pr.

Fitzpatrick, Sheila. Commissariat of Enlightenment. (Soviet & East European Studies). (Illus.). 1971. 47.95 (ISBN 0-521-07919-5). Cambridge U Pr.

--Education & Social Mobility in the Soviet Union: 1921-1934. LC 78-58788. (Soviet & East European Studies). 1979. 39.95 (ISBN 0-521-22325-3). Cambridge U Pr.

Fitzpatrick, William J. Monarch Notes on Austen's Emma & Mansfield Park. (Orig.). pap. 1.95 (ISBN 0-671-00704-1). Monarch Pr.

Fitz-Randolph, Jane. How to Write for Children. rev. ed. LC 79-2747. (Everyday Handbook Ser.). 288p. 1980. pap. 4.95 (ISBN 0-06-463491-4, EH 491, EH). Har-Row.

Fitzsimmons, Muriel. Cooking for Absolute Beginners. LC 75-35405. Orig. Title: You Can Cook If You Can Read. 380p. 1976. pap. 3.95 (ISBN 0-486-23311-1). Dover.

Fitzsimmons, R. W. & Wrigley, C. W. Australian Barley. 1980. 20.00x (ISBN 0-643-00344-4, Pub. by CSIRO Australia). State Mutual Bk.

--Australian Barleys. 86p. 1980. 9.95x (ISBN 0-643-00344-4, Pub. by CSIRO Australia). Intl Schol Bk Serv.

Fitzsimmons, S. J., et al. Guidance Manual to Providing Neighborhood Services. LC 77-5225. 1977. PLB 12.50x (ISBN 0-89158-242-8). Westview.

--Social Assessment Manual: A Guide to the Preparation of the Social Well-Being Account for Planning Water Resource Projects. LC 76-58332. 1977. lib. bdg. 21.00x (ISBN 0-89158-228-2). Westview.

Fitzsimons, Christopher. Early Warning. 256p. 1981. pap. 2.25 (ISBN 0-380-50179-1, 50179). Avon.

Fitzsimons, J. T. The Physiology of Thirst & Sodium Appetite. LC 78-16212. (Physiological Society Monographs: No. 35). 1979. 83.50 (ISBN 0-521-22292-3). Cambridge U Pr.

FitzSimons, Raymund. Death & the Magician. LC 80-21071. 1981. 10.95 (ISBN 0-689-11122-3). Atheneum.

Fitzsimons, Virginia, jt. auth. see Forbes, Elizabeth.

Fitzwilliam Museum. All for Art: The Ricketts & Shannon Collection. Darracott, J., ed. LC 79-51597. (Illus.). 1979. 36.00 (ISBN 0-521-22841-7); pap. 9.95 (ISBN 0-521-29674-9). Cambridge U Pr.

--Drawings & Watercolours by Peter De Wint. LC 79-4652. (Illus.). 32.50 (ISBN 0-521-22745-3); pap. 8.95 (ISBN 0-521-29631-5). Cambridge U Pr.

Fivars, Grace, ed. The Critical Incident Technique: A Bibliography. 2nd ed. 1980. pap. 7.50 (ISBN 0-89785-662-7). Am Inst Res.

Fixel, Lawrence. Time to Destroy - to Discover. 1972. regular ed 1.50 (ISBN 0-915572-58-3); ltd. signed, numbered ed 3.00 (ISBN 0-915572-58-3). Panjandrum.

Fixler, Alvin. Family River Rafting Guide: 1979. LC 79-83686. (Illus.). 1979. pap. write for info. o.p. (ISBN 0-89803-006-4). Caroline Hse.

Fixx, James. More Games for the Super-Intelligent. 1977. pap. 2.25 (ISBN 0-445-04114-5). Popular Lib.

Fixx, James F. The Complete Book of Running. (Illus.). 1977. 10.00 (ISBN 0-394-41159-5). Random.

--Games for the Super-Intelligent. 128p. 1974. pap. 1.75 (ISBN 0-445-08518-5). Popular Lib.

--Jim Fixx's Second Book of Running. 320p. 1980. 10.95 (ISBN 0-394-50898-X). Random.

Fizdale, Robert, jt. auth. see Gold, Arthur.

Fizer, John. Psychologism & Psychoaesthetics: A Historical & Critical View of Their Relations. (Linguistic & Literary Studies in Eastern Europe Ser.: No. 6). 300p. 1980. text ed. 37.25x (ISBN 90-272-1506-5). Humanities.

Fizzell, James A., jt. auth. see Jarabak, Joseph R.

Fjelde, Rolf, tr. see Ibsen, Henrik.

Flach, Frederic. Choices: Coping Creatively with Personal Change. LC 77-22923. 1977. 8.95 o.p. (ISBN 0-397-01234-9). Lippincott.

--The Secret Strength of Depression. LC 74-3097. 1974. 7.95 o.s.i. (ISBN 0-397-01031-1). Lippincott.

Flach, Frederic F. & Draghi, Suzanne C. The Nature & Treatment of Depression. LC 74-28265. 448p. 1975. 38.95 (ISBN 0-471-26271-4, Pub. by Wiley Medical). Wiley.

Flach, George W. Changes in the 1981 National Electrical Code. 144p. 1981. pap. 6.95 (ISBN 0-13-127852-5). P-H.
Flachmann, K. Time In: A Guide to Communication Skills. 1973. 8.95 (ISBN 0-201-43031-2); tchrs' guide 4.25 (ISBN 0-201-43032-0, 43032). A-W.
Flachmann, Kim. Focus: A College English Handbook. (Illus.). 448p. 1981. pap. text ed. 6.95 (ISBN 0-395-29728-1); instrs' manual 0.75. HM.
Flack, Dora B. Monumental Experiences: Biography of Florence Hansen, Sculptor. Bennett, Heather, ed. 90p. 1980. pap. 5.95 o.p. (ISBN 0-913420-84-0). Olympus Pub Co.
Flack, Dora D. Fun with Fruit Preservation: Leather, Drying, & Other Methods. LC 74-78025. (Illus.). 98p. 1973. pap. 4.50 (ISBN 0-88290-023-4). Horizon Utah.
Flack, Marjorie. Angus Lost. (ps-k). 1941. 5.95a (ISBN 0-385-07214-7); PLB (ISBN 0-385-07601-0); pap. 1.49 (ISBN 0-385-08009-3). Doubleday.
--Angus y el Gato. LC 76-40263. (ps-k). 1977. PLB 4.95 (ISBN 0-385-11697-7). Doubleday.
--Ask Mister Bear. (gr. k-3). 1958. 6.95 (ISBN 0-02-735390-7). Macmillan.
--Story About Ping. (Illus.). (ps-2). 1933. PLB 7.95 (ISBN 0-670-67223-8). Viking Pr.
--Tim Tadpole & the Great Bullfrog. (ps-1). 4.95a o.p. (ISBN 0-385-07530-8); PLB (ISBN 0-385-07658-4). Doubleday.
Flagel, Clarice. Avoiding Burnout: Time Management for D. R.E.'s. 60p. (Orig.). 1981. pap. 4.95 (ISBN 0-697-01782-6). Wm C Brown.
Flageul, G., jt. auth. see Elbaz, Jean S.
Flagg, Fannie. Coming Attractions. 320p. 1981. 11.95 (ISBN 0-688-00472-5). Morrow.
Flagg, Isaac, ed. see Autenrieth, Georg.
Flagg, Jared B. Life & Letters of Washington Allston. LC 68-27719. (Library of American Art Ser). 1969. Repr. of 1892 ed. lib. bdg. 42.50 (ISBN 0-306-71168-0). Da Capo.
Flagg, Jim. The British Ornithologist's Guide to Bird Life. (Illus.). 284p. 1980. 32.50 (ISBN 0-7137-0996-0, Pub. by Blandford Pr England). Sterling.
Flagg, John S. Prometheus Unbound & Hellas: An Approach to Shelley's Lyrical Dramas. (Salzburg Studies in English Literature, Romantic Reassessment: No. 14). 1972. pap. text ed. 25.00x (ISBN 0-391-01375-0). Humanities.
Flagg, William G. The Clam Lover's Cookbook. 2nd ed. LC 80-10619. (Illus., Orig.). 1980. pap. 5.95 (ISBN 0-88427-041-6, Dist. by Caroline Hse). North River.
Flaherty, Bernard E., ed. Psychophysiological Aspects of Spaceflight. LC 60-15809. 1961. 22.50x (ISBN 0-231-02456-8). Columbia U Pr.
Flaherty, Bernard E., ed. see Symposium on Psychophysiological Aspects of Space Flight, Brooks Air Force Base, Texas, 1960.
Flaherty, Daniel, jt. auth. see Ciszek, Walter J.
Flaherty, Daniel L., Fr., S.J., jt. auth. see Ciszek, Walter J., Fr., S.J.
Flaherty, David H. Privacy in Colonial New England, 1630-1776. LC 76-154804. (Illus.). 350p. 1972. 17.50x (ISBN 0-8139-0339-4). U Pr of Va.
Flaherty, James C. Johann Georg Harmann. (World Authors Ser.: No. 527). 1979. lib. bdg. 14.95 (ISBN 0-8057-6371-6). Twayne.
Flaherty, John E. Managing Change: Today's Challenge to Management. 12.50 (ISBN 0-8424-0115-6). Green Hill.
Flaherty, John E., jt. ed. see Bonaparte, Tony H.
Flaherty, Maureen O. The Care of the Elderly Person: A Guide for the Licensed Practical Nurse. 3rd. ed. LC 80-11236. (Illus.). 1980. pap. text ed. 9.95 (ISBN 0-8016-3706-6). Mosby.
Flaherty, Patrick F. & Ziegler, Richard S. Estate Planning for Everyone. rev. ed. LC 78-4761. (Funk & W Bk.). 1979. 14.95 o.s.i. (ISBN 0-308-10346-7, TYC-T). T Y Crowell.
Flaherty, Patrick F. & Ziegler, Richard. Estate Planning for Everyone. rev. ed. LC 80-8314. (Illus.). 1981. 14.95 (ISBN 0-690-01943-2, HarpT). Har-Row.
Flamholtz, Eric. Human Resource Accounting. LC 73-92477. 1974. text ed. 17.95 (ISBN 0-8221-0129-7). CBI Pub.
Flamholtz, Eric G. & Lacey, John M. Personnel Management, Human Resource Accounting & Human Capital Theory. (Monograph: No. 27). 100p. 1980. 7.50 (ISBN 0-89215-111-0). U Cal LA Indus Rel.
Flamm, Jerry. Good Life in Hard Times: San Francisco's '20s & '30s. LC 76-30524. (Illus.). 1977. pap. 7.95 (ISBN 0-87701-092-7). Chronicle Bks.
Flammang, C. J. Police & the Underprotected Child. 324p. 1970. 18.50 (ISBN 0-398-00583-4). C C Thomas.
--Police Juvenile Enforcement. 284p. 1972. 18.75 (ISBN 0-398-02280-1). C C Thomas.
Flammang, Robert. U. S Programs That Impede U. S. Export Competitveness: The Regulatory Environment, Vol. II. LC 80-80933. (Significant Issues Ser.: No. 3). 45p. 1980. 5.95 (ISBN 0-89206-017-4). CSI Studies.
Flammarion, Camille. Haunted Houses. LC 76-159957. (Tower Bks). 1971. Repr. of 1924 ed. 20.00 (ISBN 0-8103-3911-0). Gale.
Flammer, Philip M. Vivid Air: The Lafayette Escadrille. LC 80-22059. (Illus.). 288p. 1981. 17.50 (ISBN 0-8203-0537-5). U of Ga Pr.
Flanagan, Cathleen C. & Flanagan, John T. American Folklore: A Bibliography, 1950-1974. LC 77-23381. 1977. 19.50 (ISBN 0-8108-1073-5). Scarecrow.
Flanagan, Cathleen C. & Duane, James E., eds. Books & Other Printed Materials. LC 80-23053. (The Instructional Media Library: Vol. 1). 112p. 1981. 13.95 (ISBN 0-87778-161-3). Educ Tech Pubns.
Flanagan, Geraldine L. The First Nine Months of Life. (Illus.). 95p. 1978. Repr. of 1962 ed. 12.95x (ISBN 0-433-10600-X). Intl Ideas.
Flanagan, Henry E., Jr. & Gardner, Robert. Basic Lacrosse Strategy: An Introduction for Young Players. (Illus.). 1979. 7.95 (ISBN 0-385-14001-0). Doubleday.
Flanagan, J. L. & Rabiner, L. R., eds. Speech Synthesis. LC 73-9728. (Benchmark Papers in Acoustics Ser.). 544p. 1973. 43.50 (ISBN 0-12-786476-8). Acad Pr.
Flanagan, John T. Edgar Lee Masters: The Spoon River Poet & His Critics. LC 74-20530. 1974. 10.00 (ISBN 0-8108-0741-6). Scarecrow.
--Profile of Vachel Lindsay. LC 79-130279. (Literary Profiles Ser.). 1970. pap. text ed. 2.95x (ISBN 0-675-09287-6). Merrill.
Flanagan, John T., jt. auth. see Flanagan, Cathleen C.
Flanagan, Laurence. Ulster: Regional Archaeology. 1970. 3.95x o.p. (ISBN 0-435-32970-7). Heinemann Ed.
Flanagan, Richard. The Hunting Variety. 224p. 1975. pap. 1.25 o.p. (ISBN 0-445-00315-4). Popular Lib.
Flanagan, Robert. Maggot. 1971. pap. 2.50 (ISBN 0-446-91830-X). Warner Bks.
Flanagan, Sue. Sam Houston's Texas. LC 64-22338. (Illus.). 214p. 1973. 20.00 (ISBN 0-292-73363-1). U of Tex Pr.
Flanagan, Thomas. Beat the Races. LC 72-650. 1973. pap. 1.45 o.p. (ISBN 0-668-02644-8). Arc Bks.
--The Year of the French. 1980. pap. 3.75 (ISBN 0-671-83301-4). PB.
Flanagan, Thomas J. The Irish Novelists, 1800-1850. LC 76-21874. 362p. 1976. Repr. of 1959 ed. lib. bdg. 25.00x (ISBN 0-8371-9004-5, FLIN). Greenwood.
Flanagan, W., jt. auth. see Gugler, J.
Flanagan, William. The Chairman. (Orig.). 1981. pap. 2.50 (ISBN 0-440-11546-9). Dell.
Flanders, Allan. Collective Bargaining. 1967. 3.95 o.p. (ISBN 0-571-08232-7, Pub. by Faber & Faber). Merrimack Bk Serv.
--Management & Unions. (Orig.). 1975. pap. 4.95 (ISBN 0-571-10711-7, Pub. by Faber & Faber). Merrimack Bk Serv.
--Trade Unions. 7th ed. 1968. text ed. 5.50x (ISBN 0-09-045561-4, Hutchinson U Lib); pap. text ed. 3.00x (ISBN 0-09-045562-2, Hutchinson U Lib). Humanities.
Flanders, H. Calculus. 1970. text ed. 26.95 (ISBN 0-12-259640-4); ans. manual avail. Acad Pr.
Flanders, H. & Price, J. Calculus with Analytic Geometry. 1041p. 1978. text ed. 26.95 (ISBN 0-12-259672-2); instr's. manual 3.00 (ISBN 0-12-259673-0). Acad Pr.
Flanders, H. & Price, Justin J. Elementary Functions & Analytic Geometry. 1973. text ed. 18.95 (ISBN 0-12-259655-2); instr's manual 3.00 (ISBN 0-12-259656-0). Acad Pr.
--Introductory College Mathematics: With Linear Algebra & Finite Mathematics. 1973. text ed. 19.95 (ISBN 0-12-259660-9). Acad Pr.
Flanders, H. J. & Cresson, B. C. Introduction to the Bible. 1973. 17.95 (ISBN 0-8260-3125-0). Wiley.
Flanders, Harley. Differential Forms: With Applications to the Physical Sciences. (Mathematics in Science & Engineering Ser.). 203p. 1963. text ed. 18.95 (ISBN 0-12-259650-1). Acad Pr.
Flanders, Harley & Price, Justin. Trigonometry. 235p. 1975. text ed. 15.95 (ISBN 0-12-259667-6); instrs'. manual 3.00 (ISBN 0-12-259670-6). Acad Pr.
Flanders, Harley & Price, Justin J. Algebra. 1975. text ed. 15.95 (ISBN 0-12-259666-8); instr.s' manual 3.00 (ISBN 0-12-259669-2). Acad Pr.
--Algebra & Trigonometry. 1975. text ed. 17.95 (ISBN 0-12-259665-X); tchr's manual 3.00 (ISBN 0-12-259668-4). Acad Pr.
--A Second Course in Calculus. 1974. text ed. 19.95 (ISBN 0-12-259662-5); instrs' manual 3.00 (ISBN 0-12-259663-3). Acad Pr.
Flanders, Harley, et al. A First Course in Calculus with Analytic Geometry. 1973. 19.95 (ISBN 0-12-259657-9); instrs' manual 3.00 (ISBN 0-12-259658-7). Acad Pr.
Flanders, Helen H. & Brown, George. Vermont Folk-Songs & Ballads. LC 68-20768. iv, 256p. 1968. Repr. of 1931 ed. 18.00 (ISBN 0-8103-5010-6). Gale.
Flanders, Henry J., Jr., et al. People of the Covenant: An Introduction to the Old Testament. 2nd ed. (Illus.). 539p. 1973. 18.95 (ISBN 0-8260-3140-4). Wiley.
Flanders, M. June & Razin, Assaf, eds. Development in an Inflationary World. (Economic Theory, Econometrics & Mathematical Economics Ser.). 1981. price not set (ISBN 0-12-259750-8). Acad Pr.
Flanders, Ned A. Analyzing Teaching Behavior. (Education Ser). 1970. 19.95 (ISBN 0-201-02052-1). A-W.
Flandorffer, Tamas & Hajas, Jozsef. The Horse & Horsemanship. Kortvelyessy, Eniko, tr. (Illus.). 184p. 1979. 12.50x (ISBN 963-13-3701-4). Intl Pubns Serv.
Flandrin, J. L. Families in Former Times. LC 78-18095. (Themes in the Social Sciences Ser.). (Illus.). 1979. 39.50 (ISBN 0-521-22323-7); pap. 9.95x (ISBN 0-521-29449-5). Cambridge U Pr.
Flanigan, Patrick J., et al. Orientation to Mental Retardation: A Programmed Text. (Illus.). 216p. 1973. 13.75 (ISBN 0-398-00584-2). C C Thomas.
Flanigan, William H. & Zingale, Nancy. Political Behavior of the American Electorate. 3rd ed. 175p. 1975. pap. text ed. 5.95x o.s.i. (ISBN 0-205-04770-X). Allyn.
Flanigan, William H. & Zingale, Nancy H. Political Behavior of the American Electorate. 4th ed. 1979. pap. text ed. 8.35 (ISBN 0-205-06524-4, 7665245). Allyn.
Flanigen, E. M. & Sand, Leonard B., eds. Molecular Sieve Zeolites I & II, 2 pts. LC 77-156974. (Advances in Chemistry Ser.: Nos. 101-102). 1971. Set. 59.00 (ISBN 0-8412-0617-1); Pt. 1. 39.50 (ISBN 0-8412-0114-5); Pt. 2. 35.25 (ISBN 0-8412-0115-3). Am Chemical.
Flannagan, John F. & Marshall, K. Eric, eds. Advances in Ephemeroptera Biology. 556p. 1980. 49.50 (ISBN 0-306-40357-9, Plenum Pr). Plenum Pub.
Flanner, Hildegarde. A Vanishing Land. 60p. (Orig.). 1980. pap. 6.00 (ISBN 0-931832-15-2). No Dead Lines.
Flanner, Janet. The Cubical City: A Novel. LC 74-8655. (Lost American Fiction Ser). 440p. 1974. Repr. of 1926 ed. 13.95 (ISBN 0-8093-0700-6). S Ill U Pr.
Flannery, Edward H. Anguish of the Jews: Twenty-Three Centuries of Anti-Semitism. (Orig.). 1965. 6.95 o.p. (ISBN 0-686-66479-5); pap. 2.95 (ISBN 0-02-032280-1). Macmillan.
Flannery, Edward H., tr. see Maritain, Jacques.
Flannery, James W. Miss Annie F. Horniman & the Abbey Theatre. (Irish Theatre Ser: No. 31). 40p. 1976. pap. text ed. 3.25x (ISBN 0-85105-182-0, Dolmen Pr). Humanities.
Flannery, Melissa C. Clare's Choice. new ed. (Stories About Christian Heroes Ser.). (Illus.). (gr. 1-3). 1980. pap. 1.95 (ISBN 0-03-049431-1). Winston Pr.
Flannery, Sean. The Trinity Factor. 418p. (Orig.). 1981. pap. 2.95 (ISBN 0-441-03298-2). Charter Bks.
Flapan, Dorothy. Children's Understanding of Social Interaction. LC 67-25065. 1968. pap. text ed. 4.75x (ISBN 0-8077-1357-0). Tchrs Coll.
Flasch, Joy. Melvin B. Tolson. (U. S. Authors Ser.: No. 215). lib. bdg. 10.95 (ISBN 0-8057-0736-0). Twayne.
Flash, Edward S., Jr. Economic Advice & Presidential Leadership. LC 65-24587. 1965. 22.50x (ISBN 0-231-02827-X). Columbia U Pr.
Flatauer, S., tr. see Levy, J.
Flatauer, Susanne, tr. see Kielar, Wieslaw.
Flatt, Adrian E. Care of Cogenital Hand Anomalies. LC 77-5932. (Illus.). 1977. text ed. 39.50 (ISBN 0-8016-1586-0). Mosby.
--The Care of Minor Hand Injuries. 4th ed. LC 79-12082. (Illus.). 1979. text ed. 38.50 (ISBN 0-8016-1581-X). Mosby.
Flatte, S. M., ed. Sound Transmission Through a Fluctuating Ocean. LC 77-88676. (Cambridge Monographs on Mechanics & Applied Mathematics). (Illus.). 1979. 44.50 (ISBN 0-521-21940-X). Cambridge U Pr.
Flaubert, Gustave. The Candidate. Bd. with The Castle of Hearts. LC 76-6879. 1978. Repr. of 1904 ed. 17.00 (ISBN 0-86527-225-5). Fertig.
--A Dictionary of Platitudes. (Illus.). 1961. pap. 1.45 o.p. (ISBN 0-498-04024-0, Prpta). A S Barnes.
--The First Sentimental Education. Garman, Douglas, tr. LC 77-149947. 275p. 1972. 16.50x (ISBN 0-520-01967-9). U of Cal Pr.
--Madame Bovary. pap. 1.75. Bantam.
--Madame Bovary. De Man, Paul, ed. (Critical Editions). (gr. 9-12). 1965. pap. text ed. 5.95x (ISBN 0-393-09608-4, NortonC). Norton.
--Madame Bovary. (Classics Ser). (gr. 11 up). pap. 1.50 (ISBN 0-8049-0089-2, CL-89). Airmont.
--Madame Bovary. (Literature Ser). (gr. 10-12). 1970. pap. text ed. 3.58 (ISBN 0-87720-744-5). AMSCO Sch.
--Madame Bovary. Marmur, Mildred, tr. (Orig.). 1964. pap. 2.25 (ISBN 0-451-51365-7, CE1365, Sig Classics). NAL.
--The Temptation of Saint Anthony. LC 78-6700. 1978. Repr. of 1904 ed. 17.00 (ISBN 0-86527-312-X). Fertig.
Flaubert, Gustave, tr. Sentimental Education. pap. 1.50 o.p. (ISBN 0-451-50579-4, CW579, Sig Classics). NAL.
Flaum, Joyce. Eat to Live. LC 72-88600. 144p. 1973. pap. 1.45 o.p. (ISBN 0-668-02739-8). Arc Bks.
Flaumenhaft, Mera J., tr. see Machiavelli, Niccolo.
Flavel, John. The Mystery of Providence. 1976. pap. 2.45 (ISBN 0-85151-104-X). Banner of Truth.
Flavell, John & Ross, Lee, eds. Social Cognitive Development: Frontiers & Possible Futures. (Illus.). 336p. Date not set. price not set (ISBN 0-521-23687-8); pap. price not set (ISBN 0-521-28156-3). Cambridge U Pr.
Flavell, John H. Cognitive Development. (Illus.). 1977. 14.95x (ISBN 0-13-139774-5); pap. 9.95 (ISBN 0-13-139766-4). P-H.
Flavell, John H., jt. ed. see Elkind, David.
Flavian, C. The College Student Introduction to the World of Wall Street. (Illus.). 84p. 1974. text ed. 29.50 (ISBN 0-913314-31-5). Am Classical Coll Pr.
Flavin, Christopher. Energy & Architecture: The Solar & Conservation Potential. LC 80-54002. (Worldwatch Papers). 1980. pap. 2.00 (ISBN 0-916468-39-9). Worldwatch Inst.
--The Future of Synthetic Materials: The Petroleum Connection. (Worldwatch Papers Ser.). 1980. pap. 2.00 (ISBN 0-916468-35-6). Worldwatch Inst.
Flavin, Martin, ed. see Shirley, James.
Flavin, Matthew. Fundamental Concepts of Information Modeling. (Yourdon Press Monograph). (Illus.). 104p. (Orig.). 1981. pap. 10.00 (ISBN 0-917072-22-7). Yourdon.
Flavin, Sean, jt. auth. see Ehrman, Kenneth.
Flaviux, Josephus see Josephus, Flavius.
Flawn, P. T., jt. auth. see King, P. B.
Flax, Michael J. A Study in Comparative Urban Indicators: Conditions in 18 Large Metropolitan Areas. 1972. pap. 3.50 o.p. (ISBN 0-87766-061-1, 20006). Urban Inst.
--Survey of Urban Indicator Data, 1970-77. (An Institute Paper). 52p. 1978. pap. 3.50 (ISBN 0-87766-214-2, 21200). Urban Inst.
Flaxman, Seymour L., ed. Modern Language Teaching in Schools & Colleges. 72p. 1961. pap. 7.95x (ISBN 0-915432-61-7). NE Conf Teach Foreign.
Fleagle, Robert G. An Introduction to Atmospheric Physics. 2nd ed. LC 80-766. (International Geophysics Ser.). 1981. 29.50 (ISBN 0-12-260355-9). Acad Pr. Postponed.
Fleck, G. Peter. The Mask of Religion. LC 79-9644. (Library of Liberal Religion). 204p. 1980. 7.95 (ISBN 0-87975-125-8). Prometheus Bks.
Fleck, Ludwik. Entstehung und Entwicklung Einer Wissenschaftlichen Tatsache: Einfuehrung in Die Lehre Vom Denkstil und Denkkollektiv. (Suhrkamp Taschenbuecher Wissenschaft: Stw 312). 248p. (Ger.). 1980. pap. text ed. 7.80 (ISBN 0-686-64690-8, Pub. by Insel Verlag Germany). Suhrkamp.
Fleck, Robert & Honess, C. Brian. Data Processing & Computers: An Introduction. (Business C11 Ser.). 1978. pap. text ed. 15.95 (ISBN 0-675-08412-1); media pkg. 595.00 (ISBN 0-675-08413-X); 350.00, 2-4 sets; 250.00, 5-9 sets (ISBN 0-685-86832-X); 200.00, 10-14 sets (ISBN 0-685-86833-8); 15 or more sets 165.00. Merrill.
Flecker, James E. Hassan. LC 66-25895. (Orig.). 1968. 1.95x (ISBN 0-87830-054-6). Theatre Arts.
Flecknoe, Richard. Love's Kingdom: With a Short Treatise of the English Stage. LC 74-170431. (The English Stage Ser.: Vol. 17). lib. bdg. 50.00 (ISBN 0-8240-0600-3). Garland Pub.
Fleenor, Charles R. see Eicholz, Robert E., et al.
Fleet, A. Children's Libraries. (Grafton Books on Library Science). 1977. lib. bdg. 12.00x (ISBN 0-233-96229-8). Westview.
Fleetwood, Hugh. Fictional Lives. 166p. 1981. 13.95 (ISBN 0-241-10434-3, Pub. by Hamish Hamilton England). David & Charles.
--The Godmother. 152p. 1980. 16.95 (ISBN 0-241-10126-3, Pub. by Hamish Hamilton England). David & Charles.
Flegal, Sharon, jt. auth. see Azarnoff, Pat.
Flegmann, G. W. & George, R. A. Soils & Other Growth Media. 1978. text ed. 11.00 (ISBN 0-87055-240-6). AVI.

Flegmann, Vilma. Called to Account: The Public Accounts Committee of the House of Commons. 328p. 1980. text ed. 31.50x (ISBN 0-566-00371-6, Pub. by Gower Pub Co England). Renouf.

Fleischer, Arthur C. & James, A. Everette. Introduction to Diagnostic Sonography. LC 79-19065. 1980. 27.50 (ISBN 0-471-05473-9, Pub. by Wiley-Medical). Wiley.

Fleischer, Arthur, Jr., et al, eds. Eleventh Annual Institute on Securities Regulation. LC 70-125178. 593p. 1980. text ed. 50.00 (ISBN 0-686-69167-9, B2-1275). PLI.

Fleischer, Eugene & Goodman, Helen. Cataloguing Audiovisual Materials: A Manual Based on the AACR II. LC 80-18782. (Illus.). 1980. pap. 19.95 (ISBN 0-918212-39-1). Neal-Schuman.

Fleischer, G. A. Contingency Table Analysis for Road Safety Studies. (NAtO Advanced Study Institute Ser.: Applied Science, No. 42). 300p. 1980. 32.50x (ISBN 90-286-0960-1). Sijthoff & Noordhoff.

Fleischer, Leonore. Running. (Orig.). 1979. pap. 2.25 (ISBN 0-515-05114-4). Jove Pubns.

Fleischer, Martha H. The Iconography of the English History Play. (Salzburg Studies in English Literature, Elizabethan & Renaissance Studies: No. 10). 363p. 1974. pap. text ed. 25.00x (ISBN 0-391-01376-9). Humanities.

Fleischer, Rita M., jt. auth. see Moreland, Floyd L.

Fleischer, Robert L., et al. Nuclear Tracks in Solids. 1975. 42.50x (ISBN 0-520-02665-9); pap. 15.95x (ISBN 0-520-04096-1). U of Cal Pr.

Fleischman, H. Samuel. Gang Girl. LC 67-17269. (gr. 7-8). 1967. 5.95 o.p. (ISBN 0-385-06290-7). Doubleday.

Fleischman, Sid. The Case of Princess Tomorrow. LC 80-19518. (The Bloodhound Gang Ser.). (Illus.). 64p. (gr. 2-5). 1981. PLB 4.99 (ISBN 0-394-84674-5); pap. 1.75 (ISBN 0-394-84674-5). Random.

--The Case of the Cackling Ghost. LC 80-20059. (The Bloodhound Gang Ser.). (Illus.). 64p. (gr. 2-4). 1981. PLB 4.99 (ISBN 0-394-94673-1); pap. 1.75 (ISBN 0-394-84673-7). Random.

--Kate's Secret Riddle Book. (Easy-Read Story Books). (Illus.). (gr. k-3). 1977. PLB 6.45 s&l (ISBN 0-531-00377-9). Watts.

--McBroom & the Great Race: The McBroom Ser. (Illus.). 64p. (gr. 3-7). 1980. 7.95 (ISBN 0-316-28568-4, Atlantic-Little Brown). Little.

--Mr. Mysterious's Secrets of Magic. (Illus.). 96p. (gr. 4-6). 1975. 5.95 (ISBN 0-316-28584-6, Pub. by Atlantic Monthly Pr). Little.

Fleischmann, Glen H. Cherokee Removal 1838: An Entire Indian Nation Is Forced Out of Its Homeland. LC 75-135396. (Focus Bks). (Illus.). (gr. 7 up). 1971. PLB 4.90 o.p. (ISBN 0-531-01024-4); pap. 1.25 o.p. (ISBN 0-531-02328-1). Watts.

Fleischner, Eva. Judaism in German Christian Theology Since 1945: Christianity & Israel Considered in Terms of Mission. LC 75-22374. (ATLA Monograph: No. 8). 1975. 10.00 (ISBN 0-8108-0835-8). Scarecrow.

Fleisher, Belton M. & Kniesner, Thomas J. Labor Economics: Theory, Evidence & Policy. 2nd ed. (Illus.). 1980. text ed. 21.00 (ISBN 0-13-517433-3). P-H.

Fleisher, Martin, ed. The Clinical Biochemistry of Cancer: Proceedings of the Second Arnold O. Beckman Conference in Cliniical Chemistry. LC 79-14027. 405p. 1979. 31.95 (ISBN 0-915274-09-4). Am Assn Clinical Chem.

Fleisher, Michael L. The Encyclopedia of Comic Book Heroes: Batman, Vol. 1. LC 75-19237. (Illus.). 320p. 1976. pap. 8.95 o.s.i. (ISBN 0-02-080090-8, Collier). Macmillan.

Fleisher, Robbin. Quilts in the Attic. LC 78-3597. (Illus.). (gr. k-3). 1978. 8.95 (ISBN 0-02-735420-2, 73542). Macmillan.

Fleishman, Edwin A., jt. ed. see Alluisi, Earl A.

Fleishman, Edwin A., jt. ed. see Dunnette, Marvin D.

Fleishman, Edwin A., jt. ed. see Howell, William C.

Fleishman, Joel L. & Payne, Bruce L. Ethical Dilemmas & the Education of Policymakers. LC 80-10230. (The Teaching of Ethics Ser.). 76p. 1980. pap. 4.00 (ISBN 0-916558-05-3). Hastings Ctr Inst Soc.

Fleishman, Seymour. Printcrafts for Fun & Profit. Rubin, Caroline, ed. LC 76-78907. (How to Ser.). (Illus.). (gr. 3-6). 1977. 6.50g (ISBN 0-8075-6633-0). A Whitman.

Fleiss, Joseph L. Statistical Methods for Rates & Proportion. LC 72-8521. (Probability & Statistics Ser: Applied Section). (Illus.). 223p. 1973. 26.95 (ISBN 0-471-26370-2, Pub. by Wiley-Interscience). Wiley.

--Statistical Methods for Rates & Proportions. 2nd ed. (Probability & Statistics Ser.: Applied Probability & Statistics). 300p. 1981. 24.95 (ISBN 0-471-06428-9, Pub. by Wiley-Interscience). Wiley.

Fleissner, E. M., jt. auth. see Fleissner, Otto S.

Fleissner, Else M. Inflation. Rahmas, D. Steve, ed. LC 72-89225. (Topics of Our Times Ser.: No. 3). 32p. (Orig.). (gr. 7-12). 1973. lib. bdg. 2.75 incl. catalog cards (ISBN 0-87157-803-4); pap. 1.50 vinyl laminated covers (ISBN 0-87157-303-2). SamHar Pr.

Fleissner, Otto S. & Fleissner, E. M. Deutsches Literaturlesebuch. 4th ed. (Ger.). 1968. pap. text ed. 8.50 (ISBN 0-13-203364-X). P-H.

Flek, J., jt. auth. see Sedivec, V.

Flekenes, George T. Michigan Criminal Justice Law Manual. (Criminal Justice Ser.). 300p. 1981. pap. text ed. 18.95 (ISBN 0-8299-0369-0). West Pub.

Flemal, R. C., jt. ed. see Melhorn, W. N.

Fleming. Chitty Chitty Bang Bang. (gr. 3-5). 1980. pap. 1.50 (ISBN 0-590-03428-6, Schol Pap). Schol Bk Serv.

Fleming, Alice. Alcohol: The Delightful Poison. LC 74-22629. (Illus.). 160p. (gr. 5 up). 1975. 7.95 o.s.i. (ISBN 0-440-01796-3); PLB 7.45 (ISBN 0-440-02524-9). Delacorte.

--Contraception, Abortion, Pregnancy. LC 74-10268. 160p. 1974. 6.95 o.p. (ISBN 0-525-66396-7). Elsevier-Nelson.

--Nine Months: A Practical Guide for Expectant Mothers. Orig. Title: Nine Months: An Intelligent Woman's Guide to Pregnancy. 192p. 1974. pap. 2.95 (ISBN 0-06-463390-X, EH 390, EH). Har-Row.

--Pioneers in Print. (Adventures in Courage Ser). (Illus.). (gr. 4-7). 1971. 5.95 o.p. (ISBN 0-8092-8647-5); PLB avail. o.p. (ISBN 0-685-02311-7). Contemp Bks.

Fleming, Anne T., jt. auth. see Fleming, Karl.

Fleming, Benjamin T. Benjamin Franklin: A Biography in His Own Words. (Founding Fathers Ser.). (Illus.). 416p. (YA) 1972. 16.95 o.s.i. (ISBN 0-06-011285-7, HarpT). Har-Row.

Fleming, Berry. The Affair at Honey Hill. 104p. 1981. 5.95 (ISBN 0-9604810-2-8). Cotton Lane.

--Two Tales for Autumn. LC 79-88065. 1979. 9.95 (ISBN 0-9604810-0-1); pap. 4.95 (ISBN 0-9604810-1-X). Cotton Lane.

Fleming, D. F. The Cold War & Its Origins, 2 vols. LC 61-9193. slipcased 17.95 (ISBN 0-385-02045-7). Doubleday.

Fleming, Daniel J. & Kaput, James J. Calculus with Analytic Geometry. 1979. text ed. 26.50 scp (ISBN 0-06-382672-0, HarpC); scp study guide 6.50 (ISBN 0-06-382581-3); solutions manual avail. (ISBN 0-06-382580-5); free instructor's manual (ISBN 0-06-372860-5). Har-Row.

Fleming, David G. & Feinberg, Barry N., eds. Handbook of Engineering in Medicine & Biology, CRC. LC 75-44222. (Handbook Ser.). 1976. Vol. 1. 57.95 (ISBN 0-87819-285-9). CRC Pr.

Fleming, David L. A Contemporary Reading of the Spiritual Exercises: A Companion to St. Ignatius' Text. 2nd ed. Ganss, George E., ed. LC 80-81812. (Study Aids on Jesuit Topics Ser.: No.2). 112p. 1980. pap. 3.00 (ISBN 0-912422-47-5); smyth sewn 4.00 (ISBN 0-912422-48-3). Inst Jesuit.

Fleming, Denna F. Treaty Veto of the American Senate. LC 72-147598. (Library of War & Peace; International Law). lib. bdg. 38.00 (ISBN 0-8240-0359-4). Garland Pub.

Fleming, Donald. Science & Technology in Providence, 1760-1914: An Essay in the History of Brown University in the Metropolitan Community. (Illus.). 54p. 1952. pap. 3.00 (ISBN 0-87057-031-5, Pub. by Brown U Pr). Univ Pr of New England.

Fleming, G. H. The Unforgettable Season. LC 80-18299. (Illus.). 336p. 1981. 16.95 (ISBN 0-03-056221-X). HR&W.

Fleming, H. K. The Day They Kidnapped Queen Victoria. LC 77-18383. 1978. 7.95 o.p. (ISBN 0-312-18457-3). St Martin.

Fleming, Ian. Casino Royale. (James Bond Agent 007 Ser.). pap. 2.25 (ISBN 0-515-05895-5). Jove Pubns.

--Chitty Chitty Bang Bang. 159p. Repr. of 1964 ed. lib. bdg. 8.75x (ISBN 0-88411-983-1). Amereon Ltd.

--Chitty-Chitty-Bang-Bang. (gr. 2-4). 1964. 4.95 (ISBN 0-394-81021-X). Random.

--Diamonds Are Forever. 224p. 1980. pap. 1.95 (ISBN 0-515-05516-6). Jove Pubns.

--Doctor No. 240p. 1980. pap. 1.95 (ISBN 0-515-05517-4). Jove Pubns.

--For Your Eyes Only. (James Bond Ser.). 1981. pap. 2.25 (ISBN 0-515-06074-7). Jove Pubns.

--From Russia, with Love. 256p. 1980. pap. 1.95 (ISBN 0-515-05515-8). Jove Pubns.

--Goldfinger. 1966. 3.95 o.s.i. (ISBN 0-02-539000-7). Macmillan.

--Goldfinger. (James Bond Ser.). 272p. (Orig.). 1980. pap. 2.25 (ISBN 0-515-05839-4). Jove Pubns.

--Live & Let Die. 224p. 1980. pap. 2.25 (ISBN 0-515-05889-0). Jove Pubns.

--Moonraker. (James Bond Seer.). 1981. pap. 2.25 (ISBN 0-515-06002-X). Jove Pubns.

Fleming, J. Marcus. Essays on Economic Policy. LC 77-15991. 1978. 25.00x (ISBN 0-231-04366-X). Columbia U Pr.

Fleming, James. Interpreting the Electrocardiagram. new ed. (Illus.). 1979. text ed. 16.50 (ISBN 0-906141-05-2, Pub. by Update Pubns, England). Kluwer Boston.

Fleming, James E. The Blacksmith's Source Book: An Annotated Bibliography. 120p. 1981. write for info. (ISBN 0-8093-0989-0). S Ill U Pr.

Fleming, Jennifer B. & Washburne, Carolyn K. For Better, for Worse: A Feminist Handbook on Marriage & Other Options. LC 77-8017. (Illus.). 1977. 14.95 o.p. (ISBN 0-684-14919-2, ScribT); pap. 7.95 o.p. (ISBN 0-684-14920-6, ScribT). Scribner.

Fleming, Jo Ellen & Goplerud, Dena. Mainstreaming with Learning Sequences. 1980. pap. 9.50 (ISBN 0-8224-4260-4). Pitman Learning.

Fleming, John. The Lengthening Shadow of Slavery: A Historical Justification for Affirmative Action for Blacks in Higher Education. LC 76-21656. 158p. 1976. pap. 5.95 (ISBN 0-88258-074-4). Howard U Pr.

Fleming, John & Pevsner, Nikolaus. The Penquin Dictionary of Architecture. 1980. pap. 4.95 (ISBN 0-14-051013-3). Penguin.

Fleming, John, et al. The Penguin Dictionary of Architecture. rev. ed. (Reference Ser.). 1973. pap. 4.95 (ISBN 0-14-051013-3). Penguin.

Fleming, Joyce D. & Tiefer, Leonore. The Great American Sex Test: Who Are You, Sexually? (Illus.). 1981. 10.95 (ISBN 0-02-538720-0). Macmillan. Postponed.

Fleming, Juanita W., jt. ed. see Downs, Florence S.

Fleming, Karl & Fleming, Anne T. The First Time. pap. 1.95 o.p. (ISBN 0-425-03152-7). Berkley Pub.

Fleming, Laurence & Gore, Alan. The English Garden. (Illus.). 256p. 1981. 26.00 (ISBN 0-7181-1816-2). Merrimack Bk Serv.

Fleming, M. C. Construction & the Related Professions. (Illus.). 1980. 130.00 (ISBN 0-08-024034-8). Pergamon.

Fleming, Nicholas. August: 1939. (Illus.). 242p. 1980. 19.50x (ISBN 0-8419-7200-1). Holmes & Meier.

Fleming, P. R., ed. Twelve Hundred MCQs in Medicine. 168p. 1980. pap. text ed. 11.50 (ISBN 0-443-01571-6). Churchill.

Fleming, Phyllis J. Language of Physics. LC 77-76110. (Physics Ser.). 1978. text ed. 18.95 (ISBN 0-201-02472-1); instr's man 1.00 (ISBN 0-201-02467-5); study guide 4.95 (ISBN 0-201-02474-8). A-W.

Fleming, Quentin W. A Guide to Doing Business on the Arabian Peninsula. 225p. 1981. 29.95 (ISBN 0-8144-5666-9); comb-bound 29.95 (ISBN 0-8144-7012-2). Am Mgmt.

Fleming, Rita A., ed. Primary Care Techniques: Laboratory Tests in Ambulatory Facilities. 1st ed. LC 79-20295. (Illus.). 1980. pap. text ed. 9.50 (ISBN 0-8016-1592-5). Mosby.

Fleming, Robert E. Willard Motley. (United States Authors Ser.: No. 302). 1978. lib. bdg. 12.50 (ISBN 0-8057-7207-3). Twayne.

Fleming, Rodney R., et al, eds. American Public Works Association Directory, 1977-1980. 1978. pap. 20.00 (ISBN 0-917084-26-8). Am Public Works.

Fleming, S. J. Authenticity in Art: The Scientific Detection of Forgery. LC 75-27303. (Illus.). 150p. 1976. 16.50x (ISBN 0-8448-0752-4). Crane-Russak Co.

Fleming, Spencer. The Failure of the American Democracy: Degenerative Forces in Contemporary United States Society. enl ed. LC 72-88744. (Illus.). 65p. 1973. 37.50 (ISBN 0-913314-13-7). Am Classical Coll Pr.

--The Five Power Nuclei Which Control the Life & Destinies of the United States. (Illus.). 200p. 1976. 31.50 (ISBN 0-913314-71-4); lib. bdg. 37.50 (ISBN 0-685-59176-X). Am Classical Coll Pr.

Fleming, Susan. The Pig at Thirty-Seven Pinecrest Drive. (Illus.). (gr. 3-5). 1981. 9.95 (ISBN 0-664-32676-5). Westminster.

Fleming, Thomas. Liberty Tavern. 480p. 1977. pap. 2.50 (ISBN 0-446-91220-4). Warner Bks.

--Officer's Wives. LC 80-1063. 1981. 15.95 (ISBN 0-385-14805-4). Doubleday.

--Rulers of the City. 1980. pap. 2.25 (ISBN 0-446-82612-X). Warner Bks.

Fleming, Thomas J. & Ronalds, Francis S. Battle of Yorktown. LC 68-28247. (American Heritage Junior Library). (Illus.). 154p. (gr. 5 up). 1968. 9.95 (ISBN 0-8281-0357-7, JO20-0); PLB 6.89 o.p. (ISBN 0-06-020130-4). Am Heritage.

Fleming, W. P. Crisp County, Georgia: Historical Sketches. LC 80-13477. (Illus.). 288p. 1980. Repr. of 1932 ed. 20.00 (ISBN 0-87152-319-1). Reprint.

Fleming, Walter & Varberg, Dale. Algebra & Trigonometry. (Illus.). 1980. text ed. 18.95 (ISBN 0-13-021824-3); study guide 6.95 (ISBN 0-13-021881-2). P-H.

Fleming, Walter & Varberg, Dale E. Plane Trigonometry. 1980. text ed. 16.95 (ISBN 0-13-679043-7). P-H.

Fleming, Walter L see Johnson, Allen & Nevins, Allan.

Fleming, William. Arts & Ideas. 6th ed. LC 79-20123. 502p. 1980. pap. text ed. 14.95 (ISBN 0-03-046531-1, HoltC). HR&W.

--A Narrative of the Sufferings, & Surprizing Deliverance of William & Elizabeth Fleming, Repr. Of 1756 Ed. Incl. John Maylem: Gallic Perfidy; a Poem. Maylem, John. Repr. of 1758 ed; A Faithful Narrative of the Many Dangers & Sufferings, As Well As Wonderful Deliverances of Robert Eastburn, During His Late Captivity Among the Indians. Repr. of 1758 ed; Die Erzehlungen Von Maria le Roy und Barbara Leininger, Welche Vierthalb Jahr Unter Den Indianern Gefangen Gewesen. Repr. of 1759 ed; A Plain Narrative of the Uncommon Sufferings, & Remarkable Deliverance of Thomas Brown, of Charlestown in New-England. Repr. of 1760 ed; A Narrative of the Uncommon Sufferings, & Surprizing Deliverance of Briton Hammon, a Negro Man,...Servant to General Winslow. Repr. of 1760 ed; A Journal of the Captivity of Jean Lowry & Her Children...in Pennsylvania. Repr. of 1760 ed; Erzehlung Eines Unter Den Indianern Gewesenger Gefangenen. Repr. of 1762 ed. (Narrative of North American Indian Captivities: Vol. 8). 1978. lib. bdg. 44.00 (ISBN 0-8240-1632-7). Garland Pub.

Fleminger, A., jt. auth. see Frost, B.

Flemion, Philip F. Historical Dictionary of El Salvador. LC 78-189546. (Latin American Historical Dictionaries Ser.: No. 5). 1972. 10.00 (ISBN 0-8108-0471-9). Scarecrow.

Flemming, John. Inflation. (Illus.). 144p. 1976. 17.95x (ISBN 0-19-877085-5); pap. 4.95x (ISBN 0-19-877086-3). Oxford U Pr.

Flemming, Laraine. Reading for Results. LC 77-76422. (Illus.). 1978. pap. text ed. 9.75 (ISBN 0-395-25419-1); inst. manual 0.45 (ISBN 0-395-25430-2). HM.

Flemming, Leslie A. Another Lonely Voice: The Urdu Short Stories of Saadat Hasan Manto. 1979. 10.75. UC Ctr S&SE Asian.

Flemming, William. Artes E Ideas, Vol. 2. rev. ed. 8.75 o.p. (ISBN 0-8477-2103-5). U of PR Pr.

Flenley, D. C., ed. Recent Advances in Respiratory Medicine, No. 2. (Recent Advances Ser.). (Illus.). 272p. 1981. lib. bdg. 42.25 (ISBN 0-443-02012-4). Churchill.

Flerko, B., et al, eds. Reproduction & Development: Proceedings of the 28th International Congress of Physiological Sciences, Budapest, 1980. LC 80-41877. (Advances in Physiological Sciences: Vol. 15). (Illus.). 200p. 1981. 25.00 (ISBN 0-08-027336-X). Pergamon.

Fleron, Frederic J., Jr., ed. Technology & Communist Culture: The Socio-Cultural Impact of Technology Under Socialism. LC 77-7810. (Praeger Special Studies). 1977. text ed. 44.95 (ISBN 0-03-021821-7). Praeger.

Fleron, Frederick J., Jr., jt. ed. see Hoffman, Erik P.

Fles, Barthold. East Germany. (First Bks). (gr. 7-12). 1973. PLB 4.90 o.p. (ISBN 0-531-00807-X). Watts.

Flesch, Carl. The Memoirs of Carl Flesch. (Music Reprint Ser.). 1979. Repr. of 1957 ed. lib. bdg. 29.50 (ISBN 0-306-77574-3). Da Capo.

--Violin Fingering: It's Theory & Practice. (Music Reprint Ser.). Repr. of 1960 ed. lib. bdg. 35.00 (ISBN 0-306-79573-6). Da Capo.

Flesch, Janos. The Morra Gambit. (Algebraic Chess Openings Ser.). (Illus.). 176p. 1981. pap. 14.50 (ISBN 0-7134-2188-6, Pub. by Batsford England). David & Charles.

Flesch, Rudolf. The Art of Clear Thinking. (Illus.). 212p. 1973. pap. 2.95 (ISBN 0-06-463369-1, EH 369, EH). Har-Row.

--Why Johnny Can't Read & What You Can Do About It. 1966. pap. 1.95 (ISBN 0-06-080088-7, P88, PL). Har-Row.

--Why Johnny Still Can't Read: A New Look at the Scandal of Our Schools. LC 80-8686. 192p. 1981. 10.95 (ISBN 0-06-014842-X, HarpT). Har-Row.

Flesch, Rudolf & Lass, A. H. A New Guide to Better Writing. 1977. pap. 1.95 (ISBN 0-445-08384-0). Popular Lib.

Flesch, Yolande. Free Things for Homeowners. 96p. (Orig.). 1981. pap. 4.95 (ISBN 0-346-12533-2). Cornerstone.

Flesche, Francis La see Fletcher, Alice C. & La Flesche, Francis.

Flescher, Sharon. Zacharie Astruc: Critic, Artist & Japoniste (1883-1907) LC 77-94694. (Outstanding Dissertations in the Fine Arts Ser.). 1978. lib. bdg. 60.50 (ISBN 0-8240-3226-8). Garland Pub.

Flesher, Dale L. Accounting for Advertising Assets. 1979. pap. 4.50 (ISBN 0-938004-01-8). U MS Bus Econ.

--Operations Auditing in Hospitals. LC 75-29936. 128p. 1976. 16.95 (ISBN 0-669-00363-8). Lexington Bks.

Flesher, Dale L. & Flesher, Tonya K. Accounting for the Middle Manager. 462p. 1980. 16.95 (ISBN 0-442-23875-4). Van Nos Reinhold.

Flesher, Dale L., ed. Tax Tactics for Small Business: Pay Less Taxes Legally. 100p. (Orig.). 1980. pap. 5.00 (ISBN 0-938004-06-9). U MS Bus Econ.

Flesher, Tonya K., jt. auth. see Flesher, Dale L.

Fleshman, Bob & Fryrear, Jerry L. The Arts in Therapy. LC 80-20334. 240p. 1981. text ed. 19.95 (ISBN 0-88229-520-9); pap. text ed. 9.95 (ISBN 0-88229-762-7). Nelson-Hall.

Fleshman, Robert, jt. auth. see Fryrear, Jerry L.

Flesner, David E. & Freed, Edwin D., eds. Aging & the Aged: Problems, Opportunities, Challenges. LC 80-5869. 368p. 1980. lib. bdg. 21.00 (ISBN 0-8191-1267-4); pap. text ed. 12.75 (ISBN 0-8191-1268-2). U Pr of Amer.

Flesseman-Van Leer, E. A Faith for Today. Steely, John E., tr. LC 79-56514. (Special Studies Ser.: No. 7). 1980. 6.95 (ISBN 0-932180-06-X). Assn Baptist Profs.

Fletcher, Aaron. Blood Money. (Bounty Hunter: No. 2). 1977. pap. 1.25 (ISBN 0-8439-0471-2, Leisure Bks). Nordon Pubns.

--The Card Game. 1980. pap. 1.75 (ISBN 0-505-51456-7). Tower Bks.

--Cowboy. (Orig.). 1977. pap. 1.50 (ISBN 0-505-51152-6, BT51152). Tower Bks.

--The Flame of Chandrapore. 1979. pap. 2.25 (ISBN 0-505-51342-0). Tower Bks.

--The Labyrinth. 1977. pap. 1.95 (ISBN 0-505-51121-5, BT51121). Tower Bks.

--Treasure of the Lost City. 1976. pap. 1.25 o.p. (ISBN 0-685-73461-7, LB391, Leisure Bks). Nordon Pubns.

Fletcher, Adele W. How to Stretch Your Dollar. (Orig.). pap. 1.50 o.p. (ISBN 0-87502-001-1). Benjamin Co.

Fletcher, Alan D. & Bowers, Thomas A. Fundamentals of Advertising Research. LC 78-15516. (Advertising & Journalism Ser.). 1979. 17.95 (ISBN 0-88244-178-7). Grid Pub.

Fletcher, Alice C. & La Flesche, Francis. Omaha Tribe, 2 vols. Incl. Vol. 1. 312p (ISBN 0-8032-5756-2, BB 549, Bison); Vol. 2. viii, 347p (ISBN 0-8032-5757-0, BB 550, Bison). LC 72-175503. (Illus.). 686p. 1972. pap. 7.95 ea. U of Nebr Pr.

Fletcher, Angus. The Prophetic Moment: An Essay on Spenser. LC 73-130587. 1971. 15.00x (ISBN 0-226-25332-5). U of Chicago Pr.

Fletcher, Angus, ed. The Literature of Fact: Selected Papers from the English Institute. 1976. 12.50x (ISBN 0-231-04144-6). Columbia U Pr.

Fletcher, Anthony. A County Community in Peace & War: Sussex 1600-1660. (Illus.). 470p. 1976. text ed. 36.00x (ISBN 0-582-50024-9). Longman.

--Elizabethan Village. (Then & There Ser.). (Illus.). 1972. pap. text ed. 2.65x (ISBN 0-582-20409-7). Longman.

Fletcher, B. Universities in the Modern World. 1968. pap. 7.75 (ISBN 0-08-012762-2). Pergamon.

Fletcher, B. & Lavan, S. Civil Engineer's Technical Reference Book. 3rd ed. (Technician Ser.). (Illus.). 1980. 14.50 (ISBN 0-408-00426-6). Butterworths.

Fletcher, Barbara. Saleswoman: A Guide to Career Success. (gr. 12). 1980. pap. 2.50 (ISBN 0-671-82895-9). PB.

Fletcher, Colin. The Man from the Cave. LC 80-22548. (Illus.). 352p. 1981. 16.95 (ISBN 0-394-40695-8). Knopf.

Fletcher, Cynthia H. My Jesus Pocketbook of ABC's. (Illus.). 32p. (Orig.). (ps). pap. 0.49 (ISBN 0-937420-01-8). Stirrup Assoc.

--My Jesus Pocketbook of Nursery Rhymes. LC 80-52041. (Illus.). 32p. (Orig.). (ps). pap. 0.49 (ISBN 0-937420-00-X). Stirrup Assoc.

Fletcher, D. L., jt. auth. see Rhodes, A.

Fletcher, D. S., jt. auth. see Bradley, J. D.

Fletcher, Don. How the West Was Lost. (Illus.). 1969. pap. 2.00 (ISBN 0-87970-114-5). North Plains.

Fletcher, Dorothy. Whispers. 432p. (Orig.). 1980. pap. 2.50 (ISBN 0-89083-675-2). Zebra.

Fletcher, Edward. Antique Bottles in Color. (Color Ser.). (Illus.). 1976. 9.95 (ISBN 0-7137-0793-3, Pub by Blandford Pr England). Sterling.

Fletcher, Ella A. The Law of the Rhythmic Breath. LC 80-19750. 372p. 1980. Repr. of 1979 ed. lib. bdg. 11.95x (ISBN 0-89370-644-2). Borgo Pr.

Fletcher, F. N. Early Nevada: The Period of Exploraton Seventy-Six to Eighteen Forty-Eight. LC 80-19035. (Vintage Nevada Ser). (Illus.). xi, 195p. 1980. pap. 5.25 (ISBN 0-87417-061-3). U of Nev Pr.

Fletcher, George P. Millenium: What It Is, & What It Is Not. pap. 2.25 (ISBN 0-685-00747-2). Reiner.

Fletcher, Gilbert H. History of Radiotherapy. (Illus.). 450p. 1981. 20.00 (ISBN 0-87527-145-6). Green. Postponed.

Fletcher, Giles. English Works of Giles Fletcher, the Elder. Berry, Lloyd E., ed. (Illus.). 1964. 40.00 (ISBN 0-299-03370-8). U of Wis Pr.

Fletcher, Giles & Fletcher, Phineas. Poetical Works, 2 Vols. Boas, F. S., ed. 1970. 58.00 ea. Vol. 1 (ISBN 0-521-07773-7). Vol. 2 (ISBN 0-521-07827-X). Cambridge U Pr.

Fletcher, Gordon A. & Smoots, Vernon A. Construction Guide for Soils & Foundations. LC 73-21789. (Practical Construction Guides Ser). 420p. 1974. 32.50 (ISBN 0-471-26400-8, Pub. by Wiley-Interscience). Wiley.

Fletcher, H. & Howell, A. A. Mathematics with Understanding. Vol. 1. 19.50 (ISBN 0-08-015657-6); Vol. 2. 16.25 (ISBN 0-08-016745-4); Vol. 1. pap. 9.75 (ISBN 0-08-015656-8). Pergamon.

Fletcher, H. L. Portrait of the Wye Valley. LC 68-116674. (Portrait Bks.). (Illus.). 1968. 10.50x (ISBN 0-7091-0409-X). Intl Pubns Serv.

Fletcher, Harry. A Life of the Humber. (Illus.). 1975. 10.95 o.p. (ISBN 0-571-10723-0, Pub. by Faber & Faber). Merrimack Bk Serv.

Fletcher, Helen. Carton Crafts. (Illus.). 64p. (gr. 3-7). 1981. PLB 7.95 (ISBN 0-87460-268-8). Lion.

Fletcher, Helen J. Secret Codes. (gr. 1-3). 1980. PLB 7.90 (ISBN 0-531-04146-8). Watts.

Fletcher, Ian, ed. Decadence & the Eighteen Nineties. LC 79-20174. (Stratford-Upon-Avon Studies: Vol. 17). 1980. text ed. 32.95x (ISBN 0-8419-0568-1); pap. text ed. 15.95x (ISBN 0-8419-0569-X). Holmes & Meier.

Fletcher, Ian & Stokes, John, eds. The Book of the Rhymer's Club, Repr. Of 1892 Ed. Bd. with The Second Book of the Rhymer's Club. Repr. of 1894 ed. LC 76-20022. (Decadent Consciousness Ser.: Vol. 26). 1977. lib. bdg. 38.00 (ISBN 0-8240-2775-2). Garland Pub.

Fletcher, Ian, ed. see Adams, Francis.

Fletcher, Ian, ed. see Allen, Grant.

Fletcher, Ian, ed. see Brookfield, Charles & Glover, J. M.

Fletcher, Ian, ed. see D'Arcy, Ella.

Fletcher, Ian, ed. see Davidson, John.

Fletcher, Ian, ed. see Dixon, R. W.

Fletcher, Ian, ed. see Dowson, Ernest & Moore, Arthur.

Fletcher, Ian, ed. see Egerton, George.

Fletcher, Ian, ed. see Gissing, George.

Fletcher, Ian, ed. see Harland, Henry.

Fletcher, Ian, ed. see Henniker, Florence.

Fletcher, Ian, ed. see Hichens, Robert S.

Fletcher, Ian, ed. see Lee, Vernon.

Fletcher, Ian, ed. see Miall, A. B.

Fletcher, Ian, ed. see Moore, George.

Fletcher, Ian, ed. see O'Shaughnessy, Arthur.

Fletcher, Ian, ed. see O'Sullivan, Vincent.

Fletcher, Ian, ed. see Shiel, M. P.

Fletcher, Ian, ed. see Simcox, G. A.

Fletcher, Inglis. Bennett's Welcome. 480p. 1980. pap. 2.75 (ISBN 0-553-13448-5). Bantam.

--Lusty Wind for California. 576p. 1980. pap. 2.95 (ISBN 0-553-13393-4). Bantam.

--Men of Albemarle. 512p. 1980. pap. 2.75 (ISBN 0-553-13394-2). Bantam.

--Red Jasmine. 320p. 1976. Repr. of 1932 ed. lib. bdg. 14.95x (ISBN 0-89244-012-0). Queens Hse.

--Toil of the Brave. 560p. 1981. pap. 2.95 (ISBN 0-553-13811-1). Bantam.

--The White Leopard. 304p. 1976. Repr. of 1931 ed. lib. bdg. 14.95x (ISBN 0-89244-013-9). Queens Hse.

Fletcher, J. B., tr. see Dante Alighieri.

Fletcher, Jesse C. Bill Wallace of China. LC 63-17522. (Illus.). (gr. 7-10). 1963. pap. 1.25 (ISBN 0-8054-1113-5). Broadman.

Fletcher, John. New Directions in Literature: A Critical Approach to a Contemporary Phenomenon. 1968. text ed. 7.75x (ISBN 0-7145-0004-6). Humanities.

--Speed & Power. (gr. 5 up). 1980. PLB 7.90 (ISBN 0-531-03420-8, G21). Watts.

--The Wild-Goose Chase: A Modern Critical Edition with Commentary and Notes Based on the 1652 Folio. Lister, Rota H. & Orgel, Stephen, eds. LC 79-54349. (Renaissance Drama Second Ser.). 200p. 1980. lib. bdg. 22.00 (ISBN 0-8240-4466-5). Garland Pub.

Fletcher, John & Shakespeare, William. The Two Noble Kinsmen. Proudfoot, G. R., ed. LC 74-80902. (Regents Renaissance Drama Ser). xxvi, 141p. 1970. 9.25x (ISBN 0-8032-0286-5); pap. 2.65x (ISBN 0-8032-5287-0, BB 234, Bison). U of Nebr Pr.

Fletcher, John, jt. auth. see Beaumont, Francis.

Fletcher, John, et al. A Student Guide to the Plays of Samuel Becket. 1978. 15.00 (ISBN 0-571-10796-6, Pub. by Faber & Faber); pap. 6.95 (ISBN 0-571-10804-0). Merrimack Bk Serv.

Fletcher, L. S. & Shoup, T. E. Introduction to Engineering Including Fortran Programming. (Illus.). 1978. pap. 14.95 ref. ed. (ISBN 0-13-501858-7). P-H.

Fletcher, Margaret I. Adult & the Nursery School Child. 2nd ed. LC 59-4886. (Illus.). 1974. 7.50x o.p. (ISBN 0-8020-2167-0). U of Toronto Pr.

Fletcher, Marjorie. Thirty-Three. LC 75-32642. 72p. 1976. pap. 4.95 (ISBN 0-914086-12-X). Alicejamesbooks.

--US: Women. LC 73-86245. 72p. 1973. pap. 4.95 (ISBN 0-914086-00-6). Alicejamesbooks.

Fletcher, Max E. Economics & Social Problems. LC 78-69590. (Illus.). 1979. pap. text ed. 13.25 (ISBN 0-395-26508-8); inst. manual 0.55 (ISBN 0-395-26509-6). HM.

Fletcher, Neville. The Physics of Music. (The Fundamentals of Senior Physics Ser.: Textbook 2). 1976. pap. text ed. 4.95x (ISBN 0-686-65411-0, 00509); cassette 6.95x (ISBN 0-686-65412-9, 00510). Heinemann Ed.

Fletcher, Neville H. Chemical Physics of Ice. LC 74-75825. (Monographs on Physics). (Illus.). 1970. 41.95 (ISBN 0-521-07597-1). Cambridge U Pr.

Fletcher, Norma, jt. auth. see Ainsworth-Land, Vaune.

Fletcher, Paul & Garman, Michael, eds. Language Acquisition. LC 78-67305. 1980. 59.50 (ISBN 0-521-22521-3); pap. 14.95x (ISBN 0-521-29536-X). Cambridge U Pr.

Fletcher, Paul F. & Elson, Milton. Words You Need. 288p. (Orig.). 1981. pap. 6.00 (ISBN 0-8215-9821-X). Sadlier.

Fletcher, Phineas, jt. auth. see Fletcher, Giles.

Fletcher, R. Practical Methods of Optimization: Unconstrained Optimization, Vol. 1. LC 79-41486. 128p. 1980. 24.50 (ISBN 0-471-27711-8, Pub. by Wiley-Interscience). Wiley.

Fletcher, R., ed. Optimization. 1970. 49.00 (ISBN 0-12-260650-7). Acad Pr.

Fletcher, R. A. The Episcopate in the Kingdom of Leon in the Twelfth Century. (Historical Monographs). (Illus.). 1978. 36.00x (ISBN 0-19-821869-9). Oxford U Pr.

Fletcher, Ron & Ebert, Alan. Every Body Is Beautiful. (Illus.). 1978. 14.95 o.p. (ISBN 0-397-01312-4). Lippincott.

Fletcher, S. G., et al, eds. Turning, Vol. 2. (Engineering Craftsmen: No. H23). 1969. spiral bdg. 13.95x (ISBN 0-85083-038-9). Intl Ideas.

Fletcher, Sarah. Prayers for Little People. (Illus.). 32p. (ps-3). 1974. pap. 0.99 (ISBN 0-570-03429-9, 56-1184). Concordia.

Fletcher, Stevenson W. Pennsylvania Agriculture & Country Life: 1640-1840. LC 50-9470. 1971. 9.00 (ISBN 0-911124-33-0). Pa Hist & Mus.

--Pennsylvania Agriculture & Country Life: 1840-1940. LC 50-9470. 1955. 9.00 (ISBN 0-911124-34-9). Pa Hist & Mus.

Fletcher, Susanne. The Other Anne Fletcher. 1981. pap. 2.75 (ISBN 0-451-09805-6, E9805, Signet Bks). NAL.

Fletcher, T. J. Some Lessons in Mathematics. pap. 12.50x (ISBN 0-521-09248-5, 248). Cambridge U Pr.

Fletcher, W. W. The Pest War. LC 74-11440. 1978. pap. 11.95 (ISBN 0-470-26345-8). Halsted Pr.

Fletcher, Walter R. My Times with Dogs. LC 79-24575. (Illus.). 320p. 1980. 14.95 (ISBN 0-87605-664-8). Howell Bk.

Fletcher, William. Soviet Believers: The Religious Sector of the Population. LC 80-25495. (Illus.). 276p. 1981. 27.50x (ISBN 0-7006-0211-9). Regents Pr KS.

Flett, A. Never Shake a Skeleton. 1978. 7.95 o.s.i. (ISBN 0-8027-5392-2). Walker & Co.

Flett, T. M. Differential Analysis. Pym, J. S., ed. LC 78-67303. (Illus.). 1980. 47.50 (ISBN 0-521-22420-9). Cambridge U Pr.

Flettrich, Terry & Carr, Jan. Creole Cajun Cooking Cards from an Old New Orleans Bag. 1973. 2.95 (ISBN 0-88289-014-X). Pelican.

Fleuret, Sebastian, ed. see Schaeffer, Susan F.

Fleury, C. Rohault. La Messe: Etudes Archeologiques sur ses Monuments, 8 vols. (Illus.). 1722p. (Fr.). 1981. Repr. of 1889 ed. lib. bdg. 600.00x (ISBN 0-89241-153-8). Caratzas Bros.

Fleury, C. Rohault de see De Fleury, C. Rohault.

Fleury, C. Rohault de see Fleury, C. Rohault.

Fleuter, D. L. The Workweek Revolution: A Guide to the Changing Workweek. 1975. 9.95 o.p. (ISBN 0-201-03571-5). A-W.

Flew, A. G., ed. Logic & Language. (First Ser.). 1968. pap. 12.50x (ISBN 0-631-03420-X, Pub. by Basil Blackwell). Biblio Dist.

--Logic & Language. (Second Ser.). 1973. Repr. of 1953 ed. 12.50x (ISBN 0-631-03430-7, Pub. by Basil Blackwell England). Biblio Dist.

Flew, Antony. Introduction to Western Philosophy: Ideas & Argument from Plato to Sartre. LC 74-142179. 1971. 13.50 (ISBN 0-672-51523-7); pap. 11.95 (ISBN 0-672-61221-6). Bobbs.

--Philosophy: An Introduction. LC 79-93076. 194p. 1980. pap. text ed. 6.95 (ISBN 0-87975-127-4). Prometheus Bks.

--The Presumption of Atheism & Other Philosophical Essays on God, Freedom & Immortality. LC 75-43411. 183p. 1976. text ed. 22.50x (ISBN 0-06-492119-0). B&N.

Flew, Antony G. Hume's Philosophy of Belief. (International Library of Philosophy & Scientific Method). 1961. pap. text ed. 26.25x (ISBN 0-7100-1370-1). Humanities.

Flew, R. Newton. Idea of Perfection in Christian Theology: An Historical Study of the Christian Ideal for the Present Life. 1968. Repr. of 1934 ed. pap. text ed. 15.00x (ISBN 0-391-00507-3). Humanities.

Flew, Robert N. & Davies, Rupert E., eds. The Catholicity of Protestantism: Being a Report Presented to His Grace the Archbishop of Canterbury by a Group of Free Churchmen. LC 80-29108. 159p. 1981. Repr. of 1950 ed. lib. bdg. 17.50x (ISBN 0-313-22825-6, FLCAT). Greenwood.

Flexner, Helen T. A Quaker Childhood. 1940. 27.50x o.p. (ISBN 0-686-51294-4). Elliots Bks.

Flexner, James. World of Winslow Homer. (Library of Art). (Illus.). 1966. 15.95 (ISBN 0-8094-0235-1). Time-Life.

--World of Winslow Homer. LC 66-27562. (Library of Art Ser.). (Illus.). (gr. 6 up). 1966. 12.96 (ISBN 0-8094-0264-5, Pub. by Time-Life). Silver.

Flexner, James T. First Flowers of Our Wilderness: American Painting, the Colonial Period. (History of American Painting Ser.: Vol. 1). (Illus.). 390p. 1980. pap. 5.00 (ISBN 0-486-22180-6). Dover.

Flexner, Stuart B., jt. auth. see Wentworth, Harold.

Flibbert, Joseph. Melville & the Art of Burlesque. LC 74-80748. (Melville Studies in American Culture: No. 3). 163p. (Orig.). 1976. pap. text ed. 17.25x (ISBN 90-6203-268-0). Humanities.

Flick, E. W. Water-Based Paint Formulations. LC 75-2939. 396p. (Index of chemicals & suppliers). 1975. 28.00 o.p. (ISBN 0-8155-0571-X). Noyes.

Flick, Ernest W. Exterior Water-Based Trade Paint Formulations. LC 80-19212. 349p. 1981. 36.00 (ISBN 0-8155-0820-4). Noyes.

Flick, Maurizio, jt. auth. see Alszeghy, Zoltan.

Flick, Pauline & Jackson, Valerie. The Dollhouse Idea Book. 1976. pap. 3.50 o.p. (ISBN 0-8015-2152-1). Dutton.

Flicker, Barbara. Standards for Juvenile Justice: A Summary & Analysis. (Juvenile Justice Standards Project Ser.). 1981. softcover 7.95 (ISBN 0-88410-758-2); casebound 16.50 (ISBN 0-88410-831-7). Ballinger Pub.

--Standards for Juvenile Justice: A Summary & Analysis. (Juvenile Justice Standards Project Ser.). 1977. casebound 16.50 o.p. (ISBN 0-88410-758-2); softcover 7.95 o.p. (ISBN 0-88410-759-0). Ballinger Pub.

Fliegel, C. P., jt. ed. see Stalder, G.

Flieger, Wilhelm, jt. auth. see Keyfitz, Nathan.

Fling, Helen. Marionettes: How to Make & Work Them. (Illus.). 192p. 1973. pap. 3.50 (ISBN 0-486-22909-2). Dover.

--Marionettes: How to Make & Work Them. (Illus.). 7.25 (ISBN 0-8446-4736-5). Peter Smith.

Fling, Paul N. & Puterbaugh, Donald L. The Basic Manual of Fly Tying. LC 77-80194. (Illus.). 1979. pap. 7.95 (ISBN 0-8069-8146-6). Sterling.

Flink, James J. America Adopts the Automobile, 1895-1910. 1970. 12.00 (ISBN 0-685-16770-4). MIT Pr.

Flink, Salomon J. Israel: Chaos & Challenge: Politics vs. Economics. 265p. 1980. 18.00x (ISBN 965-20-0027-2, Pub. by Turtledove Pr Israel). Intl Schol Bk Serv.

Flinn, M. W. & Smout, T. C., eds. Essays in Social History. (Illus.). 304p. 1974. pap. 14.95x (ISBN 0-19-877017-0). Oxford U Pr.

Flinn, Michael W. The European Demographic System: 1500 to 1820. LC 80-19574. (Studies in Comparative History: No. 11). 220p. 1981. text ed. 15.00 (ISBN 0-8018-2426-5). Johns Hopkins.

--Scottish Population History: From the Seventeenth Century to the 1930s. LC 76-11060. (Illus.). 1978. 68.00 (ISBN 0-521-21173-5). Cambridge U Pr.

Flinn, Richard & Trojan, Paul K. Engineering Materials & Their Applications. 1975. 22.95 (ISBN 0-395-18916-0); instructor's manual 2.50 (ISBN 0-395-19378-8). HM.

Flinn, Richard A. Fundamentals of Metal Casting. 1963. 20.95 (ISBN 0-201-02020-3). A-W.

Flinn, Richard A. & Trojan, Paul K. Engineering Materials & Their Applications. 2nd ed. (Illus.). 753p. 1981. text ed. 22.95 (ISBN 0-395-29645-5); write for info. instr's manual (ISBN 0-395-29646-3). HM.

Flint, Austin. Insights: A Contemporary Reader. 192p. (Orig.). 1981. pap. text ed. 5.95 (ISBN 0-88377-185-3). Newbury Hse.

Flint, Charles. Charles Wesley & His Colleagues. 7.00 (ISBN 0-8183-0230-5). Pub Aff Pr.

Flint, Emily, ed. see Dincauze, Dina F.

Flint, Emily, ed. see Schaafsma, Polly.

Flint, Emily, ed. see Stone, Doris.
Flint, Emily P., ed. Creative Editing & Writing Workbook. 279p. 1979. 40.00 (ISBN 0-89964-038-9). CASE.
Flint, Jeremy & Greenwood, David. Instructions for the Defence. (Illus.). 125p. 1981. 12.50 (ISBN 0-370-30032-7, Pub. by Chatto-Bodley-Jonathan). Merrimack Bk Serv.
Flint, Kenneth C. A Storm Upon Ulster. 320p. (Orig.). 1981. pap. 2.50 (ISBN 0-553-14622-X). Bantam.
Flint, Lucy, tr. see Rowell, Margit.
Flint, R. W., tr. see Marinetti, Filippo.
Flint, R. Warren & Rabalais, Nancy N., eds. Environmental Studies of a Marine Ecosystem: South Texas Outer Continental Shelf. (Illus.). 272p. 1981. text ed. 35.00x (ISBN 0-292-72030-0). U of Tex Pr.
Flint, Richard F. Glacial & Quaternary Geology. LC 74-141198. (Illus.). 1971. 33.50 (ISBN 0-471-26435-0). Wiley.
Flint, Richard F. & Skinner, Brian J. Physical Geology. 2nd ed. LC 76-23206. 1977. text ed. 21.95x (ISBN 0-471-26442-3); study guide 7.50 (ISBN 0-471-02593-3). Wiley.
Flint, Sue. Let the Seals Live. 192p. 1980. 14.95 (ISBN 0-906191-35-1, Pub. by Thule Pr England). Intl Schol Bk Serv.
Flint, Timothy. Condensed Geography & History of the Western States or the Mississippi Valley 1828, 2 Vols. LC 70-119865. 1970. Repr. of 1828 ed. 90.00x set (ISBN 0-8201-1076-0). Schol Facsimiles.
--Recollections of the Last Ten Years in the Valley of the Mississippi. 2nd ed. LC 68-24891. (American Scene Ser). 1968. Repr. of 1826 ed. lib. bdg. 39.50 (ISBN 0-306-71136-2). Da Capo.
Flippo, Chet. Your Cheatin' Heart: A Biography of Hank Williams. 1981. 12.95 (ISBN 0-671-24114-1). S&S.
Flitman, Malcolm. Upholstering. LC 77-72396. 1977. pap. 4.95 o.p. (ISBN 0-8069-8756-1). Sterling.
Flitter, Hessel H. An Introduction to Physics in Nursing. 7th ed. (Illus.). 294p. 1976. pap. 13.95 (ISBN 0-8016-1597-6). Mosby.
Flnt, Emily, ed. see Phillips, Philip & Brown, James A.
Floan, Howard R. William Saroyan. (U. S. Authors Ser.: No. 100). 1966. lib. bdg. 10.95 (ISBN 0-8057-0652-6). Twayne.
Floberg, Marilyn. Practice in Real Estate Mathematics. 3rd ed. 1975. text ed. 13.50 scp (ISBN 0-06-453617-3, HarpC). Har-Row.
Floch, Martin H. Nutrition & Diet Therapy in Gastrointestinal Diseases. (Topics in Gastroenterology Ser.). 390p. 1981. 35.00 (ISBN 0-306-40508-3, Plenum Pr). Plenum Pub.
Flock, Warren L. Electromagnetics & the Environment: Remote Sensing & Telecommunications. (Illus.). 1979. ref. 28.00 (ISBN 0-13-248997-X). P-H.
Flocker, William J. & Hartmann, Hudson T. Plant Science: Growth, Development & Utilization of Cultivated Plants. (Illus.). 688p. 1981. text ed. 25.95 (ISBN 0-13-681056-X). P-H.
Flodin, N. W. Vitamin - Trace Mineral - Protein Interactions, Vol. 2. Horrobin, D. F., ed. (Annual Research Reviews). 1980. 30.00 (ISBN 0-88831-062-5, Dist. by Pergamon). Eden Med Res.
--Vitamin, Trace Mineral, Protein Interactions, Vol. 1. Horrobin, D. F., ed. (Annual Research Reviews). 1979. 26.40 (ISBN 0-88831-042-0). Eden Med Res.
Flodin, Nestor W. Vitamin-Trace Mineral-Protein Interactions, Vol. 3. Horribin, David F., ed. (Annual Research Reviews). 362p. 1980. 38.00 (ISBN 0-88831-085-4). Eden Med Res.
Floethe, Louise L. Farmer & His Cows. (Illus.). (gr. 1-5). 1957. reinforced bdg. 5.95 (ISBN 0-684-12396-7, ScribJ). Scribner.
--Fishing Around the World. LC 72-498. (Illus.). 40p. (gr. 1-3). 1972. write for info. (ISBN 0-684-12948-5, ScribJ). Scribner.
Flood, C. R., jt. auth. see Parkin, N.
Flood, Charles B. Rise, & Fight Again. LC 76-29619. (Illus.). 1976. 12.95 (ISBN 0-396-07356-5). Dodd.
Flood, Charles R. Welding & Metal Fabrication. 1981. text ed. price not set (ISBN 0-408-00448-7). Butterworths.
Flood, J. The Moth Hunters: Aboriginal Prehistory of the Australian Alps. (AIAS New Ser.). (Illus.). 1980. text ed. 22.00x (ISBN 0-391-00993-1); pap. text ed. 15.50x (ISBN 0-391-00994-X). Humanities.
Flood, Kenneth U., ed. Research in Transportation: Legal-Legislative & Economic Sources & Procedures. LC 72-118792. (Management Information Guides Ser.: No. 20). 1970. 30.00 (ISBN 0-8103-0820-7). Gale.
Flood, R. B. Home Fruit & Vegetable Production. LC 78-4214. 1978. 10.00 (ISBN 0-8108-1132-4). Scarecrow.
Flood, Robert. Graduation: A New Start. 128p. 1981. pap. 5.95. Moody.
Flora, James. Grandpa's Ghost Stories. 1980. pap. 1.95 (ISBN 0-689-70469-0, Aladdin). Atheneum.
--Kangaroo for Christmas. LC 62-14243. (Illus.). (gr. k-3). 1962. 5.95 o.p. (ISBN 0-15-242026-6, HJ); PLB 4.95 o.p. (ISBN 0-15-242027-4). HarBraceJ.
Flora, Joseph M. Vardis Fisher. (U. S. Authors Ser.: No. 76). 1965. lib. bdg. 12.50 (ISBN 0-8057-0252-0). Twayne.
Flora, Peter & Heidenheimer, Arnold J., eds. Development of Welfare States in Europe & America. 264p. 1981. 16.95 (ISBN 0-87855-357-6). Transaction Bks.
Flora, Snowden D. Tornadoes of the United States. (Illus.). 1953. pap. 3.95 (ISBN 0-8061-1057-0). U of Okla Pr.
Florance, Cheri L., jt. auth. see Shames, George H.
Florczyk, Sandra E., jt. auth. see Bednarski, Mary W.
Florea, J. H. ABC of Poultry Raising: A Complete Guide for the Beginner or Expert. 8.00 (ISBN 0-8446-5186-9). Peter Smith.
Floren, Lee. Bonanza at Wishbone. 1977. pap. 1.50 (ISBN 0-505-51183-5). Tower Bks.
--The Bushwackers. (Orig.). 1980. pap. 1.75 (ISBN 0-505-51531-8). Tower Bks.
--Callahan Rides Alone. 1977. pap. 1.50 (ISBN 0-505-51206-8). Tower Bks.
--Hangman's Range. 1975. pap. 0.95 o.p. (ISBN 0-685-53131-7, LB279NK, Leisure Bks). Nordon Pubns.
--Pinon Mesa. 1978. pap. 1.50 (ISBN 0-505-51266-1). Tower Bks.
--Rimrock Renegade. 1978. pap. 1.25 (ISBN 0-505-51247-5). Tower Bks.
--Rope the Wild Wind. (Orig.). 1979. pap. 1.75 (ISBN 0-532-23149-X). Manor Bks.
--Rough Country. 1976. pap. 0.95 o.p. (ISBN 0-685-69149-7, LB362NK, Leisure Bks). Nordon Pubns.
Floren, Myron, jt. auth. see Elwood, Roger.
Florence, Gene. The Collector's Encyclopedia of Occupied Japan Collectibles II. (Illus.). 1979. 12.95 (ISBN 0-89145-004-1). Collector Bks.
Florence, Mal. Trojan Heritage: A Pictorial History of USC Football. LC 80-84556. (Illus.). 184p. 1980. 16.95 (ISBN 0-938694-01-4). JCP Corp VA.
Florence, P. S. Atlas of Economic Structure & Policies, Vol. 2. LC 68-30840. 1970. 14.50 (ISBN 0-08-013218-9). Pergamon.
Florence, P. Sargant, ed. C. K. Ogden: A Collective Memoir. 1978. 12.95 o.p. (ISBN 0-301-76061-6, Pub. by Paul Elek); pap. 5.95 o.p. (ISBN 0-301-76062-4). Merrimack Bk Serv.
Florentz, C. So Wild a Dream. (Pacesetters Ser.). (Illus.). 64p. (gr. 4 up). 1978. PLB 7.95 (ISBN 0-516-02172-9). Childrens.
Flores, Angel, ed. Anthology of German Poetry from Holderlin to Rilke. 8.50 (ISBN 0-8446-1185-9). Peter Smith.
Flores, Angel, tr. see Subercaseaux, Benjamin.
Flores, Ernest Y. The Mini-Guide to Leadership. LC 80-83627. 90p. 1981. perfect bdg. 5.50 (ISBN 0-86548-037-0). Century Twenty One.
--The Nature of Leadership for Hispanics & Other Minorities. LC 80-69239. 140p. 1981. perfect bdg. 10.95 (ISBN 0-86548-036-2). Century Twenty One.
Flores, F., jt. auth. see Garcia-Moliner, F.
Flores, Frances. Desperate Longings. (Candlelight Romance Ser.). (Orig.). Date not set. pap. 1.50 (ISBN 0-440-12015-2). Dell.
Flores, Ivan. Data Structure & Management. 2nd ed. 1977. 23.95 (ISBN 0-13-197335-5). P-H.
Flores, Jose, tr. see Collins, Gary.
Flores, Jose, tr. see Karo, Nancy & Mickelson, Alvera.
Flores, Jose, tr. see Manley, G. T.
Flores, Jose, tr. see Manley & Robinson.
Flores, Rhode, tr. see Eareckson, Joni & Estes, Stephen.
Flores, Rhode, tr. see Marosi, Esteban.
Flores, Rhode, tr. see Mercado, Benjamin.
Flores, Rhode, tr. see Neimark, Paul.
Flores, Rosa. Caracolitos, 54 bks. (Crossties Ser.). (gr. k-3). 1979. Set. pap. text ed. 129.90 (ISBN 0-8332-1135-8). Economy Co.
Florescu, Radu & McNally, Raymond T. In Search of Dracula. (Illus.). 256p. 1973. pap. 2.50 (ISBN 0-446-91630-7). Warner Bks.
Florey, Francis G. Elementary Linear Algebra with Applications. LC 78-9412. (Illus.). 1979. ref. ed. 18.95 (ISBN 0-13-258251-1). P-H.
Florey, Klaus, ed. Analytical Profiles of Drug Substances, Vol. 9. 1981. 34.00 (ISBN 0-12-260809-7). Acad Pr.
Florey, Klaus, et al, eds. Analytical Profiles of Drug Substances, Vols. 1-3 & 5-6. Vol. 1, 1972. 41.00 (ISBN 0-12-260801-1); Vol. 2. 1973. 39.00 (ISBN 0-12-260802-X); Vol. 3, 1974. 36.00 (ISBN 0-12-260803-8); Vol. 4, 1975. 43.00 (ISBN 0-12-260804-6); Vol. 5, 1976. 37.50 (ISBN 0-12-260805-4); Vol. 6, 1977. 41.00 (ISBN 0-12-260806-2). Acad Pr.
Florey, R. A. General Strike. 1981. 28.95 (ISBN 0-7145-3698-9). Riverrun NY.
Florian, Douglas, jt. auth. see Linklater, Kristin.
Florian, Michael & Gaudry, Marc, eds. Transportation Supply Models. 225p. 1981. 30.00 (ISBN 0-08-026075-6). Pergamon.
Florida State University Conference on Literature & Films, Fourth. Ideas of Order in Literature & Film: Selected Papers. Ruppert, Peter, et al, eds. LC 80-2601. xiii, 135p. (Orig.). 1981. pap. 8.00 (ISBN 0-8130-0699-6). U Presses Fla.
Florin, Gustav. Interpretation of Shear & Bond in Reinforced Concrete. (Structural Engineering Ser.: Vol. 1). (Illus.). 86p. 1980. pap. 24.00x (ISBN 0-87849-033-7). Trans Tech.
--Theory & Design of Surface Structures Slabs & Plates. (Structural Engineering Ser.: Vol. 2). (Illus.). 222p. 1980. 38.00x (ISBN 0-87849-034-5); pap. 30.00 (ISBN 0-87849-035-3). Trans Tech.
Florin, John W., jt. auth. see Birdsall, Stephen S.
Florio, Anthony. Two to Get Ready. 1978. pap. 3.95 (ISBN 0-88207-635-3). Victor Bks.
Florio, Carol. Collegiate Programs for Older Adults: A Summary Report on a 1976 Survey. 52p. 1978. pap. 3.00 (ISBN 0-89192-241-5). Interbk Inc.
Florio, Carol, jt. auth. see Murphy, Judith.
Florio, J., tr. see Cartier, Jacques.
Floristan, Casiano & Duquoc, Christian, eds. Charisms in the Church Concilium, Vol. 109. 1978. pap. 4.95 (ISBN 0-8164-2168-4). Crossroad NY.
--Christian Experience, Concilium 139. (New Concilium 1980). 128p. 1980. pap. 5.95 (ISBN 0-8245-4772-1). Crossroad NY.
Floristan, Casiano, jt. ed. see Duquoc, Christian.
Florit, E. & Jemenez, J., eds. La Poesia Hispanoamericano Desde el Modernismo. 1968. 17.95 o.p. (ISBN 0-13-521807-1). P-H.
Florkin, Marcel & Mason, Howard S., eds. Comparative Biochemistry: A Comprehensive Treatise, 7 vols. Incl. Vol. 1. Sources of Free Energy. 1960. 50.50 (ISBN 0-12-261001-6); Vol. 2. Free Energy & Biological Function. 1960. 50.50 (ISBN 0-12-261002-4); Vol. 3. Constituents of Life. 1962. 71.50 (ISBN 0-12-261003-2); Vol. 4. Constituents of Life. 1962. 66.25 (ISBN 0-12-261004-0); Vol. 5. Constituents of Life. 1963. 50.50 (ISBN 0-12-261005-9); Vol. 6. Cells & Organisms. 1963. 50.50 (ISBN 0-12-261006-7); Vol. 7. Supplementary Volume. 1964. 48.50 (ISBN 0-12-261007-5). LC 67-23158. Set. 315.00 (ISBN 0-685-23113-5). Acad Pr.
Florkin, Marcel & Sheer, Bradley T., eds. Chemical Zoology, 11 vols. Incl. Vol. 1. 1967. 72.50 (ISBN 0-12-261031-8); Vol. 2. 1968. 62.50 (ISBN 0-12-261032-6); Vol. 3. 1968. 68.50 (ISBN 0-12-261033-4); Vol. 4. 1969. 58.50 (ISBN 0-12-261034-2); Vol. 5. 1970. 52.50 (ISBN 0-12-261035-0); Vol. 6. 1971. 58.50 (ISBN 0-12-261036-9); Vol. 7. 1972. 57.00 (ISBN 0-12-261037-7); Vol. 8. 1974. 75.00 (ISBN 0-12-261038-5); Vol. 9. 1974. 72.50 (ISBN 0-12-261039-3); Vol. 10. 1978. 56.50 (ISBN 0-12-261040-7); Vol. 11. Mammalia. 1979. 49.50 (ISBN 0-12-261041-5). LC 67-23158. Set. 588.75. Acad Pr.
Florman, Samuel C. Engineering & the Liberal Arts: A Technologist's Guide to History, Literature, Philosophy, Art & Music. 1968. 24.50 o.p. (ISBN 0-07-021385-2, P&RB). McGraw.
Florovsky, Georges. Ways of Russian Theology: Pt. 2. Haugh, Richard S., et al, eds. (Collected Works of Georges Florovsky). 400p. (Orig.). 1980. pap. 27.50 (ISBN 0-913124-24-9). Nordland Pub.
Flory, David, jt. auth. see Van Name, Frederick W.
Flory, Jane. We'll Have a Friend for Lunch. (gr. k-3). 1981. pap. 3.45x (ISBN 0-395-31126-8). HM.
Flory, M. A. A Book About Fans: The History of Fans & Fan-Painting. LC 72-174940. (Illus.). xiv, 141p. 1975. Repr. of 1895 ed. 20.00 (ISBN 0-8103-4049-6). Gale.
Flory, Thomas. Judge & Jury in Imperial Brazil, 1808-1871: Social Control & Political Stability in the New State. 288p. 1981. text ed. 25.00x (ISBN 0-292-74015-8). U of Tex Pr.
Flory, Thomas, tr. see Petras, James & Zemelman Merino, Hugo.
Flota, Estelle Y. Golden Nuggets. LC 80-51806. 60p. 1981. 5.95 (ISBN 0-533-04721-8). Vantage.
Floud, R. The British Machine-Tool Industry, 1850-1914. LC 75-46205. (Illus.). 180p. 1976. 29.95 (ISBN 0-521-21203-0). Cambridge U Pr.
Floud, R. & McCloskey, D., eds. The Economic History of Britain Since Seventeen Hundred: Volume 2: 1860 to the 1970s. LC 79-41645. (Illus.). 504p. Date not set. price not set (ISBN 0-521-23167-1); pap. text ed. price not set (ISBN 0-521-29843-1). Cambridge U Pr.
Flournoy, Don M., et al. The New Teachers. LC 77-184957. (Higher Education Ser.). 1972. 11.95x o.p. (ISBN 0-87589-117-9). Jossey-Bass.
Flournoy, Valerie. The Best Time of Day. LC 77-91641. (Pictureback Ser.). (Illus.). (ps-2). 1979. PLB 4.99 (ISBN 0-394-93799-6, BYR); pap. 1.25 (ISBN 0-394-83799-1). Random.
--Too Many Monkeys Paint the Town. (Golden Storytime Bks.). (Illus.). 24p. 1981. 1.95 (ISBN 0-307-11951-3, Golden Pr); PLB 1.56 (ISBN 0-686-69207-1). Western Pub.
Flower, Dean, ed. see Thoreau, Henry D.
Flower, Desmond & Reeves, James, eds. The Taste of Courage: The War 1939-45. Incl. Vol. 1. The Blitzkrieg. 1971 (ISBN 0-425-03374-0); Vol. 2. The Axis Triumphant. 1971. o.p. (ISBN 0-425-01976-4); Vol. 3. The Tide Turns. 1971. o.p. (ISBN 0-425-01991-8); Vol. 4. The Allies Advance. 1971. o.p. (ISBN 0-425-02008-8); Vol. 5. Victory & Defeat. 1971. o.p. (ISBN 0-425-02018-5). (gr. 9 up). pap. 1.75 o.p. (ISBN 0-685-24476-8, Medallion). Berkley Pub.
Flower, J. R., jt. auth. see Hurlbut, Lyman.
Flower, John, jt. auth. see Daiches, David.
Flower, John E. Literature & the Left in France. LC 76-2895. 1980. text ed. 28.50x (ISBN 0-06-492135-2). B&N.
Flowerdew, Phyllis. Pedro Books Series. Incl. A Hat for Pedro; Hats for Donkeys; Mr. Carlos & the Baby; Mrs. Carlos Wants a Car; Pedro; Pedro & the Cars; Pedro & the Kitten; The Wrong Donkey. (Illus., Ea. bk 24p.). (gr. k-2). 1978. pap. 53.40 5 ea. of 8 titles incl. reproducible shts. (ISBN 0-8372-2590-6). Bowmar-Noble.
Flowers, Ann M. Big Book of Language Through Sounds. 2nd ed. LC 79-92515. 1980. pap. text ed. 6.95x (ISBN 0-8134-2114-4, 2114). Interstate.
--The Big Book of Sounds. 3rd ed. LC 80-81413. 1980. pap. text ed. 6.95x (ISBN 0-8134-2142-X, 2142). Interstate.
Flowers, B. H. & Mendoza, E. Properties of Matter. LC 70-11815. (Manchester Physics Ser.). 1970. 34.75 (ISBN 0-471-26497-0, Pub. by Wiley-Interscience). Wiley.
Flowers, Charles M., jt. ed. see Callaway, Cason J., Jr.
Flowers, Damon B., ed. The Photography Index for 1980, Vol. IV. LC 80-640225. 160p. (Orig.). 1981. pap. 8.95 (ISBN 0-934918-03-1). Photo Res.
Flowers, John H., ed. Nebraska Symposium on Motivation, 1980: Human Cognition. LC 53-11655. (Nebraska Symposium on Motivation: Vol. 28). 264p. 1981. 16.50x (ISBN 0-8032-0620-8); pap. 9.95x (ISBN 0-8032-0621-6). U of Nebr Pr.
Flowers, Marilyn R., jt. auth. see Buchanan, James M.
Floy, Michael. The Diary of Michael Floy Jr., Bowery Village, Eighteen Thirty-Three to Eighteen Thirty-Seven. Brooks, R. A., ed. 1941. 47.50 (ISBN 0-686-51371-1). Elliots Bks.
Floyd, Ann. Cognitive Development in the School Years. LC 78-9155. 1979. 24.95 (ISBN 0-470-26429-2). Halsted Pr.
Floyd, C. M., jt. ed. see Berry, M. F.
Floyd, Charles F. Real Estate Principles. 592p. 1981. text ed. 19.95 (ISBN 0-394-32263-0). Random.
Floyd, John A., Jr. Trees & Shrubs: Ground Covers Vines. LC 79-92605. (Illus.). 256p. 1980. 17.95 (ISBN 0-8487-0512-2). Oxmoor Hse.
Floyd, John A., Jr., jt. auth. see Southern Living Gardening Staff.
Floyd, Thomas L. Digital Logic Fundamentals. (Electronics Technology Ser.). 1977. text ed. 20.95 (ISBN 0-675-08495-4); instructor's manual 3.95 (ISBN 0-685-74279-2). Merrill.
--Principles of Electric Circuits. (Illus.). 768p. 1981. text ed. 19.95 (ISBN 0-675-08081-9); tchr's. ed. 3.95 (ISBN 0-686-69499-6). Merrill.
Fluck, E. & Goldanskii, V. I. Modern Physics in Chemistry, Vol. 1. 1977. 58.00 (ISBN 0-12-261201-9). Acad Pr.
Fluck, Richard C. & Baird, C. Direlle. Agricultural Energetics. (Illus.). 1980. text ed. 19.50 (ISBN 0-87055-346-1). AVI.
Fluckiger, W. Lynn. Unique Advantages of Being a Mormon. pap. 3.95 (ISBN 0-89036-138-X). Hawkes Pub Inc.
Fluegelman, Andrew, ed. see New Games Foundation.
Fluegge, W. Stresses in Shells. 2nd ed. LC 74-183604. (Illus.). 525p. 1973. 28.30 (ISBN 0-387-05322-0). Springer-Verlag.
Flugaur, Florence, ed. The Formation of Christian Europe: An Illustrated History of the Church. Drury, John, tr. (gr. 5-9). 1980. text ed. 16.95 (ISBN 0-03-056827-7). Winston Pr.
Flugaur, Florence & Brokering, Mark, eds. The First Christians: An Illustrated History of the Church. Drury, John, tr. from Ital. (Illus.). 124p. (gr. 4-9). 1980. 16.95 (ISBN 0-03-056823-4). Winston Pr.
Flugel, J. C. The Psychology of Clothes. (Illus.). 1969. Repr. text ed. 13.50x o.p. (ISBN 0-8236-5580-6). Intl Univs Pr.

Flugge, Wilhelm, ed. Handbook of Engineering Mechanics. 1962. 69.50 o.p. (ISBN 0-07-021392-5, P&RB). McGraw.

Fluharty, George & Ross, Harold R. Public Speaking. (Orig.). 1966. pap. 3.95 o.p. (ISBN 0-06-463207-5, 207, EH). Har-Row.

Fluharty, George W & Ross, Harold R. Public Speaking. 2nd ed. (Illus.). 416p. (Orig.). 1981. pap. 5.95 (ISBN 0-06-463525-2, EH 525, EH). Har-Row.

Fluidized Combustion Conference, 1975. Proceedings. 1976. 47.50x (ISBN 0-8002-1847-7). Intl Pubns Serv.

Flumiani, C. M. The Collapse of Gold & the Tragic Dilemma of the Swiss Banks. (Illus.). 205p. 1976. 39.50 (ISBN 0-918968-18-6). Am Classical Coll Pr.

--The Decline & Decay of American Education. (Illus.). 200p. 1976. 37.50 (ISBN 0-913314-79-X). Am Classical Coll Pr.

--Economics: The Essential Knowledge Which Everybody, but Absolutely Everybody Ought to Possess of Economics & Economic Forecasting. (Essential Knowledge Ser.). (Illus.). 1978. plastic spiral bdg. 21.45 (ISBN 0-89266-115-1). Am Classical Coll.

--The Financial Education of Children & Teenagers. (Idea Books Ser.). (Illus.). 1978. 24.50 (ISBN 0-89266-127-5). Am Classical Coll Pr.

--The Large Corporation, the Perversion of the Democratic Order & the Corporate State. (Illus.). 1977. 39.50 (ISBN 0-89266-073-2). Am Classical Coll Pr.

--The Laws of History & the Caprice of Men. (Illus.). 1977. 49.75 (ISBN 0-89266-018-X). Am Classical Coll Pr.

--The New Dictionary of Strange & Ingenious Stock Market Tricks the Experts Follow in Their Search for Wealth. 215p. 1976. 37.50 (ISBN 0-89266-002-3). Am Classical Coll Pr.

--The New Expanded Dictionary of Stock Market Charts. new ed. (Illus.). 1977. 43.25 (ISBN 0-89266-050-3). Am Classical Coll Pr.

--The Physiology & Psychology of Stock Market Charts. (Illus.). 103p. 1981. 47.85 (ISBN 0-918968-84-4). Inst Econ Finan.

--Seven Unusual Business Careers: Guaranteed Maximal Profit Potential for the Intelligent College Graduate & the Daring Businessman. LC 76-115460. (Illus.). 90p. 1974. 37.50 (ISBN 0-913314-47-1). Am Classical Coll Pr.

--Stock Market & Wall Street: The Essential Knowledge Which Everybody, but Absolutely Everybody Ought to Have of the Stock Market & Wall Street. (The Essential Knowledge Ser. Books.). (Illus.). 1978. plastic spiral bdg. 28.75 (ISBN 0-89266-115-1). Am Classical Coll Pr.

--Stock Market Charts: The Essential Knowledge of Stock Market Charts, How to Interpret & Apply Them Which Everyone, but Absolutely Everybody Who Is Interested in Speculation Ought to Know. (Essential Knowldge Ser. Books). (Illus.). 1978. plastic spiral dg. 28.95 (ISBN 0-89266-119-4). Am Classical Coll Pr.

--Stock Market Manual for Teenagers. LC 72-89684. (Illus.). 70p. (YA) 1973. 14.75 (ISBN 0-913314-14-5). Am Classical Coll Pr.

--The Teenager's Life Extension Financial Test. (The Seminar for Human Development Books). (Illus.). 1978. plastic spiral bdg. 12.00 (ISBN 0-89266-124-0). Am Classical Coll Pr.

--The Teenager's Life Extension Test. (Illus.). 40p. (YA) (gr. 6 up). 1974. 12.00 (ISBN 0-913314-40-4). Am Classical Coll Pr.

--The Wall Street Manual for Teenagers. (Illus.). 80p. (gr. 7-12). 1973. 19.75 (ISBN 0-913314-24-2). Am Classical Coll Pr.

--The Wall Street Manual for Teenagers. (Illus.). 99p. 1981. 13.75 (ISBN 0-89266-287-5). Am Classical Coll Pr.

Flumiani, Carlo M. The Economic Philosophy of History & Basic Patterns in the Growth & Decline of Nations. (Illus.). 117p. 1981. 59.85 (ISBN 0-930008-77-4). Inst Econ Finan.

--The Teenager's Guidebook to Wall Street & the Stock Market. 1979. 27.75 (ISBN 0-89266-162-3). Am Classical Coll Pr.

Flumiani, Carlo M., jt. auth. see Fibonacci, Leonardo.

Flumiani, Carlo M., ed. The Best Critical Chart Studies Issued by the Stock Market Chartists Club of America. (Illus.). 1978. 47.50 (ISBN 0-89266-104-6). Am Classical Coll Pr.

Flumiani, Carlo Maria De see De Flumiani, Carlo M.

Flurry, Robert L., Jr. Symmetry Groups: Theory & Chemical Applications. (Illus.). 1980. text ed. 28.95 (ISBN 0-13-880013-8). P-H.

Flury, Patricia A. Environmental Health & Safety in the Hospital Laboratory. (Illus.). 200p. 1978. 23.75 (ISBN 0-398-03773-6). C C Thomas.

Fly Fisherman Magazine, ed. Fly Fisherman's Complete Guide to Fishing with the Fly Rod. (Illus.). 1978. 14.95 (ISBN 0-87165-013-4); pap. 7.95 (ISBN 0-87165-094-0). Ziff-Davis Pub.

Flygare, W. H. Molecular Structure & Dynamics. LC 77-16786. (Illus.). 1978. ref. 29.95 (ISBN 0-13-599753-4). P-H.

Flying Magazine, ed. America's Flying Book. LC 72-1213. (Illus.). 320p. 1972. 14.95 o.p. (ISBN 0-684-12929-9, ScribT). Scribner.

--America's Soaring Book. LC 74-32016. 1975. 12.95 o.p. (ISBN 0-684-14208-2, ScribT). Scribner.

Flying Magazine Editors, jt. auth. see Sorensen, Chris.

Flynn, Bernice, jt. auth. see Flynn, Leslie.

Flynn, Beverly. Current Perspectives in Nursing: Social Issues & Trends, Vol. 2. LC 76-57746. (Current Perspectives Ser.). (Illus.). 1979. pap. text ed. 10.50 (ISBN 0-8016-3466-0). Mosby.

Flynn, Beverly, jt. ed. see Miller, Michael H.

Flynn, Charles & McCarthy, Todd, eds. The King of the B's: Working Within the Hollywood System: an Anthology of Film History & Criticism. LC 74-10478. 1975. pap. 6.95 o.p. (ISBN 0-525-47378-5). Dutton.

Flynn, Charles P. Insult & Society: Patterns of Comparative Interaction. 1976. 11.50 (ISBN 0-8046-9152-5, National University Pub). Kennikat.

Flynn, Edith E. & Conrad, John P., eds. The New & the Old Criminology. LC 76-14130. (Praeger Special Studies). 1978. 25.95 (ISBN 0-03-040891-1). Praeger.

Flynn, Elizabeth & La Faso, John. Group Discussion As Learning Process: Sourcebook, Student Edition. LC 74-170013. 1972. pap. 8.95 (ISBN 0-8091-1589-1). Paulist Pr.

Flynn, Elizabeth G. Memories of the Industrial Workers of the World (IWW) (Occasional Papers: No. 24). 1977. 1.00 (ISBN 0-89977-025-8). Am Inst Marxist.

Flynn, Errol. Beam Ends. 1976. Repr. of 1937 ed. lib. bdg. 13.35x (ISBN 0-89966-092-4). Buccaneer Bks.

--My Wicked, Wicked Ways. 1981. pap. 2.75. Berkley Pub.

--My Wicked, Wicked Ways. 1976. Repr. of 1959 ed. lib. bdg. 17.95x (ISBN 0-89966-093-2). Buccaneer Bks.

--My Wicked, Wicked Ways. 1979. pap. 2.75 (ISBN 0-425-04686-9). Berkley Pub.

--Showdown. 1976. Repr. of 1946 ed. lib. bdg. 16.95x (ISBN 0-89966-094-0). Buccaneer Bks.

Flynn, G. Spanish for Urban Workers. LC 72-78445. 1975. pap. 7.95x o.p. (ISBN 0-87108-186-5). Pruett.

Flynn, George Q. American Catholics & the Roosevelt Presidency, 1932-1936. LC 68-12968. 288p. 1968. 11.00x (ISBN 0-8131-1165-X). U Pr of Ky.

Flynn, Gerard. Manuel Breton De los Herreros. (World Authors Ser.: No. 487). 1978. lib. bdg. 11.95 (ISBN 0-8057-6328-7). Twayne.

--Manuel Tamayo y Baus. (World Authors Ser.: Spain: No. 263). 1973. lib. bdg. 10.95 (ISBN 0-8057-2880-5). Twayne.

Flynn, Gregory A., et al, eds. The Internal Fabric of the Atlantic Alliance. 350p. 1981. text ed. 32.50 (ISBN 0-86598-039-X). Allanheld.

Flynn, J. M. Danger Zone. 1977. pap. 1.50 (ISBN 0-505-51171-1). Tower Bks.

Flynn, James R. Race, IQ, & Jensen. 320p. 1980. 27.50 (ISBN 0-7100-0651-9). Routledge & Kegan.

Flynn, Jay. Bannerman. 1976. pap. 1.25 o.p. (ISBN 0-685-72574-X, LB389, Leisure Bks). Nordon Pubns.

--Bannerman Border Incident. 1976. pap. 1.25 o.p. (ISBN 0-685-72573-1, LB401, Leisure Bks). Nordon Pubns.

--Blood on Frisco Bay. 1976. pap. 1.25 o.p. (ISBN 0-685-69143-8, LB36OZK, Leisure Bks). Nordon Pubns.

--Trouble Is My Business. 1976. pap. 1.25 o.p. (ISBN 0-685-72358-5, LB384ZK, Leisure Bks). Nordon Pubns.

Flynn, Joe B. The Design of Executive Protection Systems. (Illus.). 100p. 1979. text ed. 12.75 (ISBN 0-398-03894-5). C C Thomas.

Flynn, John Thomas. Country Squire in the White House. LC 77-167846. (FDR & the Era of the New Deal Ser). 122p. 1972. Repr. of 1940 ed. lib. bdg. 17.50 (ISBN 0-306-70324-6). Da Capo.

Flynn, Joyce. About the House. 6.95 (ISBN 0-916752-08-9). Green Hill.

Flynn, Leslie. Joseph: God's Man in Egypt. 1979. pap. 2.50 (ISBN 0-88207-788-0). Victor Bks.

Flynn, Leslie & Flynn, Bernice. God's Will: You Can Know It. 1979. pap. 2.95 (ISBN 0-88207-779-1). Victor Bks.

Flynn, Leslie B. From Clay to Rock: Personal Insights into Life from Simon Peter. LC 80-69307. 176p. 1981. pap. 5.95 (ISBN 0-915684-79-9). Christian Herald.

--Great Church Fights. 1976. pap. 1.95 o.p. (ISBN 0-88207-743-0). Victor Bks.

--Man: Ruined & Restored. 1978. pap. 3.95 (ISBN 0-88207-762-7). Victor Bks.

--Ninteen Gifts of the Spirit. LC 74-91027. 204p. 1974. pap. 3.95 (ISBN 0-88207-701-5). Victor Bks.

--Now a Word from Our Creator. 144p. 1976. pap. 2.25 o.p. (ISBN 0-88207-728-7). Victor Bks.

--You Don't Have to Go It Alone. LC 80-66722. 160p. (Orig.). 1981. pap. 4.95 (ISBN 0-89636-058-X). Accent Bks.

Flynn, Patricia, jt. auth. see Burbach, Roger.

Flynn, Patricia A. The Healing Continuum: Journeys in the Philosophy of Holistic Health. (Illus.). 568p. 1980. 14.95 (ISBN 0-87619-670-9). R J Brady.

--Holistic Health: The Art & Science of Care. (Illus.). 259p. 1980. pap. text ed. 12.95 (ISBN 0-87619-626-1). R J Brady.

Flynn, Peter. Brazil: A Political Analysis. LC 77-16243. (Nations of the Modern World Ser.). 1978. lib. bdg. 40.00x (ISBN 0-89158-747-0). Westview.

--Brazil: A Political Analysis. (Nations of the Modern World Ser.). (Illus.). 1979. pap. text ed. 12.50x (ISBN 0-89158-694-6). Westview.

Flynt, Candace. Chasing Dad. 274p. 1980. 9.95 (ISBN 0-8037-1392-4). Dial.

Flynt, Henry N., jt. auth. see Chamberlain, Samuel.

Fo, Dario. Gli Imbianchini Non Hanno Ricordi. (Easy Readers). 1979. pap. 2.90 (ISBN 0-88436-296-5). EMC.

Foa, Edna B., jt. auth. see Foa, Uriel G.

Foa, Edna B., jt. auth. see Goldstein, Alan.

Foa, Piero P., jt. ed. see Cohen, Margo P.

Foa, Uriel G. & Foa, Edna B. Societal Structures of the Mind. (Illus.). 468p. 1974. pap. 37.50 (ISBN 0-398-02932-6). C C Thomas.

Foakes, R. A. Shakespeare: From the Dark Comedies to the Last Plays. 1971. 19.00x (ISBN 0-7100-6963-4). Routledge & Kegan.

--Shakespeare, the Dark Comedies to the Last Plays: From Satire to Celebration. LC 70-146536. 200p. 1971. 9.95x (ISBN 0-8139-0327-0). U Pr of Va.

Foakes, R. A., ed. see Henslowe, Philip.

Focal Editorial Staff, ed. Cameras: The Facts, a Collector's Guide, 1957-1964. LC 80-41969. (Illus.). 528p. 1981. 45.00 (ISBN 0-240-51062-3). Focal Pr.

Fochs, Arnold, ed. Best Local-Retail Ads. 248p. 1975. pap. 14.92 (ISBN 0-685-99089-3). A J Pub.

Fock, V. A. The Theory of Space, Time & Gravitation. 2nd ed. 1964. 52.00 (ISBN 0-08-010061-9). Pergamon.

Focsa, Marcela, jt. auth. see Irimie, Cornel.

Foda, Ezzeldin. The Projected Arab Court of Justice: A Study in Regional Jurisdiction with Specific Reference to the Muslim Law of Nations. LC 79-2858. 258p. 1981. Repr. of 1957 ed. 22.50 (ISBN 0-8305-0031-6). Hyperion Conn.

Fodor. Fodor's Budget Europe, 1980. 1979. 10.95 o.p. (ISBN 0-679-00487-4); pap. 7.95 o.p. (ISBN 0-679-00488-2). McKay.

--Fodor's Budget France, 1980. 1980. pap. 4.95 o.p. (ISBN 0-679-00484-X). McKay.

--Fodor's Farwest, 1980. 1979. 10.95 o.p. (ISBN 0-679-00451-3); pap. 7.95 o.p. (ISBN 0-679-00452-1). McKay.

--Fodor's Iran, 1979. 1979. 12.95 o.p. (ISBN 0-679-00368-1). McKay.

--Fodor's People's Republic of China. 1979. 14.95 o.p. (ISBN 0-679-00397-5); pap. 10.95 o.p. (ISBN 0-679-00398-3). McKay.

Fodor, Eugene. Fodor's Great Britain: 1980. (Fodor's Travel Guide Ser.). (Illus.). 1980. 12.95 o.p. (ISBN 0-679-00510-2); pap. 9.95 o.p. (ISBN 0-679-00511-0). McKay.

--Fodor's Greece: 1980. (Fodor's Travel Guide Ser.). (Illus.). 1980. 12.95 o.p. (ISBN 0-679-00560-9); pap. 9.95 o.p. (ISBN 0-679-00561-7). McKay.

--Fodor's Israel: 1980. (Fodor's Travel Guide Ser.). (Illus.). 1980. 12.95 o.p. (ISBN 0-679-00520-X); pap. 9.95 o.p. (ISBN 0-679-00521-8). McKay.

--Fodor's Italy: 1980. (Fodor's Travel Guide Ser.). (Illus.). 1980. 12.95 o.p. (ISBN 0-679-00512-9); pap. 9.95 o.p. (ISBN 0-679-00513-7). McKay.

--Fodor's Portugal: 1980. (Fodor's Travel Guide Ser.). (Illus.). 1980. 11.95 o.p. (ISBN 0-679-00527-7). McKay.

--Fodor's South 1980. (Fodor's Travel Guide Ser.). 1979. 11.95 o.p. (ISBN 0-679-00463-7); pap. 7.95 o.p. (ISBN 0-679-00464-5). McKay.

--Fodor's Southwest 1980. (Fodor's Travel Guide Ser.). 1979. 10.95 o.p. (ISBN 0-679-00465-3); pap. 7.95 o.p. (ISBN 0-679-00466-1). McKay.

--Fodor's Spain 1980. (Fodor's Travel Guide Ser.). 1979. 12.95 o.p. (ISBN 0-679-00537-4); pap. 9.95 o.p. (ISBN 0-679-00538-2). McKay.

Fodor, Eugene, ed. Fodor's Brazil. (Fodor Travel Guides). (Illus.). 1979. 8.95 o.p. (ISBN 0-679-00550-1); pap. 5.95 o.p. (ISBN 0-679-00551-X). McKay.

Fodor, J. A. Semantics: Theories of Meaning in Generative Grammer. 1977. text ed. 18.50 scp o.p. (ISBN 0-690-00866-X, HarpC). Har-Row.

Fodor, Janet D. The Linguistic Description of Opaque Contexts. Hankamer, Jorge, ed. LC 78-66537. (Outstanding Dissertations in Linguistics Ser.). 1979. lib. bdg. 42.00 (ISBN 0-685-94397-6). Garland Pub.

--Semantics: Theories of Meaning in Generative Grammar. (Language & Thought Ser.). 240p. 1980. pap. 7.95 (ISBN 0-674-80134-2). Harvard U Pr.

Fodor, Jerry & Katz, J. J. Structure of Language. 1964. 19.95 (ISBN 0-13-854703-3). P-H.

Fodor, Jerry A. Psychological Explanation: An Introduction to the Philosophy of Psychology. 1968. pap. text ed. 5.50 (ISBN 0-394-30663-5). Random.

--Representations: Philosophical Essays on the Foundations of Cognitive Science. (Illus.). 368p. 1980. text ed. cancelled (ISBN 0-89706-011-3). Bradford Bks.

--Representations: Philosophical Essays on the Foundations of Cognitive Science. LC 81-24313. (Illus.). 384p. 1981. text ed. 20.00 (ISBN 0-89706-011-3). Bradford Bks.

Fodor, John T. & Dalis, Gus T. Health Instruction: Theory & Application. 3rd ed. LC 80-24484. (Illus.). 150p. 1981. text ed. write for info. (ISBN 0-8121-0776-4). Lea & Febiger.

Fodor, Nandor. Haunted Mind: A Psychoanalyst Looks at the Supernatural. LC 59-15675. 5.00 o.p. (ISBN 0-912326-05-0). Garrett-Helix.

Fodor, Nandor, jt. ed. see Gaynor, Frank.

Fodor, R. V. Earth in Motion: The Concept of Plate Tectonics. LC 77-12568. (Illus.). (gr. 3-7). 1978. 6.95 (ISBN 0-688-22135-1); PLB 6.67 (ISBN 0-688-32135-6). Morrow.

Fodor, R. V. & Taylor, G. J. Growing Strong. LC 79-65073. (Illus.). (gr. 4 up). 1979. 7.95 (ISBN 0-8069-4142-1); PLB 7.49 (ISBN 0-8069-4143-X). Sterling.

Fodor, Ronald. Frozen Earth: Explaining the Ice Ages. (Illus.). 64p. (gr. 6-12). 1981. PLB 7.95 (ISBN 0-89490-036-6). Enslow Pubs.

Fodor, Ronald V. Competitive Weightlifting. LC 77-93307. (Illus.). 1978. 9.95 (ISBN 0-8069-4124-3); lib. bdg. 9.29 (ISBN 0-8069-4125-1). Sterling.

--What to Eat & Why: The Science of Nutrition. LC 78-24086. (Illus.). (gr. 4-6). 1979. 6.50 (ISBN 0-688-22189-0); PLB 6.24 (ISBN 0-688-32189-5). Morrow.

Foerster, Norman. Toward Standards. LC 66-13476. 1928. 9.00x (ISBN 0-8196-0166-7). Biblo.

Foerster, Norman, et al, eds. American Poetry & Prose, 3 Vols. 5th ed. LC 70-137981. 1970. pap. 13.25 ea.; Vol. 1. pap. (ISBN 0-395-04460-X); Vol. 2. pap. (ISBN 0-395-04461-8); Vol. 3. pap. (ISBN 0-395-04462-6). HM.

--American Poetry & Prose, 2 pts. 5th ed. LC 70-137981. 1970. pap. 15.50 ea. Pt. 1 (ISBN 0-395-04458-8). Pt. 2 (ISBN 0-395-04459-6). text ed. 18.50 2 pts in one vol. (ISBN 0-686-57582-2). HM.

--Eight American Writers. 1963. 19.95x (ISBN 0-393-09524-X, NortonC). Norton.

--Introduction to American Poetry & Prose. LC 72-140999. 1971. text ed. 17.50 (ISBN 0-395-04457-X). HM.

Foerster, Werner. From the Exile to Christ: Historical Introduction to Palestinian Judaism. Harris, Gordon E., ed. LC 64-18151. 264p. 1964. pap. 7.50 (ISBN 0-8006-0978-6, 1-978). Fortress.

Fogarty, Michael. Forty to Sixty- How We Waste the Middle Aged. 250p. 1975. pap. text ed. 8.75x (ISBN 0-7199-0904-X, Pub. by Bedford England). Renouf.

Fogarty, Michael P., et al. Sex, Career & Family. LC 70-158823. 1970. 20.00x (ISBN 0-8039-0121-6); pap. 9.95x (ISBN 0-8039-0348-0). Sage.

Fogarty, Nancy. Shelley in the Twentieth Century: A Study of the Development of Shelley Criticism in England & America, 1916-71. (Salzburg Studies in English Literature, Romantic Reassessment: No. 56). 179p. 1976. pap. text ed. 25.00x (ISBN 0-391-01377-7). Humanities.

Fogdall, Richard P., jt. auth. see Fischbach, David P.

Foged, N. Diatoms in New Zealand, the North Island. (Bibliotheca Phycologica: No. 47). (Illus.). 1979. pap. text ed. 30.00x (ISBN 3-7682-1253-X). Lubrecht & Cramer.

Fogedby, Hans C. Theoretical Aspects of Mainly Low Dimensional Magnetic Systems. (Lecture Notes in Physics Ser.: Vol. 131). 163p. 1981. pap. 12.00 (ISBN 0-387-10238-8). Springer Verlag.

Fogel, Barbara R., jt. auth. see Thompson, Kenneth W.

Fogel, Catherine I. & Woods. Health Care of Women: A Nursing Perspective. LC 80-17400. (Illus.). 394p. 1981. pap. text ed. 24.95 (ISBN 0-8016-1605-0). Mosby.

Fogel, Danny & Howe, Randolph. Real Estate Is Now...Investment Analysis & Exchange. 2nd ed. 256p. (Orig.). 1979. pap. text ed. 18.95 (ISBN 0-8403-2113-9). Kendall-Hunt.

Fogel, David & Hudson, Joe, eds. Justice As Fairness: Perspectives on the Justice Model. 300p. 1981. pap. text ed. price not set (ISBN 0-87084-287-0). Anderson Pub Co.

Fogel, Joshua A. & Rowe, William T., eds. Perspectives on a Changing China: Essays in Honor of Prof. C. Martin Wilbur. (Westview Special Studies on China & East Asia). 1979. lib. bdg. 26.50x (ISBN 0-89158-091-3, Dawson). Westview.

Fogel, Marvin & Walker, Mort. How to Get into Medical School: A Comprehensive Guide. 196p. 1981. pap. 6.95 (ISBN 0-8015-3670-7, Hawthorn). Dutton.

--The Medical School Admission Adviser. 1976. pap. 5.95 o.p. (ISBN 0-8015-1628-5). Dutton.

Fogel, Seymour, jt. ed. see Gabriel, Mordecai L.

Fogelin, Maria B. The Vow. 272p. (Orig.). 1980. pap. 2.50 (ISBN 0-89083-653-1). Zebra.

Fogelin, Robert J. Wittgenstein. (Arguments of the Philosophers Ser.). 1976. 16.00x (ISBN 0-7100-8426-9). Routledge & Kegan.

Fogelman, E., jt. auth. see Ebenstein, W.

Fogelman, K. R. Leaving the Sixth Form: A Selection of Opinions. 1972. pap. text ed. 4.50x (ISBN 0-85633-002-7, NFER). Humanities.

--Piagetian Tests for the Primary School. (General Ser.). 72p. 1970. pap. text ed. 5.75x (ISBN 0-901225-50-9, NFER). Humanities.

Fogelson, Raymond D. Cherokees: A Critical Bibliography. LC 78-3254. (The Newberry Library Center for the History of the American Indian Bibliographical Ser.). 112p. 1978. pap. 4.95x (ISBN 0-253-31346-5). Ind U Pr.

Fogelson, Robert M. Violence As Protest: A Study of Riots & Ghettos. LC 80-36808. xviii, 265p. 1980. Repr. of 1971 ed. lib. bdg. 22.50x (ISBN 0-313-22642-3, FOVP). Greenwood.

Fogerty, James E., compiled by. Manuscripts Collections of the Minnesota Regional Research Centers: Guide No. 2. 92p. 1980. pap. 4.50 (ISBN 0-87351-150-6). Minn Hist.

--Preliminary Guide to the Holdings of the Minnesota Regional Research Centers. LC 76-1287. (Guide Ser.: No. 1). 1975. 1.00x (ISBN 0-87351-093-3). Minn Hist.

Fogg, G. E. Algal Cultures & Phytoplankton Ecology. 2nd ed. LC 74-27308. 144p. 1975. 15.00 (ISBN 0-299-06760-2). U of Wis Pr.

Fogg, Walter. One Thousand Sayings of History, Presented As Pictures in Prose. LC 79-143634. 1971. Repr. of 1929 ed. 28.00 (ISBN 0-8103-3779-7). Gale.

Fogg, Walter L. & Richter, Peyton E. Philosophy Looks to the Future: Confrontation, Commitment & Utopia. 2nd ed. 1978. pap. text ed. 13.95 (ISBN 0-205-06030-7, 6060307). Allyn.

Fogle, Richard H. Hawthorne's Imagery: The Proper Light & Shadow in the Major Romances. 8.95 o.p. (ISBN 0-8061-0855-X). U of Okla Pr.

Fogler, H. Russell. Analyzing the Stock Market: Statistical Evidence & Methodology. 2nd ed. LC 77-75801. (Finance & Real Estate Ser.). 1978. pap. text ed. 10.50 (ISBN 0-88244-138-8). Grid Pub.

Fogler, H. Scott. The Elements of Chemical Kinetics & Reactor Calculations: A Self-Paced Approach. (Illus.). 512p. 1974. pap. 24.95 ref. ed. (ISBN 0-13-263442-2). P-H.

Foglio, Frank, tr. Ei, Deus. (Portuguese Bks.). 1979. 1.25 (ISBN 0-8297-0791-3). Life Pubs Intl.

--Oye Dios. (Spanish Bks.). (Span.). 1978. 1.65 (ISBN 0-8297-0588-0). Life Pubs Intl.

Foh, Susan. Women & the Word of God. 6.95 (ISBN 0-87552-268-8). Presby & Reformed.

Foh, Susan T. Women & the Word of God: A Response to Biblical Feminism. 280p. 1981. pap. 6.95. Baker Bk.

Foin, Theodore C., Jr. Ecological Systems & the Environment. LC 75-25010. (Illus.). 640p. 1976. text ed. 19.50 (ISBN 0-395-20666-9); inst. manual 1.00 (ISBN 0-395-20667-7). HM.

Folan, Lilias M. Lilia's Yoga & Your Life. 1981. 8.95 (ISBN 0-02-080060-6, Collier). Macmillan.

Folb, P. I. Safety of Medicines: Evaluation & Prediction. (Illus.). 120p. 1980. pap. 12.90 (ISBN 0-387-10143-8). Springer-Verlag.

Foldvary, Fred E. The Soul of Liberty: The Universal Ethic of Freedom & Human Rights. LC 79-56782. (Illus.). 330p. 1980. pap. 6.75 (ISBN 0-9603872-1-8). Gutenberg.

Foley. The Gazelle & the Hunter. (Folk Tales Ser.). PLB 7.35 (ISBN 0-516-06480-0). Childrens.

Foley, et al. Building Math Skills. Incl. Level 1. text ed. 8.32 (ISBN 0-201-13350-4); tchr's manual with ans. 6.00 (13359); test & practice dupl. masters avail.; Level 2. text ed. 8.32; tchr's manual with ans. 6.00 (13379); test & practice dupl. masters avail.. (Gr. 7-12 Basal, Gr. 9-12 Remedial, Gr. 7-12 Supplemental). 1981. A-W.

Foley, Albert S. Dream of an Outcaste: Patrick F. Healy. 1981. 12.50 (ISBN 0-916620-31-X). Portals Pr.

Foley, Augusta E., ed. see Vega Capiro, Lope F.

Foley, Daniel J. Nursing Home Estimates for California, Illinois, Massachusetts, New York & Texas from the 1977 National Nursing Home Survey. Olmsted, Mary, ed. (Ser. 13-48). 50p. 1980. pap. text ed. 1.75 (ISBN 0-8406-0190-5). Natl Ctr Health Stats.

Foley, Donald L. Controlling London's Growth: Planning the Great Wen, 1940-1960. (Illus.). 1963. 18.50x (ISBN 0-520-00424-8). U of Cal Pr.

--Governing the London Region: Reorganization & Planning in the 1960's. LC 76-157822. (Institute of Governmental Studies, UC Berkeley & Lane Studies in Regional Environment). 1972. 18.50x (ISBN 0-520-02040-5); pap. 5.75x (ISBN 0-520-02248-3, CAMPUS81). U of Cal Pr.

Foley, Doris, jt. auth. see Morely, Jim.

Foley, Frederic J. The Great Formosan Imposter. 126p. 1980. 7.50 (ISBN 0-89955-148-3, Pub. by Mei Ya Pub Taiwan). Intl Schol Bk Serv.

Foley, Gerald & Van Buren, E. Ariane. Nuclear or Not? Choices for Our Energy Future. 1978. text ed. 18.95x o.p. (ISBN 0-435-54770-4). Heinemann Ed.

Foley, Helen S. Abstracts of Wills & Estates, Barbour County, Ala. Eighteen Fifty-Two to Eighteen Fifty-Six, Vol. 3. 122p. 1976. pap. 12.50 (ISBN 0-89308-183-3). Southern Hist Pr.

Foley, J. M., jt. auth. see De Palma, D. J.

Foley, James. Foundations of Theoretical Phonology. LC 76-27904. (Cambridge Studies in Linguistics Monographs: No. 2). 1977. 26.95 (ISBN 0-521-21466-1). Cambridge U Pr.

Foley, James W., jt. auth. see Hunter, John M.

Foley, Joan, jt. auth. see Foley, Joseph.

Foley, John F. Self-Assessment of Current Knowledge in Oncology. 1975. spiral bdg. 14.00 (ISBN 0-87488-284-2). Med Exam.

Foley, Joseph & Foley, Joan. The Chesapeake Bay Fish & Fowl Cookbook: A Treasury of Old & New Recipes from Maryland's Eastern Shore. (Illus.). 192p. 1981. 13.95 (ISBN 0-02-539560-2). Macmillan.

Foley, Rae. The Brownstone House. 1978. Repr. 1.75 o.s.i. (ISBN 0-515-04491-1). Jove Pubns.

--The Girl Who Had Everything. 1978. pap. 1.75 o.s.i. (ISBN 0-515-04806-2). Jove Pubns.

--One O'Clock at the Gotham. 1978. pap. 1.75 o.s.i. (ISBN 0-515-04494-6). Jove Pubns.

--Put Out the Light. 1978. pap. 1.50 o.s.i. (ISBN 0-515-04493-8). Jove Pubns.

--Suffer a Witch. 1978. pap. 1.75 o.s.i. (ISBN 0-515-04492-X). Jove Pubns.

--Where Helen Lies. 1978. pap. 1.75 o.s.i. (ISBN 0-515-04490-3). Jove Pubns.

Foley, Tom, illus. Sakshi Gopal: A Witness for the Wedding. (Illus.). 16p. (gr. 1-4). 1981. pap. 2.95 (ISBN 0-89647-010-5). Bala Bks.

Folger, Karen. The Story of a Young Gymnast: Tracee Talavera. 192p. (Orig.). (gr. 6 up). 1980. pap. 2.25 (ISBN 0-553-14134-1). Bantam.

Foligno, Angela Da see Da Foligno, Angela.

Folino, Joseph. Contemporary World Horoscopes, No. 1. Date not set. pap. cancelled (ISBN 0-88231-061-5). ASI Pubs Inc.

Folio Magazine Editors, ed. Handbook of Magazine Publishing. 1977. 59.95 (ISBN 0-918110-00-9). Folio.

--Magazine Publishing Management. 1977. loose leaf ed. 49.95 o.p. (ISBN 0-918110-01-7). Folio.

Folk, Karen R., jt. auth. see Wolf, Carolyn E.

Folk, R. L., et al. Field Excursion, Central Texas: Tertiary Bentonites of Central Texas. 53p. 1973. Repr. of 1961 ed. 1.25 (GB 3). Bur Econ Geology.

Folk, Robert L. Petrology of Sedimentary Rocks. 4th ed. (Illus.). 1980. pap. 11.95x (ISBN 0-914696-14-9). Hemphill.

Folkers, George F., et al, trs. The Complete Narrative Prose of Conrad Ferdinand Meyer, 2 vols. 640p. 1976. Vol. 1, 1872-1879. 27.50 (ISBN 0-8387-1036-0); Vol. 2, 1881-1891. 27.50 (ISBN 0-8387-1547-8). Bucknell U Pr.

Folks, J. Leroy. Ideas of Statistics. LC 80-14723. 352p. 1981. text ed. 15.95 (ISBN 0-471-02099-0); tchr's ed. avail. (ISBN 0-471-07969-3); write for info. study guide (ISBN 0-471-07972-3). Wiley.

Follain, James & Struyk, Raymond. Homeownership Effects of Alternate Mortgage Instruments. (An Institute Paper). 95p. 1977. pap. 6.00 (ISBN 0-87766-193-6, 18900). Urban Inst.

Follain, Jean. Canisy. Guiney, Louise & Follain, Madeleine, trs. from Fr. 80p. 1981. text ed. 9.00 (ISBN 0-937406-06-6); pap. 4.00 (ISBN 0-937406-05-8); lib. bdg. 50.00 (ISBN 0-937406-07-4). Logbridge-Rhodes.

--A World Rich in Anniversaries. rev. ed. Feeney, Mary & Matthews, William, trs. (Illus.). 96p. (Fr.). 1981. text ed. 10.00 (ISBN 0-937406-01-5); deluxe ed. 50.00 (ISBN 0-937406-02-3); pap. 5.00 (ISBN 0-937406-00-7). Logbridge-Rhodes.

Follain, Jean, jt. auth. see Graziano, Frank.

Follain, Madeleine, tr. see Follain, Jean.

Follett, B. K., jt. ed. see Reiter, R. J.

Follett, Barbara Lee. Checklist for a Perfect Wedding. rev. ed. LC 72-97272. 120p. 1973. pap. 1.95 (ISBN 0-385-04251-5, Dolp). Doubleday.

Follett, James. Churchill's Gold. 228p. 1981. 9.95 (ISBN 0-395-30526-8). HM.

--Crown Court. LC 77-24773. 1978. 7.95 o.p. (ISBN 0-312-17737-2). St Martin.

--The Wotan Warhead. 224p. 1981. pap. 2.50 (ISBN 0-445-04629-5). Popular Lib.

Follett, Ken. Eye of the Needle. (Illus.). 1981. pap. 3.50 (ISBN 0-451-09913-3, E9913, Sig). NAL.

--The Key to Rebecca. LC 80-16760. 1980. 12.95 (ISBN 0-688-03734-8). Morrow.

--The Key to Rebecca. 1981. lib. bdg. 16.95 (ISBN 0-8161-3151-1, Large Print Bks). G K Hall.

Follett, Ken, jt. auth. see Maurice.

Follett, Mary P. Creative Experience. 8.00 (ISBN 0-8446-1186-7). Peter Smith.

Follett, Muriel. New England Year: A Journal of Vermont Farm Life. LC 73-145711. 1971. Repr. of 1939 ed. 15.00 (ISBN 0-8103-3393-7). Gale.

Follett, Robert. How to Keep Score in Business: Accounting & Financial Analysis for the Non-Accountant. 1980. pap. 2.50 (ISBN 0-451-61860-2, ME1860, Ment). NAL.

Follett, Wilson. Modern American Usage: A Guide. Barzun, Jacques, ed. 443p. 1979. 12.95 (ISBN 0-8090-6950-4); pap. 6.95 (ISBN 0-8090-6950-4). Hill & Wang.

Follette, Daniel. Machining Fundamentals. Williams, Roy & Weller, E. J., eds. LC 80-51218. (Illus.). 400p. 1980. 27.50 (ISBN 0-87263-054-4). SME.

Follette, P. La see Hunter, W. F. & La Follette, P.

Folliott, Rosemary. De Bever Hall. (Illus.). 75p. 1976. 8.95 (ISBN 0-7156-1018-X, Pub. by Duckworth England). Biblio Dist.

Folliott, Rosemary, jt. auth. see De Breffney, Brian.

Follis, Anne B. I'm Not a Women's Libber, but... 128p. 1981. 7.95 (ISBN 0-687-18687-0). Abingdon.

Follmann, Joseph F. Helping the Troubled Employee. 1979. 17.95 (ISBN 0-8144-5488-7). Am Mgmt.

Folmsbee, Beulah. Little History of the Horn-Book. LC 42-36336. (Illus.). 1942. 7.50 (ISBN 0-87675-085-4). Horn Bk.

Folmsbee, Stanley J., et al. Tennessee, a Short History. LC 69-20114. (Illus.). 1969. o.p. 15.00 o.p. (ISBN 0-87049-095-8); pap. text ed. 10.00x o.p. (ISBN 0-87049-103-2). U of Tenn Pr.

Folon, Jean-Michel. The Eyewitness. 64p. 1980. 55.00 (ISBN 0-8109-0906-5). Abrams.

--Folon: The Eyewitness. (Illus.). 64p. 1980. 55.00 (ISBN 0-686-62699-0, 0906-5); limited edition aquatint with signed book 500.00 (ISBN 0-686-62700-8, 84909-1). Abrams.

Folsch, D. W., ed. The Ethology & Ethics of Farm Animal Production. (Animal Management Ser.: No. 6). 144p. (Ger. & Eng.). 1978. pap. 19.50 (ISBN 3-7643-1004-9). Birkhauser.

Folsom, Burton W., Jr. Urban Capitalists: Entrepreneurs & City Growth in the Lackawanna & Lehigh Valleys, 1800-1920. LC 80-8864. (Studies in Industry & Society: No. 1). (Illus.). 208p. 1981. text ed. 16.50x (ISBN 0-8018-2520-2). Johns Hopkins.

Folsom, Franklin. Red Power on the Rio Grande: The Native American Revolution of 1680. LC 72-85581. 160p. (gr. 7-9). 1973. 5.95 o.p. (ISBN 0-695-80374-3, T0374); lib. ed. 5.97 o.p. (ISBN 0-695-40374-5, L0374). Follett.

Folsom, James K., jt. ed. see Slotkin, Richard.

Folsom, Kenneth E. Friends, Guests & Colleagues: The Mufu System of the Late Ch'ing Period. 1968. 18.50x (ISBN 0-520-00425-6). U of Cal Pr.

Folsom, Le Roi & Culinary Inst. of America. Instructor's Guide for the Teaching of Professional Cooking. rev. ed. 272p. 1967. pap. 16.00 spiral bdg. (ISBN 0-8436-2048-X). CBI Pub.

Folsom, LeRoi A. Professional Chef & the Recipe Cards. 1974. 44.95 (ISBN 0-8436-0586-3). CBI Pub.

Folsom, LeRoj, ed. see Culinary Institute of America.

Folsom, M. M. & Kirschner, L. H. By Women. 1975. pap. text ed. 11.32 (ISBN 0-395-20500-X); instr's. resource bk. 4.64 (ISBN 0-395-20494-1). HM.

Folsom, Merrill. More Great American Mansions: And Their Stories. (Illus.). 1979. 1.50 (ISBN 0-8038-4635-5); pap. 7.95 (ISBN 0-8038-4723-8). Hastings.

Folsom, Michael, jt. auth. see Elting, Mary.

Folsom, Ralph H. Corporate Competition Law in the European Communities. LC 76-40404. (Illus.). 1978. 17.95 (ISBN 0-669-01043-X). Lexington Bks.

Folsome, Clair E. The Origin of Life: A Warm Little Pond. LC 78-10809. (Biology Ser.). (Illus.). 1979. text ed. 16.95x (ISBN 0-7167-0294-0); pap. text ed. 8.95x (ISBN 0-7167-0293-2). W H Freeman.

Folsome, Clair E., intro. by. Life: Origin & Evolution: Readings from Scientific American. LC 78-15129. (Illus.). 1979. text ed. 16.95x (ISBN 0-7167-1033-1); pap. text ed. 8.95x (ISBN 0-7167-1032-3). W H Freeman.

Folta, J. & Deck, E. Sociological Framework for Patient Care. 2nd ed. LC 78-12073. 1979. pap. 14.95 (ISBN 0-471-04496-2, Pub. by Wiley Medical). Wiley.

Foltin, L. B. Aus Nah und Fern. 2nd ed. 1963. pap. text ed. 7.70 (ISBN 0-395-04464-2). HM.

Foltman, Felician F. Manpower Information for Effective Management, 2 pts. Incl. Pt. 1. Collecting & Managing Employee Information (ISBN 0-87546-217-0); Pt. 2. Skills Inventories & Manpower Planning (ISBN 0-87546-218-9). (Key Issues Ser.: Nos. 10 & 14). 1973. pap. 2.00 ea. NY Sch Indus Rel.

Foltman, Felician F., jt. ed. see Briggs, Vernon M., Jr.

Folts, Betty, ed. see Nisbet, James D.

Folz, Joe. Psychic Healers of the Philippines. 1981. pap. 2.95 (ISBN 0-88270-508-3). Logos.

Folz, Robert. The Concept of Empire in Western Europe from the Fifth to the Fourteenth Century. Ogilvie, Sheila A., tr. from French. LC 80-18796. xv, 250p. 1980. Repr. of 1969 ed. lib. bdg. 27.50x (ISBN 0-313-22453-6, FOCO). Greenwood.

Fomin, S. V., jt. auth. see Gelfand, Izrail M.

Fonblanque, John. A Treatise of Equity. Ballow, Henry, et al, eds. LC 77-86649. (Classics of English Legal History in the Modern Era Ser.: Vol. 34). 775p. 1979. lib. bdg. 40.00 (ISBN 0-8240-3083-4). Garland Pub.

Fondane, Benjamin. La Conscience Malheureuse. LC 78-65073. (Phenomenology-Background, Foreground & Influences Ser.). 1980. lib. bdg. 33.55 (ISBN 0-8240-9565-0). Garland Pub.

Fondation des Sciences Politiques, Paris, France. Bibliographie Courante D'Articles de Periodiques Posterieurs a 1944 Sur les Problems Politiques, Economiques et Sociaux: Dixieme Supplement, 2 vols. (Library Catalogs Bib.Guides). Orig. Title: Index to Post-1944 Periodical Articles on Political Economic & Social Problems - Tenth Supplement. 1979. Set. lib. bdg. 275.00 (ISBN 0-8161-0298-8). G K Hall.

Fondiller, Harvey V., ed. The Best of Popular Photography. (Illus.). 1979. 29.95 (ISBN 0-87165-037-1); deluxe ed. 35.00 (ISBN 0-87165-037-1); deluxe ed. 100.00 signed (ISBN 0-685-96576-7). Ziff-Davis Pub.

Fondu, M., ed. Lipics & Bioprotein. (Journal: Nutrition & Metabolism: Vol. 24, Supplement 1). (Illus.). iv, 212p. 1980. 29.50 (ISBN 3-8055-1266-X). S Karger.

Fone, Byrne R., ed. Hidden Heritage: History & the Gay Imagination, an Anthology. 323p. 1979. 18.95 (ISBN 0-686-66021-8); pap. 9.95 (ISBN 0-8290-0401-7). Irvington.

Foner, Anne & Schwab, Karen. Aging & Retirement. LC 80-24765. (Social Gerontology Ser.). 192p. (Orig.). 1981. pap. text ed. 8.95 (ISBN 0-8185-0444-7). Brooks-Cole.

Foner, Anne, ed. Age in Society. LC 76-41105. (Sage Contemporary Social Science Issues: Vol. 30). 1976. 4.95x (ISBN 0-8039-0731-1). Sage.

Foner, Eric. Free Soil, Free Labor, Free Men. LC 70-97024. 1970. 17.95 (ISBN 0-19-500548-1). Oxford U Pr.

--Free Soil, Free Labor, Free Men: The Ideology of the Republican Party Before the Civil War. 1971. pap. 5.95 (ISBN 0-19-501352-2, 342, GB). Oxford U Pr.

--Politics & Ideology in the Age of the Civil War. 256p. 1981. pap. 5.95 (ISBN 0-19-502926-7, GB 646, GB). Oxford U Pr.

--Tom Paine & the American Revolution. 250p. 1976. 17.50 (ISBN 0-19-501986-5). Oxford U Pr.

Foner, Eric, ed. see Sitkoff, Harvard.

Foner, Moe. Images of Labor. (Illus.). 96p. 1981. 25.00 (ISBN 0-8298-0433-1); pap. 12.95 (ISBN 0-8298-0452-8). Pilgrim NY.

Foner, Nancy. Jamaica Farewell: Jamaican Migrants in London. LC 77-80471. 1978. 20.00x (ISBN 0-520-03544-5). U of Cal Pr.

--Status & Power in Rural Jamaica: A Study of Educational & Political Change. LC 72-5943. (Illus.). 1973. text ed. 9.25x (ISBN 0-8077-2366-5); pap. text ed. 5.75x (ISBN 0-8077-2408-4). Tchrs Coll.

Foner, P., ed. Formation of the Workingmen's Party of the U. S. 1876. (Occasional Papers: No.18). 1976. 1.25 (ISBN 0-89977-017-7). Am Inst Marxist.

Foner, Philip S. American Socialism & Black Americans: From the Age of Jackson to World War II. LC 77-71858. (Contributions in Afro-American & African Studies: No. 33). 1977. lib. bdg. 25.00 (ISBN 0-8371-9545-4, FAS/). Greenwood.

--Frederick Douglass on Women's Rights. LC 76-5326. (Contributions in Afro-American & African Studies: No. 25). (Orig.). 1976. lib. bdg. 16.95 (ISBN 0-8371-8895-4, FFD/). Greenwood.

--History of the Labor Movement in the United States, 4 vols. Incl. Vol. 1. From Colonial Times to the Founding of the American Federation of Labor. 576p. 1947. 15.00 (ISBN 0-7178-0091-1); pap. 3.95 (ISBN 0-7178-0376-7); Vol. 2. From the Founding of the American Federation of Labor to the Emergence of American Imperialism. 480p. 1955. 15.00 (ISBN 0-7178-0092-X); pap. 4.95 (ISBN 0-7178-0388-0); Vol. 3. Policies & Practices of the A. F. of L. 1900-1909. 480p. 1964. 15.00 (ISBN 0-7178-0093-8); pap. 3.95 (ISBN 0-7178-0389-9); Vol. 4. Industrial Workers of the World. 608p. 1965. 15.00 (ISBN 0-7178-0094-6); pap. 4.95 (ISBN 0-7178-0396-1). LC 47-19381. Intl Pub Co.

--History of the Labor Movement in the United States: The AFL in the Progressive Era (1910-1915, Vol. 5. 15.00 (ISBN 0-7178-0570-0); pap. 4.95 (ISBN 0-7178-0562-X). Intl Pub Co.

--Women & the American Labor Movement: From World War I to the Present. LC 80-753. (Illus.). 1980. 22.50 (ISBN 0-02-910380-0). Free Pr.

Foner, Philip S. & Lewis, Ronald L. The Black Worker: From Nineteen Hundred to Nineteen Nineteen, Vol. V. 1980. 17.50x (ISBN 0-87722-184-7). Temple U Pr.

Foner, Philip S., ed. Black Panthers Speak. LC 76-134927. 1970. pap. 2.95 o.s.i. (ISBN 0-397-00636-5). Lippincott.

--The Black Worker: The Era of Post-War Prosperity & the Great Depression, 1920 to 1936, Vol. VI. Lewis, Ronald L. 400p. 1981. 17.50x (ISBN 0-87722-196-0). Temple U Pr.

Foner, Philip S., ed. see Du Bois, William E.

Foner, Phillip S. Labor & the American Revolution. LC 76-18034. 1976. lib. bdg. 17.95 (ISBN 0-8371-9003-7, FLA/). Greenwood.

Fones, Kathy, ed. see Editors of Bicycling.

Fong, B. & Resnick, M. The Child: Development Through Adolescence. 1980. 16.95 (ISBN 0-8053-9010-3); instrs guide-test item file 3.95 (ISBN 0-8053-9011-1); study guide 6.95 (ISBN 0-8053-9012-X); project & film guide 1.95 (ISBN 0-686-65168-5). A-W.

Fong, Bernadine & Resnick, Miriam. The Child: Development Through Adolescence. 1980. 16.95 (ISBN 0-8053-9010-3); study guide 6.95 (ISBN 0-8053-9012-X). Benjamin-Cummings.

Fong, Leo T. Choy Lay Fut Kung-Fu. Alston, Pat, ed. LC 70-181999. (Series 307). (Illus.). 1972. pap. text ed. 6.95 (ISBN 0-89750-035-0). Ohara Pubns.

Fong, Paul, ed. see Brauer, Richard.

Fong, Wen, ed. The Great Bronze Age of China: An Exhibition from the People's Republic of China. (Illus.). xviii, 404p. 1980. 25.00 (ISBN 0-87099-226-0). Metro Mus Art.

Fong, Wen, intro. by see Fong Wen.

Fong Wen, tr. from Chinese. Returning Home: Tao-Chi's Album of Landscapes and Flowers. Fong, Wen, intro. by. LC 76-15911. (Illus.). 92p. 1976. slipcase 25.00 (ISBN 0-8076-0827-0). Braziller.

Fonnum, Frade, ed. Amino Acids As Chemical Transmitters. LC 78-2362. (NATO Advanced Study Institutes Ser.: Series A, Life Sciences, Vol. 16). 759p. 1978. 49.50 (ISBN 0-306-35616-3, Plenum Pr). Plenum Pub.

Fonseca, A. J., ed. The Marxian Dilemma: Transformation of Values to Prices. 1980. 10.00x (ISBN 0-8364-0654-0, Pub. by Manohar India). South Asia Bks.

Fonseca, F. Peixoto Da see Da Fonseca, F. Peixoto.

Fonseca, John R. Consumer Credit Compliance Manual. LC 74-31560. (Commercial Law Library). 1975. 47.50 (ISBN 0-686-20647-9). Lawyers Co-Op.

Fonseca, John R., jt. auth. see Clark, Barkley.

Fonseca, John R., jt. auth. see Squillante, Alphonse M.

Fonseca, John R., jt. auth. see Woodroof, M. G., 3rd.

Fonstad, Karen W. The Atlas of the Middle-Earth. 224p. 1981. 14.95 (ISBN 0-686-69045-1). HM.

Fontaine, Joan. No Bed of Roses. 1979. pap. 2.75 (ISBN 0-425-05028-9). Berkley Pub.

Fontaine, Margaret. Love Among the Butterflies: The Secret Life of a Victorian Lady. 256p. 1981. 19.95 (ISBN 0-316-28942-6). Little.

Fontaine, P. Basic Formal Structures in Music. 1967. text ed. 17.95 (ISBN 0-13-061416-5). P-H.

Fontaine, Robert. Humorous Monologues for Teen-Agers. (YA) 1975. Repr. 8.95 (ISBN 0-8238-0125-X). Plays.

Fontaine, Roger W. The Andean Pact: A Political Analysis. LC 76-54540. (The Washington Papers Ser.: No. 45). 1977. 3.50x (ISBN 0-8039-0790-7). Sage.

Fontana, Bernard L. Tarahumara: Where Night Is the Day of the Moon. LC 78-71375. (Illus.). 1979. 37.50 (ISBN 0-87358-183-0). Northland.

Fontana, Frank, jt. auth. see Gross, Nancy D.

Fontana, Vincent J. Maltreated Child: The Maltreatment Syndrome in Children - A Medical, Legal & Social Guide. 4th ed. (Illus.). 192p. 1979. 17.50 (ISBN 0-398-03904-6). C C Thomas.

Fontane, Theodor. Die Poggenpuhls. Barlow, Derrick, ed. pap. 10.00x (ISBN 0-631-01640-6, Pub. by Basil Blackwell). Biblio Dist.

--Sir Ribbeck of Ribbeck of Havelland. Shub, Elizabeth, tr. LC 69-12746. (Illus.). (gr. k-3). 1969. 4.95g o.s.i. (ISBN 0-02-735630-2). Macmillan.

Fontanella De Weinberg, M. B., ed. Vicus, Linguistica, Vol. 1. (Illus.). 1979. text ed. 34.25x (ISBN 0-391-01248-7). Humanities.

--Vicus, Linguistica, Vol. 2. (Illus.). 1979. text ed. 34.25x (ISBN 0-391-01247-9). Humanities.

Fonteneau, et al, eds. Larousse Illustrated French-English, English-French Dictionary for Young Readers. 1974. 21.25 o.p. (ISBN 2-03-051431-4, 3794). Larousse.

Fonteneau, M. & Theureau, S. Mon Premier Larousse en couleurs. (Illus., Fr.). 27.25 (ISBN 2-03-051403-9, 3795). Larousse.

Fonteneau, Marthe. Mon Larousse en Images. (Illus.). 16.75 (ISBN 0-686-65648-2). Larousse.

Fontenelle. La Republique des Philsophes du Histoire des Ajaoiens. (Fr.). 1977. Repr. of 1768 ed. lib. bdg. 27.50x o.p. (ISBN 0-8287-0352-3). Clearwater Pub.

Fontenelle, Don. How to Live with Your Children. LC 80-21261. (Illus.). 264p. (Orig.). 1981. write for info. (ISBN 0-930256-07-7); pap. 9.95. Almar.

Fontenelle, Maurice De see De Fontenelle, Maurice.

Fontenot, Mary A. Clovis Crawfish & the Singing Cigales. 48p. 1981. 6.95 (ISBN 0-88289-270-3). Pelican.

Fontenot, Peggy Joan. I Almost Burned in Hell. 1978. 5.50 o.p. (ISBN 0-682-49078-4). Exposition.

Fontenrose, Joseph. The Delphic Oracle: Its Responses & Operations. LC 76-47969. 1978. 30.00x (ISBN 0-520-03360-4). U of Cal Pr.

--The Delphic Oracle: Its Responses & Operations. 1981. pap. 10.95 (ISBN 0-520-04359-6, CAL 490). U of Cal Pr.

--Python. 1959. 27.00x (ISBN 0-8196-0285-X). Biblo.

--Python: A Study of Delphic Myth & Its Origins. 637p. 1980. 30.00x (ISBN 0-520-04106-2); pap. 8.95 (ISBN 0-520-04091-0, CAL 449). U of Cal Pr.

Fontes, Norman E., jt. auth. see Miller, Gerald R.

Fontes, Rick, jt. auth. see Wright, Sharon.

Fonteyn, Margot. Margot Fonteyn: Autobiography. (Illus.). 1977. pap. 2.50 o.s.i. (ISBN 0-446-81380-X). Warner Bks.

Fonts, Alfredo R. Histology & Embryology Notes for Dental Assistants & Dental Hygienists. 1980. pap. text ed. 8.50 (ISBN 0-89669-029-6). Collegium Bk Pubs.

Food & Nutrition Board. Folic Acid: Biochemistry & Physiology in Relation to the Human Nutrition Requirement. LC 77-8182. 1977. pap. text ed. 13.50 (ISBN 0-309-02605-9). Natl Acad Pr.

--Human Vitamin B-Six Requirements. 1978. pap. 13.25 (ISBN 0-309-02642-3). Natl Acad Pr.

--Laboratory Indices of Nutritional Status in Pregnancy. 1978. pap. 9.25 (ISBN 0-309-02729-2). Natl Acad Pr.

--Nutrition and Fertility Interrelationships. 1975. pap. 4.50 (ISBN 0-309-02341-6). Natl Acad Pr.

--Radionuclides in Foods. 2nd rev. ed. LC 62-60075. (Illus.). 104p. 1973. pap. 5.25 (ISBN 0-309-02113-8). Natl Acad Pr.

--Toxicants Occurring Naturally in Foods. rev. 2nd ed. (Illus.). 704p. 1973. 17.25 (ISBN 0-309-02117-0). Natl Acad Pr.

Food & Nutrition Board, jt. auth. see Dietary Allowances Committee.

Food And Nutrition Board, jt. auth. see Food Protection Committee.

Food and Nutrition Board - Division of Biology and Agriculture. Maternal Nutrition & the Course of Pregnancy. LC 72-605179. (Illus., Orig.). 1970. pap. text ed. 8.25 (ISBN 0-309-01761-0). Natl Acad Pr.

Food & Nutrition Board, National Research Council. Prevention of Microbial & Parasitic Hazard Associated with Processed Foods: A Guide for the Food Processor. 1975. pap. 5.75 (ISBN 0-309-02343-5). Natl Acad Pr.

--A Selected Annotated Bibliography on Breast Feeding 1970-1977. 1978. pap. text ed. 6.50 (ISBN 0-309-02796-9). Natl Acad Pr.

Food & Nutrition Board, Natl Research Council. Technology of Fortification of Foods. 114p. 1975. pap. 7.25 (ISBN 0-309-02415-3). Natl Acad Pr.

Food & Nutrition Board, Natural Research Council, jt. auth. see Agricultural & Renewable Resources Board.

Food Processors Institute. Canned Foods: Principles of Thermal Process Control, Acidification & Container Closure Evaluation. rev. 3rd ed. 224p. 1979. pap. 35.00 (ISBN 0-937774-02-2). Food Processors.

--A Guide for Waste Management in the Food Processing Industry, Vol. 1. Katsuyama, Allen M., ed. LC 79-115086. 276p. 1979. pap. text ed. 50.00 (ISBN 0-937774-00-6). Food Processors.

--Principles of Food Processing Sanitation. Katsuyama, Allen, ed. LC 79-57624. 303p. (Orig.). 1980. pap. 40.00 (ISBN 0-937774-03-0). Food Processors.

Food Protection Committee. Food Chemicals Codex. 2nd ed. (Illus.). 1088p. 1972. 28.00 (ISBN 0-309-01949-4). Natl Acad Pr.

--Use of Human Subjects in Safety Evaluation of Food Chemicals. 1967. pap. 6.25 (ISBN 0-309-01491-3). Natl Acad Pr.

Food Protection Committee & Food And Nutrition Board. Food Colors. LC 70-176233. 1971. pap. 3.25 o.p. (ISBN 0-309-01930-3). Natl Acad Pr.

Food Safety Council, Columbia, U. S. A., ed. Proposed System for Food Safety Assessment: A Comprehensive Report on the Issues of Food Ingredient Testing. new ed. LC 78-40901. (Illus.). 1978. pap. text ed. 23.00 (ISBN 0-08-023752-5). Pergamon.

Foodservice Editors of CBI. The Professional Host. LC 80-15609. (Illus.). 496p. 1980. 24.95 (ISBN 0-8436-2154-0). CBI Pub.

Fooner, Michael. Interpol. 1977. pap. 1.95 o.p. (ISBN 0-445-08580-0). Popular Lib.

Foose, Sandra L. More Scrap Savers Stitchery. LC 80-2740. 1981. 12.95 (ISBN 0-385-17526-4). Doubleday.

Fooshee, George & Fooshee, Marjean. You Can Beat the Money Squeeze. 1980. pap. 4.95 (ISBN 0-8007-5030-6). Revell.

Fooshee, Marjean, jt. auth. see Fooshee, George.

Foot, David K. Public Employment & Compensation in Canada: Myths & Realities. 188p. 1978. pap. text ed. 10.95x (ISBN 0-409-88600-9, Pub. by Inst Res Pub Canada). Renouf.

--Public Employment in Canada: Statistical Series. 217p. 1979. pap. text ed. 15.00x (ISBN 0-409-88603-3, Pub. by Inst Res Pub Canada). Renouf.

Foot, Hugh C., jt. auth. see Chapman, Antony J.

Foot, Hugh C., et al. Friendship & Social Relations in Children. LC 79-40637. 1980. 51.25 (ISBN 0-471-27628-6, Pub. by Wiley-Interscience). Wiley.

Foot, M. R., ed. see Gladstone, William E.

Foot, Philippa. Virtues & Vices & Other Essays in Moral Philosophy. 1981. pap. 5.95 (ISBN 0-520-04396-0, CAL 494). U of Cal Pr.

Foot, Philippa, ed. Theories of Ethics. 1967. pap. 5.95x (ISBN 0-19-875005-6). Oxford U Pr.

Foot, Philippa R. Virtues & Vices & Other Essays in Moral Philosophy. 1979. 20.00x (ISBN 0-520-03686-7). U of Cal Pr.

Foote, ed. Thesaurus of Entomology. 1977. 9.00 (ISBN 0-686-22689-5). Entomol Soc.

Foote, Alexander. Handbook for Spies. 12.50x (ISBN 0-392-07888-0, SpS). Soccer.

Foote, Andrea & Erfurt, John C. Occupational Employee Assistance Programs for Substance Abuse & Mental Health Problems. 1977. pap. 3.50x (ISBN 0-87736-327-7). U of Mich Inst Labor.

Foote, Arthur. Arthur Foote, 1853-1937: An Autobiography. LC 78-2021. (Music Reprint Ser.,1978). (Illus.). 1978. Repr. of 1946 ed. lib. bdg. 25.00 (ISBN 0-306-77531-X). Da Capo.

--Suite in E, Serenade in E. (Early American Music Ser.: No. 60). 60p. 1980. 18.50. Da Capo.

Foote, Caleb & Meyer, Henry. The Culture of the University: Governance & Education. LC 68-54947. (Higher Education Ser). 1968. 13.95x o.p. (ISBN 0-87589-027-X). Jossey-Bass.

Foote, Caleb, et al. Cases & Materials on Family Law. 2nd ed. 1976. 24.50 (ISBN 0-316-28850-0); pap. 5.95 1980 suppl. (ISBN 0-316-28852-7). Little.

Foote, Gary L, et al. Hydrologic Inventory of the Great Salt Lake Desert Area. 1971. 2.50 o.p. (ISBN 0-87421-062-3). Utah St U Pr.

Foote, Henry W. John Smilbert, Painter. LC 78-87537. (Library of American Art Ser). 1969. Repr. of 1930 ed. lib. bdg. 29.50 (ISBN 0-306-71453-1). Da Capo.

--Robert Feke, Colonial Portrait Painter. LC 72-75357. (Library of American Art Ser). 1969. Repr. of 1950 ed. lib. bdg. 29.50 (ISBN 0-306-71319-5). Da Capo.

Foote, Henry W., jt. auth. see Clarke, Herman F.

Foote, Nancy, et al. Drawings: The Pluralist Decade. LC 80-83653. (Illus.). 1979. pap. 8.00 (ISBN 0-88454-057-X). U of Pa Contemp Art.

Foote, R. B. Prehistory & Protohistoric Antiquities of India. 1979. text ed. 21.50x (ISBN 0-391-01865-5). Humanities.

Foote, Richard H. & Blanc, F. L. The Fruit Flies or Tephritidae of California. (Bulletin of the California Insect Survey: Vol. 7). 1963. pap. 8.50x (ISBN 0-520-09032-2). U of Cal Pr.

Foote, Shelby. September, September. 1979. pap. 2.25 o.p. (ISBN 0-345-26027-9). Ballantine.

Foote, Ted. Jewelry Making: A Guide for Beginners. LC 80-67547. (Illus.). 112p. 1981. 14.95 (ISBN 0-87192-130-8). Davis Mass.

Foote, Timothy. World of Bruegel. (Library of Art). (Illus.). 1968. 15.95 (ISBN 0-8094-0246-7). Time-Life.

--World of Bruegel. LC 68-31677. (Library of Art Ser.). (Illus.). (gr. 6 up). 1968. 12.96 (ISBN 0-8094-0275-0, Pub. by Time-Life). Silver.

Foote, Wilder, jt. ed. see Cordier, Andrew W.

Footman, Robert. Once a Spy. LC 80-15748. 224p. 1980. 8.95 (ISBN 0-396-07864-8). Dodd.

Footner, Hulbert. Maryland Main & the Eastern Shore. LC 67-1719. 1967. Repr. of 1942 ed. 15.00 (ISBN 0-8103-5034-3). Gale.

Foott, Sydney, et al. Kitchen Sense for Disabled People of All Ages. rev. ed. (Illus.). 218p. 1976. spiral bdg. 11.00x (ISBN 0-433-10665-4). Intl Ideas.

Forastieri-Braschi, Eduardo & Guiness, Gerald. On Text & Context: Methodological Approaches to the Context of Literature. LC 79-18001. 1980. pap. write for info. (ISBN 0-8477-3194-4). U of PR Pr.

Foray, Cyril P. Historical Dictionary of Sierra Leone. LC 77-3645. (African Historical Dictionaries Ser.: No. 12). 1977. 16.00 (ISBN 0-8108-1035-2). Scarecrow.

Forbath, Peter. The River Congo: The Discovery, Exploration, & Exploitation of the World's Most Dramatic River. 1979. pap. 7.95 o.p. (ISBN 0-525-47573-7). Dutton.

Forbes, Alec. Try Being Healthy. 184p. 1976. pap. 5.50x (ISBN 0-8464-1057-5). Beekman Pubs.

Forbes, Calvin. Blue Monday. LC 73-15011. (Wesleyan Poetry Program: Vol. 70). 1974. pap. 4.95 (ISBN 0-8195-1070-X, Pub. by Wesleyan U Pr). Columbia U Pr.

Forbes, Christopher, jt. auth. see Waterfield, Hermoine.

Forbes, Claudia A. How to Leave Home & Survive. LC 76-56832. (Illus.). 1978. pap. 3.95 (ISBN 0-89430-031-8). Morgan-Pacific.

Forbes, Colin. The Stone Leopard. 288p. 1977. pap. 1.95 o.p. (ISBN 0-449-23129-1, Crest). Fawcett.

--The Year of the Golden Ape. 320p. 1975. pap. 1.50 o.p. (ISBN 0-449-22563-1, Q2563, Crest). Fawcett.

Forbes, Crosby & Lee, Henry. Massachusetts Help to Ireland During the Great Famine. LC 67-24085. (Illus.). 1967. 6.00x (ISBN 0-686-10827-2). Mus Am China.

Forbes, D. Hume's Philosophical Politics. LC 75-9282. 400p. 1975. 47.95 (ISBN 0-521-20754-1). Cambridge U Pr.

Forbes, D., ed. see Hegel, Georg W.

Forbes, Duncan. Life Before Man: The Story of Fossils. 2nd ed. (Illus.). 64p. (gr. 4-9). 1974. 6.95 (ISBN 0-7136-1300-9). Transatlantic.

Forbes, Duncan see Milne, John.

Forbes, Elizabeth. Opera from A to Z. LC 76-44554. 1977. 8.95 o.p. (ISBN 0-498-02046-0). A S Barnes.

Forbes, Elizabeth & Fitzsimons, Virginia. The Older Adult: A Process for Care. 300p. 1981. pap. text ed. 11.50 (ISBN 0-8016-1631-X). Mosby.

Forbes, Elliot, jt. auth. see Jacobs, David.

Forbes, Grace P., ed. see Azbel, Mark Y.

Forbes, Harriette M. Gravestones of Early New England: And the Men Who Made Them. (Thanatology Service Ser.). 150p. 1981. Repr. of 1980 ed. 15.00 (ISBN 0-686-64831-5). Highly Specialized.

Forbes, Henry O. A Handbook to the Primates, 2 vols. LC 78-72715. Repr. of 1894 ed. Set. 84.50 (ISBN 0-404-18288-7). Vol. 1 (ISBN 0-404-18289-5). Vol. 2 (ISBN 0-404-18290-9). AMS Pr.

Forbes, Jack E. & Eicholz, Robert E. Mathematics for Elementary Teachers. LC 75-137839. (Mathematics Ser). 1971. text ed. 16.95 (ISBN 0-201-01853-5); instr's manual 2.50 (ISBN 0-201-01854-3). A-W.

Forbes, James G. Sketches, Historical & Topographical, of the Floridas. Covington, James W., ed. LC 64-19158. (Floridiana Facsimile & Reprint Ser). 1964. Repr. of 1821 ed. 9.50 (ISBN 0-8130-0078-5). U Presses Fla.

Forbes, Kathryn. Mama's Bank Account. (gr. 10 up). 1968. pap. 2.50 (ISBN 0-15-656377-0, HPL27, HPL). HarBraceJ.

Forbes, Malcolm S. Fact & Comment. 1974. 7.95 o.p. (ISBN 0-394-49187-4). Knopf.

Forbes, Robert J. Short History of the Art of Distillation from the Beginnings up to the Death of Cellier Blumenthal. LC 79-8608. Repr. of 1948 ed. 37.50 (ISBN 0-404-18470-7). AMS Pr.

Forbes, Rosalind. Corporate Stress: How to Manage Stress & Make It Work for You. LC 78-55849. 1979. pap. 4.95 (ISBN 0-385-14440-7, Dolp). Doubleday.

--Life Stress. LC 78-55848. 1979. pap. 3.95 (ISBN 0-385-14441-5, Dolp). Doubleday.

Forbes, William R. Engaging in Mission: A Study-Action Guide. (Orig.). 1980. pap. 2.25 (ISBN 0-377-00102-3). Friend Pr.

Forbis, Judith E. Hoofbeats Along the Tigris. (Illus.). 14.00 (ISBN 0-85131-018-4, Dist. by Sporting Book Center). J A Allen.

Forbis, W. The Cowboys. LC 72-87680. (Old West Ser). (Illus.). (gr. 5 up). 1973. kivar 12.96 (ISBN 0-8094-1451-1, Pub. by Time-Life). Silver.

--The Cowboys. (The Old West Ser.). (Illus.). 1973. 12.95 (ISBN 0-8094-1450-3). Time-Life.

Forbush, Gabrielle. Puppies. (Illus.). 2.95 (ISBN 0-87666-674-8, KW-023). TFH Pubns.

Force, Edward, jt. auth. see Wieland, James.

Force, Robert, jt. ed. see Gallant, Donald M.

Forcese, D. & Richter, S. Social Research Methods. (Illus.). 1973. text ed. 16.95 (ISBN 0-13-818237-X). P-H.

Forcucci, Samuel L. Let There Be Music. new ed. (gr. 9-12). 1973. text ed. 14.40 (ISBN 0-205-03768-2, 5837685); tchrs'. guide 2.40 (ISBN 0-205-03794-1, 5837944). Allyn.

Ford. A Time to Heal. pap. 2.95 (ISBN 0-425-04693-1). Berkley Pub.

Ford, Alice E. John James Audubon. (Illus.). 1964. 24.95x (ISBN 0-8061-0630-1); pap. 9.95x o.p. (ISBN 0-8061-1115-1). U of Okla Pr.

Ford, Alphonse. The Cleaning, Repairing, Lining & Restoring of Oil Paintings: A Practical Guide for Their Better Care & Preservation. (Library of the Arts). (Illus.). 1977. Repr. of 1867 ed. 55.25 (ISBN 0-89266-074-0). Am Classical Coll Pr.

Ford, Anthony, ed. see Arnold, Denis.

Ford, Arthur L. Robert Creeley. (United States Authors Ser.: No. 310). 1978. lib. bdg. 10.95 (ISBN 0-8057-7220-0). Twayne.

Ford, B. G. Do You Know? One Hundred Fascinating Facts. LC 78-62132. (Picture Ser.). (Illus.). (ps-1). 1979. PLB 3.99 (ISBN 0-394-94070-9, BYR); pap. 1.25 (ISBN 0-394-84070-4). Random.

Ford, Barbara. Alligators, Raccoons, & Other Survivors: The Wildlife of the Future. LC 80-28193. (Illus.). 96p. (gr. 4-6). 1981. 8.95 (ISBN 0-688-00369-9); PLB 8.59 (ISBN 0-688-00370-2). Morrow.

--Black Bear. (gr. 7 up). 1981. 8.95 (ISBN 0-395-30444-X). HM.

--Country & Growing with Nature. Date not set. 4.95 (ISBN 0-8062-1134-2). Carlton.

--How Birds Learn to Sing. LC 74-28482. (Illus.). (gr. 4-6). 1975. PLB 5.79 o.p. (ISBN 0-671-32729-1). Messner.

--The Island Ponies: An Environmental Study of Their Life on Assateague. LC 79-11026. (Illus.). (gr. 4-6). 1979. 7.50 (ISBN 0-688-22179-3); PLB 7.20 (ISBN 0-688-32179-8). Morrow.

Ford, C. Quentin, ed. Space Technology & Earth Problems. (Science & Technology Ser.: Vol. 23). (Illus.). 1970. lib. bdg. 35.00 (ISBN 0-87703-051-0); microfiche suppl. 20.00 (ISBN 0-87703-134-7). Am Astronaut.

Ford, Charles H. Om Krishna II: From the Sickroom of the Walking Eagles. LC 80-13972. (Orig.). 1981. 35.00x (ISBN 0-916156-48-6); pap. 4.00x (ISBN 0-916156-47-8). Cherry Valley.

Ford, Charles W. Clinical Education for the Allied Health Professions. LC 78-3620. 1978. text ed. 15.95 (ISBN 0-8016-1623-9). Mosby.

--Learning from Hebrews. LC 80-67467. (Radiant Life Ser.). 128p. (Orig.). 1981. 1.95 (ISBN 0-88243-915-4, 02-0915); teacher's ed 2.50 (ISBN 0-88243-188-9, 32-0188). Gospel Pub.

Ford, Charles W. & Morgan, Margaret K. Teaching in Health Professions. LC 75-37571. (Illus.). 250p. 1976. text ed. 16.95 (ISBN 0-8016-1622-0). Mosby.

Ford, D., jt. auth. see Eckenfelder, W. W.

Ford, Desmond. The Abomination of Desolation in Biblical Eschatology. LC 79-64195. 1979. pap. text ed. 11.50 (ISBN 0-8191-0757-3). U Pr of Amer.

--Answers on the Way. LC 76-17704. (Dimension Ser). 1976. pap. 5.95 (ISBN 0-8163-0253-7, 01636-0). Pacific Pr Pub Assn.

--Daniel. LC 78-8172. (Anvil Ser.). 1978. pap. 6.95 (ISBN 0-8127-0174-7). Southern Pub.

--Physicians of the Soul. LC 79-25555. (Horizon Ser.). 1980. pap. 4.95 (ISBN 0-8127-0262-X). Southern Pub.

Ford, Donald H. Standard Fortran Programming. 3rd ed. (Irwin-Dorsey Ser. in Information Processing). 1978. pap. text ed. 11.50 (ISBN 0-256-01998-3). Irwin.

Ford, Donald H. & Urban, Hugh B. Systems of Psychotherapy: A Comparative Study. LC 63-20630. 1963. 35.95 (ISBN 0-471-26580-2). Wiley.

Ford, Doug. Start Golf Young. LC 77-93324. (gr. 5 up). 1978. 7.95 (ISBN 0-8069-4126-X); PLB 7.49 (ISBN 0-8069-4127-8). Sterling.

--The Wedge. 160p. 1965. pap. 2.95 (ISBN 0-346-12357-7). Cornerstone.

Ford, E. H. Human Chromosomes. 1973. 54.00 o.s.i. (ISBN 0-12-262150-6). Acad Pr.

Ford, Ford M. Critical Writings of Ford Madox Ford. MacShane, Frank, ed. LC 64-11356. (Regents Critics Ser). 1964. 9.75x (ISBN 0-8032-0455-8); pap. 2.65x (ISBN 0-8032-5454-7, B*B 401, Bison). U of Nebr Pr.

Ford, Ford Madox. Fifth Queen. LC 63-13786. (Consists of: Fifth Queen, Privy Seal, & Fifth Queen Crowned). 1963. 15.00 (ISBN 0-8149-0099-2). Vanguard.

--The Queen Who Flew. LC 65-23176. (Illus.). (gr. 4-6). 1965. 4.35 (ISBN 0-8076-0324-4). Braziller.

--Return to Yesterday. 1972. 12.95 (ISBN 0-87140-563-6); pap. 4.45 (ISBN 0-87140-071-5). Liveright.

Ford Foundation. Litigation on Behalf of Women: A Review for the Ford Foundation. Berger, Margaret A., ed. LC 80-66052. 1980. pap. 4.50 (ISBN 0-916584-15-1). Ford Found.

Ford, Francis. The Jobbers. (Illus.). 1980. pap. 9.95 o.p. (ISBN 0-930490-26-6). Future Shop.

Ford, Franklin L. Europe Seventeen Eighty to Eighteen Thirty. (General History of Europe Ser.). 1971. pap. text ed. 10.50x (ISBN 0-582-48346-8). Longman.

Ford, G., jt. auth. see Ford, P.

Ford, G. A., jt. auth. see Ford, P.

Ford, George A. & Lippitt, Gordon L. Planning Your Future: A Workbook for Personal Goal Setting. LC 76-11357. Orig. Title: Life Planning Workbook. 50p. 1976. 8.50 (ISBN 0-88390-120-X). Univ Assocs.

Ford, George B. A Degree of Difference. 1969. 5.95 o.p. (ISBN 0-374-13640-8). FS&G.

Ford, Gerald R. A Vision for America. (YA) 1981. limited signed ed. 50.00 (ISBN 0-935716-08-4). Lord John.

Ford, Gertrude. Eighty-One Sheriff Street. 272p. 1981. 10.95 (ISBN 0-8119-0343-5). Fell.

Ford, Gordon B., Jr. The Old Lithuanian Catechism of Baltramiejus Vilentas 1579: A Phonological, Morphological, & Syntactical Investigation. LC 68-23807. 1969. 40.00 o.p. (ISBN 0-910198-20-9). Baltica Pr.

Ford, Gordon B., Jr., ed. Baltramiejus Vilentas' Lithuanian Translation of the Gospels & Epistles (1579, 2 vols. LC 66-1610. 1966. 100.00 ea. o.p. Vol. 1 (ISBN 0-910198-18-7). Vol. 2 (ISBN 0-910198-19-5). Baltica Pr.

--The Letters of St. Isidore of Seville: Isidore of Seville. 2nd ed. LC 71-498089. 1970. 15.00 o.p. (ISBN 0-916760-03-0). Medieval Latin.

--Old Lithuanian Texts of the Sixteenth & Seventeenth Centuries with a Glossary. LC 68-17875. 1969. 10.00 o.p. (ISBN 0-910198-13-6). Baltica Pr.

--The Wolfenbuettel Lithuanian Postile Manuscript of the Year 1573, 3 vols. LC 66-4719. 1966. 200.00 ea. o.p. Vol. 1 (ISBN 0-910198-14-4). Vol. 2 (ISBN 0-910198-15-2). Vol. 3 (ISBN 0-910198-16-0). Baltica Pr.

Ford, Gordon B., Jr., tr. see Isidore of Seville.

Ford, Harold. Shakespeare, His Ethical Teaching. 112p. 1980. Repr. lib. bdg. 30.00 (ISBN 0-89987-257-3). Century Bookbindery.

Ford, Henry. The International Jew. 1978. pap. 5.00x (ISBN 0-911038-45-0). Noontide.

Ford, Henry, jt. auth. see Heneage, Simon.

Ford, Henry J. The Natural History of the State: An Introduction to Political Science. LC 79-1628. 1981. Repr. of 1915 ed. 18.00 (ISBN 0-88355-932-3). Hyperion Conn.

--Rise & Growth of American Politics. 2nd ed. LC 67-23377. (Law, Politics, & History Ser). 1967. Repr. of 1898 ed. lib. bdg. 25.00 (ISBN 0-306-70946-5). Da Capo.

Ford, Henry J see Johnson, Allen & Nevins, Allan.

Ford, Herta J. Herta's Viennese Kitchen. LC 78-71096. (Illus.). 160p. (Orig.). 1980. pap. 8.95 (ISBN 0-930048-06-7). Prologue.

Ford, High & Alexander, J. M. Advanced Mechanics of Materials. 2nd ed. 1977. 34.95 (ISBN 0-470-99065-1). Halsted Pr.

Ford, Hilary. Castle Malindine. 1977. pap. 1.75 o.p. (ISBN 0-345-25315-9). Ballantine.

--Sarnia. 256p. 1975. pap. 1.50 o.p. (ISBN 0-345-24551-2). Ballantine.

Ford, Hugh D. Poets' War: British Poets & the Spanish Civil War. LC 64-10899. 1964. 10.00x o.p. (ISBN 0-8122-7484-9). U of Pa Pr.

Ford, Ian. Buying & Running Your Own Business. 2nd ed. 210p. 1977. text ed. 21.00x (ISBN 0-220-66336-X, Pub. by Busn Bks England). Renouf.

Ford, Ira W. Traditional Music of America. (Music Reprint Ser., 1978). 1978. Repr. of 1940 ed. lib. bdg. 35.00 (ISBN 0-306-77588-3). Da Capo.

Ford, James A. A Comparison of Formative Cultures in the Americas. (Illus.). 211p. 1969. 45.00x (ISBN 0-87474-159-9). Smithsonian.

Ford, James C., jt. auth. see Haner, F. T.

Ford, James L. Ohlin-Heckscher Theory of the Basis & Effects of Commodity Trade. 6.00x (ISBN 0-210-27110-8). Asia.

Ford, James L. & Ford, Mary K., eds. Every Day in the Year: A Political Epitome of the World's History. LC 68-17941. 1969. Repr. of 1902 ed. 18.00 (ISBN 0-8103-3105-5). Gale.

Ford, Jeremiah D. Main Currents of Spanish Literature. LC 68-13689. 1968. Repr. of 1919 ed. 12.00x (ISBN 0-8196-0213-2). Biblo.

Ford, Jesse H. The Raider. 1976. pap. 1.95 o.p. (ISBN 0-345-25214-4). Ballantine.

Ford, Jo Ann G., et al. Applied Decision Making for Nurses. LC 78-15713. (Illus.). 1979. pap. text ed. 9.50 (ISBN 0-8016-1624-7). Mosby.

Ford, John. Broken Heart. Anderson, Donald K., Jr., ed. LC 68-10354. (Regents Renaissance Drama Ser). 1968. 7.95x (ISBN 0-8032-0259-8); pap. 1.65x (ISBN 0-8032-5259-5, BB 227, Bison). U of Nebr Pr.

--Ford: Five Plays. Ellis, Havelock, ed. Incl. The Lover's Melancholy; 'Tis Pity She's a Whore; The Broken Heart; Love's Sacrifice; Perkin Warbeck. (Orig.). 1957. pap. 2.95 o.p. (ISBN 0-8090-0704-5, Mermaid). Hill & Wang.

--Perkin Warbeck. Anderson, Donald K., Jr., ed. LC 65-15338. (Regents Renaissance Drama Ser). 1965. 7.50x (ISBN 0-8032-0260-1); pap. 1.65x (ISBN 0-8032-5260-9, BB 213, Bison). U of Nebr Pr.

--Tis Pity She's a Whore. Bawcutt, N. W., ed. LC 65-15339. (Regents Renaissance Drama Ser). 1966. 7.50x o.p. (ISBN 0-8032-0262-8); pap. 3.50x (ISBN 0-8032-5261-7, BB 215, Bison). U of Nebr Pr.

Ford, John, jt. auth. see Webster, John.

Ford, John K. A Framework for Financial Analysis. 176p. 1981. pap. text ed. 9.95 (ISBN 0-13-330241-5). P-H.

Ford, Kenneth. Classical & Modern Physics, 3 vols. Incl. Vol. 1. 1972. text ed. 19.95x (ISBN 0-471-00723-4); Vol. 2. text ed. 19.95x (ISBN 0-471-00724-2); answer manual 5.95 (ISBN 0-471-00945-8); Vol. 3. 1974. text ed. 21.95x (ISBN 0-471-00878-8); answer manual 5.95 (ISBN 0-471-00946-6). LC 76-161385. combined ed. for vols. 1 & 2 27.95 (ISBN 0-471-00666-1). Wiley.

Ford, Leighton. Gran Minoria. Blanch, Jose M., tr. from Eng. Orig. Title: The Christian Persuader. 170p. (Orig., Span.). 1969. pap. write for info. o.p. (ISBN 0-89922-005-3). Edit Caribe.

Ford, Leroy. Pedagogia Ilustrada: Tomo I Principios Generales. Orig. Title: A Primer for Teachers & Leaders. (Illus.). 1979. pap. 2.10 (ISBN 0-311-11001-0, Edit Mundo). Casa Bautista.

--Primer for Teachers & Leaders. LC 63-19069. (Orig.). 1963. pap. 3.50 (ISBN 0-8054-3404-6). Broadman.

--Sugerencias Para Ayudas Visuales. Campbell, Viola D., tr. from Eng. Orig. Title: Tool for Teaching & Training. (Illus.). 72p. (Span.). 1980. pap. 1.35 (ISBN 0-311-24302-9). Casa Bautista.

--Tools for Teaching & Training. LC 61-5630. (Orig.). 1961. pap. 3.50 (ISBN 0-8054-3411-9). Broadman.

--Using Problem Solving in Teaching & Training. LC 77-178060. (Multi-Media Teaching & Training Ser.). (Orig.). 1972. pap. 3.25 (ISBN 0-8054-3415-1). Broadman.

--Using the Case Study in Teaching & Training. LC 71-105324. (Multi-Media Teaching & Training Ser.). (Illus.). 1970. pap. 3.25 (ISBN 0-8054-3413-5). Broadman.

--Using the Lecture in Teaching & Training. LC 68-20673. (Multi-Media Teaching & Training Ser.). (Orig.). 1968. pap. 3.25 (ISBN 0-8054-3412-7). Broadman.

--Using the Panel in Teaching & Training. McCormick, Joe, tr. LC 79-127196. (Multi-Media Teaching & Training Ser.). (Orig.). 1971. pap. 3.25 (ISBN 0-8054-3414-3). Broadman.

Ford, Lester R. Automorphic Functions. LC 52-8647. 14.95 (ISBN 0-8284-0085-7). Chelsea Pub.

Ford, Lewis S., ed. Two Process Philosophers: Hartshorne's Encounter with Whitehead. LC 73-85592. (American Academy of Religion. Studies in Religion). 1973. pap. 7.50 (ISBN 0-88420-104-X, 010005). Scholars Pr Ca.

Ford, Marcia. The Sycamores. (YA) 1972. 5.95 (ISBN 0-685-25148-9, Avalon). Bouregy.

Ford, Mary F. Roswell Heritage. (YA) 1968. 4.95 o.p. (ISBN 0-685-07458-7, Avalon). Bouregy.

Ford, Mary K., jt. ed. see Ford, James L.

Ford, Michael J. & Munro, John F. Practical Procedures in Clinical Medicine. (Illus.). 144p. 1981. pap. text ed. 9.95 (ISBN 0-443-02120-1). Churchill.

Ford, Miriam A. de see De Ford, Miriam A. & Jackson, Joan S.

Ford Motor Company, ed. Ford Model T Manual: 1922. (Illus.). 1949. pap. 4.00 o.p. (ISBN 0-89287-255-1, H505). Clymer Pubns.

Ford, Nick A., ed. Black Insights: Significant Literature by Black-Americans, 1760 to the Present. LC 77-127525. (Orig.). 1971. pap. text ed. 13.50 (ISBN 0-471-00168-6). Wiley.

--Language in Uniform: A Reader on Propaganda. LC 67-18746. (Orig.). 1967. pap. 3.95 (ISBN 0-672-63054-0). Odyssey Pr.

Ford, Norman D. Good Health Without Drugs: Get Well & Stay Well the Natural Way. LC 77-9226. 1978. 8.95 o.p. (ISBN 0-312-33868-6). St Martin.

Ford, P. Social Theory & Social Practice: An Exploration of Experience. (Bibliography on Parliamentary Papers Ser.). 335p. 1968. 24.00x (ISBN 0-7165-0500-2, Pub. by Irish Academic Pr Ireland). Biblio Dist.

Ford, P. & Ford, G. Select List of British Parliamentary Papers 1833-1899. 188p. 1969. Repr. of 1953 ed. 20.00x (ISBN 0-7165-0574-6, Pub. by Irish Academic Pr Ireland). Biblio Dist.

--A Select List of Reports of Inquiries of the Irish Dail & Senate: Fifty Years of Policy Making, 1922-72. 64p. 1974. 15.00x (ISBN 0-7165-2254-3, Pub. by Irish Academic Pr Ireland). Biblio Dist.

Ford, P. & Ford, G. A. Breviate of Parliamentary Papers 1900-1916. 520p. 1970. Repr. of 1957 ed. 36.00x (ISBN 0-7165-0575-4, Pub. by Irish Academic Pr Ireland). Biblio Dist.

--Breviate of Parliamentary Papers 1917-1939. 624p. 1970. Repr. of 1951 ed. 36.00x (ISBN 0-7165-0576-2, Pub. by Irish Academic Pr Ireland). Biblio Dist.

Ford, P., et al. Select List of British Parliamentary Papers 1955-1964. 128p. 1970. 17.00x (ISBN 0-7165-0884-2, Pub. by Irish Academic Pr Ireland). Biblio Dist.

Ford, P. L., ed. see Dickinson, John.

Ford, Pam, illus. Funny Friends in Mother Goose Land. (Tell-a-Tale Readers). (Illus.). (gr. k-3). 1979. PLB 4.77 (ISBN 0-307-68647-7, Whitman). Western Pub.

Ford, Patrick K. The Poetry of Llywarch Hen: Introduction, Text & Translation. LC 73-87249. 1974. 15.75x (ISBN 0-520-02601-2). U of Cal Pr.

Ford, Patrick K., ed. Mabinogi & Other Medieval Welsh Tales. 1977. 16.50x (ISBN 0-520-03205-5); pap. 3.95 (ISBN 0-520-03414-7). U of Cal Pr.

Ford, Paul. Companion to Narnia. LC 80-7734. (Illus.). 304p. 1980. 12.95 (ISBN 0-06-250340-5, HarpR). Har-Row.

Ford, Paul L. Pamphlets on the Constitution of the United States. LC 68-22228. (American History, Politics & Law Ser). 1968. Repr. of 1888 ed. lib. bdg. 25.00 (ISBN 0-306-71144-3). Da Capo.

Ford, Paul L., ed. New England Primer. LC 62-20977. (Orig.). 1962. pap. text ed. 4.00x (ISBN 0-8077-1368-6). Tchrs Coll.

Ford, Percy. Social Theory & Social Practice. 1968. text ed. 9.50x (ISBN 0-7165-0500-2). Humanities.

Ford, Peter, jt. auth. see Howell, Michael.

Ford, Peter, ed. Catalytic Activation of Carbon Monoxide. (ACS Symposium Ser.: No. 152). 1981. price not set (ISBN 0-8412-0620-1). Am Chemical.

Ford, Phyllis M. Principles & Practices of Outdoor-Environment Education. LC 80-23200. 350p. 1981. text ed. 15.95 (ISBN 0-471-04768-6). Wiley.

Ford, R. D. Introduction to Acoustics. (Illus.). 1970. pap. text ed. 15.00x (ISBN 0-444-20078-9). Intl Ideas.

Ford, Richard. The Ultimate Good Luck. 216p. 1981. 9.95 (ISBN 0-686-69063-X). HM.

Ford, Robert. Children's Rhymes, Children's Games, Children's Songs, Children's Stories. LC 69-16067. 1968. Repr. of 1904 ed. 18.00 (ISBN 0-8103-3526-3). Gale.

Ford, Robert N. Motivation Through the Work Itself. LC 77-77749. 1969. 15.95 (ISBN 0-8144-5173-X). Am Mgmt.

--Why Jobs Die & What to Do About It: Job Redesign & Future Productivity. 1979. 15.95 (ISBN 0-8144-5502-6). Am Mgmt.

Ford, Robert S. Red Trains Remembered. Sebree, Mac, ed. LC 80-81976. (Interurbans Special Ser.: 75). 120p. 1980. 16.95 (ISBN 0-916374-44-0). Interurban.
--Stale Food vs. Fresh Food: Cause & Cure of Choked Arteries. 6th ed. 48p. 1977. pap. 4.40 (ISBN 0-686-09051-9). Magnolia Lab.
Ford, T. D., jt. ed. see Sylvester-Bradley, P. C.
Ford, Tamara de see De Ford, Tamara.
Ford, Thomas R., ed. Rural U.S.A. Persistence & Change. (Illus.). 1978. text ed. 10.95 (ISBN 0-8138-1345-X). Iowa St U Pr.
Ford, W. C., ed. Defences of Philadelphia in 1777. LC 71-146145. (Era of the American Revolution Ser). 1971. Repr. of 1897 ed. lib. bdg. 32.50 (ISBN 0-306-70140-5). Da Capo.
Ford, W. E., jt. auth. see Dana, E. S.
Ford, W. Herschel. Seven Simple Sermons on the Savior's Last Words. pap. 3.95 (ISBN 0-310-24621-0). Zondervan.
--Seven Simple Sermons on the Second Coming. pap. 3.95 (ISBN 0-310-24631-8). Zondervan.
--Simple Sermons for Funeral Services. pap. 3.95 (ISBN 0-310-24461-7). Zondervan.
--Simple Sermons for Midweek Services. pap. 3.95 (ISBN 0-310-24531-1). Zondervan.
--Simple Sermons for Modern Man. pap. 2.95 (ISBN 0-310-24541-9). Zondervan.
--Simple Sermons for Special Days & Occasions. pap. 2.95 (ISBN 0-310-24661-X). Zondervan.
--Simple Sermons for Sunday Evening. 1967. 3.95 (ISBN 0-310-24671-7). Zondervan.
--Simple Sermons for Time & Eternity. pap. 3.95 (ISBN 0-310-24701-2). Zondervan.
--Simple Sermons from the Book of Acts. pap. 6.95 (ISBN 0-310-24401-3). Zondervan.
--Simple Sermons on Conversion & Commitment. pap. 3.95 (ISBN 0-310-24441-2). Zondervan.
--Simple Sermons on Evangelistic Themes. pap. 3.95 (ISBN 0-310-24451-X). Zondervan.
--Simple Sermons on Grace & Glory. 1977. pap. 3.95 (ISBN 0-310-24751-9). Zondervan.
--Simple Sermons on Heaven, Hell, & Judgment. pap. 2.95 (ISBN 0-310-24481-1). Zondervan.
--Simple Sermons on Life & Living. pap. 3.95 (ISBN 0-310-24511-7). Zondervan.
--Simple Sermons on Old Testament Texts. 112p. 1975. pap. 3.95 (ISBN 0-310-24561-3). Zondervan.
--Simple Sermons on Prayer. pap. 3.95 (ISBN 0-310-24581-8). Zondervan.
--Simple Sermons on Prophetic Themes. pap. 3.95 (ISBN 0-310-24591-5). Zondervan.
--Simple Sermons on Sevens Churches of the Revelation. pap. 3.95 (ISBN 0-310-24431-5). Zondervan.
--Simple Sermons on Simple Themes. pap. 2.95 o.p. (ISBN 0-310-24641-5). Zondervan.
--Simple Sermons on the Ten Commandments. pap. 3.95 (ISBN 0-310-24691-1). Zondervan.
Ford, Walter B. Divergent Series; Asymptotic Series, 2 Vols. in 1. LC 60-16836. 14.95 (ISBN 0-8284-0143-8). Chelsea Pub.
Ford, Wendell H. Public Papers of Governor Wendell H. Ford, Nineteen Seventy-One to Nineteen Seventy-Four. Jones, W. Landis, ed. LC 77-73702. 1978. 28.00x o.p. (ISBN 0-8131-0602-8). U Pr of Ky.
Ford, Wendy W., jt. auth. see Resnick, Lauren B.
Ford, William W. Bacteriology. (Illus.). 1964. pap. 8.25 o.s.i. (ISBN 0-02-844800-6). Hafner.
Forde, Daryll, ed. African Worlds. 1954. pap. 11.50x (ISBN 0-19-724156-5). Oxford U Pr.
Forde, Nels W. Cato the Censor. LC 74-28128. (World Leaders Ser: No. 49). 1975. lib. bdg. 10.95 (ISBN 0-8057-3017-6). Twayne.
Forder, Anthony. Concepts in Social Administration: A Framework for Analysis. 200p. 1974. 11.75x (ISBN 0-7100-7869-2); pap. 7.50 (ISBN 0-7100-7870-6). Routledge & Kegan.
--Social Casework & Administration. 1969. 6.95 (ISBN 0-571-04641-X, Pub. by Faber & Faber). Merrimack Bk Serv.
Forder, Henry G. Calculus of Extension. LC 59-1178. 19.50 (ISBN 0-8284-0135-7). Chelsea Pub.
Fordham, jt. auth. see Cooper, W. F.
Fordham, Adrian & Ainley, John. Evalution of Staff Development in Technical & Further Education: A Proposed Methodology. (Australian Council for Educational Research Monograph: No. 7). 266p. 1980. pap. text ed. 22.50 (ISBN 0-85563-207-0). Verry.
Fordham, David, jt. auth. see Todd, Pamela.
Fordham, Edward W., ed. Notable Cross-Examinations. LC 79-98759. Repr. of 1951 ed. lib. bdg. 15.00x (ISBN 0-8371-3099-9, FOCE). Greenwood.
Fordham, Monroe. Major Themes in Northern Black Religious Thought, 1800-1860. LC 75-10618. 1975. 8.50 o.p. (ISBN 0-682-48256-0, University). Exposition.
Fordham, Sheldon L. & Leaf, Carol A. Physical Education & Sports: An Introduction to Alternative Careers. LC 77-19115. 1978. text ed. 18.95 (ISBN 0-471-26622-1). Wiley.
Fordney, Marilyn T. Insurance Handbook for the Medical Office. 2nd ed. (Illus.). 475p. 1981. pap. text ed. price not set (ISBN 0-7216-3814-7). Saunders.
Ford-Smith, J., tr. see Heinisch, K. F.
Fordwor, Kwame D. The African Development Bank: Problems of International Cooperation. LC 80-24607. (Pergamon Policy Studies on International Development). 300p. 1980. 30.00 (ISBN 0-08-026339-9). Pergamon.
Fordyce, Beth see Eldridge, James, pseud.
Fordyce, C. J., ed. Catullus: A Commentary. 1961. 22.50x (ISBN 0-19-814430-X). Oxford U Pr.
Fordyce, Jack K. & Weil, Raymond. Managing with People: A Manager's Handbook of Organization Development. 2nd ed. 1979. pap. text ed. 8.95 (ISBN 0-201-02031-9). A-W.
Fordyce, M. W., jt. auth. see Darlison, John L.
Fordyce, Wilbert E. Behavioral Methods for Control of Chronic Pain & Illness. LC 75-31782. (Illus.). 256p. 1976. 12.95 (ISBN 0-8016-1621-2). Mosby.
Fordyce, Wilbert E., jt. auth. see Berni, Rosemarian.
Fordyee. Organization Development Overview. 1976. 15.95 o.p. (ISBN 0-201-02104-8). A-W.
Foreign & Commonwealth Office, London. Catalogue of the Colonial Office Library: Third Supplement, 4 vols. 1979. Set. lib. bdg. 520.00 (ISBN 0-8161-0010-1). G K Hall.
Foreign Policy Association. Foreign Policy Priorities 1970-1971. 1970. pap. 0.95 o.s.i. (ISBN 0-02-073500-6, Collier). Macmillan.
--Great Decisions Nineteen Eighty-One. (Illus.). 96p. (Orig.). 1981. pap. 5.00 (ISBN 0-87124-066-1). Foreign Policy.
--Great Decisions 1976. (gr. 10-12). 1976. pap. text ed. 5.20 (ISBN 0-205-05383-1, 7653832); tchrs' guide 2.20 (ISBN 0-205-06115-X). Allyn.
--Great Decisions 1978. (gr. 9-12). 1978. pap. 5.20 (ISBN 0-205-06076-5, 7660766); tchrs'. ed 2.20 (ISBN 0-205-06077-3, 7660774). Allyn.
--Great Decisions 1979. rev. ed. 1979. text ed. 5.20 (ISBN 0-205-06428-0, 7664281). Allyn.
--U. S. Foreign Policy 1972-1973. 1972. pap. 1.25 o.s.i. (ISBN 0-02-073510-3, Collier). Macmillan.
Foreign Service Institute. Advanced French, 2 pts. 567p. 1980. Pt. A. text & cassettes 170.00x (ISBN 0-88432-067-7, Audio-Forum); Pt. B. text & cassettes 160.00 (ISBN 0-88432-068-5). J Norton Pubs.
--Advanced German Course. 375p. 1980. plus 18 audio-cassettes 160.00x (ISBN 0-88432-043-X, G160). J Norton Pubs.
--Advanced Spanish, Part B. 614p. 1980. plus 12 audio-cassettes 135.00x (ISBN 0-88432-058-8, S 153). J Norton Pubs.
--Advanced Spanish, Pt. A. 699p. 1980. plus 16 audio cassettes 155.00x (ISBN 0-88432-057-X, S 131). J Norton Pubs.
--French Phonology. 394p. (Fr.). 1980. 60.00x (ISBN 0-88432-032-4, F250); 8 audiocassettes incl. J Norton Pubs.
--Greek Basic Course, Vol. 1. 328p. (Gr.). 1980. 12 cassettes plus text 115.00x (ISBN 0-88432-034-0, R301, Audio-Forum). J Norton Pubs.
--Greek Basic Course, Vol. 2. 200p. (Gr.). 12 cassettes plus text 98.00x (ISBN 0-88432-035-9, R318, Audio-Forum). J Norton Pubs.
--Hebrew Basic Course. 552p. (Hebrew.). 1980. 185.00x (ISBN 0-88432-040-5, H345); 24 audiocassettes incl. J Norton Pubs.
--Modern Written Arabic. 419p. (Arabic.). 1980. 165.00x (ISBN 0-88432-039-1, A269); 18 audiocassettes incl. J Norton Pubs.
Forell, Betty. El Nino Benjamin y la Primera Navidad. Villalobos, Fernando, tr. from Eng. (Libros Arco). (Illus.). 32p. (Orig., Span.). (gr. 1-3). 1974. pap. 0.95 o.s.i. (ISBN 0-89922-042-8). Edit Caribe.
Forell, George W. & McCue, James F. Confessing One Faith: A Joint Commentary on the Augsburg Confession by Lutheran & Catholic Theologians. LC 80-65557. 368p. 1981. pap. 15.00 (ISBN 0-8066-1802-7, 10-1637). Augsburg.
Forell, George W. & Lazareth, William H., eds. Corporation Ethics: The Quest for Moral Authority. rev. ed. LC 79-8899. (Justice Bks.). 1980. pap. 2.25 (ISBN 0-8006-1556-5, 1-1556). Fortress.
--Population Perils. LC 78-54548. (Justice Books Ser.). 64p. 1978. pap. 2.25 (ISBN 0-8006-1554-9, 1-1554). Fortress.
Forell, George W. & Lehmann, Helmut T., eds. Luther's Works: Career of the Reformer II, Vol. 32. LC 55-9893. 1958. 10.00 (ISBN 0-8006-0332-X, 1-332). Fortress.
Foreman, Alexa. Women Make Movies. (Illus.). 1981. 20.00 (ISBN 0-685-94786-6); pap. 10.00 (ISBN 0-685-94787-4). Booklegger Pr.
Foreman, Dale I. & Allen, Sally. Reading Skills for Social Studies: Understanding Concepts, Level C. (Skillbooster Ser.). 64p. (gr. 3). 1980. wkbk. 2.80 (ISBN 0-87895-351-5). Modern Curr.
--Reading Skills for Social Studies: Understanding Concepts, Level E. (Skillbooster Ser.). 64p. (gr. 5). 1981. wkbk. 2.80 (ISBN 0-87895-555-0). Modern Curr.
--Reading Skills for Social Studies: Understanding Concepts, Level F. (Skillbooster Ser.). 64p. (gr. 6). 1981. wkbk. 2.80 (ISBN 0-87895-657-3). Modern Curr.
--Reading Skills for Social Studies: Understanding Concepts, Level D. (Skillbooster Ser.). 64p. (gr. 4). 1980. wkbk. 2.80 (ISBN 0-87895-452-X). Modern Curr.
--Reading Skills for Social Studies: Using Maps, Charts & Graphs, Level C. (Skillbooster Ser.). 64p. (gr. 3). 1980. wkbk. 2.80 (ISBN 0-87895-350-7). Modern Curr.
--Reading Skills for Social Studies: Using Maps, Charts & Graphs, Level D. (Skillbooster Ser.). 64p. (gr. 4). 1980. wkbk. 2.80 (ISBN 0-87895-452-X). Modern Curr.
--Reading Skills for Social Studies: Using Maps, Charts & Graphs, Level E. (Skillbooster Ser.). 64p. (gr. 5). 1981. 2.80 (ISBN 0-87895-554-2). Modern Curr.
--Reading Skills for Social Studies: Using Maps, Charts & Graphs, Level F. (Skillbooster Ser.). 64p. (gr. 6). 1981. wkbk. 2.80 (ISBN 0-87895-656-5). Modern Curr.
Foreman, Gail H., jt. auth. see Zollers, Frances E.
Foreman, Grant. Five Civilized Tribes. (Civilization of the American Indian Ser.: No. 8). (Illus.). 1971. 14.95 o.p. (ISBN 0-8061-0033-8); pap. 7.95 (ISBN 0-8061-0923-8). U of Okla Pr.
--Indians & Pioneers: The Story of the American Southwest Before 1830. (Civilization of the American Indian Ser.: No. 14). (Illus.). 1967. 15.95 (ISBN 0-8061-0057-5); pap. 8.95 (ISBN 0-8061-1262-X). U of Okla Pr.
--Sequoyah. (Civilization of the American Indian Ser.: No. 16). (Illus.). 1938. pap. 2.95 (ISBN 0-8061-1056-2). U of Okla Pr.
Foreman, J. K. & Stockwell, P. B. Automatic Chemical Analysis. LC 74-14671. (Series in Analytical Chemistry). 346p. 1974. 54.95 (ISBN 0-470-26619-8). Halsted Pr.
Foreman, J. K. & Stockwell, P. B., eds. Topics in Automatic Chemical Analysis, Vol. 1. LC 79-40239. (Series in Analytical Chemistry). 1979. 62.95x (ISBN 0-470-26600-7). Halsted Pr.
Foreman, John, jt. auth. see Zizmor, Jonathan.
Foreman, Ken & Husted, Virginia. Track & Field. (Physical Education Ser.). 1966. pap. text ed. 3.25x (ISBN 0-697-07033-6); teacher's manual available. Wm C Brown.
Foreman, L. L. Desperado's Gold. 1979. pap. 1.50 (ISBN 0-505-51431-1). Tower Bks.
--The Road to San Jancinto. 1977. pap. 1.25 (ISBN 0-505-51117-7). Tower Bks.
Foreman, Michael. War & Peas. LC 74-10368. (Illus.). (ps-3). 1974. 7.95 (ISBN 0-690-00628-4, TYC-J); PLB 8.74 (ISBN 0-690-00629-2). T Y Crowell.
Foreman, Michael, jt. auth. see Fagg, William.
Foreman, Michael, jt. auth. see Wright, Freire.
Foreman, Michael, jt. auth. see Wright, Friere.
Foreman, Richard L. Indian Water Rights. 1980. pap. text ed. 8.95x (ISBN 0-8134-2160-8, 2160). Interstate.
Foreman, Roger. The U. S. Strategic Bomber. 1979. 8.95 (ISBN 0-88254-562-0, Pub by Macdonald & Jane's England). Hippocrene Bks.
Foreman, Walter C., Jr. The Music of the Close: The Final Scenes of Shakespeare's Tragedies. LC 77-75484. 240p. 1979. 16.50x (ISBN 0-8131-1366-0). U Pr of Ky.
Foren, R. & Bailey, R. Authority in Social Casework. 1968. 11.25 (ISBN 0-08-012962-5). Pergamon.
Forer, Eric, ed. see Sitkoff, Harvard.
Forer, Lucille K. Birth Order & Life Roles. 184p. 1969. pap. 14.75 photocopy ed. spiral (ISBN 0-398-00596-6). C C Thomas.
Forest, Antonia. The Attic Term. (gr. 5 up). 1976. 10.95 (ISBN 0-571-10970-5, Pub. by Faber & Faber). Merrimack Bk Serv.
--The Cricket Term. (gr. 5 up). 1974. 9.95 (ISBN 0-571-10632-3, Pub. by Faber & Faber). Merrimack Bk Serv.
--Falconer's Lure. (Illus.). (gr. 5 up). 1957. 6.50 (ISBN 0-571-06548-1, Pub. by Faber & Faber). Merrimack Bk Serv.
--The Marlows & the Traitor. (Illus.). (gr. 5 up). 1953. 6.50 (ISBN 0-571-06769-7, Pub. by Faber & Faber); pap. 2.95 (ISBN 0-571-05911-2). Merrimack Bk Serv.
--The Ready-Made Family. (Fanfares Ser.). (gr. 4 up). 1980. pap. 3.25 (ISBN 0-571-11494-6, Pub. by Faber & Faber). Merrimack Bk Serv.
Forest, Dael. Haesel the Slave No. 2. 1978. pap. 1.75 o.p. (ISBN 0-345-25671-9). Ballantine.
Forest, Grant E. De see De Forest, Grant E.
Forest, James H. Thomas Merton: A Pictorial Biography. LC 80-82249. (Illus., Orig.). 1980. pap. 5.95 (ISBN 0-8091-2284-7). Paulist Pr.
Forest, Jean see Otten, Anna.
Forestell, J. T. Targumic Traditions & the New Testament. LC 79-19293. (Society of Biblical Literature Aramaic Studies: No. 4). pap. 12.00 (06 13 04). Scholars Pr CA.
Forestell, J. T., jt. auth. see Macleod, Donald.
Forester, C. S. Brown on Resolution. 1978. 6.95 (ISBN 0-370-00680-1, Pub. by Chatto Bodley Jonathan). Merrimack Bk Serv.
--The Gun. 1978. 6.95 (ISBN 0-370-00681-X, Pub. by Chatto Bodley Jonathan). Merrimack Bk Serv.
--Payment Deferred. 1978. 7.95 (ISBN 0-370-00657-7, Pub. by Chatto Bodley Jonathan). Merrimack Bk Serv.
--Plain Murder. 1978. 7.95 (ISBN 0-370-00650-X, Pub. by Chatto Bodley Jonathan). Merrimack Bk Serv.
Foreyt, John P., jt. auth. see Davis, Julian C.
Foreyt, John P., ed. Behavioral Treatments of Obesity: A Practical Handbook. 1977. text ed. 21.00 (ISBN 0-08-019902-X). Pergamon.
Foreyt, John P., jt. ed. see Rathjen, Diana P.
Forgan, Harry W. & Mangrum, Charles T. Teaching Content Area Reading Skills. 2nd ed. (Illus.). 336p. 1981. pap. text ed. 12.95 (ISBN 0-675-08037-1); instr's. manual 3.75 (ISBN 0-686-69501-1). Merrill.
--Teaching Content Area Reading Skills: A Modular Preservice & Inservice Program. new ed. (Elementary Education Ser.). 384p. 1976. pap. text ed. 14.95 (ISBN 0-675-08597-7); instructor's manual 3.95 (ISBN 0-686-67333-6). Merrill.
Forgan, Harry W., jt. auth. see Mangrum, Charles T.
Forgie, George B. Patricide in the House Divided: A Psychological Interpretation of Lincoln & His Age. 320p. 1981. pap. 5.95 (ISBN 0-393-00035-4). Norton.
Forgione, Albert G. & Bauer, Frederic M. Fearless Flying: The Complete Program for Relaxed Air Travel. 1980. 11.95 (ISBN 0-395-29123-2); pap. 6.95. HM.
Forgue, Guy J., ed. Letters of H. L. Mencken. 506p. Date not set. price not set (ISBN 0-930350-17-0); pap. price not set (ISBN 0-930350-18-9). NE U Pr.
Forgus, Ronald, jt. auth. see Shulman, Bernard H.
Forier, Louis C. Motor Auto Repair Manual: Fifth Early Model Edition, Nineteen Sixty-Eight to Nineteen Seventy-Four. (Illus.). 1979. 16.95 (ISBN 0-87851-510-0). Hearst Bks.
--Motor Nineteen Eighty Auto Repair Manual. (Illus.). 1979. 16.95 (ISBN 0-87851-508-9). Hearst Bks.
Forisha, Barbara L. Sex Roles & Personal Awareness. 1978. pap. text ed. 9.95x (ISBN 0-673-15307-X). Scott F.
Forisha, Barbara L. & Goldman, Barbara. Outsiders on the Inside: Women & Organizations. (Illus.). 352p. 1981. 14.95 (ISBN 0-13-645382-1, Spectrum); pap. 6.95 (ISBN 0-13-645374-0). P-H.
Forkel, Johann N. Johann Sebastian Bach: His Life, Art, & Work. LC 75-125044. (Music Ser). 1970. Repr. of 1920 ed. lib. bdg. 27.00 (ISBN 0-306-70010-7). Da Capo.
Forker, Charles, jt. auth. see Calder, Daniel G.
Forker, Dom. The Ultimate Baseball Quiz Book. (Orig.). 1981. pap. 1.95 (ISBN 0-451-09679-7, J9679, Sig). NAL.
Forkner, Ben, ed. Modern Irish Short Stories. 512p. 1980. 15.95 (ISBN 0-670-48324-9). Viking Pr.
--Modern Irish Short Stories. 1980. pap. 5.95 (ISBN 0-14-005669-6). Penguin.
Forkner, Hamden L., jt. auth. see Brown, Frances A.
Forkner, Hamden L., jt. auth. see Brown, Francis A.
Forkner, Hamden L., et al. Forkner Shorthand. 4th ed. 11.20x (ISBN 0-912036-10-9); pap. 9.20x (ISBN 0-912036-11-7). Forkner.
--Study Guide for Forkner Shorthand. 4th ed. 121p. pap. 6.64x (ISBN 0-912036-12-5). Forkner.
Forkner, Irvine F. Basic Programming for Business. (Illus.). 288p. 1978. pap. text ed. 13.95x (ISBN 0-13-066423-5). P-H.
Forkner, Irvine H. Computerized Business Systems: An Introduction to Data Processing. LC 73-19. 501p. 1973. text ed. 21.95 (ISBN 0-471-26620-5); instructors' manual avail. (ISBN 0-471-26621-3). Wiley.
Forkner, Jerry & Schatz, Gail. Consumer Education Learning Activities. 64p. (Orig.). 1981. pap. 10.95 (ISBN 0-89994-252-0). Soc Sci Ed.
Forkosch, Morris D. Essays in Legal History in Honor of Felix Frankfurter. 1966. 17.50 (ISBN 0-672-80026-8, Bobbs-Merrill Law). Michie.
Forland, Marvin. Nephrology-A Review of Clinical Nephrology. 1977. pap. 16.00 (ISBN 0-87488-622-8). Med Exam.
Forlines, Leroy. Biblical Systematics. 1975. 7.95 (ISBN 0-89265-025-7); pap. 4.95 (ISBN 0-89265-038-9). Randall Hse.
Form, William H., jt. auth. see Huber, Joan.

Forman, B. Fred. Local Stresses in Pressure Vessels. 2nd ed. 1979. 60.00 (ISBN 0-914458-05-1). Pressure.

Forman, Bedrich. Borobudur: The Buddhist Legend in Tone. (Illus.). 1980. 16.95. Mayflower Bks.

Forman, Brenda. America's Place in the World Economy. LC 69-11494. (Curriculum Related Bks). (gr. 9-12). 1969. 5.50 o.p. (ISBN 0-15-203168-5, HJ). HarBraceJ.

Forman, Brenda Lu & Forman, Harrison. The Land & People of Nigeria. rev. ed. LC 77-37925. (Portraits of the Nations Ser.). (Illus.). (gr. 6 up). 8.79 (ISBN 0-397-31205-9). Lippincott.

Forman, George E. & Hill, D. Fleet. Constructive Play: Applying Piaget in the Preschool. LC 79-21316. 1980. pap. text ed. 10.95 (ISBN 0-8185-0391-2). Brooks-Cole.

Forman, George E. & Sigel, Irving E. Cognitive Development: A Life-Span View. Rabelsky, Freda & Dorman, Lynn, eds. LC 78-31176. (Life-Span Human Development Ser.). (Illus.). 1979. pap. text ed. 8.95 (ISBN 0-8185-0275-4). Brooks-Cole.

Forman, H. Chandlee. Old Buildings, Gardens & Furniture in Tidewater, Maryland. LC 67-17538. (Illus.). 1967. 12.50 (ISBN 0-87033-075-6, Pub. by Tidewater). Cornell Maritime.

Forman, Harrison. Report from Red China. LC 74-28417. (China in the 20th Century Ser). (Illus.). iv, 250p. 1975. Repr. of 1945 ed. lib. bdg. 22.50 (ISBN 0-306-70676-8). Da Capo.

Forman, Harrison, jt. auth. see Forman, Brenda Lu.

Forman, Henry J. & Gammon, Roland. Truth Is One. (Illus.). 1954. 10.00 o.s.i. (ISBN 0-06-001680-9, HarpT). Har-Row.

Forman, J. Making of Black Revolutionaries: A Memoir. 1972. 12.50 o.s.i. (ISBN 0-02-539700-1). Macmillan.

Forman, James. Code Name Valkyrie: Count Claus von Stauffenberg & the Plot to Kill Hitler. LC 72-12581. (Illus.). 256p. (gr. 9-12). 1973. PLB 10.95 (ISBN 0-87599-188-2). S G Phillips.

--Inflation. (gr. 6 up). 1977. PLB 7.90 s&l (ISBN 0-531-00392-2). Watts.

--My Enemy, My Brother. (Illus.). 256p. (gr. 7 up). 1981. 9.95 (ISBN 0-525-66735-0). Elsevier-Nelson.

--The Pumpkin Shell. 246p. (gr. 7 up). 1981. 9.95 (ISBN 0-374-36159-2). FS&G.

Forman, James D. Anarchism: Political Innocence or Social Violence. LC 74-13436. (Studies in Contemporary Politics Ser.). 160p. (gr. 7 up). 1975. PLB 5.90 o.p. (ISBN 0-531-02790-2). Watts.

--Capitalism: Economic Individualism to Today's Welfare State. LC 72-6739. (Studies in Contemporary Politics). 128p. (gr. 7-12). 1972. 5.90 o.p. (ISBN 0-531-02570-5). Watts.

--Communism. 2nd ed. (Studies in Contemporary Politics). (gr. 9 up). 1979. PLB 7.90 s&l (ISBN 0-531-02933-6). Watts.

--Nazism. (gr. 6 up). 1978. PLB 6.90 s&l (ISBN 0-531-01473-8). Watts.

--Socialism: Its Theoretical Roots & Present-Day Development. LC 72-6736. (Studies in Contemporary Politics). 128p. (gr. 7-12). 1972. PLB 5.90 o.p. (ISBN 0-531-02581-0). Watts.

--That Mad Game: War & the Chances for Peace. LC 80-11500. (gr. 7 up). 1980. 10.95 (ISBN 0-684-16509-0). Scribner.

Forman, Joan. The Princess in the Tower. (Illus.). (gr. 1-4). 1978. 7.50 (ISBN 0-571-09911-4, Pub. by Faber & Faber). Merrimack Bk Serv.

Forman, Joan & Strongman, Harry. The Romans. LC 77-86188. (Peoples of the Past Ser.). (Illus.). 1977. lib. bdg. 7.95 (ISBN 0-686-51160-3). Silver.

Forman, Louis H. & Ramsburg, Janelle S. Hello Sigmund, This Is Eric! 1978. 12.95 o.p. (ISBN 0-8362-0754-8); pap. 5.95 o.p. (ISBN 0-8362-5202-0). Andrews & McMeel.

Forman, Phillip M., ed. see Sigel, Bernard.

Forman, R. C. Public Speaking Made Easy. (Speaker's & Toastmaster's Library). 1977. pap. 2.95 o.p. (ISBN 0-8010-3476-0). Baker Bk.

Forman, Robert. How to Control Your Allergies. 256p. (Orig.). 1979. pap. 1.95 (ISBN 0-915962-29-2). Larchmont Bks.

Forman, Shepard. The Brazilian Peasantry. LC 75-16156. 336p. 1975. 20.00x (ISBN 0-231-03106-8); pap. 10.00x (ISBN 0-231-08366-1). Columbia U Pr.

Forman, William & Gavurin, Lester L. Elements of Arithmetic, Algebra, & Geometry. LC 78-159159. 1972. text ed. 18.95 (ISBN 0-471-00654-8); solns. manual & tchr's guide 6.95 (ISBN 0-471-00731-5). Wiley.

Formanek, Ruth & Gurian, Anita. Charting Intellectual Development: A Practical Guide to Piagetian Tasks. 2nd ed. write for info. (ISBN 0-398-04476-7). C C Thomas.

--Charting Intellectual Development: A Practical Guide to Piagetian Tasks. protocopy ed. (Illus.). 120p. 1976. 13.50 (ISBN 0-398-03449-4); pap. 8.00 o.p. (ISBN 0-398-03450-8). C C Thomas.

Formann, J. D. Fascism: The Meaning & Experience of Reactionary Revolution. LC 73-11480. (gr. 7 up). 1974. 6.90 o.p. (ISBN 0-685-47544-1); pap. 3.95. Watts.

Fornander, Abraham. An Account of the Polynesian Race: Its Origin & Migration, 3 vols. in 1. LC 69-13505. (Illus.). 1980. Repr. of 1878 ed. Set. 37.50 (ISBN 0-8048-0002-2). C E Tuttle.

Fornari, Harry. Bread Upon the Waters. LC 73-76524. (Illus.). 1973. 10.00 o.s.i. (ISBN 0-87695-166-3). Aurora Pubs.

Fornatale, Peter & Mills, Joshua E. Radio in the Television Age. LC 79-67675. 1980. 12.95 (ISBN 0-87951-106-0). Overlook Pr.

Fornell, Claes. Consumer Input for Marketing Decisions: A Study of Corporate Departments for Consumer Affairs. LC 76-14397. 1976. text ed. 21.95 (ISBN 0-275-23480-0). Praeger.

Fornell, Earl W. The Galveston Era: The Texas Crescent on the Eve of Secession. (Illus.). 355p. 1976. pap. 9.95 (ISBN 0-292-72710-0). U of Tex Pr.

Forness, Steven R., jt. auth. see Hewett, Frank M.

Forney, J. W. Anecdotes of Public Men. LC 70-87540. (American Scene Ser). 1970. Repr. of 1873 ed. lib. bdg. 25.00 (ISBN 0-306-71456-6). Da Capo.

Forney, Robert & Hughes, Francis. Combined Effects of Alcohol & Other Drugs. 132p. 1968. pap. 11.75 photocopy ed. spiral (ISBN 0-398-00597-4). C C Thomas.

Forrai, Katalin, et al. Music Education in Hungary. 3rd, enl. ed. Macnicol, Fred, tr. from Hungarian. LC 80-123375. 310p. 1975. 12.00 (ISBN 0-85162-025-6). Boosey & Hawkes.

Forrer, Matthi. Egoyomi & Surimono: Their History & Development. (Illus.). 1977. pap. text ed. 23.00x (ISBN 90-70265-01-X). Humanities.

Forrer, Matthi, et al, eds. A Sheaf of Japanese Papers: In Tribute to Heinz Kaempfer on His Seventy-Fifth Birthday. 1980. 20.00x (ISBN 90-70265-71-0). Humanities.

Forrest, Alan. Society & Politics in Revolutionary Bordeaux. (Oxford Historical Monographs). 320p. 1975. 42.00x (ISBN 0-19-821859-1). Oxford U Pr.

Forrest, David M. Eel Capture, Culture, Processing & Marketing. (Illus.). 206p. 20.25 (ISBN 0-85238-070-4, FN). Unipub.

Forrest, Gary G. The Diagnosis & Treatment of Alcoholism. 2nd ed. 364p. 1978. 22.50 (ISBN 0-398-03779-5); pap. 15.75 (ISBN 0-398-03780-9). C C Thomas.

Forrest, Irene S., et al, eds. Phenothiazines & Structurally Related Drugs. LC 73-88571. (Advances in Biochemical Psychopharmacology Ser.: Vol. 9). 840p. 1974. 61.50 (ISBN 0-911216-61-8). Raven.

Forrest, James F., ed. see Bunyan, John.

Forrest, John C., et al. Principles of Meat Science. LC 75-8543. (Food & Nutrition Ser.). (Illus.). 1975. text ed. 26.95x (ISBN 0-7167-0743-8). W H Freeman.

Forrest, Mary & Olson, Margot. Exploring Speech Communication: An Introduction. 320p. 1981. pap. text ed. 9.56 (ISBN 0-8299-0381-X). West Pub.

Forrest, R. A. The Chinese Language. 3rd ed. (Great Language Ser.). 1973. text ed. 19.50x (ISBN 0-571-04815-3). Humanities.

Forrester, A. R., et al. Organic Chemistry of Stable Free Radicals. 1968. 48.00 o.s.i. (ISBN 0-12-262050-X). Acad Pr.

Forrester, Andrew, jt. auth. see Moss, Michael.

Forrester, Andrew, jt. ed. see Moss, Michael.

Forrester, Donald J., et al, eds. Pediatric Dental Medicine. LC 80-10694. (Illus.). 692p. 1981. text ed. write for info. (ISBN 0-8121-0663-6). Lea & Febiger.

Forrester, Helen. Minerva's Stepchild. LC 80-26968. 320p. 1981. 9.95 (ISBN 0-8253-0017-7). Beaufort Bks NY.

Forrester, Jay. World Dynamics. 2nd ed. 1979. text ed. 15.00x (ISBN 0-262-06066-3); pap. 7.95 (ISBN 0-262-56018-6). MIT Pr.

Forrester, Jay W. Industrial Dynamics. (Illus.). 1961. pap. 19.95x (ISBN 0-262-56001-1). MIT Pr.

Forrester, John. Language & the Origins of Psychoanalysis. 304p. 1980. 22.50x (ISBN 0-231-05136-0). Columbia U Pr.

Forrester, Marian. Farewell to Thee. 1978. pap. 2.25 (ISBN 0-505-51309-9). Tower Bks.

Forsberg, Foy. Beginner's Guide to Shorecasting. (Illus.). 183p. 1975. 10.95 (ISBN 0-7207-0753-6). Transatlantic.

Forsberg, Sara J., jt. auth. see Cartwright, Carol.

Forscutt, Mark H., ed. Saints' Harmony. (Heritage Reprint Ser.). 566p. 1974. Repr. of 1889 ed. 19.95 o.p. (ISBN 0-8309-0120-5). Herald Hse.

Forsdale, Louis. Perspectives on Communication. LC 80-16616. (Speech Ser.). (Illus.). 400p. 1981. text ed. 12.95 (ISBN 0-201-04571-0). A-W.

Forshaw, Joseph M. Australian Parrots. 2nd ed. (Illus.). 224p. 1980. 75.00 (ISBN 0-686-62188-3); write for ltd. ed. Eastview.

Forsky, V., ed. see Romen, A. S.

Forslin, Jan, et al. Automation & Industrial Workers: A Fifteen Nation Study--Vol. 1, Pt. 1. (Illus.). 1979. 61.00 (ISBN 0-08-023339-2). Pergamon.

Forsling, Mary L. Anti-Diuretic Hormone, Vol. 1. (Annual Research Reviews Ser.). 1977. 19.20 (ISBN 0-904406-51-2). Eden Med Res.

--Anti-Diuretic Hormone, Vol. 2, 1977. LC 78-309279. (Annual Research Reviews). 1978. 24.00 (ISBN 0-88831-016-1). Eden Med Res.

Forssberg, Arne, jt. ed. see Errera, Maurice.

Forst, Martin L. Civil Commitment & Social Control. LC 77-14626. (Illus.). 1978. 17.95 (ISBN 0-669-01988-7). Lexington Bks.

Forstenzer, Thomas R. French Provincial Police & the Fall of the Second Republic: Social Fear & Counterrevolution. LC 80-8549. 384p. 1981. 25.00x (ISBN 0-691-05318-9). Princeton U Pr.

Forster, C., jt. auth. see Calleley, A.

Forster, D. Lynn & Erven, Bernard L. Foundations for Managing the Farm Business. LC 80-20832. (Agricultural Economics Ser.). 320p. 1981. text ed. 20.95 (ISBN 0-88244-230-9). Grid Pub.

Forster, E. M. Alexandria: A History & a Guide. new ed. LC 74-78549. 243p. 1974. 11.95 (ISBN 0-87951-023-4). Overlook Pr.

--Artic Summer & Other Fiction. (The Abinger Edition of E. M. Forster: Vol. 9). 342p. 1981. 35.00x (ISBN 0-8419-0670-X). Holmes & Meier.

--E. M. Forster's Letters to Donald Windham. 1975. wrappers. ltd. ed. 35.00x (ISBN 0-917366-04-2). S Campbell.

--Goldsworthy Lowes Dickinson. Stallybrass, Oliver, ed. (Abinger Edition of E. M. Forster Ser.). 1978. text ed. 17.75x (ISBN 0-8419-5810-6). Holmes & Meier.

--Howards End. Stallybrass, Oliver, ed. (Abinger Edition of E. M. Forster Ser.). 1978. text ed. 20.50x (ISBN 0-8419-5806-8). Holmes & Meier.

--Maurice. 256p. 1981. pap. 4.95 (ISBN 0-393-00026-5). Norton.

--A Room with a View. Stallybrass, Oliver, ed. (Abinger Edition of E. M. Forster Ser.). 1978. text ed. 24.50x (ISBN 0-8419-5804-1). Holmes & Meier.

Forster, Edward S., tr. see Busbecq, Ogier G. De.

Forster, Francis M. Clinical Neurology. 4th ed. LC 78-7343. 1978. pap. text ed. 10.95 (ISBN 0-8016-1637-9). Mosby.

Forster, Klaus. Pronouncing Dictionary of English-Place Names. 308p. 1981. 30.00 (ISBN 0-7100-0756-6). Routledge & Kegan.

Forster, Lancelot. The New Culture in China. LC 79-2823. 240p. 1981. Repr. of 1936 ed. 19.75 (ISBN 0-8305-0003-0). Hyperion Conn.

Forster, Leonard W. Icy Fire: Four Studies in European Petrarchism. LC 71-77288. (Illus.). 1969. 29.50 (ISBN 0-521-07495-9); pap. 8.95x (ISBN 0-521-29521-1). Cambridge U Pr.

Forster, M. C., jt. auth. see Beck, P. G.

Forster, Margaret. The Bride of Lowther Fell. LC 80-69370. 1981. 11.95 (ISBN 0-689-11129-0). Atheneum.

Forster, Marianne. Making Furry Toys. 1972. pap. 4.95 (ISBN 0-236-15424-9, Pub. by Paul Elek). Merrimack Bk Serv.

Forster, O. Analysis. 2nd ed. Incl. No. 1. Differential & Integralrechnung Einer Veranderlichen. 208p. 1976 (ISBN 3-528-07224-5); No. 2. Differentialrechnung im Rn Gewohnliche Differentialgleichungen. 1977. (Mathematik Grundkurs Ser.). (Ger.). pap. 9.00 ea. Birkhauser.

Forster, Werner, et al. Prostaglandins & Thromboxins: Proceedings of the Third International Symposium on Prostaglandins & Thromboxanes in the Cardiovascular System, Halle-Salle, GDR, 5-7 May 1980. LC 80-41802. (Illus.). 500p. 1981. 80.00 (ISBN 0-08-027369-6). Pergamon.

Forstman, Jack. A Romantic Triangle: Schleiermacher & Early German Romanticism. LC 76-55709. (American Academy of Religion. Dissertation Ser.). 1977. pap. 7.50 (ISBN 0-89130-124-0, 010013). Scholars Pr Ca.

Forsyth, Cecil. Music & Nationalism: A Study of English Opera. LC 80-2276. 1981. Repr. of 1911 ed. 37.00 (ISBN 0-404-18844-3). AMS Pr.

Forsyth, Elizabeth, jt. auth. see Hyde, Margaret.

Forsyth, Ella M. Building a Chamber Music Collection: A Descriptive Guide to Published Scores. LC 79-4587. 1979. 10.00 (ISBN 0-8108-1215-0). Scarecrow.

Forsyth, Frederick. Forsyth's Three. 1152p. 1980. 15.95 (ISBN 0-670-52410-7). Viking Pr.

Forsyth, Ilene H. The Throne of Wisdom: Wood Sculptures of the Madonna in Romanesque France. LC 72-166372. (Illus.). 336p. 1972. 38.50x o.p. (ISBN 0-691-03837-6). Princeton U Pr.

Forsyth, J., ed. see Vinokur, G. O.

Forsyth, James. Tyrone Guthrie: The Authorized Biography. (Illus.). 1978. 22.50 (ISBN 0-241-89471-9, Pub. by Hamish Hamilton England). David & Charles.

Forsyth, Patrick. Running an Effective Sales Office. 160p. 1980. text ed. 37.25x (ISBN 0-566-02185-4, Pub. by Gower Pub Co England). Renouf.

Forsyth, Phyllis Y. Atlantis: The Making of Myth. (Illus.). 256p. 1980. 19.50x (ISBN 0-7735-0355-2). McGill-Queens U Pr.

Forsyth, Robert A., jt. auth. see Blommers, Paul J.

Forsythe, A. I., et al. Computer Science: A First Course. 2nd ed. LC 74-34244. 876p. 1975. pap. text ed. 23.95 (ISBN 0-471-26681-7). Wiley.

Forsythe, Alan B., ed. Control Language Summary. (BMDP Statistical Software). 56p. (Orig.). 1980. pap. 3.00 (ISBN 0-935386-01-7). UCLA Dept Biomath.

Forsythe, Alexander I., et al. Computer Science: Programming in BASIC. 1976. pap. 8.95 (ISBN 0-471-26684-1). Wiley.

Forsythe, Alexandra I., et al. Computer Science: A Primer. LC 74-76053. 403p. 1969. 21.50 o.p. (ISBN 0-471-26680-9). Wiley.

Forsythe, Charles E. & Keller, Irwin A. Administration of High School Athletics. 6th ed. (Illus.). 1977. 17.95x (ISBN 0-13-005710-X). P-H.

Forsythe, Elizabeth. The Low-Fat Gourmet. 156p. 1981. 14.95 (ISBN 0-7207-1226-2). Merrimack Bk Serv.

Forsythe, George E. & Moler, C. Computer Solution of Linear Algebraic Systems. 1967. ref. ed. 17.95 (ISBN 0-13-165779-8). P-H.

Forsythe, George E., et al. Computer Methods for Mathematical Computations. (Illus.). 1977. ref. ed. 22.50x (ISBN 0-13-165332-6). P-H.

Fort, Joel. The Addicted Society. LC 80-8918. 256p. 1981. pap. 3.95 (ISBN 0-394-17889-0, B454, BC). Grove.

Forte, Allen. The Compositional Matrix. LC 73-4337. 1974. Repr. of 1961 ed. lib. bdg. 14.00 (ISBN 0-306-70577-X). Da Capo.

Forte, David F. The Supreme Court. (American Government Ser.). (Illus.). (gr. 7 up). 1979. PLB 6.90 s&l (ISBN 0-531-02267-6). Watts.

Forte, Imogene. Think About It-Kindergarten. LC 80-84619. (Think About It Ser.). (Illus.). 80p. (ps-k). 1981. pap. text ed. 5.95 (ISBN 0-913916-96-X, IP-96X). Incentive Pubn.

--Think About It: Middle Grades. LC 80-84619. (Think About It Ser.). (Illus.). 96p. (gr. 4-6). 1981. pap. text ed. 5.95 (ISBN 0-913916-98-6, IP 98-6). Incentive Pubn.

--Think About It: Primary. LC 80-84619. (Think About It Ser.). (Illus.). 88p. (gr. 1-3). 1981. pap. text ed. 5.95 (ISBN 0-913916-97-8, IP 97-8). Incentive Pubn.

Forte, Imogene & MacKenzie, Joy. Skillstuff: Reasoning. LC 80-81737. (The Skillstuff Ser.). (Illus.). 232p. (gr. 2-6). 1981. pap. text ed. 10.95 (ISBN 0-913916-81-1). Incentive Pubns.

Forten, Charlotte L. The Journal of Charlotte L. Forten. Billington, Ray A., ed. 286p. 1981. pap. 4.95 (ISBN 0-393-00046-X). Norton.

Forter, Elizabeth T., ed. see Shaw, George B.

Fortes, Meyer. Kinship & the Social Order: The Legacy of Lewis Henry Morgan. LC 80-67927. (Lewis Henry Morgan Lectures). 368p. Date not set. cancelled; pap. cancelled (ISBN 0-521-28211-X). Cambridge U Pr.

--Time & Social Structure & Other Essays. (Monographs on Social Anthropology Ser: No.40). (Illus.). 1970. text ed. 19.50x (ISBN 0-391-00112-4, Athlone Pr). Humanities.

Fortescue, John. De Laudibus Legum Anglie. Chrimes, S. B., intro. by. LC 78-62331. 1979. Repr. of 1942 ed. 26.50 (ISBN 0-88355-793-2). Hyperion Conn.

--De Natura Legis Naturae, et De Ejus Censura in Succesione Regnorum Suprema: The Works of Sir John Fortescue, London, 1869. (Classics of the Modern Era: Vol. 1). 296p. 1980. lib. bdg. 50.00 (ISBN 0-8240-4600-5). Garland Pub.

Fortescue, Michael D. A Discourse Production Model for Twenty Quesations. (Pragmatics & Beyond Ser.: No.2). 145p. 1980. pap. text ed. 17.25x (ISBN 90-272-2505-2). Humanities.

Fortey, R. A. The Ordovician Trilobites of Spitsbergen I. Olenidae. (Norsk Polarinstitutt Ser: No. 160). 1974. 16.00x (ISBN 8-200-29180-4, Dist. by Columbia U Pr). Universitet.

--The Ordovician Trilobites of the Spitsbergen. (Norsk Polarinstitutt Skrifter: Vol. 171). (Illus.). 163p. 1980. pap. text ed. 18.00x (ISBN 82-00-29189-8). Universitet.

Forth, W. & Rummel, W., eds. Pharmacology of Intestinal Absorption: Gastrointestinal Absorption of Drugs. 1976. text ed. 140.00 (ISBN 0-08-016210-X). Pergamon.

Forthofer, Ronald N., jt. auth. see Lehnen, Robert G.

Fortin, Joseph P. Get Out of Debt. 160p. 1980. pap. text ed. 6.95 (ISBN 0-936256-00-1). Omega Pub Co.

Fortini, Arnaldo. Francis of Assisi. Moak, Helen, tr. 900p. 1980. 29.50 (ISBN 0-8245-0116-0). Crossroad NY.

Fortman, Jan. Creatures of Mystery. LC 77-24705. (Great Unsolved Mysteries Ser.). (Illus.). (gr. 4-5). 1977. PLB 9.65 (ISBN 0-8172-1063-6). Raintree Pubs.

--First to Sail the World Alone: Joshua Slocum. LC 78-13720. (Famous Firsts Ser.). (Illus.). 1978. lib. bdg. 7.35 (ISBN 0-686-51105-0). Silver.

--Houdini & Other Masters of Magic. LC 77-12638. (Myth, Magic & Superstition Ser.). (Illus.). (gr. 4-5). 1977. PLB 9.65 (ISBN 0-8172-1032-6). Raintree Pubs.

Fortner, Irene. Western Adventure. Date not set. 4.95 (ISBN 0-8062-1647-6). Carlton.

Fortnum, Charles D. Maiolica: A Historical Treatise on the Glazed & Enamelled Earthenwares of Italy. Freitag, Wolfgang M., ed. LC 78-50321. (Ceramics & Glass Ser.: Vol. 7). (Illus.). 1979. lib. bdg. 55.00 (ISBN 0-8240-3393-0). Garland Pub.

Fortson, Walter L., jt. auth. see Rogers, Jean L.

Fortuna, James L., Jr. The Unsearchable Wisdom of God: A Study of Providence in Richardson's Pamela. LC 80-14919. (University of Florida Humanities Monograph: No. 49). vii, 130p. 1980. pap. 5.50 (ISBN 0-8130-0676-7). U Presses Fla.

Fortunato, Donald J. Two Thousand Miles on the Appalachian Trail. 1981. 5.50 (ISBN 0-686-26176-3). D J Fortunato.

Fortunato, P. When We Were Young: An Album of Stars. 1980. 8.95 (ISBN 0-13-956482-9); pap. 2.50 (ISBN 0-13-956474-8). P-H.

Fortunato, Pat. Dino-Mite Foozles. (YA) (gr. 6 up). 1979. pap. 1.25 (ISBN 0-440-91950-9, LFL). Dell.

Fortunatus, Venantius. From the Miscellania of Venantius Fortunatus. Cook, Geoffrey, tr. LC 79-17109. (Lat.). 1981. 12.00x (ISBN 0-916156-38-9); pap. 5.00x (ISBN 0-916156-40-0). Cherry Valley.

Fortune, Dion. Cosmic Doctrine. 5.95 (ISBN 0-87728-455-5). Weiser.

--Demon Lover. pap. 6.00 (ISBN 0-87728-173-4). Weiser.

--Esoteric Philosophy of Love & Marriage. pap. 4.95 (ISBN 0-685-01081-3). Weiser.

--The Machinery of the Mind. 1980. pap. 4.95 (ISBN 0-87728-505-5). Weiser.

--Mystical Qabalah. 5.95 (ISBN 0-685-22174-1). Weiser.

--The Problem of Purity. 1980. pap. 4.95 (ISBN 0-87728-506-3). Weiser.

Fortune, George, jt. ed. see Hodza, Aaron C.

Fortune Magazine & Davenport, Russell W. U. S. A., the Permanent Revolution. LC 80-15776. 267p. 1980. Repr. of 1951 ed. lib. bdg. 22.50x (ISBN 0-313-22500-1, FMUS). Greenwood.

Fortune, Nigel & Lewis, Anthony, eds. New Oxford History of Music, Vol. 5: Opera & Church Music 1630-1750. (Illus.). 800p. 1975. 49.95x (ISBN 0-19-316305-5). Oxford U Pr.

Fortune, Robert & Myers, Ramon H. Three Years' Wanderings in the Northern Provinces of China. LC 78-74307. (Modern Chinese Economy Ser.: Vol. 4). 1979. 44.00 (ISBN 0-8240-4253-0). Garland Pub.

Forty, George. Chieftan. (Illus.). 1980. 14.95 (ISBN 0-684-16433-7, ScribT). Scribner.

--Desert Rats at War: Europe. (Illus.). 1977. 16.95 o.p. (ISBN 0-7110-0733-0). Hippocrene Bks.

--Fifth Army at War. (Illus.). 144p. 1980. 17.50 (ISBN 0-684-16615-1, ScribT). Scribner.

--Patton's Third Army at War. (Illus.). 1979. 17.50 (ISBN 0-684-16076-5, ScribT). Scribner.

Forty, Ralph. Sayonara Streetcar. Sebree, Mac, ed. (Special Ser.: No. 70). 1978. pap. 8.00 (ISBN 0-916374-33-5). Interurban.

Forwald, Haakon. Mind, Matter, & Gravitation. LC 72-97212. (Parapsychological Monograph No. 11). 1969. pap. 3.50 (ISBN 0-912328-15-0). Parapsych Foun.

Fosbenner, Al. The Westphal Empire. (Orig.). 1980. pap. 2.75 (ISBN 0-440-19492-X). Dell.

Fosberg, F. Raymond, jt. auth. see Sachet, Marie-Helene.

Fosburgh, Hugh. The Hunter. 1977. pap. 1.50 (ISBN 0-505-51182-7). Tower Bks.

FOSECO, see Foundry Services Ltd.

Foshay, Arthur W., ed. Professional As Educator. LC 73-120602. 1970. pap. text ed. 6.00x (ISBN 0-8077-1378-3). Tchrs Coll.

Foskett, D. Classification for a General Indexing Language. 1970. pap. 4.50x (ISBN 0-85365-032-2, Pub. by Lib Assn England). Oryx Pr.

Foskett, Daphne. A Dictionary of British Miniature Painters, 2 vols. 1972. Set. 145.00 o.p. (ISBN 0-686-16376-1, Pub. by Faber & Faber); Vol. 1. (ISBN 0-571-08295-5); Vol. 2. (ISBN 0-571-09746-4). Merrimack Bk Serv.

--Samuel Cooper: 1609-1672. 1974. 25.00 (ISBN 0-571-10346-4, Pub. by Faber & Faber). Merrimack Bk Serv.

Foss. Armour & Artillery Nineteen Seventy-Nine to Nineteen Eighty. 1980. 99.50 (ISBN 0-531-03916-1). Watts.

--Artillery of the World. 3rd ed. 1981. 12.95 (ScribT). Scribner.

--Artillery of the World. 2nd, rev. ed. 1980. 12.95 o.p. (ISBN 0-684-16722-0, ScribT). Scribner.

--Basic Metallurgy. Date not set. text ed. price not set (ISBN 0-685-67274-3). Bennett IL. Postponed.

--Combat Support Equipment Nineteen Eighty to Nineteen Eighty-One. 1980. 125.00 (ISBN 0-531-03954-4). Watts.

Foss, Brian, ed. Psychology Survey, Vol. 1. (Psychology Yearbook Ser.). 1978. text ed. 17.95x (ISBN 0-04-150065-2); pap. text ed. 7.95x (ISBN 0-04-150066-0). Allen Unwin.

Foss, Charles R. Evening Before the Diesel: A History of the Grand Trunk Western Railroad. (Illus.). 1980. 44.95 (ISBN 0-87108-552-6). Pruett.

Foss, Christopher. Artillery of the World. 2nd ed. LC 76-6642. (Illus.). 192p. 1976. 8.95 o.p. (ISBN 0-684-14787-4, ScribT). Scribner.

Foss, Christopher F. Armoured Fighting Vehicles of the World. rev. ed. LC 77-74717. (Illus.). 1978. 8.95 o.p. (ISBN 0-684-15225-8, ScribT). Scribner.

--The Illustrated Guide to Modern Tanks & Fighting Vehicles. LC 80-65165. (Illustrated Military Guides Ser.). (Illus.). 160p. 1980. 7.95 (ISBN 0-668-04965-0, 4965-0). Arco.

Foss, Donald J. & Hakes, David T. Psycholinguistics: An Introduction to the Psychology of Language. LC 77-27826. (Experimental Psychology Ser.). (Illus.). 1978. ref. 18.95 (ISBN 0-13-732446-4). P-H.

Foss, E. W. Construction & Maintenance for Farm & Home. 1960. text ed. 18.50x o.p. (ISBN 0-471-26763-5). Wiley.

Foss, George R. What the Author Meant. 196p. 1980. Repr. of 1932 ed. lib. bdg. 25.00 (ISBN 0-89984-204-6). Century Bookbindery.

Foss, J. F., jt. auth. see Potter, M. C.

Foss, Lukas. Quintets for Orchestra: Study Score. 60p. (Orig.). 1980. pap. 15.00 (ISBN 0-686-64720-3, PCB115). Fischer Inc NY.

Foss, Merle L. & Garrick, James G. Ski Conditioning. LC 77-24553. (American College of Sports Medicine Ser.). 1978. text ed. 14.95 (ISBN 0-471-26764-3). Wiley.

Foss, Phillip, Jr. Somata. 1981. pap. price not set (ISBN 0-931460-18-2). Bieler.

Fossen, Richard W. Van see Marlowe, Christopher.

Fosson, Abe R. & Kaak, H. Otto. Child Abuse & Neglect Case Studies. 1977. 13.00 (ISBN 0-87488-062-9). Med Exam.

Fossum, John A. Labor Relations: Development Structure Process. 1979. 19.50x (ISBN 0-256-02088-4). Business Pubns.

Foster, ed. see Nee, Watchman.

Foster, et al. Let the Sunshine in: Learning Activities for Multiply Handicapped Deaf Children, Pt. 1. 1973. pap. 4.50 (ISBN 0-913072-15-X). Natl Assn Deaf.

Foster, Adriance S. & Gifford, Ernest M. Comparative Morphology of Vascular Plants. 2nd ed. LC 73-22459. (Illus.). 1974. text ed. 28.95x (ISBN 0-7167-0712-8). W H Freeman.

Foster, Alan D. The Black Hole. LC 79-53894. (Illus., Orig.). 1979. pap. 1.95 (ISBN 0-345-28538-7). Ballantine.

--Bloodhype. 1977. pap. 2.25 (ISBN 0-345-29476-9). Ballantine.

--Dark Star. 1978. pap. 1.95 (ISBN 0-345-28871-8, Del Rey Bks). Ballantine.

--Icerigger. 1978. pap. 2.25 (ISBN 0-345-29454-8, Del Rey Bks). Ballantine.

--Midworld. 1976. pap. 1.50 o.p. (ISBN 0-345-25364-7). Ballantine.

--Outland. (Orig.). 1981. pap. 2.75 (ISBN 0-446-95829-8). Warner Bks.

--The Tar-Aiym Krang. 1979. pap. 2.45 (ISBN 0-345-29232-4, Del Rey Bks). Ballantine.

Foster, Albert B. Approved Practices in Soil Conservation. 5th ed. (Illus.). 1981. 13.00 (ISBN 0-8134-2170-5, 2170); text ed. 9.75x. Interstate.

--Approved Practices in Soil Conservation. 4th ed. LC 72-81495. (Illus.). 1973. 14.00 o.p. (ISBN 0-8134-1486-5, 1486); text ed. 10.50x o.p. (ISBN 0-685-42162-7). Interstate.

Foster, Arthur L., ed. The House Church Evolving. LC 76-4198. (Studies in Ministry & Parish Life). 126p. 1976. 12.95x (ISBN 0-913552-04-6); pap. 5.50x (ISBN 0-913552-05-4). Exploration Pr.

Foster, Arthur R. & Wright, Robert L., Jr. Basic Nuclear Engineering. 3rd ed. 1977. text ed. 26.95x (ISBN 0-205-05697-0); sol. manual free (ISBN 0-205-05698-9). Allyn.

Foster, Arthur R., jt. auth. see Mark, Melvin.

Foster, C. A., et al. Introduction to the Administration of Justice. 2nd ed. LC 78-13498. 347p. 1979. 17.50 (ISBN 0-471-04079-7). Wiley.

Foster, C. D., et al. Local Government Finance in a Unitary State. (Illus.). 640p. 1980. text ed. 60.00x (ISBN 0-04-336066-1, 2473). Allen Unwin.

Foster, C. E. How to Prepare Stamp Exhibits. LC 75-14662. 1970. 21.00 o.s.i. (ISBN 0-917922-04-2); plastic binding 12.00 (ISBN 0-917922-06-9); pap. 10.50 (ISBN 0-917922-05-0). Hobby Pub Serv.

Foster, C. R., et al. Modern Guidance Practices in Teaching. (Illus.). 294p. 1980. 19.75 (ISBN 0-398-03990-9); pap. 14.50 (ISBN 0-398-04040-0). C C Thomas.

Foster, Carol. Developing Self-Control. 136p. 1980. pap. text ed. 7.00 (ISBN 0-917472-02-0). F Fournies.

Foster, Catharine O. The Ecological Garden. Ingraham, Erick, tr. (Illus.). 188p. (Orig.). 1981. 12.50 (ISBN 0-8159-5407-7); pap. 6.95 (ISBN 0-8159-5408-5). Devin.

Foster, Charles. First Steps: Bible Stories for Children. (Illus.). (gr. 5-8). 1960. pap. 2.50 (ISBN 0-8024-0023-X). Moody.

Foster, Charles R., ed. Comparative Public Policy & Citizen Participation: Energy, Education, Health & Local Governance in the U. S. A. & Germany. (Pergamon Policy Studies). 1980. 29.50 (ISBN 0-08-024624-9). Pergamon.

--Nations Without a State: Ethnic Minorities of Western Europe. 304p. 1980. 22.95 (ISBN 0-03-056807-2). Praeger.

Foster, Dave, ed. Jerusalem: The Christian Herald Photoguide. LC 79-57167. (Illus.). 128p. 1980. 14.95 (ISBN 0-915684-60-8). Christian Herald.

Foster, David. Innovation & Employment. 1980. 27.00 (ISBN 0-08-022500-4); pap. 11.25 (ISBN 0-08-022499-7). Pergamon.

Foster, David E. Revision of North American Trichodes (Herbst) (Coleoptera: Cleridae) (Special Publications: No. 11). (Illus.). 1976. 4.00 (ISBN 0-89672-037-3). Tex Tech Pr.

Foster, David W. Augusto Roa Bastos. (World Authors Ser.: No. 507 (Paraguay)). 1978. 12.50 (ISBN 0-8057-6348-1). Twayne.

--The Early Spanish Ballad. (World Authors Ser.: Spain: No. 185). lib. bdg. 10.95 (ISBN 0-8057-2288-2). Twayne.

--Twentieth Century Spanish-American Novel: A Bibliographic Guide. LC 75-25787. 1975. 10.00 (ISBN 0-8108-0871-4). Scarecrow.

Foster, David W. & Foster, Virginia R. Luis de Gongora. (World Authors Ser.: Spain: No. 226). 1973. lib. bdg. 10.95 (ISBN 0-8057-2386-2). Twayne.

--Research Guide to Argentine Literature. LC 70-9731. 1970. 10.00 (ISBN 0-8108-0298-8). Scarecrow.

Foster, David W. & Foster, Virginia R., eds. Modern Latin American Literature, 2 vols. LC 72-81710. (A Library of Literary Criticism). 1100p. 1975. Set. 60.00 (ISBN 0-8044-3139-6). Ungar.

Foster, Donald. Managing the Catalog Department. LC 75-19081. 1975. 10.00 (ISBN 0-8108-0836-6). Scarecrow.

Foster, Donald L. Prints in the Public Library. LC 72-13056. (Illus.). 1973. 10.00 (ISBN 0-8108-0579-0). Scarecrow.

Foster, Donna. Building a Child's Self-Esteem. 1977. pap. 1.25 (ISBN 0-8307-0489-2, 90-702-06). Regal.

Foster, Doris V. Tell Me, Mister Owl. LC 56-9155. (Illus.). (ps-3). 1957. PLB 7.92 o.p. (ISBN 0-688-51071-X). Lothrop.

Foster, Durwood, jt. ed. see Bryant, Darrol.

Foster, Edward H. Catharine Maria Sedgwick. (U. S. Authors Ser.: No. 233). 1974. lib. bdg. 10.95 (ISBN 0-8057-0658-5). Twayne.

--The Civilized Wilderness: Backgrounds to American Literature, 1817-1860. LC 74-33091. (Illus.). 1975. 12.95 (ISBN 0-02-910350-9). Free Pr.

--Susan & Anna Warner. (United States Authors Ser.: No. 312). 1978. lib. bdg. 12.50 (ISBN 0-8057-7232-4). Twayne.

Foster, Eugene S. Understanding Broadcasting. LC 77-74323. (Mass Communication Ser.). (Illus.). 1978. text ed. 16.95 (ISBN 0-201-02468-3). A-W.

Foster, F. Blanche. First Book of Kenya. LC 77-87928. (First Bks). (Illus.). (gr. 7 up). 1969. PLB 4.90 o.p. (ISBN 0-531-00706-5). Watts.

Foster, F. Gordon & Goyette, Richert E., eds. Medical Psychiatry Journal Articles. 1974. spiral bdg. 15.50 (ISBN 0-87488-530-2). Med Exam.

Foster, Frederick. The Up & Outer. 1980. pap. 4.95 (ISBN 0-8423-7799-9). Tyndale.

Foster, G. M. Tzintzuntzan. 416p. 1979. pap. 7.95 (ISBN 0-444-99070-4). Elsevier.

Foster, Genevieve. Abraham Lincoln's World. (Illus.). (gr. 5-11). 1944. lib. rep. ed. 20.00x (ISBN 0-684-14855-2, ScribJ). Scribner.

--Seventeen Seventy-Six: Year of Independence. LC 75-106531. (Illus.). (gr. 2-6). 1970. 4.50 (ISBN 0-684-20822-9, ScribJ). Scribner.

--Theodore Roosevelt: An Initial Biography. (Illus.). (gr. 5-7). 1954. write for info. (ISBN 0-684-12690-7, ScribJ). Scribner.

--Year of Columbus, 1492. LC 77-85268. (Illus.). (gr. 2-6). 1969. write for info. (ISBN 0-684-12695-8, ScribJ). Scribner.

Foster, H. D. Disaster Planning: The Preservation of Life & Property. (Springer Series on Environmental Management). (Illus.). 275p. 1981. 29.80 (ISBN 0-387-90498-0). Springer-Verlag.

Foster, H. H., Jr. A Bill of Rights for Children. (Amer. Lec Behavioral Science & Law Ser.). 96p. 1974. pap. 7.75 (ISBN 0-398-02986-5). C C Thomas.

Foster, Herbert L. Ribbin', Jivin', & Playin' the Dozens: The Unrecognized Dilemma of Inner-City Schools. LC 74-7393. 304p. 1974. text ed. 16.50 o.s.i. (ISBN 0-88410-150-9); pap. 9.95 (ISBN 0-88410-163-0). Ballinger Pub.

Foster, Hope S., jt. auth. see Halper, H. Robert.

Foster, J. & Nightingale, J. D. A Short Course in General Relativity. (Illus.). 1979. pap. text ed. 14.95 (ISBN 0-582-44194-3). Longman.

Foster, J. Bristol, jt. auth. see Dagg, Anne I.

Foster, J. R., tr. see Gernet, Jacques.

Foster, Jack S. Structure & Fabric, 2 pts. (Mitchell's Building Construction Ser.). 1978. Pt. 1. pap. 13.95 (ISBN 0-470-26348-2); Pt. 2. pap. 13.95 (ISBN 0-470-26349-0). Halsted Pr.

Foster, James H. & Berman, Martin M. Solid Liver Tumors. LC 76-28938. (Major Problems in Clinical Surgery Ser.: Vol. 22). 1977. text ed. 25.00 (ISBN 0-7216-3824-4). Saunders.

Foster, Jeanne R. Awakening Grace, Poems at the Feet of the Silent Master. Shaw, Jeanne & Shaw, Darwin, eds. (Illus.). 1977. 4.95 (ISBN 0-913078-28-X). Sheriar Pr.

Foster, John. The Influences of Rudolph Laban. 1978. 16.95 (ISBN 0-86019-015-3). Transatlantic.

Foster, John L., jt. auth. see Henderson, Thomas A.

Foster, John T. The Flight of the Lone Eagle: Charles Lindbergh Flies Nonstop from New York to Paris. LC 74-898. (Focus Bks). (Illus.). 72p. 1974. PLB 6.45 (ISBN 0-531-02723-6). Watts.

Foster, John W. American Diplomacy in the Orient. LC 74-112309. (Law, Politics, & History Ser). 1970. Repr. of 1903 ed. lib. bdg. 42.50 (ISBN 0-306-71915-0). Da Capo.

--Arbitration & the Hague Court. 148p. 1980. Repr. of 1904 ed. lib. bdg. 18.50x (ISBN 0-8377-0535-5). Rothman.

--Century of American Diplomacy. LC 79-87542. (American History, Politics & Law Ser). 1970. Repr. of 1900 ed. lib. bdg. 45.00 (ISBN 0-306-71458-2). Da Capo.

Foster, Joseph W., 3rd, et al. Reliability, Availability & Maintainability: RAM. 300p. 1981. 39.95 (ISBN 0-930206-05-3). M-a Pr.

Foster, Julia A., jt. auth. see Lund, Shirley.

Foster, K. Neill. Help! I Believe in Tongues. LC 75-2518. 160p. (Orig.). 1975. pap. 2.45 (ISBN 0-87123-211-1, 210211). Bethany Fell.

--Revolution of Love. 96p. 1973. pap. 0.95 (ISBN 0-87123-486-6, 200486). Bethany Fell.

Foster, Kenelm. The Two Dantes & Other Studies. 1978. 20.00x (ISBN 0-520-03326-4). U of Cal Pr.

Foster, Lawrence. Religion & Sexuality: Three American Communal Experiments of the Nineteenth Century. 400p. 1981. 19.95 (ISBN 0-19-502794-9). Oxford U Pr.

Foster, Lawrence J., et al. Teaching Preschool Language Arts. (Illus.). 272p. 1981. pap. text ed. 15.95 (ISBN 0-8425-1933-5). Brigham.

Foster, Lee. Adventures in California Country. Shangle, Robert D., ed. LC 79-28673. (Illus.). 64p. 1981. pap. 4.95 (ISBN 0-89802-063-8). Beautiful Am.

--Backyard Farming. (Urban Life Practical Solutions to the Challenges of the 80's Ser.). 96p. (Orig.). pap. 4.95 (ISBN 0-87701-224-5). Chronicle Bks.

--The Beautiful California Missions. Shangle, Robert D., ed. LC 78-102341. (Illus.). 72p. 1977. 14.95 (ISBN 0-915796-23-6); pap. 7.95 (ISBN 0-915796-22-8). Beautiful Am.

--Beautiful San Francisco. Shangle, Robert D., ed. LC 78-102340. (Illus.). 72p. 1977. 14.95 (ISBN 0-915796-19-8); pap. 7.95 (ISBN 0-915796-18-X). Beautiful Am.

--Beautiful Southern California. Shangle, Robert D., ed. LC 78-8532. (Illus.). 72p. 1978. 14.95 (ISBN 0-915796-38-4); pap. 7.95 (ISBN 0-915796-37-6). Beautiful Am.

--Portrait of the Bay Area. Pfeiffer, Douglas A., ed. (Portrait of America Ser.). (Illus.). 80p. (Orig.). 1981. pap. text ed. 5.95 (ISBN 0-912856-69-6). Graphic Arts Ctr.

Foster, Lowell W. Geo-Metrics: The Metric Application of Geometric Tolerancing. (Illus.). 300p. 1974. 14.95 (ISBN 0-201-01989-2); pocket guide 9.95 (ISBN 0-201-01987-6). A-W.

--Geometrics Two: The Application of Geometric Tolerancing Techniques. LC 78-67959. 1979. pap. text ed. 14.95 (ISBN 0-201-01936-1). A-W.

Foster, Lynn & Boast, Carol. Subject Compilations of State Laws: Research Guide & Annotated Bibliography. LC 80-1788. 480p. 1981. lib. bdg. 45.00 (ISBN 0-313-21255-4, FOS). Greenwood.

Foster, Marcia S. OJT Payroll Clerk Resource Materials. 2nd ed. (Gregg Office Job Training Program). (Illus.). 112p. (gr. 11-12). 1980. soft cover 4.80 (ISBN 0-07-021641-X); training manual 3.56 (ISBN 0-07-021641-X). McGraw.

Foster, Mary. Learning to Cook. 1971. pap. text ed. 4.95x o.p. (ISBN 0-435-42501-3). Heinemann Ed.

Foster, Michael B. Mystery & Philosophy. LC 79-8721. (The Library of Philosophy & Theology). 96p. 1980. Repr. of 1957 ed. lib. bdg. 18.75x (ISBN 0-313-20792-5, FOMP). Greenwood.

Foster, Muriel. Days on Sea, Loch & River. (Illus.). 124p. 1981. 4.95 (ISBN 0-7181-1788-3). Merrimack Bk Serv.

Foster, Myles B. Anthems & Anthem Composers. LC 76-125047. (Music Ser). 1970. Repr. of 1901 ed. lib. bdg. 19.50 (ISBN 0-306-70012-3). Da Capo.

Foster, Phillips. Plaid for Introduction to Environmental Science. 1977. pap. 5.50 (ISBN 0-256-01262-8, 08-0313-00). Learning Syst.

Foster, R. Organic Charge-Transfer Complexes. (Organic Chemistry Ser.). 1969. 65.00 o.s.i. (ISBN 0-12-262650-8). Acad Pr.

Foster, R. L. The Nature of Enzymology. 384p. 1980. 79.00x (ISBN 0-85664-434-X, Pub. by Croom Helm England). State Mutual Bk.

Foster, R. R. Charles Stewart Parnell: The Man & His Family. 320p. 1976. text ed. 31.25x (ISBN 0-391-00909-5). Humanities.

Foster, R. W. Twelve Hundred Multiple Choice Questions in Pharmacology. LC 79-42816. (Illus.). 188p. 1980. pap. write for info. Butterworths.

Foster, R. W. & Cox, Barry. Basic Pharmacology. LC 80-49873. (Illus.). 296p. 1980. text ed. 18.95 (ISBN 0-407-00170-0). Butterworths.

Foster, Richard, jt. ed. see Sutton, Walter.

Foster, Richard J. Freedom of Simplicity. LC 80-8351. 192p. 1981. 9.95 (ISBN 0-06-062832-4, HarpR). Har-Row.

Foster, Rick, ed. West Coast Plays, No. 6. Incl. Dinosauer. Hopkins, Glenn & Lindberg, Wayne.; Jacob's Ladder. Graham, Barbara; Pizza. Linfante, Michele; Sylvester the Cat vs. Galloping Billy Bronco. Lynch, Michael. 1980. pap. 5.00. West Coast Plays.

Foster, Robert. A Guide to Middle Earth. 1975. pap. 1.95 o.p. (ISBN 0-345-24936-4). Ballantine.

Foster, Robert J. Physical Geology. 3rd ed. (Science Ser.). 1979. text ed. 19.95 (ISBN 0-675-08312-5); study guide avail. Merrill.

Foster, Roy A., jt. auth. see Mayshark, Cyrus.

Foster, Ruel E. Jesse Stuart. LC 68-24298. (U. S. Authors Ser.: No. 140). 1968. lib. bdg. 10.95 (ISBN 0-8057-0704-2). Twayne.

Foster, Ruth S. Homeowner's Guide to Landscaping That Saves Energy Dollars. (Illus.). 1978. 10.95 o.p. (ISBN 0-679-50863-5); pap. 5.95 o.p. (ISBN 0-679-50866-X). McKay.

Foster, Stephen. Household Songs: Eighteen Forty-Four to Eighteen Sixty-Four. LC 76-169647. (Earlier American Music Ser.: No. 12). (Illus.). 1973. Repr. of 1862 ed. lib. bdg. 19.50 (ISBN 0-306-77312-0). Da Capo.

--The Social Orchestra: A Collection of Popular Melodies Arranged As Duets, Trios, & Quartets. Hitchcock, H. Wiley, ed. LC 79-169645. (Earlier American Music Ser: Vol. 13). (Illus.). 96p. 1973. Repr. of 1854 ed. lib. bdg. 18.50 (ISBN 0-306-77313-9). Da Capo.

Foster, Stephen C. The Critics of Abstract Expressionism. Kuspit, Donald B., ed. (Studies in Fine Arts: Criticism: No. 13). 130p. 1980. 21.95 (ISBN 0-8357-1088-2, Pub. by UMI Res Pr). Univ Microfilms.

Foster, Steven. Minstrel-Show Songs. (Early American Music Ser.). 1979. Repr. of 1863 ed. lib. bdg. 18.50 (ISBN 0-306-77314-7). Da Capo.

Foster, Steven & Little, Meredith. The Book of the Vision Quest. (Illus.). 192p. (Orig.). 1981. pap. 10.00 (ISBN 0-933280-03-3). Island CA.

Foster, Sue B. Self-Assessment of Current Knowledge in Cardiopulmonary Nursing. 1975. spiral bdg. 9.50 (ISBN 0-87488-288-5). Med Exam.

Foster, Timothy D. Dare to Lead. LC 76-57013. 1977. pap. 3.25 o.p. (ISBN 0-8307-0519-8, 54-054-08); study guide 1.39 o.p. (ISBN 0-8307-0530-9, 61-006-00). Regal.

Foster, Timothy R. The Aviator's Catalog: A Source Book of Aeronautica. 288p. 1980. 24.95 (ISBN 0-442-21201-1); pap. 16.95 (ISBN 0-442-22465-6). Van Nos Reinhold.

Foster, V., jt. auth. see Walkley, Christina.

Foster, Virginia R. Baltasar Gracian. (World Authors Ser.: Spain: No. 337). 176p. 1975. lib. bdg. 12.50 (ISBN 0-8057-2398-6). Twayne.

Foster, Virginia R., jt. auth. see Foster, David W.

Foster, Virginia R., jt. ed. see Foster, David W.

Foster, William. Homeowner's Guide to Solar Heating & Cooling. LC 76-24786. (Illus.). 1976. pap. 4.95 (ISBN 0-8306-5906-4, 906). TAB Bks.

Foster, William L. & Urquhart, Kenneth T. Vicksburg: Southern City Under Siege. LC 80-84685. (Illus.). xxv, 82p. 1980. 15.00x (ISBN 0-917860-02-0). Historic New Orleans.

Foster, William Z. Great Steel Strike & Its Lessons. LC 70-139202. (Civil Liberties in American History Ser). (Illus.). 1971. Repr. of 1920 ed. lib. bdg. 29.50 (ISBN 0-306-70079-4). Da Capo.

--More Pages from a Worker's Life. Zipser, Arthur, ed. (Occasional Papers: No. 32). 1979. 1.50 (ISBN 0-89977-026-6). Am Inst Marxist.

Foster-Harris, William. Basic Formulas of Fiction. rev. ed. 1977. Repr. of 1960 ed. 7.95x (ISBN 0-8061-0135-0). U of Okla Pr.

Fosu, Kojo. Trends in African Contemporary Art. LC 79-51527. (Illus.). 1980. 45.00 (ISBN 0-933184-02-6); pap. 35.00 (ISBN 0-933184-03-4). Flame Intl.

Foth, H. & Jacobs, H. S. Field Guide to Soils. (Earth Science Curriculum Project Pamphlet Ser). 1971. pap. 3.20 (ISBN 0-395-02616-4). HM.

Foth, Henry D. Fundamentals of Soil Science. 6th ed. LC 77-86509. 1978. 22.95 (ISBN 0-471-26792-9). Wiley.

Fothergill, Brian. The Mitred Earl. (Illus.). 1974. 8.95 o.p. (ISBN 0-571-09736-7, Pub. by Faber & Faber). Merrimack Bk Serv.

--Sir William Hamilton: Envoy Extraordinary. (Illus.). 1969. 9.95 o.p. (ISBN 0-571-08958-5, Pub. by Faber & Faber); pap. 3.95 o.p. (ISBN 0-571-10291-3). Merrimack Bk Serv.

Fothergwill, Brian, ed. Essays by Divers Hands: Being the Transactions of the Royal Society of Literature. (New Series: Vol. XLI). 147p. 1980. 22.50x (ISBN 0-8476-3530-9). Rowman.

Fotheringham, John & Morris, Joan. Understanding the Preschool Retarded Child. 1976. pap. text ed. 4.25x (ISBN 0-8077-8006-5). Tchrs Coll.

Fotheringham, Nick. Beachcomber's Guide to Gulf Coast Marine Life. LC 80-10607. (Illus.). 1980. pap. 6.95 (ISBN 0-88415-496-3). Pacesetter Pr.

Fotheringham, Nick & Brunenmeister, Susan L. Beachcomber's Guide to Gulf Coast Marine Life. rev. ed. Orig. Title: Common Marine Invertebrates of the Northwestern Gulf Coast. (Illus.). 176p. (Orig.). 1980. pap. 6.95 (ISBN 0-88415-062-3). Gulf Pub.

Fotheringham, Peter, et al. American Government & Politics. 2nd ed. 1978. 19.95 o.p. (ISBN 0-571-04973-7, Pub. by Faber & Faber); pap. 9.95 (ISBN 0-571-04889-7). Merrimack Bk Serv.

Fotine, Larry. Contemporary Musician's Handbook & Dictionary. (Illus.). 1981. softcover 10.00 (ISBN 0-933830-03-3). Poly Tone.

Fotinis, Athanasios P. The De Anima of Alexander of Aphrodisias: A Translation & Commentary. LC 80-5062. 362p. 1980. text ed. 20.00 (ISBN 0-8191-1032-9); pap. text ed. 12.00 (ISBN 0-8191-1033-7). U Pr of Amer.

Fotinos, S. Douglas, jt. auth. see Carver, Tina K.

Fotion, N. Moral Situations. LC 68-31034. 1968. 7.00x (ISBN 0-87338-076-2); pap. 3.50x (ISBN 0-87338-077-0). Kent St U Pr.

Fototeca. Ancient Roman Architecture. 141p. 1979. binder 725.00 (ISBN 0-89664-008-6, Pub. by K G Saur); write for info. microfiche (Pub. by K G Saur). Gale.

Fotre, Vincent. Why You Lose at Tennis. 128p. pap. 1.95 o.p. (ISBN 0-06-463326-8, 326, EH). Har-Row.

Fouad, A. A., jt. auth. see Anderson, P. M.

Foucault, Michel. Archaeology of Knowledge: Includes the Discourse on Language. Sheridan-Smith, A. M., tr. LC 72-1135. 1972. 28.50x (ISBN 0-394-47118-0). Irvington.

--Power Knowledge: Selected Interviews & Other Writings, 1972-1977. 1981. 12.95 (ISBN 0-394-51357-6); pap. 5.95 (ISBN 0-394-73954-X). Pantheon.

--Language, Counter-Memory, Practice: Selected Essays & Interviews. Bouchard, Donald F., ed. Simon, Sherry, tr. from Fr. LC 77-4561. (Cornell Paperbacks Ser.). 240p. 1980. pap. 5.95 (ISBN 0-8014-9204-1). Cornell U Pr.

--Mental Illness & Psychology. Smith, A. M., tr. 1976. pap. 3.95x (ISBN 0-06-131801-9, TB 1801, CN). Har-Row.

Foucault, Michel, intro. by see McDougall, Richard.

Foudraine, Jan. Not Made of Wood: A Psychiatrist Discovers His Profession. LC 73-6057. 480p. 1974. 9.95 o.s.i. (ISBN 0-02-540200-5). Macmillan.

Fought, John G. Chorti (Mayan) Texts: I. LC 72-80380. (Folklore & Folklife Ser). 592p. 1973. 18.00x (ISBN 0-8122-7667-1). U of Pa Pr.

Fouk al-Ada. English-French-Arabic Dictionary of Diplomacy & International Terms. 30.00x (ISBN 0-685-54026-X). Intl Bk Ctr.

Foulds, Jervis. The Lady Dudley Challenge Cup. (Illus.). 1978. 17.50 (ISBN 0-85131-294-2, Dist. by Sporting Book Center). J A Allen.

Foulds, L. Neoplastic Development. Vol. 1. 1969. 58.50 (ISBN 0-12-262801-2); Vol. 2. 1975. 96.00 (ISBN 0-12-262802-0). Acad Pr.

Foulis, David, jt. auth. see Munem, Mustafa.

Foulke, Adrienne, tr. see Condominas, Georges.

Foulke, Adrienne, tr. see Sciascia, Leonardo.

Foulke, J. Focusing on Gebruder Heubach Dolls. 1980. pap. 6.95 (ISBN 0-87588-148-3). Hobby Hse.

Foulke, William D., tr. see Paul The Deacon.

Foulkes, A. Peter & Lohner, Edgar, eds. Deutsche Drama Von Kleist Bis Hauptmann. LC 76-185793. 680p. 1973. text ed. 21.80 (ISBN 0-395-12742-4). HM.

Foulkes, E. Tamez de see De Foulkes, E. Tamez & De Foulkes, I. W.

Foulkes, Fred K. Personnel Policies in Nonunion Companies. 350p. 1981. 19.95 (ISBN 0-686-69329-9). P-H.

Foulkes, I. W. de see De Foulkes, E. Tamez & De Foulkes, I. W.

Foulkes, Irene. Griego Del Nuevo Testamento: Texto Programado, Tomo III. 220p. (Span.). 1973. pap. text ed. 7.00 (ISBN 0-89922-054-1). Edit Caribe.

--Griego Del Nuevo Testamento: Texto Programado, Tomo II. 203p. (Span.). 1973. pap. 7.00 (ISBN 0-89922-053-3). Edit Caribe.

--Griego Del Nuevo Testamento: Texto Programado, Tomo I. 194p. (Span.). 1973. pap. 7.00 (ISBN 0-89922-052-5). Edit Caribe.

Foulkes, Richard. Panorama del Nuevo Testamento. LC 75-15161. 112p. (Orig., Span.). 1975. pap. 2.50 (ISBN 0-89922-048-7). Edit Caribe.

Found, Peter, ed. European Direct Mail Databook: 1976. 1976. pap. 27.00 o.p. (ISBN 0-7161-0284-6, Gower). Unipub.

--International Literary Market Place 1981. 15th ed. LC 77-70295. 500p. 1981. pap. 42.50 (ISBN 0-8352-1345-5). Bowker.

Foundation Center. COMSEARCH: Geographic. (COMSEARCH Printouts). (Orig.). 1980. write for info. (ISBN 0-87954-030-3); pap. write for info. (ISBN 0-87954-033-8). Foundation Ctr.

--COMSEARCH: Special Topics. (COMSEARCH Printouts). (Orig.). 1980. pap. 12.00 (ISBN 0-87954-031-1); microfiche 4.00 (ISBN 0-87954-034-6). Foundation Ctr.

--Comsearch: Subjects. (COMSEARCH Printouts). (Orig.). 1980. pap. 12.00 (ISBN 0-87954-029-X); microfiche 4.00 (ISBN 0-87954-032-X). Foundation Ctr.

--Corporate Foundation Profiles. LC 80-69622. 512p. (Orig.). 1980. pap. 50.00 (ISBN 0-87954-038-9). Foundation Ctr.

--Foundation Center National Data Book, 2 vols. 4th ed. 846p. (Orig.). 1979. pap. 45.00 (ISBN 0-87954-027-3). Foundation Ctr.

--The Foundation Center National Data Book, 2 vols. 840p. (Orig.). 1981. pap. 45.00 (ISBN 0-87954-039-7). Foundation Ctr.

--Foundation Center Source Book Profiles. Goldstein, Sherry E., ed. LC 77-79015. (Ser. 3). (Orig.). 1980. pap. 200.00 (ISBN 0-87954-024-9). Foundation Ctr.

--The Foundation Grants Index Nineteen Eighty. LC 72-76018. 540p. (Orig.). 1981. pap. 30.00 (ISBN 0-87954-040-0). Foundation Ctr.

Foundation for San Francisco's Architectural Heritage. Splendid Survivors: San Francisco's Downtown Architectural Heritage. Charles Hall Page & Assocs., ed. LC 79-53196. (Illus.). 1979. 32.50 (ISBN 0-89395-037-8); pap. 19.95 (ISBN 0-89395-031-9). Cal Living Bks.

Foundation for the Advancement of Artists. Artists USA Nineteen Eighty One to Nineteen Eighty Two. 7th ed. LC 78-134303. (Illus.). 1981. 30.00 (ISBN 0-912916-07-9). Foun Adv Artists.

Foundry Services Ltd. Foundryman's Handbook. 8th ed. 1976. text ed. 13.75 (ISBN 0-08-018020-5). Pergamon.

Foundyller, Charles M. Turnkey CAD-CAM Computer Graphics: A Survey & Buyers' Guide for Manufacturers, Pts. 1 & 2. Incl. Pt. 1. 254p. 84.00x (ISBN 0-938484-01-X); Pt. 2. 120p. 69.00x (ISBN 0-938484-02-8). (Illus.). 374p. 1980. Set. spiral with laminated covers 153.00x (ISBN 0-938484-00-1). Daratech.

--Turnkey CAD-CAM Computer Graphics: A Survey & Buyers' Guide for Manufacturers, 3 pts, Pts. 1,2, & 3. (Illus.). 476p. 1980. Set. spiral with laminated covers 199.00x (ISBN 0-938484-04-4). Daratech.

--Turnkey CAD-CAM Computer Graphics: A Survey & Buyers' Guide for Manufacturers, Pt. 3. (Illus.). 102p. 1980. spiral with laminated covers 46.00x (ISBN 0-938484-03-6). Daratech.

Fountaine, George La see La Fountaine, George.

Fourel, M. Exercices de Verbes. Incl. No. 1. 60p. 1969 (ISBN 0-87774-031-3); No. 2. 86p. 1969; No. 3. 102p. 1969 (ISBN 0-87774-033-X); No. 4. 75p. 1967 (ISBN 0-87774-034-8). (Fr.). pap. text ed. 3.50 ea. Schoenhof.

Fournier. Le Grand Meaulnes. (Easy Reader, B). pap. 3.75 (ISBN 0-88436-110-1, FRA201056). EMC.

Fournier, Alfred, tr. see Hamby, Wallace B.

Fournier, William & O'Malley, Sarah A. Age & Grace. (Orig.). 1980. 6.95 (ISBN 0-8146-1127-3). Liturgical Pr.

Fournies, Ferdinand F. Management Performance Appraisal: A National Study. 1977. 12.00 (ISBN 0-917472-03-9). F Fournies.

--Salesman Performance Appraisal: A National Study. 1975. 25.00 (ISBN 0-917472-01-2). F Fournies.

Fourrier, M., jt. auth. see Auvray, J.

Fourth Cranfield Fluidics Conference. Proceedings. 1970. text ed. 60.00 (ISBN 0-900983-08-6, Dist. by Air Science Co.). BHRA Fluid.

Fourth Fluid Power Symposium. Proceedings. 1975. text ed. 56.00 (ISBN 0-900983-45-0, Dist. by Air Science Co.). BHRA Fluid.

Fourth Franklin Conference. Innovation & the American Economy. 140p. 1980. pap. text ed. 8.95 (ISBN 0-89168-030-0). Franklin Inst Pr.

Fourth International Conference on Jet Cutting Technology. Proceedings, 2 vols. Stephens, H. S., ed. (Illus.). 1979. Set. pap. text ed. 68.00 (ISBN 0-900983-79-5, Dist. by Air Science Co.). BHRA Fluid.

Fourth International Conference on the Pneumatic Transport of Solids in Pipes. Proceedings. Stephens, H. S. & Stapleton, C. A., eds. (Illus.). 1979. pap. text ed. 71.00 (ISBN 0-900983-86-8, Dist by Air Science Co.). BHRA Fluid.

Fourth Symposium of the International Research Society for Children's Literature, Held at the University of Exeter, September 9-12, 1978 & Fox, Geoff. Responses to Children's Literature: Proceedings. 150p. 1980. text ed. 17.80 (ISBN 0-89664-949-0). K G Saur.

Foust. The Economic Landscape: A Theoretical Introduction. (Geography Ser.). 1978. text ed. 18.95 (ISBN 0-675-08432-6). Merrill.

Foust, A. S., et al. Principles of Unit Operations. 2nd ed. 768p. 32.95 (ISBN 0-471-26897-6). Wiley.

Fout, John C. German History & Civilization - 1806-1914: A Bibliography of Scholarly Periodical Literature. LC 74-10803. 1974. 15.00 (ISBN 0-8108-0742-4). Scarecrow.

Fowke, Edith & Carpenter, Carole H. A Bibliography of Canadian Folklore in English. 232p. 1981. 15.00x (ISBN 0-8020-2394-0). U of Toronto Pr.

Fowke, Edith F. Traditional Singers & Songs from Ontario. LC 65-26777. (Illus.). x, 210p. Repr. of 1965 ed. 18.00 (ISBN 0-8103-5011-4). Gale.

Fowkes, Robert A., jt. auth. see Brody, Elaine.

Fowle, T. W. The Poor Law: The English Citizen: His Rights & Responsibilities. vi, 175p. 1980. Repr. of 1893 ed. lib. bdg. 17.50x (ISBN 0-8377-0534-7). Rothman.

Fowler, A., ed. see Lewis, C. S.

Fowler, A., ed. see Lewis, Clive S.

Fowler, Alastair. John Milton: Paradise Lost. (Longman Annotated English Poets Ser.). (Illus.). 1974. pap. text ed. 9.95x (ISBN 0-582-48455-3). Longman.

--Triumphal Forms, Structural Patterns in Elizabethan Poetry. LC 75-105498. (Illus.). 1970. 42.00 (ISBN 0-521-07747-8). Cambridge U Pr.

Fowler, Austin. Monarch Notes on Camus' Major Works. (Orig.). pap. 1.75 (ISBN 0-671-00552-9). Monarch Pr.

Fowler, Barney. Adirondack Album, No. 1. (Illus.). 200p. (Orig.). 1981. pap. 10.25 (ISBN 0-9605556-1-7). Outdoor Assocs.

--Adirondack Album, No. 2. (Illus.). 200p. (Orig.). 1980. pap. 10.25 (ISBN 0-9605556-0-9). Outdoor Assocs.

Fowler, Carol. Contributions of Women: Art. LC 76-3479. (Contributions of Women Ser.). (Illus.). (gr. 6 up). 1976. PLB 8.95 (ISBN 0-87518-115-5). Dillon.

--Contributions of Women: Dance. LC 78-10313. (Contributions of Women Ser.). (Illus.). (gr. 6 up). 1979. PLB 8.95 (ISBN 0-87518-169-4). Dillon.

Fowler, Charles W. & Smith, Tim D. Dynamics of Large Mammal Populations. 525p. 1981. 40.00 (ISBN 0-471-05160-8, Pub.by Wiley Interscience). Wiley.

Fowler, D. H., tr. see Thom, R.

Fowler, Douglas. A Guide to Pynchon's Gravity's Rainbow. 1980. 17.50 (ISBN 0-88233-404-2); pap. 7.50 (ISBN 0-88233-405-0). Ardis Pubs.

Fowler, E. P., tr. see Benedikt, Moriz.

Fowler, Elaine, jt. ed. see Wright, Louis B.

Fowler, Ethel L., ed. For Your Delight. (gr. 4-6). 1924. 5.95 o.p. (ISBN 0-571-06514-7, Pub. by Faber & Faber). Merrimack Bk Serv.

Fowler, F. G., jt. auth. see Fowler, Henry W.

Fowler, Frank P. & Sandberg, E. W. Basic Mathematics for Administration. LC 62-15189. 1962. text ed. 19.95 (ISBN 0-471-26976-X). Wiley.

Fowler, Gene. Good Night, Sweet Prince. 1978. Repr. of 1944 ed. 16.05x (ISBN 0-89966-095-9). Buccaneer Bks.

--Return of the Shaman. Winans, A. D., ed. (Illus.). 64p. (Orig.). 1981. pap. 4.00 (ISBN 0-915016-29-X). Second Coming.

Fowler, H. W., et al. Metaphor. Commager, Steele, ed. Incl. English Idioms; English Influence on the French Vocabulary; Briton, British, Britisher; The Split Infinitive; Logic & Grammar; Four Words; Subjunctives; Medium Aevum & the Middle Age; Index to Tracts I-XIX. (Society for Pure English Ser.: Vol. 2). 1979. lib. bdg. 42.00 (ISBN 0-8240-3666-2). Garland Pub.

Fowler, Harlan D. Three Caravans to Yuma: The Untold Story of Bactrian Camels in Western America. LC 80-66268. (Illus.). 173p. 1980. 25.00 (ISBN 0-87062-131-9). A H Clark.

Fowler, Harold. The Gospel of Matthew, Vol. I. LC 78-1064. (The Bible Study Textbook Ser.). (Illus.). 1975. 13.50 (ISBN 0-89900-029-0). College Pr Pub.

--The Gospel of Matthew, Vol. III. (The Bible Study Textbook Ser.). (Illus.). 1978. 12.95 (ISBN 0-89900-031-2). College Pr Pub.

Fowler, Heather T. see Tiger, Lionel.

Fowler, Henry W. & Fowler, F. G. King's English. 3rd ed. 1931. 12.95x (ISBN 0-19-869105-X). Oxford U Pr.

Fowler, James W. Stages of Faith: The Psychology of Human Development & the Quest for Meaning. LC 80-7757. 224p. 1981. 10.95 (ISBN 0-06-062840-5, HarpR). Harper Row.

Fowler, John & Cornforth, John. English Decoration in the 18th Century. (Illus.). 1978. 29.95 o.p. (ISBN 0-214-20033-7, 8057, Dist. by Arco). Barrie & Jenkins.

Fowler, John F. Nuclear Particles in Cancer Treatment. (Medical Physics Handbook: No. 8). 216p. 1981. 28.00 (ISBN 0-9960020-7-3, Pub. by a Hilger England). Heyden.

Fowler, John M. Energy-Environment Source Book. rev. ed. 1978. pap. 5.00 o.p. (ISBN 0-686-53816-1, 471-14692). Natl Sci Tchrs.

Fowler, Kathryn M. Hunger: The World Food Crisis, An NSTA Environmental Materials Guide. 1977. pap. 2.50 (ISBN 0-87355-005-6). Natl Sci Tchrs.

--Population Growth: The Human Dilemma, An NSTA Environmental Materials Guide. 1977. pap. 3.50 (ISBN 0-87355-008-0). Natl Sci Tchrs.

Fowler, Kenneth. The Age of Plantagenet & Valois. 1967. 19.95 o.p. (ISBN 0-236-30832-7, Pub. by Paul Elek). Merrimack Bk Serv.

--Jackal's Gold. 1981. pap. 1.95 (ISBN 0-440-14237-7). Dell.

Fowler, L. N. Phrenology Applied to Marriage & to the Major Social Relations of Mankind. (Illus.). 1978. Repr. of 1842 ed. 39.75 (ISBN 0-89266-109-7). Am Classical Coll Pr.

Fowler, Mark, jt. auth. see Felton, Bruce.

Fowler, P. J., ed. Archaeology & the Landscape: Essays for L. V. Grinsell. (Illus.). 1972. text ed. 12.00x (ISBN 0-212-98398-9). Humanities.

Fowler, Peter. Wessex: Regional Archaeology. 1967. 3.95x o.p. (ISBN 0-435-32965-0). Heinemann Ed.

Fowler, Peter J. Approaches to Archaeology. LC 77-81910. (Illus.). 1977. 18.95x (ISBN 0-312-04665-0). St Martin.

Fowler, R. S. & Dick, A. J. English: A Literary Foundation Course. 1975. text ed. 18.95x o.p. (ISBN 0-04-428032-7); pap. text ed. 9.50x o.p. (ISBN 0-04-428033-5). Allen Unwin.

Fowler, Ralph H. Statistical Mechanics. rev., 2nd ed. 96.00 (ISBN 0-521-05025-1); pap. 29.50 (ISBN 0-521-09377-5). Cambridge U Pr.

Fowler, Raymond E. Casebook of a UFO Investigator. 1980. 11.95 (ISBN 0-13-117432-0). P-H.

Fowler, Robert B. & Orenstein, Jeffrey R. Contemporary Issues in Political Theory. LC 76-7410. 288p. 1977. pap. text ed. 9.95x (ISBN 0-471-27032-6). Wiley.

Fowler, Robert H. Jim Mundy. 1978. pap. 2.25 o.s.i. (ISBN 0-515-04707-4). Jove Pubns.

Fowler, Roger. Understanding Language: An Introduction to Linguistics. 1974. 12.50x (ISBN 0-7100-7755-6); pap. 7.95 (ISBN 0-7100-7756-4). Routledge & Kegan.

Fowler, Ron. Flying Precision Maneuvers in Light Airplanes. (Illus.). 224p. 1980. 10.95 (ISBN 0-440-02598-2). Delacorte.

Fowler, Stewart H. Beef Production in the South. LC 78-55815. (Illus.). (gr. 9-12). 1979. 29.95 (ISBN 0-8134-2035-0); text ed. 22.95x (ISBN 0-685-12569-6, 2035). Interstate.

Fowler, Will. The Second Handshake. (Illus.). 1980. 12.50 (ISBN 0-8184-0287-3). Lyle Stuart.

Fowler, William & Coyle, E. Wallace. The American Revolution: Changing Perspectives. 2nd ed. LC 79-88424. (Illus.). 231p. 1981. pap. text ed. 9.95x (ISBN 0-930350-21-9). NE U Pr.

Fowler, William M., Jr. Rebels Under Sail: The American Navy During the Revolution. LC 75-38556. (Encore Edition). (Illus.). 384p. 1976. 6.95 o.p. (ISBN 0-684-15406-4, ScribT). Scribner.

--William Ellery: A Rhode Island Politico & Lord of Admiralty. LC 72-12673. (Illus.). 1973. 10.00 (ISBN 0-8108-0576-6). Scarecrow.

Fowler, William W. Religious Experience of the Roman People: From the Earliest Times to the Age of Augustus. LC 71-145870. 1971. Repr. of 1911 ed. lib. bdg. 37.50x (ISBN 0-8154-0372-0). Cooper Sq.

--Woman on the American Frontier. LC 73-12867. 1974. Repr. of 1878 ed. 30.00 (ISBN 0-8103-3702-9). Gale.

Fowler, Wilton B. British-American Relations, 1917-1918: The Role of Sir William Wiseman. 1969. 18.50 (ISBN 0-691-04594-1). Princeton U Pr.

Fowles, jt. auth. see Cartmell.

Fowles, Diane E., jt. auth. see Willmott, Alan S.

Fowles, John. The Magus. rev. ed. 1979. pap. 3.50 (ISBN 0-440-15162-7). Dell.

Fowles, John & Brukoff, Barry. The Enigma of Stonehenge. LC 80-11472. (Illus.). 128p. 1980. 19.95 (ISBN 0-671-40116-5). Summit Bks.

Fowles, John, tr. see Durfort, Claire de.

Fowles, Robert B. Mass Advertising As Social Forecast: A Method for Futures Research. LC 75-35344. (Illus.). 160p. 1976. lib. bdg. 13.95 (ISBN 0-8371-8595-5, FMA/). Greenwood.

Fowlie, Wallace. Lautreamont. (World Authors Ser.: France: No. 284). 1974. lib. bdg. 10.95 (ISBN 0-8057-2511-3). Twayne.

--A Reading of Dante's Inferno. LC 80-19025. 248p. 1981. lib. bdg. 18.00 (ISBN 0-226-25887-4); pap. 6.50 (ISBN 0-226-25888-2). U of Chicago Pr.

--Stendhal. Kronenberger, Louis, ed. (Masters of World Literature Ser.: Vol. 12). 1969. 5.95 o.s.i. (ISBN 0-02-540390-7). Macmillan.

Fowlie, Wallace, tr. see Rimbaud, Arthur.

Fox. Readings on the Research Process in Nursing. 1979. 16.50 (ISBN 0-8385-8266-4). ACC.

Fox, jt. auth. see Dixson.

Fox, A. F. World of Oil. 1964. 12.25 (ISBN 0-08-010687-0); pap. 7.00 (ISBN 0-08-010686-2). Pergamon.

Fox, Aileen. Roman Britain. (Illus.). (gr. 7 up). 1968. 7.50 (ISBN 0-8023-1143-1). Dufour.

Fox, Alan. Beyond Contract. (Society Today and Tomorrow Ser.). 1974. 16.95 o.p. (ISBN 0-571-10469-X, Pub. by Faber & Faber). Merrimack Bk Serv.

Fox, Allen & Evans, Richard. If I'm the Better Player, Why Can't I Win. LC 79-63332. (Tennis Magazine Bks.). 160p. 1979. 8.95. Golf Digest Bks.

--If I'm the Better Player, Why Can't I Win? LC 79-63332. 160p. 1979. 8.95 (ISBN 0-914178-28-8, 24924, Pub. by Tennis Mag). Golf Digest.

Fox, Annette B. The Politics of Attraction: Four Middle Powers & the United States. LC 76-27291. (Institute of War & Peace Studies of Columbia). 1977. 21.00x (ISBN 0-231-04116-0). Columbia U Pr.

Fox, Annette B., jt. auth. see Fox, William T.

Fox, Anthony. Kingfisher Scream. LC 80-51769. 228p. 1981. 10.95 (ISBN 0-670-41352-6). Viking Pr.

Fox, Betsy. Visions of Sugar Plums. 1980. 6.95 (ISBN 0-935746-00-5). Green Hill.

Fox, Brian A. & Cameron, Allan G. Food Science: A Chemical Approach. 3rd ed. 1977. 10.50x (ISBN 0-8448-0938-1). Crane-Russak Co.

Fox, C. A., et al. Education in Nineteenth Century Britain. (Government & Society in Nineteenth Century Britain Ser.). 246p. 1977. 25.00x (ISBN 0-7165-2211-X, Pub. by Irish Academic Pr Ireland). Biblio Dist.

Fox, C. Fred, jt. ed. see Alberts, Bruce.

Fox, C. Fred, jt. ed. see Gale, Robert P.

Fox, C. Fred, jt. ed. see Hynes, R.

Fox, C. Fred, ed. see ICN-UCLA Symposium, Keystone, Colo., February 1979.

Fox, C. Fred, jt. ed. see Oxender, Dale.

Fox, Cedering-Siv. The Blue Horse & Other Night Poems. LC 78-12793. (Illus.). (gr. 1-4). 1979. 8.95 (ISBN 0-395-28952-1, Clarion). HM.

Fox, Charles. The Noble Enemy. 1980. 12.50 (ISBN 0-385-14526-8). Doubleday.

--The Noble Enemy. LC 78-22770. 1980. 12.50 o.p. (ISBN 0-385-14526-8). Doubleday.

Fox, Charles K. Rising Trout. rev., 2nd ed. LC 77-92364. 1978. 11.95 (ISBN 0-8015-6394-1, Hawthorn); pap. 6.95 (ISBN 0-8015-6395-X, Hawthorn). Dutton.

Fox, Clayton. Prairie Empire. 1977. pap. 1.50 (ISBN 0-505-51215-7). Tower Bks.

Fox, D. J. & Leeser, I. Readings on the Research Process in Nursing. 232p. 1981. pap. 16.50 (ISBN 0-686-69604-2). ACC.

Fox, Danny G., jt. auth. see Minish, Gary L.

Fox, Denis. Animal Biochromes & Structural Colours. 1976. 33.75x (ISBN 0-520-02347-1). U of Cal Pr.

Fox, Denis L. Biochromy: Natural Coloration of Living Things. (Illus.). 1979. 26.75x (ISBN 0-520-03699-9). U of Cal Pr.

Fox, Denton, ed. The Poems of Robert Henryson. (Oxford English Texts Ser.). 704p. 1980. 89.00 (ISBN 0-19-812703-0). Oxford U Pr.

Fox, Dickie L. Directory of Dividend Reinvestment Plans. LC 80-19078. 240p. (Orig.). 1980. pap. 15.00 (ISBN 0-930256-06-9). Almar.

Fox, Douglas J. The Matthew-Luke Commentary of Philoxenus. LC 78-12852. 1979. 13.50 (ISBN 0-89130-350-2); pap. 9.00 (ISBN 0-89130-266-2, 060143). Scholars Pr Ca.

Fox, Edward J. & Moore, Malcolm T. Junior Words, Phrases, Clauses: Exercises in Elementary Grammar. 89p. (Orig.). (gr. 4-6). 1980. pap. 3.25x (ISBN 0-88334-127-1). Ind Sch Pr.

--Words, Phrases, Clauses: Exercises in English Grammar. 3rd ed. 120p. (gr. 6-12). 1980. pap. text ed. 3.50 (ISBN 0-88334-128-X). Ind Sch Pr.

Fox, Edward J. & Wheatley, Edward W. Modern Marketing: Principles & Practice. 1978. 16.95x (ISBN 0-673-15045-3). Scott F.

Fox, Edward J., Jr. & Moore, Malcolm T. Words, Phrases, Clauses. 3rd ed. 120p. (gr. 6-10). 1980. pap. text ed. 3.50x (ISBN 0-686-67158-9). Ind Sch Pr.

Fox, Frank W. J. Reuben Clark: The Public Years. LC 80-17903. (J. Reuben Clark Three Vol. Ser.). (Illus.). 706p. 1980. 10.95 (ISBN 0-8425-1832-0). Brigham.

--J. Reuben Clark: The Public Years. LC 80-17903. (Illus.). 702p. 12.95 (ISBN 0-87747-834-1). Deseret Bk.

Fox, Fred. Essentials of Brass Playing. LC 77-85127. 1978. pap. 6.00 (ISBN 0-913650-03-X). Volkwein Bros.

Fox, Gail. Making Your Children's Clothes. (Penny Pinchers Ser.). 1978. 2.95 (ISBN 0-7153-7549-0). David & Charles.

Fox, Gardner. Blood Trail. 1979. pap. 1.50 (ISBN 0-505-51367-6). Tower Bks.

--The Bold Ones. 1976. pap. 1.25 o.p. (ISBN 0-685-72571-5, LB398, Leisure Bks). Nordon Pubns.

--Hurricane. 1976. pap. 1.50 o.p. (ISBN 0-685-69510-7, LB375DK, Leisure Bks). Nordon Pubns.

--Savage Passage. 1978. pap. 1.95 (ISBN 0-505-51270-X). Tower Bks.

Fox, Gardner F. Kyrik & the Lost Queen. 1976. pap. 1.25 o.p. (ISBN 0-685-74571-6, LB420ZK, Leisure Bks). Nordon Pubns.

--Kyrik & the Wizards Swords. (Orig.). 1976. pap. 1.25 o.p. (ISBN 0-685-64011-6, Leisure Bks). Nordon Pubns.

--Kyrik Fights the Demon World. (Orig.). 1975. pap. 0.95 o.p. (ISBN 0-685-53902-4, LB284NK, Leisure Bks). Nordon Pubns.

--Kyrik: Warlock Warrior. (Orig.). 1975. pap. 0.95 o.p. (ISBN 0-685-52180-X, LB252NK, Leisure Bks). Nordon Pubns.

--The Liberty Sword. 1976. pap. 1.25 o.p. (ISBN 0-685-69145-4, LB358ZK, Leisure Bks). Nordon Pubns.

Fox, Geoff, jt. auth. see Fourth Symposium of the International Research Society for Children's Literature, Held at the University of Exeter, September 9-12, 1978.

Fox, H. & Langley, F. A. Postgraduate Obstetrical & Gynaecological Pathology. 596p. 1973. 90.00 (ISBN 0-08-016992-9). Pergamon.

Fox, Harrison W., Jr. & Hammond, Susan W. Congressional Staffs: The Invisible Force in American Lawmaking. LC 77-72041. (Illus.). 1979. pap. text ed. 7.95 (ISBN 0-02-910430-0). Free Pr.

Fox, Harrison W., Jr. & Schnitzer, Martin. Doing Business in Washington: How to Win Friends & Influence Governemnt. LC 80-2313. (Illus.). 1981. 14.95 (ISBN 0-02-910460-2). Free Pr.

Fox, Helen M. Gardening for Good Eating. (Illus.). 278p. 1973. pap. 1.95 o.s.i. (ISBN 0-686-66736-0, Collier). Macmillan.

Fox, Hero N., et al. Canada & the United States: Transnational & Transgovernmental Relations. 1976. 26.00x (ISBN 0-231-04025-3); pap. 10.00x (ISBN 0-231-04026-1). Columbia U Pr.

Fox, Howard N. Directions. LC 79-14499. (Illus.). 103p. 1979. 17.50 (ISBN 0-87474-434-2). Smithsonian.

Fox, Howard N., jt. ed. see Messerli, Douglas.

Fox, Hugh. First Fire: Central & South American Indian Poetry. LC 77-11528. 1978. pap. 5.95 o.p. (ISBN 0-385-03815-1, Anchor Pr). Doubleday.

--Keep It Peaking. (Rockbottom Proseworks Ser.). Date not set. 15.00 o.p. (ISBN 0-930012-17-8, 79-87598); pap. 5.00 o.p. (ISBN 0-930012-16-X). Mudborn. Postponed.

--Leviathan. 1981. pap. 5.00 (ISBN 0-914140-10-8). Carpenter Pr.

Fox, Hugh see Smith Experimental Fiction Project.

Fox, J., ed. Microwave Research Institute Symposia. Incl. Vol. 1. Modern Network Synthesis. 1952. 19.95 (ISBN 0-470-27093-4); Vol. 4. Modern Advances in Microwave Techniques. LC 55-12897. 1955. o.p. (ISBN 0-470-27192-2); Vol. 5. Modern Network Synthesis. LC 56-2590. 1956. o.p. (ISBN 0-470-27225-2); Vol. 6. Nonlinear Circuit Analysis. LC 55-3575. 1956. o.p. (ISBN 0-470-27258-9); Vol. 9. Millimeter Waves. LC 60-10073. 1960. o.p. (ISBN 0-470-27357-7); Vol. 11. Electromagnetics & Fluid Dynamics of Gaseaous Plasma. LC 62-13174. 1962. 25.95 (ISBN 0-470-27423-9); Vol. 13. Optical Lasers. LC 63-22084. o.p. (ISBN 0-470-27428-X); Vol. 15. System Theory. LC 65-28522. 1965. 26.50 (ISBN 0-470-27430-1); Vol. 17. Modern Optics. LC 67-31757. 1967. o.p. (ISBN 0-470-27433-6); Vol. 19. Computer Processing in Communications. LC 77-122632. 1970. o.p. (ISBN 0-471-27436-4); Vol. 20. Submillimeter Waves. 1971. o.p. (ISBN 0-471-27437-2); Vol. 21. Computers & Automata. 1972. 33.95 (ISBN 0-471-27438-0); Vol. 22. **Computer Communications. 1972. 37.95 (ISBN 0-471-27439-9); Vol. 24. Computer Software Engineering. 1977. 44.95 (ISBN 0-470-98948-3). Pub. by Wiley-Interscience). Wiley.**

Fox, J. D., jt. ed. see Robson, D.

Fox, James A. Forecasting Crime Data. LC 77-8720. (Illus.). 1978. 16.95 (ISBN 0-669-01639-X). Lexington Bks.

Fox, James A., ed. Frontiers in Quantitative Criminology. (Quantitative Studies in Social Relations). 1981. price not set (ISBN 0-12-263950-2). Acad Pr.

Fox, Jane. Primary Health Care of the Young. (Illus.). 1024p. 1980. text ed. 25.95 (ISBN 0-07-021741-6). McGraw.

Fox, Jerome. Microwave Research Institute Symposia: Computer Communications, Vol. 22. LC 72-92508. 1972. 37.95 (ISBN 0-470-27439-5). Halsted Pr.

Fox, Jerome, ed. Computer Software Engineering: Symposium 24. (Microwave Research Institute Symposia Ser.: Vol. 24). 1977. 44.95 o.p. (ISBN 0-470-98948-3). Halsted Pr.

Fox, Joan. Poems to the Eighties. 1979. 6.95 (ISBN 0-533-04540-1). Vantage.

Fox, John. Crittenden: A Kentucky Story of Love & War. 1976. lib. bdg. 12.95x (ISBN 0-89968-035-6). Lightyear.

--The Kentuckians. 1976. lib. bdg. 13.50x (ISBN 0-89968-038-0). Lightyear.

--The Little Shepherd of Kingdom Come. 1976. lib. bdg. 17.75x (ISBN 0-89968-039-9). Lightyear.

--The Trail of the Lonesome Pine. 1976. lib. bdg. 18.25x (ISBN 0-89968-040-2). Lightyear.

Fox, K. A., et al, eds. Economic Models, Estimation & Risk Programming: Essays in Honor of Gerhard Tintner. LC 72-98260. (Lecture Notes in Operations Research & Mathematical Economics: Vol. 15). 1969. pap. 21.90 o.p. (ISBN 0-387-04638-0). Springer-Verlag.

Fox, Karl A. Social Indicators & Social Theory: Elements of an Operational System. LC 74-16255. (Urban Research Ser). 328p. 1974. 23.95 (ISBN 0-471-27060-1, Pub. by Wiley-Interscience). Wiley.

Fox, Karl A. & Kaul, Tej K. Intermediate Economic Statistics, 2 vols. 2nd ed. Incl. Vol. 1. An Integration of Economic Theory & Statistical Methods. Repr. of 1968 ed. 23.50 (ISBN 0-88275-521-8); Vol. 2. A Guide to Recent Developments & Literature, 1968-1978. 186p. 10.50 (ISBN 0-88275-987-6). LC 76-30914. 584p. 1980. 30.00 set (ISBN 0-686-64856-0). Krieger.

Fox, Karl A., jt. auth. see Ezekiel, Mordecai.

Fox, L., ed. Advances in Programming Non-Numerical Applications to Computing Machines. 1965. 16.80 o.p. (ISBN 0-08-011356-7). Pergamon.

Fox, Lay C., ed. see De Alcantara, Shimon.

Fox, Leslie. Introduction to Numerical Linear Algebra. (Monographs on Numerical Analysis Ser.). 1965. 12.95x (ISBN 0-19-500325-X). Oxford U Pr.

Fox, M. & Schnabel, T. It's Your Body - Know What the Doctor Ordered: Your Complete Guide to Medical Testing. 1979. 10.00 (ISBN 0-13-507624-2). P-H.

Fox, M. W. Canine Behavior. (Illus.). 152p. 1978. 11.50 (ISBN 0-398-00599-0). C C Thomas.

--Canine Pediatrics: Development, Neonatal & Congenital Diseases. 160p. 1966. pap. 14.75 photocopy ed, spiral (ISBN 0-398-00600-8). C C Thomas.

Fox, M. W., ed. The Wild Canids: Their Systematics, Behavioral Ecology & Evolution. 508p. 1975. 22.50 (ISBN 0-442-22430-3). Krieger.

Fox, Margaret, ed. Biological Basis for Cancer Diagnosis, Vol. 4. (Illus.). 1979. 68.00 (ISBN 0-08-024387-8). Pergamon.

Fox, Mary V. Jane Goodall: Living Chimp Style. LC 80-27542. (Taking Part Ser.). (Illus.). 48p. (gr. 3 up). 1981. PLB 6.95 (ISBN 0-87518-204-6). Dillon.

--Janet Guthrie: Foot to the Floor. LC 80-28309. (Taking Part Bks.). (Illus.). 48p. (gr. 3 up). 1981. PLB 6.95 (ISBN 0-87518-202-X). Dillon.

--The Skating Heidens. LC 80-23066. (Illus.). 128p. (gr. 5-12). 1980. PLB 7.95 (ISBN 0-89490-046-3). Enslow Pubs.

Fox, Matthew, intro. By. Breakthrough: Meister Eckhart's Creation Spirituality. LC 80-909. 600p. 1980. 15.95 (ISBN 0-385-17045-9). Doubleday.

--Breakthrough: Meister Eckhart's Creation Spirituality in New Translation. LC 80-909. 600p. 1980. pap. 7.95 (ISBN 0-385-17034-3, Im). Doubleday.

Fox, Matthew, ed. Western Spirituality: Historical Roots & Ecumenical Routes. 1979. 9.95 o.p. (ISBN 0-8190-0635-1). Fides Claretian.

Fox, Michael, ed. Schopenhauer: His Philosophical Achievement. 276p. 1980. 28.50x (ISBN 0-389-20097-2). B&N.

Fox, Michael W. Returning to Eden: Animal Rights & Human Responsibility. LC 79-56281. 300p. 1980. 13.95 (ISBN 0-670-12722-1). Viking Pr.

--The Touchlings: Fantasy Creatures That Live on Love, Sunshine & Giving. 1981. 7.95 (ISBN 0-87491-293-8). Acropolis.

Fox, Nell N. How to Raise & Train an Australian Terrier. (Orig.). pap. 2.00 (ISBN 0-87666-238-6, DS1050). TFH Pubns.

Fox, Nicholas J., jt. auth. see Hunter, Eric J.

Fox, Paula. How Many Miles to Babylon? LC 79-25802. (Illus.). (gr. 5-7). 1980. 7.95 (ISBN 0-87888-164-6). Bradbury Pr.

--King's Falcon. LC 69-13322. (Illus.). (gr. 6-8). 1969. 6.95 (ISBN 0-87888-005-4). Bradbury Pr.

--The Little Swineherd & Other Tales. (gr. k-6). 1981. pap. 1.75 (ISBN 0-440-45302-X, YB). Dell.

--Maurice's Room. (Illus.). (gr. 3-5). 1966. 4.95g o.s.i. (ISBN 0-02-735730-9). Macmillan.

--Maurice's Room. LC 66-10167. (gr. 3-5). 1972. pap. 1.50 o.s.i. (ISBN 0-02-043200-3, Collier). Macmillan.

--Slave Dancer. LC 73-80642. (Illus.). 192p. (gr. 6-8). 1973. 9.95 (ISBN 0-87888-062-3). Bradbury Pr.

--The Widow's Children. 1977. pap. 1.75 (ISBN 0-380-01791-1, 35352). Avon.

Fox, R. The Tory Islanders. LC 77-83992. (Illus.). 1978. 27.95 (ISBN 0-521-21870-5); pap. 7.95x (ISBN 0-521-29298-0). Cambridge U Pr.

Fox, R. M. & Real, H. G. A Monograph of the Ithomiidae: Napeogenini, Pt. 4. (Memoirs Ser: No. 15). (Illus.). 358p. 1971. 25.00 (ISBN 0-686-01270-4). Am Entom Inst.

Fox, Renee C. Essays in Medical Sociology: Journeys into the Field. LC 79-10413. (Health, Medicine & Society: a Wiley Interscience Ser.). 1979. 22.95 (ISBN 0-471-27040-7, Pub. by Wiley-Interscience). Wiley.

--Experiment Perilous. LC 59-6816. 264p. 1974. pap. 6.50x (ISBN 0-8122-1040-9). U of Pa Pr.

Fox, Richard G. Kin, Clan, Raja, & Rule: State-Hinterland Relations in Preindustrial India. LC 76-129614. (Center for South & Southeast Asia Studies, UC Berkeley). 1971. 17.50x (ISBN 0-520-01807-9). U of Cal Pr.

--Urban Anthropology: Cities in Their Cultural Setting. (Illus.). 1977. pap. text ed. 9.95 (ISBN 0-13-939462-1). P-H.

Fox, Richard L. Optimization Methods for Engineering Design. LC 78-127891. (Engineering Ser). 1971. 23.95 (ISBN 0-201-02078-5). A-W.

Fox, Richard W. So Far Disordered in Mind: Insanity in California, 1870-1930. LC 77-93479. 1979. 11.95x (ISBN 0-520-03620-4). U of Cal Pr.

Fox, Robert & Weisz, George, eds. The Organisation of Science & Technology in France 1808-1914. LC 80-40227. (La Maison Des Sciences De L'homme). (Illus.). 336p. 1980. 37.50 (ISBN 0-521-23234-1). Cambridge U Pr.

Fox, Robert J. Saints & Heroes Speak. LC 77-70206. 1977. pap. 7.95 o.p. (ISBN 0-87973-640-2). Our Sunday Visitor.

Fox, Robert W. & McDonald, Alan T. Introduction to Fluid Mechanics. 2nd ed. LC 77-20839. 1978. text ed. 25.95 (ISBN 0-471-01909-7); solutions manual 15.00 (ISBN 0-471-03681-1). Wiley.

Fox, Robin. Keresan Bridge: A Problem in Pueblo Ethnology. (Monographs on Social Anthropology: No. 35). 1967. text ed. 20.75x (ISBN 0-485-19535-6, Athlone Pr). Humanities.

--The Red Lamp of Incest: What the Taboo Can Tell Us About Who We Are & How We Got That Way. (Illus.). 288p. 1980. 12.95 (ISBN 0-525-18943-2). Dutton.

Fox, Robin, ed. Biosocial Anthropology. LC 75-4110. (Association of Social Anthropologists, Ser. No. 1). 1975. 22.95 (ISBN 0-470-27033-0). Halsted Pr.

Fox, Ruth. The Tangled Chain: The Structure of Disorder in the Anatomy of Melancholy. 1976. 16.50x (ISBN 0-520-03085-0). U of Cal Pr.

Fox, Siv C. & Brauer, Bil. The Juggler. (Illus.). 1977. pap. 4.95 (ISBN 0-915298-08-2). Sagarin Pr.

Fox, Stephen R. John Muir & His Legacy: The American Conservation Movement. (Illus.). 416p. 1981. 16.95 (ISBN 0-316-29110-2). Little.

Fox, Stuart I. Laboratory Guide to Human Physiology: A Concepts & Clinical Applications. 2nd ed. 285p. 1980. wire coil bdg. avail. (ISBN 0-697-04595-1); answers to questions available (ISBN 0-697-04596-X). Wm C Brown.

Fox, Theodore. Crisis in Communication: The Functions & Future of Medical Journals. (Heath Clark Lectures 1963). 1965. text ed. 2.50x (ISBN 0-485-26316-5, Athlone Pr). Humanities.

Fox, Uffa. More Joys of Living. 180p. 1980. 12.00x (ISBN 0-245-50796-5, Pub. by Nautical England). State Mutual Bk.

Fox, V. Community-Based Corrections. 1977. 15.95 (ISBN 0-13-153254-5). P-H.

Fox, Vernon. Introduction to Criminology. (Illus.). 416p. 1976. 17.95 (ISBN 0-13-480053-2). P-H.

Fox, Vernon B. Introduction to Corrections. 2nd ed. (Illus.). 1977. text ed. 17.95 (ISBN 0-13-479485-0). P-H.

Fox, Vivian, jt. auth. see Quitt, Martin.

Fox, W. J., jt. auth. see McBirnie, S. C.

Fox, W. Randolph. After the Apocalypse. (Orig.). 1980. pap. 1.95 (ISBN 0-532-23118-X). Manor Bks.

Fox, Walter. Writing the News: Print Journalism in the Electronic Age. 1977. 8.95 (ISBN 0-8038-8081-2); pap. text ed. 4.50 (ISBN 0-8038-8082-0). Hastings.

Fox, Wesley. Golden State Rails. (Illus.). 76p. 1980. pap. 8.95 (ISBN 0-9604122-0-4). W Fox.

Fox, William J., jt. auth. see Berkley, George.

Fox, William L., jt. auth. see Walsh, Richard.

Fox, William P. Dixiana Moon. LC 80-51770. 256p. 1981. 11.95 (ISBN 0-670-27453-4). Viking Pr.

--Ruby Red. LC 75-146686. 1971. 6.95 o.s.i. (ISBN 0-397-00710-8). Lippincott.

Fox, William T. & Fox, Annette B. NATO & the Range of American Choice. LC 67-11560. 1967. 22.50x (ISBN 0-231-03001-0). Columbia U Pr.

Fox, William T. & Schilling, Warner R, eds. European Security & the Atlantic System. LC 72-4248. (Institute for War & Peace Studies). 276p. 1973. 17.00x (ISBN 0-231-03640-X). Columbia U Pr.

Foxall, Raymond. Highwayman No. One: Society of the Dispossessed. pap. 1.25 (ISBN 0-451-07216-2, Y7216, Sig). NAL.

Fox-Davies, A. C. The Mauleverer. 1976. lib. bdg. 14.95x (ISBN 0-89968-163-8). Lightyear.

Fox-Davies, Arthur C., ed. Armorial Families: A Directory of Gentlemen of Coat-Armour, Vol. 1 & 2. LC 76-94029. (Illus.). 1970. Repr. Set. 38.50 (ISBN 0-8048-0721-3). C E Tuttle.

Foxe. Foxe's Book of Martyrs. Repr. 7.95 (ISBN 0-686-12388-3). Church History.

Foxe, John. Foxe's Book of Martyrs. 400p. 1981. pap. 2.95 (ISBN 0-686-69320-5). Whitaker Hse.

Foxley, A., ed. Income Distribution in Latin America. LC 75-20835. 1976. 35.50 (ISBN 0-521-21029-1). Cambridge U Pr.

Foxley, A., et al. Redistributive Effects of Government Programmes: The Chilean Case. (Illus.). 1979. 32.00 (ISBN 0-08-023130-6). Pergamon.

Foxley, Alejandro & Whitehead, Laurence, eds. Economic Stabilization in Latin America: Political Dimensions. 120p. 1980. pap. 16.50 (ISBN 0-08-026788-2). Pergamon.

Fox-Lockert, Lucia. Women Novelists in Spain & Spanish America. LC 79-23727. 356p. 1979. 19.00 (ISBN 0-8108-1270-3). Scarecrow.

Foxon, D. F. English Verse, 1701-50. Incl. Vol. 1. Catalogue; Vol. 2. Indexes. 1975. 540.00 (ISBN 0-521-08144-0). Cambridge U Pr.

Fox Strangeways, A. H. The Music of Hindustan. LC 75-905015. 1975. 20.00x (ISBN 0-88386-638-2). South Asia Bks.

Foxton, Thomas see Bunyan, John.

Foxworth, Jo. Boss Lady: An Executive Woman Talks About Making It. LC 77-2514. 1978. 9.95 o.s.i. (ISBN 0-690-01398-1, TYC-T). T Y Crowell.

--Wising up. 1980. 9.95 (ISBN 0-440-09605-7). Delacorte.

Foxworth, Thomas, ed. see Matt, Paul, et al.

Foy, Elizabeth. Decoupage, the Ancient Art of Surface Finishing & Antiquing. new ed. LC 73-185673. (Handicraft Ser.). (Illus.). 32p. (Orig.). (gr. 7-12). 1971. lib. bdg. 2.45 incl. catalog cards (ISBN 0-87157-905-7); pap. 1.25 vinyl laminated covers (ISBN 0-87157-405-5). SamHar Pr.

Foy, Elizabeth & Schurer, John. Construction of Assemblages. new ed. Rahmas, D. Steve, ed. (Handicraft Ser.: No. 7). (Illus.). 32p. (Orig.). (gr. 7-12). 1973. lib. bdg. 2.45 incl. catalog cards (ISBN 0-87157-907-3); pap. 1.25 vinyl laminated covers (ISBN 0-87157-407-1). SamHar Pr.

Foy, J. G. Gone Is Shadow's Child. 1972. pap. 1.25 (ISBN 0-89129-205-5). Jove Pubns.

Foy, Jessie G. Gone Is Shadow's Child. 1976. pap. 1.25 (ISBN 0-89129-205-5). Jove Pubns.

Foy, Nancy. The Yin & Yang of Organizations. LC 80-18558. 1980. 11.95 (ISBN 0-688-03769-0). Morrow.

Foy, Tom. A Guide to Archery. (Illus.). 176p. 1981. 14.95 (ISBN 0-7207-1245-9). Merrimack Bk Serv.

Foye, Raymond, jt. auth. see Poe, Edgar A.

Foye, Raymond, ed. Edgar Allan Poe: The Unknown Poe. LC 80-2431. 1980. pap. 5.95 (ISBN 0-87286-110-4). City Lights.

Foye, Raymond, ed. see Kaufman, Bob.

Foye, William O., ed. Principles of Medicinal Chemistry. 2nd ed. (Illus.). 931p. 1981. text ed. write for info. (ISBN 0-8121-0722-5). Lea & Febiger.

Foyle, Christina, ed. see Beak, Linda.

Foyle, Christina, ed. see Birchall, M. Joyce.

Foyle, Christina, ed. see Daglish, E. Fitch.

Foyle, Christina, ed. see Evans, Anthony.

Foyle, Christina, ed. see Genders, Roy.

Foyle, Christina, ed. see Gill, Joan.

Foyle, Christina, ed. see Gordon, John F.

Foyle, Christina, ed. see Gore, Catherine.

Foyle, Christina, ed. see Harmar, Hilary.

Foyle, Christina, ed. see Hayes, Irene E.

Foyle, Christina, ed. see Hill, Frank W.

Foyle, Christina, ed. see Hill, Herminie W.

Foyle, Christina, ed. see Keeling, Jill A.

Foyle, Christina, ed. see Pond, Grace.

Foyle, Christina, ed. see Rogers, Cyril H.

Foyle, Christina, ed. see Shelton, Margaret R., et al.

Foyle, Christina, ed. see Stenning, Eiliah M.

Foyle, Christina, ed. see Wiley, Constance & Wiley, Wilson.

Foyle, W. G., ed. see Chenuz, Frida J.

Foyles, Christina, ed. see Noel-Hume, Ivor & Noel-Hume, Audrey.

Fozdar, Jamshed. Buddha Maitrya-Amitabha Has Appeared. LC 75-6131. (Illus.). 1976. 24.00 (ISBN 0-87743-119-1, 7-32-25); pap. 12.50 (ISBN 0-87743-120-5, 7-32-26). Baha'i.

Frable, William J., jt. auth. see Johnston, William W.

Fracchia, Charles A. Junk Bonds. (Illus.). 1980. 10.95 (ISBN 0-07-021766-1). McGraw.

--Second Spring: U. S. Catholicism in the 1980s. LC 79-3599. 208p. 1980. 9.95 (ISBN 0-06-063012-4, HarpR, HarpR). Har-Row.

Fraccia, Charles A. So This Is Where You Work! A Guide to Unconventional Working Environments. (Illus.). 1979. pap. 9.95 o.p. (ISBN 0-14-005219-4). Penguin.

Frackenpohl, Arthur. Harmonization at the Piano. 4th ed. 275p. 1981. pap. text ed. write for info. (ISBN 0-697-03559-X). Wm C Brown.

Fraczek, Adam, jt. ed. see Feshbach, Seymour.

Fradenburg, Leo G. United States Airlines: Trunk & Regional Carriers, Their Operations & Management. (Orig.). 1980. pap. text ed. 18.95 (ISBN 0-8403-2128-7). Kendall-Hunt.

Fradin, Dennis. Cara. (Illus.). (gr. 2-4). 1977. PLB 7.95 o.p. (ISBN 0-516-03438-3). Childrens.

--Delaware in Word & Pictures. LC 80-5842. (Young Peoples Stories of Our States Ser.). (Illus.). 48p. (gr. 2-5). 1980. PLB 8.95 (ISBN 0-516-03908-3). Childrens.

--Florida: In Words & Pictures. LC 80-16681. (Young People's Stories of Our States Ser.). (Illus.). 48p. (gr. 2-5). 1980. PLB 8.65 (ISBN 0-516-03909-1). Childrens.

--Georgia: In Words & Pictures. LC 80-26768. (Young People's Stories of Our States Ser.). (Illus.). 48p. (gr. 2-5). 1981. PLB 8.65g (ISBN 0-516-03910-5, Time Line). Childrens.

--Kentucky: In Words & Pictures. LC 80-25810. (Young People's Stories of Our States Ser.). 48p. (gr. 2-5). 1981. PLB 8.65g (ISBN 0-516-03917-2, Time Line). Childrens.

--Louisiana: In Words & Pictures. (Young People's Stories of Our States Ser.). (Illus.). 48p. (gr. 2-5). 1981. PLB 8.65g (ISBN 0-516-03918-0, Time Line). Childrens.

--Massachusetts: In Words & Pictures. LC 80-26161. (Young People's Stories of Our States Ser.). (Illus.). 48p. (gr. 2-5). 1981. PLB 8.65g (ISBN 0-516-03921-0, Time Line). Childrens.

--Montana: In Words & Pictures. LC 80-25023. (Young People's Stories of Our States Ser.). (Illus.). 48p. (gr. 2-5). 1981. PLB 8.65g (ISBN 0-516-03926-1, Time Line). Childrens.

--Nevada: In Words & Pictures. LC 80-24179. (Young People's Stories of Our States Ser.). (Illus.). 48p. (gr. 2-5). 1981. PLB 8.65g (ISBN 0-516-03928-8, Time Line). Childrens.

--New Hampshire: In Words & Pictures. LC 80-25421. (Young People's Stories of Our States Ser.). (Illus.). 48p. (gr. 2-5). 1981. PLB 8.65g (ISBN 0-686-69455-4, Time Line). Childrens.

--New Mexico: In Words & Pictures. (Young People's Stories of Our States Ser.). (Illus.). 48p. (gr. 2-5). 1981. PLB 8.65g (ISBN 0-516-03931-8, Time Line). Childrens.

--North Dakota: In Words & Pictures. LC 80-26480. (Young People's Stories of Our States Ser.). (Illus.). 48p. (gr. 2-5). 1981. PLB 8.65g (ISBN 0-516-03934-2, Time Line). Childrens.

--Oklahoma: In Words & Pictures. LC 80-26961. (Young People's Stories of Our States Ser.). (Illus.). 48p. (gr. 2-5). 1981. PLB 8.65g (ISBN 0-516-03936-9, Time Line). Childrens.

--Rhode Island: In Words & Pictures. LC 80-22669. (Young People's Stories of Our States Ser.). (Illus.). 48p. (gr. 2-5). 1981. PLB 8.65g (ISBN 0-516-03939-3, Time Line). Childrens.

--South Dakota: In Words & Pictures. LC 80-25349. (Young People's Stories of Our States Ser.). (Illus.). 48p. (gr. 2-5). 1981. PLB 8.65g (ISBN 0-516-03941-5, Time Line). Childrens.

Fradkin, Philip L. A River, No More: The Colorado River & the West. LC 80-2713. (Illus.). 384p. 1981. 15.95 (ISBN 0-394-41579-5). Knopf.

Fraenkel, C. E., ed. see Brecht, Bertolt.

Fraenkel, C. E., ed. see Grass, Gunter.

Fraenkel, Eduard. Horace. (Oxford Paperbooks Ser). 1957. 34.00x (ISBN 0-19-814310-9). Oxford U Pr.

--Horace. 478p. 1981. pap. 23.95 (ISBN 0-19-814376-1). Oxford U Pr.

Fraenkel, Heinrich & O'Connell, Kevin J. Prepared Variations. 1981. 15.61 (ISBN 0-08-024095-X); pap. 7.71 (ISBN 0-08-024096-8). Pergamon.

Fraenkel, J. Helping Students Think & Value: Strategies for Teaching the Social Studies. 1973. 16.95 (ISBN 0-13-386557-6). P-H.

Fraenkel, Jack, ed. see Wolf, Alvin.

Fraenkel, Jack R. How to Teach About Values: An Analytic Approach. (Illus.). 176p. 1977. text ed. 11.95x (ISBN 0-13-435446-X); pap. text ed. 8.95x (ISBN 0-13-435453-2). P-H.

Fraenkel, Jack R., ed. see Czarra, Fred R. & Heaps, Joseph F.

Fraenkel, Jack R., ed. see Durfee, David A.

Fraenkel, Jack R., ed. see Eckenrod, James S.

Fraenkel, Jack R., ed. see Pratt, Francis.

Fraenkel, Jack R., ed. see Selakovich, Daniel.

Fraenkel, Jack R., et al. Decision-Making in American Government. (gr. 9-12). 1980. text ed. 16.40 (ISBN 0-205-06845-6, 7668457); tchrs'. guide 6.12 (ISBN 0-205-06852-9, 766852-X). Allyn.

Fraenkel, Osmond K. The Rights We Have. rev. ed. 256p. 1974. 6.95 o.s.i. (ISBN 0-690-00585-7, TYC-T). T Y Crowell.

Fraenkel, Peter. Namibians of Southwest Africa. (Minority Rights Group: No. 19). 1974. pap. 2.50 (ISBN 0-89192-105-2). Interbk Inc.

--Overland. LC 75-26358. (Illus.). 160p. 1976. 6.50 (ISBN 0-7153-7040-5). David & Charles.

Fraenkel, Richard, et al, eds. American Agriculture & U.S. Foreign Policy. LC 78-19761. 1979. 19.95 (ISBN 0-03-043101-8). Praeger.

Fraenkel-Conrat, H. & Wagner, R. R., eds. Comprehensive Virology, Vol. 1: Descriptive Catalogue of Viruses. LC 74-5493. (Illus.). 200p. 1974. 22.50 (ISBN 0-306-35141-2, Plenum Pr). Plenum Pub.

--Comprehensive Virology, Vol. 7: Reproduction-Bacterial DNA Viruses. (Illus.). 300p. 1977. 25.00 (ISBN 0-306-35147-1, Plenum Pr). Plenum Pub.

--Comprehensive Virology, Vol. 8: Regulation & Genetics-Bacterial Dna Viruses. (Illus.). 350p. 1977. 29.50 (ISBN 0-306-35148-X, Plenum Pr). Plenum Pub.

Fraenkel-Conrat, Heinz. Design & Function at the Threshold of Life: The Viruses. (Orig.). 1962. o. p. 20.50 (ISBN 0-12-265162-6); pap. 10.50 (ISBN 0-12-265168-5). Acad Pr.

Fraenkel-Conrat, Heinz & Wagner, Robert, eds. Comprehensive Virology: Volume 16, Virus-Host Interactions. 385p. 1980. 39.50 (ISBN 0-306-40488-5, Plenum Pr). Plenum Pub.

Fraenkel Von Velson, Ruth, tr. see Ehrenberg, Victor.

Fragasso, Philip M. Good News-Bad News. LC 80-15582. 176p. (gr. 4-8). 1980. PLB 7.95 (ISBN 0-201-03197-3). A-W.

Frager, Ruth L., jt. auth. see Paternoster, Lewis M.

Fragomen, Austin L., ed. see Annual Legal Conference on the Representation of Aliens 1978.

Fraiberg, Selma. Clinical Studies in Infant Mental Health: The First Year of Life. (Illus.). 279p. 1980. text ed. 17.50x (ISBN 0-465-01170-5). Basic.

--Magic Years. LC 59-6073. 1968. 12.95 (ISBN 0-684-10166-1, ScribT); pap. 4.95 (ISBN 0-684-71768-9, SL161, ScribT). Scribner.

Fraissard, Jacques P. & Resing, Henry A., eds. Magnetic Resonance in Colloid & Interface Science. (NATO Advanced Study Institutes C. Mathematical & Physical Sciences Ser.: No. 61). 710p. 1980. lib. bdg. 76.00 (ISBN 90-277-1153-4, Pub. by D. Reidel). Kluwer Boston.

Fraizer, Dale W. Alain Robbe-Grillet: An Annotated Bibliography of Critical Studies, 1953-1972. LC 73-13874. (Author Bibliographies Ser.: No. 13). 1973. 10.00 (ISBN 0-8108-0645-2). Scarecrow.

Frajese, G., et al, eds. Oligozoospermia. 1981. text ed. price not set (ISBN 0-89004-589-5). Raven.

Frake, Charles O. Language & Cultural Description: Essays by Charles O. Frake. Dil, Anwar S., ed. LC 79-67771. (Language Science & National Development Ser.). 360p. 1980. 17.50x (ISBN 0-8047-1074-0). Stanford U Pr.

Frakes, George E. Laboratory for Liberty: The South Carolina Legislative Committee System, 1719-1776. LC 74-94066. (Illus.). 218p. 1970. 14.50x (ISBN 0-8131-1219-2). U Pr of Ky.

Frakes, James R. & Traschen, Isadore. Short Fiction: A Critical Collection. 2nd ed. LC 69-11382. 1968. pap. text ed. 9.95 (ISBN 0-13-809178-1). P-H.

Fraknoi, Andrew. Resource Book for the Teaching of Astronomy & Instructor's Manual for Ivan King's Text, "The Universe Unfolding". 1977. pap. text ed. 6.95x (ISBN 0-7167-0288-6). W H Freeman.

Fraleigh, John B. Calculus with Analytic Geometry. LC 79-18693. (Illus.). 1980. text ed. 26.95 (ISBN 0-201-03041-1). A-W.

--A First Course in Abstract Algebra. 2nd ed. LC 75-9010. 1976. 19.95 (ISBN 0-201-01984-1). A-W.

Fraleigh, John B., jt. auth. see Beauregard, Raymond A.

Fraleigh, Patrick W., jt. auth. see Gilmore, Susan K.

Fraley, Angela E. Schooling & Innovation: The Rhetoric & the Reality. 288p. 1981. text ed. write for info. (ISBN 0-9605520-0-6). Gibson Pubs.

Fralin, Richard. Rousseau & Representation. LC 78-15903. 1979. 17.50x (ISBN 0-231-04474-7). Columbia U Pr.

Fram, Eugene H. & Mossien, Herbert J. Before the Economy Dips: Planning Protective Action. (Presidents Association Special Studies: No. 66). 1977. 20.00 o.p. (ISBN 0-8144-4066-5). Am Mgmt.

Frame, Donald M. & McKinley, Mary B., eds. Columbia Montaigne Conference: Papers. (French Forum Monographs: No. 27). 120p. (Orig.). 1981. pap. 11.50 (ISBN 0-917058-26-7). French Forum.

Frame, Donald M., ed. & tr. see Montaigne, Michel De.

Frame, George & Frame, Lory. Swift & Enduring: Cheetahs & Wild Dogs of the Serengeti. 1981. 15.95 (ISBN 0-525-93060-4). Dutton.

--Swift & Enduring: Cheetahs & Wilddogs of the Serengeti. (Illus.). 256p. 1980. 15.95 (ISBN 0-525-93060-4). Dutton.

Frame, J. E. Thessalonians. LC 12-23430. (International Critical Commentary Ser.). 336p. Repr. of 1912 ed. 17.50x (ISBN 0-567-05032-7). Attic Pr.

Frame, Janet. The Adaptable Man. LC 65-19327. 1965. 4.95 o.s.i. (ISBN 0-8076-0302-3). Braziller.

--The Edge of the Alphabet. LC 62-16268. 1962. 4.95 o.p. (ISBN 0-8076-0194-2). Braziller.

--Faces in the Water. 1961. 4.95 o.s.i. (ISBN 0-8076-0149-7). Braziller.

--Intensive Care. LC 78-110305. 1970. 6.95 o.s.i. (ISBN 0-8076-0555-7). Braziller.

--Owls Do Cry. 4.50 o.s.i. (ISBN 0-8076-0116-0). Braziller.

--Scented Gardens for the Blind. LC 64-10786. 1964. 4.50 o.s.i. (ISBN 0-8076-0268-X). Braziller.

--A State of Siege. LC 66-20188. 1966. 5.00 o.p. (ISBN 0-8076-0373-2). Braziller.

--Stories & Fables: The Reservoir (With Snowman Snowman) 2 vols. boxed 7.00 o.s.i. (ISBN 0-8076-0233-7). Braziller.

Frame, Jean & Frame, Paul. How to Give a Party. LC 74-183296. (First Bks). (Illus.). 96p. (gr. 4-7). 1972. PLB 4.90 o.p. (ISBN 0-531-00759-6). Watts.

Frame, Linda J. Folk & Forign Costume Dolls. (Illus.). 1980. pap. 9.95 (ISBN 0-89145-143-9). Collector Bks.

Frame, Lory, jt. auth. see Frame, George.

Frame, Paul. Drawing Dogs & Puppies. (How to Draw Ser.). (Illus.). (gr. 4-6). 1978. PLB 6.90 s&l (ISBN 0-531-01452-5). Watts.

Frame, Paul, jt. auth. see Frame, Jean.

Frame, R., jt. auth. see Jedamus, Paul.

Frame, Robert & Curry, Dudley. Financial Management. LC 73-89292. (Business Ser.). 576p. 1974. text ed. 17.95 (ISBN 0-675-08852-6); media: audiocassettes & filmstrips 450.00, 2-7 sets, 380.00 ea., 8-15 sets, 340.00 ea., 16 or more sets, 275.00 ea. (ISBN 0-675-08807-0); instructor's manual 3.95 (ISBN 0-686-66911-8). Merrill.

Frame, Robert, jt. auth. see Curry, Dudley.

Framo, James L., jt. ed. see Green, Robert J.

Frampton, Kenneth, ed. Five Houses: Gwathmy Siegel Architects. (IAUS Catalogues Ser.). 96p. (Orig.). 1980. pap. 12.00 (ISBN 0-932628-05-2). IAUS.

--A New Wave of Japanese Architecture. (IAUS Exhibition Catalogues Ser.). (Illus.). 96p. 1978. pap. 12.00 (ISBN 0-932628-00-1). IAUS.

Frampton, Kenneth, ed. see Eisenman, Peter D. & Rossi, Aldo.

Frampton, Kenneth, ed. see Eisenman, Peter & Hejduk, John.

Frampton, P., et al, eds. First Workshop on Grand Unification. (Lie Groups; History, Frontiers & Applications: Vol. XI). 250p. 1980. text ed. 30.00x (ISBN 0-915692-31-7). Math Sci Pr.

Francatelli, Charles E. A Plain Cookery Book for the Working Classes. 105p. 1978. pap. 1.95 (ISBN 0-85967-390-1, Pub. by Scolar Pr England). Biblio Dist.

France, Anatole. Le Livre De Mon Ami. Thomas, J. Heywood, ed. (French Texts Ser.). 1957. pap. text ed. 9.95x (ISBN 0-631-00380-0, Pub. by Basil Blackwell). Biblio Dist.

France, Anna K. Boris Pasternak's Translations of Shakespeare. LC 76-52027. 1978. 18.50x (ISBN 0-520-03432-5). U of Cal Pr.

France, Charles E., ed. see Baryshnikov, Mikhail.

France, Joseph B. Crisis Therapy. LC 80-83967. 1980. pap. text ed. 8.75x (ISBN 0-918970-28-8). Intl Gen Semantics.

France, Marie de. Lais. Ewert, A., ed. (French Texts Ser). 1976. pap. text ed. 5.00x o.p. (ISBN 0-631-00470-X, Pub. by Basil Blackwell). Biblio Dist.

France, Marie de see De France, Marie.

France, Peter. Rhetoric & Truth in France: Descartes to Diderot. 1972. 24.95x (ISBN 0-19-815709-6). Oxford U Pr.

Frances, Carol. The Short-Run Economic Outlook for Higher Education. 64p. 1980. 7.95 (ISBN 0-8268-1395-X). ACE.

Frances, E. Ladies Home Journal Family Diet Book. 1973. 6.95 o.s.i. (ISBN 0-02-571700-6). Macmillan.

Frances, Margaret. Education of a Memoir. 1981. 13.95 (ISBN 0-533-04673-4). Vantage.

Franchere, Hoyt C. Edwin Arlington Robinson. LC 68-24295. (U. S. Authors Ser.: No. 137). 1968. lib. bdg. 9.95 (ISBN 0-8057-0632-1). Twayne.

Franchere, Ruth. Westward by Canal. LC 71-185217. (Illus.). (gr. 5-9). 1972. 8.95 (ISBN 0-02-735700-7). Macmillan.

--The Wright Brothers. LC 70-158689. (Biography Ser). (Illus.). (gr. 1-5). 1972. PLB 7.89 (ISBN 0-690-90701-X, TYC-J). T Y Crowell.

Franchi, G., jt. ed. see Garattini, S.

Franchimont, P., jt. auth. see Van Cauwenberge, H.

Francia, Arthur J. & Strawser, Robert H. Managerial Accounting. 3rd ed. (Illus.). 565p. 1980. pap. text ed. 18.95 (ISBN 0-931920-20-5); practice problems 4.95x; study guide 5.95x; work papers 6.95x. Dame Pubns.

Francillon, Rene. Japanese Aircraft of the Pacific War. (Illus.). 1980. 31.95 (ISBN 0-370-30251-6, Pub. by Chatto Bodley Jonathan). Merrimack Bk Serv.

Francis. Cement Industry: 1796-1914. 1978. 25.00 (ISBN 0-7153-7386-2). David & Charles.

--Manual of Socialpsychologic Assessment. 1976. pap. 11.95 (ISBN 0-8385-6127-6). ACC.

Francis, A. D. Methuens & Portugal. 1966. 53.50 (ISBN 0-521-05028-6). Cambridge U Pr.

--The Wine Trade. (Merchant Adventurers). (Illus.). 1972. text ed. 11.25x (ISBN 0-7136-1308-4). Humanities.

Francis, A. J. Introducing Structures. (International Series in Structure & Solid Body Mechanics). 1980. 34.00 (ISBN 0-08-022701-5); pap. 12.00 (ISBN 0-08-022702-3). Pergamon.

Francis, Andre. Jazz. LC 76-6983. (Roots of Jazz Ser.). 1976. Repr. of 1960 ed. lib. bdg. 19.50 (ISBN 0-306-70812-4). Da Capo.

Francis, Austin. Smart Squash. 1979. pap. 2.95 (ISBN 0-346-12385-2). Cornerstone.

--Smart Squash: Using Your Head to Win. LC 77-22011. (Illus.). 1977. 10.00 o.s.i. (ISBN 0-397-01238-1). Lippincott.

Francis, Carl C. & Martin, Alexander H. Introduction to Human Anatomy. 7th ed. LC 75-2455. (Illus.). 1975. text ed. 19.95 (ISBN 0-8016-1646-8). Mosby.

Francis, Carol A. Study Skills. pap. text ed. 2.95x (ISBN 0-933892-14-4). Child Focus Co.

Francis, Carol B. Europe Dimensions: A Study-Activity Guide. (Orig.). 1981. pap. 3.95 (ISBN 0-377-00108-2). Friend Pr.

Francis, Clark & Archer, Stephen H. Portfolio Analysis. 2nd ed. (Foundations of Finance Ser.). (Illus.). 1979. text ed. 19.95 (ISBN 0-13-686675-1). P-H.

Francis, D. Pitt. Statistical Method for Accounting Students. 1978. pap. text ed. 15.95x (ISBN 0-434-90580-1). Intl Ideas.

Francis, Dave & Young, Don. Improving Work Groups: A Practical Manual for Team Building. LC 78-64978. 262p. 1979. pap. 16.95 (ISBN 0-88390-149-8). Univ Assocs.

Francis, Dave, jt. auth. see Woodcock, Mike.

Francis, David, ed. see Permanent International Altaistic Conference, Indiana University, 1962.

Francis, Dick. Across the Board: Three Harper Novels of Suspense. Incl. Enquiry; Flying Finish; Blood Sport. LC 74-15869. 1975. 14.95 o.s.i. (ISBN 0-06-011318-9, HarpT). Har-Row.

--Bonecrack. LC 79-181670. (Harper Novel of Suspense). 208p. 1972. 8.95 o.s.i. (ISBN 0-06-011319-7, HarpT). Har-Row.

--For Kicks. 1980. pap. write for info. (ISBN 0-671-83499-1). PB.

--Reflex. 288p. 1981. 11.95 (ISBN 0-399-12598-1). Putnam.

--Slayride. LC 73-14311. (Harper Novel of Suspense). 256p. (YA) 1974. 8.95 o.p. (ISBN 0-06-011336-7, HarpT). Har-Row.

--Smokescreen. LC 72-9095. (Harper Novel of Suspense). 224p. (YA) 1973. 8.95 o.p. (ISBN 0-06-011334-0, HarpT). Har-Row.

--Whip Hand. 336p. 1981. pap. 2.75 (ISBN 0-671-41903-X). PB.

Francis, Dorothy & Dixon, Daphne. Diets for Sick Children. 3rd ed. 432p. 1975. 25.00 (ISBN 0-397-60319-3, Blackwell). Mosby.

Francis, Dorothy B. The Legacy of Merton Manor. 192p. (YA) 1976. 4.95 o.p. (ISBN 0-685-61055-1, Avalon). Bouregy.

--Nurse at Playland Park. 192p. (YA) 1976. 4.95 o.p. (ISBN 0-685-67079-1, Avalon). Bouregy.

Francis, F. G. & Clydesdale, F. M. Food Colorimetry: Theory & Applications. (Illus.). 1975. text ed. 39.50 (ISBN 0-87055-183-3). AVI.

Francis, F. J., jt. auth. see Clydesdale, Fergus S.

Francis, Fred O. Conflict at Colossae: A Problem in the Interpretation of Early Christianity, Illustrated by Selected Modern Studies. LC 75-15737. (Society of Biblical Literature. Sources for Biblical Study). 1975. pap. 7.50 (ISBN 0-89130-009-0, 060304). Scholars Pr Ca.

Francis, Fred O. & Sampley, J. Paul, eds. Pauline Parallels. LC 74-26346. 400p. 1975. pap. 10.95x spiral bdg. (ISBN 0-8006-1206-X, 1-1206). Fortress.

Francis, Fred O., ed. see American Academy of Religion, 1974.

Francis, G. James. Organization Development: A Practical Approach. 200p. 1982. text ed. 17.95 (ISBN 0-8359-5301-7). Reston.

Francis, Gary S., jt. auth. see Alpert, Joseph S.

Francis, H. E. Naming Things. LC 80-19543. (Illinois Short Fiction Ser.). 140p. 1980. 10.00 (ISBN 0-252-00830-8); pap. 3.95 (ISBN 0-252-00831-6). U of Ill Pr.

Francis, Hywel & Smith, David. The Fed: A History of the South Wales Miners in the Twentieth Century. (Illus.). 530p. 1980. text ed. 33.75x (ISBN 0-85315-489-9). Humanities.

Francis, J. A. History of the English Railway: Its Social Relations & Revelations 1820-1845, Vols. 1 & 2. 1972. Repr. of 1851 ed. 13.50 o.p. (ISBN 0-7153-4238-X). David & Charles.

Francis, J. D., ed. see Raudkivi, A. J.

Francis, Mac, jt. auth. see Darbee, Harry.

Francis, Marjorie. Three R's of Life Language. (gr. k-6). 1971. 3.25x (ISBN 0-933892-11-X). Child Focus Co.

Francis, Nelson. English Language: An Introduction. (gr. 12). 1965. 4.95x (ISBN 0-393-09629-7, NortonC); pap. text ed. 6.95x (ISBN 0-393-09925-3). Norton.

--History of English. (Orig.). 1963. pap. text ed. 2.95x (ISBN 0-393-09709-9, NortonC). Norton.

Francis, P., ed. Ricardo Palma: Tradiciones Peruanas. LC 72-92110. 1970. 5.40 (ISBN 0-08-006665-8); pap. 4.30 (ISBN 0-08-006666-6). Pergamon.

Francis, Paul. Beyond Control? A Study of Discipline in the Comprehensive School. (Unwin Education Books). 1975. text ed. 16.50x o.p. (ISBN 0-04-371033-6); pap. text ed. 8.95x o.p. (ISBN 0-04-371034-4). Allen Unwin.

Francis, Peter. Volcanoes. 1976. pap. 5.95 (ISBN 0-14-021897-1, Pelican). Penguin.

Francis, Richard, jt. auth. see Bacon, Francis.

Francis, Robert. The Orb Weaver. LC 60-7255. (Wesleyan Poetry Program: Vol. 5). (Orig.). 1960. 10.00x (ISBN 0-8195-2005-5, Pub. by Wesleyan U Pr); pap. 4.95 (ISBN 0-8195-1005-X). Columbia U Pr.

Francis, Valerie, jt. auth. see MacDonald, Janet.

Francis, W. Fuels & Fuel Technology, 2 Vols. 1965. Vol. 1. 27.00 (ISBN 0-08-010754-0); Vol. 2. 28.00 (ISBN 0-08-010756-7); Vol. 1. pap. 11.75 (ISBN 0-08-010753-2); Vol. 2. pap. 11.75 (ISBN 0-08-010755-9). Pergamon.

Francis, W. & Peters, M. C. Fuels & Fuel Technology. 2nd ed. (Illus.). 608p. 1980. 105.00 (ISBN 0-08-025249-4); pap. 34.50 (ISBN 0-08-025250-8). Pergamon.

Francis, William H., jt. auth. see Choate, Robert A.

Francisco, C. T. Introduccion Al Antiguo Testamento. Lacue, Juan J., tr. Orig. Title: Introducing the Old Testament. 350p. (Span.). 1980. pap. 4.25 (ISBN 0-311-04010-1). Casa Bautista.

Francisco, Garcia & Pavon. Las Hermanas Coloradas. (Easy Readers, C). 1979. pap. 3.75 (ISBN 0-88436-295-7). EMC.

Francisco, Ronald A. & Laird, Betty A. Agricultural Policies in the USSR & Eastern Europe. (Westview Special Studies on the Soviet Union & Eastern Europe Ser.). (Illus.). 332p. 1980. lib. bdg. 26.50x (ISBN 0-89158-687-3). Westview.

Francis de Sales, St. Introduction to the Devout Life. rev. ed. 1972. pap. 2.45 (ISBN 0-385-03009-6, Im). Doubleday.

Francis De Sales, Saint Introduction to the Devout Life. Day, M., tr. 1961. 10.50x (ISBN 0-460-00324-0, Evman). Dutton.

Francis Of Assisi, St. An Instrument of Your Peace. LC 77-70404. 1977. pap. 2.95 o.p. (ISBN 0-385-13159-3). Doubleday.

Francis-Williams, Jesse. Children with Specific Learning Difficulties. 2nd ed. LC 74-4021. 240p. 1974. text ed. 23.00 (ISBN 0-08-017967-3); pap. text ed. 10.75 (ISBN 0-08-017968-1). Pergamon.

Franck. U. S. Foreign Relations Law, Vol. 1. 1980. 40.00 (ISBN 0-379-20355-3). Oceana.

Franck, Carl L. Villas of Frascati, 1650-1750. (Illus.). 1966. 20.00 (ISBN 0-85458-669-5). Transatlantic.

Franck, Frederick. Everyone: The Timeless Myth of Everyman Reborn. LC 77-25590. 1978. 12.50 o.p. (ISBN 0-385-14357-5); pap. 6.95 o.p. (ISBN 0-385-13329-4). Doubleday.

Franck, Lavina M. History of Costume. 1977. spiral bdg. 9.95x (ISBN 0-916434-27-3). Plycon Pr.

Franck, Richard. The Admirable & Indefatigable Adventures of the Nine Pious Pilgrims... Written in America. LC 72-170515. (Foundations of the Novel Ser.: Vol. 11). lib. bdg. 50.00 (ISBN 0-8240-0523-6). Garland Pub.

Franck, Thomas M. Structure of Impartiality. LC 68-20264. 1968. 8.95 o.s.i. (ISBN 0-02-540580-2). Macmillan.

Franck, Thomas M. & Weisband, Edward. Word Politics: Verbal Strategy Among the Superpowers. 1971. 12.95 (ISBN 0-19-501460-X); pap. 4.95x (ISBN 0-19-501459-6). Oxford U Pr.

Franck, Thomas M., jt. auth. see Glennon, Michael J.

Franck, Thomas M., ed. The Tethered Presidency: A Study of New Congressional Restraints on Presidential Power & Their Effect on America's Ability to Conduct an Effective Foreign Policy. 272p. 1981. text ed. 17.50x (ISBN 0-8147-2567-8). NYU Pr.

Francke, A. H. Antiquities of Indian Tibet, 2 vols. 1972. Repr. Set. 35.00x (ISBN 0-8364-0382-7). South Asia Bks.

Francke, Donald E., ed. Handbook of I.V. Additive Reviews. Incl. 1970. (Illus.). 50p (ISBN 0-914768-03-4); 1971. (Illus.). 60p (ISBN 0-914768-04-2); 1972. (Illus.) (ISBN 0-914768-05-0); 1973. (Illus.). 68p (ISBN 0-914768-06-9). pap. 3.75 ea. Drug Intl Pubns.

Franco, Jean. Introduction to Spanish-American Literature. LC 69-12927. 1969. 42.00 (ISBN 0-521-07374-X); pap. 9.95x (ISBN 0-521-09891-2). Cambridge U Pr.

Franco, Jean, ed. see Quiroga, Horacio.

Franco, Sylvia, et al. The World of Cosmetology, A Professional Text: Student Activities Manual. (Illus.). 352p. 1980. 7.96 (ISBN 0-07-021792-0, G); instructor's planning manual 17.00 (ISBN 0-07-021793-9). McGraw.

--Cosmetology: A Professional Text. (Illus.). 1980. text ed. 14.96 (ISBN 0-07-021791-2). McGraw.

--The World of Cosmetology: A Professional Text. LC 79-20678. (Illus.). 512p. 1980. text ed. 14.96 (ISBN 0-07-021791-2). McGraw.

Francois, D. Advances in Fracture Research: Proceedings of the 5th International Conference on Fracture, 1981, Cannes, France. LC 80-41879. (International Series on the Strength & Fracture of Materials & Structures). 3000p. 1981. 450.00 (ISBN 0-08-025428-4); pap. 375.00 (ISBN 0-08-024776-8). Pergamon.
Francois, Guy Le see Le Francois, Guy.
Francois, H., et al, eds. see International Conference, 10th, Lyon, July 2-6, 1979.
Francois, J., et al, eds. Proceedings of the Symposium of the International Society for Corneal Research. (Documenta Ophthalmologica Proceedings Ser.: No. 20). 1979. pap. text ed. 47.40 (ISBN 90-6193-157-6, Dr. W. Junk Pub). Kluwer Boston.
Francois, Michel, et al, eds. International Bibliography of Historical Sciences: 1976-1977, Vols. 45-46. 492p. 1980. 58.00 (ISBN 3-598-20402-7, Dist. by Gale Research Co.). K G Saur.
Francois, William E. Beginning News Writing. LC 74-16752. (Journalism & Advertising Ser.). 1975. pap. text ed. 9.50 (ISBN 0-88244-065-9). Grid Pub.
--Introduction to Mass Communications & Mass Media. LC 76-46059. (Advertising & Journalism Ser.). 1977. pap. text ed. 14.95 (ISBN 0-88244-141-8). Grid Pub.
--Mass Media Law & Regulation. 2nd ed. LC 77-92582. (Law Ser.). 1978. 20.50 (ISBN 0-88244-168-X). Grid Pub.
Francoise. Minou. LC 62-9646. (Illus.). (gr. k-3). 1962. 5.95 (ISBN 0-684-13153-6, ScribJ). Scribner.
Francois-Poncet, Andre. The Fateful Years: Memoirs of a French Ambassador in Berlin, 1931-1938. LC 76-80549. 295p. 1973. Repr. of 1949 ed. 18.00 (ISBN 0-86527-066-X). Fertig.
Francombe, Maurice H., jt. ed. see Hass, Georg.
Francovich, Allan, tr. see Salles Gomes, P. E.
Frandon, Ramona & Hunt, Dave. The Story of Superman: Four Little Library Books. LC 79-67574. (Illus.). (ps). 1980. Set. 4.95 (ISBN 0-394-84416-5, BYR). Random.
Frandson, R. D. Anatomy & Physiology of Farm Animals. 3rd ed. LC 80-25775. (Illus.). 494p. 1981. text ed. write for info. (ISBN 0-8121-0759-4). Lea & Febiger.
Frane, Jeff. Fritz Leiber. (Starmont Reader's Guide Ser.: No. 8). 64p. 1980. lib. bdg. 9.95 (ISBN 0-89370-039-8). Borgo Pr.
--Reader's Guide to Fritz Leiber. Scholbin, Roger C., ed. LC 80-22107. (Starmont Reader's Guides to Contemporary Science Fiction & Fantasy Authors Ser.: Vol. 8). (Illus.). 1980. pap. text ed. 3.95 (ISBN 0-916732-10-X). Starmont Hse.
Franey, Pierre. The New York Times Sixty Minute Gourmet. 352p. 1981. pap. 6.95 (ISBN 0-686-69133-4, Columbine). Fawcett.
Franey, Pierre, jt. auth. see Claiborne, Craig.
Frangia, George W., jt. auth. see Wolf, Harvey J.
Frank. Alcohol & the Family: Three Sure Ways to Solve the Problem. 1978. pap. 1.50 (ISBN 0-89243-086-9). Liguori Pubns.
--Message Dimensions of Television News. LC 73-8791. (Illus.). 1973. 14.95 (ISBN 0-669-90274-8). Lexington Bks.
Frank & Porges, Peter P. Mad Around the World. (Mad Ser.). (Illus.). 1979. pap. 1.50 (ISBN 0-446-88390-5). Warner Bks.
Frank, A. G. Mexican Agriculture: Fifteen Twenty-One to Sixteen Thirty. LC 78-6201. (Studies in Modern Capitalism Ser.). 1979. 16.95 (ISBN 0-521-22209-5). Cambridge U Pr.
Frank, Adolph F. Animated Scale Models Handbook. LC 80-22858. (Illus.). 160p. 1981. lib. bdg. 10.00 (ISBN 0-668-05118-3, 5118). Arco.
Frank, Alan, jt. auth. see Stratton, George.
Frank, Andre F. On Capitalist Underdevelopment. 1976. pap. 3.95x (ISBN 0-19-560475-X). Oxford U Pr.
Frank, Andre G. Akkumulation: Abhaengigkeit und Unterentwicklung. (Edition Suhrkamp: 706). 256p. (Orig., Ger.). 1980. pap. text ed. 6.50 (ISBN 3-518-10706-2, Pub. by Insel Verlag Germany). Suhrkamp.
--Crisis: In the Third World. LC 80-239444. 1981. text ed. 29.50x (ISBN 0-8419-0584-3); pap. text ed. 9.75x (ISBN 0-8419-0597-5). Holmes & Meier.
--Crisis: In the World Economy. LC 80-14540. 1980. text ed. 28.50x (ISBN 0-8419-0583-5); pap. text ed. 9.75x (ISBN 0-8419-0596-7). Holmes & Meier.
Frank, Anne. Anne Frank: The Diary of a Young Girl. rev. ed. (YA) 1967. 9.95a (ISBN 0-385-04019-9); PLB (ISBN 0-385-09190-7). Doubleday.
--Anne Frank: The Diary of a Young Girl. pap. 2.50 (ISBN 0-671-80243-7); enriched classic edition 2.25 (ISBN 0-671-82748-0). PB.
Frank, Barbara, jt. auth. see Frank, Jerome.
Frank, Benjamin, ed. Contemporary Corrections: A Concept in Search of Content. LC 73-20072. 272p. 1974. pap. 10.95 (ISBN 0-87909-151-7). Reston.
Frank, Bernhard, tr. from Heb. & intro. by. Modern Hebrew Poetry. LC 80-20037. (Iowa Translations Ser.). 240p. 1980. text ed. 15.00x (ISBN 0-87745-106-0); pap. 9.95 (ISBN 0-87745-107-9). U of Iowa Pr.
Frank, C. W. Maximizing Hospital Cash Resources. LC 78-14271. (Illus.). 1978. text ed. 25.95 (ISBN 0-89443-076-9). Aspen Systems.
Frank, C. W., jt. auth. see Drickamer, H. G.
Frank, Charles R., Jr. Adjustment Assistance: American Jobs & Trade with the Developing Countries. LC 73-84869. (Development Papers: No. 13). 50p. 1973. pap. 1.00 (ISBN 0-686-28678-2). Overseas Dev Council.
--Foreign Trade & Domestic Aid. LC 76-51821. 1977. 10.95 (ISBN 0-8157-2914-6). Brookings.
Frank, Charles R., Jr. & Webb, Richard C., eds. Income Distribution & Growth in the Less-Developed Countries. LC 77-86494. 1977. pap. 13.95 (ISBN 0-8157-2915-4). Brookings.
Frank, Clyde, jt. auth. see Pietrzyk, Donald J.
Frank, Edward R. Veterinary Surgery. 7th ed. LC 59-12462. 1964. text ed. 34.95 (ISBN 0-8087-0606-3). Burgess.
Frank, Elke, jt. auth. see Irish, Marion D.
Frank, F. Capitalism & Underdevelopment in Latin America. 1979. 24.50 o.p. (ISBN 0-685-67803-2). Porter.
Frank, Gelya F., jt. auth. see Langness, L. L.
Frank, George. Eighty-Eight Rue de Charonne: Adventures in Wood Finishing. LC 80-54431. (Illus.). 128p. 1981. 9.95 (ISBN 0-918804-06-X, Dist. by Van Nostrand Reinhold). Taunton.
--Psychiatric Diagnosis: A Review of Research. LC 74-13884. 1975. text ed. 23.00 (ISBN 0-08-017712-3). Pergamon.
Frank, Gerold. The Deed. 1979. pap. 2.25 o.p. (ISBN 0-425-03913-7). Berkley Pub.
Frank, Grace. Medieval French Drama. 1954. 29.50x (ISBN 0-19-815317-1). Oxford U Pr.
Frank, Harold H. Women in the Organization. LC 76-20167. 1977. 13.50x (ISBN 0-8122-7715-5). U of Pa Pr.
Frank, Harry. Introduction to Probability & Statistics: Concepts & Principles. LC 73-19852. 448p. 1974. 19.95 o.p. (ISBN 0-471-27500-X). Wiley.
Frank, Harry T. Discovering the Biblical World. LC 74-25082. (Illus.). 288p. 1975. 19.95 o.p. (ISBN 0-06-063014-0, HarpR). Har-Row.
--Discovering the Biblical World. LC 74-7044. (Illus.). 1977. pap. 11.95 (ISBN 0-8437-3625-9). Hammond Inc.
Frank, Helmut & Schanz, John T. US-Canadian Energy Trade Relationships: Past Perspectives & Future Opportunities. (Westview Special Studies in Natural Resources & Energy Management). 1978. lib. bdg. 16.50 o.p. (ISBN 0-89158-250-9). Westview.
Frank, Howard & Frisch, Ivan T. Communication, Transmission, & Transportation Networks. LC 78-119666. (Engineering Ser). 1971. text ed. 25.95 (ISBN 0-201-02081-5). A-W.
Frank, Jerome & Frank, Barbara. Not Guilty. LC 72-138495. (Civil Liberties in American History Ser.). 1971. Repr. of 1957 ed. lib. bdg. 25.00 (ISBN 0-306-70072-7). Da Capo.
Frank, Jerome D. Persuasion & Healing: A Comparative Study of Psychotherapy. rev. ed. LC 72-4015. (Illus.). 398p. 1973. 18.50x o.p. (ISBN 0-8018-1443-X). Johns Hopkins.
Frank, Jerome D. & Hoehn-Saric, Rudolph. Effective Ingredients of Successful Psychotherapy. LC 78-937. 1978. 17.50 (ISBN 0-87630-168-5). Brunner-Mazel.
Frank, John. Complete Guide to Co-Curricular Programs & Activities for the Middle Grades. 1976. 11.95 o.p. (ISBN 0-13-160051-6). P-H.
Frank, Josette, adapted by see Barrie, James M.
Frank, Larry & Harlow, Francis. Historic Pottery of the Pueblo Indians, 1600-1880. LC 73-89957. (Illus.). 224p. 1975. 27.50 (ISBN 0-8212-0586-2, 365017). NYGS.
Frank, Leonard R., jt. auth. see Chaudhuri, Haridas.
Frank, Leonard R., ed. The History of Shock Treatment. LC 78-13550. (Illus.). 206p. 1978. 6.00 (ISBN 0-9601376-1-0). L R Frank.
Frank, Manfred. Das Sagbare und das Unsagbare: Studien Zur Neueren Franzoesischen Hermeneutik. (Suhrkamp Taschenbuecher Wissenschaft: 317). 224p. (Orig., Ger.). 1980. pap. text ed. 7.15 (ISBN 3-518-07917-4, Pub. by Insel Verlag Germany). Suhrkamp.
Frank, Marcella. Modern English: A Practical Reference Guide. (Illus.). 1972. pap. text ed. 10.95 (ISBN 0-13-594002-8). P-H.
Frank, Marjorie, ed. see Ozaeta, Pablo.
Frank, Marjorie S. & Hutchins, P. J. Building Language Power with Cloze: Level C. (Skillbooster Ser.). 64p. (gr. 3). 1981. write for info. wkbk. (ISBN 0-87895-516-X). Modern Curr.
--Building Language Power with Cloze: Level D. (Skillbooster Ser.). 64p. (gr. 4). 1981. write for info. (ISBN 0-87895-517-8). Modern Curr.
--Building Language Power with Cloze: Level E. (Skillbooster Ser.). 64p. (gr. 5). 1981. write for info. wkbk. (ISBN 0-87895-518-6). Modern Curr.
--Building Language Power with Cloze, Level F. (Skillbooster Ser.). 64p. (gr. 6). 1981. write for info. (ISBN 0-87895-519-4). Modern Curr.
Frank, Michael B., ed. see Blair, Walter.
Frank, Nathaniel H., jt. auth. see Slater, John C.
Frank, P., et al, eds. Selected Papers of Richard von Mises, 2 vols. (Illus.). Vol. 1 (Geometry, Mechanics, Analysis) 19.60 o.p. (ISBN 0-8218-0043-4, VM-1); Vol. 1, 1963. 17.20 o.p. (ISBN 0-8218-0044-2, VM-2). Am Math.
Frank, Phil. Travels with Farley. (Illus.). 96p. 1980. pap. 6.95 (ISBN 0-89844-023-8). Troubador Pr.
Frank, Richard A., jt. ed. see Wilcox, Francis O.
Frank, Robert, jt. auth. see Norton, Thomas E.
Frank, Robert G., Jr. Harvey & the Oxford Physiologists: A Study of Scientific Ideas & Social Interaction. (Illus.). 1981. 27.50x (ISBN 0-520-03906-8). U of Cal Pr.
Frank, Ted & Ray, David. Basic Business & Professional Speech Communication. (Speech Communication Ser.). (Illus.). 1979. pap. text ed. 14.95 (ISBN 0-13-057273-X). P-H.
Frank, William L. Sherwood Bonner (Catherine McDowell) LC 76-6900. (U. S. Authors Ser.: No. 267). 1976. lib. bdg. 10.95 (ISBN 0-8057-7169-7). Twayne.
Frank, Wolfgang. The Sea Wolves. 224p. 1981. pap. 2.50 (ISBN 0-345-29504-8). Ballantine.
Frankcom, G. & Musgrave, J. H. The Irish Giant. (Illus.). 128p. 1976. 15.50x (ISBN 0-7156-1021-X, Pub. by Duckworth England). Biblio Dist.
Franke, Herbert W. Zone Null. (Suhrkamp Taschenbuecher: Phantastische Bibliothek, Vol. 35). 208p. (Orig.). 1980. pap. text ed. 4.55 (ISBN 3-518-37085-5, Pub. by Insel Verlag Germany). Suhrkamp.
Franke, Lois & Udell, William L. Handwrought Jewelry. (gr. 7 up). 1962. text ed. 16.00 (ISBN 0-87345-175-9). McKnight.
Franke, M. E., jt. ed. see Drzewiecki, T. M.
Franke, Richard & Chasin, Barbara. The Seeds of Famine: Ecological Destruction & the Development Dilemma in the West African Sahel. LC 79-52471. 284p. 1980. text ed. 19.50 (ISBN 0-916672-26-3). Allanheld.
Frankel & Richard. Be Alive As Long As You Live: The Older Person's Guide to Exercise for Joyful Living. 1981. 11.95 (ISBN 0-690-01892-4). Lippincott & Crowell.
Frankel, Aaron. Writing the Broadway Musical. LC 76-58925. 1977. pap. text ed. 10.00x (ISBN 0-910482-82-9). Drama Bk.
Frankel, B. G. & Whitehead, P. C. Drinking & Damage: Theoretical Advances & Implications for Prevention. (Rutgers Center for Alcohol Studies Monograph: No. 14). 1981. 10.00x (ISBN 0-911290-09-5). Rutgers Ctr Alcohol.
Frankel, Charles. Case for Modern Man. 1959. pap. 2.95 o.p. (ISBN 0-8070-5089-X, BP74). Beacon Pr.
--Morality & U. S. Foreign Policy. (Headline Ser.: No. 224). (Orig.). 1975. pap. 2.00 (ISBN 0-87124-029-7). Foreign Policy.
--The Neglected Aspect of Foreign Affairs: American Educational & Cultural Policy Abroad. 1966. 9.95 (ISBN 0-8157-2918-9). Brookings.
Frankel, F. H. & Zamansky, H., eds. Hypnosis at Its Bicentennial: Selected Papers. LC 78-16605. 320p. 1978. 27.50 (ISBN 0-306-40029-4, Plenum Pr). Plenum Pub.
Frankel, Godfrey, jt. auth. see Frankel, Lillian.
Frankel, Haskel. Big Band. LC 65-19867. (gr. 7-9). 1965. 5.95 o.p. (ISBN 0-385-05863-2). Doubleday.
--Pro Football Rookie. LC 64-19297. (gr. 7-9). 5.95 o.p. (ISBN 0-385-04061-X). Doubleday.
Frankel, Haskel, jt. auth. see Hagen, Uta.
Frankel, Jonathan. Prophecy & Politics: Socialism, Nationalism, & the Russian Jews, 1862-1917. LC 80-14414. (Illus.). 816p. Date not set. price not set (ISBN 0-521-23028-4). Cambridge U Pr.
Frankel, Lillian & Frankel, Godfrey. Bikeways: One Hundred One Things to Do with a Bike. rev. ed. LC 61-15857. (Illus.). 128p. (gr. 8 up). 1972. 6.95 (ISBN 0-8069-4004-2); PLB 7.49 (ISBN 0-8069-4005-0). Sterling.
Frankel, Marvin. Partisan Justice. 142p. 1980. 9.95 (ISBN 0-8090-6478-2). Hill & Wang.
Frankel, Marvin E. Criminal Sentences: Law Without Order. LC 72-95111. 144p. 1973. 5.95 (ISBN 0-8090-3709-2, AmCen); pap. 5.25 (ISBN 0-8090-1374-6, AmCen). Hill & Wang.
--Partisan Justice. 1981. pap. 4.95 (ISBN 0-8090-1395-9). Hill & Wang.
Frankel, Maurice. Social Audit Pollution Handbook: How to Assess Environmental & Workplace Pollution. 1978. text ed. 26.00x (ISBN 0-333-21646-6); pap. text ed. 10.00x (ISBN 0-333-21647-4). Humanities.
Frankel, Max G., et al. Functional Teaching of the Mentally Retarded. 2nd ed. (Illus.). 288p. 1975. 18.50 (ISBN 0-398-03361-7). C C Thomas.
Frankel, Nat & Smith, Laurence J. Patton's Best: An Informal History of the Fourth Armored Division. LC 77-79918. (Illus.). 1978. 9.95 o.p. (ISBN 0-8015-5797-6). Dutton.
Frankel, Neville. The Third Power. LC 80-21723. 384p. 1980. 12.95 (ISBN 0-8253-0026-6). Beaufort Bks NY.
Frankel, O. H. & Soule, M. E. Conservation & Evolution. LC 80-40528. (Illus.). 300p. Date not set. 49.50 (ISBN 0-521-23275-9); pap. 17.95 (ISBN 0-521-29889-X). Cambridge U Pr.
Frankel, O. H. & Hawkes, J. G., eds. Crop Genetic Resources for Today & Tomorrow. LC 74-82586. (International Biological Programme Ser.: Vol. 2). (Illus.). 544p. 1975. 75.00 (ISBN 0-521-20575-1). Cambridge U Pr.
Frankel, Paul H. Essentials of Petroleum: A Key to Oil Economics. 2nd, rev. ed. 188p. 1969. 24.00x (ISBN 0-7146-1220-0, F Cass Co). Biblio Dist.
Frankel, S. Herbert. Capital Investment in Africa: Its Course & Effects. LC 68-9593. (Illus.). 1970. Repr. 22.50 (ISBN 0-86527-021-X). Fertig.
--Money & Banking. 1980. pap. 4.25 (ISBN 0-8447-3398-9). Am Enterprise.
Frankel, Sandor & Mews, Webster. The Aleph Solution. 1981. pap. 2.50 (ISBN 0-425-04654-0). Berkley Pub.
Frankel, Tamar. The Regulation of Money Managers, 4 vols. 1980. Vol. 1. (ISBN 0-316-29191-9); Vol. 2. text ed. (ISBN 0-316-29192-7); text ed. write for info. (ISBN 0-316-29193-5); Vol. 4. text ed. 50.00 ea. (ISBN 0-316-29194-3); 195.00 set (ISBN 0-316-29190-0). Little.
Frankel, Theodore T. Gravitational Curvature: An Introduction to Einstein's Theory. LC 78-12092. (Illus.). 1979. pap. text ed. 11.95x (ISBN 0-7167-1062-5). W H Freeman.
Frankel, Tobia. The Russian Artist. (Russia Old & New Ser.). (Illus.). 224p. 1972. 5.95 o.s.i. (ISBN 0-02-540650-7). Macmillan.
Frankel, Victor H. & Nordin, Margareta, eds. Basic Biomechanics of the Skeletal System. LC 79-24593. (Illus.). 303p. 1980. text ed. 20.00 (ISBN 0-8121-0708-X). Lea & Febiger.
Frankena, M. W. & Scheffman, D. T. Economic Analysis of Provincial Land Use Policies in Ontario. (Ontario Economic Council Research Studies). 1980. pap. 7.50 (ISBN 0-8020-3364-4). U of Toronto Pr.
Frankena, William K. & Granrose, John T. Introductory Readings in Ethics. 496p. 1974. text ed. 18.95 (ISBN 0-13-502112-X). P-H.
Frankena, William K., ed. see Edwards, Jonathan.
Frankenberg, Lloyd. The Stain of Circumstance: Selected Poems. LC 73-85448. 237p. 1974. 10.95 (ISBN 0-8214-0138-6). Ohio U Pr.
Frankenburg, W. G., et al. Advances in Catalysis & Related Subjects, Vol. 29. Date not set. 45.00 (ISBN 0-12-007829-5). Acad Pr.
Frankenstein, Alfred. After the Hunt. LC 68-31417. (Illus.). 1975. 45.00 (ISBN 0-520-02936-4). U of Cal Pr.
--Painter of Rural America: William Sidney Mount. LC 68-57955. (Illus.). 72p. (Orig.). 1968. pap. 5.00 (ISBN 0-88397-062-7). Intl Exhibit Foun.
--World of Copley. LC 74-113381. (Library of Art Ser.). (Illus.). (gr. 6 up). 1970. 12.96 (ISBN 0-8094-0284-X, Pub. by Time-Life). Silver.
--World of John Singleton Copley. (Library of Art). (Illus.). 1969. 15.95 (ISBN 0-8094-0255-6). Time-Life.
Frankenstein, Diane, jt. auth. see Frankenstein, George.
Frankenstein, George & Frankenstein, Diane. Brand Names: Who Owns What. 384p. 1981. lib. bdg. 45.00 (ISBN 0-87196-420-1). Facts on File.
Frankfather, Dwight. The Aged in the Community: Managing Senility & Deviance. LC 77-8327. (Praeger Special Studies). 1977. text ed. 22.95 (ISBN 0-03-021936-1); pap. 9.95 (ISBN 0-03-021931-0). Praeger.
Frankforter, A. Daniel. A History of the Christian Movement: The Development of Christian Institutions. LC 77-8071. 1978. text ed. 18.95 (ISBN 0-88229-292-7); pap. 8.95 (ISBN 0-88229-568-3). Nelson-Hall.
Frankfurt, Harry. Demons, Dreamers, & Madmen: The Defense of Reason in Descartes Meditations. LC 70-75142. 1970. 10.95 (ISBN 0-672-51136-3). Bobbs.
Frankfurter, Felix, ed. Mr. Justice Brandeis. LC 73-37766. (American Constitutional & Legal History Ser). (Illus.). 232p. 1972. Repr. of 1932 ed. lib. bdg. 22.50 (ISBN 0-306-70430-7). Da Capo.
Frankhauser, Eduard. Nudism, Obscenity & the Law. Knapp, Alozis, tr. (Illus.). 1.95 (ISBN 0-910550-09-3). Elysium.

Frankis, G., jt. auth. see Anderson, R. C.
Frankl, George. The Failure of the Sexual Revolution. 190p. 1974. text ed. 6.75x o.p. (ISBN 0-900707-35-6). Humanities.
Frankl, Paul T. New Dimensions: The Decorative Arts of Today in Words and Pictures. LC 75-15851. (Architecture and Decorative Arts Ser.). (Illus.). 122p. 1975. Repr. of 1928 ed. lib. bdg. 37.50 (ISBN 0-306-70741-1). Da Capo.
Frankland, A. W., ed. see European Congress of Allergology & Clinical Immunology, 9th.
Frankland, Noble. Prince Henry: Duke of Gloucester. (Illus.). 343p. 1980. 25.00x (ISBN 0-297-77705-X, Pub. by Weidenfeld & Nicolson England). Biblio Dist.
--Prince Henry: Duke of Gloucester. (Illus.). 343p. 1980. 25.00x (ISBN 0-297-77705-X). Biblio Dist.
Frankland, Noble, ed. see Bond, Brian.
Frankland, Noble, ed. see Jackson, William.
Frankle, Judith, jt. auth. see Cotter, John.
Frankle, Reva T. & Owen, Anita Y. Nutrition in the Community: The Art of Delivering Services. LC 78-9144. 1978. text ed. 17.95 (ISBN 0-8016-1666-2). Mosby.
Franklin, A. C., jt. auth. see Stigant, S. Austin.
Franklin, A. White, ed. see International Congress on Child Abuse & Neglect, 2nd, London 1978.
Franklin, Aubrey A. Teatime. LC 80-70953. (Illus.). 196p. 1981. 9.95 (ISBN 0-8119-0334-6, 1902). Fell.
Franklin, Benjamin. The Autobiography & Selected Writings. Lemisch, Jesse, ed. & intro. by. Date not set. pap. 2.50 (ISBN 0-451-51463-7, CJ1332, Sig Classics). NAL.
--Autobiography of Benjamin Franklin. 1962. pap. 2.95 (ISBN 0-02-002910-1, Collier). Macmillan.
--Autobiography of Benjamin Franklin. (Keith Jennison Large Type Bks). (gr. 6 up). PLB 7.95 o.p. (ISBN 0-531-00159-8). Watts.
--The Autobiography of Benjamin Franklin: A Genetic Text. Lemay, J. A. & Zall, P. M., eds. 328p. 1981. 23.50x (ISBN 0-87049-256-X). U of Tenn Pr.
--Benjamin Franklin Autobiography & Selections from his Other Writings. Schneider, Herbert W., ed. LC 52-14644. pap. 5.50 (ISBN 0-672-60003-X, AHS2). Bobbs.
Franklin, Benjamin & Schneider, Duane. Anais Nin: An Introduction. LC 79-10635. 309p. 1980. pap. 8.50x (ISBN 0-8214-0432-6). Ohio U Pr.
--Anais Nin: An Introduction. LC 79-10635. 1980. 16.00x (ISBN 0-8214-0395-8). Ohio U Pr.
Franklin, Benjamin, ed. Poetry of the Minor Connecticut Wits, 1791-1818. LC 68-17015. 1970. 85.00x (ISBN 0-8201-1066-3). Schol Facsimiles.
Franklin, Clyde W., jt. auth. see Martin, James G.
Franklin, D. A. & Newman, G. B. A Guide to Medical Mathematics. LC 73-15859. (Illus.). 453p. 1973. 26.95 (ISBN 0-470-27520-0). Halsted Pr.
Franklin, Edward. It's Cold in Pongo-Ni. LC 65-17368. 1965. 6.95 (ISBN 0-8149-0100-X). Vanguard.
Franklin, George E. From Cotswolds to High Sierras. LC 66-20373. (Illus.). 167p. 1966. 4.00 (ISBN 0-87004-046-4). Caxton.
Franklin, Grace A., jt. auth. see Ripley, Randall B.
Franklin, Grace A., jt. ed. see Ripley, Randall B.
Franklin, H. Bruce. Robert A. Heinlein: America As Science Fiction. (Science Fiction Writers Ser.: No. Gb 610). (Illus.). 250p. 1980. 18.95 (ISBN 0-19-502746-9, GB); pap. 4.95 (ISBN 0-19-502747-7). Oxford U Pr.
--The Victim As Criminal & Artist: Literature from the American Prison. 1978. 15.95 (ISBN 0-19-502244-0). Oxford U Pr.
Franklin, H. Bruce, ed. Future Perfect: American Science Fiction of the Nineteenth Century. 1978. 17.50x (ISBN 0-19-502322-6). Oxford U Pr.
Franklin, H. Bruce, ed. see Melville, Herman.
Franklin, Howard. A Flowers Arrangers Guide to Showing. 1979. 14.95 (ISBN 0-7134-3321-3). David & Charles.
Franklin Institute. ENGUIDE: A Guide to Bibliographic Data for Users of Environmental Information. 100p. 1980. pap. text ed. 14.95. Franklin Inst Pr.
Franklin Institute Gmbh, ed. see Gillepsie, Paul D.
Franklin, J. L., ed. Ion-Molecule Reactions, 2 vols. LC 77-179758. 1972. Vol. 1, 362p. 42.50 (ISBN 0-306-30551-8, Plenum Pr); Vol. 2. 42.50 (ISBN 0-306-30552-6). Plenum Pub.
Franklin, Jerome L., jt. auth. see Bowers, David G.
Franklin, Jerome L., ed. Human Resource Development in the Organization: A Guide to Information Sources. LC 76-28289. (Management Information Guide Ser.: No. 35). 1978. 30.00 (ISBN 0-8103-0835-5). Gale.
Franklin, Jerome L., et al. Survey-Guided Development III: A Manual for Concepts Training. rev. ed. LC 77-75523. 118p. 1977. pap. 11.50 (ISBN 0-88390-139-0). Univ Assocs.
Franklin, Jill. The Gentleman's Country House & Its Plan 1835-1914. (Illus.). 272p. 1981. 40.00 (ISBN 0-7100-0622-5). Routledge & Kegan.
Franklin, Jon & Doelp, Alan. Shocktrauma. 256p. 1981. pap. 2.95 (ISBN 0-449-24387-7, Crest). Fawcett.
Franklin, Julian H., ed. & tr. Constitutionalism & Resistance in the Sixteenth Century: Three Treatises by Heltman, Beza & Mornay. LC 71-77131. (Orig.). 1969. 4.95 (ISBN 0-672-63519-4). Pegasus.
Franklin, Julian H., ed. Constitutionalism & Resistance in the Sixteenth Century: Three Treatises by Holtman, Beza & Mornay. LC 71-77131. 1969. 22.50x (ISBN 0-672-53519-X). Irvington.
Franklin, Linda. Antiques & Collectibles: A Bibliography of Works in English, 16th Century to 1976. LC 77-25026. (Illus.). 1978. 40.00 (ISBN 0-8108-1092-1). Scarecrow.
Franklin, Linda C. From Hearth to Cookstove. LC 73-93247. (Collector Ser.). (Illus.). 1978. 15.00 (ISBN 0-87637-339-2, 339-02). Hse of Collectibles.
--Library Display Ideas. LC 80-17036. (Illus.). 243p. 1980. lib. bdg. 11.95x (ISBN 0-89950-008-0); pap. 7.95x (ISBN 0-89950-009-9). McFarland & Co.
Franklin, M. & Dotts, Maryann J. Clues to Creativity, Vol. 2: J-P. (Orig.). 1975. pap. 4.50 (ISBN 0-377-00041-8). Friend Pr.
Franklin, Max. Charlie's Angels, No. 4. 1977. pap. 1.50 o.p. (ISBN 0-345-27182-3). Ballantine.
--Charlie's Angels, No. 3: Angels on a String. 1977. pap. 1.50 o.p. (ISBN 0-345-25691-3). Ballantine.
--The Dark. (Illus., Orig.). 1978. pap. 1.75 o.p. (ISBN 0-451-08242-7, E8242, Sig). NAL.
--Starsky & Hutch, No. 7. 1978. pap. 1.75 o.p. (ISBN 0-345-27340-0). Ballantine.
Franklin, Miriam A. Rehearsal: The Principles & Practice of Acting for the Stage. 5th ed. (Illus.). 256p. 1972. pap. 14.95 ref. ed. (ISBN 0-13-771592-7). P-H.
Franklin, Neville, compiled by. Lancaster Photo Album. (Illus.). 96p. 1981. pap. 17.95 (ISBN 0-85059-477-4). Aztex.
Franklin, Olga, tr. see Vassilyeva, Larissa.
Franklin, P., ed. see Bauer-Lechner, Natalie.
Franklin, Ralph W., ed. see Dickinson, Emily.
Franklin, Raoul N. Plasma Phenomena in Gas Discharges. (Oxford Engineering Science Ser.). (Illus.). 1976. 59.00x (ISBN 0-19-856113-X). Oxford U Pr.
Franklin, Shirley A. Perilous Homecoming. 192p. (YA) 1975. 5.95 (ISBN 0-685-53497-9, Avalon). Bouregy.
Franklin, Vincent P. The Education of Black Philadelphia: The Social & Educational History of a Minority Community, Nineteen Hundred to Nineteen Fifty. LC 79-5045. (Illus.). 1979. 19.95 (ISBN 0-8122-7769-4). U of Pa Pr.
Franklin, Woodman B. Guatemala. (World Bibliographical Ser.: No. 9). 1981. write for info. (ISBN 0-903450-24-0). Abc-Clio.
Franklyn, Julian, ed. A Dictionary of the Occult. Repr. of 1935 ed. 18.00 (ISBN 0-685-32596-2). Gale.
Franklyn, Robert A. Instant Beauty. LC 72-87046. 180p. 1973. pap. 1.45 o.p. (ISBN 0-668-02735-5). Arc Bks.
Franko, Lawrence & Stephenson, Sherry. French Export Behavior in Third World Markets, Vol. II. LC 80-66695. (Significant Issues Ser.: No. 6). 96p. 1980. 4.00. CSI Studies.
Franko, Lawrence G. & Seiber, Marilyn J. Developing Country Debt. 1979. text ed. 44.00 (ISBN 0-08-023864-5). Pergamon.
Franks, B. Don & Deutsch, Helga. Evaluating Performance in Physical Education. 1973. text ed. 14.95 (ISBN 0-12-266050-1). Acad Pr.
Franks, C. E. The Canoe & White Water: From Essential to Sport. LC 77-2611. 1977. 15.00x (ISBN 0-8020-2236-7); pap. 8.95 (ISBN 0-8020-6294-6). U of Toronto Pr.
Franks, F., ed. Physico-Chemical Processes in Mixed Aqueous Solvents. 1967. text ed. 14.95x o.p. (ISBN 0-435-66320-8). Heinemann Ed.
Franks, Hugh. Will to Live. 1979. 14.00 (ISBN 0-7100-0181-9). Routledge & Kegan.
Franks, Kenny A. The Oklahoma Petroleum Industry. LC 80-5242. (Oklahoma Horizons Ser.). (Illus.). 320p. 1980. 17.50 (ISBN 0-8061-1625-0). U of Okla Pr.
--Stand Watie & the Agony of the Cherokee Nation. LC 79-124380. 1979. 14.95x (ISBN 0-87870-063-3). Memphis St Univ.
Franks, Lloyd W. The Journal of Elder William Conrad: Pioneer Preacher. 1976. pap. text ed. 6.50x o.p. (ISBN 0-8191-0054-4). U Pr of Amer.
Franks, Margaret L. & Graves, Joy D. Mathematical Concepts in Pharmacology. (A Skills Work Book for the Health Sciences). 1973. 3.95x (ISBN 0-88236-600-9). Anaheim Pub Co.
Franks, R. & Swartz, H. Simplified Medical Dictionary. 1977. 14.50 (ISBN 0-87489-054-3). Med Economics.
Franks, Relix. Polywater: The History of an Artifact. 100p. 1981. 17.50x (ISBN 0-262-06073-6). MIT Pr.
Franks, Richard. Simplified Medical Dictionary. 1977. pap. text ed. 12.52 (ISBN 0-8273-1786-7). Delmar.
Franks, Steve. Sundays. 1972. 1.00 o.p. (ISBN 0-685-67927-6). Windless Orchard.
Fransella, F. Personal Change & Reconstruction: Research on a Treatment of Stuttering. 1973. 34.50 (ISBN 0-12-266150-8). Acad Pr.
Fransella, F. & Bannister, D. A Manual for Repertory Grid Technique. 1977. 27.00 (ISBN 0-12-265450-1); pap. 12.00 (ISBN 0-12-265456-0). Acad Pr.
Fransella, F., jt. auth. see Beech, H. R.
Fransen, Peter. The New Life of Grace. 384p. 1972. pap. 6.95 (ISBN 0-8164-2559-0). Crossroad NY.
Franson, John K., ed. Milton Reconsidered: Essays in Honour of Arthur E. Baker. (Salzburg Studies in English Literature: Elizabethan & Renaissance Studies: No. 49). (Illus.). 215p. 1976. pap. text ed. 25.00x (ISBN 0-391-01378-5). Humanities.
Frantz, Forest H. Successful Small Business Management. LC 77-14385. 1978. text ed. 17.95 (ISBN 0-13-872119-X). P-H.
Frantz, Harper W. & Malm, Lloyd E. Laboratory Studies in General Chemistry, 1001-1062, 62 studies. 1966-68. loose-leaf 0.50 ea. o.p. W H Freeman.
Frantz, Joe B. LBJ: Thirty-Seven Years of Public Service. LC 73-91025. (Illus.). 120p. 1974. 3.95 o.p. (ISBN 0-88319-018-4). Shoal Creek Pub.
--Texas. (States & the Nation). (Illus.). 1976. 12.95 (ISBN 0-393-05580-9, Co-Pub by AASLH). Norton.
Franz, Barbara, jt. auth. see Franz, William.
Franz, Carl. The People's Guide to Camping in Mexico. (Illus.). 400p. (Orig.). 1981. pap. 9.50 (ISBN 0-912528-18-4). John Muir.
Franz, David R., jt. auth. see Jacobson, Morris.
Franz, David R., jt. auth. see Jacobson, Morris K.
Franz, M-L Von see Von Franz, M-L.
Franz, Marie-Louise Von see Von Franz, Marie-Louise.
Franz, Marie Louise Von see Von Franz, Marie-Louise.
Franz, Marie-Louise Von see Von Franz, Marie-Louise & Hillman, James.
Franz, Mary-Louise Von see Von Franz, Marie-Louise.
Franz, Mary-Louise Von see Von Franz, Mary-Louise.
Franz, William & Franz, Barbara. To Eat or Not to Eat: A Young People's Guide to Dietary Goals for the United States. (Illus.). 160p. (gr. 9-12). 1981. PLB price not set (ISBN 0-671-42563-3). Messner.
Franzen, Nils-Clof. Agaton Sax & the Diamond Thieves. LC 79-64183. (Illus.). (gr. 2-7). 1980. 7.95 (ISBN 0-233-95724-3). Andre Deutsch.
Franzen, Nils-Olof. Agaton Sax & Lispington's Grandfather Clock. (gr. 2-7). 1979. PLB 8.95 (ISBN 0-233-96964-0). Andre Deutsch.
--Agaton Sax & the Big Rig. LC 80-2693. 128p. (gr. 2-7). 1981. 8.95 (ISBN 0-233-96754-0). Andre Deutsch.
--Agaton Sax & the Big Rig. LC 80-2693. (Illus.). 128p. (gr. 2-7). 1981. 8.95 (ISBN 0-233-96754-0). Andre Deutsch.
Franzmann, Martin. Alive with the Spirit. 94p. 1974. pap. 2.95 (ISBN 0-570-03174-5, 12-2577). Concordia.
Franzmann, Martin H. Pray for Joy. LC 73-98298. 1970. 2.95 (ISBN 0-570-03001-3, 12-2910). Concordia.
--Romans. LC 68-19990. (Concordia Commentary Ser). 1968. 10.95 (ISBN 0-570-06284-5, 15-2061). Concordia.
--Word of the Lord Grows. 1961. 10.95 (ISBN 0-570-03222-9, 15-1861). Concordia.
Franzmann, Werner H. Bible History Commentary: Old Testament. LC 80-53145. (Illus.). 616p. 1981. 15.95 (ISBN 0-938272-04-7). Wis Ev Luth.
Franzosini, P. & Sanesi, P., eds. Thermodynamic & Transport Properties of Organic Salts. (IUPAC Chemical Data Ser.: No. 28). 376p. 1980. 105.00 (ISBN 0-08-022378-8). Pergamon.
Franzwa, Gregory M. The Old Cathedral. 2nd ed. LC 80-15885. (Illus.). 1980. 14.95 (ISBN 0-935284-18-4). Patrice Pr.
Frasca, Albert J. & Hill, Robert H. The Forty Five - Seventy Springfield. Suydam, Charles R., ed. LC 80-51230. (Illus.). 396p. 1980. 49.50 (ISBN 0-937500-11-9); deluxe ed. 9.50 deluxe edition (ISBN 0-937500-10-0). Springfield Pub Co.
Frasche, Dean F. Southeast Asian Ceramics: Ninth Through Seventeenth Centuries. LC 76-20204. (Illus.). 144p. 1976. 25.00 (ISBN 0-87848-047-1). Asia Soc.
Frascona, Joseph L. Business Law: Text & Cases. 900p. 1980. text ed. write for info. (ISBN 0-697-08209-1); instructor's manual avail. (ISBN 0-697-08213-X); student study guide avail. (ISBN 0-697-08214-8); transparencies avail. (ISBN 0-697-08212-1). Wm C Brown.
--CPA Law Review. 5th ed. 1977. text ed. 22.95 (ISBN 0-256-01891-X). Irwin.
Frasconi, Antonio, ed. see Melville, Herman.
Frase, Robert W., jt. auth. see McKinley, Charles.
Fraser, Al, jt. auth. see Gillespie, Dizzy.
Fraser, Alistair & Thear, Katie, eds. Small Farmer's Guide to Raising Livestock & Poultry. (Illus.). 240p. 1981. 25.00 (ISBN 0-668-04687-2). Arco.
Fraser, Amy S. The Hills of Home. (Illus.). 250p. 1973. 15.00 (ISBN 0-7100-7414-X). Routledge & Kegan.
--Roses in December: Edwardian Recollections. (Illus.). 1981. price not set (ISBN 0-7100-0823-6). Routledge & Kegan.
Fraser, Andrew F. Farm Animal Behaviour. 2nd ed. (Illus.). 291p. 1980. pap. 14.75 (ISBN 0-8121-0739-X). Lea & Febiger.
Fraser, Angus M. The People's Liberation Army: Communist China's Armed Forces. LC 73-76898. 72p. 1973. pap. 2.45x (ISBN 0-8448-0223-9). Crane-Russak Co.
Fraser, Antonia. Royal Charles. 1980. pap. 8.95 (ISBN 0-440-56960-5, Delta). Dell.
Fraser, C. M. China: Past, Present & Personal. LC 80-67728. 141p. 1980. 8.95 (ISBN 0-8059-2736-0). Dorrance.
Fraser, Colin. Avalanches & Snow Safety. (Illus.). 1978. 14.95 o.p. (ISBN 0-684-14794-7, ScribT). Scribner.
--Tractor Pioneer: The Life of Harry Ferguson. LC 73-85451. (Illus.). vi, 294p. 1973. 12.95x (ISBN 0-8214-0134-3). Ohio U Pr.
Fraser, D. Wales in History: The Adventurers, 1485-1760, 3 vols. Bk. 3. 1976. 12.50 (ISBN 0-7083-0610-1). Verry.
Fraser, D. A. The Physics of Semiconductor Devices. 2nd ed. (Oxford Physics Ser.). 1979. 29.95x (ISBN 0-19-851850-1); pap. 11.95x (ISBN 0-19-851851-X). Oxford U Pr.
Fraser, D. G., jt. auth. see Wood, B. J.
Fraser, Derek. Urban Politics in Victorian England: The Structure of Politics in Victorian Cities. 320p. 1976. text ed. 30.00x (ISBN 0-7185-1145-X, Leicester). Humanities.
Fraser, Donald R., jt. auth. see Rose, Peter S.
Fraser, Donald R. & Rose, Peter S., eds. Financial Institutions & Markets in a Changing World. 1980. pap. 12.95x (ISBN 0-256-02201-1). Business Pubns.
Fraser, Dorothy M. & West, Edith. Social Studies in Secondary Schools: Curriculum & Methods. 1961. 11.95 o.p. (ISBN 0-8260-3215-X). Wiley.
Fraser, Douglas. Village Planning in the Primitive World. LC 68-24701. (Planning & Cities Ser). (Illus., Orig.). (YA) (gr. 9-12). 1968. pap. 5.95 o.p. (ISBN 0-8076-0468-2). Braziller.
Fraser, Douglas F. Torres Straits Sculpture: A Study in Oceanic Primitive Art. LC 77-94696. (Outstanding Dissertations in the Fine Arts Ser.). 1978. lib. bdg. 48.50 (ISBN 0-8240-3228-4). Garland Pub.
Fraser, Edward & Gibbons, John. Soldier & Sailor Words & Phrases. LC 68-30635. 1968. Repr. of 1925 ed. 22.00 (ISBN 0-8103-3281-7). Gale.
Fraser, G. Ezra Pound. 1979. cancelled (ISBN 0-685-99623-9). Chips.
Fraser, G. M. & Blockley, J. The Language Disordered Child. Berse, P. A., ed. (General Ser.). 56p. 1973. pap. text ed. 6.75x (ISBN 0-85633-031-0, NFER). Humanities.
Fraser, G. S. Lawrence Durrell: A Study. 1973. pap. 4.95 (ISBN 0-571-04790-4, Pub. by Faber & Faber). Merrimack Bk Serv.
--A Short History of English Poetry. 250p. 1981. 23.50x (ISBN 0-389-20174-X); pap. 9.95x (ISBN 0-389-20175-8). B&N.
Fraser, G. S; see Bradbrook, M. C.
Fraser, Gordon H. Is Mormonism Christian? 1977. pap. 2.50 (ISBN 0-8024-4169-6). Moody.
Fraser, Hamish, jt. auth. see Ward, J. T.
Fraser, Hugh, jt. ed. see Barnett, Herbert E.
Fraser, Ian. The Stranger Warrior. 208p. 1980. 19.50x (ISBN 0-7050-0073-7, Pub. by Skilton & Shaw England). State Mutual Bk.
Fraser, J. Violence in the Arts. LC 73-84319. 208p. 1976. 27.00 (ISBN 0-521-20331-7); pap. 7.95x (ISBN 0-521-29029-5). Cambridge U Pr.

Fraser, J. D. & Allbutt, Mary E., eds. Prayer of Faith. pap. 0.90 (ISBN 0-85363-106-9). OMF Bks.
Fraser, J. M. Industrial Psychology. 1962. 16.50 (ISBN 0-08-009649-2); pap. 7.75 (ISBN 0-08-009648-4). Pergamon.
Fraser, J. T., ed. The Voices of Time. 12.50 o.s.i. (ISBN 0-8076-0318-X). Braziller.
Fraser, James. A Wreath of Lords & Ladies. LC 75-5261. (Crime Club Ser). 192p. 1975. 5.95 o.p. (ISBN 0-385-11074-X). Doubleday.
Fraser, James F. Dr. Jimmy: Some Reminiscences by James Fowler Fraser 1893-1979. 150p. 1980. pap. 10.90 (ISBN 0-08-025737-2). Pergamon.
Fraser, Janet, jt. auth. see May, Ernest R.
Fraser, John. The Chinese: Portrait of a People. LC 80-26314. (Illus.). 463p. 1980. 14.95 (ISBN 0-671-44873-0). Summit Bks.
--Imperial India: Dr. John Murray of Agra. (Oresko-Jupiter Art Bks). (Illus.). 96p. 1981. 17.95 (ISBN 0-933516-89-4, Pub. by Oresko-Jupiter England). Hippocrene Bks.
Fraser, John M. Employment Interviewing. 5th ed. (Illus.). 224p. 1978. pap. 13.95 (ISBN 0-7121-0570-0, Pub. by Macdonald & Evans England). Intl Ideas.
Fraser, John W., tr. see Calvin, John.
Fraser, Kathleen & Levy, Miriam. Adam's World: San Francisco. LC 71-150801. (Illus.). (gr. k-2). 1971. 5.75g o.p. (ISBN 0-8075-0174-3). A Whitman.
Fraser, Marshall. College Algebra & Trigonometry: A Functions Approach. 1978. 18.95 (ISBN 0-8053-2590-5); instr's guide 5.95 (ISBN 0-8053-2591-3). Benjamin-Cummings.
Fraser, Maryna, ed. see Phillips, Lionel.
Fraser, Maxwell & Elmsley, Kenneth. Northumbria. 1978. 27.00 (ISBN 0-7134-1140-6, Pub. by Batsford England). David & Charles.
Fraser, Mowat G. Education & Western Civilization-the Long View: An Attempt to Gain Perspective. LC 73-91097. 1974. 9.00 o.p. (ISBN 0-682-47867-9, University); pap. 3.50 o.p. (ISBN 0-682-47868-7). Exposition.
Fraser, N. M., jt. auth. see Bates, R. W.
Fraser, Nicholas & Navarro, Marysa. Eva Peron. (Illus.). 1981. 14.95 (ISBN 0-393-01457-6). Norton.
Fraser, Nicholas, et al. Aristotle Onassis. LC 77-24417. (Illus.). 1977. 12.50 o.p. (ISBN 0-397-01218-7). Lippincott.
Fraser, P. M. see Lehmann, Karl & Lehmann, P. W.
Fraser, P. M., ed. see Butler, Alfred J.
Fraser, Peter. Puppets & Puppetry. (Illus.). 168p. 1980. 24.00 (ISBN 0-7134-2073-1, Pub. by Batsford England). David & Charles.
Fraser, R. D., et al. Keratins: Their Composition, Structure & Biosynthesis. (Amer. Lec. Living Chemistry Ser.). (Illus.). 320p. 1972. 24.75 (ISBN 0-398-02283-6). C C Thomas.
Fraser, Raymond. Fighting Fisherman: The Life of Yvon Durelle. LC 80-703. (Illus.). 288p. 1981. 11.95 (ISBN 0-385-15863-7). Doubleday.
Fraser, Richard G. Marketing One & Two. 1977. No. 1, 224p. text ed. 13.27 (ISBN 0-7715-0870-0); No. 2, 208p. text ed. 13.27 (ISBN 0-7715-0872-7); tchr's. guide 6.60 (ISBN 0-7715-0871-9). Forkner.
Fraser, Robert D. International Banking & Finance: Vol. 1 - Comprehensive Overview. 5th ed. (A Comprehensive Overview: Vol. 1). 700p. 1979. 26.00 (ISBN 0-686-66081-1). R & H Pubs.
--International Banking & Finance: Vol. 2 - Global Funds Management of Assets Liabilities, Vol. 2. 1st ed. 500p. 1978. 35.00 (ISBN 0-686-66082-X). R & H Pubs.
Fraser, Ronald. Consolidations: A Simplified Approach. LC 80-83431. 128p. 1981. pap. text ed. 9.15 (ISBN 0-8403-2303-4). Kendall-Hunt.
Fraser, Ronald, tr. see Schwaller De Lubicz, Isha.
Fraser, Russell. The Language of Adam: On the Limits and Systems of Discourse. LC 77-3528. 1977. 17.50x (ISBN 0-231-04256-6). Columbia U Pr.
Fraser, Russell A. Court of Virtue. 1961. 27.50 (ISBN 0-8135-0388-4). Rutgers U Pr.
Fraser, Stewart E., jt. auth. see Bjork, Robert M.
Fraser, Sylvia. The Emperor's Virgin. LC 80-1064. 408p. 1980. 12.95 (ISBN 0-385-17237-0). Doubleday.
--The Emperor's Virgin. 320p. 1981. pap. 2.95 (ISBN 0-686-68903-8). Bantam.
Fraser, T. G. The Middle East: 1914-1979. 1980. 19.95 (ISBN 0-312-53181-8). St Martin.
Fraser, T. M. Ergonomic Principles in the Design of Hand Tools. International Labour Office, ed. (Occupational Safety & Health Ser.: No. 44). (Illus.). vii, 93p. (Orig.). 1980. pap. 8.55 (ISBN 0-686-69012-5). Intl Labour Office.
Fraser, Theodore P. & Whipple, Alan L. Le Pot au Feu. (Illus.). 218p. (gr. 7-10). 1975. pap. text ed. 4.75x (ISBN 0-88334-068-2). Ind Sch Pr.
Fraser, Theodore P., jt. auth. see Kopp, Richard D.
Fraser, Thomas B., ed. see Wheeler, Alwynne.
Fraser, W. R. Reforms & Restraints in Modern French Education. (World Education Ser). 1971. 16.50 (ISBN 0-7100-7174-4). Routledge & Kegan.
--Residential Education. LC 68-24064. 1968. 25.00 (ISBN 0-08-012909-9); pap. 12.75 (ISBN 0-08-012908-0). Pergamon.
Fraser-Tytler, William K., Sr. Afghanistan: A Study of Political Developments in Central and Southern Asia. 5th ed. LC 80-1931. 1981. 42.50 (ISBN 0-404-18962-8). AMS Pr.
Frasier, S. Douglas. Pediatric Endocrinology. 1980. 29.50 (ISBN 0-8089-1272-0). Grune.
Frassanito, William. Gettysburg: A Journey in Time. LC 74-10597. 1976. pap. 8.95 (ISBN 0-684-14696-7, ScribT). Scribner.
Frassanito, William A. Antietam: The Photographic Legacy of America's Bloodiest Day. LC 78-2336. (Encore Edition). (Illus.). 1978. 5.95 (ISBN 0-684-16835-9, ScribT). Scribner.
Frassica, Pietro & Carrara, Antonio. Per Modo Di Dire: A First Course in Italian. 1981. text ed. 16.95 (ISBN 0-669-02068-0); wkbk. 5.95 (ISBN 0-669-02069-9); cassette 65.00 (ISBN 0-669-02073-7); tapes-reels 65.00 (ISBN 0-669-02072-9); instructor's guide (ISBN 0-669-02069-9); tapescript (ISBN 0-669-02074-5); demo tape (ISBN 0-669-02075-3). Heath.
Frasure, David W. Bluebirds. 1981. 3.95 (ISBN 0-932298-08-7). Green Hill.
Frasure, William, jt. auth. see Rossell, James H.
Frates, Jeffrey & Moldrup, William. Introduction to the Computer: An Integrative Approach. (Illus.). 1980. text ed. 18.95 (ISBN 0-13-480301-9); pap. 5.95 study guide (ISBN 0-13-480285-3). P-H.
Fratianni, Michele & Peeters, Theo, eds. One Money for Europe. LC 78-67228. (Praeger Special Studies). 1979. 24.95 (ISBN 0-03-047526-0). Praeger.
Fratter, David G. Aere Perennius. (Lat. & Eng.). 1969. 4.95 (ISBN 0-312-00735-3). St Martin.
Frauchiger, Fritz & Van Buskirk, William R. Spoken Swedish. 261p. 1980. pap. text ed. 20.00x (ISBN 0-87950-704-7); cassettes 24 dual track 145.00x (ISBN 0-87950-705-5); bk. & cassettes 160.00 (ISBN 0-87950-706-3). Spoken Lang Serv.
Frauenfelder, Hans & Henley, Ernest M. Subatomic Physics. (Illus.). 544p. 1974. 29.95 (ISBN 0-13-859082-6). P-H.
Frauenfelder, P. & Huber, P. Introduction to Physics, Vol. 1: Mechanics, Hydrodynamics, Thermodynamics. 1966. text ed. 27.00 (ISBN 0-08-011603-5); pap. 21.00 (ISBN 0-08-013521-8). Pergamon.
Frauenthal, J. C. Mathematical Modeling in Epidemiology. (Universitexts Ser.). 118p. 1980. pap. 16.80 (ISBN 0-387-10328-7). Springer-Verlag.
Fraunce, Abraham see Batman, Stephen.
Fraunce, Abraham, et al. Insignium Armorum, Emblematum, Hieroglyphicorum et Symbolorum; Discours Ou Traicte Des Devises; The Art of Making Devises. Orgel, Stephen, ed. LC 78-68183. (Philosophy of Images Ser.: Vol. 7). (Illus.). 1980. lib. bdg. 66.00 (ISBN 0-8240-3681-6). Garland Pub.
Fraunfelder, F. T. & Roy, F. Hampton. Current Ocular Therapy. 600p. 1980. text ed. 42.50 (ISBN 0-7216-3860-0). Saunders.
Fraunhofer, J. A. Von see Von Fraunhofer, J. A.
Fray, G. I. & Saxton, R. G. The Chemistry of Cyclo-Octatetraene & Its Derivatives. LC 76-57096. 1978. 95.00 (ISBN 0-521-21580-3). Cambridge U Pr.
Frayer, William C., ed. Lancaster Course in Ophthalmic Histopathology. (Illus.). 325p. 1980. Text, Slides & Fourteen Units With Lectures. 936.00 (ISBN 0-686-65874-4). Davis Co.
Frayling, Christopher. Spaghetti Westerns: Cowboys & Europeans from Karl May to Sergio Leone. (Cinema & Society Ser.). (Illus.). 352p. 1980. 40.00 (ISBN 0-7100-0503-2); pap. 20.00 (ISBN 0-7100-0504-0). Routledge & Kegan.
Frayling, Christopher, ed. The Vampyre: A Bedside Companion. LC 78-53006. 1978. 9.95 o.p. (ISBN 0-684-15813-2, ScribT). Scribner.
Frayne, John P. Columbia Essays on Modern Writers, No. 73: Sean O'Casey. 1976. pap. 2.00 (ISBN 0-231-03655-8). Columbia U Pr.
Frayne, John P., ed. see Yeats, W. B.
Frayne, Trent. Famous Women Tennis Players. LC 78-22428. (Famous Biographies Ser.). (Illus.). 1979. 6.95 (ISBN 0-396-07681-5). Dodd.
Frazee, Steve. He Rode Alone. 1979. pap. 1.75 o.p. (ISBN 0-449-14103-9, GM). Fawcett.
--Lassie: Lost in the Snow. (gr. 3 up). 1979. pap. 1.25 (ISBN 0-307-21504-0, Golden Pr). Western Pub.
--Lassie: The Mystery of Bristlecone Pine. (gr. 3 up). 1979. pap. 1.25 (ISBN 0-307-21505-9, Golden Pr). Western Pub.
--Lassie: The Secret of the Smelter's Cave. (gr. 3 up). 1979. pap. 1.25 (ISBN 0-307-21514-8, Golden Pr). Western Pub.
--Lassie: Trouble at Panter's Lake. (gr. 3 up). 1979. pap. 1.25 (ISBN 0-307-21515-6, Golden Pr). Western Pub.
--Many Rivers to Cross. 176p. 1981. pap. 1.75 (ISBN 0-449-14012-1, GM). Fawcett.
Frazee, W. D. Ransom & Reunion: Through the Sanctuary. LC 77-76135. (Horizon Ser.). 1977. pap. 4.50 (ISBN 0-8127-0138-0). Southern Pub.
Frazer, J. F. & Frazer, O. H. Amphibians. (Wykeham Science Ser.: No. 25). 1972. 9.95x (ISBN 0-8448-1152-1). Crane Russak Co.
Frazer, J. G., tr. see Pausanias.
Frazer, James E. Tales of Pudding Hill: True Animal Stories from New Hampshire. 1975. 5.00 o.p. (ISBN 0-682-48096-7). Exposition.
Frazer, James G. Golden Bough. abr ed. 19.95 (ISBN 0-02-095560-X); pap. 8.95 (ISBN 0-685-15196-4). Macmillan.
--The Golden Bough, 13 vols. 5380p. 1980. Repr. of 1890 ed. Set. 375.00 (ISBN 0-312-33215-7). St Martin.
--New Golden Bough. abridged ed. Gaster, Theodor H., ed. LC 59-6125. 1959. 19.95 (ISBN 0-87599-036-3). S G Phillips.
Frazer, James George, Sir. The Illustrated Golden Bough. LC 78-3229. 1978. 14.95 o.p. (ISBN 0-385-14515-2). Doubleday.
Frazer, Joan, jt. auth. see Blockcolsky, Valeda.
Frazer, O. H., jt. auth. see Frazer, J. F.
Frazer, Ray & Kelling, Harold D., eds. Literature in Four Aspects. 1965. pap. text ed. 13.95x (ISBN 0-669-20628-8). Heath.
Frazer, Robert W. Forts of the West: Military Forts & Presidios & Posts Commonly Called Forts West of the Mississippi to 1898. (Illus.). 1977. 11.95 o.p. (ISBN 0-8061-0674-3); pap. 5.95 (ISBN 0-8061-1250-6). U of Okla Pr.
Frazer, Robert W., ed. see Mansfield, Joseph K.
Frazer, William. Expectations, Forecasting & Control--a Provisional Textbook of Macroeconomics: Volume II, Prices, Market & Turning Points. LC 80-1361. 439p. 1980. lib. bdg. 25.50 (ISBN 0-8191-1290-9); pap. text ed. 16.25 (ISBN 0-8191-1291-7). U Pr of Amer.
Frazer, William & Henyey, Frank, eds. Quantum Chromodynamics. LC 79-54969. (AIP Conference Ser.; Particles & Fields Sub-Ser.: No. 55; No. 18). (Illus.). 1979. lib. bdg. 20.50 (ISBN 0-88318-154-1). Am Inst Physics.
Frazier, A. Eugene. Glamorize with Lighting. Ide, Arthur F., ed. LC 79-9441. (Good Taste Begins with You Ser.). (Illus.). iii, 50p. 1980. Repr. of 1969 ed. pap. text ed. 5.00 (ISBN 0-86663-224-7). Ide Hse.
Frazier, Alexander. Values, Curriculum & the Elementary School. LC 79-87862. 1980. pap. text ed. 9.50 (ISBN 0-395-26739-0). HM.
Frazier, Alton E. Good Taste Begins with You. Ide, Arthur F., ed. LC 79-9441. (Illus., Orig.). 1980. pap. 39.00x set (ISBN 0-86663-250-6). Ide Hse.
Frazier, Anitra & Eckroate, Norma. The Natural Cat: A Holistic Guide for Finnicky Owners. (Illus.). 208p. 1981. 11.95 (ISBN 0-936602-12-0); pap. 7.95 (ISBN 0-936602-13-9). Harbor Pub CA.
Frazier, Beverly. Nature Crafts & Projects. (Illus.). 40p. (gr. 1-8). 1979. pap. 2.25 (ISBN 0-912300-23-X). Troubador Pr.
--Small World Cook & Color Book. 40p. (gr. 1-8). 1979. pap. 2.25 (ISBN 0-912300-15-9). Troubador Pr.
Frazier, Carl & Frazier, Rosalie. The Lincoln Country-In Pictures. (Illus.). (gr. 4-6). 1963. 5.95 (ISBN 0-8038-4238-4). Hastings.
Frazier, Carla. To the South Pole. LC 78-26274. (Raintree Great Adventures). (Illus.). (gr. 3-6). 1979. PLB 8.95 (ISBN 0-8393-0153-7). Raintree Child.
Frazier, Claude A. Annual Review of Allergy 1977-1978. 1978. spiral bdg. 22.50 (ISBN 0-87488-329-6). Med Exam.
--Insect Allergy: Allergic & Toxic Reactions to Insects & Other Arthropods. 2nd ed. LC 67-30896. (Illus.). 508p. 1980-81. 26.50 (ISBN 0-87527-010-7). Green.
--Self-Assessment of Current Knowledge in Allergy. 1976. spiral bdg. 14.00 (ISBN 0-87488-296-6). Med Exam.
--Sniff, Sniff Al-er-gee. new ed. LC 76-27985. (Illus.). (gr. k-3). 1978. 6.35 (ISBN 0-910812-19-5); pap. 3.00 (ISBN 0-910812-24-1). Johnny Reads.
Frazier, Claude A. & Brown, F. K. Insects & Allergy: And What to Do About Them. LC 79-6706. (Illus.). 350p. 1980. 14.95 (ISBN 0-8061-1518-1); pap. 8.95 (ISBN 0-8061-1706-0). U of Okla Pr.
Frazier, Claude A., ed. Current Therapy of Allergy. 2nd ed. 1978. spiral bdg. 21.00 (ISBN 0-87488-745-3). Med Exam.
--Dentistry & the Allergic Patient. (Illus.). 456p. 1973. text ed. 28.75 (ISBN 0-398-02585-1). C C Thomas.
--Games Doctors Play. (Illus.). 424p. 1973. 29.75 (ISBN 0-398-02586-X). C C Thomas.
--Is It Moral to Modify Man? 252p. 1973. 15.75 (ISBN 0-398-02632-7). C C Thomas.
Frazier, E. Franklin. Black Bourgeoisie. 1965. pap. text ed. 6.95 (ISBN 0-02-910580-3). Free Pr.
Frazier, Greg. San Francisco Scenes. (City Scenes Ser.). (Illus.). 32p. 1972. pap. 3.50 (ISBN 0-912300-29-9, 29-9). Troubador Pr.
Frazier, Jane see Meredith, Grace E.
Frazier, Kendrick, ed. Borderlands Beyond Science: Skeptical Inquiries into the Paranormal. LC 80-84403. (Critiques of the Paranormal Ser.). 400p. 1981. 19.95 (ISBN 0-87975-147-9); pap. 9.95 (ISBN 0-87975-148-7). Prometheus Bks.
Frazier, Rosalie, jt. auth. see Frazier, Carl.
Frazier, Shervert, ed. Aggression. (ARNMD Research Publications Ser.: Vol. 52). 1974. 34.50 (ISBN 0-683-00246-5). Raven.
Frazier, Walt & Berkow, Ira. Rockin' Steady: A Guide to Basketball & Cool. LC 73-20933. (Illus.). 160p. 1974. 3.50 o.p. (ISBN 0-13-782235-9). P-H.
Frean, David. The Board & Management Development. 188p. 1980. text ed. 30.75x (ISBN 0-220-66304-1, Pub. by Busn Bks England). Renouf.
Freas, Kelly, ed. see Adams, Robert.
Freas, Kelly, ed. see Asprin, Robert.
Freas, Kelly, ed. see Garrett, Randall.
Freas, Kelly, ed. see MacClean, Katherine.
Freas, Kelly, ed. see Whelan, Michael.
Freas, Polly, ed. see Adams, Robert.
Freas, Polly, ed. see Asprin, Robert.
Freas, Polly, ed. see Garrett, Randall.
Freas, Polly, ed. see MacClean, Katherine.
Freas, Polly, ed. see Whelan, Michael.
Frechette, V. D., et al, eds. Quality Assurance in Ceramic Industries. 1979. 39.50 (ISBN 0-306-40183-5, Plenum Pr). Plenum Pub.
Frechtman, Bernard, tr. see Genet, Jean.
Fred R. Weber Co. Real Estate Math Using the Pocket Calculator-Computer. 1979. pap. 8.95 (ISBN 0-8359-6554-6). Reston.
Fredborg, K. M., et al. An Unedited Part of Roger Bacon's Opus maius: De signis. (Illus.). 62p. (Orig.). 1978. pap. 6.00 (ISBN 0-8232-0095-7). Fordham.
Frederic, Helene & Malinsky, Martine. Martin. McGreal, John & Lipshitz, Susan, trs. from Fr. Orig. Title: Martin: un Enfant Battait Sa Mere. 108p. 1981. price not set (ISBN 0-7100-0814-7). Routledge & Kegan.
Frederick, jt. auth. see Gaertner.
Frederick, Brooks, pseud. A Happy Christmas Carol. (Writers Workshop Redbird Book Ser.). 35p. 1975. 9.00 (ISBN 0-88253-554-4); pap. text ed. 4.00 (ISBN 0-88253-553-6). Ind-US Inc.
--Rocket to the Moon. (Redbird Ser). 118p. 1975. 15.00 (ISBN 0-88253-616-8); pap. text ed. 4.80 (ISBN 0-88253-615-X). Ind-US Inc.
Frederick, Carl. EST: Playing the Game the New Way. 1976. 7.95 o.p. (ISBN 0-440-02364-5). Delacorte.
Frederick, D., jt. auth. see Pletta, D. H.
Frederick, Dean K. & Carlson, A. Bruce. Linear Systems in Communication & Control. LC 71-155118. 1971. 33.50 (ISBN 0-471-27721-5). Wiley.
Frederick, Dean K., jt. auth. see Close, Charles M.
Frederick, Engels, jt. auth. see Marx, Karl.
Frederick, Filis, ed. see Schloss, Malcolm & Purdom, Charles.
Frederick, Franz J. Guide to Microcomputers. Assn Ed Comm Tech, ed. LC 80-68716. (Orig.). 1980. pap. 11.50 (ISBN 0-89240-038-2). Assn Ed Comm T.
Frederick, Guy. One Hundred One Best Magic Tricks. (Illus.). (gr. 8 up). 6.95 (ISBN 0-8069-4510-9); PLB 6.69 (ISBN 0-8069-4511-7). Sterling.
Frederick, J. George. The Long Island Seafood Cookbook. Joyce, Jean, ed. 1971. pap. 4.00 (ISBN 0-486-22677-8). Dover.
--Pennsylvania Dutch Cook Book. 7.00 (ISBN 0-8446-0099-7). Peter Smith.
--The Pennsylvania Dutch Cookbook. abr. ed. Orig. Title: Pennsylvania Dutch & Their Cookery. 1971. pap. 2.75 (ISBN 0-486-22676-X). Dover.
Frederick, John T. William Henry Hudson. (English Authors Ser.: No. 130). 10.95 (ISBN 0-8057-1276-3). Twayne.
Frederick, Lee. Crash Dive. LC 78-15596. (Pacesetters Ser.). (Illus.). (gr. 4 up). 1978. PLB 7.95 (ISBN 0-516-02167-2). Childrens.
Frederick, Peter. Creative Sunprinting. (Illus.). 192p. 1980. 35.00 (ISBN 0-240-51045-3). Focal Pr.
Frederick, Peter J. Knights of the Golden Rule: The Intellectual as Christian Social Reformer in the 1890s. LC 76-9497. 344p. 1976. 19.50x (ISBN 0-8131-1345-8). U Pr of Ky.
Frederick, Richard G., jt. auth. see Roe, Keith E.

Frederick The Great. Musical Works of Frederick the Great, 4 Vols. Spitta, Philip, ed. LC 67-27453. (Music Ser). 1967. Repr. of 1889 ed. lib. bdg. 115.00 (ISBN 0-306-70980-5). Da Capo.

Frederick, Wayne A. & Lyons, Thomas T. The Expansion of the Federal Union Eighteen Hundred & One to Eighteen Forty-Eight. (Illus.). 296p. (Orig.). (gr. 10-12). 1978. pap. text ed. 4.50x (ISBN 0-88334-116-6). Ind Sch Pr.

Frederick Of Prussia. The Refutation of Machiavelli's Prince or Anti-Machiavel. Sonnino, Paul, tr. LC 80-15801. viii, 173p. 1981. 13.95x (ISBN 0-8214-0559-4); pap. 5.95 (ISBN 0-8214-0598-5). Ohio U Pr.

Fredericks, Claude see Corrigan, Robert W.

Fredericks, H. D. & Baldwin, Victor. The Teaching Research Curriculum for Moderately & Severely Handicapped. (Illus.). 340p. 1978. pap. 23.75 photocopy ed. spiral (ISBN 0-398-03330-7). C C Thomas.

Fredericks, H. D., et al. The Teaching Research Curriculum for Moderately & Severely Handicapped: Gross & Fine Motor. (Illus.). 264p. 1980. pap. 17.75 (ISBN 0-398-04035-4); developmental chart 3.50. C C Thomas.

--The Teaching Research Curriculum for Moderately & Severely Handicapped: Gross & Fine Motor. (Illus.). 1980. pap. 17.75 o.p. (ISBN 0-398-04035-4); developmental chart 3.50 o.p. (ISBN 0-686-65145-6). C C Thomas.

--The Teaching Research Curriculum for Moderately & Severely Handicapped: Self-Help & Cognitive. (Illus.). 288p. 1980. pap. 15.75 o.p. (ISBN 0-398-04034-6). C C Thomas.

--The Teaching Research Curriculum for Moderately & Severely Handicapped: Self-Help & Cognitive. (Illus.). 280p. 1980. pap. 17.75 (ISBN 0-398-04034-6); developmental chart 3.50 (ISBN 0-686-65146-4). C C Thomas.

--Teaching Research Motor-Development Scale: For Moderately & Severely Retarded Children. (Illus.). 80p. 1972. 9.75 (ISBN 0-398-02284-4). C C Thomas.

Fredericks, Leo Brooks see Frederick, Brooks, pseud.

Fredericks, Marcel A., et al. Dental Care in Society: The Sociology of Dental Health. LC 80-15985. (Illus.). 194p. 1980. text ed. 15.95x (ISBN 0-89950-001-3). McFarland & Co.

Fredericks, Robert F., jt. auth. see Lipner, Barbara E.

Fredericksen, Carl H., et al, eds. Variation in Writing: Functional & Linguistic-Cultural Differences, Vol. 1. 240p. 1981. prof. - refer. 16.50 (ISBN 0-89859-099-X). L Erlbaum Assocs.

Fredericksen, Hazel & Mulligan, Raymond A. The Child & His Welfare. 3rd ed. LC 70-172242. (Illus.). 1972. text ed. 21.95x (ISBN 0-7167-0905-8). W H Freeman.

Fredericksen, Thomas M. Intuitive IC Electronics: A Sophisticated Primer for Engineers & Technicians. (Illus.). 208p. 1981. 18.50 (ISBN 0-07-021923-0, P&RB). McGraw.

Frederickson, H. George. New Public Administration. LC 80-10569. (Illus.). 144p. 1980. 10.50 (ISBN 0-8173-0040-6); pap. 5.50 (ISBN 0-8173-0041-4). U of Ala Pr.

Frederickson, H. George & Wise, Charles, eds. Public Administration & Public Policy. LC 76-14280. (Policy Studies Organization Bk.). (Illus.). 1977. 19.95 (ISBN 0-669-00738-2). Lexington Bks.

Frederickson, Jaye & Gibb, Sandra. The Covenant Chain: Indian Ceremonial & Trade Silver. (Illus.). 168p. 1980. 24.95 (ISBN 0-660-10347-8, 56313-8, Pub. by Natl Gallery Canada); pap. 19.95 (ISBN 0-660-10348-6, 56314-6). U of Chicago Pr.

Fredericq, P; see Luria, S. E.

Frederiksen, A. K. The Finer Points of Riding. rev. ed. (Illus.). pap. 8.75 (ISBN 0-85131-323-X, Dist. by Sporting Book Center). J A Allen.

Frederiksen, Lee W., jt. auth. see Eisler, Richard M.

Frederiksen, N., et al. Prediction of Organizational Behavior. 344p. 1972. text ed. 27.00 (ISBN 0-08-016967-8); pap. text ed. 14.50 (ISBN 0-08-017189-3). Pergamon.

Frederique & Papy. Graph Games. LC 72-157647. (Young Math Ser). (Illus.). (gr. 1-4). 1971. PLB 7.89 (ISBN 0-690-34965-3, TYC-J). T Y Crowell.

Fredgant, Don. Electrical Collectibles: Relics of the Electrical Age. (Illus.). 1981. pap. 9.95 (ISBN 0-914598-04-X). Padre Prods.

Fredland, J. Eric & Macrae, C. Duncan. Econometric Models of the Housing Sector: A Policy-Oriented Survey. (An Institute Paper). 109p. 1978. pap. 5.00 (ISBN 0-87766-232-0, 23600). Urban Inst.

Fredland, Richard A. Africa Faces the World. LC 80-81101. (Scholarly Monograph Ser.). 212p. 1980. pap. 15.00 (ISBN 0-8408-0502-0); pap. text ed. 15.00 o.p. (ISBN 0-686-64869-2). Carrollton Pr.

Fredland, Richard A., jt. ed. see Potholm, Christian P.

Fredman, Alice. Anthony Trollope. LC 74-136496. (Columbia Essays on Modern Writers Ser.: No. 56). 48p. 1971. pap. 2.00 (ISBN 0-231-03081-9, MW56). Columbia U Pr.

Fredman, Donna R., ed. see Tessier, Mitzi.

Fredman, John. The Wolf of Masada. 416p. 1979. pap. 2.50 (ISBN 0-380-49049-8, 49049). Avon.

Fredman, Ruth G. The Passover Seder: Afikoman in Exile. 1980. 18.00x (ISBN 0-8122-7788-0). U of Pa Pr.

Fredoville, Jean C. Dictionnaire civilisation romaine. (Dictionnaires de l'homme du vingtieme siecle). (Illus., Fr.). 1968. 8.50 (ISBN 0-685-13862-3, 3716). Larousse.

Fredrick, Laurence & Baker, Robert. An Introduction to Astronomy. 9th ed. 1980. text ed. 22.95 (ISBN 0-442-22422-2); instr's. manual 3.95 (ISBN 0-442-22421-4). D Van Nostrand.

Fredrick, Len. Fast Food Gets an "A" in School Lunch. LC 76-54649. 1977. 17.95 (ISBN 0-685-74393-4). CBI Pub.

Fredricks, Simon & Brody, Garry S., eds. Symposium on the Neurologic Aspects of Plastic Surgery. LC 78-7355. (Symposia of the Educational Foundaion of the American Society of Plastic & Reconstructive Surgeons, Inc. Ser.: Vol. 17). 1978. text ed. 51.50 (ISBN 0-8016-1679-4). Mosby.

Fredrickson, George M. The Black Image in the White Mind: The Debate on Afro-American Character & Destiny, 1817-1914. 1977. pap. text ed. 8.50x (ISBN 0-06-131688-1, TB 1688, Torch). Har-Row.

Fredrickson, Olive A. & East, Ben. Silence of the North. 224p. 1981. pap. 2.50 (ISBN 0-446-81559-4). Warner Bks.

Free, Anne R. Social Usage. 2nd ed. (Illus.). 1969. pap. text ed. 9.50 (ISBN 0-13-819607-9). P-H.

--Social Usage: A Guide to Good Manners. 2nd ed. (Illus.). 1969. 18.95x (ISBN 0-89197-585-3). Irvington.

Free, James L. Just One More. LC 77-86272. 1977. pap. 5.95 (ISBN 0-915950-12-X). Bull Pub.

Free, Joseph P. Archeology & Bible History. LC 69-15256. (Illus.). 1950. pap. text ed. 5.95 o.p. (ISBN 0-88207-801-1). Victor Bks.

Free, Lloyd A., jt. auth. see Watts, William.

Free Stuff Editors, ed. Free Stuff for Home & Garden. (Illus.). 120p. (Orig.). 1981. pap. 2.95 (ISBN 0-915658-27-5). Meadowbrook Pr.

--Free Stuff for Travelers. 120p. (Orig.). 1981. pap. 2.95 (ISBN 0-915658-29-1). Meadowbrook Pr.

Freebairen-Smith, S. J. & Littlejohn, G. N. Winner Take All: From Trial to Triumph, Vol. 1. 1977. pap. text ed. 5.25x (ISBN 0-435-36320-4). Heinemann Ed.

Freebairn-Smith, S. J. & Littlejohn, G. N. Chief Factors for the Gods: From Trial to Triumph, Vol. 2. 1977. pap. text ed. 5.25x (ISBN 0-435-36321-2). Heinemann Ed.

Freeborn, R. The Rise of the Russian Novel: Studies in the Russian Novel from Eugene Onegin to War & Peace. LC 75-190417. 250p. 1973. 49.50 (ISBN 0-521-08588-8); pap. 12.95x (ISBN 0-521-09738-X). Cambridge U Pr.

Freed, Alvyn. TA for Tots (and Other Prinzes) LC 76-19650. (Transactional Analysis for Everybody Ser.). (Illus.). 256p. (Orig.). 1973. buckram 11.95 o.p. (ISBN 0-915190-11-7). Jalmar Pr.

Freed, Alvyn M. TA for Tots (and Other Prinzes) LC 76-19650. (Transactional Analysis for Everybody Ser.). (Illus.). (ps-3). 1973. pap. 7.95 (ISBN 0-915190-12-5). Jalmar Pr.

--TA for Tots Coloring Book. (Transactional Analysis for Everybody Ser.). 1976. pap. 1.95 (ISBN 0-915190-33-8); spirit masters 3.95. Jalmar Pr.

Freed, Alvyn M. & Michelson, Herb. Please Keep on Smoking: We Need the Money. (Orig.). 1980. pap. 2.95 saddle stitch (ISBN 0-915190-27-3). Jalmar Pr.

Freed, Barbara F. From the Community to the Classroom: Gathering Second Language Speech Samples. (Language in Education Ser.: No. 6). 1978. pap. 2.95 (ISBN 0-87281-085-2). Ctr Appl Ling.

Freed, Daniel J. & Terrell, Timothy P. Standards Relating to Interim Status: The Release, Control & Detention of Accused Juvenile Offenders Between Arrest & Disposition. (Juvenile Justice Standards Project Ser.). 1980. softcover 7.95 (ISBN 0-88410-812-0); casebound 16.50 (ISBN 0-88410-244-0). Ballinger Pub.

--Standards Relating to Interim Status: The Release, Control, & Detention of Accused Juvenile Offenders Between Arrest & Disposition. LC 77-2318. (Juvenile Justice Standards Project Ser.). 1977. softcover 7.95 o.p. (ISBN 0-88410-770-1); 16.50, casebound o.p. Ballinger Pub.

Freed, Donald. China Card. 1980. 12.95 (ISBN 0-87795-281-7). Arbor Hse.

--Inquest. (Illus., Orig.). 1970. 4.50 o.p. (ISBN 0-8090-5845-6, New Mermaid); pap. 1.95 o.p. (ISBN 0-8090-1221-9, New Mermaid). Hill & Wang.

Freed, Donald & Landis, Fred S. Death in Washington: The Murder of Orlando Letelier. 256p. 1980. 12.95 (ISBN 0-88208-123-3); pap. 6.95 (ISBN 0-88208-124-1). Lawrence Hill.

Freed, Earl X., ed. Interfaces Between Alcoholism & Mental Health. (NIAAA-RUCAS Alcoholism Treatment Ser.: No. 4). 1981. pap. 8.00 (ISBN 0-911290-50-8). Rutgers Ctr Alcohol.

Freed, Edwin D., jt. ed. see Flesner, David E.

Freed, Leonard. Police Work. 1981. 19.95 (ISBN 0-671-25202-X, Touchstone Bks); pap. 9.95 (ISBN 0-671-25203-8). S&S.

Freed, Paul. Let the Earth Hear. 1980. 8.95 (ISBN 0-8407-5188-5). Nelson.

Freed, Ruth, jt. auth. see Freed, Stanley A.

Freed, Stanley A. & Freed, Ruth. Man from the Beginning. LC 65-28357. (Creative Science Ser). (Illus., Orig.). (gr. 6 up). 1967. PLB 7.95 (ISBN 0-87191-008-X). Creative Ed.

Freedberg, S. J. Paintings of the High Renaissance in Rome & Florence, 2 vols. (Icon Eds.). (Illus.). 1232p. 1972. Vol. 1. pap. 11.00x o.s.i. (ISBN 0-06-430013-7, IN-13, HarpT); Vol. 2. pap. 10.00x o.s.i. (ISBN 0-06-430014-5, IN-14). Har-Row.

Freedberg, Sydney J., ed. see Baudelaire, Charles.

Freedberg, Sydney J., ed. see Burckhardt, Jakob.

Freedberg, Sydney J., ed. see Chevreul, M. E.

Freedberg, Sydney J., ed. see Crowe, J. A. & Cavalcaselle, G. B.

Freedberg, Sydney J., ed. see Delacroix, Eugene.

Freedberg, Sydney J., ed. see De Quincy, A. C.

Freedberg, Sydney J., ed. see Erhart, Katherine P.

Freedberg, Sydney J., ed. see Fuseli, Henry.

Freedberg, Sydney J., ed. see Hildebrand, Adolf.

Freedberg, Sydney J., ed. see Lamoureux, Richard E.

Freedberg, Sydney J., ed. see Landau, Sarah B.

Freedberg, Sydney J., ed. see Lichtenstein, Sara.

Freedberg, Sydney J., ed. see Morris, William.

Freedberg, Sydney J., ed. see Ottley, William Y.

Freedberg, Sydney J., ed. see Passavant, Johann D.

Freedberg, Sydney J., ed. see Quatremere de Quincy, A. C.

Freedberg, Sydney J., ed. see Ruskin, John.

Freedberg, Sydney J., ed. see Sale, J. Russell.

Freeden, Michael. The New Liberalism: An Ideology of Social Reform. 1978. 37.50x (ISBN 0-19-822463-X). Oxford U Pr.

Freedland, Mark, jt. auth. see Davies, Paul.

Freedland, Mark R. The Contract of Employment. 400p. 1975. 39.50x (ISBN 0-19-825306-0). Oxford U Pr.

Freedland, Michael. Gregory Peck. LC 80-82359. (Illus.). 320p. 1980. 10.95 (ISBN 0-688-03619-8). Morrow.

--Jerome Kern. (Illus.). 182p. 1978. 13.25x (ISBN 0-8476-3126-5). Rowman.

--Jerome Kern: A Biography. LC 80-6160. 200p. 1981. 12.95 (ISBN 0-8128-2776-7). Stein & Day.

Freedley, Edwin T. A Treatise on the Principal Trades & Manufactures of the United States: Showing the Progress, State & Prospects of Business, & Illustrated by Sketches of Distinguished Mercantile & Manufacturing Firms. (The Neglected American Economists Ser.). 1974. lib. bdg. 50.00 (ISBN 0-8240-1012-4). Garland Pub.

Freedman, Alfred M. & Kaplan, Harold I. Comprehensive Textbook of Psychiatry. 3rd ed. (Illus.). 1975. 100.00 o.p. (ISBN 0-683-03357-3). Williams & Wilkins.

Freedman, Ben. Sanitarian's Handbook: Theory & Administrative Practice for Environmental Health. 1977. 69.50 (ISBN 0-930234-02-2). Peerless.

Freedman, D. X., ed. see Association for Research in Nervous & Mental Disease.

Freedman, David H., ed. see International Labour Office, Geneva.

Freedman, David N., jt. auth. see Cross, Frank M., Jr.

Freedman, David Noel & Campbell, Edward F., Jr. Biblical Archaeologist Reader, Vol. 3. LC 61-7649. 1970. pap. 2.45 o.p. (ISBN 0-385-05178-6, A250C, Anch). Doubleday.

Freedman, Estelle B. Their Sister's Keepers: Women's Prison Reform in America, 1830-1930. LC 80-24918. (Women & Culture Ser.). 256p. 1981. text ed. 18.50 (ISBN 0-472-10008-4). U of Mich Pr.

Freedman, Gabriel F., et al, eds. Scholastic Aptitude Test (SAT) LC 80-88. 512p. 1981. lib. bdg. 12.00 (ISBN 0-668-04916-2, 4916). Arco.

Freedman, H. F. Super Marriage, Super Sex. 1975. pap. 1.75 o.p. (ISBN 0-345-24949-6). Ballantine.

Freedman, Jacob. Polychrome Historical Prayerbook: Siddur 'bet Yosef' (Illus.). 400p. Date not set. 75.00 (ISBN 0-686-12113-9). J Freedman Liturgy. Postponed.

Freedman, James O. Crisis & Legitimacy. LC 78-51683. 352p. 1980. pap. 9.95 (ISBN 0-521-29380-4). Cambridge U Pr.

--Crisis & Legitimacy. LC 78-5183. 1978. 27.50 (ISBN 0-521-22063-7); pap. 9.95 (ISBN 0-521-29380-4). Cambridge U Pr.

Freedman, Jill, jt. auth. see Smith, Dennis.

Freedman, Joel. On Both Sides of the Gate. LC 79-67518. 1981. 6.95 (ISBN 0-533-04466-9). Vantage.

Freedman, Jonathan. Crowding & Behavior. LC 75-20217. (Psychology Ser.). 1975. pap. text ed. 7.95x (ISBN 0-7167-0750-0). W H Freeman.

Freedman, Jonathan, et al. Social Psychology. 4th ed. (Illus.). 656p. 1981. text ed. 18.95 (ISBN 0-13-817783-X). P-H.

Freedman, Jonathan L. Introductory Psychology. LC 76-15461. 1978. text ed. 17.95 (ISBN 0-201-05788-3); instr's manual o.p. avail. (ISBN 0-201-05791-3); tests o.p. 4.00 (ISBN 0-685-85890-1). A-W.

Freedman, Kenneth. Management of the Geriatric Dental Patient. (Illus.). 148p. 1980. 42.00 (ISBN 0-931386-05-5). Quint Pub Co.

Freedman, Lawrence. Britain & Nuclear Weapons. 1981. text ed. 27.50x (ISBN 0-333-30494-2). Humanities.

Freedman, M. Chinese Lineage & Society: Fukien & Kwangtung. (Monographs on Social Anthropology: No. 33). (Illus.). 206p. 1971. pap. text ed. 10.00x (ISBN 0-391-00199-X, Athlone Pr). Humanities.

Freedman, Marcia & Maclachlan, Gretchen. Labor Markets: Segments & Shelters. LC 76-470. (Conservation of Human Resources Ser: No. 1). 224p. 1976. 18.50 (ISBN 0-916672-00-X). Allanheld.

Freedman, Matthew. Radiology of the Postoperative Hip. LC 79-12411. 1979. 38.95 (ISBN 0-471-04416-4, Pub. by Wiley Medical). Wiley.

Freedman, Maurice. Lineage Organization in Southeastern China. rev. ed. (Monographs on Social Anthropology: No. 18). 1965. pap. text ed. 9.50x (ISBN 0-485-19618-2, Athlone Pr). Humanities.

Freedman, Mervin B. The College Experience. LC 67-13280. (Higher Education Ser.). 1967. 11.95x o.p. (ISBN 0-87589-004-0). Jossey-Bass.

Freedman, Michael. The Diamond Book: The Investors Guide to Value, Price & Liquidity. LC 80-70145. 222p. 1981. 14.95 (ISBN 0-87094-223-9). Dow Jones-Irwin.

Freedman, Miriam & Perl, Teri. A Sourcebook for Substitutes...& Other Teachers. (gr. k-8). 1974. 10.25 (ISBN 0-201-05786-7). A-W.

Freedman, Nancy. The Immortals. 1977. pap. 2.25 o.s.i. (ISBN 0-446-82271-X). Warner Bks.

--Prima Donna. LC 80-21568. 320p. 1981. 10.95 (ISBN 0-688-03730-5). Morrow.

Freedman, Philip, et al. Nephrology. (Medical Examination Review Book: Vol. 34). 1976. spiral bdg. 15.00 (ISBN 0-87488-176-5). Med Exam.

Freedman, Robert, ed. Marxist Social Thought. LC 68-13362. (Orig.). 1968. pap. 4.95 o.p. (ISBN 0-15-657650-3, HB137, Harv). HarBraceJ.

Freedman, Robert O. Soviet Policy Toward the Middle East Since 1970. rev. ed. LC 78-19457. 1978. 28.95 (ISBN 0-03-046601-6); student ed. 10.95 (ISBN 0-03-046606-7). Praeger.

Freedman, Robert O., ed. World Politics & the Arab-Israeli Conflict. (Pergamon Policy Studies). 1979. 39.00 (ISBN 0-08-023380-5). Pergamon.

Freedman, Russell. Animal Architects. LC 79-141404. (Illus.). 126p. (gr. 4-7). 1971. 5.95 (ISBN 0-8234-0182-0). Holiday.

--When Winter Comes. LC 80-22831. (Illus.). (gr. 1-3). 1981. PLB 7.95 (ISBN 0-525-42583-7). Dutton.

Freedman, Russell & Morriss, James E. The Brains of Animals & Man. LC 71-151754. (Illus.). 160p. (gr. 4-6). 1972. 8.95 (ISBN 0-8234-0205-3). Holiday.

Freedman, Ruth, jt. auth. see Doucette, John.

Freedomways Editors, ed. Paul Robeson: The Great Forerunner. LC 78-7917. (Illus.). 1978. 12.95 (ISBN 0-396-07545-2). Dodd.

Freehling, William. Prelude to Civil War: The Nullification Controversy in South Carolina, 1816-1836. (Illus.). 1968. pap. 5.95x (ISBN 0-06-131359-9, TB1359, Torch). Har-Row.

Freehof, Soloman B. Book of Isaiah: A Commentary. Syme, Daniel B., ed. LC 72-2156. (Jewish Commentary for Bible Readers Ser.). 1972. 15.00 (ISBN 0-8074-0042-4, 383015). UAHC.

Freehof, Solomon. Isaiah: A Commentary. 1972. 15.00 (ISBN 0-8074-0042-4, 383015). UAHC.

Freehof, Solomon B. The Book of Ezekiel: A Commentary. Syme, Daniel B., ed. (Jewish Commentary for Bible Readers Ser.). 1979. 15.00 (ISBN 0-8074-0033-5, 380010). UAHC.

--Preface to Scripture: A Guide to the Understanding of the Bible in Accordance with the Jewish Tradition. 1950. pap. 4.95x o.p. (ISBN 0-87441-261-7, Union of American Hebrew Congregations). Behrman.

Free John, Da. The Paradox of Instruction: An Introduction to the Esoteric Spiritual Teaching of Da Free John. 10.95 (ISBN 0-913922-28-5); pap. 5.95 o.p. (ISBN 0-913922-32-3). Dawn Horse Pr.

Freeland, Howard J., et al, eds. Fjord Oceanography. (NATO Conference Ser., Ser. IV: Marine Science: Vol. 4). 713p. 1980. 69.50 (ISBN 0-306-40439-7, Plenum Pr). Plenum Pub.

Freeland, J. M. Architecture in Australia: A History. (Illus.). 1968. 15.00 o.p. (ISBN 0-8426-1262-9). Verry.

Freeland, Kenneth H. High School Work Study Program for the Retarded: Practical Information for Teacher Preparation & Program Organization & Operation. (Illus.). 120p. 1974. text ed. 11.50 (ISBN 0-398-00611-3). C C Thomas.

Freeley, Austin J. Argumentation & Debate: Rational Decision-Making. 4th ed. 1976. 15.95x (ISBN 0-534-00420-2). Wadsworth Pub.

Freeling, Nicolas. Arlette. 1981. 10.95 (ISBN 0-394-51454-8). Pantheon.

--A Dressing of Diamond. LC 73-18710. (Harper Novel of Suspense). 256p. 1974. 7.95 o.p. (ISBN 0-06-011352-9, HarpT). Har-Row.

--The King of the Rainy Country. 160p. 1975. pap. 1.95 o.p. (ISBN 0-14-002853-6). Penguin.

--Love in Amsterdam. 192p. 1975. pap. 1.95 o.p. (ISBN 0-14-002281-3). Penguin.

--The Night Lords. LC 78-55242. 1978. 7.95 (ISBN 0-394-50281-7). Pantheon.

--Sabine. LC 74-15871. (Harper Novel of Suspense). 1978. 7.95 o.p. (ISBN 0-06-011356-1, HarpT). Har-Row.

Freely, John, jt. auth. see Sumner-Boyd, Hilary.

Freely, Maureen. Mother's Helper. 1981. pap. 2.95 (ISBN 0-440-15696-3). Dell.

Freeman. Plaid for Writing Resumes, Locating Jobs, Handling Job Interviews. 1976. pap. 4.95 (ISBN 0-256-01871-5, 11-1219-00). Learning Syst.

--TV '80. (gr. 7-12). 1980. pap. 1.25 (ISBN 0-590-30877-7, Schol Pap). Schol Bk Serv.

--Vitreous Surgery & Advances in Fundus Diagnosis & Management. (Illus.). 1976. 65.00 o.p. (ISBN 0-8385-9485-9). ACC.

Freeman, A. Myrick, 3rd, jt. ed. see Enthoven, Alain C.

Freeman, Arnold. Boy Life & Labour: The Manufacture of Inefficiency, London Nineteen Fourteen. LC 79-56956. (The English Working Class Ser.). 1980. lib. bdg. 25.00 (ISBN 0-8240-0110-9). Garland Pub.

Freeman, Arthur, ed. The English Stage Ser. Attack & Defense, 1577-1730, 50 vols. lib. bdg. 50.00 ea.; lib. bdg. 1600.00 set (ISBN 0-685-41743-3). Garland Pub.

Freeman, Cecilia, jt. auth. see Dieterich, Thomas G.

Freeman, Charles. Terrorism in Today's World. LC 79-56474. (Illus.). 96p. 1980. 16.95 (ISBN 0-7134-1230-5, Pub. by Batsford England). David & Charles.

Freeman, Christopher. Measurement of Output of Research & Experimental Development. 1970. pap. 2.50 (ISBN 92-3-100760-2, U376, UNESCO). Unipub.

Freeman, Christopher J. Encyclopedia of World Air Power. (Illus.). 1980. 17.95 (ISBN 0-517-53754-0). Crown.

Freeman, Cynthia. Portraits. 608p. 1980. pap. 3.50 (ISBN 0-553-13641-0). Bantam.

Freeman, Dan. Elephants: The Vanishing Giants. (Illus.). 192p. 1981. 20.00 (ISBN 0-399-12567-1). Putnam.

Freeman, David. Philosophical Study of Religion. 1976. pap. 4.95 o.p. (ISBN 0-934532-12-5). Presby & Reformed.

Freeman, David S. Techniques of Family Therapy. LC 80-69669. 350p. 1981. 25.00 (ISBN 0-87668-431-2). Aronson.

Freeman, Derek. Report on the Iban. 2nd ed. (Monographs on Social Anthropology Ser: No. 41). (Illus.). 1970. text ed. 26.25x (ISBN 0-391-00113-2, Athlone Pr). Humanities.

Freeman, Don. Beady Bear. (Illus.). (gr. 3-6). 1977. pap. 1.95 o.p. (Puffin); cassette o.p. 17.95 o.p. (ISBN 0-670-15058-4). Penguin.

--Dandelion. LC 54-21472. (Illus.). (ps-2). 1977. pap. 2.50 (ISBN 0-14-050218-1, VS4, Puffin). Penguin.

--Hattie, the Backstage Bat. (Illus.). (gr. k-3). 1970. PLB 4.95 o.p. (ISBN 0-670-36253-0). Viking Pr.

--Hattie the Backstage Bat. (Illus.). (gr. k-1). 1973. pap. 0.95 o.p. (ISBN 0-670-05082-2, Puffin). Penguin.

--In a Flea's Navel: A Critic's Love Affair with Television. LC 80-16781. 224p. 1980. 8.95 (ISBN 0-498-05030-0). A S Barnes.

--Inspector Peckit. (Viking Seafarer Ser.). (Illus.). (gr. 1-3). 1976. pap. 0.95 o.p. (ISBN 0-670-05101-2, Puffin). Penguin.

--Norman the Doorman. (Illus.). (ps-2). 1959. PLB 6.95 o.s.i. (ISBN 0-670-51515-9). Viking Pr.

--Norman the Doorman. (Picture Puffins Ser.). (Illus.). (ps-3). 1981. pap. 1.95 (ISBN 0-14-050288-2, Puffin). Penguin.

--Rainbow of My Own. (Illus.). (gr. k-3). 1966. PLB 6.95 o.s.i. (ISBN 0-670-58928-4). Viking Pr.

--Space Witch. (Illus.). (gr. k-3). 1959. PLB 7.95 (ISBN 0-670-65995-9). Viking Pr.

--Will's Quill. (Illus.). 32p. (gr. k-3). 1975. PLB 7.95 (ISBN 0-670-76922-3). Viking Pr.

Freeman, Donald E. & Perry, Olney R. I-O Design: Data Management in Operating Systems. (Illus.). 1977. text ed. 19.95x (ISBN 0-8104-5789-X). Hayden.

Freeman, Donald M., ed. Foundation of Political Science: Research, Methods & Scope. LC 76-43130. 1978. 35.00 (ISBN 0-02-910670-2). Free Pr.

Freeman, Douglas S. Lee's Lieutenants, 3 vols. 1942-1944. Set. lib. rep. ed. 90.00x (ISBN 0-684-15630-X, ScribT). Scribner.

--R. E. Lee: An Abridgement. (Illus.). 1961. lib. rep. ed. 30.00x (ISBN 0-684-15489-7, ScribT). Scribner.

Freeman, E., ed. see Cocteau, Jean.

Freeman, E. M., ed. Campfire Chillers. LC 79-28318. (Illus.). 192p. (Orig.). 1980. lib. bdg. 10.25 o.p. (ISBN 0-686-26886-5). East Woods.

Freeman, Elinor Illus. by see Brown, Alfred G.

Freeman, Eugene, jt. ed. see Reese, William L.

Freeman, Grace & Sugarman, Joan G. Inside the Synagogue. LC 62-19996. (Illus.). (gr. 3-5). 1963. 4.00 (ISBN 0-8074-0041-6, 301782). UAHC.

Freeman, Henry G. Dictionary of Mechanical Engineering. 8th rev. ed. LC 72-347328. (Eng. Ger.). 1971. 45.00x (ISBN 3-7736-5031-0). Intl Pubns Serv.

Freeman, Herbert. Discrete-Time Systems. LC 80-15357. 256p. 1980. Repr. of 1965 ed. lib. bdg. 19.25 (ISBN 0-89874-228-5). Krieger.

Freeman, Herbert & Lewis, P. M., II, eds. Software Engineering. 1980. 21.00 (ISBN 0-12-267160-0). Acad Pr.

Freeman, Herbert & Pieroni, Goffredo G., eds. Map Data Processing. 1980. 26.00 (ISBN 0-12-267180-5). Acad Pr.

Freeman, Hobart. Introduction to the Old Testament Prophets. 10.95 (ISBN 0-8024-4145-9). Moody.

Freeman, Howard E., et al. Handbook of Medical Sociology. 3rd ed. 1979. 21.95 (ISBN 0-13-380253-1). P-H.

--Evaluating Social Projects in Developing Countries. 239p. (Orig.). 1980. pap. text ed. 9.00x (ISBN 92-64-12040-8). OECD.

Freeman, Ira M. All About the Atom. (gr. 4-6). 1956. 2.95 o.p. (ISBN 0-394-80210-1, BYR). Random.

--Look-It-up Book of Space. LC 71-84840. (Look-It-up Books Ser.: No. 7). (Illus.). (gr. 3-5). 1969. PLB 5.99 (ISBN 0-394-90840-6, BYR). Random.

--Physics Made Simple. rev. ed. LC 65-13090. pap. 3.50 (ISBN 0-385-08727-6, Made). Doubleday.

Freeman, Ira M., jt. auth. see Freeman, Mae B.

Freeman, James A. Milton & the Martial Muse: Paradise Lost & European Traditions of War. LC 80-7519. 1980. 17.50x (ISBN 0-691-06435-0). Princeton U Pr.

Freeman, James M. Scarcity & Opportunity in an Indian Village. LC 76-4423. (Kiste-Ogan Social Change Ser.). 1976. pap. text ed. 6.95 (ISBN 0-8465-2115-6). Benjamin-Cummings.

--Untouchable: An Indian Life History. LC 78-55319. (Illus.). 1979. 19.50x (ISBN 0-8047-1001-5); pap. 8.95 (ISBN 0-8047-1103-8, SP40). Stanford U Pr.

Freeman, Jim. Fishing with Small Fry: A Parent's Guide to Teaching Children How to Fish. LC 73-77333. (Illus.). 128p. 1973. pap. 2.95 o.p. (ISBN 0-87701-035-8). Chronicle Bks.

--How to Catch California Trout. (Illus.). 80p. 1972. pap. 1.95 o.p. (ISBN 0-87701-027-7). Chronicle Bks.

Freeman, Jo. The Politics of Women's Liberation: A Case Study of an Emerging Social Movement & Its Relation to the Policy Process. LC 74-25208. 1975. 9.95x (ISBN 0-679-30284-0); pap. 9.95x (ISBN 0-582-28009-5). Longman.

Freeman, John. Creative Writing. (gr. 9-12). pap. 3.95 (ISBN 0-584-62006-3). Transatlantic.

Freeman, John, jt. auth. see Consumer Guide.

Freeman, Julian. Arthritis: The New Treatments. rev. ed. (Illus.). 1981. pap. 5.95 (ISBN 0-8092-5960-5). Contemp Bks.

Freeman, Kathleen. Murder of Herodes & Other Trials from the Athenian Law Courts. 1963. pap. 2.95 o.p. (ISBN 0-393-00201-2, Norton Lib). Norton.

Freeman, Kathleen, tr. see Untersteiner, Mario.

Freeman, Kenneth J., ed. Schools of Hellas. LC 73-7994. (Illus.). 1969. text ed. 10.50 (ISBN 0-8077-1391-0); pap. text ed. 5.25x (ISBN 0-8077-1390-2). Tchrs Coll.

Freeman, Leonard, ed. Nuclear Medicine Annual, 1980. Weissmann, Heidi. 440p. 1980. text ed. 42.50 (ISBN 0-89004-472-4). Raven.

Freeman, Leslie G., jt. ed. see Tax, Sol.

Freeman, Leslie J. Nuclear Witnesses: Insiders Speak Out. (Illus.). 1981. 14.95 (ISBN 0-393-01456-8). Norton.

Freeman, Linton C. Elementary Applied Statistics: For Students in Behavioral Science. LC 65-14256. 1965. text ed. 18.95x (ISBN 0-471-27780-0). Wiley.

Freeman, Louis. Guide to Typewriting. (Orig.). (gr. 7-12). 1974. wkbk 4.00 (ISBN 0-87720-401-2). AMSCO Sch.

--Modular Typewriting. (gr. 10-11). 1978. wkbk. 7.58 (ISBN 0-87720-405-5). AMSCO Sch.

Freeman, Lucy, jt. auth. see Herman, Melvin.

Freeman, Lucy, jt. auth. see Williams, Edwina D.

Freeman, Lucy, et al. Too Deep for Tears. 1980. 12.95 (ISBN 0-8015-7820-5, Hawthorn). Dutton.

Freeman, M. A., ed. Arthritis of the Knee. (Clinical Features & Surgical Management Ser.). (Illus.). 320p. 1980. 110.00 (ISBN 0-387-09699-X). Springer-Verlag.

Freeman, M. A., jt. ed. see Swanson, S. A.

Freeman, M. D. The Legal Structure. (Aspects of Modern Sociology Ser: Social Structure of Modern Britain). 1977. text ed. 8.50x (ISBN 0-582-48761-7); pap. text ed. 7.95x (ISBN 0-582-48762-5). Longman.

--Violence in the Home: A Socio-Legal Study. 1979. 19.95 (ISBN 0-566-00129-2, 00407-3, Pub. by Saxon Hse England). Lexington Bks.

Freeman, M. H., jt. auth. see Fincham, W. H.

Freeman, Mae. The Real Magnet Book. (gr. k-3). 1970. pap. 1.50 (ISBN 0-590-01660-1, Schol Pap). Schol Bk Serv.

--Undersea Base. LC 73-9996. (Illus.). 64p. (gr. 3-4). 1974. PLB 4.90 o.p. (ISBN 0-531-02664-7). Watts.

Freeman, Mae B. Do You Know About Stars. LC 70-123070. (Illus.). (gr. k-3). 1970. PLB 3.99 (ISBN 0-394-90620-9). Random.

--Finding Out About the Past. (Gateway Ser.: No. 44). (Illus.). (gr. 4-8). 1967. 2.95 o.p. (ISBN 0-394-80144-X, BYR); PLB 5.99 (ISBN 0-394-90144-4). Random.

--Fun with Cooking. rev ed. (Illus.). (gr. 4-6). 1947. 3.95 (ISBN 0-394-80278-0, BYR); PLB 4.99 (ISBN 0-394-90278-5). Random.

Freeman, Mae B. & Freeman, Ira M. Fun with Scientific Experiments. (Illus.). (gr. 4-7). 1960. 3.95 o.p. (ISBN 0-394-80281-0, BYR); PLB 4.99 (ISBN 0-394-90281-5). Random.

Freeman, Marian, ed. Legal Secretary's Handbook. 11th ed. LC 76-52065. 1980. incl. 1979 suppl. 45.00 (ISBN 0-911110-22-4). Parker & Son.

Freeman, Michael. Edmund Burke & the Critique of Political Radicalism. LC 80-16266. 264p. 1980. lib. bdg. 21.00 (ISBN 0-226-26175-1). U of Chicago Pr.

--The Thirty-Five Millimeter Handbook. (Illus.). 320p. 1980. 25.00 (ISBN 0-87165-093-2). Ziff-Davis Pub.

Freeman, Neil J., jt. auth. see Waite, Thomas D.

Freeman, R. Austin. John Thorndykes Cases. 1976. lib. bdg. 12.95x (ISBN 0-89968-169-7). Lightyear.

--The Singing Bone. LC 75-44972. (Crime Fiction Ser). 1976. Repr. of 1912 ed. lib. bdg. 17.50 (ISBN 0-8240-2367-6). Garland Pub.

--The Singing Bone. 1976. lib. bdg. 12.95x (ISBN 0-89968-168-9). Lightyear.

Freeman, R. B. British Natural History Books from the Beginning to 1900: A Handlist. 350p. 1980. 39.50 (ISBN 0-686-62545-5, Archon). Shoe String.

Freeman, R. B. & Wertheimer, Douglas. P. H. Gosse: A Bibliography. 148p. 1980. 30.00 (ISBN 0-7129-0935-4, Dist. by Shoe String). Dawson Pub.

Freeman, Robert. Hidden Treasure: Public Sculpture in Providence, Rhode Island. (Illus.). 50p. (Orig.). 1981. pap. 4.95 (ISBN 0-917012-23-2). RI Pubns Soc.

Freeman, Robert N. Franz Schneider (Seventeen Thirty-Seven to Eighteen Twelve) A Thematic Catalogue of His Works. (Thematic Catalogues Ser.: No. 5). 1979. lib. bdg. 27.50 (ISBN 0-918728-13-4). Pendragon NY.

Freeman, Roger. B-Twenty Six Marauder at War. LC 78-7161. (Illus.). 1979. 17.95 (ISBN 0-684-15998-8, ScribT). Scribner.

--Telecommunication System Engineering: Analog & Digital Network. LC 79-26661. 1980. 32.50 (ISBN 0-471-02955-6, Pub. by Wiley-Interscience). Wiley.

--The Wayward Welfare State. (Publications Ser.: No. 249). (Illus.). 415p. 1981. price not set. Hoover Inst Pr.

Freeman, Roger & Garite, Thomas. Fetal Monitoring. (Illus.). 187p. 1980. lib. bdg. 27.00 (ISBN 0-683-03378-6). Williams & Wilkins.

Freeman, Roger A. B-Seventeen Fortress at War. LC 76-39858. (Illus.). 1977. 20.00 (ISBN 0-684-14872-2, ScribT). Scribner.

Freeman, Roger L. English-Spanish, Spanish-English Dictionary of Communications & Electronic Terms. 1972. 37.50 (ISBN 0-521-08080-0). Cambridge U Pr.

--Telecommunications Transmission Handbook. LC 75-1134. 587p. 1975. 37.50 (ISBN 0-471-27789-4, Pub. by Wiley-Interscience). Wiley.

Freeman, Ronald G. Intercambios: An Activities Manual. 209p. 1980. pap. text ed. 7.95 (ISBN 0-394-32425-0). Random.

Freeman, Rosemary see Muir, Kenneth.

Freeman, Ruth B. & Heinrich, Janet. Community Health Nursing Practice. 2nd ed. (Illus.). 500p. 1981. text ed. price not set (ISBN 0-7216-3877-5). Saunders.

Freeman, Stephen A; see Bishop, G. Reginald, Jr.

Freeman, Stephen A; see Kellenberger, Hunter.

Freeman, Stephen W. Does Your Child Have a Learning Disability? Questions Answered for Parents. 128p. 1974. pap. 7.50 (ISBN 0-398-03073-1). C C Thomas.

Freeman, T. Field Guide to Layered Rocks. (Earth Science Curriculum Project Pamphlet Ser). 1971. pap. 3.20 (ISBN 0-395-02617-2). HM.

Freeman, T. W. Geography & Regional Administration: England & Wales: 1830-1968. 3rd ed. 1967. text ed. 5.50x (ISBN 0-09-086610-X, Hutchinson U Lib). Humanities.

--A History of Modern British Geography. (Illus.). 288p. 1980. lib. bdg. 33.00 (ISBN 0-582-30030-4). Longman.

Freeman, Thomas W. Geography & Planning. (Repr. of 1958 ed.). 1968. pap. text ed. 2.25x (ISBN 0-09-028604-9, Hutchinson U Lib). Humanities.

Freeman, Tony. Aircraft That Work for Us. LC 80-23078. (On the Move Ser.). (Illus.). 48p. (gr. 3-6). 1981. PLB 9.25 (ISBN 0-516-03888-5). Childrens.

Freeman, W. H. & Bracegirdle, Brian. An Advanced Atlas of Histology. (Heinemann Biology Atlases Ser.). 1976. text ed. 16.95x (ISBN 0-435-60317-5). Heinemann Ed.

Freeman, William. Physical Education in a Changing Society. LC 76-10898. (Illus.). 1977. text ed. 15.75 (ISBN 0-395-24408-0); inst. manual 1.25 (ISBN 0-395-24409-9). HM.

Freeman-Grenville, G. S. The Mombasa Rising Against the Portuguese, Sixteen Thirty-One: From Sworn Evidence. (British Academy-Fontes Historiae Africanae). (Illus.). 224p. 98.00x (ISBN 0-19-725992-8). Oxford U Pr.

Freeman-Moir, D. John, jt. ed. see Broughton, John M.

Freemantle, Brian. Charlie M. LC 77-75383. 1977. 7.95 o.p. (ISBN 0-385-13021-X). Doubleday.

--The Man Who Wanted Tomorrow. 1978. pap. 1.75 o.s.i. (ISBN 0-515-04437-7). Jove Pubns.

Freemantle, M. H. The Chemist in Industry (3) Management & Economics. (Oxford Chemistry Ser). (Illus.). 96p. 1975. 14.95x (ISBN 0-19-855497-4). Oxford U Pr.

Freemon, B. M., jt. ed. see Bell, D. J.

Freemon, Frank R. Organic Mental Disease. LC 79-23180. (Illus.). 248p. 1981. text ed. 30.00 (ISBN 0-89335-109-1). Spectrum Pub.

--Sleep Research: A Critical Review. (Illus.). 220p. 1974. 19.75 (ISBN 0-398-02540-1). C C Thomas.

Freere, Roy H., tr. see Gander, Ralph.

Frees, Jane A. Dear Dad, Love, Jane. (Illus.). 1980. 9.95 (ISBN 0-8323-0361-5). Binford.

Freese, Arthur. GRIEF: Living Through It & Growing with It. 1978. pap. 3.50 (ISBN 0-06-464024-8, BN 4024, BN). Har-Row.

Freese, Arthur, jt. auth. see Lauton, Barry.

Freese, Arthur J. The Miracle of Vision. LC 76-26226. 1977. 11.95 (ISBN 0-06-011371-5, HarpT). Har-Row.

Freese, Arthur S. How Hypnosis Can Help You. 1976. pap. 1.75 o.p. (ISBN 0-445-08540-1). Popular Lib.

--The Prime of Your Life: The Book That Makes Old Age Obsolete. Orig. Title: The End of Senility. 192p. 1981. pap. 5.95 (ISBN 0-87795-316-3). Arbor Hse.

Freese, Arthur S., jt. auth. see Lauton, Barry.

Freese, Lee, ed. Theoretical Methods in Sociology: Seven Essays. LC 79-3998. 1980. 19.95x (ISBN 0-8229-3402-7). U of Pittsburgh Pr.

Freeston, Ewart C. Prisoner of War Ship Models 1775-1825. LC 73-77883. 1973. 22.50 o.s.i. (ISBN 0-87021-858-1). Naval Inst Pr.

Freeston, Ewart Co & Kent, Bernard. Modelling Thames Sailing Barges. 96p. 1980. 15.00x (ISBN 0-85177-091-6, Pub. by Cornell England). State Mutual Bk.

Freestone, Basil. Good English. LC 71-375014. (Pegasus Books: No. 11). (Illus.). 1968. 7.50x (ISBN 0-234-77962-4). Intl Pubns Serv.

Freethy, Ron. The Making of the British Countryside. LC 80-68688. (Illus.). 192p. 1981. 24.00 (ISBN 0-7153-8012-5). David & Charles.

Frege, Gottlob. The Basic Laws of Arithmetic: Exposition of the System. Furth, Montgomery, ed. & tr. (gr. 9-12). 1965. 12.00x o.p. (ISBN 0-520-00432-9). U of Cal Pr.

--The Philosophical & Mathematical Correspondence. McGuinness, Brian, ed. Kaal, Hans, tr. LC 79-23199. 1980. lib. bdg. 31.00x (ISBN 0-226-26197-2). U of Chicago Pr.

--Translations from the Philosophical Writings of Gottlob Frege. Geach, Peter & Black, Max, eds. 1977. Repr. of 1952 ed. 19.00x o.p. (ISBN 0-87471-325-0). Rowman.

--Translations from the Philosophical Writings of Gottlob Frege. 3rd ed. Geach, Peter & Black, Max, eds. 228p. 1980. 25.00x (ISBN 0-8476-6286-1); pap. 10.95x (ISBN 0-8476-6287-X). Rowman.

Fregly, Bert. Help Wanted: Everything You Need to Get the Job You Deserve. pap. 9.95 (ISBN 0-88280-071-X). Chicago Review.

Fregosi, Claudia. Are There Spooks in the Dark? LC 76-9789. (Illus.). 32p. (gr. k-3). 1977. 5.95 (ISBN 0-590-07451-2, Four Winds). Schol Bk Serv.

--The Happy Horse. LC 76-54894. (Illus.). (ps-3). 1977. 8.25 (ISBN 0-688-80087-4); PLB 7.92 (ISBN 0-688-84087-6). Greenwillow.

--The Mammoth, the Owl, & the Crab. LC 74-13836. (Illus.). 32p. (ps-2). 1975. 8.95 (ISBN 0-02-735690-6). Macmillan.

--Sun Grumble. LC 73-6046. (Illus.). 32p. (ps-2). 1974. 4.95g o.s.i. (ISBN 0-02-735740-6). Macmillan.

Frehse, H. & Geissbuhler, H., eds. Pesticide Residues: A Contribution to Their Interpretation, Relevance & Legislation. (International Union of Pure & Applied Chemistry). 1979. text ed. 37.00 (ISBN 0-08-023931-5). Pergamon.

Frei, Daniel. International Crisis & Crisis Management. LC 78-58474. 1978. 24.95 (ISBN 0-03-046346-7). Praeger.

Frei, Daniel, ed. Definitions & Measurement of Detente: East & West Perspectives. LC 80-27960. 256p. 1981. lib. bdg. 22.50 (ISBN 0-89946-080-1). Oelgeschlager.

Frei, Ernest J. The Historical Development of the Philippine National Language. LC 77-86950. (Anthro Ser.). 104p. 1980. Repr. of 1959 ed. cancelled (ISBN 0-404-16710-1). AMS Pr.

Freiberg, J. W. The French Press: Class, State, & Ideology. 255p. 1981. 31.95 (ISBN 0-03-058309-8). Praeger.

Freiberger, Robert H. & Kaye, Jeremy J. Arthrography. 1979. 48.50x (ISBN 0-8385-0423-X). ACC.

Freiberger, Stephen & Chew, Paul, Jr. A Consumer's Guide to Personal Computing & Microcomputers. 2nd ed. 208p. 1980. pap. 8.95 (ISBN 0-8104-5116-6). Hayden.

Freiberger, W. & Grenander, U. A Course in Computational Probability & Statistics. LC 76-176272. (Applied Mathematical Sciences: Vol. 6). 168p. 1971. pap. 14.50 (ISBN 0-387-90029-2). Springer-Verlag.

Freidberg & Hanawalt. DNA Repair, Pt. 1A. 312p. 1981. 29.75 (ISBN 0-8247-6848-5). Dekker.

Freidel, Frank, ed. The Golden Age of American History. LC 59-12230. (Golden Age Ser). 8.50 o.s.i. (ISBN 0-8076-0091-1). Braziller.

Freidel, Frank & Showman, Richard K., eds. Harvard Guide to American History, 2 vols. rev. ed. LC 72-81272. 1312p. 1974. 45.00x (ISBN 0-674-37560-2, Belknap Pr); pap. 12.50 one-vol. ed. (ISBN 0-674-37555-6). Harvard U Pr.

Freidel, Frank, ed. see Allen, Donald R.

Freidel, Frank, ed. see Bannister, Robert C., Jr.

Freidel, Frank, ed. see Carlisle, Rodney P.

Freidel, Frank, ed. see Cramer, C. H.

Freidel, Frank, ed. see Curry, E. R.

Freidel, Frank, ed. see Daniels, Jonathan.

Freidel, Frank, ed. see Davis, Polly Ann.

Freidel, Frank, ed. see Dizikes, John.

Freidel, Frank, ed. see Ferrell, Robert H., et al.

Freidel, Frank, ed. see Hand, Samuel B.

Freidel, Frank, ed. see Heinrichs, Waldo H., Jr.

Freidel, Frank, ed. see Hoover, Clark H.

Freidel, Frank, ed. see Johnson, Walter.

Freidel, Frank, ed. see Kesselman, Steven.

Freidel, Frank, ed. see Killigrew, John W.

Freidel, Frank, ed. see Macdonald, Dwight.

Freidel, Frank, ed. see McGeary, M. Nelson.

Freidel, Frank, ed. see Moley, Raymond.

Freidel, Frank, ed. see Mulder, Ronald A.

Freidel, Frank, ed. see Myers, William S.

Freidel, Frank, ed. see Nordhauser, Norman.

Freidel, Frank, ed. see Smith, Glenn H.

Freidel, Frank, ed. see Stoneman, William E.

Freidel, Frank, ed. see Walker, Forrest A.

Freidel, Frank, ed. see Warken, Philip W.

Freidel, Frank, ed. see Wickens, James F.

Freiden, R., jt. auth. see Rosen, A.

Freidheim, Robert L., ed. Managing Ocean Resources: A Primer. LC 79-53772. (Westview Special Studies in Natural Resources & Energy Management). 1979. lib. bdg. 22.00x (ISBN 0-89158-572-9). Westview.

Freidlina, R. Kh., ed. Organic Sulfer Chemistry: Ninth International Symposium on Organic Sulfur Chemistry, Riga, USSR, 9-14 June 1980. (IUPAC Symposium Ser.). (Illus.). 270p. 1981. 81.00 (ISBN 0-08-026180-9). Pergamon.

Freidrich, Otto. Going Crazy. 1976. pap. 1.95 (ISBN 0-380-00888-2, 31567). Avon.

Freidson, Eliot. Doctoring Together: A Study of Professional Social Control. LC 80-15513. 312p. 1980. pap. 7.95 (ISBN 0-226-26222-7, P911, Phoen). U of Chicago Pr.

--Patient's Views of Medical Practice. (Midway Reprint Ser.). 268p. 1980. pap. text ed. 10.00x (ISBN 0-226-26223-5). U of Chicago Pr.

--Professional Dominance: The Social Structure of Medical Care. LC 72-116538. 1970. 15.95x (ISBN 0-202-30203-2). Aldine Pub.

Freidson, Eliot, ed. Hospital in Modern Society. LC 63-10648. (Illus.). 1963. 19.95 (ISBN 0-02-910690-7). Free Pr.

--The Professions & Their Prospects. LC 72-84048. 1977. pap. 9.95x (ISBN 0-8039-0937-3). Sage.

Freidson, Eliot & Lorber, Judith, eds. Medical Men & Their Work: A Sociological Reader. LC 70-140627. 1972. 22.95x (ISBN 0-202-30231-8); pap. text ed. 12.95x (ISBN 0-202-30230-X). Aldine Pub.

Freier, Jerold L. Acquisition Search Programs. LC 80-26356. 1981. pap. 3.95 (ISBN 0-87576-094-5). Pilot Bks.

Freifelder, David. The DNA Molecule: Structure & Properties. LC 77-2768. (Illus.). 1978. text ed. 27.95x (ISBN 0-7167-0287-8); pap. text ed. 16.95x (ISBN 0-7167-0286-X). W H Freeman.

--Molecular Biology & Biochemistry: Problems & Applications. LC 78-18712. (Biology Ser.). (Illus.). 1978. pap. text ed. 10.95x (ISBN 0-7167-0068-9). W H Freeman.

--Physical Biochemistry: Applications to Biochemistry & Molecular Biology. LC 76-6495. (Illus.). 1976. text ed. 31.95x (ISBN 0-7167-0560-5); pap. text ed. 17.95x (ISBN 0-7167-0559-1). W H Freeman.

Freifelder, David, intro. by. Recombinant DNA: Readings from Scientific American. LC 77-29159. (Illus.). 1978. pap. text ed. 8.95x (ISBN 0-7167-0092-1). W H Freeman.

Freilich, Gerald & Greenleaf, Frederick P. Algebraic Methods in Business, Economics, & the Social Sciences: A Short Course. (Mathematics Ser.). (Illus.). 1977. pap. text ed. 7.95x (ISBN 0-7167-0470-6). W H Freeman.

--Calculus: A Short Course with Applications to Business, Economics, & the Social Sciences. LC 75-37569. (Illus.). 1976. 18.95x (ISBN 0-7167-0466-8). W H Freeman.

Freiman, Grigori. It Seems I Am a Jew: A Samizdat Essay. Nathanson, Melvyn B., ed. & tr. from Russian. LC 80-404. (Science & International Affairs Ser.). 120p. 1980. 9.95 (ISBN 0-8093-0962-9). S Ill U Pr.

Freire, Paulo. Pedagogy of the Oppressed. Ramos, Myra B., tr. from Port. LC 70-110074. 1970. pap. 4.95 (ISBN 0-8164-9132-1). Continuum.

Freis, Edward C. Introduction to Nature & Management of Hypertension. (Illus.). 1974. pap. 16.95 (ISBN 0-87618-030-6). R J Brady.

Freiser, H., ed. see Jeffery, P. G.

Freiser, Henry, ed. Ion-Selective Electrodes in Analytical Chemistry, Vol. 2. (Modern Analytical Chemistry Ser.). (Illus.). 290p. 1980. 35.00 (ISBN 0-306-40500-8, Plenum Pr). Plenum Pub.

Freislich, Richard. The Last Tribal War: A History of the Bondelswart Uprising Which Took Place in Southwest Africa in 1922. 117p. 1964. 19.50x (ISBN 0-686-28314-7, F Cass Co). Biblio Dist.

Freitag, Jeffrey J., ed. see Washington University Dept. of Medicine.

Freitag, Wolfgang M., ed. Encyclopedie Des Arts Decoratifs et Industriels Modernes Au XXeme Siecle, 12 vols. Incl. Vol. 1. Preface (ISBN 0-8240-2488-5); Vol. 2. Architecture (ISBN 0-8240-2489-3); Vol. 3. Architectural Ornamentation & Sculpture (ISBN 0-8240-2490-7); Vol. 4. Furniture (ISBN 0-8240-2491-5); Vol. 5. Furniture Hardware & Accessories (ISBN 0-8240-2492-3); Vol. 6. Textiles & Paper Products (ISBN 0-8240-2493-1); Vol. 7. The Art of the Book (ISBN 0-8240-2494-X); Vol. 8. Toys, Scientific & Musical Instruments, Vehicles of Transportation (ISBN 0-8240-2495-8); Vol. 9. Costume & Fashion Design (ISBN 0-8240-2496-6); Vol. 10. Stage Design, Photography & Film (ISBN 0-8240-2497-4); Vol. 11. The Environment - Street & Garden (ISBN 0-8240-2498-2); Vol. 12. The Teaching of the Decorative Arts (ISBN 0-8240-2499-0). LC 76-29204. (Illus.). Set. lib. bdg. 660.00 (ISBN 0-685-76428-1); lib. bdg. 55.00 ea. Garland Pub.

Freitag, Wolfgang M., ed. see Fortnum, Charles D.

Freitus, Joe. The Natural World Cookbook: Complete Gourmet Meals from Wild Edibles. (Illus.). 320p. 1980. 15.00 (ISBN 0-913276-33-2). Stone Wall Pr.

Frelden, R., jt. auth. see Rosen, A.

Frelinghuysen, Joseph, jt. auth. see Kiell, Paul J.

Fremantle, Anne. Age of Faith. (Great Ages of Man Ser). (Illus.). 1965. 12.95 (ISBN 0-8094-0343-9). Time-Life.

Fremantle, Francesca & Trungpa, Chogyam, trs. from Tibetan. The Tibetan Book of the Dead: The Great Liberation Through Hearing in the Bardo. LC 74-29615. (Clear Light Ser.). (Illus.). 256p. 1975. pap. 4.50 (ISBN 0-394-73064-X). Shambhala Pubns.

Fremgen, James M. Accounting for Managerial Analysis. 3rd ed. (Illus.). 1976. text ed. 18.95 (ISBN 0-256-01777-8). Irwin.

Fremlin, D. H. Topological Riesz Spaces & Measure Theory. LC 72-95410. 300p. 1974. 42.00 (ISBN 0-521-20170-5). Cambridge U Pr.

Fremlin-Key, Hermyone. More Toys & Gifts for You to Make. (Illus.). 96p. 1971. 3.75 (ISBN 0-8231-5027-5). Branford.

--Toys & Gifts for You to Make. LC 70-108784. (Illus.). 1970. 8.75 (ISBN 0-8231-5022-4). Branford.

Fremon, George & Fremon, Suzanne. Why Trade It In? Your Mechanic Can Save You Money. LC 76-42603. (Illus.). 1980. pap. 5.95 (ISBN 0-89709-016-0). Liberty Pub.

--Your First Car. (Illus.). 176p. (Orig.). 1981. pap. 3.95 (ISBN 0-89709-024-1). Liberty Pub.

Fremon, Suzanne, jt. auth. see Fremon, George.

Fremon, Suzanne, ed. Women & Men. (Reference Shelf Ser.). 1977. 6.25 (ISBN 0-8242-0607-X). Wilson.

Fremon, Suzanne, jt. ed. see Wilson, Morrow.

Fremont, Theodore S., et al. Informal Diagnostic Assessment of Children. (Illus.). 176p. 1977. 16.75 (ISBN 0-398-03646-2). C C Thomas.

Fremy, Pierre. Cyanophycees des Cotes d'Europe. (Memoires of the National Society of Natural Sciences & Mathematics of Cherborg Ser.). (Illus.). 1972. 49.00 (ISBN 90-6123-274-0). Lubrecht & Cramer.

Frenaye, Frances, tr. see Pons, Maurice.

French, A. L. Shakespeare & the Critics. LC 75-183221. 224p. 1972. 42.00 (ISBN 0-521-08470-9). Cambridge U Pr.

French, A. P., ed. Einstein: A Centenary Volume. LC 78-25968. (Illus.). 1979. text ed. 20.00 (ISBN 0-674-24230-0); pap. 8.95 (ISBN 0-674-24231-9). Harvard U Pr.

French, Alfred & Berlin, Irving. Depression in Children & Adolescents. 300p. 1979. text ed. 29.95 (ISBN 0-87705-390-1). Human Sci Pr.

French, Alfred D. & Gardner, Kenncorwin H., eds. Fiber Diffraction Methods. LC 80-21566. (ACS Symposium Ser.: No. 141). 1980. 34.50 (ISBN 0-8412-0589-2). Am Chemical.

French, Benjamin I., Jr. Customer Service Manual with Model Letters & Forms. 1976. 17.95 o.p. (ISBN 0-13-196568-9). P-H.

French, Brian & Squire, Stan. Human & Economic Geography. (Illus.). 216p. (Orig.). 1973. pap. text ed. 4.50x (ISBN 0-19-519769-0). Oxford U Pr.

French, Bryant M., ed. see Twain, Mark.

French, Frances. OJT Mail Clerk Resource Materials. 2nd ed. (Gregg Office Job Training Program Ser.). (Illus.). 112p. (gr. 11-12). 1980. soft cover 4.80 (ISBN 0-07-022190-1); training manual 3.56 (ISBN 0-07-022191-X). McGraw.

French, Francis G. & Jacobs, Zeney. Communicating with the Computer: Introductory Experiences, Basic. (Orig.). (gr. 9-12). 1975. pap. text ed. 10.96 (ISBN 0-205-04470-0, 2044706); tchrs'. guide 4.40 (ISBN 0-205-04471-9, 2044714). Allyn.

French, Frank S., et al, eds. Hormonal Regulation of Spermatogenesis. LC 75-32541. (Current Topics in Molecular Endocrinology Ser.: Vol. 2). 526p. 1975. 45.00 (ISBN 0-306-34002-X, Plenum Pr). Plenum Pub.

French Government Public. Association Internationale Des Travailleurs, Vol. 1. 1976. lib. bdg. 12.00x o.p. (ISBN 0-8287-1329-4); pap. text ed. 5.00x o.p. (ISBN 0-685-71492-6). Clearwater Pub.

--Association Internationale Des Travailleurs, Vol. 2. 1976. lib. bdg. 15.00x o.p. (ISBN 0-8287-1330-8); pap. text ed. 7.50x o.p. (ISBN 0-685-71490-X). Clearwater Pub.

French, H. W. Art & Artists in Connecticut. LC 70-87543. (Library of American Art Ser). 1970. Repr. of 1879 ed. lib. bdg. 19.50 (ISBN 0-306-71459-0). Da Capo.

French, Hajjar. Christiarisme en Orient. 9.00x (ISBN 0-685-85421-3). Intl Bk Ctr.

French, Henri, ed. Heat Transfer & Fluid Flow in Nuclear Systems. 300p. 1981. 30.01 (ISBN 0-08-027181-2). Pergamon.

French, Hollis. Jacob Hurd & His Sons, Silversmiths. LC 70-175722. (Architecture & Decorative Art Ser.: Vol. 39). 158p. 1972. Repr. of 1939 ed. lib. bdg. 32.50 (ISBN 0-306-70406-4). Da Capo.

--Silver Collector's Glossary & a List of Early American Silversmiths & Their Marks. LC 67-27454. (Architecture & Decorative Art Ser). 1967. lib. bdg. 17.50 (ISBN 0-306-70969-4). Da Capo.

French Institute of Petroleum, Paris, 1971, et al. Rapid Methods for the Analysis of Used Oils: Proceedings. (Illus.). 96p. 1973. text ed. 25.00x (ISBN 0-900645-10-5). Scholium Intl.

French, J. H. Historical & Statistical Gazetteer of New York State. (Illus.). 782p. 1980. Repr. of 1860 ed. deluxe ed. 22.50 deluxe (ISBN 0-932334-31-8); pap. 17.50 (ISBN 0-932334-32-6). Heart of the Lakes.

French, Jane, jt. auth. see French, Joel.

French, Joel & French, Jane. Straight Is the Way. LC 79-169. 1979. pap. 2.95 (ISBN 0-87123-497-1, 210497). Bethany Fell.

--War Beyond the Stars. LC 79-90267. 1979. pap. 3.50 (ISBN 0-89221-067-2). New Leaf.

French, Laura. Cats. (Illus.). 24p. (gr. k-2). 1976. PLB 5.00 (ISBN 0-307-60150-1, Golden Pr). Western Pub.

--Fat Albert & the Cosby Kids: Getting It Together. (Tell-a-Tale Readers). (Illus.). (gr. k-3). 1975. PLB 4.77 (ISBN 0-307-68598-5, Whitman). Western Pub.

French, Marilyn. The Bleeding Heart. 416p. 1981. pap. 3.50 (ISBN 0-345-28896-3). Ballantine.

--Shakespeare's Division of Experience. LC 80-23147. 384p. 1981. 15.95 (ISBN 0-671-44865-X). Summit Bks.

--The Women's Room. 1980. pap. 3.50 (ISBN 0-515-05933-1). Jove Pubns.

French, Michael. Rhythms. 1981. pap. 2.75 (ISBN 0-425-05023-8). Berkley Pub.

French, P. M., jt. ed. see McCall, J. L.

French, Parker H. Overland Expedition to California. 1970. pap. 2.25 (ISBN 0-917420-03-9). Buck Hill.

French, Paul see Asimov, Isaac, pseud.

French, Peter, et al, eds. Foundations of Analytic Philosophy. (Midwest Studies in Philosophy: Vol. 6). 576p. 1981. 35.00 (ISBN 0-8166-1033-9); pap. 15.00 (ISBN 0-8166-1036-3). U of Minn Pr.

French, Peter A., et al, eds. Contemporary Perspectives in the Philosophy of Language. (Midwest Studies in Philosophy). 1977. 25.00x (ISBN 0-8166-0865-2); pap. 8.95x (ISBN 0-8166-0866-0). U of Minn Pr.

French, Peter J. John Dee: The World of an Elizabethan Magus. 256p. 1980. 25.00 (ISBN 0-7100-7158-2). Routledge & Kegan.

French, Ray. My Kind of Rugby: Union & League. LC 80-670268. (Illus.). 160p. 1980. 14.95 (ISBN 0-571-11422-9, Pub. by Faber & Faber). Merrimack Bk Serv.

--Running Rugby. (Illus.). 80p. 1980. 13.95 (ISBN 0-571-11597-7, Pub. by Faber & Faber); pap. 5.95 (ISBN 0-571-11600-0, Pub. by Faber & Faber). Merrimack Bk Serv.

French, Reginald M., tr. from Rus. Way of a Pilgrim. (Illus.). 242p. 1974. 7.50 (ISBN 0-8164-0259-0); pap. 3.95 (ISBN 0-8164-2069-6, SP18). Crossroad NY.

French, Richard & Beliveau, Andre. The R. C. M. P. & the Management of National Security. 77p. 1979. pap. text ed. 6.95x (ISBN 0-920380-18-2, Pub. by Inst Res Pub Canada). Renouf.

French, Robert. Vietnam: Both Sides. (Orig.). 1979. pap. 2.25 (ISBN 0-532-23177-5). Manor Bks.

French, T. L., ed. Cahiers Du Cinema. (Thousand Eyes Ser.). (Illus.). 1978. pap. 3.50 o.p. (ISBN 0-918432-18-9). NY Zoetrope.

French, Thomas E. & Vierck, Charles J. Engineering Drawing & Graphic Technology. 12th ed. (Illus.). 1978. lib. bdg. 19.95 (ISBN 0-07-022158-8, C); problems 10.50 (ISBN 0-07-022160-X); tchr. manual 3.95 (ISBN 0-07-022159-6). McGraw.

French, Valerie, jt. auth. see Lichtman, Allan J.

French, Warren. J. D. Salinger. 2nd rev. ed. (U. S. Author Ser.: No. 40). 1976. lib. bdg. 9.95 (ISBN 0-8057-7163-8). Twayne.

--John Steinbeck. 2nd ed. (U. S. Authors Ser.: No. 2). 1975. lib. bdg. 12.50 (ISBN 0-8057-0693-3). Twayne.

--Twentieth Century American Literature. 672p. 1981. pap. 12.95 (ISBN 0-312-82401-7). St Martin.

French, Warren, ed. J. D. Salinger. (Twayne's U. S. Authors Ser.). 187p. 1963. pap. text ed. 4.95 (ISBN 0-672-61505-3). Bobbs.

--John Steinbeck. (Twayne's U. S. Authors Ser.). 189p. pap. text ed. 4.95 (ISBN 0-672-61501-0). Bobbs.

--The Twenties: Fiction, Poetry, Drama. rev. ed. LC 74-24534. 1976. lib. bdg. 16.00 o.p. (ISBN 0-912112-05-0). Everett-Edwards.

French, Wendell L. The Personnel Management Process. 4th ed. LC 77-73992. (Illus.). 1978. text ed. 18.95 (ISBN 0-395-25529-5); inst. manual 0.50 (ISBN 0-395-25530-9). HM.

French, Wendell L. & Bell, Cecil H., Jr. Organization Development: Behavioral Science Interventions for Organization Improvement. 2nd ed. 1978. ref. 15.95 (ISBN 0-13-641688-8); pap. 10.95 (ISBN 0-13-641670-5). P-H.

French, Wendell L., et al. The Personnel Management Process: Cases on Human Resources Administration. LC 77-74422. (Illus.). 1977. pap. text ed. 9.25 (ISBN 0-395-25531-7); inst. manual 0.50 (ISBN 0-395-26087-6). HM.

French, Wendell L., Jr., et al. Organization Development: Theory, Practice, & Research. 1978. pap. 16.50 (ISBN 0-256-02089-2). Business Pubns.

French, William. Further Recollections of a Western Ranchman: New Mexico 1883-1889, Vol. II. (Illus.). 1965p. 20.00 (ISBN 0-87266-011-7). Argosy.

--Some Recollections of a Western Ranchman, New Mexico 1883-1899, 2 Vols. 1965. Set. 35.00 (ISBN 0-87266-011-7). Argosy.

French, William B. & Lusk, Harold F. Law of the Real Estate Business. 4th ed. 1979. 18.95 (ISBN 0-256-02167-8). Irwin.

French, William L. Your Handwriting & What It Means. (Newcastle Self-Enrichment Ser). (Illus.). 228p. 1976. pap. 2.95 o.p. (ISBN 0-87877-036-4, G-36). Newcastle Pub.

--Your Handwriting & What It Means. LC 80-19831. 226p. 1980. Repr. of 1976 ed. lib. bdg. 9.95x (ISBN 0-89370-636-1). Borgo Pr.

French, William M. America's Educational Tradition: An Interpretive History. 1964. text ed. 8.95x o.p. (ISBN 0-669-20107-3). Heath.

French-Hodges, Peter & Althaus, Catherine. Cook Now, Dine Later. 1972. 9.50 (ISBN 0-571-08815-5, Pub. by Faber & Faber); pap. 4.95 (ISBN 0-571-09895-9). Merrimack Bk Serv.

--Fork, Spoon & Finger Food. (Illus.). 1975. 6.95 o.p. (ISBN 0-571-10613-7, Pub. by Faber & Faber). Merrimack Bk Serv.

Frend, W. H. Martydom & Persecution in the Early Church. (Twin Brooks Ser.). 645p. 1981. pap. 12.95 (ISBN 0-8010-3502-3). Baker Bk.

--The Rise of the Monophysite Movement: Chapters in the History of the Church in the Fifth & Sixth Centuries. LC 72-75302. (Illus.). 400p. 1972. 69.50 (ISBN 0-521-08130-0). Cambridge U Pr.

Freneau, Philip. Poems. Clark, Harry H., ed. (Library of Classics Ser.: No. 19). 1960. pap. text ed. 8.75 o.s.i. (ISBN 0-02-844850-2). Hafner.

Freneau, Philip M. The Writings in Prose & Verse of Hezekiah Salem, Late of New England. LC 75-15901. (Illus.). 88p. 1975. lib. bdg. 20.00x (ISBN 0-8201-1156-2). Schol Facsimiles.

Freniere, H. Francis, et al, trs. see People's Court, Munich & Hitler, Adolph.

Frenkel, Jacob A. & Johnson, Harry G. Economics of Exchange Rates. (Economics Ser.). 1978. text ed. 14.95 (ISBN 0-201-02374-1); pap. text ed. 9.50 (ISBN 0-201-02376-8). A-W.

Frenkel, Robert E. Ruderal Vegetation Along Some California Roadsides. (California Library Reprint Ser.: No. 92). 1978. Repr. of 1970 ed. 13.75x (ISBN 0-520-03589-5). U of Cal Pr.

Frenkel, Stephen J., ed. Industrial Action in Australia. 184p. 1981. text ed. 24.95x (ISBN 0-86861-122-0, 2513); pap. text ed. 12.50x (ISBN 0-86861-130-1, 2514). Allen Unwin.

Frenkiel, F. N. see Landsberg, H. E.

Frentz, Brand, tr. see Turchin, Valentin F.

Frentz, Henry J., jt. auth. see Chelius, Carl R.

Frenyo, V. L., jt. auth. see Pethes, G.

Frenz, Horst. Eugene O'Neill. Sebba, Helen, tr. LC 79-143188. (Modern Literature Ser.). 1971. 10.95 (ISBN 0-8044-2211-7); pap. 3.45 (ISBN 0-8044-6159-7). Ungar.

Frenz, Horst, jt. ed. see Hibbard, Addison.

Frenz, Horst, ed. see O'Neill, Eugene, et al.

Frenzel, Louis E., Jr. The Howard W. Sams Crash Course in Microcomputers. LC 79-65750. 1980. pap. 17.50 (ISBN 0-672-21634-5, 21634). Sams.

Frere, John H. Prospectus & Specimen of an Intended National Work by William & Robert Whistlecraft of Stowmarket. Reiman, Donald H., ed. LC 75-31204. (Romantic Context Ser.: Poetry 1789-1830: Vol. 55). 1978. lib. bdg. 47.00 (ISBN 0-8240-2154-1). Garland Pub.

Frere, Paul. Porsche Nine Eleven Story. 2nd ed. (Illus.). 200p. 1981. 37.95 (ISBN 0-85059-482-0). Aztex.

--Porsche Racing Cars of the Seventies. LC 80-23773. (Illus.). 256p. 1981. 16.95 (ISBN 0-668-05113-2, 5113). Arco.

Frere, Sheppard. Britannia: A History of Roman Britain. rev. ed. (Illus.). 1978. 32.00x (ISBN 0-7100-8916-3). Routledge & Kegan.

Frere-Cook, Gervis & Macksey, Kenneth. History of Sea Warfare. (Illus.). 245p. 1980. 14.95 (ISBN 0-8069-9214-X, Pub by Guinness Superlatives England). Sterling.

Freschet, Berniece. Black Bear Baby. (See & Read Book). (Illus.). 48p. (gr. 6-9). 1981. PLB 6.99 (ISBN 0-399-61151-7). Putnam.

--Skunk Baby. LC 72-83781. (Illus.). (gr. 2-5). 1973. PLB 7.89 (ISBN 0-690-74194-4, TYC-J). T Y Crowell.

--Year on Muskrat Marsh. LC 73-19559. (Illus.). 56p. (gr. 1-4). 1974. write for info. (ISBN 0-684-13748-8, ScribJ). Scribner.

Fresener, Patricia A., jt. ed. see Fresener, Scott O.

Fresener, Scott O. & Fresener, Patricia A., eds. How to Print T-Shirts for Fun & Profit. (Illus.). 176p. (Orig.). 1979. pap. text ed. 19.95 (ISBN 0-9603530-0-3). Southwest Screen Print.

Freshwater Biological Association, Cumbria England. Catalogue of the Library of the Freshwater Biological Association. 1979. lib. bdg. 630.00 (ISBN 0-8161-0289-9). G K Hall.

Fresno City & County Historical Society. Fresno California Illustrated. LC 80-68522. (Illus.). 192p. 1980. Repr. 13.95 (ISBN 0-914330-35-7). Pioneer Pub Co.

Fresquet, G., jt. auth. see Parramon, J. M.

Fretz, Bruce R. & Mills, David H. Licensing & Certification of Psychologists & Counselors: A Guide to Current Policies, Procedures, & Legislation. LC 80-8011. (Social & Behavioral Science Ser.). 1980. text ed. 13.95x (ISBN 0-87589-470-4). Jossey-Bass.

Fretz, Bruce R., jt. auth. see Whiteley, John M.

Fretz, Thomas A., et al. Plant Propagation Laboratory Manual. 3rd rev. ed. 1979. text ed. 9.95 (ISBN 0-8087-0668-3). Burgess.

Freuchen, Peter. Book of the Eskimos. 1977. pap. 1.75 o.p. (ISBN 0-449-30802-2, Prem). Fawcett.

Freud, Geza. Orthogonal Polynomials. LC 76-134028. 1971. 42.00 (ISBN 0-08-016047-6). Pergamon.

Freud, Sigmund. General Psychological Theory. 1963. pap. 2.95 (ISBN 0-02-076350-6, Collier). Macmillan.

--General Selection from the Works of Sigmund Freud. LC 57-11436. 1957. pap. 2.95 (ISBN 0-385-09325-X, A115, Anch). Doubleday.

--Group Psychology & the Analysis of the Ego. Strachey, James, ed. & tr. 1975. 6.95 (ISBN 0-393-01117-8, Norton Lib); pap. 2.95 (ISBN 0-393-00770-7). Norton.

--Outline of Psychoanalysis. rev. ed. Strachey, James, ed. & tr. 1970. pap. 1.95 (ISBN 0-393-00151-2, Norton Lib). Norton.

--Question of Lay Analysis. Strachey, James, ed. & tr. (Standard ed.). 1969. pap. 3.95 (ISBN 0-393-00503-8, Norton Lib). Norton.

--Three Case Histories. 1963. pap. 2.95 (ISBN 0-02-076650-5, Collier). Macmillan.

--Totem & Taboo. Brill, Abraham A., tr. 1960. pap. 2.95 (ISBN 0-394-70124-0, Vin, V124). Random.

Freudberg, Judy. Many Faces of Ernie. (A Young Reader Ser.). (Illus.). (gr. k-3). 1979. PLB 5.00 (ISBN 0-307-60108-0, Golden Pr). Western Pub.

Freudenberger, Herbert & Richelson, Geraldine. Burn Out: The High Cost of High Achievement. LC 79-6596. 240p. 1980. 9.95 (ISBN 0-385-15664-2, Anchor Pr). Doubleday.

Freudenberger, Herman. The Waldstein Woolen Mill. (Kress Library of Business & Economics: No. 18). (Illus.). 1963. pap. 5.00x (ISBN 0-678-09912-X, Baker Lib). Kelley.

Freudenstein, Reinhold, ed. Teaching Foreign Languages to the Very Young. LC 79-42885. (Pergamon Institute of English - Symposium). (Illus.). 112p. 1979. 7.50 (ISBN 0-08-024576-5). Pergamon.

Freudenthal, Alfred M., et al, eds. Structural Safety & Reliability: Proceedings of the International Conference. 1972. 115.00 (ISBN 0-08-016566-4). Pergamon.

Freudenthal, Ralph I. & Jones, Peter, eds. Polynuclear Aromatic Hydrocarbons: Chemistry, Metabolism, & Carcinogenesis. LC 75-43194. 1976. 48.00 (ISBN 0-89004-103-2). Raven.

Freudenthal, Ralph I., ed. see International Symposium on Analysis, Chemistry, & Biology, No. 2.

Freund, Bill. Capital & Labour in the Nigerian Tin Mines. (Ibadan History Ser.). 1980. text ed. write for info. (ISBN 0-391-02155-9). Humanities.

Freund, Eric C., jt. ed. see Goodman, William I.

Freund, H. R. Principles of Head & Neck Surgery. 2nd ed. (Illus.). 1979. 43.50 (ISBN 0-8385-7922-1). ACC.

Freund, J., jt. auth. see Miller, I.

Freund, John E. College Mathematics with Business Applications. 2nd ed. (Illus.). 720p. 1975. ref. ed. 19.95 (ISBN 0-13-146464-7). P-H.

--Modern Elementary Statistics. 5th ed. 1979. text ed. 18.95 (ISBN 0-13-593491-5); pap. 5.95 study guide (ISBN 0-13-593517-2). P-H.

--Statistics: A First Course. 2nd ed. (Illus.). 1976. pap. 17.95 (ISBN 0-13-846055-8); wkbk. 5.50 (ISBN 0-13-846014-0). P-H.

Freund, John E. & Walpole, Ronald E. Mathematical Statistics. 3rd ed. 1980. text ed. 20.95 (ISBN 0-13-562066-X). P-H.

Freund, John E. & Williams, F. J. Elementary Business Statistics: The Modern Approach. 3rd ed. (Illus.). 1977. 19.95 (ISBN 0-13-253062-7). P-H.

Freund, Paul A. On Understanding the Supreme Court: A Series of Lectures Delivered Under the Auspices of the Julius Rosenthal Foundation at Northwestern University, School of Law. LC 77-23550. (Illus.). 1977. Repr. of 1949 ed. lib. bdg. 13.50x (ISBN 0-8371-9699-X, FROU). Greenwood.

Freund, Philip. Three Poetic Plays: Jocasta, Flame & Cedar, the Bacchae. 216p. 1973. 5.75 (ISBN 0-693-01607-8); pap. 4.95 (ISBN 0-693-01608-6). Transatlantic.

Freund, Roberta B. Open the Book. 2nd ed. LC 66-13739. (Illus.). 1966. 10.00 (ISBN 0-8108-0107-8). Scarecrow.

Freundlich, Charles I. College Vacabulary Builder. 256p. (Orig.). 1981. pap. 5.95 (ISBN 0-671-41337-6). Monarch Pr.

--Latin for the Grades, 3 Bks. (gr. 4-6). 1970. Bk. 1. pap. text ed. 3.75 (ISBN 0-87720-562-0); Bk. 2. pap. text ed. 3.75 (ISBN 0-87720-564-7); Bk. 3. pap. text ed. 3.75 (ISBN 0-87720-566-3). AMSCO Sch.

--Review Text in Latin First Year. 2nd ed. (Illus., Orig.). (gr. 7-12). 1966. pap. text ed. 5.33 (ISBN 0-87720-551-5). AMSCO Sch.

--Review Text in Latin Three & Four Years. (Orig.). (gr. 7-12). 1967. pap. text ed. 6.42 (ISBN 0-87720-558-2). AMSCO Sch.

--Review Text in Latin Two Years. (gr. 7-12). 1966. pap. text ed. 5.75 (ISBN 0-87720-555-8). AMSCO Sch.

--Workbook in Latin First Year. (Illus., Orig.). (gr. 8-11). 1963. wkbk 6.75 (ISBN 0-87720-553-1). AMSCO Sch.

--Workbook in Latin Two Years. (Illus., Orig.). (gr. 9-12). 1965. wkbk 6.75 (ISBN 0-87720-556-6). AMSCO Sch.

Freundlich, Irwin, jt. auth. see Friskin, James.

Freundlich, Irwin M. Diffuse Pulmonary Disease: A Radiologic Approach. LC 77-27745. (Illus.). 1979. pap. text ed. 15.95 o.p. (ISBN 0-7216-3866-X). Saunders.

Frevert, Patricia. Why Does the Weather Change? (Creative's Questions & Answer Library). (Illus.). (gr. 3-4). Date not set. PLB 5.75 (ISBN 0-87191-748-3); pap. 2.75 (ISBN 0-89812-214-7). Creative Ed. Postponed.

Frevert, Patricia D. Beatrix Potter, Children's Storyteller. Redpath, Ann, ed. (People to Remember Ser.). (Illus.). 32p. (gr. 5-9). 1981. PLB 5.95 (ISBN 0-87191-801-3). Creative Ed.

--Margaret Mead Herself. Redpath, Ann, ed. (People to Remember Ser.). (Illus.). 32p. (gr. 5-9). 1981. PLB 5.95 (ISBN 0-87191-799-8). Creative Ed.

--Mark Twain, an American Voice. Redpath, Ann, ed. (People to Remember Ser.). (Illus.). 32p. (gr. 5-9). 1981. PLB 5.95 (ISBN 0-87191-802-1). Creative Ed.

--Muppet Magic. (TV-Movie Tie-Ins Ser.). 32p. (gr. 4-8). 1980. PLB 5.95 (ISBN 0-87191-755-6); pap. 2.95 (ISBN 0-89812-224-4). Creative Ed.

--Pablo Picasso, Twentieth Century Genius. Redpath, Ann, ed. (People to Remember Ser.). (Illus.). 32p. (gr. 5-9). 1981. PLB 5.95 (ISBN 0-87191-800-5). Creative Ed.

Frew, David R. Management of Stress: Using TM at Work. LC 76-18164. 1977. 15.95 (ISBN 0-88229-254-4). Nelson-Hall.

Frew, David R., jt. auth. see Frew, Mary A.

Frew, Mary A. & Frew, David R. Fundamentals of Medical Assisting, Administrative & Clinical. 1981. 16.95 (ISBN 0-8036-3858-2). Davis Co.

Frew, Robert M., et al. A Guidebook for Writers. 200p. (gr. 9-12). 1981. pap. text ed. 6.95 (ISBN 0-917962-69-9). Peek Pubns.

Frewer, Glyn see Milne, John.

Frey, Albert R. Sobriquets & Nicknames. LC 66-22671. 1966. Repr. of 1888 ed. 18.00 (ISBN 0-8103-3003-2). Gale.

Frey, Albert W. & Halterman, Jean C. Advertising. 4th ed. 593p. 1970. 24.50x (ISBN 0-8260-3245-1, 33291). Wiley.

Frey, Berta. Designing & Drafting for Handweavers. 240p. 1975. 10.95 (ISBN 0-02-541460-7). Macmillan.

Frey, Bruno S. Modern Political Economy, Paper. 166p. 1980. pap. text ed. 13.95 (ISBN 0-470-26999-5). Halsted Pr.

Frey, Christine L., ed. Aging in Culture & Society: Comparative Viewpoints & Strategies. LC 79-13198. 29.95 (ISBN 0-03-052726-0). Praeger.

Frey, D. G., jt. ed. see Wright, Herbert E.

Frey, G. Donald & Klobukowski, Christopher J. Nuclear Medicine Technology Examination Review Book. 1980. pap. 14.50 (ISBN 0-87488-457-8). Med Exam.

Frey, Jay J. How to Fly Floats: Seaplane Flying. (Illus.). Date not set. pap. 4.95x (ISBN 0-911721-71-1, Pub. by Edo-Aire). Aviation.

Frey, Karl, et al, eds. Research in Science Education in Europe: Report of a Cooperative Study & a European Contact Workshop Organised by the Council of Europe & the Institute for Science Education, FRG (Kiel) 394p. 1977. pap. text ed. 25.50 (ISBN 90-265-0266-4, Pub. by Swets Serv Pub Holland). Swets North Am.

Frey, Kenneth J., ed. Plant Breeding II. 1981. 30.00 (ISBN 0-8138-1550-9). Iowa St U Pr.

Frey, Leonard H., ed. Readings in Early English Language History. LC 66-13894. (Orig.). 1966. pap. 4.50 (ISBN 0-672-63100-8). Odyssey Pr.

Frey, Paul R. Chemistry Problems & How to Solve Them. 7th ed. (Illus., Orig.). 1969. pap. 4.95 (ISBN 0-06-460046-7, CO 46, COS). Har-Row.

Frey, R. & Safer, P., eds. Resuscitation & Life Support in Disasters: Relief of Pain & Suffering in Disaster Situations. (Disaster Medicine Ser.: Vol. 2). (Illus.). 320p. 1980. pap. 49.60 (ISBN 0-387-09044-4). Springer-Verlag.

Frey, R. G. Interests & Rights: The Case Against Animals. (Clarendon Library of Logic & Philosophy Ser.). 188p. 1980. 24.95x (ISBN 0-19-824421-5). Oxford U Pr.

Frey, R. W., ed. The Study of Trace Fossils: A Synthesis of Principles, Problems, & Procedures in Ichnology. LC 74-30164. (Illus.). xxiii, 570p. 1975. 66.50 o.p. (ISBN 0-387-06870-8). Springer-Verlag.

Frey, Richard L., et al. New Complete Hoyle. rev. ed. LC 55-11330. 1956. 9.95 (ISBN 0-385-00126-6). Doubleday.

Frey, Robert W., ed. Excursions in Southeastern Geology: Field Trip Guidebooks, 2 vols. Incl. Vol. I. Field Trips-1-13. pap. 25.00 (ISBN 0-913312-48-7); Vol. II. Field Trips-14-23. pap. 25.00 (ISBN 0-913312-49-5). (Illus., Orig.). 1980. Set. pap. 40.00 (ISBN 0-913312-50-9). Am Geol.

Frey, Shaney. Complete Beginner's Guide to Skin Diving. LC 65-11061. (gr. 7-11). 5.95 o.p. (ISBN 0-385-04523-9). Doubleday.

--The Complete Beginners Guide to Swimming. LC 74-9651. 208p. (gr. 5-9). 1975. PLB 5.95 (ISBN 0-385-00354-4). Doubleday.

Frey, Sylvia R. The British Soldier in America: A Social History of Military Life in the Revolutionary Period. 240p. 1981. text ed. 25.00x (ISBN 0-292-78040-0). U of Tex Pr.

Frey, T., ed. Computational Linguistics & Computer Languages Nine. Vamos, T. (Orig.). 1979. pap. text ed. 24.00x (ISBN 0-391-01690-3). Humanities.

Frey, T. & Vamos, T., eds. Computational Linguistics & Computer Languages Eleven. 1979. pap. text ed. 24.00x (ISBN 0-686-58500-3). Humanities.

Freyberger, H., ed. see European Conference on Psychosomatic Research, 12th July 1978.

Freycinet, Charles L. Souvenirs, Eighteen Seventy-Eight to Eighteen-Ninety-Three. LC 73-258. (Europe 1815-1945 Ser.). 524p. 1973. Repr. of 1913 ed. lib. bdg. 49.50 (ISBN 0-306-70560-5). Da Capo.

Freyha, Anis. Dictionary of Modern Lebanese Proverbs. (Arabic-Eng.). 1974. 23.00x (ISBN 0-685-77118-0). Intl Bk Ctr.

--Dictionary of Non-Classical Vocables in Spoken Arabic. 1973. 14.00x (ISBN 0-685-77117-2). Intl Bk Ctr.

Freyha, Annis. Arabic-Arabic Dictionary of the Names of Towns & Villages in Lebanon. 1974. 15.00x (ISBN 0-685-72040-3). Intl Bk Ctr.

Freyhan, F. A., jt. ed. see Ban, T. A.

Freyhardt, H. C., ed. Organic Crystals, Germanates, Semiconductors. (Crystals, Growth, Properties & Applications: Vol. 4). (Illus.). 250p. 1980. 55.50 (ISBN 0-387-10298-1). Springer-Verlag.

--Three to Five Semiconductors. (Crystals. Growth, Properties & Applications Ser.: Vol. 3). (Illus.). 180p. 1980. 39.80 (ISBN 0-387-09957-3). Springer-Verlag.

Freyman, Jay M., tr. see Mahaney, William E. & Sherwin, Walter K.

Freyne, Sean V. Galilee from Alexander the Great to Hadrian, 323 B. C. E. to 135 C. E. 27.50 (ISBN 0-89453-099-2). M. Glazier.

Freyre, De Matos. ABC De Puerto Rico. 1966. 8.95 (ISBN 0-87751-005-9, Pub by Troutman Press). E Torres & Sons.

Freytag, George W. Lexicon Arabico-Latimun. 70.00x. Intl Bk Ctr.

Freytag, Joseph. The Mercenary. (Orig.). 1977. pap. 1.25 o.p. (ISBN 0-685-77273-X). Pinnacle Bks.

Frey-Wyssling, A. Comparative Organellography of the Cytoplasm. (Protoplasmatologia: Vol. 3g). (Illus.). vii, 106p. 1973. 31.30 o.p. (ISBN 0-387-81139-7). Springer-Verlag.

Friant, Ray J., Jr. Preparing Effective Presentations. rev. ed. LC 74-133853. 1980. pap. 3.50 (ISBN 0-87576-033-3). Pilot Bks.

Friar, John G. & Kelly, George W. Practical Spanish Grammar. 1960. pap. 3.50 (ISBN 0-385-00977-1). Doubleday.

Friar, Kimon, tr. see Sahtouris, Miltos.

Friar, Natasha, jt. auth. see Friar, Ralph.

Friar, Ralph & Friar, Natasha. The Only Good Indian...the Hollywood Gospel. LC 72-78907. (Illus.). 346p. 1973. 5.00 o.p. (ISBN 0-910482-21-7). Drama Bk.

Friberg, Barbara, jt. ed. see Friberg, Timothy.

Friberg, Timothy & Friberg, Barbara, eds. Analytical Greek New Testament. 1000p. 1981. 16.95 (ISBN 0-8010-3496-5). Baker Bk.

Frick, C. H. Patch. LC 57-6559. (gr. 7 up). 4.50 o.p. (ISBN 0-15-259570-8, HJ). HarBraceJ.

Frick, Elizabeth. Library Research Guide to History. (Library Research Guides Ser.: No. 4). 1980. 9.95 (ISBN 0-87650-119-6); pap. 5.95 (ISBN 0-87650-123-4). Pierian.

Frick, Frank S. The City in Ancient Israel. LC 77-21984. (Society of Biblical Literature. Dissertation Ser.: No. 36). 1977. pap. 7.50 (ISBN 0-89130-149-6, 060136). Scholars Pr Ca.

Frick, G. William, ed. Environmental Glossary. LC 80-67274. 1980. 19.50 (ISBN 0-86587-080-2). Gov Insts.

--Environmental Glossary. LC 80-67274. 225p. 19.50 (ISBN 0-86587-080-2). Gov Insts.

Frick, Grace, tr. see Yourcenar, Marguerite.

Frick, Henry C., II, jt. ed. see Nahas, Gabriel G.

Fricke, Charles W. & Alarcon, Arthur L. California Criminal Procedure. 8th ed. LC 73-80491. 1981. 16.00x (ISBN 0-910874-26-3). Legal Bk Corp.

Fricke, Peter H., ed. Seafarer & Community. 164p. 1973. bds. 17.50x (ISBN 0-87471-197-5). Rowman.

Frid, Tage. Tage Frid Teaches Woodworking, Bk. 1-Joinery. LC 78-65178. (Illus.). 1979. 15.95 (ISBN 0-918804-03-5, Dist. by Van Nostrand Reinhold). Taunton.

Friday, Nancy. Forbidden Flowers: More Women's Sexual Fantasies. pap. 3.50 (ISBN 0-671-81166-5). PB.

--Men in Love, Male Sexual Fantasies: The Triump of Love Over Rage. 1981. pap. 3.50 (ISBN 0-440-15404-9). Dell.

--My Mother, My Self. 1978. boxed gift edition 14.95 o.s.i. (ISBN 0-440-06010-9). Delacorte.

--My Mother, Myself. 1981. pap. 3.25 (ISBN 0-440-15663-7). Dell.

Friday, Paul C. & Stewart, V. Lorne, eds. Youth Crime & Juvenile Justice: International Perspectives. LC 77-7820. (Praeger Special Studies). 1977. text ed. 23.95 (ISBN 0-03-022646-5). Praeger.

Friday, William. How to Sell Your Product Through (Not to) Wholesalers. LC 79-90315. (Illus.). 1980. 14.50 (ISBN 0-934432-05-8). Prudent Pub Co.

Friddell, Guy & Burda, Franz. Washington the Open City. 250p. 1974. 14.95 o.p. (ISBN 0-914962-01-9). Burda Pubns.

Fridriksson, S. Surtsey: Evolution of Life on a Volcanic Island. LC 74-30850. 198p. 1975. 21.95 (ISBN 0-470-28000-X). Halsted Pr.

Friebert, Stuart, et al, trs. from Ger. Valuable Nail: The Selected Poems of Gunter Eich. LC 80-85332. (Field Translation Ser.: No. 5). 150p. 1981. 9.95 (ISBN 0-932440-08-8); pap. 4.95 (ISBN 0-932440-09-6). Field-Oberlin.

Fried & Oxern. Smoking for Two: Cigarettes & Pregnancy. 102p. Date not set. 8.95 (ISBN 0-02-910720-2). Macmillan.

Fried, Albert. John Brown's Journey: Notes & Reflections on His America & Mine. LC 72-79388. 1978. 10.00 o.p. (ISBN 0-385-05511-0, Anchor Pr). Doubleday.

Fried, Albert & Sanders, Ronald, eds. Socialist Thought: A Documentary History. LC 64-11312. 1964. pap. 3.95 o.p. (ISBN 0-385-01638-7, A384, Anch). Doubleday.

Fried, Barbara. Concerto in the Key of Death. (Orig.). 1980. pap. 1.75 (ISBN 0-505-51508-3). Tower Bks.

--The Middle-Age Crisis. LC 75-36729. 160p. 1976. pap. 3.95 o.p. (ISBN 0-06-063016-7, RD137, HarpR). Har-Row.

Fried, Bryan A., jt. auth. see Hibbard, Jack.

Fried, D. V., jt. auth. see Younker, Lucas.

Fried, Edward R. & Schultze, Charles L., eds. Higher Oil Prices & the World Economy: The Adjustment Problem. 1975. 14.95 (ISBN 0-8157-2932-4); pap. 5.95 (ISBN 0-8157-2931-6). Brookings.

Fried, Edward R., et al. Setting National Priorities: E the 1974 Budget. LC 73-1076. 446p. 1973. 14.95 (ISBN 0-8157-2934-0); pap. 5.95 (ISBN 0-8157-2933-2). Brookings.

Fried, Elliot, ed. Amorotica: A New Collection of Erotic Poetry. (Illus.). 144p. 1981. 12.95 (ISBN 0-935232-05-2); pap. 8.95 (ISBN 0-935232-04-4). Deep River Pr. Postponed.

Fried, Erich. On Pain of Seeing. Rapp, Georg, tr. LC 74-97025. (Poetry Europe Ser.: No. 11). 72p. 1969. 6.95 (ISBN 0-8040-0234-7). Swallow.

Fried, Ilana. The Chemistry of Electrode Processes. 1974. 30.50 (ISBN 0-12-267650-5). Acad Pr.

Fried, Isaac. Numerical Solution of Differential Equations. (Computer Science & Applied Math. Ser.). 1979. 26.50 (ISBN 0-12-267780-3). Acad Pr.

Fried, J. J., jt. auth. see Dietrich, E. B.

Fried, Jacob & Molnar, Paul. Technological & Social Change: A Transdisciplinary Model. 1979. text ed. 17.50 (ISBN 0-89433-074-8). Petrocelli.

Fried, John J., jt. auth. see Younker, Lucas.

Fried, Lawerence A. Anatomy of the Head, Neck, Face, & Jaws. 2nd ed. LC 80-16800. (Illus.). 299p. 1980. text ed. 17.50 (ISBN 0-8121-0717-9). Lea & Febiger.

Fried, Maurice & Broeshart, Hans. Soil-Plant System in Relation to Inorganic Nutrition. (Atomic Energy Commission Monographs). 1967. 22.50 o.s.i. (ISBN 0-12-268050-2). Acad Pr.

Fried, Morton. Evolution of Political Society: An Evolutionary View. (Orig.). 1968. pap. text ed. 4.95x (ISBN 0-394-30787-9, RanC). Random.

Fried, Morton H. The Notion of Tribe. 1975. pap. 4.95 o.p. (ISBN 0-8465-1548-2). Benjamin-Cummings.

Fried, Peter A., ed. Readings in Perception. 1974. pap. text ed. 8.95x o.p. (ISBN 0-669-89367-6). Heath.

Fried, Richard M. Men Against McCarthy. 376p. 1976. 22.50x (ISBN 0-231-03872-0); pap. 10.00x (ISBN 0-231-08360-2). Columbia U Pr.

Fried, William & Watson, Edward B. New York in Aerial Views: Eighty-Six Photographs. (Illus.). 176p. (Orig.). 1981. pap. 6.50 (ISBN 0-486-24018-5). Dover.

Friedan, Betty. The Feminine Mystique. 1977. pap. 2.50 (ISBN 0-440-12498-0). Dell.

--It Changed My Life. 1977. pap. 2.25 o.s.i. (ISBN 0-440-13936-8). Dell.

--The Second Stage. 320p. 1981. 12.95 (ISBN 0-671-41034-2). Summit Bks.

Friedan, Leon, compiled by. The Law of War: A Documentary History, 2 vols. LC 72-765. 1972. Set. lib. bdg. 85.00 (ISBN 0-313-20133-1). Greenwood.

Friedberg, Erhard, jt. auth. see Crozier, Michel.

Friedberg, Maurice. Decade of Euphoria: Western Literature in Post-Stalin Russia, 1954-1964. LC 76-11932. 384p. 1977. 17.50x (ISBN 0-253-31675-8). Ind U Pr.

Friedberg, Robert. Paper Money of the United States. 10th ed. LC 78-66813. (Illus.). 1981. write for info. (ISBN 0-87184-210-6). Coin & Curr.

Friede, Eleanor, ed. see Sutton, M. & Sutton, A.

Friede, Reinhard L. Histochemical Atlas of Tissue Oxidation in the Brain Stem of the Cat. (Illus., Eng. & Ger.). 1961. 19.75 o.s.i. (ISBN 0-02-844860-X). Hafner.

Friedel, Kathy. Pelicans Are Scarce. Date not set. 5.95 (ISBN 0-533-04865-6). Vantage.

Frieden, B. R., ed. The Computer in Optical Research: Methods & Applications. (Topics in Applied Physics: Vol. 41). (Illus.). 400p. 1980. 58.00 (ISBN 0-387-10119-5). Springer-Verlag.

Frieden, Carl & Nichol, Lawrence. Protein-Protein Interactions. 400p. 1981. 30.00 (ISBN 0-471-04979-4, Pub. by Wiley-Interscience). Wiley.

Frieden, Edward H. Basic Chemistry Experiments for the Life Sciences. 1977. spiral bdg. o.p. 3.95 o.p. (ISBN 0-88252-066-0). Paladin Hse.

Frieden, Julian & Rubin, Ira. ECG Case Studies. 2nd ed. LC 77-94387. 1974. pap. 9.50 (ISBN 0-87488-003-3). Med Exam.

Friedenberg, Robert M. Unexplored Model Systems in Modern Biology. (Pioneering Concepts in Modern Science Ser.: No. 1). 1968. 9.75 o.s.i. (ISBN 0-02-844870-7). Hafner.

Friedenreich, Kenneth. Christopher Marlowe: An Annotated Bibliography of Criticism Since 1950. LC 79-17646. (Scarecrow Author Bibliographies Ser.: No. 43). 1979. 10.00 (ISBN 0-8108-1239-8). Scarecrow.

--Henry Vaughan. (English Authors Ser.: No. 226). 1978. lib. bdg. 12.50 (ISBN 0-8057-6697-9). Twayne.

Friedenwald, Herbert. The Declaration of Independence: An Interpretation & an Analysis. LC 77-166325. (American Constitutional & Legal History Ser.). xii, 299p. 1974. Repr. of 1904 ed. lib. bdg. 29.50 (ISBN 0-306-70230-4). Da Capo.

Friederichsen, Mrs. Paul. God's Word Made Plain. (Span). 1958. pap. 2.50 (ISBN 0-8024-3041-4). Moody.

Friedheim, P. First-Year Harmony Workbook. 1966. pap. text ed. 5.95 (ISBN 0-02-910710-5). Free Pr.

Friedhoff, Herman & Lenthall, Ben. The University Desk Encyclopedia. 59.95 (ISBN 0-525-93001-9). Gaylord Prof Pubns.

Friedl, Ernestine see Bishop, G. Reginald, Jr.

Friedl, John. The Human Portrait: An Introduction to Cultural Anthropology. (Illus.). 464p. 1981. pap. text ed. 13.95 (ISBN 0-13-445353-0); pap. 5.95 (ISBN 0-13-445387-5). P-H.

Friedlaender, Ann F. Approaches to Controlling Air Pollution. LC 77-25484. (MIT Bicentennial Ser.: Vol. 3). 1978. 27.50x (ISBN 0-262-06064-7). MIT Pr.

--The Dilemma of Freight Transport Regulation. LC 69-18820. (Studies in the Regulation of Economic Activity). 216p. 1969. 11.95 (ISBN 0-8157-2936-7). Brookings.

Friedlaender, Ann F. & Spady, Richard H. Regulation of Rail & Trucking Industries. 512p. 1980. text ed. 30.00x (ISBN 0-262-06072-8). MIT Pr.

Friedlaender, Ann F., jt. auth. see Due, John F.

Friedlaender, Jonathan S., jt. ed. see Giles, Eugene.

Friedland, Bea. Louise Farrenc, Eighteen Hundred Four to Eighteen Seventy-Five: Composer, Performer, Scholar. Buelow, George, ed. (Studies in Musicology). 270p. 1981. 34.95 (ISBN 0-8357-1111-0, Pub. by UMI Res Pr). Univ Microfilms.

Friedland, Edward P. Antique Houses: Their Construction & Restoration. Nelson, Cyril L., ed. (Illus.). 288p. 1981. 14.95 (ISBN 0-525-93076-0). Dutton.

Friedland, Joyce & Gross, Irene. Reading for Mathematics. 1977. pap. 2.25x (ISBN 0-88323-129-8, 218); tchrs answer key 3.00 (ISBN 0-88323-142-5, 231). Richards Pub.

Friedland, M. L., ed. Courts & Trials: A Multidisciplinary Approach. LC 75-5672. 1975. pap. 4.95 (ISBN 0-8020-6273-3). U of Toronto Pr.

Friedland, Robert P., jt. ed. see Weinstein, Edwin A.

Friedland, Ronnie & Kort, Carol, eds. The Mother's Book. 384p. 1981. 14.95 (ISBN 0-686-69055-9). HM.

Friedlander, et al. Concepts & Methods of Social Work. 2nd ed. LC 75-45164. (Illus.). 288p. 1976. text ed. 15.95 (ISBN 0-13-165488-3). P-H.

Friedlander, Albert H. Leo Baeck: Teacher of Theresienstadt. LC 68-11829. 1968. 8.95 o.p. (ISBN 0-03-068555-9). HR&W.

Friedlander, Barbara, et al. The Great Garlic Cookbook. LC 75-16359. (Illus.). 160p. 1975. 12.95 o.s.i. (ISBN 0-02-541500-X, 54150). Macmillan.

Friedlander, Benjamin. Shorthand in Four Days. rev. ed. LC 52-3478. 24p. 1974. pap. 2.98 o.p. (ISBN 0-917520-02-5). Fineline.

Friedlander, Dov & Goldscheider, Calvin. The Population of Israel. 1979. 20.00x (ISBN 0-231-04572-7). Columbia U Pr.

Friedlander, F. G. The Wave Equation on a Curved Space-Time. LC 74-14435. (Cambridge Monographs on Mathematical Physics). (Illus.). 328p. 1976. 65.50 (ISBN 0-521-20567-0). Cambridge U Pr.

Friedlander, Gerhart. Nuclear & Radiochemistry. 3rd ed. 650p. 1981. price not set (ISBN 0-471-28021-6, Pub. by Wiley-Interscience). Wiley.

Friedlander, Gerhart, et al. Nuclear & Radiochemistry. 2nd ed. 1964. 29.95 (ISBN 0-471-28020-8). Wiley.

Friedlander, Ira. The Ninety-Nine Names of Allah. (Orig.). 1978. pap. 3.50 (ISBN 0-06-090621-9, CN 621, CN). Har-Row.

--The Whirling Dervishes. LC 74-30416. (Illus.). 1975. 15.00 o.s.i. (ISBN 0-02-541540-9). Macmillan.

Friedlander, Ira, jt. auth. see Speeth, Kathleen R.

Friedlander, Janet & Grunden, Elizabeth H. Early Reading Development. 1981. text ed. 52.80 (ISBN 0-06-318161-4, IntlDept). Har-Row.

Friedlander, Judith N. Being Indian in Hueyapan: A Study of Forced Identity in Contemporary Mexico. LC 74-23047. (Illus.). 224p. (Orig.). 1975. text ed. 14.95 (ISBN 0-312-07280-5); pap. text ed. 6.95 (ISBN 0-312-07315-1). St Martin.

Friedlander, Robert A., jt. ed. see Alexander, Yonah.

Friedlander, S. K. Smoke, Dust & Haze: Fundamentals of Aerosol Behavior. LC 76-26928. 1977. 26.50 (ISBN 0-471-01468-0, Pub. by Wiley Interscience). Wiley.

Friedlander, Saul. History & Psychoanalysis. Suleiman, Susan, tr. from Fr. LC 77-18524. 1978. text ed. 27.50x (ISBN 0-8419-0339-5); pap. text ed. 15.50x (ISBN 0-8419-0611-4). Holmes & Meier.

--When Memory Comes. 1980. pap. 2.75 (ISBN 0-686-69240-3, 50807, Discus). Avon.

Friedlander, Stanley L., jt. ed. see Leiter, Robert D.

Friedlander, W., ed. Current Reviews. LC 75-14572. (Advances in Neurology Ser.: Vol. 13). 415p. 1975. 36.00 (ISBN 0-89004-000-1). Raven.

Friedlander, Walter A. International Social Welfare. (Illus.). 256p. 1975. 16.95 (ISBN 0-13-470906-3). P-H.

Friedlander, Walter A. & Apte, Robert Z. Introduction to Social Welfare. 5th ed. (Illus.). 1980. text ed. 17.95 (ISBN 0-13-497032-2). P-H.

Friedlander, Walter J., ed. Current Reviews of Higher Nervous System Dysfunction. LC 74-15667. (Advances in Neurology Ser.: Vol. 7). 1975. 24.50 (ISBN 0-911216-78-2). Raven.

Friedman. Meet Elvis Presley. (gr. 7-12). pap. 1.25 (ISBN 0-590-11875-7, Schol Pap). Schol Bk Serv.

Friedman & Macaulay. Law & the Behavioral Sciences. (Contemporary Legal Education Ser.). 1977. 25.00 (ISBN 0-672-82025-0, Bobbs-Merrill Law). Michie.

Friedman, A. J. Basketball: Picking Winners Against the Spread. (Orig.). 1978. pap. 2.95 (ISBN 0-89650-620-7, Gambler's Book Shelf). Gamblers.

--Football: Picking Winners Against the Spread. 64p. (Orig.). 1980. pap. 2.95 (ISBN 0-89650-703-3). Gamblers.

Friedman, Ada J., ed. Roads to Extinction: Essays on the Holocaust. 616p. 1980. 27.50 (ISBN 0-8276-0170-0, 446). Jewish Pubn.

Friedman, Alan W., jt. ed. see Rossman, Charles.

Friedman, Alexander Z. Wellsprings of Torah. Hirchter, Gertrude, tr. from Yiddish. 584p. 1980. 13.95 (ISBN 0-910818-04-5); pap. 10.95 (ISBN 0-910818-20-7). Judaica Pr.

Friedman, Andrew L. Industry & Labour: Class Struggle at Work & Monopoly Capitalism. 1977. text ed. 26.00x (ISBN 0-333-23031-0); pap. text ed. 12.50x (ISBN 0-333-23032-9). Humanities.

Friedman, Arthur, ed. see Goldsmith, Oliver.

Friedman, Arthur, ed. see Wycherley, William.

Friedman, Avner. Differential Games. LC 75-155119. (Pure & Applied Mathematics Ser.). 1971. 38.95 (ISBN 0-471-28049-6, Pub. by Wiley-Interscience). Wiley.

--Stochastic Differential Equations & Applications, 2 vols. (Probability & Mathematical Statistics Ser.). 1975. 75.00 set (ISBN 0-685-72447-6); Vol. 1, 1975. 40.50 (ISBN 0-12-268201-7); Vol. 2, 1976. 51.50 (ISBN 0-12-268202-5). Acad Pr.

Friedman, B. H. The Polygamist. 228p. 1981. 11.95 (ISBN 0-316-29357-1, An Atlantic Monthly Press Bk). Little.

Friedman, Benjamin M., ed. New Challenges to the Role of Profit: The Fourth Series of the John Diebold Lectures. 1978. 14.95 (ISBN 0-669-02171-7). Lexington Bks.

Friedman, Delores L. Education Handbook for Black Families. LC 79-6537. (Illus.). 456p. 1980. 14.95 (ISBN 0-385-14881-X). Doubleday.

Friedman, Donna R., ed. see Bird, Roy.

Friedman, Donna R., ed. see Boss, Judith A.

Friedman, Donna R., ed. see Bronwell, Nancy.

Friedman, Donna R., ed. see Clark, Nancy.

Friedman, Donna R., ed. see Conley, Patrick T.

Friedman, Donna R., ed. see Hoffecker, Carol E.

Friedman, Donna R., ed. see Hoffman, Roslyn.

Friedman, Donna R., ed. see Kirkman, Kay & Stinnett, Roger.

Friedman, Donna R., ed. see Naske, Claus M. & Rowinski, Ludwig J.

Friedman, Donna R., ed. see Pierce, Bess.

Friedman, Donna R., ed. see Reap, James.

Friedman, Donna R., ed. see Walker, Carroll.

Friedman, Donna R., ed. see Weiner, Melissa.

Friedman, Donna R., ed. see Willoughby, Larry.

Friedman, Donna R., ed. see Wilson, Ann Q.

Friedman, Edward. Backward Toward Revolution: The Chinese Revolutionary Party. 1974. pap. 5.95x (ISBN 0-520-03279-9). U of Cal Pr.

Friedman, Eli A. Strategy in Renal Failure. LC 77-11003. (Nephrology & Hypertension Ser.). 1978. 44.00 (ISBN 0-471-01597-0, Pub. by Wiley Medical). Wiley.

Friedman, Eli A. & L'Esperance, Frances, eds. Diabetic Renal-Retinal Syndrome. 1980. 39.50 (ISBN 0-8089-1302-6). Grune.

Friedman, Ellen G. Joyce Carol Oates. LC 79-4828. (Modern Literature Ser.). 1980. 13.50 (ISBN 0-8044-2221-4). Ungar.

Friedman, Emanuel A. Labor: Clinical Evaluation & Management. 2nd ed. (Illus.). 1978. 32.00 (ISBN 0-8385-5580-2). ACC.

Friedman, Emanuel A., jt. auth. see Plentl, Albert A.

Friedman, Emanuel A., ed. Blood Pressure, Edema & Proteinuria in Pregnancy. LC 76-10262. (Progress in Clinical & Biological Research: Vol. 7). 296p. 1976. 29.00x (ISBN 0-8451-0007-6). A R Liss.

Friedman, Favius, ed. What's in a Name. (gr. 7-12). 1976. pap. 1.25 (ISBN 0-590-00090-X, Schol Pap). Schol Bk Serv.

Friedman, Frank & Koffman, Elliot. Problem Solving & Structured Programming in Fortran. 2nd ed. LC 80-20943. (First Course in Computers Ser.). 450p. 1981. pap. text ed. 11.95 (ISBN 0-201-02461-6). A-W.

Friedman, Frank L., jt. auth. see Koffman, Elliot B.

Friedman, Frieda. Dot for Short. (Illus.). (gr. 4-6). 1947. 8.25 (ISBN 0-688-21242-5). Morrow.

--Ellen & the Gang. (Illus.). (gr. 3-7). 1963. PLB 7.44 o.p. (ISBN 0-688-31263-2). Morrow.

--The Janitor's Girl. (Illus.). (gr. 3-7). 1956. PLB 7.44 (ISBN 0-688-31708-1). Morrow.

Friedman, Gary D. A Primer of Epidemiology. (Illus.). 256p. 1974. pap. text ed. 8.50 o.p. (ISBN 0-07-022425-0, HP). McGraw.

Friedman, George. The Political Philosophy of the Frankfurt School. LC 80-66890. 320p. 1981. 17.50x (ISBN 0-8014-1279-X). Cornell U Pr.

Friedman, H., jt. ed. see Escobar, M. R.

Friedman, H., jt. ed. see Rose, N. R.

Friedman, Herman & Prier, James E., eds. Rubella: Proceedings. (American Lectures in Clinical Microbiology Ser). (Illus.). 164p. 1973. 14.75 (ISBN 0-398-02650-5). C C Thomas.

Friedman, Howard M. Securities & Commodities Enforcement: Criminal Prosecutions & Civil Injunctions. LC 79-9685. 1981. price not set (ISBN 0-669-03617-X). Lexington Bks.

Friedman, Irving S. Inflation: A World-Wide Disaster. 2nd ed. 320p. 1980. write for info.; pap. 5.95 (ISBN 0-395-29847-4). HM.

Friedman, Jack & Ordway, Nicholas. Income Property Appraisal & Analysis. 300p. 1981. text ed. 17.95 (ISBN 0-8359-3057-2); instr's. manual free (ISBN 0-8359-3058-0). Reston.

Friedman, Jack P., jt. auth. see Lindeman, J. Bruce.

Friedman, James M. Dancer & Other Aesthetic Objects: San Francisco: Balletmonographs, 1980. LC 80-65960. (Illus.). xii, 144p. (Orig.). 1980. pap. 5.95 (ISBN 0-9604232-0-6). J M Friedman.

Friedman, Jean E. & Shade, William G. Our American Sisters: Women in American Life & Thought. 2nd ed. 317p. 1976. pap. 11.95 o.p. (ISBN 0-205-05578-8, 7855788). Allyn.

Friedman, John B. The Monstrous Races in Medieval Art & Thought. LC 80-23181. (Illus.). 272p. 1981. text ed. 20.00 (ISBN 0-674-58652-2). Harvard U Pr.

Friedman, Joy T. The Important Thing About. LC 80-83936. (Illus.). 96p. (gr. k-2). 1981. PLB 10.15 (ISBN 0-448-13947-2); pap. 3.95 (ISBN 0-448-14754-8). G&D.

--Sounds All Around. LC 80-83935. Orig. Title: Look Around & Listen. (Illus.). 80p. (gr. k-2). 1981. PLB 10.15 (ISBN 0-448-13945-6); pap. 3.95 (ISBN 0-448-14755-6). G&D.

Friedman, Judi. The Eels Strange Journey. LC 75-20136. (A Let's Read & Find Out Science Bk). (Illus.). 40p. (gr. k-3). 1976. PLB 7.89 (ISBN 0-690-01007-9, TYC-J). T Y Crowell.

--Puffins, Come Back! LC 80-2786. (Illus.). 80p. (gr. 3-7). 1981. PLB 6.95 (ISBN 0-396-07940-7). Dodd.

Friedman, Judith C. The ABC of a Summer Pond. new ed. LC 73-92631. (Illus.). (gr. k-4). 1975. 5.45 (ISBN 0-910812-14-4); pap. 2.35 (ISBN 0-910812-15-2). Johnny Reads.

Friedman, Julius, jt. auth. see Felde, Nathan.

Friedman, Kenneth M. & Rakoff, Stuart H. Toward a National Health Policy: Public Policy & the Control of Health Care Costs. 1977. 20.50 (ISBN 0-669-00563-0). Lexington Bks.

Friedman, Laura, jt. auth. see Coryell, Julie.

Friedman, Lawrence M. Contract Law in America: A Social & Economic Case Study. 1965. 17.50x (ISBN 0-299-03570-0). U of Wis Pr.

Friedman, Lawrence M., et al. Fundamentals of Clinical Trials. 320p. 1981. 24.50 (ISBN 0-88416-296-6). PSG Pub.

Friedman, Lenemaja. Shirley Jackson. LC 74-31244. (U. S. Authors Ser.: No. 253). 1975. lib. bdg. 9.95 (ISBN 0-8057-0402-7). Twayne.

Friedman, Lenemaja, ed. Shirley Jackson. LC 74-31244. (Twayne's U. S. Authors Ser.). 182p. 1975. pap. text ed. 4.95 (ISBN 0-672-61507-X). Bobbs.

Friedman, Leon. The Law of War, 2 vols. 1972. Set. text ed. 65.00 o.p. (ISBN 0-394-47240-3). Random.

Friedman, Leon, ed. Argument: Brown vs. Board of Education of Topeka, 1925-55, 2 vols. 2nd ed. LC 70-75118. (Oral Arguments Before the Supreme Court Ser.). 610p. 1981. Set. pap. 12.95 (ISBN 0-87754-210-4). Chelsea Hse.

--Episodes of Violence in U.S. History, 3 vols. Incl. Vol. 1. Dynamite. Adamic, Louis. LC 80-21964; Vol. 2. The Dorr War. Mowry, Arthur M. LC 80-21969; Vol. 3. The Molly Maguires. Broehl, Wayne G., Jr. LC 80-21794. (Illus.). 750p. 1981. Repr. of 1970 ed. Set. 50.00 (ISBN 0-87754-133-7). Chelsea Hse.

--Obscenity. 2nd ed. (Oral Arguments Before the Supreme Court Ser.). 365p. 1981. pap. 8.95 (ISBN 0-87754-211-2). Chelsea Hse.

--Oral Arguments Before the Supreme Court, 2 vols. LC 80-29337. 975p. 1981. Set. pap. 20.00 (ISBN 0-87754-147-7). Chelsea Hse.

--United States Vs. Nixon: The President Before the Supreme Court. LC 74-16403. 644p. 1980. pap. 11.95 (ISBN 0-87754-144-2). Chelsea Hse.

Friedman, Leon & Israel, Fred L., eds. The Justices of the United States Supreme Court, 1789-1978, 5 vols. LC 69-13699. 1980. pap. 75.00 set (ISBN 0-87754-130-2). Chelsea Hse.

Friedman, Lewis B. Budgeting Municipal Expenditures: A Study in Comparative Policy Making. LC 74-11600. (Special Studies). (Illus.). 266p. 1975. text ed. 19.95 o.p. (ISBN 0-275-09630-0). Praeger.

Friedman, M. A Beginner's Guide to Sightsinging & Musical Rudiments. 1981. pap. 12.95 (ISBN 0-13-074088-8). P-H.

--Dollars & Deficits: Inflation, Monetary Policy & the Balance of Payments. 1968. pap. 10.95 (ISBN 0-13-218289-0). P-H.

Friedman, M. & Schwartz, A. From New Deal Banking Reform to World War Two Inflation. 1980. pap. 3.95 (ISBN 0-691-00363-7). Princeton U Pr.

Friedman, M. & Schwartz, A. J. Monetary History of the United States: 1867-1960. (National Bureau of Economic Research, B.12). 1963. 33.00x (ISBN 0-691-04147-4); pap. 11.95 (ISBN 0-691-00354-8). Princeton U Pr.

Friedman, Marilyn M. Family Nursing: Theory & Assessment. 337p. 1981. pap. 16.50 (ISBN 0-8385-2532-6). ACC.

Friedman, Maurice. The Hidden Human Image. 1974. 12.50 o.s.i. (ISBN 0-440-03509-0). Delacorte.

--Martin Buber: The Life of Dialogue. 3rd, rev. ed. 1976. pap. 9.00 (ISBN 0-226-26356-8). U of Chicago Pr.

Friedman, Mendel. Chemistry & Biochemistry of the Sulfhydryl Group in Amino Acids, Peptides & Proteins. 1973. text ed. 72.00 (ISBN 0-08-016845-0). Pergamon.

Friedman, Michael H. The Making of a Tory Humanist. LC 79-10968. 1979. 22.50x (ISBN 0-231-04668-5). Columbia U Pr.

Friedman, Milton. An Adult Guide to Beginning Piano & Basic Musicianship. (Illus.). 1979. pap. 11.50 ref. (ISBN 0-13-008797-1). P-H.

--Optimum Quantity of Money & Other Essays. LC 68-8148. 1969. 19.95x (ISBN 0-202-06030-6). Aldine Pub.

Friedman, Milton & Friedman, Rose. Free to Choose: A Personal Statement. 352p. 1981. pap. 2.95 (ISBN 0-380-52548-8, 52548). Avon.

Friedman, Milton, ed. Studies in the Quantity Theory of Money. LC 56-10999. (Economic Research Ser). 1956. 10.50x o.s.i. (ISBN 0-226-26404-1). U of Chicago Pr.

Friedman, Milton, et al. Milton Freidman's Monetary Framework: A Debate with His Critics. Gordon, Robert J., ed. LC 73-92599. xii, 192p. 1975. pap. 4.50 (ISBN 0-226-26408-4, P619, Phoen). U of Chicago Pr.

Friedman, Morton P., jt. ed. see Carterette, Edward C.

Friedman, Myles I. & Rowls, Michael D. Teaching Reading & Thinking Skills. (Illus.). 1979. pap. 12.95x (ISBN 0-582-29006-6). Longman.

Friedman, Norman. E. E. Cummings: The Growth of a Writer. LC 80-17081. (Arcturus Books Paperbacks Ser.). 208p. 1980. pap. 5.95 (ISBN 0-8093-0978-5). S Ill U Pr.

--Modern Warship Design & Development. (Illus.). 192p. 1980. 22.50 (ISBN 0-686-65676-8). Mayflower Bks.

Friedman, Philip & Eisen, Gail. The Pilates Method of Physical & Mental Conditioning. 1981. pap. 7.95 (ISBN 0-446-97859-0). Warner Bks.

Friedman, Renee, jt. auth. see Goodall, Harrison.

Friedman, Renee C., jt. auth. see Ikenberry, Stanley O.

Friedman, Richard, jt. auth. see Fischler, Stan.

Friedman, Robert, ed. Family Roots of School Learning & Behavior Disorders. 360p. 1973. 19.75 (ISBN 0-398-02469-3); pap. 11.50 (ISBN 0-398-02472-3). C C Thomas.

Friedman, Robert M. Interferons: A Primer. 1981. price not set (ISBN 0-12-268280-7). Acad Pr.

Friedman, Rose, jt. auth. see Friedman, Milton.

Friedman, Samy. Expropriation in International Law. rev. ed. Jackson, Ivor C., tr. from Fr. LC 80-26295. (The Library of World Affairs: No. 20). 236p. 1981. Repr. of 1953 ed. lib. bdg. 29.75x (ISBN 0-313-20840-9, FREI). Greenwood.

Friedman, Sandor. Vascular Diseases: A Concise Guide to Diagnosis, Management, Pathogenesis, & Prevention. 1981. write for info. (ISBN 0-88416-283-4). PSG Pub.

Friedman, Sandra C. & Love Set, Inc. Staff, eds. A Complete Guide to Tennis Camps, Clinics & Reports in the U.S., with Special Listings for the Caribbean & Europe. LC 78-6966. (All Seasons Travel Ser.). Date not set. pap. 5.95 o.p. (ISBN 0-87491-255-5). Acropolis.

Friedman, Sanford. Rip Van Winkle. LC 80-66016. 1980. 12.95 (ISBN 0-689-11099-5). Atheneum.

Friedman, Sarah L. & Sigman, Marian, eds. Preterm Birth & Psychological Development. LC 80-980. (Developmental Psychology Ser.). 1980. 34.00 (ISBN 0-12-267880-X). Acad Pr.

Friedman, Saul S. Amcha: An Oral Testament of the Holocaust. LC 79-67054. 1979. pap. text ed. 14.25 (ISBN 0-8191-0867-7). U Pr of Amer.

Friedman, Stanford & Hoekelman, Robert. Behavioral Pediatrics: Psychological Aspects of Child Health Care. (Illus.). 448p. 1980. text ed. 19.95 (ISBN 0-07-022426-9, HP). McGraw.

Friedman, Sydney M. Visual Anatomy, Vol. 1: Head & Neck. (Illus.). 1970. 20.50x o.p. (ISBN 0-06-140836-0, Harper Medical). Har-Row.

--Visual Anatomy, Vol. 3: Back & Limbs. (Illus.). 1972. 21.50x o.p. (ISBN 0-06-140835-2, Harper Medical). Har-Row.

Friedman, William F. Military Cryptanalysis, 4 vols. 1980. lib. bdg. 500.00 (ISBN 0-87700-271-1). Revisionist Pr.

--The Riverbank Publications, 3 vols. (Cryptographic Ser.). 1979. 16.80 ea. Vol. 1 (ISBN 0-89412-032-8). Vol. 2 (ISBN 0-89412-033-6). Vol. 3 (ISBN 0-89412-034-4). Aegean Park Pr.

Friedman, Winnifred H. Boydell's Shakespeare Gallery. LC 75-23791. (Outstanding Dissertations in the Fine Arts - 17th & 18th Century). (Illus.). 1976. lib. bdg. 45.00 (ISBN 0-8240-1987-3). Garland Pub.

Friedman, Wolfgang see Jessup, Philip C.

Friedman, Wolfgang & Nalmanoff, George, eds. Joint International Business Ventures. LC 61-7173. 1961. 25.00x (ISBN 0-231-02465-7). Columbia U Pr.

Friedman, Yona. Toward a Scientific Architecture. Lang, Cynthia, tr. LC 75-8769. 208p. 1975. 14.50x o.p. (ISBN 0-262-06058-2). MIT Pr.

--Toward a Scientific Architecture. Lang, Cynthia, tr. from Fr. 208p. 1980. pap. 4.95 (ISBN 0-262-56019-4). MIT Pr.

Friedmann, Arnold. Commonsense Design. LC 76-15179. (Encore Edition). (Illus.). 1976. encore ed. 5.95 o.p. (ISBN 0-684-16191-5, ScribT); pap. 6.95 o.p. (ISBN 0-684-14688-6, SL650, ScribT). Scribner.

Friedmann, Herbert. A Bestiary for St. Jerome: A Study of Animal Symbolism in European Religious Art. LC 79-607804. (Illus.). 378p. 1980. 35.00 (ISBN 0-87474-446-6). Smithsonian.

Friedmann, J., et al. Fortran Four. 2nd ed. (Wiley Self Teaching Guide Ser.). 544p. 1980. pap. 10.95 (ISBN 0-471-07771-2). Wiley.

Friedmann, Jehosua. Complete Fortran, 3 vols. Set. pap. text ed. 23.85 (ISBN 0-471-06452-1). Wiley.

Friedmann, Jehosua, et al. Fortran IV. LC 74-34044. (Self-Teaching Guides Ser). 464p. 1975. pap. text ed. 8.95 (ISBN 0-471-28082-8). Wiley.

Friedmann, John & Weaver, Clyde. Territory & Function. 1979. 22.50x (ISBN 0-520-03928-9); pap. 6.95x (ISBN 0-520-04105-4). U of Cal Pr.

Friedmann, Lawrence W. The Psychological Rehabilitation of the Amputee. (Illus.). 176p. 1978. 18.50 (ISBN 0-398-03707-8). C C Thomas.

--The Surgical Rehabilitation of the Amputee. (Illus.). 576p. 1978. 54.50 (ISBN 0-398-03763-9). C C Thomas.

Friedmann, Wolfgang, ed. Public & Private Enterprise in Mixed Economies. LC 73-12406. 440p. 1974. 25.00x (ISBN 0-231-03776-7). Columbia U Pr.

Friedmann, Wolfgang G. Law in a Changing Society. 2nd ed. LC 67-26509. 550p. 1972. 27.50x (ISBN 0-231-03653-1). Columbia U Pr.

--Legal Theory. 5th ed. LC 67-26509. 1967. 27.50x (ISBN 0-231-03100-9). Columbia U Pr.

Friedmann, Wolfgang G. & Garner, J. F., eds. Government Enterprise. 1971. 22.50x (ISBN 0-231-03448-2). Columbia U Pr.

Friedmann, Wolfgang G., et al. International Financial Aid. LC 66-20494. 1966. 25.00x (ISBN 0-231-02953-5). Columbia U Pr.

Friedmann, Wolfgang G., et al, eds. Transnational Law in a Changing Society: Essays in Honor of Philip C. Jessup. LC 71-187029. 290p. 1972. 20.00x (ISBN 0-231-03619-1). Columbia U Pr.

Friedrich, et al. Experiments in Atomic Physics. (gr. 12). text ed. 6.95 (ISBN 0-7195-0467-8). Transatlantic.

Friedrich, Carl J. Constitutional Reason of State: The Survival of the Constitutional Order. LC 57-10150. 131p. 1957. 6.50x (ISBN 0-87057-046-3, Pub. by Brown U Pr). Univ Pr of New England.

--Limited Government: A Comparison. LC 74-802. (Contemporary Comparative Politics Ser.). 176p. 1974. ref. ed. 7.95 (ISBN 0-13-537167-8); pap. 6.95 (ISBN 0-13-537159-7). P-H.

--Pathology of Politics: Violence, Betrayal, Corruption, Secrecy & Propaganda. Repr. of 1972 ed. text ed. 28.50x (ISBN 0-8290-0343-6). Irvington.

--Philosophy of Law in Historical Perspective. rev. ed. LC 57-9546. 1963. 11.50x o.s.i. (ISBN 0-226-26465-3). U of Chicago Pr.

Friedrich, Carl J. & McCloskey, Robert G., eds. From the Declaration of Independence to the Constitution: The Roots of American Constitutionalism. 1954. pap. 4.50 (ISBN 0-672-60006-4, AHS6). Bobbs.

Friedrich, Gustav W., jt. auth. see Brooks, William D.

Friedrich, Lynette K. see Hetherington, E. Mavis.

Friedrich, Manfred & Bull, D. The Register of United States Breweries: 1876-1976, Vol. 1. LC 76-23156. 1976. pap. 10.95 (ISBN 0-9601190-1-9). D Bull.

Friedrich, Manfred & Bull, Donald. The Register of United States Breweries: 1876 to 1976: an Alphabetical Index, Vol. 2. LC 76-23150. 1976. pap. 10.95 (ISBN 0-9601190-2-7). D Bull.

Friedrich, Paul. Poetry & Anthropology. 1978. 1.00 (ISBN 0-934528-01-2). B & M Waite Pr.

Friedrichs, K. O. Perturbation of Spectra in Hilbert Space. LC 60-12712. (Lectures in Applied Mathematics Ser.: Vol. 3). 1967. Repr. of 1965 ed. 15.20 (ISBN 0-8218-1103-7, LAM-3). Am Math.

Friedrichs, Robert W. A Sociology of Sociology. LC 77-91882. 1972. pap. text ed. 7.95 (ISBN 0-02-910880-2). Free Pr.

Friedrichson, Carol. Pooh Craft Book. (Illus.). (gr. 4 up). 1976. 6.95 o.p. (ISBN 0-525-37410-8). Dutton.

Friedt, Joseph H. Patriarchs of Outer Space. 1978. 5.95 o.p. (ISBN 0-533-03814-6). Vantage.

Friel, Brian. Translations. 72p. 1981. pap. 8.50 (ISBN 0-571-11742-2). Merrimack Bk Serv.

--Two Plays. Incl. Crystal & Fox; The Mundy Scheme. 317p. 1970. 6.50 o.p. (ISBN 0-374-13248-8); pap. 2.45 o.p. (ISBN 0-374-50796-1). FS&G.

Friel, Theodore W. & Carkhuff, Robert R. The Art of Developing a Career. LC 74-75375. (Career Skills Ser.). (Illus.). 229p. 1974. pap. text ed. 8.95x student's guide o.p. (ISBN 0-914234-40-4). Human Res Dev Pr.

--The Art of Developing a Career: A Helper's Guide. LC 74-75375. (Illus., Prog. Bk.). 1974. teachers' ed. 11.95x (ISBN 0-914234-41-2). Human Res Dev Pr.

Frieling, Rudolf. Christianity & Islam: A Battle for the True Image of Man. 1978. 8.95 (ISBN 0-903540-11-8, Pub. by Floris Bks). St George Bk Serv.

--Christianity & Reincarnation. 1977. pap. 7.95 (ISBN 0-903540-05-3, Pub. by Floris Books). St George Bk Serv.

--Hidden Treasures in the Psalms. 1967. Repr. of 1954 ed. 8.50 (ISBN 0-900285-02-8, Pub. by Floris Books). St George Bk Serv.

Frieman, Donald G. Milestones in the Life of a Jew. LC 65-15710. 1980. pap. 3.95x (ISBN 0-8197-0002-9). Bloch.

Friend, Charles E. The Law of Evidence in Virginia. 1977. 40.00 (ISBN 0-87215-197-2); 1980 suppl. 10.00 (ISBN 0-87215-323-1). Michie.

Friend, Diane, jt. auth. see Dubane, Janet.

Friend, Diane, jt. ed. see DuBane, Janet.

Friend, Ed. Scalphunters. 1970. pap. 0.60 o.p. (ISBN 0-685-88321-3, R2351, GM). Fawcett.

Friend, Hilderic. The Flowers & Their Story. LC 78-175751. (Illus.). 300p. 1972. Repr. of 1907 ed. 18.00 (ISBN 0-8103-3868-8). Gale.

Friend, Irwin, jt. auth. see Blume, Marshall E.

Friend, J. A., ed. Australian Conference on Electrochemistry, 1st. 1964. 44.00 o.p. (ISBN 0-08-010501-7). Pergamon.

Friend, J. N. Man & the Chemical Elements. 354p. 1961. 19.50x (ISBN 0-85264-053-6, Pub. by Griffin England). State Mutual Bk.

--Science Data. 4th ed. 120p. 1960. 10.00x (ISBN 0-85264-090-0, Pub. by Griffin England). State Mutual Bk.

Friend, J. Newton. Numbers: Fun & Facts. 1972. 5.95 (ISBN 0-684-10186-6, ScribT); pap. 2.45 o.p. (ISBN 0-684-13082-3, SL399, ScribT). Scribner.

Friend, Jewell A. Writing English As a Second Language. 1971. pap. 6.95x (ISBN 0-673-07536-2). Scott F.

Friend, Jewell A., ed. Language Programs in the Public Schools. LC 76-58879. 160p. 1977. pap. 4.95x (ISBN 0-8093-0811-8). S Ill U Pr.

Friend, Llerena B. Sam Houston: The Great Designer. LC 54-13252. (Illus.). 1954. pap. 7.95x (ISBN 0-292-78422-8). U of Tex Pr.

Friend, Llerena B., ed. see Webb, Walter P.

Friend, Oscar. Lobo Brand. 256p. (YA) 1973. 5.95 (ISBN 0-685-32414-1, Avalon). Bouregy.

Friend, Paul D. The Great Frame-Up: The Consumer's Guide to Eyeglasses. Hammond, Debbie, ed. 1980. 11.95 (ISBN 0-87949-181-7). Ashley Bks.

Friend, W. L. Anglo-American Legal Bibliographies. 1966. 15.00x (ISBN 0-8377-2128-8). Rothman.

Friendly, Alfred. Israel's Oriental Immigrants & Druzes. (Minority Rights Group: No. 12). 1972. pap. 2.50 (ISBN 0-89192-101-X). Interbk Inc.

Friendly, Fred. The Good Guys, the Bad Guys & the First Amendment: Free Speech Vs. Fairness in Broadcasting. 1976. 10.00 o.p. (ISBN 0-394-49725-2). Random.

Friendly, Henry J. Federal Jurisdiction: A General View. 199p. 1973. 15.00x (ISBN 0-231-03741-4). Columbia U Pr.

Friends of the Earth Staff. Earthworks: Ten Years on the Environmental Front. Vander Vender, Mary Lou, ed. LC 79-56910. (Orig.). 1980. pap. 8.95 (ISBN 0-913890-39-1). Friends Earth.

Frier, Bruce W. Landlords & Tenants in Imperial Rome. LC 79-3207. (Illus.). 248p. 1980. 17.50x (ISBN 0-691-05299-9). Princeton U Pr.

Fries, Chloe. The Full of the Moon. (Challenge Bks). (Illus.). (gr. 4-8). 1979. PLB 5.95 (ISBN 0-87191-686-X). Creative Ed.

Fries, Fritz R. Das Nackte Maedchen Auf der Strasse Erzaehlungen. (Suhrkamp Taschenbuecher: St 577). 192p. (Ger.). 1980. pap. text ed. 3.90 (ISBN 3-518-37077-4, Pub. by Insel Verlag Germany). Suhrkamp.

Fries, James F. & Crapo, Lawrence M. Vitality & Aging: Implications of the Rectangular Curve. 1981. text ed. price not set (ISBN 0-7167-1308-X); pap. text ed. price not set (ISBN 0-7167-1309-8). W H Freeman.

Fries, James F. & Ehrlich, George E. Prognosis: Contemporary Outcomes of Disease. (Illus.). 600p. 1980. 34.95 (ISBN 0-89303-005-8). Charles.

Fries, James F. & Holman, Halsted R. Systematic Lupus Erythematosus: A Clinical Analysis, Vol. 6. LC 74-31837. (Major Problems in Internal Medicine Ser.). (Illus.). 199p. 1975. text ed. 20.00 (ISBN 0-7216-3917-8). Saunders.

Fries, James F., jt. auth. see Calin, Andrei.

Fries, James F., jt. auth. see Loring, Kate.

Friese, John F. & Williams. Course Making in Industrial Education. 3rd ed. 1966. 11.96 (ISBN 0-87002-251-2). Bennett IL.

Friese, Ralf, tr. see Kiefer, H. & Maushart, R.

Friese, U. Erich. Aquarium Fish. (Illus.). 96p. 1980. 2.95 (ISBN 0-87666-512-1, KW026). TFH Pubns.

Friese, U. Erich, tr. see Enehjelm, Curt A.

Friesen, et al. Managing the Courts. 1971. text ed. 14.00 (ISBN 0-672-81533-8, Bobbs-Merrill Law). Michie.

Friesen, Connie M. The Political Economy of East-West Trade. LC 76-14395. 1976. text ed. 23.95 (ISBN 0-275-56920-9). Praeger.

Friesen, Garry & Maxson, J. Robin. Decision Making & the Will of God. LC 80-24592. (Critical Concern Bks.). 1981. 9.95 (ISBN 0-930014-47-2). Multnomah.

Friesen, John W., jt. auth. see Carson, Robert B.

Friesen, Raymond L. From Furrows to Freeways. 1981. 6.95 (ISBN 0-533-04712-9). Vantage.

Frieser, H. Photographic Information Recording. 1975. 80.00 (ISBN 0-240-50754-1). Focal Pr.

Frieser, Hellmut. Photographic Information Recording. LC 75-20097. 592p. 1975. 82.95 (ISBN 0-470-28117-0). Halsted Pr.

Friesner, Arlyne. Maternity Nursing. 2nd ed. Raff, Beverly, ed. LC 77-80106. (Nursing Outline Ser.). 1977. pap. 8.50 (ISBN 0-87488-377-6). Med Exam.

Friess, Horace L. Felix Adler & Ethical Culture. (Illus.). 320p. 1981. 20.00x (ISBN 0-231-05184-0). Columbia U Pr.

Frigerio, A. & Castagnoli, N., Jr., eds. Mass Spectrometry in Biochemistry & Medicine. LC 73-91164. (Monographs of the Mario Negri Institute for Pharmacological Research). 379p. 1974. 48.00 (ISBN 0-911216-53-7). Raven.

Frigerio, Alberto & Ghisalberti, Emilio L. Mass Spectrometry in Drug Metabolism. LC 76-53013. 532p. 1977. 49.50 (ISBN 0-306-31018-X, Plenum Pr). Plenum Pub.

Frigidaire. Microwave Cooking in Multiple Speeds. 256p. 1980. 12.95 (ISBN 0-385-13233-6). Doubleday.

Friguglietti, James see Lefebvre, Georges.

Frigyesi, T., et al, eds. Corticothalamic Projections & Sensorimotor Activities. LC 74-181303. (Illus.). 601p. 1972. 43.50 (ISBN 0-911216-35-9). Raven.

Friis, Herman R., ed. see Porter, Russell W.

Frik, Seigina M., et al. Chronic Care Nursing. 304p. 1981. text ed. price not set (ISBN 0-8261-3010-0); pap. text ed. price not set (ISBN 0-8261-3011-9). Springer Pub.

Frimann-Dahl, J. Roentgen Examinations in Acute Abdominal Diseases. 3rd ed. (Illus.). 632p. 1974. text ed. 49.50 (ISBN 0-398-02939-3). C C Thomas.

Frings, Hubert & Frings, Mable. Animal Communication. LC 76-50562. 1977. 9.95 o.p. (ISBN 0-8061-1392-8); pap. 5.95 (ISBN 0-8061-1393-6). U of Okla Pr.

Frings, Keti see Watson, E. Bradlee & Pressey, Benfield.

Frings, Mable, jt. auth. see Frings, Hubert.

Frink, Maurice. Fort Defiance & the Navajos. (Illus.). 150p. (Orig.). 1981. pap. 5.95 (ISBN 0-87108-585-2). Pruett.

Frinternational Symposium on X-Ray Optics & X-Ray Microanalysis - 3rd - Stanford - California - 1962. Proceedings. Pattee, Howard H., Jr., et al, eds. 1964. 58.50 (ISBN 0-12-547050-9). Acad Pr.

Fripiat, J. J., jt. ed. see Van Olphen, H.

Frisancho, A. Roberto. Human Adaptation: A Functional Interpretation. LC 78-31913. (Illus.). 1979. text ed. 14.95 (ISBN 0-8016-1693-X). Mosby.

Frisbee, Richard. Basic Boat Building. LC 74-6890. (Illus.). 288p. 1975. 6.95 (ISBN 0-8092-8390-5); pap. 6.95 o.p. (ISBN 0-8092-8342-5). Contemp Bks.

Frisbie, Charlotte J., ed. Southwestern Indian Ritual Drama. LC 79-2308. (School of American Research Advanced Seminar Ser.). (Illus.). 384p. 1980. 30.00 (ISBN 0-8263-0521-0). U of NM Pr.

Frisbiewhicher, George. This Was a Poet: A Critical Biography of Emily Dickinson. 337p. 1980. 17.50 (ISBN 0-208-01900-6, Archon); pap. 9.50 tchr.'s ed. (ISBN 0-208-01901-4). Shoe String.

Frisby, David, tr. see Simmel, Georg.

Frisch, jt. ed. see Frisch, K. C.

Frisch, Ivan T., jt. auth. see Frank, Howard.

Frisch, K. C. & Frisch, eds. Polymer Alloys: Blends, Grafts, & Interpenetrating Networks. (Polymer Science & Technology Ser.: Vol. 10). 501p. 1977. 47.50 (ISBN 0-306-36410-7, Plenum Pr). Plenum Pub.

Frisch, K. C., jt. ed. see Klempner, D.

Frisch, Kurt C., et al. Polyelectrolytes. LC 76-177446. (Illus.). 1976. 25.00x (ISBN 0-87762-076-8). Technomic.

Frisch, Max. Biedermann und Die Brandstifter. Ackermann, Paul K., ed. (gr. 10-12). 1963. pap. text ed. 7.20 (ISBN 0-395-04090-6). HM.

--Herr Biedermann und Die Brandstifter: Rip Van Winkle, Zwei Hoerspiele. (Suhrkamp Taschenbucher: No. 599). 128p. 1980. pap. text ed. 3.25 (ISBN 3-518-37099-5, Pub. by Insel Verlag Germany). Suhrkamp.

--Homo Faber. Ackermann, Paul K., ed. LC 72-9379. 300p. (Orig.). 1973. pap. text ed. 8.05 (ISBN 0-395-14402-7). HM.

--Triptych: Three Scenic Panels. Skelton, Geoffrey, tr. (Helen & Kurt Wolff Bk.). 1981. 8.95 (ISBN 0-15-191157-6). HarBraceJ.

Frisch, Michael H. Town into City: Springfield, Massachusetts & the Meaning of Community, 1840-1880. LC 72-178075. (Studies in Urban History). (Illus.). 464p. 1972. 15.00x (ISBN 0-674-89820-6); pap. 6.95x (ISBN 0-674-89826-5). Harvard U Pr.

Frisch, Morton J. Franklin D. Roosevelt. LC 74-16425. (World Leaders Ser.: No. 43). 1975. lib. bdg. 9.95 (ISBN 0-8057-3708-1). Twayne.

Frisch, Morton J. & Stevens, Richard G., eds. The Political Thought of American Statesmen: Selected Writings & Speeches. LC 72-89723. 350p. 1973. 11.00 o.p. (ISBN 0-87581-141-8); pap. text ed. 10.95 (ISBN 0-87581-142-6). Peacock Pubs.

Frisch, O. R., ed. Progress in Nuclear Physics, Vols. 2 & 5-9. Vol. 2. 1952. 81.00 (ISBN 0-08-013329-0); Vol. 5. 1956. 81.00 (ISBN 0-08-009043-5); Vol. 6. 1957. 81.00 (ISBN 0-08-009066-4); Vol. 7. 1959. 81.00 (ISBN 0-08-009186-5); Vol. 8. 1960. 81.00 (ISBN 0-08-009479-1); Vol. 9. 1963. 81.00 (ISBN 0-08-010063-5). Pergamon.

Frisch, Otto R. What Little I Remember. LC 78-18096. (Illus.). 227p. 1980. pap. 9.95 (ISBN 0-521-28010-9). Cambridge U Pr.

Frisch, Robert A. ESOP for the Eighties. 1981. 14.95 (ISBN 0-87863-003-1). Farnswth Pub.

--The Magic of ESOT: The Fabulous New Instrument of Corporate Finance. rev. ed. LC 75-13780. (Illus.). 200p. 1976. 14.95 o.p. (ISBN 0-87863-108-9). Farnswth Pub.

Frishman, Austin M. & Schwartz, Arthur P. The Cockroach Combat Manual. LC 80-288. (Illus.). 1980. 9.95 (ISBN 0-688-03613-9, Quill); pap. 4.95 (ISBN 0-688-08613-6). Morrow.

Frishman, Bernard L. & Loshak, Lionel. Metric Architectural Drawing: A Manual for Designers & Draftsmen. 160p. 1981. 20.00 (ISBN 0-471-07724-0, Pub. by Wiley-Interscience). Wiley.

Frishman, William H. Clinical Pharmacology of the Beta-Adrenocepter Blocking Drugs. 288p. 1980. 16.95x (ISBN 0-8385-1143-0). ACC.

Frisk, Peter D., jt. auth. see Gustafson, R. David.

Friskey, Margaret. Indian Two Feet & His Horse. (Illus.). (gr. 2-3). pap. 1.25 (ISBN 0-590-08056-3, Schol Pap); pap. 3.95 indian two feet & witch next door (2 bks.) & record (ISBN 0-590-04394-3). Schol Bk Serv.

--Indian Two Feet & the Wolf Cubs. (Illus.). 64p. (gr. k-3). 1971. PLB 7.95 (ISBN 0-516-03501-0). Childrens.

--True Book of the Moon Ride Rock Hunt. LC 72-1457. (True Bks). (Illus.). 48p. (gr. 3-5). 1972. PLB 8.65 o.p. (ISBN 0-516-01144-8). Childrens.

Friskin, James & Freundlich, Irwin. Music for the Piano: A Handbook of Concert & Teaching Material from 1580 to 1952. rev. ed. LC 72-93608. 443p. 1973. pap. 5.00 (ISBN 0-486-22918-1). Dover.

Frisling, B. W., ed. Social Change in Europe. 146p. 1974. pap. text ed. 20.75x (ISBN 90-04-03778-0). Humanities.

Frison, George, ed. The Casper Site: A Hell Gap Bison Kill on the High Plains. 1974. 25.00 (ISBN 0-12-268550-4). Acad Pr.

Frisoni, Gaetano. Dizionario Moderno Spagnuolo-Italiano--Italiano-Spagnuolo, 2 vols. 1865p. Set. 44.00x (ISBN 0-913298-51-4). S F Vanni.

Fritch, Bruce E. & Reisman, Albert F., eds. Equipment Leasing. LC 80-8348C. 1980. 75.00 (ISBN 0-685-85340-3, A1-1273). PLI.

Fritch, Elizabeth. Richmond, Vol. 1: The Flame. 480p. (Orig.). 1980. pap. 2.75 (ISBN 0-89083-654-X). Zebra.

--Richmond Volume 2: The Fire. 1980. pap. 2.75 (ISBN 0-89083-679-5, Kable News Co). Zebra.

Frith, D. New Priorities & Developments in the Construction Market in Saudi Arabia & Iran. 206p. 1979. 209.00x (ISBN 0-86010-135-5, Pub. by Graham & Trotman England). State Mutual Bk.

Frith, Francis. Egypt & the Holy Land in Historic Photographs: Seventy-Seven Views. Van Haaften, Julia, ed. 112p. 1981. pap. 7.00 (ISBN 0-486-24048-7). Dover.

Frith, Henry. Graphology: The Science of Handwriting. (Illus.). 128p. pap. 4.50 (ISBN 0-8334-1756-8). Steinerbks.

Frith, James R., ed. Measuring Spoken Language Proficiency. 69p. (Orig.). 1980. pap. text ed. 3.95 (ISBN 0-87840-188-1). Georgetown U Pr.

Frith, William P. John Leech: His Life & Work, 2 Vols. LC 69-17491. 1969. Repr. of 1891 ed. Set. 32.00 (ISBN 0-8103-3831-9). Gale.

Fritsch, Al, ed. see Center for Science in the Public Interest.

Fritsch, Charles T. Qumran Community: Its History & Scrolls. 1973. Repr. of 1956 ed. 12.00x (ISBN 0-8196-0279-5). Biblo.

Fritsch, Felix E. Structure & Reproduction of the Algae, 2 Vols. Vol. 1. 75.00 (ISBN 0-521-05041-3); Vol. 2. 90.00 (ISBN 0-521-05042-1). Cambridge U Pr.

Fritschka, E., jt. ed. see Cervos-Navarro, J.

Fritschler, A. Lee. Smoking & Politics: Policy Making & the Federal Bureaucracy. 2nd ed. LC 74-12381. 208p. 1975. pap. text ed. 6.95 (ISBN 0-13-815019-2). P-H.

Fritz, Carl. Combating Nutritional Blindness in Children: A Case Study of Technical Assistance in Indonesia. (Pergamon Policy Studies). 1980. 28.00 (ISBN 0-08-024636-2). Pergamon.

Fritz, Irving, ed. see Symposium on Insulin Action, Toronto, 1971.

Fritz, James S. Acid-Base Titration in Non-Aqueous Solvents. new ed. 156p. 1973. pap. text ed. 10.95x o.p. (ISBN 0-205-03735-6). Allyn.

Fritz, James S. & Schenk, George H., Jr. Quantitative Analtical Chemistry. 4th ed. (Illus.). 1979. text ed. 23.95x (ISBN 0-205-06527-9, 6865275). Allyn.

--Quantitative Analytical Chemistry. 3rd ed. (Illus.). 704p. 1974. text ed. 17.95x o.s.i. (ISBN 0-205-04464-6, 6942032); sol. manual 1.95x o.s.i. (ISBN 0-685-34568-8); answer bk. avail. o.s.i. (ISBN 0-685-34569-6). Allyn.

Fritz, Jean. The Man Who Loved Books. (Illus.). 48p. (gr. 7-11). 1981. 8.95 (ISBN 0-399-20715-5). Putnam.

Fritz, John H., ed. Champion Horses & Riders of North America: A Picture Yearbook. (Illus.). 1975. 10.00 o.p. (ISBN 0-397-01083-4). Lippincott.

Fritz, Kurt Von. Antike und moderne Tragoedie: Neun Abhandlungen. (Ger). 1962. 45.90x (ISBN 3-11-005039-0). De Gruyter.

Fritz, N. Business Recordkeeping Practice Set. 2nd ed. 1974. text ed. 5.48 o.p. (ISBN 0-07-022482-X, G); tchr's. manual & key 1.50 o.p. (ISBN 0-07-022487-0). McGraw.

--Service Station Operation & Management. 1968. text ed. 7.96 o.p. (ISBN 0-07-022475-7, G). McGraw.

Fritze, David, ed. see Kirby, Colleen & Roberts, Laura.

Fritzell, B., et al, eds. see Internaional Associaion of Logopedics & Phoniatrics, 18th Congress, Washington, D.C., August 1980.

Fritzhand, James. Blood Island. 1981. pap. 2.75 (ISBN 0-671-83012-0). PB.

--Third Avenue. (Orig.). 1979. pap. 2.75 (ISBN 0-515-05787-8). Jove Pubns.

Fritzhand, James & Glickman, Frank. The Unicorn Affair. (Orig.). 1981. pap. 2.50 (ISBN 0-451-09605-3, E9605, Sig). NAL.

Frizzell, D. D., jt. ed. see Thompson, W. Scott.

Frizzell, Lawrence, tr. see Thoma, Clemens.

Frobisher, Martin, et al. Fundamentals of Microbiology. 9th ed. LC 73-88259. (Illus.). 850p. 1974. text ed. 18.95 o.p. (ISBN 0-7216-3922-4). Saunders.

Froboess, Harry. Fell's Official Guide to Diving. pap. 4.95 (ISBN 0-8119-0368-0). Fell.

--Fell's Official Guide to Diving: Plain, High, Fancy, Platform, Comedy & Acrobatic. LC 65-15502. (gr. 7 up). 1965. 8.95 (ISBN 0-8119-0052-5). Fell.

Frocht, M. M. Photoelasticity, Vol. 2. 1948. 49.50 (ISBN 0-471-28281-2, Pub. by Wiley-Interscience). Wiley.

Frodesen, A. G., et al. Probability & Statistics in Particle Physics. 1979. pap. 39.00x (ISBN 8-2000-1906-3, Dist. by Columbia U. Pr.). Universitet.

Frodsham, J. D., tr. The First Chinese Embassy to the West: The Journals of Kuo Sung-Tao, Liu Hsi-Hung & Chang Te-Yi. (Illus.). 266p. 1974. 24.00x (ISBN 0-19-821555-X). Oxford U Pr.

Frodsham, J. D., tr. see Li Ho.

Froeb, Herman. Ernst Koch's Prinz Rosa-Stramin: Ein Beitrag Zur Hessischen Literaturgeschichte. pap. 7.00 (ISBN 0-384-17029-3). Johnson Repr.

Froebel, Fred. Selection from His Writings. Lilley, Irene M., ed. (Cambridge Texts & Studies in Education). 22.50 (ISBN 0-521-05043-X). Cambridge U Pr.

Froebel, Frederich. Educations of Man. Hailmann, W. N., tr. from German. (Contributions to the History of Psychology B, I: Psychometrics Ser.). 1978. Repr. of 1887 ed. write for info. (ISBN 0-89093-161-5). U Pubns Amer.

Froehlich, John F. The Companion to Cornucopia. 1980. 6.50 (ISBN 0-8233-0321-7). Golden Quill.

Froehlich, Ronald B. Food Additives, Student Syllabus. pap. text ed. 4.85 (ISBN 0-89420-076-3, 168008); cassette recordings 39.00 (ISBN 0-89420-205-7, 168000). Natl Book.

Froelich, Robert E., et al. Communication in the Dental Office: A Programmed Manual for the Dental Professional. (Illus.). 128p. 1976. pap. 10.95 (ISBN 0-8016-1698-0). Mosby.

Froer, Hans. I Will Tell You About God. Bachmann, E. Theodore, tr. from Ger. LC 78-14666. 80p. (gr. k up). 1979. pap. 3.50 (ISBN 0-8006-1350-3, 1-1350). Fortress.

Frohn, Peggy, ed. Successful Home Plans for the Eighties. LC 80-7498. (Successful Ser.). (Illus.). 1980. 15.95 (ISBN 0-89999-002-9); pap. 6.95 (ISBN 0-89999-003-7). Structures Pub.

Frohn, Peggy, ed. see Derven, Ronald & Nichols, Carol.

Frohn, Peggy, ed. see Ritchie, James D.

Frohn, Peggy, ed. see Schram, Joseph.

Frohock, Fred M. Normative Political Theory. (Foundations of Modern Political Science Ser). 128p. 1973. pap. 7.95 (ISBN 0-13-623710-X). P-H.

--Public Policy: Scope & Logic. LC 78-8382. 1979. 16.95 (ISBN 0-13-737932-3). P-H.

Frohock, Wilbur. Andre Malraux. (Columbia Essays on Modern Writers Ser.: No. 71). 1974. pap. 2.00 (ISBN 0-231-03441-5). Columbia U Pr.

Frohock, Wilbur M. French Literature: An Approach Through Close Reading. 4th ed. 1970. 5.50 (ISBN 0-87774-000-3). Schoenhof.

Frohse, Franz, et al. Atlas of Human Anatomy. 6th rev. & enl. ed. LC 61-15471. (Illus.). 180p. 1961. pap. text ed. 9.00x (ISBN 0-06-480289-2). B&N.

Froissart, Jean. Here Begynneth the First Volum of Sir J. Froyssart. Bourchier, J., tr. LC 72-26004. (English Experience Ser.: No. 257). 644p. 1970. Repr. of 1523 ed. 104.00 (ISBN 90-221-0257-2). Walter J Johnson.

Frolich, J. C., ed. Methods in Prostaglandin Research. LC 78-66346. (Advances in Prostaglandin & Thromboxane Research: Vol. 5). 1978. 29.00 (ISBN 0-89004-204-7). Raven.

Frolick, N. J. & Oppenheimer, J. Modern Political Economy. 1978. pap. 7.95 (ISBN 0-13-597120-9). P-H.
From, Franz. Perception of Other People. Maher, Brendan A. & Kvan, Erik, trs. from Dan. LC 76-138295. 1971. 15.00x (ISBN 0-231-03402-4). Columbia U Pr.
From the Pages of Interiors Magazine. The Interiors Book of Shops & Restaurants. 144p. 1981. 25.00 (ISBN 0-8230-7284-3, Whitney Lib). Watson-Guptill.
Froman, Robert. Angles Are Easy As Pie. LC 75-6608. (Young Math Ser). (Illus.). 40p. (gr. k-3). 1976. PLB 7.89 (ISBN 0-690-00916-X, TYC-J). T Y Crowell.
--A Game of Functions. LC 74-2266. (Young Math Ser). (Illus.). 40p. (gr. k-3). 1974. 6.95 o.p. (ISBN 0-690-00544-X, TYC-J); PLB 6.89 (ISBN 0-690-00545-8). T Y Crowell.
--The Greatest Guessing Game. LC 77-5463. (A Young Math Book). (Illus.). (gr. 1-3). 1978. PLB 7.89 (ISBN 0-690-01376-0, TYC-J). T Y Crowell.
--Less Than Nothing Is Really Something. LC 72-7546. (Young Math Ser). (Illus.). (gr. 1-5). 1973. 7.95 (ISBN 0-690-48862-9, TYC-J). T Y Crowell.
--Mushrooms & Molds. LC 71-187936. (A Let's-Read-&-Find-Out Science Book). (Illus.). (gr. k-3). 1972. PLB 7.89 (ISBN 0-690-56603-4, TYC-J). T Y Crowell.
--Rubber Bands, Baseballs & Doughnuts: A Book About Topology. LC 74-158690. (Young Math Ser). (Illus.). (gr. 1-4). 1972. 7.95 (ISBN 0-690-71353-3, TYC-J); PLB 7.89 (ISBN 0-690-71354-1). T Y Crowell.
--Seeing Things: A Book of Poems. LC 73-18494. 64p. (gr. 5-9). 1974. 7.95 (ISBN 0-690-00291-2, TYC-J). T Y Crowell.
--Venn Diagrams. LC 75-187937. (Young Math Ser). (Illus.). (gr. 1-5). 1972. 4.50 o.p. (ISBN 0-690-85996-1, TYC-J); PLB 7.89 (ISBN 0-690-85997-X). T Y Crowell.
Fromberg, Doris P. Early Childhood Education: A Perceptual Models Curriculum. LC 76-45390. 1977. text ed. 18.95x (ISBN 0-471-28286-3). Wiley.
Frome, Michael. National Park Guide, 1981. LC 77-4075. 1981. pap. 7.95 (ISBN 0-528-84544-6). Rand.
--The National Parks. rev.. ed. (Illus.). 160p. (Orig.). 1981. pap. 9.95 (ISBN 0-528-88045-4). Rand.
Frome, Michael, intro. by. Hosteling U. S. A. The Offical American Youth Hostels Handbook. rev. ed. (Illus.). 250p. (Orig.). 1981. pap. 6.95 (ISBN 0-914788-33-7). East Woods.
Frome, Robert L. & Rosenzweig, Victor M. Sales of Securities by Corporate Insiders: The Impact of the 140 Series. 2nd ed. 1975. 20.00 o.p. (ISBN 0-685-85359-4, B1-1216). PLI.
Froment, Diana de see De Froment, Diana.
Froment, Gilbert F. & Bischoff, Kenneth B. Chemical Reactor Analysis & Design. LC 78-12465. 1979. text ed. 35.95 (ISBN 0-471-02447-3). Wiley.
Fromenteau, A. Painting with Cold Enamel. LC 73-3716. (Illus.). 96p. 1980. Repr. of 1973 ed. 4.95 (ISBN 0-8069-8550-X); lib. bdg. 4.59 (ISBN 0-8069-8551-8). Sterling.
Fromentin, Eugene. Dominique. Wright, Barbara, ed. (French Texts Ser.). 1965. pap. text ed. 7.00x o.p. (ISBN 0-631-00650-8, Pub. by Basil Blackwell). Biblio Dist.
Fromer, Margaret & Keyes, Sharrel. Let's Pray Together: Eight Studies on Prayer. LC 74-76160. (Fisherman Bible Study Guide). 1974. pap. 1.95 (ISBN 0-87788-801-9). Shaw Pubs.
--Letters to the Thessalonians. LC 75-33441. (Fisherman Bible Studyguides). 1975. pap. 1.25 saddle-stich (ISBN 0-87788-489-7). Shaw Pubs.
Fromer, Margaret & Nystrom, Carolyn. James: Roadmap for Down-to-Earth Christians (Student & Teacher) (Young Fisherman Bible Studyguide). (Illus.). 80p. 1981. tchr.'s ed. 4.95 (ISBN 0-87788-420-X, 420-X); wkbk. 3.95 (ISBN 0-87788-419-6, 419-X). Shaw Pubs.
Fromer, Margot J. Ethical Issues in Health Care. LC 80-25058. 350p. 1981. pap. text ed. 14.95 (ISBN 0-8016-1728-6). Mosby.
Fromhold, A. T. Quantum Mechanics for Applied Physics & Engineering. LC 80-19001. 1981. 34.50 (ISBN 0-12-269150-4). Acad Pr.
Fromkin, Howard L., jt. auth. see Snyder, C. R.
Fromkin, Howard L. & Sherwood, John J., eds. Integrating the Organization: A Social Psychological Analysis. LC 73-21306. (Illus.). 1974. 19.95 (ISBN 0-02-910920-5). Free Pr.
Fromm, David. Complications of Gastric Surgery. LC 77-9313. (Clinical Gastroenterology Monographs). 1977. 28.95 (ISBN 0-471-28291-X, Pub. by Wiley Medical). Wiley.
Fromm, Erich. The Art of Loving. 128p. 1974. pap. 1.95 (ISBN 0-06-080291-X, P291, PL). Har-Row.
--Art of Loving: An Enquiry into the Nature of Love. pap. 3.50 (ISBN 0-06-090001-6, CN 1, CN). Har-Row.
--Crisis of Psychoanalysis. 1977. pap. 1.50 o.p. (ISBN 0-449-30792-1, Prem). Fawcett.
--Dogma of Christ & Other Essays. 1974. pap. 1.25 o.p. (ISBN 0-449-30715-8, P715, Prem). Fawcett.
--Escape from Freedom. 1971. pap. 3.50 (ISBN 0-380-01167-0, 54296, Discus). Avon.
--The Heart of Man: Its Genius for Good & Evil. LC 64-18053. 1980. pap. 3.95 (ISBN 0-06-090119-5, CN 795, CN). Har-Row.
--Sane Society. 320p. 1977. pap. 2.50 (ISBN 0-449-30821-9, Prem). Fawcett.
--To Have or to Be? 256p. 1981. pap. 2.95 (ISBN 0-553-10949-9). Bantam.
Fromm, Erich & Xirau, Ramon, eds. Nature of Man: A Reader. (Problems of Philosophy Series, Vol. 5). 1968. 7.95 o.s.i. (ISBN 0-02-541530-1); pap. 2.95 o.s.i. (ISBN 0-02-084960-5). Macmillan.
Fromm, Erika & Shor, Ronald E. Hypnosis: Developments in Research & New Perspectives. 2nd ed. LC 79-89279. (Illus.). 1979. 42.95 (ISBN 0-202-26085-2). Aldine Pub.
Fromm, Gary & Taubman, Paul. Policy Simulations with an Econometric Model. 1968. 10.95 (ISBN 0-8157-2944-8). Brookings.
Fromm, Gary, et al, eds. Tax Incentives & Capital Spending. (Studies of Government Finance). 301p. 1971. 14.95 (ISBN 0-8157-2942-1); pap. 5.95 (ISBN 0-8157-2941-3). Brookings.
Fromm, Lilo. Muffel & Plums. LC 72-85184. (Illus.). 64p. (ps-3). 1973. 4.95g o.s.i. (ISBN 0-02-735710-4). Macmillan.
Fromme, Allan. The Book for Normal Neurotics. 1981. 10.95 (ISBN 0-374-11544-3). FS&G.
--Doctor Fromme's Book on Sex & Marriage. 1950. pap. 2.25 (ISBN 0-06-463264-4, EH 264, EH). Har-Row.
Fromme, Babbette B. Curators' Choice: From the Collections of the Art Museums of the U. S. (Midwestern Edition) Aymar, Brandt, ed. (Illus.). 160p. 1981. pap. 6.95 (ISBN 0-517-54199-8). Crown.
--Curators' Choice: From the Collections of the Art Museums of the U. S. (Northeastern Edition) Aymar, Brandt, ed. (Illus.). 288p. 1981. pap. 8.95 (ISBN 0-517-54197-1). Crown.
--Curators' Choice: From the Collections of the Art Museums of the U. S. (Southern Edition) Aymar, Brandt, ed. (Illus.). 160p. 1981. pap. 6.95 (ISBN 0-686-69482-1). Crown.
--Curators' Choice: From the Collections of the Art Museums of the U. S. (Western Edition) (Illus.). 160p. 1981. pap. 6.95 (ISBN 0-517-54200-5). Crown.
Frommer, E. A. Voyage Through Childhood to the Adult World. 1969. 22.00 (ISBN 0-08-006496-5); pap. 10.75 (ISBN 0-08-006495-7). Pergamon.
Frommer, Eva A. Diagnosis & Treatment in Clinical Child Psychiatry. (Illus.). 1972. 24.00x (ISBN 0-433-10910-6). Intl Ideas.
Frommer, Herbert H. Radiology for Dental Auxiliaries. 2nd ed. LC 77-15473. (Illus.). 1978. text ed. 14.50 (ISBN 0-8016-1706-5). Mosby.
Frompovich, Catherine J. Attacking Hay Fever & Winning. Koppenhaver, April M., ed. (Orig.). 1981. pap. 2.00. C J Frompovich.
--The Fox in Shangri-La. (ps-2). 1978. tchr's. ed. 0.75x (ISBN 0-935322-01-9). C J Frompovich.
--Kids Cooking Naturally. (Illus.). 32p. (gr. 2-5). 1979. pap. 1.29x (ISBN 0-935322-04-3). C J Frompovich.
--Nutrition Workbook for Children. 32p. (gr. 1-5). 1978. pap. 1.50x (ISBN 0-935322-00-0). C J Frompovich.
--Preventing Burnout: The Nutritional Approach. (Illus.). 145p. Date not set. pap. 50.00 course materials (ISBN 0-935322-14-0). C J Frompovich.
Frompovich, Catherine J. & Hays, Joanne M. Everyday Herbs for Cooking & Healing. 1980. 100 frame filmstrips, cassette, text 15.00 (ISBN 0-935322-11-6). C J Frompovich.
Frompovich, Catherine J., ed. see Pack-Miller, Lisa, et al.
Froncek, Thomas. Northmen. LC 74-77815. (Emergence of Man Ser.). (gr. 6 up). 1974. lib. bdg. 9.63 o.p. (ISBN 0-8094-1275-6, Pub. by Time-Life). Silver.
--The Northmen. (The Emergence of Man Ser). (Illus.). 1974. 9.95 (ISBN 0-8094-1324-8); lib. bdg. avail. (ISBN 0-685-49690-2). Time-Life.
Froncek, Thomas, ed. see Horizon Magazine Editors.
Frondel, Judith W. Lunar Mineralogy. LC 75-9786. 323p. 1975. 33.00 (ISBN 0-471-28289-8, Pub. by Wiley-Interscience). Wiley.
Frontera, Jose G. Neuroanatomy Laboratory Guide. 7.50 o.p. (ISBN 0-8477-2309-7); pap. 6.25 (ISBN 0-8477-2310-0). U of PR Pr.
Frontier Press Company. Lincoln Library of Language Arts, 2 vols. 5th ed. LC 80-54173. 1981. Set. 54.95 (ISBN 0-912168-06-4). Frontier Pr Co.
Fronval, George & Dubois, Daniel. Indian Signs & Signals. Egan, E. W., tr. LC 78-57792. (Illus.). (gr. 3 up). 1978. 14.95 (ISBN 0-8069-2720-8); PLB 13.29 (ISBN 0-8069-2721-6). Sterling.
Frosch, John & Ross, Nathaniel, eds. The Annual Survey of Psychoanalysis: A Comprehensive Survey of Current Psychoanalytic Practice & Theory, 10 vols. Incl. Vol. 1. 1952 (ISBN 0-8236-0160-9); Vol.2. 1953 (ISBN 0-8236-0180-3); Vol. 3. 1956 (ISBN 0-8236-0200-1); Vol. 4. 1958 (ISBN 0-8236-0220-6); Vol. 5. 1959 (ISBN 0-8236-0240-0); Vol. 6. 1961 (ISBN 0-8236-0260-5); Vol. 7. 1963 (ISBN 0-8236-0280-X); Vol. 8. 1965 (ISBN 0-8236-0300-8); Vol. 9. 1967 (ISBN 0-8236-0320-2); Vol. 10 (ISBN 0-8236-0340-7). LC 52-12082. text ed. 25.00 ea. o.p. Intl Univs Pr.
Frost, Alan. Convicts & Empire: A Naval Question, 1776-1811. (Illus.). 280p. 1980. 45.00 (ISBN 0-19-554261-4). Oxford U Pr.
--Convicts & Empire: A Naval Question Seventeen Seventy-Six-Eighteen Eleven. (Illus.). 280p. 1980. 39.50 (ISBN 0-19-554261-4). Oxford U Pr.
Frost, Anne & Howard, Coral. Representation & Administrative Tribunals. (Direct Editions Ser). (Orig.). 1977. pap. 10.00 (ISBN 0-7100-8701-2). Routledge & Kegan.
Frost, Arthur A. & Pearson, R. G. Kinetics & Mechanism: A Study of Homogeneous Reactions. 2nd ed. LC 61-6773. 1961. 23.95 o.p. (ISBN 0-471-28347-9). Wiley.
Frost, B. & Fleminger, A. A Revision of the Genus Clausocalanus (Copepoda: Calanoida) with Remarks on Distributional Patterns in Diagnostic Characters. (Bulletin of the Scripps Institution of Oceanography: Vol. 12). 1968. pap. 10.00x (ISBN 0-520-09317-8). U of Cal Pr.
Frost, D. L. School of Shakespeare. LC 68-11283. 1968. 49.50 (ISBN 0-521-05044-8). Cambridge U Pr.
Frost, D. L., ed. Selected Plays of Thomas Middleton. LC 77-23339. (Plays by Renaissance & Restoration Dramatists Ser.). 1978. 47.50 (ISBN 0-521-21698-2); 11.50x (ISBN 0-521-29236-0). Cambridge U Pr.
Frost, Frank J. Greek Society. 2nd ed. 1980. pap. text ed. 7.95 (ISBN 0-669-02452-X). Heath.
--Plutarch's Themistocles: A Historical Commentary. LC 79-3208. 1980. 17.50x (ISBN 0-691-05300-6). Princeton U Pr.
Frost, Gerhard. Homing in the Presence: Meditations for Daily Living. 1978. pap. 4.95 (ISBN 0-03-043921-3). Winston Pr.
Frost, Gerhard E. Blessed Is the Ordinary. (Illus.). 96p. pap. 4.95 (ISBN 0-03-056662-2). Winston Pr.
Frost, H. Gordon & Jenkins, John H. I'm Frank Hamer: The Life of a Texas Peace Officer. LC 68-31953. (Illus.). 12.50 (ISBN 0-8363-0051-3); limited ed. 150.00 (ISBN 0-685-13275-7). Jenkins.
Frost, Harold M. Bone Modeling & Skeletal Modeling Errors: Orthopaedic Lectures, Vol. 4. (Illus.). 224p. 1973. 19.75 (ISBN 0-398-02667-X). C C Thomas.
--Bone Remodeling & Its Relationship to Metabolic Bone Diseases: Orthopaedic Lectures, Vol. 3. (Illus.). 225p. 1973. 22.50 (ISBN 0-398-02588-6). C C Thomas.
--An Introduction to Biomechanics. 160p. 1971. pap. 14.75 photocopy ed. spiral (ISBN 0-398-00622-9). C C Thomas.
--Orthopaedic Biomechanics: Orthopaedic Lectures, Vol. 5. (Illus.). 664p. 1973. 49.50 (ISBN 0-398-02824-9). C C Thomas.
--The Physiology of Cartilaginous, Fibrous, & Bony Tissue: Orthopaedic Lectures, Vol. 2. (Illus.). 264p. 1972. 29.75 (ISBN 0-398-02562-2). C C Thomas.
Frost, Jane C. Your Future As a Dental Assistant. rev. ed. LC 70-114128. (Career Guidance Ser.). 160p. 1976. pap. 3.50 (ISBN 0-668-02238-8). Arco.
--Your Future in Dental Assisting. LC 75-84955. (Careers in Depth Ser). (Illus.). (gr. 7 up). 1976. PLB 5.97 o.p. (ISBN 0-8239-0175-0). Rosen Pr.
Frost, Jens. World Radio & TV Handbook 1980. 34th ed. 1980. pap. 14.95 o.p. (ISBN 0-8230-5906-5). Watson-Guptill.
Frost, Jens M., ed. World Radio TV Handbook Nineteen Eighty-One. 35th ed. 560p. (Orig.). 1980. pap. 16.50 (ISBN 0-8230-5907-3). Watson-Guptill.
Frost, Joe L. & Hawkes, Glenn R. Disadvantaged Child: Issues & Innovations. 2nd ed. LC 70-16422. (Illus., Orig.). 1970. pap. text ed. 12.95 (ISBN 0-395-04475-8). HM.
Frost, Joe L. & Klein, Barry L. Children's Play & Playgrounds. 1979. pap. text ed. 10.50 (ISBN 0-205-06586-4). Allyn.
Frost, John. Heroic Women of the West: Comprising Thrilling Examples of Courage, Fortitude, Devotedness, & Self-Sacrifice, Among the Pioneer Mothers of the Western Country. LC 75-7090. (Indian Captivities Ser.: Vol. 66). 1976. Repr. of 1854 ed. lib. bdg. 44.00 (ISBN 0-8240-1690-4). Garland Pub.
Frost, John, jt. auth. see Wold, Tina.
Frost, Kelman. Men of the Mirage. LC 69-14323. (gr. 7-12). 1969. 5.25 o.p. (ISBN 0-688-41602-0); PLB 6.00 (ISBN 0-688-51602-5). Lothrop.
Frost, Marie. Action Rhymes for Preschoolers. (Peter Panda Ser.). 1977. pap. 1.25 (ISBN 0-87239-142-6, 42034). Standard Pub.
--Characteristics of Preschoolers. (Peter Panda Ser.). 1977. pap. 1.25 (ISBN 0-87239-143-4, 42035). Standard Pub.
--Crafts for Preschoolers. (Peter Panda Ser.). 1977. pap. 1.25 (ISBN 0-87239-144-2, 42036). Standard Pub.
--Effective Visitation. (Peter Panda Ser.). 1977. pap. 1.25 (ISBN 0-87239-145-0, 42037). Standard Pub.
--Songs for Preschoolers. (Peter Panda Ser.). 1977. pap. 1.25 (ISBN 0-87239-146-9, 42038). Standard Pub.
--Teaching Preschoolers. (Peter Panda Ser.). 1977. pap. 1.25 (ISBN 0-87239-147-7, 42039). Standard Pub.
Frost, Miriam, ed. see Emmons, Michael & Richardson, David.
Frost, Miriam, ed. see Mandel, Evelyn.
Frost, Miriam, ed. see Pilch, John J.
Frost, N. E., et al. Metal Fatigue. (Oxford Engineering Science Ser). 1975. 55.00x (ISBN 0-19-856114-8). Oxford U Pr.
Frost, Percival. Curve Tracing. 5th ed. LC 60-10348. 9.95 (ISBN 0-8284-0140-3). Chelsea Pub.
Frost, Peter. Exploring Cuzco. (Illus.). 139p. 1981. pap. 7.95 (ISBN 0-933982-05-4). Bradt Ent.
Frost, R. A. Birds of Derbyshire. 182p. 1980. 30.00x (ISBN 0-903485-46-X, Pub. by Moorland England). State Mutual Bk.
Frost, Reuben B. Physical Education: Foundations, Principles, & Practices. LC 74-10351. 528p. 1975. text ed. 17.95 (ISBN 0-201-02107-2). A-W.
Frost, Reuben B. & Marshall, Stanley J. Administration of PE & Athletics. 2nd ed. 432p. 1981. text ed. 17.25 (ISBN 0-697-07171-5). Wm C Brown.
Frost, Richard. The Circus Villains: Poems. LC 65-24647. 55p. 1965. 5.95 (ISBN 0-8214-0010-X). Ohio U Pr.
--Getting Drunk with the Birds. LC 72-141385. 49p. 1971. 5.95 (ISBN 0-8214-0088-6). Ohio U Pr.
--Race Against Time: Human Relations & Politics in Kenya Before Independence. (Illus.). 292p. 1978. 24.50x (ISBN 0-8476-3102-8). Rowman.
Frost, Robert. New Enlarged Anthology of Robert Frost's Poems. enl. ed. Untermeyer, Louis, ed. pap. 2.50 (ISBN 0-671-48149-5). WSP.
--North of Boston Poems. Lathem, Edward C., ed. LC 77-1401. (Illus.). 1977. 8.95 (ISBN 0-396-07440-5). Dodd.
--Robert Frost: Farm-Poultryman--the Story of Robert Frost's Carreer As a Breeder & Fancier of Hens. Thompson, Lawrance & Lathem, Edward C., eds. LC 64-638. 116p. 1981. pap. 5.00 (ISBN 0-87451-202-6). U Pr of New Eng.
--Selected Prose of Robert Frost. Cox, Hyde & Lathem, Edward C., eds. LC 66-10268. 1968. pap. 1.95 o.s.i. (ISBN 0-02-051000-4, Collier). Macmillan.
--Stopping by Woods on a Snowy Evening. LC 78-8134. (Illus.). 1978. PLB 8.95 (ISBN 0-525-40115-6). Dutton.
Frost, Robert, ed. see Thompson, L.
Frost, Robert, tr. Vida Desbordante. (Spanish Bks.). (Span.). 1978. 1.95 (ISBN 0-8297-0606-2). Vida Pub.
--Vida Transbordante. (Portugese Bks.). (Port.): 1979. write for info. (ISBN 0-8297-0919-3). Vida Pub.
Frost, S. E. Masterworks of Philosophy, Vol. 3. (Masterworks Ser.). 192p. 1972. Pts. 1-2. pap. 1.95 (ISBN 0-07-040803-3, SP). McGraw.
Frost, S. E., Jr. The Basic Teachings of the Philosophers. 314p. 1980. Repr. of 1942 ed. lib. bdg. 25.00 (ISBN 0-89987-256-5). Darby Bks.
Frost, S. E., Jr., B.D., Ph.D. Basic Teachings of the Great Philosophers. LC 62-15320. pap. 2.95 (ISBN 0-385-03007-X, C398, Dolp). Doubleday.
Frost, T. H. Technical Aspects of Renal Dialysis. LC 78-40089. 1978. 32.50 (ISBN 0-471-04524-1, Pub. by Wiley Medical). Wiley.
Frost, William S. Marlin History: Collectors Edition. 5.95 (ISBN 0-685-48801-2). Nortex Pr.
Frostick, M., jt. auth. see Hough, Richard.
Frothingham, Octavius B. Transcendentalism in New England: A History. LC 59-10346. 1972. pap. 6.50x (ISBN 0-8122-1038-7, Pa. Paperbacks). U of Pa Pr.
Frothingham, R. Life & Times of Joseph Warren. LC 72-146148. (Era of the American Revolution Ser). 1971. Repr. of 1865 ed. lib. bdg. 49.50 (ISBN 0-306-70133-2). Da Capo.

Frothingham, Richard. History of the Siege of Boston & of the Battles of Lexington, Concord & Bunker Hill. LC 77-115680. (Era of the American Revolution Ser). 1970. Repr. of 1903 ed. lib. bdg. 37.50 (ISBN 0-306-71932-0). Da Capo.

Frothingham, Thomas E, et al. Pediatric Infectious Diseases Case Studies. 1978. pap. 15.00 (ISBN 0-87488-048-3). Med Exam.

Froud, Nina. The World Book of Soups. 224p. 1975. pap. 1.50 o.p. (ISBN 0-345-24357-9). Ballantine.

Froude, James A. The Nemesis of Faith, 1849. Wolff, Robert L., ed. Bd. with Shadows of the Clouds, 1847. LC 75-1519. (Victorian Fiction Ser.). 1975. lib. bdg. 66.00 (ISBN 0-8240-1592-4). Garland Pub.

Frowen, S. F., et al, eds. Monetary Policy & Economic Activity in West Germany. LC 77-2403. 1977. 52.95 (ISBN 0-470-99131-3). Halsted Pr.

Frucht, Phyllis, et al, eds. The Best of Jewish Cooking. 1981. pap. 9.95 (ISBN 0-686-69080-X). Dial.

Fruchtman, Bernard & Newman, Harry R. Urology Case Studies. 1979. pap. 15.50 (ISBN 0-87488-017-3). Med Exam.

Frude, Neil, ed. Psychological Approaches to Child Abuse. 200p. 1981. 19.50x (ISBN 0-8476-6925-4). Rowman.

Fruhan, William E., Jr. Financial Strategy. 1979. 17.95 (ISBN 0-256-02228-3). Irwin.

Frumkin, Gene. Loops. (Orig.). 1980. pap. 3.00x (ISBN 0-88235-039-0). San Marcos.

Frumkin, V., ed. see Okudzhava, Bulat.

Frungel, Frank. High Speed Pulse Technology, 4 vols. Incl. Vol. 1. Capacitor Discharges, Magneto-Hydrodynamics, X-Rays, Ultrasonics. 1965. 55.25, by subscription 47.50 o.s.i. (ISBN 0-12-269001-X); Vol. 2. Optical Pulses, Lasers, Measuring Techniques. 1965. 51.00, by subscription 44.00 (ISBN 0-12-269002-8); Vol. 3. 1975. 55.25, by subscription 47.50 (ISBN 0-12-269003-6); Vol. 4. 1978. write for info. (ISBN 0-12-269004-4). Acad Pr.

Frutiger, Adrian. Type Sign Symbol. 156p. 1980. 67.50 (ISBN 0-8038-7221-6, Visual Communications). Hastings.

Fruton, Joseph S. Molecules & Life: Historical Essays on the Interplay of Chemistry & Biology. LC 72-3095. 579p. 1972. 17.00 (ISBN 0-471-28448-3, Pub. by Wiley-Interscience). Wiley.

Fry, Bernard M. & White, Herbert S. Publishers & Libraries: The Study of Scholarly & Research Journals. (Illus.). 1976. 18.95 (ISBN 0-669-00886-9). Lexington Bks.

Fry, C. Boat That Mooed. (Illus.). (ps-2). 1965. 4.75g o.s.i. (ISBN 0-02-735720-1). Macmillan.

Fry, Carroll L. Charlotte Smith, Popular Novelist. Varma, Devendra P., ed. LC 79-8453. (Gothic Studies & Dissertations Ser.). 1980. lib. bdg. 24.00x (ISBN 0-405-12667-0). Arno.

Fry, Charles R. Art Deco Interiors in Color. LC 77-75887. (Illus.). 1977. pap. 5.00 (ISBN 0-486-23527-0). Dover.

Fry, Christine L., ed. Dimensions of an Anthropology of Aging. LC 79-13198. (Illus.). 1980. 23.95 (ISBN 0-03-052971-9). Praeger.

Fry, Christopher. The Lady's Not for Burning, a Phoenix Too Frequent, & an Essay, "an Experience of Critics". 1977. pap. 4.95 (ISBN 0-19-519916-2, 507, GB). Oxford U Pr.

Fry, Christopher see Ibsen, Henrik.

Fry, D. B. Acoustic Phonetics: A Course of Basic Reading. (Illus.). 1976. 35.00 (ISBN 0-521-21393-2). Cambridge U Pr.

--The Physics of Speech. LC 78-56752. (Textbooks in Linguistics Ser.). (Illus.). 1979. 27.95 (ISBN 0-521-22173-0); pap. 8.95x (ISBN 0-521-29379-0). Cambridge U Pr.

Fry, Daniel W. The White Sands Incident. 120p. 1967. 3.95 o.s.i. (ISBN 0-910228-05-1). Best Bks.

Fry, Dennis B. Homo Loquens. LC 77-5134. (Illus.). 1977. 24.50 (ISBN 0-521-21705-9); pap. 6.95x (ISBN 0-521-29239-5). Cambridge U Pr.

Fry, E. A., jt. auth. see Phillimore, W. P.

Fry, Earl H. Canadian Government & Politics in Comparative Perspective. LC 78-61913. (Illus.). 1978. pap. text ed. 9.25 (ISBN 0-8191-0627-5). U Pr of Amer.

Fry, Earl H. & Raymond, Gregory A. The Other Western Europe: A Political Analysis of the Smaller Democracies. (Studies in International & Comparative Politics Ser.: No. 14). 251p. 1980. 24.75 (ISBN 0-87436-267-9). Abc-Clio.

Fry, Edward. Skimming & Scanning. (Illus.). (gr. 9-12). 1978. pap. text ed. 4.00x (ISBN 0-89061-123-8, 781). Jamestown Pubs.

--Teaching Faster Reading: A Manual. 1963. text ed. 7.95x (ISBN 0-521-05047-2). Cambridge U Pr.

Fry, Edward B. Dictionary Drills. 128p. (gr. 9 up). 1980. pap. text ed. 4.00x (ISBN 0-89061-206-4, 752). Jamestown Pubs.

--The Emergency Reading Teacher's Manual. 107p. (Orig.). 1979. pap. text ed. 6.00x (ISBN 0-89061-207-2, 752S). Jamestown Pubs.

--Reading Drills. (Illus.). 192p. (gr. 9 up). 1975. pap. text ed. 4.80x (ISBN 0-89061-039-8). Jamestown Pubs.

--Sailboat: Barco De Vela, Bk. 3. Gunning, Monica, tr. (Storybooks for Beginners Ser.). (Illus.). 15p. (Eng. & Span.). 1980. pap. 12.50 set (ISBN 0-89061-214-5). Jamestown Pubs.

--Sailboat in the Wind: Barco De Vela En el Viento, Bk. 4. Gunning, Monica, tr. (Storybooks for Beginners Ser.). (Illus.). 15p. (Eng. & Span.). (gr. 1). 1980. pap. 12.50 (ISBN 0-89061-215-3). Jamestown Pubs.

Fry, Edward F. Cubism. (World of Art Ser.). (Illus.). 1978. pap. 9.95 (ISBN 0-19-520069-1). Oxford U Pr.

Fry, Edward F., jt. ed. see Schultz, Douglas G.

Fry, Eric C. & Wilson, Peter. Shell Book of Practical & Decorative Ropework. (Illus.). 1979. 12.95 (ISBN 0-7153-7615-2). David & Charles.

Fry, George. The Varnishes of the Italian Violin-Makers of the Sixteenth, Seventeenth & Eighteenth Centuries & Their Influence on Tone. (Illus.). 1977. Repr. of 1904 ed. text ed. 16.00 (ISBN 0-918624-02-9). Virtuoso.

Fry, Gladys-Marie. Night Riders in Black Folk History. LC 74-34268. (Illus.). 264p. 1975. pap. 7.95x (ISBN 0-87049-238-1). U of Tenn Pr.

Fry, Jack, jt. auth. see Garretson, Rose A.

Fry, Joan & Denby-Wrightson, Kathryn. The Beginning Dressage Book: A Guide to the Basics for Horse & Rider. LC 80-16950. (Illus.). 224p. 1981. 10.95 (ISBN 0-668-04969-3, 4969). Arco.

Fry, John. Common Diseases. 2nd ed. LC 79-88209. 1979. text ed. 24.00 (ISBN 0-397-58256-0). Lippincott.

--Limits of the Welfare State. 240p. 1979. text ed. 24.00x (ISBN 0-566-00235-3, Pub. by Gower Pub Co England). Renouf.

--Winners on the Ski Slopes. LC 78-16443. (Picture Life Bks.). (Illus.). (gr. k-3). 1979. PLB 6.45 s&l (ISBN 0-531-02292-7). Watts.

Fry, John A. Industrial Democracy & Labour Market Policy in Sweden. 1979. 35.00 (ISBN 0-08-022462-8); pap. 17.75 (ISBN 0-08-022498-9). Pergamon.

Fry, John R. The Great Apostolic Blunder Machine. LC 78-3137. 1978. pap. 4.95 o.p. (ISBN 0-06-063072-8, RD 277, HarpR). Har-Row.

Fry, Lionel. Dermatology: An Illustrated Guide. 2nd ed. (Illus.). 1978. text ed. 19.00x (ISBN 0-906141-02-8, Pub. by Update Pubns England). Kluwer Boston.

Fry, Maxwell & Drew, Jane. Tropical Architecture in the Dry & Humid Zones. 2nd ed. 1980. lib. bdg. 22.50 (ISBN 0-89874-126-2). Krieger.

Fry, N., jt. ed. see Adkinson, A. Wyle.

Fry, P. Spirits of Protest. LC 75-20832. (Cambridge Studies in Social Anthropology: No. 14). 134p. 1976. 19.95 (ISBN 0-521-21052-6). Cambridge U Pr.

Fry, P. Eileen, jt. auth. see Irvine, Betty J.

Fry, Patricia B. & Rubinstein, Ronald A. Of a Homosexual Teacher: Beneath the Mainstream of Constitutional Equalities. (Scholarly Monographs). 180p. 1981. pap. 15.00 (ISBN 0-8408-0508-X). Carrollton Pr.

Fry, Plantagenet S. The David & Charles Book of Castles. LC 80-69352. (Illus.). 496p. 1981. 33.00 (ISBN 0-7153-7976-3). David & Charles.

Fry, Richard. Bankers in West Africa: The Story of the Bank of British West Africa Limited. (Illus.). 1976. text ed. 14.50x (ISBN 0-09-126910-5). Humanities.

Fry, Robin. The VW Beetle. LC 80-67583. (Illus.). 160p. 1980. 22.50 (ISBN 0-7153-7859-7). David & Charles.

Fry, Roger. Vision & Design. (Illus.). pap. 3.95 o.p. (ISBN 0-452-00033-5, FM33, Mer). NAL.

Fry, Rosalie K. Whistler in the Mist. LC 68-29467. (Illus.). 144p. (gr. 4 up). 1968. 3.75 (ISBN 0-374-38382-0). FS&G.

Fry, Sam, Jr., ed. see Watson, Louis H.

Fry, Timothy, et al, eds. The Rule of Saint Benedict RB 1980: In Latin and English with Notes. 650p. 1981. 21.95 (ISBN 0-8146-1211-3); pap. 16.95 (ISBN 0-8146-1220-2). Liturgical Pr.

Fryatt, Norma R. Horn Book Sampler on Children's Books & Reading. LC 59-15028. 1959. 9.50 (ISBN 0-87675-030-7); pap. 6.50 (ISBN 0-87675-031-5). Horn Bk.

Fryde, Natalie. The Tyranny & Fall of Edward II: 1321-1326. LC 78-56179. 1979. 32.95 (ISBN 0-521-22201-X). Cambridge U Pr.

Frye, Charles A. Values in Conflict: Blacks & the American Ambivalence Toward Violence. LC 79-5516. 1980. pap. text ed. 9.00 (ISBN 0-8191-0899-5). U Pr of Amer.

Frye, Charles A., ed. Level Three: A Black Philosophy Reader. LC 80-5801. 217p. 1980. lib. bdg. 18.00 (ISBN 0-8191-1241-0); pap. text ed. 9.75 (ISBN 0-8191-1242-9). U Pr of Amer.

Frye, Jerry K. FIND: Frye's Index to Nonverbal Data. LC 80-51053. 344p. 1980. 39.95 (ISBN 0-936992-01-8); pap. 29.95 (ISBN 0-936992-02-6). U of Minn Comp Ctr.

Frye, John T. Basic Radio Course. LC 61-16513. (Illus.). 1961. 8.95 o.p. (ISBN 0-8306-1104-5); pap. 5.95 (ISBN 0-8306-0104-X, 104). TAB Bks.

Frye, Keith. Modern Minerology. (Illus.). 336p. 1973. ref. ed. 21.95 (ISBN 0-13-595686-2). P-H.

Frye, Northrop. Anatomy of Criticism. 1957. 19.50x (ISBN 0-691-06004-5); pap. 4.95 (ISBN 0-691-01298-9). Princeton U Pr.

--Critical Path: An Essay on the Social Context of Literary Criticism. LC 70-143246. (Midland Bks.: No. 158). 176p. 1971. 8.95x (ISBN 0-253-31568-9); pap. 3.50x (ISBN 0-253-20158-6). Ind U Pr.

--Fools of Time: Studies in Shakespearean Tragedy. LC 67-5748. 1967. pap. 3.95 (ISBN 0-8020-6215-6). U of Toronto Pr.

--The Return of Eden: Five Essays on Milton's Epics. 1975. 10.00x (ISBN 0-8020-1353-8); pap. 4.50 (ISBN 0-8020-6281-4). U of Toronto Pr.

Frye, Northrop, ed. Romanticism Reconsidered. LC 63-18020. (English Institute). 1963. 12.50x (ISBN 0-231-02671-4); pap. 5.00x (ISBN 0-231-08589-3, 89). Columbia U Pr.

--Sound & Poetry. LC 57-11003. (English Institute Essay). 1957. 12.50x (ISBN 0-231-02209-3). Columbia U Pr.

Frye, Northrop, et al. Morality of Scholarship. Black, Max, ed. (Studies in Humanities Ser.). 101p. 1967. 12.50 (ISBN 0-8014-0042-2). Cornell U Pr.

--Myth & Symbol: Critical Approaches & Applications. Slote, Bernice, ed. LC 63-9960. 1963. pap. 4.25x (ISBN 0-8032-5065-7, BB 141, Bison). U of Nebr Pr.

Frye, Prosser H. Romance & Tragedy: A Study of the Classic & Romantic Elements in the Great Tragedies of European Literature. LC 61-10518. (Landmark Edns.). xiv, 372p. 1980. 21.00x (ISBN 0-8032-1955-5). U of Nebr Pr.

--Visions & Chimeras. LC 66-23517. 1929. 9.00x (ISBN 0-8196-0179-9). Biblo.

Frye, Richard N. Islamic Iran & Central Asia (7th-12th Centuries) 380p. 1980. 75.00x (ISBN 0-86078-044-9, Pub. by Variorum England). State Mutual Bk.

Fryene, Sean. The World of the New Testament. (New Testament Message Ser.). 9.00 (ISBN 0-89453-125-5); pap. 5.95 (ISBN 0-89453-190-5). M Glazier.

Fryer. Weed Control Handbook, Vol. II. (Illus.). 1978. Vol. 2. 36.50 (ISBN 0-8016-1716-2, Blackwell). Mosby.

Fryer, Bob, et al, eds. Law, State & Society. Hunt, Alan & McBarret, Doreen. 224p. 1981. 31.00x (ISBN 0-7099-1004-5, Pub. by Croom Helm LTD England). Biblio Dist.

Fryer, D. W. & Jackson, James C. Indonesia. LC 76-3707. (Nations of the Modern World Ser). 1977. 29.75x (ISBN 0-89158-028-X). Westview.

Fryer, Douglas, et al. General Psychology. 4th ed. (Orig.). 1954. pap. 3.95 (ISBN 0-06-460024-6, CO 24, COS). Har-Row.

Fryer, G. & Iles, T. D. The Cichlid Fishes of the Great Lakes of Africa, Their Biology & Evolution. (Illus.). 641p. 1981. Repr. of 1972 ed. lib. bdg. 104.50x (ISBN 3-87429-169-3). Lubrecht & Cramer.

Fryer, K. D., jt. auth. see Berman, Gerald.

Fryer, Russell G. Recent Conservative Political Thought: American Perspectives. LC 78-68568. 1979. pap. text ed. 11.75 (ISBN 0-8191-0694-1). U Pr of Amer.

Frykenberg, Robert E. Guntur District 1788-1848: A History of Local Influence & Central Authority in South India. 1965. 24.95x (ISBN 0-19-821532-0). Oxford U Pr.

Frykenberg, Robert E., ed. Land Control & Social Structure in Indian History. LC 69-16111. 1969. 21.50x (ISBN 0-299-05240-0). U of Wis Pr.

Fryklund, Verne C. & Kepler, Frank R. General Drafting. 4th ed. LC 78-81375. (Illus.). (gr. 9-10). 1969. text ed. 11.16 (ISBN 0-87345-095-7). McKnight.

Fryklund, Verne C. & LaBerge, Armand J. General Shop Bench Woodworking. rev. ed. (Illus.). (gr. 9-10). 1955. pap. 5.80 (ISBN 0-87345-001-9). McKnight.

--General Shop Woodworking. rev. ed. (gr. 9-10). 1972. text ed. 12.60 (ISBN 0-87345-031-0). McKnight.

Fryling, Robert. Urbana Praise. (Orig.). 1979. pap. 2.95 o.p. (ISBN 0-87784-585-9). Inter-Varsity.

Frym, Gloria. Second Stories. LC 79-9390. (Illus.). 1980. pap. 7.95 (ISBN 0-87701-152-4). Chronicle Bks.

Fryman, Elizabeth D. How to Raise & Train a Welsh Terrier. (Illus.). 1960. pap. 1.79 o.p. (ISBN 0-87666-407-9, ...036). TFH Pubns.

Frymier, Jack R. School for Tomorrow. LC 72-10647. 286p. 1973. 17.50x (ISBN 0-8211-0505-1); text ed. 15.75x (ISBN 0-685-28804-8). McCutchan.

Fryrear, Jerry L. & Fleshman, Robert. Videotherapy in Mental Health. (Illus.). 312p. 1981. pap. text ed. 36.50 (ISBN 0-398-04117-2). C C Thomas.

Fryrear, Jerry L., jt. auth. see Fleshman, Bob.

Fryxell, Fritiof. Mountaineering in the Tetons: The Pioneer Period, Eighteen Ninety-Eight to Nineteen Forty. 2nd ed. Smith, Phil D., ed. LC 79-83648. (Illus.). 1978. 8.95 (ISBN 0-933160-00-3); pap. 5.95 (ISBN 0-933160-01-1). Teton Bkshop.

Fu, K. S. & Yu, T. S. Statistical Pattern Classification Using Contextual Information. (Patterns Recognition & Image Processing Ser.). 208p. 1981. write for info. (ISBN 0-471-27859-9, Pub. by Wiley-Interscience). Wiley.

Fu, K. S., ed. Digital Pattern Recognition. 2nd ed. (Communication & Cybernetics: Vol. 10). (Illus.). 234p. 1980. pap. 29.80 (ISBN 0-387-10207-8). Springer-Verlag.

Fu, Shen C. Y., et al. Traces of the Brush: Studies in Chinese Calligraphy. LC 79-24080. 1980. text ed. 45.00 (ISBN 0-300-02487-8); pap. 17.50x (ISBN 0-300-02490-8). Yale U Pr.

Fuchs, Daniel. The Williamsburg Trilogy. 1977. pap. 4.95 (ISBN 0-380-01468-8, 13672). Avon.

Fuchs, Erich. Journey to the Moon. LC 74-103151. (Illus.). (ps-3). 1970. 5.95 (ISBN 0-440-04277-1, Sey Lawr); PLB 5.47 o.s.i. (ISBN 0-440-04278-X, Sey Lawr). Delacorte.

--What Makes a Nuclear Power Plant Work? Edite, Kroll, tr. from Ger. LC 73-182237. (Illus.). 32p. (gr. 3-7). 1972. 5.95 o.s.i. (ISBN 0-440-09723-1, Sey Lawr). Delacorte.

Fuchs, Ernst. Ernst Fuchs. (Contemporary Art Ser.). (Illus.). 1979. 65.00 (ISBN 0-8109-0903-0). Abrams.

Fuchs, Estelle, Ph.D. The Second Season: Life, Love & Sex in the Middle Years. LC 77-70897. 1977. 3.95 (ISBN 0-385-09761-1, Anchor Pr). Doubleday.

Fuchs, Jacob, tr. Horace's Satires & Epistles. 1980. pap. 3.95 (ISBN 0-393-04479-3). Norton.

Fuchs, Jerome H. Making the Most of Management Consulting Services. LC 74-6808. 224p. 1975. 15.95 (ISBN 0-8144-5371-6). Am Mgmt.

Fuchs, Lucy. Wild Winds of Mayaland. (YA) 1978. 5.95 (ISBN 0-685-85784-0, Avalon). Bouregy.

Fuchs, M., jt. auth. see Bass, F. G.

Fuchs, P. L. & Bunnell, C. A. Carbon-Thirteen NMR Based Organic Spectral Problems. LC 78-20668. 1979. pap. text ed. 13.95 (ISBN 0-471-04907-7); answer booklet avail. (ISBN 0-471-05138-1). Wiley.

Fuchs, Peter C. Epidemiology of Hospital Associated Infections. LC 79-17036. 1980. text ed. 25.00 (ISBN 0-89189-072-6, 45-7-011-00). Am Soc Clinical.

Fuchs, R. H. Dutch Painting. (World of Art Ser.). (Illus.). 1978. 17.95 (ISBN 0-19-520060-8); pap. 9.95 (ISBN 0-19-520061-6). Oxford U Pr.

Fuchs, Stephen. Rebellious Prophets: A Study of Messianic Movements in Indian Religions. 1965. 8.95x (ISBN 0-210-27136-1). Asia.

Fuchs, Victor R. Changes in Location of Manufacturing in the United States Since 1929. 1962. 65.00x o.p. (ISBN 0-685-69819-X). Elliots Bks.

Fuchshuber, Annegert. The Wishing Hat. Crawford, Elizabeth D., tr. (ps-3). 1977. 7.25 (ISBN 0-688-22100-9); PLB 6.96 (ISBN 0-688-32100-3). Morrow.

Fuchtbauer, Hans & Muller, G. Sediments & Sedimentary Rocks, Vol. 2, Pt. 1. LC 67-28575. (Sedimentary Petrology Ser.). (Illus.). 1974. 64.95 (ISBN 0-471-28500-5). Halsted Pr.

Fucik, Svatopluk. Solvability of Nonlinear Equations & Boundry Value Problems. (Mathematics & Its Applications Ser.: No. 4). 400p. 1980. lib. bdg. 29.95 (ISBN 90-277-1077-5, Pub. by D. Reidel). Kluwer Boston.

Fu...lla, Joseph G., tr. see Metastasio, Pietro.

Fu...enberg, Hugh H. & Graber, Charles D. Microbiology & Immunology: A Positive Statement Manual. 1977. spiral bddg. 9.75 (ISBN 0-87488-242-7). Med Exam.

Fuechtbauer, H., ed. Stability of Heavy Minerals. LC 74-342080. (Contributions to Sedimentology Ser.: Vol. I). (Illus.). 125p. (Orig.). 1973. pap. 37.50x (ISBN 3-510-57001-4). Intl Pubns Serv.

Fuechtbauer, H., ed. see Gwinner, M. P.

Fuell, A. J. see Von Wiesner, J. & Von Regel, C.

Fuellenbach, John. Ecclesiastical Office & the Primacy of Rome: An Evaluation of Recent Theological Discussion of 1 Clement. (Studies in Christian Antiquity: Vol. 20). 278p. 1980. 25.00x (ISBN 0-8132-0551-4, Pub. by Cath U of America Pr). Intl Schol Bk Serv.

Fuenllana, Miguel De. Orphenica Lyra (Seville, 1554) Jacobs, Charles, ed. (Illus.). 1978. 98.00x (ISBN 0-19-816128-X). Oxford U Pr.

Fuente, Tomas de ha see De La Fuente, Tomas.

Fuente, Tomas De La see Cowan, Marvin W.

Fuentes, Carlos. Burnt Water. Peden, Margaret S., tr. from Span. 295p. 1980. 11.95 (ISBN 0-374-11741-1). FS&G.

--Holy Place. Levine, Suzanne J., tr. 1978. pap. 3.95 o.p. (ISBN 0-525-47528-1). Dutton.

--The Hydra Head. Peden, Margaret S., tr. from Sp. 292p. 1978. 9.95 (ISBN 0-374-17397-4); pap. 6.95 (ISBN 0-374-51563-8). FS&G.

--Where the Air Is Clear. Hileman, Sam, tr. 1971. pap. 7.95 (ISBN 0-374-50919-0, N405). FS&G.

Fuentes, Milma M. & Edito T. De La Cruz, trs. A Treasury of Mandaya & Mansaka Folk Literature. (Illus.). 130p. (Mandaya, Mansaka.). 1980. pap. 8.25x (ISBN 0-686-28808-4). Cellar.

Fuerst, Elinor V., et al. Fundamentals of Nursing: The Humanities & the Sciences in Nursing. 5th ed. LC 74-519. 450p. 1974. text ed. 10.95 o.p. (ISBN 0-397-54152-X). Lippincott.

Fuerst, J. S., ed. Public Housing in Europe & America. LC 73-10890. 1974. 19.95 (ISBN 0-470-28515-X). Halsted Pr.

Fuess, Claude M. Daniel Webster, 2 Vols. 2nd ed. LC 68-8722. (American Scene Ser). (Illus.). 1968. Repr. of 1930 ed. lib. bdg. 65.00 (ISBN 0-306-71186-9). Da Capo.

Fugate, Francis L. Viewpoint: Key to Fiction Writing. 1968. 8.95 (ISBN 0-87116-025-0). Writer.

Fugate, Francis L. & Fugate, Roberta B. Secrets of the World's Best-Selling Writer: The Storytelling Techniques of Erle Stanley Gardner. LC 80-82544. (Illus.). 352p. 1980. 12.95 (ISBN 0-688-03701-1). Morrow.

Fugate, Roberta B., jt. auth. see Fugate, Francis L.

Fugate, Stephen. Hard Summer. 224p. (Orig.). 1981. pap. 1.95 (ISBN 0-449-14389-9, GM). Fawcett.

Fugitt, Glen V., jt. auth. see Harley, Johansen.

Fuguitt, Glenn V., et al. Growth & Change in Rural America. LC 79-65329. (Management & Control of Growth Ser.). 101p. 1979. pap. text ed. 14.50 (ISBN 0-87420-586-7). Urban Land.

Fuhr, Sr. Mary T. Clinical Experience Record & Nursing Care Planning: A Guide for Student Nurses. 2nd ed. LC 77-22532. 1978. pap. text ed. 9.50 (ISBN 0-8016-1711-1). Mosby.

Fuhrmann. Salads. 1981. 8.95 (ISBN 0-8120-5398-2). Barron.

Fuhrmann, Barbara, jt. auth. see Curwin, Richard.

Fuhrmann, Brigita. Bobbin Lace. (Illus., Orig.). 1976. 15.95 o.p. (ISBN 0-8230-0520-8). Watson-Guptill.

--Bobbin Lace. (Illus.). 1979. pap. cancelled o.p. (ISBN 0-8230-0521-6). Watson-Guptill.

Fuhrmann, Paul A. Linear Systems & Operators in Hilbert Space. 336p. 1981. text ed. 44.95 (ISBN 0-07-022589-3). McGraw.

Fuhs, G. W. Nuclear Structures of Protocaryotic Organisms. (Protoplasmatologia: Vol. 5, Pt. 4). (Illus.). 1969. 54.30 o.p. (ISBN 0-387-80917-1). Springer-Verlag.

Fujii, Setsuro, et al, eds. Kinins IIB: Systemic Proteases & Cellular Function. LC 79-9079. (Advances in Experimental Medicine & Biology: Vol. 120B). 733p. 1979. 69.50 (ISBN 0-306-40197-5, Plenum Pr). Plenum Pub.

Fujii, Shinichi. Essentials of Japanese Constitutional Law. (Studies in Japanese Law & Government). 459p. 1979. Repr. of 1940 ed. 32.50 (ISBN 0-89093-214-X). U Pubns Amer.

--Tenno Seiji: Direct Imperial Rule. (Studies in Japanese History & Civilization). 415p. 1979. Repr. of 1944 ed. 30.00 (ISBN 0-89093-263-8). U Pubns Amer.

Fujikawa, Gyo. Come Out & Play. (Gyo Fujikawa Tiny Board Books). (Illus.). 14p. (ps-k). 1981. 1.95 (ISBN 0-448-15115-4). G&D.

--Fairyland. (Gyo Fujikawa Tiny Board Books). (Illus.). 14p. (ps-k). 1981. 1.95 (ISBN 0-448-15139-1). G&D.

--Faraway Friends. (Gyo Fujikawa Tiny Board Books). (Illus.). 14p. (ps-k). 1981. 1.95 (ISBN 0-448-15103-0). G&D.

--The Flyaway Kite. LC 80-3353. (Gyo Fujikawa Ser.). (Illus.). 32p. (gr. k-3). 1981. 3.95 (ISBN 0-448-11747-9); PLB 9.30 (ISBN 0-448-13652-X). G&D.

--Make-Believe. (Gyo Fujikawa Tiny Board Books). (Illus.). 14p. (ps-k). 1981. 1.95 (ISBN 0-448-15127-8). G&D.

--Mother Goose. (Gyo Fujikawa Tiny Board Books). (Illus.). 14p. (ps-k). 1981. 1.95 (ISBN 0-448-15091-3). G&D.

--My Animal Friend. (Gyo Fujikawa Tiny Board Books). (Illus.). 14p. (ps-k). 1981. 1.95 (ISBN 0-448-15079-4). G&D.

--Shags Has a Dream. LC 80-3352. (Gyo Fujikawa Ser.). (Illus.). (gr. k-3). 1981. 3.95 (ISBN 0-448-11749-5); PLB 9.30 (ISBN 0-448-13653-8). G&D.

Fujimura, Kobon. The Tokyo Puzzles. Gardner, Martin, ed. Adachi, Fumie, tr. (Illus.). 1978. 8.95 o.p. (ISBN 0-684-15536-2, ScribT). Scribner.

Fujimura, Thomas H., ed. see Wycherley, William.

Fujioka, Ryoichi. Shino & Oribe Ceramics. Morse, Samuel C., tr. from Jap. LC 76-9357. (Japanese Arts Library: Vol. 1). 1977. 16.95 (ISBN 0-87011-284-8). Kodansha.

Fujisawa, Chikao. Zen & Shinto: The Story of Japanese Philosophy. LC 78-139133. 92p. Repr. of 1959 ed. lib. bdg. 13.50x (ISBN 0-8371-5749-8, FUZS). Greenwood.

Fujita, H., tr. see Kurata, M.

Fujiwara no Nagako. The Emperor Horikawa Diary: Sanuki no Suke Nikki. Brewster, Jennifer, tr. from Japanese. LC 77-89194. 1978. text ed. 14.00x (ISBN 0-8248-0605-0). U Pr of Hawaii.

Fukuda, Tsuneari, ed. Future of Japan & the Korean Peninsula. Jahng, K., tr. from Japanese. LC 78-71337. (Illus.). 1979. 12.40 (ISBN 0-930878-14-0). Hollym Intl.

Fukushima, Sho & Russell, Wrio. Men's Gymnastics. (Illus.). 1980. 25.00 (ISBN 0-571-11478-4, Pub. by Faber & Faber). Merrimack Bk Serv.

Fukuzawa, Yukichi. Autobiography. Kiyooka, E., tr. LC 66-15468. (Illus.). 1966. 122.50 (ISBN 0-231-02884-9); pap. 10.00x (ISBN 0-231-08373-4). Columbia U Pr.

Fulbecke, William. A Booke of Christian Ethicks or Moral Philosophie. LC 74-28856. (English Experience Ser.: No. 737). 1975. Repr. of 1587 ed. 6.00 (ISBN 90-221-0737-X). Walter J Johnson.

--A Direction or Preparative to the Study of the Lawe: London, 1600. (Classics of English Legal History in the Modern Era Ser.: Vol. 3). 99p. 1980. lib. bdg. 60.50 (ISBN 0-8240-4602-1). Garland Pub.

--The Pandectes of the Law of Nations. LC 79-84109. (English Experience Ser.: No.928). 192p. 1979. Repr. of 1602 ed. lib. bdg. 18.00 (ISBN 90-221-0928-3). Walter J Johnson.

Fulbright, J. William. Arrogance of Power. 1967. pap. 1.95 o.p. (ISBN 0-394-70378-2, V378, Vin). Random.

--Old Myths & New Realities: And Other Commentaries. 1964. 8.95 o.p. (ISBN 0-394-43741-1). Random.

Fulcanelli. Fulcanelli: Master Alchemist, le Mystere Des Cathedrales. 2nd ed. Sworder, Mary, tr. (Illus.). 1977. Repr. of 1971 ed. 14.00 (ISBN 0-685-01095-3). Bro Life Bks.

Fulcher, Jane M., ed. Medical Librarian Examination Review Book, Vol. 1. 2nd ed. 1972. spiral bdg. 8.50 o.s.i. (ISBN 0-87488-495-0). Med Exam.

Fulcher Of Chartres. History of the Expedition to Jerusalem, 1095-1127. Fink, Harold S., ed. Ryan, Frances R., tr. from Lat. LC 78-77847. 1969. 18.50x (ISBN 0-87049-097-4). U of Tenn Pr.

Fulco, Armand J., jt. auth. see Mead, James F.

Fulda, Hans F., et al. Kritische Darstellung der Metaphysik. (Suhrkamp Taschenbuecher Wissenschaft: Vol. 315). 152p. (Orig.). 1980. pap. text ed. 5.85 (ISBN 3-518-07915-8, Pub. by Insel Verlag Germany). Suhrkamp.

Fulder, Stephen. Tao of Medicine. (Illus.). 1981. pap. 8.95. Inner Tradit.

Fuldheim, Dorothy. Three-&-a-Half Husbands. 1977. pap. 1.75 o.p. (ISBN 0-451-07793-8, E7793, Sig). NAL.

Fulenwider, Claire K. Feminism in American Politics: A Study of Ideological Influence. LC 79-25131. 182p. 1980. 20.95 (ISBN 0-03-053461-5). Praeger.

Fulford, Paula. Island Destiny. (Sihouette Ser.: No. 20). pap. 1.50 (ISBN 0-686-68328-5). PB.

--Island Destiny. 192p. (Orig.). 1980. pap. 1.50. S&S.

Fulker, Mary, jt. auth. see Fulker, Wilber H.

Fulker, Wilber H. & Fulker, Mary. Techniques with Tangibles: A Manual for Teaching the Blind. 84p. 1968. 9.50 (ISBN 0-398-00628-8). C C Thomas.

Fulkerson, Katherine. The Merchandise Buyers' Game. 1981. pap. text ed. 2.95 (ISBN 0-933836-13-9). Simtek.

Fulkerson, W. J. Hormonal Control of Lactation, Vol. 1. Horrobin, D. F., ed. (Annual Research Reviews). 1980. 18.00 (ISBN 0-88831-061-7). Eden Med Res.

Fulks, Bryan. Black Struggle: A History of the Negro in America. LC 77-107211. (Illus.). (gr. 7 up). 1970. Repr. of 1970 ed. 5.95 o.s.i. (ISBN 0-440-00678-3). Delacorte.

Fulks, Danny G. Informal Learning in Elementary Schools. LC 78-61303. 1978. pap. text ed. 7.50 (ISBN 0-8191-0606-2). U Pr of Amer.

Fulks, Watson. Advanced Calculus: An Introduction to Analysis. 3rd ed. LC 78-5268. 1978. text ed. 27.95 (ISBN 0-471-02195-4); solns. manual 3.00 (ISBN 0-471-05125-X). Wiley.

Fullam, Everett L. & Slosser, Bob. Living the Lords Prayer. 120p. 1980. pap. 4.95 (ISBN 0-912376-62-7). Chosen Bks Pub.

Fullard, Harold & Darby, H. C. Atlas general Larousse. Reynaud-Dulaurier, Georges, ed. (Illus.). 312p. (Fr.). 1973. 85.50 (ISBN 2-03-000922-9, 997). Larousse.

Fullard, Harold, ed. see Muir, Ramsey.

Fullenbach. European Environmental Policy East & West. 1981. text ed. price not set (ISBN 0-408-10689-1). Butterworth.

Fuller, A. T., ed. see Routh, E. J.

Fuller, Chet. I Hear Them Calling My Name: A Journey Through the New South. 320p. 1981. 12.95 (ISBN 0-395-30528-4). HM.

Fuller, Curtis. Proceedings of the First International UFO Congress. 1980. pap. 2.75 (ISBN 0-446-95159-5). Warner Bks.

Fuller, Daniel P. Gospel & Law: Contrast or Continuum? the Hermeneutics of Dispensationalism & Covenant Theology. (Orig.). 1980. pap. 10.95 (ISBN 0-8028-1808-0). Eerdmans.

Fuller, Dudley D. Theory & Practice of Lubrication for Engineers. LC 56-6483. 1956. 42.50 (ISBN 0-471-28710-5, Pub. by Wiley-Interscience). Wiley.

Fuller, E. G. & Hayward, E., eds. Photonuclear Reactions. (Benchmark Papers in Nuclear Physics: Vol. 2). 1976. 48.50x (ISBN 0-12-786495-4). Acad Pr.

Fuller, Edmund & Davis, O. B. Introduction to the Essay. (Introduction to Ser.). 1972. pap. 7.15x (ISBN 0-8104-5824-1). Hayden.

Fuller, Elizabeth. Poor Elizabeth's Almanac. 1980. pap. 2.25 (ISBN 0-425-04603-6). Berkley Pub.

Fuller, Emeline L. see Miller, Pierre.

Fuller, Frank. Deep Foundations. LC 80-69155. 540p. 1981. pap. text ed. 25.00 (ISBN 0-87262-256-8). Am Soc Civil Eng.

Fuller, George D. Projects in Biofeedback. (Orig.). 1980. pap. 9.95 (ISBN 0-686-27974-3). Biofeed Pr.

Fuller, George W., ed. A Bibliography of Bookplate Literature. LC 72-178635. 151p. 1971. Repr. of 1926 ed. 24.00 (ISBN 0-8103-3190-X). Gale.

Fuller, Harold Q., et al. Physics: Including Human Application. 1978. text ed. 20.50 scp (ISBN 0-06-042214-9, HarpC); scp lab manual 6.50 (ISBN 0-06-042212-2); scp study guide 6.50 (ISBN 0-06-042213-0). Har-Row.

Fuller, Harry J. & Ritchie, Donald D. General Botany. 5th ed. (Illus.). 1967. pap. 4.95 (ISBN 0-06-460033-5, CO 33, COS). Har-Row.

Fuller, Iola. Loon Feather. LC 40-27210. (gr. 10 up). 1940. 9.50 o.p. (ISBN 0-15-153201-X). HarBraceJ.

Fuller, Jack W. Continuing Education & the Community College. LC 78-10905. 1979. 14.95 (ISBN 0-88229-371-0). Nelson-Hall.

Fuller, Jack W. & Whealon, Terry O., eds. Career Education: A Lifelong Process. LC 78-1994. 1978. text ed. 19.95 (ISBN 0-88229-200-5). Nelson-Hall.

Fuller, Jan. Space: The Scrapbook of My Divorce. 176p. 1975. pap. 1.50 o.p. (ISBN 0-449-22450-3, Q2450-150, Crest). Fawcett.

Fuller, John. Chef's Manual of Kitchen Management. 1977. pap. 22.50 (ISBN 0-7134-0551-1, Pub. by Batsford England). David & Charles.

--Gueridon & Lamp Cookery. 2nd ed. 1975. 21.95 (ISBN 0-685-88360-4). Radio City.

Fuller, John, ed. see Pellaprat, H. P.

Fuller, John G. The Ghost of Flight 401. (YA) 1978. 2.25 (ISBN 0-425-03553-0, Dist. by Putnam). Berkley Pub.

--Incident at Exeter. 272p. Date not set. pap. 1.95 (ISBN 0-425-03929-3). Berkley Pub.

--The Interrupted Journey. 1980. pap. 2.50 (ISBN 0-686-62913-2). Berkley Pub.

--We Almost Lost Detroit. 1976. pap. 1.95 o.p. (ISBN 0-345-25266-7). Ballantine.

Fuller, John L. & Thompson, William R. Foundations of Behavior Genetics. LC 78-4199. (Illus.). 1978. text ed. 23.95 (ISBN 0-8016-1712-X). Mosby.

Fuller, Joseph V. Bismarck's Diplomacy at Its Zenith. 1922. 19.50 (ISBN 0-86527-011-2). Fertig.

Fuller, M. F. & Lury, D. A. Statistics Workbook for Social Science Students. 256p. 1977. 30.00x (ISBN 0-86003-016-4, Pub. by Allan Pubs England); pap. 15.00x (ISBN 0-86003-117-9). State Mutual Bk.

Fuller, M. M. & Martin, C. A. The Older Woman. 368p. 1980. pap. 16.75 (ISBN 0-398-03974-7). C C Thomas.

Fuller, Millard & Scott, Diane. Love in the Mortar Joints: The Story of Habitat for Humanity. 150p. 1980. pap. 4.95 (ISBN 0-695-81444-3, Assn Pr). Follett.

Fuller, Neil, ed. Rush. (Australian Theatre Workshop Ser.). 1975. pap. text ed. 5.95x (ISBN 0-686-65418-8, 00537). Heinemann Ed.

Fuller, Nelson & Miller, Rex. Experiments for Electricity & Electronics. 2nd ed. LC 78-7708. 1978. pap. 3.33 (ISBN 0-672-97260-3); tchr's guide 7.50 (ISBN 0-685-91575-1). Bobbs.

Fuller, Nicholas. The Argument of Master Nicholas Fuller, in the Case of Thomas Lad, & Richard Maunsell...Proved That the Ecclesiasticall Commissioners Have No Power...to Imprison...His Maiesties Subjects. LC 74-28857. (English Experience Ser.: No. 738). 1975. Repr. of 1607 ed. 3.50 (ISBN 90-221-0738-8). Walter J Johnson.

Fuller, Paul E. Laura Clay & the Woman's Rights Movement. LC 74-7875. (Illus.). 240p. 1975. 15.00x (ISBN 0-8131-1299-0). U Pr of Ky.

Fuller, Persis, jt. auth. see Miller, Amy B.

Fuller, R., ed. Microbial Ultrastructure. 1977. 47.00 (ISBN 0-12-269450-3). Acad Pr.

Fuller, R. Buckminster. And It Came to Pass - Not to Stay. 1976. 9.95 o.s.i. (ISBN 0-02-541810-6). Macmillan.

--Critical Path. 448p. 1981. 15.95 (ISBN 0-312-17488-8). St Martin.

--Earth, Inc. LC 73-75587. 192p. 1973. pap. 2.95 (ISBN 0-385-01825-8, Anch). Doubleday.

Fuller, R. Buckminster & Marks, Robert W. The Dymaxion World of Buckminster Fuller. LC 74-164727. 256p. 1973. pap. 5.95 (ISBN 0-385-01804-5, Anch). Doubleday.

Fuller, R. W., jt. auth. see Byron, F. W.

Fuller, Reginald H. Advent-Christmas. Achtemeier, Elizabeth, et al, eds. LC 79-7377. (Proclamation 2: Aids for Interpreting the Lessons of the Church Year, Ser. C). 64p. 1979. pap. 2.50 (ISBN 0-8006-4079-9, 1-4079). Fortress.

--The Formation of the Resurrection Narratives. LC 79-8885. 240p. 1980. pap. 5.95 (ISBN 0-8006-1378-3, 1-1378). Fortress.

--Foundations of New Testament Christology. 1965. lib. rep. ed. 17.50x (ISBN 0-684-15532-X, ScribT); pap. 3.95 o.p. (ISBN 0-684-15537-0, SL772, ScribT). Scribner.

--New Testament in Current Study. (Hudson River Editions). 1976. 12.50x (ISBN 0-684-14843-9, ScribT). Scribner.

--The Use of the Bible in Preaching. LC 80-2377. 80p. (Orig.). 1981. pap. 3.50 (ISBN 0-8006-1447-X, 1-1447). Fortress.

Fuller, Reginald H., jt. auth. see McFadden, William C.

Fuller, Richard R. Constipation Control: An Exercise Program to Achieve Regularity. 64p. 1981. 5.00 (ISBN 0-682-49690-1). Exposition.

Fuller, Ronald. Pilgrim: John Bunyan's Pilgrim's Progress Retold. LC 80-156. (Illus.). 48p. (gr. 5 up). 1980. 10.95 (ISBN 0-916144-44-5); pap. 5.95 (ISBN 0-916144-45-3). Stemmer Hse.

Fuller, Thomas. History of the Worthies of England, 3 vols. 66.50 o.p. (ISBN 0-686-12340-9). Church History.

Fuller, W. H. Small-Bore Target Shooting. rev. ed. Palmer, A. J., ed. 1978. 11.95 o.p. (ISBN 0-214-20334-4, 8031, Dist. by Arco). Barrie & Jenkins.

Fuller, W. Harold. Mission-Church Dynamics. LC 80-83659. (Orig.). 1980. pap. 8.95 (ISBN 0-87808-176-3). William Carey Lib.

Fuller, Wallace H. Dust of Old Adobe. 40p. 1980. 3.50 (ISBN 0-8059-2765-4). Dorrance.

Fuller, Wayne A. Introduction to Statistical Time Series. LC 76-6954. (Probability & Mathematical Statistics Ser.). 1976. 32.95 (ISBN 0-471-28715-6, Pub. by Wiley-Interscience). Wiley.

Fuller, Wayne F. The American Mail: Enlarger of the Common Life. LC 72-78254. (History of American Civilization Ser.). 390p. 1980. pap. 12.00x (ISBN 0-226-26885-3, Midway). U of Chicago Pr.

Fullerton, Georgiana. Ellen Middleton, a Tale, 1844. Wolff, Robert L., ed. LC 75-471. (Victorian Fiction Ser). 1975. lib. bdg. 66.00 (ISBN 0-8240-1549-5). Garland Pub.

--Grantley Manor: A Tale, 1847. Wolff, Robert L., ed. LC 75-451. (Victorian Fiction Ser.). 1975. lib. bdg. 66.00 (ISBN 0-8240-1531-2). Garland Pub.

--Mrs. Gerald's Niece: A Novel, 1869. (Victorian Fiction Ser.). 1975. lib. bdg. 66.00 (ISBN 0-8240-1534-7). Garland Pub.

Fullick, Roy, jt. auth. see Powell, Geoffery.

Fulling, Stephen, tr. see Bogolubov, Nikolai N., et al.

Fullinwider, Robert K. The Reverse Discrimination Controversy: A Moral & Legal Analysis. (Philosophy & Society Ser.). 300p. 1980. 22.50x (ISBN 0-8476-6273-X); pap. 9.95x (ISBN 0-8476-6901-7). Rowman.

Fullman, James B., jt. auth. see Shuldener, Henry L.

Fullmer, Daniel W. Counseling: Group Theory & System. 2nd ed. LC 78-9058. 1978. 27.00 (ISBN 0-910328-12-9); pap. 16.50 (ISBN 0-686-52428-4). Carroll Pr.

Fulmer, Robert M. Management & Organization. LC 78-15830. 1980. pap. 4.95 (ISBN 0-06-460176-5, CO 176, COS). Har-Row.

--Practical Human Relations. 1977. 16.95x (ISBN 0-256-01908-8). Irwin.

--Supervision: Principles of Management. 1976. text ed. 14.95x (ISBN 0-02-473070-X). Macmillan.

Fulmer, Robert M., jt. auth. see Koontz, Harold.

Fulmer, William E. Problems in Labor Relations: Text & Cases. 1980. 22.00x (ISBN 0-256-02366-2). Irwin.

Fulop. Alloantigen Systems of Human Leucocytes & Platelets. 1979. 32.00 (ISBN 0-9960015-2-2, Pub. by Kaido Hungary). Heyden.

Fulrath, Richard M., ed. Ceramic Microstructures 1976: With Emphasis on Energy Related Applications. Pask, Joseph A. LC 77-5232. 1977. lib. bdg. 75.00x (ISBN 0-89158-307-6). Westview.

Fulton, A. R. Motion Pictures: The Development of an Art. rev. ed. LC 79-6711. (Illus.). 443p. 1980. 14.95x (ISBN 0-8061-1633-1). U of Okla Pr.

Fulton, Albert R. Motion Pictures: The Development of an Art from Silent Films to the Age of Television. (Illus.). 1970. Repr. of 1960 ed. 14.95 (ISBN 0-8061-0467-8). U of Okla Pr.

Fulton, Elmer B. Maritime Poems of World War II. 1981. 5.75 (ISBN 0-8062-1665-4). Carlton.

Fulton, Gwen. Did You Ever? Traditional Verse. 24p. (gr. k up). 1981. 8.95 (ISBN 0-224-01740-3, Pub. by Chatto-Bodley-Jonathan). Merrimack Bk Serv.

Fulton, Janet. Raggedy Ann Book. (Illus.). (ps-1). 1969. PLB 5.38 (ISBN 0-307-68951-4, Golden Pr). Western Pub.

Fulton, John A. & Gordon, Steven M. Diving West. rev. ed. (Updated Every 2 to 4 Years Ser.). (Illus.). 96p. (Orig.). 1980. pap. 4.95 (ISBN 0-938206-01-X). ChartGuide.

Fulton, John F. Harvey Cushing: A Biography. Cohen, I. Bernard, ed. LC 79-7961. (Three Centuries of Science in America Ser.). (Illus.). 1980. Repr. of 1946 ed. lib. bdg. 62.00x (ISBN 0-405-12542-9). Arno.

Fulton, Len & Ferber, Ellen, eds. International Directory of Little Magazines & Small Presses. 16th ed. (Dustbooks Small Press Info. Library). 580p. 1980. 17.95 (ISBN 0-913218-94-4); pap. 13.95 (ISBN 0-913218-93-6). Dustbooks.

--Small Press Record of Books in Print. 9th ed. (Dustbooks Small Press Info. Library). 680p. 1980. 17.95 (ISBN 0-913218-95-2). Dustbooks.

Fulton, Martin W. A Chronology of Substances of Abuse. LC 78-62253. 1978. pap. text ed. 8.50 (ISBN 0-8191-0566-X). U Pr of Amer.

Fulton, Mary. Raggedy Ann & Andy Go Flying. Hunt, Judith, tr. 24p. (ps). 1.50 (ISBN 0-307-11986-6); PLB 6.08 (ISBN 0-307-61986-9). Western Pub.

Fulton, Mary J. Detective Arthur, Master Sleuth. 1974. PLB 9.15 o.p. (ISBN 0-307-65790-6, Golden Pr). Western Pub.

--Detective Arthur on the Scent. (Scratch & Sniff Ser.). (Illus.). (ps-3). 1971. 4.95 o.p. (ISBN 0-307-13535-7, Golden Pr); PLB 9.92 (ISBN 0-307-64535-5). Western Pub.

Fulton, Maurice G. Charles Lamb in Essays & Letters. 349p. 1980. Repr. of 1930 ed. lib. bdg. 30.00 (ISBN 0-89984-203-8). Century Bookbindery.

Fulton, Renee J; see Bottiglia, William F.

Fulton, Richard M., ed. The Revolution That Wasn't: A Contemporary Assessment of 1776. (National University Publication, American Studies). 1981. 19.50 (ISBN 0-8046-9259-9). Kennikat.

Fulton, Robert, ed. Death & Dying: Challenge & Change. (Illus.). 1978. lib. bdg. 12.00 o.p. (ISBN 0-201-07724-8); pap. 5.95 o.p. (ISBN 0-201-07723-X); pap. text ed. 9.95 o.p. (ISBN 0-201-07722-1); tchr's ed. 1.95 o.p. (ISBN 0-201-07727-2). A-W.

Fulton, Robin, jt. auth. see Reynolds, E. G.

Fulton, Robin, tr. see Barkan, Stanley H.

Fulton, Robin, tr. see Harding, Gunnar & Barkan, Stanley H.

Fulton, Robin, tr. see Transtromer, Tomas.

Fulves, Karl. The Children's Magic Kit: Sixteen Easy-to-Do Tricks Complete with Cardboard Cutouts. (Illus.). 32p. (Orig.). (gr. 3-6). Date not set. pap. price not set (ISBN 0-486-24019-3). Dover. Postponed.

--Self-Working Card Tricks: Seventy-Two Foolproof Card Miracles for the Amateur Magician. (Illus.). 113p. (Orig.). 1976. pap. 2.00 (ISBN 0-486-23334-0). Dover.

--Self-Working Table Magic: Ninety-Seven Foolproof Tricks with Everyday Objects. (Illus.). 128p. (Orig.). 1981. pap. price not set (ISBN 0-486-24116-5). Dover.

Fulwiler, Kyle D. The Berry Cookbook. 120p. 1981. pap. 5.95 (ISBN 0-914718-59-2). Pacific Search.

Funai, M., jt. auth. see Polhamus, J.

Funai, Mamoru. Cartoons for Kids. LC 76-44273. (Illus.). (gr. 1-4). 1977. 7.95 (ISBN 0-13-115154-1); pap. 1.95 (ISBN 0-13-115147-9). P-H.

Funakoshi, Gichin. Karate-Do-Kyohan: The Master Text. Oshima, Tsutomu, tr. from Japanese. LC 72-90228. (Illus.). 370p. 1973. 22.50 (ISBN 0-87011-190-6). Kodansha.

Funatsu, M., et al. Proteins: Structure & Function, 2 bks. 1972. Vol. 1. 27.95 (ISBN 0-470-28770-5); Vol. 2. o.p. (ISBN 0-470-28771-3). Halsted Pr.

Funck, R. Recent Developments in Regional Science. (Karlsruhe Papers in Regional Science). 153p. 1980. pap. text ed. 10.00x (ISBN 0-85086-034-2, Pub. by Pion). Methuen Inc.

Funck-Brentano, Frantz. The Old Regime in France. LC 68-9656. 1970. Repr. 17.50 (ISBN 0-86527-141-0). Fertig.

Funcken, Fred, jt. auth. see Funcken, Liliane.

Funcken, Liliane & Funcken, Fred. Ancient Egypt to the Eighteenth Century. (Arms & Uniforms: Vol. 1). (Illus.). 155p. (gr. 6-10). 1972. 11.95x (ISBN 0-7063-1814-5). Intl Pubns Serv.

Fundaburk, Emma L. Reference Materials & Periodicals in Economics: An International List, Agriculture. LC 78-142232. 1971. 21.00 (ISBN 0-8108-0349-6). Scarecrow.

--Reference Materials & Periodicals in Economics: An International List, Major Manufacturing Industries - Automotive, Chemical, Iron & Steel, Petrole. LC 78-142232. 1972. 23.50 (ISBN 0-8108-0453-0). Scarecrow.

Fundaburk, Emma L. & Davenport, Thomas. Art at Educational Institutions in the United States: A Handbook of Permanent, Semi-Permanent & Temporary Works of Art at Elementary & Secondary Schools, Colleges & Universities. LC 74-3187. (Illus.). 1974. 45.00 (ISBN 0-8108-0715-7). Scarecrow.

Funes, Marilyn & Lazarus, Alan. Popular Careers. Piltch, Benjamin, ed. 64p. (gr. 5-12). 1980. wkbk 3.50 (ISBN 0-934618-01-1). Skyview Pub.

Fung, Kwok, jt. auth. see Ahmad, S. I.

Fung, Y., jt. ed. see Greenwood, Donald T.

Fung, Y. C. Biomechanics: Mechanical Properties of Living Tissues. (Illus.). 400p. 1980. 29.80 (ISBN 0-387-90472-7). Springer-Verlag.

--Foundations of Solid Mechanics. 1965. ref. ed. 26.95 (ISBN 0-13-329912-0). P-H.

Fung, Y. C., jt. ed. see Sechler, E. E.

Fung, Yu-Lan. Short History of Chinese Philosophy. abr. ed. Bedde, Derk, ed. Orig. Title: History of Chinese Philosophy. 1966. pap. text ed. 5.95 (ISBN 0-02-910980-9). Free Pr.

Fung, Yuan-Cheng. A First Course in Continuum Mechanics. 2nd ed. (International Series in Dynamics). (Illus.). 1977. 26.95 (ISBN 0-13-318311-4). P-H.

Funigiello, Philip J. The Challenge to Urban Liberalism: Federal-City Relations During World War II. LC 78-2670. (Twentieth-Century America Ser). 1978. 14.50x (ISBN 0-87049-228-4). U of Tenn Pr.

Funk. Business Mathematics. 416p. 1980. pap. text ed. 15.95 (ISBN 0-205-06849-9, 1068490). Allyn.

Funk And Wagnalls Editors. Funk & Wagnalls Standard College Dictionary. new updated ed. LC 72-13007. (Funk & W Bk.). 1632p. 1977. 9.95 o.s.i. (ISBN 0-308-10309-2, TYC-T); thumb indexed 10.95 o.s.i. (ISBN 0-308-10310-6). T Y Crowell.

Funk, Berverley M., jt. auth. see Schatz, Anne E.

Funk, Beverley M., jt. auth. see Schatz, Anne E.

Funk, Charles E. Heavens to Betsy & Other Curious Sayings. LC 55-8053. (Illus.). 1955. 10.95 o.p. (ISBN 0-06-001740-6, HarpT). Har-Row.

Funk, Charles E. & Funk, Charles E., Jr. Horsefeathers & Other Curious Words. LC 58-8870. (Illus.). 1958. 10.95 o.p. (ISBN 0-06-001830-5, HarpT). Har-Row.

Funk, David A. Group Dynamic Law. LC 80-84733. 1981. 29.50 (ISBN 0-686-68867-8). Philos Lib.

Funk, Georg. Die Algenvegetation Des Golfes Von Neapel. (Pubbl. d. Stazione Zool. di Napoli). (Illus., Ger.). Repr. of 1927 ed. lib. bdg. 95.40 (ISBN 3-87429-142-1). Lubrecht & Cramer.

--Beitraege zur Kenntnis der Meeresalgen von Neapel, zugleich mikrophotographischer Atlas. (Pubbl. d. Stazione Zool. di Napoli). (Illus., Ger.). 1978. Repr. of 1935 ed. lib. bdg. 48.60 (ISBN 3-87429-146-4). Lubrecht & Cramer.

Funk, Jerry. Sportset: A Math Practice Set. 100p. pap. text ed. 5.95 (ISBN 0-686-69610-7); free. Allyn.

Funk, Merle M. Wes Weatherby, Gunfighter. (YA) 1979. 5.95 (ISBN 0-685-93883-2, Avalon). Bouregy.

Funk, Peter, jt. auth. see Gordon, Ernest.

Funk, Robert W. A Beginning-Intermediate Grammar of Hellenistic Greek, 3 vols. 2nd, rev. ed. Incl. Vol. 1. Morphology; Vol. 2. Syntax; Vol. 3. Appendices. LC 72-88769. (Society of Biblical Literature. Sources for Biblical Studies). (Orig.). 1977. Set. pap. text ed. 18.00 (ISBN 0-89130-148-8). Scholars Pr Ca.

--Language Hermeneutic, & Word of God. LC 66-20776. (Scholars Press Reprint Ser.: No. 1). 1966. pap. 9.00 (ISBN 0-89130-225-5, 000701). Scholars Pr Ca.

Funk, Robert W., ed. see Bultmann, Rudolf.

Funk, Wilfred. Word Origins & Their Romantic Stories. LC 50-42316. (Funk & W Bk.). (gr. 9-12). 1950. text ed. 6.95 o.s.i. (ISBN 0-308-40069-0, TYC-T); pap. 4.75 o.s.i. (ISBN 0-308-90048-0, F39, TYC-T). T Y Crowell.

Funk, Wilfred & Lewis, Norman. Thirty Days to a More Powerful Vocabulary. LC 72-94340. (Funk & W Bk.). (gr. 9-12). 1970. text ed. 8.95 (ISBN 0-308-40079-8, 430180, TYC-T). T Y Crowell.

Funnell, B. M. & Riedel, W. R. Micropalaeontology of Oceans. 1971. 145.00 (ISBN 0-521-07642-0). Cambridge U Pr.

Funnell, Bertha. Walt Whitman on Long Island. LC 78-134275. (Empire State Historical Publications Ser). 1971. 8.50 (ISBN 0-8046-8091-4). Friedman.

Funt, Marilyn. Are You Anybody? 352p. 1981. pap. 2.75 (ISBN 0-523-41413-7). Pinnacle Bks.

Fuori, William M. Introduction to the Computer: The Tool of Business. 2nd ed. (Illus.). 1977. text ed. 18.95 (ISBN 0-13-480103-2). P-H.

--Introduction to the Computer: The Tool of Business. 3rd ed. (Illus.). 720p. 1981. text ed. 17.95 (ISBN 0-13-480343-4); pap. 5.95 study guide (ISBN 0-13-480368-X). P-H.

Fuoss, D. E. & Troppman, R. J. Creative Management Techniques in Interscholastic Athletics. LC 76-46500. 1977. 19.95 (ISBN 0-471-28815-2). Wiley.

Fuoss, Donald E. & Smith, Rowland. Effective Football Coaching. 264p. 1980. text ed. 14.95 (ISBN 0-205-07125-2). Allyn.

Fu Pei Mei. Chinese Cookbook. (Eng. & Chinese.). 1969. deluxe ed. 17.50 (ISBN 0-911268-14-6). Rogers Bk.

--Chinese Cookbook, Vol. 2. 1974. 17.50 (ISBN 0-911268-18-9). Rogers Bk.

Fuquay, jt. auth. see Maddox.

Fuquay, John W. & Bearden, H. Joe. Applied Animal Reproduction. (Illus.). 352p. 1980. text ed. 16.95 (ISBN 0-8359-0249-8); instr's. manual free. Reston.

Furbank, P. N. Italo Svevo: The Man & the Writer. 1966. 16.50x (ISBN 0-520-00436-1). U of Cal Pr.

Furbank, P. N., tr. see Svevo, Italo.

Furbee, Louanna, ed. Mayan Texts III. LC 76-15159. (International Journal of American Linguistics Native American Texts Ser.: No. 5). 122p. (Orig.). 1980. pap. 10.75 (ISBN 0-8357-0567-6, IS-00115, Pub. by U of Chicago Pr). Univ Microfilms.

Furbee-Losee, Louanna. The Correct Language, Tojolabal: A Grammar with Ethnographic Notes. LC 75-25115. (American Indian Linguistics Ser.). 1976. lib. bdg. 42.00 (ISBN 0-8240-1966-0). Garland Pub.

Furchgott, Terry & Dawson, Linda. Phoebe & the Hot Water Bottles. LC 78-74756. (Illus.). (gr. k-3). 1979. 7.95 (ISBN 0-233-96860-1). Andre Deutsch.

Furfey, Paul H. Love & the Urban Ghetto. LC 77-16700. 1978. pap. 3.95x o.p. (ISBN 0-88344-292-2). Orbis Bks.

Furia, Thomas E., ed. & tr. Fenaroli's Handbook of Flavor Ingredients, 2 vols. 2nd ed. LC 72-152143. (Handbk. Ser). 1975. Vol. 1, 560p. 59.95 (ISBN 0-87819-534-3); Vol. 2, 944p. 69.95 (ISBN 0-87819-532-7). CRC Pr.

Furia, Thomas E., ed. Handbook of Food Additives, Vol. 2. 2nd ed. (Handbook Ser.). 1980. 59.95 (ISBN 0-8493-0543-8). CRC Pr.

Furio Ceriol, Fadrique. Of Councils & Counselors, 1570: An English Reworking by Thomas Blundeville of el Consejo I Consejeros Del Principe, 1559. LC 63-7083. 1963. 20.00x (ISBN 0-8201-1018-3). Schol Facsimiles.

Furley, David J. & Allen, R. E., eds. Studies in Pre-Socratic Philosophy, Vol. 1. (International Library of Philogophy & Scientific Method). 1970. text ed. 24.75x (ISBN 0-391-00077-2). Humanities.

Furlong, Charles W. Let'er Buck: A Story of the Passing of the Old West. LC 77-159961. 280p. 1971. Repr. of 1921 ed. 18.00 (ISBN 0-8103-3405-4). Gale.

Furlong, William B., jt. auth. see Diamond, Seymour.

Furlonge, Geoffrey. Lands of Barbary. (Illus.). 1968. 9.95 (ISBN 0-7195-0470-8). Transatlantic.

Furlow, Bill, ed. Circuit Design Idea Handbook. LC 73-76440. 1972. 21.50 (ISBN 0-8436-0205-8). CBI Pub.

Furlow, Elaine. Love with No Strings: The Human Touch in Christian Social Ministries. Hullum, Everett, ed. (The Human Touch Photo-Text Ser.: Volume Iv). (Illus.). 1977. 6.95 (ISBN 0-937170-15-1). Home Mission.

Furlow, Elaine S., jt. auth. see Rutledge, Don.

Furlow, Elaine S., ed. see Knight, Walker & Wall, Steve.

Furlow, Elaine S., ed. see Loucks, Celeste, et al.

Furlow, Elaine S., ed. see Loucks, Celeste & Hullum, Everett.

Furlow, Elaine S., ed. see Nicholas, Tim & Touchton, Ken.

Furman, A. L., ed. More Horse Stories. (gr. 5-7). 1979. pap. 1.75 (ISBN 0-671-56009-3). Archway.

Furman, Abraham L., ed. Everygirls Companion. LC 68-11184. (Everygirls Library). (gr. 5-9). 1968. 4.25 o.p. (ISBN 0-8313-0051-5); PLB 6.19 (ISBN 0-685-13773-2). Lantern.

--Everygirls Mystery Stories. (Illus.). (gr. 6-10). PLB 6.19 o.p. (ISBN 0-8313-0061-2). Lantern.

--Teen-Age Party Time Stories. (gr. 6-10). 1966. PLB 6.19 (ISBN 0-8313-0039-6). Lantern.

Furman, Erna. A Child's Parent Dies: Studies in Childhood Bereavement. LC 73-86894. 1974. 25.00x (ISBN 0-300-01719-7). Yale U Pr.

--A Child's Parent Dies: Studies in Childhood Bereavement. LC 73-86894. 352p. 1981. pap. 7.95x (ISBN 0-300-02645-5). Yale U Pr.

Furman, Laura. The Glass House. 204p. 1980. 10.95 (ISBN 0-670-34179-7). Viking Pr.

Furman, Victoria. Five in a Tent. LC 66-1334. (gr. 3-7). 1966. 5.95 o.s.i. (ISBN 0-8193-0133-7, Four Winds); PLB 5.41 o.s.i. (ISBN 0-8193-0134-5). Schol Bk Serv.

Furneaux, Barbara, jt. ed. see Roberts, Brian.

Furneaux, Rupert. The Battle of Saratoga. LC 69-17940. 320p. 1981. pap. 7.95 (ISBN 0-8128-6125-6). Stein & Day.

Furneaux Jordan, Robert. Concise History of Western Architecture. LC 79-99555. 1970. 9.95 o.p. (ISBN 0-15-121275-9). HarBraceJ.

Furnell, Dennis L. The Country Book of the Year. LC 79-56061. (Illus.). 192p. 1980. 22.50 (ISBN 0-7153-7878-3). David & Charles.

Furner, Mary O. Advocacy & Objectivity: A Crisis in the Professionalization of American Social Science, 1865-1905. LC 73-86403. 376p. 1975. 19.50x (ISBN 0-8131-1309-1). U Pr of Ky.

Furness, E. L. Introduction to Financial Economics. 1972. pap. 13.95x (ISBN 0-434-90596-8). Intl Ideas.

Furnham, A. & Argyle, M., eds. The Psychology of Social Situations: Selected Readings. 350p. 1981. 40.00 (ISBN 0-08-024319-3); pap. 15.70 (ISBN 0-08-023719-3). Pergamon.

Furnish, Dorothy J. Living the Bible with Children. LC 79-12297. 1979. pap. 4.95 (ISBN 0-687-22368-7). Abingdon.

Furnish, Victor P. Theology & Ethics in Paul. LC 68-17445. 1978. pap. 8.95 (ISBN 0-687-41499-7). Abingdon.

Furnish, Victor P. & Thulin, Richard L. Pentecost 3. Achtemeier, Elizabeth, et al, eds. LC 79-7377. (Proclamation 2: Aids for Interpreting the Lessons of the Church Year, Ser. A). 64p. (Orig.). 1981. pap. 2.50 (ISBN 0-8006-4098-5, 1-4098). Fortress.

Furnish, Victor P., jt. auth. see Snow, John H.

Furniss, Norman & Tilton, Timothy. Case for the Welfare State: From Social Security to Social Equality. LC 76-26414. 256p. 1977. 14.00x (ISBN 0-253-31322-8); pap. 5.95x (ISBN 0-253-20230-2). Ind U Pr.

Furniss, Tim. Man in Space. (Today's World Ser.). (Illus.). 72p. (gr. 7-9). 1981. 15.95 (ISBN 0-7134-3582-8, Pub. by Batsford England). David & Charles.

Furnival, Frederick J., ed. Early English Meals & Manners. LC 73-81154. 1969. Repr. of 1868 ed. 32.00 (ISBN 0-8103-3853-X). Gale.

Furrer, Dieter. Modusprobleme bei Notker: Die modalen Werte in den Nebensaetzen der Consolatio-Uebersetzung. 201p. 1971. 34.75x (ISBN 3-11-001808-X). De Gruyter.

Furriack, William de see Reppy, William A. & De Funiack, William Q.

Furrow, Barry R. Malpractice in Psychotherapy. LC 79-3253. 192p. 1980. 18.95x (ISBN 0-669-03399-5). Lexington Bks.

Furse, Chris. Elephant Island: An Antarctic Expedition. (Illus.). 1979. 27.50 (ISBN 0-904614-02-6, Pub. by Anthony Nelson Ltd, England). Buteo.

Furst, Arnold. Post Hypnotic Instructions. pap. 3.00 (ISBN 0-87980-119-0). Wilshire.

Furst, Arthur. Chemistry of Chelation in Cancer. 160p. 1963. pap. 14.75 photocopy ed. spiral (ISBN 0-398-00633-4). C C Thomas.

Furst, Bruno. Stop Forgetting. Furst, Lotte & Storm, Gerrit, eds. LC 79-7401. (Illus.). 1979. pap. 6.95 (ISBN 0-385-15401-1). Doubleday.

Furst, Jeffrey, ed. Edgar Cayce's Story of Jesus. 1970. pap. 1.95 o.p. (ISBN 0-425-03225-6, Medallion). Berkley Pub.

Furst, Lilian R. Romanticism in Perspective. 2nd ed. 1979. text ed. 13.00x (ISBN 0-391-00003-9). Humanities.

Furst, Lotte, ed. see Furst, Bruno.

Furst, Merrick L., jt. auth. see Morse, Donald R.

Furst, Susanna & Knoll, J., eds. Opiate Receptors & the Neurochemical Correlates of Pain: Proceedings of the Third Congress of the Hungarian Pharmacological Society, Budapest, 1979. LC 80-41281. (Advances in Pharmacological Research & Practice Ser.: Vol. V). 240p. 1981. 45.00 (ISBN 0-08-026390-9). Pergamon.

Furstenberg, Frank, et al, eds. Teenage Sexuality, Pregnancy & Childbearing. 1980. 22.95x; pap. 10.50x. U of Pa Pr.

Furstenberg, Frank F., Jr. Unplanned Parenthood: The Social Consequences of Teenage Childbearing. LC 76-8144. 1976. 15.95 (ISBN 0-02-911010-6). Free Pr.

--Unplanned Parenthood: The Social Consequences of Teenage Childbearing. LC 76-8144. 1979. pap. text ed. 7.95 (ISBN 0-02-911030-0). Free Pr.

Furstenberg, Friedrich. Why the Japanese Have Been So Successful in Business. LC 73-77702. 110p. 1974. 15.00 (ISBN 0-900537-11-6). Hippocrene Bks.

Furstenberg, H. Recurrence in Ergodic Theory & Combinatorial Number Theory. LC 80-7518. (Rice University, Dept. of Mathematics, M. B. Porter Lectures). 228p. 1981. 19.50 (ISBN 0-691-08269-3). Princeton U Pr.

Furstenberg, Ira Von see Von Furstenberg, Ira.

Furtado, C. Economic Development of Latin America. 2nd ed. LC 74-121365. (Latin American Studies: No.8). (Illus.). 280p. 1977. 37.50 (ISBN 0-521-21197-2); pap. 9.95x (ISBN 0-521-29070-8). Cambridge U Pr.

Furtado, Celso. Diagnosis of the Brazilian Crisis. Macedo, Suzette, tr. 1965. 16.50x (ISBN 0-520-00444-2). U of Cal Pr.

Furtado, R. D. The Oleanders. (Redbird Bk.). 1976. lib. bdg. 8.00 (ISBN 0-89253-094-4); flexible bdg. 4.00 (ISBN 0-89253-131-2). Ind-US Inc.

Furter, Pierre. Possibilities & Limitations of Functional Literacy: The Iranian Experiment. LC 73-781021. (Educational Studies & Documents, No. 9). (Illus.). 59p. (Orig.). 1973. pap. 2.50 (ISBN 92-3-101075-1, U472, UNESCO). Unipub.

Furth, Hans G. Deafness & Learning: A Psycho-Social Approach. 140p. 1973. pap. 7.95x (ISBN 0-534-00231-5). Wadsworth Pub.

--Piaget & Knowledge: Theoretical Foundations. LC 80-26284. (Illus., Orig.). 1981. pap. price not set (ISBN 0-226-27420-9). U of Chicago Pr.

--Piaget for Teachers. (Illus.). 1970. 10.95 o.p. (ISBN 0-13-674945-3); pap. text ed. 13.95 (ISBN 0-13-674937-2). P-H.

--Thinking Without Language. LC 66-10958. 1966. 15.95 (ISBN 0-02-911000-9). Free Pr.

Furth, John L., jt. auth. see Knowlton, Winthrop.

Furth, Montgomery, ed. & tr. see Frege, Gottlob.

Furubotn, Eirik G. & Pejovich, Svetozar. The Economics of Property Rights. LC 73-14644. 1975. 25.00 (ISBN 0-88410-251-3); pap. 12.50 (ISBN 0-88410-278-5). Ballinger Pub.

Fusaro, A. Daniel, ed. Rules of the U.S. Courts in New York. rev. ed. LC 78-83771. 1978. with 1979 rev. pages 35.00 (ISBN 0-87632-070-1). Boardman.

Fusayama, Takao. Two Layers of Carious Dentin & New Conservative Restoration. 190p. 1981. 42.00. Quint Pub Co.

Fuscaldo, Anthony A., et al, eds. Laboratory Safety: Theory & Practice. LC 80-762. 1980. 39.50 (ISBN 0-12-269980-7). Acad Pr.

Fusch, Otto. Building Cost Composites. 208p. (Orig.). 1981. pap. 14.25 (ISBN 0-910460-79-5). Craftsman.

Fusco, Luigi. The Piazza of the Decameron. Fusco, Marion & Fusco, Luigi, trs. from It. LC 76-56615. 1977. 8.95 o.p. (ISBN 0-8076-0862-9). Braziller.

Fusco, Luigi, tr. see Fusco, Luigi.

Fusco, Marina, jt. auth. see Fusco, Patricia S.

Fusco, Marion, tr. see Fusco, Luigi.

Fusco, P., jt. auth. see Horwitz, G.

Fusco, Patricia S. & Fusco, Marina. Marina & Ruby. (Illus.). 1977. 17.50 o.p. (ISBN 0-688-03229-X). Morrow.

Fusco, Peter, et al. The Romantics to Rodin: French Nineteenth-Century Sculpture from North American Collections. LC 79-27101. (Illus.). 1980. pap. 11.95 (ISBN 0-87587-091-0). LA Co Art Mus.

Fusco, Sylvia. Tamara. 1979. 4.75 o.p. (ISBN 0-8062-1225-X). Carlton.

Fuseli, Henry. The Lectures of Henry Fuseli- in "Lectures on Paintings by the Royal Academicians". Freedberg, Sydney J., ed. LC 77-19376. (Connoisseurship Criticism & Art History Ser.: Vol. 10). 450p. 1979. lib. bdg. 40.00 (ISBN 0-8240-3268-3). Garland Pub.

Fusfeld, Daniel R. The Age of the Economist. 3rd ed. 1977. pap. 7.95x (ISBN 0-673-15071-2). Scott F.

--Economics. 2nd ed. 928p. 1976. 19.95x (ISBN 0-669-90571-2); instructor's manual free (ISBN 0-669-90589-5); study guide 7.95x (ISBN 0-669-90597-6); transparency masters 15.00 (ISBN 0-669-00244-5); test item file to adopters free (ISBN 0-669-00081-7). Heath.

Fuson, Henry H. Ballads of the Kentucky Highlands. 219p. 1980. Repr. of 1931 ed. text ed. 25.00 (ISBN 0-8492-4706-3). R West.

Fuss, Peter, jt. ed. see Wheelwright, Philip.

Fuss, Werner. Die Deuteronomistische Pentateuchredaktion in Exodus 3-17. (Beiheft 126 zur Zeitschrift fuer die alttestamentliche Wissenschaft). xii, 406p. 1972. 60.60x (ISBN 3-11-003854-4). De Gruyter.

Fussell, Paul, Jr. Poetic Meter & Poetic Form. LC 78-14548. 1978. pap. text ed. 4.50 (ISBN 0-394-32120-0). Random.

--Theory of Prosody in Eighteenth Century England. 1966. Repr. of 1954 ed. 12.50 o.p. (ISBN 0-208-00581-1, Archon). Shoe String.

Fussey, Joyce. Milk My Ewes & Weep. (YA) 1977. 9.95 (ISBN 0-236-40031-2, Pub. by Paul Elek). Merrimack Bk Serv.

Fussler, Herman H. Research Libraries & Technology. 1974. 10.00x (ISBN 0-226-27558-2). U of Chicago Pr.

Fussler, Herman H. & Jenck, John E., eds. Management Education: Implications for Libraries & Library Schools. LC 73-92600. vi, 116p. 1974. 10.00x (ISBN 0-226-27560-4). U of Chicago Pr.

Fuster, Joaquin M. The Prefrontal Cortex. 232p. 1980. text ed. 22.00 (ISBN 0-89004-524-0). Raven.

Futrell, Charles M. Cases in Sales Management. LC 80-65797. 320p. 1981. pap. text ed. 10.95 (ISBN 0-03-054736-9). Dryden Pr.

--Sales Management. LC 80-65796. 528p. 1981. text ed. 17.95 (ISBN 0-03-049276-9). Dryden Pr.

Futrelle, Jacques. Elusive Isabel. 1976. lib. bdg. 14.95x (ISBN 0-89968-164-6). Lighthouse Pr NY.

Futuyma, Douglas J. Evolutionary Biology. LC 78-27902. (Illus.). 1979. text ed. 19.50x (ISBN 0-87893-199-6). Sinauer Assoc.

Fuxe, K., ed. Dopaminergic Ergot Derivatives & Motor Function: Proceedings of an International Symposium, Stockholm, 1978. (Wenner-Gren Center International Symposium Series: Vol. 31). (Illus.). 1979. 75.00 (ISBN 0-08-024408-4). Pergamon.

Fuxe, K., et al, eds. Dynamics of Degeneration & Growth in Neurons. 1974. text ed. 115.00 (ISBN 0-08-017917-7). Pergamon.

Fuxe, Kjell, et al, eds. Central Adrenaline Neurons: Basic Aspects & Their Role in Cardiovascular Disease: Proceedings of an International Symposium 27-28 August 1979, Wenner-Gren Center, Stockholm. (Wenner-Gren Ser.: Vol. 33). (Illus.). 356p. 1980. 53.00 (ISBN 0-08-025927-8). Pergamon.

Fuze, M. M. The Black People & Whence They Came: A Zulu View. Cope, A. T., ed. Lugg, H. C., tr. from Zulu. (Killie Campbell Africana Library Translation Ser.: No. 1). 206p. 1979. text ed. 21.00 (ISBN 0-86980-167-8). Verry.

Fyfe, C., ed. see Blyden, Edward.

Fyfe, Christopher. Short History of Sierra Leone. (Illus., Orig.). 1962. pap. text ed. 3.25x (ISBN 0-582-60251-3). Humanities.

--A Short History of Sierra Leone. new ed. (Illus.). 1979. pap. text ed. 5.50 (ISBN 0-582-60358-7). Longman.

Fyfe, Christopher, ed. African Studies Since 1945: A Tribute to Basil Davidson. 1976. text ed. 15.00x o.p. (ISBN 0-8419-6700-8). Holmes & Meier.

Fyfe, Thomas A. Who's Who in Dickens. LC 73-142011. 1971. Repr. of 1912 ed. 24.00 (ISBN 0-8103-3630-8). Gale.

--Who's Who in Dickens. 352p. Repr. of 1913 ed. lib. bdg. 30.00 (ISBN 0-8495-1713-3). Arden Lib.

Fyfe, W. Hamilton, ed. see Aristotle.

Fyfe, W. S., ed. see Royal Society of London, et al.

Fyffe, David E., jt. auth. see Clifton, David S., Jr.

Fyle, Clifford M., jt. auth. see Prakash, Om.

Fynn. Mister God, This Is Anna. 192p. 1976. pap. 2.25 (ISBN 0-345-28910-2). Ballantine.

Fynn, G. W. & Powell, W. J. The Cutting & Polishing of Electro-Optic Materials. LC 78-21139. 1979. 74.95 (ISBN 0-470-26607-4). Halsted Pr.

Fyson, Anthony, jt. auth. see Ward, Colin.

Fyson, Nance L. Growing up in Edwardian Britain. LC 79-56456. (Growing up Ser.). (Illus.). 72p. (gr. 7-9). 1980. text ed. 14.95 (ISBN 0-7134-3372-8, Pub. by Batsford England). David & Charles.

--Growing up in the Eighteenth Century. (Growing up Ser.). 1977. 14.95 (ISBN 0-7134-0481-7, Pub. by Batsford England). David & Charles.

--Growing up in the Second World War. (Growing up Ser.). (Illus.). 72p. (gr. 6 up). 1981. 14.95 (ISBN 0-7134-3574-7, Pub. by Batsford England). David & Charles.

Fyvel, T. R., ed. Frontiers of Sociology. 1965. text ed. 4.25x (ISBN 0-7100-1436-8); pap. text ed. 2.50x (ISBN 0-7100-6093-9). Humanities.

G

G-Jo Institute. Arthritis Self-Help Program. 1980. pap. 4.50 (ISBN 0-916878-10-4). Falkynor Bks.

--Permanent Weight Loss Program. 1980. pap. 4.50 (ISBN 0-916878-11-2). Falkynor Bks.

--Sexual Pleasure Enhancement Program. 1980. pap. 4.50 (ISBN 0-916878-12-0). Falkynor Bks.

--Stop Smoking Soon. 1980. pap. 4.50 (ISBN 0-916878-09-0). Falkynor Bks.

Gaal, O., et al. Electrophoresis in the Separation of Biological Macromolecules. LC 77-28502. 1980. 72.75 (ISBN 0-471-99602-5, Pub. by Wiley-Interscience). Wiley.

Gaarder, A. Bruce see Bishop, G. Reginald, Jr.

Gabaldon, Jacqueline, jt. auth. see Fedder, Ruth.

Gabarro, J., jt. auth. see Athos, A.

Gabasov, R. & Kirillova, F. M., eds. Optimal Linear Systems: Methods of Functional Analysis. (Mathematical Concepts & Methods in Science & Engineering Ser.: Vol. 15). 300p. 1978. 29.50 (ISBN 0-306-40119-3, Plenum Pr). Plenum Pub.

Gabay, Sabit, jt. ed. see Grenell, Robert.

Gabba, Emilio. Republican Rome, the Army & the Allies. Cuff, P. J., tr. 1977. 30.00x (ISBN 0-520-03259-4). U of Cal Pr.

Gabbay, S. M. Elementary Mathematics for Basic Chemistry & Physics. 128p. (Orig.). 1980. pap. 9.95 (ISBN 0-9604722-0-7). Basic Science Prep Ctr.

Gabbot, Mabel J. Have a Very Merry Christmas. LC 80-83034. 56p. (Orig.). 1981. pap. 2.50 (ISBN 0-88290-163-X, 2044). Horizon Utah.

Gabe, D. R. Principles of Metal Surface Treatment & Protection. 2nd ed. (International Ser. on Materials Science & Technology: Vol. 28). (Illus.). 1978. text ed. 36.00 (ISBN 0-08-022703-1); pap. text ed. 14.00 (ISBN 0-08-022707-4). Pergamon.

Gabe, M. Histological Techniques. Blackith, R. E. & Kovoor, A., trs. from Fr. (Illus.). 1976. 62.70 (ISBN 0-387-90162-0). Springer-Verlag.

Gabe, Peter. Clerical & Commercial Training Handbook. 1974. 21.00x o.p. (ISBN 0-8464-0249-1). Beekman Pubs.

Gabel, Creighton. Stone Age Hunters of the Kafue: The Gwisho A Site. LC 65-22281. (Pub. by Boston U Pr). 1965. 9.50x (ISBN 0-8419-8707-6, Africana). Holmes & Meier.

Gabel, Creighton & Bennett, Norman R., eds. Reconstructing African Culture History. LC 67-25932. (Pub. by Boston U Pr). 1967. 9.50x (ISBN 0-8419-8704-1, Africana). Holmes & Meier.

Gabel, Robert A. & Roberts, Richard A. Signals & Linear Systems. 2nd ed. LC 80-14811. 480p. 1980. text ed. 29.95 (ISBN 0-471-04958-1). Wiley.

Gabel, Stewart & Erickson, Marilyn T. Child Development & Developmental Disabilities. (Little, Brown Ser. in Clinical Pediatrics). 1980. text ed. 24.50 (ISBN 0-316-30100-0). Little.

Gabel, Stewart, ed. Behavioral Problems of Childhood. 1981. price not set (ISBN 0-8089-1336-0). Grune.

Gabelnick, Henry L. & Litt, Mitchell. Rheology of Biological Systems. (Illus.). 320p. 1973. 24.50 (ISBN 0-398-02589-4). C C Thomas.

Gaber, Norman H. Your Future in Oceanography. LC 76-114108. 143p. 1975. pap. 2.95 o.p. (ISBN 0-668-02258-2). Arco.

Gaber, Susan. Favorite Poems for Children Coloring Book. (Illus.). 48p. (Orig.). (ps-3). 1980. pap. 2.00 (ISBN 0-486-23923-3). Dover.

--A Treasury of Flower Designs for Artists, Embroiderers & Craftsmen: 100 Garden Favorites. (Illus.). 80p. (Orig.). 1981. pap. price not set (ISBN 0-486-24096-7). Dover.

Gabert, Glen, Jr. In Hoc Signo? A Brief History of Catholic Parochial Education in America. LC 72-89992. 1973. 9.95 (ISBN 0-8046-9028-6, Natl U). Kennikat.

Gabhart, Ann. A Heart Divided. (Orig.). 1980. pap. 2.50 (ISBN 0-446-91250-6). Warner Bks.

Gabin, Sanford B. Judicial Review & the Reasonable Doubt Test. (National University Publications, Multi-Disciplinary Studies in the Law). 1980. 17.50 (ISBN 0-8046-9248-3). Kennikat.

Gabis, Stanley T. Selected Problems of State Administration. 1979. write for info. (ISBN 0-87543-151-8). Lucas.

Gable, John A. The Bull Moose Years: Theodore Roosevelt & the Progressive Party. (National University Publications in American Studies). 1978. 17.50 (ISBN 0-8046-9187-8). Kennikat.

Gable, R. W., jt. auth. see Finkle, J. L.

Gable, Richard W. & Springer, J. Fred. Administering Agricultural Development in Asia: A Comparative Analysis of Four National Programs. new ed. LC 76-41210. (Illus.). 1977. lib. bdg. 32.00x (ISBN 0-89158-206-1). Westview.

Gabler, Hans W., ed. Chamber Music, Pomes Penyeach, & Occasional Verse: A Facsimile of Manuscripts by James Joyce, Typescripts & Proofs, Vol. 1. LC 78-10445. (James Joyce Archive Ser.). 1979. lib. bdg. 74.00 (ISBN 0-8240-2800-7). Garland Pub.

Gabler, Ray. New England White Water River Guide. 2nd ed. (Illus.). 250p. 1981. pap. 7.95 (ISBN 0-910146-33-0). Appalach Mtn.

Gabo, Naum. Of Divers Arts. (Bollingen Ser. Vol. 35; A. W. Mellow Lecture Ser. No. 8). (Illus.). 1962. 21.00x (ISBN 0-691-09794-1, 224). Princeton U Pr.

Gabor, Andre. Pricing: Principles & Practices. 1977. text ed. 36.95x (ISBN 0-435-84365-6); pap. text ed. 15.95x (ISBN 0-435-84366-4). Heinemann Ed.

Gabor, D., et al. Beyond the Age of Waste. LC 77-30309. 1978. text ed. 37.00 (ISBN 0-08-021835-0); pap. text ed. 17.00 (ISBN 0-08-021834-2). Pergamon.

--Beyond the Age of Waste: A Report to the Club of Rome. 2nd ed. LC 80-41614. (Illus.). 265p. 1981. lib. bdg. 42.00 (ISBN 0-08-027303-3); pap. 19.00 (ISBN 0-08-027304-1). Pergamon.

Gabor, Mark, jt. auth. see Revien, Leon.

Gaboriau, Emile. The Mystery of Orcival. 320p. 1977. Repr. of 1900 ed. lib. bdg. 14.25x (ISBN 0-89968-183-2). Lightyear.

--The Widow LeRouge. 293p. 1980. Repr. of 1900 ed. lib. bdg. 12.50x (ISBN 0-89968-184-0). Lightyear.

Gabriel, E., ed. Ueber Kie Beeinflussbarkeit Psychiatrischer Krankheitsverlaeufe, 1980, Vol. 13, No. 3-4. (Illus.). iv, 136p. 1981. pap. write for info. (ISBN 3-8055-2336-X). S Karger.

Gabriel, Judy M., jt. auth. see Sack, John.

Gabriel, M. C. Poems. 8.00 (ISBN 0-89253-479-6); flexible cloth 4.00 (ISBN 0-89253-480-X). Ind-US Inc.

Gabriel, Mordecai L. & Fogel, Seymour, eds. Great Experiments in Biology. 1955. pap. text ed. 14.95x (ISBN 0-13-363549-X). P-H.

Gabriel, P., jt. ed. see Dlab, V.

Gabriel, Ralph H. American Values: Continuity & Change. LC 74-24. (Contributions in American Studies: No. 15). 230p. 1974. lib. bdg. 17.95 (ISBN 0-8371-7355-8, GAV/). Greenwood.

--The Course of American Democratic Thought. 2nd ed. (gr. 10-12). 1956. text ed. 18.95 (ISBN 0-8260-3275-3). Wiley.

--Religion & Learning at Yale: Church of Christ in the College & University, 1757-1957. 1958. 27.50x (ISBN 0-685-69820-3). Elliots Bks.

Gabriel, Ralph H. see Gabriel, Ralph H.

Gabriel, Ralph H., ed. Pageant of America, 15 vols. Incl. Vol. 1. Adventurers in the Wilderness. Wissler, Clark & Skinner, Constance L. (ISBN 0-911548-56-4); Vol. 2. The Lure of the Frontier. Gabriel, Ralph H (ISBN 0-911548-57-2); Vol. 3. Toilers of Land & Sea. Gabriel, Ralph H (ISBN 0-911548-58-0); Vol. 4. The March of Commerce. Keir, Malcolm (ISBN 0-911548-59-9); Vol. 5. The Epic of Industry. Keir, Malcolm (ISBN 0-911548-60-2); Vol. 6. The Winning of Freedom. Wood, William & Gabriel, Ralph H. (ISBN 0-911548-61-0); Vol. 7. In Defense of Liberty. Wood, William & Gabriel, Ralph H. (ISBN 0-911548-62-9); Vol. 8. Builders of the Republic. Ogg, Frederic A (ISBN 0-911548-63-7); Vol. 9. Makers of a New Nation. Bassett, John S (ISBN 0-911548-64-5); Vol. 10. American Idealism. Weigle, Luther A (ISBN 0-911548-65-3); Vol. 11. The American Spirit in Letters. Williams, Stanley T (ISBN 0-911548-66-1); Vol. 12. The American Spirit in Art. Mather, Frank J., Jr., et al. (ISBN 0-911548-67-X); Vol. 13. The American **Spirit in Architecture. Hamlin, Talbot F (ISBN 0-911548-68-8); Vol. 14. The American Stage. Coad, Oral S. & Mims, Edwin, Jr. (ISBN 0-911548-69-6); Vol. 15. Annals of American Sport. Krout, John A (ISBN 0-911548-70-X). (Illus.). 22.95 ea.; Set. 330.00 (ISBN 0-911548-72-6). US Pubs.**

Gabriel, Ralph H., ed. see Royce, Sarah.

Gabriel, Richard A. The New Red Legions: A Survey Data Source Book. LC 79-24458. (Contributions in Political Science: No. 44). (Illus.). xii, 252p. 1980. lib. bdg. 40.00 (ISBN 0-313-21497-2, GAP/). Greenwood.

--The New Red Legions: An Attitudinal Portrait of the Soviet Soldier. LC 79-8956. (Contributions in Political Science: No. 44). (Illus.). xiv, 246p. 1980. lib. bdg. 22.50 (ISBN 0-313-21496-4, GAO/). Greenwood.

Gabrieli, Francesco, ed. Arab Historians of the Crusades. (The Islamic World Ser.). 1978. 20.00x (ISBN 0-520-03616-6). U of Cal Pr.
Gabriels, D. see De Boodt, M.
Gabriels, D., jt. auth. see DeBoodt, M.
Gabrielson, Ira N., jt. auth. see Zim, Herbert S.
Gabrovsek, John. Concepts Concerning Dental Caries Prevention. 200p. 1981. 16.50 (ISBN 0-87527-209-6). Green.
Gaburo, Kenneth. Whole Language, Language. (Illus.). 41p. 1981. softcover 9.75. Lingua Pr.
Gaburo, Kenneth, jt. auth. see Brun, Herbert.
Gaburo, Kenneth, ed. see Lingua Press.
Gaburo, Kenneth, et al, eds. Allos: 41 Writings by 41 Writers. LC 80-80809. (Illus.). 448p. 1980. softcover 20.95. Lingua Pr.
Gaburo, Virginia. Notation. LC 77-75432. (Illus.). 176p. 1977. soft-cover 14.45. Lingua Pr.
--Who Is Bruce Simonds. 44p. 1978. saddle-sticed 13.95, soft cover, lP recording. Lingua Pr.
Gabuzda, Thomas G., jt. auth. see Ersley, Allan J.
Gaby, D. & Treusch, M. Election Campaign Handbook. 1976. 35.00 o.p. (ISBN 0-13-247098-5). P-H.
Gace Brule. Gace Bule, Trouvere Champenois. LC 80-2158. (Societe Neo-Philologique De Helsingfors Ser.: Memoires, Vol. 16). 1981. Repr. of 1951 ed. 59.50 (ISBN 0-404-19022-7). AMS Pr.
Gackenbach. Harry y el Terrible Quiensabeque (Harry & the Terrible Whatzit) (ps-3). pap. 1.95 (ISBN 0-590-12116-2, Schol Pap). Schol Bk Serv.
Gackenbach, Dick. Claude & Pepper. LC 75-25507. (Illus.). 32p. (ps-2). 1976. 6.95 (ISBN 0-395-28793-6, Clarion). HM.
--Claude the Dog. LC 74-3403. (Illus.). 32p. (ps-2). 1974. 6.95 (ISBN 0-395-28792-8, Clarion). HM.
--Crackle Gluck & the Sleeping Toad. LC 78-12635. (Illus.). (gr. 1-3). 1979. 7.95 (ISBN 0-395-28953-X, Clarion). HM.
--Do You Love Me? LC 74-34104. (Illus.). 48p. (ps-4). 1975. 6.95 (ISBN 0-395-28794-4, Clarion). HM.
--Harry & the Terrible Whatzit. LC 76-40205. (Illus.). (ps-2). 1977. 6.95 (ISBN 0-395-28795-2, Clarion). HM.
--Hound & Bear. LC 76-3525. (Illus.). 32p. (ps-3). 1976. 6.95 (ISBN 0-395-28796-0, Clarion). HM.
--The Leatherman. LC 77-2584. (Illus.). (gr. 2-5). 1977. 6.95 (ISBN 0-395-28855-X, Clarion). HM.
--Little Bug. (Illus.). 32p. (ps-2). 1981. 7.95 (ISBN 0-395-30080-0, Clarion). HM.
--McGoogan Moves the Mighty Rock. LC 80-8455. (Illus.). 48p. (gr. 1-4). 1981. 8.95 (ISBN 0-06-021967-X, HarpJ); PLB 8.79g (ISBN 0-06-021968-8). Har-Row.
--Pepper & All the Legs. LC 78-5084. (ps-3). 1978. 6.95 (ISBN 0-395-28797-9, Clarion). HM.
--The Pig Who Saw Everything. LC 77-12741. (Illus.). 1978. 6.95 (ISBN 0-395-28798-7, Clarion). HM.
Gadbois, Robert, jt. auth. see Peterson, Mike.
Gadbois, Robert, jt. auth. see Roberts, David.
Gadbois, Robert, jt. auth. see Sadowski, Karen.
Gadbois, Robert, jt. auth. see Woldum, Thomas.
Gadda, Carlo Emilio. That Awful Mess on Via Merulana. Weaver, W., tr. LC 65-19320. 1965. 5.95 o.s.i. (ISBN 0-8076-0305-8). Braziller.
Gaddes, W. H. Learning Disabilities & Brain Function: A Neuropsychological Approach. (Illus.). 350p. 1980. 26.90 (ISBN 0-387-90486-7). Springer-Verlag.
Gaddis, Ben. How to Repair Home Kitchen Appliances. LC 76-45052. (Illus.). 1976. 8.95 o.p. (ISBN 0-8306-6885-3); pap. 5.95 (ISBN 0-8306-5885-8, 885). TAB Bks.
Gaddis, John L. The United States & the Origins of the Cold War, 1941-1947. LC 75-186388. (Contemporary American History Ser). 448p. 1972. text ed. 22.50x (ISBN 0-231-03289-7); pap. 7.50x (ISBN 0-231-08302-5, 133). Columbia U Pr.
Gaddis, John L., jt. auth. see Etzold, Thomas.
Gaddis, Robert S., jt. auth. see Coker, Lawrence T.
Gaddis, Thomas E. Killer. 1970. 7.95 o.s.i. (ISBN 0-02-542100-X). Macmillan.
Gaddis, Vincent H. American Indian Myths & Mysteries. (RL 10). 1978. pap. 1.95 o.p. (ISBN 0-451-08086-6, J8086, Sig). NAL.
Gaddy, C. Welton. Easter Proclamation: Remembrance & Renewal. LC 73-87065. pap. 1.95 (ISBN 0-8054-1921-7). Broadman.
Gaddy, Wade & Hart, Robert. Real Estate Fundamentals. 250p. (Orig.). 1981. pap. 13.95 (ISBN 0-88462-425-0). Real Estate Ed Co.
Gade, D. New Dimensions in Creativity. LC 74-78396. 1974. pap. 5.00 (ISBN 0-686-14991-2, 261-08418). Home Econ Educ.
Gaden, Eileen, jt. auth. see Seranne, Ann.
Gadgil, D. R. Writings & Speeches of Professor D. R. Gadgil on Co-operation. 1975. 8.00x o.p. (ISBN 0-88386-018-X). South Asia Bks.
Gadney, Alan. Gadney's Guide to One Thousand Eight Hundred International Contests, Festivals & Grants in Film & Video, Photography, TV-Radio Broadcasting, Writing, Poetry, Playwriting & Journalism: Updated Address Edition. rev. ed. LC 80-66803. 610p. 1980. 22.95 (ISBN 0-930828-03-8); pap. 15.95 (ISBN 0-930828-02-X). Festival Pubns.
Gadon, Herman, jt. auth. see Cohen, Allan R.
Gadow, Kenneth D. & Loney, Jan, eds. Psychosocial Aspects of Drug Treatment for Hyperactivity. (AAAS Selected Symposium: No. 44). 460p. 1981. lib. bdg. 26.50x (ISBN 0-89158-834-5). Westview.
Gaebelein, Arno C. Ezekiel. LC 72-88419. 1918. 5.50 (ISBN 0-87213-217-X). Loizeaux.
--Psalms. rev. ed. 1939. 6.75 (ISBN 0-87213-222-6). Loizeaux.
Gaebelein, Frank. Letters of Samuel Rutherford. 480p. 1980. pap. 8.95 (ISBN 0-8024-4673-6). Moody.
Gaeddert, Lou Ann. Noisy Nancy Norris. LC 65-10180. (ps-1). 1971. Repr. of 1965 ed. PLB 7.95 (ISBN 0-385-04749-5). Doubleday.
Gaeddert, LouAnn. A New England Love Story: Nathaniel Hawthorne & Sophia Peabody. LC 80-16329. (Illus.). 160p. (gr. 7 up). 1980. 8.95 (ISBN 0-8037-6153-8). Dial.
--Your Night to Make Dinner. (Illus.). 1977. lib. bdg. 6.90 (ISBN 0-531-01297-2). Watts.
Gaede, Marc, jt. auth. see Gaede, Marnie.
Gaede, Marnie & Gaede, Marc. Camera, Spade & Pen: An Inside View of Southwestern Archaeology. LC 80-23751. 1980. 25.00 (ISBN 0-8165-0663-9). U of Ariz Pr.
Gaehtgens, P., ed. Recent Advances in Microcirculatory Research. (Bibliotheca Anatomica Ser.: No. 20). (Illus.). xiv, 746p. 1980. soft cover 149.25 (ISBN 3-8055-2272-X). S Karger.
Gaer, Joseph. How the Great Religions Began. rev. ed. pap. 1.75 (ISBN 0-451-07764-4, E7764, Sig). NAL.
Gaerny, Arnold. Removable Closure of the Interdental Space. (Illus.). 196p. 1972. 52.50. Quint Pub Co.
Gaertner & Frederick. Alsatian Cooking. 1981. 16.95 (ISBN 0-8120-5403-2). Barron.
Gafencu, Grigore. Prelude to the Russian Campaign: From the Moscow Pact (August 21st 1939) to the Opening of Hostilities in Russia (June 22nd 1941) LC 79-5207. 348p. 1981. Repr. of 1945 ed. 26.50 (ISBN 0-8305-0072-3). Hyperion Conn.
Gaff, Jerry, et al. The Cluster College. LC 77-110641. (Higher Education Ser.). 1970. 12.95x o.p. (ISBN 0-87589-062-8). Jossey-Bass.
Gaffin, Richard B., Jr., ed. Redemptive History & Biblical Interpretation: The Shorter Writings of Geerhardus Vos. 1980. 17.50 (ISBN 0-87552-270-X). Presby & Reformed.
Gaffin, Richard B., Jr., ed. see Vos, Geerhardus.
Gaffney, Edward M. & Moots, Philip R. Government & Campus: Federal Regulation of Religiously Affiliated Higher Education. LC 80-53164. 210p. 1981. text ed. 15.95 (ISBN 0-268-01003-X); pap. text ed. 8.95 (ISBN 0-268-01005-6). U of Notre Dame Pr.
Gaffney, James, ed. Essays in Morality & Ethics. LC 80-80578. 224p. (Orig.). 1980. pap. 8.95 (ISBN 0-8091-2248-0). Paulist Pr.
Gaffney, Judith H., jt. auth. see Toye, Randall.
Gaffney, Walter J., jt. auth. see Nouwen, Henri J. M.
Gafney, Leo & Beers, John C. Essential Math Skills. Devine, Peter, ed. 224p. 1980. pap. text ed. 5.20 (ISBN 0-07-010260-0, W); tchr's ed. 6.08 (ISBN 0-07-010261-9); Webstermasters tests 4.52 (ISBN 0-07-010262-7). McGraw.
Gafney, Leo, ed. see Gurau, Peter K. & Lieberthal, Edwin M.
Gafney, Leo, ed. see Maher, Carolyn A., et al.
Gagala, Kenneth. Economics of Minorities: A Guide to Information Sources. LC 73-17573. (Economics Information Guide Ser: Vol. 2). 339p. 1976. 30.00 (ISBN 0-8103-1294-8). Gale.
Gagarin, Michael. Aeschylean Drama. LC 74-30520. 1976. 18.00x (ISBN 0-520-02943-7). U of Cal Pr.
Gage, John T. In the Arresting Eye: The Rhetoric of Imagism. LC 80-24893. 208p. 1981. 17.95x (ISBN 0-8071-0790-5). La State U Pr.
Gage, Joy P. Broken Boundaries-Broken Lives. 1981. pap. 3.95 (ISBN 0-89636-068-7). Accent Bks.
Gage, Matilda J. Woman, Church & State. LC 80-13639. 336p. 1980. pap. 7.95 (ISBN 0-930436-04-0). Persephone.
Gage, Michael. Guide to Exposed Concrete Finishes. LC 72-552437. (Illus.). 161p. (Orig.). 1970. pap. 18.50x (ISBN 0-85139-263-6). Intl Pubns Serv.
Gage, Michael & Vandenberg, M. Hard Landscape in Concrete. LC 75-31700. 167p. 1975. 27.95 (ISBN 0-470-28913-9). Halsted Pr.
Gage, Michael & Kirkbridge, T., eds. Design in Blockwork. 3rd ed. (Illus.). 1980. 25.00 (ISBN 0-686-60663-9, Pub. by Architectural Pr). Nichols Pub.
Gage, N. L. The Scientific Basis of the Art of Teaching. LC 78-6250. 1978. pap. text ed. 6.50x (ISBN 0-8077-2537-4). Tchrs Coll.
Gage, N. L., ed. The Psychology of Teaching Methods: Seventy-Fifth Yearbook Part I. LC 6-16938. (National Society for the Study of Education). 1976. lib. bdg. 13.00x o.s.i. (ISBN 0-226-60119-6). U of Chicago Pr.
Gage, Richard L., tr. see Ikeda, Daisaku.
Gage, Richard L., tr. see Ikeda, Daisaku & Inoue, Yasushi.
Gage, Thomas. Thomas Gage's Travels in the New World. rev. ed. enl. ed. Thompson, J. Eric, ed. LC 58-6856. (American Exploration & Travel Ser.: Vol. 58). (Illus.). 1958. 15.95 (ISBN 0-8061-0881-9). U of Okla Pr.
Gage, William & Duong Thanh Binh. Vietnamese-English Phrase Book with Useful Word List: For English Speakers. LC 75-24857. (Vietnamese Refugee Education Ser.: No. 2). 1975. pap. text ed. 3.00x (ISBN 0-87281-044-5). Ctr Appl Ling.
Gage, William W. English for Speakers of Vietnamese. (English As a Foreign Language Ser.). 366p. 1981. text & 9 cassettes 85.00 (ISBN 0-87950-617-2); cassettes separate 80.00 (ISBN 0-87950-616-4). Spoken Lang Serv.
Gage, Wilson. Down in the Boondocks. (gr. k-6). 1980. pap. 0.95 (ISBN 0-440-41745-7, YB). Dell.
--The Ghost of Five Owl Farm. (gr. 4-6). 1980. pap. 1.75 (ISBN 0-671-56085-9). Archway.
--Miss Osborne the Mop. (Illus.). (gr. 4-6). 1975. pap. 1.50 (ISBN 0-671-29895-X). PB.
Gagen, T. M. Topic in Finite Groups. LC 75-17116. (London Mathematical Society Lecture Note Ser.: No. 16). 80p. 1976. 11.95 (ISBN 0-521-21002-X). Cambridge U Pr.
Gagg, J. C. The Countryside. 7.50x (ISBN 0-392-07745-0, SpS). Soccer.
Gagliardelli, Giancarlo, jt. auth. see Ragazzini, Giuseppe.
Gagliardi, R. & Valenza, S. W., Jr., eds. The Mathematics of the Energy Crises. LC 78-53592. 96p. (gr. 7-12). 1978. 6.96 (ISBN 0-936918-01-2). Intergalactic NJ.
Gagliardi, Robert. Introduction to Communications Engineering. LC 77-18531. 1978. 34.00 (ISBN 0-471-03099-6, Pub. by Wiley-Interscience). Wiley.
Gagliardo, John G. Enlightened Despotism. LC 67-14301. (AHM Europe Since 1500 Ser.). (Orig.). 1967. pap. 5.95x (ISBN 0-88295-735-X). AHM Pub.
--From Pariah to Patriot: The Changing Image of the German Peasant, 1770-1840. LC 72-80091. 352p. 1969. 15.00x (ISBN 0-8131-1187-0). U Pr of Ky.
--Reich & Nation: The Holy Roman Empire As Idea & Reality, 1763-1806. LC 79-2170. 416p. 1980. 25.00x (ISBN 0-253-16773-6). Ind U Pr.
Gagliostro, Vincenza. Am I OK - If I Feel the Way I Do? LC 80-2077. 128p. 1981. pap. 2.75 (ISBN 0-385-17437-3, Im). Doubleday.
Gagliostro, Sr. Vincenzia. Am I Ok--If I Feel the Way I Do? (Illus.). 128p. (Orig.). (gr. 5-9). 1980. pap. 2.45 (ISBN 0-529-05779-4). Collins Pubs.
Gagnadre, Marius F. Condensation of Decimal & Metrical Systems: Jumelex Method. 1980. 5.95 (ISBN 0-533-04392-1). Vantage.
Gagnon, Dennis R. Exploring the Santa Barbara Backcountry. LC 73-77044. (Illus.). 150p. (Orig.). 1981. pap. 5.95 (ISBN 0-934136-13-0). Western Tanager.
Gagnon, Francois-Marc. Paul-Emile Borduas. (Canadian Artists Ser.). (Illus.). 1980. pap. 3.95 (ISBN 0-88884-386-0, 56470-3, Pub. by Natl Gallery Canada). U of Chicago Pr.
Gagnon, John H. Human Sexualities. 1977. pap. 12.95x (ISBN 0-673-15033-X). Scott F.
Gagnon, John H. & Greenblat, Cathy S. Life Designs: Individuals, Marriages, & Families. 1978. 16.95x (ISBN 0-673-07911-2). Scott F.
Gaherty, Sherry, jt. ed. see Katz, William A.
Gahndi, Mohandas K. The Collected Works of Mahatma Gandi: 04/01/1942 to 12/17/1942, Vol. 76. LC 58-36286. (Illus.). 491p. 1979. 10.00x o.p. (ISBN 0-8002-2465-5). Intl Pubns Serv.
Gaier, Claude. Four Centuries of Liege Gunmaking. (Illus.). 368p. 1977. 106.00x (ISBN 0-85667-028-6, Pub. by Sotheby Parke Bernet England). Biblio Dist.
Gaige, Frederick H. Regionalism & National Unity in Nepal. LC 74-30520. 1975. 21.50x (ISBN 0-520-02728-0). U of Cal Pr.
Gaikwad, V. R. Anglo-Indians. 1968. 10.00x (ISBN 0-210-27090-X). Asia.
Gail, Marzieh. Dawn Over Mount Hira & Other Essays. 1976. 9.50 (ISBN 0-85398-063-2, 7-32-18, Pub. by G Ronald England); pap. 5.50 (ISBN 0-85398-064-0, 7-32-19, Pub. by G Ronald England). Baha'i.
--Life in the Renaissance. (gr. 6-10). 1969. PLB 7.99 o.p. (ISBN 0-394-90298-X, BYR). Random.
--The Sheltering Branch. 1959. 4.75 (ISBN 0-87743-058-6, 7-31-33, Pub. by George Ronald England). Baha'i.
Gail, Marzieh, tr. see Abdu'l-Baha.
Gail, Marzieh, tr. see Baha'U'llah.
Gail, Meredith D. Handbook for Evaluating & Selecting Curriculum Materials. 190p. 1981. pap. text ed. 9.95 (ISBN 0-205-07301-8, 2373017). Allyn.
Gailey, Harry A. Historical Dictionary of the Gambia. LC 75-5882. (African Historical Dictionaries Ser.: No. 4). 180p. 1975. 10.00 (ISBN 0-8108-0810-2). Scarecrow.
--A History of the Gambia. rev. ed. 256p. 1980. text ed. 28.50x (ISBN 0-8290-0350-9); pap. text ed. 16.95x (ISBN 0-8290-0351-7). Irvington.
--Lugard & the Abeokuta Uprising: The Demise of Egba Independence. 1981. 27.50x (ISBN 0-7146-3114-0, F Cass Co). Biblio Dist.
Gailey, Harry A., Jr. History of Africa: From Earliest Times to 1800, Vol. 1. LC 80-15898. (Illus., Orig.). 1980. pap. text ed. 9.95 (ISBN 0-89874-032-0). Krieger.
--History of Africa: From 1800 to Present, Vol. 2. rev. ed. LC 80-15898. (Orig.). 1980. pap. text ed. 12.95 (ISBN 0-89874-033-9). Krieger.
Gaillard, Bob, et al. Handbook for the Young Athlete. 1978. pap. 5.95 (ISBN 0-915950-18-9). Bull Pub.
Gaillard, Dawson & Mosier, John. Women & Men Together: An Anthology of Short Fiction. (Illus., LC 77-078566). 1977. pap. text ed. 9.75 (ISBN 0-395-25032-3); inst. manual 0.50 (ISBN 0-395-25033-1). HM.
Gaillard, Frye. Watermelon Wine: The Spirit of Country Music. LC 76-62766. (Illus.). 240p. 1977. 10.00 o.p. (ISBN 0-312-85697-0). St Martin.
Gailloud, C., ed. Developments in Ophthalmology, Vol. 2. (Illus.). viii, 492p. 1981. 180.00 (ISBN 3-8055-1672-X). S Karger.
Gain, D. B., ed. The Aratus Ascribed to Germanicus Caesar. (University of London Classical Studies Ser.: No. 8). (Illus.). 200p. 1976. text ed. 36.50x (ISBN 0-485-13708-9, Athlone Pr). Humanities.
Gainer, Bernard. The Alien Invasion: The Origins of the Aliens Act of 1905. LC 72-80307. 302p. 1972. 17.50x (ISBN 0-8448-0050-3). Crane-Russak Co.
Gaines, Arleigh, ed. United Nations Philately. LC 80-53294. (Illus.). 704p. 1980. write for info. looseleaf (ISBN 0-938152-00-9). R & D Pubns.
Gaines, Charles & Butler, George. Staying Hard. (Orig.). 1980. pap. 8.95 (ISBN 0-671-41265-5, Kenan Pr). S&S.
Gaines, Edith & Jenkins, Dorothy H. Woman's Day Dictionary of Antique Furniture. (Illus.). 1979. pap. 4.95 (ISBN 0-8015-8792-1, Hawthorn). Dutton.
Gaines, F. P. The Southern Plantation: A Study in the Development & the Accuracy of a Tradition. 7.50 (ISBN 0-8446-1193-X). Peter Smith.
Gaines, Helen F. Cryptanalysis: A Study of Ciphers & Their Solutions. (Illus.). 1939. pap. text ed. 4.00 (ISBN 0-486-20097-3). Dover.
Gaines, J. H., jt. auth. see Volterra, Enrico.
Gaines, John S., jt. auth. see Rolle, Andrew F.
Gaines, Patricia E. The Fabric Decoration Book. LC 75-4543. (Illus.). 240p. 1975. 14.95 o.p. (ISBN 0-688-02903-5). Morrow.
Gaines, Pierce W. William Cobbett & the United States, 1792-1835: Bibliographies with Notes & Extracts. LC 79-168901. 1971. 15.95x (ISBN 0-912296-00-3, Dist. by U Pr of Va). Am Antiquarian.
Gaines, Price, ed. Interest-Adjusted Index: Nineteen Eighty-One Edition. LC 76-6788. 410p. 1980. pap. 18.00 (ISBN 0-87218-012-3). Natl Underwriter.
--Life Financial Reports, Nineteen Eighty Edition. LC 76-6785. 816p. 1980. pap. 24.00 (ISBN 0-87218-011-5). Natl Underwriter.
--Who Writes What: Nineteen Eighty-One Edition. LC 76-6787. 498p. 1980. pap. 10.50 (ISBN 0-87218-013-1). Natl Underwriter.
Gaines, Steven & Cohen, Robert J. The Club. 288p. 1980. pap. 2.50 (ISBN 0-553-13746-8). Bantam.
Gaines, Sylvia W. Data Bank Applications in Archaeology. 1980. pap. write for info. (ISBN 0-8165-0686-8). U of Ariz Pr.
Gainesborough, Louis. Of Dope & Dervishes. 1981. 8.95. Green Hill.
Gainham, Sarah. To the Opera Ball. 1978. pap. 2.25 o.s.i. (ISBN 0-446-82592-1). Warner Bks.
Gaither, Edmund B. Lois Mailou Jones, Reflective Moments. (Illus.). 1973. pap. 3.50 o.p. (ISBN 0-87846-172-8). Mus Fine Arts Boston.
Gaither, Norman. Production & Operations Management. 784p. 1980. text ed. 21.95 (ISBN 0-03-042701-0). Dryden Pr.

Gaither, Robert. Alcohol Fuel Book. (Illus.). 55p. (Orig.). Date not set. pap. price not set (ISBN 0-89196-084-8, Domus Bks). Quality Bks IL.
Gajda, Walter J., Jr. & Biles, William E. Engineering: Modeling & Computation. LC 77-74378. (Illus.). 1977. text ed. 19.95 (ISBN 0-395-25585-6); solutions manual 0.50 (ISBN 0-395-25584-8). HM.
Gajdusek, D. Carleton, jt. ed. see Farquhar, Judith.
Gajdusek, Robert E. Hemingway's Paris. LC 78-17214. (Illus.). 1978. 14.95 o.p. (ISBN 0-684-15799-3, ScribT). Scribner.
Gakenheimer, Ralph A., jt. ed. see Miller, John.
Gakwandi, Shatto A. The Novel & Contemporary Experience in Africa. LC 77-1273. 1981. text ed. 22.50x (ISBN 0-8419-0306-9, Africana); pap. text ed. 8.95x (ISBN 0-8419-0642-4). Holmes & Meier.
Gal, Hans. Johannes Brahms: His Work & Personality. Stein, Joseph, tr. from Ger. LC 76-55410. (Illus.). Repr. of 1963 ed. lib. bdg. 21.00x (ISBN 0-8371-9367-2, GABR). Greenwood.
--Schumann Orchestral Music. LC 79-52145. (BBC Music Guides Ser.: No. 40). (Illus.). 64p. (Orig.). 1980. pap. 2.95 (ISBN 0-295-95696-8). U of Wash Pr.
Gal, Hans, ed. see Brahms, Johannes.
Gal, Susan. Language Shift: Social Determinants of Linguistic Change in Bilingual Austria. (Language, Thought & Culture Ser.). 1979. 21.00 (ISBN 0-12-273750-4). Acad Pr.
Galambos, Janos. The Asymptotic Theory of Extreme Order Statistics. LC 78-1916. (Series in Probability & Mathematical Staistics: Applied Probability & Statistics). 1978. 33.50 (ISBN 0-471-02148-2, Pub. by Wiley-Interscience). Wiley.
Galamian, Ivan. Principles of Violin Playing & Teaching. 1962. text ed. 13.95 (ISBN 0-13-710780-3). P-H.
Galana, Laurel, jt. ed. see Covina, Gina.
Galand, Rene. Saint-John Perse. (World Authors Ser.: France: No. 244). lib. bdg. 10.95 (ISBN 0-8057-2690-X). Twayne.
Galanoy, Terry. Charge It: Inside the Credit Card Conspiracy. 264p. 1981. 11.95 (ISBN 0-399-12555-8). Putnam.
Galant, Stanley P., et al. Pediatric Allergy Case Studies. LC 80-18937. 1980. pap. 14.50 (ISBN 0-87488-195-1). Med Exam.
Galantay, Ervin Y. New Towns: Planned Towns Throughout History. LC 74-81216. (Planning & Cities Ser.). (Illus.). 192p. 1975. 15.00 o.s.i. (ISBN 0-8076-0766-5); pap. 5.95 o.s.i. (ISBN 0-8076-0767-3). Braziller.
Galante, Cosmo. The Degeneration of the Female of the Species & the Decay of the Human Society. enl. ed. (Illus.). 68p. 1973. 39.45 (ISBN 0-913314-18-8). Am Classical Coll Pr.
Galante, Lawrence. Tai Chi: The Supreme Ultimate. 1981. pap. 8.95 (ISBN 0-87728-497-0). Weiser.
Galanter, Marc, ed. Currents in Alcoholism: Treatment, Rehabilitation & Epidemiology, Vol. 6. 1979. 33.50 (ISBN 0-8089-1201-1). Grune.
Galantiere, Lewis, tr. see Cocteau, Jean.
Galantiere, Lewis, tr. see De Saint-Exupery, Antoine.
Galarza, Ernesto. Barrio Boy. 1971. pap. 4.95x (ISBN 0-268-00441-2); 8.95x o.p. (ISBN 0-268-00440-4). U of Notre Dame Pr.
Galasiewicz, Z. M. Helium Four. 1971. 25.00 (ISBN 0-08-015816-1). Pergamon.
--Superconductivity & Quantum Fluids. 1970. 32.00 (ISBN 0-08-013089-5). Pergamon.
Galassi, Jonathan, ed. Understand the Weapon Understand the Wound: Selected Writings of John Cornford. (Essays, Prose, & Scottish Literature). 1979. 12.50 o.s.i. (ISBN 0-85635-152-0, Pub. by Carcanet New Pr England). Persea Bks.
Galasso, F. S. Structure & Properties of Inorganic Solids. LC 70-104123. 1970. 42.00 (ISBN 0-08-006873-1). Pergamon.
--Structure, Properties & Preparation of Perovskite-Type Compounds. 1969. 25.00 (ISBN 0-08-012744-4). Pergamon.
Galasso, George J., et al, eds. Antivirals & Virus Diseases of Man. LC 78-67025. 1979. 62.50 (ISBN 0-89004-222-5). Raven.
Galaty, Fillmore W., et al. Modern Real Estate Practice Teacher's Manual. 96p. (Orig.). 1978. pap. 13.95 (ISBN 0-88462-263-0). Real Estate Ed Co.
Galavaris, George. Bread & the Liturgy: The Symbolism of Early Christian & Byzantine Bread Stamps. LC 75-98120. 1970. 21.50x (ISBN 0-299-05310-5). U of Wis Pr.
Galaway, Burt, jt. auth. see Compton, Beulah.
Galaway, Burt & Hudson, Joe, eds. Offender Restitution in Theory & Action. LC 78-54700. 1978. 18.95 (ISBN 0-669-02328-0). Lexington Bks.
Galaway, Burt, jt. ed. see Hudson, Joe.
Galaway, Burt, et al, eds. Community Corrections: A Reader. (Illus.). 324p. 1976. 22.50 (ISBN 0-398-03533-4). C C Thomas.
Galaway, Burton & Hudson, Hamilton C. Perspectives on Crime Victims. (Illus.). 435p. 1980. pap. 16.95 (ISBN 0-8016-1733-2). Mosby.
Galaway, Burton, jt. auth. see Hudson, Joe.
Galbraith, J. K., ed. see United States National Resources Planning Board, Public Works Committee.
Galbraith, Jay. Designing Complex Organizations. LC 72-11887. 1973. pap. text ed. 6.50 (ISBN 0-201-02559-0). A-W.
--Organization Design. LC 76-10421. (Illus.). 1977. text ed. 18.95 (ISBN 0-201-02558-2). A-W.
Galbraith, Jean. Collinsfield Guide to the Wild Flowers of Southeast Australia. 450p. 1980. 13.95x (ISBN 0-00-219246-2, Pub. by W Collins Australia). Intl Schol Bk Serv.
Galbraith, John K. Economics & the Public Purpose. 1975. pap. 2.50 o.p. (ISBN 0-451-08428-4, E8428, Sig). NAL.
--Economics & the Public Purpose. 1980. pap. 2.95 (ISBN 0-451-61864-5, ME1864, Ment). NAL.
--Economics, Peace & Laughter. 288p. 1972. pap. 1.75 (ISBN 0-451-04954-3, E4954, Sig). NAL.
--The Galbraith Reader. LC 75-19930. 1977. 15.00 (ISBN 0-87645-091-5). Gambit.
--The Great Crash of Nineteen Twenty-Nine. 1980. pap. 2.75 (ISBN 0-686-69255-1, 50799, Discus). Avon.
--Liberal Hour. pap. 0.95 o.p. (ISBN 0-451-60873-9, MQ873, Ment). NAL.
--A Life in Our Times. 576p. 1981. 15.95 (ISBN 0-686-69050-8). HM.
--A Theory of Price Control. (HP Ser.: No. 173). 1980. text ed. 7.95x (ISBN 0-674-88170-2); pap. text ed. 2.95 (ISBN 0-674-88175-3). Harvard U Pr.
Galbraith, John S. Crown & Charter: The Early Years of the British South Africa Company. LC 73-93050. (Perspectives on Southern Africa Ser.). 1974. 21.50x (ISBN 0-520-02693-4). U of Cal Pr.
Galbraith, Madelyn. There Is a Book. LC 75-147021. 1971. 8.50 o.p. (ISBN 0-8309-0043-8). Herald Hse.
Galbraith, Ronald E. & Jones, Thomas M. Moral Reasoning: A Teaching Handbook for Adapting Kohlberg to the Classroom. (Illus.). 1976. lib. bdg. 11.95 (ISBN 0-912616-23-7); pap. 6.95 (ISBN 0-912616-22-9). Greenhaven.
Galbraith, Vivian H. Domesday Book: Its Place in Administrative History. 232p. 1975. 24.50x (ISBN 0-19-822424-9). Oxford U Pr.
--Introduction to the Use of the Public Records. 1934. 12.95x (ISBN 0-19-821221-6). Oxford U Pr.
--The Making of Domesday Book. LC 80-2224. 1981. Repr. of 1961 ed. 36.50 (ISBN 0-404-18761-7). AMS Pr.
Galbreath, Donald L. Papal Heraldry. 2nd ed. (Illus.). 156p. 1972. 34.00 (ISBN 0-685-29193-6). Gale.
Galdon, Joseph A., ed. Essays on the Philippine Novel in English. 168p. 1980. 17.50x (ISBN 0-686-28638-3); pap. 8.50x (ISBN 0-686-28639-1). Cellar.
Galdone. Henny Penny. (ps-3). 1980. pap. 1.50 (ISBN 0-590-08732-0, Schol Pap). Schol Bk Serv.
--The Three Little Pigs. (ps-3). pap. 1.25 (ISBN 0-590-09272-3, Schol Pap). Schol Bk Serv.
Galdone, Joanna. Gertrude, the Goose Who Forgot. LC 73-19583. (Illus.). (gr. k-3). 1975. PLB 5.90 o.p. (ISBN 0-531-02735-X). Watts.
--The Tailypo. LC 77-23289. (ps-4). 1977. 8.95 (ISBN 0-395-28809-6, Clarion). HM.
Galdone, Paul. The Amazing Pig. (Illus.). 32p. (ps-3). 1981. 8.95 (ISBN 0-395-29101-1, Clarion). HM.
--Henny Penny. LC 68-24735. (Illus.). (ps-2). 1968. 6.95 (ISBN 0-395-28800-2, Clarion). HM.
--Horse, the Fox, & the Lion. LC 68-14085. (Illus.). (ps-1). 1968. 6.95 (ISBN 0-395-28802-9, Clarion). HM.
--The Little Red Hen. LC 72-97770. (Illus.). (ps-2). 1973. 6.95 (ISBN 0-395-28803-7, Clarion). HM.
--Little Tuppen. LC 67-10364. (Illus.). (ps-1). 1967. 6.95 (ISBN 0-395-28805-3, Clarion). HM.
--The Magic Porridge Pot. LC 76-3531. (Illus.). (ps-3). 1976. 7.95 (ISBN 0-395-28805-3, Clarion). HM.
--Monkey & The Crocodile. LC 78-79939. (Illus.). (ps-2). 1969. 8.95 (ISBN 0-395-28806-1, Clarion). HM.
--Obedient Jack. LC 72-131155. (Illus.). (gr. k-3). 1971. PLB 4.90 o.p. (ISBN 0-531-01970-5). Watts.
--Puss in Boots. LC 75-25505. (Illus.). 32p. (ps-4). 1976. 7.95 (ISBN 0-395-28808-8, Clarion). HM.
--Three Aesop Fox Fables. LC 79-133061. (ps-2). 1971. 6.95 (ISBN 0-395-28810-X, Clarion). HM.
--Three Little Pigs. LC 75-123456. (Illus.). (ps-1). 1970. 6.95 (ISBN 0-395-28813-4, Clarion). HM.
Galdone, Paul, retold by. & illus. The Gingerbread Boy. LC 74-11461. 40p. (ps-3). 1975. 7.95 (ISBN 0-395-28799-5, Clarion). HM.
Galdone, Paul, ed. & illus. The Three Bears. LC 78-158833. (Illus.). 32p. (ps-2). 1972. 8.95 (ISBN 0-395-28811-8, Clarion). HM.
Galdone, Paul, retold by. & illus. Three Billy Goats Gruff. LC 72-85338. (Illus.). 32p. (ps-2). 1973. 6.95 (ISBN 0-395-28812-6, Clarion). HM.
Galdone, Paul, illus. History of Mother Twaddle & the Marvelous Achievements of Her Son Jack. LC 73-9726. (Illus.). (ps-2). 1974. 6.95 (ISBN 0-395-28801-0, Clarion). HM.
Galdos, Benita Perez see Perez Galdos, Benita.
Galdos, Benito P. The Shadow. Austin, Karen O., tr. from Sp. LC 80-10549. Orig. Title: La Sombra. 65p. 1980. 7.95 (ISBN 0-8214-0553-5, 0553E). Ohio U Pr.
Galdos, Benito Perez see Perez Galdos, Benito.
Galdos, Benito Perez see Rodgers, Eamon J.
Galdston, Iago. The Social & Historical Foundations of Modern Medicine. 250p. 1981. 25.00 (ISBN 0-87630-259-2). Brunner-Mazel.
Gale, Bill. Mature Man's Guide to Style. LC 80-13843. (Illus.). 320p. 1980. 12.95 (ISBN 0-688-03688-0). Morrow.
Gale, Bill, jt. auth. see Baker, Oleda.
Gale, Cedric. Building an Effective Vocabulary. LC 79-1496. (Orig.). 1979. pap. 3.95 (ISBN 0-8120-2041-3); answer bklet, 1 for every 25 ordered avail. (ISBN 0-8120-2167-3). Barron.
Gale, E. F., et al. The Molecular Basis of Antibiotic Action. 2nd ed. 640p. 1981. 98.00 (ISBN 0-471-27915-3, Pub. by Wiley-Interscience). Wiley.
Gale, Frederick. Mortuary Science. (Illus.). 240p. 1960. pap. 14.50 photocopy ed., spiral (ISBN 0-398-04166-0). C C Thomas.
Gale, J. S. Population Genetics. LC 80-12675. (Tertiary Level Biology Ser.). 189p. 1980. 41.95x (ISBN 0-470-26970-7); pap. text ed. 19.95x (ISBN 0-470-26969-3). Halsted Pr.
Gale, Jack. How About a Career in Real Estate? 34p. (Orig.). 1979. pap. 2.95 (ISBN 0-88462-374-2). Real Estate Ed Co.
Gale, Janice & Gale, Stephen. Guide to Fairs, Festivals & Fun Events. (Illus.). 190p. 1981. pap. 6.95 (ISBN 0-937928-00-3). Sightseer.
Gale, Joseph. Behind Barres: The Mystique of Masterly Teaching. LC 79-56900. (Illus.). 96p. 12.95 (ISBN 0-87127-115-X). Dance Horiz.
Gale, June. SNOW: Twice Orphaned-Once Rescued. LC 80-21941. (Illus.). 168p. 1980. 10.00 (ISBN 0-914016-74-1). Phoenix Pub.
Gale, Leah. Animals of Farmer Jones. (ps-1). 1970. PLB 5.00 (ISBN 0-307-60282-6, Golden Pr). Western Pub.
Gale, M. T. Surface Relief Images for Color Reproduction. (Illus.). 200p. 1980. pap. 25.00 (ISBN 0-240-51068-2). Focal Pr.
Gale, Mort. Instant Astrology. (Illus., Orig.). 1980. pap. 6.95 (ISBN 0-446-97355-6). Warner Bks.
--Moon Power. (Orig.). 1980. pap. 2.25 (ISBN 0-446-82988-9). Warner Bks.
Gale Research Co. Library of Congress & National Union Catalogue Author Lists, 1942-1962: A Master Cummulation, 152 vols. LC 73-82135. 1969. fiche only 1390.00 (ISBN 0-8103-0950-5); fiche only 125.00 (ISBN 0-8103-0951-3). Gale.
Gale Research Company, jt. auth. see United States. Nautical Almanac Office.
Gale, Richard M. Language of Time. (International Library of Philosophy & Scientific Method). 1968. text ed. 14.50x (ISBN 0-7100-3637-X). Humanities.
Gale, Robert L. Francis Parkman. (U. S. Authors Ser.: No. 220). 1973. lib. bdg. 10.95 (ISBN 0-8057-0582-1). Twayne.
--John Hay. (United States Authors Ser.: No. 296). 1978. lib. bdg. 12.50 (ISBN 0-8057-7199-9). Twayne.
--Richard Henry Dana. LC 68-24301. (U. S. Authors Ser.: No. 143). 1969. lib. bdg. 10.95 (ISBN 0-8057-0184-2). Twayne.
Gale, Robert P. & Fox, C. Fred, eds. Biology of Bone Marrow Transplantation. (ICN-UCLA Symposia on Molecular & Cellular Biology Ser.: Vol. 17). 1980. 40.00 (ISBN 0-12-273960-4). Acad Pr.
Gale, Roger W. The Americanization of Micronesia: A Study of the Consolidation of the U. S. Role in the Pacific. LC 78-68800. 1979. pap. text ed. 12.00 (ISBN 0-8191-0703-4). U Pr of Amer.
Gale, Stephen, jt. auth. see Gale, Janice.
Gale, Steven H. Readings for Todays Writers. LC 79-21312. 1980. pap. text ed. 9.95 (ISBN 0-471-05127-6); tchrs'. manual avail. (ISBN 0-471-07846-8). Wiley.
Gale, W. A., ed. Life in the Universe: The Ultimate Limits to Growth. (AAAS Selected Symposium: No. 31). 1979. lib. bdg. 14.50x (ISBN 0-89158-378-5). Westview.
Galeener, Janet see McNall, Leota K.
Galejs, J. Terrestrial Propagation of Long Electromagnetic Waves. 376p. 1972. 82.00 (ISBN 0-08-016710-1). Pergamon.
Galen, P. S. & Gambino, S. R. Beyond Normality: The Predictive Value & Efficiency of Medical Diagnosis. LC 75-25915. 1975. 23.95 (ISBN 0-471-29047-5, Pub. by Wiley Medical). Wiley.
Galena, J. N. Sex in Groups. 1974. pap. 1.25 o.p. (ISBN 0-685-51414-5, LB221ZK, Leisure Bks). Nordon Pubns.
Galerie St. Etienne. Egon Schiele: Watercolors & Drawings. (Illus.). 155p. 1968. pap. 12.00 o.p. (ISBN 0-910810-01-X). Johannes.
Galerstein, Carolyn L., ed. see LaForet, Carmen.
Galerstein, David H. Mastering Fundamental Mathematics. (Orig.). (gr. 7). 1976. pap. text ed. 5.83 (ISBN 0-87720-226-5). AMSCO Sch.
Galet, Pierre. A Practical Ampelography: Grapevine Indentification. Morton, Lucie, tr. LC 78-59631. (Illus.). 192p. 1979. 28.50x (ISBN 0-8014-1240-4). Comstock.
Galewitz, Herb, ed. see Gould, Chester.
Galilea, Segundo. Following Jesus. Phillips, Helen, tr. 128p. (Orig.). 1981. pap. 4.95 (ISBN 0-88344-136-5). Orbis Bks.
Galilei, Galileo. Dialogue Concerning the Two Chief World Systems- Ptolemaic & Copernican. 3rd ed. Drake, Stillman, tr. & intro. by. 1980. 30.00x (ISBN 0-520-04104-6). U of Cal Pr.
--Dialogue Concerning the Two Chief World Systems-Ptolemaic & Copernican. 2nd rev. ed. Drake, Stillman, tr. 1967. 25.00x (ISBN 0-520-00449-3); pap. 7.95x (ISBN 0-520-00450-7, CAL66). U of Cal Pr.
--Dialogues Concerning Two New Sciences. (Illus.). 1914. pap. text ed. 4.00 (ISBN 0-486-60099-8). Dover.
Galileo. Discoveries & Opinions of Galileo. LC 57-6305. 1957. pap. 2.95 (ISBN 0-385-09239-3, A94, Anch). Doubleday.
Galileo, Galilei. Dialogues Concerning Two New Sciences. (Illus.). 8.50 (ISBN 0-8446-0636-7). Peter Smith.
Galindo, Sergio. Precipice. Brushwood, John & Brushwood, Carolyn, trs. (Texas Pan American Series). Orig. Title: El Bordo. (Illus.). 1969. 9.95x (ISBN 0-292-78408-2); pap. 4.95x (ISBN 0-292-76426-X). U of Tex Pr.
Galinkin, George B., ed. Readings on Social Services in the Health Professions. 1976. pap. text ed. 9.50x (ISBN 0-8191-0083-8). U Pr of Amer.
Galinsky, Ellen. Between Generations: The Six Stages of Parenthood. 320p. 1981. 14.95 (ISBN 0-8129-0924-0). Times Bks.
--Six Stages of Parenthood: Between Generations. 1981. 12.95 (ISBN 0-686-62160-3). Times Bks.
Galinsky, G. Karl. Ovid's Metamorphoses: An Introduction to Its Basic Aspects. LC 74-84146. 1975. 20.00x (ISBN 0-520-02848-1). U of Cal Pr.
Galinsky, M. David, jt. auth. see Shaffer, John B.
Galjart, B. F. Peasant Mobilization & Solidarity. (Studies of Developing Countries: No. 19). (Illus.). 1976. pap. text ed. 14.00x (ISBN 90-232-1381-5). Humanities.
Gall, A. Le see Le Gall, A., et al.
Gall, Donald A., ed. Resource Directory on Rural America. 51p. (Orig.). 1981. pap. 4.95 (ISBN 0-8298-0446-3). Pilgrim NY.
Gall, Edward A. & Mostofi, F. K., eds. The Liver. 2nd ed. LC 79-28745. (I.A.P. Ser.). 540p. 1980. Repr. lib. bdg. cancelled (ISBN 0-89874-122-X). Krieger.
Gall, Franz J. On the Functions of the Brain & Each of Its Parts. Lewis, W., tr. from Ger. (Contributions to the History of Psychology Ser.). 1980. Repr. of 1835 ed. 30.00 ea. U Pubns Amer.
Gall, Herbert. Deleatur. (Suhrkamp Taschenbuecher: St 639). 244p. (Orig.). 1980. pap. text ed. 5.20 (ISBN 3-518-37139-8, Pub. by Insel Verlag Germany). Suhrkamp.
Gall, Meredith, jt. auth. see Acheson, Keith.
Gall, Meredith D., jt. auth. see Borg, Walter R.
Gall, Morris, ed. see Stone, David.
Gall, Pirie M., et al. Municipal Development Programs in Latin America: An Intercountry Evaluation. LC 76-23401. (Illus.). 1976. 22.95 (ISBN 0-275-23280-8). Praeger.
Gallager, H. Stephen, et al, eds. The Breast. LC 78-14811. (Illus.). 1978. text ed. 69.50 (ISBN 0-8016-1727-8). Mosby.
Gallagher. Medical Care of the Adolescent. 3rd ed. (Illus.). 1975. 38.50 o.p. (ISBN 0-8385-6199-3). ACC.
Gallagher, Bernard J., III. Sociology of Mental Illness. (Ser. in Sociology). (Illus.). 1980. text ed. 14.95 (ISBN 0-13-820928-6). P-H.
Gallagher, Chuck, Fr., S.J. Love Is a Couple. 1978. pap. 2.95 (ISBN 0-385-13595-5, Im). Doubleday.
--Parents Are Lovers. 1977. pap. 2.45 (ISBN 0-385-12697-2, Im). Doubleday.

Gallagher, D. P. Modern Latin American Literature. 210p. 1973. pap. 3.95 (ISBN 0-19-888071-5, 400, GB). Oxford U Pr.
Gallagher, Donat, ed. see Waugh, Evelyn.
Gallagher, Eugene B. Infants, Mothers, & Doctors. LC 78-2071. 1978. 19.95 (ISBN 0-669-02269-1). Lexington Bks.
Gallagher, I. J. The Case of the Ancient Astronauts. LC 77-10822. (Great Unsolved Mysteries Ser.). (Illus.). (gr. 4-5). 1977. PLB 9.65 (ISBN 0-8172-1059-8). Raintree Pubs.
Gallagher, James J. Study Guide for Educating Exceptional Children. 3rd ed. (Illus.). 208p. 1980. pap. text ed. write for info. (ISBN 0-395-28690-5). HM.
Gallagher, James J. & Nathan, Kurt C. The Trees Jobs Grow on: And How to Find the One for You. LC 80-70399. (Illus.). 80p. (Orig.). 1980. 9.95 (ISBN 0-938176-00-5). Wendover.
Gallagher, James J., jt. auth. see Kirk, Samuel A.
Gallagher, James J., jt. ed. see Haskins, Ron.
Gallagher, Jeanette & Reid, D. Kim. The Learning Theory of Piaget & Inhelder. LC 80-24410. (Orig.). 1981. pap. text ed. 7.95 (ISBN 0-8185-0343-2). Brooks-Cole.
Gallagher, Joseph, ed. East African Culture History. LC 76-50927. (Foreign & Comparative Studies-Eastern Africa Ser.: No. 25). 93p. 1976. pap. text ed. 4.50x (ISBN 0-915984-22-9). Syracuse U Foreign Comp.
Gallagher, Joseph V. To Be a Catholic. LC 73-137884. 1970. pap. 1.45 (ISBN 0-8091-5143-X). Paulist Pr.
Gallagher, Neil. Don't Go Overseas Until You've Read This Book. LC 77-2643. 1977. pap. 3.50 (ISBN 0-87123-105-0, 210105). Bethany Fell.
--How to Save Money on Almost Everything. LC 78-19113. 1978. pap. 2.95 (ISBN 0-87123-234-0, 210234). Bethany Fell.
--How to Stop the Porno Plague. LC 77-21992. (Illus.). 1977. pap. 3.50 (ISBN 0-87123-231-6, 210231). Bethany Fell.
Gallagher, Patricia. Shadows of Passion. 1976. pap. 1.75 (ISBN 0-380-00928-5, 31906). Avon.
--Shannon. 1976. pap. 1.50 (ISBN 0-380-00918-8, 31807). Avon.
--The Thicket. 1977. pap. 1.75 (ISBN 0-380-01578-1, 33316). Avon.
Gallagher, R. H. Optimum Structural Design: Theory & Applications. LC 72-8600. (Numerical Methods in Engineering Ser.). 400p. 1973. 44.25 (ISBN 0-471-29050-5, Pub. by Wiley-Interscience). Wiley.
Gallagher, R. H., et al, eds. Finite Elements in Fluids, 3 vols. Incl. Vol. 1. Viscous Flow & Hydrodynamics. 290p. 1975. 55.75 (ISBN 0-471-29045-9); Vol. 2. Mathematical Foundations, Aerodynamics, & Lubrication. 287p. 1975. 55.75 (ISBN 0-471-29046-7); Vol. 3. 1978. 55.75 (ISBN 0-471-99630-0). LC 74-13573 (Pub. by Wiley-Interscience). Wiley.
Gallagher, Raymond R. The Ballad of Mich-o-Tta-Wa. 64p. 1979. 2.95 (ISBN 0-8059-2595-3). Dorrance.
Gallagher, Richard & Remsberg, Charles. Hostage Negotiation for Police: Officer Reference. 1977. 2.50 (ISBN 0-686-52997-9). MTI Tele.
Gallagher, Richard H. Finite Element Analysis: Fundamentals. (Civil Engr. & Engr. Mechanics Ser.). (Illus.). 416p. 1975. 26.95 (ISBN 0-13-317248-1). P-H.
Gallagher, Richard H., jt. auth. see McGuire, William.
Gallagher, T. J. Simple Dielectric Liquids: Mobility, Conduction, & Breakdown. (Oxford Science Research Papers Ser). (Illus.). 180p. 1975. pap. 24.95x (ISBN 0-19-851933-8). Oxford U Pr.
Gallagher, Tess. Under Stars. LC 77-95331. 1978. 9.00 (ISBN 0-915308-19-3); pap. 5.00 (ISBN 0-915308-20-7). Graywolf.
Gallagher, Thomas B. Private Pilot Written Exam Course. LC 80-70132. (Illus.). 68p. (Orig.). 1981. pap. 19.95 (ISBN 0-938706-00-4). Fed Aviation.
Gallagher, William D., ed. Selections from the Poetical Literature of the West. LC 68-29083. 1968. Repr. of 1841 ed. 29.00x (ISBN 0-8201-1019-1). Schol Facsimiles.
Gallagher, William J. Report Writing for Management. (Orig.). 1969. pap. 8.95 (ISBN 0-201-02256-7). A-W.
--Writing the Business & Technical Report. LC 80-19781. 120p. 1980. pap. 8.95 (ISBN 0-8436-0796-3). CBI Pub.
Gallaher, Art, Jr. Plainville Fifteen Years Later. LC 61-15104. 1961. 17.50x (ISBN 0-231-02481-9). Columbia U Pr.
Gallaher, John G. The Iron Marshal: A Biography of Louis N. Davout. LC 75-37956. 432p. 1976. 24.95x (ISBN 0-8093-0691-3). S Ill U Pr.
Gallahue, David L. Motor Development & Movement Experiences for Young Children. LC 75-37676. 1976. text ed. 19.95x (ISBN 0-471-29042-4). Wiley.
Gallahue, David L., et al. A Conceptual Approach to Moving & Learning. LC 75-2369. 423p. 1975. text ed. 20.95 (ISBN 0-471-29043-2); tchrs' resource bk. avail. (ISBN 0-471-29039-4). Wiley.
Galland, China. Women in the Wilderness. LC 80-7830. (Illus.). 256p. (Orig.). 1980. pap. 7.95 (ISBN 0-06-090817-3, CN 817, CN). Har-Row.
Galland, Joseph S. Ten Favorite French Stories. (Fr.). 1935. 12.50x (ISBN 0-89197-506-3); pap. text ed. 6.95x (ISBN 0-89197-962-X). Irvington.
Gallant, Donald M. & Force, Robert, eds. Legal & Ethical Issues in Human Research & Treatment: Psychopharmacologic Considerations. 1978. 15.00 (ISBN 0-470-26354-7). Halsted Pr.
Gallant, Gladys S. Living Image. LC 77-15178. 1978. 7.95 o.p. (ISBN 0-385-13651-X). Doubleday.
Gallant, Robert W. & Railey, Jay M. Physical Properties of Hydrocarbons, Vol. 2. 2nd ed. 1981. cancelled (ISBN 0-87201-690-0). Gulf Pub.
Gallant, Roy A. Astrology: Sense or Nonsense? LC 73-15340. (Illus.). 256p. (gr. 7-9). 1974. PLB 6.95 (ISBN 0-385-08673-3). Doubleday.
--Exploring the Planets. LC 67-17267. (gr. 7-9). 1967. 7.95a (ISBN 0-385-07430-1); PLB (ISBN 0-385-07432-8). Doubleday.
--Fires in the Sky: The Birth & Death of Stars. LC 78-4339. (Illus.). 176p. (gr. 5-9). 1978. 8.95 (ISBN 0-590-07475-X, Four Winds). Schol Bk Serv.
--Memory: How It Works & How to Improve It. LC 79-6342. (Illus.). 128p. (gr. 7 up). 1980. 8.95 (ISBN 0-590-07613-2, Four Winds). Schol Bk Serv.
Gallant, Roy A. & Sedeen, Magaret. National Geographic Picture Atlas of Our Universe. (Illus.). 276p. (gr. 6 up). 1980. 14.95 (ISBN 0-87044-356-9); PLB 16.95 (ISBN 0-87044-357-7). Natl Geog.
Gallatin, Judith E. Adolescence & Individuality: A Conceptual Approach to Adolescent Psychology. 364p. 1975. pap. text ed. 15.50 scp (ISBN 0-06-042227-0, HarpC); instructor's manual free (ISBN 0-06-362233-5). Har-Row.
Gallaway, Francis. Reason, Rule & Revolt in English Classicism. 384p. 1966. pap. 5.75x (ISBN 0-8131-0105-0). U Pr of Ky.
Galle, William P., Jr., jt. auth. see Level, Dale A., Jr.
Gallegos, Frederick, jt. auth. see Dawson, Peter P.
Gallegos, Louisa M., ed. see Crane, Barbara J.
Gallender, D. Symbol Communication for the Severely Handicapped. (Illus.). 272p. 1980. pap. 24.75 spiral (ISBN 0-398-04018-4). C C Thomas.
Gallender, Demos. Teaching Eating & Toileting Skills to the Multi-Handicapped in the School Setting. (Illus.). 384p. 1980. text ed. 22.75 (ISBN 0-398-03879-1). C C Thomas.
Galler & Perlis. A View of Programming Languages. 1976. 18.95 (ISBN 0-201-02324-5). A-W.
Galler, Meyer & Marquess, Harlan E., eds. Soviet Prison Camp Speech: A Survivor's Glossary. LC 75-176411. 216p. 1972. 19.50x (ISBN 0-299-06080-2). U of Wis Pr.
Gallery, Daniel V. Stand by-y-y to Start Engines. 1967. pap. 1.50 (ISBN 0-446-88921-0). Warner Bks.
Gallet, Jeffrey H., et al. Rent Stabilization & Control Laws in N. Y. (Supplemented annually). 25.00 (ISBN 0-87526-082-9). Gould.
Galley, Howard, ed. The Prayer Book Office. 800p. 1980. 24.50 (ISBN 0-8164-0370-8). Crossroad NY.
Galley, J. N. The Board & Computer Management. 185p. 1978. text ed. 23.50x (ISBN 0-220-67000-5, Pub. by Busn Bks England). Renouf.
Galli, C. & Avogaro, P., eds. Polyunsaturated Fatty Acids in Nutrition: Proceedings of a Round Table in Polyunsaturated Fatty Acids in Nutrition, Milan, Italy, April 1979. (Progress in Food & Nutrition Sciences Ser.: Vol. 4, No. 5). (Illus.). 80p. 1980. pap. 26.00 (ISBN 0-08-027362-9). Pergamon.
Galli, C., et al, eds. Dietary Lipids & Postnatal Development. LC 73-79580. (Illus.). 286p. 1973. 27.00 (ISBN 0-911216-50-2). Raven.
Galli, Claudio, et al, eds. Phospholipases & Prostaglandins. LC 77-87457. (Advances in Prostaglandin & Thromboxane Research Ser.: Vol. 3). 1978. 27.00 (ISBN 0-89004-201-2). Raven.
Galli, Nicholas. Foundations & Principles of Health Education. LC 77-21586. 1978. text ed. 18.95 (ISBN 0-471-29065-3). Wiley.
Galliart, William F., jt. auth. see Wheeler, James E.
Gallico, Paul. The Boy Who Invented the Bubble Gun. 272p. 1974. 6.95 o.s.i. (ISBN 0-440-01789-0). Delacorte.
--The House That Wouldn't Go Away. LC 79-53599. 1980. 8.95 (ISBN 0-440-03496-5); PLB 8.44 (ISBN 0-440-03497-3). Delacorte.
--Matilda. 1978. pap. 1.95 o.p. (ISBN 0-425-03556-5, Medallion). Berkley Pub.
--Miracle in the Wilderness. 48p. 1975. 4.95 o.s.i. (ISBN 0-440-05714-0). Delacorte.
--Thomasina. 256p. 1981. pap. 2.25 (ISBN 0-380-51524-5, 51524). Avon.
Gallie, D. In Search of the New Working Class. LC 77-80834. (Studies in Sociology: No. 9). (Illus.). 1978. 36.00 (ISBN 0-521-21771-7); pap. 10.95x (ISBN 0-521-29275-1). Cambridge U Pr.
Gallier, James. Autobiography of James Gallier, Architect. LC 69-13715. (Architecture & Decorative Art Ser.). 1973. Repr. of 1864 ed. lib. bdg. 25.00 (ISBN 0-306-71247-4). Da Capo.
Galliher, John F. & McCartney, James. Criminology: Power, Crime & Criminal Law. 1977. 15.50x (ISBN 0-256-01942-8). Dorsey.
Gallimore, Laurene, jt. auth. see Joyce, Gayle.
Gallimore, Ronald, et al. Culture, Behavior & Education: A Study of Hawaiian-Americans. LC 74-75863. (Sage Library of Social Research: Vol. 11). 1974. 18.00x (ISBN 0-8039-0380-4); pap. 8.95x (ISBN 0-8039-0446-0). Sage.
Gallin, Bernard. Hsin Hsing, Taiwan: A Chinese Village in Change. 1966. 19.50x (ISBN 0-520-00451-5). U of Cal Pr.
Gallin, John I. & Quie, Paul G., eds. Leukocyte Chemotaxis: Methods, Physiology, & Clinical Implications. LC 76-58053. 1978. 42.50 (ISBN 0-89004-198-9). Raven.
Gallo & Sedwick. French for Careers: Conversational Perspectives. (Illus., Orig.). 1980. pap. text ed. 8.95 (ISBN 0-442-23883-5). D Van Nostrand.
Gallo, Ezequiel. Farmers in Revolt: The Revolutions of 1893 in the Province of Santa Fe, Argentina. (Institute of Latin American Studies Monograph: No. 7). (Illus.). 108p. 1976. text ed. 21.00x (ISBN 0-485-17707-2, Athlone Pr). Humanities.
Gallo, May, jt. auth. see Gray, Martin.
Gallo, Michael & Kiehl, Charles. Basic Arithmetic. 1981. write for info. (ISBN 0-8302-0756-2). Goodyear.
Gallo, Patrick J. Old Bread, New Wine: A Portrait of the Italiann-Americans. LC 80-20401. 360p. 1981. 16.95 (ISBN 0-88229-146-7). Nelson-Hall.
Gallo, Robert C., ed. Recent Advances in Cancer Research: Cell Biology, Molecular Biology & Tumor Virology. (Uniscience Ser.). 1977. Vol. 1, 280p. 64.95 (ISBN 0-8493-5138-3); Vol. 2, 240p. 59.95 (ISBN 0-8493-5139-1). CRC Pr.
Gallo, Robert C., jt. ed. see Sarin, Prem S.
Gallo, Rose A. F. Scott Fitzgerald. LC 76-15650. (Modern Literature Ser.). 1978. 10.95 (ISBN 0-8044-2225-7). Ungar.
Gallon, Arthur J. Coaching: Ideas & Ideals. 400p. 1974. pap. text ed. 9.50 o.p. (ISBN 0-395-17624-7). HM.
--Coaching: Ideas & Ideals. 2nd ed. LC 79-90061. (Illus.). 1980. text ed. 10.95 (ISBN 0-395-28693-X). HM.
Gallop, David, tr. & notes by see Plato.
Galloway, Anne, jt. auth. see Saubel, Katherine S.
Galloway, David. Edward Lewis Wallant. (United States Authors Ser.: No. 319). 1979. lib. bdg. 13.50 (ISBN 0-8057-7250-2). Twayne.
--A Family Album. 1980. 12.95 (ISBN 0-7145-3682-2); pap. 6.95 (ISBN 0-7145-3785-3). Riverrun NY.
--A Family Album: A Novel. LC 77-84387. 1978. 8.95 o.p. (ISBN 0-15-130153-0). HarBraceJ.
--Lamaar Ransom. 250p. 1981. 11.95 (ISBN 0-7145-3686-5). Riverrun NY.
--Melody Jones. 1981. 9.95 (ISBN 0-7145-3807-8); pap. 4.95 (ISBN 0-7145-3733-0). Riverrun NY.
--Teaching & Counselling. 192p. 1981. pap. 13.50 (ISBN 0-582-48987-3). Longman.
Galloway, David, et al. New Writers Twelve. 1980. pap. 6.00 (ISBN 0-7145-3545-1). Riverrun NY.
Galloway, David D. The Absurd Hero in American Fiction: Updike, Styron, Bellow, Salinger. 2nd, rev. ed. 288p. 1981. text ed. 22.50x (ISBN 0-292-70356-2); pap. text ed. 8.95x (ISBN 0-292-70355-4). U of Tex Pr.
Galloway, David M. Case Studies in Classroom Management. 1976. pap. text ed. 7.95 (ISBN 0-582-48562-2). Longman.
Galloway, Joseph. Selected Tracts, 3 vols. LC 70-166326. (Era of the American Revolution Ser.). 1974. lib. bdg. 125.00 (ISBN 0-306-70222-3). Da Capo.
Galloway, Sylvia, et al, eds. Guide to Professional Development Opportunities for College & University Administrators. rev. ed. 1977. 5.75 o.p. (ISBN 0-685-77228-4). ACE.
Galloway, Terry. Buncha Crocs in Surch of Snac. LC 80-65065. 1980. 5.95 (ISBN 0-931604-04-4); pap. 2.95 (ISBN 0-931604-05-2). Curbstone Pub NY TX.
Galloway, W. E., et al. South Texas Uranium Province, Geologic Perspective. (Illus.). 81p. 1979. 3.00 (GB 18). Bur Econ Geology.
Gallucci, Ed, jt. auth. see Grumley, Michael.
Gallup, Dick. Where I Hang My Hat. LC 70-123977. (A Full Court Rebound Bk.). 1978. 14.95 (ISBN 0-685-60029-7). Full Court NY.
Gallup, Donald. T. S. Eliot: A Bibliography. 19.95 (ISBN 0-571-08928-3, Pub. by Faber & Faber). Merrimack Bk Serv.
Gallup, George H., ed. The Gallup Poll: Public Opinion, 1980. LC 79-56557. 320p. 1981. lib. bdg. 49.50 (ISBN 0-8420-2181-7). Scholarly Res Inc.
--The International Gallup Polls: Public Opinion, 1979. LC 79-3844. 350p. 1981. lib. bdg. 49.50 (ISBN 0-8420-2180-9). Scholarly Res Inc.
Gallup, George, Jr., jt. auth. see Linkletter, Art.
Gallwey, W. Timothy. The Inner Game of Tennis. 1974. 8.95 (ISBN 0-394-49154-8). Random.
Galm, John A. Sidney's Arcadian Poems. (Salzburg Studies in English Literature,Elizabethan & Renaissance Studies: No. 1). 229p. 1973. pap. text ed. 25.00x (ISBN 0-391-01379-3). Humanities.
Galonska, Michael. Connecticut Supplement. 2nd ed. 196p. 1980. pap. 7.95 (ISBN 0-695-81499-0). Follett.
Galonska, Michael L. Connecticut Supplement for Modern Real Estate Practice. 2nd ed. 184p. (Orig.). 1981. pap. 7.95 (ISBN 0-88462-319-X). Real Estate Ed Co.
Gal-Or, B., ed. Modern Developments in Thermodynamics. LC 74-2399. 458p. 1974. text ed. 34.95 (ISBN 0-470-29044-7). Halsted Pr.
Galper, Jeffrey. The Politics of Social Services. 272p. 1975. pap. text ed. 10.95 (ISBN 0-13-685214-9). P-H.
--Social Work Practice: A Radical Perspective. (P-H Ser. Sociology & Social Work). 1980. pap. text ed. 10.95 (ISBN 0-13-819508-0). P-H.
Galper, Miriam. The Joint Custody & Co-Parenting Handbook. rev. ed. 207p. 1980. lib. bdg. 12.90 (ISBN 0-89471-116-4); pap. 5.95 (ISBN 0-89471-117-2). Running Pr.
Galpin, Francis W. Music of the Sumerians. LC 78-87458. (Music Reprint Ser). 1970. Repr. of 1937 ed. lib. bdg. 25.00 (ISBN 0-306-71462-0). Da Capo.
Galster, Georg. Sylloge of Coins of the British Isles-National Museum, Copenhagen, Royal Collection of Coins & Metals: Anglo-Saxon Coins, Aethelred II, Vol. 2. 1966. 25.75x (ISBN 0-19-725896-4). Oxford U Pr.
Galston, A., et al. Life of the Green Plant. 3rd ed. 1980. 17.95 (ISBN 0-13-536326-8); pap. 13.95 (ISBN 0-13-536318-7). P-H.
Galston, A. W., ed. see Mayer, A. M., et al.
Galston, Arthur. Green Wisdom. LC 80-68183. 1981. 12.95 (ISBN 0-465-02712-1). Basic.
Galston, Arthur W. & Davies, Peter J. Control Mechanisms in Plant Development. (Foundations of Developmental Biology Ser). 1970. pap. 11.95x ref. ed. (ISBN 0-13-171801-0). P-H.
Galston, James, tr. see Walter, Bruno.
Galston, James A., tr. see Walter, Bruno.
Galsworthy, John. End of the Chapter. (Encore Edition). 1970. 5.95 o.p. (ISBN 0-684-15944-9, ScribT). Scribner.
--Forsyte Saga. 1933. lib. rep. ed. 25.00x (ISBN 0-684-15368-8, ScribT). Scribner.
--The Plays of John Galsworthy. 1150p. 1980. Repr. of 1929 ed. lib. bdg. 40.00 (ISBN 0-8492-4960-0). R West.
Galsworthy, John see Salerno, Henry F.
Galton, Francis. Francis Galton's Art of Travel. LC 79-53734. (Illus.). 1979. 19.95 (ISBN 0-7153-5139-7). David & Charles.
--Inquiries into Human Faculty & Its Development. 261p. 1980. Repr. lib. bdg. 20.00 (ISBN 0-89984-230-5). Century Bookbindery.
--Natural Inheritance. Bd. with Darwinism. (Contributions to the History of Psychology Ser., Vol. IV, Pt. D: Comparative Psychology). 1978. Repr. of 1889 ed. 30.00 (ISBN 0-89093-173-9). U Pubns Amer.
Galton, Francis see Angell, J. R., et al.
Galton, Laurence. The Patient's Guide to Surgery. 1977. pap. 2.50 o.p. (ISBN 0-380-00683-9, 32987). Avon.
Galton, Lawrence. How Long Will I Live? And 434 Other Questions Your Doctor Doesn't Have Time to Answer & You Can't Afford to Ask. LC 76-2440. 1976. 9.95 o.s.i. (ISBN 0-02-542390-8, 54239). Macmillan.
--Save Your Stomach. 1978. pap. 2.25 o.s.i. (ISBN 0-515-04485-7). Jove Pubns.
Galton, Lawrence, jt. auth. see Barnes, Broda.
Galton, Lawrence, jt. auth. see Roth, Oscar.

Galton, Maurice & Simon, Brian. Progress & Performance in the Primary Classroom. 240p. 1980. 25.00 (ISBN 0-7100-0669-1); pap. 15.50 (ISBN 0-7100-0670-5). Routledge & Kegan.
Galton, Maurice, ed. Curriculum Change. 120p. 1980. pap. text ed. 10.50x (ISBN 0-7185-1183-2, Leicester). Humanities.
Galtung, J., jt. auth. see First International Working Conference on Violence & Non-Violent Action in Industrialized Societies, Brussels, March 13-15th, 1974, Part II.
Galtung, Johan. Theory & Methods of Social Research. LC 67-26343. (Illus.). 1967. 17.00x (ISBN 0-231-03088-6). Columbia U Pr.
--The True Worlds: A Transnational Experience. LC 79-7351. (Preferred World for the 1990's Ser.). (Illus.). 469p. 1981. pap. text ed. 9.95 (ISBN 0-02-911070-X). Free Pr.
Galtung, Johan, jt. ed. see Jungk, Robert.
Galub, Jack. The U. S. Air Force Academy Fitness Program for Women. LC 78-21218. (Illus.). 1979. 14.95 o.p. (ISBN 0-13-938142-2); pap. 7.95 o.p. (ISBN 0-13-938134-1). P-H.
Galuppi, Baldassare. Six Keyboard Sonatas. Serafine, Mary L., ed. 62p. (gr. 6-12). pap. 7.95 (ISBN 0-686-64721-1, 05052). Fischer Inc NY.
Galus, Z. Fundamentals of Electrochemical Analysis. Reynolds, G. F., tr. from Pol. LC 76-5838. (Series in Analytical Chemistry). 1976. 84.95 (ISBN 0-470-15080-7). Halsted Pr.
Galvez, Bernardo de see De Galvez, Bernardo.
Galvin, E. Michael, ed. Potato World Handbook. 400p. 1980. perfect bdg 19.95 (ISBN 0-937358-45-2). G D L Inc.
Galvin, James. Imaginary Timber. LC 79-6746. 96p. 1980. pap. 4.95 (ISBN 0-385-15776-2). Doubleday.
Galvin, John R. Three Men of Boston. LC 75-20331. 348p. 1976. 10.00 o.s.i. (ISBN 0-690-01018-4, TYC-T). T Y Crowell.
Galvin, Michael E. Oilseed World Handbook. 450p. 1981. 50.00 (ISBN 0-937358-52-5). G D L Inc.
Galvin, Miles. The Organized Labor Movement in Puerto Rico. LC 77-74389. 1979. 16.50 (ISBN 0-8386-2009-4). Fairleigh Dickinson.
Galvin, Patricia, tr. see Decarpentry.
Galvin, Patrick J. Book of Successful Kitchens. 2nd ed. LC 77-25375. (Illus.). 136p. 1978. 13.95 (ISBN 0-912336-58-7); pap. 6.95 (ISBN 0-912336-59-5). Structures Pub.
--Finishing off. LC 77-24521. (A Successful Book). (Illus.). 1977. 13.95 (ISBN 0-912336-50-1); pap. 6.95 (ISBN 0-912336-51-X). Structures Pub.
--Successful Space Saving at Home. LC 76-27683. (Illus.). 1976. 12.00 (ISBN 0-912336-30-7); pap. 5.95 (ISBN 0-912336-31-5). Structures Pub.
Galway, Alberic De see De Galway, Alberic.
Galyon, Aubrey E. The Art of Versification: Matthew of Vendome. 135p. 1980. pap. 8.50 (ISBN 0-8138-1370-0). Iowa St U Pr.
Galzigna, L., jt. ed. see Burlina, A.
Gaman, P. M. & Sherrington, K. B. The Science of Food: An Introduction to Food Science, Nutrition & Microbiology. 2nd ed. (Illus.). 224p. 1980. 30.00 (ISBN 0-08-025896-4); pap. 12.50 (ISBN 0-08-025895-6). Pergamon.
Gaman, Pamela D. & Shernington, Kathleen B. The Science of Food an Introduction to Food Science, Nutrition & Microbiology. LC 76-27697. 1977. text ed. 32.00 (ISBN 0-08-019948-8); pap. text ed. 12.50 (ISBN 0-08-019947-X). Pergamon.
Gamba, Pietro. A Narrative of Lord Byron's Last Journey to Greece. 314p. 1980. Repr. of 1945 ed. lib. bdg. 45.00 (ISBN 0-8495-2046-0). Arden Lib.
Gambaccini, Paul. Paul McCartney: In His Own Words. LC 76-8068. 1976. pap. 5.95 (ISBN 0-8256-3910-7, Quick Fox). Music Sales.
Gambaccini, Peter. Bill Joel: A Photo Biography. 192p. (Orig.). 1980. pap. 2.50 (ISBN 0-515-05317-1). Jove Pubns.
--Bruce Springsteen: A Photo Bio. 1979. pap. 2.25 (ISBN 0-515-05220-5). Jove Pubns.
--Photographer's Assistant. (Illus.). Date not set. pap. 10.95 o.p. (ISBN 0-8256-3201-3, Quick Fox). Music Sales. Postponed.
Gambaryan, P. R. How Mammals Run: Anatomical Adaptations. Hardin, H., tr. from Rus. LC 74-16190. 367p. 1974. 39.95 (ISBN 0-470-29059-5). Halsted Pr.
Gambee, Robert. Exeter Impressions. new ed. (Illus.). 206p. 1980. 14.95 (ISBN 0-8038-1961-7). Hastings.
Gambell, Ray. The Life of Sea Mammals. LC 78-56582. (Easy Reading Edition of Introduction to Nature Ser.). (Illus.). 1978. lib. bdg. 7.95 (ISBN 0-686-51146-8). Silver.
Gambhirananda, Swami, tr. see Shivananda, Swami.
Gambill, Edward L. Conservative Ordeal: Northern Democrats & Reconstruction, 1865 to 1868. 208p. 1981. text ed. 13.50 (ISBN 0-8138-1385-9). Iowa St U Pr.
Gambino, Richard. Blood of My Blood: The Dilemma of the Italian Americans. LC 73-11705. 360p. 1974. 4.50. Doubleday.
--Blood of My Blood, the Dilemma of the Italian-Americans. 400p. 1975. pap. 4.50 (ISBN 0-385-07564-2, Anch). Doubleday.
--Bread & Roses. LC 79-67598. 480p. 1981. 13.95 (ISBN 0-87223-651-X). Seaview Bks.
Gambino, S. R., jt. auth. see Galen, P. S.
Gambit Editors, jt. auth. see Coon, Carleton S.
Gamble, Andrew. The Politics of Decline. (Critical Social Studies). 1980. text ed. write for info. (ISBN 0-391-01179-0); pap. text ed. write for info. (ISBN 0-391-01180-4). Humanities.
Gamble, Eliza B. The God-Idea of the Ancients: Or Sex in Religion. LC 79-66997. 339p. 1981. Repr. of 1897 ed. 27.50 (ISBN 0-8305-0110-X). Hyperion Conn.
Gamble, Geoffrey. Wikchamni Grammar. LC 77-8566. (Publications in Linguistics Ser.: Vol. 89). 1978. 11.00x (ISBN 0-520-09589-8). U of Cal Pr.
Gamble, Sidney D. North China Villages: Social, Political & Economic Activities Before 1933. 1963. 16.50x o.p. (ISBN 0-520-00452-3). U of Cal Pr.
Gamble, Thomas. Savannah Duels & Duellists: 1733-1877. LC 74-2325. (Illus.). 322p. 1974. Repr. of 1923 ed. 18.00 (ISBN 0-87152-169-5). Reprint.
Gamble, Thomas, Jr. Bethesda, an Historical Sketch of Whitefield's House of Mercy in Georgia, & of the Union Society, His Associate & Successor in Philanthropy. LC 78-187383. (Illus.). 150p. 1972. Repr. of 1902 ed. 13.50 (ISBN 0-87152-078-8). Reprint.
Gamble, W. Music Engraving & Printing: Historical & Technical Treatise. LC 70-155576. (Music Ser). 1971. Repr. of 1923 ed. lib. bdg. 25.00 (ISBN 0-306-70168-5). Da Capo.
Gamble, W. L., jt. auth. see Park, R.
Gambling, Trevor. A One Year Accounting Course, 2 pts. 1969. Pt. 1. text ed. 11.75 (ISBN 0-08-013025-9); Pt. 2. text ed. o.p. (ISBN 0-08-013027-5); pap. text ed. 6.00 ea.; Pt. 1. pap. text ed. (ISBN 0-08-013024-0); Pt. 2. pap. text ed. (ISBN 0-08-013026-7). Pergamon.
Gambogi, P., jt. auth. see Verona, O.
Gambrell, Linda B. & Wilson, Robert M. Focusing on the Strengths of Children. LC 73-80404. 1973. pap. 4.50 (ISBN 0-8224-2900-4). Pitman Learning.
Gambs, John S. John Kenneth Galbraith. (World Leaders Ser.: No. 37). 1975. lib. bdg. 9.95 (ISBN 0-8057-3681-6). Twayne.
Gamec, Hazel S. The Disappearing ABC Game Book. (Illus.). 12p. write for info. (ISBN 0-938042-02-5). Printek.
--Looking Out of the Window. (Illus.). 12p. 1980. write for info. (ISBN 0-938042-01-7). Printek.
--The Magic Pencil Counting Book. (Illus.). 12p. 1980. write for info. (ISBN 0-938042-00-9). Printek.
Gamelin, T. W. Uniform Algebras & Jensen Measures. LC 78-16213. (London Mathematical Society Lecture Note Ser.: No. 32). 1979. pap. 17.95x (ISBN 0-521-22280-X). Cambridge U Pr.
Gamer, Robert E. The Developing Nations: A Comparative Perspective. 651p. 1976. pap. text ed. 12.95x (ISBN 0-205-05418-8). Allyn.
Gamlin, A. T., et al, eds. Mechanical Maintenance & Installation: Supplementary Training Manual. (Engineering Craftsmen: No. J21S). (Illus.). 1976. pap. 21.50x (ISBN 0-85083-332-9). Intl Ideas.
Gammage, Allen Z. Basic Police Report Writing. 2nd ed. (Police Science Ser.). (Illus.). 344p. 1978. 15.75 (ISBN 0-398-03204-1). C C Thomas.
Gammage, Allen Z. & Sachs, Stanley L. Police Unions. 204p. 1972. 14.75 (ISBN 0-398-02467-7). C C Thomas.
Gammage, Allen Z., et al. Alcoholism Skid Row & the Police. 96p. 1972. photocopy ed. spiral 9.75 (ISBN 0-398-02288-7). C C Thomas.
Gammage, B. An Australian in the First World War. (Cambridge Introduction to the History of Mankind Ser.). (Illus.). 1976. pap. text ed. 3.95 (ISBN 0-521-21018-6). Cambridge U Pr.
Gammell, Stephen. Once Upon MacDonald's Farm. LC 80-23956. (Illus.). 32p. (gr. k-3). 1981. 7.95 (ISBN 0-590-07792-9, Four Winds). Schol Bk Serv.
Gammon, C. L. Poems. 1981. 4.50 (ISBN 0-8062-1710-3). Carlton.
Gammon, Clive. A Tide of Fish. 10.00x (ISBN 0-392-06417-0, SpS). Soccer.
Gammon, Margaret & Read, Carol I. Edgar Cayce on Diet & Health. 192p. (Orig.). 1969. pap. 2.25 (ISBN 0-446-92690-6). Warner Bks.
Gammon, Margaret, compiled by. Normal Diet. 1976. pap. 1.95 (ISBN 0-87604-010-5). ARE Pr.
Gammon, Margaret H. Astrology & the Edgar Cayce Readings. rev. ed. 1973. pap. 2.95 (ISBN 0-87604-067-9). ARE Pr.
Gammon, Roland. Nirvana Now: Higher Consciousness in the Dawning Aquarian Age. 555p. 1980. 14.95 (ISBN 0-89975-003-6). World Authors.
Gammon, Roland, jt. auth. see Forman, Henry J.
Gammon, Samuel R., Jr. Presidential Campaign of Eighteen Thirty-Two. LC 78-96952. (Law, Politics & History Ser). 1969. Repr. of 1922 ed. lib. bdg. 20.00 (ISBN 0-306-71830-8). Da Capo.
Gammond, Peter. Music on Record: Brass Bands. (Illus.). 184p. 1981. 39.00 (ISBN 0-85059-366-2). Aztex.
--Musical Instruments in Color. LC 75-17604. (Illus.). 176p. 1976. 6.95 o.s.i. (ISBN 0-02-542410-6). Macmillan.
Gammond, Peter, ed. Duke Ellington: His Life & Music. LC 77-1927. (The Roots of Jazz Ser.). 1977. Repr. of 1958 ed. lib. bdg. 22.50 (ISBN 0-306-70874-4). Da Capo.
Gamon, Richard Louis. The Thoughts of Thomas Robert Malthus As They Apply to the Economic Complexities of Our Present Age. (The Living Thoughts of the Great Economists Ser.). (Illus.). 97p. 1981. 17.55 (ISBN 0-918968-87-9). Inst Econ Finan.
Gamoran, Mamie G. Fun Ways to Holidays. (gr. 5-9). 1951. pap. 2.00 (ISBN 0-8074-0136-6, 321400). UAHC.
--Hillel's Calendar. (Illus.). (gr. 1-3). 1960. text ed. 3.25 o.p. (ISBN 0-685-20740-4, 101610). UAHC.
Gamow, G. & Cleveland, John. Physics: Foundations & Frontiers. 3rd ed. 640p. 1976. 21.95 (ISBN 0-13-672535-X). P-H.
Gamow, George. Gravity. LC 62-8840. 1962. pap. 2.50 o.p. (ISBN 0-385-01577-1, S22, Anch). Doubleday.
--Mister Tompkins in Paperback. (Illus., Orig.). 1967. bds. 17.95 (ISBN 0-521-06905-X); pap. 5.95x (ISBN 0-521-09355-4). Cambridge U Pr.
Gamow, George, tr. see Khinchin, Alexander I.
Gams, W., jt. auth. see Domsch, K. H.
Gamson, William A. Power & Discontent. (Orig.). 1968. pap. text ed. 9.50x (ISBN 0-256-01101-X). Dorsey.
--The Strategy of Social Protest. 1975. pap. text ed. 10.50x (ISBN 0-256-01684-4). Dorsey.
Gamson, William A., ed. SIMSOC (Simulated Society) 3rd ed. LC 77-84285. 1978. pap. text ed. 7.95 (ISBN 0-02-911170-6). Free Pr.
Gamst, Frederick C. Hoghead. (Case Studies in Cultural Anthropology). 128p. 1980. pap. text ed. 4.95 (ISBN 0-03-052636-1, HoltC). HR&W.
Gamwell, Lynn. Cubist Criticism. Kuspit, Donald B., ed. (Studies in Fine Arts - Criticism). 229p. 1980. 24.95 (ISBN 0-8357-1089-0, Pub. by UMI Res Pr). Univ Microfilms.
Gander & Gardiner. Child & Adolescent Development. 1981. text ed. 16.95 (ISBN 0-316-30322-4); tchrs'. manual free (ISBN 0-316-30319-4); study guide 5.95 (ISBN 0-316-30318-6). Little.
Gander, Ralph. Photomicrographic Technique for Medical & Biological Scientists. Freere, Roy H., tr. from Ger. (Illus., Eng.). 1969. 9.75 o.s.i. (ISBN 0-02-845100-7). Hafner.
Gander, Terry. The Modern British Army. (Illus.). 280p. 1980. 59.95 (ISBN 0-85059-435-9). Aztex.
Gandert, Slade R. Protecting Your Collection: A Handbook, Survey, & Guide for the Security of Rare Books, Manuscripts, Archives, Works of Art, & the Circulating Library Collection. (Library & Archival Security Ser.: No. 4). 192p. 1981. text ed. 19.95 (ISBN 0-917724-78-X). Haworth Pr.
Ganderton, M. A., ed. see European Congress of Allergology & Clinical Immunology, 9th.
Gandhi. Microwave Design Engineering & Applications. 400p. Date not set. text ed. price not set (ISBN 0-08-025589-2); pap. text ed. price not set (ISBN 0-08-025588-4). Pergamon.
Gandhi, Hans. A Novel Approach to Losing Weight. 1981. 10.00 (ISBN 0-533-04724-2). Vantage.
Gandhi, Indira. Eternal India. LC 80-51191. Orig. Title: Inde. (Illus.). 260p. 1980. 50.00 (ISBN 0-86565-003-9). Vendome.
--India & Bangla Desh: Selected Speeches & Statements, March-December, 1971. 200p. 1972. text ed. 4.50x (ISBN 0-391-00508-1). Humanities.
Gandhi, Kishore. Aldous Huxley: Vedantic & Buddhistic Influences. 256p. 1980. text ed. write for info. (ISBN 0-391-02024-2). Humanities.
Gandhi, Kishore, ed. Contemporary Relevance of Sri Aurobundo. 1973. text ed. 10.50x (ISBN 0-391-00497-2). Humanities.
Gandhi, M. K. Satyagraha in South Africa. Desai, V. G., tr. 1980. 8.00 (ISBN 0-934676-15-1). Greenlf Bks.
Gandhi, Mohanad K. The Collected Works of Mahatma Gandi: 12/17/1942 to 07/31/1944, Vol. 77. LC 58-36286. (Illus.). 508p. 1979. 10.00x o.p. (ISBN 0-8002-2466-3). Intl Pubns Serv.
Gandhi, Mohandas. Gandhi on Non-Violence: Selected Texts from Gandhi's Non-Violence in Peace & War. Merton, Thomas, ed. LC 65-15672. (Orig.). 1965. pap. 2.95 (ISBN 0-8112-0097-3, NDP197). New Directions.
Gandhi, Mohandas K. All Men Are Brothers. LC 59-426. 1969. 15.00x (ISBN 0-231-02919-5). Columbia U Pr.
--Collected Works: Vols. 1-77. LC 58-36286. 1958-1979. Set. 10.00x ea. (ISBN 0-8002-0138-8). Intl Pubns Serv.
--The Essential Gandhi. 1963. text ed. 6.50x o.p. (ISBN 0-04-320009-5). Allen Unwin.
--For Pacifists. Kumarappa, Bharatan, ed. 130p. (Orig.). 1981. pap. 1.50 (ISBN 0-934676-28-3). Greenlf Bks.
--Hind Swaraj, or Indian Home Rule. 110p. (Orig.). 1981. pap. 1.50 (ISBN 0-934676-25-9). Greenlf Bks.
--Man v. Machine. Hingorani, A. T., ed. 113p. (Orig.). 1980. pap. 2.00 (ISBN 0-934676-18-6). Greenlf Bks.
--Socialism of My Conception. Hingorani, Anand T., ed. 290p. (Orig.). 1981. pap. 4.00 (ISBN 0-934676-29-1). Greenlf Bks.
--To the Perplexed. Hingorani, Anand T., ed. 229p. 1981. 6.00 (ISBN 0-934676-27-5). Greenlf Bks.
Gandhi, Om P. Microwave Engineering & Applications. (Illus.). 543p. 1981. 60.00 (ISBN 0-08-025589-2); pap. 24.50 (ISBN 0-08-025588-4). Pergamon.
Gandhi, Ramchandra. Presuppositions of Human Communication. 156p. 1974. 4.50x o.p. (ISBN 0-19-560310-9). Oxford U Pr.
Gandia, Delsie. Benefits in Development for Less Developed Countries Under the EEC's Generalized Scheme of Preferences & Yaounde Agreement. LC 79-91005. 160p. 1980. text ed. 20.00 (ISBN 0-916672-47-6). Allanheld.
Gandin, L. S., jt. auth. see Anapol'Skaya, L. E.
Gandini, A. & Cheradame, H. Cationic Polymerisation. (Advances in Polymer Science Ser.: Vol. 34, 35). (Illus.). 360p. 1980. 79.80 (ISBN 0-387-10049-0). Springer-Verlag.
Gandy, Charles & Zimmerman-Stidham, Susan. Contemporary Classics: Furniture of the Masters. (Architectural Record Ser.). (Illus.). 160p. 1981. 19.75 (ISBN 0-07-022760-8, P&RB). McGraw.
Gandy, Richard E., ed. Theories & Observation in Science. vii, 184p. 1980. lib. bdg. 22.00 (ISBN 0-917930-39-8); pap. 7.50x (ISBN 0-917930-19-3). Ridgeview.
Gane, Christopher. Managing the Training Function. (Professional Management Library). (Illus.). 183p. 1972. text ed. 11.25x o.p. (ISBN 0-04-658045-X). Allen Unwin.
Ganesan, Jayalakshmi, jt. auth. see Sampath, R. K.
Gangadharan, N. Lingapurana: A Study. 1980. 22.50x (ISBN 0-8364-0618-4, Pub. by Ajanta). South Asia Bks.
Gangal, S. C. Gandhian Way to World Peace. 1960. 4.50x o.p. (ISBN 0-8426-1266-1). Verry.
Gangemi, Kenneth. Corroboree. LC 76-27241. 96p. 1977. pap. 2.95 (ISBN 0-685-56012-0). Assembling Pr.
--OLT. LC 75-476287. 1979. pap. 5.95 (ISBN 0-7145-0660-5, Pub. by M Boyars). Merrimack Bk Serv.
--The Volcanoes from Puebla. 192p. 1979. 11.95 (ISBN 0-7145-2577-4, Pub. by M Boyars). Merrimack Bk Serv.
Gangloff, Eric J., tr. & intro. by see Kinoshita Junji.
Gangopadhyaya, Mrinalkanti. Indian Atomosm: History & Sources. 384p. 1980. pap. text ed. write for info. (ISBN 0-391-02177-X). Humanities.
Gangrade, Kesharichand D. Challenge & Response: Study of Famines in India. LC 73-903461. xiii, 124p. 1973. 8.00x o.p. (ISBN 0-88386-406-1). South Asia Bks.
Gangstad, John E. The Great Pyramid: Signs in the Sun. LC 76-24077. (Illus.). 200p. 1976. lib. bdg. 9.95 (ISBN 0-9603374-0-7); pap. 5.95 (ISBN 0-9603374-1-5); 1980 supplement 2.50 (ISBN 0-9603374-2-3). Di-Tri Bks.
Ganguli, B. N. Integration of International Economic Relations. pap. 3.00x o.p. (ISBN 0-210-22217-4). Asia.
Ganguli, H. C. Some Thoughts on Planning in India. pap. 1.75x o.p. (ISBN 0-210-27181-7). Asia.
--Structure & Processes of Organization. 1964. 6.50 o.p. (ISBN 0-210-27005-5). Asia.
Ganguly, Shivaji, jt. ed. see Rajan, M. S.
Gani, J. & Rohatgi, V. K., eds. Contributions to Probability: A Collection of Papers Dedicated to Eugen Lukacs. LC 80-768. 1981. 40.00 (ISBN 0-12-274460-8). Acad Pr.
Ganjemi, Kenneth. The Interceptor Pilot. 128p. 1981. 11.50 (ISBN 0-7145-2699-1, Pub. by M. Boyars). Merrimack Bk Serv.

Ganley, Albert C., et al. After Hiroshima: America Since Nineteen Forty-Five. (Illus.). 320p. (Orig.). (gr. 11-12). 1979. pap. text ed. 4.75x (ISBN 0-88334-121-2). Ind Sch Pr.

Gann. Masada. pap. 2.75 (ISBN 0-515-05443-7). BJ Pub Group.

Gann, Ernest K. The Aviator. LC 80-68543. 1981. 10.95 (ISBN 0-87795-299-X). Arbor Hse.

--In the Company of Eagles. 240p. (Orig.). 1981. pap. 2.50 (ISBN 0-515-05484-4). Jove Pubns.

--Island in the Sky. 224p. 1981. pap. 2.50 (ISBN 0-515-05483-6). Jove Pubns.

--Masada. Orig. Title: The Antagonists. 320p. 1981. pap. 2.95 (ISBN 0-515-05443-7). Jove Pubns.

--Song of the Sirens. 256p. 1981. pap. 2.50 (ISBN 0-515-05482-8). Jove Pubns.

Gann, L. H. & Duigan, Peter. The Stability of South Africa-or Why South Africa Will Survive. 320p. 1980. write for info. St Martin.

Gann, L. H. & Duignan, Peter. Africa South of the Sahara: The Challenge to Western Security. LC 80-82750. (Publication Ser.: No. 238). 155p. 1980. pap. 9.95 (ISBN 0-8179-7382-6). Hoover Inst Pr.

--Why South Africa Will Survive. 329p. 1980. write for info. St Martin.

Gann, L. H., jt. auth. see Duignan, Peter.

Gann, Lewis H. Birth of a Plural Society: The Development of Northern Rhodesia Under the British South African Company. 1958. text ed. 18.00x (ISBN 0-685-12359-6). Humanities.

Gann, Pamela B., jt. auth. see Kahn, Douglas A.

Gann, William D. The Subtle Art of Choosing Early & Late Leaders in the Operations of the Stock Market. (Illus.). 123p. 1981. 49.85 (ISBN 0-918968-97-6). Inst Econ Finan.

--Successful Stock Selecting Methods in Wall Street. (The New Stock Market Reference Library). (Illus.). 118p. 1981. 49.85 (ISBN 0-918968-96-8). Inst Econ Finan.

Gannaway, Dave. Buying a Secondhand Boat. 104p. 1980. 15.00x (ISBN 0-245-53446-6, Pub. by Nautical England). State Mutual Bk.

--Small Boat Building. 1980. 6.00x (ISBN 0-245-52656-0, Pub. by Nautical England). State Mutual Bk.

Gannett, Henry. Origin of Certain Place Names in the United States. LC 68-23159. 1971. Repr. of 1902 ed. 15.00 (ISBN 0-8103-3382-1). Gale.

Gannett, Lewis, tr. see Schacht, Hjalmar.

Gannett, Ruth. Elmer & the Dragon. (Orig.). (gr. k-6). 1980. pap. 1.25 (ISBN 0-440-41761-9, Pub. by YB). Dell.

Gannett, Ruth S. Elmer & the Dragon. (Illus.). (gr. 4-6). 1950. PLB 5.99 o.s.i. (ISBN 0-394-91120-2). Random.

Gannett, Stiles. My Father's Dragon. (gr. k-6). 1980. pap. 1.25 (ISBN 0-440-45628-2, YB). Dell.

Gannon, Edmund C. Sub-Saharan Africa: An Introduction. 1978. pap. 10.00 (ISBN 0-685-59451-3). Coun Am Affair.

Gannon, Francis X. Biographical Dictionary of the Left, 4 vols. Incl. Vol. 1. LC 78-113035. 624p. 1969. 8.00 (ISBN 0-88279-216-4); Vol. 2. 632p. 1971. 9.00 (ISBN 0-88279-223-7); Vol. 3. LC 76-12821. 1972. 9.00 (ISBN 0-88279-224-5); Vol. 4. LC 72-12821. 1973. 11.95 (ISBN 0-88279-226-1). Set. 32.95. Western Islands.

Gannon, Frank. Drugs, What They Are- How They Look- What They Do. LC 70-148361. 1971. 8.95 (ISBN 0-89388-005-1). Okpaku Communications.

Gannon, Franklin R. British Press & Germany, 1936-1939. 1971. 16.50x o.p. (ISBN 0-19-821490-1). Oxford U Pr.

Gannon, Jack. Deaf Heritage: A Narrative History of Deaf America. 1981. text ed. 19.00x (ISBN 0-913072-38-9); pap. text ed. 12.00x (ISBN 0-913072-39-7). Natl Assn Deaf.

Gannon, Robert. How to Raise & Train a Scottish Terrier. (Illus.). pap. 2.00 (ISBN 0-87666-383-8, DS1032). TFH Pubns.

--How to Raise & Train an English Cocker Spaniel. pap. 2.00 (ISBN 0-87666-291-2, DS1014). TFH Pubns.

--How to Raise & Train an Irish Setter. (Illus.). pap. 2.00 (ISBN 0-87666-319-6, DS1024). TFH Pubns.

--Start Right with Goldfish. (Orig.). pap. 2.00 (ISBN 0-87666-081-2, M504). TFH Pubns.

Gannon, Robert I. After More Black Coffee. 1964. 3.50 o.p. (ISBN 0-374-10196-5). FS&G.

Ganoczy, Alexander. Becoming Christian: A Theology of Baptism As the Sacrament of Human History. Lynch, John G., tr. from Fr. LC 76-23530. 1976. pap. 2.95 (ISBN 0-8091-1980-3). Paulist Pr.

Ganong, Joan & Ganong, Warren. Nursing Management. LC 76-29787. 1976. 15.95 o.p. (ISBN 0-912862-30-0). Aspen Systems.

Ganong, Joan, jt. auth. see Ganong, Warren.

Ganong, W. F., jt. ed. see Martini, L.

Ganong, Warren & Ganong, Joan. Cases in Nursing Management. LC 79-2572. 1979. text ed. 23.95 (ISBN 0-89443-152-8). Aspen Systems.

--Nursing Management. 2nd ed. 350p. 1980. text ed. 19.95 (ISBN 0-89443-278-8). Aspen Systems.

Ganong, Warren, jt. auth. see Ganong, Joan.

Ganong, William F. & Martini, Luciano, eds. Frontiers in Neuroendocrinology, Vol. 5. LC 77-82030. 1978. 31.00 (ISBN 0-89004-135-0). Raven.

Ganong, William F., jt. ed. see Martini, Luciano.

Gans, Benjamin J. Atlas of Oral Surgery. LC 73-187485. (Illus.). 232p. 1972. 34.50 o.p. (ISBN 0-8016-1723-5). Mosby.

Gans, Bruce, jt. auth. see Cohen, Steven.

Gans, Eric. The Origin of Language: A Formal Theory of Representation. 1981. 19.95x (ISBN 0-520-04202-6). U of Cal Pr.

Gans, Eric L. The Discovery of Illusion: Flaubert's Early Works, 1835-1837. (U. C. Publ. in Modern Philology: Vol. 100). 1971. pap. 8.50x (ISBN 0-520-09371-2). U of Cal Pr.

Gans, Herbert, et al, eds. On the Making of Americans: Essays in Honor of David Riesman. LC 78-65118. (Illus.). 1979. 19.95x (ISBN 0-8122-7754-6). U of Pa Pr.

Gans, Herbert J. Urban Villagers. LC 62-15362. 1965. pap. text ed. 7.95 (ISBN 0-02-911120-X). Free Pr.

Gans, Irvin. The Gourmet Doggie Bag Cookbook. Date not set. 6.95 (ISBN 0-533-04764-1). Vantage.

Gans, Roma. Bird Talk. LC 71-132298. (A Let's-Read- and- Find-Out Science Bk). (Illus.). (gr. k-3). 1971. PLB 7.89 (ISBN 0-690-14593-4, TYC-J). T Y Crowell.

--Birds Eat & Eat & Eat. LC 63-9213. (A Let's-Read-&-Find-Out Science Bk). (Illus.). (gr. k-3). 1963. bds. 7.95 (ISBN 0-690-14514-4, TYC-J); PLB 6.89 o.p. (ISBN 0-690-14515-2); filmstrip with record 11.95 (ISBN 0-690-14516-0); filmstrip with cassette 14.95 (ISBN 0-690-14518-7). T Y Crowell.

--Caves. LC 76-4881. (Let's Read & Find Out Science Book Ser.). (Illus.). (gr. k-3). 1977. PLB 7.89 (ISBN 0-690-01070-2, TYC-J). T Y Crowell.

--Guiding Children's Reading Through Experience. LC 79-16407. 1979. pap. 6.50x (ISBN 0-8077-2569-2). Tchrs Coll.

--Hummingbirds in the Garden. LC 69-11083. (A Let's Read- & Find-Out Science Bk). (Illus.). (gr. k-3). 1969. PLB 7.89 (ISBN 0-690-42562-7, TYC-J). T Y Crowell.

--Icebergs. LC 64-18163. (A Let's-Read-&-Find-Out Science Bk). (Illus.). (gr. k-3). 1964. PLB 7.89 (ISBN 0-690-42775-1, TYC-J). T Y Crowell.

--It's Nesting Time. LC 64-10861. (A Let's-Read-&-Find-Out Science Bk). (Illus.). (gr. k-3). 1964. PLB 6.89 o.p. (ISBN 0-690-45544-5, TYC-J); filmstrip with record 11.95 o.p. (ISBN 0-690-45545-3); filmstrip with cassette 14.95 o.p. (ISBN 0-690-45547-X). T Y Crowell.

--It's Nesting Time. LC 64-10861. (Crocodile Paperbacks Ser.). (Illus.). 33p. (gr. k-3). 1972. pap. 1.45 o.p. (ISBN 0-690-45549-6, TYC-J). T Y Crowell.

--Millions & Millions of Crystals. LC 72-7547. (A Let's Read & Find Out Science Bk). (Illus.). (gr. k-3). 1973. PLB 7.89 (ISBN 0-690-54030-2, TYC-J). T Y Crowell.

--Oil: The Buried Treasure. LC 74-7375. (A Let's-Read-&-Find-Out Science Bk). (Illus.). (gr. k-3). 1975. PLB 7.89 (ISBN 0-690-00613-6, TYC-J). T Y Crowell.

--Water for Dinosaurs & You. LC 78-158691. (A Let's-Read-&-Find-Out Science Bk). (Illus.). (gr. k-3). 1972. PLB 7.89 (ISBN 0-690-87027-2, TYC-J); pap. 2.95 crocodile paperback ser. (ISBN 0-690-00202-5, TYC-J). T Y Crowell.

--When Birds Change Their Feathers. LC 78-20627. (Let's-Read-&-Find-Out Science Books). (Illus.). 40p. (gr. k-3). 1980. 7.95 (ISBN 0-690-03947-6, TYC-J); PLB 7.89 (ISBN 0-690-03948-4). T Y Crowell.

Gansberg, Judith M. Stalag: U.S.A. The Remarkable Story of German POWs in America. LC 76-51407. (Illus.). 1977. 10.95 o.s.i. (ISBN 0-690-01223-3, TYC-T). T Y Crowell.

Ganschow, Thomas W., jt. ed. see Bertsch, Gary K.

Ganshof, F. L. Carolingians & the Frankish Monarchy: Studies in Carolingian History. Sondheimer, Janet, tr. LC 72-147074. (Illus.). 1971. 22.50x o.p. (ISBN 0-8014-0635-8). Cornell U Pr.

Ganshof, Francois L. Etude Sur les Ministeriales En Flandre et En Lotharingie. LC 80-2029. 1981. Repr. of 1926 ed. 44.50 (ISBN 0-404-18563-0). AMS Pr.

--Frankish Institutions Under Charlemagne. Lyon, Bryce & Lyon, Mary, trs. LC 68-29166. 191p. 1968. 8.50x (ISBN 0-87057-108-7, Pub. by Brown U Pr). Univ Pr of New England.

Gansler, Jacques S. The Defense Industry. 432p. 1980. text ed. 19.95 (ISBN 0-262-07078-2). MIT Pr.

Ganss, George E., ed. Jesuit Religious Life Today. LC 77-78816. (Jesuit Primary Sources in English Translation Ser.: No. 3). 190p. 1977. pap. 3.00 (ISBN 0-912422-27-0); pap. 4.00 smyth sewn o.s.i. (ISBN 0-912422-29-7). Inst Jesuit.

Ganss, George E., ed. see Fleming, David L.

Ganss, George E., ed. see Gruenberg, Gladys W.

Ganss, George E., tr. & commentary by see Ignatius Of Loyola, St.

Gant, Jonathan. Long Vendetta. (YA) 4.95 o.p. (ISBN 0-685-07442-0, Avalon). Bouregy.

Gant, Margaret E. The Raven's Story. LC 80-105389. (Illus.). 1979. 9.95 (ISBN 0-9603138-0-X). M E Gant.

Gant, Michael S., ed. see De la Perouse.

Gant, Michael S., ed. see Rowland, Leon.

Gant, Michael S., ed. see Young, John V.

Gant, Norman F. & Worley, Richard. Hypertensions in Pregnancy. 224p. 1980. 18.50x (ISBN 0-8385-4002-3). ACC.

Gant, R., tr. see Zola, Emile.

Gant, Roland, ed. & intro. by. Edward Thomas in the Countryside. 1977. 14.95 (ISBN 0-571-10799-0, Pub. by Faber & Faber). Merrimack Bk Serv.

Gant, Roland, ed. see Thomas, Edward.

Gant, Thomas & Vasconez, Luis. Post-Mastectomy Reconstruction. (Illus.). 196p. 1980. softcover 27.00 (ISBN 0-683-03419-7). Williams & Wilkins.

Ganter, et al. Retrieval from Limbo: The Intermediary Group Treatment of Inaccessible Children. LC 67-14602. 117p. 1967. pap. 2.40 o.p. (ISBN 0-87868-026-8, CW-23). Child Welfare.

Gantmacher, Felix R. Theory of Matrices, 2 Vols. LC 59-11779. Vol. 1. 15.95 (ISBN 0-8284-0131-4); Vol. 2. 12.95 (ISBN 0-8284-0133-0). Chelsea Pub.

Gantos, Jack. Swampy Alligator. (Illus.). (gr. 3-5). Date not set. 7.95 (ISBN 0-671-96092-X). Dial.

Gantt, W. H., et al. Pavlovian Approach to Psychopathology. 1970. 52.00 (ISBN 0-08-013016-X). Pergamon.

Ganz, Arthur. Realms of the Self: Variations on a Theme in Modern Drama. (The Gotham Library). 256p. 1981. 17.95x (ISBN 0-8147-2979-7); pap. 8.95x (ISBN 0-8147-2980-0). NYU Pr.

Ganz, Raffael, ed. George Mikes Introduces Switzerland. (Illus.). 1978. 15.95 (ISBN 0-233-96757-5). Transatlantic.

Ganzer, Nick. How to Vertical Fish for Great Lakes Salmon & Trout. (Orig.). 1981. pap. write for info. (ISBN 0-9602648-1-7). Merganzer Pr. Postponed.

Ganzevoort, Herman, tr. see De Gelder, Willem.

Gaona, Francisco. Basic Spanish One, 6 vols. 1971. Set. 12.75 (ISBN 0-86589-032-3). Vol. 1, Units 1,2 (ISBN 0-86589-033-1). Vol. 2, Units 3-4 (ISBN 0-86589-034-X). Vol. 3, Units 5-6 (ISBN 0-86589-035-8). Vol. 4, Units 7-8 (ISBN 0-86589-036-6). Vol. 5, Units 9-10 (ISBN 0-86589-037-4). Vol. 6, Unit 11-12 (ISBN 0-86589-038-2). Student Guide I (ISBN 0-86589-039-0). Individual Learn.

GAP Ad Hoc Committee. Crisis in Child Mental Health: Critical Assessment, Vol. 8. LC 72-184968. (Report No. 82). 1972. pap. 2.00 (ISBN 0-87318-115-8). Adv Psychiatry.

GAP Committee on Adolescence. Normal Adolescence: Its Dynamics & Impact, Vol. 6. LC 62-2872. (Report: No. 68). 1968. pap. 4.00 (ISBN 0-87318-093-3). Adv Psychiatry.

GAP Committee on Aging. Toward a Public Policy on Mental Health Care of the Elderly, Vol. 7. LC 62-2872. (Report No. 79). 1970. pap. 2.00 (ISBN 0-87318-110-7). Adv Psychiatry.

GAP Committee on Child Psychiatry. The Diagnostic Process in Child Psychiatry, Vol. 3. (Report No. 38). 1957. pap. 2.00 (ISBN 0-87318-048-8). Adv Psychiatry.

--Psychopathological Disorders in Childhood: Theoretical Considerations & a Proposed Classification, Vol. 6. LC 62-2872. (Report No. 62). 1966. pap. 6.00 (ISBN 0-87318-087-9). Adv Psychiatry.

GAP Committee on Family. Case History Method in the Study of Family Process, Vol. 7. LC 62-2872. (Report No. 76). 1970. pap. 5.00 (ISBN 0-87318-105-0). Adv Psychiatry.

GAP Committee on Governmental Agencies. Preventive Psychiatry in the Armed Forces: With Some Implications for Civilian Use, Vol. 4. (Report No. 47). 1960. pap. 2.00 (ISBN 0-87318-062-3). Adv Psychiatry.

GAP Committee on International Relations. Psychiatrist & Public Issues, Vol. 7. LC 62-2872. (Report No. 74). 1969. pap. 2.00 (ISBN 0-87318-103-4). Adv Psychiatry.

GAP Committee on Med. Education. Education for Community Psychiatry, Vol. 6. LC 62-2872. (Report No. 64). 1967. pap. 2.00 (ISBN 0-87318-089-5). Adv Psychiatry.

GAP Committee on Medical Education. Assessment of Sexual Function: A Guide to Interviewing, Vol. 8. LC 74-158143. (Report No. 88). 1973. pap. 4.00 (ISBN 0-87318-122-0). Adv Psychiatry.

--The Preclinical Teaching of Psychiatry, Vol. 5. (Report: No. 54). 1962. pap. 2.00 (ISBN 0-87318-073-9). Adv Psychiatry.

GAP Committee on Mental Health Services. Drug Misuse: a Psychiatric View of a Modern Dilemma, Vol. 7. LC 62-2872. (Report No. 80). 1970. pap. 2.00 (ISBN 0-87318-112-3). Adv Psychiatry.

GAP Committee on Mental Retardation. Basic Considerations in Mental Retardation: A Preliminary Report, Vol. 4. LC 62-2872. (Report No. 43). 1959. pap. 2.00 (ISBN 0-87318-056-9). Adv Psychiatry.

--Mental Retardation: A Family Crisis; the Therapeutic Role of the Physician, Vol. 5. (Report No. 56). 1963. pap. 1.00 o.p. (ISBN 0-87318-075-5). Adv Psychiatry.

--Mild Mental Retardation: A Growing Challenge to the Physician, Vol. 6. LC 62-2872. (Report No. 66). 1967. pap. 2.00 (ISBN 0-87318-091-7). Adv Psychiatry.

GAP Committee on Preventive Psychiatry. Dimensions of Community Psychiatry, Vol. 6. LC 62-2872. (Report No. 69). 1968. pap. 2.00 (ISBN 0-87318-094-1). Adv Psychiatry.

--Mental Health & Primary Medical Care, Vol. 10. LC 80-19016. (Publication Ser.: No. 105). pap. 4.00 (105, Mental Health Materials Center). Adv Psychiatry.

--Problems of Estimating Changes in Frequency of Mental Disorders, Vol. 4. (Report No. 50). 1961. pap. 2.00 (ISBN 0-87318-067-4). Adv Psychiatry.

GAP Committee on Psychiatry & Community. On Psychotherapy & Casework, Vol. 7. LC 62-2872. (Report No. 71). 1969. pap. 2.00 (ISBN 0-87318-099-2). Adv Psychiatry.

--Psychiatrists As Teachers in Schools of Social Work, Vol. 4. (Report No. 53). 1962. pap. 2.00 (ISBN 0-87318-071-2). Adv Psychiatry.

GAP Committee on Psychiatry & Law. Misuse of Psychiatry in the Criminal Courts: Competency to Stand Trial, Vol. 8. LC 74-170397. (Report No. 89). 1974. pap. 4.00 (ISBN 0-87318-124-7). Adv Psychiatry.

--Right to Abortion: a Psychiatric View, Vol. 7. LC 62-2872. (Report No. 75). 1969. pap. 2.00 (ISBN 0-87318-104-2). Adv Psychiatry.

GAP Committee on Psychiatry & Social Work. The Welfare System & Mental Health, Vol. 8. LC 73-178268. (Report No. 85). 1973. pap. 2.00 (ISBN 0-87318-119-0). Adv Psychiatry.

GAP Committee on Psychiatry & the Community. The Chronic Mental Patient in the Community: Vol. 10. LC 78-55381. (Publication No. 102). 1978. pap. 4.00 (ISBN 0-87318-139-5). Adv Psychiatry.

--Psychiatrist & Public Welfare Agencies, Vol. 9. LC 75-37889. (Report no. 94). 1975. pap. 3.00 (ISBN 0-87318-131-X). Adv Psychiatry.

GAP Committee on Psychopathology. The Recruitment & Training of the Research Psychiatrist, Vol. 6. LC 62-2872. (Report No. 65). 1967. pap. 2.00 (ISBN 0-87318-090-9). Adv Psychiatry.

GAP Committee on Public Education. Medical Practice & Psychiatry: The Impact of Changing Demands, Vol. 5. (Report No. 58). 1964. pap. 2.00 (ISBN 0-87318-077-1). Adv Psychiatry.

GAP Committee on Research. Psychiatric Research & the Assessment of Change, Vol. 6. LC 62-2872. (Report No. 63). 1966. pap. 3.00 (ISBN 0-87318-088-7). Adv Psychiatry.

GAP Committee on Social Issues. Psychiatric Aspects of School Desegregation, Vol. 3. LC 57-7606. (Report No. 37). 1957. pap. 2.00 (ISBN 0-87318-045-3). Adv Psychiatry.

--Psychiatric Aspects of the Prevention of Nuclear War, Vol. 5. LC 64-7800. (Report No. 57). 1964. pap. 4.00 (ISBN 0-87318-076-3). Adv Psychiatry.

GAP Committee on the College Student. A College Experience: The Focus for Psychiatric Research, Vol. 4. (Report No. 52). 1962. pap. 2.00 (ISBN 0-87318-070-4). Adv Psychiatry.

--Sex & the College Student, Vol. 6. LC 65-28363. (Report No. 60). 1965. pap. 2.00 (ISBN 0-87318-085-2). Adv Psychiatry.

Gap Committee on the Family. Divorce, Child Custody & the Family, Vol. 10. LC 80-25935. (Publications Ser.: No. 106). 1980. pap. 12.95 (ISBN 0-910958-10-6, 106, Mental Health Materials Center). Adv Psychiatry.

--Integration & Conflict in Family Behavior, Vol. 6. (Report No. 27A). 1968. pap. 2.00 (ISBN 0-87318-096-8). Adv Psychiatry.

GAP Committee on Therapeutic Care. Crisis in Psychiatric Hospitalization, Vol. 7. LC 62-2872. (Report No. 72). 1969. pap. 2.00 (ISBN 0-87318-101-8). Adv Psychiatry.

GAP Committee on Therapy. Problems of Psychiatric Leadership, Vol. 8. LC 74-170958. (Report No. 90). 1974. pap. 2.00 (ISBN 0-87318-125-5). Adv Psychiatry.

--Psychotherapy & the Dual Research Tradition, Vol. 7. LC 62-2872. (Report No. 73). 1969. pap. 2.00 (ISBN 0-87318-102-6). Adv. Psychiatry.

Gapany-Gapana, Vicius B. Otosclerosis: Genetics & Surgical Rehabilitation. LC 75-8545. 1975. 34.95 (ISBN 0-470-29080-3). Halsted Pr.

Gapen, D. Kaye & Library & Information Technology Association, eds. Authority Control: Proceedings of the LITA Institute. 1981. price not set (ISBN 0-912700-85-8). Oryx Pr.

Gapen, D. Kaye, ed. see Library & Information Technology Association.

Gappa, Sylvia & Glenn, Deirdre. Room to Grow. LC 80-81681. (Learning Handbooks Ser.). 1981. pap. 5.95 (ISBN 0-8224-5875-6). Pitman Learning.

Gappert, Gary & Rose, Harold M., eds. The Social Economy of Cities. LC 73-88911. (Urban Affairs Annual Reviews: Vol. 9). 1975. 25.00x (ISBN 0-8039-0326-X). Sage.

Gara, Larry. The Liberty Line: The Legend of the Underground Railroad. LC 61-6552. 216p. 1967. pap. 5.50x (ISBN 0-8131-0115-8). U Pr of Ky.

Gara, Otta G. & Naegeli, Bruce A. Technological Changes & the Law: A Reader. LC 92-276. 1979. lib. bdg. 25.00 (ISBN 0-930342-97-6). W S Hein.

Garabedian, Paul R. Partial Differential Equations. LC 64-11505. 1964. 35.95 (ISBN 0-471-29088-2). Wiley.

Garabedian, Peter G. & Gibbons, Don C., eds. Becoming Delinquent: Young Offenders & the Correctional Process. LC 73-91727. (Illus.). 1970. text ed. 16.95x (ISBN 0-202-30103-6). Aldine Pub.

Garam, Katalin, jt. ed. see Simai, Mihaly.

Garard, Ira. The Story of Food. LC 73-94093. (Illus., Orig.). 1974. pap. 11.00 (ISBN 0-87055-155-8). AVI.

Garard, Ira D. Introductory Food Chemistry. (Illus.). 1976. lib. bdg. 27.00 (ISBN 0-87055-206-6); pap. text ed. 17.00 (ISBN 0-87055-288-0). AVI.

Garas, F. K. & Armer, G. S. T., eds. Reinforced & Prestressed Microconcrete Models. (Illus.). 400p. 1980. text ed. 55.00 cased (ISBN 0-86095-880-9). Longman.

Garas, F. K., jt. ed. see Armer, G. S.

Garattini, S. & Berendes, H. W., eds. Pharmacology of Steroid Contraceptive Drugs. LC 77-6100. (Monographs of the Mario Negri Institute for Pharmacological Research). 1977. 35.00 (ISBN 0-89004-187-3). Raven.

Garattini, S. & Franchi, G., eds. Chemotherapy of Cancer Dissemination & Metastasis. LC 72-96335. (Monographs of the Mario Negri Institute for Pharmacological Research). (Illus.). 400p. 1973. 34.50 (ISBN 0-911216-46-4). Raven.

Garattini, S. & Samanin, R., eds. Central Mechanisms of Anorectic Drugs. LC 77-17749. (Monographs of the Mario Negri Institute for Pharmacological Research). 1978. 40.00 (ISBN 0-89004-219-5). Raven.

Garattini, S., et al, eds. Interactions Between Putative Neurotransmitters in the Brain. LC 77-83686. (Monographs of the Mario Negri Institute for Pharmacological Research). 1978. 34.50 (ISBN 0-89004-196-2). Raven.

--Benzodiazepines. LC 78-181304. (Monograph of the Mario Negri Institute for Pharmacological Research). (Illus.). 707p. 1973. 60.00 (ISBN 0-911216-25-1). Raven.

Garattini, Silvio, jt. ed. see De Gaetano, Giovanni.

Garb, Forrest A. Waterflood Calculations for Hand-Held Computers. (Illus.). 200p. 1981. 19.95 (ISBN 0-87201-895-4). Gulf Pub.

Garber, A. Brent & Sparks, Leroy. Hospital Crisis Management: A Casebook. LC 79-25691. 1978. text ed. 27.00 (ISBN 0-89443-079-3). Aspen Systems.

--Learn-a-Term. LC 77-82026. 1977. pap. text ed. 16.50 (ISBN 0-912862-48-3). Aspen Systems.

Garber, Aubrey. Mountain-Ese. LC 76-3278. 105p. 1976. 4.95 (ISBN 0-89227-004-7); pap. 2.95 (ISBN 0-89227-038-1). Commonwealth Pr.

Garber, Eugene K. Metaphysical Tales: Short Fiction by Eugene K. Garber. 128p. 1981. text ed. 10.00x (ISBN 0-8262-0325-6). U of Mo Pr.

Garber, Frederick. Thoreau's Redemptive Imagination. LC 77-73031. (Gotham Library). 229p. 1977. pap. 6.00x (ISBN 0-8147-2965-7); pap. 4.95x (ISBN 0-8147-2966-5). NYU Pr.

Garber, Frederick, ed. see Radcliffe, Ann.

Garber, Janet. High Action Reading for Comprehension, D. Incl. Study Skills. Hansen, Merrily. pap. text ed. 2.40 (ISBN 0-87895-428-7); Vocabulary. Christensen, Barbara. pap. text ed. 2.40 (ISBN 0-87895-426-0). (Skillbooster Ser.). (gr. 4). 1979. pap. text ed. 2.40 (ISBN 0-87895-427-9). Modern Curr.

--High Action Reading for Comprehension, E. Incl. Study Skills. Hansen, Merrily. pap. text ed. 2.40 (ISBN 0-87895-531-3); Vocabulary. Christensen, Barbara. pap. text ed. 2.40 (ISBN 0-87895-529-1). (Skillbooster Ser.). (gr. 5). 1979. pap. text ed. 2.40 (ISBN 0-87895-530-5). Modern Curr.

--High Action Reading for Study Skills-F. Incl. Study Skills. Hansen, Merrily. pap. text ed. 2.40 (ISBN 0-87895-634-4); High Action Reading for Vocabulary. Christensen, Barbara. pap. text ed. 2.40 (ISBN 0-87895-632-8). (Skillbooster Ser.). (gr. 6). 1979. pap. text ed. 2.40 (ISBN 0-87895-633-6). Modern Curr.

Garber, Judy & Seligman, Martin E., eds. Human Helplessness: Theory & Applications. LC 79-6773. 1980. 18.50 (ISBN 0-12-275050-0). Acad Pr.

Garber, Lee O., ed. Current Legal Concepts in Education. LC 65-22382. 1966. 9.00x o.p. (ISBN 0-8122-7497-0). U of Pa Pr.

Garber, Max B. & Bond, P. S. A Modern Military Dictionary: Ten Thousand Technical & Slang Terms of Military Usage. 2nd ed. LC 74-31354. 1975. Repr. of 1942 ed. 20.00 (ISBN 0-8103-4208-1). Gale.

Garber, Patty J., et al. Kinder-Fun Insect Series. rev. ed. Incl. Funny Little Ant; Ladybug, Ladybug; Fly, Fly; The Little Yellow Butterfly; The Little Mosquito; The Bad Little Cricket. (Illus.). 16p. (For partially-sighted & partially-hearing children). (ps-2). 1973. Set. pap. text ed. 16.00x (ISBN 0-89039-055-X). Ann Arbor Pubs.

--Kinder-Fun Sports Series. Incl. Fun Balls; Jump, Jump, Jump; A Home Run; Joey (Basketball; Football; Snow Fun. (Illus.). 16p. (For partially-sighted & partially-hearing children). (ps-2). 1973. Set. pap. text ed. 16.00 (ISBN 0-89039-056-8). Ann Arbor Pubs.

Garbett, Thomas. Corporate Advertising: The What, the Why, & the How. (Illus.). 224p. 1981. 24.95 (ISBN 0-07-022787-X, C). McGraw.

Garbicz, Adam & Klinowski, Jacek. Cinema, the Magic Vehicle-A Guide to Its Achievement-Journey One: The Cinema Through 1949. LC 75-2183. 551p. 1975. 22.50 (ISBN 0-8108-0801-3). Scarecrow.

--Cinema, the Magic Vehicle-A Guide to Its Achievement-Journey Two: The Cinema in the Fifties. LC 75-2183. 551p. 1979. 27.50 (ISBN 0-8108-1241-X). Scarecrow.

Garbo, Norman. Cabal. 1980. pap. 2.95 (ISBN 0-440-10883-7). Dell.

Garbuny, Max. Optical Physics. 1965. text ed. 22.95 (ISBN 0-12-275350-X). Acad Pr.

Garbus, Martin. Ready for the Defense. 320p. 1971. write for info. FS&G.

Garbutt, Bernard. The Day of the Horse. (Illus.). 67p. 1976. 10.50 o.p. (ISBN 0-87358-145-8). Northland.

Garbutt, J. W. & Bartlett, A. J. Experimental Biology with Micro-Organisms. 1972. pap. text ed. 4.95 (ISBN 0-408-70228-1); teachers' guide 12.95 (ISBN 0-408-70240-0). Butterworths.

Garchik, Morton. Art Fundamentals. LC 78-10336. (Illus.). 1979. 14.95 (ISBN 0-87396-082-3). Stravon.

Garcia. Diagnostic Neuropathology. 1981. price not set. Masson Pub.

Garcia, Carlos. Guzman, Hinde & Hannam Outstript: Being a Discovery of the Whole Art, Mistery & Antiquity of Theeves & Theeving. LC 80-2480. 1981. Repr. of 1657 ed. 49.50 (ISBN 0-404-19114-2). AMS Pr.

Garcia, Carmen I. Raffucci De see Raffucci de Garcia, Carmen I.

Garcia, Cisneros F. Jose Marti y las Artes Plasticas. 1972. 9.95 (ISBN 0-88303-996-6); pap. 7.95 (ISBN 0-685-73207-X). E Torres & Sons.

Garcia, Clarita. Clarita's Cocina: Great Traditional Recipes from a Spanish Kitchen. LC 74-113069. (Illus.). 1970. 10.95 (ISBN 0-385-04657-X). Doubleday.

Garcia, David. Fairy Tales of Puerto Rico. (Children's Bks: No. 166). (Illus.). 50p. (gr. 1-5). 1981. 6.95 (ISBN 0-934642-02-8). Puerto Rico Almanacs.

Garcia, David, jt. auth. see Ogletree, Earl J.

Garcia, Elvira F. A Critical Edition of Tirso De Molina's Marta la Piadosa. (Salzburg Studies in English Literature: Elizabethan & Renaissance Studies: No. 78). 1978. pap. text ed. 25.00x (ISBN 0-391-01380-7). Humanities.

Garcia, F. Chris & Hain, Paul. New Mexico Government. rev. ed. 360p. 1981. 12.95 (ISBN 0-686-68597-0). U of NM Pr.

Garcia, Hazel D., jt. auth. see Stevens, John D.

Garcia, Juan R. Operation Wetback: The Mass Deportation of Mexican Undocumented Workers in 1954. LC 79-6189. (Contributions in Ethnic Studies: No. 2). (Illus.). xvii, 268p. 1980. lib. bdg. 25.00 (ISBN 0-313-21353-4, GOW/). Greenwood.

Garcia, Lynne S. & Ash, Lawrence R. Diagnostic Parasitology: Clinical Laboratory Manual. 2nd ed. LC 78-31497. (Illus.). 1979. pap. text ed. 14.95 (ISBN 0-8016-1741-3). Mosby.

Garcia, Manuel, II. A Complete Treatise on the Art of Singing, Pt. 2. Paschke, V., tr. from Span. & pref. by. LC 74-23382. xii, 261p. 1975. Repr. of 1972 ed. lib. bdg. 25.00 (ISBN 0-306-70660-1). Da Capo.

Garcia, Mario R. Contemporary Newspaper Design: A Structural Approach. (Illus.). 240p. 1981. text ed. 25.95 (ISBN 0-13-170381-1); pap. text ed. 12.95 (ISBN 0-13-170373-0). P-H.

Garcia, Mary H. & Gonzalez-Mena, Janet. The Big E: Learning Package One. Ragan, Lise B., ed. LC 75-27579. (Prog. Bk.). (gr. 1-2). 1976. tchr's ed. 9.95 (ISBN 0-88499-228-4); workbook 1.95 (ISBN 0-88499-230-6); pkg. of 10 tests 9.95 (ISBN 0-88499-229-2); program package 35.00 (ISBN 0-88499-231-4). Inst Mod Lang.

Garcia, Ricardo. Ensenanza Bilingue. LC 76-16879. (Fastback Ser.: No. 84s). (Sp.). 1976. pap. 0.75 (ISBN 0-87367-084-1). Phi Delta Kappa.

Garcia, Rolando V. Nature Pleads Not Guilty: An IFIAS Report. (Illus.). 330p. Date not set. 54.01 (ISBN 0-08-025823-9). Pergamon.

Garcia, Salvador. Las Ideas Literarias en Espana entre 1840 y 1850. (U. C. Publ. in Modern Philology: Vol. 98). (Span). 1971. pap. 7.50x (ISBN 0-520-09365-8). U of Cal Pr.

Garcia-Barron, Carlos. Cancionero De la Hisapno-Peruana De 1866. LC 79-51156. (Coleccion De Estudios Hispanicos: Hispanic Studies Collection). (Illus.). 226p. (Span.). 1980. pap. 12.95 (ISBN 0-89729-225-1). Ediciones.

Garcia-Cortez, Julio. Pataki: Leyendas Y Misterios De los Orishas Africanos. LC 79-54684. (Coleccion Ebano Y Canela Ser.). (Illus.). 250p. (Span.). 1980. pap. 14.95 (ISBN 0-89729-236-7). Ediciones.

Garcia De Leon, Luis, tr. see Didactic Systems Staff.

Garcia de Serrano, Irma, compiled by. (Resoluciones De la Junta De Personal De Puerto Rico, Vols. 1, 3 & 4. (Illus., Sp.). 1980. Set. write for info. (ISBN 0-8477-2218-X). Vol. I (ISBN 0-8477-2221-X). Vol. II (ISBN 0-8477-2223-6). Vol. III. Vol. IV (ISBN 0-8477-2224-4). U of PR Pr.

Garcia-Diaz, Alberto, jt. auth. see Phillips, Don T.

Garcia-Granados, Jorge. The Birth of Israel: The Drama As I Saw It. (Return to Zion Ser.). viii, 291p. 1980. Repr. of 1948 ed. lib. bdg. 20.00x (ISBN 0-87991-141-7). Porcupine Pr.

Garcia Lorca, Federico see Lorca, Federico Garcia.

Garcia-Marquez, Gabriel. Innocent Erendira & Other Stories. Rabassa, Gregory, tr. from Span. LC 74-15873. 1979. pap. 3.95 (ISBN 0-06-090701-0, CN 701, CN). Har-Row.

--Leaf Storm & Other Stories. Rabassa, Gregory, tr. from Span. LC 76-138784. 192p. 1972. 10.95 o.s.i. (ISBN 0-06-012779-1, HarpT). Har-Row.

--No One Writes to the Colonel & Other Stories. Bernstein, J. S., tr. from Span. LC 68-15977. 1979. pap. 3.95 (ISBN 0-06-090700-2, CN 700, CN). Har-Row.

Garcia-Moliner, F. & Flores, F. Introduction to the Theory of Solid Surfaces. LC 78-17617. (Cambridge Monographs on Physics). (Illus.). 1979. 71.50 (ISBN 0-521-22294-X). Cambridge U Pr.

Garcia-Pelayo, R. & Testas, J. Dictionnaire moderne Larousse, francais-espagnol et espagnol-francais. (Span. & Fr.). 39.95 (ISBN 2-03-020601-6, 3773). Larousse.

Garcia-Prada, Carlos & Wilson, William E. Entendamonos: Manual de Conversacion. 2nd ed. (Span). 1959. pap. text ed. 9.15 (ISBN 0-395-04481-2). HM.

--Tres Cuentos. 2nd ed. LC 59-4973. (Span). 1959. pap. text ed. 7.20 (ISBN 0-395-04482-0). HM.

Garcia-Zamor, Jean-Claude, ed. Politics & Administration in Brazil. LC 78-58823. 1978. pap. text ed. 17.50 (ISBN 0-8191-0544-9). U Pr of Amer.

Gard, Donald H. The Exegetical Method of the Greek Translator of the Book of Job. (Society of Biblical Literature Monographs: No. 8). 1952. pap. 7.50 (ISBN 0-89130-178-X, 060008). Scholars Pr Ca.

Gard, Richard A., ed. Buddhism. LC 61-15499. (Great Religions of Modern Man Ser). 8.95 (ISBN 0-8076-0166-7). Braziller.

Gard, Robert E., et al, eds. We Were Children Then: Ninety Wisconsin Writers, Age Sixty to Ninety-Six. LC 76-22967. 1976. pap. 8.95 (ISBN 0-88361-041-8). Stanton & Lee.

Gard, Roger, ed. Henry James: The Critical Heritage. (The Critical Heritage Ser.). 1976. Repr. of 1968 ed. 38.50x (ISBN 0-7100-6068-8). Routledge & Kegan.

Gard, Roger M. Du see Du Gard, Roger.

Gard, Spencer A. Jones on Evidence, Civil & Criminal, 4 vols. 6th ed. LC 72-76892. 1972. Set. 170.00 (ISBN 0-686-14505-4). Lawyers Co-Op.

Gard, Wayne. The Chisholm Trail. (Illus., Orig.). 1954. 13.50 (ISBN 0-8061-0291-8); pap. 6.95 (ISBN 0-8061-1536-X). U of Okla Pr.

--Frontier Justice. (Illus.). 324p. 1981. 17.50 (ISBN 0-8061-0194-6); pap. 8.95 (ISBN 0-8061-1755-9). U of Okla Pr.

--Great Buffalo Hunt. LC 59-11049. (Illus.). 1968. pap. 5.95 (ISBN 0-8032-5067-3, BB 390, Bison). U of Nebr Pr.

--Sam Bass. LC 36-17302. (Illus.). x, 262p. 1969. 10.50x (ISBN 0-8032-0868-5); pap. 3.65 (ISBN 0-8032-5068-1, BB 391, Bison). U of Nebr Pr.

Gardair, J. M. Pirandello: Fantasmes et logique du double. new ed. (Collection themes et textes). 160p. (Orig., Fr.). 1972. pap. 6.75 (ISBN 2-03-035003-6, 2688). Larousse.

Gardam, Jane. Bilgewater. LC 77-2890. (gr. 7 up). 1977. 8.25 (ISBN 0-688-80108-0); PLB 7.92 (ISBN 0-688-84108-2). Greenwillow.

--A Few Fair Days. LC 71-187794. (Illus.). (gr. 5 up). 1972. 4.95g o.s.i. (ISBN 0-02-735790-2). Macmillan.

--Long Way from Verona. LC 76-171923. 192p. (YA) (gr. 7-12). 1972. 4.95 o.s.i. (ISBN 0-02-735780-5). Macmillan.

--A Long Way from Verona. LC 76-171923. 256p. (gr. 7 up). 1974. pap. 1.25 o.s.i. (ISBN 0-02-043220-8, 04322, Collier). Macmillan.

--The Sidmouth Letters. LC 80-23940. 163p. 1980. 8.95 (ISBN 0-688-00134-3). Morrow.

Garde, R. J. & Raju, K. Ranga. Mechanics of Sediment Transportation & Alluvial Stream Problems. LC 77-13628. 1978. 22.95 (ISBN 0-470-99329-4). Halsted Pr.

Gardel, A. Energie: Economie et Prospective. LC 79-40986. (Illus.). 1979. 82.00 (ISBN 0-08-024782-2). Pergamon.

--Energy: Economy & Prospective: A Handbook for Engineers & Economists. (Illus.). 480p. 1981. 82.00 (ISBN 0-08-025427-6). Pergamon.

Gardell, Bertil & Johansson, Bunn. Working Life: Social Science Contribution to Work Reform. 352p. 1981. write for info. (ISBN 0-471-27801-7, Pub. by Wiley-Interscience). Wiley.

Gardell, Bertil & Johansson, Gunn. Working Life: A Social Science Contribution to Work Reform. LC 80-40289. 352p. 1981. 46.95 (ISBN 0-471-27801-7, Pub. by Wiley-Interscience). Wiley.

Gardella, Lawrence. Sing a Song to Jenny Next. 1981. 12.95 (ISBN 0-525-20462-8). Dutton.

Garden Center of Greater Cleveland. Flowering Plant Index of Illustration & Information. 1979. lib. bdg. 200.00 (ISBN 0-8161-0301-1). G K Hall.

Garden, Nancy. The Kid's Code & Cipher Book. LC 80-10434. (Illus.). 176p. (gr. 5 up). 1981. 10.95 (ISBN 0-03-053856-4); pap. 4.95 (ISBN 0-03-059267-4). HR&W.

Gardener, Leslie, ed. Mechanical Plant in Construction. (Illus.). 138p. 1979. 55.00 (ISBN 0-7114-4306-8). Transatlantic.

Gardener, Nico, jt. auth. see Mollo, Victor.

Gardenhour, Nancy D., jt. auth. see Harris, Charles M.

Gardette, Charles D. & Poe, Edgar A. The Fire-Fiend & the Raven. 1973. 7.50 (ISBN 0-938192-03-5). De La Ree.

Gardier, R., jt. auth. see Saunders, W.

Gardine, Michael. Lamia. (Orig.). 1981. pap. 2.25 o.s.i. (ISBN 0-440-14236-9). Dell.

Gardiner, jt. auth. see Gander.

Gardiner, A. G. The War Lords. (Wayfarer's Library). 328p. lib. bdg. 20.00 (ISBN 0-89984-232-1). Century Bookbindery.

Gardiner, Alan. Egypt of the Pharaohs: An Introduction. (Illus.). 1966. pap. 7.95 (ISBN 0-19-500267-9, 165, GB). Oxford U Pr.

Gardiner, Anne M. Women & Catholic Priesthood: An Expanded Vision. LC 76-12357. 1976. pap. 5.95 (ISBN 0-8091-1955-2). Paulist Pr.

Gardiner, C. Harvey, ed. see Prescott, William H.

Gardiner, Duncan B. Intonation & Music: The Semantics of Czech Prosody. LC 79-67358. (Physsardt Series in Prague Linguistics: No. 2). (Illus.). 1980. pap. 10.00 (ISBN 0-916062-04-X). Physsardt.

Gardiner, James J. & Roberts, J. Deotis, eds. Quest for a Black Theology. LC 76-151250. 128p. 1971. 6.95 (ISBN 0-8298-0196-0). Pilgrim NY.

Gardiner, John A. & Lyman, Theodore R. Decisions for Sale: Corruption & Reform in Localland-Use & Building Regulation. LC 78-19758. 1978. 23.95 (ISBN 0-03-044691-0). Praeger.

Gardiner, John A., ed. Public Law & Public Policy. LC 76-12851. (Special Studies). 1977. text ed. 24.95 o.p. (ISBN 0-275-23320-0); pap. 9.95 o.p. (ISBN 0-275-85750-6). Praeger.

Gardiner, John R. Stone Fox. LC 79-7895. (Illus.). 96p. (gr. 2-6). 1980. 7.95 (ISBN 0-690-03983-2, TYC-J); PLB 7.89 (ISBN 0-690-03984-0). T Y Crowell.
Gardiner, Nancy. Yesterday's House. (YA) 1977. 4.95 o.p. (ISBN 0-685-74269-5, Avalon). Bouregy.
Gardiner, P. A. Development of Vision, Vol.4. 240p. 1981. 17.50 (ISBN 0-88416-379-2). PSG Pub.
Gardiner, Patrick, ed. Theories of History. LC 58-6481. 1959. text ed. 16.95 (ISBN 0-02-911210-9). Free Pr.
Gardiner, Paul B. The Abysmal Failure of the German Philosophers. (Illus.). 157p. 1981. 39.75 (ISBN 0-89266-285-9). Am Classical Coll Pr.
Gardiner, Peter, et al, eds. Aspects of Developmental & Paediatric Ophthalmology. (Clinics in Developmental Medicine Ser. No. 32). 126p. 1969. 10.75 o.p. (ISBN 0-685-24727-9). Lippincott.
Gardiner, S. C. Old Church Slavonic: An Elementary Grammar. Date not set. price not set (ISBN 0-521-23674-6). Cambridge U Pr.
Gardner, A. L., jt. ed. see Wilson, D. E.
Gardner, Alfred L. The Systematics of the Genus Didelphis (Marsupialia: Didelphidae) in North & Middle America. (Special Publications: No. 4). (Illus., Orig.). 1973. pap. 4.00 (ISBN 0-89672-029-2). Tex Tech Pr.
Gardner, Alvin F., ed. Dental Examination Review Book. Vol. 1, 5th Ed. 1977. spiral bdg. 14.50 (ISBN 0-87488-431-4); Vol. 2, 4th Ed. 1978. spiral bdg. 14.50 (ISBN 0-87488-432-2); Vol. 3, 3rd Ed. 1978. spiral bdg. 14.50 (ISBN 0-87488-433-0). Med Exam.
Gardner, Averil, jt. auth. see Gardner, Philip.
Gardner, Bruce. Optimal Stockpiling of Grain. LC 78-24768. 192p. 1979. 21.00 (ISBN 0-669-02829-0). Lexington Bks.
Gardner, Carl. Andrew Young: A Biography. LC 77-88945. (Illus.). 1978. 10.95 o.p. (ISBN 0-8069-8118-0, 002700). Sterling.
Gardner, Carl, ed. Media, Politics, & Culture: A Socialist View. (Communications & Culture). 1979. text ed. 23.00x (ISBN 0-333-23588-6); pap. text ed. 10.50x (ISBN 0-333-23589-4). Humanities.
Gardner, Clifford L. Black Caesar, Pirate. (Illus.). 96p. (gr. 9 up). 1980. 7.95 (ISBN 0-931948-09-6). Peachtree Pubs.
Gardner, David C. & Beatty, Grace J. Dissertation Proposal Guidebook: How to Prepare a Research Proposal & Get It Accepted. (Illus.). 112p. 1980. 9.50 (ISBN 0-398-04086-9); pap. 5.75 (ISBN 0-398-04087-7). C C Thomas.
Gardner, David C. & Warren, Sue A. Careers & Disabilities: A Career Education Approach. LC 78-62312. (Orig.). 1978. text ed. 9.95x (ISBN 0-89223-020-7). Greylock Pubs.
Gardner, David M. & Belk, Russell W. A Basic Bibliography on Experimental Design in Marketing. LC 80-19563. (Bibliography Ser.: No. 37). 59p. 1980. pap. 6.00 (ISBN 0-87757-142-2). Am Mktg.
Gardner, David M., jt. auth. see Jones, Mary G.
Gardner, David P. The California Oath Controversy. 1967. 17.50x (ISBN 0-520-00455-8). U of Cal Pr.
Gardner, E. Clinton. Biblical Faith & Social Ethics. 1960. text ed. 19.50 scp (ISBN 0-06-042240-8, HarpC). Har-Row.
Gardner, E. L. Fairies. 11.95 (ISBN 0-8356-5090-1). Theos Pub Hse.
--Web of the Universe. 2nd ed. 1960. 3.00 o.p. (ISBN 0-7229-5086-1). Theos Pub Hse.
Gardner, Eldon J. & Snustad, D. Peter. Principles of Genetics. 6th ed. LC 80-12114. 704p. 1980. text ed. 23.95 (ISBN 0-471-04412-1). Wiley.
Gardner, Elton J. & Mertens, Thomas R. Genetics Laboratory Investigations. 7th rev. ed. 1980. 7.95 (ISBN 0-8087-0786-8). Burgess.
Gardner, Eric K. & Shelton, Brenda. The Intensive Therapy Unit & the Nurse. 2nd ed. 1967. text ed. 3.95 o.p. (ISBN 0-571-08148-7, Pub. by Faber & Faber). Merrimack Bk Serv.
Gardner, Erle S. The Case of the Crimson Kiss. 1971. 6.95 (ISBN 0-688-01275-2). Morrow.
--The Case of the Crying Swallow. 1971. 6.95 (ISBN 0-688-01274-4). Morrow.
--The Case of the Daring Divorcee. 192p. 1981. pap. 1.95 (ISBN 0-345-29499-8). Ballantine.
--The Case of the Deadly Toy. LC 80-27287. 288p. Repr. of 1959 ed. lib. bdg. 10.00x (ISBN 0-8376-0397-8). Bentley.
--The Case of the Fabulous Fake. LC 70-90761. 1969. 6.95 (ISBN 0-688-01276-0). Morrow.
--The Case of the Fenced-in Woman. 1972. 6.95 (ISBN 0-688-00059-2). Morrow.
--The Case of the Fiery Fingers. 1981. pap. 1.95 (ISBN 0-345-29494-7). Ballantine.
--The Case of the Gilded Lily. LC 80-27291. 256p. Repr. of 1956 ed. lib. bdg. 10.00x (ISBN 0-8376-0396-X). Bentley.
--The Case of the Horrified Heirs. 1964. 4.50 o.p. (ISBN 0-688-01264-7). Morrow.
--The Case of the Ice Cold Hands. 1980. lib. bdg. 11.95 (ISBN 0-8161-3174-0, Large Print Bks). G K Hall.
--The Case of the Irate Witness. 1972. 6.95 (ISBN 0-688-00102-5). Morrow.
--The Case of the Mischievous Doll. 1981. lib. bdg. 11.95 (ISBN 0-8161-3215-1, Large Print Bks). G K Hall.
--The Case of the Murderer's Bride. Queen, Ellery, intro. by. LC 77-81936. 1977. pap. 1.50 o.p. (ISBN 0-89559-003-4). Davis Pubns.
--The Case of the Mythical Monkeys. LC 80-27190. 288p. Repr. of 1959 ed. lib. bdg. 10.00x (ISBN 0-8376-0398-6). Bentley.
--The Case of the Postponed Murder. LC 72-1344. 1973. 6.95 (ISBN 0-688-00033-9). Morrow.
--The. Case of the Queenly Contestant. 1967. 6.95 (ISBN 0-688-01280-9). Morrow.
--The Case of the Shapely Shadow. 1981. pap. 1.95 (ISBN 0-345-29498-X). Ballantine.
--The Case of the Singing Skirt. LC 80-27263. 256p. Repr. of 1959 ed. lib. bdg. 10.00x (ISBN 0-8376-0399-4). Bentley.
--Ellery Queen Presents. Bd. with Erle Stanley Gardner; The Amazing Adventures of Lester Leith. 192p. 1981. 9.95. Davis Pubns.
Gardner, Ernest, et al. Anatomy: A Regional Study of Human Structure. 4th ed. LC 74-17753. (Illus.). 881p. 1975. text ed. 26.00 (ISBN 0-7216-4018-4). Saunders.
Gardner, Frank. Racing Driver's Manual. LC 73-93418. (Illus.). 1974. 8.50 o.p. (ISBN 0-668-03458-0). Arco.
Gardner, Frank M., ed. Sequels. 6th ed. 1974. 39.00 o.p. (ISBN 0-934598-75-4). Am Lib Pub Co.
Gardner, Gerald & Caruso, Dee. The World's Greatest Athlete. (gr. 7-12). 1975. pap. 1.50 (ISBN 0-590-03755-2, Schol Pap). Schol Bk Serv.
Gardner, Gilbert, tr. see Brutzkus, Boris.
Gardner, Helen. King Lear. (John Cofin Memorial Lectures 1966). 1967. pap. text ed. 2.50x (ISBN 0-485-16205-9, Athlone Pr). Humanities.
Gardner, Helen, ed. see Donne, John.
Gardner, Helen, ed. see Wilson, Frank P.
Gardner, Hershal. How to Troubleshoot & Repair Your Stereo System. (Illus.). 240p. 1976. 17.95 (ISBN 0-87909-349-8); pap. 6.95 (ISBN 0-8359-2976-0). Reston.
Gardner, Hope P. & Gunnell, Sally. Teach Me in My Way: A Collection for L.D.S. Children. LC 80-84147. 1980. soft cover 5.95 (ISBN 0-913420-85-9). Olympus Pub Co.
Gardner, Horace J. Let's Celebrate Christmas: Parties, Plays, Legends, Carols, Poetry, Stories. (Illus.). (gr. 6-12). 1940. 9.50 o.p. (ISBN 0-8260-3320-2). Ronald Pr.
Gardner, Howard. Echoes in My Mind. Date not set. 7.95 (ISBN 0-533-04727-7). Vantage.
Gardner, Jack I. Gambling: A Guide to Information Sources. LC 79-23797. (Sports, Games, & Pastimes Information Guide Ser.: Vol. 8). 1980. 30.00 (ISBN 0-8103-1229-8). Gale.
Gardner, James A. Lead King: Moses Austin. 256p. 1980. 9.95 (ISBN 0-86629-004-4). Sunrise MO.
--Legal Imperialism: A Critical History of American Legal Assistance to the Third World. LC 79-5406. 259p. 1981. 20.00 (ISBN 0-299-08130-3). U of Wis Pr.
Gardner, James E. Safety Training for the Supervisor. 3rd ed. LC 78-52505. 1979. pap. text ed. 8.95 (ISBN 0-201-03090-X). A-W.
--Training Interventions in Job Skill Development. LC 80-23810. (Illus.). 224p. 1981. text ed. 12.95 (ISBN 0-201-03097-7). A-W.
Gardner, James F., et al, eds. Program Issues in Developmental Disabilities: A Resource Manual for Surveyors & Reviewers. LC 80-12555. (Illus.). 176p. (Orig.). 1980. pap. text ed. 12.95 (ISBN 0-933716-05-2). P H Brookes.
Gardner, James S. Physical Geography: An Introduction. (Illus.). 1977. text ed. 21.50 scp (ISBN 0-06-167411-7, HarpC); inst. manual free (ISBN 0-06-167414-1). Har-Row.
Gardner, Jerry G. Contract Food Service-Vending. LC 73-76359. 1973. 16.95 (ISBN 0-8436-0568-5). CBI Pub.
Gardner, John. The Art of Living & Other Stories. LC 80-20988. (Illus.). 320p. 12.95 (ISBN 0-394-51674-5). Knopf.
--The Dancing Dodo. 336p. 1980. pap. 2.25. Bantam.
--The Dancing Dodo. LC 77-80888. 1978. 8.95 o.p. (ISBN 0-385-12462-7). Doubleday.
--Freddy's Book. 1981. pap. 2.95 (ISBN 0-345-29544-7). Ballantine.
--The Last Trump. LC 80-16560. 256p. 1981. 11.95 (ISBN 0-07-022852-3, GB). McGraw.
Gardner, John C. The Alliterative Morte Arthure, the Owl & the Nightingale, & Five Other Middle English Poems: In a Modernized Version with Comments on the Poems & Notes. LC 73-7728. (Arcturus Books Paperbacks). 310p. 1973. pap. 7.95 (ISBN 0-8093-0648-4). S Ill U Pr.
--Grendel. 1975. pap. 2.25 (ISBN 0-345-28865-3). Ballantine.
--The Poetry of Chaucer. LC 76-22713. 445p. 1977. 15.00 (ISBN 0-8093-0772-3); pap. 9.95 (ISBN 0-8093-0871-1). S Ill U Pr.
Gardner, John W. In Common Cause. rev. ed. 1974. o.p. (ISBN 0-393-06403-4); pap. write for info. Norton.
--Self-Renewal: The Individual & the Innovative Society. 1964. pap. 1.75 o.p. (ISBN 0-06-090054-7, CN54, CN). Har-Row.
Gardner, John W., ed. see Kennedy, John F.
Gardner, Joseph L. & Weisberger, Bernard A. Labor on the March: The Story of America's Unions. LC 74-88864. (American Heritage Junior Library). (Illus.). 153p. (gr. 5 up). 1969. PLB 12.89 (ISBN 0-06-021938-6, J0210, Dist. by Har-Row); 9.95 (ISBN 0-8281-5015-X). Am Heritage.
Gardner, Joseph M., Jr. How to Sell Your Own Home Without a Real Estate Agent & Save Thousands of Dollars. 1975. 6.50 o.p. (ISBN 0-682-48180-7, Banner). Exposition.
Gardner, Joyce. Basic Writing Skills with Activities & Tests. (gr. k-6). 1978. spiral bdg. 6.50x (ISBN 0-933892-00-4). Child Focus Co.
Gardner, Joyce & La Fleur, Ida. Oral Language Continuum Book. (gr. k-3). 1975. 9.00x (ISBN 0-933892-08-X). Child Focus Co.
--Psychomotor Continuum. (gr. k-2). 1977. 7.00x (ISBN 0-933892-09-8). Child Focus Co.
Gardner, Kenncorwin H., jt. ed. see French, Alfred D.
Gardner, Kenneth D., Jr., ed. Cystic Diseases of the Kidney. LC 75-31626. (Perspectives in Nephrology & Hypertension Ser.). 1976. 43.50 (ISBN 0-471-29146-3, Pub. by Wiley Medical). Wiley.
Gardner, L. I. & Amacher, P., eds. Endocrine Aspects of Malnutrition: Marasmus, Kwashiorkor & Psychosocial Deprivation. LC 73-88110. 1973. 27.00 (ISBN 0-685-48386-X). Raven.
Gardner, Laurence B., jt. auth. see Sanders, Jay H.
Gardner, Lewis, ed. English Teacher's Companion: A Survey of the Media. LC 74-82110. 160p. 1975. pap. 3.95 (ISBN 0-590-09588-9, Citation). Schol Bk Serv.
Gardner, Lionel. Further Pavement Reflections. (Writers Workshop Redbird Book Ser.). 42p. 1975. 12.00 (ISBN 0-88253-544-7); pap. text ed. 4.80 (ISBN 0-88253-543-9). Ind-US Inc.
--Pavement Relections. 6.75 (ISBN 0-89253-688-8). Ind-US Inc.
Gardner, Lloyd, ed. American Foreign Policy, Present to Past: A Narrative with Readings & Documents. LC 74-2651. (Urgent Issues in American Society Ser). 1975. pap. text ed. 7.95 (ISBN 0-02-911300-8). Free Pr.
Gardner, Lloyd C., et al, eds. Origins of the Cold War. 1970. pap. 9.95 (ISBN 0-471-00188-0). Wiley.
Gardner, Lytt I., ed. Endocrine & Genetic Diseases of Childhood & Adolescence. LC 74-4561. (Illus.). 1404p. 1975. text ed. 75.00 o.p. (ISBN 0-7216-3991-7). Saunders.
Gardner, Marjorie & Heikkinen, Henry, eds. Interdiscplinary Approaches to Chemistry: An Instructional Program for High School Chemistry, 7 vols. Incl. Delicate Balance: Environmental Chemistry Module. 4.00 (ISBN 0-06-561106-3); tchr's ed. 5.20 (ISBN 0-06-561215-9); tests 15.88 (ISBN 0-06-561606-5); Heart of Matter: Nuclear Chemistry Module; Molecules in Living Systems: Biochemistry Module. 4.00 (ISBN 0-06-561103-9); tchr's ed. 5.20 (ISBN 0-06-561213-2); tests 15.40 (ISBN 0-06-561604-9); Form & Function: An Organic Chemistry Module. 4.00 (ISBN 0-06-561102-0); tchr's ed. 5.20 (ISBN 0-06-561212-4); tests 14.80 (ISBN 0-06-561603-0); Diversity & Periodicity: An Inorganic Chemistry Module. 4.00 (ISBN 0-06-561101-2); tchr's ed. 5.20 (ISBN 0-06-561211-6); tests 15.88 (ISBN 0-06-561602-2); Reactions & Reason: An Introductory Chemistry Module. 4.00 (ISBN 0-06-561100-4); tchr's ed. 5.20 (ISBN 0-06-561210-8); tests 19.32 (ISBN 0-06-561601-4); Communities of Molecules: Physical Chemistry Module. 4.00 (ISBN 0-06-561107-1); tchr's **ed. 5.20 (ISBN 0-06-561216-7); tests 15.40 (ISBN 0-06-561607-3). text ed. 25.88 set (ISBN 0-06-561110-1, SchDept). Har-Row.**
Gardner, Martin. Aha! Insight. LC 78-51259. (Illus.). 1978. pap. text ed. 7.95x (ISBN 0-89454-001-7). W H Freeman.
--The Ambidextrous Universe: Mirror Asymmetry & Time-Reversed Worlds. rev. ed. (Illus.). 1979. 12.50 (ISBN 0-684-15789-6, ScribT). Scribner.
--The Buffooneries of Modern Science. LC 80-84405. (Critiques of the Paranormal Ser.). 450p. 1981. 19.95 (ISBN 0-87975-144-4); pap. 9.95 (ISBN 0-87975-145-2). Prometheus Bks.
--Codes, Ciphers, & Secret Writing. (gr. 5-7). 1973. pap. 1.25 (ISBN 0-671-29954-9). Archway.
--Codes, Ciphers & Secret Writing. (gr. 5-7). 1979. pap. 1.25 (ISBN 0-671-29954-9). PB.
--The Incredible Dr. Matrix. LC 76-16860. (Illus.). 265p. 1977. 8.95 o.p. (ISBN 0-684-14669-X, ScribT). Scribner.
--Mathematical Carnival: A New Round-up of Tantalizers & Puzzles from "Scientific American". 1977. pap. 3.95 o.p. (ISBN 0-394-72349-X, Vin). Random.
--Mathematical Puzzles. LC 61-6142. (Illus.). (gr. 7 up). 1961. 7.95 (ISBN 0-690-52360-2, TYC-J). T Y Crowell.
--More Perplexing Puzzles & Tantalizing Teasers. (gr. 3-6). 1981. pap. price not set. Archway.
--More Perplexing Puzzles & Teasers. (Illus.). (gr. 3-6). 1977. pap. 1.25 (ISBN 0-671-29832-1). PB.
--Perplexing Puzzles & Tantalizing Teasers. (Illus., Orig.). (gr. 3-6). 1971. pap. 1.25 (ISBN 0-671-29927-1). PB.
--Perplexing Puzzles & Tantalizing Teasers. 1981. pap. 1.50 (ISBN 0-686-69007-9). Archway.
--Science Fiction Puzzle Tales. Novograd, Nancy, ed. (Illus.). 128p. 1981. 10.95 (ISBN 0-517-54380-X); pap. 4.95 (ISBN 0-517-54381-8). Potter.
--Space Puzzles: Curious Questions & Answers About the Solar System. (Illus.). (YA) (gr. 7-9). 1972. pap. 1.25 (ISBN 0-671-29838-0). PB.
Gardner, Martin, ed. see Carroll, Lewis.
Gardner, Martin, ed. see Dudeney, Henry E.
Gardner, Martin, ed. see Fujimura, Kobon.
Gardner, P. S. & McQuillan, J. Rapid Virus Diagnosis. 2nd ed. LC 80-40239. (Illus.). 336p. 1980. text ed. 79.95 (ISBN 0-407-38441-3). Butterworths.
Gardner, P. S., ed. see Symposium Held by European Group for Rapid Virus Diagnosis, London, Jan. 1978.
Gardner, Paul, jt. auth. see Woosnam, Phil.
Gardner, Philip. Kingsley Amis. (English Authors Ser.: No. 319). 1981. lib. bdg. 11.95 (ISBN 0-8057-6809-2). Twayne.
--Norman Nicholson. (English Authors Ser.: No. 153). 1973. lib. bdg. 10.95 (ISBN 0-8057-1418-9). Twayne.
Gardner, Philip & Gardner, Averil. The God Approached: A Commentary on the Poems of William Empson. 226p. 1978. 17.50x (ISBN 0-8476-6059-1). Rowman.
Gardner, Philip, ed. E. M. Forster: The Critical Heritage. (The Critical Heritage Ser). 518p. 1973. 38.50x (ISBN 0-7100-7641-X). Routledge & Kegan.
Gardner, Ralph D., intro. by. Horatio Alger: A Fancy of Hers-The Disagreeable Woman. 160p. 1981. 14.95 (ISBN 0-442-24716-8). Van Nos Reinhold.
Gardner, Richard A. Dr. Gardner's Fables for Our Times, Vol. 1. LC 80-26098. (Illus.). 125p. (gr. k-6). 10.95 (ISBN 0-933812-06-X). Creative Therapeutics.
--Dr. Gardner's Stories About the Real World, Vol. II. (Illus.). 110p. (gr. k-6). write for info. Creative Therapeutics.
--Dorothy & the Lizard of Oz. LC 80-12787. (Illus.). 108p. (gr. 1-6). 1980. 9.95 (ISBN 0-933812-03-5). Creative Therapeutics.
--Therapeutic Communication with Children: The Mutual Storytelling Technique in Child Psychotherapy. LC 71-155063. 1238p. 1971. 35.00x (ISBN 0-87668-042-2). Aronson.
Gardner, Richard A., M.D. The Parents Book About Divorce. LC 76-23762. 1977. 9.95 o.p. (ISBN 0-385-12237-3). Doubleday.
Gardner, Richard K. Library Collections: Their Origin, Selection, & Development. (Library Education Ser.). 384p. 1981. text ed. 17.95 (ISBN 0-07-022850-7, C). McGraw.
Gardner, Richard S., jt. auth. see McDonough, James L.
Gardner, Robert. Magic Through Science. LC 77-76239. (gr. 3-5). 1978. 6.95 (ISBN 0-385-12437-6); PLB (ISBN 0-385-12438-4). Doubleday.
--Save That Energy. (Illus.). 192p. (gr. 8-12). 1981. PLB price not set (ISBN 0-671-34066-2). Messner.
Gardner, Robert & Webster, David. Moving Right Along: A Book of Science Experiments & Puzzlers About Motion. LC 77-15149. (gr. 3-5). 1978. 7.95a (ISBN 0-385-11642-X); PLB (ISBN 0-385-11643-8). Doubleday.
Gardner, Robert, jt. auth. see Flanagan, Henry E., Jr.
Gardner, Roy. To Serve Where Sent. 1978. 6.95 o.p. (ISBN 0-533-02962-7). Vantage.
Gardner, Samantha. The Voyage of the Wanderer. 1977. 6.50 o.p. (ISBN 0-533-03045-5). Vantage.
Gardner, Stanley, ed. see Blake, William.

Gardner, Thomas J. Criminal Evidence: Principles, Cases & Readings. (Criminal Justice Ser.). (Illus.). 1978. text ed. 17.95 (ISBN 0-8299-0148-5); instrs.' maual avail. (ISBN 0-8299-0589-8). West Pub.

Gardner, W. H. Some Thoughts on the Mayor of Casterbridge. 52p. 1980. Repr. of 1930 ed. lib. bdg. 6.00 (ISBN 0-8492-4959-7). R West.

Gardner, Warren H. Laryngectomee Speech & Rehabilitation. (Illus.). 260p. 1978. 22.50 (ISBN 0-398-00643-1). C C Thomas.

Gardner, William E., et al. Selected Case Studies in American History, 2 vols. new ed. (gr. 8-12). 1975. Vol. 1. pap. text ed. 5.40 (ISBN 0-205-04902-8, 7849028); Vol. 2. pap. text ed. 5.20 (ISBN 0-205-03771-2, 7837712); Tchrs.' Guide. Vol. 1. 2.40 (ISBN 0-205-02165-4, 7821654); Tchrs.' Guide. Vol. 2. 2.40 (ISBN 0-205-03772-0, 7837720). Allyn.

Gardner, William I. Behavior Modification in Mental Retardation: The Education & Rehabilitation of the Mentally Retarded Adolescent & Adult. LC 79-149839. 1971. 21.95x (ISBN 0-202-25000-8). Aldine Pub.

--Children with Learning & Behavior Problems: A Behavior Management Approach. 2nd ed. 1978. text ed. 19.95 (ISBN 0-205-06067-6); pap. text ed. 12.50 (ISBN 0-205-06066-8). Allyn.

--Learning & Behavior Characteristics of Exceptional Children & Youth: A Humanistic Behavioral Approach. 1977. text ed. 18.50x (ISBN 0-205-05586-9). Allyn.

Gardner, Wyland. Government Finance: National, State & Local. LC 77-3572. 1978. 17.95 (ISBN 0-13-360743-7). P-H.

Gardner, Wynelle. Church That Glowed. 1978. pap. 2.95 o.p. (ISBN 0-88270-129-0). Logos.

Gardocki, Gloria J. & Pokras, Robert. Utilization of Short-Stay Hospitals by Persons with Heart Disease & Malignant Neoplasms. Shipp, Audrey, ed. (Ser. Thirteen: No. 52). 50p. 1981. pap. 1.75 (ISBN 0-8406-0214-6). Natl Ctr Health Stats.

Garee, Betty, ed. Ideas for Making Your Home Accessible. (Illus.). 1979. 6.50 (ISBN 0-915708-08-6). Cheever Pub.

Garehime, Ed D. Mr. Jelly Bean. LC 77-82261. (Mr. Jelly Bean Adventure Ser.: No. 1). (Illus.). 64p. (gr. k-5). PLB 6.95 (ISBN 0-918822-01-7). Deem Corp.

Garelick, May. What's Inside: The Story of an Egg That Hatched. (Illus.). (gr. k-3). 1970. pap. 1.25 (ISBN 0-590-02947-9, Schol Pap). Schol Bk Serv.

Gareth Jones, E. B. Recent Advances in Aquatic Mycology. LC 74-27179. 1976. 64.95 (ISBN 0-470-29176-1). Halsted Pr.

Garey, Michael R. & Johnson, David S. Computers & Intractability: A Guide to the Theory of NP-Completeness. LC 78-12361. (Mathematical Sciences Ser.). (Illus.). 1979. pap. text ed. 12.95x (ISBN 0-7167-1045-5). W H Freeman.

Garfias, Robert. Music of One Thousand Autumns: The Togaku Style of Japanese Courtly Music. LC 75-13865. 1976. 35.00x (ISBN 0-520-01977-6). U of Cal Pr.

Garfield, Brian. Deep Cover. 1978. pap. 1.95 o.p. (ISBN 0-449-23601-3, Crest). Fawcett.

--Hit. LC 75-93719. (Cock Robin Mystery). 1970. 4.50 o.s.i. (ISBN 0-02-542640-0). Macmillan.

--Line of Succession. 1972. 7.95 o.s.i. (ISBN 0-440-04847-8). Delacorte.

--The Paladin. 1980. 12.95 (ISBN 0-686-60899-2, 24704). S&S.

--The Paladin. 352p. 1981. pap. 2.95 (ISBN 0-553-14261-5). Bantam.

--Recoil. 1978. pap. 1.95 o.p. (ISBN 0-449-23552-1, Crest). Fawcett.

--Wild Times. 1980. pap. 2.50 o.s.i. (ISBN 0-440-19457-1). Dell.

Garfield, Charles A., ed. Stress & Survival: The Emotional Realities of Life Threatening Illness. LC 78-31341. (Illus.). 1979. text ed. 16.95 (ISBN 0-8016-1743-X). Mosby.

Garfield, Eugene. Essays of an Information Scientist, 3 vols. LC 77-602. Vols. 1 & 2 (1962-1976) 25.00 (ISBN 0-89495-001-0); Vol. 3 (1977-1978) 15.00 (ISBN 0-89495-000-2, EOIS2W). Vol. 3 (ISBN 0-89495-000-2). ISI Pr.

Garfield, Evelyn P. Julio Cortazar. LC 74-78440. (Modern Literature Ser.). 184p. 1975. 10.95 (ISBN 0-8044-2224-9). Ungar.

Garfield, Leon. The House of Hanover England in the Eighteenth Century. LC 75-42422. (Illus.). (gr. 6 up). 1976. 8.95 (ISBN 0-395-28904-1, Clarion). HM.

--Jack Holborn. (Windward Bks.). (gr. 7 up). 1965. pap. 0.75 o.p. (ISBN 0-394-82175-0, BYR). Random.

Garfield, Leon, jt. auth. see Dickens, Charles.

Garfield, Patricia. Creative Dreaming. 256p. 1976. pap. 2.50 (ISBN 0-345-28468-2). Ballantine.

--Pathway to Ecstasy: The Way of the Dream Mandala. LC 78-16806. (Illus.). 1979. 12.95 o.p. (ISBN 0-03-041996-4). HR&W.

Garfield, Paul & Lovejoy, W. Public Utility Economics. (Illus.). 1963. text ed. 21.95 (ISBN 0-13-739367-9). P-H.

Garfield, Sol L. Clinical Psychology: The Study of Personality & Behavior. LC 73-89520. 1974. lib. bdg. 22.95x (ISBN 0-202-26073-9); pap. text ed. 12.95x (ISBN 0-202-26077-1). Aldine Pub.

Garfield, Sol. L. Psychotherapy: An Eclectic Approach. LC 79-17724. (Personality Processes Ser.). 1980. 22.95 (ISBN 0-471-04490-3, Pub. by Wiley-Interseience). Wiley.

Garfield, Sol L. & Bergin, Allen E. Handbook of Psychotherapy & Behavior Change: An Empirical Analysis. 2nd ed. LC 78-8526. 1978. text ed. 47.95 (ISBN 0-471-29178-1). Wiley.

Garfink, Christine, jt. auth. see Pizer, Hank.

Garfinkel, Alan. Forms of Explanation: Rethinking the Questions in Social Theory. LC 80-2341. 192p. 1981. 16.00x (ISBN 0-300-02136-4). Yale U Pr.

Garfinkel, Bernie. Liv Ullman & Ingmar Bergman. 1978. pap. 1.75 o.p. (ISBN 0-425-03653-7). Berkley Pub.

Garfinkel, Harold. Studies in Ethnomethodology. 1967. text ed. 16.95 (ISBN 0-13-858381-1). P-H.

Garfinkel, Perry. Retreats: Away-to-Pray Weekends. (Illus.). 1977. 0.25 (ISBN 0-89570-140-5). Claretian Pubns.

Garfinkel, Robert & Nemhauser, George L. Integer Programming. LC 72-3881. (Decision & Control Ser.). 528p. 1972. 33.95 (ISBN 0-471-29195-1, Pub. by Wiley-Interscience). Wiley.

Garforth, F. W. Scope of Philosophy: An Introductory Study-Book. 1971. text ed. 8.75x (ISBN 0-391-00186-8); pap. text ed. 5.00x (ISBN 0-391-00187-6). Humanities.

Garforth, F. W., ed. see Locke, John.

Garforth, Francis W., ed. John Locke's of the Conduct of the Understanding. LC 66-20498. 1966. text ed. 8.75 (ISBN 0-8077-1401-1); pap. text ed. 4.00x (ISBN 0-8077-1398-8). Tchrs Coll.

--John Stuart Mill on Education. LC 75-115230. 1971. text ed. 10.50 (ISBN 0-8077-1403-8); pap. 4.50x (ISBN 0-8077-1402-X). Tchrs Coll.

Garforth, John. A Day in the Life of a Victorian Policeman. (Victorian Day Ser.). 1974. pap. text ed. 5.95x (ISBN 0-04-942123-9). Allen Unwin.

Garg, Prem C. Optimal Economic Growth with Exhaustible Resources. LC 78-75019. (Outstanding Dissertations on Energy Ser.). 1979. lib. bdg. 12.00 (ISBN 0-8240-4054-6). Garland Pub.

Gargi, Balwant. The Naked Triangle. 1980. text ed. cancelled o.p. (Pub. by Vikas India). Advent Bk.

Garigan, Catherine, jt. ed. see Carter, Virginia L.

Garigliano, Leonard J. & Knape, Beth J., eds. Environmental Education in the Elementary School: A Selection of Articles Reprinted from "Science & Children". rev. ed. 1977. pap. 4.75 (ISBN 0-87355-007-2). Natl Sci Tchrs.

Garite, Thomas, jt. auth. see Freeman, Roger.

Garitee, Jerome R. The Republic's Private Navy: The American Privateering Business As Practiced by Baltimore During the War of 1812. LC 76-41487. (American Maritime Library: Vol. 8). (Illus.). 356p. 1977. 17.50 (ISBN 0-8195-5004-3); limited ed. 35.00 (ISBN 0-8195-5005-1). Mystic Seaport.

Garland, D. David. Hosea. 128p. 1975. pap. 3.50 (ISBN 0-310-24843-4). Zondervan.

--Job: A Study Guide Commentary. 160p. 1971. pap. 2.95 (ISBN 0-310-24863-9). Zondervan.

Garland, G. D. Earth's Shape & Gravity. 1965. 21.00 (ISBN 0-08-010823-7); pap. 9.75 (ISBN 0-08-010822-9). Pergamon.

Garland, H. G. Schiller: Dramatic Writer: a Study of Style in the Plays. 1969. 29.95x (ISBN 0-19-815387-2). Oxford U Pr.

Garland, Hamlin. Boy Life on the Prairie. LC 61-16185. (Illus.). 1961. pap. 5.50 (ISBN 0-8032-5070-3, BB 120, Bison). U of Nebr Pr.

--Main-Travelled Roads. 1962. pap. 1.95 (ISBN 0-451-51378-9, CJ1378, Sig Classics). NAL.

--Rose of Dutcher's Coolly. Pizer, Donald, ed. LC 79-82509. 1970. pap. 3.95 (ISBN 0-8032-5071-1, BB 506, Bison). U of Nebr Pr.

Garland, Henry. The Berlin Novels of Theodor Fontane. 296p. 1980. 42.00 (ISBN 0-19-815765-7). Oxford U Pr.

Garland, J. National Electrical Code Questions & Answers, 1978. 1979. pap. 5.95 o.p. (ISBN 0-13-622779-1). P-H.

Garland, J. D. National Electrical Code Reference Book, 1981. 3rd ed. (Illus.). 640p. 1981. 21.95 (ISBN 0-13-609321-3). P-H.

Garland, James A. The Private Stable. 50.00 (ISBN 0-88427-018-1). Green Hill.

Garland, John S. Financing Foreign Trade in Eastern Europe: Problems of Bilateralism & Currency Inconvertibility. LC 76-24351. 1977. text ed. 23.95 (ISBN 0-275-23800-8). Praeger.

Garland, Joseph E. Guns off Gloucester. LC 75-21650. (Illus.). 1975. pap. 3.95 (ISBN 0-930352-06-8). Nelson B Robinson.

Garland, Martha M. Cambridge Before Darwin. LC 80-40327. 224p. 1980. 34.50 (ISBN 0-521-23319-4). Cambridge U Pr.

Garland, Mary. Hebbel's Prose Tragedies. LC 72-88621. (Anglica Germanica Ser.: No. 2). 364p. 1973. 60.00 (ISBN 0-521-20090-3). Cambridge U Pr.

Garland, Sarah. Henry & Fowler. LC 76-42160. (Illus.). 1976. 6.95 (ISBN 0-684-14866-8, ScribJ). Scribner.

--Potter Brownware. LC 77-70271. (Illus.). (gr. k-3). 1977. 6.95 (ISBN 0-684-15044-1, ScribJ). Scribner.

--Rose & Her Bath. (Illus.). (ps-5). 1970. 6.95 (ISBN 0-571-08728-0, Pub. by Faber & Faber); pap. 2.45 (ISBN 0-571-11017-7). Merrimack Bk Serv.

--Rose, the Bath & the Merboy. (Illus.). (ps-5). 6.95 (ISBN 0-571-09581-X, Pub. by Faber & Faber). Merrimack Bk Serv.

Garlick, J. P. & Keay, R.. Human Ecology in the Tropics: Symposia of the Society for the Study of Human Biology, Vol. 16. LC 76-18781. 1977. 15.95 (ISBN 0-470-15165-X). Halsted Pr.

Garlick, J. P., jt. ed. see Clegg, E. J.

Garlick, Kenneth & MacIntyre, Angus, eds. The Diary of Joseph Farington, R.A, 2 vols. (Studies in British Art Ser.). 1979. Set. 60.00x (ISBN 0-300-02314-6); Vol 1. write for info. (ISBN 0-300-02294-8); Vol. 2. write for info. (ISBN 0-300-02295-6). Yale U Pr.

Garlin, Sender. John Swinton: American Radical, 1829-1901. (Occasional Paper: No. 20). 1976. pap. 1.50 (ISBN 0-89977-022-3). Am Inst Marxist.

Garma, Angel. The Psychoanalysis of Dreams. LC 73-17741. 224p. (Orig.). 1974. 20.00x (ISBN 0-87668-118-6). Aronson.

Garmaise, Freda. Love Bites. 11.95 (ISBN 0-671-42036-4). S&S.

Garman, Douglas, tr. see Flaubert, Gustave.

Garman, Michael, jt. ed. see Fletcher, Paul.

Garmire, Bernard L., ed. Local Government Police Management. LC 77-3926. (Municipal Management Ser). (Illus.). 1977. text ed. 28.00 (ISBN 0-87326-016-3). Intl City Mgt.

Garmo, Murshed. School of Heroes. (Arabic.). pap. 12.00x. Intl Bk Ctr.

Garmon, Gerald R. John Reuben Thompson. (United States Authors Ser.: No. 346). 1979. lib. bdg. 13.50 (ISBN 0-8057-7284-7). Twayne.

Garmonsway. Anglo-Saxon Chronicle. 1975. pap. 4.50 (ISBN 0-460-11624-X, Evman). Dutton.

Garms, Walter I. Financing Community Colleges. LC 76-54165. 1977. text ed. 9.25x (ISBN 0-8077-2510-2). Tchrs Coll.

Garms, Walter I., et al. School Finance: The Economics & Politics of Public Education. (Illus.). 1978. text ed. 18.95 (ISBN 0-13-793315-0). P-H.

Garn, Harvey A. & Wilson, Robert H. A Critical Look at "Urban Dynamics". 38p. 1970. pap. 2.00 o.p. (ISBN 0-87766-096-4, 30009). Urban Inst.

Garn, Harvey A., et al. Models for Indicator Development: A Framework for Policy Analysis. (An Institute Paper). 61p. 1976. pap. 2.50 o.p. (ISBN 0-685-99538-0, 89000). Urban Inst.

Garn, Paul D., jt. ed. see Kambe, H.

Garn, Stanley M. Human Races. 3rd ed. 216p. 1971. pap. 14.75 photocopy ed. spiral (ISBN 0-398-00646-6). C C Thomas.

--Writing the Biomedical Research Paper. 76p. 1970. pap. 6.95 (ISBN 0-398-00648-2). C C Thomas.

Garn, Stanley M., ed. Readings on Race. 2nd ed. (Illus.). 1968. photocopy ed. spiral 24.75 (ISBN 0-398-00647-4). C C Thomas.

Garnel, Donald. The Rise of Teamster Power in the West. 1971. 25.00x (ISBN 0-520-01733-1). U of Cal Pr.

Garnell, P & East, D. J. Guided Weapon Control Systems. LC 76-40061. 1977. text ed. 33.00 o.p. (ISBN 0-08-019691-8). Pergamon.

Garner, Alan. Conversationally Speaking: Tested New Ways to Increase Your Personal & Social Effectiveness. 164p. (Orig.). 1980. pap. 4.95 (ISBN 0-938044-00-1). Psych Res Assoc.

--The Guizer. LC 75-42040. (Illus.). 224p. (gr. 7 up). 1976. 9.50 (ISBN 0-688-86001-X). Greenwillow.

--Red Shift. LC 73-584. 256p. (gr. 10 up). 1973. 5.95g o.s.i. (ISBN 0-02-735870-4). Macmillan.

Garner, Art. Why Winners Win. 128p. 1981. 6.95 (ISBN 0-88289-267-3). Pelican.

Garner, Dwight L. Idea to Delivery: A Handbook of Oral Communication. 3rd ed. 1979. pap. 7.95x (ISBN 0-534-00599-3). Wadsworth Pub.

Garner, F. H. & Archer, Michael. English Delftware. 2nd ed. 1972. 28.00 (ISBN 0-571-04756-4, Pub. by Faber & Faber). Merrimack Bk Serv.

Garner, Gerald W. The Police Role in Alcohol-Related Crises. 168p. 1979. text ed. 14.75 (ISBN 0-398-03853-8). C C Thomas.

--Police Supervision: A Common Sense Approach. 296p. 1981. write for info. (ISBN 0-398-04127-X). C C Thomas.

Garner, Harry. Chinese Ceramics. LC 75-18991. 1976. 20.00 o.p. (ISBN 0-312-13370-7). St Martin.

--Oriental Blue & White. 3rd ed. 1970. 35.00 (ISBN 0-571-04702-5, Pub. by Faber & Faber). Merrimack Bk Serv.

Garner, Harry M. Chinese & Japanese Cloisonne Enamels. (Illus.). 1962. 41.50 (ISBN 0-8048-0093-6). C E Tuttle.

Garner, Herschel W. Population Dynamics, Reproduction, & Activities of the Kangaroo Rat, Dipodomys ordii, in Western Texas. (Graduate Studies: No. 7). (Illus.). 28p. 1974. pap. 2.00 (ISBN 0-89672-014-4). Tex Tech Pr.

Garner, J. F., jt. ed. see Friedmann, Wolfgang G.

Garner, James W. Reconstruction in Mississippi. LC 12-1798. 1968. pap. text ed. 7.95x (ISBN 0-8071-0137-0). La State U Pr.

Garner, John. How to Make & Set Nets: The Technology of Netting. (Illus.). 96p. 10.00 (ISBN 0-85238-031-3, FN). Unipub.

--Modern Inshore Fishing Gear. 2nd ed. 13.75 (FN). Unipub.

Garner, June B. June Brown's Guide to Let's Read. 55p. 1980. pap. 2.50 (ISBN 0-8143-1667-0). Wayne St U Pr.

Garner, K. C. Introduction to Control Systems Performance Measurements. 1968. 23.00 (ISBN 0-08-012499-2); pap. 11.25 (ISBN 0-08-012498-4). Pergamon.

Garner, K. C., jt. auth. see Wass, C. A.

Garner, Kathryn F. & Young, Christa G. My Prayer Diary. LC 78-17345. 1978. pap. 5.95 spiral bd (ISBN 0-8407-5657-7). Nelson.

Garner, Philippe. Contemporary Decorative Arts. 224p. 1980. 27.50 (ISBN 0-87196-472-4). Facts on File.

--Twentieth Century Furniture. 224p. 1980. 24.95 (ISBN 0-442-25421-0). Van Nos Reinhold.

Garner, Robert H. The Way of St. Francis. 1981. 6.95 (ISBN 0-8062-1605-0). Carlton.

Garner, S. Paul. Evolution of Cost Accounting. LC 76-41238. (Accounting History Classics Ser.: Vol. 1). (Illus.). 432p. 1976. pap. 11.95 (ISBN 0-8173-8900-8). U of Ala Pr.

Garner, Sam, ed. see Scribbs, Buck.

Garner, Stanton, ed. see Lawrence, Mary C.

Garner, William R. Letters from California, 1846-1847. Craig, Donald M., ed. LC 71-124736. (Illus.). 1970. 17.50 (ISBN 0-520-01565-7). U of Cal Pr.

Garnet, Eva D. Exercise & Tape Manual for Movement Is Life. (Illus.). 200p. 1981. spiral bdg. 15.00 (ISBN 0-916622-20-7). Princeton Bk Co.

--Movement Is Life: A Holistic Approach to Exercise for Older Adults. (Illus.). 150p. (Orig.). 1981. pap. text ed. 12.50 (ISBN 0-916622-19-3). Princeton Bk Co.

Garnet, J. Ros. Wild Flowers of Wilson's Promontory National Park. (Illus.). 1979. 7.95x (ISBN 0-85091-111-7, Pub. by Lothian). Intl Schol Bk Serv.

Garnett, Angelica. Mosaics. (Oxford Paperbacks Handbooks for Artists Ser.). 1967. pap. 4.00x o.p. (ISBN 0-19-289901-5). Oxford U Pr.

Garnett, Constance, tr. see Dostoyevsky, Fedor.

Garnett, Constance, tr. see Tolstoy, Leo.

Garnett, Constance, et al, trs. see Chekhov, Anton.

Garnett, Emmeline. Madame Prime Minister: The Story of Indira Gandhi. LC 67-15005. (Illus.). (gr. 7 up). 1967. 4.50 o.p. (ISBN 0-374-34686-0). FS&G.

Garnett, Eve. Further Adventures of the Family from One End Street. LC 56-12040. (Illus.). (gr. 4-7). 6.95 (ISBN 0-8149-0303-7). Vanguard.

--Holiday at the Dew Drop Inn. LC 62-11218. (Illus.). (gr. 7 up). 1962. 5.95 (ISBN 0-8149-0304-5). Vanguard.

Garnett, Henry. Know About the Armada. (Illus.). (gr. 7 up). 1967. 7.95 (ISBN 0-8023-1121-0). Dufour.

Garnett, James L. Reorganizing State Government: The Executive Branch. (Westview Special Studies in Public Policy & Public Systems Management). (Illus.). 320p. 1980. lib. bdg. 25.00x (ISBN 0-89158-835-3). Westview.

Garnett, John B. Bounded Analytic Functions. (Pure & Applied Mathematics Ser.). 1981. price not set (ISBN 0-12-276150-2). Acad Pr.

Garnett, Richard. Coleridge. 111p. 1980. Repr. of 1904 ed. lib. bdg. 12.50 (ISBN 0-89987-307-3). Darby Bks.

Garnham, P. C. Progress in Parasitology. 1971. text ed. 12.50x (ISBN 0-485-26321-1, Athlone Pr). Humanities.

Garnica, Olga K. Mother-Child Interaction Strategies. (Humanist Psychobiology & Psychiatry Ser.). Date not set. price not set (ISBN 0-08-024302-9). Pergamon.

Garnica, Olga K. & King, Martha L., eds. Language, Children & Society: The Effect of Social Patterns on Children Learning to Communicate. new ed. (International Series in Psychobiology & Learning (Pal)). 1979. text ed. 60.00 (ISBN 0-08-023716-9). Pergamon.

Garnier, Robert. Two Tragedies: Hippolyte and Marc Antoine. Hill, Christine M. & Morrison, Mary G., eds. (Renaissance Ser). 181p. 1975. text ed. 14.25x (ISBN 0-485-13809-3, Athlone Pr); pap. text ed. 6.75x (ISBN 0-485-12809-8). Humanities.

Garnsey, P. D. & Whittaker, C. R., eds. Imperialism in the Ancient World. LC 77-85699. (Cambridge Classical Studies). (Illus.). 1979. 42.50 (ISBN 0-521-21882-9). Cambridge U Pr.

Garoche, Pierre. Dictionary of Commodities Carried by Ship. 1952. pap. 6.00x (ISBN 0-87033-019-5). Cornell Maritime.

Garofalo, Reebee & Chapple, Steve. Rock 'n' Roll Is Here to Pay: The History & Politics of the Music Industry. LC 77-10488. 1978. 17.95 (ISBN 0-88229-395-8); pap. 10.95 (ISBN 0-88229-437-7). Nelson-Hall.

Garon, Paul. Blues & the Poetic Spirit. LC 78-2025. (Roots of Jazz Ser.). (Illus.). 1978. Repr. of 1975 ed. lib. bdg. 19.50 (ISBN 0-306-77542-5). Da Capo.

--The Devil's Son-in-Law. (The Paul Oliver Blues Ser.). pap. 2.95 (ISBN 0-913714-34-8). Legacy Bks.

Garon, Philip A. Advertising Law Anthology, Vol. LC 73-87656. 1981. 59.95 (ISBN 0-686-69402-3). Intl Lib.

--Banking Law Anthology, Vol.1. 1981. 59.95. Intl Lib.

--Zoning Law Anthology, Vol. Ii. LC 78-66283. 1980. 59.95. Intl Lib.

Garon, Philip A., ed. Advertising Law Anthology: 1973, Vol. I-VI. LC 73-87656. (National Law Anthology Ser.). 1973. 59.95 ea.; Vol. 1, 1973. (ISBN 0-914250-01-9). Vol.II, 1974 (ISBN 0-914250-07-8). Vol. III, 1975 (ISBN 0-914250-09-4). Vol. IV, 1976 (ISBN 0-914250-11-6). Vol. V, 1977-78 (ISBN 0-914250-15-9). Vol. VI, 1979 (ISBN 0-914250-18-3). Vol VII, 1980-81 (ISBN 0-914250-22-1). complete set 344.90 (ISBN 0-914250-05-1). Intl Lib.

--Zoning Law Anthology, Vol. 2. LC 78-66283. (National Law Anthology Ser.). 1979-80. text ed. 59.95 (ISBN 0-914250-20-5). Intl Lib.

Garon, Phillip A., ed. Insurance Law Anthology, Vol. 1. (National Law Anthology Ser.). 1981. text ed. 59.95. Intl Lib.

Garoutte, Bill. A Survey of Functional Neuroanatomy. (Illus.). 240p. 1981. pap. text ed. 9.00x (ISBN 0-930010-04-3). Jones Med.

Garrad, Larch S. The Naturalist in the Isle of Man. (Naturalist in...Ser.). (Illus.). 232p. 1973. 5.95 (ISBN 0-7153-5628-3). David & Charles.

--Present from...Holiday Souvenirs of the British Isles. (Illus.). 157p. 1976. 5.95 (ISBN 0-7153-7080-4). David & Charles.

Garrand, Victor. Augustine Laure, S.J., Missionary to the Yakimas. 1977. 6.95 (ISBN 0-87770-176-8); pap. 4.95 (ISBN 0-87770-187-3). Ye Galleon.

Garrard & Boyd. Practical Problems in Mathematics for Electricians. LC 79-56247. 1981. pap. text ed. 5.00 (ISBN 0-8273-1277-6); instructor's guide 2.00 (ISBN 0-8273-1278-4). Delmar.

Garrard, J., et al, eds. The Middle Class in Politics. 380p. 1978. text ed. 24.00x (ISBN 0-566-00225-6, Pub. by Gower Pub Co England). Renouf.

--The Middle Class in Politics. 1978. text ed. 24.00x (ISBN 0-566-00225-6, Pub. by Gower Pub Co England). Renouf.

Garrard, J. G., ed. The Eighteenth Century in Russia. (Illus.). 348p. 1973. 29.95x (ISBN 0-19-815638-3). Oxford U Pr.

Garrard, Lewis H. Wah-To-Yah and the Taos Trail. (Western Frontier Library: No. 5). 1966. 6.95 (ISBN 0-8061-0322-1); pap. 7.95 (ISBN 0-8061-1016-3). U of Okla Pr.

Garrard, Timothy H. Akan Weights & the Gold Trade. (Legon History Ser.). (Illus.). 1980. text ed. 50.00 (ISBN 0-582-64631-6). Longman.

Garratt, Bob, ed. see Association of Teachers of Management.

Garratt, Colin. The Last of Steam: Steam Locomotives Today. LC 76-43194. (Illus.). 128p. 1980. 24.95 (ISBN 0-8040-0754-3). Swallow.

--A Popular Guide to the Preserved Steam Railways of Britain. (Illus.). 1979. 12.95 (ISBN 0-7137-0978-2, Pub by Blandford Pr England). Sterling.

Garratt, Mary A. The Duchess of Asherwood. (Orig.). 1981. pap. 2.95 o.s.i. (ISBN 0-440-12157-4). Dell.

Garratty, G., jt. auth. see Delaney, J. W.

Garraty, John A. The American Nation: A History of the United States, 2 vols. 4th ed. LC 78-10712. 1979. pap. text ed. 13.50 ea. scp (ISBN 0-06-044711-7, HarpC); Vol. 1, To 1877. (ISBN 0-06-042267-X); Vol. 2, Since 1865. (ISBN 0-06-042268-8); inst. manual free (ISBN 0-06-362235-1); Set. scp student review manuals 6.50 (ISBN 0-686-67507-X). Vol. I (ISBN 0-06-044709-5). Vol. II. Har-Row.

--A Short History of the American Nation. 2nd, abr. ed. (Illus.). 1977. pap. text ed. 14.95 scp o.p. (ISBN 0-06-042266-1, HarpC); instructor's manual avail. o.p. (ISBN 0-685-71546-9); scp student's review manual 6.50 o.p. (ISBN 0-06-044708-7). Har-Row.

--Theodore Roosevelt, the Strenuous Life. LC 67-17820. (American Heritage Junior Library). (Illus.). 153p. (gr. 5 up). 1967. 9.95 (ISBN 0-06-021931-9, Dist. by Har-Row); PLB 12.89 o.p. (ISBN 0-06-021932-7). Am Heritage.

Garraty, John A. & Von Klemperer, Lily. The New Guide to Study Abroad: 1981 to 1982. LC 77-11533. 464p. 1980. 15.95 (ISBN 0-06-011423-1, CN849, HarpT); pap. 7.95 (ISBN 0-06-090849-1). Har-Row.

Garraty, John A., et al. The New Guide to Study Abroad, 1978-1979. rev., 6th ed. LC 77-11533. 1978. 15.95 o.s.i. (ISBN 0-06-011458-4, HarpT); pap. 5.95 o.s.i. (ISBN 0-06-011424-X, TD-299, HarpT). Har-Row.

Garreau, Joel. Nine Nations of North America. 1981. 14.00 (ISBN 0-395-29124-0). HM.

Garrels, Robert M. & Mackenzie, Fred T. Evolution of Sedimentary Rocks. (Illus.). 1971. text ed. 14.95x (ISBN 0-393-09959-8, NortonC). Norton.

Garret, Maxwell R. & Poulson, Mary H. Foil Fencing: Skills, Safety, Operations, & Responsibilities for the 1980s. LC 80-18426. (Illus.). 160p. 1981. text ed. 9.75x (ISBN 0-271-00273-5). Pa St U Pr.

Garret, Robert, et al. The Valuation of Shopping Centers. 1976. pap. 8.00 (ISBN 0-911780-38-6). Am Inst Real Estate Appraisers.

Garretson, Lucy, jt. auth. see Selby, Henry.

Garretson, R. L. Music in Childhood Education. 2nd ed. (Illus.). 336p. 1976. ref. ed. 14.95x (ISBN 0-13-606988-6); pap. text ed. 11.95x (ISBN 0-13-606970-3). P-H.

Garretson, Robert. Currents of Change. 83p. 1980. 5.95 (ISBN 0-8059-2758-1). Dorrance.

Garretson, Rose A. & Fry, Jack. The Positive Power of Sex. LC 80-68666. 120p. 1980. pap. 5.95 (ISBN 0-89708-025-4). And Bks.

Garrett, Alfred B., et al. Semimicro Qualitative Analysis. 3rd ed. 1966. pap. 16.95 (ISBN 0-471-00192-9). Wiley.

Garrett, Arthur. The Folk of Christendom. LC 79-92433. 1981. 49.95 (ISBN 0-8022-2363-X). Philos Lib.

Garrett, Betty. Columbus: America's Crossroads. Blakey, Ellen S. & Silvey, Larry P., eds. LC 80-66337. (The American Portrait Ser.). (Illus.). 256p. 1980. 24.95 (ISBN 0-932986-10-2). Continent Herit.

Garrett, Bill, jt. ed. see Randolph, David J.

Garrett, E. R., jt. ed. see Hirtz, Jean L.

Garrett, Eileen J. Adventures in the Supernormal: A Personal Memoir. 1949. 4.95 o.p. (ISBN 0-912326-02-6). Garrett-Helix.

--Awareness. LC 60-53468. 1947. 5.00 o.p. (ISBN 0-912326-01-8). Garrett-Helix.

--Life Is the Healer. LC 57-13489. 3.75 o.p. (ISBN 0-685-57230-7). Garrett-Helix.

--Telepathy. 1941. 4.00 o.p. (ISBN 0-912326-00-X). Garrett-Helix.

Garrett, G. G. & Marriott, D. L., eds. Engineering Applications of Fracture Analysis: Proceeedings of the First National Conference on Fracture Held in Johannesburg, South Africa, 7-9 November 1979. LC 80-41074. (International Ser. on the Strength & Fractures of Materials & Structures). (Illus.). 440p. 1980. 60.00 (ISBN 0-08-025437-3). Pergamon.

Garrett, Garet. Where the Money Grows. 1966. Repr. of 1911 ed. flexible cover 2.50 (ISBN 0-87034-024-7). Fraser Pub Co.

Garrett, Garet & Rothbard, Murray N. The Great Depression & New Deal Monetary Policy: Two Essays. LC 80-36791. (Cato Paper Ser.: No. 13). 148p. 1980. pap. 4.00 (ISBN 0-932790-19-4). Cato Inst.

Garrett, George, et al, eds. see Douglas, Nathan, et al.

Garrett, George P., et al, eds. Film Scripts Four: A Hard Day's Night, The Best Man, Darling. LC 71-135273. (Orig.). 1972. Set. 18.95x (ISBN 0-89197-162-9); pap. text ed. 8.95x ea.; instruc. manual free avail. Irvington.

--Film Scripts Three: The Apartment, The Misfits, Charade. LC 71-135273. (Orig.). 1972. pap. 18.95x set (ISBN 0-89197-165-3); pap. text ed. 8.95x ea.; instructor's manual free avail. (ISBN 0-685-26613-3). Irvington.

--Film Scripts Two: High Noon, Twelve Angry Men, The Defiant Ones. LC 71-135273. (Orig.). 1971. pap. 16.50x set (ISBN 0-89197-165-3); pap. text ed. 6.95x ea.; instructor's manual free avail. (ISBN 0-8290-0137-9). Irvington.

Garrett, George P., et al, eds. see Cunningham, John M.

Garrett, George P., et al, eds. see Rose, Reginald.

Garrett, H. E. Surface Active Chemicals. 177p. 1973. pap. text ed. 21.00 (ISBN 0-08-016422-6). Pergamon.

Garrett, Henry E. Great Experiments in Psychology. 3rd ed. (Century Psychology Ser.). (Illus.). 1981. 29.50x (ISBN 0-89197-190-4); pap. text ed. 16.50x (ISBN 0-89197-776-7). Irvington.

Garrett, James & Levine, Edna. Rehabilitation Practices with the Physically Disabled. 500p. 1973. text ed. 25.00x (ISBN 0-231-03523-3). Columbia U Pr.

Garrett, Jane. The Triumphs of Providence. (Illus.). 250p. 1981. 19.50 (ISBN 0-521-23346-1). Cambridge U Pr.

Garrett, Jessie A., ed. Camp & Community: Manzanar & the Owens Valley. Larson, Ronald C. 1977. pap. 7.95 (ISBN 0-930046-00-5). CSUF Oral Hist.

Garrett, John. Gothic Strains & Bourgeois Sentiments in the Novels of Mrs. Ann Radcliffe & Her Imitations. Varma, Devendra P., ed. LC 79-8454. (Gothic Studies & Dissertations Ser.). 1980. lib. bdg. 40.00x (ISBN 0-405-12668-9). Arno.

Garrett, Julia K. Green Flag Over Texas: The Last Years of Spain in Texas. 2nd ed. LC 40-3613. (Texas Heritage Ser). (Illus.). 1969. Repr. of 1939 ed. 12.50 (ISBN 0-8363-0038-6). Jenkins.

Garrett, Leonard J., jt. auth. see McDonough, Adrian M.

Garrett, Leroy. The Stone-Campbell Movement. LC 80-65965. 1981. 13.50 (ISBN 0-89900-059-2). College Pr Pub. Postponed.

Garrett, Patrick. Analog I-O Design: Acquisition, Conversion, Recovery. (Illus.). 1981. text ed. 21.95 (ISBN 0-8359-0208-0); solutions manual avail. Reston.

Garrett, Patrick H. Analog Systems for Microprocessors & Minicomputers. (Illus.). 1978. 21.95 (ISBN 0-87909-035-9); instructor's manual free. Reston.

Garrett, Randall. Takeoff. Freas, Polly & Freas, Kelly, eds. LC 79-9140. (Illus.). 1980. pap. 4.95 (ISBN 0-915442-84-1, Starblaze). Donning Co.

Garrett, Randall & Heydron, Vicki A. The Steel of Raithskar. 192p. (Orig.). 1981. pap. 2.25 (ISBN 0-553-14607-6). Bantam.

Garrett, Richard. The Raiders. 224p. 1980. 18.95 (ISBN 0-442-25873-9). Van Nos Reinhold.

Garrett, Roger. Starship Simulation. LC 78-60612. 1978. pap. 7.95 (ISBN 0-918398-10-X). Dilithium Pr.

Garrett, S. D. Pathogenic Root-Infecting Fungi. LC 72-10024. (Illus.). 1970. 42.50 (ISBN 0-521-07786-9). Cambridge U Pr.

--Soil Fungi & Soil Fertility. 1963. pap. 15.00 (ISBN 0-08-010475-4). Pergamon.

--Soil Fungi & Soil Fertility: An Introduction to Soil Mycology. 2nd ed. (Illus.). 150p. 1981. 19.21 (ISBN 0-08-025507-8); pap. 9.51 (ISBN 0-08-025506-X). Pergamon.

Garrett, Sean. The Suez Canal. Yapp, Malcolm, et al, eds. (World History Ser.). (Illus.). 32p. (gr. 10). 1980. Repr. of 1977 ed. lib. bdg. 5.95 (ISBN 0-686-59707-9); pap. text ed. 1.95 (ISBN 0-89908-205-X). Greenhaven.

Garrett, Stephen A. Ideals & Reality: An Analysis of the Debate Over Viet-Nam. LC 78-59852. 1978. pap. text ed. 10.00 (ISBN 0-8191-0555-4). U Pr of Amer.

Garrett, Thomas M. Cases in Business Ethics. 1968. pap. text ed. 10.95 (ISBN 0-13-118703-1). P-H.

Garrett, W. N., jt. ed. see Cole, H. H.

Garrett, William J. & Robinson, David E. Ultrasound in Clinical Obstetrics. (Illus.). 128p. 1970. 16.50 (ISBN 0-398-00652-0). C C Thomas.

Garrett, William R. The Early Political Caricature in America & the History of the United States. (Illus.). 1979. 31.45 (ISBN 0-89266-164-X). Am Classical Coll Pr.

Garrett, Willis O. Church Ushers' Manual. pap. 1.95 (ISBN 0-8007-0048-1). Revell.

Garrett, Yvonne. The Newlywed Handbook. 1981. 8.95 (ISBN 0-8499-0276-2). Word Bks.

Garrey, Matthew M., et al. Obstetrics Illustrated. 3rd ed. (Illus.). 550p. 1980. pap. text ed. 22.00 (ISBN 0-443-02223-2). Churchill.

--Obstetrics Illustrated: 2nd Edition. LC 73-91453. (Illus.). 536p. 1974. pap. 18.75 o.p. (ISBN 0-443-01118-4). Churchill.

Garrick, Barbara L., ed. Hematology for Medical Technologists PreTest Self-Assessment & Review. LC 78-51704. (PreTest Self-Assessment & Review Ser.). (Illus.). 1979. pap. 9.95 (ISBN 0-07-051573-5). McGraw-Pretest.

Garrick, James G., jt. auth. see Foss, Merle L.

Garrido, L., ed. Systems Far from Equilibrium: Sitges Conference. (Lecture Notes in Physics Ser.: Vol. 132). 403p. 1981. pap. 27.70 (ISBN 0-387-10251-5). Springer Verlag.

Garrigan, Kristine O. Ruskin on Architecture: His Thought & Influence. LC 73-2045. 368p. 1973. 19.50x (ISBN 0-299-06460-3). U of Wis Pr.

Garrigue, Jean. Studies for an Actress & Other Poems. 1973. pap. 1.95 o.s.i. (ISBN 0-02-069370-2, Collier). Macmillan.

Garrigue, Jean, ed. Translations by American Poets. LC 76-86309. 371p. 1970. 15.00x (ISBN 0-8214-0062-2). Ohio U Pr.

Garrigue, Sheila. Between Friends. LC 77-90952. (gr. 5-7). 1978. 8.95 (ISBN 0-87888-133-6). Bradbury Pr.

Garris, Kathleen W. The Santa Casa di Loreto: Problems in Cinquecento Sculpture. LC 76-23653. (Outstanding Dissertations in the Fine Arts Ser.). 1977. lib. bdg. 133.00x (ISBN 0-8240-2735-3). Garland Pub.

Garrison, A. Joseph. Solar Projects: Working Solar Devices to Cut Out & Assemble. (Illus.). 128p. (Orig.). 1981. lib. bdg. 12.90 (ISBN 0-89471-129-6); pap. 6.95 (ISBN 0-89471-130-X). Running Pr.

Garrison, Carolyn L., jt. auth. see Brasher, Ruth E.

Garrison, Chester A. The Vast Venture: Hardy's Epic-Drama The Dynasts. (Salzburg Studies in English Literature, Poetic Drama & Poetic Theory: No. 18). 250p. 1973. pap. text ed. 25.00x (ISBN 0-391-01381-5). Humanities.

Garrison, Christian. The Dream Eater. LC 78-55213. (Illus.). (ps-2). 1978. 9.95 (ISBN 0-87888-134-4). Bradbury Pr.

--Little Pieces of the West Wind. LC 75-887. (Illus.). 32p. (ps-3). 1975. 8.95 (ISBN 0-87888-105-0). Bradbury Pr.

--Snakedoctor. 1980. pap. 1.95 (ISBN 0-686-69263-2, 76232). Avon.

Garrison, Chuck. Offshore Fishing in Southern California & Baja. (Illus.). 1977. pap. 4.95 (ISBN 0-87701-166-4). Chronicle Bks.

--Offshore Fishing: In Southern California & Baja. (Illus., Orig.). 1980. pap. 4.95 (ISBN 0-87701-166-4). Chronicle Bks.

Garrison, Ernest R. The Art & Science of Breeding Dogs. 1979. 29.75 (ISBN 0-89266-163-1). Am Classical Coll Pr.

Garrison, James. The Plutonium Culture from Hiroshima to Harrisburg. 224p. 1981. 14.95 (ISBN 0-8264-0029-9). Continuum.

Garrison, James D. Dryden & the Tradition of Panegyric. LC 73-91676. 1975. 16.50x (ISBN 0-520-02682-9). U of Cal Pr.

Garrison, Jim. A Heritage of Stone. pap. 1.50 o.p. (ISBN 0-425-02953-0). Berkley Pub.

--The Star-Spangled Contract. 272p. 1977. pap. 1.95 o.s.i. (ISBN 0-446-89259-9). Warner Bks.

Garrison, Juanita B. Piedmont Garden: How to Grow by the Calendar. LC 80-23218. 1981. pap. text ed. 4.95 mechanical (ISBN 0-87249-403-9). U of SC Pr.

Garrison, Karl C. Psychology of Adolescence. 7th ed. 448p. 1975. 18.95 (ISBN 0-13-734996-3). P-H.

Garrison, Linda & Read, Ann K. Fitness for Every Body. LC 79-91831. (Illus.). 138p. 1980. pap. text ed. 3.95 (ISBN 0-87484-444-4). Mayfield Pub.

Garrison, Marjorie K. Happy Families Are Homemade. LC 75-18922. 144p. (Orig.). 1976. pap. 1.50 o.p. (ISBN 0-912692-80-4). Cook.

Garrison, Paul. Cross-Country Flying. (Illus.). 192p. 1980. 9.95 (ISBN 0-8306-9966-X); pap. 5.95 (ISBN 0-8306-2284-5, 2284). TAB Bks.

Garrison, Peter. CV: Carrier Aviation. (Illus.). 1980. cancelled (ISBN 0-89141-117-8); pap. 8.95 (ISBN 0-89141-074-0). Presidio Pr.

Garrison, Ray H. Managerial Accounting: Concepts for Planning, Control, Decision Making. rev. ed. 1979. 18.95x (ISBN 0-256-02209-7); study guide 5.95x (ISBN 0-256-02249-6). Business Pubns.

Garrison, Roger H. How the Writer Works: Through the Composing Room. 112p. 1980. pap. 5.95 scp (ISBN 0-06-042276-9, HarpC); avail. Har-Row.

Garrison, Tom, jt. auth. see Lebow, Ruth.

Garrison, V., jt. auth. see Crapanzano, V.

Garrison, Webb. Strange Facts About the Bible. 1976. pap. 1.95 (ISBN 0-89129-174-1). Jove Pubns.

Garrison, William E. Selling Your Handcrafts. LC 74-16304. (Creative Crafts Series). 1974. 10.95 (ISBN 0-8019-6042-8); pap. 6.95 (ISBN 0-8019-6043-6). Chilton.

Garrison, William E & Dowd, Merle E. Handcrafting Jewelry: Designs & Techniques. LC 71-183815. (Illus.). 256p. 1973. 14.95 o.p. (ISBN 0-8092-8851-6). Contemp Bks.

Garrod, Claude, jt. auth. see Hurley, James P.

Garrod, D. J., ed. see Zoological Society of London - 29th Symposium.

Garrod, H. W., ed. see Horace.

Garrod, H. W., ed. see Keats, John.

Garrod, Heathcote W., ed. see Keats, John.

Garrod, L. P., et al. Antibiotic & Chemotherapy. 5th ed. (Illus.). 480p. (Orig.). 1981. text ed. write for info. (ISBN 0-443-02143-0). Churchill.

Garronsky, Serge, jt. auth. see Terry, Patricia.

Garronsky, Serge, tr. see Terry, Patricia & Garronsky, Serge.
Garry, Charles & Goldberg, Art. Streetfighter in the Courtroom. 1977. 11.95 o.p. (ISBN 0-525-21110-1). Dutton.
Garsee, Lee. New Dimensions in Puppet Ministry. 1981. pap. write for info. (ISBN 0-89137-607-0). Quality Pubns.
Garside, R. G. The Architecture of Digital Computers. (Oxford Applied Mathematics & Computing Science Ser.). (Illus.). 376p. 1980. text ed. 74.00x (ISBN 0-19-859627-8); pap. text ed. 34.50x (ISBN 0-19-859638-3). Oxford U Pr.
Garside, W. R. The Measurement of Unemployment: Methods & Sources in Great Britain. 300p. 1981. 37.50x (ISBN 0-631-12643-0). Biblio Dist.
Garsoian, Nina G., ed. see Phaustos Of Byzantium.
Garson, G. David, ed. Worker Self-Management in Industry: The West European Experience. LC 77-2774. (Praeger Special Studies). 1977. text ed. 29.95 (ISBN 0-03-022406-3). Praeger.
Garson, G. David & Smith, Michael P., eds. Organizational Democracy: Participation & Self-Management. LC 75-32375. (Sage Contemporary Social Science Issues: Vol. 22). 1976. 4.95x (ISBN 0-8039-0580-7). Sage.
Garson, Helen S. Truman Capote. LC 80-5336. (Modern Literature Ser.). (Illus.). 160p. 1980. 10.95 (ISBN 0-8044-2229-X); pap. 4.95 (ISBN 0-8044-6172-4). Ungar.
Garson, Michel. Mystery at the Summit of the Himalayas. 1981. 8.95 (ISBN 0-8062-1625-5). Carlton.
Garson, N. G. Louis Botha or John X. Merriman: The Choice of South Africa's First Prime Minister. (Commonwealth Papers: No. 12). 1969. pap. text ed. 2.25x (ISBN 0-485-17612-2, Athlone Pr). Humanities.
Garst, Shannon. Buffalo Bill. (Biography Ser.). (Illus.). (gr. 7 up). 1948. PLB 4.79 o.p. (ISBN 0-671-03840-0). Messner.
Garstang, Walter. Larval Forms & Other Zoological Verses. 1966. Repr. of 1951 ed. 7.50x o.p. (ISBN 0-631-07090-7, Pub. by Basil Blackwell). Biblio Dist.
Garstein, Oskar. Rome & the Counter-Reformation in Scandinavia. 630p. 1980. 40.00x (ISBN 82-00-06165-5). Universitet.
Garten, Hugh P. Gerhart Hauptmann. 1954. 22.50x o.p. (ISBN 0-686-51393-2). Elliots Bks.
Gartenberg, Leo. Torah Thoughts, Vol. 6. LC 64-15745. 1971. 5.95 o.p. (ISBN 0-8246-0125-4). Jonathan David.
Gartenberg, Michael & Shaw, Barry. Mathematics for Financial Analysis. 240p. 1976. text ed. 23.00 (ISBN 0-08-019599-7). Pergamon.
Garth, et al, trs. see Ovid.
Garth, Bryant. Neighborhood Law Firms for the Poor: A Comparative Study of Recent Developments in Legal Aid & in the Legal Profession. LC 80-51739. 282p. 1980. 40.00x (ISBN 90-286-0180-5). Sijthoff & Noordhoff.
Garth, Samuel. The Dispensary: With a Short Account of the Proceedings of the College of Physicians, London, in Relation to the Sick Poor (1697) & Claremont (1715) LC 74-23391. 160p. 1975. Repr. lib. bdg. 20.00x (ISBN 0-8201-1145-7). Schol Facsimiles.
Garthoff, Raymond L. Soviet Military Policy. 1966. 8.95 o.p. (ISBN 0-571-06788-3, Pub. by Faber & Faber). Merrimack Bk Serv.
Gartner. Consumer Education in the Human Services. (Pergamon Policy Studies). 1979. 25.00 (ISBN 0-08-023708-8). Pergamon.
Gartner, Alan. Paraprofessionals in Education: Paraprofessionals Today, Vol. 1. LC 76-12419. 272p. 1977. text ed. 22.95 (ISBN 0-87705-258-1). Human Sci Pr.
--The Preparation of Human Service Professionals. LC 75-11004. 272p. 1976. 22.95 (ISBN 0-87705-259-X). Human Sci Pr.
Gartner, Alan, et al, eds. A Full Employment Program for the 1970's. LC 75-36408. (Praeger Special Studies Ser.). 160p. 1976. text ed. 11.95 (ISBN 0-275-22810-X). Praeger.
Gartner, Lloyd P., ed. Jewish Education in the United States. LC 73-112708. 1970. pap. text ed. 4.25x (ISBN 0-8077-1404-6). Tchrs Coll.
Garton, Alison, jt. ed. see Bruner, Jerome S.
Garton, George. Colt's SAA: Post War Models. 166p. 17.95 (ISBN 0-917714-23-7). Beinfeld Pub.
Garton, George S. How to Really Save Money & Energy in Cooling Your Home. pap. 9.95 (ISBN 0-931624-00-2). Green Hill.
Garton, Malinda D. Teaching the Educable Mentally Retarded: Practical Methods. 3rd ed. (Illus.). 356p. 1974. 14.75 (ISBN 0-398-00654-7). C C Thomas.
Garton-Springer, J., et al. Encounters. (Orig.). 1980. pap. text ed. 8.95x (ISBN 0-435-28477-0); tchrs. bk. 17.95 (ISBN 0-435-28476-2); tapes 144.00 (ISBN 0-435-28474-6); cassettes 128.00 (ISBN 0-435-28473-8). Heinemann Ed.
Gartside, I. Model Business Letters. 2nd ed. 416p. 1974. pap. 13.95x (Pub. by Macdonald & Evans England). Intl Ideas.
Gartside, L. Modern Business Correspondence. 3rd ed. (Illus.). 480p. 1976. pap. 14.95x (ISBN 0-7121-1392-4, Pub. by Macdonald & Evans England). Intl Ideas.
Garve, Andrew. Counterstroke. LC 78-378. 1978. 8.95 o.s.i. (ISBN 0-690-01748-0, TYC-T). T Y Crowell.
Garver. At Wit's End Corner. (Illus.). pap. 0.50 o.p. (ISBN 0-686-12326-3). Christs Mission.
--Watch Your Teaching: Home Study. pap. 3.95 (ISBN 0-686-12324-7). Christs Mission.
Garvey, Gerald. Nuclear Power & Social Planning: The City of the Second Sun. LC 76-54556. 1977. 18.95 (ISBN 0-669-01303-X). Lexington Bks.
Garvey, Sr. M. Patricia, tr. see Augustine, Saint.
Garvey, Mona. Library Displays. LC 79-86918. 1969. 10.00 (ISBN 0-8242-0395-X). Wilson.
--Library Public Relations. 1980. 14.00 (ISBN 0-8242-0651-7). Wilson.
Garvey, William D. Communication: The Essence of Science Facilitating Information Exchange Among Librarians, Scientists, Engineers, & Students. 1978. text ed. 49.00 (ISBN 0-08-022254-4); pap. text ed. 19.50 (ISBN 0-08-023344-9). Pergamon.
Garvie, A. E. The Joy of Finding: An Exposition of Luke 15: 11-32. (Short Course Ser.). 146p. 1914. text ed. 2.95 (ISBN 0-567-08313-6). Attic Pr.
--The Master's Comfort & Hope. (Scholar As Preacher Ser.). 253p. 1917. text ed. 7.75 (ISBN 0-567-04416-5). Attic Pr.
Garvie, A. F. Aeschylus' Supplices: Play & Trilogy. LC 69-10195. 1969. 48.00 (ISBN 0-521-07182-8). Cambridge U Pr.
Garvie, Edie M. Breakthrough to Fluency: English As a Second Language for Young Children. 1977. pap. 8.50x (ISBN 0-631-93970-9, Pub. by Basil Blackwell). Biblio Dist.
Garvin, Andrew & Bermont, Hubert. How to Win with Information or Lose Without It. (Bermont Bks.). 196p. 1980. 26.00 (ISBN 0-89696-110-9). Everest Hse.
Garvin, Charles, et al. The Work Incentive Experience. LC 77-83926. 243p. 1978. text ed. 19.50x (ISBN 0-916672-99-9). Allanheld.
Garvin, Charles D. Contemporary Group Work. (P-H Ser. in Social Work Practice). (Illus.). 304p. 1981. text ed. 15.95 (ISBN 0-13-170233-5). P-H.
Garvin, David. The Economics of University Behavior. 1980. 17.50 (ISBN 0-12-276550-8). Acad Pr.
Garvin, Harry, ed. Romanticism, Modernism, Postmodernism: Vol. 25, No. 2. LC 79-50103. (Bucknell Review Ser.). 192p. 1980. 12.00 (ISBN 0-8387-5004-4). Bucknell U Pr.
Garvin, Harry R., ed. The Arts & Their Interrelations: Bucknell Review, Fall 1978. LC 78-62038. 192p. 1979. 12.00 (ISBN 0-8387-2355-1). Bucknell U Pr.
--Shakespeare: Contemporary Critical Approaches: Bucknel Review, Spring 1979. LC 79-50103. 192p. 1980. 12.00 (ISBN 0-8387-2376-4). Bucknell U Pr.
--Theories of Reading, Looking, & Listening. LC 80-20475. (Bucknell Review Ser.). 192p. 1981. 12.00 (ISBN 0-8387-5007-9). Bucknell U Pr.
Garvin, Mary H. Bible Study Can Be Exciting! 192p. 1976. pap. 3.95 o.p. (ISBN 0-310-24911-2). Zondervan.
Garvin, Richard M. & Burger, Robert E. Where They Go to Die. 1968. 4.95 o.p. (ISBN 0-440-09511-5). Delacorte.
Garvy, G. An Appraisal of the Nineteen-Fifty Census Income Data. (National Bureau of Economic Research: F.23). 1958. 23.50 (ISBN 0-691-04102-4). Princeton U Pr.
Garwood, S. Gray. Educating Young Handicapped Children: A Developmental Approach. LC 79-13200. 1979. text ed. 24.75 (ISBN 0-89443-099-8). Aspen Systems.
Garwood, William R. Kill Him, Again. LC 80-66355. 315p. 1980. 9.95 (ISBN 0-937618-00-4). Bath St Pr.
Gary, A. L. & Glover, John A. Eye Color, Sex, & Children's Behavior. LC 76-3642. 208p. 1976. 14.95 (ISBN 0-88229-213-7). Nelson-Hall.
Gary, Charles E., ed. see Hegel, Georg W.
Gary, James H., ed. see Oil Shale Symposium, 11th.
Gary, Joseph H., ed. Thirteenth Oil Shale Symposium: Proceedings. (Oil Shale Ser.). (Illus.). 400p. (Orig.). 1980. pap. 16.00x (ISBN 0-918062-39-X). Colo Sch Mines.
Garza, Hedda, compiled by. The Watergate Hearings: Index to the Senate Select Committee Reports. LC 80-53886. 625p. 1981. lib. bdg. price not set (ISBN 0-8420-2175-2). Scholarly Res Inc.
Garza, Roberto J. Contemporary Chicano Theatre. 1975. 16.95x (ISBN 0-268-00709-8); pap. 5.95x (ISBN 0-268-00710-1). U of Notre Dame Pr.
Garzke, William H., Jr., jt. auth. see Dulin, Robert O., Jr.
Gas Dynamics Symposium - 5th Biennial - 1964. Physico-Chemical Diagnostics of Plasma: Proceedings. Anderson, Thomas P., et al, eds. 1964. 8.95x o.s.i. (ISBN 0-8101-0041-X). Northwestern U Pr.
Gas Dynamics Symposium - 7th Biennial - 1968. Energy: Proceedings. Holmes, Lawrence B., ed. 1968. 12.75x o.s.i. (ISBN 0-8101-0123-8). Northwestern U Pr.
Gascar, Pierre. The Best Years. LC 66-25398. 1966. 5.00 o.p. (ISBN 0-8076-0378-3). Braziller.
Gasciogne, Christina. Castles of Britain. (Illus.). 224p. 1980. 19.95 (ISBN 0-500-24098-1). Thames Hudson.
Gasco, Hugo. Despierta, Continente Mio. LC 78-50624. 159p. (Orig., Span.). 1978. pap. 3.50 (ISBN 0-89922-108-4). Edit Caribe.
Gascoigne. World List Annual 1979. (World List Ser.). 1980. text ed. 29.95 (ISBN 0-408-70858-1). Butterworths.
Gascoigne, ed. British Union Catalogue of Periodicals 1979. 1980. text ed. 31.50 (ISBN 0-408-70857-3). Butterworths.
Gascoigne, George. The Posies of G. Gascoigne, Corrected & Augmented. LC 79-84110. (English Experience Ser.: No. 929). 532p. 1979. Repr. of 1575 ed. lib. bdg. 50.00 (ISBN 90-221-0929-1). Walter J Johnson.
--The Steele Glas & The Complainte of Phylomene: A Critical Edition with Introduction. Wallace, William I., ed. (Salzburg Studies in English Literature, Elizabethan & Renaissance Studies Ser.: No. 24). 240p. 1975. pap. text ed. 25.00x (ISBN 0-391-01382-3). Humanities.
Gash, John. Caravaggio. (Oresko-Jupiter Art Bks). (Illus.). 96p. 1981. 17.95 (ISBN 0-933516-83-5, Pub. by Oresko-Jupiter England). Hippocrene Bks.
Gash, Jonathan. Spend Game. LC 80-26266. 204p. 1981. 9.95 (ISBN 0-89919-030-8). Ticknor & Fields.
Gash, Norman. Peel. LC 75-25695. (Illus.). 328p. 1976. 21.00x (ISBN 0-582-48083-3). Longman.
--Politics in the Age of Peel: A Study in the Technique of Parliamentary Representation, 1830-1850. 2nd ed. 518p. 1977. text ed. 23.50x (ISBN 0-391-00676-2). Humanities.
Gash, Norman, ed. Age of Peel. 1969. pap. 5.95x (ISBN 0-312-01260-8). St Martin.
Gashutz, W. Lectures on Subgroups of Sylow Type in Finite Soluble Groups. Kuhn, U., tr. (Notes on Pure Mathematics Ser.: No. 11). 100p. (Orig.). 1980. pap. text ed. 7.95 (ISBN 0-908160-22-4, 0571). Bks Australia.
Gasiorowicz, Stephen. Structure of Matter: A Survey of Modern Physics. LC 78-18645. (Physics Ser.). (Illus.). 1979. text ed. 23.95 (ISBN 0-201-02511-6). A-W.
Gaskell, David R. Metallurgical Thermodynamics. 2nd ed. (Materials Engineering Ser.). 560p. 1981. text ed. 29.95 (ISBN 0-07-022946-5). McGraw.
Gaskell, Elizabeth. Cousin Phillis & Other Tales. 1970. 5.00x o.p. (ISBN 0-460-00615-0, Evman). Dutton.
--Life of Charlotte Bronte. 1958. 12.95x (ISBN 0-460-00318-6, Evman); pap. 2.95 (ISBN 0-460-01318-1). Dutton.
--Mary Barton. 1961. 7.50x (ISBN 0-460-00598-7, Evman); pap. 4.50 (ISBN 0-460-01598-2). Dutton.
--Sylvia's Lovers. 1964. 15.50x (ISBN 0-460-00524-3, Evman). Dutton.
Gaskell, Elizabeth C. The Life of Charlotte Bronte. (World's Classics Ser: No. 214). 1975. 14.95 (ISBN 0-19-250214-X). Oxford U Pr.
--Ruth. Wolff, Robert L., ed. LC 75-1507. (Victorian Fiction Ser.). 1975. Repr. of 1853 ed. lib. bdg. 66.00 (ISBN 0-8240-1581-9). Garland Pub.
Gaskell, Jane. The City. LC 77-23530. 1978. 8.95 o.p. (ISBN 0-312-13982-9). St Martin.
--The Serpent. LC 76-62771. 1977. 8.95 o.p. (ISBN 0-312-71312-6). St Martin.
--Some Summer Lands. LC 77-9179. (The Atlan Saga: Vol. V). 1979. 8.95 o.p. (ISBN 0-312-74362-9). St Martin.
Gaskell, P. Morvern Transformed. (Illus.). 300p. 1980. 37.50 (ISBN 0-521-05060-X); pap. 14.95 (ISBN 0-521-29797-4). Cambridge U Pr.
--Trinity College Library. LC 79-41415. (Illus.). 256p. Date not set. 67.50 (ISBN 0-521-23100-0). Cambridge U Pr.
Gaskell, Ronald. Drama & Reality: The European Theatre Since Ibsen. 1972. 12.75x (ISBN 0-7100-7145-0); pap. 6.95 (ISBN 0-7100-7146-9). Routledge & Kegan.
Gaskin, Catherine. A Falcon for a Queen. 336p. 1981. pap. 2.50 (ISBN 0-553-14543-6). Bantam.
--A Falcon for a Queen. 320p. 1977. pap. 1.75 o.p. (ISBN 0-449-23074-0, Crest). Fawcett.
--Family Affairs. LC 79-8832. 528p. 1980. 12.95 (ISBN 0-385-13468-1). Doubleday.
--Fiona. 288p. 1977. pap. 1.75 o.p. (ISBN 0-449-23238-7, Crest). Fawcett.
--The Lynmara Legacy. 1977. pap. 1.95 o.p. (ISBN 0-449-23060-0, Crest). Fawcett.
--Property of a Gentleman. 320p. 1975. pap. 1.75 o.p. (ISBN 0-449-22542-9, X2542, Crest). Fawcett.
--Sara Dane. 1978. pap. 1.95 o.p. (ISBN 0-449-23528-9, Crest). Fawcett.
--The Summer of the Spanish Woman. LC 76-56292. 1977. 10.00 o.p. (ISBN 0-385-07414-X). Doubleday.
--Tilsit Inheritance. 1976. pap. 1.75 o.p. (ISBN 0-449-22852-5, X2852, Crest). Fawcett.
--The Tilsit Inheritance. 384p. 1981. pap. 2.50 (ISBN 0-553-14833-8). Bantam.
Gaskin, Cathering. Edge of Glass. 240p. 1981. pap. 2.50 (ISBN 0-553-14362-X). Bantam.
Gaskin, Maxwell, ed. The Political Economy of Tolerable Survival. 224p. 1981. 30.00x (ISBN 0-7099-0266-2, Pub. by Croom Helm Ltd England). Biblio Dist.
Gaskin, Stephen. Amazing Dope Tales. (Illus.). 1980. pap. 7.00 (ISBN 0-913990-29-9). Book Pub Co.
Gasnick, Roy, compiled By. The Francis Book: A Celebration of the Universal Saint. (Illus.). 320p. 1980. 19.95 (ISBN 0-02-542760-1, Collier); pap. 12.95 (ISBN 0-02-003200-5). Macmillan.
Gaspar, Edmund. United States-Latin America: A Special Relationship? 1978. pap. 4.25 (ISBN 0-8447-3287-7). Am Enterprise.
Gasparic, Jiri. Laboratory Handbook of Paper & Thin-Layer Chromatography. Churacek, Jaroslov, ed. LC 77-14168. 1978. 71.95 (ISBN 0-470-99298-0). Halsted Pr.
Gasparini, Francesco. The Practical Harmonist at the Harpsichord. Burrows, David L., ed. Stillings, Frank S., tr. from It. (Music Reprint Ser.: 1980). (Illus.). 1980. Repr. of 1963 ed. lib. bdg. 17.50 (ISBN 0-306-76017-7). Da Capo.
Gasparini, Graziano & Margolies, Luise. Inca Architecture. Lyon, Patricia J., tr. from Sp. LC 79-3005. (Illus.). 352p. 1980. 32.50x (ISBN 0-253-30443-1). Ind U Pr.
Gasparov, M. L. Russkij Narodnyj Stix V Literaturnyx Imitacijax. (PDR Press Publications on Russian Poetics Ser.). (Orig., Russian.). 1976. pap. text ed. 4.50x (ISBN 90-316-0013-X). Humanities.
Gasperini, Riechard E. Digital Troubleshooting: Practical Digital Theory & Troubleshooting Tips. 1976. pap. 10.95x (ISBN 0-8104-5708-3). Hayden.
Gasque, Ward & Lasor, William. Scripture, Tradition, Interpretation. 12.95 o.p. (ISBN 0-8028-3507-4). Eerdmans.
Gasquet, Cardinal, tr. see Benedict, Saint.
Gass, J. Donald. Differential Diagnosis of Intracocular Tumors: A Stereoscopic Presentation. (Illus.). 1974. text ed. 79.50 o.p. (ISBN 0-8016-1750-2). Mosby.
Gass, William. In the Heart of the Heart of the Country. LC 68-11820. 1968. 10.00 o.s.i. (ISBN 0-06-011468-1, HarpT). Har-Row.
Gass, William H. In the Heart of the Heart of the Country. 1981. pap. 7.95 (ISBN 0-87923-374-5). Godine.
Gassan, Arnold. A Chronology of Photography: A Critical Survey of the History of Photography As a Medium of Art. 380p. (Orig.). 1981. text ed. 19.95 (ISBN 0-87992-022-X); pap. text ed. 12.95 (ISBN 0-87992-021-1). Light Impressions.
--The Color Print Book: A Survey of Contemporary Photographic Printmaking Methods for the Creative Photographer. (The Extended Photo Media Ser.: No. 3). (Illus., Orig.). 1980. pap. 9.95 (ISBN 0-87992-023-8); 16.95 o.p. (ISBN 0-87992-024-6). Light Impressions.
Gassan, Arnold H. Handbook for Contemporary Photography. 4th ed. LC 77-14576. (Illus.). 1977. 14.95 (ISBN 0-87992-009-2); pap. 8.95x (ISBN 0-87992-008-4). Light Impressions.
Gassel, W. D., ed. Cultivation of Harmatopoetic Stem Cells & of Comitted Leucocyte Progenitor Cells. (Vol. 62, No. 5-6). (Illus.). 58p. 1980. pap. cancelled o.p. (ISBN 3-8055-0697-X). S Karger.
Gasser, J. K., ed. Modelling Nitrogen from Farm Wastes. (Illus.). 1979. 26.00x (ISBN 0-85334-869-3). Intl Ideas.
Gasser, J. K., et al, eds. Effluents from Livestock. (Illus.). v, 712p. 1980. 80.00x (ISBN 0-85334-895-2). Burgess-Intl Ideas.
Gasser, R. P. & Richards, W. G. Entropy & Energy Levels. (Oxford Chemistry Ser.). (Illus.). 150p. 1974. pap. text ed. 7.95x (ISBN 0-19-855490-7). Oxford U Pr.
Gassick, Trevor Le see Mahfouz, Naguib.
Gassner, John. Masters of the Drama. 3rd ed. (Illus.). 1953. 10.00 o.p. (ISBN 0-486-20100-7). Dover.
Gassner, John, ed. Ideas in the Drama. LC 64-21201. 1964. 12.50x (ISBN 0-231-02733-8). Columbia U Pr.
Gasson, Raphael. Food for God's Children. 1977. pap. 3.95 o.p. (ISBN 0-88270-255-6). Logos.

Gast, Kelly P. Last Stage from Opal. LC 77-26525. 1978. 7.95 o.p. (ISBN 0-385-13473-8). Doubleday.

Gastaut, Henri & Broughton, Roger. Epileptic Seizures: Clinical & Electrographic Features, Diagnosis & Treatment. 304p. 1972. pap. 32.50 photocopy ed. spiral (ISBN 0-398-02290-9). C C Thomas.

Gaster, Bertha, ed. see Szigethi, Agnes.

Gaster, Moses. The Ketubah. new ed. LC 68-9532. (Illus.). 90p. 1974. 7.95 (ISBN 0-87203-029-6). Hermon.

Gaster, Theodor H., ed. see Frazer, James G.

Gasteyger, Curt, et al. Energy, Inflation & International Economic Relations: Atlantic Institute Studies - Two. LC 75-19764. (Special Studies). (Illus.). 256p. 1975. text ed. 24.95 (ISBN 0-275-01250-6). Praeger.

Gastil, R. Gordon, et al. Reconnaissance Geology of the State of Baja California. LC 74-83806. (Memoir: No. 140). (Illus.). 1975. 25.00x (ISBN 0-8137-1140-1); pap. 21.00x (ISBN 0-685-56041-4). Geol Soc.

Gastil, Raymond D. Freedom in the World: Political Rights & Civil Liberties, 1980. LC 80-66430. (Illus.). 1980. lib. bdg. 24.95 (ISBN 0-932088-02-3). Freedom Hse.

Gastil, Raymond D., ed. Freedom in the World: Political Rights & Civil Liberties. 321p. (Orig.). 1981. pap. 8.95 (ISBN 0-87855-819-5). Transaction Bks.

Gastmann, Albert. Historical Dictionary of the French & Netherlands Antilles. LC 78-19070. (Latin American Historical Dictionaries Ser.: No. 18). 1978. lib. bdg. 10.00 (ISBN 0-8108-1153-7). Scarecrow.

Gaston, A. G. Green Power: The Successful Way of A. G. Gaston. (Illus.). 1977. Repr. of 1968 ed. 8.95 (ISBN 0-916624-09-9). TSU Pr.

--Green Power: The Successful Way of A. G. Gaston. (Illus.). 1978. pap. 2.95 (ISBN 0-916624-10-2). TSU Pr.

Gaston, Desmond. The Care & Repair of Furniture. LC 78-55622. 1978. 9.95 o.p. (ISBN 0-385-14466-0). Doubleday.

Gaston, Jerry. The Reward System in British & American Science. LC 77-17404. (Science, Culture & Society Ser.). 1978. 24.50 (ISBN 0-471-29293-1, Pub. by Wiley-Interscience). Wiley.

Gaston, Jerry, jt. ed. see Merton, Robert K.

Gaston, Mary F. Collector's Encyclopedia of Limoges Porcelain. (Illus.). 1980. 19.95 (ISBN 0-89145-132-3). Collector Bks.

Gaston, Paul L. W. D. Snodgrass. (United States Authors Ser.: No. 316). 1978. lib. bdg. 12.50 (ISBN 0-8057-7242-1). Twayne.

Gaston, Thomas, jt. auth. see Peacock, Frederick.

Gastonguay, Paul R. Evolution for Everyone. LC 73-5809. (BSCS Ser.). 320p. 1974. pap. 5.95 (ISBN 0-672-63642-5). Pegasus.

Gastwirt, Harold P. Fraud Corruption & Holiness: The Controversy Over the Supervision of Jewish Dietary Practice in New York City. LC 74-77649. 1974. 15.00 (ISBN 0-8046-9056-1, Natl U). Kennikat.

Gatchel, Robert J. & Price, Kenneth P., eds. Clinical Applications of Biofeedback: Appraisal & Status. LC 78-26959. (Pergamon General Psychology Ser.: Vol. 75). (Illus.). 1979. text ed. 33.00 (ISBN 0-08-022978-6); pap. text ed. 11.00 (ISBN 0-08-022977-8). Pergamon.

Gatell, Frank O. & McFaul, John M., eds. Jacksonian America, 1815-1840: New Society, Changing Politics. 1970. 5.95 o.p. (ISBN 0-13-509604-9); pap. 2.95 o.p. (ISBN 0-13-509596-4, S218). P-H.

Gatell, Frank O., jt. ed. see Weinstein, Allen.

Gatell, Frank O., et al. The Growth of American Politics: A Modern Reader. Incl. Vol. 1. Through Reconstruction. o.p.; pap. 6.95x (ISBN 0-19-501545-2); Vol. 2. Since the Civil War. o.p.; pap. 6.95x (ISBN 0-19-501547-9). 1972. Oxford U Pr.

Gately, George. Heathcliff. (Heathcliff Cartoon Ser.: No. 1). (Illus.). 128p. (gr. 5 up). 1981. pap. 1.50 (ISBN 0-448-12616-8, Tempo). G&D.

--Heathcliff Rides Again. 128p. 1981. pap. 1.50 (ISBN 0-448-12629-X, Tempo). G&D.

Gatenby, Greg, ed. Whale Sound. (Illus.). 1977. pap. 6.95 (ISBN 0-88894-135-8, Pub. by Douglas & McIntyre). Madrona Pubs.

Gatenby, Rosemary. Hanged for a Sheep. 1977. pap. 1.50 o.s.i. (ISBN 0-515-04418-0). Jove Pubns.

--The Season of Danger. 1977. pap. 1.50 o.s.i. (ISBN 0-515-04429-6). Jove Pubns.

Gates, ed. see Makkai, Adam.

Gates, Bruce L. Social Program Administration: The Implementation of Social Policy. (Illus.). 1980. text ed. 15.95 (ISBN 0-13-817767-8). P-H.

Gates, D. M. & Papian, U. N. Atlas of Energy Budgets of Plant Leaves. 1971. 38.00 (ISBN 0-12-277250-4). Acad Pr.

Gates, Doris. Blue Willow. LC 40-32435. (gr. 4-6). 1976. pap. 2.50 (ISBN 0-14-030924-1, VS30, Puffin). Penguin -

--Two Queens of Heaven: Aphrodite & Demeter. (Greek Myths Ser). (Illus.). 96p. (gr. 4-6). 1974. PLB 7.95 (ISBN 0-670-73680-5). Viking Pr.

Gates, Eleanor. The Poor Little Rich Girl. LC 75-32203. (Classics of Children's Literature, 1621-1932: Vol. 64). (Illus.). 1976. Repr. of 1912 ed. PLB 38.00 (ISBN 0-8240-2313-7). Garland Pub.

Gates, Gilman C. Saybrook at the Mouth of the Connecticut River: The First One Hundred Years. 1935. 42.50x (ISBN 0-685-89040-6). Elliots Bks.

Gates, Hill see Ahern, Emily M.

Gates, John D. The Astor Family: A Unique Exploration of One of America's First Families. LC 79-6580. 288p. 1981. 12.95 (ISBN 0-385-14909-3). Doubleday.

--The Du Pont Family. LC 78-7753. 1979. 11.95 o.p. (ISBN 0-385-13043-0). Doubleday.

Gates, John E. An Analysis of the Lexicographic Resources Used by American Biblical Scholars Today. LC 72-88670. (Society of Biblical Literature. Dissertation Ser.). (Illus.). 1972. pap. text ed. 7.50 (ISBN 0-89130-164-X, 060108). Scholars Pr Ca.

Gates, John K. A Touch of Nostalgia: A Glimpse of America's Past. LC 80-84010. (Illus.). 192p. (Orig.). 1980. pap. 14.95 (ISBN 0-9605168-0-8). Photographit.

Gates, Robert J. Awntyrs off Arthure at the Terne Wathelyne: A Critical Edition. LC 69-16539. (Haney Foundation Ser). 1969. 12.00x (ISBN 0-8122-7587-X). U of Pa Pr.

Gatewood, Willard B., Jr., jt. ed. see Donovan, Timothy P.

Gatewood, Willard B., Jr., ed. see Knox, George L.

Gatewood, Worth, ed. Fifty Years-The New York Daily News in Pictures. LC 78-24843. (Illus.). 1979. 17.95 o.p. (ISBN 0-385-15025-3); pap. 8.95 o.p. (ISBN 0-385-15024-5, Dolp). Doubleday.

Gatfield, George. Guide to Printed Books & Manuscripts Relating to English & Foreign Heraldry & Genealogy. 1966. Repr. of 1892 ed. 26.00 (ISBN 0-8103-3121-7). Gale.

Gathercole, Peter, et al. Art of the Pacific Islands. LC 79-3637. (Illus.). 368p. 1980. 45.00x (ISBN 0-253-10145-X). Ind U Pr.

Gathje, Curtis. The Disco Kid No. 1. (Hi Lo Ser.). 96p. (gr. 6 up). 1981. pap. 1.50 (ISBN 0-553-14618-1). Bantam.

Gathorne-Hardy, Jonathan. Jane's Adventures in & Out of the Book. LC 80-29185. (Illus.). 192p. 1981. 10.95 (ISBN 0-87951-122-2). Overlook Pr.

Gathorne-Hardy, Robert. Amalfi: Aspects of the City & Her Ancient Territories. (Illus.). 1968. 8.95 (ISBN 0-571-08576-8, Pub. by Faber & Faber). Merrimack Bk Serv.

Gati, Charles. Caging the Bear: Containment & the Cold War. LC 73-19522. 1974. pap. text ed. 5.95 (ISBN 0-672-61351-4). Bobbs.

Gati, Charles & Gati, Toby T. The Debate Over Detente. (Headline Ser.: 234). (Illus.). 1977. pap. 2.00 (ISBN 0-87124-039-4, 76-55300). Foreign Policy.

Gati, Charles, ed. The International Politics of Eastern Europe. LC 75-23963. (Illus.). 1976. text ed. 29.95 (ISBN 0-275-55960-2); pap. text ed. 10.95 (ISBN 0-275-89500-9). Praeger.

--The Politics of Modernization in Eastern Europe: Testing the Soviet Model. LC 73-15185. (Special Studies). (Illus.). 410p. 1974. text ed. 32.95 (ISBN 0-275-09440-5). Praeger.

Gati, Toby T., jt. auth. see Gati, Charles.

Gatje, Charles T. & Gatje, John F. A MAP for Fractions. Marcos, Rafael, tr. (Orig., Span.). (gr. 5 up). 1981. pap. text ed. 1.75 (ISBN 0-937534-07-2). G & G Pubs.

--A Math Activity Packet for Fractions. (Orig.). 1976. pap. text ed. 1.50 (ISBN 0-937534-01-3). G&G Pubs.

Gatje, Helmut. The Qur'an & Its Exegesis: Selected Texts with Classical & Modern Muslim Interpretations. Welch, Alford T., ed. (Islamic World Ser). 1977. 26.50x (ISBN 0-520-02833-3). U of Cal Pr.

Gatje, John F., jt. auth. see Gatje, Charles T.

Gatland, Bruce, jt. auth. see Fisher, Jack.

Gatland, H. B. Electronic Engineering Applications of Two Port Systems. 1976. text ed. 32.00 (ISBN 0-08-018069-8); pap. 16.00 (ISBN 0-08-019866-X). Pergamon.

Gatland, Kenneth. Manned Spacecraft. (YA) (gr. 9 up). 1967. 3.50 o.s.i. (ISBN 0-02-542890-X). Macmillan.

--Missiles and Rockets. LC 75-15641. (Illus.). 256p. 1975. 9.95 (ISBN 0-02-542860-8, 54286). Macmillan.

--The Robot Explorers. LC 72-78611. 1972. 5.95 o.s.i. (ISBN 0-02-542870-5). Macmillan.

--Rockets & Space Travel. LC 78-64661. (Fact Finders Ser.). (Illus.). 1979. lib. bdg. 3.96 (ISBN 0-686-51130-1). Silver.

--The Young Scientist Book of Spaceflight. (Young Scientist Ser.). (gr. 4-5). text ed. 6.95 (ISBN 0-88436-526-3). EMC.

Gatland, Kenneth, jt. auth. see Bono, Philip.

Gatland, Kenneth, jt. auth. see Bono, Phillip.

Gatlin, Carl. Petroleum Engineering: Drilling & Well Completion. 1960. ref. ed. 31.95 (ISBN 0-13-662155-4). P-H.

Gatlin, Lila L. Information Theory & the Living System. LC 76-187030. (Molecular Biology Ser.). 208p. 1972. 16.00x (ISBN 0-231-03634-5). Columbia U Pr.

Gatschet, Albert. An Extract from the Klamath Indians of SW Oregon. Repr. of 1890 ed. pap. 4.50 (ISBN 0-8466-0118-4, SJS118). Shorey.

Gattegno, Caleb. Towards a Visual Culture. 1971. pap. 1.65 o.s.i. (ISBN 0-380-01455-6, 11940, Discus). Avon.

Gattegno, Jean. Lewis Carroll: Fragments of a Looking Glass. Sheed, Rosemary, tr. from Fr. LC 75-23388. (Illus.). 320p. 1976. 8.95 o.s.i. (ISBN 0-690-01028-1, TYC-T). T Y Crowell.

Gatti, David. Ready-to-Use Sale Announcements. (Dover Clip Art Pictorial Archive Ser.). (Illus.). 64p. (Orig.). 1980. pap. 2.50 (ISBN 0-486-24012-6). Dover.

Gatti-Casazza, Guilio. Memories of the Opera. 1980. 19.95 (ISBN 0-7145-3518-4); pap. 9.95 (ISBN 0-7145-3665-2). Riverrun NY.

Gattinoni, C. T., tr. see Jones, E. Stanley.

Gatty, Margaret. Parables from Nature. LC 75-32180. (Classics of Children's Literature, 1621-1932: Vol. 43). (Illus.). 1977. Repr. of 1880 ed. PLB 38.00 (ISBN 0-8240-2292-0). Garland Pub.

Gatz, Konrad & Achtenberg, Gerhard. Color & Architecture. Date not set. 22.50 o.p. (ISBN 0-8038-0039-8). Hastings.

Gatzke, Hans W., jt. auth. see Strayer, Joseph R.

Gauba, K. L. The Assassination of Mahatma Gandhi. 1969. pap. 3.50 (ISBN 0-88253-140-9). Ind-US Inc.

Gaubert, Henri B. Isaac & Jacob, God's Chosen Ones. (Bible in History Ser.). Date not set. 5.95 o.p. (ISBN 0-8038-3356-3). Hastings.

Gauch, Hugh. Inorganic Plant Nutrition. LC 72-76542. 528p. 1972. 40.00 (ISBN 0-12-786518-7). Acad Pr.

Gauch, Patricia L. Kate Alone. 112p. (YA) (gr. 5-12). 1980. 7.95 (ISBN 0-399-20738-4). Putnam.

Gaudin, Anthony J., jt. auth. see Jones, Kenneth C.

Gaudin, C., ed. see Bachelard, Gaston.

Gaudry, Marc, jt. ed. see Florian, Michael.

Gaudy, Anthony & Gaudy, Elizabeth. Microbiology for Environment Science Engineers. (Water Resources & Environmental Engineering Ser.). (Illus.). 704p. 1980. 25.95 (ISBN 0-07-023035-8); solutions manual 16.50 (ISBN 0-07-023036-6). McGraw.

Gaudy, Elizabeth, jt. auth. see Gaudy, Anthony.

Gaugas, Joseph M., ed. Polyamines in Biomedical Research. LC 79-40651. 1980. 85.00 (ISBN 0-471-27629-4, Pub. by Wiley-Interscience). Wiley.

Gaughan, Edward D. College Algebra. LC 73-81779. (Contemporary Undergraduate Mathematics Ser.). 1974. text ed. 16.95 o.p. (ISBN 0-8185-0097-2). Brooks-Cole.

--College Algebra. 2nd ed. LC 79-22247. 1980. text ed. 16.95 (ISBN 0-8185-0351-3). Brooks-Cole.

Gaughan, J. A. The Knights of Glin. 1980. text ed. 19.50x (ISBN 0-391-01181-2). Humanities.

Gauhar, Altaf, ed. The Challenge of Islam. 393p. 1980. 35.00x (ISBN 0-906041-02-3, Pub. by Islamic Council of Europe England); pap. 14.95x (ISBN 0-906041-03-1). Intl Schol Bk Serv.

Gaukroger, Stephen, ed. Descartes: Philosophy, Mathematics & Physics. (Harvester Readings in the History of Science & Philosophy Ser.: No. 1). 329p. 1980. 30.00x (ISBN 0-389-20084-0). B&N.

Gauld & Shotter. Human Action & Its Psychological Investigation. 1977. 16.00 (ISBN 0-7100-8568-0). Routledge & Kegan.

Gauld, Alan & Shotter, John. Human Action & Its Psychological Investigation. 248p. 1980. pap. 12.95 (ISBN 0-7100-0589-X). Routledge & Kegan.

Gauld, Charles A. The Last Titan, Percival Farquhar: American Entrepreneur in Latin America. 446p. 1972. 5.50 o.p. (ISBN 0-912098-04-X). Cal Inst Intl St.

Gaulden, Ray. High Country Showdown. 1979. pap. 1.50 (ISBN 0-505-51438-9). Tower Bks.

--Shadow of the Rope. 1979. pap. 1.50 (ISBN 0-505-51439-7). Tower Bks.

Gauldie, Sinclair. Architecture. (Appreciation of the Arts Ser). (Illus., Orig.). 1969. pap. 6.95 o.p. (ISBN 0-19-211902-8). Oxford U Pr.

Gaulke, Earl H. You Can Have a Family Where Everybody Wins. LC 75-23574. 104p. 1975. pap. 2.50 (ISBN 0-570-03723-9, 12-2625). Concordia.

Gault, C. & Gault, G. Harlem Globetrotters Funniest Games. (ps-3). pap. 0.95 (ISBN 0-590-03000-0, Schol Pap). Schol Bk Serv.

Gault, Clare & Gault, Frank. Four Stars from the World of Sports. LC 75-3909. (Illus.). 112p. (gr. 3-7). 1975. 4.95 (ISBN 0-8027-6221-2); PLB 4.83 o.s.i. (ISBN 0-8027-6222-0). Walker & Co.

--Home Run Kings. LC 74-31903. (Illus.). (gr. 3-5). 1975. 4.95 (ISBN 0-8027-6217-4); PLB 4.85 o.s.i. (ISBN 0-8027-6216-6). Walker & Co.

Gault, Clare, jt. auth. see Gault, Frank.

Gault, Frank & Gault, Clare. Stories from the Olympics. LC 75-42823. (Illus.). 96p. 1976. 5.95 (ISBN 0-8027-6255-7); PLB 5.85 o.s.i. (ISBN 0-8027-6256-5). Walker & Co.

Gault, Frank, jt. auth. see Gault, Clare.

Gault, G., jt. auth. see Gault, C.

Gault, Jan, et al. Laboratory Investigations in Zoology. 176p. 1980. pap. 8.95 (ISBN 0-8403-2261-5). Kendall-Hunt.

Gault, John C. Public Utility Regulation of an Exhaustible Resource: The Case of Natural Gas. LC 78-75016. (Outstanding Dissertations in Economics). 1980. lib. bdg. 31.00 (ISBN 0-8240-4051-1). Garland Pub.

Gault, Lila & Sestrap, Betsy. The Cider Book. LC 80-18267. 200p. 1980. pap. 5.95 (ISBN 0-914842-48-X). Madrona Pubs.

Gault, Lila, jt. auth. see Weiss, Jeffrey.

Gault, William C. Dirt Track Summer. (gr. 7-9). 1961. PLB 6.95 o.p. (ISBN 0-525-28752-3). Dutton.

--Drag Strip. (gr. 5-8). pap. 0.95 o.p. (ISBN 0-425-03014-8, Highland). Berkley Pub.

--Gasoline Cowboy. LC 73-15784. 160p. (gr. 5-7). 1974. PLB 7.95 o.p. (ISBN 0-525-30352-9). Dutton.

--Quarterback Gamble. LC 72-102743. (gr. 4 up). 1973. op o.p. (ISBN 0-525-37940-1, Anytime Bks); pap. 0.95 o.p. (ISBN 0-525-45015-7, Anytime Bks). Dutton.

--Speedway Challenge. (gr. 5-8). 1965. pap. 0.95 o.p. (ISBN 0-685-06915-X, Highland). Berkley Pub.

--Stubborn Sam. (gr. 5 up). 1969. PLB 7.95 o.p. (ISBN 0-525-40433-3). Dutton.

Gaumann, T. & Hoigne, J., eds. Aspects of Hydrocarbon Radiolysis. LC 68-19261. 1968. 38.00 (ISBN 0-12-277650-X). Acad Pr.

Gaumnitz, Jack E., jt. auth. see Dougall, Herbert E.

Gaunt & Petzold. Focal Encyclopedia of Photography. 1980. desk ed. 24.95 (ISBN 0-240-50680-4). Focal Pr.

Gaunt, Joan, jt. auth. see Lancaster, Janet.

Gaunt, Leonard. Focalguide to Camera Accessories. (Focalguide Ser.). (Illus.). 216p. 1980. pap. 7.95 (ISBN 0-240-51043-7). Focal Pr.

--Practical Exposure. LC 80-40793. (Practical Photography Ser.). (Illus.). 192p. 1981. 19.95 (ISBN 0-240-51058-5). Focal Pr.

--Praktica Book. 2nd ed. 120p. 1979. 8.95 (ISBN 0-240-50749-5). Focal Pr.

--Zoom & Special Lenses. LC 80-41245. (Illus.). 128p. 1981. pap. 9.95 (ISBN 0-240-51069-0). Focal Pr.

Gaunt, William. Turner. (Illus.). 96p. 1976. pap. text ed. 5.95 (ISBN 0-8120-0704-2). Barron.

Gauquelin, Michel. Cosmic Influences on Human Behavior. LC 77-28405. (Illus.). 1978. 8.95 (ISBN 0-88231-050-X). ASI Pubs Inc.

--Your Personality & the Planets. LC 80-5499. (Illus.). 262p. 1980. 11.95 (ISBN 0-8128-2737-6). Stein & Day.

Gaurico, Pomponio. De sculptura. (Documents of Art & Architectural History Series 2: Vol. 2). 104p. (Latin.). 1981. Repr. of 1504 ed. 25.00x (ISBN 0-89371-202-7). Broude Intl Edns.

Gaus, John M. & Wolcott, Leon O. Public Administration & the Department of Agriculture. LC 75-8788. (FDR & the Era of the New Deal Ser.). 1975. Repr. of 1940 ed. lib. bdg. 45.00 (ISBN 0-306-70704-7). Da Capo.

Gausch, John P. Balanced Involvement: Safety, Production Motivation. (Monographs: No.3). cancelled (ISBN 0-686-21671-7); cancelled (ISBN 0-686-21672-5). ASSE.

Gause, John T. Complete University Word Hunter. (Apollo Eds.). (YA) (gr. 9-12). pap. 2.45 o.s.i. (ISBN 0-8152-0140-0, A140, TYC-T). T Y Crowell.

Gauss, H. E. Introduction to Physics. LC 66-12756. (Illus.). 1966. pap. 1.65 o.p. (ISBN 0-668-01411-3). Arc Bks.

Gauss, Karl. Briefwechsel Zwischen Carl Friedrich Gauss und W. Bolyai. 1971. Repr. of 1899 ed. 18.50 (ISBN 0-384-17765-4); 12.00 (ISBN 0-686-66286-5). Johnson Repr.

Gaustad, Edwin S., ed. see American Academy of Religion, 1974.

Gautam, Vinayshil. Enterprise & Society. 1979. text ed. 8.00x (ISBN 0-391-01861-2). Humanities.

Gautard, Raymond. The Beautiful String Art Book. LC 78-58375. (Illus.). 1978. 19.95 (ISBN 0-8069-5386-1); lib. bdg. 16.79 (ISBN 0-8069-5387-X). Sterling.

Gautheaux, S. A., Jr., ed. Animal Migration, Orientation & Navigation. 1981. 39.00 (ISBN 0-12-277750-6). Acad Pr.
Gautherie, M., et al. Thermographie und Brustkrebs: Diagnose, Prognose, Ueberwachung. Pusterla, E. & Gros, C. M., eds. (Gynaekologische Rundschau: Vol. 19, No. 4). (Illus.). 1980. pap. 19.75 (ISBN 3-8055-0716-X). S Karger.
Gauthier, Howard L., jt. auth. see Taaffe, Edward.
Gauthier, J. D., ed. French Twenty Bibliography: Provencal Upplement No. 1, Critical & Biographical References to Provencal Literature Since 1850. (Orig.). 1976. pap. 12.00 (ISBN 0-933444-32-X). French Inst.
Gauthier-Pilters, Hilde & Dagg, Anne I. The Camel: Its Evolution, Ecology, Behavior, & Relationship to Man. LC 80-23822. 1981. lib. bdg. 26.00x (ISBN 0-226-28453-0). U of Chicago Pr.
Gautier, Theophile. Charles Baudelaire. Thorne, Guy, tr. LC 77-10264. (Illus.). 1977. Repr. of 1915 ed. 27.50 (ISBN 0-685-87692-6). Ams Pr.
--Mademoiselle De Maupin. Richardson, Joanna, tr. from Fr. & intro. by. 304p. 1981. pap. 4.95 (ISBN 0-14-044398-3). Penguin.
--Poesies: 1830. Cockerham, H., ed. 1973. text ed. 10.25x (ISBN 0-485-14705-X, Athlone Pr). Humanities.
--The Romantic Ballet as Seen by Theophile Gautier. LC 79-7764. (Dance Ser.). (Illus.). 1980. Repr. of 1932 ed. lib. bdg. 14.00x (ISBN 0-8369-9292-X). Arno.
Gautot, Henri J., jt. ed. see Crawford, O. William.
Gautruche, Pierre. The Poetical Histories, Repr. Of 1671 Ed. D'Assigny, Marius, tr. Bd. with Appendix De Diis et Heroibus Poeticis. Jouvency, Joseph de. Repr. of 1705 ed. LC 75-27877. (Renaissance & the Gods Ser.: Vol. 32). (Illus.). 1976. lib. bdg. 73.00 (ISBN 0-8240-2081-2). Garland Pub.
Gautschi, Theodore F. Management Forum. (Illus.). 271p. 1979. pap. 16.00 (ISBN 0-536-03096-0). Herman Pub.
G. A. Van, Der Knaap see Van Der Knaap, G. A.
Gaventa, John. Power & Powerlessness: Quiescence & Rebellion in an Appalachian Valley. LC 80-12988. (Illus.). 284p. 1980. 16.50 (ISBN 0-252-00772-7). U of Ill Pr.
Gaver, Jessyca R. The Golden Dozen. 1976. pap. 1.25 o.p. (ISBN 0-685-69151-9, LB348ZK, Leisure Bks). Nordon Pubns.
--How Deep the Cup. (Orig.). 1975. pap. 1.50 o.p. (ISBN 0-685-53125-2, LB280DK, Leisure Bks). Nordon Pubns.
Gaverluk, Emil. Did Genesis Man Conquer Space? LC 74-1262. (Illus.). 192p. 1974. pap. 2.95 o.p. (ISBN 0-8407-5553-8). Nelson.
Gavin, Frank. Seven Centuries of the Problem of Church & State. 1938. 11.50 (ISBN 0-86527-180-1). Fertig.
Gavin, Jim. Club Motor Racing. 1977. 17.95 (ISBN 0-7134-0893-6, Pub. by Batsford England). David & Charles.
Gavin, William F. Street Corner Conservative. 1975. 7.95 o.s.i. (ISBN 0-87000-325-9). Arlington Hse.
Gavin, William G. Accoutrement Plates North & South, 1861-1865. 2nd enl. ed. LC 74-24432. (Illus.). 400p. 1975. casebound 22.00 o.p. (ISBN 0-87387-068-9); pap. 15.00 o.p. (ISBN 0-87387-050-6). Shumway.
Gavins, Raymond. The Perils & Prospects of Southern Black Leadership: Gordon Blaine Hancock, 1884-1970. LC 76-44090. 1977. 11.75 (ISBN 0-8223-0381-7). Duke.
Gavoty, Bernard. Chopin. Sokolinsky, Martin, tr. LC 77-3966. (Illus.). 1977. encore edition 5.95 o.p. (ISBN 0-684-16354-3, ScribT). Scribner.
Gavrilov, M. A. & Zakrevsky, A. D., eds. LYAPAS: A Programming Language for Logic & Coding Algorithms. (ACM Monograph Ser). 1969. 55.25 (ISBN 0-12-277850-2). Acad Pr.
Gavron, Hannah. Captive Wife. (International Library of Sociology & Social Reconstruction Ser.). 1966. text ed. 17.00x (ISBN 0-7100-3457-1). Humanities.
Gavronsky, Serge, tr. Francis Ponge: The Power of Language. 1979. 16.95x (ISBN 0-520-03441-4). U of Cal Pr.
Gavronsky, Serge, tr. see Ponge, Francis.
Gavurin, Lester L., jt. auth. see Forman, William.
Gaw. It Depends: Appropriate Interpersonal Communication. 1981. 9.95 (ISBN 0-88284-124-6). Alfred Pub.
Gaw, Albert, ed. Cross-Cultural Psychiatry. 475p. 1981. text ed. 37.50 (ISBN 0-88416-338-5). PSG Pub.
Gaw, Beverly & Sayer, James E. May I Join You? LC 78-23300. (Illus.). 1979. pap. text ed. 9.95x (ISBN 0-88284-069-X). Alfred Pub.
Gawel, M., jt. auth. see Rose, Clifford F.
Gawne, Eleanor & Oerke. Dress. rev. ed. 672p. (gr. 9-12). 1975. 17.96 (ISBN 0-87002-069-2); tchr's guide 3.80 (ISBN 0-87002-900-2). Bennett IL.
Gawne, Eleanor J. Fabrics for Clothing. (gr. 10-12). 1973. pap. text ed. 4.60 (ISBN 0-87002-149-4). Bennett IL.
Gaworski, Michael E. & Warming, Wanda. The World of Indonesian Textiles. LC 80-82526. (Illus.). 280p. 1981. 50.00 (ISBN 0-87011-432-8). Kodansha.
Gawrilov, G. G. Chemical (Electroless) Nickel Plating. (Illus.). 189p. 1979. 42.50x (ISBN 0-86108-023-8). Intl Pubns Serv.
Gawronski, Donald V. Out of the Past: A Topical History of the United States. 2nd ed. 1975. pap. text ed. 9.95x (ISBN 0-02-474410-7, 47441); tchrs' manual free (ISBN 0-02-474420-4). Macmillan.
Gawryn, Marvin. Reaching High: The Psychology of Spiritual Living. LC 80-24306. 200p. 1981. 11.95 (ISBN 0-938380-00-1); pap. 7.95 (ISBN 0-938380-01-X). Spiritual Renaissance.
Gawthrop, Louis C. Administrative Politics & Social Change. LC 76-145413. (American Politics Ser). 1971. pap. text ed. 5.95 (ISBN 0-312-00455-9). St Martin.
--Bureaucratic Behavior in the Executive Branch. LC 69-10568. 1969. pap. text ed. 6.95 (ISBN 0-02-911400-4). Free Pr.
Gay, Andrew J., et al. Eye Movement Disorders. LC 74-10747. 1974. 23.00 o.p. (ISBN 0-8016-1763-4). Mosby.
Gay, George R., jt. ed. see Smith, David E.
Gay, J., jt. ed. see Lloyd, Barbara.
Gay, Jeanne, ed. The Travel & Tourism Bibliography & Resource Handbook. 1342p. 1980. pap. 35.00 (ISBN 0-935638-00-8). Travel & Tourism.
--The Travel & Tourism Personnel Directory. (Orig.). 1981. pap. 10.00x (ISBN 0-935638-03-2). Travel & Tourism.
Gay, Jeanne & Mead, Bernard, eds. The Travel & Tourism Audiovisual Guide. 530p. (Orig.). 1980. pap. 15.00x (ISBN 0-935638-01-6). Travel & Tourism.
--The Travel & Tourism Education Guide. (Orig.). 1980. pap. cancelled (ISBN 0-935638-02-4). Travel & Tourism.
Gay, John. Beggar's Opera. Griffith, Benjamin W., Jr., ed. LC 61-18353. 1962. pap. text ed. 3.25 (ISBN 0-8120-0032-3). Barron.
--Beggar's Opera. Roberts, Edgar V., ed. LC 68-21878. (Regents Restoration Drama Ser). 1969. 11.50x (ISBN 0-8032-0362-4); pap. 3.65x (ISBN 0-8032-5361-3, BB 269, Bison). U of Nebr Pr.
--The Brightening Shadow. LC 80-81852. (Illus., Orig.). (gr. 10-12). 1980. pap. text ed. write for info. (ISBN 0-933662-09-2). Intercult Pr.
--Fables. facsimile ed. 1969. 20.00x (ISBN 0-85417-056-1, Pub. by Scolar Pr England). Biblio Dist.
Gay, John E., jt. auth. see Wantz, Molly S.
Gay, Kathleen. Eating What Grows Naturally. LC 80-68745. (Illus.). 120p. 1980. pap. 5.95 (ISBN 0-89708-031-9). And Bks.
Gay, Kathlyn. Money Isn't Everything. LC 67-10677. (Illus.). (gr. 4-6). 1967. PLB 4.58 o.s.i. (ISBN 0-440-05784-1). Delacorte.
Gay, Kathlyn & Barnes, Ben. Your Fight Has Just Begun: The Sport of Boxing. LC 79-28242. (Illus.). 192p. (gr. 7-12). 1980. PLB 8.29 (ISBN 0-671-33005-5). Messner.
Gay, L. R. Educational Research. 2nd ed. (Illus.). 464p. 1981. write for info student guide (ISBN 0-675-08021-5); price not set student guide (ISBN 0-675-08020-7); instr's. manual 3.95 (ISBN 0-686-69490-2). Merrill.
--Educational Research: Competencies for Analysis & Application. (Illus.). 368p. 1976. text ed. 17.95 (ISBN 0-675-08636-1); student suppl. 7.50 (ISBN 0-675-08600-0); instructor's manual 3.95 (ISBN 0-686-67249-6). Merrill.
Gay, Larry. Central Heating with Wood & Coal. (Illus.). 128p. 1980. write for info. (ISBN 0-8289-0419-7); pap. write for info. (ISBN 0-8289-0420-0). Greene.
Gay, P., ed. see Voltaire, F. M.
Gay, Peter. Age of Enlightenment. LC 66-18266. (Great Ages of Man). (Illus.). (gr. 6 up). 1966. PLB 11.97 (ISBN 0-8094-0368-4, Pub. by Time-Life). Silver.
--Freud, Jews & Other Germans: Masters & Victims in Modernist Culture. 1978. 15.95x (ISBN 0-19-502258-0). Oxford U Pr.
--A Loss of Mastery: Puritan Historians in Colonial America. (Jefferson Memorial Lectures). 1966. 14.00x (ISBN 0-520-00456-6). U of Cal Pr.
Gay, Peter, ed. John Locke on Education. LC 64-14307. 1964. text ed. 8.75 (ISBN 0-8077-1419-4); pap. text ed. 4.00x (ISBN 0-8077-1416-X). Tchrs Coll.
Gay, Peter & Cavanaugh, Gerald J., eds. Historians at Work, Vol. 1. LC 75-123930. 1972. 20.00 o.s.i. (ISBN 0-06-011473-8, HarpT). Har-Row.
--Historians at Work, Vol. 4. LC 75-123930. 1975. 20.00 o.s.i. (ISBN 0-06-011476-2, HarpT). Har-Row.
Gay, Peter & Wexler, Victor G., eds. Historians at Work, Vol. 2. LC 75-123930. 1972. 20.00 o.s.i. (ISBN 0-06-011472-X, HarpT). Har-Row.
--Historians at Work, Vol. 3. LC 75-123930. 1975. 20.00 o.s.i. (ISBN 0-06-011474-6, HarpT). Har-Row.
Gay, Robert M. Emerson: A Study of the Poet As Seer. LC 80-2533. 1981. Repr. of 1928 ed. 32.75 (ISBN 0-404-19259-9). AMS Pr.
Gay Sunshine Press, compiled by. Meat: How Men Look, Act, Talk, Walk, Dress, Undress, Taste & Smell: True Homosexual Experiences from S.T.H. (Illus.). 192p. (Orig.). 1981. pap. 10.00 (ISBN 0-917342-78-X, Pub by Gay Sunshine). Bookpeople.
Gay, Sydney H. James Madison. LC 80-25344. (American Statesmen Ser.). 350p. 1981. pap. 5.95 (ISBN 0-87754-196-5). Chelsea Hse.
Gay, Volney P. Freud on Ritual: Reconstruction & Critique. LC 79-11385. (American Academy of Religion, Dissertation Ser.: No. 26). 1979. 12.00 (ISBN 0-89130-282-4, 010126); pap. 7.50 (ISBN 0-89130-301-4). Scholars Pr Ca.
Gaya, S. D. Gili see Gili Gaya, S. D.
Gayarre, Charles. Historical Sketch of Pierre & Jean Lafitte, the Famous Smugglers of Louisiana. pap. 4.50 wrappers (ISBN 0-685-13272-2). Jenkins.
Gay-Crosier, Raymond. Albert Camus Nineteen Eighty. LC 80-22240. 330p. (Orig., Fr.). 1981. pap. 16.00 (ISBN 0-8130-0691-0). U Presses Fla.
Gaydar, Arkadiy. Tchuck & Gyek. Scott, Grahame, ed. (Oxford Rapid-Reading Russian Texts Ser). 1969. pap. 1.75x o.p. (ISBN 0-19-832805-2). Oxford U Pr.
Gaydasch, Alex. Principles of Electronic Data Processing Management. 300p. 1982. text ed. 18.95 (ISBN 0-8359-5604-0); instr's. manual free (ISBN 0-8359-5605-9). Reston.
Gaydon, A. G., jt. auth. see Pearse, R. W.
Gaydos, Alice G. Please Quote Me: Selected Poems. 64p. 1980. 5.00 (ISBN 0-682-49626-X). Exposition.
Gaydos, Michael. Eyes to Behold. 1980. pap. 2.50 o.p. (ISBN 0-89221-069-9). New Leaf.
Gayford, M. L. Modern Relay Techniques. (Illus.). 149p. 1975. 15.00x (ISBN 0-408-06843-4). Transatlantic.
Gayle, Addison. Richard Wright: Ordeal of a Native Son. LC 77-12854. (Illus.). 1980. 14.95 (ISBN 0-385-08877-9, Anchor Pr). Doubleday.
Gayle, Addison, Jr The Way of the New World: The Black Novel in America. LC 74-9449. 336p. 1975. 10.00 o.p. (ISBN 0-385-04103-9, Anchor Pr). Doubleday.
--The Way of the New World: The Black Novel in America. LC 74-9449. 440p. 1976. pap. 3.95 (ISBN 0-385-04135-7, Anch). Doubleday.
Gayle, Addison, Jr., ed. Black Aesthetic. LC 71-123692. 1972. pap. 3.50 o.p. (ISBN 0-385-06951-0, Anch). Doubleday.
--Bondage Freedom & Beyond: The Prose of Black Americans. (Illus.). 1971. 4.95 (ISBN 0-385-08951-1, Zenith); pap. 2.50 (ISBN 0-385-08960-0). Doubleday.
Gayley, Charles M. Classic Myths in English Literature & in Art. rev. & enlarged ed. 1939. 18.50 (ISBN 0-471-00191-0). Wiley.
--Plays of Our Forefathers & Some of the Traditions Upon Which They Were Founded. LC 68-25810. (Illus.). 1968. Repr. of 1907 ed. 15.00x (ISBN 0-8196-0209-4). Biblo.
Gaylin, Evelyn. Doll Repair. 1976. 11.95 o.p. (ISBN 0-87588-121-1); pap. 7.95 o.p. (ISBN 0-87588-122-X). Hobby Hse.
Gaylord, Elizabeth B. & Abercrombie, V. T. Places to Take a Crowd: Three to Three Thousand. LC 79-66213. (Orig.). 1979. pap. 5.95 (ISBN 0-933988-01-X). Brown Rabbit.
Gaylord, Louise, jt. auth. see Abercrombie, V. T.
Gaylord, M. W. Reinforced Plastics: Theory & Practice. 2nd ed. LC 74-9842. 213p. 1974. 17.95 o.p. (ISBN 0-8436-1210-X). CBI Pub.
Gayn, Mark. Japan Diary. LC 80-51196. 530p. 1981. pap. 9.50 (ISBN 0-8048-1369-8). C E Tuttle.
Gayner, Jeffrey. Namibia: The Road to Independence. 1979. pap. 10.00 (ISBN 0-686-60259-5). Coun Am Affairs.
Gaynes, David. Artisans-Appalachia-USA. 1977. pap. 4.95 (ISBN 0-686-27863-1). Appalach Consortium.
Gaynes, N. I. Testing of Organic Coatings. LC 76-24148. (Illus.). 1977. 24.00 o.p. (ISBN 0-8155-0650-3). Noyes.
Gaynor, Frank, jt. auth. see Pei, Mario.
Gaynor, Frank & Fodor, Nandor, eds. Freud: Dictionary of Psychoanalysis. 1976. pap. 1.25 o.p. (ISBN 0-449-30725-5, P725, Prem). Fawcett.
Gazda, George M. Group Counseling: A Developmental Approach. 2nd ed. 1978. pap. text ed. 18.95 (ISBN 0-205-05958-9). Allyn.
Gazda, George M., ed. Basic Approaches to Group Psychotherapy & Group Counseling. 2nd ed. (Illus.). 560p. 1979. 21.50 (ISBN 0-398-03212-2). C C Thomas.
Gazda, George M., et al. Human Relations Development: A Manual for Educators. 2nd ed. 1977. text ed. 14.95x (ISBN 0-205-05566-4); pap. text ed. 9.95x (ISBN 0-685-71782-8). Allyn.
Gazenko, O. G., ed. Man in Space: Chelovek V Kosmose. Bjurstedt, H. A., tr. (Illus., Eng., Fr., Rus.). 1974. 20.00 o.p. (ISBN 0-87703-122-3). Univelt Inc.
Gazey, B. K., jt. auth. see Tucker, D. G.
Gazis, Denos C. Traffic Science. LC 73-21947. 304p. 1974. 37.95 (ISBN 0-471-29480-2, Pub. by Wiley-Interscience). Wiley.
Gazzaniga, Michael. Fundamentals of Psychology: An Introduction. 1973. text ed. 18.95 (ISBN 0-12-278650-5). Acad Pr.
Gazzaniga, Michael S. The Bisected Brain. LC 77-105426. 172p. 1970. 18.50 (ISBN 0-306-50040-X, Plenum Pr). Plenum Pub.
GBC Editorial Staff, ed. More Blue Ribbon Systems. (Gambler's Book Shelf). (Orig.). 1979. pap. 2.95 (ISBN 0-89650-801-3). Gamblers.
--One Hundred Fifty Blue Ribbon Systems. (Gambler's Book Shelf). (Orig.). 1979. pap. 2.95 (ISBN 0-89650-813-7). Gamblers.
Gdowski, Charles, jt. auth. see Lachar, David.
Geach, P. T. Logic Matters. 1972. 17.50x (ISBN 0-520-01851-6, CAMPUS 222); pap. 5.95 (ISBN 0-686-66341-1). U of Cal Pr.
--Providence of Evil. LC 76-28005. 1977. 18.95 (ISBN 0-521-21477-7). Cambridge U Pr.
--Reason & Argument. LC 76-19961. 1977. pap. 4.95x (ISBN 0-520-03289-6). U of Cal Pr.
--Truth, Love, & Immortality: An Introduction to McTaggart's Philosophy. 1979. 15.95x (ISBN 0-520-03755-3). U of Cal Pr.
--The Virtues. LC 76-19627. 1977. 20.50 (ISBN 0-521-21350-9). Cambridge U Pr.
Geach, Peter, ed. see Frege, Gottlob.
Geach, Peter T. Reference & Generality: An Examination of Some Medieval & Modern Theories. 3rd ed. LC 80-10977. (Contempory Philosophy Ser.). 256p. 1980. 19.50x (ISBN 0-8014-1315-X). Cornell U Pr.
Geach, Peter T., ed. see Descartes, Rene.
Geach, Peter T., tr. see Descartes, Rene.
Geahigan, George, ed. Career Education in the Visual Arts: Representative Programs & Projects. 127p. 1980. 6.75 (ISBN 0-686-27492-X). Natl Art Ed.
Gealy, Fred D., et al. Companion to the Hymnal. 1970. 14.95 (ISBN 0-687-09259-0). Abingdon.
Geanakoplos, Deno J. Western Medieval Civilization. 1978. text ed. 16.95x (ISBN 0-669-00868-0). Heath.
Geanangel, Russell A. & Wendlandt, Wesley W. Experimental Chemistry. 5th ed. 1979. pap. text ed. 8.95 (ISBN 0-8403-2355-7). Kendall-Hunt.
Geaney, Dennis. Emerging Lay Ministries. 1979. 9.95 o.p. (ISBN 0-8362-3305-0). Andrews & McMeel.
--Living with Sorrow. 1977. pap. 4.95 (ISBN 0-88347-074-8). Thomas More.
Geaney, Dennis J. A Guide for Parents Who Aren't Sure What to Believe Anymore. (Illus.). 40p. pap. 1.50 (ISBN 0-89570-096-4). Claretian Pubns.
Geankoplis. Transport Processes & Unit Operations. 1978. text ed. 29.95 (ISBN 0-205-05939-2, 3259390). Allyn.
Gear, Felix B. Our Presbyterian Belief. LC 79-23421. 90p. (Orig.). 1980. pap. 4.95 (ISBN 0-8042-0676-7). John Knox.
Gear, G. W. Introduction to Computer Science. LC 72-86105. 1975. text ed. 15.95 (ISBN 0-574-18045-1, 13-4035); instr's guide avail. (ISBN 0-574-18471-6, 13-1471); transparency masters 46.00 (ISBN 0-574-18472-4, 13-1472). SRA.
Gear, Josephine. Masters or Servants? A Study of Selected English Painters & Their Patrons of the Late 18th & Early 19th Centuries. LC 76-23619. (Outstanding Dissertations in the Fine Arts - 18th Century). (Illus.). 1977. Repr. lib. bdg. 56.00 (ISBN 0-8240-2690-X). Garland Pub.
Gear, Michael, jt. auth. see Gough, Malcolm.
Gearey, John. Goethes's Faust: The Making of Part I. LC 80-5826. 256p. 1981. 19.00x (ISBN 0-300-02571-8). Yale U Pr.
Gearhart, Sally & Rennie, Susan. A Feminist Tarot: A Guide to Intrapersonal Communication. 4th ed. (Illus.). 1981. pap. write for info. (ISBN 0-930436-01-6). Persephone.
Gearheart, Bill. Learning Disabilities: Educational Strategies. 3rd ed. (Illus.). 345p. 1981. text ed. 17.95 (ISBN 0-8016-1768-5). Mosby.
Gearheart, Bill R. Special Education for the Eighties. LC 79-20647. (Illus.). 1980. text ed. 17.95 (ISBN 0-8016-1759-6). Mosby.
Gearheart, Bill R. & Litton, Freddie W. The Trainable Retarded: A Foundations Approach. 2nd ed. LC 78-13959. (Illus.). 1979. 16.95 (ISBN 0-8016-1761-8). Mosby.
Gearheart, Bill R. & Weishahn, Mel. The Handicapped Child in the Regular Classroom. LC 75-31543. (Illus.). 272p. 1976. 15.50 o.p. (ISBN 0-8016-1764-2). Mosby.
Gearheart, Bill R. & Weishahn, Mel W. The Handicapped Student in the Regular Classroom. 2nd ed. LC 79-23706. 1980. text ed. 17.95 (ISBN 0-8016-1760-X). Mosby.

Gearheart, George, ed. see Hawley, Newton & Suppes, Patrick.

Gearing, Catherine. Field Guide to Wilderness Living. LC 72-97849. 224p. 1973. pap. 3.95 (ISBN 0-8127-0057-0). Southern Pub.

Gearing, P. & Brunson, E. Breaking into Print: How to Get Your Work Published. 1977. 11.95 (ISBN 0-13-081687-6, Spec); pap. 3.45 (ISBN 0-13-081679-5, Spec). P-H.

Geary, D. P., jt. auth. see Mayhall, P. D.

Geary, Don. The How-to Book of Floors & Ceilings. (Illus.). 1978. 8.95 o.p. (ISBN 0-8306-8998-2); pap. 5.95 (ISBN 0-8306-7998-7, 998). TAB Bks.

--Roofs & Siding: A Practical Guide. (Illus.). 1978. 10.95 (ISBN 0-87909-752-3). Reston.

--The Welder's Bible. (Illus.). 420p. 1980. 16.95 (ISBN 0-8306-9938-4); pap. 10.95 (ISBN 0-8306-1244-0, 1244). Tab Bks.

Geary, Edward J., ed. Solitudes: Premieres Lectures Modernes. (Integral French Eds. Ser). (Fr). 1965. pap. text ed. 2.75x o.p. (ISBN 0-685-20247-X). Schoenhof.

Geary, Michael. Pictorial Encyclopedia of Dogs. (Illus.). 192p. 1979. 14.95 (ISBN 0-528-81092-8). Rand.

Geary, Rosemary J., jt. auth. see Blustein, Lotte.

Geaugue, Pierre. Cappy Dee Stories. 1979. cancelled o.p. (ISBN 0-685-96676-3). Wake-Brook.

Gebbard, David. Schindler. (Illus.). 240p. 1980. pap. 9.95 (ISBN 0-87905-077-2). Peregrine Smith.

Gebbie, Kristine M., jt. auth. see Deloughery, Grace L.

Gebbie, Kristine M. & Lavin, Mary A., eds. Classification of Nursing Diagnoses. LC 74-14869. 1975. pap. text ed. 9.50 (ISBN 0-8016-1769-3). Mosby.

Geber, B. Piaget & Knowing. 1977. 20.00 (ISBN 0-7100-8500-1). Routledge & Kegan.

Gebert, Rosemary, tr. see Jaffke, Freya.

Gebhardt, Chuck. Inside Death Valley. rev. 3rd ed. LC 80-83123. (Illus.). 166p. 1980. pap. 5.95 (ISBN 0-9601410-1-4). C Gebhardt.

Gebhardt, Eike, ed. Science As Behavior: Sociological Approaches to the Sciences. 320p. 1981. 24.50 (ISBN 0-8264-0015-9); pap. 12.95 (ISBN 0-8264-0024-8). Continuum.

Gebhardt, Louis P. & Nicholes, Paul S. Microbiology. 5th ed. LC 74-10691. 1975. text ed. 15.95 (ISBN 0-8016-1784-7); lab manual 8.50 (ISBN 0-8016-1773-1). Mosby.

Gebregziabher, Betru. Integrated Development in Rural Ethiopia. 1975. pap. text ed. 3.00 (ISBN 0-89249-029-2). Intl Development.

Geckle, George L. John Marston's Plays: Themes, Images, Sources. LC 77-89777. 1979. 18.50 (ISBN 0-8386-2157-0). Fairleigh Dickinson.

Geckle, George L., ed. Twentieth Century Interpretations of Measure for Measure. 7.95 o.p. (ISBN 0-13-567727-0, Spec); pap. 1.25 o.p. (ISBN 0-13-567719-X, Spec). P-H.

Gecoma, Richard M., et al. Energy Efficient Purchasing: A Guide for Local Governments. 75p. 1980. pap. 7.50 (ISBN 0-89854-064-X). U of GA Inst Govt.

Geczi, Mike. Futures: The Anti-Inflation Investment. 1980. pap. 2.95 (ISBN 0-686-69239-X, 75713, Discus). Avon.

Geda, Carolyn L., et al. Archivists & Machine-Readable Records. Austin, Erik W. & Blouin, Francis X., eds. 1980. pap. text ed. 10.00 (ISBN 0-931828-19-8). Soc Am Archivists.

Gedai, I., ed. see Internaional Numismatic Symposium, Warsaw & Budapest, 1976.

Gedda, Luigi & Brenci, Gianni. Chronogenetics: The Inheritance of Biological Time. (Illus.). 232p. 1978. 27.75 (ISBN 0-398-03641-1). C C Thomas.

Gedde, Palmer. One Plus One Equals. Kujath, Mentor, ed. 1979. pap. 4.95 (ISBN 0-8100-0103-9, 12-1712). Northwest Pub.

Geddes, Ann E. Trends in Relief Expenditures, 1910-1935. LC 74-166327. (FDR & the Era of the New Deal Ser). 1971. Repr. of 1937 ed. lib. bdg. 15.00 (ISBN 0-306-70342-4). Da Capo.

Geddes, Candida, ed. The Concise Book of the Horse. LC 76-1874. (Illus.). 1976. 9.95 o.p. (ISBN 0-668-03965-5). Arco.

Geddes, Dolores. Physical Activities for Individuals with Handicapping Conditions. 2nd ed. LC 77-26228. (Illus.). 1978. pap. text ed. 10.50 (ISBN 0-8016-1793-6). Mosby.

Geddes, James D. Large Ground Movements & Structures. LC 78-19092. 1978. 64.95 (ISBN 0-470-26460-8). Halsted Pr.

Geddes, L. A. & Baker, L. E. Principles of Applied Biomedical Instrumentation. 2nd ed. LC 74-34390. (Biomedical Engineering & Health Systems Ser.). 616p. 1975. 31.95 (ISBN 0-471-29496-9, Pub. by Wiley-Interscience). Wiley.

Geddes, L. A., jt. auth. see Tacker, W. A.

Geddes, M. & Sturtridge, G. Listening Links. 1979. pap. text ed. 3.95x (ISBN 0-435-28051-1); tchrs. ed. 7.95x (ISBN 0-435-28052-X); of three tapes 60.00 set (ISBN 0-435-28053-8); of three cassettes 54.00 set (ISBN 0-435-28054-6). Heinemann Ed.

Geddes, Robert N. & Mead, Daniel R. Encyclopedia of Slot Machines. (Illus.). 300p. 1980. write for info. (ISBN 0-934422-17-6). Mead Co.

Geddes, William R. Migrants of the Mountains: The Cultural Ecology of the Blue Miao (Hmong Nyua) or Thailand. (Illus.). 1976. 37.50x (ISBN 0-19-823187-3). Oxford U Pr.

Geddie, William. Bibliography of Middle Scots Poets. (Scottish Text Society Publications Ser: No. 61). 1969. Repr. of 1912 ed. 35.50 (ISBN 0-384-17975-4). Johnson Repr.

Gedo, John E. Advances in Clinical Psychoanalysis. (Illus.). 250p. 1981. text ed. 29.95 (ISBN 0-8236-0125-0, 00-0125). Intl Univs Pr.

Gedo, Mary M. Picasso: Art As Autobiography. LC 80-11126. (Illus.). 288p. 1980. lib. bdg. 20.00 (ISBN 0-226-28482-4). U of Chicago Pr.

Gedraitis, A. Worship & Politics. 1973. pap. 2.75 o.p. (ISBN 0-686-11980-0). Wedge Pub.

Geduld, Carolyn. Bernard Wolfe. LC 78-187612. (U. S. Authors Ser.: No. 211). lib. bdg. 10.95 (ISBN 0-8057-0832-4). Twayne.

--Filmguide to Two Thousand One: A Space Odyssey. LC 72-88635. (Filmguide Ser.: No. 3). 96p. 1973. 5.00x (ISBN 0-253-39305-1); pap. 1.75x (ISBN 0-253-39306-X). Ind U Pr.

Geduld, Harry M. Filmguide to Henry V. LC 73-75788. (Filmguide Ser: No. 7). 96p. 1973. 5.00x (ISBN 0-253-39313-2); pap. 1.75x (ISBN 0-253-29314-6). Ind U Pr.

Geduld, Harry M., ed. Film Makers on Film Making. LC 67-25134. (Midland Bks.: No. 104). 1967. Repr. 10.00x o.p. (ISBN 0-253-12600-2). Ind U Pr.

Gedzelman, Stanley D. The Science & Wonders of the Atmosphere. LC 79-23835. 1980. text ed. 22.95 (ISBN 0-471-02972-6); avail. tchrs' manual (ISBN 0-471-08013-6). Wiley.

Gee, D. J., jt. auth. see Polson, C. J.

Gee, Don A., tr. Pentecostes. (Spanish Bks.). 1979. 1.25 (ISBN 0-8297-0552-X). Life Pubs Intl.

Gee, Donald. The Fruit of the Spirit. 80p. 1975. pap. 1.25 (ISBN 0-88243-501-9, 02-0501, Radiant Bks). Gospel Pub.

Gee, Edwin A. & Tyler, Chaplin. Managing Innovation. LC 76-7056. (Systems & Controls for Financial Management Ser). 1976. 31.50 (ISBN 0-471-29503-5). Ronald Pr.

Gee, J. M., tr. see Napoleoni, Claudio.

Gee, John & Selby, Elliot. Triumph of Tchaikovsky. LC 60-15068. (Illus.). 1960. 8.95 (ISBN 0-8149-0103-4). Vanguard.

Gee, Maurice. The World Around the Corner. (Illus.). 80p. (gr. 4-6). 1981. 9.95 (ISBN 0-19-558061-3). Oxford U Pr.

Gee, Ralph C., jt. auth. see Townley, Helen M.

Gee, Sherman. Technology Transfer, Innovation, & International Competitiveness. 240p. 1980. 21.00 (ISBN 0-471-08468-9, Pub. by Wiley-Interscience). Wiley.

Geeenberg, Reesa. The Drawings of Alfred Pellan. (National Gallery of Canada Ser.). (Illus.). 192p. 1981. pap. 15.95 (ISBN 0-88884-458-1, 56319-7, Pub. by Natl Mus Canada). U of Chicago Pr.

Geelhaar, Christian. Klee, Paul. (Pocket Art Ser.). (Illus.). 112p. (gr. 9-12). 1981. pap. 3.50 (ISBN 0-8120-2186-X). Barron.

Geels, B. H., jt. auth. see Appels, J. T.

Geen, Fox. Fitting Out a Moulded Hull. (Illus.). 176p. 1976. pap. 10.95 (ISBN 0-685-69131-4). Transatlantic.

--Improved Keelboat Performance. (Illus.). 224p. 1976. 7.95 (ISBN 0-370-10318-1); pap. 7.95 (ISBN 0-370-10342-4). Transatlantic.

Geen, Russell G. Personality: The Skein of Behavior. LC 75-4786. (Illus.). 292p. 1976. text ed. 15.50 (ISBN 0-8016-1794-4). Mosby.

Geer, Blanche, ed. Learning to Work. LC 73-87855. (Sage Contemporary Social Science Issues: Vol. 4). 1974. 4.95x (ISBN 0-8039-0320-0). Sage.

Geer, Russel M., tr. see Lucretius.

Geer, Russell, tr. see Epicurus.

Geeraerts, Gustaff, ed. see Polemological Centre of the Free University of Brussels.

Geering, R. G. Christina Stead. (World Authors Ser.: Australia: No. 95). lib. bdg. 12.50 (ISBN 0-8057-2858-9). Twayne.

Geertz, C. Negara: Theatre-State in 19th Century Bali. LC 80-7520. 256p. 1980. 18.50 (ISBN 0-691-05316-2); pap. 5.95 (ISBN 0-691-00778-0). Princeton U Pr.

Geertz, C., et al. Meaning & Order in Moroccan Society. LC 78-54327. (Illus.). 1979. 49.50 (ISBN 0-521-22175-7). Cambridge U Pr.

Geertz, Clifford. Agricultural Involution: The Processes of Ecological Change in Indonesia. 1963. 16.50x (ISBN 0-520-00458-2); pap. 4.25x (ISBN 0-520-00459-0, CAMPUS11). U of Cal Pr.

--Islam Observed: Religious Development in Morocco & Indonesia. 1971. pap. 3.95 (ISBN 0-226-28511-1, P439, Phoen). U of Chicago Pr.

--Islam Observed: Religious Development in Morocco & Indonesia. LC 68-27753. (Terry Lectures Ser). (Illus.). 1968. 10.00x o.p. (ISBN 0-300-00483-4). Yale U Pr.

Geeslin, Campbell. What Ever Became of the Bonner Boys. 1981. 10.95 (ISBN 0-671-42430-0). S&S.

Geest, A. J. Van Der see Van Der Geest, A. J.

Geeting, Baxter & Geeting, Corinne. How to Listen Assertively. (Illus.). 1978. 7.95 o.p. (ISBN 0-671-18365-6, Sovereign). Monarch Pr.

--How to Listen Assertively. (Illus.). 1976. 8.95 (ISBN 0-671-18336-2); pap. 3.95 (ISBN 0-671-18336-2). Sovereign Bks.

--How to Listen Assertively. (Illus.). 1978. pap. 3.95 (ISBN 0-671-18336-2). Monarch Pr.

Geeting, Corinne, jt. auth. see Geeting, Baxter.

Geevarghese, P. K. A Changing Small-Town in South India. LC 78-71371. (Illus.). 1979. pap. text ed. 11.50 (ISBN 0-8191-0666-6). U Pr of Amer.

Geffner, Saul & Lauren, Paul. Experimental Chemistry. 2nd ed. (gr. 10-12). 1968. pap. text ed. 6.17 (ISBN 0-87720-113-7); wkbk ed. 7.00 (ISBN 0-87720-115-3). AMSCO Sch.

Geffner, Saul L. Fundamental Concepts of Modern Chemistry. (Illus.). (gr. 10-12). 1968. text ed. 11.58 (ISBN 0-87720-102-1); pap. text ed. 6.58 (ISBN 0-87720-101-3). AMSCO Sch.

Geffner, Saul L. & Kass, Gerard A. Contemporary Chemistry. (Orig.). (gr. 10-12). 1981. pap. text ed. price not set (ISBN 0-87720-100-5). AMSCO Sch.

Geffner, Saul L., jt. auth. see Mould, J. Albert.

Geffre, Claude. The Churches of Africa. (Concilium Ser.: Vol. 106). pap. 4.95 (ISBN 0-8164-2150-1). Crossroad NY.

--Humanism & Christianity. (Concilium Ser.: Religion in the Seventies: Vol. 86). 156p. 1973. pap. 4.95 (ISBN 0-8164-2542-6). Crossroad NY.

--Mystical & Political Dimension of the Christian Faith. (Concilium Ser.: Religion in the Seventies: Vol. 96). pap. 4.95 (ISBN 0-8164-2580-9). Crossroad NY.

Geffre, Claude & Jossua, Jean-Pierre, eds. True & False Universality of Christianity, Concilium 135. (New Concilium 1980). 128p. 1980. pap. 5.95 (ISBN 0-8245-4768-3). Crossroad NY.

Geffre, Claude, jt. ed. see Duquoc, Christian.

Gefter, Y. Organophosphorus Monomers & Polymers. 1962. 32.00 (ISBN 0-08-009655-7). Pergamon.

Geherin, David. Sons of Sam Spade: The Private Eye Novel in the 70s. LC 79-4823. (Recognitions Ser.). 1980. 10.95 (ISBN 0-8044-2231-1). Ungar.

Gehlmann, John & Eisman, Philip. Say What You Mean: The Paragraph, Bk 2. LC 66-19065. 1968. 5.85 o.p. (ISBN 0-672-73231-9). Odyssey Pr.

--Say What You Mean: The Sentence, Bk 1. LC 66-19065. 1967. 6.50 (ISBN 0-672-73232-7). Odyssey Pr.

Gehlmann, John, ed. Challenge of Ideas: An Essay Reader. rev. ed. LC 61-1143. 1961. 5.50 (ISBN 0-672-73247-5). Odyssey Pr.

Gehman, H. S., jt. auth. see Montgomery, J. A.

Gehrig, Eleanor & Durso, Joseph. My Luke & I. (RL 10). 1977. pap. 1.75 o.p. (ISBN 0-451-07818-7, E7818, Sig). NAL.

Gehring, Robert E. Basic Behavioral Statistics. LC 77-78447. (Illus.). 1978. text ed. 19.95 (ISBN 0-395-24684-9); study guide 6.95 (ISBN 0-395-24683-0); inst. manual 0.65 (ISBN 0-395-25511-2). HM.

Gehrke, Ralph D. Samuel One & Two. (Concordia Commentary Ser). 1968. 10.95 (ISBN 0-570-06280-2, 15-2029). Concordia.

Gehu, J. M., ed. Colloques Phytosociologiques VII: Lille 1978, le Vegetation Des Sois Tourbeux. 556p. (Fr.). 1981. lib. bdg. 75.00x (ISBN 3-7682-1260-2, Pub. by Cramer Germany). Lubrecht & Cramer.

Gehweiler, John A., et al. The Radiology of Vertebral Trauma. LC 78-65376. (Monograph in Clinical Radiology: No. 16). (Illus.). 496p. 1980. text ed. 39.00 (ISBN 0-7216-4065-6). Saunders.

Geiberger, Al & Dennis, Larry. Tempo (Golf's Master Key: How to Find It, How to Keep It) LC 79-52550. (Illus.). 160p. 1980. 9.95 (ISBN 0-914178-34-2). Golf Digest Bks.

Geier, Alvin E. & Lamm, Nathaniel. Mathematics & Your Career. (gr. 10-12). 1978. pap. text ed. 6.58 (ISBN 0-87720-241-9). AMSCO Sch.

Geier, Annette. Hyperactivity: Research & Treatment Alternatives. 1978. pap. 9.50 o.p. (ISBN 0-686-00910-X, D-112). Essence Pubns.

--Tenure: Research Evidence & Practical & Philosophical Considerations. 47p. 1977. pap. 10.00 o.p. (ISBN 0-686-00914-2, D-106). Essence Pubns.

Geiger, Adolph, jt. auth. see Jackson, Eugene.

Geiger, Dana F. Phaselock Loops for DC Motor Control. 140p. 1981. 22.00 (Pub. by Wiley-Interscience). Wiley.

Geiger, F. M., jt. auth. see Geiger, Theodore.

Geiger, G. H. & Poirier, D. R. Transport Phenomena in Metallurgy. LC 75-164648. 1973. text ed. 27.95 (ISBN 0-201-02352-0). A-W.

Geiger, H. Kent. National Development 1776-1966: A Selective & Annotated Guide to the Most Important Articles in English. LC 77-5813. 1969. 10.00 (ISBN 0-8108-0248-1). Scarecrow.

Geiger, Theodore & Geiger, F. M. Welfare & Efficiency: Their Interactions in Western Europe & Implications for International Economic Relations. (Illus.). 1979. text ed. 31.25x (ISBN 0-333-26864-4). Humanities.

Geiger, Wilhelm. Culture of Ceylon in Mediaeval Times. LC 60-39625. (Illus.). 309p. 1960. 42.50x (ISBN 3-447-00278-6). Intl Pubns Serv.

Geijsbeek, John B. Ancient Double-Entry Bookkeeping. 1975. Repr. text ed. 15.00 (ISBN 0-914348-16-7). Scholars Bk.

Geilikman, B. T. & Kresin, V. Z. Kinetic & Nonsteady-State Effects in Superconductors. Shelnitz, P., tr. from Rus. LC 73-22089. 170p. 1974. 29.95 o.p. (ISBN 0-470-29513-9). Halsted Pr.

Geiogamah, Hanay, ed. New Native American Drama. LC 79-4733. (Illus.). 1980. 9.95 (ISBN 0-8061-1586-6); pap. 4.95 (ISBN 0-8061-1697-8). U of Okla Pr.

Geipel, John. Great Adventures of the Vikings. LC 77-72486. (Illus.). 48p. (gr. 5-9). 1977. 3.95 (ISBN 0-528-82204-7); PLB 3.97 o.p. (ISBN 0-528-80052-3). Rand.

Geiringer, Karl. The Bach Family: Seven Generations of Creative Genius. (Music Reprint 1980 Ser.). (Illus.). 1980. Repr. of 1954 ed. lib. bdg. 35.00 (ISBN 0-306-79596-5). Da Capo.

--Brahms: His Life & Work. 2nd ed. (Illus.). 400p. 1948. 19.95 (ISBN 0-04-780006-2). Allen Unwin.

Geiringer, Karl, ed. & pref. by. Haydn: Symphony No. One Hundred & Three in E-Flat Major (Drum Roll) LC 73-20231. (Illus.). 116p. 1974. pap. 4.95x (ISBN 0-393-09349-2). Norton.

Geis, F. L. Personality Research Manual. 227p. 1978. 10.95 (ISBN 0-471-29519-1). Wiley.

Geis, Gilbert & Meier, Robert S. White-Collar Crime: Offenses in Business, Politics, & Professions. rev. ed. LC 76-27223. 1977. pap. text ed. 8.95 (ISBN 0-02-911600-7). Free Pr.

Geis, Gilbert & Stotland, Ezra, eds. White-Collar Crime: Theory & Research. LC 79-26672. (Sage Criminal Justice System Annuals: Vol. 13). (Illus.). 320p. 1980. 20.00x (ISBN 0-8039-1404-0); pap. 9.95x (ISBN 0-8039-1405-9). Sage.

Geis, Irving, jt. auth. see Dickerson, Richard E.

Geise, Judie. The Northwest Kitchen: A Seasonal Cookbook. LC 78-64741. 1978. 12.95 (ISBN 0-685-91736-3, Pub. by B Wright & Co). Madrona Pubs.

Geiser, Elizabeth & Brewer, Annie. Book Publishers Directory. 3rd ed. 500p. 1981. 160.00 (ISBN 0-8103-0191-1). Gale.

Geiser, Elizabeth, jt. ed. see Brewer, Annie.

Geiser, Elizabeth A. & Brewer, Annie M., eds. Book Publishers Directory. 2nd ed. LC 77-74820. 1979. 124.00 (ISBN 0-8103-0189-X). Gale.

Geiskopf, Susan. Putting It Up with Honey. LC 78-59871. 1979. pap. 6.95 (ISBN 0-930356-13-6). Quicksilver Prod.

Geisler, Ellen, et al. How to Make a Book. LC 77-83346. 1978. pap. 10.00 o.s.i. (ISBN 0-930638-03-4). Cal-Syl Pr.

Geisler, Norman. Biblical Errancy. 1981. pap. cancelled (ISBN 0-310-39291-8, 18158P). Zondervan.

--La Etica Christiana del Amor. Canclini, Arnoldo, tr. from Eng. LC 77-15813. 126p. (Orig., Span.). 1977. pap. 2.50 (ISBN 0-89922-103-3). Edit Caribe.

Geisler, Norman L. Options in Contemporary Christian Ethics. 128p. (Orig.). 1981. pap. 4.95 (ISBN 0-8010-3757-3). Baker Bk.

--A Popular Survey of the Old Testament. LC 77-78578. 1977. pap. 7.95 (ISBN 0-8010-3684-4). Baker Bk.

Geisler, Norman L. & Nix, William E. From God to Us. 302p. (Orig.). 1974. pap. 5.50 (ISBN 0-8024-2878-9). Moody.

Geisler, Rolf. Aquarium Fish Diseases. (Illus., Orig.). 1963. pap. 2.00 (ISBN 0-87666-008-1, M516). TFH Pubns.

Geisman, Miriam S., jt. auth. see Radics, Stephen P., Jr.

Geismar, Ludwig & Krisberg, Jane. Forgotten Neighborhood: Site of an Early Skirmish in the War on Poverty. LC 67-12067. 1967. 11.00 o.p. (ISBN 0-8108-0048-9). Scarecrow.

Geismar, Ludwig L. Family & Community Functioning: A Manual of Measurement for Social Work Practice & Policy. LC 77-163429. 1971. 8.00 o.p. (ISBN 0-8108-0415-8). Scarecrow.
--Family & Community Functioning: A Manual of Measurement for Social-Work Practice & Policy. 2nd, rev. ed. LC 80-17785. 317p. 1980. 15.00 (ISBN 0-8108-1332-7); pap. 9.75 (ISBN 0-8108-1341-6). Scarecrow.
Geismar, Ludwig L. & Geismar, Shirley. Families in an Urban Mold: Policy Implications of an Australian-U.S. Comparison. (Pergamon Policy Studies). 1979. 27.00 (ISBN 0-08-023379-1). Pergamon.
Geismar, Ludwig L., et al. Early Supports for Family Life: A Social Work Experiment. LC 70-188665. 1972. 10.00 (ISBN 0-8108-0476-X). Scarecrow.
Geismar, Maxwell. Ring Lardner & the Portrait of Folly. LC 77-175105. (Twentieth-Century American Writers Ser). (gr. 6-9). 1972. 7.95 (ISBN 0-690-70234-5, TYC-J). T Y Crowell.
Geismar, Maxwell, ed. The Higher Animals: A Mark Twain Bestiary. LC 76-6563. (Illus.). 1976. 8.95 o.s.i. (ISBN 0-690-01149-0, TYC-T). T Y Crowell.
Geismar, Maxwell, ed. see Lardner, Ring.
Geismar, Shirley, jt. auth. see Geismar, Ludwig L.
Geiss, Imanuel. German Foreign Policy, 1871-1914. (Orig.). 1976. pap. 18.00 (ISBN 0-7100-8303-3). Routledge & Kegan.
--The Pan-African Movement: A History of Pan-Africanism in America, Europe & Africa. LC 74-78310. 546p. 1974. text ed. 37.50x (ISBN 0-8419-0161-9, Africana); pap. text ed. 15.95x (ISBN 0-8419-0215-1). Holmes & Meier.
Geiss, Tony. Four Seasons. (Illus.). (ps-3). 1979. PLB 5.00 (ISBN 0-307-60179-X, Golden Pr). Western Pub.
--The Four Seasons. (Big Picture Bks.). (Illus.). (ps-k). 1979. 1.95 (ISBN 0-307-10820-1, Golden Pr); PLB 7.62 (ISBN 0-307-60820-4). Western Pub.
Geissbuehler, H., et al, eds. see International Congress of Pesticide Chemistry, 4th, Zurich, 1978.
Geissbuehler, H., et al, eds. see International Congress of Pesticides Chemistry, 4th, Zurich, July 1978.
Geissbuhler, Elisabeth C., tr. see Rodin, Auguste.
Geissbuhler, H., jt. ed. see Frehse, H.
Geissler, Eugene S., ed. Bible Prayerbook. LC 80-71052. 528p. (Orig.). 1981. pap. 4.95 (ISBN 0-87793-218-2). Ave Maria.
Geissman, T. A. Principles of Organic Chemistry. 4th ed. LC 76-13891. (Illus.). 1977. 29.95x (ISBN 0-7167-0177-4); tchrs. manual avail. W H Freeman.
--Workbook in Organic Chemistry: Exercises in the Properties, Behavior, & Synthesis of Organic Compounds. (Illus.). 1972. pap. text ed. 9.95x (ISBN 0-7167-0167-7). W H Freeman.
Geisst, Charles R. Raising International Capital: International Markets & the European Institutions. 176p. 1979. 20.95x (ISBN 0-566-00282-5, 03296-4, Pub. by Saxon Hse England). Lexington Bks.
Geist, Harold. The Psychological Aspects of the Aging Process with Sociological Implications. 2nd ed. LC 80-13233. 174p. 1980. Repr. of 1968 ed. text ed. 11.50 (ISBN 0-89874-073-8). Krieger.
Geist, Harold & Martinez, Cecelia. Tennis Psychology. LC 75-17651. (Illus.). 136p. 1976. 10.95 (ISBN 0-88229-120-3). Nelson-Hall.
Geist, Kenneth L. Pictures Will Talk: The Life & Films of Joseph L. Mankiewicz. LC 78-1104. (Encore Edition). (Illus.). 1978. 4.95 (ISBN 0-684-16560-0, ScribT). Scribner.
Geist, Sidney. Brancusi: the Sculpture & Drawings. (Contemporary Artists Ser.). 1975. 65.00 o.p. (ISBN 0-8109-0124-2). Abrams.
Geist, Valerius. Mountain Sheep: A Study in Behavior & Evolution. LC 77-149596. (Wildlife Behavior & Ecology Ser). (Illus.). 1971. 15.50x o.s.i. (ISBN 0-226-28572-3). U of Chicago Pr.
--Mountain Sheep: A Study in Behavior & Evolution. LC 77-149596. (Wildlife Behavior & Ecology Ser.). (Illus.). xvi, 384p. 1976. pap. 9.00 (ISBN 0-226-28573-1, P666, Phoen). U of Chicago Pr.
Geiwitz, James. Psychology: Looking at Ourselves. 2nd ed. (Illus.). 1980. 16.95 (ISBN 0-316-30706-8); instr's manual by P.S.Assocs. free (ISBN 0-316-30707-6); student guide by Syrdal-lasky 5.95 (ISBN 0-316-30710-6); test bank by P.S.Assocs. free (ISBN 0-316-30708-4). Little.
Gekas, Alexandra B. & Countryman, Kathleen M. Development & Implementation of a Patient's Bill of Rights in Hospitals. LC 80-11366. 24p. 1980. pap. 7.50 (ISBN 0-87258-306-6, 1580). Am Hospital.
Gelatt. Nijinsky: The Film. 29.95 (ISBN 0-345-28899-8). Ballantine.
Gelatt, Kirk N., ed. Textbook of Veterinary Opthalmology. LC 80-17291. (Illus.). 788p. 1981. text ed. write for info. (ISBN 0-8121-0686-5). Lea & Febiger.
Gelatt, Roland. Music Makers: Some Outstanding Musical Performers of Our Day. LC 72-2334. (Music Ser.). Repr. of 1953 ed. lib. bdg. 25.00 (ISBN 0-306-70519-2). Da Capo.
Gelb, Arthur & Gelb, Barbara. O'Neill. enl. ed. LC 73-6760. (Illus.). 1088p. 1974. 25.00 o.p. (ISBN 0-06-011487-8, HarpT); pap. 7.95 o.p. (ISBN 0-06-011484-3, TD-202, HarpT). Har-Row.
Gelb, Barbara. On the Track of Murder. 1976. pap. 1.95 o.p. (ISBN 0-345-25228-4). Ballantine.
Gelb, Barbara, jt. auth. see Gelb, Arthur.
Gelb, Barbara L. The Dictionary of Food & What's in It for You. 1979. pap. 3.50 (ISBN 0-345-29479-3). Ballantine.
Gelb, Lawrence. Your Future in Beauty Culture. rev. ed. (Careers in Depth Ser.). (Illus.). 128p. 1980. lib. bdg. 5.97 (ISBN 0-8239-0201-3). Rosen Pr.
Gelb, Leslie H. & Betts, Richard K. The Irony of Vietnam: The System Worked. 1979. 16.95 (ISBN 0-8157-3072-1); pap. 7.95 (ISBN 0-8157-3071-3). Brookings.
Gelber, Lynne L. In-Stability: The Shape & Space of Claudel's Art Criticism. Kuspit, Donald B., ed. (Studies in Fine Arts: Criticism: Vol. 15). 99p. 1980. 19.95 (ISBN 0-8357-1090-4, Pub. by UMI Res Pr). Univ Microfilms.
Gelber, S. M. Job Stands Up: Play with Music & Lyrics. (Orig.). 1975. pap. 6.00 (ISBN 0-8074-0189-7, 382660). UAHC.
Gelber, Steven M. Black Men & Businessman: The Growing Awareness of a Social Responsibility. LC 74-77654. 320p. 1974. 17.50 (ISBN 0-8046-9062-6, Natl U). Kennikat.
Gelboin, Harry V., ed. Polycyclic Hydrocarbons & Cancer, 2 vols. Incl. Vol. 1. Environment, Chemistry & Metabolism. 46.50 (ISBN 0-12-279201-7); Vol. 2. Molecular & Cell Biology. 51.50 (ISBN 0-12-279202-5). 1978. Acad Pr.
Geldard, Frank A. Human Senses. 2nd ed. LC 72-37432. 1972. text ed. 30.95 (ISBN 0-471-29570-1). Wiley.
--Sensory Saltation: Metastability in the Perceptual World. LC 75-22269. 133p. 1975. 10.00 (ISBN 0-470-29571-6). Halsted Pr.
Geldart, Graham. Hand Lapidary Craft. LC 79-56446. (Illus.). 144p. 1980. 19.95 (ISBN 0-7134-1536-3, Pub. by Batsford England). David & Charles.
Geldart, W. M., ed. see Aristophanes.
Gelder, Patricia Van see Van Gelder, Patricia.
Gelder, Richard G. Van see Bancroft, Henrietta & Van Gelder, Richard G.
Gelder, Willem De see De Gelder, Willem.
Gelderman, Carol. Henry Ford: The Wayward Capitalist. (Illus.). 416p. 1981. 14.95 (ISBN 0-8037-3436-0). Dial.
Gelderman, Carol W. George Fitzmaurice. (English Authors Ser.: No. 252). 1979. lib. bdg. 11.95 (ISBN 0-8057-6741-X). Twayne.
Gelender, Maxwell. Review Text in Chemistry. (Illus., Orig.). (gr. 10-12). 1964. pap. text ed. 5.67 (ISBN 0-87720-104-8). AMSCO Sch.
Gelfand. Hearing Science. Date not set. price not set (ISBN 0-8247-1189-0). Dekker.
Gelfand, Donna L. & Hartmann, Donald P. Child Behavior Analysis & Therapy. LC 74-14707. 1975. text ed. 23.00 (ISBN 0-08-018229-1); pap. text ed. 12.50 (ISBN 0-08-018228-3). Pergamon.
Gelfand, Erwin W. & Dosch, Hans-Michael, eds. Biological Basis of Immunodeficiency. 1979. text ed. 35.00 (ISBN 0-89004-361-2). Raven.
Gelfand, I. M., jt. auth. see Vasiliev, J. M.
Gelfand, Israel M., et al. Commutative Normed Rings. LC 61-15024. 1964. 13.95 (ISBN 0-8284-0170-5). Chelsea Pub.
Gelfand, Izrail M. & Fomin, S. V. Calculus of Variations. Silverman, R., tr. (Illus.). 1963. ref. ed. 23.95 (ISBN 0-13-112292-4). P-H.
Gelfand, Morris A. University Libraries for Developing Countries. (Manuals for Libraries, Vol. 14). (Photos). 1971. pap. 7.00 (ISBN 92-3-100654-1, U708, UNESCO). Unipub.
Gelfand, Toby. Professionalizing Modern Medicine: Paris Surgeons & Medical Science & Institutions in the Eighteenth Century. LC 79-8955. (Contributions in Medical History: No. 6). (Illus.). xviii, 271p. 1980. lib. bdg. 29.95 (ISBN 0-313-21488-3, GPM/). Greenwood.
Gelfano. Hearing. 392p. Date not set. 29.75 (ISBN 0-8247-1189-0). Dekker.
Gelfant, Blanche H. American City Novel. 1970. Repr. of 1954 ed. 8.95 o.p. (ISBN 0-8061-0293-4). U of Okla Pr.
Gelfman, Judith S. Women in Television News. LC 75-33167. (Illus.). 213p. 1976. 15.00x (ISBN 0-231-03994-8). Columbia U Pr.
Gelfond, Rhoda. Laughing Past History. (Illus., Orig.). 1976. pap. 3.50 (ISBN 0-914278-09-6). Copper Beech.
Gelinas, Paul. Coping with Sexual Problems. (Coping with Ser.). 140p. 1981. lib. bdg. 7.97 (ISBN 0-8239-0542-X). Rosen Pr.
--Teenagers & Their Hang-Ups. (YA) 1975. PLB 5.97 o.p. (ISBN 0-8239-0328-1). Rosen Pr.
Geline, Robert & Turner, Priscilla. Forward: Rick Barry. LC 75-42339. (Sports Profile Ser.). (Illus.). (gr. 4-11). 1976. PLB 8.50 (ISBN 0-8172-0146-7). Raintree Pubs.
Gell, Alfred. Metamorphosis of the Cassowaries: Umeda Society, Language & Ritual. (London School of Economics Monographs on Social Anthropology Ser). (Illus.). 385p. 1975. text ed. 25.25x (ISBN 0-391-00388-7, Athlone Pr). Humanities.
Gella, Aleksander. Humanism in Sociology: Its Historical Roots & Contemporary Problems. LC 78-61394. 1978. pap. text ed. 10.25 (ISBN 0-8191-0598-8). U Pr of Amer.
Gellar, Sheldon. Senegal. (Nations of Contemporary Africa Ser.). 128p. 1981. lib. bdg. 16.50x (ISBN 0-89158-837-X). Westview.
Gellatly, Peter, ed. Sex Magazines in the Library Collection: Serials Librarian Monographic Supplement to Vol. 4. LC 80-15011. 1981. text ed. 14.95 (ISBN 0-917724-16-X). Haworth Pr.
Gellens, Jay, ed. Twentieth Century Interpretations of A Farewell to Arms. (Twentieth Century Interpretations Ser). 1970. 8.95 (ISBN 0-13-303180-2, Spec). P-H.
Geller, Efim. King's Indian Defence. LC 79-56453. (Illus.). 288p. 1980. pap. 17.95 (ISBN 0-7134-2531-8, Pub. by Batsford England). David & Charles.
Geller, Evelyn, ed. Communism: End of the Monolith? (Reference Shelf Ser.: Vol. 50, No. 3). 1978. 6.25 (ISBN 0-8242-0624-X). Wilson.
--Saving America's Cities. (Reference Shelf Ser.). 1979. 6.25 (ISBN 0-8242-0631-2). Wilson.
Geller, Harriet, jt. auth. see Rosenfeld, Erwin.
Geller, Judith. Inner Space: The Wonders of You. rev. ed. (Student Scientist Ser.). (Illus.). (gr. 7-12). 1979. PLB 7.97 (ISBN 0-8239-0446-6). Rosen Pr.
Geller, L. D. Between Concord & Plymouth: The Transcendentalists & the Watsons. (Illus.). 255p. 1973. 10.00 (ISBN 0-87451-999-3). U Pr of New Eng.
Geller, Larry, jt. auth. see Stearn, Jess.
Geller, Louis & Shim, Jae K. Readings in Cost & Managerial Accounting. 448p. 1980. pap. text ed. 9.95 (ISBN 0-8403-2266-6). Kendall-Hunt.
Geller, Michael. Corpse for a Candidate. (Bud Dugan Ser.: No. 2). 1980. pap. text ed. 1.75 (ISBN 0-505-51478-8). Tower Bks.
--The Man Who Needed Action. 1979. pap. 1.75 (ISBN 0-505-51436-2). Tower Bks.
--Mayhem on the Coney Beat. (Bud Dugan Ser.: No. 1). 1979. pap. 1.75 (ISBN 0-505-51353-6). Tower Bks.
--Thoroughbreds. 1981. pap. 2.75 (ISBN 0-8439-0901-3, Leisure Bks). Nordon Pubns.
Geller, Ruth. Pictures from the Past. LC 80-82075. 205p. 1980. pap. 7.95 (ISBN 0-9603008-1-3). Imp Pr.
Geller, Stephen A. Parallelism in Early Biblical Poetry. LC 78-27255. (Harvard Semitic Monographs: No. 20). 1979. 12.00 (ISBN 0-89130-275-1, 040020). Scholars Pr Ca.
Gellerman. Management of Human Resources. 1976. 10.95 (ISBN 0-03-080485-X). Dryden Pr.
--Manager & Subordinates. 1976. 13.95 (ISBN 0-03-089928-1). Dryden Pr.
Gellerman, Saul W. Management by Motivation. LC 68-12699. (Illus.). 1968. 16.95 (ISBN 0-8144-5157-8). Am Mgmt.
--Motivation & Productivity. LC 63-16332. 1963. 15.95 (ISBN 0-8144-5084-9). Am Mgmt.
--Motivation & Productivity. (AMACOM Executive Books). 1978. pap. 6.95 (ISBN 0-8144-7502-7). Am Mgmt.
Gellermann, William. Martin Dies. LC 77-151620. (Civil Liberties in American History Ser.). 1972. Repr. of 1944 ed. lib. bdg. 29.50 (ISBN 0-306-70200-2). Da Capo.
Gelles, Richard J. Family Violence. LC 79-14813. (Sage Library of Social Research: Vol. 84). (Illus.). 1979. 18.00x (ISBN 0-8039-1234-X); pap. 8.95x (ISBN 0-8039-1235-8). Sage.
Gellhorn, Ernest. Antitrust Law & Economics in a Nutshell. 2nd ed. (Nutshell Ser.). 426p. 1981. pap. text ed. write for info. (ISBN 0-8299-2117-6). West Pub.
Gellhorn, Martha. Travels with Myself & Another. LC 79-15274. 1979. 8.95 (ISBN 0-396-07736-6). Dodd.
--Weather in Africa. LC 79-23763. 236p. 1980. 8.95 (ISBN 0-396-07781-1). Dodd.
Gellhorn, Walter. Federal Administrative Proceedings. LC 70-138237. 150p. 1972. Repr. of 1941 ed. lib. bdg. 13.50x (ISBN 0-8371-5594-0, GEFA). Greenwood.
Gellin, William. Moved by Love. LC 80-52633. 272p. 1980. 10.00 (ISBN 0-88400-070-2). Shengold.
Gelling, Margaret. Early Charters of the Thames Valley. (Studies in Early English History). (Illus.). 208p. 1980. text ed. 35.00x (ISBN 0-7185-1132-8, Leicester). Humanities.
Gellis, Roberta. The Dragon & the Rose. LC 76-43400. 1977. pap. 1.95 o.p. (ISBN 0-87216-364-4). Playboy Pbks.
Gellner, E. Legitimation of Belief. LC 74-14337. 240p. 1975. 29.95 (ISBN 0-521-20467-4). Cambridge U Pr.
--Legitimation of Belief. LC 74-14337. 1979. pap. 9.95 (ISBN 0-521-29587-4). Cambridge U Pr.
Gellner, Ernest. Cause & Meaning in the Social Sciences. Jarvie, I. C. & Agassi, Joseph, eds. 240p. 1973. 20.00x (ISBN 0-7100-7599-5). Routledge & Kegan.
--Muslim Society. LC 80-41103. (Cambridge Studies in Social Anthropology: No. 32). 280p. Date not set. price not set (ISBN 0-521-22160-9). Cambridge U Pr.
--Spectacles & Predicaments: Essays in Social Theory. LC 78-67304. 1980. 41.00 (ISBN 0-521-22486-1). Cambridge U Pr.
--Words & Things: An Examination of, & an Attack on, Linguistic Philosophy. 1979. 24.00 (ISBN 0-7100-0260-2); pap. 12.50 (ISBN 0-7100-0285-8). Routledge & Kegan.
Gellner, Ernest, ed. Soviet & Western Anthrpology. LC 80-11676. 300p. 1980. 37.50x (ISBN 0-231-05120-4). Columbia U Pr.
Gelman. Hello, Cat, You Need a Hat. (ps-3). 1980. pap. 1.25 (ISBN 0-590-05793-6, Schol Pap). Schol Bk Serv.
Gelman, Howard. The Films of John Garfield. 1977. pap. 6.95 (ISBN 0-8065-0620-2). Citadel Pr.
Gelman, Rita. Hey Kid. (Easy-Read Storybooks). (Illus.). (gr. k-3). 1977. PLB 4.90 s&l o.p. (ISBN 0-531-00376-0); 3.95. Watts.
--Why Can't I Fly? (gr. k-3). 1977. pap. 1.50 (ISBN 0-590-10331-8, Schol Pap). Schol Bk Serv.
Gelman, Rita, jt. auth. see Gelman, Steve.
Gelman, Steve. Evans of the Army. LC 64-11699. 3.95 o.p. (ISBN 0-385-03986-7). Doubleday.
--Football Fury. LC 62-8954. (gr. 6-9). 5.95 o.p. (ISBN 0-385-01428-7). Doubleday.
--Pro Football Heroes. (gr. 4-6). 1969. pap. 0.95 o.p. (ISBN 0-590-02965-7, Schol Pap). Schol Bk Serv.
Gelman, Steve & Gelman, Rita. America's Favorite Sports Stars. (gr. 4-6). 1978. pap. 1.50 o.p. (ISBN 0-590-05355-8, Schol Pap). Schol Bk Serv.
Gelman, Steve, ed. see Jordan, Henry, et al.
Gelman, Woody, ed. see Raymond, Alex & Hammett, Dashiell.
Gelong, Karma S., ed. see Rinpoche, Namgyal.
Gelperin, Abraham & Gelperin, Eve A. Emergency Room Journal Articles. 2nd ed. 244p. 1977. spiral bdg. 14.00 o.p. (ISBN 0-87488-795-X). Med Exam.
Gelperin, Alan, jt. ed. see Jacobs, Barry L.
Gelperin, Eve A., jt. auth. see Gelperin, Abraham.
Gelpi, Albert, jt. ed. see Gelpi, Barbara.
Gelpi, Barbara & Gelpi, Albert, eds. Adrienne Rich's Poetry. (Critical Editions Ser). 150p. 1975. 7.95 (ISBN 0-393-04399-1); pap. text ed. 4.95x (ISBN 0-393-09241-0). Norton.
Gelsen, H., jt. auth. see Fennel, T. G.
Gelsinger, Bruce E. Icelandic Enterprise: Economy & Commerce in the Middle Ages. LC 80-26116. (Illus.). 1981. text ed. 19.50 (ISBN 0-87249-405-5). U. of SC Pr.
Gelsthorpe, Annie L. Wings for Nurse Karen. (YA) 1978. 5.95 (ISBN 0-685-86417-0, Avalon). Bouregy.
Geltner, Gerson, jt. auth. see Aspaklaria, Shelley.
Gelwick, Richard. The Way of Discovery: An Introduction to the Thought of Michael Polanyi. LC 76-47429. 1977. 14.95 (ISBN 0-19-502192-4). Oxford U Pr.
--Way of Discovery: An Introduction to the Thought of Michael Polanyi. 1977. pap. 4.95 (ISBN 0-19-502193-2, GB492, GB). Oxford U Pr.
Gembleton, jt. auth. see Windrow, M.
Gemignami, Michael. Law & the Computer: A Guide for Computer Professionals. 320p. 1981. 18.95 (ISBN 0-8436-1604-0). CBI Pub.
Gemignani, Michael C. Elementary Topology. 2nd ed. LC 73-168763. (Mathematics Ser). 1972. text ed. 17.95 (ISBN 0-201-02340-7). A-W.
Gemme, Leila B. King on the Court: Billie Jean King. LC 75-42488. (Sports Profiles Ser.). (Illus.). 48p. (gr. 4-11). 1976. PLB 8.50 (ISBN 0-8172-0128-9). Raintree Pubs.
--Ten-Speed Taylor. Pacini, Kathy, ed. LC 78-1263. (Springboard Bks.). (Illus.). (gr. 3-6). 1978. 5.75g (ISBN 0-8075-7771-5). A Whitman.
Gemmel, Charlotte M. Modern Mathematics. LC 68-55295. (Rapid Reviews Ser.). pap. text ed. 2.75 o.s.i. (ISBN 0-8220-1757-1). Cliffs.
Gemmel, Charlotte M., jt. auth. see Nielsen, Kaj L.

Gemmer, Thomas V. An Introduction to Computers. 1975. coil bdg. 5.95 o.p. (ISBN 0-88252-036-9). Paladin Hse.

Gemmett, Robert J. William Beckford. (English Authors Ser.: No. 204). 1977. lib. bdg. 12.50 (ISBN 0-8057-6674-X). Twayne.

Gemmill, G. T. ICCH Commodities Yearbook 1980-81. 304p. 1980. 75.00x (ISBN 0-85941-071-4, Pub. by Woodhead-Faulkner England). State Mutual Bk.

Gemmill, Paul F. Britain's Search for Health. LC 60-11500. 1961. 9.00x o.p. (ISBN 0-8122-7286-2). U of Pa Pr.

Genazzani, A. R., et al, eds. Adrenal Androgens. 400p. 1980. text ed. 35.00 (ISBN 0-89004-488-0). Raven.

Genazzani, E., et al, eds. Pharmacological Modulation of Steroid Action. 1980. text ed. 32.00 (ISBN 0-89004-373-6). Raven.

Genders, Roy. Complete Book of Herbs. LC 79-93206. (Illus.). 160p. 1980. 14.95 (ISBN 0-8069-3928-1); pap. 8.95 (ISBN 0-8069-3930-3). Sterling.

--Greyhounds. Foyle, Christina, ed. (Foyle's Handbks). 1973. 3.95 (ISBN 0-685-55807-X). Palmetto Pub.

--Mushroom Growing for Everyone. 1970. 11.50 (ISBN 0-571-08992-5). Transatlantic.

--Pears Encyclopedia of Gardening: Flowers, Trees & Shrubs, Vol. 1. 1972. 9.95 (ISBN 0-7207-0249-6, Pub. by Michael Joseph). Merrimack Bk Serv.

--Pears Encyclopedia of Gardening: Fruits & Vegetables, Vol. 2. 1973. 9.95 (ISBN 0-7207-0537-1, Pub. by Michael Joseph). Merrimack Bk Serv.

Gendlin, Eugene. Focusing. 192p. (Orig.). 1981. pap. 3.50 (ISBN 0-553-14526-6). Bantam.

Gendrop, Paul & Heyden, Doris. Pre-Columbian Architecture of Mesoamerica. LC 75-8993. (History of World Architecture Ser.). (Illus.). 340p. 1976. 45.00 (ISBN 0-8109-1018-7). Abrams.

Gendzier, Irene. Frantz Fanon: A Critical Study. 1973. 10.00 o.p. (ISBN 0-394-46205-X). Pantheon.

General Electric Company. Data Processing Self-Study Kit. Incl. An Introduction to Electronic Data Processing. 256p. (ISBN 0-932078-38-9); An Introduction to Magnetic Discs. 98p. (ISBN 0-932078-39-7); An Introduction to Integrated Data Store. 97p. (ISBN 0-932078-40-0); Time-Sharing's BASIC Language. 250p. (ISBN 0-932078-41-9). 1970. pap. 8.50 ea. GE Tech Prom & Train.

--G-MAP Training Manual. 1970. pap. 14.95 (ISBN 0-932078-42-7). GE Tech Prom & Train.

--Work Effectiveness. 94p. 1973. pap. 7.00 (ISBN 0-932078-01-X). GE Tech Prom & Train.

General Electric Marketing Consulting Services. Sales Situation Elements. 1973. 55.00 (ISBN 0-932078-02-8). GE Tech Prom & Train.

General Fisheries Council for the Mediterranean. Report of the First Session of the Working Party on Acoustic Methods for Fish Detection & Abundance Estimation of the General Fisheries Council for the Mediterranean. (FAO Fisheries Report: No. 231). 27p. 1980. pap. 6.00 (ISBN 92-5-100928-7, F2039, FAO). Unipub.

General Mills. Betty Crocker's International Cookbook. (Illus.). 1980. 12.95 (ISBN 0-394-50453-4). Random.

Generous, William T., Jr. Swords & Scales: The Development of the Uniform Code of Military Justice. LC 72-91173. 1973. 17.50 (ISBN 0-8046-9039-1, Natl U). Kennikat.

Genest, Emile. L' Opera-Comique Connu et Inconnu: Son Histoire Depuis l'origine Jusqu'a Nos Jours. LC 80-2277. 1981. Repr. of 1925 ed. 39.50 (ISBN 0-404-18845-1). AMS Pr.

Genestal, Robert. La Tutelle: Etudes De Droit Prive Normand, Vol. 3. LC 80-2027. 1981. Repr. of 1930 ed. 26.00 (ISBN 0-404-18564-9). AMS Pr.

Genet, Jean. Poems. 1980. pap. 6.95 (ISBN 0-686-28714-2). Man-Root.

--The Screens. Frechtman, Bernard, tr. from Fr. 1962. pap. 4.95 (ISBN 0-394-17245-0, E374, Ever). Grove.

--Treasures of the Night: Collected Poems of Jean Genet. Finch, Steven, tr. from Fr. (Illus.). 120p. (Orig.). 1981. 25.00 (ISBN 0-917342-75-5, Pub. by Gay Sunshine); pap. 5.95 (ISBN 0-917342-76-3). Bookpeople.

Genetski, Robert J., jt. auth. see Sprinkel, Beryl W.

Genett, Ann. Contributions of Women: Aviation. LC 74-19004. (Contributions of Women Ser.). (Illus.). (gr. 6 up). 1975. PLB 8.95 (ISBN 0-87518-089-2). Dillon.

Genette, Gerard. Narrative Discourse: An Essay in Method. Lewin, Jane E., tr. from Fr. LC 79-13499. (Illus.). 1979. 17.50 (ISBN 0-8014-1099-1). Cornell U Pr.

Genicot, Leopold. L' Economie Rurale Namuroise au Bas Moyen Age (1199-1429, 2 vols. LC 80-2028. 1981. Repr. of 1943 ed. Set. 79.50 (ISBN 0-404-18565-7). Vol. 1 (ISBN 0-404-18566-5). Vol. 2 (ISBN 0-404-18567-3). AMS Pr.

Genin, Joseph, jt. auth. see Ginsberg, Jerry H.

Genin, Salomea, tr. see Hoerz, Herbert, et al.

Genishi, Celia, jt. auth. see Almy, Millie.

Gennes, P. G. De see De Gennes, P. G.

Gennes, Pierre-Gilles De see De Gennes, Pierre-Gilles.

Genno, Charles N. & Wetzel, Heinz, eds. The First World War in German Narrative Prose. LC 79-26625. 1980. 17.50x (ISBN 0-8020-5490-0). U of Toronto Pr.

Geno. Today's Barbarian. 1978. 4.50 o.p. (ISBN 0-533-02959-7). Vantage.

Geno, Thomas H., ed. Foreign Languages & International Studies 1981: Toward Cooperation & Integration. LC 55-34379. 200p. 1981. pap. 7.95 (ISBN 0-915432-81-1). NE Conf Teach Foreign.

--Our Profession: Present Status & Future Directions. 1980. pap. 7.95x (ISBN 0-915432-80-3). NE Conf Teach.

Geno, Thomas H., jt. ed. see Born, Warren C.

Genouvrier. Linguistique et enseignement du francais. 13.95 (ISBN 2-03-042171-5, 4539). Larousse.

Genovese, Eugene D. From Rebellion to Revolution: Afro-American Slave Revolts in the Making of the Modern World. LC 80-11386. 208p. 1981. pap. 2.95 (ISBN 0-394-74485-3, Vin). Random.

--Roll, Jordan, Roll: The World the Slaves Made. 1976. pap. 8.95 (ISBN 0-394-71652-3, Vin). Random.

Genovese, Michael A. The Supreme Court, the Constitution, & Presidential Power. LC 80-5695. 345p. 1980. lib. bdg. 20.50 (ISBN 0-8191-1322-0); pap. text ed. 11.75 (ISBN 0-8191-1323-9). U Pr of Amer.

Genoways, Hugh H. Systematics & Evolutionary Relationships of Spiny Pocket Mice, Genus Liomys. (Special Publications: No. 5). (Illus., Orig.). 1973. pap. 10.00 (ISBN 0-89672-030-6). Tex Tech Pr.

Genser, Cynthia. Taking on the Local Color. LC 76-41486. (Wesleyan Poetry Program: Vol. 85). 1977. 10.00x (ISBN 0-8195-2085-3, Pub. by Wesleyan U Pr); pap. 4.95 (ISBN 0-8195-1085-8). Columbia U Pr.

Gensini, Goffredo G., ed. Coronary Arteriography. 2nd ed. 1981. write for info. (ISBN 0-87993-130-2). Futura Pub.

Gensler, Kinereth. Without Roof. LC 80-70829. 64p. (Orig.). 1981. pap. 4.95 (ISBN 0-914086-32-4). Alicejamesbooks.

Gent, Peter. North Dallas Forty. 1973. 7.95 o.p. (ISBN 0-688-00183-1). Morrow.

Gent, Thomas. Poetic Sketches; a Collection of Miscellaneous Poems, Repr. Of 1808 Ed. 2nd ed. Reiman, Donald H., ed. Bd. with Poems. Repr. of 1820 ed; Poems. Repr. of 1828 ed. LC 75-31205. (Romantic Context Ser.: Poetry 1789-1830). 1979. lib. bdg. 47.00 (ISBN 0-685-63648-8). Garland Pub.

Gentel, William D., jt. auth. see Hanna, Donald G.

Genthe, Arnold. Isadora Duncan. LC 79-5300. (Dance Ser.). (Illus.). 1980. Repr. of 1929 ed. lib. bdg. 24.00x (ISBN 0-8369-9306-3). Arno.

Genthon, Istvan. From Romanticism to Post-Impressionism. (Illus.). 1966. 7.50 (ISBN 0-8283-1124-2). Branden.

Gentile, A. G. & Bailey, S. F. A Revision of the Genus Thrips Linnaeus in the New World with a Catalogue of the World Species (Thysanoptera: Thripidae) (U. C. Publ. in Entomology: Vol. 51). 1968. pap. 8.00x (ISBN 0-520-09124-8). U of Cal Pr.

Gentile, Gennaro L. The Mouse in the Manger. LC 78-72944. (Illus.). 80p. (gr. k-4). 1978. pap. 3.95 (ISBN 0-87793-165-8). Ave Maria.

Gentili, Bruno. Theatrical Performances in the Ancient World: Hellenistic & Early Roman Theatre. (London Studies in Classical Philology: No. 2). 1978. pap. text ed. 17.25x (ISBN 0-391-01164-2). Humanities.

Gentilini, P., et al, eds. Intrahepatic Cholestasis. LC 75-10551. 199p. 1975. 24.50 (ISBN 0-89004-049-4). Raven.

Gentle, E. J. & Reithmaier, L. W. Aviation - Space Dictionary. 6th ed. LC 80-67567. (Illus.). 1980. 18.95 (ISBN 0-8168-3002-9). Aero.

Gentle, Ernest J., et al. FAA Flight Test Guides. rev. ed. LC 74-77533. 112p. 1976. pap. 2.95 (ISBN 0-8168-5702-4). Aero.

Gentleman, Francis. A Trip to the Moon: Containing an Account of the Island of Noibla, 2 vols. in 1. Shugrue, Michael F., ed. (Flowering of the Novel, 1740-1775 Ser.: Vol. 68). 1974. lib. bdg. 50.00 (ISBN 0-8240-1167-8). Garland Pub.

Gentry, Alwyn H. Bignoniaceae: Crescentieae & Tourretieae, Pt. 1. LC 80-10846. (Flora Neotropica Monograph: No. 25). (Illus.). 132p. 1980. pap. 15.75 (ISBN 0-89327-222-1). NY Botanical.

Gentry, Curt. Dolphin Guide to San Francisco & the Bay Area. rev. ed. LC 69-11017. 1969. pap. 2.50 (ISBN 0-385-05489-0, C205, Dolp). Doubleday.

Gentry, Curt, jt. auth. see Bugliosi, Vincent.

Gentry, Deborah, jt. auth. see Brewster, John W.

Gentry, Francis G. Triuwe & Vriunt in the Nibelungenlied. Minis, Cola, ed. (Amsterdamer Publikationen Zur Sprache und Literatur: Vol. 19). 94p. 1975. pap. text ed. 17.25x (ISBN 90-6203-368-7). Humanities.

Gentry, Gardiner. Bus Them in. 1976. pap. 2.95 o.p. (ISBN 0-8010-3705-0). Baker Bk.

Gentry, J., jt. auth. see Johnson, G.

Gentry, J & Johnson, G., eds. Principles of Accounting: Advanced. 6th ed. 1971. 17.95 o.p. (ISBN 0-13-317578-2). P-H.

Gentry, John T. Introduction to Health Services & Community Health Systems. new ed. LC 77-78899. 1978. text ed. 20.50 (ISBN 0-8211-0612-0); text ed. 18.00 in ten or more copies (ISBN 0-685-48956-6). McCutchan.

Gentry, Rodney D. Introduction to Calculus for the Biological & Life Sciences. LC 77-79470. (Illus.). 1978. text ed. 20.95 (ISBN 0-201-02477-2); instr's man. avail. (ISBN 0-201-02478-0); key avail. (ISBN 0-201-02479-9). A-W.

Gentry, W. Doyle. Applied Behavior Modification. LC 74-28290. (Illus.). 164p. 1975. pap. text ed. 9.50 (ISBN 0-8016-1803-7). Mosby.

Gentry, W. Doyle & Williams, Redford B. Psychological Aspects of Myocardial Infarction & Coronary Care. LC 75-2461. 1975. pap. text ed. 7.50 o.p. (ISBN 0-8016-1799-5). Mosby.

--Psychological Aspects of Myocardial Infarction & Coronary Care. 2nd ed. LC 79-2554. (Illus.). 1979. pap. text ed. 12.95 (ISBN 0-8016-1796-0). Mosby.

Gentz, Friedrich Von. The Origin & Principles of the American Revolution, Compared with the Origin & Principles of the French Revolution. Loss, Richard, ed. LC 77-16175. 1977. Repr. of 1800 ed. lib. bdg. 20.00 (ISBN 0-8201-1302-6). Schol Facsimiles.

Gentz, William H. & Colvin, Elaine W. Religious Writers Marketplace. 221p. 1980. 12.95 (ISBN 0-89471-132-6); lib. bdg. 19.80 (ISBN 0-89471-106-7). Running Pr.

Gentzler, J. Mason. A Syllabus of Chinese Civilization. rev. 2nd ed. LC 68-55814. (Companions to Asian Studies). 120p. 1972. pap. text ed. 6.00x (ISBN 0-231-03676-0). Columbia U Pr.

Genua, Robert L. The Employer's Guide to Interviewing, Strategies & Tactics for Picking a Winner. (Illus.). 1979. 12.95 (ISBN 0-13-274696-4, Spec); pap. 5.95 (ISBN 0-13-274688-3, Spec). P-H.

Genuys, F., ed. Programming Languages. 1969. 54.50 (ISBN 0-12-279750-7). Acad Pr.

Genyea, Julien, jt. auth. see Callewaert, Denis M.

Genzel, Peter, jt. auth. see Allardyce, Alex.

Geoffrey Of Monmouth. Geoffrey of Monmouth: Historia Regum Brittaniae. Hammer, Jacob, ed. 1951. 15.00 o.p. (ISBN 0-910956-31-6). Medieval Acad.

Geoffroy, Gregory & Elial, Ernest L. Topics in Inorganic & Organometallic Stereochemistry, Vol. 12. (Topics in Stereochemistry Ser.). 344p. 1981. 50.00 (ISBN 0-471-05292-2, Pub. by Wiley-Interscience). Wiley.

Geoffroy-Dechaume, Claude. Craft Jewelery. (Illus.). 144p. 1980. 16.95 (ISBN 0-571-11486-5, Pub. by Faber & Faber); pap. 6.95 (ISBN 0-571-11309-5, Pub. by Faber & Faber). Merrimack Bk Serv.

--Simple Craft Jewellery. 3rd ed. 1963. 6.95 (ISBN 0-571-05733-0, Pub. by Faber & Faber). Merrimack Bk Serv.

Geoghegan, Sheilah. Dining Out & Dining in: Memorable Menus & Recipes from Washington's Finest Restaurants. 128p. 1981. 10.00 (ISBN 0-914440-47-0). EPM Pubns.

Geographics Editors. World Directory of Engineering Schools. 2nd ed. LC 80-66864. 1980. pap. 28.95 (ISBN 0-930722-02-7). Geographics.

Geological Society Of America. Ten Year Index to Vols. 61-70 of Geological Society of America Bulletin. LC 1-23380. (Orig.). 1962. pap. 10.50x o.p. (ISBN 0-8137-9061-1). Geol Soc.

Geological Society of America, ed. Memorials: Nineteen Seventy-Seven Decedents. LC 73-76887. (Vol. 9). (Illus.). 1979. pap. 9.00 (ISBN 0-8137-8077-2). Geol Soc.

Geophysics Research Board. Climate, Climatic Change & Water Supply. 1977. pap. 7.75 (ISBN 0-309-02625-3). Natl Acad Pr.

--Continental Scientific Drilling. 1979. pap. 5.50 (ISBN 0-309-02872-8). Natl Acad Pr.

--Continental Tectonics. (Studies in Geophysics). xii, 197p. 1980. pap. text ed. 13.50 (ISBN 0-309-02928-7). Natl Acad Pr.

--Impact of Technology on Geophysics. xii, 121p. 1979. pap. 10.25 (ISBN 0-309-02887-6). Natl Acad Pr.

Geophysics Research Board & Division Of Earth Sciences. Solid-Earth Geophysics: Survey & Outlook. 1964. pap. 5.00 (ISBN 0-309-01231-7). Natl Acad Pr.

Geophysics Research Board, National Research Council. Geophysical Predictions. LC 78-8147. (Studies in Geophysics Ser.). 1978. pap. text ed. 12.75 (ISBN 0-309-02741-1). Natl Acad Pr.

Geophysics Study Committee. Estuaries, Geophysics, & the Environment. LC 77-82812. (Studies in Geophysics). (Illus.). 1977. pap. text ed. 8.50 (ISBN 0-309-02629-6). Natl Acad Pr.

--Upper Atmosphere & Magnetosphere. 1977. pap. 10.00 (ISBN 0-309-02633-4). Natl Acad Pr.

Georgakas, Dan. The Methuselah Factors: Living Long & Living Well. 1981. 14.95 (ISBN 0-671-24064-1). S&S.

Georgano, G. N. The Complete Encyclopedia of Commercial Vehicles. 1979. 29.95 (ISBN 0-87341-024-6). Motorbooks Intl.

--Complete Encyclopedia of Motorcars. rev. ed. 1973. 30.00 o.p. (ISBN 0-525-08351-0). Dutton.

Georgano, G. N. & Demand, Carlo. Trucks: An Illustrated History 1892-1921. (Illus.). 1978. 24.95 (ISBN 0-8467-0500-1, Pub. by Two Continents). Hippocrene Bks.

George. Modern Interstitial & Intracavitary Radiation Cancer Management, Vol. 6. (Cancer Management Ser.). 1981. write for info. Masson Pub.

George, A. G. Critics & Criticism. 1971. lib. bdg. 8.75x (ISBN 0-210-22347-2). Asia.

George, A. G., ed. see Hawthorne, Nathaniel.

George, A. G., jt. ed. see Rajan, B.

George A. Talland Memorial Conference. New Directions in Memory & Aging: Proceedings. Poon, Leonard W., et al, eds. LC 79-27548. (Illus.). 592p. 1980. text ed. 36.00 (ISBN 0-89859-035-3). L Erlbaum Assocs.

George, Abraham M. Foreign Exchange Management & the Multinational Corporation: A Manager's Guide. LC 78-19738. 1978. 28.95 (ISBN 0-03-046641-5). Praeger.

George, Ajax E. Neuroradiology Case Studies. 1977. sprial bdg. 17.50 (ISBN 0-87488-037-8). Med Exam.

George, Albert. Books by Balzac: A Checklist of Books by Honore De Balzac, Compiled from the Papers of William Hobart Royce Presently in the Syracuse University Collection. 1960. text ed. 10.50x (ISBN 0-391-01606-7). Humanities.

George, Alexander. Presidential Decisionmaking in Foreign Policy. (Westview Special Studies in International Relations). 1980. lib. bdg. 24.50x (ISBN 0-89158-380-7); pap. text ed. 10.50x (ISBN 0-89158-510-9). Westview.

George, Alexander, et al. Deterrence in American Foreign Policy: Theory & Practice. LC 74-7120. 656p. 1974. 25.00x (ISBN 0-231-03837-2); pap. 10.00x (ISBN 0-231-03838-0). Columbia U Pr.

George, Alexander L. The Chinese Communist Army in Action: The Korean War & Its Aftermath. LC 67-12659. 1969. 20.00x (ISBN 0-231-03020-7); pap. 7.50x (ISBN 0-231-08595-8). Columbia U Pr.

George, Andrew J., ed. The Complete Poetical Works of William Wordsworth, 10 vols. 1981. Repr. of 1919 ed. Set. lib. bdg. 350.00 (ISBN 0-89987-862-8). Darby Bks.

George, Anthea, jt. ed. see Cisek, James D.

George, B. J., Jr., tr. see Dando, S.

George, Bernard. Edouard Boubat: Great Contemporary Photographer. LC 73-7351. (Men & Movements Ser.: Vol. 3). (Illus.). 96p. 1974. 10.95 o.s.i. (ISBN 0-02-542980-9). Macmillan.

--Edouard Boubat: Great Contemporary Photographer. (Photography, Men & Movements Ser.: Vol. 3). (Illus.). 96p. 1974. pap. 5.95 o.s.i. (ISBN 0-02-000350-1, Collier). Macmillan.

George, Carol V. Segregated Sabbaths: Richard Allen & the Rise of Independent Black Churches, 1760-1840. 225p. 1973. 11.95 (ISBN 0-19-501678-5); pap. 3.95x (ISBN 0-19-501677-7). Oxford U Pr.

George, Claude S., Jr. The History of Management Thought. 2nd ed. 256p. 1972. pap. text ed. 11.95 (ISBN 0-13-390187-4). P-H.

--Management for Business & Industry. Orig. Title: Management in Industry. 1970. text ed. 20.95 (ISBN 0-13-548578-9). P-H.

George, D. V. Principles of Quantum Chemistry. 280p. 1973. text ed. 21.00 (ISBN 0-08-016925-2). Pergamon.

George, Dan, jt. auth. see Mortimer, Hilda.

George, David, jt. auth. see Olgilvie, Eric.

George, David L. (Compiler) Family Book of Best Loved Poems. 1952. 9.95 (ISBN 0-385-01421-X). Doubleday.

George, David Lloyd see Lloyd George, David.

George, Denise. How to Be a Seminary Student-& Survive. 1981. pap. 3.95 (ISBN 0-8054-6930-3). Broadman.

George, Emery. Kate's Death: Poems. 1980. 8.95 (ISBN 0-88233-583-9); pap. 3.95 (ISBN 0-88233-584-7). Ardis Pubs.

George, Emery E. Gift of Nerve - Poems, 1966-1977. 1978. 6.95 (ISBN 0-914408-06-2); pap. 3.95 (ISBN 0-685-89712-5). Kylix Pr.

George, Eric. Life & Death of Benjamin Robert Haydon, Historical Painter, 1786-1846. 2nd ed. 1967. 16.95x (ISBN 0-19-817156-0). Oxford U Pr.

George, F. H. Computer Arithmetic. 1966. 17.25 (ISBN 0-08-011464-4); pap. 7.75 (ISBN 0-08-011463-6). Pergamon.

--An Introduction to Computer Programming. (Illus.). 1968. 12.10 o.p. (ISBN 0-08-012394-5); pap. 5.50 o.p. (ISBN 0-08-012393-7). Pergamon.

--An Introduction to Digital Computing. 1966. pap. 7.75 (ISBN 0-08-011280-3). Pergamon.

--Precision, Language & Logic. 224p. 1977. text ed. 29.00 (ISBN 0-08-019650-0). Pergamon.

--Problem Solving. 194p. 1980. 19.50x (ISBN 0-7156-1004-X, Pub. by Duckworth England). Biblio Dist.

--The Science of Philosophy. 1981. price not set (ISBN 0-677-05550-1). Gordon.

George, Garfield J. A Surprise for Cashimere. Bd. with Cashimere Learns to Skate. Date not set. pap. 4.95 (ISBN 0-533-04770-6). Vantage.

George, Gerald S. Biomechanics of Women's Gymnastics. 1980. text ed. 15.95 (ISBN 0-13-077461-8). P-H.

George, Henry, Jr. Henry George. Aaron, Daniel, ed. (American Men & Women of Letters Ser.). Orig. Title: The Life of Henry George. 640p. 1981. pap. 8.95 (ISBN 0-87754-164-7). Chelsea Hse.

George, J. Socialism for the Dead. LC 79-67320. 354p. 1980. 12.95 (ISBN 0-533-04454-5). Vantage.

George, J. C. & Berger, Andrew J. Avian Myology. 1966. 49.00 (ISBN 0-12-280150-4). Acad Pr.

George, J. David & George, Jennifer. Marine Life: An Illustrated Encyclopedia of Invertebrates in the Sea. LC 79-10976. 1979. 45.95 (ISBN 0-471-05675-8, Pub. by Wiley-Interscience). Wiley.

George, James E. Law & Emergency Care. LC 80-14606. 1980. 24.95 (ISBN 0-8016-1834-7). Mosby.

George, Jean C. All Upon a Stone. LC 75-101929. (Illus.). (gr. 2-5). 1971. PLB 7.49 o.p. (ISBN 0-690-05533-1, TYC-J). T Y Crowell.

--Gull Number 737. LC 64-16531. (Illus.). (gr. 5-10). 1964. 8.95 (ISBN 0-690-36171-8, TYC-J). T Y Crowell.

--My Side of the Mountain. (Illus.). (gr. 4-9). 1975. PLB 7.95 (ISBN 0-525-35530-8, Anytime Bks); pap. 3.25 (ISBN 0-525-45030-0, Anytime Bk). Dutton.

--The Wentletrap Trap. (Illus.). (ps-3). 1978. PLB 7.95 o.p. (ISBN 0-525-42310-9). Dutton.

George, Jennifer, jt. auth. see George, J. David.

George, John A., jt. auth. see Daellenbach, Hans G.

George, Judith St. see St. George, Judith.

George, K. D. & Joll, Caroline. Competition Policy in the UK & EEC. LC 75-9285. 1975. 39.00 (ISBN 0-521-20943-9). Cambridge U Pr.

George, K. M. Survey of Malayalam Literature. 10.00x (ISBN 0-210-22735-4). Asia.

George, Kathleen. Rhythm in Drama. LC 79-24432. 1980. 9.95 (ISBN 0-8229-3416-7); pap. 4.95 (ISBN 0-8229-5316-1). U of Pittsburgh Pr.

George, Kenneth D., et al. Science Investigations for Elementary School Teachers. 1973. pap. text ed. 4.95x (ISBN 0-669-83154-9). Heath.

--Elementary School Science: Why & How. 1973. pap. text ed. 7.95x (ISBN 0-669-83162-X). Heath.

George, L. O., jt. auth. see Baur, G. R.

George, Linda K. Role Transitions in Later Life. LC 79-25239. (Social Gerontology Ser.). (Orig.). 1980. pap. text ed. 6.95 (ISBN 0-8185-0382-3). Brooks-Cole.

George, Llewellyn. The A to Z Horoscope Maker & Delineator. 13th, rev. ed. Bytheriver, Marylee, ed. (Illus.). 600p. (Orig.). 1981. 17.95 (ISBN 0-87542-263-2). Llewellyn Pubns.

George, M. Dorothy. English Political Caricature: A Study of Opinion & Propaganda, 2 vols. Incl. Vol. 1. To 1792. 42.00x (ISBN 0-19-817130-7); Vol. 2. 1793-1832. 42.00x (ISBN 0-19-817131-5). 1959. Oxford U Pr.

George, Michael, jt. ed. see Greenbeg, Alan.

George, Prince of Wales. The Correspondence of George, Prince of Wales, 1770-1812, 8 vols. Aspinall, A., ed. Incl. Vol. 1. 1770-1789. 1963. o.p. (ISBN 0-19-519464-0); Vol. 2. 1789-1794. 1964. 29.00x (ISBN 0-19-519465-9); Vol. 5. 1804-1806. 1968. 30.00x (ISBN 0-19-519468-3); Vol. 6. 1806-1809. 1969. 30.00x (ISBN 0-19-519469-1); Vol. 7. 1810-1811. 454p. 1970. 30.00x (ISBN 0-19-519516-7); Vol. 8. 1811-1812. 588p. 1971. 33.75 (ISBN 0-19-519517-5). Oxford U Pr.

George, R., jt. ed. see Zimmermann, E.

George, R., et al, eds. Annual Review of Pharmacology & Toxicology, Vol. 21. LC 61-5649. (Illus.). 1981. 20.00 (ISBN 0-8243-0421-7). Annual Reviews.

George, R. A., jt. auth. see Flegmann, G. W.

George, Richard T. De see De George, Richard T.

George, Robert & Okun, Ronald, eds. Annual Review of Pharmacology & Toxicology, Vol. 20. LC 61-5649. (Illus.). 1980. text ed. 17.00 (ISBN 0-8243-0420-9). Annual Reviews.

George, Rolf, ed. & tr. see Bolzano, Bernhard.

George, Rolf, tr. see Brentano, Franz.

George, Rolf A., tr. see Carnap, Rudolf.

George, Sally. Frog Salad. 256p. 1981. 9.95 (ISBN 0-684-16766-2, ScribT). Scribner.

George, Ted. The Lives You Live As Revealed in the Heavens. LC 77-73594. 1977. 12.00 (ISBN 0-932782-00-0). Arthur Pubns.

George, Terry, jt. ed. see Doll, John.

George, V. Foster Care: Theory & Practice. (International Library of Sociology & Social Reconstruction). 1970. text ed. 11.25x (ISBN 0-7100-6800-X). Humanities.

George, V. N. Social Security: Beveridge & After. (International Library of Sociology & Social Reconstruction). 1968. text ed. 13.00x (ISBN 0-7100-6205-2). Humanities.

George, Vic & Manning, Nick. Socialism, Social Welfare, & the Soviet Union. (Radical Social Policy Ser.). 224p. (Orig.). 1980. pap. 15.95 (ISBN 0-7100-0608-X). Routledge & Kegan.

George, Vic & Lawson, Roger, eds. Poverty & Inequality in Common Market Countries. 1980. 27.00x (ISBN 0-7100-0424-9); pap. 15.00 (ISBN 0-7100-0517-2). Routledge & Kegan.

George, Victor & Wilding, Paul. Motherless Families. (International Library of Sociology). 1972. 20.00x (ISBN 0-7100-7305-4). Routledge & Kegan.

George, W. N., jt. auth. see Willis, Arthur J.

George, Waldemar & Nouaille-Rouault, Genevieve. Rouault. (Artists Ser.). (Illus.). 1976. pap. 5.95 (ISBN 0-8120-0713-1). Barron.

George Washington University, Biological Sciences Communications Project. The Millets: A Bibliography of the World Literature Covering the Years 1930-1963. 1967. 10.00 (ISBN 0-8108-0095-0). Scarecrow.

George Washington University, Biological Sciences Communication Project. Sorghum: A Bibliography of the World Literature Covering the Years 1930-1963. LC 67-12060. 1967. 10.00 (ISBN 0-8108-0135-3). Scarecrow.

George, Wesley C. The Biology of the Race Problem. 72p. 1979. pap. 2.00x (ISBN 0-911038-76-0, 132). Noontide.

George, Wilfred R. The Profit Box System of Forecasting Stock Prices. LC 76-15737. (Illus.). 1976. 19.95 o.p. (ISBN 0-87094-129-1). Dow Jones-Irwin.

George, William C., et al, eds. Educating the Gifted: Acceleration & Enrichment. LC 79-7559. (Hyman Blumberg Symposium on Research in Early Childhood Education). 1980. text ed. 16.00x o.p. (ISBN 0-8018-2260-2); pap. text ed. 4.95x (ISBN 0-8018-2266-1). Johns Hopkins.

George, William J., ed. see International Conference on Cyclic Nucleotide, 3rd, New Orleans, la., July 1977.

George, Wilma. Animal Geography. 1962. pap. text ed. 9.95 (ISBN 0-435-60345-0). Heinemann Ed.

--Animals & Maps. (Illus.). 1969. 25.00x (ISBN 0-520-01480-4). U of Cal Pr.

Georges, Daniel E. The Geography of Crime & Violence: A Spatial & Ecological Perspective. Natoli, Salvatore, ed. LC 78-50967. (Resource Papers for College Geography Ser.). 1978. pap. text ed. 4.00 (ISBN 0-89291-128-X). Assn Am Geographers.

Georges, Rip & Heimann, Jim. California Crazy: Roadside Vernacular Architecture. LC 79-24181. (Illus.). 144p. (Orig.). 1980. pap. 7.95 (ISBN 0-87701-171-0). Chronicle Bks.

Georges, Robert A. & Jones, Michael O. People Studying People: The Human Element in Fieldwork. 1980. 14.95x (ISBN 0-520-03989-0); pap. 3.95x (ISBN 0-520-04067-8, CAMPUS NO. 250). U of Cal Pr.

George Third. Later Correspondence of George Third, 5 vols. Aspinall, A., ed. Incl. Vol. 1. 1783-1793 (ISBN 0-521-04066-3); Vol. 2. 1793-1797 (ISBN 0-521-04067-1); Vol. 3. 1798-1801 (ISBN 0-521-04068-X); Vol. 4. 1802-1807 (ISBN 0-521-06918-1); Vol. 5. 1807-1810, with Index to Vols. 1-5 (ISBN 0-521-07451-7). LC 61-52516. 700p. 120.00 ea. Cambridge U Pr.

Georgi, Charlotte. The Arts & the World of Business. 2nd ed. LC 78-12103. 1979. lib. bdg. 10.00 (ISBN 0-8108-1174-X). Scarecrow.

Georgiade, Nicholas G. Breast Reconstruction Following Mastectomy. LC 79-15679. (Illus.). 1979. text ed. 44.50 (ISBN 0-8016-1807-X). Mosby.

Georgiades, Thrasybulos. Greek Music, Verse & Dance. LC 73-4336. 156p. 1973. Repr. of 1955 ed. lib. bdg. 17.50 (ISBN 0-306-70561-3). Da Capo.

Georgiou, Constantine. Children & Their Literature. LC 69-10223. (Education Ser). 1969. text ed. 18.95x (ISBN 0-13-132167-6). P-H.

Georgiou, Hara. The Late Minoan I Destruction of Crete: Metal Groups & Stratigraphic Considerations. (Monograph: IX). (Orig.). 1979. pap. text ed. 5.00 (ISBN 0-917956-06-0). UCLA Arch.

Georis, Walter. French Windows. 1981. 19.95 (ISBN 0-89396-029-2); pap. 9.95 (ISBN 0-89396-030-6). Urizen Bks.

Geosset, Philip, ed. see Le Seur, Jean F.

Geothermal Resources Council, ed. Commercial Uses of Geothermal Heat. (Special Report: No. 9). (Illus.). 143p. 1980. pap. 3.50 (ISBN 0-934412-09-X). Geothermal.

--Direct Utilization of Geothermal Energy: A Symposium, January 31-February 2, 1978, San Diego, California. (Illus., Orig.). pap. 2.50 o.p. (ISBN 0-934412-74-X). Geothermal.

--Proceedings: State-Federal Geothermal Regulatory Interface Workshop, November 17-18, 1976, Asilomar, California. (Orig.). 1977. pap. 3.50 (ISBN 0-934412-73-1). Geothermal.

--A Symposium on Geothermal Energy & Its Direct Uses in the Eastern United States, April Fifth to Seventh, Nineteen Seventy-Nine, Roanoke, Virginia. (Special Report Ser.: No. 5). (Illus., Orig.). 1979. pap. 3.50 (ISBN 0-934412-05-7). Geothermal.

Gephart, William & Ingle, Robert. Educational Research: Selected Readings. 1969. text ed. 15.95x (ISBN 0-675-09521-2). Merrill.

Gephart, William, ed. Accountability: A State, a Process, or a Product? LC 74-84288. 82p. 1975. pap. 3.50 (ISBN 0-87367-702-1). Phi Delta Kappa.

Gephart, William J., jt. ed. see Cunningham, Luvern L.

Gephart, William J., ed. see Phi Delta Kappa Symposium on Educational Research, 12th.

Geraci, Philip C. Photojournalism: Making Pictures for Publication. 2nd ed. (Illus.). 1978. pap. text ed. 13.95 (ISBN 0-8403-1422-1). Kendall-Hunt.

Geradin, M. B. M. Fraeijs De Veubeke Memorial Volume of Selected Papers. 79p. 1980. 57.50x (ISBN 90-286-0900-8). Sijthoff & Noordhoff.

Geraghty, Tony. Inside the SAS. (Elite Unit Ser.: No. 2). (Illus.). 249p. 1981. 17.95 (ISBN 0-89839-039-7). Battery Pr.

Gerald, Curtis F. Applied Numerical Analysis. 2nd ed. LC 77-79469. (Illus.). 1978. text ed. 21.95 (ISBN 0-201-02696-1). A-W.

Gerald, Mark & Eyman, William. Thinking Straight & Talking Sense. LC 78-71008. 1981. pap. 10.00 (ISBN 0-917476-14-X). Rational Living.

Gerald, Michael C. Pharmacology: An Introduction to Drugs. (Illus.). 576p. 1974. 18.95 (ISBN 0-13-662080-9). P-H.

--Pharmacology: An Introduction to Drugs. (Illus.). 720p. 1981. 19.95 (ISBN 0-13-662098-1). P-H.

Gerald, Michael C. & O'Bannon, Freda V. Nursing Pharmacology. (Illus.). 544p. 1981. text ed. 22.95 (ISBN 0-13-627505-2). P-H.

Gerard, Albert S. The African Language Literatures South of the Sahara: An Introduction. LC 79-3103. (Illus.). 396p. 1981. 30.00x (ISBN 0-914478-65-6); pap. 12.00x (ISBN 0-914478-66-4). Three Continents.

--Four African Literatures: Xhosa, Sotho, Zulu, Amharic. LC 74-126763. 1971. 26.50x (ISBN 0-520-01788-9). U of Cal Pr.

Gerard, David E., ed. Libraries in Society: A Reader. 1979. 16.00 (ISBN 0-89664-402-2, Pub. by K G Saur). Shoe String.

Gerard, F. A., jt. auth. see Bowman, Frank.

Gerard, John. The Herball or General Historie of Plants, 2 vols. LC 74-80179. (English Experience Ser.: Nos. 660a-660b). 1974. Repr. of 1597 ed. Set. 214.00 (ISBN 90-221-0660-8). Walter J Johnson.

Gerard, Max & Orizet, Louis. Dali: The Wines of Gala. LC 77-8625. (Illus.). 1978. 50.00 o.p. (ISBN 0-8109-0802-6). Abrams.

Gerard, Yves, ed. Thematic, Bibliographical & Critical Catalogue of the Works of Luigi Boccherini. Mayor, Andreas, tr. 1969. 74.00x (ISBN 0-19-711616-7). Oxford U Pr.

Gerard Of Cremona, tr. see Muhammad Ibn Zakariya.

Geras, Adele. The Girls in the Velvet Frame. LC 79-12352. (gr. 4-7). 1979. 8.95 (ISBN 0-689-30729-2). Atheneum.

Gerasimov, I. P., et al, eds. Natural Resources of the Soviet Union: Their Use & Renewal, English Edition. LC 74-138667. (Illus.). 1971. text ed. 31.95x (ISBN 0-7167-0248-7). W H Freeman.

Geraty, Lawrence, ed. God's Hand in My Life. LC 77-12585. (Horizon Ser.). 1977. pap. 4.95 (ISBN 0-8127-0151-8). Southern Pub.

Gerbault, Alain. Firecrest Round the World. 1981. 12.50 (ISBN 0-679-51026-5). McKay.

Gerbeaux, Jacques. Pediatric Respiratory Disease. 875p. 1981. 45.00 (ISBN 0-471-03456-8, Pub. by Wiley-Med). Wiley.

Gerber & Storzer. French Conversation Through Idioms. Date not set. pap. 6.95 (ISBN 0-8120-2107-X). Barron. Postponed.

Gerber, Aaron. Abraham: The First Hebrew. 180p. 1981. 12.50 (ISBN 0-89962-208-9). Todd & Honeywell.

Gerber, Barbara & Storzer, Gerald. French Idioms on the Way. (Illus.). Date not set. pap. 4.95 (ISBN 0-8120-2108-8). Barron. Postponed.

Gerber, Dan. Indy: The World's Fastest Carnival Ride. LC 76-28812. (Illus.). 1977. pap. 8.95 o.p. (ISBN 0-13-464156-6). P-H.

Gerber, Douglas E. Pindar's Olympian I: A Commentary. (Phoenix Supplementary Volumes Ser.). 264p. 1981. 47.50 (ISBN 0-8020-5507-9). U of Toronto Pr.

Gerber, Ellen W., et al. The American Woman in Sport. 1974. text ed. 16.95 (ISBN 0-201-02353-9). A-W.

Gerber, Hans U. An Introduction to Mathematical Risk Theory. LC 79-89749. (S. S. Huebner Foundation Monographs: No. 8). (Illus.). 1980. pap. 15.95 (ISBN 0-918930-08-1). Huebner Foun Insur.

Gerber, Irving. Albert Einstein: World Scientist. 1979. of 10 6.75 set (ISBN 0-87594-185-0). Book Lab.

--Emma Lazarus: Poet of Liberty. 1979. of 10 6.75 set (ISBN 0-87594-183-4). Book Lab.

--Haym Solomon: Patriot of Liberty. 1979. of six 6.75 set (ISBN 0-87594-182-6). Book Lab.

Gerber, Irwin, jt. ed. see Schoenberg, Bernard.

Gerber, John C., ed. Twentieth Century Interpretations of The Scarlet Letter. LC 68-23438. (Twentieth Century Interpretations Series). (Orig.). 1968. 8.95 (ISBN 0-13-791582-9, Spec). P-H.

Gerber, John C., et al, eds. see Twain, Mark.

Gerber, Lane A., jt. ed. see Duffy, John C.

Gerber, Linda L., jt. auth. see Haines, B. Joan.

Gerber, Merrill J. Please Don't Kiss Me Now. 224p. (YA) (gr. 8 up). 1981. 9.95 (ISBN 0-8037-6792-7). Dial.

Gerber, Philip L. Robert Frost. (U. S. Authors Ser.: No. 107). 1966. lib. bdg. 9.95 (ISBN 0-8057-0296-2). Twayne.

--Theodore Dreiser. (U. S. Authors Ser.: No. 52). 1963. lib. bdg. 9.95 (ISBN 0-8057-0212-1). Twayne.

--Willa Cather. LC 75-2287. (U. S. Authors Ser.: No. 258). 1975. lib. bdg. 9.95 (ISBN 0-8057-7155-7). Twayne.

Gerber, Phillip L., ed. Willa Cather. LC 75-2287. (Twayne's U. S. Authors Ser.). 187p. 1975. pap. text ed. 4.95 (ISBN 0-672-61508-8). Bobbs.

Gerber, Ruth. A Marriageable Asset. (Orig.). 1981. pap. 1.50 o.s.i. (ISBN 0-440-14974-6). Dell.

Gerber, Sanford, jt. auth. see Mencher, George T.

Gerber, Sanford E. Introductory Hearing Science: Physical & Psychological Concepts. LC 73-89177. (Illus.). 305p. 1974. text ed. 17.00 (ISBN 0-7216-4104-0). Saunders.

Gerber, Sanford E. & Mencher, George T. Auditory Dysfunction. (Illus.). 256p. 1980. text ed. 19.95 (ISBN 0-933014-60-0). College-Hill.

Gerber, William. American Liberalism. LC 74-32118. (World Leaders Ser.: No. 51). 1975. lib. bdg. 10.95 (ISBN 0-8057-3604-2). Twayne.

Gerbers, Teresa. The Laughing Willows. (YA) 1977. 5.95 (ISBN 0-685-71793-3, Avalon). Bouregy.

Gerbert, Joshua, ed. Textbook of Bunion Surgery. LC 80-68895. (Illus.). 300p. 1981. monograph 24.50 (ISBN 0-87993-153-1). Futura Pub.

Gerbino, Philip P., ed. Self-Assessment of Current Knowledge in Clinical Pharmacy. 2nd ed. 1978. pap. 9.50 (ISBN 0-87488-281-8). Med Exam.

Gerbner, G., et al. Communications Technology & Social Policy: Understanding the New Cultural Revolution. LC 73-7563. 1973. 34.00 (ISBN 0-471-29670-8, Pub. by Wiley-Interscience). Wiley.

Gerbner, George, ed. Mass Media Policies in Changing Cultures. LC 77-2399. 1977. 27.50 (ISBN 0-471-01514-8, Pub. by Wiley-Interscience). Wiley.

Gerbracht, Carl & Robinson, Frank E. Understanding America's Industries. (gr. 7-9). 1971. text ed. 14.64 (ISBN 0-87345-499-5). McKnight.

Gerdes. Seeing the Real San Francisco. 1981. pap. 7.95 (ISBN 0-8120-2244-0). Barron.

Gerdine, Leigh, tr. see Keller, Hermann.

Gereboff, Joel. Rabbi Tarfon: The Tradition, the Man & Early Rabbinic Judaism. LC 78-15220. (Brown Judaic Studies: No. 7). 1979. 16.50 (ISBN 0-89130-257-3, 140007); pap. 12.00 (ISBN 0-89130-300-6). Scholars Pr Ca.

Gerevas, Lawrence E. Basic Drafting Problems. 1972. pap. 7.30 o.p. (ISBN 0-672-97612-9); pap. 5.00 answer bk o.p. (ISBN 0-672-97613-7). Bobbs.

--Drafting Technology Problems. 2nd ed. 1981. pap. write for info. (ISBN 0-672-97701-X); write for info. answer bk. (ISBN 0-672-97864-4). Bobbs.

Gergely, J., ed. Immunology 1978. (Illus.). 532p. 1978. 45.00x (ISBN 963-05-1878-3). Intl Pubns Serv.

Gergely, J., jt. ed. see Baum, H.

Gergely, T. E., ed. see IUA Symposium, College Park, Md., Aug. 7-10, 1979.

Gergely, Tibor. Scuffy the Tugboat. (Illus.). (ps-1). 1972. PLB 5.38 (ISBN 0-307-68928-X, Golden Pr). Western Pub.

Gergely, Tibor, illus. Great Big Book of Bedtime Stories. (Illus.). (ps-2). 1972. 7.95 (ISBN 0-307-16529-9, Golden Pr); PLB 7.62 o.p. (ISBN 0-307-66529-1). Western Pub.

--Great Big Fire Engine Book. (Illus.). (gr. k-2). 1950. 1.95 (ISBN 0-307-10470-2, Golden Pr); PLB 7.62 (ISBN 0-307-60470-5). Western Pub.

Gergen, K. J., jt. auth. see Bauer, R. A.

Gergen, Kenneth J. Psychology of Behavior Exchange. Kiesler, Charles A., ed. (Topics in Social Psychology Ser). 1969. pap. text ed. 6.95 (ISBN 0-201-02350-4). A-W.

Gergen, Kenneth J., et al, eds. Social Exchange: Advances in Theory & Research. 320p. 1980. 24.50 (ISBN 0-306-40395-1, Plenum Pr). Plenum Pub.

Gerger, Dawn. Tempo World Finds, No. 6. 128p. pap. 1.50 (ISBN 0-448-05777-8, Tempo). G&D.

Gerhard, H. Harris, jt. auth. see Horvitz, Leslie.

Gerhard, P. A Guide to the Historical Geography of New Spain. (Latin America Studies: No. 14). 1972. 84.50 (ISBN 0-521-08073-8). Cambridge U Pr.

Gerhard, Poul. Pornography in Art. 1969. 18.50 (ISBN 0-910550-11-5). Elysium.

Gerhardstein, Virginia B. Dickinson's American Historical Fiction. 4th ed. LC 80-23450. 328p. 1981. 15.00 (ISBN 0-8108-1362-9). Scarecrow.

Gerhardt, Philipp, ed. Manual of Methods for General Bacteriology. (Illus.). 1981. pap. 25.00 (ISBN 0-914826-29-8); flexible bdg. 21.00 (ISBN 0-914826-30-1). Am Soc Microbio.

Gerhardt, Philipp, et al, eds. see International Spores Conference, Michigan State University.

Gerhart, Eugene C., ed. Quote It! Memorable Legal Quotations. LC 78-83771. 1969. 30.00 (ISBN 0-87632-001-9). Boardman.

Gerhart, Gail M. Black Power in South Africa: The Evolution of an Ideology. LC 75-13149. (Perspectives on Southern Africa Ser.: Vol. 19). 1978. 16.50x (ISBN 0-520-03022-2, CAL 423); pap. 5.95 (ISBN 0-520-03933-5). U of Cal Pr.

Gerhold, H. D., et al, eds. The Breeding of Pest Resistant Trees. 1966. 64.00 (ISBN 0-08-011764-3). Pergamon.

Gerin, Winifred. Elizabeth Gaskell. (Ser. K). (Illus.). 352p. 1980. pap. 9.95 (ISBN 0-19-281296-3). Oxford U Pr.

--Horatia Nelson. 1970. 19.50x (ISBN 0-19-822331-5). Oxford U Pr.

Geringer, Laura. Lincoln Institute of Land Policy. (Illus.). (gr. 2-5). 1978. 6.95 (ISBN 0-8038-6747-6). Hastings.

Gerischer, Heinz. Advances in Electrochemistry & Electrochemical Engineering, Vol. 12. Tobias, Charles W., ed. 40404p. 1981. write for info. (ISBN 0-471-87530-9, Pub. by Wiley-Interscience). Wiley.

Gerischer, Heinz & Tobias, Charles W., eds. Advances in Electrochemistry & Electrochemical Engineering. LC 61-15021. Vol. 10, 1977. 42.50 (ISBN 0-471-87527-9, Pub. by Wiley-Interscience); Vol. 11, 1978. 37.50 (ISBN 0-471-87528-7). Wiley.

Gerking, Shelby D., ed. Ecology of Freshwater Fish Production. LC 77-92407. 1978. 61.95 (ISBN 0-470-99362-6). Halsted Pr.

Gerlach, J., jt. auth. see Kuhlenbeck, H.

Gerlach, J., ed. see Kuhlenbeck, H.

Gerlach, John & Gerlach, Lana. The Critical Index: A Bibliography of Articles on Film in English, 1946-1973 - Arranged by Names & Topics. Milic, Louis T., ed. LC 74-1959. 1974. text ed. 20.00 o.p. (ISBN 0-8077-2442-4); pap. text ed. 9.25x (ISBN 0-8077-2438-6). Tchrs Coll.

Gerlach, Lana, jt. auth. see Gerlach, John.

Gerlach, Larry R. Prologue to Independence: New Jersey in the Coming of the American Revolution. 1976. 33.00 (ISBN 0-8135-0801-0). Rutgers U Pr.

Gerlach, Luther P. & Hine, Virginia H. People, Power, Change: Movements of Social Transformation. LC 70-109434. 1970. pap. 6.50 (ISBN 0-672-60613-5). Bobbs.

Gerlach, Rex. Creative Fly Tying & Fishing. 1974. 13.95 (ISBN 0-87691-122-X). Winchester Pr.

Gerlach, Vernon S. & Ely, Donald P. Teaching & Media: A Systematic Approach. LC 71-138476. (Illus.). 1971. ref. ed. 17.95x o.p. (ISBN 0-13-891333-1). P-H.

--Teaching & Media: A Systematic Approach. 2nd ed. (Illus.). 1980. text ed. 18.95 (ISBN 0-13-891358-7). P-H.

Gerli, E. Michael. Alfonso Martinez De Toledo. LC 76-4556. (World Authors Ser: No. 398). 1976. lib. bdg. 12.50 (ISBN 0-8057-9239-2). Twayne.

Gerloch, M. & Slade, R. C. Ligand-Field Parameters. LC 72-93139. (Illus.). 250p. 1973. 42.50 (ISBN 0-521-20137-3). Cambridge U Pr.

Gerlovich, Jack A., ed. Better Science Through Safety. 160p. 1981. text ed. 6.00 (ISBN 0-8138-1780-3). Iowa St U Pr.

Germain, Carel B., ed. Social Work Practice: People & Environments. Orig. Title: Ecological Perspective in Social Work Practice. 1979. 22.50x (ISBN 0-231-04332-5); pap. 10.00x (ISBN 0-231-04333-3). Columbia U Pr.

Germain, Carol P., jt. auth. see Smith, Dorothy.

Germain, Edward, ed. Blues Anthology. 1981. 15.00x (ISBN 0-916156-50-8); pap. 6.50x (ISBN 0-916156-49-4). Cherry Valley.

Germain, Edward, ed. see Crosby, Harry.

Germain, Jocelyn P. & Turvey, David J. Preparatory Techniques in Histology. 1981. text ed. price not set. Butterworth.

Germain, Saint. Intermediate Studies in Alchemy. new ed. LC 74-82295. (Alchemy Ser.). (Illus.). 132p. 1975. pap. 3.95 (ISBN 0-916766-01-2). Summit Univ.

German, Donald R. & German, Joan W. How to Find a Job When Jobs Are Hard to Find. 387p. 1981. 14.95 (ISBN 0-8144-5677-4). Am Mgmt.

German, Gene A., jt. auth. see Leed, Theodore W.

German, Jerry B. Polluted Nursery Rhymes. 1974. pap. 2.50 o.p. (ISBN 0-682-47864-4). Exposition.

German, Joan W. The Money Book. (Illus.). 32p. (ps-2). 1981. 5.95 (ISBN 0-525-66726-1). Elsevier-Nelson.

--What Am I? LC 78-73531. (Illus.). (ps-2). Date not set. price not set (ISBN 0-89799-163-X); pap. price not set (ISBN 0-89799-081-1). Dandelion Pr. Postponed.

German, Joan W., jt. auth. see German, Donald R.

German, Paul M. How to Win the Small Business Game. (Illus.). 182p. (Orig.). 1981. 16.95 (ISBN 0-9605436-1-9); pap. 12.95 (ISBN 0-9605436-0-0). Small Busn Pubns.

German Section of Oxford Pr Dictionary Department, ed. see Pheby, John.

German Society for Documentation. International Symposium on Patent Information & Documentation, May 16 to May 18, 1977, Munich. 479p. 1978. 65.00 (ISBN 0-89664-047-7, Pub. by K G Saur). Gale.

Germann, A. C., et al. Introduction to Law Enforcement & Criminal Justice. rev. ed. (Illus.). 400p. 1980. 11.75 (ISBN 0-398-03799-X). C C Thomas.

Germano, Joseph & Schmitt, Conrad. Schaum's Outline of Italian Grammar. 2nd ed. (Schaum's Outline Ser.). 288p. 1981. pap. 4.95 (ISBN 0-07-023031-5, SP). McGraw.

Germano, William P. & Lecyn, Nancy, eds. Directory of Social & Health Agencies of New York City: 1981-1982. 576p. 1981. 32.50x (ISBN 0-231-05134-4); pap. text ed. 24.00x (ISBN 0-231-05135-2). Columbia U Pr.

Germany, Jo. City of Golden Cages. LC 78-3967. 1978. 7.95 o.p. (ISBN 0-312-14115-7). St Martin.

Germany, Lucille, jt. auth. see Sumrall, Velma.

Germino, Dante. Machiavelli to Marx: Modern Western Political Thought. LC 77-181415. 1979. 8.50x (ISBN 0-226-28850-1, Midway). U of Chicago Pr.

Germino, Dante L. The Italian Fascist Party in Power: A Study in Totalitarian Rule. LC 74-80551. 1971. Repr. 16.50 (ISBN 0-86527-108-9). Fertig.

Germogenova, O. A., tr. see Pozhela, J.

Gernet, Jacques. Daily Life in China in the Thirteenth Century. 1962. 4.95 o.s.i. (ISBN 0-02-543060-2). Macmillan.

--A History of Chinese Civilization. Foster, J. R., tr. (Illus.). 750p. (Orig.). 1980. lib. bdg. cancelled (ISBN 0-89158-992-9); pap. cancelled (ISBN 0-89158-995-3). Westview.

Gernhardt, Robert. One More Makes Four. Taylor, Elizabeth W., tr. (Illus.). 32p. (gr. k up). 1981. 9.95 (ISBN 0-224-01577-X, Pub. by Chatto-Bodley-Jonathan). Merrimack Bk Serv.

Gernsheim, Helmut. Julia Margaret Cameron: Her Life & Photographic Work. LC 73-85258. (Illus.). 128p. 1974. 25.00 o.p. (ISBN 0-912334-50-9); pap. 14.50 o.p. (ISBN 0-912334-51-7). Aperture.

Gero, Ihan. Il Prime Libre de' Madrigali Italiani et Canzoni Francese a due Voci: Masters & Monuments of the Renaissance, Vol. 1. Bernstein, Lawrence F. & Haar, James, eds. xliv, 213p. 1980. 35.00x (ISBN 0-8450-7301-X). Broude.

Gero, John S. & Cowan, H. J. Design of Building Frames. LC 75-28388. 1976. 57.95 (ISBN 0-470-29683-6). Halsted Pr.

Gero, John S., ed. Computer Applications in Architecture. (Illus.). 1977. 77.70x (ISBN 0-85334-737-9, Pub. by Applied Science). Burgess-Intl Ideas.

Geroch, Robert. General Relativity from A to B. (Illus.). 238p. 1981. pap. 4.95 (ISBN 0-226-28864-1). U of Chicago Pr.

--General Relativity from A to B. pap. 4.95 (ISBN 0-226-28864-1). U of Chicago Pr.

Gerold, T. Histoire De la Musique Des Origines a la Fin Du 14th Siecle. LC 78-162869. (Music Ser). (Fr). 1971. Repr. of 1936 ed. lib. bdg. 49.00 (ISBN 0-306-70196-0). Da Capo.

Gerold, William. College Hill: A Photographic Study of Brown University in Its Two Hundredth Year. LC 65-20874. (Illus.). 120p. 1965. 10.00 (ISBN 0-87057-089-7, Pub. by Brown U Pr). Univ Pr of New England.

Gerolde, Steven. Universal Conversion Factors. LC 71-164900. 1971. 14.00 (ISBN 0-87814-005-0). Pennwell Pub.

Gerould, Daniel. Witkacy: A Critical Study of Stanislaw Ignacy Witkiewicz As an Imaginative Writer. LC 79-3872. (Illus.). 400p. 1981. 25.00 (ISBN 0-295-95714-X). U of Wash Pr.

Gerould, Daniel, ed. Melodrama. LC 79-52615. (New York Literary Forum Ser.). (Illus.). 296p. (Orig.). 1980. pap. 12.50x (ISBN 0-931196-06-X). NY Lit Forum.

Gerould, Daniel C., jt. auth. see Dukore, Bernard F.

Gerould, Daniel C., ed. Twentieth-Century Polish Avant-Garde Drama: Plays, Scenarios, Documents. LC 76-13659. (Illus.). 1977. 18.50x (ISBN 0-8014-0952-7). Cornell U Pr.

Gerould, G. H., tr. Beowulf & Sir Gawain & the Green Knight. rev ed. 1935. 11.95 (ISBN 0-8260-3380-6). Wiley.

Gerould, Katharine F. Vain Obliations. 324p. 1980. Repr. of 1915 ed. lib. bdg. 25.00 (ISBN 0-89987-306-5). Century Bookbindery.

Gerow, Maurice, jt. auth. see Tanner, Paul.

Gerrard, Brian, et al. Interpersonal Skills for Health Professionals. (Illus.). 272p. 1980. text ed. 15.95 (ISBN 0-8359-3138-2); pap. text ed. 12.95 (ISBN 0-8359-3136-6). Reston.

Gerrard, Brian A., jt. auth. see Gray, William A.

Gerrard, Don. One Bowl: A Simple Concept for Controlling Body Weight. 1974. 5.95 o.p. (ISBN 0-394-49285-4); pap. 1.45 (ISBN 0-394-70690-0). Random.

Gerrard, Frank. Meat Technology: Practical Textbook for Student & Butcher. 5th ed. (Illus.). 1977. 27.50x (ISBN 0-7198-2607-1). Intl Ideas.

--Sausage & Small Goods Production: Practical Handbook on the Manufacture of Sausages & Other Meat-Based Products. 6th ed. (Illus.). 1976. 19.95x (ISBN 0-7198-2587-3). Intl Ideas.

Gerrard, J. W. Food Allergy. (Illus.). 312p. 1980. 28.50 (ISBN 0-398-04038-9); pap. 19.75 (ISBN 0-398-04041-9). C C Thomas.

Gerrard, James W., jt. auth. see Beck, Harry S.

Gerrard, John W. Understanding Allergies. 88p. 1977. pap. 6.95 (ISBN 0-398-02768-4). C C Thomas.

Gerras, Charles, ed. Feasting on Raw Foods. (Illus.). 1980. 14.95 (ISBN 0-87857-271-6); pap. 9.95 o.p. (ISBN 0-87857-271-6). Rodale Pr Inc.

--Rodale's Soups & Salads Cookbook & Kitchen Album. (Illus.). 352p. 1981. 14.95 (ISBN 0-87857-332-1). Rodale Pr Inc.

Gerras, Charlie, ed. see Brewer, Gail S. & Greene, Janice P.

Gerras, Charlie, ed. see Kindelehrer, Jane.

Gerrath, Jean, et al. A Plant Biology Lab Manual for a One Semester Course Form & Function. 144p. 1980. pap. text ed. 6.95 (ISBN 0-8403-2272-0). Kendall-Hunt.

Gerraughty, Robert J., ed. Pharmacy Examination Review Book Vol. 1. 7th ed. 1979. pap. 9.50 (ISBN 0-87488-421-7). Med Exam.

Gerrick, David J. Footnotes to Medicine. 172p. 1980. 10.95 (ISBN 0-686-68569-5). Dayton Labs.

--Gold Prospecting in Ohio. 84p. 1980. pap. 5.95 (ISBN 0-686-68570-9). Dayton Labs.

--Kissing Games: A Study in Fokelore. 1978. 3.00 o.p. (ISBN 0-685-30120-6). Dayton Labs.

Gerrick, David J. & Dietsche, Doreen. Old Time Cures - Farmers Folklore. 104p. (Orig.). 1980. pap. 3.95 (ISBN 0-686-68571-7). Dayton Labs.

Gerrish, Brian, ed. Reformatio Perennis: Essays on Calvin & the Reformation in Honor of Ford Lewis Battles. (Pittsburgh Theological Monograph Ser.: No. 32). 1981. pap. 12.95 (ISBN 0-915138-41-7). Pickwick.

Gerrish, F. Pure Mathematics, a University & College Course: Calculus. 1960. text ed. 28.95 (ISBN 0-521-05069-3). Cambridge U Pr.

Gerrish, H. & Dugger, W., Jr. Exploring Electricity & Electronics: Basic Fundamentals. rev. ed. LC 80-20830. (Illus.). 208p. 1981. text ed. 9.96 (ISBN 0-87006-308-1). Goodheart.

Gerrish, Howard H. Electricity. LC 77-95064. 1978. text ed. 4.80 (ISBN 0-87006-259-X). Goodheart.

Gerrish, Howard H. & Dugger, William E., Jr. Electricity & Electronics. LC 79-6345. (Illus.). 1980. text ed. 11.96 (ISBN 0-87006-310-3); lab manual 4.96 (ISBN 0-87006-263-8). Goodheart.

Gerritzen, L. & Van Der Put, M. Schottky Groups & Mumford Curves. (Lecture Notes in Mathematics: Vol. 817). 317p. 1980. pap. 19.50 (ISBN 0-387-10229-9). Springer-Verlag.

Gerrold, David. Deathbeast. 1978. pap. 1.75 o.p. (ISBN 0-445-04245-1). Popular Lib.

--The Galactic Whirlpool. (Star Trek Ser.). 240p. (Orig.). 1980. pap. 2.25 (ISBN 0-553-14242-9). Bantam.

--SF Yearbook. LC 79-63463. 1979. pap. 4.95 (ISBN 0-931064-10-4). Starlog.

--Trouble with Tribbles. pap. 2.25 (ISBN 0-345-27671-X). Ballantine.

--When Harlie Was One. 288p. 1975. pap. 1.50 o.p. (ISBN 0-345-24390-0). Ballantine.

Gerrold, David & Niven, Larry. The Flying Sorcerers. (A Del Rey Bk.). 1977. pap. 1.95 (ISBN 0-345-28039-3). Ballantine.

Gerrold, David, ed. Ascents of Wonder. 1977. pap. 1.50 o.p. (ISBN 0-445-04128-5). Popular Lib.

Gerry De La Ree, ed. The Art of the Fantastic. (Illus.). 1978. 15.50 (ISBN 0-938192-00-0). De La Ree.

--Beauty & the Beasts: The Art of Hannes Bok. 1978. 15.50 o.p. (ISBN 0-686-12087-6). De La Ree.

--Fifth Book of Virgil Finlay. (Illus.). 1979. 15.75 (ISBN 0-938192-02-7). De La Ree.

--The Fourth Book of Virgil Finlay. (Illus.). 1979. 15.50 o.p. (ISBN 0-686-15703-6). De La Ree.

--More Fantasy by Fabian. (Illus.). 1979. 15.75 (ISBN 0-938192-05-1). De La Ree.

--Third Book of Virgil Finlay. (Illus.). 1979. 15.50 (ISBN 0-938192-07-8). De La Ree.

Gerry De La Ree & Nigra, Gene, eds. A Hannes Bok Sketchbook. 1976. 7.50 o.p. (ISBN 0-938192-04-3). De La Ree.

Gerschenkron, Alexander. Europe in the Russian Mirror. LC 76-96090. 1970. 23.95 (ISBN 0-521-07721-4). Cambridge U Pr.

Gersh, Harry. Animals Next Door: A Guide to Zoos & Aquariums of the Americas. LC 71-104745. (Orig.). 1971. pap. 4.50x (ISBN 0-8303-0088-0, Acad Edns). Fleet.

Gersh, Isidore, ed. Submicroscopic Cytochemistry, 2vols. Incl. Vol. 1. Protein & Nucleic Acids. 1974. 49.25 (ISBN 0-12-281401-0); Vol.2. Membranes,Mitochondria, & Connective Tissue. 1974. 36.50 (ISBN 0-12-281402-9). Set. 70.50 (ISBN 0-685-40610-5). Acad Pr.

Gersh, Marvin J. & Litt, Iris F. The Handbook of Adolescence: A Medical Guide for Parents & Teenagers. LC 77-151288. 256p. (Orig.). 1980. pap. 5.95 (ISBN 0-8128-6070-5). Stein & Day.

Gershator, David. Play Mas. 92p. (Orig.). 1981. pap. 3.00 (ISBN 0-917402-14-6). Downtown Poets.

Gershator, Phillis. A Bibliographic Guide to the Literature of Contemporary American Poetry, 1970-1975. LC 76-41812. 1976. 10.00 (ISBN 0-8108-0987-7). Scarecrow.

--Honi & His Magic Circle. (Illus.). (gr. k-4). 1979. 6.95 (ISBN 0-8276-0167-0). Jewish Pubn.

Gershenfeld, Matti, jt. auth. see Napier, Rodney.

Gershenfeld, Matti K., jt. auth. see Napier, Rodney W.

Gershenfeld, Walter J, et al. Scope of Public Sector Bargaining. LC 76-53904. 1977. 18.95 (ISBN 0-669-01298-X). Lexington Bks.

Gershenson, Milton G. & Birzon, Paul I., eds. New York Matrimonial Practice Under Equitable Distribution: Course Handbook. LC 80-83148. 364p. 1980. pap. 25.00 (ISBN 0-686-69170-9, F4-3706). PLI.
Gershenzon, M. O. Mechta I Mysl I. S. Turgeneva. LC 74-119760. (Slavic Reprint Ser.: No. 8). 169p. (Rus.). 1970. pap. 4.00 (ISBN 0-87057-124-9, Pub. by Brown U Pr). Univ Pr of New England.
Gershman, Carl. The Foreign Policy of American Labor. LC 75-33469. (The Washington Papers: No. 29). 1975. 3.50x (ISBN 0-8039-0572-6). Sage.
Gershon, Anne A., ed. see Symposium by the New York University Medical Center & the National Foundation-March of Dimes, New York City, Mar. 1975.
Gershon, Michael & Biller, Henry B. The Other Helpers. LC 76-55535. (Illus.). 1977. 22.95 (ISBN 0-669-01317-X). Lexington Bks.
Gershon, S. & Raskin, A., eds. Genesis & Treatment of Psychologic Disorders in the Elderly: Aging, Vol. 2. LC 75-14573. 288p. 1975. 27.00 (ISBN 0-89004-004-4). Raven.
Gershon-Cohen, Jacob, jt. auth. see Ingleby, Helen.
Gershoy, Leo. Bertrand Barere: A Reluctant Terrorist. 1962. 25.00 o.p. (ISBN 0-691-05105-4). Princeton U Pr.
Gershuni, G. Z. & Zhukovitskii, E. M. Convective Stability of Incompressable Fluids. 1976. 41.95 o.p. (ISBN 0-470-98981-5). Halsted Pr.
Gershuny, J. After Industrial Society? The Emerging Self-Service Economy. 1978. text ed. 20.75x (ISBN 0-391-00837-4); pap. text ed. 7.75x (ISBN 0-391-00847-1). Humanities.
Gershwin, M. Eric. Bronchial Asthma: Principles of Diagnosis & Treatment. 1981. write for info. (ISBN 0-8089-1331-X). Grune.
Gershwin, M. Eric, ed. see International Symposium of the American Society of Zoologists, Toronto, December 27-30, 1977.
Gersmehl, Phillip, et al. Physical Geography. LC 78-12212. 415p. 1980. text ed. 15.95 (ISBN 0-03-014476-0, HoltC). HR&W.
Gerson & Ter Kuile. Art & Architecture in Belgium: 1600 to 1800. (Pelican History of Art Ser.: No. 18). 1978. 40.00 (ISBN 0-670-13380-9). Viking Pr.
Gerson, Benjamin & Anhalt, John P. High Pressure Liquid Chromatography & Therapeutic Drug Monitoring. LC 80-16443. (Illus.). 1980. pap. text ed. 35.00 (ISBN 0-89189-077-7, 45-2-037-00). Am Soc Clinical.
Gerson, Corinne. Choices. (Orig.). 1980. pap. 1.75 (ISBN 0-505-51476-1). Tower Bks.
--How I Put My Mother Through College. LC 80-21681. 144p. (gr. 4-8). 1981. PLB 8.95 (ISBN 0-689-30810-8). Atheneum.
Gerson, Corrine. Passing Through. (YA) (gr. 7-12). 1980. pap. 1.50 (ISBN 0-440-96958-1, LFL). Dell.
Gerson, Cyrelle K. More Than Dispensing. LC 80-65958. 120p. 1980. 24.00 (ISBN 0-917330-31-5). Am Pharm Assn.
Gerson, Menachem. Family, Women, & Socialization in the Kibbutz. LC 78-57188. (Illus.). 1978. 17.95 (ISBN 0-669-02371-X). Lexington Bks.
Gerson, Noel. The Smugglers. LC 77-8162. 1977. 8.95 o.s.i. (ISBN 0-690-01468-6, TYC-T). T Y Crowell.
--The Swamp Fox, Francis Marion. 1980. pap. 2.25 (ISBN 0-89176-001-6, 6001). Mockingbird Bks.
Gerson, Noel B. Franklin, America's "Lost State". LC 68-19819. (Illus.). (gr. 7-10). 1968. 3.50 o.s.i. (ISBN 0-02-735920-4, CCPr). Macmillan.
--The Glorious Scoundrel: A Biography of Captain John Smith. LC 78-1357. (Illus.). 1978. 7.95 (ISBN 0-396-07518-5). Dodd.
Gersoni-Edelman, Diane. Work-Wise: Learning Bout the World from Books--Critical Guide to Bool Selection & Usage. LC 79-11920. (Selection Guide Ser.: No. 3). 258p. 1980. 16.50 (ISBN 0-87436-264-4, Co-Pub. by Neal-Schuman). ABC-Clio.
Gerstacker, Friedrich. Die Flussbpiraten Des Mississippi. (Insel Taschenbuecher: It 435). (Illus.). 551p. (Ger.). 1980. pap. text ed. 7.80 (ISBN 3-458-32135-7, Pub. by Insel Verlag Germany). Suhrkamp.
Gerstein, Melvin see Heat Transfer & Fluid Mechanics Institute.
Gersten, Irene & Bliss, Betsy. Ecidujerp-Prejudice: Either Way It Doesn't Make Sense. LC 73-10371. (Illus.). 96p. (gr. 4-7). 1974. PLB 3.90 o.p. (ISBN 0-531-02669-8). Watts.
Gerstenberg, Alice. Overtones. (Playbooks). 1.25 o.p. (ISBN 0-679-39054-5). McKay.
Gerstenberger, Donna. The Complex Configuration: Modern Verse Drama. (Salzburg Studies in English Literature, Poetic Drama & Poetic Theory: No. 5). 178p. 1973. pap. text ed. 25.00x (ISBN 0-391-01383-1). Humanities.
--John Millington Synge. (English Authors Ser.: No. 12). 1964. lib. bdg. 10.95 (ISBN 0-8057-1532-0). Twayne.
Gerstenberger, Donna & Hendrick, George. The American Novel, 1789 to 1959, 2 vols. LC 61-9356. 333p. 1961. Vol. 1. 12.50 o.p. (ISBN 0-8040-0007-7); Vol. 1. pap. 9.95x (ISBN 0-8040-0006-9). Swallow.
--Fourth Directory of Periodicals: Publishing Articles in English & American Literature & Language- LC 74-21506. 234p. 1974. 18.95x (ISBN 0-8040-0675-X); pap. 9.95x (ISBN 0-8040-0676-8). Swallow.
Gerstenfeld, Arthur. Innovation: A Study of Technological Policy. 1976. pap. text ed. 9.75x (ISBN 0-8191-0037-4). U Pr of Amer.
Gerstenzang, Adolph. Learn Touch Typing in Four Easy Lessons. (Secretarial Paperback Ser). (Illus.). 1968. pap. 1.50 o.p. (ISBN 0-8069-7404-4). Sterling.
Gerster, Patrick & Cords, Nicholas. Myth in American History. 1977. pap. text ed. 7.95x (ISBN 0-02-473290-7). Macmillan.
Gerster, Patrick, jt. auth. see Cords, Nicholas.
Gersting, Judith L. & Kuczkowski. Yes-No, Stop-Go: Some Patterns in Mathematic Logic. LC 76-46376. (Young Math Ser.). (Illus.). (gr. k-3). 1977. PLB 7.89 (ISBN 0-690-01130-X, TYC-J). T Y Crowell.
Gerstl, Joel & Jacobs, G., eds. Professions for the People: The Politics of Skill. 1976. text ed. 11.95 (ISBN 0-470-29702-6); pap. 5.95 o.p. (ISBN 0-470-29703-4). Halsted Pr.
Gerstle, Kurt H. Basic Structural Analysis. (Civil Engineering & Engineering Mechanics Ser). (Illus.). 560p. 1973. ref. ed. 27.95 (ISBN 0-13-069393-6). P-H.
Gerstner, Hugo. Mankind's Quest for Identity. 1981. 22.50 (ISBN 0-930376-23-4). Pathotox Pubs.
Gerstner, John. Bible Inerrancy Primer. Date not set. pap. 1.95 (ISBN 0-88469-144-6). BMH Bks.
--Predestination Primer. Date not set. pap. 1.95 (ISBN 0-88469-145-4). BMH Bks.
--Reconciliation Primer. Date not set. pap. 1.95 (ISBN 0-88469-143-8). BMH Bks.
Gerstner, Karl. Compendium for Literates: The Systematics of Writing. Stephenson, Dennis Q., tr. from Ger. LC 73-21246. 180p. 1974. 17.50 (ISBN 0-262-07061-8); pap. 10.00 (ISBN 0-262-57055-6). MIT Pr.
Gersuni, G. V., ed. Sensory Processes at the Neuronal & Behavioral Levels. 1971. 46.50 (ISBN 0-12-281350-2). Acad Pr.
Gersuny, Carl. Work Hazards & Industrial Conflict. LC 80-51506. (Illus.). 200p. 1981. 12.00 (ISBN 0-87451-189-5). U Pr of New Eng.
Gersuny, Carl, jt. auth. see Poggie, John J.
Gersuny, Carl, et al. Some Effects of Technological Change on New England Fishermen. (Marine Technical Report Ser.: No. 42). 1975. pap. 1.00 (ISBN 0-938412-14-0). URI MAS.
Gert, Bernard, ed. Man & Citizen: Thomas Hobbes De Homine. Wood, Charles T., tr. 1972. pap. text ed. 5.95x (ISBN 0-391-00849-8). Humanities.
Gerth, Donald R. & Haehn, James O. An Invisible Giant: The California State Colleges. LC 79-173855. (Higher Education Ser.). 1971. 14.95x o.p. (ISBN 0-87589-110-1). Jossey-Bass.
Gertler, M. & White, P. D. Coronary Heart Disease: A Twenty-Five Year Study in Retrospect. 1976. 29.95 (ISBN 0-87489-093-4). Med Economics.
Gertman, Paul M., jt. auth. see Egdahl, Richard H.
Gertman, Paul M., jt. ed. see Egdahl, Richard H.
Gertman, Stuart A. And You Shall Teach Them Diligently: A Study of the Current State of Religious Education in the Reform Movement. 1977. pap. 5.00 (ISBN 0-8074-0052-1, 383760). UAHC.
Gertner, Richard, ed. Motion Picture Almanac, 1981, Vol. 52. 716p. 1981. 38.00 (ISBN 0-900610-23-9). Quigley Pub Co.
--Television Almanac, 1981, Vol. 26. 650p. 1981. 38.00 (ISBN 0-900610-25-5). Quigley Pub Co.
Gertz, Elmer & Pisciotte, Joe. Charter for a New Age: An Inside View of the Sixth Illinois Constitutional Convention. LC 80-10837. (Studies in Illinois Constitution Making Ser.). 368p. 1980. 15.00 (ISBN 0-252-00820-0). U of Ill Pr.
Gertzel, Cherry. Party & Locality in Northern Uganda, 1945-1962. (Commonwealth Papers Ser: No. 16). (Illus.). 100p. 1974. pap. text ed. 8.75x (ISBN 0-485-17616-5, Athlone Pr). Humanities.
Gertzog, Irvin N. Readings on State & Local Government. (Foundation of Modern Political Science Ser). 1970. pap. 10.95 ref. ed. (ISBN 0-13-761106-4). P-H.
Gert zur Heide, Karl. Deep South Piano. (The Paul Oliver Blues Ser.). pap. 2.95 (ISBN 0-913714-32-1). Legacy Bks.
Gerulskis-Estes, Susan. The Book of Tarot. 96p. 1981. pap. 5.95 (ISBN 0-87100-162-4). Morgan.
Gervasi, Tom. Arsenal of Democracy: American Weapons Available for Export. rev. ed. LC 80-993. (Illus.). 1981. pap. 9.95 (ISBN 0-394-17662-6, E760, Ever). Grove.
Gervers, Michael, ed. The Cartulary of the Order of St. John of Jerusalem (Hospitalers) in England. (Records of Social & Economic History Ser.). 618p. 1980. 169.00 (ISBN 0-19-725996-0). Oxford U Pr.
Gerwick, Ben C. Construction of Prestressed Concrete Structures. LC 71-140176. (Practical Construction Guides Ser). 1971. 28.95 (ISBN 0-471-29710-0, Pub. by Wiley-Interscience). Wiley.
Gerwig, Norma, jt. auth. see King, Virginia.
Gerwin, Donald. Budgeting Public Funds: The Decision Process in the Urban School District. LC 69-17326. 1969. 17.50x (ISBN 0-299-05270-2). U of Wis Pr.
--The Employment of Teachers. LC 73-20854. 1974. 20.00x (ISBN 0-8211-0610-4); text ed. 18.00x (ISBN 0-685-42632-7). McCutchan.
Gerwin, K. S. & Glorig, A. Detection of Hearing Loss & Ear Disease in Children. (Illus.). 208p. 1974. 16.75 (ISBN 0-398-03175-4). C C Thomas.
Gerwin, Kenneth S., ed. see Glorig, Aram.
Gery, Jacques. Characoids of the World. (Illus.). 1978. 20.00 (ISBN 0-87666-458-3, H-961). TFH Pubns.
Gerzon, Mark F., jt. ed. see Hiatt, Thomas A.
Geschickter, Charles F. & Cannon, Albert. Color Atlas of Pathology, Vol. 3. LC 50-58214. 1963. 41.00 o.p. (ISBN 0-397-50091-2). Lippincott.
Geschwender, J. A. Class, Race & Worker Insurgency: LC 76-62581. (ASA Rose Monographs). (Illus.). 1977. 22.95 (ISBN 0-521-21584-6); pap. 6.95x (ISBN 0-521-29191-7). Cambridge U Pr.
Gesell, Arnold. Atlas of Infant Behavior, Vol. 2. (Illus.). 1934. 125.00x (ISBN 0-685-69821-1). Elliots Bks.
Gesenius, William. Hebrew & Chaldee Lexicon, Tregelles Translation. 1949. 11.95 (ISBN 0-8028-8029-0). Eerdmans.
Gesner, Carol. Shakespeare & the Greek Romance: A Study of Origins. LC 70-11509. 232p. 1970. 11.00x (ISBN 0-8131-1220-6). U Pr of Ky.
Gesner, Clark. You're a Good Man, Charlie Brown. 1978. pap. 1.50 (ISBN 0-449-23354-5, Crest). Fawcett.
Gessa, G. L., jt. ed. see Costa, E.
Gessa, G. L., jt. ed. see Sandler, M.
Gessner, Robert. Massacre: A Survey of Today's American Indian. LC 72-38831. (Civil Liberties in American History Ser). 418p. 1972. Repr. of 1931 ed. lib. bdg. 35.00 (ISBN 0-306-70445-5). Da Capo.
Gessner, Urs, jt. auth. see Talbot, Samuel A.
Gesualda Of The Holy Spirit, Sr. Saint Theresa, the Little Flower. (Illus.). 1960. 4.95 o.s.i. (ISBN 0-8198-0142-9). Dghtrs St Paul.
Getchell, Robert. Alice Doesn't Live Here Anymore. 128p. 1975. pap. 1.50 o.s.i. (ISBN 0-446-88418-9). Warner Bks.
Getches, David H., et al. Cases & Materials on Federal Indian Law. LC 79-3906. (American Casebook Ser.). 600p. 1979. text ed. 19.95 (ISBN 0-8299-2027-7). West Pub.
Gethers, Judith. The Fabulous Food Processor. 384p. (Orig.). 1981. pap. 7.95 (ISBN 0-345-29586-2). Ballantine.
Gethers, Peter S. The Dandy. 1978. 8.95 o.p. (ISBN 0-525-08852-0). Dutton.
Getis, A. & Boots, B. Models of Spatial Processes. LC 75-17118. (Cambridge Geographical Studies Ser.: No.8). 1978. 29.95x (ISBN 0-521-20983-8). Cambridge U Pr.
Getlein, Frank. Mary Cassatt: Paintings & Prints. LC 80-66523. (Illus.). 160p. 1980. 22.50 (ISBN 0-89659-181-6); pap. 14.95 (ISBN 0-89659-155-7). Abbeville Pr.
Getsi, Lucia, tr. Georg Trakl: Poems. LC 73-79473. xi, 173p. 1973. pap. 11.00 (ISBN 0-8214-0174-2). Ohio U Pr.
Gettens, Rutherford J. & Stout, George L. Painting Materials: A Short Encyclopedia. (Illus.). 1965. pap. 4.50 (ISBN 0-486-21597-0). Dover.
Gettings, Fred. Arthur Rackham. LC 75-21767. (Illus.). 192p. 1976. 20.00 o.s.i. (ISBN 0-02-543080-7). Macmillan.
--Dictionary of Occult, Hermetic & Alchemical Sigils. 1981. 34.95 (ISBN 0-7100-0095-2). Routledge & Kegan. Postponed.
Gettleman, Barry, jt. auth. see Prager, Audrey.
Gettleman, Marvin E. The Dorr Rebellion: A Study in American Radicalism: 1833-1849. LC 79-1205. 296p. 1980. Repr. of 1973 ed. lib. bdg. 11.50 (ISBN 0-88275-894-2). Krieger.
--An Elusive Presence: The Discovery of John H. Finley & His America. LC 79-10547. (Illus.). 1979. 15.95 (ISBN 0-88229-312-5); pap. 8.95 (ISBN 0-88229-695-7). Nelson-Hall.
Getty, David J. & Howard, James H., Jr. Auditory & Visual Pattern Recognition. 240p. 1981. professional ref. text 16.50 (ISBN 0-89859-087-6). L Erlbaum Assocs.
Getty, Kathleen & Humphries, Winifred. Understanding the Family. 608p. 1981. pap. 12.95 (ISBN 0-8385-9265-1). ACC.
Getty, Mary A. Philippians & Philemon. (New Testament Message Ser.). 9.95 (ISBN 0-89453-137-9); pap. 4.95 (ISBN 0-89453-202-2). M Glazier.
Getz, Arthur. Hamilton Duck. (Illus.). 32p. (ps-2). 1972. PLB 7.62 (ISBN 0-307-62055-7, Golden Pr). Western Pub.
--Hamilton Duck's Springtime Story. (Illus.). 32p. (gr. k-3). 1974. PLB 7.62 (ISBN 0-307-62048-4, Golden Pr). Western Pub.
Getz, Donald J. & McGraw, Lora. Vision Training for Better Learning. 1981. spiral bound 12.95 (ISBN 0-87804-430-2). Mafex.
Getz, Gene. Loving One Another. 1979. pap. 3.50 (ISBN 0-88207-786-4). Victor Bks.
--A Profile for a Christian Life Style: Titus. pap. 2.95 (ISBN 0-310-25092-7). Zondervan.
Getz, Gene, tr. Vers la Stature Parfaite De Jesus-Christ. (French Bks.). (Fr.). 1979. 1.95 (ISBN 0-8297-0820-0). Vida Pub.
Getz, Gene A. Building up One Another. 1976. pap. 3.50 (ISBN 0-88207-744-9). Victor Bks.
--Encouraging One Another. 1981. pap. 3.95 (ISBN 0-88207-256-0). Victor Bks.
--Measure of a Family. LC 76-46872. (Orig.). 1977. pap. 2.95 (ISBN 0-8307-0445-0, 50-150-06). Regal.
--Measure of a Man: A Practical Guide to Christian Maturity. LC 74-175983. (Orig.). 1974. pap. 2.95 (ISBN 0-8307-0291-1, 50-121-04). Regal.
--The Measure of a Marriage Workbook. 96p. 1980. lab manual 5.95 (ISBN 0-8307-0756-5). Regal.
--The Measure of a Woman. LC 77-7433. (Orig.). 1977. pap. 2.50 (ISBN 0-8307-0537-6, 50-161-18). Regal.
--Moses: Moments of Glory, Feet of Clay. LC 75-23519. (Orig.). 1976. pap. 3.25 o.p. (ISBN 0-8307-0400-0, 54-032-00); study guide 1.39 o.p. (ISBN 0-8307-0514-7, 61-003-09). Regal.
--Nehemiah: A Man of Prayer & Persistence. LC 80-53102. 1981. pap. 4.95 (ISBN 0-8307-0778-6). Regal.
Getz, Jerome L., tr. see Nelson, Alvar.
Getz, Lorine M. Flannery O'Connor: Her Life, Library & Book Reviews. (Studies in Women & Religion: Vol. 5). 1980. soft cover 24.95x (ISBN 0-88946-997-0). E Mellen.
Getz, Malcolm, jt. auth. see Watson, Donald S.
Getzels, Jacob W. & Csikszentmihalyi, Mihaly. The Creative Vision: A Longitudinal Study of Problem Finding in Art. LC 76-16862. 304p. 1976. 24.95 (ISBN 0-471-01486-9, Pub. by Wiley-Interscience). Wiley.
Getzels, Jacob W., jt. ed. see Taylor, Irving A.
Getzels, Judith, et al, eds. Rural & Small Town Planning. LC 79-93345. (Illus.). 326p. (Orig.). 1980. pap. 12.95 (ISBN 0-918286-19-0). Planners Pr.
Geumlek, Lois. Stranger in Town. (YA) 4.95 o.p. (ISBN 0-685-07460-9, Avalon). Bouregy.
Geurts, Reiner. Hair Colour in the Horse. Dent, Anthony, tr. from Dutch. (Illus.). pap. 8.75 (ISBN 0-85131-290-X). J A Allen.
Gewehr. The Great Awakening in Virginia. Repr. 12.00 (ISBN 0-686-12354-9). Church History.
Gewirth, Alan. Reason & Morality. 416p. 1981. pap. 9.95x (ISBN 0-226-28876-5). U of Chicago Pr.
--Reason & Morality. pap. 9.95 (ISBN 0-226-28876-5). U of Chicago Pr.
Gewirth, Alan, tr. see Marsilius Of Padua.
Gewirtz, Herman. Essentials of Physics. rev. ed. LC 67-30941. (gr. 9-12). 1974. 12.95 (ISBN 0-8120-6062-8); pap. text ed. 6.95 (ISBN 0-8120-0278-4). Barron.
--Physics. LC 56-39359. (Regents Exams & Answer Ser.). (gr. 10-12). 1976. pap. 3.95 (ISBN 0-8120-0201-6). Barron.
Geyer, Dick. Wreck Diving. 192p. Date not set. pap. 6.95 (ISBN 0-695-81567-9, Assn Pr). Follett. Postponed.
Geyer, Grant B., jt. auth. see Bollens, John C.
Geyer, R. F. & Zouwen, J. van der, eds. Sociocybernetics, Vols. 1 & 2. 1978. Vol. 1. pap. 17.25 (ISBN 90-207-0854-6, Martinus Nijhoff Pubs); Vol. 2. pap. 17.25 (ISBN 90-207-0855-4). Kluwer Boston.
Geyman. Family Practice: Foundation of Changing Health Care. LC 79-18290. 1979. 28.50 (ISBN 0-8385-2537-7). ACC.
--Family Practice in the Medical School. 1977. 8.00 o.p. (ISBN 0-686-51335-5). ACC.
Geyman, John P. Archives of Family Practice, 1981. 448p. 1981. 36.00 (ISBN 0-8385-0325-X). ACC.
Geyman, John P., ed. Archives of Family Practice 1980. 416p. 1980. 34.50x (ISBN 0-8385-0324-1). ACC.
--Profile of the Residency-Trained Family Physician in the United States 1970-1979. 72p. 1980. pap. 7.00x (ISBN 0-8385-7961-2). ACC.

Gezi, Kal & Bradford, Ann. Beebi, the Little Blue Bell. LC 75-34179. (Illus.). (ps-3). 1976. 5.50 (ISBN 0-913778-29-X). Childs World.

Gezi, Kal, jt. auth. see Bradford, Ann.

Ghadar, Fariborz. The Evolution of OPEC Strategy. LC 76-48377. 1977. 20.50 (ISBN 0-669-01147-9). Lexington Bks.

Ghadially, F. N. Diagnostic Electron Microscopy of Tumors. LC 79-42839. 1980. text ed. 98.95 (ISBN 0-407-00156-5). Butterworths.

Ghadially, F. N., Dr. Advanced Aquarist Guide. 6.98 o.p. (ISBN 0-385-01556-9). Doubleday.

Ghadially, Feroze N. Ultrastructural Pathology of the Cell. new ed. 530p. 1975. 149.00 (ISBN 0-407-00011-9). Butterworths.

Ghadimi, Hossein. Total Parenteral Nutrition: Premises & Promises. LC 74-17152. (Clinical Pediatrics, Maternal & Child Health Ser.). 672p. 1975. 56.95 (ISBN 0-471-29719-4, Pub. by Wiley Medical). Wiley.

Ghai, O. P. & Taneja, P. N. Current Topics in Pediatrics: Abstracts of Papers from the International Congress of Pediatrics, New Delhi, India, Oct 23-29 1977. 350p. 1980. pap. 12.50x (ISBN 0-89955-324-9, Pub. by Interprint India). Intl Schol Bk Serv.

Ghai, O. P., ed. New Developments in Pediatric Research, 3 vols. 1330p. 1980. Set. 42.50x (ISBN 0-89955-325-7, Pub. by Interprint India); Set. pap. 25.00x (ISBN 0-89955-326-5). Intl Schol Bk Serv.

--Perspectives in Pediatrics. 158p. 1980. 8.50x (ISBN 0-89955-323-0, Pub. by Interprint India). Intl Schol Bk Serv.

Ghai, S. K., ed. see Powell, James N.

Ghalib, Mirza. Lighter Verses. (Translated from Urdu). 8.00 (ISBN 0-89253-756-6); flexible cloth 4.80 (ISBN 0-89253-757-4). Ind-US Inc.

--Love Poems. (Translated from Urdu). 6.75 (ISBN 0-89253-758-2); flexible cloth 4.80 (ISBN 0-89253-759-0). Ind-US Inc.

--Twenty-Five Verses. (Translated from Urdu). 6.75 (ISBN 0-89253-754-X); flexible cloth 4.80 (ISBN 0-89253-755-8). Ind-US Inc.

Ghalib, Mirza A. Whispers of the Angel (Nawa-E-Sarosh) (Illus.). 56p. 1969. 3.00 (ISBN 0-88253-384-3). Ind-US Inc.

Ghandhi, Mohandas K. The Teaching of the Gita. Hingorani, Anand T., ed. 103p. (Orig.). 1981. pap. 2.00 (ISBN 0-934676-26-7). Greenlf Bks.

Ghandhi, Sorab K. Semiconductor Power Devices: Physics of Operation & Fabrication Technology. LC 77-8019. 1977. 26.95 (ISBN 0-471-02999-8, Pub by Wiley-Interscience). Wiley.

--Theory & Practice of Microelectronics. LC 68-28501. (Illus.). 1968. 38.00 (ISBN 0-471-29718-6, Pub. by Wiley-Interscience). Wiley.

Ghandour, Mounir. Arabic Conversation. pap. 5.00; book & cassettes 30.00. Intl Bk Ctr.

--Learn Arabic Reading & Writing I. pap. 5.00; book & cassettes 30.00. Intl Bk Ctr.

Ghanem, Fathy. The Man Who Lost His Shadow. Stewart, Desmond, tr. from Arabic. 352p. (Orig.). 1980. 12.00x (ISBN 0-89410-206-0); pap. 6.00x (ISBN 0-89410-207-9). Three Continents.

Ghani, Noordin & Farrell, Edward. Microprocessor System Debugging. (Computer Engineering Ser.). 160p. 1981. 28.00 (ISBN 0-471-27860-2, Pub. by Wiley-Interscience). Wiley.

Ghatak, A. K. & Kothari, L. S. Introduction to Lattice Dynamics. 1972. 22.50 (ISBN 0-201-02363-6, Adv Bk Prog). A-W.

Ghatak, A. K., jt. auth. see Sodha, M. S.

Ghatak, Subrata. Development Economics. (Modern Economics). (Illus.). 1978. pap. text ed. 12.95 (ISBN 0-582-44874-3). Longman.

--Developmental Economics. 1979. text ed. 21.00x (ISBN 0-582-44873-5). Longman.

--Monetary Economics in Developing Countries. Date not set. 25.00 (ISBN 0-312-54418-9). St Martin.

Ghauri, M. S. The Morphology & Taxonomy of Male Scale Insects (Homoptera: Coccoidea) (Illus.). vii, 221p. 1962. 19.50x (ISBN 0-565-00580-4, Pub. by British Mus Nat Hist England). Sabbot-Natural Hist Bks.

Ghausi, M. & Laker, K. Modern Filter Design: Active RC & Switched Capacitor. 1980. 34.95 (ISBN 0-13-594663-8). P-H.

Ghazali. Book of Counsel for Kings. I, Jalal Huma & Isaacs, H. D., eds. Bagley, F. R., tr. 1964. 24.95x (ISBN 0-19-713129-8). Oxford U Pr.

Ghazanfar, S. M. Idaho Statistical Abstract, 1980. 3rd ed. 1980. 30.00x (ISBN 0-686-28924-2). Ctr Bus Devel.

Gheddo, Pierro. Why Is the Third World Poor? Sullivan, Kathryn, tr. from It. LC 72-85793. 196p. 1973. pap. 4.95x o.p. (ISBN 0-88344-757-6). Orbis Bks.

Ghelardi, Robert. Economics, Culture & Society. 1976. 12.95 o.s.i. (ISBN 0-440-02341-6). Delacorte.

Ghelderode, Michel De. Ghelderode: Seven Plays, Vol. 1. Incl. Chronicles of Hell; Barabbas; The Women at the Tomb; Pantagleize; The Blind Men; Three Actors & Their Drama; Lord Halewyn. 304p. (Orig.). 1960. pap. 4.95 (ISBN 0-8090-0719-3, Mermaid). Hill & Wang.

Ghent, Dorothy Van see Van Ghent, Dorothy.

Gheorghiu, A. & Dragomir, V., eds. Geometry of Structural Forms. (Illus.). 1978. 51.30x (ISBN 0-85334-683-6, Pub. by Applied Science). Burgess-Intl Ideas.

Ghidalia, Vic, jt. ed. see Elwood, Roger.

Ghirardo, Diane, tr. see Eisenman, Peter D. & Rossi, Aldo.

Ghirelli, Michael, ed. List of Emigrants from England to America 1682-1692. LC 68-15793. 1968. 10.00 (ISBN 0-685-32673-X). C E Tuttle.

Ghiretti, F., ed. Physiology & Biochemistry of Haemocyanins. LC 68-17675. (Illus.). 1968. 18.00 (ISBN 0-12-281550-5). Acad Pr.

Ghisalberti, Emilio L., jt. auth. see Frigerio, Alberto.

Ghiselin, Brewster. Windrose. (University of Utah Press Poetry Series). 252p. 1980. 15.00 (ISBN 0-87480-167-2). U of Utah Pr.

Ghiselin, Michael T. The Economy of Nature & the Evolution of Sex. 1974. 21.50x (ISBN 0-520-02474-5). U of Cal Pr.

Ghiselli, Edwin E., et al. Measurement Theory for the Behavioral Sciences. LC 80-27069. (Psychology Ser.). (Illus.). 1981. text ed. 21.95x (ISBN 0-7167-1048-X); pap. text ed. 13.95 (ISBN 0-7167-1252-0). W H Freeman.

Ghista, D. Biomechanics of Medical Devices. 1981. 95.00 (ISBN 0-8247-6848-5). Dekker.

Ghista, D. N., et al, eds. Perspective in Biomechanics, Vol. I. (Perspectives in Biomechanics Ser.). 902p. 1981. 205.00 (ISBN 3-7186-0006-4). Harwood Academic.

Ghosal, Amitaval. Some Aspects of Queueing & Storage Systems. LC 78-114016. (Lecture Notes in Operations Research & Mathematical Systems: Vol. 23). 1970. pap. 10.70 o.p. (ISBN 0-387-04947-9). Springer-Verlag.

Ghose, M. Selected Poems. 8.00 (ISBN 0-89253-546-6); flexible cloth 4.00 (ISBN 0-89253-547-4). Ind-US Inc.

Ghose, S. K. Mystics & Society. 5.00x (ISBN 0-210-98132-6). Asia.

Ghose, Sankar. Political Ideas & Movements in India. LC 75-908962. 1975. 13.00x o.p. (ISBN 0-88386-732-X). South Asia Bks.

Ghose, Sisirkumar. Metaesthetics & Other Essays. 67p. 1975. 8.00 (ISBN 0-88253-719-9); pap. 4.00 (ISBN 0-88253-843-8), Ind-US Inc.

--The Mystic As a Force for Change. rev. ed. LC 80-53954. 144p. 1980. pap. 4.75 (ISBN 0-8356-0547-7, Quest). Theos Pub Hse.

Ghosh, Arun. Indian Political Movements, 1919-1971: A Systematic Bibliography. 1976. 36.00x o.p. (ISBN 0-88386-697-8). South Asia Bks.

Ghosh, Asok K. Paleolithic Cultures of Singhbhum. (Transactions Ser.: Vol. 60, Pt. 1). (Illus.). 1970. pap. 1.00 o.p. (ISBN 0-87169-601-0). Am Philos.

Ghosh, Debapriya, et al. The Economics of Personal Injury. LC 75-28611. (Illus.). 1975. 17.00 o.p. (ISBN 0-347-01111-X, 00312-3, Pub. by Saxon Hse). Lexington Bks.

Ghosh, S. L., tr. see Basu, Manoje.

Ghosh, Sachindra L., tr. see Basu, Manoje.

Ghosh, Sadhan K. My English Journey. 12.00 (ISBN 0-89253-670-5). Ind-US Inc.

Ghosh, Sakti P., ed. see National Computer Conference, 1978.

Ghosh, Sanjib K. Analytical Photogrammetry. LC 79-1063. (Illus.). 1979. 28.00 (ISBN 0-08-023883-1). Pergamon.

Ghuman, Paul A. The Cultural Context of Thinking: A Comparative Study of Punjabi & English Boys. (General Ser.). 139p. 1975. pap. text ed. 13.25x (ISBN 0-85633-078-7, NFER). Humanities.

Ghurye, G. S. Vedic India. 1979. 44.00x (ISBN 0-8364-0455-6). South Asia Bks.

Giacconi, Richard & Setti, Giancarlo, eds. X-Ray Astronomy. (NATO Advanced Study Institutes Series, C. Mathematical & Physical Sciences: No. 60). 400p. 1980. lib. bdg. 47.50 (ISBN 90-277-1156-9, Pub. by D. Reidel). Kluwer Boston.

Giachery, Ugo. Shoghi Effendi: Recollections. (Illus.). 1973. 9.95 (ISBN 0-85398-050-0, 7-31-65, Pub. by George Ronald England). Baha'i.

Giachino, Joseph W. Basic General Metals. (gr. 9-12). 1969. text ed. 6.96 (ISBN 0-02-817070-9). Macmillan.

Giacobini, Ezio, et al, eds. Tissue Culture in Neurobiology. 536p. 1980. text ed. 52.00 (ISBN 0-89004-461-9). Raven.

Giacomo, M., jt. auth. see Dubois, J.

Giallombardo, Rose. The Social World of Imprisoned Girls. 314p. 1981. Repr. text ed. price not set (ISBN 0-89874-285-4). Krieger.

--Society of Women: A Study of a Women's Prison. LC 66-14132. 1966. pap. text ed. 9.95x (ISBN 0-471-29729-1). Wiley.

Giallombardo, Rose, ed. Juvenile Delinquency: A Book of Readings. 3rd ed. LC 75-35887. 1976. pap. text ed. 15.95 (ISBN 0-471-29726-7). Wiley.

Giam, C. S. Pollutant Effects on Marine Organisms. LC 77-2475. (Illus.). 1977. 19.95 (ISBN 0-669-01518-0). Lexington Bks.

Giammatteo, Michael C. Beyond Relevancy: A Book for Teachers of the Future. (Illus.). 1973. pap. 10.00 (ISBN 0-918428-09-2). Sylvan Inst.

--Rings Around Your Mind: How to Program Your Mind to Control Stress, Fear, & Self-Destructive Behavior Patterns. (Illus.). 1976. pap. text ed. 10.00 (ISBN 0-918428-08-4). Sylvan Inst.

--The Thin Fine Line. (Illus., Orig.). 1975. pap. 5.00 (ISBN 0-918428-05-X). Sylvan Inst.

Giammatteo, Michael C., et al. Forces on Leadership. 80p. 1981. pap. 4.00 (ISBN 0-88210-116-1). Natl Assn Principals.

Giammatteo, Mike & Mattox, Phil. Paths of Life. (Illus.). 1977. 5.00 (ISBN 0-918428-10-6). Sylvan Inst.

Gianakaris, C. J. Foundations of Drama. 1975. pap. 9.75 (ISBN 0-395-18611-0); instr's. manual 1.75 (ISBN 0-395-18800-8). HM.

--Plutarch. (World Authors Ser.: Greece: No. 111). lib. bdg. 9.95 (ISBN 0-8057-2706-X). Twayne.

Gianakos, Larry J. Television Drama Series Programming: A Comprehensive Chronicle, 1947-1959. LC 80-17023. 581p. 1980. 29.50 (ISBN 0-8108-1330-0). Scarecrow.

--Television Drama Series Programming: A Comprehensive Chronicle, 1959-1975. LC 78-650. 1978. 32.50 (ISBN 0-8108-1116-2). Scarecrow.

Gianakoulis, Theodore. The Land & People of Greece. rev. ed. LC 75-37745. (Portraits of the Nations Ser.). (Illus.). (gr. 6 up). 1972. 8.79 (ISBN 0-397-31523-6). Lippincott.

Gianaris, Larry. Reality. LC 78-68900. 1980. 5.95 (ISBN 0-533-04184-8). Vantage.

Gian-Carlo Rota, jt. auth. see Birkhoff, Garrett.

Giancoli, Douglas C. Physics: Principle with Applications. 1979. text ed. 21.95 (ISBN 0-13-672600-3). P-H.

Gianelli, Stanley, Jr., jt. auth. see Greenbaum, Dennis.

Giangreco, C. Joseph & Giangreco, Marianne R. Education of the Hearing Impaired. (Illus.). 204p. 1976. pap. 15.50 (ISBN 0-398-00673-3). C C Thomas.

Giangreco, Marianne R. Canoe Country Poems. 1974p. 1981. 4.95 (ISBN 0-935054-05-7). Webb-Newcomb.

Giangreco, Marianne R., jt. auth. see Giangreco, C. Joseph.

Giannella, Donald A., ed. Religion & the Public Order, 3 Vols. LC 64-17164. 1964-66. Vol. 1. 10.00x o.s.i. (ISBN 0-226-29046-8); Vol. 2. 9.50x o.s.i. (ISBN 0-226-29047-6); Vol. 3. 11.00x o.s.i. (ISBN 0-226-29048-4). U of Chicago Pr.

Giannetti, Louis. The American Cinema: The Art, the Industry, the Audience, the Artists. 255p. 1981. text ed. 17.95 (ISBN 0-13-024687-5); pap. text ed. 11.95 (ISBN 0-13-024679-4). P-H.

Giannetti, Louis D. Understanding Movies. 2nd ed. (Illus.). 512p. 1976. ref. ed. 16.95 (ISBN 0-13-936302-5); pap. 11.95x (ISBN 0-13-936294-0). P-H.

Giannini, A. James. Psychitric, Psychologenic, & Somatopsychic Disorders Handbook. 1978. pap. 14.50 (ISBN 0-87488-596-5). Med Exam.

Giannini, Allan V. The Best Guide to Allergy. (Appleton Consumer Health Guides). 160p. 1981. 12.95 (ISBN 0-8385-0645-3); pap. 5.95 (ISBN 0-8385-0644-5). ACC.

Giannini, Vera, tr. see Silvan, Matthew.

Giannone, Richard. Vonnegut: A Preface to His Novels. LC 76-54943. (National University Pubns. Literary Criticism Ser.). 1977. 11.50 (ISBN 0-8046-9167-3). Kennikat.

Giannotti, John B. & Smith, Richard W. International Treasury Management for the 1980's: A Practical Approach to Treasury Management in the Multinatioanl Corporation. 600p. 1981. 39.50 (ISBN 0-471-08062-4, Pub. by Wiley Interscience). Wiley.

Gianos, Mary P., ed. Introduction to Modern Greek Literature. LC 67-30722. 1969. text ed. 29.50x (ISBN 0-8057-3125-3); pap. text ed. 16.50x (ISBN 0-89197-801-1). Irvington.

Gianpietri, Peter. The Successful Rules of Artistic Composition. (Illus.). 1979. deluxe ed. 49.75 (ISBN 0-930582-42-X). Gloucester Art.

Gianturco, Daniel T. & Smith, Harmon L. The Promiscuous Teenager. (Illus.). 128p. 1974. text ed. 12.75 (ISBN 0-398-03117-7). C C Thomas.

Giap, Vo Nguyen. Military Art of People's War: Selected Writings. Stetler, Russell, ed. LC 75-105317. (Illus.). 1970. 8.50 o.p. (ISBN 0-85345-129-X, CL-129X); pap. 5.95 (ISBN 0-85345-193-1, PB-1931). Monthly Rev.

Giarda, Christophoro. Bibliothecae Alexandrinae Icones Symbolicae. Orgel, Stephen, ed. LC 78-68230. (Philosophy of Images Ser.: Vol. 14). (Illus.). 1980. lib. bdg. 66.00 (ISBN 0-8240-3688-3). Garland Pub.

Giarini, Orio. Dialogue on Wealth & Welfare: An Alternative View of World Capital Formation, a Report to the Club of Rome. (Illus.). 368p. 1980. 48.00 (ISBN 0-08-026088-8); pap. 24.00 (ISBN 0-08-026087-X). Pergamon.

Giarini, Orio & Louberge, Henri. The Diminishing Returns to Technology: An Essay on the Crisis in Economic Growth. 1978. text ed. 23.00 (ISBN 0-08-023338-4); pap. text ed. 8.50 (ISBN 0-08-023337-6). Pergamon.

Gibaldi, Joseph & Achtert, Walter S. MLA Handbook for Writers of Research Papers, Theses & Dissertations. LC 77-76954. 163p. (Orig.). 1977. 6.25 (ISBN 0-87352-450-0); pap. 4.75x (ISBN 0-87352-000-9). Modern Lang.

Gibaldi, Joseph, jt. auth. see Clements, Robert J.

Gibaldi, Joseph, ed. Approaches to Teaching Chaucer's Canterbury Tales. LC 80-22909. (Approaches to Teaching Masterpieces of World Literature Ser.: No. 1). xvi, 175p. (Orig.). 1980. 13.50x (ISBN 0-87352-476-4); pap. 6.50x (ISBN 0-87352-475-6). Modern Lang.

Gibaldi, Joseph & Mirollo, James V., eds. Teaching Apprentice Programs in Language & Literature. (Options for Teaching Ser.: No. 4). 160p. (Orig.). 1981. pap. 7.00x (ISBN 0-87352-303-2). Modern Lang.

Gibaldi, Joseph, ed. see Lehmann, Winfred P., et al.

Gibb, H. A. & Kramers, J. H., eds. Shorter Encyclopedia of Islam. (Illus.). 1957. 45.00x (ISBN 0-8014-0150-X). Cornell U Pr.

Gibb, H. A., et al see Lewis, B., et al.

Gibb, Hamilton A. Mohammedanism: An Historical Survey. 2nd ed. 1953. pap. 3.95x (ISBN 0-19-500245-8, 90). Oxford U Pr.

Gibb, Jack R. The Omicron Process. LC 80-67898. 1981. pap. 8.95 (ISBN 0-89615-025-9). Guild of Tutors.

--Trust: A New View of Personal & Organizational Development. LC 77-93139. 1978. 15.00 (ISBN 0-89615-002-X); pap. 8.95 (ISBN 0-89615-006-2). Guild of Tutors.

Gibb, Robert. Whalesongs. 2nd ed. 42p. 1979. 30.00 o.p. (ISBN 0-918824-17-6); pap. cancelled o.p. (ISBN 0-918824-16-8). Turkey Pr.

Gibb, Sandra, jt. auth. see Frederickson, Jaye.

Gibbes, Phoebe. The Life & Adventures of Mr. Francis Clive, 1764, 2 vols. in 1. LC 75-1172. (Novel in England, 1700-1775 Ser). 1974. lib. bdg. 50.00 (ISBN 0-8240-1168-6). Garland Pub.

Gibbings, J. C. Thermomechanics. 1970. 21.00 (ISBN 0-08-006334-9); pap. 9.75 (ISBN 0-08-006333-0). Pergamon.

Gibbins, Robert J., et al, eds. Research Advances in Alcohol & Drug Problems, 3 vols. LC 73-18088. 384p. 1974-76. Vol. 1. 45.95 (ISBN 0-471-29737-2); Vol. 2. 47.95 (ISBN 0-471-29738-0); Vol. 3. 51.95 (ISBN 0-471-29736-4, Pub. by Wiley-Medical). Wiley.

Gibbon, D. L. Aeration of Activated Sludge in Sewage Treatment. LC 74-8138. 126p. 1975. text ed. 23.00 (ISBN 0-08-018156-2). Pergamon.

Gibbon, Edward. Autobiography. (World's Classics, No. 139). 14.95 (ISBN 0-19-250139-9). Oxford U Pr.

--Decline & Fall of the Roman Empire, 6 vols. 1954 (Evman). Vol. 1. 5.00x (ISBN 0-460-00434-4); Vol. 2. 12.95x (ISBN 0-460-00435-2); Vol. 3. 12.95x (ISBN 0-460-00436-0); Vol. 4. 9.00x (ISBN 0-460-00474-3); Vol. 5. 10.00x (ISBN 0-460-00475-1); Vol. 6. 10.00x (ISBN 0-460-00476-X). Dutton.

--The English Essays of Edward Gibbon. Craddock, Patricia B., ed. 1972. 59.00 (ISBN 0-19-812496-1). Oxford U Pr.

--Gibbon's Autobiography. Reese, M. M., ed. (Routledge English Texts). 1970. 7.95 (ISBN 0-7100-6923-5); pap. 4.95 (ISBN 0-7100-6925-1). Routledge & Kegan.

Gibbon, Guy E. The Mississippian Occupation of the Red Wing Area: Microfiche Edition. (Minnesota Prehistoric Archaeology Ser.: No. 13). 394p. 1979. 12.50 (ISBN 0-87351-137-9). Minn Hist.

Gibbon, Lewis G. A Scots Quair: A Trilogy of Sunset Song, Cloud Howe, & Grey Granite. LC 77-75288. 1977. 10.95 (ISBN 0-8052-3661-9). Schocken.

Gibbon, Monk. Red Shoes Ballet & the Tales of Hoffman, Vol. 14. Kupelnick, Bruce S., ed. LC 76-52106. (Classics of Film Literature Ser.). 1978. lib. bdg. 39.00 (ISBN 0-8240-2878-3). Garland Pub.

Gibbon, Vivian, jt. auth. see Sealey, Leonard G.

Gibboney, Charles. Worth Thinking About. 1976. pap. 1.25 (ISBN 0-8272-4210-7). Bethany Pr.

Gibbons. Basic Math, 9 bks. Incl. Gr. K. pap. text ed. 2.92 (ISBN 0-8009-1401-5); tchr's. ed. 4.40 (ISBN 0-8009-1403-1); Gr. 1 & 2. pap. text ed. 4.64 ea.; Gr. 1. pap. text ed. (ISBN 0-8009-1406-6); Gr. 2. pap. text ed. (ISBN 0-8009-1410-4); tchr's. eds, 6.16 ea. Gr. 1 (ISBN 0-8009-1408-2). Gr. 2 (ISBN 0-8009-1412-0); Gr. 3-6. Gr. 3. pap. text ed. 4.64 (ISBN 0-8009-1414-7); Gr. 4. pap. text ed. 4.64 (ISBN 0-8009-1425-2); Gr. 5. 4.64 (ISBN 0-8009-1433-3); Gr. 6. tchr's. eds. 6.16 ea. (ISBN 0-8009-1443-0); tchr's. ed. gr. 3 6.16 (ISBN 0-8009-1416-3); tchr's. ed. gr. 4 6.16 (ISBN 0-8009-1427-9); tchr's. ed. gr. 5 6.16 (ISBN 0-8009-1437-6); tchr's. ed. gr. 6 6.16 (ISBN 0-8009-1445-7); tests for gr. 3-6 1.12 ea.; Gr. 7 & 8. pap. text ed. 5.08 ea.; Gr. 7. pap. text ed. (ISBN 0-8009-1462-7); Gr. 8. pap. text ed. (ISBN 0-8009-1472-4); tchr's. eds. 6.60 ea. Gr. 7 (ISBN 0-8009-1464-3). Gr. 8 (ISBN 0-8009-1474-0). tests for gr. 7-8 1.12 ea. Gr. 7 (ISBN 0-8009-1468-6). Gr. 8 (ISBN 0-8009-1476-7). **(gr. k-8). 1977-78. McCormick-Mathers.**

Gibbons, Cardinal. Faith of Our Fathers. LC 80-51331. 1980. write for info. o.p. (ISBN 0-89555-158-6). Tan Bks Pubs.

Gibbons, Don. The Clout. 1974. pap. 1.95 o.s.i. (ISBN 0-380-00005-9, 28126). Avon.

--The Criminological Enterprise: Theories & Perspectives. (P-H Series in Sociology). 1979. pap. text ed. 9.95 (ISBN 0-13-193615-8). P-H.

Gibbons, Don C. Changing the Lawbreaker. 1981. pap. text ed. 8.95 (ISBN 0-86598-017-9). Allanheld.

--Delinquent Behavior. 2nd ed. (Illus.). 1976. text ed. 17.95 (ISBN 0-13-197939-6). P-H.

--Delinquent Behavior. 3rd ed. (Illus.). 1980. text ed. 17.95 (ISBN 0-13-197962-0). P-H.

--Society, Crime & Criminal Careers. 3rd ed. (Illus.). 1977. 18.95 (ISBN 0-13-820100-5). P-H.

Gibbons, Don C. & Jones, John F. The Study of Deviance: Perspectives & Problems. (Illus.). 192p. 1975. pap. text ed. 10.95 (ISBN 0-13-858936-4). P-H.

Gibbons, Don C., jt. ed. see Garabedian, Peter G.

Gibbons, Don C., et al. Criminal Justice Planning: An Introduction. (Illus.). 192p. 1977. text ed. 15.95x (ISBN 0-13-193037-0). P-H.

Gibbons, Euell. Stalking the Blue-Eyed Scallop. (Illus.). 1964. 9.95 o.p. (ISBN 0-679-50088-X); pap. 3.95 o.p. (ISBN 0-679-50236-X). McKay.

--Stalking the Wild Asparagus. 1970. pap. 3.95 Field Guide ed. (ISBN 0-679-50223-8). McKay.

Gibbons, Gail. Locks & Keys. LC 79-7825. (Illus.). 32p. (gr. 1-4). 1980. 7.95 (ISBN 0-690-04058-X, TYC-J); PLB 7.89 (ISBN 0-690-04059-8). T Y Crowell.

--Things to Make & Do for Columbus Day. (Things to Make & Do Ser.). (Illus.). (gr. 1-3). 1977. PLB 7.90 s&l (ISBN 0-531-01274-3). Watts.

--Things to Make & Do for Halloween. LC 75-19396. (Things to Make & Do Ser.). (Illus.). 48p. (gr. k-2). 1976. PLB 7.90 (ISBN 0-531-01103-8). Watts.

--Things to Make & Do for Your Birthday. (Things to Make & Do Ser.). (Illus.). (gr. 1-3). 1978. 3.95 (ISBN 0-531-02380-X); PLB 7.90 s&l (ISBN 0-531-01462-2). Watts.

Gibbons, Jean D. Nonparametric Methods for Quantitative Analysis. LC 74-28910. 1976. text ed. 29.95 (ISBN 0-03-007811-3). Am Sciences Pr.

Gibbons, John, jt. auth. see Fraser, Edward.

Gibbons, John T., jt. auth. see Smith, Douglas C.

Gibbons, Joseph C. Whatever Happened to Friday? and Other Questions Catholics Ask. LC 79-91275. (Orig.). 1980. pap. 2.95 (ISBN 0-8091-2278-2). Paulist Pr.

Gibbons, Julie. My Secret Place. (Illus.). 20p. (Orig.). (gr. 1-4). 1975. pap. 2.50 (ISBN 0-911336-61-3). Sci of Mind.

--There Is Only One Me. 20p. (gr. 1-4). 1974. pap. 2.50 (ISBN 0-911336-56-7). Sci of Mind.

Gibbons, Mary, illus. Invite Me Again. 300p. (Orig.). 1979. pap. 6.95x plastic cone spine (ISBN 0-9605174-0-5). IMA Ed.

Gibbons, Reginald, tr. see Cernuda, Luis.

Gibbons, Robert. Yellow & Black. (Illus.). 24p. 1980. 25.00; pap. 6.00. Four Zoas Pr.

Gibbons, Thomas. The Exhibition: Scenes from the Life of John Merrick. 1980. pap. 1.25 (ISBN 0-686-68848-1). Dramatists Play.

Gibbs, A. M., ed. see Davenant, William.

Gibbs, Alan G., tr. see Plesner, A. I.

Gibbs, Alonzo. A Man's Calling. (gr. 7-12). 1966. 6.00 o.p. (ISBN 0-688-41236-X); PLB 6.24 (ISBN 0-688-51236-4). Lothrop.

Gibbs, Angela, tr. see Kallberg, Sture.

Gibbs, Anthony. Passion for Cars. (Encore Ed.). (Illus.). 1974. 2.95 o.p. (ISBN 0-684-14974-5, Scribner-T). Scribner.

Gibbs, C. E., jt. auth. see Gibbs, R. S.

Gibbs, Charles H., jt. ed. see Lundeen, Harry C.

Gibbs, Erna L., jt. auth. see Gibbs, Frederic A.

Gibbs, Errol A. The Dilemma of Our Society: A Proposal for Moral Maturity. (Illus.). 336p. 1980. 15.00 (ISBN 0-682-49650-2). Exposition.

Gibbs, Frederic A. & Gibbs, Erna L. Medical Electroencephalography. 1967. 18.95 (ISBN 0-201-02365-2). A-W.

Gibbs, Frederic A., jt. auth. see Boshes, Louis D.

Gibbs, G. W. & Pintus, P. Health & Safety in the Canadian Mining Industry. 249p. (Orig.). 1978. pap. text ed. 12.00x (ISBN 0-88757-003-8, Pub. by Ctr Resource Stud Canada). Renouf.

Gibbs, H. G. & Richards, T. H., eds. Stress, Vibration & Noise Analysis in Vehicles. LC 75-14389. 1975. 61.95 (ISBN 0-470-29742-5). Halsted Pr.

Gibbs, J. Willard. Scientific Papers, 2 vols. Set. 16.00 (ISBN 0-8446-2127-7). Peter Smith.

Gibbs, James, ed. Critical Perspectives on Wole Soyinka. LC 79-89931. (Critical Perspectives Ser.). (Illus.). 274p. (Orig.). 1980. 20.00 (ISBN 0-914478-49-4); pap. 9.00 (ISBN 0-914478-50-8). Three Continents.

Gibbs, James A. Oregon's Salty Coast. LC 78-11899. (Illus.). 1978. 15.95 o.p. (ISBN 0-87564-222-5). Superior Pub.

--West Coast Lighthouses. Pfeiffer, Douglas A., ed. (Illus.). 96p. (Orig.). 1981. pap. 5.95 (ISBN 0-912856-72-6). Graphic Arts Ctr.

Gibbs, Jerry. Bass Myths Exploded: Newest Ways to Catch Largemouths. (Illus.). 1978. 10.95 o.p. (ISBN 0-679-50859-7). McKay.

Gibbs, Jesse B. Transformer Principles & Practice. 2nd ed. (Engineering Books for Industry Ser). (Illus.). 1950. 24.50 o.p. (ISBN 0-07-023179-6, P&RB). McGraw.

Gibbs, Joan. Jewelry for Everyone: Soft Jewelry to Create at Home from Twine & Wool, Bone & Shell, Fur & Feather, Clay & Leather, Beads, Recyclables, Other Easy-to-Find Materials. (Illus.). 128p. 1981. 15.95 (ISBN 0-916144-74-7); pap. 7.95 (ISBN 0-916144-73-9). Stemmer Hse.

Gibbs, Josiah W. The Collected Works of Josiah Willard Gibbs, 2 vols. 1948. Set. 100.00x o.p. (ISBN 0-686-51355-X). Elliots Bks.

Gibbs, Katherine. Travelin' Woman. (Orig.). 1980. pap. 1.95 (ISBN 0-8439-0728-2, Leisure Bks). Nordon Pubns.

Gibbs, Lee & Stevenson, Taylor. Myth & the Crisis of Historical Consciousness. LC 75-33049. (American Academy of Religion. Section Papers). 1975. pap. 7.50 (ISBN 0-89130-053-8, 010915). Scholars Pr Ca.

Gibbs, Lee W., tr. see Ames, William.

Gibbs, Margaret S. & Lachenmeyer, Juliana R. Community Psychology: Theoretical & Empirical Approaches. Sigal, Janet, ed. LC 79-13755. 1980. 24.95x (ISBN 0-470-26787-9). Halsted Pr.

Gibbs, Mark, ed. see Mouw, Richard J.

Gibbs, Mary A. The Romantic Frenchman. 208p. 1976. pap. 1.25 o.p. (ISBN 0-449-22869-X, P2869, Crest). Fawcett.

--A Young Lady of Fashion. 1979. pap. 1.75 o.p. (ISBN 0-449-23843-1, Crest). Fawcett.

Gibbs, R. S. & Gibbs, C. E. Ambulatory Obstetrics: A Clinical Guide. LC 79-18554. 1979. pap. text ed. 10.95 (ISBN 0-471-05227-2, Pub. by Wiley Medical). Wiley.

Gibbs, Ronald S. Antibiotic Therapy in Obstetrics & Gynecology. 224p. 1981. 16.50 (ISBN 0-471-06003-8, Pub. by Wiley Med). Wiley.

Gibbs, Terry R. & Popolato, Alphonse, eds. LASL Explosive Property Data. (Los Alamos Scientific Laboratory Series on Dynamic Material Properties). 1980. 40.00x (ISBN 0-520-04012-0). U of Cal Pr.

Gibbs, Tony. Backpacking. LC 74-11326. (Career Concise Guide Ser.). (Illus.). 72p. (gr. 7 up). 1975. PLB 4.90 o.p. (ISBN 0-531-02786-4). Watts.

--Navigation: Finding Your Way on Sea & Land. LC 75-12541. (Impact Bks). 96p. (gr. 8 up). 1975. PLB 6.90 (ISBN 0-531-00838-X). Watts.

Gibbs, Tony & Sports Illustrated Editors. Sports Illustrated Power Boating. LC 72-13277. 1973. 5.95 (ISBN 0-397-00971-2); pap. 2.95 (ISBN 0-397-00972-0, LP81). Lippincott.

Gibbs-Smith, Charles. The Inventions of Leonardo Da Vinci. LC 77-94117. (Illus.). 1978. pap. 7.95 o.p. (ISBN 0-684-15746-2, ScribT). Scribner.

Gibert, Stephen P. Northeast Asia in U. S. Foreign Policy. LC 79-67647. (The Washington Policy Papers: No. 71). 88p. 1979. pap. 3.50 (ISBN 0-8039-1427-X). Sage.

--Soviet Images of America. LC 76-28569. 1977. pap. 9.95x (ISBN 0-8448-1075-4). Crane-Russak Co.

Gibian, George, ed. Daniil Kharms: Izbrannoe. (Colloquium Shavicum: No. 5). (Eng & Rus.). 1974. pap. text ed. 16.50x (ISBN 3-7778-0115-1). Humanities.

Giblett, Eloise R. Genetic Markers in Human Blood. (Illus.). 1969. 22.75 (ISBN 0-632-05290-2, Blackwell). Mosby.

Gibney, Frank, jt. ed. see Timmons, Christine.

Gibor, Aharon, intro. by. Conditions for Life: Readings from Scientific American. LC 76-22196. (Illus.). 1976. text ed. 19.95x (ISBN 0-7167-0480-3); pap. text ed. 9.95x (ISBN 0-7167-0479-X). W H Freeman.

Gibra, Isaac. Probability & Statistical Inference for Scientists & Engineers. (Industrial Engineering Ser.). (Illus.). 608p. 1973. ref. ed. 23.95 o.p. (ISBN 0-13-711622-5). P-H.

Gibran, Kahlil. Between Night & Morn. 1972. 3.75 o.p. (ISBN 0-8022-2081-9). Philos Lib.

--Kahlil Gibran Diary for Nineteen Eighty-One. LC 80-7662. (Illus.). 224p. 1980. ivory bdg. 5.95 (ISBN 0-394-51329-0); blue bdg. 5.95 (ISBN 0-394-51327-4); red bdg. 5.95 (ISBN 0-394-51328-2). Knopf.

--Twenty Drawings. LC 74-9154. 1974. pap. 4.95 o.p. (ISBN 0-394-71123-8, V-123, Vin). Random.

Gibson, Alexander D., ed. Anthologie. LC 66-28097. (Orig., Fr.). 1967. pap. 5.95 (ISBN 0-672-63008-7). Odyssey Pr.

Gibson, Arrell. Canadian River Valley. LC 73-96758. 1971. pap. 2.95 (ISBN 0-8077-1422-4). Tchrs Coll.

--West in the Life of the Nation. 1976. 15.95x (ISBN 0-669-61515-3). Heath.

Gibson, Arrell M. The Chickasaws. (Civilization of the American Indian Ser.: Vol. 109). (Illus.). 320p. 1971. 16.95 o.p. (ISBN 0-8061-0945-9); pap. 7.95 (ISBN 0-8061-1042-2). U of Okla Pr.

--Kickapoos: Lords of the Middle Border. (Civilization of the American Indian Ser.: No. 70). (Illus.). 1976. pap. 6.95 (ISBN 0-8061-1264-6). U of Okla Pr.

Gibson, Arthur, et al. Truth in Advertising. 1981. Repr. of 1972 ed. soft cover 4.95x (ISBN 0-88946-912-1). E Mellen.

Gibson, Bess. Glowing Embers. 26p. 1980. 2.95 (ISBN 0-8059-2761-1). Dorrance.

Gibson, Betty S. Pride of the Golden Bear. 560p. 1981. text ed. 23.75 (ISBN 0-8403-2397-2). Kendall-Hunt.

Gibson, C., ed. Selected Plays of Philip Massinger. LC 77-80835. (Plays by Renaissance & Restoration Dramatists Ser.). 1978. 47.50 (ISBN 0-521-21728-8); pap. 10.50x (ISBN 0-521-29243-3). Cambridge U Pr.

Gibson, Catherine, ed. see Monroe City County Fine Arts Council.

Gibson, Cyrus F. Managing Organizational Behavior. 1980. 18.50 (ISBN 0-256-02237-2). Irwin.

Gibson, Cyrusf., jt. auth. see Lucas, Henry.

Gibson, D. Down's Syndrome: The Psychology of Mongolism. LC 77-87381. 1979. 45.00 (ISBN 0-521-21914-0). Cambridge U Pr.

Gibson, David & Brown, Roy I. Managing the Severely Retarded: A Sampler. (Illus.). 500p. 1976. 32.75 (ISBN 0-398-03513-X). C C Thomas.

Gibson, E. J., ed. Developments in Building Maintenance, Vol. 1. (Illus.). 1979. 38.90x (ISBN 0-85334-801-4, Pub. by Applied Science). Burgess-Intl Ideas.

Gibson, Edgar. The Book of Job. 1978. 9.75 (ISBN 0-686-12949-0). Klock & Klock.

Gibson, Elsa. The Christians for Christians Inscriptions of Phrygia. LC 78-12688. (Harvard Theological Studies: No. 32). 1978. pap. 7.50 (ISBN 0-89130-262-X, 020032). Scholars Pr Ca.

Gibson, Elsie. Honest Prayer. LC 80-39570. (Orig.). 1981. pap. price not set (ISBN 0-664-24348-7). Westminster.

Gibson, Evan K. C. S. Lewis: Spinner of Tales. (Orig.). 1980. pap. 8.95 (ISBN 0-8028-1826-9). Eerdmans.

Gibson, Francis. Gibby: The Memoirs 0f a Horsey Man. 1978. pap. 8.75 (ISBN 0-85131-277-2). J A Allen.

Gibson, Frank F., jt. auth. see Dunfee, Thomas W.

Gibson, George. Captain Incognito. 224p. 1980. 12.00x (ISBN 0-245-53040-1, Pub. by Nautical England). State Mutual Bk.

Gibson, George H. Public Broadcasting: The Role of the Federal Government, 1912-76. LC 77-24422. (Praeger Special Studies). 1977. 25.95 (ISBN 0-03-022831-X). Praeger.

Gibson, Glenn A. & Liu, Yu-Cheng. Microcomputers for Engineers & Scientists. (Illus.). 1980. text ed. 28.95 (ISBN 0-13-580886-3). P-H.

Gibson, Guy. Enemy Coast Ahead. 1976. 9.95 o.p. (ISBN 0-7181-1519-8, Pub. by Michael Joseph). Merrimack Bk Serv.

Gibson, Helen. An Australian Christmas. (Illus.). 32p. (ps-1). 1980. Repr. of 1961 ed. cancelled o.s.i. (ISBN 0-934680-01-9). Cobbers.

Gibson, Ian. The English Vice: Beating, Sex & Shame in Victorian England & After. (Illus.). 364p. 1978. 27.50 (ISBN 0-686-26719-2, Pub. by Duckworth England). Biblio Dist.

Gibson, J. Psychology for the Classroom. 1976. pap. text ed. 17.95 (ISBN 0-13-733287-4); study guide & wkbk. 4.95 (ISBN 0-13-733329-3). P-H.

Gibson, J. B. Histological Typing of Tumors of the Liver, Biliary Tract & Pancreas. (World Health Organization: International Histological Classification of Tumours Ser.). (Illus.). 1978. text ed. 40.00 (ISBN 92-4-176020-6, 70-0-020-20); text & slides 122.00 (ISBN 0-685-96476-0, 70-1-020-00). Am Soc Clinical.

Gibson, J. E. Thin Shells: Computing & Theory. (International Series in Structure & Solid Body Mechanics). (Illus.). 1980. 40.00 (ISBN 0-08-023275-2); pap. 18.00 (ISBN 0-08-024204-9). Pergamon.

Gibson, J. T. Growing up: A Study of Children. 1978. 17.95 (ISBN 0-201-02914-6); wkbk. 4.95 (ISBN 0-201-02917-0). A-W.

Gibson, Jack E. Managing Research Development. 450p. 1981. 35.00 (ISBN 0-471-08799-8, Pub. by Wiley-Interscience). Wiley.

Gibson, James, jt. auth. see Boeri, David.

Gibson, James, ed. see Hardy, Thomas.

Gibson, James J. The Ecological Approach to Visual Perception. LC 78-69585. (Illus.). 1979. text ed. 29.95 (ISBN 0-395-27049-9). HM.

--Senses Considered As Perceptual Systems. LC 66-7132. 1966. text ed. 29.95 (ISBN 0-395-04494-4). HM.

Gibson, James L., et al. Organizations: Behavior, Structure, Processes. 3rd ed. 1979. 18.50x (ISBN 0-256-02210-0). Business Pubns.

--Readings in Organizations: Behavior, Structure, Processes. 3rd ed. 1979. pap. 9.95x (ISBN 0-256-02247-X). Business Pubns.

Gibson, James R. Feeding the Russian Fur Trade: Provisionment of the Okhotsk Seaboard & the Kamchatka Peninsula, 1639-1856. LC 79-81319. (Illus.). 1969. 27.50x (ISBN 0-299-05230-3). U of Wis Pr.

--Imperial Russia in Frontier America: The Changing Geography of Supply of Russian America, 1784-1867. (The Andrew H. Clark Ser in the Historical Geography of North America). (Illus.). 300p. 1976. text ed. 10.95x (ISBN 0-19-501876-1); pap. text ed. 7.95x (ISBN 0-19-501875-3). Oxford U Pr.

Gibson, James W. & Hanna, Michael. Audience Analysis: A Programmed Approach to Receiver Behavior. (Illus.). 1976. pap. 10.95 (ISBN 0-13-050724-5). P-H.

Gibson, Jane, jt. auth. see Padzensky, Herbert R.

Gibson, Janice. Psychology for the Classroom. 2nd ed. (Illus.). 640p. 1981. pap. text ed. 17.95 (ISBN 0-13-733352-8). P-H.

Gibson, Janice T. Educational Psychology. 2nd ed. (Illus.). 1972. text ed. 13.95 (ISBN 0-13-236968-0). P-H.

Gibson, Janice T. & Blumberg, Phyllis. Growing up: Readings on the Study of Children. LC 77-83026. (Education Ser.). 1978. 7.95 (ISBN 0-201-02915-4); instr's man. 4.00 (ISBN 0-201-02916-2). A-W.

Gibson, Jean. Advanced Christian Training. (Believer's Bible Lessons Ser.). (Orig.). Date not set. pap. 5.95 (ISBN 0-937396-04-4). Walterick Pubs. Postponed.

--Intermediate Christian Training. 1981. pap. 6.50 (ISBN 0-937396-60-5). Walterick Pubs.

Gibson, Jeffry R., jt. auth. see Anderson, Charles H.

Gibson, John. Health, Personal & Communal. 4th ed. (Illus.). 1976. 8.95 (ISBN 0-571-04908-7, Pub. by Faber & Faber); pap. 4.95 (ISBN 0-571-04909-5). Merrimack Bk Serv.

Gibson, John C. Canaanite Myths and Legends. 2nd ed. 208p. 1978. text ed. 32.00x (ISBN 0-567-02351-6). Attic Pr.

--Textbook of Syrian Semitic Inscriptions: Aramaic Inscriptions, Including Inscriptions in the Dialect of Zenjirli, Vol. 2. (Illus.). 160p. 1975. 34.50x (ISBN 0-19-813186-0). Oxford U Pr.

Gibson, John C. L. Textbook of Syrian Semitic Inscription: Vol. 1, Hebrew & Moabite Inscriptions. 1971. text ed. 22.50x (ISBN 0-19-813159-3). Oxford U Pr.

Gibson, John E. How to Size up People. 1980. pap. write for info. (ISBN 0-671-83334-0). PB.

Gibson, John R. Human Biology. 3rd ed. 1979. pap. 7.50 (ISBN 0-571-04974-5, Pub. by Faber & Faber). Merrimack Bk Serv.

Gibson, Karon W., et al. On Our Own. Catterson, Joy S. & Skalka, Patricia, eds. 256p. 1981. 10.95 (ISBN 0-312-58455-5). St Martin.

Gibson, Katherine. The Tall Book of Bible Stories. LC 57-10952. (Tall Bks.). (Illus.). 128p. (gr. k-3). 1980. 5.95 (ISBN 0-06-021935-1, HarpJ); PLB 6.89 (ISBN 0-06-021936-X). Har-Row.

Gibson, L., jt. auth. see Alexander, John W.

Gibson, Litzka R. How to Read Palms. LC 77-2290. 1977. 7.95 o.p. (ISBN 0-8119-0278-1); pap. 4.95 (ISBN 0-8119-0278-1). Fell.

Gibson, M. T., jt. ed. see Alexander, J. J. G.

Gibson, McGuire, et al. Excavations at Nippur: Twelfth Season. LC 78-59117. (Oriental Institute Communications Ser.: No. 23). (Illus.). 1978. pap. 22.00x (ISBN 0-918986-22-2). Oriental Inst.

Gibson, Madelaine. Rake's Reward. 176p. (Orig.). 1981. pap. 1.95 (ISBN 0-553-13191-5). Bantam.

Gibson, Margaret. The Butterfly Ward. LC 79-67815. 135p. 1980. 8.95 (ISBN 0-8149-0834-9). Vanguard.

--Lanfranc of Bec. 1978. 37.50x (ISBN 0-19-822462-1). Oxford U Pr.

Gibson, Margaret, jt. auth. see David, William.

Gibson, Margaret, ed. see Lanfranc.

Gibson, Michael. Gods, Men & Monsters from the Greek Myths. (Illus.). 1978. 12.95 (ISBN 0-85654-027-7, Pub. by Two Continents). Hippocrene Bks.

Gibson, Michael & Strongman, Harry. The Vikings. LC 77-86712. (Peoples of the Past Ser.). (Illus.). 1977. lib. bdg. 7.95 (ISBN 0-686-51161-1). Silver.

Gibson, Miles E. AG Aviation. pap. 7.00 (ISBN 0-685-46361-3, Pub. by Diversified). Aviation.

--AG Pilot & Chemicals. pap. 7.00 (ISBN 0-685-46362-1, Pub. by Diversified). Aviation.

--AG Pilot Employment Guide. pap. 7.00 (ISBN 0-685-46363-X, Pub. by Diversified). Aviation.

--All About Crop Dusting. pap. 7.00 (ISBN 0-685-46364-8, Pub. by Diversified). Aviation.

Gibson, Parke D. Seventy Billion in the Black: America's Black Consumers. 1978. 12.95 (ISBN 0-02-543160-9). Macmillan.

Gibson, R., compiled by. Modern French Poets on Poetry. LC 78-73241. 1979. 32.50 (ISBN 0-521-05078-2). Cambridge U Pr.

Gibson, Ray. Nemerteans. (Illus.). 1972. text ed. 10.50x (ISBN 0-09-111990-1, Hutchinson U Lib); pap. text ed. 5.50x (ISBN 0-09-111991-X, Hutchinson U Lib). Humanities.

Gibson, Raymond W. Forever in Debt. (Orig.). 1980. pap. text ed. 5.00 (ISBN 0-89536-461-1). CSS Pub.

Gibson, Robert W., ed. The Special Library Role in Networks: Proceedings of a Conference. spiral bdg. 10.50 (ISBN 0-87111-279-5). SLA.

Gibson, Robert W., Jr. & Kunkel, Barbara K. Japanese Scientific & Technical Literature: A Subject Guide. LC 80-39693. (Illus.). 480p. 1981. lib. bdg. 75.00 (ISBN 0-313-22929-5, GJS/). Greenwood.

Gibson, Sandra. Beyond the Body. 1979. pap. 2.25 (ISBN 0-505-51340-4). Tower Bks.

Gibson, Scott L., jt. auth. see Castel, Albert.

Gibson, Susan. Voice Audience Content. 1979. pap. text ed. 8.95 (ISBN 0-582-28108-3); instrs.' manual free (ISBN 0-582-28133-4). Longman.

Gibson, W. L., Jr., et al, eds. Methods for Land Economics Research. LC 66-19269. 1967. pap. 3.95x (ISBN 0-8032-5225-0, BB 352, Bison). U of Nebr Pr.

Gibson, W. M. Basic Electricity. 2nd ed. LC 76-7398. 1976. pap. text ed. 11.50x (ISBN 0-582-44181-1). Longman.

Gibson, W. M. & Pollard, B. R. Symmetry Principles in Elementary Particle Physics. LC 74-31796. (Cambridge Monographs on Physics). (Illus.). 395p. 1980. 22.50 (ISBN 0-521-29964-0). Cambridge U Pr.

Gibson, W. Martin. The Physics of Nuclear Reactions. LC 79-40063. (Illus.). 288p. 1980. 45.00 (ISBN 0-08-023078-4); pap. 16.75 (ISBN 0-08-023077-6). Pergamon.

Gibson, Walker. Persona: A Style Study for Readers & Writers. 1969. pap. text ed. 3.95 (ISBN 0-394-30198-6). Random.

Gibson, Walter. Fell's Guide to Winning Backgammon. LC 74-75381. 1974. pap. 4.95 (ISBN 0-8119-0365-6). Fell.

--Fell's Official Guide to Knots & How to Tie Them. LC 61-9266. 1961. pap. 4.95 (ISBN 0-8119-0369-9). Fell.

--The Shadow Scrapbook. LC 78-22277. (Orig.). 1979. pap. 8.95 (ISBN 0-15-681475-7, Harv). HarBraceJ.

Gibson, Walter see Grant, Maxwell, pseud.

Gibson, Walter, ed. see Houdini, Harry.

Gibson, Walter B. Bunko Book. (Gambler's Book Shelf). 64p. 1976. pap. 2.95 (ISBN 0-89650-565-0). Gamblers.

--Carnival Gaffs. (Gambler's Book Shelf). 64p. 1976. pap. 2.95 (ISBN 0-89650-566-9). Gamblers.

--Complete Illustrated Book of Card Magic: The Principles & Techniques Fully Revealed in Text & Photographs. LC 69-10988. 1969. 15.95 o.p. (ISBN 0-385-06314-8). Doubleday.

--Fell's Beginner's Guide to Magic. LC 76-17125. 160p. 1976. 7.95 (ISBN 0-8119-0271-4); pap. 4.95 (ISBN 0-8119-0364-8). Fell.

--Houdini's Escapes & Magic. LC 75-30523. (Funk & W Bk.). (Illus.). 656p. 1976. 12.50 o.s.i. (ISBN 0-308-10220-7, TYC-T); pap. 6.95 o.s.i. (ISBN 0-308-10235-5, TYC-T). T Y Crowell.

--How to Bet the Harness Races. (Gambler's Book Shelf). 80p. 1975. pap. 2.95 (ISBN 0-89650-557-X). Gamblers.

--How to Play Winning Solitaire. LC 63-7724. 160p. 1976. 8.95 (ISBN 0-8119-0268-4); pap. 4.95 (ISBN 0-8119-0382-6). Fell.

--Hoyle's Modern Encyclopedia of Card Games, Rules of All the Basic Games & Popular Variations. LC 73-163085. 408p. 1974. pap. 5.95 (ISBN 0-385-07680-0, Dolp). Doubleday.

--Junior Magic. LC 76-58624. (Illus.). (gr. 5 up). 7.95 (ISBN 0-8069-4546-X); PLB 7.49 (ISBN 0-8069-4547-8). Sterling.

--Mastering Magic: Secrets of the Great Magicians Revealed. LC 77-1535. 1977. pap. 4.95 (ISBN 0-8119-0277-3). Fell.

--Professional Magic for Amateurs. (Illus.). 225p. 1974. pap. 3.50 (ISBN 0-486-23012-0). Dover.

--Walter Gibson's Big Book of Magic for All Ages. LC 80-496. (Illus.). 240p. 1980. 12.95 (ISBN 0-385-14808-9). Doubleday.

--Winning the Two-Dollar Bet. (Gambler's Book Shelf). 1975. pap. 2.95 (ISBN 0-89650-556-1). Gamblers.

Gibson, Walter B. & Young, Morris N. Houdini on Magic. LC 53-13518. 1953. lib. bdg. 11.50x (ISBN 0-88307-538-5). Gannon.

Gibson, Walter S. Bruegel. (Illus.). 1977. 17.95 (ISBN 0-19-519952-9); pap. 9.95 (ISBN 0-19-519953-7). Oxford U Pr.

--Hieronymous Bosch. (World of Art Ser.). (Illus.). 1973. pap. 9.95 (ISBN 0-19-519945-6). Oxford U Pr.

--The Paintings of Cornelis Engebrechtsz. LC 76-23620. (Outstanding Dissertations in the Fine Arts - 16th Century). (Illus.). 1977. Repr. of 1969 ed. lib. bdg. 56.00 (ISBN 0-8240-2691-8). Garland Pub.

Gibson, William. Dinny & the Witches: Two Plays. Bd. with The Miracle Worker. LC 60-7778. 1960. 4.50 (ISBN 0-689-10095-7). Atheneum.

--Family Life & Morality: Studies in Black & White. LC 79-57076. 116p. 1980. pap. text ed. 7.50 (ISBN 0-8191-0969-X). U Pr of Amer.

Gibson, William M. The Art of Mark Twain. LC 75-25455. 225p. 1976. 14.95x (ISBN 0-19-501993-8). Oxford U Pr.

--Theodore Roosevelt Among the Humorists: W. D. Howells, Mark Twain, & Mr. Dooley. LC 79-17592. (John C. Hodges Lecture Ser.). 1980. 7.50x (ISBN 0-87049-263-2). U of Tenn Pr.

Gibson, William M., ed. see Twain, Mark.

Gibson-Jarvie, Robert. The City of London: A Financial & Commercial History. (Illus.). 128p. 1980. 17.50 (ISBN 0-85941-090-0). Herman Pub.

Gicovate, Bernard. Garcilaso De la Vega. LC 74-28304. (World Authors Ser.: Spain: No. 349). 1975. lib. bdg. 12.50 (ISBN 0-8057-2342-0). Twayne.

Gidal, Sonia & Gidal, Tim. My Village in Spain. (Illus.). (gr. 4-6). 1962. PLB 5.69 o.p. (ISBN 0-394-91922-X). Pantheon.

Gidal, Tim, jt. auth. see Gidal, Sonia.

Gidal, Tim N. Modern Photo-Journalism: Origin & Evolution, 1910-1933. Oberli-Turner, Maureen, tr. (Men & Movements Ser.: Vol. 1). (Illus.). 96p. 1974. 10.95 o.s.i. (ISBN 0-02-544300-3). Macmillan.

--Modern Photo-Journalism: Origin & Evolution, 1910-1933. Oberli-Turner, Maureen, tr. (Photography, Men & Movements Ser.: Vol. 1). (Illus.). 96p. 1974. pap. 5.95 o.s.i. (ISBN 0-02-000400-1, Collier). Macmillan.

Gidbeau, Kenneth W., jt. auth. see Miller, George H.

Giddens, A., jt. ed. see Stanworth, P.

Giddens, Anthony. Capitalism & Modern Social Theory: An Analysis of the Writings of Marx, Durkheim & Max Weber. LC 70-161291. 1971. 29.95 (ISBN 0-521-08293-5); pap. 8.95x (ISBN 0-521-09785-1). Cambridge U Pr.

--Central Problems in Social Theory: Action, Structure & Contradiction in Social Analysis. 1979. 23.75x (ISBN 0-520-03972-6); Campus No. 241. pap. 8.95x (ISBN 0-520-03975-0). U of Cal Pr.

Gidding, Joshua. The Old Girl. LC 79-26850. 264p. 1980. 12.95 (ISBN 0-03-052196-3); pap. 5.95 (ISBN 0-03-057998-8). HR&W.

Giddings. Advances in Chromatography, Vol. 19. 336p. Date not set. 39.75. Dekker.

Giddings, et al. Advances in Chromatography, Vol. 17. 1979. 36.00 (ISBN 0-8247-6902-3). Dekker.

Giddings, J. C. Dynamics of Chromatography, Pt. 1: Principles & Theory. (Chromatographic Science Ser.: Vol. 1). 1965. 39.75 o.p. (ISBN 0-8247-1225-0). Dekker.

Giddings, James L. Archeology of Cape Denbigh. LC 63-10231. (Illus.). 331p. 1964. 25.00 (ISBN 0-87057-080-3, Pub. by Brown U Pr). Univ Pr of New England.

Giddings, John A., jt. ed. see Greenspan, Kalman.

Giddings, Joshua R. Exiles of Florida. Thompson, Arthur W., intro. by. LC 64-19159. (Floridiana Facsimile & Reprint Ser). (Illus.). 1964. Repr. of 1858 ed. 10.75 (ISBN 0-8130-0085-8). U Presses Fla.

Giddings, L. E., jt. auth. see Mani, M. S.

Giddings, P. J. Marketing Boards & Ministries: A Study of Agricultural Marketing Boards As Political & Administrative Instruments. 1974. 19.50 (ISBN 0-347-01033-4, 93484-4, Pub. by Saxon Hse England). Lexington Bks.

Giddings, Robert. You Should Se Me in Pyjamas. 192p. 1981. 27.00 (ISBN 0-241-10534-X, Pub. by Hamish Hamilton England). David & Charles.

Giddins, Gary. Riding on a Blue Note: Jazz & American Pop. 275p. 1981. 16.95 (ISBN 0-19-502835-X). Oxford U Pr.

Giddy, Ian H., jt. auth. see Dufey, Gunter.

Gide, Andre. Lafcadio's Adventures. Bussy, Dorothy, tr. from Fr. LC 79-24000. 1980. Repr. of 1925 ed. lib. bdg. 10.00x (ISBN 0-8376-0452-4). Bentley.

--Notebooks of Andre Walter. LC 67-24573. 1968. 4.75 o.p. (ISBN 0-8022-0586-0). Philos Lib.

--Porte Etroite. Shackleton, M., ed. 1962. pap. text ed. 4.95x o.p. (ISBN 0-669-27391-0). Heath.

--The School for Wives-Robert-Genevieve or the Unfinished Confidence. Bussy, Dorothy, tr. from Fr. LC 79-23993. 1980. Repr. of 1929 ed. lib. bdg. 10.00x (ISBN 0-8376-0454-0). Bentley.

--Strait Is the Gate. Bussy, Dorothy, tr. from Fr. LC 79-23999. Orig. Title: La Porte Etroite. 1980. Repr. of 1924 ed. lib. bdg. 10.00x (ISBN 0-8376-0453-2). Bentley.

Gidley, J. A., jt. auth. see Elwell, W. T.

Gidley, James W. Paleocene Primates of the Fort Union, with Discussion of Relationships of Eocene Primates. Bd. with The Fort Union of the Crazy Mountain Field, Montana, & Its Mammalian Faunas. Simpson, George G. Repr. of 1937 ed. LC 78-72717. Date not set. Repr. of 1923 ed. 42.50 (ISBN 0-404-18292-5). AMS Pr.

Gidley, Mick. Kopet: Chief Joseph's Last Years, a Documentary Narrative. LC 80-54428. (Illus.). 168p. 1981. 16.95 o.p. (ISBN 0-295-95794-8). U of Wash Pr.

Gidley, Richard, jt. auth. see Seymour, Dale.

Gidney, James B., jt. auth. see Weeks, Philip.

Gidney, James B., tr. see Romains, Jules.

Gido, Jack. An Introduction to Project Planning. 1974. pap. 6.75 (ISBN 0-932078-48-6). GE Tech Prom & Train.

Gidwin, William. The Adventures of Caleb Williams. LC 80-2481. 1981. Repr. of 1926 ed. 49.50 (ISBN 0-404-19115-0). AMS Pr.

Gidwitz, Betsy. Politics of International Air Transport. LC 79-2706. 1980. 23.95 (ISBN 0-669-03234-4). Lexington Bks.

Gie, Daphne. Afghan Hounds: A Complete Guide. 1978. 19.95 (ISBN 0-7153-7423-0). David & Charles.

Gieber, Robert L. An English-French Glossary of Educational Terminology. LC 80-5652. 212p. 1980. lib. bdg. 18.00 (ISBN 0-8191-1344-1); pap. text ed. 9.25 (ISBN 0-8191-1345-X). U Pr of Amer.

Giedon, Sigfried. The Beginnings of Architecture: The Eternal Present, a Contribution on Constancy & Change, Vol. 2. LC 80-8733. (The A. W. Mellon Lectures in the Fine Arts, 1957, Bolligen Ser.: XXXV: 6,11). (Illus.). 604p. 1981. 42.50x (ISBN 0-691-09945-6); pap. 15.00 (ISBN 0-691-09945-6). Princeton U Pr.

Giedt, Warren H. see Heat Transfer & Fluid Mechanics Institute.

Giegel, Joseph L., jt. auth. see Henry, John B.

Giehl, Dudley. Vegetarianism: A Way of Life. 272p. 1981. pap. 3.95 (ISBN 0-06-464045-0, BN). Har-Row.

Giele, Janet Z. Women & the Future: Changing Sex Roles in Modern America. LC 77-2472. 1979. pap. text ed. 7.95 (ISBN 0-02-911690-2). Free Pr.

Giele, Janet Z. & Smock, Audrey C. Woman: Roles & Status in Eight Countries. LC 76-39950. 1977. 26.50 (ISBN 0-471-01504-0, Pub. by Wiley-Interscience). Wiley.

Gielgud, John. Gielgud: An Actor & His Time, a Memoir. (Illus.). 1980. 14.95 (ISBN 0-517-54179-3). Potter.

--Stage Directions. 1979. pap. 6.85 (ISBN 0-87830-568-8). Theatre Arts.

Gielgud, John, ed. see Chekhov, Anton.

Gielnik, S. J. & Gossling, W. F., eds. Input, Output & Marketing: Proceedings of the 1977 London Conference & the 1979 Toledo Ohio Workshop. (I.-O.P.C. Conference Ser.: No. 4). (Illus.). 400p. 1980. 50.00x (ISBN 0-904870-14-6, Pub. by Input-Output England). Kelley.

Giere, Ronald, jt. ed. see Asquith, Peter D.

Gierl, Irmgard. Cross Stitch Patterns. LC 77-75315. (Illus.). 1977. encore ed. o.p. 2.95 (ISBN 0-684-16192-3, ScribT); pap. 3.95 (ISBN 0-684-15232-0, ScribT). Scribner.

Gierz, G., et al. A Compendium of Continuous Lattices. 380p. 1980. 19.80 (ISBN 0-387-10111-X). Springer-Verlag.

Gies, David T. Nicholas Fernandez de Moratin. (World Authors Ser.: No. 558). 1979. lib. bdg. 14.50 (ISBN 0-8057-6400-3). Twayne.

Gies, Frances. Joan of Arc: The Legend & the Reality. LC 80-7900. (Illus.). 256p. 1981. 12.95 (ISBN 0-690-01942-4, HarpT). Har-Row.

Gies, Frances & Gies, Joseph. Women in the Middle Ages. LC 77-25832. (Illus.). 1978. 10.95 o.s.i. (ISBN 0-690-01724-3, TYC-T). T Y Crowell.

Gies, Frances, jt. auth. see Gies, Joseph.

Gies, Joseph & Gies, Frances. The Ingenious Yankees. (Illus.). 1976. 12.95 o.s.i. (ISBN 0-690-01150-4, TYC-T). T Y Crowell.

--Life in a Medieval Castle. LC 74-13058. (Medieval Life Ser). (Illus.). 320p. (Bibl., index). 1974. 9.95 o.s.i. (ISBN 0-690-00561-X, TYC-T). T Y Crowell.

--Life in a Medieval City. LC 74-13058. (Apollo Eds.). 274p. 1973. pap. 3.95 o.s.i. (ISBN 0-8152-0345-4, A345, TYC-T). T Y Crowell.

Gies, Joseph, jt. auth. see Gies, Frances.

Gies, Thomas G., jt. ed. see Sichel, Werner.

Giese, A. C., ed. Photophysiology. Incl. Vol. 1. General Principles - Action of Light on Plants. 1964. 46.50 (ISBN 0-12-282601-9); Vol. 2. Action of Light on Animals & Microorganisms, Photobiochemical Mechanisms, Bioluminescence. 1964. 46.50 (ISBN 0-12-282602-7); Vols. 3 & 4. Current Topics. 1968. Vol. 3. 46.50 (ISBN 0-12-282603-5); Vol. 4. 46.50 (ISBN 0-12-282604-3); Vols. 5-7. Current Topics in Photobiology & Photochemistry. 1970-72. Vol. 5. 46.50 (ISBN 0-12-282605-1); Vol. 6. 46.50 (ISBN 0-12-282607-8); Vol. 7. 46.50 (ISBN 0-12-282608-6); Vol. 8. 1973. 46.50 (ISBN 0-12-282608-6). Acad Pr.

Giese, Frank S. & Wilder, Warren F. French Lyric Poetry: An Anthology. LC 64-7849. 1965. pap. 5.50 (ISBN 0-672-63038-9). Odyssey Pr.

Giese, Vincent M. You Got It All: A Personal Account of a White Priest in a Chicago Ghetto. LC 79-92505. (Illus.). 252p. 1980. pap. 5.95 (ISBN 0-87973-526-0, 526). Our Sunday Visitor.

Giesecke, Minnie. The Genesis of Hand Preference. LC 78-72795. Repr. of 1936 ed. 18.00 (ISBN 0-686-63637-6). AMS Pr.

Gieseke, Carl L. & Schikaneder, Emanuel. Magic Flute. Dent, Edward J., tr. 1937. 1.50 o.p. (ISBN 0-19-313310-5). Oxford U Pr.

Gieseking, Audrey, jt. auth. see Joseph, Marjory.

Gieseking, Audrey G., jt. auth. see Joseph, Marjory.

Giesel, James T. The Biology & Adaptability of Natural Populations. LC 73-18288. 1974. pap. text ed. 7.95 o.p. (ISBN 0-8016-1812-6). Mosby.

Gieson, Susan Van see Kurtz, Regina & Van Gieson, Susan.

Giesy, J. U. Jason, Son of Jason. (YA) 5.95 (ISBN 0-685-07439-0, Avalon). Bouregy.

Giff, Patricia G. Next Year I'll Be Special. LC 79-19174. 32p. (gr. k-3). 1980. PLB 7.95 (ISBN 0-525-35810-2). Dutton.

Giff, Patricia R. The Fourth Grade Celebrity. (gr. k-6). 1981. pap. 1.25 (ISBN 0-440-42676-6, YB). Dell.

--The Girl Who Knew It All. (gr. k-6). 1981. pap. 1.25 (ISBN 0-440-42855-6, YB). Dell.

--Have You Seen Hyacinth Macaw: A Mystery. LC 80-68729. (Illus.). 128p. (gr. 4-7). 1981. 7.95 (ISBN 0-440-03467-1); PLB 7.45 (ISBN 0-440-03472-8). Delacorte.

--Left-Handed Shortstop. LC 80-65835. (Illus.). 128p. (gr. 5-8). 1980. 7.95 (ISBN 0-440-04553-3); PLB 7.45 (ISBN 0-440-04554-1). Delacorte.

Giffard, Ann, jt. auth. see Greenhill, Basil.

Giffen, Daniel H. New Hampshire Colony. LC 76-93178. (Forge of Freedom Ser). (Illus.). (gr. 5-8). 1970. 7.95 (ISBN 0-02-735890-9, CCPr). Macmillan.

Giffen, Robert. Economic Inquiries & Studies, 2 vols. (The Development of Industrial Society Ser.). 916p. 1981. Repr. 65.00x (ISBN 0-7165-1758-2, Pub. by Irish Academic Pr). Biblio Dist.

Giffen, Walter C. Queueing: Basic Theory & Application. LC 76-44996. (Industrial Engineering Ser.). 1978. text ed. 28.95 (ISBN 0-88244-133-7). Grid Pub.

Giffin, Frederick C. Six Who Protested: Radical Opposition to the First World War. (National University Publications Ser. in American Studies). 1977. 12.50 (ISBN 0-8046-9193-2). Kennikat.

Giffin, Kim & Barnes, Richard. Trust of Self & Others. (Interpersonal Communication Ser.). (Illus.). 96p. 1976. pap. text ed. 5.95 (ISBN 0-675-08647-7). Merrill.

Giffin, Kim, jt. auth. see Patton, Bobby R.

Gifford, Ann, jt. auth. see Greenhill, Basil.

Gifford, Barry. Beautiful Phantoms. 1981. pap. 5.00 (ISBN 0-686-28912-9). Tombouctou.

--The Neighborhood of Baseball. 1981. 12.95 (ISBN 0-525-16457-X). Dutton.

--Port Tropique. LC 80-15440. (Black Lizard Bks, Fiction Ser.). 200p. 1980. pap. 5.95 (ISBN 0-916870-31-6). Creative Arts Bk.

--Port Tropique. LC 80-15440. (Black Lizard Fiction Ser.). 200p. 1980. 9.95 (ISBN 0-916870-32-4). Creative Arts Bk.

Gifford, Denis. The Illustrated Who's Who in British Films. (Illus.). 1980. 32.00 (ISBN 0-7134-1434-0). David & Charles.

Gifford, Douglas & Hoggarth, Pauline. Carnival & Coca-Leaf: Some Traditions of the Quechua Ayllu. LC 76-1302. 200p. 1976. 18.95 (ISBN 0-312-12215-2). St Martin.

Gifford, E. W., jt. auth. see Kroeber, A. L.

Gifford, Ernest M., jt. auth. see Foster, Adriance S.

Gifford, Frank & Mangel, Charles. Gifford on Courage. LC 76-21862. 320p. 1976. 9.95 (ISBN 0-87131-223-9). M Evans.

Gifford, Frank D. The Christian Way: A Book of Instructions & Devotions for Members of the Episcopal Church. (Orig.). pap. 3.25 (ISBN 0-8192-1033-1). Morehouse.

Gifford, George E., ed. Dear Jeffie: Being the Letters from Jeffries Wyman to His Son Jeffries Wyman, Jr. LC 78-58830. (gr. 6 up). 1978. 10.00 (ISBN 0-87365-796-9). Peabody Harvard.

Gifford, H. Boris Pasternak. LC 76-9735. (Illus.). 1977. 38.50 (ISBN 0-521-21288-X). Cambridge U Pr.

Gifford, James C. Archaeological Explorations in Caves of the Point of Pines Region, Arizona. LC 79-9180. (Anthropological Papers: No. 36). 1980. 8.95x (ISBN 0-8165-0360-5). U of Ariz Pr.

--Prehistoric Pottery Analysis & the Ceramics of Barton Ramie in the Belize Valley. LC 75-40772. (Peabody Museum Memoirs: Vol. 18). 1976. pap. text ed. 35.00 (ISBN 0-87365-691-1). Peabody Harvard.

Gifford, James C. & Smith, S. Watson. Gray Corrugated Pottery from Awatovi. LC 78-50909. (Peabody Museum Papers: Vol. 69). 1978. pap. 20.00 (ISBN 0-87365-194-4). Peabody Harvard.

Gifford, Thomas. The Cavanaugh Quest. 1977. pap. 2.50 (ISBN 0-345-29065-8). Ballantine.

--Hollywood Gothic. 1980. pap. 2.50 (ISBN 0-345-29084-4). Ballantine.

--The Wind Chill Factor. 384p. 1976. pap. 2.75 (ISBN 0-345-29728-8). Ballantine.

Gifford-Jones, W. What Every Woman Should Know About Hysterectomy. LC 76-45747. (Funk & W Bk.). 1977. 8.95 o.p. (ISBN 0-308-10275-4, TYC-T). T Y Crowell.

Gifft, Helen, et al. Nutrition, Behavior & Change. LC 79-170033. 1972. ref. ed. 17.95 (ISBN 0-13-627836-1). P-H.

Gifis, Steven H. Dictionary of Legal Terms. 1981. pap. 2.95 (ISBN 0-8120-2013-8). Barron. Postponed.

Giggins, L. W. & Shoebridge, D. J. Tense Drills. 1975. pap. text ed. 5.00x (ISBN 0-582-52173-4). Longman.

Giglio, Richard. Ambulatory Care Systems, Vol. 2: Location, Layout, & Information Systems for Efficient Operations. LC 76-55865. 1977. 19.50 (ISBN 0-669-01324-2). Lexington Bks.

Gignac, Louis & Warsaw, Jacqueline. Everything You Need to Know to Have Great Looking Hair. LC 80-51999. (Illus.). 144p. 1981. 14.95 (ISBN 0-670-30040-3). Viking Pr.

Gihman, I. I. & Skorohod, A. V. The Theory of Stochastic Processes, Vol. 1. (Grundlehren der Mathematischen Wissenschaften: Vol. 210). 570p. 1981. 89.00 (ISBN 0-387-06573-3). Springer-Verlag.

Gil, Carlos A., ed. Age of Porfirio Diaz: Selected Readings. LC 76-57535. (Illus.). 191p. 5.95 (ISBN 0-8263-0284-X). U of NM Pr.

Gil, David G. Violence Against Children: Physical Child Abuse in the United States. LC 77-130809. (Commonwealth Fund Publications Ser). (Illus.). 1970. 8.50x (ISBN 0-674-93941-7); pap. 3.50 (ISBN 0-674-93942-5). Harvard U Pr.

Gilbar, Steven. The Book Book. 224p. 1981. 10.95 (ISBN 0-312-08803-5). St Martin.

Gilberg, Laura S., jt. auth. see Buchholz, Barbara.

Gilberg, Trond. Modernization in Romania Since World War 2. LC 73-15187. (Special Studies). 195p. 1975. text ed. 24.95 (ISBN 0-275-09520-7). Praeger.

Gilbert. Criminal Investigation. (Public Service Technology Ser.). 496p. 1980. text ed. 17.95 (ISBN 0-675-08186-6). Merrill.

Gilbert, Alan. Marx's Politics: Communists & Citizens. 320p. 1981. 19.00 (ISBN 0-8135-0903-3). Rutgers U Pr.

Gilbert, Alan D. The Making of Post-Christian Britain. 192p. 1980. text ed. 23.00 cased (ISBN 0-582-48563-0). Longman.

--Religion & Society in Industrial England. (Themes in British Social History Ser.). (Illus.). 260p. 1976. pap. text ed. 12.95x (ISBN 0-582-48323-9). Longman.

Gilbert, Allan H., ed. Literary Criticism: Plato to Dryden. LC 61-12266. (Waynebooks Ser: No. 1). 1962. pap. 6.50x (ISBN 0-8143-1160-1). Wayne St U Pr.

Gilbert, B. The Trailblazers. LC 73-76268. (Old West Ser). (Illus.). 1973. kivar 12.96 (ISBN 0-8094-1459-7, Pub. by Time-Life). Silver.

Gilbert, Bil. The Trailblazers. (The Old West Ser.). (Illus.). 1973. 12.95 (ISBN 0-8094-1458-9). Time-Life.

Gilbert, Bill. This City, This Man: The Cookingham Era in Kansas City. LC 78-13401. (Illus.). 1978. 14.00 (ISBN 0-87326-021-X). Intl City Mgt.

Gilbert, Bruce. Remembering. LC 80-54370. 96p. 1981. 3.95 (ISBN 0-87159-139-1). Unity Bks.

Gilbert, Brynn. Love's Bold Embrace. 1979. pap. 2.25 (ISBN 0-505-51402-8). Tower Bks.

Gilbert, C. Italian Art: Fourteen Hundred to Fifteen Hundred. 1980. pap. 10.95 (ISBN 0-13-507947-0). P-H.

Gilbert, C. M. The Ozine Conquest. 1981. pap. 1.75 (ISBN 0-8439-0891-2, Leisure Bks). Nordon Pubns.

Gilbert, Charles, jt. auth. see Krooss, Herman E.

Gilbert, Claude. Histoire De Calejava, ou De. (Utopias in the Enlightenment Ser.). 332p. (Fr.). 1976. Repr. of 1700 ed. 47.50x o.p. (ISBN 0-8287-0376-0). Clearwater Pub.

Gilbert, Creighton, tr. from It. The Complete Poems & Selected Letters of Michelangelo. LC 79-87767. 1980. 22.00x (ISBN 0-691-03925-9); pap. 5.95 (ISBN 0-691-00324-6). Princeton U Pr.

Gilbert, Dennis A., jt. auth. see Weber, Paul J.

Gilbert, Doris W. Breaking the Reading Barrier. 1959. text ed. 9.50 (ISBN 0-13-081471-7). P-H.

--Breaking the Word Barrier. LC 77-173596. (Illus.). 240p. 1972. pap. text ed. 8.95 (ISBN 0-13-081661-2). P-H.

--Power & Speed in Reading. 1956. text ed. 10.95 (ISBN 0-13-685040-5). P-H.

Gilbert, Douglas. American Vaudeville: Its Life & Times. (Illus.). 10.00 (ISBN 0-8446-2128-5). Peter Smith.

Gilbert, Douglas L. Natural Resources & Public Relations. LC 76-143896. (Illus.). 320p. 1971. 8.00 (ISBN 0-933564-03-1). Wildlife Soc.

Gilbert, Douglas L., ed. see Wildlife Management Institute.

Gilbert, Edith. Tabletop the Right Way: An Information & Training Guide for the Professional in the Hospitality Industry. rev ed. LC 80-81206. (Illus.). 54p. 1980. 15.00x (ISBN 0-9600786-4-9). Jet'iquette.

Gilbert, Elliot L. The Good Kipling. LC 73-122098. ix, 216p. 1970. 11.95x (ISBN 0-8214-0085-1). Ohio U Pr.

Gilbert, Fontelle, ed. Minorities & Community Colleges. 1979. pap. 7.50 (ISBN 0-87117-091-4). Am Assn Comm Jr Coll.

Gilbert, G. G., ed. Pidgin & Creole Languages. LC 79-15866. 320p. 1980. 32.95 (ISBN 0-521-22789-5). Cambridge U Pr.

Gilbert, G. M. Nuremberg Diary. pap. 1.50 (ISBN 0-451-04551-3, W4551, Sig). NAL.

Gilbert, Sir Gefrey & Peake, Thomas. The Law of Evidence: A Compendium of the Law of Evidence, Vol. 35A & B. Berkowitz, David S. & Thorne, Samuel E., eds. LC 77-86648. (Classics of English Legal History in the Modern Era Ser.: Vol. 97). 1979. lib. bdg. 55.00 (ISBN 0-8240-3084-2). Garland Pub.

Gilbert, George. The Photographica Collector's Price Guide. LC 75-28698. (Illus.). 1977. pap. 4.95 o.p. (ISBN 0-8015-1409-6). Dutton.

--Photography: The Early Years a Historical Guide for Collectors. LC 78-20163. (Illus.). 181p. 1980. 19.95 (ISBN 0-06-011497-5, HarpT). Har-Row.

Gilbert, Harvey A. & Kagan, Robert A. Radiation Damage to the Nervous System: A Delayed Therapeutic Hazard. (Illus.). 225p. 1980. text ed. 27.00 (ISBN 0-89004-418-X). Raven.

Gilbert, Harvey A. & Kagan, A. Robert, eds. Modern Radiation Oncology: Classic Literature & Current Management. (Illus.). 1978. text ed. 52.50x (ISBN 0-06-140910-3, Harper Medical). Har-Row.

Gilbert, J., see Hills, P. J.

Gilbert, Jack G. Edmund Waller. (English Authors Ser.: No. 266). 1979. lib. bdg. 13.50 (ISBN 0-8057-6763-0). Twayne.

Gilbert, James, ed. see Antique Airplane Association.

Gilbert, James, ed. see Bridgeman, William & Hazard, Jacqueline.

Gilbert, James, ed. see Caproni, Gianni.

Gilbert, James, ed. see Coppens de Houthulst, Willy.

Gilbert, James, ed. see Farre, Henry.

Gilbert, James, ed. see Hall, James N.

Gilbert, James, ed. see Haydon, Frederick S.

Gilbert, James, ed. see Lockheed Aircraft Corporation.

Gilbert, James, ed. see Luukkanen, Eino.

Gilbert, James, ed. see Royal Aeronautical Society.

Gilbert, James, ed. see Wykeham, Peter.

Gilbert, John. Dinosaurs Discovered. LC 80-82756. (Illus.). 96p. 1981. 8.95 (ISBN 0-88332-252-8). Larousse.

--An Interview with Bobby Clarke. (Interviews Ser.). (Illus.). (gr. 3-8). 1977. PLB 6.75 (ISBN 0-87191-573-1). Creative Ed.

--An Interview with Bobby Unser. (Interviews Ser.). (Illus.). (gr. 3-8). 1977. PLB 6.75 (ISBN 0-87191-572-3). Creative Ed.

Gilbert, John, tr. see Taglianti, Augusto V.

Gilbert, John H., ed. Speech & Cortical Functioning. (Based upon a symposium). 1972. 24.50 (ISBN 0-12-282850-X). Acad Pr.

Gilbert, Julie Goldsmith. Ferber: A Biography of Edna Ferber. LC 76-57512. 1978. 10.50 o.p. (ISBN 0-385-03960-3). Doubleday.

Gilbert, Kay, jt. auth. see Tolman, Newton F.

Gilbert, Kitty S., compiled by. Treasures from the Great Bronze Age of China: An Exhibition from the People's Republic of China. (Illus.). 192p. 1980. pap. 9.95 (ISBN 0-87099-230-9). Metro Mus Art.

Gilbert, Lawrence I., jt. ed. see Etkin, William.

Gilbert, Leopold & Daniel, Sol, eds. Medical State Board Examination Review Book, 2 pts. 6th ed. Incl. Vol. 1. Basic Sciences. 287p; Vol. 2. Clinical Sciences. 239p. 1976. spiral bdg. 12.00 ea. o.p. Med Exam.

Gilbert, Lynn & Moore, Gaylen. Who Shaped Our Time. Southern, Carol, ed. 1981. 17.95 (ISBN 0-517-54371-0). Potter.

Gilbert, M. S. Biography of the Unborn. 2nd ed. 1963. 12.95 (ISBN 0-02-845260-7). Hafner.

Gilbert, Marilyn B. Communicating by Letter. LC 72-11879. (Self-Teaching Guides Ser.). 192p. 1973. 6.95 (ISBN 0-471-29897-2). Wiley.

Gilbert, Marilyn B., jt. auth. see Gilbert, Thomas F.

Gilbert, Marjorie. Faith at an Early Age. (Illus.). 1973. pap. 1.50 (ISBN 0-89570-078-6). Claretian Pubns.

Gilbert, Martin. British History Atlas. 1969. 4.95 o.s.i. (ISBN 0-02-543270-2). Macmillan.

--The Coming of War. (Jackdaw Ser: No. 64). (Illus.). 1973. 5.95 o.p. (ISBN 0-670-23224-6, Grossman). Viking Pr.

--Exile & Return: The Struggle for a Jewish Homeland. LC 78-9780. (Illus.). 1978. 12.95 o.s.i. (ISBN 0-397-01249-7). Lippincott.

--Jerusalem History Atlas. (Illus.). 1977. 12.95 (ISBN 0-02-543410-1). Macmillan.

--Jewish History Atlas. (Illus.). 1969. 11.95 (ISBN 0-02-543280-X). Macmillan.

--Roots of Appeasement. pap. 3.50 o.p. (ISBN 0-452-25024-2, Z5024, Plume). NAL.

--Russian History Atlas. LC 72-80174. (Illus.). 160p. 1972. 12.95 (ISBN 0-02-543320-2). Macmillan.

Gilbert, Mary E., ed. see Hofmannsthal, Hugo Von.

Gilbert, Michael. The Empty House. (Penguin Crime Monthly Ser.). 1980. pap. 2.50 (ISBN 0-14-005142-2). Penguin.

--The Killing of Katie Steelstock. LC 79-3409. (A Harper Novel of Suspense Ser.). 304p. 1980. 12.95 (ISBN 0-06-011494-0, HarpT). Har-Row.

Gilbert, Michael, jt. auth. see Norton, Andre.

Gilbert, Milton. Quest for World Monetary System: Gold-Dollar System & It's Aftermath. LC 80-17865. 255p. 1980. 19.95 (ISBN 0-471-07998-7, Pub. by Wiley-Interscience). Wiley.

Gilbert, Miriam, jt. auth. see Guy, May.

Gilbert, Miriam, jt. auth. see Warner, Marie P.

Gilbert, Mitchell. An Owner's Manual for the Human Being. 1980. pap. 4.95 (ISBN 0-686-69316-7). Weiser.

Gilbert, N. & Specht, H. Planning for Social Welfare: Issues, Models & Tasks. 1977. text ed. 17.95 (ISBN 0-13-679555-2). P-H.

Gilbert, N., et al. Ecological Relationships. (Illus.). 1976. text ed. 13.95x (ISBN 0-7167-0486-2). W H Freeman.

Gilbert, Neil. Biometrical Interpretation. (Illus.). 130p. 1973. text ed. 11.50x o.p. (ISBN 0-19-854122-8). Oxford U Pr.

Gilbert, Neil & Specht, Harry. Dimensions of Social Welfare Policy. (Illus.). 208p. 1974. 15.95 (ISBN 0-13-214486-7). P-H.

--The Emergence of Social Work. 2nd ed. LC 80-83097. 484p. 1981. pap. text ed. 12.95 (ISBN 0-87581-266-X). Peacock Pubs.

Gilbert, Neil, et al. An Introduction to Social Work Practice. (P-H Ser. in Social Work Practice). (Illus.). 1980. text ed. 16.95 (ISBN 0-13-479105-3). P-H.

Gilbert, R. P. Function Theoretic Methods in Partial Differential Equations. (Mathematics in Science & Engineering Ser: Vol. 54). 1969. 46.00 (ISBN 0-12-283050-4). Acad Pr.

Gilbert, Robert. Business Practice Set: SAAL Manufacturing Limited Financial Operating Budget. 64p. 1981. pap. text ed. 6.95 (ISBN 0-8403-2346-8). Kendall-Hunt.

Gilbert, Rodney V. The Unequal Treaties: China & the Foreigner. (Studies in Chinese History & Civilzation). 248p. 1977. Repr. of 1929 ed. 19.50 (ISBN 0-89093-075-9). U Pubns Amer.

Gilbert, S. M. Monarch Notes on Woolf's Mrs. Dalloway & to the Lighthouse. (Orgi). pap. 1.95 (ISBN 0-671-00883-8). Monarch Pr.

Gilbert, Sandra. In the Fourth World: Poems. LC 78-11144. 80p. 1979. 7.95 o.p. (ISBN 0-8173-8528-2); pap. 3.95 (ISBN 0-8173-8527-4). U of Ala Pr.

--Monarch Notes on Lawrence's Sons & Lovers & Other Works. (Orig.). pap. 1.95 (ISBN 0-671-00716-5). Monarch Pr.

Gilbert, Sara. Fat Free: Common Sense for Young Weight Worriers. 112p. (gr. 6 up). 1975. 7.95 (ISBN 0-02-736410-0). Macmillan.

--Feeling Good: A Book About You & Your Body. LC 78-5306. 192p. (gr. 7 up). 1979. 7.95 (ISBN 0-590-07510-1, Four Winds). Schol Bk Serv.

--Trouble at Home. 192p. (gr. 7 up). 1981. 7.95 (ISBN 0-688-41995-X); PLB 7.63 (ISBN 0-688-51995-4). Morrow.

--You Are What You Eat: A Common-Sense Guide to the Modern American Diet. LC 76-39806. (gr. 5 up). 1977. 8.95 (ISBN 0-02-736020-2, 73602). Macmillan.

Gilbert, Stuart. James Joyce's Ulysses. 1955. pap. 2.95 (ISBN 0-394-70013-9, V13, Vin). Random.

Gilbert, Stuart, tr. see De Saint-Exupery, Antoine.

Gilbert, Stuart, tr. see Valery, Paul.

Gilbert, Thomas F. & Gilbert, Marilyn B. Thinking Metric. 2nd ed. LC 77-20190. (Self-Teaching Guide Ser.). 1978. pap. text ed. 5.95 (ISBN 0-471-03427-4). Wiley.

Gilbert, W. S. Additional Adventures of Messrs. Box & Cox: A Continuation of the Dramatic History of Box & Cox. MacPhail, Ralph, Jr., ed. Bd. with Penelope Anne. Burnand, F. C. LC 75-304933. (Illus.). 74p. 1974. pap. 7.50x (ISBN 0-9601580-0-6). Parenthesis Pr.

--Bab Ballads. Ellis, James, ed. LC 77-102668. 1970. 17.50x (ISBN 0-674-05800-3, Belknap Pr); pap. 8.95 (ISBN 0-674-05801-1). Harvard U Pr.

Gilbert, W. S. & Sullivan, Arthur. The Complete Plays of Gilbert & Sullivan. (Illus.). 640p. 1976. pap. 8.95 (ISBN 0-393-00828-2, Norton Lib). Norton.

Gilbert, Wilfred C., ed. see U. S. Library of Congress Legislative Reference Service.

Gilbert, William H., ed. Public Relations in Local Government. LC 75-29400. (Municipal Management Ser.). 1975. text ed. 22.00 (ISBN 0-87326-012-0). Intl City Mgt.

Gilbert, William J. Modern Algebra with Applications. LC 76-22756. 1976. 25.95 (ISBN 0-471-29891-3, Pub by Wiley-Interscience). Wiley.

Gilbert, Zoe. Fruit Growing in Southern Africa. 1980. 25.00x (Pub. by Bailey & Swinton South Africa). State Mutual Bk.

Gilbertie, Sal & Sheehan, Larry. Herb Gardening at Its Best: Everything You Need to Know About Growing Your Favorite Herbs. LC 77-23678. (Illus.). 1980. pap. 6.95 (ISBN 0-689-70595-6, 255). Atheneum.

Gilbertson, M. P., jt. auth. see Scrutton, D. R.

Gilbertson, R. L., jt. auth. see Lindsey, J. P.

Gilbey, John F. Secret Fighting Arts of the World. LC 63-7910. (Illus.). 1963. bds. 9.75 (ISBN 0-8048-0515-6). C E Tuttle.

Gilbo, Patrick F. The American Red Cross--the First Century: A Pictorial History. LC 80-8204. (Illus.). 256p. 1981. 25.00 (ISBN 0-06-011461-4, HarpT). Har-Row.

Gilborn, Alice. What Do You Do with a Kinkajou? LC 75-29195. 1976. 8.95 o.s.i. (ISBN 0-397-01109-1). Lippincott.

Gilboy, Robert C. Spell It Fast. 1981. pap. 4.95 (ISBN 0-87491-071-4). Acropolis.

Gilbreath, Alice. Beginning Crafts for Beginning Readers. LC 71-184461. (Picture Bk). (Illus.). 32p. (gr. 1-4). 1972. 2.95 o.p. (ISBN 0-695-80317-4); PLB 5.97 o.p. (ISBN 0-695-40317-6). Follett.

--Candles for Beginners to Make. LC 74-14968. (Illus.). 64p. (gr. 3-7). 1975. 7.25 (ISBN 0-688-22010-X); PLB 6.96 (ISBN 0-688-32010-4). Morrow.

--Fun with Weaving. (Illus.). 96p. (gr. 3-7). 1976. 6.25 (ISBN 0-688-22064-9); PLB 6.00 o.p. (ISBN 0-688-32063-5). Morrow.

--Making Costumes for Parties, Plays & Holidays. LC 73-13996. (Illus.). 96p. (gr. 3-7). 1974. PLB 6.96 (ISBN 0-688-30103-7). Morrow.

--Simple Decoupage: Having Fun with Cutouts. LC 77-22088. (Illus.). (gr. 3-7). 1978. 6.50 (ISBN 0-688-22134-3); PLB 6.24 (ISBN 0-688-32134-8). Morrow.

--Slab, Coil, & Pinch: A Beginners Pottery Book. (Illus.). (gr. 3-7). 1977. 6.75 (ISBN 0-688-22105-X); PLB 6.48 (ISBN 0-688-32105-4). Morrow.

Gilbreath, Glenn H., jt. auth. see Van Matre, Joseph G.

Gilbreth, Frank B. & Carey, Ernestine G. Cheaper by the Dozen. rev. ed. LC 63-20411. (Illus.). 1963. 10.95 (ISBN 0-690-18632-0, TYC-T). T Y Crowell.

Gilbreth, Frank B., Jr. & Carey, Ernestine G. Belles on Their Toes. LC 50-13907. (Illus.). 1950. 8.95 (ISBN 0-690-13023-6, TYC-T). T Y Crowell.

Gilby, Thomas. Poetic Experience. 114p. 1980. Repr. of 1934 ed. lib. bdg. 20.00 (ISBN 0-8492-4976-7). R West.

Gilby, Thomas, ed. see Thomas Aquinas, St.

Gilchrist, Agnes A. William Strickland-Architect & Engineer 1788-1854. enl. ed. LC 69-13714. (Architecture & Decorative Art Ser). (Illus.). 1969. Repr. of 1950 ed. lib. bdg. 29.50 (ISBN 0-306-71235-0). Da Capo.

Gilchrist, Alexander. Life of William Blake: With Selections from His Poems & Other Writings, 2 vols. enl. ed. (Illus.). 993p. 1969. Set. 35.00. Phaeton.

Gilchrist, Bruce & Wessel, Milton R. Government Regulation of the Computer Industry. LC 72-83726. ix, 247p. 1972. 12.50 (ISBN 0-88283-028-7). AFIPS Pr.

Gilchrist, Bruce, jt. ed. see Leininger, Joseph E.

Gilchrist, J. D. Extraction Metallurgy. 2nd ed. 1978. 50.00 (ISBN 0-08-021711-7); pap. 17.00 (ISBN 0-08-021712-5). Pergamon.

--Fuels & Refractories. 1963. 9.90 (ISBN 0-08-009780-4); pap. 4.95 (ISBN 0-08-009779-0). Pergamon.

Gilchrist, James S., tr. see Wright, J. Stafford.

Gilchrist, Joelyn & Wood, Jacqueline. The Campus Survival Cookbook. (Illus.). 160p. 1973. 5.95 (ISBN 0-688-00030-4); pap. 4.95 (ISBN 0-688-05030-1). Morrow.

Gilchrist, Peter S. My Amateur World. (Illus.). 200p. 1975. text ed. 10.00. Gilchem Corp.

Gilchrist, Robert S. & Roberts, Bernice R. Curriculum Development: A Humanized Systems Approach. LC 72-93705. 1974. pap. 3.95 (ISBN 0-8224-1687-5). Pitman Learning.

Gilchrist, T. L. & Storr, R. C. Organic Reactions & Orbital Symmetry. 2nd ed. LC 78-54578. (Cambridge Texts in Chemistry & Biochemistry Ser.). (Illus.). 1979. 59.50 (ISBN 0-521-22014-9); pap. 18.95x (ISBN 0-521-29336-7). Cambridge U Pr.

Gilchrist, Theo E. Halfway up the Mountain. LC 77-29020. (Illus.). (gr. k-2). 1978. 6.89 (ISBN 0-397-31805-7). Lippincott.

Gilchrist, W. & Murray, W. J., eds. Press in the French Revolution. LC 77-150256. 1971. 28.50x (ISBN 0-89197-596-9). Irvington.

Gilchrist, Warren. Statistical Forecasting. LC 76-13504. 1976. 42.95 (ISBN 0-471-99402-2, Pub. by Wiley-Interscience); pap. 18.50 (ISBN 0-471-99403-0). Wiley.

Gildas. Gildas: The Ruin of Britain & Other Works. Winterbottom, Michael, ed. 162p. 1978. 16.00x (ISBN 0-8476-6079-6). Rowman.

Gilder, George. Wealth & Poverty. LC 80-50556. 1981. 16.95 (ISBN 0-465-09105-9). Basic.

Gilder, Jules. One Hundred & Ten IC Timer Projects. 1979. pap. 6.35 (ISBN 0-8104-5688-5). Hayden.

--Telephone Accessories You Can Build. (Illus.). 1976. pap. 6.50 (ISBN 0-8104-5748-2). Hayden.

Gilder, Jules H. Basic Computer Programs in Science & Engineering. 256p. 1980. pap. 9.95 (ISBN 0-8104-0761-2). Hayden.

Gilder, Rosamond. Enter the Actress. (Illus.). 1959. pap. 1.95 (ISBN 0-87830-502-5, 2). Theatre Arts.

Gilderbloom, John I., ed. Rent Control: A Source Book. 314p. (Orig.). 1981. pap. 9.95 (ISBN 0-938806-00-9). Foun Natl Prog.

Gilderman, Martin S. Juan Rodriguez de la Camara. (World Authors Ser.: No. 423). 1977. lib. bdg. 12.50 (ISBN 0-8057-6195-0). Twayne.

Gildersleeve, Thomas R. Organizing & Documenting Data Processing Information. 1977. pap. text ed. 9.95x (ISBN 0-8104-5739-3). Hayden.

Gildin, Hilail, ed. see Strauss, Leo.

Gildon, Charles. The Deist's Manual; or a Rational Enquiry into the Christian Religion. Wellek, Rene, ed. LC 75-11220. (British Philosophers & Theologians of the 17th & 18th Centuries: Vol. 23). 1976. Repr. of 1705 ed. lib. bdg. 42.00 (ISBN 0-8240-1774-9). Garland Pub.

--The Golden Spy. LC 77-170519. (Foundations of the Novel Ser.: Vol. 14). lib. bdg. 50.00 (ISBN 0-8240-0526-0). Garland Pub.

--The Post-Man Robb'd of His Mail: Or, the Packet Broke Open. LC 73-170542. (Foundations of the Novel Ser.: Vol. 31). lib. bdg. 50.00 (ISBN 0-8240-0543-0). Garland Pub.

--Remarks on Mr. Rowes Tragedy of Lady Jane Grey & All His Other Plays. LC 74-7279. (The English Stage Ser.). lib. bdg. 50.00 (ISBN 0-685-41744-1). Garland Pub.

Gildon, Charles see Collier, Jeremy.

Gildon, Charles see Dennis, John.

Gildrie, Richard P. Salem, Massachusetts, 1626-1683: A Covenant Community. LC 74-20841. (Illus.). 1975. 9.95x (ISBN 0-8139-0532-X). U Pr of Va.

Gile, Joanne, jt. auth. see Wilson, Eunice.

Gileadi, E., et al. Interfacial Chemistry: An Experimental Approach. 1975. text ed. 30.50 (ISBN 0-201-02398-9, Adv Bk Prog); pap. text ed. 18.50 (ISBN 0-201-02399-7). A-W.

Giles, Anne E. Merwan: Stories of Meher Baba for Children. LC 80-53858. (Illus.). 96p. (Orig.). (gr. 3-7). 1980. pap. 4.95 (ISBN 0-913078-41-7). Sheriar Pr.

Giles, Carl H. & Williams, Barbara A. Bewitching Jewelry. LC 74-30726. (Illus.). 1976. 12.00 o.p. (ISBN 0-498-01654-4). A S Barnes.

Giles, Eugene & Friedlaender, Jonathan S., eds. The Measures of Man: Methodologies in Biological Anthropology. LC 76-28638. (Peabody Museum Press Ser.). (Illus.). 1976. 32.00 (ISBN 0-87365-782-9); pap. 25.00 (ISBN 0-685-84631-8). Peabody Harvard.

Giles, F. A. Herbaceous Perennials. (Illus.). 1980. text ed. 15.95 (ISBN 0-8359-2822-5). Reston.

Giles, Floyd, jt. auth. see Turgeon, A. J.

Giles, Floyd H., et al. Developing Human Brain: Growth & Epidemiologic Neuropathology. Date not set. write for info. (ISBN 0-88416-254-0). PSG Pub.

Giles, Herbert A. A Glossary of Reference on Subjects Connected with Far East. 328p. 1978. Repr. 17.50 (ISBN 0-89684-134-0, Pub. by Cosmo Pubns India). Orient Bk Dist.

Giles, Herbert A., tr. from Chinese. Chuang Tzu. (Unwin Paperbacks Ser.). 336p. (Orig.). 1980. pap. 7.50x (ISBN 0-04-299009-2, 2572). Allen Unwin.

Giles, Howard & Robinson, W. Peter. Language: Social Psychological Perspectives: Selected Papers from the First International Conference on Social Psychology & Language Held at the University of Bristol, England, July 1979. Smith, Philip M., ed. LC 80-40714. 450p. 1980. 60.00 (ISBN 0-08-024696-6). Pergamon.

Giles, Howard & Saint-Jacques, Bernard. Language & Ethnic Relations: Language & Ethnic Interaction Section of the Sociolinguistics Program of the 9th World Congress of Sociology. LC 79-40709. (Illus.). 1979. 33.00 (ISBN 0-686-58671-9). Pergamon.

Giles, Howard, jt. ed. see Scherer, Klaus R.

Giles, Jacob, jt. auth. see Hale, Matthew.

Giles, James E. Esto Creemos los Bautistas. Date not set. pap. 1.90 (ISBN 0-311-09091-5). Casa Bautista.

--La Psicologia y el Ministerio Cristiano. 1978. 2.50 (ISBN 0-311-42059-1). Casa Bautista.

Giles, James R. Claude McKay. LC 76-10154. (U.S. Authors Ser.: No. 271). 1976. lib. bdg. 10.95 (ISBN 0-8057-7171-9). Twayne.

--James Jones. (United States Authors Ser.: No. 366). 1981. lib. bdg. 9.95 (ISBN 0-8057-7293-6). Twayne.

Giles, James V., jt. auth. see Smith, A. Robert.

Giles, Janice H. Hannah Fowler. 1980. lib. bdg. 16.95 (ISBN 0-8161-3051-5, Large Print Bks). G K Hall.

--Johnny Osage. 1980. lib. bdg. 15.95 (ISBN 0-8161-3053-1, Large Print Bks). G K Hall.

--Run Me a River. 1976. pap. 1.75 (ISBN 0-380-00875-0, 31427). Avon.

--Six-Horse Hitch. 408p. 1980. pap. 2.75 (ISBN 0-380-51532-6, 51532). Avon.

--Voyage to Santa Fe. 1977. pap. 1.75 (ISBN 0-380-00965-X, 32417). Avon.

Giles, Ken & Smith, Clive. Match Fishing Our Way. 1978. 13.50 (ISBN 0-7153-7692-6). David & Charles.

Giles, Lionel, jt. tr. see Johnston, Charles.

Giles, Marian T., jt. auth. see Bush, Wilma J.

Giles, Raymond. Rogue Black. 208p. 1978. pap. 2.25 (ISBN 0-449-13809-7, GM). Fawcett.

Giles, Robert H., Jr. Wildlife Management. LC 78-15700. (Animal Science Ser.). (Illus.). 1978. text ed. 23.95x (ISBN 0-7167-0082-4). W H Freeman.

Gilfond, Henry. Genealogy: How to Find Your Roots. (Impact Bks.). (Illus.). (gr. 7 up). 1978. PLB 6.90 s&l (ISBN 0-531-01455-X). Watts.

--The New Ice Age. (Impact Bks). (Illus.). (gr. 7 up). 1978. PLB 6.90 s&l (ISBN 0-531-01458-4). Watts.

--The Reichstag Fire, February, 1933: Hitler Utilizes Arson to Extend His Dictatorship. LC 78-8182. (World Focus Bks.). (Illus.). 96p. 1973. PLB 4.90 o.p. (ISBN 0-531-02168-8). Watts.

--Syria. (First Bks.). (Illus.). (gr. 4-6). 1978. PLB 6.45 s&l (ISBN 0-531-02238-2). Watts.

--Voodoo: Its Origins & Practices. (Illus.). 160p. (gr. 6 up). 1976. PLB 5.90 o.p. (ISBN 0-531-00347-7). Watts.

--Water: A Scarce Resource. LC 78-3563. (Impact Bks.). (Illus.). 1978. lib. bdg. 6.90 s&l (ISBN 0-531-02205-6). Watts.

Gilford, Henry. How to Give a Speech. (gr. 7 up). 1980. PLB 6.45 (ISBN 0-531-04130-1). Watts.

Gilg, Andrew, jt. auth. see Blacksell, Mark.

Gilg, Andrew W. Countryside Planning: The First Three Decades 1945-76. LC 77-85036. (Illus.). 1978. 30.00 (ISBN 0-7153-7499-0). David & Charles.

Gilge, Jeanette. City-Kid Farmer. LC 75-4454. (Illus.). 128p. (Orig.). (gr. 6-7). 1975. pap. 1.95 (ISBN 0-912692-67-7). Cook.

Gilgun, John. Everything That Has Been Shall Be Again. (Illus.). 1981. 100.00 (ISBN 0-931460-11-5); pap. 7.50 (ISBN 0-931460-13-1). Bieler.

Gilhooley, Leonard, ed. No Divided Allegiance: Essays in Brownson's Thought. LC 79-56139. xiv, 193p. 1980. 20.00 (ISBN 0-8232-1056-1); pap. 8.00 (ISBN 0-8232-1057-X). Fordham.

Gili Gaya, S. D. Curso Superior De Sinaxtis Espanola. 12.50x (ISBN 0-686-00849-9). Colton Bk.

Giljlstra, D. J., et al, eds. Legal Isssues of European Integration 1979. 2nd ed. 130p. 1980. pap. 21.50 (ISBN 90-2681-178-0, Pub. by Kluwer Law & Taxation). Kluwer Boston.

Gilkerson, William. Maritime Arts by William Gilkerson. (Illus.). 100p. (Orig.). 1981. pap. write for info. (ISBN 0-87577-061-4). Peabody Mus Salem.

Gilkey, Landgon. Naming the Whirlwind: The Renewal of God-Language. LC 68-11146. 1969. pap. 8.60 o.p. (ISBN 0-672-60796-4). Bobbs.

Gilkey, Langdon. Catholocism Confronts Modernity: A Protestant View. 1975. 8.95 (ISBN 0-8164-1163-8). Crossroad NY.

--Message & Existence: An Introduction to Christian Theology. 272p. 1980. pap. 4.95 (ISBN 0-8164-2023-8). Crossroad NY.

--Reaping the Whirlwind: A Christian Interpretation of History. 1977. 17.50 (ISBN 0-8164-0308-2). Crossroad NY.

--Shantung Compound. LC 75-9312. 272p. 1975. pap. 4.95x (ISBN 0-06-063112-0, RD101, HarpR). Har-Row.

Gill, Arthur. Applied Algebra for the Computer Sciences. (Illus.). 416p. 1976. 23.95 (ISBN 0-13-039222-7). P-H.

--Machine & Assembly Language Programming of the PDP-Eleven. LC 78-9690. (Illus.). 1978. 19.95 (ISBN 0-13-541870-4). P-H.

Gill, B. M. Suspect. 192p. 1981. 9.95 (ISBN 0-684-16885-5, ScribT). Scribner.

Gill, Barry, ed. Motor Sport Yearbook 1974. LC 74-2649. (Illus.). 448p. 1974. pap. 5.95 o.s.i. (ISBN 0-02-029660-6, Collier). Macmillan.

Gill, Bartholomew. McGarr at the Dublin Horse Show. 1981. pap. 2.25 (ISBN 0-440-15379-4). Dell.

--McGarr on the Cliffs of Moher. LC 78-2645. 1978. 7.95 o.p. (ISBN 0-684-15570-2, ScribT). Scribner.

Gill, Bob. Forget All the Rules You Ever Learned About Graphic Design: Including the Ones in This Book. 168p. 1981. 22.50. Watson-Guptill.

Gill, Brendan. The Dream Come True: Great Houses of Los Angeles. 1980. 40.00 (ISBN 0-690-01893-2); ltd. ed 100.00 (ISBN 0-690-01961-0). Har-Row.

Gill, C. B. Non-Ferrous Extractive Metallurgy. LC 79-28696. 1980. 39.50 (ISBN 0-471-05980-3, Pub. by Wiley-Interscience). Wiley.

Gill, Colin, et al. Industrial Relations in the Chemical Industry. 1978. text ed. 30.00x (ISBN 0-566-00215-9, Pub. by Gower Pub Co England). Renouf.

Gill, Corrington. Wasted Manpower. LC 72-2371. (FDR & the Era of the New Deal Ser). 316p. 1973. Repr. of 1939 ed. lib. bdg. 32.50 (ISBN 0-306-70467-6). Da Capo.

Gill, Crispin. Countryman's Britain in Pictures. (Countryman Books). 1977. 11.95 (ISBN 0-7153-7450-8). David & Charles.

--The Isles of Scilly. LC 75-12. (Island Series). (Illus.). 208p. 1975. 16.95 (ISBN 0-7153-6957-1). David & Charles.

--Plymouth: A New History, 2 vols. Incl. Vol. 1. Ice Age of Elizabethans (ISBN 0-7153-4018-2); Vol. 2. Sixteen Hundred & Three to Present Day (ISBN 0-7153-7617-9). LC 66-6718. (Illus.). 1979. 22.50 ea. David & Charles.

Gill, Crispin, ed. Countryman's Britain. LC 76-20122. (Countryman Books). 1976. 17.95 (ISBN 0-7153-7284-X). David & Charles.

Gill, Dan & Merriam, Daniel F. Geomathematical & Petrophysical Studies in Sedimentology, an International Symposium: Proceedings of Papers Presented at Sessions Sponsored by the International Association for Mathematical Geology at the Tenth International Congress on Sedimentology in Jerusalem, July 1979. (Computers & Geology Ser.: Vol. 3). (Illus.). 285p. 1979. 41.00 (ISBN 0-08-023832-7). Pergamon.

Gill, Deemster, et al. The Manx National Songbook, Vol. 1. 1979. text ed. 14.50x (ISBN 0-904980-30-8). Humanities.

Gill, Derek. Illegitimacy, Sexuality & the Status of Women. 1977. 36.00x (ISBN 0-631-17020-0, Pub. by Basil Blackwell). Biblio Dist.

--Quest: The Life of Elisabeth Kubler-Ross. LC 78-19823. (Illus.). 1980. 11.95 (ISBN 0-06-011543-2, HarpT). Har-Row.

--Tom Sullivan's Adventures in Darkness. (Illus., Orig.). 1977. pap. 1.50 o.p. (ISBN 0-451-07698-2, W7698, Sig). NAL.

Gill, Derek, jt. auth. see Graham, Robin L.

Gill, Derek, jt. auth. see Sullivan, Tom.

Gill, Donald F. Canvases & Cathedrals. 1977. 4.50 o.p. (ISBN 0-685-86616-5). Vantage.

Gill, Eric. Eric Gill - Autobiography. LC 68-54231. (Illus.). 1969. Repr. of 1941 ed. 12.00x (ISBN 0-8196-0220-5). Biblo.

Gill, F. W. & Bates, G. L. Airline Competition: A Study of the Effects of Competition on the Quality & Price of Airline Service & the Self-Sufficiency of the United States Domestic Airlines. 1970. 51.00 (ISBN 0-08-018738-2). Pergamon.

Gill, Flora. Economics & the Black Exodus: An Analysis of Negro Emigration from the Southern United States; 1910-70. LC 78-75070. (Outstanding Dissertations in Economics Ser.). 1979. lib. bdg. 22.00 (ISBN 0-8240-4144-5). Garland Pub.

Gill, Frances M. & Abbe, Kathryn M. Twins on Twins. 1980. 17.95 (ISBN 0-517-54149-1, 541491). Potter.

Gill, Gordon N., ed. Pharmacology of Adrenal Cortical Hormones. LC 78-40135. 1978. text ed. 55.00 (ISBN 0-08-019619-5). Pergamon.

Gill, Harjeet S. A Phulkari from Bhatinda. 1980. 17.50x (ISBN 0-89955-322-2, Pub. by Interprint India). Intl Schol Bk Serv.

Gill, Harold E., jt. ed. see Subitzky, Seymour.

Gill, Harold, Jr. The Apothecary in Colonial Virginia. LC 76-187597. (Williamsburg Research Studies Ser.). 1972. pap. 3.00 o.p. (ISBN 0-910412-99-5). Williamsburg.

Gill, Jack C. Mathematics & the Liberal Arts. LC 72-95501. 1973. pap. text ed. 15.95 (ISBN 0-675-08981-6); media: audiocassettes 89.50, 2-4 sets, 65.00 ea., 5 or more sets, 49.50 ea. (ISBN 0-675-08973-5); instructor's manual 3.95 (ISBN 0-686-66864-2). Merrill.

Gill, Jerry H. Ian Ramsey: To Speak Responsibly of God. 1976. text ed. 16.95x (ISBN 0-04-230014-2). Allen Unwin.

Gill, Jill. Tiger & Leopard. LC 73-134673. (Illus.). 4.95 (ISBN 0-8149-0679-6). Vanguard.

Gill, Joan. Golden Retrievers. Foyle, Christina, ed. (Foyles Handbks). 1973. 3.95 (ISBN 0-685-55801-0). Palmetto Pub.

Gill, John. Cause of God & Truth. (Giant Summit Ser.). 336p. 1981. pap. 7.95 (ISBN 0-8010-3761-1). Baker Bk.

--The Listener. 1977. pap. 1.95 o.p. (ISBN 0-445-08555-X). Popular Lib.

Gill, John L. Design & Analysis of Experiments in the Animal & Medical Sciences, Vol. 1. (Illus.). 1978. text ed. 16.50 (ISBN 0-8138-0020-X). Iowa St U Pr.

Gill, Joseph. Byzantium & the Papacy, Eleven Ninety Eight - Fourteen Hundred. 1979. 25.00 (ISBN 0-8135-0864-9). Rutgers U Pr.

Gill, K. F., jt. auth. see Schwarzenbach, J.

Gill, Merton M. Analysis of Transference. LC 80-15652. (Psychological Issues, Monograph: No. 53). 1981. text ed. 25.00 (ISBN 0-8236-0144-7, 00-0144). Intl Univs Pr.

Gill, N. T. & Vear, K. C. Agricultural Botany 1: Dicotyledonous Crops. 3rd ed. (Illus.). 268p. 1980. 45.00x (ISBN 0-7156-1250-6, Pub. by Duckworth England). Biblio Dist.

--Agricultural Botany 2: Monocotyledonous Crops. 3rd ed. Barnard, A. D., rev. by. (Illus.). 259p. 1980. 45.00x (ISBN 0-7156-1251-4, Pub by Duckworth England). Biblio Dist.

Gill, Paul. Electrical Equipment Testing & Maintenance Handbook. 350p. 1981. text ed. 16.95 (ISBN 0-8359-1625-1). Reston.

Gill, Richard & Sherman, Ernest. The Fabric of Existentialism: The Philisophical & Literary Sources. 1973. text ed. 20.95 (ISBN 0-13-298216-1). P-H.

Gill, Robert W. Creative Perspective. (Illus.). 1980. pap. 5.95 (ISBN 0-500-27056-2). Thames Hudson.

Gill, S. S. The Stress Analysis of Pressure Vessels & Pressure Vessel Components. 1970. 90.00 (ISBN 0-08-006729-8). Pergamon.

Gill, Sam D. Sacred Words: A Study of Navajo Religion & Prayer. LC 80-659. (Contributions in Intercultural & Comparative Studies: No. 4). (Illus.). 272p. 1981. lib. bdg. 29.95 (ISBN 0-313-22165-0, GSW/). Greenwood.

Gill, Spencer. Washington Shores. (Illus.). 128p. 1981. 27.50 (ISBN 0-912856-68-8). Graphic Arts Ctr.

Gill, Suzanne L. File Management & Information Retrieval Systems: A Manual for Managers & Technicians. LC 80-22785. (Illus.). 300p. 1981. lib. bdg. 16.50 (ISBN 0-87287-229-7). Libs Unl.

Gillam, Tony. Simple Checkmates. 1978. pap. 5.95 (ISBN 0-7134-1482-0, Pub. by Batsford England). David & Charles.

--Simple Chess Tactics. 1978. pap. 5.95 (ISBN 0-7134-1480-4, Pub. by Batsford England). David & Charles.

--Starting Chess. 1978. pap. 5.95 (ISBN 0-7134-1478-2, Pub. by Batsford England). David & Charles.

Gillard, David. The Struggle for Asia 1828-1914. 1978. text ed. 31.50x (ISBN 0-8419-7000-9); pap. 13.95 o.p. (ISBN 0-8419-7003-3). Holmes & Meier.

Gillard, William H. & Tooke, Thomas R. The Niagara Escarpment: From Tobermory to Niagara Falls. LC 73-84434. (Illus.). 1974. pap. 4.95 (ISBN 0-8020-6214-8). U of Toronto Pr.

Gillebaud, John. The Pill. (Illus.). 196p. 1980. 16.95 (ISBN 0-19-217675-7); pap. 6.95 (ISBN 0-19-286002-X). Oxford U Pr.

Gillelan, G. Howard. The Complete Book of Bow & Arrow. rev., 3rd ed. (Illus.). 330p. 1981. pap. 9.95 (ISBN 0-8117-2118-3). Stackpole.

--Complete Book of the Bow & Arrow. rev. ed. LC 76-30484. (Illus.). 330p. 1981. 9.95 (ISBN 0-8117-2118-3). Stackpole.

Gillemot, L. F. Material Testing Laboratories. 1970. pap. 2.50 (ISBN 92-3-100826-9, U373, UNESCO). Unipub.

Gillen, Charles H. H. H. Munro (Saki) (English Authors Ser.: No. 102). lib. bdg. 9.95 (ISBN 0-8057-1408-1). Twayne.

Gilleo, Alma. About Grams. LC 77-23285. (Metric Bk.). (Illus.). (gr. 1-4). 1977. 5.50 (ISBN 0-913778-84-2); pap. 2.75 (ISBN 0-89565-061-4). Childs World.

--About Liters. LC 77-23260. (Metric Bk.). (Illus.). (gr. 1-4). 1977. 5.50 (ISBN 0-913778-85-0); pap. 2.75 (ISBN 0-89565-062-2). Childs World.

--About Meters. LC 77-23261. (Metric Bk.). (Illus.). (gr. 1-4). 1977. 5.50 (ISBN 0-913778-86-9); pap. 2.75 (ISBN 0-89565-063-0). Childs World.

--About the Thermometer. LC 77-23182. (A Metric Book). (Illus.). (gr. 1-4). 1977. PLB 5.50 (ISBN 0-913778-87-7); pap. 2.75 (ISBN 0-89565-064-9). Childs World.

--Air Travel from the Beginning. LC 77-24134. (From the Beginning Ser.). (Illus.). (gr. 1-4). 1977. PLB 5.50 (ISBN 0-89565-002-9). Childs World.

--Communications from the Beginning. LC 77-24211. (From the Beginning Ser.). (Illus.). (gr. 1-4). 1977. PLB 5.50 (ISBN 0-89565-003-7). Childs World.

--Dinosaurs & Other Reptiles from the Beginning. LC 77-24957. (From the Beginning Ser.). (Illus.). (gr. 1-4). 1977. PLB 5.50 (ISBN 0-89565-004-5). Childs World.

--From the Beginning, 5 bks. Incl. Air Travel from the Beginning (65002-9); Communications from the Beginning (ISBN 0-89565-003-7); Dinosaurs & Other Reptiles from the Beginning (ISBN 0-89565-004-5); Land Travel from the Beginning (ISBN 0-89565-000-2); Water Travel from the Beginning (ISBN 0-89565-000-2). (Illus.). (gr. 1-4). 1977. 27.50 set (ISBN 0-685-86290-9); 5.50 ea. Childs World.

--Land Travel from the Beginning. LC 77-24068. (From the Beginning Ser.). (Illus.). (gr. 1-4). 1977. PLB 5.50 (ISBN 0-89565-000-2). Childs World.

--Water Travel from the Beginning. LC 77-22822. (From the Beginning Ser.). (Illus.). (gr. 1-4). 1977. PLB 5.50 (ISBN 0-89565-001-0). Childs World.

Gilleo, Alma, ed. The Elves & the Shoemaker. LC 65-2642. (Holiday Tales). (Illus.). (ps). 1977. pap. 21.00 10 bks. & 1 casette (ISBN 0-89290-013-X). Soc for Visual.

--The Four Servants. LC 74-734828. (Fairy Tales of the Brothers Grimm Cassette Bks). (Illus.). 16p. 1976. pap. 21.00 incl. 10 bks. & one cassette (ISBN 0-89290-009-1). Soc for Visual.

--The Golden Buttons. LC 74-734827. (Fairy Tales of the Brothers Grimm Cassette Bks). (Illus.). 16p. (ps). 1976. pap. 21.00 10 bks. & one cassette (ISBN 0-89290-008-3); cassette incl. (ISBN 0-685-70098-4). Soc for Visual.

--It's Perfectly True. LC 76-730153. (Hans Christian Andersen Cassette Bks). (Illus.). 16p. 1976. 10 bks. & one cassette 21.00 (ISBN 0-89290-001-6). Soc for Visual.

--King Grisly-Beard, 10 bks. & one cassette. LC 74-734822. (Fairy Tales of the Brothers Grimm Cassette Bks). (Illus.). 16p. (ps). 1976. 10 bks. & one cassette 21.00 (ISBN 0-89290-004-0). Soc for Visual.

Gillepsie, Janet. Growing Natural. 224p. 1976. pap. 1.75 o.p. (ISBN 0-345-24872-4). Ballantine.

Gillepsie, Paul D. Problems of Document Delivery for the Euronet User. Franklin Institute GmbH, ed. 1979. 20.00 (Pub. by K G Saur). Shoe String.

Gillerman, Dorothy. The Cloture of Notre-Dame & Its Role in the 14th Century Choir Program. LC 76-23623. (Outstanding Dissertations in the Fine Arts - 2nd Series - Medieval). (Illus.). 1977. Repr. of 1973 ed. lib. bdg. 57.00 (ISBN 0-8240-2693-4). Garland Pub.

Gillers, Stephen. The Rights of Lawyers & Clients. 1978. pap. 1.95 (ISBN 0-380-42382-0, 42382, Discus). Avon.

Gilles, Jean, ed. How to Run Your House. LC 72-97091. 1973. 7.95 (ISBN 0-89795-007-0). Farm Journal.

Gilles, R., ed. see First Conference of the European Society for Comparative Physiology & Biochemistry, 27-31 August, 1979, Liege, Belgium.

Gillespie, Abraham L. The Syntactic Revolution. Milazzo, Richard, ed. LC 75-22994. (Illus.). 190p. 1981. pap. 12.95 (ISBN 0-915570-05-X). Oolp Pr.

Gillespie, Angus K. Folklorist of the Coal Fields: George Korson's Life & Work. LC 79-25839. (Illus.). 1980. 16.95 (ISBN 0-271-00255-7). Pa St U Pr.

Gillespie, D. H., jt. auth. see Strayer, D. R.

Gillespie, Daniel T. A Quantum Mechanics Primer: An Elementary Introduction to the Formal Theory of Non-Relativistic Quantum Mechanics. LC 74-3107. 137p. (Orig.). 1973. pap. text ed. 15.95 (ISBN 0-470-29912-6). Halsted Pr.

Gillespie, David F. & Mileti, Dennis S. Technostructures & Inter-Organizational Relations. LC 78-19543. (Illus.). 1978. 17.95 (ISBN 0-669-02542-9). Lexington Bks.

Gillespie, Dizzy & Fraser, Al. To Be or Not to Bop: Memoirs. LC 77-76237. (Illus.). 1979. 15.95 (ISBN 0-385-12052-4). Doubleday.

Gillespie, George T. A Catalogue of Persons Named in Germanic Heroic Literature 700-1600, Including Named Animals & Objects & Ethnic Names. 1973. 33.75x o.p. (ISBN 0-19-815718-5). Oxford U Pr.

Gillespie, Gerald, ed. & tr. see Tieck, Ludwig.

Gillespie, Gilbert. Public Access Cable Television in the United States & Canada: With an Annotated Bibliography. LC 75-15644. (Special Studies). 172p. 1975. text ed. 18.95 o.p. (ISBN 0-275-09980-6). Praeger.

Gillespie, James. Modern Livestock & Poultry Production. LC 79-50918. (Agriculture Ser.). 1981. pap. 18.20 (ISBN 0-8273-1688-7); instr's guide 3.15 (ISBN 0-8273-1689-5). Delmar.

Gillespie, James E., Jr. Solos for Unaccompanied Clarinet: An Annotated Bjbliography. LC 73-87277. (Detroit Studies in Music Bibliography Ser.: No. 28). 1973. 7.00 (ISBN 0-685-30213-X); pap. 5.50 (ISBN 0-685-30213-X). Info Coord.

Gillespie, James H. & Timoney, John F. Hagan & Bruner's Infectious Diseases of Domestic Animals. 7th rev. ed. LC 80-15937. (Illus.). 912p. 1981. 39.50x (ISBN 0-8014-1333-8). Cornell U Pr.

Gillespie, John. The Musical Experience. 2nd ed. 576p. 1972. 14.95x o.p. (ISBN 0-534-00161-0); record album 14.95x o.p. (ISBN 0-534-00674-4). Wadsworth Pub.

Gillespie, John T. & Spirt, Diana L. Creating a School Media Program. LC 77-164032. (Illus.). 236p. 1973. 16.25 o.p. (ISBN 0-8352-0484-7). Bowker.

Gillespie, John V., jt. ed. see Zinnes, Dina A.

Gillespie, Laroux K., ed. Deburring Capabilities & Limitations. LC 76-47179. (Illus.). text ed. 15.95 (ISBN 0-87263-038-2). SME.

Gillespie, Laurel, jt. auth. see Ungrue, Dawn.

Gillespie, Mabel. Where the Birds Are. LC 76-55062. (Illus., Orig.). 1976. pap. 4.95 (ISBN 0-932384-03-X). Tashmoo.

Gillespie, Neal C. Collapse of Orthodoxy: The Intellectual Ordeal of George Frederick Holmes. LC 70-163978. 1972. 9.95x (ISBN 0-8139-0345-9). U Pr of Va.

Gillespie, Netta. Circus. Bensen, Robert, ed. (Chapbook: No. 6). 1980. pap. 3.50. Red Herring.

Gillespie, Patricia. Teaching Reading to the Special Needs Child: An Ecological Approach. (Special Education Ser.). 1979. text ed. 17.95 (ISBN 0-675-08274-9). Merrill.

Gillespie, R. D., jt. auth. see Henderson, David.

Gillespie, Robert. Tempo Daily Crosswords, No. 4. 128p. (gr. 4 up). 1981. pap. 1.50 (ISBN 0-448-05727-1, Tempo). G&D.

Gillespie, Robert, jt. ed. see Kostuik, J. P.

Gillespie, V. Bailey. Religious Conversion & Personal Identity. LC 79-15605. 264p. (Orig.). 1979. pap. 8.95 (ISBN 0-89135-018-7). Religious Educ.

Gillespy, Rosalynne H. Space Wars. LC 78-730966. 1978. pap. text ed. 175.00 (ISBN 0-89290-111-X, CM-31). Soc for Visual.

Gillet, Margaret, jt. ed. see Grozier, Edwin A.

Gillet, Pamela. Career Edition for Exceptional Children & Youth: Career Edition for Excepional Children & Youth. LC 80-84931. 340p. 1981. text ed. 18.95 (ISBN 0-913420-90-5). Olympus Pub Co.

Gillet, Philip. Calculus & Analytic Geometry. 928p. 1981. text ed. 28.95 (ISBN 0-669-00641-6); instr's. guide avail. (ISBN 0-669-02702-2); solutions guide vol. 1 6.95 (ISBN 0-669-00642-4); solutions guide vol. 2 6.95 (ISBN 0-669-03212-3); solutions guides vol. 3 6.95 (ISBN 0-669-03213-1). Heath.

Gillett, B. E., jt. auth. see Carlile, R. E.

Gillett, Dorothy. Comprehensive Musicianship Through Classroom Music: Zone 3, Book A. Burton, Leon & Thomson, William, eds. (University of Hawaii Music Project). (gr. 3). 1974. pap. text ed. 6.84 (ISBN 0-201-00858-0, Sch Div); tchr's ed. 11.48 (ISBN 0-201-00859-9). A-W.

Gillett, Edward & MacMahon, Kenneth A., eds. A History of Hull. (Illus.). 448p. 1980. 45.00x (ISBN 0-19-713436-X). Oxford U Pr.

Gillett, James B. Six Years with the Texas Rangers, 1875 to 1881. Quaife, Milo M., ed. LC 76-4495. (Illus.). 1976. 14.95x (ISBN 0-8032-0889-8); pap. 3.95 (ISBN 0-8032-5844-5, BB 624, Bison). U of Nebr Pr.

Gillett, John M. & White, David J. Checklist of Vascular Plants of the Ottawa-Hull Region, Canada. (Illus.). 1978. pap. text ed. 4.50x (ISBN 0-660-00091-1, 56300-6, Pub. by Natl Mus Canada). U of Chicago Pr.

Gillett, Keith. The Australian Great Barrier Reef in Colour. rev. ed. (Illus.). 96p. 1980. Repr. of 1968 ed. 11.95 (ISBN 0-589-50199-2, Pub. by Reed Books Australia). C E Tuttle.

Gillett, Keith, jt. auth. see Wilson, Barry R.

Gillett, Margaret & Kehoe, Monika. Laurel & the Poppy. LC 66-10681. 1967. 7.95 (ISBN 0-8149-0106-9). Vanguard.

Gillett, Margaret & Laska, John A. Foundation Studies in Education: Justifications & New Directions: A Source Book. LC 73-7899. 1973. 13.50 (ISBN 0-8108-0671-1). Scarecrow.

Gillett, Philip W. Introduction to Linear Algebra. 1975. text ed. 19.50 (ISBN 0-395-18574-2); solutions manual 3.00 (ISBN 0-395-18809-1). HM.

Gillette, A. D. Minutes of the Philadelphia Baptist Association from AD 1707 to AD 1807. Repr. 15.00 (ISBN 0-686-12341-7). Church History.

Gillette, Harriet E. Systems of Therapy in Cerebral Palsy. (American Lecture in Cerebral Palsy Ser.). (Illus.). 96p. 1974. text ed. 9.75 (ISBN 0-398-00680-6). C C Thomas.

Gillette, Paul C., et al, eds. Pediatric Cardiac Dysrhythmias. (Clinical Cardiology Monographs). 1981. price not set (ISBN 0-8089-1332-8). Grune.

Gilley, Jeanne M., et al. Early Childhood: Development & Education. LC 78-73823. 1980. pap. 12.20 (ISBN 0-8273-1579-1); instructor's guide 1.50 (ISBN 0-8273-1580-5). Delmar.

Gillha, Bill. Problem Behaviour in the Secondary School. 192p. 1981. 26.00x (ISBN 0-7099-0129-1, Pub. by Croom Helm LTD England). Biblio Dist.

Gillham, Bill. The First Words Language Programme. 96p. 1980. 20.00x (Pub. by Beaconsfield England). State Mutual Bk.

--First Words Language Programme. (Illus.). 1979. text ed. 15.95x (ISBN 0-04-371059-X). Allen Unwin.

--Septimus Fry or How Mrs Fry Had the Cleverest Baby in the World. LC 80-65661. (Illus.). 32p. (ps-3). 1980. 8.95 (ISBN 0-233-97253-6). Andre Deutsch.

Gillham, Charles E. Medicine Men of Hooper Bay. (Illus.). (gr. 4-6). 1966. 3.95g o.s.i. (ISBN 0-02-735990-5). Macmillan.

Gillham, D. G. Keats-Poems of Eighteen Twenty. 224p. 1969. pap. text ed. 9.95x (ISBN 0-7121-0141-1, Pub. by Macdonald & Evans England). Intl Ideas.

Gillham, David G. William Blake. LC 72-80296. (British Authors Ser). (Illus.). 224p. 1973. 32.50 (ISBN 0-521-08680-9); pap. 8.95x (ISBN 0-521-09735-5). Cambridge U Pr.

Gillham, Nicholas W. Organelle Heredity. LC 75-43195. 1978. 53.50 (ISBN 0-89004-102-4). Raven.

Gillham, W. E., jt. ed. see Howath, C. I.

Gillhoff, Gerd A. University Spanish-English & English-Spanish Dictionary. (Apollo Eds.). (YA) (gr. 9-12). pap. 6.95 o.s.i. (ISBN 0-8152-0129-X, A129, TYC-T). T Y Crowell.

Gilliam, Dorothy B. Paul Robeson: All American. LC 76-23233. (Illus.). 1976. 8.95 o.p. (ISBN 0-915220-15-6); pap. 3.95 o.si. o.p. (ISBN 0-915220-39-3). New Republic.

Gilliam, Harold. Weather of the San Francisco Bay Region. (California Natural History Guides: No. 6). (Illus., Orig.). 1962. 12.95x (ISBN 0-520-03425-2); pap. 3.95 (ISBN 0-520-00469-8). U of Cal Pr.

Gilliam, Olivia L., jt. ed. see Morey, Sylvester M.

Gillie, C. Movements in English Literature, 1900-1940. LC 74-16993. 200p. 1975. 36.00 (ISBN 0-521-20655-3); pap. 8.95x (ISBN 0-521-09922-6). Cambridge U Pr.

Gillie, Christopher. Character in English Literature. 1965. text ed. 6.25x (ISBN 0-7011-0715-4). Humanities.

Gillies, A., ed. see Herder, Johann G.

Gillies, A., ed. see Wackenroder, William H. & Tiek, Ludwig.

Gillies, Dee A. & Alyn, Irene B. Saunders Tests for Self-Evaluation of Nursing Competence. rev. ed. 1980. text ed. write for info. (ISBN 0-7216-4157-1). Saunders.

Gillies, Jerry. Moneylove. 1979. pap. 2.50 (ISBN 0-446-91009-0). Warner Bks.

--Psychological Immortality: Using Your Mind to Extend Your Life. 225p. 1981. 11.95 (ISBN 0-399-90103-5). Marek.

Gillies, John. A Guide to Caring for & Coping with Aging Parents. 1981. pap. 4.95 (ISBN 0-8407-5772-7). Nelson.

Gillies, M. T., ed. Powder Coating: Recent Developments. LC 80-26426. (Chemical Tech. Rev. Ser.: 183). (Illus.). 326p. 1981. 48.00 (ISBN 0-8155-0836-0). Noyes.

--Solventless & High Solids Industrial Finishes: Recent Developments. LC 80-21553. (Chemical Technology Review: No. 179). (Illus.). 342p. 1981. 48.00 (ISBN 0-8155-0828-X). Noyes.

Gillies, Marilyn. Tracings. LC 80-67934. 84p. 1981. pap. 4.95 (ISBN 0-9605170-0-6). Earth-Song.

Gillies, R. F. Lecture Notes on Medical Microbiology. 2nd ed. (Illus.). 1978. softcover 13.00 (ISBN 0-632-00062-7, Blackwell). Mosby.

Gilligan, C. & Crowther, G. Advertising Management. 1976. 33.00x (ISBN 0-86003-500-X, Pub. by Allan Pubs England); pap. 16.50x (ISBN 0-86003-600-6). State Mutual Bk.

Gilligan, Lawrence & Nenno, Robert. College Algebra & Trigonometry: College Algebra. 1981. text ed. write for info. (ISBN 0-8302-1996-X). Goodyear.

--College Algebra & Trigonometry: Precalculus Math. 1981. text ed. write for info. (ISBN 0-8302-1992-7). Goodyear.

Gilliland, Alexis A. Revolution from Rosinante. 192p. (Orig.). 1981. pap. 2.25 (Del Rey). Ballantine.

Gilliland, Burl E., jt. ed. see Mayo, G. Douglas.

Gilliland, Hap. Practical Guide to Remedial Reading. 2nd ed. Heilman, Arthur, ed. (Elementary Education Ser.). 1978. text ed. 15.95 (ISBN 0-675-08359-1). Merrill.

Gilliland, Jean. The Fourteenth Day Conspiracy. LC 80-51212. 224p. 1980. pap. 6.95 (ISBN 0-934616-09-4). Valkyrie Pr.

Gilliland, Ken & Millard, J. Trucking: A Truck Driver's Training Handbook. McFadden, S. Michele, ed. LC 79-90760. 1981. pap. 19.50x (ISBN 0-89262-025-0). Career Pub.

--Trucking: A Truck Driver's Workbook. McFadden, S. Michele, ed. 1981. pap. text ed. 16.50 (ISBN 0-89262-029-3). Career Pub. Postponed.

--Trucking: Instructor's Guide. McFadden, S. Michele, ed. 1981. pap. text ed. 12.50 (ISBN 0-89262-030-7). Career Pub. Postponed.

Gilliland, Martha W., ed. Energy Analysis: A New Public Policy Tool. LC 77-15895. (AAAS Selected Symposium Ser.: No. 9). (Illus.). 1978. lib. bdg. 17.00x (ISBN 0-89158-437-4). Westview.

Gillingham, F. J. Advances in Stereotactic & Functional Neurosurgery Four: Proceedings. (Acta Neurochirurgica Supplementum: Vol. 30). (Illus.). 444p. 1981. pap. 146.40 (ISBN 0-387-90501-4). Springer-Verlag.

Gillingham, John, tr. see Mayer, Hans E.

Gillingwater, David & Hart, D. A., eds. The Regional Planning Process. 1978. 22.95 (ISBN 0-347-01130-6, 00412-X, Pub. by Saxon Hse). Lexington Bks.

Gilliom. Practical Methods for Social Studies. 1977. 11.95x (ISBN 0-534-00486-5). Wadsworth Pub.

Gilliom, Richard D. Introduction to Physical Organic Chemistry. LC 75-99483. (Chemistry Ser). 1970. text ed. 20.95 (ISBN 0-201-02375-X). A-W.

Gillion, K. L. Ahmedabad: A Study in Indian Urban History. 1968. 18.75x (ISBN 0-520-00473-6). U of Cal Pr.

Gillis, Daniel. Furtwangler in America. LC 75-125028. (Illus.). 1980. Repr. of 1971 ed. 7.95 (ISBN 0-87867-079-3). Ramparts.

Gillis, Don. Unfinished Symphony Conductor. LC 68-1408. (Illus.). 1967. 6.95 o.p. (ISBN 0-8363-0098-X). Jenkins.

Gillis, Everett A. Far Beyond Distance. 64p. 1981. 8.00 (ISBN 0-938328-01-8). Pisces Pr TX.

--South by West: A Galaxy of Southwestern & Western Scences & Portraits. 48p. (Orig.). 1981. pap. write for info. Pisces Pr TX.

--The Waste Land As Grail Romance: Eliot's Use of the Medieval Grail Legends. (Graduate Studies: No. 6). 26p. 1974. pap. 2.00 (ISBN 0-89672-013-6). Tex Tech Pr.

Gillis, Jackson. The Killers of Starfish. LC 77-6231. 1977. 8.95 o.p. (ISBN 0-397-01201-2). Lippincott.

Gillis, John R. The Development of European Society: 1770-1870. LC 76-10891. (Illus.). 1977. pap. text ed. 14.25 (ISBN 0-395-24482-X). HM.

Gillis, John S. The Psychology of Human Height. 200p. 1981. pap. 9.95 (ISBN 0-918296-15-3). Inst Personality & Ability.

Gillis, Lynn. Human Behavior in Illness. 1972. pap. text ed. 4.95 o.p. (ISBN 0-571-04788-2, Pub. by Faber & Faber). Merrimack Bk Serv.

--Human Behavior in Illness: Psychology & Interpersonal Relationships. 3rd ed. 224p. 1980. pap. 9.95 (ISBN 0-571-18025-6, Pub. by Faber & Faber). Merrimack Bk Serv.

Gillis, Lynn & Egert, Stella. The Psychiatric Outpatient. 1973. text ed. 10.95x (ISBN 0-571-10202-6, Pub. by Faber & Faber). Merrimack Bk Serv.

Gillis, M. T., ed. Water-Based Industrial Finishes: Recent Developments. LC 80-17520. (Chemical Technology Review: No. 167). 435p. 1980. 48.00 (ISBN 0-8155-0812-3). Noyes.

Gillis, Phyllis, jt. auth. see Lichtendorf, Susan.

Gillis, William, ed. see Durrenmatt, Friedrich.

Gillispie, Charles C. Science & Polity in France at the End of the Old Regime. LC 80-7521. (Illus.). 472p. 1980. 40.00x (ISBN 0-691-08233-2). Princeton U Pr.

Gillispie, Charles C., ed. Dictionary of Scientific Biography, 8 vols. 1981. lib. bdg. 595.00 set (ISBN 0-684-16962-2); lib. bdg. 80.00 ea. Scribner.

--Dictionary of Scientific Biography: Compact Edition, 8 vols. LC 69-18090. 1970-1980. Set. text ed. 695.00 (ISBN 0-684-16962-2, ScribR). Scribner.

Gillispie, John V. & Zinnes, Dina A., eds. Mathematical Systems in International Relations Research. LC 75-23964. 1977. text ed. 45.95 (ISBN 0-275-55620-4). Praeger.

Gillium, James E. Autism: Diagnosis, Instruction, Management, & Research. write for info. (ISBN 0-398-04072-9). C C Thomas.

Gillman, Gavin P., jt. auth. see Uehara, Goro.

Gillman, L. & Jerison, M. Rings of Continuous Functions. LC 60-14787. xi, 300p. 1975. 11.50 o.p. (ISBN 0-387-90120-5). Springer-Verlag.

Gillman, Neil. Gabriel Marcel on Religious Knowledge. LC 80-5061. 315p. 1980. text ed. 19.50 (ISBN 0-8191-1034-5); pap. text ed. 11.50 (ISBN 0-8191-1035-3). U Pr of Amer.

Gillmor. Agriculture in the Republic of Ireland. 1977. 15.00 (ISBN 0-686-28201-9, Pub. by Kaido Hungary). Heyden.

Gillmor, Donald M. & Barron, Jerome A. Mass Communications Law, Cases & Comment. 3rd ed. LC 79-15306. (American Casebook Ser.). 1008p. 1979. text ed. 19.95 (ISBN 0-8299-2050-1). West Pub.

Gillmor, Frances. Windsinger. LC 75-17380. (Zia Bks). 226p. 1976. pap. 3.95 o.p. (ISBN 0-8263-0397-8). U of NM Pr.

Gillmore, Eunice, jt. auth. see Gillmore, John.

Gillmore, John & Gillmore, Eunice. Give Your Child a Future: How to Develop a Productive Personality. 1981. pap. 6.95 (ISBN 0-89803-038-2). Caroline Hse.

Gillon, Adam & Krzyzanowski, Ludwik, eds. Introduction to Modern Polish Literature. 480p. 1981. pap. 6.95 (ISBN 0-88254-516-7, Pub. by Ars Polona Poland). Hippocrene Bks.

Gillon, Aitken, tr. see Solzhenitsyn, Alexander.

Gillon, Edmund V., ed. A New England Town in Early Photographs: Illustrations of Southbridge, Massachusetts 1878 - 1930. LC 75-463. (Illus.). 176p. (Orig.). 1976. pap. 6.00 (ISBN 0-486-23286-7). Dover.

Gillon, Edmund V., Jr. Decorative Frames & Borders: 396 Examples from the Renaissance to the Present Day. LC 72-96186. (Illus.). 224p. (Orig.). 1973. pap. 5.00 (ISBN 0-486-22928-9). Dover.

--Early Illustrations & Views of American Architecture. (Illus.). 1971. pap. 8.95 (ISBN 0-486-22750-2). Dover.

--Pennsylvania Dutch Farm: To Cut Out & Assemble. (Orig.). 1979. pap. 6.95 (ISBN 0-684-16341-1). Scribner.

Gillot, Cedric. Entomology. 690p. 1980. 49.50 (ISBN 0-306-40366-8, Plenum Pr); pap. text ed. 22.50 (ISBN 0-306-40514-8, Plenum Pr). Plenum Pub.

Gillsater, Pia, jt. auth. see Gillsater, Sven.

Gillsater, Sven & Gillsater, Pia. Pia's Journey to the Holy Land. MacMillan, Annabelle, tr. LC 61-2285. (Illus.). (gr. 1 up). 1961. bds. 4.95 o.p. (ISBN 0-15-261360-9, HJ). HarBraceJ.

Gilluly, James, et al. Principles of Geology. 4th ed. LC 74-23076. (Geology Ser.). (Illus.). 1975. text ed. 21.95x (ISBN 0-7167-0269-X). W H Freeman.

Gilman, Alfred G., et al, eds. Goodman & Gilman's The Pharmacological Basis of Therapeutics. 6th ed. 1980. text ed. 45.00 (ISBN 0-02-344720-6). Macmillan.

Gilman, Antonio. A Later Prehistory of Tangier, Morocco. LC 75-20595. (American School of Prehistoric Research Bulletins Ser.: No. 29). (Illus.). 1976. pap. 17.00 (ISBN 0-87365-531-1). Peabody Harvard.

Gilman, C. Malcolm. Blazing Star. LC 72-5188. (Illus.). 240p. 1973. 7.95 o.p. (ISBN 0-498-01220-4). A S Barnes.

Gilman, Daniel C. James Monroe. LC 80-24500. (American Statesmen Ser.). 315p. 1981. pap. 4.95 (ISBN 0-87754-187-6). Chelsea Hse.

Gilman, Dorothy. The Amazing Mrs. Pollifax. 1978. pap. 1.95 (ISBN 0-449-23447-9, Crest). Fawcett.

--The Clairvoyant Countess. 224p. 1978. pap. 1.95 (ISBN 0-449-23561-0, Crest). Fawcett.

--Unexpected Mrs Pollifax. 1978. pap. 1.95 (ISBN 0-449-23923-3, Crest). Fawcett.

Gilman, Dugan. Upstate. LC 79-142724. (Wesleyan Poetry Program: Vol. 55). 1971. 10.00x (ISBN 0-8195-2055-1, Pub. by Wesleyan U Pr); pap. 4.95 (ISBN 0-8195-1055-6). Columbia U Pr.

Gilman, Esther, jt. auth. see De Regniers, Beatrice.

Gilman, George. Death Drive. (Edge Ser.: No. 27). 1978. pap. 1.75 (ISBN 0-523-41309-2, Dist. by Independent News Co.). Pinnacle Bks.

Gilman, George C. Edge No. Thirty: Towering Nightmare. 1979. pap. 1.75 (ISBN 0-523-41312-2). Pinnacle Bks.

Gilman, George G. Death's Bounty. (Edge Ser.: No. 12). 1974. pap. 1.75 (ISBN 0-523-41290-8). Pinnacle Bks.

--Edge, Number Thirty-Six: Town on Trial. 160p. 1981. pap. 1.75 (ISBN 0-523-40867-6). Pinnacle Bks.

--Frightened Gun, No. Thirty Two. (Edge Ser.). (Orig.). 1979. pap. 1.75 (ISBN 0-523-41314-9). Pinnacle Bks.

--The Guilty Ones. (Edge Ser.: No. 31). 1979. pap. 1.75 (ISBN 0-523-41313-0). Pinnacle Bks.

--Red Fury. (Edge Ser.: No. 33). 160p. 1980. pap. 1.75 (ISBN 0-523-41315-7). Pinnacle Bks.

--Sioux Uprising. (Edge Ser.: No. 11). 1974. pap. 1.75 (ISBN 0-523-41289-4). Pinnacle Bks.

--Violence Trail. (The Edge Ser.: No. 25). 1978. pap. 1.75 (ISBN 0-523-41303-3). Pinnacle Bks.

Gilman, J. J., ed. Metallic Glasses. (TN 693.m4m37). 1977. 58.00 (ISBN 0-87170-051-4). ASM.

Gilman, John J. Art & Science of Growing Crystals. LC 63-11432. (Wiley Science & Technology of Materials Ser.). 1963. 49.95 (ISBN 0-471-30177-9, Pub. by Wiley-Interscience). Wiley.

Gilman, Lawrence. Edward MacDowell: A Study. 2nd ed. LC 67-27455. (Music Ser). 1969. Repr. of 1908 ed. lib. bdg. 17.50 (ISBN 0-306-70979-1). Da Capo.

Gilman, Margaret, ed. Foreign Language Tests & Techniques. 136p. 1956. pap. 7.95x (ISBN 0-915432-56-0). NE Conf Teach Foreign.

Gilman, Rachel & Bess, Nancy. Basketry. (Step-by-Step Crafts Ser.). (Illus.). 1977. PLB 9.15 o.p. (ISBN 0-307-62021-2, Golden Pr); pap. 2.95 (ISBN 0-307-42021-3). Western Pub.

Gilman, Richard. Decadence: The Strange Life of an Epithet. 192p. 1979. 8.95 (ISBN 0-374-13567-3); pap. 4.95 (ISBN 0-374-51553-0). FS&G.

--The Making of Modern Drama. LC 74-1171. 292p. 1974. 10.00 o.p. (ISBN 0-374-20018-1); pap. 4.50 (ISBN 0-374-51148-9). FS&G.

Gilman, Sander, jt. auth. see Von Eckardt, Wolf.

Gilman, Sander L. Seeing the Insane: A Cultural History of Psychiatric Illustration. (Illus.). 500p. 1981. 50.00 (ISBN 0-87630-233-9). Brunner-Mazel.

Gilman, Sander L., ed. see Agricola, Johannes.

Gilman, Sid, et al, eds. Disorders of the Cerebellum. LC 80-23393. (Contemporary Neurology Ser.: No. 21). (Illus.). 415p. 1981. text ed. 40.00 (ISBN 0-8036-4150-8). Davis Co.

Gilman, Stephen. Galdos & the Art of the European Novel, Eighteen Sixty-Seven to Eighteen Eighty-Seven. LC 80-8550. 416p. 1981. 27.50x (ISBN 0-691-06456-3). Princeton U Pr.

Gilman, Stuart, jt. auth. see Luhman, Reid.

Gilmartin, Jean. The Bromeliaceae of Ecuador. (Monographiae Phanerogamarum Ser.: No. 5). (Illus.). 1972. 60.00 (ISBN 3-7682-0725-0). Lubrecht & Cramer.

Gilmer, Ann. Skyscraper Nurse. (YA) 1976. 4.95 o.p. (ISBN 0-685-69516-6, Avalon). Bouregy.

Gilmer, B. Von Haller. Psicologia General. (Span.). 1975. 9.40 (ISBN 0-06-313150-1, IntlDept). Har-Row.

Gilmer, Harry. The If-You Form an Israelite Law. LC 75-23136. (Society of Biblical Literature. Dissertation Ser.). 140p. 1975. pap. 7.50 (ISBN 0-89130-004-X, 060115). Scholars Pr Ca.

Gilmer, Wesley. Cochran's Law Dictionary. LC 72-95860. 1978. pap. text ed. 6.00 (ISBN 0-87084-147-5). Anderson Pub Co.

--The Law Dictionary: Criminal Justice Ed. LC 72-95860. pap. text ed. 6.00 (ISBN 0-87084-149-1). Anderson Pub Co.

Gilmore, Al-Tony. Bad Nigger! The National Impact of Jack Johnson. LC 74-80590. 1975. 12.95 (ISBN 0-8046-9061-8, Natl U). Kennikat.

Gilmore, Al-Tony, ed. Revisiting Blassingame's "The Slave Community". The Scholar's Respond. LC 77-84765. (Contributions in Afro-American & African Studies: No. 37). 1978. lib. bdg. 17.50 (ISBN 0-8371-9879-8, GJB/). Greenwood.

Gilmore, Alden S. & Rich, Thomas A. Mental Retardation: A Programmed Manual for Volunteer Workers. (Illus.). 152p. 1973. 9.75 (ISBN 0-398-00681-4). C C Thomas.

Gilmore, Alec. Tomorrow's Pulpit. LC 74-18108. 96p. 1975. pap. 3.50 o.p. (ISBN 0-8170-0641-9). Judson.

Gilmore, C. P. Exercising for Fitness. Time-Life Books, ed. (Health Ser.). (Illus.). 176p. 1981. 12.95 (ISBN 0-8094-3754-6). Time Life.

Gilmore, Cecile. Hold Me Fast. (YA) 1972. 5.95 (ISBN 0-685-28627-4, Avalon). Bouregy.

--The Lesser Love. (YA) 1971. 5.95 (ISBN 0-685-23396-0, Avalon). Bouregy.

--Web of Honey. (YA) 1970. 5.95 (ISBN 0-685-07463-3, Avalon). Bouregy.

--Wedding Is Destiny. 256p. (YA) 1973. 5.95 (ISBN 0-685-30371-3, Avalon). Bouregy.

Gilmore, Charles. Understanding & Using Modern Signal Generators. LC 76-45060. (Illus.). 1976. 9.95 o.p. (ISBN 0-8306-6877-2); pap. 6.95 (ISBN 0-8306-5877-7, 877). TAB Bks.

Gilmore, Charles M. Introduction to Microprocessors. LC 80-26115. (Basic Skills in Electricity & Electronics). 320p. 1981. pap. 14.96. McGraw.

--Introduction to Microprocessors: Activities Manual. (Basic Skills in Electricity & Electronics Ser.). 96p. 1981. lab manual 8.96 (ISBN 0-07-023302-0). McGraw.

--Understanding & Using Modern Electronic Servicing Test Equipment. LC 76-45062. (Illus.). 1976. 8.95 o.p. (ISBN 0-8306-6777-6); pap. 5.95 (ISBN 0-8306-5777-0, 777). TAB Bks.

Gilmore, D. E., ed. see Crouse, William H. & Anglin, Donald L.

Gilmore, D. E., ed. see Schulz, Erich J.

Gilmore, Elaine & MacDonald, Lachlan, eds. The Collector's Book of Doll Poems. (Illus.). 1981. pap. 5.95 (ISBN 0-914598-37-6). Padre Prods.

Gilmore, Gene & Root, Robert. Modern Newspaper Editing. 2nd ed. 1976. 14.95x (ISBN 0-87835-054-3). Boyd & Fraser.

Gilmore, Grant. Security Interests in Personal Property, 2 Vols. 1508p. 1965. 75.00 (ISBN 0-316-31374-2). Little.

Gilmore, Grant, jt. auth. see Kessler, Friedrich.

Gilmore, H. William, et al. Operative Dentistry. 3rd ed. LC 76-30465. (Illus.). 1977. text ed. 32.95 (ISBN 0-8016-1822-3). Mosby.

Gilmore, Iris, jt. auth. see Talmadge, Marian.

Gilmore, John S. & Duff, Mary K. Boom Town Growth Management: A Case Study of Rock Springs, Green River, Wyoming. LC 75-25905. 200p. 1975. 26.25x (ISBN 0-89158-010-7). Westview.

Gilmore, M., ed. Twentieth Century Interpretations of Moby Dick. 1977. 8.95 (ISBN 0-13-586057-1, Spec); pap. 2.45 (ISBN 0-13-586032-6, Spec). P-H.

Gilmore, Maeve, ed. see Peake, Mervyn.

Gilmore, Melvin. Notes on the Gynecology & Obstetrics of the Arikara Tribe of Indians, Vol. 14, No. 1. 1980. pap. 2.50 (ISBN 0-686-69103-2). Acoma Bks.

Gilmore, Melvin R. Uses of Plants by the Indians of the Missouri River Region. LC 77-89833. (Illus.). 1977. 11.95x (ISBN 0-8032-0935-5); pap. 3.50 (ISBN 0-8032-5872-0, BB 644, Bison). U of Nebr Pr.

Gilmore, Michael T. American Literature: A Collection of Critical Essays. (Twentieth Century Interpretations Ser.). 192p. 1980. text ed. 10.95 o.p. (ISBN 0-13-222513-1, Spec); pap. 3.95 o.p. (ISBN 0-13-222463-1). P-H.

--Middle Way: Puritanism & Ideology in American Romantic Fiction. 1977. 16.00 (ISBN 0-8135-0837-1). Rutgers U Pr.

Gilmore, Robert. Catastrophe Theory for Scientists & Engineers. LC 80-22154. 700p. 1981. 45.00 (ISBN 0-471-05064-4, Pub. by Wiley-Interscience). Wiley.

Gilmore, Robert L. Caudillism & Militarism in Venezuela, 1810-1910. LC 64-22887. 1964. 12.00 o.p. (ISBN 0-8214-0003-7). Ohio U Pr.

Gilmore, Susan K. The Counselor-in-Training. (Illus.). 1973. 15.95x (ISBN 0-13-183293-X). P-H.

Gilmore, Susan K. & Fraleigh, Patrick W. Communication at Work. LC 80-69467. (Illus.). 150p. (Orig.). 1980. 6.95 (ISBN 0-938070-00-2). Friendly Pr.

Gilmour, D. Biochemistry of Insects. 1961. 36.50 (ISBN 0-12-284050-X). Acad Pr.

Gilmour, H. B. All That Jazz. (Orig.). pap. 2.25 (ISBN 0-515-05374-0). Jove Pubns.

Gilmour, John S., tr. see Tournier, Paul.

Gilmour, R. Business Systems Handbook: Analysis, Designs & Documentation Standards. 1979. 24.95 (ISBN 0-13-107755-4). P-H.

Gilmurray, Susan. Weaving Tricks. 128p. 1981. 12.95 (ISBN 0-442-26132-2). Van Nos Reinhold.

Giloi, W. K. Principles of Continuous System Simulation. (Illus.). 1976. pap. 19.50 (ISBN 3-5190-2336-9). Adler.

Giloi, W. K., jt. ed. see Berg, H. K.

Gilpatrick, Gil. Building a Strip Canoe: Easy Step-by-Step Instructions & Patterns for 5 Canoe Models. (Illus.). 96p. (Orig.). 1979. pap. 8.95 (ISBN 0-89933-000-2). DeLorme Pub.

--Building Snowshoes: Easy Step-by-Step Instructions & Patterns for 4 Snowshoe Styles. (Illus.). 96p. 1979. pap. 8.95 (ISBN 0-89933-001-0). DeLorme Pub.

--The Canoe Guide's Handbook: Planning a Trip for 2 to 20 People. (Illus., Orig.). 1981. pap. price not set (ISBN 0-89933-011-8). DeLorme Pub.

--The Canoe Guide's Handbook: Planning a Trip for 2 to 20 People. (Illus., Orig.). 1981. pap. 7.95 (ISBN 0-89933-011-8). DeLorme Pub.

Gilpin, Alan. Environmental Policy in Australia. (Australian Environment Ser.: No. 8). (Illus.). 380p. 1981. text ed. 36.25x (ISBN 0-7022-1366-7); pap. text ed. 21.75x (ISBN 0-7022-1367-5). U of Queensland Pr.

Gilpin, Arthur, jt. auth. see Singleton, Val.

Gilpin, Doris C., jt. ed. see Anthony, James E.

Gilpin, George H. The Strategy of Joy: An Essay on the Poetry of Samuel Taylor Coleridge. (Salzburg Studies in English Literature, Romantic Reassessment: No.3). 1972. pap. text ed. 25.00x (ISBN 0-391-01384-X). Humanities.

Gilpin, Laura. The Hocus-Pocus of the Universe. LC 76-2746. 1977. 7.95 o.p. (ISBN 0-385-11600-4). Doubleday.

Gilpin, William. Mission of the North American People. 2nd ed. LC 68-16234. (American Scene Ser.). (Illus.). 218p. 1974. Repr. of 1874 ed. lib. bdg. 25.00 (ISBN 0-306-71013-7). Da Capo.

Gilreath, Esmarch S. Elementary Quantitative Chemistry. (Illus.). 1969. pap. 10.95x (ISBN 0-7167-0146-4). W H Freeman.

Gilreath, Kenneth J., jt. auth. see Cushenbery, Donald C.

Gilroy, Thomas, jt. ed. see Eppler, Klaus.

Gilsenan, Michael. Saint & Sufi in Modern Egypt: An Essay in the Sociology of Religion. (Monographs in Social Anthropology). (Illus.). 258p. 1973. 22.50x (ISBN 0-19-823181-4). Oxford U Pr.

Gilson, Barbara, jt. ed. see Charlton, James.

Gilson, Etienne. Heloise & Abelard. 1960. pap. 3.95 (ISBN 0-472-06038-4, 38, AA). U of Mich Pr.

--Reason & Revelation in the Middle Ages. pap. text ed. 4.95x (ISBN 0-684-15026-3, ScribC). Scribner.

--Spirit of Medieval Philosophy. 1936. lib. rep. ed. 22.50x (ISBN 0-684-14835-8, ScribT). Scribner.

Gilson, Jamie. Can't Catch Me, I'm the Gingerbread Man. LC 80-39748. 160p. (gr. 5-9). 1981. 7.95 (ISBN 0-688-00435-0); PLB 7.63 (ISBN 0-688-00436-9). Morrow.

--Dial Leroi Rupert, DJ. 1981. pap. 1.75 (ISBN 0-671-56099-9). Archway.

--Do Bananas Chew Gum? LC 80-11414. 160p. (gr. 5-9). 1980. 6.95 (ISBN 0-688-41960-7); PLB 6.67 (ISBN 0-688-51960-1). Lothrop.

Gilson, Thomas. How to Screen Print on Cylindrical & Contoured Surfaces. rev. ed. (Illus.). 1970. pap. 5.00 (ISBN 0-911380-10-8). Signs of Times.

Gilstrap, Frank. How to Do Your Own Texas Divorce for Under Forty Dollars. 80p. (Orig.). 1980. pap. 7.95 (ISBN 0-938356-00-3). How-to Pr.

Gilsvik, Bob. All Season Hunting. 1976. 11.95 (ISBN 0-87691-181-5). Winchester Pr.

Giltsoff, Natalie. Fashion Bead Embroidery. 88p. 1971. 8.75 (ISBN 0-8231-4025-3). Branford.

Gilula, Norton B., ed. Membrane-Membrane Interactions. (Society of General Physiologists Ser.: Vol. 34). 1980. text ed. 29.00 (ISBN 0-89004-377-9). Raven.

Gimbel, Ann. Lenora. LC 77-71894. (Destiny Ser.). 1977. pap. 4.95 (ISBN 0-8163-0303-7, 12121-0). Pacific Pr Pub Assn.

Gimbel, Mary, jt. ed. see Cott, Jonathan.

Gimbel, Theo. Healing Through Colour. 108p. 1980. 23.95x (ISBN 0-8464-1017-6). Beekman Pubs.

Gimbutas, Marija. The Prehistory of Eastern Europe: Part I: Mesolitic, Neolitic & Copper Age Cultures in Russia & the Baltic Area. LC 57-1393. (ASPR Bulletin: No. 20). 1956. pap. text ed. 25.00 (ISBN 0-87365-521-4). Peabody Harvard.

Gimingham, C. H. Ecology of the Heathlands. LC 73-3968. 266p. 1972. text ed. 21.95x o.p. (ISBN 0-412-14980-X, Pub. by Chapman & Hall). Methuen Inc.

--Ecology of the Heathlands. LC 73-3968. 266p. 1972. 21.95 o.p. (ISBN 0-470-30210-0). Halsted Pr.

Gimmestad, Victor E. John Trumbull. (U. S. Authors Ser.: No. 240). lib. bdg. 10.95 (ISBN 0-8057-0746-8). Twayne.

Gimondo, Angelo. Italian First Year. (gr. 8-11). 1978. wkbk. 7.17 (ISBN 0-87720-593-0). AMSCO Sch.

--Italian First Year. (Orig.). (gr. 7-12). 1975. pap. text ed. 6.00 (ISBN 0-87720-590-6). AMSCO Sch.

Gimpel, James F. Algorithms in SNOBOL 4. LC 75-33850. 487p. 1976. 30.00 (ISBN 0-471-30213-9, Pub. by Wiley-Interscience). Wiley.

Gimpel, Jean. The Medieval Machine: The Industrial Revolution of the Middle Ages. 1977. pap. 3.95 (ISBN 0-14-004514-7). Penguin.

Gimson, A. C. An Introduction to the Pronunciation of English. 3rd ed. 352p. 1980. 19.00x (Pub. by Arnold Pubs England). State Mutual Bk.

Gin, Margaret, jt. auth. see Allen, Jana.

Ginandes, Shepard. Coming Home. LC 76-8866. 1976. 7.95 o.s.i. (ISBN 0-440-01447-6, Sey Lawr). Delacorte.

Ginder, Geri, jt. auth. see Blevin, Margo.

Gindin, James, ed. see Hardy, Thomas.

Gine, Evarist, jt. auth. see Araujo, Aloisio.

Giner, Salvador. Sociology. 296p. 1981. 30.50x (ISBN 0-85520-008-1, Pub. by Martin Robertson England); pap. 12.50x (ISBN 0-85520-007-3). Biblio Dist.

Giner, Salvador & Archer, Margaret S., eds. Contemporary Europe: Social Structures & Cultural Patterns. (International Library of Sociology). 1978. 26.00x (ISBN 0-7100-8790-X); pap. 14.00 (ISBN 0-7100-8926-0). Routledge & Kegan.

Ginever, C. A., tr. see Riedl, Frederick.

Ginger, Ann, ed. Human Rights Casefinder 1953-1969: The Warren Court Era. 1972. 17.50x o.p. (ISBN 0-913876-02-X). Meiklejohn Civil Lib.

Ginger, John. The Notable Man: The Life & Times of Oliver Goldsmith. (Illus.). 1978. 25.00 (ISBN 0-241-89626-6, Pub. by Hamish Hamilton England). David & Charles.

Ginger, Ray & Ginger, Victoria. People on the Move: A United States History, 2 vols. Incl. Vol. 1. To 1877. pap. text ed. 9.50x o.p. (ISBN 0-205-04732-7); Vol. 2. Since 1860. pap. text ed. 9.50x o.p. (ISBN 0-685-99087-7). 1975. Combined Ed. text ed. 14.95x o.p. (ISBN 0-685-50569-3). Allyn.

Ginger, Victoria, jt. auth. see Ginger, Ray.

Gingerich, Duane, jt. ed. see Research Group.

Gingerich, Owen, intro. by. Cosmology Plus One: Readings from Scientific American. LC 77-1448. (Illus.). 1977. text ed. 15.95x (ISBN 0-7167-0043-3); pap. text ed. 7.95x (ISBN 0-7167-0042-5). W H Freeman.

--New Frontiers in Astronomy: Readings from Scientific American. LC 75-8902. (Illus.). 1975. text ed. 19.95x (ISBN 0-7167-0520-6); pap. text ed. 9.95x (ISBN 0-7167-0519-2). W H Freeman.

Gingery, David J. The Dividing Head & Deluxe Accessories. LC 80-66142. (Build Your Own Metal Working Shop from Scrap: Bk. 6). (Illus.). 112p. (Orig.). 1981. pap. 7.95 (ISBN 0-9604330-5-8). D J Gingery.

--The Drill Press. LC 80-66142. (Build Your Own Metal Working Shop from Scrap Ser.: Bk. 5). (Illus.). 72p. (Orig.). 1981. pap. 6.95 (ISBN 0-9604330-4-X). D J Gingery.

--The Metal Lathe. LC 80-66142. (Build Your Own Metal Working Shop from Scrap Ser.: Bk. 2). (Illus.). 128p. (Orig.). 1980. pap. 7.95 (ISBN 0-9604330-1-5). D J Gingery.

--The Metal Shaper. LC 80-66142. (Build Your Own Metal Working Shop from Scrap: Bk. 3). (Illus.). 84p. (Orig.). 1980. pap. 6.95 (ISBN 0-9604330-2-3). D J Gingery.

--The Milling Machine. LC 80-66142. (Build Your Own Metal Working Shop from Scrap Ser.: Bk. 4). (Illus.). 96p. (Orig.). 1981. pap. 7.95 (ISBN 0-9604330-3-1). D J Gingery.

Gingold, Diane J., ed. Corporate Collections in Montgomery. LC 76-15913. (Illus.). 1976. pap. cancelled (ISBN 0-89280-002-X). Montgomery Mus.

Gingras, Rosario C., ed. Second-Language Acquisition & Foreign Language Teaching. LC 78-74014. 1978. pap. text ed. 7.25x (ISBN 0-87281-090-9). Ctr Appl Ling.

Gingrich. Relating the Arts. write for info. (ISBN 0-87628-216-8). Ctr Appl Res.

Gingrich, F. Wilbur, tr. from Ger. A Greek-English Lexicon of the New Testament. Arndt, William F., et al, eds. Danker, F. W., tr. from Ger. LC 78-14293. (2nd rev. & augmented edition). 1979. lib. bdg. 30.00x (ISBN 0-226-03932-3). U of Chicago Pr.

Gingrich, Harold W. Electrical Machinery, Transformers, & Control. (Illus.). 1978. ref. 19.95 (ISBN 0-13-247320-8). P-H.

Gingrich, Wilbur F. & Danker, Frederick W. Greek-English Lexicon of the New Testament. rev 2nd. ed. 1979. 30.00 o.p. (ISBN 0-310-20570-0). Zondervan.

Giniger, Ken S., compiled by. Compact Treasury of Inspiration. (Orig.). pap. 1.95 (ISBN 0-89129-229-2). Jove Pubns.

Ginott, Haim G. Between Parent & Child. 1965. 10.95 (ISBN 0-02-543300-8). Macmillan.

--Teacher & Child. Markel, Robert, ed. LC 70-182448. 228p. 1972. 9.95 (ISBN 0-02-543340-7). Macmillan.

Ginoux, Jean J. Two Phase Flows & Heat Transfer with Application to Nuclear Reactor Design Problems. LC 77-2090. (McGraw-Hill - Hemisphere Thermal & Fluids Engineering Ser). (Illus.). 1978. text ed. 39.50x (ISBN 0-07-023305-5, C). McGraw.

Ginsberg, Allen. The Fall of America: Poems of These States, 1965-1971. LC 72-84228. (Pocket Poets Ser.: No. 30). 190p. 1972. pap. 4.00 (ISBN 0-87286-063-9). City Lights.

--Mostly Sitting Haiku. 2nd rev., exp. ed. (Xtras Ser.: No. 6). 36p. (Orig.). 1981. pap. 2.00 (ISBN 0-89120-014-2). From Here.

--Plutonium Ode: Poems 1977-1980. (Pockets Poets Ser.: No. 40). 80p. 1981. 8.50 (ISBN 0-87286-125-2); pap. 3.50 (ISBN 0-87286-126-0). City Lights.

Ginsberg, Allen & Orlovsky, Peter. Straight Hearts' Delight: Love Poems & Selected Letters. Leyland, Winston, ed. (Illus.). 240p. 1980. 20.00 (ISBN 0-917342-64-X); pap. 8.95 (ISBN 0-917342-65-8). Gay Sunshine.

Ginsberg, Frances, et al. Manual of Operating Room Technology. LC 66-17293. (Illus., Orig.). pap. 5.75 o.p. (ISBN 0-397-54052-3). Lippincott.

Ginsberg, Gerlad L. A User's Guide to Selecting Electronic Components. LC 80-25197. 250p. 1981. 25.00 (ISBN 0-471-08308-9, Pub. by Wiley-Interscience). Wiley.

Ginsberg, Harold, jt. auth. see Dulbecco, Renato.

Ginsberg, Jerry H. & Genin, Joseph. Statics & Dynamics Combined Edition. LC 76-30664. 1977. text ed. 28.95 (ISBN 0-471-01795-7). Wiley.

Ginsberg, Leon H., jt. auth. see Harbert, Anita S.

Ginsberg, Linda. Family Financial Survival. LC 80-70436. (Illus.). 192p. (Orig.). 1981. pap. 8.95 (ISBN 0-89087-315-1). Celestial Arts.

Ginsborg, Paul. Daniele Manin & the Venetian Revolution of 1848-49. LC 78-56180. (Illus.). 1979. 41.50 (ISBN 0-521-22077-7). Cambridge U Pr.

Ginsburg. Ysaye. Paradise, ed. (Illus.). 576p. 1980. text ed. 20.00 (ISBN 0-87666-620-9, Z-31). Paganiniana Pubns.

Ginsburg, Douglas H. Regulation of Broadcasting: Law & Policy Towards Radio, Television & Cable Communications. LC 78-11973. (American Casebook Ser.). 741p. 1978. text ed. 20.95 (ISBN 0-8299-2017-X). West Pub.

Ginsburg, Helen, ed. Poverty, Economics, & Society. LC 80-6115. 361p. 1981. lib. bdg. 21.50 (ISBN 0-8191-1385-9); pap. text ed. 11.95 (ISBN 0-8191-1386-7). U Pr of Amer.

Ginsburg, Herbert. Myth of the Deprived Child: Poor Children's Intellect & Education. LC 76-166042. 1972. pap. text ed. 10.95 (ISBN 0-13-609149-0). P-H.

Ginsburg, Herbert & Opper, Sylvia. Piaget's Theory of Intellectual Development. 2nd ed. (Illus.). 1979. 13.95 (ISBN 0-13-675140-7); pap. 8.95 (ISBN 0-13-675132-6). P-H.

Ginsburg, Mirra. The Chick & the Duckling. LC 74-188773. (ps-1). 1972. 9.95 (ISBN 0-02-735940-9). Macmillan.

--The Fisherman's Son. LC 78-31852. (Illus.). (gr. k-3). 1979. 7.95 (ISBN 0-688-80216-8); PLB 7.63 (ISBN 0-688-84216-X). Greenwillow.

--Good Morning, Chick. LC 70-11352. (Illus.). 24p. (ps). 1980. 7.95 (ISBN 0-688-80284-2); PLB 7.63 (ISBN 0-688-84284-4). Greenwillow.

--How the Sun Was Brought Back to the Sky: Adapted from a Slovenian Folk Tale. LC 74-19060. (Illus.). 32p. (ps-2). 1975. 8.95 (ISBN 0-02-735750-3). Macmillan.

--Little Rystu. LC 76-30485. (Illus.). (gr. k-3). 1978. 7.95 (ISBN 0-688-80097-1); PLB 7.63 (ISBN 0-688-84097-3). Greenwillow.

--Striding Slippers: Adapted from an Udmurt Tale. LC 77-12035. (Illus.). (gr. k-3). 1978. 8.95 (ISBN 0-02-736370-8, 73637). Macmillan.

--The Strongest One of All. LC 76-44326. (Illus.). 1977. 8.25 (ISBN 0-688-80081-5); PLB 7.92 (ISBN 0-688-84081-7). Greenwillow.

--Two Greedy Bears: Adapted from a Hungarian Folk Tale. LC 76-8819. (Illus.). 32p. (ps-2). 1976. 8.95 (ISBN 0-02-736450-X, 73645). Macmillan.

--Which Is the Best Place: Adapted from the Russian of Pyotr Dudochkin. LC 75-31946. (Illus.). 32p. (ps-1). 1976. 8.95 (ISBN 0-02-735980-8, 73598). Macmillan.

Ginsburg, Mirra, ed. & tr. from Rus. The Air of Mars: And Other Stories of Time & Space. LC 75-34279. 160p. (gr. 5 up). 1976. 6.95 o.s.i. (ISBN 0-02-736160-8, 73616). Macmillan.

--The Lazies: Tales of the Peoples of Russia. LC 72-92437. (Illus.). 80p. (gr. 3-6). 1973. 7.95 (ISBN 0-02-735840-2). Macmillan.

Ginsburg, Mirra, adapted by. & tr. The Proud Maiden, Tungak & the Sun. LC 73-19060. (Illus.). 32p. (gr. k-2). 1974. 7.95 (ISBN 0-02-736260-4). Macmillan.

Ginsburg, Mirra, tr. Last Door to Aiya: A Selection of the Best New Science Fiction from the Soviet Union. LC 68-16347. (YA) 1968. 9.95 (ISBN 0-87599-135-1). S G Phillips.

Ginsburg, Mirra, tr. see Bulgakov, Mikhail.

Ginsburg, Mirra, tr. see Bulychev, Kirill.

Ginsburg, Mirra, tr. see Obukhova, Lydia.

Ginsburg, Norton, jt. ed. see Borgese, Elisabeth M.

Ginsburg, R. N., jt. auth. see James, N. P.

Ginsburg, Ruth R., et al. Nueva vista. (gr. 7-12). 1978. text ed. 14.80 (ISBN 0-205-05878-7, 4258789); 4.40 (ISBN 0-205-05880-9, 4258800); 4.96 (ISBN 0-205-03662-7, 4236629). Allyn.

--Vista Hispanica. (gr. 9-12). 1978. text ed. 15.40 (ISBN 0-205-05875-2, 4258754); tchr's ed. 4.40 (ISBN 0-205-05870-1, 4258770). Allyn.

Ginsburg, Victor. Biology of Carbohydrates, Vol. 1. LC 80-20758. 336p. 1981. 35.00 (ISBN 0-471-03905-5, Pub. by Wiley-Interscience). Wiley.

Ginsburgs, George. Soviet Foreign Policy Toward Western Europe. Rubinstein, Alvin Z, ed. LC 78-17925. (Praeger Special Studies). 1978. 24.95 (ISBN 0-03-044331-8). Praeger.

Ginsburgs, George & Pinkele, Carl F. The Sino-Soviet Territorial Dispute: 1949-64. LC 78-19458. 1978. 20.95 (ISBN 0-275-99990-3). Praeger.

Ginsburgs, George, jt. auth. see Slusser, Robert M.

Ginsbury, Norman, tr. see Ibsen, Henrik.

Ginter, Donald E., ed. Whig Organization in the General Election of 1790: Selections from the Blair Adam Papers. 1967. 20.00x (ISBN 0-520-00477-9). U of Cal Pr.

Ginter, Jay J., jt. ed. see Rettig, R. Bruce.

Ginther, John R. But You Look So Well! LC 77-26009. 1978. 11.95 (ISBN 0-88229-399-0). Nelson-Hall.

Ginzberg, Eli. American Jews: The Building of a Voluntary Community. (Texts & Studies Ser.). 1980. write for info. Am Jewish Hist Soc.

--Development of Human Resources. 1966. 13.95 o.p. (ISBN 0-07-023277-6, C); pap. 9.95 o.p. (ISBN 0-07-023276-8). McGraw.

--Effecting Change in Large Organizations. LC 57-13484. 1957. 15.00x (ISBN 0-231-02249-2). Columbia U Pr.

--The Negro Potential. LC 56-9606. 1956. pap. 5.00x (ISBN 0-231-08546-X). Columbia U Pr.

--Occupational Choice. LC 51-10961. 1951. 17.50x (ISBN 0-231-01846-0). Columbia U Pr.

--Urban Health Services: The Case of New York. LC 70-134987. 1970. 16.00x (ISBN 0-231-03515-2). Columbia U Pr.

--School Work Nexus. LC 80-82882. (Foundation Monograph Ser.). 100p. (Orig.). 1981. pap. 5.00 (ISBN 0-87367-425-1). Phi Delta Kappa.

Ginzberg, Eli & Berman, H. American Worker in the Twentieth Century. LC 63-10647. 1963. 14.95 (ISBN 0-02-911730-5). Free Pr.

Ginzberg, Eli & Conservation of Human Resources Staff. Manpower Strategy for the Metropolis. LC 68-27290. 1968. 18.50x (ISBN 0-231-03161-0). Columbia U Pr.

--New York Is Very Much Alive: A Manpower View. LC 73-2674. 287p. 1973. 12.95 o.p. (ISBN 0-07-023286-5, P&RB). McGraw.

Ginzberg, Eli & Ostow, Miriam. Men, Money & Medicine. LC 79-101134. 1970. 17.50x (ISBN 0-231-03366-4). Columbia U Pr.

Ginzberg, Eli & Yohalem, Alice M. Educated American Women: Life-Styles & Self-Portraits. LC 66-28964. 1966. 14.50x (ISBN 0-231-03027-4); pap. 5.00x (ISBN 0-231-03604-3). Columbia U Pr.

Ginzberg, Eli, ed. Jobs for Americans. (The American Assembly Ser.). 1976. pap. 4.50 (ISBN 0-13-510016-X, Spec) (ISBN 0-13-510016-X). P-H.

Ginzberg, Eli, et al. Democratic Values & the Rights of Management. LC 63-20227. 1963. 20.00x (ISBN 0-231-02664-1). Columbia U Pr.

--The Middle-Class Negro in the White Man's World. LC 67-26364. 1969. 15.00x (ISBN 0-231-03096-7); pap. 5.00x (ISBN 0-231-08596-6). Columbia U Pr.

Ginzberg, V. L. Theoretical Physics & Astrophysics. Haar, D. Ter, tr. (International Series in Natural Philosophy: Vol. 99). (Illus.). 1979. 75.00 (ISBN 0-08-023067-9); pap. 32.00 (ISBN 0-08-023066-0). Pergamon.

Ginzburg, Eugenia. Within the Whirlwind. Boland, Ian, tr. (Helen & Kurt Wolff Bk.). 1981. 14.95 (ISBN 0-15-197517-5). HarBraceJ.

Ginzburg, S. I., et al. Analytical Chemistry of the Platinum Metals. Shelnitz, P., ed. Kaner, N., tr. from Rus. LC 74-34394. (Analytical Chemistry of the Elements Ser). 673p. 1975. 79.95 (ISBN 0-470-30220-8). Halsted Pr.

Ginzburg, V. L. Propagation of Electromagnetic Waves in Plasmas. 2nd rev. ed. 1971. 60.00 (ISBN 0-08-015569-3). Pergamon.

Gioello, Debbie A. Fairchild's Designer: Stylist Handbook, 2 vols. (Illus.). 1979. Vol. 1. (ISBN 0-87005-332-9); Vol. 2. (ISBN 0-87005-333-7); Set. 35.00; tracing pad 7.95 (ISBN 0-87005-334-5). Fairchild.

--Profiling Fabrics: Properties, Performance, & Construction Techniques. (Language of Fashion Ser.). (Illus.). 325p. 1980. text ed. 27.50 (ISBN 0-87005-259-4). Fairchild.

Gioncu, Victor. Thin Reinforced Concrete Shells: Special Analysis Problems. LC 78-10338. 1980. 57.00 (ISBN 0-471-99735-8, Pub. by Wiley-Interscience). Wiley.

Giono, Jean. Angelo. Murch, Alma E., tr. 1960. 10.95 o.p. (ISBN 0-7206-0440-0). Dufour.

--Battle of Pavia. 15.00 (ISBN 0-7206-0780-9). Dufour.

--Joy of Man's Desiring. Clarke, Katherine A., tr. from Fr. 464p. 1980. pap. 9.50 (ISBN 0-86547-015-4). N Point Pr.

--To the Slaughterhouse. 11.95 (ISBN 0-7206-3602-7). Dufour.

--Two Riders of the Storm: A Novel. Brown, Alan, tr. 1967. 11.95 (ISBN 0-7206-9198-2). Dufour.

Giordani, Igino. St. Catherine of Siena. LC 75-1624. 1975. 5.95 o.s.i. (ISBN 0-8198-0493-2). Dghtrs St Paul.

--Saint Paul, Apostle & Martyr. 1941. 7.00 o.s.i. (ISBN 0-8198-0138-0); pap. 6.00 o.s.i. (ISBN 0-8198-0139-9). Dghtrs St Paul.

Giordano, Al. Business Mathematics - Electronic Calculation. (Illus.). 304p. 1981. text ed. 17.95 (ISBN 0-13-105163-6); pap. text ed. 13.95 (ISBN 0-13-105155-5). P-H.

Giordano, Albert. Business Machine Calculation: Vol. I, Adding Machines & Printing Calculators. (Orig.). 1964. Vol. 1. pap. text ed. 9.95 (ISBN 0-13-104943-7). P-H.

Giordano, Albert G. Concise Dictionary of Business Terminology. 464p. 1981. text ed. 14.95 (ISBN 0-13-166553-7, Spec); pap. text ed. 5.95 (ISBN 0-13-166546-4). P-H.

Giordano, Joseph. Ethnicity & Mental Health: Research & Recommendations. 1980. pap. 2.00 (ISBN 0-87495-006-6). Am Jewish Comm.

Giorgi, Louis P. The Windows of Saint Justin Martyr. LC 80-67119. (Illus.). 128p. 1981. 25.00 (ISBN 0-87982-034-9). Art Alliance.

Gioseffi, Daniela. Earth Dancing. (Illus.). 224p. 1980. pap. 13.95 o.p. (ISBN 0-8117-2116-7). Stackpole.

--Earth Dancing: Mother Nature's Oldest Rite. 224p. 1980. pap. 13.95 (ISBN 0-8117-2116-7). Stackpole.

Giovacchini, Peter. The Urge to Die: Why Young People Commit Suicide. LC 80-24435. 256p. 1981. 12.95 (ISBN 0-02-543440-3). Macmillan.

Giovacchini, Peter L., jt. auth. see Feinstein, Sherman C.

Giovanelli, G., et al, eds. Hypertension in Children & Adolescents. 364p. 1981. text ed. 33.00 (ISBN 0-89004-523-2). Raven.

Giovanni, Nikki. Cotton Candy on a Rainy Day. LC 78-16897. 1978. 5.95 (ISBN 0-688-03365-2); pap. 3.95 (ISBN 0-688-08365-X). Morrow.

--Cotton Candy on a Rainy Day. LC 78-16897. 1980. pap. 3.95 (ISBN 0-688-08365-X, Quill). Morrow.

--My House. LC 72-116. 96p. 1972. 7.95 (ISBN 0-688-00021-5); pap. 3.95 (ISBN 0-688-05021-2). Morrow.

Giovanni, Norman T. Di see Borges, Jorge L.

Gipe, George. Coney Island Quickstep. 1979. pap. 2.25 o.p. (ISBN 0-345-27978-6). Ballantine.

--Coney Island Quickstep. 1977. 8.95 o.s.i. (ISBN 0-690-01197-0, TYC-T). T Y Crowell.

--The Great American Sports Book. LC 78-4707. (Illus.). 1978. 15.95 (ISBN 0-385-13091-0); pap. 7.95 o.p. (ISBN 0-385-13092-9). Doubleday.

Gipe, George & Winokur, Alice. Melvin & Howard. 224p. 1980. pap. 2.25 (ISBN 0-515-05442-9). Jove Pubns.

Gippius, V. V. Gogol. Maguire, R., tr. 1981. 17.50 (ISBN 0-88233-612-6). Ardis Pubs.

Gippius, Vasily. Gogol. LC 63-7522. (Slavic Reprint Ser.: No. 1). 246p. (Rus). 1971. pap. 4.75 (ISBN 0-87057-069-2, Pub. by Brown U Pr). Univ Pr of New England.

Gips, James, jt. auth. see Stiny, George.

Gipson, Fred. Hound-Dog Man. LC 49-7116. 1949. PLB 9.89 o.s.i. (ISBN 0-06-011540-8, HarpT); lib. bdg. 9.89 (ISBN 0-06-011541-6). Har-Row.

--Hound-Dog Man. LC 80-10995. viii, 247p. 1980. pap. 4.95 (ISBN 0-8032-7005-4, BB 748, Bison). U of Nebr Pr.

--Old Yeller. 1964. pap. 1.95 (ISBN 0-06-080002-X, P2, PL). Har-Row.

--Savage Sam. (gr. 1-5). 1976. pap. 1.95 (ISBN 0-06-080377-0, P377, PL). Har-Row.

Gipson, Leland F. How to Use the Tremendous Power of Creative Prayer. 120p. (Orig.). 1981. pap. 3.95x (ISBN 0-9605014-0-1). Levada.

Gipson, R. McCandless. The Life of Emma Thursby. (Music Reprint Ser.). 1980. Repr. of 1940 ed. lib. bdg. 32.50 (ISBN 0-306-76016-9). Da Capo.

Giraldi, Lilio G. De Deis Gentium. LC 75-27850. (Renaissance & the Gods Ser.: Vol. 8). (Illus.). 1976. Repr. of 1548 ed. lib. bdg. 73.00 (ISBN 0-8240-2057-X). Garland Pub.

Giraldi Cinthio. Giraldi Cinthio on Romances. Snuggs, Henry L., tr. LC 68-12971. 216p. 1968. 9.75x (ISBN 0-8131-1158-7). U Pr of Ky.

Giraldo, Z. I. Public Policy & the Family: Wives & Mothers in the Labor Fource. LC 80-7692. 240p. 1980. 22.95x (ISBN 0-669-03762-1). Lexington Bks.

Giraldus Cambrensis. Speculum Duorum: Or, a Mirror of Two Men. (University of Wales, History & Law Ser.: No. 27). 1974. 25.00 (ISBN 0-7083-0544-X). Verry.

Girard, Hazel B. & Girard, Marvin E. Rail Fences & Roosters. 1978. 6.00 (ISBN 0-8233-0276-8). Golden Quill.

Girard, Joe. How to Sell Yourself. 352p. 1981. pap. 5.95 (ISBN 0-446-97336-X). Warner Bks.

Girard, Joe & Brown, Stanley H. How to Sell Anything to Anybody. 240p. 1979. pap. 2.75 (ISBN 0-446-95810-7); pap. 4.95 (ISBN 0-446-97719-5). Warner Bks.

Girard, Louis J. Advanced Techniques in Ophthalmic Microsurgery: Corneal Surgery, Vol. II. LC 78-31773. (Illus.). 305p. 1980. text ed. 82.50 (ISBN 0-8016-1835-5). Mosby.

--Ultrasonic Fragmentation for Intraocular Surgery. LC 78-20733. (Illus.). 1979. text ed. 79.50 (ISBN 0-8016-1837-1). Mosby.

Girard, Marvin E., jt. auth. see Girard, Hazel B.

Girard, Paul F. A Short History of Roman Law: Being the First Part of His "Manuel Elementaire De Droit Romain.". Lefrox, A. H. & Cameron, J. H., trs. LC 79-1603. 1981. Repr. of 1906 ed. 18.50 (ISBN 0-88355-906-4). Hyperion Conn.

Girard, R. M. Texas Rocks & Minerals: An Amateur's Guide. (Illus.). 109p. 1964. Repr. 2.00 (GB 6). Bur Econ Geology.

Girard, Raphael. Esotericism of the Popol Vuh. LC 78-74712. 1979. softcover 7.50 (ISBN 0-911500-14-6). Theos U Pr.

Girard, Robert C. Brethren, Hang Together. 1980. pap. 6.95 (ISBN 0-310-39071-0). Zondervan.

--My Weakness--His Strength: The Personal Face of Renewal. 208p. 1981. pap. 5.95 (ISBN 0-310-39081-8, 15607P). Zondervan.

Girard, Victor. Proto-Takanan Phonology. (U. C. Publ. in Linguistics: Vol. 70). 1971. pap. 9.50x (ISBN 0-520-09369-0). U of Cal Pr.

Girardi, Guilio. Marxism & Christianity. 1968. 5.95 o.s.i. (ISBN 0-02-543940-5). Macmillan.

Girardi, Wolfgang. Olympic Games. LC 72-173604. (International Library). (Illus.). 128p. (gr. 7 up). 1972. PLB 6.90 o.p. (ISBN 0-531-02111-4). Watts.

Giraud. Mots dans le vent. 11.25 (ISBN 0-685-36202-7, 2727). Larousse.

Giraud, J. & Pamart, J. Riverain. Les Nouveaux mots dans le vent. 271p. (Fr.). 1974. pap. 11.95 (ISBN 2-03-070334-6, 2717). Larousse.

Giraudoux see Bentley, Eric.

Giraudoux, Jean. Electre. Patty, James S., ed. LC 65-19222. (Fr.). 1965. pap. text ed. 4.95x (ISBN 0-89197-138-6). Irvington.

--Giraudoux: Four Plays, Vol. 1. Incl. Ondine; The Enchanted; The Madwoman of Chaillot; The Apollo of Bellac. 255p. (Orig.). 1958. pap. 5.95 (ISBN 0-8090-0712-6, Mermaid). Hill & Wang.

--Giraudoux: Three Plays, Vol. 2. La Farge, Phyllis & Judd, Peter H., trs. Incl. Siegfried; Amphitryon 38; Electra. 247p. (Orig.). 1964. pap. 5.95 (ISBN 0-8090-0731-2, Mermaid). Hill & Wang.

--Intermezzo. Reilly, John H., ed. LC 67-14570. (Fr.). 1967. pap. text ed. 6.95x (ISBN 0-89197-232-3). Irvington.

--Suzanne & the Pacific. Redman, Ben R., tr. from Fr. 286p. 1975. Repr. of 1923 ed. 17.00 (ISBN 0-86527-311-1). Fertig.

Girault, Rene, jt. auth. see Bouvier, Jean.

Girdano, D. A. & Girdano, D. D. Drug Education. alt. ed. 1972. pap. 5.95 o.p. (ISBN 0-201-02372-5). A-W.

Girdano, D. D., jt. auth. see Girdano, D. A.

Girdano, Daniel, jt. auth. see Dusek, Dorothy.

Girdano, Daniel, jt. auth. see Everly, George.

Girdano, Daniel A. Better Late Than Never: How Men Can Avoid a Midlife Fitness Crisis. (Illus.). 256p. 1981. 12.95t (ISBN 0-13-074773-4, Spec); pap. 5.95b (ISBN 0-13-074765-3). P-H.

Girdano, Daniel A. & Dusek, Dorothy. Drug Education: Content & Methods. 3rd ed. LC 79-21100. (Health Education Ser.). (Illus.). 1980. text ed. 9.50 (ISBN 0-201-02963-4); overlay masters 6.50 (ISBN 0-201-02389-X). A-W.

Girdano, Daniel A. & Everly, George S., Jr. Controlling Stress & Tension: A Holistic Approach. (Illus.). 1979. 12.95 (ISBN 0-13-172114-3); pap. 6.95 (ISBN 0-13-172106-2). P-H.

Girdano, Daniel A. & Girdano, Dorothy D. Drug Education: Content & Methods. 2nd ed. LC 75-20986. (Health Education Ser.). 224p. 1976. pap. text ed. 10.75 o.p. (ISBN 0-201-02381-4); overlay masters 6.50 o.p. (ISBN 0-201-02389-X). A-W.

Girdano, Daniel A., jt. auth. see Girdano, Dorothy D.

Girdano, Dorothy D. & Girdano, Daniel A. Drugs - A Factual Account. 2nd ed. LC 75-18154. (Health Education Ser.). 224p. 1976. pap. text ed. 9.95 o.p. (ISBN 0-201-02379-2). A-W.

Girdano, Dorothy D., jt. auth. see Girdano, Daniel A.

Girdler, Allan, jt. ed. see Mitchell, William L.

Girdlestone, Cuthbert. Mozart & His Piano Concertos. Orig. Title: Mozart's Piano Concertos,Il. 1952. pap. 7.50 (ISBN 0-486-21271-8). Dover.

Girdlestone, Cuthbert, ed. see Racine, Jean.

Girdoux, Jean. My Friend from Limousin. Willcox, L. C., tr. from Fr. LC 76-27657. 1977. Repr. of 1923 ed. 15.75 (ISBN 0-86527-279-4). Fertig.

Girgensohn, Herbert. Teaching Luther's Catechism, Vol. II. Doberstein, John W., tr. from Ger. LC 59-8463. 1960. 6.00 (ISBN 0-8006-0866-6, 1-866). Fortress.

Girgis, Makram. Neural Substrates of Limbix Epilepsy. (Illus.). 320p. 1981. 35.00 (ISBN 0-87527-238-X). Green.

Girgus, Sam B., ed. The American Self: Myth, Ideology, & Popular Culture. 288p. 1980. 20.00x (ISBN 0-8263-0557-1). U of NM Pr.

Giri, V. V. Labour Problems in Indian Industry. 3rd rev. ed. 564p. 1973. pap. text ed. 10.00x (ISBN 0-210-33692-7). Asia.

Girion, Barbara. Like Everybody Else. LC 80-21850. 192p. (gr. 6-8). 1980. 8.95 (ISBN 0-684-16715-8). Scribner.

--A Tangle of Roots. (gr. 7-12). pap. 1.75 (ISBN 0-440-98889-6, LE). Dell.

--A Tangle of Roots. 192p. (YA) (gr. 7 up). 1979. 7.95 (ISBN 0-684-16074-9). Scribner.

Girl Scouts of the U. S. A. Girl Scout Cookbook. List, Ely, ed. LC 70-144349. (Illus.). 192p. 1971. 6.95 o.p. (ISBN 0-8092-9144-4); PLB avail o.p. (ISBN 0-685-28671-1). Contemp Bks.

Girl Scouts of the USA. The Beginner's Cookbook. (gr. 1-6). 1972. pap. 0.95 (ISBN 0-88441-442-6, 26-114, Pub. by Dell). GS.

--Cooking Out-of-Doors: For Juniors, Brownies Cadettes, Seniors & Leaders. (Illus.). (gr. 1-12). 1960. spiral bdg. 4.00 (ISBN 0-88441-128-1, 19-984). GS.

--Sing Together: A Girl Scout Songbook. (Illus.). (gr. 1-12). 1973. 4.50 (ISBN 0-88441-309-8, 20-206). GS.

--The Story of the Four World Centres: For Girls & Leaders. (Illus.). 51p. (gr. 4-8). 1976. pap. 1.75 (ISBN 0-900827-27-0, 23-123). GS.

Girl Scouts of the U.S.A., Our Chalet Committee of Waggs. Our Chalet Songbook. 2nd ed. 1978. 2.00 (ISBN 0-88441-364-0, 23-929); in 7 languages avail. GS.

Girl Scouts of the U.S.A. Program Department. Girl Scout Badges & Signs: Leaders Guide. 1980. pap. text ed. 2.50 (ISBN 0-88441-327-6, 20-712). GS.

Girl Scouts of the U.S.A. Program Dept. Careers to Explore for Brownie & Junior Girl Scouts. (GS Catalogue: No. 20-813). 80p. (Orig.). (gr. 6-12). 2.75 (ISBN 0-88441-324-1). GS.

--Let's Make It Happen. (GS Catalogue: No. 20-815). (gr. 9-12). 2.50 (ISBN 0-88441-322-5). GS.

Girl Scouts of the U.S.A. Training Department. You Make the Difference: Leaders Guide. (Orig.). 1980. pap. text ed. 2.00 (ISBN 0-88441-330-6, 20-705). GS.

Girma-Selassie, Asfaw see Asfaw, Girma-Selassie, et al.

Girolami, Anne-Marie, jt. auth. see Martineau, Richard.

Girolamo, Costanzo Di see Di Girolamo, Costanzo.

Giron, Jose, tr. Testigos De Jehova y Sus Doctrinas. (Spanish Bks.). 1978. 1.50 (ISBN 0-8297-0604-6). Life Pubs Intl.

Girouard, Mark. Alfred Waterhouse & the Natural History Museum. LC 80-53742. (Illus.). 1981. 12.95x (ISBN 0-300-02578-5). Yale U Pr.

Giroux, Henry A., et al, eds. Curriculum & Instruction: Alternatives in Education. LC 80-84142. 1981. price not set (ISBN 0-8211-0615-5); text ed. price not set. McCutchan.

Giroux, James A. Drawing a Conclusion: Advanced Level. Spargo, Edward, ed. (Comprehension Skills Ser). (Illus.). (gr. 9-12). 1974. pap. text ed. 2.40x (ISBN 0-89061-015-0). Jamestown Pubs.

Giroux, James A. & Twining, James E. Making a Judgment: Advanced Level. Spargo, Edward, ed. (Comprehension Skills Ser). (Illus.). (gr. 9-12). 1974. pap. text ed. 2.40x (ISBN 0-89061-013-4). Jamestown Pubs.

Giroux, James A. & Williston, Glenn R. Appreciation of Literary Forms: Advanced Level. Spargo, Edward, ed. (Comprehension Skills Ser). (Illus.). 1974. pap. text ed. 2.40x (ISBN 0-89061-018-5). Jamestown Pubs.

--Making an Inference: Advanced Level. Spargo, Edward, ed. (Comprehension Skills Ser). (Illus.). (gr. 9-12). 1974. pap. text ed. 2.40x (ISBN 0-89061-016-9). Jamestown Pubs.

--Recognizing Tone: Advanced Level. Spargo, Edward, ed. (Comprehension Skills Ser). (Illus.). (gr. 9-12). 1974. pap. text ed. 2.40x (ISBN 0-89061-017-7). Jamestown Pubs.

--Retaining Concepts & Organizing Facts: Advanced Level. (Comprehension Skills Ser). (Illus.). (gr. 9-12). 1974. pap. text ed. 2.40x (ISBN 0-89061-019-3). Jamestown Pubs.

--Understanding Characters: Advanced Level. (Comprehension Skills Ser). (Illus.). (gr. 12 up). 1974. pap. text ed. 2.40x (ISBN 0-89061-014-2). Jamestown Pubs.

--Understanding the Main Idea: Advanced Level. (Comprehension Skills Ser). (Illus.). (gr. 9-12). 1974. pap. text ed. 2.40x (ISBN 0-89061-012-6). Jamestown Pubs.

Giroux, Joan. The Haiku Form. LC 73-86135. 176p. 1974. 6.50 o.p. (ISBN 0-8048-1110-5). C E Tuttle.

Girsanov, I. V. Lectures on Mathematical Theory of Extremum Problems. Louvish, D., tr. from Rus. LC 72-80360. (Lecture Notes in Economics & Mathematical Systems: Vol. 67). (Illus.). 139p. 1972. pap. 7.40 (ISBN 0-387-05857-5). Springer-Verlag.

Girshick, M. A., jt. auth. see Blackwell, David A.

Girtin, Tom. The Mark of the Sword: A Narrative History of the Cutler's Company, 1189 - 1975. (Illus.). 1975. text ed. 15.75x (ISBN 0-09-124790-X). Humanities.

Girvan, Norman. Corporate Imperialism: Conflict & Expropriation Transnational Corporations & Economic Nationalism in the Third World. LC 75-46112. 1976. 22.50 o.p. (ISBN 0-87332-073-5). M E Sharpe.

Gisbert, jt. auth. see De Toro, M.

Gisborne, Maria & Williams, Edward E. Maria Gisborne & Edward E. Williams, Shelley's Friends: Their Journals & Letters. Jones, Frederick L., ed. (Illus.). 1951. 11.95 o.p. (ISBN 0-8061-0232-2). U of Okla Pr.

Gisborne, Thomas. An Enquiry into the Duties of the Female Sex. Luria, Gina, ed. LC 74-8236. (The Feminist Controversy in England, 1788-1810 Ser.). 1974. lib. bdg. 50.00 (ISBN 0-8240-0860-X). Garland Pub.

Gischler, Christian. Water Resources in the Arab Middle East & North Africa. (Illus.). 1979. lib. bdg. 23.00x (ISBN 0-906559-00-6). Westview.

Gise, Peter. Microprocessor Interfacing. 288p. 1982. text ed. 19.95 (ISBN 0-8359-4364-X). Reston.

Gish, Ira M. & Christman, H. K. Madison, God's Beautiful Farm. LC 78-70891. (Redwood Ser.). 1979. pap. 3.95 (ISBN 0-8163-0243-X). Pacific Pr Pub Assn.

Gish, Oscar. Doctor Migration & World Health. 151p. 1971. pap. text ed. 6.90x (ISBN 0-7135-1611-9, Pub. by Bedford England). Renouf.

--Planning the Health Sector: The Tanzanian Experience. 209p. 1976. text ed. 24.50x (ISBN 0-8419-9722-5). Holmes & Meier.

Gisselquist, David. Oil Prices & Trade Deficits: U. S. Conflicts with Japan & West Germany. LC 79-20632. (Praeger Special Studies Ser.). 158p. 1980. 21.95 (ISBN 0-03-052381-8). Praeger.

Gisser, David G., jt. auth. see Carlson, A. Bruce.

Gisser, Micha. Intermediate Price Theory: Analysis, Issues & Applications. (Illus.). 608p. 1981. text ed. 17.95 (ISBN 0-07-023312-8, C); instructor's manual 4.95 (ISBN 0-07-023313-6). McGraw.

Gissing, George. Eve's Ransom. 125p. 1980. pap. 3.00 (ISBN 0-486-24016-9). Dover.

--The House of Cobwebs. 300p. 1980. Repr. of 1914 ed. lib. bdg. 25.00 (ISBN 0-89760-315-X). Telegraph Bks.

--Human Odds & Ends. Fletcher, Ian & Stokes, John, eds. LC 76-20076. (Decadent Consciousness Ser.). 1978. lib. bdg. 38.00 (ISBN 0-8240-2759-0). Garland Pub.

--Sleeping Fires. (Society & the Victorians: No. 24). 1974. text ed. 17.00x (ISBN 0-85527-032-2). Humanities.

--Thyrza: A Tale. Korg, Jacob, ed. (Society & Victorians: No. 21). 1974. text ed. 19.50x (ISBN 0-901759-94-5). Humanities.

--The Town Traveller. 247p. 1980. Repr. of 1927 ed. lib. bdg. 25.00 (ISBN 0-89984-231-3). Century Bookbindery.

--Workers in the Dawn. Wolff, Robert L., ed. LC 75-1527. (Victorian Fiction Ser.). 1975. Repr. of 1880 ed. lib. bdg. 66.00 (ISBN 0-8240-1599-1). Garland Pub.

Gissing, George R. The Letters of George Gissing to Eduard Bertz: 1887-1903. Young, Arthur C., ed. LC 80-12936. xl, 337p. 1980. Repr. of 1961 ed. lib. bdg. 28.25x (ISBN 0-313-22454-4, GILE). Greenwood.

Gist, Noel P. & Wright, Roy D. Marginality & Identity. (Monographs & Studies in Sociology & Anthropology in Honour of Nels Anderson Ser: Vol. 3). (Illus.). 161p. 1973. text ed. 31.00x (ISBN 90-040-3638-5). Humanities.

Giteau, Cecile. Dictionnaire Des Arts Du Spectacle. LC 79-499699. 455p. (Fr, Eng. & Ger.). 1970. 25.00x (ISBN 0-8002-1364-5). Intl Pubns Serv.

Githens, Marianne & Prestage, Jewel L., eds. A Portrait of Marginality: The Political Behavior of the American Woman. LC 76-58484. 1977. pap. 11.95x (ISBN 0-582-28129-6). Longman.

Gitler, I. Jazz Masters of the Forties. 1966. 5.95 o.p. (ISBN 0-02-543950-2). Macmillan.

Gitlin, Todd. The Whole World Is Watching: Mass Media in the Making & Unmaking of the New Left. 1980. 12.95 (ISBN 0-520-03889-4). U of Cal Pr.

Gitlow, Abraham L. Labor & Manpower Economics. 3rd ed. 1971. text ed. 14.95x o.p. (ISBN 0-256-00173-1). Irwin.

Gitman. Personal Finance. 1978. 18.95 (ISBN 0-03-020821-1). Dryden Pr.

Gitman, Larry & Moses, Edward A. Financial Management: Cases. 1978. text ed. 19.50 (ISBN 0-8299-0167-1); instrs.' manual avail. (ISBN 0-8299-0480-8). West Pub.

Gitman, Lawrence J. Fundamentos De Administracion Financiera. Herrera, Jesus V. & Mei Mei Alicia Chu Polido, eds. Restrepo, Carlos S., tr. from Eng. (Span.). 1978. text ed. cancelled (ISBN 0-06-313160-9, Pub. HarLA Mexico). Har-Row.

--Personal Finance. 2nd ed. LC 80-65798. 672p. 1981. text ed. 18.95 (ISBN 0-03-058094-3). Dryden Pr.

Gitnick, Gary L. Practical Diagnosis: Gastrointestinal & Liver Disease. 1979. kouverflex bdg. 14.00x (ISBN 0-89289-202-1). HM Prof Med Div.

Gitnick, Gary L., ed. Current Gastroenterology, Vol. 1. (Current Ser). (Illus.). 464p. 1980. 35.00 (ISBN 0-89289-115-7). HM Prof Med Div.

--Current Gastroenterology & Hepatology. (Illus.). 1979. 35.00 (ISBN 0-89289-108-4). HM Prof Med Div.

--Current Hepatology, Vol. 1. (Current Ser). (Illus.). 384p. 1980. 35.00x (ISBN 0-89289-114-9). HM Prof Med Div.

Gittell, Marilyn, et al. Limits to Citizen Participation: The Decline of Community Organizations. LC 80-15950. (Sage Library of Social Research: Vol. 109). (Illus.). 280p. 1980. 18.00 (ISBN 0-8039-1478-4); pap. 8.95 (ISBN 0-8039-1479-2). Sage.

Gittelsohn, Roland B. Love, Sex & Marriage: A Jewish View. (Illus.). (gr. 6-10), 1980. pap. 7.95x (ISBN 0-8074-0046-7, 142683). UAHC.

--Wings of the Morning: Little Lower Than the Angels. rev. ed. (Illus.). (gr. 10). 1969. text ed. 7.00 (ISBN 0-8074-0194-3, 161850). wkbk. 2.25 (ISBN 0-8074-0196-X, 161852). UAHC.

Gittelson, Bernard. Biorhythm: A Personal Science. rev. ed. 1978. pap. 2.95 (ISBN 0-446-93469-0). Warner Bks.

--Biorhythm Sports Forecasting. 1978. pap. 2.95 o.s.i. (ISBN 0-446-83799-7). Warner Bks.

Gittelson, Roland B. Modern Jewish Problems. rev. ed. (gr. 9-12). text ed. 5.00 (ISBN 0-8074-0099-8, 163303); tchrs'. guide 2.50 (ISBN 0-685-04890-X, 203303); wkbk. 1.75 (ISBN 0-685-04891-8, 163312). UAHC.

Gitter, A. George & Grunin, Robert, eds. Communication: A Guide to Information Sources. LC 79-54692. (Psychology Information Guide Ser.: Vol. 3). 1980. 30.00 (ISBN 0-8103-1443-6). Gale.

Gitterman, M. & Halpern, V., eds. Qualitative Analysis of Physical Problems. LC 80-767. 1981. 24.50 (ISBN 0-12-285150-1). Acad Pr.

Gittinger, J. Price. Economic Analysis of Agricultural Projects. (World Bank Ser). (Illus.). 240p. 1972. 15.00x (ISBN 0-8018-1386-7); pap. 5.50x (ISBN 0-8018-1403-0). Johns Hopkins.

Gittinger, J. Price, ed. Compounding & Discounting Tables for Project Evaluation. LC 73-19353. (International Bank for Reconstruction & Development Ser.). (Illus.). 143p. 1973. pap. 5.50x (ISBN 0-8018-1604-1). Johns Hopkins.

Gittings, Clare. Brasses & Brass Rubbings. (Illus.). 1979. 6.95 (ISBN 0-7137-0520-5, Pub. by Blandford Pr England). Sterling.

Gittings, James A. Bread, Meat & Raisins After the Dance. LC 77-83883. 1977. 7.00 (ISBN 0-89430-006-7). Morgan-Pacific.

Gittings, Robert, jt. ed. see Reeves, James.

Gittins, Anne. Tales from the South Pacific Islands. LC 76-5411. (Illus.). 96p. (gr. 3 up). 1977. 4.95 (ISBN 0-916144-02-X). Stemmer Hse.

Gittins, L., ed. see Fifth International Conference on the Hydraulic Transport of Solids in Pipes.

Gittins, L., jt. ed. see Stephens, H. S.

Gittins, Lavinia. Wear in Slurry Pipelines. (BHRA Information Ser.). (Illus.). 173p. (Orig.). Date not set. pap. 45.00 (ISBN 0-906085-45-4). BHRA Fluid.

Gittleman, Arthur. History of Mathematics. new ed. 304p. 1975. text ed. 18.95x (ISBN 0-675-08784-8). Merrill.

Gittleman, Edwin. Jones Very: The Effective Years, 1833-1840. LC 67-16202. 1967. 22.50x (ISBN 0-231-03043-6). Columbia U Pr.

Gittleman, Sol. From Shtetl to Suburbia: The Family in Jewish Literary Imagination. LC 78-53646. 1979. 10.95 (ISBN 0-8070-6364-9, BP-591); pap. 4.95 (ISBN 0-8070-6365-7). Beacon Pr.

Gittler, Josephine. Standards Relating to Juvenile Probation Function: Intake & Predisposition Investigative Services. (Juvenile Justice Standards Project Ser.). 1980. softcover 7.95 (ISBN 0-88410-828-7); casebound 14.50 (ISBN 0-88410-248-3). Ballinger Pub.

--Standards Relating to Juvenile Probation Function: Intake & Predisposition Investigative Services. LC 77-3257. (Juvenile Justice Standards Project Ser.). 1977. 7.95 o.p. (ISBN 0-88410-771-X); casebound 16.50 o.p. Ballinger Pub.

Gittner, Louis. Listen Listen Listen. Farish, Starr, ed. 320p. (Orig.). 1980. pap. 7.95 (ISBN 0-9605492-0-X). Louis Found.

Gittus, Elizabeth. Flats, Families & the Under-Fives. (International Library of Social Policy). 1976. 20.00 (ISBN 0-7100-8284-3). Routledge & Kegan.

Gittus, J. Irradiation Effects in Crystalline Solids. (Illus.). 1978. 102.60x (ISBN 0-85334-778-6). Intl Ideas.

Gittus, John. Creep, Viscoelasticity & Creep Fracture in Solids. LC 74-26524. 725p. 1975. 98.95 (ISBN 0-470-30265-8). Halsted Pr.

Giucharhaud, J., ed. Moliere: A Collection of Critical Essays. 1964. 10.95 (ISBN 0-13-599712-7, Spec). P-H.

Giuffey, George R. see Dryden, John.

Giuliano, William, jt. auth. see DeLuca, A. Michael.

Giumarra, Nancy, ed. see Curran, June.

Giurgea, Corneliu E. Fundamentals to a Pharmacology of the Mind. (American Lectures on Objective Psychiatry). (Illus.). 376p. 1981. text ed. 37.75 (ISBN 0-398-04130-X). C C Thomas.

Given, Barbara A. & Simmons, Sandra J. Gastroenterology in Clinical Nursing. 3rd ed. LC 79-13048. (Illus.). 1979. pap. text ed. 17.95 (ISBN 0-8016-1855-X). Mosby.

Givens, Ellen D., jt. auth. see Ehrlich, Ruth A.

Givens, Harold. Landscape It Yourself. LC 76-14436. (Illus.). 1977. pap. 8.95 (ISBN 0-15-147689-6, Harv). HarBraceJ.

Givens, John. Living Alone. LC 80-69366. 1981. 9.95 (ISBN 0-689-11147-9). Atheneum.

--Sons of the Pioneers. LC 77-73052. 1977. 10.00 o.p. (ISBN 0-15-183775-9); pap. 3.95 o.p. (ISBN 0-15-683815-X, Harv). HarBraceJ.

Gividen, Edith H. End of Tether. 1981. 6.95 (ISBN 0-8062-1609-3). Carlton.

Givone, Donald D. & Roesser, Robert P. Microprocessors - Microcomputers: An Introduction. (Illus.). 1979. text ed. 22.95 (ISBN 0-07-023326-8); solns. manual 4.95 (ISBN 0-07-023327-6). McGraw.

Givoni, B. Man, Climate & Architecture. 2nd ed. (Illus.). 1976. 74.50x (ISBN 0-85334-678-X). Intl Ideas.

Gjelle, S, et al. Geological Survey of Norway. (No. 343, Bulletin 48). pap. 16.00x (ISBN 82-00-31377-8, Dist. by Columbia U Pr.). Universitet.

Gjelsvik, Atle. The Theory of Thin Walled Bars. 272p. 1981. 27.95 (ISBN 0-471-08594-4, Pub. by Wiley-Interscience). Wiley.

Gjelsvik, Tore. Results from Norwegian Antartic Research, Nineteen Seventy Four to Nineteen Seventy Seven. (Norsk Polarinstitutt Skrifter: Vol. 169). (Illus.). 117p. 1980. pap. text ed. 7.50x (ISBN 82-90307-03-9). Universitet.

Gjesdahl, Maurice S., jt. auth. see Niebel, Benjamin W.

Gjessing, Lieve. Contribution to the Somatology of Periodic Catatonia. Marshall, H., tr. 1976. text ed. 75.00 (ISBN 0-08-015650-9). Pergamon.

Gjorgov, A. N. Barrier Contraception & Breast Cancer. (Contributions to Gynecology & Obstetrics Ser.: Vol. 8). (Illus.). 1980. soft cover 49.75 (ISBN 3-8055-0330-X). S Karger.

G. J. Van, Der Plaats see Van Der Plaats, G. J.

Glab, Stanislaw, jt. ed. see Hulanicki, Adam.

Glad, Paul W. Trumpet Soundeth: William Jennings Bryan & His Democracy, 1896-1912. LC 60-12259. (Illus.). 1966. pap. 3.75x (ISBN 0-8032-5073-8, BB 344, Bison). U of Nebr Pr.

Gladden, Edgar N. Civil Services of the United Kingdom, 1855-1970. LC 67-16352. 1967. 17.50x (ISBN 0-678-05048-1). Kelley.

Gladieux, Lawrence E. & Wolanin, Thomas R. Congress & the Colleges: The National Politics of Higher Education. LC 75-22881. (Politics of Education Ser.). 288p. 1976. 21.95 (ISBN 0-669-00183-X). Lexington Bks.

Gladson, Deek. Encyclopedia of Dowsing. 4.00 o.s.i. (ISBN 0-89316-606-5). Exanimo Pr.

--The Midas Manual. 1981. pap. 4.00 (ISBN 0-89316-623-5); plastic bdg. 6.00 (ISBN 0-89316-624-3). Exanimo Pr.

--The Miser's Manual: A Guide to Frofitable Self-Employment. 1981. pap. 4.00 (ISBN 0-686-69465-1); plastic bdg. 6.00 (ISBN 0-89316-626-X). Exanimo Pr.

Gladstone Associates, jt. auth. see ULI Research Division.

Gladstone, Bernard. New York Times Guide to Simple Home Repairs. LC 75-45764. (Illus.). 177p. 1976. pap. 2.95 o.p. (ISBN 0-89104-040-4). A & W Pubs.

Gladstone, F. J. Voluntary Action in a Changing World. 137p. 1979. pap. text ed. 9.90x (ISBN 0-7199-1033-1, Pub. by Bedford England). Renouf.

Gladstone, Francis. The Politics of Planning. 1977. 15.00 (ISBN 0-85117-106-0). Transatlantic.

Gladstone, Irving. Confessions of a Golf Duffer in Search of No Fault Insurance. LC 77-10114. 1977. 6.95 (ISBN 0-8119-0286-2). Fell.

Gladstone, John. Air Conditioning & Mechanical Trades: Preparing for the Contractor's License Examination. LC 74-18258. (Illus.). 425p. 1980. pap. 18.95 (ISBN 0-930644-04-2). Engineers Pr.

--Air Conditioning Testing & Balancing: A Field Practice Manual. 1974. cancelled (ISBN 0-685-92593-5). Engineers Pr.

Gladstone, M. J. A Report on Professional Salaries in New York State Museums. 48p. 1972. pap. 3.00x (ISBN 0-89062-020-2, Pub. by NYS Assn Mus). Pub Ctr Cult Res.

Gladstone, Penelope. Travels of Alexine. (Illus.). 1971. 12.50 (ISBN 0-7195-2044-4). Transatlantic.

Gladstone, Robert M., jt. auth. see Wilburn, Michael D.

Gladstone, T. H. Englishman in Kansas; or, Squatter Life & Border Warfare. LC 74-155700. 1971. 14.95x (ISBN 0-8032-0800-6); pap. 3.95 (ISBN 0-8032-5742-2, BB 536, Bison). U of Nebr Pr.

Gladstone, W. E. Midlothian Speeches, 1879. (Victorian Library). 1971. Repr. of 1879 ed. text ed. 9.00x (ISBN 0-391-00110-8, Leicester). Humanities.

Gladstone, William. Real Estate License Examination: Salesman & Broker. 2nd ed. LC 74-27434. 1976. pap. 6.00 o.p. (ISBN 0-668-03755-5). Arco.

Gladstone, William E. Gladstone Diaries, Vols. 1 & 2# 1825-39. Foot, M. R., ed. 1968. 89.00x (ISBN 0-19-821370-0). Oxford U Pr.

--The Gladstone Diaries: Volumes V & VI, 1844-1868. Matthew, H. C., ed. (Gladstone Diaries Ser.). (Illus.). 1978. 139.00x set (ISBN 0-19-822445-1). Oxford U Pr.

--The Gladstone Diaries: 1840-1854, Vols. 3 & 4. Foot, M. R. & Foot, M. R., eds. (Illus.). 1450p. 1975. Set. 109.00x (ISBN 0-19-822425-7). Oxford U Pr.

Gladstone, William J. Test Your Own Mental Health: A Self-Evaluation Workbook. LC 77-4678. 1978. lib. bdg. 9.95 o.p. (ISBN 0-668-04192-7, 4192); pap. 4.95 o.p. (ISBN 0-668-04186-2, 4186). Arco.

Gladwell, G. M. Contact Problems in the Classical Theory of Elasticity. (Mechanics of Elastic & Viscoelastic Solids Ser.). 716p. 1980. 60.00x (ISBN 9-0286-0440-5); pap. 35.00x (ISBN 9-0286-0760-9). Sijthoff & Noordhoff.

Gladwell, I. & Wait, R., eds. A Survey of Numerical Methods for Partial Differential Equations. (Illus.). 1980. 39.95x (ISBN 0-19-853351-9). Oxford U Pr.

Gladwin, D. D. The Waterways of Britain: A Social Panorama. 1976. 22.50 (ISBN 0-7134-3159-8). David & Charles.

Gladwin, David. A Pictorial History of Canals. 1977. 19.95 (ISBN 0-7134-0554-6, Pub. by Batsford England). David & Charles.

Gladwin, John. God's People in God's World. LC 80-7726. 1980. pap. 5.95 (ISBN 0-87784-607-3). Inter-Varsity.

Gladwin, Thomas & Saidin, Ahmad. Slaves of the White Myth: The Psychology of Neocolonialism. LC 80-14939. 1981. text ed. 12.50 (ISBN 0-391-01936-8). Humanities.

Gladwin, Thomas N. & Walter, Ingo. Multinationals Under Fire: Lessons in the Management of Conflict. LC 79-21741. 1980. 34.95 (ISBN 0-471-01969-0, Pub. by Wiley-Interscience). Wiley.

Gladwyn, Hubert. Halfway to Nineteen Eighty-Four. LC 66-27476. 1966. 10.00x (ISBN 0-231-02991-8). Columbia U Pr.

Glaeser, W. A., jt. ed. see Rigney, D. A.

Glaister, E., jt. auth. see Lockwood, M. S.

Glaister, Geoffrey. Glaister's Glossary of the Book: Terms Used in Paper-Making, Printing, Bookbinding, & Publishing. 1979. 75.00 (ISBN 0-520-03364-7). U of Cal Pr.

Glaister, Stephen. Mathematical Methods for Economists. rev. ed. 1978. pap. 14.50x (ISBN 0-631-19050-3, Pub. by Basil Blackwell England). Biblio Dist.

Glanfield, P., compiled by. Applied Cook-Freezing. (Illus.). xii, 203p. 1980. 35.00x (ISBN 0-85334-888-X). Burgess-Intl Ideas.

Glansdorff, P. & Prigogine, I. Thermodynamic Theory of Structure, Stability & Fluctuations. LC 78-147070. 1971. 48.50 (ISBN 0-471-30280-5, Pub. by Wiley-Interscience). Wiley.

Glantz, Michael. Desertification. LC 77-3901. (Westview Special Studies in Natural Resources & Energy Management). 1977. lib. bdg. 28.00x (ISBN 0-89158-115-4). Westview.

Glantz, Michael H., ed. Politics of Natural Disaster: The Case of the Sahel Drought. LC 75-8474. (Illus.). 1976. text ed. 25.95 o.p. (ISBN 0-275-01180-1). Praeger.

Glantz, Micheal H. & Thompson, J. Dana, eds. Resource Management & Environmental Uncertainty: Lessons from Coastal Upwelling Fisheries. LC 80-16645. (Advances in Environmental Science & Technology Ser.). 550p. 36.50 (ISBN 0-471-05984-6, Pub. by Wiley-Interscience). Wiley.

Glantz, Stanton A. Mathematics for Biomedical Applications. LC 77-20320. 1979. 32.50x (ISBN 0-520-03599-2). U of Cal Pr.

Glanvill, A. B. & Denton, E. N. Injection-Mould Design Fundamentals. (Illus.). 1965. 18.00 (ISBN 0-8311-1033-3). Indus Pr.

Glanvill, John & Martin, Henry. The Copies of Two Speeches in Parliament. The One by John Glanvill, Esquire. The Other by Sir Henry Martin, Knight. LC 74-28858. (English Experience Ser.: No. 739). 1975. Repr. of 1628 ed. 3.50 (ISBN 90-221-0739-6). Walter J Johnson.

Glanvill, Joseph. Joseph Glanvill: Scepsis Scientifica, or Confest Ignorance, the Way to Science, 1664. Wellek, Rene, ed. LC 75-11222. (British Philosophers & Theologians of the 17th & 18th Centuries Ser.). 1978. lib. bdg. 42.00 (ISBN 0-8240-1776-5). Garland Pub.

--Saducismus Triumphatus: Or, Full & Plain Evidence Concerning Witches & Apparitions. LC 66-60009. 1966. Repr. of 1689 ed. 65.00x (ISBN 0-8201-1021-3). Schol Facsimiles.

Glanville, Brian. A Book of Soccer. (Illus.). 1979. 14.95 (ISBN 0-19-502585-7). Oxford U Pr.

--History of the Soccer World Cup. LC 73-8089. (Illus.). 256p. 1974. pap. 4.95 o.s.i. (ISBN 0-02-028840-9, Collier). Macmillan.

Glanville, Joseph. Some Discourse, Sermons & Remains. Wellek, Rene, ed. LC 75-11221. (British Philosophers & Theologians of the 17th & 18th Centuries Ser.). lib. bdg. 42.00 (ISBN 0-8240-1775-7). Garland Pub.

--Two Choice & Useful Treatises. Wellek, Rene, ed. LC 75-11223. (British Philosophers & Theologians of the 17th & 18th Centuries Ser.). 1978. lib. bdg. 42.00 (ISBN 0-8240-1777-3). Garland Pub.

Glanville, Ranulph de. Translation of Glanville: (A Treatise on the Laws & Customs of the Kingdom of England) Beames, John, tr. from Latin. xl, 362p. 1980. Repr. of 1812 ed. lib. bdg. 30.00x (ISBN 0-8377-0313-1). Rothman.

Glanz, Edward C. Guidance: Foundations, Principles & Techniques. 2nd ed. 1974. text ed. 15.95x o.s.i. (ISBN 0-205-04280-5, 224280X). Allyn.

Glapthorne, Henry. The Hollander: A Comedy Written Sixteen Thirty-Five. LC 79-84112. (English Experience Ser.: No.931). 76p. 1979. Repr. of 1640 ed. lib. bdg. 9.50 (ISBN 90-221-0931-3). Walter J Johnson.

Glare, G. P., ed. Oxford Latin Dictionary, Fascicle IV: Gorgonia-Libero. 260p. 1973. pap. 39.00x (ISBN 0-19-864217-2). Oxford U Pr.

Glare, P. G., ed. Oxford Latin Dictionary, Fascicle 5. 260p. 1975. pap. 42.00x (ISBN 0-19-864218-0). Oxford U Pr.

--Oxford Latin Dictionary: Fascicle VII. 256p. (Orig.). 1980. pap. 49.50x (ISBN 0-19-864220-2). Oxford U Pr.

--Oxford Latin Dictionary: Fascicle 1, a-Calcitro. 1968. pap. 42.00x (ISBN 0-19-864209-1). Oxford U Pr.

--Oxford Latin Dictionary: Fascicle 2, Calcitro-Demitto. 1969. pap. 39.00x (ISBN 0-19-864215-6). Oxford U Pr.

--Oxford Latin Dictionary, Fascicle 3: Demiurgus-Gorgoneus. 264p. 1971. pap. 42.00x (ISBN 0-19-864216-4). Oxford U Pr.

Glare, P. G. W., ed. Oxford Latin Dictionary: Fascicle VI-a-Calcitro. 1978. pap. 42.00x (ISBN 0-19-864219-9). Oxford U Pr.

Glasauer, Franz E., jt. auth. see Bakay, Louis.

Glasby, J. S., ed. Encyclopedia of the Alkaloids, Vol. 1, (a-h), Vol. 2, (i-z) LC 75-17753. 1423p. 1975. Set. 95.00 (ISBN 0-306-30845-2, Plenum Pr). Plenum Pub.

Glasby, John S. The Nebular Variables. LC 74-3354. 220p. 1974. text ed. 42.00 (ISBN 0-08-017949-5). Pergamon.

Glasco, Grodon. Second Nature. 432p. (Orig.). 1980. pap. cancelled (ISBN 0-446-83954-X). Warner Bks.

Glase, Jon C., ed. see Association for Biology Laboratory Education, 1st Workshop.

Glasenapp, C. F., jt. auth. see Ellis, William A.

Glasenapp, C. P., jt. auth. see Ellis, William A.

Glaser, Anton. History of Binary & Other Nondecimal Numeration. LC 71-149293. (Illus., Orig.). 1971. 7.50 o.p. (ISBN 0-9600324-2-8); pap. 4.00 o.p. (ISBN 0-9600324-1-X). A Glaser.

Glaser, Arthur & Subak-Sharpe, Gerald E. Integrated Circuit Engineering: Fabrication, Design, Application. LC 77-73945. 1977. text ed. 28.95 (ISBN 0-201-07427-3, 0-201-07428). A-W.

Glaser, Barbara, jt. auth. see Kirschenbaum, Howard.

Glaser, Barney G. & Straus, Anselm L. Discovery of Grounded Theory: Strategies for Qualitative Research. LC 66-28314. 1967. text ed. 18.95x (ISBN 0-202-30028-5); pap. text ed. 7.50x (ISBN 0-202-30260-1). Aldine Pub.

Glaser, Barney G. & Strauss, Anselm L. Awareness of Dying. LC 65-12454. 1965. 15.95x (ISBN 0-202-30001-3). Aldine Pub.

Glaser, Christine, jt. auth. see Glaser, Rollin.

Glaser, Daniel. Effectiveness of a Prison & Parole System. abr ed. LC 79-93448. 1969. pap. 7.95 (ISBN 0-672-60842-1). Bobbs.

Glaser, Dianne. Amber Wellington, Daredevil. LC 74-78854. (Illus.). 128p. (gr. 3-7). 1975. 5.95 o.s.i. (ISBN 0-8027-6197-6). Walker & Co.

--The Diary of Trilby Frost. LC 75-37080. 192p. (gr. 6 up). 1976. 8.95 (ISBN 0-8234-0277-0). Holiday.

Glaser, Edward M., jt. auth. see Greenberg, Paul D.

Glaser, G. Temporal Lobe Psychomotor Seizures. 1981. pap. text ed. write for info. (ISBN 0-443-08000-3). Churchill.

Glaser, G. H., et al, eds. Antiepileptic Drugs: Mechanisms of Action. Penry, J. Kiffin. 1980. text ed. 74.50 (ISBN 0-89004-251-9). Raven.

Glaser, Herman. The Cultural Roots of National Socialism. Menze, Ernest A., tr. LC 77-89144. Orig. Title: Spiesser-ideologie. 1978. 15.00x (ISBN 0-292-71044-5). U of Tex Pr.

Glaser, Hermann, ed. The German Mind of the Nineteenth Century: A Literary & Historical Anthology. 416p. 1981. 19.50 (ISBN 0-8264-0041-8); pap. 8.95 (ISBN 0-8264-0044-2). Continuum.

Glaser, Joel S. Neuro Ophthalmology: Symposium of the University of Miami & the Bascom Palmer Eye Institute, Vol. 10. LC 64-18729. (Illus.). 242p. 1980. text ed. 45.00 (ISBN 0-8016-1876-2). Mosby.

Glaser, Joel S. & Smith, J. Lawton. Neuro-Ophthalmology: Symposium of the University of Miami & the Bascom Palmer Eye Institute, Vol. 8. (Illus.). 1975. text ed. 37.50 o.p. (ISBN 0-8016-1846-0). Mosby.

Glaser, Joel S., ed. Neuro-Ophthalmology: Symposium of the University of Miami & the Bascom Palmer Eye Institute, Vol. 9. LC 64-18729. (Illus.). 1977. 39.50 o.p. (ISBN 0-8016-1843-6). Mosby.

Glaser, Kurt. Learning Difficulties: Causes & Psychological Implications - A Guide for Professionals. (Illus.). 112p. 1974. 11.25 (ISBN 0-398-03157-6). C C Thomas.

Glaser, Kurt & Possony, Stefan T. Victims of Politics. LC 78-5591. (Illus.). 1979. 37.50x (ISBN 0-231-04442-9). Columbia U Pr.

Glaser, Milton. Milton Glaser: Graphic Design. LC 73-79228. (Illus.). 240p. 1973. 45.00 (ISBN 0-87951-013-7). Overlook Pr.

Glaser, Milton, jt. auth. see Weymouth, Lally.

Glaser, R. O., jt. auth. see Otto, C. P.

Glaser, Rollin & Glaser, Christine. Managing by Design. LC 80-22455. 192p. 1981. text ed. 9.95 (ISBN 0-201-02717-8). A-W.

Glaser, William A. The Brain Drain: Emigration & Return-A UNITAR Study. LC 77-30576. 1978. text ed. 22.00 (ISBN 0-08-022415-6); pap. text ed. 50.00 (ISBN 0-08-022419-9). Pergamon.

Glaser-Wohrer, Evelyn. An Analysis of John Barth's Weltanschauung: His View of Life & Literature. (Salzburg Studies in English Literature: No. 5). 1977. pap. text ed. 31.25x (ISBN 0-391-01385-8). Humanities.

Glasgow, G. H. A Modern View of Conveyancing. 1969. 22.00 (ISBN 0-08-013063-1); pap. 10.75 (ISBN 0-08-013062-3). Pergamon.

Glasgow, Mary. Weekend a Paris. (Choucas (Jackdaw in French) Ser: No. CH2). 1973. 5.95 o.p. (ISBN 0-670-75625-3, Grossman). Viking Pr.

Glasgow University Media Group. Bad News, Vol.1. 326p. 1981. price not set (ISBN 0-7100-0792-2). Routledge & Kegan.

--More Bad News, Vol. 2. (Illus.). 1980. 50.00x (ISBN 0-7100-0414-1). Routledge & Kegan.

Glashagel, Jerry, ed. Young Winners Flag Football. (Illus.). 65p. 1980. spiral bdg. 29.95 (ISBN 0-936446-04-8). Youth Sports.
--Young Winners Soccer. (Illus.). 57p. 1980. spiral bdg. 29.95 (ISBN 0-936446-03-X). Youth Sports.
Glashow, Judith, et al. Shoot the Works. (Illus.). 128p. 1980. 14.95 (ISBN 0-87165-058-4); pap. 7.95 (ISBN 0-87165-059-2). Ziff-Davis Pub.
Glasier. Falconry & Hawking. 53.00 (ISBN 0-7134-0232-6). David & Charles.
Glasman, Ronald M., jt. ed. see Vidich, Arthur J.
Glasrud, Bruce A., jt. ed. see Halseth, James A.
Glass, Amee & Hackett, Dorothy. Ngaanyatjarra Texts. rev. ed. (AIAS New Ser.: No. 16). 144p. 1979. pap. text ed. 9.25x (ISBN 0-391-01683-0). Humanities.
Glass, D. V. & Taylor, P. A. Population & Emigration in Nineteenth Century Britain. (Commentaries on British Parlimentary Papers). 132p. 1976. 15.00x (ISBN 0-7165-2219-5, Pub. by Irish Academic Pr Ireland). Biblio Dist.
Glass, E. W. Integrated Pest Management: Rationale, Potential Needs & Implementation. 1975. 5.85 (ISBN 0-686-18864-0). Entomol Soc.
Glass, Gene V. & Stanley, Julian C. Statistical Methods in Education & Psychology. (Educational Measurement, Research & Statistics Ser). 1970. text ed. 19.95x (ISBN 0-13-844928-7). P-H.
Glass, Gene V., jt. auth. see Hopkins, Kenneth D.
Glass, George. Your Book of Judo. (Your Book Ser). (Illus.). 1978. 5.95 o.p. (ISBN 0-571-11054-1, Pub. by Faber & Faber). Merrimack Bk Serv.
Glass, George B., ed. Gastrointestinal Hormones. (Comprehensive Endocrinology Ser.). 1980. text ed. 92.00 (ISBN 0-89004-395-7). Raven.
Glass, J. Colin. Introduction to Mathematical Methods in Economics. 352p. 1980. text ed. 18.95 (ISBN 0-07-084116-0, C). McGraw.
Glass, Marion & Atchison, Evelyn. Integrated Studies in Patient Care. LC 76-46127. 1978. pap. text ed. 9.00 (ISBN 0-8273-1608-9); instructor's guide 1.60 (ISBN 0-8273-1609-7). Delmar.
Glass, Mary E. Nevada's Turbulent Fifties: Decade of Political & Economic Change. LC 80-25651. (Nevada Studies in History & Political Science: No. 15). (Illus.). ix, 138p. (Orig.). 1981. pap. price not set (ISBN 0-87417-062-1). U of Nev Pr.
Glass, Philip, jt. auth. see De Jong, Constance.
Glass, Robert E. Gene Function: E. coli & Its Heritable Elements. 450p. 1980. 60.00x (Pub. by Croom Helm England). State Mutual Bk.
Glass, Robert L. Software Reliability Guidebook. (Illus.). 1979. text ed. 21.95 (ISBN 0-13-821785-8). P-H.
--Software Soliloquies. 1981. 9.95. Computing Trends.
Glass, Robert L. & Noiseux, Ronald A. Software Maintenance Guidebook. (Illus.). 208p. 1981. text ed. 21.95 (ISBN 0-13-821728-9). P-H.
Glasscock, Michael E., jt. auth. see Shambaugh, George E.
Glasscoe, Marion, ed. The Medieval Mystical Tradition in England. 249p. 1981. pap. 12.00x (Pub. by U Exeter, England). Humanities.
Glasscote, R. M. Partial Hospitalization for the Mentally Ill: A Study of Programs & Problems. 187p. 1969. pap. 5.00 (ISBN 0-685-24873-9, P204-1). Am Psychiatric.
--The Psychiatric Emergency - a Study of Patterns of Service. 111p. 1966. pap. 3.50 (ISBN 0-685-24858-5, P179-0). Am Psychiatric.
Glasscote, R. M. & Fishman, M. E. Mental Health on the Campus: A Field Study. 216p. 1973. 8.50 (ISBN 0-685-77454-6, P202-0). Am Psychiatric.
Glasscote, R. M. & Gudeman, Jon E. The Staff of the Mental Health Center: A Field Study. 207p. 1969. 7.50- (ISBN 0-685-24872-0, P155-0). Am Psychiatric.
Glasscote, R. M. & Kanno, C. K. General Hospital Psychiatric Units - a National Survey. pap. 1.50 o.p. (ISBN 0-685-24856-9, 154). Am Psychiatric.
Glasscote, R. M. & Sussex, J. N. Community Mental Health Center-an Interim Appraisal, 1969. 156p. 1969. text ed. 8.00 (ISBN 0-685-31185-6, P206-0); pap. 5.00 (ISBN 0-685-31186-4, P206-1). Am Psychiatric.
Glasscote, R. M., jt. auth. see Kanno, C. K.
Glasscote, R. M., et al. Halfway Houses for the Mentally Ill: A Study of Programs & Problems. 244p. 1971. 7.50 (ISBN 0-685-24870-4, P203-0). Am Psychiatric.
--Old Folks at Home: A Field Study of Nursing & Board-&-Care Facilities. 148p. 1976. 8.00 (ISBN 0-685-76789-2, P222-0). Am Psychiatric.
--Rehabilitating the Mentally Ill in the Community: A Study of Psychosocial Rehabilitation Centers. 214p. 1971. 7.50 (ISBN 0-685-24869-0, P-157-0). Am Psychiatric.
--Creative Mental Health Services for the Elderly. 189p. 1977. 10.00 (ISBN 0-685-86111-2). Am Psychiatric.
--Treatment of Drug Abuse: Programs, Problems, Prospects, 1972. 250p. 1972. pap. 8.00 (ISBN 0-686-57639-X, P197-0). Am Psychiatric.
Glasscote, Raymond M. & Fishman, M. E. Mental Health Programs for Preschool Children: A Field Study. 182p. 1974. pap. 8.50 (ISBN 0-685-65571-7, P208-0). Am Psychiatric.
Glasscote, Raymond M., et al. Alternate Services - Their Role in Mental Health: A Field Study of Free Clinics, Runaway Houses, Counseling Centers & the Like. 1975. pap. 10.00 (ISBN 0-685-63942-8, P209-0). Am Psychiatric.
--Children & Mental Health Centers: Programs, Problems, Prospects, 1972. 257p. 1972. pap. 7.50 (P172-0). Am Psychiatric.
Glassenapp, C. F., jt. auth. see Ellis, William A.
Glasser, et al. Explorations in National Cinema. Lawton, Ben & Staiger, Janet, eds. (Film Studies Annual, 1977: Pt. 1). (Illus.). 1977. pap. 6.00 (ISBN 0-913178-52-7). Redgrave Pub Co.
Glasser, Hannelore. Artist's Contracts of the Early Renaissance. LC 76-23624. (Outstanding Dissertations in the Fine Arts - 2nd Series - 15th Century). (Illus.). 1977. Repr. of 1965 ed. lib. bdg. 56.00 (ISBN 0-8240-2694-2). Garland Pub.
Glasser, Morton & Pelto, Gretel H. Medical Merry-Go-Round: A Plea for Reasonable Medicine. 1980. pap. 6.90 (ISBN 0-913178-54-3). Redgrave Pub Co.
Glasser, Otto. Doctor W. C. Rontgen. 2nd ed. (Illus.). 192p. 1972. 10.75 (ISBN 0-398-02196-1). C C Thomas.
Glasser, Paul H., et al, eds. Individual Change Through Small Groups. LC 73-14113. (Illus.). 1974. 16.95 (ISBN 0-02-911810-7); pap. text ed. 9.95 (ISBN 0-02-911800-X). Free Pr.
Glasser, Selma. Complete Guide to Prize Contests, Sweepstakes, & How to Win Them. new ed. LC 80-14523. 192p. 1980. 9.95 (ISBN 0-8119-0327-3). Fell.
Glasser, William. Mental Health or Mental Illness. LC 60-15216. (Illus.). 1961. 7.95 o.s.i. (ISBN 0-06-002010-5, HarpT). Har-Row.
--Schools Without Failure. 256p. 1975. pap. 2.50 (ISBN 0-06-080349-5, P349, PL). Har-Row.
Glasser, William & Powers, William T. Stations of the Mind: New Directions for Reality Therapy. LC 80-8205. (Illus.). 288p. 1981. 11.95 (ISBN 0-06-011478-9, HarpT). Har-Row.
Glassheim, Eliot & Cargille, Charles, eds. Key Issues in Population & Food Policy: Capon Springs Public Policy Conference No. 2. LC 78-63063. (Illus.). 1978. pap. text ed. 14.00 (ISBN 0-8191-0613-5). U Pr of Amer.
Glassheim, Eliot, et al, eds. see Capon Springs Public Policy Conference, No. 1.
Glassie, Henry. Folk Housing in Middle Virginia: A Structural Analysis of Historic Artifacts. LC 75-11653. (Illus.). 1975. 16.50x (ISBN 0-87049-173-3); pap. 9.50x (ISBN 0-87049-268-3). U of Tenn Pr.
--Pattern in the Material Folk Culture of the Eastern United States. rev. ed. LC 75-160630. (Folklore & Folklife Ser). (Illus.). 1971. 12.50x (ISBN 0-8122-7569-1); pap. 5.95x (ISBN 0-8122-1013-1, Pa Paperbks). U of Pa Pr.
Glassie, Henry, jt. auth. see Leach, MacEdward.
Glassman. Dangerous Lives. (gr. 7-12). 1980. pap. 1.25 (ISBN 0-590-30875-0, Schol Pap). Schol Bk Serv.
Glassman, Alan M. The Challenge of Management: A Behavioral Orientation. LC 77-16095. 1978. text ed. 9.95 (ISBN 0-471-02767-7); tchrs. manual avail. (ISBN 0-471-02766-9). Wiley.
Glassman, Carl. Hocus Focus: The World's Weirdest Cameras. (Illus.). 96p. (gr. 5 up). 1976. PLB 5.90 o.p. (ISBN 0-531-00350-7). Watts.
Glassman, Craig. Off the Wall. (Illus.). 277p. 1980. 12.95 (ISBN 0-8119-0410-5, Pegasus Rex). Fell.
Glassman, Eugene H. The Translation Debate. 128p. (Orig.). 1981. pap. 4.25 (ISBN 0-87784-467-4). Inter Varsity.
Glassman, Henry S. Lead the Way, Rangers - Fifth Ranger Bn. (Illus.). 104p. 1980. pap. 5.95 (ISBN 0-934588-03-1). Ranger Assocs.
Glassman, Judith. Beadcraft, Step by Step. (Step by Step Craft Ser). 1974. PLB 9.15 o.p. (ISBN 0-307-62012-3, Golden Pr); pap. 2.95 (ISBN 0-307-42012-4). Western Pub.
Glassman, Paul. Guatemala Guide. LC 77-74034. (Illus.). 1978. 10.00 (ISBN 0-930016-00-9). Passport Pr.
--Guatemala Guide. (Orig.). 1982. pap. 12.95 (ISBN 0-930016-02-5). Passport Pr.
Glassman, Peter J. Language & Being: Joseph Conrad & the Literature of Personality. LC 75-29092. 294p. 1976. 17.50x (ISBN 0-231-03999-9). Columbia U Pr.
Glassman, Samuel. Epic of Survival: The Story of Anti-Semitism. LC 80-69018. 400p. 20.00 (ISBN 0-8197-0481-4). Bloch.
Glassner, Herman M., ed. see Bicks, Alexander.
Glassner, Lester & Harris, Brownie. Dime Store Dreams. 128p. 1981. write for info. (ISBN 0-670-27279-5, Studio). Viking Pr.
--Dime Store Dreams. 1981. pap. 12.95 (ISBN 0-14-005668-8). Penguin. Postponed.
Glassner, Martin I. Bibliography on Land-Locked States. LC 80-51737. 60p. 1980. 20.00x (ISBN 90-286-0290-9). Sijthoff & Noordhodf.
Glassner, Martin I. & Deblij, Harm J. Systematic Political Geography. 3rd ed. LC 79-26750. 1980. text ed. 26.95 (ISBN 0-471-05228-0). Wiley.
Glassow, Ruth B., jt. auth. see Cooper, John M.
Glasspool, John. Boats of the Longshoremen. 136p. 1980. 18.00x (ISBN 0-245-53111-4, Pub. by Nautical England). State Mutual Bk.
Glasstone, Richard. Better Ballet. LC 78-55577. (Better Sport Ser.). (Illus.). 95p. 1977. 8.50x (ISBN 0-7182-1453-6). Intl Pubns Serv.
Glasstone, Samuel & Jordan, Walter H. Nuclear Power & Its Environmental Effects. LC 80-67303. (Illus.). 400p. 1980. 25.95 (ISBN 0-89448-022-7); pap. 17.95 (ISBN 0-89448-024-3). Am Nuclear Soc.
Glasstone, Samuel & Sesonske, Alexander. Nuclear Reactor Engineering. 2nd ed. 800p. 1980. text ed. 39.50 (ISBN 0-442-20057-9). Van Nos Reinhold.
Glastonbury, Bryan, et al, eds. Social Work in Conflict: The Practitioner & Bureaurcrat. Cooper, David & Hawkins, Pearl. 178p. 1980. 27.50x (ISBN 0-7099-0314-6, Pub. by Croom Helm Ltd England). Biblio Dist.
Glatstein, Jacob, et al. Anthology of Holocaust Literature. LC 68-19609. (Temple Bks). 1972. pap. text ed. 5.95x (ISBN 0-689-70343-0, T23). Atheneum.
Glatt, M. M. A Guide to Addiction & Its Treatment. LC 74-8421. 346p. 1974. 17.95 o.p. (ISBN 0-470-30322-0). Halsted Pr.
Glatter, Ron, jt. auth. see Piper, David W.
Glatthorn, Allan A. A Guide for an English Curriculum for the Eighties. 1980. pap. 6.50 (ISBN 0-8141-1922-0). NCTE.
Glatzer, Nahum N., ed. see Josephus.
Glatzer, Paula. The Complaint of the Poet: The Parnassus Plays. (Salzburg Studies in English Literature: Elizabethan & Renaissance Studies: No. 60). 1977. pap. text ed. 25.00x (ISBN 0-391-01386-6). Humanities.
Glauber, R. J., ed. Quantum Optics. (Italian Physical Society: Course 42). 1970. 67.00 (ISBN 0-12-368842-6). Acad Pr.
Glauert, Earl T. & Langley, Lester D., eds. The United States & Latin America. LC 79-133376. (History Ser). 1971. pap. 5.95 (ISBN 0-201-02404-7). A-W.
Glauert, M. B. Principles of Dynamics. (Library of Mathematics). 1969. pap. 5.00 (ISBN 0-7100-4348-1). Routledge & Kegan.
Glaves-Smith, J. R., jt. auth. see Melly, George.
Glaz, Edith & Vecsei, Paul. Aldosterone. LC 70-138666. 628p. 1971. 87.00 (ISBN 0-08-013368-1). Pergamon.
Glaze, Andrew. The Trash Dragon of Shensi. (Illus., Orig.). 1978. pap. 4.50 (ISBN 0-914278-15-0). Copper Beech.
Glaze, Ralph, ed. Guns & Ammo Annual 1980. LC 72-1758. (Illus.). 1979. pap. 6.95 o.p. (ISBN 0-8227-3015-4). Petersen Pub.
Glazebrook, G. P. Story of Toronto. LC 78-163815. (Illus.). 1971. 20.00 o.p. (ISBN 0-8020-1791-6); pap. 6.50 o.p. (ISBN 0-8020-6256-3). U of Toronto Pr.
Glazer, Joan I. Literature for Early Childhood. (Illus.). 240p. 1981. pap. text ed. 8.95 (ISBN 0-686-69494-5). Merrill.
Glazer, Nathan. Mediating Structures & Welfare. 250p. Date not set. price not set (ISBN 0-88410-823-6). Ballinger Pub. Postponed.
Glazer, Nathan & Moynihan, Daniel P. Beyond the Melting Pot: The Negroes, Puerto Ricans, Jews, Italians, & Irish of New York City. 2nd rev ed. 1970. 17.00x (ISBN 0-262-07039-1); pap. 4.95 (ISBN 0-262-57022-X). MIT Pr.
Glazer, Nathan, jt. ed. see Gorham, William.
Glazer, Tom. All About Your Name Anne, Anna, Annie, Annette, Anita, Hannah, Nan. LC 77-82444. (gr. 1 up). 1978. 4.95a o.p. (ISBN 0-385-04279-5); PLB (ISBN 0-385-04299-X). Doubleday.
--All About Your Name David, Dave, Davy, Davis, Davies, Davidson. LC 77-82443. (gr. 1 up). 1978. 4.95a o.p. (ISBN 0-385-06388-1); PLB (ISBN 0-385-06397-0). Doubleday.
--All About Your Name Elizabeth, Eliza, Betsy, Beth, Bette, Betty, Lizzie, Liz. LC 77-82442. (gr. 1 up). 1978. 4.95a o.p. (ISBN 0-385-06399-7); PLB (ISBN 0-385-06404-7). Doubleday.
--All About Your Name James, Jim, Jamie, Jimmy. LC 77-15153. (gr. 1 up). 1978. 4.95 o.p. (ISBN 0-385-06436-5); PLB (ISBN 0-385-06449-7). Doubleday.
--All About Your Name John, Johnny, Jack, Jackie. LC 77-15154. (gr. 1 up). 1978. 4.95 o.p. (ISBN 0-385-06424-1); PLB (ISBN 0-385-06428-4). Doubleday.
--All About Your Name Joseph, Joe, Joey, Jo-Jo. LC 77-15155. (gr. 1 up). 1978. 4.95a o.p. (ISBN 0-385-06554-X); PLB (ISBN 0-385-06558-2). Doubleday.
--All About Your Name Katherine, Catherine, Cathy, Kate, Katie, Kathy. LC 77-15151. (gr. 1 up). 1978. 4.95a o.p. (ISBN 0-385-06476-4); PLB (ISBN 0-385-06536-1). Doubleday.
--All About Your Name Mary, Marion, Maria, Marie, Miriam, Maureen, Molly. LC 77-82441. (gr. 1 up). 1978. 4.95a o.p. (ISBN 0-385-06405-5); PLB (ISBN 0-385-06406-3). Doubleday.
--All About Your Name Susan, Susie, Susanna, Suzanne, Sue. LC 77-15156. (gr. 1 up). 1978. 4.95a o.p. (ISBN 0-385-06579-5); PLB (ISBN 0-385-06643-0). Doubleday.
--All About Your Name William, Willie, Billy, Will, Bill, Willy. LC 76-23763. (gr. 1 up). 1978. 4.95a o.p. (ISBN 0-385-06419-5); PLB (ISBN 0-385-06420-9). Doubleday.
--Eye Winker, Tom Tinker, Chin Chopper. (Illus.). 1978. pap. 1.95 o.p. (ISBN 0-385-13344-8). Doubleday.
Glazier, Lyle. Stills from a Moving Picture: Paunch No. 39. 1974. pap. 2.00 (ISBN 0-9602478-3-1). Paunch.
Glazier, Richard. A Manual of Historic Ornament: Treating Upon the Evolution, Tradition & Development of Architecture & the Applied Arts. 5th ed. LC 70-163174. (Tower Bks). (Illus.). vi, 183p. 1972. Repr. of 1933 ed. 24.00 (ISBN 0-8103-3937-4). Gale.
Glazier, Stephen D., ed. Perspectives on Pentecostalism: Case Studies from the Caribbean & Latin America. LC 80-7815. 207p. 1980. lib. bdg. 17.25 (ISBN 0-8191-1071-X); pap. text ed. 9.50 (ISBN 0-8191-1072-8). U Pr of Amer.
Glazner, Joseph M. Dirty Money Can't Wash Both Hands at Once. (Orig.). 1980. pap. 1.95 (ISBN 0-446-90165-2). Warner Bks.
--Fast Money Shoots from the Hip. (Orig.). 1980. pap. 1.95 (ISBN 0-446-90164-4). Warner Bks.
Gleaolow, Rupert, tr. see De Lubicz, Isha S.
Gleasner, Bill & Gleasner, Diana. Sea Islands of the South. LC 79-24730. (Illus.). 176p. 1980. lib. bdg. 12.25 o.p. (ISBN 0-914788-21-3). East Woods.
Gleasner, Diana, jt. auth. see Gleasner, Bill.
Gleasner, Diana C. Illustrated Swimming, Diving & Surfing Dictionary for Young People. LC 79-93358. (Illustrated Dictionary Ser.). (Illus.). 128p. (gr. 4 up). 1980. lib. bdg. 6.79 (ISBN 0-8178-0001-8). Harvey.
--Illustrated Swimming, Diving & Surfing Dictionary for Young People. (Illus.). (gr. 9 up). pap. 2.50 (ISBN 0-13-451195-6). P-H.
Gleason, G. H. Introduction a la linguistique. (Sciences humaines et sociales). (Fr). pap. 20.95 (ISBN 2-03-070351-6, 3652). Larousse.
Gleason, Gary N. & Horn, Lister W. Structured COBOL. LC 78-31566. (Illus.). 1979. pap. 10.95x (ISBN 0-87835-079-9). Boyd & Fraser.
Gleason, Harold & Becker, Warren. Early American Music. (Music Literature Outlines Ser. III). 1980. write for info. (ISBN 0-89917-265-2, Frangipani Pr). TIS Inc.
Gleason, Harold, jt. auth. see Marrocco, W. Thomas.
Gleason, Harole. Methods of Organ Playing. 6th ed. 1979. 18.95 (ISBN 0-13-579466-8). P-H.
Gleason, Henry A. & Cronquist, Arthur. Natural Geography of Plants. LC 64-15448. (Illus.). (gr. 9 up). 1964. 25.00x (ISBN 0-231-02668-4). Columbia U Pr.
Gleason, Herbert P., ed. Getting Better: A Report on Health Care from the Salzbug Seminar. LC 80-23486. 192p. Date not set. text ed. 22.50 (ISBN 0-89946-053-4). Oelgeschlager.
Gleason, John J., Jr. Consciousness & the Ultimate. LC 80-21397. 192p. (Orig.). 1981. pap. 6.95 (ISBN 0-687-09470-4). Abingdon.
Gleason, John M. see Alexander, Yonah.
Gleason, Judith. Leaf & Bone: African Praise Poems. LC 79-56265. 228p. 1980. 14.95 (ISBN 0-670-42178-2). Viking Pr.
Gleason, Norma. Cryptograms & Spygrams. 128p. (Orig.). 1981. pap. price not set. Dover.
Gleason, Robert W., ed. Contemporary Spirituality. 1968. 9.95 o.s.i. (ISBN 0-02-544030-6). Macmillan.
Gleason, Walter J. Moral Idealists, Bureaucracy, & Catherine the Great. 320p. 1981. 21.00 (ISBN 0-8135-0917-3). Rutgers U Pr.
Gleave, M. B., jt. auth. see White, H. P.
Gleazer, Edmund J., Jr. The Community College: Values, Vision & Vitality. 1980. pap. 6.50 (ISBN 0-87117-097-3). Am Assn Comm J Coll.

Gledhill, Alan. Pakistan: The Development of Its Laws & Constitution. LC 80-20180. (The British Commonwealth, the Development of Its Laws & Constitutions: Vol. 8). x, 263p. 1980. Repr. of 1957 ed. lib. bdg. 29.75x (ISBN 0-313-20842-5, GLPA). Greenwood.
Gleeson, Denis & Whitty, Geoff. Developments in Social Studies Teaching. (Changing Classroom). 1976. text ed. 11.75x (ISBN 0-7291-0099-5); pap. text ed. 4.75x (ISBN 0-7291-0094-4). Humanities.
Gleeson, Geoff. All About Judo. (Sports Library). (Illus.). 1979. 12.95 (ISBN 0-8069-9100-3); pap. 6.95 (ISBN 0-8069-9102-X). Sterling.
Glegg, G. L. The Science of Design. (Illus.). 112p. 1973. 16.95 (ISBN 0-521-20327-9). Cambridge U Pr.
Glegg, Gordon L. Design of Design. LC 69-12432. (Cambridge Engineering Pubns.). (Illus.). 1969. 14.50 (ISBN 0-521-07447-9). Cambridge U Pr.
--The Selection of Design. LC 72-80591. (Illus.). 96p. 1972. 14.50 (ISBN 0-521-08686-8). Cambridge U Pr.
Gleit, J., jt. auth. see Eckstein, J.
Gleit, Joyce, jt. auth. see Eckstein, Joan.
Gleitman, Henry. Psychology. (Illus.). 1981. 18.95x (ISBN 0-393-95102-2); study guide 7.95x (ISBN 0-393-95110-3). Norton.
Glen, Ann & Williams, Michael. Scotland from the Air. 1975. pap. text ed. 7.95x o.p. (ISBN 0-435-34363-7). Heinemann Ed.
Glen, Jan, jt. auth. see Glen, Simon.
Glen, Simon & Glen, Jan. Sahara Handbook. (Illus.). 316p. (Orig.). 1980. pap. 19.95 (ISBN 0-903909-10-3, Roger Lascelles). Bradt Ent.
Glen, Thomas L. Rubens & the Counter Reformation: Studies in His Religious Paintings Between 1609 & 1620. LC 76-23621. (Outstanding Dissertations in the Fine Arts Ser.). 1977. lib. bdg. 56.00x (ISBN 0-685-38855-7). Garland Pub.
Glen, William. Continental Drift & Plate Tectonics. (Physics & Physical Science Ser.). 192p. 1975. pap. text ed. 8.95 (ISBN 0-675-08799-6). Merrill.
Glendening, Frank S. Business Interruption Insurance: What Is Covered. LC 79-92558. 245p. 1980. pap. text ed. 20.00 (ISBN 0-87218-304-1). Natl Underwriter.
Glendening, Parris N. & Reeves, Mavis M. Pragmatic Federalism: An Intergovernmental View of American Government. LC 76-29891. (Illus.). 1977. 13.50 (ISBN 0-913530-10-7); pap. 8.50x (ISBN 0-913530-09-3). Palisades Pub.
Glendinning, Eric H. English in Mechanical Engineering. (English in Focus Ser). 1975. pap. text ed. 6.95x (ISBN 0-19-437512-9); tchr's ed. 11.95x (ISBN 0-19-437501-3). Oxford U Pr.
Glendinning, Nigel. Goya & His Critics. LC 76-49697. 1977. 40.00x (ISBN 0-300-02011-2). Yale U Pr.
Glendinning, Ralph. The Ultimate Game. 1981. 13.95 (ISBN 0-671-42016-X, Wyndham Bks). S&S.
Glendinning, Sally. Doll: Bottle-Nosed Dolphin. LC 80-13660. (Young Animal Adventures Ser.). 40p. (gr. 2). 1980. PLB 5.88 (ISBN 0-8116-7501-7). Garrard.
--Little Blue & Rusty: Red Kangaroos. LC 80-13935. (Young Animal Adventures Ser.). 40p. (gr. 2). 1980. PLB 5.88 (ISBN 0-8116-7502-5). Garrard.
--Pen: Emperor Penguin. LC 80-13212. (Young Animal Adventures Ser.). 40p. (gr. 2). 1980. PLB 5.88 (ISBN 0-8116-7500-9). Garrard.
Glendinning, Victoria. Edith Sitwell: A Unicorn Among Lions. LC 80-2721. (Illus.). 384p. 1981. 17.95 (ISBN 0-394-50439-9). Knopf.
Glenister, T. W. & Ross, Jean R., eds. Anatomy & Physiology for Nurses. 3rd ed. (Illus.). 630p. 1980. pap. text ed. 27.00x (ISBN 0-433-12102-5). Intl Ideas.
Glenn. Thoracic & Cardiovascular Surgery with Related Pathology. 3rd ed. (Illus.). 1975. 65.00 o.p. (ISBN 0-8385-8955-3). ACC.
Glenn, Alfred A. Taking Your Faith to Work. (Orig.). 1980. pap. 4.95 (ISBN 0-8010-3748-4). Baker Bk.
Glenn, Constance, ed. Kathe Kollwitz - Jake Zeitlin: Jake Zetlin Bookshop & Gallery-1937; The Art Museum & Galleries, California State University, Long Beach-1979. (Illus.). 64p. (Orig.). 1979. pap. 8.00 (ISBN 0-936270-14-4). Art Mus Gall.
Glenn, Constance W. Jim Dine Figure Drawings, Nineteen Seventy Five-Nineteen Seventy Nine. LC 79-3060. (Icon Edns.). (Illus.). 1980. pap. 12.95 (ISBN 0-06-430102-8, HarpT). Har-Row.
--Roy Lichtenstein Ceramic Sculpture. (Illus.). 64p. (Orig.). 1977. pap. 8.00 (ISBN 0-936270-05-5). Art Mus Gall.
Glenn, Constance W. & Rice, Leland. Frances Benjamin Johnston: Women of Class & Station. (Illus.). 96p. (Orig.). 1979. pap. 8.00 (ISBN 0-936270-12-8). Art Mus Gall.
Glenn, Constance W., ed. The Frederick Weisman Company Collection of California Art. 2nd ed. (Illus.). 64p. 1979. pap. 8.00 (ISBN 0-936270-11-X). Art Mus Gall.
Glenn, Deirdre, jt. auth. see Gappa, Sylvia.
Glenn, Edmund S. Man & Mankind: Conflict & Communication Between Cultures. 300p. 1981. price not set (ISBN 0-89391-068-6). Ablex Pub.
Glenn, F., ed. Prescription Drugs. 287p. 1981. 28.50 o.p. (ISBN 0-686-68308-0). Porter.
Glenn, Frank, et al. Surgery of the Adrenal Glands. (Illus.). 1968. 14.00 o.s.i. (ISBN 0-02-344260-3). Macmillan.
Glenn, George D. & Scholz, Charles B. Super Eight Handbook. 1980. pap. 9.95 (ISBN 0-672-21743-0). Bobbs.
Glenn, Harold. Automechanics. rev. ed. (gr. 9-12). 1976. text ed. 14.64 (ISBN 0-87002-169-9); wkbk & ans. sheets 3.96 (ISBN 0-87002-180-X); avail. tchr's guide. Bennett IL.
Glenn, Harold T. Exploring Power Mechanics. (Illus.). (gr. 7-12). 1973. 11.96 (ISBN 0-87002-119-2); prog. wkbk. 3.32 (ISBN 0-87002-150-8). Bennett IL.
--Glenn's Datsun. 1975. pap. 7.95 o.p. (ISBN 0-8092-8319-0). Contemp Bks.
--Glenn's Diesel & Gasoline Fuel-Injection Manual. (Illus.). 128p. 1973. 8.95 o.p. (ISBN 0-8092-9069-3, 1085). Contemp Bks.
--Glenn's Jaguar Repair & Tune-up Guide. (Illus.). 1965. 8.95 (ISBN 0-8019-5083-X). Chilton.
--Glenn's Triumph Repair & Tune-up Guide. (Illus.). 1965. 8.95 (ISBN 0-8019-1433-7). Chilton.
--Glenn's Volvo Repair & Tune-up Guide. (Illus.). 1965. 8.95 (ISBN 0-8019-1434-5). Chilton.
Glenn, J. Si Units for Nursing. 1981. pap. text ed. 5.15 (ISBN 0-06-318180-0, Pub. by Har-Row Ltd England). Har-Row.
Glenn, J. A. Teaching Primary Mathematics: Strategy & Evaluation. 1977. text ed. 9.50 (ISBN 0-06-318071-5, IntlDept); pap. text ed. 6.65 (ISBN 0-06-318072-3, IntlDept). Har-Row.
--The Third R: Towards a Numerate Society. 1978. text ed. 11.95 (ISBN 0-06-318075-8, IntlDept); pap. text ed. 6.60 (ISBN 0-06-318076-6, IntlDept). Har-Row.
Glenn, Jerry. Paul Celan. (World Authors Ser.: Germany: No. 262). 1973. lib. bdg. 10.95 (ISBN 0-8057-2205-X). Twayne.
Glenn, Jules. Child Analysis & Therapy. LC 78-65122. 1978. 35.00 (ISBN 0-87668-356-1). Aronson.
Glenn, Kathleen M. Azorin. (World Authors Ser: No. 604). 1981. lib. bdg. 14.95 (ISBN 0-8057-6446-1). Twayne.
Glenn, Morton B. How to Get Thinner Once & for All. 1979. pap. 1.95 o.p. (ISBN 0-449-23849-0, Crest). Fawcett.
Glenn, Paul J. Apologetics. LC 80-51330. 298p. 1980. write for info. o.p. (ISBN 0-89555-157-8). Tan Bks Pubs.
--Tour of the Summa. LC 78-66307. 1978. pap. 9.00 (ISBN 0-89555-081-4, 127). TAN Bks Pubs.
Glenn, Peter, jt. ed. see Brill, Chip.
Glenn, Peter, et al, eds. Madison Avenue Handbook 1981. 1981. price not set (ISBN 0-87314-011-7). Peter Glenn.
--National Radio Publicity Directory, 1980-81. 10th ed. 400p. 1981. ring-binder 75.00 (ISBN 0-87314-046-X). Peter Glenn.
--National Radio Publicity Directory, 1981. 11th ed. 320p. 1981. 85.00 (ISBN 0-87314-047-8). Peter Glenn.
Glenn, Richard F. Juan de la Cueva. (World Authors Ser.: Spain: No. 273). 1973. lib. bdg. 10.95 (ISBN 0-8057-2258-0). Twayne.
Glenn, Robert W. Black Rhetoric: A Guide to Afro-American Communication. LC 75-38912. 1976. 16.50 o.p. (ISBN 0-8108-0889-7). Scarecrow.
Glenn, Stanley. The Complete Actor. 1977. text ed. 15.95 (ISBN 0-205-05580-X). Allyn.
Glenn, William E., jt. auth. see Conrad, William R., Jr.
Glenn, William H., jt. auth. see Johnson, Donovan A.
Glennerster, Howard. Social Service Budgets & Social Policy. 1977. pap. text ed. 9.95x (ISBN 0-04-360042-5). Allen Unwin.
Glennon, Canon J. Your Healing Is Within You. 1980. pap. 4.95 (ISBN 0-88270-457-5). Logos.
Glennon, Lynda M. Women & Dualism. 1979. pap. text ed. 9.95 (ISBN 0-582-28076-1). Longman.
Glennon, Michael J & Franck, Thomas M. United States Foreign Relations Law, Documents & Sources, 3 vols. Bowman, Ronald C., ed. Incl. Vol. 1. Executive Agreements. 1200p. (ISBN 0-379-20355-3); Vol. 2. Treaties. 1200p. (ISBN 0-379-20356-1); Vol. 3. The War Power. 1200p. (ISBN 0-379-20357-X). LC 80-18165. 40.00 set (ISBN 0-686-68787-6). Oceana.
Glennon, Micheal, ed. Researcher's Guide to Washington: Fifth Edition. LC 77-95197. 1981. pap. 45.00 (ISBN 0-686-26089-9). Wash Res.
--Washington Information Workbook. 5th ed. LC 79-63792. 1981. pap. 45.00 (ISBN 0-686-25747-2). Wash Res.
Glenny, Lyman A., ed. Funding Higher Education: A Six Nation Analysis. LC 79-4557. 1979. 25.95 (ISBN 0-03-049616-0). Praeger.
Glenny, Michael, tr. see Grzimek, Bernhard.
Glenny, Michael, tr. see Schoeck, Helmut.
Glenny, Tamara, tr. see Aleshkovsky, Yuz.
Glenwick, David & Jason, Leonard, eds. Behavioral Community Psychology: Progress & Prospects. LC 79-21457. 1979. 23.95 (ISBN 0-03-052111-4). Praeger.
Gleser, Goldine C., et al. Buffalo Creek Revisted: Prolonged Psychological Effects of a Disaster. (Personality & Psychopathology Ser.). 1981. price not set (ISBN 0-12-286260-0). Acad Pr.
Gless, Eleanor G. Murder at Tall Tip. (YA) 5.95 (ISBN 0-685-07449-8, Avalon). Bouregy.
Gleve, Paul & Shulman, Julius. The Architecture of Los Angeles. LC 80-28988. 1981. 35.00 (ISBN 0-8310-7142-7). Howell-North.
Glew, G. Catering Equipment & Systems Design. (Illus.). 1977. 102.60x (ISBN 0-85334-730-1, Pub. by Applied Science). Burgess-Intl Ideas.
Glew, G., ed. Advances in Catering Technology. (Illus.). xii, 450p. 1980. 99.00x (ISBN 0-85334-844-8). Burgess-Intl Ideas.
Glezen, G. William, jt. auth. see Taylor, Donald H.
Glick. Human Lymphoid Cell Cultures: The Fundamentals. Date not set. 22.50 (ISBN 0-8247-6988-0). Dekker.
Glick, Carl. Shake Hands with the Dragon. LC 75-162513. 334p. 1971. Repr. of 1941 ed. 20.00 (ISBN 0-8103-3765-7). Gale.
Glick, Clarence E. Sojourners & Settlers: Chinese Migrants in Hawaii. LC 80-13799. 480p. 1980. text ed. 20.00x (ISBN 0-8248-0707-3). U Pr of Hawaii.
Glick, David. Methods of Biochemical Analysis, Vol. 27. 464p. 1981. 29.50 (ISBN 0-471-06503-X, Pub. by Wiley-Interscience). Wiley.
Glick, David, ed. Methods of Biochemical Analysis. LC 54-7273. Vol. 23, 1976. 35.00 (ISBN 0-471-01413-3, Pub. by Wiley Interscience); Vol. 25, 1979. 33.95 (ISBN 0-471-04397-4); Vol. 26, 1980. 32.50 (ISBN 0-471-04798-8). Wiley.
--Methods of Biochemical Analysis, Vol. 21. 582p. 1981. Repr. of 1973 ed. lib. bdg. write for info. (ISBN 0-89874-130-0). Krieger.
Glick, David M. Biochemistry Review. LC 80-19927. (Basic Science Review Bks.). 1980. pap. 8.50. Med Exam.
Glick, David M., ed. Biochemistry Review. 6th ed. (Basic Science Review Bks.). 1975. spiral bdg. 8.00 o.p. (ISBN 0-87488-202-8). Med Exam.
Glick, Ira D. & Hargreaves, William A. Psychiatric Hospital Treatment for the Nineteen Eighties. LC 77-26995. 1979. 18.95 (ISBN 0-669-01502-4). Lexington Bks.
Glick, Ira O., et al. The First Year of Bereavement. LC 74-12499. 536p. 1974. 20.95 (ISBN 0-471-30421-2, Pub. by Wiley-Interscience). Wiley.
Glick, Joyce, jt. auth. see Wiener, Joan.
Glick, Leonard & Hebding, Daniel E. Introduction to Social Problems. LC 78-67953. (Sociology Ser.). 1980. pap. text ed. 12.95 (ISBN 0-201-02600-7). A-W.
Glick, Leonard, jt. auth. see Hebding, Daniel E.
Glick, Leslie A. Trading with Saudi Arabia: A Guide to the Shipping, Trade, Investment & Tax Laws of Saudi Arabia. LC 79-55002. 620p. 1980. text ed. 55.00 (ISBN 0-916672-43-3). Allanheld.
Glick, Marianne, ed. see Basile, Frank M.
Glick, Rush G. & Newsom, Robert S. Fraud Investigation: Fundamentals for Police. (Illus.). 358p. 1974. text ed. 17.75 (ISBN 0-398-03070-7). C C Thomas.
Glick, Stanley D. & Goldfarb, Joseph. Behavioral Pharmacology. 1st ed. 1977. text ed. 19.50 o.p. (ISBN 0-8016-1851-7). Mosby.
Glick, Wendell, ed. Recognition of Henry David Thoreau: Selected Criticism Since 1848. LC 69-15845. 1969. 9.50 o.p. (ISBN 0-472-37200-9). U of Mich Pr.
Glickman, Albert S., jt. auth. see Sheppard, David I.
Glickman, Carl D. & Esposito, James P. Leadership Guide for Elementary School Improvement: Procedures for Assessment & Change. new ed. 1979. text ed. 17.75 (ISBN 0-205-06443-4). Allyn.
Glickman, Carl D., jt. auth. see Wolfgang, Charles H.
Glickman, Esther. Child Placement Through Clinically Oriented Casework. LC 56-10783. 1957. 20.00x (ISBN 0-231-02127-5). Columbia U Pr.
Glickman, Frank, jt. auth. see Fritzhand, James.
Glickman, Irving & Smulow, Jerome B. Periodontal Disease: Clinical Radiographic & Histopathologic Features. LC 71-145558. (Illus.). 230p. 1974. 47.00 o.p. (ISBN 0-7216-4138-5). Saunders.
Glickman, Linda. Inpatient Utilization of Short-Stay Hospitals by Diagnosis: United States, 1974. Stevenson, Taloria, ed. (Ser. 13: No. 32). 1977. pap. text ed. 1.50 (ISBN 0-8406-0002-X). Natl Ctr Health Stats.
Glickman, Norman, jt. auth. see Adams, F. Gerard.
Glickman, Paul. Magic Tricks. (gr. 1-3). 1980. PLB 7.90 (ISBN 0-531-04141-7). Watts.
Glickman, Robert J., ed. Poetry of Julian Del Casal: A Critical Edition, 3 vols. Incl. Vol. 1. 1976. 15.00 (ISBN 0-8130-0540-X); pap. 6.50 (ISBN 0-8130-0572-8); Vol. 2. 1978. 20.00 (ISBN 0-8130-0596-5); Vol.III. 1977. 17.50 (ISBN 0-8130-0576-0). LC 76-22800. U Presses Fla.
Glickman, S. Craig. Knowing Christ. 200p. 1980. pap. 4.95 (ISBN 0-8024-3502-5). Moody.
Glickman, William G. Winners on the Tennis Court. (Picture Life Books Ser.). (Illus.). (gr. 2 up). 1978. PLB 6.45 s&l (ISBN 0-531-02912-3). Watts.
Glickson. Biomycin: Chemistry & Clinical Applications. Date not set. price not set (ISBN 0-8247-1289-7). Dekker.
Glickstein, Cyrus, jt. auth. see Ewen, Sol J.
Glidden, Hope H. The Storyteller As Humanist: The Serees of Guillaume Bouchet. (French Forum Monographs: No. 25). 200p. (Orig.). 1981. pap. 11.50 (ISBN 0-917058-24-0). French Forum.
Gliddon, Richard. Units of Life. (Investigations in Biology Ser.). 1970. text ed. 3.95x o.p. (ISBN 0-435-60282-9). Heinemann Ed.
Glidewell, John C., ed. The Social Context of Learning & Development. LC 76-8867. 239p. 1976. 18.95 (ISBN 0-470-15078-5). Halsted Pr.
Glie, Rowen, ed. Speaking of Standards. LC 70-185561. 350p. 1972. 18.00 (ISBN 0-8436-0307-0). CBI Pub.
Glieberman, Herbert A. & Neimark, Paul. Confessions of a Divorce Lawyer. 1977. pap. 1.75 o.p. (ISBN 0-345-25119-9). Ballantine.
--Four Weekends to an Ideal Marriage. 1981. 8.95 (ISBN 0-938814-00-1). Barrington.
Gligoric, S. & Sokolov, V. The Sicilian Defence, Bk. 1. 1970. pap. 10.50 (ISBN 0-08-017276-8). Pergamon.
Glimcher, Arnold. Louise Nevelson. 1976. pap. 13.95 o.p. (ISBN 0-525-47439-0). Dutton.
Glimcher, Sumner & Johnson, Warren. Movie Making: A Guide to Film Production. new ed. (Illus.). 256p. 1975. 15.00x (ISBN 0-231-03962-X). Columbia U Pr.
Glines, Carrol V., ed. see Kilbourne, James W.
Glines, Carroll V. Doolittle's Tokyo Raiders. 464p. 1981. pap. 7.95 (ISBN 0-442-21925-3). Van Nos Reinhold.
--Jimmy Doolittle: Master of the Calculated Risk. 208p. 1980. pap. 4.95 (ISBN 0-442-23102-4). Van Nos Reinhold.
Glines, Carroll V., ed. see Carter, William T.
Glinka, N. General Chemistry. MIR Publishers, tr. from Rus. 710p. 1975. 18.00x o.p. (ISBN 0-8464-0446-X). Beekman Pubs.
Glinz, W. Chest Trauma: Diagnosis & Management. (Illus.). 310p. 1981. 58.00 (ISBN 0-387-10409-7). Springer-Verlag.
Glitz, Maurice L., jt. auth. see Borror, Donald.
Gloag, John. A Short Dictionary of Furniture. 1976. pap. 14.95 (ISBN 0-04-749009-8). Allen Unwin.
--Victorian Comfort: A Social History of Design 1830-1900. (Illus.). 268p. 1980. Repr. 28.00 (ISBN 0-7153-6329-8). David & Charles.
--Victorian Taste. (Illus.). 168p. 1980. Repr. 28.00 (ISBN 0-7153-5739-5). David & Charles.
Gloag, Julian. Sleeping Dogs Lie. 1981. pap. price not set (ISBN 0-671-42494-7). PB.
Globerson, Amiela, jt. ed. see Feldman, Michael.
Globerson, Arye. Higher Education & Employment: A Case Study of Israel. LC 78-60131. (Praeger Special Studies). 1979. 22.95 (ISBN 0-03-046226-6). Praeger.
Glock, jt. auth. see Ahmann.
Glock, Charles Y., jt. auth. see Stark, Rodney.
Glock, Charles Y. & Bellah, Robert N., eds. The New Religious Consciousness. LC 75-17295. 1976. 21.50x (ISBN 0-520-03083-4); pap. 6.95 (ISBN 0-520-03472-4). U of Cal Pr.
Glock, Charles Y., et al. To Comfort & to Challenge: The Dilemma of the Contemporary Church. 1967. 17.50x (ISBN 0-520-00486-8). U of Cal Pr.
--Adolescent Prejudice. LC 74-15824. (Patterns of American Prejudice Ser.). (Illus.). 248p. 1975. 12.50x o.p. (ISBN 0-06-011567-X, HarpT). Har-Row.

Glock, Marvin D. & Bender, David. Probe. abridged ed. (Communication Skills Ser.). 1978. pap. text ed. 6.95x (ISBN 0-675-08373-7); instructor's manual 3.95 (ISBN 0-675-08372-9); 1 set 80.00 (ISBN 0-675-08372-9); 2-7 sets 55.00 (ISBN 0-686-67985-7); 8 or more 45.00 (ISBN 0-686-67986-5). Merrill.
Glock, Marvin D., jt. auth. see Ahmann, J. Stanley.
Glock, Waldo S., jt. auth. see Agerter, Sharlene.
Gloede, Wolfgang, jt. auth. see Wunderlich, Klaus.
Gloede, Wolfgang, jt. auth. see Wunderluch, Klaus.
Glogan, Joseph. Sportsmans Book of U.S. Records. (Illus.). 96p. (Orig.). 1980. pap. text ed. 2.50 (ISBN 0-937328-00-6). NY Hunting.
Glorfeld, Louis E. Short Unit on General Semantics. LC 69-17339. 125p. 1969. pap. text ed. 3.95x (ISBN 0-02-474210-4, 47421). Macmillan.
Glorig, A., jt. auth. see Gerwin, K. S.
Glorig, Aram. Otitis Media: Proceedings. Gerwin, Kenneth S., ed. (Illus.). 328p. 1972. 22.50 (ISBN 0-398-02294-1). C C Thomas.
Glorioso, Robert M. & Hill, F. S., Jr. Introduction to Engineering. (Illus.). 448p. 1975. ref. ed. 21.95x (ISBN 0-13-482398-2). P-H.
Glorioso, Robert M. & Osorio, Fernando C. Engineering Intelligent Systems: Concepts, Theory, & Applications. (Illus.). 512p. 1980. 27.00 (ISBN 0-932376-06-1). Digital Pr.
Glossbrenner, Alfred, jt. auth. see Costanza, Betty.
Glossop, R. H. Method Study & the Furniture Industry. LC 75-112711. 1970. 21.00 (ISBN 0-08-015653-3). Pergamon.
Gloster, Jesse E. Minority Economic, Political & Social Development. LC 78-62738. 1978. pap. text ed. 17.25 (ISBN 0-8191-0593-7). U Pr of Amer.
Glovach, Linda. Little Witch's Black Magic Book of Disguises. (gr. k-6). 1973. 5.95 (ISBN 0-13-537910-5); pap. 1.95 (ISBN 0-13-537944-X). P-H.
--Little Witch's Halloween Book. LC 75-11713. (Illus.). (gr. 1-4). 1975. 7.95 (ISBN 0-13-537985-7). P-H.
Glover, A. S, ed. Shelley: Selected Poetry, Prose & Letters. 1978. 11.95 (ISBN 0-370-00516-3, Pub. by Chatto Bodley Jonathan). Merrimack Bk Serv.
Glover, Dennis W. & Glover, Margaret M. Respiratory Therapy: Basics for Nursing & Allied Health Professions. LC 78-6500. (Illus.). 1978. pap. 10.50 (ISBN 0-8016-1863-0). Mosby.
Glover, Donald E. C. S. Lewis: The Art of Enchantment. LC 80-21421. xii, 235p. 1981. 15.00x (ISBN 0-8214-0566-7); pap. 6.95 (ISBN 0-8214-0609-4). Ohio U Pr.
Glover, Elizabeth. The Gold & Silver Wyre-Drawers. (Illus.). 91p. 1979. 47.50x (ISBN 0-8476-3144-3). Rowman.
Glover, Fred & Mulvey, John M. Network-Related Scheduling Models for Problems with Quasi-Adjacency & Block Adjacency Structures. 1976. 2.50 (ISBN 0-686-64194-9). U CO Busn Res Div.
Glover, J. C. B., ed. The Philosophy of Mind. (Oxford Readings in Philosophy). 1977. pap. text ed. 5.95x (ISBN 0-19-875038-2). Oxford U Pr.
Glover, J. M., jt. auth. see Brookfield, Charles.
Glover, J. N. Laws of the Turks & Caicos, Vol. 7. 1980. 47.50 (ISBN 0-379-12707-5). Oceana.
Glover, Jane. Cavalli. LC 77-23638. (Illus.). 1978. 18.95 (ISBN 0-312-12546-1). St Martin.
Glover, John. London's Railways Today. LC 80-70293. (Illus.). 96p. 1981. 17.95 (ISBN 0-7153-8070-2). David & Charles.
Glover, John A. A Parent's Guide to Intelligence Testing. LC 78-25991. 1979. 16.95 (ISBN 0-88229-423-7); pap. 8.95 (ISBN 0-88229-670-1). Nelson-Hall.
Glover, John A., jt. auth. see Gary, A. L.
Glover, John A., jt. auth. see Sautter, Frederic J.
Glover, John D. The Revolutionary Corporations: Engines of Plenty, Engines of Growth, Engines of Change. LC 80-66021. 350p. 1980. 35.00 (ISBN 0-87094-217-4). Dow Jones-Irwin.
Glover, John D., et al. The Administrator: Cases on Human Aspects in Management. 5th ed. 1973. text ed. 19.50 (ISBN 0-256-00170-7). Irwin.
Glover, Jonathan. Responsibility. (International Library of Philosophy and Scientific Method). 1970. text ed. 23.25x (ISBN 0-391-00097-7). Humanities.
Glover, Judith. Batsford Colour Book of Kent. 1976. 11.95 (ISBN 0-7134-3153-9, Pub. by Batsford England). David & Charles.
--Batsford Colour Book of Sussex. (Illus.). 64p. 1980. pap. 8.95 (ISBN 0-7134-3275-6, Pub. by Batsford England). David & Charles.
Glover, Margaret M., jt. auth. see Glover, Dennis W.
Glover, Rhoda, et al. Plantagenet "Rich & Beautiful...". A History of the Shire of Plantagenet, Western Australia. 429p. 1980. 21.00x (ISBN 0-85564-175-4, Pub. by U of West Australia Pr Australia). Intl Schol Bk Serv.
Glover, Robert W. Minority Enterprise in Construction. LC 77-10650. (Praeger Special Studies). 22.95 (ISBN 0-275-24070-3). Praeger.
Glover, S. W. & Hopwood, D. A., eds. Genetics As a Tool in Microbiology. (Society for General Microbiology Symposium: No. 31). (Illus.). 450p. Date not set. text ed. price not set (ISBN 0-521-23748-3). Cambridge U Pr.
Glover, Terrot R. The Conflicts of Religion in the Early Roman Empire. LC 74-20182. vii, 358p. 1975. Repr. of 1909 ed. lib. bdg. 32.50x (ISBN 0-8154-0510-3). Cooper Sq.
Gloversmith, Frank. Class, Culture & Social Change: A Reconsideration of the 1930's. 1980. text ed. 42.50x (ISBN 0-391-01739-X). Humanities.
Glowinski, R., jt. auth. see Lions, J. L.
Gloxhuber, C. Anionic Surfactants: Biology. (Surfactant Ser.: Vol. 9). 59.75 (ISBN 0-8247-6946-5). Dekker.
Glubb, Faris. Zionist Relations with Nazi Germany. 3.00. New World Press NY.
Glubb, John, jt. auth. see Churchill, Winston S.
Glubb, John B. The Story of the Arab Legion. LC 76-7060. (The Middle East in the 20th Century Ser.). 1976. Repr. of 1948 ed. lib. bdg. 32.50 (ISBN 0-306-70763-2). Da Capo.
--War in the Desert: An R. A. F. Frontier Campaign. LC 80-1929. 1981. Repr. of 1961 ed. 38.00 (ISBN 0-404-18964-4). AMS Pr.
--The Way of Love. LC 75-44945. 1976. 7.95 (ISBN 0-916624-01-3). TSU Pr.
Glubetich, Dave. Double Your Money in Real Estate Every Two Years. Moretz, Judy, ed. (Illus.). 232p. 1980. 12.95 (ISBN 0-9601530-4-7). Impact Pub.
--How to Grow a Moneytree. Wigginton, Dave, ed. 1977. pap. 6.95 (ISBN 0-9601530-0-4). Impact Pub.
Glubetich, Dave & Wigginton, Dave. How to Grow a Moneytree. 112p. 1977. pap. 7.95 o.p. (ISBN 0-9601530-0-4). Impact Pub.
Glubok, Shirley. The Art of America from Jackson to Lincoln. LC 72-81066. (Illus.). 48p. (gr. 4-8). 1973. 9.95 (ISBN 0-02-736250-7). Macmillan.
--The Art of America in the Early Twentieth Century. LC 74-6329. (Illus.). 48p. (gr. 4 up). 1974. 9.95 (ISBN 0-02-736180-2). Macmillan.
--The Art of America in the Gilded Age. LC 73-6048. (Art of America Ser). (Illus.). 48p. (gr. 4 up). 1974. 9.95 (ISBN 0-02-736100-4). Macmillan.
--The Art of America Since World War II. LC 75-34453. (Art History Ser.: Vol. 6). (Illus.). 48p. (gr. 3 up). 1976. 10.95 (ISBN 0-02-736310-4, 73631). Macmillan.
--The Art of China. LC 72-81059. (Illus.). 48p. (gr. 4 up). 1973. 9.95 (ISBN 0-02-736170-5). Macmillan.
--Art of Colonial America. LC 77-102964. (Art of Bks). (Illus.). (gr. 4 up). 1970. 10.95 (ISBN 0-02-736070-9). Macmillan.
--The Art of India. LC 72-78087. (Illus.). (gr. 5-8). 1969. 5.95g o.s.i. (ISBN 0-02-736040-7). Macmillan.
--The Art of Japan. LC 75-89584. (Art of Bks). (Illus.). (gr. 4 up). 1970. 5.95g o.s.i. (ISBN 0-02-736080-6). Macmillan.
--The Art of Photography. LC 77-4985. (Art of...Ser.). (Illus.). (gr. 4 up). 1977. 10.95 (ISBN 0-02-736680-4, 73668). Macmillan.
--The Art of the Comic Strip. LC 78-24342. (Illus.). (gr. 4 up). 1979. 10.95 (ISBN 0-02-736500-X). Macmillan.
--The Art of the New American Nation. LC 76-160073. (Art of Ser). (Illus.). (gr. 4 up). 1972. 9.95 (ISBN 0-02-736140-3). Macmillan.
--The Art of the Northwest Coast Indians. LC 74-22384. (Illus.). 48p. (gr. 4 up). 1975. 9.95 (ISBN 0-02-736150-0). Macmillan.
--Art of the Old West. LC 79-123138. (Illus.). (gr. 4 up). 1971. 5.95g o.s.i. (ISBN 0-02-736090-3). Macmillan.
--The Art of the Plains Indians. LC 75-14064. (Illus.). 48p. (gr. 4 up). 1975. 9.95 (ISBN 0-02-736360-0, 73636). Macmillan.
--The Art of the Southeastern Indians. LC 77-20850. (Illus.). (gr. 4 up). 1978. 9.95 (ISBN 0-02-736480-1, 73648). Macmillan.
--The Art of the Southwest Indians. LC 78-133558. (Art of Ser). (Illus.). (gr. 4 up). 1971. 9.95 (ISBN 0-02-736120-9). Macmillan.
--The Art of the Spanish in the United States & Puerto Rico. LC 75-185218. (Illus.). (gr. 4up). 1972. 9.95 (ISBN 0-02-736130-6). Macmillan.
--The Art of the Vikings. LC 78-6849. (Illus.). (gr. 4 up). 1978. 10.95 (ISBN 0-02-736460-7, 73646). Macmillan.
--The Art of the Woodland Indians. LC 76-12434. (Illus.). (gr. 4 up). 1976. 10.95 (ISBN 0-02-736440-2, 73644). Macmillan.
--Fall of the Incas. (gr. 4 up). 1967. 5.95 o.s.i. (ISBN 0-02-736000-8). Macmillan.
Glubok, Shirley, ed. Digging in Assyria. LC 79-103679. (Illus.). (gr. 7 up). 1970. 7.95g o.s.i. (ISBN 0-02-736110-1). Macmillan.
--Discovering the Royal Tombs at Ur. LC 76-78088. (Illus.). (gr. 7 up). 1969. 7.95g o.s.i. (ISBN 0-02-736050-4). Macmillan.
--Discovering Tut-Ankh-Amen's Tomb. LC 68-12069. (Illus.). (gr. 5 up). 1968. 14.95 (ISBN 0-02-736030-X). Macmillan.
Glubok, Shirley, ed. see Earle, Alice M.
Gluck, Herb. Baseball's Great Moments. LC 74-23539. (Major League Library Ser.: No. 23). (Illus.). 160p. (gr. 5 up). 1975. 2.50 o.p. (ISBN 0-394-83030-X, BYR); PLB 3.69 (ISBN 0-394-93030-4). Random.
Gluck, Herb, jt. auth. see Karas, Alex.
Gluck, Jay. Zen Combat. 224p. 1976. pap. 1.75 o.p. (ISBN 0-345-25030-3). Ballantine.
Gluck, Jay, ed. Ukiyo: Stories of "The Floating World" of Postwar Japan. LC 63-21851. 1964. 6.95 (ISBN 0-8149-0108-5). Vanguard.
Gluck, P., tr. see Kulik, I. O. & Yanson, I. K.
Gluckman, Max. The Ideas in Barotse Jurisprudence. (Institute for African Studies). (Illus.). 299p. (Orig.). text ed. 17.50x (ISBN 0-7190-1030-6); pap. text ed. 16.75x (ISBN 0-7190-1031-4). Humanities.
--Judicial Process Among the Barotse of Northern Rhodesia. (Rhodes Livingston Institute Bks). 1955. pap. text ed. 15.00x (ISBN 0-7190-1040-3). Humanities.
--Politics, Law & Ritual in Tribal Society. 1977. pap. 15.95x (ISBN 0-631-08750-8, Pub. by Basil Blackwell). Biblio Dist.
Gluckman, Max, ed. The Allocation of Responsibility. 321p. 1972. text ed. 19.50x (ISBN 0-7190-0491-8). Humanities.
Gluckman, Max, jt. ed. see Colson, Elizabeth.
Glucksberg, S. & Danks, J. H. Experimental Psycholinguistics. LC 75-2408. 250p. 1975. 10.00 o.p. (ISBN 0-470-30840-0). Halsted Pr.
Glucksman, Miriam. Structuralist Analysis in Contemporary Social Thought: A Comparison of the Theories of Claude Levi-Strauss & Louis Althusser. (International Library of Sociology). 1974. 26.00 (ISBN 0-7100-7773-4). Routledge & Kegan.
Glueck. Managing Essentials. 1979. 13.95 (ISBN 0-03-045416-6). Dryden Pr.
Glueck, B. C., jt. ed. see Solomon, P.
Glueck, E., jt. auth. see Glueck, S.
Glueck, Eleanor, jt. auth. see Glueck, Sheldon.
Glueck, S. & Glueck, E. Of Delinquency & Crime: A Panorama of Years of Search & Research. (Criminal Law Education & Research Center Ser.). 384p. 1974. 17.50 (ISBN 0-398-02989-X). C C Thomas.
Glueck, Sheldon. Continental Police Practice: In the Formative Years. (Criminal Law Education and Research Center Ser.). 88p. 1974. 9.75 (ISBN 0-398-02880-X). C C Thomas.
--Lives of Labor-Lives of Love: Fragments of Friendly Autobiographies. LC 76-24259. (Illus.). 1977. 8.50 o.p. (ISBN 0-682-48632-9, Banner). Exposition.
Glueck, Sheldon & Glueck, Eleanor. Delinquents in the Making. LC 51-11917. 1952. 7.95x o.p. (ISBN 0-06-032370-1, HarpT). Har-Row.
Glueck, William F. Business Policy & Strategic Management. 3rd ed. (Management Ser.). (Illus.). 1980. text ed. 19.95x (ISBN 0-07-023519-8, C). McGraw.
--Business Policy: Strategy, Formation & Executive Action. 1976. text ed. 18.95 o.p. (ISBN 0-07-023514-7, C). McGraw.
--Cases & Excercises in Personnel. rev. ed. 1978. pap. 9.95x (ISBN 0-256-01952-5). Business Pubns.
--Foundations of Personnel. 1979. 18.50x (ISBN 0-256-02202-X). Business Pubns.
--Personnel: A Diagnostic Approach. rev. ed. 1978. 18.95x (ISBN 0-256-01951-7). Business Pubns.
Glueck, William F. & Wall, Jerry A. Student Involvement Manual for Personnel Management. 1979. pap. 6.95x (ISBN 0-256-02253-4). Business Pubns.
Glueck, William F., ed. Personnel: A Book of Readings. 1979. pap. 11.95x (ISBN 0-256-02078-7). Business Pubns.
Glueck, William G. Management. 2nd ed. 640p. 1980. text ed. 20.95 (ISBN 0-03-050906-8). Dryden Pr.
Gluhbegovic, Nedzad & Williams, Terence H. The Human Brain. (Illus.). 176p. 1980. text ed. 27.50 (ISBN 0-06-140945-6, Harper Medical). Har-Row.
Glusker, Irwin, ed. see Morris, Willie.
Glusker, Jenny P. & Trueblood, Kenneth N. Crystal Structure Analysis: A Primer. (Illus.). 1972. 12.95x (ISBN 0-19-501425-1); pap. 6.95x (ISBN 0-19-501426-X). Oxford U Pr.
Glut, Don, ed. Clash of the Titans. (Big Little Book Special Ser.). (Illus.). 256p. (gr. 3-7). 2.50 (Golden Pr). Western Pub.
Glut, Donald F. Classic Movie Monsters. LC 77-16014. (Illus.). 1978. 18.00 (ISBN 0-8108-1049-2). Scarecrow.
--The Dinosaur Scrapbook. 1980. 19.95 (ISBN 0-8065-0671-7). Lyle Stuart.
--The Dracula Book. LC 75-4917. (Illus.). 410p. 1975. 15.00 (ISBN 0-8108-0804-8). Scarecrow.
--The Empire Strikes Back. 1980. pap. 2.25 (ISBN 0-345-28392-9, Del Rey). Ballantine.
--The Frankenstein Legend: A Tribute to Mary Shelley & Boris Karloff. LC 73-944. (Illus.). 1973. 13.50 (ISBN 0-8108-0589-8). Scarecrow.
Gluyas, Constance. Born to Be King. 1977. pap. 1.95 o.s.i. (ISBN 0-515-04297-8). Jove Pubns.
--Lord Sin. 1980. pap. 2.75 (ISBN 0-451-09521-9, E9521, Sig). NAL.
Glymour, Clark. Theory & Evidence. LC 79-3209. 1980. 25.00x o.s.i. (ISBN 0-691-07240-X); pap. 9.95 o.s.i. (ISBN 0-691-10077-2). Princeton U Pr.
Glyn, Elinor. The Great Moment. (Barbara Cartland's Library of Love: Vol. 14). 214p. 1980. 12.95x (ISBN 0-7156-1474-6, Pub. by Duckworth England). Biblio Dist.
--His Hour. (Barbara Cartland's Library of Love: Vol. 2). 182p. 1979. 12.95x (ISBN 0-7156-1378-2, Pub. by Duckworth England). Biblio Dist.
--Man & Maid. (Barbara Cartland's Library of Love: Vol. 10). 182p. 1979. 12.95x (ISBN 0-7156-1386-3, Pub. by Duckworth England). Biblio Dist.
--The Reason Why. (Barbara Cartland's Library of Love: Vol. 6). 246p. 1979. 12.95x (ISBN 0-7156-1382-0, Pub. by Duckworth England). Biblio Dist.
--The Sequence. (Barbara Cartland's Library of Love: Vol. 17). 213p. 1980. 12.95x (ISBN 0-7156-1477-0, Pub. by Duckworth England). Biblio Dist.
--Six Days. (Barbara Cartland's Library of Love: Vol. 12). 213p. 1980. 12.95x (ISBN 0-7156-1471-1, Pub. by Duckworth England). Biblio Dist.
--The Vicissitudes of Evangeline. (Barbara Cartland's Library of Love: Vol. 8). 182p. 1979. 12.95x (ISBN 0-7156-1385-5, Pub. by Duckworth England). Biblio Dist.
Glyn, Erica. Formulacion Quimica. (Span). 1970. pap. text ed. 2.70 (ISBN 0-06-313340-7, IntlDept). Har-Row.
Glynn, L. E. Structure & Fuction of Antibodies. Steward, M. W., ed. 150p. 1981. pap. 15.00 (ISBN 0-471-27917-X, Pub. by Wiley-Interscience). Wiley.
Glynn, L. E. & Steward, M. W., eds. Antibody Production. 1981. 15.00 (ISBN 0-471-27916-1, Pub. by Wiley-Interscience). Wiley.
Glynn, Maryanne C. Student Guide to the Registered Nurse (R.N.) Examination. Tarlow, David M., ed. (Illus.). 1978. pap. 7.00 (ISBN 0-931572-03-7). Datar Pub.
Glynn, Prudence. In Fashion: Dress in the Twentieth Century. (Illus.). 252p. 1978. 22.50 (ISBN 0-04-391003-3). Allen Unwin.
Glynn, Sean & Oxborrow, John. Interwar Britain: A Social & Economic History. 1976. pap. text ed. 9.95x o.p. (ISBN 0-04-942041-0, 1974). Allen Unwin.
Glyph. Johns Hopkins Textual Studies. 1980. No. 6, 224p. 14.50 (ISBN 0-8018-2296-3); pap. 3.95 (ISBN 0-8018-2297-1); No. 7 240p. 16.50 (ISBN 0-8018-2365-X); pap. 5.95 (ISBN 0-8018-2366-8). Johns Hopkins.
Gmehling, J., et al. Aromatic Hydrocarbons: Vol. I, Pt. 7, Vapor-Liquid Equilibrium Data Collection. Behrens, D. & Eckermann, R., eds. (Dechema Chemistry Data Ser.). 564p. 1980. text ed. 106.00x (ISBN 3-9215-6723-8, Pub. by Dechema Germany). Scholium Intl.
Gmelin, Otto. Mom Is an Elephant. Hermann, Judith M., tr. from Ger. LC 80-80651. (Illus.). Date not set. price not set (ISBN 0-89793-026-6). Hunter Hse.
Gmelin, Wolfgang, jt. ed. see Bucholz, Hans.
Gnade, Michael. People in My Camera. 1978. 21.95 o.p. (ISBN 0-8038-5876-0, Pub. by Fountain). Morgan.
Gnanadesikan, Ramanathan. Methods for Statistical Data Analysis of Multivariate Observations. LC 76-14994. (Probability & Mathematical Statics Ser.). 1977. 29.95 (ISBN 0-471-30845-5, Pub. by Wiley-Interscience). Wiley.
Gnarowski, Michael, intro. by. New Provinces: Poems of Several Authors. (Literature of Canada Ser., Poetry & Prose in Reprint). 1976. pap. 5.50 (ISBN 0-8020-6299-7). U of Toronto Pr.
Gnedenko, B. V. Theory of Probability: With Answers to Exercises. 4th ed. LC 67-8772. 14.95 (ISBN 0-8284-0132-2). Chelsea Pub.
Gnedenko, Boris V. & Khinchin, Alexander Y. Elementary Introduction to the Theory of Probability. 5th ed. Boron, Leon F., tr. 1961. pap. text ed. 3.00 (ISBN 0-486-60155-2). Dover.

Gneist, Rudolph. The History of the English Constitution, 2 vols. Ashworth, Philip A., tr. from Ger. 1980. Repr. of 1886 ed. Set. lib. bdg. 75.00x (ISBN 0-8377-0613-0). Rothman.

Gnnick, Harvey C., ed. Current Nephrology, Vol. 4. (Current Ser.). (Illus.). 500p. 1980. text ed. 48.00 (ISBN 0-89289-110-6). HM Prof Med Div.

Goadby, Robert, tr. see Cervantes Saavedra, Miguel De.

Goaman, Muriel. Never So Good or How Children Were Treated. 1974. 7.95 o.p. (ISBN 0-7207-0627-0, Pub. by Michael Joseph). Merrimack Bk Serv.

Goatsend, Slim. Thor's Goats & Other Crazy Ways to Ride Around. (Odd Books for Odd Moments Ser.). (Illus.). 72p. (Orig.). 1981. pap. 3.95 (ISBN 0-938338-07-2). Winds World Pr.

Gobbel, A. Roger & Huber, Phillip C. Creative Designs with Children at Worship. LC 80-82225. 96p. (Orig.). 1981. pap. 4.95 (ISBN 0-8042-1526-X). John Knox.

Gobble, Bill & Harwood, Bruce. North Carolina Real Estate. 1981. text ed. 16.95 (ISBN 0-8359-4951-6). Reston.

Gobel, E. F. Rubber Springs Design. Brichta, A. M., ed. & tr. LC 74-9997. 211p. 1974. 39.95 (ISBN 0-470-30855-9). Halsted Pr.

Gobel, F., tr. see Schuh, Fred.

Goble, Alfred T. & Baker, D. K. Elements of Modern Physics. 2nd ed. (Illus.). 1971. 19.95 (ISBN 0-8260-3425-X). Wiley.

Goble, Dorothy, jt. auth. see Goble, Paul.

Goble, E. A., et al. Rehabilitation of the Severely Disabled-1: Evaluation of a Disabled Living Unit. 268p. 1971. 15.95 (ISBN 0-407-38510-X). Butterworths.

Goble, Paul. The Gift of the Sacred Dog. LC 80-15843. (Illus.). 32p. (gr. k-2). 9.95 (ISBN 0-87888-165-4). Bradbury Pr.

--The Girl Who Loved Wild Horses. LC 77-20500. (gr. k-2). 1978. 9.95 (ISBN 0-87888-121-2). Bradbury Pr.

Goble, Paul & Goble, Dorothy. Friendly Wolf. LC 74-77664. (Illus.). 32p. (gr. 1-3). 1975. 9.95 (ISBN 0-87888-104-2). Bradbury Pr.

--Lone Bull's Horse Raid. LC 73-76546. (Illus.). 64p. (gr. 4-6). 1973. 9.95 (ISBN 0-87888-059-3). Bradbury Pr.

Goble, Phillip E. Everything You Need to Grow a Messianic Synagogue. LC 74-28017. (Orig.). 1974. pap. 3.95 (ISBN 0-87808-421-5). William Carey Lib.

Goble, Ross & Shaw, Roy. Controversy & Dialogue in Marketing. (Illus.). 480p. 1975. pap. text ed. 10.95 (ISBN 0-13-172320-0). P-H.

Gocan, S., jt. auth. see Liteanu, C.

Gochnour, Elizabeth. Gochnour Idiom Screening Test (GIST) 1977. pap. text ed. 3.95x (ISBN 0-8134-2049-0, 1970). Interstate.

Gochnour, Elizabeth A. & Smith, Theresa B. Language of Life. 2nd ed. (Illus.). 1981. pap. 6.50x (ISBN 0-8134-2162-4, 2162). Interstate.

--Language of Life. (Illus.). 1973. pap. 6.50x o.p. (ISBN 0-8134-1539-X, 1539). Interstate.

Gochros, Harvey L. & Fischer, Joel. Treat Yourself to a Better Sex Life. (Illus.). 1980. 16.95 (ISBN 0-13-930685-4, Spec); pap. 7.95 (ISBN 0-13-930677-3). P-H.

Gochros, Harvey L., jt. auth. see Fischer, Joel.

Gochros, Harvey L. & Schultz, Leroy G., eds. Human Sexuality & Social Work. LC 71-129436. 1972. 9.95 o.p. (ISBN 0-8096-1808-7, Assn Pr). Follett.

Gockel, H. Cross & Common Man. 1980. 5.95 (ISBN 0-8100-0119-5). Northwest Pub.

Gockel, Herman W. Answer to Anxiety. 1965. pap. 4.95 (ISBN 0-570-03704-2, 12-2254). Concordia.

--What Jesus Means to Me. 1956. 4.50 (ISBN 0-570-03021-8, 6-1008). Concordia.

Gockel, Herman W. & Saleska, Edward J., eds. Child's Garden of Prayer. (Illus.). (gr. k-2). 1981. pap. 0.99 (ISBN 0-570-03412-4, 56-1016). Concordia.

God, Phyllis. God. Date not set. 7.95 (ISBN 0-533-04754-4). Vantage.

Goday, Dale. Dressing Thin. 1980. 3.95 (ISBN 0-671-25471-5, 25471, Fireside). S&S.

Godby, Joyce G. God Makes the Difference. 128p. 1981. 5.00 (ISBN 0-8059-2764-6). Dorrance.

Goddard. Information Sources in Geographical Science. (Butterworths Guides to Information Sources Ser.). 1981. text ed. price not set (ISBN 0-408-10690-5). Butterworth.

Goddard, Anthea. The Aztec Skull. LC 76-56606. 1977. 5.95 o.s.i. (ISBN 0-8027-6285-9). Walker & Co.

--Time for Violence. 1978. 7.95 o.s.i. (ISBN 0-8027-5369-8). Walker & Co.

--The Vienna Pursuit. LC 75-42826. 192p. 1976. 6.95 o.s.i. (ISBN 0-8027-5346-9). Walker & Co.

Goddard, Carrie Lou. Isn't It a Wonder! LC 75-15664. (Illus.). (gr. k-3). 1976. 7.95 (ISBN 0-687-19715-5). Abingdon.

Goddard, Donald. All Fall Down. 384p. 1980. 12.95 (ISBN 0-686-62157-3). Times Bks.

--All Fall Down: One Man Against the Waterfront Mob. 320p. 1980. 14.95 (ISBN 0-8129-0938-0). Times Bks.

Goddard, Dwight, ed. A Buddhist Bible, the Favorite Scriptures of the Zen Sect: History of Early Buddhism. 2nd rev. & enl. ed. LC 78-72434. 1980. Repr. of 1938 ed. 57.50 (ISBN 0-404-17297-0). AMS Pr.

Goddard, Gloria, jt. ed. see Wood, Clement.

Goddard, Harold C. Chaucer's Legend of Good Women. 107p. 1980. Repr. of 1908 ed. lib. bdg. 20.00 (ISBN 0-8495-1959-4). Arden Lib.

--Studies in New England Transcendentalism. 1960. text ed. 12.50x (ISBN 0-391-00599-5). Humanities.

Goddard, Ives. Delaware Verbal Morphology: A Descriptive & Comparative Study. Hankamer, Jorge, ed. LC 78-66556. (Outstanding Dissertations in Linguistics Ser.). 1979. lib. bdg. 26.50 (ISBN 0-8240-9685-1). Garland Pub.

Goddard, J. B., ed. Industrial Innovation & Regional Economic Development. 120p. 1980. pap. 15.60 (ISBN 0-08-026102-7). Pergamon.

Goddard, John, jt. auth. see Clarke, Brian.

Goddard, John B. Office Location in Urban & Regional Development. (Theory & Practice in Geography Ser.). (Illus.). 1975. pap. text ed. 5.95x (ISBN 0-19-874033-6). Oxford U Pr.

Goddard, K. Crime Scene Investigation. 1977. 13.00 (ISBN 0-87909-172-X); students manual avail. Reston.

Goddard, L. & Routley, R. The Logic of Significance & Context, Vol. 1. LC 73-8025. 641p. 1973. 44.95 (ISBN 0-470-30865-6). Halsted Pr.

Goddard, Ruth & Dobie, J. Frank. Ralph Ogden & the Seven Mustangs. LC 73-15099. 8.50 (ISBN 0-8363-0082-3). Jenkins.

Godden, Geoffrey. Godden's Guide to English Porcelain. (Illus.). 286p. 1980. text ed. 31.25x (ISBN 0-686-61566-2). Humanities.

--Oriental Export Market Porcelain & Its Influence on European Wares. (Illus.). 384p. 1980. text ed. 65.00x (ISBN 0-246-11057-0). Humanities.

--Oriental Export Porcelain & Its Influence on European Wares. (Illus.). 1979. 69.95x (ISBN 0-8464-0052-9). Beekman Pubs.

Godden, Geoffrey A. Godden's Guide to English Porcelain. 1978. 70.00x (ISBN 0-246-11002-3, Pub. by Granada England). State Mutual Bk.

--Jewett's Ceramic Art of Great Britain, 1800-1900. LC 76-184414. (Illus.). 300p. 1972. 25.00 o.p. (ISBN 0-668-02595-6). Arco.

--Minton Pottery & Porcelain of the First Period: 1783-1850. 1978. 29.95 o.p. (ISBN 0-686-01036-1, 8034, Dist. by Arco). Barrie & Jenkins.

Godden, John O., ed. see Symposium, Roswell Park Memorial Institute, Buffalo, Sept. 1974.

Godden, Jon. In Her Garden. LC 80-19849. 192p. 1981. 10.95 (ISBN 0-394-51361-4). Knopf.

Godden, Malcolm, ed. see AElfric.

Godden, Rumer. The Butterfly Lions: The Story of the Pekingese in History, Legend & Art. (Illus.). 1978. 13.95 o.p. (ISBN 0-670-19788-2, Studio). Viking Pr.

--China Court. 1974. pap. 1.25 o.s.i. (ISBN 0-380-00114-4, 20412). Avon.

--Five for Sorrow, Ten for Joy. 256p. 1981. pap. 2.75 (ISBN 0-449-24372-9, Crest). Fawcett.

--Gulbadan: Portrait of a Rose Princess at the Mughal Court. LC 80-51752. (Illus.). 160p. 1981. 14.95 (ISBN 0-670-35756-1, Studio). Viking Pr.

--The Rocking Horse Secret. (gr. 4-6). 1979. pap. 1.25 (ISBN 0-590-03168-6, Schol Pap). Schol Bk Serv.

Godden, Rumer, ed. see Dickinson, Emily.

Gode, Alexander, tr. see Petersen, Carol.

Gode, Merlin. Winter Outdoor Living. 1978. pap. text ed. 2.75 (ISBN 0-89832-008-9). Brighton Pub.

Godechot, Jacques. Counter-Revolution, Doctrine & Action, Seventeen Eighty-Nine to Eighteen Four. LC 70-159820. 1971. 24.00 (ISBN 0-86527-035-X). Fertig.

Godel, Jules B. Sources of Construction Information: An Annotated Guide to Reports, Books, Periodicals, Standards, and Codes. LC 77-4671. 1977. 30.00 (ISBN 0-8108-1030-1). Scarecrow.

Godel, Jules B., jt. auth. see Berger, Seymour.

Godelier, M. Perspectives in Marxist Anthropology. Brain, R., tr. LC 76-11081. (Studies in Social Anthropology: No. 18). (Illus.). 1977. 29.95 (ISBN 0-521-21311-8); pap. 8.95x (ISBN 0-521-29098-8). Cambridge U Pr.

Godet, F. Commentary on the Gospel of Saint Luke, 2 vols. 5th ed. 920p. 1976. pap. text ed. 27.50x (ISBN 0-567-27446-2). Attic Pr.

Godet, Frederic L. Commentary John's Gospel, 2 vols. in 1. LC 78-59145. (Kregel Reprint Library). 1979. 22.95 (ISBN 0-8254-2714-2). Kregel.

--Commentary on Luke. LC 80-8068. 918p. 1981. 16.95 (ISBN 0-8254-2720-7). Kregel.

Godet, Michel. The Crisis in Forecasting & the Emergence of the "Prospective" Approach: With Case Studies in Energy & Air Transport. LC 78-10548. (Pergamon Policy Studies). 1979. 16.50 (ISBN 0-08-022487-3). Pergamon.

Godfrey, Elbert D. Unforgetable Sounds. (The Mental Therapy Ser.). 128p. Date not set. 6.50 (ISBN 0-89962-030-2). Todd & Honeywell.

Godfrey, James. Revolutionary Justice: A Study of the Organization, Personnel & Procedure of the Paris Tribunal 1793-1795. (Perspectives in Europen History Ser.: No. 42). vi, 166p. 1981. Repr. of 1951 ed. lib. bdg. 15.00x (ISBN 0-87991-640-0). Porcupine Pr.

Godfrey, John. Twelve Hundred & Four - the Unholy Crusade. (Illus.). 256p. 1980. 28.50 (ISBN 0-19-215834-1). Oxford U Pr.

Godfrey, Michael. A Closer Look. LC 75-8961. (Illus.). 160p. 1975. 14.95 o.p. (ISBN 0-87156-143-3). Sierra.

Godfrey, Michael A. A Sierra Club Naturalist's Guide to the Piedmont. LC 79-22328. (Naturalists Guide Ser.). (Illus.). 1980. 19.95 (ISBN 0-87156-268-5); pap. 9.95 (ISBN 0-87156-269-3). Sierra.

Godfrey, Robert K. & Wooten, Jean W. Aquatic & Wetland Plants of Southeastern United States: Dicotyledons. LC 80-16452. (Illus.). 864p. 1981. lib. bdg. 40.00x (ISBN 0-8203-0532-4). U of Ga Pr.

Godfrey, Robert S. Appraisal Manual, 1981. 2nd ed. 320p. 1981. pap. 33.00 (ISBN 0-911950-35-4). Means.

--Building Construction Cost Data, 1981. 39th ed. LC 55-20084. 1981. pap. 24.50 (ISBN 0-911950-29-X). Means.

--Building Systems Cost Guide: 1980. 3rd ed. LC 76-17689. (Illus.). 1980. pap. 29.50 (ISBN 0-911950-24-9). Means.

--Building Systems Cost Guide: 1981. 6th ed. LC 76-17689. 375p. 1981. pap. 32.00 (ISBN 0-911950-30-3). Means.

--Mechanical & Electrical Cost Data, 1980. 3rd ed. 360p. 1980. pap. 27.50 (ISBN 0-911950-23-0). Means.

--Mechanical & Electrical Cost Data, 1981. 4th ed. LC 79-643328. 400p. 1981. pap. 29.50 (ISBN 0-911950-31-1). Means.

--Nineteen Eighty-One Labor Rates for the Construction Industry. 8th ed. LC 74-75990. 300p. 1981. pap. 26.75 (ISBN 0-911950-33-8). Means.

--Repair & Remodeling Cost Data Nineteen Eighty. 325p. 1980. pap. 32.00 (ISBN 0-911950-28-1). Means.

--Repair & Remodeling Cost Data, 1981. 2nd ed. 325p. 1981. pap. 32.00 (ISBN 0-911950-34-6). Means.

Godfrey, S., jt. ed. see Clark, T. J.

Godfrey, Simon. Your Child with Asthma. 1975. pap. text ed. 10.00x (ISBN 0-433-12300-1). Intl Ideas.

Godfrey, W. Earl. Birds of Canada. Crosby, John A., tr. (Illus.). 1966. 27.50 (ISBN 0-660-00126-8, 56282-4, Pub. by Natl Mus Canada). U of Chicago Pr.

Godfriaux, Bruce L., ed. Power Plant Waste Heat Utilization in Aquaculture. LC 78-73590. 288p. 1979. text ed. 35.00 (ISBN 0-916672-24-7). Allanheld.

Godin, Alfred J. Wild Mammals of New England: Field Guide Edition. rev. ed. Vanderweide, Harry, ed. (Illus.). 200p. 1981. pap. 6.95 (ISBN 0-89933-012-6). DeLorme Pub.

Godiwalla, Yezdi M., et al. Corporate Strategy & Functional Management. LC 79-65182. 1979. 20.95 (ISBN 0-03-049781-7). Praeger.

Godlas, Alan, tr. see Nurbaksh, Javad.

Godley, Michael R. The Mandarin-Capitalists from Nanyang: Overseas Chinese Enterprise in the Modernisation of China 1893-1911. (Cambridge Studies in Chinese History, Literature & Institutions Ser.). (Illus.). 288p. Date not set. price not set (ISBN 0-521-23626-6). Cambridge U Pr.

Godley, Wynne. Cambridge Economic Policy Review. 76p. (Orig.). 1979. pap. 12.95 (ISBN 0-686-62424-6, Pub. by Gower Pub Co England). Lexington Bks.

Godman, A. & Payne, E. M. F. Longman Dictionary of Scientific Usage. (Illus.). 1979. pap. text ed. 13.50x (ISBN 0-582-52587-X). Longman.

Godman, Stanley, tr. see Blume, Friedrich.

Godnick, Newton E., jt. auth. see Tepper, Bette.

Godson, Joseph, jt. ed. see Schapiro, Leonard.

Godson, Roy. American Labor and European Politics: The AFL As a Transnational Force. LC 76-491. 1976. 17.50x (ISBN 0-8448-0919-5); pap. 9.95x (ISBN 0-8448-0920-9). Crane-Russak Co.

--The Kremlin & Labor: A Study in National Security Policy. LC 77-85317. 1977. 9.95x (ISBN 0-8448-1274-9); pap. 3.25x (ISBN 0-8448-1225-0). Crane-Russak Co.

Godson, Roy, jt. auth. see Lefever, Ernest W.

Godward, Maud B. Chromosomes of the Algae. (Illus.). 1969. 21.95 (ISBN 0-312-13440-1). St Martin.

Godwin, E. W. Art Furniture. Stansky, Peter & Shewan, Rodney, eds. Incl. Artistic Conservatories. Adams, Maurice. LC 76-18322. (Aesthetic Movement & the Arts & Crafts Movement Ser.: Vol. 14). 1978. Repr. of 1880 ed. lib. bdg. 44.00x (ISBN 0-8240-2463-X). Garland Pub.

Godwin, Gail. The Odd Woman. pap. 1.95 o.p. (ISBN 0-425-03167-5). Berkley Pub.

Godwin, George. Town Swamps & Social Bridges. (Victorian Library). 110p. 1972. Repr. of 1859 ed. text ed. 8.25x (ISBN 0-391-00158-2, Leicester). Humanities.

Godwin, H. Fenland: Its Ancient Past & Uncertain Future. LC 77-8824. (Illus.). 1978. 32.50 (ISBN 0-521-21768-7). Cambridge U Pr.

Godwin, Harry. The Archives of the Peat Bogs. (Illus.). Date not set. price not set (ISBN 0-521-23784-X). Cambridge U Pr.

--The History of the British Flora. 2nd ed. LC 73-84324. (Illus.). 500p. 1975. 125.00 (ISBN 0-521-20254-X). Cambridge U Pr.

Godwin, Herbert J., jt. auth. see Weston, J. D.

Godwin, Jocelyn. Schirmer Scores: A Repertory of Western Music. LC 75-557. 1975. pap. text ed. 12.95 o.s.i. (ISBN 0-02-870700-1). Schirmer Bks.

Godwin, Parke. Firelord. LC 80-497. (Science Fiction Ser.). 416p. 1980. 12.95 (ISBN 0-385-17070-X). Doubleday.

Godwin, William. Essays. 293p. 1980. Repr. of 1873 ed. lib. bdg. 35.00 (ISBN 0-8492-4974-0). R West.

--Fables, Ancient & Modern: Adapted for the Use of Children, 2 vols. in 1. LC 75-32153. (Classics of Children's Literature, 1621-1932: Vol. 19). 1976. Repr. of 1805 ed. PLB 38.00 (ISBN 0-8240-2267-X). Garland Pub.

--Fleetwood: or, The New Man of Feeling, 3 vols. Paulson, Ronald, ed. LC 78-60852. (Novel 1720-1805 Ser.: Vol. 14). 1979. Set. lib. bdg. 93.00 (ISBN 0-8240-3663-8). Garland Pub.

--Memoirs of the Author of a Vindication of the Rights of Woman. (The Feminist Controversy in England, 1788-1810 Ser.). 1974. lib. bdg. 50.00 (ISBN 0-8240-0861-8). Garland Pub.

--St. Leon: A Tale of the Sixteenth Century, 4 vols. (The Feminist Controversy in England, 1788-1810 Ser.). 1974. Set. lib. bdg. 152.00 (ISBN 0-8240-0862-6); lib. bdg. 50.00 ea. Garland Pub.

--Uncollected Writings 1785-1822. LC 68-24208. (Illus.). 1968. 52.00x (ISBN 0-8201-1023-X). Schol Facsimiles.

Godwin, William, ed. see Wollstonecraft, Mary.

Goebbels, Joseph. My Part in Germany's Fight. Fiedler, Kurt, tr. from Ger. LC 76-27871. 1979. Repr. of 1935 ed. 18.50 (ISBN 0-86527-137-2). Fertig.

Goebel, jt. auth. see Banas.

Goebel, Ulrich, jt. auth. see McDonald, William C.

Goederf, Jeanne E. Generalizing from the Experimental Housing Allowance Program: An Assessment of Site Characteristics. (An Institute Paper). 67p. 1978. pap. 4.50 (ISBN 0-87766-224-X, 22900). Urban Inst.

Goedert, Jeanne E. & Goodman, John L., Jr. Indicators of the Quality of U. S. Housing. (An Institute Paper). 55p. 1977. pap. 5.50 (ISBN 0-87766-204-5, 20200). Urban Inst.

Goedsche, C. R. Sag's Auf Deutsch: A First Book for German Conversation. (Illus., Ger.). (gr. 10 up). 1979. text ed. 21.00x o.p. (ISBN 0-89197-387-7); pap. text ed. 6.95x (ISBN 0-8290-0026-7). Irvington.

Goehle, Donna G. Decision Making in Multinational Corporations. Dufey, Gunter, ed. (Research for Business Decisions). 237p. 1980. 26.95 (ISBN 0-8357-1102-1, Pub. by UMI Res Pr). Univ Microfilms.

Goehlert, Robert & Hoffmeister, Elizabeth R. The CIA: A Bibliography. (Public Administration Ser.: Bibliography P-498). 79p. 1980. pap. 8.50. Vance Biblios.

Goei, Jacques S. How to Be Your Own Hairdresser for Fun or Profit. Date not set. 7.50 (ISBN 0-682-49128-4). Exposition. Postponed.

Goel, N. S., et al. On the Volterra & Other Nonlinear Models of Interacting Populations. (Reviews of Modern Physics Monographs). 1971. 21.00 (ISBN 0-12-287450-1). Acad Pr.

Goel, S. C. Education & Economic Growth in India. LC 75-904970. 1975. 9.50x o.p. (ISBN 0-333-90101-0). South Asia Bks.

Goeldner, C. R. The Airline Skier: 1977-78. 77p. 1978. 15.00 (ISBN 0-89478-045-X). U CO Busn Res Div.

--The Aspen Skier: (1977-78) 80p. 1978. 15.00 (ISBN 0-89478-043-3). U CO Busn Res Div.

--The Colorado Skier. 92p. 1978. 25.00 (ISBN 0-89478-044-1). U CO Busn Res Div.

Goeldner, C. R. & Courteney, Sally. Colorado Ski & Winter Recreation Statistics, 1977: (1976-77 Season) 124p. 1977. 20.00 (ISBN 0-89478-036-0). U CO Busn Res Div.

Goeldner, C. R. & Dicke, Karen. Bibliography of Skiing Studies. 5th ed. 1980. 10.00 (ISBN 0-89478-050-6). U CO Busn Res Div.

--Bibliography of Skiing Studies. 1978. 10.00 (ISBN 0-89478-039-5). U CO Busn Res Div.

--Colorado Ski & Winter Recreation Statistics, 1978: (1977-78 Season) 117p. 1978. 20.00 (ISBN 0-89478-048-4). U CO Busn Res Div.

--Colorado Ski Industry Characteristics & Financial Analysis. 54p. 1979. 25.00 o.p. (ISBN 0-686-64150-7). U CO Busn Res Div.

Goeldner, C. R. & Farwell, Ted. NSAA Economic Analysis of North American Ski Areas (79-80 Season) 139p. 1980. 35.00 (ISBN 0-89478-054-9). U CO Busn Res Div.

Goeldner, C. R. & Fellhauer, Cheryl. The Aspen Summer Visitor. 97p. 1976. 10.00 (ISBN 0-89478-028-X). U CO Busn Res Div.

--Colorado Ski & Winter Recreation Statistics, 1976: (1975-76 Season) 123p. 1977. 10.00 (ISBN 0-89478-030-1). U CO Busn Res Div.

Goeldner, C. R. & Gortmaker, Gwen. The Aspen Design Conference Visitor. 56p. 1976. 10.00 (ISBN 0-89478-029-8). U CO Busn Res Div.

Goeldner, C. R. & Sletta, Yvonne. The Breckenridge Skier. 97p. 1975. 10.00 (ISBN 0-89478-021-2). U CO Busn Res Div.

Goeldner, C. R., jt. auth. see Dicke, Karen.

Goeller, Carl. Writing & Selling Greeting Cards. 1980. 10.95 (ISBN 0-87116-124-9). Writer.

Goeltz, Judith. Jet Stress: What It Is & How to Cope with It. Donsbach, Kurt W., ed. LC 79-89366. 350p. 1980. 9.95 (ISBN 0-86664-000-2). Inst Pubs.

Goen, Ted, Jr. Smile or I'll Kick Your Bed. (Illus.). 1981. 12.95 (ISBN 0-393-01433-9). Norton.

Goergen, Don. The Sexual Celibate. 256p. 1975. 8.95 (ISBN 0-8164-0268-X). Crossroad NY.

Goergen, Donald. The Sexual Celibate. 1979. pap. 3.95 (ISBN 0-385-14902-6, Im). Doubleday.

Goerlick, Sherry. City College & the Jewish Poor: Education in New York, 1880-1924. (Illus.). 256p. 1981. 14.95 (ISBN 0-8135-0905-X). Rutgers U Pr.

Goertz, Christopher, et al. Experiments in Mechanics, Wave Motion, & Heat, Laboratory Manual. 1977. pap. text ed. 5.50 o.p. (ISBN 0-8403-1750-6). Kendall-Hunt.

Goerzen, Janice L. & Chinn, Peggy L. Review of Maternal & Child Nursing. LC 74-20973. 1975. text ed. 9.00 (ISBN 0-8016-1852-5). Mosby.

Goes. Das Brandopfer. (Easy Readers, C). pap. 3.75 (ISBN 0-88436-057-1, GEA301051). EMC.

Goes, Albrecht. Loffelchen: Eine Erzahlung. Schweitzer, Christoph E., ed. LC 68-13150. (Orig., Ger.). 1968. pap. text ed. 1.95x (ISBN 0-89197-280-3). Irvington.

Goeschel, Joachim. Strukturelle und instrumentalphonetische Untersuchungen zur gesprochenen Sprache. LC 72-76054. (Studia Linguistica Germanica Vol. 9). (Illus.). 1973. 51.00x (ISBN 3-11-003624-X). De Gruyter.

Goetchius, E. V. Language of the New Testament. 1966. text ed. 9.95x (ISBN 0-684-41263-2, ScribC); wkbk. 8.95x (ISBN 0-684-41264-0). Scribner.

Goethals, Eric J., ed. Polymeric Amines & Ammonium Salts: International Symposium on Polymeric Amines & Ammonium Salts, Ghent, Belgium, 24-26 September 1979. LC 80-40324. (IUPAC Symposium Ser). 424p. 1980. 98.00 (ISBN 0-08-023941-2). Pergamon.

Goethals, G., jt. auth. see Worchel, S.

Goethals, Gregor. The TV Ritual: Worship at the Video Altar. LC 80-66072. (Illus.). 192p. 1981. 11.95 (ISBN 0-8070-3222-0). Beacon Pr.

Goetham, Larry Van see Van Goetham, Larry.

Goethe, Johann W. Egmont. Waidson, H. M., ed. (German Text Ser.). 1960. pap. 9.95x (ISBN 0-631-01670-8, Pub. by Basil Blackwell). Biblio Dist.

--The Eternal Feminine: Selected Poems of Goethe. Ungar, Frederick, ed. LC 76-15651. 192p. 1980. 14.50 (ISBN 0-8044-2256-7). Ungar.

--Goethe's World View: Presented in His Reflections & Maxims. Ungar, Frederick, ed. Norden, Heinz, tr. LC 63-18513. pap. 3.45 (ISBN 0-8044-6192-9). Ungar.

--Die Leiden Des Jungen Werthers. 2nd ed. Stahl, E. L., ed. 1972. pap. 9.95x (ISBN 0-631-01900-6, Pub. by Basil Blackwell). Biblio Dist.

Goethe, Johann W. Von. The Fairy Tale of the Green Snake & the Beautiful Lily. 80p. 1980. pap. 3.50 (ISBN 0-8334-1769-X). Steinerbks.

--Faust. new ed. Hamlin, Cyrus, ed. Arndt, Walter, tr. from Ger. (Critical Edition Ser). 24p. 1976. pap. text ed. 5.45x (ISBN 0-393-09208-9). Norton.

--Faust, Pts. 1 & 2. abr. ed. MacNiece, Louis, tr. 1960. pap. 4.95 (ISBN 0-19-500410-8). Oxford U Pr.

Goethe, Johann W. Von see Von Goethe, Johann W.

Goethe, Johann W. von see Von Goethe, Johann W.

Goethe, Johann W. Von see Von Goethe, Johann W.

Goettinger, H., ed. Diagnostik und Therapie des Prostatakarzinoms. (Beitraece zur Urologie: Vol. 1). 1979. soft cover 24.00 (ISBN 3-8055-0294-X). S Karger.

Goetz, Abraham. Introduction to Differential Geometry. (Intermediate Mathematics Ser). 1970. text ed. 18.95 (ISBN 0-201-02431-4). A-W.

Goetz, Delia. Deserts. (Illus.). (gr. 3-7). 1956. PLB 6.48 (ISBN 0-688-31232-2). Morrow.

--Lakes. LC 72-7226. (Illus.). 64p. (gr. 3-7). 1973. 6.75 (ISBN 0-688-21866-0). Morrow.

--Neighbors to the South. rev. ed. LC 56-5874. (Illus.). (gr. 7-9). 1956. 4.95 o.p. (ISBN 0-15-256885-9, HJ). HarBraceJ.

--Rivers. (Illus.). (gr. 3-7). 1969. PLB 6.48 (ISBN 0-688-31480-5). Morrow.

--State Capital Cities. LC 70-155991. (Illus.). (gr. 5-9). 1971. PLB 7.92 (ISBN 0-688-31955-6). Morrow.

--Valleys. LC 75-26980. (Illus.). 64p. (gr. 3-7). 1976. 6.25 (ISBN 0-688-22059-2); PLB 6.00 (ISBN 0-688-32059-7). Morrow.

Goetz, Delia, jt. tr. see Recinos, Adrian.

Goetze, A. Heights. 3.00 (ISBN 0-8283-1438-1). Branden.

Goetze, Joan. El Amor & la Juventud. Montero, Lidia D., tr. from Eng. Orig. Title: Let's Look at Love. (Illus.). 1979. Repr. of 1975 ed. 1.70 (ISBN 0-311-46058-5, Edit Mundo). Casa Bautista.

Goetzmann, William H. When the Eagle Screamed: The Romantic Horizon in American Diplomacy, 1800-1860. (Illus., Orig.). 1966. pap. 7.95x (ISBN 0-471-31001-8). Wiley.

Goff, Beatrice L. Symbols of Ancient Egypt in the Late Period (21st Dynasty) (Religion & Society Ser.). 1979. text ed. 91.75x (ISBN 90-279-7622-8). Mouton.

Goff, C. & Reasons, C. Corporate Crime in Canada: A Critical Analysis of Anti-Combines Legislation. 1978. pap. 8.50 (ISBN 0-13-173302-8). P-H.

Goff, Georgeanna, jt. auth. see Guth, Phyllis.

Goff, Harry. Inventions Wanted. 1981. 5.95 (ISBN 0-914960-24-5). Green Hill.

--Inventions Wanted! LC 79-56695. (Illus.). 160p. (Orig.). 1980. text ed. 8.95 (ISBN 0-914960-27-X, Dist. by Caroline Hse); pap. 5.95 (ISBN 0-914960-24-5). Academy Bks.

Goff, Jacques Le see Le Goff, Jacques.

Goff, James & Goff, Margaret. In Every Person Who Hopes... (Orig.). 1980. pap. 3.75 (ISBN 0-377-00096-5). Friend Pr.

Goff, James F., jt. auth. see Dooley, Mary T.

Goff, Margaret, jt. auth. see Goff, James.

Goff, Martyn. The Royal Pavilion Brighton. (Folio Miniature Ser.). 1976. 4.95 (ISBN 0-7181-1477-9, Pub. by Michael Joseph). Merrimack Bk Serv.

--Why Conform? (Liberal Studies Ser.). 1968. pap. text ed. 1.75x o.p. (ISBN 0-435-46538-4). Heinemann Ed.

Goff, Nancy, jt. auth. see Collier, Diana.

Goff, T. J. Le see Le Goff, T. J.

Goff, Walter S. Finance for Managers. 296p. 1980. pap. text ed. 14.95x (ISBN 0-7121-0636-7). Intl Ideas.

Goffart, M. Function & Form in the Sloth. 1971. 37.00 (ISBN 0-08-016090-5). Pergamon.

Goffart, Walter. Barbarians & Romans, A. D. Four Hundred Eighteen to Five Hundred Eighty-Four: The Techniques of Accomodation. LC 80-7522. 240p. 1980. 25.00 (ISBN 0-691-05303-0). Princeton U Pr.

Goffe, Thomas. The Courageous Turk. O'Malley, Susan G. & Orgel, Stephen, eds. LC 78-66772. (Renaissance Drama Ser.). 1979. lib. bdg. 33.00 (ISBN 0-8240-9737-8). Garland Pub.

Goffee, Robert, jt. auth. see Scase, Richard.

Goffin, Robert. Horn of Plenty: The Story of Louis Armstrong. LC 77-8050. (Roots of Jazz). 1977. Repr. of 1947 ed. lib. bdg. 25.00 (ISBN 0-306-77430-5). Da Capo.

--Jazz: From the Congo to the Metropolitan. Schaap, Walter & Feather, Leonard G., trs. from Fr. LC 74-23384. (Roots of Jazz Ser). xii, 254p. 1975. Repr. of 1944 ed. lib. bdg. 22.50 (ISBN 0-306-70680-6). Da Capo.

Goffinet, Donald R., jt. auth. see Portlock, Carol S.

Goffman, Erving. Asylums: Essays on the Social Situation of Mental Patients & Other Inmates. LC 61-13812. 1961. 22.95x o.p. (ISBN 0-202-30000-5). Aldine Pub.

--Asylums: Essays on the Social Situation of Mental Patients & Other Inmates. LC 61-13812. pap. 4.50 (ISBN 0-385-00016-2, A277, Anch). Doubleday.

--Behavior in Public Places: Notes on Social Organization of Gatherings. LC 80-19005. viii, 248p. 1980. Repr. of 1963 ed. lib. bdg. 22.25x (ISBN 0-313-22390-4, GOBP). Greenwood.

--Behavior in Public Places: Notes on the Social Organization of Gatherings. LC 62-11850. 1963. 15.95 (ISBN 0-02-911930-8); pap. 4.50 (ISBN 0-02-911940-5). Free Pr.

--Encounters: Two Studies in the Sociology of Interaction. LC 61-16844. (Orig.). 1961. pap. 4.95 (ISBN 0-672-60818-9). Bobbs.

--Gender Advertisements. (Illus., Orig.). 1979. pap. 5.95 (ISBN 0-06-090633-2, CN 633, CN). Har-Row.

--Interaction Ritual: Essays on Face-To-Face Behavior. LC 67-22457. pap. 2.95 o.p. (ISBN 0-385-08850-7, A596, Anch). Doubleday.

--Presentation of Self in Everyday Life. LC 59-9138. 1959. pap. 3.50 (ISBN 0-385-09402-7, A174, Anch). Doubleday.

--Relations in Public. 390p. 1972. pap. 7.95x (ISBN 0-06-131957-0, TB 1957, Torch). Har-Row.

--Strategic Interaction. LC 74-92857. (Conduct & Communication Ser). 1971. 12.00x (ISBN 0-8122-7607-8); pap. 3.95x (ISBN 0-8122-1011-5, Pa Paperbks). U of Pa Pr.

--Strategic Interaction. 1975. pap. 1.95 o.p. (ISBN 0-345-24842-2). Ballantine.

Goffman, I. J., ed. Federal Taxation As an Instrument of Social & Economic Policy: A Symposium. LC 72-5017. 104p. 1972. Repr. of 1968 ed. lib. bdg. 15.00 (ISBN 0-306-70501-X). Da Capo.

Goffman, William & Warren, Kenneth. Scientific Information Systems & the Principle of Selectivity. 20.95 (ISBN 0-03-056081-0). Praeger.

Goffstein, M. B. An Artist. LC 79-2663. (Illus.). 32p. 1980. 7.95 (ISBN 0-06-022012-0, HarpJ); PLB 7.89 (ISBN 0-06-022013-9). Har-Row.

--Brookie & Her Lamb. rev. ed. 32p. (ps up). 1981. 6.95 (ISBN 0-374-30990-6). FS&G.

--Goldie the Dollmaker. rev. ed. (Illus.). 64p. (ps-3). 1980. 6.95 (ISBN 0-374-32739-4). FS&G.

Goforth, Ellen. Path of Desire. 192p. (Orig.). 1980. pap. 1.50 (ISBN 0-671-57005-6). S&S.

Goforth, Jonathan. By My Spirit. 1967. pap. 2.95 (ISBN 0-87123-034-8, 210034). Bethany Fell.

Goforth, Rosalind. Goforth of China. 1969. pap. 3.95 (ISBN 0-87123-181-6, 200181). Bethany Fell.

--How I Know God Answers Prayer. pap. 1.50 (ISBN 0-8024-3593-9). Moody.

Gogarty, Oliver S. Many Lines to Thee: Letters to G. K. A. Bell from the Martello Tower at Sandycove, Rutland Square & Trinity College, Dublin, 1904-7. Carens, James F., ed. & intro. by. (Illus.). 168p. 1971. text ed. 13.75x (ISBN 0-85105-198-7, Dolmen Pr). Humanities.

Gogna, Ruth M. Hollywood Nineteen Eighty Crossword Puzzle. 80p. (Orig.). (gr. 7 up). 9.95 (ISBN 0-686-64482-4). Alchemy Bks.

Gogol, Nicolai V. The Overcoat, & Other Tales of Good & Evil. Magarshack, David, tr. from Rus. LC 79-17318. 1979. Repr. of 1965 ed. lib. bdg. 10.00x (ISBN 0-8376-0442-7). Bentley.

Gogol, Nikolai. Arabesques. Tulloch, Alexander, tr. from Rus. 1981. 17.50 (ISBN 0-88233-435-2). Ardis Pubs.

--Mirgorad: Four Tales. Magarshack, David, tr. (Funk & W Bk.). 1969. pap. 2.50 o.s.i. (ISBN 0-308-60067-3, M62, TYC-T). T Y Crowell.

Gogol, Nikolai V. The Government Inspector. LC 73-187162. (Drama Editions Ser: No. 7). 1972. 2.45x (ISBN 0-8166-0640-4); pap. 1.95x (ISBN 0-8166-0642-0). U of Minn Pr.

--Taras Bulba & Other Tales. 1977. 7.50x (ISBN 0-460-00740-8, Evman); pap. 2.75 o.p. (ISBN 0-460-01740-3). Dutton.

Gogos, Costas G., jt. auth. see Tadmor, Zehev.

Goguel, Jean. Tectonics. Thalmann, H. E., tr. LC 62-7477. (Geology Ser.). (Illus.). 1962. 29.95x (ISBN 0-7167-0217-7). W H Freeman.

Gohagan, John K. Quantitative Analysis for Public Policy. (Quantitative Methods for Management). (Illus.). 1980. text ed. 25.00x (ISBN 0-07-023570-8); instructor's manual 8.95 (ISBN 0-07-023571-6); solutions manual 8.95 (ISBN 0-07-023571-6). McGraw.

Gohlke, Annette & Gohlke, Annette, eds. Sweets 'n' Treats. (Illus.). 68p. (Orig.). 1980. pap. 2.95 (ISBN 0-89821-034-8). Reiman Assocs.

Gohm, Richard De De see Van De Gohm, Richard.

Gohmann, John W. Arbitration & Representation: Applications in Air & Rail Labor Relations. LC 80-84183. 336p. 1981. text ed. 22.50 (ISBN 0-8403-2335-2). Kendall-Hunt.

Gohn, Jack B., ed. see Benoit, Emile.

Goh Poh Seng. If We Dream Too Long. (Writing in Asia Ser.). 1972. text ed. 5.50x (ISBN 0-686-60439-3, 00225). Heinemann Ed.

Goin, Coleman J., et al. Introduction to Herpetology. 3rd ed. LC 77-13554. (Illus.). 1978. text ed. 20.95x (ISBN 0-7167-0020-4). W H Freeman.

Goin, John M. & Goin, Maria K. Changing the Body: Psychological Effects of Plastic Surgery. 240p. 1981. write for info. soft cover (3630-0). Williams & Wilkins.

Goin, Kenneth, jt. ed. see Cross, Lee.

Goin, Maria K., jt. auth. see Goin, John M.

Goines, David L. A Constructed Roman Alphabet. 1981. 40.00 (ISBN 0-87923-391-5); ltd. ed. 140.00 (ISBN 0-87923-376-1). Godine.

Goins, Charles R. & Morris, John W. Oklahoma Homes: Past & Present. LC 80-5239. (Illus.). 288p. 1981. 25.00 (ISBN 0-8061-1668-4). U of Okla Pr.

Goins, W. C. & Sheffield, Riley. Blowout Prevention. 2nd ed. 300p. 1981. 19.95 (ISBN 0-87201-073-2). Gulf Pub.

Goirand, Roger, jt. auth. see Cohen, Jean P.

Goitein, H. Primitive Ordeal & Modern Law. xvii, 302p. 1980. Repr. of 1923 ed. lib. bdg. 32.50x (ISBN 0-8377-0612-2). Rothman.

Goitein, S. D. A Mediterranean Society: The Jewish Communities of the Arab World As Portrayed in the Documents of the Cairo Geniza. Incl. Vol. I. Economic Foundations. 1968. 21.50x (ISBN 0-520-00484-1); Vol. 2. The Community. 1971. 30.00x (ISBN 0-520-01867-2); Vol. 3. The Family. 1978. 27.50x (ISBN 0-520-03265-9). (Near Eastern Center, UCLA). U of Cal Pr.

Gojmerac, Walter L. Bees, Bee Keeping, Honey & Pollination. (Illus.). 1980. lib. bdg. 19.50 (ISBN 0-87055-342-9). AVI.

Gokak, Vinayak K. English in India. 1964. 7.50x (ISBN 0-210-34041-X). Asia.

Gokhale, B. G. Surat in the Seventeenth Century: A Study in Urban Hstory of Pre-Modern India. (Scandinavian Inst. of Asian Studies: No. 28). 1977. pap. text ed. 12.50x (ISBN 0-7007-0099-4). Humanities.

Gokhfeld, D. A. & Cherniavsky, O. F. Limit Analysis of Structures at Thermal Cycling. (Mechanics of Plastic Solids Ser.: No. 4). 576p. 1980. 110.00x (ISBN 90-286-0455-3). Sijthoff & Noordhoff.

Golan, Aviezier & Pinkas, Danny. Shula: Code Name the Pearl. 1981. pap. 3.50 (ISBN 0-440-17805-3). Dell.

Golan, Galia. The Soviet Union & the Palestinian Liberation Organization: Uneasy Alliance. LC 80-18760. 304p. 1980. 24.95 (ISBN 0-03-057319-X). Praeger.

--Yom Kippur & After. LC 76-2278. (Soviet & East European Studies). 1977. 38.50 (ISBN 0-521-21090-9). Cambridge U Pr.

Golan, Matti. The Geneva Crisis. 288p. 1981. 11.95 (ISBN 0-89479-073-0). A & W Pubs.

Golan, Naomi. Treatment in Crisis Situations. LC 77-85350. (Treatment Approaches in the Human Services Ser., Gen. Ed. Francis J. Turner). 1978. text ed. 15.95 (ISBN 0-02-912060-8). Free Pr.

Golany, Gideon. Housing in Arid Lands Design & Planning. LC 80-41108. 257p. 1980. 104.95 (ISBN 0-470-27055-1). Halsted Pr.

--Innovations for Future Cities. LC 75-36410. (Illus.). 1976. text ed. 28.95 (ISBN 0-275-22860-6). Praeger.

--International Urban Growth Policies: New-Town Contributions. LC 77-28274. 1978. 40.00 (ISBN 0-471-03748-6, Pub. by Wiley-Interscience). Wiley.

--New-Town Planning: Principles & Practice. LC 76-15958. 1976. 37.50 (ISBN 0-471-31038-7, Pub. by Wiley-Interscience). Wiley.

--New Towns Planning & Development: A Worldwide Bibliography. LC 72-93819. (Research Reports: No. 20). (Illus.). 1973. pap. 4.75 (ISBN 0-87420-320-1). Urban Land.

Golany, Gideon, ed. Arid Zone Settlement Planning: The Israeli Experience. (Pergamon Policy Studies). 1979. 53.00 (ISBN 0-08-023378-3). Pergamon.

Golay, Frank H. Philippines: Public Policy & National Economic Development. 473p. 1968. 25.00x (ISBN 0-8014-0153-4); pap. 5.95 1968 ed. (ISBN 0-8014-9075-8, CP75). Cornell U Pr.

Golbus, Mitchell S. & Hall, Bryan D., eds. Diagnosti Approaches to Malformed Fetus, Abortus, Stillborn & Deceased Newborn. LC 79-2369. (Alan R. Liss Ser.: Vol. 15, No. 5a). 1979. 22.00 (ISBN 0-8451-1028-4). March of Dimes.

Gold, Annalee. How to Sell Fashion. 2nd ed. LC 78-51903. (Illus.). 1978. 12.50 (ISBN 0-87005-201-2). Fairchild.

Gold, Arthur & Fizdale, Robert. Misia: The Life of Misia Sert. (Illus.). 340p. 1981. Repr. pap. price not set (ISBN 0-688-00391-5, Quill). Morrow.

Gold, Avie. Hoshanos. (Art Scroll Mesorah Ser.). 160p. 1980. 8.95 (ISBN 0-89906-162-1); pap. 5.95 (ISBN 0-89906-163-X). Mesorah Pubns.

Gold, B. Brown. The Organization of Afferents from the Brain Stem Nuclei to the Cerebellar Cortex in the Cat. (Advances in Anatomy, Embryology & Cell Biology: Vol. 62). (Illus.). 100p. 1980. pap. 28.30 (ISBN 0-387-09960-3). Springer-Verlag.

Gold, Bela. Productivity, Technology, & Capital Economic Analysis, Managerial Strategies, & Government Policies. LC 79-4749. 1979. 26.95 (ISBN 0-669-02957-2). Lexington Bks.

Gold, Bela, ed. Research, Technological Change & Economic Analysis. LC 76-50496. (Illus.). 1977. 21.95 (ISBN 0-669-01286-6). Lexington Bks.

--Technological Change: Economics, Management & Environment. LC 74-17112. 1975. 28.00 (ISBN 0-08-018012-4). Pergamon.

Gold, Don. The Priest. LC 80-22752. 320p. 1981. 13.95 (ISBN 0-03-053981-1). Hr&W.

Gold, Eddie. Eddie Gold's White Sox & Cubs Trivia Book. 144p. 1981. pap. 3.95 (ISBN 0-695-81574-1). Follett.

Gold, Edgar. Maritime Transport: The Evolution of International Marine Policy & Shipping Law. LC 80-8641. (Illus.). 1981. write for info. (ISBN 0-669-04338-9). Lexington Bks.

Gold, F., tr. see Bichat, Xavier.

Gold, Faye, et al. Modern Supermarket Operations. 3rd. rev. ed. (Illus.). 260p. 1981. text ed. 18.50 (ISBN 0-87005-263-2). Fairchild.

Gold, H., jt. auth. see Calmon, C.

Gold, Harvey J. Mathematical Modeling of Biological Systems: An Introductory Guidebook. LC 77-8193. 1977. 27.95 (ISBN 0-471-02092-3, Pub. by Wiley-Interscience). Wiley.

Gold, Herbert. My Last Two Thousand Years. 1972. 8.95 o.p. (ISBN 0-394-47098-2). Random.

--A Walk on the West Side: California on the Brink. LC 80-70216. 208p. 1981. 10.95 (ISBN 0-87795-305-8); pap. 4.95 (ISBN 0-87795-322-8). Arbor Hse.

Gold, Jay J. & Josimovich, John B. Gynecological Endocrinology. 3rd ed. (Illus.). 918p. 1980. pap. 62.50 (ISBN 0-06-140954-5, Harper Medical). Har-Row.

Gold, Jeffrey S., ed. see Schain, George M.

Gold, Louise, jt. auth. see Kane, Kay.

Gold, Marc. Marc Gold: "Did I Say That?". Articles & Commentary on the Try Another Way System. LC 80-51793. (Illus.). 347p. 1980. pap. text ed. 15.95 (ISBN 0-87822-219-7, 2197). Res Press.

--Try Another Way Training Manual. LC 80-52142. 105p. (Orig.). 1980. pap. 5.95 (ISBN 0-87822-222-7, 2227). Res Press.

Gold, Marvin, jt. auth. see Leslie, Glenn F.

Gold, Robert. Point of Departure. (gr. 7-12). 1981. pap. 1.50 (ISBN 0-440-96983-2, LE). Dell.

Gold, Robert, ed. Stepping Stones. (Orig.). (YA) (gr. 7-12). 1981. pap. 1.50 (ISBN 0-440-98269-3, LE). Dell.

Gold, Ronald & Yankaskas, Bonnie C., eds. Epidemiology & Public Health. 2nd ed. LC 79-83719. (Clinical Sciences PreTest Self-Assessment & Review Ser.). (Illus.). 1980. 9.95 (ISBN 0-07-050967-0). McGraw-Pretest.

Gold, Sharlya. Amelia Quackenbush. LC 73-7129. (gr. 3-6). 1973. 5.95 (ISBN 0-395-28856-8, Clarion). HM.

--Time to Take Sides. LC 76-8265. (gr. 5 up). 1976. 6.95 (ISBN 0-395-28905-X, Clarion). HM.

Gold, Sharon. The Woman's Day Book of Beauty, Health & Fitness Hints. LC 80-12022. (Illus.). 166p. 1980. pap. 5.95 (ISBN 0-688-08611-X, Quill). Morrow.

Gold, Victor, ed. Advances in Physical Organic Chemistry. Incl. Vol. 1. 1963. 59.00 (ISBN 0-12-033501-8); Vol. 2. 1964. 40.50 (ISBN 0-12-033502-6); Vol. 3. 1965. 39.00 (ISBN 0-12-033503-4); Vol. 4. 1966. 49.50 (ISBN 0-12-033504-2); Vol. 5. 1967. 54.00 (ISBN 0-12-033505-0); Vol. 6. 1968. 50.00 (ISBN 0-12-033506-9); Vol. 7. 1969. 48.50 (ISBN 0-12-033507-7); Vol. 8. 1970. 58.50 (ISBN 0-12-033508-5); Vol. 9. 1972. 41.00 (ISBN 0-12-033509-3); Vol. 10. 1973. 34.50 (ISBN 0-12-033510-7). Acad Pr.

Gold, Winifred A., jt. auth. see Bash, Deborah M.

Goldanskii, V. I., jt. auth. see Fluck, E.

Goldbach, John & Ross, Michael J. Politics, Parties & Power. LC 79-47991. 382p. 1980. 15.95 (ISBN 0-913530-21-2); pap. 10.95 (ISBN 0-686-64356-9). Palisades Pub.

Goldbach, Joseph. The Other Mafia. 1977. 5.00 o.p. (ISBN 0-682-48307-9). Exposition.

Goldbarth, Albert. Eurekas. 24p. 1981. pap. 3.95 (ISBN 0-918518-21-0). St Luke TN.

--January Thirty-First. LC 73-22534. 120p. 1974. pap. 5.95 (ISBN 0-385-05955-8). Doubleday.

Goldbeck, David, jt. auth. see Goldbeck, Nikki.

Goldbeck, Nikki & Goldbeck, David. The Supermarket Handbook: Access to Whole Foods. LC 73-4084. (Illus.). 432p. 1973. 9.95 o.p. (ISBN 0-06-011581-5, HarpT). Har-Row.

Goldbeck, W. B. Mental Illness Programs for Employees. (Springer Ser. in Industry & Health Care: Vol. 9). 250p. 1980. pap. 12.00 (ISBN 0-387-90479-4). Springer-Verlag.

Goldberg, jt. auth. see Schwarz.

Goldberg, Alan M. & Hanin, Israel, eds. Biology of Cholinergic Function. LC 74-14473. 730p. 1976. 48.00 (ISBN 0-911216-98-7). Raven.

Goldberg, Alvin & Larson, Carl. Group Communication: Discussion Processes & Application. LC 74-5295. (Speech Communication Ser.). (Illus.). 224p. 1975. ref. ed. 15.95x (ISBN 0-13-365221-1). P-H.

Goldberg, Art, jt. auth. see Garry, Charles.

Goldberg, Arthur J. Equal Justice: The Supreme Court in the Warren Era. LC 72-167921. (Julius Rosenthal Memorial Lecture Ser.: 1971). 100p. 1971. 7.95x o.s.i. (ISBN 0-8101-0363-X). Northwestern U Pr.

Goldberg, Barry B. Abdominal Gray Scale Ultrasonography. LC 77-5889. (Wiley Series in Diagnostic & Therapeutic Radiology). 1977. 45.00 (ISBN 0-471-01510-5, Pub. by Wiley Medical). Wiley.

--Ultrasound in Cancer. (Clinics in Diagnostic Ultrasound Ser.: Vol. 6). (Illus.). 224p. 1980. 20.50 (ISBN 0-443-08144-1). Churchill.

Goldberg, Carl & Goldberg, Merle C. The Human Circle: An Existential Approach to the New Group Therapies. LC 73-75523. 1973. 16.95 (ISBN 0-911012-67-2). Nelson-Hall.

Goldberg, David M. Clinical Biochemistry Review, Vol. 2. 416p. 1981. 24.00 (ISBN 0-471-08297-X, Pub. by Wiley Med). Wiley.

Goldberg, David M., ed. Annual Review of Clinical Biochemistry, Vol. 1. LC 80-15463. 1980. 19.95 (ISBN 0-471-04036-3, Pub. by Wiley Med). Wiley.

Goldberg, David M. & Werner, Mario, eds. Progress in Clinical Enzymology. LC 80-80965. (Illus.). 304p. 1980. 45.00 (ISBN 0-89352-091-8). Masson Pub.

Goldberg, E. P. & Nakajima, A. Biomedical Polymers: Polymeric Materials & Pharmaceuticals for Biomedical Use. LC 80-17691. 1980. 32.00 (ISBN 0-12-287580-X). Acad Pr.

Goldberg, Edward D., ed. The Sea: Ideas & Observations on Progress in the Study of the Seas, Vol. 5, Marine Chemistry. LC 62-18366. 896p. 1974. 65.00 (ISBN 0-471-31090-5, Pub. by Wiley-Interscience). Wiley.

--Strategies for Marine Pollution Monitoring. LC 76-12490. 1976. 35.00 (ISBN 0-471-31070-0, Pub. by Wiley-Interscience). Wiley.

Goldberg, Edward D., et al, eds. The Sea; Ideas & Observations on Progress in the Study on the Seas, Vol. 6: Marine Modeling. LC 62-18366. 992p. 1977. 69.95 (ISBN 0-471-31091-3, Pub. by Wiley-Interscience). Wiley.

Goldberg, Edward M., jt. auth. see Dial, O. E.

Goldberg, Enid A. How to Run a School Newspaper. LC 74-101898. (Illus.). (gr. 7 up). 1970. 8.95 o.p. (ISBN 0-397-31124-9). Lippincott.

--How to Write an Essay. 1981. pap. text ed. 8.95x (ISBN 0-673-15181-6). Scott F.

Goldberg, Gale, jt. auth. see Middleman, R.

Goldberg, Gerald J. Fate of Innocence. 1965. pap. text ed. 7.50x (ISBN 0-13-308189-3). P-H.

Goldberg, H., jt. auth. see DiMascio, A.

Goldberg, Harold. Extending the Limits of Reliability Theory. 300p. 1981. 30.00 (ISBN 0-471-07799-2, Pub. by Wiley Interscience). Wiley.

Goldberg, Harvey E., ed. & tr. from Hebrew. The Book of Mordechai: A Study of the Jews of Libya - Selections from the Highid Mordekhai of Mordechai Hakohen. LC 80-11470. 1980. text ed. 19.50x (ISBN 0-89727-005-3). Inst Study Human.

Goldberg, Henry I. see Moss, Albert A.

Goldberg, Herb. The Hazards of Being Male: Surviving the Myth of Masculine Privilege. 1977. pap. 2.25 (ISBN 0-451-09437-9, E9437, Sig). NAL.

--The New Male: From Self-Destruction to Self-Care. 1980. pap. 2.95 (ISBN 0-451-09339-9, E9339, Sig). NAL.

Goldberg, Hyman J. Your Mouth Is Your Business: The Dentists' Guide to Better Health. (Appleton Consumer Health Guides). (Illus.). 215p. 1980. 12.95 (ISBN 0-8385-9943-5); pap. 5.95 (ISBN 0-8385-9942-7). ACC.

Goldberg, I. Ignacy. Selected Bibliography of Special Education. LC 67-19388. (Orig.). 1967. pap. 3.25x (ISBN 0-8077-1434-8). Tchrs Coll.

Goldberg, Isaac. Tin Pan Alley. LC 60-63364. (Illus.). 1961. pap. 3.95 (ISBN 0-8044-6196-1). Ungar.

--Wonder of Words: An Introduction to Language for Every Man. LC 74-164294. 1971. Repr. of 1938 ed. 22.00 (ISBN 0-8103-3777-0). Gale.

Goldberg, Isaac, jt. auth. see Witmark, Isidore.

Goldberg, Isaac, ed. & tr. see Assis, Joaquim M.

Goldberg, Isaac, tr. see Kobrin, Leon.

Goldberg, Ivan K., jt. auth. see Kutscher, Austin H.

Goldberg, Jack L. & Schwartz, Arthur J. Systems of Ordinary Differential Equations: An Introduction. (Herstein-Rota Ser). 1972. text ed. 20.50 o.p. (ISBN 0-06-042384-6, HarpC). Har-Row.

Goldberg, Joe. Jazz Masters of the Fifties. (The Roots of Jazz Ser.). 246p. 1980. Repr. of 1965 ed. lib. bdg. 22.50 (ISBN 0-306-76031-2). Da Capo.

Goldberg, Kenneth P., jt. auth. see Weinberg, Sharon L.

Goldberg, Larry. Goldberg's Diet Catalog. (Illus.). 1977. 17.50 (ISBN 0-02-544480-8). Macmillan.

Goldberg, Lawrence G. & White, Lawrence J. The Deregulation of the Banking & Securities Industries. LC 78-19705. 1979. 23.95 (ISBN 0-669-02720-0). Lexington Bks.

Goldberg, Lazer. Children & Science. LC 70-106554. 1970. 6.95 o.p. (ISBN 0-684-10207-2, ScribT). Scribner.

--Learning to Choose: Stories & Essays About Science, Technology, & Human Values. LC 76-13919. (Encore Edition). 224p. (gr. k-12). 1976. 3.95 o.p. (ISBN 0-684-15692-X, ScribT). Scribner.

Goldberg, Louis P. Lawless Judges. LC 74-97451. Repr. of 1935 ed. 17.50x (ISBN 0-8371-2696-7). Negro U Pr.

Goldberg, Louis P. & Levenson, Eleanore. Lawless Judges. LC 73-138498. (Civil Liberties in American History Ser). 1970. Repr. of 1935 ed. lib. bdg. 29.50 (ISBN 0-306-70070-0). Da Capo.

Goldberg, M. Hirsh. Just Because They're Jewish: The Incredible, Ironic, Bizarre, Funny, & Provocative in the Way Jews Are Seen by Other People. LC 78-6400. 264p. 1981. pap. 6.95 (ISBN 0-8128-6122-1). Stein & Day.

Goldberg, Martin. A Guide to Psychiatric Diagnosis & Understanding for the Helping Professions. LC 73-77747. 1973. 15.95 (ISBN 0-88229-104-1). Nelson-Hall.

Goldberg, Maxwell H. Design in Liberal Learning. LC 71-110645. (Higher Education Ser.). 1971. 11.95x o.p. (ISBN 0-87589-102-0). Jossey-Bass.

Goldberg, Merle C., jt. auth. see Goldberg, Carl.

Goldberg, Morton E., ed. Pharmacological & Biochemical Properties of Drug Substances. LC 77-88184. 30.00 (ISBN 0-917330-17-X). Am Pharm Assn.

Goldberg, Morton H., jt. auth. see Topazian, Richard G.

Goldberg, Moses. The Analysis of Mineral Number Four. (Orig.). 1981. playscript 2.00 (ISBN 0-87602-234-4). Anchorage.

--The Men's Cottage. (Orig.). 1980. playscript 2.00 (ISBN 0-87602-229-8). Anchorage.

Goldberg, Philip & Rubin, Richard. The Small Business Guide to Borrowing Money. (Illus.). 1980. 19.95 (ISBN 0-07-054198-1). McGraw.

Goldberg, Philip, jt. auth. see Hegarty, Christopher.

Goldberg, Phyllis Z. So What If You Can't Chew, Eat Hearty! Recipes & a Guide for the Healthy & Happy Eating of Soft & Pureed Foods. (Illus.). 152p. 1980. pap. 13.95 (ISBN 0-398-04065-6). C C Thomas.

Goldberg, Reuben. Rube Goldberg Vs. the Machine Age. LC 68-31688. (Illus.). 1968. 12.95 (ISBN 0-8038-6305-5). Hastings.

Goldberg, Richard A., jt. auth. see Herman, John R.

Goldberg, Richard R. Methods of Real Analysis. 2nd ed. LC 75-30615. 1976. text ed. 25.95 (ISBN 0-471-31065-4). Wiley.

Goldberg, Robert L. A Systems Approach to Library Program Development. LC 76-18157. 1976. 10.00 (ISBN 0-8108-0944-3). Scarecrow.

Goldberg, S. L. An Essay on King Lear. LC 73-84318. 212p. 1974. 33.50 (ISBN 0-521-20200-0); pap. 10.50x (ISBN 0-521-09831-9). Cambridge U Pr.

Goldberg, Samuel. Introduction to Difference Equations: With Illustrative Examples from Economics, Psychology & Sociology. LC 58-10223. (Illus.). 1958. pap. 14.50 (ISBN 0-471-31051-4). Wiley.

--Probability: An Introduction. (gr. 11 up). 1960. ref. ed. 19.95 (ISBN 0-13-711580-6); pap. 0.50 ans. bk. (ISBN 0-13-711572-5). P-H.

Goldberg, Samuel, jt. auth. see Bishop, Richard.

Goldberg, Sander M. The Making of Menander's Comedy. 1980. 17.50 (ISBN 0-520-04250-6). U of Cal Pr.

Goldberg, Stanley J., et al. Pediatric & Adolescent Echocardiography: A Handbook. 2nd ed. (Illus.). 480p. 1980. 39.50 (ISBN 0-8151-3720-6). Year Bk Med.

Goldberg, Stanley M., et al. Essentials of Anorectal Surgery. (Illus.). 416p. 1980. text ed. 37.50 (ISBN 0-397-50417-9). Lippincott.

Goldberg, Stuart C. Private Placements & Restricted Securities, 2 vols. rev. ed. LC 70-163723. 1978. looseleaf with 1979 rev. pages 110.00 (ISBN 0-87632-078-7). Boardman.

Goldberg, Vicki, ed. Thinking About Photography: Writings from 1816 to the Present. 1981. 14.95 (ISBN 0-671-25034-5, Touchstone); pap. 6.95 (ISBN 0-686-68487-7). S&S.

Goldberger, Arthur S. Econometric Theory. LC 64-10370. (Wiley Series in Probability & Mathematical Statistics). (Illus.). 1964. 29.95 (ISBN 0-471-31101-4). Wiley.

Goldberger, Ary L. Myocardial Infarction. 2nd ed. LC 78-31981. (Illus.). 1979. text ed. 29.50 (ISBN 0-8016-1860-6). Mosby.

Goldberger, Ary L. & Goldberger, Emanuel. Clinical Electrocardiography: A Simplified Approach. 2nd ed. LC 80-27024. (Illus.). 278p. 1981. text ed. 14.95 (ISBN 0-8016-1865-7). Mosby.

Goldberger, Emanuel. A Textbook of Clinical Cardiology. (Illus.). 934p. 1981. text ed. 35.00 (ISBN 0-8016-1864-9). Mosby.

Goldberger, Emanuel, jt. auth. see Goldberger, Ary L.

Goldbeter, A., jt. ed. see Lefever, R.

Goldblatt, Burt, jt. auth. see Devaney, John.

Goldblatt, Burt, jt. auth. see Green, Stanley.

Goldblatt, Burt, jt. auth. see Messick, Hank.

Goldblatt, Harold, tr. see Halbwachs, Maurice.

Goldblatt, Howard. Hsiao Hung. LC 75-30650. (World Authors Ser.: China: No. 386). 1976. lib. bdg. 12.50 (ISBN 0-8057-6228-0). Twayne.

Goldblatt, Howard, tr. see Chen, Jo-hsi.

Goldblatt, Howard, tr. see Chun-ming, Hwang.

Goldblatt, Howard, tr. see Hsiao Hung.

Goldblatt, R. Topoi: The Categorial Analysis of Logic. (Studies in Logic & the Foundations of Mathematics Ser.: Vol. 98). 1980. 68.50 (ISBN 0-444-85207-7, North Holland). Elsevier.

Goldblith, S. A., et al, eds. Freeze Drying & Advanced Food Technology. 1975. 98.00 (ISBN 0-12-288450-7). Acad Pr.

Goldblith, Samuel A. & Decareau, Robert V. An Annotated Bibliography on Microwaves: Their Properties, Production, & Application to Food Processing. 1973. 21.50x (ISBN 0-262-07049-9). MIT Pr.

Goldblum, N., et al, eds. Rift Valley Fever. (Contributions to Epidemiology & Biostatistics Ser.: Vol. 3). (Illus.). 200p. 1981. pap. 60.00 (ISBN 3-8055-1770-X). S Karger.

Golde, Roger A. Muddling Through: The Art of Properly Unbusinesslike Management. LC 76-888. 1976. 12.95 (ISBN 0-8144-5411-9). Am Mgmt.

Golden, Bruce. Ocular Inflammatory Disease. (Illus.). 352p. 1974. 32.00 (ISBN 0-398-02792-7). C C Thomas.

Golden, Charles A., et al. Interpretation of the Halstead Reitan Neuropsychological Test Battery: A Casebook Approach. 1980. 26.50 (ISBN 0-8089-1298-4). Grune.

Golden, Dean W. & Wright, A. J. Dancing in Your Ear: Poems of Protest, Humor & Love. (Doctor Jazz Press Chapbook Ser.: No. 1). (Illus.). 40p. (Orig.). 1980. pap. 2.50 (ISBN 0-934002-00-2). Doctor Jazz.

Golden, Duke L. Statics & Strengths of Materials. LC 76-105328. 1970. text ed. 21.95 (ISBN 0-675-09366-X). Merrill.

Golden, Edward J. The Art & Science of Real Estate Investment Analysis. 300p. 1980. pap. text ed. 15.00 (ISBN 0-9604532-0-2). Adv Prof Seminars.

Golden, Frederic. Quasars, Pulsars, & Black Holes: A Scientific Detective Story. LC 75-37646. (Illus.). 128p. 1976. 9.95 o.p. (ISBN 0-684-14501-4, ScribJ). Scribner.

Golden, Harry, jt. auth. see Metzker, Isaac.

Golden, Hilda. Urbanization & Cities: A Historical & Comparitive Perspective on Our Urbanizing World. 384p. 1981. text ed. 18.95 (ISBN 0-669-03175-5). Heath.

Golden, Jim & Baldwin, Bob. Economics & Public Policy: Principles, Problems & Applications. 1979. pap. text ed. 8.95 (ISBN 0-89529-098-7). Avery Pub.

Golden, Joseph. Olympus on Main Street: A Process for Planning a Community Arts Facility. LC 80-16479. 248p. 1980. 9.95 (ISBN 0-8156-0156-5). Syracuse U Pr.

Golden, Richard. The Godly Rebellion: Parisian Cures & the Religious Fronde, 1652-1662. LC 80-25282. 264p. 1981. 22.50x (ISBN 0-8078-1466-0). U of NC Pr.

Golden, Samuel A. Frederick Goddard Tuckerman. (U. S. Authors Ser.: No. 104). 1966. lib. bdg. 10.95 (ISBN 0-8057-0748-4). Twayne.

--Jean Le Clerc. (World Authors Ser.: Netherlands: No. 209). lib. bdg. 10.95 (ISBN 0-8057-2232-7). Twayne.

Goldenberg, Herbert, jt. auth. see Goldenberg, Irene.

Goldenberg, I. Ira. Oppression & Social Intervention: The Human Condition & the Problems of Change. LC 78-6869. (Illus.). 1978. 13.95 (ISBN 0-88229-349-4); pap. 6.95 (ISBN 0-88229-601-9). Nelson-Hall.

Goldenberg, Irene & Goldenberg, Herbert. A Family Therapy Workbook. 1980. pap. text ed. 4.95 (ISBN 0-8185-0412-9). Brooks-Cole.

Goldenberg, Leon & Weese, Harry. Housing for the Elderly: New Trends in Europe. 1981. lib. bdg. 29.50 (ISBN 0-8240-7139-5). Garland Pub.

Goldenberg, Naomi R. Changing of the Gods: Feminism & the End. LC 78-19602. 1979. 9.95 (ISBN 0-8070-1110-X); pap. 5.95 (ISBN 0-8070-1111-8, BP600). Beacon Pr.
Goldenberg, Robert. The Sabbath-Law of R. Meir. LC 78-14370. (Brown University. Brown Judaic Studies: No. 6). 1978. pap. 9.00 (ISBN 0-89130-249-2, 140006). Scholars Pr Ca.
Goldenson, Dan, jt. auth. see Sandman, Peter.
Goldenson, Robert M. All About the Human Mind: An Introduction to Psychology for Young People. (Allabout Ser.: No. 47). (Illus.). (gr. 4 up). 1963. PLB 5.39 (ISBN 0-394-90247-5, BYR). Random.
Goldenson, Robert M., jt. auth. see Hartley, Ruth E.
Goldenthal, Allan B. Think Chinese, Speak Chinese. (Illus.). (gr. 10-12). 1978. 16.95 (ISBN 0-88345-367-3); pap. text ed. 12.95 (ISBN 0-88345-358-4); cassettes 40.00 (ISBN 0-686-67814-1). Regents Pub.
Golden-Wolfe, Malka. Malka - A Total Celebration (a survival manual) LC 80-53000. (Illus., Orig.). 1980. pap. 5.85 (ISBN 0-937946-00-1). Univ Goddess.
Golder, Diane. The Newspaper & You. (Orig.). (gr. 9). 1980. wkbk. 5.83 (ISBN 0-87720-300-8). AMSCO Sch.
Gol'dfarb, D. M., jt. ed. see Dubinin, N. P.
Goldfarb, I. William & Yates, Anthony P. Critical Care Medicine. 1980. Repr. of 1977 ed. write for info. (ISBN 0-935170-01-4). Synapse Pubns.
Goldfarb, Johanna & Tibbetts, Edith. Breastfeeding Handbook: A Practical Reference for Physicians, Nurses & Other Health Professionals. LC 72-29691. (Illus.). 256p. 1980. pap. text ed. 14.95x (ISBN 0-89490-030-7). Enslow Pubs.
Goldfarb, Joseph, jt. auth. see Glick, Stanley D.
Goldfarb, Leo. The Weather Book for Pilots. (Illus.). Date not set. spiral bdg. 8.95 (ISBN 0-911721-72-X, Pub. by Weather Book). Aviation.
Goldfarb, Ronald L. Contempt Power. LC 63-20342. 1963. 22.50x (ISBN 0-231-02654-4). Columbia U Pr.
--Migrant Farm Workers: A Culture of Despair. 232p. 1981. text ed. 16.00 (ISBN 0-8138-1790-0). Iowa St U Pr.
Goldfarb, Sally. Inside the Law Schools. 1980. pap. 8.95 (ISBN 0-525-47638-5). Dutton.
Goldfarb, Sidney. Messages. LC 74-143298. 96p. 1971. 6.95 (ISBN 0-374-20861-1); pap. 2.95 o.p. (ISBN 0-374-50933-6). FS&G.
--Speech, for Instance. LC 69-13743. 1969. pap. 1.95 o.p. (ISBN 0-374-50788-0, N371). FS&G.
Goldfarb, Theodore, jt. auth. see Swartz, Clifford.
Goldfarb, W. Office Gynecology: An Audiovisual Book. 1971. including three cassettes 37.95 (ISBN 0-685-54393-5). Krieger.
Goldfein, Donna. Every Woman's Guide to Getting Ready for the Career You Want. LC 80-83692. 128p. (Orig.). 1981. pap. 5.95 (ISBN 0-89087-935-4). Celestial Arts.
Goldfield, David R. & Brownell, Blaine A. Urban America: From Downtown to No Town. LC 78-69562. (Illus.). 1979. pap. text ed. 11.50 (ISBN 0-395-27397-8). HM.
Goldfield, David R. & Lane, James B., eds. The Enduring Ghetto: Sources & Readings. 1973. pap. text ed. 3.95 o.p. (ISBN 0-397-47285-4). Lippincott.
Goldfield, David R., jt. ed. see Brownell, Blaine A.
Goldfinger, Erno. British Furniture Today. (Illus.). 1951. 2.75 o.p. (ISBN 0-85458-899-X). Transatlantic.
Goldfrank, Walter L., ed. The World-System of Capitalism: Past & Present. LC 78-26935. (Political Economy of the World-System Annuals: Vol. 2). 1979. 20.00x (ISBN 0-8039-1105-X); pap. 9.95x (ISBN 0-8039-1106-8). Sage.
Goldgar, Bertrand A., ed. see Pope, Alexander.
Goldhaber, C. Information Strategies: New Pathways to Corporate Power. 1979. 18.95 (ISBN 0-13-464651-7). P-H.
Goldhaber, Gerald M. & Goldhaber, Marylynn B. Transactional Analysis: Principles & Applications. 368p. 1976. pap. text ed. 6.95x o.p. (ISBN 0-205-05424-2). Allyn.
Goldhaber, Marylynn B., jt. auth. see Goldhaber, Gerald M.
Goldhaber, Nat & Denniston, Denise. TM: An Alphabetical Guide to the Transcendental Meditation Program. (Illus.). 1976. pap. 3.95 (ISBN 0-345-24096-0). Ballantine.
Goldhaber, Stanley, et al. Construction Management: Principles & Practices. LC 76-58397. (Construction Management & Engineering Ser.). 450p. 1977. 28.95 (ISBN 0-471-44270-4, Pub. by Wiley-Interscience). Wiley.
Goldhamer, Herbert. The Soviet Soldier: Soviet Military Management at the Troop Level. LC 74-26727. 1975. 22.50x (ISBN 0-8448-0615-3); pap. 8.75x (ISBN 0-8448-0652-8). Crane-Russak Co.
Goldhammer, Arthur, tr. see Crozier, Michel & Friedberg, Erhard.
Goldhammer, Arthur, tr. see Le Goff, Jacques.
Goldhammer, Arthur, tr. see Rodinson, Maxime.
Goldhawk, Norman, tr. see Schmidt, Martin.
Goldhirsch, A., ed. Mammakarzinom: Neue Aspekte Fuer Die Praxis, 1981. (Journal: Gynaekologische Rundschau: Vol. 21, No. 1). (Illus.). 68p. 1981. pap. write for info. (ISBN 3-8055-2188-X). S Karger.
Goldie, I., ed. Surgery in Rheumatoid Arthritis. (Reconstruction Surgery & Traumatology Ser.: Vol. 18). (Illus.). 200p. 1981. 60.00 (ISBN 3-8055-1445-X). S Karger.
Goldin, Augusta. Bottom of the Sea. LC 66-10194. (A Let's-Read-&-Find-Out Science Bk). (Illus.). (ps-3). 1967. bds. 7.95 (ISBN 0-690-15863-7, TYC-J); PLB 7.89 (ISBN 0-690-15864-5). T Y Crowell.
--Ducks Don't Get Wet. LC 65-11647. (A Let's-Read-&-Find-Out Science Bk). (Illus.). (gr. k-3). PLB 7.89 (ISBN 0-690-24668-4, TYC-J); filmstrip with cassette 14.95 (ISBN 0-690-24671-4); filmstrip with record 11.95 (ISBN 0-690-24669-2). T Y Crowell.
--Geothermal Energy: A Hot Prospect. LC 80-8800. (Illus.). (gr. 7 up). 1981. 10.95 (ISBN 0-15-230662-5, HJ). HarBraceJ.
--Oceans of Energy: Reservoir of Power for the Future. LC 79-3767. (Illus.). 114p. (gr. 7 up). 8.95 (ISBN 0-15-257688-6, HJ). HarBraceJ.
--Pelo Lacio, Pelo Rizo. Palmer, Richard J., tr. LC 68-27324. (A Let's-Read-&-Find-Out Science Bk). (Illus., Span.). (gr. k-3). 1968. PLB 7.89 (ISBN 0-690-77923-2, TYC-J). T Y Crowell.
--Salt. LC 65-18696. (A Let's-Read-&-Find-Out Science Bk). (Illus.). (gr. k-3). 1966. PLB 7.89 (ISBN 0-690-71815-2, TYC-J). T Y Crowell.
--Spider Silk. LC 64-18164. (A Let's-Read-&-Find-Out Science Bk). (Illus.). (gr. k-3). 1964. bds. 6.95 o.p. (ISBN 0-690-76074-4, TYC-J); PLB 7.89 (ISBN 0-690-76075-2); film with records 11.95 (ISBN 0-690-76076-0); filmstrip with cassette 14.95 (ISBN 0-690-76078-7). T Y Crowell.
--Straight Hair, Curly Hair. LC 66-12669. (A Let's-Read-&-Find-Out Science Bk). (Illus.). (gr. k-3). 1966. PLB 7.89 (ISBN 0-690-77921-6, TYC-J); filmstrip with record 11.95 (ISBN 0-690-77924-0); filmstrip with cassette 14.95 (ISBN 0-690-77926-7). T Y Crowell.
--Sunlit Sea. LC 68-17075. (A Let's-Read-&-Find-Out Science Bk). (Illus.). (gr. k-3). 1968. bds. 7.95 (ISBN 0-690-79411-8, TYC-J); PLB 7.89 (ISBN 0-690-79412-6). T Y Crowell.
--Where Does Your Garden Grow? (A Let's-Read-&-Find-Out Science Bk). (Illus.). (gr. k-3). 1967. bds. 7.95 (ISBN 0-690-88357-9, TYC-J); PLB 7.89 (ISBN 0-690-88358-7). T Y Crowell.
Goldin, Frederick, tr. The Song of Roland. 1978. 10.00 (ISBN 0-393-04523-4); pap. 3.95x (ISBN 0-393-09008-6). Norton.
Goldin, Grace. Come Under the Wings: A Midrash on Ruth. 2nd ed. LC 79-91327. 85p. 1980. pap. 4.95 (ISBN 0-8276-0171-9, 451). Jewish Pubn.
Goldin, Milton. Why They Give: American Jews & Their Philanthropies. LC 75-17655. 1976. 10.95 o.s.i. (ISBN 0-02-544560-X, 54456). Macmillan.
Goldin, Stephen. A World Called Solitude. LC 78-22611. (Science Fiction Ser.). 192p. 1981. 9.95 (ISBN 0-385-14375-3). Doubleday.
Goldin, Stephen, jt. auth. see Smith, E. E.
Goldina, Miriam, tr. see Gorchakov, Nikolai M.
Golding, Elliot. Making the News. (Illus.). 241p. 1979. text ed. 35.00x (ISBN 0-582-50460-0). Longman.
Golding, J., et al, eds. Access to Law: The Second Seminar on Australian Lawyers & Social Change. 336p. (Orig.). 1980. pap. text ed. 16.95 (ISBN 0-7081-1305-2, 0581). Bks Australia.
Golding, John. Cubism: A History & an Analysis, 1907-1914. rev. ed. (Icon Edition Ser). (Illus.). 1972. pap. 5.95x o.s.i. (ISBN 0-06-430008-0, IN-8, HarpT). Har-Row.
Golding, Martin P. Philosophy of Law. (Foundation of Philosophy Ser.). 176p. 1975. text ed. 13.50 (ISBN 0-13-664136-9); pap. text ed. 7.95x (ISBN 0-13-664128-8). P-H.
Golding, Martin P., ed. Nature of Law. 1966. 11.95 (ISBN 0-394-30213-3). Random.
Golding, Stephen L., jt. auth. see Roesch, Ronald.
Golding, William. The Brass Butterfly. 1969. pap. 4.95 (ISBN 0-571-09073-7, Pub. by Faber & Faber). Merrimack Bk Serv.
--Darkness Visible. 265p. 1979. 10.95 (ISBN 0-374-13502-9). FS&G.
--Free Fall. LC 60-5431. (YA) (gr. 9-12). 1962. pap. 2.95 (ISBN 0-15-633468-2, H010, Hbgr). HarBraceJ.
--Pincher Martin. LC 57-10059. Orig. Title: Two Deaths of Christopher Martin. 1968. pap. 2.95 (ISBN 0-15-671833-2, HPL32, HPL). HarBraceJ.
--Rites of Passage. 278p. 1980. 10.95 (ISBN 0-374-25086-3). FS&G.
Golding, William G. Inheritors. LC 62-16724. 1963. pap. 3.95 (ISBN 0-15-644379-1, HB64, Harv). HarBraceJ.
Goldkuhl, G., jt. auth. see Sundburg, M.
Goldman. Hydraulics of Multiple Mains. 8.50 o.p. (ISBN 0-686-00161-3). Columbia Graphs.
--Sizing of Services, Meters & House Pipes. 6.00 o.p. (ISBN 0-686-00163-X). Columbia Graphs.
--Water Hammer. 7.00 o.p. (ISBN 0-686-00162-1). Columbia Graphs.
Goldman, jt. auth. see Yardley.
Goldman, Alan H. The Moral Foundations of Professional Ethics. (Philosophy & Society Ser.). 305p. 1980. 22.50x (ISBN 0-8476-6274-8); pap. 9.95x (ISBN 0-8476-6285-3). Rowman.
Goldman, Albert. Carnival in Rio. LC 78-52280. (Illus.). 1978. 19.95 o.p. (ISBN 0-8015-1000-7). Dutton.
--Grass Roots. (Orig.). 1980. pap. 2.75 (ISBN 0-446-85465-4). Warner Bks.
Goldman, Alvin I. Theory of Human Action. 1977. 14.50 (ISBN 0-691-07216-7); pap. 4.95 (ISBN 0-691-01974-6). Princeton U Pr.
Goldman, Alvin L. The Supreme Court & Labor-Management Relations Law. LC 75-42953. 1976. 19.95 (ISBN 0-669-00496-0). Lexington Bks.
Goldman, Barbara, jt. auth. see Forisha, Barbara L.
Goldman, Bernard S., jt. ed. see Adelman, Allen G.
Goldman, Charles R., ed. Primary Productivity in Aquatic Environments. 1966. 22.50x (ISBN 0-520-01425-1). U of Cal Pr.
Goldman, Charles R., et al, eds. Environmental Quality & Water Development. LC 72-83739. (Illus.). 1973. 34.95x (ISBN 0-7167-0256-8). W H Freeman.
Goldman, David, jt. auth. see LaRouche, Lyndon H., Jr.
Goldman, Emma. Living My Life, 2 Vols. LC 73-109546. (Civil Liberties in American History Ser.). Repr. of 1931 ed. lib. bdg. 75.00 (ISBN 0-306-71900-2). Da Capo.
--My Disillusionment in Russia. 8.25 (ISBN 0-8446-0115-2). Peter Smith.
Goldman, George D. & Milman, Donald S., eds. Psychoanalytic Psychotherapy. LC 77-79454. (Topics in Clinical Psychology: 3). 1978. pap. text ed. 7.50 (ISBN 0-201-02513-2). A-W.
Goldman, George D. & Stricker, George, eds. Practical Problems of a Private Psychotherapy Practice. (Illus.). 284p. 1972. 13.25 o.p. (ISBN 0-398-02296-8). C C Thomas.
Goldman, George D., jt. ed. see Milman, Donald S.
Goldman, Guido. German Political System. (Patterns of Government Ser). 1974. pap. text ed. 5.95 (ISBN 0-394-31820-X). Random.
Goldman, Harold L. Student Resource & Activity Manual to Accompany Koontz & Fulmer's a Practical Introduction to Business. rev. ed. 1978. pap. text ed. 6.95x (ISBN 0-256-02044-2). Irwin.
Goldman, Heinz. How to Win Customers. pap. 4.95 (ISBN 0-8015-3898-X, Hawthorn). Dutton.
Goldman, Henry M. & Cohen, D. Walter. Periodontal Therapy. 6th ed. LC 77-22523. (Illus.). 1979. 47.50 (ISBN 0-8016-1875-4). Mosby.
Goldman, Henry M., et al, eds. Current Therapy in Dentistry, Vols. 4-6. (Illus.). Vol. 4, 1970. 37.50 (ISBN 0-8016-1193-8); Vol. 5, 1974. 39.50 (ISBN 0-8016-1194-6); Vol. 6, 1977. 43.50 (ISBN 0-8016-1195-4). Mosby.
Goldman, I. & Krivchenkov, V. D. Problems in Quantum Mechanics. 1961. text ed. 24.00 (ISBN 0-08-009462-7). Pergamon.
Goldman, Irving. The Mouth of Heaven: An Introduction to Kwakiutl Religious Thought. LC 80-11163. 284p. 1981. Repr. of 1975 ed. lib. bdg. write for info. (ISBN 0-89874-136-X). Krieger.
Goldman, J., ed. Health Care Technology Evaluation. (Lecture Notes in Medical Informatics: Vol. 6). 1980. pap. 12.50 (ISBN 0-387-09561-6). Springer-Verlag.
Goldman, Jacquelin. Becoming a Psychotherapist. (Amer. Lec. Psychology Ser.). (Illus.). 140p. 1976. 12.75- (ISBN 0-398-03497-4). C C Thomas.
Goldman, Judith. Windows at Tiffany's: The Art of Gene Moore. (Illus.). 280p. 1980. 50.00 (ISBN 0-686-62688-5, 1655-X). Abrams.
Goldman, Leo, ed. Research Methods for Counselors: Practical Approaches in Field Settings. LC 77-10950. (Counseling & Human Development Ser.). 1978. text ed. 21.95 (ISBN 0-471-02339-6). Wiley.
Goldman, Leon, et al. Laboratory Diagnosis in Dermatology. LC 70-176170. 300p. 1981. 37.50 (ISBN 0-87527-194-4). Green.
Goldman, Marshall. Enigma of Soviet Petroleum: Half Empty or Half Full? (Illus.). 216p. (Orig.). 1980. text ed. 19.95x (ISBN 0-04-333015-0, 2509); pap. 7.95 (ISBN 0-04-333016-9, 2510). Allen Unwin.
Goldman, Myra F., jt. auth. see Kalakian, Leonard H.
Goldman, R. F., tr. see Eca de Queiroz.
Goldman, Richard, jt. auth. see Wallat, Cynthia.
Goldman, Robert P. God's Priests & Warriors. LC 76-41255. 1977. 15.00x (ISBN 0-231-03941-7). Columbia U Pr.
Goldman, Ronald. Readiness for Religion. 1970. pap. 3.95 (ISBN 0-8164-2060-2, SP70). Crossroad NY.
--Religious Thinking from Childhood to Adolescence. 1968. pap. text ed. 3.95 (ISBN 0-8164-2061-0, SP53). Crossroad NY.
Goldman, Sheldon & Sarat, Austin, eds. American Court Systems: Readings in Judicial Process & Behavior. LC 78-19160. (Illus.). 1978. text ed. 24.95x (ISBN 0-7167-0061-1); pap. text ed. 12.95x (ISBN 0-7167-0060-3). W H Freeman.
Goldman, Shifra M. Contemporary Mexican Painting in a Time of Change. LC 80-17107. 272p. 1981. text ed. 30.00x (ISBN 0-292-71061-5). U of Tex Pr.
Goldman, Susan. Cousins Are Special. Rubin, Caroline, ed. LC 75-11924. (Self-Starter Bks). (Illus.). (ps-2). 1978. 6.50g (ISBN 0-8075-1317-2). A Whitman.
--Grandma Is Somebody Special. Rubin, Caroline, ed. LC 76-18980. (Self-Starter Bks.). (Illus.). 32p. (ps-1). 1976. 6.50g (ISBN 0-8075-3034-4). A Whitman.
--Grandpa & Me Together. Tucker, Kathleen, ed. LC 79-18244. (Self-Starter Ser.). (Illus.). (ps-2). 1980. 6.50g (ISBN 0-8075-3036-0). A Whitman.
Goldman, William. Magic. 1976. 7.95 o.s.i. (ISBN 0-440-05159-2). Delacorte.
--The Princess Bride. 1977. pap. 2.50 (ISBN 0-345-29412-2, 345-25483-X-195). Ballantine.
--Tinsel. 1980. pap. 2.75 o.s.i. (ISBN 0-440-18735-4). Dell.
Goldmann, Lucien. Cultural Creation in Modern Society. Grahl, Bart, tr. from Fr. LC 75-46394. 150p. 1976. 9.50 (ISBN 0-914386-08-5); pap. 3.00 (ISBN 0-914386-09-3). Telos Pr.
--Lukacs & Heidegger: Towards a New Philosophy. Boelhower, William Q., tr. 1979. pap. 7.95 (ISBN 0-7100-8794-2). Routledge & Kegan.
--Lukacs & Heidegger: Towards a New Philosophy. Boelhower, William Q., tr. 15.00x (ISBN 0-7100-8625-3). Routledge & Kegan.
Goldmann, Robert B., ed. Roundtable Justice: Case Studies in Conflict Resolution. (Westview Special Studies in Peace, Conflict, & Conflict Resolution). 231p. 1980. lib. bdg. 24.50x (ISBN 0-89158-962-7); pap. text ed. 9.00x (ISBN 0-86531-139-0). Westview.
Goldoni, Carlo. Comic Theatre: A Comedy in Three Acts. Miller, John W., tr. LC 69-14867. 1969. 7.50x (ISBN 0-8032-0056-0). U of Nebr Pr.
Goldovsky, B. Bringing Opera to Life: Operatic Acting & Stage Direction. 1968. 19.95 (ISBN 0-13-083105-0). P-H.
Goldreich, Esther, jt. auth. see Goldreich, Gloria.
Goldreich, Gloria. Season of Discovery. LC 76-40482. (gr. 6-12). 1977. 6.95 o.p. (ISBN 0-525-66523-4). Elsevier-Nelson.
Goldreich, Gloria & Goldreich, Esther. What Can She Be? A Computer Scientist. LC 78-31988. (What Can She Be Ser.). (Illus.). (gr. 2-5). 1979. 7.50 (ISBN 0-688-41887-2); PLB 7.20 (ISBN 0-688-51887-7). Lothrop.
--What Can She Be? A Farmer. LC 76-12474. (What Can She Be? Ser.). (Illus.). 48p. (gr. k-5). 1976. PLB 7.20 (ISBN 0-688-51768-4). Lothrop.
--What Can She Be? A Film Producer. LC 77-8889. (What Can She Be? Ser.). (Illus.). (gr. 1-5). 1977. 6.25 o.p. (ISBN 0-688-41815-5); PLB 7.20 (ISBN 0-688-51815-X). Lothrop.
--What Can She Be? A Geologist. LC 76-10316. (What Can She Be? Ser.). (Illus.). 48p. (gr. 1-5). 1976. 7.20 (ISBN 0-688-51767-6). Lothrop.
--What Can She Be? A Lawyer. LC 72-10587. (What Can She Be? Ser.). (Illus.). 40p. (gr. k-5). 1973. PLB 7.20 (ISBN 0-688-51521-5). Lothrop.
--What Can She Be? a Legislator. (What Can She Be? Ser). (Illus.). (gr. 1-5). 1978. 7.50 (ISBN 0-688-41865-1); PLB 7.20 (ISBN 0-688-51865-6). Lothrop.
--What Can She Be? A Musician. LC 74-28461. (What Can She Be? Ser.). (Illus.). 48p. (gr. k-5). 1975. 7.50 (ISBN 0-688-41701-9); PLB 7.20 (ISBN 0-688-51701-3). Lothrop.
--What Can She Be? A Newscaster. LC 73-4940. (What Can She Be? Ser.). (Illus.). 48p. (gr. k-5). 1973. PLB 7.20 (ISBN 0-688-51540-1). Lothrop.
--What Can She Be? A Police Officer. LC 75-7442. (What Can She Be? Ser.). (Illus.). 48p. (gr. k-5). 1975. PLB 7.20 (ISBN 0-688-51706-4). Lothrop.

--What Can She Be? A Scientist. LC 80-25011. (What Can She Be Ser.). (Illus.). 32p. (gr. 3-6). 1981. 7.95 (ISBN 0-03-055671-6). HR&W.
--What Can She Be? a Veterinarian. LC 76-177324. (What Can She Be? Ser.). (Illus.). 48p. (gr. k-5). 1972. PLB 7.20 (ISBN 0-688-51501-0). Lothrop.
--What Can She Be? An Architect. LC 73-17710. (What Can She Be? Ser.). (Illus.). 48p. (gr. k-5). 1974. PLB 7.20 (ISBN 0-688-51579-7). Lothrop.
Goldring, Sidney, jt. ed. see O'Leary, James L.
Goldring, Winifred. Handbook of Paleontology for Beginners & Amateurs: The Fossils, Pt. 1. (Illus.). 1960. Repr. 6.75 (ISBN 0-87710-363-1). Paleo Res.
Goldrosen, John. Buddy Holly. 1979. pap. 7.95 (ISBN 0-8256-3936-0, Quick Fox). Music Sales.
Goldsack. World Railways & Rapid Transit Systems 1980-81. 1980. 125.00 (ISBN 0-531-03938-2). Watts.
--World Railways & Rapid Transit Systems 1979-80. 1980. 89.50 (ISBN 0-531-03906-4). Watts.
Goldsack, Paul, ed. Jane's World Railways 1977. 1977. 72.50 o.p. (ISBN 0-531-03268-X). Watts.
Goldsborough, June. Happy Helper A B C. (Illus.). (ps-1). 1971. PLB 5.38 (ISBN 0-307-68925-5, Golden Pr). Western Pub.
Goldsborough, June, illus. I Can Do It by Myself. (Golden Sturdy Shape Bk.). (Illus.). 22p. 1981. 3.50 (ISBN 0-307-12123-2, Golden Pr). Western Pub.
--Mother Goose on the Farm. (Tell-a-Tale Readers). (Illus.). (ps-1). 1975. PLB 4.77 (ISBN 0-307-68587-X, Whitman). Western Pub.
Goldsby, Richard A. Biology. 2nd ed. (Illus.). 1979. text ed. 21.50 scp (ISBN 0-06-162409-8, HarpC); instr. manual avail. (ISBN 0-06-162402-0); scp study guide 6.50 (ISBN 0-685-63467-1). Har-Row.
Goldscheider, Calvin, jt. auth. see Friedlander, Dov.
Goldscheider, Robert, jt. auth. see Eckstrom, Lawrence J.
Goldscheider, Robert, jt. auth. see Finnegan, Marcus B.
Goldschmid, Harvey J., et al, eds. Industrial Concentration: The New Learning. 1974. pap. 7.95 (ISBN 0-316-31941-4). Little.
Goldschmidt, Arthur, Jr. A Concise History of the Middle East. 1979. lib. bdg. 28.50x (ISBN 0-89158-251-7); pap. text ed. 11.50x (ISBN 0-89158-289-4). Westview.
Goldschmidt, E. P. Medieval Texts & Their First Appearance in Print. LC 68-54232. 1969. Repr. of 1943 ed. 9.50x (ISBN 0-8196-0226-4). Biblo.
Goldschmidt, Victor M. Geochemistry. Muir, Alex, ed. (International Ser. of Monographs on Physics). 1954. 62.00x (ISBN 0-19-851210-4). Oxford U Pr.
Goldschmidt, Walter. Culture & Behavior of the Sebei: A Study in Continuity & Adaptation. LC 74-82848. 1976. 34.50x (ISBN 0-520-02828-7). U of Cal Pr.
--Kambuya's Cattle: The Legacy of an African Herdsman. 1968. 19.50x (ISBN 0-520-01472-3). U of Cal Pr.
--Sebei Law. 1967. 19.50x (ISBN 0-520-00489-2). U of Cal Pr.
Goldschmidt, Walter, ed. see Alkire, William.
Goldschmidt, Walter, ed. see Sutlive, Vinson H., Jr.
Goldschmidt, Y. & Admon, K. Profit Measurement During Inflation: Accounting, Economic & Financial Aspects. LC 77-4500. (Wiley Series in Operations Management). 1977. 29.95 (ISBN 0-471-01983-6, Pub. by Wiley-Interscience). Wiley.
Goldschmiedt, Henry. Practical Formulas for Hobby & Profit. LC 77-21301. (Illus.). 1978. pap. 5.95 o.p. (ISBN 0-668-04495-0). Arco.
Goldsmid, Charles & Wilson, Everett. Passing on Sociology: The Teaching of Discipline. 448p. 1980. text ed. 21.95x (ISBN 0-534-00914-X). Wadsworth Pub.
Goldsmid, Paula. Did You Ever. (Illus.). 30p. (ps-k). 1971. pap. 2.50 (ISBN 0-914996-01-0). Lollipop Power.
Goldsmith. Toto the Timid Turtle. 1980. 8.95 (ISBN 0-87705-525-4). Human Sci Pr.
Goldsmith, jt. auth. see Davies.
Goldsmith, Arnold I. American Literary Criticism: Vol. III, 1905-1965. (United States Author Ser.: No. 341). 1979. lib. bdg. 12.50 (ISBN 0-8057-7265-0). Twayne.
Goldsmith, Barbara. Little Gloria: Happy at Last. Date not set. pap. 3.50 (ISBN 0-440-15109-0). Dell.
--The Straw Man. 1981. pap. 2.75 (ISBN 0-345-29423-8). Ballantine.
Goldsmith, D. & Owen, T. The Search for Life in the Universe. 1980. pap. 12.95 (ISBN 0-8053-3325-8). A-W.
Goldsmith, Donald. The Evolving Universe. 1981. 18.95 (ISBN 0-8053-3327-4). Benjamin-Cummings.
--The Quest for Extraterrestrial Life: A Book of Readings. LC 79-57423. (Illus.). 308p. 1980. 18.00 (ISBN 0-935702-08-3); pap. text ed. 12.00 (ISBN 0-935702-02-4). Univ Sci Bks.
--The Universe. LC 75-28643. 1976. 18.95 o.p. (ISBN 0-8053-3324-X). Benjamin-Cummings.
Goldsmith, Elisabeth E. Ancient Pagan Symbols. LC 68-18025. (Illus.). xxxix, 220p. 1976. Repr. of 1929 ed. 15.00 (ISBN 0-8103-4140-9). Gale.
Goldsmith, G. A., ed. Clinical Nutrition & Dietetics. 1976. text ed. write for info. o.p. (ISBN 0-08-016469-2). Pergamon.
Goldsmith, Howard, jt. ed. see Elwood, Roger.
Goldsmith, Ilse. Anatomy for Children. LC 64-15111. (Illus.). (gr. 3-8). 1964. 7.95 (ISBN 0-8069-3000-4); PLB 7.49 (ISBN 0-8069-3001-2). Sterling.
--Why You Get Sick & How You Get Well. LC 70-115448. (Illus.). (gr. 4-6). 1970. 7.95 (ISBN 0-8069-3036-5); PLB 7.49 (ISBN 0-8069-3037-3). Sterling.
Goldsmith, Jack & Goldsmith, Sharon. Crime & the Elderly. (Illus.). 1976. 19.95 (ISBN 0-669-00561-4). Lexington Bks.
Goldsmith, Joel S. The Gift of Love. Sinkler, Lorraine, ed. LC 75-9330. 96p. (Gift format). 1975. 4.95 (ISBN 0-06-063172-4, HarpR). Har-Row.
--Man Was Not Born to Cry. 1977. pap. 4.95 (ISBN 0-8065-0569-9). Citadel Pr.
--The World Is New. LC 62-7953. 1978. 8.95 (ISBN 0-06-063291-7, HarpR). Har-Row.
Goldsmith, John A. Autosegmental Phonology. Hankamer, Jorge, ed. LC 78-67735. (Outstanding Dissertations in Linguistics Ser.). 1979. lib. bdg. 22.00 (ISBN 0-8240-9673-8). Garland Pub.
Goldsmith, M. M. Hobbes's Science of Politics. LC 66-18860. 1966. 17.50x (ISBN 0-231-02803-2). Columbia U Pr.
--Hobbes's Science of Politics. 1978. pap. 7.00x (ISBN 0-231-02804-0). Columbia U Pr.
Goldsmith, Margaret. Frederick the Great. 218p. 1980. Repr. of 1929 ed. lib. bdg. 20.00 (ISBN 0-89760-314-1). Telegraph Bks.
Goldsmith, Margot, jt. auth. see Wolfe, Maxine G.
Goldsmith, Maurice. Frederic Joliot-Curie. 1976. text ed. 15.75x (ISBN 0-85315-342-6). Humanities.
Goldsmith, Maurice, ed. see International Symposium on Science & Technology for Development, Singapore, 1979.
Goldsmith, Maurice, et al, eds. Einstein: The First Hundred Years. (Illus.). 188p. 1980. 19.95 (ISBN 0-08-025019-X). Pergamon.
Goldsmith, Oliver. The Belles Letters Series, the English Drama. 283p. 1980. Repr. of 1905 ed. lib. bdg. 30.00 (ISBN 0-89987-324-3). Century Bookbindery.
--History of Little Goody Two Shoes. (Illus.). (gr. 2-4). 1924. 4.95 (ISBN 0-02-736280-9). Macmillan.
--She Stoops to Conquer. Hopper, Vincent F. & Lahey, Gerald B., eds. (Illus.). (gr. 9 up). 1958. pap. text ed. 2.50 (ISBN 0-8120-0158-3). Barron.
--She Stoops to Conquer. Balderston, Katherine G., ed. LC 51-6755. (Crofts Classics Ser.). 1951. pap. text ed. 2.75x (ISBN 0-88295-039-8). AHM Pub.
--Traveller,Or,a Prospect of Society. Incl. The Deserted Village; A Prospect of Society: Preliminary Version of the "Traveller", Dating from 1964. 1975. text ed. 8.50x o.p. (ISBN 0-8277-3845-5); pap. text ed. 5.95x o.p. (ISBN 0-8277-2197-8). British Bk Ctr.
--Vicar of Wakefield. 1956. 11.50x (ISBN 0-460-00295-3, Evman); pap. 4.95 (ISBN 0-460-01295-9). Dutton.
--The Vicar of Wakefield. Friedman, Arthur, ed. (Oxford English Novels Ser.). 250p. 1974. 16.50x (ISBN 0-19-255345-3). Oxford U Pr.
Goldsmith, Robert H. Nutrition & Learning. LC 80-82680. (Fastback Ser.: No. 147). (Orig.). 1980. pap. 0.75 (ISBN 0-87367-147-3). Phi Delta Kappa.
Goldsmith, S. J. Twenty Twentieth Century Jews. LC 62-21948. (Illus.). 142p. 1962. 6.95 (ISBN 0-88400-021-4). Shengold.
Goldsmith, Seth. Health Care Management: Perspectives for Today. 300p. 1981. text ed. price not set (ISBN 0-89443-336-9). Aspen Systems.
Goldsmith, Seth B. Ambulatory Care: Theory & Practice. LC 77-10315. 1977. 21.50 (ISBN 0-912862-46-7). Aspen Systems.
Goldsmith, Sharon, jt. auth. see Goldsmith, Jack.
Goldsmith, Ulrich K. Stefan George. LC 78-110601. (Columbia Essays on Modern Writers Ser.: No. 50). 48p. 1970. pap. 2.00 (ISBN 0-231-03204-8, MW50). Columbia U Pr.
Goldsmith, V. F. A Short Title Catalogue of French Books 1601-1700 in the Library of the British Museum. 1973. 90.00 (ISBN 0-7129-0575-8, Dist. by Shoe String). Dawson Pub.
Goldsmith, William M., ed. The Growth of Presidential Power: A Documented History, 3 vols. LC 74-9623. 1981. Repr. of 1974 ed. 96.50 set (ISBN 0-87754-125-6). Chelsea Hse.
Goldsmith, William W., jt. ed. see Clavel, Pierre.
Goldspink, D. F., ed. The Development & Specialisation of Skeletal Muscle. (Society for Experimental Biology Seminar Ser.: No. 7). (Illus.). 200p. Date not set. 45.00 (ISBN 0-521-23317-8); pap. 19.95 (ISBN 0-521-29907-1). Cambridge U Pr.
Goldstain, Leonard. George Chapman: Aspects of Decadence in Early 17th Century Drama, 2 vols. (Salzburg Studies in English Literature, Jacobean Drama Studies Ser.: No. 31). 440p. 1975. Set. pap. text ed. 50.25x (ISBN 0-391-01387-4). Humanities.
Goldstein & Baker. Readings in Abnormal Psychology. (Orig.). 1981. pap. text ed. 8.95 (ISBN 0-316-07830-1). Little.
Goldstein, A., jt. auth. see Goldstein, J.
Goldstein, A. P., jt. auth. see Kanfer, F. H.
Goldstein, A. P., ed. see Hersen, Michel & Barlow, David H.
Goldstein, Alan & Foa, Edna B. Handbook of Behavioral Interventions. LC 79-16950. (Ser. on Personality Processes). 1980. 30.95 (ISBN 0-471-01789-2, Pub. by Wiley-Interscience). Wiley.
Goldstein, Allan L., jt. ed. see Bergsma, Daniel.
Goldstein, Arnold P. Prescriptions for Child Mental Health & Education. 1978. text ed. 44.00 (ISBN 0-08-022250-1); pap. text ed. 10.95 (ISBN 0-08-022249-8). Pergamon.
--Psychotherapeutic Attraction. LC 79-119598. 260p. 1971. 15.25 (ISBN 0-08-016398-X). Pergamon.
Goldstein, Arnold P. & Sorcher, Melvin. Changing Supervisor Behavior. LC 73-10059. 1974. text ed. 12.75 (ISBN 0-08-017742-5); pap. text ed. 6.75 (ISBN 0-08-017769-7). Pergamon.
Goldstein, Arnold P. & Stein, Norman. Prescriptive Psychotherapies. LC 75-5620. 1977. text ed. 32.00 (ISBN 0-08-019506-7, 75-5620); pap. text ed. 14.50 (ISBN 0-08-019505-9). Pergamon.
Goldstein, Arnold P., jt. auth. see Miron, Murray S.
Goldstein, Arnold P., jt. ed. see Kanfer, Frederick H.
Goldstein, Arnold P., et al. In Response to Aggression: Controls & Alternatives. (Pergamon General Psychology Ser.). 500p. Date not set. 42.51 (ISBN 0-08-025580-9); pap. 14.91 (ISBN 0-08-025579-5). Pergamon.
--Police Crisis Intervention. LC 76-48283. (Pergamon General Psychology Ser.: Vol. 80). 175p. 1979. 22.00 (ISBN 0-08-023873-4); pap. 8.75 (ISBN 0-08-023874-2). Pergamon.
Goldstein, Arnold P., et al, eds. Police & the Elderly. LC 78-27400. (Pergamon General Psychology Ser.: Vol. 78). 1979. 16.50 (ISBN 0-08-023894-7); pap. 8.00 (ISBN 0-08-023893-9). Pergamon.
Goldstein, Auram. Biostatistics. (Illus.). 1964. text ed. 18.95 (ISBN 0-02-344440-1). Macmillan.
Goldstein, Avram. VFR Flight Review. (Illus.). 1979. pap. 6.50 (ISBN 0-911721-67-3, Pub. by Airguide). Aviation.
Goldstein, Avram, ed. The Opiate Narcotics: Neurochemical Mechanisms of Analgesia & Dependence. 270p. 1976. text ed. 30.00 (ISBN 0-08-019869-4). Pergamon.
Goldstein, Avram, et al. Principles of Drug Action: The Basis of Pharmacology. 2nd ed. LC 73-15871. 1974. 35.00 (ISBN 0-471-31260-6, Pub. by Wiley-Medical). Wiley.
Goldstein, Benjamin & Davis, Ross, eds. Neighborhoods in the Urban Economy. LC 77-166. (Illus.). 1977. 14.95 (ISBN 0-669-01459-1). Lexington Bks.
Goldstein, Catherine, jt. auth. see Kohl, Sam.
Goldstein, David I. Dostoyevsky & the Jews, Vol. 3, Vol 3. (University of Texas Press Slavic Ser: Vol. 3). 224p. 1980. 17.50x (ISBN 0-292-71528-5). U of Tex Pr.
Goldstein, E. Bruce. Sensation & Perception. 512p. 1980. text ed. 22.95x (ISBN 0-534-00760-0). Wadsworth Pub.
Goldstein, Frances. Children's Treasure Hunt Travel to Belgium & France. LC 80-85012. (Children's Treasure Hunt Travel Guide Ser.). (Illus.). 230p. (Orig.). (gr. k-12). 1981. pap. 4.95 (ISBN 0-933334-02-8). Paper Tiger Pap.
Goldstein, Gerald. A Clinician's Guide to Research Design. LC 79-18818. 288p. 1981. text ed. 24.95 (ISBN 0-88229-340-0). Nelson-Hall.
Goldstein, Harold M. & Horowitz, Morris A. Utilization of Health Personnel: A Five Hospital Study. LC 78-12011. 1978. text ed. 22.00 (ISBN 0-89443-080-7). Aspen Systems.
Goldstein, Harold M., et al. Health Personnel: Meeting the Explosive Demand for Medical Care. LC 76-55042. 1977. text ed. 22.50 (ISBN 0-912862-36-X). Aspen Systems.
Goldstein, Harris K. Research Standards & Methods for Social Workers. rev. ed. LC 70-84001. 1980. pap. 12.50x (ISBN 0-87655-551-2). Whitehall Co.
Goldstein, Herbert. Classical Mechanics. 2nd ed. LC 79-23456. (Illus.). 1980. text ed. 25.95 (ISBN 0-201-02918-9). A-W.
Goldstein, Herbert & Goldstein, Marjorie T. The Reasoning Ability of Mildly Retarded Learners. LC 80-65500. 80p. (Orig.). 1980. pap. 6.25 (ISBN 0-86586-102-1). Coun Exc Child.
Goldstein, Howard. Social Learning & Change: A Cognitive Approach to Human Services. LC 80-23446. 1981. 19.50 (ISBN 0-87249-402-0). U of SC Pr.
Goldstein, Inge, jt. auth. see Goldstein, Martin.
Goldstein, Irving S. Organic Chemicals from Biomass. 304p. 1981. 74.95 (ISBN 0-8493-5531-1). CRC Pr.
Goldstein, J. & Goldstein, A. Crime, Law & Society. LC 77-136009. 1971. 14.50 (ISBN 0-02-912270-8); pap. text ed. 10.95 (ISBN 0-02-912260-0). Free Pr.
Goldstein, Jack. Triumph Over Disease: By Fasting & Natural Diet. LC 76-44863. 1978. pap. 2.50 o.p. (ISBN 0-668-04140-4, 4140). Arco.
Goldstein, Jeffrey H. Aggression & Crimes of Violence. Lana, Robert & Rosnow, Ralph, eds. (Reconstruction of Society Ser.). (Illus.). 208p. 1975. 12.95 (ISBN 0-19-501935-0); pap. 3.95x (ISBN 0-19-501936-9). Oxford U Pr.
--Social Psychology. LC 78-64447. 1980. 17.95 (ISBN 0-12-287050-6); text ed. 11.50 international ed. (ISBN 0-12-287055-7). Acad Pr.
Goldstein, Joseph. Government of British Trade Unions. 1953. 7.95 o.s.i. (ISBN 0-02-912250-3). Free Pr.
Goldstein, Joseph, et al. Criminal Law: Theory & Process. 2nd ed. LC 73-22533. (Illus.). 1974. text ed. 45.00 (ISBN 0-02-912310-0). Free Pr.
Goldstein, K., jt. ed. see Ben-Amos, D.
Goldstein, Kenneth M. & Blackman, Sheldon. Cognitive Style: Five Approaches & Relevant Research. LC 78-1378. 1978. 21.50 (ISBN 0-471-31275-4, Pub. by Wiley-Interscience). Wiley.
Goldstein, Kenneth S. A Guide for Field Workers in Folklore. LC 64-24801. xx, 199p. Repr. of 1964 ed. 15.00 (ISBN 0-8103-5000-9); pap. 6.00 (ISBN 0-8103-5041-6). Gale.
Goldstein, L. Calculus & It's Applications. 1980. 21.95 (ISBN 0-13-111963-X). P-H.
Goldstein, L. & Prescott, David, eds. Cell Biology: A Comprehensive Treatise, 2 vols. Incl. Vol. 1. 1978. 47.00 (ISBN 0-12-289501-0); by subscription 40.50 (ISBN 0-686-61588-3); Vol. 2. The Structure & Replication of Genetic Material. 1979. 47.00, by subscription 40.50 (ISBN 0-12-289502-9). LC 78-10457. Acad Pr.
Goldstein, Larry J. Abstract Algebra: A First Course. LC 72-12790. (Illus.). 1973. 21.95x (ISBN 0-13-000851-6). P-H.
Goldstein, Laurence & Kaufman, Jay. Into Film, 2 vols. 1976. Set. pap. 12.95 (ISBN 0-525-47315-7). Dutton.
Goldstein, Leslie F. The Constitutional Rights of Women. 1979. pap. text ed. 10.95 (ISBN 0-582-28063-X). Longman.
Goldstein, Louis A. Atlas of Orthopaedic Surgery. 2nd ed. LC 80-23987. (Illus.). 1000p. 1981. text ed. 90.00 (ISBN 0-8016-1884-3). Mosby.
Goldstein, Malcolm. George S. Kaufman: His Life, His Theater. (Illus.). 1979. 25.00 (ISBN 0-19-502623-3). Oxford U Pr.
Goldstein, Malcolm, ed. see Rowe, Nicholas.
Goldstein, Malcolm L. Art of Thornton Wilder. LC 65-10239. 1965. 9.95x (ISBN 0-8032-0057-9); pap. 2.95x (ISBN 0-8032-5074-6, BB 308, Bison). U of Nebr Pr.
Goldstein, Marjorie T., jt. auth. see Goldstein, Herbert.
Goldstein, Martin & Goldstein, Inge. How We Know. (Da Capo Quality Paperbacks Ser.). (Illus.). 376p. 1981. pap. 8.95 (ISBN 0-306-80140-X). Da Capo.
Goldstein, Mary. Teaching in the First School. 1975. pap. 14.95 (ISBN 0-7134-3026-5, Pub. by Batsford England). David & Charles.
Goldstein, Melvyn C. Modern Literary Tibetan. 1977. 13.95x (ISBN 0-685-89513-0). Himalaya Hse.
--Tibetan-English Dictionary of Modern Tibetan. 1975. 24.95x (ISBN 0-685-89505-X). Himalaya Hse.
Goldstein, Menek, et al. Ergot Compounds & Brain Function: Neuroendocrine & Neuropsychiatric Aspects. 1980. text ed. 44.50 (ISBN 0-89004-450-3). Raven.
Goldstein, Michael J., et al. Pornography & Sexual Deviance. 1973. 16.50x (ISBN 0-520-02406-0); pap. 2.45 (ISBN 0-520-02619-5). U of Cal Pr.
Goldstein, Murray, et al, eds. Cerebrovascular Disorders & Stroke. LC 76-62496. (Advances in Neurology Ser.: Vol. 25). 1979. text ed. 41.50 (ISBN 0-89004-294-2). Raven.

Goldstein, N. Figure Drawing: Structure, Anatomy & Expressive Design of Human Form. 1976. 18.95 (ISBN 0-13-314765-7). P-H.

Goldstein, Nathan. The Art of Responsive Drawing. 2nd ed. LC 76-25001. (Illus.). 1977. 18.95 (ISBN 0-13-048629-9). P-H.

--Figure Drawing: The Structure, Anatomy, & Expressive Design of Human Form. (Illus.). 330p. 1981. text ed. 20.95 (ISBN 0-13-314518-2); pap. text ed. 17.95 (ISBN 0-13-314435-6). P-H.

--Painting: Visual & Technical Fundamentals. LC 78-15907. 1979. 17.95 (ISBN 0-13-647800-X). P-H.

Goldstein, Paul. Changing the American Schoolbook. LC 77-13572. (Politics of Education Ser.). 160p. 1978. 15.95 (ISBN 0-669-01984-4). Lexington Bks.

--Real Estate Transactions: Cases & Materials on Land Transfer, Development & Finance. LC 80-11638. (University Casebook Ser.). 842p. 1980. write for info. (ISBN 0-88277-005-5). Foundation Pr.

Goldstein, Paul J. Prostitution & Drugs. LC 78-24766. 208p. 1979. 19.95 (ISBN 0-669-02833-9). Lexington Bks.

Goldstein, Philip. Wonders of Parasites. LC 69-15171. (Illus.). (gr. 5-10). 1969. 4.25 o.p. (ISBN 0-8313-0064-7); PLB 6.19 (ISBN 0-685-13791-0). Lantern.

Goldstein, Philip, jt. auth. see Nason, Alvin.

Goldstein, R. J. Introduction to Cichlids. 1970. pap. 7.95 (ISBN 0-87666-019-7, PS-662). TFH Pubns.

Goldstein, Robert J. Anabantoids Gouramis & Related Species. (Illus.). 7.95 (ISBN 0-87666-750-7, PS672). TFH Pubns.

--Cichlids of the World. (Illus.). 382p. 1973. 20.00 (ISBN 0-87666-032-4, H-945). TFH Pubns.

--Political Repression in Modern America. (Orig.). 1978. pap. 6.95 o.p. (ISBN 0-8467-0511-7, Pub. by Two Continents). Hippocrene Bks.

Goldstein, Ruth M. & Zornow, Edith. Movies for Kids: A Guide for Parents & Teachers on the Entertainment Film for Children. rev. ed. LC 79-6149. (Illus.). 300p. 1980. 14.95 (ISBN 0-8044-2267-2); pap. 5.95 (ISBN 0-8044-6194-5). Ungar.

--The Screen Image of Youth: Movies About Children & Adolescents. LC 80-14053. (Illus.). xxi, 363p. 1980. 20.00 (ISBN 0-8108-1316-5). Scarecrow.

Goldstein, Sam. The Birdicide of Cock Robin, & Other Murderous Words Ending in Cide. (Illus.). 68p. (Orig.). 1981. pap. 3.95 (ISBN 0-938338-04-8). Winds World Pr.

--Goliath to Gog: A Gallery of Giants from Fable, Fact, Fiction & Folklore. (Odd Books for Odd Moments Ser.). (Illus.). 72p. (Orig.). 1980. pap. 3.95 (ISBN 0-938338-00-5). Winds World Pr.

--What Are You Afraid of? An Illustrated Dictionary of Fearful Words Ending in Phobia. (Weirdictionaries Ser.). (Illus.). 72p. (Orig.). 1981. pap. 3.95 (ISBN 0-938338-05-6). Winds World Pr.

Goldstein, Sanford, tr. see Mori, Ogai.

Goldstein, Sherry E., ed. see Foundation Center.

Goldstein, Sidney. Patterns of Mobility. LC 57-7221. 1958. 9.00x o.p. (ISBN 0-8122-7092-4). U of Pa Pr.

Goldstein, Sidney, jt. auth. see Mayer, Kurt B.

Goldstein, Stephen R. Law & Public Education, Cases & Materials. (Contemporary Legal Education Ser). 944p. 1974. 22.00 (ISBN 0-672-81784-5, Bobbs-Merrill Law); 1978 suppl 5.50 (ISBN 0-672-83546-0). Michie.

Goldstein, Stephen R., jt. auth. see Buss, William G.

Goldstein, Susan B. & Sies, Luther F. The Communication Contract. (Illus.). 384p. 1974. text ed. 18.75 (ISBN 0-685-49058-0). C C Thomas.

Goldstein, Sydney, ed. Modern Developments in Fluid Dynamics, 2 Vols. (Illus.). 1938. pap. text ed. 5.50 ea.; Vol. 1. pap. text ed. (ISBN 0-486-61357-7); Vol. 2. pap. text ed. (ISBN 0-486-61358-5). Dover.

Goldstein, Waller, ed. Planning, Politics, & the Public Interest. LC 78-1720. 1978. 15.00x (ISBN 0-231-04538-7). Columbia U Pr.

Goldstein, William. Controversial Issues in Our Schools. LC 80-82679. (Fastback Ser.: No. 146). (Orig.). 1980. pap. 0.75 (ISBN 0-87367-146-5). Phi Delta Kappa.

Goldstein-Jackson, Kevin, et al. Experiments with Everyday Objects: Science Activities for Children, Parents & Teachers. LC 77-13232. (Illus.). 1978. 13.95 (ISBN 0-13-295287-4, Spec); pap. 3.95 (ISBN 0-13-295279-3, Spec). P-H.

Goldstene, Paul N. The Collapse of Liberal Empire: Science & the Revolution in the Twentieth Century. (Political Science Ser.). 160p. 1980. pap. 5.95 (ISBN 0-88316-540-6). Chandler & Sharp.

Goldstern, W. Steam Storage Installations. 1970. 28.00 (ISBN 0-08-015560-X). Pergamon.

Goldstine, H. H. A History of the Calculus of Vatriations from the Seventeenth Through the Nineteenth Century. (Studies in the History of Mathematics & Physical Sciences Ser.: Vol. 5). (Illus.). 410p. 1981. 48.00 (ISBN 0-387-90521-9). Springer-Verlag.

Goldstine, Herman H. The Computer from Pascal to Von Neumann. LC 70-173755. (Illus.). 400p. 1980. 22.50x (ISBN 0-691-08104-2); pap. 6.95 (ISBN 0-691-02367-0). Princeton U Pr.

Goldston, Robert. Battles of the Constitution: Old Ironsides & the Freedom of the Sea. LC 71-78084. (Battle Books Ser). (Illus.). (gr. 5-9). 1969. 7.95 (ISBN 0-02-736330-9). Macmillan.

--Coming of the Civil War. LC 72-123139. (gr. 6 up). 1972. 8.95 (ISBN 0-02-736270-1). Macmillan.

--Coming of the Cold War. LC 79-89585. (Illus.). (gr. 7 up). 1970. 4.50 o.s.i. (ISBN 0-02-736320-1). Macmillan.

--Long March, Nineteen Thirty-Four to Thirty-Five: A Red Army Survives to Bring Communism to China. LC 74-157748. (World Focus Bks). (Illus.). (gr. 7 up). 1971. PLB 4.47 o.p. (ISBN 0-531-02153-X). Watts.

--Negro Revolution: From Its African Genesis to the Death of Martin Luther King. (Illus.). (gr. 7-12). 1968. pap. text ed. 2.96 o.s.i. (ISBN 0-02-296870-9). tchrs' manual 0.60 o.s.i. (ISBN 0-686-66484-1). Macmillan.

--New York: Civic Exploitation. LC 72-89586. (Portraits in Urban Civilization Ser). (Illus.). (gr. 9 up). 1970. 5.95g o.s.i. (ISBN 0-02-736400-3). Macmillan.

--Spain. (Illus.). (gr. 7 up). 1967. 8.95 (ISBN 0-02-736340-6). Macmillan.

--Suburbia: Civic Denial. LC 76-99120. (Portraits in Urban Civilization Ser). (gr. 9 up). 1970. 5.95g o.s.i. (ISBN 0-02-736380-5). Macmillan.

--The Sword of the Prophet. 224p. 1981. pap. 2.50 (ISBN 0-449-24393-1, Crest). Fawcett.

Goldston, Robert C. The Death of Gandhi: January 30, 1948: India's Spiritual Leader Helps His Nation Win Independence. LC 72-6074. (World Focus Bks.). (Illus.). 96p. 1973. PLB 6.45 (ISBN 0-531-02160-2). Watts.

--The Siege of the Alcazar, July-September, 1936: Facism Defeats Democracy in the Spanish Civil War. LC 75-188689. (World Focus Bks.). (Illus.). 72p. (gr. 7-12). 1972. PLB 6.45 (ISBN 0-531-02164-5). Watts.

--Spain. LC 72-3717. (First Bks). (Illus.). 72p. (gr. 7-12). 1972. PLB 4.90 o.p. (ISBN 0-531-00781-2). Watts.

Goldston, Robert G. Pearl Harbor December 7, 1941. LC 72-1339. (World Focus Bks). (Illus.). (gr. 7-12). 1972. PLB 4.47 o.p. (ISBN 0-531-02163-7). Watts.

Goldstone, Robert, ed. Health Care & Industrial Relations: Costs, Conflicts & Controversy. 120p. 1981. price not set (ISBN 0-89215-112-9). U Cal LA Indus Rel.

Goldstucker, Jac L., ed. Marketing Information: A Professional Reference Guide. 1981. 29.95 (ISBN 0-88406-132-9). Ga St U Busn Pub.

Goldstucker, Jac L., et al. New Developments in Retail Trading Area Analysis & Site Selection. LC 78-8033. (Research Monograph: No. 78). 1978. pap. 9.95 (ISBN 0-88406-115-9). Ga St U Busn Pub.

Goldsworth, Maureen. New Fashion from Old. 1978. pap. 8.95 (ISBN 0-7134-0913-4, Pub. by Batsford England). David & Charles.

Goldsworthy, Maureen. Dressmaking with Leather. 1977. 17.95 (ISBN 0-7134-3240-3, Pub. by Batsford England). David & Charles.

Goldthorpe, J. E. An Introduction to Sociology. 2nd ed. LC 73-83107. (Illus.). 200p. 1974. text ed. 29.95 (ISBN 0-521-20338-4); pap. text ed. 8.95x (ISBN 0-521-09826-2). Cambridge U Pr.

--The Sociology of the Third World. LC 74-12979. (Illus.). 336p. 1975. 39.95 (ISBN 0-521-20521-2); pap. 9.95x (ISBN 0-521-09924-2). Cambridge U Pr.

Goldthorpe, John H. & Hope, Keith. The Social Grading of Occupations: A New Approach & Scale. (Oxford Studies in Social Mobility). (Illus.). 196p. 1974. pap. 17.95x (ISBN 0-19-827220-0). Oxford U Pr.

Goldthorpe, John H., et al. Affluent Worker, in the Class Structure. (Studies in Sociology: No. 3). 1969. 29.95 (ISBN 0-521-07231-X); pap. 9.95x (ISBN 0-521-09533-6). Cambridge U Pr.

--Affluent Worker: Industrial Attitudes. LC 68-21192. (Cambridge Studies in Sociology: No. 1). 1968. 24.00 (ISBN 0-521-07109-7); pap. 9.95x (ISBN 0-521-09466-6). Cambridge U Pr.

Goldthwaite, Richard A. The Building of Renaissance Florence: A Social & Economic History. LC 80-7995. (Illus.). 448p. 1981. text ed. 25.00x (ISBN 0-8018-2342-0). Johns Hopkins.

Goldwasser, Janet & Dowty, Stuart. Huan-Ying: Workers' China. LC 74-7790. 400p. 1975. 12.50 o.p. (ISBN 0-85345-337-3, CL3373). Monthly Rev.

Goldwater, Barry M. Delightful Journey: Down the Green & Colorado Rivers. LC 77-94876. 1970. 15.00 (ISBN 0-685-67965-9). AZ Hist Foun.

Goldwater, Robert. Gauguin. (Library of Great Painters Ser). (Illus.). 1957. 35.00 (ISBN 0-8109-0137-4). Abrams.

Goldwater, Robert, jt. auth. see Jordan, Jim M.

Goldwert, Marvin. Democracy, Militarism, & Nationalism in Argentina, 1930-1966: An Interpretation. (Latin American Monographs: No. 25). 286p. 1972. 10.00 (ISBN 0-292-71500-5). U of Tex Pr.

--History As Neurosis: Paternalism and Machismo in Spanish America. LC 80-5640. 85p. 1980. lib. bdg. 12.50 (ISBN 0-8191-1226-7); pap. text ed. 6.50 (ISBN 0-8191-1227-5). U Pr of Amer.

Goldwhite, H. Introduction to Phosphorus Chemistry. LC 79-27141. (Cambridge Texts in Chemistry & Biochemistry). 175p. Date not set. 30.00 (ISBN 0-521-22978-2); pap. text ed. 12.95 (ISBN 0-521-29757-5). Cambridge U Pr.

Goldwhite, Harold & Moynihan, Cornelius T. Experiments for College Chemistry. 1971. pap. text ed. 10.95 scp (ISBN 0-06-042388-9, HarpC). Har-Row.

Goldwhite, Harold see Chang, Raymond.

Goldwin, Robert A., ed. Political Parties in the Eighties. 1980. 10.25 (ISBN 0-8447-3377-6); pap. 5.25 (ISBN 0-686-64315-1). Am Enterprise.

Goldwin, Robert A. & Schambra, William A., eds. How Democratic Is the Constitution? 1980. 12.25 (ISBN 0-8447-3400-4); pap. 5.25. Am Enterprise.

Goldworthy, Graham J. Endocrinology. LC 80-18704. 184p. 1981. 34.95 (ISBN 0-470-27034-9). Halsted Pr.

Goldwurm, Hersh. Daniel. (The Art Scroll Tanach Ser.). 352p. 1979. 12.95 (ISBN 0-89906-079-X); pap. 9.95 (ISBN 0-89906-080-3). Mesorah Pubns.

Goldwurm, Hersh, et al. Mishnah-Moed, Vol. 3. (Art Scroll Mishnah Ser.). 1980. 16.95 (ISBN 0-89906-256-3); pap. 13.95 (ISBN 0-89906-257-1). Mesorah Pubns.

Goldwyn, Robert M. Long Term Results in Plastic & Reconstruction Surgery. 1980. text ed. 95.00 (ISBN 0-316-31972-4, Little Med Div). Little.

Goldziher, Ignaz. Introduction to Islamic Theology & Law. Lewis, Bernard, ed. Hamori, Andras & Hamori, Ruth, trs. from Ger. LC 80-7523. (Modern Classics in Near Eastern Studies). 325p. 1981. 22.50 (ISBN 0-691-07257-4); pap. 9.95 (ISBN 0-691-10099-3). Princeton U Pr.

Golec, Anthony M. Techniques of Legal Investigation. (Illus.). 280p. 1976. 19.75 (ISBN 0-398-03522-9). C C Thomas.

Goleman, Daniel & Davidson, Richard. Consciousness: Readings. 1979. text ed. 6.95 scp (ISBN 0-06-383045-0, HarpC). Har-Row.

Golemba, Henry L. Frank R. Stockton. (United States Authors Ser.: No. 374). 1981. lib. bdg. 11.95 (ISBN 0-8057-7288-X). Twayne.

--George Ripley. (U. S. Authors Ser.: No. 281). 1977. lib. bdg. 9.95 (ISBN 0-8057-7181-6). Twayne.

Golembiewski, Robert T. & Hilles, Richard J. Toward the Responsive Organization: The Theory & Practice of Survey Feed. 1979. pap. text ed. 12.95 (ISBN 0-89832-001-1). Brighton Pub.

Golembiewski, Robert T., ed. Perspectives on Public Management: Cases & Learning Designs. 2nd ed. LC 75-17317. 1976. text ed. 12.50 (ISBN 0-87581-186-8, 186). Peacock Pubs.

--Small Group in Political Science. LC 75-36688. 519p. 1978. 27.50x (ISBN 0-8203-0405-0). U of Ga Pr.

Golenbeck, Peter, jt. auth. see Lyle, Sparky.

Golenbock, Peter, jt. auth. see Guidry, Ron.

Golenbock, Peter, jt. auth. see Martin, Billy.

Golf Digest Editors, jt. auth. see Aultman, Dick.

Golf Digest Magazine, ed. see Toski, Bob & Aultman, Dick.

Golf Digest Magazine Editors. Instant Golf Lessons. LC 77-92907. (Instant Lesson Ser.). 225p. (Orig.). 1978. pap. 4.95 (ISBN 0-914178-16-4, 24167). Golf Digest.

Golf Magazine Editors. Golf Magazine's Great Golf Courses You Can Play. LC 72-2208. (Illus.). 450p. 1973. 10.00 o.p. (ISBN 0-684-13431-4). Scribner.

--Golf Magazine's Tips from the Teaching Pros. LC 69-15310. (Illus.). 1969. 11.95 o.s.i. (ISBN 0-06-110779-4, HarpT). Har-Row.

Golfarb, Gerald, jt. auth. see Marks, Burton.

Golgi Centennial Symposium, September 1973. Golgi Centennial Symposium: Perspectives in Neurobiology. Santini, Maurizo, ed. LC 74-21985. 1975. 68.50 (ISBN 0-911216-80-4). Raven.

Golia, Jack de see De Golia, Jack.

Goliber, Paul F. Refrigeration Servicing. LC 75-6064. 112p. 1976. pap. 4.80 (ISBN 0-8273-1005-6). Delmar.

Golieb, D. E., jt. auth. see Ettinger, Richard P.

Golin, Anne K., jt. auth. see Ducanis, Alex J.

Golino, Carlo L., ed. Galileo Reappraised. (UCLA Center for Medieval & Renaissance Studies). 1966. 14.50x (ISBN 0-520-00490-6). U of Cal Pr.

Golladay, Frederick L. Economics: Problems, Principles, Priorities. LC 76-19511. 1978. 19.95 (ISBN 0-8053-3302-9); instr's man. 3.95 (ISBN 0-8053-3304-5); study guide 8.95 (ISBN 0-8053-3303-7). Benjamin-Cummings.

Gollak, B., ed. see Strogonov, B. P., et al.

Gollancz, Israel, ed. Medieval Library, 28 vols. Repr. of 1926 ed. write for info. Cooper Sq.

Golledge, Reginald G., jt. auth. see Amedeo, Douglas.

Golledge, Reginald G., jt. auth. see King, Leslie J.

Gollek, B., ed. see Zaika, V. E.

Golley, F. B., jt. ed. see Farnworth, E. G.

Golley, F. B., et al, eds. Small Mammals. LC 74-25658. (International Biological Programme Ser.: No. 5). (Illus.). 448p. 1975. 65.00 (ISBN 0-521-20601-4). Cambridge U Pr.

Gollin, Eugene S., ed. Developmental Plasticity: Behavioral & Biological Aspects of Variations in Development. (Developmental Psychology Ser.). 1981. write for info. (ISBN 0-12-289620-3). Acad Pr.

Gollin, James. The Star Spangled Retirement Dream: Why It's Going Sour & What You Can Do About It. 224p. 1981. 12.95 (ISBN 0-684-16866-9, ScribT). Scribner.

Gollmar, Robert. America's Most Bizarre Murderer: Edward Gein. (Illus.). 254p. 1981. 9.95 (ISBN 0-87319-020-3). C Hallberg.

Gollmar, Robert H. Tales of a Country Judge. LC 79-65286. (Illus.). 192p. 1981. 8.95x (ISBN 0-87319-018-1). C Hallberg.

Gollnick, Daniel A. Experimental Radiological Health Physics. LC 77-7638. (Illus.). 260p. 1978. 25.00 (ISBN 0-08-023201-9); pap. 11.25 (ISBN 0-08-020524-0). Pergamon.

Gollub, Morris, illus. That's Our Cleo. (Illus.). 1979. pap. 1.25 (ISBN 0-307-21566-0, Golden Pr). Western Pub.

Gollup, J. P., jt. ed. see Swinney, H. L.

Golomb, Harvey, jt. ed. see Coltman, Charles A., Jr.

Golomb, Morris. Know Jewish Living & Enjoy It. LC 78-54569. (gr. 3-7). 1981. 10.00 (ISBN 0-88400-054-0). Shengold.

--Know Your Festivals & Enjoy Them. 2nd ed. LC 72-90771. (Illus.). 189p. (gr. 3-6). 1973. 7.95 (ISBN 0-88400-035-4). Shengold.

Golombek, H. Capablanca's One Hundred Best Games of Chess. (Illus.). 1978. pap. 5.95 (ISBN 0-679-14044-1, Tartan). McKay.

Golombek, Harvey. Adolescent & Mood Disturbance. 1981. 22.50 (ISBN 0-8236-0085-8). Intl Univs Pr.

Golomber, H., jt. auth. see Griffith, R. C.

Golterman, H. Methods for Chemical Analysis of Fresh Waters. 2nd ed. (Blackwell Scientific Pubns.: IBP Handbk. No. 8). (Illus.). 1978. pap. 16.25 (ISBN 0-632-00459-2). Mosby.

Golub, E., jt. auth. see Dresnack, R.

Golub, Edward S. The Cellular Basis of the Immune Response: An Approach to Immunobiology. LC 77-3728. (Illus.). 1977. pap. text ed. 12.00x (ISBN 0-87893-210-0). Sinauer Assoc.

--The Cellular Basis of the Immune Response. rev. & 2nd ed. LC 80-28080. (Illus.). 325p. 1981. pap. text ed. price not set (ISBN 0-87893-212-7). Sinauer Assoc.

Golub, Gene & Oliger, James, eds. Numerical Analysis. LC 78-11096. (Proceedings of Symposia in Applied Mathematics: Vol. 22). 1978. 14.00 o.p. (ISBN 0-8218-0122-8); softcover 10.00 o.p. (ISBN 0-685-99044-3). Am Math.

Golub, Gene & Oliger, Joseph, eds. Numerical Analysis: Proceedings of a Symposia in Applied Mathematics, Vol. 22. write for info. o.p. (ISBN 0-8218-0122-8); pap. write for info. o.p. Am Math.

Golubev, G. N. & Biswas, A. K., eds. Interregional Water Transfers: Projects & Problems: Proceedings of the Task Force Meeting, International Institute for Applied Systems Analysis, Laxenburg, Austria, Oct. 1977. 1978. text ed. 27.00 (ISBN 0-08-022430-X). Pergamon.

Golubitsky, M. & Guillemin, V. W. Stable Mappings & Their Singularities: Second Corrected Printing. (Graduate Texts in Mathematics: Vol. 14). (Illus.). 209p. 1980. 22.00 o.p. (ISBN 0-387-90072-1). Springer-Verlag.

Gomaa, Ahamad M. The Foundation of the League of Arab States: Wartime Diplomacy & Inter-Arab Politics 1941-1945. 1978. text ed. 35.00x o.p. (ISBN 0-582-78073-X). Longman.

Gombas, P. & Kisdi, D. Wave Mechanics & Its Applications. LC 73-5789. 250p. 1974. text ed. 23.00 (ISBN 0-08-016979-1). Pergamon.

Gombos, George M., ed. Handbook of Ophthalmologic Emergencies. 2nd ed. LC 76-62573. (Illus.). 1977. pap. 13.75 (ISBN 0-87488-633-3). Med Exam.

Gombrich, E. H. In Search of Cultural History. 1969. pap. 5.95x (ISBN 0-19-817168-4). Oxford U Pr.

--The Story of Art. 13th rev. ed. LC 76-62643. (Illus.). 512p. 1981. 19.95 (ISBN 0-8014-1352-4); pap. 12.95 (ISBN 0-8014-9215-7). Cornell U Pr.

Gomel, Charles. Causes Financieres De la Revolution Francaise, 2 vols. 1892-93. Set. 55.00 (ISBN 0-8337-1374-4); 30.00 ea. (ISBN 0-8337-1374-4). B Franklin.

Gomer, E. Swedish Modern Pocket Dictionary: Svensk-Engelskt Engelsk-Svensk Grammatik Parlor. 1978. text ed. 8.50x (ISBN 91-518-1148-0, SW-208). Vanous.

Gomes, Celso P., jt. auth. see Keil, Klaus.

Gomes, Peter J., jt. auth. see Kee, Howard C.

Gomes, Teresa M. Friendly Correspondence: Mazes to the Mind. Kamei, Marlene, ed. 35p. (Orig.). 1978. pap. 2.00 (ISBN 0-935684-01-8). Plumbers Ink.

Gomez, A. V. The Foundation Stock. 6.95 (ISBN 0-533-01979-6). Vantage.

Gomez, Joan, jt. auth. see Dally, Peter.

Gomez, Joseph A. Peter Watkins. (Theatrical Arts Ser.). 1979. lib. bdg. 10.95 (ISBN 0-8057-9267-8). Twayne.

Gomez, June F., ed. Nursing 81: Career Directory, Vol. 3, No. 1. 3rd ed. (Illus., Orig.). 1981. pap. 10.00 (ISBN 0-916730-30-1). Intermed Comm.

Gomez, June F., ed. see Kelly, John, et al.

Gomez, Luis O. see Woodward, Hiram W.

Gomez, Luis O., jt. ed. see Lancaster, Lewis.

Gomez, Madeleine Angelique Poisson De see Poisson De Gomez, Madeleine Angelique.

Gomez, Manuel R., ed. Tuberous Sclerosis. LC 78-94312. 1979. text ed. 26.00 (ISBN 0-89004-313-2). Raven.

Gomez, Rafael A., et al. Solitary Nodular Lesions of the Lung: Contribution to Its Diagnosis & Management. (Illus.). 200p. 1981. 17.50 (ISBN 0-87527-245-2). Green.

Gomez, Victoria. Wags to Witches: More Jokes, Riddles, & Puns. LC 80-17405. (Illus.). 64p. (gr. 2-6). 1981. 6.95 (ISBN 0-688-41954-2); PLB 6.67 (ISBN 0-688-51954-7). Morrow.

Gomez De Toledo, Gaspar. Tercera Parte de la Tragicomedia de Celestina. Barrick, Mac E., ed. LC 70-137886. (Haney Foundation Ser.). (Illus.). 570p. 1973. 15.00x (ISBN 0-8122-7602-7). U of Pa Pr.

Gomez-Gil, Orlando & Stanislawczyk, Irene E., eds. Tierras, Costumbres y Tipos Hispanicos. LC 77-114675. (Span). (gr. 9-12). 1970. pap. 7.95 (ISBN 0-672-63126-1). Odyssey Pr.

Gomez-Moreno, Manuel. Renaissance Sculpture in Spain. Bevan, Bernard, tr. from Span. LC 76-116354. (Illus.). 1971. Repr. of 1931 ed. buckram 40.00 (ISBN 0-87817-042-1). Hacker.

Gomme, A. W. A Historical Commentary on Thucydides. Incl. Vol. 1. Introduction & Commentary of Book 1. 1945. 36.95x (ISBN 0-19-814126-2); Vol. 2. The Ten Years' War, Bks. 2-3. 1956. 34.00x (ISBN 0-19-814003-7); Vol. 3. The Ten Years' War, Bks. 4-5. 1956. 28.00x (ISBN 0-19-814001-0). Oxford U Pr.

Gomme, A. W. & Sandbach, F. H. Menander: A Commentary. 1973. 56.00x (ISBN 0-19-814197-1). Oxford U Pr.

Gomme, A. W., et al. Historical Commentary on Thucydides Vol. 4: Books 5-7 25. 1970. 42.00x (ISBN 0-19-814178-5). Oxford U Pr.

Gomme, A. W., et al, eds. A Historical Commentary on Thucydides, Volume V: Book VIII. (Illus.). 520p. 1981. 75.00 (ISBN 0-19-814198-X). Oxford U Pr.

Gomme, Alice B. see Gomme, George L., et al.

Gomme, George L. Ethnology in Folklore. LC 79-75802. 1969. Repr. of 1892 ed. 15.00 (ISBN 0-8103-3832-7). Gale.

Gomme, George L., et al, eds. The Gentleman's Magazine Library: Being a Classified Collection of the Chief Contents of the Gentleman's Magazine from 1731-1868, 13 vols. Incl. Vol. 1. Manners & Customs. Repr. of 1886 ed (ISBN 0-8103-3434-8); Vol. 2. Dialect, Proverbs, & Word Lore. Repr. of 1886 ed (ISBN 0-8103-3435-6); Vol. 3. Popular Superstitions. Repr. of 1884 ed (ISBN 0-8103-3436-4); Vol. 4. English Traditional Lore. Repr. of 1885 ed (ISBN 0-8103-3437-2); Vols. 5 & 6. Archaeology. Repr. of 1886 ed (ISBN 0-8103-3438-0); Vols. 7 & 8. Romano-British Remains. Repr. of 1886 ed (ISBN 0-8103-3439-9); Vol. 9. Literary Curiosities & Notes. Gomme, Alice B., ed. Repr. of 1889 ed (ISBN 0-8103-3440-2); Vol. 10. Bibliographical Notes. Bickley, A. C., ed. Repr. of 1890 ed (ISBN 0-8103-3441-0); Vols. 11 & 12. Architectural Antiquities. Repr. of 1890 ed (ISBN 0-8103-3442-9); Vol. 13. Ecclesiology. Milne, F. A., ed. Repr. of 1886 ed (ISBN 0-8103-3443-7). LC 67-23900. Vols. 1-4, 9, 10, 13. 18.00 ea.; Vols. 5 & 6, 7 & 8, 11 & 12 (two Vol. Sets) 28.00 ea. (ISBN 0-8103-3355-4). Gale.

Gomori, George. Cyprian Norwid. LC 73-17341. (World Author's Ser.: Poland: No. 305). 168p. 1974. lib. bdg. 10.95 o.p. (ISBN 0-8057-2656-X). Twayne.

Gomoyunova, M. V., jt. auth. see Dobretsov, L. N.

Gompel, Claude. Atlas of Diagnostic Cytology. LC 77-27068. 1978. text ed. 58.95 (ISBN 0-471-02278-0, Pub. by Wiley Medical). Wiley.

Gompertz, G. M. Chinese Celadon Wares. 2nd ed. (Illus.). 1980. 48.00 (ISBN 0-571-18003-5, Pub. by Faber & Faber). Merrimack Bk Serv.

--Korean Pottery & Porcelain of Yi Period. 1968. 33.00 (ISBN 0-571-08404-4, Pub. by Faber & Faber). Merrimack Bk Serv.

Gomperz, Theodor. Greek Thinkers: A History of Ancient Philosophy, 4 vols. Incl. Vol. 1. text ed. (ISBN 0-687-01947-8); pap. text ed. (ISBN 0-7195-0498-8); Vol. 2. text ed. (ISBN 0-687-01948-6); pap. text ed. (ISBN 0-7195-0499-6); Vol. 3. text ed. (ISBN 0-7195-0500-3); pap. text ed. (ISBN 0-7195-0504-6); Vol. 4. text ed. (ISBN 0-7195-0501-1); pap. text ed. (ISBN 0-7195-0505-4). 1964. text ed. 10.00x ea.; pap. text ed. 8.25x ea. Humanities.

Goncharov, Ivan. Oblomov. Hogarth, C. J., tr. from Rus. LC 79-19061. 1980. Repr. of 1915 ed. lib. bdg. 12.50x (ISBN 0-8376-0451-6). Bentley.

--The Precipice. Bryant, M., tr. from Rus. LC 73-21714. vii, 320p. 1975. Repr. of 1915 ed. 17.50 (ISBN 0-86527-295-6). Fertig.

Goncourt, Edmond De see De Goncourt, Edmond.

Goncourt, Edmond De see De Goncourt, Edmond & De Goncourt, Jules.

Goncourt, Edmond L. The Woman of the Eighteenth Century: Her Life, from Birth to Death, Her Love & Her Philosophy in the Worlds of Salon, Shop & Street. Le Clercq, Jacques & Roeder, Ralph, trs. from Fr. LC 79-2937. (Illus.). 347p. 1981. Repr. of 1927 ed. 26.50 (ISBN 0-8305-0103-7). Hyperion Conn.

Goncourt, Jules De see De Goncourt, Edmond & De Goncourt, Jules.

Gonda, J. Visnuism & Sivaism: A Comparison. 1970. text ed. 13.50x (ISBN 0-485-17409-X, Athlone Pr). Humanities.

Gonder, Peggy. Cutting Cost. 1977. pap. 8.00 (ISBN 0-87545-008-3). Natl Sch Pr.

Gondin, William R. Handbook Dictionary of Parliamentary Prodecure. (Quality Paperback: No. 234). (Orig.). 1969. pap. 2.95 (ISBN 0-8226-0234-2). Littlefield.

Gondin, William R. & Mammen, Edward W. Art of Speaking Made Simple. 1954. pap. 3.50 (ISBN 0-385-01201-2, Made). Doubleday.

Gondin, William R. & Sohmer, Bernard. Advanced Algebra & Calculus Made Simple. 1959. pap. 3.95 (ISBN 0-385-00438-9, Made). Doubleday.

--Intermediate Algebra & Analytic Geometry Made Simple. 1959. pap. 3.50 (ISBN 0-385-00437-0, Made). Doubleday.

Gonella, Ronald R., jt. ed. see Altman, Liza.

Gongora, M. Studies in the Colonial History of Spanish America. Southern, R., tr. from Span. LC 74-19524. (Latin American Studies: No. 20). 235p. 1975. 32.95 (ISBN 0-521-20686-3). Cambridge U Pr.

Gonick, Harvey C., ed. Current Nephrology, Vol. 1. (Illus.). 1977. 48.00 (ISBN 0-89289-013-4). HM Prof Med Div.

--Current Nephrology, Vol. 2. 1978. 48.00 (ISBN 0-89289-103-3). HM Prof Med Div.

--Current Nephrology, Vol. 3. 1979. 48.00 (ISBN 0-89289-106-8). HM Prof Med Div.

Gonner, Edward C. Common Land & Inclosure. 2nd ed. (Illus.). Repr. of 1912 ed. 27.50 (ISBN 0-678-05050-3). Kelley.

Gonsalves, Carol. Sermon on the Mountain. (Arch Bk. Supplement Ser.). 1981. pap. 0.79 (ISBN 0-570-06149-0, 59-1304). Concordia.

Gonsalves, Milton. Fagothey's Right & Reason: Ethics in Theory & Practice. 7th ed. 630p. 1981. text ed. 19.95 (ISBN 0-8016-1541-0). Mosby.

Gonshack, Sol. Little Stories for Big People. (Illus.). (gr. 7 up). 1976. pap. 2.95 (ISBN 0-88345-263-4). Regents Pub.

Gonzales, Dolores, ed. Canciones y Juegos de Nuevo Mexico: Songs & Games of New Mexico. LC 73-155. 128p. 1973. 4.95 o.p. (ISBN 0-498-01350-2). A S Barnes.

Gonzales, Gertrude D. & Lewis, Arthur J., eds. Modern Drug Encyclopedia & Therapeutic Index, No. 16. 16th ed. LC 34-12823. 1100p. 1981. text ed. 40.00 (ISBN 0-914316-21-4). Yorke Med.

Gonzales, Manuel G. Andrea Costa & the Rise of Socialism in the Romagna. LC 79-6771. 419p. 1980. text ed. 21.75 (ISBN 0-8191-0952-5); pap. text ed. 13.75 (ISBN 0-8191-0953-3). U Pr of Amer.

Gonzales, N. V. The Bamboo Dancers. 276p. 1961. 8.95 (ISBN 0-8040-0018-2). Swallow.

Gonzales, Pancho. Tennis. Heldman, Gladys, ed. LC 62-8027. (Illus.). 1965. 6.95 (ISBN 0-8303-0011-2). Fleet.

--Tennis. 128p. 1965. pap. 2.95 (ISBN 0-346-12328-3). Cornerstone.

Gonzales, Ronald F., jt. auth. see Edmonds, I. G.

Gonzalez, Ananias, ed. see Sisemore, J. T.

Gonzalez, Andrew B. Language & Nationalism: The Philippine Experience Thus Far. 179p. 1980. 18.25 (ISBN 0-686-28647-2); pap. 11.25x (ISBN 0-686-28648-0). Cellar.

Gonzalez, Armando E., jt. ed. see Aguilar, Juan.

Gonzalez, Carlos F., et al. Computed Brain & Orbital Tomography: Technique & Interpretation. LC 76-28530. (Wiley Series in Diagnostic & Therapeutic Radiology). 1976. 47.50 (ISBN 0-471-01692-6, Pub. by Wiley-Medical). Wiley.

Gonzalez, Catherine, jt. auth. see Gonzalez, Justo.

Gonzalez, Jean. Complete Guide to Effective Dictation. 1980. pap. text ed. 12.95 (ISBN 0-534-00811-9). Kent Pub Co.

Gonzalez, Jean, jt. auth. see Bergerud, Marly.

Gonzalez, Julio Lopez see Lopez Gonzalez, Julio.

Gonzalez, Justo. Historia de un Amor. (Illus.). 168p. (Orig., Span.). 1979. pap. 3.50 (ISBN 0-89922-151-3). Edit Caribe.

Gonzalez, Justo & Gonzalez, Catherine. In Accord-Let Us Worship. (Orig.). 1981. pap. 3.95 (ISBN 0-377-00111-2). Friend Pr.

Gonzalez, Justo L. La Era de las Tinieblas. (Y Hasta Lo Ultimo De la Tierra: una Historia Ilustrada Del Christianismo Ser.: Tomo III). (Illus.). 199p. (Orig., Span.). 1978. pap. 4.50 (ISBN 0-89922-128-9). Edit Caribe.

--La Era de los Altos Ideales. (Y Hasta Lo Ultimo De la Tierra: una Historia Ilustrada Del Christianismo Ser.: Tomo IV). (Illus.). 197p. (Orig., Span.). 1979. pap. 4.50 (ISBN 0-89922-135-1). Edit Caribe.

--La Era De los Conquistadores. (Y Hasta Lo Ultimo de la Tierra: una Historia Ilustrada del Cristianismo: Tomo VII). (Illus.). 218p. (Span.). 1981. pap. 4.50 (ISBN 0-89922-162-9). Edit Caribe.

--La Era de los Gigantes. (Y Hasta Lo Ultimo De la Tierra: una Historia Ilustrada Del Christianismo Ser.: Tomo II). (Illus.). 184p. (Orig., Span.). 1978. pap. 4.50 (ISBN 0-89922-117-3). Edit Caribe.

--La Era de los Martires. (Y Hasta Lo Ultimo De la Tierra: una Historia Ilustrada Del Christianismo Ser.: Tomo I). (Illus.). 189p. (Orig., Span.). 1978. pap. 4.50 (ISBN 0-89922-109-2). Edit Caribe.

--La Era de los Reformadores. (Y Hasta Lo Ultimo De la Tierra: una Historia Ilustrada Del Christianismo Ser.: Tomo VI). (Illus.). 219p. (Orig., Span.). 1980. pap. 4.50 (ISBN 0-89922-154-8). Edit Caribe.

--La Era de los Suenos Frustrados. (Y Hasta Lo Ultimo De la Tierra: una Historia Ilustrada Del Christianismo Ser.: Tomo V). (Illus.). 182p. (Orig., Span.). 1979. pap. 4.50 (ISBN 0-89922-139-4). Edit Caribe.

--History of Christian Thought, 3 vols. 1975. Set. 43.95 (ISBN 0-687-17177-6). Abingdon.

--A History of Christian Thought, Vol. 3: From the Protestant Reformation to the Twentieth Century. LC 74-109679. 416p. 1975. 16.95 (ISBN 0-687-17176-8). Abingdon.

--Luces Bajo el Almud. LC 77-11753. 76p. (Orig., Span.). 1977. pap. 1.95 (ISBN 0-89922-102-5). Edit Caribe.

Gonzalez, Justo L., tr. see Carson, Mary F. & Duba, Arlo D.

Gonzalez, Justo L., tr. see Farrior, Louise H.

Gonzalez, Mike, tr. see Vazquez, Adolfo S.

Gonzalez, Nancie L., ed. Social & Technological Management in Dry Lands: Past & Present, Indigenous & Imposed. LC 77-93023. (AAAS Selected Symposium Ser.: No. 10). (Illus.). 1978. lib. bdg. 18.75x (ISBN 0-89158-438-2). Westview.

Gonzalez, R. C., jt. auth. see Tou, J. T.

Gonzalez, Rafael C. & Thomason, Michael G. Syntactic Pattern Recognition: An Introduction. (Applied Mathematics & Computation Ser.: No. 14). 1978. text ed. 33.50 (ISBN 0-201-02930-8, Adv Bk Prog); pap. text ed. 21.50 (ISBN 0-201-02931-6). A-W.

Gonzalez, Rafael C. & Wintz, Paul. Digital Image Processing & Recognition. LC 77-10317. (Applied Mathematics & Computation Ser.: No. 13). 1977. text ed. 33.50 (ISBN 0-201-02596-5, Adv Bk Prog); pap. text ed. 19.50 (ISBN 0-201-02597-3). A-W.

Gonzalez, Richard F. & McMillan, Claude, Jr. Machine Computation: An Algorithmic Approach. (Irwin-Dorsey Information Processing Ser). 1971. text ed. 16.95x (ISBN 0-256-00234-7). Irwin.

Gonzalez, Richard F., jt. auth. see Harris, Roy D.

Gonzalez, Richard F., jt. auth. see McMillan, Claude.

Gonzalez-Balado, Jose. Always the Poor: Mother Teresa, Her Life & Message. Diaz, Olimpia, Sr., tr. from Span. 112p. (Orig.). 1980. pap. 2.50 (ISBN 0-89243-134-2). Liguori Pubns.

Gonzalez Del Valle, L. & Cabrera, Vicente. La Nueva Ficcion Hispanoamericana A Traves De Miguel Angel Asturias Y Gabriel Garcia Marquez. 1972. 9.95 (ISBN 0-88303-008-X); pap. 6.95 (ISBN 0-685-73212-6). E Torres & Sons.

Gonzalez Gordon, Manuel M. Sherry: The Noble Wine. LC 73-151683. (Illus.). 237p. 1972. 15.00 (ISBN 0-304-93472-0). Intl Pubns Serv.

Gonzalez-Mena, Frank & Gonzalez-Mena, Janet. Experiencias En Espanol. Medrano, A., ed. Gonzalez-Mena, Frank & Gonzalez-Mena, Janet, trs. from Eng. (Illus.). 192p. (Orig., Span.). (gr. k-3). 1976. pap. text ed. 12.95 tchrs ed. (ISBN 0-88499-232-2); wkbk. 2.95 (ISBN 0-88499-234-9); program package 38.95 (ISBN 0-88499-233-0). Inst Mod Lang.

Gonzalez-Mena, Frank, tr. see Gonzalez-Mena, Frank & Gonzalez-Mena, Janet.

Gonzalez-Mena, Janet. English Experiences. Incl. Program for English Experiences. (Illus.). 142p. pap. 12.95 (ISBN 0-88499-225-X); My Book. (Illus.). 48p. pap. 2.95 (ISBN 0-88499-238-1). LC 75-5307. (gr. 4 up). 1975. Set. 38.95 (ISBN 0-88499-238-1). Inst Mod Lang.

Gonzalez-Mena, Janet & Eyer, Dianne W. Infancy & Caregiving. LC 79-91838. (Illus.). 163p. (Orig.). 1980. pap. text ed. 6.95 (ISBN 0-87484-515-7). Mayfield Pub.

Gonzalez-Mena, Janet, jt. auth. see Garcia, Mary H.

Gonzalez-Mena, Janet, jt. auth. see Gonzalez-Mena, Frank.

Gonzalez-Mena, Janet, tr. see Gonzalez-Mena, Frank & Gonzalez-Mena, Janet.

Gonzalez Torres, Rafael A. La Obra poetica de Felix Franco Oppenheimer: Estudio Tematico-Analitico-Estilistico. LC 79-17993. (Coleccion UPREX; Ser. Estudios Literarios: No. 59). 150p. (Orig., Sp.). 1980. pap. 1.85x (ISBN 0-8477-0059-3). U of PR Pr.

Gonzalo, Cespedes & Gonzalo, Meneses. Gerardo the Unfortunate Spaniard: A Pattern for Lascivious Lovers. Digges, Leonard, tr. LC 80-2475. 1981. Repr. of 1622 ed. 142.40 (ISBN 0-404-19107-X). AMS Pr.

Gonzalo, Meneses, jt. auth. see Gonzalo, Cespedes.

Gooberman, Lawrence A. Operation Intercept. 1976. 23.00 (ISBN 0-08-017837-5); pap. 10.00 (ISBN 0-08-017836-7). Pergamon.

Gooch, A. Diminutive, Augumentative & Pejorative Suffixes in Modern Spanish. 2nd ed. 1970. 21.00 (ISBN 0-08-015808-0); pap. text ed. 3.50 (ISBN 0-08-011960-3). Pergamon.

Gooch, Bill, jt. auth. see Stadt, Ronald.

Gooch, Bob. Conveys & Singles. LC 78-75306. (Illus.). 192p. 1980. 10.95 (ISBN 0-498-02342-7). A S Barnes.

--Spinning for Trout. (Illus.). 192p. 1981. 12.50 (ISBN 0-684-16843-X, ScribT). Scribner.

Gooch, Brison D., ed. Interpreting Western Civilization, 2 vols. Incl. Vol. 1. From Antiquity to the Sun King. pap. text ed. o.p. (ISBN 0-256-01094-3); Vol. 2. From the Enlightenment to the Present. pap. text ed. 9.95x (ISBN 0-256-01095-1). 1969. Dorsey.

Gooch, George P; see Hobson, John A.

Gooch, John. The Plans of War: The General Staff & British Military Strategy c. 1900-1916. LC 74-511. 348p. 1974. 21.95 (ISBN 0-470-31321-8). Halsted Pr.

--The Prospect of War: British Defence Policy Eighteen Forty-Seven to Nineteen Forty-Two. 150p. 1981. 25.00x (ISBN 0-7146-3128-0, F Cass Co). Biblio Dist.

Gooch, Ken & Caroline, John. Construction for Profit. (Illus.). 240p. 1980. text ed. 21.95 (ISBN 0-8359-0938-7). Reston.

Gooch, Peter H. Ideas for Art Teachers. 1972. pap. 16.95 (ISBN 0-7134-2304-8, Pub. by Batsford England). David & Charles.

Gooch, Stan & Pringle, M. L. Four Years On: A Follow-up Study at School Leaving Age of Children Formerly Attending a Traditional & Progessive Junior School. (Studies in Child Development). (Orig.). 1966. pap. text ed. 3.50x (ISBN 0-582-32392-4). Humanities.

Goock, Roland. The World's One Hundred Best Recipes. Culinary Arts Institute, tr. from Ger. LC 73-9341. (Illus.). 1973. 14.95 (ISBN 0-8326-0542-5, 1650); pap. 7.95 (ISBN 0-686-67697-1, 2650). Delair.

Good, Carter V. Essentials of Educational Research: Methodology & Design. 2nd ed. (Orig.). 1972. pap. text ed. 18.95 (ISBN 0-13-285841-X). P-H.

Good Housekeeping Editors. Family Health & Medical Guide. LC 78-51129. (Illus.). 928p. 1979. 19.95 (ISBN 0-87851-023-0). Hearst Bks.

Good, Judith, ed. Skillseekers 3: Decimal Computation Kit. (gr. 5-8). 1978. kit 185.00 (ISBN 0-201-23200-6, Sch Div). A-W.

Good, Maurice. John Synge Comes Next. 48p. (Orig.). 1973. pap. text ed. 3.75x (ISBN 0-85105-225-8, Dolmen Pr). Humanities.

Good, Merle. Hazel's People. 1975. pap. 1.25 (ISBN 0-89129-008-7). Jove Pubns.

Good, Paul. The Individual. (Human Behavior Ser.). 1974. 9.95 (ISBN 0-8094-1904-1); lib. bdg. avail. (ISBN 0-685-50285-6). Time-Life.

--The Individual. LC 74-83977. (Human Behavior Ser.). (Illus.). 1974. lib. bdg. 9.99 o.p. (ISBN 0-686-51077-1). Silver.

Good, Richard. Watches in Color. (Illus.). 218p. 1981. pap. 6.95 (Pub. by Blandford Pr England). Sterling.

--Watches in Color. (Illus.). 1979. 12.95 (ISBN 0-7137-0831-X, Pub. by Blandford Pr England). Sterling.

Good, Robert A., jt. ed. see Lieberman, Philip H.

Good, Robert A., jt. ed. see Safai, Bijan.

Good, Robert A., et al, eds. Molecular Pathology. (Illus.). 888p. 1975. text ed. 85.50 (ISBN 0-398-02944-X). C C Thomas.

Good, Ronald. The Geography of Flowering Plants. 4th ed. LC 73-85684. (Illus.). 584p. 1974. text ed. 33.00x (ISBN 0-582-46611-3). Longman.

Good, Shirley R. & Rodgers, Susan S. Analysis for Action: Nursing Care of the Elderly. (Illus.). 1980. pap. text ed. 10.95 (ISBN 0-13-032623-2). P-H.

Good, Stephen M. How to Get a Job with the Post Office. LC 79-2240. 1980. pap. 4.95 (ISBN 0-06-463500-7, EH 500, EH). Har-Row.

Good Thing Inc. & Burstein, John. Slim Goodbody: Your Health & Feelings. (gr. 1-3). 1978. pap. text ed. 125.00 (ISBN 0-89290-098-9, CM-43). Soc for Visual.

Goodacre, Clive, ed. Penrose Seventy-Nine to Eighty. (International Review of the Graphic Arts Ser.: Vol. 72). 1979. 49.50 o.p. (ISBN 0-8038-5881-7). Hastings.

--Penrose 1980-1981: International Review of the Graphic Arts, Vol.73. (Illus.). 200p. 1981. 59.50 (ISBN 0-8038-5892-2, Visual Communication). Hastings.

Goodacre, Elizabeth J. School & Home. 1970. pap. text ed. 5.00x (ISBN 0-391-02083-8, NFER). Humanities.

Goodall, Blake. The Homilies of St. John Chrysostom on the Letters of St. Paul to Titus & Philemon. (Univ. of California Publications in Classical Studies: Vol. 20). 1979. 11.00x (ISBN 0-520-09596-0). U of Cal Pr.

Goodall, D. W. & Perry, R. A., eds. Arid-Land Ecosystems: Structure, Functioning & Management, Vol. 2. LC 77-84810. (International Biological Programme Ser.: No. 17). 550p. Date not set. 110.00 (ISBN 0-521-22988-X). Cambridge U Pr.

Goodall, Daphne M. Horses of the World. rev. ed. LC 73-7480. (Illus.). 272p. 1974. 14.95 (ISBN 0-02-544650-9). Macmillan.

--Zebras. LC 77-608273. (Animals of the World Ser). (Illus.). (gr. 4-8). 1978. PLB 10.65 (ISBN 0-8172-1080-6). Raintree Pubs.

Goodall, Daphne M., tr. see Klimke, Reiner.

Goodall, David, ed. Evolution of Desert Biota. (Illus.). 1976. 12.95x (ISBN 0-292-72015-7). U of Tex Pr.

Goodall, E. G., tr. see Von Cube, Hans L. & Staimle, Fritz.

Goodall, Harrison & Friedman, Renee. Log Structures, Preservation & Problem-Solving. 120p. 1980. pap. 10.95 (ISBN 0-910050-46-5). AASLH.

Goodall, Helen S. & Cooper, Ella G. Daily Lessons Received at 'Akka January 1908. rev. ed. LC 79-19806. 1979. pap. 5.00 (ISBN 0-87743-135-3, 7-32-41). Baha'i.

Goodall, John S. An Edwardian Season. LC 79-89479. (Illus.). 64p. 1980. 7.95 (ISBN 0-689-50155-2, McElderry Bk). Atheneum.

--Paddy's New Hat. LC 80-80129. (Illus.). 64p. (ps up). 1980. 6.95 (ISBN 0-689-50172-2, McElderry Bk). Atheneum.

--Victorians Abroad. LC 80-67431. (Illus.). 64p. 1981. 8.95 (ISBN 0-689-50191-9, McElderry Bk). Atheneum.

Goodall, John S., illus. John S. Goodall's Theatre: The Sleeping Beauty. McElderry, Margaret K. (Illus.). 1980. 3.95 (ISBN 0-689-50161-7, McElderry Bk). Atheneum.

--The Midnight Adventures of Kelly, Dot, & Esmeralda. LC 75-190555. (ps-12). 1973. 4.95 (ISBN 0-689-30505-2, McElderry Bk). Atheneum.

Goodall, Merrill, et al. California Water: A New Political Economy. LC 77-88255. 128p. 1978. text ed. 18.00 (ISBN 0-916672-86-7). Allanheld.

Goodavage, Joseph. Magic: Science of the Future. (Orig.). 1976. pap. 1.50 o.p. (ISBN 0-451-07081-X, W7081, Sig). NAL.

Goodavage, Joseph F. Our Threatened Planet. 1980. pap. write for info. (ISBN 0-671-81640-3). PB.

Goodban, Dale F., jt. auth. see Mehaffy, Robert E.

Goodbar, Joseph E. Managing the People's Money. 1935. 47.50x (ISBN 0-685-89765-6). Elliots Bks.

Goodbody, John. Judo: How to Become a Champ. (Illus.). 1976. pap. 7.50 (ISBN 0-86002-128-9). Transatlantic.

Goodbody, John, jt. ed. see Kirkley, George.

Goodboy, Eadie, jt. auth. see Lawless, Agnes.

Goodboy, Eadie, ed. Jesus Es el Senor. Fast, Todd H., tr. Orig. Title: Jesus Is Lord. 113p. (Span.). 1979. pap. 3.50 (ISBN 0-930756-50-9, 4230-G01(S)). Women's Aglow.

--Jesus Is Lord. 130p. 1977. 3.50 (ISBN 0-930756-27-4, 4230-G01). Women's Aglow.

Goodchild, Peter. J. Robert Oppenheimer: Shatterer of Worlds. (Illus.). 320p. 1981. 15.00 (ISBN 0-686-69049-4). HM.

Goodden, Robert. British Butterflies: A Field Guide. 13.50 (ISBN 0-7153-7594-6, Pub. by Batsford England). David & Charles.

Goode. The Nuclear Energy Controversy. (gr. 7 up). 1980. PLB 6.90 (ISBN 0-531-04165-4, G05). Watts.

Goode, Erich. Deviant Behavior: An Interactionist Approach. LC 77-20487. (P-H Ser. in Sociology). (Illus.). 1978. 17.95 (ISBN 0-13-208306-X). P-H.

--The Drug Phenomenon: Social Aspects of Drug Taking. LC 73-920. (Studies in Sociology Ser.). 66p. 1973. pap. text ed. 3.50 (ISBN 0-672-61326-3). Bobbs.

Goode, James B. Poets of Darkness. LC 80-29653. (The Center for the Study of Southern Culture Ser.). 1981. price not set (ISBN 0-87805-133-3). U Pr of Miss.

Goode, John. George Gissing. (Barnes & Noble Critical Study Ser). 205p. 1979. text ed. 18.50x (ISBN 0-06-492488-2). B&N.

Goode, John, ed. George Gissing: The Nether World. LC 74-499. 432p. 1974. 20.00 o.p. (ISBN 0-8386-1543-0). Fairleigh Dickinson.

Goode, Judith G., jt. auth. see Eames, Edwin.

Goode, Patrick, jt. ed. see Bottomore, Tom.

Goode, Richard. The Individual Income Tax. rev. ed. (Studies of Government Finance). 1976. 15.95 (ISBN 0-8157-3198-1); pap. 6.95 (ISBN 0-8157-3197-3). Brookings.

Goode, Ruth. A Book for Grandmothers. 1976. 7.95 o.s.i. (ISBN 0-02-544620-7). Macmillan.

--People of the First Cities. LC 77-6279. (gr. 5-9). 1977. 9.95 (ISBN 0-02-736430-5, 73643). Macmillan.

--People of the Ice Age. LC 72-85191. (Illus.). 144p. (gr. 5-8). 1973. 8.95 (ISBN 0-02-736420-8, CCPr). Macmillan.

Goode, Stephen. Assassination! Kennedy, King, Kennedy. LC 78-10227. (Illus.). (gr. 6 up). 1979. PLB 7.90 s&l (ISBN 0-531-02213-7). Watts.

--Guerrilla Warfare & Terrorism. (gr. 8 up). 1977. PLB 6.90 s&l o.p. (ISBN 0-531-00383-3). Watts.

--The National Defense System. (Career Concise Guides Ser.). (Illus.). (gr. 7 up). 1977. PLB 6.90 s&l (ISBN 0-531-00398-1). Watts.

--The New Congress. LC 80-19111. 224p. (gr. 7 up). 1980. PLB 9.49 (ISBN 0-671-34031-X). Messner.

--The Prophet & the Revolutionary: Arab Socialism in the Modern East. LC 75-6816. 160p. (gr. 7 up). 1975. PLB 6.90 (ISBN 0-531-02840-2). Watts.

Goode, William J. The Celebration of Heroes: Prestige As a Social Control System. LC 77-20322. 1979. 20.00x (ISBN 0-520-03602-6); pap. 7.95x (ISBN 0-520-03811-8). U of Cal Pr.

--Religion Among the Primitives. 1951. 10.95 o.s.i. (ISBN 0-02-912410-7); pap. text ed. 3.50 o.s.i. (ISBN 0-02-912420-4). Free Pr.

--Women in Divorce. LC 78-14243. 1978. Repr. of 1965 ed. lib. bdg. 27.50x (ISBN 0-313-21026-8, GOWD). Greenwood.

--World Revolution & Family Patterns. LC 63-13538. 1970. pap. text ed. 8.95 (ISBN 0-02-912460-3). Free Pr.

Goode, William J., et al. Social Systems & Family Patterns: A Propositional Inventory. LC 75-158851. 1971. 38.50x (ISBN 0-672-61151-1). Irvington.

Goodearl, K. R., et al. Affine Representations of Grothendieck Groups & Applications to Rickart C -Algebras & Aleph O-Continuous Regular Rings. (Memoirs: No. 234). 1980. 6.00 (ISBN 0-8218-2234-9). Am Math.

Goodell, Helen, jt. auth. see Wolf, Stewart.

Goodell, William. American Slave Code in Theory & Practice. LC 68-55888. Repr. of 1853 ed. 19.75x (ISBN 0-8371-0450-5). Negro U Pr.

Goodenough, Donald R., jt. auth. see Witkin, Herman A.

Goodenough, Erwin R. Church in the Roman Empire. LC 77-122754. 1970. Repr. of 1931 ed. lib. bdg. 12.50x (ISBN 0-8154-0337-2). Cooper Sq.

Goodenough, Erwin R. & Goodhart, H. L. Politics of Philo Judaeus. 1938. 50.00x (ISBN 0-685-69822-X). Elliots Bks.

Goodenough, Florence. Anger in Young Children. LC 77-141547. (University of Minnesota Institute of Child Welfare Monographs: No. 9). (Illus.). 278p. 1975. Repr. of 1931 ed. lib. bdg. 22.00x (ISBN 0-8371-5894-X, CWGA). Greenwood.

Goodenough, Florence & Maurer, Katharine. The Mental Growth of Children from Two to Fourteen Years: Study of the Predictive Value of the Minnesota Pre-School Scales. LC 70-141548. (Univ. of Minnesota Institute of Child Welfare Monographs: No. 20). (Illus.). 130p. 1975. Repr. of 1942 ed. lib. bdg. 15.75x (ISBN 0-8371-5895-8, CWGM). Greenwood.

Goodenough, Ursula. Genetics. LC 77-26245. 840p. 1978. text ed. 19.95 (ISBN 0-03-019716-3, HoltC). HR&W.

Goodenough, Ward. Culture, Language & Society. 1981. 9.95; pap. 5.95. Benjamin-Cummings.

Goodenough, Ward H. Description & Comparison in Cultural Anthropology. LC 80-67925. (Lewis Henry Morgan Lectures). 192p. 1981. 22.50 (ISBN 0-521-23740-8); pap. 6.95 (ISBN 0-521-28196-2). Cambridge U Pr.

Goodenough, Ward H. & Sugita, Hiroshi. Trukese-English Dictionary. LC 79-54277. (Memoir Ser.: Vol. 141). 1980. 10.00 (ISBN 0-87169-141-8). Am Philos.

Goodenow, Ronald, jt. ed. see Ravitch, Diane.

Gooder, Eileen A. Latin for Local History: An Introduction. 2nd ed. (Illus.). 1978. pap. text ed. 11.95x (ISBN 0-582-48728-5). Longman.

Gooders, John, jt. auth. see Alden, Peter.

Gooderson, P. J. A History of Lancashire. (Illus.). 144p. 1980. 17.95 (ISBN 0-7134-2588-1, Pub. by Batsford England). David & Charles.

Goodfellow, Ron. Underwater Engineering. 1977. 23.00 (ISBN 0-87814-065-4). Pennwell Pub.

Goodfield, June. An Imagined World: A Story of Scientific Discovery. LC 79-1664. (Illus.). 288p. 1981. 12.95 (ISBN 0-06-011641-2, HarpT). Har-Row.

--Playing God: Genetic Engineering & the Manipulation of Life. 1977. 8.95 o.p. (ISBN 0-394-40692-3). Random.

Goodfriend. The Ages of Woman: Female Lives in American History. (Orig.). 1981. pap. text ed. 7.95 (ISBN 0-316-32005-6). Little.

Goodfriend, Ronnie S. Power in Perception for the Young Child: A Comprehensive Program for the Development of Pre-Reading Visual Perceptual Skills. LC 72-189232. 1972. pap. text ed. 7.75x (ISBN 0-8077-1430-5); pap. text ed. 5.25x suppl. (ISBN 0-8077-1429-1). Tchrs Coll.

Goodger, E. M. Alternative Fuels: Chemical Energy Resources. LC 80-11796. 238p. 1980. 43.95x (ISBN 0-470-26952-9). Halsted Pr.

--Hydrocarbon Fuels: Production Properties & Performance of Liquids & Gases. LC 74-30837. 270p. 1975. 15.95 o.p. (ISBN 0-470-31365-X). Halsted Pr.

--Principles of Spaceflight Propulsion. LC 77-88306. 1970. 19.55 o.p. (ISBN 0-08-013884-5). Pergamon.

Goodgold, Edwin & Carlinsky, Dan. The Compleat Beatles Quiz Book. (Orig.). 1975. pap. 1.75 o.s.i. (ISBN 0-446-84644-9). Warner Bks.

Goodhardt, G. J., et al. The Television Audience: Patterns of Viewing. (Illus.). 174p. 1975. 18.95 (ISBN 0-347-01102-0, 00179-1, Pub. by Saxon Hse). Lexington Bks.

Goodhart, Arthur L. Law of the Land. LC 66-16914. 1966. pap. 1.95x (ISBN 0-8139-0108-1). U Pr of Va.

Goodhart, H. L., jt. auth. see Goodenough, Erwin R.

Goodhew, P. J. & Cartwright, L. E. Electron Microscopy & Analysis. LC 74-32449. (Wykeham Science Ser.: No. 33). 1975. 9.95x (ISBN 0-8448-1160-2). Crane Russak Co.

Goodich, Michael. The Unmentionable Vice. LC 78-13276. 179p. 1980. pap. 6.95 (ISBN 0-87436-300-4). Ross-Erikson.

Goodier, J. H. Dictionary of Painting & Decorating. 308p. 1974. 39.50x (ISBN 0-85264-224-5, Pub. by Griffin England). State Mutual Bk.

--Painting & Decorating: A Guide for Houseowner & Decorator. (Illus.). 1977. 16.95x (ISBN 0-7114-4612-1). Intl Ideas.

Goodier, J. M., jt. auth. see Hurst, A. E.

Gooding, Charles A., jt. ed. see Margulis, Alexander R.

Gooding, D. W. Relics of Ancient Exegesis. LC 74-19523. (Society for Old Testament Studies Monograph No. 4). 100p. 1976. 28.50 (ISBN 0-521-20700-2). Cambridge U Pr.

Gooding, D. W., ed. see Walters, Peter.

Gooding, David. Monarch Notes on Defoe's Moll Flanders. (Orig.). pap. 1.95 (ISBN 0-671-00705-X). Monarch Pr.

Gooding, Earl. The West Indies at the Crossroads. 256p. 1981. text ed. 12.95x (ISBN 0-87073-052-5); pap. text ed. 6.95x (ISBN 0-87073-053-3). Schenkman.

Gooding, John D. Durango South Project: Archaeological Salvage of Two Basketmaker III Sites in the Durango District. (Anthropological Papers Ser.: No. 34). 1980. write for info. (ISBN 0-8165-0705-8). U of Ariz Pr.

Goodisman, Jerry. Diatomic Interaction Potential Theory, 2 vols. Incl. Vol. 1. Fundamentals. 1973. 47.00 (ISBN 0-12-290201-7); Vol. 2. Applications. 1973. 52.25 (ISBN 0-12-290202-5). (Physical Chemistry Ser.). Set. 80.00 (ISBN 0-12-290202-5). Acad Pr.

Goodisman, Leonard D. Quantitative Methods in Public Administration. LC 79-52724. 1979. pap. text ed. 12.25 (ISBN 0-8191-0782-4). U Pr of Amer.

Goodjohn, Albert J. & Pomraning, Gerald C., eds. Reactor Physics in the Resonance & Thermal Regions, 2 vols. Incl. Vol. 1. Neutron Thermalization. 450p (ISBN 0-262-07023-5); Vol. 2. Resonance Absorbtion. 450p (ISBN 0-262-07024-3). 1966. text ed. 30.00x ea. MIT Pr.

Goodkin, Marie, jt. auth. see Billingham, Richard.

Goodlad. The Conventional & the Alternative in Education. new ed. LC 75-2780. 288p. 1975. 16.60x (ISBN 0-8211-0611-2); text ed. 15.00x (ISBN 0-685-53835-4). McCutchan.

Goodlad, J. B. Accounting for Construction Management. 1975. 16.95x (ISBN 0-434-90680-8). Intl Ideas.

Goodlad, John I. What Schools Are For. LC 79-54644. (Foundation Monograph Ser.). 136p. 1979. pap. 5.50 (ISBN 0-87367-422-7). Phi Delta Kappa.

Goodland, Robert. Itumbiara Hydroelectric Project: Environmental Impact Reconnaissance. (Illus.). 1972. pap. 5.00 o.p. (ISBN 0-89327-217-5). NY Botanical.

Goodland, Robert, jt. auth. see Tillman, Robert.

Goodlin, Robert C. Care of the Fetus. LC 78-62542. (Illus.). 580p. 1979. 43.50 (ISBN 0-89352-021-7). Masson Pub.

Goodman, A. W. Analytic Geometry & the Calculus: Student Study Guide, 2 vols. 4th ed. (Illus.). 1980. pap. text ed. 6.95 ea. Vol. I (ISBN 0-02-344970-5). Vol. II (ISBN 0-02-344980-2). Macmillan.

--Mainstream of Algebra & Trigonometry. LC 72-5241. 475p. 1973. text ed. 17.95 o.p. (ISBN 0-395-16004-9, 3-19075); solutions manual. pap. 4.75 o.p. (ISBN 0-395-16005-7, 3-19076). HM.

Goodman, A. W., et al. The Mainstream of Algebra & Trigonometry. 2nd ed. LC 79-90059. (Illus.). 1980. text ed. 18.95 (ISBN 0-395-26765-X); solutions manual 2.25 (ISBN 0-395-26761-7). HM.

Goodman, Allan E. The Lost Peace: America's Search for a Negotiated Settlement of the Vietnam War. LC 77-77566. (Publication Ser: No. 173). (Illus.). 1978. 22.50 (ISBN 0-8179-6731-1). Hoover Inst Pr.

Goodman, Allan E., jt. ed. see Abramowski, Luise.

Goodman, Ann, jt. auth. see Elting, Mary.

Goodman, Anthony. A History of England from Edward II to James I. LC 76-51405. (Illus.). 1977. text ed. 21.00x (ISBN 0-582-48281-X); pap. text ed. 12.95x (ISBN 0-582-48282-8). Longman.

Goodman, Anthony A., jt. auth. see Shapero, Lucy.

Goodman, Bernice. The Lesbian: A Celebration of Difference. 1977. pap. 3.50 (ISBN 0-918314-04-6). Out & Out.

Goodman, Charles D., et al, eds. The p,n Reaction & the Nucleon-Nucleon Force. 550p. 1980. 55.00 (ISBN 0-306-40351-X, Plenum Pr). Plenum Pub.

Goodman, David, tr. see Domes, Jurgen.

Goodman, David M. Arizona Odyssey: Bibliographic Adventures in Nineteenth Century Magazines. LC 73-94875. 1969. 20.00 (ISBN 0-685-67969-1). AZ Hist Foun.

Goodman, David S. Beijing Street Voices. (Illus.). 192p. 1981. 20.00 (ISBN 0-7145-2703-3, Pub. by M Boyars). Merrimack Bk Serv.

--Emotional Well-Being Through Rational Behavior Training. 3rd rev. ed. (Illus.). 256p. 1978. pap. 12.50 (ISBN 0-398-03750-7). C C Thomas.

Goodman, Edward. Study of Liberty & Revolution. 1975. 19.95x (ISBN 0-7156-0870-3); pap. 11.95x (ISBN 0-685-88347-7). Intl Ideas.

Goodman, Elaine, jt. auth. see Goodman, Walter.

Goodman, Ellen. Close to Home. 1980. pap. 2.50 (ISBN 0-449-24351-6, Crest). Fawcett.

Goodman, Elliot R. Soviet Design for a World State. LC 60-7625. 1960. 25.00x (ISBN 0-231-02339-1). Columbia U Pr.

Goodman, Felicitas D. The Exorcism of Anneliese Michel. LC 80-910. 312p. 1981. 12.95 (ISBN 0-385-15789-4). Doubleday.

Goodman, G. & Ross, M., eds. Laser Applications: Video Disc, Vol. 4. 1980. 32.00 (ISBN 0-12-431904-1). Acad Pr.

Goodman, G. T., jt. auth. see Chadwick, M. J.

Goodman, G. T. & Chadwick, M. H., eds. Environmental Management of Mineral Wastes. 382p. 1978. 42.50x (ISBN 90-286-0728-5). Sijthoff & Noordhoff.

Goodman, George J. see Smith, Adam, pseud.

Goodman, Grant K. & Moos, Felix, eds. The United States & Japan in the Western Pacific. (Westview Replica Edition Ser.). (Illus.). 225p. 1980. lib. bdg. 20.00x (ISBN 0-89158-840-X). Westview.

Goodman, Helen, jt. auth. see Fleischer, Eugene.

Goodman, Irving & Schein, Martin, eds. Birds: Brain & Behavior. 1974. 31.00 o.s.i. (ISBN 0-12-290350-1). Acad Pr.

Goodman, J. F., et al. Ideology & Shopfloor Industrial Relations. 224p. 1981. 37.50x (ISBN 0-7099-0465-7, Pub. by Croom Helm Ltd England). Biblio Dist.

Goodman, Jack, ed. While You Were Gone: A Report on Wartime Life in the United States. LC 73-19969. (FDR & the Era of the New Deal Ser). 625p. 1974. Repr. of 1946 ed. lib. bdg. 49.50 (ISBN 0-306-70605-9). Da Capo.

Goodman, James A., ed. Dynamics of Racism in Social Work Practice. LC 73-88446. 388p. 1973. pap. 10.00 (ISBN 0-87101-068-2, CBA-068-C). Natl Assn Soc Wkrs.

Goodman, Jay S. Democrats & Labor in Rhode Island, 1952-1962: Changes in the Old Alliance. LC 67-26817. (Illus.). 154p. 1967. 7.50 (ISBN 0-87057-104-4, Pub. by Brown U Pr). Univ Pr of New England.

Goodman, Jeffrey. American Genesis: The American Indian & the Origins of Modern Man. LC 80-18652. (Illus.). 288p. 1981. 11.95 (ISBN 0-671-25139-2). Summit Bks.

--Psychic Archeology: Time Machine to the Past. (YA) 1980. 2.50 (ISBN 0-425-05000-9). Berkley Pub.

--We Are the Earthquake Generation. 1980. pap. 2.75 (ISBN 0-425-04991-4). Berkley Pub.

Goodman, Joel, jt. auth. see Weinstein, Matt.

Goodman, John. The Regulation of Medical Care: Is the Price Too High? LC 80-25397. (Cato Public Policy Research Monograph: No. 3). (Orig.). 1980. pap. 5.00 (ISBN 0-932790-23-2). Cato Inst.

Goodman, John C. & Dolan, Edwin G. Economics of Public Policy: The Micro View. (Illus.). 1979. pap. text ed. 8.50 (ISBN 0-8299-0238-4); instrs.' manual avail. (ISBN 0-8299-0481-6). West Pub.

Goodman, John L., Jr., jt. auth. see Goedert, Jeanne E.

Goodman, Jonathan. The Killing of Julia Wallace. LC 76-9918. 1977. 7.95 o.p. (ISBN 0-684-14793-9, ScribT). Scribner.

Goodman, Joseph I. & Biggers, W. Watts. Diabetes Without Fear. 1980. pap. 5.95 (ISBN 0-87795-294-9). Arbor Hse.

Goodman, L. J., et al, eds. Low-Cost Housing Technology: An East-West Perspective. (Illus.). 500p. 1980. 69.00 (ISBN 0-08-023250-7). Pergamon.

Goodman, Lawrence R. & Putman, Charles E. Intensive Care Radiology: Imaging of the Critically Ill. LC 78-64. 1978. text ed. 36.50 (ISBN 0-8016-1894-0). Mosby.

Goodman, Lawrence R. & Putnam, C. The Radiographic Evaluation of the Intensive Care Unit Patient. LC 78-50186. 1981. write for info. (ISBN 0-87527-172-3). Green.

Goodman, Leo A. Analyzing Qualitative-Categorical Data: Log-Linear Models & Latentstructure Analysis. Magidson, Jay, ed. 1978. text ed. 18.50 (ISBN 0-89011-513-3). Abt Assoc.

--Analyzing Qualitative-Categorical Data. Magidson, Jay, ed. 1978. text ed. 30.00 o.p. (ISBN 0-201-02505-1). A-W.

Goodman, Leonard H., ed. Current Career & Occupational Literature,1973-1977. 1978. 12.00 (ISBN 0-8242-0616-9). Wilson.

--Current Career & Occupational Literature, 1977-1979. 1980. 15.00. Wilson.

Goodman, Linda. Linda Goodman's Love Signs: A New Approach to the Human Heart. (Illus.). 1980. pap. 7.95 (ISBN 0-449-90043-6, Columbine). Fawcett.

--Linda Goodman's Sun Signs for Aries to Pisces, 12 bks. 96p. 1979. pap. 1.25 o.s.i. (ISBN 0-686-65662-8). Bantam.

Goodman, Lisl M. Death & the Creative Life. 1981. text ed. price not set (ISBN 0-8261-3500-5). Springer Pub.

Goodman, Louis J. & Love, Ralph N., eds. Biomass Energy Projects: Planning & Management. (Pergamon Policy Studies). 300p. Date not set. price not set (ISBN 0-08-025564-7). Pergamon.

--Geothermal Energy Projects: Planning & Management. (Policy Studies). 1980. 33.00 (ISBN 0-08-025095-5). Pergamon.

--Management of Development Projects: An International Case Study Approach. LC 78-26673. (Pergamon Policy Studies: No. 11). 272p. 1979. 29.50 (ISBN 0-08-022493-8). Pergamon.

--Project Planning & Management: An Integrated Approach. LC 79-25990. (Pergamon Policy Studies). 312p. 1980. 33.00 (ISBN 0-08-024667-2); pap. 11.95 (ISBN 0-08-025962-6). Pergamon.

--Small Hydroelectric Projects for Rural Development: Planning & Management. (Pergamon Policy Studies). 250p. Date not set. price not set (ISBN 0-08-025966-9). Pergamon.

Goodman, Louis W., jt. ed. see Davis, Stanley M.

Goodman, M., jt. auth. see Falcaro, Joe.

Goodman, M. C. Junior History of the American Negro, 2 vols. Incl. Vol. 1. Discovery to Civil War. 1969 (ISBN 0-8303-0072-4); Vol. 2. Civil War to Civil Rights War. LC 73-76026. 1970 (ISBN 0-8303-0073-2). (Illus.). (gr. 6-12). 6.50 ea.; text ed. avail. (ISBN 0-8303-0162-3); teaching manual 0.50 ea. Fleet.

Goodman, M. W., jt. auth. see Penzias, Walter.

Goodman, Martin, tr. see Renchlin, Johannes.

Goodman, Mary E. Culture of Childhood: Child's-Eye Views of Society & Culture. LC 75-106992. 1970. pap. 6.50x (ISBN 0-8077-1444-5). Tchrs Coll.

Goodman, Michael J. & Sparberg, Marshall. Ulcerative Colitis. LC 78-8686. (Clinical Gastroenterology Monographs). 1978. 26.95 (ISBN 0-471-48895-X, Pub. by Wiley Medical). Wiley.

Goodman, Miriam, jt. auth. see Aguero, Kathleen.

Goodman, Mitchell. The End of It. LC 79-66117. 286p. 1980. 15.95 (ISBN 0-933256-10-8); pap. 7.95 (ISBN 0-933256-11-6). Second Chance.

Goodman, Morris C. Astrology & Sexual Analysis. 1973. pap. 1.95 o.s.i. (ISBN 0-446-89501-6). Warner Bks.

Goodman, Murray & Meienhofer, Johannes, eds. Peptides: Proceedings. American Peptide Symposium, Fifth. LC 77-88855. 1977. 39.95 (ISBN 0-470-99384-7). Halsted Pr.

Goodman, Nathan G., ed. The Ingenious Dr. Franklin: Selected Scientific Letters of Benjamin Franklin. LC 74-81751. 256p. 1974. 14.00 (ISBN 0-8122-7680-9); pap. 3.95x (ISBN 0-8122-1067-0). U of Pa Pr.

Goodman, Paul. The Break-up of Our Camp, Stories 1932-1935: The Collected Stories, Vol. 1. Stoehr, Taylor, ed. 300p. 1978. 14.00 (ISBN 0-87685-330-0); deluxe ed. 25.00 (ISBN 0-87685-331-9); pap. 7.50 (ISBN 0-87685-329-7). Black Sparrow.

--A Ceremonial, Stories 1936-1940: The Collected Stories of Paul Goodman, Vol. 2. Stoehr, Taylor, ed. 273p. 1978. 14.00 (ISBN 0-87685-354-8); deluxe ed. 25.00 (ISBN 0-87685-355-6); pap. 7.50 (ISBN 0-87685-353-X). Black Sparrow.

--Don Juan: Or, the Continuum of the Libido. Stoehr, Taylor, ed. 225p. 1979. 14.00 (ISBN 0-87685-422-6); deluxe ed. 25.00 (ISBN 0-87685-423-4); pap. 5.00 (ISBN 0-87685-421-8). Black Sparrow.

--The Galley to Mytilene, Stories 1949-1960: Collected Stories of Paul Goodman. Stoehr, Taylor, ed. (Vol. 4). 315p. (Orig.). 1980. 14.00 (ISBN 0-87685-360-2); deluxe ed. 25.00 (ISBN 0-87685-361-0); pap. 7.50 (ISBN 0-87685-359-9). Black Sparrow.

--Nature Heals: The Psychological Essays of Paul Goodman. Stoehr, Taylor, ed. 1979. pap. 4.95 o.p. (ISBN 0-525-47569-9). Dutton.

--Speaking & Language: Defense of Poetry. 1971. 8.95 o.p. (ISBN 0-394-47089-3). Random.

Goodman, Paul, ed. Seeds of Liberation. 1962. 7.50 o.s.i. (ISBN 0-8076-0291-4). Braziller.

Goodman, Paul S. Assessing Organizational Change: Rushton Quality of Work Experiment. LC 78-31857. (Organizational Behavior Assessment & Change Ser.). 1979. 27.95 (ISBN 0-471-04782-1, Pub. by Wiley-Interscience). Wiley.

Goodman, Percival. The Double E. LC 76-50873. 1977. pap. 3.50 (ISBN 0-385-12868-1, Anch). Doubleday.

Goodman, Richard. Modern Statistics. LC 63-19414. (Orig.). 1964. pap. 1.45 o.p. (ISBN 0-668-01108-4). Arc Bks.

Goodman, Richard M. Automobile Design Liability. LC 74-94828. 1970. 85.00 (ISBN 0-686-14535-6, 052A). Lawyers Co-Op.

Goodman, Richard M. & Motulsky, Arno G., eds. Genetic Diseases Among Ashkenazi Jews. LC 77-90594. 1979. text ed. 39.00 (ISBN 0-89004-262-4). Raven.

Goodman, Robert B. & Spicer, Robert A. Kaguya Hime: The Shimmering Princess. Johnson, Victor, ed. LC 75-18791. (Illus.). (gr. 1-7). 1974. 5.95 (ISBN 0-89610-005-7). Island Her.

--The Secret of Beaver Valley. LC 73-77781. (Illus.). (gr. 1-7). 1963. 5.95 (ISBN 0-89610-017-0). Island Her.

--Urashima Taro. Tabrah, Ruth, ed. LC 73-79570. (Illus.). (gr. 1-7). 1973. 5.95 (ISBN 0-89610-013-8). Island Her.

Goodman, Robert L. Simplified TV Trouble Diagnosis. LC 72-94810. 224p. 1973. 8.95 o.p. (ISBN 0-8306-3633-1); pap. 5.95 o.p. (ISBN 0-8306-2633-6, 633). TAB Bks.

--Zenith Color TV Service Manual, Vol. 1. LC 75-85325. (Schematic Servicing Manual Ser.). (Illus.). 1969. vinyl o.p. 8.95 (ISBN 0-8306-9502-8); pap. 7.95 (ISBN 0-8306-8502-2, 502). TAB Bks.

Goodman, Stanley, jt. auth. see Winters, Arthur A.

Goodman, Stephen H., ed. Financing & Risk in Developing Countries. LC 78-63013. (Praeger Special Studies). 1978. 22.50 (ISBN 0-03-042281-7). Praeger.

Goodman, Walter. The Committee: The Extraordinary Career of the House Committee on un-American Activities. LC 68-13010. (Illus.). 564p. 1968. 15.00 (ISBN 0-374-12688-7). FS&G.

Goodman, Walter & Goodman, Elaine. The Family: Yesterday, Today, Tomorrow. LC 74-32069. 128p. (gr. 7 up). 1975. 7.95 (ISBN 0-374-32260-0). FS&G.

--The Rights of the People: The Major Decisions of the Warren Court. LC 79-157926. (gr. 7 up). 1971. 4.95 (ISBN 0-374-36279-3). FS&G.

Goodman, William I. & Freund, Eric C., eds. Principles & Practice of Urban Planning. 4th ed. LC 67-30622. (Municipal Management Ser.). 1968. text ed. 22.00 (ISBN 0-87326-006-6). Intl City Mgt.

Goodnough, David. Cherry Valley Massacre, November 11, 1778: The Frontier Atrocity That Shocked a Young Nation. LC 68-24489. (Focus Bks). (Illus.). (gr. 7 up). 1968. PLB 4.90 o.p. (ISBN 0-531-00998-X). Watts.

--The Colony of New York. LC 72-7087. (First Bks). (Illus.). 96p. (gr. 5-7). 1973. PLB 4.90 o.p. (ISBN 0-531-00783-9). Watts.

--John Cabot & Son. new ed. LC 78-18054. (gr. 4-9). 1979. PLB 4.89 (ISBN 0-89375-172-3); pap. 1.75 (ISBN 0-89375-164-2). Troll Assocs.

Goodpaster, Andrew J. For the Common Defense. LC 77-4562. 1977. 18.95 (ISBN 0-669-01620-9). Lexington Bks.

Goodrich, Chauncey. A Pocket Dictionary: Chinese-English, & Pekingese Syllabary. 341p. 1981. pap. 2.50 (ISBN 0-85656-131-2). Great Eastern.

Goodrich, Leland M. The United Nations in a Changing World. (Columbia University Studies in International Organization). 280p. 1976. 20.00x (ISBN 0-231-03824-0); pap. 7.50x (ISBN 0-231-08343-2). Columbia U Pr.

Goodrich, Leland M. & Kay, David A., eds. International Organization: Politics & Process. 1973. 25.00 (ISBN 0-299-06250-3); pap. 9.95x (ISBN 0-299-06254-6). U of Wis Pr.

Goodrich, Leland M., et al. Charter of the United Nations: Commentary & Documents. 3rd ed. LC 79-87146. 1969. 27.50x (ISBN 0-231-03218-8). Columbia U Pr.

Goodrich, Lloyd. Winslow Homer. (Illus.). 144p. 1976. pap. 6.95 o.p. (ISBN 0-89104-017-X). A & W Pubs.

Goodrich, Roy G. Physics Laboratory Textbook. (Illus.). 442p. 1980. pap. text ed. 13.95 (ISBN 0-89892-031-0). Contemp Pub Co of Raleigh.

Goodrich, Samuel G. Recollections of a Lifetime, or Men & Things I Have Seen. LC 67-23886. 1967. Repr. of 1857 ed. 20.00 (ISBN 0-8103-3041-5). Gale.

--Tales of Peter Parley About America, Repr. Of 1827 Ed. Bd. with Tales of Travels West of the Mississippi, by Solomon Bell. Snelling, William J. Repr. of 1830 ed. LC 75-32158. (Classics of Children's Literature, 1621-1932: Vol. 23). 1976. PLB 38.00 (ISBN 0-8240-2272-6). Garland Pub.

Goodrich, Warren. Change at Jamaica: A Commuter's Guide to Survival. LC 57-12254. (Illus.). 5.95 (ISBN 0-8149-0109-3). Vanguard.

Goodrich, William D. The Sherlock Holmes Reference Guide. LC 80-67701. (Sherlock Holmes Reference Ser.). Date not set. price not set (ISBN 0-934468-06-0). Gaslight.

Goodrick, A. T., tr. see Grimmelshausen, H. J. Von.

Goodrick, Edward W. Do It Yourself Hebrew & Greek: Everybody's Guide to the Language Tools. 256p. (Orig.). 1980. pap. 9.95 (ISBN 0-310-41741-4). Zondervan.

Goodrick, Edward W. & Kohlenberger, John P. The NIV Complete Concordance. 1056p. 1981. 19.95 (ISBN 0-310-43650-8). Zondervan.

Goodridge, J. F., tr. see Langland, William.

Goodrum, Charles A. Treasures of the Library of Congress. (Illus.). 456p. 1980. 50.00 (ISBN 0-8109-1661-4, 1661-4); pre-Jan 45.00 (ISBN 0-686-62680-X). Abrams.

Goodryder, Ernest. How to Earn Money As a Consultant: Including Specimen Contracts. rev. & 5th ed. LC 78-58276. (Frontiers of Industry Ser.). (Illus.). 1978. pap. 31.00 (ISBN 0-931918-01-4). Busn Psych.

--How to Earn Money As an Internal-Consultant: Including Employment Contract. rev. 2nd ed. (Frontiers of Industry Ser). 1977. pap. 27.00 (ISBN 0-931918-00-6). Busn Psych.

Goodsell, Charles T. Administracion De una Revolucion: La Reforma Del Poder Ejecutivo En Puerto Rico Bajo el Gobernador Tugwell, 1941-1946. 5.00 o.p. (ISBN 0-8477-2206-6); pap. 3.75 (ISBN 0-8477-2207-4). U of PR Pr.

Goodsell, Jane. Daniel Inouye. LC 77-1405. (Biography Ser.). (Illus.). (gr. 1-4). 1977. PLB 7.89 (ISBN 0-690-01358-2, TYC-J). T Y Crowell.

--Eleanor Roosevelt. LC 71-106573. (Biography Ser.). (Illus.). (gr. 2-5). 1970. PLB 7.89 (ISBN 0-690-25626-4, TYC-J). T Y Crowell.

--Mayo Brothers. LC 70-139104. (Biography Ser). (Illus.). (gr. 2-5). 1972. PLB 6.49 o.p. (ISBN 0-690-52751-9, TYC-J). T Y Crowell.

Goodslall, jt. auth. see Cozens.

Goodson, Gar. Many Splendored Fishes of the Atlantic Coast. LC 76-3231. 1976. pap. 4.95 (ISBN 0-916240-01-0). Marquest Colorguide.

Goodspeed. This Is the Life. (gr. 7-12). 1981. text ed. price not set. Bennett Co.

Goodspeed, Edgar J. How Came the Bible. 1976. pap. 1.75 (ISBN 0-89129-125-3). Jove Pubns.

--Story of the Bible. LC 36-21666. 1936. 5.00 o.s.i. (ISBN 0-226-30375-6). U of Chicago Pr.

Goodspeed, Edgar J., jt. auth. see Owen, William B.

Goodspeed, T. Harper. Plant Hunters in the Andes. 2nd rev. & enl. ed. 1961. 21.50x (ISBN 0-520-00495-7). U of Cal Pr.

Goodstadt, Leo. China's Watergate: Political & Economic Conflicts in China 1969-1977. 1979. text ed. 15.00x (ISBN 0-7069-0725-6). Humanities.

--China's Watergate: Political & Economic Conflicts, 1969-1977. LC 79-902871. 219p. 1979. 13.50x (ISBN 0-7069-0725-6). Intl Pubns Serv.

Goodstein, L. D., jt. auth. see Lanyon, R. I.

Goodstein, Leonard D. & Lanyon, Richard I. Adjustment, Behavior, & Personality. 2nd ed. LC 78-62553. (Illus.). 1979. text ed. 17.95 (ISBN 0-201-02455-1); wkbk. 6.50 (ISBN 0-201-02456-X). A-W.

Goodstein, Leonard D., jt. ed. see Burke, W. Warner.

Goodstein, Leonard D., et al, eds. Organizational Change Sourcebook Ii: Cases in Conflict Management. LC 79-63006. 234p. 1979. pap. 12.95 (ISBN 0-88390-151-X). Univ Assocs.

Goodstein, R. L. Essays in the Philosophy of Mathematics. 1965. text ed. 12.50x (ISBN 0-7185-1044-5, Leicester). Humanities.

--Fundamental Concepts of Mathematics. 2nd ed. 1978. text ed. 45.00 (ISBN 0-08-021665-X); pap. text ed. 19.25 (ISBN 0-08-021666-8). Pergamon.

--Mathematical Logic. 2nd ed. 1965. text ed. 6.50x (ISBN 0-7185-1010-0, Leicester). Humanities.

Goodwater, Leanna. Women in Antiquity: An Annotated Bibliography. LC 75-23229. 1975. 10.00 (ISBN 0-8108-0837-4). Scarecrow.

Goodwin, Barbara. Social Science & Utopia: Harvester Studies in Philosophy. (No. 4). (Illus.). 1978. text ed. 30.00x (ISBN 0-391-00855-2). Humanities.

Goodwin, Brian C. Temporal Organization in Cells. 1964. 23.00 (ISBN 0-12-289350-6). Acad Pr.

Goodwin, Craufurd D. Exhortation & Controls: The Search for a Wage - Price Policy, 1945-1971. (Studies in Wage-Price Policy). 1975. 16.95 (ISBN 0-8157-3208-2); pap. 7.95 (ISBN 0-8157-3207-4). Brookings.

Goodwin, Craufurd D., ed. Energy Policy in Perspective: Today's Problems, Yesterday's Solution. LC 80-22859. 600p. 1980. 29.95 (ISBN 0-8157-3202-3); pap. 14.95 (ISBN 0-8157-3201-5). Brookings.

Goodwin, David. Delivering Educational Services. LC 76-54166. 1977. pap. text ed. 8.25x (ISBN 0-8077-2507-2). Tchrs Coll.

Goodwin, Del & Chaffee, Dorcas, eds. Perspectives Seventy Six, a Compendium of Useful Knowledge About Old-Time Vermont & New Hampshire. (Illus.). (gr. 6-12). 1975. pap. text ed. 4.95 (ISBN 0-915892-02-2); 6.95 (ISBN 0-686-64804-8). Regional Ctr Educ.

Goodwin, Derek. Birds of Man's World. LC 77-74922. (Illus.). 190p. 1978. 12.50 (ISBN 0-8014-1167-X). Comstock.

--Crows of the World. LC 76-20194. (Illus.). 352p. 1976. 32.50x (ISBN 0-8014-1057-6). Comstock.

--Pigeons & Doves of the World. 2nd ed. LC 76-55484. (Illus.). 464p. 1977. 32.50x (ISBN 0-8014-1100-9). Comstock.

Goodwin, Donald W. & Erickson, Carlton K., eds. Alcoholism & Affective Disorders: Clinical, Genetic, & Biochemical Studies with Emphasis on Alcohol-Lithium Interaction. new ed. (Illus.). 1979. 29.95 (ISBN 0-89335-073-7). Spectrum Pub.

Goodwin, Dwight L. & Coates, Thomas J. Helping Students Help Themselves: How You Can Put Behavior Analysis into Action in Your Classroom. (Illus.). 256p. 1976. 14.95 (ISBN 0-13-386490-1); pap. text ed. 9.95 (ISBN 0-13-386482-0). P-H.

Goodwin, Harold L. All About Rockets & Space Flight. (Allabout Bk). (gr. 5-9). 1970. PLB 4.39 (ISBN 0-394-90259-9). Random.

Goodwin, Harold L., jt. ed. see Hanson, Joe A.

Goodwin, Hope. Home for the Heart. (Orig.). 1980. pap. 1.95 (ISBN 0-532-23135-X). Manor Bks.

Goodwin, Irene & Silvers, Ruth. Polka Dotted Pencil Pushers: Math. LC 79-63129. 156p. (Orig.). 1979. pap. 8.95 (ISBN 0-932970-08-7). Prinit Pr.

Goodwin, Jean M. Sexual Abuse: Clinical Problems & Practical Approaches. 1981. write for info. (ISBN 0-88416-326-1). PSG Pub.

Goodwin, John C. Insanity & the Criminal. (Historical Foundations of Forensic Psychiatry & Psychology Ser.). 308p. 1980. Repr. of 1924 ed. lib. bdg. 29.50 (ISBN 0-306-76061-4). Da Capo.

Goodwin, John F., jt. ed. see Krikler, Dennis M.

Goodwin, John F., jt. ed. see Yu, Paul N.

Goodwin, John R. Business Law: Principles, Documents & Cases. 3rd ed. 1980. 18.50x (ISBN 0-256-02266-6). Irwin.

--Business Law: U.C.C. & C.C.P.A. Principles, Documents & Cases. rev. ed. 1976. text ed. 15.95x o.p. (ISBN 0-256-01781-6); pap. text ed. 5.50x workbk. o.p. (ISBN 0-256-01782-4). Irwin.

--Student Workbook to Accompany Business Law. 3rd ed. 1980. pap. 6.50x (ISBN 0-256-02267-4). Irwin.

Goodwin, John R. & Rovelstad, James M. Travel & Lodging Law. LC 79-12189. (Grid Series in Law). 1980. text ed. 24.50 (ISBN 0-88244-188-4). Grid Pub.

Goodwin, John W. Agricultural Economics. (Illus.). 400p. 1977. text ed. 15.95 (ISBN 0-87909-020-0); instructor's manual free. Reston.

Goodwin, Kenneth, ed. National Identity. 1970. text ed. 10.50 o.p. (ISBN 0-435-18370-2). Heinemann Ed.

Goodwin, Leonard. Do the Poor Want to Work? A Social-Psychological Study of Work Orientations. 170p. 1972. 11.95 (ISBN 0-8157-3206-6); pap. 4.95 (ISBN 0-8157-3205-8). Brookings.

Goodwin, Mary J. The Ghost of Bennett's Villa. LC 79-88506. (Illus.). (gr. 5 up). 1981. 10.00 (ISBN 0-932632-05-X); pap. 3.95 (ISBN 0-932632-03-3). MJG Co.

Goodwin, Mary T. & Pollen, Gerry. Creative Food Experiences for Children. rev. ed. (Illus.). 256p. 1980. text ed. 12.95 (ISBN 0-89329-028-9). Ctr Sci Public.

Goodwin, Mathew O. Numerology: The Complete Guide. 1981. Repr. Set. lib. bdg. 33.00 (ISBN 0-89370-999-9); Vol. 1. lib. bdg. 16.95 ea. (ISBN 0-89370-653-1). Vol. 2 (ISBN 0-89370-654-X). Borgo Pr.

Goodwin, Matthew O. Numerology: The Complete Guide. (Orig.). 1981. Set. pap. 17.50 (ISBN 0-87877-999-X); Vol. 1. pap. 8.95 (ISBN 0-87877-053-4); Vol. 2. pap. 8.95 (ISBN 0-87877-054-2). Newcastle Pub.

Goodwin, Nancy & Manilla, James. Make Your Own Professional Movies. LC 70-152286. 1971. 9.95 (ISBN 0-02-544700-9). Macmillan.

Goodwin, R. M. Elementary Economics from the Higher Standpoints. LC 72-116842. 1970. 35.50 (ISBN 0-521-07923-3). Cambridge U Pr.

Goodwin, Reason A. Troika: Introduction to Russian Letters & Sounds. LC 80-817888. (Orig.). (gr. 11-12). 1980. text ed. 14.50 (ISBN 0-936368-00-4); pap. text ed. 6.95 (ISBN 0-936368-01-2). Lexik Hse.

Goodwin, Robert P., tr. see Thomas Aquinas, St.

Goodwin, Ruby B. It's Good to Be Black. LC 53-11462. (Arcturus Books Paperbacks). 256p. 1976. pap. 4.95 (ISBN 0-8093-0757-X). S Ill U Pr.

Goodwin, Stanley J. Black Destiny. 60p. 1981. pap. 1.95 (ISBN 0-686-28004-0). Northland Pubns WA.

--The Book of Desire. 1979. pap. 2.40 (ISBN 0-686-10271-1). Northland Pubns WA.

--Can Ice Cream & Oranges Prevent the Common Cold & Influenza? (Illus.). 1979. pap. 2.40 (ISBN 0-686-24961-5). Northland Pubns WA.

--The Devastating Eighties. 80p. 1980. pap. 2.40 (ISBN 0-686-27500-4). Northland Pubns WA.

Goodwin, Stephen. The Blood of Paradise. 1979. 8.95 o.p. (ISBN 0-525-06846-5). Dutton.

Goodwin, T. W. & Mercer, E. I. Introduction to Plant Biochemistry. 1972. 18.00 (ISBN 0-08-016223-1). Pergamon.

Goodwin, T. W., ed. see I U B - I U B S Joint Symposium - 1st - Stockholm - 1960.

Goodwin, T. W., ed. see International Symposium on Carotenoids, Madison, 5th, U. S. A., July 23-28 1978.

Goodwin, Thomas. Holy Spirit in Salvation. 1979. 12.95 (ISBN 0-85151-279-8). Banner of Truth.

Goodwin, Thomas, jt. auth. see Bunyan, John.

Goodwin, William, jt. auth. see Klausmeier, Herbert J.

Goodwin-Gill, Guy S. International Law & the Movement of Persons Between States. 1978. 49.50x (ISBN 0-19-825333-8). Oxford U Pr.

Goodworth, C. T. Effective Interviewing for Employment Selection. 138p. 1979. text ed. 22.00x (ISBN 0-220-67005-6, Pub. by Busn Bks England). Renouf.

Goodworth, Clive T. Effective Speaking & Presentation for the Company Executive. 204p. 1980. text ed. 12.25x (Pub. by Busn Bks England). Renouf.

Goodwyn, Floyd L., Jr. Image Pattern & Moral Vision in John Webster. (Salzburg Studies in English Literature: Jacobean Drama Ser: 71). 1977. pap. text ed. 25.00x (ISBN 0-391-01389-0). Humanities.

Goodwyn, Lawrence. The Populist Moment: A Short History of the Agrarian Revolt in America. 1978. pap. 6.95 (ISBN 0-19-502417-6, GB 536, GB). Oxford U Pr.

Goody, Esther N. Questions & Politeness. LC 77-6577. (Cambridge Papers in Social Anthropology Ser: No. 8). 1978. 32.50 (ISBN 0-521-21749-0); pap. 10.95x (ISBN 0-521-29250-6). Cambridge U Pr.

Goody, J., et al, eds. Family & Inheritance. LC 76-10402. (Past & Present Publications Ser.). (Illus.). 1976. 45.00 (ISBN 0-521-21246-4); pap. 13.95x (ISBN 0-521-29354-5). Cambridge U Pr.

Goody, J. R. & Tambiah, S. J. Bridewealth & Dowry. LC 72-95407. (Papers in Social Anthropology Ser.: No. 7). (Illus.). 128p. 1973. 19.95 (ISBN 0-521-20169-1); pap. 7.95x (ISBN 0-521-09805-X). Cambridge U Pr.

Goody, Jack. Developmental Cycle in Domestic Groups. LC 78-160087. (Papers in Social Anthropology: No. 1). (Illus.). 1972. 19.95 (ISBN 0-521-05116-9); pap. 9.95x (ISBN 0-521-09660-X). Cambridge U Pr.

--Succession to High Office. LC 79-52487. (Cambridge Papers in Social Anthropology: No. 4). (Illus.). 1979. pap. 7.95x (ISBN 0-521-29732-X). Cambridge U Pr.

Goody, Jack R., ed. Literacy in Traditional Societies. LC 69-10427. 1969. 29.95 (ISBN 0-521-07345-6); pap. 11.95x (ISBN 0-521-29005-8). Cambridge U Pr.

Goody, Peter. Horse Anatomy. (Illus.). 17.50 (ISBN 0-85131-230-6, Dist. by Sporting Book Center). J A Allen.

Goody, Roy W. Microcomputer Fundamentals. 300p. 1979. pap. text ed. 13.95 (ISBN 0-574-21540-9, 13-4540); instr's. guide avail. (ISBN 0-574-21541-7, 13-4541). SRA.

Goodyear, Carmen. The Sheep Book. 26p. (ps-1). 1972. pap. 2.75 (ISBN 0-914996-02-9). Lollipop Power.

Goodyear, F. R., jt. ed. see Diggle, J.

Goodyear, Imogene, jt. auth. see Brunson, Madelon.

Goodyear, Imogene, ed. The Beauty of Wholeness: Program Resource for Women 1981. 1980. pap. 4.00 (ISBN 0-8309-0294-5). Herald Hse.

Goodyear, William H. Greek Refinements. (Illus.). 1912. 100.00x (ISBN 0-685-69823-8). Elliots Bks.

Goodzeit, Jack M. Foundations for Serving Those Wth Severe & Multiple Handicaps. 300p. 1981. text ed. 24.50x (ISBN 0-8290-0268-5); pap. text ed. 12.95x (ISBN 0-8290-0269-3). Irvington.

Googe, Barnabe. Eglogs, Epytaphes, & Sonettes, (1563) LC 68-24209. (Illus.). 1969. Repr. of 1563 ed. lib. bdg. 20.00x (ISBN 0-8201-1060-4). Schol Facsimiles.

--Selected Poems of Barnabe Googe. Stephens, Alan, ed. LC 80-29155. (Books of the Renaissance Ser.). 60p. 1981. Repr. of 1961 ed. lib. bdg. 17.50x (ISBN 0-313-22830-2, GOSEP). Greenwood.

Gooneratne, Y. Alexander Pope. LC 76-4758. (British Authors Ser). 160p. 1976. 27.50 (ISBN 0-521-21127-1); pap. 7.95x (ISBN 0-521-29051-1). Cambridge U Pr.

Gooneratne, Yasmine. Jane Austen. LC 75-123669. (British Authors Ser.: Introductory Critical Studies). 1970. 28.50 (ISBN 0-521-07843-1); pap. 7.95x (ISBN 0-521-09630-8). Cambridge U Pr.

Goonetileke, H. A. Bibliography of Ceylon, 3 vols. 2nd ed. LC 77-851302. 954p. 1973. Set. 140.00x (ISBN 3-85750-015-8). Intl Pubns Serv.

--Sri Lanka. (World Bibliographical Ser.: No. 20). 1981. price not set (ISBN 0-903450-33-X). ABC Clio.

Gooque, Ray. Hook, Line & Sinker. 14.50x (ISBN 0-392-07163-0, SpS). Soccer.

Goor, A. Y. & Barney, C. W. Forest Tree Planting in Arid Zones. 2nd ed. LC 76-22314. (Illus.). 1976. 27.50 (ISBN 0-8260-3441-1, 39153, Pub. by Wiley-Interscience). Wiley.

Goosens, Leon & Roxburgh, Edwin. Oboe. LC 77-15886. (The Yehudi Menuhin Music Guides Ser.). (Illus.). 1978. 12.95 (ISBN 0-02-871450-4); pap. 6.95 (ISBN 0-02-871460-1). Schirmer Bks.

Goospeed, Robert C. From Greek to Graffiti. (Illus.). 288p. (Orig.). 1981. 15.00 (ISBN 0-682-49696-0, University); pap. 10.00 (ISBN 0-682-49706-1, University). Exposition.

Goossen, C. Herbert Ferber. LC 80-66531. (Illus.). 1981. 75.00 (ISBN 0-89659-148-4). Abbeville Pr.

Goossen, E. C. Kelly. (Derriere le Miroir: No. 110). (Illus.). 1978. pap. 19.95 (ISBN 0-8120-2000-6). Barron.

Gootzeit, Michael J. David Ricardo. (Essays on the Great Economists Ser). 96p. 1975. 12.50x (ISBN 0-231-03524-1); pap. 5.00x (ISBN 0-231-03916-6). Columbia U Pr.

Goozner, Calman. Arithmetic Skills. (gr. 7-12). 1973. text ed. 11.17 (ISBN 0-87720-238-9); pap. text ed. 5.83 (ISBN 0-87720-237-0); wkbk 7.08 (ISBN 0-87720-236-2). AMSCO Sch.

--Clerical Practice Skills. (gr. 10 up). 1978. pap. text ed. 7.08 (ISBN 0-87720-403-9). AMSCO Sch.

--Computational Skills for College Students. 1976. pap. text ed. 7.58 (ISBN 0-87720-976-6). AMSCO Sch.

Gopal, E. S. Statistical Mechanics & Properities of Matter: Theory & Applications. LC 74-3382. 1976. pap. 24.95 (ISBN 0-470-15168-4). Halsted Pr.

Gopal, M., jt. auth. see Nagrath, I. J.

Gopal, M. H. Introduction to Research Procedure in Social Sciences. 2nd ed. 1970. pap. 6.00x o.p. (ISBN 0-210-27013-6). Asia.

Gopal, Madan. Tulasi Das. 120p. 1980. 6.95x (ISBN 0-89955-320-6, Pub. by Interprint India). Intl Schol Bk Serv.

Gopal, R. Indian Muslims: A Political History 1858-1947. 10.00 (ISBN 0-210-33673-0). Asia.

Gopal, R., ed. Energy Conservation in Building Heating & Air Conditioning Systems. 1978. 18.00 (ISBN 0-685-66798-7, H00116). ASME.

Gopal, Ram. India, China, Tibet Triangle. 1966. pap. 2.00 (ISBN 0-88253-139-5). Ind-US Inc.

--Linguistic Affairs of India. 1967. 8.50x (ISBN 0-210-27158-2). Asia.

--Lokmanya Tilak. 9.75x o.p. (ISBN 0-210-22661-7). Asia.

Gopal, Sarvepalli, ed. A Nehru Anthology. 648p. 1980. 29.95x (ISBN 0-19-561220-5). Oxford U Pr.

Gopalakrishnan, Chennat. Natural Resources & Energy: Theory & Policy. (Illus.). 120p. 1980. 12.50 (ISBN 0-250-40385-4). Ann Arbor Science.

Gopalakrishnan, K. Developmental & Growth Studies of the Euphausiid Nematoscelis Difficilis (Crustacea) Based on Rearing. (Bulletin of the Scripps Institution of Oceanography: Vol. 20). 1973. pap. 7.00x (ISBN 0-520-09463-8). U of Cal Pr.

Gopalan, S. Outlines of Jainism. LC 73-13196. 205p. 1973. pap. 8.95 (ISBN 0-470-31530-X). Halsted Pr.

Gopen, George D. Writing from a Legal Perspective. 250p. 1981. text ed. 11.95 (ISBN 0-8299-2123-0). West Pub.

Gopinath. Pakistan in Transition. LC 75-907273. 1975. 9.00x o.p. (ISBN 0-88386-710-9). South Asia Bks.

Gopinath, Santha. Customer Satisfaction in the Postal Services. 105p. 1980. text ed. 10.25x (ISBN 0-391-02125-7). Humanities.

Goplerud, Dena, jt. auth. see Fleming, Jo Ellen.

Gopnik, Adam & Huberman, Jack. Voila Careme! The Gastronomic Adventures of History's Greatest Chef. 1980. pap. 4.95 (ISBN 0-312-85098-0). St Martin.

Goppelt, Leonard. Theology of the New Testament: Jesus & the Gospels, Vol I. Alsup, John E., tr. LC 80-28947. 316p. 1981. 15.95 (ISBN 0-8028-2384-X). Eerdmans.

Gora, Thomas, tr. see Kristeva, Julia.

Goralski, Robert. World War Two Almanac: Nineteen Thirty-One to Nineteen Forty-Five A Political & Military Record. new ed. (Illus.). 484p. 1981. 17.95 (ISBN 0-399-12548-5). Putnam.

Goran, Lester. This New Land. (The Heritage Ser.: Pt. 1). (Orig.). 1980. pap. 2.75 (ISBN 0-451-09480-8, E9480, Sig). NAL.

Goran, Morris. Ten Lessons of the Energy Crisis. LC 80-130511. 1980. 19.80 (ISBN 0-915250-35-7). Environ Design.

Gorbachev, V. M. & Zamyatnin, A. A. Nuclear Reactions in Heavy Elements: A Data Handbook. LC 79-40928. 460p. 1980. 115.00 (ISBN 0-08-023595-6). Pergamon.

Gorbet, Larry P. A Grammar of Diegueno Nominals. LC 75-25116. (American Indian Linguistics Ser.). 1976. lib. bdg. 42.00 (ISBN 0-8240-1967-9). Garland Pub.

Gorchakov, Nikolai M. Stanislavsky Directs. Goldina, Miriam, tr. (Funk & W Bk.). 1968. pap. 4.95 o.s.i. (ISBN 0-308-60064-9, M60, TYC-T). T Y Crowell.

Gordan, Phyllis G., ed. Two Renaissance Book Hunters: The Letters of Poggius Bracciolini to Nicolaus De Niccolis. (Records of Civilization, Sources & Studies: No. 91). 384p. 1974. 25.00x (ISBN 0-231-03777-5). Columbia U Pr.

Gorden, Raymond L. Unidimensional Scaling of Social Variables: Concepts and Procedures. LC 76-26443. 1977. 15.95 (ISBN 0-02-912580-4). Free Pr.

Gorden, William I. Communication: Personal & Public. LC 76-30803. (Illus.). 325p. 1978. 11.50 (ISBN 0-88284-041-X). Alfred Pub.

Gordenker, Leon. International Aid & National Decisions: Developmental Programs in Malawi, Tanzania & Zambia. (Center of International Studies). 200p. 1976. text ed. 16.00 (ISBN 0-691-05662-5). Princeton U Pr.

Gordenker, Leon, ed. The United Nations in International Politics. LC 71-132239. (Center of International Studies Ser.). 224p. 1971. 14.50x (ISBN 0-691-05615-3). Princeton U Pr.

Gordenker, Leon, jt. ed. see Davison, W. Phillips.

Gordian Associates for the U. S. Department of Energy. Heat Pump Technology: A Survey of Technical Developments, Market Prospects & Research Needs. 464p. 1980. 44.95 (ISBN 0-89934-016-4); pap. 29.95 (ISBN 0-89934-017-2). Solar Energy Info.

Gordimer, Nadine. Burger's Daughter. 362p. 1980. pap. 3.95 (ISBN 0-14-005593-2). Penguin.

--July's People. LC 80-24877. 192p. 1981. 10.95 (ISBN 0-670-41048-9). Viking Pr.

Gordis, Leon, jt. auth. see Markowitz, Milton.

Gordis, Robert. Faith for Moderns. 2nd rev. ed. LC 76-136424. 1971. pap. 6.95x (ISBN 0-8197-0001-0, 10001). Bloch.

Gordon A. Friesen International, Inc. The Ready Foods Systems for Health Care Facilities. LC 72-95360. 1973. 12.95 (ISBN 0-8436-0562-6). CBI Pub.

Gordon, Adoniran J. Ministry of the Spirit. 1964. pap. 2.45 (ISBN 0-87123-366-5, 210366). Bethany Fell.

Gordon, Albert S., jt. ed. see LoBue, Joseph.

Gordon, Andrew, jt. auth. see Barr, David.

Gordon, Archie. Towers. LC 79-52374. (Illus.). 1979. 17.95 (ISBN 0-7153-7787-6). David & Charles.

Gordon, Arthur. Touch of Wonder. (Orig.). pap. 1.75 (ISBN 0-515-04811-9). Jove Pubns.

Gordon, Arthur E. The Inscribed Fibula Praenestina: Problems of Authenticity. LC 75-620010. (Publications in Classical Studies: Vol. 16). 1975. 8.00x (ISBN 0-520-09537-5). U of Cal Pr.

--The Letter Names of the Latin Alphabet. (U. C. Publ. in Classical Studies: Vol. 9). 1973. pap. 9.00x (ISBN 0-520-09422-0). U of Cal Pr.

Gordon, B. L., et al. Apache Indians VI. Horr, David A., ed. (American Indian Ethnohistory Ser.). 1978. lib. bdg. 42.00 (ISBN 0-8240-0708-5). Garland Pub.

Gordon, Barbara & Gordon, Elliott. How to Survive in the Free Lance Jungle. (Illus.). 150p. 1980. pap. write for info. (ISBN 0-917168-06-2). Executive Comm.

Gordon, Barbara B. Improving Your Tennis Game. 1973. pap. 2.95 o.p. (ISBN 0-8015-3978-1). Dutton.

Gordon, Barry J. Non-Ricardian Political Economy. (Kress Library of Business & Economics: No. 20). 1967. pap. 5.00x (ISBN 0-678-09914-6, Baker Lib). Kelley.

Gordon, Bernard, jt. auth. see Gordon, Esther.

Gordon, Bernard L. Once There Was a Giant Sea Cow. (Illus.). (gr. k-3). 1977. 5.95 o.p. (ISBN 0-679-20410-5). McKay.

--Secret Lives of Fishes. rev. ed. (Illus.). 306p. 1980. pap. text ed. 7.95 (ISBN 0-910258-12-0). Book & Tackle.

Gordon, Bernard L. & Gordon, Esther S. If an Auk Could Talk. (Illus.). (gr. k-3). 1977. 5.95 o.p. (ISBN 0-8098-0002-0). Walck.

Gordon, Bernard L., jt. auth. see Charlier, Roger H.
Gordon, Burgess. Untapped Resources of Aging People. 1980. 5.50 (ISBN 0-682-49599-9). Exposition.
Gordon, Caroline. Aleck Maury, Sportsman: A Novel. LC 80-14493. (Lost American Fiction Ser.). 312p. 1980. 12.95 (ISBN 0-8093-0972-6); pap. 6.95 (ISBN 0-8093-0988-2). S Ill U Pr.
--The Collected Stories of Caroline Gordon. 1981. 17.50 (ISBN 0-374-12630-5). FS&G.
Gordon, Chad & Johnson, Gayle, eds. Readings in Human Sexuality: Contemporary Perspectives. 2nd ed. 1980. pap. text ed. 10.50 scp (ISBN 0-06-042399-4, HarpC); instructor's manual avail. (ISBN 0-685-60893-X). Har-Row.
Gordon, Coco. Raw Hands & Bagging. (Illus.). 1978. pap. 2.50 (ISBN 0-931956-00-5). Water Mark.
Gordon, Colin. By Gaslight in Winter: A Victorian Family History Through the Magic Lantern. (Illus.). 128p. 1981. 30.00 (ISBN 0-241-10474-2, Pub. by Hamish Hamilton England). David & Charles.
--A Richer Dust: Echoes from an Edwardian Album. 1979. 15.00 o.s.i. (ISBN 0-397-01350-7). Lippincott.
Gordon, Cyrus H. Ancient Near East. 1965. pap. 6.95 (ISBN 0-393-00275-6, Norton Lib). Norton.
--Common Background of Greek & Hebrew Civilizations. (Illus.). 1965. pap. 7.95 (ISBN 0-393-00293-4, Norton Lib). Norton.
--Ugaritic Textbook. 1965. pap. 56.00 (ISBN 0-911566-08-2). Ventnor.
Gordon, D. I. Regional History of the Railway of Great Britain, Vol. 5. 1976. 19.95 (ISBN 0-7153-7431-1). David & Charles.
Gordon, D. L., jt. auth. see Smyth, D. S.
Gordon, David. Labor Market Segmentation. 350p. 1975. pap. text ed. 8.95x o.p. (ISBN 0-669-95547-7). Heath.
Gordon, David, tr. from Chinese. Equinox: A Gathering of T'ang Poets. LC 73-181682. xx, 88p. 1975. 9.95 (ISBN 0-8214-0162-9); pap. 3.50 o.s.i. (ISBN 0-8214-0173-4). Ohio U Pr.
Gordon, David C. Overcoming the Fear of Death. 1970. 8.95 (ISBN 0-02-544790-4). Macmillan.
Gordon, David J. Literary Art & the Unconscious. LC 75-27662. 1976. 12.50 (ISBN 0-8071-0197-4). La State U Pr.
Gordon, Debbie, jt. auth. see Adler-Golden, Rachel.
Gordon, Dellanna. The Boy King & the Witch. (Illus.). 124p. (Orig.). 1980. pap. 3.95 (ISBN 0-89260-180-9). Hwong Pub.
Gordon, Donald. New Literacy. LC 71-163816. 1971. pap. 3.50 (ISBN 0-8020-6120-6). U of Toronto Pr.
Gordon, Dorothy. You & Democracy. (Illus.). (gr. 5-9). 1951. PLB 5.95 o.p. (ISBN 0-525-43491-7). Dutton.
Gordon, E. D., tr. see Bykhovskii, B. E.
Gordon, E. V., ed. The Battle of Maldon, with a Supplement. Scragg, D. G. LC 76-28820. (Old and Middle English Texts Ser.). 1976. pap. text ed. 5.25x (ISBN 0-06-492494-7). B&N.
Gordon, E. V., jt. ed. see Tolkien, J. R.
Gordon, Edmund I. Sumerian Proverbs: Glimpses of Everyday Life in Ancient Mesopotamia. LC 69-10100. 1969. Repr. of 1959 ed. lib. bdg. 39.75x o.p. (ISBN 0-8371-0086-0, GOSP). Greenwood.
Gordon, Edwin. Musical Aptitude Profile. write for info. (ISBN 0-395-09344-9). HM.
Gordon, Elayne, jt. auth. see Haydon, Dorothy.
Gordon, Elinor. Collecting Chinese Export Porcelain. LC 77-70474. (Illus.). 1977. 17.50x (ISBN 0-87663-295-9). Universe.
Gordon, Elliott, jt. auth. see Gordon, Barbara.
Gordon, Eric V. Introduction to Old Norse. 2nd ed. Taylor, A. R., ed. 1957. 17.95x (ISBN 0-19-811105-3). Oxford U Pr.
Gordon, Ernest & Funk, Peter. What's Next? 1978. pap. 3.95 o.p. (ISBN 0-88270-282-3). Logos.
Gordon, Esther & Gordon, Bernard. Once There Was a Giant Sea Cow. (Illus.). (gr. k-3). 1980. pap. 1.95 o.p. (ISBN 0-679-20851-8). McKay.
Gordon, Esther S., jt. auth. see Gordon, Bernard L.
Gordon, Ethel. The Chaperone. (Orig.). 1981. pap. 1.50 o.s.i. (ISBN 0-440-12076-4). Dell.
--Freer's Cove. (Candlelight Romance Ser.). 1981. pap. 1.50 (ISBN 0-440-12704-1). Dell.
Gordon, Everett J. Practical Medico-Legal Guide for the Physician. (Illus.). 360p. 1973. 14.95 (ISBN 0-398-02688-2). C C Thomas.
Gordon, F. L., ed. see Delibes, Miguel.
Gordon, F. L., ed. see Ugarte, Francisco.
Gordon, G., ed. Active Touch-The Mechanism of Recognition of Objects by Manipulation: A Multidisciplinary Approach. 1978. text ed. 59.00 (ISBN 0-08-022647-7); pap. text ed. 34.00 (ISBN 0-08-022667-1). Pergamon.
Gordon, G. E. & Zoller, W. H. Chemistry in Modern Perspective. 1975. 18.95 (ISBN 0-201-02561-2); lab manual 6.95 (ISBN 0-201-03154-X). A-W.
Gordon, Gary J. Product Liability Litigation. 200p. 1980. pap. 24.50 (ISBN 0-917126-20-3). Mason Pub.
Gordon, Geoffrey. The Application of GPSS Five to Discrete System Simulation. (Illus.). 336p. 1975. 23.95 (ISBN 0-13-039057-7). P-H.
--System Simulation. 2nd ed. LC 77-24579. (Illus.). 1978. ref. ed. 23.50 (ISBN 0-13-881797-9). P-H.
Gordon, George. Persuasion: Theory & Practice of Manipulative Communication. (Studies in Public Communication). 1971. 16.50 o.s.i. (ISBN 0-8038-5774-8); pap. text ed. 10.00x (ISBN 0-8038-5777-2). Hastings.
Gordon, George G. & Cummins, Walter. Managing Management Climate. (Illus.). 1979. 19.95 (ISBN 0-669-02545-3). Lexington Bks.
Gordon, George N., et al. Idea Invaders. (Communication Arts Bks.). 1963. 4.95 o.p. (ISBN 0-8038-3338-5). Hastings.
Gordon, Gilbert & Pressman, Israel. Quantitative Decision-Making for Business. LC 77-25831. (Illus.). 1978. ref. ed. 21.00 (ISBN 0-13-746701-X). P-H.
Gordon, Giles, ed. Prevailing Spirits: A Book of Scottish Ghost Stories. 1979. 17.95 (ISBN 0-241-89403-4, Pub. by Hamish Hamilton England). David & Charles.
Gordon, Giles, jt. ed. see Urquhart, Fred.
Gordon, Gua N. Red Are the Embers. 1980. 8.50 (ISBN 0-8233-0317-9). Golden Quill.
Gordon, Hampden. Antiques, the Amateur's Questions. (Illus.). 1951. pap. 3.95 (ISBN 0-7195-0511-9). Transatlantic.
--Old English Furniture. pap. 1.95 o.p. (ISBN 0-7195-0509-7). Transatlantic.
Gordon, Harvey C. Grime & Punnishment. (Orig.). 1981. pap. 3.95 (ISBN 0-446-97026-3). Warner Bks.
--Punishment: The Art of Punning. 1980. pap. 2.95 (ISBN 0-446-97263-0). Warner Bks.
Gordon, I. R. A Preface to Pope. LC 75-25572. (Preface Books). (Illus.). 136p. 1976. text ed. 11.95x (ISBN 0-582-31505-0); pap. text ed. 5.95x (ISBN 0-582-31506-9). Longman.
Gordon, Ian A; see Blackstone, Bernard.
Gordon, Ian A., intro. by see Mansfield, Katherine.
Gordon, Irving. World History Review Text. 2nd ed. (gr. 10-12). 1979. text ed. 14.75 (ISBN 0-87720-625-2); pap. text ed. 8.92 (ISBN 0-87720-624-4). AMSCO Sch.
Gordon, Irving L. American Studies: A Conceptual Approach. (gr. 11). 1975. text ed. 15.34 (ISBN 0-87720-600-7); pap. text ed. 9.33 (ISBN 0-87720-603-1). AMSCO Sch.
--Review Text in American History. (Illus., Orig.). (gr. 10-12). 1968. pap. text ed. 6.75 (ISBN 0-87720-606-6). AMSCO Sch.
--Review Text in World History. rev. ed. (Illus., Orig.). (gr. 10-12). 1968. pap. text ed. 6.75 (ISBN 0-87720-604-X). AMSCO Sch.
Gordon, Isabel, jt. auth. see De Regniers, Beatrice S.
Gordon, J. California Real Estate Law: Text & Cases. (Illus.). 1980. pap. text ed. 14.50 (ISBN 0-13-112524-9). P-H.
Gordon, J., et al, eds. Protein Phoporylation & Bio-Regulaion. (Illus.). x, 234p. 1980. 49.25 (ISBN 3-8055-1168-X). S Karger.
Gordon, Jaimy. The Bend, the Lip, the Kid: Real Life Stories. LC 78-15579. 1978. pap. 4.00 (ISBN 0-915342-25-1). SUN.
Gordon, Joan. Joe Haldeman. LC 80-25936. (Starmont Reader's Guide: No. 4). 80p. 1980. Repr. lib. bdg. 9.95x (ISBN 0-89370-035-5). Borgo Pr.
--Reader's Guide to Joe Haldeman. Schlobin, Roger C., ed. LC 80-21388. (Reader's Guide to Contemporary Science Fiction & Fantasy Author Ser.: Vol. 4). (Illus., Orig.). 1980. pap. text ed. 3.95 (ISBN 0-916732-06-1). Starmont Hse.
Gordon, Joanne J., jt. auth. see Solmen, Lewis C.
Gordon, John, jt. auth. see Whitely, J. Stuart.
Gordon, John F. All About the Boxer. 1970. 9.95 (ISBN 0-7207-0317-4, Pub. by Michael Joseph). Merrimack Bk Serv.
--All About the Cocker Spaniel. 1971. 8.95 (ISBN 0-7207-0424-3, Pub. by Michael Joseph). Merrimack Bk Serv.
--Beagle Guide. 6.98 o.p. (ISBN 0-385-01558-5). Doubleday.
--Miniature Schnauzer Guide. 6.98 o.p. (ISBN 0-385-01579-8). Doubleday.
--Miniature Schnauzers. Foyle, Christina, ed. (Foyle's Handbks). 1972. 3.95 (ISBN 0-685-55812-6). Palmetto Pub.
--The Staffordshire Bull Terrier Owner's Encyclopedia. 2nd ed. (Illus.). 1977. 12.95 (ISBN 0-7207-0944-X, Pub. by Michael Joseph). Merrimack Bk Serv.
--Staffordshire Bull Terriers. (Foyle's Handbks). (Illus.). 1973. 3.95 (ISBN 0-685-55791-X). Palmetto Pub.
Gordon, Julius & Weeks, Townsend E. Seashells of the S. E. Coast. Campbell, Margaret, ed. (Illus.). 50p. (Orig.). 1981. pap. 4.95 (ISBN 0-88839-080-7). Hancock Hse.
Gordon, Karen E. The Garden of Eternal Swallows. LC 80-50745. (Illus.). 176p. (Orig.). 1980. pap. 5.95 (ISBN 0-394-73948-5). Shambhala Pubns.
Gordon, Katherine, jt. auth. see Gordon, Richard E.
Gordon, Kathleen M. The Psychic & the Swamp Man. 1981. 12.95 (ISBN 0-670-58188-7). Viking Pr.
Gordon, Kermit, ed. Agenda for the Nation. 1968. 15.95 (ISBN 0-8157-3210-4). Brookings.
Gordon, Laura B. Behavioral Intervention in Health Care. (Behavioral Sciences for Health Care Professionals Ser.). 128p. 1981. lib. bdg. 15.00x (ISBN 0-86531-018-1); pap. text ed. 6.00x (ISBN 0-86531-019-X). Westview.
Gordon, Leland & Lee, Stewart. Economics for Consumers. 7th ed. 693p. 1977. text ed. 16.95 (ISBN 0-442-22242-4). Van Nos Reinhold.
Gordon, Leonard. Bengal: The Nationalist Movement, 1876-1940. 1974. 20.00x (ISBN 0-231-03753-8). Columbia U Pr.
Gordon, Leonard & Harvey, Patricia. Sociology & American Social Issues. LC 77-78577. (Illus.). 1978. pap. text ed. 18.95 (ISBN 0-395-25369-1); study guide 6.95 (ISBN 0-395-25371-3); inst. manual 0.70 (ISBN 0-395-25370-5). HM.
Gordon, Leonard A. & Miller, Barbara S. Syllabus of Indian Civilization. LC 70-168868. (Companions to Asian Studies). 1971. pap. 7.50x (ISBN 0-231-03560-8). Columbia U Pr.
Gordon, Leonard H., ed. Taiwan: Studies in Chinese Local History. LC 78-108096. (East Asian Institute Ser). 1970. 12.50x (ISBN 0-231-03376-1). Columbia U Pr.
Gordon, Leonard V. Measurement of Interpersonal Values. LC 74-22623. 122p. (Orig.). 1975. text ed. 12.00 (ISBN 0-574-72770-1); pap. text ed. 8.20 (ISBN 0-574-72764-7). SRA.
Gordon, Lesley. A Country Herbal. (Illus.). 208p. 1980. 19.95 (ISBN 0-8317-4446-4). Mayflower Bks.
Gordon, M. Sick Cities. 1963. 6.95 o.s.i. (ISBN 0-02-544730-0). Macmillan.
Gordon, Margaret, illus. A Paper of Pins. LC 74-8767. (Illus.). 32p. (ps-3). 1975. 6.95 (ISBN 0-395-28814-2, Clarion). HM.
Gordon, Margaret S. Economics of Welfare Policies. LC 63-14113. 1964. 15.00x (ISBN 0-231-02639-0). Columbia U Pr.
Gordon, Marilyn K., jt. auth. see Shampine, Lawrence F.
Gordon, Marshall, ed. Reflections on the Mathematics Experience. LC 79-83694. (Educational Ser.). 1979. text ed. cancelled (ISBN 0-8211-0614-7). McCutchan.
Gordon, Marshall S., jt. auth. see Simonsen, Clifford E.
Gordon, Mary. The Company of Women. 1981. 12.95 (ISBN 0-394-50508-5). Random.
--Final Payments. 320p. 1981. pap. 2.75 (ISBN 0-345-29554-4). Ballantine.
Gordon, Maurice R. Aesculapius Comes to the Colonies. LC 70-101590. (Illus.). 1969. Repr. of 1949 ed. 17.50. Argosy.
Gordon, Maxwell, ed. Psychopharmacological Agents, 3 vols. Incl. Vol. 1. 1964. 69.50 (ISBN 0-12-290550-4); Vol. 2. 1967. 69.50 (ISBN 0-12-290556-3); Vol. 3. 1974. 54.00 (ISBN 0-12-290558-X). (Medicinal Chemistry Ser.). Acad Pr.
Gordon, Michael. The American Family in Social-Historical Perspective. 2nd ed. LC 77-86000. 1978. text ed. 16.95 (ISBN 0-312-02311-1); pap. text ed. 9.95 (ISBN 0-312-02312-X). St Martin.
--The American Family: Past, Present, & Future. 1977. text ed. 1.95x (ISBN 0-394-31722-X). Random.
--Old Enough to Feel Better: A Medical Guide for Seniors. LC 80-70351. 384p. 1981. 14.95 (ISBN 0-686-69523-2). Chilton.
Gordon, Mildred, jt. auth. see Yates, Robert.
Gordon, Milton M. Human Nature, Class, & Ethnicity. (Illus.). 1978. 14.95 (ISBN 0-19-502236-X); pap. 4.95 (ISBN 0-19-502237-8). Oxford U Pr.
Gordon, Milton M. & Lambert, Richard D., eds. America As a Multicultural Society. (Annals of the American Academy of Political & Social Science Ser.: No. 454). 250p. 1981. 7.50 (ISBN 0-87761-260-9); pap. 6.00 (ISBN 0-87761-261-7). Am Acad Pol Soc Sci.
Gordon, Myron & Axelrod, Herbert R. Siamese Fighting Fish. pap. 2.00 (ISBN 0-87666-145-2, M536). TFH Pubns.
Gordon, Neal J., jt. ed. see Farley, Frank.
Gordon, Neil & McKinlay, Ian, eds. Helping Clumsy Children. (Illus.). 200p. 1980. pap. text ed. 16.00x (ISBN 0-443-01868-5). Churchill.
Gordon, P. J. The Renaissance Imagination: Essays & Lectures. Orgel, Stephen, ed. LC 74-81432. 1976. 33.75x (ISBN 0-520-02817-1). U of Cal Pr.
Gordon, Pearl S. Simply Elegant: A Guide for Elegant but Simple Entertaining. rev. 8th ed. LC 77-13166. (Illus.). 208p. 1981. lib. bdg. 12.95 (ISBN 0-9600492-3-1). Simply Elegant.
Gordon, Peter. Study of Curriculum. 192p. 1981. 27.00 (ISBN 0-686-69077-X, Pub. by Batsford England); pap. 13.50 (ISBN 0-7134-2092-8). David & Charles.
Gordon, Peter & Lawton, Denis. Curriculum Change in the 19th & 20th Centuries. LC 78-23803. 1979. pap. 18.00x (ISBN 0-8419-6216-2). Holmes & Meier.
Gordon, Peter & White, John. Philosophers As Educational Reformers: The Influence of Idealism on British Educational Thought & Practice, 1875-1925. (International Library of the Philosophy of Education). (Illus.). 1979. 26.00x (ISBN 0-7100-0214-9). Routledge & Kegan.
Gordon, Peter, ed. The Study of Education: A Collection of Inaugural Lectures, Vol. I--Early & Modern, Vol. II--The Last Decade. (The Woburn Education Ser.). 662p. 1980. Set. 60.00x (ISBN 0-7130-0169-0, Pub. by Woburn Pr England); Set. pap. 30.00x (ISBN 0-7130-4004-1). Biblio Dist.
Gordon, R. A., et al, eds. International Symposium on Malignant Hyperthermia. (Illus.). 512p. 1973. 32.75 (ISBN 0-398-02549-5). C C Thomas.
Gordon, R. L. Interviewing: Strategy, Techniques & Tactics. 3rd ed. 1980. 18.50x (ISBN 0-256-02370-0). Dorsey.
--The Lady Who Loved New York. LC 76-28359. 1977. 10.00 o.s.i. (ISBN 0-690-01213-6, TYC-T). T Y Crowell.
--You'll Hear Me Laughing. LC 78-69534. 1979. 8.95 o.s.i. (ISBN 0-690-01791-X, TYC-T). T Y Crowell.
Gordon, R. L., ed. Myth, Religion & Society: Structuralist Essays by M. Detienne, L. Gernet, J. P. Vernant & P. Vidal-Naquet. (Illus.). 250p. Date not set. text ed. price not set (ISBN 0-521-22780-1); pap. text ed. price not set (ISBN 0-521-29640-4). Cambridge U Pr.
Gordon, Rex. First on Mars, No. 18. (Science Fiction Rediscovery Ser.). 1976. pap. 2.25 o.p. (ISBN 0-380-00572-7, 28084). Avon.
Gordon, Richard. World Energy Problems: An Economic Analysis. (Illus.). 320p. 1981. text ed. 30.00x (ISBN 0-262-07080-4). MIT Pr.
Gordon, Richard E. & Gordon, Katherine. Systems of Treatment for the Mentally Ill: Filling the Gaps. 1981. price not set (ISBN 0-8089-1338-7). Grune.
Gordon, Richard L. Coal & Canada-U.S. Energy Relations. LC 76-20420. 76p. 1976. 3.00 (ISBN 0-88806-017-3). Natl Planning.
--Coal in the U.S. Energy Market. LC 77-14625. (Illus.). 1978. 19.95 (ISBN 0-669-01987-9). Lexington Bks.
Gordon, Richard S. Issues in Health Care Regulation. (Regulation of American Business & Industry). (Illus.). 400p. 1980. 35.00 (ISBN 0-07-023780-8, C). McGraw.
Gordon, Robert. Changing Channels: On Channeling the Direction of Your Life. LC 79-66609. 111p. 1980. 12.00 (ISBN 0-936654-00-7). Wilmington Pr.
--Forensic Psychology. 1977. 7.95 (ISBN 0-88229-477-6). Nelson-Hall.
--John Butler Yeats & John Sloan. (New Yeats Papers: Vol. 14). 1978. pap. text ed. 9.25x (ISBN 0-85105-322-X, Dolmen Pr). Humanities.
Gordon, Robert & Spaulding, Malcolm. A Bibliography of Numerical Models for Tidal Rivers, Estuaries & Coastal Waters. (Marine Technical Report Ser.: No. 32). 1974. pap. 2.00 (ISBN 0-938412-03-5). URI MAS.
Gordon, Robert A. Business Leadership in the Large Corporation. 1945. pap. 2.25 o.p. (ISBN 0-520-00502-3, CAL43). U of Cal Pr.
Gordon, Robert J. Macroecomomics. 2nd ed. 1981. text ed. 16.95 (ISBN 0-316-32125-7); wkbk. 6.95 (ISBN 0-316-32127-3). Little.
Gordon, Robert J., ed. see Friedman, Milton, et al.
Gordon, Ronni L., jt. auth. see Stillman, David M.
Gordon, Ruth. My Side: The Autobiography of Ruth Gordon. LC 76-5124. (Illus.). 576p. 1976. 12.95 o.p. (ISBN 0-06-011618-8, HarpT). Har-Row.
Gordon, Sanford D. & Dawson, George G. Introductory Economics. 4th ed. 1980. text ed. 14.95x (ISBN 0-669-02425-2); instrs' manual avail. (ISBN 0-669-02427-9); study guide 5.95 (ISBN 0-669-02426-0); test file avail. (ISBN 0-669-02429-5). Heath.
Gordon, Scott. Welfare, Justice, & Freedom. LC 80-14571. 256p. 1980. 17.50x (ISBN 0-231-04976-5). Columbia U Pr.
Gordon, Sharon. Christmas Surprise. (Illus.). 32p. (gr. k-2). 1980. PLB 2.96 (ISBN 0-89375-373-4); pap. 0.95 (ISBN 0-89375-273-8). Troll Assocs.
--Easter Bunny's Lost Egg. (Illus.). 32p. (gr. k-3). 1980. PLB 2.96 (ISBN 0-89375-375-0); pap. 0.95 (ISBN 0-89375-275-4). Troll Assocs.
--Friendly Snowman. (Illus.). 32p. (gr. k-2). 1980. PLB 2.96 (ISBN 0-89375-377-7); pap. 0.95 (ISBN 0-89375-277-0). Troll Assocs.

--Pete the Parakeet. (Illus.). 32p. (gr. k-2). 1980. PLB 2.96 (ISBN 0-89375-384-X); pap. 0.95 (ISBN 0-89375-284-3). Troll Assocs.
--Three Little Witches. (Illus.). 32p. (gr. k-2). 1980. PLB 2.96 (ISBN 0-89375-390-4); pap. 0.95 (ISBN 0-89375-290-8). Troll Assocs.
--What a Dog. (Illus.). 32p. (gr. k-2). 1980. PLB 2.96 (ISBN 0-89375-393-9); pap. 0.95 (ISBN 0-89375-293-2). Troll Assocs.
Gordon, Shirley. Me & the Bad Guys. LC 79-9611. (Illus.). 80p. (gr. 3-6). 1980. 7.95 (ISBN 0-06-022116-X, HarpJ); PLB 7.89 (ISBN 0-06-022117-8). Har-Row.
Gordon, Shirley C., jt. ed. see Augier, F. R.
Gordon, Sid. How to Fish from Top to Bottom. (Illus.). 384p. 1978. 21.95 (ISBN 0-8117-0931-0); deluxed slipcased ed. 30.00 (ISBN 0-8117-0931-0). Stackpole.
Gordon, Sol. Sexual Rights for People Who Happen to Be Handicapped. 1979. 1.00 (ISBN 0-937540-03-X, HPP-10). Human Policy Pr.
Gordon, Sol, jt. ed. see Williams, Gertrude.
Gordon, Steven M., jt. auth. see Fulton, John A.
Gordon, Stewart. Gunswift. 1979. pap. 1.50 (ISBN 0-505-51347-1). Tower Bks.
Gordon, Stuart. Gordonstown, a New Design for America. (Illus.). 288p. 1980. pap. 10.95 (ISBN 0-9603942-0-6). Gordonstown.
--Smile on the Void. 264p. 1981. 12.95 (ISBN 0-399-12503-5). Putnam.
Gordon, Theodore J. Life-Extending Technologies: A Technology Assessment. 1980. 33.00 (ISBN 0-08-023132-2). Pergamon.
Gordon, Vivian V., ed. Lectures: Black Scholars on Black Issues. LC 79-63259. 1979. pap. text ed. 11.25 (ISBN 0-8191-0709-3). U Pr of Amer.
Gordon, W. J. The Horse World of London. (Illus.). 7.00 (ISBN 0-85131-144-X, Dist. by Sporting Book Center). J A Allen.
Gordon, Walter K., jt. ed. see Sanderson, James L.
Gordon, Wendell C. Political Economy of Latin America. LC 65-19444. 1965. 20.00x (ISBN 0-231-02675-7); pap. write for info. (ISBN 0-231-08572-9). Columbia U Pr.
Gordon, William C., jt. auth. see Logan, Frank A.
Gordon, William J. Synectics: The Development of Creative Capacity. 1968. pap. 1.95 o.s.i. (ISBN 0-02-008250-9, Collier). Macmillan.
Gordons. Night After the Wedding. LC 78-20073. 288p. 1979. 8.95 (ISBN 0-385-14012-6). Doubleday.
Gordons, The. Catnapped! the Further Adventures of Undercover Cat. LC 74-5915. 192p. 1974. 5.95 o.p. (ISBN 0-385-08901-5). Doubleday.
--Night Before the Wedding. LC 68-22621. 1969. 5.50 o.p. (ISBN 0-385-04130-6). Doubleday.
Gordus, Jeanne P. Leaving Early: Perspectives & Problems in Current Retirement Practice & Policy. LC 80-39653. 88p. (Orig.). 1980. pap. text ed. 4.00 (ISBN 0-911558-78-0). Upjohn Inst.
Gordy, W. Techniques of Chemistry: Vol. 15 Theory & Application of Electron Spin Resonance. 625p. 1980. 39.95 (ISBN 0-471-93162-4). Wiley.
Gore, jt. auth. see Kiesel.
Gore, Alan, jt. auth. see Fleming, Laurence.
Gore, Catherine. Dalmatians. Foyle, Christina, ed. (Foyle's Handbks). (Illus.). 1973. 3.95 (ISBN 0-685-55792-8). Palmetto Pub.
--Dalmatians. LC 76-11029. (Illus.). 1976. bds. 2.25 o.p. (ISBN 0-668-03983-3). Arco.
Gore, D. Bibliography for Beginners. 2nd ed. 1973. pap. text ed. 7.95 (ISBN 0-13-076109-5). P-H.
Gore, Daniel. To Know a Library: Essays & Annual Reports, 1970-1976. LC 77-84769. (New Directions in Librarianship: No. 1). 1978. lib. bdg. 19.95 (ISBN 0-8371-9881-X, GTK/). Greenwood.
Gore, Daniel, ed. Farewell to Alexandria: Solutions to Space, Growth & Performance Problems of Libraries. LC 75-35345. 224p. 1976. lib. bdg. 15.00 (ISBN 0-8371-8587-4, GGP/). Greenwood.
Gore, Daniel, et al, eds. Requiem for the Card Catalog: Management Issues in Automated Cataloging. LC 78-7129. (New Directions in Librarianship: No. 2). 1979. lib. bdg. 18.95 (ISBN 0-313-20608-2, GMI/). Greenwood.
Gore, Elizabeth. Child Psychiatry Observed. Nursten, Jean, ed. LC 75-6926. 264p. 1975. text ed. 26.00 (ISBN 0-08-017277-6); pap. text ed. 14.00 (ISBN 0-08-017278-4). Pergamon.
Gore, Norman C. Tzeena U-Reenah of Jacob ben Isaac Ashkenazy. 1965. 10.00 (ISBN 0-685-22508-9). Ktav.
Gore, William, et al. Rails in the North Woods. rev. ed. 1978. Repr. of 1973 ed. 13.95 (ISBN 0-932052-16-9). North Country.
Gore, William J. & Dyson, James. Making of Decisions. LC 64-23084. 1964. 15.95 (ISBN 0-02-912590-1). Free Pr.
Goreau, Angeline. Reconstructing Aphra: A Social Biography of Aphra Behn. (Illus.). 339p. 1980. 14.95 (ISBN 0-8037-7478-8). Dial.
Goreau, Eloise K. Integrity of Life: Allegorical Imagery in the Plays of John Webster. (Salzburg Studies in English Literature, Jacobean Drama Studies: No. 32). 194p. 1974. pap. text ed. 25.00x (ISBN 0-391-01390-4). Humanities.
Gore-Booth, Lord, ed. Satow's Guide to Diplomatic Practice. 5th ed. LC 77-12580. 1979. text ed. 36.00x (ISBN 0-582-50109-1). Longman.
Gorecki, Henryk, et al. Analysis & Synthesis of Time Delay Systems. LC 79-40508. 1980. write for info. (ISBN 0-471-27622-7, Pub by Wiley-Interscience). Wiley.
Gorecki, Jan. A Theory of Criminal Justice. 1979. 17.50x (ISBN 0-231-04670-7). Columbia U Pr.
Gorecki, P. K. & Stanbury, W. T. Perspectives on the Royal Commission on Corporate Concentration. 308p. 1979. pap. text ed. 15.95x (ISBN 0-409-88606-8, Pub. by Inst Res Pub Canada). Renouf.
Goree, Lynn, ed. Puppets for Bible Discovery. LC 79-55016. (Bible Discovery Bks.). 1979. pap. 4.25 (ISBN 0-8344-0112-6). Sweet.
Gorelik, A. G., jt. ed. see Vinnichenko, N. K.
Goren, Arthur A. New York Jews & the Quest for Community. LC 76-129961. 1979. pap. 10.00 (ISBN 0-231-08368-8). Columbia U Pr.
--New York Jews' Quest of Community: The Kehillah Experiment, 1908-1922. LC 76-129961. 1970. 22.50 (ISBN 0-231-03422-9). Columbia U Pr.
Goren, Charles H. Goren on Play & Defense. LC 73-16506. 448p. 1974. 9.95 o.p. (ISBN 0-385-06753-4). Doubleday.
--Goren's Bridge Complete. rev. ed. LC 73-75161. 9.95 o.p. (ISBN 0-385-04355-4). Doubleday.
--Goren's Bridge Complete. LC 80-2247. 736p. 1981. 14.95 (ISBN 0-385-17441-1). Doubleday.
--Modern Backgammon Complete. 208p. 1975. pap. 2.95 (ISBN 0-346-12296-1). Cornerstone.
--The Precision System of Contract Bridge Bidding. 225p. 1972. pap. 2.95 (ISBN 0-346-12061-6). Cornerstone.
Goren, Charles H. & Wei, C. C. Precision Bridge for Everyone. LC 78-62636. 1978. 6.95 o.p. (ISBN 0-385-14709-0). Doubleday.
Goren, Leyla. Elements of Brahmanism in the Transcendentalism of Emerson. LC 80-2534. 1981. Repr. of 1959 ed. 18.50 (ISBN 0-404-19260-2). AMS Pr.
Goren, Richard, ed. see Nicolaisen, Age.
Gorenflo, Louise, et al. Farm & Rural Energy Planning Manual. (Illus.). 80p. (Orig.). 1981. pap. 5.00 (ISBN 0-937786-04-7). Inst Ecological.
Gorenstein, Daniel. Finite Groups. 2nd ed. xvii, 517p. 1980. 22.50 (ISBN 0-8284-0301-5). Chelsea Pub.
Gorer, Geoffrey. Exploring English Character. LC 55-11159. 14.95 (ISBN 0-87599-040-1). S G Phillips.
--Sex & Marriage in England Today: A Study of the Views & Experience of the Under 45's. 318p. 1971. text ed. 10.00x (ISBN 0-391-00236-8). Humanities.
Gorer, Richard. Development of Garden Flowers. 1970. 12.25 o.p. (ISBN 0-8231-6036-X). Branford.
--The Flower Garden in England. (Illus.). 1975. 11.50 o.s.i. (ISBN 0-7134-2858-9). Hippocrene Bks.
--Trees & Shrubs: A Complete Guide. (Illus.). 240p. 1976. 25.00 (ISBN 0-7153-6850-8). David & Charles.
Gorer, Richard & Rochford, Thomas. The Rochford Book of Flowering Pot Plants. 2nd ed. (Illus.). 1974. 9.95 (ISBN 0-571-04853-6, Pub. by Faber & Faber). Merrimack Bk Serv.
--Rochford's House-Plants for Everyone. (Illus., Orig.). 1978. pap. 4.95 (ISBN 0-571-08827-9, Pub. by Faber & Faber). Merrimack Bk Serv.
Gores, Joe. Dead Skip. 1981. pap. 2.25 (ISBN 0-345-29206-5). Ballantine.
Gorey, Edward. Blue Aspic. (Illus.). 1969. 4.95 (ISBN 0-8015-0738-3, Hawthorn). Dutton.
--The Curious Sofa. LC 61-12368. 64p. 1980. 5.95 (ISBN 0-396-07861-3). Dodd.
--Curious Sofa, Ogdred Weary. (Illus.). 1961. pap. 3.50 (ISBN 0-8392-1020-5). Astor-Honor.
--The Doubtful Guest. LC 57-10200. (Illus.). 1978. 5.95 (ISBN 0-396-07628-9). Dodd.
--Fatal Lozenge. (Illus.). 1960. pap. 3.50 (ISBN 0-8392-1031-0). Astor-Honor.
--The Gilded Bat. LC 66-22413. (Illus.). 1979. 5.95 (ISBN 0-396-07688-2). Dodd.
--Gorey Posters. 1979. pap. 8.95 (ISBN 0-8109-2179-0). Abrams.
--Hapless Child. 1961. pap. 3.50 (ISBN 0-8392-1044-2). Astor-Honor.
--Hapless Child. LC 61-6959. (Illus.). 64p. 1980. 5.95 (ISBN 0-396-07817-6). Dodd.
--Sinking Spell. (Illus.). 1965. pap. 7.95 (ISBN 0-8392-1150-3). Astor-Honor.
--Utter Zoo. (Illus.). 1967. 4.95 (ISBN 0-8015-8268-7, Hawthorn). Dutton.
--The Willowdale Handcar. LC 62-17515. (Illus.). 1979. 5.95 (ISBN 0-396-07767-6). Dodd.
Gorey, Edward & Chess, Victoria. Fletcher & Zenobia. LC 67-14746. (Illus.). 1967. 4.95 o.p. (ISBN 0-8015-2670-1). Dutton.
Gorga, Francisco V. Cell Three Fifty. LC 73-93096. (Stories That Win Ser.). 1974. pap. 0.95 o.p. (ISBN 0-8163-0130-1, 03075-9). Pacific Pr Pub Assn.
Gorges, A., tr. see Bacon, Frances.
Gorges, Arthur see Bacon, Francis.
Gorham, Charles. Leader at Large: The Long & Fighting Life of Norman Thomas. LC 72-119548. (Illus.). (gr. 7 up). 1970. 4.95 o.p. (ISBN 0-374-34372-1). FS&G.
Gorham, Georgia & Warth, Jeanne. A Treasury of Charted Designs for Needleworkers. (Dover Needlework Ser.). (Illus.). 1978. pap. 1.75 (ISBN 0-486-23558-0). Dover.
Gorham, M. Ireland from Old Photographs. 1979. pap. 11.95 (ISBN 0-7134-2195-9, Pub. by Batsford England). David & Charles.
Gorham, Maurice, ed. Dublin from Old Photographs. (Illus.). 1975. 11.50 o.s.i. (ISBN 0-7134-0122-2). Hippocrene Bks.
Gorham, William & Glazer, Nathan, eds. The Urban Predicament. 363p. 1976. 12.50 (ISBN 0-87766-161-8, 14700); pap. 6.95 (ISBN 0-87766-160-X, 14500). Urban Inst.
Gorin, Ralph E. Introduction to DECsystem 20: Assembly Language Programming. 1981. pap. 21.00 (ISBN 0-932376-12-6). Digital Pr.
Goringe, Michael J., jt. auth. see Thomas, Gareth.
Gorki, Maxim. Reminiscences of My Youth. 334p. 1980. Repr. of 1924 ed. lib. bdg. 25.00 (ISBN 0-8492-4961-9). R West.
Gorky, Maxim. The Autobiography of Maxim Gorky, 3 vols. in 1. Schneider, Isidore, tr. Incl. My Childhood; In the World; My Universities. 10.00 (ISBN 0-8446-2143-9). Peter Smith.
--My Childhood. Wilks, Ronald, tr. (Classics Ser.). (Orig.). 1966. pap. 2.95 (ISBN 0-14-044178-6). Penguin.
--On Literature. LC 72-11682. 400p. 1975. pap. 3.95 (ISBN 0-295-95453-1). U of Wash Pr.
--Through Russia. 1959. 5.00x o.p. (ISBN 0-460-00741-6, Evman). Dutton.
Gorlick, S. Now That You've Incorporated. 1977. 14.95 (ISBN 0-87489-138-8). Med Economics.
--The Whys & Wherefores of Corporate Practice. 3rd ed. 1978. 14.50 (ISBN 0-87489-209-0). Med Economics.
Gorlin, Robert J., ed. Morphogenesis & Malformation of the Ear. LC 80-18892. (Birth Defects: Original Article Ser.: Vol XVI, No. 4). 367p. 1980. 44.00 (ISBN 0-8451-1038-1). A R Liss.
--Morphogenesis & Malformation of the Ear. LC 80-18892. (Alan R. Liss: Vol. 16,No. 4). 1980. 44.00 (ISBN 0-8451-1038-1). March of Dimes.
Gorlitz, Dietmar, ed. Perspectives on Attribution Research & Theory: The Bielefeld Symposium. 1981. 19.50 (ISBN 0-88410-375-7). Ballinger Pub.
Gorlitz, Walter. History of the German General Staff, 1657-1945. Battershaw, Brian, tr. from Ger. LC 75-3867. (Illus.). 508p. 1975. Repr. of 1953 ed. lib. bdg. 33.00x (ISBN 0-8371-8092-9, GOGG). Greenwood.
Gorman, D. J. Free Vibration Analysis of Beams & Shafts. LC 74-20504. 448p. 1975. 35.00 (ISBN 0-471-31770-5, Pub. by Wiley-Interscience). Wiley.
Gorman, George. The Society of Friends. 1978. pap. 2.90 (ISBN 0-08-021412-6). Pergamon.
Gorman, George, jt. auth. see Licht, Paul.
Gorman, Herbert S. Hawthorne. LC 66-13474. 1927. 9.50x (ISBN 0-8196-0170-5). Biblo.
Gorman, James E. Simplified Guide to Construction Management for Architects & Engineers. LC 75-34480. 288p. 1976. 17.95 (ISBN 0-8436-0160-4). CBI Pub.
Gorman, John A. Western Horse. LC 66-12997. (Illus.). (gr. 9-12). 1967. 14.60 (ISBN 0-8134-0126-7); text ed. 10.95 (ISBN 0-685-03940-4). Interstate.
Gorman, Kenneth A., jt. auth. see Crowningshield, Gerald.
Gorman, M. Island Ecology. LC 79-41166. (Outline Studies in Ecology). 79p. 1979. pap. 5.95x o.p. (ISBN 0-412-15540-0, Pub. by Chapman & Hall). Methuen Inc.
--Island Ecology. LC 79-41166. 79p. 1979. pap. 4.95x o.p. (ISBN 0-470-26751-8). Halsted Pr.
Gorman, Margaret. General Semantics & Contemporary Thomism. LC 62-9136. 1962. pap. 2.95x (ISBN 0-8032-5075-4, BB 146, Bison). U of Nebr Pr.
Gorman, Michael & Height, Frank, eds. Design for Tourism: An I.C.S.I.D. Interdesign Report. 64p. 1977. text ed. 15.00 (ISBN 0-08-021481-9). Pergamon.
Gorman, Peter. Pythagoras: A Life. 1978. 18.00 (ISBN 0-7100-0006-5). Routledge & Kegan.
Gorman, Stephen M., jt. auth. see Maghroori, Ray.
Gorman, Tom & Holtzman, Jerome. Three & Two: The Autobiography of Tom Gorman, the Great National League Umpire. (Encore Edition). (Illus.). 1979. 3.95 (ISBN 0-684-16751-4, ScribT). Scribner.
Gormican, Annette. Controlling Diabetes with Diet. (Illus.). 232p. 1976. pap. 10.75 spiral (ISBN 0-398-00705-5). C C Thomas.
Gormly, James L., jt. auth. see Bain, Kenneth R.
Gornall, Allan G., ed. Applied Biochemistry of Clinical Disorders. (Illus.). 544p. 1981. pap. text ed. write for info. (ISBN 0-06-141010-1, Harper Medical). Har-Row.
Gornall, Thomas. The Letters & Diaries of John Henry Newman: Liberalism in Oxford, January 1835 to December 1836, Vol. 5. 464p. 1981. 65.00 (ISBN 0-19-920117-X). Oxford U Pr.
Gorney, Len. Queueing Theory: A Solving Approach. (Illus.). 300p. 1981. 20.00 (ISBN 0-89433-128-0). Petrocelli.
Gornick, Vivian. Essays in Feminism. LC 77-6884. 1978. 12.95 o.s.i. (ISBN 0-06-011627-7, HarpT). Har-Row.
Gornick, Vivian & Moran, Barbara K. Woman in Sexist Society. 1972. pap. 2.50 (ISBN 0-451-61351-1, ME1883, Ment). NAL.
Gorodetsky. The Precarious Truce. LC 76-2279. (Soviet & East European Studies). 1977. 36.00 (ISBN 0-521-21226-X). Cambridge U Pr.
Gorodezky, Sarah, jt. auth. see Lauffer, Armand.
Gorove, Stephen. Legal Aspects of International Investment. (L. Q. C. Lamar Society of International Law, University of Mississippi Law Center, Monograph: No. 1). viii, 79p. (Orig.). 1977. pap. text ed. 10.00x (ISBN 0-8377-0607-6). Rothman.
Gorovitz, Samuel. Moral Problem in Medicine. 500p. 1976. 18.95 (ISBN 0-13-600817-8). P-H.
Gorovitz, Samuel, ed. see Mill, John S.
Gorowara, Krishna, tr. see Pritam, Amrita.
Gorree, Georges & Barbier, Jean. Love Without Boundaries: Mother Teresa of Calcutta. LC 75-37364. 1976. pap. 3.95 (ISBN 0-87973-679-8). Our Sunday Visitor.
Gorrell, Robert & Laird, Charlton. Modern English Handbook. 6th ed. 1976. text ed. 12.95 (ISBN 0-13-594283-7); tchr's man. free (ISBN 0-13-594275-6). P-H.
Gorrell, Robert M. & Laird, Charlton. Writing Modern English. (Illus.). 288p. 1973. pap. text ed. 8.95 (ISBN 0-13-970632-1). P-H.
Gorshkov, S. G. Sea Power of the State. (Illus.). 1979. text ed. 39.00 (ISBN 0-685-93645-7). Pergamon.
--World Ocean Atlas, Vol. 2: Atlantic & Indian Oceans. 3504p. 1979. 400.00 (ISBN 0-08-021953-5). Pergamon.
Gorshkov, Sergei. Sea Power of the State. Crozey, Alan, tr. from Rus. LC 77-88875. 1979. 18.95 o.s.i. (ISBN 0-87021-961-8). Naval Inst Pr.
Gorski, Roger A. & Whalen, Richard E., eds. Brain & Behavior: Brain & Gonadal Function, Vol. 3. (UCLA Forum in Medical Sciences). 1966. 50.00x (ISBN 0-520-00506-6). U of Cal Pr.
Gorsky, Benjamin H. Pain: Origin & Treatment -- Discussions in Pain Management. LC 80-15857. 1980. 18.00 (ISBN 0-87488-448-9); pap. 10.00 (ISBN 0-87488-447-0). Med Exam.
Gorsky, Susan R. Virginia Woolf. (English Authors Ser.: No. 243). 1978. 12.50 (ISBN 0-8057-6712-6). Twayne.
Gorsline, Douglas, jt. auth. see Gorsline, Marie.
Gorsline, G. W. Computer Organization: Hardware-Software. (Illus.). 1980. text ed. 21.95 (ISBN 0-13-165290-7). P-H.
Gorsline, Marie & Gorsline, Douglas. Cowboys. LC 78-1131. (Picturebacks Ser.). (Illus.). 32p. (ps-2). 1980. PLB 4.99 o.p. (ISBN 0-394-93935-2, BYR); pap. 1.25 (ISBN 0-394-83935-8). Random.
--North American Indians. LC 77-79843. (Picturebacks Ser.). (ps-2). 1978. PLB 4.99 (ISBN 0-394-93702-3, BYR); pap. 1.25 (ISBN 0-394-83702-9). Random.
Gorsuch, Richard L. & Malony, H. Newton. The Nature of Man: A Social Psychological Perspective. (Illus.). 228p. 1976. 18.75 (ISBN 0-398-03327-7). C C Thomas.
Gortler, Leon B. & Tripp, Robert C., eds. Techniques & Experiments in Organic Chemistry. 2nd ed. (Illus.). 1978. lab manual 8.95 (ISBN 0-89529-016-2). Avery Pub.
Gortmaker, Gwen, jt. auth. see Goeldner, C. R.
Gortner, Harold J. Administration in the Public Sector. 2nd ed. LC 80-19757. 400p. 1981. text ed. 15.95 (ISBN 0-471-06320-7). Wiley.
Gorton, Ron. The Lawyers of Hell. LC 78-27011. 1979. 9.95 (ISBN 0-8119-0319-2). Fell.
Gorun, Joel R. Focus on Growth in the Church: School Ed. (To Live Is Christ Ser.). 1980. teacher's manual 3.85 (ISBN 0-697-01722-2). Wm C Brown.
Gorvine, Beverly, jt. ed. see Watson, Joellen.

Gorz, Andre, ed. The Division of Labour: The Labour Process & Class-Struggle in Modern Capitalism. Mepham, John, et al, trs. from Fr. (Marxist Theory & Contemporary Capitalism 2 Ser.). 208p. 1976. 12.50x (ISBN 0-85527-124-8); pap. text ed. 10.00x (ISBN 0-85527-781-5). Humanities.

Gorzelany, James A. North Dakota Supplement for Modern Real Estate Practice. 120p. (Orig.). 1980. pap. 7.95 (ISBN 0-88462-377-7). Real Estate Ed Co.

Gorzelany, James A. & Reus, Violet. Indiana Supplement for Modern Real Estate Practice. 128p. (Orig.). 1980. pap. 7.95 (ISBN 0-88462-379-3). Real Estate Ed Co.

Gos, Francois & Baldausky, Karen. Alpine Flower Designs for Artists & Craftsmen. (Illus.). 64p. (Orig.). 1980. pap. 4.00 (ISBN 0-486-23982-9). Dover.

Gosal, Gurdev S. & Ojha, B. S. Agricultural Land-Use in Punjab: A Spatial Analysis. (Illus.). 87p. 1967. 7.50x (ISBN 0-8002-0430-1). Intl Pubns Serv.

Goschie, Susan. Fashion Direction & Coordination. 1980. 9.90 (ISBN 0-672-97267-0); pap. 3.33 (ISBN 0-672-97266-2). Bobbs.

Goscinny & Uderzo. Asterix & Caesar's Gift. Bell, Anthea & Hockridge, Derek, trs. from Fr. (Illus.). 1979. pap. 4.95 (ISBN 2-205-06920-9, Pub. by Dargaud Canada). C Berke.

--Asterix & Cleopatra. Bell, Anthea & Hockridge, Derek, trs. from Fr. (Illus.). 1979. pap. 4.95 (ISBN 0-340-17220-7, Pub. by Dargaud Canada). C Berke.

--Asterix & the Big Fight. Bell, Anthea & Hockridge, Derek, trs. from Fr. (Illus.). 1979. pap. 4.95 (ISBN 0-340-19167-8, Pub. by Dargaud Canada). C Berke.

--Asterix & the Cauldron. Bell, Anthea & Hockridge, Derek, trs. from Fr. (Illus.). 1979. pap. 4.95 (ISBN 2-205-06912-8, Pub. by Dargaud Canada). C Berke.

--Asterix & the Chieftain's Shield. Bell, Anthea & Hockridge, Derek, trs. from Fr. (Illus.). 1979. pap. 4.95 (ISBN 2-205-06910-1, Pub. by Dargaud Canada). C Berke.

--Asterix & the Golden Sickle. Bell, Anthea & Hockridge, Derek, trs. from Fr. (Illus.). 1979. pap. 4.95 (ISBN 0-685-92306-1, Pub. by Dargaud Canada). C Berke.

--Asterix & the Great Crossing. Bell, Anthea & Hockridge, Derek, trs. from Fr. (Illus.). 1979. pap. 4.95 (ISBN 2-205-06921-7, Pub. by Dargaud Canada). C Berke.

--Asterix & the Laurel Wreath. Bell, Anthea & Hockridge, Derek, trs. from Fr. (Illus.). 1979. pap. 4.95 (ISBN 2-205-06917-9, Pub. by Dargaud Canada). C Berke.

--Asterix & the Mansions of the Gods. Bell, Anthea & Hockridge, Derek, trs. from Fr. (Illus.). 1979. pap. 4.95 (ISBN 2-205-06916-0, Pub. by Dargaud Canada). C Berke.

--Asterix & the Normans. Bell, Anthea & Hockridge, Derek, trs. from Fr. (Illus.). 1979. pap. 4.95 (ISBN 2-205-06908-X, Pub. by Dargaud Canada). C Berke.

--Asterix & the Roman Agent. Bell, Anthea & Hockridge, Derek, trs. from Fr. (Illus.). 1979. pap. 4.95 (ISBN 0-340-19168-6, Pub. by Dargaud Canada). C Berke.

--Asterix & the Soothsayer. Bell, Anthea & Hockridge, Derek, trs. from Fr. (Illus.). 1979. pap. 4.95 (ISBN 2-205-06918-7, Pub. by Dargaud Canada). C Berke.

--Asterix at the Olympic Games. Bell, Anthea & Hockridge, Derek, trs. from Fr. (Illus.). 1979. pap. 4.95 (ISBN 2-205-06911-X, Pub. by Dargaud Canada). C Berke.

--Asterix in Britain. Bell, Anthea & Hockridge, Derek, trs. from Fr. (Illus.). 1979. pap. 4.95 (ISBN 2-205-06907-1, Pub. by Dargaud Canada). C Berke.

--Asterix in Spain. Bell, Anthea & Hockridge, Derek, trs. from Fr. (Illus.). 1979. pap. 4.95 (ISBN 0-340-18326-8, Pub. by Dargaud Canada). C Berke.

--Asterix in Switzerland. Bell, Anthea & Hockridge, Derek, trs. from Fr. (Illus.). 1979. pap. 4.95 (ISBN 2-205-06915-2, Pub. by Dargaud Canada). C Berke.

--Asterix the Gaul. Bell, Anthea & Hockridge, Derek, trs. from Fr. (Illus.). 1979. pap. 4.95 (ISBN 0-340-17210-X, Pub. by Dargaud Canada). C Berke.

--Asterix the Gladiator. Bell, Anthea & Hockridge, Derek, trs. from Fr. (Illus.). 1979. pap. 4.95 (ISBN 0-340-18320-9, Pub. by Dargaud Canada). C Berke.

--Asterix the Goths. Bell, Anthea & Hockridge, Derek, trs. from Fr. (Illus.). 1979. pap. 4.95 (ISBN 2-205-06902-0, Pub. by Dargaud Canada). C Berke.

--Asterix the Legionary. Bell, Anthea & Hockridge, Derek, trs. from Fr. (Illus.). 1979. pap. 4.95 (ISBN 0-340-18321-7, Pub. by Dargaud Canada). C Berke.

Gosden, P. H. & Sharp, P. R. The Development of an Education Service: The West Riding, 1889-1974. 273p. 1978. 36.00x (ISBN 0-85520-150-9, Pub by Martin Robertson England). Biblio Dist.

Goshen, Charles E. Drinks, Drugs, & Do-Gooders. LC 72-93309. (Illus.). 1973. 10.95 (ISBN 0-02-912620-7). Free Pr.

Goshen-Gottstein, Moshe H. Syriac Manuscripts in the Harvard College Library: A Catalog. LC 77-13132. (Harvard Semitic Studies: No. 23). 1979. 15.00 (ISBN 0-89130-189-5, 040423). Scholars Pr Ca.

Goslett, Dorothy. The Professional Practice of Design. 1978. 19.95 (ISBN 0-7134-1176-7, Pub. by Batsford England). David & Charles.

Goslich, Siegfried. Beitrage Zur Geschicte der Deutschen Romantischen Oper Zwischen Spohrs "Faust" und Wagner's "Lohengrin". LC 80-2281. 1981. Repr. of 1937 ed. 31.50 (ISBN 0-404-18846-X). AMS Pr.

Goslin, David A. School in Contemporary Society. 1965. 7.95x o.p. (ISBN 0-673-05538-8); pap. 4.95x o.p. (ISBN 0-673-05535-3). Scott F.

Gosling, J. C. Plato. (Arguments of the Philosophers Ser). 1973. 21.00x (ISBN 0-7100-7664-9). Routledge & Kegan.

Gosling, J. C., tr. & notes by see Plato.

Gosling, Nalda. Herbs for Colds & Flu. LC 80-53450. (Everybody's Home Herbal Ser.). (Illus.). 64p. (Orig.). 1981. pap. 1.95 (ISBN 0-394-74834-4). Shambhala Pubn.

--Herbs for Headaches & Migraine. LC 80-50750. (Everybody's Home Herbal Ser.). (Illus.). 64p. (Orig.). 1980. pap. 1.95 (ISBN 0-394-73946-9). Shambhala Pubns.

Gosling, Nigel. Adventurous World of Paris Nineteen Hundred to Nineteen Fourteen. LC 78-52477. (Illus.). 1978. 17.95 o.p. (ISBN 0-688-03366-0). Morrow.

Gosling, P. E. Beginning BASIC. 104p. 1977. pap. 10.95 (ISBN 0-333-22304-7). Robotics Pr.

--Continuing BASIC. 160p. 1980. pap. 10.95 (ISBN 0-333-26286-7). Robotics Pr.

Gosman, Martin L. Accounting Graffiti. LC 75-4144. (Illus.). 152p. 1975. pap. text ed. 6.95 (ISBN 0-8299-0058-6). West Pub.

Gosnell, Harold F. Negro Politicians: The Rise of Negro Politics in Chicago. LC 66-30216. 1935. 7.95x (ISBN 0-226-30493-0). U of Chicago Pr.

Gosnell, Harold F. & Smolka, Richard G. American Parties & Elections. new ed. (Political Science Ser.). 288p. 1976. pap. text ed. 15.95 (ISBN 0-675-08620-5). Merrill.

Gosner, K. L. Guide to Identification of Marine & Estuarine Invertebates: From Cape Hatteras to the Bay of Fundy. 693p. 1971. pap. 22.50 (ISBN 0-471-31901-5). Wiley.

Gosner, Pamela. Caribbean Georgian: The Great Houses & Small of the Caribbean. LC 78-72966. (Illus.). 324p. (Orig.). 1981. 30.00x (ISBN 0-89410-011-4); pap. 12.00x (ISBN 0-89410-012-2). Three Continents.

Goss, B. & Yamey, B. S. Economics of Future Trading. LC 75-6266. 1976. 27.95 (ISBN 0-470-97115-0). Halsted Pr.

Goss, B. A. The Theory of Futures Trading. (Students Library of Economics). (Illus.). 128p. 1972. 12.50 (ISBN 0-7100-7217-1). Routledge & Kegan.

Goss, Clav see Harrison, Paul C.

Goss, Gordon J. National Square Dance Directory. rev. ed. 128p. 1981. pap. 8.50 (ISBN 0-9605494-2-0). Natl Sq Dance.

Goss, Michael, compiled by. Poltergeists: An Annotated Bibliography of Works in English, Circa 1880-1975. LC 78-11492. 1979. 16.50 (ISBN 0-8108-1181-2). Scarecrow.

Goss, R. O. Studies in Maritime Economics. LC 68-29328. (Illus.). 1968. 35.50 (ISBN 0-521-07329-4). Cambridge U Pr.

Goss, R. O., ed. Advances in Maritime Economics. LC 76-1135. (Illus.). 1977. 49.50 (ISBN 0-521-21232-4). Cambridge U Pr.

Goss, Richard J. Adaptive Growth. 1965. 39.00 (ISBN 0-12-292750-8). Acad Pr.

Gosse, Edmund. Father & Son. 1963. pap. 4.95 (ISBN 0-393-00195-4, Norton Lib). Norton.

Gosse, Edmund, ed. Restoration Plays. 1953. 6.00x (ISBN 0-460-00604-5, Evman); pap. 4.95 (ISBN 0-460-01604-0). Dutton.

Gosse, Philip. The History of Piracy. LC 75-16396. (Illus.). xvi, 349p. 1976. Repr. of 1934 ed. 22.00 (ISBN 0-8103-4156-5). Gale.

Gosselin, Chris, jt. auth. see Wilson, Glenn.

Gosset, Philip, ed. see Bellini, Vincenzio.

Gossett, et al. La Cenerentola: Rossini. Jacobs, Arthur, tr. 1980. pap. 4.95 (ISBN 0-7145-3819-1). Riverrun NY.

Gossett, Don. How to Conquer Fear. Orig. Title: How You Can Rise Above Fear. 160p. 1981. pap. 2.95 (ISBN 0-88368-092-0). Whitaker Hse.

--What You Say Is What You Get. 192p. 1976. pap. 2.50 (ISBN 0-88368-066-1). Whitaker Hse.

Gossett, Don, tr. Avenida Alabanza. (Spanish Bks.). (Span.). 1978. 1.60 (ISBN 0-8297-0902-9). Life Pubs Intl.

Gossett, Philip, ed. see Bellini, Vincenzo.

Gossett, Philip, ed. see Cherubini, Maria L.

Gossett, Philip, ed. see Donizetti, Gaetano.

Gossett, Philip, ed. see Halevy, Jacques-Francois.

Gossett, Philip, ed. see Mehul, Etienne.

Gossett, Philip, ed. see Meyerbeer, Giacomo.

Gossett, Philip, ed. see Rossini, Gioachino.

Gossett, Philip, ed. see Scribe, Eugene & Delestre-Poirson, Charles-Gaspard.

Gossett, Phillip, ed. see Cherubini, Maria L.

Gossett, Phillip, ed. see Mehul, Etienne N.

Gossett, Phillip, ed. see Meyerbeer, Giacomo.

Gossett, Phillip, ed. see Rossini, Gioachino.

Gossett, Phillip, ed. see Spontini, Gasparo.

Gossett, Suzanne, ed. Hierarchomachia, or the Antibishop. LC 78-75201. 300p. 1981. 14.50 (ISBN 0-8387-2151-6). Bucknell U Pr.

Gossip, A. J. Experience Worketh Hope. (Scholar As Preacher Ser.). 206p. 1945. text ed. 7.75 (ISBN 0-567-04423-8). Attic Pr.

--From the Edge of the Crowd. (Scholar As Preacher Ser.). 316p. 1924. text ed. 7.75 (ISBN 0-567-04420-3). Attic Pr.

--The Galilean Accent. (Scholar As Preacher Ser.). 302p. 1926. text ed. 7.75 (ISBN 0-567-04421-1). Attic Pr.

Gossip, C. J. An Introduction to French Classical Tragedy. 1981. 29.50x (ISBN 0-389-20163-4). B&N.

Gossling, W. F., jt. ed. see Gielnik, S. J.

Gossman, Lionel. The Empire Unpossess'd: An Essay on Gibbon's "Decline & Fall of the Roman Empire". LC 80-24008. (Illus.). 176p. Date not set. price not set (ISBN 0-521-23453-0). Cambridge U Pr.

Gossman, N. J., jt. ed. see Baylen, J. O.

Gosson, Stephen. The Ephemerides of Phialo. LC 73-170404. (The English Stage Ser.: Vol. 3). lib. bdg. 50.00 (ISBN 0-8240-0586-4). Garland Pub.

--Playes Confuted in Fiue Actions. LC 74-170407. (The English Stage Ser.: Vol. 6). lib. bdg. 50.00 (ISBN 0-8240-0589-9). Garland Pub.

--The Schoole (Sic) of Abuse. Bd. with A Reply to Gosson's Schoole of Abuse. Lodge, Thomas. (The English Stage Ser.: Vol. 2). lib. bdg. 50.00 (ISBN 0-8240-0585-6). Garland Pub.

Gossop, M. Theories of Neurosis. (Illus.). 261p. 1981. 35.00 (ISBN 0-387-10370-8). Springer-Verlag.

Gostelow, Mary. Embroidery of All Russia. (Encore Edition). (Illus.). 1978. 3.95 (ISBN 0-684-16542-2, ScribT). Scribner.

--Embroidery South Africa. (Illus.). 1977. 20.00 (ISBN 0-263-06232-5). Transatlantic.

Gostin, Larry O., jt. auth. see Weisstub, David N.

Gostling, E. P. & Ambrose, K. Case Studies from the Distribution Trades. 1972. text ed. 14.95x (ISBN 0-07-002016-7). Intl Ideas.

Goswami, Amit. The Concepts of Physics. 1979. text ed. 19.95x (ISBN 0-669-01897-X). Heath.

Gotch, A. F. Mammals: Their Latin Names Explained. (Illus.). 1979. 18.95 (ISBN 0-7137-0939-1, Pub. by Blandford Pr England). Sterling.

Gotch, Christopher, jt. auth. see Scutt, R. W. B.

Goth, Andres. Medical Pharmacology: Principles & Concepts. 9th ed. LC 78-4107. 1978. text ed. 26.50 (ISBN 0-8016-1948-3). Mosby.

Gothmann, W. Electronics: A Contemporary Approach. 1980. 18.95 (ISBN 0-13-252254-3). P-H.

Gothmann, William H. Digital Electronics: An Introduction to Theory & Practice. LC 76-18258. (Illus.). 1977. 19.95 (ISBN 0-13-212217-0). P-H.

Gotlieb, C. C. Computers in the Home. 65p. 1978. pap. text ed. 3.00x (ISBN 0-920380-10-7, Pub. by Inst Res Pub Canada). Renouf.

Gotlieb, C. C. & Borodin, A. Social Issues in Computing. (Computer Science & Applied Mathematics Ser.). 1973. 17.95 (ISBN 0-12-293750-3). Acad Pr.

Gotlieb, C. C. & Gotlieb, Leo R. Data Types & Structures. (Illus.). 1978. ref. ed. 22.95 (ISBN 0-13-197095-X). P-H.

Gotlieb, Leo R., jt. auth. see Gotlieb, C. C.

Gotlieb, Phyllis. O Master Caliban! LC 76-5540. 256p. (YA) 1976. 8.95 o.p. (ISBN 0-06-011621-8, HarpT). Har-Row.

Goto, Toshio, et al. Problems in Advanced Organic Chemistry. LC 67-13842. (Illus.). 1968. pap. 8.95x (ISBN 0-8162-3411-6). Holden-Day.

Gotobed, Jabez. Darts: Fifty Ways to Play the Game. (Illus.). 1979. 9.95 (ISBN 0-900891-71-8); pap. 4.95 (ISBN 0-900891-72-6). Oleander Pr.

Gotshall, Daniel W. Fishwatchers' Guide to the Inshore Fishes of the Pacific Coast. LC 77-73915. (Illus.). 1977. pap. 8.95 o.p. (ISBN 0-930118-01-4). Sea Chall.

--Pacific Coast Inshore Fishes. (Illus.). 112p. 1980. pap. 11.50 (ISBN 0-930118-01-4). Western Marine.

--Pacific Coast Inshore Fishes. LC 80-53027. (Illus.). 96p. pap. 11.50 (ISBN 0-930118-06-5). Sea Chall.

Gotshall, Daniel W. & Laurent, Laurence L. Pacific Coast Subtidal Marine Invertebrates. (Illus.). 112p. pap. 11.50 (ISBN 0-686-62677-X). Western Marine Ent.

Gottesfeld, Harry. Alternative to Psychiatric Hospitalization. LC 77-7318. 1979. 12.95 (ISBN 0-470-99188-7). Halsted Pr.

Gottesfeld, Mary & Pharis, Mary. Profiles in Social Work. LC 76-20697. 1977. text ed. 19.95 (ISBN 0-87705-296-4). Human Sci Pr.

Gottesfeld, Mary, ed. Case Studies in Clinical Social Work. LC 78-71807. 1979. pap. 6.95x (ISBN 0-87705-397-9). Human Sci Pr.

--Education for Clinical Social Work: A Special Issue of Clinical Social Work Journal. LC 77-81412. 1977. text ed. 12.95 (ISBN 0-87705-323-5). Human Sci Pr.

Gottesman, Irving I. & Shields, James. Schizophrenia & Genetics. (Personality & Psychopathology Ser.: Vol. 13). 1972. 39.00 (ISBN 0-12-293450-4). Acad Pr.

Gottesman, Rita S. Arts & Crafts in New York, Seventeen Twenty-Six to Seventeen Seventy-Six. LC 70-127254. (Architecture & Decorative Art Ser.: Vol. 35). 1970. Repr. of 1938 ed. lib. bdg. 39.50 (ISBN 0-306-71129-X). Da Capo.

Gottesman, Ronald, ed. see Seidman, Steve.

Gottesman, Ronald, ed. see Van Wert, William.

Gottesman, Ronald, ed. see Wead, George & Lellis, George.

Gottfredson, Don M., jt. auth. see Gottfredson, Michael R.

Gottfredson, Michael, jt. ed. see Hirshi, Travis.

Gottfredson, Michael R. & Gottfredson, Don M. Decision Making in Criminal Justice: Toward the Rational Exercise of Discretion. 424p. 1980. 28.50 (ISBN 0-88410-234-3). Ballinger Pub.

Gottfried, John & Gottfried, Patricia. A Wine-Tasting Course: The Practical Way to Know & Enjoy Wine. (Illus.). 1978. 14.95 o.p. (ISBN 0-679-51451-1); pap. 6.95 o.p. (ISBN 0-679-50810-4). McKay.

Gottfried, Nathan, jt. auth. see Seay, Bill M.

Gottfried, Patricia, jt. auth. see Gottfried, John.

Gottfried, Paul. Conservative Millenarians: The Romantic Experience in Bavaria. LC 74-20028. 1979. 22.50 (ISBN 0-8232-0982-2). Fordham.

Gottfried, Robert S. Epidemic Disease in Fifteenth Century England: The Medical Response & the Demographic Consequences. (Illus.). 1978. 19.50 (ISBN 0-8135-0861-4). Rutgers U Pr.

Gottfried, Rosalie. Getting into American Medical-Veterinary Schools: A Practical "How to" Guide. LC 77-93397. (gr. 8 up). 1978. pap. text ed. 5.50x (ISBN 0-931084-01-6). Argee Pub.

Gottheil, E. L., et al, eds. see Coatesville-Jefferson Conference on Addiction, 1st, October 1977.

Gottheil, Edward, et al, eds. Substance Abuse & Psychiatric Illness: Proceedings of the Second Annual Coatesville--Jefferson Conference on Addiction. LC 79-25407. 224p. 1980. 28.00 (ISBN 0-08-025547-7). Pergamon.

Gotthelf, Jeremias. Black Spider. Waidson, H. M., tr. 1980. pap. 5.95 (ISBN 0-7145-0125-5). Riverrun NY.

--Die Schwarze Spinne. Waidson, H. M., ed. 1976. pap. 9.95x (ISBN 0-631-01620-1, Pub. by Basil Blackwell). Biblio Dist.

Gottinger, Hans W. Elements of Bayesian Statistics. (De Gruyter Lehrbuch). 288p. 1979. pap. text ed. 28.25x (ISBN 3-11-007169-X). De Gruyter.

Gottleib, A. A History of Transfusion & Blood Banking Practices. Date not set. 25.00 (ISBN 0-8391-1468-0). Univ Park.

Gottleib, Elaine, et al, trs. see Singer, Isaac B.

Gottleib, Richard M., jt. auth. see Thompson, Waite.

Gottlieb, Arlan J., et al. The Whole Internist Catalog: A Compendium of Clues to Diagnosis & Management. LC 79-66034. (Illus.). 509p. 1980. pap. text ed. 19.50 (ISBN 0-7216-4179-2). Saunders.

Gottlieb, Carla. From the Window of God to the Vanity of Man: A Study of Window Symbolism in Western Painting. LC 80-53355. (Illus.). 500p. 1980. 35.00 (ISBN 0-9604420-1-4); pap. 25.00 (ISBN 0-9604420-2-2). Boian Bks.

--The Restoration of the 'Nereid Monument' at Xanthos. (Illus.). 340p. 1980. 30.00 (ISBN 0-9604420-0-6); pap. 25.00 (ISBN 0-686-28889-0). Boian Bks.

Gottlieb, David. Babes in Arms: Youth in the Army. LC 80-15830. (Illus.). 173p. 1980. 14.95 (ISBN 0-8039-1499-7). Sage.

Gottlieb, David, et al. Emergence of Youth Societies. LC 66-13598. 1966. 10.50 o.s.i. (ISBN 0-02-912600-2). Free Pr.
Gottlieb, E., ed. see Hemley, Cecil.
Gottlieb, Gerald. Adventures of Ulysses. (World Landmark Ser.: No. 40). (Illus.). (gr. 5-9). 1959. PLB 4.39 o.p. (ISBN 0-394-90540-7, BYR). Random.
Gottlieb, Gilbert, ed. Studies on the Development of Behavior & the Nervous System, 4 vols. Incl. Vol. 1. Behavioral Embryology. 1973. 39.50 o.s.i. (ISBN 0-12-609301-6); Vol. 2. Aspects of Neurogenesis. 1973. 37.57 (ISBN 0-12-609302-4); Vol. 3. Development of Neural & Behavioral Specificity. 1976. 43.00 (ISBN 0-12-609303-2); Vol. 4. Early Influences. 1978. 28.50 (ISBN 0-12-609304-0). Acad Pr.
Gottlieb, Irving. Switching Regulators & Power Supplies with Practical Inverters & Converters. LC 75-41722. (Illus.). 252p. 1976. 12.95 o.p. (ISBN 0-8306-6828-4); pap. 6.95 (ISBN 0-8306-5828-9, 828). TAB Bks.
Gottlieb, Jean S., ed. Directory of Planning & Urban Affairs Libraries in the United States & Canada. 4th ed. 112p. 1980. pap. 15.00 (ISBN 0-86602-000-4). CPL Biblios.
Gottlieb, Lois C. Rachel Crothers. (United States Authors Ser.: No. 332). 1979. lib. bdg. 12.50 (ISBN 0-8057-7222-7). Twayne.
Gottlieb, Manuel. Health Care Financing in Mainland Tanzania. LC 75-30548. (Foreign and Comparative Studies Eastern African Series XX). 104p. 1975. pap. text ed. 4.50x (ISBN 0-915984-17-2). Maxwell Schl Citizen.
Gottlieb, Marvin, jt. auth. see Cohn, Sidney A.
Gottlieb, Marvin I., jt. auth. see Cohn, Sidney A.
Gottlieb, Marvin I., et al, eds. Pediatrics Specialty Board Review. 4th ed. 1974. spiral bdg. 16.50 (ISBN 0-87488-301-6). Med Exam.
Gottlieb, Marvine I., jt. auth. see Holmes, Marguerite C.
Gottlieb, Naomi. The Welfare Bind. LC 73-17259. 240p. 1974. 17.50x (ISBN 0-231-03762-7). Columbia U Pr.
Gottlieb, Naomi, ed. Alternative Social Services for Women. LC 80-164. 1980. 22.50x (ISBN 0-231-04212-4). Columbia U Pr.
Gottlieb, Nathan. A Jewish Child Is Born. LC 60-16833. 1976. pap. 4.95 (ISBN 0-8197-0017-7). Bloch.
--Stinger. 1978. pap. 1.75 o.s.i. (ISBN 0-685-54635-7, 04749-X). Jove Pubns.
Gottlieb, Nora & Chapman, Raymond, eds. Letters to an Actress: The Story of Turgenev & Savina. LC 73-92898. 155p. 1973. 8.95 (ISBN 0-8214-0146-7). Ohio U Pr.
Gottman, John, jt. ed. see Asher, Steven.
Gottmann, Jean. Virginia in Our Century. LC 68-8541. 1969. 9.95 (ISBN 0-8139-0109-X). U Pr of Va.
Gottmann, Jean, ed. Centre & Periphery: Spatial Variation in Politics. LC 79-21564. (Sage Focus Editions: Vol. 19). 1980. 18.95x (ISBN 0-8039-1344-3); pap. 9.95x (ISBN 0-8039-1345-1). Sage.
Gotto, Antonio & Panoletti, Rodolfo, eds. Atherosclerosis Reviews, Vol. 6. LC 75-14582. 1979. text ed. 28.00 (ISBN 0-89004-276-4). Raven.
Gotto, Antonio M., jt. ed. see Paoletti, Rodolfo.
Gotto, Antonio M., Jr., jt. ed. see Paoletti, Rodolfo.
Gottschalk, Fruma, tr. see Wiles, Timothy J.
Gottschalk, H. B. Heraclides of Pontus. 192p. 1980. 37.50x (ISBN 0-19-814021-5). Oxford U Pr.
Gottschalk, Louis A., ed. The Content Analysis of Verbal Behavior: Further Studies. 1979. 45.00 (ISBN 0-470-26367-9). Halsted Pr.
Gottschalk, Louis A., et al. Manual of Instructions for Using the Gottschalk-Gleser Content Analysis Scales: Anxiety, Hostility, Social Alienation-Personal Disorganization. 1969. 8.50 o.p. (ISBN 0-520-01483-9). U of Cal Pr.
--Manual of Instructions for Using the Gottschalk-Gleser Content Analysis Scales: Anxiety, Hostility, Social Alienation - Personal Disorganization. 1979. Repr. of 1969 ed. 12.00x (ISBN 0-520-03814-2). U of Cal Pr.
Gottschang, Jack L. Guide to the Mammals of Ohio. (Illus.). 276p. 1981. 35.00 (ISBN 0-8142-0242-X). Ohio St U Pr.
Gottschling, E. see Siegel, C. L.
Gottsdanker, Robert. Experimenting in Psychology. (P-H Ser. in Experimental Psychology). (Illus.). 1978. ref. ed. 17.95x (ISBN 0-13-295501-6). P-H.
Gottsegen, Abby J., jt. ed. see Gottsegen, Gloria B.
Gottsegen, Gloria B., ed. Group Behavior: A Guide to Information Sources. LC 79-63744. (Psychology Information Guide Ser.: Vol. 2). 1979. 30.00 (ISBN 0-8103-1439-8). Gale.
Gottsegen, Gloria B. & Gottsegen, Abby J., eds. Humanistic Psychology: A Guide to Information Sources. (Psychology Information Guide Ser.: Vol. 6). 175p. 1980. 30.00 (ISBN 0-8103-1462-2). Gale.
Gottshall, Franklin H. Masterpiece Furniture Making. LC 79-12. (Illus.). 224p. 1979. 24.95 (ISBN 0-8117-0974-4). Stackpole.
--Wood Carving & Whittling for Everyone. LC 77-23224. (Illus.). 1980. pap. 9.95 (SL 921, ScribT). Scribner.
--Wood Carving & Whittling for Everyone. LC 77-23224. (Illus.). 1977. 12.95 o.p. (ISBN 0-684-14886-2, ScribT). Scribner.
--Wood Carving & Whittling Made Easy. 1963. 9.95 (ISBN 0-02-544860-9). Macmillan.
Gottstein, G. & Luecke, K., eds. Textures of Materials: Proceedings of the 5th Int'l. Conf. on Texture of Materials, March 29-April 1, 1978, Aachen, Germany, 2 vols. 1979. pap. 116.90 o.p. (ISBN 0-387-09220-X). Springer-Verlag.
Gottwald, Paul, tr. see Luthi, Max.
Gotz, Ignacio L. Creativity: Theoretical & Socio-Cosmic Reflections. LC 78-59126. 1978. pap. text ed. 7.75 (ISBN 0-8191-0548-1). U Pr of Amer.
Gotze, Hans. Prints: Processing & Enlarging in Black & White. Mason, R. H., ed. Shields, Mike, tr. from Ger. (Illus.). 83p. (Orig.). 1980. pap. 7.50x (ISBN 0-85242-704-2). Intl Pubns Serv.
Gotzkowsky, Bodo, ed. see Adelphus, Johannes.
Goudey, Alice E. Good Rain. (Illus.). (gr. 1-5). 1950. PLB 5.95 o.p. (ISBN 0-525-30856-3). Dutton.
--Here Come the Bears. LC 54-5924. (Illus.). 96p. (gr. 1-5). 1954. 5.95 (ISBN 0-684-13365-2, ScribJ). Scribner.
Goudge, Elizabeth. A Book of Faith. 336p. 1980. pap. 2.50 (ISBN 0-553-11052-7). Bantam.
--The Rosemary Tree. 1976. pap. 1.75 o.s.i. (ISBN 0-515-04147-5). Jove Pubns.
Goudge, Thomas A. Ascent of Life: A Philosophical Study of the Theory of Evolution. LC 61-65468. 1961. 12.50x o.p. (ISBN 0-8020-1152-7). U of Toronto Pr.
Goudie, A. & Wilkinson, J. The Warm Desert Environment. LC 76-9731. (Topics in Geography Ser). (Illus.). 1977. 14.50 (ISBN 0-521-21330-4); pap. 7.95 (ISBN 0-521-29105-4); 26.50x (ISBN 0-521-21912-4). Cambridge U Pr.
Goudie, Andrew. Environmental Change. (Contemporary Problems in Geography Ser.). (Illus.). 1977. 29.95x (ISBN 0-19-874073-5); pap. 9.50x (ISBN 0-19-874074-3). Oxford U Pr.
Goudie, Andrew S. Duricrusts in Tropical & Sub-Tropical Landscapes. (Oxford Research Studies in Geography). (Illus.). 192p. 1973. 19.95x o.p. (ISBN 0-19-823212-8). Oxford U Pr.
Goudket, Michael. Audiovisual Primer. rev. ed. LC 72-93755. (Illus.). 77p. 1974. pap. text ed. 3.25x (ISBN 0-8077-2437-8). Tchrs Coll.
Goudsblom, Johan. Nihilism & Culture. 213p. 1980. 27.50x (ISBN 0-8476-6766-9). Rowman.
--Sociology in the Balance. LC 77-4368. 1977. 17.50x (ISBN 0-231-04290-6). Columbia U Pr.
Goudsmit, Samuel, jt. auth. see Claiborne, Robert.
Goudy, Frederic W. Alphabet & Elements of Lettering. rev. ed. 8.50 (ISBN 0-8446-2145-5). Peter Smith.
--Typologia: Studies in Type Design & Type Making with Comments on the Invention of Typography, the First Types, Legibility & Fine Printing. 1978. 17.50x (ISBN 0-520-03308-6); pap. 3.95 (ISBN 0-520-03278-0, CAL 334). U of Cal Pr.
Goudzwaard, B. A Christian Political Option. 1973. pap. 2.75 o.p. (ISBN 0-686-11981-9). Wedge Pub.
Goudzwaard, Bob. Capitalism & Progress: A Diagnosis of Western Society. 1979. pap. 9.95 (ISBN 0-88906-106-8). Radix Bks.
Gouedy, Terrence. Everything You Never Wanted to Know About Yourself or the Cancer Syndrome. (Illus.). 64p. 1980. 12.50 (ISBN 0-682-49640-5). Exposition.
Gouge, William. Commentary on Hebrews. LC 79-2541. (Kregel Limited Edition Library). 1980. Repr. of 1866 ed. 29.95 (ISBN 0-686-52558-2). Kregel.
Gough, Aidan. Standards Relating to Non-Criminal Misbehavior. (Juvenile Justice Standards Project Ser.). Date not set. softcover 6.95 (ISBN 0-88410-832-5). Ballinger Pub.
--Standards Relating to Non-Criminal Misbehavior. LC 76-14394. (Juvenile Justice Standards Project Ser.). 1977. soft cover 6.95 o.p. (ISBN 0-88410-772-8); 14.00, casebound o.p. (ISBN 0-88410-232-7). Ballinger Pub.
Gough, Chester R. & Srikantaiah, Taverekere. Systems Analysis in Libraries: A Question & Answer Approach. 1980. pap. cancelled o.p. (ISBN 0-85157-278-2). K G Saur.
Gough, Henry & Parker, James. Glossary of Terms Used in Heraldry. (Illus.). 1966. Repr. of 1894 ed. 15.00 (ISBN 0-8103-3126-8). Gale.
Gough, John. Into Print. 1979. 19.95 (ISBN 0-7134-0739-5, Pub. by Batsford England). David & Charles.
Gough, Kathleen, jt. ed. see Schneider, David M.
Gough, Malcolm & Gear, Michael. Plain X-Ray in the Diagnosis of the Acute Abdomen. (Illus.). 194p. 1971. 9.50 (ISBN 0-632-08380-8, Blackwell). Mosby.
Gough, Richard. The History of Myddle. 1979. Repr. text ed. 19.50x (ISBN 0-686-58501-1). Humanities.
--History of Myddle, 17th Century England. 35.00 (ISBN 0-87556-105-5). Saifer.
Gough, Vera & Grier, B. R. Better Telephoning: A Plan to Improve Your Telephone Technique. 1970. pap. text ed. 3.90 o.p. (ISBN 0-08-006822-7). Pergamon.
--Planned Speaking & Your Career. 1967. 12.25 (ISBN 0-08-012589-1); pap. 4.20 (ISBN 0-08-012588-3). Pergamon.
Gougher, Ronald L; see Dodge, James W.
Goulart, Frances S. Eating to Win. LC 77-8756. 1978. 25.00x (ISBN 0-8128-2322-2); pap. 6.95 (ISBN 0-686-67964-4). Stein & Day.
--The Ecological Eclair: And Other Sugarless Treats. 144p. 1975. 9.50 o.s.i. (ISBN 0-02-544910-9). Macmillan.
Goulart, Francis S. Ecological Eclair. 1975. pap. 3.50 o.s.i. (ISBN 0-02-009650-X, Collier). Macmillan.
Goulart, Ron. The Adventurous Decade: Comic Strips in the Thirties. 1975. 8.95 o.p. (ISBN 0-87000-252-X). Arlington Hse.
--Broke Down Engine. 1971. 10.95 (ISBN 0-02-544880-3). Macmillan.
--Capricorn One. 1978. pap. 1.75 o.p. (ISBN 0-449-14024-5, GM). Fawcett.
--The Emperor of the Last Days. (Orig.). 1977. pap. 1.50 o.p. (ISBN 0-445-03201-4). Popular Lib.
--The Robot in the Closet. 1981. pap. 1.75 (ISBN 0-87997-626-8, UE1626, Daw Bks). NAL.
--Vampirella, No. 1: Bloodstalk. (Orig.). 1975. pap. 1.25 o.s.i. (ISBN 0-446-76928-2). Warner Bks.
--Vampirella, No. 3: Deadwalk. (Orig.). 1976. pap. 1.25 o.s.i. (ISBN 0-446-76930-4). Warner Bks.
--Vampirella No. 6: Snakegod. 144p. (Orig.). 1976. pap. 1.25 o.s.i. (ISBN 0-446-86090-5). Warner Bks.
Goulart, Ron, jt. auth. see Preiss, Byron.
Gould, Beryl M. Buy Wisely, Eat Well. 1969. 10.95 (ISBN 0-571-10328-6, Pub. by Faber & Faber); pap. 4.95 (ISBN 0-571-10665-X). Merrimack Bk Serv.
Gould, Bryan, jt. auth. see Topliss, Eda.
Gould, Carol C. Marx's Social Ontology. 1978. 15.00x (ISBN 0-262-07071-5); pap. 5.95 (ISBN 0-262-57056-4). MIT Pr.
Gould, Charles. Mythical Monsters. LC 74-75474. 1969. Repr. of 1886 ed. 20.00 (ISBN 0-8103-3834-3). Gale.
Gould, Chester. The Celebrated Cases of Dick Tracy Nineteen Thirty-One to Nineteen Fifty-One. abr. ed. Galewitz, Herb, ed. LC 70-127010. (Illus.). 290p. 1981. pap. 12.50 (ISBN 0-87754-220-1). Chelsea Hse.
Gould, David J. Bureaucratic Corruption in the Third World. (Policy Studies). 1980. 22.50 (ISBN 0-08-025084-X). Pergamon.
--Law & the Administrative Process: Analytic Frameworks for Understanding Public Policy Making. LC 79-63850. 1979. pap. text ed. 11.25 (ISBN 0-8191-0746-8). U Pr of Amer.
Gould, Douglas, jt. auth. see Dockrill, Michael.
Gould, E. P. Saint Mark. LC 25-17683. (International Critical Commentary Ser.). 376p. 1896. text ed. 20.00x (ISBN 0-567-05022-X). Attic Pr.
Gould Editorial Staff. Administrative Law 1981. 1981. pap. text ed. 6.50x (ISBN 0-87526-190-6). Gould.
--Agency Law of U. S., 1981. 1981. pap. text ed. 5.75x (ISBN 0-87526-191-4). Gould.
--Crime Codes of Pennsylvania. 400p. (Supplemented annually). 1980. looseleaf 13.00 (ISBN 0-87526-216-3). Gould.
--Criminal Laws of Illinois. (Annual). 1981. text ed. 9.95x (ISBN 0-87526-199-X). Gould.
--Criminal Laws of Ohio. (Annual). 1981. looseleaf 10.50x (ISBN 0-87526-202-3). Gould.
--Criminal Procedure Law of New York Quizzer, 1978-79. 1978. looseleaf 5.50x o.p. (ISBN 0-685-80905-6). Gould.
--Evidence Code-Federal. (Supplemented annually). 1981. looseleaf 8.50 (ISBN 0-87526-207-4). Gould.
--Evidence Law of New York Quizzer 1981. 1981. text ed. 7.50x (ISBN 0-87526-220-1). Gould.
--Law Digest of New York. (Supplemented annually). looseleaf 7.50 (ISBN 0-87526-252-X). Gould.
--Motor Vehicle & Traffic Laws of New Jersey. (Supplemented annually). looseleaf 12.50x (ISBN 0-87526-232-5). Gould.
--Motor Vehicle Laws of Massachusetts. (Supplemented annually). looseleaf 12.50x (ISBN 0-87526-231-7). Gould.
--Patents. 1981. 77.50 (ISBN 0-87526-078-0). Gould.
--Penal Law of New York Quizzer. 1981. looseleaf 5.50 (ISBN 0-87526-225-2). Gould.
--Surrogate's Court Procedure Act (N. Y.) (Supplemented annually). looseleaf 8.00 (ISBN 0-87526-129-9). Gould.
--Vehicle & Traffic Law (N.Y.) 250p. (Supplemented annually). looseleaf 10.00 (ISBN 0-87526-130-2). Gould.
--Vehicle Laws of Pennsylvania. Date not set. looseleaf 12.00 (ISBN 0-87526-233-3). Gould.
Gould, Elaine & Gould, Loren. Arts & Crafts for Physically & Mentally Disabled: The How, What & Why of It. (Illus.). 368p. 1978. 38.00 (ISBN 0-398-03783-3). C C Thomas.
--Crafts for the Elderly. (Illus.). 224p. 1976. 14.75 (ISBN 0-398-00710-1). C C Thomas.
Gould, Ezra P. see Hovey, Alvah.
Gould, F. J., jt. auth. see Eppen, Gary D.
Gould, Frederick J. The Agnostic Island: A Tale. Wolff, Robert L., ed. Bd. with The Individualist. Mallock, W. H. Repr. of 1899 ed. LC 75-1536. (Victorian Fiction Ser.). 1975. lib. bdg. 66.00 (ISBN 0-8240-1608-4). Garland Pub.
Gould, Heywood. Fort Apache, the Bronx. 224p. (Orig.). 1981. pap. 2.50 (ISBN 0-446-91618-8). Warner Bks.
--One Dead Debutante. LC 75-9483. 256p. 1975. 7.95 o.p. (ISBN 0-312-58520-9). St Martin.
--One Dead Debutante. 1979. pap. 1.95 o.p. (ISBN 0-345-25520-8). Ballantine.
--Sir Christopher Wren: Renaissance Architect, Philosopher, & Scientist. LC 75-101752. (Biography Ser). (Illus.). (gr. 7 up). 1970. PLB 5.90 o.p. (ISBN 0-531-00946-7). Watts.
Gould, J. P. & Ferguson, C. E. Microeconomic Theory. 5th ed. 1980. 18.95x (ISBN 0-256-02157-0). Irwin.
Gould, James A. Classic Philosophical Questions. 3rd ed. (Philosophy Ser.). 1979. pap. text ed. 12.95 (ISBN 0-675-08308-7); instructor's manual free. Merrill.
Gould, James A. & Iorio, John J. Violence in Modern Literature. LC 71-182676. 208p. 1972. pap. 4.95x (ISBN 0-87835-037-3). Boyd & Fraser.
Gould, Jay M. Input-Output Databases. 1978. lib. bdg. 22.50 (ISBN 0-8240-7058-5). Garland Pub.
Gould, Jean. All About the Old English Sheepdog. 1973. 8.95 (ISBN 0-7207-0619-X, Pub. by Michael Joseph). Merrimack Bk Serv.
--American Women Poets: Pioneers of Modern Poetry. LC 79-25670. (Illus.). 352p. 1980. 10.95 (ISBN 0-396-07828-1). Dodd.
--Amy: The World of Amy Lowell & the Imagist Movement. LC 75-11563. 350p. 1975. 12.50 (ISBN 0-396-07022-1). Dodd.
Gould, Jean & Lorena, Hickok. Walter Reuther: Labour's Rugged Individualist. LC 71-39225. 1972. 8.95 (ISBN 0-396-06409-4). Dodd.
Gould, John. The Greenleaf Fires. LC 77-17824. 1978. 8.95 o.p. (ISBN 0-684-15478-1, ScribT). Scribner.
Gould, John & Bittlingmayer, George. Economics of the Davis-Bacon Act: An Analysis of Prevailing Wage Laws. 1980. pap. 4.25 (ISBN 0-8447-3381-4). Am Enterprise.
Gould, John P., jt. auth. see Ferguson, Charles E.
Gould, Julius & Kolb, W. J. UNESCO Dictionary of the Social Sciences. LC 64-20307. 1964. 35.00 (ISBN 0-02-917490-2). Free Pr.
Gould, Julius & Smith, J. H., eds. Teaching of the Social Sciences in Higher Technical Education: An International Survey. (Teaching in the Social Sciences, Vol. 5). 1968. pap. 7.00 (ISBN 92-3-100692-4, U660, UNESCO). Unipub.
Gould, Karen, jt. ed. see Birn, Randi.
Gould, Leonard A. Chemical Process Control: Theory & Applications. (Chemical Engineering Ser). 1969. text ed. 21.95 (ISBN 0-201-02562-0). A-W.
Gould, Lewis L. The Presidency of William McKinley. LC 80-16022. (The American Presidency Ser.). 298p. 1981. 15.00x (ISBN 0-7006-0206-2). Regents Pr KS.
--Progressives & Prohibitionists: Texas Democrats in the Wilson Era. (Illus.). 380p. 1973. 17.95x (ISBN 0-292-76407-3); pap. 8.95x (ISBN 0-292-76428-6). U of Tex Pr.
--Reform & Regulations: American Politics, 1900-1916. LC 77-21058. (Critical Episodes in American Policy Ser.). 1978. pap. text ed. 7.95 (ISBN 0-471-31914-7). Wiley.
Gould, Lois. Necessary Objects. 1972. 6.95 o.p. (ISBN 0-394-46847-3). Random.
--La Presidenta. 1981. price not set (ISBN 0-671-24930-4, Linden). S&S.
--Such Good Friends. 1970. 6.95 o.p. (ISBN 0-394-43855-8). Random.
Gould, Loren, jt. auth. see Gould, Elaine.
Gould, Loyal N. E N D C & the Press. (Stockholm International Peace Research Institute: No. 3). (Orig.). 1969. pap. text ed. 4.50x (ISBN 0-391-00028-4). Humanities.
Gould, Marjorie, jt. auth. see Larson, Carroll B.

Gould, P. R. Spatial Diffusion. LC 79-94260. (CCG Resource Papers Ser.: No. 4). (Illus.). 1969. pap. text ed. 4.00 (ISBN 0-89291-051-8). Assn Am Geographers.

Gould, Phillip L. Static Analysis of Shell Structure. LC 76-47142. (Illus.). 1977. 45.95 (ISBN 0-669-00966-0). Lexington Bks.

Gould, Phillip L. & Abu-Sitta, S. H. Dynamic Response of Structures to Wind & Earthquake Loading. LC 79-23741. 175p. 1980. 39.95x (ISBN 0-470-26905-7). Halsted Pr.

Gould, Richard A. Archaeology of the Point St. George Site, & Tolowa Prehistory. (U. C. Publ. in Anthropology: Vol. 4). 1966. pap. 7.00x (ISBN 0-520-09003-9). U of Cal Pr.

Gould, Richard A. & Schiffer, Michael, eds. The Archaeology of U. S. LC 80-2332. (Studies in Archaeology). 1981. price not set (ISBN 0-12-293580-2). Acad Pr.

Gould, Roberta. Writing Air, Written Water. 96p. (Orig.). 1980. write for info. (ISBN 0-936628-00-6). Waterside.

Gould, Rupert T. The Case for the Sea Serpent. LC 72-75791. 1969. Repr. of 1930 ed. 15.00 (ISBN 0-8103-3833-5). Gale.

Gould, S. E., ed. Pathology of the Heart & Blood Vessels. 3rd ed. (Illus.). 1218p. 1968. 59.75 (ISBN 0-398-00708-X). C C Thomas.

Gould, S. H. Contemporary Chinese Research Mathematics, Vol. 2: A Report on Chinese-English Mathematical Dictionaries. 1964. 1.00 (ISBN 0-8218-0016-7, CED). Am Math.

--A Manual for Translaters of Mathematical Russian. 1980. Repr. of 1973 ed. 4.00 (ISBN 0-8218-0028-0, MTR). Am Math.

--Report on Chinese-English Mathematical Dictionaries. 1969. 1.00 o.p. (ISBN 0-686-67535-5, CED). Am Math.

Gould, S. H. & Obreanu, P. E., eds. Romanian-English Dictionary & Grammar for the Mathematical Sciences. 60p. (Eng & Romanian.). 1979. Repr. of 1969 ed. 6.00 (ISBN 0-8218-0038-8, ROMA). Am Math.

Gould, Saundra, jt. auth. see Berkley.

Gould, Shirley. The Challenge of Achievement: Helping Your Child Succeed. LC 78-53400. 1979. 7.95 o.p. (Hawthorn); pap. 4.95 (ISBN 0-8015-3386-4). Dutton.

--Challenge of Friendship: Helping Your Child Become a Friend. 124p. 1981. 16.95 (ISBN 0-8015-1172-0, Hawthorn). Dutton.

Gould, Shirley G. Teenagers: The Continuing Challenge. 1977. 7.95 (ISBN 0-8015-5800-X, Hawthorn); pap. 3.95 (ISBN 0-8015-5801-8, Hawthorn). Dutton.

Gould Staff Editors. Estates. (Supplemented annually). 1980. looseleaf 7.50 (ISBN 0-87526-140-X). Gould.

Gould, Stephen J. The Panda's Thumb: More Reflections in Natural History. (Illus.). 1980. 12.95 (ISBN 0-393-01380-4). Norton.

Gould, Stephen J., ed. see Department of the Interior, U. S. Geological Survey, Monograph & Osborn, Henry F.

Gould, Tony. In Limbo: The Story of Stanley's Rear Column. (Illus.). 269p. 1980. 27.00 (ISBN 0-241-10125-5, Pub. by Hamish Hamilton England). David & Charles.

Gould, Wilbur A. Food Quality Assurance. (Illus.). 1977. text ed. 29.50 (ISBN 0-87055-219-8); pap. text ed. 18.50 (ISBN 0-87055-294-5). AVI.

--Tomato Production Processing & Quality Evaluation. (Illus.). 1974. text ed. 42.00 (ISBN 0-87055-162-0). AVI.

Goulden, Joseph C. The Benchwarmers: The Private World of the Powerful Federal Judges. 416p. 1976. pap. 1.95 o.p. (ISBN 0-345-24852-X). Ballantine.

Goulden, Shirley. Royal Book of Ballet. LC 64-16319. (Illus.). (gr. 5 up). 1964. 7.95 (ISBN 0-695-90040-4). Follett.

Goulden, Steven L., jt. ed. see Turner, Roland.

Gouldie, Andrew, ed. Geomorphological Techniques. (Illus.). 320p. 1981. text ed. 60.00x (ISBN 0-04-551042-3, 2632-3); pap. text ed. 29.95x (ISBN 0-04-551043-1). Allen Unwin.

Goulding, Daniel J., jt. ed. see Wolfe, W. Dean.

Goulding, Michael. The Fishes & the Forest: Explorations in Amazonian Natural History. LC 80-41201. (Illus.). 250p. 1981. 20.00x (ISBN 0-520-04131-3). U of Cal Pr.

Gouldman, W. Clyde & Hess, Amy M. Virginia Forms. 1978. 60.00 (ISBN 0-87215-205-7). Michie.

Gould-Marks, Beryl. Eating in the Open. 1974. 9.95 (ISBN 0-571-09299-3, Pub. by Faber & Faber). Merrimack Bk Serv.

--The Home Book of Italian Cookery. (Orig.). 1974. pap. 3.95 o.p. (ISBN 0-571-10590-4, Pub. by Faber & Faber). Merrimack Bk Serv.

Gouldner, Alvin W. Coming Crisis of Western Sociology. 1971. pap. text ed. 5.45 o.s.i. (ISBN 0-380-01109-3, 22186). Avon.

--Patterns of Industrial Bureaucracy: A Case Study of Modern Factory Administration. 1954. 12.95 (ISBN 0-02-912730-0); pap. text ed. 6.95 (ISBN 0-02-912740-8). Free Pr.

Gouldner, Helen. Teacher's Pets, Troublemakers, & Nobodies: Black Children in Elementary School. LC 78-53660. (Contributions in Afro-American & African Studies: No. 41). (Illus.). 1978. lib. bdg. 18.50 (ISBN 0-313-20417-9, GOE/). Greenwood.

Goulet, Denis. Looking at Guinea-Bissau: A New Nation's Development Strategy. LC 78-55460. (Occasional Papers: No. 9). 72p. 1978. 2.50 (ISBN 0-686-28695-2). Overseas Dev Council.

--The Uncertain Promise: Value Conflicts in Technology Transfer. LC 77-80314. 324p. 1977. 12.95 (ISBN 0-89021-045-4); pap. 5.95 (ISBN 0-686-28704-5). Overseas Dev Council.

Goulet, Denis & Kallab, Valeriana, eds. Tradition, Values & Development. 322p. 1981. write for info. Overseas Dev Council.

Goulet, Larry, ed. see Jackson, Nancy E., et al.

Goulet, Robert. The Violent Season. 1961. 4.50 o.s.i. (ISBN 0-8076-0143-8). Braziller.

Goulian, Dicran & Courtiss, Eugene H., eds. Symposium of Surgery of the Aging Face. LC 78-12298. (Symposia of the Educational Foundation of the American Society of Plastic & Reconstructive Surgeons Inc. Ser.). 1978. text ed. 46.50 (ISBN 0-8016-1941-6). Mosby.

Goulson, Cary F. A Source Book of Royal Commissions & Other Major Governmental Inquiries in Canadian Education 1787-1978. 248p. 1981. 20.00x (ISBN 0-8020-2408-4). U of Toronto Pr.

Goulston, S. J. & McGovern, V. J. The Basic Facts About Colitis. (Illus.). 144p. 1981. 25.00 (ISBN 0-08-026862-5); pap. 11.20 (ISBN 0-08-026861-7). Pergamon.

Goult, R. J. Applied Linear Algebra. LC 78-40608. 1979. pap. text ed. 16.95x (ISBN 0-470-26864-6). Halsted Pr.

Goult, R. J., et al. Computational Methods in Linear Algebra. LC 75-19054. 201p. 1975. 16.95 (ISBN 0-470-31920-8). Halsted Pr.

Gounaud, Karen J. A Very Nice Joke Book. 1981. 6.95 (ISBN 0-395-30445-8); pap. text ed. 2.95 (ISBN 0-395-30442-3). HM.

Goundry, J. H., jt. auth. see Thiery, P.

Gounod, Charles. Autobiographical Reminiscences: With Family Letters & Notes on Music. LC 68-16235. (Music Ser). 1970. Repr. of 1896 ed. lib. bdg. 25.00 (ISBN 0-306-71081-1). Da Capo.

Goupil, Armand. Jules Verne. new ed. Barberis, Pierre & Jean, Georges, eds. (Textes pour aujourd'hui). (Illus.). 191p. (Orig., Fr.). 1975. pap. 3.95 (ISBN 2-03-038006-7). Larousse.

Gourand, Henri. Computer Display of Curved Surfaces. LC 79-50558. (Outstanding Dissertations in the Computer Sciences). 1980. lib. bdg. 11.00 (ISBN 0-8240-4412-6). Garland Pub.

Gourdie, Tom. Handwriting for Today. 1978. pap. 3.50 (ISBN 0-8008-3812-2, Pentalic). Taplinger.

--Handwriting Made Easy: A Simple Modern Approach. (Illus.). 64p. 1981. pap. 3.95 (ISBN 0-8008-4597-8). Taplinger.

--Improve Your Handwriting. (Illus.). 80p. 1975. 8.95x (ISBN 0-8464-0505-9); pap. 7.50x (ISBN 0-686-60815-1). Beekman Pubs.

Goure, Leon, et al. The Emerging Strategic Environment: Implications for Ballistic Missile Defense. LC 79-53108. 75p. 1979. 6.50. Inst Foreign Policy Anal.

Gourevitch, D. & Stadler, E. M. Premiers Textes Litteraires. 2nd ed. LC 74-83346. 242p. 1975. text ed. 8.95 (ISBN 0-471-00811-7). Wiley.

Gourevitch, Peter A. Paris & the Provinces: The Politics of Local Government Reform in France. 256p. 1981. 18.50x (ISBN 0-520-03971-8). U of Cal Pr.

Gourguechon, Charlene. Journey to the End of the World: A Three-Year Adventure in the New Hebrides. LC 76-46360. (Encore Edition). (Illus.). 1977. 3.95 o.p. (ISBN 0-684-16193-1, ScribT). Scribner.

Gourley, Douglas, ed. see Roberts, Willis J. & Bristow, Allen P.

Gourley, G. Douglas. Effective Municipal Police Organization. (Criminal Justice Ser). 1970. pap. text ed. 3.95x (ISBN 0-02-474610-X, 47461). Macmillan.

Gourley, Jay. The Great Lakes Triangle. 1977. pap. 1.75 o.p. (ISBN 0-449-13827-5, GM). Fawcett.

Gourley, R., jt. auth. see Yeager, D.

Gourman, Jack. The Gourman Report: A Rating of Graduate & Professional Programs in American & International Universities. LC 79-91882. 119p. (Orig.). 1980. pap. 21.50 (ISBN 0-918192-03-X). Natl Ed Stand.

--The Gourman Report: A Rating of Undergraduate Programs in American & International Universities. 3rd ed. LC 79-91881. 124p. 1980. pap. 21.50 (ISBN 0-918192-02-1). Natl Ed Stand.

Gourmont, Remy De see De Gourmont, Remy.

Gourou, Pierre. The Tropical World: Its Social & Economic Conditions & Its Future Status. 4th ed. Beaver, S. H. & Laborde, E. D., trs. from Fr. (Geography for Advanced Study Ser.). (Illus.). 200p. 1974. pap. 11.95 o.p. (ISBN 0-470-31919-4). Halsted Pr.

Gouwenius, Peder. Power to the People: A Pictorial History. (Illus.). 240p. (Orig.). 1981. cancelled (ISBN 0-905762-72-X, Pub. by Zed Pr); pap. 6.95 (ISBN 0-905762-66-5). Lawrence Hill.

Gouy, Louis P. De see De Gouy, Louis P.

Govan, et al. Pathology Illustrated. (Illus.). 1981. text ed. 35.00 (ISBN 0-443-01647-X). Churchill.

Govan, Alastair D., et al. Pathology Illustrated. (Illus.). 880p. (Orig.). 1981. pap. text ed. 35.00 (ISBN 0-443-01647-X). Churchill.

Gove, Samuel K. & Wirt, Frederick M., eds. Political Science & School Politics: The Princes & Pundits. (A Policy Studies Organization Bk). 1976. 16.95 (ISBN 0-669-00739-0). Lexington Bks.

Gove, Samuel K., et al. Illinois Legislature: Structure & Process. LC 76-21238. 208p. 1976. pap. 5.95 (ISBN 0-252-00621-6). U of Ill Pr.

Gove, Walter R., ed. The Labelling of Deviance: Evaluating a Perspective. 2nd ed. LC 80-50397. (Illus.). 428p. 1980. 20.00x (ISBN 0-8039-1470-9); pap. 9.95x (ISBN 0-8039-1471-7). Sage.

Goveia, Elsa V. A Study on the Historiography of the British West Indies to the End of the Nineteenth Century. LC 75-20036. 192p. 1981. pap. 8.95 (ISBN 0-88258-048-5). Howard U Pr.

Gover, Harvey R. Keys to Library Research on the Graduate Level: A Guide to Guides. LC 80-5841. 75p. 1981. pap. text ed. 5.75 (ISBN 0-8191-1370-0). U Pr of Amer.

Gover, Robert. One Hundred Dollar Misunderstanding. LC 62-20506. 256p. 1980. pap. 2.95 (ISBN 0-394-17764-9, B448, BC). Grove.

Govinda, Lama A. The Way of the White Clouds. (Clear Light Ser). (Illus.). 1970. pap. 8.95 (ISBN 0-394-73005-4). Shambhala Pubns.

Govindagraj. Poems of Govindagraj. 2nd ed. Namjoshi, Sarojini & Namjoshi, Suniti, trs. 1976. lib. bdg. 8.00 (ISBN 0-89253-099-5); flexible bdg. 4.80 (ISBN 0-89253-145-2). Ind-US Inc.

Govindarajulu, Zakkula. The Sequential Statistical Analysis of Hypothesis Testing, Point & Interval Estimation, & Decision Theory. LC 80-68287. (The American Sciences Press Ser. in Mathematical & Management Sciences: Vol. 5). 1981. text ed. write for info. (ISBN 0-935950-02-8). Am Sciences Pr.

Govoni, Laura E. & Hayes, Janice E. Drugs & Nursing Implications. 3rd ed. 1978. 25.00 (ISBN 0-8385-1785-4); pap. 14.95 (ISBN 0-8385-1784-6). ACC.

Govoni, Norman, jt. auth. see Kleppner, Otto.

Govoni, Norman A., et al. Marketing Problems: Cases for Analysis. LC 76-19946. (Marketing Ser.). 1977. pap. text ed. 9.50 (ISBN 0-88244-128-0). Grid Pub.

Gow, A. S., tr. see Theocritus.

Gow, Andrew S. & Page, D. L. Greek Anthology: Garland of Philip & Other Contemporary Epigrams, 2 Vols. LC 68-10149. (Eng. & Gr.). 1968. 130.00 set (ISBN 0-521-05874-0). Cambridge U Pr.

--Greek Anthology: Hellenistic Epigrams, 2 Vols. 1965. Set. 130.00 set (ISBN 0-521-05124-X). Cambridge U Pr.

Gow, Andrew S., ed. Bucolici Graeci. (Oxford Classical Texts). 1952. 14.95x (ISBN 0-19-814517-9). Oxford U Pr.

Gow, Bonar A. Madagascar & the Protestant Impact. LC 78-11216. (Dalhousie African Studies). 1979. text ed. 37.50x (ISBN 0-8419-0463-4, Africana). Holmes & Meier.

Gow, J. G. & Hopkins, H. H. Handbook of Urological Endoscopy. (Illus.). 1978. text ed. 35.00x (ISBN 0-443-01419-1). Churchill.

Gow, James. Short History of Greek Mathematics. LC 68-21639. 1968. 11.95 (ISBN 0-8284-0218-3). Chelsea Pub.

Gow, K. M. Yes Virginia, There Is Right & Wrong! Values Education Survival Kit. 248p. 1980. 15.95 (ISBN 0-471-79954-8); pap. 9.95 (ISBN 0-471-79953-X). Wiley.

Gow, Lesley & McPherson, Andrew. Tell Them from Me. 137p. 1980. 30.65 (ISBN 0-08-025738-0); pap. 13.45 (ISBN 0-08-025739-9). Pergamon.

Gowan, Donald E. Bridge Between the Testaments: Reappraisal of Judaism from the Exile to the Birth of Christianity. 2nd ed. LC 76-49996. (Pittsburgh Theological Monographs: No. 14). 1980. text ed. 12.95 (ISBN 0-915138-47-6). Pickwick.

Gowan, J. C. Operations of Increasing Order. 408p. (Orig.). 1980. pap. 5.00x (ISBN 0-686-28154-3). Gowan.

Gowan, John C., et al. The Guidance of Exceptional Children. 2nd ed. LC 70-185135. 1980. pap. 10.95x (ISBN 0-582-28169-5, Pub. by MacKay). Longman.

--Educating the Ablest. 2nd ed. LC 78-61876. 1979. pap. text ed. 12.50 (ISBN 0-87581-235-X). Peacock Pubs.

Gowan, Susan, et al. Moving Toward a New Society. 296p. 1976. pap. 5.00 (ISBN 0-86571-007-4). Movement New Soc.

Gowanlock, Theresa. Two Months in the Camp of Big Bear: The Life & Adventures of Theresa Gowanlock & Theresa Delaney, Repr. Of 1885 Ed. Bd. with Cynthia Ann Parker, the Story of Her Capture at the Massacre of the Inmates of Parker's Fort: Of Her Quarter of a Century Spent Among the Comanches As the Wife of the War Chief Peta Nocona: and of Her Recapture at the Battle of Pease River by Captain L. S. Ross of the Texian Rangers. Repr. of 1886 ed. LC 75-7121. (Indian Captivities Ser.: Vol. 95). 1976. lib. bdg. 44.00 (ISBN 0-8240-1719-6). Garland Pub.

Gowans, Fred R. & Campbell, Eugene E. Fort Supply: Brigham Young's Green River Experiment. 1976. pap. 3.25 o.s.i. (ISBN 0-8425-0248-3). Brigham.

Gowar, Norman. An Invitation to Mathematics. (Illus.). 214p. 1979. text ed. 27.50x (ISBN 0-19-853002-1); pap. 11.50x (ISBN 0-19-853001-3). Oxford U Pr.

Gowar, R. G., ed. Developments in Fire Protection of Offshore Platforms, Vol. 1. (Illus.). 1978. text ed. 42.80 (ISBN 0-85334-792-1, Pub. by Applied Science). Burgess-Intl Ideas.

Gowda, K. Venkatagiri. International Currency Plans & Expansion of World Trade. 1964. 7.75x o.p. (ISBN 0-210-27039-X). Asia.

Gowen, James A. English Review Manual. 2nd ed. 1970. text ed. 10.95 (ISBN 0-07-023881-2, C); pap. text ed. 10.95 o.p. (ISBN 0-07-023880-4); instructor's guide & test answers 5.95 (ISBN 0-07-023883-9). McGraw.

Gower, A. M. Water Quality in Catchment Ecosystems. LC 79-42907. (Institution of Environmental Sciences Ser.). 335p. 1980. 50.00 (ISBN 0-471-27692-8, Pub. by Wiley-Interscience). Wiley.

Gower, D. B. Steroid Hormones. 120p. 1980. 35.00x (ISBN 0-85664-838-8, Pub. by Croom Helm England). State Mutual Bk.

--Steroid Hormones. 1980. pap. 6.95 (ISBN 0-8151-3832-6). Year Bk Med.

Gower, D. M., jt. auth. see Lewis, D. B.

Gower, John. Confessio Amantis. Peck, Russell A., ed. (Medieval Academy Reprints for Teaching Ser.). 570p. 1981. pap. 7.95x (ISBN 0-8020-6438-8). U of Toronto Pr.

Gower, R. Life in New Testament Times. (Ladybird Ser). 1969. lib. bdg. 1.49 (ISBN 0-87508-844-9). Chr Lit.

Gowin, D., jt. auth. see Millman, Jason.

Gowing, Lawrence. Matisse. (World of Art Ser.). (Illus.). 1979. 17.95 (ISBN 0-19-520157-4); pap. 9.95 (ISBN 0-19-520158-2). Oxford U Pr.

--Vermeer. rev. ed. LC 71-114356. (Icon Editions). (Illus.). 240p. 1975. pap. 5.95x o.s.i. (ISBN 0-06-430066-8, IN-66, HarpT). Harrow.

Gowing, Lawrence, ed. see Stokes, Adrian.

Gowing, Margaret & Arnold, Lorna. The Atomic Bomb. (Science in a Social Context Ser.). 1979. pap. text ed. 3.95 (ISBN 0-408-71311-9). Butterworths.

Gowland, David. Monetary Policy & Credit Control: The Uk Experience. 1978. 30.00x (ISBN 0-85664-327-0, Pub. by Croom Helm Ltd England). Biblio Dist.

Gowland, Peter. The Secrets of Photographing Women. Michelman, Herbert, ed. (Illus.). 224p. 1981. 12.95 (ISBN 0-517-54180-7, Michelman Books). Crown.

Gowler, Dan & Legge, Karen, eds. Managerial Stress. LC 74-20107. 236p. 1975. 14.95 (ISBN 0-470-31985-2). Halsted Pr.

Goyan De Laplombania, H. De see De Goyon De La Plombanie, H.

Goyder, D. G., jt. auth. see Neale, A. D.

Goyen, Judith & Philip, Hugh. Innovation in Reading in Britain. LC 73-77398. (Experiments & Innovations in Education Ser., No. 3). 52p. (Orig.). 1973. pap. 2.50 (ISBN 92-3-101112-X, U312, UNESCO). Unipub.

Goyen, William. The House of Breath. LC 74-23987. 1975. 8.95 (ISBN 0-394-49699-X); pap. 4.95 (ISBN 0-394-73053-4). Random.

Goyette, Richert E. Hematologic & Reticuloendothelial Pathology & Pathophysiology Case Studies. 1976. spiral bdg. 12.00 o.p. (ISBN 0-87488-076-9). Med Exam.

--Renal, Genitourinary, & Breast Pathology & Pathophysiology Case Studies. 1976. spiral bdg 12.00 o.p. (ISBN 0-87488-077-7). Med Exam.

Goyette, Richert E., jt. ed. see Foster, F. Gordon.

Goyette, Rickert E. Cardiopulmonary Pathology & Pathophysiology Case Studies. 1976. spiral bdg. 12.00 o.p. (ISBN 0-87488-075-0). Med Exam.

Goytortua, Jesus. Pensativa. Walsh, Donald D., ed. (Orig., Span.). (gr. 10-12). 1962. pap. text ed. 8.95 (ISBN 0-13-655605-1). P-H.

Goyvaerts, D. Phonology of the Nineteen Eighties. (Story-Scientia Linguistics Ser.: No. 4). 1980. text ed. write for info. (ISBN 90-6439-150-5). Humanities.

Goyvaerts, D. L. Present-Day Historical & Comparative Linguistics: An Introductory Guide to Theory & Method Part One General Background-Phonological Change. 231p. 1975. pap. text ed. 21.75x (ISBN 0-391-01588-5). Humanities.

Goyvaerts, Didier & Pullum, Geoffrey, eds. Essays on the Sound Pattern of English. (Illus.). 1975. text ed. 82.25x (ISBN 0-685-95917-1). Humanities.

Gozmany, Laszlo, ed. Septemlingual Dictionary of the Names of European Animals, 2 vols. 2228p. 1979. Set. 200.00x (ISBN 963-05-1381-1). Intl Pubns Serv.

Gozzi, Raymond. Tropes and Figures: A Psychological Study of Henry David Thoreau. LC 80-2506. 1981. 62.50 (ISBN 0-404-19054-5). AMS Pr.

Graaff, John H. Van De see Van De Graaff, John H., et al.

Grabar, Andre. Christian Iconography: A Study of Its Origins. LC 67-31114. (A. W. Mellon Lectures in the Fine Arts Bollingen Ser: No. XXXV: 10). (Illus.). 432p. (Orig.). 1980. 30.00x (ISBN 0-691-09716-X); pap. 8.95 (ISBN 0-691-01830-8). Princeton U Pr.

--Early Christian Art. LC 68-10414. (Arts of Mankind Ser). 30.00 o.s.i. (ISBN 0-8076-0506-9). Braziller.

Grabau, Richard F., tr. see Jaspers, Karl.

Grabb, William C. & Myers, M. Bert, eds. Skin Flaps. LC 74-20219. 440p. 1975. 60.00 (ISBN 0-316-32267-9). Little.

Grabb, William C., jt. ed. see Feller, Irving.

Grabbe see Bentley, Eric.

Grabbe, Lester L. Comparative Philology & the Text of Job: A Study in Methodology. LC 77-23489. (Society of Biblical Literature. Dissertation Ser.). 1977. pap. 7.50 (ISBN 0-89130-139-9, 060134). Scholars Pr Ca.

Graber, Benjamin, jt. auth. see Kline-Graber, Georgia.

Graber, Charles D., jt. auth. see Fudenberg, Hugh H.

Graber, Doris. Crime News & the Public. LC 80-16032. 256p. 1980. 24.95 (ISBN 0-03-055756-9). Praeger.

Graber, Edward A., jt. ed. see Schaefer, George.

Graber, Kay, compiled by. Nebraska Pioneer Cookbook. LC 74-77089. (Illus.). x, 164p. 1974. 8.95 (ISBN 0-8032-0945-2); pap. 3.75 (ISBN 0-8032-5801-1, BB 573, Bison). U of Nebr Pr.

Graber, Kay, ed. see Tibbles, Thomas H.

Graber, R. Pay Your Respects. (gr. 7 up). 1981. pap. 1.95 (ISBN 0-440-97317-1, LE). Dell.

Graber, Richard. Black Cow Summer. LC 80-7767. 224p. (YA) (gr. 7 up). 1980. 8.95 (ISBN 0-06-022118-6, HarpJ); PLB 8.79 (ISBN 0-06-022119-4). Har-Row.

Graber, T. M. Orthodontics: Principles & Practice. 3rd ed. LC 73-186950. (Illus.). 953p. 1972. text ed. 32.00 (ISBN 0-7216-4182-2). Saunders.

Grabianski, Janusz. Grabianski's Birds. LC 68-11332. (Illus.). (gr. k-3). 1968. PLB 3.95 o.p. (ISBN 0-531-01365-0). Watts.

--Grabianski's Cats. LC 67-10577. (Illus.). (gr. k-3). 1967. PLB 4.95 o.p. (ISBN 0-531-01366-9). Watts.

Grabill, James & Fiely, Douglas. Clouds Blowing Away. 1977. pap. 2.00 o.p. (ISBN 0-87711-093-X). Kayak.

Grabiner, Judith. The Origins of Cauchy's Rigorous Calculus. 368p. 1981. text ed. 27.50x (ISBN 0-262-07079-0). MIT Pr.

Grabo, Carl H. Prometheus Unbound: An Interpretation. LC 68-19149. 1968. Repr. of 1935 ed. 7.50 (ISBN 0-87752-045-3). Gordian.

--Technique of the Novel. LC 64-8178. 1964. Repr. of 1928 ed. 6.50 (ISBN 0-87752-046-1). Gordian.

Grabo, Norman S. Edward Taylor. (U. S. Authors Ser.: No. 8). lib. bdg. 12.95 (ISBN 0-8057-0720-4). Twayne.

Graboff, Abner, illus. Old Macdonald Had a Farm. (Illus.). (gr. k-3). 1970. pap. 1.25 (ISBN 0-590-01622-9, Schol Pap); pap. 3.50 bk. & record (ISBN 0-590-09098-4). Schol Bk Serv.

Grabois, Ayreh. The Illustrated Encyclopedia of Medeival Civilization. (Illus.). 752p. 1980. 25.00 (ISBN 0-7064-0856-X). Mayflower Bks.

Grabowski, John G., jt. ed. see Thompson, Travis.

Grabowski, Stanley M. & Loague, Nehume, eds. Adult Education Dissertation Abstracts Nineteen Sixty-Eight to Sixty Nine. 1972. 7.50 o.p. (ISBN 0-88379-001-7). Adult Ed.

Grace, Alicia. The Terrified Heart. 1976. pap. 1.25 o.p. (ISBN 0-685-72357-7, LB383ZK, Leisure Bks). Nordon Pubns.

Grace, Alonzo G; see Bree, Germaine.

Grace, Clive & Wilkinson, Philip. Negotiating the Law: Social Work & Legal Services. (Direct Editions Ser.). 1978. pap. 14.00 (ISBN 0-7100-8851-5). Routledge & Kegan.

Grace, Evelyn. Introduction to Fashion Merchandising. LC 78-1318. (Illus.). 1978. ref. ed. 16.95 (ISBN 0-13-483206-X). P-H.

Grace, George. An Essay on Language. 1981. write for info.; pap. price not set. Hornbeam Pr.

Grace, Gerald. Teachers, Ideology & Control: A Study in Urban Education. 1978. 22.50x (ISBN 0-7100-0014-6); pap. 12.00 (ISBN 0-7100-0015-4). Routledge & Kegan.

Grace, Gerald R. Role Conflict & the Teacher. (International Library of Sociology). 1972. 14.00x (ISBN 0-7100-7353-4). Routledge & Kegan.

Grace, Helen K. & Camilleri, Dorothy. Mental Health Nursing: A Socio-Psychological Approach. 2nd ed. 592p. 1981. text ed. write for info. (ISBN 0-697-05517-5); instrs.' manual avail. (ISBN 0-697-05518-3). Wm C Brown.

Grace, J., et al. Plants & Their Atmospheric Enviroment. (British Ecological Society Symposia Ser.). 428p. 1981. 89.95 (ISBN 0-470-27125-6). Halsted Pr.

Grace, John A. & Young, Alfred. The Algebra of Invariants. LC 65-11860. 1965. 13.95. Chelsea Pub.

Grace, John P. Hearing His Voice. LC 79-54696. (Illus.). 160p. (Orig.). 1979. pap. 3.50 (ISBN 0-87793-187-9). Ave Maria.

Grace, Joyce, jt. auth. see Grace, Mike.

Grace, Mike & Grace, Joyce. A Joyful Meeting: Sexuality in Marriage. (Illus.). 100p. (Orig.). 1980. pap. 3.00 (ISBN 0-936098-14-7). Natl Marriage.

Grace, Patricia. Mutuwhenua: The Moon Sleeps. 155p. (Orig.). 1978. pap. 6.00x (ISBN 0-582-71762-0, Pub. by Longman Paul New Zealand). Three Continents.

Grace, Princess & Robyns, Gwen. My Book of Flowers. LC 78-68361. (Illus.). 224p. 1980. 24.95 (ISBN 0-385-14076-2). Doubleday.

Grace, Robert A. Marine Outfall Systems: Planning, Design, & Construction. LC 77-20980. (P-H Environmental Engineering Ser.). 1978. ref. 38.50 (ISBN 0-13-556951-6). P-H.

Grace, Vilma J. Latin American & Cholesterol Conscious Cooking. (Illus.). 1979. pap. 5.95 (ISBN 0-87491-280-6). Acropolis.

Grace, Virginia R. Amphoras & the Ancient Wine Trade. (Excavations of the Athenian Agora Picture Bks.: No. 6). (Illus.). 1979. pap. 1.50x (ISBN 0-87661-619-8). Am Sch Athens.

Gracenin, Carolyn T. Thoughts, Troubles & Things About Reading from the Cradle Through Grade Three. LC 80-65611. 180p. 1981. perfect bdg. 14.95 (ISBN 0-86548-038-9). Century Twenty One.

Graces, R. W., Jr. Geology of Hood Spring Quadrangle, Brewster County, Texas. (Illus.). 51p. 1954. 2.25 (RI 21). Bur Econ Geology.

Gracey, Douglas R. Tuberculosis. Addington, Whitney W., ed. LC 79-88043. (Discussions in Patient Management Ser.). 1979. pap. 9.50 (ISBN 0-87488-875-1). Med Exam.

Gracey, William. Measurement of Aircraft Speed & Altitude. 300p. 1980. 30.00 (ISBN 0-471-08511-1, Pub. by Wiley-Interscience). Wiley.

Gracia, Mario T. Desert Immigrants: The Mexican of El Paso, 1880-1920. LC 80-36862. (Western Americana Ser.: No. 32). (Illus.). 328p. 1981. text ed. 23.00x (ISBN 0-300-02520-3). Yale U Pr.

Gracia Lorca, Federico see Watson, E. Bradlee & Pressey, Benfield.

Gracie, Gordon, jt. auth. see Mikhail, Edward M.

Gracy, David B., 2nd. Littlefield Lands: Colonization on the Texas Plains, 1912-1920. (M. K. Brown Range Life Ser.: No. 8). (Illus.). 1968. 9.95 (ISBN 0-292-78359-0). U of Tex Pr.

Gracy, David B., 2nd, ed. see Austin, Stephen F.

Grad, Arthur see Schaeffer, A. C. & Spencer, D. C.

Grad, Bonnie L., ed. Milton Avery. (Illus.). 132p. 1981. 95.00 (ISBN 0-931554-19-5). Strathcona.

Grad, Burton, et al. Management Systems. 2nd ed. 504p. 1979. text ed. 21.95 (ISBN 0-03-047541-4). Dryden Pr.

Grad, Frank P. & Marti, Noelia. Physicians' Licensure & Discipline. LC 79-21925. 471p. 1980. lib. bdg. 45.00 (ISBN 0-379-20463-0). Oceana.

Grad, Frank P., et al. Environmental Control: Priorities, Policies & the Law. LC 79-155361. 1971. 17.50x (ISBN 0-231-03563-2). Columbia U Pr.

Grad, Marcia. A Taste for Life: A High Protein Diet Especially Suited for Hypoglycemia, Diabetes, & Weight Reduction. LC 75-22217. (Encore Edition). 160p. 1976. 3.50 o.p. (ISBN 0-684-15678-4, ScribT). Scribner.

Graddy, Duane B. The Band Holding Company Performance Controversy. LC 78-65842. 1979. pap. text ed. 24.50 (ISBN 0-8191-0678-X). U Pr of Amer.

Gradidge, Roderick. Dragon Horses: The Edwardian Ideal. LC 80-17866. 272p. 30.00 (ISBN 0-8076-0988-9). Braziller.

Gradman, Barry. Metamorphosis in Keats. LC 79-3756. 160p. 1980. 13.95x (ISBN 0-8147-2977-0); pap. 5.95x (ISBN 0-8147-2978-9). NYU Pr.

Gradshteyn, I. S. & Ryshik, I. M. Table of Integrals, Series & Products. 1966. 21.50 o.p. (ISBN 0-12-294750-9). Acad Pr.

Gradus, Ben. Directing the Television Commercial. (Communication Arts Books). 228p. 1981. 16.95x (ISBN 0-8038-1575-1, Communications Arts); pap. 9.95x (ISBN 0-8038-1577-8). Hastings.

Grady & Lim. Biological Wastewater Treatment: Theory & Applications. 984p. 1980. 75.00 (ISBN 0-8247-1000-2). Dekker.

Grady, Bo. Resurrection Two. 80p. 1981. 5.50 (ISBN 0-682-49698-7). Exposition.

Grady, James H; see O'Neal, William B.

Grady, John C., Jr., jt. auth. see Felmy, Bradford K.

Grady, Michael. A la New Orleans: Restaurant Recipes. (Orig.). 1980. pap. 6.50 (ISBN 0-937070-02-5). Crabtree.

Grady, Michael J. Evolution & Education. 1977. pap. text ed. 10.75x (ISBN 0-8191-0135-4). U Pr of Amer.

Grady, Mike, et al. Precalculus. 464p. 1979. text ed. 18.95x (ISBN 0-534-00733-3); solns. manual for students 5.95x (ISBN 0-534-00831-3). Wadsworth Pub.

Grae, Ida. Nature's Colors: Dyes from Plants. LC 73-11836. (Illus.). 1974. 14.95 o.s.i. (ISBN 0-02-544950-8). Macmillan.

--Nature's Colors: Dyes from Plants. (Illus.). 1979. pap. 8.95 (ISBN 0-02-012390-6, Collier). Macmillan.

Graebner, Norman A., compiled by. American Diplomatic History Before 1900. LC 77-85991. (Goldentree Bibliographies in American History). 1978. text ed. 16.95x (ISBN 0-88295-573-X); pap. text ed. 12.95x (ISBN 0-88295-543-8). AHM Pub.

Graebner, William. Coal-Mining Safety in the Progressive Period: The Political Economy of Reform. LC 75-38215. 256p. 1976. 18.00x (ISBN 0-8131-1339-3). U Pr of Ky.

Graedon, Joe. The People's Pharmacy - Two. 1980. pap. 5.95 (ISBN 0-380-76059-2, 76059). Avon.

Graef, Hilda C. Mary: A History of Doctrine & Devotion, 2 Vols. (Illus.). 1963-66. Vol. 1. 5.95 o.p. (ISBN 0-8362-0118-3, Pub. by Sheed); Vol. 2. 4.00 o.p. (ISBN 0-8362-0072-1, Pub. by Sheed). Guild Bks.

Graef, John W., ed. see Children's Hospital Medical Center, Boston.

Graeff, H. & Kuhn, W. Coagulation Disorders in Obstetrics: Pathobiochemistry-Pathophysiology-Diagnosis-Treatment. Davis, A., tr. from Ger. LC 79-48020. (Major Problems in Obstetrics & Gynecology Ser.: No. 13). 1980. write for info. (ISBN 0-7216-4192-X). Saunders.

Graeme, Lynn, jt. auth. see Powell, Marcia.

Graendorf, Werner, ed. Introduction to Biblical Christian Education. 1981. text ed. 11.95 (ISBN 0-8024-4128-9). Moody.

Graendorf, Werner & Mattson, Lloyd, eds. An Introduction to Christian Camping. 1979. 6.95 (ISBN 0-8024-4131-9). Moody.

Graeser, Andreas. Zenon von Kition: Positionen und Probleme. 1975. 51.00x (ISBN 3-11-004673-3). De Gruyter.

Graeser, Kathi, ed. Harris-Indiana Industrial Directory 1981. (Illus., Annual). 1981. 36.40 (ISBN 0-916512-26-6). Harris Pub.

Graetz, Heinrich. The Structure of Jewish History & Other Essays. 15.00x (ISBN 0-87068-466-3); pap. 8.95x (ISBN 0-685-56206-9). Ktav.

Graetz, Rick. Beautiful Montana. Shangle, Robert D., ed. LC 78-102354. (Illus.). 1977. 14.95 (ISBN 0-915796-25-2); pap. 7.95 (ISBN 0-915796-24-4). Beautiful Am.

--Beautiful Montana, Vol. II. LC 78-102354. 72p. 1979. text ed. 14.95 (ISBN 0-89802-006-9); pap. 7.95 (ISBN 0-89802-005-0). Beautiful Am.

Graf, Alfred B. Exotica Series Three: Pictorial Cyclopedia of Exotic Plants. 10th, rev. ed. LC 72-90669. (Illus.). 1980. 78.00 (ISBN 0-911266-15-1). Roehrs.

--Tropica: Color Cyclopedia of Exotic Plants. (Illus.). 1978. 115.00x (ISBN 0-684-15568-0, ScribT). Scribner.

--Tropica: Color Encyclopedia of Exotic Plants. 2nd ed. LC 77-82461. (Illus.). 1981. 115.00x (ISBN 0-911266-16-X). Roehrs.

Graf, Herbert. Opera for the People. LC 68-23811. (Music Reprint Ser.). 1973. Repr. of 1951 ed. lib. bdg. 27.00 (ISBN 0-306-70984-8). Da Capo.

Graf, LeRoy P. & Haskins, Ralph W., eds. Papers of Andrew Johnson, 5 vols. Incl. Vol. 1. 1822-1851. (Illus.). 744p. 1967. 20.00x (ISBN 0-87049-079-6); Vol. 2. 1852-1857. (Illus.). 608p. 1970. 20.00x (ISBN 0-87049-098-2); Vol. 3. 1858-1860. (Illus.). 800p. 1972. 20.00x (ISBN 0-87049-141-5); Vol. 4. 1860-1861. 1976. 20.00x (ISBN 0-87049-183-0); Vol. 5. 1861-1862. 1979. text ed. 20.00x (ISBN 0-87049-273-X). LC 67-25733. U of Tenn Pr.

Graf, R. & Whalen, G. Home Wiring. 1981. 14.95 (ISBN 0-13-392977-9). P-H.

Grafe, Louis. Get Rich in Spite of Yourself. pap. 1.50 (ISBN 0-912576-10-3). R Collier.

Graff, Gerald. Literature Against Itself: Literary Ideas in Modern Society. LC 78-9879. x, 250p. 1981. pap. 5.95 (ISBN 0-226-30598-8). U of Chicago Pr.

--Poetic Statement & Critical Dogma. LC 80-14318. 208p. 1980. lib. bdg. 7.00x (ISBN 0-226-30601-1). U of Chicago Pr.

Graff, Harvey J. & Monaco, Paul, eds. Quantification & Psychology: Toward a 'new' History. LC 79-3854. 526p. 1980. pap. text ed. 15.25 (ISBN 0-8191-0942-8). U Pr of Amer.

Graff, Henry F., jt. auth. see Barzun, Jacques.

Graff, Henry F., jt. auth. see Morris, Richard B.

Graff, Polly A., jt. auth. see Graff, Stewart.

Graff, Richard A. Elements of Non-Linear Functional Analysis. LC 78-14727. (Memoirs: No. 206). 1980. Repr. of 1978 ed. 8.40 (ISBN 0-8218-2206-3). Am Math.

Graff, Stewart & Graff, Polly A. Helen Keller. (Illus.). (gr. 2-7). 1966. pap. 1.25 (ISBN 0-440-43566-8, YB). Dell.

Graffigny, Francoise. Letters Written by a Peruvian Princess, 1748. Shugrue, Michael F., ed. LC 74-16070. (Novel in England, 1700-1775 Ser.). 1974. lib. bdg. 50.00 (ISBN 0-8240-1121-X). Garland Pub.

Graffis, Herb. The PGA: The Official History of the Professional Golfers' Association of America. LC 75-9967. 1975. 16.95 o.s.i. (ISBN 0-690-00919-4, TYC-T). T Y Crowell.

Graffman, Gary. I Really Should Be Practicing. LC 80-1119. 288p. 1980. 14.95 (ISBN 0-385-15559-X). Doubleday.

Grafstein, Paul & Schwarz, Otto B. Pictorial Handbook of Technical Devices. LC 77-15620. (Illus.). 1978. pap. 6.95 o.p. (ISBN 0-668-04494-2, 4494). Arco.

Grafton, Carol. Historic Alphabets & Initials. (Dover Pictorial Archive Ser.). (Illus.). 1977. pap. 5.00 (ISBN 0-486-23480-0). Dover.

Grafton, Carol B. Bizarre & Ornamental Alphabets. (Illus.). 128p. (Orig.). 1981. pap. price not set (ISBN 0-486-24105-X). Dover.

--Traditional Patchwork Patterns: Full-Size Cut-Outs & Instructions for 12 Quilts. (Illus.). 64p. (Orig.). 1974. pap. 3.00 (ISBN 0-486-23015-5). Dover.

--Treasury of Art Nouveau Design & Ornament. (Pictorial Archive Ser.). (Illus.). 144p. (Orig.). 1980. pap. 4.50 (ISBN 0-486-24001-0). Dover.

Grafton, Carol B., jt. auth. see Verneuil, M. P.

Grafton, John, jt. auth. see Sugar, Bert.

Gragg, Rod. Bobby Bagley POW. 1978. pap. 2.95 (ISBN 0-89728-022-9, 678434). Omega Pubns OR.

Graham & Lipscomb. Dr. George Wasington Carver: Scientist. (gr. 7-9). pap. 1.25 o.p. (ISBN 0-686-68475-3, 29796). Archway.

Graham, A. Richard. An Introduction to Engineering Measurements. (Illus.). 224p. 1975. ref. ed 19.95 (ISBN 0-13-482406-7). P-H.

Graham, Ada & Graham, Frank. Alligators. LC 79-50671. (Audubon Readers Ser.: No. 5). (Illus.). (gr. 5 up). 1979. 7.95 (ISBN 0-440-00390-3); PLB 7.45 (ISBN 0-440-00391-1). Delacorte.

--Bears in the Wild. LC 80-68732. (Audubon Reader: No. 6). (Illus.). 128p. (gr. 4-7). 1981. 8.95 (ISBN 0-440-00532-9); PLB 8.44 (ISBN 0-440-00538-8). Delacorte.

--Birds of the Northern Seas. (Illus.). 96p. 1981. 8.95a (ISBN 0-385-12565-8); PLB (ISBN 0-385-12566-6). Doubleday.

--Careers in Conservation: Profiles of People Working for the Environment. LC 79-20793. (Illus.). (gr. 5 up). 1980. 9.95 (ISBN 0-684-16472-8). Scribner.

Graham, Ada & Graham, Frank, Jr. The Careless Animal. LC 73-14222. 112p. (gr. 3-5). 1975. PLB 4.95 (ISBN 0-385-01828-2). Doubleday.

Graham, Aelred. Contemplative Christianity. 1975. 6.95 (ISBN 0-8164-0269-8). Crossroad NY.

Graham, Alexander. Matrix Theory & Applications for Engineers & Mathematicians. LC 79-40988. (Mathematics & Its Applications Ser.). 295p. 1979. 49.95x (ISBN 0-470-26713-5). Halsted Pr.

--Matrix Theory & Applications for Engineers & Mathematicians. LC 79-40988. (Mathematics & Its Applications). 295p. 1980. pap. 24.95 (ISBN 0-470-27072-1). Halsted Pr.

Graham, Alistair. British Prosobranch & Other Operculate Gastropod Molluscs. (Synopses of the British Fauna: No. 2). 1972. 7.50 (ISBN 0-12-294850-5). Acad Pr.
Graham, Barbara see Foster, Rick.
Graham, Ben S., Jr., jt. auth. see Titus, Parvin S.
Graham, Billy. Los Angeles: Agentes Secretos de Dios. Rojas, Juan, tr. from Eng. LC 76-20259. 168p. (Orig., Span.). 1976. pap. 2.75 (ISBN 0-89922-069-X). Edit Caribe.
--Angels. 1976. pap. 2.50 (ISBN 0-671-43281-8). PB.
--Billy Graham Talks to Teenagers. (Orig.). (YA) pap. 1.25 (ISBN 0-89129-153-9). Jove Pubns.
--El Espiritu Santo. Sipowicz, A. Edwin, tr. from Eng. Orig. Title: The Holy Spirit. 252p. (Span.). 1980. pap. 3.95 (ISBN 0-311-09096-6). Casa Bautista.
--Finding Freedom. pap. 1.25 o.p. (ISBN 0-310-25062-5). Zondervan.
--Holy Spirit. 336p. 1980. pap. 2.75 (ISBN 0-446-95038-6). Warner Bks.
--Nacer a Una Nueva Vida. Ward, Rhode, tr. from Eng. LC 78-52622. 191p. (Orig., Span.). 1978. pap. 3.50 (ISBN 0-89922-110-6). Edit Caribe.
--Paz Con Dios. Muntz, Carrie, tr. from Eng. Orig. Title: Peace with God. 272p. 1980. pap. 2.95 (ISBN 0-311-43037-6). Casa Bautista.
--El Secreto de la Felicidad. Orig. Title: The Secret of Happiness. 192p. (Span.). Date not set. pap. price not set (ISBN 0-311-04352-6). Casa Bautista.
--Till Armageddon. 1981. 8.95 (ISBN 0-8499-0195-2). Word Bks.
Graham, Brenda K. The Pattersons & the Goat Men. (gr. 5-9). 1981. 5.95 (ISBN 0-8054-4803-9). Broadman.
--The Pattersons & the Mysterious Airplane. LC 79-6022. (gr. 5-9). 1980. 5.95 (ISBN 0-8054-4802-0). Broadman.
Graham, Carolyn. Jazz Chants. 1978. pap. text ed. 3.95 (ISBN 0-19-502407-9); cassette 6.95x (ISBN 0-19-502410-9); text & cassette 9.00x (ISBN 0-19-502429-X). Oxford U Pr.
Graham, Charles E., ed. Reproductive Biology of the Great Apes: Comparative & Biomedical Perspectives. 1981. write for info. (ISBN 0-12-295020-8). Acad Pr.
Graham, Clarence H., et al, eds. Vision & Visual Perception. LC 65-12711. 1965. 54.95 (ISBN 0-471-32170-2). Wiley.
Graham, Colin, jt. auth. see Lane, Billy.
Graham, D., jt. auth. see Thomas, D.
Graham, Daniel & Thomson, John. Grenz Rays: An Illustrated Guide to the Theory & Practical Applications of Soft X-Rays. LC 79-42745. (Illus.). 164p. 1980. 24.00 (ISBN 0-08-025525-6). Pergamon.
Graham, David. Down to a Sunless Sea. 1981. 13.95 (ISBN 0-671-41217-5). S&S.
Graham, David W., ed. The Bible's Teachings for the Happy Life. (Illus.). 1980. deluxe ed. 37.75 (ISBN 0-930582-57-8). Gloucester Art.
Graham, Don, jt. ed. see Pilkington, William T.
Graham, Dougal. Collected Writings of Dougal Graham, Skellat Bellman of Glasgow, 2 Vols. LC 69-16478. 1968. Repr. of 1883 ed. Set. 18.00 (ISBN 0-8103-3535-2). Gale.
Graham, Douglas. Moral Learning & Development. 1974. pap. 17.95 (ISBN 0-7134-2842-2, Pub. by Batsford England). David & Charles.
Graham, Douglas J., tr. see Pogony, G. E.
Graham, Elizabeth. Come Next Spring. (Harlequin Romances Ser.). (Orig.). 1980. pap. 1.25 o.p. (ISBN 0-373-02326-X, Pub. by Harlequin). PB.
--Jacintha Point. (Harlequin Romances Ser.). 192p. 1980. pap. 1.25 (ISBN 0-373-02374-X, Pub. by Harlequin). PB.
--Thief of Copper Canyon. (Harlequin Presents Ser.). 192p. (Orig.). 1981. pap. 1.50 (ISBN 0-373-10403-0, Pub. by Harlequin). PB.
Graham, Frank. Power Plant Engineers Guide. 2nd ed. LC 74-98686. (Illus.). 816p. 1974. 15.95 (ISBN 0-672-23329-0). Audel.
Graham, Frank & Schank, Kenneth. Questions & Answers for Engineers & Firemen's Examinations. 3rd ed. 1979. 10.95 (ISBN 0-672-23327-4). Audel.
Graham, Frank, jt. auth. see Graham, Ada.
Graham, Frank, Jr. Great Hitters of the Major Leagues. (Major League Baseball Library). (Illus.). (gr. 5-9). 1969. 2.50 o.p. (ISBN 0-394-80180-6, BYR). Random.
--Great No Hit Games of the Major Leagues. (Major League Baseball Library: No. 9). (Illus.). (gr. 1-6). 1968. 2.50 (ISBN 0-394-80189-X, BYR); PLB 3.69 (ISBN 0-394-90189-4). Random.
--Great Pennant Races of the Major Leagues. (Major League Baseball Library). (Illus.). 1967. 2.50 o.p. (ISBN 0-394-80187-3, BYR). Random.
--Potomac: The Nation's River. (Illus.). 1976. 15.95 o.p. (ISBN 0-397-01139-3). Lippincott.
--Since Silent Spring. 1977. pap. 1.75 o.p. (ISBN 0-449-23141-0, Crest). Fawcett.
Graham, Frank, Jr., jt. auth. see Graham, Ada.
Graham, George, et al. Children Moving: A Reflective Approach to Teaching Physical Education. LC 79-91832. (Illus.). 497p. 1980. text ed. 15.95 (ISBN 0-87484-467-3). Mayfield Pub.
Graham, George P., jt. auth. see Easton, Richard J.
Graham, Gerald H. Business: The Process of Enterprise. LC 76-45808. 580p. 1977. text ed. 16.95 (ISBN 0-574-19300-6, 13-2300); instr's guide avail. (ISBN 0-574-19301-4, 13-2301); study guide 6.50 (ISBN 0-574-19302-2, 13-2302); lecture resource & trans. masters 7.95 (ISBN 0-685-93533-7, 13-2304); filmstrip-tape 35.00 (ISBN 0-685-93534-5, 13-2306); test bank 5.75 (ISBN 0-574-19311-1, 13-2305). SRA.
Graham, Gerald S. The China Station: War & Diplomacy 1830-1860. (Illus.). 1978. 54.00x (ISBN 0-19-822472-9). Oxford U Pr.
Graham, Gordon. Automated Inventory Management for the Distributor. LC 80-17655. 350p. 1980. 19.95 (ISBN 0-8436-0794-7). CBI Pub.
Graham, Gregory S. Metalworking: An Introduction. 1980. text ed. write for info. (ISBN 0-534-00843-7, Breton Pubs). Wadsworth Pub.
Graham, H. D. Food Colloids. (Illus.). 1977. lib. bdg. 39.50 (ISBN 0-87055-201-5). AVI.
Graham, Horace D. The Safety of Foods. 2nd ed. (Illus.). 1980. lib. bdg. 49.00 (ISBN 0-87055-337-2). AVI.
Graham, Hugh, jt. auth. see Carlson, Jack.
Graham, Hugh D., jt. auth. see Bartley, Numan V.
Graham, Hugh D. & Gurr, Ted R., eds. Violence in America: Historical & Comparative Perspectives. rev., college ed. LC 78-21934. (Illus.). 1979. 20.00x (ISBN 0-8039-0963-2); pap. 9.95x (ISBN 0-8039-0964-0). Sage.
Graham, Hugh F., ed. see Skrynnikov, R. G.
Graham, Ian. The Art of Maya Hieroglyphic Writing. 1971. pap. 2.50 (ISBN 0-87365-998-8). Peabody Harvard.
--Corpus of Maya Hieroglyphic Inscriptions: Xultun, la Honradex, Vol. 5, No. 2. 1981. pap. cancelled o.s.i. (ISBN 0-686-64360-7). Peabody Harvard.
Graham, J. A., ed. Use of Computers in Managing Material Property Data. (MPC: No. 14). 64p. 1980. 18.00 (G00192). ASME.
Graham, James W. Palaces of Crete. (Illus.). 1962. 25.00 o.p. (ISBN 0-691-03524-5); pap. 6.95 (ISBN 0-691-00206-1, 154). Princeton U Pr.
Graham, Jerry & Johnson, M. L. Where Flies Don't Land. (Illus.). 1977. pap. 3.95 o.p. (ISBN 0-88270-222-X). Logos.
Graham, Jo-Ann, jt. auth. see Schmidt, Wallace V.
Graham, John. Fast Reactor Safety. (Nuclear Science & Technology Ser.: Vol. 8). 1971. 48.00 (ISBN 0-12-294950-1). Acad Pr.
--The Shetland Dictionary. 144p. 1980. 13.95x (ISBN 0-906191-33-5, Pub. by Thule Pr England). Intl Schol Bk Serv.
Graham, John A. The Hieroglyphic Inscriptions & Monumental Art of Alter De Sacrificios. LC 70-186984. (Peabody Museum Papers: Vol. 64, No. 2). 1972. pap. text ed. 15.00 (ISBN 0-87365-184-7). Peabody Harvard.
Graham, John R. Constitutional History of the Military Draft. 5.95 (ISBN 0-87018-065-7); pap. 2.95 (ISBN 0-87018-070-3). Ross.
Graham, Jorie. Hybrids of Plants & Ghosts. LC 79-3210. (Princeton Series of Contemporary Poets). 1980. 8.75x (ISBN 0-691-06421-0); pap. 3.95 (ISBN 0-691-01335-7). Princeton U Pr.
Graham, Jory. In the Company of Others. LC 78-22252. 288p. 1981. 10.95 (ISBN 0-15-144642-3). HarBraceJ.
Graham, Katherine A., jt. auth. see Feldman, Lionel D.
Graham, Katherine A., et al. The Administration of Mineral Exploration in the Yukon & Northwest Territories. 60p. (Orig.). 1979. pap. text ed. 3.00x (ISBN 0-686-63144-7, Pub. by Ctr Resource Stud Canada). Renouf.
Graham, Keith. J. L. Austin: A Critique of Ordinary Language Philosophy. 1977. text ed. 22.25x (ISBN 0-391-00747-5). Humanities.
Graham, Kennard C. Industrial & Commercial Wiring. 2nd ed. (Illus.). 1963. 12.50 o.p. (ISBN 0-8269-1500-0). Am Technical.
Graham, Kenneth. The Wind in the Willows. (gr. k-6). 1981. pap. 1.50 (ISBN 0-440-49555-5, YB). Dell.
Graham, Kennon. Bugs Bunny-Kingdom of Dimly. (Illus.). 24p. (ps-k). 1.95 (ISBN 0-307-10827-9, Golden Pr). Western Pub.
--Lassie & the Secret Friend. (Illus.). 32p. (ps-1). 1972. PLB 7.62 (ISBN 0-307-60059-9, Golden Pr). Western Pub.
--Lassie's Big Clean-up Day. (Young Reader Ser.). 24p. (ps-3). 1980. PLB 5.00 (ISBN 0-307-60311-3, Golden Pr). Western Pub.
--My Little Book About Flying. (Tell-a-Tale Readers). (Illus.). (gr. k-3). 1979. PLB 4.77 (ISBN 0-307-68646-9, Whitman). Western Pub.
--My Little Book of Cars & Trucks. (Tell-a-Tale Readers). (Illus.). (gr. k-3). 1973. PLB 4.77 (ISBN 0-307-68473-3, Whitman). Western Pub.
--Smokey Bear Saves the Forest. (Tell-a-Tale Readers). (Illus.). (gr. k-3). 1971. PLB 4.77 (ISBN 0-307-68463-6, Whitman). Western Pub.
Graham, L. R. Soviet Academy of Sciences & the Communist Party, 1927-1932. (Studies of the Russian Institute). 1968. 15.00 (ISBN 0-691-08038-0). Princeton U Pr.
Graham, Lawrence S. Civil Service Reform in Brazil: Principles Versus Practice. (Latin American Monographs: No. 13). 1968. 9.95x (ISBN 0-292-78356-6). U of Tex Pr.
--Romania: A Profile. (Nations of Contemporary Eastern Europe Ser.). 128p. 1981. lib. bdg. 16.50x (ISBN 0-89158-925-2). Westview.
Graham, Lawrence S., jt. auth. see Thurber, Clarence E.
Graham, Lillian S., jt. auth. see Wackerbarth, Marjorie.
Graham, Lloyd A. Surprise Attack in Mathematical Problems. (Illus., Orig.). 1968. pap. 3.00 (ISBN 0-486-21846-5). Dover.
Graham, Lorenz. Every Man Heart Lay Down. LC 75-109899. (Illus.). (gr. 2-5). 1970. 8.95 (ISBN 0-690-27134-4, TYC-J). T Y Crowell.
--God Wash the World & Start Again. LC 75-109900. (Illus.). (gr. 2-5). 1971. 6.95 o.p. (ISBN 0-690-33295-5, TYC-J); PLB 6.89 o.p. (ISBN 0-690-33296-3). T Y Crowell.
--Return to South Town. LC 75-33712. (gr. 7 up). 1976. 8.95 (ISBN 0-690-01081-8, TYC-J). T Y Crowell.
--Whose Town? LC 69-13639. (gr. 5 up). 1969. 8.95 (ISBN 0-690-88783-3, TYC-J). T Y Crowell.
Graham, M. A., jt. auth. see Burghes, D. N.
Graham, Malcolm. Modern Elementary Mathematics. 3rd ed. 470p. 1979. text ed. 15.95 (ISBN 0-15-561041-4, HC); instructor's manual avail. (ISBN 0-15-561042-2). HarBraceJ.
Graham, Margaret A. Katie. 1981. pap. 2.95 (ISBN 0-8423-2028-8). Tyndale.
Graham, Munir & De La Torre Bueno, Laura, eds. Index to the Sayings of Hazrat Inayat Khan. (The Collected Works of Hazrat Inayat Khan). 144p. (Orig.). 1981. pap. 3.95 (ISBN 0-930872-23-1, 1009P). Sufi Order Pubns.
Graham, Neil. Introduction to PASCAL. 272p. 1980. pap. text ed. 10.95 (ISBN 0-8299-0334-8). West Pub.
Graham, Neill. Introduction to Computer Science: A Structured Approach. (Illus.). 1979. text ed. 18.50 (ISBN 0-8299-0187-6); instrs.' manual avail. (ISBN 0-8299-0482-4). West Pub.
--The Mind Tool: Computers & Their Impact on Society. 2nd ed. (Illus.). 1980. pap. 13.50 (ISBN 0-8299-0272-4); instrs.' manual avail. (ISBN 0-8299-0483-2); study guide avail. (ISBN 0-8299-0350-X). West Pub.
Graham, Norman A. & Jordan, Robert S., eds. The Changing Role & Concepts of the International Civil Service. (Pergamon Policy Studies). 1980. 27.00 (ISBN 0-08-024643-5). Pergamon.
Graham, Otis, jt. auth. see Borden, Morton.
Graham, Otis L., jt. auth. see Borden, Morton.
Graham, Otis L., Jr. Encore for Reform: The Old Progressives & the New Deal. (Orig.). 1967. pap. 4.95 (ISBN 0-19-500745-X, GB). Oxford U Pr.
--Toward a Planned Society: From Roosevelt to Nixon. LC 75-10189. 1977. pap. 4.95 (ISBN 0-19-502181-9, 486, GB). Oxford U Pr.
Graham, Otis L., Jr. & Litwack, Leon. The Great Campaigns-- Reform & War in America Nineteen Hundred to Nineteen Twenty-Eight. LC 79-24302. 400p. 1980. pap. 9.95 (ISBN 0-89874-022-3). Krieger.
Graham, Otis L., Jr., ed. From Roosevelt to Roosevelt, 1901-1941. LC 70-151116. (Literature of History Ser). (Orig.). 1971. 18.95x (ISBN 0-89197-181-5); pap. text ed. 6.95x (ISBN 0-89197-182-3). Irvington.
Graham, Patricia A. Progressive Education: From Arcady to Academe: A History of the Progressive Education Association: 1919-1955. LC 67-26480. (Teachers College Studies in Education Ser.). 1967. text ed. 10.25x (ISBN 0-8077-1452-6). Tchrs Coll.
Graham, R. Britain & the Onset of Modernization in Brazil, 1850-1914. LC 68-21393. (Latin American Studies: No. 4). (Illus.). 1972. 42.50 (ISBN 0-521-07078-3); pap. 10.95x (ISBN 0-521-09681-2). Cambridge U Pr.
Graham, R. Cunninghame. Reincarnation: The Best Short Stories of Cunninghame Graham. LC 79-28208. 160p. 1980. 8.95 (ISBN 0-89919-004-9). Ticknor & Fields.
Graham, R. M., jt. ed. see Bayer, R.
Graham, R. W. Secondary Batteries-Recent Advances. LC 77-94228. (Chemical Technology Review 106; Energy Technology Review 26). (Illus.). 1978. 42.00 o.p. (ISBN 0-8155-0696-1). Noyes.
Graham, Richard. The Good Dog's Cook Book. LC 79-92259. (Illus., Orig.). 1980. pap. 4.95 (ISBN 0-932966-06-3). Permanent Pr.
Graham, Richard, jt. auth. see Beer, Alice S.
Graham, Robert. Iran: The Illusion of Power. LC 78-65258. (Illus.). 272p. 1980. 17.95x (ISBN 0-312-43587-8); pap. 6.95 (ISBN 0-312-43589-4). St Martin.
Graham, Robert W., ed. Rechargable Batteries: Advances Since 1977. LC 80-13152. (Energy Technology Review Ser. No. 55; Chemical Technology Review Ser. No.160). 452p. 1980. 54.00 (ISBN 0-8155-0802-6). Noyes.
Graham, Robin L. & Gill, Derek. The Boy Who Sailed Around the World Alone. (Illus.). 144p. (gr. 6 up). 1973. 6.95 o.p. (ISBN 0-307-16510-8, Golden Pr); PLB 12.23 o.p. (ISBN 0-307-66510-0). Western Pub.
Graham, Ronald, et al. Ramsey Theory. LC 80-14110. (Wiley Interscience Ser. in Discrete Mathematics). 240p. 1980. 21.95 (ISBN 0-471-05997-8, Pub. by Wiley Interscience). Wiley.
Graham, Sandra, ed. Glip, Glop, Gloop: The Common School Children's Cookbook. Hawley, Isabel L. LC 74-80786. (Illus.). 128p. (ps-6). Date not set. cancelled (ISBN 0-913636-05-3). Educ Res MA. Postponed.
Graham, Sheila. Confessions of a Hollywood Columnist. 1969. 5.95 o.p. (ISBN 0-688-05017-4). Morrow.
Graham, Sheila Y. Sentencecraft. (Illus.). 128p. 1976. pap. text ed. 6.95 (ISBN 0-13-806224-2). P-H.
--Writingcraft: The Paragraphs & the Essays. (Illus.). 192p. 1976. pap. text ed. 7.50x (ISBN 0-13-970152-4). P-H.
Graham, Shirley. Booker T. Washington. LC 55-9855. (Biography Ser.). (gr. 7 up). 1955. PLB 5.29 o.p. (ISBN 0-671-32562-0). Messner.
Graham, Susan. Quick Simple Meals. (Leisure Plan Bks). 1971. pap. 2.95 (ISBN 0-600-01354-5). Transatlantic.
Graham, Terry. Let Loose on Mother Goose. (Illus.). 96p. (ps-k). 1981. pap. text ed. 6.95 (ISBN 0-86530-030-5, IP 305). Incentive Pubns.
Graham, Thomas. Impact of Tokyo Round Agreements on U. S. Export Competitiveness, Vol. II. LC 80-67709. (Significant Issues Ser.: No. 10). 30p. 1980. 5.95 (ISBN 0-89206-024-7). CSI Studies.
Graham, Thomas R., jt. ed. see Rubin, Seymour J.
Graham, Victor E. & Johnson, W. McAllister. Estienne Jodelle, Le Recueil de Inscriptions, 1558: A Literary & Iconographical Exegesis. LC 79-163818. (Illus.). 1972. 20.00x (ISBN 0-8020-1752-5). U of Toronto Pr.
Graham, Victor E., ed. Representative French Poetry. rev. ed. LC 67-55719. 1965. 3.50x o.p. (ISBN 0-8020-1338-4). U of Toronto Pr.
Graham, W. S. Implements in Their Places. 1978. pap. 4.95 o.p. (ISBN 0-571-10955-1, Pub. by Faber & Faber). Merrimack Bk Serv.
Graham, Walter W. & Rowan, William H. Plane Analytic Geometry. (Quality Paperback: No. 47). (Orig.). 1968. pap. 3.50 (ISBN 0-8226-0047-1). Littlefield.
Graham, William H. What Is a Woman. 2nd ed. (Illus.). 1967. 12.50 (ISBN 0-910550-16-6). Elysium.
Graham, Winston. The Black Moon. (Poldark Ser.: No.5). 1977. pap. 2.25 (ISBN 0-345-27735-X). Ballantine.
--Jeremy Poldark, No. 3. (Poldark Ser). 1977. pap. 2.25 (ISBN 0-345-27733-3). Ballantine.
Graham-Cameron, Mike. Home Sweet Home. (Illus.). 32p. 1980. pap. 1.60 ea. (Pub. by Dinosaur Pubns); pap. in 5 pk. avail. (ISBN 0-85122-174-2). Merrimack Bk Serv.
Grahame, Kenneth. Dream Days. (Illus.). 1975. pap. 4.95 o.p. (ISBN 0-380-00288-4, 23994). Avon.
--Dream Days. LC 75-32201. (Classics of Children's Literature, 1621-1932: Vol. 62). (Illus.). 1976. Repr. of 1902 ed. PLB 38.00 (ISBN 0-8240-2311-0). Garland Pub.
--The Golden Age. LC 75-32198. (Classics of Children's Literature, 1621-1932: Vol. 59). (Illus.). 1976. Repr. of 1900 ed. PLB 38.00 (ISBN 0-8240-2308-0). Garland Pub.
--The Open Road. LC 79-22614. (Illus.). (gr. 1 up). 1980. 9.95 (ISBN 0-684-16471-X). Scribner.
--Reluctant Dragon. (Illus.). 58p. (gr. 3-6). 1953. 5.95 (ISBN 0-8234-0093-X). Holiday.
--Wayfarers All. (Illus.). 32p. (gr. 1 up). 1981. 10.95 (ISBN 0-684-16876-6). Scribner.
--The Wind in the Willows. LC 80-197. (Illus.). 216p. (gr. 2-7). 1980. 16.95 (ISBN 0-03-056294-5). HR&W.
--The Wind in the Willows. 253p. Repr. of 1908 ed. lib. bdg. 11.60x (ISBN 0-88411-877-0). Amereon Ltd.

Grahame, R. & Anderson, J. A. Low Back Pain, Vol. 2. (Annual Research Reviews). 83p. 1981. 14.00 (ISBN 0-88831-095-1). Eden Med Res.

Graham-Helwig, H. How to Take Minutes. 8th ed. 136p. 1975. 6.95x o.p. (ISBN 0-8464-0496-6). Beekman Pubs.

Graham-Pole, John, ed. Non-Hodgkin's Lymphomas in Children. LC 80-81990. (Pochedly & Miller Series in Pediatric Hematology Oncology). (Illus.). 192p. 1980. 26.50 (ISBN 0-89352-068-3). Masson Pub.

Grahams, Betty L., tr. Ministrando Con Musica. (Portugese Bks.). (Port.). 1979. write for info. (ISBN 0-8297-0732-8). Life Pubs Intl.

Grahl, Bart, ed. see International Telos Conference, 1st, Waterloo, Ont., Oct. 8-11, 1970.

Grahl, Bart, tr. see Goldmann, Lucien.

Grahl-Madsen, Atle. Territorial Asylum. LC 80-10498. (Monograph in the Uppsala University Swedish Institute of International Law). 231p. 1980. lib. bdg. 28.00 (ISBN 0-379-20706-0). Oceana.

Grahman, Lorenz. Song of the Boat. LC 74-5183. (Illus.). (gr. 2-5). 1975. 8.95 (ISBN 0-690-75231-8, TYC-J); PLB 7.89 o.p. (ISBN 0-690-75232-6). T Y Crowell.

Grahn, Judy, ed. Lesbians Speak Out. (Illus.). 1974. pap. 5.00 (ISBN 0-88447-028-8). Diana Pr.

Graig, M. J. The Man Whose Name Was Not Thomas. (Illus.). 32p. (gr. k-3). 1981. 7.95a (ISBN 0-385-15064-4); PLB (ISBN 0-385-15065-2). Doubleday.

Grainger, J. F., jt. auth. see Clarke, D.

Grainger, Stuart. Creative Papercraft. (Illus.). 128p. 1980. 12.95 (ISBN 0-7137-1008-X, Pub. by Blandford Pr England). Sterling.

Gralla, E. J., ed. Scientific Considerations in Monitoring & Evaluating Toxicological Research. LC 80-21367. (CIIT Ser.). (Illus.). 221p. 1980. 24.50 (ISBN 0-89116-209-7). Hemisphere Pub.

Gram, Dewey. Boulevard Nights. (Orig.). 1979. pap. 1.95 o.s.i. (ISBN 0-446-90106-7). Warner Bks.

--Foxes. (Orig.). 1979. pap. 2.25 (ISBN 0-446-92156-4). Warner Bks.

Grambs, Jean D. Schools, Scholars & Society. rev. ed. LC 77-12417. 1978. pap. 10.95 (ISBN 0-13-793802-0). P-H.

Grambs, Jean D., jt. auth. see Amos, William E.

Grambsch, Paul V. see Carnegie Commission on Higher Education.

Gramiak, Raymond & Waag, Robert C. Cardiac Ultrasound. LC 75-29250. (Illus.). 308p. 1975. 41.50 o.p. (ISBN 0-8016-1956-4). Mosby.

Gramiak, Raymond, jt. auth. see Nanda, Navin C.

Gramlich, Edward M. Benefit-Cost Analysis of Government Programs. (Illus.). 304p. 1981. text ed. 15.95 (ISBN 0-13-074757-2). P-H.

Gramlich, Edward M. & Koshel, Patrica P. Educational Performance Contracting: An Evaluation of an Experiment. (Studies in Social Experimentation). 76p. 1975. pap. 3.95 (ISBN 0-8157-3239-2). Brookings.

Gramm, W. Phillip see Anders, Gerhard, et al.

Grammel, Richard, ed. see International Union of Theoretical & Applied Mechanics Colloquium, Madrid, 1955.

Gramophone, ed. The Gramophone Classical Catalogue. LC 79-53740. (Illus.). 1980. 13.50 (ISBN 0-7153-7883-X). David & Charles.

Grams, Betty J. Women of Grace. LC 77-93409. 1978. pap. 1.95 (ISBN 0-88243-751-8, 02-0751, Radiant Books); teacher's ed 2.50 (ISBN 0-88243-226-5, 32-0226). Gospel Pub.

Grams, Betty J., tr. Ministrando Con Musica. (Spanish Bks.). 1978. 2.50 (ISBN 0-8297-0584-8). Life Pubs Intl.

Grams, Ralph Raymond. Problem Solving, Systems Analysis, & Medicine. (Illus.). 244p. 1972. Set. 31.00 (ISBN 0-398-02298-4); companion volume - Systems Analysis wkbk. incl. (ISBN 0-398-02566-5). C C Thomas.

Gramsci, Antonio. Modern Prince & Other Writings. LC 67-25646. 1959. 5.95 o.p. (ISBN 0-7178-0134-9); pap. 2.25 (ISBN 0-7178-0133-0). Intl Pub Co.

Gran, Guy. Zaire: The Political Economy of Underdevelopment. LC 79-19512. (Praeger Special Studies). 352p. 1979. 25.95 (ISBN 0-03-048916-4). Praeger.

Grana, Cesar. Fact & Symbol: Essays in the Sociology of Art & Literature. 1971. 12.95 (ISBN 0-19-501285-2). Oxford U Pr.

Granacher, Robert P., jt. auth. see Mason, Aaron S.

Granbeck, Marilyn. Celia. 1977. pap. 1.95 (ISBN 0-515-03951-9). Jove Pubns.

--Elena. (Orig.). pap. 2.25 (ISBN 0-515-04420-2). Jove Pubns.

--Lorielle. (Historical Romance Ser.). 1980. pap. 2.75 (ISBN 0-515-04627-2). Jove Pubns.

--Social Work Careers. (Career Concise Guides Ser.). (Illus.). (gr. 7 up). 1977. lib. bdg. 6.45 s&l (ISBN 0-531-01310-3). Watts.

--Winds of Desire. (Orig.). pap. 1.95 (ISBN 0-515-04337-0). Jove Pubns.

Granberg, Millianne, jt. auth. see Cruse, Allan.

Grand, Evalyne S. The Fifty Dollar Gift. 178p. 1979. 11.95 (ISBN 0-86629-017-6). Sunrise MO.

--Oliver & Jonathan. 32p. 1980. 8.95 (ISBN 0-86629-014-1). Sunrise MO.

Grand, Samuel, jt. auth. see Grand, Tamar.

Grand, Sarah. The Beth Book. (Virago Modern Classics Ser.). 1981. pap. 6.95. Dial.

Grand, Tamar. Holiday-Craft Kit for the Jewish Child. (Illus.). (ps). 1976. pap. text ed. 5.00 (ISBN 0-8074-0138-2, 103901). UAHC.

Grand, Tamar & Grand, Samuel. Children of Israel. (gr. 3-4). 1972. text ed. 5.50 (ISBN 0-8074-0131-5, 121320); tchr's guide 2.25 (ISBN 0-8074-0132-3, 201320); fun & act bk. 3.00 (ISBN 0-8074-0133-1, 121322). UAHC.

Grandbois, Mildred, ed. Cumulative Index to Nursing & Allied Health Literature, Vol. 22. LC 78-643434. 1977. 50.00 (ISBN 0-910478-13-9). Glendale Advent Med.

Grande, Hypolite La see La Grande, Hypolite.

Grande, Hyppolite La see La Grande, Hyppolite.

Grande, J. J. Del see Del Grande, J. J. & Duff, G. F.

Grandgenett, Myrna, jt. auth. see Clifford, Margaret M.

Grandilli, Peter A. Technician's Handbook of Plastics. 272p. 1981. text ed. 19.95 (ISBN 0-442-23870-3). Van Nos Reinhold.

Grandis, Sue L. Instrumentation for Coronary Care. (Techniques of Measurement in Medicine: No. 5). (Illus.). 150p. Date not set. price not set (ISBN 0-521-23548-0); pap. price not set (ISBN 0-521-28024-9). Cambridge U Pr.

Grandjean, E. Ergonomics of the Home. LC 73-13221. 344p. 1973. 34.95 (ISBN 0-470-32180-6). Halsted Pr.

--Sitting Posture. 1976 ed. 34.95 (ISBN 0-470-15176-5). Halsted Pr.

Grandjean, Etienne. Fitting the Task to the Man: An Ergonomic Approach. 3rd ed. LC 77-447838. 379p. 1980. 35.00 (ISBN 0-85066-192-7); pap. 22.50 (ISBN 0-8002-2225-3). Intl Pubns Serv.

Grandjean, Etienne, ed. see International Workshop on Ergonomic Aspects of Visual Display Terminals, Milan, March 1980.

Grandjean, Serge. Empire Furniture 1800 to 1825. 1966. 26.00 o.p. (ISBN 0-571-06666-6, Pub. by Faber & Faber). Merrimack Bk Serv.

Grandower, Elissa. Rivergate House. large print ed. LC 80-29028. 1981. Repr. of 1980 ed. 11.95 (ISBN 0-89621-268-8). Thorndike Pr.

--Rivergate House. LC 79-6036. 288p. 1980. 10.95 (ISBN 0-385-15420-8). Doubleday.

Grandy, Richard E. Theories & Observation in Science. (Central Issues in Philosophy Ser.). (Illus.). 224p. 1973. pap. 8.50 o.p. (ISBN 0-13-913392-5). P-H.

Graneau, Peter. Underground Power Transmission: The Science, Technology, & Economics of High Voltage Cables. LC 79-15746. 1979. 34.50 (ISBN 0-471-05757-6, Pub. by Wiley-Interscience). Wiley.

Granet, Irving. Thermodynamics & Heat Power. 2nd ed. (Illus.). 1980. text ed. 21.95 (ISBN 0-8359-7672-6); instrs' manual avail. Reston.

Granfield, David. Abortion Decision. LC 69-12185. 1969. 6.95 o.p. (ISBN 0-385-03304-4). Doubleday.

Granfield, Patrick. Ecclesial Cybernetics: A Study of Democracy in the Church. LC 72-87158. 320p. 1973. 8.95 o.s.i. (ISBN 0-02-545030-1). Macmillan.

Grange, John. The Golden Aphroditis. LC 37-5556. 1978. Repr. of 1577 ed. 22.00 (ISBN 0-8201-1177-5). Schol Facsimiles.

Grange, Roger T., Jr. Archeological Investigations at the Red Willow Reservoir. (Publications in Anthropology Ser.: No. 9). (Illus.). 238p. (Orig.). 1980. pap. 10.00 (ISBN 0-686-28124-1). Nebraska Hist.

Grange, William J. & Woodbury, Thomas C. Manual of Real Estate: Law, Procedures, & Forms. 2nd ed. (Illus.). 461p. 1968. 26.50 (ISBN 0-8260-3500-0, 39381). Ronald Pr.

Grange, William J., et al. Manual for Corporation Officers: The Law, Procedures, & Forms. (Illus.). 1967. 30.50 (ISBN 0-8260-3485-3). Ronald Pr.

Granger, Bill. Public Murders. 288p. (Orig.). 1980. pap. 1.95 (ISBN 0-515-05130-6). Jove Pubns.

Granger, Bill & Granger, Lori. Fighting Jane: Mayor Jane Byrne & the Chicago Machine. 1980. 12.95 (ISBN 0-8037-2470-5). Dial.

Granger, Bruce I. American Essay Serials from Franklin to Irving. LC 78-4120. 1978. 14.50x (ISBN 0-87049-221-7). U of Tenn Pr.

Granger, C. W. Forecasting in Business & Economics. LC 79-91742. (Economic Theory, Econometrics, & Mathematical Econometrics Ser.). 1979. text ed. 18.95 (ISBN 0-12-295180-8). Acad Pr.

Granger, Clive W., jt. auth. see Labys, Walter.

Granger, Colin & Hicks, Tony. Contact English: Contact 1. 1977. 5.95x (ISBN 0-435-28371-5); tchr's manual 14.95x (ISBN 0-435-28370-7); three tapes 72.00 (ISBN 0-435-28372-3); three cassettes 60.00 (ISBN 0-435-28373-1). Heinemann Ed.

Granger, Jean. Mushroom Matings: The Best in Mushroom Cookery. LC 78-5407. 1978. pap. 2.95 (ISBN 0-89666-000-1). Cragmont Pubns.

Granger, John V. Technology & International Relations. LC 78-15363. (Illus.). 1979. text ed. 19.95x (ISBN 0-7167-1004-8); pap. text ed. 9.95x (ISBN 0-7167-1003-X). W H Freeman.

Granger, Lori, jt. auth. see Granger, Bill.

Granger, Neil & Bulkley, Gregory B. Measurement of Blood Flow: Applications to the Splanchnic Circulation. (Illus.). 496p. 1981. write for info. (3730-7). Williams & Wilkins.

Granger, Peggy. Everywoman's Guide to a New Image. LC 75-37070. 1976. pap. 3.95 o.p. (ISBN 0-89087-916-8). Les Femmes Pub.

Granit, R., ed. see IBRO Symposium, Italy, September 1978.

Grannes, Alf. Loan Compounds in Bulgarian Reflecting the Turkish Indefinite Izafet-Construction. 70p. 1980. pap. 16.00x (ISBN 82-00-01951-9). Universitet.

Grannis, Chandler B., ed. What Happens in Book Publishing. 2nd ed. LC 67-19875. 1967. 22.50x (ISBN 0-231-02948-9). Columbia U Pr.

Grannis, G. F., jt. ed. see Dietz, A. A.

Grannis, Gary E., jt. auth. see Groneman, Chris H.

Granof, Michael H. Financial Accounting: Principles & Issues. 2nd ed. (Illus.). 1980. text ed. 19.95 (ISBN 0-13-314153-5). P-H.

Granowsky, Alvin & Mumford, Janice H. Building Life Skills, Level D. (Skillbooster Ser.: Bk. 1). 64p. (gr. 4). 1981. write for info. wkbk. (ISBN 0-87895-418-X). Modern Curr.

--Building Life Skills, Level E. (Skillbooster Ser.: Bk. 2). 64p. (gr. 5). 1981. rite for info. wkbk. (ISBN 0-87895-523-2). Modern Curr.

--Building Life Skills, Level F. (Skillbooster Ser.: Bk. 3). 64p. (gr. 6). 1981. write for info. wkbk. (ISBN 0-87895-617-4). Modern Curr.

Granrose, John T., jt. auth. see Frankena, William K.

Grant, Alexander T. Study of the Capital Market in Britain from 1919-1936. LC 67-16365. Repr. of 1937 ed. 26.00x (ISBN 0-678-05052-X). Kelley.

Grant, Alice, et al. Shindano-Swahili Essays & Other Stories. (Foreign & Comparative Studies-African Special Publications Ser.: No.6). 55p. 1971. pap. 2.50x. Syracuse U Foreign Comp.

Grant, Aline. Susan Ferrier of Edinburgh: A Biography. 174p. 1957. 4.95 (ISBN 0-8040-0286-X). Swallow.

Grant, Allan. A Preface to Coleridge. (Preface Bks.). (Illus.). 1977. pap. text ed. 5.95x (ISBN 0-582-31516-6). Longman.

Grant, Barbara M. & Hennings, Dorothy G. The Teacher Moves: An Analysis of Non-Verbal Activity. LC 71-148592. 1971. pap. text ed. 5.95x (ISBN 0-8077-1456-9). Tchrs Coll.

--Written Expression in the Language Arts. LC 80-25532. (Orig.). 1981. pap. 11.95 (ISBN 0-8077-2604-4). Tchrs Coll.

Grant, Barra. Slow Dancing in the Big City. 1978. pap. 1.95 o.s.i. (ISBN 0-446-89630-6). Warner Bks.

Grant, Barry K., ed. Film Genre: Theory & Criticism. LC 77-8908. 1977. 12.00 (ISBN 0-8108-1059-X). Scarecrow.

Grant, Bruce. Encyclopedia of Rawhide & Leather Braiding. LC 72-10407. (Illus.). 1972. 22.50 (ISBN 0-87033-161-2). Cornell Maritime.

--Leather Braiding. (Illus.). 1950. 6.00 (ISBN 0-87033-039-X). Cornell Maritime.

Grant, Bruce & Rice, Lee W. How to Make Cowboy Horse Gear. 2nd ed. LC 56-10884. (Illus.). 1956. pap. 6.00 (ISBN 0-87033-034-9). Cornell Maritime.

Grant, Bruce K. A Guide to Korean Characters: Reading & Writing Hangul & Hanja. 400p. 1979. 15.50 (ISBN 0-930878-13-2). Hollym Intl.

Grant, C. H. The Making of Modern Belize. LC 75-36022. (Cambridge Commonwealth Ser.). (Illus.). 400p. 1976. 49.50 (ISBN 0-521-20731-2). Cambridge U Pr.

Grant, C. L. A Quiet Night of Fear. (Orig.). 1981. pap. 2.25 (ISBN 0-425-04844-6). Berkley Pub.

--The Shadow of Alpha. pap. 1.25 o.p. (ISBN 0-425-03143-8). Berkley Pub.

Grant, Campbell. Rock Art of the American Indian. (Illus.). 192p. 1981. pap. 9.95 (ISBN 0-89646-060-6). Outbooks.

Grant, Carl A. Community Participation in Education. 1978. text ed. 16.95x (ISBN 0-205-06052-8). Allyn.

Grant, Carolyn, jt. auth. see Wakeman, Frederic.

Grant, Charles F. Introductory Accounting: An Audio-Tutorial Approach. (Business Ser.). 1977. pap. text ed. 15.95 (ISBN 0-675-08502-0); audio cassettes 140.00 (ISBN 0-675-08501-2); 2-5 sets 90.00, 6 or more sets 60.00 (ISBN 0-685-74284-9); instructor's manual 3.95 (ISBN 0-686-67615-7). Merrill.

Grant, Charles L. Tales from the Nightside. (Illus.). 250p. 1981. 11.95 (ISBN 0-87054-091-2). Arkham.

Grant, Clay. Demon Samurai. 1978. pap. 1.50 (ISBN 0-505-51244-0). Tower Bks.

Grant, Cynthia D. Joshua Fortune. LC 80-11983. 156p. (gr. 6-9). 1980. 8.95 (ISBN 0-689-30777-2). Atheneum.

Grant, D. J., jt. auth. see Wallwork, S. C.

Grant, Damian, ed. see Smollet, Tobias.

Grant, Daniel A., et al. Periodontics in the Tradition of Orban & Gottlieb: A Concept-Theory & Practice. 5th ed. LC 79-10615. (Illus.). 1979. text ed. 39.50 (ISBN 0-8016-1961-0). Mosby.

Grant, Daniel R. & Nixon, H. C. State & Local Government in America. 3rd ed. 608p. 1975. text ed. 18.95x (ISBN 0-205-04574-X, 7645740); instr's manual o.p. free (ISBN 0-205-05473-0). Allyn.

Grant, Daniel T. Who Should Survive the Purge in American Education & Why. (Illus.). 1978. 7.50 o.p. (ISBN 0-682-48659-0). Exposition.

Grant, Douglas & Grant, Douglas, eds. Dryden: Poetry & Prose. 1979. 10.95x (ISBN 0-8464-0085-5). Beekman Pubs.

Grant, Douglas, ed. see Churchill, Charles.

Grant, E. Physical Science in the Middle Ages. LC 77-8393. (History of Science Ser.). (Illus.). 1978. 19.95 (ISBN 0-521-21862-4); pap. 6.50x (ISBN 0-521-29294-8). Cambridge U Pr.

Grant, E. H., et al. Dielectric Behaviour of Biological Molecules in Solution. (Monographs on Physical Biochemistry). (Illus.). 1978. 39.95x (ISBN 0-19-854621-1). Oxford U Pr.

Grant, Edward. Much Ado About Nothing. LC 80-13876. (Illus.). 545p. Date not set. 59.50 (ISBN 0-521-22983-9). Cambridge U Pr.

Grant, Edward, ed. Nicole Oresme & the Kinematics of Circular Motion: Tractatus De Commensurabilitate Vel Incommensurabilitate Motuum Celi. LC 79-133238. (Medieval Science Ser). 1971. 50.00 (ISBN 0-299-05830-1). U of Wis Pr.

Grant, Elliott M. Emile Zola. (World Authors Ser.: France: No. 10). 1966. lib. bdg. 9.95 (ISBN 0-8057-2996-8). Twayne.

Grant, Eugene L. & Leavenworth, Richard. Statistical Quality Control. 5th ed. (Industrial Engineering & Management Science Ser.). (Illus.). 1979. text ed. 25.95x o.p. (ISBN 0-07-024114-7); solutions manual 6.95 o.p. (ISBN 0-685-95714-4). McGraw.

Grant, Eva. Will I Ever Be Older? LC 80-24782. (Life & Living from a Child's Point of View Ser.). (Illus.). (gr. k-5). 1981. PLB 9.65 (ISBN 0-8172-1363-5). Raintree Child.

Grant, F. W., ed. The Numerical Bible, 7 vols. Incl. Vol. 1. Genesis to Deuteronomy (ISBN 0-87213-262-5); Vol. 2. Joshua to Second Samuel (ISBN 0-87213-263-3); Vol. 3. Psalms (ISBN 0-87213-264-1); Vol. 4. Ezekiel (ISBN 0-87213-265-X); Vol. 5. Matthew to John (ISBN 0-87213-266-8); Vol. 6. Acts to Philemon (ISBN 0-87213-267-6); Vol. 7. Hebrews to Revelation (ISBN 0-87213-268-4). 1890-1932. Set. 52.95 (ISBN 0-87213-261-7); 7.95 ea. Loizeaux.

Grant, Francis J. The Manual of Heraldry. LC 75-23365. (Illus.). 1976. Repr. of 1929 ed. 15.00 (ISBN 0-8103-4252-9). Gale.

Grant, Frederick C., ed. Ancient Roman Religion. 1957. 6.50 (ISBN 0-672-61171-6, LLA138). Bobbs.

--Hellenistic Religions: The Age of Syncretism. 1953. 8.95 (ISBN 0-672-60342-X, LLA134). Bobbs.

Grant, G. F., jt. ed. see Brett, R. I.

Grant, George. The Master Fly Weaver (the Art of Weaving Hair Hackles) 150p. 1980. 50.00x (ISBN 0-918400-03-1, Pub. by Champoeg Pr). Intl Schol Bk Serv.

Grant, H. Vehicle Rescue. (Illus.). 1975. pap. 16.95 (ISBN 0-87618-137-X); instructor's guide 7.95 (ISBN 0-87618-611-8); systems chart 7.95 (ISBN 0-87618-610-X). R J Brady.

Grant, H. & Murray, R., Jr. Emergency Care. 2nd ed. LC 78-17756. (Illus.). 1978. 12.50 (ISBN 0-87618-886-2). R J Brady.

Grant, I. F. Highland Folk Ways. (Illus.). 1961. 22.50 (ISBN 0-7100-1466-X); pap. 11.95 (ISBN 0-7100-8064-6). Routledge & Kegan.

Grant, I. S. & Phillips, W. R. Electromagnetism. LC 73-17668. (Manchester Physics Ser). 1975. 45.25 (ISBN 0-471-32245-8); pap. 19.25 (ISBN 0-471-32246-6, Pub. by Wiley-Interscience). Wiley.

Grant, Ian. Cameraman at War. (Illus.). 200p. 1981. 31.95 (ISBN 0-85059-489-8). Aztex.

Grant, J., jt. auth. see Stevens, J.

Grant, J. F. Along a Highland Road. 208p. 1980. 25.00x (ISBN 0-85683-048-8, Pub. by Shepheard-Walwyn England). State Mutual Bk.

Grant, James. Island of Gold. 1978. 7.95 o.s.i. (ISBN 0-8027-5400-7). Walker & Co.

--The Mysteries of All Nations. LC 79-150243. 1971. Repr. of 1880 ed. 36.00 (ISBN 0-8103-3391-0). Gale.

Grant, James J. More Single Shot Rifles. (Illus.). 15.00 (ISBN 0-88227-006-0). Gun Room.

Grant, James P. Disparity Reduction Rates in Social Indicators: A Proposal for Measuring & Targeting Progress in Meeting Basic Needs. LC 78-61153. (Monographs: No. 11). 88p. 1978. 3.00 (ISBN 0-686-28684-7). Overseas Dev Council.

Grant, Jim. A Thief in the Night. 128p. 1974. pap. 2.50 (ISBN 0-8024-8688-6). Moody.

Grant, Joan. So Moses Was Born. 1976. pap. 1.50 (ISBN 0-380-00828-9, 30940). Avon.

Grant, John, ed. Aries I. LC 79-53731. 192p. 1979. 15.95 (ISBN 0-7153-7777-9). David & Charles.

Grant, John & Wilson, Colin, eds. The Book of Time. (Illus.). 320p. 1980. 32.00 (ISBN 0-7153-7764-7). David & Charles.

Grant, John C., jt. auth. see Legros, Lucien.

Grant, John J. & Pirtle, Wayne. Social Problems As Human Concerns. LC 75-38062. (Illus.). 400p. 1976. text ed. 13.95x (ISBN 0-87835-051-9). Boyd & Fraser.

Grant, John P., jt. ed. see Cusine, Douglas J.

Grant, Joseph M. & Crum, Lawrence L. The Development of State-Chartered Banking in Texas from Predecessor Systems Until 1970. (Studies in Banking & Finance: No. 11). 1978. 10.00 (ISBN 0-87755-219-3); pap. 6.00 (ISBN 0-87755-238-X). U of Tex Busn Res.

Grant, Joy. Harold Monro & the Poetry Bookshop. 1967. 18.50x (ISBN 0-520-00512-0). U of Cal Pr.

Grant, Julius. Books & Documents: Dating, Permanence & Preservation. 1980. lib. bdg. 59.95 (ISBN 0-8490-3157-5). Gordon Pr.

Grant, Karen A. & Grant, Verne. Flower Pollination in the Phlox Family. LC 65-19809. 1965. 17.50x (ISBN 0-231-02843-1). Columbia U Pr.

Grant, Kenneth, jt. ed. see Symonds, John.

Grant, Lester, jt. ed. see Lee, Si D.

Grant, Lewis, jt. ed. see Davis, Ray J.

Grant, Lorenzo G. The Weight of the Historical Inevitabilities at the End of the 20th Century & the Future of Humanity. (Illus.). 141p. 1981. 41.75 (ISBN 0-930008-76-6). Inst Econ Finan.

Grant, Louise. The Fort & the Flag. (N. H.-Vermont Historiettes). (Illus.). 73p. (Orig.). (gr. 3-4). 1977. pap. 2.45 (ISBN 0-915892-09-X). Regional Ctr Educ.

Grant, M., jt. auth. see Edwards, G.

Grant, M. D., jt. auth. see Davies, R.

Grant, Marcus & Gwinner, Paul. Alcoholisms in Perspective. 176p. 1980. 27.00x (ISBN 0-85664-790-X, Pub. by Croom Helm England). State Mutual Bk.

Grant, Margaret. Your Child & the Piano: How to Enrich & Share in Your Child's Musical Experience. 104p. 1980. pap. 5.95 (ISBN 0-8253-0027-4). Beaufort Bks NY.

Grant, Matthew G. Buffalo Bill. LC 73-10073. 1974. PLB 5.95 (ISBN 0-87191-255-4). Creative Ed.

--Champlain. LC 73-13714. 1974. PLB 5.95 (ISBN 0-87191-287-2). Creative Ed.

--Chief Joseph. LC 73-9816. 1974. PLB 5.95 (ISBN 0-87191-251-1). Creative Ed.

--Clara Barton. LC 73-15869. 1974. PLB 5.95 (ISBN 0-87191-306-2). Creative Ed.

--Columbus. LC 73-13959. 1974. PLB 5.95 (ISBN 0-87191-286-4). Creative Ed.

--Coronado. LC 73-13957. 1974. PLB 5.95 (ISBN 0-87191-285-6). Creative Ed.

--Crazy Horse. LC 73-12403. 1974. PLB 5.95 (ISBN 0-87191-269-4). Creative Ed.

--Daniel Boone. LC 73-10070. 1974. PLB 5.95 (ISBN 0-87191-256-2). Creative Ed.

--Davy Crockett. LC 73-10072. 1974. PLB 5.95 (ISBN 0-87191-258-9). Creative Ed.

--DeSoto. LC 73-13917. 1974. PLB 5.95 (ISBN 0-87191-283-X). Creative Ed.

--Dolley Madison. LC 73-15848. 1974. PLB 5.95 (ISBN 0-87191-308-9). Creative Ed.

--Elizabeth Blackwell. LC 73-15858. 1974. PLB 5.95 (ISBN 0-87191-307-0). Creative Ed.

--Francis Marion. LC 73-10061. 1974. PLB 5.95 (ISBN 0-87191-257-0). Creative Ed.

--Geronimo. LC 73-12203. 1974. PLB 5.95 (ISBN 0-87191-267-8). Creative Ed.

--Harriet Tubman. LC 73-15849. 1974. PLB 5.95 (ISBN 0-87191-309-7). Creative Ed.

--Jim Bridger. LC 73-10071. 1974. PLB 5.95 (ISBN 0-87191-254-6). Creative Ed.

--John Paul Jones. LC 73-18212. 1974. PLB 5.95 (ISBN 0-87191-300-3). Creative Ed.

--Kit Carson. LC 73-10063. 1974. PLB 5.95 (ISBN 0-87191-253-8). Creative Ed.

--Lafayette. LC 73-18155. 1974. PLB 5.95 (ISBN 0-87191-301-1). Creative Ed.

--Leif Ericson. LC 73-14531. 1974. PLB 5.95 (ISBN 0-87191-278-3). Creative Ed.

--Lewis & Clark. LC 73-14582. 1974. PLB 5.95 (ISBN 0-87191-277-5). Creative Ed.

--Osceola. LC 73-12407. 1974. PLB 5.95 (ISBN 0-87191-266-X). Creative Ed.

--Paul Revere. LC 73-18076. 1974. PLB 5.95 (ISBN 0-87191-303-8). Creative Ed.

--Pontiac. LC 73-12193. 1974. PLB 5.95 (ISBN 0-87191-268-6). Creative Ed.

--Robert E. Lee. LC 73-18078. 1974. PLB 5.95 (ISBN 0-87191-302-X). Creative Ed.

--Sam Houston. LC 73-18080. 1974. PLB 5.95 (ISBN 0-87191-299-6). Creative Ed.

--Squanto. LC 73-12813. 1974. PLB 5.95 (ISBN 0-87191-270-8). Creative Ed.

--Susan B. Anthony. LC 73-15911. 1974. PLB 5.95 (ISBN 0-87191-305-4). Creative Ed.

Grant, Maurice H. A Dictionary of British Landscape Painters: From the 16th to the 20th Century. (Illus.). 236p. 1970. 40.00x (ISBN 0-85317-250-1). Intl Pubns Serv.

Grant, Maxwell. Charg, Monster, No. 20. 1977. pap. 1.25 o.s.i. (ISBN 0-515-04284-6). Jove Pubns.

--The Death Giver: Shadow No. 23. 1978. pap. 1.25 o.s.i. (ISBN 0-515-04282-X). Jove Pubns.

--Murder Trail: Shadow No. 18. 1977. pap. 1.25 o.s.i. (ISBN 0-515-04280-3). Jove Pubns.

--Norgil: More Tales of Prestidigitection. LC 78-53497. (Illus.). 1979. 10.00 (ISBN 0-89296-041-8); limited ed. o.p. 25.00 (ISBN 0-89296-042-6). Mysterious Pr.

Grant, Maxwell, pseud. Norgil the Magician. LC 76-16891. 1977. 10.00 (ISBN 0-89296-006-X). Mysterious Pr.

Grant, Maxwell. The Silent Death: Shadow No. 22. 1978. pap. 1.25 o.s.i. (ISBN 0-515-04281-1). Jove Pubns.

--The Wealth Seeker: Shadow No. 21. 1978. pap. 1.25 o.p. (ISBN 0-515-04283-8). Jove Pubns.

--Zemba: Shadow No. 19. 1977. pap. 1.25 o.p. (ISBN 0-515-04285-4). Jove Pubns.

Grant, Michael. Civilizations of Europe. 4.95 o.p. (ISBN 0-452-25039-0, Z5039, Plume). NAL.

--Jews in the Roman World. LC 72-11118. 1973. lib. rep. ed. 20.00x (ISBN 0-684-15494-3, ScribT). Scribner.

--Roman History from Coins. (Illus.). 1968. pap. 5.95 (ISBN 0-521-09549-2). Cambridge U Pr.

Grant, Michael, ed. Greek Literature: An Anthology. (Classics Ser.). 1977. pap. 2.50 o.p. (ISBN 0-14-044323-1). Penguin.

Grant, Michael, tr. see Cicero.

Grant, Michael, tr. see Tacitus.

Grant, Micheal. Ancient History Atlas. LC 73-654430. (Illus.). 112p. 1972. 6.95 o.s.i. (ISBN 0-02-545130-8). Macmillan.

Grant, Murray. Handbook of Community Health. 2nd ed. LC 74-3029. 1975. pap. 7.50 o.p. (ISBN 0-8121-0495-1). Lea & Febiger.

--Handbook of Community Health. 3rd ed. LC 80-26182. (Illus.). 368p. 1981. pap. write for info. (ISBN 0-8121-0760-8). Lea & Febiger.

Grant, Myrna. Ivan & the Moscow Circus. (gr. 4-8). 1980. pap. write for info. (ISBN 0-8423-1843-7). Tyndale.

--Vanya. LC 73-89729. 1974. pap. 2.45 (ISBN 0-88419-009-9). Creation Hse.

Grant, Nancy. Time to Care. (Royal College of Nursing Research Ser.). 186p. 1980. pap. text ed. 10.00x (ISBN 0-443-02330-1). Churchill.

Grant, Neil. Benjamin Disraeli: Prime Minister Extraordinary. LC 69-11143. (Biography Ser.). (Illus.). (gr. 7 up). 1969. PLB 5.90 o.p. (ISBN 0-531-00867-3). Watts.

--Cathedrals. LC 79-183939. (First Bks). (Illus.). 96p. (gr. 4-6). 1972. PLB 4.90 o.p. (ISBN 0-531-00755-3). Watts.

--Charles Fifth. LC 79-104187. (Biography Ser). (gr. 7 up). 1970. PLB 5.90 o.p. (ISBN 0-531-00937-8). Watts.

--The Easter Rising: Dublin, 1916. LC 72-3532. (World Focus Bks). (Illus.). 96p. (gr. 7-12). 1972. PLB 6.45 (ISBN 0-531-02161-0). Watts.

--A First Book of the Renaissance. LC 72-134366. (First Bks). (Illus.). (gr. 7 up). 1971. PLB 4.90 o.p. (ISBN 0-531-00737-5). Watts.

--Guilds. LC 72-3616. (First Bks). (Illus.). 96p. (gr. 4-7). 1972. PLB 4.90 o.p. (ISBN 0-531-00771-5). Watts.

--The Industrial Revolution. LC 73-5705. (First Bks). (Illus.). (gr. 7-12). 1973. PLB 4.90 o.p. (ISBN 0-531-00808-8). Watts.

--Munich: Nineteen Thirty-Eight Appeasement Fails to Bring Peace for Our Time. LC 70-16185. (World Focus Bks). (Illus.). (gr. 7 up). 1971. PLB 6.45 (ISBN 0-531-02154-8). Watts.

--The Partition of Palestine, 1947: Jewish Triumph, British Failure, Arab Disaster. LC 73-4279. (World Focus Bks). (Illus.). (gr. 7-12). 1973. PLB 4.47 o.p. (ISBN 0-531-01044-9). Watts.

Grant, Nellie. Nellie's Story. Huxley, Elspeth, ed. 352p. 1981. Repr. 12.95 (ISBN 0-688-00475-X). Morrow.

Grant, Nigel, jt. auth. see Bell, Robert.

Grant, P. J. Nuclear Science. (Illus.). 1971. pap. text ed. 11.95x (ISBN 0-245-50419-2). Intl Ideas.

Grant, R. E., ed. Sing Along-Senior Citizens. 108p. 1973. pap. 7.50 (ISBN 0-398-02722-6). C C Thomas.

Grant, R. M. & Shaw, G. K. Current Issues in Economic Policy. 320p. 28.50x (ISBN 0-86003-029-6, Pub. by Allan Pubs England); pap. 14.25x (ISBN 0-86003-128-4). State Mutual Bk.

Grant, Raymond J. S. Cambridge, Corpus Christi College Forty One: The Loricas & the Missal. (Costerus New Ser.: No. XVII). 1979. pap. 17.25x (ISBN 90-6203-762-3). Humanities.

Grant, Richard B. The Goncourt Brothers. (World Authors Ser.: France: No. 183). lib. bdg. 10.95 (ISBN 0-8057-2384-6). Twayne.

--Theophile Gautier. LC 75-4819. (World Authors Ser.: France: No. 362). 1975. lib. bdg. 10.95 (ISBN 0-8057-6213-2). Twayne.

Grant, Robert B. Black Man Comes to the City: A Documentary Account from the Great Migration to the Great Depression, 1915-1930. LC 72-83821. 1972. 17.95 (ISBN 0-911012-45-1). Nelson-Hall.

Grant, Robert M. Eusebius As Church Historian. 192p. 1980. 29.95 (ISBN 0-19-826441-0). Oxford U Pr.

Grant, Roderick. A Private Vendetta. 1979. 7.95 o.p. (ISBN 0-684-15801-9, ScribT). Scribner.

Grant, Ron. Where the Light Was Burning. 192p. 1981. 8.95 (ISBN 0-89962-044-2). Todd & Honeywell.

Grant, Roy E., jt. auth. see Jordan, Myra J.

Grant, Sea. First Aid for Boaters & Divers. 128p. 1980. pap. 4.95 (ISBN 0-695-81425-7). Follett.

Grant, Sister Marie, jt. auth. see Ashlock, Patrick.

Grant, Stan. Jimmy Carter's Odyssey to Black Africa: Part One. (Illus.). 9.50. Courier Pr FL.

Grant, Steven A., jt. auth. see Brown, John H.

Grant, Thomas M. The Comedies of George Chapman: A Study in Development. (Salzburg Studies in English Literature, Jacobean Drama Studies: No. 5). 1972. pap. text ed. 25.00x (ISBN 0-391-01391-2). Humanities.

Grant, Ulysses S. The Papers of Ulysses S. Grant: Vol. 5 - April 1 to August 31, 1862. Simon, John Y. & Alexander, Thomas G., eds. LC 67-10725. (Illus.). 488p. 1973. 30.00x (ISBN 0-8093-0636-0). S Ill U Pr.

--The Papers of Ulysses S. Grant: Vol. 6 - September 1 to December 8, 1862. Simon, John Y., ed. LC 67-10725. (Illus.). 516p. 1977. 30.00x (ISBN 0-8093-0694-8). S Ill U Pr.

--The Papers of Ulysses S. Grant, Vol. 7: December Ninth, Eighteen Sixty-Two to March Thirty First, Eighteen Sixty-Three. Simon, John Y., ed. LC 67-10725. (Illus.). 612p. 1979. 35.00x (ISBN 0-8093-0880-0). S Ill U Pr.

Grant, Ulysses S. & Simon, John Y., eds. The Papers of Ulysses S. Grant, Vol. 8: April First to July Sixth, Eighteen Sixty-Three. LC 67-10725. (Illus.). 634p. 1979. 35.00x (ISBN 0-8093-0884-3). S Ill U Pr.

Grant, Verne. Genetics of Flowering Plants. LC 74-13555. (Illus.). 1975. 27.50x (ISBN 0-231-03694-9); pap. 12.50x (ISBN 0-231-08363-7). Columbia U Pr.

--Organismic Evolution. LC 76-54175. (Illus.). 1977. text ed. 24.95x (ISBN 0-7167-0372-6). W H Freeman.

--Origin of Adaptations. LC 63-11695. (Illus.). 1963. 27.50x (ISBN 0-231-02529-7); pap. 12.50x (ISBN 0-231-08648-2). Columbia U Pr.

--Plant Speciation. 1971. 25.00x (ISBN 0-231-03208-0); pap. 12.50x (ISBN 0-231-08326-2). Columbia U Pr.

Grant, Verne, jt. auth. see Grant, Karen A.

Grant, W. A., jt. auth. see Carter, G.

Grant, W. Morton. Toxicology of the Eye: Drugs, Chemicals, Plants, Venoms, 2 vols. 2nd ed. (Illus.). 1216p. 1974. pap. 60.25 photocopy (ISBN 0-398-02299-2). C C Thomas.

Grant, W. Parks. Handbook of Music Terms. LC 67-10187. 1967. 22.50 (ISBN 0-8108-0054-3). Scarecrow.

Grant, Walter, tr. see Fastenrath, Fritz.

Grant, Wyn. Independent Local Politics in England. (Illus.). 1977. 19.95 (ISBN 0-566-00183-7, 01608-X, Pub. by Saxon Hse England). Lexington Bks.

Grant-Duff, Mountstuart E. Studies in European Politics. LC 72-110901. 1970. Repr. of 1866 ed. 16.50 (ISBN 0-8046-0884-9). Kennikat.

Grantham, Alexandra E. Manchu Monarch: An Interpretation of Chia Ch'ing. (Studies in Chinese History & Civilization). 1977. Repr. of 1934 ed. 19.00 (ISBN 0-89093-076-7). U Pubns Amer.

Grantham, Walter J., jt. auth. see Vincent, Thomas L.

Grantz, Gerald J. Home Book of Taxidermy & Tanning. LC 77-85651. (Illus.). 160p. 1970. 10.95 (ISBN 0-8117-0805-5). Stackpole.

Granville, W. A., et al. Elements of the Differential & Integral Calculus. new & rev. ed. 1962. text ed. 25.50 (ISBN 0-471-00206-2). Wiley.

Granville-Baker, Harley. Preface to Shakespeare: Volume 1, Hamlet. 1977. pap. 10.50 (ISBN 0-7134-2050-2, Pub. by Batsford England). David & Charles.

Granville-Barker, Harley. Prefaces to Shakespeare, 6 vols. in 1. 1972. 42.50 o.p. (ISBN 0-7134-2070-7, Pub. by Batsford England). David & Charles.

Granville-Barker, Harley & Harrison, George B. Companion to Shakespeare Studies. 1934. 63.00 (ISBN 0-521-05132-0). Cambridge U Pr.

Granzer, F., et al, eds. see Nuclear Track Detection Conference, Neuherberg Munich, Sept. 30 to Oct. 6, 1976.

Graphic Arts Trade Journal Intl Inc. Export Grafics USA 1980-81. Humphrey, G. A. & Miura, Lydia, eds. (Illus.). 94p. (Orig.). 1980. pap. 10.00 (ISBN 0-910762-06-6). Graph Arts Trade.

Grappel, Robert D. & Hemenway, Jack E. Link Sixty-Eight: An M6800 Linking Loader. LC 78-17819. 1979. pap. 8.00 (ISBN 0-931718-09-0, BYTE Bks). McGraw.

Grappin, P. Dictionnaire moderne Larousse, francais-allemand et allemand-francais. (Fr. & Ger.). 39.95 (ISBN 2-03-020603-2, 3778). Larousse.

Grases, Pedro J. & Beker G., Simon. Color Atlas of Liver Biopsy: A Clinical Pathological Guide. Orig. Title: Guia Practica De Biopsia Hepatica En el Adulto. (Illus.). 125p. 1981. write for info. (ISBN 0-8451-0209-5). A R Liss.

Grashey, R. & Schwarz, G. S. X-Ray Chart of the Human Skeleton. 1957. 6.50 o.s.i. (ISBN 0-02-845430-8). Hafner.

Grass, Guenter. Four Plays. Manheim, Ralph & Willson, A. Leslie, trs. Incl. Flood; Mister, Mister; Only Ten Minutes to Buffalo; The Wicked Cooks. LC 67-11968. 289p. 1968. pap. 3.25 o.p. (ISBN 0-15-633150-0, HB138, Harv). HarBraceJ.

Grass, Gunter. From the Diary of a Snail. Manheim, Ralph, tr. from Ger. LC 73-6680. 1973. 7.95 o.p. (ISBN 0-15-133800-0). HarBraceJ.

--The Meeting at Telgte. Manheim, Ralph, tr. from Ger. (Helen & Kurt Wolff Bk.). 1981. 9.95 (ISBN 0-15-162138-1). HarBraceJ.

--Die Plebejer Proben Den Aufstand. Brookes, H. F. & Fraenkel, C. E., eds. 1971. pap. text ed. 4.50x (ISBN 0-435-38372-8). Heinemann Ed.

--Tin Drum. Manheim, Ralph, tr. 1971. pap. 3.95 (ISBN 0-394-70300-6, V-300, Vin). Random.

Grasse, Pierre-Paul, ed. Larousse Encyclopedia of the Animal World. LC 75-7569. Orig. Title: Vie Des Animaux. (Illus.). 1975. 50.00 o.p. (ISBN 0-88332-028-2). Larousse.

Grasselli, J. & Ritchey, W., eds. Atlas of Spectral Data & Physical Constants for Organic Compounds, 6 vols. 2nd ed. LC 72-2452. 1975. Set. 700.00 (ISBN 0-87819-317-0). CRC Pr.

Grassi, Carlo, ed. see International Congress of Chemotherapy, 11th & Interscience Conference on Antimicrobial Agents & Chemotherapy, 19th.

Grassi, Carlo, ed. see Symposium Milan, Italy, November 1978.

Grassi, Joseph R. Grassi Block Substitution Test for Measuring Organic Brain Pathology. 2nd ed. (American Lecture Psychology Ser.). (Illus.). 96p. 1970. text ed. 9.75 (ISBN 0-398-00717-9). C C Thomas.

Grassian, Victor. Moral Reasoning: Ethical Theory & Some Contemporary Moral Problems. 400p. 1981. pap. text ed. 10.95 (ISBN 0-13-600759-7). P-H.

Grassie, N., ed. Developments in Polymer Degradation, Vol. 2. (Illus.). 1979. 50.00x (ISBN 0-85334-854-5, Pub. by Applied Science). Burgess-Intl Ideas.

Grassman, Peter. Physical Principles of Chemical Engineering. 928p. 1971. text ed. 105.00 (ISBN 0-08-012817-3). Pergamon.

Grasso, Joseph E., jt. auth. see Miller, Ernest L.

Grasty, William K. & Newman, Mary T. Introduction to Basic Speech. (Illus., Orig.). 1969. text ed. 7.95x (ISBN 0-02-474180-9, 47418). Macmillan.

Grastyan, E. & Molnar, P., eds. Sensory Functions: Proceedings of the 28th International Congress of Physiological Sciences, Budapest, 1980. LC 80-41852. (Advances in Physiological Sciences). (Illus.). 350p. 1981. 40.00 (ISBN 0-08-027337-8). Pergamon.

Gratch, Alan S. Board Members Are Child Advocates. (Orig.). 1980. pap. text ed. 4.95 (ISBN 0-87868-198-1). Child Welfare.

Grater, Michael. Cut & Color Paper Masks. (Dover Coloring Book Ser.). 32p. (Orig.). 1975. pap. 1.75 (ISBN 0-486-23171-2). Dover.

--Cut & Fold Paper Spaceships That Fly. (Illus.). 48p. (Orig.). (gr. 1-5). Date not set. pap. price not set (ISBN 0-486-23978-0). Dover. Postponed.

--Paper Things. (Make & Play Ser.). (Illus.). 48p. (gr. k-6). 1976. pap. 1.50 (ISBN 0-263-05899-9). Transatlantic.

Grathoff, Richard, ed. Theory of Social Action: The Correspondence of Alfred Schutz & Talcott Parsons. LC 77-15761. (Studies in Phenomenology and Existential Philosophy). 176p. (04#176). 1978. 12.50x (ISBN 0-253-35957-0). Ind U Pr.

Gratsch, Edward, et al. Principles of Catholic Theology: A Synthesis of Dogma & Morals. LC 80-26272. 401p. (Orig.). 1981. pap. 10.95 (ISBN 0-8189-0407-0). Alba.

Gratsch, Edward J. Where Peter Is: A Survey of Ecclesiology. LC 74-34578. 290p. 1975. pap. 5.95 (ISBN 0-8189-0302-3). Alba.

Grattan, C. H. Why We Fought. Nelson, Keith, ed. LC 70-84163. 1969. 24.50x (ISBN 0-672-60944-4). Irvington.

Grattan, C. Hartley, ed. American Ideas About Adult Education Sevventeen Ten to Nineteen Fifty-One. LC 59-8042. (Classics in Education Ser.: No. 2). (Orig.). 1959. 7.90 o.p. (ISBN 0-8077-1461-5); pap. text ed. 3.75 o.p. (ISBN 0-8077-1458-5). Tchrs Coll.

Grattan, Gurney A., jt. auth. see Willett, Roderick.

Grattan, Virginia L. Mary Colter: Builder Upon the Red Earth. LC 79-52507. (Illus.). 1980. 15.50 (ISBN 0-87358-197-0); pap. 9.95 (ISBN 0-87358-198-9). Northland.

Grattan-Guinness, I., ed. Dear Russell-Dear Jourdain. LC 77-9431. 1977. 22.50x (ISBN 0-231-04460-7). Columbia U Pr.

Gratton, Livio, ed. Star Evolution. (Italian Physical Society: Course 28). (Illus.). 1974. 55.00 (ISBN 0-12-368828-0). Acad Pr.

Gratton, Marilyn. It's a Good Thing I'm Not Married. 1975. 1.95 o.p. (ISBN 0-686-17211-6). Sandollar Pr.

Gratz, David B. Fire Department Management: Scope & Method. (Fire Science Ser). 1972. text ed. 13.95x (ISBN 0-02-474620-7, 47462). Macmillan.

Gratzek, J. B., jt. auth. see Brown, E. Evan.

Gratzer, G. H. Lattice Theory: First Concepts & Distributive Lattices. LC 75-151136. (Mathematics Ser). (Illus.). 1971. text ed. 25.95x (ISBN 0-7167-0442-0). W H Freeman.

Grau, Joseph J. Criminal & Civil Investigation Handbook. (Illus.). 1088p. 1982. 39.50 (ISBN 0-07-024130-9). McGraw.

Grau, Shirley A. Evidence of Love. 1978. pap. 1.95 o.p. (ISBN 0-449-23766-4, Crest). Fawcett.

--The Keepers of the House. 1976. pap. 1.50 o.p. (ISBN 0-449-23031-7, Crest). Fawcett.

--Wind Shifting West. 1977. pap. 1.95 o.p. (ISBN 0-449-23349-9, Crest). Fawcett.

Graubard, Mark. Campustown in the Throes of the Counterculture. 420p. 1974. pap. 4.95. Campus Scope.

--Campustown U.S.A. at Midcentury. 308p. 1971. pap. 3.95. Campus Scope.

Graubard, Stephen R. Kissinger: Portrait of a Mind. new ed. 288p. 1973. text ed. 9.95 (ISBN 0-393-05481-0); pap. text ed. 5.95x (ISBN 0-393-09278-X). Norton.

Graubard, Stephen R., ed. A New America? 1979. pap. text ed. 6.95x (ISBN 0-393-95019-0). Norton.

--The State. 1981. 12.95 (ISBN 0-393-01387-1); pap. text ed. 4.95x (ISBN 0-393-95098-0). Norton.

Graubard, Stephen R. & Holton, Gerald, eds. Excellence & Leadership in a Democracy. LC 62-20743. 1962. text ed. 20.00x (ISBN 0-231-02567-X). Columbia U Pr.

Grauer, R. Cobol: A Vehicle for Information Systems. 1981. 18.95 (ISBN 0-13-139709-5). P-H.

Grauer, Robert T. A Cobol Book of Practice & Reference. (P-H Software Ser.). (Illus.). 352p. 1981. pap. text ed. 15.95 (ISBN 0-13-139717-6). P-H.

Grauer, Robert T. & Crawford, Marshal A. Structured COBOL: A Pragmatic Approach. (Illus.). 544p. 1981. pap. text ed. 19.95 (ISBN 0-13-854455-7). P-H.

Grauerholz, James, ed. see Burroughs, William.

Grault, Donald. Student Rights & Responsibilities. 1976. pap. text ed. 8.00 (ISBN 0-87545-003-2). Natl Sch Pr.

Graumnitz, Jack E., jt. auth. see Dougall, Herbert E.

Graumont, Raoul & Hensel, John. Encyclopedia of Knots & Fancy Rope Work. 4th ed. (Illus.). 1953. 22.50 (ISBN 0-87033-021-7). Cornell Maritime.

Grava, Sigurd. Urban Planning Aspects of Water Pollution Control. LC 72-87147. (Institute of Urban Environment Ser). (Illus.). 1969. text ed. 17.50x (ISBN 0-231-03280-3). Columbia U Pr.

Gravalos, Elizabeth, tr. see Parodi, Pierre.

Gravas, jt. auth. see Brunner.

Grave, Gilman. Thyroid Hormones & Brain Development. LC 76-52899. 1977. 36.00 (ISBN 0-89004-146-6). Raven.

Grave, Gilman, ed. Early Detection of Potential Diabetes: The Problems & the Promise. 1979. 28.00 (ISBN 0-89004-301-9). Raven.

Gravel, Fern, pseud. Oh Millersville! Andrews, Clarence A., tr. 100p. (gr. 6-12). 1980. Repr. of 1940 ed. PLB price not set (ISBN 0-934582-01-7). Midwest Heritage.

Gravelle, H. & Rees, R. Microeconomics. 2nd ed. (Modern Economic Series). (Illus.). 1981. pap. text ed. 25.00 (ISBN 0-582-44075-0). Longman.

Gravelle, H. F. E., jt. auth. see Rees, R.

Gravelles, William D. De see De Gravelles, William D. & Kelley, John H.

Gravely, William. Gilbert Haven: Methodist Abolitionist. LC 72-14179. 272p. 1973. 8.95 o.p. (ISBN 0-687-14702-6). Abingdon.

Gravenstein, J. S., et al. Monitoring Surgical Patients in the Operating Room. (Illus.). 288p. 1979. 25.75 (ISBN 0-398-03774-4). C C Thomas.

Graver, B. D. Advanced English Practice. 2nd ed. 1971. pap. text ed. 3.50x with key o.p. (ISBN 0-19-432190-8). Oxford U Pr.

Graver, Fred, ed. see Bowie, Donald.

Graver, Fred, ed. see Lewis, Tom.

Graver, Fred, ed. see Olsen, Paul.

Graver, Fred, ed. see Scher, Paula.

Graver, Jane. Please, Lord, Don't Put Me on Hold! 1979. pap. 2.25 (ISBN 0-570-03790-5, 12-2753). Concordia.

--Puppets. (A Nice Place to Live Ser.). 1978. pap. 2.25 (ISBN 0-570-07757-5, 12-2716). Concordia.

Graver, Lawrence. Conrad's Short Fiction. LC 69-14302. 1968. 16.50x (ISBN 0-520-00513-9). U of Cal Pr.

Graver, Lawrence & Federman, Raymond, eds. Samuel Beckett. (The Critical Heritage Ser.). 1979. 27.00x (ISBN 0-7100-8948-1). Routledge & Kegan.

Graves, Arthur H. Illustrated Guide to Trees & Shrubs. rev. ed. 1956. 12.95x o.p. (ISBN 0-06-070870-0, HarpT). Har-Row.

Graves, Charles E., ed. see Aristophanes.

Graves, Donald H., jt. ed. see De Vore, R. William.

Graves, Edgar B., ed. Bibliography of British History to Fourteen Eighty-Five, 2 vols. 2nd ed. 1080p. 1974. Set. 98.00x (ISBN 0-19-822391-9). Oxford U Pr.

Graves, Edward C. Our Search for Wilderness: The Story of a Sixty-Year Marriage. 224p. 1975. 8.00 o.p. (ISBN 0-682-48321-4, Lochinvar). Exposition.

Graves, F. Windows of Tarot. LC 73-85990. 1973. pap. 4.95 (ISBN 0-87100-027-X). Morgan.

Graves, Harold F. & Hoffman, L. Report Writing. 4th ed. 1965. text ed. 12.95 (ISBN 0-13-773671-1). P-H.

Graves, Harvey W. Nuclear Fuel Management. LC 78-19119. 1979. text ed. 28.95 (ISBN 0-471-03136-4). Wiley.

Graves, Herbert S., jt. auth. see Ficker, Victor.

Graves, Ian D. Enneagrams: A Game of Nine Letter-Words. (Oleander Games & Pastimes Ser.: Vol. 4). (Illus.). 64p. 1981. 9.95 (ISBN 0-900891-78-5); pap. 4.75 (ISBN 0-900891-79-3). Oleander Pr.

Graves, John. From a Limestone Ledge. LC 80-7641. (Illus.). 256p. 1980. 11.95 (ISBN 0-394-51238-3). Knopf.

--Goodbye to a River. LC 77-7198. (Illus.). 1977. pap. 4.95 (ISBN 0-8032-5876-3, BB 642, Bison). U of Nebr Pr.

--Hard Scrabble: Observations on a Patch of Land. 1976. autographed 6.95 o.p. (ISBN 0-685-77042-7). Encino Pr.

Graves, John, jt. auth. see Bones, Jim, Jr.

Graves, John, illus. Landscapes of Texas. LC 79-5274. (Louise Lindsey Merrick Texas Environment Ser.: No. 3). (Illus.). 162p. 1980. 24.95 (ISBN 0-89096-088-7). Tex A&M Univ Pr.

Graves, Joy D., jt. auth. see Franks, Margaret L.

Graves, Norman. Curriculum Planning in Geography. 1979. text ed. 29.95 (ISBN 0-435-35313-6); pap. text ed. 10.50 (ISBN 0-435-35312-8). Heinemann Ed.

Graves, Norman, ed. New Movements in the Study & Teaching of Geography. (Illus.). 248p. 1972. text ed. 11.75x (ISBN 0-685-30108-7). Humanities.

Graves, Oliver F., ed. see Pape, Ambrosius.

Graves, Perceval. A. E. Housman: The Scholar-Poet. 15.95 (ISBN 0-684-16106-0). Scribner.

Graves, Richard. Bushcraft: A Serious Guide to Survival & Camping. (Illus.). 1978. pap. 3.50 (ISBN 0-446-96807-2). Warner Bks.

--The Spiritual Quixote; or, the Summer's Ramble of Mr. Geoffrey Wildgoose, 1773, 3 vols. Shugrue, Michael F., ed. (The Flowering of the Novel 1740-1775 Ser: Vol. 102). 1974. Set. lib. bdg. 114.00 (ISBN 0-8240-1201-1); lib. bdg. 50.00 ea. Garland Pub.

Graves, Richard L. Rhetoric & Composition: A Sourcebook for Teachers. (English Language Ser). 1976. pap. text ed. 9.50x (ISBN 0-8104-5984-1). Hayden.

Graves, Richard P. Lawrence of Arabia & His World. LC 76-7183. (Encore Edition). (Illus.). 128p. 1976. 3.95 (ISBN 0-684-16543-0, ScribT). Scribner.

Graves, Robert. The Greek Myths. LC 55-8278. 1959. 10.00 o.p. (ISBN 0-8076-0054-7). Braziller.

--Poems, Nineteen Thirty-Three to Nineteen Forty-Five. 58p. 1946. 4.95 (ISBN 0-374-23472-8). FS&G.

--Poetic Unreason & Other Studies. LC 68-59244. 1968. Repr. of 1925 ed. 12.00x (ISBN 0-8196-0227-2). Biblo.

--The White Goddess: A Historical Grammar of Poetic Myth. rev. & enl. ed. 511p. 1966. pap. 7.95 (ISBN 0-374-50493-8, N295). FS&G.

Graves, Robert, tr. see Tranquillus, Gaius S.

Graves, W. Brooke, ed. see Pi Sigma Alpha Committee on Publications.

Graves, William H. Conference on Integration, Topology and Geometry in Linear Spaces: Proceedings, Vol. 2. LC 80-25417. (Contemporary Mathematics Ser.). 1980. 14.00 (ISBN 0-8218-5002-4). Am Math.

Graveson, R. H., ed. Law: An Outline for the Intending Student. (Outlines Ser). 1967. cased 15.00x (ISBN 0-7100-2999-3); pap. 8.95 (ISBN 0-7100-6028-9). Routledge & Kegan.

Gravie, Francisca, tr. see Von Albertini, Rudolf.

Grawoig, Dennis E. Decision Mathematics. (Accounting Ser.). 1967. text ed. 18.95 (ISBN 0-07-024177-5, C); solutions manual 3.00 (ISBN 0-07-024178-3). McGraw.

Grawoig, Dennis E. & Hubbard, Charles L. Strategic Financial Planning with Simulation. (Illus.). 1980. 35.00 (ISBN 0-89433-115-9). Petrocelli.

Grawoig, Dennis E., jt. auth. see Hughes, Ann J.

Grawoig, Dennis E., et al. Mathematics: A Foundation for Decisions. LC 75-12097. (Illus.). 542p. 1976. text ed. 18.95 (ISBN 0-201-02598-1); instr's guide 4.50 (ISBN 0-201-02595-7). A-W.

Gray. Calculus with Finite Mathematics for Social Science. 1972. 17.95 (ISBN 0-201-02573-6); instr's man. 2.00 (ISBN 0-201-02574-4). A-W.

Gray & Rees. Pediatric Anesthesia. 1981. text ed. price not set (ISBN 0-407-00114-X). Butterworths.

Gray, A. & Thompson, A. E. The Development of Economic Doctrine. 496p. 1980. pap. text ed. 17.95 (ISBN 0-582-44871-9). Longman.

Gray, A. H., jt. auth. see Markel, J. E.

Gray, A. William & Ulm, Otis M. Applications of College Mathematics. 1970. text ed. 11.95x (ISBN 0-02-474540-5, 47454). Macmillan.

--Mathematics for the College Student: Elementary Concepts. 2nd ed. LC 73-7359. 1975. text ed. 9.95x (ISBN 0-02-474700-9, 47470). Macmillan.

Gray, Al. Alegebra; Beginning: Syllabus. 2nd ed. 1976. pap. text ed. 6.90 (ISBN 0-89420-033-X, 367015); cassette recordings 164.00 (ISBN 0-89420-125-5, 367007). Natl Book.

Gray, Al & Matousek, Clifford H. General Mathematics: Syllabus. 2nd ed. 1972. pap. text ed. 5.75 (ISBN 0-89420-019-4, 350899); cassette recordings 102.55 (ISBN 0-89420-148-4, 350900). Natl Book.

Gray, Alice & Kasahara, Kunihiko. Magic of Origami. LC 77-74654. (Illus.). 1977. 12.50 (ISBN 0-87040-390-7). Japan Pubns.

Gray, Allan W., jt. auth. see Bryson, Carlton W.

Gray, Allan W., jt. auth. see Williams, Lloyd B.

Gray, Allan W., ed. see Brunelle, Wallace & O'Neill, Robert.

Gray, Andrew. Absolute Measurements in Electricity & Magnetism. 2nd ed. (Illus.). 1921. pap. text ed. 6.00 (ISBN 0-486-61787-4). Dover.

Gray, Angela. The Love of the Lion. 1980. pap. 2.50 (ISBN 0-671-41464-X). PB.

Gray, Asa, jt. auth. see Torrey, John.

Gray, B. F. Measurements, Instrumentation & Data Transmission. LC 76-49922. (Illus.). 1977. text ed. 13.50x (ISBN 0-582-41065-7); pap. text ed. 9.50x (ISBN 0-582-41066-5). Longman.

Gray, Basil. The World History of Rashid Al-Din. (Illus.). 1979. 42.00 (ISBN 0-571-10918-7, Pub. by Faber & Faber). Merrimack Bk Serv.

Gray, Betty, jt. auth. see Gray, William B.

Gray, Cecil. Forty-Eight Preludes & Fugues of J. S. Bach. (Music Reprint Ser.). 1979. Repr. of 1938 ed. 16.00 (ISBN 0-306-79559-0). Da Capo.

Gray, Charles. Explorations in Chemistry. (Illus.). (gr. 5 up). 1965. PLB 8.95 o.p. (ISBN 0-525-29433-3). Dutton.

Gray, Charles E., jt. auth. see Pierce, Walter D.

Gray, Charles H. & Bacharach, Alfred L., eds. Hormones in Blood, 2 Vols. 2nd ed. Vol. 1, 1967. 38.50 (ISBN 0-12-296101-3); Vol. 2, 1968. 42.00 (ISBN 0-12-296102-1). Acad Pr.

Gray, Charles M., ed. The Costs of Crime. LC 79-18871. (Sage Criminal Jusice System Annuals: Vol. 12). (Illus.). 1979. 20.00x (ISBN 0-8039-1198-X); pap. 9.95x (ISBN 0-8039-1199-8). Sage.

Gray, Colin S. The Soviet-American Arms Race. LC 75-28542. 208p. 1976. 23.95 (ISBN 0-685-67535-1, 00318-2, Pub. by Saxon Hse). Lexington Bks.

Gray, Daniel S. In the Words of Napoleon. LC 77-71468. 1977. pap. 8.50 (ISBN 0-916624-07-2). TSU Pr.

Gray, Donald J., ed. see Carroll, Lewis.

Gray, Donald P. A New Creation Story: The Creative Spirituality of Teilhard de Chardin. 1979. pap. 2.00 (ISBN 0-89012-014-5). Anima Pubns.

Gray, Dorothy, jt. auth. see Butler, Phyllis.

Gray, Douglas. Themes & Images in the Medieval English Religious Lyric. (Illus.). 1972. 23.00x (ISBN 0-7100-7253-8). Routledge & Kegan.

Gray, Eden. The Tarot Revealed: A Modern Guide to Reading the Tarot Cards. 239p. Date not set. pap. 1.75 o.p. (ISBN 0-451-09510-3, E9510, Sig). NAL.

Gray, Edwyn. Fighting Submarine. 192p. Date not set. pap. 2.25 (ISBN 0-523-41399-8). Pinnacle Bks.

Gray, Eileen. Everywoman's Guide to College. LC 75-10576. 1975. pap. 3.95 o.p. (ISBN 0-89087-903-6). Les Femmes Pub.

Gray, Ernest. Successful Business Resumes. 265p. 1981. 10.95 (ISBN 0-8436-0771-8). CBI Pub.

Gray, Farnum & Mager, George C. Liberating Education. LC 73-7240. 1973. 15.50x (ISBN 0-8211-0609-0); text ed. 14.00x (ISBN 0-685-42638-6). McCutchan.

Gray, Floyd, ed. Anthologie de la Poesie Francaise du Seizieme Siecle. LC 67-10343. (Fr.). 1977. 29.50x (ISBN 0-89197-026-6); pap. text ed. 18.95x (ISBN 0-89197-659-0). Irvington.

Gray, G. Buchanan. Isaiah: Chapters 1-39. (International Critical Commentary Ser.). 576p. 1912. text ed. 23.00x (ISBN 0-567-05015-7). Attic Pr.

--Numbers. LC 3-31887. (International Critical Commentary Ser.). 544p. 1930. text ed. 23.00x (ISBN 0-567-05002-5). Attic Pr.

Gray, G. Buchanan, jt. auth. see Driver, S. R.

Gray, G. W. & Winsor, P. A., eds. Liquid Crystals & Plastic Crystals, Vol. 1: Preparation, Constitution & Applications. LC 73-11504. (Illus.). 383p. 1974. 59.95 (ISBN 0-470-32339-6). Halsted Pr.

--Liquid Crystals & Plastic Crystals, Vol. 2: Physico-Chemical Properties & Methods of Investigation. LC 73-11505. (Illus.). 314p. 1974. 59.95 (ISBN 0-470-32340-X). Halsted Pr.

Gray, Gordon, jt. auth. see Linn, Jo W.

Gray, H. J. High Speed Digital Memories & Circuits. LC 75-14790. (University of Pennsylvania Advances in Modern Engineering Ser.: Vol.5). (Illus.). 151p. 1976. pap. text ed. 8.95 (ISBN 0-201-02579-5). A-W.

Gray, H. J., jt. ed. see Isaacs, A.

Gray, H. Peter. International Trade, Investment & Payments. LC 78-69573. (Illus.). 1979. text ed. 19.50 (ISBN 0-395-26659-9). HM.

Gray, Harold. Little Orphan Annie & Little Orphan Annie in Cosmic City. (Illus.). 1974. pap. 2.75 (ISBN 0-486-23107-0). Dover.

Gray, Henry L. & Odell, Patrick. Probability for Practicing Engineers. LC 78-109531. 1970. 11.95 (ISBN 0-389-00501-0); pap. 9.95 (ISBN 0-8436-0315-1). CBI Pub.

Gray, Howard L. English Field Systems. 1981. Repr. of 1915 ed. lib. bdg. 20.00x (ISBN 0-678-08069-0). Kelley.

Gray, Hugh, tr. & compiled by see Bazin, Andre.

Gray, Hugh, tr. see Bazin, Andre.

Gray, I. Engineer in Transition to Management. LC 78-61533. (IEEE Reprint Ser.). 1979. pap. 18.95 (ISBN 0-471-05212-4); pap. 12.50 (ISBN 0-471-05213-2, Pub. by Wiley-Interscience). Wiley.

Gray, Ilse. Designing & Making Dolls. LC 72-1449. (Illus.). 96p. 1972. 9.95 o.p. (ISBN 0-8230-2991-3). Watson-Guptill.

Gray, Irwin, et al. Product Liability: A Management Response. LC 75-1261. 256p. 1975. 14.95 (ISBN 0-8144-5373-2). Am Mgmt.

Gray, J. A. & Lovet, Mrs. Heather M. Take Care of Your Elderly Relative. (Illus., Orig.). 1980. 23.95 (ISBN 0-04-618015-X); pap. 13.50 (ISBN 0-04-618016-8). Allen Unwin.

Gray, J. H. China: A History of the Laws, Manners & Customs of the People, 2 vols. Gregor, W. G., ed. (Illus.). 800p. 1972. Repr. of 1878 ed. 70.00x (ISBN 0-7165-2030-3, Pub. by Irish Academic Pr Ireland). Biblio Dist.

Gray, J. Malcolm, jt. ed. see Rothwell, A. B.

Gray, J. Muir & Wilcock, Gordon. Our Elders. (Illus.). 224p. 1981. text ed. 19.95x (ISBN 0-19-217698-6); pap. text ed. 10.95x (ISBN 0-19-286012-7). Oxford U Pr.

Gray, J. S. The Ecology of Marine Sediments. (Cambridge Studies in Modern Biology: No. 2). (Illus.). 170p. Date not set. price not set (ISBN 0-521-23553-7); pap. price not set (ISBN 0-521-28027-3). Cambridge U Pr.

Gray, J. S., jt. auth. see McCulla, Dorothy.

Gray, Jack. Striker Schneiderman. LC 72-954459. 1973. pap. 2.50 (ISBN 0-8020-6172-9). U of Toronto Pr.
Gray, Jane. Medicine. LC 74-76181. (Professions Ser.). (Illus.). 168p. 1974. 11.95 (ISBN 0-7153-6623-8). David & Charles.
Gray, Jane, ed. see Biology Colloquium, 37th, Oregon State University, 1976.
Gray, Janet G. The French Huguenots. 200p. (Orig.). 1981. pap. 6.95 (ISBN 0-8010-3758-1). Baker Bk.
Gray, Jeffrey A. Ivan Pavlov. (Modern Masters Ser.). 1981. pap. 3.95. Penguin.
Gray, Jenny, ed. see Stevenson, Robert L.
Gray, Jeremy. Ideas of Space: Euclidean, Non-Euclidean & Relativistic. (Illus.). 1980. 28.50x (ISBN 0-19-853352-7). Oxford U Pr.
Gray, Jerry & Starke, Frederick. Readings in Organizational Behavior: Concepts and Applications. (Business Ser.). 1976. pap. text ed. 12.95 (ISBN 0-675-08522-5). Merrill.
Gray, Jerry L. & Starke, Frederick A. Organizational Behavior. 2nd ed. (Marketing & Management Ser.). 464p. 1980. text ed. 18.95 (ISBN 0-675-08141-6); instructor's manual 3.95 (ISBN 0-686-63343-1). Merrill.
Gray, Jerry L., ed. The Glacier Project: Concepts & Critiques-Selected Readings on the Glacier Theories of Organization & Management. LC 75-27252. (Illus.). 350p. 1976. 27.50x (ISBN 0-8448-0716-8). Crane-Russak Co.
Gray, John. The Biblical Doctrine of the Reign of God. 414p. Repr. of 1979 ed. text ed. 21.50x (ISBN 0-567-09300-X). Attic Pr.
Gray, John E., ed. see Atlantic Council Working Group on Nuclear Fuels Policy.
Gray, Kevin, jt. auth. see Pearl, David.
Gray, Laman A. Vaginal Hysterectomy: Indications, Technique & Complications. 2nd ed. (American Lectures in Gynecology & Obstetrics Ser.). (Illus.). 240p. 1963. 14.75 (ISBN 0-398-00721-7). C C Thomas.
Gray, Laman A., Sr. Endometrial Carcinoma & Its Treatment: The Role of Irradiation, Extent of Surgery & Approach to Chemotherapy. (Illus.). 240p. 1977. 29.75 (ISBN 0-398-03608-X). C C Thomas.
Gray, Lawrence, jt. ed. see Serfaty, Simon.
Gray, Lee L. How We Chose A President. 5th ed. 1980. 8.95 (ISBN 0-312-39411-X). St Martin.
Gray, Les. Happy Helper One-Two-Three. (Illus.). (ps-2). 1971. PLB 5.38 (ISBN 0-307-68926-3, Golden Pr). Western Pub.
Gray, Linda C. Satyr. LC 81-80085. 224p. (Orig.). 1981. pap. 2.50 (ISBN 0-87216-849-2). Playboy Pbks.
Gray, Madeline. The Changing Years: The Menopause Without Fear. rev. ed. LC 77-16917. 280p. 1981. 12.95 (ISBN 0-385-12635-2). Doubleday.
Gray, Malcom. The Fishing Industries of Scotland 1790-1914: A Study in Regional Adaptation. LC 78-40244. 1978. 26.00x (ISBN 0-19-714105-6). Oxford U Pr.
Gray, Margaret, ed. see Swami Sivananda Radha.
Gray, Marjorie. Soul-Winning Helps for Members of the Healing Profession. LC 75-18268. 1976. pap. 2.95 o.p. (ISBN 0-8163-0219-7, 19467-0). Pacific Pr Pub Assn.
Gray, Martin & Gallo, May. For Those I Loved. (RL 10). 1974. pap. 1.95 (ISBN 0-451-06942-0, J6942, Sig). NAL.
Gray, Mary Jane, jt. auth. see Burleigh, Robert.
Gray, Mary Jane, jt. auth. see Lutgendorf, Philip.
Gray, Mary W. Calculus with Finite Math for Social Sciences. LC 74-174335. 1972. text ed. 17.95 (ISBN 0-201-02573-6); instructor's manual 2.00 (ISBN 0-201-02574-4). A-W.
Gray, Mayo L. The Savage Season. 1978. pap. 1.95 o.p. (ISBN 0-449-14036-9, GM). Fawcett.
Gray, Muir & McKenzie, Heather. Take Care of Your Elderly Relative. 208p. 1980. 25.00x (Pub. by Beaconsfield England). State Mutual Bk.
Gray, Nicholas S. The Further Adventures of Puss in Boots. (Illus.). (ps-5). 1971. 3.95 o.p. (ISBN 0-571-09641-7, Pub. by Faber & Faber). Merrimack Bk Serv.
Gray, P. R., et al, eds. Analog MOS Integrated Circuits. LC 80-22116. 1980. 30.95 (ISBN 0-87942-141-X). Inst Electrical.
Gray, Paul. Analog MOS Integrated Circuits. 400p. 1980. 28.00 (ISBN 0-471-08966-4, Pub. by Wiley-Interscience); pap. 18.00 (ISBN 0-471-08964-8). Wiley.
Gray, Paul E. & Searle, Campbell L. Electronic Principles: Physics, Models & Circuits. LC 78-107884. 1969. text ed. 34.95x (ISBN 0-471-32398-5). Wiley.
Gray, Paul S. Unions & Leaders in Ghana: A Model of Labor & Development. LC 80-18482. 1981. 35.00 (ISBN 0-914970-57-7); pap. text ed. 17.50 (ISBN 0-914970-58-5). Conch Mag.
Gray, Paula G. Dramatics for the Elderly: A Guide for Directors of Dramatics Groups in Senior Centers & Residential Care Settings. LC 74-3185. 1974. pap. text ed. 3.50x (ISBN 0-8077-2400-9). Tchrs Coll.
Gray, Peter. Encyclopedia of the Biological Sciences. LC 80-28590. 1056p. 1981. Repr. lib. bdg. price not set (ISBN 0-89874-326-5). Krieger.
Gray, Peter, ed. A. I. B. S. Directory of Bioscience Departments & Facilities in the United States & Canada. 2nd ed. LC 75-33761. 1975. 43.50 (ISBN 0-12-786589-6). Acad Pr.
Gray, R. Brecht the Dramatist. LC 75-19575. 240p. 1976. 36.50 (ISBN 0-521-20937-4); pap. 10.50 (ISBN 0-521-29003-1). Cambridge U Pr.
--Christopher Wren & St. Paul's Cathedral. LC 77-94370. (Cambridge Introduction to the History of Mankind Ser.). (Illus.). (YA) 1980. pap. 3.95 (ISBN 0-521-21656-4). Cambridge U Pr.
--German Poetry: A Guide to Free Appreciation. rev. ed. LC 75-20834. 120p. 1976. 27.50 (ISBN 0-521-20931-5); pap. 8.95x (ISBN 0-521-29000-7). Cambridge U Pr.
--Ibsen: A Dissenting View. LC 77-5653. 1977. 28.50 (ISBN 0-521-21702-4). Cambridge U Pr.
Gray, Ralph & Peterson, John M. Economic Development of the United States. rev. ed. 1974. text ed. 15.95x o.p. (ISBN 0-256-01549-X). Irwin.
Gray, Ralph D., ed. The Hoosier State: A Documentary of Indiana, 2 vols. LC 80-12496. 448p. 1981. Vol. 1. pap. 14.95 (ISBN 0-8028-1842-0); Vol. 2. pap. 14.95 (ISBN 0-8028-1843-9). Eerdmans.
Gray, Robert. Rolls on the Rocks: The History of Rolls-Royce. (Illus.). 96p. 1971. 4.95 o.p. (ISBN 0-900193-01-8, Pub. by Compton Pr England). Motorbooks Intl.
Gray, Robert Emmert. The Bard's Theme. 1977. 5.00 o.p. (ISBN 0-682-48961-1). Exposition.
Gray, Robert M. & Davisson, Lee D., eds. Ergodic & Information Theory. (Benchmark Papers in Electrical Engineering & Computer Science: Vol. 19). 1977. 40.50 (ISBN 0-12-786590-X). Acad Pr.
Gray, Robert Q. The Labour Aristocracy in Victorian Edinburgh. (Illus.). 1976. text ed. 29.50x (ISBN 0-19-822442-7). Oxford U Pr.
Gray, Roland P., ed. Songs & Ballads of the Maine Lumberjacks. LC 73-75944. 1969. Repr. of 1924 ed. 15.00 (ISBN 0-8103-3835-1). Gale.
Gray, Ronald D. Francis Kafka. LC 72-83576. 192p. 1973. 36.00 (ISBN 0-521-20007-5); pap. 10.50x (ISBN 0-521-09747-9). Cambridge U Pr.
--German Tradition in Literature. LC 65-17206. 1966. 48.00 (ISBN 0-521-05133-9); pap. 17.50 (ISBN 0-521-29278-6). Cambridge U Pr.
--Goethe: A Critical Introduction. (Orig.). 44.50 (ISBN 0-521-05134-7); pap. text ed. 14.50x (ISBN 0-521-09404-6). Cambridge U Pr.
Gray, Ruth, jt. auth. see Rudy, Ellen.
Gray, Simon. Stage Struck. 64p. 1981. pap. 4.95 (ISBN 0-394-17882-3). Seaver Bks.
Gray, Stephen W. & Skandalakis, John E. Embryology for Surgeons. LC 72-126453. (Illus.). 1972. 44.00 (ISBN 0-7216-4220-9). Saunders.
Gray, Susan, jt. auth. see Morse, Dean.
Gray, Susan W., et al. Before First Grade: Training Project for Culturally Disadvantaged Children. LC 66-24872. (Orig.). 1966. pap. text ed. 4.95x (ISBN 0-8077-1464-X). Tchrs Coll.
Gray, T. C. & Nunn, J. General Anesthesia, 2 vols. 4th ed. Incl. Vol. 1. text ed. 94.95 (ISBN 0-407-00144-1); Vol. 2. text ed. 94.95 (ISBN 0-407-00145-X). LC 79-42889. (Illus.). 1979. Set. text ed. 189.00 (ISBN 0-407-00146-8). Butterworths.
Gray, T. G. & Postgate, J. R., eds. The Survival of Vegetative Microbes. LC 75-31399. (Society for General Microbiology Symposium: N0. 26). (Illus.). 450p. 1976. 57.50 (ISBN 0-521-21094-1). Cambridge U Pr.
Gray, T. R. & Williams, S. T. Soil Micro-Organisms. LC 75-9595. (Illus.). 240p. 1975. pap. text ed. 14.95x (ISBN 0-582-44160-9). Longman.
Gray, Tony. The Orange Order. 292p. 1974. 12.00 (ISBN 0-370-10371-8). Transatlantic.
Gray, Truman S. Applied Electronics. 2nd ed. (Illus.). 1954. 26.00x (ISBN 0-262-07002-2). MIT Pr.
Gray, Virginia & Williams, Bruce. The Organizational Politics of Criminal Justice: Policy in Context. LC 77-18590. 1980. 17.50x (ISBN 0-669-02108-3). Lexington Bks.
Gray, W. A. & Muller, R. Engineering Calculations in Radiative Heat Transfer. LC 73-17321. 176p. 1974. text ed. 29.00 (ISBN 0-08-017786-7); pap. text ed. 13.25 (ISBN 0-08-017787-5). Pergamon.
Gray, William A. & Gerrard, Brian A. Learning by Doing: Developing Teaching Skills. (Education Ser.). 1977. pap. text ed. 8.95 (ISBN 0-201-02547-7); instr's manual 2.75 (ISBN 0-201-02548-5). A-W.
Gray, William B. & Gray, Betty. Episcopal Church Welcomes You: An Introduction to Its History, Worship & Mission. LC 73-17898. 168p. 1974. 6.95 o.p. (ISBN 0-8164-0253-1); pap. 2.95 (ISBN 0-8164-2087-4). Crossroad NY.
Gray, William G. Magical Ritual Methods. pap. 6.95 (ISBN 0-87728-498-9). Weiser.
--An Outlook on Our Inner Western Way. 1980. pap. 6.95 (ISBN 0-87728-493-8). Weiser.
Gray, William R. Voyages to Paradise: In the Wake of Captain Cook, No. XV. LC 78-21187. (Illus.). 1981. 6.95 (ISBN 0-87044-284-8); lib. bdg. 8.50 (ISBN 0-87044-289-9). Natl Geog.
Gray, Wood, et al. Historian's Handbook: A Key to the Study & Writing of History. 2nd ed. (Orig.). 1964. pap. text ed. 3.95 (ISBN 0-395-04537-1, 3-19750). HM.
Graybar, Lloyd J. Albert Shaw of the Review of Reviews: An Intellectual Biography. LC 73-80464. (Illus.). 256p. 1974. 14.00x (ISBN 0-8131-1300-8). U Pr of Ky.
Graybill, F. A., jt. auth. see Krumbein, William C.
Graybill, Florence C. & Boesen, Victor. Edward Sheriff Curtis: Visions of a Vanishing Race. LC 76-16579. (Illus.). 1976. 35.00 o.s.i. (ISBN 0-690-01162-8, TYC-T). T Y Crowell.
Graybill, Florence C., jt. auth. see Boesen, Victor.
Graybill, Michael, jt. auth. see Johnson, David A.
Grayling, Tony. Introduction to Philosophical Logic. (Harvester Studies in Philosophy Ser.: No. 15). 1980. text ed. write for info. (ISBN 0-391-01791-8). Humanities.
Graymore, Clive N., ed. Biochemistry of the Retina. (Illus.). 1966. 23.50 (ISBN 0-12-297150-7). Acad Pr.
Grayson. Diseases of the Cornea. LC 79-16021. 1979. 79.50 (ISBN 0-8016-1964-5). Mosby.
Grayson, Benson L. The Unknown President: The Administration of President Millard Fillmore. LC 80-5962. 179p. 1981. lib. bdg. 17.75 (ISBN 0-8191-1456-1); pap. text ed. 8.75 (ISBN 0-8191-1457-X). U Pr of Amer.
Grayson, Cary T., Jr., jt. ed. see Lukowski, Susan.
Grayson, Cecil. The World of Dante: Essays on Dante & His Times. (Illus.). 204p. 1980. text ed. 36.00x. Oxford U Pr.
Grayson, Esther C., jt. auth. see Rockwell, F. F.
Grayson, George W. The Politics of Mexican Oil. LC 80-5253. (Pitt Latin American Ser.). (Illus.). 1981. 21.95 (ISBN 0-8229-3425-6); pap. 6.95 (ISBN 0-8229-5323-4). U of Pittsburgh Pr.
Grayson, H. W. The Theory of Relativity Revisited. 272p. 1978. 10.00 (ISBN 0-8059-2529-5). Dorrance.
Grayson, Henry, ed. Short-Term Approaches to Psychotheraphy, Vol. 3. LC 78-27605. (New Directions in Psychotherapy). 1979. 22.95 (ISBN 0-87705-345-6). Human Sci Pr.
Grayson, Jane. Nabokov Translated: A Comparison of Nabokov's Russian & English Prose. (Oxford Modern Languages & Literature Monographs). 1977. 36.00x (ISBN 0-19-815527-1). Oxford U Pr.
Grayson, Janet. Structure & Imagery in Ancrene Wisse. LC 73-77480. 256p. 1974. text ed. 15.00x (ISBN 0-87451-081-3). U Pr of New Eng.
Grayson, L. Library & Information Services to Local Government. 1979. pap. 12.50x (ISBN 0-85365-810-2, Pub. by Lib Assn England). Oryx Pr.
Grayson, L. E. European National Oil Companies. 256p. 1981. price not set (ISBN 0-471-27861-0, Wiley-Interscience). Wiley.
Grayson, Linda M. & Bliss, Michael, eds. Wretched of Canada: Letters to R. B. Bennett, 1930-35. LC 73-163838. (Social History of Canada Ser.). 199p. 1971. pap. 5.00 (ISBN 0-8020-6127-3). U of Toronto Pr.
Grayson, Martin & Griffith, Edward J. Topics in Phosphorus Chemistry, Vol. 10. 1980. 70.00 (ISBN 0-471-05890-4, Pub. by Wiley-Interscience). Wiley.
Grayson, Richard. Death of Abbe Didier. 180p. 1981. 9.95 (ISBN 0-312-18648-7). St Martin.
Grayson, Stan, ed. Ferrari. (Automobile Quarterly Lib.). (Illus.). 300p. 1975. 27.50 o.p. (ISBN 0-525-10445-3). Dutton.
Grayson, T. J., ed. see Ivanov, E. K.
Grazer, Frederick M. & Klingbeil, Jerome R. Body Image: A Surgical Perspective. LC 79-23858. 1979. text ed. 74.50 (ISBN 0-8016-1965-3). Mosby.
Graziani, Vicenzo G. De see De Graziani, Vincenzo G.
Graziano, Anthony M. Behavior Therapy with Children, Vol. 3. 1981. write for info. (ISBN 0-202-26087-9). Aldine Pub.
--Child Without Tomorrow. LC 73-3394. 1974. 23.00 (ISBN 0-08-017085-4). Pergamon.
Graziano, Anthony M., ed. Behavior Therapy with Children, Vol. 1. LC 79-80906. 1971. text ed. 27.95x (ISBN 0-202-26046-1). Aldine Pub.
--Behavior Therapy with Children, Vol. 2. LC 74-29461. 1975. lib. bdg. 28.95 (ISBN 0-202-26082-8). Aldine Pub.
Graziano, Frank & Follain, Jean. Follain Initiation. Feeney, Mary, tr. 1979. pap. 24.00x (ISBN 0-931460-07-7). Bieler.
Graziano, Frank, ed. Homage to Robert Penn Warren. 80p. (Orig.). 1981. price not set (ISBN 0-937406-12-0); pap. price not set (ISBN 0-937406-11-2); price not set limited ed. (ISBN 0-937406-13-9). Logbridge-Rhodes.
Grear, A. C. & Oxborough, J. Commercial Property Management. 1970. 24.00x o.p. (ISBN 0-8464-0258-0). Beekman Pubs.
Great Britain, Census Office. Abstract of the Answers & Returns: The Census Report for 1801, 2 vols. LC 79-366591. 1981. Repr. of 1802 ed. Set. lib. bdg. 90.00x (ISBN 0-678-05225-5). Vol. 1, Enumeration. Vol. 2, Parish Registers. Kelley.
Great Britain, Factories Inquiry Commission. First Report of the Central Board of His Majesty's Commissioners Appointed to Collect Information in the Manufacturing Districts: As to the Employment of Children in Factories. LC 71-367641. 1981. Repr. of 1833 ed. lib. bdg. 75.00x (ISBN 0-678-05226-3). Kelley.
Great Britain Historical Manuscripts Commission. Report on Manuscripts in Various Collections. Manuscripts of Captain H. V. Knox (from Vol. VI) Billias, George, ed. LC 72-8832. (American Revolutionary Ser.). Repr. of 1901 ed. lib. bdg. 18.00x (ISBN 0-8398-0804-6). Irvington.
Great Britain Historical Manuscripts Commission. Manuscripts of the Earl of Dartmouth, 3 vols. Billias, George, ed. LC 72-8795. (American Revolutionary Ser.). Repr. of 1896 ed. Set. lib. bdg. 85.00x (ISBN 0-8398-0802-X). Irvington.
--Report on American Manuscripts in the Royal Institution of Great Britain, 4 vols. Billias, George, ed. LC 72-8703. (American Revolutionary Ser.). 1979. Repr. of 1909 ed. Set. lib. bdg. 94.00x (ISBN 0-8398-0801-1). Irvington.
Great Britain, Parliament, House of Commons, Secret Committee on Joint Stock Banks. Report from the Secret Committee on Joint Stock Banks, 20 August 1836. LC 70-363560. 1981. Repr. of 1836 ed. lib. bdg. 25.00x (ISBN 0-678-05228-X). Kelley.
Great Britain, Parliament, House of Commons, Select Committee on Public Libraries. Report from the Select Committee on Public Libraries, 23 July 1849. LC 74-366370. 1981. Repr. of 1849 ed. lib. bdg. 27.50x (ISBN 0-678-05231-X). Kelley.
Great Britain, Parliament, House of Commons, Select Committee on the Health of Towns. Report from the Select Committee on the Health of Towns. LC 68-111978. 1981. Repr. of 1840 ed. lib. bdg. 25.00x (ISBN 0-678-05230-1). Kelley.
Great Britain, Parliament, House of Commons. Report from the Select Committee to Whom the Several Petitions Complaining of the Distressed State of the Agriculture in the United Kingdom Were Referred, 18 June 1821. LC 68-112457. 1981. Repr. of 1821 ed. lib. bdg. 35.00x (ISBN 0-678-05227-1). Kelley.
Great Britain, Parliament, House of Commons, Select Committee on Artizans & Machinery. Six Reports from the Select Committee on Artizans & Machinery, 23 February - 21 May 1824. LC 68-110405. 1981. Repr. of 1824 ed. lib. bdg. 45.00x (ISBN 0-678-05229-8). Kelley.
Great Britain, Royal Commission on Capital Punishment, 1949-1953. Report: Presented to Parliament by Command of Her Majesty, Sept, 1953. LC 79-25707. 505p. 1980. Repr. of 1953 ed. lib. bdg. 35.00x (ISBN 0-313-22121-9, GBCP). Greenwood.
Greater London Council. Survey of London. Incl. Vol. 31-32. St. James, Westminister, Pt. 2. text ed. 47.50x (ISBN 0-485-41831-2); Vol. 33-34. St. Anne, Soho. text ed. 53.75x (ISBN 0-485-48233-9); Vol. 35. Theatre Royal, Drury Lane, & the Royal Opera House, Covent Garden. text ed. o.p. (ISBN 0-485-48235-5); Vol. 36. St. Paul, Covent Garden. text ed. 75.00x (ISBN 0-485-48236-3); Vol. 37. Northern Kensington. text ed. 46.25x (ISBN 0-485-48237-1). Athlone Pr). Humanities.
--Survey of London, Vol. 38: The Museum Area of South Kensington & Westminster. (Illus.). 480p. 1975. text ed. 80.00x (ISBN 0-485-48238-X, Athlone Pr). Humanities.
--Survey of London, Vol. 39: The Grosvenor Estate in Mayfair, Part. 1, General History. (Survey of London Ser.). 1977. text ed. 75.00x (ISBN 0-485-48239-8, Athlone Pr). Humanities.

Greater Portland Landmarks Research Committee, ed. Researching the Old House. (Illus.). 70p. 1980. price not set o.p. (ISBN 0-9600612-9-0). Greater Portland.

Greaves, A. A. Maurice Barres. (World Authors Ser.: No. 454). 1978. lib. bdg. 12.50 (ISBN 0-8057-6291-4). Twayne.

Greaves, C. Desmond. Sean O'Casey: Politics & Art. 1980. text ed. 18.25x (ISBN 0-391-01023-9). Humanities.

Greaves, Griselda, ed. Burning Thorn. (gr. 7 up). 1971. 5.95 o.s.i. (ISBN 0-02-736740-1). Macmillan.

Greaves, Margaret. Cat's Magic. LC 80-8451. 192p. (gr. 5 up). 1981. 8.95 (ISBN 0-06-022122-4, HarpJ); PLB 8.79g (ISBN 0-06-022123-2). Har-Row.

Greaves, Richard. The Puritan Revolution & Education Thought: Background for Reform. 1970. 13.00 (ISBN 0-8135-0616-6). Rutgers U Pr.

Greaves, Richard L. Society & Religion in Elizabethan England. 832p. 1981. 32.50x (ISBN 0-8166-1030-4). U of Minn Pr.

--Theology & Revolution in the Scottish Reformation. 336p. 1980. pap. 10.95 (ISBN 0-8028-1847-1, Chr Univ Pr). Eerdmans.

Greaves, Roger, tr. see Grendel, Frederick.

Grebanier, Bernard. English Literature, 2 Vols. (Orig.). (gr. 9 up). text ed. 7.00 ea. Vol. 1 1959 (ISBN 0-8120-5037-1). Vol. 2 1948. Vol. 1. pap. 3.95 (ISBN 0-8120-0065-X); Vol. 2. pap. 4.50 (ISBN 0-8120-0066-8). Barron.

--Playwriting. (Apollo Eds.). pap. 4.95 o.s.i. (ISBN 0-8152-0111-7, A111, TYC-T). T Y Crowell.

--Truth About Shylock: The Jew of Venice Revisited. 1962. 8.95 o.p. (ISBN 0-394-44978-9). Random.

Grebel, Rosemary & Pogrund, Phyllis. Becoming a Driver. new ed. Katz, Elaine, ed. (Survival Guides Ser.). (Illus.). 64p. (Orig.). (gr. 7 up). 1980. pap. text ed. 2.85 (ISBN 0-915510-43-X). Janus Bks.

Greben, Stanley E., et al, eds. A Method of Psychiatry. LC 80-10348. (Illus.). 375p. 1980. text ed. 20.00 (ISBN 0-8121-0710-1). Lea & Febiger.

Grebene, A. B. Analog Integrated Circuits. (IEEE Reprint Ser.). 1978. 28.95 (ISBN 0-471-05210-8, Pub. by Wiley-Interscience); pap. 19.00x (ISBN 0-686-67364-6). Wiley.

Grebler, L., jt. auth. see Burns, L. S.

Grebler, Leo & Mittelbach, Frank G. The Inflation of House Prices: Its Extent, Causes & Consequences. LC 78-20272. (Special Ser. in Real Estate & Urban Land Economics). 1979. 25.95 (ISBN 0-669-02708-1). Lexington Bks.

Grebler, Leo, et al. Mexican American People: The Nation's Second Largest Minority. LC 73-81931. 1970. 30.00 (ISBN 0-02-912800-5). Free Pr.

Grebstein, Sheldon N. Sinclair Lewis. (U. S. Authors Ser.: No. 14). lib. bdg. 9.95 (ISBN 0-8057-0448-5). Twayne.

Greco, Ben. How to Get the Job That's Right for You: A Career Guide for the 80's. rev. ed. LC 79-56085. 210p. (Orig.). 1981. pap. 6.95 (ISBN 0-87094-194-1). Dow Jones-Irwin.

Greco, F. Anthony, et al. Small Cell Lung Cancer. (Clinical Oncolgy Monograph). 1981. write for info. (ISBN 0-8089-1345-X). Grune.

Greco, Marshall C. Group Life: The Nature & Treatment of Its Specific Conflicts. 357p. 1980. Repr. of 1950 ed. lib. bdg. 35.00 (ISBN 0-89984-229-1). Century Bookbindery.

Gree & Camps. La Pandilla En el Zoo. 1980. 8.95 (ISBN 0-88332-253-6). Larousse.

--La Pandilla En la Carretera. 1980. 8.95 (ISBN 0-686-69157-1). Larousse.

Gree, Alain. Les Farfeluches aiment les Animaux-Love the Animals. (Illus., Fr.). 1980. 8.95 (ISBN 2-203-12313-3). Larousse.

--Les Farfeluches font des achats. (Illus., Fr.). (gr. k-3). 1979. 8.95 (ISBN 0-88332-114-9). Larousse.

Gree, Alain & Camps, Luis. Les Farfeluches a la campagne. (Illus.). 1973. 8.95 (ISBN 0-88332-234-X, 2914). Larousse.

--Les Farfeluches a la maison. (Illus.). 1973. 8.95 (ISBN 0-88332-235-8, 2915). Larousse.

--Les Farfeluches a l'ecole. (Illus.). 1973. 8.95 (ISBN 0-88332-236-6, 2907). Larousse.

--Les Farfeluches au bord de la mer. (Illus.). 1973. 8.95 (ISBN 0-88332-237-4, 2913). Larousse.

--Les Farfeluches au cirque. (Illus.). 1973. 8.95 (ISBN 0-88332-238-2, 2916). Larousse.

--Les Farfeluches au marche. (Illus.). 1973. 8.95 (ISBN 0-88332-239-0, 2909). Larousse.

--Les Farfeluches prennent le train. (Illus.). 1973. 8.95 (ISBN 0-88332-242-0, 2918). Larousse.

--Les Farfeluches sur la route. (Illus.). 1973. 8.95 (ISBN 0-88332-243-9, 2917). Larousse.

--La Pandilla En el Circo. (Illus., Span.). (gr. 3). 1979. 8.95 (ISBN 0-88332-112-2). Larousse.

--La Pandilla Va a las Tiendas. (Illus., Span.). (gr. 2). 1979. 8.95 (ISBN 0-88332-111-4). Larousse.

Greeley, A. M. Ethnicity. (Concilium Ser.: Vol. 101). 1977. pap. 4.95 (ISBN 0-8164-2145-5). Crossroad NY.

--May the Wind Be at Your Back: The Prayer of St. Patrick. (Orig.). 1976. pap. 4.95 (ISBN 0-8164-2595-7). Crossroad NY.

Greeley, Andrew. The Cardinal Sins. (Orig.). 1981. 12.95 (ISBN 0-446-51236-2). Warner Bks.

--Death & Beyond. 1976. pap. 5.95 (ISBN 0-88347-062-4). Thomas More.

--Young Catholic Family. (Illus.). 1980. pap. 12.95 (ISBN 0-88347-122-1). Thomas More.

Greeley, Andrew & McCready, William C. Ethnic Drinking Subcultures. LC 79-13904. 144p. 1980. 18.95 (ISBN 0-03-052731-7). Praeger.

Greeley, Andrew, jt. auth. see Baum, Gregory.

Greeley, Andrew & Baum, Gregory, eds. The Persistence of Religion. (Concilium Ser.: Religion in the Seventies: Vol. 81). 156p. 1973. pap. 4.95 (ISBN 0-8164-2537-X). Crossroad NY.

Greeley, Andrew, jt. ed. see Baum, Gregory.

Greeley, Andrew M. The Communal Catholic: A Personal Manifesto. 220p. 1976. 8.95 (ISBN 0-8164-0299-X). Crossroad NY.

--The Devil, You Say: Man & His Personal Devils & Angels. 200p. 1975. pap. 1.45 o.p. (ISBN 0-385-12069-9, Im). Doubleday.

--Ethnicity in the United States: A Preliminary Reconnaissance. LC 74-11483. (Urban Research Ser). 384p. 1974. 23.95 (ISBN 0-471-32465-5, Pub. by Wiley-Interscience). Wiley.

--Friendship Game. LC 79-117979. 1971. pap. 1.95 (ISBN 0-385-04230-2, Im). Doubleday.

--The Great Mysteries: An Essential Catechism. (Orig.). 1976. 8.95x (ISBN 0-8164-0309-0); pap. 3.95x (ISBN 0-8164-2128-5). Crossroad NY.

--Life for a Wanderer: A New Look at Christian Spirituality. LC 70-78701. 1971. pap. 1.45 (ISBN 0-385-02961-6, Im). Doubleday.

--Love & Play. LC 77-5798. (Orig.). 1977. pap. 3.95 (ISBN 0-8164-1222-7). Crossroad NY.

--The Mary Myth: On the Femininity of God. 1977. 12.95 (ISBN 0-8164-0333-3). Crossroad NY.

--Sexual Intimacy. 199p. 1975. pap. 3.95 (ISBN 0-8164-2591-4). Crossroad NY.

--The Sinai Myth. LC 72-79390. 200p. 1975. pap. 2.45 (ISBN 0-385-08824-8, Im). Doubleday.

--Why Can't They Be Like Us? Facts & Fallacies About Ethnic Differences & Group Conflicts in America. LC 73-81091. (Institute of Human Relations Press Paperback Ser). x, 76p. (Orig.). 1980. pap. 1.50 (ISBN 0-87495-009-0). Am Jewish Comm.

Greeley, Andrew M., jt. auth. see McCready, William C.

Greeley, Andrew M., ed. The Family - in Crisis or in Transition. (Concilium: Vol. 121). (Orig.). 1979. pap. 4.95 (ISBN 0-8164-2201-X). Crossroad NY.

Greeley, Andrew M., et al. Catholic Schools in a Declining Church. (Illus.). 488p. 1975. 15.00 o.p. (ISBN 0-8362-0648-7). Andrews & McMeel.

Greeley, Horace. Essays Designed to Elucidate the Science of Political Economy, While Serving to Explain & Defend the Policy of Protection to Home Industry, As a System of National Cooperation for the Elevation of Labor. (The Neglected American Economists Ser.). 1974. lib. bdg. 50.00 (ISBN 0-8240-1006-X). Garland Pub.

Greeley, Horace, ed. The American Laborer, Devoted to the Cause of Protection to Home Industry, Embracing the Arguments, Reports & Speeches of the Ablest Civilians of the United States in Favor of the Policy of Protection to American Labor. (The Neglected American Economists Ser.). 1974. lib. bdg. 50.00 (ISBN 0-8240-1005-1). Garland Pub.

--The Great Industries of the United States: Being an Historical Summary of the Origin, Growth, & Perfection of the Chief Industrial Arts of This Country, 2 vols. (The Neglected American Economists Ser.). 1974. Set. lib. bdg. 76.00 (ISBN 0-8240-1007-8); lib. bdg. 50.00 ea. Garland Pub.

Greeley, R., jt. auth. see Guest, J. E.

Greeley, R. G., jt. auth. see Piermattei, D. L.

Greeley, Richard S., et al. Solar Heating & Cooling of Buildings. 1981. 47.50 (ISBN 0-250-40353-6). Ann Arbor Science.

Greelis, Michael T. & Haarmann, Betsy S. ABC's of Video Therapy. (Illus.). 96p. 1980. pap. text ed. 7.00 (ISBN 0-87879-243-0). Acad Therapy.

Green & Morphet. Research & Technology As Economic Activities. (Sicon Bks.). 1977. 3.95 (ISBN 0-408-71300-3). Butterworths.

Green, jt. auth. see Weiner.

Green, A. E. & Bourne, A. J. Reliability Technology. LC 73-161691. 400p. 1972. 79.25 (ISBN 0-471-32480-9, Pub. by Wiley-Interscience). Wiley.

Green, A. E., ed. Coal Burning Issues. LC 79-25376. (Illus.). x, 390p. (Orig.). 1980. pap. 10.00 (ISBN 0-8130-0667-8). U Presses Fla.

Green, A. Wigfall. Sir Francis Bacon. (English Authors Ser.: No. 40). 1966. lib. bdg. 10.95 (ISBN 0-8057-1016-7). Twayne.

Green, Alan, jt. auth. see Green, Barry.

Green, Albert E. & Zerna, Wolfgang. Theoretical Elasticity. 2nd ed. 1968. 55.00x (ISBN 0-19-853329-2). Oxford U Pr.

Green, Andre. The Tragic Effect. Sheridan, Alan, tr. LC 76-12629. 1979. 28.50 (ISBN 0-521-21377-0). Cambridge U Pr.

Green, Anna K. Circular Study. 1976. lib. bdg. 12.95x (ISBN 0-89968-170-0). Lightyear.

--The Leavenworth Case. 1976. lib. bdg. 12.95x (ISBN 0-89968-171-9). Lightyear.

Green, Anthony, jt. auth. see Sharp, Rachel.

Green, Arthur. Tormented Master: A Life of Rabbi Nahman of Bratslav. LC 80-14668. 408p. 1981. pap. 11.95 (ISBN 0-8052-0663-9). Schocken.

Green, B. S. & Johns, E. A. An Introduction to Sociology. 1966. 11.25 (ISBN 0-08-012155-1); pap. 6.25 (ISBN 0-08-012154-3). Pergamon.

Green, Barry & Green, Alan. The Directory of Athletic Scholarships: Where They Are & How to Get Them. 312p. 1981. 14.95 (ISBN 0-399-12620-1, Perigee); pap. 6.95 (ISBN 0-399-50533-4). Putnam.

Green, Benjamin. The Basic Guide to Pictorial Perspective. (A Promotion of the Arts Library Book). (Illus.). 97p. 1981. 27.75 (ISBN 0-86650-001-4). Gloucester Art.

Green, Benny. Shaw's Champions: G. B. S. & Prize Fighting from Cashel Byron to Gene Tunney. (Illus.). 1978. 19.95 (ISBN 0-241-89735-1, Pub. by Hamish Hamilton England). David & Charles.

Green, Bernard & Schwarz, Ted. Goodbye Blues. 224p. 1981. 10.95 (ISBN 0-07-024337-9, GB). McGraw.

Green, Bette. Summer of My German Soldier. 208p. 1981. pap. 2.25 (ISBN 0-553-14687-4). Bantam.

Green, Bill. Welcome to the Tax Revolt. (Illus.). 192p. 1981. 11.95 (ISBN 0-936602-10-4). Harbor Pub CA.

Green, Bob, jt. auth. see Bryant, Anita.

Green, C. & Bourgue, R. Theory & Servicing of AM, FM & FM Stereo Receivers. 1980. 25.95 (ISBN 0-13-913590-1). P-H.

Green, C. J., et al, eds. Airframe & Systems Fitting. 2nd ed. (Engineering Craftsmen: No. H9). (Illus.). 1973. spiral bdg. 14.95x (ISBN 0-85083-218-7). Intl Ideas.

Green, Carl R., jt. auth. see Sanford, William R.

Green, Christopher. Leger & the Avant-Garde. LC 75-11499. 1976. 40.00x (ISBN 0-300-01800-2). Yale U Pr.

--Negative Taxes & the Poverty Problem. (Studies of Government Finance). 1967. 11.95 (ISBN 0-8157-3264-3); pap. 4.95 (ISBN 0-8157-3263-5). Brookings.

Green, Cliff. Marion. (Australian Theatre Workshop Ser.). 1974. pap. text ed. 6.95x (ISBN 0-686-65322-X, 00526). Heinemann Ed.

Green, Clifford J. The Sociality of Christ & Humanity: Dietrich Bonhoeffer's Early Theology, 1927-1933. LC 75-33816. (American Academy of Religion. Dissertation Ser.). 1975. pap. 9.00 (ISBN 0-89130-055-4, 010106). Scholars Pr Ca.

Green, Constance M. Washington: a History of the Capital. 1976. pap. 7.50 (ISBN 0-691-00585-0). Princeton U Pr.

Green, D. H. Irony in the Medieval Romance. LC 78-14930. 1979. 69.00 (ISBN 0-521-22458-6). Cambridge U Pr.

Green, David. Fabric Printing & Dyeing. (Illus.). (gr. 7 up). 1972. 12.00 (ISBN 0-8231-7025-X). Branford.

--The Irish Language: Great Languages. 1980. text ed. write for info. (ISBN 0-391-01135-9). Humanities.

--Pottery: Materials & Techniques. 1967. 13.95 (ISBN 0-571-08080-4, Pub. by Faber & Faber). Merrimack Bk Serv.

--Understanding Pottery Glazes. 1963. 11.95 (ISBN 0-571-06987-8, Pub. by Faber & Faber). Merrimack Bk Serv.

Green, David & Ashburner, Jenni. Dyes from the Kitchen. 1979. 17.95 (ISBN 0-7134-1565-7, Pub. by Batsford England). David & Charles.

Green, David, jt. auth. see Butler, Anne.

Green, David, ed. Hemophilia: A Manual of Outpatient Management. (Illus.). 132p. 1973. 12.75 (ISBN 0-398-02853-2). C C Thomas.

Green, David C. Julius Caesar & It's Sources. (Salzburg Institute for English Literature Jacobean Drama Studies: No. 86). (Orig.). 1980. pap. text ed. 25.00x (ISBN 0-391-01715-2). Humanities.

Green, David E. & Baum, Harold. Energy & the Mitochondrion. 1970. 12.95 (ISBN 0-12-297950-8). Acad Pr.

Green, David E., tr. see Becker, Joachim.

Green, David E., tr. see Hahn, Ferdinand.

Green, David E., tr. see Schweizer, Eduard.

Green, David E., tr. see Westermann, Claus.

Green, David G. Plutarch Revisited. A Study of Shakespeare's Last Roman Tragedies & Their Source. (SSEL Jacobean Drama Studies: No. 78). (Orig.). pap. text ed. 25.00x (ISBN 0-391-01608-3). Humanities.

--Power & Party in an English City. (New Local Government Ser.: No. 20). 256p. 1981. text ed. 37.50x (ISBN 0-04-352094-4, 2548). Allen Unwin.

Green, Dennis H. Carolingian Lord. 1965. 90.00 (ISBN 0-521-05138-X). Cambridge U Pr.

--Millstatter Exodus: A Crusading Epic. 1966. 78.00 (ISBN 0-521-05139-8). Cambridge U Pr.

Green, Donald. Mirror, Mirror. 192p. 1980. 17.95 (ISBN 0-241-10248-0, Pub. by Hamish Hamilton England). David & Charles.

Green, Earl L. Genetics & Probability. (Illus.). 1981. text ed. 29.50x (ISBN 0-19-520159-0). Oxford U Pr.

Green, Edward. Judicial Attitudes in Sentencing. LC 74-17589. (Cambridge Studies in Criminology: Vol. 15). 149p. 1975. Repr. of 1961 ed. lib. bdg. 15.00x (ISBN 0-8371-7834-7, GRJA). Greenwood.

Green, Edward J. Psychology for Law Enforcement. LC 75-15634. 167p. 1976. text ed. 13.95 o.p. (ISBN 0-471-32474-4); pap. text ed. 9.95 (ISBN 0-471-32475-2). Wiley.

Green, Elizabeth & Malko, Nicolai. The Conductor & His Score. LC 74-13718. (Illus.). 208p. 1975. 13.95 (ISBN 0-13-167312-2). P-H.

Green, Elizabeth A. The Modern Conductor. 3rd ed. (Illus.). 288p. 1981. text ed. 18.95 (ISBN 0-13-590216-9). P-H.

Green, Elizabeth B., jt. auth. see Bittinger, Morton N.

Green, Elton. Tuscarora Language. 1969. 4.95 (ISBN 0-930230-27-2). Johnson NC.

Green, Ely. Ely: Too Black, Too White. abr. ed. Chitty, Arthur & Chitty, Elizabeth, eds. (RL 10). 1971. pap. 1.95 o.p. (ISBN 0-451-61075-X, MJ1075, Ment). NAL.

Green, Eric. Don't Speak Now. 121p. 1981. 6.95 (ISBN 0-533-04650-5). Vantage.

Green, Eric F., et al. Profitable Food & Beverage Management: Planning. 1978. text ed. 17.95x (ISBN 0-8104-9480-9). Hayden.

--Profitable Food & Beverage Management: Operations. 1978. text ed. 19.95 (ISBN 0-8104-9466-3). Hayden.

Green, Fletcher. The Role of the Yankee in the Old South. LC 68-54086. (Mercer University Lamar Lecture Ser: No. 11). 156p. 1972. 9.95x (ISBN 0-8203-0233-3). U of Ga Pr.

Green, Fletcher M. & Copeland, J. Isaac, eds. The Old South. LC 79-55730. (Goldentree Bibliographies in American History Ser.). 1980. text ed. 16.95 (ISBN 0-88295-539-X); pap. text ed. 12.95x (ISBN 0-88295-580-2). AHM Pub.

Green, Fletcher M., ed. see Smedes, Susan D.

Green, Floyd & Meyer, Susan E. You Can Renovate Your Own Home: A Step-by-Step Guide to Major Interior Improvements. (Illus.). 304p. 1980. pap. 8.95 (ISBN 0-385-17006-8, Dolp). Doubleday.

Green, Francis & Nore, Petter, eds. Economics: An Anti Text. 1977. text ed. 20.75x (ISBN 0-333-21201-0); pap. text ed. 7.75x (ISBN 0-333-21202-9). Humanities.

--Issues in Political Economy: A Critical Approach. 294p. 1980. text ed. 31.25x (ISBN 0-333-25376-0). Humanities.

Green, G. D., ed. Assessment & Performance of Implanted Cardiac Pacemakers. 1975. 35.95 (ISBN 0-407-00015-1). Butterworths.

Green, G. D., tr. see Fichte, J. G.

Green, George. Mathematical Papers. LC 70-92316. 15.00 o.p. (ISBN 0-8284-0229-9). Chelsea Pub.

Green, George, jt. auth. see Mooney, Sean.

Green, Gerald. The Chains. 528p. 1981. pap. 3.50 (ISBN 0-553-13419-1). Bantam.

--The Last Angry Man. 1980. pap. 3.50 (ISBN 0-425-04993-0). Berkley Pub.

--The Lotus Eaters. 1980. pap. 2.95 (ISBN 0-425-04571-4). Berkley Pub.

--Murphy's Men. LC 80-52409. 352p. 1981. 12.95 (ISBN 0-87223-662-5). Seaview Bks.

Green, Gion & Farber, Raymond C. Introduction to Security. 2nd ed. LC 78-7318. 1978. 15.95 (ISBN 0-913708-31-3). Butterworths.

--Introduction to Security: Principles & Practices. 3rd ed. 1981. text ed. 17.95 (ISBN 0-409-95036-X). Butterworth.

Green, Gordon. Read, Think & Answer. 1969. tchrs ed. 2.50x (ISBN 0-19-432771-X). Oxford U Pr.

Green, H. Benedict. The Gospel According to Matthew in the Revised Standard Version. (New Clarendon Bible Ser). 314p. 1975. 15.50x o.p. (ISBN 0-19-836918-2); pap. 7.95 (ISBN 0-19-836911-5). Oxford U Pr.

Green, Harry L. Echoes of Thunder. LC 80-66322. 167p. 1980. 10.95 (ISBN 0-936958-00-6); pap. 5.95 (ISBN 0-936958-01-4). Emerald Hse.

Green, Henry. Back. 256p. 1981. pap. 5.95 (ISBN 0-8112-0798-6, NDP517). New Directions.

--Nothing-Doting-Blindness. 1980. pap. 6.95 (ISBN 0-14-005664-5). Penguin.
Green, Hollis. Why Churches Die. 224p. (Orig.). 1972. pap. 3.95 (ISBN 0-87123-642-7, 210642). Bethany Fell.
Green, I. M. The Re-Establishment of the Church of England, 1660-1663. (Oxford Historical Monographs). 1978. 33.00x (ISBN 0-19-821867-2). Oxford U Pr.
Green, Ira, et al, eds. Mechanisms of Tumor Immunity. LC 76-48047. (Basic & Clinical Immunology Ser.). 1977. 45.00 (ISBN 0-471-32481-7, Pub. by Wiley Medical). Wiley.
Green, J. see Barnes, R. S.
Green, J., jt. ed. see Dumont, H. J.
Green, J. A. Polynomial Representations of GLN. (Lecture Notes in Mathematics: Vol. 830). 118p. 1981. pap. 9.80 (ISBN 0-387-10258-2). Springer-Verlag.
--Sets & Groups. (Library of Mathematics). 1971. pap. 5.00 (ISBN 0-7100-4356-2). Routledge & Kegan.
Green, J. H. Basic Clinical Physiology. 3rd ed. (Illus.). 1979. pap. text ed. 10.95x (ISBN 0-19-263331-7). Oxford U Pr.
Green, J. H. & Silver, P. H. An Introduction to Human Anatomy. (Illus.). 400p. 1981. pap. text ed. 16.95x (ISBN 0-19-261196-8). Oxford U Pr.
Green, J. Keith & Perkins, Philip H. Concrete Liquid Retaining Structures. (Illus.). 1979. 55.00x (ISBN 0-85334-856-1, Pub. by Applied Science). Burgess-Intl Ideas.
Green, J. R., jt. ed. see Thompson, Richard A.
Green, Janet C. & Janssen, Robert B. Minnesota Birds: Where, When, & How Many. LC 74-16980. (Illus.). 1980. pap. 6.95 (ISBN 0-8166-0959-4). U of Minn Pr.
Green, John A., tr. see Pestalozzi, Johann H.
Green, John H. An Introduction to Human Physiology. 4th ed. (Illus.). 1976. pap. text ed. 16.50x (ISBN 0-19-263328-7). Oxford U Pr.
--Speak to Me. LC 62-14943. (Orig.). 1962. pap. 3.95 (ISBN 0-672-63116-4). Odyssey Pr.
Green, John H. & Kramer, Amihud. Food Processing Waste Management. (Illus.). 1979. text ed. 39.00 (ISBN 0-87055-331-3). AVI.
Green, John L. Pioneer Evangelists of the Church of God in the Pacific Northwest. 164p. pap. 2.00. Faith Pub Hse.
Green, John R. Short History of the English People, 2 Vols. 1960. Vol. 1. 21.00x (ISBN 0-460-00727-0, Evman); Vol. 2. 5.00x (ISBN 0-460-00728-9). Dutton.
Green, John R., jt. ed. see Thompson, Richard A.
Green, Joseph, tr. see Guareschi, Giovanni.
Green, Judith. Winners. 240p. 1981. pap. 2.75. Ballantine.
Green, Judith & Wallat, Cynthia, eds. Ethnography & Language in Educational Settings, Vol. 5. (Advances in Discourse Processes Ser.). 368p. 1980. text ed. 29.50 (ISBN 0-89391-035-X). Ablex Pub.
Green, Judith A. The Man Who Stopped Time. (Adult Learner Ser.). (Illus.). 189p. (Orig.). 1979. pap. text ed. 3.60x (ISBN 0-89061-173-4, 201). Jamestown Pubs.
--The Man with the Scar. (Adult Learner Ser.). (Illus.). 203p. (Orig.). 1979. pap. text ed. 3.60x (ISBN 0-89061-153-X, 202). Jamestown Pubs.
--Murder by Radio. (Adult Learner Ser.). (Illus.). 191p. (Orig.). 1979. pap. text ed. 3.60x (ISBN 0-89061-152-1, 200). Jamestown Pubs.
Green, Julien. Memories of Evil Days. Piriou, Jean-Pierre J., ed. LC 75-44037. 200p. 1976. 13.95x (ISBN 0-8139-0553-2). U Pr of Va.
Green, Justin J., jt. ed. see Chipp, Sylvia A.
Green, K. Family Life Education: Focus on Student Involvement. LC 75-4098. 1975. pap. 4.00 (ISBN 0-686-14989-0, 261-08420). Home Econ Educ.
Green, K. & Coombs, Rod. The Effects of Microelectronic Technologies on Employment Prospects. 240p. 1980. text ed. 36.75x (ISBN 0-566-00418-6, Pub. by Gower Pub Co England). Renouf.
Green, Karen. Winner's: Recipes That Won the Contests & How You Can Be a Winner Too! LC 79-24003. 256p. 1980. 12.95 (ISBN 0-688-03566-3). Morrow.
Green, Karen & Black, Betty. How to Cook His Goose. 1977. pap. 6.95 (ISBN 0-87691-229-3). Winchester Pr.
--How to Cook His Goose: And Other Wild Games. 1973. 8.95 (ISBN 0-87691-106-8). Winchester Pr.
Green, Kathleen. Leprechaun Tales. LC 68-10771. (Illus.). (gr. 4-7). 1968. 4.50 o.p. (ISBN 0-397-31025-0). Lippincott.
Green, L. F., ed. Developments in Soft Drinks Technology, Vol. 1. (Illus.). 1978. text ed. 51.30x (ISBN 0-85334-767-0, Pub. by Applied Science). Burgess-Intl Ideas.
Green, L. F., jt. ed. see Birch, G. G.
Green, Lawrence & Kansler, Connie, eds. Professional & Scientific Literature on Patient Education: A Guide to Information Sources. (Health Affairs Information Guide Ser.: Vol. 5). 330p. 1980. 30.00 (ISBN 0-8103-1422-3). Gale.
Green, Lawrence S. & Johnston, Francis S., eds. Social & Biological Predictors of Nutritional Status, Physical Growth & Neurological Development. 1980. 25.00 (ISBN 0-12-299750-6). Acad Pr.
Green, Lila. Tales from Africa. LC 78-54623. (The World Folktale Library). (Illus.). 1979. lib. bdg. 7.65 (ISBN 0-686-51162-X). Silver.
--Tales from Hispanic Lands. LC 78-54624. (The World Folktale Library). (Illus.). 1979. lib. bdg. 7.65 (ISBN 0-686-50009-1). Silver.
Green, Louis. Chronicle into History: An Essay on the Interpretation of History in Florentine Fourteenth Century Cronicles. LC 71-186249. (Cambridge Studies in Early Modern History). 180p. 1972. 26.95 (ISBN 0-521-08517-9). Cambridge U Pr.
Green, M. Organo-Metallic Compounds, Vol. 2. 3rd ed. 376p. 1968. 35.00x o.p. (ISBN 0-412-11580-8, Pub. by Chapman & Hall). Methuen Inc.
--Organo-Metallic Compounds, Vol. 2. 3rd ed. 1968. 29.95 o.p. (ISBN 0-470-32471-6). Halsted Pr.
Green, M., jt. ed. see Domb, C.
Green, M., et al, eds. Engineering Woodworking, Vol. 2. (Engineering Craftsmen: No. K21). (Illus.). 1977. spiral bdg. 21.00x (ISBN 0-85083-340-X). Intl Ideas.
Green, M. B. see Rose, J. & Weidener, E. W.
Green, M. M. Human Genetics Notes. LC 74-28814. (Illus.). 240p. 1975. text ed. 8.95 (ISBN 0-201-02599-X). A-W.
Green, M. S., ed. Critical Phenomena. (Italian Physical Society: Course 51). 1973. 56.00 (ISBN 0-12-368851-5). Acad Pr.
Green, Marge. A Life with Wings. 1966. 6.45 (ISBN 0-89137-403-5); pap. 3.75 (ISBN 0-89137-402-7). Quality Pubns.
--Martha, Martha! 1964. 6.45 (ISBN 0-89137-401-9); pap. 3.75 (ISBN 0-89137-400-0). Quality Pubns.
Green, Marilyn L. & Harry, Joann. Nutrition in Contemporary Nursing Practice. 752p. 1981. 17.95 (ISBN 0-471-03892-X, Pub. by Wiley Med). Wiley.
Green, Mark, jt. auth. see Nader, Ralph.
Green, Mark & Massie, Robert K, Jr., eds. The Big Business Reader. LC 80-13542. 640p. (Orig.). 1980. pap. 4.95 (ISBN 0-8298-0398-X). Pilgrim NY.
Green, Martin. The Home Pet Vet Guide: Dogs. 1980. 7.95 (ISBN 0-345-28944-7). Ballantine.
--The Home Pet Vet Guide for Cats. pap. cancelled (ISBN 0-686-68438-9, 43406). Avon.
--The Home Pet Vet Guide for Dogs. pap. cancelled (ISBN 0-686-68439-7, 43414). Avon.
Green, Marvin, jt. auth. see Behrendt, Hans.
Green, Mary J., jt. auth. see Ansberger, Carolyn.
Green, Mary J., jt. auth. see Ausberger, Carloyn.
Green, Mary J., jt. auth. see Ausberger, Carolyn.
Green, Mary M. Is It Hard? Is It Easy? LC 60-50169. (ps-1). 1960. PLB 6.95 (ISBN 0-201-09243-3, A-W Childrens). A-W.
Green, Maurice B. Eating Oil: Energy Use in Food Production. 1978. lib. bdg. 22.50x (ISBN 0-89158-244-4). Westview.
Green, Maurice R., ed. Violence & the Family. (AAAS Selected Symposium: No. 47). 200p. 1980. lib. bdg. 17.50x (ISBN 0-89158-841-8); pap. text ed. 8.00 (ISBN 0-86531-141-2). Westview.
Green, Melinda. Bembelman's Bakery. LC 77-22858. (Illus.). 40p. (ps-3). 1978. 6.95 (ISBN 0-590-07719-8, Four Winds); PLB 5.41 o.p. (ISBN 0-8193-0914-1). Schol Bk Serv.
Green, Michael. The Art of Coarse Acting. rev. ed. LC 80-20310. (Illus.). 136p. 1981. tchrs' ed. 10.00 (ISBN 0-89676-041-3). Drama Bk.
--Creo en el Espiritu Santo. Vilela, Ernesto S., tr. from Eng. LC 77-164. (Serie Creo). 267p. (Orig., Span.). 1977. pap. 3.95 (ISBN 0-89922-090-8). Edit Caribe.
--Evangelism in the Early Church. 1970. pap. 5.95 (ISBN 0-8028-1612-6). Eerdmans.
--I Believe in the Holy Spirit. (I Believe Ser). 224p. 1975. pap. 3.95 (ISBN 0-8028-1609-6). Eerdmans.
--Runaway World. LC 74-78819. (Orig.). 1969. pap. 2.25 o.p. (ISBN 0-87784-688-X). Inter-Varsity.
--A Walk Through the Shire: Wherin We Discover Some Rare Drawings of Hobbit Life. (Illus., Orig.). 1980. lib. bdg. 12.90 (ISBN 0-89471-114-8); pap. 4.95 (ISBN 0-89471-115-6). Running Pr.
Green, Michael, jt. auth. see Green, Sally.
Green, Michael, ed. The Daily Telegraph: The Peterborough Book. LC 80-69341. 64p. 1981. 8.95 (ISBN 0-7153-8082-6). David & Charles.
--Truck Facts Buyer's Guide, 1981. rev. ed. 96p. (Orig.). write for info. DMR Pubns.
Green, Michael, illus. A Hobbits Journal: Being a Blank Book with Some Curious Illustrations of Friends & Foes of the Nine Companions. LC 79-20203. (Illus.). 1979. lib. bdg. 12.90 (ISBN 0-89471-089-3); pap. 4.95 (ISBN 0-89471-090-7). Running Pr.
--A Hobbit's Travels: Being the Hitherto Unpublished Travel Sketches of Sam Gamgee with Space for Notes. LC 78-15318. (Illus.). 1978. lib. bdg. 12.90 (ISBN 0-89471-041-9); pap. 4.95 (ISBN 0-89471-040-0). Running Pr.
Green, Michael D. Creeks: A Critical Bibliography. LC 79-2166. (Newberry Library Center for the History of the American Indian Bibliographical Ser.). 132p. (Orig.). 1980. pap. 4.95x (ISBN 0-253-31776-2). Ind U Pr.
Green, Michael L., ed. Car Facts, 1981. rev. ed. (Buyer's Guide Ser.). 96p. (Orig.). Date not set. pap. 2.50 (ISBN 0-89552-069-9). DMR Pubns.
--Economy Cars, 1981. rev. ed. (Buyer's Guide Ser.). 96p. (Orig.). Date not set. pap. 2.50 (ISBN 0-89552-073-7). DMR Pubns.
--Franchise Handbook. rev. ed. Date not set. 12.00 (ISBN 0-89552-027-3); pap. text ed. 7.95 (ISBN 0-89552-026-5). DMR Pubns.
--New & Used Foreign Car Prices. rev. ed. (Buyer's Guide Ser.). 96p. (Orig.). Date not set. pap. 2.50 (ISBN 0-89552-067-2). DMR Pubns.
--New Car Prices Buyer's Guide, 1981. rev. ed. (Buyer's Guide Ser.). 128p. (Orig.). Date not set. pap. 2.50 (ISBN 0-89552-068-0). DMR Pubns.
--New Truck & Van Prices, 1981. rev. ed. (Buyer's Guide Ser.). 96p. (Orig.). Date not set. pap. 2.50 (ISBN 0-89552-070-2). DMR Pubns.
--Nineteen Eighty Autos: Rating, Specifications & Best Buys. (Buyer's Guide Ser.). 1979. pap. 2.25 (ISBN 0-89552-060-5). DMR Pubns.
--Nineteen Eighty Car Facts. (Buyer's Guide Ser.). 1979. pap. 2.25 (ISBN 0-89552-059-1). DMR Pubns.
--Nineteen Eighty Economy Cars. (Buyer's Guide Ser.). 1979. pap. 2.25 (ISBN 0-89552-063-X). DMR Pubns.
--Nineteen Eighty New Car Prices. (Buyer's Guide Ser.). 1979. pap. 2.25 (ISBN 0-685-95267-3). DMR Pubns.
--Nineteen Eighty New Truck & Van Prices. (Buyer's Guide Ser.). 1979. pap. 2.25 (ISBN 0-89552-061-3). DMR Pubns.
--Nineteen Eighty U. S. Income Tax Guide. (Buyer's Guide Ser.). 1979. pap. 2.25 (ISBN 0-89552-064-8). DMR Pubns.
--U. S. Income Tax Guide, 1981. rev. ed. (Buyer's Guide Ser.). 80p. (Orig.). Date not set. pap. 2.50 (ISBN 0-89552-074-5). DMR Pubns.
--Used Car Prices. rev. ed. (Buyer's Guide Ser.). 96p. (Orig.). Date not set. pap. 2.50 (ISBN 0-89552-065-6). DMR Pubns.
--Used Truck & Van Prices. rev. ed. (Buyer's Guide Ser.). 96p. (Orig.). Date not set. pap. 2.25 (ISBN 0-89552-066-4). DMR Pubns.
Green, Morris. Green & Richmond Pediatric Diagnosis: Interpretation of Symptoms & Signs in Different Age Periods. 3rd ed. LC 79-65454. (Illus.). 658p. 1980. text ed. 29.00 (ISBN 0-7216-4242-X). Saunders.
Green, Norma, retold by. The Hole in the Dike. (Illus.). (gr. k-3). 1975. pap. 1.50 (ISBN 0-590-08127-6, Schol Pap); pap. 3.50 bk. & record (ISBN 0-590-20742-3). Schol Bk Serv.
Green Note Music Publications Staff. Country Rock Guitar. Straw Dog, ed. (Contemporary Guitar Styles Ser.). (Illus.). 1978. pap. 8.95 (ISBN 0-912910-07-0). Green Note Music.
--Country Rock Guitar, Vol. 2. (Guitar Transcription Ser.). 1980. pap. 7.25 (ISBN 0-912910-10-0). Green Note Music.
--Electric Blues Guitar. (Contemporary Guitar Styles Ser). (Illus.). 96p. (Orig., Prog. Bk.). 1977. pap. 8.95 (ISBN 0-912910-05-4). Green Note Music.
--Improvising Blues Guitar, Vol. 2. (Guitar Transcription Ser.). 1980. pap. 7.25 (ISBN 0-912910-11-9). Green Note Music.
--Improvising Rock Guitar, Vol. 2. (Guitar Transcription Ser.). 1980. pap. 7.25 (ISBN 0-912910-08-9). Green Note Music.
--Improvising Rock Guitar, Vol. 3. (Guitar Transcription Ser.). 1980. pap. 7.25 (ISBN 0-912910-09-7). Green Note Music.
Green, P. & Barban. Analyzing Multivariate Data. 1978. 28.95 (ISBN 0-03-020786-X). Dryden Pr.
Green, Percy B. History of Nursery Rhymes. LC 68-31082. 1968. Repr. of 1899 ed. 18.00 (ISBN 0-8103-3481-X). Gale.
Green, Peter. Design Education. (Illus.). 137p. 1974. 12.50x (ISBN 0-7134-2321-8). Intl Pubns Serv.
--Design Education: Problem Solving & Visual Experience. 1974. pap. 17.95 (ISBN 0-7134-2325-0, Pub. by Batsford England). David & Charles.
--Essays in Antiquity. 1960. 12.95 (ISBN 0-7195-0558-5). Dufour.
--The Shadow of the Parthenon: Studies in Ancient History & Literature. LC 72-87205. 1973. 17.50x (ISBN 0-520-02322-6). U of Cal Pr.
Green, Philip. The Pursuit of Inequality. 1981. 14.95 (ISBN 0-394-50676-6). Pantheon.
Green, Phyllis. Bagdad Ate It. (gr. k-3). 1980. 3.95 (ISBN 0-531-03429-1); PLB 6.45 (ISBN 0-531-02855-0). Watts.
--The Empty Seat. LC 79-21813. (gr. 4 up). 1980. 7.50 o.p. (ISBN 0-525-66660-5). Elsevier-Nelson.
--Gloomy Louie. Fay, Ann, ed. LC 79-28533. (Illus.). (gr. 3-6). 1980. 5.75 (ISBN 0-8075-2962-1). A Whitman.
--Mildred Murphy How Does Your Garden Grow. (gr. k-6). 1980. pap. 1.75 (ISBN 0-440-45590-1, YB). Dell.
--Wild Violets. (gr. k-6). 1980. pap. 1.25 (ISBN 0-440-49671-3, YB). Dell.
Green, R. D. Hydrogen Bonding by C-H Groups. LC 74-11310. 207p. 1974. 39.95 (ISBN 0-470-32478-3). Halsted Pr.
Green, R. F. Chess. rev. ed. (Illus.). 113p. 1974. 7.50 (ISBN 0-7135-0506-0). Transatlantic.
Green, R. L. The Tale of Thebes. LC 76-22979. (Illus.). 1977. 14.95 (ISBN 0-521-21410-6); pap. 5.50 (ISBN 0-521-21411-4). Cambridge U Pr.
Green, Richard & Money, John, eds. Transsexualism & Sex Reassignment. LC 69-15761. (Illus.). 534p. 1969. 32.50x o.p. (ISBN 0-8018-1038-8). Johns Hopkins.
Green, Richard H., tr. see Boethius.
Green, Robert C., Jr., et al. The Care & Management of the Sick & Incompetent Physician. (Illus.). 116p. 1978. 12.75 (ISBN 0-398-03727-2). C C Thomas.
Green, Robert H., jt. auth. see Hsiung, Gueh-Djen.
Green, Robert J. & Framo, James L., eds. Family Therapy: The Major Approaches. 620p. 1981. text ed. 30.00 (ISBN 0-8236-1885-4). Intl Univs Pr.
Green, Robert L. The Urban Challenge: Poverty & Race. 1978. pap. 7.95 o.p. (ISBN 0-695-81145-2). Follett.
Green, Robert T. & Lutz, James. The United States & World Trade: Changing Patterns & Dimensions. LC 78-19762. 336p. 1979. 29.95 (ISBN 0-03-045351-8). Praeger.
Green, Roger L. Adventures of Robin Hood. (Orig.). (gr. 2-5). 1956. pap. 2.50 (ISBN 0-14-030101-1, Puffin). Penguin.
--A Book of Myths. (Childrens Illustrated Classics Ser). (Illus.). 1976. Repr. of 1965 ed. 9.00x o.p. (ISBN 0-460-05066-4, Pub. by J. M. Dent England). Biblio Dist.
--King Arthur & His Knights of the Round Table. (Orig.). (gr. 5-7). 1974. pap. 2.95 (ISBN 0-14-030073-2, Puffin). Penguin.
--King Arthur & the Knights of the Round Table. 1980. pap. 2.95 o.p. (ISBN 0-14-030073-2). Penguin.
--Myths of the Norsemen. 1970. pap. 2.50 (ISBN 0-14-030464-9, Puffin). Penguin.
--Tales of Ancient Egypt. (gr. k-3). 1972. pap. 2.25 (ISBN 0-14-030438-X, Puffin). Penguin.
Green, Roger L. & Hooper, Walter. C. S. Lewis: A Biography. 320p. 1974. 6.95 o.p. (ISBN 0-15-123190-7). HarBraceJ.
Green, Roger L., ed. see Carroll, Lewis.
Green, Roger L., ed. & suppl. by see Dodgson, Charles L.
Green, Ronald M. Population Growth & Justice: An Examination of Moral Issues Raised by Rapid Population Growth. LC 76-44233. (Harvard Dissertations in Religion). 1976. pap. 7.50 (ISBN 0-89130-099-6, 020105). Scholars Pr Ca.
--Religious Reason: The Rational & Moral Basis of Religious Belief. 1978. text ed. 13.95 (ISBN 0-19-502388-9); pap. text ed. 4.50 (ISBN 0-19-502389-7). Oxford U Pr.
Green, Sally & Green, Michael. Welcome to the Planet Earth: A Five Year Baby Journal. (Illus.). 96p. (Orig.). 1981. lib. bdg. 12.90 (ISBN 0-89471-125-3); pap. 6.95 (ISBN 0-89471-126-1). Running Pr.
Green, Samuel & Long, John V. Modern Family Law, 3 vols. 1800p. Date not set. Set. 180.00 (ISBN 0-07-024275-5). McGraw.
Green, Sheila M. Selected Writings of Teresa of Avila. 4.50 o.p. (ISBN 0-685-58944-7). Vantage.
Green, Stanford J. The Classification & Cataloging of Picture & Slides. 200p. (Orig.). pap. write for info. (ISBN 0-9604656-0-X). S Green.
Green, Stanley. Encyclopedia of the Musical Theatre. LC 76-21069. 1976. 17.50 (ISBN 0-396-07221-6). Dodd.
--The World of Musical Comedy. 4th, rev. ed. LC 80-16915. 448p. 1980. 19.95 (ISBN 0-498-02344-3). A S Barnes.
Green, Stanley & Goldblatt, Burt. Starring Fred Astaire. 436p. 1973. 22.50 o.p. (ISBN 0-396-06877-4). Dodd.
Green, Stuart A. Complications of External Skeletal Fixation: Causes, Prevention, & Treatment. write for info. (ISBN 0-398-04482-7). C C Thomas.
Green, Ted & Hirshberg, Al. High Stick. LC 77-179695. (Illus.). 1971. 5.95 (ISBN 0-396-06427-2). Dodd.

Green, Thaddeus B. & Lee, Sang M. The Decision Science Process. (Illus.). 1979. text ed. 23.00 (ISBN 0-89433-060-8). Petrocelli.
Green, Thomas, et al. Predicting the Behavior of the Educational System. (Illus.). 224p. 1980. 15.95x (ISBN 0-8156-2223-6); pap. 8.95x (ISBN 0-8156-2224-4). Syracuse U Pr.
Green, Thomas J. The Flowered Box: A Novel of Suspense. LC 80-22442. 192p. 1980. 9.95 (ISBN 0-8253-0010-X). Beaufort Bks NY.
Green Tiger Staff. The Green Tiger's Caravan. (Illus.). 1981. pap. 8.95 (ISBN 0-914676-58-X). Green Tiger.
Green, Timothy S. The World of Diamonds. LC 80-26196. (Illus.). 1981. price not set (ISBN 0-688-03731-3). Morrow.
Green, Tina. Until the Jaguar Sings. (YA) 1977. 4.95 o.p. (ISBN 0-685-71792-5, Avalon). Bouregy.
Green, Tom & Wooton, William. Intermediate Algebra. 608p. 1980. pap. text ed. 16.95x (ISBN 0-534-00788-0). Wadsworth Pub.
Green, V. H. A History of Oxford University. 1974. 28.00 (ISBN 0-7134-1132-5, Pub. by Batsford England). David & Charles.
Green, Vera. Migrants in Aruba: Interethnic Integration. 154p. 1974. pap. text ed. 18.50x (ISBN 90-232-1126-X). Humanities.
Green, Victor. The Story of Red Rum & Brian Fletcher. 1974. 6.95 o.p. (ISBN 0-7207-0800-1, Pub. by Michael Joseph). Merrimack Bk Serv.
Green, Walter L., jt. auth. see Speckhart, Frank H.
Green, William & Swanborough, Gordon. The Observer's World Airlines Directory. LC 74-21043. 374p. 1975. 15.00 o.p. (ISBN 0-7232-1547-2). Warne.
--U. S. Navy & Marine Corps Fighters. (World War II Aircraft Fact Files Ser.). (Illus.). 1977. 6.95 o.p. (ISBN 0-668-04174-9); pap. 4.95 o.p. (ISBN 0-668-04121-8). Arco.
Green, William, ed. see Luukkanen, Eino.
Green, William A. British Slave Emancipation: The Sugar Colonies & the Great Experiment, 1830-1865. (Illus.). 1976. 49.50x (ISBN 0-19-822436-2). Oxford U Pr.
Green, William A., jt. auth. see DeLo, James S.
Green, William B. & L'Engle, Madeleine, eds. Spirit & Light: Essays in Historical Theology. 1976. 8.95 (ISBN 0-8164-0310-4). Crossroad NY.
Green, William H. The Argument of the Book of Job Unfolded. 10.75 (ISBN 0-686-12967-9). Klock & Klock.
--Key to Cribbage. (Gambler's Book Shelf). 1965. pap. 2.95 (ISBN 0-89650-501-4). Gamblers.
Green, William M. The Man Who Called Himself Devlin. (Orig.). pap. 1.95 (ISBN 0-515-05245-0). Jove Pubns.
Green, William S., ed. Persons & Institutions in Early Rabbinic Judaism. LC 76-52503. (Brown University. Brown Judaic Studies: No. 3). 1977. pap. 9.00 (ISBN 0-89130-131-3, 140003). Scholars Pr Ca.
Greenawalt, R. Kent & Low, Peter W., eds. Model Penal Code & Commentaries, 3 vols, Pt. II. 1427p. 105.00 set (ISBN 0-686-69005-2); postage & handling 9.00 (ISBN 0-686-69006-0). Am Law Inst.
Greenaway, D. L. & Harbeke, G. Optical Properties & Band Structures of Semiconductors. 1968. 34.00 (ISBN 0-08-012648-0). Pergamon.
Greenaway, J. R., jt. auth. see Chapman, Richard A.
Greenaway, Kate. Birthday Book for Children. (Illus.). (gr. 3-6). 1880. 6.95 (ISBN 0-7232-0216-8); lea. 9.95 (ISBN 0-7232-0217-6). Warne.
Greenbank, Anthony. The Book of Survival. (Illus.). 1968. 12.95 o.s.i. (ISBN 0-06-070873-5, HarpT). Har-Row.
--A Handbook for Emergencies: Coming Out Alive. LC 74-25104. 192p. (gr. 7 up). 1976. 8.95 (ISBN 0-385-09842-1); pap. 3.95 (ISBN 0-385-09822-7). Doubleday.
Greenbaum, Dennis & Gianelli, Stanley, Jr. Acute Cardiovascular Failure. (Clinics in Critical Care Medicine Ser.). (Illus.). 224p. 1981. lib. bdg. 22.50 (ISBN 0-443-08111-5). Churchill.
Greenbaum, Everett. The Goldenberg Who Couldn't Dance. LC 79-3353. 168p. 1980. 8.95 (ISBN 0-15-136174-6). HarBraceJ.
Greenbaum, Fred. Robert Marion la Follette. LC 74-26675. (World Leaders Ser. No. 44). 1975. lib. bdg. 12.50 (ISBN 0-8057-3057-5). Twayne.
Greenbaum, Howard H. & Falcione, Raymond L. Organizational Communication Nineteen Seventy-Seven: Abstracts, Analysis, & Overview. new ed. 1979. pap. 9.00 o.p. (ISBN 0-931874-08-4). Am Busn Comm Assn.
Greenbaum, Howard H., jt. auth. see Falcione, Raymond L.
Greenbaum, S., et al, eds. Studies in English Linguistics: For Randolph Quirk. (Illus.). 320p. 1980. lib. bdg. 45.00 (ISBN 0-582-55079-3). Longman.
Greenbeg, Alan & George, Michael, eds. Student's Edition of Monograph of the Work of McKim, Mead & White--1879-1915. (Illus.). 160p. 1981. 18.95 (ISBN 0-8038-6774-3); pap. 10.95 (ISBN 0-8038-6775-1). Hastings.
Greenberg, Alan, tr. see Herzog, Werner.
Greenberg, Allan M. Standards Relating to Architecture of Facilities. LC 77-14495. (Juvenile Justice Standards Project Ser.). 1977. soft cover 7.59 o.p. (ISBN 0-88410-778-7); casebound 12.50 o.p. (ISBN 0-88410-249-1). Ballinger Pub.
Greenberg, B., ed. Significant References in Psychiatry & Mental Health. 1979. lib. bdg. 25.00 o.p. (ISBN 0-89495-004-5). ISI Pr.
Greenberg, Barbara, jt. auth. see Greenberg, Herbert A.
Greenberg, Barbara L. The Spoils of August. LC 73-15012. (Wesleyan Poetry Program: No. 71). 72p. 1974. 10.00x (ISBN 0-8195-2071-3, Pub. by Wesleyan U Pr); pap. 4.95 (ISBN 0-8195-1071-8). Columbia U Pr.
Greenberg, Barnett A., jt. auth. see Bellenger, Danny N.
Greenberg, Bette, ed. How to Find Out in Psychiatry: A Guide to Sources of Mental Health Information. LC 78-16005. 1978. text ed. 14.75 (ISBN 0-08-021860-1). Pergamon.
Greenberg, Bradley S. Life on Television: Content Analysis of U.S. TV Drama. LC 80-14478. (Communication & Information Science Ser.). 224p. 1980. text ed. 22.50 (ISBN 0-89391-039-2); pap. text ed. 12.95 (ISBN 0-89391-062-7). Ablex Pub.
Greenberg, Bruce. Model Railroading: A Complete Guide. LC 78-61847. (Illus.). 1979. 14.95 o.p. (ISBN 0-13-586149-7). P-H.
Greenberg, Bruce C. Greenberg's Price Guide to Lionel Trains: 1901-1942 2nd ed. Greenberg, Linda, ed. (Illus.). 1979. 19.95 (ISBN 0-89778-088-4); pap. 12.95 (ISBN 0-89778-072-8). Greenberg Pub Co.
--Greenberg's Price Guide to Lionel Trains: O & O-27 Trains, 1945-1977. (Illus.). 1977. pap. 12.95 o.p. (ISBN 0-89778-500-2, Pub. by Crown). Greenberg Pub Co.
--Greenberg's Repair & Operating Manual for Lionel Trains. 736p. 1980. pap. 9.95 (ISBN 0-442-21363-8). Van Nos Reinhold.
Greenberg, Bruce C., ed. Lionel Nineteen Thirty-Eight Catalogue. (Illus.). 1975. pap. 6.00 o.p. (ISBN 0-89778-313-1). Greenberg Pub Co.
--Lionel 1932 Catalogue. (Illus.). 1975. pap. 6.00 o.p. (ISBN 0-89778-317-4). Greenberg Pub Co.
--Lionel 1933 Catalogue. (Illus.). 1975. pap. 6.00 o.p. (ISBN 0-89778-309-3). Greenberg Pub Co.
Greenberg, Bruce C., ed. see Hubbard, John.
Greenberg, Dan & Jacobs, Marcia. How to Make Yourself Miserable. 1976. pap. 3.95 (ISBN 0-394-73168-9). Random.
Greenberg, David, jt. auth. see Kessler, Ronald.
Greenberg, David, ed. The Malibu Tiles Coloring Book. (Illus.). 128p. 1980. lib. bdg. cancelled (ISBN 0-89471-118-0); pap. cancelled (ISBN 0-89471-144-X). Running Pr.
Greenberg, David F. Mathematical Criminology. (Illus.). 1979. text ed. 22.50x (ISBN 0-8135-0873-8). Rutgers U Pr.
Greenberg, David F., ed. Crime & Class: Essays in Marxist Criminology. 350p. (Orig.). 1981. write for info (ISBN 0-87484-505-X). Mayfield Pub.
Greenberg, Dolores. A Study of Morton, Bliss & Company. LC 78-66830. 288p. 1980. 22.50 (ISBN 0-87413-148-0). U Delaware Pr.
Greenberg, E. S. Serving the Few: Corporate Capitalism & the Bias of Government Policy. 1974. pap. 8.95x (ISBN 0-471-32487-6). Wiley.
Greenberg, Edward, et al. Regulation, Market Prices, & Process Innovation: The Case of the Ammonia Industry. (Westview Replica Edition). 1979. lib. bdg. 25.50x (ISBN 0-89158-381-5). Westview.
Greenberg, Edward S. Understanding Modern Government: The Rise & Decline of the American Political Economy. LC 78-10104. 1979. pap. text ed. 8.95x (ISBN 0-470-26879-4). Wiley.
Greenberg, Eliezer, jt. ed. see Howe, Irving.
Greenberg, Evelyn. Reference Services: A Guide to Information Sources. LC 74-11553. (Books, Publishing & Libraries Information Guide Ser.). 30.00 (ISBN 0-8103-1285-9). Gale.
Greenberg, Florence & Heffley, Anne P. Tradition & Dissent: A Rhetoric Reader. 2nd ed. LC 76-145858. 1971. pap. 8.50 (ISBN 0-672-61179-1). Bobbs.
Greenberg, H. M. Teaching with Feeling. 1969. 11.95 (ISBN 0-02-545460-9). Macmillan.
Greenberg, Harold I. & Nadler, Samuel. Poverty in Israel: Economic Realities & the Promise of Social Justice. LC 76-58558. (Special Studies). 1977. text ed. 22.95 (ISBN 0-275-24300-1). Praeger.
Greenberg, Harvey, jt. ed. see Maybee, John.
Greenberg, Hazel, ed. see Equal Rights Amendment Project.
Greenberg, Herbert A. & Greenberg, Barbara. Sabbath, a Kit. 1971. boxed 11.00 (ISBN 0-8074-0149-8, 101075). UAHC.
Greenberg, Herbert J., jt. auth. see Dorn, William S.
Greenberg, Herbert M. Teaching with Feeling: Compassion & Self-Awareness in the Classroom Today. LC 69-13393. 1969. pap. 5.50 (ISBN 0-672-63601-8). Pegasus.
--To Educate with Love. LC 73-10562. 228p. 1974. 6.95 o.s.i. (ISBN 0-02-545470-6). Macmillan.
Greenberg, Idaz. Field Guide to Marine Invertebrates. (Illus.). 1980. plastic card 3.95 (ISBN 0-913008-11-7). Seahawk Pr.
--Fishwatcher's Field Guide. (Illus.). 1979. plastic card 3.95 (ISBN 0-913008-10-9). Seahawk Pr.
--Guide to Corals & Fishes. (Illus.). 1977. saddlestitched 4.95 (ISBN 0-913008-08-7). Seahawk Pr.
Greenberg, Idaz & Greenberg, Jerry. Sharks & Other Dangerous Sea Creatures. (Illus.). 1981. saddlestiched 4.95 (ISBN 0-913008-09-5). Seahawk Pr.
Greenberg, Ira A., ed. Group Hypnotherapy & Hypnodrama. LC 76-17012. 320p. 1977. 19.95 (ISBN 0-88229-256-0). Nelson-Hall.
Greenberg, Jack. Race Relations & American Law. LC 59-11179. 1959. 17.50x (ISBN 0-231-02313-8). Columbia U Pr.
Greenberg, James B. Santiago's Sword: Chatino Peasant Religion & Economics. 250p. 1981. 16.95x (ISBN 0-520-04135-6). U of Cal Pr.
Greenberg, Jan. The Iceberg & Its Shadow. 132p. 1980. 8.95 (ISBN 0-374-33624-5). FS&G.
Greenberg, Jan W. Theatre Facts: From Putting the Show Together Through Opening Night. LC 80-20295. 1981. 10.95 (ISBN 0-03-051451-7). HR&W.
Greenberg, Janelle R., jt. auth. see Weston, Corin.
Greenberg, Jean, et al. Guide to Current Research. (Resources in Bilingual Education Ser.). (Orig.). 1981. pap. write for info. (ISBN 0-89763-052-1). Natl Clearinghse Bilingual Ed.
Greenberg, Jerrold S. Student-Centered Health Instruction: A Humanistic Approach. LC 76-55642. (Illus.). 1978. pap. text ed. 7.95 (ISBN 0-201-02627-9). A-W.
Greenberg, Jerrold S., jt. auth. see Dintiman, George B.
Greenberg, Jerry. The Coral Reef. (Orig.). saddlestiched 4.95 (ISBN 0-913008-06-0). Seahawk Pr.
Greenberg, Jerry, jt. auth. see Greenberg, Idaz.
Greenberg, Joanne. Founder's Praise. LC 76-3968. 1976. 8.95 o.p. (ISBN 0-03-015391-3). HR&W.
--In This Sign. 1972. pap. 1.95 (ISBN 0-380-38414-0, 38414). Avon.
--A Season of Delight. LC 80-20421. 240p. 1981. 11.95 (ISBN 0-03-057627-X). HR&W.
Greenberg, Joel, jt. auth. see Higham, Charles.
Greenberg, Joseph H. A New Invitation to Linguistics. LC 76-42422. 1977. pap. 2.95 (ISBN 0-385-07550-2, Anch). Doubleday.
Greenberg, Kathy, jt. auth. see Kyte, Barbara.
Greenberg, Kenneth R. A Tiger by the Tail: Parenting in a Troubled Society. LC 73-93103. 1974. 14.95 (ISBN 0-911012-77-X). Nelson-Hall.
Greenberg, L. M., et al, eds. see Velikovsky, et al.
Greenberg, Lewis M., et al, eds. see Velikovsky, et al.
Greenberg, Linda, ed. see Barker, Thomas.
Greenberg, Linda, ed. see Greenberg, Bruce C.
Greenberg, M., jt. auth. see Olander, J.
Greenberg, Marshall, ed. see Annual Attitude Research Conference, 7th, Hilton Head, S.C., Feb. 1976.
Greenberg, Martin & Olander, Joseph. Science Fiction of the Fifties. 1979. pap. 4.95 (ISBN 0-380-46409-8, 46409). Avon.
Greenberg, Martin & Waugh, Charles, eds. Tantalizing Locked Room Mysteries. LC 80-54817. 224p. 1981. 12.95 (ISBN 0-8027-0680-0). Walker & Co.
Greenberg, Martin H., jt. auth. see Waugh, Charles G.
Greenberg, Martin H., ed. Astounding Science Fiction, July, Nineteen Thirty-Nine. 184p. 1981. Repr. of 1939 ed. write for info. (ISBN 0-8093-0991-2). S Ill U Pr.
--Fantastic Lives: Autobiographical Essays by Notable Science Fiction Writers. (Alternatives Ser.). 216p. 1981. 15.00 (ISBN 0-8093-0987-4). S Ill U Pr.
Greenberg, Martin H. & Waugh, Charles G., eds. The Human Zero: The Science Fiction Stories of Erle Stanley Gardner. 432p. Date not set. 12.95 (ISBN 0-688-00122-X). Morrow.
Greenberg, Martin H., jt. ed. see Asimov, Isaac.
Greenberg, Martin H., jt. ed. see Ferman, Edward L.
Greenberg, Martin H., jt. ed. see Nolan, William Fl.
Greenberg, Martin H., jt. ed. see Waugh, Charles G.
Greenberg, Martin H., et al, eds. Anthropology Through Science Fiction. 350p. (Orig.). 1974. 16.95 (ISBN 0-312-04305-8); pap. text ed. 8.95 (ISBN 0-312-04340-6). St Martin.
--The Future, Vol. I. 384p. (Orig.). 1981. pap. 2.50 (ISBN 0-449-24366-4, Crest). Fawcett.
Greenberg, Marvin J. Euclidean & Non-Euclidean Geometries: Development & History. 2nd ed. LC 79-19348. (Illus.). 1980. text ed. 19.95x (ISBN 0-7167-1103-6); instrs. manual & answer book avail. W H Freeman.
Greenberg, Michael, et al. Environmental Impact Statements. Natoli, Salvatore J., ed. LC 78-59102. (Resource Papers for College Geography Ser.). (Illus.). 1978. pap. text ed. 4.00 (ISBN 0-89291-131-X). Assn Am Geographers.
Greenberg, Michael D. Foundations of Applied Mathematics. LC 77-11125. (Illus.). 1978. ref. ed. 27.95x (ISBN 0-13-329623-7). P-H.
Greenberg, Michael I. & Roberts, James R. Uncommon Problems in Emergency Medicine. 1981. 15.00 (ISBN 0-8036-4331-4). Davis Co.
Greenberg, Moshe. The Hab-Piru. (American Oriental Ser.: Vol. 39). 1955. pap. 5.00x (ISBN 0-686-00020-X). Am Orient Soc.
--Introduction to Hebrew. 1964. text ed. 14.95 (ISBN 0-13-484469-6). P-H.
--Understanding Exodus. 1969. pap. 5.95x o.p. (ISBN 0-87441-029-0). Behrman.
Greenberg, Noah, ed. see Auden, W. H. & Kallman, Chester.
Greenberg, P., ed. see Anapol'Skaya, L. E. & Gandin, L. S.
Greenberg, P., ed. see Dukhin, S. S. & Shilov, V. N.
Greenberg, P., ed. see Sedunov, Yu. S.
Greenberg, Paul D. & Glaser, Edward M. Some Issues in Joint Union-Management Quality of Worklife Improvement Efforts. LC 80-14044. 80p. 1980. pap. 4.00 (ISBN 0-911558-70-5). Upjohn Inst.
Greenberg, Polly. Oh Lord, I Wish I Was a Buzzard. LC 68-24103. (Illus.). (gr. k-2). 1968. 10.95 (ISBN 0-02-736730-4). Macmillan.
Greenberg, Robert A., ed. see Swift, Jonathan.
Greenberg, Samuel. Taxes, Government & You. 58p. 1980. 6.95 (ISBN 0-533-04424-3). Vantage.
Greenberg, Sheldon F. & Valletutti, Peter J. Stress & the Helping Professions. LC 80-20328. 156p. (Orig.). 1980. pap. text ed. 9.95 (ISBN 0-933716-09-5). P H Brookes.
Greenberg, Warren, ed. Competition in the Health Care Sector: Past, Present & Future. LC 78-24573. 1978. text ed. 35.00 (ISBN 0-89443-081-5). Aspen Systems.
Greenberger, Howard. Bogey's Baby. LC 77-9178. (Illus.). 1978. 8.95 o.p. (ISBN 0-312-08740-3). St Martin.
Greenblat, Cathy & Cottle, Thomas J. Getting Married. LC 80-16369. 276p. 1980. 11.95 (ISBN 0-07-024330-1). McGraw.
Greenblat, Cathy & Dressler, David. An Introduction to Sociology. 4th ed. 592p. 1981. pap. text ed. 15.95 (ISBN 0-394-32656-3); wkbk 6.95 (ISBN 0-394-32711-X). Knopf.
Greenblat, Cathy S., jt. auth. see Duke, Richard D.
Greenblat, Cathy S., jt. auth. see Gagnon, John H.
Greenblat, Cathy S., et al. The Marital Game: Personal Growth & Fulfillment. 2nd ed. 1977. pap. text ed. 6.95x (ISBN 0-685-86656-4). Random.
Greenblatt, Bernard S. Doctor's Sex Guide for Patients. (Illus.). 1976. pap. 2.50 (ISBN 0-685-07679-2). Budlong.
Greenblatt, David J., jt. auth. see Miller, Russell R.
Greenblatt, M., et al, eds. Poverty & Mental Health: PRR 21. 275p. 1967. pap. 5.00 (ISBN 0-685-24868-2, P021-0). Am Psychiatric.
Greenblatt, M. H. Multiple Sclerosis & Me. (Illus.). 86p. 1972. 8.75 (ISBN 0-398-02300-X). C C Thomas.
Greenblatt, Michael & Richmond, Steven. Public Welfare: Notes from Underground. 1979. text ed. 9.50 (ISBN 0-87073-767-8); pap. text ed. 5.95 (ISBN 0-686-66209-1). Schenkman.
Greenblatt, Robert B. Geriatric Endocrinology. LC 75-43196. (Aging Ser.: Vol. 5). 1978. 24.50 (ISBN 0-89004-112-1). Raven.
--Search the Scriptures: Modern Medicine & Biblical Personages. 3rd enl. ed. LC 76-50054. 1977. 10.50 o.p. (ISBN 0-397-59060-1). Lippincott.
Greenblatt, Stephen. Renaissance Self-Fashioning: More to Shakespeare. LC 80-13837. 272p. 1980. 20.00 (ISBN 0-226-30653-4). U of Chicago Pr.
Greenburg, Dan. Porno-Graphics: The Shame of Our Art Museums. (Illus.). 1969. 2.95 o.p. (ISBN 0-394-42483-2). Random.
Greenburg, Joanne. Jack in the Beanstalk. (Illus.). 48p. (gr. 3 up). 1980. write for info. (ISBN 0-8299-1033-6). West Pub.
Greendyke, Robert M. Introduction to Blood Banking. 3rd ed. LC 79-91979. 1980. pap. 14.50 (ISBN 0-87488-975-8). Med Exam.

Greendyke, Robert M. & Banzhaf, Jane C. Blood Bank Policies & Procedures. 1976. spiral bdg. 12.00 o.p. (ISBN 0-87488-652-X). Med Exam.
Greene, A. C. A Christmas Tree. (Illus.). 40p. 1973. 9.50 o.p. (ISBN 0-88426-035-6). Encino Pr.
--Dallas: The Deciding Years - a Historical Portrait. (Illus.). 192p. 1974. 12.50 o.p. (ISBN 0-88426-034-8). Encino Pr.
--The Last Captive. (Illus.). 185p. (gr. 6-9). 1972. 8.95 o.p. (ISBN 0-88426-004-6). Encino Pr.
Greene, Amsel. Word Clues. (Honor Groups). (gr. 11-12). 1962. text ed. 6.32 (ISBN 0-06-538011-8, SchDept); study guide 1.44 (ISBN 0-06-538203-X). Har-Row.
Greene, Bernard L. A Clinical Approach to Marital Problems: Diagnosis, Prevention & Treatment. 2nd ed. (Illus.). 528p. 1981. text ed. 53.75 (ISBN 0-398-04138-5). C C Thomas.
Greene, Bette. Get on Out of Here, Philip Hall. LC 79-50151. 160p. (gr. 3-6). 1981. 9.95 (ISBN 0-8037-2871-9); PLB 9.43 (ISBN 0-8037-2872-7). Dial.
--Morning Is a Long Time Coming. (Illus.). (YA) (gr. 7-9). 1979. pap. 1.75 (ISBN 0-671-56005-0). PB.
--Morning Is a Long Time Coming. (gr. 7-9). 1979. pap. 1.95 (ISBN 0-671-42456-4). Archway.
Greene, Bill. Win Your Personal Tax Revolt. (Illus.). 192p. 1981. 11.95 (ISBN 0-936602-10-4). Harbor Pub CA.
Greene, Bob. Billion Dollar Baby. 1975. pap. 1.95 o.p. (ISBN 0-451-06713-4, J6713, Sig). NAL.
--Johnny Deadline Reporter: The Best of Bob Greene. LC 76-6932. 1976. 14.95 (ISBN 0-88229-361-3). Nelson-Hall.
Greene, Bruce L., jt. auth. see Baughman, Kenneth L.
Greene, Bruce M., jt. auth. see Baughman, Kenneth L.
Greene, Carla. How Man Began. LC 73-172346. (gr. 2-6). 1972. 6.95 o.p. (ISBN 0-672-51612-8). Bobbs.
--Manuel, Young Mexican-American. (Illus.). (gr. 3-6). 1969. 4.25 o.p. (ISBN 0-8313-0069-8, 8313); PLB 6.19 (ISBN 0-685-13776-7). Lantern.
Greene, Carol. Give Us This Day. 1980. pap. 6.50 (ISBN 0-570-03496-5, 56-1713). Concordia.
--Seven Baths for Naaman. (I Can Read a Bible Story Ser.: No. 2). (Illus.). 48p. (gr. 2-4). 1977. 4.95 (ISBN 0-570-07321-9, 56-1512); pap. 1.95 (ISBN 0-570-07315-4, 56-1412). Concordia.
Greene, Constance C. Beat the Turtle Drum. (gr. 4 up). 1979. pap. 1.75 (ISBN 0-440-40875-X, YB). Dell.
--Dotty's Suitcase. 168p. (gr. 5-9). 1980. 8.95 (ISBN 0-670-28050-X). Viking Pr.
--A Girl Called Al. (Illus.). (gr. 6-8). 1969. 7.95 (ISBN 0-670-34153-3). Viking Pr.
Greene, David. The Irish Language. (Irish Life & Culture). 1977. pap. 2.25 o.p. (ISBN 0-85342-283-4). Irish Bk Ctr.
Greene, David B. Temporal Processes in Beethoven's Music. 1981. price not set (ISBN 0-677-05600-1). Gordon.
Greene, David L. & Martin, Dick. The Oz Scrapbook. (Illus.). 1977. 10.00 o.p. (ISBN 0-394-41054-8). Random.
Greene, Diane S. Sunrise, a Whole Grain, Natural Food Breakfast Cook Book. LC 80-20749. 240p. 1980. 12.95 (ISBN 0-89594-041-8); pap. 6.95 (ISBN 0-89594-040-X). Crossing Pr.
Greene, Donald. Samuel Johnson. (English Authors Ser.: No. 95). lib. bdg. 10.95 (ISBN 0-8057-1296-8). Twayne.
Greene, Donald A. The Politics of Samuel Johnson. LC 72-85311. 376p. 1973. Repr. of 1960 ed. 17.50 o.p. (ISBN 0-8046-1697-3). Kennikat.
Greene, Douglas, ed. Diaries of the Popish Plot. LC 77-938. 1977. 40.00 (ISBN 0-8201-1288-7). Schol Facsimilies.
Greene, E. L. Landmarks of Botanical History, 2 parts in 2 vols. Egerton, F. N., ed. 1981. Set. slipcased 65.00 (ISBN 0-686-65497-8). Hunt Inst Botanical.
Greene, Ellin. Clever Cooks: A Ready-Mix of Stories, Recipes, & Riddles. (gr. 4-6). 1977. pap. 1.25 o.p. (ISBN 0-590-02352-7, Schol Pap). Schol Bk Serv.
Greene, Ethel J., jt. auth. see Robinson, Kitty K.
Greene, Eunice G. Anatomy of the Rat. (Illus.). 1971. Repr. of 1935 ed. 65.00 (ISBN 0-02-845440-5). Hafner.
Greene, Fayal. Crepes. 1977. pap. 1.25 o.p. (ISBN 0-445-08560-6). Popular Lib.
--The Food Processor Cookbook. 1977. pap. 1.50 o.p. (ISBN 0-445-08598-3). Popular Lib.
Greene, Fred. Stresses in U.S. - Japanese Security Relations. (Studies in Defense Policy). 120p. 1975. pap. 3.95 (ISBN 0-8157-3271-6). Brookings.
Greene, Graham. Brighton Rock. LC 38-15724. 316p. 1981. 14.95 (ISBN 0-670-19153-1). Viking Pr.
--A Burnt-Out Case. 1977. pap. 2.50 (ISBN 0-14-001894-8). Penguin.
--The Comedians. 1981. 14.95 (ISBN 0-670-23208-4). Viking Pr.
--The Confidential Agent. 208p. 1981. pap. 2.95 (ISBN 0-14-001895-6). Penguin.
--The Heart of the Matter. 1981. 14.95 (ISBN 0-670-36459-2). Viking Pr.
--The Human Factor. 1978. pap. 2.75 (ISBN 0-380-41491-0, 50302). Avon.
--In Search of a Character. 112p. 1981. pap. 2.50 (ISBN 0-14-002822-6). Penguin.
--The Little Fire Engine. 48p. (gr. 1-3). 1973. PLB 5.95 o.p. (ISBN 0-385-08908-2). Doubleday.
--Loser Takes All. 1977. pap. 2.95 (ISBN 0-14-003277-0). Penguin.
--Our Man in Havana. LC 58-11735. 248p. 1981. 14.95 (ISBN 0-670-53141-3). Viking Pr.
--The Third Man; bd. with The Fallen Idol. 1981. pap. 3.95 (ISBN 0-14-003278-9). Penguin.
--The Third Man: Loser Takes All. Date not set. 14.95 (ISBN 0-670-70084-3). Viking Pr.
--Travels with My Aunt. LC 72-94848. 324p. 1981. 14.95 (ISBN 0-670-72524-2). Viking Pr.
--Twenty-One Stories. 200p. 1981. pap. 2.95 (ISBN 0-14-003093-X). Penguin.
--Ways of Escape. Date not set. 12.95 (ISBN 0-671-41219-1). S&S.
Greene, Harry A. & Petty, Walter T. Developing Language Skills in the Elementary Schools. 5th ed. 480p. 1975. text ed. 15.95x o.p. (ISBN 0-205-04670-3, 2246708); student guide 5.95x o.p. (ISBN 0-205-04672-X); instr's manual free o.p. (ISBN 0-205-04671-1). Allyn.
Greene, Herb. Mind & Image: An Essay on Art & Architecture. LC 74-18932. (Illus.). 224p. 1976. 23.50x (ISBN 0-8131-1323-7). U Pr of Ky.
Greene, Herb & Greene, Nanine H. Building to Last. (Illus.). 168p. 1981. 24.95. Architectural.
Greene, Hugh, ed. Cosmopolitan Crimes: The Foreign Rivals of Sherlock Holmes. 1972. pap. 1.95 o.p. (ISBN 0-14-003571-0). Penguin.
Greene, Iohn see Heywood, Thomas.
Greene, Jack. The Mudgrump. LC 80-68130. (Illus.). 56p. (Orig.). pap. text ed. 3.95 perfect inding (ISBN 0-9601258-3-3). Golden Owl Pub.
Greene, Jack P. Landon Carter: An Inquiry into the Personal Values & Social Imperatives of the Eighteenth-Century Virginia Gentry. LC 64-19201. 1976. pap. 3.95x (ISBN 0-8139-0111-1). U Pr of Va.
Greene, Jack P., ed. Settlements to Society, 1607-1763: A Documentary History of Colonial America. 400p. 1975. pap. 5.95x (ISBN 0-393-09232-1). Norton.
Greene, Jacqueline. A Classroom Hanukah. (Illus., Orig.). (gr. k-4). 1980. pap. 3.00x (ISBN 0-938836-01-3). Pascal Pubs.
Greene, Jacqueline D. The Hanukah Tooth. (Illus.). 24p. (ps-2). 1980. pap. 2.00 (ISBN 0-938836-00-5). Pascal Pubs.
Greene, James H. Production & Inventory Control: Systems & Decisions. rev. ed. 1974. text ed. 19.95 (ISBN 0-256-01431-0). Irwin.
Greene, Janice P., jt. auth. see Brewer, Gail S.
Greene, John C. Science, Ideology, & World View: Essays in the History of Evolutionary Ideas. 1981. 14.00 (ISBN 0-520-04217-4); pap. 4.95 (ISBN 0-520-04218-2). U of Cal Pr.
Greene, Joshua, retold by. Krishna, Master of All Mystics. (Illus.). 16p. (gr. 1-4). 1981. pap. 2.95 (ISBN 0-89647-010-5). Bala Bks.
Greene, Kenyon De see De Greene, Kenyon.
Greene, Laura. Change. 32p. 1980. 8.95 (ISBN 0-87705-401-0). Human Sci Pr.
Greene, Lawrence S., ed. Malnutrition, Behavior & Social Organization. 1977. 29.50 (ISBN 0-12-298050-6). Acad Pr.
Greene, Lee S., et al. Government in Tennessee. 3rd ed. LC 75-12587. 418p. 1975. 12.50x (ISBN 0-87049-178-4); pap. 7.95 o.p. (ISBN 0-87049-180-6). U of Tenn Pr.
Greene, Liz. The Dreamer of the Vine: A Novel About Nostramus. 1981. 12.95 (ISBN 0-393-01434-7). Norton.
--Looking at Astrology. LC 77-83149. (Illus.). 30p. (gr. 2-7). 1981. pap. 4.95 (ISBN 0-916360-13-X). CRCS Pubns WA.
--Star Signs for Lovers. LC 80-5890. (Illus.). 480p. 1980. 14.95 (ISBN 0-8128-2765-1). Stein & Day.
Greene, M., ed. see Nekrasov, V.
Greene, M. Louise. Development of Religious Liberty in Connecticut. LC 74-99858. (Civil Liberties in American History Ser). 1970. Repr. of 1905 ed. lib. bdg. 49.50 (ISBN 0-306-71861-8). Da Capo.
Greene, Margaret. Disorders of Voice. LC 77-183113. (Studies in Communicative Disorders Ser.). 1972. pap. 2.95 (ISBN 0-672-61279-8). Bobbs.
--The Voice & Its Disorders. 4th ed. 446p. 1980. 47.50. Lippincott.
Greene, Margaret C. The Voice & Its Disorders. 3rd ed. LC 72-560. (Illus.). 512p. 1972. 22.50 o.p. (ISBN 0-397-50300-8). Lippincott.
Greene, Maxine. Landscapes of Learning. LC 78-6571. 1978. pap. text ed. 11.50x (ISBN 0-8077-2534-X). Tchrs Coll.
--Teacher As Stranger: Educational Psychology for the Modern Age. 256p. 1973. 10.95x (ISBN 0-534-00205-6). Wadsworth Pub.
Greene, Nanine H., jt. auth. see Greene, Herb.
Greene, Nathanael. From Versailles to Vichy: The Third French Republic 1919-1940. LC 75-101945. (AHM Europe Since 1500 Ser.). 1970. pap. 5.95x (ISBN 0-88295-737-6). AHM Pub.
Greene, Nathanael, ed. Fascism: An Anthology. LC 67-30582. (Orig.). 1968. pap. 8.95x (ISBN 0-88295-736-8). AHM Pub.
Greene, Nicholas M. Physiology of Spinal Anesthesia. 3rd ed. 265p. 1981. write for info. (3554-1). Williams & Wilkins.
Greene, Ralph L. Dynamic & Inspirational Sermons for Today. 128p. 1980. 7.95 (ISBN 0-89962-021-3). Todd & Honeywell.
Greene, Raymond, ed. Current Concepts in Migraine Research. LC 77-83690. 1978. 22.50 (ISBN 0-89004-199-7). Raven.
Greene, Richard L., ed. The Early English Carols. 2nd ed. 1977. 85.00x (ISBN 0-19-812715-4). Oxford U Pr.
Greene, Richard M., Jr. The Management Game. 1973. pap. 4.95 (ISBN 0-8015-4866-7, Hawthorn). Dutton.
Greene, Robert. Ciceronis Amor: Tullie's Love, a Critical Edition. Larson, Charles H., ed. (Salzburg Studies in English Literature, Elizabethan & Renaissance Studies: No. 36). 216p. 1974. pap. text ed. 25.00x (ISBN 0-391-01392-0). Humanities.
--Friar Bacon & Friar Bungay. Seltzer, Daniel, ed. LC 63-14697. (Regents Renaissance Drama Ser). 1963. 6.95x (ISBN 0-8032-0263-6); pap. 1.85x (ISBN 0-8032-5262-5, BB 200, Bison). U of Nebr Pr.
Greene, Robert F. Tennis Drills: On & off Court Drills & Exercises to Improve Your Game. (Illus.). 1977. pap. 8.95 (ISBN 0-8015-7527-3, Hawthorn). Dutton.
Greene, Robert W. The Sting Man. (Illus.). 256p. 1981. 12.95 (ISBN 0-525-20985-9). Dutton.
Greene, Roberta M. A Question in Search of an Answer: Learning Disability in Jewish Education. LC 8-18059. (Illus.). 262p. 1981. pap. 5.95 (ISBN 0-8074-0029-7). UAHC.
Greene, Roger L. The MMPI: An Interpretive Manual. 1980. 21.00 (ISBN 0-8089-1279-8). Grune.
Greene, Samuel S. First Lessons in Grammar. Repr. of 1848 ed. write for info. (ISBN 0-8201-1349-2). Schol Facsimil.
Greene, Shep. The Boy Who Drank Too Much. (YA) 1980. pap. 1.50 (ISBN 0-440-91066-8, LFL). Dell.
Greene, Sylvia W. Longings. 352p. (Orig.). 1981. pap. 2.50 (ISBN 0-89083-706-6). Zebra.
Greene, Theodora W. Protective Groups in Organic Synthesis. LC 80-25348. 325p. 1981. 80.00 (ISBN 0-471-05764-9, Pub. by Wiley-Interscience). Wiley.
Greene, Thomas H. Comparative Revolutionary Movements. LC 74-793. (Contemporary Comparative Politics Ser). (Illus.). 176p. 1974. pap. text ed. 7.95 (ISBN 0-13-154179-X). P-H.
Greene, Vivian. Chip, Oh Brother! (Illus.). (gr. 3-5). 1979. 2.95 (ISBN 0-531-02510-1); PLB 5.90 s&l (ISBN 0-531-04089-5). Watts.
--Cleveland, the Disco King. (Illus.). (gr. 3-5). 1979. 2.95 (ISBN 0-531-02513-6); PLB 5.90 s&l (ISBN 0-531-04095-X). Watts.
Greene, Vivien. Family Dolls' Houses. 176p. 1974. 23.00 (ISBN 0-8231-3030-4). Branford.
Greene, William C., ed. see Plato.
Greenebaum, Louise G. Contributions of Women: Politics & Government. LC 77-9593. (Contributions of Women Ser.). (Illus.). (gr. 6 up). 1977. PLB 8.95 (ISBN 0-87518-144-9). Dillon.
Greener. The Everything Book of Floors, Walls, & Ceilings. (Illus.). 250p. 1980. 14.95 (ISBN 0-8359-1803-3); pap. 7.95 (ISBN 0-8359-1802-5). Reston.
Greenewalt, C. H., Jr. Ritual Dinners in Early Historic Sardis. (Publications in Classical Studies: Vol. 17). 1978. pap. 11.50x (ISBN 0-520-09563-4). U of Cal Pr.
Greenfeld, Howard. Marc Chagall: An Introduction. LC 80-14277. 192p. 1980. Repr. of 1967 ed. 13.95 (ISBN 0-87951-115-X). Overlook Pr.
Greenfield. Greek & English Lexicon to the New Testament. 5.95 (ISBN 0-310-20350-3). Zondervan.
Greenfield, Concetta C. Humanist & Scholastic Poetics, 1250-1500. LC 76-49779. 341p. 1981. 22.50 (ISBN 0-8387-1991-0). Bucknell U Pr.
Greenfield, Edward, et al. Penguin Stereo Record Guide. 2nd ed. (Handbooks Ser). 1978. pap. 8.95 o.p. (ISBN 0-14-046223-6). Penguin.
Greenfield, Eloise. First Pink Light. LC 75-45478. (Illus.). 40p. (gr. k-3). 1976. PLB 7.89 (ISBN 0-690-01087-7, TYC-J). T Y Crowell.
--Honey, I Love: And Other Love Poems. LC 77-2845. (Illus.). (gr. 1-3). 1978. 7.95 (ISBN 0-690-01334-5, TYC-J); PLB 7.89 (ISBN 0-690-03845-3). T Y Crowell.
--Mary McLeod Bethune. LC 76-11522. (Biography Ser.). (Illus.). (gr. 2-5). 1977. PLB 7.89 (ISBN 0-690-01129-6, TYC-J). T Y Crowell.
--Me & Neesie. LC 74-23078. (Illus.). 40p. (gr. 1-4). 1975. PLB 7.89 (ISBN 0-690-00715-9, TYC-J). T Y Crowell.
--Paul Robeson. LC 74-13663. (Biography Ser.). (Illus.). (gr. 1-5). 1975. PLB 7.89 (ISBN 0-690-00660-8, TYC-J). T Y Crowell.
--Rosa Parks. LC 72-83782. (Biography Ser.). (Illus.). (gr. 1-5). 1973. 7.95 (ISBN 0-690-71210-3, TYC-J); PLB 7.89 (ISBN 0-690-71211-1). T Y Crowell.
--She Come Bringing Me That Little Baby Girl. LC 74-8104. (gr. k-3). 1974. 8.79 (ISBN 0-397-31586-4). Lippincott.
--Sister. LC 73-22182. (gr. 5-12). 1974. 8.95 (ISBN 0-690-00497-4, TYC-J). T Y Crowell.
Greenfield, Eloise, jt. auth. see Little, Lessie J.
Greenfield, Eric V. German Grammar. 3rd ed. (Orig., Ger.). 1968. pap. 3.95 (ISBN 0-06-460034-3, CO 34, COS). Har-Row.
--Spanish Grammar. 4th ed. (Orig.). 1972. pap. 3.95 (ISBN 0-06-460042-4, CO 42, COS). Har-Row.
Greenfield, Eric V., jt. auth. see D'Eca, Raul.
Greenfield, Harry I. Allied Health Manpower. LC 75-76249. (Illus.). 1969. 20.00x (ISBN 0-231-03226-9). Columbia U Pr.
--Manpower & the Growth of Producer Services. LC 66-28265. 1967. 20.00x (ISBN 0-231-03028-2). Columbia U Pr.
Greenfield, Irving. High Terror. 1978. pap. 1.95 o.p. (ISBN 0-445-04244-3). Popular Lib.
Greenfield, Jeff. Tiny Giant: Nate Archibald. LC 75-42035. (Sports Profiles Ser.). (Illus.). 48p. (gr. 4-11). 1976. PLB 8.50 (ISBN 0-8172-0124-6). Raintree Pubs.
--The World's Greatest Team: A Portrait of the Boston Celtics 1957-69. 1976. 7.95 o.p. (ISBN 0-394-49560-8). Random.
Greenfield, Joseph D. Practical Digital Design Using ICs. LC 76-54282. (Electronic Engineering Technology Ser.). 1977. text ed. 22.95 (ISBN 0-471-32505-8); tchr's manual avail. (ISBN 0-471-02532-1). Wiley.
--Using Microprocessors & Microcomputers: The 6800 Family. LC 80-18090. (Electronic Technology Ser.). 512p. 1981. text ed. 18.95 (ISBN 0-471-02727-8). Wiley.
Greenfield, Josh & Mazursky, Paul. Harry & Tonto. 1974. pap. 1.25 o.p. (ISBN 0-445-00214-X). Popular Lib.
Greenfield, Natalee. First Do No Harm. 176p. 1981. pap. 1.95 (ISBN 0-448-17227-5, Tempo). G&D.
Greenfield, Natalee S. First Do No Harm... A Dying Woman's Battle Against the Physicians & Drug Companies Who Misled Her About the Hazards of the Pill. 1976. 7.95 (ISBN 0-8467-0198-7, Pub. by Two Continents). Hippocrene Bks.
Greenfield, Pete. The First Ferro Boat Book. Desoutter, Denny, ed. (Practical Handbooks for the Yachtsman Ser.). (Illus.). 1979. 15.00 (ISBN 0-370-30066-1); pap. 10.50 (ISBN 0-370-30090-4). Transatlantic.
Greenfield, Richard. The Wretched of the Horn: Forgotten Refugees in Black Africa. LC 80-13204. (Illus.). 72p. (Orig.). 1981. pap. 5.95 (ISBN 0-936508-01-9). Barber Pr.
Greenfield, Robert. S. T. P. A Journey Through America with the Rolling Stones. LC 73-16346. 352p. 1974. pap. 3.95 o.p. (ISBN 0-8415-0323-0). Dutton.
Greenfield, S. & Clift, S. Analytic Chemistry of the Condensed Phosphates. LC 74-32261. 1975. text ed. 27.00 (ISBN 0-08-018174-0). Pergamon.
Greenfield, Stanley B. The Interpretation of Old English Poems. 1972. 16.00 (ISBN 0-7100-7340-2). Routledge & Kegan.
Greenfield, Stanley B. & Robinson, Fred C. Bibliography of Publications on Old English Literature to the End of Nineteen Seventy-Two. LC 78-4989. 1980. 75.00x (ISBN 0-8020-2292-8). U of Toronto Pr.
Greenfield, Sumner M., ed. La Generacion de 1898 ante Espana: Antologia de literatura de temas nacionales y universales. LC 80-80146. 400p. 1981. pap. 25.00 (ISBN 0-89295-013-7). Society Sp & Sp-Am.
Greenfield, William. The Greek-English Lexicon to the New Testament. 216p. 1981. pap. 5.95 (ISBN 0-310-20351-1). Zondervan.
Greengard, P. & Costa, E., eds. Role of Cyclic AMP in Cell Function. LC 73-84113. (Advances in Biochemical Psychopharmacology Ser.: Vol. 3). 1970. 24.50 (ISBN 0-911216-15-4). Raven.
Greengard, P. & Robison, G. A., eds. Advances in Cyclic Nucleotide Research, Vol. 6. LC 71-181305. 368p. 1975. 34.50 (ISBN 0-89004-042-7). Raven.

--Advances in Cyclic Nucleotide Research Series, 2 vols. Incl. Vol. 2. New Assay Methods for Cyclic Nucleotides. 145p. 1972. 19.00 (ISBN 0-911216-21-9); Vol. 3. 250p. 1973. 32.00 (ISBN 0-911216-38-3). LC 71-181305. Raven.

Greengard, P., jt. ed. see Costa, E.

Greengard, Paul. Cyclic Nucleotides, Phosphorylated Proteins, & Neuronal Function. LC 78-66349. (Distinguished Lecture Series of the Society of General Physiologists). 1978. 15.00 (ISBN 0-89004-281-0). Raven.

Greengard, Paul & Robison, G. Alan, eds. Advances in Cyclic Nucleotide Research, Vol. 4. LC 71-181305. 498p. 1974. 39.00 (ISBN 0-911216-76-6). Raven.

--Advances in Cyclic Nucleotide Research, Vol. 7. LC 71-181305. 1976. 34.50 (ISBN 0-89004-107-5). Raven.

--Advances in Cyclic Nucleotide Research, Vol. 8. LC 71-181305. 1977. 43.50 (ISBN 0-89004-169-5). Raven.

--Advances in Cyclic Nucleotide Research, Vol. 11. LC 71-181305. 1979. text ed. 39.00 (ISBN 0-89004-363-9). Raven.

Greengard, Paul, jt. ed. see Robison, G. Alan.

Greengarten, I. M. Thomas Hill Green & the Social Assumptions of Liberal-Democratic Thought. 194p. 1981. 25.00x (ISBN 0-8020-5503-6). U of Toronto Pr.

Greengerg, Allan M. Standards Relating to Architecture of Facilities. (Juvenile Justice Standards Project Ser.). 1980. softcover 6.95 (ISBN 0-88410-813-9); casebound 14.50. Ballinger Pub.

Greenhalgh, John. Practitioner's Guide to School Business Management. new ed. 1978. 15.95 (ISBN 0-205-07128-7). Allyn.

Greenhalgh, Michael & Megaw, Vincent, eds. Art in Society: Studies in Style, Culture & Aesthetics. LC 78-69954. 1978. 29.95 (ISBN 0-312-05267-7). St Martin.

Greenhalgh, P. A. Early Greek Warfare. LC 72-87437. 228p. 1973. 32.50 (ISBN 0-521-20056-3). Cambridge U Pr.

Greenhalgh, Peter. Pompey, Vol. I: The Roman Alexander. 288p. 1981. text ed. 23.00 (ISBN 0-8262-0335-3). U of Mo Pr.

Greenhill, Basil. A Quayside Camera, 1845-1917. LC 74-20469. (Illus.). 112p. 1975. 14.95x (ISBN 0-8195-4088-9, Pub. by Wesleyan U Pr). Columbia U Pr.

--Schooners. LC 79-91086. (Illus.). 168p. 1980. 24.95 (ISBN 0-87021-960-X). Naval Inst Pr.

Greenhill, Basil & Giffard, Ann. Travelling by Sea in the Nineteenth Century. (Illus.). 1974. 12.50 o.s.i. (ISBN 0-8038-7151-1). Hastings.

Greenhill, Basil & Gifford, Ann. Victorian & Edwardian Sailing Ships. 1976. 16.95 (ISBN 0-7134-3146-6). David & Charles.

Greenhill, Frank. Incised Effigial Slabs, 2 vols. 1976. Set. 98.00 (ISBN 0-571-10880-6, Pub. by Faber & Faber); Vol. 1. (ISBN 0-571-10741-9); Vol. 2. Merrimack Bk Serv.

Greenhill, George. Gyroscopic Theory. LC 66-30616. 17.50 (ISBN 0-8284-0205-1). Chelsea Pub.

Greenhill, Richard. Employee Remuneration & Profit Sharing. 224p. 1980. 45.00x (ISBN 0-85941-123-0, Pub. by Woodhead-Faulkner England). State Mutual Bk.

Greenhill, Richard, et al. Photography. (Ideals Guidelines). (Illus.). 1980. pap. 2.95 (ISBN 0-89542-900-4). Ideals.

Greenhouse, Jean. Making Miniature Toys & Dolls. 1980. 19.95 (ISBN 0-7134-3271-3). David & Charles.

Greenhowe, Jean. Dolls in National & Folk Costume. (Illus.). 112p. 1978. 11.75 (ISBN 0-8231-3033-9). Branford.

--Fancy Dress from Nursery Tales. (Illus.). 88p. 1976. 10.50 o.s.i. (ISBN 0-7134-2918-6). Hippocrene Bks.

--Making Costume Dolls. 1974. 14.95 (ISBN 0-7134-2313-7, Pub. by Batsford England). David & Charles.

--Making Musical Miniatures. (Illus.). 120p. 1980. 17.95 (ISBN 0-7134-1631-9, Pub. by Batsford England). David & Charles.

Green-Hughes, Evan. A History of Firefighting. 158p. 1980. 37.50x (ISBN 0-903485-61-3, Pub. by Mooreland England). State Mutual Bk.

Greenhut, M. L. & Colberg, Marshall R. Factors in the Location of Florida Industry. LC 62-63440. (FSU Studies: No. 36). (Illus.). 108p. 1962. 5.25 (ISBN 0-8130-0649-X). U Presses Fla.

Greenidge, Gordon & Symes, Patrick. Gordon Greenidge: The Man in the Middle. LC 80-66424. (Illus.). 208p. 1980. 19.95 (ISBN 0-7153-8044-3). David & Charles.

Greening, John R. Fundamentals of Radiation Dosimetry. (Medical Physics Handbook: No. 6). 190p. 1980. 27.00 (ISBN 0-9960020-5-7, Pub. by a Hilger England). Heyden.

Greenland, Cyril. Mental Illness & Civil Liberty. 126p. 1970. pap. text ed. 5.00x (ISBN 0-7135-1826-X, Pub. by Bedford England). Renouf.

Greenland, D. J. Characterization of Soils in Relation to Their Classification & Management. 450p. 1981. 98.00x (ISBN 0-19-854538-X). Oxford U Pr.

Greenland, D. J. & Hayes, M. H. The Chemistry of Soil Processes. LC 79-42908. 618p. 1981. 92.95 (ISBN 0-471-27693-6, Pub. by Wiley-Interscience). Wiley.

Greenland, D. J. & Lal, R., eds. Soil Conservation & Management in the Humid Tropics. LC 76-8908. 1977. 58.75 (ISBN 0-471-99473-1, Pub. by Wiley-Interscience). Wiley.

Greenlaw. Modern Personnel Management. 1979. 19.95 (ISBN 0-03-020806-8). Dryden Pr.

Greenlaw, Jean & Barton, Gretchen. Springboards. (Design for Reading Ser). (Illus., Personal reading). (gr. 3). 1972. text ed. 10.28 (ISBN 0-06-516031-2, SchDept); tchrs.' ed. 5.12 (ISBN 0-06-516231-5); wkbk. 3.20 (ISBN 0-06-516331-1); tchr's ed. wkbk. 6.36 (ISBN 0-06-516431-8). Har-Row.

--Stepping Stones. (Design for Reading Ser). (Illus., Personal reading). (gr. 2). 1972. text ed. 8.68 (ISBN 0-06-516030-4, SchDept); tchr's ed. 5.12 (ISBN 0-06-516230-7); wkbk. 3.20 (ISBN 0-06-516330-3); tchr's ed. wkbk. 6.36 (ISBN 0-06-516430-X). Har-Row.

Greenlaw, Jean & VanRoekel, Byron. Really Reading. (Design for Reading Ser). (Illus.). (gr. 1). 1972. pap. 3.60 (ISBN 0-06-516300-1, SchDept); tchrs. ed. 6.44 (ISBN 0-06-516400-8). Har-Row.

Greenlaw, Jean, jt. auth. see Hamp, Eric P.

Greenlaw, P. S. & Hottenstein, M. P. Prosim: A Production Management Simulation. 1969. pap. text ed. 11.50 scp (ISBN 0-685-88947-5, HarpC); instructor's manual avail. (ISBN 0-06-362455-9); scp 360 computer deck 35.95 (ISBN 0-685-88949-1); scp 700-7000 computer deck 18.50 (ISBN 0-685-88950-5). Har-Row.

Greenlaw, Paul S., jt. auth. see Richards, Max D.

Greenlaw, Paul S., et al. Finansim: A Financial Management Simulation. 2nd ed. 1979. pap. text ed. 11.50 (ISBN 0-8299-0248-1); instrs.' maual avail. (ISBN 0-8299-0613-4). West Pub.

Greenleaf, Elisabeth, ed. Ballads & Sea Songs of Newfoundland. LC 68-20767. (Illus.). xix, 395p. 1968. Repr. of 1933 ed. 15.00 (ISBN 0-8103-5013-0). Gale.

Greenleaf, Frederick P., jt. auth. see Freilich, Gerald.

Greenleaf, Peter. Experiments in Space Science. rev. ed. LC 79-13299. (Illus.). 176p. 1980. lib. bdg. 8.95 (ISBN 0-668-05104-3, 4812-3); pap. 4.95 (ISBN 0-668-04812-3). Arco.

Greenleaf, Richard E. & Meyer, Michael C., eds. Research in Mexican History: Topics, Methodology, Sources, & a Practical Guide to Field Research. LC 72-86020. (Illus.). xiv, 226p. 1973. pap. 3.75x (ISBN 0-8032-5773-2, BB 516, Bison). U of Nebr Pr.

Greenleaf, Stephen. Death Bed. 306p. 1980. 10.95 (ISBN 0-686-69082-6). Dial.

Greenler, Robert. Rainbows, Halos & Glories. LC 80-143722. (Illus.). 304p. 1980. 24.95 (ISBN 0-521-23605-3). Cambridge U Pr.

Greeno, James G., et al. Associative Learning: A Cognitive Analysis. LC 77-17096. (Century Psychology Ser.). (Illus.). 1978. 18.95 (ISBN 0-13-049650-2). P-H.

Greenough, Frances, ed. Letters of Horatio Greenough. LC 70-96437. (Library of American Art Ser.). 1970. Repr. of 1887 ed. lib. bdg. 29.50 (ISBN 0-306-71828-6). Da Capo.

Greenough, Horatio. Form & Function: Remarks on Art, Design & Architecture. Small, Harold A., ed. 1947. pap. 3.95x (ISBN 0-520-00514-7, CAMPUS26). U of Cal Pr.

--The Miscellaneous Writings of Horatio Greenough. LC 75-1118. 1975. lib. bdg. 20.00x (ISBN 0-8201-1152-X). Schol Facsimiles.

Greenough, William C. & King, Francis P. Benefit Plans in American Colleges. LC 77-79995. 1969. 22.50x (ISBN 0-231-03287-0); pap. 9.00x (ISBN 0-231-08632-6). Columbia U Pr.

--Pension Plans & Public Policy. 336p. 1976. 17.50x (ISBN 0-231-04070-9). Columbia U Pr.

Greenough, William T., jt. ed. see Walsh, Roger N.

Greenough, William T., intro. by. The Nature & Nurture of Behavior: Developmental Psychobiology: Readings from Scientific American. LC 72-11800. (Illus.). 1973. pap. text ed. 7.95x (ISBN 0-7167-0867-1); multiple choice questions avail. (ISBN 0-685-99777-4). W H Freeman.

Greenslade, M. W., ed. Victoria History of the Counties of England: Stafford, Vol. 17. (Illus.). 1976. text ed. 69.00x o.p. (ISBN 0-19-722743-0). Oxford U Pr.

Greenslade, Roy. Goodbye to the Working Class. LC 76-373483. 1979. 11.95 (ISBN 0-7145-2511-1, Pub. by M Boyars); pap. 6.95 (ISBN 0-7145-2523-5). Merrimack Bk Serv.

Greenslade, Stanley L. Church & State from Constantine to Theodosius. LC 79-8712. 93p. 1981. Repr. of 1954 ed. lib. bdg. 19.50x (ISBN 0-313-20793-3, GRCS). Greenwood.

Greenslet, Ferris. James Russell Lowell: His Life & Work. LC 77-77162. 1969. Repr. of 1905 ed. 18.00 (ISBN 0-8103-3893-9). Gale.

Greensmith, J. T. Petrology of the Sedimentary Rocks. 6th ed. (Textbook of Petrology Ser.). (Illus.). 1978. text ed. 27.50x (ISBN 0-04-552011-9); pap. text ed. 14.95x (ISBN 0-04-552012-7). Allen Unwin.

Greenspan, Alice. Granny's Special Moments Book. (Florida Grandparents Guide Ser.). (Illus., Orig.). (ps-4). 1980. pap. 1.95 (ISBN 0-936076-01-1). Aaron Pubs.

Greenspan, Bud. Numero Uno. Date not set. pap. 1.75 o.p. (ISBN 0-451-08686-4, E8686, Sig). NAL. Postponed.

Greenspan, Donald. Arithmetic Applied Mathematics. LC 80-40295. (Illus.). 172p. 1980. 29.00 (ISBN 0-08-025047-5); pap. 12.00 (ISBN 0-08-025046-7). Pergamon.

Greenspan, E., ed. Clinical Cancer Chemotherapy. LC 75-14575. 432p. 1975. 26.00 (ISBN 0-89004-069-9). Raven.

Greenspan, Ezra. Clinical Interpretation & Practice of Cancer Chemotherapy. 1981. text ed. price not set (ISBN 0-89004-566-6). Raven.

Greenspan, H. P. Theory of Rotating Fluids. LC 68-12058. (Cambridge Monographs on Mechanics & Applied Mathematics). (Illus.). 1968. text ed. 44.50 (ISBN 0-521-05147-9). Cambridge U Pr.

--The Theory of Rotating Fluids. (Cambridge Monographs on Mechanics & Applied Mathematics). (Illus.). 328p. 1980. pap. 17.95 (ISBN 0-521-29956-X). Cambridge U Pr.

Greenspan, Jack. Accountability & Quality Assurance. LC 80-11308. (Illus.). 288p. 1980. text ed. 29.95 (ISBN 0-89303-007-4). Charles.

Greenspan, Kalman & Fischer, John, eds. Cardiovascular Diseases. (Medical Examination Review Ser.: No. 28). 1973. spiral bdg. 15.00 o.s.i. (ISBN 0-87488-138-2). Med Exam.

Greenspan, Kalman & Giddings, John A., eds. Physiology Review. 5th ed. 1972. spiral bdg. 8.50 (ISBN 0-87488-206-0). Med Exam.

Greenspan, Stanley I. Intelligence & Adaptation. LC 78-13893. (Psychological Issues Monograph: No. 47/48). (Illus.). 412p. 1980. text ed. 22.50x (ISBN 0-8236-2717-9, 002718); pap. 17.50x (ISBN 0-8236-2718-7). Intl Univs Pr.

Greensted, C. S., et al. Essentials of Statistics in Marketing. 1974. 17.95 (ISBN 0-470-32630-1). Halsted Pr.

Greenstein, Blanche, jt. auth. see Woodard, Thomas K.

Greenstein, F. I. & Polsby, N. W. The Handbook of Political Science, 8 vols. Incl. Vol. 1. Political Science: Scope & Theory. 18.95 (ISBN 0-201-02601-5); Vol. 2. Micropolitical Theory. 17.75 (ISBN 0-201-02602-3); Vol. 3. Macropolitical Theory. 22.95 (ISBN 0-201-02603-1); Vol. 4. Nongovernmental Politics. 17.95 (ISBN 0-201-02604-X); Vol. 5. Governmental Institutions & Processes. 21.95 (ISBN 0-201-02605-8); Vol. 6. Politics & Policymaking. 20.95 (ISBN 0-201-02606-6); Vol. 7. Strategies of Inquiry. 18.95 (ISBN 0-201-02607-4); Vol. 8. International Politics. 20.95 (ISBN 0-201-02608-2). 1975. Set With Index. boxed 160.00 (ISBN 0-201-02611-2). A-W.

Greenstein, Fred L. American Party System & the American People. 2nd ed. LC 73-110080. (Foundations of Modern Political Science Ser.). 1970. pap. 6.95 ref. ed. (ISBN 0-13-028415-7). P-H.

Greenstein, Jesse P. & Haddow, Alexander, eds. Advances in Cancer Research. Incl. Vol. 1. 1953. 47.00 (ISBN 0-12-006601-7); Vol. 2. 1954. 47.00 (ISBN 0-12-006602-5); Vol. 3. 1955. 47.00 (ISBN 0-12-006603-3); Vol. 4. 1956. 47.00 (ISBN 0-12-006604-1); Vol. 5. 1958. 47.00 (ISBN 0-12-006605-X); Vol. 6. Haddow, Alexander & Weinhouse, Sidney, eds. 1962. 47.00 (ISBN 0-12-006606-8); Vol. 7. 1963. 47.00 (ISBN 0-12-006607-6); Vol. 8. 1964. 47.00 (ISBN 0-12-006608-4); Vol. 9. 1965. 47.00 (ISBN 0-12-006609-2); Vol. 10. 1967. 47.00 (ISBN 0-12-006610-6); Vol. 11. 1969. 47.00 (ISBN 0-12-006611-4); Vol. 12. Klein, George & Weinhouse, Sidney, eds. 1969. 47.00 (ISBN 0-12-006612-2); Vol. 13. 1970. 47.00 (ISBN 0-12-006613-0); Vol. 14. 1971. 47.00 (ISBN 0-12-006614-9); Vol. 15. 1972. 47.00 (ISBN 0-12-006615-7); Vol. 16. 1972. 47.00 (ISBN 0-12-006616-5); Vol. 17. 1973. 47.00 (ISBN 0-12-006617-3); Vol. 18. 1973. 47.00 (ISBN 0-12-006618-1). Acad Pr.

Greenstone, James L. & Leviton, Sharon. Hotline: The Crisis Intervention Directory. 350p. 1981. lib. bdg. 45.00 (ISBN 0-87196-373-6). Facts on File.

Greenstreet, Robert, jt. auth. see Porter, Tom.

Greenvale School, Ninth Grade English Class. Bulldozers, Loaders, & Spreaders. LC 73-10799. (Illus.). 64p. (gr. k-3). 1974. PLB 4.95 (ISBN 0-385-02376-6). Doubleday.

Greenwald, Anthony G., et al. Psychological Foundations of Attitudes. (Social Psychology Ser). 1968. text ed. 19.95 (ISBN 0-12-300750-X). Acad Pr.

Greenwald, Bruce C. Adverse Selection in the Labor Market. LC 78-75052. (Outstanding Dissertations in Economics Ser.). 1979. lib. bdg. 30.00 (ISBN 0-8240-4130-5). Garland Pub.

Greenwald, Edward S. Cancer Chemotherapy. 2nd ed. (Medical Outline Ser.). 1973. spiral bdg. 13.50 (ISBN 0-87488-631-7). Med Exam.

Greenwald, Edward S., et al. Cancer Chemotherapy: Supplement. 2nd. ed. 1974. pap. 4.00 (ISBN 0-87488-630-9). Med Exam.

Greenwald, Harold. Active Psychotherapy. new ed. LC 73-22473. 384p. 1974. Repr. 25.00x (ISBN 0-87668-136-4). Aronson.

--Direct Decision Therapy. LC 73-75565. 1973. text ed. 10.95 (ISBN 0-912736-15-1). EDITS Pubs.

--The Happy Person. LC 80-6154. 192p. 1981. 10.95 (ISBN 0-8128-2783-X). Stein & Day.

Greenwald, Howard P. Social Problems in Cancer Control. LC 79-15385. 304p. 1979. reference 24.50 (ISBN 0-88410-708-6). Ballinger Pub.

Greenwald, Jerry. Creative Intimacy. 1977. pap. 2.75 (ISBN 0-515-05971-4). Jove Pubns.

Greenwald, Maurine W. Women, War, & Work: The Impact of World War I on Women Workers in the United States. LC 80-540. (Contributions in Women's Studies: No. 12). (Illus.). xxvii, 309p. 1980. lib. bdg. 27.50 (ISBN 0-313-21355-0, GWW/). Greenwood.

Greenwald, Nancy. Ladycat. 1981. pap. 2.75 (ISBN 0-451-09762-9, E9762, Sig). NAL.

Greenwald, Sheila. Give Us a Great Big Smile, Rosy Cole. (Illus.). 80p. (gr. 3 up). 1981. 7.95 (ISBN 0-316-32672-0, Pub. by Atlantic). Little.

--It All Began with Jane Eyre: Or, the Secret Life of Franny Dillman. (Illus.). (gr. 3-7). 1980. 7.95 (ISBN 0-316-32671-2, Pub. by Atlantic-Little Brown). Little.

--The Secret in Miranda's Closet. (gr. 4-6). 1978. pap. 0.95 o.p. (ISBN 0-590-11895-1, Schol Pap). Schol Bk Serv.

Greenwalt, Tibor J., ed. see American Red Cross Seventh Annual Scientific Symposium, Washington, D.C., May 1975.

Greenway, Ambrose. Comecon Merchant Ships. 2nd ed. (Illus.). 150p. 1981. text ed. 20.00x (ISBN 0-911378-34-0). Sheridan.

--Soviet Merchant Ships. 4th ed. (Illus.). 220p. 1981. text ed. 20.00x (ISBN 0-911378-33-2). Sheridan.

Greenway, Cornelius, frwd. by. This Is for You. 68p. 1974. Repr. of 1949 ed. text ed. 3.75. Pen-Art.

Greenway, Hawk. The Trail North. (Illus.). 180p. (Orig.). 1981. pap. 6.00 (ISBN 0-933280-04-1). Island CA.

Greenway, James C., Jr. Extinct & Vanishing Birds of the World. 2nd ed. (Illus.). 11.00 (ISBN 0-8446-2164-1). Peter Smith.

Greenway, John. Literature Among the Primitives. LC 64-13289. xviii, 346p. 1964. Repr. of 1964 ed. 15.00 (ISBN 0-8103-5001-7). Gale.

--The Primitive Reader: An Anthology of Myths, Tales, Songs, Riddles, & Proverbs of Aboriginal Peoples Around the World. LC 65-21986. viii, 211p. Repr. of 1965 ed. 15.00 (ISBN 0-8103-5014-9). Gale.

--Tales from the British Isles. LC 78-56058. (The World Folktale Library). (Illus.). 1979. lib. bdg. 7.65 (ISBN 0-686-51163-8). Silver.

--Tales from the United States. LC 78-54626. (The World Folktale Library). (Illus.). 1979. lib. bdg. 7.65 (ISBN 0-686-51166-2). Silver.

Greenway, K. Marigold Garden. LC 72-3992. (Peter Possum Paperbacks Ser). 1967. pap. 0.95 o.p. (ISBN 0-531-05120-X). Watts.

Greenwood, B. & Dowell, J. Masculine Focus in Home Economics. LC 75-10815. 1975. pap. 2.50 (ISBN 0-686-14990-4, 261-08422). Home Econ Educ.

Greenwood, C. T., jt. auth. see MacGregor, A.

Greenwood, Colin. Firearms Control: A Study of Armed Crime & Firearms Control in England & Wales. (Illus.). 272p. 1972. 25.00 (ISBN 0-7100-7435-2). Routledge & Kegan.

Greenwood, D. Classical Dynamics. 1977. 26.95 (ISBN 0-13-136036-1). P-H.

Greenwood, David, jt. auth. see Flint, Jeremy.

Greenwood, David C. Nature of Science. 1960. 3.75 o.p. (ISBN 0-685-77487-2). Philos Lib.

Greenwood, Donald T. & Fung, Y., eds. Principles of Dynamics. 1965. text ed. 27.95 (ISBN 0-13-708974-0). P-H.

Greenwood, Douglas C. Product Engineering Design Manual. (Illus.). 342p. 1981. Repr. text ed. write for info. (ISBN 0-89874-273-0). Krieger.

Greenwood, Ernest, jt. auth. see Mayer, K.

Greenwood, Isaac J. Circus, Its Origin & Growth Prior to 1835. (Illus.). 1962. 5.00 o.p. (ISBN 0-87588-021-5). Hobby Hse.

Greenwood, J. A., jt. auth. see Charlier, C. V.

Greenwood, James W., III & Greenwood, James W., Jr. Managing Executive Stress: A Systems Approach. LC 79-4100. 1979. 19.95 (ISBN 0-471-04084-3, Pub. by Wiley-Interscience). Wiley.

Greenwood, John D. Namesakes of the Eighties. 1980. 22.00. Freshwater.

Greenwood, John O. Greenwood's Guide to Great Lakes Shipping. rev. ed. 700p. 1979. text ed. 30.00 (ISBN 0-685-52168-0). Freshwater.

--Namesakes Nineteen Fifty-Six to Ninety Eighty. 1981. casebound 27.00 (ISBN 0-686-69468-6). Freshwater.

Greenwood, Larry. How to Search for Information: A Beginner's Guide to the Literature of Psychology. LC 80-53708. (Basic Tools Ser.: No. 1). 50p. (Orig.). 1980. pap. text ed. 3.95 (ISBN 0-938376-00-4). Willowood Pr.

Greenwood, Michael. Migration & Economic Growth in the United States: National, Regional & Metropolitan Perspectives. (Studies in Urban Economics). 1981. price not set (ISBN 0-12-300650-3). Acad Pr.

Greenwood, N. N. The Chemistry of Boron. (Pergamon Texts in Inorganic Chemistry: Vol. 8). 328p. 1975. text ed. 46.00 (ISBN 0-08-018790-0); pap. text ed. 26.00 (ISBN 0-08-018789-7). Pergamon.

Greenwood, P. H. & Norman, J. R. A History of Fishes. 3rd ed. 1976. pap. 18.95 (ISBN 0-470-99012-0). Halsted Pr.

Greenwood, Royston, et al. Patterns of Management in Local Government. (Government & Administration Ser.). 192p. 1981. 27.50x (ISBN 0-85520-244-0, Pub. by Martin Robertson England). Biblio Dist.

Greenwood, William T. Issues in Business & Society. 3rd ed. LC 76-12021. (Illus.). 576p. 1976. pap. text ed. 12.75 (ISBN 0-395-21410-6). HM.

Greep, J. M., et al, eds. Pain in Shoulder & Arm: An Integrated View. (Developments in Surgery Ser.: No. 1). 306p. 1980. lib. bdg. 47.35 (ISBN 90-247-2146-6, Pub. by Martinus Nijhoff). Kluwer Boston.

Greep, Roy, ed. Recent Progress in Hormone Research, Vol. 37. (Serial Publication). 1981. price not set (ISBN 0-12-571137-9). Acad Pr.

Greep, Roy O. see Laurentian Hormone Conferences.

Greer, Archie, jt. ed. see Clift, Charles, III.

Greer, Art. The Sacred Cows Are Dying: Exploding the Myths We Try to Live by. LC 77-70123. 1978. 6.95 (ISBN 0-8015-6509-X, Hawthorn). Dutton.

Greer, Arthur E. No Grown-Ups in Heaven. 1977. pap. 3.95 (ISBN 0-8015-5403-9, Hawthorn). Dutton.

Greer, Colin. Cobweb Attitudes: Essays on Educational & Cultural Mythology. LC 76-94368. 1970. pap. text ed. 4.75x (ISBN 0-8077-1468-2). Tchrs Coll.

Greer, Colin, jt. ed. see Shields, James J.

Greer, Donald. The Incidence of Emigration During the French Revolution. 1951. 7.00 (ISBN 0-8446-1210-3). Peter Smith.

Greer, Douglas. Design for Music Learning. LC 79-21117. 1980. pap. text ed. 12.95x (ISBN 0-8077-2573-0). Tchrs Coll.

Greer, Frances & Greer, Frances. Stenospeed Shorthand 25,000 Word Dictionary. (Illus.). 384p. 1971. 8.50 o.p. (ISBN 0-911744-26-6). Intl Educ Systems.

Greer, Frances A. Instant Notetaking. (Illus.). 1974. 7.95 o.p. (ISBN 0-911744-28-2). Intl Educ Systems.

--Stenospeed Shorthand. 300p. 1974. 8.75 o.p. (ISBN 0-911744-31-2). Intl Educ Systems.

--Stenospeed Workbook. 150p. 1974. pap. 3.45 o.p. (ISBN 0-911744-32-0). Intl Educ Systems.

Greer, Frances A. & Mitchell, W. M. Advanced Dictation & Transcription. 384p. 1974. 9.45 o.p. (ISBN 0-911744-27-4). Intl Educ Systems.

Greer, Francesca. First Fire. (Orig.). 1979. pap. 2.50 o.s.i. (ISBN 0-446-81915-8). Warner Bks.

--Second Sunrise. 284p. (Orig.). 1981. pap. 2.50 (ISBN 0-446-91214-X). Warner Bks.

Greer, Gaylon E. The Real Estate Investor & the Federal Income Tax. LC 78-569. (Real Estate for Professional Practitioners Ser.). 1978. 26.50 (ISBN 0-471-01882-1, Pub. by Wiley-Interscience). Wiley.

Greer, Germaine. The Female Eunuch. (McGraw-Hill Paperback Ser.). 360p. 1980. pap. 5.95 (ISBN 0-07-024375-1). McGraw.

--The Obstacle Race: The Fortunes of Women Painters & Their Work. (Illus.). 373p. 1979. 25.00 (ISBN 0-374-22412-9); pap. 15.00 (ISBN 0-374-51582-4). FS&G.

Greer, Michael. Your Future in Interior Design. rev. ed. LC 79-95600. (Illus.). (gr. 7 up). 1980. PLB 5.97 o.p. (ISBN 0-8239-0200-5). Rosen Pr.

--Your Future in Interior Design. (Careers in Depth Ser.). 1980. lib. bdg. 5.97 (ISBN 0-8239-0524-1). Rosen Pr.

Greer, Roger C. Illustration Index. 3rd ed. LC 72-10918. 1973. 10.00 (ISBN 0-8108-0568-5). Scarecrow.

Greer, Scott. The Urbane View: Life & Politics in Metropolitan America. (Illus.). 352p. 1972. 14.95 (ISBN 0-19-501544-4). Oxford U Pr.

--The Urbane View: Life & Politics in Metropolitan America. LC 71-182424. 364p. 1973. pap. 4.95 (ISBN 0-19-501728-5, 397, GB). Oxford U Pr.

Greer, Scott, ed. Ethnics, Machines, & the American Urban Future. 1981. pap. text ed. 14.25x (ISBN 0-87073-227-7); pap. text ed. 7.95x (ISBN 0-87073-228-5). Schenkman.

Greer, Scott A. Emerging City. LC 62-11851. 1965. pap. text ed. 5.95 (ISBN 0-02-912960-5). Free Pr.

Greer, William J., jt. auth. see Baker, James K.

Greet, Anne H., tr. see Apollinaire, Guillaume.

Greet, Anne Hyde, tr. & annotations by see Apollinaire, Guillaume.

Greeve, Alec. Build Your Boat with Me. 14.95x (ISBN 0-392-07731-0, SpS). Soccer.

Greever, William S. The Bonanza West: The Story of the Western Mining Rushes 1848-1900. 1963. 18.95 (ISBN 0-8061-0556-9). U of Okla Pr.

Greg, Philo see Beharrel, Peter.

Greg, Walter W., ed. Companion to Arber: Being a Calendar of Documents in Edward Arber's Transcript of the Registers of the Company of Stationers of London, 1554-1640. 1967. 20.50x o.p. (ISBN 0-19-818125-6). Oxford U Pr.

Greger, Debora. Cartography. 1980. signed 35.00 (ISBN 0-686-28114-4). Penumbra Press.

Gregg, Davis W. & McGill, Dan M., eds. World Insurance Trends: Proceedings of the 1st International Insurance Conference. LC 58-11409. 1960. 22.00 o.p. (ISBN 0-8122-7220-X). U of Pa Pr.

Gregg, Davis W., jt. ed. see Long, John D.

Gregg, Elizabeth M. & Boston Children's Medical Center Staff, eds. What to Do When There's Nothing to Do: A Mother's Handbook. 1968. 5.95 o.s.i. (ISBN 0-440-09466-6, Sey Lawr). Delacorte.

Gregg, James. The Sportman's Eye. (Illus.). 224p. 1974. pap. 2.95 o.s.i. (ISBN 0-02-028850-6, Collier). Macmillan.

Gregg, James R. How to Communicate in Optometric Practice. LC 69-17435. 1969. text ed. 5.95x o.p. (ISBN 0-8019-5374-X). Chilton.

--Your Future in Optometry. LC 72-114107. (Career Guidance Ser). 1971. pap. 3.50 (ISBN 0-668-02259-0). Arco.

Gregg, Joan. Communication & Culture: A Reading-Writing Text. (Orig.). 1980. pap. text ed. 8.95 (ISBN 0-442-23895-9); instr's. manual 2.95. D Van Nostrand.

Gregg, John R., et al. Gregg Shorthand. (Diamond Jubilee Ser). 1963. text ed. 9.80 (ISBN 0-07-024591-6, G); student transcript 3.40 (ISBN 0-07-024525-8); wkbk. 4.40 (ISBN 0-07-037308-6) (ISBN 0-686-60795-3). McGraw.

--Gregg Shorthand. 2nd ed. (Diamond Jubilee Ser). 1972. 7.95 (ISBN 0-07-024625-4, G); text ed. 9.80 (ISBN 0-686-66105-2); instructor's handbk. 3.90 (ISBN 0-07-024626-2); students transcript 3.40 (ISBN 0-07-024627-0); wkbk 4.40 (ISBN 0-07-037250-0); key to wkbk. 2.70 (ISBN 0-07-037251-9). McGraw.

Gregg, Josiah. Commerce of the Prairies. Quaife, Milo M., ed. LC 27-1450. (Illus.). 1967. pap. 4.75 (ISBN 0-8032-5076-2, BB 324, Bison). U of Nebr Pr.

Gregg, Lee W. & Steinberg, Erwin, eds. Cognitive Processes in Writing. LC 80-18624. (Illus.). 208p. 1980. text ed. 19.95 (ISBN 0-89859-032-9). L Erlbaum Assocs.

Gregg, Linda. Too Bright to See. 72p. 1981. 9.00. Graywolf.

Gregg, Philip M. Problems of Theory in Policy Analysis. LC 75-16626. (Policy Studies Organization Ser.). 208p. 1976. 18.95 (ISBN 0-669-00057-4). Lexington Bks.

Gregg, Robert E. The Ants of Colorado: Their Ecology, Taxonomy & Geographic Distribution. LC 62-63446. (Illus.). 1963. 19.50x (ISBN 0-87081-027-8). Colo Assoc.

Gregg, Robert S. Influence of Border Troubles on Relations Between the United States & Mexico, 1876-1910. LC 72-98181. (American Scene Ser). 1970. Repr. of 1937 ed. lib. bdg. 25.00 (ISBN 0-306-71833-2). Da Capo.

Gregg, Rosalie, ed. see Wise County Historical Survey Committee.

Gregg, Thomas G., jt. auth. see Mettler, Lawrence E.

Gregg, W. David. Analog & Digital Communications: Concepts, Systems & Applications, & Services in Electrical Dissemination of Aural, Visual & Data Information. LC 76-58417. 1977. text ed. 30.95 (ISBN 0-471-32661-5). Wiley.

Grego, Joseph. A History of Parliamentary Elections & Electioneering: From the Stuarts to Queen Victoria. LC 73-141755. (Illus.). 403p. 1974. Repr. of 1892 ed. 36.00 (ISBN 0-8103-4030-5). Gale.

Gregor, A. J. Ideology of Fascism. LC 69-16920. 1969. 13.95 o.s.i. (ISBN 0-02-913030-1). Free Pr.

Gregor, A. James. The Fascist Persuasion in Radical Politics. LC 73-2463. 424p. 1974. 21.50 (ISBN 0-691-07556-5). Princeton U Pr.

--Young Mussolini & the Intellectual Origins of Fascism. 1979. 18.50x (ISBN 0-520-03799-5). U of Cal Pr.

Gregor, Arthur S. Adventure of Man. (gr. 7 up). 1966. 4.95g o.s.i. (ISBN 0-02-736970-6). Macmillan.

--Galileo Galilei, Space Pioneer. (gr. 2-5). 1965. 3.95 o.s.i. (ISBN 0-02-736800-9). Macmillan.

--How the World's First Cities Began. (Illus.). (gr. 3-7). 1967. PLB 6.50 o.p. (ISBN 0-525-32417-8). Dutton.

--Life Styles: An Introduction to Cultural Anthropology. LC 78-3416. (Illus.). 1978. 9.95 (ISBN 0-684-15599-0, ScribT). Scribner.

--Witchcraft & Magic: The Supernatural World of Primitive Man. LC 72-1166. (Illus.). 160p. (gr. 5-9). 1972. pap. 2.45 o.p. (ISBN 0-684-14537-5, SL 619, ScribT). Scribner.

Gregor, Douglas B. Celtic: A Comparative Study. (Language & Literature Ser.). 1980. 36.00 (ISBN 0-900891-41-6). Oleander Pr.

Gregor, Hugh. Armor. LC 78-64662. (Fact Finders Ser.). (Illus.). 1979. lib. bdg. 3.96 (ISBN 0-686-51124-7). Silver.

--Warships. LC 78-64660. (Fact Finders Ser.). (Illus.). 1979. lib. bdg. 3.96 (ISBN 0-686-51132-8). Silver.

Gregor, Ian, ed. see Arnold, Matthew.

Gregor, Joseph. Kulturgeschichte der Oper. 2nd, rev. & enl. ed. LC 80-2282. 1981. Repr. of 1950 ed. 57.50 (ISBN 0-404-18847-8). AMS Pr.

Gregor, Richard see McNeal, Robert H.

Gregor, W. G., ed. see Gray, J. H.

Gregoratos, Gabriel, jt. ed. see Karliner, Joel.

Gregoriadis, G. & Allison, A. C. Liposomes in Biological Systems. LC 79-40507. 1980. 68.50 (ISBN 0-471-27608-1, Pub. by Wiley-Interscience). Wiley.

Gregorich, Barbara. Expanding Your Vocabulary. LC 78-730053. (Illus.). 1978. pap. text ed. 99.00 (ISBN 0-89290-126-8, 327-SATC). Soc for Visual.

Gregorich, Barbara & Odom, Clark. Fractions. LC 79-730045. (Illus.). 1978. 99.00 (ISBN 0-89290-094-6, A510-SATC). Soc for Visual.

Gregorich, Barbara & Waldowski, Therese F. Punctuation Through Proofreading. LC 78-730056. (Illus.). 1977. pap. text ed. 99.00 (ISBN 0-89290-124-1, A325). Soc for Visual.

--The Research Paper. LC 78-730060. (Illus.). 1977. pap. text ed. 99.00 (ISBN 0-89290-124-1, A323). Soc for Visual.

Gregorich, Barbara & Zack, Carol. The Newspaper: Reading Skills. LC 78-730963. (Illus.). 1978. pap. text ed. 99.00 (ISBN 0-89290-114-4, A160). Soc for Visual.

Gregorio, M. Pauline, ed. Medical Record Library Science Examination Review Book, Vol. 1. 3rd ed. 1976. spiral bdg. 10.00 (ISBN 0-87488-496-9). Med Exam.

Gregorius I. Life & Miracles of Saint Benedict: Book Two of Dialogues. Zimmermann, Odo J. & Avery, Benedict R., trs. from Latin. LC 80-19624. xv, 87p. 1980. Repr. of 1949 ed. lib. bdg. 13.75x (ISBN 0-313-22766-7, GRLI). Greenwood.

Gregorvich, Barbara & Manoni, Mary H. Learning to Spell Correctly. LC 78-730054. (Illus.). 1978. pap. text ed. 99.00 (ISBN 0-89290-127-6, 331-SATC). Soc for Visual.

Gregorvich, Barbara, jt. auth. see Mahoney, Susan.

Gregory. Go Ahead Series, Gr. 1. Incl. Bk. 1. Tom's Little Feet. pap. text ed. (ISBN 0-8009-0819-8); pkg. of 10 copies 9.28 (ISBN 0-8009-0917-8); Bk. 2. Big Egg. pap. text ed. (ISBN 0-8009-0822-8); Bk. 3. Red Kite. pap. text ed. (ISBN 0-8009-0824-4); pkg. of 10 copies 9.28 (ISBN 0-8009-0921-6); Bk. 4. Grandma the Kitten. pap. text ed. (ISBN 0-8009-0826-0); pkg. of 10 copies 9.28 (ISBN 0-8009-0923-2); Bk. 5. Dog Who Wanted a Boy. pap. text ed. (ISBN 0-8009-0828-7); pap. text ed. 9.28 pkg. of 10 copies (ISBN 0-8009-0925-9). 1969. pap. text ed. 1.04 ea.; tchr's. ed. for Go Ahead Ser, Gr. 1-3 9.28 (ISBN 0-8009-0919-4). McCormick-Mathers.

--Go Ahead Series, Gr. 2. Incl. Bk. 1. Bill & I. (ISBN 0-8009-0830-9); pkg. of 10 (ISBN 0-8009-0927-5); Bk. 2. Blue Weed. pap. text ed. (ISBN 0-8009-0832-5); pkg. of 10 (ISBN 0-8009-0929-1); Bk. 3. House on Wheels. pap. text ed. (ISBN 0-8009-0834-1); pkg. of 10 (ISBN 0-8009-0931-3); Bk. 4. New Shoes. pap. text ed. (ISBN 0-8009-0836-8); pkg. of 10 (ISBN 0-8009-0934-8); Bk. 5. Balloon Book. pap. text ed. (ISBN 0-8009-0838-4); pkg. of 10 (ISBN 0-8009-0936-4); Bk. 6. An Umbrella for May. (ISBN 0-8009-0840-6); pap. text ed. kpkg. of 10 (ISBN 0-8009-0938-0); Bk. 7. Boat. pap. text ed. (ISBN 0-8009-0842-2); pkg. of 10 (ISBN 0-8009-0940-2). 1969-70. pap. text ed. 1.04 ea.; pkgs. of 10 of same title 9.28 ea.; tchr's. ed. for Go Ahead 8ser, Gr. 1-3 9.25 (ISBN 0-8009-0919-4). McCormick-Mathers.

--Go Ahead Series, Gr. 3. Incl. Bk. 2. Little Clown. pap. text ed. (ISBN 0-8009-0844-9); pkg. of 10 (ISBN 0-8009-0942-9); Bk. 2310#10#.00. Yellow Horse. pap. text ed. (ISBN 0-8009-0846-5); pkg. of 10 (ISBN 0-8009-0944-5); Bk. 3. Sue's Tree. pap. text ed. (ISBN 0-8009-0850-3); pkg. of 10 (ISBN 0-8009-0946-1); Bk. 4. Mr. Long's Long Feet. pap. text ed. (ISBN 0-8009-0853-8); pkg. of 10 (ISBN 0-8009-0948-8); Bk. 5. Nine on Team. pap. text ed. (ISBN 0-8009-0855-4); pkg. of 10 (ISBN 0-8009-0951-8); Bk. 6. Happy the Merry-Go-Round. pap. text ed. (ISBN 0-8009-0857-0); pkg. of 10 (ISBN 0-8009-0953-4). pap. text ed. 1.16 ea.; pkgs. of 10 of same title 10.60 ea.; tchr's. ed. for Go Ahead Ser, Gr. 1-3 9.28 (ISBN 0-8009-0919-4). McCormick-Mathers.

Gregory, Augusta. Seventy Years, 1852-1922. Smythe, Colin, ed. (Illus.). 608p. 1976. 15.00 o.s.i. (ISBN 0-02-545550-8). Macmillan.

Gregory, B. A. An Introduction to Electric Instrumentation & Measurement. LC 80-22869. 435p. 1981. pap. 29.95 (ISBN 0-470-27092-6). Halsted Pr.

Gregory - Bishop Of Tours. History of the Franks. Brehaut, Ernest, tr. (Columbia University Records of Civilization Ser). 1969. pap. 6.95x (ISBN 0-393-09845-1, NortonC). Norton.

Gregory, C., jt. auth. see Jarvis, A. C.

Gregory, C. R., jt. auth. see Jarvis, A. C.

Gregory, Cedric E. A Concise History of Mining. LC 80-13925. 1980. 30.00 (ISBN 0-08-023882-3). Pergamon.

Gregory, D., jt. auth. see Fetter, F. W.

Gregory, Diana. Dairy Goats. LC 76-235. 1976. o. p. 7.95 (ISBN 0-668-03938-8); pap. 3.95 (ISBN 0-668-03941-8). Arco.

--The Fog Burns off by Eleven O'clock. LC 80-26790. 134p. (gr. 4-8). 1981. PLB 7.95 (ISBN 0-201-04139-1, 4139, A-W Childrens). A-W.

--Owning a Horse: A Practical Guide. LC 76-9192. (Illus.). 1977. 11.95 o.s.i. (ISBN 0-06-011622-6, HarpT). Har-Row.

--There's a Caterpillar in My Lemonade. LC 80-17067. 176p. (gr. 4-8). 1980. PLB 7.95 (ISBN 0-201-03603-7, 3603, A-W Childrens). A-W.

Gregory, Dick. Nigger: An Autobiography. Lipsyte, Robert, ed. 1964. 7.95 o.p. (ISBN 0-525-16697-1). Dutton.

--Up from Nigger. 1978. pap. 1.95 o.p. (ISBN 0-449-23416-9, Crest). Fawcett.

Gregory, Elizabeth. Alfred's Alphabet Antics. (Illus.). 1981. 6.95 (ISBN 0-933184-07-7); pap. 4.95 (ISBN 0-933184-08-5). Flame Intl.

--Beach Colors & Beach Creatures. (Illus.). 1981. 6.95 (ISBN 0-933184-17-4); pap. 5.50 (ISBN 0-933184-18-2). Flame Intl.

--Blinky & the Blends. (Illus.). 1981. 6.95 (ISBN 0-933184-11-5); pap. 4.95 (ISBN 0-933184-12-3). Flame Intl.

--The Short & Long. (Illus.). 1981. 6.95 (ISBN 0-933184-09-3); pap. 4.95 (ISBN 0-933184-10-7). Flame Intl.

Gregory, G. Robinson. Forest Resource Economics. 512p. 1972. 22.95 (ISBN 0-8260-3605-8, 40503). Wiley.

Gregory, Gus. Animals & Things. (Illus.). 36p. (gr. k-3). 1979. 2.95 (ISBN 0-8059-2435-3). Dorrance.

Gregory, H. F. The Helicopter. LC 74-30720. (Illus.). 224p. 1976. 15.00 o.p. (ISBN 0-498-01670-6). A S Barnes.

Gregory, Horace & Zaturenska, Marya. Crystal Cabinet. 1967. pap. 1.50 o.s.i. (ISBN 0-02-069540-3, Collier). Macmillan.

--Silver Swan. LC 66-12031. (Illus.). 1968. pap. 1.50 o.s.i. (ISBN 0-02-069550-0, Collier). Macmillan.

Gregory, Hugo H. Stuttering: Differential Evaluation & Therapy. LC 73-4549. (Studies in Communicative Disorders Ser.). 1973. pap. text ed. 2.95 (ISBN 0-672-61291-7). Bobbs.

Gregory, J. W., ed. The Structure of Asia. LC 75-31680. 240p. 1976. Repr. of 1929 ed. 14.50 o.p. (ISBN 0-88275-361-4). Krieger.

Gregory, Janice, jt. auth. see Gregory, Neal.

Gregory, John. A Father's Legacy to His Daughters. Luria, Gina, ed. LC 73-22031. (The Feminist Controversy in England, 1788-1810 Ser.). 1974. lib. bdg. 50.00 (ISBN 0-8240-0863-4). Garland Pub.

Gregory, John, ed. Quadratic Form Theory & Differential Equations. LC 80-520. (Mathematics in Science & Engineering Ser.). 1981. 29.50 (ISBN 0-12-301450-6). Acad Pr.

Gregory, John D., ed. see International Symposium on Glycoconjugates, Fourth.

Gregory, John M. Seven Laws of Teaching. 3rd ed. 1976. 6.00 (ISBN 0-8010-3652-6). PBBC Pr.

Gregory, Joseph L., et al. Bibliography of Fossil Vertebrates, 1978. 384p. (Orig.). 1981. 50.00 (ISBN 0-913312-52-5). Am Geol.

Gregory, Julia, jt. auth. see Bartlett, Hazel.

Gregory, Justina, et al. Survival of Antiquity. LC 80-53219. (Studies in History Ser.: No. 48). (Illus.). 1980. pap. 10.00 (ISBN 0-87391-019-2). Smith Coll.

Gregory, K. J. & Walling, D. E. Drainage Basin Form & Process: A Geomorphological Approach. 1976. pap. text ed. 16.95 (ISBN 0-470-15198-6). Halsted Pr.

Gregory, K. J. & Walling, D. E., eds. Man & Environmental Processes. (Studies in Physical Geography Ser.). 224p. 1980. lib. bdg. 27.50x (ISBN 0-89158-696-2, Pub. by Dawson England); pap. text ed. 13.50x (ISBN 0-89158-865-5). Westview.

Gregory, Laura A. A Study of Data Base Processor Technology. (Data Base Monograph: No. 8). (Illus.). 77p. (Orig.). pap. 15.00 (ISBN 0-89435-035-8). QED Info Sci.

Gregory, Lisa. Analise. 304p. (Orig.). 1981. pap. 2.75 (ISBN 0-515-05469-0). Jove Pubns.

--Bonds of Love. (Orig.). 1978. pap. text ed. 1.95 (ISBN 0-515-04646-9). Jove Pubns.

--The Rainbow Season. (Orig.). pap. 2.25 (ISBN 0-515-05350-3). Jove Pubns.

Gregory, Mary, jt. auth. see Ary, Sheila.

Gregory, Michael & Carroll, Susanne. Language & Situation: Language Varieties & Their Social Contexts. (Language & Sociaty Ser). 1978. 12.50x (ISBN 0-7100-8756-X); pap. 6.25 (ISBN 0-7100-8773-X). Routledge & Kegan.

Gregory, Neal & Gregory, Janice. When Elvis Died. LC 80-19862. (Illus.). 300p. 1980. 13.95 (ISBN 0-89461-032-5). Comm Pr Inc.

Gregory, Norma, jt. auth. see Watling, Roy.

Gregory, P. H. Phytophthora Disease of Cocoa. LC 73-85686. (Illus.). 300p. 1974. text ed. 53.00x (ISBN 0-582-46658-X). Longman.

Gregory, Paul & Stuart, Robert. Comparative Economic Systems. LC 79-87859. 1980. 17.75 (ISBN 0-395-28183-0); inst. manual 0.40 (ISBN 0-395-28184-9). HM.

Gregory, Paul R. & Stuart, Robert C. Soviet Economic Structure & Performance. (Illus.). 1974. pap. text ed. 16.95 scp o.p. (ISBN 0-06-042509-1, HarpC). Har-Row.

Gregory, Peter. Deafness & Public Responsibility. 56p. 1964. pap. text ed. 3.75x (Pub. by Bedford England). Renouf.

--Polluted Homes. 64p. 1965. pap. text ed. 3.75x (Pub. by Bedford England). Renouf.

--Telephones for the Elderly. 128p. 1973. pap. text ed. 5.00x (ISBN 0-7135-1889-8, Pub. by Bedford England). Renouf.

Gregory, R. L. Concepts & Mechanisms of Perception. LC 74-7511. (Encore Edition). (Illus.). 712p. 1974. 14.95 o.p. (ISBN 0-684-15474-9, ScribT). Scribner.

Gregory, R. P. Biochemistry of Photosynthesis. 2nd ed. 1977. 29.75 (ISBN 0-471-32676-3). Wiley.

Gregory, Robert T. Error-Free Computation: Why It Is Needed & Methods for Doing It. LC 80-23923. 148p. (Orig.). 1980. 6.50 (ISBN 0-89874-240-4). Krieger.

Gregory, Robert T., jt. auth. see Young, David M.

Gregory, Ross. Origins of American Intervention in First World War. LC 70-141588. (Essays in American History Ser). 1972. pap. 4.95x (ISBN 0-393-09980-6). Norton.

--Walter Hines Page: Ambassador to the Court of St. James's. LC 78-94067. (Illus.). 252p. 1970. 12.00x (ISBN 0-8131-1198-6). U Pr of Ky.

Gregory, S. Statistical Methods & the Geographer. (Geographies for Advanced Study Ser). (Illus.). 1968. pap. text ed. 7.25x (ISBN 0-391-00185-X). Humanities.

--Statistical Methods & the Geographer. 4th ed. LC 77-7025. (Geographies for Advanced Study Ser). (Illus.). 1978. pap. text ed. 10.95x (ISBN 0-582-48186-4). Longman.

Gregory, S., jt. auth. see Chandler, T. J.

Gregory, S. A. Creativity & Innovation in Engineering. 313p. 1973. 19.50x o.p. (ISBN 0-408-70339-3). Transatlantic.

Gregory, Sadie, jt. auth. see McKenzie, George A.

Gregory, Susan. The Deaf Child & His Family. LC 75-39523. 1976. 19.95 (ISBN 0-470-32662-X). Halsted Pr.

Gregory, Tappan. Nature Photography at Night. (Museum Pictorial: No. 14). 1952. pap. 1.10 o.p. (ISBN 0-916278-41-7). Denver Mus Natl Hist.

Gregory, Thomas W. Adolescence in Literature. LC 77-17719. (English & Humanities Ser.). 1978. pap. text ed. 10.95 (ISBN 0-582-28045-1). Longman.

Gregory, William A., jt. auth. see Reuschlein, Harold G.

Gregory, William K. The Orders of Mammals. LC 78-72718. Repr. of 1910 ed. 67.50 (ISBN 0-404-18293-3). AMS Pr.

--The Structure & Relationships of Notharctus, an American Eocene Primate. LC 78-72719. Repr. of 1920 ed. 47.50 (ISBN 0-404-18294-1). AMS Pr.

Gregory Of Tours see Peters, Edward.

Gregory The Great. The Life of Saint Benedict: Book II of the Dialogues of Gregory the Great. Uhlfelder, Myra L., tr. LC 66-30611. (Orig.). 1967. pap. 2.50 (ISBN 0-672-60468-X, LLA216). Bobbs.

Gregory The Great, St. Dialogues. (Fathers of the Church Ser.: Vol. 39). 15.00 (ISBN 0-8132-0039-3). Cath U Pr.

Gregoy, Robert G., et al. The Guide to the Kenya National Archives. (Foreign & Comparative Studies-Eastern African Bibliographic Ser.: No. 3). 452p. 1969. 16.00. Syracuse U Foreign Comp.

Greidanus, Sidney. Sola Scriptura: Problems & Principles in Preaching Historical Texts. 1979. pap. 10.95x (ISBN 0-88906-103-3). Radix Bks.

Greidanus, T. B. Van Wimersma see Van Wimersma Greidanus, T. B. & Rees, L. H.

Greider, Janice E. & Beadles, William T. Law & the Life Insurance Contract. 4th ed. 1979. text ed. 17.95 (ISBN 0-256-02158-9). Irwin.

--Principles of Life Insurance, Vol. 1. rev. ed. 1973. pap. text ed. 9.00 (ISBN 0-256-01396-9). Irwin.

Greif, Edwin C. Store Talk: An Introduction to Retail Merchandising. LC 78-60034. (gr. 9 up). 1979. pap. 8.60 (ISBN 0-8224-6530-2); pap. 2.40 tchrs'. manual, 1981 (ISBN 0-8224-6531-0). Pitman Learning.

Greif, Martin. Depression Modern: The Thirties Style in America. LC 75-11140. (Illus.). 1977. pap. 7.95 o.s.i. (ISBN 0-87663-925-2). Universe.

--The St. Nicholas Book. LC 76-5089. (Illus.). 60p. 1976. 5.95 o.s.i. (ISBN 0-87663-234-7). Universe.

Greifer, et al. CAPD Update: Continuous Ambulatory Peritoneal Dialysis, Vol. 1. (Modern Problems in Kidney Disease Ser.). 1981. price not set (ISBN 0-89352-134-5). Masson Pub.

Greiff, Barrie S. & Munter, Preston K. Tradeoffs: Executive, Family, & Organizational Life. 1981. pap. 3.50 (ISBN 0-451-61960-9, ME1960, Ment). NAL.

Greig, C., tr. from Lat. Pliny. LC 77-91088. (Illus.). 1979. 3.95x (ISBN 0-521-21978-7). Cambridge U Pr.

Greig, J. C., tr. see Wrede, William.

Greig, W. Smith. Economics of Food Processing. (Illus.). 1971. text ed. 28.50 o.p. (ISBN 0-87055-096-9). AVI.

Greimas, A. Essais de semiotique poetique: Avec des etudes sur Apollinaire, Bataille, Hugo, Jarry, Mallarme, Michaux, Nerval, Rimbaud, Roubaud. (Collection L). 240p. (Orig., Fr.). 1972. pap. 13.95 (ISBN 2-03-036002-3, 2666). Larousse.

Greimas, A. J. L' Ancien Francais. 271p. (Orig.). 1974. bds. 27.50 (ISBN 2-03-070335-4, 3609). Larousse.

Greinacher, Norbert. The Poor & the Church. Muller, Alois, ed. (Concilium Ser: Vol. 104). 1978. pap. 4.95 (ISBN 0-8164-2147-1). Crossroad NY.

Greinacher, Norbert, ed. Evangelization in the World Today. (Concilium Ser.: Vol. 114). 1979. pap. 4.95 (ISBN 0-8164-2610-4). Crossroad NY.

Greinacher, Norbert & Mueller, Alois, eds. Political Commitment & Christian Community. (Concilium Ser.: Religion in the Seventies: Vol. 84). 156p. 1973. pap. 4.95 (ISBN 0-8164-2540-X). Crossroad NY.

Greinacher, Norbert & Muller, Alois, eds. The Church & Human Rights. (Concilium Ser.: Vol. 124). 1979. pap. 4.95 (ISBN 0-8164-2232-X). Crossroad NY.

Greinacher, Norbert, jt. ed. see Elizondo, Virgil.

Greiner, Donald J. Comic Terror: The Novels of John Hawkes. rev. ed. LC 78-16886. 1978. pap. 6.95x (ISBN 0-87870-044-7). Memphis St Univ.

Greiner, Donald J., ed. American Poets Since World War II, 2 vols. (Dictionary of Literary Biography Ser.: Vol. 5). (Illus.). 1980. 108.00 set (ISBN 0-8103-0924-6, Bruccoli Clark). Gale.

Greiner, Gretchen. More of the Best. (gr. 3 up). 1978. pap. 1.25 (ISBN 0-307-21520-2, Golden Pr). Western Pub.

Greiner, James. The Red Snow: Story of the Alaska Gray Wolf. LC 77-82943. 240p. 1980. 10.95 (ISBN 0-385-13169-0). Doubleday.

Greiner, John & Hatry, Harry. Productivity & Motivation: A Review of State & Local Government Initiatives. LC 80-53981. 1981. 18.00 (ISBN 0-87766-283-5, 29600). Urban Inst.

Greiner, John M., et al. Monetary Incentives & Work Standards in Five Cities: Impacts & Implications for Management & Labor. 94p. 1977. pap. 3.95 (ISBN 0-87766-187-1, 17300). Urban Inst.

Greiner, N. Gretchen. My Little Book of Cats. (Tell-a-Tale Readers). (Illus.). (gr. k-3). PLB 4.77 (ISBN 0-307-68626-4, Whitman). Western Pub.

Greiner, N. Gretchen, ed. Best Stories for Girls. (gr. 9 up). 1980. Box Set. pap. 3.75 (ISBN 0-307-13620-5, Golden Pr). Western Pub.

--Still More of the Best. (gr. 3 up). 1979. pap. 1.25 (ISBN 0-307-21519-9, Golden Pr). Western Pub.

Greiner, Vivian. German Achievement Test. (gr. 11-12). 1968. lib. bdg. 4.50 o.p. (ISBN 0-668-01697-3). Arco.

Grejda, Edward S. The Common Continent of Men: Racial Equality in the Novels of Herman Melville. LC 74-80067. 1974. 12.00 (ISBN 0-8046-9073-1, Natl U). Kennikat.

Grell, E., ed. Membrane Spectroscopy. (Molecular Biology, Biochemistry, & Biophysics Ser.: Vol. 31). (Illus.). 512p. 1981. 87.40 (ISBN 0-387-10332-5). Springer-Verlag.

Grell, K. G. Protozoology. 2nd, rev. ed. LC 73-77394. (Illus.). vii, 554p. 1973. 26.20 (ISBN 0-387-06239-4). Springer-Verlag.

Grenander, M. E. Ambrose Bierce. (U. S. Authors Ser.: No. 180). lib. bdg. 8.50 o.p. (ISBN 0-8057-0056-0). Twayne.

Grenander, U., jt. auth. see Freiberger, W.

Grenander, Ulf. Abstract Inference. LC 80-22016. (Probability & Mathematical Statistics Ser.). 528p. 1980. 30.00 (ISBN 0-471-08267-8, Pub. by Wiley Interscience). Wiley.

Grenard, jt. auth. see Krause.

Grendel, Frederick. Beaumarchais: A Biography. Greaves, Roger, tr. (Illus.). 344p. 1977. 14.95 o.s.i. (ISBN 0-690-01210-1, TYC-T). T Y Crowell.

Grene, David & Lattimore, Richmond, eds. Greek Tragedies. Incl. Vol. 1. Agamemnon, Prometheus Bound, Oedipus the King, Antigone. 1960. pap. 4.50 (ISBN 0-226-30774-3, P41); Vol. 2. The Libation Bearers, Electra (Sophocles), Iphigenia in Tauris, Electra (Euripides), the Trojan Women. 1960. pap. text ed. 3.95 (ISBN 0-226-30775-1, P42); Vol. 3. The Eumenides, Philoctetes, Oedipus at Colonus, the Bacchae, Alcestis. 1960. pap. text ed. 3.95 (ISBN 0-226-30777-8, P43). LC 60-950. 1960 (Phoen). U of Chicago Pr.

Grene, David, ed. see Euripides.

Grene, Marjorie. Philosophy in & Out of Europe & Other Essays. LC 75-27924. 1976. 12.50x (ISBN 0-520-03121-0). U of Cal Pr.

Grene, Nicholas. Shakespeare, Jonson, Moliere: The Comic Contract. 246p. 1980. 26.50x (ISBN 0-389-20093-X). B&N.

Grenell, Robert & Gabay, Sabit, eds. Biological Foundations of Psychiatry, 2 vols. LC 74-15664. 690p. 1976. 43.50 ea.; Vol. 1. (ISBN 0-911216-96-0); Vol. 2. (ISBN 0-89004-126-1). Raven.

Grenez-Brovender, Jacqueline, tr. see Clastres, Helene.

Grenier, Albert. Roman Spirit in Religion, Thought & Art. Dobie, M. R., tr. LC 76-118639. (Illus.). 1970. Repr. of 1926 ed. lib. bdg. 29.50x (ISBN 0-8154-0330-5). Cooper Sq.

Grenier, Lise & Wieser-Benedetti, Hans. Les Chateaux de l'Industrie: Lille, 1830-1930, Vol. 2. (Archives d'Architecture Moderne Ser.). (Illus.). 250p. (Fr.). 1979. pap. 27.50x (ISBN 0-8150-0920-8). Wittenborn.

Grennell, Dean A. Home Workshop Digest. 256p. 1981. pap. 7.95 (ISBN 0-910676-14-3). DBI.

Grennen, Joseph. Monarch Notes on Donne & the Metaphysical Poets. (Orig.). pap. 1.95 (ISBN 0-671-00731-9). Monarch Pr.

Grennes, Thomas, et al. Economics of World Grain Trade. LC 77-13715. (Praeger Special Studies). 1978. 22.95 (ISBN 0-03-022836-0). Praeger.

Grenon, M. The Nuclear Apple & the Solar Orange: Alternatives in World Energy. LC 80-40836. (Illus.). 200p. 1980. 36.00 (ISBN 0-08-026157-4); pap. 15.75 (ISBN 0-08-026156-6). Pergamon.

Grenon, M., ed. Future Coal Supply for the World Energy Balance. (International Institute for Applied Systems Analysis. Proceedings). 1979. 125.00 (ISBN 0-08-023437-2). Pergamon.

--Methods & Models for Assessing Energy Resources: First IIASA Conference on Energy Resources, 20-21 May, 1975, Laxenburg, Austria. (IIASA Proceedings: Vol. 5). (Illus.). 1979. 89.00 (ISBN 0-08-024443-2). Pergamon.

Grenvik, Ake, jt. auth. see Safar, Peter.

Grenville, J. A. Europe Reshaped Eighteen Forty-Eight to Eighteen Seventy-Eight. LC 80-66910. (History of Europe Ser.; Cornell Paperbacks Ser.). 412p. 1980. pap. 5.95 (ISBN 0-8014-9207-6). Cornell U Pr.

--A World History of the Twentieth Century: Western Dominance 1900-45, Vol. 1. (Illus.). 605p. 1981. 32.50x (ISBN 0-389-20171-5). B&N.

Grenville, Peter. Kurt Tucholsky: The Ironic Sentimentalist. (German Literature & Society Ser.: Vol. 1). 1980. pap. text ed. write for info. (ISBN 0-85496-074-0). Humanities.

Gresh, Sean. Becoming a Father: A Handbook for Expectant Fathers. Leedham, L., ed. 160p. 1980. 12.95 (ISBN 0-88421-099-5). Butterick Pub.

Gresham, Perry D. With Wings As Eagles. LC 80-66183. 1980. 10.95 (ISBN 0-89305-025-3); pap. 5.95 (ISBN 0-89305-026-1). Anna Pub.

Gresham, Stephen, et al. SPWAO Showcase. Warren, David, ed. Raney, Ken, tr. (Illus.). 72p. (Orig.). 1981. pap. 3.00 (ISBN 0-916176-14-2). Sproing.

Gresham, William L. Houdini: The Man Who Walked Through Walls. LC 59-10470. (Illus.). 1959. 8.95 o.p. (ISBN 0-03-027260-2). HR&W.

Gresley, William. Portrait of an English Churchman, 1838. Wolff, Robert L., ed. Bd. with Charles Lever; or, the Man of the Nineteenth Century, 1841; Church Clavering; or, the Schoolmaster, 1843. LC 75-468. (Victorian Fiction Ser). 1975. lib. bdg. 66.00 (ISBN 0-8240-1546-0). Garland Pub.

Gress, James R. & Purpel, David E., eds. Curriculum: An Introduction to the Field. LC 77-23651. (National Society for the Study of Education Series on Contemporary Educ. Issues). 1978. 17.90 (ISBN 0-8211-0613-9); text ed. 16.20 ten copies (ISBN 0-686-52368-7). McCutchan.

Gresser, Julian, et al. Environmental Law in Japan: An International Perspective. (Illus.). 1980. text ed. 60.00x (ISBN 0-262-07076-6). MIT Pr.

Greteman, Jim. Coping with Divorce. (Illus.). 80p. 1981. spiralbound 3.95 (ISBN 0-87793-226-3). Ave Maria.

Gretler, Armin. The Training of Adult Middle-Level Personnel. LC 72-89860. (Illus.). 164p. (Orig.). 1973. pap. 7.00 (ISBN 92-3-100935-4, U685, UNESCO). Unipub.

Gretor, William, tr. see Bode, Wilhelm.

Gretz, Susanna. The Bears Who Went to the Seaside. LC 72-86763. (Picture Bk). (Illus.). 32p. (gr. k-2). 1973. 4.95 o.p. (ISBN 0-695-80375-1); PLB 5.97 lib. ed. o.p. (ISBN 0-695-40375-3). Follett.

--Teddy Bears, One to Ten. LC 68-9563. (Picture Bk). (Illus.). (ps-3). 1968. 5.95 o.p. (ISBN 0-695-88460-3); PLB 5.97 lib. ed. o.p. (ISBN 0-695-48460-5). Follett.

Greub, Werner, et al. Connections, Curvature, & Cohomology, 2 vols. Incl. Vol. 1. De Rham Cohomology of Manifold & Vector Bundles. 1972. 48.50 (ISBN 0-12-302701-2); Vol. 2. Lie Groups, Principal Bundles & Characteristic Classes. 1973. 55.25 (ISBN 0-12-302702-0); Vol. 3. Cohomology of Principle Bundles & Homogeneous Spaces. 1976. 68.00 (ISBN 0-12-302703-9). (Pure & Applied Mathematics Ser.). Acad Pr.

Greulach, Victor A. & Chiappetta, Vincent J. Biology: The Science of Life. 1977. text ed. 17.95x (ISBN 0-673-15301-0); study guide 5.95x (ISBN 0-673-15302-9). Scott F.

Greulach, Victor A., Ph.D. Botany Made Simple. LC 68-11764. 1968. pap. 2.50 o.p. (ISBN 0-385-01188-1, Made). Doubleday.

Greve, Alice W. Shadow on the Plains. 1944. 6.50 o.p. (ISBN 0-8323-0113-2). Binford.

Greve, John. London's Homeless. 76p. 1964. pap. text ed. 3.75x (Pub. by Bedford England). Renouf.

--Private Landlords in England. 54p. 1965. pap. text ed. 3.75x (Pub. by Bedford England). Renouf.

Grevel, H., ed. see Bouchot, Henri.

Greves, Beryl, jt. auth. see Butler, Margaret.

Greville, Fulke. Selected Writings of Fulke Greville. Rees, ed. (Athlone Renaissance Library). 1973. text ed. 23.50x (ISBN 0-485-13603-1, Athlone Pr); pap. text ed. 13.00x (ISBN 0-686-66967-3). Humanities.

Greville, G. D., jt. ed. see Campbell, Paul N.

Grevisse, M. Le Bon Usage. (Fr). 59.95 (ISBN 0-685-20226-7). Schoenhof.

Grevisse, Maurice. Grevisse's Correct French: A Practical Guide. Kendris, Christopher, tr. from Fr. (gr. 11-12). 1981. pap. text ed. 8.95 (ISBN 0-8120-2169-X). Barron.

Grew, Eva M. & Grew, Sydney. Bach. (The Master Musicians Ser.: No. M113). (Illus.). 1979. pap. 4.50 (ISBN 0-8226-0703-4). Littlefield.

Grew, James H; see Bottiglia, William F.

Grew, Sydney, jt. auth. see Grew, Eva M.

Grewe, Horst-Eberhard & Kremer, Karl. Atlas of Surgery, Vol 1. 2nd ed. Hirsch, H. J., tr. from Ger. LC 77-84671. 1980. write for info. (ISBN 0-7216-4273-X). Saunders.
Grewell, Joy see Stortz, Diane, et al.
Grewen, J., ed. see International Symposium Clausthal - Zellerfeld, 1968.
Grey, A., tr. see Svetloff, V.
Grey, Arthur, jt. auth. see Elliott, John E.
Grey, C. G. & Bridgeman, Leonard, eds. Jane's All the World's Aircraft, 1938. facsimile ed. LC 10-8268. 1972. lib. bdg. 35.00 o.p. (ISBN 0-668-02646-4). Arco.
Grey, David, jt. auth. see McCombs, Maxwell.
Grey, Gene W. & Deneke, Frederick J. Urban Forestry. LC 78-5275. 1978. text ed. 20.95 (ISBN 0-471-01515-6). Wiley.
Grey, Herman. Tales from the Mohaves. LC 69-16731. (Civilization of the American Indian Ser.: Vol. 107). 96p. 1980. pap. 5.95 (ISBN 0-8061-1655-2). U of Okla Pr.
Grey, Loren, jt. auth. see Dreikurs, Rudolf.
Grey, Loren, ed. see Grey, Zane.
Grey, Louis D. Course in APL with Applications. 2nd ed. LC 76-5079. 300p. 1976. pap. text ed. 13.95 (ISBN 0-201-02563-9). A-W.
Grey, Robert W., jt. ed. see Stone, Nancy.
Grey, Romer Z. Zane Grey's Arizona Ames: King of the Outlaw Horde. (Orig.). 1980. pap. 1.95 (ISBN 0-505-51509-1). Tower Bks.
--Zane Grey's Buck Duane: King of the Range. (Orig.). 1980. pap. 1.95 (ISBN 0-505-51499-0). Tower Bks.
--Zane Grey's Buck Duane: The Rider of Distant Trails. 1980. pap. 2.25 (ISBN 0-505-51469-9). Tower Bks.
--Zane Grey's Laramie Nelson. 1980. pap. 2.25 (ISBN 0-505-51458-3). Tower Bks.
--Zane Grey's Nevada Jim Lacy: Beyond the Mogollon Rim. (Orig.). 1980. pap. 1.95 (ISBN 0-505-51529-6). Tower Bks.
--Zane Grey's Yaqui: Siege at Forlorn River. (Orig.). 1980. pap. 1.95 (ISBN 0-505-51519-9). Tower Bks.
--Zane's Grey Arizona Ames: Gun Trouble in Tonto Basin. (Orig.). 1980. pap. 2.25 (ISBN 0-505-51479-6). Tower Bks.
Grey, Rowland, jt. auth. see Dark, Sidney.
Grey, Zane. Buffalo Hunter. 1979. pap. 1.75 (ISBN 0-505-51334-X). Tower Bks.
--The Dude Ranger. 1981. pap. 1.95 (ISBN 0-671-83591-2). PB.
--Fresh Water Fishing. 298p. Repr. lib. bdg. 12.75x (ISBN 0-89190-762-9). Am Repr-Rivercity Pr.
--Greatest Indian Stories. 1978. pap. 1.50 (ISBN 0-505-51303-X). Tower Bks.
--Heritage of the Desert. 1976. lib. bdg. 12.95x (ISBN 0-89968-151-4). Lightyear.
--Light of Western Stars. 1980. pap. write for info. (ISBN 0-671-83498-3). PB.
--Nevada. 304p. 1980. pap. 1.95 (ISBN 0-553-12383-1). Bantam.
--Rainbow Trail. 1980. pap. write for info. (ISBN 0-671-83540-8). PB.
--Savage Kingdom. 1978. pap. 1.50 (ISBN 0-505-51293-9). Tower Bks.
--Seafishing Yarns. 276p. Repr. lib. bdg. 12.15x (ISBN 0-89190-766-1). Am Repr-Rivercity Pr.
--Shark. Grey, Loren, ed. 1978. pap. 1.50 (ISBN 0-505-51265-3). Tower Bks.
--Spirit of the Border. 288p. 1980. pap. 1.95 (ISBN 0-448-12393-2, Tempo). G&D.
--Tales of the Great Game Fish. 304p. Repr. of 1928 ed. lib. bdg. 12.95x (ISBN 0-89190-767-X). Am Repr-Rivercity Pr.
--The Westerner. (Large Print Bks.). 1980. lib. bdg. 10.95 (ISBN 0-8161-3125-2). G K Hall.
--Wildfire. 1981. pap. price not set (ISBN 0-671-43194-3). PB.
Greydanus, Rose. Mike's New Bike. (Illus.). 32p. (gr. k-2). 1980. PLB 2.96 (ISBN 0-89375-382-3); pap. 0.95 (ISBN 0-89375-282-7). Troll Assocs.
--My Secret Hiding Place. (Illus.). 32p. (gr. k-2). 1980. PLB 2.96 (ISBN 0-89375-383-1); pap. 0.95 (ISBN 0-89375-085-9). Troll Assocs.
--Susie Goes Shopping. (Illus.). 32p. (gr. k-2). 1980. PLB 2.96 (ISBN 0-89375-389-0); pap. 0.95 (ISBN 0-89375-289-4). Troll Assocs.
--Tree House Fun. (Illus.). 32p. (gr. k-2). 1980. PLB 2.96 (ISBN 0-89375-391-2); pap. 0.95 (ISBN 0-89375-291-6). Troll Assocs.
--Willie the Slowpoke. (Illus.). 32p. (gr. k-2). 1980. PLB 2.96 (ISBN 0-89375-394-7); pap. 0.95 (ISBN 0-89375-294-0). Troll Assocs.
Greyser, Stephen A. Cases in Advertising & Communications Management. 2nd ed. 300p. 1981. text ed. 19.95 (ISBN 0-13-118513-6). P-H.
--Cases in Advertising & Communications Management. LC 74-158911. (Illus.). 1972. ref. ed. 19.95 (ISBN 0-13-118497-0). P-H.
Greysmith, Brenda. Wallpaper. (Illus.). 1976. 12.95 o.s.i. (ISBN 0-02-545610-5). Macmillan.
Greysmith, David. Richard Dadd: The Rock & Castle of Seclusion. LC 74-2648. (Illus.). 192p. 1975. 17.95 o.s.i. (ISBN 0-02-545600-8). Macmillan.
Grez, Zane. Majesty's Rancho. 1980. pap. write for info. (ISBN 0-671-83506-8). PB.
Gribben, John, jt. auth. see Orgill, Douglas.
Gribben, Trish. Pajamas Don't Matter (or: What Your Baby Really Needs) LC 79-90081. (Illus.). 1980. pap. 5.95 (ISBN 0-915190-21-4). Jalmar Pr.
Gribbin, J., ed. Climatic Change. LC 76-52185. 1978. 68.50 (ISBN 0-521-21594-3); pap. 19.50x (ISBN 0-521-29205-0). Cambridge U Pr.
Gribbin, John. Death of the Sun. 1981. pap. price not set (ISBN 0-440-51854-7, Delta). Dell.
--Galaxy Formation: A Personal View. LC 75-31706. 1976. 24.95 (ISBN 0-470-32775-8). Halsted Pr.
--Genesis: The Origins of Man & the Universe. 1981. 13.95 (ISBN 0-440-02832-9). Delacorte.
--Our Changing Planet. LC 77-5547. (Illus.). 1977. 7.95 o.s.i. (ISBN 0-690-01693-X, TYC-T). T Y Crowell.
--What's Wrong with Our Weather? The Climatic Threat of the 21st Century. 1979. 9.95 o.p. (ISBN 0-684-15807-8, ScribT). Scribner.
Gribble, Charles E. Russian Root List with a Sketch of Russian Word Formation. 1981. soft cover 3.95 (ISBN 0-89357-052-4). Slavica.
Gribble, Colin, jt. auth. see McLean, Adam.
Gribble, James. Introduction to the Philosophy of Education. 1969. pap. text ed. 7.95x o.p. (ISBN 0-205-02397-5, 222397X). Allyn.
Gribble, Leonard. Famous Mysteries of Modern Times. 1977. 9.50 (ISBN 0-584-10240-2). Transatlantic.
Gribble, McPhee. Cooking: Making Things to Eat. (Practical Puffins Ser.). 32p. (gr. 5 up). 1976. pap. 1.50 o.p. (ISBN 0-14-049142-2, Puffin). Penguin.
Gribble, Mary. Eighties Odes. 1981. 4.75 (ISBN 0-8062-1662-X). Carlton.
Gribbon, R. T. Students, Churches & Higher Education. 128p. 1981. pap. 6.95 (ISBN 0-8170-0931-0). Judson.
Gribbons, Warren D. & Lohnes, Paul R. Emerging Careers. LC 68-20557. 1968. text ed. 11.00x (ISBN 0-8077-1474-7). Tchrs Coll.
Grice, Charles R., Jr. Fifteen Tips on Handling Job Interviews. McFadden, S. Michele, ed. 1981. pap. text ed. 0.65 (ISBN 0-89262-043-9). Career Pub.
Grice, E. B. Le see Le Grice, E. B.
Grice, Julia. Cry for the Demon. 400p. (Orig.). 1980. pap. 2.75 (ISBN 0-446-95497-7). Warner Bks.
--Lovefire. 1977. pap. 2.25 (ISBN 0-380-01741-5, 42499). Avon.
--Passion Star. 1980. pap. 2.50 (ISBN 0-446-91498-3). Warner Bks.
Grice, R. J. Vehicle Recovery: A Practical Manual for the Heavy-Vehicle Driver, Fleet Operator and Recovery Specialist. (Illus.). 1977. 25.00 (ISBN 0-685-75855-9). Transatlantic.
Grice, Tony. Badminton. 2nd ed. (Illus.). 71p. 1980. pap. text ed. 3.95x (ISBN 0-89641-053-6). American Pr.
Gridley, Mark C. Jazz Styles. (Illus.). 352p. 1978. text ed. 16.95 (ISBN 0-13-509885-8); pap. text ed. 11.95 (ISBN 0-13-509877-7). P-H.
Gridley, Roy E. Browning. (Routledge Author Guides). 1972. 16.00x (ISBN 0-7100-7368-2); pap. 7.95 (ISBN 0-7100-7369-0). Routledge & Kegan.
Grieb, Kenneth J. Guatemalan Caudillo: The Regime of Jorge Ubica, Guatemala, 1931-1944. LC 78-14339. 384p. 1979. 18.00x (ISBN 0-8214-0379-6). Ohio U Pr.
Grieb, Lyndal C. The Operas of Gian Carlo Menotti, 1937-1972: A Selective Bibliography. LC 74-16310. 1974. 10.00 (ISBN 0-8108-0743-2). Scarecrow.
Grieco, Victor A. Management of Small Business. new ed. (Business Ser). 1975. text ed. 18.95 (ISBN 0-675-08731-7); instructors manual 3.95 (ISBN 0-685-50983-4). Merrill.
Grieder, Terence, jt. ed. see Catlin, Stanton L.
Griego, Jose & Maestas. Cuentos: Tales from the Hispanic Southwest. Anaya, Rudolfo, tr. from Sp. (Illus.). 1980. 12.95 (ISBN 0-89013-110-4); pap. 6.95 (ISBN 0-89013-111-2). Museum NM Pr.
Griem, Hans R. see Marton, L.
Grier, B. R., jt. auth. see Gough, Vera.
Grier, W. J. The Momentous Event. 1976. pap. 2.45 (ISBN 0-85151-020-5). Banner of Truth.
Grierson, Edward. The Second Man. LC 80-8411. 320p. 1981. pap. 2.25 (ISBN 0-06-080528-5, P 528, PL). Har-Row.
Grierson, George A., ed. Linguistic Survey of India, 1903-28, 11 Vols. in 19. 1967. 600.00x set (ISBN 0-8426-1284-X). Verry.
Grierson, H. J; see Doughty, Oswald.
Grierson, Herbert J., ed. see Donne, John.
Grierson, John. Grierson on Documentary. Hardy, Forsyth, ed. 1979. pap. 6.95 (ISBN 0-571-11367-2, Pub. by Faber & Faber). Merrimack Bk Serv.
--Grierson on the Movies. Hardy, H. Forsyth, ed. 200p. 1981. 22.00 (ISBN 0-571-11665-5, Pub. by Faber & Faber). Merrimack Bk Serv.
Grierson, Philip. Later Medieval Numismatics (11th-16th Centuries) 1980. 60.00x (ISBN 0-86078-043-0, Pub. by Variorum England). State Mutual Bk.
--The Origins of Money. 1977. pap. text ed. 4.50x (ISBN 0-485-14115-9, Athlone Pr). Humanities.
Griesbach, Heinz, jt. auth. see Schulz, Dora.
Griese, Arnold. At the Mouth of the Luckiest River. LC 72-7548. (Illus.). 80p. (gr. 2-5). 1973. 8.95 o.p. (ISBN 0-690-10786-2, TYC-J); PLB 8.79 (ISBN 0-690-10787-0). T Y Crowell.
--Your Philosophy of Education- What Is It? (Illus.). 350p. (Orig.). 1981. pap. 12.95x (ISBN 0-8302-9857-6). Goodyear.
Griese, Arnold A. The Wind Is Not a River. LC 77-5082. (Illus.). (gr. 4-7). 1978. 8.95 (ISBN 0-690-03807-0, TYC-J); PLB 8.79 (ISBN 0-690-03842-9). T Y Crowell.
Grieser, E. H., jt. auth. see Sturm, Mary M.
Grieson, Ronald E., ed. Public & Urban Economics. LC 74-31877. 288p. 1976. 27.95 (ISBN 0-669-98400-0). Lexington Bks.
Griest, W. H., et al, eds. Health Effects Investigation of Oil Shale Development. 1981. text ed. 29.50. Ann Arbor Science.
Grieve, B. J. & Blackall, W. E., eds. How to Know Western Australian Wildflowers: A Key to the Flore of the Flora of the Extratropical Regions of Western Australia, Pt. IIIA. 350p. 1980. 39.50x (ISBN 0-85564-160-6, Pub. by U of West Australia Pr Australia). Intl Schol Bk Serv.
Grieve, M. A Modern Herbal. Leyel, Mrs. C. F., ed. LC 72-169784. (Illus.). 1971. pap. 6.00 ea.; Vol. 1. pap. (ISBN 0-486-22798-7); Vol. 2. pap. (ISBN 0-486-22799-5). Dover.
Grieve, Mrs. M. A Modern Herbal, 2 vols. (Illus.). Set. 22.00 (ISBN 0-8446-0302-3). Peter Smith.
Grieve, Nichol. The Scottish Metrical Psalter (1650) A Revision. 183p. pap. text ed. 2.95 (ISBN 0-567-02127-0). Attic Pr.
Grieves, Forest L., ed. Transnationalism in World Politics & Business. LC 79-1397. (Pergamon Policy Studies). 240p. 1979. 33.00 (ISBN 0-08-023892-0). Pergamon.
Griffen, Dana T., jt. auth. see Phillips, Wm. Revell.
Griffen, Edmund & Dodge, Daniel. Washington Playland. 1976. pap. 1.95 o.p. (ISBN 0-685-73463-3, LB403, Leisure Bks). Nordon Pubns.
Griffen, Ward O., Jr., jt. auth. see Maull, Kimball I.
Griffen, William L. & Marciano, John. Teaching the Vietnam War: A Critical Examination of School Texts. LC 78-73553. 203p. 1980. text ed. 14.50 (ISBN 0-916672-23-9); pap. text ed. 6.50 (ISBN 0-916672-27-1). Allanheld.
Griffeth, Bill, ed. see Hayes, Stephen K.
Griffin, et al. Welding Processes. LC 76-28745. (gr. 9-12). 1978. 15.00 (ISBN 0-8273-1257-1); instructor's guide 1.60 (ISBN 0-8273-1259-8). Delmar.
Griffin, A. Clark, ed. see Annual Symposium on Fundamental Cancer Research, No. 31.
Griffin, A. J. How to Avoid People Problems & Increase Lab Productivity. 112p. 1980. pap. 12.00 (ISBN 0-931386-17-9). Quint Pub Co.
Griffin, Adelaide, jt. auth. see Adams, Sexton.
Griffin, Appleton P. Bibliography of American Historical Societies. 2nd ed. rev. ed. LC 67-480. 1966. Repr. of 1907 ed. 42.00 (ISBN 0-8103-3080-6). Gale.
Griffin, Betty F. Family to Family. 78p. 1980. pap. text ed. 5.75 (ISBN 0-88200-140-X, 16008). Alexander Graham.
Griffin, C. F. Haakon. LC 77-26043. 1978. 9.95 o.s.i. (ISBN 0-690-01703-0, TYC-T). T Y Crowell.
Griffin, Charles H., et al. Advanced Accounting. 4th ed. 1980. 22.95x (ISBN 0-256-02328-X). Irwin.
Griffin, Daniel. The Life of Gerald Griffin by His Brother. (Nineteenth Century Fiction Ser.: Ireland: Vol. 32). 422p. 1979. lib. bdg. 46.00 (ISBN 0-8240-3481-3). Garland Pub.
Griffin, David R. & Cobb, John B., Jr., eds. Mind in Nature: Essays on the Interface of Science & Philosophy. 1977. pap. text ed. 8.75x (ISBN 0-8191-0157-5). U Pr of Amer.
Griffin, Donald R. Bird Migration. LC 74-76321. (Illus.). 192p. 1974. pap. 3.00 (ISBN 0-486-20529-0). Dover.
Griffin, Donald R., intro. by. Animal Engineering: Readings from Scientific American. LC 74-12112. (Illus.). 1974. pap. text ed. 7.95x (ISBN 0-7167-0508-7). W H Freeman.
Griffin, Dustin H. Satires Against Man: The Poems of Rochester. 1974. 18.50x (ISBN 0-520-02394-3). U of Cal Pr.
Griffin, Frank M., Jr., jt. auth. see Cobbs, C. Glenn.
Griffin, G. G. The Silent Misery-Why Marriages Fail. (American Lecture in Social & Rehabilitation Psychology). 296p. 1974. 13.75 (ISBN 0-398-03214-9); pap. 8.75 (ISBN 0-398-03237-8). C C Thomas.
Griffin, Gary W., jt. auth. see Tsang, Wing-Sum.
Griffin, George, jt. auth. see Osler, Jack.
Griffin, Gerald. The Collegians. (Nineteenth Century Fiction Ser.: Ireland: Vol. 28). 1014p. 1979. lib. bdg. 46.00 (ISBN 0-8240-3477-5). Garland Pub.
--Gabriele D'Annunzio. LC 77-113312. 1970. Repr. of 1935 ed. 12.50 (ISBN 0-8046-0995-0). Kennikat.
--Holland-Tide; or, Munster Popular Tales. (Nineteenth Century Fiction Ser.: Ireland: Vol. 26). 382p. 1979. lib. bdg. 46.00 (ISBN 0-8240-3475-9). Garland Pub.
--The Rivals & Tracy's Ambition. (Nineteenth Century Fiction Ser.: Ireland: Vol. 29). 976p. 1979. lib. bdg. 46.00 (ISBN 0-8240-3478-3). Garland Pub.
--Tales of My Neighbourhood. (Nineteenth Century Fiction Ser.: Ireland: Vol. 30). 956p. 1979. lib. bdg. 46.00 (ISBN 0-8240-3479-1). Garland Pub.
--Tales of the Munster Festivals. (Nineteenth Century Fiction Ser.: Ireland: Vol. 27). 1044p. 1979. lib. bdg. 46.00 (ISBN 0-8240-3476-7). Garland Pub.
--Talis Qualis; or, Tales of the Jury Room. (Nineteenth Century Fiction Ser.: Ireland: Vol. 31). 942p. 1979. lib. bdg. 46.00 (ISBN 0-8240-3480-5). Garland Pub.
Griffin, Gerald C., jt. auth. see Dittmer, Paul R.
Griffin, Glen C. You Were Smaller Than a Dot. LC 72-90685. 31p. (gr. k-6). 1980. pap. 3.95 (ISBN 0-87747-817-1). Deseret Bk.
Griffin, H. W., ed. see Dobson, Christopher.
Griffin, Howard. Conversations with W. H. Auden. LC 80-24381. 128p. 1981. 12.95 (ISBN 0-912516-55-0); pap. 4.95 (ISBN 0-912516-56-9). Grey Fox.
Griffin, I. H., et al. Basic Tig & Mig Welding. 2nd ed. LC 76-14085. 1977. pap. text ed. 5.20 (ISBN 0-8273-1260-1); instructor's guide 1.00 (ISBN 0-8273-1262-8). Delmar.
--Pipe Welding Techniques. 2nd ed. LC 76-51121. 1978. pap. text ed. 5.80 (ISBN 0-8273-1256-3). Delmar.
Griffin, Ivan H., et al. Basic Arc Welding. LC 76-4309. 1977. pap. text ed. 5.00 (ISBN 0-8273-1250-4); instructor's guide 1.00 (ISBN 0-8273-1251-2). Delmar.
Griffin, James A. Sackcloth & Ashes: Liturgical Reflections for Lenten Weekdays. LC 74-44463. 1976. pap. 2.50 (ISBN 0-8189-0336-8). Alba.
Griffin, James E. & Karselis, Terence C. Physical Agents for Physical Therapists. (Illus.). 388p. 1979. 26.25 (ISBN 0-398-03706-X). C C Thomas.
Griffin, James M. & Steele, Henry B. Energy Economics & Policy. 1980. text ed. 18.95 (ISBN 0-12-303950-9). Acad Pr.
Griffin, Jasper. Homer on Life & Death. 248p. 1980. 37.50x (ISBN 0-19-814016-9). Oxford U Pr.
--Pastmasters Series: Homer. 1981. 7.95 (ISBN 0-8090-5523-6); pap. 2.95 (ISBN 0-8090-1413-0). Hill & Wang.
Griffin, Joanne K., et al. Maternal & Child Health Nursing. 3rd ed. (Nursing Examination Review Books: Vol. 3). 1972. pap. 6.00 spiral bdg. (ISBN 0-87488-503-5). Med Exam.
Griffin, John H. A Time to Be Human. LC 76-47468. (Illus.). (gr. 5 up). 1977. 8.95 (ISBN 0-02-737200-6). Macmillan.
Griffin, John I. Statistics Essential for Police Efficiency. (Illus.). 248p. 1972. 12.75 (ISBN 0-398-00734-9). C C Thomas.
Griffin, John R. Newman: A Bibliography of Secondary Studies. 150p. (Orig.). 1980. pap. text ed. 12.00 (ISBN 0-931888-04-2). Christendom Pubns.
Griffin, Keith. Land Concentration & Rural Poverty. LC 75-34149. 300p. 1976. 29.50x o.p. (ISBN 0-8419-0246-1). Holmes & Meier.
--Under-Development in Spanish America. 1969. text ed. 16.95x (ISBN 0-04-330150-9). Allen Unwin.
Griffin, Keith, jt. ed. see Robinson, E. A.
Griffin, LaDean. Escape the Drug Scene. pap. 3.95 (ISBN 0-89036-141-X). Hawkes Pub Inc.
--Hierbas Al Rescate. Orig. Title: Herbs to the Rescue. (Spa.). 2.00 (ISBN 0-89557-006-8). Bi World Indus.
Griffin, Margaret P. Practical Approach to Communicating in Writing & Speech. 1969. text ed. 7.95x (ISBN 0-02-474220-1, 47422); tchrs' manual free (ISBN 0-685-03677-4). Macmillan.
Griffin, Marvin A., et al. A Beginning Course in Computer Science Using UBASIC. 1978. pap. text ed. 11.95 (ISBN 0-8403-1965-7, 40196502). Kendall-Hunt.
Griffin, Merv & Barsocchini, Peter. Merv. 1980. 11.95 (ISBN 0-671-22764-5). S&S.
Griffin, N. B., ed. see Dummer, Geoffrey W.
Griffin, Peg, ed. see Dieterich, T., et al.

Griffin, Robert. Clement Marot & the Inflections of Poetic Voice. 1976. 22.50x (ISBN 0-520-02586-5). U of Cal Pr.
--Coronation of the Poet: Joachim Du Bellay's Debt to the Trivium. (U. C. Publ. in Modern Philology: Vol. 96). 1969. pap. 8.50x (ISBN 0-520-09291-0). U of Cal Pr.
--I Never Said I Didn't Love You. LC 76-24442. (Emmuas Book Ser.). 1977. pap. 1.95 (ISBN 0-8091-1989-7). Paulist Pr.
--John Webster: Politics & Tragedy. (Salzburg Studies in English Literature, Jacobean Drama Studies: No. 12). 179p. 1972. pap. text ed. 25.00x (ISBN 0-391-01394-7). Humanities.
--Ludovico Ariosto. (World Authors Ser.: Italy: No. 301). 1974. lib. bdg. 10.95 (ISBN 0-8057-2063-4). Twayne.

Griffin, Robert, jt. auth. see Thaine, Marina.

Griffin, Roger & Sacharow, Stanley. Principles of Package Development. (Illus.). 1972. text ed. 28.50 (ISBN 0-87055-118-3). AVI.

Griffin, Roger C., jt. auth. see Sacharow, Stanley.

Griffin, Roger C., Jr., jt. auth. see Sacharow, Stanley.

Griffin, Steven. The Seekers. 1978. 4.95 (ISBN 0-533-03321-7). Vantage.

Griffin, Stuart. Japanese Food & Cooking. LC 55-10617. 1955. pap. 5.25 (ISBN 0-8048-0299-8). C E Tuttle.

Griffin, Susan. Pornography & Silence: Culture's Revolt Against Nature. LC 80-8206. 320p. 1981. 11.95 (ISBN 0-06-011647-1, HarpT). Har-Row.
--Woman & Nature: The Roaring Inside Her. LC 77-3752. 1978. 9.95 o.s.i. (ISBN 0-06-011511-4, HarpT). Har-Row.

Griffin, Thomas K. Pelican Guide to New Orleans. 4th, rev. ed. LC 74-182889. (Pelican Guide Ser.). (Illus.). 160p. 1980. pap. 3.95 (ISBN 0-88289-010-7). Pelican.

Griffin, Tom, jt. auth. see Svendson, Roger.

Griffing, Marie F. Fitness for the Working Woman. 1979. 9.95 o.p. (ISBN 0-8092-7425-6); pap. 5.95 (ISBN 0-8092-7424-8). Contemp Bks.

Griffinn, S. G. & Whitcomb, M. A. A History of the Town of Keene (N.H.), Seventeen Thirty-Two to Nineteen Hundred & Four. (Illus.). 792p. (Orig.). 1980. Repr. of 1904 ed. 38.00 (ISBN 0-917890-21-3). Heritage Bk.

Griffith, Belver C., ed. Key Papers in Information Science. LC 79-24288. 439p. 1980. text ed. 25.00 (ISBN 0-914236-50-4, ASIS). Knowledge Indus.

Griffith, Benjamin W., Jr. Barron's How to Prepare for the Graduate Record Examination in Literature: With 3 Model Examinations & a Complete Survey of the Elements of Literature. Date not set. pap. text ed. 3.95 (ISBN 0-686-62943-4). Barron.

Griffith, Benjamin W., Jr., ed. see Gay, John.

Griffith, C. Quiet Times. 1979. 4.00 o.p. (ISBN 0-8062-1208-X). Carlton.

Griffith, D. A., jt. auth. see Schiff, S. O.

Griffith, Edward J., jt. auth. see Grayson, Martin.

Griffith, Ernest S. History of American City Government. LC 72-3615. (Law, Politics & History Ser.). Repr. of 1938 ed. lib. bdg. 42.50 (ISBN 0-306-70526-5). Da Capo.

Griffith, G. T., jt. auth. see Hammond, N. G. L.

Griffith, Grosvenor T. Population Problems of the Age of Malthus. LC 67-16350. Repr. of 1926 ed. 25.00x (ISBN 0-678-05054-6). Kelley.

Griffith, Gwilym O. Mazzini: Prophet of Modern Europe. LC 78-80552. 1970. Repr. 19.50 (ISBN 0-86527-124-0). Fertig.

Griffith, H. D., tr. see Zimmer, K. G.

Griffith, H. Winter. Drug Information for Patients. LC 76-58602. 1978. 39.00 (ISBN 0-7216-4275-6). Saunders.

Griffith, H. Winter, jt. auth. see Lewis, Thomas E.

Griffith, H. Winter, et al. Information & Instructions for Pediatric Patients. LC 80-51712. 320p. 1980. 35.00 (ISBN 0-938372-00-9). Winter Pub Co.

Griffith, Helen V. Mine Will, Said John. LC 79-27886. (Illus.). 32p. (ps). 1980. 7.95 (ISBN 0-688-80267-2); PLB 7.63 (ISBN 0-688-84267-4). Greenwillow.

Griffith, J. A. The Politics of the Judiciary. LC 77-88391. (Political Issues of Modern Britain). 1977. text ed. 19.50x (ISBN 0-391-00551-0). Humanities.

Griffith, Jack D. Electron Microscopy in Biology, Vol.1. (Electron Microscopy in Biology Ser.). 325p. 1981. 32.50 (ISBN 0-471-05525-5, Pub. by Wiley-Interscience). Wiley.

Griffith, Jack S., et al. Biology One Hundred & Twenty: Laboratory Manual for Man & His Environment. 128p. 1980. pap. text ed. 7.95 (ISBN 0-8403-2228-3). Kendall-Hunt.

Griffith, Jerry & Miner, Lynn E. Phonetic Context Drill Book. 1979. pap. 11.95 (ISBN 0-13-665398-7). P-H.

Griffith, John L. & Weston, Edward G. Programmed Newswriting. (Basic Skills in Journalism Ser.). (Illus.). 1978. pap. text ed. 6.95 (ISBN 0-13-730630-X). P-H.

Griffith, John R. Quantitative Techniques for Hospital Planning & Control. LC 72-3550. (Illus.). 308p. 1972. 18.95 (ISBN 0-669-84087-4). Lexington Bks.

Griffith, John R., et al. Cost Control in Hospitals. 450p. 1976. 17.50 (ISBN 0-686-68582-2, 14916). Hospital Finan.
--Cost Control in Hospitals. LC 75-28579. 375p. 1976. text ed. 17.50x (ISBN 0-914904-12-4). Health Admin Pr.

Griffith, John S. Theory of Transition-Metal Ions. 1961. 83.50 (ISBN 0-521-05150-9). Cambridge U Pr.

Griffith, Lucille, ed. see Royall, Anne N.

Griffith, Mark. The Authenticity of Prometheus Bound. LC 76-14031. (Cambridge Classical Studies). 1977. 44.00 (ISBN 0-521-21099-2). Cambridge U Pr.

Griffith, Paul. My Stillness. LC 72-83347. 212p. 1972. 7.95 (ISBN 0-8149-0724-5). Vanguard.

Griffith, Peter. The School Play: A Complete Handbook. (Illus.). 168p. 1981. 14.95 (ISBN 0-7134-3541-0, Pub. by Batsford England). David & Charles.

Griffith, R. C. & Golomber, H. A Pocket Guide to Chess Openings. (Illus.). 128p. 1974. 9.50 (ISBN 0-7135-0515-X). Transatlantic.

Griffith, Richard. The World of Robert Flaherty. LC 72-166104. 1972. Repr. of 1953 ed. lib. bdg. 25.00 (ISBN 0-306-70296-7). Da Capo.

Griffith, Robert W. Politics of Fear: Joseph R. McCarthy & the Senate. 1971. pap. 8.35 (ISBN 0-8104-6100-5). Hayden.

Griffith, Samuel B., tr. & intro. by see Sun Tzu.

Griffith, Samuel B., 2nd. Battle for Guadalcanal. (Bantam War Book Ser.). 352p. 1980. pap. 2.50 (ISBN 0-553-13643-7). Bantam.

Griffith, W. Adventures of Pryderi: Taken from the Mabinogion. 1962. 7.50x (ISBN 0-7083-0418-4). Verry.

Griffith, Wickham. Young Wives Encyclopedia. 7.95 (ISBN 0-392-08135-0, SpS). Soccer.

Griffith, William E. Peking, Moscow & Beyond. LC 72-10375. (The Washington Papers: No. 6). 1973. 3.50x (ISBN 0-8039-0280-8). Sage.

Griffith, William E., ed. Communism in Europe: Continuity, Change & the Sino-Soviet Dispute, 1 vol. Incl. Vol. 2. East Germany, Czechoslovakia, Sweden, Norway, Finland. pap. 5.95x (ISBN 0-262-57009-2). 1967. MIT Pr.
--The European Left: Italy, France, & Spain. LC 79-7711. 272p. 1979. 25.95 (ISBN 0-669-03199-2). Lexington Bks.

Griffiths, A. J., jt. auth. see Suzuki, David T.

Griffiths, A. Philips, ed. Knowledge & Belief. 1967. pap. 4.95x (ISBN 0-19-500328-4). Oxford U Pr.

Griffiths, Alison. Fire in the Islands! The Acts of the Holy Spirit in the Solomon Islands. LC 77-71627. (Illus.). 1977. pap. 3.95 (ISBN 0-87788-264-9). Shaw Pubs.

Griffiths, Anthony J. F., jt. auth. see Suzuki, David T.

Griffiths, Antony. Prints & Printmaking: An Introduction to the History & Techniques. 152p. 1981. text ed. 12.95 (ISBN 0-394-32673-3). Knopf.

Griffiths, Brian, ed. Monetary Targets. Wood, Geoffrey E. 27.50 (ISBN 0-312-54421-9). St Martin.

Griffiths, C. Auditory Techniques. (Illus.). 232p. 1974. 22.75 (ISBN 0-398-03047-2). C C Thomas.

Griffiths, D. H. & King, R. F. Applied Geophysics for Engineers & Geologists. 1965. 27.00 (ISBN 0-08-010750-8); pap. 9.50 (ISBN 0-08-010749-4). Pergamon.
--Applied Geophysics for Geologists & Engineers: The Elements of Geophysical Prospecting. (Illus.). 224p. Date not set. 30.00 (ISBN 0-08-022071-1); pap. 14.50 (ISBN 0-08-022072-X). Pergamon.

Griffiths, Daniel E. & McCarty, Donald J., eds. The Dilemma of Deanship. LC 78-61237. 1980. 11.95x (ISBN 0-8134-2041-5, 2041). Interstate.

Griffiths, E. H. Weighing Machines: Application of Electricity & Electronics to Weighting Machines, Vol. 3. 248p. 1970. 49.75x (ISBN 0-85264-160-5, Pub. by Griffin England). State Mutual Bk.

Griffiths, Franklyn & Polanyi, John C., eds. The Dangers of Nuclear War. LC 79-18825. 1979. 15.00 (ISBN 0-8020-2356-8); pap. 5.95 (ISBN 0-8020-6389-6). U of Toronto Pr.

Griffiths, G. D. Abandoned. LC 74-18131. 96p. (gr. 4 up). 1975. 4.95 o.p. (ISBN 0-695-80537-1); lib. ed. 4.98 o.p. (ISBN 0-695-40537-3). Follett.

Griffiths, Gareth. A Double Exile: African & West Indian Writing Between Two Cultures. (Critical Appraisals). 1978. text ed. 18.25x (ISBN 0-7145-2622-3). Humanities.

Griffiths, Garth. Boating in Canada: Practical Piloting & Seamanship. 2nd ed. LC 77-163820. (Illus.). 1971. 16.95 o.p. (ISBN 0-8020-1817-3). U of Toronto Pr.

Griffiths, H. B. Surface. LC 74-25660. (Illus.). 128p. 1976. 19.95 (ISBN 0-521-20696-0). Cambridge U Pr.

Griffiths, H. B. & Howson, A. G. Mathematics: Society & Curricula. (Illus.). 400p. 1974. 49.50 (ISBN 0-521-20287-6); pap. 17.50x (ISBN 0-521-09892-0). Cambridge U Pr.

Griffiths, Harry. Basic Bone Radiology. 182p. 1980. text ed. 15.50x (ISBN 0-8385-0535-X). ACC.

Griffiths, Helen. Adventures of Moshie Cat. (gr. 4-6). 1977. pap. 1.25 o.s.i. (ISBN 0-671-29816-X). Archway.
--Grip, a Dog Story. 1981. pap. price not set (ISBN 0-671-56034-4). Archway.
--Grip, a Dog Story. LC 78-6819. (Illus.). (gr. 5-9). 1978. 8.95 (ISBN 0-8234-0335-1). Holiday.
--Just a Dog. (gr. 5-7). 1976. pap. 1.95 (ISBN 0-671-42166-2). Archway.
--Just a Dog. (gr. 5-7). 1976. pap. 1.75 (ISBN 0-671-56036-0). PB.
--Moshie Cat. (Illus.). (gr. 4-6). 1977. pap. 1.25 (ISBN 0-686-68484-2). PB.
--Moshie Cat. (Illus.). (gr. 4-6). 1977. pap. 1.25 o.s.i. (ISBN 0-671-29816-X). Archway.
--The Mysterious Appearance of Agnes. LC 74-21793. (Illus.). 160p. (gr. 7 up). 1975. 8.95 (ISBN 0-8234-0267-3). Holiday.

Griffiths, J. A., ed. From Policy to Administration: Essays in Honour of William A.Robson. 1976. text ed. 42.50x (ISBN 0-686-67889-3). Allen Unwin.

Griffiths, John. Complete Word Game Finisher. 1980. pap. 7.95 (ISBN 0-446-97582-6). Warner Bks.
--A Loyal Servant. 352p. 1981. 11.95 (ISBN 0-87223-659-5). Seaview Bks.
--Three Tomorrows: American, British & Soviet Science Fiction. 217p. 1980. 23.50x (ISBN 0-389-20008-5); pap. 8.95x (ISBN 0-389-20009-3). B&N.

Griffiths, John, ed. see Rahner, Karl.

Griffiths, John C. Afganistan: Key to a Continent. 200p. 1981. 16.00 (ISBN 0-86531-080-7). Westview.
--Clinical Enzymology. LC 79-84461. (Illus.). 222p. 1979. 22.50 (ISBN 0-89352-030-6). Masson Pub.

Griffiths, John F. & Driscoll, Dennis M. Survey of Climatology. 352p. 1981. text ed. 19.95 (ISBN 0-675-09994-3); instr's. manual 3.95 (ISBN 0-686-69500-3). Merrill.

Griffiths, John F. see Rose, J. & Weidener, E. W.

Griffiths, L., jt. auth. see Young, A. P.

Griffiths, M. Echidnas. LC 68-21385. 1968. 42.00 (ISBN 0-08-012650-2). Pergamon.

Griffiths, Mary. Economy Cook Book. LC 77-91748. 1978. 8.95 (ISBN 0-7153-7542-3). David & Charles.

Griffiths, Maurice. Dream Ships. 290p. 1980. 29.95x (ISBN 0-85177-076-2, Pub. by Cornell England). State Mutual Bk.
--The Hidden Menace. 160p. 1980. 20.75x (ISBN 0-85177-186-6, Pub. by Conway Maritime England). State Mutual Bk.
--The Magic of the Swatchways. 236p. 1980. 18.95x (ISBN 0-85177-045-2, Xpub. by Cornell England). State Mutual Bk.

Griffiths, P. C. The Endings: In Modern Theory & Practice. LC 76-46161. (Encore Edition). (Illus.). 1977. 3.95 o.p. (ISBN 0-684-16194-X, ScribT). Scribner.

Griffiths, Patricia B. Tennessee Blue. Southern, Carol, ed. 192p. 1981. 10.95 (ISBN 0-517-54187-4). Potter.

Griffiths, Paul. Boulez. (Oxford Studies of Composers). (Illus.). 1979. pap. 10.50x (ISBN 0-19-315442-0). Oxford U Pr.
--Concise History of Avant Garde Music: From Debussy to Boulez. LC 77-25056. (World of Art Ser.). (Illus.). 1978. pap. 9.95 (ISBN 0-19-520045-4). Oxford U Pr.
--A Guide to Electronic Music. 128p. pap. 6.95 (ISBN 0-500-27203-4). Thames Hudson.
--A Guide to Electronic Music. 1979. 11.95 (ISBN 0-500-01224-5). Thames Hudson.
--Modern Music: The Avant Garde Since 1945. (Illus.). 308p. 1981. 37.50x (ISBN 0-460-04365-X, Pub. by J. M. Dent England). Biblio Dist.

Griffiths, Percival. Modern India. 1962. pap. 2.00 (ISBN 0-88253-203-0). Ind-US Inc.

Griffiths, Peter. Improving Your Chess. (Illus.). 72p. 1980. pap. 6.95 (ISBN 0-8069-9024-4, Pub. by EP Publishing England). Sterling.
--Understanding Your Dog. 1977. 11.50 o.p. (ISBN 0-7153-7353-6). David & Charles.

Griffiths, Phillip A. An Introduction to the Theory of Special Divisors on Algebraic Curves. LC 80-16415. (Conference Board of Mathematical Sciences Ser.). 1980. 5.60 (ISBN 0-8218-1694-2). Am Math.

Griffiths, R. A., ed. Boroughs Olf Medieval Wales. (Illus.). 1979. text ed. 50.00x (ISBN 0-7083-0681-0). Verry.

Griffiths, Ralph, ed. Patronage, the Crown & the Provinces in Later Medieval England. 224p. 1980. text ed. 20.00x (ISBN 0-391-02096-X). Humanities.

Griffiths, Rees. God in Idea & Experience: The Apriori Elements of Religious Consciousness; an Epistemological Study. 316p. Repr. of 1931 ed. text ed. 4.95 (ISBN 0-567-02128-9). Attic Pr.

Griffiths, Richard, ed. see Montherlant, Henry de.

Griffiths, Trevor. Occupations. new ed. 74p. 1981. pap. 7.50 (ISBN 0-571-11667-1, Pub. by Faber & Faber). Merrimack Bk Serv.
--The Party. 1974. 8.50 (ISBN 0-571-10629-3, Pub. by Faber & Faber); pap. 4.95 (ISBN 0-571-10647-1). Merrimack Bk Serv.
--Through the Night & Such Impossibilities. 1977. pap. 5.95 (ISBN 0-571-11158-0, Pub. by Faber & Faber). Merrimack Bk Serv.

Griffiths, V. L. Problems of Rural Education. (Fundamentals of Educational Planning Ser). (Orig.). 1968. pap. 6.00 (ISBN 92-803-1022-4, U484, UNESCO). Unipub.

Grigalunas, Thomas A. Offshore Petroleum & New England. (Marine Technical Report Ser.: No. 39). 1975. pap. 5.00 (ISBN 0-938412-12-4). URI MAS.

Grigarick, A. A. & Schuster, R. O. Reichenbachia Found in the United States West of the Continental Divide (Coleoptera: Pselaphidae) (U. C. Publ. in Entomology: Vol. 47). 1967. pap. 6.00x (ISBN 0-520-09119-1). U of Cal Pr.

Grigarick, A. A. & Stange, L. A. The Pollen-Collecting Bees of the Anthidiini of California (Hymenoptera: Megachilidae) (Bulletin of the California Insect Survey: Vol. 9). 1968. pap. 6.50x (ISBN 0-520-09034-9). U of Cal Pr.

Grigarick, Albert A. & Schuster, Robert O. A Revision of Actium Casey & Actiastes Casey (Coleoptera: Pselaphidae) (U. C. Publ. in Entomology: Vol. 67). 1971. pap. 6.00x (ISBN 0-520-09398-4). U of Cal Pr.

Grigg, D. B. Population Growth & Agrarian Change. LC 79-4237. (Cambridge Geographical Studies: No. 13). 368p. 1981. 47.50 (ISBN 0-521-22760-7); pap. 17.95 (ISBN 0-521-29635-8). Cambridge U Pr.

Grigg, David B. Agricultural Revolution in South Lincolnshire. (Cambridge Studies in Economic History). 1966. 41.50 (ISBN 0-521-05152-5). Cambridge U Pr.

Grigg, E. C., jt. auth. see Chiswell, B.

Grigg, E. R. Traii of the Invisible Light: From X-Strahlen to Radiobiology. (American Lectures in Roentgen Diagnosis Ser.). (Illus.). 1106p. 1965. 49.75 (ISBN 0-398-00739-X). C C Thomas.

Grigg, Jessie S. Of Roots & Petals. LC 79-57290. 1980. 10.95 (ISBN 0-89754-009-3); pap. 3.50 (ISBN 0-89754-008-5). Dan River Pr.

Grigg, John. Lloyd George: The People's Champion, 1902-1911. 1979. 29.50x (ISBN 0-520-03634-4). U of Cal Pr.
--Nancy Astor. (Illus.). 192p. 1981. 15.00 (ISBN 0-316-32870-7). Little.
--Nancy Astor: A Lady Unashamed. (Illus.). 192p. 1981. 15.00 (ISBN 0-316-32870-7). Little.
--Nineteen Forty-Three: The Victory That Never Was. 234p. 1980. 12.50 (ISBN 0-8090-7377-3). Hill & Wang.

Grigg, Richard W. Hawaii's Precious Corals. LC 77-78113. (Illus.). 1977. 5.95 (ISBN 0-89610-068-5); pap. 4.95 (ISBN 0-89610-069-3). Island Her.

Griggs, Donald & Griggs, Patricia. Generations Learning Together. (Griggs Educational Resources Ser.). 1980. pap. 6.95 (ISBN 0-687-14050-1). Abingdon.

Griggs, M., jt. auth. see Spitze, H.

Griggs, Patricia, jt. auth. see Griggs, Donald.

Griggs, Patricia, jt. auth. see Williams, Doris.

Griggs, Patricia R. Using Storytelling in Christian Education. LC 80-26468. 64p. (Orig.). 1981. pap. 4.95 (ISBN 0-687-43117-4). Abingdon.

Griggs, Robert C. & Moxley, R. T., eds. Treatment of Neuromuscular Diseases. LC 75-43197. (Advances in Neurology Ser: Vol. 17). 1977. 32.00 (ISBN 0-89004-113-X). Raven.

Grigorenko, Peter. The Grigorenko Papers: Writings by General P. G. Grigorenko & Documents on His Case. LC 76-5912. 1976. 22.00x (ISBN 0-89158-603-2). Westview.

Grigoriev, V. J., jt. ed. see Whetstone, G. W.

Grigsby, Hugh B. History of the Virginia Convention of 1788, 2 Vols. LC 70-75319. (American History, Politics & Law Ser). 1969. Repr. of 1890 ed. Set. lib. bdg. 65.00 (ISBN 0-306-71280-6). Da Capo.
--Virginia Convention of 1776. LC 75-75320. (American History, Politics & Law Ser). 1969. Repr. of 1855 ed. lib. bdg. 25.00 (ISBN 0-306-71281-4). Da Capo.
--Virginia Convention of 1829-1830. LC 79-75321. (American History, Politics & Law Ser). 1969. Repr. of 1854 ed. lib. bdg. 19.50 (ISBN 0-306-71282-2). Da Capo.

Grigson, Geoffrey. Shapes & People. LC 76-11954. (gr. 9 up). 7.95 (ISBN 0-8149-0662-1). Vanguard.

--Shapes & Stories: A Book About Pictures. LC 65-25262. (Illus.). (gr. 5 up). 7.95 (ISBN 0-8149-0311-8). Vanguard.
--Shapes, Animals & Special Creatures. LC 72-77789. (Illus.). (gr. 5 up). Date not set. 6.95 (ISBN 0-8149-0717-2). Vanguard. Postponed.
Grigson, Geoffrey, ed. The Oxford Book of Satirical Verse. 480p. 1980. 22.50 (ISBN 0-19-214110-4). Oxford U Pr.
Grigson, Geoffrey, ed. see Morris, William.
Grigson, Geoffrey, ed. see Southey, Robert.
Grigson, Geoffrey, intro. by. The Faber Book of Poems & Places. 408p. 1980. 19.95 (ISBN 0-571-11647-7, Pub. by Faber & Faber). Merrimack Bk Serv.
Grigson, Jane. Jane Grigson's Vegetable Book. 1981. pap. 6.95 (ISBN 0-14-046352-6). Penguin.
Grijalva, Josue, tr. see Sisemore, J. T.
Grijalva, Maria C., jt. auth. see Bailey, Helen M.
Grijpstra, B. G. Common Efforts in the Development of Rural Sarawak, Malaysia. (Studies of Developing Countries: No. 20). (Illus.). 1976. text ed. 28.25x (ISBN 90-232-1408-0). Humanities.
Grikscheit, Gary M., et al. Handbook of Selling: Psychological, Managerial & Marketing Basis. LC 80-19371. (Marketing Management Ser.). 650p. 1981. 29.95 (ISBN 0-471-04482-2, Pub. by Ronald). Wiley.
Griliches, Zvi, et al, eds. Income Distribution & Economic Inequality. 1978. 34.95 (ISBN 0-470-26331-8). Halsted Pr.
Grill, Tom & Scanlon, Mark. Taking Better Pictures with Your Thirty-Five MM SLR. (Illus.). 1980. 14.95 (ISBN 0-690-01920-3, H&R); pap. 7.95 (ISBN 0-690-01921-1). Lippincott.
--Taking Better Pictures with Your 35mm SLR: A Practial Guide--with Special Emphasis on 35mm Automatic Cameras. LC 80-7855. (Illus.). 128p. 1981. 15.95 (ISBN 0-690-01920-3, HarpT). Har-Row.
--Taking Better Pictures with Your 35mm SLR: A Practial Guide--with Special Emphasis on 35mm Automatic Cameras. LC 80-7855. (Illus.). 128p. 1981. pap. 7.95 (ISBN 0-690-01921-1, CN 864, CN). Har-Row.
Grilli, Enzo R., et al. The World Rubber Economy: Structure, Changes, & Prospects. LC 80-554. (World Bank Occasional Papers). (Illus.). 224p. 1981. pap. text ed. 6.50x (ISBN 0-8018-2421-4). Johns Hopkins.
Grilli, Sam. Sam Grilli's Complete Guide to Lake Erie Walleye. (Illus.). 160p. (gr. 4-12). 1980. 5.95 (ISBN 0-9604304-0-7); pap. 5.95 (ISBN 0-686-64677-0). Sport Fishing.
Grilliot, Harold J. Introduction to Law & the Legal System. 2nd ed. LC 78-69579. (Illus.). 1979. text ed. 18.50 (ISBN 0-395-26866-4); inst. manual 0.80 (ISBN 0-395-26865-6). HM.
Grillmeier, Aloys. Christ in Christian Tradition: From the Apostolic Age to Chalcedon, Vol. 1. rev. ed. Bowden, John S., tr. from Ger. LC 75-13456. 451p. 1975. 28.00 (ISBN 0-8042-0492-6). John Knox.
Grillo, Francesco. Tomaso Campanella in America: A Critical Bibliography & a Profile. 109p. 1954. 5.75x (ISBN 0-913298-43-3). S F Vanni.
--Tommaso Campanella in America: A Supplement to the Critical Bibliography. 48p. 1957. 5.00x (ISBN 0-913298-49-2). S F Vanni.
Grillot De Givry. Witchcraft, Magic & Alchemy. Locke, J. Courtney, tr. from Fr. (Illus.). 395p. 1971. pap. 6.50 (ISBN 0-486-22493-7). Dover.
Grillparzer, F. Traum Ein Leben. Yates, W. E., ed. 1968. text ed. 7.50x (ISBN 0-521-05154-1). Cambridge U Pr.
Grillparzer, Franz. Des Meeres und der Liebe Wellen. Yates, Douglas, ed. (German Text Ser.). 1947. pap. 9.95x (ISBN 0-631-01400-4, Pub. by Basil Blackwell). Biblio Dist.
Grimal, Henri. Decolonization of the British, French, Dutch & Belgian Empires: 1919-1963. LC 77-922. 1978. lib. bdg. 33.50x (ISBN 0-89158-732-2). Westview.
Grimaldi, John V. & Simonds, Rollin H. Safety Management. 3rd ed. 1975. 19.95 (ISBN 0-256-01564-3). Irwin.
Grimaldi, Paul L. Supplemental Security Income: New Federal Program Aged, Blind, & Disabled. 1980. pap. 5.25 (ISBN 0-8447-3356-3). Am Enterprise.
Grimaldi, William M. Aristotle, Rhetoric I: A Commentary. LC 79-53372. 1980. 45.00 (ISBN 0-8232-1048-0). Fordham.
Grimes, Alan P. Democracy & the Amendments to the Constitution. LC 78-4342. (Illus.). 1978. 19.95 (ISBN 0-669-02344-2). Lexington Bks.
--The Puritan Ethic & Woman Suffrage. LC 80-21799. xiii, 159p. 1980. Repr. of 1967 ed. lib. bdg. 19.50x (ISBN 0-313-22689-X, GRPE). Greenwood.
Grimes, D. M. Electromagnetism & Quantum Theory. (Electrical Science Ser). 1969. 25.00 o.p. (ISBN 0-12-303150-8). Acad Pr.
Grimes, Frances H. Good Night! LC 79-87669. (Illus.). (ps-3). Date not set. price not set (ISBN 0-89799-181-8); pap. price not set (ISBN 0-89799-182-6). Dandelion Pr. Postponed.
Grimes, George H., jt. auth. see Doyle, James M.
Grimes, Harriette H. & Knack, John W., Sr. Games Book. (gr. 1-8). 1976. wkbk. 5.00 (ISBN 0-89039-163-7). Ann Arbor Pubs.
Grimes, Janet & Daims, Diva. Novels in English by Women, 1891 to 1920: A Preliminary Checklist. Robinson, Doris, ed. LC 79-7911. 800p. 1981. lib. bdg. 75.00 (ISBN 0-8240-9522-7). Garland Pub.
Grimes, John, et al. The New Vision: Forty Years of Photography at the Institute of Design. (Illus.). Date not set. 20.00 (ISBN 0-89381-067-3). Aperture. Postponed.
Grimes, John S. Henry's Probate Law & Practice. 7th ed. 5500p. Date not set. text ed. 125.00 (ISBN 0-672-83934-2). Michie.
--Thompson on Real Property, 24 vols. Set. 350.00 (ISBN 0-672-83972-5, Bobbs-Merrill Law); 1980 suppl. 95.00 (ISBN 0-672-84139-8). Michie.
Grimes, Ronald L. The Divine Imagination: William Blake's Major Prophetic Visions. LC 72-6437. (ATLA Monograph: No. 1). 1972. 10.00 (ISBN 0-8108-0539-1). Scarecrow.
Grimes, Ruby M., jt. auth. see Minnear, Festus L.
Grimes, William A. Criminal Law Outline. (Ser. 1050). 1980. pap. 8.00 (ISBN 0-686-08768-2). Natl Judicial Coll.
Grimeston, E., tr. see Le Petit, Jean Francois.
Grimm. Grimm's Fairy Tales. (Illustrated Classics Ser.). (Illus.). (gr. 7-12). 1980. Repr. cancelled o.p. (ISBN 0-19-274503-4). Oxford U Pr.
Grimm & Sage, Jacquelyn. Many Furs: A Grimm's Fairy Tale. Sage, Jacquelyn, tr. from Ger. (Illus.). 32p. (gr. 1-4). 1981. 12.95 (ISBN 0-89742-041-1). Dawne-Leigh.
Grimm Brothers. About Wise Men & Simpletons: Twelve Tales from Grimm. Shub, Elizabeth, tr. from Ger. LC 79-146628. (Illus.). (gr. 3-6). 1971. 8.95 (ISBN 0-02-737290-1). Macmillan.
--The Best of Grimm's Fairy Tales. LC 79-63439. (Illus.). (gr. k-3). 1980. 9.95 (ISBN 0-88332-150-5); PLB 10.95 (ISBN 0-88332-122-X). Larousse.
--The Brave Little Tailor. LC 78-74631. (Illus.). (gr. k-3). 1980. PLB 6.95 (ISBN 0-88332-124-6). Larousse.
--German Folk Tales. Magoun, Francis P., Jr. & Krappe, Alexander H., trs. LC 59-5095. (Arcturus Books Paperbacks). 682p. (gr. 5 up). 1969. pap. 11.95 (ISBN 0-8093-0356-6). S Ill U Pr.
--Golden Bird & Other Fairy Tales. Jarrell, Randall, tr. (Illus.). (gr. k-3). 1963. 4.50 o.s.i. (ISBN 0-02-737280-4). Macmillan.
--Hansel & Gretel. (Illus.). (gr. k-3). 1976. PLB 5.00 (ISBN 0-307-60419-5, Golden Pr). Western Pub.
--The Musicians of Bremen. LC 74-78599. (Illus.). 6.95 (ISBN 0-88332-060-6). Larousse.
--Rapunzel. Hoffmann, Felix, ed. & illus. LC 61-2865. (Illus.). (gr. k-3). 1961. 5.50 o.p. (ISBN 0-15-265656-1, HJ). HarBraceJ.
Grimm, Ede, jt. auth. see Edney, Margon.
Grimm, G. Those Who Remember. 6.50 o.p. (ISBN 0-8062-1059-1). Carlton.
Grimm, Gary & Mitchell, Don. Creative Writing. (gr. 3-8). 1976. 7.95 (ISBN 0-916456-04-8, GA61). Good Apple.
--Dandylions Never Roar Book. (gr. k-8). 1976. 5.95 (ISBN 0-916456-03-X, GA53). Good Apple.
--Good Apple Math Book. (gr. 3-8). 1975. 10.95 (ISBN 0-916456-00-5, GA59). Good Apple.
--Mostly Me. (gr. k-6). 1976. 10.50 (ISBN 0-916456-07-2, GA64). Good Apple.
--Spelling Book. (gr. 3-8). 1976. 7.95 (ISBN 0-916456-05-6, GA60). Good Apple.
Grimm, Gary, jt. auth. see Mitchell, Don.
Grimm, George. Buddhist Wisdom: The Mystery of the Self. 2nd, rev. ed. Keller-Grimm, M., ed. Aikins, Carrol, tr. from Ger. 1978. 6.50 (ISBN 0-89684-041-7, Pub. by Motilal Banarsidass India). Orient Bk Dist.
Grimm, Harold J. & Lehmann, Helmut T., eds. Luther's Works: Career of the Reformer I, Vol. 31. LC 55-9893. 1957. 14.95 (ISBN 0-8006-0331-1, 1-331). Fortress.
Grimm, Jacob & Grimm, Wilhelm. The Juniper Tree & Other Tales from Grimm, 2 vols. Lore, Segal & Jarrell, Randall, trs. LC 73-82698. 384p. (gr. 4 up). 1973. boxed set 15.00 (ISBN 0-374-18057-1). FS&G.
--Snow-White & the Seven Dwarfs: A Tale from the Brothers Grimm. Jarrell, Randall, tr. from Ger. LC 72-81489. (Illus.). 32p. (ps-3). 1972. 8.95 (ISBN 0-374-37099-0). FS&G.
Grimm, Jacob & Wilhelm see Manheim, Ralph.
Grimm, Jakob L. Grimm's Household Tales, 2 Vols. Hunt, Margaret, tr. LC 68-31090. 1968. Repr. of 1884 ed. 40.00 (ISBN 0-8103-3463-1). Gale.
Grimm, Robert H., jt. ed. see Care, Norman S.
Grimm, Wilhelm, jt. auth. see Grimm, Jacob.
Grimm, William C. Book of Trees. 1974. pap. 6.95 (ISBN 0-8015-0812-6, Hawthorn). Dutton.
Grimm Brothers. Grimm's Fairy Tales. Dobbs, Rose, ed. (Illus.). (gr. k-3). 1955. PLB 4.39 (ISBN 0-394-80657-3, BYR); PLB 4.39 (ISBN 0-394-90657-8). Random.
--Grimm's Fairy Tales: Twenty Stories. (Large Format Ser.). (Illus.). 1978. pap. 5.95 o.p. (ISBN 0-14-004908-8). Penguin.
--Hansel & Gretel. LC 75-117296. (Illus.). (gr. k-3). 1971. 6.95 (ISBN 0-440-03465-5); PLB 6.46 o.s.i. (ISBN 0-440-03466-3). Delacorte.
--Rumpelstiltskin. LC 74-2139. (Illus.). 48p. (gr. k-3). 1974. 3.95g o.s.i. (ISBN 0-590-07393-1, Four Winds). Schol Bk Serv.
Grimmelshausen, H. J. Von. Adventurous Simplicissimus. Goodrick, A. T., tr. LC 62-8406. (Illus.). 1962. pap. 3.95x (ISBN 0-8032-5077-0, BB 134, Bison). U of Nebr Pr.
Grimmelshausen, Johann. Simplicius Simplicissimus. Schulz-Behrend, George, tr. LC 63-16934. (Orig.). 1965. pap. 6.95 (ISBN 0-672-60424-8, LLA186). Bobbs.
Grimshaw. Union Rule in the Schools: Big-City Politics in Transformation. LC 78-24631. (Politics of Education Ser.). (Illus.). 1979. 18.95 (ISBN 0-669-02769-3). Lexington Bks.
Grimshaw, Allen D. Language As a Social Resource: Essays by Allen D. Grimshaw. (Language Science & National Development). 400p. 1981. text ed. 18.75x (ISBN 0-8047-1108-9). Stanford U Pr.
Grimshaw, Nigel. Bluntstone & the Wildkeepers. (gr. 5-7). 1978. 7.95 (ISBN 0-571-10533-5, Pub. by Faber & Faber). Merrimack Bk Serv.
--The Wildkeepers' Guest. (gr. 5-7). 1978. 9.95 (ISBN 0-571-10899-7, Pub. by Faber & Faber). Merrimack Bk Serv.
Grimshaw, R. W. The Chemistry & Physics of Clays. 4th ed. LC 76-178139. 1032p. 1971. 49.95 (ISBN 0-471-32780-8). Halsted Pr.
Grimsley, Ronald, ed. see Rousseau, Jean-Jacques.
Grimsted, David, ed. Notions of the Americans. LC 77-132199. (American Culture Ser). 1970. 8.95 o.s.i. (ISBN 0-8076-0568-9); pap. 6.95 o.s.i. (ISBN 0-8076-0567-0). Braziller.
Grimsted, Patricia K. Archives & Manuscript Repositories in the USSR: Estonia, Latvia & Belorussia. LC 79-15427. (Studies of the Russian Institute, Columbia University). 1981. 60.00x (ISBN 0-691-05279-4). Princeton U Pr.
--The Foreign Ministers of Alexander First: Political Attitudes & the Conduct of Russian Diplomacy, 1801-1825. LC 69-11615. (Illus.). 1969. 20.50x (ISBN 0-520-01387-5). U of Cal Pr.
Grimstone, A. V. & Skaer, R. J. A Guidebook to Microscopical Methods. LC 70-182027. (Illus.). 150p. 1972. 29.95 (ISBN 0-521-08445-8); pap. 8.95x (ISBN 0-521-09700-2). Cambridge U Pr.
Grimwade, Arthur. London Goldsmiths, 1697-1837. 1976. 108.00 (ISBN 0-571-10550-5, Pub. by Faber & Faber). Merrimack Bk Serv.
Grimwood, Ken. Breakthrough. 1977. pap. 2.25 o.p. (ISBN 0-345-25470-8). Ballantine.
Grimwood-Jones, Diana, et al, eds. Arab-Islamic Bibliography: Based on Giuseppe Gabrieli's Manvale Di Bibliografia Muselmana. 1977. text ed. 52.00x (ISBN 0-391-00691-6). Humanities.
Grinaker, Robert L. & Barr, Ben B. Audit Practice Case: Midwestern Products, Inc. 1967. text ed. 13.50x (ISBN 0-256-00172-3). Irwin.
Grinaker, Robert L., jt. auth. see Barr, Ben.
Grindal, Bruce T. & Warren, Dennis M. Essays in Humanistic Anthropology: Festschrift in Honor of Davis Bidney. LC 78-66121. (Orig.). 1979. pap. text ed. 13.75 (ISBN 0-8191-0682-8). U Pr of Amer.
Grinder, Robert E. Adolescence. 2nd ed. LC 77-7239. 1978. text ed. 20.95x (ISBN 0-471-32767-0); 2.00 (ISBN 0-471-03798-2). Wiley.
Grinder, Walter E., ed. & intro. by see Lachmann, Ludwig M.
Grindlay, J. An Introduction to the Phenomenological Theory of Ferroelectricity. LC 72-90455. 1970. 36.00 (ISBN 0-08-006362-4). Pergamon.
Grindle, Juliet, jt. ed. see Clements, Patricia.
Grindle, Merilee S. Bureaucrats, Politicians, & Peasants in Mexico: A Case Study in Public Policy. LC 76-7759. 1977. 18.00x (ISBN 0-520-03238-1). U of Cal Pr.
Grindle, Merilee S., ed. Politics & Policy Implementation in the Third World. LC 79-3213. 1980. 20.00x (ISBN 0-691-07617-0); pap. 7.95 (ISBN 0-691-02195-3). Princeton U Pr.
Grindley, J. H. Principles of Electrical Transmission Lines in Power & Communication. 1967. 25.00 (ISBN 0-08-012111-X); pap. 13.25 (ISBN 0-08-012112-8). Pergamon.
Grindrod, Muriel, tr. see Chabod, Federico.
Grinfelds, Vesma & Hultstrand, Bonnie. Right Down Your Alley: The Complete Book of Bowling. LC 80-82071. (Illus.). 208p. (Orig.). 1980. pap. text ed. 4.95 (ISBN 0-918438-58-6). Leisure Pr.
Gringhuis, Dirk. The Eagle Pine. LC 58-7206. (Illus., Orig.). (gr. 5-8). 1969. pap. text ed. 2.75 (ISBN 0-910726-81-7). Hillsdale Educ.
--Lore of the Great Turtle: Indian Legends of Mackinac Retold. LC 73-636148. (Illus.). 96p. (Orig.). 1970. pap. 2.50 (ISBN 0-911872-11-6). Mackinac Island.
--Were-Wolves & Will-O-the-Wisps: French Tales of Mackinac Retold. (Illus., Orig.). 1974. pap. 2.50 (ISBN 0-911872-14-0). Mackinac Island.
--Young Voyageur: Trade & Treachery at Michilimackinac. rev. ed. (Illus.). 202p. (gr. 9 up). 1969. pap. 2.50 (ISBN 0-911872-34-5). Mackinac Island.
Gringhuis, Dirk, jt. auth. see Holman, J. Allan.
Grinker, Roy R., Sr. Psychiatry in Broad Perspective. LC 74-13012. 256p. 1975. deluxe ed. 22.95 (ISBN 0-87705-231-X). Human Sci Pr.
Grinker, Roy R., Sr. & Speigel, John. Men Under Stress. 1979. Repr. of 1945 ed. 28.50x (ISBN 0-89197-645-0). Irvington.
Grinker, Roy R., Sr. & Werble, Beatrice. The Borderline Patient. LC 77-44789. 1977. 25.00x (ISBN 0-87668-315-4). Aronson.
Grinnell & Carter. Destination Saturn. (YA) 4.95 o.p. (ISBN 0-685-07429-3, Avalon). Bouregy.
Grinnell, Alan & Barber, Albert A. Laboratory Experiments in Physiology. 9th ed. (Illus.). 208p. 1976. pap. 8.95 (ISBN 0-8016-2978-0). Mosby.
Grinnell, Alan D., et al, eds. The Regulation of Muscle Contraction: Excitation-Contraction Coupling. (UCLA Forum in Medical Sciences: Vol. 22). 1981. price not set (ISBN 0-12-303780-8). Acad Pr.
Grinnell, George B. Blackfoot Lodge Tales: The Story of a Prairie People. LC 62-4146. 1962. pap. 3.50 (ISBN 0-8032-5079-7, BB 129, Bison). U of Nebr Pr.
--By Cheyenne Campfires. LC 79-158083. (Illus.). 1971. pap. 3.95 (ISBN 0-8032-5746-5, BB 541, Bison). U of Nebr Pr.
--Pawnee Hero Stories & Folktales with Notes on the Origin, Customs & Character of the Pawnee People. LC 61-10153. (Illus.). 1961. 14.95x (ISBN 0-8032-0896-0); pap. 7.50 (ISBN 0-8032-5080-0, BB 116, Bison). U of Nebr Pr.
--Two Great Scouts & Their Pawnee Battalion. LC 29-2718. (Illus.). vi, 299p. 1973. pap. 3.45 (ISBN 0-8032-5775-9, BB 564, Bison). U of Nebr Pr.
--When Buffalo Ran. (Western Frontier Library: No. 31). (Illus.). 1966. 6.95 (ISBN 0-8061-0715-4); pap. 2.95 (ISBN 0-8061-1271-9). U of Okla Pr.
Grinnell, Richard. Social Work Research & Evaluation. LC 80-52448. 600p. 1981. text ed. 19.50 (ISBN 0-87581-261-9). Peacock Pubs.
Grinsell, L. V., et al. Sylloge of Coins of the British Isles, No. 19: Ancient British Coins & Coins of the Bristol & Gloucestershire. (Illus.). 162p. 1973. 22.50x o.p. (ISBN 0-19-725932-4). Oxford U Pr.
Grinsell, Leslie V. Folklore of Prehistoric Sites in Britain. LC 76-8624. (Illus.). 304p. 1976. 24.00 (ISBN 0-7153-7241-6). David & Charles.
Grinspoon, Lester & Bakalar, James B. Psychedelic Drugs Reconsidered. 1981. pap. 7.95 (ISBN 0-465-06451-5). Basic.
Grinspoon, Lester & Hedblom, Peter. The Speed Culture: Amphetamine Use & Abuse in America. LC 74-27257. 368p. 1975. 17.50x (ISBN 0-674-83192-6); pap. 5.95 (ISBN 0-674-83194-2). Harvard U Pr.
Grinstead, David. The Earth Movers. 1980. 10.95 (ISBN 0-316-32892-8, Pub. by Atlantic Little Brown). Little.
Grinstead, Eric. Analysis of the Tangut Script. (Scandinavian Inst. of Asian Studies: No. 10). 376p. 1975. pap. text ed. 21.00x (ISBN 0-7007-0059-5). Humanities.
Grinstead, J. E. Maverick Guns. 1978. pap. 1.25 (ISBN 0-505-51269-6). Tower Bks.
Grinstein, Alexander. On Sigmund Freud's Dreams. 484p. 1968. 19.95x o.p. (ISBN 0-8143-1351-5). Wayne St U Pr.
--Sigmund Freud's Dreams. LC 79-2485. 475p. 1980. text ed. 22.50x (ISBN 0-8236-6074-5). Intl Univs Pr.
Grinter, H. C., tr. see Rudolph, Joachim.
Gripe, Maria. Elvis & His Friends. LC 75-8002. (Illus.). 224p. 1976. 6.95 o.s.i. (ISBN 0-440-02272-X, Sey Lawr); PLB 6.46 o.s.i. (ISBN 0-440-02273-8). Delacorte.
--The Glassblower's Children. La Farge, Sheila, tr. from Swedish. LC 73-949. (Illus.). 160p. (gr. 3-7). 1973. PLB 6.46 o.s.i. (ISBN 0-440-03065-X, Sey Lawr). Delacorte.
--Hugo & Josephine. Austin, Paul B., tr. from Swedish. LC 79-18438. (Illus.). (gr. 4-6). 1970. 4.95 o.s.i. (ISBN 0-440-04283-6, Sey Lawr). Delacorte.

--Hugo & Josephine. Austin, Paul B., tr. from Swedish. LC 69-18438. (Illus.). (gr. 4-6). 1969. 4.95 o.s.i. (ISBN 0-440-03929-0, Sey Lawr). Delacorte.

Grippando, Gloria M. Nursing Perspectives & Issues. LC 76-14090. 1977. pap. text ed. 11.60 (ISBN 0-8273-1314-4); instructor's guide 2.75 (ISBN 0-8273-1315-2). Delmar.

Grise, Jeanette. Robert Benjamin & the Disappearing Act. LC 80-19519. (Illus.). (gr. 3-5). 1980. 8.95 (ISBN 0-664-32673-0). Westminster.

Grisez, Germain & Boyle, Joseph M., Jr. Life & Death with Liberty & Justice: A Contribution to the Euthanasia Debate. LC 78-31249. 544p. 1980. pap. text ed. 9.95 (ISBN 0-268-01263-6). U of Notre Dame Pr.

Grisez, Germain & Shaw, Russell. Beyond the New Morality: The Responsibilities of Freedom. rev. ed. LC 80-18293. 240p. 1980. text ed. 10.95 (ISBN 0-268-00663-6); pap. 4.95 (ISBN 0-268-00665-2). U of Notre Damepr.

Grisham, Noel. A Serpent for a Dove: The Suppression of the American Indian. (Illus.). 168p. 7.50 (ISBN 0-8363-0089-0). Jenkins.

--Tame the Restless Wind: The Life & Legends of Sam Bass. (Illus.). 6.95 (ISBN 0-685-13279-X). Jenkins.

Grisham, Roy A., Jr. & McConaughy, Paul D., eds. The Encyclopedia of U. S. Government Benefits. new ed. LC 66-22903. (Illus.). 1977. 11.95 o.s.i. (ISBN 0-308-10335-1, TYC-T). T Y Crowell.

Grismer, Raymond L., ed. see Altamirano, Ignacio M.

Grisolia, Santiago, et al. The Urea Cycle. LC 76-7382. 656p. 1976. 47.50 (ISBN 0-471-32791-3, Pub. by Wiley-Interscience). Wiley.

Grissell, E. E., jt. auth. see Bohart, R. M.

Grisso, Thomas. Juveniles Waiver of Righs: Legal & Psychological Competence. (Perspectives in Law & Psychology Ser.: Vol. 3). 285p. 1981. 32.50 (ISBN 0-306-40526-1, Plenum Pr). Plenum Pub.

Grissum, Marlene & Spengler, Carol. Womanpower & Health Care. LC 75-41571. 1976. pap. 8.95 (ISBN 0-316-32895-2). Little.

Griswold, H. D. Religion of the Rigveda. 1971. 7.50 (ISBN 0-89684-305-X). Orient Bk Dist.

Griswold, P. R. Colorado's Loneliest Railroads: The San Luis Southern. (Illus.). 200p. 1980. 29.95 (ISBN 0-87108-554-2). Pruett.

Griswold, Ralph C. String & List Processing in Snobol 4: Techniques & Applications. (Illus.). 304p. 1975. text ed. 14.95 (ISBN 0-13-853010-6). P-H.

Griswold, Ralph E. The Macro Implementation of SNOBOL4: A Case Study of Machine-Independent Software Development. LC 72-184097. 1972. text ed. 30.95x (ISBN 0-7167-0447-1). W H Freeman.

Griswold, Ralph E., jt. auth. see Nichols, Frederick D.

Griswold, Ralph E., et al. Snobol Four Programming Language. 2nd ed. (Automatic Computation Ser). 1971. pap. 15.95 (ISBN 0-13-815373-6). P-H.

Griswold, Whit. Berkshire Trails for Walking & Ski Touring. LC 79-4901. (Illus.). 224p. 1978. lib. bdg. 10.25 o.p. (ISBN 0-914788-13-2). East Woods.

Griswold, Whit, jt. auth. see Mitchell, John H.

Griswold del Castillo, Richard. Los Angeles Barrio, Eighteen Fifty to Eighteen Ninety: A Social History. 1980. 18.50x (ISBN 0-520-03816-9). U of Cal Pr.

Gritsch, Eric W. & Jenson, Robert W. Lutheranism: The Theological Movement & Its Confessional Writings. LC 76-7869. 228p. 1976. pap. 7.50 (ISBN 0-8006-1246-9, 1-1246). Fortress.

Gritsch, Eric W. & Lehmann, Helmut T., eds. Luther's Works: Church & Ministry I, Vol. 39. LC 55-9893. 1970. 15.95 (ISBN 0-8006-0339-7, 1-339). Fortress.

Gritsch, Eric W., jt. ed. see Lehmann, Helmut T.

Gritzen, Edward F. Introduction to Naval Engineering. LC 79-90773. 448p. 1980. text ed. 13.95x (ISBN 0-87021-319-9). Naval Inst Pr.

Grivet, P. Electron Optics, 2 pts. 2nd ed. Incl. Pt. 1. Optics. pap. 14.50 (ISBN 0-08-016226-6); Pt. 2. Instruments. pap. 16.00 (ISBN 0-08-016228-2). 1972. Set. 67.00 (ISBN 0-08-016086-7). Pergamon.

Grmela, M., ed. Global Analysis. (Lecture Notes in Mathematics: Vol. 755). 1980. pap. 20.00 (ISBN 0-387-09703-1). Springer-Verlag.

Groak, S. & Koenigsberger, O. H., eds. Housing. 140p. 1980. pap. 32.00 (ISBN 0-08-026082-9). Pergamon.

Grob, G. N., jt. auth. see Billias, G. A.

Grob, Gerald N. Edward Jarvis & the Medical World of Nineteenth-Century America. LC 78-3771. 1978. 15.00x (ISBN 0-87049-239-X). U of Tenn Pr.

--Mental Institutions in America: Social Policy to 1875. LC 72-92868. 1973. 15.95 (ISBN 0-02-913040-9). Free Pr.

Grob, Gerald N. & Billias, George A. Historical Interpretations, 3 vols. Incl. Vol. 1. From Puritanism to the First Party System (ISBN 0-02-912900-1); Vol. 2. From Jacksonian Democracy to the Gilded Age. pap. text ed. o.s.i. (ISBN 0-02-912910-9); Vol. 3. From Progressivism to the Cold War. pap. text ed. o.s.i. (ISBN 0-02-912920-6). LC 67-12834. 1972. pap. text ed. 5.95 ea. Free Pr.

Grob, Gerald N., compiled by. American Social History Before 1860. LC 72-102037. (Goldentree Bibliographies in American History Ser). (Orig.). 1970. pap. 6.95x (ISBN 0-88295-515-2). AHM Pub.

Grob, Mollie C. & Singer, Judith E. Adolescent Patients in Transition: Impact & Outcome of Psychiatric Hospitalization. LC 73-22379. 224p. 1974. text ed. 19.95 (ISBN 0-87705-137-2). Human Sci Pr.

Grob, Regula, et al, trs. see Dietl, Walter.

Grobstein, Clifford. A Double Image of the Double Helix: The Recombinant-DNA Debate. LC 78-26093. (Biology Ser.). (Illus.). 1979. text ed. 16.95x (ISBN 0-7167-1056-0); pap. text ed. 8.95x (ISBN 0-7167-1057-9). W H Freeman.

--The Strategy of Life. 2nd ed. LC 73-18061. (Biology Ser.). (Illus.). 1974. text ed. 16.95x (ISBN 0-7167-0591-5); pap. text ed. 8.95x (ISBN 0-7167-0590-7). W H Freeman.

Groch, Dick. Mastering Baseball. LC 77-91156. 1978. 9.95 o.p. (ISBN 0-8092-7816-2); pap. 6.95 (ISBN 0-8092-7815-4). Contemp Bks.

Grochla, E., jt. ed. see Szperski, N.

Grocott, Allan M. Convicts, Clergymen & Churches. 356p. 1980. 27.50x (ISBN 0-424-00072-5, Pub. by Sydney U Pr Australia). Intl Schol Bk Serv.

Groddeck, Georg W. The World of Man. LC 51-13247. (Illus.). 272p. 1951. 12.50x o.p. (ISBN 0-85478-030-0). Intl Pubns Serv.

Grodecki, Louis. Gothic Architecture. (History of World Architecture). (Illus.). 1977. 45.00 (ISBN 0-8109-1008-X). Abrams.

Groden, James, ed. see Joyce, James.

Groden, Michael, ed. Ulysses: "Ithaca" & "Penelope." A Facsimile of Manuscripts & Typescripts for Episodes 17 & 18. LC 77-10882. (James Joyce Archive Ser.: Vol. 16). 1979. lib. bdg. 104.00 (ISBN 0-8240-2826-0). Garland Pub.

--Ulysses: "Sirens," "Cyclops," "Nausicaa," & "Oxen of the Sun." A Facsimile of Placards for Episodes 11-14. LC 78-11931. (James Joyce Archive Ser.: Vol. 19). 1979. lib. bdg. 104.00 (ISBN 0-8240-2813-9). Garland Pub.

--Ulysses: "Wandering Rocks," "Sirens," "Cyclops," "Nausicaa": Facsimile of Drafts & Typescripts for Episodes 10-13. LC 77-10196. (James Joyce Archive Ser.). 1978. lib. bdg. 104.00 (ISBN 0-8240-2823-6). Garland Pub.

Groden, Michael, ed. see Joyce, James.

Groden, Michael, ed. see Joyce, James, et al.

Groden, Michael, ed. see Joyce, James.

Groden, Suzy Q., tr. see Sappho.

Groder, Martin G. & Von Hartz, John. Business Games. LC 80-19095. 250p. 1980. 50.00 (ISBN 0-932648-14-2). Boardroom.

Grodin, Joseph R. & Grodin, Sharon. High Sierra Hiking Guide to Silver Lake. 2nd ed. LC 78-50994. (High Sierra Hiking Guide Ser.: Vol. 17). (Illus., Orig.). 1970. pap. 3.95 (ISBN 0-911824-73-1). Wilderness.

Grodin, Sharon, jt. auth. see Grodin, Joseph R.

Grodins, Fred S. Control Theory & Biological Systems. LC 63-10521. 1963. 15.00x (ISBN 0-231-02517-3). Columbia U Pr.

Grodins, Fred S. & Yamashiro, Stanley M. Respiratory Function of the Lung & Its Control. (Illus.). 1978. text ed. 13.50 (ISBN 0-02-348190-0); pap. text ed. 9.95 (ISBN 0-02-348120-X). Macmillan.

Grodinsky, Julius. Transcontinental Railway Strategy, 1869-1893: A Study of Businessmen. LC 61-6624. 1962. 15.00x o.p. (ISBN 0-8122-7268-4). U of Pa Pr.

Grodzinsky, Stephen, jt. auth. see Kirwin, Gerald J.

Groebner, David & Shannon, Patrick. Business Statistics: A Decision-Making Approach. (Illus.). 800p. 1981. text ed. 20.95 (ISBN 0-675-08083-5); tchr's. manual avail.; lab manual avail. (ISBN 0-675-08084-3); test bank avail. Merrill.

Groebner, David F. & Shannon, Patrick W. Statistics for Decision Makers. (General Business Ser.). 800p. 1981. text ed. 20.95 (ISBN 0-675-08083-5); student guide 6.95 (ISBN 0-675-08084-3). Merrill.

Groeg, Otto J., ed. Who's Who in Germany, 2 vols. 7th ed. (Who's Who Ser.). 1600p. 1980. 147.00x (ISBN 3-921220-28-9, Pub. by Who's Who Germany). Standing Orders.

--Who's Who in Germany, 1980, 2 vols. 7th ed. LC 56-3621. 1500p. 1980. Set. 175.00 (ISBN 3-921220-28-9). Intl Pubns Serv.

--Who's Who in Technology: Austria, Germany, Switzerland, 2 vols. 1055p. 1979. Set. 195.00x (ISBN 3-921220-24-6). Intl Pubns Serv.

Groen, B. M. A Structural Description of the Macedonian Dialect of Dihovo. (PDR Press Publication on Macedonian: No. 2). 1977. pap. text ed. 22.75x (ISBN 9-0316-0143-8). Humanities.

Groene, Janet. Cooking on the Go. rev. ed. (Illus.). 1980. 13.95 (ISBN 0-393-03259-0). Norton.

Groenewegen Frankfort, Mrs. H. & Ashmole, Bernard. Art of the Ancient World. (Janson Art History Ser). (Illus.). 512p. 1972. text ed. 21.95x (ISBN 0-13-047001-5). P-H.

Groer, Maureen E. & Shekleton, Maureen E. Basic Pathophysiology: A Conceptual Approach. LC 78-21170. (Illus.). 1979. pap. 18.95 (ISBN 0-8016-1983-1). Mosby.

Grof, P., ed. Recent Advances in Canadian Neuropsychopharmacology. 132p. 1981. pap. 30.00 (ISBN 3-8055-1459-X). S Karger.

Grof, Stanislav & Cayce, Hugh L. Dimensions of Dying & Rebirth. 1977. pap. 2.50 o.p. (ISBN 0-87604-099-7). ARE Pr.

Groff, Betty & Wilson, Jose. Betty Groff's Country Goodness Cookbook. LC 80-1093. (Illus.). 336p. 1981. 17.95 (ISBN 0-385-12120-2). Doubleday.

--Good Earth & Country Cooking. 2nd ed. LC 73-23128. (Illus.). 256p. 1974. pap. 8.95 (ISBN 0-8117-2066-7). Stackpole.

Groff, Diller B., ed. Handbook of Pediatric Surgical Emergencies. 2nd. ed. 1980. write for info. (ISBN 0-87488-642-2). Med Exam.

Groff, John W. The Mystic Journey. 1980. 1.45 (ISBN 0-686-28785-1). Forward Movement.

Groff, Russell E. Two Hundred Patterns for Multiple Harness Looms. (Illus.). 1980. 14.95 (ISBN 0-686-27272-2); pap. 9.95 (ISBN 0-686-28458-5). Robin & Russ.

Groft, Tammis K. The Folk Spirit of Albany. (Illus.). 1978. pap. 6.00 (ISBN 0-939072-00-9). Albany Hist & Art.

Grogan, Denis. Practical Reference Work. (Outlines of Modern Librarianship Ser.). 144p. 1979. text ed. 12.00 (ISBN 0-686-65492-7, Pub. by K G Saur). Shoe String.

Grogan, Raymond G., et al, eds. Annual Review of Phytopathology, Vol. 18. LC 63-8847. (Illus.). 1980. text ed. 20.00 (ISBN 0-8243-1318-6). Annual Reviews.

Grogg, Evelyn. Bible Lessons for Little People: Revised with Learning Centers. rev. ed. Eberle, Sarah, rev. by. LC 80-53878. 144p. 1981. pap. 6.95 (ISBN 0-87239-430-1, 3368). Standard Pub.

--Kindergarten Pattern Book. Eberle, Sarah, rev. by. (Illus.). 48p. (Orig.). 1981. pap. 3.95 (ISBN 0-87239-431-X, 2159). Standard Pub.

Grogono, Peter. Programming in Pascal. rev. ed. LC 79-24640. 384p. 1980. pap. text ed. 13.95 (ISBN 0-201-02775-5). A W.

--Programming in Pascal. LC 77-90175. 1978. pap. text ed. 11.50 o.p. (ISBN 0-201-02473-X). A-W.

Groh, John E. & Smith, Robert H., eds. The Lutheran Church in North American Life: 1776-1976, 1580-1980. LC 78-71233. 1979. 5.95 (ISBN 0-915644-17-7, Clayton). Luth Acad.

Grohman, Joan S. Keeping a Family Cow. (Illus.). 192p. 1981. 9.95 (ISBN 0-684-16867-7, ScribT). Scribner.

Grohmann, Will, ed. see Klee, Paul.

Grolier, jt. ed. see Associated Press.

Grolier Incorporated. Encyclopedia Science Supplement, 1980. Kondo, Herbert, ed. LC 64-7603. (Illus.). 1979. write for info. o.p. (ISBN 0-7172-1510-5). Grolier Ed Corp.

--Encyclopedia Science Supplement, 1981. Kondo, Herbert, ed. LC 64-7603. (Illus.). 1980. write for info. (ISBN 0-7172-1511-3). Grolier Ed Corp.

Grollenberg, Lucas, et al. Minister? Pastor? Prophet? Grassroots Leadership in the Churches. 112p. (Dutch.). 1981. 9.95 (ISBN 0-8245-0017-2). Crossroad NY.

Grollman, Earl A. Living - When a Loved One Has Died. LC 76-48508. (Illus.). 1977. 7.95 (ISBN 0-8070-2740-5); pap. 4.95 (ISBN 0-8070-2741-3, BP560). Beacon Pr.

Grollman, Earl A., ed. Concerning Death: A Practical Guide for the Living. LC 73-17117. 384p. 1974. 9.95 o.p. (ISBN 0-8070-2764-2); pap. 5.95 (ISBN 0-8070-2765-0, BP484). Beacon Pr.

--What Helped Me: When My Loved One Died. LC 80-68166. 160p. 1981. 9.95 (ISBN 0-8070-3228-X). Beacon Pr.

Grollman, Sharon H. More Time to Grow. LC 76-48513. (gr. k-5). 1977. 7.95 o.p. (ISBN 0-8070-2370-1). Beacon Pr.

Gromacki, Robert. Is Salvation Forever? 1973. pap. 3.95 (ISBN 0-8024-7506-X). Moody.

--Is Salvation Forever? 1981. pap. 4.95 (ISBN 0-8024-7507-8). Moody.

--The Virgin Birth of Christ. 200p. 1981. pap. 5.95 (ISBN 0-8010-3765-4). Baker Bk.

Grombach, John V. The Saga of the Fist. LC 75-20594. 1977. 19.95 (ISBN 0-498-01681-1). A S Barnes.

Gromisch, Donald S., jt. auth. see Wasserman, Edward.

Gromisch, Donald S., jt. auth. see Wasserman, Edward D.

Gromme, Owen J. Birds of Wisconsin. (Illus.). 1963. 37.50 (ISBN 0-299-03001-6). U of Wis Pr.

Gromyko, A. A. Only for Peace. (Illus.). 1979. text ed. 46.00 (ISBN 0-08-023582-4); pap. text ed. 19.00 (ISBN 0-08-024513-7). Pergamon.

Gronbech, Kaare. The Structure of the Turkic Languages. Sinor, Denis, ed. Krueger, John R., tr. (Indiana University Uralic & Altaic Ser.: Vol. 136). 189p. pap. text ed. 8.00 (ISBN 0-933070-04-7). Ind U Res Inst.

Gronbech, Vilhelm. Preliminary Studies in Turkic Historical Phonology. Sinor, Denis, ed. Krueger, John R., tr. from Danish. (Indiana University Uralic & Altaic Ser.: Vol. 135). Orig. Title: Forstudier Til Turkisk Lyndhistorie. 162p. 1979. pap. text ed. 8.00 (ISBN 0-933070-03-9). Ind U Res Inst.

--Preliminary Studies in Turkic Historical Phonology. Krueger, John, tr. (Indiana University Uralic & Altaic Ser.: Vol. 135). 162p. 1979. 8.00. Ind U Res Inst.

--Religious Currents in the Nineteenth Century. Mitchell, P. M. & Paden, W. D., trs. from Danish. LC 72-11829. (Arcturus Bks. Paperbacks). 206p. 1973. lib. bdg. 7.00x (ISBN 0-8093-0629-8); pap. 2.45 (ISBN 0-8093-0630-1). S Ill U Pr.

Gronbjerg, Kirsten, et al. Poverty & Social Change. LC 78-876. viii, 248p. 1980. lib. bdg. 9.00x (ISBN 0-226-30963-0). U of Chicago Pr.

Grondahl, Carl H., intro. by. The Literary Masters of Norway. LC 79-309381. (Tokens of Norway Ser.). (Illus.). 89p. (Orig.). 1978. pap. 12.50x (ISBN 82-518-0727-1). Intl Pubns Serv.

Groneman, Chris. Leathercraft. (gr. 9-12). 1963. pap. 7.96 (ISBN 0-87002-204-0). Bennett IL.

Groneman, Chris H. & Grannis, Gary E. Exploring the Industries. LC 79-55313. 1980. pap. text ed. 14.40 (ISBN 0-8273-1757-3); instr's manual 1.55 (ISBN 0-8273-1758-1). Delmar.

Groner, Alex, et al. The American Heritage History of American Business & Industry. LC 72-80699. 384p. 1972. deluxe ed. 20.00 o.p. (ISBN 0-8281-0313-5, BO52DI-00). Am Heritage.

Groner, Pat N. Cost Containment Through Employee Incentives Program. LC 77-72514. 1977. 22.00 (ISBN 0-912862-42-4). Aspen Systems.

Gronicka, Andre Von see Von Gronicka, Andre & Bates-Yakobson, Helen.

Groninger, Vicki, ed. see Holbrook, Charles & Holbrook, Linda.

Gronlie, Gisle. Geophysical Studies in the Norwegian-Greenland Sea. (Norsk Polarinstitutt Skrifter: Vol. 170). (Illus.). 117p. 1980. pap. text ed. 10.00 (ISBN 82-90307-05-5). Universitet.

Gronlund, Norman E. Constructing Achievement Tests. 2nd ed. 1977. pap. 8.95 ref. ed. (ISBN 0-13-169235-6). P-H.

Gronneberg, Roy. Island Futures. 96p. 1980. pap. 5.95 (ISBN 0-686-68846-5, Pub. by Thule Pr England). Intl Schol Bk Serv.

Gronowicz, Anthony, ed. Oswald Garrison Villard: The Dilemmas of the Absolute Pacifist in Two World Wars. LC 72-147764. (Library of War & Peace; Documentary Anthologies). lib. bdg. 38.00 (ISBN 0-8240-0504-X). Garland Pub.

Gronsky, Paul P. & Astrov, Nicholas J. The War & the Russian Government. 17.50 (ISBN 0-86527-207-7). Fertig.

Gronwall, Anders. Dextran & Its Use in Colloidal Infusion Solutions. (Illus.). 1957. 23.50 (ISBN 0-12-304050-7). Acad Pr.

Groom, Bob. The Blues Revival. (The Paul Oliver Blues Ser.). pap. 2.95 (ISBN 0-913714-28-3). Legacy Bks.

Groom, Kathe, ed. see Sonnenberg, David E. & Birnbaum, Michael.

Groom, N. S. Frankincense & Myrrh: A Study of the Arabian Incense Trade. (Arab Background Ser.). (Illus.). 328p. 1981. text ed. 37.00 (ISBN 0-582-76476-9). Longman.

Groom, Winston. As Summers Die. LC 80-17451. 319p. 1980. 12.95 (ISBN 0-671-40072-X). Summit Bks.

--Better Times Than These. 1979. pap. 2.75 (ISBN 0-425-04098-4). Berkley Pub.

Groome, Thomas H. Christian Religious Education: Sharing Our Story & Vision. LC 80-7755. 288p. 1980. 12.95 (ISBN 0-06-063491-X, HarpR). Har-Row.

Groomer, Vera. Good Friends Again: Two - Three. (Come Unto Me Ser.: Year 2, Bk. 3). 32p. (ps). 1980. pap. 1.50 (ISBN 0-8127-0272-7). Southern Pub.

--Growing Stronger: Two - Two. (Come Unto Me Ser.: Year 2, Bk. 2). 32p. (ps). 1980. pap. 1.50 (ISBN 0-8127-0271-9). Southern Pub.

--Talking to My Friend Jesus: Two - Four. (Come Unto Me Ser.: Year 2, Bk. 4). 32p. (ps). 1980. pap. 1.50 (ISBN 0-8127-0273-5). Southern Pub.

Grooms, Kathe, ed. see Audette, Vicki.

Grooms, Kathe, ed. see Consumer-Aid Group.

Grooms, Kathe, ed. see Olson, Craig.

Grooms, Kathe, ed. see Whitman, John.

Groot, Georg Van Der see Van Der Groot, Georg.

Groot, J. J. De see De Groot, J. J.

Groot, Jan J. The Religion of the Chinese. LC 79-2824. 230p. 1981. Repr. of 1910 ed. 19.50 (ISBN 0-8305-0004-9). Hyperion Conn.

Groot, Silvia W. De see De Groot, Silvia W.

Gropius, et al. Four Great Makers of Modern Architecture: Gropius, le Corbusier, Mies Van der Rohe, Wright. LC 78-130312. (Architecture & Decorative Art Ser.: Vol. 37). 1970. Repr. of 1963 ed. lib. bdg. 29.50 (ISBN 0-306-70065-4). Da Capo.

Gropius, Ise see O'Neal, William B.

Gropius, Walter. Scope of Total Architecture. 1962. pap. 1.25 o.s.i. (ISBN 0-02-000500-8, Collier). Macmillan.

Gropius, Walter, ed. The Theater of the Bauhaus. Wensinger, Arthur S., tr. from Ger. LC 61-14239. (Illus.). 109p. 1971. pap. 10.95 (ISBN 0-8195-6020-0, Pub. by Wesleyan U Pr). Columbia U Pr.

Gropman, Donald, jt. auth. see DiOrio, Ralph A.

Gropp, Arthur E. Bibliography of Latin American Bibliographies. LC 68-9330. 1968. 40.00 (ISBN 0-8108-0011-X). Scarecrow.

--Bibliography of Latin American Bibliographies Published in Periodicals, 2 vols. LC 75-32552. 1976. Set. 40.00 o.p. (ISBN 0-8108-0838-2). Scarecrow.

--Bibliography of Latin American Bibliographies: Supplement 1965-1969. LC 68-9330. 1971. 10.00 (ISBN 0-8108-0350-X). Scarecrow.

Gropper, Rena C. The Practice of Anthropology: A Manual for Professionals. LC 76-19136. 1981. 20.00 (ISBN 0-87850-029-4). Darwin Pr.

Gros, C. M., ed. see Gautherie, M., et al.

Gros, J. H. De see De Gros, J. H.

Grosch, Robert, jt. auth. see Hullinger, Robert.

Groseclose, Elgin. Money & Man: A Survey of Monetary Experience. LC 75-40960. 326p. 1976. 14.95 (ISBN 0-8061-1338-3); pap. 6.95 (ISBN 0-8061-1339-1). U of Okla Pr.

--Olympia. 1981. pap. 9.95 (ISBN 0-89191-290-8). Cook.

Grose-Hodge, Humfrey, ed. see Cicero.

Grosheide, Frederick W. Commentary on First Corinthians. (New International Commentary on the New Testament). 1953. 12.95 (ISBN 0-8028-2185-5). Eerdmans.

Grosicki. Watsons Advanced Textile Design. 4th ed. Watson, ed. 1977. 42.95 (ISBN 0-408-00250-6). Butterworths.

Grosicki, Z. J., ed. see Watson, William.

Grosjean, Ardis, tr. see Stang, Ragna.

Grosklos, Jacqueline R., jt. auth. see Heasley, Bernice E.

Groskreutz, Donna J. Spook & the Giant Ant. LC 79-64491. 1980. 4.50 (ISBN 0-533-04298-4). Vantage.

Gross. If You Were a Ballet Dancer. (gr. 3). 1979. pap. 1.50 (ISBN 0-590-05746-4, Schol Pap). Schol Bk Serv.

--Los Musicos De Brema (the Bremen-Town Musicians) (ps-3). pap. 1.95 (ISBN 0-590-10446-2, Schol Pap). Schol Bk Serv.

Gross, Alan J. & Clark, Virginia A. Survival Distributions: Reliability Applications in the Biomedical Sciences. LC 75-6806. (Probability & Mathematical Statistics Ser). 331p. 1975. 32.95 (ISBN 0-471-32817-0, Pub. by Wiley-Interscience). Wiley.

Gross, Arthur W. Child's Garden of Bible Stories. (Concordia Primary Religion Ser.). (gr. 1-3). 1981. 6.50 (ISBN 0-570-03414-0, 56-1001); pap. 4.95 (ISBN 0-570-03402-7, 56-1012). Concordia.

Gross, Barbara & Shuman, Bernard. Essentials of Parenting in the First Years of Life. LC 79-23739. (Orig.). 1980. pap. text ed. 3.95 (ISBN 0-87868-184-1). Child Welfare.

Gross, Barry R. Discrimination in Reverse: Is Turn-About Fair Play? LC 77-14672. 1978. pap. 5.00x (ISBN 0-8147-2967-3); pap. 4.95x (ISBN 0-8147-2970-3). NYU Pr.

Gross, Beatrice & Gross, Ronald, eds. The Children's Rights Movement: Overcoming the Oppression of Young People. LC 75-40753. 1977. 9.95 (ISBN 0-385-11027-8, Anchor Pr); pap. 3.95 (ISBN 0-385-11028-6). Doubleday.

Gross, Bertram M. Organizations & Their Managing. LC 68-22642. 1968. text ed. 19.95 (ISBN 0-02-913140-5). Free Pr.

Gross, Charles W. & Peterson, Robin T. Business Forecasting. LC 75-31029. (Illus.). 320p. 1976. text ed. 20.95 (ISBN 0-395-19505-5). HM.

Gross, Charles W., jt. auth. see Verma, Harish L.

Gross, D. R., jt. ed. see Hwang, N. H.

Gross, David. The Writer & Society: Heinrich Mann & Literary Politics in Germany, 1890-1940. 316p. 1980. text ed. 15.00x (ISBN 0-391-00972-9). Humanities.

Gross, David C., ed. see Isaacson, Ben.

Gross, Donald & Harris, Carl M. Fundamentals of Queueing Theory. LC 73-20084. (Probability & Mathematical Statistics Ser.). 576p. 1974. 34.95 (ISBN 0-471-32812-X, Pub. by Wiley-Interscience). Wiley.

Gross, E. T., et al, eds. Coil Spring Making. 2nd ed. (Engineering Craftsmen: No. H6). (Illus.). 1974. spiral bdg. 25.00x (ISBN 0-85083-172-5). Intl Ideas.

Gross, Edward, ed. see Carnegie Commission on Higher Education.

Gross, Erhard, ed. The Peptides: Analysis, Synthesis, Biology: Vol. 3 Protection of Functional Groups in Peptides Synthesis. 1980. 45.00 (ISBN 0-12-304203-8). Acad Pr.

Gross, Erhard & Meienhofer, Johannes, eds. The Peptides: Analysis, Synthesis, Biology, Part A, Major Methods Of Peptide Bond Formation. LC 78-31958. 1979. 42.50, by subscription 36.50 (ISBN 0-12-304201-1). Acad Pr.

Gross, Ernest, et al. New Jersey Police & Fire Arbitration Databook, 1980, 2 vols. 2000p. 1980. Set. 100.00. Inst Mgmt & Labor.

Gross, F., jt. ed. see Zbinden, G.

Gross, Feliks. Ethnics in a Borderland: An Inquiry into the Nature of Ethnicity & Reduction of Ethnic Tensions in a One-Time Genocide Area. LC 77-94741. (Contributions in Sociology: No. 32). 1978. lib. bdg. 19.95 (ISBN 0-313-20310-5, GET/). Greenwood.

Gross, Franz, et al, eds. Enzymatic Release of Vasoactive Peptides: Workshop Conferences HOECHST. (Illus.). 430p. 1980. text ed. 41.00 (ISBN 0-89004-458-9). Raven.

Gross, H. Privacy, Its Legal Protection. rev. ed. 1976. 5.95 (ISBN 0-379-11099-7). Oceana.

Gross, Henry. Pure Magic! LC 77-15069. (Illus.). 1978. 12.50 o.p. (ISBN 0-684-15338-6, SL 751, ScribT); pap. 6.95 o.p. (ISBN 0-684-15337-8, SL 751, ScribJ). Scribner.

Gross, Hyman, jt. auth. see Feinberg, Joel.

Gross, Hyman & Von Hirsch, Andrew, eds. Sentencing. 416p. 1981. text ed. 19.95x (ISBN 0-19-502763-9); pap. text ed. 9.95x (ISBN 0-19-502764-7). Oxford U Pr.

Gross, Irena, jt. ed. see Gross, Jan.

Gross, Irene, jt. auth. see Friedland, Joyce.

Gross, Irman H., et al. Management for Modern Families. 4th ed. (Illus.). 1980. text ed. 16.95 (ISBN 0-13-549477-X). P-H.

Gross, J. F., et al, eds. Modern Techniques in Physiological Sciences. 1974. 66.00 (ISBN 0-12-304450-2). Acad Pr.

Gross, Jan & Gross, Irena, eds. War Through the Children's Eyes: The Soviet Occupation of Poland & the Deportations, 1939-1941. LC 80-83832. (Publications Ser.: No.247). 300p. 1981. 21.95. Hoover Inst Pr.

Gross, Jim, et al. April Fourth, Nineteen Eighty-One: Pivotal Day in a Critical Year. (Illus.). 1980. pap. 7.00 (ISBN 0-933646-12-7). Aries Pr.

Gross, Joel. The Books of Rachel. 1981. 3.50 (ISBN 0-451-09561-8, E9561, Sig). NAL.

--Maura's Dream. LC 80-52416. 416p. 1981. 12.95 (ISBN 0-87223-654-4). Seaview Bks.

Gross, John J. John P. Marquand. (U. S. Authors Ser.: No. 33). 1962. lib. bdg. 10.95 (ISBN 0-8057-0476-0). Twayne.

Gross, Joseph F., ed. Mathematics of Microcirculation Phenomena. 189p. 1980. text ed. 24.00 (ISBN 0-89004-449-X). Raven.

Gross, Joy. The Thirty-Day to a Born-Again Body. 1981. pap. 2.75 (ISBN 0-425-04733-4). Berkley Pub.

Gross, L. Oncogenic Viruses. 2nd ed. 1970. 57.00 (ISBN 0-08-013236-7). Pergamon.

Gross, Leo, ed. see American Society Of International Law.

Gross, Leonard. The Golden Years of the Hutterites. LC 80-10711. (Studies in Anabaptist & Mennonite History Ser.: Vol. 23). 1980. 12.95x (ISBN 0-8361-1227-X). Herald Pr.

--Mirror. LC 80-8229. 352p. 1981. 10.95 o.p. (ISBN 0-06-011642-0, HarpC). Har-Row.

--The Terrible Teens: A Guide for Bewildered Parents. 256p. 1981. 10.95 (ISBN 0-02-545820-5). Macmillan.

Gross, Lynne S., jt. auth. see Hunter, Julius.

Gross, M. Grammaire transformationelle du francais: Syntaxe du verbe. (Fr). pap. 14.50 (ISBN 0-685-13931-X). Larousse.

Gross, M. Grant. Oceanography: A View of the Earth. 2nd ed. (Illus.). 1977. 19.95 (ISBN 0-13-629675-0). P-H.

Gross, Malvern J. & Jablonsky, Stephen F. Principles of Accounting & Financial Reporting for Nonprofit Organizations. LC 79-4559. 1979. 21.95 (ISBN 0-471-05719-3, Pub. by Wiley-Interscience); instr's manual avail. Wiley.

Gross, Malvern J., Jr. & Warshauer, William, Jr. Financial & Accounting Guide for Nonprofit Organizations. 3rd ed. 1979. 32.50 (ISBN 0-471-04974-3). Ronald Pr.

Gross, Martin L. The Psychological Society. 1978. 10.95 (ISBN 0-394-46233-5). Random.

Gross, Mary P. Mrs. NCO. 1980. pap. 3.45. Beau Lac.

--Mrs. NCO. LC 71-101333. 1969. pap. 1.25 o.p. (ISBN 0-911980-02-4). Beau Lac.

Gross, Maurice. Grammaire transformationelle du francais: Syntaxe du nom. 1978. pap. text ed. 20.95 (ISBN 2-03-070343-5, 3633). Larousse.

Gross, Michael. Selling Strategy for Getting Orders. LC 73-80141. 196p. 1974. pap. 1.50 o.p. (ISBN 0-668-03322-3). Arc Bks.

Gross, Nancy D. & Fontana, Frank. Shishi Embroidery: Traditional Mirrorwork of India, Pakistan & Afghanistan. (Illus.). 80p. (Orig.). Date not set. pap. price not set (ISBN 0-486-24043-6). Dover.

Gross, Neal & Trask, Anne E. The Sex Factor & the Management of Schools. LC 75-34337. 304p. 1976. 24.95 (ISBN 0-471-32800-6, Pub. by Wiley-Interscience). Wiley.

Gross, Neal, jt. ed. see Herriott, Robert E.

Gross, Nicholas, ed. Self-Assessment of Current Knowledge in Pulmonary Diseases. 1973. spiral bdg. 12.00 o.s.i. (ISBN 0-87488-271-0). Med Exam.

Gross, Richard E., et al. Social Studies for Our Times. LC 78-2733. 1978. text ed. 21.95x (ISBN 0-471-02340-X); tchrs. ed. 72.50 (ISBN 0-471-04051-7). Wiley.

Gross, Rita M., ed. Beyond Androcentrism: New Essays on Women & Religion. LC 77-13312. (AAR Aids for the Study of Religion: No. 6). 1977. pap. 7.50 (ISBN 0-89130-196-8, 010306). Scholars Pr Ca.

Gross, Robert. A Veterinarian's Limerick Book. 1979. 4.50 o.p. (ISBN 0-8062-1213-6). Carlton.

Gross, Robert A. The Minutemen & Their World. 1976. 8.95 (ISBN 0-8090-6933-4, AmCen); pap. 4.95 (ISBN 0-8090-0120-9). Hill & Wang.

Gross, Robert E. Atlas of Children's Surgery. LC 70-108366. (Illus.). 1970. 24.00 (ISBN 0-7216-4287-X). Saunders.

Gross, Robin & Cullen, Jean. Help! The Basics of Borrowing Money. 160p. 1980. 9.95 (ISBN 0-8129-0899-6). Times Bks.

Gross, Ronald, jt. ed. see Gross, Beatrice.

Gross, Ronald, et al. The New Old: Struggling for Decent Aging. LC 77-12857. 1978. pap. 5.95 (ISBN 0-385-12763-4, Anch). Doubleday.

Gross, Ruth B. Alligators & Other Crocodilians. LC 77-18310. (Illus.). 64p. (gr. 1-5). 1978. 7.95 (ISBN 0-590-07556-X, Four Winds). Schol Bk Serv.

--A Book About Your Skeleton. (Illus.). (gr. k-4). 1979. 6.95g (ISBN 0-8038-0794-5). Hastings.

--Snakes. LC 74-13227. (Illus.). 64p. (gr. k-3). 1975. 7.95 (ISBN 0-590-07385-0, Four Winds). Schol Bk Serv.

Gross, Ruth B., retold by. The Bremen-Town Musicians. (Illus.). (gr. k-3). 1975. pap. 1.95 (ISBN 0-590-09894-2, Schol Pap); pap. 3.50 bk. & record (ISBN 0-590-20713-X). Schol Bk Serv.

Gross, S. An Elephant Is Soft & Mushy. LC 79-28642. (Illus.). 128p. 1980. pap. 6.95 (ISBN 0-396-07823-0). Dodd.

--I Am Blind & My Dog Is Dead. LC 77-7314. 1977. 7.95 (ISBN 0-396-07473-1). Dodd.

Gross, Seymour L., ed. see Hawthorne, Nathaniel.

Gross, Seymour L, jt. ed. see Stern, Milton R.

Gross, Sidney & Gross, Sue. Recipes from a Brooklyn Childhood. 1979. pap. write for info. cancelled (ISBN 0-917234-14-6). Kitchen Harvest.

Gross, Sue, jt. auth. see Gross, Sidney.

Gross, Susan E. The Midnight Fury. 320p. 1981. pap. 2.75 (ISBN 0-449-14392-9, GM). Fawcett.

Gross, Theodore L. Literature of American Jews. LC 72-93311. 1973. 12.95 (ISBN 0-02-913190-1). Free Pr.

Gross, Theodore L. & Wertheim, S. Hawthorne, Melville, Stephen Crane: A Critical Bibliography. LC 75-142364. 1971. 12.95 (ISBN 0-02-913220-7). Free Pr.

Gross, Theodore L., jt. ed. see Emanuel, James A.

Gross, Theodore L., et al. America in Literature, 2 vols. LC 76-49486. 1978. Vol. 1. pap. text ed. 13.95 (ISBN 0-471-32808-1); Vol. 2. pap. text ed. 13.95 (ISBN 0-471-32809-X); tchrs. manual 3.00 (ISBN 0-471-04050-9). Wiley.

Gross, Theodore. Readings in English, Bk. 2: Travel. (gr. 9-12). 1981. pap. text ed. price not set (ISBN 0-88345-418-1, 18883). Regents Pub.

Gross, William & Matsch, Lee A. Fluid Film Lubrication. Vohr, John H. & Wildman, Manfred, eds. LC 80-36889. 773p. 1980. 35.00 (ISBN 0-471-08357-7, Pub. by Wiley-Interscience). Wiley.

Grossack, Irvin M. International Economy & the National Interest. LC 78-13817. (Illus.). 272p. 1980. 17.95x (ISBN 0-253-36775-1). Ind U Pr.

Grossbach, Robert. Going in Style. (Orig.). 1979. 2.25 (ISBN 0-446-92485-7). Warner Bks.

--Neil Simon's Chapter Two. (Orig.). 1980. pap. 2.25 (ISBN 0-446-92279-X). Warner Bks.

Grossbard, E., ed. Straw Decay & Its Effect on Disposal & Utilization. LC 79-42841. 1979. 50.25 (ISBN 0-471-27694-4, Pub. by Wiley Interscience). Wiley.

Grossberg, Kenneth A., ed. Japan Today. (Illus., Orig.). 1981. 12.95 (ISBN 0-89727-018-5); pap. 5.95 (ISBN 0-89727-019-3). Inst Study Human.

Grossberg, Milton. Family Bike Rides. (Illus.). 128p. (Orig.). 1981. pap. 5.95 (ISBN 0-87701-148-6). Chronicle Bks.

Grosse, Arthur E., jt. auth. see Butler, Ian S.

Grosse, Robert E. Foreign Investment Codes & Location of Direct Investment. LC 80-15194. (Praeger Special Studies). 174p. 1980. 20.95 (ISBN 0-03-057024-7). Praeger.

Grossen, Neal E., jt. auth. see Meyers, Lawrence S.

Grosser, Arthur E. The Cookbook Decoder: or, Culinary Alchemy Explained. 192p. 1981. 9.95 (ISBN 0-8253-0033-9). Beaufort Bks NY.

Grosser, Charles, et al, eds. Nonprofessionals in the Human Services. LC 76-92887. (Social & Behavioral Science Ser.). 1969. 14.95x o.p. (ISBN 0-87589-041-5). Jossey-Bass.

Grosser, Morton. Gossamer Odyssey: The Triumph of Human-Powered Flight. (Illus.). 288p. 1981. 14.95 (ISBN 0-686-69048-6). HM.

Grossett, Philip, ed. see Auber, Daniel F.

Grossett, Philip, ed. see Meyerbeer, Giacomo.

Grossett, Philip, ed. see Spontini, Gasparo.

Grossfeld, Bernard & Aberbach, Moses. Targum Onqelos on Genesis 49. LC 76-27271. (Society of Biblical Literature. Aramaic Studies). 1976. pap. 6.00 (ISBN 0-89130-078-3, 061301). Scholars Pr Ca.

Grosshandler, William L. see Heat Transfer & Fluid Mechanics Institute.

Grossi, John A., jt. ed. see Jordan, June B.

Grossinger, Richard. Book of the Cranberry Islands. 1975. pap. 5.95 o.p. (ISBN 0-06-090373-2, CN373, CN). Har-Row.

Grossinger, Richard, ed. Alchemy: Pre-Egyptian Legacy, Millennial Promise. (Io Ser.: No. 26). (Illus., Orig.). 1979. pap. 8.95 (ISBN 0-913028-62-2). North Atlantic.

--Ecology & Consciousness. 2nd ed. 226p. (Orig.). 1980. pap. 6.95 (ISBN 0-913028-71-1). North Atlantic.

Grossinger, Tania. Weekend. Date not set. pap. 2.95 (ISBN 0-440-19375-3). Dell.

Grossman, Alvin. The Standard Book of Dog Breeding. LC 76-56010. (Other Dog Bk.). (Illus.). 1981. price not set (ISBN 0-87714-054-5). Denlingers.

Grossman, David A. The Future of New York City's Capital Plant. (America's Urban Capital Stock Ser.: Vol. 1). 112p. (Orig.). 1979. pap. text ed. 4.50 (ISBN 0-87766-249-5, 25700). Urban Inst.

Grossman, Edith, tr. see Segre, Roberto & Katz, Fernando K.

Grossman, Eli A. Life Reinsurance. 79p. (Orig.). 1980. pap. text ed. 4.50 (ISBN 0-915322-38-2). Loma.

Grossman, Frances K., et al. Pregnancy, Birth, & Parenthood: Adaptations of Mothers, Fathers, & Infants. LC 80-16518. (Social & Behavioral Science Ser.). 1980. text ed. 15.95x (ISBN 0-87589-465-8). Jossey-Bass.

Grossman, Gary. Saturday Morning TV. (Orig.). 1981. pap. 9.95 (ISBN 0-440-52397-4, Delta). Dell. Postponed.

Grossman, H. I., jt. auth. see Barro, R. J.

Grossman, Harold J. Grossman's Guide to Wines, Beers, & Spirits. 6th rev. ed. (Illus.). 1977. 27.50 (ISBN 0-684-15033-6, ScribT). Scribner.

Grossman, Irwin & Wolania, Ron. Twenty-Five Ski Tours in & Around Greater Boston. (Illus.). Date not set. pap. 5.95 (ISBN 0-89725-007-9). NH Pub Co. Postponed.

Grossman, J. B., et al. Social Science Approaches to the Judicial Process. LC 74-153371. (Symposia on Law & Society Ser). 1971. Repr. of 1966 ed. lib. bdg. 14.50 (ISBN 0-306-70135-9). Da Capo.

Grossman, Joan D., ed. The Diary of Valery Bryusov (1893-1905) With Reminiscences by V. F. Khodasevich & Marina Tsvetaeva. (Documentary Studies in Modern Russian Poetry). 200p. 1980. 15.75x (ISBN 0-520-03858-4). U of Cal Pr.

Grossman, Karl. Cover Up: What You Are Not Supposed to Know About Nuclear Power. 1980. 11.95 (ISBN 0-531-07405-6, Permanent Pr). Watts.

Grossman, Larry. Galaxy World Postage Stamp Album. (Illus.). 1980. 2.95 (ISBN 0-685-78367-7). Grossman Stamp.

--Liberty Bell U. S. Album. (Illus.). 1980. 2.95 (ISBN 0-685-99702-2). Grossman Stamp.

--Topicals World Stamp Album. (Illus.). 1980. 2.00 o.p. (ISBN 0-685-99700-6). Grossman Stamp.

--Universe World Stamp Album. (Illus.). 1980. 11.95 (ISBN 0-685-99699-9). Grossman Stamp.

Grossman, Larry, ed. America U.S. Stamp Album. (Illus.). 1980. 12.95 (ISBN 0-685-78366-9). Grossman Stamp.

--Seven Seas World Stamp Album. (Illus.). 1979. 7.95 (ISBN 0-686-64403-4). Grossman Stamp.
--Victory U. S. Stamp Album. (Illus.). 1980. 2.95 (ISBN 0-686-64402-6). Grossman Stamp.
Grossman, Louis I., ed. Mechanism & Control of Pain. LC 79-84476. (Masson Monographs in Dentistry: Vol. 1). 256p. 1979. 26.00 (ISBN 0-89352-048-9). Masson Pub.
Grossman, Mary L. & Hamlet, John. Birds of Prey of the World. (Illus.). 500p. 1964. 25.00 (ISBN 0-517-52181-4). Crown.
Grossman, Michael B. & Kumar, Martha J. Portraying the President: The White House & the News Media. 380p. 1981. text ed. 26.50 (ISBN 0-8018-2375-7); pap. 9.95 (ISBN 0-8018-2537-7). Johns Hopkins.
Grossman, Morris. For-Hhundred Ideas for Ddesign, Vol.4. 376p. 1980. 13.95 (ISBN 0-8104-0950-X). Hayden.
--Technician's Guide to Solid State Electronics. 1976. 14.95 o.p. (ISBN 0-13-898585-5). P-H.
Grossman, Morris, ed. see Electronic Design.
Grossman, N. J., jt. auth. see Baylen, J. O.
Grossman, Reinhardt. Meinong. (Arguments of the Philosophers Ser.). 1974. 19.00 (ISBN 0-7100-7831-5). Routledge & Kegan.
Grossman, Richard. Choosing & Changing: A Guide to Self Reliance. 1978. 7.95 o.p. (ISBN 0-525-07940-8). Dutton.
Grossman, Robert G., jt. auth. see Willis, William D., Jr.
Grossman, Ronald. Italians in America. rev. ed. LC 66-10149. (In America Bks.). (Illus.). (gr. 5-11). 1979. PLB 5.95 (ISBN 0-8225-0202-X). Lerner Pubns.
Grossman, Stanley. Calculus. 1977. 26.95 (ISBN 0-12-304350-6). Acad Pr.
--Calculus: Instructor's Manual. 120p. 1977. 3.00 (ISBN 0-12-304352-2). Acad Pr.
--Elementary Linear Algebra. 400p. 1980. text ed. 19.95x (ISBN 0-534-00746-5). Wadsworth Pub.
Grossman, Stanley I., jt. auth. see Derrick, William R.
Grossman, Steven D., jt. auth. see Lindhe, Richard.
Grossman, Stewart, jt. auth. see Vye, George.
Grossman, William & Farrell, Jack. The Heart of Jazz. LC 76-75730. (Roots of Jazz Ser.). 1976. Repr. of 1956 ed. lib. bdg. 25.00 (ISBN 0-306-70811-6). Da Capo.
Grossman, William, ed. Cardiac Catheterization & Angiography. 2nd ed. LC 80-10331. (Illus.). 427p. 1980. text ed. 34.50 (ISBN 0-8121-0714-4). Lea & Febiger.
Grossman, William L., ed. Modern Brazilian Short Stories. LC 67-13379. 1974. 14.00x (ISBN 0-520-00523-6); pap. 2.25 (ISBN 0-520-02766-3). U of Cal Pr.
Grossmith, George & Grossmith, Weedon. Diary of a Nobody. 1962. 8.00x o.p. (ISBN 0-460-00963-X, Evman); pap. 3.50 (ISBN 0-460-01963-5). Dutton.
Grossmith, Weedon, jt. auth. see Grossmith, George.
Grossvogel, David I. Twentieth Century French Drama. LC 65-7487. Orig. Title: Self-Conscious Stage in Modern French Drama. 1958. pap. 6.00x (ISBN 0-231-08522-2). Columbia U Pr.
Grosswirth, Marvin. Beginners Guide to Home Computers. LC 77-16918. 1978. pap. 4.50 (ISBN 0-385-13572-6, Dolp). Doubleday.
--The Heraldry Book: A Guide to Designing Your Own Coat of Arms. LC 78-22321. (Illus.). 240p. 1981. 11.95 (ISBN 0-385-14157-2). Doubleday.
Grosvenor, Charles. The Portraits of T.E. Lawrence. (Illus.). 1975. pap. 15.00 o.s.i. (ISBN 0-918868-00-9). Otterden.
Grosvenor, Peter, ed. We Are Amused: The Cartoonist's View of Royalty. 1979. 9.95 (ISBN 0-370-30139-0, Pub. by Chatto Bodley Jonathan). Merrimack Bk Serv.
Grotch, Howard, jt. auth. see McKelvey, John P.
Grote, Jeanette, jt. auth. see Pape, Donna L.
Grotenhuis, Elizabeth T., tr. see Okazaki, Joji.
Grotenhuis, Elizabeth Ten see Rosenfield, John M. & Ten Grotenhuis, Elizabeth.
Groth, A. N. Men Who Rape: The Psychology of the Offender. LC 79-18624. 245p. 1979. 15.00 (ISBN 0-306-40268-8, Plenum Pr). Plenum Pub.
Groth, Patricia C. & Druck, Kitty, eds. Foothpath. LC 78-71325. (Illus.). 72p. (Orig.). 1978. pap. 5.00 (ISBN 0-937158-00-3). Del Valley.
Grothendieck, Alexander. Produits Tensoriels Topologiques et Espaces Nucleaires. LC 52-42839. (Memoirs: No. 16). 1979. pap. 12.00 (ISBN 0-8218-1216-5, MEMO-16). Am Math.
Grotjahn, Martin. The Art & Technique of Analytic Group Therapy. LC 76-22916. 1977. 25.00x (ISBN 0-87668-252-2). Aronson.
Grotpeter, John J. Historical Dictionary of Swaziland. LC 75-4734. (African Historical Dictionaries Ser.: No. 3). 265p. 1975. 12.00 (ISBN 0-8108-0805-6). Scarecrow.
--Historical Dictionary of Zambia. LC 79-342. (African Historical Dictionaries Ser.: No. 19). 1979. 18.50 (ISBN 0-8108-1207-X). Scarecrow.
Grotpeter, John J., jt. auth. see Weinstein, Warren.
Grott, J. J. De see De Groot, J. J.
Grotty, Robert B., jt. auth. see Hunt, Arnold D.
Grotz, George. The Current Antique Furniture Style & Price Guide. LC 77-27673. 1979. 9.95 (ISBN 0-385-13165-8, Dolp). Doubleday.
--Staining & Finishing Unfinished Furniture & Other Naked Woods. LC 68-25596. 1968. pap. 2.95 (ISBN 0-385-01906-8, Dolp). Doubleday.
Grouch, Colin. The Politics of Industrial Relations. (Political Issues of Modern Britain Ser.). 1979. text ed. 5.00x (ISBN 0-391-01163-4). Humanities.
Grouchy, Jean De see De Grouchy, Jean & Turleau, Catherine.
Groueff, S. L' Homme et la mer. (Collection maitrise du monde). 64.50x (ISBN 0-685-36200-0, 2278). Larousse.
Groueff, S. & Cartier, J. P. L' Homme et le cosmos. new ed. Cartier, Raymond, ed. (Collection maitrise du monde). (Illus.). 396p. (Fr.). 1975. 64.50x (ISBN 2-03-013369-8). Larousse.
Grounds, Roger. Growing Vegetables & Herbs. (Orig.). 1980. pap. 6.95x (ISBN 0-8464-1016-8). Beekman Pubs.
--Ornamental Grasses. 216p. 1981. 16.95 (ISBN 0-442-24707-9). Van Nos Reinhold.
Grounds, Roger, ed. The Complete Handbook of Pruning. LC 74-2865. (Illus.). 160p. 1975. 15.95 (ISBN 0-02-546000-5). Macmillan.
Grounds, Vernon. Emotional Problems & the Gospel. 160p. 1976. pap. text ed. 2.95 o.p. (ISBN 0-310-25311-X). Zondervan.
Group-Effort. California Manufacturers Register 1980. 33rd ed. Newman, Phyllis, ed. LC 48-3418. 1980. 77.50 o.s.i. (ISBN 0-911510-80-X). Times-M Pr.
Group for the Advancement of Psychiatry Conference. Application of Psychiatric Insights to Cross-Cultural Communication, Vol. 4. LC 62-2872. (Symposium No. 7). 1961. pap. 0.75 o.p. (ISBN 0-87318-065-8). Adv Psychiatry.
Group For The Advancement Of Psychiatry. Clinical Psychiatry: Problems of Treatment, Research & Prevention. LC 67-8140. 1967. 25.00x (ISBN 0-87668-003-1). Aronson.
--Factors Used to Increase the Susceptibility of Individuals to Forceful Indoctrination; Observations & Experiments, Vol. 3. (Symposium: No. 3). 1956. pap. 2.00 (ISBN 0-87318-043-7). Adv Psychiatry.
--Illustrative Strategies for Research on Psychopathology in Mental Health, Vol. 3. (Symposium No. 2). 1956. pap. 1.00 o.p. (ISBN 0-87318-041-0). Adv Psychiatry.
--Joys & Sorrows of Parenthood. LC 73-1365. 1975. pap. 2.95 o.p. (ISBN 0-684-14438-7, SL 609, ScribT). Scribner.
--Methods of Forceful Indoctrination; Observations & Interviews, Vol. 3. (Symposium No. 4). 1957. pap. 1.00 o.p. (ISBN 0-87318-046-1). Adv Psychiatry.
Group for the Advancement of Psychiatry Conference. Pavlovian Conditioning & American Psychiatry, Vol. 5. (Symposium No. 9). 1964. pap. 3.00 (ISBN 0-87318-079-8). Adv Psychiatry.
Group for the Advancement of Psychiatry. Psychological & Medical Aspects of the Use of Nuclear Energy, Vol. 4. (Symposium No. 6). 1960. pap. 2.00 (ISBN 0-87318-059-3). Adv Psychiatry.
--Right to Abortion: A Psychiatric View. 1970. 5.95 o.p. (ISBN 0-684-10200-5, ScribT). Scribner.
--The Right to Die: Decision & Decision Makers. LC 73-17780. 90p. 1974. 15.00x (ISBN 0-87668-127-5). Aronson.
--Some Considerations of Early Attempts in Cooperation Between Religion & Psychiatry, Vol. 3. (Symposium No. 5). 1958. pap. 2.00 (ISBN 0-87318-049-6). Adv Psychiatry.
--Treatment of Families in Conflict: The Clinical Study of Family Process. LC 78-130635. 1970. 30.00x (ISBN 0-87668-036-8). Aronson.
--The VIP with Psychiatric Impairment. LC 76-37208. 160p. 1973. 4.95 o.p. (ISBN 0-684-12778-4, ScribT). Scribner.
Grousset, Rene. The Empire of the Steppes. LC 77-108759. 1970. 37.50 (ISBN 0-8135-0627-1). Rutgers U Pr.
Grout, Donald J. Alessandro Scarlatti: An Introduction to His Operas. 1979. 14.00x (ISBN 0-520-03682-4). U of Cal Pr.
--History of Western Music. rev. ed. (Illus.). 1973. text ed. 18.95x (ISBN 0-393-09416-2). Norton.
--History of Western Music. rev. ed. (Illus.). 540p. 1973. pap. text ed. 15.95x (ISBN 0-393-09358-1). Norton.
--Short History of Opera. 2nd ed. LC 64-11043. (gr. 9 up). 1965. text ed. 20.00x (ISBN 0-231-02422-3). Columbia U Pr.
Grout, Jack. The Golden Age of Yachting. Chamier, John, tr. LC 80-51188. Orig. Title: C'etait Au Temps Des Yachtsmen. (Illus.). 240p. (Fr.). Date not set. 29.95 (ISBN 0-86565-006-3). Vendome. Postponed.
Grout, Phil. A Spell in Plains. LC 78-2230. (Illus.). 1978. 19.95 (ISBN 0-916144-17-8); pap. 9.95 (ISBN 0-916144-18-6). Stemmer Hse.
Grove, A. T. & Klein, F. Rural Africa. LC 77-82496. (Topics in Geography Ser.). (Illus.). 1979. 22.50 (ISBN 0-521-21825-X); pap. 6.95x (ISBN 0-521-29282-4). Cambridge U Pr.
Grove, E. J., jt. auth. see Davies, E. L.
Grove, Edward A. & Ladas, Gerasimbs E. Introduction to Complex Variables. 1974. 19.50 (ISBN 0-395-17087-7). HM.
Grove, Frank W. The Coins of Mexico. 1981. lib. bdg. 60.00 (ISBN 0-88000-123-2). Quarterman.
Grove, Fred. The Landseekers. 1974. pap. 0.95 o.p. (ISBN 0-345-23798-6). Ballantine.
Grove, Hugh D., jt. auth. see Mock, Theodore J.
Grove, Joseph, jt. auth. see Webb, Philip C.
Grove, Judi. A Vacationer's Guide to Orlando. (Illus.). 150p. (Orig.). 1981. pap. 4.95x (ISBN 0-914788-39-6). East Woods.
Grove, Lilly. Dancing: A Handbook of the Terpsichorean Arts in Diverse Places & Times, Savage & Civilized. LC 76-76138. (Illus.). xviii, 454p. 1969. Repr. of 1895 ed. 18.00 (ISBN 0-8103-3469-0). Gale.
Grove, Martin A. Visions. 496p. (Orig.). 1980. pap. 2.75 (ISBN 0-89083-695-7). Zebra.
Grove, Richard. The Cambridgeshire Coprolite Mining Rush. (Cambridge Town, Gown & County Ser.: Vol. 1). (Illus.). 1976. pap. 4.25 (ISBN 0-902675-61-3). Oleander Pr.
Grove, Robert B. Communication Monitoring & Communications Projects. 128p. 1979. pap. 5.95 (ISBN 0-8104-0894-5). Hayden.
Grove, Theodore S. Experiences in Interpersonal Communication. (Illus.). 224p. 1976. pap. 11.95 (ISBN 0-13-294975-X). P-H.
Grove, Wendell E. Brief Numerical Methods. 1966. text ed. 17.95x (ISBN 0-13-082917-X). P-H.
Grover, Eulalie O. Robert Louis Stevenson, a Teller of Tales. LC 71-164308. x, 265p. (YA) 1975. Repr. of 1940 ed. 20.00 (ISBN 0-8103-4080-1). Gale.
Grover, F & Wallace, P. Laboratory Organization & Management. (Illus.). 1979. text ed. 19.95 (ISBN 0-408-70793-3). Butterworths.
Grover, Frances. Poems for Holidays & Special Days. LC 80-52667. (Illus.). 90p. 1980. 6.95 (ISBN 0-533-04779-X). Vantage.
--Poems of Nature. 1981. 7.95 (ISBN 0-533-04780-3). Vantage.
Grover, Frederic J. Drieu la Rochelle & the Fiction of Testimony. 1958. 17.50x (ISBN 0-520-00526-0). U of Cal Pr.
Grover, Lee, jt. auth. see Grover, Ray.
Grover, Marshall. Feud at Mendoza. 1977. pap. 1.25 (ISBN 0-505-51187-8). Tower Bks.
Grover, Philip L. Chemical Carcinogens & DNA, 2 vols. 1979. Vol. 1, 256p. 59.95 (ISBN 0-8493-5303-3); Vol. 2, 224p. 59.95 (ISBN 0-8493-5304-1). CRC Pr.
Grover, R. F. New Zealand. (World Biliographical Ser.: No. 13). 1981. write for info. (ISBN 0-903450-31-3). ABC-Clio.
Grover, Ray & Grover, Lee. Carved & Decorated European Art Glass. LC 71-94025. (Illus.). 1970. 55.00 (ISBN 0-8048-0707-8). C E Tuttle.
--English Cameo Glass. (Illus.). 1980. 30.00 (ISBN 0-517-53815-6). Crown.
Groves, David N. & Poirot, James L. Computers & Data Processing. (Illus.). 1978. text ed. 14.95 (ISBN 0-88408-101-X); avail. tchrs. ed. Sterling Swift.
Groves, David N., et al. Practice in Data Processing. 217p. (Orig.). (gr. 11-12). 1979. wkbk 4.95x (ISBN 0-88408-114-1). Sterling Swift.
Groves, G. W., jt. auth. see Kelly, Anthony.
Groves, Harold M. Federal Tax Treatment of the Family. LC 76-55946. (Brookings Institution, Studies of Government Finance Ser). 1977. Repr. of 1963 ed. lib. bdg. 15.00x (ISBN 0-8371-9425-3, GRFT). Greenwood.
--Tax Philosophers: Two Hundred Years of Thought in Great Britain & the United States. Curran, Donald J., ed. LC 74-5901. 256p. 1974. 17.50 (ISBN 0-299-06660-6). U of Wis Pr.
Groves, John, jt. ed. see Ballantyne, John.
Groves, L., ed. Physical Education for Special Needs. LC 78-68389. 1979. 19.95 (ISBN 0-521-22391-1); pap. 8.95 (ISBN 0-521-29471-1). Cambridge U Pr.
Groves, Leslie R. Now It Can Be Told: The Story of the Manhattan Project. LC 75-1001. (FDR & the Era of the New Deal Ser.). 465p. 1975. Repr. of 1962 ed. lib. bdg. 35.00 (ISBN 0-306-70738-1). Da Capo.
Groves, Martha, jt. ed. see Warden, Rob.
Groves, Philip, jt. auth. see Cox, Anthony.
Groves, R. H., ed. Australian Vegetation. LC 80-40421. (Illus.). 350p. Date not set. price not set (ISBN 0-521-23436-0); pap. price not set (ISBN 0-521-29950-0). Cambridge U Pr.
Groves, Wanda J. Precious Parables for Tiny Tots. 27p. 1980. 4.50 (ISBN 0-533-04417-0). Vantage.
Grow, Douglas, jt. auth. see Barnidge, Thomas.
Grow, Laurence. The Old House Book of Outdoor Living Places. (Illus., Orig.). 1981. 15.00 (ISBN 0-446-51219-2). Warner Bks.
--The Old House Book of Outdoor Spaces. (Orig.). 1981. 8.95 (ISBN 0-446-97556-7). Warner Bks.
Grow, Lawrence. The Old House Book of Bedrooms. (The Old House Book Ser.). (Illus.). 96p. 1980. 15.00 (ISBN 0-446-51216-8); pap. 7.95 (ISBN 0-446-97553-2). Warner Bks.
--The Old House Book of Living Rooms & Parlors. (The Old House Book Ser.). (Illus.). 150p. 1980. 15.00 (ISBN 0-446-51215-X); pap. 7.95 (ISBN 0-446-97552-4). Warner Bks.
Grow, Lawrence, ed. The Brand New Old House Catalogue. (Illus.). 224p. 1980. 17.95 (ISBN 0-446-51214-1); pap. 9.95 (ISBN 0-446-97557-5). Warner Bks.
Grow, Lucille, jt. auth. see CWLA Research Center.
Grow, Lynn M. The Prose Style of Samuel Taylor Coleridge. (Salzburg Studies in English Literature, Romantic Reassessment: No. 54). 161p. 1976. pap. text ed. 25.00x (ISBN 0-391-01395-5). Humanities.
Groza, Mavis A. Everywoman's Guide to Financial Independence. LC 76-11371. 128p. 1976. pap. 3.95 o.p. (ISBN 0-89087-918-4). Les Femmes Pub.
Grozier, Edwin A. & Gillet, Margaret, eds. Plot Outlines of One Hundred One Best Novels. 1962. pap. 4.95 (ISBN 0-06-463215-6, EH 215, EH). Har-Row.
Grub & Ellis Commercial Brokerage Co., jt. auth. see Real Estate Education Company.
Grubb & Ellis Commercial Brokerage Co., jt. auth. see Real Estate Education Co.
Grubb & Ellis Company. Successful Industrial Real Estate Brokerage. 2nd ed. 327p. (Orig.). 1980. pap. 49.95 (ISBN 0-88462-317-3). Real Estate Ed Co.
Grubb & Ellis Company, jt. auth. see Real Estate Education Company Staff.
Grubb, Chandra. Colour Atlas of Gynaecological Cytopathology. (Illus.). 1977. text ed. 29.50 o.p. (ISBN 0-8016-8353-X). Mosby.
Grubb, Davis. Twelve Tales of Suspense & the Supernatural. 144p. 1977. pap. 1.25 o.p. (ISBN 0-449-13727-9, GM). Fawcett.
Grubb, Norman. Key to Everything. 1975. pap. 3.50 (ISBN 0-8024-4545-4). Moody.
Grubb, Norman P. Rees Howells: Intercessor. 1964-1967. 4.95 o.p. (ISBN 0-87508-220-3); pap. 3.95 (ISBN 0-87508-219-X). Chr Lit.
Grubb, R. & Samuelsson, G. Human Anti-Human Gammaglobulins: Their Specificity & Function. 240p. 1971. 42.00 (ISBN 0-08-016451-X). Pergamon.
Grubb, Reba D. & Mueller, Carolyn J. Designing Hospital Training Programs. (Illus.). 216p. 1975. 20.50 (ISBN 0-398-03316-1). C C Thomas.
Grubb, Reba D. & Ondov, Geraldine. Operating Room Guidelines: An Illustrated Manual. LC 78-31422. (Illus.). 1979. pap. text ed. 17.95 (ISBN 0-8016-1985-8). Mosby.
--Planning Ambulatory Surgery Facilities. LC 79-10123. (Illus.). 1979. 17.95 (ISBN 0-8016-1986-6). Mosby.
Grubb, Reba D., jt. auth. see Dubay, Elaine C.
Grubb, Reba G., jt. auth. see Vukovich, Virginia C.
Grubb, W. Norton, jt. ed. see Lazerson, Marvin.
Grubbs, H. A. & Kneller, J. W. Introduction a la Poesie Francaise. 1962. 14.95x (ISBN 0-471-00217-8). Wiley.
Grube, G. M. Plato's Thought. Zeyl, Donald J., ed. 240p. 1980. 18.50 (ISBN 0-915144-79-4); pap. text ed. 7.95 (ISBN 0-915144-80-8). Hackett Pub.
Grube, G. M., tr. see Aristotle.
Grube, G. M., tr. see Aurelius, Marcus.
Grube, G. M., tr. see Longinus.
Grube, Oswald. One Hundred Years of Architecture in Chicago. 1977. 14.95 o.p. (ISBN 0-695-80837-0). Follett.
Grubel, H. G. & Lloyd, P. J. Intra-Industry Trade. LC 74-13576. 205p. 1975. 34.95 (ISBN 0-470-33000-7). Halsted Pr.
Grubel, Herbert G. International Economics. 1977. 18.95x (ISBN 0-256-01793-X). Irwin.
Gruber, et al. The Multistate Bar Examination. rev. ed. (Exam Prep. Ser.). 256p. 1981. pap. text ed. 6.95 (ISBN 0-671-18965-4). Monarch Pr.
Gruber, Alan R. Children in Foster Care: Destitute, Neglected...Betrayed. LC 77-521. 1977. 19.95 (ISBN 0-87705-265-4). Human Sci Pr.

Gruber, Edward C. Graduate Management Admission Test. 1976. pap. 6.95 (ISBN 0-671-18995-6). Monarch Pr.
--Preparation for the New Mathematics Test (GED) rev. ed. (Exam Preparation Ser.). (gr. 11). 1980. pap. text ed. 5.95 (ISBN 0-671-09240-5). Monarch Pr.
--Preparation for the New Science Test (GED) rev ed. (Exam Preparation Ser.). (gr. 11). 1980. pap. text ed. 5.95 (ISBN 0-671-09241-3). Monarch Pr.
--Preparation for the New Social Studies Test: (GED) (Orig.). 1980. pap. 5.95 (ISBN 0-671-09246-4). Monarch Pr.
--Test of English As a Foreign Language (TOEFL) rev. ed. (Exam Preparation Ser.). 528p. (gr. 12). 1981. pap. text ed. 6.95 (ISBN 0-671-18987-5). Monarch Pr.
--Twenty Three Hundred Steps to Word Power. LC 62-20285. (Orig.). 1963. pap. 2.95 (ISBN 0-668-01032-0). Arc Bks.
Gruber, Edward C., jt. auth. see Strand, Stanley.
Gruber, Elmar. Metal & Wire Sculpture. LC 69-19489. (Little Craft Book Ser). (Illus.). (gr. 8 up). 1969. 4.95 o.p. (ISBN 0-8069-5128-1); PLB 5.89 o.p. (ISBN 0-8069-5129-X). Sterling.
Gruber, Frank. Fort Starvation. 160p. 1980. pap. 1.75 o.s.i. (ISBN 0-553-14180-5). Bantam.
--Lonesome River. 1979. pap. 1.75 o.p. (ISBN 0-451-08844-1, E8856, Sig). NAL.
--Peace Marshal. 160p. (Orig.). 1981. pap. 1.75 (ISBN 0-553-14539-8). Bantam.
--Quantrell's Raiders. 1981. pap. 1.95 (ISBN 0-451-09735-1, J9735, Sig). NAL.
--This Gun Is Still. 1979. pap. 1.50 o.p. (ISBN 0-685-93870-0, T8773-8). Bantam.
Gruber, Frederick C., ed. Good Education of Youth. 1957. 12.00x o.p. (ISBN 0-8122-7049-5). U of Pa Pr.
Gruber, Gary R. High School Equivalency Test. (Exam Prep. Ser.). pap. 6.95 (ISBN 0-671-18998-0). Monarch Pr.
Gruber, Harvey, ed. see Bush, Loren S. & McLaughlin, James.
Gruber, Harvey, ed. see Erven, Lawrence.
Gruber, Harvey, ed. see Meidl, James.
Gruber, Howard E. Darwin on Man: A Psychological Study of Scientific Creativity. 2nd ed. LC 80-28453. 1981. lib. bdg. price not set (ISBN 0-226-31008-6); pap. price not set (ISBN 0-226-31007-8). U of Chicago Pr.
Gruber, James & Pryor, Judith. Materials & Methods for Sociology Research. LC 79-14814. (Bibliographic Instruction Ser.). 1980. lib. bdg. 14.95x (ISBN 0-918212-13-8); wkbk. 5 or more 4.95x (ISBN 0-918212-12-X). Neal-Schuman.
Gruber, James, jt. auth. see Benson, Tedd.
Gruber, M. J., jt. auth. see Elton, E. J.
Gruber, Martin J., jt. auth. see Elton, Edwain J.
Gruber, Murray L., ed. Management Systems in the Human Services: An Introduction to New Technologies. 325p. 1981. 19.50x (ISBN 0-87722-207-X): Temple U Pr.
Gruberg, Edward & Raymond, Stephen. Beyond Cholesterol. 208p. 1981. 9.95 (ISBN 0-312-07779-3). St Martin.
Grubman, Barbara J. Introduction to Terrariums. (Illus.). 128p. 1973. pap. 1.50 o.p. (ISBN 0-445-08488-X). Popular Lib.
Gruchy, Allan G. Comparative Economic Systems: Competing Ways to Stability, Growth & Welfare. 2nd ed. LC 76-10899. (Illus.). 1977. text ed. 20.95 (ISBN 0-395-18606-4). HM.
Grudin, Robert. Mighty Opposites: Shakespeare & Renaissance Contrariety. 1979. 15.75x (ISBN 0-520-03666-2). U of Cal Pr.
Gruelle, Johnny. Raggedy Ann & the Wonderful Witch. (Illus.). (gr. 1-4). 1977. 1.95 o.s.i. (ISBN 0-685-86227-5). Dell.
Gruen, Erich S. The Last Generation of the Roman Republic. LC 72-89244. 1974. 33.75x (ISBN 0-520-02238-6). U of Cal Pr.
Gruen, Ernest J. Freedom to Choose. 224p. 1976. pap. 2.95 (ISBN 0-88368-072-6). Whitaker Hse.
Gruen, F. H., ed. Surveys of Australian Economics, Vol. 1. LC 78-55055. 1978. text ed. 21.00x (ISBN 0-86861-208-1); pap. text ed. 12.50x (ISBN 0-86861-216-2). Allen Unwin.
Gruen, John. Menotti: A Biography. LC 77-9304. (Illus.). 1978. 16.95 (ISBN 0-02-546320-9). Macmillan.
--The Private World of Ballet. 1976. pap. 4.95 o.p. (ISBN 0-14-004343-8). Penguin.
Gruenbaum, Thelma, jt. auth. see Rivera, A. Ramon.
Gruenberg, Gladys, jt. auth. see Kugel, Yerachmiel.
Gruenberg, Gladys W. Labor Peacemaker: The Life & Works of Father Leo. C. Brown, S. J. Ganss, George E., ed. (Original Studies Composed in English Ser.: No. 4). (Illus.). 176p. 1981. 7.50 (ISBN 0-912422-54-8); pap. 6.00 smythsewn paperbound (ISBN 0-912422-53-X); pap. 5.00 (ISBN 0-912422-52-1). Inst Jesuit. Postponed.
Gruenberg, Gladys W., jt. auth. see Kugel, Yerachmiel.
Gruenberg, Sidonie M. Wonderful Story of How You Were Born. rev. ed. LC 71-92055. (Illus.). (gr. 3-5). 1970. 6.95a (ISBN 0-385-03674-4); PLB (ISBN 0-385-03680-9); pap. 1.49 o.p. (ISBN 0-385-05383-5). Doubleday.
Gruenberger, F. J. & Jaffray, G. Problems for Computer Solution. LC 65-24303. 1965. pap. 16.95 (ISBN 0-471-32908-8). Wiley.
Gruenberger, Fred & Babcock, David. Computing with Mini Computers. LC 73-4793. 88p. 1973. 22.00 (ISBN 0-471-33005-1, Pub. by Wiley-Interscience). Wiley.
Gruendemann, Barbara J., jt. auth. see Rhodes, Marie J.
Gruendemann, Barbara J., et al. The Surgical Patient: Behavioral Concepts for the Operating Room Nurse. 2nd ed. LC 76-51725. (Illus.). 1977. pap. text ed. 10.50 (ISBN 0-8016-1981-5). Mosby.
Gruenfeld, Elaine F. Promoton: Practices, Policies, & Affirmative Action. (Key Issues Ser.: No. 17). 1975. pap. 3.00 (ISBN 0-87546-222-7). NY Sch Indus Rel.
Gruenhagen, Robert W. Mustang: Story of the P-Fifty-One Fighter. LC 75-30278. (Illus.). 1980. pap. 9.95 (ISBN 0-668-04884-0). Arco.
Gruening, Ernest. The Public Pays - & Still Pays: A Study of Power Propaganda. rev. ed. LC 64-16420. pap. 2.25 (ISBN 0-8149-0112-3). Vanguard.
Gruenwald, Oskar. The Yugoslav Search for Man: Marxist Humanism in Contemporary Yugoslavia. 400p. 1981. 24.95x (ISBN 0-89789-005-1). J F Bergin.
Grugel, Lee E. Society & Religion During the Age of Industrialization: Christianity in Victorian England. LC 78-65844. (Illus.). 1979. pap. text ed. 7.50 (ISBN 0-8191-0671-2). U Pr of Amer.
Grugeon, E., jt. ed. see Cashdan, A.
Gruhn, William T. & Douglass, Harl R. The Modern Junior High School. 3rd ed. LC 78-110549. 424p. 1971. 18.95 (ISBN 0-8260-3695-3, 41985). Wiley.
Gruhn, William T., jt. auth. see Anderson, Vernon E.
Gruits, Patricia B. Understanding God. 2nd ed. 415p. 1972. pap. 7.95 (ISBN 0-88368-011-4). Whitaker Hse.
Gruliou, Leo. Moscow. (The Great Cities Ser.). (Illus.). (gr. 6 up). 1977. PLB 11.97 (ISBN 0-8094-2275-1, Pub. by Time-Life). Silver.
Gruliow, Leo, ed. Moscow. (The Great Cities Ser.). 1977. 14.95 (ISBN 0-8094-2274-3). Time-Life.
Grumbach, Doris. The Missing Person. 256p. 1981. 11.95 (ISBN 0-399-12587-6). Putnam.
Grumbach, Jane & Emerson, Robert. Actors Guide to Monologues, Vol. I. rev ed. LC 74-23335. 35p. 1972. pap. text ed. 2.95x (ISBN 0-910482-41-1). Drama Bk.
--Actor's Guide to Monologues, Vol. 2. rev ed. LC 73-21893. 1981. pap. 2.95x (ISBN 0-89676-043-X). Drama Bk.
--Actors Guide to Scenes. LC 73-75346. 28p. 1973. pap. text ed. 2.95x (ISBN 0-910482-42-X). Drama Bk.
--More Actors Guide to Monologues, Vol. 2. rev. ed. LC 73-21893. pap. text ed. 1.95x o.p. (ISBN 0-89676-043-X). Drama Bk.
Grumbach, Melvin M., et al, eds. Control of the Onset of Puberty. LC 73-18091. (Clinical Pediatrics, Maternal & Child Health Ser.). 512p. 1974. 46.95 (ISBN 0-471-32265-2, Pub. by Wiley Medical). Wiley.
Grumelli, Antonio, jt. ed. see Caporale, Rocco.
Grumet, Priscilla H. How to Dress Well: A Complete Guide for Women. (Illus., Orig.). 1980. pap. 6.95 (ISBN 0-346-12510-3). Cornerstone.
Grumet, Robert S. Native Americans of the Northwest Coast: A Critical Bibliography. LC 79-2165. (Newberry Library Center for the History of the American Indian Bibliographical Ser.). 128p. (Orig.). 1980. pap. 4.95x (ISBN 0-253-30385-0). Ind U Pr.
Grumley, Michael & Gallucci, Ed. Hard Corps: Studies in Leather & Sado Masochism. LC 76-47487. (Illus.). 1977. pap. 7.95 o.p. (ISBN 0-525-47457-9). Dutton.
Grumm, John & Wasby, Stephen, eds. The Analysis of Policy Impact. 1980. pap. 5.00 (ISBN 0-918592-39-9). Policy Studies.
Grumm, John G. & Wasby, Stephen L., eds. The Analysis of Policy Impact. (A Policy Studies Orgnization Bk.). 224p. 1981. 23.95x (ISBN 0-669-03951-9). Lexington Bks.
Grumman, Joan, jt. auth. see Webber, Jeanette.
Grummer, Arnold E. Paper by Kids. LC 79-22904. (Doing & Learning Bks.). (Illus.). (gr. 5 up). 1980. PLB 7.95 (ISBN 0-87518-191-0). Dillon.
Grun, Max Von Der see Von Der Grun, Max.
Grun, Paul. Cytoplasmic Genetics and Evolution. (Illus.). 384p. 1976. 30.00x (ISBN 0-231-03975-1). Columbia U Pr.
Grunbaum, B. Arrangements & Spreads. LC 71-38926. (CBMS Regional Conference Series in Mathematics: No. 10). 1980. Repr. of 1974 ed. 7.60 (ISBN 0-8218-1659-4, CBMS-10). Am Math.
Grunberger, Richard. Twelve-Year Reich: A Social History of Nazi Germany, 1933-1945. (Illus.). 1971. 10.00 o.p. (ISBN 0-03-076435-1). HR&W.
Grunden, Elizabeth H., jt. auth. see Friedlander, Janet.
Grundin, Elizabeth H. Literacy. 1979. text ed. 14.25 (ISBN 0-06-318128-2, IntlDept); pap. text ed. 9.25 (ISBN 0-06-318140-1). Har-Row.
Grundler, Horst. The Study of Tooth Shapes: A Systematic Procedure. (Illus.). 104p. 1976. 24.00 (ISBN 3-87652-561-6). Quint Pub Co.
Grundmann, E., ed. Drug Induced Pathology. (Current Topics in Phathology Ser.: Vol. 69). (Illus.). 384p. 1981. 70.00 (ISBN 0-387-10415-1). Springer-Verlag.
Grundy, J. T. Construction Technology, Vol. 1. (Illus.). 1977. pap. 12.95x (ISBN 0-7131-3387-2). Intl Ideas.
--Construction Technology, Vol. 2. (Illus.). 200p. 1979. pap. 13.95x (ISBN 0-7131-3403-8). Intl Ideas.
Grundy, Julia M. Ten Days in the Light of 'Akka. rev. ed. LC 79-12177. 1979. pap. 5.00 (ISBN 0-87743-131-0, 7-32-40). Baha'i.
Grundy, Kenneth W. Confrontation & Accomodation in Southern Africa. (Perspectives on Southern Africa Ser., No. 10). 1973. 22.50x (ISBN 0-520-02271-8). U of Cal Pr.
Grundy, Kenneth W., et al, eds. Evaluating Transnational Programs in Government & Business. 1980. 29.50 (ISBN 0-08-025101-3). Pergamon.
Grundy, R. F. Magnetohydrodynamic Energy for Electric Power Generation. LC 77-15220. (Energy Technology Review Ser.: No. 20). (Illus.). 1978. 36.00 (ISBN 0-8155-0689-9). Noyes.
Grunebaum, Gustave E. Von see Von Grunebaum, Gustave E. & Caillois, Roger.
Grunebaum, Henry U., jt. auth. see Cohler, Bertram J.
Gruneberg, Michael M. Understanding Job Satisfaction. LC 78-20782. 1979. 27.95x (ISBN 0-470-26610-4). Halsted Pr.
Gruneberg, Michael M., ed. Job Satisfaction. LC 75-43852. 1976. 29.95 (ISBN 0-470-32911-4). Halsted Pr.
Grunelius, Elizabeth M. Early Childhood Education & the Waldorf School Plan. 1974. pap. 2.95 o.p. (ISBN 0-916786-06-4, Pub by Waldorf School Monographs). St George Bk Serv.
Gruner, Charles R. Understanding Laughter: The Workings of Wit & Humor. LC 78-16759. 1978. 17.95 (ISBN 0-88229-186-6). Nelson-Hall.
Gruner, Charles R., et al. Speech Communication in Society. 2nd ed. 1977. text ed. 13.95 (ISBN 0-205-05732-2, 4857321); instr's manual o.p. free (ISBN 0-205-05733-0). Allyn.
Gruner, Rolf. Theory & Power: On the Character of Modern Science. 1977. pap. text ed. 17.25x (ISBN 90-6032-087-5). Humanities.
Grunewald, Alan E., jt. auth. see Nemmers, Erwin E.
Grunfeld. The Jewish Dietary Laws, 2 vols. 1973. Set. 31.50x (ISBN 0-685-32987-9). Bloch.
Grunfeld, Frederic V. Prophets Without Honor: A Background to Freud, Kafka, Einstein & Their World. 1980. 5.95x (ISBN 0-07-025087-1). McGraw.
--Vienna. Bayrd, Edwin, ed. LC 79-3538. (Illus.). 176p. 1981. 16.95 (ISBN 0-88225-304-2). Newsweek.
Grunfeld, Frederic V. & Time-Life Editors. Berlin. new ed. (Great Cities Ser.). (Illus.). 1977. 14.95 (ISBN 0-8094-2282-4). Time-Life.
Grunfeld, Frederick V. Art & Times of the Guitar: From the Hittites to the Hippies. 1969. 9.95 o.s.i. (ISBN 0-02-546290-3). Macmillan.
--Berlin. (The Great Cities Ser.). (Illus.). (gr. 6 up). 1977. PLB 14.94 (ISBN 0-8094-2283-2, Pub by Time-Life). Silver.
Grunfeld, Joseph. Science & Values. 210p. 1980. text ed. 23.00x (ISBN 90-6032-018-2). Humanities.
Grunin, Robert, jt. ed. see Gitter, A. George.
Grunlan, Stephen A. & Mayers, Marvin K. Cultural Anthropology: A Christian Perspective. 1979. 8.95 (ISBN 0-310-36321-7). Zondervan.
Grunmann-Gaudet, Minnette & Jones, Robin F., eds. The Nature of Medieval Narrative. LC 80-66330. (French Forum Monographs: No. 22). 218p. (Orig.). 1980. pap. 12.50 (ISBN 0-917058-21-6). French Forum.
Grunwald, Joseph, ed. Latin America & World Economy: A Changing International Order. LC 77-17031. (Latin American International Affairs Ser.: Vol. 2). 1978. 20.00x (ISBN 0-8039-0864-4); pap. 9.95x (ISBN 0-8039-0966-7). Sage.
Grunwald, Joseph, et al. Latin American Economic Integration & United States Policy. 1972. 10.95 (ISBN 0-8157-3300-3). Brookings.
Grunwald, Stefan. The Renderings of Stefanos: Book I, Science & Technology. LC 79-10680. 1980. pap. 4.95 (ISBN 0-915442-91-4, Unilaw). Donning Co.
--Voices, Voices. (Orig.). 1980. pap. 4.95 (ISBN 0-89865-040-2). Donning Co.
Grunwald, Stefan, ed. see Nau, Erika S.
Grunwald, Stefan, ed. see Noyle, Ken.
Grunze, Richard. Paul: An Example for Christian Teachers. 1979. pap. text ed. 2.50 (ISBN 0-8100-0108-X). Northwest Pub.
--The Young Christian's Life. (gr. 7-8). 1979. 8.50 (ISBN 0-8100-0104-7, 06N0557). Northwest Pub.
Gruppe, M. The Frigates. (The Seafarers Ser.). (Illus.). 1979. lib. bdg. 11.97 (ISBN 0-8094-2716-8); kivar bdg. 9.96 (ISBN 0-8094-2717-6). Silver.
Grusec, Joan E., jt. auth. see Walters, Gary C.
Grusky, O. & Miller, G. A. Sociology of Organizations. LC 69-20286. 1970. text ed. 16.95 (ISBN 0-02-913180-4). Free Pr.
Grusky, Oscar & Miller, George A., eds. The Sociology of Organizations: Basic Studies. LC 80-1060. (Illus.). 1981. 18.95 (ISBN 0-02-913060-3); pap. text ed. 12.95 (ISBN 0-02-912930-3). Free Pr.
Gruss, Edmund C. Cults & the Occult. rev. ed. pap. 2.95 (ISBN 0-87552-308-0). Presby & Reformed.
Gruver, Rebecca B. An American History. 3rd ed. LC 75-14794. 1981. text ed. write for info. (ISBN 0-201-05051-X); Vol. 1. pap. text ed. 12.95 (ISBN 0-201-05052-8); Vol. 2. pap. text ed. 12.95 (ISBN 0-201-05053-6); write for info. mstr's manual (ISBN 0-201-05054-4); Vol. 1. write for info. study guide (ISBN 0-201-05055-2); Vol. 2. write for info. study guide (ISBN 0-201-05056-0). A-W.
--American History. 3rd ed. (Illus.). 1076p. 1981. One Vol. Ed. text ed. 17.95 (ISBN 0-201-05051-X); Vol. I. pap. 12.95 (ISBN 0-201-05052-8); Vol. II. pap. 12.95 (ISBN 0-201-05053-6). A-W.
--American History: Brief Edition, 2 vols. 1978. Set. pap. text ed. 12.95 o.p. (ISBN 0-201-02699-6); Vol. 1. pap. text ed. 8.95 o.p. (ISBN 0-201-02697-X); Vol. 2. pap. text ed. 8.95 o.p. (ISBN 0-201-02698-8). A-W.
Grygier, Tadeusz. Oppression. LC 73-14194. (International Library of Sociology & Social Reconstruction: A Study in Social & Criminal Psychology). 362p. 1974. Repr. of 1954 ed. lib. bdg. 27.50x (ISBN 0-8371-7145-8, GROP). Greenwood.
--Social Protection Code: A New Model of Criminal Justice. (American Series of Foreign Penal Codes: Vol. 22). 1977. text ed. 15.00x (ISBN 0-8377-0605-X). Rothman.
Grymeston, Elizabeth. Miscelanea, Meditations, Memoratives. LC 79-84114. (English Experience Ser.: No. 933). 68p. 1979. Repr. of 1604 ed. lib. bdg. 8.00 (ISBN 90-221-0933-X). Walter J Johnson.
Gryphius, Andreas. Cardenio und Celine. 2nd ed. Powell, Hugh, ed. (Ger.). 1967. pap. text ed. 4.75x (ISBN 0-7185-1028-3, Leicester). Humanities.
--Carolus Stuardus. 1963. Repr. of 1955 ed. text ed. 6.50x (ISBN 0-7185-1004-6, Leicester). Humanities.
Gryski, Gerard S. Bureaucratic Policy Making in a Technological Society. 320p. 1981. pap. text ed. 8.95x (ISBN 0-87073-829-1). Schenkman.
Gryst, Gary. Eden Hotel. 1980. 1.50 (ISBN 0-917554-08-6). Maelstrom.
Grzebien, Albert E. Contemporary College Speech. LC 74-6010. (Illus.). 229p. 1974. pap. text ed. 10.15 (ISBN 0-913310-35-2). PAR Inc.
Grzimek, Bernhard. He & I & the Elephants. Figes, Eva, tr. (Illus.). 1967. 5.00 o.p. (ISBN 0-8090-5435-3). Hill & Wang.
--Wild Animal, White Man. Glenny, Michael, tr. (Illus.). 1966. 8.95 o.p. (ISBN 0-8090-9725-7). Hill & Wang.
Grzybowski, Stefan. Tuberculosis & Its Prevention. (Illus.). 224p. 1981. 19.75 (ISBN 0-87527-210-X). Green.
Grzynkowicz, Wineva. Meeting the Needs of Learning Disabled Children in the Regular Class. 208p. 1975. pap. 16.50 photocopy ed. spiral (ISBN 0-398-03159-2). C C Thomas.
Grzynkowicz, Wineva M. Teaching Inefficient Learners. 148p. 1971. 12.75 (ISBN 0-398-00743-8). C C Thomas.
Gschwend, N. & Debrunner, H. U. Total Hip Prosthesis. (Illus.). 31.00 o.p. (ISBN 0-683-03777-3). Williams & Wilkins.
Guadalupe, Alma. Sea of Sadness. 64p. 1981. 5.95 (ISBN 0-89962-041-8). Todd & Honeywell.
Guadalupi, Gianni, jt. ed. see Manguel, Alberto.
Guala, F., jt. auth. see Marinone, N.
Guangzhou Conference on Theoretical Particle Physics 1980. Proceedings, Vols. 1 & 2. 1980. text ed. 89.50 (ISBN 0-442-20273-3, Pub. by Sci Pr China). Van Nos Reinhold.

Guarasci, Richard. The Theory & Practice of American Marxism, Nineteen Fifty-Seven to Nineteen Seventy. LC 80-1376. 170p. 1980. lib. bdg. 19.50 (ISBN 0-8191-1148-1); pap. text ed. 10.50 (ISBN 0-8191-1149-X). U Pr of Amer.
Guard, Charles. The Manx National Songbook, Vol. 2. 1980. text ed. 22.25x (ISBN 0-904980-32-4). Humanities.
Guard, David. Deirdre: A Celtic Legend. LC 80-69774. (Illus.). 118p. (gr. 6). 1981. Repr. of 1977 ed. 9.95 (ISBN 0-89742-047-0). Dawne-Leigh.
--Deirdre: A Celtic Legend. LC 77-23492. (Illus.). (gr. k-12). 1977. pap. 4.95 o.p. (ISBN 0-89087-201-5). Celestial Arts.
--Hale-Ano: A Legend of Hawaii. LC 80-69773. (Illus.). 118p. (gr. 6). 1981. 9.95 (ISBN 0-89742-048-9). Dawne-Leigh.
Guardino, Joseph R. Accounting, Legal & Tax Aspects of Corporate Acquisitions. 1973. 27.95 o.p. (ISBN 0-13-002105-9). P-H.
Guardo, Carol J. The Adolescent As Individual: Issues & Insights. 352p. 1975. pap. text ed. 10.95 (ISBN 0-06-042228-9, HarpC). Har-Row.
Guaresch, Giovanni. Dunlan & Clotilda. Conrad, L. K., tr. 1968. 4.95 o.p. (ISBN 0-686-63532-9). FS&G.
Guareschi. Don Camillo. (Easy Reader, B). pap. 3.75 (ISBN 0-88436-121-7, ITA201052). EMC.
Guareschi, Giovanni. Don Camillo Omnibus. 1981. 20.00 (ISBN 0-374-29290-6); pap. 12.95 (ISBN 0-374-51646-4). FS&G.
--The Family Guareschi: Chronicles of the Past & Present. Conrad, L. K., tr. from It. 1970. 6.50 o.p. (ISBN 0-374-15233-0). FS&G.
--A Husband in Boarding School. 1967. 4.50 o.p. (ISBN 0-374-17392-3). FS&G.
--My Home, Sweet Home. Green, Joseph, tr. 1966. 4.50 o.p. (ISBN 0-374-21708-4). FS&G.
Guarnaschelli, Maria, ed. see Faderman, Lillian.
Guay, Terrie. The Personal Fertitlity Guide: How to Avoid or Achieve Pregnancy Naturally. 192p. (Orig.). 1980. pap. 7.95 (ISBN 0-936602-04-X). Harbor Pub CA.
Guba, Egon G. & Lincoln, Yvonna S. Effective Evaluation: Improving the Usefulness of Evaluation Results Through Responsive & Naturalistic Approaches. LC 80-8909. (Social & Behavioral Science Ser.). 1981. text ed. price not set (ISBN 0-87589-493-3). Jossey-Bass.
Gubb, F. Points to Watch in 'o' Level French. (Fr.). 1965. pap. text ed. 3.50x (ISBN 0-435-37380-3). Heinemann Ed.
Gubbay, Sasson S. The Clumsy Child. LC 75-12487. (MPN: Vol. 5). (Illus.). 275p. 1975. text ed. 20.00 (ISBN 0-7216-4340-X). Saunders.
Guberlet, Muriel L. Animals of the Seashore. 4th ed. LC 62-142921. (Illus.). 1981. 12.50 o.p. (ISBN 0-8323-0121-3); pap. 8.95 (ISBN 0-8323-0386-0). Binford.
Guberman, Reuben. Handbook of Retail Promotion Ideas. LC 80-12276. 192p. 1981. text ed. 24.95 (ISBN 0-201-02720-8). A-W.
Gubernatis, Angelo De. Zoological Mythology, 2 Vols. LC 68-58904. 1968. Repr. of 1872 ed. Set. 32.00 (ISBN 0-8103-3527-1). Gale.
Gubernick, David J. & Klopfer, Peter H., eds. Parental Care in Mammals. 460p. 1981. 39.50 (ISBN 0-306-40533-4, Plenum Pr). Plenum Pub.
Gubrium, Jaber F. Late Life: Communities & Environmental Policy. (Illus.). 304p. 1975. 19.75 (ISBN 0-398-03249-1); pap. 15.25 (ISBN 0-398-03248-3). C C Thomas.
--The Myth of the Golden Years: A Socio-Environmental Theory of Aging. (Illus.). 244p. 1973. 14.75 (ISBN 0-398-02703-X); pap. 9.75 (ISBN 0-398-02757-9). C C Thomas.
Gubrium, Jaber F., jt. auth. see Buckholdt, David R.
Guck, Dorothy. Danger Rides the Forest. LC 68-30261. (Illus.). (gr. 6-8). 1968. 5.95 (ISBN 0-8149-0312-6). Vanguard.
Gucker, Frank T. & Seifert, Ralph T. Physical Chemistry. (Illus.). 1966. 16.95x (ISBN 0-393-09691-2, NortonC). Norton.
Guckin, John P., jt. auth. see Kaufman, Fredrick.
Guddat, Kurt H., jt. ed. see Easton, Lloyd.
Gudeman, Jon E., jt. auth. see Glasscote, R. M.
Gudeman, Stephen. The Demise of a Rural Economy: From Subsistence to Capitalism in a Latin American Village. (International Library of Anthropology). 1978. 21.00x (ISBN 0-7100-8835-3); pap. 8.95 (ISBN 0-7100-8836-1). Routledge & Kegan.
Guder, Eileen. More Than Just Me: Looking Beyond No. One. (Orig.). 1981. pap. cancelled (ISBN 0-88449-039-4). Vision Hse.
Guder, Robert F. Managing for Productivity: Motivating Employees. Reilly, Harry, ed. 100p. 1980. binder 110.00 (ISBN 0-89290-090-3, SUB 111); participant 45.00 (ISBN 0-89290-089-X). Soc for Visual.
Guder, W. G., jt. ed. see Ross, D. B.
Gudgin, G. Industrial Location Processes & Employment Growth. 352p. 1978. text ed. 30.75x (ISBN 0-566-00144-6, Pub. by Gower Pub Co England). Renouf.
Gudiol, J. Goya. (Library of Great Painters Ser). 1965. 35.00 (ISBN 0-8109-0149-8). Abrams.
Gue. Increased Profits Through Control of Work in Process. (Illus.). 1980. text ed. 18.95 (ISBN 0-8359-3062-9). Reston.
Guedj, R. A., ed. see IFIP Workshop on Methodology in Computer Graphics, France, May 1976.
Guehenno, Jean. Jean-Jacques Rousseau, 2 vols. Weightman, John & Weightman, Doreen, trs. from Fr. LC 66-12112. 1966. Set. 35.00x (ISBN 0-231-08961-9). Columbia U Pr.
Guelich, Robert A. Unity & Diversity in the New Testament. 1978. 9.95 o.p. (ISBN 0-8028-3504-X). Eerdmans.
Guelph. Biophysics Handbook II. 208p. 1980. pap. text ed. 8.95 (ISBN 0-8403-2281-X). Kendall-Hunt.
Guemple, D. L., ed. Alliance in Eskimo Society. LC 72-3423. 1972. 7.50 o.p. (ISBN 0-295-95236-9). U of Wash Pr.
Guenter, Clarence A., et al. Clinical Aspects of Respiratory Physiology. LC 78-498. 1978. soft cover 12.95 (ISBN 0-397-50400-4). Lippincott.
Guenther, Ernest. Essential Oils: Individual Essential Oils of the Plant Families, 6 vols. Vol. 1, 444p. 25.20 (ISBN 0-88275-073-9); Vol. 2, 866p. 46.50 (ISBN 0-88275-338-X); Vol. 3, 794p. 39.75 (ISBN 0-88275-163-8); Vol. 4, 766p. 36.50 (ISBN 0-88275-074-7); Vol. 5, 526p. 25.50 (ISBN 0-88275-354-1); Vol. 6, 498p. 28.50 (ISBN 0-88275-092-5); 180.00 set (ISBN 0-88275-953-1). Krieger.
Guenther, H. V. Philosophy & Psychology in the Abhidharma. 2nd rev. ed. 1974. 12.50 o.p. (ISBN 0-87773-048-2). Orient Bk Dist.
Guenther, Herbert, et al. Questions & Answers on Guru & Disciple. (Illus.). 1978. pap. text ed. 3.00 (ISBN 0-931454-02-6). Timeless Bks.
Guenther, Herbert V. Philosophy & Psychology in the Abhidharma. LC 75-40259. 282p. 1981. pap. 6.95 (ISBN 0-87773-081-4). Great Eastern.
--Treasures on the Tibetan Middle Way. LC 75-40260. 166p. 1981. pap. 5.95 (ISBN 0-87773-002-4). Great Eastern.
Guenther, Herbert V., tr. see Klong-Chen Rab-'Byams-Pa.
Guenther, Herbert V., tr. see SGam po pa.
Guenther, Horst, ed. see Moritz, Karl P.
Guenther, John. Pearl Harbor: A Narrative Poem. (Illus.). 64p. (Orig.). 1980. pap. 4.95 (ISBN 0-938266-00-4). Purchase Pr.
Guenther, William C. Scientific Sampling for Statistical Quality Control. LC 77-72042. (Griffin Statistical Monographs: No. 37). 1977. 16.25 (ISBN 0-02-845560-6). Macmillan.
Guerard, A., ed. Hardy: A Collection of Critical Essays. 1963. pap. 2.95 o.p. (ISBN 0-13-384065-4, Spec). P-H.
Guerard, Albert. France: A Modern History. rev. & enl. ed. LC 69-19782. (Illus.). 632p. 1969. 12.50x (ISBN 0-472-08390-2). U of Mich Pr.
Guerber, Helene A. Myths & Legends of the Middle Ages: Their Origin & Influence on Literature & Art. LC 72-2464. (Illus.). xvi, 405p. 1974. Repr. of 1909 ed. 18.00 (ISBN 0-8103-3873-4). Gale.
--Myths of Northern Lands: Narrated with Special Reference to Literature & Art. 1970. Repr. 26.00 (ISBN 0-8103-3862-9). Gale.
Guercio, E., et al. Reading Interpretation in Social Sciences, Natural Sciences, & Literature: Preparation & Review for the Reading Parts of the High School Equivalency Diploma Test. LC 74-19739. (GED Preparation Ser.). 224p. (Orig.). 1975. lib. bdg. 7.00 (ISBN 0-668-03843-8); pap. 5.00 (ISBN 0-668-03690-7). Arco.
Gueriguian, J. L., et al, eds. Insulins, Growth Hormone, & Recombinant DNA Technology. 250p. 1981. 25.00 (ISBN 0-89004-544-5). Raven.
Guerin, Daniel. Class Struggle in the First French Republic: Bourgeois & Bras Nus 1793-1795. Patterson, Ian, tr. from Fr. 1977. text ed. 17.25x (ISBN 0-904383-03-X). Humanities.
--West Indies & Their Future. 1961. text ed. 8.50x (ISBN 0-391-02067-6). Humanities.
Guerin, Marcel, ed. see Degas, Edgar G.
Guerin, Philip J. Making Good Marriages Better. 1973. pap. 0.95 o.p. (ISBN 0-89570-083-2). Claretian Pubns.
Guerin, Philip J., Jr. Family Therapy: Theory & Practice. 516p. 1976. lib. bdg. 24.50 o.p. (ISBN 0-470-15089-0). Halsted Pr.
Guerin, Polly. Fashion Writing. 1972. text ed. 15.00 (ISBN 0-672-96033-8); tchr's manual 5.00 (ISBN 0-672-96034-6). Bobbs.
Guerini, V. A History of Dentistry from the Most Ancient Times Until the End of the 18th Century. 1967. Repr. of 1909 ed. text ed. 71.25x (ISBN 90-6041-129-3). Humanities.
Gueritz, Caroline, tr. see Broger, Achim.
Guerman, Mikhail, compiled by. Art of the October Revolution. (Illus.). 1979. 30.00 o.p. (ISBN 0-8109-0675-9). Abrams.
Guern, M. Le see Le Guern, M. & Le Guern, M. R.
Guern, M. R. Le see Le Guern, M. & Le Guern, M. R.
Guernelli, Giovanni. Gaspara Stampa, Louise Labe y Sor Juana Ines de la Cruz: Triptico Renacentista Barroco. 4.65 (ISBN 0-8477-3132-4). U of PR Pr.
Guerney, Bernard G., ed. Anthology of Russian Literature in the Soviet Period from Gorki to Pasternak. (Russian Library Ser). (Orig.). 1960. pap. 2.95 o.p. (ISBN 0-394-70717-6, Vin). Random.
--Treasury of Russian Literature. LC 43-17369. (Illus.). 15.00 (ISBN 0-8149-0113-1). Vanguard.
Guernsey, Elwood W. Social Research & Basic Computer Programming. (Illus.). 336p. 1973. 21.75 (ISBN 0-398-02591-6). C C Thomas.
--Workbook in Basic Computer Programming (Fortran 4) (Illus.). 192p. 1973. pap. 17.75 (ISBN 0-398-02592-4). C C Thomas.
Guernsey, Otis L., Jr. The Best Plays of 1975-1976. (The Burns Mantle Yearbook of the Theater Ser.). (Illus.). 1976. 20.00 (ISBN 0-396-07380-8). Dodd.
Guernsey, Otis L., Jr., ed. The Best Plays of 1964-1969, 5 Vols. (The Burns Mantle Yearbook of the Theater Ser.). Set. 20.00 (ISBN 0-686-66398-5). Vol. 1 (ISBN 0-396-05211-8). Vol. 2 (ISBN 0-396-05435-8). Vol. 3. o.p. (ISBN 0-396-05634-2). Vol. 4 (ISBN 0-396-05843-4). Vol. 5 (ISBN 0-396-06028-5). Dodd.
--The Best Plays of 1969-1970. (The Burns Mantle Yearbook of the Theater Ser.). (Illus.). 1970. 20.00 (ISBN 0-396-06249-0). Dodd.
--The Best Plays of 1971-1972. LC 20-21432. (The Burns Mantle Yearbook of the Theater Ser.). (Illus.). 492p. 1972. 20.00 (ISBN 0-396-06698-4). Dodd.
--The Best Plays of 1972-1973. (The Burns Mantle Yearbook of the Theater Ser.). (Illus.). 492p. 1973. 20.00 (ISBN 0-396-06878-2). Dodd.
--The Best Plays of 1973-1974. (The Burns Mantle Yearbook of the Theater Ser.). (Illus.). 492p. 1974. 20.00 (ISBN 0-396-07017-5). Dodd.
--The Best Plays of 1974-1975. (The Burns Mantle Yearbook of the Theater Ser.). (Illus.). 492p. 1975. 20.00 (ISBN 0-396-07220-8). Dodd.
--The Best Plays of 1976-1977. (The Burns Mantle Yearbook of Theater Ser.). (Illus.). 1977. 20.00 (ISBN 0-396-07501-0). Dodd.
--The Best Plays of 1977-1978. (The Burns Mantle Yearbook of the Theater Ser.). (Illus.). 1979. 20.00 (ISBN 0-396-07637-8). Dodd.
--The Best Plays of 1978-1979. LC 20-21432. (The Burns Mantle Yearbook of the Theater Ser.). (Illus.). 1980. 20.00 (ISBN 0-396-07723-4). Dodd.
--The Best Plays of 1979-1980. (The Burns Mantle Yearbook of the Theatre Ser.). (Illus.). 550p. 1981. 20.00 (ISBN 0-396-07907-5). Dodd.
Guerra, F. The Pre-Columbian Mind. LC 75-183465. 350p. 1972. 46.50 (ISBN 0-12-785286-7). Acad Pr.
Guerra, Julio J., jt. auth. see Cotler, Sherwin B.
Guerra, Mario. The Naturalist's Handbook -- Collecting & Preparing Animals, Plants & Minerals. LC 79-91396. (Illus.). 96p. (gr. 10 up). Date not set. cancelled (ISBN 0-8069-3114-0); PLB 9.29 (ISBN 0-8069-3115-9). Sterling.
Guerreiro, Miriam, jt. auth. see Packard, Sidney.
Guerry, jt. auth. see Malone.
Guertin, Carolyn W., jt. auth. see Blank, Florence W.
Guertin, Richard L. Introduction to Pl360 Programming. 1977. pap. text ed. 13.95x (ISBN 0-534-00524-1). Wadsworth Pub.
Guertner, Beryl. Australian Book of Flower Arrangements. (Illus.). 12.50x (ISBN 0-392-06790-0, ABC). Soccer.
--Gregory's Two Hundred Home Plan Ideas. pap. 7.50x (ISBN 0-392-05865-0, ABC). Soccer.
Guesde, Jules. Le Livre Rouge De la Justice Rurale. Documents Pour Servir L'histoire D'une Republique Sans Republicains. (Fr.). 1977. lib. bdg. 17.50x o.p. (ISBN 0-8287-0404-X); pap. text ed. 7.50x o.p. (ISBN 0-685-77013-3). Clearwater Pub.
Guest, Arthur. Advanced Practical Geography. 5th ed. 1977. text ed. 14.95x (ISBN 0-435-35356-X). Heinemann Ed.
Guest, Barbara. Poems: The Location of Things. 1962. 7.95 (ISBN 0-911660-06-2). Yankee Peddler.
Guest, C. Z. & McDonald, Elvin. C.Z. & Elvin's Week-by-Week Garden Guide. LC 80-67097. (Illus.). 180p. (Orig.). 1980. pap. 5.95 (ISBN 0-87754-137-X). Chelsea Hse.
Guest, Carol L. Space Trip. 48p. 1981. 5.95 (ISBN 0-89962-047-7). Todd & Honeywell.
Guest, David. Worker Participation: Individual Control & Performance. 252p. 1974. 15.00x (ISBN 0-85292-097-0). Intl Pubns Serv.
Guest, David & Knight, Kenneth. Putting Participation into Practice. 1979. text ed. 26.50x (ISBN 0-566-02086-6, Pub. by Gower Pub Co England). Renouf.
Guest, Dean. Discovering, the Word of God. 64p. (Orig.). 1980. Repr. pap. 1.95 (ISBN 0-89841-011-8). Zoe Pubns.
--Tabernacle, God's Dwelling Place. 64p. (Orig.). Date not set. pap. 1.95 (ISBN 0-89841-012-6). Zoe Pubns.
Guest, Edgar. A Heap O'Living. 1976. lib. bdg. 10.95x (ISBN 0-89968-041-0). Lightyear.
--Just Folks. 192p. 1980. Repr. of 1917 ed. lib. bdg. 11.95x (ISBN 0-89968-190-5). Lightyear.
--Over Here. 192p. 1980. Repr. of 1918 ed. lib. bdg. 11.95x (ISBN 0-89968-192-1). Lightyear.
--Passing Through. 190p. 1980. Repr. of 1923 ed. lib. bdg. 11.95x (ISBN 0-89968-191-3). Lightyear.
Guest, Elissa H. The Handsome Man. LC 80-66247. 192p. (gr. 7 up). 1980. 7.95 (ISBN 0-590-07661-2, Four Winds). Schol Bk Serv.
Guest, G. Martin. Brief History of Engineering. (Illus.). 1974. pap. text ed. 11.00x (ISBN 0-245-52337-5). Intl Ideas.
Guest, Ivor. The Ballet of the Second Empire. LC 73-15010. (Illus.). 332p. 1974. 20.00x (ISBN 0-8195-4067-6, Pub. by Wesleyan U Pr). Columbia U Pr.
--Fanny Elssler. LC 74-105507. (Illus.). 1970. 20.00x (ISBN 0-8195-4022-6, Pub. by Wesleyan U Pr). Columbia U Pr.
--The Romantic Ballet in England: Its Development, Fulfillment & Decline. 2nd ed. LC 77-172138. (Illus.). 176p. 1972. 20.00x (ISBN 0-8195-4050-1, Pub. by Wesleyan U Pr). Columbia U Pr.
Guest, J. E. & Greeley, R. Geology on the Moon. LC 77-371984. (Wykeham Science Ser.: No. 43). 1977. 17.95x (ISBN 0-8448-1170-X); pap. 12.50x (ISBN 0-8448-1346-X). Crane-Russak Co.
Guest, Judith. Ordinary People. 1980. pap. 2.75 (ISBN 0-345-29132-8). Ballantine.
--Ordinary People. LC 76-2368. 1980. pap. 2.75 o.p. (ISBN 0-345-25755-3). Ballantine.
Guest, Lo. Random Thoughts & Dialogues. 1978. 5.95 o.p. (ISBN 0-533-03064-1). Vantage.
Guest, R., et al. Organizational Change Through Effective Leadership. 1977. 14.95 (ISBN 0-13-641316-1); pap. text ed. 9.95 (ISBN 0-13-641308-0). P-H.
Guest, Richard. Compendious History of the Cotton Manufacture. LC 68-108209. (Illus.). Repr. of 1823 ed. 18.00x (ISBN 0-678-05170-4). Kelley.
Gueulette, Thomas S. Mogul Tales: or the Dreams of Man Awake, Pt. 2. LC 73-170593. (Novel in England, 1700-1775). lib. bdg. 50.00 (ISBN 0-8240-0576-7). Garland Pub.
--Mogul Tales: or the Dreams of Men Awake, Pt. 1. LC 73-170593. (Novel in England, 1700-1775). lib. bdg. 50.00 (ISBN 0-8240-0575-9). Garland Pub.
Guezou, J & Nilsen, O. Geological Survey of Norway. (No. 340, Bulletin 47). 1979. pap. 19.00x (ISBN 82-00-31373-5, Dist. by Columbia U Pr.). Universitet.
Guffey, George R. Concordance to the Poetry of Thomas Traherne. 1974. 45.00x (ISBN 0-520-02449-4). U of Cal Pr.
Guffridge, Len, jt. auth. see Smith, Jay D.
Guggenbuhl, Craig A. Die Ehe Ist Tot: Lang Lebe Die Ehe! 1976. pap. 6.00 o.p. (ISBN 0-89192-086-2). Interbk Inc.
Guggenbuhl-Craig, A. Marriage - Dead or Alive? 1977. pap. 6.00 (ISBN 0-88214-309-3). Spring Pubns.
Guggenbuhl-Craig, Adolf. Eros on Crutches. Hartman, Gary V., tr. from Ger. 126p. (Orig.). 1980. pap. text ed. 7.00 (ISBN 0-88214-315-8). Spring Pubns.
--Power in the Helping Professions. Hillman, James, ed. 155p. 1971. text ed. 7.00 (ISBN 0-88214-304-2). Spring Pubns.
Guggenheim, E. A. & Stokes, R. H. Equilibrium Properties of Aqueous Solutions of Single Strong Electrolytes. LC 79-20329. 1970. 28.00 (ISBN 0-08-013445-9). Pergamon.
Guggenheim, Hans G. Around the World in Eighty Ways. 64p. (Orig.). 1981. pap. 6.00 (ISBN 0-682-49683-9). Exposition.
Guggenheim, Martin, jt. auth. see Sussman, Alan.
Guggenheimer, Heinrich. Differential Geometry. pap. text ed. 6.00 (ISBN 0-486-63433-7). Dover.
Guggenmos, Josef. Wonder-Fish from the Sea. Tresselt, Alvin, tr. LC 78-148165. (Illus.). (gr. k-3). 1971. 5.95 o.s.i. (ISBN 0-8193-0483-2, Four Winds); PLB 5.41 o.s.i. (ISBN 0-8193-0484-0). Schol Bk Serv.
Guggenmos, Josef, jt. auth. see Konopka, Ursula.

Gugler, J. & Flanagan, W. Urbanization & Social Changes in West Africa. LC 76-9175. (Urbanisation in Developing Countries Ser.). (Illus.). 1978. 24.95 (ISBN 0-521-21348-7); pap. 7.95x (ISBN 0-521-29118-6). Cambridge U Pr.

Guha, Nikhiles, tr. see Bhattacharya, Lokenath.

Guha, Nikhiles, tr. see Roy, Rammohun.

Guha Majumdar, Rupendra see Majumdar, Rupendra G.

Guhin, Michael A. John Foster Dulles: A Statesman & His Times. LC 72-5873. (Illus.). 435p. 1972. 22.50x (ISBN 0-231-03664-7). Columbia U Pr.

Guiart, Jean. The Arts of the South Pacific. LC 63-7331. (Arts of Mankind Ser). 30.00 o.s.i. (ISBN 0-8076-0500-X). Braziller.

Guiasu, S. & Malitza, M. Coalition & Connection in Games. 1980. text ed. 33.00 (ISBN 0-08-023033-4). Pergamon.

Guicciardini, Francesco. History of Italy. Alexander, Sidney, tr. (Illus.). 1969. 12.50 o.s.i. (ISBN 0-02-500830-7). Macmillan.

--The History of Italy. Alexander, Sidney, tr. 496p. 1972. pap. 3.95 o.s.i. (ISBN 0-02-032980-6, Collier). Macmillan.

--Maxims & Reflections. LC 64-23752. 1972. pap. 4.95x (ISBN 0-8122-1037-9, Pa. Paperbacks). U of Pa Pr.

Guichard, Ami. Automobile Year, No. 18: 1970-1971. (Illus.). 1970. 19.95 o.p. (ISBN 0-8019-6389-3). Chilton.

--Automobile Year, No. 21: 1973-1974. (Illus.). 1973. 25.00 o.p. (ISBN 0-8019-6392-3). Chilton.

Guicharnaud, Jacques. Raymond Queneau. LC 65-26340. (Columbia Ser.: No. 14). (Orig.). 1965. pap. 2.00 (ISBN 0-231-02706-0, MW14). Columbia U Pr.

Guicharnaud, June, tr. see Halevy, Daniel.

Guidepost Associates. Guideposts Treasury of Love. (Illus.). 352p. 1981. 12.95 (ISBN 0-385-14973-5). Doubleday.

Guidepost Magazine, ed. The Guideposts Treasury of Hope. 320p. 1980. pap. 2.50 (ISBN 0-553-13678-X). Bantam.

Guideposts Associates. Guideposts Treasury of Hope. LC 78-22228. (Illus.). 1979. 9.95 (ISBN 0-385-14975-1). Doubleday.

Guidetti, Geri. A Seneca Garden. (Illus.). 26p. (Orig.). (gr. 2-8). 1981. pap. 3.95 (ISBN 0-938928-00-7). KMG Pubns OR.

Guido, Dennis, ed. see Martin, Philip R.

Guido, Raymond. Calculating with Basic. (Da Capo Quality Paperbacks Ser.). (Illus.). 80p. 1981. pap. text ed. 8.95 (ISBN 0-306-80144-2). Da Capo.

Guidoni, Enrico. Primitive Architecture. (History of World Architecture Ser.). (Illus.). 1978. 45.00 (ISBN 0-8109-1026-8). Abrams.

Guidry, Ron & Golenbock, Peter. Guidry. LC 80-13732. 1980. 8.95 (ISBN 0-13-371609-0). P-H.

Guie, H. Dean. Bugles in the Valley: Garnett's Fort Simcoe. rev. ed. LC 77-88149. (Illus.). 216p. 1977. pap. 5.95 (ISBN 0-87595-057-4); 11.95 (ISBN 0-87595-090-6). Oreg Hist Soc.

Guieu, J. D., jt. ed. see Houdas, Y.

Guigo II. Guigo II: The Ladder of Monks & Twelve Meditations. Colledge, Edmund & Walsh, James, trs. (Cistercian Studies: No. 48). 1981. pap. write for info. (ISBN 0-87907-748-4). Cistercian Pubns.

Guilbault, G. G. Enzymatic Methods of Analysis. 1970. 45.00 (ISBN 0-08-006989-4). Pergamon.

Guilbert, L. La Formation du vocabulaire de l'aviation. (Fr). pap. 23.75x o.p. (ISBN 0-685-13923-9). Larousse.

Guilbert, Louis. La Creativite lexicale. (Collection langue et langage). 285p. (Fr.). 1975. pap. 23.95 (ISBN 2-03-070340-0). Larousse.

Guild, Frank, Jr. Action of the Tiger: The Four Hundred & Thirty Seventh Troop Carrier Group in World War II. LC 80-65181. (Aviation Ser.: No. 2). (Illus.). 177p. 1980. Repr. 15.00 (ISBN 0-89839-028-1). Battery Pr.

Guild, Nicholas. The Favor. 320p. 1981. 12.95 (ISBN 0-312-28512-4). St Martin.

--Old Acquaintance. (Orig.). pap. 2.50 (ISBN 0-515-05229-9). Jove Pubns.

--Summer Soldier. 1979. pap. 1.95 o.s.i. (ISBN 0-515-05228-0). Jove Pubns.

Guild, Reuben A. The Librarian's Manual: A Treatise on Bibliography, Comprising a Select & Descriptive List of Bibliographical Works; to Which Are Added, Sketches of Public Libraries. LC 70-174942. (Illus.). x, 304p. 1972. Repr. of 1858 ed. 22.00 (ISBN 0-8103-3811-4). Gale.

Guild, W., et al. Science of Health. 1969. 16.95 (ISBN 0-13-794818-2). P-H.

Guile, A. E. & Paterson, W. Electrical Power Systems, Vol. 1. 2nd ed. LC 77-1789. 1977. text ed. 52.00 (ISBN 0-08-021728-1); pap. text ed. 17.00 (ISBN 0-08-021729-X). Pergamon.

Guiles, Cecil R. Ministering to Youth. 1973. 4.50 (ISBN 0-87148-551-6); pap. 3.50 (ISBN 0-87148-552-4); instrs. kit 4.50 (ISBN 0-87148-834-5). Pathway Pr.

Guiles, Fred L. Stan. (Illus.). 1980. cancelled (ISBN 0-7181-1908-8, Pub. by Michael Joseph). Merrimack Bk Serv.

--Stan: The Life of Stan Laurel. LC 80-5806. (Illus.). 272p. 1980. 12.95 (ISBN 0-8128-2762-7). Stein & Day.

Guilford, C., jt. auth. see Mackenzie, W. S.

Guilford, J. P. Intelligence, Creativity & Their Educational Implications. LC 68-26627. 1968. pap. text ed. 8.95 (ISBN 0-912736-09-7). EDITS Pubs.

Guilford, Joy P. Nature of Human Intelligence. (Psychology Ser.). (Illus.). 1967. text ed. 34.00 o.p. (ISBN 0-07-025135-5, C). McGraw.

Guillano, Edward. Lewis Carroll: An Annotated International Bibliography, 1960-1977. LC 80-13975. 1981. 15.00x (ISBN 0-8139-0862-0). U Pr of Va.

Guillaume De, Bertier De Sauvigny see De Bertier De Sauvigny, Guillaume.

Guillaumin, Colette. L' Idelogie Reciste: Genese et Langage Actuel. (Publications De L'institut D'etudes et De Recherches Interethinques et Interculturelles: No. 2). 1972. pap. 17.75x (ISBN 90-2796-993-0). Mouton.

Guillebaud, C. W. The Social Policy of Nazi Germany. LC 71-80553. 1971. Repr. 13.00 (ISBN 0-86527-183-6). Fertig.

Guillebon, Regine P. De see De Guillebon, Regine P.

Guillemain, B. L' Eveil de l'Europe. (Histoire universelle Larousse de poche). (Fr). pap. 3.50 (ISBN 0-685-13913-1). Larousse.

Guillemin, Jeanne. Urban Renegades: The Cultural Strategy of American Indians. new ed. LC 74-30434. 240p. 1975. 17.50x (ISBN 0-231-03884-4). Columbia U Pr.

Guillemin, V. W., jt. auth. see Golubitsky, M.

Guillemin, Victor. Story of Quantum Mechanics. LC 68-17354. (Illus.). 1968. pap. 3.95 o.p. (ISBN 0-684-71790-5, SL230, ScribT). Scribner.

Guillemin, Victor & Pollack, Alan. Differential Topology. (Math. Ser). (Illus.). 324p. 1974. 21.95x (ISBN 0-13-212605-2). P-H.

Guilleminault, Christian & Guilleminault, Christian, eds. Sleep Apnea Syndromes: Proceedings. LC 78-416. (Kroc Foundation Ser.: Vol. 11). 1978. 39.00 (ISBN 0-8451-0301-6). A R Liss.

Guillen, Nicolas. Man-making Words: Selected Poems of Nicolas Guillen. Marquez, Robert & McMurray, David, eds. LC 78-181363. 248p. (Span. & Eng.). 1972. pap. 5.95x (ISBN 0-87023-101-4). U of Mass Pr.

Guillermaz, Jacques. Chinese Communist Party in Power, Nineteen Forty-Nine to Nineteen Seventy-Eight. LC 76-7593. 1976. 32.50x (ISBN 0-89158-041-7); pap. 14.50x (ISBN 0-89158-348-3). Westview.

Guillermo, E. & Hernandez, J. A. La Novelistica Espanola De los Sesenta. 1971. 12.45 (ISBN 0-88303-002-0); pap. 9.00 (ISBN 0-685-73208-8). E Torres & Sons.

Guillet, Edwin C. Pioneer Arts & Crafts. 2nd ed. LC 72-415879. (Photos). 1968. pap. 2.95 (ISBN 0-8020-6081-1). U of Toronto Pr.

--Pioneer Settlements in Upper Canada. (Illus.). 1970. pap. 4.50 (ISBN 0-8020-6110-9). U of Toronto Pr.

Guillim, John. A Display of Heraldrie. LC 79-84115. (English Experience Ser.: No. 934). 308p. 1979. Repr. of 1611 ed. lib. bdg. 46.00 (ISBN 90-221-0934-8). Walter J Johnson.

Guillory, William A. Introduction to Molecular Structure & Spectroscopy. 1977. text ed. 27.95 (ISBN 0-205-05718-7). Allyn.

Guillot, Rene. Three Hundred Ninety-Seventh White Elephant. LC 57-6246. (Illus.). (gr. 4-6). 1957. 8.95 (ISBN 0-87599-043-6). S G Phillips.

Guilmartin, J. F., Jr. Gunpowder & Galleys. LC 73-83109. (Early Modern History Studies). (Illus.). 380p. 1975. 46.50 (ISBN 0-521-20272-8). Cambridge U Pr.

Guin, Ursula K. Le see Le Guin, Ursula K.

Guinan, Michael D. Gospel Poverty: Witness to the Risen Christ. 96p. (Orig.). 1981. pap. 3.95 (ISBN 0-8091-2377-0). Paulist Pr.

Guinard, Frances De see De Guinard, Frances.

Guindon, Richard. Cartoons by Guindon. (Illus.). 1980. pap. 6.95 (ISBN 0-8256-3180-7, Quick Fox). Music Sales.

Guiness, Desmond. Georgian Dublin. 1979. 45.00 (ISBN 0-7134-1908-3, Pub. by Batsford England). David & Charles.

Guiness, Gerald, jt. auth. see Forastieri-Braschi, Eduardo.

Guiney, Louise, tr. see Follain, Jean.

Guinier, A. X-Ray Diffraction: In Crystals, Imperfect Crystals, & Amorphous Bodies. Lorrain, Paul & Lorrain, Dorothee, trs. LC 62-13298. (Physics Ser.). (Illus.). 1963. text ed. 27.95x (ISBN 0-7167-0307-6). W H Freeman.

Guinness, Os. The Dust of Death. LC 72-94670. 430p. 1973. pap. 8.95 (ISBN 0-87784-911-0). Inter-Varsity.

Guinsburg, T. N. & Reuber, Grant, eds. Perspectives on the Social Sciences in Canada. LC 74-78508. 1974. pap. 4.00 (ISBN 0-8020-6248-2). U of Toronto Pr.

Guinther, John. The Malpractitioners. LC 77-92215. 1978. 10.00 o.p. (ISBN 0-385-12898-3, Anchor Pr). Doubleday.

--Winning Your Personal Injury Suit. LC 79-6575. 312p. (Orig.). 1980. pap. 6.95 (ISBN 0-385-15005-9, Anch). Doubleday.

Guiraud, Jean. The Medieval Inquisition. Messenger, E. C., tr. LC 78-63181. (Hereseis 2 Ser.). 216p. 1980. Repr. of 1929 ed. 19.00 (ISBN 0-404-16222-3). AMS Pr.

Guiraud, Pierre. Semiology. 1975. 12.00x (ISBN 0-7100-8005-0); pap. 6.95 (ISBN 0-7100-8011-5). Routledge & Kegan.

Guirdham, M. Marketing: The Management of Distribution Channels. 222p. 1972. text ed. 32.00 (ISBN 0-08-016964-3); pap. text ed. 18.00 (ISBN 0-08-016965-1). Pergamon.

Guisewite, Cathy. What Do You Mean, I Still Don't Have Equal Rights? 128p. pap. 3.95 (ISBN 0-8362-1158-8). Andrews & McMeel.

--What's a Nice Girl Like You Doing with a Double Bed. 160p. 1981. pap. 4.95 (ISBN 0-553-01316-5). Bantam.

Guitar Player Editors. Blues Guitarists. (Illus.). 3.95 o.p. (ISBN 0-8256-9518-X). Guitar Player.

Guitar Player Magazine, ed. Jazz Guitarists. (Illus.). 120p. 5.95 (ISBN 0-8256-9508-2). Guitar Player.

--Putting a Band Together. 1.95 (ISBN 0-8256-9509-0). Guitar Player.

--Rock Guitarists, Vol. I. LC 74-25845. (Illus.). 176p. (Orig.). 1975. pap. 6.95 (ISBN 0-8256-9505-8). Guitar Player.

Guitar Player Magazine & Kriss, Eric, eds. Fix Your Axe: Easy Guitar Repairs You Can Do at Home. LC 75-27790. (Illus.). 72p. (Orig.). 1976. pap. 5.95 (ISBN 0-8256-9503-1). Guitar Player.

Guitard, Lucien & Marandet, Leon. French Pronunciation Illustrated. text ed. 3.25x (ISBN 0-521-05156-8). Cambridge U Pr.

Guithues, Henry J., jt. auth. see Kim, Suk H.

Guiton, Shirley. A World by Itself: Tradition & Change in the Venetian Lagoon. (Illus.). 1978. 17.95 (ISBN 0-241-89434-4, Pub. by Hamish Hamilton). David & Charles.

Guizot, Francois P. Democracy in France. LC 74-19357. v, 82p. 1974. Repr. of 1849 ed. 10.00 (ISBN 0-86527-040-6). Fertig.

Gukhman, A. A. Introduction to the Theory of Similarity. 1965. 33.50 o.p. (ISBN 0-12-305450-8). Acad Pr.

Gulati, Basia, tr. see Dumont, Louis.

Gulati, Bodh R. A Short Course in Calculus. LC 79-67409. 560p. 1981. text ed. 17.95 (ISBN 0-03-047466-3). Dryden Pr.

Gulati, I. S. & Gulati, K. S. Undivided Hindu Family: A Study of Its Tax Privileges. 4.50x o.p. (ISBN 0-210-34070-3). Asia.

Gulati, K. S., jt. auth. see Gulati, I. S.

Gulcher, Conrad. Racing Techniques Explained. rev. ed. (Illus.). 1972. 7.50 (ISBN 0-8286-0062-7). De Graff.

Guldmann, Jean-Michel & Shefer, Daniel. Industrial Location & Air Quality Control: A Planning Approach. LC 80-15380. (Environmental Science & Technology Monograph). 225p. 1980. 32.00 (ISBN 0-471-05377-5, Pub. by Wiley-Interscience). Wiley.

Guldseth, G. J. God Is for the Emotionally Ill: A Doctor's Spiritual-Medical Approach. 108p. 1969. pap. 1.95 o.p. (ISBN 0-912106-72-7). Logos.

Gulezian. Elements of Business Statistics. 1979. 18.95 (ISBN 0-7216-4351-5). Dryden Pr.

--Statistics for Decision Making. 1979. 19.95 (ISBN 0-7216-4350-7). Dryden Pr.

Guli, Francesca. Poems in Praise of the Man. 1980. 6.50 (ISBN 0-8233-0309-8). Golden Quill.

Gulick, Bill. The Hallelujah Trail. 176p. 1976. pap. 1.25 o.p. (ISBN 0-445-00336-7). Popular Lib.

Gulick, Charles A. Austria from Habsburg to Hitler, 2 vols. Incl. Vol. I. Labor's Workshop of Democracy; Vol. II. Facism's Subversion of Democracy (ISBN 92-0159-280-9). (California Library Reprint Ser.: No. 109). 1980. Repr. of 1948 ed. Set. 85.00x o.p. (ISBN 0-520-04211-5). U of Cal Pr.

--Austria from Habsburg to Hitler, 2 vols. Incl. Vol. I. Labor's Workshop of Democracy; Vol. II. Fascism's Subversion of Democracy. (California Library Reprint Ser.: No. 109). 1936p. 1981. Repr. of 1948 ed. Set. 85.00x (ISBN 0-520-04211-5). U of Cal Pr.

Gulick, Frances F., jt. auth. see Davidson, Neil A.

Gulick, W. Lawrence. Hearing: Physiology & Psychophysics. (Illus.). 1971. 16.95x (ISBN 0-19-501299-2). Oxford U Pr.

Gulick, W. Lawrence & Lawson, Robert B. Human Stereopsis: A Psychophysical Approach. (Illus.). 320p. 1976. text ed. 16.95x (ISBN 0-19-501971-7). Oxford U Pr.

Gulik, Robert H. Van see Van Gulik, Robert H.

Gullace, Giovanni, tr. from Ital. see Croce, Benedetto.

Gullahorn, Jeanne E. Psychology & Women: In Transition. LC 78-16794. (In Transition Scripts Series in Personality & Social Psychology). 1979. 15.95 (ISBN 0-470-26459-4). Halsted Pr.

Gulland, John A., ed. Fish Population Dynamics. LC 75-45094. 1977. 50.75 (ISBN 0-471-01575-X, Pub by Wiley-Interscience). Wiley.

Gullberg, Ingvar E. Swedish-English Fact Ordbok (Technical Terms) 2nd ed. 1977. 200.00x (ISBN 91-1-775052-0, SW-207). Vanous.

Gullen, Karen, ed. see Sunday, Billy.

Gullett, C. Ray, jt. auth. see Hicks, Herbert G.

Gullett, Jane Fellows, jt. auth. see Gullett, Walter.

Gullett, Walter & Gullett, Jane Fellows. Everyone's Guide to Food Self-Sufficiency. 1980. 7.95 (ISBN 0-87961-096-4); pap. 3.95 (ISBN 0-87961-095-6). Naturegraph.

Gullette, Margaret M. The Lost Bellybutton. LC 76-26377. (Illus.). 31p. (ps-2). 1976. pap. 2.50 (ISBN 0-914996-11-8). Lollipop Power.

Gulley, Norman R. Final Events on Planet Earth. LC 77-24206. (Horizon Ser.). 1977. pap. 4.50 (ISBN 0-8127-0144-5). Southern Pub.

Gullick, John. Malaysia: Economic Expansion & National Unity. (Illus.). 272p. 1980. lib. bdg. 25.00x (ISBN 0-86531-089-0). Westview.

Gulliford, R. Helping the Handicapped Child, No. 2: At School. (Illus.). 40p. 1975. pap. text ed. 2.50x (ISBN 0-85633-059-0, NFER). Humanities.

Gulliford, R., jt. auth. see Tansley, A. E.

Gullikson, Sandra S., ed. see Ambrosek, Jim, et al.

Gullino, Pietro M., jt. ed. see Jain, Rakesh K.

Gulliver, P. H. Neighbours & Networks: The Idiom of Kinship Among the Ndendeuli of Tanzania. LC 71-115491. 1971. 21.50x (ISBN 0-520-01722-6). U of Cal Pr.

Gulliver, P. H., ed. Tradition & Transition in East Africa: Studies of the Tribal Factor in the Modern Era. LC 78-84787. 1969. 21.50x (ISBN 0-520-01402-2). U of Cal Pr.

Gumaer, J., jt. auth. see Duncan, J. A.

Gumbel, Emil J. Statistics of Extremes. LC 57-10160. 1959. 20.50x (ISBN 0-231-02190-9). Columbia U Pr.

Gumbiner, Joseph H. Leaders of Our People, 2 Bks. (Illus.). (gr. 4-6). Bk. 1. 1963. text ed. 5.00 (ISBN 0-8074-0141-2, 122921); Bk. 2. 1965. text ed. 5.00 (ISBN 0-8074-0142-0, 123921); tchrs'. guide 3.25 (ISBN 0-8074-0143-9, 202922). UAHC.

Gumina, Deanna P. The Italians of San Francisco, Eighteen Fifty to Nineteen Thirty: (Gli Italiani Di San Francisco, 1850 to 1930) dual language ed. Are, Ennio T., tr. LC 77-89342. 1978. pap. text ed. 9.95x (ISBN 0-913256-28-5, Dist. by Ozer). Ctr Migration.

Gummere, John F; see Bird, Thomas E.

Gummere, Richard M. Seneca, the Philosopher & His Modern Message. LC 63-10274. (Our Debt to Greece & Rome Ser). 145p. 1963. Repr. of 1930 ed. 15.00x (ISBN 0-8154-0098-5). Cooper Sq.

Gummett, P. Scientists in Whitehall. 1980. text ed. 38.00x (ISBN 0-7190-0791-7). Humanities.

Gummett, P., jt. auth. see Johnston, R.

Gumowski, I. & Mira, C. Recurrence & Discrete Dynamic Systems. (Lecture Notes in Mathematics: Vol. 809). (Illus.). 272p. 1980. pap. 16.80 (ISBN 0-387-10017-2). Springer-Verlag.

Gumowski, Igor & Mira, C. Optimization in Control Theory & Practice. LC 68-12059. (Illus.). 1968. 40.75 (ISBN 0-521-05158-4). Cambridge U Pr.

Gump, Margaret. Adalbert Stifter. (World Authors Ser.: Austria: No. 274). 1974. lib. bdg. 10.95 (ISBN 0-8057-2864-3). Twayne.

Gump, Patricia L., ed. see Wallower, Lucille.

Gump, Paul V. see Hetherington, E. Mavis.

Gump, Richard. Jade: Stone of Heaven. LC 62-12100. 1962. 10.95 (ISBN 0-385-01705-7). Doubleday.

Gunatilaka, Ananda, jt. auth. see Bowen, Robert.

Gunda, Bela. Ethnographica Carpatho-Balcanica. (Illus.). 427p. (Eng, Fr & Ger.). 1979. 45.00x (ISBN 963-05-1747-7). Intl Pubns Serv.

Gunders, Henry, jt. auth. see Hoffman, Raymond A.

Gundersen, Joan R., jt. auth. see Smelser, Marshall.

Gunderson, E. K. & Rahe, Richard H., eds. Life Stress & Illness. (Illus.). 274p. 1979. 17.50 (ISBN 0-398-03003-0). C C Thomas.

Gunderson, Robert G. Old Gentlemen's Convention: The Washington Peace Conference of 1861. LC 80-24747. (Illus.). xiii, 168p. 1981. Repr. of 1961 ed. lib. bdg. 17.50x (ISBN 0-313-22584-2, GUOG). Greenwood.

Gundrey, Elizabeth. Painting & Decorating. (Orig.). 1980. pap. 6.95x (ISBN 0-8464-1036-2). Beekman Pubs.

--Simple Home Repairs. (Orig.). 1980. pap. 6.95x (ISBN 0-8464-1050-8). Beekman Pubs.

Gundry, Patricia. The Complete Woman. LC 79-8928. 240p. 1981. 10.95 (ISBN 0-385-15521-2, Galilee). Doubleday.

Gundry, R. Soma, in Biblical Theology, with Emphasis on Pauline Anthropology. LC 75-22927. (Society for New Testament Studies: No. 29). 300p. 1976. 42.00 (ISBN 0-521-20788-6). Cambridge U Pr.

Gundry, Robert H. The Church & the Tribulation. 224p. 1973. text ed. 6.95 (ISBN 0-310-25401-9). Zondervan.

Gundry, Stanley N. & Johnson, Alan F., eds. Tensions in Contemporary Theology. 384p. 1979. 12.95 (ISBN 0-8024-8585-5). Moody.

Gundy, Arthur B. Van see Van Gundy, Arthur B.

Gundy, Elizabeth. Bliss. 1978. pap. 1.95 (ISBN 0-515-04706-6). Jove Pubns.

Gundy, H. Pearson, ed. Letters of Bliss Carman. (Illus.). 500p. 1981. 55.00 (ISBN 0-7735-0364-1). McGill-Queens U Pr.

Gundy, John H. Assessment of the Child in Primary Health Care. (Illus.). 208p. 1981. pap. text ed. 7.95 (ISBN 0-07-025197-5). McGraw.

Gunji, Masakatsu. Kabuki. LC 70-82658. (Illus.). 265p. 1965. 85.00 (ISBN 0-87011-090-X). Kodansha.

Gunlicks, Arthur B., ed. Local Government Reform & Reorganization: An International Perspective. (National University Publications, Political Science Ser.). 1981. 17.50 (ISBN 0-8046-9272-6). Kennikat.

Gunn, Alan M. The Mirror of Love: A Reinterpretation of the "Romance of the Rose". 1952. 24.00 (ISBN 0-89672-005-5). Tex Tech Pr.

Gunn, Angus M. Habitat: Human Settlements in an Urban Age. 1978. text ed. 27.00 (ISBN 0-08-021487-8); pap. 15.00 (ISBN 0-08-021486-X); tchr's. ed. 9.25 (ISBN 0-08-022998-0). Pergamon.

Gunn, Anita & Courrier, Kathleen, eds. Shining Examples: Model Projects Using Renewable Resources. LC 80-67831. (Illus.). 210p. 1980. 6.95 (ISBN 0-937446-00-9). Ctr Renewable.

Gunn, Clare A. Tourism Planning. LC 79-15931. 1979. 19.50x (ISBN 0-8448-1301-X). Crane-Russak Co.

Gunn, D. M. The Story of King David: Genre & Interpretation. (JSOT Supplement Ser.: No. 6). 164p. 1978. text ed. 29.95x (ISBN 0-905774-11-6, Pub. by JSOT Pr England); pap. text ed. 16.75x (ISBN 0-905774-05-1, Pub. by JSOT Pr England). Eisenbrauns.

Gunn, Donald L. & Stevens, John G. R. Pesticides & Human Welfare. (Illus.). 1977. text ed. 19.95x (ISBN 0-19-854522-3); pap. text ed. 9.95x (ISBN 0-19-854526-6). Oxford U Pr.

Gunn, Drewey W. Mexico in American & British Letters: A Bibliography of Fiction & Travel Books Citing Original Editions. LC 73-20354. 1974. 10.00 (ISBN 0-8108-0692-4). Scarecrow.

Gunn, Elizabeth. Ella's Dream. 1979. 14.95 (ISBN 0-241-89847-1, Pub. by Hamish Hamilton England). David & Charles.

Gunn, Gertrude E. Political History of Newfoundland, 1832-1864. LC 67-397. 1966. pap. 8.50 (ISBN 0-8020-6323-3). U of Toronto Pr.

Gunn, Giles. The Interpretation of Otherness: Literature Religion & the American Imagination. 1979. 15.95 (ISBN 0-19-502453-2). Oxford U Pr.

Gunn, Jack W. & Castle, Gladys C. A Pictorial History of Delta State University. LC 80-19085. 216p. 1980. 25.00 (ISBN 0-87805-112-0). U Pr of Miss.

Gunn, James. Alternate Worlds: An Illustrated History of Science Fiction. (Illus.). 224p. 1976. pap. 8.95 o.p. (ISBN 0-89104-049-8). A & W Pubs.

--The Dreamers. 1981. 10.95 (ISBN 0-671-25280-1). S&S.

--This Fortress World. 1979. pap. 1.75 o.p. (ISBN 0-425-03881-5). Berkley Pub.

Gunn, James, ed. Nebula Award Stories No. 10, Anniversary Issue. LC 66-20974. 268p. (YA) 1975. 10.95 o.s.i. (ISBN 0-06-011628-5, HarpT). Har-Row.

Gunn, L. Ray, jt. auth. see Eakle, Arlene H.

Gunn, Mary K. Guide to Academic Protocol. LC 70-76250. 1969. 15.00x (ISBN 0-231-03036-3). Columbia U Pr.

Gunn, Peter. Napoleon's "Little Pest" The Dutchess of Abrantes. (Illus.). 1979. 24.00 (ISBN 0-241-10183-2, Pub. by Hamish Hamilton England). David & Charles.

Gunn, Thom. Fighting Terms. 39p. 1970. pap. 1.95 o.p. (ISBN 0-571-09390-6, Pub. by Faber & Faber). Merrimack Bk Serv.

--The Menace. 1980. signed ed. 15.00 (ISBN 0-686-28715-0). Man-Root.

--Poems, Nineteen Fifty to Nineteen Sixty-Six: A Selection. 41p. 1969. pap. 3.95 (ISBN 0-571-08845-7, Pub. by Faber & Faber). Merrimack Bk Serv.

--Selected Poems, Nineteen Fifty to Nineteen Seventy-Five. 1979. 12.95 (ISBN 0-374-25865-1). FS&G.

--The Sense of Movement. 1968. pap. 3.95 (ISBN 0-571-08530-X, Pub. by Faber & Faber). Merrimack Bk Serv.

Gunn, Thom & Hughes, Ted. Selected Poems. 1962. pap. 3.95 (ISBN 0-571-05019-0, Pub. by Faber & Faber). Merrimack Bk Serv.

Gunnell, Sally, jt. auth. see Gardner, Hope P.

Gunnerson, James H. The Fremont Culture: A Study in Culture Dynamics on the Northern Anasazi Frontier. LC 79-76014. (Peabody Museum Papers: Vol. 59, No. 2). 1969. pap. text ed. 15.00 (ISBN 0-87365-172-3). Peabody Harvard.

Gunneweg, Antonius H. & Schmithals, Walter. Achievement. Smith, David, tr. LC 80-26977. (Biblical Encounter Ser.). 208p. (Orig.). 1981. pap. 7.95 (ISBN 0-687-00690-2). Abingdon.

Gunning, B. E. & Steer, M. Plant Cell Biology: An Ultrastructural Approach. LC 75-13749. 1975. 10.50x o.p. (ISBN 0-8448-0669-2). Crane-Russak Co.

Gunning, Monica, tr. see Fry, Edward B.

Gunning, Monica, tr. see Mountain, Lee.

Gunnis, Rupert, jt. auth. see Whinney, Margaret.

Gunnufson, Kent, photos by. Tracking the Snow-Shoe Itinerant. LC 80-54041. (Illus.). 128p. 1981. text ed. 18.95 (ISBN 0-9605366-0-4); pap. text ed. 11.95 (ISBN 0-9605366-1-2). Snowstorm.

Guns & Ammo Magazine Editors, ed. Guns & Ammo Annual, 1981. (Illus.). 320p. 1980. pap. 6.95 (ISBN 0-8227-3017-0). Petersen Pub.

Gunson, Niel. Messengers of Grace: Evangelical Missionaries in the South Seas 1797-1860. (Illus.). 1978. 41.00x (ISBN 0-19-550517-4). Oxford U Pr.

Gunston, Bill. The F-Four Phantom. (Illus.). 1977. 9.95 o.p. (ISBN 0-684-15298-3, ScribT). Scribner.

--The Illustrated Guide to Bombers of World War II. LC 80-67628. (Illustrated Military Guides). (Illus.). 4094p. 1981. 7.95 (ISBN 0-668-05094-2, 5094). Arco.

--The Illustrated Guide to German, Italian & Japanese Fighters of World War II. LC 80-67627. (Illustrated Military Guides). (Illus.). 160p. 1981. 7.95 (ISBN 0-668-05093-4, 5093). Arco.

--The Illustrated Guide to Modern Fighters & Attack Aircraft. LC 80-65164. (Illustrated Military Guides Ser.). (Illus.). 160p. 1980. 7.95 (ISBN 0-668-04964-2, 4964-2). Arco.

--The Philatelist's Companion. (Illus.). 240p. 1975. 8.95 (ISBN 0-7153-6384-0). David & Charles.

--Transportation: Problems & Prospects. Clarke, Robin, ed. (The World of Science Lib.). 1973. 7.95 o.p. (ISBN 0-525-22228-6). Dutton.

Gunston, C. A. & Corner, C. M. German-English Glossary of Financial & Commercial Terms. new ed. (Ger. & Eng.). 1977. 57.50 (ISBN 3-7819-2008-9). Adler.

Gunstone, F. D. Guidebook to Stereochemistry. LC 75-12762. (Illus.). 128p. 1975. pap. text ed. 10.95x (ISBN 0-582-44170-6). Longman.

Gunstone, John. Living Together. LC 76-57794. 1977. pap. 1.95 (ISBN 0-87123-325-8, 200325). Bethany Fell.

Gunter, A. Y. Big Thicket: A Challenge for Conservation. LC 73-184310. 1972. 14.95 (ISBN 0-8363-0120-X); pap. 8.50 (ISBN 0-685-02984-0). Jenkins.

Gunter, Altner. The Nature of Human Behaviour. Van Amerongen, Charles, tr. 1976. text ed. 21.00x o.p. (ISBN 0-04-573012-1). Allen Unwin.

Gunter, Laurie M. & Ryan, Joanne E. Self-Assessment of Current Knnowledge in Geriatric Nursing. 1976. spiral bdg. 9.50 (ISBN 0-87488-295-8). Med Exam.

Gunter, P. A., ed. & tr. Bergson & the Evolution of Physics. LC 77-77844. 1969. 19.50x (ISBN 0-87049-092-3). U of Tenn Pr.

Gunter, Pete A., jt. ed. see Sibley, Jack R.

Guntermann, Karl L., jt. auth. see Cooper, James R.

Gunther, Albert. Catalogue of Colubrine Snakes in the Collection of the British Museum. xvi, 281p. 1971. Repr. of 1858 ed. 4.50x (ISBN 0-565-00709-2, Pub. by British Mus Nat Hist England). Sabbot-Natural Hist Bks.

Gunther, Bernard. Love View. 1971. pap. 2.95 o.s.i. (ISBN 0-02-076830-3, Collier). Macmillan.

--Sense Relaxation Below Your Mind. 1968. 6.95 o.s.i. (ISBN 0-02-546600-3). Macmillan.

Gunther, Bernard & Kent, Corita. High Cards. 4.95 o.p. (ISBN 0-06-061585-0, HarpR). Har-Row.

Gunther, Bernard, et al. The Book of Knowledge. (The Essence Books Ser). (YA) 1973. pap. 0.50 o.s.i. (ISBN 0-02-080190-4, Collier). Macmillan.

--Meditations. (The Essence Books Ser.). (Illus.). (YA) 1973. pap. 0.50 o.s.i. (ISBN 0-02-080240-4, Collier). Macmillan.

--Symbols & Sounds. (The Essence Books Ser). (YA) 1973. pap. 0.50 o.s.i. (ISBN 0-02-080260-9, Collier). Macmillan.

--Wholley Man. (The Essence Books Ser.). (Illus.). (YA) 1973. pap. 0.50 o.s.i. (ISBN 0-02-080230-7, Collier). Macmillan.

Gunther, Erna. The Permanent Collection, Vol. 1. LC 75-32053. (Whatcom Museum). (Illus.). 64p. 1975. pap. 5.00 (ISBN 0-295-95579-1). U of Wash Pr.

Gunther, Erna, tr. see Krause, Aurel.

Gunther, F. A., ed. Residue Reviews, Vol. 75. (Illus.). 189p. 1981. 29.80 (ISBN 0-387-90534-0). Springer-Verlag.

--Residue Reviews, Vol. 76. (Illus.). 218p. 1981. 29.80 (ISBN 0-387-90535-9). Springer-Verlag.

--Residue Reviews, Vol. 79. (Illus.). 280p. 1981. 39.80 (ISBN 0-387-90539-1). Springer-Verlag.

Gunther, Gerald. Cases & Materials on Constitutional Law. 10th ed. LC 80-20484. (University Casebook Ser.). 1839p. 1980. text ed. write for info. (ISBN 0-88277-010-1). Foundation Pr.

--Cases & Materials on Individual Rights in Constitutional Law. 3rd, abr. ed. LC 80-70238. (University Casebook Ser.). 1337p. 1980. text ed. write for info. (ISBN 0-88277-021-7). Foundation Pr.

Gunther, H. G. The Desert Doctor. (H. G. Gunther Ser.). pap. 1.95 (ISBN 0-515-05675-8). Jove Pubns.

--Dr. Erica Werner. (H. G. Gunther Ser.: No. 4). 224p. 1981. pap. 1.95 (ISBN 0-515-05673-1). Jove Pubns.

--Natasha. (Gunther Romance Ser.: No. 6). 224p. (Orig.). 1981. pap. 1.95 o.p. (ISBN 0-515-05680-4). Jove Pubns.

--Private Hell. (Gunther Romance Ser.: No. 5). 208p. (Orig.). 1981. pap. 1.95 (ISBN 0-515-05677-4). Jove Pubns.

--The Ravishing Doctor. (Gunther Ser.). pap. 1.95 (ISBN 0-515-05676-6). Jove Pubns.

--Summer with Danica. (Gunther Ser.: No. 3). 224p. (Orig.). 1981. pap. 1.95 (ISBN 0-515-05674-X). Jove Pubns.

Gunther, John. Inside Europe Today. rev. ed. LC 62-9889. 1962. 12.50 o.s.i. (ISBN 0-06-011670-6, HarpT). Har-Row.

--Inside Russia Today. new, rev. ed. LC 62-17196. 1962. 12.50 o.p. (ISBN 0-06-011685-4, HarpT). Har-Row.

Gunther, Richard. Public Policy in a No-Party State: Spanish Planning & Budgeting in the Twilight of the Franquist Era. 1980. 18.50x (ISBN 0-520-03752-9). U of Cal Pr.

Gunther, Werner A. Physics of Modern Electronics. rev. ed. Antin, David, tr. (Illus.). 1966. pap. text ed. 3.50 (ISBN 0-486-61749-1). Dover.

Gunther, Wolfgang H., jt. auth. see Klayman, Daniel L.

Gunton, Sharon, ed. Contemporary Literary Criticism: Excerpts from Criticism of the Works of Today's Novelists, Poets, Playwrights, & Other Creative Writers. LC 76-38938. (Contemporary Literary Criticism Ser.: Vol. 17). 600p. 1981. 58.00 (ISBN 0-8103-0107-5). Gale.

--Contemporary Literary Criticism: Excerpts from the Criticism of the Works of Today's Novelists, Poets,, Playwrights & Other Creative Writers, 15 vols. Incl. Vol. 1. 1973. (ISBN 0-8103-0100-8); Vol. 2. 1974. (ISBN 0-8103-0102-4); Vol. 3. 1975. (ISBN 0-8103-0104-0); Vol. 4. 1975. (ISBN 0-8103-0106-7); Vol. 5. 1976. (ISBN 0-8103-0108-3); Vol. 6. 1976. (ISBN 0-8103-0110-5); Vol. 7. 1977. (ISBN 0-8103-0112-1); Vol. 8. 1978. (ISBN 0-8103-0114-8); Vol. 9. 1978. (ISBN 0-685-92122-0); Vol. 10. 1979. (ISBN 0-8103-0118-0); Vol. 11. 1979 (ISBN 0-8103-0120-2); Vol. 12. 1979 (ISBN 0-8103-0122-9); Vol. 13. 1979 (ISBN 0-8103-0124-5); Vol. 14. 1980 (ISBN 0-8103-0101-6); Vol. 15. 1980 (ISBN 0-8103-0103-2). LC 76-38938. (Contemporary Literary Criticism Ser.). 58.00 ea. Gale.

--Contemporary Literary Criticism, Vol. 16: Excerpts from Criticism of the Works of Today's Novelists, Poets, Playwrights & Other Creative Writers. LC 76-38938. (Contemporary Literary Criticism Ser.: Vol. 16). 600p. 1980. 58.00 (ISBN 0-8103-0105-9). Gale.

--Contemporary Literary Criticism: Vol. 18, Excerpts from Criticism of the Works of Today's Novelists, Poets, Playwrights & Other Creative Writers. LC 76-38938. (Contemporary Literary Criticism Ser.: Vol. 17). 600p. 1981. 58.00 (ISBN 0-8103-0123-7). Gale.

Gunzel, Dave, ed. see Lien, David A.

Gunzel, David, ed. see Lieh, David A.

Gunzel, David, ed. see Lien, David A.

Gup, Benton E. The Basics of Investing. LC 78-17521. (Ser. in Finance). 1979. text ed. 21.50 (ISBN 0-471-33620-3); tchrs. manual avail. (ISBN 0-471-04813-5); tests avail. (ISBN 0-471-05663-4); study guide avail. (ISBN 0-471-05573-5). Wiley.

--Financial Intermediaries: An Introduction. LC 75-31005. (Illus.). 416p. 1976. text ed. 18.50 o.p. (ISBN 0-395-19828-3); inst. manual 2.25 o.p. (ISBN 0-395-19827-5). HM.

--Financial Intermediaries: An Introduction. 2nd ed. LC 79-87858. 1979. text ed. 19.50 (ISBN 0-395-28138-5); instrs' manual 1.50 (ISBN 0-395-28157-1). HM.

Gupa, Brijen K. & Lopatin, Arthur D. Starting & Succeeding in Small Business: A Guide for the Innercity Businessman. LC 78-58105. iv, 100p. (Orig.). 1978. pap. 15.00 (ISBN 0-936876-14-X). Learn Res Intl Stud.

Guppy, Alice. Children's Clothes Nineteen Thirty Nine to Nineteen Seventy: The Advent of Fashion. (Illus.). 1978. 23.95 (ISBN 0-7137-0896-4, Pub. by Blandford Pr England). Sterling.

Guppy, James G., jt. ed. see Agrawal, Ashok K.

Gupta, ed. Entomology in the U. S. A. 1976. 5.00 (ISBN 0-686-17552-2). Entomol Soc.

Gupta, A. P. Insect Hemocytes. LC 78-10477. 1979. 95.00 (ISBN 0-521-22364-4). Cambridge U Pr.

Gupta, Anirudha. Revolution Through Ballot: India, January - March 1977. 1977. 8.00x o.p. (ISBN 0-8364-0460-2). South Asia Bks.

Gupta, B. D. Mathematical Physics. 1977. 35.00 (ISBN 0-7069-0514-8, Pub. by Vikas India). Advent Bk.

Gupta, B. K., jt. auth. see Agnihotri, O. P.

Gupta, B. N. Government Budgeting with Special Reference to India. 1967. 10.00 (ISBN 0-210-27103-5). Asia.

Gupta, Bhabani Ser see Sen Gupta, Bhabani.

Gupta, Bhagwan Das. Life & Times of Maharaja Chhatrasal Bundela. 178p. 1980. text ed. 10.00x (ISBN 0-391-01771-3). Humanities.

Gupta, Brijan K. & Lopatin, Arthur D. Small Business Development in the Inner City Areas of Rochester. LC 78-58110. (Illus.). xx, 231p. (Orig.). 1978. pap. 22.50 (ISBN 0-936876-15-8). Learn Res Intl Stud.

Gupta, Brijen K. India in English Fiction, 1800-1970: An Annotated Bibliography. LC 73-4194. 1973. 10.00 (ISBN 0-8108-0612-6). Scarecrow.

Gupta, D. C. Indian Government & Politics. 1978. 20.00 (ISBN 0-7069-0521-0, Pub. by Vikas India). Advent Bk.

Gupta, Derek. Radioimmunoassay of Steroid Hormones. 2nd ed. (Illus.). 1980. 48.80 (ISBN 3-5272-5863-9). Verlag Chemie.

Gupta, Derek & Voelter, Wolfgang. Hypothalamic Hormones: Chemistry, Physiology & Clinical Applications. (Illus.). 1978. 75.30 (ISBN 3-527-25712-8). Verlag Chemie.

--Hypothalamic Hormones: Structure, Synthesis, & Biological Activity. (Illus.). 1975. 34.20 (ISBN 3-527-25589-3). Verlag Chemie.

Gupta, G. R. Marriage, Religion, & Society: Tradition & Change in an Indian Village. LC 73-5903. 180p. 1974. 12.95 (ISBN 0-470-33648-X). Halsted Pr.

Gupta, H. Selected Topics in Number Theory. 1980. 55.00x (ISBN 0-85626-177-7, Pub. by Abacus Pr). Intl Schol Bk Serv.

Gupta, H. C., tr. see Bongard-Levin, G. M.

Gupta, H. C., tr. see Stcherbatsky, T.

Gupta, J. N. D. Postal Applications of Operations Research. 1978. text ed. 34.50 (ISBN 0-08-023011-3). Pergamon.

Gupta, K. Balasundara. Cumulative Index to the Proceedings of the British Academy, 1903-1968. 1971. 8.00 o.p. (ISBN 0-8108-0383-6). Scarecrow.

Gupta, K. C. Microwaves. LC 80-11904. 256p. 1980. 14.95x (ISBN 0-470-26966-9). Halsted Pr.

Gupta, K. C. & Singh, A., eds. Microwave Integrated Circuits. LC 74-8772. 380p. 1974. 18.95 (ISBN 0-470-33640-4). Halsted Pr.

Gupta, Marie & Brandon, Frances. A Treasury of Witchcraft & Devilry. LC 74-6571. 1974. 8.95 o.p. (ISBN 0-685-50510-3). Jonathan David.

Gupta, Pranati Sen. The Art of Indian Cuisine: Everday Menus, Feasts, & Holiday Banquets. Backman, Beth, ed. 240p. 1980. pap. 5.95 o.p. (ISBN 0-8015-0367-1, Hawthorn). Dutton.

Gupta, R. M., ed. Personnel Management in India: The Practical Approach to Human Relations in Industry. 2nd ed. 346p. 1974. pap. text ed. 5.95x o.p. (ISBN 0-210-33913-6). Asia.

Gupta, Rohini. Karna & Other Poems. 1976. 8.00 (ISBN 0-89253-825-2); flexible cloth 4.80 (ISBN 0-89253-826-0). Ind-US Inc.

Gupta, S. C. & Majid, A. Producers' Response to Changes in Prices & Marketing Policies. 5.25x o.p. (ISBN 0-210-22628-5). Asia.

Gupta, S. K. Madhusudan Saraswati on the Bhagavaddita. 1977. 25.00 (ISBN 0-89684-246-0, Pub. by Motilal Banarsidass India). Orient Bk Dist.

Gupta, S. L. & Rani, Nisha. Fundamental Real Analysis. 1976. 15.00 (ISBN 0-686-63607-4, Pub. by Vikas India). Advent Bk.

Gupta, S. P. Archaeology of Central Asia & the Indian Border Lands, 3 vols. 1979. text ed. 28.00 ea. (ISBN 0-391-02092-7). Humanities.

--India: a Study in Futurism. LC 76-904615. 1976. 6.75x o.p. (ISBN 0-88386-824-5). South Asia Bks.

--Modern India & Science & Technology. 166p. 1979. 13.95 (ISBN 0-7069-0743-4, Pub by Vikas India). Advent Bk.

--The Roots of Indian Art. (Illus.). Date not set. 102.50 (ISBN 0-391-02172-9). Humanities.

Gupta, Shanti C. & Panchapakesan, S. Multiple Decision Procedures: Theory & Methodology of Selecting & Ranking Populations. LC 79-13119. (Probability & Mathematical Statistics: Applied Section). 1979. 39.95 (ISBN 0-471-05177-2, Pub. by Wiley-Interscience). Wiley.

Gupta, Shashikant, jt. auth. see McIntosh, Robert W.

Gupta, Shiv K. & Cozzolino, John M. Fundamentals of Operations Research for Management. LC 73-94384. (Illus.). 1975. text ed. 22.95x (ISBN 0-8162-3476-0); solutions manual 6.50x (ISBN 0-8162-3486-8). Holden-Day.

Gupta, Shiv K. & Hamman, Ray T. Starting a Small Business: A Simulation Game. (Illus.). 64p. 1974. pap. text ed. 10.95 (ISBN 0-13-842963-4). P-H.

Gupta, Sipra Das see Das Gupta, Sipra.

Gupta, Suraj B. Monetary Planning for India. 252p. 1979. text ed. 14.95x (ISBN 0-19-561145-4). Oxford U Pr.

Gupta, U. S. Physiological Aspects of Dryland Farming. LC 76-42138. 392p. 1977. text ed. 18.00 (ISBN 0-916672-94-8). Allanheld.

Gupta, Virendra K., jt. auth. see Townes, Henry.

Guptara, Prabhu. Beginnings. 8.00 (ISBN 0-89253-689-6); flexible cloth 4.80 (ISBN 0-89253-690-X). Ind-US Inc.

Gupton, James A. Microcomputer for External Control Devices. LC 80-67640. 1980. pap. 13.95 (ISBN 0-918398-28-2). Dilithium Pr.

Gur, Arieh. From Kiev to Tel Aviv: Escape from Russia. 1981. 14.00x (ISBN 0-931556-02-3). Translation Pr.

Gura, Philip F. The Wisdom of Words: Language, Theology, & Literature in the New England Renaissance. 192p. 1981. 17.50 (ISBN 0-8195-5053-1). Wesleyan U Pr.

Guraedy, Ila. Illustrated Gymnastics Dictionary for Young People. LC 79-93357. (Illustrated Dictionary Ser.). (Illus.). 120p. (gr. 4 up). 1980. lib. bdg. 6.79 (ISBN 0-8178-0002-6). Harvey.

--Illustrated Gymnastics Dictionary for Young People. (Illus., Orig.). pap. 2.50 (ISBN 0-13-450932-3). P-H.

Guratzsch, Herwig. Dutch Paintings. (Alpine Fine Arts Collection). (Illus.). 304p. 1981. 50.00 (ISBN 0-933516-09-6, Pub by Alpine Fine Arts). Hippocrene Bks.

Gurau, Peter K. & Lieberthal, E. A. Fingermath, Bk. 1. (Fingermath Ser.). 1979. pap. 4.00 pupil's ed. (ISBN 0-07-025221-1, W); tchr's. ed. 8.00 (ISBN 0-07-025231-9). McGraw.

Gurau, Peter K. & Lieberthal, Edwin M. Fingermath Book. Gafney, Leo, ed. (Fingermath Ser.: Bk. 3). 192p. (gr. 3-8). 1980. pap. text ed. 4.40 (ISBN 0-07-025223-8, W); tchrs. ed. 8.80 (ISBN 0-07-025233-5). McGraw.

Gurdjian, E. S. Head Injury from Antiquity to the Present with Special Reference to Penetrating Head Wounds. (Beaumont Lecture Ser.). (Illus.). 148p. 1973. 16.75 (ISBN 0-398-02689-0). C C Thomas.

Gurdjian, E. S. & Thomas, L. M. Neckache & Backache: Proceedings. (Illus.). 296p. 1970. 14.50 (ISBN 0-398-00747-0). C C Thomas.

Gurdjieff, G. I. Beelzebub's Tales to His Grandson, 3 vols. 1973. Set. pap. 13.95 (ISBN 0-525-47351-3); pap. 3.95 ea. o.p.; Vol. 1. o.p. (ISBN 0-525-47348-3); Vol. 2. o.p. (ISBN 0-525-47349-1); Vol. 3. o.p. (ISBN 0-525-47350-5). Dutton.

--Life Is Real Only Then, When "I Am". 1981. 12.95 (ISBN 0-525-14547-8); pap. 6.95 o.p. (ISBN 0-525-47661-X). Dutton.

Gurel, Lee. A Survey of Academic Resources in Psychiatric Residency Training. 117p. 1973. pap. 3.25 o.p. (ISBN 0-685-65570-9, 187). Am Psychiatric.

Gurel, Lee, ed. Descriptive Directory of Psychiatric Training Programs in the U. S., 1972-1973. 144p. 1973. 3.25 o.p. (ISBN 0-685-38354-7, 186). Am Psychiatric.

Gurel, Lois M., jt. auth. see Horn, Marilyn J.

Guren, Pamela, et al. Life & Times in Shoe City: The Shoe Workers of Lynn. Farnam, Anne, ed. (Illus.). 1979. pap. 4.00 (ISBN 0-88389-100-X). Essex Inst.

Gurevich, David A., tr. see Schneersohn, Y. Y.

Gurian, Anita, jt. auth. see Formanek, Ruth.

Gurin, Arnold, jt. auth. see Perlman, Robert.

Gurin, Patricia & Epps, Edgar G. Black Consciousness, Identity & Achievement: A Study of Students in Historically Black Colleges. LC 75-5847. 545p. 1975. text ed. 25.50 (ISBN 0-471-33670-X). Wiley.

Gurko, Leo. Joseph Conrad: Giant in Exile. 1979. 12.95 (ISBN 0-02-546700-X). Macmillan.

--Thomas Wolfe: Beyond the Romantic Ego. LC 74-34204. (Twentieth Century American Writers Ser.). 153p. (gr. 6 up). 1975. 8.95 (ISBN 0-690-00751-5, TYC-J). T Y Crowell.

--Two Lives of Joseph Conrad. LC 65-16180. (gr. 7 up). 1965. 8.95 (ISBN 0-690-84310-0, TYC-J). T Y Crowell.

Gurko, Miriam. Clarence Darrow. LC 65-13138. (gr. 7 up). 1965. 8.95 o.p. (ISBN 0-690-19484-6, TYC-J). T Y Crowell.

Gurland, A. R., et al. The Fate of Small Business in Nazi Germany. LC 74-12275. 160p. 1975. Repr. of 1943 ed. 14.25 (ISBN 0-86527-065-1). Fertig.

Gurley, John G. & Shaw, Edward S. Money in a Theory of Finance. 1960. 18.95 (ISBN 0-8157-3322-4). Brookings.

Gurman, Alan S. & Kniskern, David P. Handbook of Family Therapy. LC 80-20357. 800p. 1981. 39.95 (ISBN 0-87630-242-8). Brunner Mazel.

Gurman, Alan S. & Razin, Andrew M. Effective Psychotherapy: A Handbook of Research. LC 76-23300. 1977. pap. 35.75 (ISBN 0-08-019508-3). Pergamon.

Gurman, Alan S., ed. Questions & Answers in the Practice of Family Therapy. 544p. 1981. 25.00 (ISBN 0-87630-246-0). Brunner-Mazel.

Gurman, Alan S. & Rice, David G., eds. Couples in Conflict. LC 74-6951. 372p. 1975. 30.00x (ISBN 0-87668-150-X). Aronson.

Gurnall, William. The Christian in Complete Armour. 1979. 22.95 (ISBN 0-85151-196-1). Banner of Truth.

Gurnee, Jeanne, jt. auth. see Gurnee, Russell.

Gurnee, Russell & Gurnee, Jeanne. Gurnee Guide to American Caves. 1980. 9.95 (ISBN 0-914264-29-X); pap. 5.95 (ISBN 0-914264-30-3). Caroline Hse.

Gurney, Claire, jt. auth. see Gurney, Gene.

Gurney, Clare, jt. auth. see Gurney, Gene.

Gurney, Edmund. Phantasms of the Living, 2 Vols. LC 71-119868. (Hist. of Psych. Ser.). 1970. Repr. of 1886 ed. Set. 120.00x set (ISBN 0-8201-1075-2). Schol Facsimiles.

Gurney, Eric. The Calculating Cat Returns. LC 78-61782. (Illus.). 1978. 5.95 (ISBN 0-13-110213-3); pap. 2.95 (ISBN 0-13-110205-2). P-H.

--Eric Gurney's Pop-up Book of Cats. LC 74-19317. (Pop-up Bks). (Illus.). (ps-2). 1974. 4.95 (ISBN 0-394-82825-9, BYR). Random.

Gurney, Gene. Americans to the Moon: The Story of Project Apollo. LC 77-103405. (Landmark Giant Ser.: No. 20). (gr. 5-9). 1970. 4.95 (ISBN 0-394-81853-9); PLB 5.99 (ISBN 0-394-91853-3). Random.

--Space Technology Spinoffs. (Impact Ser.). (Illus.). (gr. 7 up). 1979. PLB 6.90 s&l (ISBN 0-531-02290-0). Watts.

--Walk in Space: The Story of Project Gemini. (gr. 5 up). 1967. PLB 5.99 (ISBN 0-394-90417-6, BYR). Random.

Gurney, Gene & Gurney, Claire. North & South Korea: First Bks. LC 73-4278. (gr. 7 up). 1973. PLB 4.47 o.p. (ISBN 0-531-00804-5). Watts.

Gurney, Gene & Gurney, Clare. Agriculture Careers. (Career Concise Guides Ser.). (Illus.). (gr. 7 up). 1978. PLB 6.45 s&l (ISBN 0-531-01418-5). Watts.

--The Colony of Maryland. LC 76-182897. (First Bks). (Illus.). 72p. (gr. 4-6). 1972. PLB 4.90 o.p. (ISBN 0-531-00757-X). Watts.

--Cosmonauts in Orbit: The Story of the Soviet Space Program. LC 76-189516. (Illus.). 192p. (gr. 7 up). 1972. PLB 8.87 o.p. (ISBN 0-531-02572-1). Watts.

--The Launching of Sputnik, October 4, 1957. LC 75-5545. (World Focus Bks). 72p. (gr. 6-10). 1975. PLB 4.47 o.p. (ISBN 0-531-02175-0). Watts.

Gurney, J. D. & Cotter, I. A. Cooling Towers in Refrigeration. (Illus.). 1966. 20.50x (ISBN 0-85334-390-X, Pub. by Applied Science). Burgess-Intl Ideas.

Gurney, Jason. Crusade in Spain. (Illus.). 1974. 7.95 o.p. (ISBN 0-571-10310-3, Pub. by Faber & Faber). Merrimack Bk Serv.

Gurney, Joseph J. Journey in North America. LC 71-159795. (The American Scene Ser.). 422p. 1973. Repr. of 1841 ed. lib. bdg. 39.50 (ISBN 0-306-70572-9). Da Capo.

Gurney, Oliver R. Some Aspects of Hittite Religion. (British Academy - Schweich Lectures). (Illus.). 94p. 1977. text ed. 24.95x (ISBN 0-19-725974-X). Oxford U Pr.

Gurney, Oliver R. & Kramer, Samuel N., eds. Sumerian Literary Texts in the Ashmolean Museum. (Oxford Editions of Cuneiform Texts). (Illus.). 1976. pap. 45.00x (ISBN 0-19-815450-X). Oxford U Pr.

Gurney, T. R. Fatigue of Welded Structures. 2nd ed. LC 78-21885. (British Welding Research Association Ser.). (Illus.). 1980. 66.00 (ISBN 0-521-22558-2). Cambridge U Pr.

Gurnick, Stanley & Dias, Robert M. Bradley CPA Review Quantitative Methods. 6th ed. LC 78-50970. 1978. pap. 8.00 (ISBN 0-932788-03-3). Bradley CPA.

Guro, Elena. The Little Camels of the Sky. O'Brien, Kevin, tr. from Rus. 1981. 11.00 (ISBN 0-88233-437-9). Ardis Pubs.

Gurock, Jeffrey. When Harlem Was Jewish, Eighteen Seventy to Nineteen Thirty. 1979. 17.50x (ISBN 0-231-04666-9). Columbia U Pr.

Gurr, A. The Shakespearean Stage, 1574-1642. 2nd ed. LC 80-40085. (Illus.). 220p. 1981. 49.50 (ISBN 0-521-23029-2); pap. 12.95 (ISBN 0-521-29772-9). Cambridge U Pr.

Gurr, Andrew. Shakespearean Stage, Fifteen Seventy-Four - Sixteen Forty-Two. LC 72-116747. (Illus.). 1970. 36.00 (ISBN 0-521-07816-4); pap. 8.95x (ISBN 0-521-09632-4). Cambridge U Pr.

--Writers in Exile: The Creative Use of Home in Modern Literature. 220p. 1981. 21.00x (ISBN 0-389-20189-8). B&N.

Gurr, David. Troika. 1980. pap. 2.75 (ISBN 0-425-04662-1). Berkley Pub.

--A Woman Called Scylla. LC 80-51998. 324p. 1981. 13.95 (ISBN 0-670-77775-7). Viking Pr.

Gurr, Ted R. Why Men Rebel. LC 74-84865. (Center of International Studies). 1970. 21.00x (ISBN 0-691-07528-X); pap. 5.95 (ISBN 0-691-02167-8). Princeton U Pr.

Gurr, Ted R., jt. auth. see Eckstein, Harry.

Gurr, Ted R., ed. Handbook of Political Conflict: Theory & Research. LC 79-6145. (Free Press Ser. on Political Behavior). (Illus.). 1980. 39.95 (ISBN 0-02-912760-2). Free Pr.

Gurr, Ted R., jt. ed. see Graham, Hugh D.

Gurry, Edward J. Quantative Methods. 6th ed. LC 78-50970. 8.00 (ISBN 0-932788-03-3). Bradley CPA.

Gurti & Nash. Philanthropy in the Shaping of American Higher Education. LC 65-19399. 8.50 (ISBN 0-910294-27-5). Brown Bk.

Gurtin, Morton E. An Introduction to Continuum Mechanics. (Mathematics in Science & Engineering Ser.). 1981. write for info. (ISBN 0-12-309750-9). Acad Pr.

Gurtler, Mary. Let's Look at Thailand. 1974. pap. 1.25 (ISBN 0-85363-104-2). OMF Bks.

--Nid's Exciting Day. 1961. pap. 0.90 (ISBN 0-85363-033-X). OMF Bks.

Guruge, Ananda W. P. Buddhism: The Religion & Its Culture. (Cultural & Religious Patterns in India: No. 2). 248p. 1976. pap. text ed. 5.00 (ISBN 0-89253-050-2). Ind-US Inc.

Gurvitch, Georges. Sociology of Law. (International Library of Sociology). 264p. 1973. 18.00x (ISBN 0-7100-7519-7). Routledge & Kegan.

Gur'Yanova, E. N., et al. The Donor-Acceptor Bond. Slutzkin, D., ed. Kondor, R., tr. from Rus. LC 75-12804. 366p. 1975. 57.95 (ISBN 0-470-33680-3). Halsted Pr.

Gusdorf, Georges. Speaking. Brockelman, Paul T., tr. (Studies in Phenomenology & Existential Philosophy Ser). 1965. 10.95x (ISBN 0-8101-0111-4); pap. 4.25x (ISBN 0-8101-0531-4). Northwestern U Pr.

Gusev, N. G. & Dimitriev, P. P. Quantum Radiation of Radioactive Nuclides. new ed. 1979. text ed. 140.00 (ISBN 0-08-023058-X). Pergamon.

Gusfield, Joseph R. The Culture of Public Problems: Drinking-Driving & the Symbolic Order. LC 80-17007. 1981. lib. bdg. 20.00x (ISBN 0-226-31093-0). U of Chicago Pr.

--Symbolic Crusade: Status Politics & the American Temperance Movement. LC 80-13342. viii, 198p. 1980. Repr. of 1963 ed. lib. bdg. 18.00x (ISBN 0-313-22423-4, GUSC). Greenwood.

Gushee, Charles H., ed. see Financial Publishing Company Staff.

Guskin, Alan E. & Guskin, Samuel L. A Social Psychology of Education. LC 73-104968. 1970. pap. text ed. 5.95 (ISBN 0-201-02631-7). A-W.

Guskin, Samuel L., jt. auth. see Guskin, Alan E.

Gussman, Edmund. Studies in Abstract Phonology. (Linguistic Inquiry Monographs). 160p. (Orig.). 1980. 22.50x (ISBN 0-262-07081-2); pap. text ed. 13.50x (ISBN 0-262-57057-2). MIT Pr.

Gussow, Mel. Don't Say Yes Until I Finish Talking. (Illus.). 318p. Date not set. pap. 7.95 (ISBN 0-306-80132-9). Da Capo.

Gussow, Zachary, et al. Sac, Fox & Iowa Indians, Vol. 1. Horr, David A., ed. (American Indian Ethnohistory Ser.). 1978. lib. bdg. 42.00 (ISBN 0-8240-0789-1). Garland Pub.

Gustafson, Alrik. History of Swedish Literature. LC 61-7722. (Illus.). 1961. 25.00x (ISBN 0-89067-035-8). Am Scandinavian.

--Six Scandinavian Novelists: Lie, Jacobsen, Heidenstam, Selma Lagerlof, Hamsun, Sigrid Undset. LC 69-19835. 1968. Repr. of 1940 ed. 12.00x (ISBN 0-8196-0230-2). Biblo.

Gustafson, Anita. Burrowing Birds. LC 80-29058. (Illus.). 64p. (gr. 4-6). 1981. 7.95 (ISBN 0-688-41977-1); PLB 7.63 (ISBN 0-688-51977-6). Morrow.

Gustafson, Clair, jt. auth. see Becker, Leonard, Jr.

Gustafson, Daniel R. Physics: Health & the Human Body. 528p. 1979. text ed. 17.95x (ISBN 0-534-00756-2). Wadsworth Pub.

Gustafson, James M. Can Ethics Be Christian? LC 74-11622. 1977. pap. 4.95 (ISBN 0-226-31102-3, P734, Phoen). U of Chicago Pr.

--Church As Moral Decision-Maker. LC 74-124454. 1970. 5.95 o.p. (ISBN 0-8298-0178-2). Pilgrim NY.

--The Contributions of Theology to Medical Ethics. (Pere Marquette Theology Lectures). 1975. 6.95 (ISBN 0-87462-507-6). Marquette.

--Theology & Christian Ethics. LC 74-510. 320p. 1974. 9.95 (ISBN 0-8298-0270-3). Pilgrim NY.

Gustafson, Jim. Shameless. 1979. pap. 4.00 (ISBN 0-686-28245-0). Tombouctou.

Gustafson, Milton O., ed. The National Archives & Foreign Relations Research. LC 74-82494. (National Archives Conferences Ser.: Vol. 4). xvii, 292p. 1974. 15.00x (ISBN 0-8214-0163-7). Ohio U Pr.

Gustafson, R. David & Frisk, Peter D. Elementary Plane Geometry. LC 72-5840. 320p. 1973. text ed. 17.95x (ISBN 0-471-33700-5); tchrs'. manual avail. (ISBN 0-471-33701-3). Wiley.

Gustafson, Robert J. Fundamentals of Electricity for Agriculture. (Illus.). 1980. pap. 16.50 (ISBN 0-87055-327-5). AVI.

Gustafson, Thane. Reform in Soviet Politics: The Lessons of Recent Policies on Land & Water. LC 80-24286. (Illus.). 224p. Date not set. price not set (ISBN 0-521-23377-1). Cambridge U Pr.

Gustafson, W. Eric, ed. Pakistan & Bangladesh: Bibliographic Essays in Social Science. 1976. 12.00x o.p. (ISBN 0-88386-794-X); text ed. 7.50x o.p. (ISBN 0-8364-0442-4). South Asia Bks.

Gustafsson, Lars. Warm Rooms & Cold. Sandstroem, Yvonne, tr. (Orig.). 1975. pap. 3.50 (ISBN 0-914278-05-3). Copper Beech.

Gustason, G. & Zaevolkow, E., eds. Using Signing Exact English in Total Communication. LC 80-84549. 62p. 1980. 4.50 (ISBN 0-916708-04-7). Modern Signs.

Gustason, Gerilee, ed. Using Signing Exact English in Total Communication: A Collection of Articles. LC 80-84549. (Illus.). 68p. (Orig.). 1980. pap. 4.50x (ISBN 0-916708-04-7). Modern Signs.

Gustason, Gerilee, et al. Signing Exact English: 1980 Edition. (Illus.). xix, 460p. (gr. k-12). 1980. 21.00 (ISBN 0-916708-02-0); pap. 16.00 (ISBN 0-916708-03-9). Modern Signs.

Gustaveson, David. Personal Life Notebook. 1980. pap. 8.95 spiral bdg. (ISBN 0-87123-467-X, 210467). Bethany Fell.

Gustavson, Bjorn & Hunius, Gerry. Improving the Quality of Life: The Case of Norway. 112p. 1981. pap. 25.00x (ISBN 82-00-05525-6). Universitet.

Gustavson, Carl G. The Institutional Drive: A Study in Pluralistic Democracy. LC 66-14029. 1966. 12.95x (ISBN 0-8214-0019-3). Ohio U Pr.

Gustavson, Frances & Sackson, Marian. Problem Solving in Basic: A Modular Approach. LC 78-21904. 1979. pap. text ed. 9.95 (ISBN 0-574-21240-X, 13-4240); instr's guide avail. (ISBN 0-574-21241-8, 13-4241). SRA.

Gustavus, Susan O., jt. auth. see Nam, Charles B.

Guste, Roy F., Jr. Antoine's Restaurant Cookbook. (Illus.). 1980. pap. 9.95 (ISBN 0-393-00027-3). Norton.

Gustin, Lawrence R. Billy Durant: Creator of General Motors. 1973. 8.95 o.p. (ISBN 0-8028-3435-3). Eerdmans.

Gustin, Lawrence R., jt. auth. see Dunham, Terry B.

Gutch, C. F. & Stoner, Martha H. Mosby's Review Series: Review of Hemodialysis for Nurses & Dialysis Personnel. 3rd ed. LC 79-16882. (Illus.). 1979. pap. text ed. 15.95 (ISBN 0-8016-1994-7). Mosby.

--Review of Hemodialysis for Nurses and Dialysis Personnel. 2nd ed. LC 75-4637. (Illus.). 1975. pap. 12.50 o.p. (ISBN 0-8016-1993-9). Mosby.

Gutcheon, Beth. The New Girls. 336p. 1981. pap. 2.50 (ISBN 0-380-50831-1, 50831). Avon.

--Still Missing. 252p. 1981. 10.95 (ISBN 0-399-12578-7). Putnam.

Gutcho, M. H. Microcapsules & Other Capsules: Advances Since 1975. LC 79-15917. (Chemical Technology Review Ser.: No. 135). (Illus.). 1980. 40.00 (ISBN 0-8155-0776-3). Noyes.

Gutcho, M. H., ed. Cement & Mortar Technology & Additives: Developments Since 1977. LC 80-19343. (Chemical Tech. Rev. 173). 540p. (Orig.). 1981. 54.00 (ISBN 0-8155-0822-0). Noyes.

--Inorganic Pigments: Manufacturing Processes. LC 80-16319. (Chemical Technology Review No. 166). 488p. 1980. 54.00 (ISBN 0-8155-0811-5). Noyes.

Gutcho, S. J. Surfactants & Sequestrants-Recent Advances. LC 77-72960. (Chemical Technology Review Ser.: No. 89). (Illus.). 1977. 39.00 o.p. (ISBN 0-8155-0661-9). Noyes.

Gutek, Gerald L. A History of the Western Educational Experience. 448p. 1972. text ed. 13.95x (ISBN 0-394-31355-0, RanC). Random.

--Philosophical Alternatives in Education. LC 73-76802. 1974. pap. 11.50x (ISBN 0-675-08926-3). Merrill.

Guter, Marvin & Serafini, Aldo. Chest Nuclear Medicine Case Studies. 1979. spiral bdg. 14.50 (ISBN 0-87488-083-1). Med Exam.

Guterbock, Hans G., jt. ed. see Hoffner, Harry A., Jr.

Guterman, Norbert, ed. see Schelling, Friedrich.

Guterman, Norbert, tr. see Raphael, Max.

Guterman, Norbert see Zuckerland, Victor.

Guterman, Simeon L. From Personal to Territorial Law: Aspects of the History & Structure of the Western Legal - Constitutional Tradition. 1972. 12.50 o.p. (ISBN 0-8108-0405-0). Scarecrow.

Gutfreund, H. Biochemical Evolution. 320p. Date not set. text ed. price not set (ISBN 0-521-23549-9); pap. text ed. price not set (ISBN 0-521-28025-7). Cambridge U Pr.

Gutfreund, H., et al. Felix Bloch & Twentieth Century Physics. Chodorow, M., et al, eds. (Rice University Studies: Vol. 66, No. 3). 247p. 1980. pap. 5.50x (ISBN 0-89263-246-1). Rice Univ.

Guth, Bernard. Be Your Own Television Repairman. new ed. LC 65-1629. (Illus.). 1965. pap. 1.95 o.p. (ISBN 0-8019-0370-X). Chilton.

Guth, DeLloyd J. & Wrone, David R.compiled By. The Assassination of John F. Kennedy: A Comprehensive Historical & Legal Bibliography, 1963-1979. LC 79-6184. (Illus.). lvi, 442p. 1980. lib. bdg. 37.50 (ISBN 0-313-21274-0, GJK/). Greenwood.

Guth, Hans P. Literature. 2nd ed. (Orig.). 1968. pap. 12.95x (ISBN 0-534-00667-1). Wadsworth Pub.

--Wadsworth English Workbook. 160p. 1980. pap. text ed. 5.95x (ISBN 0-534-00848-8). Wadsworth Pub.

--Words & Ideas. 5th ed. 528p. 1980. text ed. 11.95x (ISBN 0-534-00815-1). Wadsworth Pub.

--Words & Ideas: A Handbook for College Writing. 4th ed. 1975. 10.95x o.p. (ISBN 0-534-00371-0). Wadsworth Pub.

Guth, Hans P. & Schuster, Edgar H. Our Common Language. 3rd ed. (American English Today Ser.). (Illus.). 480p. (gr. 8). 1980. text ed. 10.88 (ISBN 0-07-025018-9, W); tchrs. manual 9.60 (ISBN 0-07-025028-6). McGraw.

Guth, Paul. Le Naif Aux Guarante Enfants. (Easy Readers, C). 1979. pap. 3.75 (ISBN 0-88436-294-9). EMC.

Guth, Phyllis. Crafts for Kids. LC 75-4287. 182p. (gr. 4-8). 1975. 7.95 (ISBN 0-8306-5766-5); pap. 6.95 (ISBN 0-8306-4766-X, 766). TAB Bks.

Guth, Phyllis & Goff, Georgeanna. Sewing with Scraps. (Illus.). (YA) (gr. 10 up). 1977. 8.95 (ISBN 0-8306-7878-6); pap. 5.95 (ISBN 0-8306-6878-0, 878). TAB Bks.

Guth de Lloyd, J. Late-Medieval England, 1377-1485. LC 75-23845. (Conference on British Studies Bibliographical Handbooks Ser.). 164p. 1976. 17.95 (ISBN 0-521-20877-7). Cambridge U Pr.

Guthean, Beth. Still Missing. 336p. 1981. 11.95 (ISBN 0-399-12578-7). Putnam.

Guthkelch, A. C., et. ed. see Swift, Jonathan.

Guthman, William, ed. Guns & Other Arms. (Illus.). 160p. 1980. pap. 7.95 (ISBN 0-8317-4182-1). Mayflower Bks.

Guthorn, Peter J. John Hills, Assistant Engineer: With a Collection of Plans of the Provinces of New Jersey. LC 76-1497. 1977. pap. text ed. 24.75 (ISBN 0-916762-01-7). Portolan.

Guthrie, A. B., Jr. The Big It & Other Stories. (Western Fiction Ser.). 1980. lib. bdg. 9.95 (ISBN 0-8398-2680-X). Gregg.

--The Last Valley. LC 75-17598. 304p. 1975. 8.95 o.s.i. (ISBN 0-395-21899-3). HM.

Guthrie, Andrew. Vacuum Technology. LC 63-20631. 1963. 36.95 (ISBN 0-471-33722-6, Pub. by Wiley-Interscience). Wiley.

Guthrie, Arlo. Arlo Guthrie Book. 1969. pap. 2.95 o.s.i. (ISBN 0-02-060680-X, Collier). Macmillan.

Guthrie, Art, et al. Accounting: The Canadian Scene. 144p. 1980. pap. text ed. 8.95 (ISBN 0-8403-2234-8). Kendall-Hunt.

Guthrie, D. M. Neuroethology: An Introduction. 200p. 1981. pap. 24.95x (ISBN 0-470-26993-6). Halsted Pr.

Guthrie, Diana W. & Guthrie, Richard A., eds. Nursing Management of Diabetes Mellitus. LC 76-27828. (Illus.). 1977. pap. 12.95 (ISBN 0-8016-1995-5). Mosby.

Guthrie, Donald. The Apostles. 432p. 1981. pap. 10.95 (ISBN 0-310-25421-3). Zondervan.

--New Bible Commentary. rev. ed. 1970. 19.95 (ISBN 0-8028-2281-9). Eerdmans.

--New Testament Theology. 1056p. 1981. text ed. 24.95 (ISBN 0-87784-965-X). Inter-Varsity.

--Shorter Life of Christ. LC 71-120039. (Contemporary Evangelical Perspectives Ser). 1970. kivar 4.95 (ISBN 0-310-25441-8). Zondervan.

Guthrie, E. R., tr. see Janet, Pierre.

Guthrie, H. M., tr. see Janet, Pierre.

Guthrie, Harvey H. Israel's Sacred Songs: A Study of Dominant Themes. 1978. pap. 4.95 (ISBN 0-8164-2178-1). Crossroad NY.

Guthrie, Helen. Introductory Nutrition. 4th ed. LC 78-16649. (Illus.). 1979. text ed. 19.95 (ISBN 0-8016-2001-5). Mosby.

Guthrie, Helen A. & Braddock, Karen S. Programmed Nutrition. 2nd ed. (Illus.). 1978. pap. text ed. 12.95 (ISBN 0-8016-2003-1). Mosby.

Guthrie, J. T., jt. auth. see Hebeisch, A.

Guthrie, Jack S., jt. auth. see Guthrie, Ruby C.

Guthrie, James W., ed. School Finance Policies & Practices: The Nineteen-Eighties: Decade of Conflict. 312p. 1981. 22.50 (ISBN 0-88410-195-9). Ballinger Pub.

Guthrie, Lorna & Mattinson, Janet. Brief Casework with a Marital Problem. 64p. 1971. 5.00x (ISBN 0-901882-03-8, CBO-901-I). Natl Assn Soc Wkrs.

Guthrie, Motyer, et al. Nuevo Comentario Bible. Orig. Title: The New Bible Commentary Revised. 136p. 1980. pap. 29.95 (ISBN 0-311-03001-7). Casa Bautista.

Guthrie, Ramon. Maximum Security Ward. 1970. 7.50 o.p. (ISBN 0-374-20468-3). FS&G.

Guthrie, Richard A., jt. ed. see Guthrie, Diana W.

Guthrie, Ruby C. & Guthrie, Jack S. A Primer for Pickles & a Reader for Relishes. LC 74-18029. (Illus.). 144p. 1974. 4.95 (ISBN 0-912238-53-4); pap. 4.95 (ISBN 0-912238-52-6). One Hund One Prods.

Guthrie, Rufus K. Food Sanitation. 1972. text ed. 21.50 o.p. (ISBN 0-87055-122-1). AVI.

--Food Sanitation. 2nd ed. (Illus.). 1980. lib. bdg. 21.50 (ISBN 0-87055-361-5). AVI.

Guthrie, Shirley C., tr. see Cullmann, Oscar.

Guthrie, Shirley C., Jr. Christian Doctrine: Teachings of the Christian Church. (Orig.). 1969. pap. 5.95 (ISBN 0-8042-9051-2). John Knox.

Guthrie, W. K. Greek Philosophers: From Thales to Aristotle. pap. 3.95x (ISBN 0-06-131008-5, TB 1008, Torch). Har-Row.

--A History of Greek Philosophy, 5 vols. LC 62-52735. 1975. 68.50 ea. Vol. 1 (ISBN 0-521-05159-2). Vol. 2 (ISBN 0-521-05160-6). Vol. 3 (ISBN 0-521-07566-1). Vol. 4 (ISBN 0-521-20002-4). Vol. 5 (ISBN 0-521-20003-2). Cambridge U Pr.

Guthrie, W. K., tr. see Plato.

Guthrie, William. The Christian's Guide Great Interest. pap. 1.95 o.p. (ISBN 0-686-12510-X). Banner of Truth.

Guthrie, William K. Socrates. 1971. pap. 9.95x (ISBN 0-521-09667-7). Cambridge U Pr.

--Sophists. 1971. pap. 11.50x (ISBN 0-521-09666-9). Cambridge U Pr.

Guthrie, William K., ed. see Cornford, Francis M.

Guthrie, Woody. Bound for Glory. LC 68-28884. 441p. 1976. 10.95 o.p. (ISBN 0-525-07025-7). Dutton.

Gutierrez, Edna L., tr. see Mandeville, Sylvia.

Gutierrez, Edna L., tr. see Mandeville, Sylvia & Pierson, Lance.

Gutierrez, Rolando. El Mensaje De los Salmos En Nuestro Contexto, Tomo II. 1980. pap. 4.45 (ISBN 0-311-04025-X). Casa Bautista.

Gutierrez, Rolando C. Mensaje De los Salmos, Tomo III. 160p. 1981. pap. write for info. (ISBN 0-311-04028-4). Casa Bautista.

--El Mensaje de los Salmos en Nuestro Contexto Tomo I. 1979. 4.45 (ISBN 0-311-04023-3). Casa Bautista.

Gutierrez De La Solana, A. Maneras De Narrar: Contraste De Lino Novas Calvo y Alfonso Hernandez Cata. 1972. 10.95 (ISBN 0-88303-017-9); pap. 8.95 (ISBN 0-685-73219-3). E Torres & Sons.

Gutkind, Erwin A. International History of City Development, 8 vols. Incl. Vol. 1. Urban Development in Central Europe. 1964 (ISBN 0-02-913250-9); Vol. 2. Urban Development in Alpine & Scandinavian Countries. 1965 (ISBN 0-02-913260-6); Vol. 3. Urban Development in Southern Europe; Spain & Portugal. 1967 (ISBN 0-02-913270-3); Vol. 4. Urban Development in Southern Europe; Italy & Greece. 1969 (ISBN 0-02-913280-0); Vol. 5. Urban Development in Western Europe; France & Belgium. 1970 (ISBN 0-02-913300-9); Vol. 6. Urban Development in Western Europe: The Netherlands & Great Britain. 1971 (ISBN 0-02-913310-6); Vol. 7. Urban Development in East-Central Europe: Poland, Czechoslavia, & Hungary. 1972 (ISBN 0-02-913320-3); Vol. 8. Urban Development in Eastern Europe: Bulgaria, Romania, & U.S.S.R. 1972 (ISBN 0-02-913330-0). LC 64-13231. 45.00 ea. Free Pr.

Gutkind, G., ed. African Social Studies. 1979. 24.50 o.p. (ISBN 0-685-67796-6). Porter.

Gutkind, Peter C., jt. auth. see Jongmans, D. G.

Gutman, Assia, tr. see Amichai, Yehuda.

Gutman, Bill. Gamebreakers of the NFL. (NFL Punt, Pass & Kick Library: No. 18). (Illus.). (gr. 5 up). 1973. 2.50 o.p. (ISBN 0-394-82501-2, BYR); PLB 3.69 (ISBN 0-394-92501-7). Random.

--More Modern Women Superstars. LC 78-22433. (High Interest-Low Vocabulary Ser.). (Illus.). (gr. 4 up). 1979. 5.95 (ISBN 0-396-07680-7). Dodd.

--The Picture Life of Reggie Jackson. (Illus.). (gr. 1 up). 1978. pap. 1.75 (ISBN 0-380-40345-5, 51631, Camelot). Avon.

--Pro Sports Champions. (Illus.). 192p. 1981. PLB price not set (ISBN 0-671-34028-X). Messner.

Gutman, Bill, ed. see Brewster, Benjamin.

Gutman, Stanley T. Mankind in Barbary: The Individual & Society in the Novels of Norman Mailer. LC 75-18290. 238p. 1975. text ed. 15.00x (ISBN 0-87451-118-6). U Pr of New Eng.

Gutmann, F. Metric Guide to Mechanical Design & Drafting. (Illus.). 1978. 12.00 (ISBN 0-8311-1122-4). Indus Pr.

Gutmann, James, tr. see Schelling, Friedrich W.

Gutmann, Joseph, ed. The Dura-Europos Synagogue: A Re-Evaluation 1932-1972. LC 73-85879. (American Academy of Religion & Society of Biblical Literature. Religion & the Arts Ser.). (Illus.). 1973. 9.00 (ISBN 0-89130-329-4, 090101). Scholars Pr Ca.

--The Image & the Word. LC 77-23470. (American Academy of Religion & Society of Biblical Literature. Religion & the Arts Ser.: Vol. 4). 1977. 9.00 (ISBN 0-89130-142-9, 090104); pap. 7.50 (ISBN 0-89130-143-7). Scholars Pr Ca.

--The Temple of Solomon: Archaeological Fact & Medieval Tradition in Christian, Islamic & Jewish Art. LC 75-19120. 1976. 9.00 (ISBN 0-89130-013-9, 090103). Scholars Pr Ca.

Gutmann, Myron P. War & Rural Life in the Early Modern Low Countries. 322p. 1980. text ed. 34.25 (ISBN 90-232-1740-3). Humanities.

Gutmann, P. T., jt. auth. see Lomax, D. F.

Gutmann, Viktor, ed. International Review of Halogen Chemistry, 3 Vols. LC 66-30147. (Illus.). Vol. 1, 1967. 64.50 (ISBN 0-12-310901-9); Vol. 2, 1967. 66.00 (ISBN 0-12-310902-7); Vol. 3, 1968. 64.50 (ISBN 0-12-310903-5). Acad Pr.

Gutnik, Martin J. Ecology & Pollution - Air. (First Experiments in Science & Nature Ser.). (Illus.). 48p. (gr. 2-4). 1973. PLB 7.95 o.p. (ISBN 0-516-00522-7). Childrens.

--How to Do a Science Project & Report. (gr. 7 up). 1980. PLB 6.45 (ISBN 0-531-04129-8). Watts.

Gutnov, Alexei. The Ideal Communist City. LC 75-129358. (I Press Ser). 1970. 6.95 o.p. (ISBN 0-8076-0576-X); pap. 2.95 o.p. (ISBN 0-8076-0575-1). Braziller.

Gutowski, Michael & Koshel, Jeffrey. Methods for Assessing Age Discrimination in Federal Programs. (An Institute Paper). 69p. 1977. pap. 3.50 (ISBN 0-87766-209-6, 20400). Urban Inst.

Gutrick, Martin J. Science of Classification: Finding Order Among Living & Nonliving Objects. (gr. 4 up). 1980. PLB 6.45 (ISBN 0-531-04160-3). Watts.

Gutridge, D. Foster, II. Your Secret Power: Creating Happiness, Vol. 2. (Your Secret Power Ser.). 96p. (Orig.). 1981. pap. 5.95 (ISBN 0-938014-02-1, 1001B). Freedom Unltd.

--Your Secret Power: Creating Harmony with Others, Vol. 4. 96p. (Orig.). 1981. pap. 5.95 (ISBN 0-938014-04-8, 301D). Freedom Unltd.

--Your Secret Power: Creating Love, Vol. 3. (Your Secret Power Ser.). 96p. (Orig.). 1981. pap. 5.95 (ISBN 0-938014-03-X, 2001C). Freedom Unltd.

--Your Secret Power: Creating Riches, Vol. 1. LC 80-69710. (Your Secret Power Ser.). 80p. (Orig.). 1980. pap. 5.95 (ISBN 0-938014-01-3, 901A). Freedom Unltd.

Gutsch, Kenneth U. & Ritenour, Jacob V. Nexus Psychotherapy: Between Humanism & Behaviorism. (Illus.). 196p. 1978. 19.75 (ISBN 0-398-03734-5). C C Thomas.

Gutsche, C. David & Pasto, Daniel G. Fundamentals of Organic Chemistry. (Illus.). 1248p. 1975. 26.95 (ISBN 0-13-333443-0); solutions manual 4.95 (ISBN 0-13-333435-X). P-H.

Gutta. Cold Platters-Cold Buffets. 1981. 8.95 (ISBN 0-8120-5400-8). Barron.

Guttchen, Robert S. Felix Adler. LC 73-15952. (World Leaders Ser.: No. 32). 1974. lib. bdg. 10.95 (ISBN 0-8057-3650-6). Twayne.

Guttentag, Marcia, jt. ed. see Struening, Elmer L.

Gutterridge, Reg. Boxing: The Great Ones. 1975. 8.95 o.p. (ISBN 0-686-26632-3, Pub. by Michael Joseph). Merrimack Bk Serv.

Gutting, Gary, ed. Paradigms & Revolutions: Appraisals & Applications of Thomas Kuhn's Philosophy of Science. LC 80-20745. 256p. 1980. text ed. 18.95 (ISBN 0-268-01542-2); pap. text ed. 7.95 (ISBN 0-268-01543-0). U of Notre Dame Pr.

Guttmacher, A. see Sanger, Margaret.

Guttman, Michael. Experiments for Chemistry: 1046L. 1976. coil bdg. 3.75 (ISBN 0-88252-047-4). Paladin Hse.

Guttmann, Allen. Freedom & Authority in Puritan New England. Brown, Richard H. & Halsey, Van R., eds. (Amherst Project Units in American History). (gr. 11-12). 1970. pap. text ed. 4.52 (ISBN 0-201-02666-X, Sch Div); tchr's manual 1.92 (ISBN 0-201-02668-6). A-W.

--From Ritual to Record: The Nature of Modern Sports. (Illus.). 1979. pap. 6.00x (ISBN 0-231-08369-6). Columbia U Pr.

--From Ritual to Record: The Nature of Modern Sport. LC 77-20886. (Illus.). 1978. 17.50 (ISBN 0-231-03993-X). Columbia U Pr.

--Wound in the Heart. LC 62-15342. 1962. 8.95 o.s.i. (ISBN 0-02-913290-8). Free Pr.

Guttmann, Allen, ed. see Rigauer, Bero.

Guttsman, W. L. The German Social Democratic Party 1875-1933. (Illus.). 1981. text ed. 40.00x (ISBN 0-04-943024-6, 2613). Allen Unwin.

Gutwirth, Madelyn, et al, eds. Sources et Reflets De l'Histoire De France. (Illus., Fr). 1972. pap. text ed. 7.95x (ISBN 0-19-501465-0). Oxford U Pr.

Gutwirth, Marcel. Stendhal. (World Authors Ser.: France: No. 174). lib. bdg. 12.50 (ISBN 0-8057-2862-7). Twayne.

Gutzke, Manford G. Plain Talk on Genesis. 160p. 1975. pap. 3.95 (ISBN 0-310-25531-7). Zondervan.

--Plain Talk on Isaiah. 1977. pap. 5.95 (ISBN 0-310-25551-1). Zondervan.

--Plain Talk on Leviticus & Numbers. 144p. 1981. pap. 4.95 (ISBN 0-310-41951-4, 9872P). Zondervan.

--Plain Talk on Luke. 1966. pap. 3.95 (ISBN 0-310-25581-3). Zondervan.

--Plain Talk on Philippians. 288p. 1973. pap. 5.95 (ISBN 0-310-25611-9). Zondervan.

--Plain Talk on the Minor Prophets. (Plain Talk Ser. of Bible Study Bks.). 160p. (Orig.). 1980. pap. 3.95 (ISBN 0-310-41941-7, 9868P). Zondervan.

Guunning, Susannah Minnifie. Barford Abbey, 1768, 2 vols. in 1. Shugrue, Michael F., ed. (The Flowering of the Novel, 1740-1775 Ser: Vol. 83). 1974. lib. bdg. 50.00 (ISBN 0-8240-1182-1). Garland Pub.

Guy, Albert G. & Hren, John J. Elements of Physical Metallurgy. 3rd ed. LC 72-9315. 1974. text ed. 25.95 (ISBN 0-201-02633-3). A-W.

Guy, Clifford M. Retail Location & Retail Planning in Britain. 208p. 1980. text ed. 30.00x (ISBN 0-566-00270-1, Pub. by Gower Pub Co England). Renouf.

Guy, Dan M. Statistical Sampling in Auditing. LC 80-17279. (Wiley Series in Accounting & Info. Systems). 224p. 1981. text ed. 17.95 (ISBN 0-471-04232-3). Wiley.

Guy, Edward T. & Merrigan, John J. Forms for Safety & Security Management. 448p. 1980. text ed. 28.95 (ISBN 0-409-95089-0). Butterworths.

Guy, Gary V. Easy to Make Candles. (Illus.). 1980. pap. 2.00 (ISBN 0-486-23881-4). Dover.

Guy, J. A. The Public Career of Sir Thomas More. LC 80-5391. 224p. 1980. 22.50x (ISBN 0-300-02546-7). Yale U Pr.

Guy, James. Metasphere: The Altered State of Word. LC 80-83463. (Illus.). 137p. (Orig.). 1980. pap. 7.00 (ISBN 0-9604918-7-2). Lampkin Pub.

Guy, Julia. Human Anatomy: Introductory Laboratory Guide. 1980. wire coil bdg. 7.95 (ISBN 0-88252-091-1). Paladin Hse.

Guy, Maxine, jt. auth. see Hickman, Mae.

Guy, May & Gilbert, Miriam. A Doctor Discusses the Care & Development of Your Baby. (Illus.). 1979. pap. 2.50 (ISBN 0-685-56949-7). Budlong.

Guy, N. G., ed. see Eighth International Conference on Fluid Sealing.

Guy, P. K., jt. auth. see Armstrong, L.

Guy, Rebecca, jt. auth. see Allen, Donald.

Guy, Rosa. Mirror of Her Own. LC 80-69448. 192p. (YA) (gr. 8-12). 1981. 8.95 (ISBN 0-440-05513-X). Delacorte.

--Mother Crocodile: An Uncle Amadou Tale from Senegal. LC 80-393. (Illus.). 32p. (gr. k-2). 1981. 10.95 (ISBN 0-440-06405-8); PLB 10.42 (ISBN 0-440-06406-6). Delacorte.

Guy, W. A; see Bucknill, John C.

Guyatt, John. The American Revolution. Yapp, Malcolm, et al, eds. (World History Ser.). (Illus.). 32p. (gr. 10). 1980. Repr. of 1977 ed. lib. bdg. 5.95 (ISBN 0-89908-135-5); pap. text ed. 1.95 (ISBN 0-89908-110-X). Greenhaven.

--Ancient America. Killingray, Margaret, et al, eds. (World History Ser.). (Illus.). 32p. (gr. 10). 1980. Repr. of 1977 ed. lib. bdg. 5.95 (ISBN 0-89908-033-2); pap. text ed. 1.95 (ISBN 0-89908-008-1). Greenhaven.

--Bolivar. Yapp, Malcolm, et al, eds. (World History Ser.). (Illus.). 32p. (gr. 10). 1980. lib. bdg. 5.95 (ISBN 0-89908-045-6); pap. text ed. 1.95 (ISBN 0-89908-020-0). Greenhaven.

Guyer, Kenneth E., jt. auth. see Seibel, Hugo.

Guynn, Denise, ed. The Crow & the Pitcher. (Aesop's Fables Bk). (Illus.). 16p. (ps). 1980. pap. 22.00 ten bks. & one cass. (ISBN 0-89290-077-6, BC14-5). Soc for Visual.

Guynn, Denise W., ed. The Boy Who Cried Wolf. (Aesop's Fable Bk). (Illus.). 16p. (ps). 1980. pap. 22.00 ten bks & one cass. (ISBN 0-89290-076-8, BC14-4). Soc for Visual.

--The Fox & the Grapes. (Aesop's Fables Bk). (Illus.). 16p. (ps). 1980. pap. 22.00 ten bks & one cass. (ISBN 0-89290-075-X, BC14-3). Soc for Visual.

Guyol, N. B. The World Electric Power Industry. 1969. 60.00x (ISBN 0-520-01484-7). U of Cal Pr.

Guyon, Madame. Selections from the Autobiography of Madam Guyon. Hutchinson, Warner A., ed. Allen, Thomas T., tr. from Fr. LC 80-82324. (Shepherd Classic Ser.). 1980. pap. 5.95 (ISBN 0-87983-234-7). Keats.

Guyon, Y. Limit-State Design of Prestressed Concrete, Vol. 2: The Design of the Member. Turner, F. H., tr. from Fr. LC 72-2655. 469p. 1974. 52.95 (ISBN 0-470-33791-5). Halsted Pr.

Guyot, J. Atlas of Human Limb Joints. (Illus.). 252p. 1981. 146.30 (ISBN 0-387-10380-5). Springer-Verlag.

Guyot, James F., jt. ed. see Wriggins, W. Howard.

Guyton, Arthur C. Basic Human Physiology: Normal Function & Mechanisms of Disease. 2nd ed. LC 76-4248. (Illus.). 1977. text ed. 22.50 (ISBN 0-7216-4383-3). Saunders.

Guyton, Arthur C., et al. Circulatory Physiology Two: Dynamics & Control of the Body Fluids. LC 74-24844. (Illus.). 397p. 1975. text ed. 27.50 (ISBN 0-7216-4361-2). Saunders.

Guyton, Emma J. W. The Wife's Trials; or, Lilian Grey, Repr. Of 1858 Ed. Wolff, Robert L., ed. Bd. with Married Life. Repr. of 1863 ed; Husbands & Wives. Repr. of 1873 ed. LC 75-492. (Victorian Fiction Ser.). 1975. lib. bdg. 66.00 (ISBN 0-8240-1568-1). Garland Pub.

Guze, Samuel B. Criminality & Psychiatric Disorders. 176p. 1976. text ed. 10.95x (ISBN 0-19-501973-3). Oxford U Pr.

Guzie, Tad. Confession for Today's Catholic. (Illus.). 24p. 1977. pap. 0.25 o.p. (ISBN 0-89570-099-9). Claretian Pubns.

Guzman, Maria O. Tagalog-English - English-Tagalog Dictionary. rev. ed. xxxix, 678p. 1977. pap. 12.50 (ISBN 0-686-68939-9). Heinman.

Guzman, Martin L. The Eagle & the Serpent. De Onis, Harriet, tr. 6.50 (ISBN 0-8446-0668-5). Peter Smith.

Gvishiani, J., ed. Science, Technology & Global Problems: Proceedings of the Symposium on the Role of Science & Technology in Solving Global Problems, Tallinn, USSR, Jan 1979. LC 79-40546. 1979. 82.00 (ISBN 0-08-024469-6). Pergamon.

Gwaltney, John L. Thrice Shy: Cultural Accommodation to Blindness & Other Disasters in a Mexican Community. LC 71-118635. 1970. 20.00x (ISBN 0-231-03237-4). Columbia U Pr.

Gwartney, James D. Economics: Private & Public Choice. 1976. 15.95 o.p. (ISBN 0-12-311050-5); coursebook 5.95 o.p. (ISBN 0-12-311051-3). Acad Pr.

--Macroeconomics: Private & Public Choice. 1977. text ed. 10.50 o.p. (ISBN 0-12-311060-2). Acad Pr.

--Microeconomics: Private & Public Choice. 1977. 10.50 o.p. (ISBN.0-12-311065-3). Acad Pr.

--Microeconomics: Public & Private Sector Choice. 2nd ed. 1980. 12.95 (ISBN 0-12-311070-X). Acad Pr.

Gwartney, James D. & Stroup, Richard. Economics: Private & Public Choice. 1980. 19.95 (ISBN 0-12-311040-8); instrs'. manual & test bank 3.00 (ISBN 0-12-311055-6). Test Bank (ISBN 0-12-311043-2). Acad Pr.

--Macroeconomics: Private & Public Choice. 2nd ed. 1980. pap. text ed. 12.95 (ISBN 0-12-311070-X). Acad Pr.

Gwartney, James D., et al. Coursebook for Economics: Private & Public Choice. 2nd ed. 1980. 7.95 (ISBN 0-12-311054-8). Acad Pr.

Gwatkin, Davidson R. A Population Strategy for the Nineteen Eighties: Health, Mortality, & Development. 224p. 1981. write for info. Overseas Dev Council.

Gwinner, M. P. Origin of the Upper Jurassic Limestones of the Swabian Alb (Southwest Germany) Fuechtbauer, H., ed. (Contributions to Sedimentology Ser.: Vol. 5). (Illus.). 75p. (Orig.). 1976. pap. 37.50x (ISBN 3-510-57005-7). Intl Pubns Serv.

Gwinner, Paul, jt. auth. see Grant, Marcus.

Gwinner, Robert F., et al. Marketing: An Environmental Perspective. (Illus.). 1977. text ed. 18.50 (ISBN 0-8299-0119-1); instrs.' manual avail. (ISBN 0-8299-0484-0). West Pub.

Gwyer, M., tr. see Cocchia, Aldo.

Gwynn, Aubrey. Medieval Province of Armagh, Fourteen Seventy-Fifteen Forty-Five. 1949. 8.50 (ISBN 0-85221-022-1). Dufour.

Gwynn, Frederick L. Sturge Moore & the Life of Art. 159p. 1980. Repr. of 1952 ed. lib. bdg. 30.00 (ISBN 0-89984-249-6). Century Bookbindery.

Gwynn, Frederick L. & Blotner, Joseph L., eds. Faulkner in the University: Class Conferences at the University of Virginia, 1957-1958. LC 59-13713. (Illus.). 1977. Repr. of 1959 ed. 13.95x (ISBN 0-8139-0843-4). U Pr of Va.

Gwynn, Mary. Love, Mary. LC 80-24996. 224p. 1981. price not set (ISBN 0-688-00429-6). Morrow.

Gwynne, G. V., jt. auth. see Miller, E. J.

Gwynne, H. A., intro. by. The Cause of World Unrest. 1978. pap. 5.00x (ISBN 0-911038-40-X). Noontide.

Gwynne, Michael. Sequence Dancing. 17.95x (ISBN 0-392-06935-0, LTB). Soccer.

Gwynne, Walker. The Christian Year; Its Purpose & Its History. LC 74-89269. xiv, 143p. 1972. Repr. of 1917 ed. 20.00 (ISBN 0-8103-3814-9). Gale.

Gyatso, Geshe. Meaningful to Behold. Landaw, Jonathan, ed. Norbu, Tenzin, tr. from Tibetan. 365p. (Orig.). 1981. pap. 12.95 (ISBN 0-86171-003-7). Great Eastern.

Gyatso, Tenzin. The Buddhism of Tibet & the Key to the Middle Way. (Wisdom of Tibet Ser.). 1975. pap. 6.95 (ISBN 0-04-294087-7). Allen Unwin.

Gyftopoulos, E. P., jt. auth. see Hatsopoulos, G. N.

Gynther, R. S. Accounting for Price Level Changes. 1966. 13.75 (ISBN 0-08-011712-0); pap. 10.75 (ISBN 0-08-011711-2). Pergamon.

Gyorffy, G. Systeme Des Residences D'hiver et D'ete Chez les Nomades et les Chefs Hongrois Au Xe Siecle. (Pdr Press Publications in Early Hungarian History: No. 2). (Illus.). 1976. pap. text ed. 14.00x (ISBN 90-316-0098-9). Humanities.

Gyorgy, Andrew & Kuhlman, James A., eds. Innovation in Communist Systems. LC 77-29048. (Westview Special Studies on the Soviet Union & Eastern Europe Ser.). 1978. lib. bdg. 24.50x (ISBN 0-89158-418-8). Westview.

Gyorgy, Paul & Burgess, Anne, eds. Protecting the Pre-School Child. 1965. 4.50 o.p. (ISBN 0-685-14254-X). Lippincott.

Gyorgy, Paul see Sebrell, W. H., Jr. & Harris, Robert S.

Gyorgyey, Clara. Ferenc Molnar. (World Author Ser.--Hungary: No. 574). 1980. lib. bdg. 13.95 (ISBN 0-8057-6416-X). Twayne.

Gyory, Richard A. The Emergence of Being: Through Indian & Greek Thought. LC 78-70692. 1978. pap. text ed. 9.50 (ISBN 0-8191-0646-1). U Pr of Amer.

Gysbers, N. & Moore, E. Improving Guidance Programs. 1981. 12.95 (ISBN 0-13-452656-2). P-H.

Gytenbeek, G. P. Van see Van Gytenbeek, G. P.

Gyure, Gerald A. The Colorado Report. LC 80-83983. (Illus.). 144p. (Orig.). 1981. pap. 6.95 (ISBN 0-938354-01-9). Hi Country Pubs.

Gywnn, Stephen L. Thomas Moore. 204p. 1980. Repr. of 1905 ed. lib. bdg. 22.50 (ISBN 0-8495-2045-2). Arden Lib.

Gzowski, Peter. The Sacrament. LC 80-51208. 1980. 9.95 (ISBN 0-689-11114-2). Atheneum.

H

H. Clarkson, Ltd., ed. The Bulk Carrier Register 1979. 11th ed. LC 71-462684. (Illus.). 1979. 160.00x (ISBN 0-8002-2203-2). Intl Pubns Serv.

H. F. M. A. Staff. Patient Account Management Techniques. 1976. 8.50 (ISBN 0-930228-01-4, 1443). Hospital Finan.

H, G. D. & Cole, Margaret. The Murder at Crome Hous. 1976. lib. bdg. 13.95x (ISBN 0-89968-167-0). Lightyear.

Ha, Tri T. see Tri T. Ha.

Ha, W. H. & Hallward, C. L. A Pictorial World History. (Illus.). 1973. Bk. 1. pap. 6.00x (ISBN 0-582-67039-X); Bk. 2. pap. 7.00x (ISBN 0-582-67040-3); Bk. 3. pap. 7.75x (ISBN 0-582-67041-1). Longman.

Haab, Armin & Haettenschweiler, Walter. Lettera 3. LC 60-50012. (Visual Communication Bks.). 1968. pap. 24.00 o.p. (ISBN 0-8038-4231-7). Hastings.

Haab, Armin & Hattenschweiler, Walter. Lettera 4. (Visual Communication Bks.). 1972. pap. 25.00 o.p. (ISBN 0-8038-4282-1). Hastings.

Haab, Armin, et al. Lettera 1. (Visual Communication Bks.). 1960. pap. 24.00 o.p. (ISBN 0-8038-4233-3). Hastings.

Haab, Armin, et al, eds. Lettera 2. (Visual Communication Bks.). (Illus., Eng.,.). 1961. pap. 24.00 o.p. (ISBN 0-8038-4232-5). Hastings.

Haac, Oscar A. Marivaux. (World Authors Ser.: France: No. 294). 1974. lib. bdg. 10.95 (ISBN 0-8057-2593-8). Twayne.

Haac, Oscar A. & Bieler, Arthur. Actualite et Avenir: A Guide to France & to French Conversation. LC 74-30489. (Illus.). 256p. 1975. pap. text ed. 9.50 (ISBN 0-13-003855-5). P-H.

Haack, Herman. Oriental Rugs. 12.25 o.p. (ISBN 0-8231-3012-6). Branford.

Haack, Hermann. Oriental Rugs. (Illus.). 1960. 14.95 o.p. (ISBN 0-571-07018-3, Pub. by Faber & Faber). Merrimack Bk Serv.

Haack, Susan. Deviant Logic. LC 74-76949. 208p. 1975. 23.95 (ISBN 0-521-20500-X). Cambridge U Pr.

--Philosophy of Logics. LC 77-17071. (Illus.). 1978. 42.00 (ISBN 0-521-21988-4); pap. 10.95x (ISBN 0-521-29329-4). Cambridge U Pr.

Haack, W. & Wendland, W. Lectures on Partial & Pfaffian Differential Equations. 1972. 86.00 (ISBN 0-08-016553-2); pap. 25.00 (ISBN 0-08-018997-0). Pergamon.

--Vorlesungen Uber Partielle und Pfaffsche Diggerentialgleichungen. (Mathematische Reihe Ser.: No. 39). (Illus.). 555p. (Ger.). 1969. 73.50 (ISBN 3-7643-0159-7). Birkhauser.

Haaften, Julia Van see Frith, Francis.

Haag, J., ed. see Coan, James S.

Haag, Michael Von see Von Haag, Michael.

Haag, Michael Von see Von Haag, Michael & Crew, Anna.

Haag, Vincent H., et al. Elementary Geometry. 1970. text ed. 14.95 (ISBN 0-201-02658-9); instructor's manual 2.00 (ISBN 0-201-02659-7). A-W.

Haaga, John & Reich, Norbert E. Computed Tomography of Abdominal Abnormalities. LC 77-20661. (Illus.). 1978. 52.50 (ISBN 0-8016-2006-6). Mosby.

Haagen, C. Hess. Venturing Beyond the Campus: Students Who Leave College. LC 77-2541. 1977. pap. 10.00 (ISBN 0-8195-8027-9, Pub. by Wesleyan U Pr); pap. 5.00x o.p. (ISBN 0-685-79916-6). Columbia U Pr.

Haak, B., jt. auth. see Munnz, Ludwig.

Haak, Bob. Rembrandt. (Illus.). 1981. pap. 2.95 (ISBN 0-8120-2103-7). Barron.

Haaker, Ann, ed. see Brome, Richard.

Haakonsen, Daniel. Contemporary Approaches to Ibsen, Vol. II. (Ibsen Yearbook). 210p. 1980. 22.00x (ISBN 82-00-01937-3). Universitet.

Haal, Bob. Rembrandt: His Life, His Work, His Times. 125.00 (ISBN 0-8109-4750-1). Abrams.

Haam, Emmerich Von see Von Haam, Emmerich.

Haan, C. T. Statistical Methods in Hydrology. 1977. text ed. 13.50 (ISBN 0-8138-1510-X). Iowa St U Pr.

Haan, Charles T., jt. ed. see De Vore, R. William.

Haan, Enno R., jt. auth. see Carpenter, Allan.

Haan, Marina N. & Hammerstrom, Richard B. Graffiti in the Big Ten. 164p. (Orig.). 1980. pap. 3.95 (ISBN 0-9604534-0-7). Brown Hse Gall.

Haan, Martin R. De see De Haan, Martin R.

Haan, Martin R. De see De Haan, Martin R. & Bosch, H. G.

Haar, Charles M. Land-Use Planning: A Casebook on the Use, Misuse, & Re-Use of Urban Land. 1980. pap. 5.95 suppl. (ISBN 0-316-33681-5). Little.

Haar, D. Ter see Kapitza, P. L.

Haar, D. Ter see Ter Haar, D.

Haar, D. Ter, tr. see Ginzberg, V. L.

Haar, James, ed. see Gero, Ihan.

Haar, Jerry. The Politics of Higher Education in Brazil. LC 75-23967. 1977. text ed. 19.95 o.p. (ISBN 0-275-55630-1). Praeger.

Haard, Karen & Haard, Richard. Foraging for Edible Wild Mushrooms. rev. ed. (Illus.). 1978. lib. bdg. 11.95 (ISBN 0-88930-015-1, Pub. by Cloudburst Canada); pap. 5.95 (ISBN 0-88930-017-8). Madrona Pubs.

Haard, Karen, jt. auth. see Haard, Richard.

Haard, Norman F. & Salunkhe, D. K. Postharvest Biology & Handling of Fruits & Vegetables. (Illus.). 1975. text ed. 27.50 (ISBN 0-87055-187-6). AVI.

Haard, Richard & Haard, Karen. Poisonous & Hallucinogenic Mushrooms. 2nd ed. (Illus.). 164p. 1980. pap. 7.95 (ISBN 0-930180-05-4). Homestead Bk.

--Poisonous & Hallucinogenic Mushrooms. 2nd ed. (Illus.). 1977. lib. bdg. 11.95 (ISBN 0-88930-014-3, Pub. by Cloudburst Canada); pap. 5.95 (ISBN 0-88930-018-6, Pub. by Cloudburst Canada). Madrona Pubs.

Haard, Richard, jt. auth. see Haard, Karen.

Haarmann, Betsy S., jt. auth. see Greelis, Michael T.

Haas, Alfred. Industrial Electronics: Principles & Practice. LC 78-178690. 10.95d (ISBN 0-8306-1583-0, 583). TAB Bks.

Haas, Ben. House of Christina. 1981. pap. 2.95 (ISBN 0-440-13793-4). Dell.

Haas, C., et al. Translators Handbook on the Letters of John. (Helps for Translators Ser.). 1979. Repr. of 1972 ed. softcover 1.90 (ISBN 0-686-14401-5, 08516). United Bible.

Haas, Carolyn, et al. Backyard Vacation: Outdoor Fun in Your Own Neighborhood. (Illus.). 116p. (gr. 3-6). 1980. 9.95 (ISBN 0-316-33686-6); pap. 5.95 (ISBN 0-316-33685-8). Little.

Haas, Carolyn B. The Big Book of Recipes for Fun: Creative Learning Activities for Home and School. (Illus.). 288p. (Orig.). 1980. pap. 10.95 (ISBN 0-914090-95-X). Chicago Review.

Haas, Charles G. & Pennsylvania State Univ. Chemistry Dept. Experimental Chemistry: Laboratory Manual for Chemistry 14. 1978. pap. text ed. 4.50 (ISBN 0-8403-1913-4). Kendall-Hunt.

Haas, Charlie & Hunter, Tim. The Soul Hit. LC 76-26269. (Harper Novel of Suspense). 1977. 7.95 o.p. (ISBN 0-06-011708-7, HarpT). Har-Row.

Haas, Chuck. Rhymes O' a Driftin' Cowboy. LC 75-110942. 1970. 7.50 o.p. (ISBN 0-87358-048-6). Northland.

Haas, David F. Interaction in the Thai Bureaucracy: Structure, Culture, & Social Exchange. (A Westview Replica Edition Ser.). (Illus.). 1979. lib. bdg. 22.00x (ISBN 0-89158-578-8). Westview.

Haas, Dorothy. The Bears Upstairs. LC 78-54683. (gr. 5-9). 1978. 7.95 (ISBN 0-688-80169-2); PLB 7.63 (ISBN 0-688-84169-4). Greenwillow.

--The Bears Upstairs. (gr. k-6). 1981. pap. 1.75 (ISBN 0-440-40448-7, YB). Dell.

--Poppy & the Outdoors Cat. Tucker, Kathleen, ed. (Illus.). 100p. (gr. 2-5). 1981. 5.95g (ISBN 0-8075-6621-7). A Whitman.

Haas, Elson. Staying Healthy with the Seasons. LC 80-69469. (Illus.). 192p. (Orig.). 1981. pap. 9.95 (ISBN 0-89087-306-2). Celestial Arts.

Haas, Ernst B. Global Evangelism Rides Again: How to Protect Human Rights Without Really Trying. LC 78-620023. (Policy Papers in International Affairs Ser.: No. 5). 1978. pap. 2.50x (ISBN 0-87725-505-9). U of Cal Intl St.

Haas, Ernst B., et al. Scientists & World Order: The Uses of Technical Knowledge in International Organizations. 1978. 23.75x (ISBN 0-520-03341-8). U of Cal Pr.

Haas, Harold I. Pastoral Counseling with People in Distress. LC 77-99316. 1969. pap. 6.50 (ISBN 0-570-03794-8, 12-2776). Concordia.

Haas, Irvin. America's Historic Inns & Taverns. rev. ed. LC 76-45410. (Illus.). 1977. 8.95 o.p. (ISBN 0-668-04189-7). Arco.

Haas, J., jt. auth. see Chen Chih-Fan.

Haas, J. Eugene, et al. Reconstruction Following Disaster. LC 77-23176. (Mit Press Environmental Studies Ser). 1977. text ed. 23.00x (ISBN 0-262-08094-X). MIT Pr.

Haas, Jerome, jt. auth. see Bierman, Harold, Jr.

Haas, Joseph S. The Northeast Retreat. (Cathedral of the Beechwoods Ser.: No. 1). (Illus.). 102p. (Orig.). 1980. write for info. (ISBN 0-9605552-0-X). Haas Ent NH.

Haas, Kenneth B. & Ernest, John. Principles of Creative Selling. 1978. text ed. 14.95 (ISBN 0-02-474980-X). Macmillan.

Haas, Kenneth B. & Perry, Enos C. Sales Horizons. 3rd ed. (gr. 9-12). text ed. 10.96 o.p. (ISBN 0-685-04697-4, 78769-7); 3.68 o.p. (ISBN 0-685-04698-2, 78771-3); chapter tests 1.52 o.p. (ISBN 0-685-04699-0); tchrs' guide to text, wkbk. & tests s.p. 2.32 o.p. (ISBN 0-685-04700-8, 78770-5). P-H.

Haas, Kurt. Growth Encounter: A Guide for Groups. LC 75-2180. 1975. 15.95 (ISBN 0-88229-225-0). Nelson-Hall.
--You Can Change Your Personality--& Your Life. LC 78-11449. 1979. 11.95 (ISBN 0-88229-429-6). Nelson-Hall.
Haas, Leonard E., jt. ed. see Van Derveer, Paul D.
Haas, Lois J. Tell Me About God Kit: 12 Lessons, Vol. 1. (Tiny Steps of Faith Ser.). (ps). 1966. complete kit 9.95 (ISBN 0-86508-011-9); text only 1.95 (ISBN 0-86508-012-7); color & action book 0.60 (ISBN 0-86508-013-5). BCM Inc.
--Tell Me About Jesus Kit: 16 Lessons, Vol. 2. (Tiny Steps of Faith Ser.). (ps). 1967. complete kit 9.95 (ISBN 0-86508-014-3); text only 1.95 (ISBN 0-86508-015-1); color & action book 0.60 (ISBN 0-86508-016-X). BCM Inc.
--Tell Me How to Please God Kit: 16 Lessons, Vol. 4. (Tiny Steps of Faith Ser.). (ps). 1974. complete kit 9.95 (ISBN 0-86508-020-8); text only 1.95 (ISBN 0-86508-021-6); color & action book 0.60 (ISBN 0-86508-022-4). BCM Inc.
--Tell Me How to Trust God Kit: 16 Lessons, Vol. 3. (Tiny Steps of Faith Ser.). (ps). 1970. complete kit 9.95 (ISBN 0-86508-017-8); text only 1.95 (ISBN 0-86508-018-6); color & action book 0.60 (ISBN 0-86508-019-4). BCM Inc.
Haas, Mark, ed. see Tischler, Morris.
Haas, Merle, tr. see De Brunhoff, Jean.
Haas, Richard & Williams, David A. The Study of Oral Interpretation: Theory & Comment. LC 74-13539. 252p. 1975. pap. text ed. 5.95 (ISBN 0-672-61226-7). Bobbs.
Haas, Robert B., ed. see Stein, Gertrude.
Haas, W. Phono-Graphic Translation. 98p. 1970. 24.00x (ISBN 0-7190-0394-6, Pub. by Manchester U Pr England). State Mutual Bk.
Haas, Werner & Mathieu, Gustave B. Deutsch Fur Alle: Beginning College German: a Comprehensive Approach. LC 79-21295. 1980. text ed. 17.95 (ISBN 0-471-02210-1); tchrs. manual avail. (ISBN 0-471-04192-0); wkbk. avail. (ISBN 0-471-02211-X); tapes avail. (ISBN 0-471-05513-1). Wiley.
Haas, Werner, jt. auth. see Babbitt, Diane H.
Haas, Willy. Bertolt Brecht. LC 68-31450. (Modern Literature Ser.). 1970. 10.95 (ISBN 0-8044-2323-7); pap. 3.45 (ISBN 0-8044-6237-2). Ungar.
Haase, Rolf. Thermodynamics of Irreversible Processes. (Chemical Engineering Ser). (Illus.). 1969. text ed. 25.95 (ISBN 0-201-02651-1). A-W.
Haase, T. & Schonert, H. Solid-Liquid Equilibrium. 1969. 44.00 (ISBN 0-08-012663-4). Pergamon.
Haase, V. H., ed. see IFAC - IFIP Workshop, Leibnitz, Austria, April 1980.
Haase, Ynez D., jt. auth. see Beck, Warren A.
Haase, Ynez P., jt. auth. see Beck, Warren A.
Haasen, P., et al, eds. Strength of Metals & Alloys: International Conference on the Strength of Metals & Alloys, 5th, Aachen, 1979, 3 vols. LC 79-40131. (Illus.). 1980. Set. 260.00 (ISBN 0-08-023265-5); Set. pap. 150.00 (ISBN 0-08-024760-1). Pergamon.
Haasen, Peter. Physical Metallurgy. Mordike, Janet, tr. LC 76-53517. (Illus.). 1978. 71.50 (ISBN 0-521-21548-X); pap. 18.50x (ISBN 0-521-29183-6). Cambridge U Pr.
Haavelsrud, M. Disarmament Education. 1981. text ed. write for info. (ISBN 0-86103-043-5, Westbury Hse). Butterworth.
Haavik, Sarah F. & Menninger, Karl A., 2nd. Sexuality, Law, & the Developmentally Disabled Person: Legal & Clinical Aspects of Marriage, Parenthood, & Sterilization. 210p. (Orig.). 1981. pap. text ed. 13.95 (ISBN 0-933716-21-4). P H Brookes.
Habachi, Labib. The Obelisks of Egypt: The Skyscrapers of the Past. Van Siclen, Charles C., III, ed. LC 76-54646. (Illus.). 1977. 12.95 o.p. (ISBN 0-684-14805-6, ScribT). Scribner.
Habakkuk, H. J. American & British Technology in the Nineteenth Century. 32.95 (ISBN 0-521-05162-2); pap. 8.95x (ISBN 0-521-09447-X). Cambridge U Pr.
--Population Growth & Economic Development Since 1750. 1971. pap. text ed. 3.75x (ISBN 0-391-00211-2, Leicester). Humanities.
Habberjam, G. M. Apparent Restivity Observations & the Use of Square Array Techniques. (Geoexploration Monographs: No. 9). (Illus.). 1979. 55.00x (ISBN 3-443-13013-5). Intl Pubns Serv.
Habeeb, Virginia. Thousands of Creative Kitchen Ideas. LC 75-23318. (Funk & W Bk.). (Illus.). 256p. 1976. 13.95 o.s.i. (ISBN 0-308-10227-4, TYC-T). T Y Crowell.
Habeeb, Virginia & Treves, Ralph. Remodeling Your Kitchen & Building Your Own Cabinets. LC 79-33571. (Popular Science Skill Bks.). (Orig.). 1980. pap. 4.95 (ISBN 0-06-090781-9, CN 781, CN). Har-Row.
Habeeb, Virginia, jt. auth. see Carey, Zenja.
Habel, Norman. At the Battle of Jericho! Ho! Ho! LC 56-1219. (Purple Puzzle Tree Bk). (Illus.). (ps-5). 1971. pap. 0.85 (ISBN 0-570-06515-1). Concordia.
--Sing a Song of Solomon. (Purple Puzzle Tree Bk). (Illus.). (ps-5). 1972. pap. 0.85 (ISBN 0-570-06519-4, 56-1223). Concordia.
--This Old Man Called Moses. (Purple Puzzle Tree Ser). (Illus., Orig.). (ps-4). 1971. pap. 0.85 (ISBN 0-570-06512-7, 56-1212). Concordia.
--Trouble with Tickle the Tiger. LC 56-1218. (Purple Puzzle Tree Bk). (Illus.). (ps-5). 1972. pap. 0.85 (ISBN 0-570-06514-3). Concordia.
--Voyage to the Bottom of the Sea. (Purple Puzzle Tree Bk). (Illus.). (ps-5). 1972. pap. 0.85 (ISBN 0-570-06524-0, 56-1228). Concordia.
--When God Told Us His Name: Moses & the Burning Bush. (Purple Puzzle Tree Ser). (Illus., Orig.). (ps-4). 1971. pap. 0.85 (ISBN 0-570-06509-7, 56-1209). Concordia.
--When God Was All Alone. (Purple Puzzle Tree Ser). (Illus., Orig.). (ps-4). 1971. pap. 0.85 (ISBN 0-570-06500-3, 56-1200). Concordia.
--When Isaiah Saw the Sizzling Seraphim. (Purple Puzzle Tree Bk). (ps-5). 1972. pap. 0.85 (ISBN 0-570-06523-2, 56-1227). Concordia.
--When Jeremiah Learned a Secret from God. (Purple Puzzle Tree Bk). (Illus.). (ps-5). 1972. pap. 0.85 (ISBN 0-570-06525-9, 56-1229). Concordia.
Habel, Norman C. Job. Hayes, John, ed. LC 80-82193. (Knox Preaching Guides). 96p. (Orig.). 1981. pap. 4.50 (ISBN 0-8042-3216-4). John Knox.
--Old Rock the Fisherman. (Purple Puzzle Tree Bk.). 1972. pap. 0.85 (ISBN 0-570-06543-7, 56-1247). Concordia.
--When Jacob Buried His Treasure. (Purple Puzzle Tree Ser). (Illus., Orig.). (ps-4). 1971. pap. 0.85 (ISBN 0-570-06508-9, 56-1208). Concordia.
--When Jesus Did His Miracles of Love. (Purple Puzzle Tree Bk.). 1972. pap. 0.85 (ISBN 0-570-06541-0, 56-1245). Concordia.
--When Jesus' Friends Betrayed Him. (Purple Puzzle Tree Bk.). 1972. pap. 0.85 (ISBN 0-570-06547-X, 56-1251). Concordia.
--When Jesus Rode in the Purple Puzzle Parade. (Purple Puzzle Tree Bk.). 1972. pap. 0.85 (ISBN 0-570-06546-1, 56-1250). Concordia.
--When Jesus Told His Parables. (Purple Puzzle Tree Bk). 1972. pap. 0.85 (ISBN 0-570-06542-9, 56-1246). Concordia.
--When Laughing Boy Was Born. (Purple Puzzle Tree Ser). (Illus., Orig.). (ps-4). 1971. pap. 0.85 (ISBN 0-570-06505-4, 56-1205). Concordia.
--When the First Man Came. (Purple Puzzle Tree Ser). (Illus., Orig.). (ps-4). 1971. pap. 0.85 (ISBN 0-570-06501-1, 56-1201). Concordia.
--When the Purple Waters Came Again. (Purple Puzzle Tree Ser). (Illus., Orig.). (ps-4). 1971. pap. 0.85 (ISBN 0-570-06503-8, 56-1203). Concordia.
--A Wild Young Man Called John. 1972. pap. 0.85 (ISBN 0-570-06539-9, 56-1243). Concordia.
--Wonder Bread from a Boy's Lunch. 1972. pap. 0.85 (ISBN 0-570-06545-3, 56-1249). Concordia.
Habel, Norman C., ed. What Are We Going To Do With All These Rotting Fish? & Seven Other Short Plays for Church & Community. LC 79-119766. (Open Bks). (Illus.). 160p. (Orig.). 1970. pap. 3.25 (ISBN 0-8006-0147-5, 1-147). Fortress.
Habel, Robert E. Applied Veterinary Anatomy. 2nd ed. (Illus.). 1978. pap. text ed. 7.00x (ISBN 0-9600444-4-2). Habel.
--Guide to the Dissection of Domestic Ruminants. rev. 3rd ed. (Illus.). 165p. 1975. text ed. 4.00x (ISBN 0-9600444-1-8). Habel.
Habenstreit, Barbara. Cities in the March of Civilization. LC 73-2302. (International Library). (Illus.). 128p. (gr. 7 up). 1974. PLB 6.90 o.p. (ISBN 0-531-02114-9). Watts.
Haber, A., jt. auth. see Runyon, R.
Haber, Audrey & Runyon, Richard P. Fundamentals of Psychology. 2nd ed. LC 77-79460. (Psychology Ser.). (Illus.). 1978. text ed. 16.95 (ISBN 0-201-02766-6); wkbk 6.50 (ISBN 0-201-02767-4); instr's resource guide 4.50 (ISBN 0-201-02768-2). A-W.
--General Statistics. 3rd ed. LC 76-23985. 1977. text ed. 16.95 (ISBN 0-201-02729-1). A-W.
Haber, Barbara. Women in America: A Guide to Books, 1963-1975, with an Appendix on Books Published 1976-1979. 360p. 1981. pap. 6.95 (ISBN 0-252-00826-X). U of Ill Pr.
Haber, D. F., jt. auth. see Dransfield, P.
Haber, E. S., jt. auth. see Mahlstede, John P.
Haber, Edgar & Krause, Richard M., eds. Antibodies in Human Diagnosis & Therapy. LC 75-32089. (Royal Society of Medicine Foundation Ser.). 1977. 34.50 (ISBN 0-89004-089-3). Raven.
Haber, Eitan. Menahem Begin: The Legend & the Man. 1978. 9.95 o.p. (ISBN 0-440-05553-9). Delacorte.
Haber, F. Barry, jt. auth. see Olson, Milton C.
Haber, Fred. An Introduction to Information & Communication Theory. (Advances in Modern Engineering Ser.). (Illus.). 224p. 1974. text ed. 8.95 (ISBN 0-201-02669-4). A-W.
Haber, Heinz. Our Blue Planet: The Story of the Earth's Evolution. LC 77-85276. 1969. 6.95 o.p. (ISBN 0-684-31048-1, ScribT); pap. 1.95 (ISBN 0-684-12735-0, SL330, ScribT). Scribner.
Haber, James. Golf Made Easy. LC 73-20980. 1974. pap. 3.50 o.p. (ISBN 0-684-13791-7, SL517, ScribT). Scribner.
Haber, Joyce. The Users. 1976. 8.95 o.p. (ISBN 0-440-09220-5). Delacorte.
Haber, L. F. Chemical Industry During the Nineteenth Century: A Study of the Economic Aspect of Applied Chemistry in Europe & North America. 1958. 19.95x (ISBN 0-19-858102-5). Oxford U Pr.
Haber, Meryl H. Urine Casts: Their Microscopy & Clinical Significance. 2nd ed. LC 76-10464. (Laboratory Manual Ser). (Illus.). 1976. softbound perfect bdg. 22.00 (ISBN 0-89189-023-8); incl. slides 90.00 (15-9-002-00). Am Soc Clinical.
Haber, Tom B. A. E. Housman. (English Authors Ser.: No. 46). 1967. lib. bdg. 10.95 (ISBN 0-8057-1272-0). Twayne.
Haber, William & Murray, Merrill G. Unemployment Insurance in the American Economy. 1966. text ed. 12.50x o.p. (ISBN 0-256-00201-0). Irwin.
Haberer, Joseph. Science & Technology Policy. LC 77-70081. (Policy Studies Organization Book Ser.). (Illus.). 1977. 21.95 (ISBN 0-669-01374-9). Lexington Bks.
Haberfeld, Steven, jt. auth. see Seashore, Marjorie J.
Haberlandt, G. Physiological Plant Anatomy. 4th ed. Drummond, M., tr. from Ger. 398p. 1979. Repr. of 1928 ed. lib. bdg. 17.50x (ISBN 0-934454-89-2). Lubrecht & Cramer.
Haberlein, Bernard J., jt. ed. see Weber, George H.
Haberler, Gottfried. Economic Growth & Stability. LC 73-92965. (Principles of Freedom Ser.). 1976. Repr. of 1974 ed. 10.00x o.p. (ISBN 0-8402-1337-9, Caroline Hse Inc). Green Hill.
--Economic Growth & Stability: An Analysis of Economic Change & Policies. LC 73-92965. (Principles of Freedom Ser.). 291p. 1974. 10.00x o.p. (ISBN 0-8402-1337-9). Nash Pub.
--Economic Growth & Stability: An Analysis of Economic Change & Policies. (Principles of Freedom Ser.). 319p. 1980. text ed. 10.00x (ISBN 0-8402-1337-9). Humanities.
Haberman. Use of Digital Computers for Engineering Applications. 1966. text ed. 17.95 (ISBN 0-675-09836-X). Merrill.
--Vibration Analysis. 1968. 23.95 (ISBN 0-675-09694-4). Merrill.
Haberman, Martin & Stinnett, T. M. Teacher Education & the New Profession of Teaching. LC 73-7238. 1973. 16.00x (ISBN 0-8211-0751-8); text ed. 15.00x (ISBN 0-685-42633-5). McCutchan.
Haberman, R. Mathematical Models: Mechanical Vibrations, Population, Dynamics & Traffic Flow, An Introduction to Applied Mathematics. 1977. 23.95 (ISBN 0-13-561738-3). P-H.
Haberman, Shelby. Analysis of Qualitative Data, Vol. I: Introductory Topics (TXX) LC 77-25731. 1978. 24.50 (ISBN 0-12-312501-4). Acad Pr.
Haberman, W., jt. auth. see John, J.
Haberman, William L., jt. auth. see John, James E.
Habermann, A. N. Introduction to Operating System Design. new ed. LC 75-34073. (Computer Science Ser.). (Illus.). 480p. 1976. text ed. 25.95 (ISBN 0-574-21075-X, 13-4075). SRA.
Habermann, Gerhard. Maksim Gorki. Schlant, Ernestine, tr. LC 75-129114. (Modern Literature Ser.). 1971. 10.95 (ISBN 0-8044-2326-1); pap. 3.45 (ISBN 0-8044-6239-9). Ungar.
Habermas, J., tr. see Kortian, Garbis.
Habermas, Jurgen. Toward a Rational Society: Student Protest, Science, & Politics. Shapiro, Jeremy, tr. from Ger. LC 73-121827. 1971. pap. 3.95 (ISBN 0-8070-4177-7, BP404). Beacon Pr.
Habermehl, Laurence. Morality in the Modern World. 1976. pap. text ed. 14.95x (ISBN 0-8221-0176-9). Dickenson.
Haber-Schaim, Uri, et al. PSSC Physics. 4th ed. (gr. 11-12). 1976. text ed. 14.40 o.p. (ISBN 0-669-97451-X); tchr's res. bk. 14.40 o.p. (ISBN 0-669-97469-2); lab. guide 4.20 o.p. (ISBN 0-669-97477-3); other materials avail. write for info. o.p. (ISBN 0-685-67389-8). Heath.
Habezk, Irwin J., jt. auth. see Schuetze, Armin W.
Habib, Irfan. An Atlas of the Mughal Empire: Political & Economic Maps with Detailed Notes, Bibliography, & Index. (Illus.). 120p. 1980. 69.00x (ISBN 0-19-560379-6). Oxford U Pr.
Habib, Muhammad K. Sampling Representations & Approximations for Certain Functions & Stochastic Processes. 100p. 1980. pap. 3.15 (1260). U of NC Pr.
Haburton, Eleanor. Study Skills for College. (Illus.). 176p. 1981. pap. text ed. 6.95 (ISBN 0-87626-860-2). Winthrop.
Hachey, Thomas & Weber, Ralph E. The Awakening of a Sleeping Giant: Third World Leaders & National Liberation. LC 80-12517. 160p. 1981. pap. text ed. 6.50 (ISBN 0-89874-081-9). Krieger.
Hachey, Thomas E. & Weber, Ralph E. American Dissent from Thomas Jefferson to Cesar Chavez: The Rhetoric of Reform & Revolution. LC 80-12577. 1980. pap. 6.50. Krieger.
--The Awakening of a Sleeping Giant: Third World Leaders National Liberation. 1980. pap. 6.50 (ISBN 0-89874-081-9). Krieger.
--European Ideologies Since Seventeen Eighty-Nine: Rebels, Radicals & Political Ferment. LC 80-12562. 1980. pap. 6.50 (ISBN 0-89874-082-7). Krieger.
--European Ideologies Since Seventeen Eighty-Nine: Rebels, Radicals & Political Ferment. 200p. (Orig.). 1981. pap. text ed. 5.50 (ISBN 0-89874-082-7). Krieger.
Hachten, Harva. The Flavor of Wisconsin: An Informal History of Food & Eating in the Badger State. LC 80-26172. (Illus.). 300p. 1981. 12.95 (ISBN 0-87020-204-9). State Hist Soc Wis.
Hachten, William A. The World News Prism: Changing Media, Clashing Ideologies. 120p. 1981. pap. text ed. 6.50 (ISBN 0-8138-1580-0). Iowa St U Pr.
Hachtman, T. Gertrude's Follies. 80p. 1981. pap. 5.95 (ISBN 0-312-32630-0). St Martin.
Hack, Michel. Decidability Questions for Petri Nets. LC 79-7310. (Outstanding Dissertations in the Computer Sciences Ser.: Vol. 8). 1980. lib. bdg. 21.00 (ISBN 0-8240-4424-X). Garland Pub.
Hack, Walter G., et al. Education Futurism 1985: Challenges for Schools & Their Administrators. LC 72-158486. 1971. 16.00x (ISBN 0-8211-0720-8); text ed. 14.50x (ISBN 0-685-02004-5). McCutchan.
Hackel, Sergei. The Poet & the Revolution: Aleksandr Blok's the Twelve. 272p. 1975. 37.50x (ISBN 0-19-815645-6). Oxford U Pr.
Hackenberg, Larry M. The Green Wood House: How to Build & Own a Beautiful,Inexpensive House. rev. ed. LC 75-33166. 1978. 9.75x (ISBN 0-8139-0646-6); pap. 4.95 o.p. (ISBN 0-8139-0683-0). U Pr of Va.
Hackenbroch, Yvonne. Catalogue of the Irwin Untermyer Collection, Vols. 2, 5, 6. Incl. Vol. 1. Meissen & Other Continental Porcelain, Faience & Enamel. (Illus.). 1956. write for info. (ISBN 0-87099-103-5); Vol. 2. Chelsea & Other English Porcelain, Pottery, & Enamel. (Illus.). 1957. 12.50 (ISBN 0-87099-102-7); Vol. 5. Bronzes, Other Metalwork & Sculpture. 2nd ed. (Illus.). 1962. 27.50 (ISBN 0-87099-101-9); English & Other Silver. 2nd ed. (Illus.). 1969. Vol. 6. write for info (ISBN 0-87099-104-3). Metro Mus Art.
Hacker, Andrew. Congressional Districting: The Issue of Equal Representation. rev. ed. 1964. pap. 4.95 (ISBN 0-8157-3369-0). Brookings.
Hacker, Louis M. Shaping of the American Tradition. LC 47-1257. 1947. 37.50x (ISBN 0-231-01574-7). Columbia U Pr.
Hacker, P. M. & Raz, J., eds. Law, Morality, & Society: Essays in Honour of H. L. A. Hart. 1977. 19.95x o.p. (ISBN 0-19-824557-2). Oxford U Pr.
Hacker, Rich, jt. auth. see Myers, Earl.
Hackert, Adelbert. Finite Mathematics: From Sets to Game Theory. 1974. text ed. 15.95x o.p. (ISBN 0-669-81125-4); instructor's manual free o.p. (ISBN 0-669-90258-6). Heath.
Hackert, Adelbert F. & Duff, Charles L. Elements of Trigonometry. LC 73-140782. text ed. 15.95x o.p. (ISBN 0-669-61598-6); manual free o.p. (ISBN 0-669-61606-0). Heath.
Hackett, C. A. Rimbaud. LC 80-40455. (Major European Authors Ser.). 250p. Date not set. price not set; pap. price not set (ISBN 0-521-29756-7). Cambridge U Pr.

Hackett, C. A., ed. New French Poetry: An Anthology. 1973. 18.25x (ISBN 0-631-14490-0, Pub. by Basil Blackwell); pap. 12.50x (ISBN 0-631-14500-1, Pub. by Basil Blackwell). Biblio Dist.

Hackett, Dorothy, jt. auth. see Glass, Amee.

Hackett, John, et al. The Third World War. 1980. pap. 3.50 (ISBN 0-425-05019-X). Berkley Pub.

Hackett, Patricia, et al. The Musical Classroom: Models, Skills, & Backgrounds for Elementary Teaching. 1979. pap. 15.95 ref. (ISBN 0-13-608356-0). P-H.

Hackett, Thomas P. & Cassem, Ned H. Mass. Gen. Hosp. Handbook of General Hospital Psychiatry. LC 78-15146. (Illus.). 1978. pap. 19.95 (ISBN 0-8016-0931-3). Mosby.

Hackforth, R., ed. see Plato.

Hackforth-Jones, Jocelyn. Augustus Earle: Travel Artist: Paintings & Drawings in the Rex Nan Kivell Collection National Library of Australia. 157p. 1980. 50.00x (ISBN 0-85967-631-5, Pub. by Scolar Pr England). Biblio Dist.

Hacking, I. The Emergence of Probability. LC 74-82224. 216p. 1975. 29.95 (ISBN 0-521-20460-7). Cambridge U Pr.

--Why Does Language Matter to Philosophy. LC 75-19432. 180p. 1975. 26.95 (ISBN 0-521-20923-4); pap. 7.95x (ISBN 0-521-09998-6). Cambridge U Pr.

Hacking, Ian. Concise Introduction to Logic. (Orig.). 1971. pap. text ed. 8.95 (ISBN 0-394-31008-X). Random.

Hacking, Ian, ed. see Philosophy of Science Association, Biennial Meeting, 1978.

Hacking, Ian M. Logic of Statistical Inference. 1966. 35.50 (ISBN 0-521-05165-7); pap. 11.50x (ISBN 0-521-29059-7). Cambridge U Pr.

Hackl, C. E., ed. see Informatik Symposium, 4th, IBM Germany, Wildbad, Sept. 25-27, 1974.

Hackleman, Edwin C., jt. auth. see Boone, Louis E.

Hackleman, Michael. At Home with Alternative Energy: A Comprehensive Guide to Creating Your Own Systems. LC 79-48056. (Illus.). 152p. (Orig.). 1980. pap. 8.95 (ISBN 0-915238-38-1). Peace Pr.

--Better Use of. LC 80-9000. (Illus.). 144p. 1981. pap. 9.95 (ISBN 0-915238-50-0). Peace Pr.

Hackleman, Wauneta. How to Slay a Dragon. LC 80-65676. 1980. 9.95 (ISBN 0-89754-019-0); pap. 2.95 (ISBN 0-89754-018-2). Dan River Pr.

Hackmack, Adolf. Chinese Carpets & Rugs. LC 77-83943. (Illus.). 1981. 17.50 (ISBN 0-8048-1258-6). C E Tuttle.

Hackman, Donald J. & Caudy, Don W. Underwater Tools. (Illus.). 176p. 1981. 32.95 (ISBN 0-935470-08-5). Battelle.

Hackman, J. Richard & Oldham, Greg R. Work Redesign. LC 79-8918. 1980. pap. text ed. 7.95 (ISBN 0-201-02779-8). A-W.

Hackney, Harold L. & Cormier, Sherilyn N. Counseling Strategies & Objectives. 2nd ed. (P-H Series in Counseling & Human Development). 1979. ref. 13.95 (ISBN 0-13-183319-7); pap. 9.95 ref. (ISBN 0-13-183301-4). P-H.

Hackney, John W. Control & Management of Capital Projects. LC 65-26846. 1965. 32.50 (ISBN 0-471-33846-X, Pub. by Wiley-Interscience). Wiley.

Hackney, Louise W., rev. by see Melitz, Leo L.

Hackstaff, L. H., tr. see Augustine, Saint.

Hackston, Michael G., tr. see Esser, Karl.

Hackwood, Frederick W. Christ Lore: Being the Legends, Traditions, Myths, Symbols, Customs, & Superstitions of the Christian Church. LC 69-16064. (Illus.). 1971. Repr. of 1902 ed. 18.00 (ISBN 0-8103-3528-X). Gale.

--Good Cheer: The Romance of Food & Feasting. LC 68-9571. 1968. Repr. of 1911 ed. 18.00 (ISBN 0-8103-3508-5). Gale.

Hackworth, R., jt. auth. see Alwin, Robert H.

Hackworth, Robert D., jt. auth. see Alwin, Robert H.

Hacsi, Jacqueline. Too Rich for Her Pride. (Candlelight Romance Ser.). (Orig.). 1981. pap. 1.50 (ISBN 0-440-18619-6). Dell.

Hadad, Joseph. An Aggressive Campaign for Automatic Commodity Trading. 1980. 65.00. Windsor.

Hadamard, Jacques. Propagation Des Ondes. LC 52-9969. (Fr). 14.95 o.p. (ISBN 0-8284-0058-X). Chelsea Pub.

--Psychology of Invention in the Mathematical Field. 1945. pap. text ed. 2.50 (ISBN 0-486-20107-4). Dover.

Hadamitzky, Wolfgang & Spahn, Mark. Kanji & Kana: A Handbook & Dictionary of the Japanese Writing System. LC 81-50106. 384p. 1981. 11.50 (ISBN 0-8048-1373-6). C E Tuttle.

Hadar, Josef. Elementary Theory of Microeconomic Behavior. 2nd ed. LC 70-171435. 1974. text ed. 18.95 (ISBN 0-201-02672-4). A-W.

Hadas, Moses. Ancilla to Classical Reading. LC 54-6132. 1954. pap. 7.50x (ISBN 0-231-08517-6). Columbia U Pr.

--History of Greek Literature. LC 50-7015. 1950. 17.50x (ISBN 0-231-01767-7); pap. 4.00x o.p. (ISBN 0-231-08539-7). Columbia U Pr.

--History of Latin Literature. LC 52-7637. 1952. 27.50x (ISBN 0-231-01848-7); pap. 5.00x o.p. (ISBN 0-231-08556-7, 56). Columbia U Pr.

--History of Rome from Its Origins to 529 A.D. 7.25 (ISBN 0-8446-2182-X). Peter Smith.

--Imperial Rome. (Great Ages of Man Ser). (Illus.). 1965. 12.95 (ISBN 0-8094-0342-0); lib. bdg. avail. (ISBN 0-685-20548-7). Time-Life.

--Imperial Rome. LC 65-24363. (Great Ages of Man Ser.). 1965. lib. bdg. 11.97 (ISBN 0-8094-0364-1). Silver.

Hadas, Moses, ed. see Seneca.

Hadas, Moses, tr. Fables of the Jewish Aesop Translated from the Fox Fables of Berechiah Ha-Nakdan. LC 66-27477. (Illus.). 1966. 15.00x (ISBN 0-231-02967-5). Columbia U Pr.

Hadas, Moses, tr. see Euripides.

Hadas, Moses, tr. see Seneca.

Hadas, Pamela White. In Light of Genesis. 128p. 1980. 10.95 (ISBN 0-8276-0177-8, 462); pap. 6.95 (ISBN 0-8276-0178-6, 461). Jewish Pubn.

Haddad, Fuad I., tr. see Hashimi, Ali Ibn Sulayman al.

Haddad-Garcia, George. The Films of Jane Fonda. (Illus.). 256p. 1981. 16.95 (ISBN 0-8065-0752-7). Citadel Pr.

Hadden, Jeffrey K. Gathering Storm in the Churches. LC 68-22613. 1969. 5.95 o.p. (ISBN 0-385-03326-5). Doubleday.

Hadden, John, jt. ed. see Stewart, William E.

Hadden, Tom. Company Law & Capitalism. 2nd ed. (Law in Context Ser.). 1977. 25.00x (ISBN 0-297-77334-8, Pub. by Weidenfeld & Nicolson). Rothman.

--Company Law & Capitalism. 2nd ed. (Law in Context Ser.). 1977. 25.00x (ISBN 0-297-77334-8, Pub. by Weidenfeld & Nicolson England). Rothman.

Hadden, Wilbur C. Basic Data on Health Care Needs of Adults 25-74 Years of Age: United States, 1971-75. Cox, Klaudia, ed. (Ser. 11, No. 218). 50p. 1980. pap. text ed. 1.75 (ISBN 0-8406-0197-2). Natl Ctr Health Stats.

Haddick, Vern. Portrait of Morris. LC 78-31684. Date not set. 9.95 (ISBN 0-87949-152-3). Ashley Bks.

Haddle, Jan. The Complete Book of the Appaloosa. LC 73-10521. (Illus.). 1977. pap. 7.95 o.p. (ISBN 0-498-02049-5). A S Barnes.

Haddock, B. A. & Hamilton, W. A., eds. Microbial Energetics. LC 76-54367. (Society for General Microbiology: Symposium 27). (Illus.). 1977. 65.00 (ISBN 0-521-21494-7). Cambridge U Pr.

Haddock, Frank C. Power of Will. 9.95 (ISBN 0-912576-03-0). R Collier.

Haddon, A. C., ed. Reports of the Cambridge Anthropological Expedition to Torres Straits, 6 vols. Incl. General Ethnography. Repr. of 1935 ed. 33.00 (ISBN 0-685-27602-3); Physiology & Psychology. Repr. of 1901 ed. 19.00 (ISBN 0-685-27603-1); Linguistics. Ray, S. H. Repr. of 1907 ed. 29.00 (ISBN 0-685-27604-X); Arts & Crafts. Repr. of 1912 ed. Vols. 4-6. 33.00 ea.; Sociology, Magic & Religion of the Western Islanders. Repr. of 1904 ed. 33.00 (ISBN 0-685-27606-6); Sociology, Magic & Religion of the Eastern Islanders. Repr. of 1908 ed. 26.00 (ISBN 0-685-27607-4). (Landmarks in Anthropology Ser). 2242p. Set. 196.00 (ISBN 0-686-57612-8). Johnson Repr.

Haddon, Frank, jt. auth. see Cotton, Alan.

Haddon, Randolph J. The Basic Guidebook for Industrial Designers. (Illus.). 129p. 1981. 47.45 (ISBN 0-930582-92-6). Gloucester Art.

Haddow, Alexander, jt. ed. see Greenstein, Jesse P.

Haddow, Alexander see Greenstein, Jesse P. & Haddow, Alexander.

Haden, Peter. Elementary Knowledge: A Story of the Creation of the Hebrew Alaphabet. (Illus.). 68p. 1981. 22.50 (ISBN 0-87663-357-2). Universe.

Hader, Berta & Hader, Elmer. Big Snow. (Illus.). (gr. k-3). 1948. 8.95 (ISBN 0-02-737910-8). Macmillan.

--Cock-A-Doodle-Doo. (gr. 1-3). 1939. 5.95g o.s.i. (ISBN 0-02-738030-0). Macmillan.

--Little Appaloosa. (gr. 7 up). 1949. 8.95 (ISBN 0-02-739020-9). Macmillan.

--Little Stone House. (gr. k-3). 1944. 4.95g o.s.i. (ISBN 0-02-739380-1). Macmillan.

--Lost in the Zoo. (gr. k-3). 1951. 5.50g o.s.i. (ISBN 0-02-739680-0). Macmillan.

--Pancho. (gr. k-3). 1942. 4.95g o.s.i. (ISBN 0-02-740120-0). Macmillan.

--Quack-Quack. (Illus.). (gr. 1-3). 1961. 8.95 (ISBN 0-02-740250-9). Macmillan.

--Reindeer Trail. (Illus.). (gr. 1-3). 1959. 4.95g o.s.i. (ISBN 0-02-740560-5). Macmillan.

--Two Is Company, Three's a Crowd. (Illus.). (gr. k-3). 1965. 7.95 (ISBN 0-02-741030-7). Macmillan.

Hader, Elmer, jt. auth. see Hader, Berta.

Haders, Phyllis. Sunshine & Shadow: The Amish & Their Quilts. LC 76-5094. (Illus.). 72p. 1981. pap. 5.95 (ISBN 0-87663-556-7). Universe.

--Sunshine & Shadow: The Amish & Their Quilts. LC 76-5094. (Illus.). 72p. 1976. 5.95 o.s.i. (ISBN 0-87663-236-3). Universe.

--The Warner Collectors' Guide to American Quilts. (Orig.). 1981. pap. 9.95 (ISBN 0-446-97636-9). Warner Bks.

Hadfield, Alice M. The Chartist Land Company. 2nd ed. (Illus.). 248p. 1970. 8.95 (ISBN 0-7153-4872-8); pap. 3.95 (ISBN 0-7153-5809-X). David & Charles.

Hadfield, Alice M., jt. auth. see Hadfield, Charles.

Hadfield, Charles. British Canals: An Illustrated History. 5th ed. (Canals of the British Isles Ser.). (Illus.). 1975. 19.95 (ISBN 0-7153-6700-5). David & Charles.

--British Canals: An Illustrated History. 6th ed. LC 79-52377. (Illus.). 1979. 22.50 (ISBN 0-7153-7852-X). David & Charles.

--British Canals: An Illustrated History. 4th ed. (Canals of the British Isles Ser.). (Illus.). 8.95. David & Charles.

--The Canal Age. LC 80-69343. (Illus.). 240p. 1981. 22.50 (ISBN 0-7153-8079-6). David & Charles.

--The Canals of South Wales & the Border. 2nd ed. (Canals of the British Isles Ser.). (Illus.). 1967. 22.50 (ISBN 0-7153-4027-1). David & Charles.

--The Canals of the West Midlands. 2nd ed. (Canals of the British Isles Ser.). (Illus.). 1966. 22.50 (ISBN 0-7153-4030-1). David & Charles.

--The Canals of Yorkshire & North East England, 2 vols. (Canals of the British Isles Ser.). (Illus.). 19.95 ea. Vol. 1 (ISBN 0-7153-5719-0). Vol. 2 (ISBN 0-7153-5975-4). David & Charles.

--Inland Waterways. (Leisure & Travel Ser.). 1978. 7.50 o.p. (ISBN 0-7153-7502-4). David & Charles.

Hadfield, Charles & Biddle, Gordon. The Canals of North West England, Vols. 1 & 2. (Canals of the British Isles Ser). (Illus.). 496p. 1970. 19.95 ea. Vol. 1 (ISBN 0-7153-4956-2). Vol. 2 (ISBN 0-7153-4992-9). David & Charles.

Hadfield, Charles & Hadfield, Alice M. Afloat in America. LC 79-52986. (Illus.). 1979. 13.50 (ISBN 0-7153-7910-0). David & Charles.

--The Cotswolds: A New Study. (Illus.). 1974. 22.95 (ISBN 0-7153-6224-0). David & Charles.

Hadfield, Charles & Skempton, A. W. William Jessop, Engineer. 1979. 28.00 (ISBN 0-7153-7603-9). David & Charles.

Hadfield, J. A. Psychology & Morals. 245p. 1980. Repr. of 1926 ed. lib. bdg. 30.00 (ISBN 0-8492-5282-2). R West.

Hadfield, John, ed. Everyman's Book of English Love Poems. 234p. 1980. cancelled (ISBN 0-460-04445-1, Pub. by J M Dent). Biblio Dist.

Hadfield, Miles. A History of British Gardening. 3rd ed. (Illus.). 1979. text ed. 26.00x (ISBN 0-7195-3644-8). Humanities.

Hadgraft, C. & Wilson, R., eds. A Century of Australian Short Stories. 1964. pap. text ed. 4.50x o.p. (ISBN 0-686-65313-0). Heinemann Ed.

Hadidian, Dikran Y., ed. Intergerini Parietis Septum (Eph. 2: 14) Essays Presented to Markus Barth on His 65th Birthday. (Pittsburgh Theological Monograph Ser.: No. 33). 1980. pap. 15.95 (ISBN 0-915138-42-5). Pickwick.

Hadjinicolaou, Nicos. Art History & Class Struggle. rev. ed. Asmal, Louise, tr. from Fr. (Illus.). 1978. text ed. 19.50x (ISBN 0-904383-32-6); pap. text ed. 9.50x (ISBN 0-904383-27-X). Humanities.

Hadjiolov, A. A., jt. ed. see Cox, R. A.

Hadleigh-West, Frederick. The Archaeology of Beringia. (Illus.). 320p. 1981. 30.00x (ISBN 0-231-05172-7). Columbia U Pr.

Hadley, Arthur T. The Empty Polling Booth. 1978. 8.95 o.p. (ISBN 0-13-274928-9). P-H.

Hadley, Benjamin, et al, eds. see Encyclopedia Britannica.

Hadley, Charles D., jt. auth. see Ladd, Everett C., Jr.

Hadley, Dunstan. Hang Gliding. (Black's Picture Sports Ser.). (Illus.). 96p. 1979. 8.95 (ISBN 0-7136-1914-7). Transatlantic.

Hadley, George. Elementary Calculus. LC 68-11022. 1968. 17.95x (ISBN 0-8162-3524-4). Holden-Day.

--Elementary Statistics. LC 69-11850. (Illus.). 1969. 17.95x (ISBN 0-8162-3544-9). Holden-Day.

--Linear Algebra. (Illus.). 1961. 17.95 (ISBN 0-201-02655-4). A-W.

--Linear Programming. (Illus.). 1962. 18.95 (ISBN 0-201-02660-0). A-W.

Hadley, George & Whitin, T. M. Analysis of Inventory Systems. (Illus.). 1963. ref. ed. 21.00 (ISBN 0-13-032953-3). P-H.

Hadley, Jack, ed. Medical Education Financing: Policy Analyses & Options for the Nineteen Eighties. (Illus.). 1980. 25.00 (ISBN 0-88202-129-X). N Watson.

Hadley, Lee A. Anatomico-Roentgenographic Studies of the Spine. (Illus.). 560p. 1979. 26.75 (ISBN 0-398-02818-4). C C Thomas.

Hadley, Peter, ed. see Taylor, Henry.

Hadley, Roger, et al. Across the Generations: Old People & Young Volunteers. (National Institute Social Services Library). 1975. text ed. 35.00x (ISBN 0-04-300052-5); text ed. 11.95x (ISBN 0-04-300053-3). Allen Unwin.

Hadlich, Roger L; see Jones, George F.

Hadlock, Frank P., jt. auth. see Athey, Patricia A.

Hadlock, Richard. Jazz Masters of the Twenties. 1965. 5.95 o.p. (ISBN 0-685-15381-9); pap. 2.95 (ISBN 0-02-060770-9). Macmillan.

Hadni, A. Essentials of Modern Physics Applied to the Study of the Infrared. 1967. 64.00 (ISBN 0-08-011902-6). Pergamon.

Hadrian, Henry. How to Deal with a Bureaucrat & Best Him, 2 vols. new ed. 1979. Set. 77.50 (ISBN 0-89266-161-5). Am Classical Coll Pr.

--Wyckoff's Techniques for Stock Market Profits. (Illus.). 150p. 1972. 65.00 (ISBN 0-913314-11-0). Am Classical Coll Pr.

Hadwiger, Don, et al. New Politics of Food. LC 77-11574. (Policy Studies Organization Ser.). 1978. 21.95 (ISBN 0-669-01986-0). Lexington Bks.

Hady, Maureen E. & Danky, James P. Asian-American Periodicals & Newspapers: A Union List of Holdings in the Library of the State Historical Society of Wisconsin & the Libraries of the University of Wisconsin-Madison. LC 79-22630. 1979. pap. 2.00x (ISBN 0-87020-191-3). State Hist Soc Wis.

Hadzsits, George D. Lucretius & His Influence. LC 63-10292. (Our Debt to Greece & Rome Ser). Repr. of 1930 ed. 27.50x (ISBN 0-8154-0106-X). Cooper Sq.

Haeberli, Willy, ed. see Symposium - 3rd - Madison - 1970.

Haeckel, Ernst. Last Words on Evolution. McCabe, Joseph, tr. from Ger. Bd. with Contributions to the Study of the Behavior of Lower Organisms. Jennings, H. S; An Essay. Spencer, Herbert. (Contributions to the History of Psychology Ser.: No. 3, Pt. D). 1978. Repr. of 1906 ed. 30.00 (ISBN 0-89093-172-0). U Pubns Amer.

Haeger, John & Weber, Michael. The Bosses. rev. ed. LC 78-73266. 1979. pap. text ed. 4.50 (ISBN 0-88273-103-3). Forum Pr MO.

Haehling von Lanzenauer, Christoph. Cases in Operations Research. 1975. 12.95x (ISBN 0-8162-3546-5); manual 4.50instr's (ISBN 0-8162-3556-2). Holden-Day.

Haehn, James O., jt. auth. see Gerth, Donald R.

Haendel, Dan. Foreign Investment: The Management of Political Risk. (Westview Special Studies in International Economics). 1978. lib. bdg. 23.50x (ISBN 0-89158-253-3). Westview.

--The Process of Priority Formulation: U.S. Foreign Policy in the Indo-Pakistani War of 1971. LC 77-21372. 1978. lib. bdg. 32.50x (ISBN 0-89158-322-X). Westview.

Haenger, Heinrich. Mittelhochdeutsche Glossare und Vokabulare in Schweizerischen Bibliotheken bis 1500. (Quellen und Forschungen zur Sprach-und Kulturgeschichte der Germanischen Voelker N. F. 44). 88p. 1972. 29.50 (ISBN 3-11-003542-1). De Gruyter.

Haenni, A. O., jt. ed. see Chapeville, F.

Haerer, Armin F., ed. Self-Assessment of Current Knowledge in Neurology. 3rd ed. LC 80-81657. 1980. spiral bdg. 17.00 (ISBN 0-87488-254-0). Med Exam.

Haettenschweiler, Walter, jt. auth. see Haab, Armin.

Haeusler, Ernest F., Jr., jt. auth. see Paul, Richard S.

Hafele, W. & Kirchmayer, L. K., eds. Modeling of Large-scale Energy Systems: Proceedings of the IIASA-IFAC Symposium, Laxenburg, Austria, Feb. 25-29, 1980, Vol. 11. LC 80-41554. (IIASA Proceedings Ser.: Vol 11). 350p. 1980. 70.00 (ISBN 0-08-025696-1). Pergamon.

Hafele, Wolf, ed. Energy in a Finite World: Vol. I: Paths to a Sustainable Future. 296p. 1981. 16.50 (ISBN 0-88410-641-1). Ballinger Pub.

--Energy in a Finite World: Vol. II: Global Systems Analysis. 826p. 1981. reference 45.00 (ISBN 0-88410-642-X). Ballinger Pub.

Hafen, Ann, jt. auth. see Hafen, LeRoy.

Hafen, B., et al. Self Help Handbook. 1980. 14.95 (ISBN 0-13-803304-8); pap. 7.95 (ISBN 0-13-803296-3). P-H.

Hafen, Brent & Karren, Keith. First Aid & Emergency Care Workbook. 2nd new ed. (Illus.). 1980. 10.00x (ISBN 0-89582-024-2). Morton Pub.

Hafen, Brent Q. Nutrition, Food & Weight Control. 400p. 1980. text ed. 17.95 (ISBN 0-205-06825-1, 6268250). Allyn.

--Nutrition, Food & Weight Control. 320p. 1980. pap. text ed. 9.95 (ISBN 0-205-06826-X, 6268169); tchr's ed. free (ISBN 0-205-06828-6, 6268285). Allyn.
Hafen, Brent Q. & Karren, Keith J. Prehospital Emergency Care & Crisis Intervention. 570p. 1981. pap. 13.95x (ISBN 0-89582-057-9); wkbk. 5.95x (ISBN 0-89582-058-7); text & wkbk. 17.00x. Morton Pub.
Hafen, Brent Q., ed. Child Maltreatment: Developing a Community Team Approach. 1981. cancelled (ISBN 0-88416-320-2). PSG Pub.
Hafen, Brent Q., et al, eds. First Aid: Contemporary Practices & Principles. LC 72-82623. 1972. spiral bdg. 6.95 o.p. (ISBN 0-8087-0837-6). Burgess.
Hafen, LeRoy & Hafen, Ann. Our State: Colorado. pap. 9.95x (ISBN 0-933472-35-8). Johnson Colo.
Hafen, Leroy R. Broken Hand: The Life of Thomas Fitzpatrick, Mountain Man, Guide & Indian Agent. LC 80-23451. (Illus.). xiv, 359p. 1981. pap. 6.50 (ISBN 0-8032-7208-1, BB 753, Bison). U of Nebr Pr.
Hafen, LeRoy R., ed. see Ruxton, George F.
Hafer, Brent Q., et al. Adolescent Health. 1978. pap. text ed. 10.95 (ISBN 0-89832-009-7). Brighton Pub.
Hafer, George B., ed. A Look Back, a Look Ahead. LC 80-10370. (Proceedings Ser.). (Illus.). 207p. (Orig.). pap. text ed. 10.00 (ISBN 0-87757-134-1). Am Mktg.
Hafey, John & Shillea, Tom. The Platinum Print. LC 79-55710. (Illus.). 119p. (Orig.). 1979. pap. 14.95 (ISBN 0-89938-000-X). Graph Arts Res RIT.
Hafez, E. S. Human Reproduction: Conception & Contraception. 2nd ed. (Illus.). 932p. 1980. text ed. 47.50 (ISBN 0-06-141066-7, Harper Medical). Har-Row.
--Perspectives in Human Reproduction: Human Reproductive Physiology, Vol. 5. LC 78-50311. (Illus.). 1978. 28.00 (ISBN 0-250-40244-0). Ann Arbor Science.
Hafez, E. S., ed. Aging & Reproductive Physiology, Vol. 2. LC 75-36279. (Perspectives in Human Reproductions Ser.). 1976. 24.00 (ISBN 0-250-40108-8). Ann Arbor Science.
--Reproduction in Farm Animals. 4th ed. LC 80-10489. (Illus.). 627p. 1980. text ed. 31.00 (ISBN 0-8121-0697-0). Lea & Febiger.
--Scanning Electron Microscopy of Human Reproduction. LC 77-85087. (Perspectives in Human Reproduction Ser.: Vol. 4). (Illus.). 1978. 38.00 (ISBN 0-250-40181-9). Ann Arbor Science.
Hafez, E. S. & Peluso, J. J., eds. Sexual Maturity: Physiological & Clinical Parameters. LC 76-22248. (Perspectives in Human Reproduction: Vol. 3). 1976. 24.00 (ISBN 0-250-40112-6). Ann Arbor Science.
Hafez, E. S. & Reel, J. R., eds. Hypothalamic Hormones, Vol. 1. LC 74-28654. (Perspectives in Human Reproduction Ser.). (Illus.). 1975. 24.00 (ISBN 0-250-40089-8). Ann Arbor Science.
Hafez, E. S. & Spring-Mills, E., eds. Prostatic Carcinoma: Biology & Diagnosis. (Clinics in Andrology: No. 6). (Illus.). 200p. 1981. PLB 68.50 (ISBN 0-686-28844-0). Kluwer Boston.
Hafez, E. S. & Spring-Mills, Elinor, eds. Accessory Glands of the Male Reproductive Tract. LC 79-89654. (Perspectives in Human Reproduction Ser.: Vol. 6). (Illus.). 1979. 34.00 (ISBN 0-250-40268-8). Ann Arbor Science.
Hafez, E. S., jt. ed. see Moghissi, Kamran S.
Hafez, E. S., jt. ed. see Motta, P. M.
Haffenden, Philip S. New England in the English Nation 1689-1713. 328p. 1974. text ed. 22.50x (ISBN 0-19-821124-4). Oxford U Pr.
Haffer, Verna. Making Photograms. Date not set. 12.50 o.p. (ISBN 0-8038-4650-9). Hastings.
Haffner, Sebastian. Failure of a Revolution. LC 72-373. 221p. 1973. 10.95 o.p. (ISBN 0-912050-23-3, Library Pr). Open Court.
Hafiz. Fifty Poems (with Translation) Arberry, A. J., ed. 1947. 44.50 (ISBN 0-521-04039-6). Cambridge U Pr.
Hafner, Anne L., jt. auth. see Bailey, Robert L.
Haft, Jacob I. & Berlin, Saretta. Consultation with a Cardiologist: Coronary Heart Disease & Heart Attacks: Management. LC 78-21894. (Illus.). 1979. 15.95 (ISBN 0-88229-487-3). Nelson-Hall.
--Consultation with a Cardiologist: Coronary Heart Disease & Heart Attacks: Prevention. LC 78-26660. 1979. 19.95 (ISBN 0-88229-320-6). Nelson-Hall.
Haft, Jacob I., ed. Differential Diagnosis of Chest Pain & Other Cardiac Symptoms. LC 80-68061. (Advances in the Management of Clinical Heart Disease Monograph: Vol. 4). (Illus.). 230p. 1980. 26.50 (ISBN 0-87993-150-7). Futura Pub.
Haft, Marilyn G., jt. auth. see Hermann, Michele G.
Haft, Richard A. Investing in Securities: A Handbook for Today's Market. 1975. pap. 5.95 o.p. (ISBN 0-13-502708-X). P-H.
Haftmann, Werner. Chagall. LC 73-7657. (Library of Great Painters). (Illus.). 160p. 1974. 35.00 (ISBN 0-8109-0074-2). Abrams.
Hagan, Kenneth J., ed. In Peace & War: Interpretations of American Naval History, 1775-1978. LC 77-91108. (Contributions in Military History: No. 16). (Illus.). 1978. lib. bdg. 18.95 (ISBN 0-313-20039-4, HPW/). Greenwood.
Hagan, Ross E., jt. auth. see Wang, Jaw-Kai.
Hagan, William T. The Sac & Fox Indians. LC 58-6851. (The Civilization of the American Indian Ser.: Vol. 48). (Illus.). 320p. 1958. 14.95 (ISBN 0-8061-0397-3). U of Okla Pr.
Haganas, Knut, jt. auth. see Muther, Richard.
Hagar, Victoria, ed. Vail Epicure. (Epicure Ser.). 52p. (Orig.). 1979. pap. 2.50 (ISBN 0-89716-031-2). Peanut Butter.
Hagarty, Catherine. Revelations of an Army Nurse. 1981. 6.75 (ISBN 0-8062-1591-7). Carlton.
Hagberg, David. Flash Gordon, No. 5. 192p. (Orig.). 1981. pap. 2.25 (ISBN 0-448-17234-8, Tempo). G&D.
Hage, et al. New Strategies for Public Affairs Reporting: Investigation, Interpretation & Research. (Illus.). 336p. 1976. 13.95 (ISBN 0-13-615831-5). P-H.
Hage, Jerald. Techniques & Problems of Theory Construction in Sociology. LC 72-6447. 272p. 1972. 22.95 (ISBN 0-471-33860-5, Pub. by Wiley-Interscience). Wiley.
Hage, R. E., jt. auth. see Perkins, Courtland D.
Hagedorn, Jessica T. Dangerous Music. LC 75-32698. 1975. 10.00x o.p. (ISBN 0-917672-04-6); pap. 4.95x (ISBN 0-917672-03-8). Momos.
Hagedorn, Judy, jt. auth. see Kizziar, Janet.
Hagee, John C. Scandalous Saint. 1974. pap. 1.25 o.p. (ISBN 0-88368-056-4). Whitaker Hse.
Hagege, Claude. Critical Reflections on Transformational Grammar. rev. ed. Makkai, Valerie B., tr. from Fr. Orig. Title: La Grammaire Generative: Reflexions Critiques. 1981. pap. 12.00 (ISBN 0-933104-09-X). Jupiter Pr.
Hagel, John, III. Alternative Energy Strategies: Constraints & Opportunities. LC 75-23968. 1976. text ed. 27.95 (ISBN 0-275-56090-2). Praeger.
Hagel, William C., jt. ed. see Sims, Chester T.
Hagelganz, James W., jt. auth. see Biehl, Bobb.
Hagelstein, Isabella. Big Primer on New England's Colonial Architecture. (Regional & Recreational Guides Ser.). (Illus.). 1981. pap. 5.95 (ISBN 0-89046-074-4). Herman Pub.
Hageman, Howard G. & Beker, J. C. Easter. LC 73-88346. (Proclamation 1: Aids for Interpreting the Lessons of the Church Year, Ser. B). 64p. 1974. pap. 1.95 (ISBN 0-8006-4055-1, 1-4055). Fortress.
Hageman, L. A. & Young, D. M. Applied Iterative Methods. (Computer Science & Applied Mathematics Ser.). 1981. price not set (ISBN 0-12-313340-8). Acad Pr.
Hagemann, G. see Von Wiesner, J. & Von Regel, C.
Hagemeyer, Robert W., et al. Future Technical Needs & Trends in the Paper Industry - III. (TAPPI PRESS Reports). (Illus.). 1979. pap. 39.95 (ISBN 0-89852-378-8). TAPPI.
Hagen, A. W. Thermal Energy from the Sea. LC 75-24767. (Energy Technology Review No. 8: Ocean Technology Review No. 5). (Illus.). 150p. 1976. 24.00 (ISBN 0-8155-0597-3). Noyes.
Hagen, Anders. Rock Carving in Norway. (Tanum of Norway Tokens Ser). (Illus.). pap. 8.00x o.p. (ISBN 82-518-0004-8, N442). Vanous.
Hagen, Elizabeth. Identification of the Gifted. Tannenbaum, Abraham J., ed. (Perspectives on Gifted & Talented Education Ser.). (Orig.). 1980. pap. text ed. 5.50x (ISBN 0-8077-2588-9). Tchrs Coll.
Hagen, Elizabeth & Wolff, Luverne. Nursing Leadership Behavior in General Hospitals. LC 61-18762. 1961. pap. text ed. 4.75x (ISBN 0-8077-1482-8). Tchrs Coll.
Hagen, Everett E. The Economics of Developement. 3rd ed. 1980. 18.95x (ISBN 0-256-02318-2). Irwin.
--Economics of Development. rev. ed. 1975. text ed. 17.50x o.p. (ISBN 0-256-01735-2). Irwin.
Hagen, Lorinda. Alabama Brown. (Orig.). 1980. pap. 2.25 (ISBN 0-505-51564-4). Tower Bks.
--Amy Jean. 1976. pap. 1.75 o.p. (ISBN 0-505-51151-7). Tower Bks.
--Corrie. 1978. pap. 1.95 (ISBN 0-505-51289-0). Tower Bks.
--In the Eye of the Law. 1979. pap. 1.75 (ISBN 0-505-51392-7). Tower Bks.
--Lacey. 1977. pap. 1.95 (ISBN 0-505-51209-2). Tower Bks.
--Letitia. 1978. pap. 1.95 (ISBN 0-505-51242-4). Tower Bks.
--Mistress of Glory. 1978. pap. 1.95 (ISBN 0-505-51279-3). Tower Bks.
Hagen, Uta. Love for Cooking. LC 76-12538. (Illus.). 1976. 10.95 o.s.i. (ISBN 0-02-547380-8, 54738). Macmillan.
Hagen, Uta & Frankel, Haskel. Respect for Acting. LC 72-2328. 256p. 1973. 9.95 (ISBN 0-02-547390-5). Macmillan.
Hagen, Victor W. Von see Stephens, John L.
Hagen, Victor W. Von see Von Hagen, Victor W.
Hagen, William W. Germans, Poles, & Jews: The Nationality Conflict in the Prussian East, 1772-1914. LC 80-10557. (Illus.). 1980. lib. bdg. 17.50x (ISBN 0-226-31242-9). U of Chicago Pr.
Hagen-Ansert, Sandra L. Textbook of Diagnostic Ultrasonography. LC 78-4105. 1978. text ed. 47.50 (ISBN 0-8016-2011-2). Mosby.
Hagenbuch, W. Social Economics. (Cambridge Economic Handbook Ser). 1958. 10.95x (ISBN 0-521-08757-0). Cambridge U Pr.
Hagenmuller, P., jt. auth. see Bevan, D.
Hager, Betty. Old Jake & the Pirate's Treasure. LC 80-80606. (Illus.). 104p. (gr. 4 up). 1980. lib. bdg. 5.89 (ISBN 0-8178-0006-9). Harvey.
Hager, Jean. Captured by Love. (Orig.). 1981. pap. 1.50 (ISBN 0-440-11122-6). Dell.
--Portrait of Love. (Orig.). 1981. pap. 1.50 (ISBN 0-440-17013-3). Dell.
Hager, Stan. Lunatics & Other Lovers. 1979. 10.00 o.p. (ISBN 0-912950-14-5); pap. 4.50 o.p. (ISBN 0-912950-13-7). Blue Oak.
Hagerman, Dwain D., jt. auth. see Battagila, Frederick C.
Hagerman, Paul S. It's a Mad Mad World. LC 78-51065. (Illus.). 1978. 5.95 (ISBN 0-8069-0120-9); lib. bdg. 5.89 (ISBN 0-8069-0121-7). Sterling.
--It's an Odd World. LC 76-51184. (Illus.). (gr. 6 up). 1977. 5.95 (ISBN 0-8069-0112-8); lib. bdg. 5.89 (ISBN 0-8069-0113-6). Sterling.
Hagerman, Robert L. Mansfield: The Story of Vermont's Loftiest Mountain. LC 75-21700. (Illus.). 128p. 1975. 9.95 (ISBN 0-914016-21-0); pap. 6.95 (ISBN 0-914016-22-9). Phoenix Pub.
Hagerty, Robert & Howard, Thomas. How to Make Federal Mandatory Special Education Work for You: A Handbook for Educators & Consumers. 144p. 1978. 15.75 (ISBN 0-398-03822-8). C C Thomas.
Hagerty, W. W. & Plass, H. J., Jr. Engineering Mechanics. LC 75-4730. 672p. 1975. Repr. of 1967 ed. 19.50 o.p. (ISBN 0-88275-266-9). Krieger.
Hagerup, Inger & Tate, Joan. Helter Skelter. (Illus.). 32p. (gr. k-8). 1981. 7.95 (ISBN 0-7207-1198-3). Merrimack Bk Serv.
Haggai, J. E. Victoria Sobre las Preocupaciones. Levy, Donald L., tr. from Eng. Orig. Title: How to Win Over Worry & Care. 1980. Repr. of 1976 ed. 1.70 (ISBN 0-311-46063-1, Edit Mundo). Casa Bautista.
Haggar, Reginald & Adams, Elizabeth. Mason Porcelain & Ironstone, 1796-1853. (Illus.). 1977. 42.00 (ISBN 0-571-10945-4, Pub. by Faber & Faber). Merrimack Bk Serv.
Haggard, H. Rider. Allan Quatermain, Being an Account of His Further Adventures & Discoveries in Company with Sir Henry Curtis, Bart., Commander John Good, R.N., & One Umslopogaas. Reginald, R. & Menville, Douglas, eds. LC 80-19297. (Newcastle Forgotten Fantasy Library: Vol. 18). 278p. 1980. Repr. of 1978 ed. lib. bdg. 10.95x (ISBN 0-89370-517-9). Borgo Pr.
--Allan's Wife. Reginald, R. & Menville, Douglas, eds. LC 80-8671. (Newcastle Forgotten Fantasy Library: Vol. 24). 200p. 1980. lib. bdg. 11.95x (ISBN 0-89370-523-3). Borgo Pr.
--Ayesha: The Return of She. Reginald, R. & Menville, Douglas, eds. LC 80-19298. (Newcastle Forgotten Fantasy Library: Vol. 14). 359p. 1980. Repr. of 1977 ed. lib. bdg. 10.95x (ISBN 0-89370-513-6). Borgo Pr.
--Ayesha: The Return of She. (Illus.). 1978. pap. 3.50 (ISBN 0-486-23649-8). Dover.
--Eric Brighteyes. Reginald, R. & Menville, Douglas, eds. LC 80-24107. (Newcastle Forgotten Fantasy Library: Vol. 2). 319p. 1980. Repr. of 1974 ed. lib. bdg. 10.95x (ISBN 0-89370-501-2). Borgo Pr.
--Heart of the World. Reginald, R. & Menville, Douglas, eds. LC 80-19175. (Newcastle Forgotten Fantasy Library: Vol. 10). 347p. 1980. Repr. of 1976 ed. lib. bdg. 10.95x (ISBN 0-89370-509-8). Borgo Pr.
--Nada the Lily. Reginald, R. & Menville, Douglas, eds. LC 80-19282. (Newcastle Forgotten Fantasy Library: Vol. 20). 295p. 1980. Repr. of 1979 ed. lib. bdg. 10.95x (ISBN 0-89370-519-5). Borgo Pr.
--She. 1976. Repr. of 1887 ed. lib. bdg. 12.95 (ISBN 0-89190-705-X). Am Repr-Rivercity Pr.
--She & Allan. Reginald, R. & Menville, Douglas, eds. LC 80-19461. (Newcastle Forgotten Fantasy Library Ser.: Vol. 6). 303p. 1980. Repr. of 1977 ed. lib. bdg. 10.95x (ISBN 0-89370-505-5). Borgo Pr.
--The Spirit of Bambatse. LC 79-15278. (Forgotten Fantasy Library: Vol. 22). 1979. Repr. write for info. Newcastle Pub.
--The Spirit of Bambatse: A Romance. Reginald, R. & Menville, Douglas, eds. LC 80-19674. (Newcastle Forgotten Fantasy Library Ser.: Vol. 22). 329p. 1980. Repr. of 1979 ed. lib. bdg. 11.95x (ISBN 0-89370-521-7). Borgo Pr.
Haggard, H. W. Devils, Drugs & Doctors. (Illus.). 1976. Repr. 25.00x o.p. (ISBN 0-7158-1117-7). Charles River Bks.
Haggard, Paul W., jt. auth. see Pignani, Tullio J.
Haggard, Stephen, jt. auth. see Seyler, Athene.
Haggard, William. The Median Line. LC 80-54394. 1981. 9.95 (ISBN 0-8027-5433-3). Walker & Co.
--The Poison People. 1979. 8.95 o.s.i. (ISBN 0-8027-5401-5). Walker & Co.
Haggart, David. The Life of David Haggert, Alias John Wilson, Alias John Morison, Alias Barney M'Coul, Alias John M'Colgan, Alias Daniel O'Brien, Alias the Switcher: Written by Himself, While Under Sentence of Death. LC 80-2482. 1981. Repr. of 1821 ed. 37.50 (ISBN 0-404-19116-9). AMS Pr.
Hagger, Mark, jt. auth. see Herman, Valentine.
Haggerty, Arthur J., Capt. Dog Tricks: Teaching Your Dog to Be Useful, Fun & Entertaining. LC 77-16919. 1978. pap. 4.95 (ISBN 0-385-13493-2, Dolp). Doubleday.
Haggerty, James J. & Sebrell, William H., Jr. Food & Nutrition. (Life Science Library). (Illus.). (gr. 5 up). 1967. PLB 10.20 o.p. (ISBN 0-8094-0481-8, Pub. by Time-Life). Silver.
Haggerty, James J., jt. auth. see Stever, H. Guyford.
Haggerty, Patrick E. The Productive Society. 80p. 1974. 12.50x (ISBN 0-231-03864-X). Columbia U Pr.
Haggerty, Robert J., et al. Child Health & the Community. LC 75-1139. (Wiley Series in Health, Medicine & Society). 388p. 1975. 25.95 (ISBN 0-471-33871-0, Pub. by Wiley-Interscience). Wiley.
Haggett, Peter, et al. Locational Analysis in Human Geography, 2 vols. 2nd ed. LC 77-8967. 1977. Set. 54.95 (ISBN 0-470-99207-7); Vol. 1, Locational Models. pap. 14.95 (ISBN 0-470-99208-5); Vol. 2, Locational Methods. pap. 19.95 (ISBN 0-470-99209-3). Halsted Pr.
Haggh, Raymond, tr. see Riemann, Hugo.
Haggin, B. H. Conversations with Toscanini. 2nd ed. 1980. 11.95 (ISBN 0-8180-1244-7); pap. 5.95 (ISBN 0-8180-1220-X). Horizon.
--Discovering Balanchine. (Illus.). 196p. 1981. 19.95 (ISBN 0-8180-0404-5). Horizon.
Haggitt, T. W. Working with a Language. (Illus.). 9.50x (ISBN 0-392-01959-0, Sps). Soccer.
Hagin, F. G. A First Course in Differential Equations. (Illus.). 384p. 1975. text ed. 18.95 (ISBN 0-13-318394-7). P-H.
Hagin, Kenneth E. The Art of Intercession. 1980. pap. 3.25 (ISBN 0-89276-503-8). Hagin Ministries.
--Don't Blame God. 1979. mini bk. .50 (ISBN 0-89276-056-7). Hagin Ministries.
--Laying on of Hands. 1980. pap. 0.50 mini bk. (ISBN 0-89276-250-0). Hagin Ministries.
--El Shaddai. 1980. pap. 1.25 (ISBN 0-89276-401-5). Hagin Ministries.
--Words. 1979. mini bk. .50 (ISBN 0-89276-057-5). Hagin Ministries.
Hagin, Peter. The Epic Hero & the Decline of Heroic Poetry. 182p. 1980. Repr. of 1964 ed. lib. bdg. 25.00 (ISBN 0-89987-361-8). Darby Bks.
Hagin, Robert. Modern Portfolio Theory. 1980. pap. 10.95x (ISBN 0-256-02379-4). Irwin.
Hagin, Robert W., jt. auth. see Mader, Chris.
Hagin, Rosa. Write Right-or Left. (gr. k-3). 1981. Set Of 6. 18.50 (ISBN 0-8027-9140-9); 4.20 ea. (ISBN 0-8027-9120-4). Walker & Co.
Hagin, Rosa A., jt. auth. see Silver, Archie A.
Hagin, Rosa A., et al. Teach Manual with Task Cards. LC 76-3338. 186p. 1975. pap. text ed. 47.50 (ISBN 0-8027-9036-4). Walker Educ.
Hagiwara, M. P. & De Rocher, F. Theme et Variations. 592p. 1980. text ed. 16.95 (ISBN 0-471-05609-X); tchrs.' ed. avail. (ISBN 0-471-05612-X); wkbk. avail. (ISBN 0-471-05607-3); transcript avail. (ISBN 0-471-05613-8). Wiley.
Hagiwara, M. Peter, jt. auth. see Lindell, Anne.
Hagiwara, Michio P. & De Rocher, Francoise. Theme et variations: A Practical Introduction to French. LC 76-43036. 1977. text ed. 17.95x (ISBN 0-471-33880-X); wkbk. 6.50 (ISBN 0-471-33881-8); tchr's manual avail. (ISBN 0-471-02475-9); tapes avail. (ISBN 0-471-02476-7). Wiley.
Hagiwara, Michio P., jt. auth. see Politzer, Robert L.
Hagler, M. O. & Kristiansen, M. An Introduction to Controlled Thermonuclear Fusion. LC 74-33596. 1977. 19.95 (ISBN 0-669-99119-8). Lexington Bks.
Haglund, E. & Stevens, V. L. A Resource Guide for Mainstreaming. (Illus.). 192p. 1980. 14.75 (ISBN 0-398-04003-6). C C Thomas.

Haglund, Elizabeth, ed. Remembering: The University of Utah. (Illus.). 250p. 1981. 25.00 (ISBN 0-87480-191-5). U of Utah Pr.
Haglund, Karl T. & Notarianni, Philip F. The Avenues of Salt Lake City. LC 80-54105. (Illus.). 176p. 1980. pap. 7.50 (ISBN 0-913738-31-X). Utah St Hist Soc.
Hagman, Donald G. Cases & Materials on Public Planning & Control of Urban & Land Development. 2nd ed. LC 80-36684. (American Casebook Ser.). 1301p. 1980. text ed. 23.95 (ISBN 0-8299-2100-1). West Pub.
Hagner, Donald & Harris, Murray, eds. Pauline Studies: Essays Presented to Prof. F. F. Bruce on His 70th Birthday. LC 80-16146. 336p. 1981. 17.95 (ISBN 0-8028-3531-7). Eerdmans.
Hagood, Allen. Dinosaur: The Story Behind the Scenery. LC 75-157460. (Illus.). 1972. 7.95 (ISBN 0-916122-35-2); pap. 2.50 (ISBN 0-916122-10-7). K C Pubns.
Hagood, Allen R. This Is Zion. (Illus.). 73p. 1977. 1.75 (ISBN 0-915630-06-0). Zion.
Hagopian, Mark N. Regimes, Movements, & Ideologies: A Comparative Introduction to Political Science. LC 77-7718. (Illus.). 1978. pap. 13.50x (ISBN 0-582-28044-3); instructor's manual free (ISBN 0-582-28055-9). Longman.
Hagopian, Viola L. Italian Ars Nova Music: A Bibliographic Guide to Modern Editions & Related Literature. 2nd, rev. ed. LC 70-187748. 1973. 17.50x (ISBN 0-520-02223-8). U of Cal Pr.
Hagstrom, Julie. Traveling Games for Babies: A Handbook of Games for Infants to Five-Year-Olds. (Illus.). 96p. 1981. pap. 4.95 (ISBN 0-89104-203-2). A & W Pubs.
Hagstrum, Jean H. Sex & Sensibility: Ideal & Erotic Love from Milton to Mozart. LC 79-20657. (Illus.). 1980. text ed. 25.00 (ISBN 0-226-31289-5). U of Chicago Pr.
Hague, Hawdon. The Organic Organization & How to Manage It. LC 78-23272. 1979. 24.95x (ISBN 0-470-26563-9). Halsted Pr.
Hague, Kathleen & Hague, Michael. East of the Sun & West of the Moon. LC 80-13499. (Illus.). 48p. (gr. k-3). 1980. pap. 3.95 (ISBN 0-15-224703-3, VoyB). HarBraceJ.
--The Man Who Kept House. LC 80-26258. (Illus.). 32p. (ps-3). 1981. 11.95 (ISBN 0-15-251698-0, HJ). HarBraceJ.
Hague, Michael, jt. auth. see Hague, Kathleen.
Hague, Paul. Sea Battles in Miniature. 160p. 1980. 29.95 o.p. (ISBN 0-85059-414-6). Aztex.
Hague, Rene. Dai Greatcoat: A Self-Portrait of David Jones in His Letters. LC 80-670267. (Illus.). 320p. 1980. 37.50 (ISBN 0-571-11540-3, Pub. by Faber & Faber). Merrimack Bk Serv.
Hague, Rene, tr. see Teilhard De Chardin, Pierre.
Hague, William. Remodel, Don't Move: Make Your Home Fit Your Lifestyle. LC 80-498. (Illus.). 256p. 1981. 14.95 (ISBN 0-385-15910-2). Doubleday.
Hahm, Ben, ed. Documents of the Chilean Road to Socialism. Incl. Vol. 1. El Primer Ano del Gobierno Popular. 224p; Vol. 2. El Segundo Ano del Gobierno Popular. 400p. LC 77-26450. 1977. Set. 29.50x (ISBN 0-915980-36-3). Inst Study Human.
Hahm, Ben, intro. by. Documents of the Chilean Road to Socialism, Vol. 3. Chile 1971: Habla Fidel Castro. (Illus.). 1981. Repr. of 1971 ed. text ed. 16.75x (ISBN 0-915980-31-2). Inst Study Human.
Hahn & Springer. Canal Boat Children on the C & O, Pa., & New York Canals. 1977. 2.50 (ISBN 0-933788-57-6). Am Canal & Transport.
Hahn & Clark, eds. Life on the C & O Canal: Eighteen Fifty-Nine. 1977. 2.50 (ISBN 0-933788-54-1). Am Canal & Transport.
Hahn, B. Chekhov. 300p. 1977. 44.00 (ISBN 0-521-20951-X). Cambridge U Pr.
Hahn, Beverly. Chekhov. LC 75-22557. (Major European Authors Ser.). 1979. pap. 10.95x (ISBN 0-521-29670-6). Cambridge U Pr.
Hahn, Celia A. Minister Is Leaving: A Project Test Pattern Book in Parish Development. 1974. pap. 3.95 (ISBN 0-8164-2099-8). Crossroad NY.
Hahn, Celia A., jt. auth. see Fenhagen, James C.
Hahn, Christine. Amusement Park Machines. LC 78-26920. (Machine World Ser.). (Illus.). (gr. 2-4). 1979. PLB 9.95 (ISBN 0-8172-1330-9). Raintree Pubs.
Hahn, E. A., jt. auth. see Sturtevant, Edgar H.
Hahn, Emily. China to Me: A Partial Autobiography. LC 74-23432. (China in the 20th Century Ser). 429p. 1975. Repr. of 1944 ed. lib. bdg. 35.00 (ISBN 0-306-70695-4). Da Capo.
--Chinese Cooking. LC 68-56965. (Foods of the World Ser.). (Illus.). 200p. (gr. 6 up). 1968. lib. bdg. 11.97 (ISBN 0-8094-0062-6, Time-Life). Silver.
--Cooking of China. (Foods of the World Ser.). (Illus.). (gr. 9 up). 1968. 14.95 (ISBN 0-8094-0035-9). Time-Life.
--Lorenzo: D. H. Lawrence & the Women Who Loved Him. LC 75-11865. 368p. 1975. 12.95 o.p. (ISBN 0-397-00772-8). Lippincott.
--Love of Gold. LC 80-7877. 224p. 1980. 10.95 (ISBN 0-690-01832-0). Lippincott & Crowell.
Hahn, F. E., ed. Virus Chemotherapy. (Antibiotics & Chemotherapy Ser.: Vol. 27). (Illus.). vi, 310p. 1980. 114.00 (ISBN 3-8055-0263-X). S Karger.
Hahn, F. E., et al, eds. Progress in Molecular & Subcellular Biology, Vol. 7. (Illus.). 260p. 1980. 50.80 (ISBN 0-387-10150-0). Springer-Verlag.
Hahn, Ferdinand. The Worship of the Early Church. Reumann, John, ed. Green, David E., tr. from Ger. LC 72-87063. 144p. 1973. pap. 4.50 (ISBN 0-8006-0127-0, 1-127). Fortress.
Hahn, H. George. Henry Fielding: An Annotated Bibliography. LC 79-4498. (Author Bibliographies Ser.: No. 41). 1979. 11.00 (ISBN 0-8108-1212-6). Scarecrow.
Hahn, H. P. Von see Andrews, J. & Von Hahn, H. P.
Hahn, H. Thomas, jt. auth. see Tsai, Stephen W.
Hahn, James & Hahn, Lynn. Aim for a Job in Appliance Repair. (Aim High Ser.). 128p. 1981. lib. bdg. 5.97 (ISBN 0-8239-0541-1). Rosen Pr.
--Babe! Mildred Didrickson Zaharias. Schroeder, Howard, ed. (Sports Legends Ser.). (Illus.). 48p. (Orig.). (gr. 3-5). 1981. PLB 5.95 (ISBN 0-89686-122-8); pap. text ed. 2.95 (ISBN 0-89686-137-6). Crestwood Hse.
--Casey! Charles Stengel. Schroeder, Howard, ed. (Sports Legends Ser.). (Illus.). 48p. (Orig.). (gr. 3-5). 1981. PLB 5.95 (ISBN 0-89686-126-0); pap. text ed. 2.95 (ISBN 0-89686-141-4). Crestwood Hse.
--Environmental Careers. (Career Concise Guides Ser). (Illus.). 72p. (gr. 7 up). 1976. PLB 4.90 o.p. (ISBN 0-531-01132-1). Watts.
--Exploring a Career in Home Economics. (Careers in Depth Ser.). 140p. (gr. 7-12). 1981. lib. bdg. 5.97 (ISBN 0-8239-0530-6). Rosen Pr.
--Hamsters, Gerbils, Guinea Pigs, Pet Mice & Pet Rats. 1980. pap. 1.75 (ISBN 0-380-49239-3, 49231, Camelot). Avon.
--Hamsters, Gerbils, Guinea Pigs, Pet Mice, & Pet Rats. LC 77-1389. (Illus.). (gr. 4 up). 1977. PLB 6.45 (ISBN 0-531-01287-5). Watts.
--Henry! Henry Aaron. Schroeder, Howard, ed. (Sports Legends Ser.). (Illus.). 48p. (gr. 3-5). 1981. PLB 5.95 (ISBN 0-89686-120-1); pap. text ed. 2.95 (ISBN 0-89686-135-X). Crestwood Hse.
--The Metric System. LC 74-31386. (First Bks.). (Illus.). (gr. 3-7). 1975. PLB 4.90 o.p. (ISBN 0-531-00834-7). Watts.
--Patty! Patricia Berg. Schroeder, Howard, ed. (Sports Legends Ser.). (Illus.). 48p. (Orig.). (gr. 3-5). PLB 5.95 (ISBN 0-89686-127-9); pap. text ed. 2.95 (ISBN 0-89686-142-2). Crestwood Hse.
--Pele'! Edson do Nascimento. Schroeder, Howard, ed. (Sports Legends Ser.). (Illus.). 48p. (Orig.). (gr. 3-5). 1981. PLB 5.95 (ISBN 0-89686-125-2); pap. text ed. 2.95 (ISBN 0-89686-140-6). Crestwood Hse.
--Recycling: Reusing Our World's Solid Wastes. LC 73-4372. (First Bks.). (gr. 5 up). 1973. PLB 4.90 o.p. (ISBN 0-531-00805-3). Watts.
--Tark! Francis Tarkenton. Schroeder, Howard, ed. (Sports Legends Ser.). (Illus.). 48p. (Orig.). (gr. 3-5). 1981. PLB 5.95 (ISBN 0-89686-121-X); pap. text ed. 2.95 (ISBN 0-89686-136-8). Crestwood Hse.
--Thorpe! Jim Thorpe. Schroeder, Howard, ed. (Sports Legends Ser.). (Illus.). 48p. (Orig.). (gr. 3-5). 1981. PLB 5.95 (ISBN 0-89686-123-6); pap. text ed. 2.95 (ISBN 0-89686-138-4). Crestwood Hse.
--Wilt! Wilton Chamberlain. Schroeder, Howard, ed. (Sports Legends Ser.). (Illus.). 48p. (Orig.). (gr. 3-5). 1981. PLB 5.95 (ISBN 0-89686-124-4); pap. text ed. 2.95 (ISBN 0-89686-139-2). Crestwood Hse.
Hahn, James, jt. auth. see Hahn, Lynn.
Hahn, Lynn & Hahn, James. Plastics. LC 73-21944. (First Bks). (Illus.). 96p. (gr. 4-7). 1974. PLB 4.90 o.p. (ISBN 0-531-02702-3). Watts.
Hahn, Lynn, jt. auth. see Hahn, James.
Hahn, Lynne C., jt. auth. see McKoski, Martin M.
Hahn, Milton R; see Jones, George F.
Hahn, Robert. Creative Teachers: Who Wants Them? LC 73-6592. 272p. 1973. 16.50 (ISBN 0-471-33905-9, Pub. by Wiley). Krieger.
Hahn, Roger. The Anatomy of a Scientific Institution: The Paris Academy of Sciences, 1666-1803. LC 70-130795. (Illus.). 1971. 27.50x (ISBN 0-520-01818-4). U of Cal Pr.
Hahn, T. F. The C & O Canal Boatmen 1892 to 1929. 1980. 4.75 (ISBN 0-933788-58-4). Am Canal & Transport.
--George Washington's Canal at Great Falls, Va. 1976. 2.50 (ISBN 0-933788-55-X). Am Canal & Transport.
--Towpath Guides to the C & O Canal, 4 sections. Incl. Section 1. Georgetown to Seneca (ISBN 0-933788-50-9); Section 2. Seneca to Harper's Ferry (ISBN 0-933788-51-7); Section 3. Harper's Ferry to Ft. Frederick (ISBN 0-933788-52-5); Section 4. Ft. Frederick to Cumberland (ISBN 0-933788-53-3). 1977-78. 3.00 ea. Am Canal & Transport.
Hahn, Walter F., jt. auth. see Joshua, Wynfred.
Hahn, Walter F. & Pflatzgraff, Robert L., Jr., eds. Atlantic Community in Crisis: A Redefinition of the Transatlantic Relationship. (Pergamon Policy Studies). 386p. 1979. 42.00 (ISBN 0-08-023003-2). Pergamon.
Hahnefeld, I. W. Systematisierung von Infusionsloesungen und Grundlagen der Infusionstherapie. (Beitraege zu Infusionstherapie und klinische Ernaehrung: Band 5). (Illus.). 112p. 1980. pap. 15.00 (ISBN 3-8055-1395-X). S Karger.
Hahner, June E., ed. Women in Latin American History: Their Lives & Views. LC 75-620131. (Latin American Studies Ser.: Vol. 34). 1976. pap. text ed. 5.00 o.p. (ISBN 0-87903-034-8). UCLA Lat Am Ctr.
--Women in Latin American History: Their Lives & Views. rev. ed. LC 80-620044. (Latin American Studies: Vol. 51). 1981. pap. text ed. price not set (ISBN 0-87903-051-8). UCLA Lat Am Ctr.
Hahnewald, Harry, jt. ed. see Albert, Ronald.
Hahoda, Gloria L. Florida. (States & the Nation Ser.). (Illus.). 1976. 12.95x (ISBN 0-393-05585-X, Co-Pub by AASLH). Norton.
Haiblum, Isidore. Interworld. 1977. pap. 1.50 o.s.i. (ISBN 0-440-12285-6). Dell.
--Nightmare Express. 1979. pap. 1.95 o.p. (ISBN 0-449-14204-3, GM). Fawcett.
--Transfer to Yesterday. LC 80-2248. (Science Fiction Ser.). 192p. 1981. 9.95 (ISBN 0-385-17136-6). Doubleday.
Haiblum, Isidore, jt. auth. see Silver, Stuart.
Haich, Elisabeth. Initiation. (Illus.). 1965. 13.50 o.s.i. (ISBN 0-04-133001-3). Allen Unwin.
Haich, Elisabeth, jt. auth. see Yesudian, Selvarajan.
Haid, Helmut. Speaking of: Vein Problems. Humphries, Martha, tr. from Ger. LC 80-68765. (The Medical Adviser Ser.). (Illus.). 1980. pap. 3.95 (ISBN 0-8326-2242-7, 7456). Delair.
Haidar, Mirza M. A History of the Moghuls of Central Asia, Being the Tarikh-I-Rashidi. Elias, N., ed. Ross, E. D., tr. (Records of Asian History). (Illus.). 1972. text ed. 17.00x (ISBN 0-7007-0021-8). Humanities.
Haider, Donald H. When Governments Come to Washington: Governors, Mayors, & Intergovernmental Lobbying. LC 73-17643. (Illus.). 1974. 15.95 (ISBN 0-02-913370-X). Free Pr.
Haidinger, Timothy P. & Richardson, Dana R. A Manager's Guide to Computer Timesharing. LC 74-18413. (Manager's Guide Ser.). 192p. 1975. 18.95 (ISBN 0-471-33925-3, Pub. by Wiley-Interscience). Wiley.
Haieh, Ching-yao, et al. A Short Introduction to Modern Growth Theory. LC 78-61916. 1978. pap. text ed. 9.00 (ISBN 0-8191-0628-3). U Pr of Amer.
Haig, J. Alastair. Al Who? LC 80-52617. 270p. (Orig.). 1980. pap. 4.95 (ISBN 0-932260-05-5). Rock Harbor.
Haig-Brown, Roderick. Bright Waters, Bright Fish. (Illus.). 160p. 1980. 19.95 (ISBN 0-917304-59-4, Timber Pr). Intl Schol Bk.
--Bright Waters, Bright Fish. 1980. ltd. ed. 75.00 (ISBN 0-918400-05-8, Champoeg Pr). Intl Schol Bk.
Haig-Brown, Roderick & Wahl, Ralph. Come Wade the River. limited ed. LC 70-160188. 1971. 100.00 (ISBN 0-87564-006-0). Superior Pub.
Haigh, C. Reformation & Resistance in Tudor Lancashire. LC 73-88308. (Illus.). 416p. 1974. 42.95 (ISBN 0-521-20367-8). Cambridge U Pr.
Haigh, R. H. & Turner, P. W. Not for Glory: A Personal History of the 1914-18 War. 1969. 16.00 (ISBN 0-08-007101-5). Pergamon.
Haight, Elizabeth H. Apuleius & His Influence. LC 63-10290. (Our Debt to Greece & Rome Ser). (Illus.). 190p. 1963. Repr. of 1930 ed. 17.50x (ISBN 0-8154-0108-6). Cooper Sq.
Haight, Fulton & Cotchett, Joseph W. California Courtroom Evidence. LC 72-79475. 375p. 1981. 27.50 (ISBN 0-911110-07-0); 1979 suppl. incl. (ISBN 0-685-26721-0). Parker & Son.
Haight, M. R. A Study of Self-Deception. 1980. text ed. 20.00x (ISBN 0-391-01803-5). Humanities.
Haight, Timothy, jt. auth. see Sterling, Christopher H.
Haile, Berard. Starlore Among the Navaho. LC 76-53085. 1977. 15.00 (ISBN 0-88307-532-6); pap. 4.95 (ISBN 0-88307-533-4). Gannon.
Haile, H. G. Luther: An Experiment in Biography. LC 79-6282. (Illus.). 456p. 1980. 14.95 (ISBN 0-385-15960-9). Doubleday.
Hailes & Hubbard. Small Business Management. LC 76-3945. 1977. pap. 8.80 (ISBN 0-8273-1400-0); instructor's guide 1.60 (ISBN 0-8273-1401-9). Delmar.
Haile Sellasie I. The Autobiography of Emperor Haile Sellasis I: My Life & Ethiopia's Progress 1892-1937. Ullendorff, Edward, ed. & tr. (Illus.). 1976. 24.50x (ISBN 0-19-713589-7). Oxford U Pr.
Hailey, Anthea M., jt. ed. see Wing, J. K.
Hailey, Arthur. Hotel. 416p. 1981. pap. 3.50 (ISBN 0-553-14778-1). Bantam.
Hailey, Sheila. I Married a Best Seller. LC 77-76235. 1978. 8.95 o.p. (ISBN 0-385-12337-X). Doubleday.
Hailman, Arthur W. Phonics in Proper Perspective. 4th ed. (Illus.). 128p. 1981. pap. text ed. 6.50 (ISBN 0-675-08065-7). Merrill.
Hailman, Jack P., jt. auth. see Klopfer, Peter H.
Hailmann, W. N., tr. see Froebel, Frederich.
Hails, J. & Carr, A., eds. Nearshore Sediment Dynamics & Sedimentation. LC 75-6950. 316p. 1975. 53.50 (ISBN 0-471-33946-6, Pub. by Wiley-Interscience). Wiley.
Haim, Sylvia G., ed. Arab Nationalism: An Anthology. (California Library Reprint Ser.). 1974. 19.50x (ISBN 0-520-02645-4); pap. 3.85 (ISBN 0-520-03043-5). U of Cal Pr.
Haim, Sylvia G., jt. ed. see Kedourie, Elie.
Haiman, John. Hua: A Papuan Language of the Eastern Highlands of New Guinea. (Studies in Language Companion: No. 5). 1980. text ed. 55.00x (ISBN 90-272-3004-8). Humanities.
Haimann, Theo. Supervisory Management for Health Care Institutions. LC 72-92380. 1973. 11.00 (ISBN 0-87125-004-7). Cath Health.
Haimann, Theo, et al. Managing the Modern Organization. 3rd ed. LC 77-75879. (Illus.). 1977. text ed. 18.95 (ISBN 0-395-25512-0); inst. manual 0.95 (ISBN 0-395-25513-9); study guide 6.95 (ISBN 0-395-25514-7). HM.
Haimes, Y. & Kindler, J., eds. Water & Related Land Resource Systems: Proceedings of the IFAC Symposium, Cleveland, Ohio, U. S. A., 28-31 May 1980. LC 80-41690. (IFAC Proceedings Ser.). (Illus.). 550p. 1981. 120.00 (ISBN 0-08-027307-6). Pergamon.
Haimes, Yacov Y. Scientific, Technological & Institutional Aspects of Water Resource Policy. (AAAS Selected Symposium: No. 49). 125p. 1980. lib. bdg. 15.00x (ISBN 0-89158-842-6). Westview.
Haimes, Yacov Y., ed. Energy Auditing & Conservation: Methods, Measurement, Management, & Case Studies. LC 79-23048. 261p. 1980. pap. text ed. 22.95 (ISBN 0-89116-175-9). Hemisphere Pub.
Haimo, Oscar. Nothing Lasts Forever. 1981. deluxe ed. 9.00x (ISBN 0-686-10361-0). Haimo.
Haimovici, Henry. Vascular Emergencies. 1981. 34.50 (ISBN 0-686-69607-7). ACC.
Haims, Lawrence J. Sex Education & the Public Schools. LC 73-1014. 112p. 1973. 15.95 (ISBN 0-669-86793-4). Lexington Bks.
Haimson, Leopold H., ed. Politics of Rural Russia, 1905-1914. LC 78-62420. (Studies of the Russian Institute, Columbia University). 320p. 1979. 19.50x (ISBN 0-253-11345-8). Ind U Pr.
Hain, Paul, jt. auth. see Garcia, F. Chris.
Hainaux, Rene, ed. Stage Design Throughout the World Since 1960. 2nd ed. Bonnat, Yves. LC 72-87117. 1972. 39.95 (ISBN 0-87830-129-1). Theatre Arts.
--Stage Design Throughout the World: 1970-1975. LC 75-7879. 1976. 39.95 (ISBN 0-87830-133-X). Theatre Arts.
Haine, Edgar A. Railways Across the Andes. (Illus.). 250p. 1980. 34.95 (ISBN 0-87108-559-3). Pruett.
Hainer, K., jt. auth. see Stummel, F.
Haines, Aubrey L. Mountain Fever: Historic Conquests of Rainier. LC 62-63445. (Illus.). 1962. 8.95 (ISBN 0-87595-086-8); pap. 6.95 (ISBN 0-87595-007-8). Oreg Hist Soc.
Haines, Aubrey L., ed. see Russell, Osborne.
Haines, B. Joan & Gerber, Linda L. Guiding Young Children to Music: A Resource Book for Teachers. (Early Childhood Education Ser.: No. C24). 288p. 1980. pap. text ed. 12.95 spiral bdg. (ISBN 0-675-08161-0). Merrill.
Haines, Charles. Edgar Allan Poe: His Works & Influence. LC 74-3352. (Biography Ser). 160p. (gr. 7 up). 1974. PLB 5.90 o.p. (ISBN 0-531-02737-6). Watts.
--Florence: City of the Renaissance. LC 79-182564. (Illus.). 96p. (gr. 5-9). 1972. PLB 3.90 o.p. (ISBN 0-531-00756-1). Watts.
Haines, Charles G. The American Doctrine of Judicial Supremacy. LC 73-250. (American Constitutional & Legal History Ser.). 726p. 1973. Repr. of 1932 ed. lib. bdg. 69.50 (ISBN 0-306-70569-9). Da Capo.
--The Role of the Supreme Court in American Government & Politics 1835-1864. LC 73-604. (American Constitutional & Legal History Ser.). 544p. 1973. Repr. of 1957 ed. lib. bdg. 49.50 (ISBN 0-306-70566-4). Da Capo.

--The Role of the Supreme Court in American Government & Politics 1795-1835. LC 73-604. (American Constitutional & Legal History Ser.). 698p. 1973. Repr. of 1944 ed. lib. bdg. 69.50 (ISBN 0-306-70571-0). Da Capo.

Haines, F. The Plains Indians: Their Origins,Migrations, & Cultural Development. LC 75-23259. (Illus.). 224p. 1976. 10.95 o.s.i. (ISBN 0-690-01031-1, TYC-T). T Y Crowell.

Haines, Francis. Nez Perces: Tribesmen of the Columbia Plateau. LC 55-9626. (Civilization of American Indian Ser.: No. 42). (Illus.). 1955. 14.95 (ISBN 0-8061-0325-6); pap. 6.95 (ISBN 0-8061-0982-3). U of Okla Pr.

--Red Eagles of the Northwest: The Story of Chief Joseph & His People. LC 76-43728. (Illus.). 376p. 1980. Repr. of 1939 ed. 32.50 (ISBN 0-404-15569-3). AMS Pr.

Haines, Gail K. Baking in a Box, Cooking on a Can. LC 80-26678. (Illus.). 128p. (gr. 4-6). 1981. PLB 6.67 (ISBN 0-688-00376-1); pap. 4.95 (ISBN 0-688-00373-7). Morrow.

--Brain Power: What Does It Mean to Be Smart? (Impact Ser.). (Illus.). (gr. 7 up). 1979. PLB 6.90 s&l (ISBN 0-531-02287-0). Watts.

--Cancer. (gr. 4 up). 1980. PLB 6.45 (ISBN 0-531-04159-X). Watts.

--Explosives. LC 75-26707. (Illus.). 32p. 1976. 6.25 (ISBN 0-688-22058-4); lib. bdg. 6.00 (ISBN 0-688-32058-9). Morrow.

--Fire. LC 74-13396. (Illus.). 32p. (gr. 1-5). 1975. PLB 6.48 (ISBN 0-688-32009-0). Morrow.

--Natural & Synthetic Poisons. (Illus.). (gr. 4-6). 1978. 6.95 (ISBN 0-688-22157-2); PLB 6.67 (ISBN 0-688-32157-7). Morrow.

--Supercold - Superhot: Cryogenics & Controlled Thermonuclear Fusion. (Impact Bks.). (Illus.). 96p. (gr. 7 up). 1976. PLB 4.90 o.p. (ISBN 0-531-01203-4). Watts.

--What Makes a Lemon Sour? LC 76-28687. (Illus.). (gr. 1-5). 1978. 6.25 o.p. (ISBN 0-688-22093-2); PLB 6.96 (ISBN 0-688-32093-7). Morrow.

Haines, Gail Kay. The Elements. LC 74-180164. (First Bks). (Illus.). 96p. (gr. 4 up). 1972. PLB 4.90 o.p. (ISBN 0-531-00746-4). Watts.

Haines, George H. Consumer Behavior: Learning Models of Purchasing. LC 69-11164. (Illus.). 1969. 9.95 o.s.i. (ISBN 0-02-913390-4). Free Pr.

Haines, Gerald K. & Walker, J. Samuel, eds. American Foreign Relations: A Historiographical Review. LC 80-545. (Contributions in American History: No. 90). (Illus.). xiii, 369p. 1981. lib. bdg. 35.00 (ISBN 0-313-21061-6, HAF/). Greenwood.

Haines, Helen E. Living with Books: The Art of Book Selection. 2nd ed. LC 50-4478. 1950. 22.50x (ISBN 0-231-01803-7). Columbia U Pr.

Haines, John. Cicada. LC 77-74602. (The Wesleyan Poetry Program: Vol. 86). 1977. pap. 10.00x (ISBN 0-8195-2086-1, Pub. by Wesleyan U Pr); pap. 4.95 (ISBN 0-8195-1086-6). Columbia U Pr.

--Leaves & Ashes. 1974. pap. 2.00 o.p. (ISBN 0-87711-053-0). Kayak.

--Other Days. (Illus.). 52p. 1981. 40.00x (ISBN 0-915308-29-0); pap. 16.00x (ISBN 0-915308-30-4). Graywolf.

--The Stone Harp. LC 73-142728. (Wesleyan Poetry Program: Vol. 56). 1971. pap. 4.95 (ISBN 0-8195-1056-4, Pub. by Wesleyan U Pr). Columbia U Pr.

--Winter News. LC 66-14660. (Wesleyan Poetry Program: Vol. 29). (Orig.). 1966. 10.00x (ISBN 0-8195-2029-2, Pub. by Wesleyan U Pr); pap. 4.95 (ISBN 0-8195-1029-7). Columbia U Pr.

Haines, John, et al. Minus Thirty-One & the Wind Blowing: 9 Reflections About Living on Land. (Alaskana Book Ser.: No. 37). 150p. (Orig.). 1980. 12.95 (ISBN 0-935094-01-6); pap. 4.95 (ISBN 0-935094-03-2). Alaska Pacific.

Haines, John M. In a Dusty Light. LC 77-153718. 1978. pap. 5.00 o.p. (ISBN 0-915308-12-6). Graywolf.

Haines, Pamela. The Kissing Gate. LC 79-6581. 648p. 1981. 13.95 (ISBN 0-385-15309-0). Doubleday.

Haines, Peter G., jt. auth. see Mason, Ralph E.

Haines, R. W. Control Systems for Heating, Ventilating & Air Conditioning. LC 78-56751. 1978. pap. text ed. 8.00 (ISBN 0-8273-1804-9). Delmar.

Haines, Richard F., ed. UFO Phenomena & the Behavioral Scientist. LC 79-14878. 464p. 1979. 20.00 (ISBN 0-8108-1228-2). Scarecrow.

Haines, Robert G. Math Principles for Food Service Occupations. LC 77-88118. 1979. pap. text ed. 7.00 (ISBN 0-8273-1680-1); instructor's guide 1.60 (ISBN 0-685-91755-X). Delmar.

Haines, William W. Command Decision. LC 80-15034. (Great Classic Stories of World War II Ser.). 1980. 8.95 (ISBN 0-396-07872-9); pap. 5.95 (ISBN 0-396-07873-7). Dodd.

Haining, Peter. Ghosts: The Illustrated History. LC 74-29441. (Illus.). 128p. 1975. 9.95 o.s.i. (ISBN 0-02-547410-3). Macmillan.

--Mystery! An Illustrated History of Crime & Detective Fiction. LC 80-6170. 1981. 15.95 (ISBN 0-8128-2805-4). Stein & Day.

Haining, Peter, ed. The Ancient Mysteries Reader. LC 74-18802. 336p. 1975. 7.95 o.p. (ISBN 0-385-09867-7). Doubleday.

Hainsworth, F. Reed. Animal Physiology: Adaptations in Function. (Life Sciences Ser.). (Illus.). 600p. 1981. text ed. 19.95 (ISBN 0-201-03401-8). A-W.

Hainsworth, P. H. Agriculture, a New Approach. Bargyla & Rateaver, Gylver, eds. LC 74-33125. (Conservation Gardening & Farming Ser: Ser. C). 1976. pap. 13.00 (ISBN 0-9600698-5-2). Rateavers.

Hainsworth, R., et al, eds. Cardiac Receptors. LC 77-12404. (Illus.). 1980. 83.50 (ISBN 0-521-21853-5). Cambridge U Pr.

Hainworth, Henry. A Collector's Dictionary. (Illus.). 128p. 1981. pap. 14.95 (ISBN 0-7100-0745-0). Routledge & Kegan.

Hair, Donald S. Domestic & Heroic in Tennyson's Poetry. 272p. 1981. 25.00x (ISBN 0-8020-5530-3). U of Toronto Pr.

Hair, Michael L., jt. ed. see Bell, Alexis T.

Haire, M., ed. Modern Organization Theory: A Symposium of the Foundation for Research on Human Behavior. LC 74-30245. 334p. 1975. Repr. of 1959 ed. 15.00 o.p. (ISBN 0-88275-223-5). Krieger.

Hairston, Maxine. A Contemporary Rhetoric. 2nd ed. LC 77-78916. (Illus.). 1977. text ed. 11.95 (ISBN 0-395-25450-7); inst. manual 0.45 (ISBN 0-395-25451-5). HM.

Hairston, Maxine, jt. auth. see Trimmer, Joseph.

Hairston, Maxine C. George Sessions Perry: His Life & Works. LC 73-84416. (Illus.). 188p. 1973. 9.50 (ISBN 0-8363-0119-6). Jenkins.

Haislet, Barbara. The Rainbow Book. Blakely, Pat, ed. (Illus.). (gr. 2-6). 1977. plastic comb bdg. 3.50 o.p. (ISBN 0-930408-00-4). Parkway Pr.

--Why Are Some People Left-Handed? (Creative's Questions & Answers Ser.). (Illus.). 32p. (gr. 3-4). Date not set. PLB 5.65 (ISBN 0-87191-753-X); pap. 2.75 (ISBN 0-89812-222-8). Creative Ed. Postponed.

Haisman, Robert. Be Free: Happiness Is Owning Your Own Business. 1980. cancelled (ISBN 0-346-12464-6). Cornerstone.

Haissinsky, M., ed. Chemical & Biological Action of Radiations. 1961. Vol. 5. 38.50 (ISBN 0-12-316505-9). Acad Pr.

Haist, Grant. Modern Photographic Processing, 2 vols. LC 78-17559. (Photographic Science & Technology & Graphic Arts Ser.). 1979. Set. 85.00 (ISBN 0-471-04286-2); Vol. 1. 50.00 (ISBN 0-471-02228-4); Vol. 2. 45.00 (ISBN 0-471-04285-4, Pub. by Wiley-Interscience). Wiley.

Haitani, Kanji. The Japanese Economic System: An Institutional Overview. LC 76-11972. 1976. 18.95 (ISBN 0-669-00716-1). Lexington Bks.

Haitani, Kanji, jt. auth. see Batchelder, Alan.

Haitch, Elisabeth. Initiation. 1980. pap. write for info. PB.

Haitsma, G., jt. auth. see Mulier, Eco O.

Hajas, Jozsef, jt. auth. see Flandorffer, Tamas.

Hajdu, Eva O., jt. auth. see Hajdu, Steven I.

Hajdu, P., jt. ed. see Dezso, L.

Hajdu, Steven I. & Hajdu, Eva O. Cytopathology of Sarcomas & Other Non-Epithelial Malignant Tumors. LC 75-12488. (Illus.). 415p. 1976. text ed. 35.00 (ISBN 0-7216-4451-1). Saunders.

Hajdu, Tibor. The Hungarian Soviet Republic. De Laczay, Etelka & Fischer, Rudolph, trs. from Hungarian. LC 80-468236. (Studia Historica Academiae Scientiarum Hungaricae Ser.: No. 131). (Illus.). 172p. 1979. 20.00x (ISBN 963-05-1990-9). Intl Pubns Serv.

Hajdu, Victor. Sungates: A Testimony Carved in Wood. Stein, Rose, tr. (Illus., Hungarian.). 1980. 15.00 (ISBN 0-933652-16-X). Domjan Studio.

Hajducki, S. Maxwell. A Railway Atlas of Ireland. (Illus.). 1974. 14.95 (ISBN 0-7153-5167-2). David & Charles.

Hakanson, Lars. A Manual of Lake Morphometry. (Illus.). 100p. 1981. pap. 13.90 (ISBN 0-387-10480-1). Springer-Verlag.

Hake, Andrew. African Metropolis. LC 75-4266. 1977. 22.50 (ISBN 0-312-00980-1). St Martin.

Hake, Theodore L. Political Buttons, Bk 2: 1920-1976. LC 73-93793. (Illus.). 1977. 25.00 (ISBN 0-918708-00-1); pap. 18.00 (ISBN 0-918708-01-X). Hake.

--Political Buttons, 1789-1916, Bk 3. LC 73-93793. (Illus.). 1978. 25.00 (ISBN 0-918708-02-8); pap. 18.00 (ISBN 0-918708-03-6). Hake.

Hakeda, Yoshita S., tr. from Japanese. Kukai: Major Works, Translated with an Account of His Life & a Study of His Thought. LC 72-3124. (Records of Civilization, Sources & Studies). 328p. 1972. 17.50x (ISBN 0-231-03627-2). Columbia U Pr.

Hakeda, Yoshito, tr. Awakening of Faith. LC 67-13778. 1967. 17.50x (ISBN 0-231-03025-8). Columbia U Pr.

Hakeda, Yoshito S., tr. The Awakening of Faith, Attributed to Asvaghosha. 128p. 1974. pap. 5.00 (ISBN 0-231-08336-X). Columbia U Pr.

Haken, H. Introduction to Synergetics: Nonequilibrium Phase Transitions & Self-Organization in Physics, Chemistry & Biology. LC 76-54243. (Illus.). 1977. 33.30 o.p. (ISBN 0-387-07885-1). Springer-Verlag.

Haken, H., ed. Synergetics-A Workshop: Proceedings of the International Workshop on Synergetics at Schloss Elmau, Bavaria, Germany, May 2-7,1977. (Illus.). 1977. 34.30 (ISBN 0-387-08483-5). Springer-Verlag.

Hakes, D. T. The Development of Metalinguistic Abilities in Children. (Springer Series in Language & Communication: Vol. 9). (Illus.). 119p. 1980. 22.50 (ISBN 0-387-10295-7). Springer-Verlag.

Hakes, David T., jt. auth. see Foss, Donald J.

Hakim, Seymour. Balancing Act: A Congruence of Symbols. 55p. (Orig.). 1981. pap. 6.00x (ISBN 0-913054-12-7). Poet Gal Pr.

Hakim, Tewfik A. Fate of a Cockroach. (African Writers Ser.). 1973. pap. text ed. 3.95 (ISBN 0-435-90117-6). Heinemann Ed.

Hakki, Mamdouh. Dictionnaire Des Terms Juridiques et Commerciaux (Francais-Arabe) 1973. 20.00x (ISBN 0-685-72038-1). Intl Bk Ctr.

Hakluyt, Richard. Voyages, 8 vols. 1962. 6.00x ea. (Evman). Vol. 1 (ISBN 0-460-00264-3). Vol. 2 (ISBN 0-460-00265-1). Vol. 3 (ISBN 0-460-00313-5). Vol. 4. o.p. (ISBN 0-460-00314-3). Vol. 5 (ISBN 0-460-00338-0). Vol. 6. o.p. (ISBN 0-460-00339-9). Vol. 7 (ISBN 0-460-00388-7). Vol. 8. o.p. (ISBN 0-460-00389-5). Dutton.

Hakola, John W. Legacy of a Lifetime: The Story of Baxter State Park in Maine. (Illus.). 448p. Date not set. 16.00 (ISBN 0-931474-18-3). TBW Bks.

Haksar, Vinit. Equality, Liberty & Perfectionism. (Clarendon Library of Logic & Philosophy Ser.). 310p. 1979. text ed. 24.95x (ISBN 0-19-824418-5). Oxford U Pr.

Hakuseki, Arai. Armour Book in Honcho-Gunkiko. 35.00 (ISBN 0-87556-164-0). Saifer.

Halaby, Najeeb E. Crosswinds: An Airman's Memoir. LC 78-8210. 1978. 10.95 o.p. (ISBN 0-385-04963-3). Doubleday.

Halacy, D. S., Jr. Earthquakes: A Natural History. LC 73-13227. (Illus.). 160p. 1974. 8.50 o.p. (ISBN 0-672-51803-1). Bobbs.

--Fabulous Fireball. (Illus.). (gr. 7 up). 1957. 4.95g o.s.i. (ISBN 0-02-741340-3). Macmillan.

--Geometry of Hunger. (Illus.). 1972. 10.95 o.p. (ISBN 0-06-011746-X, HarpT). Har-Row.

--Sky on Fire. (gr. 7 up). 1965. 3.50 o.s.i. (ISBN 0-02-741720-4). Macmillan.

Halacy, Dan. Charles Babbage: Father of the Computer. LC 79-119618. (Surveyor Bks). (Illus.). (gr. 7-12). 1970. 4.95 o.s.i. (ISBN 0-02-741370-5). Macmillan.

--How to Improve Your Memory. (Career Concise Guides Ser.). (Illus.). (gr. 7 up). 1977. PLB 6.45 s&l (ISBN 0-531-00094-X). Watts.

--Nuclear Energy. LC 78-4659. (First Bks.). (Illus.). 1978. PLB 6.45 s&l (ISBN 0-531-01492-4). Watts.

Haladyna, Tom, jt. auth. see Roid, Gale.

Halamandaris, Val J., jt. auth. see Moss, Frank E.

Haland, Randi, jt. auth. see Nordstrom, Hans-Ake.

Halapy, Lili, tr. see Rozsa, Gyorgy.

Halas, Celia. Why Can't a Woman Be More Like a Man? 288p. 1981. 10.95 (ISBN 0-02-547430-8). Macmillan.

Halas, John, jt. auth. see Whitaker, Harold.

Halas, John, ed. Visual Scripting. (Library of Animation Technology). Date not set. 30.00 o.p. (ISBN 0-8038-7757-9). Hastings.

Halasa, Adnan H. The Basic Aspects of the Glaucomas. (Illus.). 244p. 1972. 19.75 (ISBN 0-398-02529-0). C C Thomas.

Halasi-Kun, ed. Pollution & Water Resources. (Columbia University Seminar Ser.). Date not set. 20.00 (ISBN 0-08-025988-X). Pergamon.

Halasi-Kun, George J. Pollution & Water Resources: Pollution & Hydrology of Surface & Groundwater -- Selected Reports. LC 78-100896. (Columbia University Seminar Ser.: Vol. XIII, Pt. 3). (Illus.). 205p. 1981. 25.00 (ISBN 0-08-027511-7). Pergamon.

Halasi-Kun, George J., ed. Pollution & Water Resourses: Pollution & Hydrology of Surface & Ground Water - Selected Reports. (Columbia University Seminar Ser.: Vol. XIII-2, 1980). (Illus.). 187p. 1981. 20.00 (ISBN 0-08-027215-0). Pergamon.

Halberg, Franz, jt. auth. see Scheving, Lawrence E.

Halberstam, David. The Powers That Be. 1980. pap. 3.50 o.s.i. (ISBN 0-440-16997-6). Dell.

Halberstam, H. & Richert, H. E. Sieve Methods. 1975. 52.00 (ISBN 0-12-318250-6). Acad Pr.

Halberstam, H., ed. see Hamilton, William R.

Halberstam, Michael. The Wanting of Levine. 1979. pap. 2.25 o.p. (ISBN 0-425-04088-7). Berkley Pub.

Halbert, Sara & Stevenson, Florence. Call Me Counselor. 1978. 8.95 o.p. (ISBN 0-397-01239-X). Lippincott.

Halbfas, Hubert. Theory of Catechetics: Language & Experience in Religious Education. LC 74-114153. 1971. 6.95 (ISBN 0-8164-1130-1). Crossroad NY.

Halbouty, Michel & Clark, James. Spindletop. 336p. 1980. 16.95 (ISBN 0-87201-791-5). Gulf Pub.

Halbritter, Kurt. Halbritter's Arms Through the Ages: An Introduction to the Secret Weapons of History. (A Richard Seaver Bk). (Illus.). 1979. 9.95 o.p. (ISBN 0-670-35908-4). Viking Pr.

Halbrook, Joyce F. A Winterthur Coloring Book. (Illus.). 1979. pap. 2.95 (ISBN 0-912724-06-4). Winterthur.

Halbroyd, L. V., jt. auth. see Hammond, Harry E.

Halbwachs, Maurice. The Causes of Suicide. Goldblatt, Harold, tr. LC 78-54110. (Illus.). 1978. 19.95 (ISBN 0-02-913540-0). Free Pr.

--The Collective Memory. Ditter, Francis J., Jr. & Ditter, Vida Y., trs. from Fr. LC 74-18576. 256p. (Orig.). 1980. pap. 5.95 (ISBN 0-06-090800-9, CN 800, CN). Har-Row.

Halcomb, Charles G., jt. auth. see Anderson, Robert P.

Halcomb, Ruth. Women Making It. 288p. 1981. pap. 2.95 (ISBN 0-345-29348-7). Ballantine.

--Women Making It. LC 79-51129. 1979. 13.95 (ISBN 0-689-10995-4). Atheneum.

Halcombe, Alvin. Find-a-Word Puzzles for Vo-Ag Students: Set 1. 1981. pap. 9.95 (ISBN 0-8134-2164-0, 2164). Interstate.

Halcroft, H. Locomotive Adventure, Vol. 2. 17.75x (ISBN 0-392-08040-0, SpS). Soccer.

Hald, A. Statistical Tables & Formulas. (Wiley Series in Probability & Mathematical Statistics). 1952. 16.50 (ISBN 0-471-34023-5, Pub. by Wiley-Interscience). Wiley.

Haldane, A. R. New Ways Through the Glens: Highland Road, Bridge & Canal Makers of the Early Nineteenth Century. (Illus.). 248p. 1973. Repr. of 1962 ed. 14.95 (ISBN 0-7153-6080-9). David & Charles.

Haldane, Bernard. Career Satisfaction & Success: A Guide to Job Freedom. (AMACOM Executive Books). 1978. pap. 4.95 (ISBN 0-8144-7501-9). Am Mgmt.

Haldane, Bernhard. How to Make a Habit of Success. 240p. 1981. pap. 2.50 (ISBN 0-446-91658-7). Warner Bks.

Haldane, E. S., ed. see Descartes, Rene.

Haldane, J. B. The Man with Two Memories. 1976. 12.95 (ISBN 0-85036-209-1). Dufour.

Haldane, Jean M., et al. Prescriptions for Parishes. 128p. 1973. pap. 2.95 (ISBN 0-8164-2080-7). Crossroad NY.

Haldane, Jolin B. Enzymes. 1965. 12.95x o.p. (ISBN 0-262-08021-4). MIT Pr.

Haldane, Sean. Applied Reichian Therapy. 1981. text ed. 34.50x (ISBN 0-8290-0121-2); audiotape cassette avail. Irvington.

Haldane, Viscount. The Reign of Relativity. 434p. 1981. Repr. lib. bdg. 35.00 (ISBN 0-8495-2354-0). Arden Lib.

Halde, du see Du Halde.

Haldeman, Joe. Infinite Dreams. 1979. pap. 2.25 (ISBN 0-380-47605-3, 47605). Avon.

--Mindbridge. 1977. pap. 1.95 (ISBN 0-380-01689-3, 33605). Avon.

--Worlds: A Novel of the Near Future. LC 80-51774. 288p. 1981. 12.95 (ISBN 0-670-78984-4). Viking Pr.

Haldeman, Linda. The Lastborn of Elvinwood. 1980. pap. 2.25 (ISBN 0-380-47985-0, 47985). Avon.

--Star of the Sea. 176p. 1981. pap. 2.25 (ISBN 0-380-54114-9, 54114). Avon.

Haldeman, Marian, ed. see Days, G. D.

Haldeman, Scott, ed. Modern Developments in the Principles & Practice of Chiropractic. 480p. 1980. 28.50x (ISBN 0-8385-6350-3). ACC.

Haldi, John F. Basic Mathematics: Skills & Structure. (Illus., LC 77-073943). 1978. pap. text ed. 14.25 (ISBN 0-395-25117-6); inst. manual 2.00 (ISBN 0-395-25114-1). HM.

Haldorsen, Sylvi. The Petrography of Tills: A Study from Ringsaker, Southeastern Norway. (Geological Survey of Norway Ser: No. 336, Bulletin 44). 32p. 1978. pap. 12.00x (ISBN 82-00-31370-0, Dist. by Columbia U Pr). Universitet.

Hale. Police Community Relations. LC 73-11827. 208p. 1974. pap. 8.80 (ISBN 0-8273-1423-X); instructor's guide 1.60 (ISBN 0-8273-1424-8). Delmar.

Hale, Arlene. Nurse Jean's Strange Case. LC 80-26058. 237p. 1980. Repr. of 1970 ed. large print ed. 8.95 (ISBN 0-89621-259-9). Thorndike Pr.

--Nurse on Leave. large print ed. LC 80-28022. 1981. Repr. of 1965 ed. 8.95 (ISBN 0-89621-270-X). Thorndike Pr.

--The Winds of Summer. 1980. lib. bdg. 13.50 (ISBN 0-8161-3168-6, Large Print Bks). G K Hall.

Hale, B. M. The Subject Bibliography of the Social Sciences & Humanities. LC 78-113358. 1970. 22.00 (ISBN 0-08-015791-2). Pergamon.

Hale, Charles D. Fundamentals of Police Administration. (Criminal Justice). 1977. text ed. 15.95 (ISBN 0-205-05688-1, 8256888); instructor's manual free (ISBN 0-205-05689-X, 825689-6). Allyn.

--Police Patrol: Operations & Management. LC 80-36814. 300p. 1981. text ed. 16.95 (ISBN 0-471-03291-3). Wiley.

Hale, Clarence E. The Stone House Murder & Other New England Tales. LC 77-88189. (Illus.). 1977. casebound 7.95 (ISBN 0-87106-090-6). Globe Pequot.

Hale, E. M., et al. Introduction to Applied Drawing. rev. ed. (gr. 7 up). 1962. pap. 4.48 (ISBN 0-87345-051-5). McKnight.

Hale, Edward E. James Russell Lowell. LC 80-20008. (American Men & Women of Letters Ser.). 310p. 1981. pap. 4.95 (ISBN 0-87754-168-X). Chelsea Hse.

--The Man Without a Country. 1976. lib. bdg. 12.95x (ISBN 0-89968-152-2). Lightyear.

Hale, Francis J. Introduction to Control System Analysis & Design. (Illus.). 400p. 1973. ref. ed. 25.95 (ISBN 0-13-479824-4). P-H.

Hale, Frederick. Danes in Wisconsin. LC 80-26088. (Illus., Orig.). 1981. pap. 2.00 (ISBN 0-87020-205-7). State Hist Soc Wis.

Hale, Frederick, jt. ed. see Sandeen, Ernest R.

Hale, Gloria, ed. The Source Book for the Disabled. 512p. 1981. pap. 3.95 (ISBN 0-553-13753-0). Bantam.

--The Source Book for the Disabled. LC 80-50722. (Illus.). 228p. Date not set. 15.95 (ISBN 0-03-057988-0); pap. 10.95 (ISBN 0-03-057654-7). HR&W. Postponed.

Hale, Helen, ed. see Klein, H. Arthur.

Hale, J. R. Renaissance Europe: The Individual & Society, 1480-1520. (Library Reprint Ser.). 1978. 18.50x (ISBN 0-520-03470-8, CAMPUS 194); pap. 5.50x (ISBN 0-520-03471-6). U of Cal Pr.

Hale, Jack K. Ordinary Differential Equations. 2nd. ed. LC 79-17238. (Pure & Applied Mathematics Ser.: Vol. 21). 350p. 1980. Repr. of 1969 ed. lib. bdg. 27.50 (ISBN 0-89874-011-8). Krieger.

Hale, Jeanne. Yesterday at the Seventh Hour. (Orig.). 1976. pap. 1.50 o.p. (ISBN 0-88368-076-9). Whitaker Hse.

Hale, Jeanne, tr. Ayer a las Siete. (Spanish Bks.). (Span.). 1977. 1.80 (ISBN 0-8297-0812-X). Life Pubs Intl.

--Hier a la Septieme Heure. (French Bks.). (Fr.). 1979. 1.80 (ISBN 0-686-28821-1). Life Pubs Intl.

--Ontem, a Hora Setima. (Portugese Bks.). (Port.). 1979. 1.50 (ISBN 0-8297-0827-8). Life Pubs Intl.

Hale, John. The Fundamentals of Radiological Science. (Illus.). 356p. 1974. text ed. 21.50 (ISBN 0-398-02805-2). C C Thomas.

Hale, John, ed. Post-War Drama: Extracts from Eleven Plays. 1967. 7.95 (ISBN 0-571-06858-8, Pub. by Faber & Faber). Merrimack Bk Serv.

Hale, John, jt. ed. see Highfield, Beryl S.

Hale, John P., jt. auth. see Arnold, Oren.

Hale, John R. Age of Exploration. LC 66-20552. (Great Ages of Man). (Illus.). (gr. 6 up). 1966. PLB 11.97 (ISBN 0-8094-0369-2, Pub. by Time-Life). Silver.

--Renaissance. LC 65-28051. (Great Ages of Man). (Illus., Fr.). (gr. 6 up). 1965. PLB 11.97 (ISBN 0-8094-0366-8, Pub. by Time-Life). Silver.

Hale, Jordan. A Typing Sourcebook. 2nd ed. LC 77-25064. 1978. pap. 6.95 (ISBN 0-672-97324-3); pap. 6.67 (ISBN 0-672-97184-4). Bobbs.

Hale, Katherine. Affinity. 1978. pap. 1.95 (ISBN 0-380-40907-0, 40907). Avon.

--Obsession. 352p. (Orig.). 1980. pap. 2.25 (ISBN 0-345-28451-8). Ballantine.

Hale, Kathleen. Orlando the Marmalade Cat & the Water Cats. LC 72-185736. (Illus.). (gr. k-3). 1979. 6.95 (ISBN 0-224-00662-2, Pub. by Chatto Bodley Jonathan). Merrimack Bk Serv.

--Orlando the Marmalade Cat Buys a Farm. (Illus.). 32p. (gr. 1-4). 1980. 6.95 (ISBN 0-224-00754-8, Pub. by Chatto Bodley Jonathan). Merrimack Bk Serv.

--Orlando the Marmalade Cat: The Frisky Housewife. (Illus.). (gr. k-3). 1979. 6.95 (ISBN 0-224-00753-X, Pub. by Chatto Bodley Jonathan). Merrimack Bk Serv.

Hale, Leon. Turn South at the Second Bridge. LC 80-5517. 224p. 1980. Repr. of 1965 ed. 12.95 (ISBN 0-89096-100-X). Tex A&M Univ Pr.

Hale, Lloyd S. & Kramer, Ruth. State Tax Liability & Compliance Manual. LC 80-21616. 350p. 1980. 37.50 (ISBN 0-471-08488-3, Pub. by Ronald Pr). Wiley.

Hale, Mabel. The Hero of Hill House. 224p. pap. 2.00. Faith Pub Hse.

--Stories of Home Folks. 160p. pap. 1.50. Faith Pub Hse.

Hale, Matthew & Giles, Jacob. The Analysis of the Law. Berkowitz, David S. & Thorne, Samuel E., eds. LC 77-86566. (Classics of English Legal History in the Modern Era Ser.: Vol. 8). 435p. 1979. lib. bdg. 40.00 (ISBN 0-8240-3057-5). Garland Pub.

Hale, Sir Matthew. Sir Matthew Hale: The Analysis of the Law: Being a Scheme or Abstract of the Several Titles & Portions of the Law of England, Digested into Method, Repr. Of 1713 Ed. Berkowitz, David & Thorne, Samuel, eds. Bd. with Giles Jacob: The Student's Companion: or, the Reason of the Laws of England, Shewing the Principal Reasons & Motives Wherein Our Laws & Statutes Are Criminal Cases; Together with the Law Itself. Jacob, Giles. Repr. of 1725 ed. LC 77-86566. (Classics of English Legal History in the Modern Era Ser.: Vol. 70). 1979. lib. bdg. 55.00 (ISBN 0-8240-3057-5). Garland Pub.

Hale, Meredith S., ed. A Practical Approach to Arm Pain. (Illus.). 116p. 1971. photocopy ed. spiral 11.75 (ISBN 0-398-00754-3). C C Thomas.

Hale, Nancy. The Life in the Studio. 1980. pap. 2.75 (ISBN 0-380-75721-4, 75721, Discus). Avon.

--The Prodigal Women. 736p. 1981. pap. 3.50 (ISBN 0-380-53553-X, 53553). Avon.

Hale, R., et al. The Principles & Practice of Health Visiting. 1968. 12.25 (ISBN 0-08-012700-2). Pergamon.

Hale, Robert B. & Coyle, Terence. Anatomy Lessons from the Great Masters. (Illus.). 1977. 21.50 (ISBN 0-8230-0222-5). Watson-Guptill.

Hale, Sara A., tr. see Mullins, Edgar Y.

Hale, Sara A., tr. see Robertson, A. T.

Hale, Sharron L. A Tribute to Yesterday. LC 80-50118. (Illus.). 224p. 1980. 25.00 (ISBN 0-913548-73-1, Valley Calif). Western Tanager.

Hale, Stu. Narragansett Bay: A Friend's Perspective. (Marine Bulletin Ser.: No. 42). 7.00 (ISBN 0-938412-19-1). URI MAS.

Hale, William H. World of Rodin. (Library of Art). (Illus.). 1969. 15.95 (ISBN 0-8094-0254-8). Time-Life.

--World of Rodin. LC 70-105511. (Library of Art Ser.). (Illus.). (gr. 6 up). 1969. 12.96 (ISBN 0-8094-0283-1, Pub. by Time-Life). Silver.

Halecki, O. Borderlands of Western Civilization: A History of East Central Europe. 1952. 18.95 (ISBN 0-8260-3740-2). Wiley.

Halen, Harry. Handbook of Oriental Collections in Finland: Manuscripts, Xylographs, Inscriptions & Russian Minority Literature. (Scandinavian Institute of Asian Studies Monograph: No. 31). 1978. pap. 15.25x (ISBN 0-7007-0105-2). Humanities.

Hales, Ann. The Children of Skylard Ward. LC 77-80836. 1978. 12.95 (ISBN 0-521-21752-0). Cambridge U Pr.

Hales, John W., et al, eds. see Percy, Bishop.

Hales, Lee, jt. auth. see Muther, Richard.

Hales, Loyde W., jt. auth. see Marshall, John C.

Hales, Mike. Living Thinwork: Where Do Labor Processes Come from? (Illus.). 192p. 1980. text ed. 26.00x (ISBN 0-906336-14-7); pap. text ed. 9.25x (ISBN 0-906336-15-5). Humanities.

Hales-Tooke, Ann, jt. auth. see Harvey, Susan.

Halet, Sydney S., ed. see Aziz, Harry.

Halevi, Z'ev. Kabbalah & Exodus. LC 80-50743. (Illus.). 234p. 1980. pap. 7.95 (ISBN 0-394-73950-7). Shambhala Pubns.

Halevi, Z'Ev B. Kabbalah & Exodus. LC 80-50743. 234p. Date not set. pap. 7.95 (ISBN 0-394-73950-7). Random.

Halevi, Z'Ev Ben Shimon. Adam & the Qabalistic Tree. 1980. pap. 7.95 (ISBN 0-87728-263-3). Weiser.

Halevy, Daniel. The End of the Notables. Silvera, Alain, ed. Guicharnaud, June, tr. from Fr. LC 73-6009. 192p. 1974. 17.50x (ISBN 0-8195-4066-8, Pub. by Wesleyan U Pr); pap. 9.00x (ISBN 0-8195-6030-8). Columbia U Pr.

Halevy, Elie. The Growth of Philosophic Radicalism. 3rd ed. (Orig.). 1972. 13.95 (ISBN 0-571-04759-9, Pub. by Faber & Faber); pap. 6.95 (ISBN 0-571-09787-1). Merrimack Bk Serv.

Halevy, Jacques-Francois. La Juive, 2 vols. Gossett, Philip & Rosen, Charles, eds. LC 76-49218. (Early Romantic Opera Ser.). 1980. 82.00 (ISBN 0-8240-2935-6). Garland Pub.

Halevy, Robyne. Knitting & Crocheting Pattern Index. LC 76-50550. 1977. 9.50 (ISBN 0-8108-0998-2). Scarecrow.

Haley, Charles W. & Schall, Larry. The Theory of Financial Decisions. 2nd ed. (Illus.). 1979. text ed. 19.95 (ISBN 0-07-025568-7, C). McGraw.

Haley, Delphine. Sleek & Savage: North America's Weasel Family. LC 75-32837. (Illus.). 128p. (YA) 1975. pap. 5.95 (ISBN 0-914718-12-6). Pacific Search.

Haley, Frances, ed. Ethnic Studies Sampler: The Best of the Title IX Project Materials. (Orig.). 1981. pap. write for info. (ISBN 0-89994-251-2). Soc Sci Ed.

Haley, George. Vicente Espinel & Marcos De Obregon: A Life & Its Literary Representation. LC 59-12056. (Brown University Studies: No. 25). (Illus.). 254p. 1959. 8.00x (ISBN 0-87057-059-5, Pub. by Brown U Pr). Univ Pr of New England.

Haley, Harold B. & Keenan, Patricia A., eds. Health Care of the Aging. 450p. 1981. write for info. (ISBN 0-8139-0869-8). U Pr of Va.

Haley, J. E., jt. auth. see Smith, Erwin E.

Haley, J. Evetts. George W. Littlefield, Texan. (Illus.). 287p. 1943. 14.95 (ISBN 0-8061-0126-1); pap. 6.95 (ISBN 0-8061-1166-6). U of Okla Pr.

--Jeff Milton: A Good Man with a Gun. (Illus.). 432p. 1981. 19.91 (ISBN 0-8061-0182-2); pap. 9.95 (ISBN 0-8061-1756-7). U of Okla Pr.

--The XIT Ranch of Texas & the Early Days of the Llano Estacado. (Western Frontier Library: No. 34). (Illus.). 1967. 8.95 (ISBN 0-8061-0728-6); pap. 3.95 (ISBN 0-8061-1428-2). U of Okla Pr.

Haley, Jay. Uncommon Therapy: The Psychiatric Techniques of Milton H. Erickson, M. D. 1977. Repr. of 1973 ed. 10.00x (ISBN 0-393-01100-3, Norton Lib); pap. 3.95 (ISBN 0-393-00846-0). Norton.

Haley, John, jt. auth. see Wilson, Dwayne.

Haley, K. Brian & Stone, Lawrence D., eds. Search Theory & Applications. (NATO Conference Ser. (Series II--Systems Science): Vol. 8). 260p. 1980. 35.00 (ISBN 0-306-40562-8, Plenum Pr). Plenum Pub.

Haley, Neale. Birds for Pets & Pleasure. LC 80-68740. (Illus.). 224p. (gr. 8). 1981. PLB 8.44 (ISBN 0-440-00476-4); pap. 4.95 (ISBN 0-440-00475-6). Delacorte.

--Judge Your Own Horsemanship. LC 74-76850. (Illus.). 169p. 1974. pap. 1.95 o.p. (ISBN 0-668-03410-6). Arco.

Haley, Ruth M., jt. auth. see Artz, Thomas.

Haley, Virginia. International English. LC 75-28718. (Illus.). 1975. pap. 7.95 (ISBN 0-8048-1151-2). C E Tuttle.

Haley-James, Shirley, ed. Perspectives on Writing in Grades 1-8. 1981. pap. price not set (ISBN 0-8141-3519-6). NCTE.

Halford, W. Wayne. NAEB History, Vol. 2. 173p. 1966. pap. 2.00 (Pub Telecomm). NAEB.

Halhuber, Carola. Cigarette End. 1978. pap. 3.95 o.s.i. (ISBN 0-7225-0423-3). Newcastle Pub.

Halhuber, M. J. & Siegrist, J., eds. Myocardial Infarction & Psychosocial Risks. (Illus.). 152p. 1981. pap. 22.50 (ISBN 0-387-10386-4). Springer-Verlag.

Haliburton, Gordon. Historical Dictionary of Lesotho. LC 76-49550. (African Historical Dictionaries Ser.: No. 10). (Illus.). 1977. 12.00 (ISBN 0-8108-0993-1). Scarecrow.

Haliburton, Thomas C. Sam Slick. Baker, Ray P., ed. 420p. 1981. Repr. of 1923 ed. lib. bdg. 45.00 (ISBN 0-8495-2373-7). Arden Lib.

Halick, Irene. A Blackberry Named Patty. 1977. pap. 1.50 o.p. (ISBN 0-917726-12-X). Hunter Bks.

Haliday, Charles. The Scandinavian Kingdom of Dublin. 300p. 1980. Repr. of 1884 ed. 15.00 (ISBN 0-7165-0052-3, Pub. by Irish Academic Pr Ireland). Biblio Dist.

Halier, William. The Rise of Puritanism. LC 57-10117. 479p. 1972. pap. 8.50x (ISBN 0-8122-1048-4, Pa Paperbks). U of Pa Pr.

Halim, A. & Das, A. C. Surface & Radiological Anatomy. 2nd rev. ed. 1980. text ed. 15.00x (ISBN 0-7069-0640-3, Pub. by Vikas India). Advent Bk.

Halima, Toure. Careers in Physical Rehabilitation Therapy. (Career Concise Guides Ser.). (Illus.). (gr. 7 up). 1977. PLB 6.45 s&l (ISBN 0-531-01306-5). Watts.

Halkerston, Ian, ed. Biochemistry. 2nd ed. LC 79-83718. (Basic Sciences PreTest Self-Assessment & Review Ser.). (Illus.). 1979. 9.95 (ISBN 0-07-050963-8). McGraw-Pretest.

Hall. Building Service & Equipment Four: Checkbook. 1981. text ed. price not set (ISBN 0-408-00613-7). Butterworth.

--Foundations of Jurisprudence. 1973. 15.00 (ISBN 0-672-81849-3, Bobbs-Merrill Law). Michie.

--Language of Advertising & Merchandising in English. (English for Careers Ser.). (gr. 10 up). 1981. pap. text ed. 3.25 (ISBN 0-88345-352-5). Regents Pub.

--The Language of Electrical & Electronic Engineering in English. (English for Careers Ser.). (gr. 10 up). 1977. pap. text ed. 3.25 (ISBN 0-88345-301-0). Regents Pub.

--Long Road to Freedom. LC 78-60562. 1978. pap. 6.50 (ISBN 0-913408-41-7). Friends United.

Hall & Davis. Course of Europe Since Waterloo, 2 vols. Schmeller, Kurt R., ed. Incl. Vol. 1. From Vienna to Sarajevo (ISBN 0-89197-203-X); Vol. 2. The Twentieth Century (ISBN 0-8290-0379-7). LC 68-15856. (Illus.). 1980. pap. text ed. 14.50x ea. Irvington.

Hall, A. Drought & Irrigation in North-East Brazil. LC 77-82497. (Latin American Studies: No. 29). (Illus.). 1978. 23.95 (ISBN 0-521-21811-X). Cambridge U Pr.

--Scandal Sensation & Social Democracy. LC 76-46856. 1977. 32.95 (ISBN 0-521-21531-5). Cambridge U Pr.

Hall, A. & Kabailo, A. P. Basic Concepts of Structural Analysis. LC 77-8289. 1977. 21.95 (ISBN 0-470-99213-1). Halsted Pr.

Hall, A. R. Philosophers at War. LC 79-15724. 1980. 29.95 (ISBN 0-521-22732-1). Cambridge U Pr.

Hall, A. R., ed. see Newton, Isaac.

Hall, Adam. The Ninth Directive. 1979. cancelled o.s.i. (ISBN 0-515-05204-3). Jove Pubns.

--The Quiller Memorandum. 1979. pap. 1.75 o.s.i. (ISBN 0-515-05211-6). Jove Pubns.

--The Scorpion Signal. LC 80-85103. 288p. 1981. pap. 2.95 (ISBN 0-87216-831-X). Playboy Pbks.

--Striker Portfolio. 1970. pap. 1.75 o.s.i. (ISBN 0-685-19679-8). Jove Pubns.

Hall, Al, ed. Datsun Tune-up & Repair. LC 79-64834. (Tune-up & Repair Ser.). (Illus.). 198p. (Orig.). 1979. pap. 4.95 (ISBN 0-8227-5050-3). Petersen Pub.

--Pinto Tune-up & Repair. LC 79-64837. (Tune-up & Repair Ser.). (Illus.). 198p. (Orig.). 1979. pap. 4.95 (ISBN 0-8227-5047-3). Petersen Pub.

--Toyota Tune-up & Repair. LC 79-64836. (Tune-up & Repair Ser.). (Illus.). 198p. (Orig.). 1979. pap. 4.95 (ISBN 0-8227-5048-1). Petersen Pub.

Hall, Alan. Conrad & the Congo. (gr. 10-12). 1972. pap. text ed. 2.75x o.p. (ISBN 0-88334-047-X). Ind Sch Pr.

Hall, Anna M. The Whiteboy: A Story of Ireland. (Nineteenth Century Fiction Ser.: Ireland: Vol. 48). 634p. 1979. lib. bdg. 46.00 (ISBN 0-8240-3497-X). Garland Pub.

Hall, Anna Maria. Lights & Shadows of Irish Life, 3 vols. Wolff, Robert L., ed. (Ireland Nineteenth Century Fiction, Ser. Two: Vol. 47). 1979. lib. bdg. 46.00 ea. (ISBN 0-8240-3496-1). Garland Pub.

--Sketches of Irish Character, 2 vols. Wolff, Robert L., ed. (Ireland Nineteenth Century Fiction, Ser. Two: Vol. 46). 1979. Set. lib. bdg. 92.00 (ISBN 0-8240-3495-3); lib. bdg. 46.00 ea. Garland Pub.

--Stories of the Irish Peasantry. Wolff, Robert L., ed. (Ireland Nineteenth Century Fiction, Ser. Two: Vol. 49). 1979. lib. bdg. 46.00 (ISBN 0-8240-3498-8). Garland Pub.

Hall, Anthony. The Point of Entry: A Study of Client Reception in the Social Services. (National Institute Social Services Library). 1974. text ed. 17.95x o.p. (ISBN 0-04-360031-X). Allen Unwin.

Hall, Archibald J. Standard Handbook of Textiles. 8th ed. 1970. 41.95 (ISBN 0-87245-596-3). Textile Bk.

Hall, B. T. Auditing the Modern Hospital. 256p. 1977. 32.95 (ISBN 0-686-68587-3, 14920). Hospital Finan.

Hall, Benjamin H. Collection of College Words & Customs. LC 68-17995. 1968. Repr. of 1856 ed. 24.00 (ISBN 0-8103-3282-5). Gale.

Hall, Brenny, jt. auth. see Peterson, Carolyn S.

Hall, Brian & Smith, Maury. Value Clarification As Learning Process: A Handbook for Christian Educators. LC 73-81108. (Educator Formation Bks). (Orig.). 1974. pap. 8.95 (ISBN 0-8091-1797-5). Paulist Pr.

Hall, Brian & Tonna, Benjamin. God's Plan for Us. LC 80-81439. 128p. 1980. pap. 8.95 (ISBN 0-8091-2311-8). Paulist Pr.

Hall, Brian K. Developmental & Cellular Skeletal Biology. 1978. 27.50 (ISBN 0-12-318950-0). Acad Pr.

Hall, Brian P. Leadership Through Values: A Study in Personal & Organizational Development. LC 80-81438. (Illus.). 112p. (Orig.). 1980. pap. 8.95 (ISBN 0-8091-2313-4). Paulist Pr.

Hall, Bryan D., jt. ed. see Golbus, Mitchell S.

Hall, Bryan D., jt. ed. see O'Donnell, James J.

Hall, Bud L. & Kidd, Roby, eds. Adult Learning: A Design for Action: A Comprehensive International Survey. 1978. text ed. 52.00 (ISBN 0-08-022245-5); pap. text ed. 15.00 (ISBN 0-08-023007-5). Pergamon.

Hall, C. F., tr. see Saakyan, G. S.

Hall, C. M. Woman Unliberated: Difficulties & Limitations in Changing Self. new ed. LC 78-21874. 1979. pap. text ed. 14.95 (ISBN 0-89116-097-3). Hemisphere Pub.

Hall, C. Margaret. The Bowen Family Theory & Its Uses. LC 79-64456. 1981. 20.00 (ISBN 0-87668-373-1). Aronson.
--Field Notes: & Butterflies Beget Butterflies. LC 77-74865. 1978. 5.00 (ISBN 0-87212-084-8). Libra.
--Giving Birth. LC 79-53198. 1979. pap. 2.25 (ISBN 0-931590-03-5). Antietam Pr.
Hall, Calvin S. & Lindzey, Gardner. Theories of Personality. 3rd ed. LC 77-26692. 1978. text ed. 23.95 (ISBN 0-471-34227-0); wkbk. 6.95 (ISBN 0-471-72926-4); test 1.00 (ISBN 0-471-03755-9). Wiley.
Hall, Calvin S. & Nordby, Vernon J. A Primer of Jungian Psychology. 144p. 1973. pap. 1.75 (ISBN 0-451-61865-3, ME1865, Ment). NAL.
Hall, Calvin S., jt. auth. see Nordby, Vernon J.
Hall, Carl. Biomass As an Alternative Fuel. LC 80-84729. 350p. 1981. 35.00 (ISBN 0-86587-087-X). Gov Insts.
Hall, Carl W. Drying & Storage of Agricultural Crops. (Illus.). 1980. pap. text ed. 21.50 (ISBN 0-87055-364-X). AVI.
Hall, Carl W. & Davis, Denny C. Processing Equipment for Agricultural Products. 2nd ed. (Illus.). 1979. lib. bdg. 19.50 (ISBN 0-87055-270-8). AVI.
Hall, Carl W. & Hedrick, T. I. Drying of Milk & Milk Products. 2nd ed. (Illus.). 1971. text ed. 29.50 (ISBN 0-87055-107-8). AVI.
Hall, Carl W., jt. auth. see Harper, W. J.
Hall, Carl W., et al. Encyclopedia of Food Engineering. (Illus.). 1971. lib. bdg. 75.00 (ISBN 0-87055-086-1). AVI.
Hall, Carol, jt. auth. see Calloway, Northern J.
Hall, Caroline, jt. auth. see Breese, Burtis B.
Hall, Carolyn V. Soft Sculpture. LC 80-67546. (Illus.). 112p. 1981. 14.95 (ISBN 0-87192-129-4). Davis Mass.
Hall, Cecil E. Introduction to Electron Microscopy. 2nd ed. LC 80-39788. 410p. 1981. Repr. of 1966 ed. lib. bdg. price not set (ISBN 0-89874-302-8). Krieger.
Hall, Charles A. & Day, John W., Jr., eds. Ecosystems Modeling in Theory & Practice: An Introduction with Case Histories. LC 76-57204. 1977. 40.00 (ISBN 0-471-34165-7, Pub. by Wiley-Interscience). Wiley.
Hall, Charles A., tr. see Cullmann, Oscar.
Hall, Chris. Southern Rock: A Climber's Guide to the South. (Illus.). 192p. 1981. pap. 7.95 (ISBN 0-914788-37-X). East Woods.
Hall, Christopher. Polymer Materials: An Introduction for Technologists & Scientists. LC 80-19341. 250p. 1981. 29.95 (ISBN 0-470-27028-4). Halsted Pr.
Hall, Christopher D., jt. auth. see Barzel, Yoram.
Hall, Clarence W. Adventurers for God. LC 75-36730. 1976. pap. 1.95 o.p. (ISBN 0-06-063571-1, HJ 18, HarpR). Har-Row.
Hall, David. Geography & the Geography Teacher. (Unwin Education Books: Teaching Today Ser.). 1976. text ed. 18.95x o.p. (ISBN 0-04-371043-3); pap. text ed. 11.50x (ISBN 0-04-371044-1). Allen Unwin.
Hall, David & Stacey, Margaret, eds. Beyond Separation: Further Studies of Children in Hospital. (Medicine, Illness & Society Ser.). 1979. 18.00x (ISBN 0-7100-0163-0). Routledge & Kegan.
Hall, David A. The Aging of Connective Tissue. 1976. 28.00 (ISBN 0-12-319150-5). Acad Pr.
Hall, David L. The Uncertain Phoenix: Adventures Toward a Post-Cultural Sensibility. LC 80-67033. 160p. 1981. 17.50x (ISBN 0-8232-1053-7); pap. 7.50 (ISBN 0-8232-1054-5). Fordham.
Hall, David O. & Hawkins, S. E. Laboratory Manual of Cell Biology. LC 74-21529. 1974. pap. 11.50x (ISBN 0-8448-0601-3). Crane-Russak Co.
Hall, David S. Elements of Estimating. 1972. 21.50 o.p. (ISBN 0-7134-0526-0, Pub. by Batsford England). David & Charles.
Hall, Dennis. Stomping Ground. 1981. pap. 2.95 (ISBN 0-440-17615-8). Dell.
Hall, Dennis, jt. auth. see Emsley, John.
Hall, Derek R. A Spatial Analysis of Urban Community Development Policy in India. (Geography & Public Policy Research Studies Ser.). 192p. 1981. 33.75 (ISBN 0-471-27862-9, Pub. by Wiley-Interscience). Wiley.
Hall, Don. Love Listens. 288p. (Orig.). 1981. pap. 2.50 (ISBN 0-523-41034-4). Pinnacle Bks.
Hall, Donald. Goatfoot Milktongue Twinbird. LC 77-3248. (Poets on Poetry Ser.). pap. 5.95 (ISBN 0-472-40000-2). U of Mich Pr.
--Marianne Moore: The Cage & the Animal. LC 71-114171. (American Authors Ser). 1970. 8.95 (ISBN 0-672-53560-2). Pegasus.
--Remembering Poets. LC 76-47266. (Illus.). 1978. 10.95 o.s.i. (ISBN 0-06-011723-0, HarpT). Har-Row.
Hall, Donald, ed. Modern Stylists: Writers on the Art of Writing. LC 68-12918. (Orig.). 1968. 5.95 o.s.i. (ISBN 0-02-913630-X); pap. text ed. 5.95 (ISBN 0-02-913640-7). Free Pr.
Hall, Donald & Pack, Robert, eds. New Poets of England & America: Second Selection. (Orig.). 1962. pap. 4.95 o.p. (ISBN 0-452-00135-8, F135, Mer). NAL.
Hall, Donald, ed. see Kinnell, Galway.
Hall, Donald, ed. see Stafford, William.
Hall, Donald, ed. see Whitman, Walt.
Hall, Donald E. Musical Acoustics: An Introduction. 528p. 1979. text ed. 17.95x (ISBN 0-534-00758-9). Wadsworth Pub.
Hall, Dorothy. The Book of Herbs. LC 74-3666. 1974. 7.95 o.p. (ISBN 0-684-13822-0, ScribT). Scribner.
--The Herb Tea Book. LC 80-84436. (Pivot Original Health Bk.). (Illus.). 120p. 1981. pap. 2.25 (ISBN 0-87983-248-7). Keats.
--The Herb Tea Book. LC 80-84436. (Pivet Original Health Bk.). (Illus.). 120p. 1981. pap. 2.25 (ISBN 0-87983-248-7). Keats.
--Iridology: How the Eyes Reveal Your Health & Personality. LC 80-84439. (Illus.). 256p. (Orig.). 1981. pap. 8.95 (ISBN 0-87983-241-X). Keats.
--Natural Health Book. LC 77-74715. (Illus.). 1977. pap. 6.95 o.p. (ISBN 0-684-15228-2, ScribT). Scribner.
Hall, Douglas J. Lighten Our Darkness: Toward an Indigenous Theology of the Cross. LC 75-38963. pap. 9.95 (ISBN 0-664-24359-2). Westminster.
Hall, Douglas K. Let'er Buck. LC 73-76497. 1973. 10.00 o.p. (ISBN 0-8415-0274-9). Dutton.
--The Master of Oakwindsor. 1976. 8.95 o.s.i. (ISBN 0-690-01171-7, TYC-T). T Y Crowell.
--Rodeo. 1976. pap. 7.95 o.p. (ISBN 0-345-24877-5). Ballantine.
--Van People: The Great American Rainbow Boogie. LC 77-451. (Illus.). 1977. 17.95 o.s.i. (ISBN 0-690-01418-X, TYC-T); pap. 8.95 o.s.i. (ISBN 0-690-01452-X, TYC-T). T Y Crowell.
Hall, Douglas T., jt. auth. see Hall, Francine S.
Hall, Douglas V. & Hall, Marybelle B. Experiments in Microprocessors & Digital Systems. (Illus.). 176p. 1981. 7.95x (ISBN 0-07-025576-8, G). McGraw.
Hall, E. C., tr. see Vignaux, Paul.
Hall, E. Raymond. Mammals of North America, 2 vols. 2nd. ed. LC 79-4109. 1981. Set. 70.00 (ISBN 0-471-05595-6, Pub. by Wiley-Interscience); Vol. 1. 40.00 (ISBN 0-471-05443-7); Vol. 2. 40.00 (ISBN 0-471-05444-5). Wiley.
Hall, E. S., ed. see Holz, R. K., et al.
Hall, Edward T. Hidden Dimension. LC 66-11173. (Illus.). 1969. pap. 3.50 (ISBN 0-385-08476-5, A609, Anch). Doubleday.
--Perspective: An Introduction to Boarding School for Prospective Candidates. (gr. 6-12). pap. text ed. 1.50x o.p. (ISBN 0-88334-083-6). Ind Sch Pr.
--The Silent Language. LC 72-97265. 240p. 1973. pap. 3.50 (ISBN 0-385-05549-8, Anch). Doubleday.
Hall, Elvajean. The Land & People of Argentina. rev. ed. LC 77-37251. (Portraits of the Nations Ser.). (Illus.). (gr. 6 up). 1972. 8.79 (ISBN 0-397-31257-1). Lippincott.
Hall, Elvajean, jt. auth. see Houlehen, Robert J.
Hall, Elvajean, ed. Proverbs: A Selection. LC 73-10094. (Illustrated Editions). (Illus.). (gr. 7 up). 1970. PLB 3.90 o.p. (ISBN 0-531-01084-8). Watts.
Hall, Eugene J. English Self-Taught. Incl. Bk. 1. 372p (ISBN 0-88345-210-3, 18140); Bk. 2. 401p (ISBN 0-88345-211-1, 18143); Bk. 3 (ISBN 0-88345-212-X, 18146); Bk. 4 (ISBN 0-88345-213-8, 18149); Bk. 5 (ISBN 0-88345-214-6, 18152); Bk. 6 (ISBN 0-88345-215-4, 18155). (gr. 7 up). 1974. wkbk. 8.25 ea.; 6-cassette album 60.00 ea. filmstrips 65.00 ea.; cassette, filmstrip & worktext sets 125.00 ea.; worktexts 1-6 & cassettes 325.00 (ISBN 0-685-48092-5). Regents Pub.
--English Self-Taught, Bk. 7. 382p. (gr. 7 up). 1974. 8.25 (ISBN 0-88345-221-9); cassettes 60.00 (ISBN 0-685-53166-X). Regents Pub.
--English Self-Taught, Bk. 8. (English Self-Taught Ser.). 358p. (gr. 7 up). 1975. 8.25 (ISBN 0-88345-223-5); cassettes 60.00 (ISBN 0-685-59324-X). Regents Pub.
--English Self-Taught, Bk. 9. (English Self-Taught Ser.). 331p. (gr. 7 up). 1975. 8.25 (ISBN 0-88345-224-3); cassettes 60.00 (ISBN 0-685-59322-3). Regents Pub.
--English Self-Taught, Bk. 10. (English Self-Taught Ser.). 318p. (gr. 7 up). 1975. 8.25 (ISBN 0-88345-225-1); cassettes 60.00 (ISBN 0-685-59326-6). Regents Pub.
--English Self-Taught, Bk. 11. (Illus.). 315p. 1975. pap. 8.25 (ISBN 0-88345-226-X); cassettes 60.00 (ISBN 0-685-62261-4). Regents Pub.
--English Self-Taught, Bk. 12. (Illus.). 308p. 1976. pap. 8.25 (ISBN 0-88345-227-8); cassettes 60.00 (ISBN 0-685-63972-X). Regents Pub.
--Estudios de Ingles: Intermedio-Avanzado. (gr. 9 up). 1965. pap. text ed. 2.95 (ISBN 0-88345-049-6, 17388); Set. records 40.00 (ISBN 0-685-48111-5); Set. cassettes 40.00 (ISBN 0-685-48112-3). ans. key 1.00 (ISBN 0-686-67014-0). Regents Pub.
Hall, Everett W. What Is Value? (International Library of Psychology, Philosophy & Scientific Method). 1961. Repr. of 1952 ed. text ed. 10.00x (ISBN 0-391-00452-2). Humanities.
Hall, F. M. Introduction to Abstract Algebra, Vol. 1. 2nd ed. (Illus.). 314p. 1980. pap. 12.50x (ISBN 0-521-29861-X). Cambridge U Pr.
--An Introduction to Abstract Algebra, Vol. 1. 2nd ed. LC 75-185565. 314p. 1972. 27.50x (ISBN 0-521-08484-9). Cambridge U Pr.
--Introduction to Abstract Algebra, Vol. 2. LC 66-10040. (Illus.). 1969. text ed. 35.50x (ISBN 0-521-07055-4). Cambridge U Pr.
--Introduction to Abstract Algebra, Vol. 2. (Illus.). 400p. 1980. pap. 15.95x (ISBN 0-521-29862-8). Cambridge U Pr.
Hall, F. W., ed. see Aristophanes.
Hall, Frances A., jt. auth. see Hall, Robert R., Jr.
Hall, Francine S. & Hall, Douglas T. Two-Career Couple. (Illus.). 1979. 10.95 (ISBN 0-201-02733-X); pap. 5.95 (ISBN 0-201-02734-8). A-W.
Hall, Francis J. Theological Outlines. 1895. 7.95 o.p. (ISBN 0-8192-1037-4). Morehouse.
Hall, Frederick. Bible Quizzes for Everybody. (Quiz & Puzzle Bks.). 150p. 1980. pap. 2.95 (ISBN 0-8010-4032-9). Baker Bk.
Hall, G. & Jones, H. Competency-Based Education: Process for Improvement of Education. LC 75-17564. (Illus.). 384p. 1975. 18.95 (ISBN 0-13-154864-6). P-H.
Hall, G. S. see Whyte, Robert.
Hall, G. Stanley & Mansfield, John M. Hints Toward a Select & Descriptive Bibliography of Education. LC 72-10907. xx, 332p. 1973. Repr. of 1886 ed. 24.00 (ISBN 0-8103-3176-4). Gale.
Hall, Gene E., jt. auth. see Butts, David P.
Hall, George, jt. auth. see Weller, Robert S.
Hall, Gerald. How to Completely Secure Your Home. (Illus.). 1978. 9.95 o.p. (ISBN 0-8306-7758-5); pap. 7.95 (ISBN 0-8306-6758-X, 758). TAB Bks.
Hall, Gerry. Offbeat Canada. (Orig.). 1981. pap. 2.50 (ISBN 0-451-09842-0, E9842, Sig). NAL.
Hall, Gertrude H., et al. Guide to Development of Protective Services for Older People. 160p. 1973. 13.75 (ISBN 0-398-02604-1); pap. 8.75 (ISBN 0-398-02758-7). C C Thomas.
Hall, Gimone. Hide My Savage Heart. 1977. pap. 1.95 o.s.i. (ISBN 0-515-04058-4). Jove Pubns.
Hall, Gladys. Prostitution in the Modern World: Prostitution Ser. Winick, Charles, ed. LC 78-60866. (Vol. 6). 200p. 1979. lib. bdg. 20.00 (ISBN 0-8240-9722-X). Garland Pub.
Hall, Grover C., Jr. Death Squadron. (World at War Ser.: No. 20). 432p. 1980. pap. 2.75 (ISBN 0-89083-636-1). Zebra.
Hall, Gus. Basics: For Peace, Democracy & Social Progress. 348p. (Orig.). 1980. 14.00 (ISBN 0-7178-0580-8); pap. 4.50 (ISBN 0-7178-0578-6). Intl Pub Co.
--Imperialism Today: An Evaluation of Major Issues & Events of Our Time. LC 72-90500. 384p. 1972. 2.50 o.p. (ISBN 0-7178-0303-1); pap. 3.50 (ISBN 0-7178-0304-X). Intl Pub Co.
Hall, H. Diseases & Parasites of Livestock in the Tropics. (Intermediate Tropical Agriculture Ser.). 1977. pap. text ed. 7.95x (ISBN 0-582-60618-7). Longman.
Hall, H. E. Solid State Physics. LC 73-10743. (Manchester Physics Ser.). 372p. 1974. 40.25 (ISBN 0-471-34280-7); pap. 16.75 (ISBN 0-471-34281-5, Pub. by Wiley-Interscience). Wiley.
Hall, H. van see Van Hall, H.
Hall, H. W. SFBRI: Science Fiction Book Review Index, 10 vols. Incl. Vol. 1. 1970 (ISBN 0-89370-066-5); Vol. 2. 1971 (ISBN 0-89370-067-3); Vol. 3. 1972 (ISBN 0-89370-068-1); Vol. 4. 1973 (ISBN 0-89370-069-X); Vol. 5. 1974 (ISBN 0-89370-070-3); Vol. 6. 1975 (ISBN 0-89370-071-1); Vol. 7. 1976 (ISBN 0-89370-072-X); Vol. 8. 1977 (ISBN 0-89370-073-8); Vol. 9. 1978 (ISBN 0-89370-074-6); Vol. 12. 1979 (ISBN 0-89370-075-4). LC 72-625320. 64p. Vols. 1-9. lib. bdg. 11.95x ea.; Vol. 12. lib. bdg. 12.95x. Borgo Pr.
--SFBRI: Science Fiction Book Review Index, Vol. 11, 1980. LC 72-625320. 54p. (Orig.). 1981. pap. text ed. 5.00 (ISBN 0-935064-06-0). H W Hall.
--SFBRI: Science Fiction Book Review Index, Vol. 5: 1974. LC 72-625320. 1975. 5.00 (ISBN 0-935064-00-1). H W Hall.
--SFBRI: Science Fiction Book Review Index, Vol. 7: 1976. LC 72-625320. 1977. 5.00 (ISBN 0-935064-02-8). H W Hall.
--SFBRI: 1975. LC 72-625320. 1976. 5.00 (ISBN 0-935064-01-X). H W Hall.
Hall, H. W., ed. Science Fiction Book Review Index 1923-1973. LC 74-29085. 1975. 70.00 (ISBN 0-8103-1054-6). Gale.
--SFBRI: Science Fiction Book Review Index, Vol. 9: 1978. LC 72-625320. 1979. pap. 4.50 (ISBN 0-935064-04-4). H W Hall.
Hall, Harrison, jt. ed. see Dreyfus, Hubert L.
Hall, Harry H. A Johnny Reb Band from Salem. (Music Reprint 1980 Ser.). (Illus.). xi, 118p. 1980. Repr. of 1963 ed. lib. bdg. 15.00 (ISBN 0-306-76014-2). Da Capo.
Hall, Howard, jt. auth. see Rabalais, Maria.
Hall, J. B. Claudian: De Raptu Proserpinae. LC 69-14395. (Cambridge Classical Texts & Commentaries Ser). 1969. 44.00 (ISBN 0-521-07442-8). Cambridge U Pr.
Hall, J. C. The Bombyliidae of Chile (Diptera: Bombyliidae) (Publications in Entomology: Vol. 76). 1975. pap. 15.00x (ISBN 0-520-09510-3). U of Cal Pr.
Hall, J. L. & Baker, D. A. Cell Membranes & Ion Transport. (Integrated Themes in Biology Ser.). (Illus.). 1978. pap. text ed. 10.50x (ISBN 0-582-44192-7). Longman.
Hall, J. L., et al. Plant Cell Structure & Metabolism. LC 73-85204. (Illus.). 360p. (Orig.). 1974. pap. text ed. 18.95x (ISBN 0-582-44119-6). Longman.
Hall, J. W., jt. auth. see Kulp, C. A.
Hall, Jack & Lessard, Victoria C. The Vocational-Technical Core Collection: Vol. I, Books. 400p. 1980. 35.00 (ISBN 0-918212-46-4). Neal-Schuman.
--The Vocational-Technical Core Collection: Vol. II, Media. 400p. 1981. 35.00 (ISBN 0-918212-47-2). Neal-Schuman.
Hall, Jack C. A Review of the Subfamily Cylleniinae with a World Revision of the Genus Thevenemyia Bigot (Eclimus Acut.) (Diptera: Bombyliidae) (U. C. Publ. in Entomology: Vol. 56). 1969. pap. 7.00x (ISBN 0-520-09129-9). U of Cal Pr.
Hall, Jacquelyn D. Revolt Against Chivalry: Jessie Daniel Ames & the Women's Campaign Against Lynching. 1979. 17.50 (ISBN 0-231-04040-7). Columbia U Pr.
Hall, James. Dictionary of Subjects & Symbols in Art. 2nd, rev. ed. LC 74-6578. (Icon Editions). (Illus.). 1979. 15.95 (ISBN 0-06-433316-7, HarpT); pap. 7.95 (ISBN 0-06-430100-1, IN-100, HarpT). Har-Row.
--Letters from the West. LC 67-10123. 1967. Repr. of 1828 ed. 41.00x (ISBN 0-8201-1024-8). Schol Facsimiles.
--Seven Stories. Burtschi, Mary, ed. 1981. 5.95. Little Brick Hse.
--Seven Stories. Burtschi, Mary, ed. LC 75-23549. 1975. 5.00 (ISBN 0-9601642-1-9). Little Brick Hse.
Hall, James, jt. auth. see Morrison, James W.
Hall, James A. Clinical Uses of Dreams: Jungian Interpretation & Enactments. 1978. 31.25 (ISBN 0-8089-1053-1). Grune.
Hall, James B. Her Name. 1980. 17.50x (ISBN 0-915316-64-1); pap. 5.00 (ISBN 0-915316-63-3). Pentagram.
--Minor White: Rites & Passages. LC 77-80023. (Illus.). 144p. 1981. 25.00 (ISBN 0-89381-069-X); pap. 15.00. Aperture.
Hall, James Baker, ed. Ralph Eugene Meatyard: An Aperture Monograph, V0l.18. LC 74-76879. (Illus.). 144p. 1974. 20.00 (ISBN 0-912334-61-4); pap. 12.50 (ISBN 0-912334-62-2). Aperture.
Hall, James H. Art Song. 1953. pap. 6.95 (ISBN 0-8061-1197-6). U of Okla Pr.
Hall, James L. & Humbertson, Albert O., Jr. Correlative Study Guide for Neuroanatomy. 2nd ed. (Illus.). 1970. pap. 10.95x o.p. (ISBN 0-06-141076-4, Harper Medical). Har-Row.
Hall, James N. High Adventure. 237p. 1980. Repr. of 1918 ed. lib. bdg. 30.00 (ISBN 0-89984-283-6). Century Bookbindery.
--High Adventure: A Narrative of Air Fighting in France. Gilbert, James, ed. LC 79-7267. (Flight: Its First Seventy-Five Years Ser.). 1979. Repr. of 1918 ed. lib. bdg. 20.00x (ISBN 0-405-12177-6). Arno.
Hall, James N. see Gravel, Fern, pseud.
Hall, James P. Peacekeeping in America: A Developmental Study of American Law Enforcement: Philosophy & Systems. 1978. pap. text ed. 11.95 (ISBN 0-8403-1143-5). Kendall-Hunt.
Hall, Jay. The Competence Process. LC 80-51211. (Illus.). 1980. text ed. 17.95 (ISBN 0-937932-01-9). Teleometrics.
Hall, Jennie. Buried Cities. rev. ed. 1964. 4.95 o.s.i. (ISBN 0-02-741940-1). Macmillan.
Hall, Jerome. General Principles of Criminal Law. 2nd ed. 1960. 17.00 (ISBN 0-672-80035-7, Bobbs-Merrill Law). Michie.
Hall, Jessie M. A Young Man Growing up. 1979. 4.00 o.p. (ISBN 0-8062-1234-9). Carlton.
Hall, Jim. The Mating Reflex. LC 80-70563. (Poetry Ser.). 1980. 9.95 (ISBN 0-915604-41-8); pap. 4.95 (ISBN 0-915604-42-6). Carnegie-Mellon.

Hall, Joanne. Mexican Tapestry Weaving. LC 77-351132. (Illus.). 1976. wrap-around spiral bdg., leatherette 9.95 (ISBN 0-9602098-0-8). J Arvidson.

Hall, John. Puzzlers Gamebook. (gr. 4 up). 1979. pap. 2.25 (ISBN 0-912300-50-7). Troubador Pr.

Hall, John C., tr. from Japanese. Japanese Feudal Law. (Studies in Japanese Law & Government). (Illus.). 266p. 1979. Repr. of 1906 ed. 24.50 (ISBN 0-89093-211-5). U Pubns Amer.

Hall, John F. Classical Conditioning & Instrumental Learning: A Contemporary Approach. LC 75-32539. 528p. 1976. text ed. 13.00 o.p. (ISBN 0-397-47346-X). Lippincott.

Hall, John R. The Ways Out: Utopian Communal Groups in an Age of Babylon. (International Library of Sociology Ser.). 1978. 22.50 (ISBN 0-7100-8807-8). Routledge & Kegan.

Hall, John W. Government & Local Power in Japan: A Study Based on the Bizen Province, 500-1700. (Illus.). 1966. 22.50x (ISBN 0-691-03019-7); pap. 8.95 (ISBN 0-691-00780-2). Princeton U Pr.

--Government & Local Power in Japan: A Study on Bizen Province, 500-1700. LC 65-14307. (Illus.). 446p. 1980. 30.00x. Princeton U Pr.

Hall, John W., jt. auth. see Kulp, C. A.

Hall, John W. & Toyoda, Takeshi, eds. Japan in the Muromachi Age. LC 74-22963. 1977. 24.00x (ISBN 0-520-02888-0); pap. 7.95x (ISBN 0-520-03214-4). U of Cal Pr.

Hall, John W., et al, eds. Japan Before Tokugawa: Political Consolidation & Economic Growth, 1500 to 1650. LC 80-7524. (Illus.). 400p. 1981. 32.50 (ISBN 0-691-05308-1). Princeton U Pr.

Hall, Joseph. The Discovery of a New World (Mundus Alter et Idem) Healey, J., tr. LC 72-6935. (English Experience Ser.: No. 119). 1969. Repr. of 1609 ed. 46.00 (ISBN 90-221-0119-3). Walter J Johnson.

--Quo Vadis? A Just Censure of Travell As It Is Commonly Undertaken by the Gentlemen of Our Nation. LC 74-28860. (English Experience Ser.: No. 740). 1975. Repr. of 1617 ed. 6.00 (ISBN 90-221-0165-7). Walter J Johnson.

Hall, Katherine R. E. B. White: A Bibliographic Catalogue of Printed Materials in the Department of Rare Books, Cornell University Library. (Garland Reference Library of the Humanities Ser.). 550p. 1979. lib. bdg. 40.00 (ISBN 0-8240-9549-9). Garland Pub.

Hall, Kathleen M., ed. see De La Taille, Jean.

Hall, Katy. Nothing but Soup. (Picture Bk). (Illus.). 32p. (gr. 1 up). 1976. 5.95 o.p. (ISBN 0-695-80670-X); lib. ed. 5.97 o.p. (ISBN 0-695-40670-1). Follett.

Hall, Katy & Eisenberg, Lisa. A Gallery of Monsters. (Illus.). 64p. (gr. 2-5). 1981. pap. 2.95 (ISBN 0-394-84743-1). Random.

Hall, Keith & Vikmyhr, Ronald. Smart Keno Play. (Gamblers Book Shelf). 64p. 1979. pap. 2.95 (ISBN 0-89650-561-8). Gamblers.

Hall, Kenneth. Trade & Statecraft in the Age of the Cholas. 1980. 16.00x (ISBN 0-8364-0597-8). South Asia Bks.

Hall, Kenneth & Miller, Isobel. Retraining & Tradition. 1975. text ed. 21.00x (ISBN 0-04-658215-0). Allen Unwin.

Hall, Kenneth R. & Whitmore, John K., eds. Explorations in Early Southeast Asian History: The Origins of Southeast Asian Statecraft. LC 76-6836. (Michigan Papers on South & Southeast Asia: No. 11). (Illus.). 350p. 1976. pap. 7.50x (ISBN 0-89148-011-0). Ctr S&SE Asian.

Hall, Kermit L. The Politics of Justice: Lower Federal Judicial Selection & the Second Party System, 1829-1861. LC 79-9238. 1979. 19.50x (ISBN 0-8032-2302-1). U of Nebr Pr.

Hall, L. Secretarial & Administrative Practice. 3rd ed. (Illus.). 304p. 1978. pap. 10.95 (ISBN 0-7121-1958-2, Pub. by Macdonald & Evans England). Intl Ideas.

Hall, Lawrence S., ed. Seeing & Describing: Selected Descriptive Writing. (Uses of English Ser.). 1966. pap. text ed. 2.95x o.p. (ISBN 0-669-21006-4). Heath.

Hall, Lenwood W., et al. Power Plant Chlorination: A Biological & Chemical Assessment. 302p. 1981. text ed. 39.95 (ISBN 0-250-40396-X). Ann Arbor Science.

Hall, Leonard. A Journal of the Seasons on an Ozark Farm. LC 57-7800. (Illus.). 242p. 1980. pap. 6.95 (ISBN 0-8262-0317-5). U of Mo Pr.

Hall, Lewis. Pruning Simplified: A Complete Guide to Pruning Trees, Bushes, Hedges, Flowers, & House Plants. 1979. 12.95 (ISBN 0-87857-248-1). Rodale Pr Inc.

Hall, Louis B. The Knightly Tales of Sir Gawain. LC 76-17866. (Illus.). 192p. 1976. 12.95 (ISBN 0-88229-350-8); pap. 7.95 (ISBN 0-88229-407-5). Nelson-Hall.

Hall, Luella J. United States & Morocco, 1776-1956. LC 71-142233. 1971. 35.00- (ISBN 0-8108-0338-0). Scarecrow.

Hall, Lynn. The Disappearing Grandad. 64p. 1980. lib. bdg. 5.39 (ISBN 0-695-41467-4). Follett.

--Dragon's Delight. (Dragon Ser.). 112p. 1980. lib. bdg. 5.97 (ISBN 0-695-41366-X). Follett.

--The Ghost of the Great River Inn. 64p. 1980. PLB 5.39 (ISBN 0-695-41465-8). Follett.

--The Haunting of the Green Bird. 64p. 1980. lib. bdg. 5.39 (ISBN 0-695-41466-6). Follett.

--The Horse Trader. 144p. (gr. 5 up). 1981. 8.95 (ISBN 0-684-16852-9). Scribner.

--Kids & Dog Shows. LC 73-93558. 160p. (gr. 4-7). 1974. 5.95 o.p. (ISBN 0-695-80482-0); lib. bdg. 5.97 o.p. (ISBN 0-695-40482-2). Follett.

--The Leaving. LC 80-18636. 128p. (gr. 7 up). 1980. 7.95 (ISBN 0-684-16716-6). Scribner.

--The Mysterious Moortown Bridge. 64p. 1980. PLB 4.39 (ISBN 0-695-41468-2). Follett.

--The Mystery of Plum Park Pony. LC 79-28125. (Mystery Ser.). 64p. (gr. 3). 1980. PLB 5.67 (ISBN 0-8116-6414-7). Garrard.

--A New Day for Dragons. 1976. pap. 1.25 (ISBN 0-380-00763-0, 30528, Camelot). Avon.

--Riff, Remember. (gr. 3-7). 1975. pap. 0.95 o.s.i. (ISBN 0-380-00186-1, 21899, Camelot). Avon.

--The Shy Ones. (YA) (gr. 9-12). 1977. pap. 1.50 (ISBN 0-380-45310-X, 45310, Camelot). Avon.

--The Siege of Silent Henry. LC 72-2789. 160p. (gr. 7 up). 1972. 4.95 o.p. (ISBN 0-695-80041-8). Follett.

--Stray. (gr. 2-4). 1975. pap. 0.95 (ISBN 0-380-00202-7, 23473, Camelot). Avon.

--To Catch a Tartar. LC 72-85582. 96p. (gr. 4-6). 1973. 4.95 o.p. (ISBN 0-695-80370-0, T0370); PLB 5.97 o.p. (ISBN 0-695-40370-2, L0370). Follett.

--Troublemaker. LC 74-78455. (Illus.). 96p. (gr. 3-6). 1974. 4.95 o.p. (ISBN 0-695-80479-0); lib. bdg. 4.98 o.p. (ISBN 0-695-40479-2). Follett.

--Troublemaker. (Illus.). (gr. 3-5). 1975. pap. 1.25 o.s.i. (ISBN 0-380-00434-8, 26203, Camelot). Avon.

Hall, M., Jr., ed. see Symposia in Applied Mathematics-New York-1958.

Hall, Malcolm. Edward, Benjamin & Butter. (Illus.). 48p. (gr. 6-9). 1981. PLB 6.99 (ISBN 0-698-30731-3). Coward.

--The Friends of Charlie Ant Bear. (A Break-of-Day Bk.). (Illus.). 64p. (gr. 3-5). 1980. PLB 6.59 (ISBN 0-698-30711-9). Coward.

Hall, Malcolm H., jt. auth. see Wilson, David H.

Hall, Mandel, jt. auth. see Sabbath, Dan.

Hall, Manly P. Healing: Divine Art. 9.90 (ISBN 0-89314-390-1); pap. 4.95 (ISBN 0-686-68489-3). Philos Res.

Hall, Marie B. Common Sense & the Battle of the Sexes. 2.50 (ISBN 0-938760-02-5). Veritas.

Hall, Marilyn C., jt. auth. see Hall, R. Vance.

Hall, Marilyn C., jt. auth. see Vance, R.

Hall, Mark A. & Lesser, Milton S. Review Text in Biology. (Illus., Orig.). (gr. 10-12). 1966. pap. text ed. 5.67 (ISBN 0-87720-051-3). AMSCO Sch.

Hall, Marryanne, jt. auth. see Wilson, Robert M.

Hall, Marshall & Hall, Sandra. The Truth: God or Evolution. 192p. 1975. pap. 3.45 (ISBN 0-8010-4139-2). Baker Bk.

Hall, Marshall see Whytt, Robert.

Hall, Marshall, Jr. The Theory of Groups. 2nd ed. LC 75-42306. xiii, 434p. text ed. 11.95 (ISBN 0-8284-0288-4). Chelsea Pub.

Hall, Marshall, Jr., ed. see Society for Industrial & Applied Mathematics - American Mathematical Society Symposia - New York - March, 1971.

Hall, Martyn T. Easy Vegetable Growing. (Penny Pinchers Ser.). 1978. 2.95 (ISBN 0-7153-7547-4). David & Charles.

Hall, Mary A. Teaching Reading As a Language Experience. 3rd ed. (Illus.). 160p. 1981. pap. text ed. 6.95 (ISBN 0-686-69503-8). Merrill.

Hall, Mary A. & Ramig, Christopher J. Linguistic Foundations for Reading. 1978. pap. text ed. 6.95 (ISBN 0-675-08448-2). Merrill.

Hall, MaryAnne. Teaching Reading As a Language Experience. 2nd ed. (Elementary Education Ser.). 128p. 1976. pap. text ed. 7.95x (ISBN 0-675-08666-3). Merrill.

Hall, Marybelle B., jt. auth. see Hall, Douglas V.

Hall, Michael G., et al, eds. Glorious Revolution in America: Documents on the Colonial Crisis of 1689. 1972. pap. text ed. 4.95x (ISBN 0-393-09398-0). Norton.

Hall, Miriam, et al. The Madison Connection: Voices of the '60s. (Harvest Bk. Ser.: Nos. 17-20). (Illus.). 180p. 1980. write for info. (0146-5414). Harvest Pubns.

Hall, N. John, ed. The Trollope Critics. 1981. 28.50x (ISBN 0-389-20044-1). B&N.

Hall, Nancy. The Big Enough Helper. (Illus.). (gr. k-3). 1978. PLB 5.00 (ISBN 0-307-60152-8, Golden Pr). Western Pub.

Hall, Nancy & Riley, Jean. Bargello Borders. (Illus.). 1977. pap. 9.95 o.p. (ISBN 0-684-15287-8, SL745, ScribT). Scribner.

Hall, Nancy A. Snowmobiles. (Illus.). (gr. 6-8). pap. 3.00 o.p. (ISBN 0-513-01315-6). Denison.

Hall, Nelson. A Complete Course in Super Ju Jitsu. pap. 13.95 (ISBN 0-911012-38-9). Nelson-Hall.

Hall, Nor. The Moon & the Virgin: Reflections on the Archetypal Feminine. LC 78-2138. (Illus.). 1981. pap. 5.95 (ISBN 0-06-090793-2, CN 793, CN). Har-Row.

Hall, P. G. & Hayde, C. C. Martingale Limit Theory & Its Application. LC 80-536. (Probability & Mathematical Statistics Ser.). 1980. 36.00 (ISBN 0-12-319350-8). Acad Pr.

Hall, Peter. London Two Thousand. (Illus., Orig.). 1971. pap. 5.95 (ISBN 0-571-09705-7, Pub. by Faber & Faber). Merrimack Bk Serv.

Hall, Peter & Hay, Dennis. Growth Centres in the European Urban System. 1980. 28.50 o.p. (ISBN 0-520-04198-4). U of Cal Pr.

Hall, Peter, jt. auth. see Ewbank, Inga-Stina.

Hall, Peter, ed. Europe Two Thousand. LC 77-9479. 1977. 16.00x (ISBN 0-231-04462-3). Columbia U Pr.

Hall, Peter, et al. The Containment of Urban England. (Political & Economic Planning Ser.). (Illus.). 1977. pap. text ed. 42.50x o.p. (ISBN 0-04-352066-9). Allen Unwin.

Hall, R. K., ed. Kokutai No Hongi. 1949. 12.50 (ISBN 0-89020-008-4). Brown Bk.

Hall, R. Vance. Applications in School & Home. (Managing Behavior Ser.: Part 3). 1974. 3.35 (ISBN 0-89079-003-5). H & H Ent.

--Basic Principles. (Managing Behavior Ser.: Part 2). 1975. 3.35 (ISBN 0-89079-002-7). H & H Ent.

--The Measurement of Behavior. (Managing Behavior Ser.: Part 1). 1974. 3.25 (ISBN 0-89079-001-9). H & H Ent.

Hall, R. Vance & Hall, Marilyn C. How to Use Planned Ignoring. 1980. 3.25 (ISBN 0-89079-045-0). H & H Ent.

--How to Use Systematic Attention & Approval. 1980. 3.25 (ISBN 0-89079-044-2). H & H Ent.

--How to Use Time Out. 1980. 3.25 (ISBN 0-89079-046-9). H & H Ent.

Hall, Radclyffe. The Unlit Lamp. (A Virago Modern Classic Ser.). 324p. 1981. pap. 5.95 (ISBN 0-8037-9171-2). Dial.

--The Well of Loneliness. 448p. 1981. pap. 3.95 (ISBN 0-380-54247-1, Bard). Avon.

Hall, Raymond L. Black Separatism & Social Reality. LC 75-34419. 1977. text ed. 35.00 (ISBN 0-08-019510-5); pap. text ed. 15.00 (ISBN 0-08-019509-1). Pergamon.

--Black Separatism in the United States. LC 77-75515. 318p. 1978. text ed. 17.50x (ISBN 0-87451-146-1). U Pr of New Eng.

Hall, Raymond L., ed. Ethnic Autonomy: Comparative Dynamics - the Americas, Europe & the Developing World. (Pergamon Policy Studies). 1979. 47.00 (ISBN 0-08-023683-9); pap. 10.95 (ISBN 0-08-023682-0). Pergamon.

Hall, Richard. Couplings: A Book of Stories. LC 80-26609. 160p. 1981. 12.00 (ISBN 0-912516-57-7); pap. 4.95 (ISBN 0-912516-58-5). Grey Fox.

--Zambia, 1890-1964: The Colonial Period. (Illus.). 1977. pap. text ed. 6.50x (ISBN 0-582-64620-0). Longman.

Hall, Richard C., ed. Psychiatric Presentation of Medical Illness: Somatopsychic Disorders. (Illus.). 428p. 1980. text ed. 35.00 (ISBN 0-89335-098-2). Spectrum Pub.

--Psychiatry in Crisis. 1981. text ed. write for info. (ISBN 0-89335-133-4). Spectrum Pub.

Hall, Richard C., jt. ed. see Levenson, Alvin J.

Hall, Richard H. Occupations & the Social Structure. 2nd ed. LC 74-23243. (Illus.). 384p. 1975. text ed. 17.95 (ISBN 0-13-629345-X). P-H.

Hall, Richard S. Organizations: Structure & Process. 2nd ed. LC 76-45743. (Illus.). 384p. 1977. text ed. 17.95 (ISBN 0-13-642025-7). P-H.

Hall, Robert A., Jr. Antonio Fogazzaro. (World Authors Ser.: No. 470). 1978. lib. bdg. 12.50 (ISBN 0-8057-6311-2). Twayne.

Hall, Robert A., Jr; see Bottiglia, William F.

Hall, Robert A., Jr., jt. auth. see Denoeu, Francois.

Hall, Robert B. Anyone Can Prophesy. LC 77-8267. 1977. pap. 3.95 (ISBN 0-8164-2158-7). Crossroad NY.

Hall, Robert E., M.D. Nine Month's Reading: Medical Guide for Pregnant Women. rev. ed. LC 72-77076. 192p. 1972. 8.95 (ISBN 0-385-03688-4). Doubleday.

Hall, Robert L. Exit Sherlock Holmes: The Great Detective's Final Days. LC 76-56152. 1977. 7.95 o.p. (ISBN 0-684-14849-8, ScribT). Scribner.

Hall, Robert R., Jr. & Hall, Frances A. Two Thousand & One Italian & English Idioms: 2001 Locuzione Italiane e Inglese. 1980. pap. text ed. 9.95 (ISBN 0-8120-0467-1). Barron.

Hall, Rosalys. Bright & Shining Breadboard. LC 69-14329. (Illus.). (gr. k-3). 1969. 8.25 (ISBN 0-688-41121-5); PLB 7.92 o.p. (ISBN 0-688-51121-X). Lothrop.

Hall, Ross H. Modified Nucleosides in Nucleic Acids. LC 73-122745. (Molecular Biology Ser). 1971. 27.50x (ISBN 0-231-03018-5). Columbia U Pr.

Hall, Ruth. Three Steps to Heaven. 1981. 4.95 (ISBN 0-8062-1560-7). Carlton.

Hall, Sandra, jt. auth. see Hall, Marshall.

Hall, Sandra P. & Hirsch, Felice L. Fingertip Reference for Dental Materials. LC 79-54689. (Dental Assisting Ser.). 121p. 1981. pap. text ed. 8.00 (ISBN 0-8273-1863-4). Delmar.

Hall, Sharon, ed. Twentieth-Century Literary Criticism. (Twentieth-Century Literary Criticism Ser.: Vol. 4). 650p. 1981. 58.00 (ISBN 0-8103-0178-4). Gale.

Hall, Sharon & Mendelson, Phyllis C., eds. Twentieth-Century Literary Criticism, Vol. 1. LC 76-46132. 1978. 54.00 (ISBN 0-8103-0175-X). Gale.

Hall, Sharon K., ed. Twentieth-Century Literary Criticism. LC 76-46132. (Vol. 3). 600p. 1980. 58.00 (ISBN 0-8103-0177-6). Gale.

Hall, Shawn. A Guide to the Ghost Towns & Mining Camps of Nye County, Nevada. (Illus.). 156p. 1981. 9.95 (ISBN 0-396-07955-5). Dodd.

Hall, Sherwood. With Stethoscope in Asia: Korea. LC 77-81765. 1978. 15.95 (ISBN 0-930696-01-8). MCL Assocs.

Hall, Stephen P. Split Rock: Epoch of a Lighthouse. LC 77-26287. (Minn. Historic Sites Pamphlet Ser.: No. 15). 24p. 1978. pap. 1.50 (ISBN 0-87351-122-0). Minn Hist.

Hall, Susan J. Africa in U. S. Schools, K-12: A Survey. 39p. (Orig.). 1978. pap. text ed. 4.00 (ISBN 0-89192-292-X). Interbk Inc.

--Africa 1974: Turning Points in American Policy. 1974. pap. 1.50 (ISBN 0-89192-074-9). Interbk Inc.

Hall, T. E., et al, eds. Semigroups. LC 80-23748. 1980. 18.00 (ISBN 0-12-319450-4). Acad Pr.

Hall, Theodore P. & Farmer, Silas. Grosse Pointe on Lake Sainte Claire. LC 73-17472. 114p. 1974. Repr. of 1886 ed. 6.00 (ISBN 0-8103-3879-3). Gale.

Hall, Thor. The State of the Arts in North America: Systematic Theology Today. LC 78-70520. 1978. pap. text ed. 9.00 (ISBN 0-8191-0645-3). U Pr of Amer.

Hall, Thor & Price, James L. Advent-Christmas. LC 74-24899. (Proclamation 1: Aids for Interpreting the Lessons of the Church Year, Ser. B). 64p. 1974. pap. 1.95 (ISBN 0-8006-4071-3, 1-4071). Fortress.

Hall, Timothy C. & Davies, Jeffrey W. Nucleic Acids in Plants, 2 vols. 1979. Vol. 1, 272p. 64.95 (ISBN 0-8493-5291-6); Vol. 2, 256p. 59.95 (ISBN 0-8493-5292-4). CRC Pr.

Hall, Tom. Academic Ropes: A Perceptual-Motor Academic Program. Alexander, Frank & Alexander, Diane, eds. (Illus.). 89p. (Orig.). 1981. pap. 5.95 (ISBN 0-915256-08-8). Front Row.

--Classroom-Made Movement Materials: A Perceptual-Motor Program with Classroom-Made Materials. Alexander, Frank & Alexander, Diane, eds. (Illus., Orig.). 1981. pap. 5.95 (ISBN 0-915256-09-6). Front Row.

--Total Sailing. LC 78-75340. (Illus.). 1980. 17.50 (ISBN 0-498-02309-5). A S Barnes.

Hall, Trevor H. Dorothy L. Sayers: Nine Literary Studies. (Illus.). 132p. 1980. 19.50 (ISBN 0-208-01877-8, Archon). Shoe String.

--Spiritualists: The Story of Florence Cook & William Crookes. 1963. 4.50 o.p. (ISBN 0-912326-06-9). Garrett-Helix.

--The Strange Case of Edmund Gurney. 2nd ed. (Illus.). 219p. 1980. 26.50x (ISBN 0-7156-1154-2, Pub. by Duckworth England). Biblio Dist.

Hall, Trish. The New Connecticut Yankees. (Illus.). (gr. 9-12). 1981. 7.95 (ISBN 0-938348-07-8); pap. 2.95 (ISBN 0-938348-08-6); limited edition 12.95 (ISBN 0-938348-06-X). Cottage Indus.

Hall, Vance, jt. ed. see Coley, Noel.

Hall, Vernon, compiled by. Literary Criticisms: Plato Through Johnson. LC 76-123515. (Goldentree Bibliographies in Language & Literature Ser). (Orig.). 1970. pap. 6.95x (ISBN 0-88295-516-0). AHM Pub.

Hall, Virginius C., Jr. Portraits in the Collection of the Virginia Historical Society: A Catalogue. LC 80-14079. 1981. price not set (ISBN 0-8139-0813-2). U Pr of Va.

Hall, W. J. Structural & Geotechnical Mechanics: A Volume Honoring Nathan M. Newmark. LC 76-28735. (Illus.). 1977. ref. ed. 32.95 (ISBN 0-13-853804-2). P-H.

Hall, W. P., et al. History of England & the Empire Commonwealth. 5th ed. 1971. text ed. 25.50 (ISBN 0-471-00225-9). Wiley.

Hall, Wayne E. Shadowy Heroes: Irish Literature of the 1890's. LC 80-21383. (Irish Studies). (Illus.). 1980. 20.00x (ISBN 0-8156-2231-7). Syracuse U Pr.

Hall, Wendy, jt. auth. see Mead, W. R.

Hall, Wendy, ed. Rare Afro-Americana: A Reconstruction of the Adger Library. (Reference Book Ser.). 1981. 25.00 (ISBN 0-8161-8175-6). G K Hall.
Hall, Wesley W., jt. auth. see Harpe, Shideler.
Hall, William, jt. auth. see Morgan, Douglas.
Hall, William D. & Landsittell, David L. A New Look at Accounting for Pension Costs. 1977. 11.50x (ISBN 0-256-01971-1). Irwin.
Hall, Willis. Christmas Crackers. 1978. pap. text ed. 2.95 (ISBN 0-435-23369-6). Heinemann Ed.
--Kidnapped at Christmas: A Play for Children. (gr. 10). 1975. pap. text ed. 2.95x (ISBN 0-435-23368-8). Heinemann Ed.
--Long & the Short & the Tall. pap. 1.35x o.s.i. (ISBN 0-87830-532-7). Theatre Arts.
--The Play of the Royal Astrologers. pap. text ed. 2.50x o.p. (ISBN 0-435-21007-6). Heinemann Ed.
Hall, Z. W., jt. ed. see Otsuka, Masanori.
Hallahan, D. & Cruickshank, W. Psychoeducational Foundations of Learning Disabilities. 1979. 8.95 (ISBN 0-13-734285-3). P-H.
Hallahan, D. & Kauffman, J. Introduction to Learning Disabilities: The Psycho-Behavioral Approach. 1976. 17.95 (ISBN 0-13-485524-8). P-H.
Hallahan, Daniel P. & Kauffman, James M. Exceptional Children: Introduction to Special Education. (Special Education Ser.). 1978. ref. ed. 18.95 (ISBN 0-13-293944-4). P-H.
Hallahan, Daniel P., jt. ed. see Cruickshank, William M.
Hallahan, William. The Trade. LC 80-22248. 384p. 1981. 11.95 (ISBN 0-688-00103-3). Morrow.
Hallak, J. Analysis of Educational Costs & Expenditure. (Fundamentals of Educational Planning Ser., No. 10). (Orig.). 1969. pap. 6.00 (ISBN 92-803-1029-1, U16, UNESCO). Unipub.
Hallak, Jacques, jt. auth. see Coombs, Philip H.
Hallam, A. Jurassic Environments. LC 74-80359. (Earth Science Ser.). (Illus.). 260p. 1975. 47.50 (ISBN 0-521-20555-7). Cambridge U Pr.
Hallam, Arthur F. Christian Capitalism. 182p. (Orig.). 1981. pap. 14.95 (ISBN 0-938770-00-4). Capitalist Pr OH.
Hallam, Elizabeth M. Capetian France Nine Hundred Thirty-Seven to Thirteen Hundred Twenty-Eight. (Illus.). 368p. 1980. text ed. 45.00 cased (ISBN 0-582-48909-1). Longman.
Hallam, Harry M. Saudi Arabia & the Economic & Political Control of the World. 1979. 55.80 (ISBN 0-930008-44-8). Inst Econ Pol.
Hallam, Henry. Constitutional History of England, from the Accession of Henry VII to the Death of George II, 2 vols, Vol. 83. Berkowitz, David & Thorne, Samuel, eds. LC 77-86590. (Classics of English Legal History in the Modern Era Ser.). 1979. lib. bdg. 110.00 (ISBN 0-8240-3070-2). Garland Pub.
Hallam, Jack. Ghosts of the North. LC 76-40612. (Ghosts Ser.). (Illus.). 1976. 4.50 o.p. (ISBN 0-7153-7320-X). David & Charles.
--Ghosts' Who's Who. 1977. 7.95 (ISBN 0-7153-7452-4). David & Charles.
Hallander, Zander, ed. Complete Handbook of Pro Basketball-1981. pap. 2.75 (ISBN 0-451-09471-9, 9471, Sig). NAL.
Hallard, Peter. Kalu & the Wild Boar. LC 72-8916. (Illus.). 96p. (gr. 2-6). 1973. PLB 4.90 o.p. (ISBN 0-531-02600-0). Watts.
--Puppy Lost in Lapland. LC 74-151890. (Illus.). (gr. 3-7). 1971. 5.90 (ISBN 0-531-01998-5). Watts.
Hallauer, Arnel R. & Miranda, J. B., Jr. Quantitative Genetics in Maize Breeding. (Illus.). 1981. write for info. (ISBN 0-8138-1520-7). Iowa St U Pr.
Hallberg, Edmond C. The Gray Itch: The Male Metapause Syndrome. 1980. pap. 2.50 (ISBN 0-446-91507-6). Warner Bks.
Hallberg, Edmond C. & Thomas, William G. When I Was Your Age... Stop. LC 73-6061. 1973. 5.95 o.s.i. (ISBN 0-02-913490-0). Free Pr.
Hallberg, Kurt, jt. ed. see Sawyer, John W.
Hallberg, Peter. Icelandic Saga. Schach, Paul, tr. LC 62-7873. (Illus.). 1962. 9.95x o.p. (ISBN 0-8032-0064-1); pap. 2.35x (ISBN 0-8032-5082-7, BB 136, Bison). U of Nebr Pr.
Halldorson, Phyllis. Temporary Bride. 192p. (Orig.). 1980. pap. 1.50 (ISBN 0-671-57031-5). S&S.
Halle, Louis J. Men & Nations. 1962. 15.00x o.p. (ISBN 0-691-07123-3); pap. 5.95 o.p. (ISBN 0-691-01954-1). Princeton U Pr.
--The Search for an Eternal Norm: As Represented by Three Classics. LC 80-5793. 220p. 1981. lib. bdg. 18.75 (ISBN 0-8191-1444-8); pap. text ed. 9.75 (ISBN 0-8191-1445-6). U Pr of Amer.
Halleck, Seymour & Bromberg, Walter. Psychiatric Aspects of Criminology. 88p. 1968. pap. 10.75 photocopy ed. spiral (ISBN 0-398-00761-6). C C Thomas.
Halleck, Seymour L. Law in the Practice of Psychiatry: A Handbook for Clinicians. (Critical Issues in Psychiatry Ser.). 310p. 1980. 21.50 (ISBN 0-306-40373-0, Plenum Pr). Plenum Pub.
--Psychiatry & the Dilemmas of Crime: A Study of Causes, Punishment & Treatment. 1971. pap. 7.95x (ISBN 0-520-02059-6, CAL237). U of Cal Pr.
Hallenbeck, Cleve. Legends of the Spanish Southwest. LC 71-164316. 1971. Repr. of 1938 ed. 20.00 (ISBN 0-8103-3799-1). Gale.
Haller, David. Swimming. (Pelham Pictorial Sports Instruction Ser.). (Illus.). 1979. 9.95 (ISBN 0-7207-0954-7). Transatlantic.
Haller, John S., Jr. American Medicine in Transition, 1840-1910. LC 80-14546. (Illus.). 334p. 1981. 27.95 (ISBN 0-252-00806-5). U of Ill Pr.
Haller, Margaret, jt. auth. see Erdsneker, Barbara.
Haller, Mark H. Eugenics: Hereditarian Attitudes in American Thought. 1963. 15.50x o.p. (ISBN 0-8135-0429-5). Rutgers U Pr.
Haller, R., jt. ed. see Chisholm, R.
Haller, Robert S., ed. & tr. see Dante Alighieri.
Haller, William. Liberty & Reformation in the Puritan Revolution. LC 54-6482. 1955. pap. 7.50x (ISBN 0-231-08547-8, 47). Columbia U Pr.
Halleran, E. E. Cimarron Thunder. 1981. pap. 1.75 (ISBN 0-345-29492-0). Ballantine.
--Devil's Canyon. 160p. 1981. pap. 1.75 (ISBN 0-345-29433-5, 01866). Ballantine.
--Shadow of the Big Horn. 160p. 1981. pap. text ed. 1.75 (ISBN 0-345-29430-0). Ballantine.
--Spanish Ridge. 160p. 1981. pap. 1.75 (ISBN 0-345-29436-X). Ballantine.
Hallet, Robin, jt. auth. see Bovill, Edward W.
Hallett, Charles A. Middleton's Cynics. (Salzburg Studies in English Literature, Jacobean Drama Studies Ser.: No. 47). 308p. 1975. pap. text ed. 25.00x (ISBN 0-391-01396-3). Humanities.
Hallett, Charles A. & Hallett, Elaine S. The Revenger's Madness: A Study of Revenge Tragedy Motifs. LC 80-13893. xii, 349p. 1981. 21.50x (ISBN 0-8032-2309-9). U of Nebr Pr.
Hallett, Elaine S., jt. auth. see Hallett, Charles A.
Hallett, F. R. & Speight, P. A. Introductory Biophysics. LC 76-21809. 1977. pap. text ed. 16.95 (ISBN 0-470-15195-1). Halsted Pr.
Hallett, Kathryn. A Guide for Single Parents: Transactional Analysis for People in Crisis. LC 73-92524. (Illus.). 96p. 1974. 7.95 (ISBN 0-912310-64-2); pap. 4.95 (ISBN 0-912310-55-3). Celestial Arts.
Hallett, R. W. Isaac Babel. LC 72-79939. (Modern Literature Ser.). 1973. 10.95 (ISBN 0-8044-2337-7). Ungar.
Halley, Anne. Between Wars & Other Poems. 1965. pap. 3.50 o.p. (ISBN 0-87023-016-6). U of Mass Pr.
Halley, Henry H. Compendio Manual De la Biblia. Denyer, C. P., tr. from Eng. (Illus.). Date not set. Repr. of 1977 ed. 9.95 (ISBN 0-311-03666-X). Casa Bautista.
--Halley's Bible Handbook. 1976. 7.95 (ISBN 0-310-25720-4); kivar 10.95 (ISBN 0-310-25727-1); large print 15.95 (ISBN 0-310-41390-7). Zondervan.
Halley, Laurence. Simultaneous Equations. LC 77-17637. 1978. 7.95 o.p. (ISBN 0-312-72595-7). St Martin.
Halley, Patrick L., jt. auth. see Nichols, Roger.
Hallgren, Soren, jt. auth. see Isaaksson, Olov.
Halliburton, John, tr. see Klauser, Theodor.
Halliburton, R., Jr. Red Over Black: Black Slavery Among the Cherokee Indians. LC 76-15329. (Illus.). 1977. lib. bdg. 17.95 (ISBN 0-8371-9034-7, HAR/). Greenwood.
Halliburton, Warren. The Fighting Redtails: America's First Black Airmen. LC 78-13173. (Famous Firsts Ser.). (Illus.). 1978. lib. bdg. 7.35 (ISBN 0-686-51098-4). Silver.
--The Picture Life of Jesse Jackson. LC 74-186937. (Picture Life Bks). (Illus.). 48p. (gr. k-3). 1972. PLB 4.90 o.p. (ISBN 0-531-00986-6). Watts.
Halliburton, Warren J. & Kaiser, Ernest. Harlem: A History of Broken Dreams. LC 72-79392. 128p. 1974. pap. 2.50 (ISBN 0-385-05840-3, Zenith). Doubleday.
Halliday, Carol & Kurzhals, Ina W. Stimulating Environments for Children Who Are Visually Impaired. (Illus.). 160p. 1976. 16.25 (ISBN 0-398-03511-3). C C Thomas.
Halliday, David & Resnick, Robert. Fundamentals of Physics. 2nd ed. LC 80-17184. 1024p. 1981. text ed. write for info. (ISBN 0-471-03363-4); write for info. wkbk. (ISBN 0-471-06463-7). Wiley.
--Fundamentals of Physics: Extended Version. 2nd extended ed. LC 80-23013. 1040p. 1981. text ed. 26.95 (ISBN 0-471-08005-5). Wiley.
Halliday, E. M. & Black, Cyril E. Russia in Revolution. LC 67-26349. (Horizon Caravel Books). (Illus.). 153p. (gr. 6 up). 1967. 9.95 (ISBN 0-8281-0393-3, J032-0); PLB 12.89 (ISBN 0-06-020123-1, Dist. by Har-Row). Am Heritage.
Halliday, Eleanore, jt. auth. see Nourse, Alan E.
Halliday, F. E. Shakespeare & His World. (And His-Her World Ser.). (Illus.). 1980. Encore Edition. 4.95 (ISBN 0-684-16898-7, ScribT). Scribner.
Halliday, Fred. Soviet Policy in the Arc of Crisis. 90p. 1981. pap. 4.95 (ISBN 0-89758-028-1). Inst Policy Stud.
Halliday, Fred, tr. see Korsch, Karl.
Halliday, H. A. Chronology of Canadian Military Aviation. (Illus.). 1975. pap. text ed. 3.00x (ISBN 0-660-00149-7, 56301-4, Pub. by Natl Mus Canada). U of Chicago Pr.
Halliday, Ian & McIntosh, Bruce A., eds. Solid Particles in the Solar System. (International Astronomical Union Symposium: No. 90). 432p. 1980. PLB 49.95 (ISBN 90-277-1164-X, Pub. by D. Reidel); pap. 26.50 (ISBN 90-277-1165-8). Kluwer Boston.
Halliday, James. Wines & Wineries of New South Wales. 165p. 1981. text ed. 10.95x (ISBN 0-7022-1570-8). U of Queensland Pr.
Halliday, M. A. & Hasan, Ruqaiya. Cohesion in English. (English Language Ser.). (Illus.). 384p. 1976. text ed. 24.00x (ISBN 0-582-55031-9); pap. text ed. 14.50x (ISBN 0-582-55041-6). Longman.
Halliday, R. J. John Stuart Mill. (Political Thinkers Ser.). 1976. text ed. 21.00x (ISBN 0-04-320113-X); pap. text ed. 9.95x o.p. (ISBN 0-04-320114-8). Allen Unwin.
Halliday, Robert & Resnick, David. Physics, Pts. 1 & 2. 3rd combined ed. 1978. text ed. 29.95x (ISBN 0-471-34530-X); answer bklt. 2.50 (ISBN 0-471-03710-9). Wiley.
Halliday, Tim. Vanishing Birds: Their Natural History & Conservation. LC 77-19010. (Illus.). 1978. 16.95 o.p. (ISBN 0-03-043561-7). HR&W.
Halliday, W. R. Folklore Studies, Ancient & Modern. LC 76-78175. 1971. Repr. of 1924 ed. 15.00 (ISBN 0-8103-3676-6). Gale.
Hallier, Amedee. The Monastic Theology of Aelred of Rievaulx: An Experiential Theology. Heaney, Columban, tr. from Fr. (Cistercian Studies: No. 2). xxxii, 180p. 1969. 7.95 o.p. (ISBN 0-87907-802-2). Cistercian Pubns.
Halligan, Marney, jt. auth. see Jackle, Mary.
Hallinan, P. K. Just Open a Book. LC 80-22099. (Self-Awareness Storybooks). (Illus.). 32p. (ps-3). 1981. PLB 7.95 (ISBN 0-516-03521-5). Childrens.
Halline, ed. Six Modern American Plays. 1951. 3.95 o.p. (ISBN 0-394-60276-5). Random.
Halling, J. Introduction to Tribology. (Wykeham Technology Ser.: Vol. 5). 1975. pap. 9.50 o.p. (ISBN 0-387-91128-6). Springer-Verlag.
Halling, J. & Smith, W. E. Introduction to Tribology. LC 75-19385. (Wykeham Technology Ser.: No. 5). 1975. 6.50x (ISBN 0-8448-1126-2). Crane-Russak Co.
Halling, J., ed. Principles of Tribology. (Illus.). 1978. pap. text ed. 27.50x (ISBN 0-333-24686-1). Scholium Intl.
Hallion, Richard P., ed. The Wright Brothers: Heirs of Prometheus. LC 78-606141. (Illus.). 146p. 1979. 19.50 (ISBN 0-87474-504-7); pap. 8.95 (ISBN 0-87474-503-9). Smithsonian.
Halliwell, David. K. D. Dufford Hears. 1970. pap. 4.95 (ISBN 0-571-09248-9, Pub. by Faber & Faber). Merrimack Bk Serv.
--Little Malcolm & His Struggle Against the Eunuchs. 1961. pap. 5.95 (ISBN 0-571-08167-3, Pub. by Faber & Faber). Merrimack Bk Serv.
--Who's Who of Flapland. 1971. pap. 4.95 (ISBN 0-571-09678-6, Pub. by Faber & Faber). Merrimack Bk Serv.
Halliwell, J. D. & Edwards, T. A. A Course in Standard Coral 66. LC 77-367227. (Illus.). 1977. text ed. 12.50x (ISBN 0-85012-187-6). Intl Pubns Serv.
Halliwell, Leslie. The Filmgoer's Companion. 1978. pap. 9.95 (ISBN 0-380-00430-5, 50419). Avon.
--Halliwell's Teleguide. 1979. 29.95 o.s.i. (ISBN 0-8464-0051-0). Beekman Pubs.
Halliwell-Phillipps, James O. Dictionary of Archaic & Provincial Words, Obsolete Phrases, Proverbs, & Ancient Customs, from the Fourteenth Century, 2 vols. LC 66-27837. 1968. Repr. of 1847 ed. Set. 58.00 (ISBN 0-8103-3283-3). Gale.
--Nursery Rhymes of England. LC 67-23936. 1969. Repr. of 1843 ed. 18.00 (ISBN 0-8103-3482-8). Gale.
--Popular Rhymes & Nursery Tales. LC 68-23470. 1968. Repr. of 1849 ed. 18.00 (ISBN 0-8103-3484-4). Gale.
Hallman, E. S. Broadcasting in Canada. (Case Studies on Broadcasting Systems). (Orig.). 1977. pap. 14.00 (ISBN 0-7100-8528-1). Routledge & Kegan.
Hallman, Howard W. The Organization & Operation of Neighborhood Councils: A Practical Guide. LC 77-1872. (Special Studies). 1977. text ed. 21.95 (ISBN 0-03-022716-X). Praeger.
Hallman, Ruth. Breakaway. LC 80-24977. (A Highway Bk). (gr. 7 up). 1981. 8.95 (ISBN 0-664-32677-3). Westminster.
--Rescue Chopper. LC 80-15593. (Hiway Bk.). 1980. 8.95 (ISBN 0-664-32667-6). Westminster.
Hallmark, Clayton. Auto Electronics Simplified. LC 74-25566. (Illus.). 256p. 1975. pap. 5.95 (ISBN 0-8306-3749-4, 749). TAB Bks.
--Computerist's Handy Manual. (Illus.). 1979. pap. 3.50 (ISBN 0-8306-1107-X, 1107). TAB Bks.
--Microwave Oven Service & Repair. (Illus.). 1977. pap. 12.95 (ISBN 0-8306-6962-0, 962). TAB Bks.
--Understanding & Using the Oscilloscope. LC 73-84546. 1973. pap. 7.95 (ISBN 0-8306-2664-6, 664). TAB Bks.
Hallmark, Clayton L. How to Repair Old-Time Radios. (Illus.). 1980. 12.95 (ISBN 0-8306-9737-3); pap. 7.95 (ISBN 0-8306-1148-7, 1148). TAB Bks.
Hallo, William W., tr. see Rosenzweig, Franz.
Hallock, David H. Good Bye World. 4.95 o.p. (ISBN 0-685-58726-6). Vantage.
Hallock, Virginia L. Business Communication: Effective Correspondence Through the Tri-Ask Technique. LC 73-80235. (Illus.). 279p. 1980. pap. text ed. 10.15 (ISBN 0-913310-31-X). PAR Inc.
Hallock, Virginia L. & Ferguson, Susan L. Charm & Charisma: A Personal Guide. LC 74-18094. (Illus.). 272p. 1974. pap. text ed. 9.55 (ISBN 0-913310-36-0). PAR Inc.
Halloran, J. Supervision: The Art of Management. 1981. 17.95 (ISBN 0-13-876276-7); pap. 6.95 study guide (ISBN 0-13-876292-9). P-H.
Halloran, J. D., et al. Television & Delinquency. (Television Research Committee Working Papers: No. 3). 1970. pap. text ed. 9.50x (ISBN 0-7185-1088-7, Leicester). Humanities.
Halloran, Jack. Applied Human Relations: An Organizational Approach. (Illus.). 1978. ref. ed. 17.95 (ISBN 0-13-040857-3); activity guide 6.95 (ISBN 0-13-040824-7). P-H.
Halloran, James D. Mass Communications. 90p. 1980. text ed. write for info. (ISBN 0-7185-1128-X, Leicester). Humanities.
Halloran, Mark, ed. see Beverly Hills Bar Association Barristers Committee for the Arts.
Halloran, Richard, jt. auth. see Time-Life Books Editors.
Hallowell, Elliot R., jt. auth. see Woolrich, Willis R.
Hallowell, Elliott R. Cold & Freezer Storage Manual. 2nd ed. (Illus.). 1980. text ed. 35.00 (ISBN 0-87055-366-6). AVI.
Hallowell, John H. The Decline of Liberalism As an Ideology. LC 75-80554. 1971. Repr. 13.75 (ISBN 0-86527-038-4). Fertig.
Hallpike, C. R. Bloodshed & Vengence in the Papuan Mountains: The Generation of Conflict in Tauade Society. (Illus.). 1977. 48.00x (ISBN 0-19-823192-X). Oxford U Pr.
Hallpike, Christopher R. The Foundations of Primitive Thought. (Illus.). 530p. 1979. text ed. 49.00x (ISBN 0-19-823196-2). Oxford U Pr.
Halls, W. D. Education, Culture & Politics in Modern France. 2nd ed. text ed. 21.00 (ISBN 0-08-018962-8); pap. text ed. 10.50 (ISBN 0-08-018961-X). Pergamon.
--International Equivalences in Access to Higher Education. (Studies on International Equivalences of Degrees). 137p. 1972. pap. 7.00 (ISBN 92-3-100909-5, U327, UNESCO). Unipub.
Hallstein, Hans P., ed. see Zweigert, Konrad & Kropholler, Jan.
Hallstein, Walter. European Community: A New Path to Peaceful Union. 1964. 6.25x (ISBN 0-210-31238-6). Asia.
Hallward, C. L., jt. auth. see Ha, W. H.
Hallwas, John, ed. The Poetry of H: A Lost Poet of Lincoln's Illinois. 192p. 1981. 16.95 (ISBN 0-933180-23-3). Kickapoo.
Hallwood, C. Paul & Sinclair, Stuart W. Oil Debt & Development: OPEC in the Third World. 208p. 1981. text ed. 29.95x (ISBN 0-04-382027-1, 2580). Allen Unwin.
Halm, C., ed. Rhetores Latini Minores. (Classical Studies Ser.). (Lat.). Repr. of 1853 ed. lib. bdg. 29.50x (ISBN 0-697-00038-9). Irvington.
Halm, George N. A Guide to International Monetary Reform. LC 74-28969. 1975. 15.95 (ISBN 0-669-98061-7). Lexington Bks.
Halman, T. S. Two Hundred & One Turkish Verbs Fully Conjugated in All the Tenses. 1980. pap. text ed. 7.95 (ISBN 0-8120-2034-0). Barron.
Halman, Talat, tr. see Anday, Melih C.

Halman, Talat S. Modern Turkish Drama: An Anthology. LC 73-79204. (Studies in Middle Eastern Literatures: No. 5). 1976. 25.00x (ISBN 0-88297-007-0). Bibliotheca.

Halman, Talat S., ed. & intro. by. Contemporary Turkish Literature: Fiction & Poetry. LC 77-74391. 550p. 1981. 22.50 (ISBN 0-8386-1360-8). Fairleigh Dickinson.

Halman, Talat S. & Barkan, Stanley H., eds. Cross-Cultural Review: Five Contemporary Turkish Poets, No. 6. 48p. 10.00 (ISBN 0-89304-610-8); pap. 4.00 (ISBN 0-89304-611-6). Cross Cult.

Halman, Talat Sait, tr. see Daglarca, Fazil Husnu.

Halmos. The Sociology of Sociology. 1970. pap. text ed. 7.75x. Humanities.

Halmos, P. R., ed. see Conway, J. B.

Halmos, Paul R. Algebraic Logic. LC 61-17955. 1962. 9.95 (ISBN 0-8284-0154-3). Chelsea Pub.

--Introduction to Hilbert Space. 2nd ed. LC 57-12834. 7.95 (ISBN 0-8284-0082-2). Chelsea Pub.

--Lectures on Ergodic Theory. LC 60-8964. 7.50 (ISBN 0-8284-0142-X). Chelsea Pub.

Halmshaw, R. Industrial Radiology Techniques. (Wykeham Technology Ser.: No. 3). 1971. 14.00x (ISBN 0-8448-1174-2). Crane Russak Co.

Halpenny, Bruce B. Action Stations Two: Military Airfields of Lincolnshire & the East Midlands. (Illus.). 232p. 1981. 37.95 (ISBN 0-85059-484-7). Aztex.

Halpenny, Frances see Halpenny, Francess.

Halpenny, Francess, ed. Dictionary of Canadian Biography. Incl. Vol. I. 1000-1700. Brown, G. W. & Trudel, Marcel, eds. xxiii, 755p. 1966. 35.00 (ISBN 0-8020-3142-0); Laurentian ed. 75.00 (ISBN 0-8020-3139-0); Vol. II. 1701-1740. Hayne, David & Vachon, Andre, eds. xli, 759p. 1969. 35.00 (ISBN 0-8020-3240-0); Laurentian ed. 75.00 (ISBN 0-8020-3249-4); Vol. III. 1741-1770. La Terreur, Marc, ed. 1974. 35.00 (ISBN 0-8020-3314-8); Laurentian ed. 75.00 (ISBN 0-8020-3315-6); Vol. IV. 1771-1800. Halpenny, Frances, ed. 1979. 35.00 (ISBN 0-8020-3351-2); laurentian ed. 100.00 (ISBN 0-8020-3352-0); Vol. IX. 1861-1870. Hamelin, Jean, ed. 1976. 35.00 (ISBN 0-8020-3319-9); Laurentian ed. 75.00 (ISBN 0-8020-3320-2); Vol. X. 1871-1880. La Terreur, Marc, ed. 1972. 35.00 (ISBN 0-8020-3287-7); laurentian ed. 75.00 (ISBN 0-8020-3288-5). LC 66-31909. U of Toronto Pr.

Halpenny, Francess G., ed. Editing Canadian Texts. (Conference on Editorial Problems Ser.). 1976. lib. bdg. 16.50 (ISBN 0-8240-2407-9). Garland Pub.

--Editing Twentieth Century Texts. (Conference on Editorial Problems Ser.). 1976. lib. bdg. 16.50 (ISBN 0-8240-2404-4). Garland Pub.

Halper. Power, Politics & American Democracy. 368p. (Orig.). 1981. pap. write for info. (ISBN 0-8302-7130-9). Goodyear.

Halper, H. Robert & Foster, Hope S. Laboratory Regulation Manual. LC 76-56666. 1977. 270.00 (ISBN 0-912862-29-7). Aspen Systems.

Halper, Joseph W., jt. auth. see Shivers, Jay S.

Halper, Roe. The Crown of Life. LC 80-19465. (Illus.). 1980. 15.00 (ISBN 0-916326-02-0). Bloch.

Halper, Thomas. Power, Politics, & American Democracy. 1981. pap. text ed. write for info. (ISBN 0-8302-7130-9). Goodyear.

Halperin, David. Merkabah in Rabbinic Literature. (American Oriental Ser.: Vol. 62). 1980. 14.00x. Am Orient Soc.

Halperin, Don A. Ancient Synagogues of the Iberian Peninsula. LC 78-62577. (Social Sciences Monographs: No. 38). (Illus.). 1969. pap. 3.25 (ISBN 0-8130-0272-9). U Presses Fla.

--Construction Funding: Where the Money Comes from. LC 74-11188. (Practical Construction Guides Ser). 256p. 1974. 22.95 (ISBN 0-471-34570-9, Pub. by Wiley-Interscience). Wiley.

--Statics & Strength of Materials for Technology. 2nd ed. LC 79-26256. 1981. deluxe ed. 18.95 text (ISBN 0-471-05651-0); tchrs'. manual avail. (ISBN 0-471-06042-9). Wiley.

Halperin, Ed, et al. Symbol Simons Too. (Orig.). (gr. 3-7). 1981. pap. 2.50 (ISBN 0-671-42537-4). Wanderer Bks.

Halperin, Ernst. Terrorism in Latin America. LC 76-4103. (The Washington Papers: No. 33). 1976. 3.50x (ISBN 0-8039-0648-X). Sage.

Halperin, J., ed. Jane Austen: Bicentenary Essays. 368p. 1975. 36.00 (ISBN 0-521-20709-6); pap. 11.50x (ISBN 0-521-09929-3). Cambridge U Pr.

Halperin, Joan U. Felix Feneon & the Language of Art Criticism. Kuspit, Donald B., ed. (Studies in Fine Arts: Criticism). 277p. 1980. 27.95 (ISBN 0-8357-1091-2, Pub. by UMI Res Pr). Univ Microfilms.

Halperin, Mark. The White Coverlet. 1979. 2.50 (ISBN 0-918116-14-7). Jawbone Pr.

Halperin, Maurice. The Taming of Fidel Castro. 1981. 16.95 (ISBN 0-520-04184-4). U of Cal Pr.

Halperin, Michael. Helping Maltreated Children: School & Community Involvement. LC 78-31527. 1979. pap. text ed. 9.50 (ISBN 0-8016-2020-1). Mosby.

Halperin, Morton H. Contemporary Military Strategy. 2nd ed. 1972. 8.95 o.p. (ISBN 0-571-04772-6, Pub. by Faber & Faber). Merrimack Bk Serv.

--National Security Policy-Making. LC 74-16941. 1975. 17.95 (ISBN 0-669-96578-2). Lexington Bks.

Halperin, Morton H. & Hoffman, Daniel N. Top Secret: National Security & the Right to Know. LC 77-5349. 1977. 8.95 o.p. (ISBN 0-915220-27-X); pap. 3.95 o.p. (ISBN 0-915220-28-8). New Republic.

Halperin, Morton H., et al. Bureaucratic Politics & Foreign Policy. LC 73-22384. 340p. 1974. 15.95 (ISBN 0-8157-3408-5); pap. 6.95 (ISBN 0-8157-3407-7). Brookings.

Halperin-Donghi, T. Politics, Economics & Society in Argentina in the Revolutionary Period. LC 74-79133. (Latin American Studies: No. 18). 552p. 1975. 63.95 (ISBN 0-521-20493-3). Cambridge U Pr.

Halpern, Abraham M., jt. ed. see Kim, Young C.

Halpern, Baruch & Levenson, Jon D., eds. Traditions in Transformation: Turning Points in Biblical Faith. 1981. text ed. write for info. (ISBN 0-931464-06-4). Eisenbrauns.

Halpern, Bomie & Larson, Kathryn. Design & Sew Children's Clothes. 1979. pap. 5.95 o.p. (ISBN 0-385-14923-9, Dolp). Doubleday.

Halpern, Florence. Survival: Black & White. 225p. 1973. text ed. 23.00 (ISBN 0-08-016994-5); pap. text ed. 10.00 (ISBN 0-08-017193-1). Pergamon.

Halpern, Frieda. Full-Color Russian Folk Needlepoint Designs Charted for Easy Use. (Needlework Ser). (Illus.). 1976. pap. 2.95 (ISBN 0-486-23451-7). Dover.

Halpern, Harvey. Adult Aphasia. LC 72-189018. (Studies in Communicative Disorders Ser). 1972. pap. 3.50 (ISBN 0-672-61280-1). Bobbs.

Halpern, John. Early Birds: An Informal Account of the Birth of Aviation. (Illus.). 96p. 1981. 19.95 (ISBN 0-525-93134-1). Dutton.

Halpern, Joseph, et al, eds. The Myths of Deinstitutionalization: Policies for the Mentally Disabled. (Westview Special Studies in Health Care & Medical Science). 152p. 1980. lib. bdg. 16.50x (ISBN 0-89158-843-4). Westview.

Halpern, M. I., ed. Annual Review in Automatic Programming. (Illus.). 222p. 1980. 55.00 (ISBN 0-08-020242-X). Pergamon.

Halpern, P. G. Keyes Papers, Vol. 2. (Illus.). 464p. 1980. text ed. 34.00x (ISBN 0-04-942165-4, 2282). Allen Unwin.

Halpern, V., jt. ed. see Gitterman, M.

Halpert, Herbert, ed. see Cox, John Harrington.

Halpert, L. H. Graduate Record Examination: Review for the Advanced Psychology Test. 1980. pap. 5.95 (ISBN 0-671-18991-3). Monarch Pr.

Halpin, Anne, ed. Gourmet Gardening. (Illus.). 256p. 1981. pap. 9.95 (ISBN 0-87857-349-6). Rodale Pr Inc.

Halpin, Anne, ed. see Bartholomew, Mel.

Halpin, Anne M., ed. Rodale's Encyclopedia of Indoor Gardening. (Illus.). 912p. 1980. 29.95 (ISBN 0-87857-319-4). Rodale Pr Inc.

Halpin, Daniel W. & Woodhead, Ronald W. Design of Construction & Process Operations. LC 76-9784. 424p. 1976. 29.95 (ISBN 0-471-34565-2). Wiley.

Halpin, James. From Columbus to Cromwell: Ireland Britain & Europe, c 1500-c.1700. (Illus.). 1978. pap. text ed. 5.25 large format limp bdg. o.p. (ISBN 0-7171-0808-2). Irish Bk Ctr.

Halporn, James, et al. The Meters of Greek & Latin Poetry. rev. ed. LC 79-6718. 138p. 1980. pap. 4.95x (ISBN 0-8061-1558-0). U of Okla Pr.

Halporn, Roberta. The Thanatology Library. (Illus.). 50p. 1980. pap. 5.75 (ISBN 0-930194-07-1). Highly Specialized.

Halprin, Lawrence. The RSVP Cycles. 1970. 15.00 o.s.i. (ISBN 0-8076-0557-3); pap. 6.95 o.s.i. (ISBN 0-8076-0628-6). Braziller.

Halsall, E. The Comprehensive School: Guidelines for the Reorganization of Secondary Education. rev ed. LC 72-10107. 248p. 1975. 25.00 o.p. (ISBN 0-08-017068-4); pap. text ed. 17.50 (ISBN 0-08-018231-3). Pergamon.

Halsall, E., ed. Becoming Comprehensive: Case Histories. 1970. 18.00 (ISBN 0-08-015820-X); pap. 12.75 (ISBN 0-08-015819-6). Pergamon.

Halsall, Eric. Sheepdogs: My Faithful Friends. (Illus.). 216p. 1980. 35.95 (ISBN 0-85059-431-6). Aztex.

Halsband, Robert. Life of Lady Mary Wortley Montagu. 1956. 23.50x (ISBN 0-19-811548-2). Oxford U Pr.

--Lord Hervey, Eighteenth Century Courtier. (Illus.). 400p. 1974. 19.95 (ISBN 0-19-501731-5). Oxford U Pr.

--The Rape of the Lock & Its Illustrations 1714-1896. 176p. 1980. 29.95x (ISBN 0-19-812098-2). Oxford U Pr.

Halsbard, Robert, ed. see Montagu, Mary W.

Halsell, Grace. Journey to Jerusalem. 256p. 1981. 9.95 (ISBN 0-02-547590-8). Macmillan.

--Peru. LC 69-11299. (Nations Today Books). (Illus.). (gr. 7 up). 1969. 4.95g o.s.i. (ISBN 0-02-742030-2). Macmillan.

Halsema, Thea B. Van see Van Halsema, Thea B.

Halseth, James A. & Glasrud, Bruce A., eds. Northwest Mosaic: Minority Conflicts in Pacific Northwest History. 1977. pap. 6.00x o.p. (ISBN 0-87108-208-X). Pruett.

Halsey, A. H., ed. Traditions of Social Policy: Essays in Honour of Violet Butler. 1976. 29.00x (ISBN 0-631-17130-4, Pub by Basil Blackwell). Biblio Dist.

Halsey, A. H., jt. ed. see Butler, David.

Halsey, A. H., et al, eds. Education, Economy, & Society: A Reader in the Sociology of Education. LC 61-9167. 1965. pap. text ed. 10.95 (ISBN 0-02-913700-4). Free Pr.

Halsey, Abigail. In Old Southampton. 3rd ed. (Illus.). 1968. pap. 3.95 (ISBN 0-911660-05-4). Yankee Peddler.

Halsey, Albert H. & Heath, Anthony F. Origins & Destinations: Family, Class & Education in Modern Britain. (Illus.). 250p. 1980. text ed. 29.50x (ISBN 0-19-827224-3); pap. 12.95x (ISBN 0-19-827249-9). Oxford U Pr.

Halsey, James H., Jr., ed. Neurology Continuing Education Review. 3rd. ed. 1981. spiral bdg. 14.00 (ISBN 0-87488-345-8). Med Exam.

Halsey, Jim. For a Time Such As This. 1976. pap. 2.95 o.p. (ISBN 0-87552-309-9). Presby & Reformed.

Halsey, Margaret. No Laughing Matter: The Autobiography of a WASP. 1977. 8.95 o.p. (ISBN 0-397-01240-3). Lippincott.

Halsey, Martha T. Antonio Buero Vallejo. (World Authors Ser.: Spain: No. 260). 1971. lib. bdg. 10.95 (ISBN 0-8057-2925-9). Twayne.

Halsey, Rosalie V. Forgotten Books of the American Nursery. LC 68-31084. 1969. Repr. of 1911 ed. 15.00 (ISBN 0-8103-3483-6). Gale.

Halsey, Van R., ed. see Baker, G.

Halsey, Van R., ed. see Bennett, P.

Halsey, Van R., ed. see Buffinton, Thomas.

Halsey, Van R., ed. see Casey, Dayle A.

Halsey, Van R., ed. see Cohan, G.

Halsey, Van R., ed. see Guttmann, Allen.

Halsey, Van R., ed. see Harris, Jonathan.

Halsey, Van R., ed. see Traverso, E.

Halsey, William & Bryan, J. Admiral Halsey's Story. (Politics & Strategy of World War II Ser.). 1976. Repr. of 1917 ed. lib. bdg. 27.50 (ISBN 0-306-70770-5). Da Capo.

Halsey, William D., jt. ed. see Barnhart, Clarence L.

Halstead, Beverly. A Closer Look at Prehistoric Mammals. (A Closer Look at Ser.). (Illus.). 32p. (gr. 5-8). 1976. 2.95 (ISBN 0-531-02435-0); PLB 6.90 (ISBN 0-531-01191-7). Watts.

--A Closer Look at the Dawn of Life. (Closer Look at Ser.). (Illus.). (gr. 5-8). 1979. PLB 6.90 s&l (ISBN 0-531-03402-X). Watts.

Halstead, Bruce W. Amgydalin (Laetrile) Therapy. (Illus.). 1977. pap. 3.00 (ISBN 0-933904-06-1). Gold Quill Pubs CA.

--Dangerous Marine Animals: That Bite, Sting, Shock, Are Non-Edible. 2nd ed. LC 80-15475. (Illus.). 1980. 15.00 (ISBN 0-87033-268-6). Cornell Maritime.

--Laetrile Poisoning & Cancer Politics. LC 79-54034. (Illus.). 1981. pap. 8.95 (ISBN 0-933904-05-3). Gold Quill Pubs CA.

Halstead, Cynthia. The Best Kept Woman in the World. 1976. pap. 1.50 (ISBN 0-505-50998-9). Tower Bks.

Halstead, George B., tr. see Saccheri, Girolamo.

Halstead, L. B. The Evolution & the Ecology of the Dinosaurs. (Illus.). 1978. 12.95 o.p. (ISBN 0-8467-0559-1, Pub. by Two Continents). Hippocrene Bks.

--The Evolution of Mammals. (Illus.). 1981. 12.95 o.p. (ISBN 0-8467-0561-3, Pub. by Two Continents). Hippocrene Bks.

Halstead, L. B. & Hill, R. Vertebrate Hard Tissues. (Wykeham Science Ser.: No. 30). 1974. 9.95x (ISBN 0-8448-1157-2). Crane Russak Co.

Halstead, Mike, jt. auth. see Killy, Jean-Claude.

Halsted, Donald L. & Bober, Anne M. Grades: Research & Reporting Procedures. 43p. 1978. pap. 9.00 o.p. (ISBN 0-686-00908-8, D-115). Essence Pubns.

Halsted, Donald L., ed. What Do Colleges Really Want for Admissions? 1977. pap. 9.00 o.p. (ISBN 0-686-00916-9, D-110). Essence Pubns.

Halsted, Donald L., jt. ed. see Streit, Fred.

Halston, Carole. Stand-in Bride. 192p. 1981. pap. 1.50 (ISBN 0-671-57062-5). S&S.

Halter, Carl. Practice of Sacred Music. 1955. 3.95 (ISBN 0-570-01319-4, 99-1095). Concordia.

Halterman, Jean C., jt. auth. see Frey, Albert W.

Halton, B., jt. auth. see Coxon, J. M.

Halty-Carrere, Maximo. Technological Development Strategies for Developing Countries: A Review for Policy Makers. 155p. 1979. pap. text ed. 12.95x (ISBN 0-920380-24-7, Pub. by Inst Res Pub Canada). Renouf.

Halver, J. E., jt. ed. see Neuhaus, O. W.

Halverhout, H. Dutch Cooking. 1975. pap. 11.00 (ISBN 0-911268-20-0). Rogers Bk.

Halverson, John, ed. see Chaucer, Geoffrey.

Halverson, Marvin & Cohen, Arthur. Handbook of Christian Theology. (Fount Paperback Ser.). pap. 4.95 (ISBN 0-529-02087-4, M361, Pub. by Collins Pubs). Abingdon.

Halverson, Marvin, ed. Religious Drama, Vol. 1: Five Plays. 8.00 (ISBN 0-8446-2792-5). Peter Smith.

--Religious Drama, Vol. 3. 8.00 (ISBN 0-8446-2794-1). Peter Smith.

Halverson, Marvin, jt. ed. see Cohen, Arthur A.

Halverson, Richard C. A Living Fellowship: A Dynamic Witness. 1977. pap. 1.50 o.p. (ISBN 0-310-25782-4). Zondervan.

--Somehow Inside of Eternity. LC 80-21687. (Illus., Orig.). 1981. pap. 8.95 (ISBN 0-930014-51-0). Multnomah.

Halverson, William H. A Concise Introduction to Philosophy. 4th ed. 493p. 1981. text ed. 16.95 (ISBN 0-394-32533-8). Random.

--Concise Readings in Philosophy. 447p. 1981. pap. text ed. 9.95 (ISBN 0-394-32551-6). Random.

Halvorsen, Robert. Econometric Models of U.S. Energy Demand. LC 77-81791. (Illus.). 1978. 18.95 (ISBN 0-669-01942-9). Lexington Bks.

Halvorson, Harlyn O. & Van Holde, Kensal E., eds. The Origins of Life & Evolution. LC 80-21901. (MBL Lectures in Biology: Vol. 1). 136p. 1980. 16.00 (ISBN 0-8451-2200-2). A R Liss.

Ham, Arthur W. & Cormack, David H. Histology. 8th ed. LC 79-13185. 1979. text ed. 39.50 (ISBN 0-397-52089-1). Lippincott.

Ham, G. E., jt. auth. see Dermer, O. C.

Ham, Inyong & Bhattacharyya, Amitabha. Design of Cutting Tools: Use of Metal Cutting Theory. LC 68-29237. (Manufacturing Data Ser). (Illus.). 1969. 11.00x (ISBN 0-87263-014-5). SME.

Ham, Richard G. & Veomett, Marilyn J. Mechanisms of Development. LC 79-9236. (Illus.). 1979. text ed. 25.95 (ISBN 0-8016-2022-8). Mosby.

Hamachek, Don E. Human Dynamics in Psychology & Education: Selected Readings. 3rd ed. 1977. pap. text ed. 12.50x (ISBN 0-205-05583-4). Allyn.

Hamada, Hirosuke. Little Mouse Who Tarried. Tresselt, Alvin, tr. from Jap. LC 72-153794. Orig. Title: Konezumi Chorochoro. (Illus.). (gr. k-4). 1971. 5.95 o.s.i. (ISBN 0-8193-0504-9, Four Winds); PLB 5.41 o.s.i. (ISBN 0-8193-0505-7). Schol Bk Serv.

Hamada, Kengi. Prince Ito. (Studies Injapanese History & Civilzation). 1979. Repr. of 1936 ed. 22.00 (ISBN 0-89093-267-0). U Pubns Amer.

Hamada, Kengi, tr. see Uyeda, Akinari.

Hamaker-Zondag, Karen. Interpretation: Jungian Symbolism & Astrology, Pt. 1. 192p. 1981. 7.95 (ISBN 0-87728-523-3). Weiser.

Hamalian, Leo. D. H. Lawrence in Italy. 224p. 1981. 10.95 (ISBN 0-8008-4572-2). Taplinger.

Hamalian, Leo & Hamalian, Linda. Solo. 1977. 10.00 o.s.i. (ISBN 0-440-08068-1). Delacorte.

Hamalian, Leo & Karl, Frederick R. The Shape of Fiction: British & American Short Stories. 2nd ed. LC 77-5839. 1978. pap. text ed. 10.95x (ISBN 0-07-025699-3, C). McGraw.

Hamalian, Leo, ed. In Search of Eden. (Orig.). 1981. pap. 3.50 (ISBN 0-451-61912-9, ME1912, Ment). NAL.

Hamalian, Leo & Karl, F. R., eds. Shape of Fiction: British & American Short Stories. 1967. pap. text ed. 7.95 o.p. (ISBN 0-07-025697-7, C). McGraw.

Hamalian, Leo & Yohannan, John D., eds. New Writing from the Middle East. LC 78-4411. 1978. 15.95 (ISBN 0-8044-2338-5). Ungar.

Hamalian, Leo, jt. ed. see Karl, Frederick.

Hamalian, Leo, jt. ed. see Karl, Frederick R.

Hamalian, Linda, jt. auth. see Hamalian, Leo.

Hamamura, John & Hamamura, Susan. Woven Works. Vandenburgh, Jane, ed. LC 78-17810. 1978. 14.95 (ISBN 0-87701-118-4, Prism Editions); pap. 6.95 (ISBN 0-87701-117-6, Prism Editions). Chronicle Bks.

Hamamura, Motoko, jt. auth. see Clarke, H. D.

Hamamura, Susan, jt. auth. see Hamamura, John.

Hamann, H. Unity & Fellowship & Ecumenicity. (Contemporary Theology Ser. II). 1973. 3.25 (ISBN 0-570-06725-1, 12RT2564). Concordia.

Hamann, H. P. A Popular Guide to New Testament Criticism. 1977. pap. 3.50 (ISBN 0-570-03760-3, 12-2671). Concordia.

Hamann, Henry P. The Bible Between Fundamentalism & Philosophy. LC 80-65558. 80p. 1980. pap. 3.50 (ISBN 0-8066-1803-5, 10-0701). Augsburg.

Hamber, Bernard. Scribble-Foolers. LC 79-92052. 175p. (Orig.). 1980. pap. 6.75 (ISBN 0-9604896-8-1). BH Ent.

Hamberg, Daniel. The U. S. Monetary System: Money, Banking, & Financial Markets. 1981. text ed. 16.95 (ISBN 0-316-34096-0). Little.

Hambidge, Jay. Elements of Dynamic Symmetry. (Illus.,). pap. text ed. 3.00 (ISBN 0-486-21776-0). Dover.

--The Greek Vase: Dynamic Symmetry. (Promotion of the Arts Library Bks.). (Illus.). 131p. Date not set. Repr. of 1917 ed. 77.45 (ISBN 0-89901-030-X). Found Class Reprints.

Hamblen, Eutha. Rim to Rim: History of Will Hamblen. 3.95 o.p. (ISBN 0-685-48812-8). Nortex Pr.

Hamblen, John W. & Landis, Carolyn R., eds. Fourth Inventory of Computers in Higher Education. (EDUCOMoser. in Computing & Telecommunications in Higher Education: No. 4). 1970. lib. bdg. 30.00x (ISBN 0-89158-568-0). Westview.

Hamblin, D. Etruscans. LC 74-25453. (Emergence of Man Ser.). (Illus.). 160p. (gr. 6 up). 1975. lib. bdg. 9.63 o.p. (ISBN 0-8094-1292-6). Silver.

Hamblin, Dora J. The Etruscans. (Emergence of Man Ser.). (Illus.). 1975. 9.95 (ISBN 0-8094-1291-8); lib. bdg. avail. (ISBN 0-685-72432-8). Time-Life.

--The First Cities. (The Emergence of Man Ser.). (Illus.). 160p. 1973. 9.95 (ISBN 0-8094-1300-0); lib. bdg. avail. (ISBN 0-685-32374-9). Time-Life.

--The First Cities. LC 73-83187. (The Emergence of Man Ser.). (Illus.). 1973. lib. bdg. 9.63 o.p. (ISBN 0-686-51071-2). Silver.

Hamblin, Douglas H. The Teacher & Counselling. 1974. 29.00x (ISBN 0-631-15230-X, Pub. by Basil Blackwell); pap. 11.25x (ISBN 0-631-19140-2). Biblio Dist.

--The Teacher & Pastoral Care. 1978. 29.00x (ISBN 0-631-18670-0, Pub. by Basil Blackwell England); pap. 11.25x (ISBN 0-631-18680-8). Biblio Dist.

Hamblin, Douglas H., ed. Problems & Practice of Pastoral Care. 1981. 29.50x (ISBN 0-631-12921-9, Pub. by Basil Blackwell); pap. 10.95x (ISBN 0-631-12931-6). Biblio Dist.

Hamblin, F. D. Abridged Thermodynamic & Thermochemical Tables in S. I. Units. 1971. 11.25 (ISBN 0-08-016456-0); pap. 5.75 (ISBN 0-08-016457-9). Pergamon.

Hamblin, Stephen F., jt. auth. see Taylor, Kathryn S.

Hamblin, T. J. Plasmapheresis & Plasma Exchange, Vol. 1. Horrobin, D. F., ed. (Annual Research Reviews). 1979. 18.00 (ISBN 0-88831-065-X, Dist. by Pergamon). Eden Med Res.

Hamblin, W. Kenneth. Atlas of Stereoscopic Aerial Photographs & Landsat Imagery of North America. LC 79-91239. (Illus.). 208p. (Orig.). 15.95 (ISBN 0-935698-00-0). Tasa Pub Co.

Hambly, Gavin, ed. Central Asia. (World History Ser). 1970. 9.95 o.p. (ISBN 0-440-01219-8). Delacorte.

Hambly, Wilfrid D. The History of Tattooing & Its Significance, with Some Account of Other Forms of Corporal Marking. LC 73-174052. (Illus.). 346p. 1975. Repr. of 1925 ed. 26.00 (ISBN 0-8103-4024-0). Gale.

Hambrick, Ralph S., Jr. & Snyder, William P. The Analysis of Policy Arguments. (Learning Packages in the Policy Sciences: No. 13). 72p. (Orig.). 1979. pap. text ed. 3.50 (ISBN 0-936826-02-9). Pol Stud Assocs.

Hambridge, Jay. The Fundamental Principles of Dynamic Symmetry As They Are Expressed in Nature & Art: A Mathematical & Geometrical Treatise. (Illus.). 1979. deluxe ed. 54.75 (ISBN 0-930582-20-9). Gloucester Art.

Hamburg, C. Bruce. Patent Fraud & Inequitable Conduct. rev. ed. LC 72-89458. 1978. looseleaf with 1978 rev. pages 60.00 (ISBN 0-87632-085-X). Boardman.

Hamburg, David A. & McGown, Elizabeth R. The Great Apes. 1979. text ed. 23.95 (ISBN 0-8053-3669-9). Benjamin-Cummings.

Hamburg, David A., et al, eds. Perception & Its Disorders. (ARNMD Research Publications Ser: Vol. 48). 1970. 24.50 (ISBN 0-683-00241-4). Raven.

Hamburg, Harold L. Sedation. (Illus.). 198p. 1980. pap. 16.00 (ISBN 0-931386-07-1). Quint Pub Co.

Hamburg, Joseph, ed. Review of Allied Health Education, No. 1. LC 74-7876. (Illus.). 244p. 1974. 9.00x (ISBN 0-8131-1322-9). U Pr of Ky.

--Review of Allied Health Education, No. 3. LC 74-7876. 167p. 1979. 9.00x (ISBN 0-8131-1367-9). U Pr of Ky.

Hamburg, Morris. Basic Statistics: A Modern Approach. 2nd ed. 496p. 1979. text ed. 18.95 (ISBN 0-15-505109-1, HC); study guide. pap. 6.95 (ISBN 0-15-505111-3); solutions manual avail. (ISBN 0-15-505110-5). HarBraceJ.

--Case Studies in Elementary School Administration. LC 57-12480. 1957. pap. text ed. 4.75x (ISBN 0-8077-1485-2). Tchrs Coll.

Hamburger, Estelle. The Fashion Business: It's All Yours. 1976. scp 11.95 (ISBN 0-06-453503-7, HarpC); pap. text ed. 11.50 scp (ISBN 0-06-453502-9). Har-Row.

Hamburger, Henry. Games As Models of Social Phenomena. LC 78-23267. (Illus.). 1979. text ed. 18.95x (ISBN 0-7167-1011-0); pap. text ed. 8.95x (ISBN 0-7167-1010-2). W H Freeman.

Hamburger, Jean. The Power & the Frailty: The Future of Medicine & the Future of Man. Neugroschel, Joachim, tr. 192p. 1973. 4.95 o.s.i. (ISBN 0-02-547600-9). Macmillan.

Hamburger, Jean, et al. Renal Transplantation: Theory & Practice. 2nd ed. (Illus.). 375p. 1981. write for info. (3872-9). Williams & Wilkins.

Hamburger, Joel I. Nontoxic Goiter: Concept & Controversy. (Illus.). 232p. 1973. 14.50 (ISBN 0-398-02723-4). C C Thomas.

Hamburger, Max. Awakening of Western Legal Thought. LC 76-79515. 1969. Repr. of 1942 ed. 12.00x (ISBN 0-8196-0246-9). Biblo.

--Awakening of Western Legal Thought. Miall, Bernard, tr. Repr. of 1942 ed. lib. bdg. 12.50x (ISBN 0-8371-3103-0, HALT). Greenwood.

--Morals & Law. LC 65-15244. 1965. 12.00x (ISBN 0-8196-0151-9). Biblo.

Hamburger, Michael & Hamburger, Michael, trs. from Ger. Paul Celan: Poems. LC 79-9117. 286p. 1980. 20.00 (ISBN 0-89255-043-0). Persea Bks.

Hamburger, Michael, tr. from Ger. see Buchner, Georg.

Hamburger, Michael, tr. see Buchner, Georg.

Hamburger, Roberta, jt. auth. see Sayre, John L.

Hamburger, Roberta see Sayre, John L.

Hamburgh, Max. Theories of Differentiation. LC 72-181848. (Contemporary Biology Ser). 181p. 1972. pap. text ed. 19.50 (ISBN 0-7131-2321-4). Univ Park.

Hamburgh, Max & Barrington, E. J., eds. Hormones in Development. LC 72-116424. 854p. 1971. 59.50 (ISBN 0-306-50028-0, Plenum Pr). Plenum Pub.

Hamby, Alonzo L. Beyond the New Deal: Harry S. Truman & American Liberalism. (Contemporary American History Ser.). 655p. 1973. 22.50x (ISBN 0-231-03335-4); pap. 10.00x (ISBN 0-231-08344-0). Columbia U Pr.

--The Imperial Years: The United States Since 1939. LC 76-5799. 1978. text ed. 16.95 (ISBN 0-582-28023-0); pap. 10.95x (ISBN 0-582-28101-6). Longman.

Hamby, Alonzo L., ed. The New Deal: Analysis & Interpretation. 2nd ed. 224p. 1980. pap. text ed. 7.95 (ISBN 0-582-28204-7). Longman.

Hamby, Wallace, tr. see Hamby, Wallace B.

Hamby, Wallace B. Jean de Vigo: Le Mal Francais Selections from Ancient Syphilographers. Fournier, Alfred & Hamby, Wallace, trs. LC 78-50191. 124p. 1981. 15.00x (ISBN 0-87527-191-X). Green.

Hamdun, Said, tr. see Battuta, Ibn.

Hamelin, Jean see Halpenny, Francess.

Hamelin, Leonce. Reconciliation in the Church. O'Connell, Matthew J., tr. from Fr. Orig. Title: La Reconciliation en Eglise. 125p. 1981. pap. text ed. 5.50 (ISBN 0-8146-1215-6). Liturgical Pr.

Hamer, Andrew M., ed. Urban Atlanta: Redefining the Role of the City. LC 79-27699. (Research Monograph: No. 84). 256p. 1980. pap. 12.95 (ISBN 0-88406-125-6). Ga St U Busn Pub.

Hamer, Barbara H., ed. see Hamer, Red.

Hamer, D. W. & Biggers, J. V. Thick Film Hybrid Microcircuit Technology. LC 72-3191. 464p. 1972. 38.50 (ISBN 0-471-34700-0, Pub by Wiley-Interscience). Wiley.

Hamer, Douglas, ed. The Works of Sir David Lindsay of the Mount, 1490-1555, 4 vols. 1931-1936. 126.00 (ISBN 0-384-32819-9). Johnson Repr.

Hamer, Irving, et al, eds. Opening the Door: Citizen Roles in Educational Collective Bargaining. 194p. (Orig.). 1979. pap. 4.50 (ISBN 0-917754-11-5). Inst Responsive.

Hamer, John & Rowlands, Derek J. Recent Advances in Cardiology, Vol. 8. (Recent Advances Ser.). (Illus.). 360p. 1980. lib. bdg. 50.00 (ISBN 0-443-01995-9). Churchill.

Hamer, P. M. Secession Movement in South Carolina, 1847-1852. LC 75-124883. (American Scene Ser). 1971. Repr. of 1918 ed. lib. bdg. 17.50 (ISBN 0-306-71036-6). Da Capo.

Hamer, R. F. Old English Sound Changes for Beginners. 1967. pap. 7.25x (ISBN 0-631-10150-0, Pub. by Basil Blackwell England). Biblio Dist.

Hamer, Red. The Four Seasons of Chester County. (Illus.). 96p. 1979. 24.95 (ISBN 0-9605400-0-8). Four Seas Bk.

--Four Seasons of the Chesapeake Bay: Fall-Winter, Vol. II. Hamer, Barbara H., ed. (Illus.). 128p. 1981. 27.50 (ISBN 0-9605400-2-4). Four Seas Bk.

--Four Seasons of the Chesapeake Bay: Spring-Summer, Vol. 1. Hamer, Barbara H., ed. (Illus.). 128p. 1980. 27.50 (ISBN 0-9605400-0-8). Four Seas Bk.

Hamer, Richard, compiled by. & intro. by. A Choice of Anglo-Saxon Verse. 207p. (Orig.). 1970. pap. text ed. 5.50x (ISBN 0-571-08765-5). Humanities.

Hamermesh, Daniel S. Unemployment: Insurance & the Older American. LC 80-18946. 117p. 1980. 4.00 (ISBN 0-911558-72-1). Upjohn Inst.

Hamermesh, Daniel S., ed. Labor in the Public & Nonprofit Sectors. 250p. 1975. 16.00x (ISBN 0-691-04203-9). Princeton U Pr.

Hamernik, Arlene. One Hundred One Microwave Favorites Plus Four. 128p. 1978. Repr. of 1977 ed. spiral bdg. 2.95 o.p. (ISBN 0-9602930-0-0). Microwave Helps.

--One Hundred One Microwave Favorites Plus Four. rev. ed. (Illus.). 82p. 1979. spiral bdg. 2.95x (ISBN 0-9602930-4-3). Microwave Help.

--One Hundred One Microwave Favorites Plus Four. (Illus.). 1978. pap. 2.95x o.p. (ISBN 0-685-99246-2). Microwave Helps.

Hamersma, Richard J. & Mark, Robert A. The Seven-Pillared Relationship. LC 79-20450. 192p. 1981. 13.95 (ISBN 0-88229-443-1). Nelson-Hall.

Hamerstrom, Frances. Strictly for the Chickens. 136p. 1980. 11.95 (ISBN 0-8138-0800-6). Iowa St U Pr.

Hamerton, John L. Human Cytogenetics, 2 vols. 1970-71. Vol. 1. 49.00 (ISBN 0-12-321001-1); Vol. 2. 52.75 (ISBN 0-12-321002-X). Acad Pr.

Hamerton-Kelly, R. G. Pre-existence, Wisdom & the Son of Man: A Study of the Idea of Pre-Existence in the New Testament. LC 72-78890. (New Testament Studies Monographs: No. 21). 340p. 1973. 42.00 (ISBN 0-521-08629-9). Cambridge U Pr.

Hamerton-Kelly, Robert. God the Father: Theology & Patriarchy in the Teaching of Jesus, No. 4. Brueggemann, Walter & Donahue, John R., eds. LC 78-54551. (Overtures to Biblical Theology Ser). 144p. 1979. pap. 5.95 (ISBN 0-8006-1528-X, 1-1528). Fortress.

Hames, Carolyn C. & Joseph, Dayle. Basic Concepts of Helping: A Wholistic Approach. 260p. 1980. pap. text ed. 9.50x (ISBN 0-8385-0558-9). ACC.

Hamet, Pavel & Sands, Howard, eds. Pathophysiological Aspects of Cyclic Nucleotides, Vol. 12. (Advances in Cyclic Nucleotide Research). 470p. 1980. text ed. 48.50 (ISBN 0-89004-454-6). Raven.

Hamil, Fred C. The Valley of the Lower Thames, 1640-1850. LC 73-86461. (Illus.). 1973. 17.50x o.p. (ISBN 0-8020-2109-3); pap. 7.50 (ISBN 0-8020-6220-2). U of Toronto Pr.

Hamil, Harold. Farmland, USA. LC 75-18756. (Illus.). 112p. 1975. 25.00 (ISBN 0-913504-24-6); deluxe ed. 100.00 (ISBN 0-913504-61-0). Lowell Pr.

Hamil, Ralph E. & Dillon, Mary E., eds. Alternative Futures: Political Choices for Tomorrow. Date not set. pap. cancelled (ISBN 0-8120-0564-3). Barron.

Hamill, B. J. & Steele, P. M. Work Measurement in the Office. (Illus.). 268p. 1974. 25.00 o.s.i. (ISBN 0-7161-0147-5). Herman Pub.

Hamill, Charlotte & Oliver, Robert C. Therapeutic Activities for the Handicapped Elderly. 295p. 1980. text ed. 24.00 (ISBN 0-89443-326-1). Aspen Systems.

Hamill, Charlotte M. The Day Hospital: Organization & Management. LC 80-607802. 192p. 1981. text ed. write for info. (ISBN 0-8261-3040-2). Springer Pub.

Hamill, Edson T. The Child Killer. (Ryker Ser: No. 5). (Orig.). 1975. pap. 1.25 o.p. (ISBN 0-685-52936-3, LB266ZK, Leisure Bks). Nordon Pubns.

--Motive for Murder. (Ryker Ser). 1975. pap. 1.25 o.p. (ISBN 0-685-61047-0, LB315, Leisure Bks). Nordon Pubns.

Hamill, Ethel. Honeymoon in Honolulu. (YA) 1970. 5.95 (ISBN 0-685-03335-X, Avalon). Bouregy.

Hamill, Pete. The Invisible City: A New York Sketchbook. LC 80-5276. (Illus.) 1980. 8.95 (ISBN 0-394-50377-5). Random.

Hamill, Pete, jt. auth. see Bennett, George.

Hamill, Sam. At Home in the World: Views & Reviews. 125p. 1981. 15.00 (ISBN 0-918116-23-6); pap. 6.00 (ISBN 0-918116-22-8). Jawbone Pr.

--Living Light. 1977. 2.50 (ISBN 0-918116-12-0). Jawbone Pr.

Hamilton. Getting in Shape to Ski. new ed. (Orig.). 1979. pap. 3.95 (ISBN 0-8015-2957-3, Hawthorn). Dutton.

Hamilton, A., tr. see Artaud, Antoain.

Hamilton, A. C., ed. Spenser: The Faerie Queene. 768p. (Orig.). 1980. pap. text ed. 19.95 (ISBN 0-582-49705-1). Longman.

--Spenser: The Faerie Queene. LC 77-2738. (Longman Annotated English Poets Ser.). 1978. text ed. 60.00x (ISBN 0-582-48106-6). Longman.

Hamilton, A. G. Logic for Mathematicians. LC 77-84802. (Illus.). 1978. 57.50 (ISBN 0-521-21838-1); pap. 14.95x (ISBN 0-521-29291-3). Cambridge U Pr.

Hamilton, Alan. Central Edinburgh & Royal Mile Visitors Map. 1977. pap. 4.50 (ISBN 0-8277-5357-8). British Bk Ctr.

--Essential Edinburgh. (Illus.). 1978. pap. 7.95 (ISBN 0-233-96984-5). Transatlantic.

Hamilton, Alastair, tr. see Artaud, Antonin.

Hamilton, Alastair, tr. see Bataille, Georges.

Hamilton, Alastair, tr. see Drieu La Rochelle, Pierre.

Hamilton, Alexander. Alexander Hamilton: A Biography in His Own Words. Kline, Mary-Jo, ed. LC 72-92140. (The Founding Fathers Ser.). (Illus.). 416p. (YA) 1973. 15.00 o.s.i. (ISBN 0-06-012417-2, HarpT). Har-Row.

--Letters of Pacificus & Helvidius. LC 76-41676. 1976. Repr. of 1845 ed. 20.00x (ISBN 0-8201-1279-8). Schol Facsimiles.

Hamilton, Alexander see Fairfield, Roy P.

Hamilton, Alice, jt. auth. see Hamilton, Kenneth.

Hamilton, Alistair. Appeal of Fascism. Bartholomew, A., ed. 1971. 7.95 o.s.i. (ISBN 0-02-547670-X). Macmillan.

Hamilton, Anne. Seven Principles of Poetry. 8.95 (ISBN 0-87116-029-3). Writer.

Hamilton, Ardith J. Critical Care Nursing Skills. 256p. 1981. pap. 12.95 (ISBN 0-8385-1242-9). ACC.

Hamilton, B. Brainteasers & Mindbenders. 1981. pap. 4.95 (ISBN 0-13-080945-4); 10.95 (ISBN 0-13-080952-7). P-H.

Hamilton, Bernard. The Latin Church in the Crusader States: The Secular Church. 402p. 1980. 40.00x (ISBN 0-86078-072-4, Pub. by Variorum England). State Mutual Bk.

--Medieval Inquisition: Foundations of Medieval History. LC 80-27997. 110p. (Orig.). 1981. pap. text ed. 13.00x (ISBN 0-8419-0695-5). Holmes & Meier.

Hamilton, Bradley. Common Man: Poems. 1981. 6.50 (ISBN 0-8062-1554-2). Carlton.

Hamilton, Carl. In No Time at All. 1974. 6.95 (ISBN 0-8138-0825-1). Iowa St U Pr.

Hamilton, Carlos D., jt. auth. see Arratia, Alejandro.

Hamilton, Charles. Collecting Autographs & Manuscripts. 2nd ed. LC 61-9007. 1961. pap. 9.95 (ISBN 0-8061-1558-0). U of Okla Pr.

Hamilton, Charles D. Sparta's Bitter Victories: Politics & Diplomacy in the Corinthian War. LC 78-58045. 1978. 19.50x (ISBN 0-8014-1158-0). Cornell U Pr.

Hamilton, Charles F. Photographing Nudes. (Illus.). 1980. 18.95 (ISBN 0-13-665273-5, Spec); pap. 9.95 (ISBN 0-13-665265-4). P-H.

Hamilton, Charles V. The Black Preacher in America. 256p. 1972. pap. 3.45 o.p. (ISBN 0-688-05006-9). Morrow.

Hamilton, Cicely M. Marriage As a Trade. LC 71-149782. 1971. Repr. of 1909 ed. 15.00 (ISBN 0-8103-3394-5). Gale.

Hamilton, Clarence H., ed. Buddhism: A Religion of Infinite Compassion. LC 52-1623. 1952. pap. 5.50 (ISBN 0-672-60340-3, LLA133). Bobbs.

Hamilton, D. Lee & Fahs, Ned C., eds. Contos do Brasil. LC 44-4280. (Port.). 1955. pap. text ed. 9.50x (ISBN 0-89197-108-4). Irvington.

Hamilton, David. Diary of Sir David Hamilton. Roberts, Philip, ed. 220p. 1975. 36.00x (ISBN 0-19-822364-1). Oxford U Pr.

Hamilton, David & Robbe-Grillet, Alain. Sisters. (Illus.). 136p. 1973. 24.95 (ISBN 0-688-00166-1); pap. 9.95 (ISBN 0-688-05166-9). Morrow.

Hamilton, David, jt. ed. see McAleese, Ray.

Hamilton, David, photos by. The Best of David Hamilton. LC 80-83280. (Illus.). 144p. 1980. pap. 10.95 (ISBN 0-688-00403-2, Quill). Morrow.

--David Hamilton's Private Collection. LC 80-83281. (Illus.). 128p. 1980. pap. 10.95 (ISBN 0-688-00402-4, Quill). Morrow.

Hamilton, David, et al, eds. Beyond the Numbers Game: A Reader in Educational Evaluation. (Education Ser.). 1977. 17.20 (ISBN 0-8211-0416-0); text ed. 15.50x (ISBN 0-685-04966-3). McCutchan.

Hamilton, David L., ed. Cognitive Processes in Stereotyping & Intergroup Behavior. 384p. 1981. prof. - refer. 24.95 (ISBN 0-89859-081-7). L Erlbaum Assocs.

Hamilton, Donald. Ambushers. 1978. pap. 1.95 (ISBN 0-449-14102-0, GM). Fawcett.

--The Betrayers. 1978. pap. 1.95 (ISBN 0-449-14060-1, GM). Fawcett.

--The Devastators. (Matt Helm Ser.). 1978. pap. 1.95 (ISBN 0-449-14084-9, GM). Fawcett.
--Interlopers. (Matt Helm Ser.). 1978. pap. 1.95 (ISBN 0-449-13994-8, GM). Fawcett.
--Intimidators. (Matt Helm Ser.). 1978. pap. 1.95 (ISBN 0-449-14110-1, GM). Fawcett.
--Murderers' Row. (Matt Helm Ser.). 1978. pap. 1.95 (ISBN 0-449-14088-1, GM). Fawcett.
--The Poisoners. (Matt Helm Ser.). 1979. pap. 1.95 (ISBN 0-449-14163-2, GM). Fawcett.
--The Shadowers. 144p. 1980. pap. 1.95 (ISBN 0-449-14006-7, GM). Fawcett.
--The Terminators. (Matt Helm Ser.). 224p. 1978. pap. 1.95 (ISBN 0-449-14035-0, GM). Fawcett.
--Texas Fever. 1979. pap. 1.75 (ISBN 0-449-14122-5, GM). Fawcett.
Hamilton, Donald R., et al, eds. Klystrons & Microwave Triodes. (Illus.). 1966. pap. text ed. 4.50 (ISBN 0-486-61558-8). Dover.
Hamilton, Donna M. After Fifty Cookbook: A Treasury of Creative Recipes for 1 or 2, Retired People, or Those on Special Diets. LC 74-16551. 377p. 1974. 13.50 (ISBN 0-8040-0667-9). Swallow.
Hamilton, Donna M. & Nemiro, Beverly A. Complete Book of High Altitude Baking. rev. ed. LC 61-18656. 370p. 1967. 12.95 (ISBN 0-8040-0054-9, SB). Swallow.
Hamilton, Donna M., jt. auth. see Anderson, Beverly M.
Hamilton, Dorothy. Amanda Fair. LC 80-25073. (Illus.). 136p. (gr. 5-10). 1981. pap. 3.25 (ISBN 0-8361-1943-6). Herald Pr.
Hamilton, Douglas M. & Robb, William. Mechanical Engineering for Public Cleansing. (Illus.). 1969. 18.60x (ISBN 0-85334-121-4). Intl Ideas.
Hamilton, E., jt. ed. see Cairns, H.
Hamilton, E. I. The Chemical Elements & Man: Measurements, Perspectives, Applications. (Am. Lec. Living Chemistry Ser.). (Illus.). 512p. 1979. 44.75 (ISBN 0-398-03732-9). C C Thomas.
Hamilton, Edith. The Greek Way. 1973. pap. 2.75 (ISBN 0-380-00816-5, 53140, Discus). Avon.
Hamilton, Edmond. Doomstar. 1979. pap. 1.25 (ISBN 0-505-51336-6). Tower Bks.
Hamilton, Edward P., tr. see Bougainville, Louis A. De.
Hamilton, Edward W. Diary of Sir Edward Walter Hamilton, Eighteen-Eighty to Eighteen-Eighty Five, 2. Bahlman, Dudley W., ed. 1972. 54.00x (ISBN 0-19-822324-2). Oxford U Pr.
Hamilton, Eleanor. Partners in Love. 3rd rev. ed. LC 79-51018. 1981. 9.95 (ISBN 0-498-02431-8). A S Barnes.
--Sex, with Love: A Guide for Young People. LC 77-75442. (Illus.). (gr. 7-10). 1978. 10.95 (ISBN 0-8070-2580-1); pap. 4.50 (ISBN 0-8070-2581-X, BP653). Beacon Pr.
Hamilton, Elizabeth. The Cottagers of Glenburnie: A Tale for the Farmer's Ingle-Nook. LC 73-22147. (The Feminist Controversy in England, 1788-1810 Ser.). 1974. lib. bdg. 50.00 (ISBN 0-8240-0864-2). Garland Pub.
--First Book of Caves. (First Bks). (Illus.). (gr. 4-6). 1956. PLB 4.90 o.p. (ISBN 0-531-00496-1). Watts.
--The Illustrious Lady: A Biography of Barbara Villiers, Countess of Castlemaine & Duchess of Cleveland. (Illus.). 248p. 1980. 38.00 (ISBN 0-241-10310-X, Pub. by Hamish Hamilton England). David & Charles.
--Letters Addressed to the Daughter of a Nobleman on the Formation of the Religious & the Moral Principle, 2 vols. Luria, Gina, ed. (The Feminist Controversy in England, 1788-1810 Ser.). 1974. Set. lib. bdg. 90.00 (ISBN 0-8240-0865-0); lib. bdg. 50.00 ea. Garland Pub.
--Memoirs of Modern Philosophers: A Novel, 3 vols. Luria, Gina, ed. (The Feminist Controversy in England, 1788-1810). 1974. lib. bdg. 50.00 ea. (ISBN 0-8240-0866-9). Garland Pub.
Hamilton, Elizabeth, ed. see Suenens, Leon J.
Hamilton, Elizabeth V. When Walls Are High. LC 72-93195. 1973. 6.00 (ISBN 0-937684-09-0). Tradd St Pr.
Hamilton, Emily, jt. auth. see Hamilton, Morse.
Hamilton, Eva M. & Whitney, Eleanor N. Nutrition: Concepts & Controversy. (Illus.). 1979. pap. text ed. 15.50 (ISBN 0-8299-0281-3, Pub by Hartnell); study guide 6.95 (ISBN 0-686-67552-5); study guide o.p. 4.95 (ISBN 0-8299-0288-0); instrs.' manual avail. (ISBN 0-8299-0485-9). West Pub.
Hamilton, Eva M., jt. auth. see Whitney, Eleanor N.
Hamilton, F. E. & Linge, G. J. Spatial Analysis, Industry & the Industrial Environment - Progess in Research & Applications: International Industrial Systems, Vol. 2. 1981. price not set (ISBN 0-471-27918-8, Pub. by Wiley-Interscience). Wiley.
Hamilton, F. E., ed. Contemporary Industrialization: Spatial Analysis & Regional Analysis. (Illus.). 1978. pap. text ed. 11.95 (ISBN 0-582-48592-4). Longman.
--Industrial Change: Industrial Experience & Public Policy. (Illus.). 1978. pap. text ed. 11.95x (ISBN 0-582-48593-2). Longman.
--Proceedings of the First British-Soviet Geographical Seminar. (Illus.). 152p. 1981. 28.60 (ISBN 0-08-025795-X). Pergamon.
Hamilton, F. J., ed. Libraries in the United Kingdom & the Republic of Ireland. 1979. pap. 7.95x (ISBN 0-85365-741-6, Pub. by Lib Assn England). Oryx Pr.
Hamilton, Frederic. Here, There & Everywhere. 332p. 1980. Repr. of 1921 ed. lib. bdg. 20.00 (ISBN 0-8492-5273-3). R West.
Hamilton, Geneva. Where the Highway Ends. LC 74-77228. (Illus.). 1977. 9.95 (ISBN 0-914598-26-0); pap. 4.95 (ISBN 0-914598-25-2). Padre Prods.
Hamilton, Geoff. Design & Build a Patio or Terrace. 4.50. David & Charles.
--Design & Build a Rockery. 4.50. David & Charles.
--Herbs: How to Grow Them. 1980. pap. 4.50 (ISBN 0-7153-7897-X). David & Charles.
Hamilton, Geoffrey, tr. see Shioda, Gozo.
Hamilton, George H. Nineteenth & Twentieth Century Art: Painting, Sculpture, Architecture. (Illus.). 492p. 1972. text ed. 21.95 (ISBN 0-13-622639-6). P-H.
Hamilton, George H. & Agee, William C. Raymond Duchamp-Villon. 7.50 o.s.i. (ISBN 0-8027-0241-4); pap. 3.50 o.s.i. (ISBN 0-8027-7073-8). Walker & Co.
Hamilton, Gordon. Psychotherapy in Child Guidance. 1947. 15.00x (ISBN 0-231-01637-9). Columbia U Pr.
--Theory & Practice of Social Case Work. 2nd ed. LC 51-12493. 1951. 15.00x (ISBN 0-231-01862-2). Columbia U Pr.
Hamilton, Henry W. & Hamilton, Jean T. The Sioux of the Rosebud: A History in Pictures. LC 78-145506. (The Civilization of the American Indian Ser.: Vol. 111). (Illus.). 320p. 1981. pap. 12.50 (ISBN 0-8061-1622-6). U of Okla Pr.
Hamilton, Holman. Prologue to Conflict: The Crisis & Compromise of 1850. LC 64-13999. 248p. 1964. 8.50x (ISBN 0-8131-1090-4). U Pr of Ky.
Hamilton, Ian. A Poetry Chronicle: Essays & Reviews. 1973. 7.95 o.p. (ISBN 0-571-10175-5, Pub. by Faber & Faber); pap. 4.95 (ISBN 0-571-10228-X). Merrimack Bk Serv.
--The Visit. 45p. 1970. 5.95 (ISBN 0-571-09369-8, Pub. by Faber & Faber). Merrimack Bk Serv.
Hamilton, James M. History of Montana: From Wilderness to Statehood, 1805-1970. 2nd. rev. & enl. ed. LC 74-92542. (Illus.). 1970. 15.00 (ISBN 0-8323-0018-7). Binford.
Hamilton, Jean T., jt. auth. see Hamilton, Henry W.
Hamilton, Jessica. Elizabeth. 1977. pap. 1.75 o.p. (ISBN 0-445-04013-0). Popular Lib.
Hamilton, Joan L. The Lion & the Cross. 1981. pap. 2.75 (ISBN 0-345-28632-4). Ballantine.
Hamilton, John & Sorrell, Alan. Saxon England. (Illus.). (gr. 6-9). 1968. 7.50 (ISBN 0-8023-1149-0). Dufour.
Hamilton, Kenneth & Hamilton, Alice. Condemned to Life. 1976. pap. 5.50 o.p. (ISBN 0-8028-1655-X). Eerdmans.
Hamilton, Kirk. The Twelve Ten from San Antone: Only the Swift. (Orig.). 1980. pap. 2.25 (ISBN 0-8439-0741-X, Leisure Bks). Nordon Pubns.
Hamilton, Louis J., jt. auth. see Duderstadt, James J.
Hamilton, Madison. Federalist: Selections. Commager, Henry S., ed. LC 49-11364. (Crofts Classics Ser.). 1949. pap. text ed. 2.75x (ISBN 0-88295-041-X). AHM Pub.
Hamilton, Malcolm C., ed. Education Literature Nineteen Hundred & Seven to Nineteen Thirty-Two, 12 vols. 1979. Set. lib. bdg. 363.00 (ISBN 0-685-94396-8). Garland Pub.
--Education Literature Nineteen Hundred & Seven to Nineteen Thirty-Two, Vol. 1. 1979. lib. bdg. 33.00 (ISBN 0-8240-3700-6). Garland Pub.
--Education Literature, Nineteen Hundred & Seven to Nineteen Thirty-Two, Vol. 7. 1979. lib. bdg. 33.00 (ISBN 0-8240-3706-5). Garland Pub.
--Education Literature, Nineteen Hundred & Seven to Nineteen Thirty-Two, Vol. 8. 1979. lib. bdg. 33.00 (ISBN 0-8240-3707-3). Garland Pub.
--Education Literature, Nineteen Hundred & Seven to Nineteen Thirty-Two, Vol. 10. 1979. lib. bdg. 33.00 (ISBN 0-8240-3709-X). Garland Pub.
--Education Literature, Nineteen Hundred & Seven to Nineteen Thirty-Two, Vol. 11. 1979. lib. bdg. 33.00 (ISBN 0-8240-3710-3). Garland Pub.
Hamilton, Marshall L. Father's Influence on Children. LC 76-41799. 1977. 13.95 (ISBN 0-88229-142-4); pap. 7.95 (ISBN 0-88229-503-9). Nelson-Hall.
Hamilton, Mary T., jt. auth. see Lorie, James H.
Hamilton, Maurice. Autocourse, Nineteen Eighty to Nineteen Eighty-One, No. 29. (Illus.). 240p. 1981. 39.95 (ISBN 0-905138-12-0, Pub. by Hazelton England). Motorbooks Intl.
Hamilton, Michael, ed. This Little Planet. 1971. pap. 2.45 o.p. (ISBN 0-684-71791-3, SL250, ScribT). Scribner.
Hamilton, Michael P. & Montgomery, Nancy S. The Ordination of Women: Pro & Con. (Orig.). 1975. pap. 4.95 o.p. (ISBN 0-8192-1203-2). Morehouse.
Hamilton, Michael P., ed. To Avoid Catastrophe: Towards a Future Nuclear Weapons Policy. 1978. pap. 4.95 o.p. (ISBN 0-8028-1703-3). Eerdmans.
Hamilton, Milton W. Sir William Johnson, Colonial American, 1715-1763. (Ser. in American Studies). 1976. 22.50 (ISBN 0-8046-9134-7, Natl U). Kennikat.
Hamilton, Morse. Big Sisters Are Bad Witches. LC 79-24907. (Illus.). 32p. (gr. k-3). 1981. 7.95 (ISBN 0-688-80268-0); PLB 7.63 (ISBN 0-688-84268-2). Greenwillow.
Hamilton, Morse & Hamilton, Emily. My Name Is Emily. LC 78-4537. (Illus.). (gr. k-3). 1979. 7.50 (ISBN 0-688-80181-1); PLB 7.20 (ISBN 0-688-84181-3). Greenwillow.
Hamilton, Neil W. & Hamilton, Peter R. Governance of Public Enterprise: A Case Study of Urban Mass Transit. LC 80-5349. 1981. 18.95. Lexington Bks.
Hamilton, Nigel. The Brother Mann. LC 78-15114. 1979. 30.00 (ISBN 0-300-02348-0). Yale U Pr.
--The Brothers Mann. LC 78-15114. 431p. pap. 9.95 (ISBN 0-300-02668-4). Yale U Pr.
Hamilton, Persis M. Basic Maternity Nursing. 4th ed. LC 78-26998. (Illus.). 1979. pap. 10.95 (ISBN 0-8016-2031-7). Mosby.
--Basic Pediatric Nursing. 3rd ed. LC 77-20662. (Illus.). 1978. pap. text ed. 13.95 (ISBN 0-8016-2039-2). Mosby.
Hamilton, Peter. Knowledge & Social Structure: An Introduction to the Classical Argument in the Sociology of Knowledge. (International Library of Sociology). 174p. 1974. 16.50x (ISBN 0-7100-7746-7); pap. 7.95 (ISBN 0-7100-7786-6). Routledge & Kegan.
Hamilton, Peter R., jt. auth. see Hamilton, Neil W.
Hamilton, R. Electrical Principles for Technicians. (Electrical & Telecommunications Technicians Ser.). (Illus.). 200p. 1980. 37.50 (ISBN 0-19-859360-0). Oxford U Pr.
Hamilton, R. F. Class & Politics in the United States. LC 72-1951. 1972. pap. 15.95x (ISBN 0-471-34709-4). Wiley.
Hamilton, Raphael. Marquette's Explorations: The Narratives Reexamined. (Illus.). 1970. 19.50 (ISBN 0-299-05570-1). U of Wis Pr.
Hamilton, Richard & Barnard, Charles N. Twenty Thousand Alarms. LC 74-33553. 256p. 1981. pap. 2.50 (ISBN 0-87216-810-7). Playboy Pbks.
Hamilton, Robert W. The Law of Corporations in a Nutshell. LC 80-21532. (Nutshell Ser.). 379p. 1980. pap. text ed. 6.95 (ISBN 0-8299-2108-7). West Pub.
Hamilton, Roberta. The Liberation of Women: A Study of Patriarchy & Capitalism. (Controversies in Sociology Ser.). 1978. text ed. 17.95x (ISBN 0-04-301085-7); pap. text ed. 7.95x (ISBN 0-04-301086-5). Allen Unwin.
Hamilton, Roger. The Life of Prehistoric Animals. LC 77-88446. (Easy Reading Edition of Introduction to Nature Ser.). (Illus.). 1978. lib. bdg. 7.95 (ISBN 0-686-50007-5). Silver.
Hamilton, Ronald. The Holiday History of France. 1978. 8.95 (ISBN 0-7011-1686-2, Pub. by Chatto Bodley Jonathan). Merrimack Bk Serv.
Hamilton, Ross. Greyhound Betting for Profit. 64p. 1980. pap. 2.95 (ISBN 0-89650-725-4). Gamblers.
Hamilton, Susan, jt. auth. see Leal, Emily B.
Hamilton, T. H., et al, eds. Ontogeny of Receptors & Reproductive Hormone Action. LC 77-92523. 1979. text ed. 42.50 (ISBN 0-89004-254-3). Raven.
Hamilton, T. M., ed. Indian Trade Guns. 10.95 (ISBN 0-913150-43-6). Pioneer Pr.
Hamilton, T. Stewart, ed. Hospital Regulation: Report of the Special Committee on the Regulatory Process. LC 77-6184. 1977. pap. 6.25 o.p. (ISBN 0-87258-218-3, 1835). Am Hospital.
Hamilton, Victoria. McDuff in the Daffodils. (Illus.). 44p. (Orig.). (gr. 4-12). 1974. pap. 2.95 (ISBN 0-939198-00-2). Blue Heron.
Hamilton, Virginia. Arilla Sun Down. LC 76-13180. 256p. (gr. 7 up). 1976. 9.25 (ISBN 0-688-80058-0); PLB 8.88 (ISBN 0-688-84058-2). Greenwillow.
--The Gathering. LC 80-12512. (Justice Cycle Ser.: Vol. 3). 192p. (gr. 7 up). 1980. 8.95 (ISBN 0-688-80269-9); PLB 8.59 (ISBN 0-688-84269-0). Greenwillow.
--House of Dies Drear. LC 8-23059. (Illus.). (gr. 5 up). 1968. 8.95 (ISBN 0-02-742500-2). Macmillan.
--Justice & Her Brothers. LC 78-54684. (gr. 7 up). 1978. 8.95 (ISBN 0-688-80182-X); PLB 8.59 (ISBN 0-688-84182-1). Greenwillow.
--M. C. Higgins, the Great. LC 72-92439. 288p. (gr. 7 up). 1974. 8.95 (ISBN 0-02-742480-4). Macmillan.
--Planet of Junior Brown. (Illus.). (gr. 7 up). 1971. 8.95 (ISBN 0-02-742510-X). Macmillan.
--Planet of Junior Brown. LC 71-155264. 224p. (gr. 5-9). 1974. pap. 0.95 o.s.i. (ISBN 0-02-043530-4, 04353, Collier). Macmillan.
--Time-Ago Lost: More Tales of Jahdu. LC 72-85187. (Illus.). 96p. (gr. 2-5). 1973. 8.95 (ISBN 0-02-742450-2). Macmillan.
--Time-Ago Tales of Jahdu. LC 70-78089. (Illus.). (gr. 2-5). 1969. 5.95g o.s.i. (ISBN 0-02-742460-X). Macmillan.
--Zeely. (gr. 5-8). 1967. 8.95 (ISBN 0-02-742470-7). Macmillan.
Hamilton, Virginia V. Alabama, a Bicentennial History. (States & the Nation Ser.). (Illus.). 1977. 12.95 (ISBN 0-393-05621-X). Norton.
Hamilton, W. A., jt. ed. see Haddock, B. A.
Hamilton, W. H. & Adair, D. The Power to Govern. LC 77-37759. (American Constitutional & Legal History Ser). 252p. 1972. Repr. of 1937 ed. lib. bdg. 27.50 (ISBN 0-306-70433-1). Da Capo.
Hamilton, W. M., ed. Surgical Treatment of Endocrine Disorders. 272p. 1976. 42.95 (ISBN 0-407-00041-0). Butterworths.
Hamilton, W. R. The Life of Animals with Hooves. LC 78-56566. (Easy Reading Edition of Introduction to Nature Ser.). (Illus.). 1979. lib. bdg. 7.98 (ISBN 0-686-51157-9). Silver.
Hamilton, Wade. Longhorn Brand. 1978. pap. 1.25 (ISBN 0-505-51248-3). Tower Bks.
--Ride the Wild Country. 1977. pap. 1.50 (ISBN 0-505-51205-X). Tower Bks.
Hamilton, Walter. Poets Laureate of England. LC 68-30621. 1968. Repr. of 1879 ed. 22.00 (ISBN 0-8103-3150-0). Gale.
Hamilton, William J., Jr. & Whitaker, John O., Jr. Mammals of the Eastern United States. 2nd ed. LC 79-12920. (HANH Ser.). (Illus.). 368p. 1979. 19.95x (ISBN 0-8014-1254-4). Comstock.
Hamilton, William L. A Social Experiment in Program Administration: The Housing Allowance Administrative Agency Experiment. LC 79-87501. 1979. text ed. 30.00 (ISBN 0-89011-533-8). Abt Assoc.
Hamilton, William P. & Lavin, Mary A. Decision Making in the Coronary Care Unit. 2nd ed. LC 75-30994. (Illus.). 184p. 1976. pap. text ed. 9.50 (ISBN 0-8016-2026-0). Mosby.
Hamilton, William R. Elements of Quaternions, 2 Vols. 3rd ed. Joly, Charles J., ed. LC 68-54711. 1969. Repr. of 1901 ed. Set. 49.50 (ISBN 0-8284-0219-1). Chelsea Pub.
--Mathematical Papers of Sir William Rowan Hamilton, Vol. 3. Halberstam, H. & Ingram, R. E., eds. 1967. 130.00 (ISBN 0-521-05183-5). Cambridge U Pr.
Hamilton-Head, Ian. Leatherwork. (Illus.). 1979. 14.95 (ISBN 0-7137-0928-6, Pub by Blandford Pr England). Sterling.
Hamilton-Paterson, James. Hostage! LC 79-25114. 192p. (gr. 7-12). 1980. 8.95 (ISBN 0-529-05596-1). Philomel.
--House in the Waves. LC 76-103043. (gr. 8 up). 1970. 9.95 (ISBN 0-87599-171-8). S G Phillips.
Hamlet, John, jt. auth. see Grossman, Mary L.
Hamlet, John N. & Carter, W. Horace. Land That I Love. (Illus.). 295p. 1980. 6.95 (ISBN 0-937866-00-8). Atlantic Pub Co.
Hamlet, Peter. Introductory Chemistry: A New View. 272p. 1975. pap. text ed. 7.95x o.p. (ISBN 0-669-83600-1); instr's manual free o.p. (ISBN 0-669-94532-3). Heath.
--Introductory Organic & Biochemistry: A New View. 416p. 1975. text ed. 14.95x o.p. (ISBN 0-669-83618-4); instructors' manual free o.p. (ISBN 0-669-94532-3). Heath.
Hamley, D. C., jt. auth. see Field, C.
Hamley, Dennis. Landings. (gr. 6 up). 1979. PLB 8.95 (ISBN 0-233-97110-6). Andre Deutsch.
--Pageants of Despair. LC 74-10841. 180p. (gr. 7-10). 1974. 9.95 (ISBN 0-87599-205-6). S G Phillips.
--Three Towneley Plays. 1963. pap. text ed. 1.95 o.p. (ISBN 0-435-21012-2). Heinemann Ed.
Hamlin, Charles E. Life & Times of Hannibal Hamlin, 2 Vols. LC 70-137914. (American History & Culture in the Nineteenth Century Ser). 1971. Repr. of 1899 ed. Set. 35.00x (ISBN 0-8046-1482-2). Kennikat.
Hamlin, Cyrus, ed. see Goethe, Johann W. Von.
Hamlin, Donna. Rapid Writing Made Easy. 1978. pap. 4.95 (ISBN 0-8119-0394-X). Fell.

Hamlin, Herbert M. Citizens' Committees in the Public Schools. (Illus.). 1952. text ed. 4.25x (ISBN 0-8134-0084-8, 84). Interstate.

Hamlin, Howard M. The Five Orders of Classic Architecture. (Illus.). 148p. 1981. 69.75 (ISBN 0-930582-95-0). Gloucester Art.

Hamlin, J. A., jt. auth. see Berci, George.

Hamlin, Jessica, jt. auth. see Hamlin, Talbot.

Hamlin, Marie C. Legends of Le Detroit. LC 68-26179. (Illus.). 1977. Repr. of 1884 ed. 18.00 (ISBN 0-8103-3330-9). Gale.

Hamlin, Marjorie, jt. auth. see Polette, Nancy.

Hamlin, Paul L. Legal Education in Colonial New York. LC 70-129082. (American Constitutional and Legal History Ser.). (Illus.). 1970. Repr. of 1939 ed. lib. bdg. 25.00 (ISBN 0-306-70062-X). Da Capo.

Hamlin, Talbot & Hamlin, Jessica. We Took to Cruising: From Maine to Florida Afloat. (Illus.). 1951. 8.95 o.p. (ISBN 0-911378-27-8). Sheridan.

Hamlin, Talbot F see Gabriel, Ralph H.

Hamlyn, D. W. Experience & the Growth of Understanding. (International Library of the Philosophy of Education Ser.). 1978. 17.50x (ISBN 0-7100-8735-7). Routledge & Kegan.

--The Theory of Knowledge. (Modern Introductions to Philosophy Ser.). 308p. 1980. pap. text ed. cancelled (ISBN 0-333-11548-1). Humanities.

Hamlyn, D. W., tr. & intro. by see Aristotle.

Hamlyn, E. C. Healing Art of Homeopathy. 111p. 1980. 15.00x (Pub. by Beaconsfield England). State Mutual Bk.

Hamlyn, Edward. The Healing Art of Homeopathy: The Organon of Samuel Hahnemann. LC 80-82321. (Orig.). 1980. pap. 4.95 (ISBN 0-87983-228-2). Keats.

Hamm, Charles, ed. see Stravinsky, Igor.

Hamm, Edward, Jr. When Fresno Rode the Rails. Sebree, Mac, ed. (Special Ser.: No. 73). (Illus.). 1979. pap. 9.50 (ISBN 0-916374-37-8). Interurban.

Hamm, Marie R. Money-in-the-Bank Cookbook. 1970. pap. 1.25 o.s.i. (ISBN 0-02-009690-9, Collier). Macmillan.

Hamm, Michael F., ed. The City in Russian History. LC 75-3544. 362p. 1976. 19.50x (ISBN 0-8131-1328-8). U Pr of Ky.

Hamm, Robert A., ed. J. Norman Heard's Bookman's Guide to Americana. 5th ed. LC 67-10190. 1969. 15.00 (ISBN 0-8108-0182-5). Scarecrow.

Hamm, Thomas Lafayette. Mirrors of the Mind. 1977. 4.00 o.p. (ISBN 0-682-48880-1). Exposition.

Hammack, ed. The Serial Literature of Entomology: A Descriptive Study. 1970. 3.35 (ISBN 0-686-18866-7). Entomol Soc.

Hamman, Ray T., jt. auth. see Gupta, Shiv K.

Hamman, Rick. California Central Coast Railways. (Illus.). 300p. 1980. 39.95 (ISBN 0-87108-553-4). Pruett.

Hammar, Russell A. Singing--An Extension of Speech. LC 78-11756. 1978. lib. bdg. 11.00 (ISBN 0-8108-1182-0). Scarecrow.

Hammar, Willie. Occupational Safety Management & Engineering. 2nd ed. (Illus.). 608p. 1981. text ed. 19.95 (ISBN 0-13-629410-3). P-H.

Hammarberg, Melvin A. & Nelson, Clifford A., eds. My Book of Prayers: A Personal Prayer Book. LC 56-10134. 192p. 1956. pap. 3.75 (ISBN 0-8006-0454-7, 1-454). Fortress.

Hammarskjold, Dag. Markings. 9th ed. 1965. 8.95 (ISBN 0-571-06015-3, Pub. by Faber & Faber); pap. 4.95 (ISBN 0-571-06591-0). Merrimack Bk Serv.

Hammarstrom, David L. Behind the Big Top. LC 78-69647. (Illus.). 1980. 19.95 (ISBN 0-498-02205-6). A S Barnes.

Hammel, Eric & Lane, John. Seventy-Six Hours: The Invasion of Tirawa. 1980. pap. 2.25 (ISBN 0-686-59463-0). Tower Bks.

Hammel, W. W. So Great Salvation. 1972. pap. 2.25 (ISBN 0-87148-751-9). Pathway Pr.

Hammell, Grandin K. The Sure Way to Get Job Interviews. Brown, Karen A., ed. (Educational Ser.). (Illus.). 78p. (Orig.). (gr. 11-12). 1980. tchrs. ed. 4.50 (ISBN 0-936510-00-5, 101); wkbk. 9.00. Diamond Pubs.

Hammelmann, Hanns, tr. see Strauss, Richard & Von Hofmannsthal, Hugo.

Hammen, Carl S. Marine Invertebrates: Comparative Physiology. LC 80-51505. (Illus.). 180p. 1980. text ed. 12.00x (ISBN 0-87451-188-7). U Pr of New Eng.

Hammen, L. Van Der see Van Der Hammen, L.

Hammer, A. G. Elementary Matrix Algebra for Psychologists & Social Scientists. LC 72-117464. 212p. 1971. 12.75 (ISBN 0-08-017502-3). Pergamon.

Hammer, Carl, Jr. Goethe & Rousseau: Resonances of the Mind. LC 72-91665. 232p. 1973. 12.00x (ISBN 0-8131-1289-3). U Pr of Ky.

Hammer, Donald P., ed. The Information Age: Its Development, Its Impact. LC 76-10603. 1976. 11.00 o.p. (ISBN 0-8108-0945-1). Scarecrow.

Hammer, Ellen J. Struggle for Indochina, 1940-1955. 1955. 15.00x (ISBN 0-8047-0458-9). Stanford U Pr.

Hammer, Emanuel F. Clinical Application of Projective Drawings. (Illus.). 688p. 1980. 28.75 (ISBN 0-398-00768-3). C C Thomas.

--House-Tree-Person (H-T-P) Clinical Research Manual. 47p. (Orig.). 1964. pap. 6.50x (ISBN 0-87424-016-6). Western Psych.

Hammer, Emanuel F., jt. ed. see Buck, John N.

Hammer, Jacob, ed. see Geoffrey Of Monmouth.

Hammer, Kenneth M. The Glory March. (Custeriana Monograph Ser.: No. 7). 1980. pap. 2.50. Monroe County Lib.

Hammer, Louis. To Burn California. LC 74-24492. 3.95 (ISBN 0-685-46996-4). Sagarin Pr.

Hammer, Mark J. Water & Waste Water Technology. LC 75-2000. 502p. 1975. text ed. 21.95 (ISBN 0-471-34726-4); solutions manual avail. (ISBN 0-471-34727-2). Wiley.

--Water & Waste-Water Technology, SI Version. LC 77-9243. 1977. text ed. 22.95 (ISBN 0-471-03787-7); solutions manual avail. (ISBN 0-471-03819-9). Wiley.

Hammer, Mark J. & Mackichan, Kenneth A. Hydrology & Quality of Water Resources. LC 80-209. 400p. 1981. text ed. 19.95 (ISBN 0-471-02681-6). Wiley.

Hammer, Max, ed. The Theory & Practice of Psychotherapy with Specific Disorders. 464p. 1972. 23.75 (ISBN 0-398-02539-8). C C Thomas.

Hammer, R. Between Life & Death. 1969. 6.95 o.s.i. (ISBN 0-02-547720-X). Macmillan.

Hammer, Richard. Mr. Jacobson's War. 1981. 9.95. HarBraceJ.

Hammer, W. Product Safety Management & Engineering. 1980. 19.95 (ISBN 0-686-51706-7). P-H.

Hammerman, Susan & Maikowski, Stephen, eds. The Economics of Disability: International Perspectives. (Illus.). 200p. (Orig.). 1981. pap. write for info. (ISBN 0-9605554-0-4). Rehab Intl.

Hammersmark, Judy. Homemaker's Response to Inflation. (Orig.). 1980. pap. 2.95 (ISBN 0-88270-454-0). Logos.

Hammerstrom, Eckart. Narzistische Figuren in Elisabethanischen Tragodien. (Salzburg Studies in English Literature Elizabethan & Renaissance Studies: No. 55). 1976. pap. text ed. 25.00x (ISBN 0-391-01397-1). Humanities.

Hammerstrom, Gary. Energy Consumption & Conservation. (Learning Packages in Policy Issues: No. 2). (Illus.). 58p. (Orig.). 1977. pap. text ed. 3.00 (ISBN 0-936826-11-8). Pol Stud Assocs.

--The Hazards of Nuclear Energy: A Policy & Planning Approach. (Learning Packages in Policy Issues: No. 3). (Illus.). 86p. (Orig.). 1977. pap. text ed. 4.00 (ISBN 0-936826-12-6). Pol Stud Assocs.

Hammerstrom, Gary & Kafton, Amy M. Descriptive Statistics for Public Policy Analysis. (Learning Packages in the Policy Sciences: No. 20). (Illus.). 110p. (Orig.). 1980. pap. text ed. 4.50 (ISBN 0-936826-09-6). Pol Stud Assocs.

Hammerstrom, Richard B., jt. auth. see Haan, Marina N.

Hammesfahr, James E. & Stong, Clair L. Creative Glass Blowing: Scientific & Ornamental. LC 68-14225. (Illus.). 1978. pap. text ed. 11.95x (ISBN 0-7167-0088-3). W H Freeman.

Hammett, Dashiell. The Continental Op. LC 74-9050. 1974. 7.95 o.p. (ISBN 0-394-48704-4). Random.

--The Dain Curse. 213p. Date not set. pap. 1.50 (ISBN 0-686-68486-9, Vin). Random.

--The Glass Key. 204p. Date not set. pap. 1.50 (ISBN 0-394-71773-2, Vin). Random.

Hammett, Dashiell, jt. auth. see Raymond, Alex.

Hammett, Evelyn A. I, Priscilla. (Illus.). (gr. 4-6). 1960. 3.00 o.s.i. (ISBN 0-02-742550-9). Macmillan.

Hammett, K. R. Fell's Guide to Plant Training, Pruning & Tree Surgery. LC 75-583. (Illus.). 1975. 8.95 (ISBN 0-8119-0260-9). Fell.

Hammett, Keith. The World of Dahlias. (Illus.). 144p. 1980. 17.50 (ISBN 0-589-01265-7, Pub. by Reed Bks Australia). C E Tuttle.

Hammett, Ralph W. Architecture in the United States: A Survey of Architectural Styles Since 1776. LC 76-4917. 1976. 28.00 (ISBN 0-471-34721-3, Pub. by Wiley-Interscience). Wiley.

Hammick, Murry, jt. auth. see Wilks, Mark.

Hammil, Donald D. & Bartel, Nettie R. Teaching Children with Learning & Behavior Problems. 2nd ed. 1978. text ed. 18.95x (ISBN 0-205-06018-8); pap. text ed. 10.95 (ISBN 0-205-06017-X). Allyn.

Hammill, Carrie E. Celestial Journey & the Harmony of the Spheres. LC 79-28416. 183p. 1980. pap. 13.50 (ISBN 0-912646-53-5). Carrollton Pr.

Hammill, Donald D., jt. auth. see Myers, Patricia L.

Hamming, R. W. Digital Filters. (Illus.). 256p. 1977. text ed. 23.95x (ISBN 0-13-212571-4). P-H.

Hamming, Richard W. Coding & Information Theory. (Illus.). 1980. text ed. 25.95 (ISBN 0-13-139139-9). P-H.

Hammitt, Frederick G. Cavitation & Multiphase Flow Phenomena. 448p. 1980. text ed. 48.00 (ISBN 0-07-025907-0). McGraw.

Hammitzch, Horst. Zen in the Art of Tea Ceremony. 104p. 1981. 7.95 (ISBN 0-312-89859-2). St Martin.

Hammon, William M., et al, eds. Immunization for Japanese Encephalitis. (Illus.). 1971. 21.25 (ISBN 0-89640-005-0). Igaku-Shoin.

Hammond, B., jt. auth. see Hammond, J. L.

Hammond, Barbara, jt. auth. see Hammond, J. L.

Hammond, Blodwen, jt. auth. see Shepardson, Mary.

Hammond, C. O. The Dragonflies of Great Britain & Ireland. 116p. 1980. 36.00x (ISBN 0-902068-06-7, Pub. by Curwen England). State Mutual Bk.

Hammond Cartographers, ed. see Hammond Incorporated.

Hammond, Charles. The Image Decade: Television Documentary 1965-1975. 256p. 1981. 16.95 (ISBN 0-8038-3431-4, Communication Arts); pap. 9.95 (ISBN 0-8038-3432-2). Hastings.

Hammond, Charlie. Charlie Hammond's Sketch-Book. (Illus.). 84p. 1980. 19.95 (ISBN 0-19-212974-0). Oxford U Pr.

Hammond, Cleon E. John Hart: The Biography of a Signer of the Declaration of Independence. LC 77-70992. (Illus.). 1977. 15.95x (ISBN 0-9603426-0-5). Pioneer VT.

Hammond, David. The Home Ownership Game & How to Win It. LC 80-68693. (Illus.). 112p. 1981. 13.50 (ISBN 0-7153-7710-8). David & Charles.

Hammond, Debbie, ed. see Beavers, Dorothy J.

Hammond, Debbie, ed. see Friend, Paul D.

Hammond, Debbie, ed. see Smolen, Maxine.

Hammond, Dorothy. Confusing Collectibles: A Guide to the Identification of Contemporary Items. (Illus.). 19.95 (ISBN 0-87069-242-9). Wallace-Homestead.

--Pictorial Price Guide to American Antiques. 3rd ed. (Illus.). 1980. pap. 9.95 (ISBN 0-525-47625-3). Dutton.

--Pictorial Price Guide to American Antiques. 4th ed. (Illus.). 224p. 1981. pap. 9.95 (ISBN 0-525-47660-1). Dutton.

--Price Guide to Country Antiques & American Primitives. (Funk & W Bk.). (Illus.). 1975. pap. 6.95 o.s.i. (ISBN 0-308-10184-7, TYC-T). T Y Crowell.

Hammond, Dorothy & Jablow, Alta. The Africa That Never Was: Four Centuries of British Writing About Africa--an Anthropological View Contrasting the Africa of Fact & the Africa of Fiction. LC 78-77035. 251p. 1978. text ed. 28.50x (ISBN 0-8290-0151-4); pap. text ed. 12.95x (ISBN 0-8290-0152-2). Irvington.

--Women in Cultures of the World. new ed. LC 75-32850. (Cummings Modular Program in Anthropology). 1976. text ed. 8.95 o.p. (ISBN 0-8465-2610-7); pap. text ed. 4.95 o.p. (ISBN 0-8465-2611-5). Benjamin-Cummings.

Hammond, Earl, et al. Elephants in the Living Room, Bears in the Canoe. LC 77-802. (gr. 5-7). 1977. 8.95 o.s.i. (ISBN 0-440-02251-7). Delacorte.

Hammond, Ed. Coming of Grace: An Illustrated Biography of Zhou Enlai. 196p. 1980. 14.95 (ISBN 0-89581-455-2); pap. 8.95 (ISBN 0-89581-503-6). Lancaster-Miller.

--To Embrace the Moon: An Illustrated Biography of Mao Zedong. 196p. 1980. 14.95 (ISBN 0-89581-455-2); pap. 8.95 (ISBN 0-89581-502-8). Lancaster-Miller.

Hammond, Frank L., jt. ed. see Ohlsen, Woodrow.

Hammond, Gerald. The Reader & Shakespeare's Young Man Sonnets. 247p. 1981. 22.50x (ISBN 0-389-20046-8). B&N.

Hammond, Harry E. & Halbroyd, L. V. Laboratory Manual of Elementary College Physics. 7th ed. 1974. text ed. 4.50x spiral bdg. (ISBN 0-87543-101-1). Lucas.

Hammond, Henry. The Lawfull Magistrate Upon Colour of Religion. Berkowitz, David S. & Thorne, Samuel E., eds. LC 77-89203. (Classics of English Legal History in the Modern Era Ser.: Vol. 58). 1979. lib. bdg. 40.00 (ISBN 0-8240-3157-1). Garland Pub.

Hammond Incorporated. The Hammond Large Type World Atlas. rev. ed. Hammond Cartographers, ed. (Illus.). (gr. 4-9). 1979. 19.95 (ISBN 0-8437-1246-5). Hammond Inc.

Hammond, J. A. An Edgar Allan Poe Companion. (Companion Ser.). (Illus.). 1981. 27.50x (ISBN 0-389-20172-3). B&N.

Hammond, J. L. & Hammond, B. The Town Labourer. new ed. Lovell, John, ed. LC 77-14533. (Illus.). 1978. text ed. 21.00x (ISBN 0-582-48519-3); pap. text ed. 11.50x (ISBN 0-582-48081-7). Longman.

--The Village Labourer. new ed. Mingay, Gordon E., ed. LC 77-21513. 1978. text ed. 22.00x (ISBN 0-582-48518-5); pap. text ed. 12.95x (ISBN 0-582-48082-5). Longman.

Hammond, J. L. & Hammond, Barbara. The Town Labourer, 1760-1832: The New Civilization. 342p. 1980. Repr. of 1932 ed. lib. bdg. 25.00 (ISBN 0-89984-293-3). Century Bookbindery.

Hammond, J. R., ed. H. G. Wells: Interviews & Recollections. LC 79-55529. (Interviews & Recollections Ser.). 121p. 1981. text ed. 26.00x (ISBN 0-06-492671-0). B&N.

Hammond, James J., et al. Woodworking Technology. rev. ed. (Illus.). (gr. 10-12). 1980. text ed. 17.28 (ISBN 0-87345-893-1); study guide 5.20 (ISBN 0-87345-894-X); ans. key avail. (ISBN 0-87345-895-8). McKnight.

Hammond, Janice M. When My Mommy Died: A Child's View of Death. (Illus.). 27p. (Orig.). (ps-5). 1980. pap. 3.95 (ISBN 0-9604690-0-1). Cranbrook Pub.

Hammond, John. Understanding Human Engineering: An Introduction to Ergonomics. 1979. 14.95 (ISBN 0-7153-7670-5). David & Charles.

Hammond, John, jt. auth. see Abell, Derek F.

Hammond, Jonathan. China. LC 75-44869. (Macdonald Countries). (Illus.). (gr. 6 up). 1976. PLB 7.95 (ISBN 0-382-06101-2, Pub. by Macdonald Ed). Silver.

Hammond, Kenneth R., ed. Psychoactive Drugs & Social Judgement: Theory & Research. Joyce, C. R. LC 80-12506. 298p. 1980. Repr. of 1975 ed. lib. bdg. write for info. (ISBN 0-89874-171-8). Krieger.

Hammond, Kenneth R., et al. Human Judgement & Decision Making: Theories, Methods & Procedures. 272p. 1980. 25.95 (ISBN 0-03-057567-2). Praeger.

Hammond, Marc. Fathom. (Orig.). 1979. pap. 2.25 o.s.i. (ISBN 0-515-05121-7). Jove Pubns.

Hammond, Mary G., ed. see University of North Carolina at Chapel Hill, Dept. of OB-GYN.

Hammond, N. G. L. & Griffith, G. T. A History of Macedonia: Volume II: 550-336 B.C. (Illus.). 1979. 79.00x (ISBN 0-19-814814-3). Oxford U Pr.

Hammond, Nicholas G. Alexander the Great: King, Commander, & Statesman. LC 80-18573. (Illus.). 358p. 1981. 24.00 (ISBN 0-8155-5058-8). Noyes.

--History of Greece to 322 B. C. 2nd ed. (Illus.). 1967. 19.50x o.p. (ISBN 0-19-814260-9). Oxford U Pr.

Hammond, Otis G., ed. see Sullivan, John.

Hammond, P. Applied Electromagnetism. 396p. 1972. text ed. 25.00 (ISBN 0-08-016381-5); pap. text ed. 11.25 (ISBN 0-08-016382-3). Pergamon.

--Electromagnetism for Engineers: In SI-Metric Units. 2nd ed. 1978. text ed. 30.00 (ISBN 0-08-022103-3); pap. text ed. 10.75 (ISBN 0-08-022104-1). Pergamon.

Hammond, P., ed. see Coekin, J. A.

Hammond, P., et al. The Structure of Human Society. 736p. 1975. text ed. 15.95x (ISBN 0-669-81315-X); instructor's manual free (ISBN 0-669-90266-7). Heath.

Hammond, Phillip E., jt. auth. see Bellah, Robert N.

Hammond, Reginald. Britain. LC 77-437537. (Red Guide Ser.). (Illus.). 256p. 1969. 7.50x (ISBN 0-7063-1082-9). Intl Pubns Serv.

Hammond, Reginald J. Complete Scotland. 13th ed. Lowther, Kenneth E., ed. (Red Guide Ser.). (Illus.). 449p. 1980. 17.50x (ISBN 0-7063-5905-4). Intl Pubns Serv.

Hammond, Reginald J., ed. Complete England. (Ward Lock Red Guides Ser.). (Illus.). 1976. 12.95 o.p. (ISBN 0-7063-1192-2). Hippocrene Bks.

--Complete Thames & Chilterns. LC 77-437537. (Red Guide Ser.). (Illus.). 1977. 11.25x (ISBN 0-7063-5502-4). Intl Pubns Serv.

Hammond, Reginald J. & Lowther, Kenneth, eds. Complete Wye Valley, Hereford & Worchester. LC 77-351996. (Red Guide Ser.). (Illus.). 1976. 11.25x (ISBN 0-7063-5134-7). Intl Pubns Serv.

Hammond, Rogers, jt. auth. see Van House, Charles.

Hammond, Sandra N. Ballet Basics. LC 73-91991. 1974. 11.95 (ISBN 0-87484-259-X); pap. text ed. 6.95 (ISBN 0-87484-258-1). Mayfield Pub.

Hammond, Susan W., jt. auth. see Fox, Harrison W., Jr.

Hammond, Tom, tr. see Deane, Forbes, et al.

Hammond, William K., jt. auth. see Rule, La Reina.

Hammonds, Michael. A Gathering of Wolves. 1976. pap. 1.25 o.p. (ISBN 0-685-72564-2, LB393, Leisure Bks). Nordon Pubns.

--Incident on the Way to a Killing. 176p. 1980. pap. 1.75 (ISBN 0-515-04681-7). Jove Pubns.

Hammond-Tooke, W. D., ed. The Bantu-Speaking Peoples of South Africa. (Illus.). 1974. 35.00x (ISBN 0-7100-7748-3). Routledge & Kegan.

--The Bantu-Speaking Peoples of Southern Africa. (Illus.). 298p. 1980. pap. 35.00 (ISBN 0-7100-0708-6). Routledge & Kegan.

Hammons, Ann R. Wild Bill Sullivan: King of the Hollow. LC 80-19625. 1980. 9.95 (ISBN 0-87805-127-9). U Pr of Miss.

Hamner, Robert D. Critical Perspectives on V. S. Naipaul. LC 77-71683. (Illus., Orig.). 1977. 20.00x (ISBN 0-914478-17-6); pap. 9.00x (ISBN 0-914478-18-4). Three Continents.

--V. S. Naipaul. (World Authors Ser.: West Indies: No. 258). 1973. lib. bdg. 10.95 (ISBN 0-8057-2647-0). Twayne.

Hamner, W. Clay & Organ, Dennis W. Organizational Behavior: An Applied Psychological Approach. 1978. 16.00x (ISBN 0-256-01811-1). Business Pubns.

Hamner, W. Clay, jt. ed. see Tosi, Henry L.

Hamnett, Michael P., ed. Research in Culture Learning: Language & Conceptual Studies. Brislin, Richard W. LC 80-21761. 195p. 1980. pap. 10.00x (ISBN 0-8248-0738-3). U Pr of Hawaii.

Hamon, Augustin F. The Technique of Bernard Shaw's Plays. 70p. 1980. Repr. of 1912 ed. lib. bdg. 12.50 (ISBN 0-8492-5274-1). R West.

Hamori, Andras, tr. see Goldziher, Ignaz.

Hamori, Ruth, tr. see Goldziher, Ignaz.

Hamp, Eric P. & Greenlaw, Jean. Like You & Me. (Design for Reading Ser). (Illus.). (preprimer 2). 1972. pap. text ed. 2.92 (ISBN 0-06-516001-0, SchDept). Har-Row.

--This Is for Me. (Design for Reading Ser). (Illus.). (preprimer 1). 1972. pap. 2.92 (ISBN 0-06-516000-2, SchDept). Har-Row.

Hamparian, Donna, et al. The Violent Few. LC 77-9128. (The Dangerous Offender Project). 1978. 18.95 (ISBN 0-669-01779-5). Lexington Bks.

Hampden, John. Ghost Stories. 1975. pap. 3.25 o.p. (ISBN 0-460-01952-X, Evman). Dutton.

Hampe, Johann C., tr. see Bonhoeffer, Dietrich.

Hamperl, H. & Ackermann, L. V. Illustrated Tumor Nomenclature. 2nd ed. (Illus., Eng. Span, Fr, Ger. & Rus.). 1969. 37.10 (ISBN 0-387-04567-8). Springer-Verlag.

Hamphill, Elizabeth. The Least of These. (Illus.). 176p. 1981. 12.50 (ISBN 0-8348-0155-8). Weatherhill.

Hampl, Patricia. A Romantic Education. 320p. 1981. 11.95 (ISBN 0-395-29697-8). HM.

Hample, Stoo. Yet Another Big Fat Funny Silly Book. LC 80-66202. (Illus.). 96p. (gr. 1-4). 1980. 4.95 (ISBN 0-440-09796-7); PLB 6.46 (ISBN 0-440-09797-5). Delacorte.

Hampshire, S. Public & Private Morality. LC 78-2839. 1978. 20.95 (ISBN 0-521-22084-X); pap. 5.95x (ISBN 0-521-29352-9). Cambridge U Pr.

Hampson, Ann. Second Tomorrow. 192p. (Orig.). 1980. pap. 1.50 (ISBN 0-671-57016-1). S&S.

Hampson, Anne. The Dawn Steals Softly. 192p. (Orig.). 1980. pap. 1.50 (ISBN 0-671-57027-7). S&S.

--Man of the Outback. 192p. (Orig.). 1980. pap. 1.50 (ISBN 0-671-57028-5). S&S.

--Man Without a Heart. 192p. 1981. pap. 1.50 (ISBN 0-671-57052-8). S&S.

--Payment in Full. 192p. (Orig.). 1980. pap. 1.50 (ISBN 0-671-57001-3). S&S.

--Second Tomorrow. (Silhouette Ser.: No. 16). pap. 1.50 (ISBN 0-686-68325-0). PB.

--Shadow of Apollo. 192p. 1981. pap. 1.50 (ISBN 0-671-57064-1). S&S.

--Stormy Masquerade. 192p. (Orig.). 1980. pap. 1.50 (ISBN 0-671-57004-8). S&S.

--Sunset Cloud. (Alpha Books). 80p. (Orig.). 1979. pap. text ed. 2.25x (ISBN 0-19-424161-0). Oxford U Pr.

--Temple of the Dawn. (Harlequin Romances Ser.). 192p. 1980. pap. 1.25 o.p. (ISBN 0-373-02353-7, Pub. by Harlequin). PB.

--Where Eagles Nest. 192p. (Orig.). 1980. pap. 1.50 (ISBN 0-671-57040-4). S&S.

Hampson, David, jt. auth. see Schaffarcick, Jon.

Hampson, Norman. The French Revolution: A Concise History. LC 74-33925. (Encore Edition). 1975. 12.50 o.p. (ISBN 0-684-14302-X, ScribT). Scribner.

Hampton, Bill R. & Lauer, Robert H. Solving Problems in Secondary School Administration: A Human Organization Approach. 336p. 1980. text ed. 16.95 (ISBN 0-205-06951-7, 2369516). Allyn.

Hampton, C. W. & Clifford, E. Planecraft. LC 79-57129. (Illus.). 1980. pap. 6.00 (ISBN 0-918036-00-3). Woodcraft Supply.

Hampton, Charles M. Dry Land Log Handling & Sorting. LC 80-80437. (A Forest Industries Bk). (Illus.). 216p. 1981. pap. 45.00 (ISBN 0-87930-081-7). Miller Freeman.

Hampton, Christopher. Moliere's Don Juan. 1974. pap. 3.95 o.p. (ISBN 0-571-10193-3, Pub. by Faber & Faber). Merrimack Bk Serv.

--The Philanthropist. 1970. pap. 5.95 o.p. (ISBN 0-571-09520-8, Pub. by Faber & Faber). Merrimack Bk Serv.

--Savages. 1974. 8.50 (ISBN 0-571-10437-1, Pub. by Faber & Faber); pap. 4.95 (ISBN 0-571-10348-0). Merrimack Bk Serv.

Hampton, Christopher, tr. see Ibsen, Henrik.

Hampton, David. Behavioral Concepts in Management. 3rd ed. (Contemporary Thought in Mngt. Ser.). 1978. pap. text ed. 8.95x (ISBN 0-534-00576-4). Wadsworth Pub.

Hampton, David R. Contemporary Management. 2nd ed. (Management Ser.). (Illus.). 528p. 1981. text ed. 19.95x (ISBN 0-07-025935-6); instructor's manual 7.95 (ISBN 0-07-025936-4); write for info study guide (ISBN 0-07-025937-2); test file 15.00 (ISBN 0-07-025938-0). McGraw.

Hampton, David R., jt. auth. see Belasco, James A.

Hampton, David R., et al. Organizational Behavior & the Practice of Management. 3rd ed. 1978. 19.95x (ISBN 0-673-15119-0). Scott F.

Hampton, Olga M. All About the English Springer Spaniel. (All About Ser.). (Illus.). 1980. 16.95 (ISBN 0-7207-1274-2, Pub. by Michael Joseph). Merrimack Bk Serv.

Hampton, Russell K. The Far Side of Despair: A Personal Account of Depression. LC 74-33177. 224p. 1975. 11.95 (ISBN 0-88229-106-8). Nelson-Hall.

Hampton, William. Everyone's Guide to Four-Wheel Drive. (Illus.). 1980. cancelled (ISBN 0-8092-7113-3); pap. cancelled (ISBN 0-8092-7112-5). Contemp Bks.

--Fell's Guide to Doubling the Performance of Your Car. 192p. 1977. 8.95 o.s.i. (ISBN 0-8119-0267-6); pap. 4.95 o.p. (ISBN 0-88391-053-5). Fell.

Hamrin, Robert D. Managing Growth in the Nineteen Eighties: Toward a New Economics. LC 79-19459. (Praeger Special Studies). (Illus.). 318p. 1980. 24.95 (ISBN 0-03-054061-5); pap. 10.95 (ISBN 0-03-054056-9). Praeger.

Hamsa, Bobbie. Your Pet Bear. LC 79-24938. (Far-Fetched Pets Ser.). (Illus.). 32p. (ps-3). 1980. PLB 7.95 (ISBN 0-516-03351-4). Childrens.

--Your Pet Kangaroo. LC 80-15764. (Far-Fetched Pets). (Illus.). 32p. (ps-3). 1980. PLB 7.95 (ISBN 0-516-03363-8). Childrens.

--Your Pet Penguin. LC 80-15588. (Far-Fetched Pets Ser.). (Illus.). 32p. (ps-3). 1980. PLB 7.95 (ISBN 0-516-03364-6). Childrens.

Hamsun, Knut. Wayfarers. McFarlane, James, tr. 1981. pap. 7.95 (ISBN 0-374-51635-9). FS&G.

--Wayfarers. McFarlane, James, tr. from Norwegian. 460p. 1980. 15.95 (ISBN 0-374-28672-8). FS&G.

Han, Henry H., ed. World in Transition: Challenges to Human Rights, Development & World Order. LC 79-66422. 1979. pap. text ed. 17.75 (ISBN 0-8191-0824-3). U Pr of Amer.

Han, Jaok, ed. Cardiac Arrhythmias: A Symposium. (Illus.). 320p. 1972. 31.50 (ISBN 0-398-02305-0). C C Thomas.

Han, Li & Tzu-Kuang, Hsu. Meng Ch'iu: Famous Episodes from Chinese History & Legend. Watson, Burton, tr. from Chinese. LC 79-89264. 184p. 1980. 15.00 (ISBN 0-87011-278-3). Kodansha.

Han, Sungjoo. The Failure of Democracy in South Korea. 1974. 18.50x (ISBN 0-520-02437-0). U of Cal Pr.

Han, Woo-Keun. The History of Korea. Mintz, Grafton K., ed. Lee, Kyung-Shik, tr. from Korean. (Illus.). 568p. 1971. 15.00 o.p. (ISBN 0-8248-0106-7, Eastwest Ctr); pap. text ed. 8.95x (ISBN 0-8248-0334-5). U Pr of Hawaii.

Hana, Nora. Embroidery. (Illus.). 1977. 6.95 (ISBN 0-8467-0239-8, Pub. by Two Continents). Hippocrene Bks.

Hana, W. J. English Lantern Clocks. (Illus.). 1979. 14.95 (ISBN 0-7137-1011-X, Pub by Blandford Pr England). Sterling.

Hanaburgh, David H. Your Future in Forestry. LC 75-114121. (Career Guidance Ser). 1971. pap. 3.50 (ISBN 0-668-02245-0). Arco.

Hanabusa, Masamichi. Trade Problems Between Japan & Western Europe. LC 79-88567. (Illus.). 138p. 1979. 24.95 (ISBN 0-03-053361-9). Praeger.

Hanagan, Mary. Me, Julie Mountain. 74p. 1979. 4.95 (ISBN 0-8059-2645-3). Dorrance.

Hanan, Mack, et al. Sales Negotiation Strategies: Building the Win-Win Customer Relationship. LC 76-44021. 1977. 11.95 (ISBN 0-8144-5431-3). Am Mgmt.

--Systems Selling Strategies: How to Justify Premium Prices for Commodity Products. 1978. 14.95 (ISBN 0-8144-5460-7). Am Mgmt.

Hanau, Laia. The Study Game. 4th ed. 1979. pap. 3.95 (ISBN 0-06-463489-2, EH 489, EH). Har-Row.

Hanauer, Elsie. Guns of the Wild West. LC 74-124202. (Illus.). 112p. Date not set. 12.00 o.p. (ISBN 0-498-07462-5). A S Barnes. Postponed.

--Rocks & Minerals of the Western United States. LC 73-144. (Illus.). 224p. 1976. 12.00 o.p. (ISBN 0-498-01273-5). A S Barnes.

Hanauer, Elsie V. The Horse Owner's Concise Guide. LC 69-14810. (Illus.). 1978. pap. 3.50 (ISBN 0-668-0466_-9, 4661). Arco.

Hanauer, Ethel R. Biology Made Simple. LC 72-76229. pap. 3.95 (ISBN 0-385-01972-6, Made). Doubleday.

Hanauer, Gary. Small Museums of the West. Vandenburgh, Jane, ed. LC 80-67476. (Illus.). 288p. (Orig.). 1981. pap. 9.95 (ISBN 0-89395-051-3). Cal Living Bks.

Hanauer, James E. Folklore of the Holy Land. 280p. 1980. Repr. of 1935 ed. lib. bdg. 30.00 (ISBN 0-8492-5272-5). R West.

Hanauer, Milton L. Chess Made Simple. 1967. pap. 3.50 (ISBN 0-385-01215-2, Made). Doubleday.

Hanawalt, jt. auth. see Freidberg.

Hanawalt, Philip C., intro. by. Molecules to Living Cells: Highlights in Molecular Biology. Readings from Scientific Americans. LC 80-10814. (Illus.). 1980. text ed. 19.95x (ISBN 0-7167-1208-3); pap. text ed. 9.95x (ISBN 0-7167-1209-1). W H Freeman.

Hanawalt, Philip C. & Haynes, Robert H.intro. by. The Chemical Basis of Life: An Introduction to Molecular & Cell Biology: Readings from Scientific American. LC 73-8899. (Illus.). 405p. 1973. text ed. 19.95x (ISBN 0-7167-0882-5); pap. text ed. 9.95x (ISBN 0-7167-0881-7). W H Freeman.

Hanbury, H. G. & Yardley, D. C. English Courts of Law. 5th ed. 1979. 14.50x (ISBN 0-19-219139-X). Oxford U Pr.

Hanbury-Tenison, Robin. Mulu: The Rain Forest. (Illus.). 176p. 1980. 22.50x (ISBN 0-297-77768-8, Pub. by Weidenfeld & Nicolson England). Biblio Dist.

Hance, Dawn. Shrewsbury, Vermont: Our Town As It Was. LC 80-69447. 328p. 1980. 20.00 (ISBN 0-914960-28-8). Academy Bks.

Hance, Kenneth G., et al. Principles of Speaking. 3rd ed. 1974. 13.95x (ISBN 0-534-00373-7). Wadsworth Pub.

Hance, William A. The Geography of Modern Africa. 2nd ed. (Illus.). 736p. 1975. 20.50x (ISBN 0-231-03869-0). Columbia U Pr.

Hance, William A., et al, eds. Southern Africa & the United States. LC 68-18147. 1969. 15.00x (ISBN 0-231-031_7-3). Columbia U Pr.

Hanchey, Marguerite, jt. auth. see Owen, Dolores.

Hancock. Introduction to Modern Mathematics Series 1. (gr. 8-12). 1972. pap. text ed. 7.50 each incl. 5 texts, 1 tchrs' manual & test (ISBN 0-8449-0220-1). Learning Line.

--Introduction to Modern Mathematics Series 2. (gr. 8-12). 1972. pap. text ed. 7.50 each incl. 4 texts, 1 tchrs' manual & test (ISBN 0-8449-0220-9). Learning Line.

Hancock, Alan. Planning for Educational Mass Media. LC 76-22496. (Illus.). 1977. text ed. 28.00x (ISBN 0-582-41055-X). Longman.

Hancock, C. V. Rod in Hand. 9.95x (ISBN 0-392-06434-0, SpS). Soccer.

Hancock, David, et al. Pacific Wilderness. 97p. 1974. pap. write for info. (ISBN 0-919654-08-8). Hancock Hse.

Hancock, Eric, ed. Benzene & Its Industrial Derivatives. LC 74-28074. 597p. 1975. 84.95 (ISBN 0-470-34730-5). Halsted Pr.

Hancock, G. B. Mormonism Exposed. 4.95 (ISBN 0-89315-157-2). Lambert Bk.

Hancock, G. F., jt. auth. see Boustead, I.

Hancock, Graham, ed. Africa Guide, Nineteen Eighty-One. 5th ed. (Annual Review Ser.). (Illus.). 1981. pap. 24.95 (ISBN 0-528-84517-9). Rand.

Hancock, Harris. Development of the Minkowski Geometry of Numbers, 2 vols. pap. text ed. 3.50 ea. Vol. 1 (ISBN 0-486-61203-1). Vol. 2 (ISBN 0-486-61204-X). Dover.

Hancock, I. F. Readings in Creole Studies. (Story-Scientia Linguistics Ser.: No. 2). 1980. text ed. 62.25x (ISBN 90-6439-163-7). Humanities.

Hancock, John C. Introduction to the Principles of Communication Theory. (Electrical & Electronic Engineering Ser.). 1961. text ed. 19.95 o.p. (ISBN 0-07-025980-1, C). McGraw.

Hancock, M., jt. auth. see Hirsch, H.

Hancock, M. Donald & Sjoberg, Gideon, eds. Politics in the Post Welfare State: Responses to the New Individualism. LC 79-165181. 1972. text ed. 22.50x (ISBN 0-231-03127-0). Columbia U Pr.

Hancock, Maxine. Love, Honor & Be Free. study ed. 5.95 (ISBN 0-8024-5015-6). Moody.

--Love, Honor & Be Free: Leader's Guide. 1979. pap. 3.25 (ISBN 0-8024-5016-4). Moody.

Hancock, Niel. Calix Stay. (Circle of Light Ser.: No. 3). 1977. pap. 2.25 (ISBN 0-445-04047-5). Popular Lib.

--Dragon Winter. 1978. pap. 2.50 (ISBN 0-445-04191-9). Popular Lib.

Hancock, Norman N. Matrix Analysis of Electrical Machinery. 2nd ed. LC 74-3286. 1974. text ed. 25.00 (ISBN 0-08-017898-7); pap. text ed. 12.50 (ISBN 0-08-017899-5). Pergamon.

Hancock, P. D. Narrow Gauge Adventure: The Story of the Craig & Mertonford Railway. (Illus.). 1978. 19.25 o.p. (ISBN 0-900586-44-3). Aztex.

--Narrow Gauge Adventure: The Story of the Craig & Mertonford Railways. 2nd ed. (Illus.). 128p. 1980. 23.50 (ISBN 0-900586-54-0). Aztex.

Hancock, Ralph. Mexico. (gr. 7 up). 1964. 5.95 o.s.i. (ISBN 0-02-742600-9). Macmillan.

Hancock, Roger N. Twentieth Century Ethics. LC 74-12023. 256p. 1974. 20.00x (ISBN 0-231-03877-1). Columbia U Pr.

Hancock, Sibyl, ed. Climbing up to Nowhere. (I Can Read a Bible Story Ser.: No. 2). (Illus.). (gr. 7-9). 1977. 3.95 (ISBN 0-570-07322-7, 56-1513); pap. 1.95 (ISBN 0-686-67848-6, 56-1413). Concordia.

Hancock, William, et al, eds. The Vermont Atlas & Gazetteer. (Illus.). 96p. (Orig.). 1978. pap. 6.95 (ISBN 0-89933-005-3). DeLorme Pub.

Hancock, William K. Ricasoli & the Risorgimento in Tuscany. LC 68-9603. 1969. Repr. of 1926 ed. 16.50 (ISBN 0-86527-171-2). Fertig.

--Smuts, 2 vols. Incl. Vol. 1. The Sanguine Years, 1870-1919. (ISBN 0-521-05187-8); Vol. 2. The Fields of Force, 1919-1950. (ISBN 0-521-05188-6). 1962. 56.00 ea. Cambridge U Pr.

Hancock, William K., ed. see Smuts, J. C.

Hancox, N. M. Biology of Bone. LC 73-169578. (Biological Structure & Function Ser). (Illus.). 1972. 57.50 (ISBN 0-521-08342-7). Cambridge U Pr.

Hand, Bruce A., et al. Traffic Investigation & Control. 2nd ed. (Public Service Technology Ser.). 272p. 1980. text ed. 15.95 (ISBN 0-675-08112-2). Merrill.

Hand, Jackson. How to Do Your Own Painting & Wall Papering. (Popular Science Skill Bk.). (Illus.). 1969. 5.95 o.s.i. (ISBN 0-06-002381-3, HarpT); pap. 3.95 2nd ed. 1976 (ISBN 0-06-011793-1, TD-283, HarpT). Har-Row.

--Walls, Floors, Ceilings. LC 75-29778. (Popular Science Bk.). (Illus.). 384p. 1976. 9.95 o.p. (ISBN 0-06-011772-9, HarpT). Har-Row.

Hand, Joan C. Entrances to Nowhere. LC 76-770231. (Poetry Ser.). (Illus.). o. p. 8.95x (ISBN 0-89304-015-0, CCC110); signed ltd. ed. 15.00x (ISBN 0-89304-044-4); pap. 3.95x (ISBN 0-89304-014-2); pap. 4.95x signed ltd. ed. o.p. (ISBN 0-89304-043-6). Cross Cult.

Hand, Lee. Nursing Supervision. (Illus.). 368p. 1980. text ed. 16.95 (ISBN 0-8359-5044-1); pap. 13.95 (ISBN 0-8359-5043-3). Reston.

Hand, Robert. Horoscope Symbols. 384p. (Orig.). 1980. pap. 14.95 (ISBN 0-914918-16-8). Para Res.

--Planets in Transit: Life Cycles for Living. LC 76-12759. (Planets Ser.). 1980. pap. 18.95 (ISBN 0-914918-24-9). Para Res.

Hand, Samuel B. Counsel & Advise: A Political Biography of Samuel I. Rosenman. Freidel, Frank, ed. LC 78-62383. (Modern American History Ser.: Vol. 8). 225p. 1979. lib. bdg. 30.00 (ISBN 0-8240-3632-8). Garland Pub.

Hand, Sherman. Carnival Glass Price Guide. 7th ed. (Illus.). 1979. pap. 3.95 o.p. (ISBN 0-89145-023-8). Collector Bks.

Hand, Wayland D. Magical Medicine: The Folkloric Component of Folk Medicine in the Folk Belief, Custom, & Ritual of Non-Primitive Peoples. 296p. 1981. 22.50 (ISBN 0-520-04129-1). U of Cal Pr.

Hand, Wayland D., ed. American Folk Legend: A Symposium. (Library Reprint Ser.: No. 98). 1979. Repr. of 1971 ed. 18.50x (ISBN 0-520-03836-3). U of Cal Pr.

Handbuck, Ein, jt. auth. see Meder, J.

Handcock, W. D., ed. English Historical Documents: 1874-1914, Vol. XII, Part 2. (English Historical Documents Ser.). (Illus.). 1978. 55.00x (ISBN 0-19-519994-4). Oxford U Pr.

Handel. Handel's "Messiah". The Conducting Score. 460p. 1979. Repr. of 1974 ed. 75.00x (ISBN 0-85967-158-5, Pub. by Scolar Pr England). Biblio Dist.

Handel, Michael. Weak States in the International System. 144p. 1980. 27.50x (ISBN 0-7146-3117-5, F Cass Co). Biblio Dist.

Handel, Warren H., jt. auth. see Lauer, Robert H.

Handelman, Ira, jt. auth. see Thompson, Gene E.

Handelsman, Judith & Baerwald, Sara. Greenworks: Tender Loving Care for Plants. LC 73-1854. 1974. pap. 1.95 o.s.i. (ISBN 0-02-062890-0); pap. cancelled o.s.i. (ISBN 0-685-31477-4). Macmillan.

Handelsman, Michael H. & Heslin, William H., Jr. La Cultura Hispanica: Dentro y Fuera de los Estados Unidos. 128p. 1981. pap. text ed. 7.95 (ISBN 0-394-32653-9). Random.

Handern, Geoff. Business Organisation & Management. 1978. 22.50x (ISBN 0-86003-023-7, Pub. by Allan Pubs England); pap. 11.25x (ISBN 0-86003-124-1). State Mutual Bk.

Handford. Professional Pattern Grading for Women's, Men's & Children's Apparel. (Illus.). 254p. 1980. spiral bdg. 14.95 (ISBN 0-686-65142-1). Burgess.

Handford, Jack. Professional Patternmaking for Designer's of Women's Wear. LC 74-78635. (Illus.). 1977. spiral bdg. 14.95x (ISBN 0-916434-21-4). Plycon Pr.

Handford, Peter. Sounds of Railways & Their Recording. LC 79-56055. (Illus.). 152p. 1980. 14.95 (ISBN 0-7153-7631-4). David & Charles.

Handford, S. A., tr. see Caesar, Julius.

Handisyde, Cecil C. Hard Landscape in Brick. (Illus.). 1977. 16.00x (ISBN 0-85139-283-0, Pub. by Architectural Pr). Nichols Pub.

Handke, Peter. Innerworld of the Outerworld of the Innerworld. Roloff, Michael, tr. from Ger. LC 73-17875. 128p. 1974. 8.95 (ISBN 0-8164-9194-1); pap. 4.50 (ISBN 0-8164-9195-X, Continuum). Continuum.

--Two Novels by Peter Handke. 1979. pap. 2.75 (ISBN 0-380-48033-6, 48033, Bard). Avon.

Handleman, Howard. Struggle in the Andes: Peasant Political Mobilization in Peru. (Latin American Monographs: No. 35). 350p. 1974. 14.95x (ISBN 0-292-77513-X). U of Tex Pr.

Handler, M., et al. Federal Trade Commission: A Fiftieth Anniversary Symposium. LC 78-152229. (Symposia on Law & Society Ser). 1971. Repr. of 1964 ed. lib. bdg. 22.50 (ISBN 0-306-70119-7). Da Capo.

Handley, George D. Personality, Learning & Teaching. (Students Library of Education). 126p. 1973. 10.00x (ISBN 0-7100-7625-8); pap. 5.00 (ISBN 0-7100-7628-2). Routledge & Kegan.

Handlin, David. The American Home: Architecture & Society 1815-1915. 1980. 20.00 (ISBN 0-316-34300-5); pap. text ed. 8.95 (ISBN 0-316-34299-8). Little.

--The American Home: Architecture & Society, 1815-1915. LC 79-14894. (Illus.). 1979. 20.00 (ISBN 0-316-34300-5); pap. 7.95 (ISBN 0-316-34299-8). Little.

Handlin, Lilian, jt. auth. see Handlin, Oscar.

Handlin, M. F., ed. see Carnegie Commission On Higher Education.

Handlin, O., ed. see Carnegie Commission On Higher Education.

Handlin, Oscar. American University As an Instrument of Republican Culture: Sir George Watson Lecture Delivered in the University of Leicester - March 1970. (Sir George Watson Lectures). 1970. pap. text ed. 1.50x (ISBN 0-7185-1097-6, Leicester). Humanities.

--John Dewey's Challenge to Education: Historical Perspectives on the Cultural Context. 59p. 1972. Repr. of 1959 ed. lib. bdg. 11.75x (ISBN 0-8371-5602-5, HAJD). Greenwood.

Handlin, Oscar & Handlin, Lilian. Abraham Lincoln & the Union. (Library of American Biography). 224p. (Orig.). 1980. 10.95 (ISBN 0-316-34315-3); pap. 4.95 (ISBN 0-316-34314-5). Little.

Handlin, Oscar, ed. Children of the Uprooted. LC 66-12905. 8.50 o.s.i. (ISBN 0-8076-0361-9). Braziller.

Handreck, K. A. When Should I Water. 1980. 10.00x (ISBN 0-643-02522-7, Pub. by CSJRO Australia). State Mutual Bk.

Hands, Rachel, ed. English Hawking & Hunting in the Boke of St. Albans. facsimile ed. (Oxford English Monographs). (Illus.). 264p. 1975. 55.00x (ISBN 0-19-811715-9). Oxford U Pr.

Handscombe, E. Electrical Measuring Instruments. (Wykeham Technology Ser.: No. 2). 1970. 9.95x (ISBN 0-8448-1173-4). Crane Russak Co.

Handwriting Institute. Better Handwriting for You. rev. ed. (gr. 1-8). 1972-75. Bk. 1. nonconsumable 2.25 (ISBN 0-8372-9509-2); Bks. 2 & 3. ea nonconsumable. 2.25 (ISBN 0-8372-9511-4); Bks. 1-3. text ed. 2.25 ea. alternate nonconsumable (ISBN 0-8372-9513-0); Bks. 2-3. text ed. 1.65 ea. transition eds.; Bks. 4-6. text ed. 2.25 ea. nonconsumable eds.; tchrs' eds. 3.90 ea.; handwriting aids avail. (ISBN 0-8372-9530-0); duplicating masters avail., wall charts. Bowmar-Noble.

Handy, D. Antoinette. Black Women in American Bands & Orchestras. LC 80-19380. 394p. 1981. 17.50 (ISBN 0-8108-1346-7). Scarecrow.

Handy, E. S. & Pukui, Mary K. The Polynesian Family System in Kau, Hawaii. LC 75-171998. 1972. 15.00 (ISBN 0-8048-1031-1). C E Tuttle.

Handy, L. J. Wage Policy in the British Coalmining Industry. LC 80-40229. (Department of Applied Economics Monograph: No. 27). 312p. Date not set. price not set (ISBN 0-521-23535-9). Cambridge U Pr.

Handy, Robert T. A History of the Churches in the United States & Canada. 1979. pap. 6.95 (ISBN 0-19-502531-8, GB577, GB). Oxford U Pr.

Handy, Robert T., ed. The Holy Land in American Protestant Life, Eighteen Hundred to Nineteen Forty Eight: A Documentary History. LC 79-1052. (Illus.). 1980. lib. bdg. 20.00 (ISBN 0-405-13466-5). Arno.

--Social Gospel in America: Gladden, Ely, & Rauschenbusch. 1966. 14.95 o.p. (ISBN 0-19-501174-0). Oxford U Pr.

Handy, W. C., ed. Blues: An Anthology. 1972. 7.95 o.s.i. (ISBN 0-02-547760-9). Macmillan.

Handy, W. C. & Silverman, Jerry, eds. Blues: An Anthology. (Illus.). 1972. pap. 4.95 o.s.i. (ISBN 0-02-060710-5, Collier). Macmillan.

Handy, William J. & Westbrook, Max. Twentieth Century Criticism: The Major Statements. LC 73-3898. (Illus.). 1974. text ed. 14.95 (ISBN 0-02-913710-1). Free Pr.

Handyside, Richard, ed. & tr. see Cabral, Amilcar.

Haneman, Dan, jt. auth. see Holt, David B.

Hanenson, Irwin B. Quick Reference to Clinical Toxicology. 1980. pap. text ed. 14.00 (ISBN 0-397-50418-7). Lippincott.

Haner, F. & Keiser, S. Introduction to Business: Concepts & Careers. 1976. 16.95 (ISBN 0-87626-392-9); student guide 6.95 (ISBN 0-87626-391-0). P-H.

Haner, F. T. & Ford, James C. Contemporary Management. LC 72-95931. 1973. text ed. 17.95 (ISBN 0-675-08987-5). Merrill.

Hanes, D. A. & Madore, B. F., eds. Globular Clusters. LC 79-41472. (Cambridge Astrophysics Ser.: No. 2). (Illus.). 288p. 1980. 62.50 (ISBN 0-521-22861-1). Cambridge U Pr.

Hanes, Mary. Lovechild. Date not set. pap. 1.50 o.p. (ISBN 0-451-07260-X, W7260, Sig). NAL.

Haney, John L. A Bibliography of Samuel Taylor Coleridge. 144p. 1980. Repr. of 1903 ed. lib. bdg. 20.00 (ISBN 0-8495-2299-4). Arden Lib.

Haney, Laura J., ed. see Knackstedt, Mary V.

Haney, Lynn. I Am a Dancer. (Illus.). 64p. (gr. 10 up). 1981. 8.95 (ISBN 0-399-20724-4); pap. 4.95 (ISBN 0-399-20792-9). Putnam.

--Naked at the Feast: A Biography of Josephine Baker. (Illus.). 360p. 1981. 15.00 (ISBN 0-396-07900-8). Dodd.

Haney, Lynn, adapted by. The Flash Gordon Book. (Illus.). 64p. 1980. 5.95 (ISBN 0-399-20782-1). Putnam.

Haney, Margaret, jt. auth. see Alpaugh, Patricia.

Haney, R. E. & Sorenson, J. S. Individually Guided Science. 1977. pap. 7.95 (ISBN 0-201-19511-9). A-W.

Haney, William V. Communication & Organizational Behavior. 4th ed. 1979. text ed. 19.50 (ISBN 0-256-02244-5). Irwin.

Han Fei Tzu. Han Fei Tzu: Basic Writings. Watson, Burton, tr. LC 64-13734. (Orig.). 1964. pap. 5.00x (ISBN 0-231-08609-1). Columbia U Pr.

Hanff, Helene. Butch Elects a Mayor. LC 78-77784. (Illus.). (gr. 1-4). 1969. 5.95 o.s.i. (ISBN 0-8193-0277-5, Four Winds); PLB 5.41 o.s.i. (ISBN 0-8193-0278-3). Schol Bk Serv.

--Movers & Shakers: Young Activists of the Sixties. LC 77-110432. (Illus.). (gr. 8 up). 1970. 10.95 (ISBN 0-87599-166-1). S G Phillips.

--Underfoot in Show Business. 192p. 1980. 10.95 (ISBN 0-316-34319-6). Little.

Hanfling, Oswald, ed. Essential Readings in Logical Positivism. 320p. 1981. pap. 14.95x (ISBN 0-631-12566-3, Dist. by Basil Blackwell). Biblio Dist.

Hanfmann, Eugenia, jt. auth. see Beier, Helen.

Hanfmann, George M. Roman Art: A Modern Survey of the Art of Ancient Rome. (Illus.). 250p. 1975. pap. text ed. 8.95x (ISBN 0-393-09222-4). Norton.

Hanford, Robert T. Complete Book of Puppets & Puppeteering. LC 80-54338. (Illus.). 160p. 1981. 12.95 (ISBN 0-8069-7032-4); lib. bdg. 11.69 (ISBN 0-8069-7033-2); pap. 7.95 (ISBN 0-8069-8970-X). Sterling.

Hanft, Ethel W. & Manley, Paula J. Outstanding Iowa Women: Past & Present. LC 80-53730. (Illus.). 135p. 1980. pap. 4.95 (ISBN 0-9605162-0-4). River Bend.

Hanft, Robert M. Red River: Paul Bunyan's Own Lumber Company & Its Railroads. LC 79-53190. (Illus.). 304p. 32.50 (ISBN 0-9602894-5-3). CSU Ctr Busn Econ.

Hangen, Patricia. Tell Him That I Heard. LC 76-40581. (Illus.). 1977. 7.95 o.p. (ISBN 0-06-011788-5, HarpT). Har-Row.

Hanh, Nhat & Vo-Dinh. Zen Poems. 2nd ed. Savory, Ted, tr. from Vietnamese & Eng. (Illus.). 1976. 10.00 (ISBN 0-87775-038-6); pap. 5.00 (ISBN 0-87775-038-6). Unicorn Pr.

Hanh, Thich Nhat. Vietnam: Lotus in a Sea of Fire. (Orig.). 1967. pap. 1.65 o.p. (ISBN 0-8090-1334-7). Hill & Wang.

Hanham, Alison. Richard Third & His Early Historians 1483-1535. 236p. 1975. 33.00x (ISBN 0-19-822434-6). Oxford U Pr.

Hanham, H. J., ed. Bibliography of British History Eighteen Fifty-One to Nineteen Fourteen. 1976. 125.00x (ISBN 0-19-822389-7). Oxford U Pr.

--Nineteenth Century Constitution, Eighteen Fifteen to Nineteen Fourteen. LC 69-11148. 1969. 44.50 (ISBN 0-521-07351-0); pap. 15.95x (ISBN 0-521-09560-3, 560). Cambridge U Pr.

Hanham, H. J., ed. see Dod, Charles.

Hanie, Robert, jt. auth. see Valentine, James.

Hanifi, M. Jamil. Historical & Cultural Dictionary of Afghanistan. LC 75-40249. (Historical & Cultural Dictionaries of Asia Ser.: No. 5). 1976. 10.00 (ISBN 0-8108-0892-7). Scarecrow.

Hanika, F. de P., jt. auth. see Pichler, F.

Hanin, Israel, ed. Choline & Acetylcholine: Handbook of Chemical Assay Methods. LC 73-79289. 246p. 1974. 24.50 (ISBN 0-911216-51-0). Raven.

Hanin, Israel & Koslow, Stephen, eds. Physico-Chemical Methodologies in Psychiatric Research. 1980. text ed. 28.50 (ISBN 0-89004-411-2). Raven.

Hanin, Israel, jt. ed. see Goldberg, Alan M.

Hanington, Edda. The Headache Book. LC 80-52621. (Illus.). 226p. 1980. 12.50 (ISBN 0-87762-292-2). Technomic.

Hanisch, jt. auth. see Ronan.

Hanissian, Aram. Pediatric Rheumatology Case Studies. 1979. pap. 19.00 (ISBN 0-87488-060-2). Med Exam.

Hankamer, Jorge, jt. auth. see Ladusaw, William A.

Hankamer, Jorge, ed. Deletion in Coordinate Structures. LC 78-67738. (Outstanding Dissertations in Linguistics Ser.). 1979. lib. bdg. 41.00 (ISBN 0-8240-9669-X). Garland Pub.

Hankamer, Jorge, ed. see Aissen, Judith.

Hankamer, Jorge, ed. see Akmajian, Adrian.

Hankamer, Jorge, ed. see Bresnan, Joan W.

Hankamer, Jorge, ed. see Fodor, Janet D.

Hankamer, Jorge, ed. see Goddard, Ives.

Hankamer, Jorge, ed. see Goldsmith, John A.

Hankamer, Jorge, ed. see Helke, Michael.

Hankamer, Jorge, ed. see Higgins, F. R.

Hankamer, Jorge, ed. see Johnson, David E.

Hankamer, Jorge, ed. see Kahn, Daniel.

Hankamer, Jorge, ed. see Kroch, Anthony S.

Hankamer, Jorge, ed. see Kuroda, S. Y.

Hankamer, Jorge, ed. see Milsark, Gary L.

Hankamer, Jorge, ed. see Partee, Barbara H.

Hankamer, Jorge, ed. see Schauber, Ellen.

Hankamer, Jorge, ed. see Seiter, William J.

Hankamer, Jorge, ed. see Shaw, Patricia A.

Hankamer, Jorge, ed. see Siegel, Dorothy.

Hankamer, Jorge, ed. see Stampe, David.

Hankamer, Jorge, ed. see Webber, Bonnie L.

Hanke, John E. & Reitsch, Arthur. Business Forecasting. new ed. 416p. 1981. text ed. 23.95 (ISBN 0-205-07139-2, 107139-4); solution's manual free (ISBN 0-205-07140-6). Allyn.

Hanke, Lewis. Bartolome Arzans de Orsua y Vela's History of Potosi. LC 65-24779. (Illus.). 81p. 1965. 8.00x (ISBN 0-87057-093-5, Pub. by Brown U Pr). Univ Pr of New England.

Hanke, Lewis, ed. see Arzans de Orsua y Vela, Bartolome.

Hankel, Wilhelm. Prosperity Amidst Crisis: Austria's Economic Policy & the Energy Crunch. Steinberg, Jean, tr. 234p. 1980. lib. bdg. 20.00x (ISBN 0-86531-101-3). Westview.

Hankey, Muriel. James Hewat Mackenzie: Pioneer of Psychical Research. 1963. 4.50 o.p. (ISBN 0-912326-07-7). Garrett-Helix.

Hankins, Cliff. Rookie Running Back. LC 68-57466. (gr. 7 up). 6.95 (ISBN 0-8149-0313-4). Vanguard.

Hankins, Frank W., jt. auth. see Barefoot, A. C.

Hankins, John E. Source & Meaning in Spenser's Allegory: A Study of the Faerie Queene. 348p. 1972. 29.95x (ISBN 0-19-812013-3). Oxford U Pr.

Hankins, Marie, jt. auth. see Hankins, Warren.

Hankins, Marie, jt. auth. see Hankins, Warren M.

Hankins, Norman E. How to Become the Person You Want to Be. LC 78-21596. 1979. 14.95 (ISBN 0-88229-297-8); pap. 7.95 (ISBN 0-88229-647-7). Nelson-Hall.

Hankins, Norman E. & Bailey, Roger C. Psychology of Effective Living. LC 79-19044. 1980. text ed. 15.95 (ISBN 0-8185-0360-2). Brooks-Cole.

Hankins, Thomas L. Sir William Rowan Hamilton: A Biography. LC 80-10627. 512p. 1980. text ed. 32.50 (ISBN 0-8018-2203-3). Johns Hopkins.

Hankins, Warren & Hankins, Marie. Introduction to Chemistry. LC 73-8600. (Illus.). 1974. text ed. 13.95 o.p. (ISBN 0-8016-2041-4). Mosby.

Hankins, Warren M. & Hankins, Marie. Introduction to Chemistry: Study Guide. (Illus.). 116p. 1975. 4.25 o.p. (ISBN 0-8016-2052-X). Mosby.

Hankinson, John & Banna, M. Pituitary & Parapituitary Tumours. LC 76-24953. (Major Problems in Neurology Ser.: Vol. 6). (Illus.). 1976. text ed. 30.00 (ISBN 0-7216-4495-3). Saunders.

Hankinson, Ken. How to Fiberglass Boats. LC 74-27715. (Illus.). pap. 7.95 (ISBN 0-686-09424-7). Glen-L Marine.

Hankinson, Ken, jt. auth. see Witt, Glen L.

Hanko, H., et al. The Five Points of Calvinism. LC 76-47146. 1976. pap. 2.95 (ISBN 0-8254-2854-8). Kregel.

Hanko, Herman. The Mysteries of the Kingdom: An Exposition of the Parables. LC 75-13930. 1975. 8.95 (ISBN 0-8254-2853-X). Kregel.

Hankoff, L. D. Emergency Psychiatric Treatment: A Handbook of Secondary Prevention. 100p. 1969. 8.75 (ISBN 0-398-00771-3). C C Thomas.

Hanks, David. Innovative Furniture in America: From 1800 to the Present. (Illus.). 250p. 1981. text ed. 30.00 (ISBN 0-8180-0450-9). Horizon.

Hanks, Geoffrey. Children of Naples. 1976. 1.55 (ISBN 0-08-017619-4). Pergamon.

Hanks, Kurt & Belliston, Larry. Draw! A Visual Approach to Thinking, Learning & Communicating. LC 77-6328. (Illus.). 242p. 1977. 19.75 o.p. (ISBN 0-913232-45-9); pap. 9.75 (ISBN 0-913232-46-7). W Kaufmann.

Hanks, Lucien M. Rice & Man: Agricultural Ecology in Southeast Asia. LC 78-169512. (Worlds of Man Ser). 1972. text ed. 11.00x (ISBN 0-88295-606-X); pap. text ed. 5.75x (ISBN 0-88295-607-8). AHM Pub.

Hanks, R. J. & Hill, R. W. Modeling Crop Responses to Irrigation in Relation to Soils, Climate & Salinity. (IIIC Publication: No. 4). 71p. 1981. 17.25 (ISBN 0-08-025513-2). Pergamon.

Hanks, Robert J. The Unnoticed Challenge: Soviet Maritime Strategy & the Global Choke Points. LC 80-83751. (Special Report Ser.). 68p. 1980. 6.50 (ISBN 0-89549-025-0). Inst Foreign Policy Anal.

Hanks, Robert J., jt. auth. see Cottrell, Alvin J.

Hanle, Paul A. & Chamberlain, Von Del, eds. Space Science Comes of Age: Perspectives in the History of the Space Sciences. (Illus.). 220p. 1981. 25.00 (ISBN 0-87474-508-X); pap. 12.50 (ISBN 0-87474-507-1). Smithsonian.

Hanley, Boniface. Ten Christians: By Their Deeds You Shall Know Them. LC 79-53836. (Illus.). 272p. (Orig.). 1979. pap. 5.95 (ISBN 0-87793-183-6). Ave Maria.

Hanley, Clifford. The Scots. 240p. 1980. 12.50 (ISBN 0-8129-0946-1). Times Bks.

Hanley, Elizabeth. The Flame & the Fire. 1978. pap. 1.95 (ISBN 0-505-51251-3). Tower Bks.

--Guilty As Charged. 1979. pap. 1.75 (ISBN 0-505-51373-0). Tower Bks.

Hanley, Gerald. See You in Yasukuni. 1978. pap. 1.50 (ISBN 0-505-51294-7). Tower Bks.

Hanley, Hope. Needlepoint. rev. ed. LC 74-14016. (Encore Edition). (Illus.). 176p. 1975. 5.95 (ISBN 0-684-16685-2, ScribT). Scribner.

--Needlework Styles for Period Furniture. LC 78-3496. (Encore Edition). (Illus.). 1978. 5.95 (ISBN 0-684-16686-0, ScribT). Scribner.

Hanley, James. Against the Stream. 256p. 1981. 10.95 (ISBN 0-8180-0629-3). Horizon.

--A Dream Journey. 1978. pap. 2.25 o.p. (ISBN 0-445-04279-6). Popular Lib.

--An End & the Beginning. 1978. pap. 1.95 o.p. (ISBN 0-445-04173-0). Popular Lib.

Hanley, Mary & Miller, Liam, eds. Thoor Ballylee: Home of William Butler Yeats. 2nd rev. ed. 1977. text ed. 3.75x (ISBN 0-85105-300-9, Dolmen Pr). Humanities.

Hanley, Mary D. A Manual of AACR 2 Examples for Early Printed Books. Swanson, Edward & McClaskey, Marilyn J, eds. 1980. pap. 6.00 (ISBN 0-936996-10-2). Soldier Creek.

Hanley, Theodore O. & Thurman, Wayne L. Developing Vocal Skills. 2nd ed. LC 79-97849. (Illus.). 1970. 29.50x (ISBN 0-03-083992-0); pap. text ed. 18.95x (ISBN 0-89197-726-0). Irvington.

Hanley, Thomas, jt. auth. see Brocklehurst, John C.

Hanley, Wayne. A Life Outdoors: A Curmudgeon Looks at the Natural World. (Illus.). 144p. 1980. cancelled (ISBN 0-8289-0417-0); pap. 5.95 (ISBN 0-8289-0403-0). Greene.

Hanlon, Al. Trade Shows in the Marketing Mix: Where They Fit & How to Make Them Pay off. 1980. 22.50 (ISBN 0-8015-1814-8). Herman Pub.

Hanlon, Emily. It's Too Late for Sorry. (gr. 7 up). Date not set. pap. 1.75 (ISBN 0-440-93905-4, LE). Dell.

--The Swing. LC 78-26400. (gr. 5-7). 1979. 8.95 (ISBN 0-87888-146-8). Bradbury Pr.

--The Wing & the Flame. LC 80-15082. 192p. (gr. 7up). 9.95 (ISBN 0-87888-168-9). Bradbury Pr.

Hanlon, John J. Public Health: Administration & Practice. 6th. ed. LC 74-8669. (Illus.). 1974. text ed. 22.50 o.p. (ISBN 0-8016-2045-7). Mosby.

Hanlon, John J. & Pickett, George E. Public Health: Administration & Practice. 7th ed. LC 79-16132. (Illus.). 1979. text ed. 27.95 (ISBN 0-8016-2046-5). Mosby.
Hanlon, Joseph, ed. Packaging Marketplace: The Practical Guide to Packaging Sources. LC 78-53442. 1978. 65.00 (ISBN 0-8103-0989-0, Norback Bk). Gale.
Hanlon, R. Brendan. A Guide to Taxes & Record Keeping for Performers, Designers & Directors. rev. ed. LC 79-25783. (Illus.). 96p. 1980. pap. text ed. 4.95x (ISBN 0-89676-032-4). Drama Bk.
Hanly, John, ed. The Letters of Saint Oliver Plunkett, Sixteen Twenty-Five to Sixteen Eighty-One: Archbishop of Armagh & Primate of All Ireland. 1979. text ed. 75.00x (ISBN 0-391-01120-0, Dolmen Pr). Humanities.
Hann, Jacquie. Big Trouble. LC 78-1712. (Illus.). 40p. (gr. k-3). 1978. 5.95 (ISBN 0-590-07557-8, Four Winds). Schol Bk Serv.
--That Man Is Talking to His Toes. LC 76-13496. (Illus.). 40p. (gr. k-3). 1976. 5.95 (ISBN 0-590-07456-3, Four Winds). Schol Bk Serv.
--Up Day, Down Day. LC 77-15936. (Illus.). 32p. (gr. k-3). 1978. 6.95 (ISBN 0-590-07519-5, Four Winds). Schol Bk Serv.
--Where's Mark? LC 76-54869. (Illus.). 40p. (gr. k-3). 1977. 5.95 (ISBN 0-590-07499-7, Four Winds). Schol Bk Serv.
Hanna, A. J. The Story of the Rhodesias & Nyasaland. 2nd ed. (Story Ser.). (Illus.). 1965. 6.95 o.p. (ISBN 0-571-06150-8, Pub. by Faber & Faber). Merrimack Bk Serv.
Hanna, Archibald, jt. auth. see Andrist, Ralph K.
Hanna, Christine A., ed. see Abraham, Nicholas A.
Hanna, David. Bogart. (Orig.). 1976. pap. 1.50 o.p. (ISBN 0-685-62586-9, LB322, Leisure Bks). Nordon Pubns.
--The Capri Affair. (Orig.). 1980. pap. 1.95 (ISBN 0-505-51547-4). Tower Bks.
--Cults in America. 1979. pap. 2.25 (ISBN 0-505-51447-8). Tower Bks.
--Hollywood Confidential. (Illus., Orig.). 1976. pap. 1.50 (ISBN 0-8439-0331-7, LB331DK, Leisure Bks). Nordon Pubns.
--The Love Goddess. 1977. pap. 1.75 (ISBN 0-505-51130-4). Tower Bks.
--The Mafia: Two Hundred Years of Terror. (Orig.). 1980. pap. 2.25 (ISBN 0-532-23131-7). Manor Bks.
--Robert Redford: The Superstar Nobody Knows. (Illus., Orig.). 1975. pap. 1.50 o.p. (ISBN 0-685-54126-6, LB291, Leisure Bks). Nordon Pubns.
--When the Clock Strikes Thirteen. 1976. pap. 1.50 o.p. (ISBN 0-685-73464-1, LB387, Leisure Bks). Nordon Pubns.
Hanna, Donald G. & Gentel, William D. Guide to Primary Police Management Concepts. (Illus.). 208p. 1971. 13.75 (ISBN 0-398-00773-X). C C Thomas.
Hanna, Donald G., jt. auth. see Cizankas, Victor I.
Hanna, Elaine, jt. auth. see Anderson, Jean.
Hanna, J. Complete Layman's Guide to the Law. 1974. 15.95 o.p. (ISBN 0-13-161232-8, Spec). P-H.
Hanna, J. Bradley, jt. auth. see Kahn, Charles H.
Hanna, Jay. Marine Carving Handbook. LC 74-33147. (Illus.). 96p. 1975. 9.95 (ISBN 0-87742-052-1). Intl Marine.
Hanna, John P. Complete Layman's Guide to the Law. (Illus.). 544p. pap. 8.95 (ISBN 0-13-161224-7, Spec). P-H.
Hanna, Judith L., jt. ed. see Hanna, William J.
Hanna, M. G., jt. ed. see Witz, Isaac.
Hanna, Mary A., jt. auth. see Sabaroff, Rose.
Hanna, Melvin. Quantum Mechanics in Chemistry. 3rd ed. 1980. pap. text ed. 12.95 (ISBN 0-8053-3705-9, 33708); pap. text ed. 9.95 (33705). Benjamin-Cummings.
Hanna, Michael, jt. auth. see Gibson, James W.
Hanna, Mike, et al. Lacrosse for Men & Women: Skills & Strategies for the Athlete & Coach. (Illus.). 160p. 1981. pap. 9.95 (ISBN 0-8015-4372-X, Hawthorn). Dutton.
Hanna, Patricia B. People Make It Happen: The Possibilities of Outreach in Every Phase of Public Library Service. LC 78-5923. 1978. lib. bdg. 10.00 (ISBN 0-8108-1136-7). Scarecrow.
Hanna, Samuel C., et al. Sets & Logic. 1971. pap. text ed. 10.50 (ISBN 0-256-00230-4). Irwin.
Hanna, Wayne, jt. auth. see Murphy, Elspeth.
Hanna, William J. & Hanna, Judith L., eds. Urban Dynamics in Black Africa: An Interdisciplinary Approach. 2nd ed. 1981. 15.95x (ISBN 0-202-24158-0). Aldine Pub.
Hannaford, Richard. Samuel Richardson: An Annotated Bibliography of Critical Studies. LC 79-7916. (Garland Reference Library of Humanities). 450p. 1980. lib. bdg. 40.00 (ISBN 0-8240-9531-6). Garland Pub.
Hannaford, William E. Jr. see Miller, George B., Jr., et al.
Hannah, Clayton L. A Collection: My Innermost Thoughts. Date not set. 5.95 (ISBN 0-533-04703-X). Vantage.
Hannah, Donald, jt. ed. see Rutherford, Anna.
Hannah, Gerald T., et al, eds. Preservation of Client Rights: A Handbook for Practitioners Providing Therapeutic, Educational, & Rehabilitative Services. LC 80-1644. (Illus.). 1981. 22.95 (ISBN 0-02-913820-5). Free Pr.
Hannah, John & Stephens, R. C. Mechanics of Machines: Advanced Theory & Examples. 2nd ed. (Illus.). 456p. 1972. pap. 18.95x (ISBN 0-7131-3254-X). Intl Ideas.
--Mechanics of Machines: Elementary Theory & Examples. 3rd ed. (Illus.). 1970. 18.95x (ISBN 0-7131-3231-0); pap. text ed. 11.95x (ISBN 0-7131-3232-9). Intl Ideas.
Hannah, Larry S. & Michaelis, John U. Comprehensive Framework for Instructional Objectives: A Guide to Systematic Planning & Evaluation. (Education Ser.). 1977. pap. text ed. 8.95 (ISBN 0-201-02757-7). A-W.
Hannah, T. Edward, et al. Study Guide for Social Psychology in the Eighties. 3rd ed. 192p. (Orig.). 1980. pap. text ed. 6.95 (ISBN 0-8185-0416-1). Brooks-Cole.
Hannah, William, jt. auth. see Cope, Robert.
Hannam, Charles. Almost an Englishman. (gr. 6 up). 1979. PLB 8.95 (ISBN 0-233-97119-X). Andre Deutsch.
Hannam, Charles L., tr. see Wolffheim, Nelly.
Hannan, Michael, ed. see Salert, Barbara & Sprague, John.
Hannan, Pamela. Runner's World Natural Foods Cookbook. LC 80-23973. 88p. (Orig.). 1981. pap. 11.95 (ISBN 0-89037-208-X). Anderson World.
Hannan, W., tr. see Moliere, Jean B.
Hannas, Warren F. Be Somebody! A Practical Philosophy for All Times. LC 80-81396. (Illus.). 165p. 1980. 11.95 (ISBN 0-936888-01-6). Pr Vision Studios.
Hannau, Hans W. Islands of the Caribbean. Date not set. 6.45 o.p. (ISBN 0-8038-3395-4). Hastings.
Hannay, Alistair, jt. ed. see Naess, Arne.
Hannay, David R. The Symptom Iceberg: A Study of Community Health. 1979. pap. 16.50 (ISBN 0-7100-8982-1). Routledge & Kegan.
Hannay, James. Essays from "The Quarterly Review". 390p. 1980. Repr. of 1861 ed. lib. bdg. 45.00 (ISBN 0-89984-282-8). Century Bookbindery.
Hannay, Margaret P. C. S. Lewis. LC 80-53700. (Modern Literature Ser.). 350p. 1981. 13.50 (ISBN 0-8044-2341-5). Ungar.
Hannay, N. Bruce, ed. Treatise on Solid State Chemistry. Incl. Vol. 1. The Chemical Structure of Solids. 540p. 1973 (ISBN 0-306-35051-3); Vol. 2, Defects in Solids. 527p. 1975 (ISBN 0-306-35052-1); Crystalline & Non Crystalline Solids. 774p. 1976 (ISBN 0-306-35053-X); Vol. 4, Reactivity of Solids. 721p. 1976 (ISBN 0-306-35054-8); Vol. 5, Changes of State. 600p. 1975 (ISBN 0-306-35055-6); Vol. 6A, Surfaces, I. 491p. 1976 (ISBN 0-306-35056-4); Vol. 6B, Surfaces, II. 418p. 1976 (ISBN 0-306-35057-2). LC 73-79421. (Illus.). 45.00 ea. (Plenum Pr). Plenum Pub.
Hannebaum, Leroy G. Landscape Operations: Management, Methods, & Materials. (Illus.). 1980. text ed. 16.95 (ISBN 0-8359-3937-5); instrs' manual avail. Reston.
Hanneman, Gerhard J. & McEwen, William J. Communication & Behavior. LC 74-19704. 464p. 1975. pap. text ed. 12.95 (ISBN 0-201-02745-3). A-W.
Hanneman, L. J. Modern Cake Decoration. 2nd ed. (Illus.). 1978. text ed. 28.50x (ISBN 0-85334-785-9). Intl Ideas.
Hanneman, L. J. & Marshall, G. I. Cake Design & Decoration. 4th ed. (Illus.). 1978. text ed. 31.30x (ISBN 0-85334-793-X, Pub. by Applied Science). Burgess-Intl Ideas.
Hannenbaum, L. Landscape Design: A Practical Approach. 1981. text ed. 16.95 (ISBN 0-8359-5577-X); instr's. manual free (ISBN 0-8359-5578-8). Reston.
Hannerz, Ulf. Soulside: Inquiries into Ghetto Culture & Community. LC 78-96865. 1969. 17.50x (ISBN 0-231-03363-X); pap. 5.00x (ISBN 0-231-08651-2). Columbia U Pr.
Hannesson, Rognvaldur. Fisheries Economics. 1979. pap. 23.00x (ISBN 82-00-05217-6, Dist. by Columbia U Pr.). Universitet.
Hannibal, Edward. Better Days. 1979. pap. 2.25 o.p. (ISBN 0-345-27979-4). Ballantine.
Hanniball, A. Aircraft, Engines & Airmen: A Selective Review of the Periodical Literature, 1930-1969. LC 70-171927. 1972. 27.50 (ISBN 0-8108-0430-1). Scarecrow.
Hannigan, Jane Anne, ed. see Vandergrift, Kay E.
Hanning, Robert, tr. see De France, Marie.
Hanning, Robert W. Vision of History in Early Britain: From Gildas to Geoffrey of Monmouth. LC 66-17856. 1966. 20.00x (ISBN 0-231-02826-1). Columbia U Pr.
Hannon, Douglas & Carter, Horace. Hannon's Field Guide for Bass Fishing. LC 80-68668. (Illus.). 208p. (Orig.). 1981. pap. 5.95 (ISBN 0-937866-01-6). D Hannon.
Hannon, Ezra. Doors. 256p. 1976. pap. write for info. (ISBN 0-446-79730-8). Warner Bks.
Hannon, Ralph H. Mathematics for Technical Careers. new ed. (Mathematics Ser.). 304p. 1976. text ed. 17.95 (ISBN 0-675-08656-6); instructor's manual 3.95 (ISBN 0-686-67254-2). Merrill.
Hannon, Sharron. Childbirth: A Source Book for Conception, Pregnancy, Birth & the First Weeks of Life. (Illus.). 256p. 1980. pap. 9.95 (ISBN 0-87131-291-3). M Evans.
--Working Woman's Beauty Book. LC 78-19959. 220p. 1981. pap. 7.95. Stein & Day.
Hannula, Reino. Computers & Programming: A System 360-370 Assembler Language Approach. 400p. 1974. text ed. 22.50 (ISBN 0-395-16796-5). HM.
Hannula, Reino N. Blueberry God: The Education of a Finnish-American. LC 80-54183. 1981. 12.00 (ISBN 0-9605044-0-0). Quality Hill.
Hannum, Alberta P. Look Back with Love: A Recollection of the Blue Ridge. LC 70-89659. (Illus.). 1969. 10.00 (ISBN 0-8149-0007-0). Vanguard.
Hannum, H. G., jt. auth. see Lohner, Edgar.
Hannum, Harold E. Let the People Sing. Davis, Tom, ed. 112p. 1981. pap. write for info. (ISBN 0-8280-0029-8). Review & Herald.
Hanrahan, Barbara. The Frangipani Garden. (Illus.). 224p. 1981. text ed. 19.25 (ISBN 0-7022-1562-7); pap. 9.75 (ISBN 0-7022-1563-5). U of Queensland Pr.
Hanrahan, J. & Dipchand, C. Fundamentals of Financial Management. 3rd ed. 1977. 21.95 (ISBN 0-13-339374-7). P-H.
Hanrahan, Mariellen. My Little Book of Trains. (Tell-a-Tale Readers). (Illus.). (gr. k-3). 1979. PLB 4.77 (ISBN 0-307-68648-5, Whitman). Western Pub.
Hanrieder, Wolfram F., ed. Arms Control & Security: Current Issues. 1979. lib. bdg. 28.50x (ISBN 0-89158-382-3); pap. text ed. 11.00x (ISBN 0-89158-385-8). Westview.
--West Germany's Foreign Policy: Nineteen Forty-Nine to Nineteen Seventy-Nine. (Special Study in West European Politics & Society). 1979. lib. bdg. 24.50x (ISBN 0-89158-579-6). Westview.
Hanrieder, Wolfram F. & Buel, Larry V., eds. Words & Arms: A Dictionary of Security & Defense Terms with Supplementary Data. 1979. lib. bdg. 27.50x (ISBN 0-89158-383-1). Westview.
Hanriot, Hugo. Mita P 'Arriba, Mita P'Abajo. SLUSA, ed. 118p. (Spanish.). 1980. pap. 4.95 (TX525-786). SLUSA.
Hans, James S. The Play of the World. LC 80-39630. 224p. 1981. lib. bdg. 15.00x (ISBN 0-87023-324-6); pap. 7.95 (ISBN 0-87023-325-4). U of Mass Pr.
Hansan, J. A., ed. see International Conference on Pressure Surges, 3rd.
Hansard Society for Parliamentary Government. The British People: Their Voice in Europe. (Illus.). 1977. 22.50 (ISBN 0-566-00174-8, 01609-8, Pub. by Saxon Hse England). Lexington Bks.
Hansburg, Henry G. Adolescent Separation Anxiety, Vol. 1. LC 79-21797. 208p. 1980. Repr. of 1972 ed. lib. bdg. 6.95 (ISBN 0-89874-042-8). Krieger.
--Adolescent Separation Anxiety: Separation Disorders, Vol. 2. LC 79-21798. (Orig.). 1980. lib. bdg. 8.95 (ISBN 0-89874-043-6). Krieger.
Hansel, C. E. ESP & Parapsychology: A Critical Re-Evaluation. LC 79-56361. (Impact Ser.). 325p. (Orig.). 1980. 16.95 (ISBN 0-87975-119-3); pap. 8.95 (ISBN 0-87975-120-7). Prometheus Bks.
Hansell, Michael H. & Aitken, John J. Experimental Animal Behavior: A Selection of Laboratory Exercises. (Illus.). 1977. 29.95x (ISBN 0-216-90325-4). Intl Ideas.
Hansell, Norris. The Person-in-Distress: On the Biosocial Dynamics of Adaptation. LC 74-8096. 252p. 1976. text ed. 22.95 (ISBN 0-87705-213-1). Human Sci Pr.
Hansen, Alvin H. Business Cycles & National Income. expanded ed. 1964. 14.95x (ISBN 0-393-09726-9, NortonC). Norton.
Hansen, Alvin J., jt. auth. see McDonough, Martin.
Hansen, Arthur A. & Mitson, Betty E., eds. Voices Long Silent: An Oral Inquiry into the Japanese American Evacuation. 1974. 7.95 (ISBN 0-930046-04-8). CSUF Oral Hist.
Hansen, B. D., jt. auth. see Evans, M. L.
Hansen, Barbara J. Good Bread. (Illus.). 1976. 9.95 o.s.i. (ISBN 0-02-547860-5). Macmillan.
Hansen, Ben. Winning of the World. 176p. (Orig.). 1980. pap. 4.95 (ISBN 0-931590-04-3). Antietam Pr.
Hansen, Chadwick. Witchcraft at Salem. LC 69-15825. (Illus.). 1969. 10.00 o.s.i. (ISBN 0-8076-0492-5). Braziller.
Hansen, Chadwick, jt. ed. see Hodes, Art.
Hansen, David A. An Analysis of Police Concepts & Programs. (Illus.). 144p. 1972. 12.75 (ISBN 0-398-02464-2). C C Thomas.
--Police Ethics. (Illus.). 96p. 1973. pap. 6.75 spiral (ISBN 0-398-02648-3). C C Thomas.
Hansen, David A. & Culley, Thomas R. The Police Leader: A Handbook. (Illus.). 128p. 1971. 10.50 (ISBN 0-398-02192-9). C C Thomas.
--The Police Training Officer. (Illus.). 244p. 1973. 13.75 (ISBN 0-398-02493-6). C C Thomas.
Hansen, Dennis R. Michigan Cross Country Skiing Atlas. 3rd ed. (Illus.). 240p. Date not set. pap. 5.95 (ISBN 0-686-65601-6). Hansen Pub MI. Postponed.
Hansen, Donald E. An Invitation to Critical Sociology: Involvement, Criticism, Exploration. LC 75-5234. (Illus.). 1976. pap. text ed. 7.95 (ISBN 0-02-913750-0). Free Pr.
Hansen, Dorothea, jt. auth. see Beaucamp, Ernest.
Hansen, Dorthea, jt. auth. see Beaucamp, Ernest.
Hansen, Eldon R. Table of Series & Products. 544p. 1975. ref. ed. 76.00 (ISBN 0-13-881938-6). P-H.
Hansen, Elo H., jt. auth. see Ruzicka, Jaromir.
Hansen, Gary E., ed. Agricultural & Rural Development in Indonesia. (Special Studies in Social, Political, & Economic Development). 312p. 1981. lib. bdg. 20.00x (ISBN 0-86531-124-2). Westview.
Hansen, Gerald. Arizona: Its Constitution & Government. LC 78-65846. (Illus.). 1979. text ed. 7.50 (ISBN 0-8191-0673-9). U Pr of Amer.
Hansen, Ginny L., et al. Caring for Patients with Chronic Renal Disease. 132p. 1974. pap. text ed. 5.75x o.p. (ISBN 0-397-54157-0). Lippincott.
Hansen, Gladys O. Word Processing Systems Manual for Support Staff. (Illus.). 1980. pap. text ed. 22.50 (ISBN 0-936512-01-6). Telecom Lib.
--Word Processing Systems Manual (1) for Originators & Support Staff. & for Support Staff. (Illus., Orig.). 1980. pap. text ed. 40.00 set (ISBN 0-936512-02-4). Telecom Lib.
Hansen, Harold A. The Witch's Garden. Crofts, Muriel, tr. from Danish. LC 78-5469. (Illus.). 1978. pap. 4.95 o.p. (ISBN 0-913300-47-0). Unity Pr.
Hansen, Harold I. America's Witness for Christ. LC 80-84565. 350p. 1981. 8.95 (ISBN 0-88290-174-5). Horizon Utah.
Hansen, Harry. New England Legends & Folklore. 1967. 6.95 o.s.i. (ISBN 0-8038-4998-2). Hastings.
Hansen, Harry, ed. California. rev. ed. Federal Writer's Project. (American Guide Ser). 1967. 12.95 (ISBN 0-8038-1073-3). Hastings.
Hansen, Harry L. Marketing: Text, Techniques, & Cases. 4th ed. 1977. text ed. 19.95 (ISBN 0-256-01642-9). Irwin.
Hansen, Henny H. Investigations in a Shi'a Village in Bahrain. (Ethnographical Ser.: No. 12). (Illus.). 1968. pap. text ed. 28.75x (ISBN 87-480-7202-8). Humanities.
Hansen, J. Perspectives on Human Learning: An Introduction to Educational Anthropology. 1979. pap. 9.95 o.p. (ISBN 0-13-660951-1). P-H.
Hansen, J., jt. auth. see Coffin, Patricia.
Hansen, J. P. & McDonald, I. R. The Theory of Simple Liquids. 1977. 54.50 (ISBN 0-12-323850-1). Acad Pr.
Hansen, James & Cramer, Stanley, eds. Group Guidance & Counseling in the Schools: Selected Readings. 1971. pap. text ed. 13.95 (ISBN 0-13-365304-8). P-H.
Hansen, James C. & Rosenthal, David. Strategies & Techniques in Family Therapy. (Illus.). 480p. 1981. 28.50 (ISBN 0-398-04435-X); pap. 19.75 (ISBN 0-398-04154-7). C C Thomas.
Hansen, James C., jt. auth. see Alabiso, Frank P.
Hansen, James C., et al. Counseling: Theory & Process. 2nd ed. 1977. text ed. 18.50x (ISBN 0-205-05626-1). Allyn.
Hansen, Joseph. A Smile in His Lifetime. LC 80-21420. 312p. 1981. 12.95 (ISBN 0-686-69127-X). HR&W.
Hansen, Joseph H. How to Breed & Whelp Dogs. (Illus.). 280p. 1973. 13.75 (ISBN 0-398-02541-X). C C Thomas.
Hansen, Joyce. The Gift-Giver. 128p. (gr. 4-8). 1980. 7.95 (ISBN 0-395-29433-9, Clarion). HM.
Hansen, Karl. War Games. LC 80-85104. 288p. (Orig.). 1981. pap. 2.50 (ISBN 0-87216-837-9). Playboy Pbks.
Hansen, Klaus J. Mormonism & the American Experience. LC 80-19312. (History of American Religion Ser.). 224p. 1981. 15.00 (ISBN 0-226-31552-5). U of Chicago Pr.
--Quest for Empire: The Political Kingdom of God & the Council of Fifty in Mormon History. LC 74-8002. xxii, 237p. 1974. pap. 3.95 (ISBN 0-8032-5769-4, BB 591, Bison). U of Nebr Pr.

Hansen, Lee D., jt. auth. see Christensen, James J.

Hansen, M. English-Arabic Dictionary of Economics & Commerce. 16.00x (ISBN 0-686-65471-4). Intl Bk Ctr.

Hansen, M. H., et al. Sample Survey Methods & Theory, 2 Vols. LC 53-8112. 1953. Vol. 1: Methods & Applications. 35.95 (ISBN 0-471-34914-3); Vol. 2: Theory. 33.50 (ISBN 0-471-34947-X, Pub. by Wiley-Interscience). Wiley.

Hansen, Mary L. Your Career As a Writer. (Arco Career Guidance Ser.). lib. bdg. 6.95 (ISBN 0-668-04500-0); pap. 3.50 (ISBN 0-668-04503-5). Arco.

Hansen, Merrily see Garber, Janet.

Hansen, Merrily see Neuman, Pearl.

Hansen, Niles. The Border Economy: Regional Development in the Southwest. (Illus.). 208p. 1981. text ed. 17.95x (ISBN 0-292-75061-7); pap. text ed. 8.95x (ISBN 0-292-75063-3). U of Tex Pr.

Hansen, Peter S. An Introduction to Twentieth Century Music. 4th ed. 1978. pap. text ed. 16.95 (ISBN 0-205-05921-X). Allyn.

Hansen, R. Gaurth & Wyse, Bonita W. Nutritional Quality Index of Foods. (Illus.). 1979. text ed. 26.50 (ISBN 0-87055-320-8). AVI.

Hansen, Roger D. Beyond the North-South Stalemate. LC 78-10607. 348p. 1979. pap. 5.95 (ISBN 0-07-026049-4). Overseas Dev Council.

Hansen, Roger D. & Overseas Development Council Staff. The U. S. & World Development: Agenda for Action, 1976. LC 76-4936. (Agenda Ser.). 240p. 1976. pap. 4.95 (ISBN 0-275-85670-4). Overseas Dev Council.

Hansen, Stephen L. The Making of the Third Party System: Voters & Parties in Illinois, Eighteen Fifty to Eighteen Seventy-Six. Berkhofer, Robert, ed. (Studies in American History & Culture). 277p. 1980. 27.95 (ISBN 0-8357-1096-3, Pub. by UMI Res Pr). Univ Microfilms.

Hansen, Terrence L. & Wilkins, Ernest J. Espanol a lo vivo: Level 1. 4th ed. LC 77-27041. 1978. text ed. 17.50x (ISBN 0-471-01807-4); wkbk 6.95 (ISBN 0-471-03453-3); tapes 16.95 (ISBN 0-471-01782-5); tchr's manual avail. (ISBN 0-471-04151-3). Wiley.

Hansen, Terrence L., et al. Beginning German: A Practical Approach. LC 73-180137. (Ger). 1972. text ed. 17.95 (ISBN 0-471-00671-8); tchr's manual avail. (ISBN 0-471-00766-8); wkbk. 6.95 (ISBN 0-471-00672-6). Wiley.

--Le Francais vivant. 2nd ed. Kaplow, Julian, ed. LC 77-27029. 1978. text ed. 17.95 (ISBN 0-471-01782-5); wkbk. 5.95 (ISBN 0-471-03539-4); tapes 1.00 (ISBN 0-471-04346-X). Wiley.

Hansen, Vaughn E., jt. auth. see Israelsen, Orson W.

Hansen, Walter A., tr. see Elert, Werner.

Hansen, William & Bigelow, Bo. Land Management Case Study: Westlake Village California. LC 77-79282. (No. 73). 1976. 17.00 (ISBN 0-87420-073-3). Urban Land.

Hansen-Krening, Nancy. Competency & Creativity in Language Arts: A Multi-Ethnic Focus. LC 78-18632. (Education Ser.). (Illus.). 1979. pap. text ed. 7.95 (ISBN 0-201-02802-6). A-W.

Hanshumaker, James, jt. auth. see Zorn, Jay.

Hanslick, Eduard. The Beautiful in Music: A Contribution to the Revisal of Musical Aesthetics. rev. ed. Cohen, Gustav, tr. LC 74-1362. (Music Ser.). 174p. 1974. Repr. of 1891 ed. lib. bdg. 19.50 (ISBN 0-306-70649-0). Da Capo.

Hanslick, Edward. Beautiful in Music. Cohen, Gustav & Weitz, Morris, trs. LC 57-14627. 1957. pap. 3.95 (ISBN 0-672-60211-3, LLA45). Bobbs.

Hanslowe, Kurt L. Procedures & Policies of the New York State Labor Relations Board. LC 63-63909. (Cornell Studies Ser.: No. 12). 224p. 1964. 4.00 o.s.i. (ISBN 0-87546-005-4). NY Sch Indus Rel.

Hanson. The Plains Rifle. 15.00 (ISBN 0-88227-015-X). Gun Room.

Hanson, jt. ed. see Bradley.

Hanson, A. & Walles, M. Governing Britain. 1970. pap. 1.95 o.p. (ISBN 0-531-06009-8, Fontana Pap). Watts.

Hanson, A. H. Public Enterprise & Economic Development. 2nd ed. 1965. 25.00x (ISBN 0-7100-1490-2). Routledge & Kegan.

Hanson, A. H. & Douglas, Janet. India's Democracy. (Introductions to Comparative Government Ser). 236p. 1972. 7.95x (ISBN 0-393-05469-1); pap. 4.95x (ISBN 0-393-09908-3). Norton.

Hanson, Agnes O., ed. Executive & Management Development for Business & Government: A Guide to Information Sources. LC 76-8337. (Management Information Guide Ser.: No. 31). 490p. 1976. 30.00 (ISBN 0-8103-0831-2). Gale.

Hanson, Allen R., jt. auth. see Maly, Kurt.

Hanson, Anthony & Hanson, Richard. Reasonable Belief: An Outline of the Christian Faith. 300p. 1981. 24.95 (ISBN 0-19-213235-0). Oxford U Pr.

Hanson, Barbara H. S. T. O. P. Smoking. 100p. (Orig.). 1981. 9.95 (ISBN 0-934400-14-8). Landmark Bks.

Hanson, C. Recent Advances in Liquid - Liquid Extraction. 1971. 65.00 o.p. (ISBN 0-08-015682-7). Pergamon.

Hanson, Carl A. Economy & Society in Baroque Portugal, 1668-1703. LC 80-17588. (Illus.). 320p. 1981. 22.50x (ISBN 0-8166-0969-1). U of Minn Pr.

Hanson, D. P. & Penrod, D. A. A Desk Reference of Legal Terms for School Psychologists & Special Educators. 224p. 1980. 19.75 (ISBN 0-398-04015-X). C C Thomas.

Hanson, Dale. Forty-Three Students, Thirty-Seven Chairs. LC 78-67253. 201p. 1978. 10.50 (ISBN 0-87527-193-6). Green.

Hanson, Earl D. Animal Diversity. 3rd ed. (Foundations of Modern Biology Ser). (Illus.). 192p. 1972. pap. 9.95 ref. ed. (ISBN 0-13-037150-5). P-H.

--Understanding Evolution. (Illus.). 560p. 1981. text ed. 19.95x (ISBN 0-19-502784-1). Oxford U Pr.

Hanson, F. Allan. Meaning in Culture. 1975. 16.50x (ISBN 0-7100-8132-4). Routledge & Kegan.

Hanson, Gilbert N., jt. ed. see Morey, G. B.

Hanson, Harry. Canal People. LC 77-91714. (Illus.). 1978. 19.95 (ISBN 0-7153-7559-8). David & Charles.

Hanson, Harvey. Game Time. LC 75-4776. (Illus.). 128p. (gr. 6-10). 1975. 5.90 (ISBN 0-531-02831-3). Watts.

Hanson, Isabel. Outwitting Arthritis: People Talk About Controlling, Conquering & Coping with Their Arthritis. 250p. 1980. pap. 7.95 (ISBN 0-916870-30-8). Creative Arts Bk.

Hanson, J. A. Growth in Open Economics. (Lecture Notes in Economics & Mathematical Systems: Vol. 59). (Illus.). 135p. 1971. pap. 10.70 o.p. (ISBN 0-387-05671-8). Springer-Verlag.

Hanson, J. L. Economics for Students. 8th ed. (Illus.). 240p. 1978. pap. text ed. 9.95x (ISBN 0-7121-0572-7, Pub. by Macdonald & Evans England). Intl Ideas.

--An Introduction to Applied Economics. 3rd ed. (Illus.). 512p. 1980. pap. text ed. 17.50x (ISBN 0-7121-0963-3). Intl Ideas.

--Monetary Theory & Practice. 6th ed. (Illus.). 352p. 1978. pap. text ed. 13.95x (ISBN 0-7121-1293-6, Pub. by Macdonald & Evans England). Intl Ideas.

--An Outline of Monetary Theory. 4th ed. 160p. 1980. pap. text ed. 9.95x (ISBN 0-7121-1533-1). Intl Ideas.

--A Textbook of Economics. 7th ed. (Illus.). 640p. 1977. pap. text ed. 15.95x (ISBN 0-7121-2020-3, Pub. by Macdonald & Evans England). Intl Ideas.

Hanson, J. L., ed. Dictionary of Economics & Commerce. 1965. 10.00 o.p. (ISBN 0-8022-0675-1). Philos Lib.

Hanson, J. R. Introduction to Steroid Chemistry. 1968. 16.50 (ISBN 0-08-012809-2); pap. 7.75 (ISBN 0-08-012808-4). Pergamon.

Hanson, Joe A. Open Sea Mariculture. LC 74-13103. 320p. 1974. 43.50 (ISBN 0-12-786625-6). Acad Pr.

Hanson, Joe A. & Goodwin, Harold L., eds. Shrimp & Prawn Farming in the Western Hemisphere: State of the Art Review & Status Assessment. 1977. 29.00 (ISBN 0-12-786626-4). Acad Pr.

Hanson, John. Music Fundamentals Workbook. 1979. pap. text ed. 13.95 (ISBN 0-582-28111-3). Longman.

--The Use of Resources. (Unwin Education Books: Teaching Today Ser.). 1975. text ed. 10.50x o.p. (ISBN 0-04-371027-1); pap. text ed. 9.50x (ISBN 0-04-371028-X). Allen Unwin.

Hanson, Judith, tr. see Kontrul, Jamgon.

Hanson, June A. Summer of the Stallion. LC 78-24212. (gr. 5-9). 1979. 8.95 (ISBN 0-02-742620-3, 74262). Macmillan.

--Winter of the Owl. LC 80-15966. (Illus.). 144p. (gr. 5-9). 1980. 8.95 (ISBN 0-02-742530-4). Macmillan.

Hanson, Kenneth. The Uncorrected World. LC 73-6012. (Wesleyan Poetry Program: Vol. 67). 1973. pap. 4.95x (ISBN 0-8195-1067-X, Pub. by Wesleyan U Pr). Columbia U Pr.

Hanson, Kermit & Roehl, Thomas, eds. The United States & the Pacific Economy in the 1980's. LC 80-16599. (ITT Key Issue Lecture Ser.). 160p. 1980. pap. text ed. 6.95. Bobbs.

Hanson, Lawrence. Renoir: The Man, the Painter, & His World. 1972. 14.95x o.p. (ISBN 0-8464-0789-2). Beekman Pubs.

Hanson, Lawrence W. Contemporary Printed Sources for British & Irish Economic History, 1701-1750. 1964. 165.00 (ISBN 0-521-05196-7). Cambridge U Pr.

Hanson, Louise G. & Davis, Lily A. Basic Beekeeping & Honey Book. 1977. 10.95 o.p. (ISBN 0-679-50746-9); pap. 6.95 (ISBN 0-679-50817-1). McKay.

Hanson, Map. Diet Management for Ulcerative Colitis: Menus, Recipes & Methods of Food Preparation for Anti-Inflammatory Treatment. 80p. 1971. pap. 10.50 spiral (ISBN 0-398-02307-7). C C Thomas.

Hanson, Mark E. Educational Administration & Organizational Behavior. 1978. text ed. 18.95 (ISBN 0-205-06164-8). Allyn.

Hanson, Marvin L., jt. auth. see Barrett.

Hanson, Nancy E. Bismarck & Mangan: A Pictorial History. (Illus.). 205p. 1981. pap. price not set (ISBN 0-89865-094-1). Donning Co.

--Fargo: A Pictorial History. (Illus.). 205p. 1981. pap. price not set. Donning Co.

--How You Can Make Twenty Thousand Dollars a Year Writing: No Matter Where You Live. LC 79-22725. 280p. 1980. 10.95x (ISBN 0-89879-011-5); pap. 6.95 (ISBN 0-89879-025-5). Writers Digest.

Hanson, Norwood R. Patterns of Discovery: An Enquiry into the Conceptual Foundations of Science. 1958-1965. 35.50 (ISBN 0-521-05197-5); pap. 9.95x (ISBN 0-521-09261-2, 261). Cambridge U Pr.

Hanson, Pamela. Resourceful Alternatives: Teaching Through Media. 1981. pap. write for info. (ISBN 0-914562-07-X). Merriam Eddy.

Hanson, Paul D. The Dawn of the Apocalyptic: The Historical & Sociological Roots of Jewish Apocalyptic Eschatology. rev. ed. LC 79-17099. 464p. 1979. 14.95 (ISBN 0-8006-0285-4, 1-285). Fortress.

Hanson, Paul D., ed. see Wolff, Hans W.

Hanson, Philip. Trade & Technology in Soviet-Western Relations. 300p. 1981. 30.00x (ISBN 0-231-05276-6). Columbia U Pr.

Hanson, Philip, jt ed. see Dawisha, Karen.

Hanson, Richard, jt. auth. see Hanson, Anthony.

Hanson, Richard J., jt. auth. see Lawson, Charles L.

Hanson, Robert N. & Rigby, D. Sue. Keyboarding for Information Processing. (Illus.). 96p. 1981. pap. text ed. 6.95 (ISBN 0-07-026105-9, G). McGraw.

Hanson, Robert P., ed. Newcastle Disease Virus: An Evolving Pathogen. (Illus.). 1964. 30.00x (ISBN 0-299-03410-0). U of Wis Pr.

Hanson, Simon G. Utopia in Uruguay: Chapters in the Economic History of Uruguay. LC 79-1579. 1981. Repr. of 1938 ed. 19.75 (ISBN 0-88355-885-8). Hyperion Conn.

Hanson, Virginia, ed. Karma. 2nd rev. ed. Stewart, Rosemarie. 200p. 1980. pap. write for info. (ISBN 0-8356-0543-4). Theos Pub Hse.

Hansson, C. B., ed. Prepare for Science. new ed. (Illus.). 1980. text ed. 30.00 (ISBN 0-08-024263-4); pap. text ed. 9.75 (ISBN 0-08-024262-6). Pergamon.

Hansson-Falk. Falk's Graphical Solutions. 8.00 o.p. (ISBN 0-686-00160-5). Columbia Graphs.

Hanten, Edward W., jt. ed. see Ma, Laurence J.

Hanus, Jerome J., ed. The Nationalization of State Government. LC 80-8635. (Illus.). 192p. 1981. 19.95x (ISBN 0-669-04334-6). Lexington Bks.

Hanway, Castner. Report of the Trial of Castner Hanway for Treason. LC 70-107508. Repr. of 1852 ed. 15.75x (ISBN 0-8371-3779-9). Negro U Pr.

Hanway, Mary Ann. Ellinor, or the World As It Is, 4 vols. LC 73-22145. (The Feminist Controversy in England, 1788-1810 Ser.). 1974. Set. lib. bdg. 80.00 (ISBN 0-8240-0867-7); lib. bdg. 50.00 ea. Garland Pub.

Hao, Wang. Popular Lectures on Mathematical Logic. 286p. 1981. text ed. 24.95 (ISBN 0-442-23109-1). Van Nos Reinhold.

Hao Yen P'ing. Comprador in Nineteenth Century China: Bridge Between East & West. LC 70-105372. (East Asian Ser: No. 45). (Illus.). 1970. 16.50x (ISBN 0-674-15525-4). Harvard U Pr.

Hapgood, Charles H. Voices of Spirit. 1975. 8.95 o.p. (ISBN 0-440-05983-6, Sey Lawr). Delacorte.

--Voices of Spirit. 1976. pap. 1.75 o.p. (ISBN 0-685-73462-5, LB404, Leisure Bks). Nordon Pubns.

Hapgood, Elizabeth R., tr. see Schwarz, Eugene.

Hapgood, Elizabeth R., tr. see Stanislavski, Constantin.

Hapgood, Fred. Why Males Exist: An Inquiry into the Evolution of Sex. 1980. pap. 2.95 (ISBN 0-451-61908-0, ME1908, Mentor). NAL.

Hapgood, I., tr. see Bunin, Ivan.

Haponski, William C. & McCabe, Charles. Back to School: A College Guide for Adults. Leedham, Linnea, ed. (Illus.). 256p. cancelled (ISBN 0-88421-095-2); pap. cancelled (ISBN 0-88421-172-X). Butterick Pub.

Happ, H. H. Diakoptics & Networks. (Mathematics in Science & Engineering Ser.: Vol. 69). 1971. 46.50 (ISBN 0-12-324150-2). Acad Pr.

Happe, Bernard. Your Film & the Lab. (Media Manuals Ser.). Date not set. pap. 8.95 (ISBN 0-8038-8595-4). Hastings.

Happe, Peter, ed. English Mystery Plays. (English Library). 714p. 1980. pap. 4.95 (ISBN 0-14-043093-8). Penguin.

Happel, J. & Brenner, H., eds. Low Reynolds Number Hydrodynamics. 556p. 1977. Repr. of 1975 ed. 45.00x (ISBN 90-01-37115-9). Sijthoff & Noordhoff.

Happel, Margaret. Healthy Eating. Machtiger, B., ed. (The Savers Ser.). (Illus.). 128p. pap. cancelled (ISBN 0-88421-152-5). Butterick Pub.

--Quick Main Courses for Two. Machtiger, B., ed. (The Savers Ser.). (Illus.). 128p. pap. cancelled (ISBN 0-88421-153-3). Butterick Pub.

Happold, D. C. Large Mammals of West Africa. LC 74-169364. (West African Nature Handbooks). (Illus.). 105p. (Orig.). 1973. pap. 5.00 (ISBN 0-582-60428-1). Intl Pubns Serv.

Happold, F. C. Religious Faith & Twentieth Century Man. 192p. 1981. 6.95 (ISBN 0-8245-0046-6). Crossroad NY.

Haq, Khadija. A New Strategy for North-South Negotiations. (Policy Studies). 1980. 25.00. Pergamon.

Haq, Khadija, ed. Equality of Opportunity Within & Among Nations. LC 77-14405. (Praeger Special Studies). 1977. 27.95 (ISBN 0-03-040856-3). Praeger.

Haq Mahbub Ul. The Poverty Curtain: Choices for the Third World. 256p. 1976. 17.50x (ISBN 0-231-04062-8); pap. 9.00x (ISBN 0-231-04063-6). Columbia U Pr.

Haque, Rizwanel & Biros, Francis J., eds. Mass Spectrometry & NMR Spectroscopy in Pesticide Chemistry. LC 73-20005. (Environmental Science Research Ser.: Vol. 4). 348p. 1974. 35.00 (ISBN 0-306-36304-6, Plenum Pr). Plenum Pub.

Harada, Joyce, illus. It's the A.B.C. Book. (Illus.). 32p. (ps). Date not set. 6.95 (ISBN 0-89346-157-1). Heian Intl. Postponed.

Haragan, Christine. Shell Designs. 1980. 9.95x (ISBN 0-85936-137-3, Pub. by Midas Bks England). Intl Schol Bk Serv.

Harakas, S. Guidelines for Marriage in the Orthodox Church. 1980. pap. 1.25 (ISBN 0-937032-21-2). Light&Life Pub Co MN.

--Living the Liturgy. 1974. pap. 3.50 (ISBN 0-937032-17-4). Light&Life Pub Co MN.

--Melody of Prayer. 1979. pap. 1.45 (ISBN 0-686-27068-1). Light&Life Pub Co MN.

--Something Is Stirring in World Orthodoxy. 1978. pap. 2.95 (ISBN 0-937032-04-2). Light & Life Pub Co MN.

Harakas, Stanley S. For the Health of Body & Soul. 48p. (Orig.). 1980. pap. 1.95 (ISBN 0-916586-42-1). Hellenic Coll Pr.

Haralambos, Michael. Right on: From Blues to Soul in Black America. (The Roots of Jazz Ser.). 1979. Repr. of 1974 ed. 19.50 (ISBN 0-306-79531-0). Da Capo.

Haraldsson, Erlendur, jt. auth. see Osis, Karlis.

Harari, Ehud. The Politics of Labor Legislation in Japan: National-International Interaction. LC 72-78945. 1973. 20.00x (ISBN 0-520-02264-5). U of Cal Pr.

Harari, Josue V., intro. by. Textual Strategies: Perspectives in Post-Structuralist Criticism. LC 79-7617. 1979. 22.50x (ISBN 0-8014-1218-8); pap. 7.95 (ISBN 0-8014-9180-0). Cornell U Pr.

Harary, Frank. Graph Theory. 1969. text ed. 20.95 (ISBN 0-201-02787-9). A-W.

Harasowski, Adam. The Skein of Legends Around Chopin. LC 77-28829. (Music Reprint Ser., 1978). (Illus.). 1978. Repr. of 1967 ed. lib. bdg. 32.50 (ISBN 0-306-77525-5). Da Capo.

Harasymiw, Bohdan, ed. Education & the Mass Media in the Soviet Union & Eastern Europe. LC 75-19789. (Special Studies). 1976. text ed. 24.95 (ISBN 0-275-56170-4). Praeger.

Haraszty, Eszter. The Embroiderer's Portfolio of Flower Designs. (Illus.). 1981. 22.95 (ISBN 0-87140-643-8). Liveright.

Harayda, Marel. Needlework Magic with Two Basic Stitches. (Illus.). (gr. 7 up). 1977. 6.95 o.p. (ISBN 0-679-20423-7). McKay.

Harbach, R. E. & Knight, Kenneth L. Taxonomists' Glossary of Mosquito Anatomy. LC 80-83112. (Illus.). 430p. 1980. 17.95 (ISBN 0-517-54149-1). Plexus Pub.

Harbage, Alfred. Annals of English Drama: Nine Seventy-Five to Seventeen Hundred. rev. ed. Schoenbaum, S., ed. LC 64-57462. 1964. 18.00x o.p. (ISBN 0-8122-7483-0). U of Pa Pr.

--Shakespeare's Audience. LC 41-26970. 1941. pap. 6.00x (ISBN 0-231-08513-3, 13). Columbia U Pr.

--William Shakespeare: A Reader's Guide. 498p. 1963. pap. 7.95 (ISBN 0-374-50288-9, N243). FS&G.

Harbage, Alfred, ed. see Shakespeare, William.

Harbaugh, William H. Lawyer's Lawyer: The Life of John W. Davis. 550p. 1973. 25.00 (ISBN 0-19-501699-8). Oxford U Pr.

Harbeck, Mary, ed. The Second Sourcebook for Science Supervisors. rev. ed. 1976. pap. 3.50 (ISBN 0-87355-004-8). Natl Sci Tchrs.
Harbeke, G., jt. auth. see Greenaway, D. L.
Harber, K., ed. Heinemann Australian Dictionary. 1976. text ed. 10.95x (ISBN 0-686-65318-1, 00511). Heinemann Ed.
Harber, K. & Payton, G., eds. Heinemann English Dictionary. 1979. text ed. 10.95x (ISBN 0-435-10378-4). Heinemann Ed.
Harberger, Arnold C. & Bailey, Martin J., eds. The Taxation of Income from Capital. (Studies of Government Finance). 331p. 1969. 12.95 (ISBN 0-8157-3456-5). Brookings.
Harbert, Anita S. Federal Grants-in-Aid: Maximizing Benefits to the States. LC 76-12854. 1976. text ed. 24.95 (ISBN 0-275-23370-7). Praeger.
Harbert, Anita S. & Ginsberg, Leon H. Human Services for Older Adults. 1979. pap. text ed. 13.95x (ISBN 0-534-00607-8). Wadsworth Pub.
Harbert, Earl N., jt. ed. see Rees, Robert A.
Harbert, John C., ed. Cisternography & Hydrocephalus: A Symposium. (Illus.). 670p. 1972. 58.75 (ISBN 0-398-02308-5). C C Thomas.
Harbert, Joseph R., jt. ed. see Finger, Seymour M.
Harbin, E. O. Old-Fashion Fun & Games. (Games & Party Books). 1978. pap. 3.45 (ISBN 0-8010-4184-8). Baker Bk.
Harbin, Elvin O. Fun Encyclopedia. (Illus.). (gr. 4 up). 1940. 8.95 (ISBN 0-687-13714-4). Abingdon.
Harbin, Gloria, et al, eds. Early Childhood Curriculum Materials: An Annotated Bibliography: Early Education for the Handicapped. (First Chance Ser). 1976. pap. 6.95 o.s.i. (ISBN 0-8027-9040-2). Walker & Co.
Harbin, Robert. New Adventures in Origami. (Funk & W Bk.). (Illus.). 192p. 1972. pap. 1.95 (ISBN 0-308-10040-9, F81, TYC-T). T Y Crowell.
--Origami: The Art of Paper-Folding. (Funk & W Bk.). (Illus.). 1969. pap. 1.75 o.s.i. (ISBN 0-308-90099-5, F67, TYC-T). T Y Crowell.
Harbison, Craig. The Last Judgment in Sixteenth Century Northern Europe: a Study of the Relation Between Art & the Reformation. LC 75-23793. (Outstanding Dissertations in the Fine Arts - 16th Century). (Illus.). 1976. lib. bdg. 45.00 (ISBN 0-8240-1988-1). Garland Pub.
Harbison, Robert. Eccentric Spaces. 192p. 1979. pap. 2.50 (ISBN 0-380-49122-2, 49122, Discus). Avon.
Harbison, Samuel A., jt. auth. see Martin, Alan.
Harborne, J. & Mabry, Helga, eds. The Flavonoids. 1975. 77.00 set (ISBN 0-685-72438-7); Pt. 1. 47.50 (ISBN 0-12-324601-6); Pt. 2. 47.50 (ISBN 0-12-324602-4). Acad Pr.
Harborne, J. B., ed. see Phytochemical Society.
Harbottle, Thomas B. Dictionary of Battles. LC 66-22672. 1966. Repr. of 1905 ed. 19.00 (ISBN 0-8103-3004-0). Gale.
--Dictionary of Historical Allusions. LC 68-23163. 1968. Repr. of 1904 ed. 18.00 (ISBN 0-8103-3088-1). Gale.
Harbsmeier, Christoph. Aspects of Classical Chinese Syntax. (Sias Monograph: No. 45). 328p. 1980. pap. text ed. 17.00x (ISBN 0-7007-0139-7). Humanities.
Harbury, Colin. Economic Behaviour: An Introduction. (Illus., Orig.). 1980. text ed. 27.50x (ISBN 0-04-330305-6, 2532); pap. 11.50x (ISBN 0-04-330306-4, 2533). Allen Unwin.
Harcleroad, Fred F., ed. Issues of the Seventies: The Future of Higher Education. LC 79-110639. (Higher Education Ser.). 1970. 11.95x o.p. (ISBN 0-87589-057-1). Jossey-Bass.
Harcourt, E. S., tr. see Sharar, Abdul H.
Harcourt, G. C. Some Cambridge Controversies in the Theory of Capital. LC 71-161294. (Illus.). 1972. 35.50 (ISBN 0-521-08294-3); pap. 14.95x (ISBN 0-521-09672-3). Cambridge U Pr.
Harcourt, G. C., ed. The Microeconomic Foundations of Macroeconomics. 1978. lib. bdg. 50.00 o.p. (ISBN 0-89158-730-6). Westview.
Harcourt, G. C., jt. ed. see Parker, R. H.
Harcourt, G. C., et al. Economic Activity. 1967. 45.00 (ISBN 0-521-05199-1); pap. 13.95x (ISBN 0-521-09427-5). Cambridge U Pr.
Harcourt, Palma. Agents of Influence. 1978. 7.95 o.s.i. (ISBN 0-8027-5374-4). Walker & Co.
--At High Risk. LC 77-91361. 1978. 7.95 o.s.i. (ISBN 0-8027-5382-5). Walker & Co.
Harcum, E. Rae. Psychology for Daily Living: Simple Guidance in Human Relations for Parents, Teachers, & Others. LC 79-1048. 1979. 14.95 (ISBN 0-88229-384-2); pap. 7.95x (ISBN 0-88229-696-5). Nelson-Hall.
Hard, Margaret. Footloose in Vermont. (Illus., orig). 1969. 3.95 o.s.i. (ISBN 0-911570-06-3); pap. 2.00 o.s.i. (ISBN 0-911570-07-1). Vermont Bks.
Hardach, Gerd. The First World War, Nineteen Fourteen to Nineteen Eighteen. (History of the World Economy in the Twentieth Century Ser.: Vol. 2). 1981. pap. 6.95 (ISBN 0-520-04397-9, CAL 495). U of Cal Pr.
--First World War, 1914-1918. (History of the World Economy in the Twentieth Century Ser: Vol. 2). 1977. 20.00x (ISBN 0-520-03060-5). U of Cal Pr.
Hardach, Karl. Political Economy of Germany in the Twentieth Century. 240p. 1980. 22.50x (ISBN 0-520-03809-6). U of Cal Pr.
Hardaway, Francine. Creative Rhetoric. 304p. 1976. pap. text ed. 9.95 (ISBN 0-13-191072-8). P-H.
Hardcastle, Michael see Milne, John.
Hardeman, Mildred, ed. Children's Ways of Knowing: Nathan Isaacs on Education, Psychology & Piaget. LC 74-3103. 1974. pap. text ed. 7.25x (ISBN 0-8077-2467-X). Tchrs Coll.
Harden, B. M. & Williams, D. L. Bulletin Boards Made the Easy Way. (Illus.). 64p. 1981. 5.00 (ISBN 0-682-49731-2). Exposition.
Harden, John. Devil's Tramping Ground & Other North Carolina Mystery Stories. 1949. 7.95 (ISBN 0-8078-0561-0). U of NC Pr.
--The Devil's Tramping Ground & Other North Carolina Mystery Stories. 178p. 1980. pap. 4.95 o.p. (ISBN 0-8078-4070-X). U of NC Pr.
--Tar Heel Ghosts. 1954. 7.95 (ISBN 0-8078-0660-9); pap. 4.95 (ISBN 0-8078-4069-6). U of NC Pr.
Harden, M. L., jt. auth. see Lamb, M. W.
Hardendorff, Jeanne B. Libraries & How to Use Them. LC 78-12992. (First Bks.). (Illus.). (gr. 4 up). 1979. PLB 6.45 s&l (ISBN 0-531-02259-5). Watts.
Hardendorff, Jeanne B., ed. Witches, Wit & a Werewolf. LC 75-153516. (Illus.). 128p. (gr. 4-6). 1971. 7.89 (ISBN 0-397-31542-2). Lippincott.
Harden-Umolu, Chinwe M. The Griot Speaks: Stories & Folktales from the Black World. 96p. (Orig.). (gr. 3 up). 1979. pap. 8.00 (ISBN 0-89062-040-7, Pub. by Medgar Evers Coll). Pub Ctr Cult Res.
Harder. Harmonic Materials in Tonal Music: A Programmed Course, Pts. 1 & 2. 4th ed. 320p. 1980. pap. 14.95 (5869250). Pt. 1 (ISBN 0-205-06925-8). Pt. 2 (ISBN 0-205-06945-2, 5869455). Allyn.
Harder, Janet. Letters from Carrie. (Illus.). 152p. (gr. 6 up). 1980. 10.95 (ISBN 0-932052-23-1). North Country.
Harder, Marvin A., jt. auth. see Palumbo, Dennis J.
Harder, Paul. Basic Materials in Music Theory: A Programmed Course. 4th ed. 1978. pap. text ed. 14.50 (ISBN 0-205-06045-5). Allyn.
Harder, Paul O. Harmonic Material in Tonal Music: A Programmed Course, 2 vols. 3rd ed. 1977. pap. text ed. 11.95 ea. o.s.i. Pt. 1 (ISBN 0-205-05708-X). Pt. 2 (ISBN 0-205-05711-X). Allyn.
Hardesty, D. L. Ecological Anthropology. 1977. 19.95x (ISBN 0-471-35144-X). Wiley.
Hardesty, Jim, jt. tr. see Tobias, Arthur.
Hardesty, Nancy A. Great Women of Faith. LC 80-65440. 200p. 1980. 7.95 (ISBN 0-8010-4223-2). Baker Bk.
Hardesty, Vida A. The Turn-of-the-Century Party. LC 77-82129. (National History Ser.). (Illus.). (gr. 4 up). 1980. 10.95 (ISBN 0-89482-001-X); write for info. ltd. ed. (ISBN 0-89482-023-0); pap. 6.95 (ISBN 0-89482-008-7). Stevenson Pr.
Hardgrave, Robert. Peasant Revolt in Malabar. 1981. Repr. 25.00x (ISBN 0-8364-0010-0). South Asia Bks.
Hardgrave, Robert L., Jr. The Nadars of Tamilnad: The Political Culture of a Community in Change. (Center for South & Southeast Asia Studies, UC Berkeley). (Illus.). 1969. 20.00x (ISBN 0-520-01471-5). U of Cal Pr.
Hardgrave, Robert L., Jr. & Hinojosa, Santiago N. The Politics of Bilingual Education: A Study of Four Southwest Texas Communities. LC 75-43748. 110p. (Orig.). 1975. pap. text ed. 4.95 (ISBN 0-88408-041-2). Sterling Swift.
Hardgrove, Carol, jt. auth. see Azarnoff, Pat.
Hardie, D. W. & Davidson Pratt, J. A History of the Modern British Chemical Industry. 1966. 22.00 (ISBN 0-08-011687-6); pap. 10.75 (ISBN 0-08-011686-8). Pergamon.
Hardie, Glenn M. Construction Contracts & Specifications. (Illus.). 1981. text ed. 21.95 (ISBN 0-8359-0923-9). Reston.
Hardie, James K. From Serfdom to Socialism (1907) Dowse, R. E., ed. Bd. with Labour & the Empire (1907) MacDonald, James R; The Socialist's Budget (1907) Snowden, Philip. LC 74-496. 385p. 1975. 18.00 (ISBN 0-8386-1540-6). Fairleigh Dickinson.
Hardie, W. F. Aristotle's Ethical Theory. 2nd ed. 472p. 1981. 49.95x (ISBN 0-19-824632-3); pap. 24.95x (ISBN 0-19-824633-1). Oxford U Pr.
Hardie, William. Scottish Painting: 1837-1939. 1977. 35.00 (ISBN 0-02-548110-X). Macmillan.
Hardigree, Peggy. The Edible Indoor Garden. 320p. 1981. 16.95 (ISBN 0-312-23689-1); pap. 7.95 (ISBN 0-312-23690-5). St Martin.
--Strike It Rich! Treasure Hunting with Metal Detectors. (Illus.). 224p. 1980. 10.95 (ISBN 0-517-54216-1, Harmony); pap. 5.95 (ISBN 0-517-54160-2, Harmony). Crown.
Hardigree, Peggy A. The Freefood Seafood Book. 224p. (Orig.). 1981. pap. 8.95 (ISBN 0-8117-2068-3). Stackpole.
Hardiman, N. J. Exploring University Mathematics, 3 Vols. Vol. 1. 1967. text ed. 15.00 (ISBN 0-08-011990-5); Vol. 2. 1966. text ed. 16.50 (ISBN 0-08-012567-0); Vol. 3. 1969. text ed. 15.00 (ISBN 0-08-012903-X); Vol. 1. pap. 7.00 (ISBN 0-08-011991-3); Vol. 2 1968. pap. 7.75 (ISBN 0-08-012566-2); Vol. 3 1969. pap. 7.00 (ISBN 0-08-012902-1). Pergamon.
Hardin, D. E. Religions of the World. (Liberal Studies Ser.). 1966. pap. text ed. 2.50x o.p. (ISBN 0-435-46531-7). Heinemann Ed.
Hardin, Evamaria. Archimedes Russell: Upstate Architect. (Illus.). 108p. 1980. pap. 5.95 (ISBN 0-8156-0165-4). Syracuse U Pr.
Hardin, Garrett. Limits of Altruism: An Ecologist's View of Survival. LC 77-74451. 160p. 1977. 10.00x (ISBN 0-253-33435-7). Ind U Pr.
--Prometiean Ethics: Living with Death, Competition, & Triage. LC 79-56592. (The Jesse & John Danz Lecture Ser.). 92p. 1980. 7.95 (ISBN 0-295-95717-4). U of Wash Pr.
--Stalking the Wild Taboo. 2nd ed. LC 78-1976. 290p. 1978. 11.95 (ISBN 0-913232-40-8); pap. 6.95 (ISBN 0-913232-41-6). W Kaufmann.
Hardin, Garrett & Bajema, Carl. Biology: Its Principles & Implications. 3rd ed. LC 77-28507. (Illus.). 1978. 21.95x (ISBN 0-7167-0028-X). W H Freeman.
Hardin, Garrett, ed. Population, Evolution, & Birth Control: A Collage of Controversial Ideas. 2nd ed. LC 69-16921. (Biology Ser.). (Illus.). 1969. pap. text ed. 10.95x (ISBN 0-7167-0670-9). W H Freeman.
Hardin, Garrett & Baden, John, eds. Managing the Commons. LC 76-40055. (Illus.). 1977. pap. text ed. 9.95x (ISBN 0-7167-0476-5). W H Freeman.
Hardin, H., tr. see Gambaryan, P. R.
Hardin, Herschel. A Nation Unaware: The Canadian Economic Culture. LC 75-302646. 384p. 1974. pap. 8.95 (ISBN 0-295-95723-9). U of Wash Pr.
Hardin, J. D. Bloody Sands. LC 80-80989. (Pinkerton Ser.: No. 8). 208p. (Orig.). 1980. pap. 1.75 (ISBN 0-87216-718-6). Playboy Pbks.
--Hard Chains, Soft Women. LC 80-83563. (Pinkerton Ser.). 224p. (Orig.). 1981. pap. 1.95 (ISBN 0-87216-799-2). Playboy Pbks.
--Raiders Gold. LC 80-85105. (J.D.Hardin Ser.). 256p. 1981. pap. 1.95 (ISBN 0-87216-861-1). Playboy Pbks.
--Raider's Revenge. LC 80-82851. (J. D. Hardin). 256p. (Orig.). 1981. pap. 1.95 (ISBN 0-87216-767-4). Playboy Pbks.
Hardin, John W. Life of John Wesley Hardin As Written by Himself. (Western Frontier Library: No. 16). (Illus.). 1977. pap. 3.95 (ISBN 0-8061-1051-1). U of Okla Pr.
Hardin, R., tr. see Vonsovskii, S. V.
Hardin, R. R., tr. see Kukarkin, B. V.
Hardin, Russel. Perhaps It Was Never the Same. 1980. write for info.; pap. write for info. Latitudes Pr.
Hardin, Veralee. Behavior Rating Scale. 1975. saddle stitched 1.50x (ISBN 0-87543-123-2); 0.75x (ISBN 0-686-65583-4). Lucas.
--Book of Readings in Diagnostic & Corrective Reading. 1974. pap. text ed. 5.00x (ISBN 0-87543-118-6). Lucas.
Hardin, Veralee & Busch, Robert L. Manual for Behavior Rating Scale. 1975. saddle stitched 19.75. Lucas.
Harding, A. J. Coleridge & the Idea of Love. 1975. 42.00 (ISBN 0-521-20639-1). Cambridge U Pr.
Harding, Alan. The Law Courts of Medieval England. (Historical Problems Studies & Documents). 1973. text ed. 17.95x (ISBN 0-04-942106-9). Allen Unwin.
Harding, Anthony, ed. Car Facts & Feats. LC 76-51170. (Guinness Family Ser.). (Illus.). 1977. 17.95 (ISBN 0-8069-0108-X); lib. bdg. 15.99 (ISBN 0-8069-0109-8). Sterling.
Harding, Beryl. Ourselves & Others. (Liberal Studies Ser.). 1965. pap. text ed. 1.75 o.p. (ISBN 0-435-46533-3). Heinemann Ed.
Harding, D. C., ed. see Nogales, Manuel C.
Harding, D. W. Social Psychology & Individual Values. 2nd ed. 1966. pap. text ed. 2.50x (ISBN 0-09-042632-0, Hutchinson U Lib). Humanities.
--Words into Rhythm. LC 76-7805. 1976. 27.50 (ISBN 0-521-21267-7). Cambridge U Pr.
Harding, E. F., jt. auth. see Kendall, D. G.
Harding, E. F. & Kendall, D. G., eds. Stochastic Geometry. LC 72-8603. (Ser. in Probability & Mathematical Statistics). 416p. 1974. 55.95 (ISBN 0-471-35141-5). Wiley.
Harding, G., tr. see D'Annunzio, Gabriele.
Harding, Gunnar & Barkan, Stanley H., eds. Cross-Cultural Review: Four Contemporary Swedish Poets, No. 5. Fulton, Robin & Hollo, Anselm, trs. 48p. 10.00 (ISBN 0-89304-608-6); pap. 4.00 (ISBN 0-89304-609-4). Cross Cult.
Harding, Harold F., ed. see Blair, Hugh.
Harding, Harry. Organizing China: The Problem of Bureaucracy, 1949-1976. LC 79-67772. 280p. 1981. text ed. 25.00x (ISBN 0-8047-1080-5). Stanford U Pr.
Harding, J. M., jt. auth. see Corballis, R.
Harding, J. M., jt. auth. see Corballis, Richard.
Harding, J. M., tr. see Descombes, Vincent.
Harding, John, jt. auth. see Corballis, Richard.
Harding, Keith A. & Welch, Kenneth R. Venomous Snakes of the World: A Checklist. 200p. 1980. 44.00 (ISBN 0-08-025495-0). Pergamon.
Harding, M. Esther. Psychic Energy: Its Source & Its Transformation. 2nd ed. (Bollingen Ser.: Vol. 10). (Illus.). 520p. 1963. 25.00 (ISBN 0-691-09817-4); pap. 6.95 (ISBN 0-691-01790-5, 296). Princeton U Pr.
Harding, P. E., et al, eds. Thyroid Research III: Eighth International Thyroid Congress 3-5 February 1980, Sydney, Australia. 800p. 1980. 130.00 (ISBN 0-08-026361-5). Pergamon.
Harding, Robert S., ed. Omnivorous Primates: Gathering & Hunting in Human Evolution. Teleki, Geza P. LC 80-23726. (Illus.). 912p. 1981. 30.00x (ISBN 0-231-04024-5). Columbia U Pr.
Harding, Robert T. & Holmes, A. L. Jacqueline Kennedy: A Woman for the World. (Illus.). 8.95 o.s.i. (ISBN 0-8149-0115-8). Vanguard.
Harding, Rosamund E. Piano-Forte. LC 69-15634. (Music Ser.). 1973. Repr. of 1933 ed. lib. bdg. 29.50 (ISBN 0-306-71084-6). Da Capo.
Harding, Samuel B. Contest Over the Ratification of the Federal Constitution in the State of Massachusetts. LC 75-98687. (American Constitutional & Legal History Ser). 1970. Repr. of 1896 ed. lib. bdg. 25.00 (ISBN 0-306-71839-1). Da Capo.
Harding, T. & Wallace, B. Cultures of the Pacific. LC 70-91883. 1970. 17.95 (ISBN 0-02-913810-8); pap. text ed. 10.95 (ISBN 0-02-913800-0). Free Pr.
Harding, T. D. Colle, London & Blackmar Diemer Systems. 1979. 17.95 (ISBN 0-7134-2110-X, Pub. by Batsford England); pap. 12.50 (ISBN 0-7134-2111-8). David & Charles.
--French: MacCutcheon & Advance Lines. (Illus.). 130p. 1980. pap. 13.95 (ISBN 0-7134-2026-X, Pub. by Batsford England). David & Charles.
--Leningrad Dutch. 1976. 18.95 (ISBN 0-7134-3129-6). David & Charles.
--Meran & Other Semi-Slav Systems. 1980. cancelled (ISBN 0-7134-2447-8); pap. cancelled (ISBN 0-686-63372-5). David & Charles.
--Queen's Gambit Declined: Semi-Slav. (Illus.). 176p. 1981. pap. 18.50 (ISBN 0-7134-2448-6, Pub. by Batsford England). David & Charles.
--Spanish (Ruy Lopez) Marshall. 1977. pap. 18.95 (ISBN 0-7134-0252-0, Pub. by Batsford England). David & Charles.
--Vienna Opening. 1978. pap. 12.50 (ISBN 0-7134-1417-0, Pub. by Batsford England). David & Charles.
Harding, T. D. & Markland, P. R. Sicilian. 1975. pap. 13.50 (ISBN 0-7134-3209-8, Pub. by Batsford England). David & Charles.
--The Sicilian Richter-Rauzer. 1975. 18.95 (ISBN 0-7134-3209-8, Pub. by Batsford England). David & Charles.
Harding, T. D., jt. auth. see Botterill, G. S.
Harding, T. D., jt. auth. see Wade, R. G.
Harding, T. D., jt. auth. see Wade, Robert.
Harding, T. D., ed. The Games of the World Correspondence Chess Championships, Nos. I-VII. (Illus.). 152p. 1980. 28.95 (ISBN 0-7134-2031-6, Pub. by Batsford England). David & Charles.
Harding, T. D., et al. Sicilian Sozin. 1974. 18.95 (ISBN 0-7134-2848-1, Pub. by Batsford England). David & Charles.
Harding, Valerie. Texturers in Embroidery. (Illus.). 1977. 10.95 o.p. (ISBN 0-8230-5341-5). Watson-Guptill.
Harding, Vincent. The Other American Revolution. Hill, Robert A., ed. LC 79-54307. (Afro-American Culture & Society Monographs: Vol. 4). 1981. pap. 8.50 (ISBN 0-934934-06-1). Ctr Afro Am St.
Harding, Walter. Thoreau on the Lecture Platform. LC 80-2681. 1981. 12.50 (ISBN 0-404-19077-4). AMS Pr.
Harding, Walter, ed. see Thoreau, Henry D.
Harding, Walter A., jt. auth. see Meltzer, Milton.

Harding, Walter R. Emerson's Library. LC 80-2535. 1981. Repr. of 1967 ed. 37.50 (ISBN 0-404-19261-0). AMS Pr.
--Threau's Library. LC 80-2507. 1981. Repr. of 1957 ed. 18.50 (ISBN 0-404-19055-3). AMS Pr.
Hardinge, George. Winter's Crimes Eleven. 1980. 9.95 (ISBN 0-312-88238-6). St Martin.
Hardison, O. B., Jr. & Mills, Jerry L. Forms of Imagination: An Anthology of Poetry, Fiction & Drama. 1972. pap. text ed. 10.95 (ISBN 0-13-329516-8). P-H.
Hardison, Theo. Poker. (Gambler's Book Shelf). pap. 2.95 (ISBN 0-89650-571-5). Gamblers.
Hardison, Thomas B. Fluid Mechanics for Technicians. (Illus.). 272p. 1977. ref. ed. 18.95 (ISBN 0-87909-297-1); students manual avail. Reston.
Hardle, Martin. Water-Colour Painting in Britain: Vol. III The Victorian Period. 1968. 120.00 (ISBN 0-7134-0718-2, Pub. by Batsford England). David & Charles.
Hardman, A. C. Equine Nutrition. (Illus.). 128p. 1981. 17.95 (ISBN 0-7207-1244-0). Merrimack Bk Serv.
Hardman, A. Leighton. The Amateur Horse Breeder. 2nd ed. (Illus.). 240p. 1980. 16.95 (ISBN 0-7207-1177-0). Transatlantic.
Hardman, Ann L. Young Horse Management. 1976. 11.95 (ISBN 0-7207-0904-0, Pub. by Michael Joseph). Merrimack Bk Serv.
Hardman, Michael. Beer Naturally. (Illus., Orig.). 1978. pap. 4.50 (ISBN 0-8467-0430-7, Pub. by Two Continents). Hippocrene Bks.
Hardman, Michael L., jt. auth. see Drew, Clifford J.
Hardman, Michael L., et al. What Will We Do in the Morning? The Exceptional Student in the Regular Classroom. 450p. 1981. pap. text ed. write for info. (ISBN 0-697-06056-X); instr's manual avail. (ISBN 0-697-06057-8). Wm C Brown.
Hardon, John A., S.J. Religions of the World, 2 Vols. (YA) 1968. Vol. 1. pap. 1.45 (ISBN 0-385-01570-4, D241B). Vol. 2 (D241B). Doubleday.
Hardorp, Detlef. All Compact Orientable Three Dimensional Manifolds Admit Total Foliations. LC 80-16612. (Memoirs: No. 233). 1980. 4.00 (ISBN 0-8218-2233-0). Am Math.
Hardoy, Jorge E. & Satterthwaite, David. Shelter - Need & Response: Housing, Land & Settlement Policies in Seventeen Third World Nations. 1981. price not set (ISBN 0-471-27919-6, Pub. by Wiley-Interscience). Wiley.
Hardoy, Jorge E., ed. Urbanization in Latin America: Approaches & Issues. LC 73-83594. 480p. 1975. pap. 4.50 o.p. (ISBN 0-385-08240-1, Anch). Doubleday.
Hardt, Dale V. Death: The Final Frontier. (Illus.). 1979. 12.50 (ISBN 0-13-197772-5); pap. 7.50 (ISBN 0-13-197780-6). P-H.
Hardt, Elaine. Four Minute Fun for Parent & Child. LC 79-90463. 1978. pap. 2.95 (ISBN 0-932960-02-2). Horizons.
Hardt, Lorraine. How to Make Money Writing Greeting Cards. LC 68-18134. (Illus.). 1968. 8.95 (ISBN 0-8119-0096-7). Fell.
Hardwick, Elizabeth. Seduction & Betrayal: Women & Literature. 1974. 6.95 o.p. (ISBN 0-394-49069-X). Random.
Hardwick, Geraline B. & Kennedy, Robert L. Fundamentals of Quantity Food Preparation: Breads, Soups & Sandwiches. LC 77-20096. (Illus.). 1978. 22.95 (ISBN 0-8436-2163-X). CBI Pub.
--Fundamentals of Quantity Food Preparation: Desserts & Beverages. LC 74-20917. (Illus.). 364p. 1975. 22.95 (ISBN 0-8436-2051-X). CBI Pub.
Hardwick, Michael & Hardwick, Mollie. The Bernard Shaw Companion. LC 73-86599. 193p. 1974. 6.50 o.p. (ISBN 0-312-07665-7). St Martin.
Hardwick, Mollie. Beauty's Daughter. 1978. pap. 1.95 o.p. (ISBN 0-425-03866-1). Berkley Pub.
--Lovers Meeting. (gr. 7-12). 1980. lib. bdg. 15.95 (ISBN 0-8161-3064-7, Large Print Bks). G K Hall.
--Thomas & Sarah. 288p. (Orig.). 1981. pap. 2.50 (ISBN 0-515-06003-8). Jove Pubns.
--The War to End War. (Upstairs, Downstairs). 244p. 1975. pap. 1.50 o.s.i. (ISBN 0-440-15987-3). Dell.
--Willowwood. 1981. lib. bdg. 16.95 (ISBN 0-8161-3154-6, Large Print Bks). G K Hall.
--The World of Upstairs, Downstairs. LC 75-21465. 1976. 12.95 o.p. (ISBN 0-03-015571-1). HR&W.
Hardwick, Mollie, jt. auth. see Hardwick, Michael.
Hardwick, Richard. Charles Richard Drew: Pioneer in Blood Research. LC 67-24049. 1967. 5.95 o.p. (ISBN 0-684-92299-1, ScribJ). Scribner.
Hardwick, Sylvia. Singing Tree & Laughing Waters. LC 71-101534. 1970. pap. 4.95 (ISBN 0-8163-0159-X, 19362-3). Pacific Pr Pub Assn.
Hardwicke, Denis, tr. see Huxley, Anthony.

Hardy. Your Money & Your Life: How to Plan Your Long Range Financial Security. Date not set. 14.95 (ISBN 0-8144-5529-8). Am Mgmt.
Hardy, A. V. The British Isles. 2nd ed. (Geography of the British Isles Ser.). (Illus.). 160p. Date not set. pap. price not set (ISBN 0-521-22258-3). Cambridge U Pr.
Hardy, A. V., jt. auth. see Monkhouse, F. J.
Hardy, Alan R. A Revision of the Genus Pelidnota of America North of Panama (Coleopera-Scarabaeidae, Rutelinae) (Publications in Entomology: Vol. 78). 1975. pap. 9.00x (ISBN 0-520-09529-4). U of Cal Pr.
Hardy, Albert V. & Monkhouse, F. J. Physical Landscape in Pictures. 1964. text ed. 6.95 (ISBN 0-521-05201-7). Cambridge U Pr.
Hardy, Arthur. New Orleans Mardi Gras Guide, Nineteen Eighty One. rev. ed. (Illus.). 82p. 1981. pap. 2.95x (ISBN 0-930892-05-4). A Hardy & Assocs.
Hardy, Barbara. Advantage of Lyric: Essays on Feeling in Poetry. LC 76-47167. 152p. 1977. 10.95x (ISBN 0-253-30130-0). Ind U Pr.
--The Appropriate Form: An Essay on the Novel. 1971. pap. 5.95x o.s.i. (ISBN 0-8101-0335-4). Northwestern U Pr.
--Dramatic Quicklyisms: Malapropic Wordplay Technique in Shakespeare's Henriad, 2 vols. (SSEL Poetic Drama Studies: No. 85, Vols. 1 & 2). 382p. 1979. Vol. 1. pap. text ed. 25.00x (ISBN 0-391-01748-9); Vol. 2. pap. text ed. 25.00x (ISBN 0-391-01749-7). Humanities.
--Tellers & Listeners: The Narrative Imagination. 279p. 1976. text ed. 27.50x (ISBN 0-485-11153-5, Athlone Pr). Humanities.
Hardy, C. & Martin, N. Your Roles As a Medical Assistant. 1974. 9.50 (ISBN 0-87489-044-6). Med Economics.
Hardy, C. Colburn. ABC's of Investing Your Retirement Funds. 1978. 22.50 (ISBN 0-87489-008-X). Med Economics.
--Dun & Bradstreet's Guide to Your Investment, Nineteen Seventy-Nine to Nineteen Eighty. 24th ed. LC 73-18050. (Illus.). 1979. 14.95 o.s.i. (ISBN 0-690-01768-5, TYC-T); pap. 8.95 o.s.i. (ISBN 0-690-01769-3, TYC-T). T Y Crowell.
--Dun & Bradstreet's Guide to Your Investments 1981. LC 73-18050. (Illus.). 192p. 1981. 12.95 (ISBN 0-690-01956-4); pap. 8.95 (ISBN 0-690-01958-0). Lippincott & Crowell.
--Dun & Bradstreet's Guide to Your Investments 1980-1981. 25th, rev. ed. (Illus.). 1980. 14.95 o.s.i. (ISBN 0-690-01853-3, TYC-T); pap. 8.95 o.s.i. (ISBN 0-690-01854-1). T Y Crowell.
--Funk & Wagnalls Guide to Personal Money Management. LC 75-17830. (Funk & W Bk.). (Illus.). 450p. 1976. 13.95 o.s.i. (ISBN 0-308-10213-4, TYC-T). T Y Crowell.
Hardy, C. De Witt, jt. auth. see Hofstadter, Richard.
Hardy, D. Elmo. Insects of Hawaii: Diptera: Cyclorrhapha IV, Vol. 14. LC 48-45482. (Illus.). 500p. (Orig.). 1981. pap. 35.00x (ISBN 0-686-69434-1). U Pr of Hawaii.
Hardy, Darel W. Basic Calculus. LC 74-83957. (Contemporary Undergraduate Mathematics Ser.). (Illus.). 1975. text ed. 14.95 o.p. (ISBN 0-8185-0138-3); instructor's manual avail. o.p. (ISBN 0-685-52375-6). Brooks-Cole.
Hardy, Dorothy, jt. auth. see Liebers, Arthur.
Hardy, Eric. The Naturalist in Lakeland. (Regional Naturalist Ser.). (Illus.). 1973. 5.95 (ISBN 0-7153-5745-X). David & Charles.
Hardy, F. Lane. Precalculus Mathematics. 2nd ed. LC 75-148246. 1971. text ed. 15.95 (ISBN 0-675-09251-5). Merrill.
Hardy, Forsyth. John Grierson: A Documentary Biography. LC 79-670273. (Illus.). 1979. 21.95 (ISBN 0-571-10331-6, Pub. by Faber & Faber). Merrimack Bk Serv.
Hardy, Forsyth, ed. see Grierson, John.
Hardy, Godfrey H. The Collected Papers of G. H. Hardy: Theory of Series, Vol. 6. London Mathematical Society Committee, ed. 1974. 49.00 (ISBN 0-19-853340-3). Oxford U Pr.
--Divergent Series. 1949. 42.00x (ISBN 0-19-853309-8). Oxford U Pr.
--Mathematician's Apology. rev. ed. LC 67-21958. 1969. 18.95 (ISBN 0-521-05207-6); pap. 5.50x (ISBN 0-521-09577-8). Cambridge U Pr.
Hardy, Godfrey H., et al. Inequalities. 2nd ed. 1952. 42.00 (ISBN 0-521-05206-8). Cambridge U Pr.
Hardy, H. Forsyth, ed. see Grierson, John.
Hardy, Helen H. & Martinez, Raymond J. Louisiana's Fabulous Foods & How to Cook Them. 80p. pap. 2.95 (ISBN 0-911116-82-6). Pelican.
Hardy, Henry, ed. see Berlin, Isaiah.
Hardy, Irene. An Ohio Schoolmistress: The Memoirs of Irene Hardy. Filler, Louis, ed. LC 80-17242. (Illus.). 321p. 1980. 14.50 (ISBN 0-87338-242-0). Kent St U Pr.
Hardy, J. P. Samuel Johnson: A Critical Study. 1979. 22.00x (ISBN 0-7100-0291-2). Routledge & Kegan.

Hardy, James. Communications Electronics. 1981. text ed. 18.95 (ISBN 0-8359-0892-5); instr's. manual free (ISBN 0-8359-0893-3). Reston.
Hardy, James D. Critical Surgical Illness. 2nd ed. (Illus.). 750p. 1980. text ed. 42.50 (ISBN 0-7216-4511-9). Saunders.
Hardy, Jean. Values in Social Policy: Nine Contradictions. (Radical Social Policy Ser.). 132p. (Orig.). 1981. pap. price not set (ISBN 0-7100-0782-5). Routledge & Kegan.
Hardy, Jim. High Frequency Circuit Design. (Illus.). 1979. ref. 21.95 (ISBN 0-8359-2824-1); students manual avail. (ISBN 0-8359-2825-X). Reston.
Hardy, John E. Katherine Anne Porter. LC 72-79929. (Modern Literature Ser.). 1973. 10.95 (ISBN 0-8044-2351-2). Ungar.
Hardy, Judith, et al. Grassroots Science: Guide to Activities Projects & Filmstrips, Sets 4 & 5. Dambry, Patricia, ed. Incl. Set 4. Earth, Air & Water. LC 78-730899 (ISBN 0-87453-045-8); Set 5. Life-Times: The Season. LC 78-730900 (ISBN 0-87453-055-5). (Illus.). (gr. k-3). 1978. 5.00 ea.; avail. activity guide (ISBN 0-685-65927-5). Denoyer.
Hardy, Margaret E., ed. Role Theory: Perspectives for the Health Professions. (Illus.). 1978. pap. 16.50 (ISBN 0-8385-8471-3). ACC.
Hardy, Martha. Tatoosh. LC 80-8174. (Illus.). 252p. 1980. pap. 6.95 (ISBN 0-89886-005-9). Mountaineers.
Hardy, Michael. World Civil Aircraft Since Nineteen Forty-Five. (Illus.). 1980. 10.95 (ISBN 0-684-16266-0, ScribT). Scribner.
Hardy, Owen B. & Lammers, Lawrence P. Hospitals: The Planning & Design Process. LC 77-76922. 1977. 38.50 (ISBN 0-912862-44-0). Aspen Systems.
Hardy, P. Muslims of British India. LC 77-184772. (South Asian Studies: No. 13). (Illus.). 300p. 1973. 39.50 (ISBN 0-521-08488-1); pap. 11.50x (ISBN 0-521-09783-5). Cambridge U Pr.
Hardy, Phil, ed. Raoul Walsh. (EIFF Ser.). (Illus., Orig.). 1980. pap. 4.00 (ISBN 0-918432-25-1). NY Zoetrope.
Hardy, R. H. Accidents & Emergencies: A Practical Handbook for Personal Use. 3rd ed. (Illus.). 240p. 1981. text ed. 14.95x (ISBN 0-19-261321-9). Oxford U Pr.
Hardy, Randall W. China's Oil Future: A Case of Modest Expectations. LC 77-27555. (Westview Special Studies on China & East Asia Ser.). 1978. lib. bdg. 23.50x (ISBN 0-89158-156-1). Westview.
Hardy, Richard, jt. ed. see Cull, John G.
Hardy, Richard, et al. International Rehabilitation: Approaches & Programs. 200p. 1980. text ed. 22.50x (ISBN 0-8290-0399-1); pap. text ed. 10.95x (ISBN 0-8290-0247-2). Irvington.
Hardy, Richard E. & Cull, John C. Social Rehabilitation Services for the Blind. 420p. 1972. pap. 32.75 photocopy ed. spiral (ISBN 0-398-02309-3). C C Thomas.
Hardy, Richard E. & Cull, John G. Drug Dependence & Rehabilitation Approaches. (Illus.). 252p. 1973. pap. 22.75 photocopy ed. spiral (ISBN 0-398-02690-4). C C Thomas.
Hardy, Richard E., jt. auth. see Cull, John G.
Hardy, Richard E. & Cull, John G., eds. Applied Psychology in Law Enforcement & Corrections. (American Lectures in Social & Rehabilitation Psychology Ser.). (Illus.). 248p. 1973. 14.50 (ISBN 0-398-02862-1). C C Thomas.
--Climbing Ghetto Walls: Disadvantagement, Delinquency & Rehabilitation. (American Lectures in Social & Rehabilitation Psychology Ser.). (Illus.). 210p. 1973. 12.75 (ISBN 0-398-02865-6). C C Thomas.
--Counseling & Rehabilitating the Cancer Patient. (American Lectures in Social & Rehabilitation Psychology Ser.). 164p. 1975. pap. 15.50 photocopy ed. spiral (ISBN 0-398-03297-1). C C Thomas.
--Drug Language & Lore. (American Lectures in Social & Rehabilitation Psychology Ser.). (Illus.). 182p. 1975. pap. 11.75 (ISBN 0-398-03245-9). C C Thomas.
--Educational & Psychosocial Aspects of Deafness. (American Lectures in Social & Rehabilitation Psychology Ser.). (Illus.). 216p. 1979. text ed. 16.75 (ISBN 0-398-03002-2). C C Thomas.
--Fundamentals of Juvenile Criminal Behavior & Drug Abuse. 276p. 1975. 18.50 (ISBN 0-398-03162-2). C C Thomas.
--Group Counseling & Therapy Techniques in Special Settings. (American Lectures in Social & Rehabilitation Psychology Ser.). 180p. 1974. text ed. 14.50 (ISBN 0-398-03001-4). C C Thomas.
--Introduction to Correctional Rehabilitation. (American Lectures in Social & Rehabilitation Psychology Ser.). 288p. 1975. 16.75 (ISBN 0-398-02649-1). C C Thomas.

--Mental Retardation & Physical Disability: A Book of Readings. (American Lectures in Social & Rehabilitation Psychology Ser.). (Illus.). 264p. 1974. 14.75 (ISBN 0-398-02879-6). C C Thomas.
--Modification of Behavior of the Mentally Ill: Rehabilitation Approaches. (American Lectures in Social & Rehabilitation Psychology Ser.). (Illus.). 248p. 1974. text ed. 18.50 (ISBN 0-398-03052-9). C C Thomas.
--Modification of Behavior of the Mentally Retarded: Applied Principles. (American Lectures in Social & Rehabilitation Psychology Ser.). 180p. 1975. text ed. 16.75 (ISBN 0-398-03136-3). C C Thomas.
--Organization & Administration of Service Programs for the Older American. (American Lectures in Social & Rehabilitation Psychology Ser.). (Illus.). 252p. 1975. 18.50 (ISBN 0-398-03286-6). C C Thomas.
--Problems of Adolescents: Social & Psychological Approach. (Amer. Lec. in Social & Rehabilitation Psychology Ser.). (Illus.). 296p. 1974. 19.75 (ISBN 0-398-03163-0). C C Thomas.
--Psychological & Vocational Rehabilitation of the Youthful Delinquent. (American Lectures in Social Rehabilitation Psychology Ser.). (Illus.). 264p. 1974. 16.50 (ISBN 0-398-03154-1). C C Thomas.
--Rehabilitation of the Drug Abuser with Delinquent Behavior. (Amer. Lec. in Social & Rehabilitation Psychology). 208p. 1974. 14.75 (ISBN 0-398-02823-0). C C Thomas.
--Severe Disabilities: Social & Rehabilitation Approaches. (American Lectures in Social & Rehabilitation Psychology Ser.). 336p. 1974. 19.75 (ISBN 0-398-02943-1). C C Thomas.
--Therapeutic Needs of the Family. (American Lectures in Social & Rehabilitation Psychology Ser.). 256p. 1974. 15.75 (ISBN 0-398-03048-0). C C Thomas.
Hardy, Richard E., jt. ed. see Cull, John G.
Hardy, Robin. The Education of Don Juan. 1981. pap. 3.50 (ISBN 0-451-09764-5, E9764, Sig). NAL.
Hardy, Thomas. The Complete Poems of Thomas Hardy. Gibson, James, ed. LC 77-15579. 1978. 24.95 (ISBN 0-02-548150-9). Macmillan.
--Jude the Obscure. pap. 1.75. Bantam.
--Jude the Obscure. Southerington, F. R., ed. LC 76-140800. (Library of Literature Ser: No. 35). 1972. pap. 8.50 (ISBN 0-672-61022-1, LL35). Bobbs.
--Jude the Obscure. Page, Norman, ed. (Norton Critical Edition Ser.). 1978. 17.50 (ISBN 0-393-04473-4); pap. 5.95x (ISBN 0-393-09089-2). Norton.
--The Mayor of Casterbridge. pap. 1.95. Bantam.
--Mayor of Casterbridge. (Literature Ser). (gr. 10-12). 1970. pap. text ed. 3.58 (ISBN 0-87720-745-3). AMSCO Sch.
--Mayor of Casterbridge. pap. 1.95 (ISBN 0-451-51230-8, CJ1230, Sig Classics). NAL.
--The Mayor of Casterbridge. Robinson, James K., ed. LC 76-57983. (Norton Critical Editions). 1977. pap. text ed. 6.95x (ISBN 0-393-09174-0). Norton.
--The Pinnacled Tower: Selected Poems of Thomas Hardy. Plotz, Helen, ed. (Illus.). 160p. (gr. 7 up). 1975. 8.95 (ISBN 0-02-742630-0). Macmillan.
--The Return of the Native. pap. 1.75. Bantam.
--Return of the Native. Gindin, James, ed. (Critical Ed. Ser). 1969. 7.00 (ISBN 0-393-04300-2); pap. 6.95 (ISBN 0-393-09791-9). Norton.
--Return of the Native. (Classics Ser). (gr. 10 up). 1964. pap. 1.95 (ISBN 0-8049-0038-8, CL-38). Airmont.
--Return of the Native. (Literature Ser). (gr. 9-12). 1969. pap. text ed. 3.58 (ISBN 0-87720-713-5). AMSCO Sch.
--Return of the Native with Reader's Guide. (AMSCO Literature Program). (gr. 10-12). 1970. pap. 4.17 (ISBN 0-87720-807-7); with model ans. s.p. 2.70 (ISBN 0-87720-907-3). AMSCO Sch.
--Tess of the D'urbervilles. pap. 1.75. Bantam.
--Tess of the D'Urbervilles. (Movie tie-in ed.). 1981. pap. 2.95 (ISBN 0-451-51522-6, CE1522, Sig Classics). NAL.
--Tess of the D'Urbervilles. (Literature Ser). (gr. 7-12). 1969. pap. text ed. 3.75 (ISBN 0-87720-717-8). AMSCO Sch.
--Tess of the D'Urbervilles. 2nd ed. Elledge, Scott, ed. (Critical Editions). 1979. 14.95 (ISBN 0-393-04507-2); pap. text ed. 4.95x (ISBN 0-393-09044-2). Norton.
--Tess of the D'urbervilles with Reader's Guide. (Amsco Literature Program). (gr. 9-12). 1972. pap. text ed. 4.33 (ISBN 0-87720-815-8); with model ans. s.p. 2.80 (ISBN 0-87720-915-4). AMSCO Sch.
--The Woodlanders. 1981. pap. 4.95 (ISBN 0-14-043153-5). Penguin.

Hardy, W. J. The Handwriting of the Kings & Queens of England. LC 78-58182. 1979. Repr. of 1893 ed. lib. bdg. 30.00 o.p. (ISBN 0-89341-472-7). Longwood Pr.
Hare, A. Paul. Handbook of Small Group Research. 2nd ed. LC 75-28569. (Illus.). 1976. 25.00 (ISBN 0-02-913840-X). Free Pr.
Hare, A. Paul & Blumberg, Herbert H. A Search for Peace & Justice: Reflections of Michael Scott. (Illus.). 255p. 1980. 19.50x. Rowman.
Hare, Cyril. Tenant for Death. 200p. 1981. pap. price not set (ISBN 0-486-24103-3). Dover.
--When the Wind Blows. LC 75-44980. (Crime Fiction Ser). 1976. Repr. of 1949 ed. lib. bdg. 17.50 (ISBN 0-8240-2373-0). Garland Pub.
Hare, D. S. Story of Peter the Fisherman. (Ladybird Ser). 1970. 1.49 (ISBN 0-87508-867-8). Chr Lit.
--The Story of St. Paul. (Ladybird Ser.). (YA) 1969. pap. 1.49 (ISBN 0-87508-869-4). Chr Lit.
Hare, David. Dreams of Leaving. 48p. (Orig.). 1980. pap. 6.95 (ISBN 0-571-11568-3, Pub. by Faber & Faber). Merrimack Bk Serv.
--Licking Hitler. 1979. pap. 5.95 (ISBN 0-571-11326-5, Pub. by Faber & Faber). Merrimack Bk Serv.
--Slag. 1971. pap. 4.95 (ISBN 0-571-09643-3, Pub. by Faber & Faber). Merrimack Bk Serv.
--Teeth 'n' Smiles. 1976. pap. 5.95 (ISBN 0-571-10995-0, Pub. by Faber & Faber). Merrimack Bk Serv.
Hare, Denise B, jt. auth. see Ashton, Dore.
Hare, Douglas. Single Ticket to China. pap. 1.55 (ISBN 0-08-017839-1). Pergamon.
Hare, F. K., jt. auth. see Hewitt, K.
Hare, Norma Q. Mystery at Mouse House. LC 79-28254. (Mystery Ser.). 48p. (gr. k-3). 1980. PLB 5.58 (ISBN 0-8116-6412-0). Garrard.
Hare, R. M. Essays on Philosophical Method. (New Studies in Practical Philosophy). 1972. 11.95x (ISBN 0-520-02178-9). U of Cal Pr.
--Essays on the Moral Concepts. LC 70-187322. (New Studies in Practical Philosophy). 150p. 1972. 11.95x (ISBN 0-520-02231-9). U of Cal Pr.
--Practical Inferences. 132p. 1972. 11.95x (ISBN 0-520-02179-7). U of Cal Pr.
Hare, Richard M. Freedom & Reason. (Oxford Paperbacks Ser.: No. 92). 1965. pap. text ed. 7.50x (ISBN 0-19-881092-X). Oxford U Pr.
Hare, Robert D. Psychopathy: Theory & Research. LC 79-120704. (Foundations of Abnormal Psychology Ser). 1970. pap. text ed. 10.95 (ISBN 0-471-35147-4). Wiley.
Har-El, Menashe. This Is Jerusalem. rev. ed. Zeevy, Rechavam, ed. (Illus.). 368p. 1980. pap. 6.95 (ISBN 0-86628-002-2). Ridgefield Pub.
Harelson, Randy. SWAK: The Complete Book of Mail Fun for Kids. LC 80-54624. (Illus.). 160p. (gr. 3-7). 1981. pap. 3.95 (ISBN 0-89480-150-3). Workman Pub.
Hare-Mustin, Rachel, jt. ed. see Brodsky, Annette M.
Harenberg, Werner. Spiegel on the New Testament. Burtness, James H., tr. 1970. 6.95 o.p. (ISBN 0-02-548160-6); pap. 1.95 (ISBN 0-02-085410-2). Macmillan.
Haresign, W., ed. Recent Advances in Animal Nutrition. LC 80-41606. (Studies in the Agricultural & Food Sciences). (Illus.). 256p. 1980. text ed. 38.25 (ISBN 0-408-71013-6). Butterworths.
Hareven, Shulamith. City of Many Days. 1978. pap. 1.95 o.p. (ISBN 0-445-04251-6). Popular Lib.
Hareven, Tamara. Eleanor Roosevelt: An American Conscience. LC 74-26539. (FDR & the Era of the New Deal Ser). (Illus.). xx, 326p. 1975. Repr. of 1968 ed. lib. bdg. 29.50 (ISBN 0-306-70705-5). Da Capo.
Hareven, Tamara K., ed. Transitions: The Family & the Life Course in Historical Perspectives. (Studies in Social Discontinuity Ser.). 1978. 24.50 (ISBN 0-12-325150-8). Acad Pr.
Harfield, Henry. Bank Credits & Acceptances. 5th ed. (Illus.). 363p. 1974. 24.95 (ISBN 0-8260-3835-2). Ronald Pr.
Harfst, Betsy P. Horace Walpole & the Unconscious: An Experiment in Freudian Analysis. Varma, Devendra P., ed. LC 79-8455. (Gothic Studies & Dissertations Ser.). 1980. lib. bdg. 25.00x (ISBN 0-405-12645-X). Arno.
Hargens, Alan R. Tissue Fluid Pressure & Composition. (Illus.). 282p. 1980. lib. bdg. 34.00 (ISBN 0-683-03891-5). Williams & Wilkins.
Harger, R. O. Synthetic Aperture Radar Systems Theory & Design. (Electrical Science Ser). 1969. 30.50 (ISBN 0-12-325050-1). Acad Pr.
Harger, Richard. The Scourge of Secrecy: A/Personal Testimony & Appeal. LC 80-50239. 218p. 1980. pap. 6.80 (ISBN 0-936472-00-6). Gordy Pr.
Harger, Robert O. Optical Communication Theory. (Benchmark Papers in Electrical Engineering & Computer Science: Vol. 18). 1977. 34.50 (ISBN 0-12-786630-2). Acad Pr.
Hargest, George E. History of Letter Post Communication Between the United States & Europe 1845-1875. LC 75-1787. (Illus.). 256p. 1975. 35.00x (ISBN 0-88000-062-7). Quarterman.
Hargie, Owen & Dickson, David. Social Skills in Interpersonal Communication. 208p. 1981. 28.00x (ISBN 0-7099-0279-4, Pub. by Croom Helm LTD England). Biblio Dist.
Hargis, Charles. English Syntax: An Outline for Clinicians & Teachers of Language Handicapped Children. (Illus.). 232p. 1977. 15.75 (ISBN 0-398-03558-X). C C Thomas.
Hargove, Robert. EST: Making Life Work. 1976. 7.95 o.p. (ISBN 0-440-02405-6). Delacorte.
Hargrave, Basil. Origins & Meanings of Popular Phrases & Names. LC 68-23164. 1968. Repr. of 1925 ed. 22.00 (ISBN 0-8103-3089-X). Gale.
Hargrave, Bettyan, jt. auth. see Stock, Albert E.
Hargrave, Francis. Collectanea Juridica: Consisting of Tracts Relative to the Law & Constitution of England, 2 vols. 1981. Repr. of 1791 ed. lib. bdg. 75.00x (ISBN 0-8377-0632-7). Rothman.
Hargrave, Leonie. Clara Reeve. 496p. 1976. pap. 1.95 o.p. (ISBN 0-345-25070-2). Ballantine.
Hargraves, R. B., ed. Physics of Magmatic Processes. LC 80-7525. (Illus.). 800p. 1980. 40.00x (ISBN 0-691-08259-6); pap. 15.00x (ISBN 0-691-08261-8). Princeton U Pr.
Hargreaves, Andy, jt. auth. see Tickle, Les.
Hargreaves, David H. Interpersonal Relations & Education. (International Library of Sociology). 1972. 25.00x (ISBN 0-7100-7245-7). Routledge & Kegan.
--Interpersonal Relations & Education. rev. ed. (International Library of Sociology). 1975. pap. 8.95 (ISBN 0-7100-8081-6). Routledge & Kegan.
Hargreaves, David H., et al. Deviance in Classrooms. 280p. 1975. 20.00x (ISBN 0-7100-8275-4); pap. 8.00 (ISBN 0-7100-8490-0). Routledge & Kegan.
Hargreaves, Eric L. National Debt. LC 66-9657. Repr. of 1930 ed. 25.00x (ISBN 0-678-05172-0). Kelley.
Hargreaves, G. R. Psychiatry & the Public Health. 1958. text ed. 3.75x (ISBN 0-485-26310-6, Athlone Pr). Humanities.
Hargreaves, J. Good Communications: What Every Good Manager Should Know. LC 76-40317. 1977. 17.95 (ISBN 0-470-98958-0). Halsted Pr.
Hargreaves, John. Expansion of Europe. (History Today Ser). 1968. 5.00 (ISBN 0-05-001655-5); pap. 3.95 (ISBN 0-685-00928-9). Dufour.
Hargreaves, John & Dauman, Jan. Business Survival & Social Change: A Practical Guide to Responsibility & Partnership. LC 75-5807. 1975. 24.95 (ISBN 0-470-35155-1). Halsted Pr.
Hargreaves, John D. West Africa Partitioned, Vol. 1: The Loaded Pause, 1885-1889. (Illus.). 288p. 1974. 19.50x (ISBN 0-299-06720-3). U of Wis Pr.
Hargreaves, Marjorie K., jt. auth. see Lieser, Marie Y.
Hargreaves, Mary W. & Hopkins, James F., eds. The Papers of Henry Clay: Secretary of State, 1827, Vol. VI. LC 59-13605. (The Papers of Henry Clay). Date not set. 35.00 (ISBN 0-8131-0056-9). U Pr of Ky. Postponed.
Hargreaves, Mary W., ed. see Clay, Henry.
Hargreaves, P. H., ed. see Quinlan, P. M. & Compton, W. V.
Hargreaves, P. H., et al. French Once a Week Book, 2 bks. 1976. pap. 5.25x ea. (Pub. by Basil Blackwell); Bk. 1, Repr. Of 1961 Ed. pap. (ISBN 0-631-97290-0); Bk. 2, Repr. Of 1962 Ed. pap. (ISBN 0-631-97300-1). Biblio Dist.
Hargreaves, Reginald, jt. auth. see Melville, Lewis.
Hargreaves, William A., jt. auth. see Glick, Ira D.
Hargreaves-Mawdsley, W. N. Oxford in the Age of John Locke. (Centers of Civilization Ser: Vol. 32). 160p. 1973. 6.95 (ISBN 0-8061-1038-4). U of Okla Pr.
Hargrove, Barbara. Religion for a Dislocated Generation. 144p. 1981. 9.95 (ISBN 0-8170-0891-8). Judson.
--The Sociology of Religion: Classical & Contemporary Approaches. LC 79-50879. 1979. pap. text ed. 11.95x (ISBN 0-88295-211-0). AHM Pub.
Hargrove, Erwin C. The Power of the Modern Presidency. 1974. pap. text ed. 6.50x o.p. (ISBN 0-394-31724-6). Random.
Hargrove, Jim & Cooper, Harry. Five Hundred Things to Do in Florida for Free. 140p. Date not set. pap. 3.95 (ISBN 0-695-81564-4). Follett. Postponed.
Hargrove, Jim, ed. see Villari, Jack & Villari, Kathleen S.
Hargrove, Jim, et al. Five Hundred Things to Do in Houston for Free. 140p. Date not set. pap. 3.95 (ISBN 0-695-81563-6). Follett. Postponed.
Hargrove, June, jt. auth. see Doezema, Marianne.
Hargrove, June E. The Life & Work of Albert Carrier-Belleuse. LC 76-23625. (Outstanding Dissertations in the Fine Arts - 19th Century). (Illus.). 1977. Repr. lib. bdg. 70.00 (ISBN 0-8240-2695-0). Garland Pub.
Hargrove, Merwin M., et al. Cases in Administrative Policies & Contemporary Issues. 4th ed. 1973. text ed. 18.50 (ISBN 0-256-01433-7). Irwin.
Haried, Andrew A., et al. Advanced Accounting. LC 78-21944. (Accounting & Information Systems Ser.). 1979. 22.95 (ISBN 0-471-02374-4); tchrs. manual (ISBN 0-471-05298-1); working papers (ISBN 0-471-05345-7); checklist avail. (ISBN 0-471-05964-1); test avail. (ISBN 0-471-05874-2). Wiley.
Harihar Das, Swami & Ito, Dee. The Healthy Body Handbook: A Basic Guide to Diet & Nutrition, Yoga for Health, & Natural Cures for a Healthy Body. LC 79-2802. (Illus.). 1980. pap. 5.95 (ISBN 0-06-090730-4, CN 730, CN). Har-Row.
Harik, Iliya, jt. ed. see Cantori, Louis J.
Harik, Iliya F. Political Mobilization of Peasants: A Study of an Egyptian Community. LC 73-16535. (International Development Research Center, Studies in Development: No. 8). 320p. 1974. 12.50x (ISBN 0-253-34535-9). Ind U Pr.
Harin, Anantham, jt. auth. see Ferrara, Angelo.
Haring. Complete Book of Growing Plants. pap. 5.95 (ISBN 0-8015-1489-4, Hawthorn). Dutton.
Haring, Bernard. Blessed Are the Pure in Heart: The Beatitudes. (Illus.). 1977. pap. 4.95 (ISBN 0-8164-2125-0). Crossroad NY.
--Embattled Witness: Memories of a Time of War. 1976. 6.95 (ISBN 0-8164-0312-0). Crossroad NY.
--The Ethics of Manipulation: Issues in Medicine, Behavior Control & Genetics. 200p. 1976. 8.95 (ISBN 0-8164-0289-2). Crossroad NY.
--The Eucharist & Our Everyday Life. (Orig.). 1979. pap. 3.95 (ISBN 0-8164-0037-7). Crossroad NY.
--Free & Faithful in Christ: General Moral Theology for Clergy & Laity, Vol. 1. 1978. 17.50 (ISBN 0-8164-0398-8). Crossroad NY.
--Free & Faithful in Christ: Light to the World, Vol. 3. 500p. 1981. 19.50 (ISBN 0-8245-0009-1). Crossroad NY.
--Free & Faithful in Christ: The Truth Will Set You Free, Vol. 2. 560p. 1979. 17.50 (ISBN 0-8164-0205-1). Crossroad NY.
Haring, Bernard, C.Ss.R. Shalom: Peace. LC 75-78750. pap. 1.95 o.p. (ISBN 0-385-07971-0, D264, Im). Doubleday.
Haring, L. Lloyd, jt. auth. see Norris, Robert E.
Haring, Norris & Bateman, Barbara. Teaching the Learning Disabled Child. LC 76-15965. (P-H Series in Education). (Illus.). 1977. 17.95 (ISBN 0-13-893503-3). P-H.
Haring, Norris G. & Phillips, E. L. Educating Emotionally Disturbed Children. (Psychology & Human Development in Education Ser.). 1962. text ed. 17.95 o.p. (ISBN 0-07-026420-1, C). McGraw.
Haring, Norris G. & Schiefelbusch, R. L. Methods in Special Education. 1967. text ed. 16.00 o.p. (ISBN 0-07-026421-X, C). McGraw.
Haring, Norris G., jt. auth. see White, Owen R.
Haring, Norris G., et al. The Fourth R: Research in the Classroom. 1978. 15.95 (ISBN 0-675-08387-7). Merrill.
Haring, Phyllis W., jt. auth. see Saxton, Dolores F.
Harita, Shigehisa, tr. see Kawamoto, Shigeo, et al.
Harju, Lorry B., ed. see Huang, Dorothy.
Harkabi, Yehoshafat. Arab Strategies & Israel's Response. LC 77-70273. 1977. 12.95 (ISBN 0-02-913760-8); pap. 4.95 (ISBN 0-02-913780-2). Free Pr.
Harkavy, Robert E. Great Power Competition for Overseas Bases. 300p. Date not set. price not set (ISBN 0-08-025089-0). Pergamon.
Harkavy, Robert E., jt. ed. see Neuman, Stephanie G.
Harken, Dwight. Cardiac Surgery One. (Illus.). 1971. 15.00 (ISBN 0-8036-4567-8). Davis Co.
Harker, Herbert. Goldenrod. pap. 1.95 (ISBN 0-451-08557-4, J8557, Sig). NAL.
Harkey, W. G. Speak Out. LC 76-56659. 7.95 (ISBN 0-87359-022-8); pap. 3.95 (ISBN 0-87359-010-4). Northwood Inst.
Harkin, Joseph B., jt. auth. see Rising, Gerald R.
Harkins, Arthur M., jt. ed. see Redd, Kathleen M.
Harkins, Dorothy, jt. auth. see Wakefield, Frances.
Harkins, Edward F. Famous Authors: Women. LC 73-173098. Date not set. Repr. of 1906 ed. 18.00 (ISBN 0-8103-4306-1). Gale.
Harkins, Paul W., tr. from Gr. John Chrysostom Saint: Discourses Against Judaizing Christians. LC 77-8466. (Fathers of the Church Ser.: Vol. 68). Orig. Title: Logoi Kata Ioudaion. 366p. 1979. 24.00 (ISBN 0-8132-0068-7). Cath U Pr.
Harkins, Philip. The Day of the Drag Race. (gr. 7 up). 1960. 7.25 (ISBN 0-688-21223-9). Morrow.
--Day of the Drag Race. (gr. 5-9). pap. 1.25 o.p. (ISBN 0-425-03705-3, Highland). Berkley Pub.
Harkins, William E. Karel Capek. LC 62-10148. 1962. 20.00x (ISBN 0-231-02512-2). Columbia U Pr.
--Modern Czech Grammar. LC 53-397. (Slavic Studies). (Illus.). 1953. 20.00x (ISBN 0-231-09937-1). Columbia U Pr.
Harkness, David J. & McMurtry, R. Gerald. Lincoln's Favorite Poets. LC 59-9718. 1959. 7.50x (ISBN 0-87049-026-5). U of Tenn Pr.
Harkness, Don, ed. Humanistic Issues in Child Abuse. 100p. (Orig.). 1981. pap. 3.50 (ISBN 0-934996-13-X). Am Stud Pr.
Harkness, Don, ed. see Sports in American Culture Conference, University of South Florida, May 8-9 1980.
Harkness, E. L. & Mehta, M. L. Solar Radiation Control in Buildings. (Illus.). 1978. text ed. 57.00x (ISBN 0-85334-764-6, Pub. by Applied Science). Burgess-Intl Ideas.
Harkness, Georgia. Mysticism: Its Meaning & Message. LC 72-10070. 192p. 1976. pap. 3.95 (ISBN 0-687-27667-5). Abingdon.
--Understanding the Christian Faith. (Series B). 1957. pap. 2.50 o.p. (ISBN 0-687-42954-4, Apex). Abingdon.
--Understanding the Christian Faith. (Festival Ser.). 192p. 1981. pap. 1.95 (ISBN 0-687-42955-2). Abingdon.
Harkness, H. W. Elementary Plane Rigid Dynamics. (Orig.). 1964. 20.00 (ISBN 0-12-325350-0); pap. 8.50 (ISBN 0-12-325356-X). Acad Pr.
Harkness, Judith. The Determined Bachelor. (Orig.). 1981. pap. 1.95 (ISBN 0-451-09609-6, J9609, Sig). NAL.
Harkness, R. OTC Handbook: What to Recommend & Why. 1977. 10.95 (ISBN 0-87489-071-3). Med Economics.
Harkness, S. D., jt. ed. see Peterson, N. L.
Harlan. Science Experiences for the Early Childhood Years. 2nd ed. (Early Childhood Education Ser.: No. C24). 256p. 1980. pap. text ed. 10.95 (ISBN 0-675-08155-6). Merrill.
Harlan, B. J., et al. Manual of Cardiac Surgery, Vol. I. (Comprehensive Manuals of Surgical Specialities Ser.). (Illus.). 204p. 1980. 140.00 (ISBN 0-387-90393-3). Springer-Verlag.
Harlan, Calvin. Vision & Invention: A Course in Art Foundamentals. 1969. ref. ed. 18.95 (ISBN 0-13-942243-9). P-H.
Harlan, David. The Clergy & The Great Awakening in New England. Berkhofer, Robert, ed. (Studies in American History & Culture). 180p. 1980. 23.95 (ISBN 0-8357-1097-1, Pub. by UMI Res Pr). Univ Microfilms.
Harlan, Douglas S., ed. Texastat '74 & '76. LC 78-52839. 1978. pap. 15.00 (ISBN 0-911536-75-2). Trinity U Pr.
Harlan, Jeff. The Rapture. 1980. pap. 2.95. Maranatha Hse.
Harlan, Louis R. & Smock, Raymond W., eds. Booker T. Washington Papers, Vol. 10: 1909-11. LC 75-186345. 525p. 1981. 20.00 (ISBN 0-252-00800-6). U of Ill Pr.
Harlan, N. E. Management Control in Airframe Subcontracting. 1970. 19.75 (ISBN 0-08-018741-2). Pergamon.
Harland, Henry, pseud. Grandison Mather. Fletcher, Ian & Stokes, John, eds. LC 76-24391. (Decadent Consciousness Ser.). 1977. lib. bdg. 38.00 (ISBN 0-8240-2768-X). Garland Pub.
Harland, Henry. Mademoiselle Miss & Other Stories. LC 76-24385. (The Decadent Consciousness Ser.: Vol. 12). 1977. Repr. of 1893 ed. lib. bdg. 38.00 (ISBN 0-8240-2760-4). Garland Pub.
--Mea Culpa: A Woman's World. Fletcher, Ian & Stokes, John, eds. LC 76-24386. (Decadent Consciousness Ser.). 1977. lib. bdg. 38.00 (ISBN 0-8240-2761-2). Garland Pub.
Harland, John. Word Controlled Humans. LC 80-52563. 120p. 1981. 8.95 (ISBN 0-914752-13-8); pap. 5.00 (ISBN 0-914752-12-X). Sovereign Pr.
Harland, Marion. Literary Hearthstones: William Cowper. 237p. 1980. Repr. of 1899 ed. lib. bdg. 30.00 (ISBN 0-89984-286-0). Century Bookbindery.
Harlap, Amiram. New Israeli Architecture. LC 73-8291. (Illus.). 355p. 1981. 40.00 (ISBN 0-8386-1425-6). Fairleigh Dickinson.
Harle, J. C. Gupta Sculpture: Indian Sculpture of the Fourth to the Sixth Centuries A.D. (Illus.). 76p. 1975. 28.50x (ISBN 0-19-817322-9). Oxford U Pr.
Harle, Louise. Who Slept There? 1979. 9.75 o.p. (ISBN 0-8062-1165-2). Carlton.

Harle, Vilho, ed. Political Economy of Food. 346p. 1978. text ed. 30.00x (ISBN 0-566-00206-X, Pub. by Gower Pub Co England). Renouf.

Harlech, David. Must the West Decline. LC 66-20135. 1966. 15.00x (ISBN 0-231-02976-4). Columbia U Pr.

Harlech, Pamela. Pamela Harlech's Practical Guide to Cooking,Entertaining & Household Management. 1981. 16.95 (ISBN 0-686-65194-4). Atheneum.

Harlen, Wynne, jt. auth. see Ennever, Len.

Harless, Dan, jt. auth. see Baxter, Batsell Barrett.

Harleston, Rebekah M. & Stoffle, Carla J. Administration of Government Documents Collections. LC 74-81960. 1974. lib. bdg. 15.00x (ISBN 0-87287-086-3). Libs Unl.

Harley, Brian. Mate in Two Moves: The Two-Move Chess Problem Made Easy. 1970. pap. 3.50 (ISBN 0-486-22434-1). Dover.

Harley, Hess. This Land Is Mine. (Orig.). 1980. pap. 1.75 (ISBN 0-532-23227-5). Manor Bks.

Harley, J. B. Maps for the Local Historian- a Guide to the British Sources. 86p. 1972. pap. text ed. 4.90x (ISBN 0-7199-0834-5, Pub. by Bedford England). Renouf.

Harley, Johansen & Fugitt, Glen V. The Changing Rural Village of America. 1981. price not set (ISBN 0-88410-692-6). Ballinger Pub.

Harley, John B., et al, eds. Hematology Case Studies, Vol. 1. 1973. spiral bdg. 12.00 o.s.i. (ISBN 0-87488-020-3). Med Exam.

Harley, Nadezhda. Russian Tales. LC 69-12163. (Illus., Rus.). 1969. text ed. 3.95x (ISBN 0-521-07357-X). Cambridge U Pr.

Harley, Randall K. & Lawrence, G. Allen. Visual Impairment in the Schools. (Illus.). 168p. 1977. 14.75 (ISBN 0-398-03587-3). C C Thomas.

Harlow, Barbara, tr. see Derrida, Jacques.

Harlow, Enid. Crashing. 1981. pap. 2.75 (ISBN 0-553-14626-2). Bantam.

Harlow, Francis, jt. auth. see Frank, Larry.

Harlow, Francis H., jt. auth. see Chapman, Kenneth M.

Harlow, Joan. The Shadow Bear. LC 80-7507. (Illus.). 32p. (gr. 3). 1981. 7.95a (ISBN 0-385-15066-0); PLB (ISBN 0-385-15067-9). Doubleday.

Harlow, Jules. Lessons from Our Living Past. LC 72-2055. (Illus.). 128p. (gr. 4-6). 1972. text ed. 6.95x (ISBN 0-87441-085-1). Behrman.

Harlow, LeRoy F. Servants of All. (Illus.). 384p. 1981. 19.95 (ISBN 0-8425-1892-4). Brigham.

Harlow, Lewis A. Covered Bridges Can Talk. (Illus.). 1963. 4.95 o.p. (ISBN 0-87482-017-0). Wake-Brook.

Harlow, Nora. Sharing the Children. 1976. pap. 2.95 o.p. (ISBN 0-06-090512-3, CN512, CN). Har-Row.

Harlow, Nora, jt. auth. see Wenk, Ernst.

Harlow, Nora, jt. ed. see Montilla, M. Robert.

Harlow, R. E. Can We Know God? pap. 1.95 (ISBN 0-89107-064-8). Good News.

Harlow, Richard R., jt. auth. see Beasley, Maurine H.

Harlow, W. Inside Wood. Date not set. 6.50 (ISBN 0-686-26732-X, 27). Am Forestry.

Harlow, William M. Art Forms from Plant Life. LC 75-25002. Orig. Title: Patterns of Life: the Unseen World of Plants. (Illus.). 1974. pap. 4.50 (ISBN 0-486-23262-X). Dover.

--Fruit Key & Twig Key to Trees & Shrubs. (Illus.). 6.00 (ISBN 0-8446-0678-2). Peter Smith.

--Trees of Eastern & Central United States & Canada. (Illus.). 7.50 (ISBN 0-8446-0679-0). Peter Smith.

Harm, Walter. Biological Effects of Ultraviolet Radiation. LC 77-88677. (IUPAB Biophysics Ser.: No. 1). (Illus.). 1980. 29.95 (ISBN 0-521-22121-8); pap. 9.95x (ISBN 0-521-29362-6). Cambridge U Pr.

Harman, Alec, et al. Man & His Music: The Story of Musical Experience in the West. 1978. 29.95 o.p. (ISBN 0-214-15665-6, 8022, Dist. by Arco). Barrie & Jenkins.

Harman, Bob & Monroe, Keith. Use Your Head in Tennis. rev. 2nd ed. LC 74-10715. 256p. 1975. 9.95 (ISBN 0-690-00584-9, TYC-T). T Y Crowell.

--Use Your Head in Tennis. 1976. pap. 4.95 (ISBN 0-684-14765-3, SL 677, ScribT). Scribner.

Harman, Cameron G., ed. see Parmelee, C. W.

Harman, Carter. A Skyscraper Goes Up. (Illus.). (gr. 5 up). 1973. 4.95 (ISBN 0-394-82147-5). Random.

Harman, David & Brim, Orville G., Jr. Learning to Be Parents: Principles, Programs, & Methods. LC 80-24030. (Illus.). 276p. 1980. 14.95 (ISBN 0-8039-1272-2). Sage.

Harman, Denham, jt. ed. see Ordy, Mark.

Harman, Earl W. Introduction to Mechanical Drawing. new ed. (gr. 7-12). 1979. pap. text ed. 6.40 (ISBN 0-205-06580-5, 3265803). Allyn.

Harman, G. S., ed. The Politics of Education: A Bibliographical Guide. LC 74-194763. 1974. 32.50x (ISBN 0-8448-0405-3). Crane-Russak Co.

Harman, Gilbert. The Nature of Morality: An Introduction to Ethics. 1977. text ed. 9.95x (ISBN 0-19-502142-8); pap. text ed. 4.95x (ISBN 0-19-502143-6). Oxford U Pr.

Harman, Gilbert, ed. On Noam Chomsky: Critical Essays. LC 74-3558. 360p. 1974. pap. 4.95 (ISBN 0-385-03765-1, Anch). Doubleday.

Harman, Ian & Vriends, Matthew M. All About Finches. (Illus.). 1978. 9.95 (ISBN 0-87666-965-8, PS-765). TFH Pubns.

Harman, J. F. Tropospheric Waves, Jet Streams & United States Weather Patterns. LC 77-182881. (CCG Resource Papers Ser.: No. 11). (Illus.). 1971. pap. text ed. 4.00 (ISBN 0-89291-058-5). Assn Am Geographers.

Harman, R. T. Gas Turbine Engineering Applications Cycles & Characteristics. LC 80-21003. 304p. 1981. 29.95 (ISBN 0-470-27065-9). Halsted Pr.

Harman, Susan E. & House, H. Descriptive English Grammar. 2nd ed. 1950. text ed. 14.95 (ISBN 0-13-199083-7). P-H.

Harman, Willis W. An Incomplete Guide to the Future. 176p. 1979. pap. text ed. 4.95 (ISBN 0-393-95006-9). Norton.

Harman, Willis W., jt. auth. see Armstrong, Joe E.

Harmar, Hilary. Chihuahua Guide. 6.98 o.p. (ISBN 0-385-01569-0). Doubleday.

--Cocker Spaniel Guide. 6.98 o.p. (ISBN 0-385-01653-0). Doubleday.

--The Pomeranian. Foyle, Christina, ed. (Foyle's Handbks). (Illus.). 1973. 3.95 (ISBN 0-685-55796-0). Palmetto Pub.

Harmer, Florence E. Anglo-Saxon Writs. LC 80-2225. 1981. Repr. of 1952 ed. 69.50 (ISBN 0-404-18762-5). AMS Pr.

Harmer, Lewis. Uncertainties in French Grammar. Rickard, P. & Combe, G. S., eds. LC 78-58793. 1980. 80.00 (ISBN 0-521-22233-8). Cambridge U Pr.

Harmin, Merrill & Sax, Saville. The Peaceable Classroom: Activities to Calm & Free Student Energies. 1977. pap. 5.95 (ISBN 0-03-021256-1). Winston Pr.

Harmon, David P., Jr., jt. auth. see Chou, Marylin.

Harmon, Jack. Texas Missions & Landmarks. 2nd ed. (Illus.). 57p. 1978. 10.00 (ISBN 0-933164-43-2); pap. 6.95 (ISBN 0-933164-17-3). U of Tex Inst Tex Culture.

Harmon, Lenore, et al. Counseling Women. LC 77-22343. 1978. pap. text ed. 9.95 o.p. (ISBN 0-8185-0240-1). Brooks-Cole.

Harmon, Lily. Freehand. 1981. 13.95 (ISBN 0-671-41452-6). S&S.

Harmon, M. Judd, ed. Essays on the Constitution of the United States. (National University Pubns. Multi-Disciplinary Studies in the Law). 1978. 15.00 (ISBN 0-8046-9210-6). Kennikat.

Harmon, Margaret. The Mistress of Corey's Landing. 256p. (Orig.). 1981. pap. 1.95 (ISBN 0-89083-711-2). Zebra.

Harmon, Maurice. The Poetry of Thomas Kinsella. 126p. 1975. text ed. 8.50x (ISBN 0-391-00386-0); pap. text ed. 4.95x (ISBN 0-391-00387-9). Humanities.

Harmon, Maurice, ed. Image & Illusion: Anglo-Irish Literature & Its Contexts. 174p. 1979. text ed. 26.00x (ISBN 0-905473-42-6). Humanities.

--J. M. Synge Centenary Papers, 1971. 1972. text ed. 13.25x (ISBN 0-85105-203-7, Dolmen Pr). Humanities.

--Richard Murphy: Poet of Two Traditions. (Interdisciplinary Studies). (Illus.). 1978. text ed. 13.75x (ISBN 0-905473-17-5). Humanities.

Harmon, Michael M. Action Theory for Public Administration. (Longman Professional Studies in Public Administration). 256p. (Orig.). 1981. text ed. 22.50 (ISBN 0-582-28254-3); pap. text ed. 9.95 (ISBN 0-582-28255-1). Longman.

Harmon, N. Paul, jt. auth. see Margolis, Neal.

Harmon, Nolan B. Ministerial Ethics & Etiquette. rev. ed. (Series C). (Illus.). 1978. pap. 5.95 (ISBN 0-687-27033-2). Abingdon.

--Understanding the United Methodist Church, 1977 Edition. 1974. pap. 4.95 (ISBN 0-687-43005-4). Abingdon.

Harmon, Paul, jt. auth. see Seyer, Philip.

Harmon, Rebecca L. Susanna: Mother of the Wesleys. 1968. 8.95 (ISBN 0-687-40765-6). Abingdon.

Harmon, Robert B. Developing the Library Collection in Political Science. LC 75-44396. 1976. 10.00 (ISBN 0-8108-0898-6). Scarecrow.

--Political Science: A Bibliographical Guide to the Literature, 2nd Supplement. LC 65-13557. 1972. 20.50 (ISBN 0-8108-0479-4). Scarecrow.

--Political Science: A Bibliographical Guide to the Literature, 3rd Supplement. LC 65-13557. 1974. 15.00 (ISBN 0-8108-0675-4). Scarecrow.

--Political Science Bibliographies, Vol. 1. LC 72-8849. 1973. 10.00 (ISBN 0-8108-0558-8). Scarecrow.

--Political Science Bibliographies, Vol. 2. LC 72-8849. 1976. 11.00 (ISBN 0-8108-0903-6). Scarecrow.

--Understanding Ernest Hemingway: A Study & Research Guide. LC 77-14893. 1977. 8.00 o.p. (ISBN 0-8108-1074-3). Scarecrow.

Harmon, T. & Allen, C. Guide to the National Electral Code R. 1981. 21.95 (ISBN 0-13-370478-5). P-H.

Harmon, William. Legion: Civic Choruses. LC 72-11053. (Wesleyan Poetry Program: Vol. 65). 1973. 10.00 (ISBN 0-8195-2065-9, Pub. by Wesleyan U Pr); pap. 4.95 (ISBN 0-8195-1065-3). Columbia U Pr.

--Treasury Holiday. LC 78-120263. (Wesleyan Poetry Program: Vol. 53). (Orig.). 1970. 10.00x (ISBN 0-8195-2053-5, Pub. by Wesleyan U Pr); pap. 4.95 (ISBN 0-8195-1053-X). Columbia U Pr.

Harmond, Paul, ed. Farmstead Book One. (Illus.). 1978. lib. bdg. 16.50 (ISBN 0-88930-020-8, Pub. by Cloudburst Canada); pap. 8.95 (ISBN 0-88930-019-4). Madrona Pubs.

Harmony, Thalia. Neurometric Assessment of Brain Dysfunction in Neurological Patients. (Functional Neuroscience: Vol. 3). 500p. 1981. profess. refer 29.95 (ISBN 0-89859-044-2). L Erlbaum Assocs.

Harms, Alvin. Jose-Maria de Heredia. LC 74-22312. (World Authors Ser.: No. 347). 1975. lib. bdg. 12.50 (ISBN 0-8057-2421-4). Twayne.

Harms, E., ed. Drugs & Youth: The Challenge of Today. 1973. text ed. 21.00 (ISBN 0-08-017063-3). Pergamon.

Harms, Edward & Zabinski, Michael P. Introduction to APL & Computer Programming. LC 76-20587. 1977. pap. text ed. 16.95 (ISBN 0-471-35201-2); instructor's manual 1.75 (ISBN 0-471-01940-2). Wiley.

Harms, L. S. Phonetic Transcription: A Programmed Introduction. 1964. pap. 5.95x (ISBN 0-673-05707-0). Scott F.

Harms, Martin J. see Crump, Ralph W.

Harms, T., jt. auth. see Veitch, B.

Harms, Thelma & Clifford, Richard M. Early Childhood Environment Rating Scale. (Orig.). 1980. pap. 5.95x (ISBN 0-8077-2632-X); 30 scoring sheets 4.95 (ISBN 0-8077-2635-4). Tchrs Coll.

Harms, William C. Who Are We & Where Are We Going: A Parish Planning Guide. 96p. (Orig.). 1981. pap. 9.00 (ISBN 0-8215-9806-6). Sadlier.

Harmuth, H. F., jt. ed. see Marton, C.

Harmuth, Henning F. see Marton, L.

Harn, Roger E. Van see Van Harn, Roger E.

Harnack, Adolph. Mission & Expansion of Christianity in the First Three Centuries. 10.00 (ISBN 0-8446-2206-0). Peter Smith.

Harnack, R. Victor, et al. Group Discussion: Theory & Technique. 2nd ed. (Illus.). 1977. text ed. 16.95 (ISBN 0-13-365247-5). P-H.

Harnad, J. P. & Shnider, S., eds. Geometrical & Topological Methods in Gauge Theories: Proceedings. (Lecture Notes in Physics: Vol. 129). 155p. 1980. pap. 14.00 (ISBN 0-387-10010-5). Springer-Verlag.

Harnecker, Marta. Cuba: Dictatorship or Democracy? 288p. 1980. 15.95 (ISBN 0-88208-100-4); pap. 7.95 (ISBN 0-88208-101-2). Lawrence Hill.

Harned, David B. Creed & Personal Identity: The Meaning of the Apostles' Creed. LC 80-8056. 120p. 1981. 6.95 (ISBN 0-8006-0645-0, 1-645). Fortress.

--Images for Self-Recognition: The Christian As Player, Sufferer, Vandal. 1977. 10.95 (ISBN 0-8164-0334-1). Crossroad NY.

Harned, Joseph W., ed. see Atlantic Council Working Group on Nuclear Fuels Policy.

Harner, James L. Michael Drayton & Samuel Daniel: A Reference Guide. (Reference Bks.). 1980. lib. bdg. 30.00 (ISBN 0-8161-8322-8). G K Hall.

Harner, Michael. The Way of the Shaman: A Guide to Power & Healing. LC 79-2995. 192p. 1980. 9.95 (ISBN 0-06-063710-2, HarpR). Har-Row.

Harner, Michael J., ed. Hallucinogens & Shamanism. (Illus.). 224p. 1973. 14.95 (ISBN 0-19-501650-5). Oxford U Pr.

Harner, Philip B. Everlasting Life in Biblical Thought. 1981. 6.95 (ISBN 0-8062-1611-5). Carlton.

--I Am of the Fourth Gospel: A Study in Johannine Usage & Thought. Reumann, John, ed. LC 72-123506. (Facet Bks.). 72p. (Orig.). 1970. pap. 1.00 (ISBN 0-8006-3060-2, 1-3060). Fortress.

Harnett, D. L. & Murphy, J. L. Introductory Statistical Analysis. 2nd ed. 1980. 19.95 (ISBN 0-201-02758-5); student's wkbk. 5.95 (ISBN 0-201-02859-X); instructor's manual 2.95 (ISBN 0-201-02759-3). A-W.

Harnett, Donald L. Introduction to Statistical Methods. 2nd ed. LC 74-10353. (Illus.). 500p. 1975. text ed. 18.50 (ISBN 0-201-02752-6). A-W.

Harney, George E., ed. see Downing, Andrew J.

Harney, Kenneth R. Beating Inflation with Real Estate. (Illus.). 1979. 12.95 (ISBN 0-394-50342-2). Random.

Harney, Malachi L. & Cross, John C. The Narcotic Officer's Notebook. 2nd ed. (Illus.). 396p. 1975. 21.75 (ISBN 0-398-02310-7). C C Thomas.

Harney, Martin P. Catholic Church Through the Ages. LC 73-76312. 1974. 12.00 (ISBN 0-8198-0500-9); pap. 11.00 (ISBN 0-8198-0501-7). Dghtrs St Paul.

Harnik, Tema. Wherewithal: A Guide to Resources for Museums & Historical Societies. 120p. (Orig.). 1981. pap. write for info. (ISBN 0-935654-01-1, Pub. by Ctr for Arts Info). Pub Ctr Cult Res.

Harning, Kerstin E. The Analytic Genitive in the Modern Arabic Dialects. (Orientalia Gothoburgensia Ser.: No. 5). 1981. pap. text ed. 17.00 (ISBN 91-7346-087-7). Humanities.

Harnisch, Herbert. Apicoectomy. (Illus.). 151p. 1975. 42.00. Quint Pub Co.

--Clinical Aspects & Treatment of Cysts of the Jaws. (Illus.). 237p. 1974. 38.00. Quint Pub Co.

Harnsberger, Caroline T. Pilot's Ready Reference. rev ed. LC 62-20288. (Illus.). 1980. pap. 4.50 (ISBN 0-8168-7402-6). Aero.

Haro, Carlos M. Mexicano-Chicano Concerns & School Desegregation in Los Angeles. (Monograph Ser.: No. 9). (Illus.). 98p. (Orig.). 1979. pap. 4.95 (ISBN 0-89551-012-X). Ucla Chicano Stud.

Haro, Michael S., et al. Explorations in Personal Health. LC 76-10900. (Illus.). 1977. text ed. 15.75 (ISBN 0-395-24478-1); inst. manual 1.25 (ISBN 0-395-24479-X). HM.

Harold, Preston. The Shining Stranger. rev. ed. LC 73-19480. 1974. 9.50 (ISBN 0-396-06931-2, Pub. by Wayfarer Pr); pap. 6.00 (ISBN 0-396-06932-0, Pub. by Wayfarer Pr.). Dodd.

Harold Shaw Publishers, ed. The Personal Promise Pocketbook. LC 80-52398. 107p. (Orig.). 1980. pap. 1.95 (ISBN 0-87788-673-3). Shaw Pubs.

Harold, Victor. A Checklist Guide to Successful Acquisitions. LC 77-180209. 54p. (Orig.). 1980. pap. 3.50 (ISBN 0-87576-039-2). Pilot Bks.

Harold, W., jt. auth. see Crossan, R. M.

Haroldsen, Mark O. How to Wake up the Financial Genius Inside of You. 192p. 1980. pap. 2.50 (ISBN 0-553-14427-8). Bantam.

Harootunian, H. D. Toward Restoration: The Growth of Political Consciousness in Tokugawa Japan. LC 79-94993. (Center for Japanese & Korean Studies, UC Berkeley). 1970. 24.50x (ISBN 0-520-01566-5). U of Cal Pr.

Harp, Richard L. Thomas Percy's Life of Dr. Oliver Goldsmith: A Critical Edition. (Salzburg Studies in English Literature, Romantic Reassessment: No. 52). 1976. pap. text ed. 25.00x (ISBN 0-391-01398-X). Humanities.

Harpe, Shideler. Arthritis: End the Agony. Date not set. 9.95 (ISBN 0-88280-057-4). ETC Pubns. Postponed.

Harpe, Shideler & Hall, Wesley W. What Teenagers Want to Know. (Illus.). 1979. pap. 2.50 (ISBN 0-910304-11-4). Budlong.

Harpe, Shideler & Salazar, Jose L. Doctor Discuss Headaches. (Illus.). 1979. pap. 2.50 (ISBN 0-686-65548-6). Budlong.

Harper. Critical Edition of Yeats' A Vision. 1980. text ed. 42.50x (ISBN 0-333-21299-1). Humanities.

Harper, jt. auth. see Auerbach.

Harper, Charles A. Handbook of Electronic Systems Design. new ed. (Handbook Ser.). (Illus.). 832p. 1979. 35.00 (ISBN 0-07-026683-2, P&RB). McGraw.

Harper, Charles G. Haunted Houses: Tales of the Supernatural with Some Account of Hereditary Curses & Family Legends. LC 79-164326. (Illus.). xvi, 283p. 1971. Repr. of 1907 ed. 24.00 (ISBN 0-8103-3928-5). Gale.

Harper, Charles L., et al. Financial Systems for Community Health Organizations: A Manager's Guide. 1981. text ed. 24.95 (ISBN 0-534-97976-9). Lifetime Learn.

Harper, David. The Green Air. 240p. 1976. pap. 1.50 o.p. (ISBN 0-445-03143-3). Popular Lib.

--The Hanged Man. pap. 1.50 o.s.i. (ISBN 0-515-04425-3). Jove Pubns.

Harper, F. A. Toward Liberty: Essays in Honor of Ludwig Von Mises on the Occasion of His 90th Birthday, 2 vols. LC 77-181817. 1976. Repr. of 1971 ed. Set. 20.00x o.p. (ISBN 0-916054-26-8, Caroline Hse Inc). Green Hill.

--Towards Liberty. (Humane Studies). 914p. 1980. text ed. 20.00x (ISBN 0-391-02090-0). Humanities.

Harper, Floyd S. & Workman, Lewis C. Fundamental Mathematics of Life Insurance. 1970. text ed. 10.75 (ISBN 0-256-00231-2). Irwin.

Harper, Francis & Presley, Delma E. Okefinokee Album. LC 80-14220. (Illus.). 235p. 1981. 14.95 (ISBN 0-8203-0530-8). U of Ga Pr.

Harper, Frederick D. Jogotherapy: Jogging As a Therapeutic Strategy. LC 79-55453. 1979. pap. 3.95 (ISBN 0-935392-00-9). Douglass Pubs.

Harper, George M. Go Back to Where You Belong: Yeats's Return from Exile. (New Yeats Papers Ser.: Vol. 6). 40p. 1973. pap. text ed. 3.75x (ISBN 0-85105-244-4, Dolmen Pr). Humanities.

--The Mingling of Heaven & Earth: Yeats' Theory of Theatre. (New Yeats Papers Ser: No. 10). 48p. 1975. pap. text ed. 5.00x (ISBN 0-85105-269-X, Dolmen Pr). Humanities.

--W. B. Yeats & W. T. Horton: The Record of an Occult Friendship. 224p. text ed. 23.25x (ISBN 0-391-01907-4). Humanities.

Harper, Howard. Episcopalian's Dictionary. 1975. 8.95 (ISBN 0-8164-1166-2); pap. 4.50 (ISBN 0-8164-2100-5). Crossroad NY.

Harper, Howard V. Profiles of Protestant Saints. LC 67-24071. 1968. 7.95 (ISBN 0-8303-0037-6). Fleet.

Harper, J. C., jt. auth. see Crimes, T. P.

Harper, J. J., jt. auth. see Pope, Alan.

Harper, J. Russell. Paul Kane's Frontier. LC 79-146522. (Illus.). 1971. 35.00 o.p. (ISBN 0-292-70110-1). Amon Carter.

Harper, James E., jt. auth. see Davisson, William I.

Harper, John C. Elements of Food Engineering. (Illus.). 1976. lib. bdg. 28.50 o.p. (ISBN 0-87055-218-X); pap. text ed. 17.00 (ISBN 0-87055-299-6). AVI.

Harper, John D. Corporate Role in Society. LC 77-75047. 1977. 7.50x (ISBN 0-915604-11-6). Columbia U Pr.

Harper, Judson M. Extrusion of Foods. 1981. Vol. 1. 59.95 (ISBN 0-8493-5203-7); Vol. 2. 46.95 (ISBN 0-8493-5204-5). CRC Pr.

Harper, Mary-Angela. Ascent to Excellence in Catholic Education: A Guide to Effective Decision-Making. 7.95. Natl Cath Educ.

Harper, Mary J., jt. auth. see Chaiken, William E.

Harper, Michael. Live by the Spirit: How to Grow in Your Relationship with God. 154p. 1980. pap. 2.25 (ISBN 0-89283-094-8). Servant.

--Walk in the Spirit: Seeking & Understanding the Baptism in the Holy Spirit. LC 78-135047. 98p. 1968. pap. 2.50 o.p. (ISBN 0-912106-70-0). Logos.

Harper, Mike. The Directory of Inland Waterway Facilities. (Illus.). 1979. pap. 5.95 o.s.i. (ISBN 0-7134-1292-5). Hippocrene Bks.

--Directory of Inland Waterway Facilities. 1978. pap. 10.50 (ISBN 0-7134-1292-5, Pub. by Batsford England). David & Charles.

Harper, N. J. & Simmonds, A. B., eds. Advances in Drug Research. Incl. Vol. 1. 1964. 28.00 (ISBN 0-12-013301-6); Vol. 2. 1966. 28.00 (ISBN 0-12-013302-4); Vol. 3. 1966. 29.50 (ISBN 0-12-013302-2); Vol. 5. 1970. o.s.i. (ISBN 0-12-013305-9); Vol. 6. 1972. 18.65 o.s.i. (ISBN 0-12-013306-7); Vol. 7. 1974. 32.50 (ISBN 0-12-013307-5). Acad Pr.

Harper, Nancy. Human Communication Theory: History of a Paraigm. 320p. 1979. pap. 9.95x (ISBN 0-8104-6091-2). Hayden.

Harper, Paula, jt. auth. see Shikes, Ralph E.

Harper, Robert A. & Schmudde, Theodore H. Between Two Worlds: An Introduction to Geography. 2nd ed. LC 77-76418. (Illus.). 1977. text ed. 21.50 (ISBN 0-395-25164-8); inst. manual 0.90 (ISBN 0-395-25165-6). HM.

Harper, Robert F., intro. by. Assyrian & Bablyonian Literature. 462p. 1980. Repr. of 1904 ed. lib. bdg. 50.00 (ISBN 0-89984-292-5). Century Bookbindery.

Harper, Robert G., et al. Nonverbal Communication: The State of the Art. LC 77-19185. (Personality Processes Ser.). 1978. 28.95 (ISBN 0-471-02672-7, Pub. by Wiley-Interscience). Wiley.

Harper, Susan, ed. see Pashdag, John & Woller, Jim.

Harper, Susan, ed. see Stokell, Marjorie.

Harper, T. A. Laboratory Guide to Disordered Hemostasis. 1970. 14.95 (ISBN 0-407-74250-6). Butterworths.

Harper, Thomas J., jt. ed. see Murakami, Hyoye.

Harper, W. J. & Hall, Carl W. Dairy Technology & Engineering. (Illus.). 1976. pap. text ed. 26.00 (ISBN 0-87055-296-1). AVI.

Harper, W. R. Amos & Hosea. LC 5-7893. (International Critical Commentary Ser.). 608p. Repr. of 1905 ed. text ed. 20.00x (ISBN 0-567-05018-1). Attic Pr.

Harper, Wilhelmina, ed. Gunniwolf. (Illus.). (ps-3). 1967. PLB 8.95 (ISBN 0-525-31139-4). Dutton.

--Harvest Feast. rev. ed. (Illus.). (gr. 5 up). 1967. PLB 7.95 o.p. (ISBN 0-525-31510-1). Dutton.

--Merry Christmas to You. rev. ed. (Illus.). (gr. 2 up). 1965. PLB 7.95 o.p. (ISBN 0-525-34852-2). Dutton.

Harper, William. Data Processing Documentation: Standards, Procedures & Applications. 1973. 27.95 o.p. (ISBN 0-13-196782-7). P-H.

--Enameling, Step by Step. (Step by Step Craft Ser). (Illus.). 80p. 1973. PLB 9.15 o.p. (ISBN 0-307-62006-9, Golden Pr); pap. 2.95 o.p. (ISBN 0-307-42010-8). Western Pub.

Harper, William A. Community, Junior, & Technical Colleges: A Public Relations Sourcebook. new ed. LC 77-1993. (Illus.). 1977. text ed. 19.95 (ISBN 0-89116-043-4). Hemisphere Pub.

Harpin, William. The Second "R". (Unwin Education Bks.: No. 31). text ed. 17.95x (ISBN 0-04-372018-8); pap. text ed. 8.95x (ISBN 0-04-372019-6). Allen Unwin.

Harpsfield, Nicholas, jt. auth. see Roper, William.

Harpstead, Milo I. & Hole, Francis D. Soil Science Simplified. (Illus.). 121p. (gr. 9-12). 1980. pap. text ed. 7.75 (ISBN 0-8138-1515-0). Iowa St U Pr.

Harr, Barbara. Mortgaged Wife. LC 77-112871. (New Poetry Ser). 85p. 1970. 5.00 o.p. (ISBN 0-8040-0215-0); pap. 3.50 (ISBN 0-8040-0216-9). Swallow.

Harr, John E., jt. auth. see Mosher, Frederick C.

Harragan, Betty L. Games Mother Never Taught You: Corporate Gamesmanship for Women. 400p. 1978. pap. 2.95 (ISBN 0-446-93685-5); pap. 6.95 (ISBN 0-446-97726-8). Warner Bks.

Harrah, Barbara K. Sports Books for Children: An Annotated Bibliography. LC 78-18510. 1978. 25.00 (ISBN 0-8108-1154-5). Scarecrow.

Harrah, Barbara K. & Harrah, David F. Alternate Sources of Energy: A Bibliography of Solar, Geothermal, Wind & Tidal Energy, & Environmental Architecture. LC 75-17853. 1975. 10.00 (ISBN 0-8108-0839-0). Scarecrow.

--Funeral Service: A Bibliography of Literature on Its Past, Present, & Future, the Various Means of Disposition, & Memorialization. LC 76-40340. 1976. 18.00 (ISBN 0-8108-0946-X). Scarecrow.

Harrah, Barbara K., jt. auth. see Harrah, David F.

Harrah, David F. & Harrah, Barbara K. Conservation-Ecology: Resources for Environmental Education. LC 74-23055. 1975. 14.50 (ISBN 0-8108-0780-7). Scarecrow.

Harrah, David F., jt. auth. see Harrah, Barbara K.

Harre, R. Matter & Method. 1979. Repr. of 1964 ed. lib. bdg. 20.00 (ISBN 0-917930-28-2); pap. text ed. 5.00x (ISBN 0-917930-08-8). Ridgeview.

Harre, R. & Eastwood, D. G. The Method of Science. LC 76-116973. (Wykeham Science Ser.: No. 8). 1970. 9.95x (ISBN 0-8448-1110-6). Crane-Russak Co.

Harre, R. & Secord, Paul F. The Explanation of Social Behaviour. (Quality Paperback: No. 269). 327p. 1979. pap. 5.95 (ISBN 0-8226-0269-5). Littlefield.

Harre, R., ed. Scientific Thought Nineteen Hundred to Nineteen Sixty: A Selective Survey. 1969. 24.95x (ISBN 0-19-858125-4); pap. 12.50x (ISBN 0-19-858126-2). Oxford U Pr.

Harre, Rom. Life Sentences: Aspects of the Social Role of Language. LC 75-40021. 1976. text ed. 25.50 (ISBN 0-471-35245-4); pap. 12.75 (ISBN 0-471-35244-6, Pub. by Wiley-Interscience). Wiley.

--Social Being: A Theory for Social Psychology. 438p. 1980. 25.00x (ISBN 0-8476-6284-5). Rowman.

Harrel, Linda. Sea Lightning. (Harlequin Romances Ser.). (Orig.). 1980. pap. text ed. 1.25 o.p. (ISBN 0-373-02337-5, Pub. by Harlequin). PB.

Harrell, Irene, jt. auth. see Hill, Harold.

Harrell, Irene, jt. auth. see Roth, Sid.

Harrell, Irene B. God Ventures. 1975. pap. 1.95 o.p. (ISBN 0-88270-136-3). Logos.

Harrell, Irene B., jt. auth. see Hill, Harold.

Harrell, Pat E. Letter of Paul to the Philippians. Ferguson, Everett, et al, eds. LC 71-79956. (Living Word New Testament Commentary Ser.: Vol. 12). 1969. 7.95 (ISBN 0-8344-0004-9). Sweet.

Harrell, Phillip A. Liquid Dawn & Crystal Fire. 40p. (Orig.). 1980. pap. 2.00 (ISBN 0-934852-51-0). Lorien Hse.

Harrell, Richard S. A Short Reference Grammar of Moroccan Arabic. (Richard Slade Harrell Arabic Ser.). 263p. 1962. pap. 8.50 (ISBN 0-87840-006-0); one cassette 5.00 (ISBN 0-87840-016-8); write for info. five-inch reel (ISBN 0-87840-017-6). Georgetown U Pr.

Harrell, Robert A., jt. auth. see Firestein, Gary S.

Harrell, Sara G. Semo: A Dolphin's Search for Christ. (Illus.). (gr. 5-7). 1977. 5.95 (ISBN 0-570-03458-2, 56-1292); pap. 2.50 (ISBN 0-570-03459-0, 56-1293). Concordia.

--Willowcat & the Chimney Sweep. LC 80-81702. (Illus.). 1980. 6.95 (ISBN 0-931948-07-X). Peachtree Pubs.

--Willowcat & the Chimney Sweep. (Illus.). 32p. 1980. 6.95 (ISBN 0-931948-07-X). Peachtree Pubs.

Harrell, Stevan, jt. ed. see Amoss, Pamela T.

Harrelson, Max, jt. ed. see Cordier, Andrew W.

Harrelson, Walter. The Ten Commandments & Human Rights. Brueggemann, Walter & Donahue, John R., eds. LC 77-15234. (Overtures to Biblical Theology). 240p. 1980. pap. 9.95 (ISBN 0-8006-1527-1, 1-1527). Fortress.

Harrelson, Walter J. From Fertility Cult to Worship. LC 66-14929. (Scholars Press Reprint Ser.: No. 4). pap. 9.00x (ISBN 0-89130-379-0, 00 07 04). Scholars Pr CA.

Harrer, G. A., jt. auth. see Howe, George.

Harrickman, Ray E. Business Failures: Causes Remedies & Cures. LC 79-84672. 1979. pap. text ed. 17.00 (ISBN 0-8191-0742-5). U Pr of Amer.

Harrier, Richard. The Canon of Sir Thomas Wyatt's Poetry. LC 74-82812. 352p. 1975. text ed. 16.50x (ISBN 0-674-09460-3). Harvard U Pr.

Harries, C., jt. auth. see Towell, D.

Harries, G. V. IBM Disk Storage Technology. (IBM Product Design & Development Ser.). (Illus.). 103p. 1980. pap. text ed. 3.80 (ISBN 0-933186-02-9, GA-26-1665-0). IBM Armonk.

Harries, Keith D. & Brunn, Stanley D. The Geography of Laws & Justice: Spatial Perspectives on the Criminal Justice System. LC 77-25460. (Praeger Special Studies). 1978. 24.95 (ISBN 0-03-022331-8). Praeger.

Harries, Phillip T., tr. from Japanese. The Poetic Memoirs of Lady Daibu. LC 79-65519. 336p. 1980. 17.50x (ISBN 0-8047-1077-5). Stanford U Pr.

Harrigan. Political Change in the Metropolis. 2nd ed. 1981. pap. text ed. 9.95 (ISBN 0-316-34744-2); training manual free (ISBN 0-316-34745-0). Little.

Harrigan, Patrick. Lyceens et Collegiens Sous le Second Empire. LC 79-15711. (Illus.). 240p. (Orig., Fr.). 1979. pap. 21.00 (ISBN 2-901725-06-6, IS-00083, Pub. by Maison Science France). Univ Microfilms.

Harriman. Leroy the Lobster & Crabby Crab. 1967. pap. 3.00 (ISBN 0-89272-000-X). Down East.

Harriman, Phillip L. Modern Psychology. (Quality Paperback: No. 20). (Orig.). 1975. pap. 3.95 (ISBN 0-8226-0020-X). Littlefield.

Harriman, Sarah. Book of Ginseng. (Health Ser.). (Orig.). 1973. pap. 1.75 (ISBN 0-515-05438-0, A2988). Jove Pubns.

Harring, Mike, jt. auth. see Jones, C. M.

Harrington, Anthony P. Every Boy's Judo. (Illus.). (YA) (RL 7). 1971. pap. 0.95 o.p. (ISBN 0-451-06407-0, Q6407, Sig). NAL.

--Science of Judo. (Illus.). 6.95 o.s.i. (ISBN 0-87523-143-8). Emerson.

Harrington, Bob. Motivating Men for the Master. LC 71-155682. 1971. 3.50 o.p. (ISBN 0-8054-2406-7). Broadman.

Harrington, Charles D. Uranium Production Technology. 584p. 1959. 27.50 (ISBN 0-442-03154-8, Pub. by Van Nos Reinhold). Krieger.

Harrington, Daniel J. God's People in Christ: New Testament Perspectives on the Church & Judaism, No. 7. Brueggemann, Walter & Donahue, John R., eds. LC 79-7380. (Overtures to Biblical Theology Ser.). 144p. 1980. pap. 6.50 (ISBN 0-8006-1531-X, 1-1531). Fortress.

--The Gospel According to Mark: An Access Guide. 128p. (Orig.). 1981. pap. 4.95 (ISBN 0-8215-9835-X). Sadlier.

--Interpreting the New Testament: A Practical Guide. Harrington, Wilfrid & Senior, Donald, eds. (New Testament Message Ser.: Vol. 1). 1979. 9.00 (ISBN 0-89453-124-7); pap. 4.95 (ISBN 0-89453-189-1). M Glazier.

Harrington, Daniel J., ed. & tr. from Heb. The Hebrew Fragments of Pseudo-Philo. LC 73-89170. (Society of Biblical Literature. Texts & Translation-Psuedepigrapha Ser.). 1974. pap. 4.50 (ISBN 0-88414-036-9, 060203). Scholars Pr Ca.

Harrington, Fred H. The Future of Adult Education: New Responsibilities of Colleges & Universities. LC 76-19499. (Higher Education Ser). 1977. 13.95x (ISBN 0-87589-301-5). Jossey-Bass.

Harrington, Geri. The College Cookbook. rev. ed. LC 72-11138. 1977. pap. 3.95 o.p. (ISBN 0-684-15269-X, SL740, ScribT). Scribner.

--Fireplace Stoves, Hearths, & Inserts. LC 80-7587. (Illus.). 192p. 1980. 20.00 (ISBN 0-06-011821-0, HarpT). Har-Row.

--Fireplace Stoves, Hearths, & Inserts: A Guide & Catalog. LC 80-7587. (Illus.). 192p. 1980. pap. 8.95 (ISBN 0-06-090804-1, CN 804, CN). Har-Row.

--Never Too Old. 256p. 1981. cancelled (ISBN 0-8129-0913-5). Times Bks.

--The Wood-Burning Stove Book. LC 77-7401. (Illus.). 1977. pap. 9.95 (ISBN 0-02-080250-1, Collier). Macmillan.

--The Woodburning Stove Book. 1977. 14.95 (ISBN 0-02-548440-0). Macmillan.

Harrington, H. D. How to Identify Grasses & Grasslike Plants. LC 76-17744. (Illus.). 142p. 1977. pap. 5.95x (ISBN 0-8040-0746-2). Swallow.

--Manual of the Plants of Colorado. rev. ed. LC 73-5952. 1964. 41.00 o.p. (ISBN 0-8040-0195-2, SB); microfilm 81.90 o.p. (ISBN 0-686-66544-9). Swallow.

Harrington, H. D. & Durrell, L. W. How to Identify Plants. LC 57-4731. (Illus.). 203p. 1957. pap. 5.95x (ISBN 0-8040-0149-9, 16). Swallow.

Harrington, James. The Political Writings of James Harrington: Representative Selections. Blitzer, Charles, ed. LC 80-21163. (The Library of Liberal Arts: No. 38). xlii, 165p. 1980. Repr. of 1955 ed. lib. bdg. 22.50x (ISBN 0-313-22670-9, HAWR). Greenwood.

--Works: The Oceana & Other Works with an Account of His Life by John Toland. LC 34-35411. (Illus.). 654p. 1980. Repr. of 1771 ed. 110.00x (ISBN 3-511-00042-4). Intl Pubns Serv.

Harrington, John. Film and-as Literature. (Illus.). 1977. pap. text ed. 11.95 (ISBN 0-13-315945-0). P-H.

Harrington, Karl P. Richard Alsop "A Hartford Wit". LC 69-17788. 1969. 12.00x (ISBN 0-8195-4000-5, Pub. by Wesleyan U Pr). Columbia U Pr.

Harrington, LaMar. Ceramics in the Pacific Northwest: A History. LC 78-4369. (Index of Art in the Pacific Northwest: No. 10). (Illus.). 128p. 1979. 15.95 (ISBN 0-295-95623-2). U of Wash Pr.

Harrington, Lyn. Australia & New Zealand: Pacific Community. LC 70-82914. (World Neighbors Ser). (Illus.). (gr. 6 up). 1969. PLB 6.80 o.p. (ISBN 0-525-67007-6). Elsevier-Nelson.

Harrington, Michael. Accidental Century. 1965. 12.95 (ISBN 0-02-548200-9). Macmillan.

--Decade of Decision. 1981. pap. 6.95 (ISBN 0-671-42808-X, Touchstone). S&S.

--Decade of Decision: The Crisis of the American System. 354p. 11.95. S&S.

--Other America. (YA) (gr. 11 up). 1971. pap. 3.50 (ISBN 0-14-021308-2, Pelican). Penguin.

--The Other America: Poverty in the United States. rev. ed. (gr. 8 up). 1970. 10.95 (ISBN 0-02-548230-0). Macmillan.

--Toward a Democratic Left. 1968. 12.95 o.s.i. (ISBN 0-02-548450-8). Macmillan.

Harrington, Michael, jt. auth. see Rodgers, Harrell R.

Harrington, R. E. The Seven of Swords. 1977. pap. 1.95 o.p. (ISBN 0-685-78261-1, 40-069-1). Pinnacle Bks.

Harrington, Richard, jt. auth. see Morgan, E. Victor.

Harrington, Rodney E. see Bloomfield, Victor A.

Harrington, T. J., jt. auth. see Earnshaw, A.

Harrington, Wilfrid. Mark. Senior, Donald, ed. (New Testament Message Ser.: Vol. 4). 270p. 1979. 10.95 (ISBN 0-89453-127-1); pap. 6.95 (ISBN 0-89453-192-1). M Glazier.

Harrington, Wilfrid, ed. see Collins, Adela Y.

Harrington, Wilfrid, ed. see Crowe, Jerome.

Harrington, Wilfrid, ed. see Harrington, Daniel J.

Harrington, Wilfrid, ed. see Karris, Robert J.

Harrington, Wilfrid, ed. see McPolin, James.

Harrington, Wilfrid, ed. see Maly, Eugene H.

Harrington, Wilfrid, ed. see Reese, James M.

Harris. Bledding Sorrow. 408p. 1977. pap. 1.95 (ISBN 0-380-00936-6, 31971). Avon.

--Manufacturing Technology, No. 3. 1981. text ed. price not set (ISBN 0-408-00493-2). Butterworth.

--Overdrive: A Human Maintenance Manual. 1978. 11.95 (ISBN 0-7153-7399-4). David & Charles.

Harris, ed. Recent Advances in Sexually Transmitted Diseases, No. 2. 1981. text ed. 45.00 (ISBN 0-443-01817-0). Churchill.

Harris, A. Bradley, ed. see Moore, Robin.

Harris, Alan. Teaching Morality & Religion. (Classroom Close-Ups Ser.). 1975. text ed. 10.95x o.p. (ISBN 0-04-371029-8); pap. text ed. 6.50x (ISBN 0-04-371030-1). Allen Unwin.

Harris, Albert J. & Sipay, Edward R. How to Increase Reading Ability. 7th ed. (Illus.). 736p. 1980. text ed. 18.95 (ISBN 0-582-28066-4). Longman.

--How to Increase Reading Ability: A Guide to Developmental & Remedial Methods. 6th ed. 1978. text ed. 16.95x o.p. (ISBN 0-582-28089-3). Longman.

--How to Teach Reading: A Competency-Based Program. LC 77-17722. 1979. pap. text ed. 14.95x (ISBN 0-582-28048-6). Longman.

Harris, Alice C. Georgian Syntax: A Study in Relational Grammar. (Cambridge Studies in Linguistics: No. 33). (Illus.). 300p. Date not set. price not set (ISBN 0-521-23584-7). Cambridge U Pr.

Harris, Andrea. Byzantine Encounter. LC 78-71422. 1979. pap. 1.50 o.p. (ISBN 0-87216-504-3). Playboy Pbks.

--An Irish Affair. LC 78-59970. 1978. pap. 1.50 o.p. (ISBN 0-87216-492-6). Playboy Pbks.
--A Scream Away. LC 78-62017. 1979. pap. 1.50 o.p. (ISBN 0-87216-510-8). Playboy Pbks.
--Windfall. LC 78-78053. 1979. pap. 1.75 o.p. (ISBN 0-87216-544-2). Playboy Pbks.
Harris, Aurand. The Arkansaw Bear. (Orig.). 1980. playscript 2.00 (ISBN 0-87602-226-3). Anchorage.
Harris, B. E., ed. A History of the County of Chester, Vol. 3. (Victoria History of the Counties of England Ser.). (Illus.). 260p. 1980. 149.00 (ISBN 0-19-722754-6). Oxford U Pr.
Harris, B. F., ed. Auckland Classical Essays: Presented to E. M. Blaiklock. 234p. 1970. 10.25x o.p. (ISBN 0-19-647597-X). Oxford U Pr.
Harris, Barbara, jt. auth. see Roland, Alan.
Harris, Barbara J. Beyond Her Sphere: Women & the Professions in American History. LC 78-4017. (Contributions in Women's Studies: No. 4). 1978. lib. bdg. 17.95x (ISBN 0-313-20415-2, HBS/). Greenwood.
Harris, Beatrice C. As I Passed by. 1977. 3.00 (ISBN 0-686-28895-5). Klassen.
--Opal Springs. 1979. 3.50 (ISBN 0-686-28896-3). Klassen.
Harris, Ben C., ed. The Compleat Herbal. LC 77-185615. 243p. (Orig.). 1972. pap. 1.75 (ISBN 0-915962-15-2). Larchmont Bks.
Harris, Ben M. Supervisory Behavior in Education. 2nd ed. LC 74-13100. (Illus.). 480p. 1975. ref. ed. 17.95x (ISBN 0-13-877118-9). P-H.
Harris, Benjamin. The Protestant Tutor. Lurie, Alison & Schiller, Justin G., eds. Incl. The New-England Primer, Enlarged. LC 75-32135. (Classics of Children's Literature 1621-1932 Ser.). PLB 38.00 (ISBN 0-8240-2252-1). Garland Pub.
Harris, Benjamin see Janeway, James.
Harris, Bernard, jt. ed. see Brown, John R.
Harris, Bernice K., ed. Southern Home Remedies. (Illus.). 1968. 6.50 (ISBN 0-930230-22-1). Johnson NC.
Harris, Bernice K., ed. see Chowan College Creative Writing Group & North Carolina Writers Conference.
Harris, Beth C. Little Green Frog. (gr. 4-6). pap. 1.50 (ISBN 0-8024-1480-X). Moody.
Harris, Beth K., jt. auth. see Robertson, Frank C.
Harris, Bill. Israel. (Illus.). 1980. 24.95 (ISBN 0-686-68761-2). Mayflower Bks.
Harris, Brice. The Poems of Charles Sackville, Sixth Earl of Dorset. LC 78-61562. 1979. lib. bdg. write for info. (ISBN 0-8240-9753-X). Garland Pub.
Harris, Brownie, jt. auth. see Glassner, Lester.
Harris, C. C. Readings in Kinship in Urban Society. 1970. 23.00 (ISBN 0-08-016039-5); pap. 12.75 (ISBN 0-08-016038-7). Pergamon.
Harris, C. Cleland. Spanish Programmatic Course, Vol. 1. LC 75-5674. (Spoken Language Ser.). xii, 464p. (Span., Prog. Bk.). (gr. 9-12). 1975. pap. 12.00 (ISBN 0-87950-354-8); cassettes 24 hr dual track 110.00x (ISBN 0-87950-358-0); cassettes with course-bk 115.00x (ISBN 0-87950-359-9). Spoken Lang Serv.
--Spanish Programmatic Course, Vol. 2. LC 75-5674. (Spoken Language Ser.). (Span. Prog. Bk.). 1978. pap. 12.00x (ISBN 0-87950-356-4); 16 dual track cassettes 80.00x (ISBN 0-87950-360-2); cassettes with course book 90.00 (ISBN 0-87950-361-0); vols. 1 & 2 & cassettes 1 & 2 200.00x (ISBN 0-87950-362-9). Spoken Lang Serv.
Harris, C. R. The Heart & the Vascular System in Ancient Greek Medicine: From Alcmaeon to Galen. (Illus.). 500p. 1971. 74.00x (ISBN 0-19-858135-1). Oxford U Pr.
Harris, Carl M., jt. auth. see Gross, Donald.
Harris, Carl V. Political Power in Birmingham, 1871-1921. LC 77-1110. (Twentieth Century America Ser.). (Illus.). 1977. 16.50x (ISBN 0-87049-211-X). U of Tenn Pr.
Harris, Catherine. Practical Pony Keeping. LC 64-16608. (Illus.). 1964. lib. bdg. 4.50 o. p. o.p. (ISBN 0-668-01191-2); pap. 2.95 o.p. (ISBN 0-668-04260-5). Arco.
Harris, Cecelia C. A Primer of Cardiac Arrhythmis: A Self Instructional Program. LC 78-27022. 1979. pap. text ed. 9.50 (ISBN 0-8016-2070-8). Mosby.
Harris, Charlaine. Sweet & Deadly. 180p. 1981. 8.95 (ISBN 0-395-30532-2). HM.
Harris, Charles. The Proofs of Christianity. LC 77-77215. (Radiant Life Ser.). 1977. pap. 1.50 (ISBN 0-88243-911-1, 02-0911); teacher's ed 2.50 (ISBN 0-88243-181-1, 320-181). Gospel Pub.
--What's Ahead? (Radiant Life Ser.). 128p. (Orig.). 1981. pap. price not set. Gospel Pub.
Harris, Charles M. & Gardenhour, Nancy D. Developmental Tasks Resource Guide for Elementary School Children. LC 75-21740. 1976. 15.00 (ISBN 0-8108-0877-3). Scarecrow.
Harris, Charles S., ed. Visual Coding & Adaptability. LC 79-26604. (Illus.). 400p. 1980. 24.95 (ISBN 0-89859-016-7). L Erlbaum Assocs.
Harris, Chauncy D. Annotated World List of Selected Current Geographical Serials. rev., 4th ed. LC 80-17561. (Research Papers: No. 194). 165p. 1980. pap. 8.00 (ISBN 0-89065-101-9). U Chicago Dept Geog.
Harris, Chauncy D. & Fellmann, Jerome D. International List of Geographical Serials. rev., 3rd ed. LC 80-16392. (Research Papers: No. 193). 457p. 1980. pap. 8.00 (ISBN 0-89065-100-0). U Chicago Dept Geog.
Harris, Chris, et al, eds. The Sociology of the Family: New Directions for Britain. (Sociological Review Monograph: No. 28). 240p. 1979. 30.00x (ISBN 0-8476-3265-2); pap. 18.95x (ISBN 0-8476-3258-X). Rowman.
Harris, Christie. Mouse Woman & the Vanished Princesses. LC 75-23147. (Illus.). 192p. (gr. 4-6). 1976. 7.95 (ISBN 0-689-30502-8). Atheneum.
Harris, Christina. Nationalism & Revolution in Egypt: The Role O the Muslim Brotherhood. LC 79-2861. 276p. 1981. Repr. of 1964 ed. 22.50 (ISBN 0-8305-0034-0). Hyperion Conn.
Harris, Clyde E., Jr., jt. auth. see Still, Richard.
Harris, Curtis, jt. ed. see Prescott, David M.
Harris, Cyril. Trees & Shrubs in the Modern Garden. 1975. 12.95 (ISBN 0-7207-0855-9, Pub. by Michael Joseph). Merrimack Bk Serv.
Harris, D. J. & Robson, P. D. The Physical Basis of Electronics. rev. ed. LC 74-996. 1974. text ed. 19.50 (ISBN 0-08-017900-2); pap. text ed. 13.25 (ISBN 0-08-017901-0). Pergamon.
--Vacuum & Solid State Electronics. 1963. 23.00 (ISBN 0-08-009960-2); pap. 10.50 o.p. (ISBN 0-08-009959-9). Pergamon.
Harris, D. J., et al. Coal, Gas & Electricity Industries. (Reviews of United Kingdom Statistical Sources Ser.: Vol. XI). 1979. 55.00 (ISBN 0-08-022461-X). Pergamon.
Harris, Dale B. & Pinder, Glenn D. Goodenough-Harris Test Examination of Intellectual Maturity of Youths 12-17 Years: Demographic & Socioeconomic Factors. (Ser. 11: No. 159). 70p. 1976. pap. text ed. 1.50 (ISBN 0-8406-0068-2). Natl Ctr Health Stats.
Harris, Daniel, jt. auth. see Schoep, Arthur.
Harris, David. I Shoulda Been Home Yesterday. 1976. 7.95 o.s.i. (ISBN 0-440-04156-2, Sey Lawr). Delacorte.
--Socialist Origins in the United States: American Forerunners of Marx, 1817-1832. (Publications on Social History). 1966. text ed. 10.50x (ISBN 90-232-0269-4). Humanities.
Harris, David P. Reading Improvement: Exercises for Students of English As a Second Language. (Orig.). 1966. pap. text ed. 7.95 (ISBN 0-13-755058-8). P-H.
Harris, Diana K. & Cole, William E. Sociology of Aging. LC 79-89741. (Illus.). 1980. text ed. 15.95 (ISBN 0-395-28528-3); inst. manual 0.75 (ISBN 0-395-28529-1). HM.
Harris, Dianne F., ed. see Schuler, Elizabeth.
Harris, Dudley. Hydroponics: Growing Without Soil. rev. ed. (Illus.). 160p. 1975. 22.50 (ISBN 0-7153-6397-2). David & Charles.
Harris, E. J., ed. see Carnegie Commission on Higher Education.
Harris, Edward M. Andover in the American Revolution: A New England Town in a Period of Crisis, 1763-1790. LC 76-13303. (Illus.). 1976. 9.50 (ISBN 0-9603160-0-0). Town of Andover.
Harris, Elizabeth F. From Oxford to Rome, & How It Fared with Some Who Lately Made the Journey, 1847. Wolff, Robert L., ed. Bd. with Rest in the Church, 1848. LC 74-449. (Victorian Fiction Ser.). 1975. lib. bdg. 66.00 (ISBN 0-8240-1529-0). Garland Pub.
Harris, Ernest E., jt. auth. see Klotman, Robert H.
Harris, Ernest E., ed. Music Education: A Guide to Information Sources. LC 74-11560. (Education Information Guide Ser.: Vol. 1). 1978. 30.00 (ISBN 0-8103-1309-X). Gale.
Harris, F. C., jt. auth. see Jessop, H. T.
Harris, Frank. ADF Fundamentals. (Avionics Technician Training Course Ser.). (Illus.). 185p. 1980. pap. 6.95 (ISBN 0-89100-120-4). Aviation Maintenance.
--Electronic Circuit Devices. (Avionics Technician Training Course Ser.). (Orig.). 1981. pap. write for info. (ISBN 0-89100-192-1). Aviation Maintenance.
Harris, Frank & McCaffer, Ronald. Modern Construction Management. (Illus.). 1977. 24.95x (ISBN 0-8464-0636-5). Beekman Pubs.
Harris, Frank E. Numbers & Units for Science. (gr. 10-12). 1972. pap. text ed. 6.00 (ISBN 0-8449-0301-9); tchr's manual & test avail. Learning Line.
--Principles of Chemistry. (gr. 10-12). 1977. pap. text ed. 15.00 each incl. 8 texts, 1 tchrs' manual & 1 test (ISBN 0-8449-0400-7). Learning Line.
Harris, G. D. Conrad's Fossil Shells of the Tertiary Formations of North America: 1832-35. (Illus.). 1971. Repr. of 1893 ed. 5.00 (ISBN 0-87710-362-3). Paleo Res.
Harris, George E. A Treatise on Sunday Laws: The Sabbath-the Lord's Day, Its History & Observance, Civil & Criminal. xxiii, 338p. 1980. Repr. of 1892 ed. lib. bdg. 32.50x (ISBN 0-8377-2232-2). Rothman.
Harris, Gordon. Apostle from Space. 1978. pap. 1.95 pocketsize o.p. (ISBN 0-88270-281-5). Logos.
--A New Command: The Story of Bruce Medaris, Maj. Gen. Retired. LC 76-10533. 1977. pap. 3.95 o.p. (ISBN 0-88270-181-9). Logos.
Harris, Gordon E., ed. see Foerster, Werner.
Harris, Grace G. Casting Out Anger. LC 77-80837. (Studies in Anthropology: No. 21). (Illus.). 1978. 24.95 (ISBN 0-521-21729-6). Cambridge U Pr.
Harris, H. G. Advanced Watch & Clock Repair. (Illus.). 9.95 (ISBN 0-87523-181-0). Wallace-Homestead.
Harris, H. R. Nineteenth Century American Clocks. (Illus.). 256p. 1981. 12.95 (ISBN 0-87523-197-7). Emerson.
Harris, H. S. Hegel's Development: Toward the Sunlight, 1770-1801. 606p. 1972. text ed. 48.00x (ISBN 0-19-824358-8). Oxford U Pr.
Harris, Harry. Prenatal Diagnosis & Selective Abortion. LC 75-3847. 112p. 1975. text ed. 7.95x (ISBN 0-674-70080-5). Harvard U Pr.
Harris, Henry. Nucleus & Cytoplasm. 3rd ed. (Illus.). 1974. text ed. 16.00x (ISBN 0-19-854124-4); pap. text ed. 7.95x o.p. (ISBN 0-19-854125-2). Oxford U Pr.
Harris, Homer I. Family Estate Planning Guide, 2 vols. 2nd ed. LC 71-114348. 1971. 95.00 (ISBN 0-686-14504-6). Lawyers Co-Op.
Harris, Homer I. & Rasch, Joseph. Handling Federal Estate & Gift Taxes, 3 vols. 2nd ed. LC 72-96007. 1972. 150.00 (ISBN 0-686-14503-8). Lawyers Co-Op.
Harris, Irving. The Breeze of the Spirit: Sam Shoemaker & the Story of Faith-at-Work. (Illus.). 1978. 8.95 (ISBN 0-8164-0399-6). Crossroad NY.
Harris, J. Donald. Anatomy & Physiology of the Peripheral Hearing Mechanism. LC 73-12474. (Studies in Communicative Disorders Ser). 1974. pap. text ed. 4.50 (ISBN 0-672-61304-2). Bobbs.
--Electrophysiology & Layout of the Auditory Nervous System. LC 73-18092. (Studies in Communicative Disorders Ser). 1974. pap. text ed. 3.95 (ISBN 0-672-61286-0). Bobbs.
--Psychoacoustics. LC 74-10512. (Studies in Communicative Disorders Ser). 1974. pap. text ed. 3.70 o.p. (ISBN 0-672-61332-8). Bobbs.
Harris, J. Milton & Wamser, Carl C. Fundamentals of Organic Reaction Mechanisms. LC 75-40275. 1976. 26.95 (ISBN 0-471-35400-7). Wiley.
Harris, J. R., ed. Legacy of Egypt. 2nd ed. (Legacy Ser.). (Illus.). 1971. 27.50x (ISBN 0-19-821912-1). Oxford U Pr.
Harris, James E. & Weeks, Kent R. X-Raying the Pharaohs. LC 72-1180. (Encore Edition). (Illus.). 265p. 1973. pap. 2.95 (ISBN 0-684-16899-5, SL 535, ScribT). Scribner.
Harris, James K., ed. The Complete Text of the Equal Rights Amendment. 132p. 1981. 3.95 (ISBN 0-9605188-0-0). Ganis & Harris.
Harris, Jana. Pin Money. 1977. 5.00 o.p. (ISBN 0-686-24337-4). Jungle Garden.
Harris, Java. Who's That Pushy Bitch? 1981. 6.50. Jungle Garden.
Harris, Jocelyn, ed. see Richardson, Samuel.
Harris, Joel C. Complete Tales of Uncle Remus. Chase, Richard, ed. (Illus.). (gr. 7 up). 1955. 24.50 (ISBN 0-395-06799-5). HM.
--Favorite Uncle Remus. Van Santvoord, George & Coolidge, Archibald C., eds. (gr. 4-8). 12.95 (ISBN 0-395-06800-2). HM.
--Nights with Uncle Remus: Myths & Legends of the Old Plantation. LC 70-164329. 1971. Repr. of 1883 ed. 26.00 (ISBN 0-8103-3866-1). Gale.
--On the Plantation: A Story of a Georgia Boy's Adventures During the War. LC 79-5189. (Brown Thrasher Bks.). (Illus.). 235p. 1980. 15.00x (ISBN 0-8203-0494-8); pap. 4.95x (ISBN 0-8203-0495-6). U of Ga Pr.
--Stories of Georgia. LC 73-174943. 1975. Repr. of 1896 ed. 18.00 (ISBN 0-8103-4082-8). Gale.
Harris, Joel C., ed. The World's Wit & Humor: An Encyclopedia of the Classic Wit & Humor of All Nations, 15 vols. in 3 mini-print vols. 1973. Repr. of 1905 ed. 120.00 (ISBN 0-8108-0543-X). Scarecrow.
Harris, John. Artist & the Country House: A History of Country House & Garden View Painting. (Illus.). 376p. 1979. 100.00 (ISBN 0-85667-053-7, Pub. by Sotheby Parke Bernet England). Biblio Dist.
--Dunkirk: The Storms of War. 1980. 19.95 (ISBN 0-7153-7857-0). David & Charles.
Harris, John & Lever, Jill. Illustrated Glossary of Architecture: Eight Fifty to Eighteen Thirty. (Illus.). 1979. 15.95 (ISBN 0-571-06883-9, Pub. by Faber & Faber); pap. 9.95 (ISBN 0-571-09074-5). Merrimack Bk Serv.
Harris, John & Pahl, Aleta. Endangered Predators. LC 75-34051. 96p. (gr. 4-7). 1976. PLB 6.95 (ISBN 0-385-08012-3). Doubleday.
Harris, John, intro. by. The Rise & Progress of the Present Taste in Planting Packs, Pleasure Grounds, Gardens, Etc. facsimile ed. 1970. 15.50 o.s.i. (ISBN 0-85362-104-7, Oriel). Routledge & Kegan.
Harris, John B. Charles Robert Maturin: The Forgotten Imitator. Varma, Devendra P., ed. LC 79-8456. (Gothic Studies & Dissertations Ser.). 1980. lib. bdg. 33.00x (ISBN 0-405-12646-8). Arno.
Harris, John B., ed. Muscular Dystrophy & Other Inherited Diseases of Skeletal Muscle in Animals, Vol. 317. LC 78-27609. (Annals Ser.). 1979. pap. 80.00x (ISBN 0-89766-005-6). NY Acad Sci.
Harris, John H., Jr. & Harris, William H. The Radiology of Emergency Medicine. 2nd ed. (Illus.). 550p. 1981. write for info. (3883-4). Williams & Wilkins.
Harris, John S. & Blake, Reed H. Technical Writing for Social Scientists. LC 75-20129. 128p. 1976. 10.95 (ISBN 0-911012-39-7); pap. 5.95 (ISBN 0-88229-362-1). Nelson-Hall.
Harris, John W. & Kellermeyer, Robert. Red Cell: Production, Metabolism, Destruction, Normal & Abnormal. rev. ed. LC 77-130344. (Commonwealth Fund Publications Ser). 1970. 25.00x (ISBN 0-674-75101-9); pap. 8.95x (ISBN 0-674-75102-7). Harvard U Pr.
Harris, Jonathan. Hiroshima: A Study in the Science, Politics, & the Ethics of War. Brown, Richard H. & Halsey, Van R., eds. (Amherst Ser). (gr. 10-12). 1970. pap. text ed. 4.52 (ISBN 0-201-02687-2, Sch Div); tchr's manual 1.92 (ISBN 0-201-02689-9). A-W.
Harris, Jose. William Beveridge: A Biography. 1977. 37.50x (ISBN 0-19-822459-1). Oxford U Pr.
Harris, Jules E. & Sinkovics, Joseph G. The Immunology of Malignant Disease. 2nd ed. LC 75-42474. (Illus.). 1976. 46.00 o.p. (ISBN 0-8016-2067-8). Mosby.
Harris, K. & Maramorosch, K., eds. Vectors of Plant Pathogens. 1980. 48.00 (ISBN 0-12-326450-2). Acad Pr.
Harris, K. W., jt. auth. see Kenlay, G.
Harris, Katerina. Colloquial Greek. (Trubners Colloquial Manuals). 336p. 1975. 14.00 (ISBN 0-7100-8069-7); pap. 8.95 (ISBN 0-7100-8070-0). Routledge & Kegan.
Harris, Katherine S., jt. auth. see Borden, Gloria J.
Harris, Kerry, jt. auth. see Maramorosch, Karl.
Harris, L. E., jt. auth. see Crampton, E. W.
Harris, L. M. Design for Reliability in Deepwater Floating Drilling Operations. 320p. 1980. 35.00 (ISBN 0-87814-082-4). Pennwell Pub.
--An Introduction to Deepwater Floating Drilling Operations. new ed. LC 72-76603. 256p. 1972. 21.00 (ISBN 0-87814-011-5). Pennwell Pub.
Harris, Lane. The Devil's Love. (Orig.). 1981. pap. 2.95 (ISBN 0-440-11915-4). Dell.
Harris, Lawrence, jt. auth. see Fine, Ben.
Harris, Leon. Merchant Princes. 1980. pap. 3.25 (ISBN 0-425-04700-8). Berkley Pub.
--Night Before Christmas-in Texas,That Is. (Illus.). (gr. k-7). 1977. Repr. of 1952 ed. 6.95 (ISBN 0-88289-175-8). Pelican.
Harris, Leonard. The Masada Plan. 1981. pap. 2.75 (ISBN 0-445-04189-7). Popular Lib.
Harris, Lester. The Frog-Eating Electric Light Bug. LC 78-3762. 1978. pap. 4.50 (ISBN 0-8127-0146-1). Southern Pub.
Harris, Lester E. Galapagos. LC 76-23727. (Crown Ser.). 128p. (gr. 8 up). 1976. pap. 4.50 (ISBN 0-8127-0125-9). Southern Pub.
Harris, Louis. The Anguish of Change. 1974. pap. text ed. 5.95x (ISBN 0-393-09315-8). Norton.
Harris, Lucien, Jr. Butterflies of Georgia. (Illus.). 326p. 1975. pap. 5.95 (ISBN 0-8061-1295-6). U of Okla Pr.
Harris, M. The Muckraker's Manual: How to Do Your Own Investigative Reporting. 1980. pap. 7.95. Loompanics.
Harris, M. & Leschot, N. Harmonium Manual. LC 79-54823. (Illus., Orig.). Date not set. pap. cancelled (ISBN 0-89793-016-9). Hunter Hse.
Harris, Madalene, jt. auth. see Cruz, Nicky.
Harris, Margaret. Sharks & Troubled Waters. LC 77-10760. (Myth, Magic & Superstition Ser.). (Illus.). (gr. 4-5). 1977. PLB 9.65 (ISBN 0-8172-1041-5). Raintree Pubs.
Harris, Maria. Portrait of Youth Ministry: Young People & the Church. 224p. (Orig.). 1981. pap. 7.95 (ISBN 0-8091-2354-1). Paulist Pr.
Harris, Maria, ed. The DRE Reader: A Sourcebook in Education & Ministry. LC 80-52059. 192p. (Orig.). 1980. pap. 6.95 (ISBN 0-88489-124-0). St Marys.

Harris, Marie. Raw Honey. LC 75-21787. 72p. 1975. pap. 4.95 (ISBN 0-914086-09-X). Alicejamesbooks.

Harris, Marilyn. The Eden Passion. 1980. pap. 2.50 (ISBN 0-345-28537-9). Ballantine.

--The Portent. 324p. 1980. 11.95 (ISBN 0-686-68352-8). Putnam.

--The Runaway's Diary. (gr. 7-9). 1974. pap. 1.75 (ISBN 0-671-41304-X). Archway.

--Runnaway's Diary. (YA) (gr. 7-9). 1974. pap. 1.75 (ISBN 0-671-41304-X). PB.

--The Women of Eden. 608p. 1981. pap. 2.95 (ISBN 0-345-28965-X). Ballantine.

Harris, Mark. Saul Bellow, Drumlin Woodchuck. LC 80-14390. 192p. 1980. 9.95 (ISBN 0-8203-0529-4). U of Ga Pr.

--Something About a Soldier. 1976. pap. 1.50 o.p. (ISBN 0-345-24099-5). Ballantine.

Harris, Marvin. Patterns of Race in the Americas. 144p. 1974. pap. 4.95 (ISBN 0-393-00727-8, Norton Lib). Norton.

--Rise of Anthropological Theory: A History of Theories of Culture. LC 68-17392. 1968. scp 22.95 (ISBN 0-690-70322-8, HarpC). Harper-Row.

Harris, Marvin, jt. auth. see Wagley, Charles.

Harris, Mary C. Crafts, Customs & Legends of Wales. LC 79-91477. (Illus.). 1980. 17.95 (ISBN 0-7153-7820-1). David & Charles.

Harris, Mary K. Seraphina. 1960. 6.50 (ISBN 0-571-07012-4, Pub. by Faber & Faber). Merrimack Bk Serv.

Harris, Max. Angry Eye: A Comment on Life & Letters. 1974. text ed. 16.00 (ISBN 0-08-017373-X). Pergamon.

Harris, Max F. Sister Act. 1981. pap. 1.95 (ISBN 0-8439-0907-2, Leisure Bks). Nordon Pubns.

Harris, Michael. Gresley's Coaches: Coaches Built for GNR, ECJS & LNER 1905-53. (Illus.). 1973. 14.95 (ISBN 0-7153-5935-5). David & Charles.

Harris, Michael H., jt. auth. see Johnson, Elmer D.

Harris, Michael H., ed. Advances in Librarianship, Vol. 10. 1980. 23.00 (ISBN 0-12-785010-4); lib. bdg. 30.00 (ISBN 0-12-785023-6); microfiche ed. 16.00 (ISBN 0-12-785024-4). Acad Pr.

--The Age of Jewett: Charles Coffin Jewett & American Librarianship, 1841-1868. LC 75-14205. (Heritage of Librarianship Ser: No. 1). 166p. 1975. lib. bdg. 20.00x (ISBN 0-87287-113-4). Libs Unl.

Harris, Michael H., ed. see Cole, J.

Harris, Michael H., jt. ed. see Cutler, Wayne.

Harris, Michael J. & Voight, Melvin J., eds. Advances in Librarianship, 8 vols. Incl. Vol. 1. 294p. 1970. 37.50 (ISBN 0-12-785001-5); Vol. 2. 388p. 1971. 37.50 (ISBN 0-12-785002-3); Vol. 3. 275p. 1972. 37.50 (ISBN 0-12-785003-1); Vol. 4. 1974. 37.50 (ISBN 0-12-785004-X); Vol. 5. 1975. 37.50 (ISBN 0-12-785005-8); lib ed. 48.00 (ISBN 0-12-785012-0); microfiche 27.50 (ISBN 0-12-785013-9); Vol. 6. 1976. 28.50 (ISBN 0-12-785006-6); lib ed. 35.50 (ISBN 0-12-785014-7); microfiche 21.00 (ISBN 0-12-785015-5); Vol. 7. 1977. lib ed. 45.00 (ISBN 0-12-785016-3); 35.50 (ISBN 0-12-785007-4); microfiche 25.50 (ISBN 0-12-785017-1); Vol. 8. 25.50 (ISBN 0-12-785008-2); lib. ed. 32.50 (ISBN 0-12-785018-X); microfiche 19.00 (ISBN 0-12-785019-8). LC 79-88675. Acad Pr.

Harris, Middleton, et al. The Black Book. 1973. 15.00 (ISBN 0-394-48388-X); pap. 8.95 (ISBN 0-394-70622-6). Random.

Harris, Murray, jt. ed. see Hagner, Donald.

Harris, Myron & Norman, Jane. American Teenager. LC 80-51249. 300p. Date not set. 12.95 (ISBN 0-89256-141-6). Rawson Wade.

Harris, Neil. The Artist in American Society. LC 66-25399. 1966. 7.50 o.s.i. (ISBN 0-8076-0382-1). Braziller.

--Humbug: The Art of P. T. Barnum. LC 80-26944. xiv, 338p. 1981. pap. 8.95 (ISBN 0-226-31752-8). U of Chicago Pr.

Harris, Neil, ed. The Land of Contrasts. LC 71-104962. (American Culture Ser). 1970. pap. 7.95 (ISBN 0-8076-0549-2). Braziller.

Harris, Oliver & Janzen, Curtis, eds. Family Treatment in Social Work Practice. LC 79-91098. 300p. 1980. pap. text ed. 7.95 (ISBN 0-87581-254-6). Peacock Pubs.

Harris, P. Buford. Modern Watch & Clock Repairing. LC 73-77479. 1972. 13.95 (ISBN 0-911012-05-2). Nelson-Hall.

Harris, Paul. Broadcasting from the High Seas: The History of Offshore Radio in Europe 1958-76. (Illus.). 1977. 20.00x (ISBN 0-904505-07-3, P Harris). Nichols Pub.

Harris, Paul, jt. auth. see Ramsay, Graham.

Harris, Paul E., Jr. So You'd Like to Know More About Soccer! A Guide for Parents. 120p. pap. 3.95 (ISBN 0-88839-107-2). Soccer for Am.

Harris, Paula. Pisces. (Sun Signs Ser.). (Illus.). (gr. 4-12). 1978. PLB 5.95 (ISBN 0-87191-652-5); pap. 2.95 (ISBN 0-89812-082-9). Creative Ed.

--Scorpio. (Sun Signs). (Illus.). (gr. 4-12). 1978. PLB 5.95 (ISBN 0-87191-648-7); pap. 2.95 (ISBN 0-89812-078-0). Creative Ed.

Harris, Peggy, jt. auth. see Hubbard, W. P.

Harris, Peter. Hong Kong: A Study in Bureaucratic Politics. 1979. pap. text ed. 8.95x (ISBN 0-686-60437-7, 00106). Heinemann Ed.

Harris, Phil. An Introduction to Law. (Law in Context Ser.). 288p. 1980. 31.00x (ISBN 0-297-77826-9, Pub. by Weidenfeld & Nicolson England). Rothman.

Harris, R. C., ed. What We Know About Cancer. 1970. pap. 4.95 o.p. (ISBN 0-04-616009-4). Allen Unwin.

Harris, R. Cole & Warkentin, John. Canada Before Confederation: A Study in Historical Geography. (Historical Geography of North America Ser). (Illus.). 368p. 1974. pap. text ed. 7.95x (ISBN 0-19-501791-9). Oxford U Pr.

Harris, R. J., ed. see International Society For Cell Biology.

Harris, R. Laird, et al, eds. Theological Wordbook of the Old Testament. 1800p. 1980. text ed. 29.95 (ISBN 0-8024-8631-2). Moody.

Harris, R. T., jt. auth. see Beckhard, R.

Harris, Rabia, tr. see Arabi, Ibn.

Harris, Ralph W. The Incomparable Story. (Radiant Life Ser.). 1977. pap. 1.50 (ISBN 0-88243-907-3, 02-0907); tchr's ed. 2.50 (ISBN 0-88243-177-3, 32-0177). Gospel Pub.

--Pictures of Truth. LC 76-58081. (Radiant Life Ser). 1977. pap. 1.50 (ISBN 0-88243-905-7, 02-0905); teacher's ed 2.50 (ISBN 0-88243-175-7, 32-0175). Gospel Pub.

--What's Next? New Life in Christ Guidebook for Children. 1972. pap. 0.35 (ISBN 0-88243-559-0, 02-0559). Gospel Pub.

Harris, Raymond. Best-Selling Chapters. (Illus.). 496p. (gr. 9 up). 1978. pap. text ed. 8.00x (ISBN 0-89061-151-3, 791). Jamestown Pubs.

--Best Short Stories. (Illus.). 560p. (Orig.). (gr. 9 up). 1980. pap. text ed. 8.00x (ISBN 0-89061-234-X, 792). Jamestown Pubs.

Harris, Raymond, jt. auth. see Spargo, Edward.

Harris, Raymond, ed. see Conan Doyle, Arthur.

Harris, Raymond, ed. see Harte, Bret.

Harris, Raymond, ed. see London, Jack.

Harris, Raymond, ed. see O'Henry.

Harris, Raymond, ed. see O. Henry.

Harris, Raymond, ed. see O'Henry.

Harris, Richard H., ed. Modern Drama in America & England, Nineteen Fifty-Nineteen Seventy: A Guide to Information Sources. (American Literature, English Literature & World Literatures in English Ser.: Vol. 34). 400p. 1981. 32.00 (ISBN 0-8103-1493-2). Gale.

Harris, Richard J. A Primer of Multivariate Statistics. 1974. text ed. 22.95 (ISBN 0-12-327250-5). Acad Pr.

Harris, Robert. Microanalytic Simulation Models for Analysis of Public Welfare Policies. (An Institute Paper). 50p. 1977. pap. 3.50 (ISBN 0-87766-223-1, 22800). Urban Inst.

Harris, Robert A., jt. auth. see Lasky, Michael S.

Harris, Robert D. Necker: Reform Statesman of the Ancien Regime. 1979. 19.50x (ISBN 0-520-03647-6). U of Cal Pr.

Harris, Robert J., ed. Cellular Basis & Aetiology of Late Somatic Effects of Ionizing Radiations: Proceedings. 1962. 50.00 (ISBN 0-12-327174-6). Acad Pr.

--Initial Effects of Ionizing Radiations on Cells. 1963. 43.00 (ISBN 0-12-327162-2). Acad Pr.

Harris, Robert S. & Karmas, Endel. Nutritional Evaluation of Food Processing. 2nd ed. (Illus.). 1975. text ed. 39.50 (ISBN 0-87055-189-2); pap. 20.50 (ISBN 0-87055-312-7). AVI.

Harris, Robert S., jt. ed. see Sebrell, W. H., Jr.

Harris, Robert S., et al, eds. Vitamins & Hormones: Advances in Research & Applications. Incl. Vols. 1-8. 1943-50. 42.00 ea. Vol. 1 (ISBN 0-12-709801-1). Vol. 2 (ISBN 0-12-709802-X). Vol. 3 (ISBN 0-12-709803-8). Vol. 4 (ISBN 0-12-709804-6). Vol. 5 (ISBN 0-12-709805-4). Vol. 6 (ISBN 0-12-709806-2). Vol. 7 (ISBN 0-12-709807-0). Vol. 8 (ISBN 0-12-709808-9); Vol. 9. 1951. 42.00 (ISBN 0-12-709809-7); Vol. 10. 1952. 42.00 (ISBN 0-12-709810-0); Vols. 11-16. 1953-58. Vols. 11-12. 42.00 ea.; Vol. 11. (ISBN 0-12-709811-9); Vol. 12. (ISBN 0-12-709812-7); Vols. 13-16. 42.00 ea.; Vol. 13. (ISBN 0-12-709813-5); Vol. 14. (ISBN 0-12-709814-3); Vol. 15. (ISBN 0-12-709815-1); Vol. 16. (ISBN 0-12-709816-X); Vol. 17. Harris, Robert S., ed. 1959. 42.00 ea. (ISBN 0-12-709817-8); Vol. 18. 1960. 42.00 (ISBN 0-12-709818-6); Vol. 19. 1961. 42.00 (ISBN 0-12-709819-4); Vol. 20. Incl. International Symposium on Vitamin E & Metabolism. Wool, I. G. 1962. 42.00 (ISBN 0-12-709820-8); Vol. 21. 1963. 42.00 (ISBN 0-12-709821-6); Vol. 22. **Incl. International Symposium on Vitamin B6. 1964. 42.00 (ISBN 0-12-709822-4); Vol. 23. 1965. 42.00 (ISBN 0-12-709823-2); Vol. 24. 1966. 42.00 (ISBN 0-12-709824-0); Vol. 25. 1967. 42.00 (ISBN 0-12-709825-9); Vol. 26. 1968. 42.00 (ISBN 0-12-709826-7); Vol. 27. 1970. 42.00 (ISBN 0-12-709827-5); Vol. 28. Munson, Paul L., ed. 1971. 42.00 (ISBN 0-12-709828-3); Vol. 29. 1971. 42.00 (ISBN 0-12-709829-1); Vol. 30. 1972. 42.00 (ISBN 0-12-709830-5); Vol. 35. Munson, Paul L., et al, eds. 1978. 42.00 (ISBN 0-12-709835-6); Vol. 36. Munson, Paul L., et al, eds. 1979. 51.50 (ISBN 0-12-709836-4). Acad Pr.**

Harris, Rosemary. The Bright & Morning Star. LC 73-171566. 264p. (gr. 7 up). 1972. 4.95 o.s.i. (ISBN 0-02-742660-2). Macmillan.

--Child in the Bamboo Grove. LC 72-4064. (Illus.). (gr. 1-3). 1972. 8.95 (ISBN 0-87599-194-7). S G Phillips.

--The Flying Ship. (Illus.). (ps-5). 1975. 6.95 (ISBN 0-571-10504-1, Pub. by Faber & Faber). Merrimack Bk Serv.

--The King's White Elephant. (Illus.). 1977. 6.95 (ISBN 0-571-10302-2, Pub. by Faber & Faber); pap. 2.95 (ISBN 0-571-11133-5). Merrimack Bk Serv.

--The Little Dog of Fo. (Illus.). (ps-5). 1976. 6.95 (ISBN 0-571-10897-0, Pub. by Faber & Faber). Merrimack Bk Serv.

--Sea Magic & Other Stories of Enchantment. 192p. (gr. 7 up). 1974. 8.95 (ISBN 0-02-742650-5). Macmillan.

--Seal-Singing. (Illus.). (gr. 7 up). 1971. 8.95 o.s.i. (ISBN 0-02-742680-7). Macmillan.

--The Seal-Singing. LC 75-155265. 288p. (gr. 7 up). 1974. pap. 1.25 o.s.i. (ISBN 0-02-043550-9, 04355, Collier). Macmillan.

--Shadow on the Sun. LC 73-120716. (gr. 7 up). 1970. 5.95 o.s.i. (ISBN 0-02-742690-4). Macmillan.

--A Wicked Pack of Cards. 2nd ed. (gr. 5 up). 1973. 6.50 (ISBN 0-571-10130-5, Pub. by Faber & Faber). Merrimack Bk Serv.

Harris, Ross. Making Photographs. 194p. 1979. pap. 9.95 (ISBN 0-442-25177-7). Van Nos Reinhold.

Harris, Roy D. & Gonzalez, Richard F. The Operations Manager. (Illus.). 450p. 1981. text ed. 14.36 (ISBN 0-8299-0332-1). West Pub.

Harris, Ruth. Kinesiology: Workbook & Laboratory Manual. (Illus.). 1977. 10.95 (ISBN 0-395-20668-5). HM.

Harris, Sara. Father Divine. 1971. pap. 1.95 o.s.i. (ISBN 0-02-033070-7, Collier). Macmillan.

Harris, Sarah. Women at Work. (History in Focus Ser.). (Illus.). 72p. (gr. 6-9). 1981. 14.95 (ISBN 0-7134-3551-8, Pub. by Batsford England). David & Charles.

Harris, Scott, jt. auth. see Rafferty, Milton D.

Harris, Seymour E. Challenge & Change in American Education. 1965. text ed. 12.50x o.p. (ISBN 0-8211-0713-5); text ed. 10.00x ten or more copies o.p. (ISBN 0-686-66475-2). McCutchan.

--The Economics of Health Care - Finance & Delivery. LC 73-17612. 1974. 25.00x (ISBN 0-8211-0725-9); text ed. 22.50x (ISBN 0-685-72313-5). McCutchan.

--Education & Public Policy. 1965. 8.75x o.p. (ISBN 0-685-92818-7); text ed. 7.00x o.p. (ISBN 0-8211-0712-7). McCutchan.

Harris, Sid. All Ends Up: Cartoons from American Scientist. (Illus.). 128p. 1980. pap. 5.95 (ISBN 0-86576-000-4). W Kaufmann.

Harris, Sidney. Chicken Soup & Other Medical Matters. (Illus.). 108p. 1979. 7.95 o.p. (ISBN 0-913232-75-0); pap. 3.95 (ISBN 0-913232-74-2). W Kaufmann.

Harris, Stephen. Fire & Ice: The Cascade Volcanoes. 2nd ed. LC 75-36435. (Illus.). 1980. pap. 7.95 (ISBN 0-89886-009-1). Mountaineers.

--The Harvest Mouse. (Mammal Society Ser.). (Illus.). 50p. 1980. 6.95 (ISBN 0-7137-0897-2, Pub. by Blandford Pr England). Sterling.

Harris, Stephen L. Fire & Ice: The Cascade Volcanoes. rev. ed. LC 75-36435. (Illus.). 320p. (YA) 1980. pap. 7.95 (ISBN 0-89886-009-1, Copublished with The Mountaineers). Pacific Search.

--Understanding the Bible: A Reader's Guide & Reference. LC 79-91833. (Illus.). 391p. 1980. pap. text ed. 9.95 (ISBN 0-87484-472-X). Mayfield Pub.

Harris, Stuart & Oshima, Keichi, eds. Australia & Japan: Nuclear Energy Issues in the Pacific. (Australia-Japan Economic Relations Research Project Monograph: No. 3). (Illus.). 245p. 1980. pap. text ed. 9.95 (ISBN 0-9596197-2-0). Bks Australia.

Harris, Styron. Charles Kingsley: A Reference Book. (Reference Books Ser.). 1981. 26.00 (ISBN 0-8161-8166-7). G K Hall.

Harris, Susan. Boats & Ships. (Easy-Read Fact Bks.). (Illus.). (gr. 2-4). 1979. PLB 6.45 s&l (ISBN 0-531-02270-6). Watts.

--Creatures That Look Alike. (Easy-Read Wildlife Bks.). (Illus.). (gr. 2 up). 1979. PLB 6.45 s&l (ISBN 0-531-01375-8). Watts.

--Crocodiles & Alligators. (gr. 2-4). 1980. PLB 6.45 (ISBN 0-531-00443-0). Watts.

--Gems & Minerals. (gr. 2-4). 1980. PLB 6.45 (ISBN 0-531-03241-8). Watts.

--Helicopters. (Easy-Read Fact Bks.). (Illus.). (gr. 2-4). 1979. s&l 6.45 (ISBN 0-531-02850-X). Watts.

--Horsemanship in Pictures. 1975. pap. 4.95 o.p. (ISBN 0-684-14337-2, SL598, ScribT). Scribner.

--Odd Animals. (Easy-Read Wildlife Books). (Illus.). (gr. 2-4). 1977. PLB 4.90 s&l o.p. (ISBN 0-531-00099-0). Watts.

--Reptiles. (Easy-Read Fact Books Ser.). (gr. 2-4). 1978. PLB 6.90 (ISBN 0-531-01335-9). Watts.

--Space. (Easy-Read Fact Bks.). (Illus.). (gr. 2-4). 1979. PLB 6.45 s&l (ISBN 0-531-02852-6). Watts.

--Swimming Mammals. (Easy-Read Wildlife Bks.). (Illus.). (gr. 2 up). 1977. lib. bdg. 6.45 s&l (ISBN 0-531-00378-7). Watts.

--Upside Down Creatures. (Easy-Read Wildlife Books Ser.). (Illus.). (gr. 2-4). 1978. PLB 6.45 s&l (ISBN 0-531-02918-2). Watts.

--Volcanoes. (Easy-Read Fact Bks.). (Illus.). (gr. 2-4). 1979. PLB 6.45 s&l (ISBN 0-531-02277-3). Watts.

--Whales. (gr. 2-4). PLB 6.45 (ISBN 0-531-00444-9). Watts.

--The World Beneath the Sea. LC 78-10880. (Easy-Read Fact Bks.). (Illus.). (gr. 2-4). 1979. PLB 6.45 s&l (ISBN 0-531-02854-2). Watts.

Harris, T. L. Unholy Pilgrimage: A Visit to Russia to Find What Twenty Years of Official Atheism Had Done for the Russian People. 195p. Repr. of 1937 ed. text ed. 2.95. Attic Pr.

Harris, Tedric A. Rolling Bearing Analysis. LC 66-25221. 1966. 59.50 (ISBN 0-471-35265-9, Pub. by Wiley-Interscience). Wiley.

Harris, Tegwyn, jt. auth. see Angel, Martin V.

Harris, Teresa. God! Please Stop Drugs. Date not set. 5.95 (ISBN 0-533-04435-9). Vantage.

Harris, Thelma B. Good Food for Good Health. LC 79-187205. (Illus.). 256p. 1971. 4.95 (ISBN 0-8127-0045-7). Southern Pub.

Harris, Theodore L. Through Happy Hours. rev. ed. (Keys to Independence in Reading Ser.). (Orig.). (gr. 2). 1973. text ed. 2.70 (ISBN 0-87892-025-0); tchrs' manual 3.96 (ISBN 0-87892-027-7); avail. wkbk. 2.64 (ISBN 0-87892-028-5). Economy Co.

Harris, Theodore L., et al. All Around. (Keys to Independence in Reading Ser.). (Illus., Orig.). (gr. 1). 1973. text ed. 2.37 (ISBN 0-87892-012-9); 4.38 (ISBN 0-87892-013-7); wkbk. avail. (ISBN 0-87892-014-5). Economy Co.

--As Days Go By. (Keys to Independence in Reading Ser.). (Illus., Orig.). (gr. 2). 1973. text ed. 2.70 (ISBN 0-87892-026-9); tchrs' manual 3.96 (ISBN 0-87892-027-7); wkbk. avail. (ISBN 0-87892-028-5). Economy Co.

--Earthrise. (Keys to Reading Ser.). (gr. 6). 1974. pap. text ed. 3.60 (ISBN 0-87892-541-4); resource book 8.85 (ISBN 0-87892-544-9); Master Key (student guide) 3.96 (ISBN 0-87892-545-7); duplicating masters 19.53 (ISBN 0-87892-547-3). Economy Co.

--The Scratch Papers. (Keys to Reading Ser.). (Illus.). (gr. 5). 1975. pap. text ed. 2.97 (ISBN 0-87892-452-3); tchr's ed. 2.97 (ISBN 0-87892-453-1); duplicating masters 15.51 (ISBN 0-87892-050-1). Economy Co.

--Spacestone. (Keys to Reading Ser.). (gr. 6). 1974. pap. text ed. 3.60 (ISBN 0-87892-543-0). Economy Co.

--Sunspinners. (Keys to Reading Ser.). (gr. 6). 1974. pap. text ed. 3.60 (ISBN 0-87892-542-2); resource bk 8.85 (ISBN 0-87892-544-9); master key (student guide) 3.96 (ISBN 0-87892-545-7); duplicating masters 19.53 (ISBN 0-87892-547-3). Economy Co.

--Tag. (Keys to Independence in Reading Ser.). (Illus., Orig.). (gr. 1). 1973. text ed. 2.07 (ISBN 0-87892-010-2); tchr's manual 4.38 (ISBN 0-87892-013-7); avail. wkbk. 2.64 (ISBN 0-87892-014-5). Economy Co.
--Wide Doors Open. (Keys to Independence in Reading Ser.). (Illus., Orig.). (gr. 3). 1973. text ed. 2.70 (ISBN 0-87892-038-2); tchrs' manual 3.96 (ISBN 0-87892-039-0); avail. wkbk. 2.64 (ISBN 0-87892-040-4). Economy Co.
--The Dopple Gang. rev. ed. (Keys to Reading Ser.). (Illus.). 160p. (gr. 6). 1975. pap. text ed. 2.97 (ISBN 0-87892-456-6); tchrs'. ed. 2.97 (ISBN 0-87892-457-4); 15.51 (ISBN 0-87892-051-X). Economy Co.
--The Kickingbird Kids' Book Factory. (Keys to Reading Ser.). (Illus.). 160p. (gr. 4). 1975. pap. text ed. 2.97 (ISBN 0-87892-448-5); tchr's. ed. 2.97 (ISBN 0-87892-449-3); dupl. masters 15.51 (ISBN 0-87892-049-8). Economy Co.
--Dreamstalkers. rev. ed. (Keys to Reading Ser.). (Illus.). 192p. (gr. 8). 1975. pap. text ed. 3.48 (ISBN 0-87892-466-3); resource bk. 9.90 (ISBN 0-87892-467-1); datalog student guide 3.96 (ISBN 0-87892-468-X); tchr's ed. 3.96 (ISBN 0-87892-469-8); 19.53 (ISBN 0-87892-499-X). Economy Co.
--Linescapes. rev. ed. (Keys to Reading Ser.). (Illus.). 192p. (gr. 7). 1975. pap. text ed. 3.99 (ISBN 0-87892-458-2); resource bk. 9.90 (ISBN 0-87892-461-2); 3.26 (ISBN 0-87892-462-0); Thoughtvault tchr's ed. 3.96 (ISBN 0-87892-462-0); dupl. masters 19.53 (ISBN 0-87892-498-1). Economy Co.
--Spindrift. rev. ed. (Keys to Reading Ser.). (Illus.). 176p. (gr. 7). 1975. pap. text ed. 3.48 (ISBN 0-87892-459-0); 9.90 (ISBN 0-87892-461-2); thoughtvault student guide 3.96 (ISBN 0-87892-462-0); thoughtvault tchrs' ed. 3.96 (ISBN 0-87892-463-9); duplicating masters 19.53 (ISBN 0-87892-498-1). Economy Co.
--Timetouchers. rev. ed. (Keys to Reading Ser.). (Illus.). 176p. (gr. 8). 1975. pap. text ed. 3.99 (ISBN 0-87892-464-7); 9.90 (ISBN 0-87892-467-1); catalog student guide 3.96 (ISBN 0-87892-468-X); catalog tchr's ed. 3.96 (ISBN 0-87892-469-8); 19.53 (ISBN 0-87892-499-X). Economy Co.
--Trajectories. rev. ed. (Keys to Reading Ser.). (Illus.). 192p. (gr. 7). 1975. pap. text ed. 3.48 (ISBN 0-87892-460-4); resource bk. 9.90 (ISBN 0-87892-461-2); thoughtvault student guide 3.96 (ISBN 0-87892-462-0); thoughtvault tchrs' ed. 3.96 (ISBN 0-87892-463-9); duplicating masters 19.53 (ISBN 0-87892-498-1). Economy Co.
--Windchange. rev. ed. (Keys to Reading Ser.). (Illus.). 192p. (gr. 8). 1975. pap. text ed. 3.48 (ISBN 0-87892-465-5); resource bk. 9.90 (ISBN 0-87892-467-1); catalog student guide 3.96 (ISBN 0-87892-468-X); tchr's ed. 3.96 (ISBN 0-87892-469-8); duplicating masters 19.53 (ISBN 0-87892-499-X). Economy Co.
Harris, Thomas. I'm OK-You're OK. 1973. pap. 2.50 (ISBN 0-380-00772-X, 46268). Avon.
Harris, Tim. Practical English One, Two, & Three, 3 bks. (Illus.). 1980. Bks. 1-3. pap. text ed. write for info. (HC); write for info. instructor's manuals 1-3; write for info. Whiting Practical English 1-3 wkbks.; write for info. tapes. HarBraceJ.
Harris, Tom see Hoffmann, William M.
Harris, Victor, tr. see Musashi, Miyamoto.
Harris, Virgil M. Ancient Curious & Famous Wills. xiii, 472p. 1981. Repr. of 1911 ed. lib. bdg. 39.50x (ISBN 0-8377-0633-5). Rothman.
Harris, Vivian J. Radiology of Jaw Bone Masses in Adults & Children. (Illus.). 220p. 1981. 22.50 (ISBN 0-87527-212-6). Green. Postponed.
Harris, W. J. Comparative Adult Education. (Illus.). 240p. 1981. pap. text ed. 14.95 (ISBN 0-582-29510-6). Longman.
Harris, W. W. Puerto Rico's Fighting Sixty-Fifth U. S. Infantry: From San Juan to Chorwan. LC 79-26889. (Illus.). 1980. 12.95 (ISBN 0-89141-056-2). Presidio Pr.
Harris, Walter. To Catch a Rat. 1978. pap. 1.50 o.p. (ISBN 0-425-03995-1, Dist. by Putnam). Berkley Pub.
Harris, Walter, jt. auth. see Antell, Gerson.
Harris, Walter D., Jr. The Growth of Latin American Cities. LC 76-141378. (Illus.). xvii, 314p. 1971. 17.95x (ISBN 0-8214-0086-X). Ohio U Pr.
Harris, William H., jt. auth. see Harris, John H., Jr.
Harris, William M. A Design for Desegregation Evaluation. 1976. pap. text ed. 5.75x (ISBN 0-8191-0006-4). U Pr of Amer.
Harris, William T. Chemical Milling: The Technology of Cutting Materials by Etching. (Oxford Series on Advanced Manufacturing). (Illus.). 1977. 59.00x (ISBN 0-19-859115-2). Oxford U Pr.
Harris, William T., jt. auth. see Sanborn, Franklin B.
Harris, William V. War & Imperialism in Republican Rome, 327-70 B.C. 1979. 45.00x (ISBN 0-19-814827-5). Oxford U Pr.
Harris, William W. Taking Root: Israeli Settlement in the West Bank, the Golan & Gaza-Sinai, 1967-1980. 256p. 1981. 39.25 (ISBN 0-471-27863-7, Pub. by Wiley-Interscience). Wiley.
Harris, Wilson. Black Marsden. 1972. 4.95 o.p. (ISBN 0-571-10104-6, Pub. by Faber & Faber). Merrimack Bk Serv.
--The Eye of the Scarecrow. (Orig.). 1974. pap. 3.95 (ISBN 0-571-10557-2, Pub. by Faber & Faber). Merrimack Bk Serv.
--The Sleepers of Roraima: A Carib Trilogy. (Illus.). 1970. 5.95 (ISBN 0-571-09272-1, Pub. by Faber & Faber). Merrimack Bk Serv.
--Whole Armor & the Secret Ladder. 1973. pap. 5.95 (ISBN 0-571-10231-X, Pub. by Faber & Faber). Merrimack Bk Serv.
Harrison. New Ways to Produce Textiles. 12.95 (ISBN 0-87245-604-8). Textile Bk.
Harrison, jt. auth. see Stelle.
Harrison, et al. Annie Oakley. (Illus.). 35p. (gr. 1-9). 1981. 2.95 (ISBN 0-86575-185-4). Dormac.
--Brigham Young. (Illus.). 35p. (gr. 1-9). 1981. 2.95 (ISBN 0-86575-188-9). Dormac.
--Chief Joseph. 35p. (gr. 1-9). 1981. 2.95. Dormac.
--Matthew Brady. (Illus.). 35p. (gr. 1-9). 1981. 2.95 (ISBN 0-86575-190-0). Dormac.
--Stonewall Jackson. 35p. (gr. 1-9). 1981. 2.95 (ISBN 0-86575-191-9). Dormac.
--Thomas Jefferson. (Illus.). 35p. (gr. 1-9). 2.95 (ISBN 0-86575-187-0). Dormac.
Harrison, A. J. The Economics of Transport Appraisal. LC 74-10625. 250p. 1974. 21.95 o.p. (ISBN 0-470-35577-8). Halsted Pr.
Harrison, A. J., jt. auth. see Atkinson, A. B.
Harrison, Amy, jt. auth. see Hutchins, Elizabeth L.
Harrison, Andrew. Making & Thinking: A Study of Intelligent Activities. LC 78-56369. 1978. text ed. 19.50 (ISBN 0-915144-55-7). Hackett Pub.
Harrison, Barbara. Rhinelander Center. 464p. (Orig.). 1981. pap. 2.75 (ISBN 0-89083-704-X). Zebra.
Harrison, Barbara G. Off Center. LC 81-80030. 320p. 1981. pap. 2.95 (ISBN 0-87216-870-0). Playboy Pbks.
--Off Center. 1980. 9.95 (ISBN 0-8037-6677-7). Dial.
Harrison, Brenda & Vesilind, P. Aarne. High Technology -- a Failure Analysis, Vol. 2. LC 80-65508. (Design & Management for Resource Recovery Ser.). (Illus.). 250p. 1981. 29.95 (ISBN 0-250-40311-0). Ann Arbor Science.
Harrison, Brian, ed. see Lowery, Robert.
Harrison, Bruce M. Dissection of the Cat & Comparisons with Man: A Laboratory Manual on Felis Domestica. 7th ed. (Illus.). 1976. pap. text ed. 7.50 (ISBN 0-8016-2075-9). Mosby.
--Manual of Comparative Anatomy: A General Laboratory Guide. rev. ed. 3rd ed. 1970. 9.50 (ISBN 0-8016-2078-3). Mosby.
Harrison, C. & Oakes, R. Basics of Librarianship. 1980. pap. 12.50x (Pub. by Lib Assn England). Oryx Pr.
Harrison, C. William. First Book of Hiking. LC 65-21648. (First Bks). (Illus.). (gr. 4-6). 1965. PLB 4.90 o.p. (ISBN 0-531-00547-X). Watts.
Harrison, Charles R. Ornamental Conifers. LC 74-11229. (Illus.). 1975. 19.75 o.s.i. (ISBN 0-02-845760-9). Hafner.
Harrison, Charles Y. Thank God for My Heart Attack. 1949. 4.50 o.p. (ISBN 0-03-027285-8). HR&W.
Harrison, Colin. Readability in the Classroom. LC 79-41794. (Illus.). 160p. 1980. 22.50 (ISBN 0-521-22712-7); pap. 7.95x (ISBN 0-521-29621-8). Cambridge U Pr.
Harrison, Dave. Sports Illustrated Canoeing. LC 80-8687. (Illus.). 192p. 1981. 8.95 (ISBN 0-06-014853-5, HarpT); pap. 5.95 (ISBN 0-06-090874-2, CN874, HarpT). Har-Row.
Harrison, David. The Boy with a Drum. (ps-1). 1971. PLB 7.15 o.p. (ISBN 0-307-63044-7, Golden Pr). Western Pub.
--Let's Go, Trucks! (Illus.). 24p. (gr. k-2). 1976. PLB 5.00 (ISBN 0-307-60185-4, Golden Pr). Western Pub.
--Little Boy & the Giant. (A Young Reader Ser.). (Illus.). (gr. k-3). 1979. PLB 5.00 (ISBN 0-307-60536-1, Golden Pr). Western Pub.
--Little Turtle's Big Adventure. (ps-2). 1969. PLB 4.99 (ISBN 0-394-90837-6, BYR). Random.
--Monster! Monster! (Eager Readers Ser). (gr. k-3). 1975. PLB 5.00 (ISBN 0-307-60808-5, Golden Pr). Western Pub.
--Patterns in Biology. LC 75-16300. 250p. 1975. text ed. 18.95 (ISBN 0-470-35555-7). Halsted Pr.
Harrison, David & Harrison, Judy. Canoe Tripping with Kids. (Illus.). 144p. (Orig.). 1981. pap. 9.95 (ISBN 0-8289-0426-X). Greene.
Harrison, David, jt. auth. see Davidson, John F.
Harrison, David E., ed. see Conference Held at Jackson Laboratory, Bar Harbor, Maine, Sept. 1976.
Harrison, David L. The Circus Is in Town. (Young Reader Ser.). (Illus.). (gr. k-3). 1979. PLB 5.00 (ISBN 0-307-60168-4, Golden Pr). Western Pub.
--Detective Bob & the Great Ape Escape. LC 80-10584. (Illus.). 48p. (ps-3). 1981. 4.95 (ISBN 0-8193-1031-X); PLB 5.95 (ISBN 0-8193-1032-8). Parents.
--My Funny Bunny Phone Book. (Golden Play & Learn Bk.). (Illus.). 14p. (ps). 1980. pap. 2.95 (ISBN 0-307-10728-0, Golden Pr). Western Pubs OH.
Harrison, E. Frank. Management & Organizations. LC 77-75476. (Illus.). 1977. text ed. 18.95 (ISBN 0-395-25481-7); inst. manual 0.50 (ISBN 0-395-25482-5). HM.
Harrison, E. J. Junior Judo. rev. ed. LC 58-10422. (gr. 4 up). 1965. 6.95 (ISBN 0-8069-4430-7); PLB 6.69 (ISBN 0-8069-4431-5). Sterling.
--Manual of Karate. LC 66-16205. (Illus.). 160p. (gr. 7 up). 1975. 6.95 (ISBN 0-8069-4092-1); PLB 6.69 (ISBN 0-8069-4093-X). Sterling.
Harrison, Edward R. Cosmology: The Science of the Universe. LC 80-18703. (Illus.). 480p. Date not set. price not set (ISBN 0-521-22981-2). Cambridge U Pr.
Harrison, Everett & Pfeiffer, Charles F., eds. Wycliffe Bible Commentary. 21.95 (ISBN 0-8024-9695-4). Moody.
Harrison, Fairfax. Landmarks of Old Prince William. (Illus.). 724p. Repr. of 1924 ed. 25.00x o.p. (ISBN 0-685-65068-5). Va Bk.
Harrison, Frank M. John Bunyan. pap. 1.95 o.p. (ISBN 0-686-12524-X). Banner of Truth.
Harrison, Fred. Hell-Holes & Hangings. 8.95 (ISBN 0-685-48825-X). Nortex Pr.
Harrison, Frederic. John Ruskin. LC 72-78229. 1971. Repr. of 1902 ed. 15.00 (ISBN 0-8103-3719-3). Gale.
Harrison, G. A., ed. Population Structure & Human Variation. LC 76-22987. (International Biological Programme Ser.: No. 11). (Illus.). 1977. 72.00 (ISBN 0-521-21399-1). Cambridge U Pr.
Harrison, G. A. & Boyce, A. J., eds. The Structure of Human Populations. (Illus.). 463p. 1972. 24.00x (ISBN 0-19-857117-8); pap. 15.50x (ISBN 0-19-857120-8). Oxford U Pr.
Harrison, G. B., ed. Anthony Munday: The English Romayne Lyfe. 105p. 1980. Repr. of 1925 ed. lib. bdg. 22.50 (ISBN 0-89760-543-8). Telegraph Bks.
--Bible for Students of Literature & Art. LC 64-13820. 1964. pap. 3.50 (ISBN 0-385-04475-5, A394, Anch). Doubleday.
--An Elizabethan Journal. 1974. 25.50x (ISBN 0-7100-7881-1). Routledge & Kegan.
--A Last Elizabethan Journal. 1974. 32.50x (ISBN 0-7100-7883-8). Routledge & Kegan.
--A Second Elizabethan Journal. 1974. 32.50x (ISBN 0-7100-7882-X). Routledge & Kegan.
Harrison, George B., jt. auth. see Granville-Barker, Harley.
Harrison, George R. First Book of Energy. LC 64-17790. (First Bks). (Illus.). (gr. 4-6). 1965. PLB 4.90 o.p. (ISBN 0-531-00523-2). Watts.
--Lasers. LC 70-156888. (First Bks). (Illus.). (gr. 7 up). 1971. PLB 4.90 o.p. (ISBN 0-531-00749-9). Watts.
Harrison, Gordon. Mosquitoes, Malaria & Man: A History of the Hostilities Since 1880. 320p. 1980. 40.00x (ISBN 0-7195-3580-8, Pub. by Murray Pubs England). State Mutual Bk.
Harrison, Gordon S., jt. auth. see Morehouse, Thomas A.
Harrison, Grant Von see Von Harrison, Grant.
Harrison, H. B. Computer Methods in Structural Analysis. (Civil Engineering & Engineering Mechanics Ser.). (Illus.). 400p. 1973. ref. ed. 25.95 (ISBN 0-13-166066-7). P-H.
--Structural Analysis & Design: Some Minicomputer Applications. (Illus.). 1980. text ed. 79.00 (ISBN 0-08-023239-6); pap. text ed. 30.00 (ISBN 0-08-023240-X). Pergamon.
Harrison, Hank. The Dead. LC 79-56661. (Illus.). 336p. (Orig.). 1980. 14.95 (ISBN 0-89087-282-1); pap. 9.95 (ISBN 0-89087-300-3). Celestial Arts.
Harrison, Harold E. & Harrison, Helen C. Disorders of Calcium & Phosphate Metabolism in Childhood & Adolescence. LC 78-64712. (MPCP Ser.: Mpcp Ser. XX). (Illus.). 314p. 1979. text ed. 35.00 (ISBN 0-7216-4537-2). Saunders.
Harrison, Harry. The California Iceberg. LC 74-78109. (Illus.). 128p. (gr. 3-7). 1975. 5.95 o.s.i. (ISBN 0-8027-6194-1). Walker & Co.
--Captive Universe. pap. 1.25 o.p. (ISBN 0-425-03072-5). Berkley Pub.
--The Deathworld Trilogy. pap. 2.50 (ISBN 0-425-04859-4). Berkley Pub.
--The Men from P.I.G. & R.O.B.O.T. LC 77-22875. (gr. 5 up). 1978. 7.95 (ISBN 0-689-30634-2). Atheneum.
--Starworld. 208p. (Orig.). 1981. pap. 2.25 (ISBN 0-553-14647-5). Bantam.
--Wheelworld. 192p. 1981. pap. 2.25 (ISBN 0-553-14339-5). Bantam.
Harrison, Harry, jt. auth. see Dickson, Gordon R.
Harrison, Harry, ed. SF Authors' Choice: 4. 192p. (YA) 1974. 5.95 o.p. (ISBN 0-399-11188-3, Dist. by Putnam). Berkley Pub.
Harrison, Harry & Aldiss, Brian W., eds. Best SF: 1973. (Fic). (YA) 1974. 6.95 o.p. (ISBN 0-399-11301-0). Berkley Pub.
Harrison, Harry, jt. ed. see Aldiss, Brian W.
Harrison, Helen A., ed. Dawn of a New Day: The New York World's Fair, 1939-1940. (Illus.). 128p. 1980. 24.95x (ISBN 0-8147-3407-3); pap. 12.95x (ISBN 0-8147-3408-1). NYU Pr.
Harrison, Helen C., jt. auth. see Harrison, Harold E.
Harrison, Helen P. Film Library Techniques: Principles of Administration. (Studies in Media Management). Date not set. 17.50 (ISBN 0-8038-2294-4). Hastings.
Harrison, Henry S. & Leonard, Margery B. Home Buying: The Complete Illustrated Guide. Berlin, Helene, ed. (Illus.). 500p. (Orig.). 1980. pap. 14.95 (ISBN 0-913652-18-0, BK128). Realtors Natl.
Harrison, Henry S., jt. auth. see Bloom, George F.
Harrison, J., jt. ed. see Ballhatchet, K.
Harrison, J. A. Do-It-Yourself Guide to Natural Stonework. (Illus.). 1979. 17.95 (ISBN 0-7153-7840-6). David & Charles.
Harrison, James, ed. Scientists As Writers. 1965. 16.00x o.p. (ISBN 0-262-08022-2); pap. 4.95x (ISBN 0-262-58004-7, 32). MIT Pr.
Harrison, James D. Community & Environmental Simulations: Annotated Guide to Over 200 Games for College & Community Education. (Public Administration Ser.: Bibliographies: P-675). 138p. 1981. 15.00. Vance Biblios.
Harrison, James M. Bird Taxidermy. LC 76-50731. (Illus.). 1977. 11.95 (ISBN 0-7153-7372-2). David & Charles.
Harrison, Jane. Ancient Art & Ritual. 1978. Repr. of 1913 ed. text ed. 13.00x (ISBN 0-239-00180-X). Humanities.
--Prolegomena to the Study of Greek Religion. 682p. 1981. text ed. 26.00x (ISBN 0-85036-262-8, Pub. by Merlin, England); pap. 13.25x. Humanities.
--Themis. (Illus.). 1963. pap. 17.95 (ISBN 0-686-23502-9, Merlin Pr). Carrier Pigeon.
Harrison, Jared F. Improving Performance & Productivity: Why Won't They Do What I Want Them to Do? (Illus.). 1978. pap. text ed. 8.95 (ISBN 0-201-02956-1). A-W.
Harrison, Jim. Letters to Yesenin. (Orig.). pap. 2.45 o.s.i. (ISBN 0-912090-32-4). Sumac Mich.
--Locations. LC 68-21703. 1968. 4.95 o.p. (ISBN 0-393-04257-X). Norton.
--Plain Song. 1965. 4.50 o.p. (ISBN 0-393-04240-5). Norton.
Harrison, John & Harrison, Shirley. Greece. LC 80-50995. (Rand McNally Pocket Guide Ser.). (Illus.). 1980. pap. 3.95 (ISBN 0-528-84307-9). Rand.
Harrison, John, et al. Akbar & the Mughal Empire. Yapp, Malcolm & Killingray, Margaret, eds. (Greenhaven World History Ser.). (Illus.). 32p. (gr. 10). lib. bdg. 5.95 (ISBN 0-89908-031-6); pap. text ed. 1.95 (ISBN 0-89908-006-5). Greenhaven.
Harrison, John F. The Second Coming: Popular Millenarianism 1780-1850. 1979. 21.00 (ISBN 0-8135-0879-7). Rutgers U Pr.
Harrison, John F., ed. Utopianism & Education: Robert Owen & the Owenites. LC 68-54675. (Orig.). 1969. pap. text ed. 5.25x (ISBN 0-8077-1498-4). Tchrs Coll.
Harrison, John S. The Teachers of Emerson. LC 80-2536. 1981. Repr. of 1910 ed. 37.00 (ISBN 0-404-19263-7). AMS Pr.
Harrison, Judy, jt. auth. see Harrison, David.
Harrison, Julius. Brahms & His Four Symphonies. LC 76-127285. (Music Ser). (Illus.). 1971. Repr. of 1939 ed. lib. bdg. 22.50 (ISBN 0-306-70033-6). Da Capo.
Harrison, June, jt. auth. see Bodo, Peter.
Harrison, K. The Framework of Anglo-Saxon History to A. D. 900. LC 75-13450. 176p. 1976. 31.95 (ISBN 0-521-20935-8). Cambridge U Pr.
Harrison, K. C. First Steps in Librarianship. (Grafton Books on Library & Information Science). 188p. 1980. lib. bdg. 26.00x (ISBN 0-233-96427-4, Pub. by Andre Deutsch). Westview.
--Libraries in Scandinavia. (Grafton Books in Library Science). 1977. lib. bdg. 12.00 o.p. (ISBN 0-233-95968-8). Westview.
--The Library & the Community. (Grafton Books on Library Service). 1977. lib. bdg. 15.00x (ISBN 0-233-96875-X). Westview.
Harrison, Louis H., jt. auth. see Pitts, Michael R.

Harrison, Lowell. The Civil War in Kentucky. LC 75-3545. (The Kentucky Bicentennial Bookshelf Ser.). (Illus.). 136p. 1980. Repr. of 1975 ed. 5.95 (ISBN 0-8131-0209-X). U Pr of Ky.
Harrison, Lowell H. & Dawson, Nelson L., eds. A Kentucky Sampler: Essays from the Filson Club History Quarterly, 1926 to 1976. LC 77-76471. 452p. 1980. Repr. of 1977 ed. 16.00x (ISBN 0-8131-1360-1). U Pr of Ky.
Harrison, M. J., et al. Aids to Anaesthesia, Vol. 1: Basic Sciences. (Illus.). 224p. 1980. pap. 15.00x (ISBN 0-443-01688-7). Churchill.
Harrison, M. John. The Pastel City. 1981. pap. 1.95 (ISBN 0-671-83584-X). PB.
Harrison, Marcus. The Memoirs of Jesus Christ. 1977. pap. 1.95 o.p. (ISBN 0-345-25466-X). Ballantine.
Harrison, Margaret A., ed. Sources Cited & Artifacts Illustrated. (Handbook of Middle American Indians Ser: Vol. 16). 350p. 1976. text ed. 25.00x (ISBN 0-292-73004-7). U of Tex Pr.
Harrison, Michael A. Introduction to Formal Language Theory. LC 77-81196. 1978. text ed. 24.95 (ISBN 0-201-02955-3). A-W.
Harrison, Molly. Homes in Britain. 1975. text ed. 10.95x (ISBN 0-04-942132-8); pap. text ed. 5.95x (ISBN 0-04-942133-6). Allen Unwin.
Harrison, Nancy S. Understanding Behavioral Research. 1979. text ed. 16.95x (ISBN 0-534-00597-7). Wadsworth Pub.
Harrison, P. M. & Hoare, R. J. Metals in Biochemistry. LC 79-41813. 80p. 1980. pap. 5.95 (ISBN 0-412-13160-9, 6361). Methuen Inc.
Harrison, P. W. The Design of Textiles for Industrial Applications. 218p. 1977. 60.00x (ISBN 0-686-63759-3). State Mutual Bk.
Harrison, Pat. Bulletin Board Ideas. (Ideas Ser). (Illus.). 1977. pap. text ed. 1.75 (ISBN 0-87239-119-1, 7959). Standard Pub.
Harrison, Paul C., ed. Kundu Drama. Incl. A Beast Story. Kennedy, Adrienne; Devil's Mask. Brown, Lennox; Great Goodness of Life. Amiri, Imanu; The Great MacDaddy. Harrison, Paul C; Kabnis. Toomer, Jean; Mars. Goss, Clav; The Owl Answers. Kennedy, Adrienne; A Season in the Congo. Cesaire, Aime. 10.00 (ISBN 0-394-48884-9, GP 717). Grove.
Harrison, Paul D. The Truth of Human Nature. (Illus.). 300p. (Orig.). Date not set. 14.95 (ISBN 0-938058-25-8); pap. 11.95 (ISBN 0-938058-26-6). Wrightwill Pub.
Harrison, Phyllis & Collins, Paul. Pendulum, Radiesthesia & You. (Illus., Orig.). 1981. pap. 6.95 (ISBN 0-89407-033-9). Strawberry Hill.
Harrison, R. & Lunt, G. Biological Membranes: Their Structure & Function. LC 75-43543. (Tertiary Level Biology Ser). 264p. 1976. pap. text ed. 18.95 (ISBN 0-470-15220-6). Halsted Pr.
Harrison, R. Cameron, jt. auth. see White, Thomas T.
Harrison, R. J. The Beaker Folk: Copper Age Archaeology in Western Europe. (Ancient People & Places Ser.). (Illus.). 180p. 1981. 19.95 (ISBN 0-500-02098-1). Thames Hudson.
--Functional Anatomy of Marine Mammals. 52.00 (ISBN 0-12-328002-8). Vol. 2, 1975. Vol. 3, 1978. 59.00 (ISBN 0-12-328003-6). Acad Pr.
Harrison, R. J. & Holmes, R. L., eds. Progress in Anatomy, Vol. 1. (Illus.). 250p. Date not set. price not set (ISBN 0-521-23603-7). Cambridge U Pr.
Harrison, R. K. & Wiseman, D. J. Leviticus: An Introduction & Commentary. LC 80-7985. (Tyndale Old Testament Commentaries Ser.). 180p. 1980. 8.95 (ISBN 0-87784-890-4). Inter-Varsity.
Harrison, Randall P. Beyond Words: An Introduction to Nonverbal Communication. LC 73-17202. (Speech Communication Ser). (Illus.). 208p. 1974. ref. ed. 14.95 (ISBN 0-13-076141-9); pap. 10.95 (ISBN 0-13-076133-8). P-H.
Harrison, Ray. A Time for Everything. 1977. 6.95 o.p. (ISBN 0-533-02907-4). Vantage.
Harrison, Rex. Rex: An Autobiography. 1975. 7.95 o.p. (ISBN 0-688-02881-0). Morrow.
Harrison, Richard A. Princetonians, Seventeen Sixty-Nine to Seventeen Seventy-Five: A Biographical Dictionary. LC 80-7526. (Illus.). 576p. 1981. 40.00x (ISBN 0-691-04675-1). Princeton U Pr.
Harrison, Richard J. Bell Beaker Cultures of Spain & Portugal. new ed. Condon, Lorna, ed. LC 76-52631. (American School of Prehistoric Research Bulletins Ser.: No. 35). (Illus.). 1977. pap. 30.00 (ISBN 0-87365-538-9). Peabody Harvard.
Harrison, Richard J. & King, Judith E. Marine Mammals. (Repr. of 1965 ed.). 1968. pap. text ed. 10.50x (ISBN 0-09-074342-3, Hutchinson U Lib). Humanities.
Harrison, Richard J., jt. ed. see Felts, William J.
Harrison, Robert. Gallic Salt: Eighteen Fabliaux Translated from the Old French. 1974. 25.00x (ISBN 0-520-02418-4). U of Cal Pr.
Harrison, Roger & Lunt, George G. Biological Membranes: Thier Structure & Function. 2nd ed. LC 80-14062. (Tertiary Level Biology Ser). 288p. 1980. pap. text ed. 21.95x (ISBN 0-470-26971-5). Halsted Pr.
Harrison, Roland K. Teach Yourself Biblical Hebrew. (Teach Yourself Ser). pap. 4.50 (ISBN 0-679-10180-2). McKay.
Harrison, Ross. On What There Must Be. (Illus.). 224p. 1974. 22.50x (ISBN 0-19-824507-6). Oxford U Pr.
Harrison, Russell S. Equality in Public School Finance. LC 76-15879. (Illus.). 1976. 19.95 (ISBN 0-669-00785-4). Lexington Bks.
Harrison, S. G. Garden Shrubs & Trees. 9.75x (ISBN 0-392-06725-0, LTB). Soccer.
Harrison, Sam. The Krone Chronicles: A True Story. (Orig.). 1980. pap. 5.95 (ISBN 0-89865-030-5). Donning Co.
Harrison, Saul I. & McDermott, John F., eds. New Directions in Childhood Psychopathology: Vol. 2, Deviations in Development. LC 78-70232. 750p. 1981. text ed. 35.00 (ISBN 0-8236-3571-6). Intl Univs Pr.
Harrison, Selig S. China, Oil, & Asia: Conflict Ahead? LC 77-8185. 1977. 15.00x (ISBN 0-231-04378-3). Columbia U Pr.
--The Widening Gulf: Asian Nationalism & American Policy. LC 76-57881. (Illus.). 1978. 17.95 (ISBN 0-02-914080-3). Free Pr.
Harrison, Shirley, jt. auth. see Harrison, John.
Harrison, Sidney. The Young Person's Guide to Playing the Piano. 2nd ed. (Illus.). 1973. 5.95 o.p. (ISBN 0-571-04787-4, Pub. by Faber & Faber). Merrimack Bk Serv.
Harrison, Stanley R. Edgar Fawcett. (U. S. Authors Ser.: No. 201). lib. bdg. 10.95 (ISBN 0-8057-0248-2). Twayne.
Harrison, T. J. Distributed Computer Control Systems: Proceedings of the IFAC Workshop, Tampa, Fla., 2-4 Oct. 1979. (IFAC Proceedings). (Illus.). 240p. 1980. 64.00 (ISBN 0-08-024490-4). Pergamon.
Harrison, T. S. Handbook of Analytical Control of Iron & Steel Production. LC 78-41222. (Series in Analytical Chemistry). 1979. 109.95 (ISBN 0-470-26538-8). Halsted Pr.
Harrison, Tony. From the School of Eloquence & Other Poems. 56p. 1978. bds. 12.50x (ISBN 0-8476-3132-X). Rowman.
--The Passion: Selected from the Fifteenth Century Cycle of York Mystery Plays in a Version by the Company with Tony Harrison. 1978. pap. 5.00x (ISBN 0-8476-3131-1). Rowman.
Harrison, Walter A. Electronic Structure & the Properties of Solids: The Physics of the Chemical Bond. LC 79-17364. (Illus.). 1980. text ed. 29.95x (ISBN 0-7167-1000-5); instr's guide avail. (ISBN 0-7167-1220-2). W H Freeman.
--Solid State Theory. 1980. pap. text ed. 8.95 (ISBN 0-486-63948-7). Dover.
Harrison, Walter T., Jr., jt. auth. see Welsch, Glenn A.
Harrison, William. Savannah Blue. 288p. 1981. 12.50 (ISBN 0-399-90081-0). Marek.
Harrison, William & Mullen, J. Passive Voice & Agreement of the Verb Predicate with a Collective Subject. (Studies in the Modern Russian Language Ser: Nos. 4 & 5). (Rus). 14.95 (ISBN 0-521-05218-1). Cambridge U Pr.
Harrison, William, et al. Colloquial Russian. (Trubners Colloquial Manuals). 1973. 17.00 (ISBN 0-7100-7021-7); pap. 9.95 (ISBN 0-7100-7025-X). Routledge & Kegan.
Harriss, Barbara. Transitional Trade & Rural Development: The Nature & Role of Agricultural Trade in a South Indian District. 400p. text ed. 35.00 (ISBN 0-7069-1036-2, Pub. by Vikas India). Advent Bk.
Harriss, C. L., ed. Government Spending & Landvalues. LC 72-9988. 320p. 1973. 21.50x (ISBN 0-299-06320-8). U of Wis Pr.
Harriss, Ernest C. Johann Mattheson's der Vollkommene Capellmeister: A Revised Translation with Critical Commentary. Buelow, George, ed. (Studies in Musicology). 875p. 1981. 59.95 (ISBN 0-8357-1134-X, Pub. by UMI Res Pr). Univ Microfilms.
Harriss, G. L. King, Parliament, & Public Finance in Medieval England to 1369. 576p. 1975. 49.50x (ISBN 0-19-822435-4). Oxford U Pr.
Harriss, G. L., ed. see McFarlane, K. B.
Harrisville, Roy A. Benjamin Wisner Bacon: Pioneer in American Biblical Criticism. LC 76-16178. (Society of Biblical Literature. Studies in Biblical Scholarship). 1976. pap. 7.50 (ISBN 0-89130-110-0, 061102). Scholars Pr Ca.
--Frank Chamberlain Porter: Pioneer in American Biblical Interpretation. LC 76-4498. (Society of Biblical Literature. Study in Biblical Scholarship). 1976. pap. 7.50 (ISBN 0-89130-104-6, 061101). Scholars Pr Ca.
Harrod, L. M. Librarian's Glossary & Reference Book. LC 76-52489. 1977. lib. bdg. 45.00x (ISBN 0-89158-727-6). Westview.
--Library Work with Children. (Grafton Books in Library Science). 1977. lib. bdg. 17.00x (ISBN 0-233-95994-7). Westview.
Harrod, Roy. International Economics. (Cambridge Economic Handbook Ser). 1957. pap. 10.95x (ISBN 0-521-08780-5). Cambridge U Pr.
Harrold, C. F., ed. see Carlyle, Thomas.
Harrold, Robert & Legg, Phyllida. Folk Costumes of the World. (Illus.). 1979. 10.95 (ISBN 0-7137-0868-9, Pub. by Blandford Pr England). Sterling.
Harrold, Robert, jt. auth. see Wingrave, Helen.
Harron, Don see Farquharson, Charlie, pseud.
Harron, Thomas. Business Law. 992p. 1981. text ed. 21.95 (ISBN 0-686-69609-3). Allyn.
--Law for Business Managers: The Regulatory Environment. 1977. text ed. 16.95 (ISBN 0-205-05743-8, 075743-8); instructor's manual free (075744-6). Allyn.
Harrop, John, jt. auth. see Cohen, Robert.
Harrop, P. J. Dielectrics. 1972. 12.95 (ISBN 0-408-70387-3); pap. 7.95 (ISBN 0-408-70388-1). Butterworths.
Harrowe, Fiona. Love's Scarlet Banner. (Orig.). 1977. pap. 1.95 o.p. (ISBN 0-449-13904-2, GM). Fawcett.
Harrower, M. R & Steiner, M. E. Large Scale Rorschach Techniques: A Manual for the Group Rorschach & Multiple Choice Tests. rev., 2nd ed. (American Lectures in Psychology Ser.). (Illus.). 376p. 1973. 19.75 (ISBN 0-398-02739-0). C C Thomas.
Harrower, Molly. The Therapy of Poetry. (Amer. Lec. Psychology Ser). 128p. 1972. 7.50 (ISBN 0-398-02311-5). C C Thomas.
Harrris, Leonard. The Hamptons. 1981. 13.95 (ISBN 0-671-61000-7, Wyndham Bks). S&S.
Harry, Joann, jt. auth. see Green, Marilyn L.
Harry, Joseph & Devall, William B. The Social Organization of Gay Males. LC 78-8381. (Praeger Special Studies). 1978. 25.95 (ISBN 0-03-044696-1). Praeger.
Harry, P., tr. see Lozina-Lozinskii, L. K.
Harsany, Peter. Energy Tomorrow. (Illus.). 1980. 17.50 (ISBN 0-686-64249-X). Heinman.
Harsanyi, J. C. Bargaining Equilibrium in Games & Social Situations. LC 75-39370. (Illus.). 352p. 1977. 47.50 (ISBN 0-521-20886-6). Cambridge U Pr.
Harsen, Ed. The Surf Club. 32p. (Orig.). 1981. pap. 3.00 (ISBN 0-935252-27-4). Street Pr.
Harsgor, Michael. Portugal in Revolution. LC 76-2250. (The Washington Papers: No. 32). 1976. 3.50x (ISBN 0-8039-0647-1). Sage.
Harsh, Ernest. South Africa: White Rule-Black Revolt. 1980. lib. bdg. 25.00 (ISBN 0-913460-78-8); pap. 6.95 (ISBN 0-913460-77-X). Monad Pr.
Harshaw, Lou. Places of Discovery I--Asheville. 1981. 10.95. Green Hill.
--Trains, Tressels, & Tunnels. 1981. 8.95 (ISBN 0-932298-10-9). Green Hill.
--Trains, Trestles & Tunnels: Railroad of the Southern Appalachians. (Illus.). pap. 5.95 (ISBN 0-686-27854-2). Appalach Consortium.
Harshaw, Ruth & Evans, Hope H. In What Book. LC 73-99122. (gr. k-12). 1970. 5.95 o.s.i. (ISBN 0-02-742780-3). Macmillan.
Harshbarger, Karl. The Burning Jungle: An Analysis of Arthur Miller's "Death of a Salesman". 1978. pap. text ed. 7.50x (ISBN 0-8191-0368-3). U Pr of Amer.
--Sophocle's Oedipus. LC 79-66476. 1979. text ed. 15.50 (ISBN 0-8191-0834-0); pap. text ed. 7.50 (ISBN 0-8191-0835-9). U Pr of Amer.
Harshbarger, Ronald J. & Reynoldds, James J. Mathematical Applications for Management, Life & Social Studies. 604p. 1981. text ed. 17.95 (ISBN 0-669-03209-3); solutions guide avail. (ISBN 0-669-03211-5). Heath.
Hart, A. B. & Cutler, A. J., eds. Deposition & Corrosion in Gas Turbines. LC 73-8187. 425p. 1973. 59.95 (ISBN 0-470-35639-1). Halsted Pr.
Hart, A. W. & Ells, M. Industrial Hygiene. (Illus.). 400p. 1976. 19.95x (ISBN 0-13-461202-7). P-H.
Hart, Albert B. Foundations of American Foreign Policy. LC 74-109549. (Law, Politics & History Ser). 1970. Repr. of 1901 ed. lib. bdg. 32.50 (ISBN 0-306-71903-7). Da Capo.
--Salmon P. Chase. LC 80-21705. (American Statesmen Ser.). 470p. 1981. pap. 6.95 (ISBN 0-87754-191-4). Chelsea Hse.
--Southern South. LC 74-96438. (American Scene Ser). 1969. Repr. of 1969 ed. lib. bdg. 45.00 (ISBN 0-306-71826-X). Da Capo.
Hart, Albert B. & Chapman, Annie B. How Our Grandfathers Lived. LC 78-164331. 1971. Repr. of 1921 ed. 20.00 (ISBN 0-8103-3795-9). Gale.
Hart, Allan H., jt. auth. see Hart, Ernest H.
Hart, Andrew W., jt. auth. see Smith, Elliott L.
Hart, Archibald. Twelve Ways to Build a Vocabulary. (Orig.). 1964. pap. 2.95 (ISBN 0-06-463293-8, EH 293, EH). Har-Row.
Hart, B. C., ed. Construction Contract Claims. LC 78-74032. (Professional Education Publications). 1979. 15.00 (ISBN 0-89707-002-X). Amer Bar Assn.
Hart, Basil H. Liddell see Liddell Hart, Basil H.
Hart, Basil L. Paris; or, the Future of War. LC 75-148368. (Library of War & Peace; the Character & Causes of War). lib. bdg. 38.00 (ISBN 0-8240-0460-4). Garland Pub.
Hart, Beatrice O. Teaching Reading to Deaf Children. 1978. 9.95 (ISBN 0-88200-117-5). Bell Assn Deaf.
Hart, Benjamin L., ed. Experimental Psychobiology: A Laboratory Manual. (Illus.). 1976. 10.95x (ISBN 0-7167-0731-4). W H Freeman.
Hart, Bernard. Psychology of Insanity. 5th ed. (Orig.). 1957. 23.50 (ISBN 0-521-05219-X). Cambridge U Pr.
Hart, C. R. The Early Charters of Northern England & the North Midlands. (Studies in Early English History Ser: No. 6). 424p. 1975. text ed. 36.50x (ISBN 0-7185-1131-X, Leicester). Humanities.
--Hidation of Cambridgeshire. (Occasional Papers in English Local History, New Ser: No. 6). (Illus.). 64p. 1973. pap. text ed. 3.75x (ISBN 0-7185-2030-0, Leicester). Humanities.
Hart, Clive. Your Book of Kites. (gr. 7 up). 1964. 6.50 (ISBN 0-571-04712-2). Transatlantic.
Hart, Cyril. The Industrial History of Dean: With an Introduction to Its Industrial Archaeology. (Illus.). 466p. 1971. 22.50 (ISBN 0-7153-5288-1). David & Charles.
Hart, D. A., jt. ed. see Gillingwater, David.
Hart, David G., jt. auth. see Lewis, Robert J.
Hart, Dennis. The Ministry of Sovereign Authority. 1978. 4.50 o.p. (ISBN 0-682-49119-5). Exposition.
Hart, Dorothy, ed. & memoir by. Thou Swell, Thou Witty: The Life & Lyrics of Lorenz Hart. LC 72-23885. (Illus.). 192p. 1976. 25.00 o.p. (ISBN 0-06-011776-1, HarpT). Har-Row.
Hart, Douglas. Strategic Planning in London: The Rise & Fall of the Primary Road Network. Urban & Regional Planning Advisory Committee, ed. 239p. 1976. text ed. 18.75 (ISBN 0-08-019780-9). Pergamon.
Hart, E. A., jt. auth. see Cotton, S. A.
Hart, Edward. The Heavy Horse at Work. (Illus.). 64p. 1981. pap. 5.95 (ISBN 0-7134-3805-3, Pub. by Batsford England). David & Charles.
--Heavy Horses Past & Present. LC 75-31325. (Illus.). 112p. 1976. 14.95 (ISBN 0-7153-7146-0). David & Charles.
--The Hill Shepherd. 1977. 13.50 (ISBN 0-7153-7483-4). David & Charles.
--Showing Livestock. LC 78-74086. 1979. 14.95 (ISBN 0-7153-7537-7). David & Charles.
Hart, Edward, jt. auth. see Longton, Tim.
Hart, Edwin J., ed. Radiation Chemistry, 2 Vols. LC 68-55363. (Advances in Chemistry Ser: Nos. 81-82). 1968. Set. 78.00 (ISBN 0-8412-0619-8); No. 81. 45.25 (ISBN 0-8412-0082-3); No. 82. 41.50 (ISBN 0-8412-0083-1). Am Chemical.
Hart, Ernest. Living with Pets. LC 76-39727. 1977. 15.00 (ISBN 0-8149-0778-4). Vanguard.
Hart, Ernest H. Cocker Spaniel Handbook. text ed. 9.95 (ISBN 0-87666-270-X, H923). TFH Pubns.
--How to Clip Your Own Poodle. (Illus.). pap. 2.00 (ISBN 0-87666-358-7, DS1040). TFH Pubns.
--How to Raise & Train a Pointer. (Illus., Orig.). 1966. pap. 2.00 (ISBN 0-87666-350-1, DS1107). TFH Pubns.
--Poodle Handbook. 7.95 (ISBN 0-87666-359-5, H924). TFH Pubns.
Hart, Ernest H. & Hart, Allan H. The Complete Guide to All Cats. 1980. 14.95 (ISBN 0-684-16493-0). Scribner.
Hart, F., et al. Multi-Story Buildings in Steel. LC 74-5513. 1978. 94.95 (ISBN 0-470-35615-4). Halsted Pr.
Hart, Francis R. The Scottish Novel: From Smollett to Spark. LC 77-20680. 1978. 20.00x (ISBN 0-674-79584-9). Harvard U Pr.
Hart, Frank D. Overcoming Arthritis. LC 80-22466. (Positive Health Guides Ser.). (Illus.). 112p. 1981. 9.95 (ISBN 0-668-04679-1); pap. 5.95 (ISBN 0-686-69380-9). Arco.
Hart, Gary. Dynamic Response of Structures. LC 80-70135. 992p. 1981. pap. text ed. 65.00 (ISBN 0-87262-261-4). Am Soc Civil Eng.
Hart, Gavin. Sexual Maladjustment & Disease: An Introduction to Modern Venereology. LC 76-29073. 1977. 18.95 (ISBN 0-88229-325-7). Nelson-Hall.
Hart, George L., III. The Poems of Ancient Tamil: Their Milieu & Their Sanskrit Counterparts. 300p. 1975. 23.75x (ISBN 0-520-02672-1). U of Cal Pr.
Hart, Gordon M. Values Clarification for Counselors: How Counselors, Social Workers, Psychologists, & Other Human Service Workers Can Use Available Techniques. (Illus.). 104p. 1978. 10.75 (ISBN 0-398-03847-3). C C Thomas.

Hart, H. The Challenge of Our Age. LC 68-9843. 1974. pap. 3.25 (ISBN 0-686-11982-7). Wedge Pub.
Hart, H. L., ed. see Bentham, Jeremy.
Hart, Harold. How to Win at Gin Rummy. (Gambler's Book Shelf Ser.). 64p. 1972. pap. 2.95 (ISBN 0-89650-528-6). Gamblers.
Hart, Harold & Schuetz, Robert D. Organic Chemistry: A Short Course. 5th ed. LC 77-75880. (Illus.). 1977. text ed. 16.95 (ISBN 0-395-25161-3); lab. manual 9.25 (ISBN 0-395-25163-X); study guide & solutions bk. 7.95 (ISBN 0-395-25162-1). HM.
Hart, Harold H., compiled by. Limericks Lewd & Lusty. 352p. 1981. pap. 3.95 (ISBN 0-89104-196-6). A & W Pubs.
--The Mammoth Book of Crossword Puzzles. 512p. 1981. pap. 8.95 (ISBN 0-89104-204-0). A & W Pubs.
Hart, Hazel C., jt. auth. see Hughes, Anne E.
Hart, Henry. Dr. Barnes of Merion. 1963. 4.95 o.p. (ISBN 0-374-14285-8). FS&G.
Hart, Henry C., ed. Indira Ghandi's India: The Political System Reappraised. LC 76-5433. (Special Studies on South & Southeast Asia Ser). 1976. 26.50x (ISBN 0-89158-042-5); pap. text ed. 10.00 o.p. (ISBN 0-89158-109-X). Westview.
Hart, Henry H., tr. from Chinese. The Charcoal Burner & Other Poems: Classical Chinese Poetry. 1974. pap. 5.95 (ISBN 0-8061-1475-4). U of Okla Pr.
Hart, Herbert L. Punishment & Responsibility: Essays in the Philosophy of Law. (Orig.). 1968. 14.95 (ISBN 0-19-500162-1); pap. 6.00x (ISBN 0-19-825181-5). Oxford U Pr.
Hart, Herbert L. & Honore, Antony M. Causation in the Law. 1959. 37.50x (ISBN 0-19-825147-5). Oxford U Pr.
Hart, Herbert M. Tour Guide to Old Forts of New Mexico, Arizona, Nevada, Utah, Colorado, Vol. 2. (Illus.). 65p. (Orig.). 1981. pap. 3.95 (ISBN 0-87108-581-X). Pruett.
--Tour Guide to Old Forts of Oregon, Idaho, Washington, California, Vol. 3. (Illus.). 65p. (Orig.). 1981. pap. 3.95 (ISBN 0-87108-582-8). Pruett.
--Tour Guide to Old Forts of Texas, Kansas, Nebraska, Oklahoma, Vol. 4. (Illus.). 65p. (Orig.). 1981. pap. 3.95 (ISBN 0-87108-583-6). Pruett.
--Tourguide to Old Forts of Montana, Wyoming North & South Dakota. (Illus.). 150p. 1980. pap. 3.95 (ISBN 0-87108-570-4). Pruett.
--Tourguide to Old Western Forts. (Illus.). 208p. 1980. 22.50 (ISBN 0-87108-568-2). Pruett.
Hart, Hornell. Toward a New Philosophical Basis for Parapsychological Phenomena. LC 65-15951. (Parapsychological Monograph No. 6). 1965. pap. 2.00 (ISBN 0-912328-09-6). Parapsych Foun.
Hart, James. Ordinance Making Powers of the President of the United States. LC 78-87482. (Law, Politics & History Ser.). 1970. Repr. of 1925 ed. lib. bdg. 29.50 (ISBN 0-306-71487-6). Da Capo.
Hart, James, jt. auth. see Clar, Lawrence.
Hart, James A., jt. auth. see Clar, Lawrence M.
Hart, James D. A Companion to California. LC 76-57286. 1978. 27.50 (ISBN 0-19-502400-1). Oxford U Pr.
--Oxford Companion to American Literature. 4th ed. (YA) 1965. 29.95 (ISBN 0-19-500565-1). Oxford U Pr.
--The Popular Book: A History of America's Literary Taste. 1950. pap. 4.95 (ISBN 0-520-00538-4, CAL49). U of Cal Pr.
Hart, James G., ed. see Heidegger, Martin.
Hart, Jerrems C. & Stone, William T. A Cruising Guide to the Caribbean & the Bahamas. LC 75-43577. (Illus.). 1979. 20.00 (ISBN 0-396-07774-9). Dodd.
Hart, John. Hiking the Bigfoot Country: Exploring the Wildlands of Northern California & Southern Oregon. LC 75-1149. (Totebook Ser). (Illus.). 398p. 1975. pap. 8.95 (ISBN 0-87156-127-1). Sierra.
--Social Work & Sexual Conduct. (Library of Social Work). 1979. 21.50x (ISBN 0-7100-0217-3). Routledge & Kegan.
Hart, John & Orman, Larry. Endangered Harvest: The Future of Bay Area Farmland. (Orig.). 1980. pap. 3.00 (ISBN 0-9605262-0-X). PFOS.
Hart, John F. The Look of the Land. LC 74-20995. (Foundations of Cultural Geography Ser.). (Illus.). 224p. 1975. text ed. 10.95 ref. ed. (ISBN 0-13-540534-3); pap. text ed. 5.95 (ISBN 0-13-540526-2). P-H.
Hart, Johnny. Back to B.C. (B.C. Ser.). (Illus.). 1978. pap. 1.50 (ISBN 0-449-13626-4, GM). Fawcett.
--B.C. Great Zot, I'm Beautiful. (B.C. Ser.). (Illus.). 1978. pap. 1.50 (ISBN 0-449-13614-0, GM). Fawcett.
--B.C. Is Alive & Well. (B.C. Ser.). (Illus.). 1978. pap. 1.50 (ISBN 0-449-13651-5, GM). Fawcett.
--B.C. One More Time. (B.C. Ser.). (Illus.). 1978. pap. 1.50 (ISBN 0-449-13646-9, GM). Fawcett.
--B.C. Where the Hell Is Heck? 1978. pap. 1.50 (ISBN 0-449-14022-9, GM). Fawcett.
--Hurray for B.C. (B.C. Ser.). (Illus.). 1978. pap. 1.50 (ISBN 0-449-13625-6, GM). Fawcett.
--Loneliness Is Rotting on a Bookrack. (B.C. Ser.). (Illus.). 1978. pap. 1.50 (ISBN 0-449-13942-5, GM). Fawcett.
--Sun Comes Up, The Sun Goes Down. (B.C. Ser.). (Illus.). 1979. pap. 1.50 (ISBN 0-449-14205-1, GM). Fawcett.
Hart, Johnny & Parker, Brant. There's a Fly in My Swill. (Wizard of Id Ser.). (Illus.). 1978. pap. 1.50 (ISBN 0-449-13687-6, GM). Fawcett.
Hart, Johnny, jt. auth. see Parker, Brant.
Hart, Jon. Black Blood. LC 80-71036. (The Mercenaries Ser.). 128p. 1981. pap. 2.95 (ISBN 0-87754-227-9). Chelsea Hse.
--Death Raid. LC 81-65241. (The Mercenaries Ser.). 128p. 1981. pap. 2.95 (ISBN 0-87754-244-9). Chelsea Hse.
--Guerrilla Attack. LC 80-71035. (The Mercenaries Ser.). 128p. 1981. pap. 2.95 (ISBN 0-87754-243-0). Chelsea Hse.
--High Slaughter. LC 80-71037. (The Mercenaries Ser.). 128p. 1981. pap. 2.95 (ISBN 0-87754-229-5). Chelsea Hse.
--Triangle of Death. LC 80-71034. (The Mercenaries Ser.). 128p. 1981. pap. 2.95 (ISBN 0-87754-228-7). Chelsea Hse.
Hart, Joseph, jt. auth. see Corriere, Richard.
Hart, Julian T. Hypertension. (Library of General Practice Ser.). 296p. 1980. text ed. 18.75x (ISBN 0-443-01665-8). Churchill.
Hart, K. M., ed. Practical Surveying. 16th ed. (Illus.). 1973. 21.00x (ISBN 0-291-39418-3). Intl Ideas.
Hart, Laura K. The Arithmetic of Dosages & Solutions. 5th ed. (Illus.). 100p. 1981. spiral bdg. 7.95 (ISBN 0-8016-2076-7). Mosby.
Hart, Lois B. Learning from Conflict: A Handbook for Trainers & Group Leaders. LC 80-17227. 224p. 1981. 8.95 (ISBN 0-201-03144-2). A-W.
Hart, M. R. How to Navigate Today. 5th ed. LC 68-23169. (Illus.). 1970. pap. 4.00 (ISBN 0-87033-035-7). Cornell Maritime.
Hart, Marie & Birrell, Susan. Sport in the Socio-Cultural Process. 3rd ed. 544p. 1981. pap. text ed. write for info. (ISBN 0-697-07099-9). Wm C Brown.
Hart, Mary B., intro. by. Journals of Convention Assembled at the City of Austin on the Fourth of July, 1845 for the Purpose of Forming a Constitution for the State of Texas. LC 74-19564. 398p. 1975. Repr. of 1845 ed. 2.95 o.p. (ISBN 0-88319-019-2). Shoal Creek Pub.
Hart, Nathan H., jt. auth. see Hopper, Arthur F.
Hart, Nicky. When Marriage Ends: A Study in Status Passage. 277p. 1976. pap. 11.95 (ISBN 0-422-74690-8, 6371). Methuen Inc.
Hart, Norman A. Industrial Advertising & Publicity. 1978. 24.95 (ISBN 0-470-99375-8). Halsted Pr.
Hart, Norman A., jt. ed. see O'Connor, James.
Hart, P. E. & Clarke, Roger. Concentration in British Industry 1935-1975. LC 79-41808. (Economic & Social Research Occasional Paper: No. 32). 163p. 1980. 29.50 (ISBN 0-521-23393-3). Cambridge U Pr.
Hart, P. E., et al. Mergers & Concentration in British Industry. (National Institute of Economic & Social Research, Occasional Papers: No. 26). (Illus.). 176p. 1973. 20.95 (ISBN 0-521-20238-8). Cambridge U Pr.
Hart, Bro. Paterick, ed. see Merton, Thomas.
Hart, Patrick, ed. The Message of Thomas Merton. (Cistercian Studies: No. 42). 1981. price not set (ISBN 0-87907-842-1). Cistercian Pub.
Hart, Patrick, ed. see Merton, Thomas.
Hart, Patrick, Bro., ed. Thomas Merton, Monk: A Monastic Tribute. 240p. 1976. pap. 1.95 (ISBN 0-385-11244-0, Im). Doubleday.
Hart, Patrick, Bro., ed. see Merton, Thomas.
Hart, Paul & Pitcher, Tony. Fisheries Ecology. 224p. 1980. 35.00x (ISBN 0-85664-894-9, Pub. by Croom Helm England). State Mutual Bk.
Hart, R. S., pseud. Hiway Sex: Women Equal the Greatest Thing on Earth. 125p. (Orig.). Date not set. pap. 5.95 (ISBN 0-9604226-1-7). R S Hart.
Hart, R. S. I Lost Them All but One. LC 80-81241. (Illus.). 200p. (Orig.). 1981. pap. 5.95 (ISBN 0-9604226-9-2). R S Hart.
Hart, R. S., pseud. Was It Incest or Child Abuse? 95p. (Orig.). 1981. pap. 5.95 (ISBN 0-9604226-0-9). R S Hart.
Hart, Robert, jt. auth. see Gaddy, Wade.
Hart, Roderick, jt. ed. see Applbaum, Ronald.
Hart, Roderick, ed. see Campbell, John A.
Hart, Roderick, ed. see Colburn, William & Weinberg, Sanford.
Hart, Roderick, ed. see Felsenthal, Norman.
Hart, Roderick, ed. see Leathers.
Hart, Roger. Children's Experience of Place: A Developmental Study. LC 77-21507. 1979. 27.50 (ISBN 0-470-99190-9). Halsted Pr.
Hart, Stan & Coker, Paul. The Mad Book of Revenge. (Mad Ser.). (Illus.). 192p. (Orig.). 1976. pap. 1.50 (ISBN 0-446-88732-3). Warner Bks.
--The Mad Guide to Careers. (Mad Ser.). (Illus., Orig.). 1978. pap. 1.50 (ISBN 0-446-88302-6). Warner Bks.
Hart, Stuart L. & Enk, Gordon A. Green Goals & Greenbacks: State-Level Environmental Review Programs & Their Associated Costs. LC 79-5229. (A Westview Replica Edition Ser.). (Illus.). 364p. 1979. lib. bdg. 27.50x (ISBN 0-89158-752-7). Westview.
Hart, Thomas N. The Art of Christian Listening. 128p. (Orig.). 1981. pap. 4.95 (ISBN 0-8091-2345-2). Paulist Pr.
Hart, Tony. Fun with Picture Projects. LC 73-174505. (Learning with Fun Ser.). 64p. (gr. 3 up). 1973. 8.50x (ISBN 0-7182-0082-9). Intl Pubns Serv.
Hart, Vivien. Distrust & Democracy. LC 77-84803. (Illus.). 1978. 27.50 (ISBN 0-521-21857-8). Cambridge U Pr.
Hart, W. A., et al. The Chemistry of Lithium, Sodium, Potassium, Rubidium, Cesium & Francium. (Pergamon Texts in Inorganic Chemistry: Vol. 13). 200p. 1975. text ed. 28.00 (ISBN 0-08-018852-4); pap. text ed. 17.50 (ISBN 0-08-018799-4). Pergamon.
Hart, William L. & Waits, Bert K. College Algebra. 6th ed. 1978. text ed. 16.95x (ISBN 0-669-01025-1); inst. manual free (ISBN 0-669-01026-X). Heath.
--College Algebra & Trigonometry. 2nd ed. 1978. text ed. 17.95x (ISBN 0-669-01460-5); inst. manual free (ISBN 0-669-01462-1). Heath.
Hartbarger, Janie C. & Hartbarger, Neil J. Eating for the Eighties. LC 80-53187. 256p. 1981. 12.95 (ISBN 0-03-059077-9); pap. 6.95 (ISBN 0-03-059076-0). HR&W.
--Eating for the Eighties: A Complete Guide to Vegetarian Nutrition. LC 80-53187. 320p. 12.95 (ISBN 0-7216-4550-X); pap. 6.95 (ISBN 0-7216-4549-6). Saunders.
Hartbarger, Neil J., jt. auth. see Hartbarger, Janie C.
Hart-Davis, Duff. The Heights of Rimring. LC 80-69379. 1981. 12.95 (ISBN 0-689-11148-7). Atheneum.
Hart-Davis, Rupert. The Arms of Time: A Memoir. (Illus.). 176p. 1979. 19.95 (ISBN 0-241-10305-3, Pub. by Hamish Hamilton England). David & Charles.
Hart-Davis, Rupert, ed. see Wilde, Oscar.
Harte, Bret. The Girl from Pike County. Pauk, Walter & Harris, Raymond, eds. (Classics Ser). (Illus.). (gr. 6-12). 1976. pap. text ed. 1.60x (ISBN 0-89061-050-9, 521); tchrs. ed. 3.00 (ISBN 0-89061-053-3, 523). Jamestown Pubs.
--The Luck of Roaring Camp. Pauk, Walter & Harris, Raymond, eds. (Classics Ser). (Illus.). (gr. 6-12). 1976. pap. text ed. 1.60x (ISBN 0-89061-054-1, 529); tchrs. ed. 3.00 (ISBN 0-89061-055-X, 531). Jamestown Pubs.
--Mliss. Pauk, Walter & Harris, Raymond, eds. (Classics Ser). (gr. 6-12). 1976. pap. text ed. 1.60x (ISBN 0-89061-048-7, 517); tchrs. ed. 3.00 (ISBN 0-89061-049-5, 519). Jamestown Pubs.
--The Outcasts of Poker Flat. Pauk, Walter & Harris, Raymond, eds. (Classics Ser). (Illus.). (gr. 6-12). 1976. pap. text ed. 1.60x (ISBN 0-89061-052-5, 525); tchrs. ed. 3.00 (ISBN 0-89061-053-3, 527). Jamestown Pubs.
--The Outcasts of Poker Flat. (Creative's Classics Ser.). (Illus.). 48p. (gr. 4-9). 1980. PLB 6.95 (ISBN 0-87191-768-6). Creative Ed.
--Outcasts of Poker Flat & Luck of Roaring Camp. rev. ed. Dixson, Robert J., ed. (American Classics Ser.: Bk. 5). (gr. 9 up). 1973. pap. text ed. 2.75 (ISBN 0-88345-201-4, 18124); cassettes 40.00 (ISBN 0-685-38996-0); tapes 40.00 (ISBN 0-685-38997-9). Regents Pub.
Harte, Bret see Disraeli, Benjamin.
Harte, N. B., ed. Study of Economic History: Collected Inaugural Lectures, 1893-1970. 385p. 1971. 29.50x (ISBN 0-7146-2905-7, F Cass Co). Biblio Dist.
Harte, Samantha. The Snows of Craggmoor. (YA) 1978. 5.95 (ISBN 0-685-87350-1, Avalon). Bouregy.
Hartelius, Margaret A. The Birthday Trombone. (ps-1). 1977. PLB 5.95 (ISBN 0-385-12293-4). Doubleday.
--The Chicken's Child. LC 74-18884. 40p. (ps-k). 1975. PLB 5.95 (ISBN 0-385-07370-4). Doubleday.
Harten, Lucille B., et al, eds. Anthropological Papers in Memory of Earl H. Swanson, Jr. (Special Publication of the Idaho Museum of Natural History). 200p. (Orig.). 1980. write for info. Idaho Mus Nat Hist.
Harter, Hugh A. Gertrudis Gomez De Avellaneda. (World Authors Ser.: No. 599). 1981. lib. bdg. 14.95 (ISBN 0-8057-6441-0). Twayne.
Harter, James & Beitzel, Wallace. Mathematics Applied to Electronics. (Illus.). 1980. text ed. 18.95 (ISBN 0-8359-4288-0); instrs'. manual avail. Reston.
Harter, Jim. Harter's Picture Archive for Collage & Illustration: Over 300 Nineteenth Century Cuts. 1978. pap. 5.00 (ISBN 0-486-23659-5). Dover.
--Music: A Pictorial Archive of Woodcuts & Engravings. (Pictorial Archive Ser.). (Illus.). 155p. (Orig.). 1981. pap. 6.00 (ISBN 0-486-24002-9). Dover.
Harter, Jim, ed. Animals: Illustrations of Mammals, Birds, Fish, Insects, Etc. A Pictorial Archive from Nineteenth-Century Sources. LC 78-73302. (Pictorial Archive Ser.). (Illus.). 1979. pap. 7.95 (ISBN 0-486-23766-4). Dover.
--Women: A Pictorial Archive from 19th Century Sources. (Pictorial Archive Ser.). 1978. pap. 4.50 (ISBN 0-486-23703-6). Dover.
Harter, Penny. Lovepoems. 56p. (Orig.). 1981. pap. 3.95 (ISBN 0-89120-016-9, Old Plate). From Here.
--The Orange Balloon. (Xtras Ser.: No. 8). 36p. (Orig.). 1980. pap. 2.00 (ISBN 0-89120-012-6). From Here.
Harter, Penny & Higginson, William J., eds. Between Two Rivers: Union County Literature Today. 112p. (Orig.). 1980. pap. 4.95 (ISBN 0-89120-017-7). From Here.
Harter, Penny, jt. ed. see Higginson, William J.
Harter, Stephen P., jt. ed. see Busha, Charles H.
Harter, W. Osceola's Head & Other American Ghost Stories. (Illus.). 1974. 4.95 (ISBN 0-13-642991-2); pap. 1.95 (ISBN 0-13-643007-4). P-H.
Harter, Walter. Birds: In Fact & Legend. LC 79-65065. (Illus.). 1979. 6.95 (ISBN 0-8069-3740-8); lib. bdg. 6.69 (ISBN 0-8069-3741-6). Sterling.
--Steel: The Metal with Muscle. (Illus.). 96p. (gr. 4-7). 1981. PLB price not set. Messner.
Hartfeld, Hermann. Faith Despite the KGB. Wagner, Henry, tr. LC 80-66491. 224p. 1980. pap. 4.95 (ISBN 0-915684-74-8). Christian Herald.
Hartford, jt. auth. see Marxer.
Hartford, Huntington. You Are What You Write. LC 72-91262. 360p. 1973. 12.95 (ISBN 0-02-548500-8). Macmillan.
Hartford, Margaret E. Groups in Social Work: Application of Small Group Theory & Research to Social Work Practice. LC 71-181782. 320p. 1972. 16.00x (ISBN 0-231-03548-9); pap. 9.00x (ISBN 0-685-23629-3). Columbia U Pr.
Hartford, Robert, ed. Bayreuth: The Early Years; an Account of the Wagner Festival, 1876-1914 As Seen by Celebrated Visitors & Participants. (Illus.). 288p. 1981. 19.95 (ISBN 0-521-23822-6). Cambridge U Pr.
Harth, Erica. Cyrano De Bergerac & the Polemics of Modernity. LC 73-9786. 1970. 20.00x (ISBN 0-231-03301-X). Columbia U Pr.
Harthan, John, ed. see Klingender, Francis D.
Hartigan, J. A. Clustering Algorithms. LC 74-14573. (Wiley Series in Probability & Mathematical Statistics). 368p. 1975. 28.50 (ISBN 0-471-35645-X, Pub. by Wiley-Interscience). Wiley.
Hartigan, Joe. To Become a Racehorse Trainer. 7.00 (ISBN 0-85131-234-9, Dist. by Sporting Book Center). J A Allen.
--Your First Point to Point Horse. pap. 5.25 (ISBN 0-85131-212-8, Dist. by Sporting Book Center). J A Allen.
Hartill, William R., ed. World Free Flight Review. (Illus.). 1978. 30.00 (ISBN 0-933066-01-5). World Free Flight.
Harting, James E. Harting's Hints on Hawks. 12.95 o.p. (ISBN 0-8231-2019-8). Branford.
Hartinger, W., jt. auth. see Eldefonso, E.
Hartjen, Clayton, jt. auth. see Duberman, Lucile.
Hartl, Daniel L. Our Uncertain Heritage: Genetics & Human Diversity. LC 76-30509. 1977. text ed. 18.50 scp (ISBN 0-397-47366-4, HarpC); scp study guide 6.50 (ISBN 0-397-47367-2). Har-Row.
--A Primer of Population Genetics. LC 80-23009. (Illus.). 175p. (Orig.). 1981. pap. text ed. 8.00x (ISBN 0-87893-271-2). Sinauer Assoc.
Hartlage, Lawrence C. & Lucas, David G. Mental Development Evaluation of the Pediatric Patient. (Illus.). 92p. 1973. 9.75 (ISBN 0-398-02522-3). C C Thomas.
Hartland, Edwin S. Science of Fairy Tales: An Inquiry into Fairy Mythology. LC 68-31149. 1968. Repr. of 1891 ed. 22.00 (ISBN 0-8103-3464-X). Gale.
Hartland, Edwin S., ed. English Fairy & Other Folktales. LC 68-21772. 1968. Repr. of 1890 ed. 18.00 (ISBN 0-8103-3465-8). Gale.
Hartland, J. Medical & Dental Hypnosis & Its Clinical Application. 2nd ed. 1971. 25.00 o.s.i. (ISBN 0-02-858000-1); pap. text ed. 26.95 (ISBN 0-02-858010-9). Macmillan.

Hartland, Robert. Design of Precast Concrete: An Introduction to Practical Design. LC 75-23528. 1976. 17.95 (ISBN 0-470-35654-5). Halsted Pr.

Hartland, S. Counter Current Extraction. LC 69-17867. 1970. 25.00 (ISBN 0-08-012976-5). Pergamon.

Hartland-Thunberg, Penelope. Botswana: An African Growth Economy. LC 78-3477. (Westview Special Studies on Africa). (Illus.). 1978. lib. bdg. 18.00x (ISBN 0-89158-171-5). Westview.

--The Political & Strategic Importance of Exports, Vol. I. LC 79-2785. (Significant Issues Ser.: No. 3). 35p. 1979. 4.00 (ISBN 0-89206-009-3). CSI Studies.

--Trading Blocs, U.S. Exports, & World Trade. (Westview Special Studies in International Economics & Business). 197p. 1980. lib. bdg. 22.00x (ISBN 0-89158-967-8). Westview.

Hartle, Douglas G. Public Policy Decision Making & Regulation. 218p. 1979. pap. text ed. 12.95x (ISBN 0-920380-20-4, Pub. by Inst Res Pub Canada). Renouf.

Hartle, Robert W., tr. see Moliere, Jean B.

Hartley, jt. auth. see Allan.

Hartley, Allan. Archie's Family Album. (Spire Comics Ser.). 1978. pap. 0.49 (ISBN 0-8007-8532-0). Revell.

--Born Again. (Spire Christian Comic). 1978. pap. 0.49 (ISBN 0-8007-8535-5). Revell.

--On the Road with Andre Crouch. 1978. pap. 0.49 o.p. (ISBN 0-8007-8529-0). Revell.

Hartley, C. W. The Oil Palm. 2nd ed. LC 76-23180. (Tropical Agriculture Ser.). 1977. text ed. 60.00x (ISBN 0-582-46809-4). Longman.

Hartley, David. Observations on Man, His Frame, His Duty & His Expectations, 2 vols. LC 66-11026. 1966. Repr. of 1749 ed. 90.00x (ISBN 0-8201-1025-6). Schol Facsimiles.

Hartley, David, ed. Freaky Fillins, No. 1. 48p. (Orig.). 1980. pap. 1.50 (ISBN 0-937518-00-X). Hartley Hse.

--Freaky Fillins, No. 3. 48p. (Orig.). 1980. pap. 1.50 (ISBN 0-937518-02-6). Hartley Hse.

Hartley, Dorothy. Lost Country Life. (Illus.). 1981. pap. 6.95 (ISBN 0-394-74838-7). Pantheon.

Hartley, F. R. Chemistry of Platinum & Palladium: With Particular Reference to Complexes of the Elements. LC 72-11319. 1973. 59.95 (ISBN 0-470-35658-8). Halsted Pr.

Hartley, Fred. Dare to Be Different. 1980. pap. 3.95 (ISBN 0-8007-5041-1). Revell.

Hartley, H. O., jt. ed. see Pearson, E. S.

Hartley, James, ed. Psychology of Written Communication. 1980. 32.50x (ISBN 0-89397-081-6). Nichols Pub.

Hartley, Joel. First Aid without Panic. 1977. pap. 2.50 o.p. (ISBN 0-445-08603-3). Popular Lib.

Hartley, John R. Management of Vehicle Production. (Illus.). 216p. 1980. text ed. 32.00 (ISBN 0-408-00396-0). Butterworths.

Hartley, Karen. Energy R & D Decision Making for Canada. 108p. 1979. pap. text ed. 3.00x (ISBN 0-920380-40-9, Pub. by Inst Res Pub Canada). Renouf.

Hartley, Keith. Problems of Economic Policy. (Economics & Society Ser.). 1977. text ed. 18.95x (ISBN 0-04-339008-0). Allen Unwin.

Hartley, L. P. The Go-Between. LC 54-7169. 320p. (Orig.). 1980. pap. 4.95 (ISBN 0-8128-6073-X). Stein & Day.

--Shrimp & Anemone. 1963. pap. 2.95 (ISBN 0-571-07061-2, Pub. by Faber & Faber). Merrimack Bk Serv.

Hartley, Leslie P. Brickfield & Betrayal. 15.00 (ISBN 0-241-02383-1). Dufour.

Hartley, Marsden. On Art. Scott, Gail R., ed. (Illus.). 360p. 1981. 19.95 (ISBN 0-8180-0130-5). Horizon.

Hartley, May L. Flitters, Tatters, & the Counsellor & Other Sketches. (Nineteenth Century Fiction Ser.: Ireland: Vol. 67). 1979. lib. bdg. 46.00 (ISBN 0-8240-3516-X). Garland Pub.

--Hogan, M. P. (Nineteenth Century Fiction Ser.: Ireland: Vol. 66). 916p. 1979. lib. bdg. 46.00 (ISBN 0-8240-3515-1). Garland Pub.

Hartley, Melissa, ed. Freaky Fillins, No. 2. 48p. (Orig.). 1980. pap. 1.50 (ISBN 0-937518-01-8). Hartley Hse.

--Freaky Fillins, No. 4. 48p. (Orig.). 1980. pap. 1.50 (ISBN 0-937518-03-4). Hartley Hse.

Hartley, Norman. Quicksilver. 240p. (Orig.). 1980. pap. 2.50 (ISBN 0-380-51482-6, 51482). Avon.

--The Viking Process. 320p. 1980. pap. 2.75 (52993). Avon.

--The Viking Process. 1976. pap. 1.95 (ISBN 0-380-00892-0, 31617). Avon.

Hartley, R. F. Marketing Fundamentals for Responsive Management. 2nd ed. 1976. text ed. 20.50 scp (ISBN 0-912212-05-5, HarpC). Har-Row.

Hartley, Robert F. Marketing Mistakes. 2nd ed. LC 80-13236. (Marketing Ser.). 220p. 1980. pap. text ed. 8.95 (ISBN 0-88244-225-2). Grid Pub.

--Retailing: Challenge & Opportunity. 1975. text ed. 16.50 o.p. (ISBN 0-395-17073-7); instructor's manual 1.75 o.p. (ISBN 0-395-18787-7). HM.

--Retailing: Challenge & Opportunity. 2nd ed. LC 79-88102. 1980. text ed. 18.95 (ISBN 0-395-28185-7); instructor's manual 2.00 (ISBN 0-395-28186-5). HM.

--Sales Management. LC 78-69614. (Illus.). 1979. text ed. 18.95 (ISBN 0-395-26511-8); inst. manual 1.10 (ISBN 0-395-26512-6); test bank 1.25 (ISBN 0-395-29301-4). HM.

Hartley, Ruth E. & Goldenson, Robert M. Complete Book of Children's Play. rev. ed. (Apollo Eds.). (Illus.). 1970. pap. 4.95 o.s.i. (ISBN 0-8152-0245-8, A245, TYC-T). T Y Crowell.

Hartley, Shirley F. Illegitimacy. LC 73-83057. 1975. 15.75x (ISBN 0-520-02533-4). U of Cal Pr.

--Population: Quantity Versus Quality. 352p. 1972. pap. text ed. 9.95 o.p. (ISBN 0-13-686600-X). P-H.

Hartley, Vicki J. Tuesday's Song. 64p. 1979. 3.50 (ISBN 0-8059-2648-8). Dorrance.

Hartley, W. Checklist of Economic Plants in Australia. 214p. 1980. pap. 7.50x (ISBN 0-643-02551-0, Pub. by CSIRO Australia). Intl Schol Bk Serv.

Hartley, W. C. Cash: Planning, Forecasting & Control. 210p. 1976. text ed. 24.50x (ISBN 0-220-66288-6, Pub. by Busn Bks England). Renouf.

--An Introduction to Business Accounting for Managers. 3rd ed. 1980. 28.00 (ISBN 0-08-024061-5); pap. 12.00 (ISBN 0-08-024062-3). Pergamon.

Hartley-Cox, Barbara. Three Little Tales. 1979. 4.50 o.p. (ISBN 0-8062-1210-1). Carlton.

Hartman, Ann. Finding Families: An Ecological Approach to Family Assessment in Adoption. LC 78-26537. (Sage Human Services Guides: Vol. 7). 1979. pap. 6.50x (ISBN 0-8039-1216-1). Sage.

Hartman, Bernard. Fundamentals of Television: Theory & Service. new ed. (Technology Ser). (Illus.). 272p. 1975. text ed. 18.95 (ISBN 0-675-08745-7). Merrill.

Hartman, Charles O. Free Verse: An Essay on Prosody. LC 80-10782. 225p. 1980. 14.00x (ISBN 0-691-06438-5). Princeton U Pr.

Hartman, Charles S., ed. & intro. by see Luccock, Halford E.

Hartman, Chester. Housing & Social Policy. (Ser. in Social Policy). 176p. 1975. ref. ed. 10.95 (ISBN 0-13-394999-0). P-H.

Hartman, Gary V., tr. see Guggenbuhl-Craig, Adolf.

Hartman, Geoffrey H. Saving the Texts: Literature-Derrida-Philosophy. LC 80-21748. (Illus.). 190p. 1981. text ed. 12.95x (ISBN 0-8018-2452-4). Johns Hopkins.

Hartman, Geoffrey H., ed. New Perspectives on Coleridge & Wordsworth: Selected Papers from the English Institute. LC 72-3738. 1972. 12.50x (ISBN 0-231-03679-5). Columbia U Pr.

Hartman, Gertrude. Medieval Days & Ways. (Illus.). (gr. 8-9). 1937. 11.95 (ISBN 0-02-743090-1). Macmillan.

Hartman, Henry L. Basic Psychiatry for Corrections Workers. 488p. 1978. 23.75 (ISBN 0-398-03663-2). C C Thomas.

Hartman, Howard L. Mine Ventilation & Air Conditioning. (Illus.). 1961. 27.50 (ISBN 0-8260-3860-3, Pub. by Wiley-Interscience). Wiley.

Hartman, Jan. The Dean's Death. (Columbo: No. 2). 1975. pap. 1.25 o.p. (ISBN 0-445-00265-4). Popular Lib.

Hartman, Jane E. Looking at Lizards. LC 78-5357. (Illus.). (gr. 5-9). 1978. 7.95 (ISBN 0-8234-0330-0). Holiday.

Hartman, Margaret & Russell, Mercer P. Laboratory Manual for Biology of Animals. 1980. coil binding 7.50 (ISBN 0-88252-108-X). Paladin Hse.

Hartman, Paul T. Collective Bargaining & Productivity: The Longshore Mechanization Agreement. (Institute of Business & Economic Research, UC Berkeley). 1969. 21.00x (ISBN 0-520-01485-5). U of Cal Pr.

Hartman, Philip, ed. see Stahl, Franklin W.

Hartman, Robert S., tr. see Hegel, Georg W.

Hartman, Robert S., tr. see Kant, Immanuel.

Hartman, Robert W. & Weber, Arnold R., eds. The Rewards of Public Service: Compensating Top Federal Officials. 1980. 14.95 (ISBN 0-8157-3494-8); pap. 5.95 (ISBN 0-8157-3493-X). Brookings.

Hartman, Susan. Satyr. Barkan, Stanley H., ed. (Cross-Cultural Review Chapbook 7). 16p. 1980. pap. 2.00 (ISBN 0-89304-806-2). Cross Cult.

Hartman, Tom, jt. ed. see Cooper, Jilly.

Hartman, W., et al. Management Information Systems Handbook. 2nd ed. 1970. 48.50 o.p. (ISBN 0-07-026957-2, P&RB). McGraw.

Hartman, Yuki. Hot Footsteps. Owen, Maureen, ed. LC 76-20487. (Illus.). 45p. (Orig.). 1976. pap. 1.50 (ISBN 0-916382-10-9). Telephone Bks.

Hartmann, Donald P., jt. auth. see Gelfand, Donna L.

Hartmann, Frank Von see Von Hartmann, Frank.

Hartmann, Franz. Magic White & Black; or, the Science of Finite & Infinite Life. LC 80-19323. 298p. 1980. Repr. of 1971 ed. lib. bdg. 11.95x (ISBN 0-89370-603-5). Borgo Pr.

Hartmann, George W. Gestalt Psychology: A Survey of Facts & Principles. LC 73-16649. (Illus.). 325p. 1974. Repr. of 1935 ed. lib. bdg. 25.00x (ISBN 0-8371-7213-6, HAGE). Greenwood.

Hartmann, H., jt. auth. see Fabian, J.

Hartmann, Hudson T., jt. auth. see Flocker, William J.

Hartmann, Hudson T., jt. auth. see Kester, Dale E.

Hartmann, Jerry. Palace Politics: An Inside Account of the Ford Years. 320p. 1980. 14.95 (ISBN 0-07-026951-3). McGraw.

Hartmann, Louis. Theatre Lighting. LC 76-115696. 1970. Repr. of 1930 ed. 5.95x o.p. (ISBN 0-910482-18-7). Drama Bk.

Hartmann, R. R. & Stork, F. C., eds. Dictionary of Language & Linguistics. LC 72-6251. 1976. 32.95 (ISBN 0-470-35667-7); pap. 24.95 (ISBN 0-470-15200-1). Halsted Pr.

Hartmann, Rudolf. Richard Strauss: The Staging of His Operas & Ballets. (Illus.). 226p. 1981. 39.95 (ISBN 0-19-520251-1). Oxford U Pr.

Hartmann, Susan. Truman & the Eightieth Congress. LC 78-149008. 1971. 15.00x (ISBN 0-8262-0105-9). U of Mo Pr.

Hartmann, Sven & Hartner, Thoman. Jacob Two: Me & My Human. Bernard, Jack, ed. Macri, Angelika, tr. 80p. (gr. k-6). 1981. pap. 7.95 (ISBN 0-8120-2391-9). Barron.

Hartmann, Von Aue. Iwein. Thomas, J. W., tr. LC 79-1139. 1979. 10.95x (ISBN 0-8032-4404-5). U of Nebr Pr.

Hartmann, William H., et al. Endocrine Pathology. LC 78-11793. (Anatomic Pathology Slide Seminar Proceedings Ser.). (Illus.). 1979. pap. text ed. 15.00 o.p. (ISBN 0-89189-054-8, 50-1-043-00); slides 84.00 o.p. (ISBN 0-686-67346-8, 01-0-077-01). Am Soc Clinical.

Hartmann, William K. Astronomy: The Cosmic Journey. 1978. text ed. 21.95x (ISBN 0-534-00546-2); study guide 1979 7.95x (ISBN 0-534-00711-2). Wadsworth Pub.

Hartmann Von Aue. Iwein: Eine Erzaehlung, 2 vols. 7th ed. Benecke, G. F., et al, eds. Incl. Vol. 1. Text. xii, 196p. 1968. 17.75x (ISBN 3-11-000329-5); Vol. 2. Handschriftenuebersicht: Anmerkungen und Lesarten. iv, 227p. 1968. 17.75 (ISBN 3-11-000330-9). (Ger.). De Gruyter.

Hartmann von Ave. Iwein. 2nd ed. Benecke, G. F., et al, eds. Cramer, Thomas, tr. & notes by. vi, 232p. (Ger.). 1974. 20.00x (ISBN 3-11-004860-4). De Gruyter.

Hartnagel, Hans L. Gunn-Effect Logic Devices. 1973. text ed. 19.50x o.p. (ISBN 0-435-71485-6). Heinemann Ed.

--Semiconductor Plasma Instabilities. 1969. text ed. 14.95x o.p. (ISBN 0-435-69390-5). Heinemann Ed.

Hartner, Thoman, jt. auth. see Hartmann, Sven.

Hartnett, Donald L., jt. auth. see Cabot, A. Victor.

Hartnett, James P., jt. auth. see Irvine, Thomas F., Jr.

Hartnett, James P., jt. ed. see Irvine, Thomas F., Jr.

Hartnett, Michael. Poems in English. 1977. text ed. 15.75x (ISBN 0-85105-313-0, Dolmen Pr). Humanities.

Hartnoll, E. G., jt. ed. see Naylor, E.

Hartnoll, Phyllis. Concise History of the Theatre. 1973. pap. 8.95 (ISBN 0-684-13521-3, SL483, ScribT). Scribner.

Hartog, Jacob P. Den see Den Hartog, Jacob P.

Hartog, Jacob P. Den see Prandtl, Ludwig & Tietjens, O. G.

Hartog, Jan de. The Peaceable Kingdom. 1978. pap. 2.50 o.p. (ISBN 0-449-23463-0, Crest). Fawcett.

--The Spiral Road. 465p. 1976. Repr. of 1957 ed. lib. bdg. 15.95x (ISBN 0-89244-092-9). Queens Hse.

Hartog, Jan de see De Hartog, Jan.

Hartog, Joop. Personal Income Distribution: A Multicapability Theory. 208p. 1980. lib. bdg. 22.00 (ISBN 0-89838-047-2). Kluwer Boston.

Hartshorn, Edward A. Handbook of Drug Interactions. 3rd ed. LC 76-27057. 225p. 1976. pap. 7.50 (ISBN 0-914768-23-9). Drug Intl Pubns.

Hartshorn, Leon R., compiled by. Inspiring Stories for Young Latter-Day Saints. LC 75-5178. 270p. 1975. 6.95 o.p. (ISBN 0-87747-547-4). Deseret Bk.

Hartshorn, S. R. Aliphatic Nucleophilic Substitution. LC 72-96675. (Chemistry Texts Ser.). (Illus.). 150p. 1973. 32.50 (ISBN 0-521-20177-2); pap. 11.95x (ISBN 0-521-09801-7). Cambridge U Pr.

Hartshorn, Truman A. Interpreting the City: Urban Geography. LC 79-19544. 1980. text ed. 21.95x (ISBN 0-471-05637-5). Wiley.

Hartshorne, Charles. Whitehead's Philosophy: Selected Essays, 1935-1970. LC 72-75343. (Landmark Ed.). 1972. 19.50x (ISBN 0-8032-0806-5). U of Nebr Pr.

Hartshorne, Charles & Peden, Creighton. Whitehead's View of Reality. 96p. (Orig.). Date not set. pap. 6.95 (ISBN 0-8298-0381-5). Pilgrim NY.

Hartshorne, Hugh & Miller, J. Q. Community Organization in Religious Education. 1932. 37.50x (ISBN 0-686-51356-8). Elliots Bks.

Hartson, William R. Benoni. 1977. 15.95 (ISBN 0-7134-0246-6, Pub. by Batsford England); pap. 12.50 (ISBN 0-7134-0247-4). David & Charles.

Hartstein, Jack. Questions & Answers on Contact Lens Practice. 2nd ed. LC 73-4658. (Illus.). 1973. 21.50 o.p. (ISBN 0-8016-2088-0). Mosby.

--Review of Refraction. (Comprehensive Review Ser). (Illus.). 1971. 17.50 o.p. (ISBN 0-8016-2091-0). Mosby.

Hartston, W. R. & Keene, R. D. Karpov-Korchnoi 1974. (Illus.). 94p. 1975. pap. 3.95 o.p. (ISBN 0-19-217530-0). Oxford U Pr.

Hartston, W. R. & Reuben, S. London Nineteen Eighty: Phillips & Drew Kings Chess Tournament. (Pergamon Chess Ser.). (Illus.). 230p. 1981. 21.60 (ISBN 0-08-024141-7); pap. 21.60 (ISBN 0-08-024140-9). Pergamon.

Hartston, William R. Grunfeld Defence. 1973. 17.50 (ISBN 0-7134-0377-2). David & Charles.

Hartstone, Robin, ed. see Symposia in Pure Mathematics, Humboldt State University, Arcata, Calif., July 29-August 16, 1974.

Hartt, Frederick. History of Italian Renaissance Art. 2nd ed. (Illus.). 1980. text ed. 21.95 (ISBN 0-13-392043-7). P-H.

Hartt, Frederick, ed. see Michelangelo.

Hartt, Frederick, et al. Chapel of the Cardinal of Portugal. LC 62-17064. (Illus.). 1964. 25.00x o.p. (ISBN 0-8122-7332-X). U of Pa Pr.

Hartt, Julian N. Theological Method & Imagination. 1977. 12.95 (ISBN 0-8164-0335-X). Crossroad NY.

Hartung, Albert E. & Severs, Burke, eds. Manual of Writings in Middle English, 1050-1500, 6 vols. Incl. Vol. 1. 338p. 1967. 17.50 (ISBN 0-208-00893-4); pap. 10.50; Vol. 2. 329p. 1970. 17.50 (ISBN 0-208-00894-2); Vol. 3. 960p. 1972. 17.50 (ISBN 0-208-01220-6); Vol. 4. 1313p. 1973. 17.50 (ISBN 0-208-01342-3); Vol. 5. 440p. 1976. 25.00 (ISBN 0-208-01459-4); Vol. 6. 500p. 1980. 25.00 (ISBN 0-208-01715-1). Shoe String.

Hartung, Rolf. Clay. 1972. 15.95 (ISBN 0-7134-2383-8, Pub. by Batsford England). David & Charles.

--Plywood. 1971. 17.95 (ISBN 0-7134-2380-3, Pub. by Batsford England). David & Charles.

Hartunian, Nelson S., et al. The Incidence & Economic Costs of Major Health Impairments: A Comparative Analysis of Cancer, Motor-Vehicle Injuries, Coronary Heart Disease, & Stroke. LC 80-8189. 1981. price not set (ISBN 0-669-03975-6). Lexington Bks.

Hartunian, Paul. Lifesavers: A Guide to Free First Aid, Health & Safety Information. 50p. (Orig.). 1981. pap. 3.95. Tri-Med.

Hartveit, Lars. Dream Within a Dream: A Thematic Approach to Scott's Vision of Fictional Reality. 1974. pap. text ed. 23.00x (ISBN 8-200-01361-8, Dist. by Columbia U Pr). Universitet.

Hartwell, A., tr. see Lopes, Duarte.

Hartwell, K. J. Making Jewellery. LC 75-512157. 80p. 1975. 7.50 (ISBN 0-7175-0466-2). Dufour.

Hartwig, Daphne M. Make Your Own Groceries. LC 79-2453. (Illus.). 1979. pap. 12.95 (ISBN 0-672-52279-9). Bobbs.

Hartwig, Frederick & Dearing, Brian E. Exploratory Data Analysis. LC 79-67621. (Quantitative Applications in the Social Sciences: No. 16). (Illus.). 1979. pap. 3.50x (ISBN 0-8039-1370-2). Sage.

Hartwig, Gerald, ed. The Africa Sketches. (Illus.). 64p. (gr. 7-10). 1980. 2.20 ea.; of 9 17.00 set (ISBN 0-686-28127-6). Ctr Intl Stud Duke.

Harty, James Q., jt. ed. see Wylie, Harry L.

Harty, Sheila. Hucksters in the Classroom: A Review of Industry Propaganda in Schools. (Illus., Orig.). 1980. pap. 10.00 o.p. (ISBN 0-686-28457-7). Ctr Responsive Law.

--Hucksters in the Classroom: A Review of Industry Propaganda in Schools. (Illus.). 190p. 1979. individuals 10.00 (ISBN 0-936758-01-5); institutions 20.00 (ISBN 0-686-28151-9). Ctr Responsive Law.

Hartzell, Dennis J. Odysseus: The Complete Adventures. (Illus.). 92p. (Orig.). (gr. 7-9). 1978. pap. text ed. 2.75x (ISBN 0-88334-110-7). Ind Sch Pr.

Hartzell, Karl D. & Sasscer, Harrison, eds. Study of Religion on the Campus of Today. 1967. 3.00 o.p. (ISBN 0-685-05154-4). ACE.

Hartzell, Warren & LaBarge, Lura. Net-Making & Knotting. LC 74-82328. (Little Craft Book Ser). (Illus.). 48p. (gr. 7 up). 1974. 4.95 o.p. (ISBN 0-8069-5310-1); PLB 5.89 o.p. (ISBN 0-8069-5311-X). Sterling.

Hartzschel, Walter. Treatise on Invertebrate Paleontology, Pt. W. Suppl.1 Miscellanea, Trace Fossils & Problematica. 2nd. rev. & enl. ed. LC 53-12913. (Illus.). 1975. 20.00x (ISBN 0-8137-3027-9). Geol Soc.

Harugi, Harith. Law Dictionary (Arabic-English) 1972. 25.00x (ISBN 0-685-72050-0). Intl Bk Ctr.

Harvard, Andrew & Thompson, Todd. Mountain of Storms: American Expeditions to Dhaulagiri, 1969 & 1973. LC 74-13925. (Illus.). 210p. (Co-published with Chelsea House). 1974. 15.00 (ISBN 0-8147-3366-2). NYU Pr.

--Mountain of Storms: The American Expeditions to Dhaulagiri. LC 74-13924. (Illus.). 220p. 1981. pap. 9.95 (ISBN 0-87754-146-9). Chelsea Hse.

Harvard, J. Bilingual Guide to Business & Professional Correspondence: English-French. 1976. 21.00 (ISBN 0-08-015973-7); pap. 10.75 (ISBN 0-08-015594-4). Pergamon.

--Bilingual Guide to Business & Professional Correspondence, English-German, German-English. 1975. 15.00 (ISBN 0-08-017654-2); pap. 7.75 (ISBN 0-08-017655-0). Pergamon.

--Bilingual Guide to Business & Professional Correspondence: Spanish-English, English-Spanish. 1970. 23.00 (ISBN 0-08-015793-9); pap. 7.75 (ISBN 0-08-015792-0). Pergamon.

Harvard Lampoon et Al. Bored of the Rings or Tolkien Revisited. 1971. pap. 1.75 (ISBN 0-451-09441-7, E9441, Sig). NAL.

Harvard Lampoon, Inc. The Harvard Lampoon: Big Book of College Life. LC 77-15165. 1978. pap. 5.95 (ISBN 0-385-13446-0, Dolp). Doubleday.

Harvard Law School Board of Student Advisers. Introduction to Advocacy: Brief Writing & Oral Argument in Moot Court Competition. 3rd ed. 100p. 1980. text ed. write for info. (ISBN 0-88277-019-5). Foundation Pr.

Harvard Medical School, Laboratory of Community Psychiatry. Competency to Stand Trial & Mental Illness. LC 74-25406. 132p. 1975. 17.50x (ISBN 0-87668-190-9). Aronson.

Harvard Student Agencies. Let's Go, Britain & Ireland: The Budget Guide 1981 to 1982 Edition. (Illus.). 550p. 1981. pap. 5.50 (ISBN 0-525-93143-0). Dutton.

--Let's Go, Britain & Ireland: The Budget Guide 1980 to 1981 Edition. (Illus.). 1980. pap. 5.50 (ISBN 0-525-93090-6). Dutton.

--Let's Go, Europe Nineteen Seventy-Nine to Nineteen Eighty. 1979. pap. 5.95 o.p. (ISBN 0-87690-301-4). Dutton.

--Let's Go, Europe: The Budget Guide 1980 to 1981 Edition. 1980. pap. 5.95 (ISBN 0-525-93091-4). Dutton.

--Let's Go, Europe 1981-82. (Illus.). 736p. 1981. pap. 6.95 (ISBN 0-525-93142-2). Dutton.

--Let's Go, France Nineteen Seventy-Nine to Nineteen Eighty. 1979. pap. 3.95 o.p. (ISBN 0-87690-303-0). Dutton.

--Let's Go, France: The Budget Guide 1980 to 1981 Edition. (Illus.). 1980. pap. 4.95 (ISBN 0-525-93088-4). Dutton.

--Let's Go, France: The Budget Guide 1981 to 1982 Edition. (Illus.). 352p. 1981. pap. 4.95 (ISBN 0-525-93144-9). Dutton.

--Let's Go, Greece, Israel & Europe: The Budget Guide 1981 to 1982 Edition. (Illus.). 352p. 1981. pap. 4.95 (ISBN 0-525-93146-5). Dutton.

--Let's Go, Italy Nineteen Seventy-Nine to Nineteen Eighty. 1979. pap. 3.95 o.p. (ISBN 0-87690-304-9). Dutton.

--Let's Go, Italy: The Budget Guide 1980 to 1981 Edition. (Illus.). 1980. pap. 5.50 (ISBN 0-525-93089-2). Dutton.

--Let's Go, Italy: The Budget Guide 1981 to 1982 Edition. (Illus.). 412p. 1981. pap. 5.50 (ISBN 0-525-93145-7). Dutton.

--Let's Go, USA: The Budget Guide 1981 to 1982 Edition. (Illus.). 556p. 1981. pap. 7.95 (ISBN 0-525-93141-4). Dutton.

Harvard University. Catalog of the Farlow Reference Library of Cryptogamic Botany. 1979. lib. bdg. 660.00 (ISBN 0-8161-0279-1). G K Hall.

--Catalogue of the Library of the Graduate School of Design, Harvard University: Third Supplement. (Library Catalogs-Bib. Guides). 1979. lib. bdg. 425.00 (ISBN 0-8161-0284-8). G K Hall.

Harvard University, Fogg Art Museum. Technical Studies in the Field of the Fine Arts, 1932-1942, 10 vols. Incl. Vol. 1, 1932. (ISBN 0-8240-1066-3); Vol. 2, 1933. (ISBN 0-8240-1067-1); Vol. 3, 1934. (ISBN 0-8240-1068-X); Vol. 4, 1935. (ISBN 0-8240-1069-8); Vol. 5, 1936. (ISBN 0-8240-1070-1); Vol. 6, 1937. (ISBN 0-8240-1071-X); Vol. 7, 1938. (ISBN 0-8240-1072-8); Vol. 8, 1939. (ISBN 0-8240-1073-6). Vol. 9, 1940 (ISBN 0-8240-1074-4); Vol. 10, 1941. (ISBN 0-8240-1075-2). (Illus.). 2665p. 1975. Repr. of 1942 ed. lib. bdg. 42.00 ea.; Set. lib. bdg. 300.00 (ISBN 0-685-51346-7). Garland Pub.

Harvard University Library. Catalogue of English & American Chap-Books & Broadside Ballads in Harvard College Library. LC 67-23932. 1968. Repr. of 1905 ed. 15.00 (ISBN 0-8103-3420-8). Gale.

Harvard-Williams, Peter, ed. see IFLA Council Meeting, 44th, Strbske, Pleso, et al.

Harvat, Robert W. Physical Education for Children with Perceptual-Motor Learning Disabilities. LC 78-158072. 1971. pap. text ed. 6.95x (ISBN 0-675-09901-3). Merrill.

Harven, Emile De see De Harven, Emile.

Harvey. Osler's Textbook Revisited. 1967. 16.50 o.p. (ISBN 0-8385-7546-3). ACC.

Harvey, A. D. Britain in the Early Nineteenth Century. LC 77-15016. 1978. 25.00x (ISBN 0-312-09747-6). St Martin.

Harvey, A. E. Companion to the New Testament the Gospels. 400p. 1972. pap. 7.95 (ISBN 0-521-09689-8). Cambridge U Pr.

--New English Bible: Companion to the New Testament. 1970. 49.50x (ISBN 0-19-826160-8). Oxford U Pr.

--The New English Bible Companion to the New Testament. rev. ed. (Illus.). 856p. 1980. pap. 19.50 (ISBN 0-19-213229-6). Oxford U Pr.

--New English Bible Companion to the New Testament. 1979. 59.50 (ISBN 0-521-07705-2); pap. 19.50 (ISBN 0-521-50539-9). Cambridge U Pr.

--The New English Bible Companion to the New Testament: The Gospels. 1972. pap. 10.95 (ISBN 0-19-826168-3). Oxford U Pr.

Harvey, Alexander. Months & Seasons. 20p. 1980. 8.00 (ISBN 0-936198-00-1); pap. 4.00 (ISBN 0-936198-01-X). Hollow Spring Pr.

Harvey, Ann, jt. ed. see Progressive Farmer Food Staff.

Harvey, Anthony, jt. auth. see Diment, Judith.

Harvey, Anthony, jt. auth. see Steel, Rodney.

Harvey, Arthur. The Apple Picker's Manual. 27p. 1968. pap. 1.00 (ISBN 0-934676-05-4). Greenlf Bks.

--Theory & Practice of Civil Disobedience. 27p. 1961. pap. 1.00 (ISBN 0-934676-04-6). Greenlf Bks.

Harvey, Barbara. Westminster Abbey & Its Estates in the Middle Ages. (Illus.). 1977. text ed. 57.00x (ISBN 0-19-822449-4). Oxford U Pr.

Harvey, Bernard G. Introduction to Nuclear Physics & Chemistry. 2nd ed. 1969. ref. ed. 26.95 (ISBN 0-13-491159-8). P-H.

Harvey, Bill. Mind Experiments. Bertisch, Jan & Bragg, Yana, eds. (Illus.). 1977. pap. 4.00 o.p. (ISBN 0-918538-04-1). Ourobourus.

--Mind Magic. 3rd ed. Orig. Title: Mind Magic: the Science of Microcosmology. (Illus.). 436p. 1980. o. p. 18.50 (ISBN 0-8290-0230-8); pap. 9.95 (ISBN 0-8290-0231-6). Irvington.

--Our Client, the Planet: The Story of Ourobourus Institute. Bertisch, Jan & Bragg, Yana, eds. (Illus.). 1977. pap. 4.50 o.p. (ISBN 0-918538-05-X). Ourobourus.

--Our Future: An Upside Opportunity Scenario. (Orig.). 1980. pap. text ed. 9.95 o.p. (ISBN 0-8290-0345-2). Irvington.

--Our Future: While We Still Have a Choice. Bertisch, Jan & Bragg, Yana, eds. (Illus.). 1979. pap. 6.95 (ISBN 0-918538-07-6). New Age Pr NM.

--Plans for America. Bertisch, Jan & Bragg, Yana, eds. (Illus.). (gr. 7-12). 1977. pap. 3.00 o.p. (ISBN 0-918538-03-3). Ourobourus.

Harvey, Brent, tr. see Tynyanov, Yury.

Harvey, Chris. Jaguar XJ Six & Twelve, Daimler, Vanden Plas, XJ-S. (AutoHistory Ser.). (Illus.). 128p. 1980. 12.95 (ISBN 0-85045-364-X, Pub. by Osprey England). Motorbooks Intl.

--MG: The A B & C. (Illus.). 1980. 36.50 (ISBN 0-902280-69-4, Pub. by Oxford Ill England). Motorbooks Intl.

Harvey, Clair & Kelly, James E. Decayed, Missing & Filled Teeth Among Persons One to Seventy-Four: United States, 1971-74, No. 11-223. Shipp, Audrey, ed. 50p. Date not set. pap. text ed. price not set (ISBN 0-8406-0209-X). Natl Ctr Health Stats.

Harvey Comics. Casper Far Out Fables. 1981. pap. 1.25 (ISBN 0-448-17251-8, Tempo). G&D.

--Casper: TV Tales. (Casper the Friendly Ghost Cartoon Bks.). 128p. (gr. 4-9). 1981. pap. text ed. 1.25 (ISBN 0-448-17119-8, Tempo). G&D.

Harvey, Curtis E. The Economics of Kentucky Coal. LC 76-51160. (Illus.). 192p. 1977. 13.00x (ISBN 0-8131-1358-X). U Pr of Ky.

Harvey, D. Society, the City & the Space-Economy of Urbanism. LC 72-77212. (CCG Resource Papers Ser.: No. 18). (Illus.). 1972. pap. text ed. 4.00 (ISBN 0-89291-065-8). Assn Am Geographers.

Harvey, D. & Brown, Donald R. An Experiential Approach to Organization Development. (Illus.). 336p. 1976. pap. text ed. 12.95 (ISBN 0-13-294983-0). P-H.

Harvey, D. & Brown, H. Experiemntal Approach to Organizational Developement. 2nd ed. 1981. pap. 10.95 (ISBN 0-13-295360-9). P-H.

Harvey, D., jt. auth. see Kelnar, G.

Harvey, D. W. A Manual of Steam Locomotive Restoration &. Preservation. LC 79-56051. (Illus.). 96p. 1980. 14.95x (ISBN 0-7153-7770-1). David & Charles.

Harvey, David C. Harvey's Law of Real Property & Title Closings, 3 vols. rev. ed. Biskind, Elliot L., ed. LC 66-23512. 1966. looseleaf with 1980 suppl. 145.00 (ISBN 0-87632-058-2). Boardman.

Harvey, Denis. The Gypsies: Waggon Time & After. (Illus.). 144p. 1980. 24.00 (ISBN 0-7134-1548-7, Pub. by Batsford England). David & Charles.

Harvey, Denis E., jt. auth. see Jackson, Ward C.

Harvey, E. C., tr. see Popp, Adelheid D.

Harvey, E. N; see Rothstein, A.

Harvey, E. Newton. History of Luminescence from the Earliest Times Until 1900. LC 57-8124. (Memoirs Ser.: Vol. 44). (Illus.). 1957. 9.00 o.s.i. (ISBN 0-87169-044-6). Am Philos.

Harvey, E. R., jt. auth. see Ashley, J. P.

Harvey, E. R., jt. auth. see Ashley, John P.

Harvey, Edward B. Industrial Society: Structures, Roles & Relations. 1975. text ed. 18.50x (ISBN 0-256-01685-2). Dorsey.

Harvey, Ethel. Athens of the Panhandle: A History of Clarendon College. 10.95 (ISBN 0-685-48816-0). Nortex Pr.

Harvey, Geoffrey. The Art of Anthony Trollope. LC 80-5088. x, 177p. 1980. 22.50 (ISBN 0-312-04998-6). St Martin.

Harvey, H. El Pastor. Treviño, Alejandro, tr. Orig. Title: The Pastor. 232p. (Span.). 1980. pap. 2.60 (ISBN 0-311-42025-7). Casa Bautista.

Harvey, Hildebrande W. Chemistry & Fertility of Sea Waters. 2nd ed. 1957. 43.00 (ISBN 0-521-05225-4). Cambridge U Pr.

Harvey, J. & Johnson, M. An Introduction to Macro-Economics. 320p. 1971. text ed. 13.00x (ISBN 0-333-12509-6); pap. text ed. 6.00x (ISBN 0-333-12511-8). Humanities.

Harvey, J. D., jt. auth. see Ramsey, Stanley C.

Harvey, J. G. Atmosphere & Ocean: Our Fluid Environments. LC 77-377903. 1978. pap. 9.95x (ISBN 0-8448-1293-5). Crane-Russak Co.

Harvey, James. Convict Guns. 1979. pap. 1.50 (ISBN 0-505-51366-8). Tower Bks.

Harvey, Joan M. Statistics America: Sources for Social, Economic, & Marketing Research. 2nd ed. 300p. 1980. write for info. Gale.

Harvey, Joan M., ed. Statistics--Africa: Sources for Social, Economic, & Market Research. 2nd ed. 1978. 98.00 (ISBN 0-900246-26-X, Pub. by CBD Research Ltd.). Gale.

--Statistics-America: Sources for Market Research (North, Central, & South America) 1973. 40.00 o.p. (ISBN 0-900246-13-8, Pub. by CBD Research Ltd). Gale.

Harvey, John. Cathedrals of England & Wales. 1974. 38.00 (ISBN 0-7134-0616-X). David & Charles.

--Mediaeval Craftsmen. 1975. 33.00 (ISBN 0-7134-2934-8, Pub. by Batsford England). David & Charles.

Harvey, John F., ed. Comparative & International Library Science. LC 77-8923. 1977. 14.50 (ISBN 0-8108-1060-3). Scarecrow.

Harvey, John H. & Smith, William P. Social Psychology: An Attributional Approach. LC 76-17113. (Illus.). 1977. pap. text ed. 13.95 (ISBN 0-8016-2079-1). Mosby.

Harvey, John H. & Weary, Gifford. Perspectives on Attributional Processes. 250p. 1981. pap. text ed. write for info. (ISBN 0-697-06637-1). Wm C Brown.

Harvey, John H., jt. auth. see Lindgren, Henry C.

Harvey, John H., et al, eds. New Directions in Attribution Research, 2 vols. LC 76-26028. (Wiley Monographs in Applied Econometrics). Vol. 1, 1976. text ed. 19.95 (ISBN 0-470-98910-6); Vol. 2, 1978. 19.95 (ISBN 0-470-26372-5). Halsted Pr.

--New Directions in Attribution Research, Vol. 3. 512p. 1981. prof. - refer. 29.95 (ISBN 0-89859-098-1). L Erlbaum Assocs.

Harvey, John L., ed. Cognition, Social Behavior, & the Environment. 600p. 1981. ref. 29.95 (ISBN 0-89859-082-5). L Erlbaum Assocs.

Harvey, John W., tr. see Otto, Rudolf.

Harvey, Jonathan. The Music of Stockhausen: An Introduction. (Illus.). 1975. 22.75x (ISBN 0-520-02311-0). U of Cal Pr.

Harvey, L. P., ed. see Stern, Samuel M.

Harvey, Marianne. The Dark Horseman. 1981. pap. 3.25 (ISBN 0-440-11758-5). Dell.

--The Proud Hunter. (Orig.). 1981. pap. 3.25 (ISBN 0-440-17098-2). Dell.

--The Wild One. (Orig.). 1981. pap. 2.95 (ISBN 0-440-19207-2). Dell.

Harvey, Milton E., jt. auth. see Holly, Brian P.

Harvey, Nancy L. Elizabeth of York: the Mother of Henry Eighth: The Mother of Henry 8. (Illus.). 324p. 1973. 6.95 o.s.i. (ISBN 0-02-548590-3). Macmillan.

--The Rose & the Thorn. (Illus.). 288p. 1975. 13.95 (ISBN 0-02-548550-4). Macmillan.

--Thomas Cardinal Wolsey. (Illus.). 256p. 1980. 19.95 o.s.i. (ISBN 0-02-548600-4). Macmillan.

Harvey, Nigel. The Industrial Archaeology of Farming in England & Wales. (Illus.). 224p. 1980. 45.00 (ISBN 0-7134-1845-1, Pub. by Batsford England). David & Charles.

Harvey, P. J., tr. see Yatsimirskii, K. B.

Harvey, Patricia, jt. auth. see Gordon, Leonard.

Harvey, Paul, ed. Oxford Companion to Classical Literature. 2nd ed. (Illus.). (YA) (gr. 9 up). 1937. 21.00 (ISBN 0-19-866103-7). Oxford U Pr.

Harvey, Paul H., jt. ed. see Clutton-Brock, T. H.

Harvey, R. J. The Kidneys & the Internal Environment. LC 74-2776. 167p. 1976. text ed. 10.95x o.p. (ISBN 0-412-12260-X, Pub. by Chapman & Hall). Methuen Inc.

--The Kidneys & the Internal Environment. LC 74-2776. 1976. 10.95 o.p. (ISBN 0-470-35775-4). Halsted Pr.

Harvey, Simon, et al, eds. Reappraisals of Rousseau: Studies in Honour of R. A. Leigh. 312p. 1980. 27.50x (ISBN 0-389-20067-0). B&N.

Harvey Society of New York. The Harvey Lectures. Incl. Ser. 47. 1951-1952. 1953 (ISBN 0-12-312047-0); Ser. 48. 1952-1953. 1954 (ISBN 0-12-312048-9); Ser. 49. 1953-1954. 1955 (ISBN 0-12-312049-7); Ser. 50. 1954-1955. 1956 (ISBN 0-12-312050-0); Ser. 51. 1955-1956. 1957 (ISBN 0-12-312051-9); Ser. 52. 1956-1957. 1958 (ISBN 0-12-312052-7); Ser. 53. 1957-1958. 1959 (ISBN 0-12-312053-5); Ser. 54. 1958-1959. 1960 (ISBN 0-12-312054-3); Ser. 55. 1959-1960. 1961 (ISBN 0-12-312055-1); Ser. 56. 1960-1961. 1961 (ISBN 0-12-312056-X); Ser. 57. 1961-1962. 1962 (ISBN 0-12-312057-8); Ser. 58. 1962-1963. 1963. 16.50 (ISBN 0-12-312058-6); Ser. 59. 1963-1964. 1965 (ISBN 0-12-312059-4); Ser. 60. 1964-1965. 1966. o.s.i. (ISBN 0-12-312060-8); Ser. 61. 1965-1966. 1967 (ISBN 0-12-312061-6); Ser. 62. 1966-1967. 1968 (ISBN 0-12-312062-4); Ser. 63. 1967-1968. 1969 (ISBN 0-12-312063-2); Ser. 64. 1968-1969. 1970 (ISBN 0-12-312064-0); Ser. 65. 1969-1970. 1971 (ISBN 0-12-312065-9); Ser. 66. 1970-1971. 1972 (ISBN 0-12-312066-7); Ser. **67. 1971-1972. 1973 (ISBN 0-12-312067-5); Ser. 68. 1972-1973. 1974. 21.50 (ISBN 0-12-312068-3); Ser. 69. 1973-1974. 1975. 20.00 (ISBN 0-12-312069-1); Ser. 70. 1974-1975. 1976. 17.50 (ISBN 0-12-312070-5); Ser. 71. 1978. 22.50 (ISBN 0-12-312071-3); Ser. 72. 1979. 25.50 (ISBN 0-12-312072-1); Ser. 73. 1979. 24.00 (ISBN 0-12-312073-X). unless otherwise indicated 17.00 ea. Acad Pr.**

Harvey, Susan & Hales-Tooke, Ann. Play in Hospital. 1972. 7.95 o.p. (ISBN 0-571-09827-4, Pub. by Faber & Faber); pap. 4.95 (ISBN 0-571-10174-7). Merrimack Bk Serv.

Harvey, Sylvia. May Sixty-Eight & Film Culture. (BFI Ser.). (Orig.). 1978. pap. 5.00 o.p. (ISBN 0-85170-081-0). NY Zoetrope.

Harvey, Van A. The Historian & the Believer: The Morality of Historical Knowledge & Christian Belief. 1981. pap. price not set (ISBN 0-664-24367-3). Westminster.

Harvey, Virginia I. Color & Design in Macrame. LC 80-25748. (Illus.). 104p. (gr. 11-12). 1980. pap. 9.95 (ISBN 0-914842-55-2). Madrona Pubs.

--Color & Design in Macrame. (Illus.). 104p. 1980. pap. 9.95 (ISBN 0-914842-55-2). Madrona Pubs.

Harvey, W. H. Nereis Boreali-Americana: 1852-1858, 3 parts in 1. (Illus.). 1976. 125.00 (ISBN 3-7682-1063-4). Lubrecht & Cramer.

Harvey, W. J., ed. Discrete Groups and Automorphic Functions. 1978. 56.00 (ISBN 0-12-329950-0). Acad Pr.

Harvey, William. De Motu Cordis: Anatomical Studies on the Motion of the Heart & Blood. 5th ed. Leake, Chauncey D., tr. (Illus.). 186p. 1978. pap. 6.75 (ISBN 0-398-00793-4). C C Thomas.

--Lectures on the Whole of Anatomy. O'Malley, C. D., et al, trs. 1961. 22.75x (ISBN 0-520-00540-6). U of Cal Pr.

Harvey, William F., tr. see Nyrop, Christopher.

Harvey-Felder, Zena, jt. ed. see Drachman, Virginia.

Harvill, Lawrence R. & Kraft, Thomas L. Technical Report Standards: How to Prepare & Write Effective Technical Reports. LC 77-70964. (Illus.). 1979. pap. 4.95 (ISBN 0-930206-01-0). M-A Pr.

Harvold, Trygve, jt. auth. see Bing, Jon.

Harward, Donald W., ed. Power: Its Nature, Its Uses, Its Limits. 1981. pap. text ed. 8.95 (ISBN 0-87073-895-X). Schenkman.

Harway, Michele & Astin, Helen S. Sex Discrimination in Career Counseling & Education. LC 77-7829. (Praeger Special Studies). 1977. 23.95 (ISBN 0-03-021826-8). Praeger.

Harwell, Ann J., jt. auth. see Harwell, Rolly M.

Harwell, C. W., jt. auth. see Dorill, J. F.

Harwell, Charles W. & McDonald, Daniel. The Bible: A Literary Survey. LC 74-13465. 307p. 1975. pap. 11.95 (ISBN 0-672-63278-0). Bobbs.

Harwell, R. B. Confederate Reader. LC 76-22465. 1976. 10.95 o.p. (ISBN 0-679-50675-6); pap. 5.95 o.p. (ISBN 0-679-50676-4). McKay.

Harwell, Richard B. More Confederate Imprints, 2 Vols. LC 57-9084. (Illus.). 1957. Vol. 1. pap. 7.50x set (ISBN 0-88490-045-2, Virginia State Library); Vol. 2. pap. (ISBN 0-88490-046-0). U Pr of Va.

Harwell, Richard B., ed. Margaret Mitchell's "Gone with the Wind" Letters: 1936-1949. (Illus.). 1976. 12.95 o.s.i. (ISBN 0-02-548650-0). Macmillan.

Harwell, Rolly M. & Harwell, Ann J. Crafts for Today: Ceramics, Glasscrafting, Leather Working, Candlemaking & Other Popular Crafts. LC 73-92979. (Spare Time Guides Ser.: No. 4). 220p. 1974. lib. bdg. 9.50 o.p. (ISBN 0-87287-067-7). Libs Unl.

Harwell, Thomas M. Keats & the Critics, 1848-1900. (Salzburg Studies in English Literature, Romantic Reassessment: No. 2). 1972. pap. text ed. 25.00x (ISBN 0-391-01399-8). Humanities.

Harwell, Thomas M., ed. Studies in Relevance: Romantic & Victorian Writers in 1972. (Salzburg Studies in English Literature, Romantic Reassessment: No. 32). 171p. 1973. pap. text ed. 25.00x (ISBN 0-391-01400-5). Humanities.

Harwick, B. L. The Frog Prints. LC 76-13840. (Read to Myself Ser.). 48p. (gr. k-2). 1976. PLB 7.75 (ISBN 0-8172-0152-1). Raintree Pubs.

Harwin, Judith, jt. ed. see Orford, Jim.

Harwit, Martin. Astrophysical Concepts. LC 73-3135. 561p. 1973. text ed. 28.95 (ISBN 0-471-35820-7). Wiley.

--Cosmic Discovery: The Search, Scope, & Heritage of Astronomy. LC 80-68172. 70p. 1981. 25.00x (ISBN 0-465-01428-3). Basic.

Harwood. Plaid for Quantitative Methods. 1979. pap. 5.50 (ISBN 0-256-02084-1, 18-1285-01). Learning Syst.

Harwood, Alan. Rx: Spiritist As Needed; a Study of a Puerto Rican Community Mental Health Resource. LC 76-54841. (Contemporary Religious Movements). 1977. 25.95 (ISBN 0-471-35828-2, Pub. by Wiley-Interscience). Wiley.

Harwood, B., jt. auth. see Ellis, J.

Harwood, Bruce & Synek, Elmer. Ohio Real Estate. (Illus.). 640p. 1980. ref. ed 19.95; pap. 16.95 (ISBN 0-8359-5189-8). Reston.

Harwood, Bruce, jt. auth. see Gobble, Bill.

Harwood, Bruce, jt. auth. see Jones, Richard O.

Harwood, Bruce, jt. auth. see New York Assn. of Realtors.

Harwood, Ellis. Real Estate Resource Handbook. (Illus.). 336p. 1980. pap. text ed. 7.95 (ISBN 0-8359-6564-3). Reston.

Harwood, Herbert. Blue Ridge Trolly: The Hagerstown & Frederick Railway. LC 73-97231. 13.95 o.p. (ISBN 0-87095-034-7). Golden West.

Harwood, Herbert H., Jr. Fifty Best of New York Central Railroad, Bk. 1. (Illus.). 1977. 12.00 (ISBN 0-934118-09-4). Barnard Robert.

Harwood, Jacobus. Texas Real Estate. (Illus.). 672p. 1980. ref. ed. 19.95; text ed. 16.95 (ISBN 0-8359-7553-3). Reston.

Harwood, Michael. The View from Hawk Mountain. LC 73-38905. 192p. 1973. pap. 2.95 o.p. (ISBN 0-684-16371-3, SL555, ScribT). Scribner.

Harwood, Michael, jt. auth. see Durant, Mary.

Harwood, Richard. Nuremberg & Other War Crimes Trials: A New Look. (Illus.). 1978. pap. 2.50 (ISBN 0-911038-34-5, Inst Hist Rev). Noontide.

Harwood, Richard, ed. see Washington Post Staff Members.

Harwood, Richard K., jt. auth. see Bachhuber, Thomas D.

Harwood, Richard R. Small Farm Development: Understanding & Improving Farming Systems in the Humid Tropics. LC 79-13169. (IAOS Development-Oriented Literature Ser.). 1979. lib. bdg. 18.50x (ISBN 0-89158-669-5). Westview.

Harwood, William. Writing & Editing School News: A Basic Project Text in Scholastic Journalism. 1977. lib. bdg. 7.50 (ISBN 0-931054-04-4). Clark Pub.

Harwood-Nash, Derek C. Neuroradiology in Infants & Children, 3 vols. LC 76-27253. (Illus., Orig.). 1976. 175.00 set o.p. (ISBN 0-8016-2086-4). Mosby.

Harz, Kurt. Trees & Shrubs. (Illus.). 144p. 1981. pap. 5.95 (ISBN 0-7011-2542-X, Pub. by Chatto-Bodley-Jonathan). Merrimack Bk Serv.

Harzem, P. & Miles, T. R. Conceptual Issues in Operant Psychology. LC 77-21280. 1978. 27.95 (ISBN 0-471-99603-3, Pub. by Wiley-Interscience). Wiley.

Harzem, Peter & Zeiler, Michael D. Predictability, Correlation & Contiguity. 400p. 1981. 48.00 (ISBN 0-471-27847-5, Pub. by Wiley-Interscience). Wiley.

Harzem, Peter, jt. auth. see Zeiler, Michael D.

Harzfeld, Lois A. Periodical Indexes in the Social Sciences & Humanities: A Subject Guide. LC 78-5230. 1978. lib. bdg. 10.00 (ISBN 0-8108-1133-2). Scarecrow.

Hasan, Amir. Folklore of Buxar. 1978. 17.00x o.p. (ISBN 0-8364-0301-0). South Asia Bks.

Hasan, Khaja S. Banking in India. Blythe, L. N., ed. 112p. (Orig.). 1979. pap. text ed. 10.95x (ISBN 0-7121-0260-4, Pub. by Macdonald & Evans England). Intl Ideas.

Hasan, M., ed. see Ansari, M. A.

Hasan, Ruqaiya, jt. auth. see Halliday, M. A.

Hasazi, Susan E. Under One Cover: Implementing the Least Restrictive Environment Concept. LC 80-68096. 208p. 1980. pap. 11.25 (ISBN 0-86586-106-4). Coun Exc Child.

Hasbach, Wilhelm. History of the English Agricultural Labourer. Kenyon, Ruth, tr. LC 67-2118. Repr. of 1908 ed. 20.00x (ISBN 0-678-05056-2). Kelley.

Hasbrouck, Jean, jt. auth. see Mirov, Nicholas T.

Hasbrouck, Marilyn, ed. see Brown, William T.

Haschemeyer, Audrey H., jt. auth. see Haschemeyer, Rudolph.

Haschemeyer, Rudolph & Haschemeyer, Audrey H. Proteins: A Guide to Study by Physical & Chemical Methods. LC 72-13134. 528p. 1973. 36.50 (ISBN 0-471-35850-9, Pub. by Wiley-Interscience). Wiley.

Hasci, Jacqueline. Paradise Isle. (Orig.). 1981. pap. 1.50 (ISBN 0-440-16966-6). Dell.

Hasebroek, Johannes. Trade & Politics in Ancient Greece. LC 65-15245. 1933. 10.00x (ISBN 0-8196-0150-0). Biblo.

Hasegawa, Goro & Brady, Maxine. How to Win at Othello. LC 77-5259. (Illus.). 1977. pap. 2.95 o.p. (ISBN 0-15-642215-8, Harv). HarBraceJ.

Hasegawa, Sam. Coaches. LC 74-23422. (Stars of the NFL Ser.). (gr. 4-12). 1975. PLB 7.95 (ISBN 0-87191-421-2). Creative Ed.

--Jackie Stewart. LC 75-1357. (New Creative Education Superstar Bks.). (Illus.). 32p. (gr. 3-6). 1975. PLB 5.95 (ISBN 0-87191-437-9); pap. 2.95 (ISBN 0-89812-178-7). Creative Ed.

--Stevie Wonder. LC 74-147456. (Rock'n Pop Stars Ser.). (Illus.). 32p. (gr. 3-6). 1974. PLB 5.95 (ISBN 0-87191-395-X); pap. 2.95 (ISBN 0-89812-099-3). Creative Ed.

--Terry Bradshaw. (Sports Superstars Ser.). (Illus.). (gr. 3-9). 1977. PLB 5.95 (ISBN 0-87191-542-1); pap. 2.95 (ISBN 0-89812-212-0). Creative Ed.

Hasegawa, T. & IFAC Workshop, Kyoto Japan, Aug. 1978. Urban, Regional & National Planning: Environmental Aspects: Proceedings. Inoue, K., ed. LC 78-40573. 1978. text ed. 50.00 (ISBN 0-08-022013-4). Pergamon.

Hasegawa, Tsuyoshi. The February Revolution: Petrograd, 1917. LC 80-50870. (Publications on Russia of the School of International Studies: No. 9). (Illus.). 675p. 1981. 25.00 (ISBN 0-295-95765-4). U of Wash Pr.

Hasek, Jaroslav. The Good Soldier Svejk & His Fortunes in the War. Parrott, Cecil, tr. from Czech. (Illus.). 752p. 1980. lib. bdg. 15.00x (ISBN 0-434-31375-0, Pub. by Heinemann England). Bentley.

Hasel, Gerhard. Jonah, Messenger of the Eleventh Hour. LC 76-12907. (Dimension Ser.). 1976. pap. 5.95 (ISBN 0-8163-0260-X, 10440-6). Pacific Pr Pub Assn.

Haselbach, Barbara. Improvisation, Dance, & Movement. Murray, Margaret, tr. from Ger. Orig. Title: Improvisation, Tanz, Bewegung. 1980. Repr. of 1976 ed. pap. 19.00 (ISBN 0-918812-15-1). Magnamusic.

Haseler, Stephen. The Tragedy of Labour. (Mainstream Ser.). 249p. 1980. 19.50x (ISBN 0-631-11341-X, Pub. by Basil Blackwell). Biblio Dist.

Haseman, William D. & Whinston, Andrew B. Introduction to Data Management. 1977. 19.95x (ISBN 0-256-01949-5). Irwin.

Hasenav, Florence A. Pinkey. (Illus.). 1975. 6.00 (ISBN 0-913042-02-1). Holland Hse Pr.

Hasenfeld, Yeheskel & English, Richard A., eds. Human Service Organizations: A Book of Readings. 1974. text ed. 15.00 c.p. (ISBN 0-472-08985-4); pap. text ed. 7.95x (ISBN 0-472-08986-2). U of Mich Pr.

Hasenohrl, Fritz, ed. see Boltzmann, Ludwig.

Hasenpflug, H., jt. auth. see Sauvant, K.

Hash, John. Light on Life's Pathway. 1977. pap. 3.95 o.p. (ISBN 0-8407-9502-5, Pub. by Action Press). Nelson.

Hash, Virginia. Values: Awareness, Significance & Action. 1975. pap. text ed. 7.95 (ISBN 0-8403-1286-5). Kendall Hunt.

Hashashe, Cedar. Cooking the Lebanese Way. (Illus.). 112p. (Orig.). 1979. pap. 7.50 (ISBN 0-589-01279-7, Pub. by Reed Books Australia). C E Tuttle.

Hashim, Dhia Al see Al Hashim, Dhia & Robertson, James W.

Hashim, George, ed. Myelin: Chemistry & Biology. LC 80-22305. (Progress in Clinical & Biological Research: Vol. 49). 130p. 1980. price not set (ISBN 0-8451-0049-1). A R Liss.

Hashimi, Ali Ibn Sulayman al. The Book of the Reasons Behind Astronomical Tables (Kitab Fi 'ilal Al-Zijat) Kennedy, E. S. & Pingree, David, eds. Haddad, Fuad I., tr. from Arabic. LC 77-14160. 400p. Date not set. 50.00x (ISBN 0-8201-1298-4). Schol Facsimiles. Postponed.

Hashimoto, Fumio. Architecture in the Shoin Style: Japanese Feudal Residences. Horton, H. Mack, tr. LC 79-91519. (Japanese Arts Library: Vol. 10). (Illus.). 220p. 1981. 16.95 (ISBN 0-87011-414-X). Kodansha.

Hashimoto, M. The Hakka Dialect. LC 72-85438. (Princeton-Cambridge Studies in Chinese Linguistics: No. 5). (Illus.). 700p. 1973. 110.00 (ISBN 0-521-20037-7). Cambridge U Pr.

Hashimoto, Oi-Kan. Studies in Yue Dialects 1. LC 78-179158. (Cambridge-Princeton Studies in Chinese Linguistics: No. 3). (Illus.). 755p. 1972. 115.00 (ISBN 0-521-08442-3). Cambridge U Pr.

Hashway, Robert M. Objective Mental Measurement: Individual & Program Evaluation Using the Rasch Model. LC 78-19739. 1978. 21.95 (ISBN 0-03-046476-5). Praeger.

Hasinbiller, Dolly, ed. Play the Game Spiritmasters. (gr. 3-8). 1977. ser. 15.84 ea. o.p.; Ser. II. write for info. o.p. Ser. I (ISBN 0-8372-3399-2). Ser. I & II. 31.68 o.p. (ISBN 0-8372-3419-0). Bowmar-Noble.

Hasinbiller, Dolly & Cebulash, Mel, eds. Crosswinds One. (Illus.). 320p. (gr. 7). 1979. text ed. 8.70 (ISBN 0-8372-3582-0); wkbk 2.52 (ISBN 0-8372-3583-9); tchrs' guide 2.52 (ISBN 0-8372-3584-7). Bowmar-Noble.

--Crosswinds, Two. (Illus.). 320p. (gr. 8). 1979. text ed. 8.70 (ISBN 0-8372-3585-5); wkbk 2.52 (ISBN 0-8372-3586-3); tchrs' guide 2.52 (ISBN 0-8372-3587-1). Bowmar-Noble.

Hasinbiller, Dolly, ed. see Emmer, Rae.

Haskel, Barbara G. The Scandinavian Option Opportunities & Opportunity Costs in Postwar Scandinavian Foreign Politics. 1976. pap. 19.50x (ISBN 8-200-01561-0, Dist. by Columbia U Pr). Universitet.

Haskel, Sebastian & Sygoda, David. Biology Investigations. (gr. 10-12). 1973. lab manual 7.08 (ISBN 0-87720-056-4). AMSCO Sch.

--Contemporary Biology. (gr. 9-12). 1977. pap. text ed. 6.00 (ISBN 0-87720-057-2). AMSCO Sch.

--Fundamental Concepts of Modern Biology. (Orig.). (gr. 10-12). 1972. text ed. 12.41 (ISBN 0-87720-055-6); pap. text ed. 7.17 (ISBN 0-87720-054-8). AMSCO Sch.

Haskelevich, B., ed. Introduction to the Talmud Study. 400p. (Rus.). 1981. pap. 6.00 (ISBN 0-938666-01-0). CHAMH.

Haskelevich, B., tr. from Hebrew. The Disputation of Nachmanides: With Introduction & Commentaries. (Rus.). 1981. pap. 3.75 (ISBN 0-938666-00-2). CHAMH.

Haskell, Charles M., jt. auth. see Cline, Martin J.

Haskell, Daniel C., jt. auth. see Stokes, I. N.

Haskell, Francis. Patrons & Painters: A Study in the Relations Between Italian Art & Society in the Age of the Baroque. rev. ed. LC 79-56891. (Illus.). 1980. 45.00x (ISBN 0-300-02537-8); pap. 14.95 (ISBN 0-300-02540-8). Yale U Pr.

--Rediscoveries in Art: Taste, Fashion & Collecting in England & France. (Wrightsman Lecture Ser.). (Illus.). 1980. pap. 14.95 o.p. (ISBN 0-8014-9187-8). Cornell U Pr.

Haskell, Francis & Penny, Nicholas. Taste & the Antique: The Lure of Classical Sculpture 1500-1900. LC 80-24951. (Illus.). 392p. 1981. 45.00x (ISBN 0-300-02641-2). Yale U Pr.

Haskell, Francis, jt. auth. see Burgess, Anthony.

Haskell, Francis, et al, eds. The Artist & the Writer in France: Essays in Honour of Jean Seznec. (Illus.). 200p. 1974. 36.00x (ISBN 0-19-817187-0). Oxford U Pr.

Haskell, Lendall L. Teaching Children Through Art in the Early Childhood Years. 1979. pap. text ed. 10.95 (ISBN 0-675-08307-9). Merrill.

Haskell, Simon H. Arithmetical Disabilities in Cerebral Palsied Children: Programmed Instruction - a Remedial Approach. 132p. 1973. 10.75 (ISBN 0-398-02537-1). C C Thomas.

Haskin, Frederic J. Ten Thousand Answers to Questions. LC 79-99074. 1970. Repr. of 1937 ed. 21.00 (ISBN 0-8103-3861-0). Gale.

Haskin, Leslie L. Wild Flowers of the Pacific Coast. 3rd ed. LC 66-28384. (Illus.). 1981. pap. 8.95 (ISBN 0-8323-0385-2). Binford.

Haskin, Marvin E., jt. auth. see Teplick, J. George.

Haskins, Charles. Renaissance of the Twelfth Century. pap. 5.95 o.p. (ISBN 0-452-00456-X, F456, Mer). NAL.

Haskins, Charles H. Norman Institutions. LC 80-2026. 1981. Repr. of 1918 ed. 39.50 (ISBN 0-404-18568-1). AMS Pr.

--The Renaissance of the Twelfth Century. x, 437p. 1971. 18.50x (ISBN 0-674-76077-8); pap. 5.95 (ISBN 0-674-76075-1). Harvard U Pr.

Haskins, Earl R., Jr., ed. see U. S. National Committee on Rock Mechanics, 15th, South Dakota School of Mines & Technology, Sept. 1973 & American Society of Civil Engineers.

Haskins, George L. The Foundations of Power: John Marshall, 1801-1815. (History of the Supreme Court of the United States: Vol. II). (Illus.). 900p. 1981. 60.00 (ISBN 0-02-541360-0). Macmillan.

--Growth of English Representative Government. 7.50 (ISBN 0-8446-2216-8). Peter Smith.

--The Growth of English Representative Government. pap. 3.95 o.p. (ISBN 0-498-04003-8, Prpta). A S Barnes.

Haskins, Ilma. Color Seems. LC 72-83356. (Illus.). 32p. (ps-3). 1974. 6.95 (ISBN 0-8149-0688-5). Vanguard.

Haskins, James. Babe Ruth & Hank Aaron: The Home Run Kings. LC 74-11018. (Illus.). 96p. (gr. 5 up). 1975. pap. 1.75 o.p. (ISBN 0-688-46654-0). Lothrop.

--I'm Gonna Make You Love Me: The Story of Diana Ross. LC 79-3586. (Illus.). 160p. (gr. 6 up). 1980. 8.95 (ISBN 0-8037-4213-4). Dial.

--Magic: A Biography of Earvin Johnson. (Illus.). (gr. 4-12). 1981. PLB 7.95 (ISBN 0-89490-044-7). Enslow Pubs.

--New Americans: Vietnamese Boat People. LC 80-14560. (Illus.). 64p. (gr. 4-6). 1980. PLB 6.95 (ISBN 0-89490-035-8). Enslow Pubs.

--Pinckney Benton Stewart Pinchback: A Biography. (Illus.). 304p. 1973. 12.95 (ISBN 0-02-548890-2). Macmillan.

--Scott Joplin: The Man Who Made Ragtime. LC 76-50768. (Illus.). 264p. (Orig.). 1980. pap. 6.95 (ISBN 0-686-64767-X). Stein & Day.

Haskins, James S. Always Movin' on: The Life of Langston Hughes. (Illus.). 128p. (gr. 7 up). 1976. PLB 6.90 o.p. (ISBN 0-531-01211-5). Watts.

--The Consumer Movement. LC 74-11351. 128p. (gr. 9 up). 1975. PLB 5.90 o.p. (ISBN 0-531-02794-5). Watts.

--Doctor J: A Biography of Julius Erving. LC 74-33645. (Illus.). 96p. (gr. 8-9). 1975. 4.95 o.p. (ISBN 0-385-09905-3); PLB write for info. o.p. (ISBN 0-385-09906-1). Doubleday.

--New Kind of Joy: The Story of the Special Olympics. LC 75-14825. 144p. 1976. 7.95 o.p. (ISBN 0-385-03902-6). Doubleday.

--The Picture Life of Malcolm X. LC 74-7441. (Picture Life Bks). (Illus.). 48p. (gr. k-3). 1975. PLB 6.45 (ISBN 0-531-02771-6). Watts.

--Snow Sculpture & Ice Carving. LC 73-20992. (Illus.). 144p. 1974. pap. 4.95 o.s.i. (ISBN 0-02-011500-8, Collier). Macmillan.

--Who Are the Handicapped? LC 76-2777. (gr. 4-7). 1978. 6.95a (ISBN 0-385-09609-7); PLB (ISBN 0-385-09610-0). Doubleday.

Haskins, Jim. Gambling: Who Really Wins? (First Bks.). (Illus.). (gr. 4 up). 1979. PLB 6.45 (ISBN 0-531-02942-5). Watts.

--James Van der Zee: The Picture-Takin' Man. LC 78-22431. (Illus.). 1979. 8.95 (ISBN 0-396-07678-5). Dodd.

--Real Estate Careers. (Career Concise Guides Ser.). (Illus.). (gr. 7 up). 1978. PLB 6.45 s&l (ISBN 0-531-01423-1). Watts.

--Teen-Age Alcoholism. 1976. 7.95 o.p. (ISBN 0-8015-7480-3, Hawthorn); pap. 3.50 (ISBN 0-8015-7481-1, Hawthorn). Dutton.

--Voodoo & Hoodoo. LC 77-17213. (Illus.). 226p. 1981. pap. 6.95 (ISBN 0-8128-6085-3). Stein & Day.

Haskins, Jim & Butts, Hugh F. The Psychology of Black Language. (College Outline Ser.). 112p. (Orig.). 1973. pap. 2.50 o.p. (ISBN 0-06-460142-0, 142, COS). Har-Row.

Haskins, Ralph W., jt. ed. see Graf, LeRoy P.

Haskins, Ron & Gallagher, James J., eds. Care & Education in Young Children in America: Policy, Politics & Social Science. LC 80-11788. (Illus.). 224p. 1980. text ed. 19.95 (ISBN 0-89391-040-6). Ablex Pub.

Haskins, Sam. Photo Graphics. (Illus.). 1981. 30.00 (ISBN 2-88046-016-6, Pub. by Roto-Vision Switzerland). Norton.

Haslam, E. The Shikimate Pathway. LC 73-18377. 316p. 1974. 43.95 (ISBN 0-470-35882-3). Halsted Pr.

Haslam, Gerald. The Wages of Sin. Robertson, Kirk, ed. (Illus.). 88p. (Orig.). 1980. pap. 4.00 (ISBN 0-916918-11-4). Duck Down.

Haslam, John. Medical Jurisprudence, As It Relates to Insanity, According to the Law of England. Berkowitz, David S. & Thorne, Samuel E., eds. LC 77-86661. (Classics of English Legal History in the Modern Era Ser.: Vol. 109). 1979. lib. bdg. 55.00 (ISBN 0-8240-3096-6). Garland Pub.

Haslam, Kenneth R. Learning in the Primary School. (Unwin Education Books). 1971. pap. text ed. 7.50x o.p. (ISBN 0-04-371018-2). Allen Unwin.

Haslam, M. T. Psychiatric Illness in Adolescence. 1975. 21.95 (ISBN 0-407-00019-4). Butterworths.

Haslam, S. M. River Plants. LC 76-46857. (Illus.). 1978. 90.00 (ISBN 0-521-21493-9); pap. 22.95x (ISBN 0-521-29172-0). Cambridge U Pr.

Haslam, S. M. & Wolseley, P. A. River Vegetation: Its Identification, Assessment & Management; a Field Guide to the Macrophytic Vegetation of British Watercourses. 96p. Date not set. text ed. price not set (ISBN 0-521-23186-8); pap. text ed. price not set (ISBN 0-521-23187-6). Cambridge U Pr.

Hasler, August B. How the Pope Became Infallible: Pius IX & the Politics of Persuasion. Heinegg, Peter, tr. LC 79-6851. (Illus.). 320p. 1981. 14.95 (ISBN 0-385-15851-3). Doubleday.

Hasling. The Audience, the Message, the Speaker. 2nd ed. 1975. 9.955 (ISBN 0-07-026990-4, C); instructor's manual 3.95 (ISBN 0-07-026991-2). McGraw.

Hasling, John. The Professional Radio Broadcaster. (Illus.). Date not set. pap. text ed. 8.95 (ISBN 0-07-026992-0). McGraw.

Hasluck, Margaret M. The Unwritten Law in Albania. LC 79-1607. 1981. Repr. of 1954 ed. 23.50 (ISBN 0-88355-910-2). Hyperion Conn.

Hasluck, Nicholas. Quarantine. LC 78-14160. 1979. 8.95 o.p. (ISBN 0-03-044201-X). HR&W.

Hasluck, Paul N. Saddlery & Harness Making. (Illus.). 12.25 (ISBN 0-85131-148-2, Dist. by Sporting Book Center). J A Allen.

Has'Minskii, R. Z. Stochastic Stability of Differential Equations. 2nd ed. 360p. 1980. 50.00x (ISBN 90-286-0100-7). Sijthoff & Noordhoff.

Haspel, Eleanor C. Marriage in Trouble: A Time of Decision. LC 76-4780. 308p. 1976. 12.95 (ISBN 0-88229-222-6); pap. 6.95 (ISBN 0-88229-428-8). Nelson-Hall.

Hasruddin Siddiqui, M. K. Bleaching Earths. 1968. 19.50 (ISBN 0-08-012738-X). Pergamon.

Hass. Curriculum Planning: A New Approach. 3rd ed. 540p. 1980. pap. text ed. 12.95 (ISBN 0-205-06869-3, 2368692). Allyn.

Hass, Georg & Francombe, Maurice H., eds. Physics of Thin Films: Advances in Research & Development, Vol. 11. (Serial Publication Ser.). 1980. 42.00 (ISBN 0-12-533011-1); lib. ed 48.50 (ISBN 0-12-533080-4); microfiche 35.50 (ISBN 0-12-533081-2). Acad Pr.

Hass, Hans. Challenging the Deep: Thirty Years of Undersea Adventure. (Illus.). 88p. 1972. 11.95 o.p. (ISBN 0-688-00140-8). Morrow.

Hass, Patricia C. Windsong Summer. LC 77-16878. (gr. 5 up). 1978. 5.95 (ISBN 0-396-07561-4). Dodd.

Hassall, K. A., jt. auth. see Edwards, N. A.

Hassall, W. O. They Saw It Happen, Vol. 1: An Anthology of Eye-Witnesses Accounts of Events in British History, 55 B. C. to A. D. 1485. 1973. pap. 6.50x o.p. (ISBN 0-631-05280-1, Pub. by Basil Blackwell). Biblio Dist.

--Treasures from the Bodleian Library. 1976. 80.00x (ISBN 0-231-04060-1). Columbia U Pr.

Hassam, Childe. Ninety-One Prints by Childe Hassam. Czestochowski, Joseph S., ed. (Illus., Orig.). 1980. 6.00 (ISBN 0-486-23981-0). Dover.

Hassan, Farooq. The Concept of State & Law in Islam. LC 80-69038. 321p. (Orig.). 1981. lib. bdg. 20.75 (ISBN 0-8191-1426-X); pap. text ed. 11.75 (ISBN 0-8191-1427-8). U Pr of Amer.

Hassan, Ihab. Dismemberment of Orpheus: Toward a Postmodern Literature. 1971. 14.95 (ISBN 0-19-501393-X). Oxford U Pr.

Hassan, Ihab, ed. Liberations: New Essays on the Humanities in Revolution. LC 77-142729. 1971. 12.50 o.p. (ISBN 0-8195-4034-X, Pub. by Wesleyan U Pr); pap. 5.95 (ISBN 0-8195-6025-1). Columbia U Pr.

Hassan, V., et al. Pipe Protection: A Review of Current Practice in the U. K. (Illus.). 183p. 1979. pap. 104.00 lib. ed. (ISBN 0-900983-92-2, Dist. by Air Sciencec Co.). BHRA Fluid.

Hassan, William E., Jr. Hospital Pharmacy. 4th ed. LC 80-20700. (Illus.). 525p. 1981. text ed. write for info. (ISBN 0-8121-0772-1). Lea & Febiger.

Hassard, D. B., et al. Theory of Applications of Hopf Bifurcation. (London Mathematical Society Lecture Notes Ser.: No. 41). (Illus.). 300p. (Orig.). Date not set. 35.00 (ISBN 0-521-23158-2). Cambridge U Pr.

Hasse, Ann F., jt. auth. see Fingarette, Herbert.

Hasse, Helmut. Mathematische Abhandlungen, 3 vols. Leopoldt, Heinrich W. & Roquette, Peter, eds. xxxvi, 1592p. 1975. 300.00x (ISBN 3-11-005931-2). De Gruyter.

Hasselberger, Francis. Uses of Enzymes & Immobilized Enzymes. LC 78-8498. (Illus.). 1978. text ed. 18.95 (ISBN 0-88229-345-1). Nelson-Hall.

Hassell, Randall G. The Karate Experience: A Way of Life. LC 80-53429. 110p. 1981. 9.95 (ISBN 0-8048-1348-5). C E Tuttle.

Hassell, T. M. Epilepsy & the Oral Manifestations of Phenytoin Therapy. (Monographs in Oral Science: Vol. 9). (Illus.). 200p. 1980. pap. 89.25 (ISBN 3-8055-1008-X). S Karger.

Hassell, Thomas, et al, eds. Phenytoin-Induced Teratology & Gingival Pathology. 252p. 1980. text ed. 27.00 (ISBN 0-89004-412-0). Raven.

Hasselmeier, H. & Spruth, W. C., eds. Data Base Systems. (Lecture Notes in Computer Science: Vol. 39). 390p. 1976. pap. 16.80 o.p. (ISBN 0-387-07612-3). Springer-Verlag.

Hasselmeyer, Eileen G., jt. auth. see Winters, Robert W.

Hasseloff, C. H. A Killer Come to Shiloh. 176p. (Orig.). 1981. pap. 1.95 (ISBN 0-553-14742-0). Bantam.

Hasselt, Carlos Van see Schatborn, Peter & Van Hasselt, Carlos.

Hassett, James. A Primer of Psychophysiology. LC 77-20913. (Psychology Ser.). (Illus.). 1978. text ed. 18.95x (ISBN 0-7167-0038-7); pap. text ed. 9.95x (ISBN 0-7167-0037-9). W H Freeman.

Hassett, Matthew, jt. auth. see Weiss, Neil.

Hassin, Vijay. The Modern Yoga Handbook. LC 77-76243. 1978. pap. 4.95 (ISBN 0-385-13001-5, Dolp). Doubleday.

Hassler, Donald M. Erasmus Darwin. (English Authors Ser.: No. 160). 1974. 10.95 (ISBN 0-8057-1138-4). Twayne.

Hassler, Gerd Von see Von Hassler, Gerd.

Hassler, Jon. Jemmy. LC 79-23091. (gr. 7 up). 1980. 7.95 (ISBN 0-689-50130-7, McElderry Bk). Atheneum.

--The Love Hunter. 320p. 1981. 12.95 (ISBN 0-688-00483-0). Morrow.

Hassler, Warren W., Jr. General George B. McClellan, Shield of the Union. LC 74-9619. (Illus.). 350p. 1974. Repr. of 1957 ed. lib. bdg. 29.75x (ISBN 0-8371-7606-9, HAGG). Greenwood.

Hassler, William T., jt. auth. see Ackerman, Bruce A.

Hassner, Pierre. Europe in the Age of Negotiation. LC 73-83410. (The Washington Papers: No. 8). 1973. 3.50x (ISBN 0-8039-0281-6). Sage.

Hasso, Anton N., jt. auth. see Thompson, Joseph R.

Hasted, John. The Metal-Benders. (Illus.). 272p. 1980. 25.00 (ISBN 0-7100-0597-0). Routledge & Kegan.

Hastenrath, Stefan & Lamb, Peter J. The Climatic Atlas of the Indian Ocean, 2 vols. LC 78-65016. (Illus.). 100.00 (ISBN 0-299-07814-0). U of Wis Pr.

--Heat Budget Atlas of the Tropical Atlantic & Eastern Pacific Oceans. LC 77-91052. (Illus.). 1978. pap. text ed. 50.00x (ISBN 0-299-07584-2). U of Wis Pr.

Hastenrath, Stefan L. & Lamb, Peter. Climatic Atlas of the Tropical Atlantic & Eastern Pacific Oceans. 1977. pap. 50.00 (ISBN 0-299-07234-7). U of Wis Pr.

Hastie, Caroline. Savoury & Sweet Dishes for Two. 1978. pap. text ed. 4.50 o.p. (ISBN 0-435-42510-2). Heinemann Ed.

Hastin, Bud. Bud Hastin's Avon Bottle Encyclopedia. 8th ed. (Illus.). 530p. 1981. 18.95. Avons Res.

Hastings, A. A History of African Christianity: 1950-1975. LC 78-16599. (Illus.). 1979. 39.95 (ISBN 0-521-22212-5); pap. 11.95x (ISBN 0-521-29397-9). Cambridge U Pr.

Hastings, A. W. & Hastings, E., eds. Important Moral Issues. LC 66-78349. 128p. Repr. of 1966 ed. pap. text ed. 4.95 (ISBN 0-567-22302-7). Attic Pr.

--Theologians of Our Time. LC 66-73626. 224p. Repr. of 1966 ed. pap. text ed. 4.95 (ISBN 0-567-22301-9). Attic Pr.

Hastings, Adrian. African Christianity. 1977. 6.95 (ISBN 0-8164-0336-8). Crossroad NY.

Hastings, Beverly. Don't Talk to Strangers. 224p. 1981. pap. 2.50 (ISBN 0-515-06001-1). Jove Pubns.

Hastings, Brooke. Desert Fire. 192p. (Orig.). 1980. pap. 1.50 (ISBN 0-671-57044-7). S&S.

--Innocent Fire. 192p. (Orig.). 1980. pap. 1.50 (ISBN 0-671-57026-9). S&S.

--Island Conquest. 192p. 1981. pap. 1.50 (ISBN 0-671-57067-6). S&S.

--Playing for Keeps. 192p. (Orig.). 1980. pap. 1.50 (ISBN 0-671-57013-7). S&S.

Hastings, C. B. Introducing Southern Baptists. 176p. (Orig.). 1981. pap. 6.95 (ISBN 0-8091-2364-9). Paulist Pr.

Hastings, Craig H., ed. see Jane, Margoe.

Hastings, De Cronin. The Alternative Society: Software for the Nineteen-Eighties. 160p. 1980. 17.95 (ISBN 0-7153-7880-5). David & Charles.

Hastings, Donald W. A Doctor Speaks on Sexual Expression in Marriage. 2nd ed. 190p. 1971. 12.95 (ISBN 0-316-35017-6). Little.

Hastings, E., jt. ed. see Hastings, A. W.

Hastings, Edward, jt. ed. see Hastings, James.

Hastings, Elizabeth H. & Hastings, Philip K., eds. Index to International Public Opinion: Nineteen Seventy-Nine to Nineteen Eighty. LC 80-643917. 510p. 1981. lib. bdg. 75.00 (ISBN 0-313-22535-4, IN80). Greenwood.

Hastings, G. W. & Williams, D. F. The Mechanical Properties of Biomaterials. LC 79-41776. (Advances in Biomaterials Ser.). 536p. 1980. 105.95 (ISBN 0-471-27761-4, Pub. by Wiley-Interscience). Wiley.

Hastings, Hester. William Ellery Channing & L'Academie Des Sciences Morales et Politques 1870: L'Etude Sur Channing & the Lost Prize Essay. LC 59-10107. (Illus.). 61p. 1959. pap. 2.00 (ISBN 0-87057-055-2, Pub. by Brown U Pr). Univ Pr of New England.

Hastings, James. The Great Texts of the Bible: Genesis-Numbers. 458p. Repr. of 1911 ed. text ed. 5.00x (ISBN 0-567-06701-7). Attic Pr.

--The Great Texts of the Bible: James-Jude. 439p. Repr. of 1912 ed. 5.00x (ISBN 0-567-06719-X). Attic Pr.

--The Great Texts of the Bible: Job-Psalm 23. 518p. Repr. of 1913 ed. text ed. 5.00x (ISBN 0-567-06703-3). Attic Pr.

--The Great Texts of the Bible: Revelation. 432p. Repr. of 1915 ed. 5.00x (ISBN 0-567-06720-3). Attic Pr.

--The Great Texts of the Bible: Romans 8-16. 479p. Repr. of 1911 ed. text ed. 5.00x (ISBN 0-567-06714-9). Attic Pr.

--The Great Texts of the Bible: Thessalonians-Hebrews. 495p. Repr. of 1914 ed. text ed. 5.00x (ISBN 0-567-06718-1). Attic Pr.

Hastings, James, ed. Dictionary of the Bible. 1963. lib. rep. ed. 45.00x (ISBN 0-684-15556-7, ScribT). Scribner.

Hastings, James & Hastings, Edward, eds. Speaker's Bible, 18 vols. 1979. 275.00 (ISBN 0-8010-4036-1). Baker Bk.

Hastings, James R. & Turner, Raymond. The Changing Mile. LC 65-25019. (Illus.). 1965. 18.00x (ISBN 0-8165-0014-2). U of Ariz Pr.

Hastings, Macdonald. Shooting - Why We Miss: Questions & Answers on the Successful Use of the Shotgun. 1977. 6.95 o.p. (ISBN 0-679-50720-5); pap. 3.95 o.p. (ISBN 0-679-50721-3). McKay.

Hastings, N. A. Dynamic Programming with Management Applications. 177p. 1973. 11.75x o.p. (ISBN 0-8448-1035-5). Crane-Russak Co.

Hastings, N. A. & Peacock, J. B. Statistical Distribution. LC 74-617. 130p. 1974. text ed. 9.95 (ISBN 0-470-35889-0). Halsted Pr.

Hastings, Phil. Chicago Great Western. (Carstens Hobby Bks.: No. C39). 1980. pap. 9.95 (ISBN 0-911868-39-9). Carstens Pubns.

Hastings, Philip K., jt. ed. see Hastings, Elizabeth H.

Hastings, Phyllis. House of the Twelve Caesars. large type ed. pap. 1.25 o.p. (ISBN 0-425-03092-X). Berkley Pub.

Hastings, Thomas. Dissertation on Musical Taste. LC 68-16237. (Music Ser.). 228p. 1974. Repr. of 1822 ed. lib. bdg. 22.50 (ISBN 0-306-71085-4). Da Capo.

Hastings, William T. Conrade Webb of Hampstead. LC 58-7622. (Illus.). 102p. 1958. 5.00x (ISBN 0-87057-050-1, Pub. by Brown U Pr). Univ Pr of New England.

Haston, Dougal. In High Places. (Illus.). 176p. 1973. 9.95 (ISBN 0-02-548980-1). Macmillan.

Hasty, Ronald W. & Will, R. Ted. Marketing. LC 74-23166. 400p. 1975. text ed. 20.50 scp (ISBN 0-06-389407-6, HarpC); scp study guide 6.50 (ISBN 0-06-389408-4). Har-Row.

Haswell & Silva. Civil Engineering Contracts. 1981. text ed. price not set (ISBN 0-408-00526-2). Butterworth.

Haswell, Harold A., jt. auth. see Eells, Walter C.

Haszonics, J. J. & Barratt, S. Wine Merchandising. (Illus.). 12.95x (ISBN 0-685-01585-8). Radio City.

Haszonics, Joseph J. Front Office Operation. LC 77-146929. 1971. text ed. 13.50 (ISBN 0-672-96074-5); tchr's manual 5.90 (ISBN 0-672-96076-1); wkbk. 6.95 (ISBN 0-672-96075-3). Bobbs.

Hata, Kazud. New Hydrogenating Catalysts: Urushibara Catalysts. LC 72-2652. 247p. 1972. 19.95 (ISBN 0-470-35890-4). Halsted Pr.

Hatab, Lawrence J. Nietzsche & Eternal Recurrence: The Redemption of Time & Becoming. LC 78-62266. 1978. pap. text ed. 7.75 (ISBN 0-8191-0564-3). U Pr of Amer.

Hatada, Takashi. A History of Korea. Smith, Warren W., Jr. & Hazard, Benjamin H., eds. LC 69-20450. Orig. Title: Chosen Shi. 1969. pap. 2.50 (ISBN 0-87436-065-X). ABC-Clio.

Hatch, Denison. The Stork. 1978. pap. 1.95 o.s.i. (ISBN 0-515-04747-3). Jove Pubns.

Hatch, Elvin. Biography of a Small Town. LC 79-313. 1979. 22.50x (ISBN 0-231-04694-4). Columbia U Pr.

Hatch, Elvin J. Theories of Man & Culture. Orig. Title: Main Theories of Man & Culture. 396p. 1973. 20.00x (ISBN 0-685-30374-8); pap. 10.00x (ISBN 0-231-03639-6). Columbia U Pr.

Hatch, Jan, ed. Public Employees Conference 1975, Hollywood, Fla. Proceedings. (Civil Service Pensions). 145p. 1976. spiral bdg 3.75 (ISBN 0-89154-044-X). Intl Found Employ.

Hatch, Janice, ed. Canadian Conference on Employee Benefit Plans, Sept.-Oct. 1975: Proceedings. (Pensions Canada). 144p. 1976. spiral bdg. 8.75 (ISBN 0-89154-041-5). Intl Found Employ.

Hatch, Lewis F. & Matar, Sami. From Hydrocarbons to Petrochemicals. (Illus.). 120p. 1981. 25.95x (ISBN 0-87201-374-X). Gulf Pub.

Hatch, M. D., jt. ed. see Stumpf, P. K.

Hatch, Mary C. Thirteen Danish Tales. LC 49-10046. (Illus.). (gr. 3-6). 1947. 4.50 o.p. (ISBN 0-15-285683-8, HJ). HarBraceJ.

Hatch, Melville H. Century of Entomology in the Pacific Northwest. (Illus.). 51p. 1949. pap. 5.00 (ISBN 0-295-73733-6). U of Wash Pr.

Hatch, Melville H., et al. Beetles of the Pacific Northwest, 5 pts. Incl. Pt. 1. Introduction & Adephaga. 348p. 1953. o.p. (ISBN 0-295-73715-8); Pt. 2. Staphyliniformia. 384p. 1957. o.p. (ISBN 0-295-73716-6); Pt. 3. Pselaphidae & Diversicornia 1. 503p. 1962. 25.00 (ISBN 0-295-73717-4); Pt. 4. Macrodactyles, Palpicornes, & Heteromera. 268p. 1965. o.p. (ISBN 0-295-73718-2); Pt. 5. Rhipiceroidea, Sternoxi, Phytophaga, Rhynchophora, & Lamellicornia. 650p. 1971. 25.00 (ISBN 0-295-73719-0). LC 53-9444. (Publications in Biology Ser.: No. 16). (Illus.). U of Wash Pr.

Hatch, Raymond N., ed. The Organization of Pupil Personnel Programs-Issues & Practices. 435p. 1974. 15.00x (ISBN 0-87013-186-9). Mich St U Pr.

Hatcher. The Book of the Garand. 15.00 (ISBN 0-88227-014-1). Gun Room.

Hatcher, et al. Firearms Investigation, Identification & Evidence. (Illus.). 548p. 1977. Repr. 24.50 (ISBN 0-8117-0612-5). Stackpole.

Hatcher, Harvey B. Holy Nativity. LC 57-10298. (Orig.). 1957. pap. 0.60 (ISBN 0-8054-9702-1). Broadman.

Hatcher, John. Plague, Population & the English Economy, 1348-1530. (Studies in Economic & Social History). 1977. pap. 4.75x (ISBN 0-333-21293-2). Humanities.

--Rural Economy & Society in the Duchy of Cornwall, 1300-1500. LC 74-105495. (Illus.). 1970. 44.50 (ISBN 0-521-07660-9). Cambridge U Pr.

Hatcher, John, jt. auth. see Miller, Edward.

Hatcher, Julian S. Hatcher's Notebook. rev. ed. LC 62-12654. (Illus.). 1962. 19.95 (ISBN 0-8117-0795-4). Stackpole.

Hatcher, Robert, jt. auth. see Stewart, Felicia.

Hatcher, Robert A. & Stewart, Gary K. Contraceptive Technology, Nineteen Eighty-Eighty-One. 10th, rev. ed. (Illus., Orig.). 1980. 12.95 (ISBN 0-8290-0083-6); pap. text ed. 6.95x (ISBN 0-8290-0084-4). Irvington.

Hatcher, William S. The Logical Foundations of Mathematics. LC 80-41253. (Foundations & Philosophy of Science & Technology Ser.). 400p. 1981. 48.00 (ISBN 0-08-025800-X). Pergamon.

--The Science of Religion. (Etudes Baha'i Studies Ser: Vol. 2). 1977. pap. 2.95 (ISBN 0-87743-124-8, 7-32-55). Baha'i.

Hatchett, Marion. Music for the Church Year. pap. 4.95 (ISBN 0-8164-0169-1). Crossroad NY.

Hatchett, Marion J. Sanctifying Life, Time & Space: An Introduction to Liturgical Study. 1976. 8.95 (ISBN 0-8164-0290-6). Crossroad NY.

Hatchimonji, Mike, ed. see Corbit, Julia.

Hatefi, D., ed. The Structural Basis of Membrane Function. 1976. 32.00 (ISBN 0-12-332450-5). Acad Pr.

Hater, Robert J. The Ministry Explosion. 96p. (Orig.). 1979. pap. 3.25 (ISBN 0-697-01709-5). Wm C Brown.

Hatfield, C. W., ed. The Complete Poems of Emily Jane Bronte. LC 41-21750. 1941. 17.50x (ISBN 0-231-01222-5). Columbia U Pr.

Hatfield, C. W., ed. see Bronte, Emily J.

Hatfield, Edwin F. Poets of the Church: A Series of Biographical Sketches of Hymn-Writers, with Notes on Their Hymns. 1979. Repr. of 1884 ed. 68.00 (ISBN 0-8103-4291-X). Gale.

Hatfield, Frederick C. Powerlifting: A Scientific Approach. (Illus.). 1981. 12.95 (ISBN 0-8092-7002-1); pap. 6.95 (ISBN 0-8092-7001-3). Contemp Bks.

Hatfield, Glen J. Are You Mad? 1963. pap. 0.75 (ISBN 0-9600216-1-2). Hatfield.

--Mister Tail Gate. (Illus.). 1969. pap. 2.00 (ISBN 0-9600216-0-4). Hatfield.

--Mysterious Cloud. 1970. pap. 4.00 (ISBN 0-9600216-3-9). Hatfield.

Hatfield, Henry. Clashing Myths in German Literature: From Heine to Rilke. LC 73-83964. 256p. 1974. text ed. 14.00x (ISBN 0-674-13375-7). Harvard U Pr.

Hatfield, Henry C. Goethe, a Critical Introduction. LC 64-24031. 1963. 12.50x (ISBN 0-674-35550-4). Harvard U Pr.

Hatfield, Henry R. Accounting: Its Principles & Problems. LC 78-12596. 1971. Repr. of 1927 ed. text ed. 15.00 (ISBN 0-914348-02-7). Scholars Bk.

Hathaway, Bo. A World of Hurt: A Novel. LC 80-18147. 272p. 1981. 11.95 (ISBN 0-8008-8586-4). Taplinger.

Hathaway, Harmon, et al. Yoga for Athletics. 1978. 12.95 o.p. (ISBN 0-8092-7561-9); pap. 5.95 o.p. (ISBN 0-8092-7560-0). Contemp Bks.

Hathaway, Winifred. Education & Health of the Partially Seeing Child. 4th ed. LC 59-65156. 1959. 18.00x (ISBN 0-231-02356-1). Columbia U Pr.

Hatheway, Allen W. & McClure, Cole R., eds. Reviews in Engineering Geology, Vol. 4: Geology in the Siting of Nuclear Power Plants. LC 62-51690. (Illus.). 1979. 41.00x (ISBN 0-8137-4104-1). Geol Soc.

Hatie, Gerd, ed. New Furniture, Vol. XI. Date not set. 24.95 o.p. (ISBN 0-8038-0186-6). Hastings.

Hatlen, Theodore W. Drama: Principles & Plays. 2nd ed. (Illus.). 768p. 1975. pap. text ed. 13.95 (ISBN 0-13-218982-8). P-H.

--Orientation to the Theater. 2nd ed. (Illus., Orig.). 1972. pap. text ed. 14.95 (ISBN 0-13-642090-7). P-H.

--Orientation to the Theatre. 3rd ed. (Speech & Theatre Ser.). (Illus.). 512p. 1981. text ed. 14.95 (ISBN 0-13-642108-3). P-H.

Hatley, Jan. Observer's Book of Zoo Animals. (Observer Bks.). (Illus.). 1977. 4.95 (ISBN 0-684-15222-3, ScribT). Scribner.

Hatmon, Paul W. Yesterday's Motorcycles. (Superwheels & Thrill Sports Bks.). (Illus.). (YA) (gr. 4 up). 1981. PLB 6.95g (ISBN 0-8225-0429-4). Lerner Pubns.

Hatoff, et al. Teacher's Practical Guide for Educating Young Children: A Growing Program. 344p. 1980. pap. text ed. 16.95 (ISBN 0-205-07126-0, 237126X). Allyn.

Hatry, Harry, jt. auth. see Greiner, John.

Hatry, Harry P. & Dunn, Diana R. Measuring the Effectiveness of Local Government Services: Recreation. 47p. 1971. pap. 1.75 o.p. (ISBN 0-87766-012-3, 70002). Urban Inst.

Hatry, Harry P., jt. auth. see Webb, Kenneth.

Hatry, Harry P., et al. How Effective Are Your Community Services: Procedures for Monitoring the Effectiveness of Municipal Services. 1977. pap. 10.00 (ISBN 0-87766-206-1, 19500). Urban Inst.

--Practical Program Evaluation for State & Local Government Officials. 1973. pap. 4.50 (ISBN 0-87766-054-9, 17000). Urban Inst.

Hatsopoulos, G. N. & Gyftopoulos, E. P. Thermionic Energy Conversion, 2 vols. Incl. Vol. 1. Processes & Duricy. text ed. 25.00x (ISBN 0-262-08060-5); Vol. 2. Theory, Technology & Application. text ed. 35.00x (ISBN 0-262-08059-1). (Illus.). 1979. MIT Pr.

Hatten, Mary L. Macroeconomics for Management. (Illus.). 384p. 1981. text ed. 18.95 (ISBN 0-13-542498-4). P-H.

Hattenschweiler, Walter, jt. auth. see Haab, Armin.

Hatter, D. & Eaton, J. Systems Analysis & Computing. 1974. 14.95 o.p. (ISBN 0-236-30898-X, Pub. by Paul Elek); pap. 7.95x o.p. (ISBN 0-236-31099-2). Merrimack Bk Serv.

Hatter, D. J. Matrix Computer Methods of Vibration Analysis. LC 73-10064. 206p. 1974. 22.95 o.p. (ISBN 0-470-35995-1). Halsted Pr.

Hatterer, Lawrence J. The Pleasure Addicts. LC 79-50769. 392p. 1981. 12.00 (ISBN 0-498-02285-4). A S Barnes.

Hattersley, Ralph. Beginner's Guide to Photographing People. LC 77-12860. 1978. pap. 4.95 (ISBN 0-385-12689-1, Dolp). Doubleday.

Hattich, William. Tombstone. LC 80-5947. (Illus.). 64p. 1981. 9.95 (ISBN 0-8061-1753-2). U of Okla Pr.

Hatto, A. T., ed. The Memorial Feast for Kokotoy-Khan: A Kirghiz Epic Poem. (London Oriental Ser.). 1977. 89.00x (ISBN 0-19-713593-5). Oxford U Pr.

Hatton, Joseph, ed. see Streeter, Edwin W.

Hatton, Thomas J. A Quiet Night: A Play for Christmas. 24p. (Orig.). 1980. pap. text ed. 2.70 (ISBN 0-89536-438-7). CSS Pub.

Hattum, Roland J. Van see Van Hattum, Rolland J.

Hatvary, George E. Horace Binney Wallace. (United States Authors Ser.: No. 287). 1977. lib. bdg. 12.95 (ISBN 0-8057-7190-5). Twayne.

Hatzopoulos, Miltiades B., ed. see Andronicos, Manolis, et al.

Hauberg, Clifford A. Puerto Rico & the Puerto Ricans. (Immigrant Heritage of America Ser). 1974. lib. bdg. 12.95 (ISBN 0-8057-3259-4). Twayne.

Haubrich, Vernon F. & Apple, Michael W., eds. Schooling & the Rights of Children. LC 74-24477. 200p. 1975. 16.00x (ISBN 0-8211-0755-0); text ed. 14.50x (ISBN 0-685-51454-1). McCutchan.

Haubrick, Judd. Scrabble Grams. Bell, Harriet, ed. 96p. 1981. pap. 2.95 (ISBN 0-517-54271-4, Harmony). Crown.

Hauch, Christine, tr. see Meyer, Niels I., et al.

Hauch, E. F., tr. see Meyer, Conrad F.

Hauck, Jo A., jt. auth. see Pelstring, Linda.

Hauenstein & Bachmeyer. Introduction to Communications Careers. (gr. 9-10). 1975. pap. text ed. 5.00 activity ed. (ISBN 0-87345-183-X). McKnight.

--World of Communications: Audiovisual Media. (gr. 9-12). 1975. text ed. 14.64 (ISBN 0-87345-662-9); teacher's guide 29.33 (ISBN 0-87345-663-7); activity manuals 4.67 ea.; filmstrip set 200.00 (ISBN 0-685-63840-5); 2 films 180.00 (ISBN 0-685-63841-3); transparency package 260.00 (ISBN 0-685-63842-1). McKnight.

Hauenstein, A. Dean & Bachmeyer, Steven A. World of Communications: Visual Media. (gr. 9-12). 1974. text ed. 14.64 (ISBN 0-87345-675-0); teacher's guide 29.33 (ISBN 0-87345-677-7); lab manual 6.33 (ISBN 0-87345-676-9); filmstrip set 200.00 (ISBN 0-685-42203-8); 2 films 170.00 (ISBN 0-685-42204-6); transparency set 325.00 (ISBN 0-685-42205-4). McKnight.

Hauer, Mary, et al. Books, Libraries, & Research. 1978. pap. text ed. 5.95 (ISBN 0-8403-1953-3, 40195301). Kendall-Hunt.

Hauerwas, Stanley. A Community of Character: Toward a Constructive Christian Social Ethic. LC 80-53072. 320p. 1981. text ed. 20.00 (ISBN 0-268-00733-0). U of Notre Dame Pr.

Hauf, H. D., jt. auth. see Parker, Harry.

Hauf, Harold D. Building Contracts for Design & Construction. 2nd ed. LC 76-2701. 304p. 1976. 27.50 (ISBN 0-471-36003-1, Pub. by Wiley-Interscience). Wiley.

Hauf, Harold D., jt. auth. see Parker, Harry.

Hauff, Wilhelm. The Adventures of Little Mouk. Shub, Elizabeth, tr. LC 74-4420. (Illus.). 36p. (gr. k-3). 1975. 6.95g o.s.i. (ISBN 0-02-743400-1). Macmillan.

Haug, Edward J. & Arora, Jasbir S. Applied Optimal Design: Mechanical & Structural Systems. LC 79-11437. 1979. 32.50 (ISBN 0-471-04170-X, Pub. by Wiley-Interscience). Wiley.

Haug, Marie. Elderly Patients & Their Doctors. 1981. text ed. price not set (ISBN 0-8261-3570-6). Springer Pub.

Haug, Olaf & Haug, Scott. Help for the Hard of Hearing: A Speech, Reading & Auditory Training Manual for Home & Professionally Guided Training. 144p. 1977. 13.00 (ISBN 0-398-03674-8); pap. 8.75 (ISBN 0-398-03675-6). C C Thomas.

Haug, Scott, jt. auth. see Haug, Olaf.

Haugaard, Erik C. Chase Me, Catch Nobody! (gr. 7 up). 1980. 7.95 (ISBN 0-395-29208-5). HM.

Haugaard, Erik Christian see Andersen, Hans Christian.

Haugaard, William P. Elizabeth & the English Reformation. LC 68-23179. 1968. 49.50 (ISBN 0-521-07245-X). Cambridge U Pr.

Haugan, Randolf E., ed. Christmas: An American Annual of Christmas Literature & Art, Vol. 45. LC 32-30914. (Illus.). 68p. (Orig.). 1975. 8.95 (ISBN 0-8066-8946-3, 17-0110); pap. 4.75 (ISBN 0-8066-8945-5, 17-0109). Augsburg.

Haugan, Randolph, ed. Christmas, Vol. 47. LC 32-30914. 1977. 8.95 (ISBN 0-8066-8951-X, 17-0115); pap. 4.75 (ISBN 0-8066-8950-1, 17-0114). Augsburg.

Haugan, Randolph E., ed. Christmas: An American Annual of Christmas Literature & Art, Vol. 46. LC 32-30914. 1976. 8.95 (ISBN 0-8066-8948-X, 17-0113); pap. 4.75 (ISBN 0-8066-8947-1, 17-0112). Augsburg.

--Christmas: An American Annual of Christmas Literature & Art, Vol. 49. LC 32-30914. (Illus.). 64p. 1979. 8.95 (ISBN 0-8066-8955-2, 17-0119); pap. 4.75 (ISBN 0-8066-8954-4, 17-0118). Augsburg.

--Christmas: An American Annual of Christmas & Art, Vol. 48. LC 32-30914. (Illus.). 1978. 8.95 (ISBN 0-8066-8953-6, 17-0117); pap. 4.75 (ISBN 0-8066-8952-8, 17-0116). Augsburg.

Hauge, Hans-Egil. Luo Religion & Folklore. (Scandinavian University Books). 154p. 1974. pap. 18.00x (ISBN 8-200-02327-3, Dist. by Columbia U Pr). Universitet.

Haugeland, John. Mind Design: Semantic Engines. 283p. 1980. text ed. cancelled (ISBN 0-89706-004-0); pap. text ed. cancelled (ISBN 0-89706-005-9). Bradford Bks.

Haugeland, John C. Mind Design: Philosophy, Psychology, Artifical Intelligence. LC 81-24275. Orig. Title: Mind Design. (Illus.). 368p. 1981. text ed. 21.50 (ISBN 0-89706-004-0); pap. text ed. 10.00 (ISBN 0-89706-005-9). Bradford Bks.

Haugen, Edward B. Probabilistic Mechanical Design. LC 80-13428. 688p. 1980. 36.95 (ISBN 0-471-05847-5, Pub. by Wiley Interscience). Wiley.

Haugen, Einar. Bilingualism in the Americas: A Research & Bibliographical Guide. (Publications of the American Dialect Society: No. 26). 159p. 1956. pap. 4.95 (ISBN 0-8173-0626-9). U of Ala Pr.

--The Ecology of Language: Essays by Einar Haugen. Dil, A. S., ed. LC 73-183888. (Language Science & National Development Ser.). xvi, 366p. 1972. 18.50x (ISBN 0-8047-0802-9). Stanford U Pr.

--Spoken Norwegian. Incl. Book 1, Units 1-12. pap. 10.00x (ISBN 0-87950-170-7); Book 2, Units 13-30. pap. 12.00x (ISBN 0-87950-171-5); Cassettes, Six Dual Track. 60.00x (ISBN 0-87950-175-8); Cassette Course, Bk. 1 & Cassettes. pap. 65.00x (ISBN 0-87950-176-6). LC 75-15152. (Spoken Language Ser.). 1977. Spoken Lang Serv.

Haugen, Einar, ed. First Grammatical Treatise: The Earliest Germanic Phonology. 2nd, rev. ed. (Classics of Linguistics Ser). (Illus.). 112p. 1973. text ed. 15.00x (ISBN 0-582-52491-1). Longman.

--Norwegian-English Dictionary. 1967. pap. 17.50 (ISBN 0-299-03874-2). U of Wis Pr.

Haugen, Einar & Bloomfield, Morton, eds. Language As a Human Problem. 1975 12.50x (ISBN 0-393-01112-7); pap. 7.95x (ISBN 0-393-09261-5). Norton.

Haugen, Einar, ed. & tr. see Dumezil, Georges.

Haugen, Einar, tr. see Beyer, Harald.

Haugen, G. Norwegian Dictionary: Norwegian-English. 1976. pap. 13.75x (ISBN 0-299-03874-2, N533). Vanous.

Haugh, James B. Power & Influence in a Southern City: Compared with the Classic Community Power Studies of the Lynds, Hunter, Vidich & Bensman, & Dahl. LC 80-5231. (Illus.). 160p. 1980. lib. bdg. 17.50 (ISBN 0-8191-1060-4); pap. text ed. 7.25 (ISBN 0-8191-1061-2). U Pr of Amer.

Haugh, Oscar M., jt. auth. see Anderson, Kenneth E.

Haugh, Richard S., et al, eds. see Florovsky, Georges.

Haugh, Robert F. Nadine Gordimer. (World Authors Ser.: South Africa: No. 315). 1974. lib. bdg. 10.95 (ISBN 0-8057-2387-0). Twayne.

Haughey, John C., S.J. Conspiracy of God: The Holy Spirit in Men. LC 73-80730. 120p. 1976. pap. 1.95 (ISBN 0-385-11558-X, Im). Doubleday.

--Should Anyone Say Forever on Making, Keeping & Breaking Commitments. LC 74-12690. 1977. pap. 2.45 (ISBN 0-385-13261-1, Im). Doubleday.

Haughey, Thomas B. The Case of the Hijacked Moon. (Baker Street Mystery Ser.). 144p. 1981. pap. 2.50 (ISBN 0-87123-143-3, 200143). Bethany Fell.

--The Case of the Kidnapped Shadow. (Baker Street Mysteries Ser.). (Orig.). 1980. pap. 2.50 (ISBN 0-87123-112-3, 200112). Bethany Fell.

--The Case of the Maltese Treasure. LC 79-54939. (Baker Street Mysteries). 1979. pap. 2.50 (ISBN 0-87123-048-8, 200048). Bethany Fell.

Haughey, Thomas Brace. The Case of the Invisible Thief. LC 78-68424. (Baker Street Mystery Ser.). 1978. pap. 2.50 (ISBN 0-87123-086-0, 200086). Bethany Fell.

Haughey, Tom B. The Case of the Frozen Scream. LC 79-50829. (Baker Street Mystery Ser.). 1979. pap. 2.50 (ISBN 0-87123-045-3, 200045). Bethany Fell.

Haught, John F. Nature & Purpose. LC 80-5738. 131p. 1980. lib. bdg. 15.75 (ISBN 0-8191-1257-7); pap. text ed. 7.75 (ISBN 0-8191-1258-5). U Pr of Amer.

--Religion & Self-Acceptance: A Study of the Relationship Between Belief in God & the Desire to Know. LC 80-5872. 195p. 1980. lib. bdg. 17.00 (ISBN 0-8191-1296-8); pap. text ed. 8.75 (ISBN 0-8191-1297-6). U Pr of Amer.

Haughton. Physical Principles of Audiology. (Medical Physics Handbook: Vol. 3). 1980. 28.00 (ISBN 0-9960019-1-3, Pub. by A Hilger England). Heyden.

Haughton, Rosemary. Carpenter's Son. (gr. 5-8). 1967. 4.95g o.s.i. (ISBN 0-02-743430-3). Macmillan.

--The Drama of Salvation. 154p. 1975. 6.95 (ISBN 0-8164-1201-4). Crossroad NY.

--The Passionate God. 308p. 1981. pap. 11.95 (ISBN 0-8091-2383-5). Paulist Pr.

--Transformation of Man. 1967. 6.95 o.p. (ISBN 0-87243-010-3). Templegate.

--Transformation of Man. rev. ed. 1980. pap. 6.95 (ISBN 0-87243-127-4). Templegate.

Hauglid & Asker. Norway: Native Art. 1977. deluxe ed. 39.50x (ISBN 82-09-01381-5, N-387). Vanous.

Hauglie-Hanssen, E. Intrinsic Neuronal Organization of the Vestibular Nuclear Complex in the Cat: A Golgi Study. LC 64-20582. (Advances in Anatomy, Embryology & Cell Biology: Vol. 40, Pt. 5). (Illus.). 1968. pap. 25.40 o.p. (ISBN 0-387-04089-7). Springer-Verlag.

Haun, Paul. Recreation: A Medical Viewpoint. LC 65-12572. (Orig.). 1965. pap. text ed. 4.50x (ISBN 0-8077-1503-4). Tchrs Coll.

Haupt, Arthur & Kane, Thomas T. Guia Rapida de Poblacion del Population Reference Bureau. LC 79-9639. (Illus.). 80p. (Orig., Span.). 1980. pap. 3.00 (ISBN 0-917136-05-5). Population Ref.

--Guide De Demographie. (Illus.). 80p. (Orig., Fr.). 1980. pap. 3.00 (ISBN 0-917136-06-3). Population Ref.

--Population Handbook: A Quick Guide to Population Dynamics for Journalists, Policymakers, Teachers, Students & Other People Interested in People. LC 77-82142. (Illus.). 64p. 1978. 3.00 (ISBN 0-917136-02-0). Population Ref.

--The Population Reference Bureau's Population Handbook, in Arabic. (Illus.). 80p. (Orig., Arabic.). 1980. pap. 3.00 (ISBN 0-917136-07-1). Population Ref.

--The Population Reference Bureau's Population Handbook: International Edition. LC 79-9638. (Illus.). 80p. (Orig.). 1980. pap. 3.00 (ISBN 0-917136-04-7). Population Ref.

Haupt, Georges. Socialism & the Great War: The Collapse of the Second International. 280p. 1972. 24.95x (ISBN 0-19-827184-0). Oxford U Pr.

Hauptman & Karle. Solution of the Phase Problem, Pt. 1: The Centrosymmetric Crystal. pap. 3.00 (ISBN 0-686-60369-9). Polycrystal Bk Serv.

Hauptmann, Gerhart. Bahnwarter Theil und Fasching. Stirk, S. D., ed. (Blackwell's German Texts Ser.). 1975. pap. 9.95x (ISBN 0-631-01540-X, Pub. by Basil Blackwell). Biblio Dist.

--The Fool in Christ, Emanuel Quint. Seltzer, T., tr. from Ger. LC 76-28694. 1977. Repr. of 1911 ed. 19.50 (ISBN 0-86527-251-4). Fertig.

Hauptmann, Tatjana. Adeline Schlime. (Illus.). 32p. (gr. k-3). 1980. 10.95 (ISBN 0-03-057979-1). HR&W.

Haurowitz, Felix. The Chemistry & Function of Proteins. 2nd ed. 455p. 1963. text ed. 19.50 (ISBN 0-12-332956-6). Acad Pr.

Haury, Emil W. Ventana Cave: Stratigraphy & Archaeology. new ed. LC 51-802. (Illus.). xxvii, 599p. 1975. text ed. 17.50x (ISBN 0-8165-0536-5). U of Ariz Pr.

Haus, Andreas. Moholy-Nagy: Photographs & Photograms. (Illus.). 1980. 35.00 (ISBN 0-394-50449-6). Pantheon.

Hauschild, Jana. Danish Cross-Stitched Zodiac Samplers: Charted Designs for the Astrological Year. (Illus.). 1980. pap. 2.25 daddlewire (ISBN 0-486-24032-0). Dover.

Hausdorf, D. Literature in America: A Century of Expansion. LC 73-139984. 1971. pap. text ed. 8.95 (ISBN 0-02-914240-7). Free Pr.

Hausdorff, Felix. Set Theory. 2nd ed. LC 57-8493. 14.95 (ISBN 0-8284-0119-5). Chelsea Pub.

Hauser, Emil D. Congenital Clubfoot. (Illus.). 104p. 1966. 9.75 (ISBN 0-398-00796-9). C C Thomas.

Hauser, Gayelord. Be Happier, Be Healthier. 1976. pap. 1.50 o.p. (ISBN 0-449-22715-4, Q2715, Crest). Fawcett.

--Look Younger, Live Longer. 1977. pap. 1.95 o.p. (ISBN 0-449-22931-9, Crest). Fawcett.

--Mirror, Mirror on the Wall. 1977. pap. 1.95 o.p. (ISBN 0-449-22952-1, Crest). Fawcett.

--New Guide to Intelligent Reducing. 1976. pap. 1.75 o.p. (ISBN 0-449-23046-5, Crest). Fawcett.

Hauser, John R., jt. auth. see Urban, Glen.

Hauser, M. M. The Economics of Medical Care. (University of York Studies in Economics). 1972. text ed. 27.50x o.p. (ISBN 0-04-330213-0). Allen Unwin.

Hauser, Philip M., ed. see UNESCO.

Hauser, Ronald. Georg Buchner. (World Authors Ser.: Germany: No. 300). 1974. lib. bdg. 10.95 (ISBN 0-8057-2183-5). Twayne.

Hauser, Stuart T. & Kasendorf, E. Black & White Identity Formation. rev. ed. 1981. write for info. (ISBN 0-89874-055-X). Krieger.

Hauser, Thomas. The Execution of Charles Horman. 272p. 1979. pap. 2.75 (ISBN 0-380-49098-6, 49098, Discus). Avon.

Hauser, Verne. River Camping: Touring by Canoe, Raft, Dory, & Kayak. (A Soltice Press Bk.). (Illus.). 1981. pap. 9.95 (ISBN 0-8037-7256-4). Dial.

Hauser, Walter. Introduction to Principles of Electromagnetism. (Physics Ser). 1971. text ed. 20.95 (ISBN 0-201-02821-2). A-W.

--Introduction to the Principles of Mechanics. 1965. 20.95 (ISBN 0-201-02806-9). A-W.

Hausman, Gerald, ed. see Pomonis, Carolyn.

Hausman, Gerald, ed. see Thompson, Waite & Gottleib, Richard M.

Hausman, Gerald A. No Witness. (Illus.). 224p. 1980. 14.95 (ISBN 0-8117-1009-2). Stackpole.

Hausman, Jim. When I Was a Boy, Vol. II. (Illus., Orig.). 1978. pap. 1.95 o.s.i. (ISBN 0-8220-1625-7). Centennial.

Hausman, Louis. Illustrations of the Nervous System: Atlas Three. (Illus.). 208p. 1971. 18.75 (ISBN 0-398-00800-0). C C Thomas.

Hausman, Patricia. Jack Sprat's Legacy: The Science & Politics of Fat & Cholesterol. 320p. 1981. 12.95 (ISBN 0-399-90111-6). Marek.

Hausman, Tim. When I Was a Boy, 2 vols. (Illus., Orig.). pap. 1.95 ea. o.s.i. Vol. 1 (ISBN 0-8220-1624-9). Vol. 2 (ISBN 0-8220-1625-7). Cliffs.

Hausman, W. H., jt. auth. see Searle, S. R.

Hausmann, Renee & Taylor, Evelyn. Practical Rhetoric for College Writers. 272p. 1980. pap. text ed. 7.95x (ISBN 0-534-00783-X). Wadsworth Pub.

Hausmann, William J. Science & the Bible in Lutheran Theology: From Luther to the Missouri Synod. LC 78-52287. 1978. pap. text ed. 8.75x o.p. (ISBN 0-8191-0482-5). U Pr of Amer.

Hausner, Henry H. Beryllium: Its Metallurgy & Properties. 1965. 25.00x (ISBN 0-520-00541-4). U of Cal Pr.

Hauss, Charles. The New Left in France: The Unified Socialist Party. LC 77-94753. (Contributions in Political Science: No. 9). (Illus.). 1978. lib. bdg. 19.95 (ISBN 0-313-20113-7, HNL/). Greenwood.

Hausser, D. L., et al. Survey-Guided Development II: A Manual for Consultants. rev. ed. LC 77-75523. 162p. 1977. pap. 11.50 (ISBN 0-88390-138-2). Univ Assocs.

Haut, F. J. History of the Electric Locomotive. LC 76-103871. (Illus.). 224p. 1980. 20.00 (ISBN 0-498-02466-0). A S Barnes.

Hautala, Rick. Moondeath. 436p. (Orig.). 1981. pap. 2.75 (ISBN 0-89083-702-3). Zebra.

Hauthal, H., jt. auth. see Martin, D.

Hautzig, Deborah. Hey Dollface. 128p. (gr. 7-9). 1980. pap. 1.75 (ISBN 0-553-13555-4). Bantam.

--Hey, Dollface. LC 78-54685. (gr. 7-9). 1978. 7.95 (ISBN 0-688-80170-6); PLB 7.63 (ISBN 0-688-84170-8). Greenwillow.

Hautzig, Esther. At Home: A Visit in Four Languages. LC 68-23063. (Illus., Eng, Fr, Span & Rus.). (gr. k-2). 1968. 8.95 (ISBN 0-02-743470-2). Macmillan.

--In School Learning in Four Languages. LC 69-18236. (Illus., Span, Eng, Fr. & Rus.). (gr. k-3). 1969. 4.95g o.s.i. (ISBN 0-02-743360-9). Macmillan.

--In the Park: An Excursion in Four Languages. LC 68-10067. (Illus., Fr, Rus, Span & Eng.). (gr. 1-3). 1968. 7.95 (ISBN 0-02-743450-8). Macmillan.

--Let's Make More Presents: Easy & Inexpensive Gifts for Every Occasion. LC 72-92445. (How-to Bk.). (Illus.). 160p. (gr. 5 up). 1973. 8.95 (ISBN 0-02-743490-7). Macmillan.

--Let's Make Presents: One Hundred Gifts for Less Than One Dollar. LC 61-14532. (Illus.). (gr. 4 up). 1962. 10.95 (ISBN 0-690-48951-X, TYC-J). T Y Crowell.

--Life with Working Parents: Practical Hints for Everyday Situations. LC 76-15223. (Illus.). (gr. 5 up). 1976. 8.25 (ISBN 0-02-743500-8, 74350). Macmillan.

Hauzig, Esther. A Gift for Mama. 64p. (gr. 3-7). 1981. 8.95 (ISBN 0-670-33976-8). Viking Pr.

Havel, Vaclav. The Memorandum. Blackwell, Vera, tr. from Czech. LC 80-485. 160p. 1980. pap. 5.95 (ISBN 0-394-17653-7, E446, Ever). Grove.

Havelick, Franklin J., ed. Collective Bargaining: New Dimensions in Labor Relations. (Westview Special Study). 1979. lib. bdg. 24.50x (ISBN 0-89158-386-6). Westview.

Havelock, Christine M. Hellenistic Art. rev. ed. (Illus.). 1981. pap. text ed. 10.95x (ISBN 0-393-95133-2). Norton.

Havelock, Eric A. The Greek Concept of Justice: From Its Shadow in Homer to Its Substance in Plato. LC 78-6064. 1978. 18.50x (ISBN 0-674-36220-9). Harvard U Pr.

Havelock, Mary C., jt. auth. see Havelock, Ronald G.

Havelock, Ronald G. & Havelock, Mary C. Training for Change Agents: A Guide to the Design of Training Programs in Education & Other Fields. LC 72-86337. 262p. 1973. cloth 10.00 (ISBN 0-87944-126-7). U of Mich Soc Res.

Havelock, Ronald G. & Huberman, A. M. Solving Educational Problems: Theory & Reality of Innovation in Developing Countries. LC 78-52224. (Praeger Special Studies). 1978. 25.95 (ISBN 0-03-044206-0). Praeger.

Haveman, Robert H. The Economics of the Public Sector. 2nd ed. LC 76-186. (Introduction to Economics Ser.). 224p. 1976. text ed. 9.50x (ISBN 0-471-36182-8, Pub. by Wiley-Hamilton). Wiley.

Havemann, Ernest, jt. auth. see Kagan, Jerome.

Havemen, Robert H. The Market System: An Introduction to Microeconomics. 4th ed. LC 80-21972. (Introduction to Economics Ser.). 304p. 1981. text ed. 11.95 (ISBN 0-471-08530-8). Wiley.

Haven, Diana. Menus for Romance. (Candlelight Romance Cookbook Ser.). (Orig.). pap. 1.50 (ISBN 0-440-16169-X). Dell.

Havener, William H. Ocular Pharmacology. 4th ed. LC 78-7208. 1978. text ed. 52.50 (ISBN 0-8016-2105-4). Mosby.

--Synopsis of Ophthalmology. 4th ed. LC 74-14772. 1975. pap. 18.95 o.p. (ISBN 0-8016-2098-8). Mosby.

--Synopsis of Opthalmology. 5th ed. LC 79-12076. (Illus.). 1979. pap. text ed. 28.50 (ISBN 0-8016-2111-9). Mosby.

Havener, William Lh. Do You Really Need Eye Surgery? 2nd ed. 1977. pap. 4.50 o.p. (ISBN 0-398-03800-7). C C Thomas.

Havenon, Andre de see De Havenon, Andre.

Havens, George R. Jean-Jacques Rousseau. (World Authors Ser.: No. 471). 1978. lib. bdg. 10.95 (ISBN 0-8057-6312-0). Twayne.

Havens, Keith. Fantanimals. (Illus.). 48p. (Orig.). (ps-3). 1980. pap. 2.95 (ISBN 0-89542-938-1). Ideals.

Havens, Thomas R. Farm & Nation in Japan: Agrarian Nationalism, 1870-1940. LC 73-16744. 352p. 1974. 22.00x (ISBN 0-691-03101-0). Princeton U Pr.

Haver, Ronald. David O. Selznick's Hollywood. LC 79-2224. (Illus.). 400p. 1980. 85.00 (ISBN 0-394-42595-2). Knopf.

Havighurst, A. F. Modern England: 1901-1970. LC 75-23844. (Conference on British Studies Bibliographical Handbooks Ser.). 118p. 1976. 15.50 (ISBN 0-521-20941-2). Cambridge U Pr.

--Radical Journalist: Henry W. Massingham, 1860-1924. LC 73-83106. (Conference on British Studies Biographical Ser). 368p. 1974. 42.00 (ISBN 0-521-20355-4). Cambridge U Pr.

Havighurst, Alfred F. Britain in Transition: The Twentieth-Century. LC 78-16052. 1979. 25.00x (ISBN 0-226-31968-7); pap. text ed. 9.95 (ISBN 0-226-31969-5, P815, Phoen). U of Chicago Pr.

Havighurst, Robert J. & Levine, Daniel U. Society & Education. 5th ed. LC 78-32024. 1979. text ed. 17.95 (ISBN 0-205-06654-2, 2366541). Allyn.

Havighurst, Robert J. & Neugarten, Bernice L. Society & Education. 4th ed. 544p. 1975. text ed. 13.95 o.s.i. (ISBN 0-205-04692-4, 2246929); study guide 4.95 o.s.i. (ISBN 0-205-04915-X). Allyn.

Havighurst, Robert J., ed. Education for the Gifted. LC 52-11216. (National Society for the Study of Education Yearbooks Ser: No. 57, Pt. 2). pap. 4.50x o.s.i. (ISBN 0-226-60047-5). U of Chicago Pr.

Havighurst, Robert J., jt. ed. see Levine, Daniel V.

Havighurst, Walter. First Book of Pioneers. (First Bks). (Illus.). (gr. 4-6). 1959. PLB 4.90 o.p. (ISBN 0-531-00611-5). Watts.

--The Heartland: Ohio, Indiana, Illinois. rev. ed. Cramer, Carl, ed. LC 74-1815. (Regions of America). (Illus.). 432p. (YA) 1974. 12.50 o.s.i. (ISBN 0-06-011781-8, HarpT). Har-Row.

--Long Ships Passing. 1961. 12.95 (ISBN 0-02-549090-7); pap. 1.65 (ISBN 0-02-033100-2). Macmillan.

--Ohio: A Bicentennial History. (States & the Nation Ser.). (Illus.). 1976. 12.95 (ISBN 0-393-05613-9, Co-Pub by AASLH). Norton.

Haviland, Diana. Defy the Storm. 352p. 1981. pap. 2.75 (ISBN 0-449-14379-1, GM). Fawcett.

--Passionate Pretenders. 1977. pap. 1.95 o.p. (ISBN 0-449-13810-0, 0-449-13810-0, GM). Fawcett.

Haviland, Henry F. The Political Role of the General Assembly. LC 78-2808. (Carnegie Endowment for International Peace, United Nation Studies: No. 7). 1978. Repr. of 1951 ed. lib. bdg. 17.75x (ISBN 0-313-20334-2, HAPG). Greenwood.

Haviland, Jeannette & Scarborough, Hollis. Adolescent Development in Contemporary Society. 1980. text ed. 16.95 (ISBN 0-442-25862-3). D Van Nostrand.

Haviland, Robert. Build-It Book of Miniature Test & Measurement Instruments. LC 75-41720. (Illus.). 238p. 1976. 7.95 o.p. (ISBN 0-8306-6792-X); pap. 4.95 (ISBN 0-8306-5792-4, 792). TAB Bks.

Haviland, Virginia. Favorite Fairy Tales Told in Scotland. (Illus.). (gr. 3 up). 1963. 6.95 (ISBN 0-316-35043-5); PLB o.p. (ISBN 0-316-35061-3). Little.

Haviland, Virginia, ed. see Bechtel, Louise S.

Haviland, William & Power, Marjory W. The Original Vermonters: Native Inhabitants, Past & Present. (Illus.). 320p. 1981. 16.50 (ISBN 0-87451-196-8). U Pr of New Eng.

Havill, Steven. The Killer. LC 80-1987. (Double D Western Ser.). 192p. 1981. 9.95 (ISBN 0-385-17287-7). Doubleday.

Havinghurst, R. J., et al, eds. Adjustment to Retirement: A Cross-National Study. (Orig.). 1969. text ed. 11.50x (ISBN 90-232-0011-X). Humanities.

Havinghurst, Walter. The Long Ships Passing: The Story of the Great Lakes. rev. ed. LC 75-16406. (Illus.). 368p. (gr. 9-12). 1975. 12.95 (ISBN 0-02-549100-8, 54910). Macmillan.

Havlice, Patricia P. Art in Time. LC 76-14885. 1970. 9.50 o.p. (ISBN 0-8108-0333-X). Scarecrow.

--Index to American Author Bibliographies. LC 73-163870. 1971. 10.00 (ISBN 0-8108-0426-3). Scarecrow.

--Index to Artistic Biography, 2 vols. LC 72-6412. 1973. Set. 45.00 (ISBN 0-8108-0540-5). Scarecrow.

--Index to Literary Biography, 2 vols. LC 74-8315. 1975. Set. 47.50 (ISBN 0-8108-0745-9). Scarecrow.

--Popular Song Index. LC 75-9896. 1975. 35.00 (ISBN 0-8108-0820-X). Scarecrow.

--Popular Song Index: First Supplement. LC 77-25219. 1978. 18.00 (ISBN 0-8108-1099-9). Scarecrow.

--World Painting Index, 2 vols. Incl. Vol. 1. Bibliography, Paintings by Unknown Artists, Painters & Their Works; Vol. 2. Titles of Works & Their Painters. LC 76-52407. 1977. 74.50 set (ISBN 0-8108-1016-6). Scarecrow.

Havlik, John. How to Enjoy Reading the Bible. 1981. 7.95 (ISBN 0-8054-1137-2). Broadman.

Havner, Vance. In Times Like These. 1969. 6.95 (ISBN 0-8007-0160-7). Revell.

--Jesus Only. rev. ed. 6.95 (ISBN 0-8007-0165-8). Revell.

--Though I Walk Through the Valley. 128p. 1974. 6.95 (ISBN 0-8007-0654-4). Revell.

Havner, Vance, tr. Buenos Dias Senor. (Spanish Bks.). (Span.). 1978. 2.25 (ISBN 0-8297-0899-5). Life Pubs Intl.

Havrella, Raymond. Heating, Ventilating & Air Conditioning Fundamentals. LC 80-17155. (Contemporary Construction Ser.). (Illus.). 288p. (gr. 10-12). 1981. text ed. 16.95x (ISBN 0-07-027281-6, G); wkbk. avail. (ISBN 0-07-027283-2). McGraw.

Havrilesky, Thomas M. & Boorman, John T. Current Perspectives in Banking: Operations, Managements & Regulation. 2nd ed. LC 79-55734. (Illus.). 1980. pap. text ed. 14.95 (ISBN 0-88295-405-9). AHM Pub.

--Monetary Macroeconomics. LC 77-85996. (Illus.). 1978. pap. text ed. 14.95x (ISBN 0-88295-401-6). AHM Pub.

Havrilesky, Thomas M., jt. auth. see Boorman, John T.

Havrilesky, Thomas M. & Boorman, John T., eds. Current Issues in Monetary Theory & Policy. 2nd ed. LC 79-55733. (Illus.). 1980. pap. text ed. 14.95x (ISBN 0-88295-406-7). AHM Pub.

Haw, James, et al. Stormy Patriot: The Life of Samuel Chase. LC 80-83807. (Illus.). 305p. 1980. 14.95 (ISBN 0-938420-00-3). Md Hist.

Haward, Lionel. Forensic Psychology. 280p. 1981. 45.00 (ISBN 0-7134-2475-3, Pub. by Batsford England). David & Charles.

Haward, R. N., ed. Developments in Polymerisation, Vol. 2. (Illus.). 1979. 64.60x (ISBN 0-85334-821-9, Pub. by Applied Science). Burgess-Intl Ideas.

--Developments in Polymerisation, Vol. 1: Ionic & Ring-Opening Polymerisation & Polymerisation of Conjugated Dienes. (Illus.). 1979. 51.80x (ISBN 0-85334-822-7, Pub. by Applied Science). Burgess-Intl Ideas.

Haweis, E. The Art of Beauty, Repr. Of 1878. Stansky, Peter & Shewan, Rodney, eds. Incl. The Art of Dress. Repr. of 1879 ed. LC 76-17760. (Aesthetic Movement & the Arts & Crafts Movement Ser.). 1978. lib. bdg. 44.00x (ISBN 0-8240-2465-6). Garland Pub.

Haweis, Mrs. E. The Art of Decoration. LC 76-17761. (Aesthetic Movement Ser.: Vol. 17). 1977. Repr. of 1889 ed. lib. bdg. 44.00x (ISBN 0-8240-2466-4). Garland Pub.

Hawes, Carolyn & Johnson, Margaret. Your Career in Art & Design. LC 76-41912. 1977. pap. 3.50 (ISBN 0-668-04141-2). Arco.

Hawes, Charles B. The Dark Frigate. rev. ed. (Illus.). (gr. 7 up). 1971. 7.95 (ISBN 0-316-35096-6, Pub. by Atlantic Monthly Pr). Little.

Hawes, Gene R. & Brownstone, David M. How to Get the Money to Pay for College. 1978. 12.95 o.p. (ISBN 0-679-50848-1); pap. 6.95 (ISBN 0-679-50849-X). McKay.

Hawes, Gordon & Knight, Stanley. Atlas of Man & Religion. 1970. 6.00 (ISBN 0-08-006999-1, Religious Educ Pr). Pergamon.

Hawes, Hampton & Asher, Don. Raise up off Me: A Portrait of Hampton Hawes. 180p. 1979. pap. 5.95 (ISBN 0-686-68925-9). Da Capo.

Hawes, J. H. Manual of United States Surveying. 1977. Repr. of 1882 ed. 12.50 (ISBN 0-686-18921-3, 612). CARBEN Survey.

Hawes, J. L., jt. auth. see Anderson, Christian.

Hawes, Judy. Bees & Beelines. LC 64-10864. (A Let's-Read-&-Find-Out Science Bk). (Illus.). (gr. k-3). 1964. bds. 6.95 (ISBN 0-690-12739-1, TYC-J); PLB 7.89 (ISBN 0-690-12740-5); filmstrip & record 11.95 (ISBN 0-690-12741-3); filmstrip with cassette 14.95 (ISBN 0-690-12743-X). T Y Crowell.

--Ladybug, Ladybug, Fly Away Home. LC 67-15399. (A Let's-Read-&-Find-Out Science Bk). (Illus.). (gr. k-3). 1967. bds. 6.95 o.p. (ISBN 0-690-48383-X, TYC-J); PLB 7.89 (ISBN 0-690-48384-8); filmstrip with record 11.95 (ISBN 0-690-48385-6); filmstrip with cassette 14.95 (ISBN 0-690-48387-2). T Y Crowell.

--Ladybug, Ladybug, Fly Away Home. LC 67-15399. (Crocodile Paperbacks Ser.). (Illus.). (ps-3). 1973. pap. 2.95 (ISBN 0-690-00200-9, TYC-J). T Y Crowell.

--My Daddy Longlegs. LC 74-175107. (A Let's-Read-&-Find-Out Science Bk). (Illus.). (gr. k-3). 1972. 7.95 (ISBN 0-690-56655-7, TYC-J); PLB 7.89 (ISBN 0-690-56656-5). T Y Crowell.

--Spring Peepers. LC 74-2038. (A Let's-Read-&-Find-Out Science Bk). (Illus.). (ps-3). 1975. 7.95 (ISBN 0-690-00522-9, TYC-J); PLB 7.89 (ISBN 0-690-00523-7). T Y Crowell.

--Watch Honeybees with Me. LC 64-19169. (A Let's-Read-&-Find-Out Science Bk). (Illus.). (gr. k-3). 1964. bds. 7.95 (ISBN 0-690-86937-1, TYC-J). T Y Crowell.

--What I Like About Toads. LC 76-78262. (A Let's Read & Find Out Science Bk). (Illus.). (gr. k-3). 1969. PLB 7.89 (ISBN 0-690-87577-0, TYC-J); filmstrip with record 11.95 (ISBN 0-690-87578-9); filmstrip with cassette 14.95 (ISBN 0-690-87580-0). T Y Crowell.

--What I Like About Toads. LC 76-78262. (Crocodile Paperbacks Ser.). (Illus.). 33p. (gr. k-3). 1972. pap. 2.95 (ISBN 0-690-87582-7, TYC-J). T Y Crowell.

Hawes, Leonard C. Analoguing: Theory & Model Construction. LC 74-19706. 1975. pap. text ed. 7.50 (ISBN 0-201-02822-0). A-W.

Hawisher, Margaret F. & Calhoun, Mary L. The Resource Room: An Educational Asset for Children with Special Needs. (Special Education Ser.). 1978. pap. text ed. 9.95x (ISBN 0-675-08354-0); instructor's manual 3.95 (ISBN 0-686-67987-3). Merrill.

Hawk, Bonnie, jt. auth. see Roberts, Joseph.

Hawk, Grace E. Pembroke College in Brown University: The First Seventy-Five Years, 1891-1966. LC 67-19656. (Illus.). 324p. 1967. 12.50 (ISBN 0-87057-101-X, Pub. by Brown U Pr). Univ Pr of New England.

Hawk, Harold W., ed. Animal Reproduction. LC 78-65535. (Beltsville Symposia in Agricultural Research Ser.: No. 3). (Illus.). 434p. 1979. text ed. 27.50. Allanheld.

--Animal Reproduction, No. 3. LC 78-65535. (Illus.). 1979. text ed. 32.95 (ISBN 0-470-26672-4). Halsted Pr.

Hawke, D. M, tr. see Pellat, Charles.

Hawke, David. Colonial Experience. LC 66-14829. 1966. 19.95 (ISBN 0-672-60688-7). Bobbs.

--In the Midst of a Revolution. LC 80-23581. 235p. 1980. Repr. of 1961 ed. lib. bdg. 23.50x (ISBN 0-313-22604-0, HAIT). Greenwood.

Hawke, David F. Paine. LC 73-14264. (Illus.). 512p. (YA) 1974. 15.00 o.s.i. (ISBN 0-06-011784-2, HarpT). Har-Row.

Hawke, David F., ed. see Smith, John.

Hawker, Geoffrey, et al. Politics & Policy in Australia. 1979. pap. 14.50 (ISBN 0-7022-1307-1). U of Queensland Pr.

Hawker, Lilian E. Fungi: An Introduction. 1966. pap. text ed. 5.75x (ISBN 0-09-078992-X, Hutchinson U Lib). Humanities.

Hawker, Ross W. Notebook of Medical Physiology: Gastroenterological. (Illus.). 1981. pap. text ed. 12.50 (ISBN 0-443-02144-9). Churchill.

--Notebook of Medical Physiology: Gastroenterology. (Notebooks of Medical Physiology Ser.). (Illus.). 256p. (Orig.). 1981. pap. text ed. 12.50 (ISBN 0-443-02144-9). Churchill.

Hawkes, Alex D. Flavors of the Caribbean & Latin America: A Personal Collection of Recipes. 1978. 14.95 o.p. (ISBN 0-670-31755-1). Viking Pr.

Hawkes, D. Models & Systems in Architecture & Building, Vol. 2. (Land Use & Built Form Studies). 1978. text ed. 38.00x (ISBN 0-904406-09-1). Longman.

Hawkes, David, tr. see Cao, Xueqin.

Hawkes, Glenn R., jt. auth. see Frost, Joe L.

Hawkes, J. G., jt. ed. see Frankel, O. H.

Hawkes, J. G., et al, eds. Computer Mapped Flora: A Study of the County of Warwickshire. 1972. 60.00 (ISBN 0-12-333360-1). Acad Pr.

Hawkes, Jaquetta. A Land. LC 78-51961. 1978. 17.95 (ISBN 0-7153-7639-X). David & Charles.

Hawkes, John. Beetle Leg. LC 51-14554. 1967. pap. 4.95 (ISBN 0-8112-0062-0). New Directions.

--Blood Oranges. LC 74-152516. 1971 ed 6.95 (ISBN 0-8112-0285-2); pap. 4.95 1972 ed. (ISBN 0-8112-0061-2, NDP338). New Directions.

--The Passion Artist. LC 79-1707. 192p. 1981. pap. 3.95 (ISBN 0-06-090837-8, CN837, CN). Har-Row.

Hawkes, Ken. Sark. 1977. 7.50 (ISBN 0-7153-7335-8). David & Charles.

Hawkes, P. W. see Marton, L.

Hawkes, Terence. Structuralism & Semiotics. 1977. 14.00x (ISBN 0-520-03398-1); pap. 3.95x (ISBN 0-520-03422-8). U of Cal Pr.

Hawkesworth, Eric. The Art of Paper Tearing. 1970. 6.50 (ISBN 0-571-09189-X, Pub. by Faber & Faber). Merrimack Bk Serv.

--A Magic Variety Show: Novelty Acts for the Amateur Entertainer. 96p. 1973. 7.95 (ISBN 0-571-10186-0). Transatlantic.

--Making a Shadowgraph Show. 1969. 5.95 o.p. (ISBN 0-571-08900-3, Pub. by Faber & Faber). Merrimack Bk Serv.

--Paper Cutting. LC 76-30461. (Illus.). (gr. 6 up). 1977. 8.95 (ISBN 0-87599-224-2). S G Phillips.

--Puppet Shows to Make. 1972. 4.95 o.p. (ISBN 0-571-09836-3, Pub. by Faber & Faber). Merrimack Bk Serv.

Hawkesworth, John. Almoran & Hamnet: An Oriental Tale 1761, 2 vols. in 1. Shugrue, Michael F., ed. (The Flowering of the Novel, 1740-1775 Ser: Vol. 57). 1974. lib. bdg. 50.00 (ISBN 0-8240-1156-2). Garland Pub.

--In My Lady's Chamber. Bd. with Upstairs Downstairs Two; Tv-Tie-in. 1974. pap. 1.25 o.s.i. (ISBN 0-440-14166-4). Dell.

Hawkey, Christine M. Comparative Mammalian Haematology: Cellular Components & Blood Coagulation in Captive Wild Animals. 1975. 60.00x (ISBN 0-433-13390-2). Intl Ideas.

Hawkey, R. B. Improving Your Squash. 2nd ed. (Illus.). 1972. 7.95 (ISBN 0-571-04783-1, Pub. by Faber & Faber); pap. 3.95 (ISBN 0-571-09949-1). Merrimack Bk Serv.

--Squash Coaching & Refereeing. (Illus.). 1975. 10.95 (ISBN 0-571-10539-4, Pub. by Faber & Faber); pap. 9.95 (ISBN 0-571-10810-5). Merrimack Bk Serv.

--Your Book of Squash. (Your Book Ser.). (Illus.). 1966. 6.95 (ISBN 0-571-06577-5, Pub. by Faber & Faber). Merrimack Bk Serv.

Hawkey, Richard. Beginner's Guide to Squash. 141p. 1973. 14.50 (ISBN 0-7207-0682-3). Transatlantic.

Hawking, F., jt. ed. see Schnitzer, Robert J.

Hawking, S. W. & Israel, W., eds. General Relativity. LC 78-62112. (Illus.). 900p. 1980. pap. 28.95 (ISBN 0-521-29928-4). Cambridge U Pr.

--General Relativity: An Einstein Centenary Survey. LC 78-62712. (Illus.). 1979. 89.50 (ISBN 0-521-22285-0). Cambridge U Pr.

Hawkins, Arthur, jt. auth. see Paul, Aileen.

Hawkins, Brett. Politics & Urban Policies. LC 77-151612. (Policy Analysis Ser). 1971. 7.95 (ISBN 0-672-51474-5); pap. 4.95 (ISBN 0-672-61060-4). Bobbs.

Hawkins, C. S., jt. auth. see Taylor, Jack R.

Hawkins, Christopher. The Race of the Century: Grundy & Bustino at Ascot. 1976. 10.95 o.p. (ISBN 0-04-796046-9). Allen Unwin.

Hawkins, Clifford W. The Dhow. 144p. 1980. 57.00x (ISBN 0-245-52655-2, Pub. by Nautical England). State Mutual Bk.

Hawkins, D. F., jt. auth. see Elder, M. G.

Hawkins, David & Pauling, Linus, eds. Orthomolecular Psychiatry: Treatment of Schizophrenia. LC 73-190182. (Illus.). 1973. text ed. 36.95x (ISBN 0-7167-0898-1). W H Freeman.

Hawkins, David F. Corporate Financial Reporting: Text & Cases. rev ed. 1977. text ed. 19.95x (ISBN 0-256-01643-7). Irwin.

Hawkins, David F. & Campbell, Walter J. Equity Valuation: Models, Analysis & Implications. LC 78-67167. 1978. 3.50 (ISBN 0-910586-26-8). Finan Exec.

Hawkins, Delbert I., et al. Consumer Behavior: Implications for Marketing Strategy. 1980. 18.50 (ISBN 0-256-02290-9). Business Pubns.

Hawkins, Denis J. The Essentials of Theism. LC 72-9373. 151p. 1973. Repr. of 1949 ed. lib. bdg. 16.75x (ISBN 0-8371-6579-2, HAET). Greenwood.

Hawkins, Donald. Online Information Retrieval Bibliography 1964-1979. 175p. 1980. 25.00x (ISBN 0-938734-00-8). Learned Info.

Hawkins, G. A., jt. auth. see Jakob, Max.

Hawkins, George A., jt. auth. see Jones, James B.

Hawkins, Gerald S. Beyond Stonehenge. LC 72-79671. (Illus.). 336p. (YA) 1973. 15.95 o.p. (ISBN 0-06-011786-9, HarpT). Har-Row.

Hawkins, Gerald S. & White, John B. Stonehenge Decoded. LC 65-19933. 1965. 7.95 o.p. (ISBN 0-385-04127-6). Doubleday.

Hawkins, Gerald S., jt. auth. see Dobson, Julia M.

Hawkins, Gordon, jt. auth. see Morris, Norval.

Hawkins, Hale. Your Old Balls. (Illus.). 80p. (Orig.). 1980. pap. 4.95 (ISBN 0-938194-00-3). Lively Hills.

Hawkins, Hugh. Pioneer: A History of the Johns Hopkins University 1874-1889. 368p. 1960. 22.50x o.p. (ISBN 0-8014-0181-X). Cornell U Pr.

Hawkins, Jim, jt. auth. see LeFlore, Ron.

Hawkins, Jim W. Cheerleading Is for Me. (Sports for Me Bks.). (Illus.). (gr. 2-5). 1981. PLB 5.95 (ISBN 0-8225-1127-4). Lerner Pubns.

Hawkins, Joellen W. Clinical Experiences in Collegiate Nursing Education: Selection of Nursing Agencies. LC 80-23401. (Springer Series on the Teaching of Nursing: Vol. 7). 128p. 1980. text ed. cancelled (ISBN 0-8261-3390-8); pap. text ed. 11.50 (ISBN 0-8261-3391-6). Springer Pub.

Hawkins, Joellen W. & Higgins, Loretta P. Nursing & the American Health Care System. (Illus., Orig.). 1981. pap. text ed. price not set (ISBN 0-913292-33-8). Tiresias Pr.

Hawkins, John C. Horae Synopticae: Contributions to the Study of the Synoptic Problem. 2nd ed. 1909. 8.95x o.p. (ISBN 0-19-826621-9). Oxford U Pr.

--This Date in Detroit Tigers History. LC 80-5435. (This Date Ser.). 288p. 1981. pap. 9.95 (ISBN 0-8128-6067-5). Stein & Day.

Hawkins, Laurence F. Notescript. (Orig.). 1964. pap. 2.95 (ISBN 0-06-463232-6, EH 232, EH). Har-Row.

Hawkins, Leslie V. Art Metal & Enameling. 234p. (gr. 9-12). 1974. text ed. 11.60 (ISBN 0-87002-157-5). Bennett IL.

Hawkins, M. F., jt. auth. see Craft, Benjamin C.

Hawkins, Martin, jt. auth. see Escott, Colin.

Hawkins, Neil M. & Mitchell, Denis, eds. Reinforced Concrete Structures in Seismic Zones: SP-53. LC 77-74267. 1977. 25.00 (ISBN 0-685-87990-9) (ISBN 0-685-87991-7). ACI.

Hawkins, P. Social Class: The Nominal Group & Verbal Strategies. (Primary Socialization, Language & Education Ser.). 1977. 22.00x (ISBN 0-7100-8375-0). Routledge & Kegan.

Hawkins, Pearl see Glastonbury, Bryan, et al.

Hawkins, R. A., jt. ed. see Lyons, F. S.

Hawkins, R. E., ed. see Corbett, Jim.

Hawkins, Richard & Tiedman, Gary. The Creation of Deviance: Interpersonal & Organizational Determinants. new ed. (Sociology Ser). 320p. 1975. text ed. 17.95x (ISBN 0-675-08693-0). Merrill.

Hawkins, Richard, jt. auth. see Akers, Ronald L.

Hawkins, Richard A., jt. auth. see Passonneau, Janet V.

Hawkins, S. E., jt. auth. see Hall, David O.

Hawkins, Thomas. Lebesgue's Theory of Integration: Its Origins & Development. 3rd ed. LC 74-8402. xv, 227p. 1975. text ed. 11.95 (ISBN 0-8284-0282-5). Chelsea Pub.

Hawkins, Tomas. Homiletica Practica. 1978. Repr. of 1975 ed. 1.50 (ISBN 0-311-42041-9). Casa Bautista.

Hawkins, William. A Treatise on the Pleas of the Crown, 2 vols. Berkowitz, David S. & Thorne, Samuel E., eds. LC 77-86643. (Classics of English Legal History in the Modern Era Ser.: Vol. 30). 874p. 1979. lib. bdg. 80.00 (ISBN 0-8240-3079-6). Garland Pub.

Hawkins, William F. & Mackin, Ronald. Physics, Mathematics, Biology & Applied Science. 1966. pap. 6.00x o.p. (ISBN 0-19-437713-X). Oxford U Pr.

Hawkinson, John. A Ball of Clay. LC 72-13350. (Illus.). 48p. (gr. 3-7). 1974. 6.50g (ISBN 0-8075-0557-9). A Whitman.

--Collect, Print & Paint from Nature. LC 63-13330. (Illus.). (gr. 3 up). 1963. 6.50g (ISBN 0-8075-1272-9). A Whitman.

--Let Me Take You on a Trail. LC 71-188428. (Activity Bks.). (Illus.). 48p. (gr. 5 up). 1972. 6.50g (ISBN 0-8075-4452-3). A Whitman.

--Old Stump. LC 65-23883. (Self Starter Bks.). (Illus.). (ps-2). 1965. 6.50g (ISBN 0-8075-5969-5). A Whitman.

--Pastels Are Great. LC 68-22193. (Activity Bks.). (Illus.). (gr. 3 up). 1968. 6.50g (ISBN 0-8075-6362-5). A Whitman.

Hawkinson, John & Faulhaber, Martha. Rhythms, Music & Instruments to Make. LC 70-91737. (Activity Bks. - Music Involvement Ser.: No. 2). (Illus.). (gr. 3 up). 1970. 6.50g (ISBN 0-8075-6958-5). A Whitman.

Hawkinson, John & Hawkinson, Lucy. Little Boy Who Lives Up High. LC 67-26515. (Self Starter Bks.). (Illus.). (ps-2). 1967. 6.50g (ISBN 0-8075-4580-5). A Whitman.

Hawkinson, Lucy, jt. auth. see Hawkinson, John.

Hawkland, William, jt. auth. see Loiseaux, Pierre R.

Hawkweed Group. The Hawkweed Passive Solar House Book. (Illus.). 192p. 1980. 14.95 (ISBN 0-528-81107-X); pap. 7.95 (ISBN 0-528-88034-9). Rand.

Hawley, Amos H. Societal Growth: Processes & Implications. LC 79-7339. (Illus.). 1979. 19.95 (ISBN 0-02-914200-8). Free Pr.

--Urban Society: An Ecological Approach. 2nd ed. LC 80-17925. 350p. 1981. 14.95 (ISBN 0-471-05753-3). Wiley.

Hawley, Amos H. & Zimmer, Basil G. The Metropolitan Community: Its People & Government. LC 77-92358. 1970. 12.50x (ISBN 0-8039-0066-X); pap. 3.50x (ISBN 0-8039-0067-8). Sage.

Hawley, Amos H. & Rock, V. P., eds. Metropolitan America in Contemporary Perspective. LC 75-8613. 450p. 1975. 25.00 o.p. (ISBN 0-470-36305-3). Halsted Pr.

Hawley, Beatrice. Making the House Fall Down. LC 77-82222. 64p. 1977. pap. 4.95 (ISBN 0-914086-19-7). Alicejamesbooks.

Hawley, Cameron. Executive Suite. 1977. pap. 1.95 o.p. (ISBN 0-445-08578-9). Popular Lib.

Hawley, Don. Come Alive! LC 75-21190. (Orig.). 1975. pap. 0.85 (ISBN 0-8280-0045-X). Review & Herald.

Hawley, Donald. The Trucial States. (Illus.). 379p. 1970. text ed. 24.50x (ISBN 0-686-66022-6); pap. text ed. 12.95x (ISBN 0-8290-0454-8). Irvington.

Hawley, Ellis W. New Deal & the Problem of Monopoly. LC 65-24273. (Orig.). 1966. 18.00 o.p. (ISBN 0-691-04528-3); pap. 6.95 (ISBN 0-691-00564-8). Princeton U Pr.

Hawley, Gloria H. Frankly Feminine: God's Idea of Womanhood. 160p. (Orig.). 1981. pap. 3.50 (ISBN 0-87239-455-7, 2969). Standard Pub.

--Laura's Psalm. 1981. pap. 4.95 (ISBN 0-86608-000-7, 14014P). Impact Tenn.

Hawley, Henry. Faberge & His Contemporaries: The India Early Minshall Collection of the Cleveland Museum of Art. LC 67-28951. (Illus.). 148p. 1967. 10.00x (ISBN 0-910386-10-2, Pub. by Cleveland Mus Art). Ind U Pr.

Hawley, Isabel I., jt. auth. see Hawley, Robert C.

Hawley, Isabel L. Common Sense Composition: A Modern Approach to Improving Written Communication. LC 73-83546. 140p. (Orig.). 1977. pap. 8.95x (ISBN 0-913636-04-5). Educ Res MA.

Hawley, Isabel L. see Graham, Sandra.

Hawley, Isabel L., jt. auth. see Hawley, Robert C.

Hawley, Mones E., ed. Coal: Social, Economics, & Environmental Aspects. (Benchmark Papers on Energy: Pt. 1). 1976. 47.00 (ISBN 0-12-786641-8); Set. 41.00. Acad Pr.

Hawley, Monroe E. Redigging the Wells. 1976. 6.95 (ISBN 0-89137-513-9); pap. 4.95 (ISBN 0-89137-512-0). Quality Pubns.

--Searching for a Better Way. 1980. pap. write for info. (ISBN 0-89137-525-2). Quality Pubns.

Hawley, Newton & Suppes, Patrick. Key to Geometry Series, 8 bks. Gearheart, George & Rasmussen, Peter, eds. Incl. Bk. 1. Lines & Segments. 56p. pap. 0.95 (ISBN 0-913684-71-6); Bk. 2. Circles. 56p. pap. 0.95 (ISBN 0-913684-72-4); Bk. 3. Constructions. 56p. pap. 0.95 (ISBN 0-913684-73-2); Bk. 4. Perpendiculars. 56p. pap. 0.95 (ISBN 0-913684-74-0); Bk. 5. Squares & Rectangles. 56p. pap. 0.95 (ISBN 0-913684-75-9); Bk. 6. Angles. 56p. pap. 0.95 (ISBN 0-913684-76-7); Bk. 7. Perpendiculars & Parallels, Chords & Tangents, Circles. 154p. pap. 2.85 (ISBN 0-913684-77-5); Bk. 8. Triangles, Parallel Lines, Similar Polygons. 139p. pap. 2.85 (ISBN 0-913684-78-3). (gr. 4 up). 1980. pap. Key Curr Project.

Hawley, R., jt. auth. see Zaky, A. A.

Hawley, Robert C. Assessing Teacher Performance: Task Analysis & Clinical Evaluation. LC 80-67945. 112p. (Orig.). 1981. pap. 9.95 (ISBN 0-913636-12-6). Educ Res MA.

--Evaluating Teaching: A Handbook of Positive Approaches. LC 75-35053. (Orig.). 1976. pap. 9.50 (ISBN 0-913636-07-X). Educ Res MA.

Hawley, Robert C. & Hawley, Isabel I. Building Motivation in the Classroom: A Structured Approach to Improving Student Achievement. LC 78-69902. 1979. pap. 8.95 (ISBN 0-913636-10-X). Educ Res MA.

Hawley, Robert C. & Hawley, Isabel L. Achieving Better Classroom Discipline. LC 80-67946. 128p. (Orig.). 1981. pap. 9.95 (ISBN 0-913636-11-8). Educ Res MA.

--Developing Human Potential: A Handbook of Activities for Personal & Social Growth. LC 75-2963. 128p. (Orig.). 1975. pap. 6.95 (ISBN 0-913636-06-1). Educ Res MA.

--Developing Human Potential: More Activities for Person & Social Growth, Vol. 2. LC 76-51467. 1977. pap. 6.95 (ISBN 0-913636-09-6). Educ Res MA.

--Writing for the Fun of It: An Experience-Based Approach to Composition. LC 73-83548. 110p. (Orig.). 1974. pap. 4.95 (ISBN 0-913636-02-9). Educ Res MA.

Hawley, Ruth. Omani Silver. LC 77-20799. (Illus.). 1977. pap. text ed. 7.50x (ISBN 0-582-78070-5). Longman.

Hawley, W. D. & Lipsky, M. Theoretical Perspectives on Urban Politics. 1976. 18.95 (ISBN 0-13-913202-3). P-H.

Hawley, Walter A. Oriental Rugs Antique & Modern. (Illus.). 1970. pap. 6.95 (ISBN 0-486-22366-3). Dover.

--Oriental Rugs, Antique & Modern. (Illus.). 12.50 (ISBN 0-8446-4551-6). Peter Smith.

Hawley, Willis. Improving Urban Management. abridged ed. Rogers, David, ed. LC 76-4682. (Urban Affairs Annual Reviews: Vol. 8). 1976. pap. 8.95x (ISBN 0-8039-0693-5). Sage.

Hawley, Willis & Rogers, David, eds. Improving the Quality of Urban Management. LC 72-98108. (Urban Affairs Annual Reviews: Vol. 8). 1974. 25.00x (ISBN 0-8039-0292-1). Sage.

Hawley, Willis D. & Svara, James H., eds. The Study of Community Power: A Bibliographic Review. LC 72-83287. 123p. 1972. text ed. 3.50 (ISBN 0-87436-088-9); pap. text ed. 2.50 (ISBN 0-87436-089-7). ABC-Clio.

Haworth, Charles, jt. auth. see Rassmussen, David.

Haworth, F., jt. auth. see Kersley, J. A.

Haworth, J. T. & Smith, M. A., eds. Work and Leisure: An Inter-Disciplinary Study in Theory, Education, and Planning. 216p. 1976. pap. text ed. 4.95x o.p. (ISBN 0-86019-009-9). Princeton Bk Co.

Hawrylyshyn, Bohdan. Condemned to Co-Exist: Road Maps to the Future. (Illus.). 200p. 1980. 31.00 (ISBN 0-08-026115-9); pap. 11.00 (ISBN 0-08-026114-0). Pergamon.

Hawrylyshyn, Oli, et al. Planning for Economic Development: The Construction & Use of a Multisectoral Model for Tunisia. LC 76-12857. 1976. text ed. 24.95 (ISBN 0-275-02300-1). Praeger.

Haws, Duncan. Merchant Fleets in Profile 4: The Ships of the Hamburg-American, Adler & Carr Lines. 248p. 1980. 37.95 (ISBN 0-85059-397-2). Aztex.

Hawthorn, G. Enlightenment & Despair. LC 76-7803. 1976. 32.95 (ISBN 0-521-21308-8); pap. 9.95x (ISBN 0-521-29093-7). Cambridge U Pr.

Hawthorn, Harry B., ed. see Doukhobor Research Committee.

Hawthorn, Jeremy. Virginia Woolf's Mrs. Dalloway: A Study in Alienation. (Text & Context Ser.). 1975. text ed. 6.50x (ISBN 0-85621-046-3); pap. text ed. 2.75x (ISBN 0-85621-047-1). Humanities.

Hawthorn, John. Foundations of Food Science. (Illus.). 1981. text ed. price not set (ISBN 0-7167-1295-4); pap. text ed. price not set (ISBN 0-7167-1296-2). W H Freeman.

Hawthorn, Ruth, jt. auth. see Davidoff, Leonore.

Hawthorne, Clive. Poems & Translations. LC 79-51457. (Illus.). 1981. pap. 8.00 (ISBN 0-912908-07-6). Tamal Land.

Hawthorne, J. & Rolfe, E. J., eds. Low Temperature Biology of Foodstuffs. 1969. 55.00 (ISBN 0-08-013294-4). Pergamon.

Hawthorne, John G., tr. see Theophilus.

Hawthorne, Mark D. John & Michael (the O'hara Brothers) A Study of the Early Development of the Anglo-Irish Novel. (Salzburg Studies in English Literature: Romantic Reassessment Ser.: No. 50). 1976. pap. text ed. 25.00x (ISBN 0-391-01401-3). Humanities.

Hawthorne, Minnie. Here We Go Again Lord. 1981. 4.50 (ISBN 0-8062-1659-X). Carlton.

Hawthorne, Nathaniel. House of the Seven Gables. Gross, Seymour L., ed. (Critical Editions). (Annotated). (gr. 9-12). 1967. pap. text ed. 4.95x (ISBN 0-393-09705-6, 9705, NortonC). Norton.

--House of the Seven Gables. (Literature Ser). (gr. 10-12). 1970. pap. text ed. 3.50 (ISBN 0-87720-728-3). AMSCO Sch.

--House of the Seven Gables. (Riverside Bookshelf Ser). (Illus.). (gr. 9 up). 1952. 7.95 (ISBN 0-395-07072-4). HM.

--House of the Seven Gabls. pap. 1.50. Bantam.

--House of the Seven Gabls. pap. 2.25 (ISBN 0-671-41373-2). WSP.

--House of the Seven Gabls. 1972. pap. 4.95 (ISBN 0-460-01176-6, Evman). Dutton.

--House of the Seven Gabls. rev. ed. Dixson, Robert J., ed. (American Classics Ser.: Bk. 1). 113p. (gr. 9 up). 1973. pap. 2.75 (ISBN 0-88345-197-2, 18120); cassettes 40.00 (ISBN 0-685-38988-X); tapes 40.00 (ISBN 0-685-38989-8). Regents Pub.
--The Scarlet Letter. Rajan, B. & George, A. G., eds. Bd. with The Life of Hawthorne. James, Henry. 7.95x (ISBN 0-210-26920-0). Asia.
--The Scarlet Letter. (Enriched Classics Ser.). (gr. 9 up). 1972. pap. 2.25 (ISBN 0-671-42142-5, RE). WSP.
--The Scarlet Letter. (gr. 7 up). 1972. pap. 1.50 (ISBN 0-590-09075-5, Schol Pap). Schol Bk Serv.
--Scarlet Letter. (Literature Ser). (gr. 9-12). 1969. pap. text ed. 3.67 (ISBN 0-87720-714-3). AMSCO Sch.
--The Scarlet Letter. LC 69-13317. (Merrill Standard Ser). 1975. 6.00 (ISBN 0-910294-31-3); pap. 4.00 (ISBN 0-910294-32-1). Brown Bk.
--The Scarlet Letter. 2nd ed. Bradley, Sculley, et al, eds. (Norton Critical Edition Ser.). 1978. 12.95 (ISBN 0-393-04495-5); pap. 3.95x (ISBN 0-393-09073-6). Norton.
--The Scarlet Letter. LC 79-52171. (Illus.). 1979. 15.00x (ISBN 0-913870-93-5). Abaris Bks.
--Scarlet Letter: A Romance. Ziff, Larzer, ed. LC 62-21260. 1963. pap. 4.50 (ISBN 0-672-60966-5, LL1). Bobbs.
--Scarlet Letter with Reader's Guide. (AMSCO Literature Program). (gr. 10-12). 1970. pap. text ed. 4.42 (ISBN 0-87720-808-5); tchr's ed. s.p. 2.85 (ISBN 0-87720-908-1). AMSCO Sch.
--Wonder Book. (Classics Ser). (gr. 5 up). pap. 1.25 (ISBN 0-8049-0118-X, CL-118). Airmont.
Hawthorne, Violet. Diary of Evil. 1976. pap. 1.25 o.p. (ISBN 0-685-69153-5, LB352ZK, Leisure Bks). Nordon Pubns.
Hawtrey, Ralph G. Art of Central Banking. 2nd ed. Repr. of 1932 ed. 25.00x (ISBN 0-678-05174-7). Kelley.
--Century of Bank Rate. Repr. of 1939 ed. 22.50x (ISBN 0-678-05175-5). Kelley.
--The Economic Problem. LC 79-1581. 1981. Repr. of 1926 ed. 27.50 (ISBN 0-88355-886-6). Hyperion Conn.
Haxby, D., jt. ed. see Klare, H. J.
Haxby, J. A. & Willey, R. C. Coins of Canada. (Whitman Coin Hobby Books). (Illus.). 1977. pap. 2.75 o.p. (ISBN 0-307-09058-2). Western Pub.
Haxthausen, Baron Von see Von Haxthausen, Baron.
Haxthausen, Charles. The Busch-Reisinger Museum: Harvard University. LC 80-65261. (Illus.). 152p. (Orig.). 1980. pap. 22.50 (ISBN 0-89659-138-7). Abbeville Pr.
Hay & Engstrom. Plaid for Accounting for Governmental & Nonprofit Entities. 1981. price not set (ISBN 0-256-02567-3, 01-1454-01). Learning Syst. Postponed.
Hay, Alan M. & Smith, Robert H. Interregional Trade & Money Flows in Nigeria, 1964. (Nigerian Institute of Social & Economic Research Ser). 1970. 12.00x o.p. (ISBN 0-19-646029-8). Oxford U Pr.
Hay, Carla H. James Burgh, Spokesman for Reform in Hanoverian England. LC 79-89204. 1979. pap. text ed. 9.00 (ISBN 0-8191-0800-6). U Pr of Amer.
Hay, David, jt. auth. see Doulton, Joan.
Hay, Dennis, jt. auth. see Hall, Peter.
Hay, Denys. The Church in Italy in the Fifteenth Century. LC 76-47409. (Birkbeck Lectures: 1971). 1977. 27.50 (ISBN 0-521-21532-3). Cambridge U Pr.
--Europe in the Fourteenth & Fifteenth Centuries. (General History of Europe Ser.). 1970. pap. text ed. 9.95x (ISBN 0-582-48343-3). Longman.
--Italian Renaissance in Its Historical Background. 2nd ed. (Illus.). 1977. 33.50 (ISBN 0-521-21321-5); pap. 7.95 (ISBN 0-521-29104-6). Cambridge U Pr.
Hay, Doddy. Hit the Silk. LC 72-85004. (gr. 5-8). 1969. 8.95 (ISBN 0-87599-163-7). S G Phillips.
Hay, Edward A., jt. auth. see McAlester, A. Lee.
Hay, Elizabeth & Bannerman, Helen. Sambo Sahib: The Story of Little Black Sambo. (Illus.). 196p. 1981. 16.50x (ISBN 0-389-20151-0). B&N.
Hay, Frank C., jt. auth. see Hudson, Leslie.
Hay, George. Architecture of Scotland. (Oriel Guides). (Illus.). 11.50 (ISBN 0-85362-038-5, Oriel). Routledge & Kegan.
Hay, George E. Vector & Tensor Analysis. 1953. pap. text ed. 3.00 (ISBN 0-486-60109-9). Dover.
Hay, George M. Samuel George Washington Jones Snake. (Illus.). 32p. (gr. 1-4). 1980. 8.95 (ISBN 0-938490-00-1). Abbincott.
Hay, Henry. The Amateur Magician's Handbook. 3rd, rev. ed. LC 72-78265. (Illus.). 400p. 1972. 12.95 (ISBN 0-690-05711-3, TYC-T). T Y Crowell.
Hay, Ian. A Safety Match. (Barbara Cartland's Library of Love: Vol. 4). 181p. 1979. 12.95x (ISBN 0-7156-1380-4, Pub. by Duckworth England). Biblio Dist.
Hay, J. Biomechanics of Sports Techniques. 2nd ed. 1978. 18.95 (ISBN 0-13-077164-3). P-H.
Hay, John. Letters of John Hay & Extracts from His Diary, 3 Vols. LC 71-93245. 1969. Repr. of 1908 ed. Set. text ed. 50.00 (ISBN 0-87752-051-8). Gordian.
--Oedipus Tyrannus: Lame Knowledge & the Homosporic Womb. LC 78-57075. 1978. pap. text ed. 8.00 (ISBN 0-8191-0518-X). U Pr of Amer.
Hay, John & Farb, P. The Atlantic Shore. (Illus.). 1966. 10.00 o.s.i. (ISBN 0-06-070743-7, HarpT). Har-Row.
Hay, K. A. Friends or Acquaintances? Canada & Japan's Other Trading Partners in the Early 1980's. 52p. 1978. pap. text ed. 3.00x (ISBN 0-920380-15-8, Pub. by Inst Res Pub Canada). Renouf.
Hay, Keith, et al. Beaver's Way. Bourne, Russell & Lawrence, Bonnie S., eds. (Ranger Rick's Best Friends Ser.: No. 1). (gr. 1-6). 1973. 2.50 o.p. (ISBN 0-912186-06-2). Natl Wildlife.
Hay, Leon E. Accounting for Government & Nonprofit Entities. 6th ed. 1980. 22.95x (ISBN 0-256-02329-8). Irwin.
Hay, Leon E. & Mikesell, R. M. Governmental Accounting. 5th ed. 1974. text ed. 17.95x o.p. (ISBN 0-256-01543-0). Irwin.
Hay, Richard L. Geology of the Olduval Gorge: A Study of Sedimentation in a Semiarid Basin. 1976. 34.50x (ISBN 0-520-02963-1). U of Cal Pr.
Hay, Robert D., jt. auth. see Broyles, J. Frank.
Hay, Rupert. The Persian Gulf States. LC 80-1926. 1981. Repr. of 1959 ed. 23.50 (ISBN 0-404-18966-0). AMS Pr.
Hay, Stephen N. Asian Ideas of East & West: Tagore & His Critics in Japan, China, & India. LC 73-89972. (East Asian Ser: No. 40). 1970. text ed. 20.00x (ISBN 0-674-04975-6). Harvard U Pr.
Hay, Suzanne. Savage Destiny. 1979. pap. 2.25 (ISBN 0-515-04891-7). Jove Pubns.
Hay, Thomas, jt. auth. see Racowsky, Dave.
Hay, Thomas R., jt. auth. see Sanger, Donald B.
Hay, W., ed. Adult Literacy in Britain: An Annotated Bibliography. 1978. 9.75x (ISBN 0-85365-811-0, Pub. by Lib Assn England). Oryx Pr.
Hay, William W. An Introduction to Transportation Engineering. 2nd ed. LC 77-9293. 1977. text ed. 29.95 (ISBN 0-471-36433-9); tchr's manual avail. (ISBN 0-471-04712-0). Wiley.
--Railroad Engineering, Vol. 1. 1953. 28.50 (ISBN 0-471-36399-5). Wiley.
Hayakawa, S. I., ed. The Use & Misuse of Language. Orig. Title: Our Language & Our World; Language, Meaning & Maturity. 1977. pap. 1.75 o.p. (ISBN 0-449-30787-5, Prem). Fawcett.
Hayakawa, S. I. & Dresser, William, eds. Dimensions of Meaning. LC 68-24164. (Composition & Rhetoric Ser). (Orig.). 1970. pap. 2.95 (ISBN 0-672-60902-9, CR16). Bobbs.
Hayakawa, S. I. & Jones, Howard M., eds. Oliver Wendell Holmes. 472p. 1980. Repr. of 1939 ed. lib. bdg. 40.00 (ISBN 0-8495-2351-6). Arden Lib.
Hayakawa, Samuel I. Language in Thought & Action. LC 78-53859. 10.95 (ISBN 0-15-148112-1). HarBraceJ.
Hayashi, Tetsumaro. An Index to Arthur Miller Criticism. 2nd ed. LC 76-10893. (Author Bibliographies Ser.: No. 3). 165p. 1976. 10.00 (ISBN 0-8108-0947-8). Scarecrow.
--A New Steinbeck Bibliography (1929-1971) LC 73-9982. (Author Bibliographies Ser.: No. 1). 1973. 10.00 (ISBN 0-8108-0647-9). Scarecrow.
--Robert Greene Criticism: A Comprehensive Bibliography. LC 79-142235. (Author Bibliographies Ser.: No. 6). 1971. 10.00 (ISBN 0-8108-0340-2). Scarecrow.
--Shakespeare's Sonnets: A Record of Twentieth Century Criticism. LC 77-184764. 1972. 10.00 (ISBN 0-8108-0462-X). Scarecrow.
--Steinbeck's Literary Dimension: A Guide to Comparative Studies. LC 72-7457. 1973. 10.00 (ISBN 0-8108-0550-2). Scarecrow.
--A Study Guide to Steinbeck, Pt. II. LC 74-735. 252p. 1979. 12.00 (ISBN 0-8108-1220-7). Scarecrow.
--Study Guide to Steinbeck: A Handbook to His Major Works. LC 74-735. 1974. 12.00 (ISBN 0-8108-0706-8). Scarecrow.
Hayashi, Tetsumaro, ed. Looking Glasse for London & England by Thomas Lodge & Robert Greene: An Elizabethan Text. LC 76-15212. 1970. 10.00 (ISBN 0-8108-0348-8). Scarecrow.
Hayashi, Tetsuro. The Theory of English Lexicography, Fifteen Thirty-Seventeen Ninety-One. (Studies in the History of Linguistics: No. 18). 1978. text ed. 25.75x (ISBN 0-391-01669-5). Humanities.
Hayashiya, Seizo & Trubner, Henry. Chinese Ceramics from Japanese Collections. LC 77-1654. (Illus.). 136p. 1977. 19.95 (ISBN 0-87848-049-8). Asia Soc.
Haycox, Ernest. Adventurers. 286p. 1975. Repr. of 1954 ed. lib. bdg. 6.95 o.p. (ISBN 0-89190-971-0). Am Repr-Rivercity Pr.
--Bugles in the Afternoon. 1981. lib. bdg. 15.95 (ISBN 0-8161-3152-X, Large Print Bks). G K Hall.
--By Rope & Lead. 174p. 1975. Repr. of 1951 ed. lib. bdg. 9.95 o.p. (ISBN 0-89190-972-9). Am Repr-Rivercity Pr.
--The Earthbreakers. 1976. Repr. of 1952 ed. lib. bdg. 9.95 o.p. (ISBN 0-89190-977-X). Am Repr-Rivercity Pr.
--Guns up. 1977. pap. 1.25 (ISBN 0-505-51125-8, BT51125). Tower Bks.
--The Last Rodeo. 165p. 1975. Repr. of 1956 ed. lib. bdg. 9.95 o.p. (ISBN 0-89190-976-1). Am Repr-Rivercity Pr.
--Rawhide Range. 192p. 1975. Repr. of 1952 ed. lib. bdg. 9.95 o.p. (ISBN 0-89190-975-3). Am Repr-Rivercity Pr.
--A Rider of High Mesa. 128p. 1975. Repr. of 1956 ed. lib. bdg. 9.95 o.p. (ISBN 0-89190-980-X). Am Repr-Rivercity Pr.
--Rough Justice. 177p. 1975. Repr. of 1950 ed. lib. bdg. 9.95 o.p. (ISBN 0-89190-978-8). Am Repr-Rivercity Pr.
--Sundown Jim. 1981. pap. 1.75 (ISBN 0-451-09676-2, E9676, Sig). NAL.
--Whispering Range. 231p. 1975. Repr. of 1931 ed. lib. bdg. 9.95 o.p. (ISBN 0-89190-979-6). Am Repr-Rivercity Pr.
--Wild Bunch. 245p. 1975. Repr. of 1943 ed. lib. bdg. 9.95 o.p. (ISBN 0-89190-973-7). Am Repr-Rivercity Pr.
Haycraft, B. The Teaching of Pronunciation. 1975. pap. text ed. 7.25x (ISBN 0-582-52434-2). Longman.
Haycraft, Brita & Lee, W. R. It Depends on How You Say It: Dialogues in Everyday Social English. LC 80-41174. (Illus.). 128p. 1981. 12.00 (ISBN 0-08-025315-6); pap. 4.95 (ISBN 0-08-025314-8). Pergamon.
Haycraft, Howard. The Art of the Mystery Story. LC 75-28263. 1975. Repr. of 1946 ed. 16.00x (ISBN 0-8196-0289-2). Biblo.
--Murder for Pleasure. LC 68-25809. 1941. 15.00x (ISBN 0-8196-0216-7). Biblo.
Haycraft, Howard, jt. ed. see Kunitz, Stanley J.
Haycraft, John. Introduction to English Language Teaching. (Longman Handbooks for Language Teachers). (Illus.). 1979. pap. text ed. 7.25x (ISBN 0-582-55604-X). Longman.
Haycroft, W. C. Book of the Royal Enfield. pap. 4.50x (ISBN 0-392-02349-0, SpS). Soccer.
Hayde, C. C., jt. auth. see Hall, P. G.
Hayden, Bob, ed. Model Railroader Cyclopedia: Diesel Locomotives. LC 61-21207. (Illus.). 160p. (Orig.). 1980. pap. 22.00 (ISBN 0-89024-547-9). Kalmbach.
--Track Planning Ideas from Model Railroader. LC 80-84022. (Illus.). 96p. (Orig.). 1981. pap. 5.95 (ISBN 0-89024-555-X). Kalmbach.
Hayden, Bob, ed. see Paine, Sheperd.
Hayden, Dolores. A Grand Domestic Revolution: Feminism, Socialism & the American Home, 1870-1930. (Illus.). 425p. 1981. text ed. 19.95x (ISBN 0-262-08108-3). MIT Pr.
Hayden, Eric W. Sermon Outlines on Christian Service. (Sermon Outline Ser.). 64p. (Orig.). 1980. pap. 1.95 (ISBN 0-8010-4239-9). Baker Bk.
--Technology Transfer to East Europe: U.S. Corporate Experience. LC 76-12855. (Illus.). 1976. text ed. 23.95 (ISBN 0-275-23240-9). Praeger.
--Traveller's Guide to Spurgeon Country. 1975. pap. 1.95 (ISBN 0-686-10527-3). Pilgrim Pubns.
Hayden, H. W., et al see Wulff, J.
Hayden, J. M. France & the Estates General of 1614. LC 73-82456. (Studies in Early Modern History). (Illus.). 320p. 1974. 42.95 (ISBN 0-521-20325-2). Cambridge U Pr.
Hayden, Jerome D. & Davis, Howard T. Mathematics for Health Careers. LC 78-59567. (Health Occupations Ser.). (gr. 10). 1980. pap. text ed. 14.40 (ISBN 0-686-59748-6); instructor's guide 1.75 (ISBN 0-8273-1717-4). Delmar.
Hayden, Jess, jt. auth. see Jorgensen, Niels B.
Hayden, John L. How to Incorporate in Tax Free Nevada for Only Fifty Dollars. LC 80-85433. 50p. 1981. text ed. 14.95. Newport Beach.
Hayden, John O., ed. Scott: The Critical Heritage. 1970. 38.50x (ISBN 0-7100-6724-0). Routledge & Kegan.
Hayden, Melissa. Dancer to Dancer: Advice for Today's Dancer. LC 80-940. (Illus.). 192p. 1981. 19.95 (ISBN 0-385-15582-4, Anchor Pr). Doubleday.
--Dancer to Dancer: Advice for Today's Dancer. LC 80-940. (Illus.). 192p. 1981. 19.95 (ISBN 0-385-15550-6, Anch). Doubleday.
Hayden, Mike. Pier Fishing on San Francisco Bay. (Illus.). 116p. (Orig.). 1981. pap. 5.95 (ISBN 0-87701-138-9). Chronicle Bks.
Hayden, Naura. Hip, High Protein, Low-Cal Easy Does It Cookbook. 1981. pap. price not set (ISBN 0-671-42390-8). PB.
Hayden, Ralston. Senate & Treaties, 1789-1817. LC 73-127295. (Law, Politics, & History Ser). 1970. Repr. of 1920 ed. lib. bdg. 27.50 (ISBN 0-306-71164-8). Da Capo.
Hayden, Shelby, jt. auth. see Zitner, Rosalind.
Hayden, Sterling. Voyage: A Novel of 1896. 1977. pap. 2.50 (ISBN 0-380-01780-6, 37200). Avon.
--Wanderer: A Reissue with a New Introduction & Illustrations. (Illus.). 1977. 10.95 (ISBN 0-393-07521-4). Norton.
Hayden, Thomas C. Handbook for College Admissions. LC 80-66009. 1981. 12.95 (ISBN 0-689-11095-2); pap. 6.95 (ISBN 0-686-69529-1). Atheneum.
Hayden, Torey L. Somebody Else's Kids. 384p. 1981. 11.95 (ISBN 0-399-12602-3). Putnam.
Hayden, Trudy & Novik, Jack. Your Rights to Privacy. (ACLU Handbook Ser.). 1980. pap. 2.50 (ISBN 0-686-69238-1, 75895). Avon.
Haydn, Joseph. Symphonies. Nos. 66, 69, 70, 71 & 75. 2nd ed. LC 65-24150. (Music Ser). 1967. text ed. 8.00 ea. (ISBN 0-306-77004-0). No. 66 (ISBN 0-306-77005-9). No. 69 (ISBN 0-306-77006-7). No. 70 (ISBN 0-306-77007-5). No. 71 (ISBN 0-306-77008-3). No. 75 (ISBN 0-306-77009-1). Da Capo.
--Twelve String Quartets: Opus 55, 64 & 71 Complete. 288p. 1980. pap. 6.95 (ISBN 0-486-23933-0). Dover.
Haydock, Ron. Deerstalker! Holmes & Watson on the Screen. LC 77-24465. 1978. 15.00 (ISBN 0-8108-1061-1). Scarecrow.
Haydocke, R., tr. see Lomazzo, Giovanni P.
Haydon, A. Eustace. Biography of the Gods. LC 67-13617. 1967. pap. 4.25 (ISBN 0-8044-6257-7). Ungar.
Haydon, D. A., jt. auth. see Aveyard, R.
Haydon, Dorothy & Gordon, Elayne. Practical Dictation & Transcription: Shorterhand Edition. Angus, M., ed. LC 75-14357. 1975. text ed. 11.20 (ISBN 0-8224-1021-4); transcript 8.60 (ISBN 0-8224-1702-2). Pitman Learning.
Haydon, Frederick S. Aeronautics in the Union & Confederate Armies: With a Survey of Military Aeronautics Prior to 1861, Vol. I. Gilbert, James, ed. LC 79-7271. (Flight: Its First Seventy-Five Years Ser.). (Illus.). 1979. Repr. of 1941 ed. lib. bdg. 38.00x (ISBN 0-405-12181-4). Arno.
Haydon, G., tr. see Jeppesen, Knud.
Haydon, Glen. Evolution of the Six-Four Chord: A Chapter in the History of Dissonant Treatment. LC 75-125052. (Music Ser). 1971. Repr. of 1933 ed. lib. bdg. 19.50 (ISBN 0-306-70017-4). Da Capo.
Hayduke, George. Get Even Two. (Get Even Ser.: Vol. 2). (Illus.). 170p. 1981. 9.95 (ISBN 0-87364-213-9). Paladin Ent.
Haye, Yves De La see Marx, Karl & Frederick, Engels.
Hayek, F. A. Law, Legislation, & Liberty: Rules & Order. 15.00 (ISBN 0-226-32080-4). U of Chicago Pr.
--Law, Legislation, & Liberty: The Mirage of Social Justice, Vol. 2. LC 73-82488. (Multi-Volumed Set Ser.). 1977. lib. bdg. 15.00x (ISBN 0-226-32082-0); pap. 5.95 (ISBN 0-226-32083-9, P799). U of Chicago Pr.
--Law, Legislation, & Liberty: The Political Order of a Free People. pap. write for info. (ISBN 0-226-32090-1). U of Chicago Pr.
--Law, Legislation, & Liberty: The Political Order of a Free People, Vol. 3. LC 78-25905. 1979. 15.00x (ISBN 0-226-32087-1). U of Chicago Pr.
Hayek, Friedrich A. A Tiger by the Tail: The Keynesian Legacy of Inflation. (The Cato Papers Ser.: No. 6). 178p. 1979. pap. 4.00 (ISBN 0-932790-06-2). Cato Inst.
Hayek, H. von. The Human Lung. rev. enl. ed. 1960. 20.75 o.s.i. (ISBN 0-02-845850-8). Hafner.
Hayes. The Gift Horse. Orig. Title: The Carousel Horse. (gr. 4-5). 1980. pap. 1.25 (ISBN 0-590-30905-6, Schol Pap). Schol Bk Serv.
Hayes, A. Wallace. Mycotoxin Teratogenicity & Mutagenicity. 160p. 1981. 59.95 (ISBN 0-8493-5651-2). CRC Pr.
Hayes, Alfred S; see Bottiglia, William F.
Hayes, Carlton. Wartime Mission in Spain. LC 76-18191. (Politics & Strategy of World War II Ser.). 1976. Repr. of 1945 ed. lib. bdg. 27.50 (ISBN 0-306-70771-3). Da Capo.
Hayes, Colin. A Practical Guide to Landscape Painting. 120p. 1981. 15.95 (ISBN 0-8230-0322-1). Watson-Guptill.

Hayes, Douglas A. & Bauman, W. Scott. Investments: Analysis & Management. 3rd ed. (Illus.). 1976. text ed. 19.95 (ISBN 0-02-352710-2). Macmillan.

Hayes, Edmund, Sr., intro. by see Boit, John.

Hayes, Elizabeth R. Dance Composition & Production. LC 80-69958. (Illus.). 210p. 1981. pap. 8.95 (ISBN 0-87127-121-4). Dance Horiz.

--An Introduction to the Teaching of Dance. LC 80-15371. 350p. 1980. Repr. of 1964 ed. lib. bdg. 14.50 (ISBN 0-89874-227-7). Krieger.

Hayes, Elizabeth S. Spices & Herbs: Their Lore & Use. (Illus.). 256p. 1980. pap. 3.50 (ISBN 0-486-24026-6). Dover.

Hayes, Ernest H., ed. Fifty Favourite Bible Stories. 1947. pap. 4.55 (ISBN 0-08-006196-6, Religious Educ Pr). Pergamon.

Hayes, Frank A., tr. see Spinoza, Baruch.

Hayes, Frederick O. Productivity in Local Government. LC 76-20400. 1977. 24.95 (ISBN 0-669-00883-4). Lexington Bks.

Hayes, Gail B. Solar Access Law: Protecting Access to Sunlight for Solar Energy Systems. LC 79-9392. (An Environmental Law Institute Bk.). (4#320). 1979. reference 18.50 (ISBN 0-88410-091-X). Ballinger Pub.

Hayes, Gerald R. King's Music: An Anthology. LC 78-66906. (Encore Music Editions Ser.). (Illus.). 1981. Repr. of 1937 ed. 14.00 (ISBN 0-88355-746-0). Hyperion Conn.

Hayes, Harold. Three Levels of Time. 1981. 12.95 (ISBN 0-525-21853-X). Dutton.

Hayes, Harold P. Realism in EEO. LC 79-2295. 1980. 27.95 (ISBN 0-471-05796-7, Pub. by Wiley-Interscience). Wiley.

Hayes, Harold T. The Last Place on Earth. LC 76-15562. (Illus.). 288p. 1980. pap. 8.95 (ISBN 0-8128-6087-X). Stein & Day.

Hayes, Heidi. Spelling Skills. Incl. Bk C. Air Mail (ISBN 0-8372-3500-6). tchr's ed. (ISBN 0-8372-9190-9); Bk D. Space-O-Grams (ISBN 0-8372-3501-4). tchr's ed. (ISBN 0-8372-9191-7); Bk E. Postmarks (ISBN 0-8372-3502-2). tchr's ed. (ISBN 0-8372-9192-5); Bk F. Fan Mail (ISBN 0-8372-3503-0). tchr's ed. (ISBN 0-8372-9193-3). (Illus.). (gr. 3-6). 1977. pap. text ed. 1.35 ea.; tchr's. eds. 1.35 ea. Bowmar-Noble.

Hayes, Heidi, ed. see Educational Challenges, Inc.

Hayes, Helen & Dody, Sandford. On Reflection: An Autobiography. LC 68-54122. (Illus.). 256p. 1968. 8.95 (ISBN 0-87131-082-1); autographed ed. 12.50 (ISBN 0-87131-293-X). M Evans.

Hayes, Irene. What's Cooking in Kentucky. 1979. 12.95 o.p. (ISBN 0-397-01357-4); pap. 7.95 o.p. (ISBN 0-397-01356-6). Lippincott.

--What's Cooking in Kentucky, 2 vols. Date not set. spiral bdg. 6.95x ea. Vol. 1, 204pp (ISBN 0-938402-02-1). Vol. 2, 196pp (ISBN 0-938402-03-X). Hayes Bk Co.

--What's Cooking in Kentucky. rev. ed. (Illus.). 1979. laminated cover 12.95 (ISBN 0-938402-01-3). Hayes Bk Co.

Hayes, Irene E. The Airdale Terrier. Foyle, Christina, ed. (Foyle's Handbks). 1973. 3.95 (ISBN 0-685-55814-2). Palmetto Pub.

Hayes, J., jt. auth. see Hopson, B.

Hayes, J., et al. The Use of Grass Filters for Sediment Control in Strip Mine Drainage, Vol. II. DeVore, R. William, ed. (Illus.). 29p. 1978. pap. text ed. 4.50 (ISBN 0-89779-008-1); microfiche 1.50 (ISBN 0-89779-009-X). OEA Pubns.

Hayes, J. E., et al. Machine Intelligence: Machine Expertise & the Human Interface. LC 79-40785. (Machine Intelligence Ser.: Vol. 9). 1979. 92.95x (ISBN 0-470-26714-3). Halsted Pr.

Hayes, J. G., ed. Numerical Approximations to Functions & Data. 1970. text ed. 21.25x (ISBN 0-485-11109-8, Athlone Pr). Humanities.

Hayes, Janice E., jt. auth. see Govoni, Laura E.

Hayes, John, ed. Corpus Vasorum Antiquorum Canada: Royal Ontario Museum, Ontario. (Corpus Vasorum Antiquorum Ser.). (Illus.). 64p. 1980. 89.00 (ISBN 0-19-726000-4). Oxford U Pr.

--First & Second Corinthians. write for info (ISBN 0-8042-3239-3). John Knox.

Hayes, John, ed. see Baird, William.

Hayes, John, ed. see Habel, Norman C.

Hayes, John H. Son of God to Superstar: Twentieth-Century Interpretation of Jesus. 256p. 1976. pap. 5.95 (ISBN 0-687-39091-5); pap. 6.95 o. p. (ISBN 0-687-39092-3). Abingdon.

Hayes, John H., ed. see Saunders, Ernest W.

Hayes, John P., jt. auth. see Brill, Peter L.

Hayes, John P., jt. auth. see Sandman, Wm. E.

Hayes, John R. Cognitive Psychology: Thinking & Creating. 1978. pap. text ed. 16.95x (ISBN 0-256-02065-5). Dorsey.

--The Complete Problem Solver. 1981. write for info. Franklin Inst Pr.

Hayes, Joseph. Winner's Circle. 1981. pap. 3.50 (ISBN 0-440-19532-2). Dell.

Hayes, Louis, jt. auth. see Woodin, J. C.

Hayes, M. H., jt. auth. see Greenland, D. J.

Hayes, M. H., tr. see Fillis, James.

Hayes, Mary R. The Yacht People. 1979. pap. 2.25 o.p. (ISBN 0-523-40377-1). Pinnacle Bks.

Hayes, Michael. The Dow Jones-Irwin Guide to Stock Market Cycles. LC 76-28903. 1977. 25.00 (ISBN 0-87094-134-8). Dow Jones-Irwin.

--Money: How to Get It, Keep It, & Make It Grow. (Illus.). 1979. 15.95 (ISBN 0-8144-5503-4). Am Mgmt.

--Supernatural Poetry. 1980. 10.95 (ISBN 0-7145-3697-0). Riverrun NY.

Hayes, Michael, ed. Ghostly Tales of Washington Irving. 1980. 9.95 (ISBN 0-7145-3739-X). Riverrun NY.

--The Haunting Tales of Nathaniel Hawthorne. 1981. 10.95 (ISBN 0-7145-3809-4). Riverrun NY.

--The Supernatural Short Stories of Charles Dickens. 1979. 9.95 (ISBN 0-7145-3678-4). Riverrun NY.

--The Supernatural Short Stories of Robert Louis Stevenson. (Scottish Library). 1976. text ed. 13.00x (ISBN 0-7145-3550-8). Humanities.

--The Supernatural Short Stories of Sir Walter Scott. (Scottish Library). 1977. text ed. 13.75x (ISBN 0-7145-3616-4). Humanities.

Hayes, Michael J. Lobbyists & Legislators: A Theory of Political Markets. 256p. 1981. 18.00 (ISBN 0-8135-0910-6). Rutgers U Pr.

Hayes, Norvel. God's Medicine of Faith. 1978. pap. 1.95 (ISBN 0-917726-20-0). Hunter Bks.

--How to Protect Your Faith. 1978. pap. 2.25 (ISBN 0-917726-19-7). Hunter Bks.

Hayes, Patrick. Mathematical Methods in the Social & Managerial Sciences. LC 74-22361. 448p. 1975. 35.50 (ISBN 0-471-36490-8, Pub. by Wiley-Interscience). Wiley.

Hayes, R. S., jt. auth. see Baker, C. R.

Hayes, Ralph. By Passion Possessed. 1978. pap. 1.95 (ISBN 0-505-51240-8). Tower Bks.

--Dark Water. 1978. pap. 1.95 (ISBN 0-505-51320-X). Tower Bks.

--The Deadly Prey. (Hunter Ser). (Orig.). 1975. pap. 1.25 o.p. (ISBN 0-685-53130-9, LB277ZK, Leisure Bks). Nordon Pubns.

--Five Deadly Guns. (Orig.). 1980. pap. write for info. (ISBN 0-505-51522-9). Tower Bks.

--Love's Dark Conquest. 1978. pap. 1.95 (ISBN 0-505-51260-2). Tower Bks.

--Sheryl. 1980. pap. 2.25 (ISBN 0-505-51452-4). Tower Bks.

Hayes, Raphael. Adventuring. (Orig.). 1979. pap. 1.75 o.s.i. (ISBN 0-515-04804-6, Jove). Jove Pubns.

Hayes, Richard L. Ten Trailer Trips in Southwest. 1.50 o.s.i. (ISBN 0-87593-013-1). Trail-R.

--Ten Trailer Trips in the Rockies. 1.50 o.s.i. (ISBN 0-87593-011-5). Trail-R.

--Trailering America's Highways & Byways. (Illus.). 1965. Vol. 1: The West. 3.95 o.s.i. (ISBN 0-87593-008-5). Trail-R.

Hayes, Rick S. Business Loans: A Guide to Money Sources & How to Approach Them Successfully. 2nd ed. LC 80-10941. 1980. 22.50 (ISBN 0-8436-0786-6). CBI Pub.

--Credit & Collections: A Practical Guide. LC 77-20141. (Illus.). 1978. 22.50 (ISBN 0-8436-0753-X). CBI Pub.

Hayes, Rick S., jt. auth. see Baker, C. Richard.

Hayes, Robert M. & Becker, Joseph. Handbook of Data Processing for Libraries. 2nd ed. LC 74-9690. (Information Sciences Ser). 712p. 1974. 38.95 (ISBN 0-471-36483-5, Pub. by Wiley-Interscience). Wiley.

Hayes, Robert M., jt. auth. see Becker, Joseph.

Hayes, Rudy, jt. auth. see Tartan, Beth.

Hayes, Sheila. Me & My Mona Lisa Smile. 128p. (gr. 7 up). 1981. 9.95 (ISBN 0-525-66731-8). Elsevier-Nelson.

Hayes, Stephen, jt. auth. see Burk, Janet L.

Hayes, Stephen K. The Ninja & Their Secret Fighting Art. LC 81-50105. (Illus.). 160p. 1981. 13.50 (ISBN 0-8048-1374-4). C E Tuttle.

--Ninja: Spirit of the Shadow Warrior. Griffeth, Bill, ed. LC 80-84678. 1980. pap. 6.95 (ISBN 0-89750-073-3). Ohara Pubns.

Hayes, Steven C., jt. auth. see Cone, John D.

Hayes, W. The Genetics of Bacteria & Their Viruses: Studies in Basic Genetics & Molecular Biology. 2nd ed. LC 69-16199. 925p. 1976. pap. text ed. 24.95 (ISBN 0-470-36474-2). Halsted Pr.

Hayes, Wallace D. & Probstein, Ronald F., eds. Hypersonic Flow Theory, Vol. 1: Inviscid Flows. 2nd ed. (Applied Mechanics & Mathematics Ser.: Vol. 5). 1966. 48.75 (ISBN 0-12-334361-5). Acad Pr.

Hayes, Walter M. & Killeen, Veronica A. Introductory French Program, 2 Bks. (Prog. Bk.). (gr. 9-12). 1970. Set. pap. 13.00 (ISBN 0-8294-0197-0); 15 tapes s.p. 85.00 (ISBN 0-685-04188-3). Loyola.

Hayes, Wayland J., Jr. see Blood, F. R.

Hayes, Will. The Complete Ballooning Book. LC 75-32444. (Illus.). 160p. 1977. Repr. of 1977 ed. handbk. 12.95 (ISBN 0-89037-111-3). Anderson World.

Hayes, William & Loudon, Rodney. Scattering of Light by Crystals. LC 78-9008. 1978. 35.95 (ISBN 0-471-03191-7, Pub. by Wiley-Interscience). Wiley.

Hayes, William C. Scepter of Egypt: A Background for the Study of Egyptian Antiquities in the Metropolitan Museum of Art. Incl. Vol. 1. From the Earliest Times to the End of the Middle Kingdom. 25.00 (ISBN 0-87099-072-1); pap. 18.50 (ISBN 0-686-60651-5); Vol. 2. The Hyksos Period & the New Kingdom (1675-1080 B.C.) 16.95 o.p. (ISBN 0-87099-074-8); pap. 18.50 (ISBN 0-87099-191-4). LC 52-7286. (Illus.). 1959. Metro Mus Art.

Hayes, Zachary. The Hidden Center: Spirituality & Speculative Christology in St. Bonaventure. 224p. (Orig.). 1981. pap. 7.95 (ISBN 0-8091-2348-7). Paulist Pr.

--What Are They Saying About Creation? LC 80-80870. 128p. 1980. pap. 2.95 (ISBN 0-8091-2286-3). Paulist Pr.

Hayford, Harrison & Parker, Hershel, eds. Moby-Dick As Doubloon. 1970. pap. text ed. 6.95x (ISBN 0-393-09883-4, NortonC). Norton.

Hayhurst, G. Mathematical Programming for Management & Business. 1976. pap. 13.50x (ISBN 0-7131-3355-4). Intl Ideas.

Hayhurst, Roy & Wills, Gordon. Organizational Designs for Marketing Futures. (Studies in Management). 1972. 18.00x o.p. (ISBN 0-8464-0692-6). Beekman Pubs.

Hayiaras, Stratis. When the Tree Sings. 192p. 1981. pap. 2.95. Ballantine.

Hayim, Gila J. The Existential Sociology of Jean-Paul Sartre. LC 80-10131. 176p. 1980. lib. bdg. 13.50x (ISBN 0-87023-298-3). U of Mass Pr.

Haykin, S. S. Active Network Theory. 1970. 24.95 (ISBN 0-201-02680-5). A-W.

Haykin, S. S., ed. Detection & Estimation: Applications to Radar. LC 75-33340. (Benchmark Papers in Electrical Engineering & Computer Science Ser.: Vol. 13). 1976. 41.00 (ISBN 0-12-786648-5). Acad Pr.

Haykin, Simon. Communication Systems. LC 77-26752. 1978. text ed. 28.95 (ISBN 0-471-02977-7); tchrs. manual 10.00 (ISBN 0-471-03045-7). Wiley.

Hayler, William B., ed. see Cornell, F. M. & Hoffman, A. C.

Hayley, Rodney, ed. The Plays of Colley Cibber, 2 vols. LC 78-66634. (Eighteenth Century English Drama Ser.). 1980. Set. lib. bdg. 50.00 (ISBN 0-8240-3582-8). Garland Pub.

Hayley, William. Essay on Epic Poetry. LC 68-17013. 1968. Repr. of 1782 ed. 31.00x (ISBN 0-8201-1026-4). Schol Facsimiles.

--An Essay on Sculpture, in a Series of Epistles to John Flaxman...with Notes...(Plates Engraved by Blake) Reiman, Donald H., ed. LC 75-31210. (Romantic Context Ser.: Poetry 1789-1830: Vol. 61). 1979. Repr. of 1800 ed. lib. bdg. 47.00 (ISBN 0-8240-2160-6). Garland Pub.

--The Eulogies of Howard, a Vision, Repr. Of 1791. Reiman, Donald H., ed. Bd. with Ballads, Founded on Anecdotes Relating to Animals, with Prints...by William Blake. Repr. of 1805 ed; Poems on Serious & Sacred Subjects, Printed Only As Private Tokens of Regard, for the Particular Friends of the Author. Repr. of 1818 ed. LC 75-31209. (Romantic Context Ser.: Poetry 1789-1830: Vol. 60). 1979. lib. bdg. 47.00 (ISBN 0-8240-2159-2). Garland Pub.

--Life of Milton. LC-78-122485. 1970. Repr. of 1796 ed. 37.00x (ISBN 0-8201-1081-7). Schol Facsimiles.

--Ode, Inscribed to John Howard, Repr. Of 1780. Reiman, Donald H., ed. Bd. with An Essay on Painting: in Two Epistles to Mr. Romney...Third Edition Corrected & Enlarged. Repr. of 1781 ed; The Triumphs of Temper; a Poem. In Six Cantos. Repr. of 1781 ed; An Essay on Epic Poetry: in Five Epistles to the Rev. Mr. Mason. With Notes... Repr. of 1782 ed. LC 75-31207. (Romantic Context Ser.: Poetry 1789-1830: Vol. 58). 1979. lib. bdg. 47.00 (ISBN 0-8240-2157-6). Garland Pub.

--A Poetical Epistle to an Eminent Painter, Repr. Of 1778. Reiman, Donald H., ed. Bd. with An Elegy, on the Ancient Greek Model. Addressed to the Right Reverend Robert Lowth. Repr. of 1779 ed; Epistle to Admiral Keppel. Repr. of 1779 ed; Epistle to a Friend, on the Death of John Thornton Esq. 2nd, corrected ed. Repr. of 1780 ed; An Essay on History; in Three Epistles to Edward Gibbon, Esq. with Notes. Repr. of 1780 ed. LC 75-31206. (Romantic Context Ser.: Poetry 1789-1830: Vol. 57). 1979. lib. bdg. 47.00 (ISBN 0-8240-2156-8). Garland Pub.

--Two Dialogues: Containing a Comparative View of the Lives, Characters, & Writings of Philip, the Late Earl of Chesterfield, & Dr. Samuel Johnson. LC 71-122486. 1970. Repr. of 1787 ed. 28.00x (ISBN 0-8201-1080-9). Schol Facsimiles.

Haymaker, Webb & Adams, Raymond D. Histology & Histopathology of the Nervous System, 2 vols. (Illus.). 3520p. 1980. Set. 295.00 (ISBN 0-398-03482-6). C C Thomas.

Haymaker, Webb & Schiller, Francis. The Founders of Neurology: One Hundred & Forty-Six Biographical Sketches by Eighty-Nine Authors. 2nd ed. (Illus.). 640p. 1970. 24.75 (ISBN 0-398-00809-4). C C Thomas.

Hayman, David. Louis Ferdinand Celine. LC 65-26339. (Columbia Ser.: No. 13). (Orig.). 1965. pap. 2.00 (ISBN 0-231-02701-X, MW13). Columbia U Pr.

Hayman, David & Anderson, Elliott, eds. In the Wake of the "Wake". 1978. 18.50 (ISBN 0-299-07600-8). U of Wis Pr.

Hayman, LeRoy. Aces, Heroes & Daredevils of the Air. 160p. (gr. 8-12). 1981. PLB price not set (ISBN 0-671-34049-2). Messner.

--The Road to Fort Sumter. LC 71-171004. (Illus.). (gr. 5-8). 1972. 8.95 (ISBN 0-690-70566-2, TYC-J). T Y Crowell.

--Up, up, & Away: All About Balloons, Blimps, & Dirigibles. LC 79-27824. (Illus.). 192p. (gr. 7-12). 1980. PLB 8.29 (ISBN 0-671-33001-2). Messner.

Hayman, Rex. Nikon F-3 Book. (Camera Book Ser.). 128p. 1980. pap. 9.95 (ISBN 0-240-51073-9). Focal Pr.

Hayman, Ronald. British Theatre Since Nineteen Fifty Five: A Reassessment. 1979. 12.95 (ISBN 0-19-219127-6). Oxford U Pr.

--De Sade: A Critical Biography. LC 78-3170. 1978. 12.95 o.s.i. (ISBN 0-690-01416-3, TYC-T). T Y Crowell.

--Tom Stoppard. 3rd ed. (Illus.). 160p. 1979. 11.75x (ISBN 0-8476-6225-X). Rowman.

Hayman, W. K. Multivalent Functions. (Cambridge Tracts in Mathematics & Mathematical Physics: No. 48). 1958. 26.50 (ISBN 0-521-05238-6). Cambridge U Pr.

Hayman, W. K., jt. ed. see Clunie, J. G.

Hayman, Walter K. Meromorphic Functions. (Oxford Mathematical Monographs Ser). 1964. 34.95x o.p. (ISBN 0-19-853510-4). Oxford U Pr.

Hayne, David see Halpenny, Francess.

Haynes, B., ed. see Clarke, H. T.

Haynes, Betsy. The Against Taffy Sinclair Club. 112p. (gr. 3-6). 1981. pap. 1.50 (ISBN 0-553-15108-8). Bantam.

--Cowslip. LC 72-13251. 160p. (gr. 5-9). 1973. 6.95 o.p. (ISBN 0-525-66266-9). Elsevier-Nelson.

--The Shadows of Jeremy Pimm. LC 80-28920. 160p. (gr. 6 up). 1981. 7.95 (ISBN 0-8253-0045-2). Beaufort Bks NY.

Haynes, David G., tr. see Akhmanova, O. S., et al.

Haynes, Denys. Greek Art & the Idea of Freedom. (Illus.). 108p. 1981. 15.95 (ISBN 0-500-23331-4). Thames Hudson.

Haynes, E S. Early Victorian & Other Papers. 78p. 1980. Repr. lib. bdg. 25.00 (ISBN 0-89984-287-9). Century Bookbindery.

Haynes, Elton. Tales of Poultney. 1977. 3.95 o.p. (ISBN 0-682-48935-2). Exposition.

Haynes, Irene W. Ghost Wineries of Napa Valley. (Illus.). 80p. (Orig.). 1980. pap. 2.40 (ISBN 0-9604904-1-8). Taylor & Friends.

Haynes, J. Popular Election of United States Senators. Bd. with Local Government in the South & Southwest. Bemis, E. W. 1973. Repr. of 1893 ed. pap. 10.00 (ISBN 0-384-03886-7). Johnson Repr.

Haynes, James D. Botany: An Introductory of the Plant Kingdom. LC 74-7084. 514p. 1975. text ed. 23.95x (ISBN 0-471-36550-5). Wiley.

Haynes, Joel B., jt. auth. see Walker, Bruce J.

Haynes, John E. Pseudonyms of Authors. LC 68-30620. 1969. Repr. of 1882 ed. 18.00 (ISBN 0-8103-3142-X). Gale.

Haynes, John M. Divorce Mediation: A/Practical Guide for Therapists & Counselors. LC 80-25065. 1981. text ed. 17.95 (ISBN 0-8261-2590-5); pap. text ed. price not set (ISBN 0-8261-2591-3). Springer Pub.

Haynes, Judy L. Organizing a Speech: A Programmed Guide. 2nd ed. (Speech Communication Ser.). (Illus.). 192p. 1981. pap. text ed. 9.95 (ISBN 0-13-641530-X). P-H.

Haynes, R. M. & Bentham, C. G. Community Hospital & Rural Accessibility. 1979. text ed. 24.00x (ISBN 0-566-00271-X, Pub. by Gower Pub Co England). Renouf.

Haynes, Robert H. see Hanawalt, Philip C.

Haynes, Robert J. Organization Theory & Local Government. (New Local Government Ser.: No. 19). (Illus.). 224p. (Orig.). 1980. text ed. 27.50x (ISBN 0-04-352088-X, 2488); pap. text ed. 12.95x (ISBN 0-04-352089-8, 2489). Allen Unwin.

Haynes, Roberta, jt. auth. see Hyland, Wende.

Haynes, Titus. Fundamentalism in Black Inner City Storefront Churches. LC 79-57584. 1980. 6.95 (ISBN 0-533-04572-X). Vantage.

Haynes, Warren W., jt. auth. see Henry, William R.

Haynes, Willaim, ed. The Stonington Chronology: 1649-1976. LC 75-25299. (Illus.). 168p. 1976. casebound 12.50 (ISBN 0-87106-059-0). Globe Pequot.

Haynie, Charles R. Caesar's Prophet. Date not set. 8.95 (ISBN 0-533-04844-3). Vantage.

Haynie, Paul J. Cabinetmaking. (Illus.). 272p. 1976. 15.95 (ISBN 0-13-110239-7). P-H.

Hays. Getting Away with Murder: The Law & Bishop Legrand. 1981. 14.95 (ISBN 0-690-01941-6). Lippincott & Crowell.

Hays, Anne M. & Hazleton, Harriet R. Chesapeake Kaleidoscope. LC 75-23447. (Illus.). 1975. pap. 5.00 (ISBN 0-87033-214-7, Pub. by Tidewater). Cornell Maritime.

Hays, Arthur G. Trial by Prejudice. LC 79-109550. (Civil Liberties in American History Ser). 1970. Repr. of 1933 ed. lib. bdg. 35.00 (ISBN 0-306-71904-5). Da Capo.

Hays, Arthur Garfield. Let Freedom Ring. LC 71-166329. (Civil Liberties in American History Ser). (Illus.). 1972. Repr. of 1937 ed. lib. bdg. 47.50 (ISBN 0-306-70227-4). Da Capo.

Hays, Brooks. Hotbed of Tranquility. 1968. 9.95 o.s.i. (ISBN 0-02-549530-5). Macmillan.

Hays, Dorothea R., et al. Psychiatric-Mental Nursing Continuing Education Review. 1973. spiral bdg. 9.50 (ISBN 0-87488-351-2). Med Exam.

Hays, Edward M. Secular Sanctity. LC 80-80872. 112p. (Orig.). 1980. pap. 3.50 (ISBN 0-8091-2314-2). Paulist Pr.

Hays, H. R. Explorers of Man. Reit, Ann, ed. LC 70-135645. (Surveyor Ser). (Illus.). (gr. 9 up). 1971. 5.95 o.s.i. (ISBN 0-02-743460-5, CCPr). Macmillan.

Hays, H. R., tr. see Vallejo, Cesar.

Hays, J. R., et al, eds. Violence & the Violent Individual. LC 80-24. (Illus.). 544p. 1981. text ed. 35.00 (ISBN 0-89335-116-4). Spectrum Pub.

Hays, Joan F. Modern Dance: A Biochemical Approach to Teaching. (Illus.). 312p. 1981. pap. text ed. 13.95 (ISBN 0-8016-2179-8). Mosby.

Hays, Joanne M., jt. auth. see Frompovich, Catherine J.

Hays, Joyce. An Apple a Day. LC 74-30978. 1976. 9.95 o.p. (ISBN 0-498-01720-6). A S Barnes.

Hays, Lee. A Deadly State of Mind. (Columbo: No. 6). 1976. pap. 1.50 o.p. (ISBN 0-445-03118-2). Popular Lib.

Hays, Mary. Appeal to the Men of Great Britain on Behalf of Women. Luria, Gina, ed. LC 74-8547. (The Feminist Controversy in England, 1788-1810 Ser.). 1974. lib. bdg. 50.00 (ISBN 0-8240-0868-5). Garland Pub.

--Letters & Essays, Moral & Miscellaneous. Luria, Gina, ed. (The Feminist Controversy in England, 1788-1810 Ser.). 1974. lib. bdg. 50.00 (ISBN 0-8240-0869-3). Garland Pub.

--Memoirs of Emma Courtney, 2 vols. (The Feminist Controversy in England, 1788-1810 Ser.). 1974. Set. lib. bdg. 76.00 (ISBN 0-8240-0870-7); lib. bdg. 50.00 ea. Garland Pub.

Hays, R., et al. International Business: An Introduction to the World of the Multinational Firm. 1972. ref. ed. 19.95 (ISBN 0-13-472472-0). P-H.

Hays, Robert. Practically Speaking: In Business, Industry, & Government. LC 71-100868. 1969. pap. 8.75 (ISBN 0-201-02825-5). A-W.

--Principles of Technical Writing. 1965. 13.95 (ISBN 0-201-02807-7). A-W.

Hays, Rolfes & Associates. The Collection: Classic Community Cookbooks. 2nd ed. (Illus.). 1980. pap. 6.50 (ISBN 0-9602448-1-6). Hays Rolfes.

Hays, Samuel P. American Political History As Social Analysis: Essays by Samuel P. Hays. LC 79-17567. (Twentieth-Century America Ser.). 1980. 25.00x (ISBN 0-87049-276-4). U of Tenn Pr.

--Conservation & the Gospel of Efficiency: The Progressive Conservation Movement, 1890-1920. LC 59-9274. 1969. pap. text ed. 4.95x (ISBN 0-689-70091-1, 139). Atheneum.

Hays, Serge. Profile Japan: A National Compendium of Facts, Figures & Essential Information. 576p. 1980. cancelled (ISBN 0-87196-433-3). Facts on File.

Hays, Steven W. Court Reform. LC 77-10348. (Illus.). 1978. 16.95 (ISBN 0-669-01841-4). Lexington Bks.

Hays, William. Twentieth Century Views of Musical History. 1972. lib. rep. ed. 22.50x (ISBN 0-684-15149-9, ScribT). Scribner.

Hays, William L. Basic Statistics. LC 67-21786. (Basic Concepts in Psychology Ser). (Orig.). 1967. pap. text ed. 5.95 o.p. (ISBN 0-8185-0294-0). Brooks-Cole.

Hays, Wilma P. The French Are Coming. LC 65-22681. (Younger Reader Ser.). (Illus.). (gr. 4-7). 1965. 3.95 o.p. (ISBN 0-910412-63-4). Williamsburg.

Hayslett, H. T., Jr. Statistics Made Simple. LC 67-10414. pap. 3.50 (ISBN 0-385-02355-3, Made). Doubleday.

Hayt, William H. & Nevdeck, Gerold W. Electronic Circuit Analysis & Design. LC 75-31032. (Illus.). 384p. 1976. text ed. 24.95 (ISBN 0-395-21919-1); ans. to selected problems incl. (ISBN 0-685-63236-9); solutions manual 1.00 (ISBN 0-395-21923-X). HM.

Hayt, William H., Jr. Engineering Electromagnetics. 4th ed. (Electrical Engineering Ser.). (Illus.). 512p. 1981. text ed. 28.95 (ISBN 0-07-027395-2, C); solutions manual 4.95 (ISBN 0-07-027396-0). McGraw.

Hayter, Alethea. A Sultry Month. 1965. 7.95 (ISBN 0-571-06214-8, Pub. by Faber & Faber). Merrimack Bk Serv.

Hayter, Roy. A Career in Catering--Choosing a Course. LC 79-41628. (Illus.). 232p. 1980. 33.00 (ISBN 0-08-024708-3); pap. 14.50 (ISBN 0-08-024707-5). Pergamon.

Haythornthwaite, Philip. Uniforms of the Civil War 1861-1865. LC 75-28111. (Macmillan Color Ser). (Illus.). 208p. 1976. 9.95 (ISBN 0-02-549200-4, 54920). Macmillan.

--Uniforms of the Retreat from Moscow, 1812. LC 76-17456. (Color Guides Ser.). (Illus.). 1976. 7.95 o.p. (ISBN 0-88254-421-7). Hippocrene Bks.

--Uniforms of Waterloo in Color. (Illus.). 190p. 1980. 9.95 (ISBN 0-7137-0714-3, Pub. by Blandford Pr England). Sterling.

--Weapons & Equipment of the Napoleonic Wars. (Illus.). 1979. 24.95 (ISBN 0-7137-0906-5, Pub by Blandford Pr England). Sterling.

Haythornthwaite, Philip J. Uniforms of the French Revolutionary Wars 1789-1802. (Illus.). 160p. 1981. 19.95 (ISBN 0-7137-0936-7, Pub. by Blandford Pr England). Sterling.

Hayum, Andree. Giovanni Antonio Bazze - "Il Sodoma". LC 75-23794. (Outstanding Dissertations in the Fine Arts - 16th Century). (Illus.). 1976. lib. bdg. 41.00 (ISBN 0-8240-1989-X). Garland Pub.

Hayward, Alan. God Is. 224p. 1980. pap. 4.95 (ISBN 0-8407-5746-8). Nelson.

Hayward, Alan T. Flowmeters: A Basic Guide & Source-Book for Users. LC 79-15530. 197p. 1979. 27.95x (ISBN 0-470-26732-1). Halsted Pr.

Hayward, Arthur H. Colonial & Early American Lighting. 3rd ed. 1962. pap. 4.50 (ISBN 0-486-20975-X). Dover.

Hayward, Bill. Cat People. LC 77-16921. 1978. 12.95 o.p. (ISBN 0-385-14313-3). Doubleday.

Hayward, C. The Courtesan: The Part She Has Played in Classical & Modern Literature & in Life. Winick, Charles, ed. LC 78-60872. (Prostitution Ser.: Vol. 7). (Illus.). 492p. 1979. lib. bdg. 40.00 (ISBN 0-8240-9721-1). Garland Pub.

Hayward, Charles. Carpentry for Beginners. LC 77-18406. (Drake Home Craftsman Ser.). (Illus.). 1978. pap. 5.95 (ISBN 0-8069-8196-2, 031250). Sterling.

--English Period Furniture. LC 77-155926. (Illus.). 1971. 10.00 o.p. (ISBN 0-684-12443-2, ScribT). Scribner.

Hayward, Charles, jt. auth. see Wheeler, William.

Hayward, Charles H. Cabinet Making for Beginners. rev. ed. LC 78-24432. (Illus.). 1980. pap. 5.95 (ISBN 0-8069-8186-5); lib. bdg. 6.39 o.p. (ISBN 0-8069-8187-3). Sterling.

--The Complete Book of Woodwork. rev. ed. LC 74-6079. (Drake Home Craftsman Ser.). (Illus.). 1974. pap. 5.95 (ISBN 0-8069-8248-9). Sterling.

--Making Toys in Wood. LC 74-6435. (Illus.). 158p. 1974. 8.95 o.p. (ISBN 0-8069-8498-8); pap. 4.95 o.p. (ISBN 0-8069-8496-1). Sterling.

--Making Toys in Wood. rev. ed. LC 80-52501. (Illus.). 168p. 1980. pap. 5.95. Sterling.

--Practical Woodwork. (Illus.). 192p. 1978. pap. 5.95 (ISBN 0-8069-8582-8). Sterling.

--Staining & Wood Polishing. (Illus.). 214p. 1980. pap. 5.95 (ISBN 0-8069-8684-0). Sterling.

Hayward, Charles H., jt. auth. see Wheeler, William.

Hayward, E., jt. ed. see Fuller, E. G.

Hayward, Helena & Kirkham, Pat. William & John Linnel: 18th Century London Furniture-Makers, 2 vols. LC 80-51404. (Illus.). 400p. 1980. slipcased 125.00 (ISBN 0-8478-0325-2). Rizzoli Intl.

Hayward, J. Fabricopedia. (Illus.). 1974. 1.45 o.p. (ISBN 0-684-14048-9, SL563, ScribT). Scribner.

Hayward, J. F. Huguenot Silver in England, 1688-1727. 1959. 26.00 (ISBN 0-571-04551-0, Pub. by Faber & Faber). Merrimack Bk Serv.

Hayward, Jack. The One & Indivisible French Republic. (Comparative Modern Government Ser.). 306p. 1974. 10.95x (ISBN 0-393-05506-X); pap. 5.95x (ISBN 0-393-09325-5). Norton.

Hayward, Jack, ed. Trade Unions & Politics in Western Europe. 138p. 1980. 25.00x (ISBN 0-7146-3155-8, F Cass Co). Biblio Dist.

Hayward, Jean. Hawkes Nest. 1979. pap. 2.25 (ISBN 0-505-51443-5). Tower Bks.

Hayward, John. A Reporte of a Discourse Concerning Supreme Power in Affaires of Religion. LC 79-84116. (English Experience Ser.: No. 935). 64p. 1979. Repr. of 1606 ed. lib. bdg. 8.00 (ISBN 90-221-0935-6). Walter J Johnson.

Hayward, John, jt. auth. see Figg, Keith.

Hayward, John, ed. Jonathan Swift. (The Nonesuch Library). 1978. 11.95 (ISBN 0-370-00517-1, Pub. by Chatto Bodley Jonathan). Merrimack Bk Serv.

Hayward, Sir John. Answer to the First Part of a Certain Conference, Concerning Succession, Published...Under the Name of R. Dolman. LC 74-28861. (English Experience Ser.: No. 741). 1975. Repr. of 1603 ed. 13.00 (ISBN 90-221-0741-8). Walter J Johnson.

--The First Part of the Life & Raigne of King Henrie the IIII. LC 74-28862. (English Experience Ser.: No. 742). 1975. Repr. of 1599 ed. 11.50 (ISBN 90-221-0742-6). Walter J Johnson.

Hayward, Linda. A Phonic Dictionary. (Illus.). 96p. (gr. k-4). 1981. PLB 11.85 (ISBN 0-448-13923-5); pap. 3.95 (ISBN 0-448-47336-4). Platt.

Hayward, Linda, ed. Hansel & Gretel. LC 73-16856. (Illus.). 32p. 1974. pap. 1.25 (ISBN 0-394-82811-9, BYR). Random.

Hayward, Linday. The Curious Little Kitten. (Golden Storytime Bks.). 1981. 1.95 (ISBN 0-307-11952-1, Golden Pr). Western Pub.

Hayward, Max, jt. auth. see Obolensky, Chloe.

Hayward, Max, tr. see Mandelstam, Nadezhda.

Hayward, Max, tr. see Mayakovsky, Vladimir.

Hayward, Robert. The Brick Book. LC 77-22. (Illus.). 1977. 12.95 o.s.i. (ISBN 0-690-01448-1, TYC-T). T Y Crowell.

Haywood, Carolyn. Annie Pat & Eddie. (Illus.). (gr. 3-7). 1960. PLB 7.92 (ISBN 0-688-31045-1). Morrow.

--Away Went the Balloons. (Illus.). (gr. 3-7). 1973. 6.95 o.p. (ISBN 0-688-20095-8); PLB 7.92 (ISBN 0-688-30095-2). Morrow.

--Betsy & Mr. Kilpatrick. (Illus.). (gr. 3-7). 1967. 7.25 o.p. (ISBN 0-688-21085-6); PLB 7.92 (ISBN 0-688-31085-0). Morrow.

--Betsy & the Circus. (Illus.). (gr. 4-6). 1954. PLB 7.92 (ISBN 0-688-31086-9). Morrow.

--Betsy's Busy Summer. (Illus.). (gr. 3-7). 1956. PLB 8.40 (ISBN 0-688-31087-7). Morrow.

--Betsy's Busy Summer. (Illus.). (gr. 3-5). 1980. pap. 1.75 (ISBN 0-671-56047-6). PB.

--Betsy's Little Star. (Illus.). (gr. k-3). 1950. PLB 7.92 (ISBN 0-688-31088-5). Morrow.

--Betsy's Play School. LC 77-1615. (Illus.). (gr. 4-6). 1977. 8.25 (ISBN 0-688-22115-7); PLB 7.92 (ISBN 0-688-32115-1). Morrow.

--Betsy's Winterhouse. (Illus.). (gr. 3-7). 1958. PLB 7.92 (ISBN 0-688-31090-7). Morrow.

--C Is for Cupcake. LC 73-9282. (Illus.). 192p. (gr. 1-5). 1974. PLB 7.44 (ISBN 0-688-30098-7). Morrow.

--A Christmas Fantasy. LC 71-184244. (Illus.). 32p. (gr. k-3). 1972. lib. bdg. 8.25 (ISBN 0-688-20094-X); PLB 7.92 (ISBN 0-688-30094-4). Morrow.

--Eddie & Gardenia. (Illus.). (gr. 3-7). 1951. PLB 7.92 (ISBN 0-688-31255-1). Morrow.

--Eddie & Louella. (Illus.). (gr. 3-7). 1959. PLB 7.92 (ISBN 0-688-31254-3). Morrow.

--Eddie & the Fire Engine. (Illus.). (gr. 1-5). 1949. PLB 7.92 (ISBN 0-688-31252-7). Morrow.

--Eddie Makes Music. (Illus.). (gr. 3-7). 1957. PLB 8.40 (ISBN 0-688-31256-X). Morrow.

--Eddie the Dog Holder. (Illus.). (gr. 3-7). 1966. PLB 7.92 (ISBN 0-688-31253-5). Morrow.

--Eddie the Dog Holder. (gr. 3-5). 1980. pap. 1.75 (ISBN 0-671-56050-6). Archway.

--Eddie's Green Thumb. (Illus.). (gr. 3-7). 1964. PLB 7.92 (ISBN 0-688-31257-8). Morrow.

--Eddie's Green Thumb. (Illus.). (gr. 3-5). 1980. pap. 1.75 (ISBN 0-671-56051-4). PB.

--Eddie's Happenings. (Illus.). (gr. 3-7). 1971. PLB 7.92 (ISBN 0-688-31258-6). Morrow.

--Eddie's Menagerie. (Illus.). (gr. 4-6). 1978. 8.95 (ISBN 0-688-22158-0); PLB 8.59 (ISBN 0-688-32158-5). Morrow.

--Eddie's Menagerie. (Illus.). (gr. 3-5). 1980. pap. 1.75 (ISBN 0-671-56049-2). PB.

--Eddie's Pay Dirt. (Illus.). (gr. 3-7). 1953. PLB 7.92 (ISBN 0-688-31259-4). Morrow.

--Eddie's Valuable Property. LC 74-17499. (Illus.). 192p. (gr. 3-7). 1975. 8.25 (ISBN 0-688-22014-2); PLB 7.92 (ISBN 0-688-32014-7). Morrow.

--Ever-Ready Eddie. LC 68-27687. (Illus.). (gr. 3-7). 1968. 7.25 o.p. (ISBN 0-688-21277-8); PLB 6.96 o.p. (ISBN 0-688-31277-2). Morrow.

--Here Comes the Bus. (Illus.). (gr. 1-5). 1963. PLB 7.92 (ISBN 0-688-31843-6). Morrow.

--Little Eddie. (Illus.). (gr. 1-5). 1947. PLB 7.92 (ISBN 0-688-31682-4). Morrow.

--Merry Christmas from Betsy. (Illus.). (gr. 4-6). 1970. PLB 7.92 (ISBN 0-688-31695-6). Morrow.

--The Mixed-up Twins. (Illus.). (ps-3). 1952. 8.25 (ISBN 0-688-21683-8). Morrow.

--Penny Goes to Camp. (Illus.). (gr. 1-5). 1948. 8.25 (ISBN 0-688-21728-1). Morrow.

--Snowbound with Betsy. (Illus.). (gr. 3-7). 1962. 7.75 o.p. (ISBN 0-688-21684-6); PLB 7.92 (ISBN 0-688-31684-0). Morrow.

--Snowbound with Betsy. (Illus.). (gr. 3-5). 1980. pap. 1.75 (ISBN 0-671-56048-4). Archway.

--Taffy & Melissa Molasess. (Illus.). (gr. 1-4). 1969. PLB 7.92 (ISBN 0-688-31690-5). Morrow.

--A Valentine Fantasy. LC 75-23083. (Illus.). 32p. (gr. k-3). 1976. 7.25 (ISBN 0-688-22055-X); PLB 6.96 (ISBN 0-688-32055-4). Morrow.

Haywood, Eliza. The Fortunate Foundlings, Seventeen Forty-Four. (The Flowering of the Novel, 1740-1775 Ser: Vol. 10). 1974. lib. bdg. 50.00 (ISBN 0-8240-1109-0). Garland Pub.

--The History of Jemmy & Jenny Jessamy, 1753, 3 vols. (The Flowering of the Novel, 1740-1775 Ser: Vol. 39). 1974. lib. bdg. 50.00 (ISBN 0-8240-1138-4). Garland Pub.

--The History of Miss Betsy Thoughtless, 4 vols. Paulson, Ronald, ed. LC 78-60837. (Novel 1720-1805 Ser.: Vol. 4). 1979. Set. lib. bdg. 124.00 (ISBN 0-8240-3653-0). Garland Pub.

--Life's Progress Through the Passions; or, the Adventures of Natura, 1748. LC 74-16053. (Novel in England, 1700-1775 Ser). 1974. lib. bdg. 50.00 (ISBN 0-8240-1123-6). Garland Pub.

--Memoirs of a Certain Island Adjacent to the Kingdom of Utopia, Vol. 45. LC 75-170564. (Novel in England, 1700-1775 Ser). lib. bdg. 50.00 (ISBN 0-8240-0557-0). Garland Pub.

--The Rash Resolve; or, the Untimely Disovery. Bd. with The Life & Adventures of the Lady Lucy. Aubin, Penelope. LC 74-170561. (Foundations of the Novel Ser.: Vol. 43). lib. bdg. 50.00 (ISBN 0-8240-0555-4). Garland Pub.

--The Secret History of the Present Intrigues of the Court of Caramania. LC 71-170571. (Foundations of the Novel Ser.: Vol. 50). lib. bdg. 50.00 (ISBN 0-8240-0562-7). Garland Pub.

Haywood, Eliza see Davys, Mary.

Haywood, Eliza see Walker, Charles.

Haywood, Eliza, tr. see Mouhy, Charles.

Haywood, Elizabeth. Adventures of Eovaai, Princess of Ijaveo. LC 70-170595. (Foundations of the Novel Ser.: Vol. 65). lib. bdg. 50.00 (ISBN 0-8240-0577-5). Garland Pub.

Haywood, Harry. Negro Liberation. 1978. pap. 3.95 (ISBN 0-930720-50-4). Liberator Pr.

Haywood, R. W. The Analysis of Engineering Cycles. 2nd ed. LC 74-7056. 1975. text ed. 21.00 o.p. (ISBN 0-08-017947-9); pap. text ed. 11.75 o.p. (ISBN 0-08-017948-7). Pergamon.

--Analysis of Engineering Cycles. 3rd ed. LC 79-41225. (Illus.). 320p. 1980. 45.00 (ISBN 0-08-025441-1); pap. text ed. 15.75 (ISBN 0-08-025440-3). Pergamon.

Haywood, S. C. Managing the Health Service. (Illus.). 1974. text ed. 18.95x (ISBN 0-04-350046-3); pap. text ed. 8.95x o.p. (ISBN 0-04-350047-1). Allen Unwin.

Haywood, Stuart & Alaszewski, Andy. Crisis in the Health Service: The Politics of Management. 154p. 1980. 30.00x (ISBN 0-7099-0013-9, Pub. by Croom Helm Ltd England). Biblio Dist.

Haywood, William D. Autobiography of Big Bill Haywood. LC 74-2407. 1966. 5.95 o.p. (ISBN 0-7178-0012-1); pap. 2.95 (ISBN 0-7178-0011-3). Intl Pub Co.

Hayworth, Don. It's the Family That Counts. 1976. 6.95 (ISBN 0-912598-14-X). Florham.

Hazan, Baruch. Soviet Impregnational Propaganda. 1981. 20.00 (ISBN 0-88233-643-6). Ardis Pubs.

Hazard, Barbara. The Tangled Web. 224p. 1981. pap. 1.95 (ISBN 0-449-50177-9, Coventry). Fawcett.

Hazard, Benjamin H., ed. see Hatada, Takashi.

Hazard, C. & Mitton, S., eds. Active Galactic Nuclei. LC 78-67426. 1979. 38.50 (ISBN 0-521-22494-2). Cambridge U Pr.

Hazard, Elizabeth. Lipreading: For the Oral Deaf & Hard-Of-Hearing Person. 228p. 1971. 14.75 (ISBN 0-398-02161-9). C C Thomas.

Hazard, Flora M. Ledge of Gold. LC 80-68079. (Illus.). (gr. 5-11). 1980. 5.95 (ISBN 0-8323-0371-2); pap. 3.95 (ISBN 0-8323-0372-0). Binford.

Hazard, Geoffrey C., Jr., jt. auth. see Ehrlich, Thomas.

Hazard, Harry W. & Setton, Kenneth M. A History of the Crusades, Vol. 3. LC 68-9837. (Illus.). 752p. 1975. 40.00x (ISBN 0-299-06670-3). U of Wis Pr.

Hazard, Harry W. see Setton, Kenneth M.

Hazard, J. N. Soviet Legal System. 3rd ed. 1977. 20.00. Oceana.

Hazard, Jacqueline, jt. auth. see Bridgeman, William.

Hazard, John L. Transportation: Management, Economics, Policy. LC 77-22414. (Illus.). 1977. 18.00x (ISBN 0-87033-229-5). Cornell Maritime.

Hazard, John N. Law & Social Change in the USSR. LC 79-1608. 1980. Repr. of 1953 ed. 23.50 (ISBN 0-88355-911-0). Hyperion Conn.

Hazard, Leland. Attorney for the Situation. LC 74-83549. 325p. 1975. 12.50x (ISBN 0-231-03898-4). Columbia U Pr.

Hazard, Paul. Books, Children & Men. (Pn 1009.a1h33). 1960. 9.00 (ISBN 0-87675-050-1); pap. 6.50 (ISBN 0-87675-051-X). Horn Bk.

Hazard, William R. Education & the Law: Cases & Materials on Public Schools. 2nd ed. LC 78-50788. 1978. text ed. 17.95 (ISBN 0-02-914230-X). Free Pr.

Hazard, William R., ed. see Stent, Madelon D.

Hazari, Bharat, et al. Non-Traded & Intermediate Goods & the Pure Theory of International Trade. 1981. 29.95 (ISBN 0-312-57728-1). St Martin.

Hazari, Bharat R. The Pure Theory of International Trade & Distortions. LC 78-9092. 1978. 27.95 (ISBN 0-470-26430-6). Halsted Pr.

Hazarika, Niru. Public Service Commissions. 1979. text ed. 9.00x (ISBN 0-391-01847-7). Humanities.

Hazel, A. C. & Reid, A. S. Enjoying a Profitable Business. 2nd ed. 251p. 1976. text ed. 18.50x (ISBN 0-220-66287-8, Pub. by Busn Bks England). Renouf.

--Managing the Survival of Smaller Companies. 2nd ed. 159p. 1977. text ed. 18.50x (ISBN 0-220-66328-9, Pub. by Busn Bks England). Renouf.

--Rapid Company Growth: How to Plan & Manage Small Company Expansion. 166p. 1979. pap. 14.75x (ISBN 0-220-67025-0, Pub. by Busn Bks England). Renouf.

Hazel, Nancy. A Bridge to Independence: The Kent Family Placement Project. (Practice of Social Work Ser.). 208p. 1981. 25.00x (ISBN 0-631-12943-X, Pub. by Basil Blackwell England); pap. 12.50x (ISBN 0-631-12596-5). Biblio Dist.

Hazel, Paul. Yearwood. 1981. pap. 2.50 (ISBN 0-671-41605-7). PB.

--Yearwood. 1980. 10.95 (ISBN 0-316-35260-8, Pub. by Atlantic-Little Brown). Little.

Hazelkorn, Ellen. Marx & Engels: On Ireland - an Annotated Checklist. (Bibliographical Ser.: No. 15). 1981. 2.00 (ISBN 0-89977-031-2). Am Inst Marxist.

Hazell, Robert. Conspiracy & Civil Liberties. 128p. 1974. pap. text ed. 6.25x (ISBN 0-7135-1909-6, Pub. by Bedford England). Renouf.

Hazelrigg, Meredith K., jt. auth. see Antico, John.

Hazelton. The Seminole Chief (Billy Bowlegs) Or the Captives of Kissimmee, Repr. Of 1865 Ed. Bd. with Old Rube, the Hunter: Or the Crow Captive. a Tale of the Great Plains. Holmes, Hamilton. Repr. of 1866 ed. LC 75-7105. (Indian Captivities Ser.: Vol. 80). 1976. lib. bdg. 44.00 (ISBN 0-8240-1704-8). Garland Pub.

Hazelton, John H. Declaration of Independence: Its History. LC 79-124892. (American Constitutional & Legal History Ser). (Illus.). 1970. Repr. of 1906 ed. lib. bdg. 39.50 (ISBN 0-306-71987-8). Da Capo.

Hazelton, Nika S. Cooking of Germany. LC 69-17198. (Foods of the World Ser). (Illus.). (gr. 6 up). 1969. PLB 14.94 (ISBN 0-8094-0064-2, Time-Life). Silver.

--Cooking of Germany. (Foods of the World Ser). (Illus.). 1969. 14.95 (ISBN 0-8094-0037-5). Time-Life.

Hazelwood, Arthur, jt. auth. see Holtham, Gerald.

Hazen, Barbara. Amelia's Flying Machine. LC 76-51861. (ps-3). 1977. PLB 6.95 (ISBN 0-385-08139-1). Doubleday.

--Raggedy Ann & the Cookie Snatcher. (Illus.). 24p. (ps-3). 1972. PLB 5.00 (ISBN 0-307-60262-1, Golden Pr). Western Pub.

Hazen, Barbara S. Animal Alphabet from A to Z. (Illus.). 24p. (gr. k-1). 1976. PLB 7.15 o.p. (ISBN 0-307-69050-4, Golden Pr). Western Pub.

--Animal Daddies & My Daddy. (Illus.). 24p. (gr. k-2). 1968. PLB 5.00 (ISBN 0-307-60756-9, Golden Pr). Western Pub.

--Animal Manners. 1974. PLB 9.15 o.p. (ISBN 0-307-63748-4, Golden Pr). Western Pub.

--The Golden Happy Birthday Book. (Illus.). 1976. 4.95 (ISBN 0-307-16809-3, Golden Pr); PLB 10.69 o.p. (ISBN 0-307-66809-6). Western Pub.

--The Gorilla Did It. (Illus.). 1974. pap. 2.95 (ISBN 0-689-70438-0, Aladdin). Atheneum.

--A Nose for Trouble. (Golden Scratch & Sniff Bk.). (Illus.). 32p. (ps-2). 1973. PLB 9.92 (ISBN 0-307-64534-7, Golden Pr). Western Pub.

--Raggedy Ann & Andy & the Rainy Day Circus. (Illus.). (ps-1). 1973. PLB 5.00 (ISBN 0-307-60401-2, Golden Pr). Western Pub.

--Step on It, Andrew. LC 80-12522. (Illus.). 32p. (ps-2). 1980. 8.95 (ISBN 0-689-30792-6). Atheneum.

--The Tiny, Tawny Kitten. (Illus.). (ps-2). 1969. PLB 5.00 (ISBN 0-307-60590-6, Golden Pr). Western Pub.

Hazen, Nancy. Grownups Cry Too: Los Adultos Tambien Lloran. 2nd ed. Cotera, Martha P., tr. LC 78-71542. (Illus.). 25p. (ps-1). 1978. pap. 2.50 (ISBN 0-914996-19-3). Lollipop Power.

Hazinga, Cynthia Van see Van Hazinga, Cynthia.

Hazlehurst, F. Hamilton. Gardens of Illusion: The Genius of Andre Le Nostre. (Illus.). 430p. 1981. 39.95 (ISBN 0-8265-1209-7). Vanderbilt U Pr.

Hazleman, Brian L., jt. auth. see Watson, Peter G.

Hazleton, Harriet R., jt. auth. see Hays, Anne M.

Hazlitt, Henry. Economics in One Lesson. 218p. 1981. pap. 4.95 (ISBN 0-87000-517-0). Arlington Hse.

--The Foundations of Morality. LC 72-81850. (Illus.). 398p. 1972. 12.00x o.p. (ISBN 0-8402-1297-6); pap. 4.95x o.p. (ISBN 0-686-65433-1). Nash Pub.

Hazlitt, William. Essay on the Principles of Human Action, 1805. LC 70-75943. (Hist. of Psych. Ser.). 1969. 28.00x (ISBN 0-8201-1053-1). Schol Facsimiles.

--Hazlitt: Selected Essays. Nabholtz, John R., ed. LC 70-91403. (Crofts Classics Ser.). 1970. pap. text ed. 1.95x (ISBN 0-88295-042-8). AHM Pub.

--Lectures on the English Comic Writers. 1963. 5.00x o.p. (ISBN 0-460-00411-5, Evman). Dutton.

--Liber Amoris: Or, the New Pygmalion. Lahey, Gerald, ed. LC 79-47996. 256p. 1980. 17.50x (ISBN 0-8147-4999-2); pap. 7.95x (ISBN 0-8147-5000-1). NYU Pr.

--Spirit of the Age: Or, Contemporary Portraits. (World's Classics Ser.). 1904. 11.95 (ISBN 0-19-250057-0). Oxford U Pr.

Hazlitt, William C. English Proverbs & Proverbial Phrases. LC 67-23914. 1969. Repr. of 1907 ed. 24.00 (ISBN 0-8103-3199-3). Gale.

--Gleanings in Old Garden Literature. LC 68-21773. 1968. Repr. of 1887 ed. 15.00 (ISBN 0-8103-3509-3). Gale.

--Old Cookery Books & Ancient Cuisine. LC 68-30612. 1968. Repr. of 1886 ed. 15.00 (ISBN 0-8103-3306-6). Gale.

--Studies in Jocular Literature. LC 67-24352. 1969. Repr. of 1890 ed. 15.00 (ISBN 0-8103-3529-8). Gale.

Hazo, Samuel. To Paris. LC 80-22685. 96p. 1981. 11.95 (ISBN 0-8112-0787-0); pap. 4.95 (ISBN 0-8112-0788-9, NDP512). New Directions.

Hazra, Tapan A. & Beachley, Michael C., eds. Recent Advances in Clinical Oncology: Proceedings of a Conference Held in Williamsburg, Va., Feb.-March 1977. LC 78-14907. (Progress in Clinical & Biological Research: Vol. 25). (Illus.). 1978. 19.00x (ISBN 0-8451-0025-4). A R Liss.

Hazrat Inayat Khan. Aphorisms. (The Collected Works of Hazrat Inayat Khan). 128p. (Orig.). 1981. pap. 4.95 (ISBN 0-930872-22-3, 1008P). Sufi Order Pubns.

--The Bowl of Saki. (The Collected Works of Hazrat Inayat Khan). 144p. (Orig.). 1981. pap. 4.95 (ISBN 0-930872-20-7, 1007P). Sufi Order Pubns.

Hazzard, Harry W. & Setton, Kenneth M., eds. A History of the Crusades, Vol. 4: The Art & Architecture of the Crusader States. LC 68-9837. 1977. 40.00x (ISBN 0-299-06820-X). U of Wis Pr.

Hazzard, Linda B. About Scientific Fasting. 1980. pap. 1.95 (ISBN 0-87904-044-0). Lust.

Hazzard, Mary E. Critical Care Nursing. (Nursing Outline Ser.). 1978. spiral bdg. 9.50 (ISBN 0-87488-384-9). Med Exam.

H. D., pseud. End to Torment: A Memoir of Ezra Pound. Pearson, Norman H. & King, Michael, eds. LC 78-27149. 1979. pap. 3.95 (ISBN 0-8112-0720-X, NDP476). New Directions.

--Helen in Egypt. LC 74-8563. 320p. 1974. 4.95 (ISBN 0-8112-0543-6); pap. 3.25 (ISBN 0-8112-0544-4, NDP380). New Directions.

--Trilogy. Incl. The Walls Do Not Fall; Tribute to the Angels; The Flowering of the Rod. LC 73-78848. 128p. 1973. 4.95 (ISBN 0-8112-0490-1); pap. 3.95 (ISBN 0-8112-0491-X, NDP362). New Directions.

H'Doubler, Margaret N. Dance: A Creative Art Experience. 2nd ed. (Illus.). 1957. 17.50 (ISBN 0-299-01520-3); pap. 6.45 (ISBN 0-299-01524-6). U of Wis Pr.

Heacox, Cecil E. The Compleat Brown Trout. 1974. 13.95 (ISBN 0-87691-129-7). Winchester Pr.

--The Education of an Outdoorsman. 1976. 9.95 (ISBN 0-87691-187-4). Winchester Pr.

Head, Bessie. Maru. (African Writers Ser.). 1972. pap. text ed. 3.75x (ISBN 0-435-90101-X). Heinemann Ed.

Head, Constance. Emperor Julian. LC 75-15724. (World Leaders Ser.: No. 53). 1976. lib. bdg. 12.50 (ISBN 0-8057-7650-8). Twayne.

--Imperial Twilight: The Palaiologos Dynasty & the Decline of Byzantium. LC 76-26527. (Illus.). 1977. 14.95 (ISBN 0-88229-368-0). Nelson-Hall.

--Justinian Two of Byzantium. (Illus.). 1972. 19.50x (ISBN 0-299-06030-6). U of Wis Pr.

Head, David. He Sent Leanness. 1959. 1.95 o.s.i. (ISBN 0-02-549630-1). Macmillan.

Head, Derek. Residential Marinas & Yachting Amenities. (Marinas Ser.: No. 3). (Illus.). 84p. (Orig.). 1980. pap. text ed. 15.00 (ISBN 0-7210-1135-7, Pub. by C & CA London). Scholium Intl.

Head, George. Home Tour Through the Manufacturing Districts of England in the Summer of 1835. LC 67-31559. Repr. of 1836 ed. 17.50x (ISBN 0-678-05057-0). Kelley.

Head, John, jt. ed. see Beatts, Anne.

Head, K. H. Manual of Soil Laboratory Testing: Vol. I, Soil Classification & Compaction Testing. (Manual of Sail Laboratory Testing Ser.). 339p. 1980. 44.95x (ISBN 0-470-26973-1). Halsted Pr.

Head, Matthew. The Cabinda Affair. LC 80-8715. 256p. 1981. pap. 2.25 (ISBN 0-06-080541-2, P541, PL). Har-Row.

--The Congo Venus. LC 75-44982. (Crime Fiction Ser). 1976. Repr. of 1950 ed. lib. bdg. 17.50 (ISBN 0-8240-2374-9). Garland Pub.

--Murder at the Flea Club. LC 80-8716. 272p. 1981. pap. 2.25 (ISBN 0-06-080542-0, P542, PL). Har-Row.

Head, R. E. Lace & Embroidery Collector. LC 74-2031. 1971. Repr. of 1922 ed. 20.00 (ISBN 0-8103-3663-4). Gale.

Head, Richard & Kirkman, Francis. The English Rogue, Described in the Life of Meriton Latroon, a Witty Extravagant: Being a Complete History of the Most Eminent Cheats of Both Sexes. LC 80-2483. 1981. Repr. of 1928 ed. 73.50 (ISBN 0-404-19117-7). AMS Pr.

Head, Richard G., et al. Crisis Resolution: Presidential Decision Making in the Mayaguez & Korean Confrontations. (A Westview Special Study). 1978. lib. bdg. 26.00x (ISBN 0-89158-163-4). Westview.

Head, Sidney W., jt. auth. see Eastman, Susan T.

Head, Sydney W. Broadcasting in America. 3rd. ed. LC 75-19534. (Illus.). 704p. 1976. text ed. 18.95 (ISBN 0-395-20644-8); inst. manual 1.75 (ISBN 0-395-20645-6). HM.

Head, Victor. Sponsorship: The Newest Marketing Skill. 160p. 1980. 39.00x (ISBN 0-85941-151-6, Pub. by Woodhead-Faulkner England). State Mutual Bk.

Heading, John. From Now to Eternity (Revelation) 1981. pap. 3.95 (ISBN 0-937396-15-X). Walterick Pubs.

--Ordinary Differential Equations-Theory & Practice. 1974. 23.95 (ISBN 0-236-17722-2, Pub. by Paul Elek); pap. 8.95 (ISBN 0-236-17723-0). Merrimack Bk Serv.

Headings, Philip R. T. S. Eliot. (U. S. Authors Ser.: No. 57). 1964. lib. bdg. 10.95 (ISBN 0-8057-0236-9). Twayne.

Headington, Christopher. The History of Western Music. LC 76-20883. 1977. 12.95 (ISBN 0-02-871090-8); pap. text ed. 8.95 (ISBN 0-02-871080-0). Schirmer Bks.

Headlam, A. C., jt. auth. see Sanday, W.

Headland, Isaac T. Home Life in China. LC 79-177278. (Illus.). xii, 319p. 1971. Repr. of 1914 ed. 26.00 (ISBN 0-8103-3822-X). Gale.

Headley, John M. Luther's View of Church History. 1963. pap. 37.50x (ISBN 0-686-51413-0). Elliots Bks.

Headley, Lee. Adults & Their Parents in Family Therapy. 193p. 1977. 14.95 (ISBN 0-306-31087-2, Plenum Pr). Plenum Pub.

Headrick, Daniel R. The Tools of Empire: Technology & European Imperialism in the Nineteenth Century. 224p. 1981. text ed. 9.95x (ISBN 0-19-502831-7); pap. text ed. 5.95x (ISBN 0-19-502832-5). Oxford U Pr.

Headstrom, Richard. Nature Discoveries with a Hand Lens. (Illus.). 425p. 1981. pap. price not set (ISBN 0-486-24077-0). Dover.

--The Weird & the Beautiful. LC 78-75309. (Illus.). 132p. Date not set. 12.00 o.p. (ISBN 0-498-02394-X). A S Barnes. Postponed.

Heady, Eleanor B. Brave Johnny O'Hare. LC 74-77791. (Illus.). (gr. k-3). 1969. 5.95 o.p. (ISBN 0-8193-0275-9, Four Winds); PLB 5.41 o.p. (ISBN 0-8193-0276-7). Schol Bk Serv.

--Safiri the Singer: East African Tales. LC 76-161551. (Illus.). 96p. (gr. 2-4). 1972. 5.95 o.p. (ISBN 0-695-80244-5); PLB 5.97 o.p. (ISBN 0-695-40244-7). Follett.

--Trees Are Forever: How They Grow from Seeds to Forests. LC 76-46541. (Finding-Out Books for Science & Social Studies, Grades 1-4). (Illus.). (gr. 2-4). 1978. PLB 6.95 (ISBN 0-8193-0897-8, Pub. by Parents). Enslow Pubs.

Heady, Ray A. Hard Head I & Other Outdoor Stories. LC 80-83551. (Illus.). 312p. 1980. 12.95 (ISBN 0-913504-59-9). Lowell Pr.

Heagarty, Margaret C., et al. Child Health: Basics for Primary Care. 454p. 1980. pap. text ed. 16.95 (ISBN 0-8385-1111-2). ACC.

Heagerty, Margaret, jt. auth. see Robertson, Leon.

Heaivilin, Annise. Grandma's Tea Leaf Ironstone. (Illus.). 19.95 (ISBN 0-87069-323-9). Wallace-Homestead.

Heal. Man in the Middle. 9.95 (ISBN 0-686-69285-3). Scribner.

Heal, Felicity. Of Prelates & Princes: A Study of the Economic & Social Position of the Tudor Episcopate. LC 79-41791. (Illus.). 368p. 1980. 47.50 (ISBN 0-521-22950-2). Cambridge U Pr.

Heal, Felicity, jt. auth. see O'Day, Rosemary.

Heal, Felicity, jt. ed. see O'Day, Rosemary.

Heal, G. M., jt. auth. see Dasgupta, P. S.

Heal, G. M., jt. auth. see Hughes, G. A.

Heal, Laird W., jt. ed. see Novak, Angela R.

Heald, F. P. Adolescent Gynecology. 173p. 1966. 10.50 o.p. (ISBN 0-683-03891-5, Pub. by Williams & Wilkins). Krieger.

Heald, Morrell & Kaplan, Lawrence S. Culture & Diplomacy: The American Experience. LC 77-71863. (Contributions in American History: No. 63). 1977. lib. bdg. 22.50 (ISBN 0-8371-9541-1, HEA/). Greenwood.

Heald, Tim. Blue Blood Will Out. 192p. 1980. pap. 2.25 (ISBN 0-345-28904-8). Ballantine.

--Just Desserts. LC 78-10856. 1979. 7.95 o.p. (ISBN 0-684-16098-6, ScribT). Scribner.

--Let Sleeping Dogs Die. 192p. 1981. pap. 2.25 (ISBN 0-345-28903-X). Ballantine.

--The Making of Space 1999. 1976. pap. 1.95 o.p. (ISBN 0-345-25265-9). Ballantine.

Heald, Tim & Mohs, Mayo. H. R. H. The Man Who Will Be King. 1980. pap. 2.75 (ISBN 0-425-04659-1). Berkley Pub.

Heald, Weldon F., jt. auth. see Wampler, Joseph.

Heale, Michael J. The Making of American Politics. LC 77-24250. 1978. text ed. 21.00x (ISBN 0-582-48735-8); pap. text ed. 12.95x (ISBN 0-582-48736-6). Longman.

Heale, William & Swinburne, Henry. An Apologie for Women. Berkowitz, David S. & Thorne, Samuel E., eds. LC 77-86658. (Classics of English Legal History in the Modern Era Ser.: Vol. 42). 322p. 1979. lib. bdg. 40.00 (ISBN 0-8240-3091-5). Garland Pub.

Healey, Denis. Healey's Eye. (Illus.). 192p. 1981. 19.95 (ISBN 0-224-01793-4, Pub. by Chatto-Bodley-Jonathan). Merrimack Bk Serv.

Healey, J., tr. see Hall, Joseph.

Healey, J. A., jt. auth. see Allsop, R. T.

Healey, James S. John E. Fogarty: Political Leadership for Library Development. LC 73-19661. 1974. 10.00 (ISBN 0-8108-0689-4). Scarecrow.

Healey, John, tr. see Augustine, Saint.

Healey, John H. & Healey, William A. Administrative Practices in Boys & Girls Interscholastic Athletics. (Illus.). 616p. 1976. 37.75 (ISBN 0-398-03475-3). C C Thomas.

--Physical Education Teaching Problems for Analysis & Solution. 196p. 1975. 14.75 (ISBN 0-398-03206-8). C C Thomas.

Healey, Joseph G. A Fifth Gospel: The Experience of Black Christian Values. LC 80-25033. (Illus.). 320p. (Orig.). 1981. pap. 7.95 (ISBN 0-88344-013-X). Orbis Bks.

Healey, Larry. The Claw of the Bear. (gr. 6 up). 1978. PLB 8.90 s&l (ISBN 0-531-01469-X). Watts.

Healey, Letitia. Summer Storm. 192p. (Orig.). 1980. pap. 1.50 (ISBN 0-671-57024-2). S&S.

Healey, Martin & Hebditch, David. Minicomputers in on-Line Systems. (Computer Systems Ser.). (Illus.). 352p. 1981. text ed. 22.95 (ISBN 0-87626-579-4). Winthrop.

Healey, William A., jt. auth. see Healey, John H.

Health Law Center. Hospital Law Manual: Administrator's & Attorney's Set, 6 vols. LC 74-80713. 350.00 (ISBN 0-912862-05-X). Aspen Systems.

--Hospital Law Manual: Administrator's Set, 3 vols. (Updated quarterly). 1974. loose-leaf metal binding 295.00 (ISBN 0-912862-06-8). Aspen Systems.

--Hospital Law Manual: Attorney's Set, 3 vols. (Updated quarterly). 1974. loose-leaf metal binding 295.00 (ISBN 0-912862-05-X). Aspen Systems.

Health Services Research Study, Institute of Medicine. Infant Death: An Analysis by Maternal Risk & Health Care. Orig. Title: Maternal & Infant Health Services. (Illus.). 192p. 1973. pap. 8.50 (ISBN 0-309-02119-7). Natl Acad Pr.

Healy, C. Career Counseling in the Community College. (Illus.). 160p. 1974. 14.75 (ISBN 0-398-03096-0); pap. 8.50 (ISBN 0-398-03097-9). C C Thomas.

Healy, David. Gunboat Diplomacy in the Wilson Era: The U.S. Navy in Haiti, 1915-1916. LC 75-32074. 1976. 21.50x (ISBN 0-299-06980-X). U of Wis Pr.
--U. S. Expansionism: The Imperialist Urge in the 1890's. LC 71-121769. (Illus.). 1970. 25.00 (ISBN 0-299-05851-4). U of Wis Pr.
Healy, David F. United States in Cuba, 1898-1902: Generals, Politicians, & the Search for Policy. (Illus.). 1963. 17.50x (ISBN 0-299-02930-1). U of Wis Pr.
Healy, G. P. A. Reminiscences of a Portrait Painter. LC 78-96439. (Library of American Art Ser). (Illus.). 1970. Repr. of 1894 ed. lib. bdg. 29.50 (ISBN 0-306-71829-4). Da Capo.
Healy, Harriet & Stainback, Susan. The Severely Motorically Impaired Student: A Handbook for the Classroom Teacher. (Illus.). 90p. 1980. 11.75 (ISBN 0-398-04050-8); pap. 7.50 (ISBN 0-398-04061-3). C C Thomas.
Healy, J. J. & DeBruzzi, D. J. Basic FORTRAN IV Programming. rev. ed. 1975. pap. 13.95 (ISBN 0-201-02827-1). A-W.
Healy, J. W. Plutonium, Health Implications for Man: Proceedings of the 2nd Los Alamos Life Sciences Symposium. 1976. 32.00 (ISBN 0-08-019751-5). Pergamon.
Healy, Juanita see Summerlin, Lee R.
Healy, R. J. Design for Security. LC 61-21179. 1968. 28.50 (ISBN 0-471-36664-1, Pub. by Wiley-Interscience). Wiley.
Healy, R. J., jt. auth. see Walsh, T. J.
Healy, Robert E., jt. auth. see McCarthy, George D.
Healy, Sean. Ideas for Teaching History. 1974. 14.95 (ISBN 0-7134-2166-5, Pub. by Batsford England). David & Charles.
Healy, Timothy. Basic Manx, Irish & Scottish Gaelic. 1977. pap. text ed. 9.25x (ISBN 90-6296-021-9). Humanities.
Healy, Timothy J. Energy & Society. (Illus.). 400p. 1976. pap. text ed. 10.95x (ISBN 0-87835-049-7). Boyd & Fraser.
Heaney, Columban, tr. see Hallier, Amedee.
Heaney, Seamus. Death of a Naturalist. 1969. 4.95 o.p. (ISBN 0-571-06665-8, Pub. by Faber & Faber); pap. 4.95 (ISBN 0-571-09024-9). Merrimack Bk Serv.
--Door into the Dark. 1972. pap. 4.95 (ISBN 0-571-08998-4, Pub. by Faber & Faber). Merrimack Bk Serv.
--Field Work. 1981. pap. 4.95 (ISBN 0-374-51620-0). FS&G.
--Hedge School. (Fine Press Poetry Ser.). (Illus.). 1979. signed ltd. ed. 50.00 o.p. (ISBN 0-931356-03-2). Seluzicki Poetry.
--North. LC 75-34888. 1976. pap. 4.95 (ISBN 0-19-519913-8, 506, GB). Oxford U Pr.
--Wintering Out. 1972. pap. 5.95x (ISBN 0-19-519820-4). Oxford U Pr.
Heap, Ken. Group Theory for Social Workers: An Introduction. 1977. text ed. 26.00 (ISBN 0-08-018956-3); pap. text ed. 11.00 (ISBN 0-08-018955-5). Pergamon.
--Process & Action in Work with Groups: The Preconditions for Treatment & Growth. 1978. text ed. 30.00 (ISBN 0-08-023023-7); pap. text ed. 11.25 (ISBN 0-08-023022-9). Pergamon.
Heaps, Joseph F., jt. auth. see Czarra, Fred R.
Heaps, Leo. Operation Morning Light. 1979. pap. 2.95 (ISBN 0-345-28101-2). Ballantine.
Heaps, Leo, ed. Log of the Centurion. LC 73-10831. (Illus.). 304p. 1974. 8.95 o.p. (ISBN 0-02-549750-2). Macmillan.
Heaps, Willard A. Juvenile Justice. LC 74-4011. 1974. 7.95 (ISBN 0-395-28906-8, Clarion). HM.
--Psychic Phenomena. LC 74-10266. 160p. 1975. 7.95 o.p. (ISBN 0-525-66418-1). Elsevier-Nelson.
--Riots, U. S. A. rev. ed. LC 69-13444. (gr. 8-12). 1970. 6.95 (ISBN 0-395-28907-6, Clarion). HM.
--Superstition! LC 72-8114. (gr. 6up). 1972. 7.95 o.p. (ISBN 0-525-66226-X). Elsevier-Nelson.
--Taxation, U. S. A. LC 71-146653. (gr. 7 up). 1971. 6.95 (ISBN 0-395-28906-8, Clarion). HM.
Heard, H. F. The Amazing Mycroft Mysteries. LC 80-52557. 768p. 1980. 14.95 (ISBN 0-8149-0840-3). Vanguard.
Heard, J. Norman. White into Red: A Study of the Assimilation of White Persons Captured by Indians. LC 72-13133. (Illus.). 1973. 10.00 (ISBN 0-8108-0581-2). Scarecrow.
Heard, J. Norman, et al. Bookman's Guide to Americana. 7th ed. LC 76-51257. 1977. 19.50 (ISBN 0-8108-1007-7). Scarecrow.
Heard, Kenneth A., jt. auth. see Shaw, Timothy M.
Heard, Nathan. The House of Slammers: A Novel. 256p. 1981. 9.95 (ISBN 0-686-68675-6). Macmillan.
Heard, Robert. Oklahoma Vs. Texas: When Football Becomes War. LC 80-82909. (Illus.). 544p. 1980. 25.00 (ISBN 0-937642-00-2). Honey Hill.
Heard, Robert, ed. Dance with Who Brung Us. new ed. LC 76-20276. 158p. 1976. 8.95 o.p. (ISBN 0-8363-0142-0). Jenkins.
Hearder, H. Europe in the Nineteenth Century 1830-1880. (General History of Europe Ser.). (Illus.). 1966. text ed. 16.00x (ISBN 0-582-48212-7); pap. text ed. 10.95x (ISBN 0-582-48344-1). Longman.
Hearder, H. & Waley, Daniel P. Short History of Italy. (Illus.). 1963. pap. 9.95 (ISBN 0-521-09394-5, 394). Cambridge U Pr.
Hearle, J. W., jt. auth. see Morton, W. E.
Hearle, J. W., ed. Mechanics of Flexible Fiber Assemblies. (NATO-Advanced Study Institute Ser.). 700p. 1980. 72.50x (ISBN 9-0286-0720-X). Sijthoff & Noordhoff.
Hearle, J. W., et al. Use of the Scanning Electron Microscope. 289p. 1972. text ed. 52.00 (ISBN 0-08-016246-0). Pergamon.
Hearn, Charles R. The American Dream in the Great Depression. LC 76-56623. (Contributions in American Studies Ser: No. 28). 1977. lib. bdg. 17.95 (ISBN 0-8371-9478-4, HAD/). Greenwood.
Hearn, E. H., tr. see Pardo Bazan, Emilia.
Hearn, Francis. Domination, Legitimation, & Resistance: The Incorporation of the Nineteenth-Century English Working Class. LC 77-84753. (Contributions in Labor History: No. 3). 1978. lib. bdg. 19.95 (ISBN 0-8371-9847-X, HDL/). Greenwood.
Hearn, Lafcadio. Boy Who Drew Cats & Other Tales. (gr. 1-3). 1963. 4.50g o.s.i. (ISBN 0-02-743480-X). Macmillan.
--Earless Ho-Ichi. LC 66-12171. (Illus.). 1966. 8.95x (ISBN 0-87011-021-7). Kodansha.
--Kwaidan: Stories & Studies of Strange Things. LC 75-138067. (Illus.). 1971. pap. 4.95 (ISBN 0-8048-0954-2). C E Tuttle.
Hearn, Michael P. The Annotated Wizard of Oz. (Illus.). 384p. 1973. 20.00 (ISBN 0-517-50086-8). Potter.
Hearn, Michael P., ed. Breakfast, Books & Dreams: A Day in Verse. LC 80-13498. (Illus.). 48p. (gr. 7-10). 1981. 9.95g (ISBN 0-7232-6189-X). Warne.
Hearn, R. B. Byron Criticism Since Nineteen Fifty-Two. (Romantic Reassessment: No. 83: 2). 1980. pap. text ed. 25.00x (ISBN 0-391-02188-5). Humanities.
Hearn, Ronald B. The Road to Rydal Mount: A Survey of William Wordsworth's Reading. (Salzburg Studies in English Literature, Romantic Reassessment: No. 6). 1973. pap. text ed. 25.00x (ISBN 0-391-01403-X). Humanities.
--Wordsworth Criticism Since 1952: A Bibliography. (Salzburg Studies in English Literature Romantic Reassessment: No. 83). 1978. pap. text ed. 25.00x (ISBN 0-391-01402-1). Humanities.
Hearnden, Arthur. Education, Culture & Politics in West Germany. King, Edmanuel J., ed. 153p. 1976. text ed. 21.00 (ISBN 0-08-019916-X); pap. text ed. 10.50 (ISBN 0-08-019915-1). Pergamon.
--Education in the Two Germanies. LC 75-46557. 1974. 23.75x (ISBN 0-89158-539-7). Westview.
Hearne, A. S., et al. Agriculture & the Planning Process. 250p. 1980. text ed. 24.75x o.p. (ISBN 0-686-66037-4). Renouf.
Hearne, Betsy. Choosing Books for Children: A Commonsense Guide. LC 80-66203. 228p. 1981. 8.95 (ISBN 0-440-01930-3). Delacorte.
Hearne, Mary see Barker, Jane.
Hearns, Rudolf S. Self-Portraits in Autographs. 1981. 7.95 (ISBN 0-8062-1550-X). Carlton.
Hearnshaw, F. J. Conservatism in England. LC 67-24582. 1968. Repr. 17.00 (ISBN 0-86527-031-7). Fertig.
Hearon, Shelby. Painted Dresses. LC 80-69644. 1981. 11.95 (ISBN 0-689-11155-X). Atheneum.
Hearsay, John. Young Mr. Pepys. LC 73-8273. (Encore Ed.). (Illus.). 1974. 3.95 o.p. (ISBN 0-684-15948-1, ScribT). Scribner.
Hearst, James. Snake in the Strawberries. 1979. 5.95 (ISBN 0-8138-0765-4). Iowa St U Pr.
Hearst, John E. & Ifft, James B. Contemporary Chemistry. LC 75-28230. (Illus.). 1976. text ed. 22.95x (ISBN 0-7167-0172-3). W H Freeman.
Hearst, John E. see Ifft, James B.
Heartwell, Charles M., Jr. & Rahn, Arthur O. Syllabus of Complete Dentures. 3rd ed. LC 80-10476. (Illus.). 558p. 1980. text ed. 28.50 (ISBN 0-8121-0711-X). Lea & Febiger.
Heartz, Daniel. Pierre Attaingnant, Royal Printer of Music: A Historical Study & Bibliographical Catalogue. LC 68-13959. 1970. 46.50x (ISBN 0-520-01563-0). U of Cal Pr.
Heaser, Eileen & Kong, Les. The Sacramento Region: Planning, Growth & Development, A Bibliographic Guide. (Public Administration Ser.: Bibliographies: P-673). 61p. 1981. 9.00. Vance Biblios.
Heasley, Bernice E. Auditory Processing Disorders & Remediation. 2nd ed. (Illus.). 168p. 1980. pap. 16.50 spiral bdg. (ISBN 0-398-04047-8). C C Thomas.
Heasley, Bernice E. & Grosklos, Jacqueline R. Programmed Language & Speech Correction Through Perceptual Activities. (Illus.). 136p. 1980. text ed. 11.50 spiral (lexotone) (ISBN 0-398-03956-9). C C Thomas.
--Programmed Lessons for Young Language-Disabled Children: A Handbook for Therapists, Educators & Parents. (Illus.). 172p. 1976. pap. text ed. 12.75 spiral (ISBN 0-398-03526-1). C C Thomas.
Heasley Cox, Martha & Chatterton, Wayne. Nelson Algren. (U. S. Authors Ser.: No. 249). 192p. 1975. lib. bdg. 10.95 (ISBN 0-8057-0014-5). Twayne.
Heaslip, George. Johnny Bench. LC 73-13862. (Creative Superstars Ser.). 1974. PLB 5.95 (ISBN 0-87191-289-9); pap. 2.95 (ISBN 0-89812-171-X). Creative Ed.
--Wilt Chamberlain. LC 73-13894. (Creative Superstars Ser.). 1974. PLB 5.95 (ISBN 0-87191-288-0); pap. 2.95 (ISBN 0-685-47498-4). Creative Ed.
Heaston, Michael D., ed. From Mississippi to California. Date not set. 9.50 (ISBN 0-8363-0157-9). Jenkins.
Heat Transfer & Fluid Mechanics Institute. Proceedings. Incl. 1958 Sessions. viii, 264p. pap. 12.50x (ISBN 0-8047-0422-8); 1959 Sessions. x, 242p. pap. 12.50x (ISBN 0-8047-0423-6); 1960 Sessions. Mason, David M, et al, eds. x, 260p. 12.50x (ISBN 0-8047-0424-4); 1961 Sessions. Binder, Raymond C., et al, eds. xi, 236p. 12.50x (ISBN 0-8047-0425-2); 1962 Sessions. Ehlers, F. Edward, et al, eds. x, 294p. 12.50x (ISBN 0-8047-0426-0); 1963 Sessions. Roshko, Anatol, et al, eds. xii, 280p. 12.50x (ISBN 0-8047-0427-9); 1964 Sessions. Giedt, Warren H. & Levy, Salomon, eds. x, 275p. 12.50x (ISBN 0-8047-0428-7); 1965 Sessions. Charwat, Andrew F., et al, eds. xii, 372p. 16.50x (ISBN 0-8047-0429-5); 1966 Sessions. Saad, Michel A. & Miller, James A., eds. xii, 444p. 17.50x (ISBN 0-8047-0430-9); 1967 Sessions. Libby, Paul A., et al, eds. x, 468p. 17.50x (ISBN 0-8047-0431-7); 1968 Sessions. Emery, Ashley F. & Depew, Creighton A., eds. ix, 272p. 12.50x (ISBN 0-8047-0438-4); 1970 Sessions. Sarpkaya, Turgut, ed. xii, 370p. 15.00x (ISBN **0-8047-0744-8); 1974 Sessions. Davis, Lorin R. & Wilson, Robert E., eds. 17.50x (ISBN 0-8047-0865-7); 1976 Sessions. McKillop, Allan A., et al, eds. 29.50x (ISBN 0-8047-0917-3); 1978 Sessions. Crowe, Clayton T. & Grosshandler, William L., eds. 344p. text ed. 28.50x (ISBN 0-8047-1002-3); 1980 Sessions. Gerstein, Melvin & Choudhury, P. Roy, eds. text ed. 22.50x (ISBN 0-8047-1087-2). (Illus.). Stanford U Pr.**
Heater, Derek & Owen, Gwyneth. Health & Wealth. Yapp, Malcolm & Killingray, Margaret, eds. (World History Ser.). (Illus.). (gr. 10). 1980. Repr. of 1977 ed. lib. bdg. 5.95 (ISBN 0-89908-142-8); pap. text ed. 1.95 (ISBN 0-89908-117-7). Greenhaven.
Heater, Sandra H. Teaching Preschool Reading. LC 80-18768. (Illus.). 128p. (Orig.). 1980. pap. text ed. 8.95x (ISBN 0-8425-1837-1). Brigham.
Heath, Adrian. Abstract Painting: Its Origin & Meaning. 1953. 3.75 (ISBN 0-85458-828-0). Transatlantic.
Heath, Ambrose. Good Sandwiches & Picnic Dishes. 1949. 4.00 (ISBN 0-693-11415-0). Transatlantic.
Heath, Anthony F., jt. auth. see Halsey, Albert H.
Heath, Christopher D. A Study of Speech Patterns in the Former Urban District of Cannock, Staffordshire. 1980. 22.00x (ISBN 0-631-11611-7, Pub. by Basil Blackwell England). Biblio Dist.
Heath, D. W., et al, eds. Cultural Factors in Alcohol Research & Treatment. (Journal of Studies on Alcohol: Suppl. No. 9). 1981. 10.00x (ISBN 0-911290-08-7). Rutgers Ctr Alcohol.
Heath, Dwight D. Historical Dictionary of Bolivia. LC 73-172476. (Latin American Historical Dictionaries Ser.: No. 4). 1972. 12.00 (ISBN 0-8108-0451-4). Scarecrow.
Heath, Edward, ed. The Joy of Christmas: A Selection of Carols by Edward Heath. (Illus.). 1978. 12.95 (ISBN 0-19-520080-2); pap. 3.95 (ISBN 0-19-520081-0). Oxford U Pr.
Heath, Edward M. Old World, New Horizons: Britain, Europe, & the Atlantic Alliance. LC 71-106959. (Godkin Lecture Ser: 1967). 1970. 6.95x (ISBN 0-674-63860-5). Harvard U Pr.
Heath, G. Louis. The Hot Campus: The Politics That Impede Change in the Technoversity. LC 73-8824. 1973. 13.50 (ISBN 0-8108-0648-7). Scarecrow.
--Vandals in the Bomb Factory: The History & Literature of the Students for a Democratic Society. LC 75-40266. 1976. 21.00 (ISBN 0-8108-0890-0). Scarecrow.
Heath, G. Louis, ed. The Black Panther Leaders Speak. LC 76-3585. 177p. 1976. 10.00 (ISBN 0-8108-0915-X). Scarecrow.
--Mutiny Does Not Happen Lightly: The Literature of the American Resistance to the Vietnam War. LC 76-4825. 636p. 1976. 27.50 (ISBN 0-8108-0922-2). Scarecrow.
--Off the Pigs! The History & Literature of the Black Panther Party. LC 75-45204. 429p. 1976. 18.00 (ISBN 0-8108-0901-X). Scarecrow.
Heath, Gordon R. Live Longer & Love It. LC 80-81595. (Illus.). 78p. (Orig.). 1980. pap. 5.95 (ISBN 0-937092-00-2). Methuselah Bks.
Heath, Henry. Flavor Technology: Profiles, Products, Applications. (Illus.). 1978. lib. bdg. 39.50 (ISBN 0-87055-258-9). AVI.
Heath, Henry B. Source Book of Flavors. (Illus.). 1981. lib. bdg. 79.50 (ISBN 0-87055-369-0). AVI.
Heath, James P., jt. auth. see Horsburgh, David B.
Heath, Patricia, jt. ed. see Meek, Brian.
Heath, Robert. Clarastella Together with Poems Occasional, Elegies, Epigrams, Satyrs, 1650. LC 74-119866. 1970. Repr. of 1650 ed. 21.00x (ISBN 0-8201-1073-6). Schol Facsimiles.
Heath, Robert W., jt. auth. see Downie, N. M.
Heath, Roy A. From the Heat of the Day. 176p. 1981. pap. 5.95 (ISBN 0-8052-8071-5, Pub. by Allison & Busby England). Schocken.
--The Murderer. 176p. 1981. pap. 5.95 (ISBN 0-8052-8072-3, Pub. by Allison & Busby England). Schocken.
Heath, Royton E. Miniature Shrubs. (Illus.). 1978. 10.95 o.p. (ISBN 0-214-20477-4, 8053, Dist. by Arco). Barrie & Jenkins.
Heath, Samuel. Coat & Skirtmaking: A Step-by-Step Approach. 1979. 12.95x (ISBN 0-8464-0047-2). Beekman Pubs.
Heath, Sandra. Mally. 224p. (Orig.). 1980. pap. 1.75 (ISBN 0-451-09342-9, E9342, Sig). NAL.
--New Harbinger Pubns. (Orig.). 1981. pap. 1.95 (ISBN 0-451-09771-8, J9771, Sig). NAL.
Heath, Shirley B. Telling Tongues: Language Policy in Mexico, Colony to Nation. LC 72-408. (Illus.). 1972. text ed. 12.95x (ISBN 0-8077-1508-5); pap. text ed. 7.95x (ISBN 0-8077-1507-7). Tchrs Coll.
Heath, Sidney. The Romance of Symbolism & It's Relation to Chureh Ornament & Architecture. LC 70-174054. (Illus.). 1976. Repr. of 1909 ed. 18.00 (ISBN 0-8103-4302-9). Gale.
Heath, Stephen, jt. ed. see DeLaurentis, Teresa.
Heath, Thomas. Mathematics in Aristotle. LC 78-66593. (Ancient Philosophy Ser.). 305p. 1980. lib. bdg. 30.00 (ISBN 0-8240-9595-2). Garland Pub.
Heath, Thomas L. A History of Greek Mathematics, 2 vols. (Illus.). 1058p. 1981. pap. price not set. Vol. I (ISBN 0-486-24073-8). Vol. II (ISBN 0-486-24074-6). Dover.
Heath, Veronica. Beginner's Guide to Riding. 1971. 8.50 (ISBN 0-7207-0440-5). Transatlantic.
Heath, W. L. The Earthquake Man. LC 80-20270. 96p. (gr. 6 up). 1980. 7.95 (ISBN 0-8253-0008-8). Beaufort Bks NY.
Heath, Wendy Y., ed. Book Auction Records: Vol. 76, Aug. 1978-July 1979. LC 5-18641. 518p. 1980. 162.50x (ISBN 0-7129-1012-3). Intl Pubns Serv.
Heathcock, Claude L. The United States Constitution in Perspective. rev. ed. (Studies in Political Science Ser.). 1972. pap. 7.20 (ISBN 0-205-03479-9, 763479X). Allyn.
Heathcote, C. R. Probability: Elements of the Mathematical Theory. LC 70-142998. 1971. 15.95 (ISBN 0-471-36675-7). Halsted Pr.
Heathcote, R. L. Australia. (World's Lanscapes Ser.). (Illus.). 240p. 1976. text ed. 19.50x o.p. (ISBN 0-582-48166-X); pap. text ed. 12.95x (ISBN 0-582-48179-1). Longman.
Heathe, Roy A. One Generation. 176p. 1981. 13.95 (ISBN 0-8052-8074-X); pap. 5.95 (ISBN 0-8052-8073-1). Schocken.
Heathers, Anne. Four Puppies. (ps-2). 1960. PLB 5.00 (ISBN 0-307-61405-0, Golden Pr). Western Pub.
Heathfield, David, ed. The Economics of Co-Determination. 1978. text ed. 20.75x (ISBN 0-8419-5029-6). Holmes & Meier.
--Perspectives on Inflation: Models & Policies. (Illus.). 1979. 21.00 (ISBN 0-582-44189-7); pap. 11.95 (ISBN 0-582-44190-0). Longman.
Heathington, Betty S., jt. auth. see Teague, Gerald V.
Heath-Stubbs, John & Wright, David, eds. The Faber Book of Twentieth Century Verse. 3rd ed. 1975. 16.95 (ISBN 0-571-04884-6, Pub. by Faber & Faber); pap. 8.95 (ISBN 0-571-04887-0). Merrimack Bk Serv.
Heaton, Charles L., jt. auth. see Pillsbury, Donald M.
Heaton, Eric W. Hebrew Kingdoms. (New Clarendon Bible Ser.). 1968. 8.95x (ISBN 0-19-836905-0). Oxford U Pr.
Heaton, Israel C. & Thorstenson, Clark T. Planning for Social Recreation. LC 77-85148. (Illus.). 1978. pap. text ed. 11.50 (ISBN 0-395-25052-8). HM.

Heaton, J. B. Beginning Composition Through Pictures. (Illus.). 1975. pap. text ed. 3.25x (ISBN 0-582-55519-1). Longman.

--Composition Through Pictures. 1975. pap. text ed. 3.25x (ISBN 0-582-52125-4). Longman.

--Practice Through Pictures. 1975. pap. text ed. 2.50x (ISBN 0-582-52135-1); teacher's bk. 2.25x (ISBN 0-582-52136-X). Longman.

--Prepositions & Adverbial Particles. 1975. pap. text ed. 5.75x (ISBN 0-582-52121-1). Longman.

--Using Prepositions & Particles. 1975. wkbk. 1 1.75x (ISBN 0-582-52122-X); wkbk. 2 1.75x (ISBN 0-582-52123-8); wkbk. 3 2.00x (ISBN 0-582-52124-6); key 2.50x (ISBN 0-582-52120-3). Longman.

--Writing English Language Tests. 1975. 8.75x (ISBN 0-582-55080-7). Longman.

Heaton, John. Better Athletics-Field. new ed. (Better Books). (Illus.). 96p. (gr. 7 up). 1974. 14.50x o.p. (ISBN 0-7182-0496-4, SpS). Soccer.

--Better Athletics: Field, (With Cross Country & Race Walking) rev. ed. (Better Bks.). (Illus.). 96p. 1980. text ed. 14.50x (ISBN 0-7182-1469-2, SpS). Soccer.

Heaton, Vernon. The Mayflower. (Illus.). 200p. 1980. 19.95 (ISBN 0-8317-5745-0). Mayflower Bks.

Heaton, William P., jt. auth. see Endicott, John E.

Heatter, Basil. Against Odds. 160p. 1970. write for info. (ISBN 0-374-30170-0). FS&G.

Heatter, Justin W. Buying a Condominium. 1981. 10.95 (ISBN 0-938602-01-2); pap. 6.95 (ISBN 0-938602-00-4). Green Hill.

Heatwole, Thelma. Ghost Towns & Historical Haunts in Arizona. (Illus.). 144p. (Orig.). 1981. pap. 4.50 (ISBN 0-914846-10-8). Golden West Pub.

Heavens, O. S. Lasers. LC 72-2053. (Illus.). 168p. 1973. 9.95 o.p. (ISBN 0-684-13399-7, ScribT). Scribner.

Heaver, Constance. The Place of Stones. 1976. pap. 1.50 o.p. (ISBN 0-451-07046-1, W7046, Sig). NAL.

Heavner, Martin L. see Hill, Richard F., et al.

Heavner, Martin L., jt. ed. see Sullivan, Thomas F.

Heavysege, Charles. Saul & Selected Poems. LC 76-17038. (Literature of Canada Ser.). 1976. pap. 7.95 (ISBN 0-8020-6262-8). U of Toronto Pr.

Heavyside, G. T. Narrow Gauge into the Eighties. LC 79-56067. (Illus.). 96p. 1980. 16.95 (ISBN 0-7153-7979-8). David & Charles.

--Steam in the Coalfields. LC 76-54079. (Illus.). 1977. 11.95 (ISBN 0-7153-7323-4). David & Charles.

--Steaming into the Eighties: The Standard Gauge Preservation Scene. 1978. 11.95 (ISBN 0-7153-7513-X). David & Charles.

Hebard, Edna L., jt. auth. see Clurman, David.

Hebart, Friedemann. One in the Gospel. 1981. pap. 4.25 (ISBN 0-570-03830-8, 12-2796). Concordia.

Hebbel, Friedrich. Herodes und Mariamne. Purdie, Edna, ed. 1965. pap. 5.00x o.p. (ISBN 0-631-01330-X, Pub. by Basil Blackwell). Biblio Dist.

--Maria Magdalena. 5th ed. Rees, G. Brychan, ed. 1968. pap. 4.50x o.p. (ISBN 0-631-01350-4, Pub. by Basil Blackwell). Biblio Dist.

Hebbert, Virginia, et al. Social Work Practice: A Philippine Casebook. abr. ed. 312p. 1980. pap. 5.00x (ISBN 0-686-28649-9). Cellar.

Hebblethwaite, B. L. The Problems of Theology. LC 79-41812. 176p. 1980. 21.50 (ISBN 0-521-23104-3); pap. 6.95 (ISBN 0-521-29811-3). Cambridge U Pr.

Hebblethwaite, Brian, jt. ed. see Hick, John.

Hebblethwaite, Paul & Ivins, J., eds. Seed Production. LC 80-40012. (Studies in the Agricultural & Food Sciences). 1980. text ed. 99.95 (ISBN 0-408-10621-2). Butterworths.

Hebblethwaite, Peter. The New Inquisition? The Case of Edward Schillebeeckx & Hans Kung. LC 80-7290. 160p. (Orig.). 1980. pap. 4.95 (ISBN 0-06-063795-1, RD 339, HarpR). Harrow.

--The Runaway Church: Post-Conciliar Growth or Decline. 250p. 1976. 8.95 (ISBN 0-8164-0291-4). Crossroad NY.

Hebblethwaite, Peter, et al. The Vatican. LC 80-50854. (Illus.). 226p. 1980. 50.00 (ISBN 0-86565-002-0). Vendome.

Hebborn, Peter, jt. auth. see Turner, Robert A.

Hebden, John & Shaw, Graham. Pathways to Participation. LC 77-8207. 1977. 24.95 (ISBN 0-470-99196-8). Halsted Pr.

Hebden, Mark. Death Set to Music. 1979. 16.95 (ISBN 0-241-10085-2, Pub. by Hamish Hamilton England). David & Charles.

--Pel & the Faceless Corpse. 1979. 17.95 (ISBN 0-241-10085-2, Pub. by Hamish Hamilton England). David & Charles.

Hebding, Daniel E. & Glick, Leonard. Introduction to Sociology. 2nd ed. (Sociology Ser.). (Illus.). 480p. 1981. pap. text ed. 12.95 (ISBN 0-201-03997-4). A-W.

Hebding, Daniel E., jt. auth. see Glick, Leonard.

Hebditch, David, jt. auth. see Healey, Martin.

Hebeisch, A. & Guthrie, J. T. The Chemistry & Technology of Cellulose Copolymers. (Polymers - Properties & Applications Ser.: Vol. 4). (Illus.). 340p. 1981. 87.30 (ISBN 0-387-10164-0). Springer-Verlag.

Hebeler, Jean R. & Reynolds, Maynard C. Casebook of Professional Practices in Special Education. 1976. pap. text ed. 4.00x o.p. (ISBN 0-86586-009-2). Coun Exc Child.

--Guidelines for Personnel in the Education of Exceptional Children. LC 76-6728. 1976. pap. text ed. 3.50x o.p. (ISBN 0-86586-038-6). Coun Exc Child.

Heber, Reginald. Poems & Translations, Repr. Of 1812 Ed. Reiman, Donald H., ed. Bd. with Hymns, Written & Adapted to the Weekly Church Service of the Year. Repr. of 1827 ed. LC 75-31212. (Romantic Context Ser.: Poetry 1789-1830). 1979. lib. bdg. 47.00 (ISBN 0-8240-2162-2). Garland Pub.

Heber, Rick. Epidemiology of Mental Retardation. (Illus.). 136p. 1970. 11.75 (ISBN 0-398-00817-5). C C Thomas.

Heberden, M. V. Engaged to Murder. LC 80-8412. 224p. 1981. pap. 2.25 (ISBN 0-06-080533-1, P 533, CN). Har-Row.

Heberle, Dave, jt. auth. see Dubbs, Chris.

Heberle, Rudolf. From Democracy to Nazism: A Regional Case Study on Political Parties in Germany. LC 72-80556. 1970. Repr. 13.50 (ISBN 0-86527-076-7). Fertig.

--Social Movements: An Introduction to Political Sociology. (Century Sociology Ser.). (Illus.). 1951. 24.00x o.p. (ISBN 0-89197-414-8); pap. text ed. 4.95x (ISBN 0-89197-415-6). Irvington.

Hebert, Jacques - Rene, ed. Le Pere Duchesne, 1790 - 1794: Reimpression Des 385 Numeros Du Celebre Journal De Jacques - Rene Hebert, 10 vols. (Fr.). 1977. Repr. of 1790 ed. lib. bdg. 687.50x o.p. (ISBN 0-8287-0679-4). Clearwater Pub.

Hebert, Joseph L., ed. Experiences in Zero Base Budgeting. LC 77-23884. 1977. text ed. 15.00 (ISBN 0-89433-033-0). Petrocelli.

Hebert, Raymond G. Florence Nightingale: Saint, Reformer, or Rebel? 120p. 1980. 6.50 (ISBN 0-89874-127-0). Krieger.

Hecht, Anthony, tr. see Aeschylus.

Hecht, Ben. Fantazius Mallare: A Mysterious Oath. LC 78-6637. (Illus.). 1978. pap. 3.95 o.p. (ISBN 0-15-630160-1, Harv). HarBraceJ.

--The Kingdom of Evil: A Continuation of the Journal of Fantazius Mallare. LC 78-7288. (Illus.). 1978. pap. 3.95 o.p. (ISBN 0-15-647123-X, Harv). HarBraceJ.

Hecht, Caroline, jt. auth. see Hecht, Miriam.

Hecht, E. & Zajac, A. Optics. 1974. 24.95 (ISBN 0-201-02835-2). A-W.

Hecht, Helen. Cold Cuisine. LC 80-69374. 1981. 11.95 (ISBN 0-689-11130-4). Atheneum.

Hecht, J. Jean. The Domestic Servant Class in Eighteenth Century England. LC 79-2938. 240p. 1981. Repr. of 1956 ed. 19.50 (ISBN 0-8305-0104-5). Hyperion Conn.

Hecht, M. K., et al, eds. Evolutionary Biology, Vols. 12 & 13. (Illus.). 1980. 32.50 ea. (Plenum Pr). Vol. 12, 388p (ISBN 0-306-40267-X). Vol. 13, 335p (ISBN 0-306-40510-5). Plenum Pub.

Hecht, Marie B. Beyond the Presidency: The Residues of Power. (Illus.). 1976. 15.95 o.s.i. (ISBN 0-02-550190-9). Macmillan.

Hecht, Max K., et al, eds. Evolutionary Biology, Vol. 9. (Illus.). 458p. 1976. 35.00 (ISBN 0-306-35409-8, Plenum Pr). Plenum Pub.

--Evolutionary Biology, Vol. 7. LC 67-11961. (Illus.). 314p. 1974. 27.95 (ISBN 0-306-35407-1, Plenum Pr). Plenum Pub.

Hecht, Miriam & Hecht, Caroline. Modumath: Arithmetic. LC 77-75447. 1978. pap. text ed. 15.25 (ISBN 0-395-24424-2); instr's. manual 0.60 (ISBN 0-395-24421-8). HM.

Hecht, Neil S., jt. auth. see Quint, Emanuel B.

Hecht, Roger. Signposts. LC 74-112873. 56p. 1973. 7.95 (ISBN 0-8040-0277-0); pap. 4.25 (ISBN 0-8040-0639-3). Swallow.

--Twenty Seven Poems. LC 66-20099. 64p. 1966. 5.95 (ISBN 0-8040-0300-9). Swallow.

Hechter, Michael. Internal Colonialism: The Celtic Fringe in British National Development. 1975. 22.75x (ISBN 0-520-02559-8); pap. 6.50x (ISBN 0-520-03512-7). U of Cal Pr.

Hechtle, Ranier, ed. see Reay, Lee.

Hechtlinger, Adelaide. Pelican Guide to Historic Homes & Sites of Revolutinary America. Incl. Vol. 1. New England. (Illus.). 1976. pap. 3.95 (ISBN 0-88289-090-5). LC 76-20434. (Pelican Guide Ser.). Pelican.

Heck, Bessie H. Cave-in at Mason's Mine. LC 80-18637. (Illus.). 64p. (gr. 2-6). 1980. 7.95 (ISBN 0-684-16718-2). Scribner.

--Golden Arrow. (Illus.). 160p. (gr. 5-9). 1981. 8.95 (ISBN 0-684-16882-0). Scribner.

Heck, Carl. Magnetic Materials & Their Applications. LC 73-77001. 1974. 65.00x o.p. (ISBN 0-8448-0206-9). Crane-Russak Co.

Heck, Shirley & Cobes, Jon P. All the Classroom Is a Stage: The Creative Classroom Environment. LC 78-7600. (Illus.). 1978. 18.25 (ISBN 0-08-022248-X); pap. 9.95 (ISBN 0-08-022247-1). Pergamon.

Hecke, Erich. Algebraische Zahlen. 2nd ed. LC 50-3732. (Ger). 1970. 11.95 (ISBN 0-8284-0046-6). Chelsea Pub.

Heckel, Frederick C., ed. see Steiner, Rudolf.

Heckelmann, Charles. The Glory Riders. 1977. pap. 1.25 o.p. (ISBN 0-445-04102-1). Popular Lib.

Heckelmann, Charles N. Deputy Marshall. 1977. pap. 1.25 o.p. (ISBN 0-445-04124-2). Popular Lib.

--Fighting Ramrod. 1977. pap. 1.25 o.p. (ISBN 0-445-04058-0). Popular Lib.

--Hell in His Holsters. 1977. pap. 1.25 o.p. (ISBN 0-445-00447-9). Popular Lib.

--Lawless Range. 1977. pap. 1.25 o.p. (ISBN 0-445-00443-6). Popular Lib.

--Let the Guns Roar. 1977. pap. 1.25 o.p. (ISBN 0-445-08609-2). Popular Lib.

Hecker, Lee, ed. see Wine Advisory Board.

Hecker, Michael, jt. ed. see Darby, John J.

Hecker, W. C., jt. auth. see Rickham, P. P.

Hecker, W. R. Auriculas & Primroses. 1971. 10.50 o.p. (ISBN 0-8231-6033-5). Branford.

Heckerman, Carole L. The Evoning Female: Woman in Psychosocial Context. LC 79-4240. 1979. text ed. 24.95 (ISBN 0-87705-392-8); pap. text ed. 9.95 (ISBN 0-87705-411-8). Human Sci Pr.

Heckert, J. Brooks & Willson, J. D. Controllership. 2nd ed. (Illus.). 1963. 29.50 (ISBN 0-8260-4025-X, Pub. by Ronald Pr); instructors' manual avail. (ISBN 0-685-19872-3, Pub. by Ronald Pr). Ronald Pr.

Heckman, Richard D., jt. auth. see Chambers, Carl D.

Heckmann, Manfred. Corkscrews: An Introduction to Their Appreciation. Sullivan, Maurice, ed. (Illus.). 124p. 1981. 12.95 (ISBN 0-686-69566-6). Wine Appreciation.

Heckner, Fritz. Practical Microscopic Hematology: A Manual for the Clinical Laboratory & Clinical Practice. Lehmann, H. Peter & Yuan Kao, eds. Lehmann, H. L., tr. from Ger. LC 79-28562. (Illus.). 127p. 1980. pap. 19.50 (ISBN 0-8067-0811-5). Urban & S.

Heclo, Hugh. A Government of Strangers: Executive Politics in Washington. LC 76-51882. 1977. 15.95 (ISBN 0-8157-3536-7); pap. 6.95 (ISBN 0-8157-3535-9). Brookings.

Heclo, Hugh & Wildavsky, Aaron. The Private Government of Public Money: Community & Policy in British Political Administration. 1974. 25.75x (ISBN 0-520-02497-4). U of Cal Pr.

Hecquet, Ignace, et al. Recent Student Flows in Higher Education. 189p. (Orig.). 1976. pap. text ed. 5.00 (ISBN 0-89192-313-6). Interbk Inc.

Hector, Derek, jt. auth. see Mathias, Michael.

Hector, M. L. EEG Recording. 2nd ed. LC 79-40117. (Illus.). 1980. text ed. 29.95 (ISBN 0-407-00136-0). Butterworths.

Hector, Winifred. Modern Nursing: Theory & Practice. 6th ed. (Illus.). 1976. 18.95x (ISBN 0-433-14212-X). Intl Ideas.

Hector, Winifred & Bourne, Gordon. Modern Gynaecology with Obstetrics for Nurses. 6th ed. (Illus.). 282p. 1980. pap. 14.95x (ISBN 0-433-14210-3). Intl Ideas.

Hector, Winifred & Malpas, J. S. Textbook of Medicine for Nurses. 3rd ed. (Illus.). 1977. pap. text ed. 19.95x (ISBN 0-433-14214-6). Intl Ideas.

Hedayetullah, Muhammad. Kabir: The Apostle of Hindu-Muslim Unity. 1978. 14.95 (ISBN 0-89684-042-5, Pub. by Motilal Banarsidass India). Orient Bk Dist.

Hedberg, Gregory. German Realism of the Twenties. (Illus.). 1980. 15.00. Minneapolis Inst Arts.

Hedberg, Stephen E., jt. auth. see Welch, Claude E.

Hedblom, Peter, jt. auth. see Grinspoon, Lester.

Hedden, Jay. Modern Plumbing for Old & New Houses. Horowitz, Shirley M., ed. LC 79-26539. (Illus.). 144p. (Orig.). 1980. 12.95 (ISBN 0-932944-13-2); pap. 4.95 (ISBN 0-932944-14-0). Creative Homeowner.

--Successful Shelves & Built-Ins. LC 78-27234. 1979. 13.95 (ISBN 0-912336-77-3); pap. 6.95 (ISBN 0-912336-78-1). Structures Pub.

Hedden, Jay W. Successful Living Rooms. LC 77-26025. (Illus.). 1978. 13.95 (ISBN 0-912336-60-9); pap. 6.95 (ISBN 0-912336-61-7). Structures Pub.

Hedden, Jay W. & Burch, Monte. Making Mediterranean Furniture. LC 72-3336. (Illus.). 1978. pap. 3.95 o.p. (ISBN 0-668-04432-2). Arco.

Hedden, Jay W., jt. auth. see Dean, Thomas Scott.

Hedgecoe, John, ed. John Hedgecoe's Complete Course in Photographing Children. 1980. 14.95 (ISBN 0-671-41220-5). S&S.

Hedgepeth, William B. The Hog Book. LC 76-23766. 1978. pap. 6.95 (ISBN 0-385-11666-7, Dolp). Doubleday.

Hedges, Bob A., jt. auth. see Mehr, Robert I.

Hedges, Elaine & Wendt, Ingrid. In Her Own Image: Women Working in the Arts. (Women's Lives-Women's Work Ser.). (Illus.). 336p. 1980. 16.95 (ISBN 0-912670-73-8); pap. 6.95 (ISBN 0-912670-62-2). Feminist Pr.

Hedges, James B. Browns of Providence Plantations: The Colonial Years. LC 52-5032. (Illus.). 379p. 1968. Repr. of 1952 ed. 15.00 (ISBN 0-87057-109-5, Pub. by Brown U Pr). Univ Pr of New England.

--Browns of Providence Plantations: The Nineteenth Century. LC 68-23790. (Illus.). 325p. 1968. 15.00 (ISBN 0-87057-110-9, Pub. by Brown U Pr). Univ Pr of New England.

Hedges, William L. Washington Irving: An American Study, 1802-1832. LC 80-23564. (The Goucher College Ser.). xiv, 274p. 1980. Repr. of 1965 ed. lib. bdg. 27.50x (ISBN 0-313-21159-0, HEWI). Greenwood.

Hedgpeth, Don. Cowboy. (Illus.). 1979. pap. 12.95 (ISBN 0-8032-6304-X, Buffalo Bill Hist. Ctr.). U of Nebr Pr.

Hedgpeth, Joel W., ed. Outer Shores One: Ed Ricketts & John Steinbeck Explore the Pacific Coast. 1978. pap. 7.95x (ISBN 0-916422-13-5). Mad River.

--Outer Shores Two: Breaking Through. 1979. pap. 9.95x (ISBN 0-916422-14-3). Mad River.

Hediger, H. Psychology & Behavior of Animals in Zoos & Circuses. Sircom, Geoffrey, tr. LC 68-55533. Orig. Title: Skizzen Zu Einer Tiorpsychologie Um und Im Zirkus. 1969. pap. text ed. 3.00 (ISBN 0-486-62218-5). Dover.

--Wild Animals in Captivity: An Outline of the Biology of Zoological Gardens. Sircom, Geoffrey, tr. Orig. Title: Wildtiere -in Gefaengschaft: ein Grundriss -Des Tiergartenbiologie. 1950. pap. text ed. 3.50 (ISBN 0-486-21260-2). Dover.

Hedin, Finn. The Thorians. LC 79-66930. 1980. 6.50 (ISBN 0-533-04423-5). Vantage.

Hedin, Robert. On the Day of the Bulls. 1979. 3.00 (ISBN 0-918116-19-8). Jawbone Pr.

Hedin, Sven. Chiang Kai-Shek: Marshal of China. Norbelle, Bernard, tr. from Swedish. LC 74-31277. (China in the 20th Century Ser). (Illus.). xiv, 290p. 1975. Repr. of 1940 ed. lib. bdg. 22.50 (ISBN 0-306-70690-3). Da Capo.

--Jehol, City of Emperors. LC 79-2827. (Illus.). 278p. 1981. Repr. of 1933 ed. 23.50 (ISBN 0-8305-0005-7). Hyperion Conn.

Hedinger, C. Histological Typing of Thyroid Tumours. (World Health Organization: International Histological Classification of Tumours Ser.). 1974. 18.50 (ISBN 92-4-176011-7, 70-1-011-20); incl. slides 48.50 (ISBN 0-685-77247-0, 70-1-011-00). Am Soc Clinical.

Hedley, John. Harry S. Truman. Cadenhead, I. E., ed. LC 76-54969. (Shapers of History Ser.). 1979. pap. text ed. 16.95 (ISBN 0-8120-5136-X). Barron.

Hedley, Patricia. Overcoming Handicap. pap. 4.50 (ISBN 0-263-05062-9). Transatlantic.

Hedlund, Roger E., ed. World Christianity: South Asia. 320p. 1980. 12.00 (ISBN 0-912552-33-6). MARC.

Hedren, Paul L. First Scalp for Custer: The Skirmish at Warbonnet Creek, Nebraska, July 17, 1876. LC 80-68844. (Hidden Springs of Custeriana Ser.: No. V). (Illus.). 106p. 1981. 38.00 (ISBN 0-87062-137-8). A H Clark.

Hedrick, Anne K., jt. auth. see Hedrick, Basil C.

Hedrick, Basil C. & Hedrick, Anne K. Historical Dictionary of Panama. Wilgus, A. Curtis, ed. (Latin American Historical Dictionaries Ser.: No. 2). 1970. 10.00 (ISBN 0-8108-0347-X). Scarecrow.

Hedrick, Basil C., jt. ed. see Riley, Carroll L.

Hedrick, Basil C., et al. A Bibliography of Nepal. LC 73-10075. 1973. 11.50 (ISBN 0-8108-0649-5). Scarecrow.

Hedrick, Basil C., et al, eds. North Mexican Frontier: Readings in Archaeology, Ethnohistory & Ethnography. LC 70-132477. 271p. 1971. 15.95x (ISBN 0-8093-0489-9). S Ill U Pr.

Hedrick, Charles W. The Apocalypse of Adam: A Literary & Source Analysis. LC 79-26013. (Society of Biblical Literature Dissertation Ser.: No. 46). Date not set. price not set (ISBN 0-89130-369-3, 060146); pap. price not set. Scholars Pr CA.

Hedrick, Hannah. Theo Van Doesburg, Propagandist & Practitioner of the Avant-Garde: Belletristic Activity in Holland, Germany & France, 1909-1923. (Studies in Fine Arts: the Avant-Garde: No. 5). 1980. 23.95x (ISBN 0-8357-1060-2). Univ Microfilms.

Hedrick, T. I., jt. auth. see Hall, Carl W.

Hedvig, Peter. Dielectric Spectroscopy of Polymers. LC 75-9653. 1977. 59.95 (ISBN 0-470-36747-4). Halsted Pr.

--Quantum Effects in Organic Chemistry. 1975. 43.50 (ISBN 0-12-336450-7). Acad Pr.

Hee, Hon-Chew. White Serpent: Hon-Chew Hee's Serigraph. (Illus.). 60p. 1979. pap. 10.50 (ISBN 0-89955-004-5, Pub. by Art Book Co). Intl Schol Bk Serv.

Heenan, Cathy & Cooper, Susan. Preparing, Designing & Leading Workshops: A Humanistic Approach. LC 79-9465. 1979. pap. 10.95 (ISBN 0-8436-0779-3). CBI Pub.

Heenan, David A. & Perlmutter, Howard V. Multinational Organization Development. 1978. pap. text ed. 6.50 (ISBN 0-201-02953-7). A-W.

Heer, C. V. Statistical Mechanics, Kinetic, Theory & Stochastic Process. 1972. 24.95 (ISBN 0-12-336550-3). Acad Pr.

Heer, E. Robots & Manipulator Systems, 2 pts. LC 77-73105. 1977. Pt. 1. pap. text ed. 29.50 (ISBN 0-08-021727-3); Pt. 2. pap. text ed. 29.50 (ISBN 0-08-022681-7). Pergamon.

Heer, Friedrich. The World of Charlemagne. LC 74-22219. (Illus.). 272p. 1975. 19.95 (ISBN 0-02-550450-9, 55045). Macmillan.

Heer, G. H. Zurich. 1973. bds. 7.50 (ISBN 0-911268-26-X). Rogers Bk.

Heerema, Elmer. Progressive Class Piano. LC 79-25220. 1980. pap. 11.50 (ISBN 0-88284-106-8). Alfred Pub.

Heeren, Gatima, jt. auth. see Lemu, B. Aisha.

Heeren, Vern E., jt. auth. see Miller, Charles D.

Heertje, Arnold. Economics & Technical Change. LC 77-76757. 1979. pap. 13.95x (ISBN 0-470-26598-1). Halsted Pr.

Heery, Joseph M., ed. Harris Postage Stamp Catalog: Fall-Winter 1980-1981. (Illus.). 362p. (Orig.). 1980. pap. 2.95 (ISBN 0-937458-02-3). Harris & Co.

--Postage Stamp Price Index U. S. & Canada from 1845: 1980-1981 Edition. (Illus.). 192p. (Orig.). 1980. pap. 2.95 (ISBN 0-937458-01-5). Harris & Co.

Heese, Fred. Canoe Racing. 1979. 12.95 o.p. (ISBN 0-8092-7630-5); pap. 6.95 (ISBN 0-8092-7629-1). Contemp Bks.

Heezen, Bruce C. & Hollister, Charles D. Face of the Deep. 1971. pap. 13.95x (ISBN 0-19-501277-1). Oxford U Pr.

Heffelfinger, Ruth J. Aesop: His Book. 1973. 6.95 (ISBN 0-87018-074-6). Ross.

Heffer, Marjorie & Porter, William. Maggot Pie: Country Dances. 2nd ed. 55p. (Orig.). (gr. 6 up). 1979. pap. 3.00 (ISBN 0-913714-51-8). Legacy Bks.

Hefferlin, J. B. Lon see Lon Hefferlin, JB & Phillips, Ellis L., Jr.

Hefferlin, JB Lon. Dynamics of Academic Reform. LC 76-92895. (Higher Education Ser.). 1969. 13.95x o.p. (ISBN 0-87589-048-2). Jossey-Bass.

Hefferlin, Jonathon. Making Inflation Pay: Jonathon's Guide to Financial Success in the 1980's. 224p. 1981. 10.95 (ISBN 0-936602-09-0). Harbor Pub CA.

Heffern, Richard. The Herb Buyers Guide. (Orig.). pap. 1.50 (ISBN 0-515-04635-3). Jove Pubns.

Heffernan, Charles W. Teaching Children to Read Music. LC 68-55077. (Illus., Orig.). 1968. pap. text ed. 4.95x (ISBN 0-89197-439-3). Irvington.

Heffernan, James A. & Lincoln, John E. Writing: A College Handbook. 1981. text ed. price not set (ISBN 0-393-95150-2); phamphlet free (ISBN 0-393-95163-4). Norton. Postponed.

Heffernan, James M. Educational & Career Services for Adults. LC 79-3279. 1981. write for info. (ISBN 0-669-03440-1). Lexington Bks.

Heffernan, John B., jt. auth. see Cross, Wilbur.

Heffernan, Joseph. Introduction to Social Welfare Policy. LC 78-61882. 1979. text ed. 12.95 (ISBN 0-87581-241-4). Peacock Pubs.

Heffernan, Thomas F. Stove by a Whale: Owen Chase & the Essex. 256p. 1981. 19.95 (ISBN 0-8195-5052-3). Wesleyan U Pr.

Heffernan, William. Caging the Raven. 1981. 12.95 (ISBN 0-671-61056-2, Wyndham Bks). S&S.

Hefferren, John J. & Moller, Mary L., eds. Patterns & Effects of Diet & Disease Today. (AAAS Selected Symposium: No. 59). 225p. 1981. lib. bdg. 18.75x (ISBN 0-89158-844-2). Westview.

Heffley, Anne P., jt. auth. see Greenberg, Florence.

Heffner, Hubert C., et al. Modern Theatre Practice: A Handbook of Play Production. 5th ed. LC 72-89404. (Illus.). 656p. 1973. 21.95 (ISBN 0-13-598805-5). P-H.

Heffner, Richard D., ed. see De Tocqueville, Alexis.

Heffner, Roe-Merrill S., et al, eds. Goethe's Faust. Incl. Vol. I. Introduction, Pts. I & II. 584p. pap. text ed. 9.25 (ISBN 0-299-06874-9, 687); Vol. II. Vocabulary & Notes. 414p. pap. text ed. 8.25 (ISBN 0-299-06884-6, 688). LC 75-12216. 1975. U of Wis Pr.

Heffron, Dan. The Million Dollar Diet Plan. (Illus.). 148p. (Orig.). 1980. pap. 10.00 (ISBN 0-9605104-1-9). Heffron Ent.

Heffron, Floyd N. Evidence for the Patrolman. (Police Science Ser). (Illus.). 192p. 1972. 12.75 (ISBN 0-398-00820-5). C C Thomas.

Hefley, Beryl F., jt. auth. see Swihart, Stanley J.

Hefley, James. How Sweet the Sound. 1981. pap. 2.95 (ISBN 0-8423-1449-0). Tyndale.

Hefley, James & Hefley, Marti. Arabs, Christians, Jews. 1978. 7.95 o.p. (ISBN 0-88270-290-4). Logos.

--The Secret File on John Birch. 1980. pap. 4.95 (ISBN 0-8423-5862-5). Tyndale.

--Unstilled Voices. LC 80-70116. 224p. 1981. 8.95 (ISBN 0-915684-85-3). Christian Herald.

Hefley, James, jt. auth. see Snow, Jimmy.

Hefley, James C. The Youthnappers. 1977. pap. 2.25 o.p. (ISBN 0-88207-754-6). Victor Bks.

Hefley, Marti, jt. auth. see Hefley, James.

Heflin, Edith H. Candle Light. (Contemporary Poets of Dorrance). 68p. 1981. 4.50 (ISBN 0-8059-2779-4). Dorrance.

Hefner, James, jt. ed. see Barnett, Marguerite R.

Hefner, Loretta L., compiled by. The W. P. A. Historical Records Survey: A Guide to the Unpublished Inventories, Indexes, & Transcripts. LC 80-51489. 1980. pap. text ed. 6.00 (ISBN 0-931828-25-2). Soc Am Archivists.

Hefter. One Bear, Two Bears: The Strawberry Number Book. 118p. Date not set. 4.95 (ISBN 0-07-027825-3). McGraw.

--The Strawberry Book of Colors. 120p. Date not set. 4.50 (ISBN 0-07-027826-1). McGraw.

--The Strawberry Look Book. 120p. Date not set. 4.95 (ISBN 0-07-027824-5). McGraw.

Hefter, G. T., jt. ed. see Bond, A. M.

Hefter, Richard & Moskof, Martin S. Christopher's Parade. LC 72-394. (Illus.). 40p. (ps-3). 1972. 5.95 o.s.i. (ISBN 0-8193-0586-3, Four Winds); PLB 5.41 o.s.i. (ISBN 0-8193-0587-1). Schol Bk Serv.

--Everything: An Alphabet, Number, Reading, Counting & Color Identification Bk. LC 72-153656. (Illus.). (gr. k-2). 1971. 5.95 o.s.i. (ISBN 0-8193-0488-3, Four Winds); PLB 5.41 o.s.i. (ISBN 0-8193-0489-1). Schol Bk Serv.

Hefti, M. L., ed. see International Congress of Life Insurance, 13th, Madrid 1979.

Hegar, Kathryn W. It's Everybody's Business: Study Guide & Readings for "Introduction to Business, Third Ed.". 3rd ed. (Illus.). 400p. 1981. 8.95 (ISBN 0-13-506659-X). P-H.

Hegar, Kathy. Study Guide to Accompany Buffa & Pletcher's Understanding Business Today. 1980. pap. 6.95x (ISBN 0-256-02282-8). Irwin.

Hegarty, Christopher & Goldberg, Philip. How to Manage Your Boss. 288p. 1981. 12.95 (ISBN 0-89256-142-4). Rawson Wade.

Hegarty, Seamus & Lucas, Dorothy. Able to Learn? the Pursuit of Culture-Fair Assessment. (General Ser.). 1979. pap. text ed. 10.00x (ISBN 0-85633-173-2, NFER). Humanities.

Hegberg, David. Flash Gordon Novel, 3 vols. Incl. No. 1 (ISBN 0-448-12963-9); No. 2 (ISBN 0-448-17215-1); No. 3 (ISBN 0-448-17231-3). (Flash Gordon Novel Ser.). 208p. 1980. pap. 2.25 (ISBN 0-686-64851-X, Tempo). G&D.

Hegedus, Louis S., jt. auth. see Collman, James P.

Hegel, Friedrich. On Christianity: Early Theological Writings. Knox, tr. 8.50 (ISBN 0-8446-0689-8). Peter Smith.

Hegel, G. W. The Difference Between the Fichtean & Schellingian Systems of Philosophy. Surber, Jere P., tr. from Ger. 1978. pap. text ed. 6.50x (ISBN 0-917930-12-6); lib. bdg. 21.00 (ISBN 0-917930-32-0). Ridgeview.

--Early Theological Writings. Knox, T. M. & Kroner, R., trs. from Ger. (Works in Continental Philosophy Ser). 1971. pap. 6.50x (ISBN 0-8122-1022-0, Pa. Paperbacks). U of Pa Pr.

--Hegel: On Tragedy. Paolucci, Anne & Paolucci, Henry, eds. 448p. (Orig.). 1975. pap. 4.95x o.p. (ISBN 0-06-131869-8, TB1869, Torch). Har-Row.

--Hegel: Phenomenology of Spirit. Miller, A. V. & Findlay, J. N., trs. 1977. 29.50x (ISBN 0-19-824530-0). Oxford U Pr.

--Natural Law. Knox, T. M., tr. from Ger. LC 75-10123. 1975. pap. 3.95x (ISBN 0-8122-1083-2, Pa Paperbks). U of Pa Pr.

--The Phenomenology of Mind. Baillie, J. B., tr. 1967. pap. 8.95x (ISBN 0-06-131303-3, TB 1303, Torch). Har-Row.

--Philosophy of Right. Knox, T. M., tr. 1942. 31.00x (ISBN 0-19-824128-3); pap. 6.95x (ISBN 0-19-500276-8). Oxford U Pr.

Hegel, Georg W. The Christian Religion. Lasson, Georg, ed. Hodgson, Peter C., tr. from Ger. LC 79-424. (American Academy of Religion, Texts & Translation Ser.: No. 2). Orig. Title: Vorlesungen Uber Die Philosophie der Religion. 1979. 13.50 (ISBN 0-89130-276-X, 010202); pap. 9.00 (ISBN 0-89130-351-0). Scholars Pr Ca.

--The Geographical Basis of History. Rittenhouse, George A., ed. (The Most Meaningful Classics in World Culture Ser.). (Illus.). 1979. 39.75 (ISBN 0-89266-198-4). Am Classical Coll Pr.

--Lectures on the Philosophy of History. Sibree, J., tr. 1956. pap. text ed. 4.50 (ISBN 0-486-20112-0). Dover.

--Lectures on the Philosophy of World History: Reason in History. Forbes, D. & Nisbet, H. B., eds. (Cambridge Studies in the History & Theory of Politics). 290p. (Ger.). 1981. pap. 12.95 (ISBN 0-521-28145-8). Cambridge U Pr.

--The Life of the Mind in Representational Charts. Gary, Charles E., ed. (Illus.). 1979. 37.75 (ISBN 0-89266-202-6). Am Classical Coll Pr.

--The Metaphysics of the Jewish, the Aegyptian & the Assyrian Spirit. (Illus.). 109p. 1981. 41.75 (ISBN 0-89266-280-8). Am Classical Coll Pr.

--The Philosophical Essence of the Oriental World. (The Most Meaningful Classics in World Culture Ser.). 1979. 49.75 (ISBN 0-89266-176-3). Am Classical Coll Pr.

--Philosophy & the Oriental Mind. (Illus.). 1980. 49.75 (ISBN 0-89266-212-3). Am Classical Coll Pr.

--Reason in History: A General Introduction to the Philosophy of History. Hartman, Robert S., tr. LC 53-4476. 1953. pap. 3.95 (ISBN 0-672-60200-8, LLA35). Bobbs.

--The Static & the Dynamic Philosophy of History & the Metaphysics of Reason. 1977. 37.50 (ISBN 0-89266-052-X). Am Classical Coll Pr.

Hegel, Robert E. The Novel in Seventeenth-Century China. (Illus.). 320p. 1981. 20.00x (ISBN 0-231-04928-5). Columbia U Pr.

Hegel Society of America Conference, 1976. Hegel's Social & Political Thought: The Philosophy of Objective Spirit Proceedings of the 1976th Hegel Society of America. Verene, Donald P., ed. LC 77-26183. 1980. text ed. 17.50x (ISBN 0-391-00543-X). Humanities.

Heger, Heinz. The Men with the Pink Triangle. Fernbach, David, tr. LC 80-69205. (Illus.). 120p. (Orig.). 1980. pap. 4.95 (ISBN 0-932870-06-6). Carrier Pigeon.

Heger, Joel. Cardiology for the House Officer. (House Officer Ser.). (Illus.). 200p. 1981. price not set softcover (ISBN 0-683-03946-6). Williams & Wilkins.

Heggelund, Per O., jt. auth. see Sullivan, Jeremiah J.

Heggie, Douglas C. Megalithic Science: Ancient Mathematics & Science in Northwest Europe. (Illus.). 256p. 1981. 27.50 (ISBN 0-500-05036-8). Thames Hudson.

Heggie, I. G., jt. auth. see Rothenberg, J.

Heggie, I. G., jt. ed. see Rothenberg, J. G.

Heggie, Ian G. Model Choice & the Value of Travel Time. (Illus.). 1976. 24.00x (ISBN 0-19-828404-7). Oxford U Pr.

Heggoy, Alf A. & Crout, Robert R. Historical Dictionary of Algeria. LC 80-24126. (African Historical Dictionaries Ser.: No. 28). x, 247p. 1981. 13.50 (ISBN 0-8108-1376-9). Scarecrow.

Heggoy, Alf A. & Cooke, James J., eds. Proceedings of the Fourth Meeting of the French Colonial Historical Society. LC 79-63751. 1979. pap. text ed. 9.50 (ISBN 0-8191-0738-7). U Pr of Amer.

Hegi, Ursula. Intrusions. 288p. 1981. 12.95 (ISBN 0-670-40065-3). Viking Pr.

Heginbotham, Stanley J. Cultures in Conflict: The Four Faces of Indian Bureaucracy. LC 74-31206. 352p. 1975. 17.50x (ISBN 0-231-03888-7). Columbia U Pr.

Heglar, Mary S. Grand Prix Champions. (Illus.). 1973. 7.95 (ISBN 0-87880-014-X). Norton.

Hegner, jt. auth. see Caldwell.

Hegner, Barbara, jt. auth. see Caldwell, Esther.

Hegner, Robert W. Parade of the Animal Kingdom. (Illus.). (gr. 7 up). 1967. 19.95 (ISBN 0-02-550660-9). Macmillan.

Hegre, T. A. Cross & Santification. LC 51-7866. Orig. Title: Three Aspects of the Cross. 1960. pap. 3.50 (ISBN 0-87123-067-4, 210067). Bethany Fell.

--How to Find Freedom from the Power of Sin. 1969. pap. 1.75 (ISBN 0-87123-217-0, 200217). Bethany Fell.

Hegwood, Mamie. My Friend Fish. LC 75-5822. (Illus.). (gr. 1-4). 1975. reinforced bdg. 4.95 o.p. (ISBN 0-03-014731-X). HR&W.

Hegyeli, Ruth J., ed. Measurement & Control of Cardiovascular Risk Factors. (Atherosclerosis Reviews: Vol. 7). 1979. 36.50 (ISBN 0-89004-396-5). Raven.

--Prostaglandins & Cardiovascular Disease. (Atherosclerosis Reviews: Vol. 8). 220p. 1980. text ed. 25.00 (ISBN 0-89004-516-X). Raven.

Hegyi, Erzsebet. Solfege According to the Kodaly Concept, Vol. I. Macnicol, Fred, tr. from Hungarian. LC 75-21981. (Illus.). 429p. 1975. 24.00 (ISBN 0-913932-09-4). Boosey & Hawkes.

Heher, J. M., ed. Great American Writers: Program Guide, Vol. 1. 100p. (gr. 9-12). 1980. pap. text ed. 7.95 (ISBN 0-667-00601-X). Microfilming Corp.

Hehn, Victor. Cultivated Plants & Domesticated Animals in Their Migration from Asia to Europe: Historico-Linguistic Studies. (Amsterdam Classics in Linguistics Ser.: No. 7). 1979. text ed. 71.25x (ISBN 90-272-0871-9). Humanities.

Hehner, Nels E. Storage Battery Manufacturing Manual. 2nd ed. 1976. 30.00 (ISBN 0-685-65141-X). IBMA Pubns.

Hehner, Nels E. & Ritchie, Everett J. Grid Metal Manual for Storage Batteries. (Avail. in eng. & span.). 1973. 15.00 (ISBN 0-685-56652-8). IBMA Pubns.

--Lead Oxides: Chemistry, Technology, Battery Manufacturing Uses, History. 1974. 15.00 (ISBN 0-685-56653-6). IBMA Pubns.

Heib, Elizabeth A., ed. Collection of Employer Contributions Institute, Las Vegas, Nevada, June 15 to 18, 1980: Proceedings. 77p. (Orig.). 1980. pap. 8.00 (ISBN 0-89154-138-1). Intl Found Employ.

Heib, Elizabeth A., jt. ed. see Brennan, Mary E.

Heiberg, Milton. Amphoto Pocket Companion: Yashica FR, FR-I & FR-II. (Illus.). 128p. 1980. spiral bdg. 4.95 (ISBN 0-8174-5534-5). Amphoto.

Heichelheim, Fritz M. & Yeo, C. A. History of the Roman People. 1962. text ed. 19.95 (ISBN 0-13-392126-3). P-H.

Heid, J. L., jt. auth. see Joslyn, Maynard A.

Heid, John L. & Joslyn, Maynard A. Fundamentals of Food Processing Operations: Ingredients, Methods & Packaging. (Illus.). 1967. 25.00 (ISBN 0-87055-014-4). AVI.

Heidbreder, Edna. Seven Psychologies. (Orig.). 1963. pap. 12.95 (ISBN 0-13-807354-6). P-H.

Heide, Florence P. Benjamin Budge & Barnaby Ball. (Illus.). (gr. k-3). 1970. pap. 1.25 (ISBN 0-590-02353-5, Schol Pap); pap. 3.50 bk. & record (ISBN 0-590-04397-8). Schol Bk Serv.

--By the Time You Count to Ten. 1981. pap. 3.50 (ISBN 0-570-07797-4, 56-1335). Concordia.

--Giants Are Very Brave People. LC 75-93857. (gr. k-3). 1970. 5.95 o.s.i. (ISBN 0-8193-0370-4, Four Winds); PLB 5.41 o.s.i. (ISBN 0-8193-0371-2). Schol Bk Serv.

--The Shrinking of Treehorn. (gr. k-3). 1979. pap. 1.75 (ISBN 0-440-47684-4, YB). Dell.

--Sound of Sunshine, Sound of Rain. LC 77-117555. (Illus.). (gr. k-3). 1970. 5.95 o.s.i. (ISBN 0-8193-0422-0, Four Winds); PLB 5.41 o.s.i. (ISBN 0-8193-0423-9). Schol Bk Serv.

--Who Taught Me. (Concept Ser. II). (Illus.). (gr. 1-4). 1978. pap. 3.50 (ISBN 0-570-07786-9, 56-1309). Concordia.

--You & Me. (Illus.). 32p. (gr. k-4). 1975. 6.95 (ISBN 0-570-03436-1, 56-1267). Concordia.

Heide, Florence P. & Heide, Roxanne. Black Magic at Brillstone. Fay, Ann, ed. (Pilot Bks.). 128p. (gr. 4-9). 1981. 6.95 (ISBN 0-8075-0782-2). A Whitman.

--Body in the Brillstone Garage. Anne, Fay, ed. LC 79-18368. (Pilot Bks.). (gr. 4-9). 1980. 6.95g (ISBN 0-8075-0825-X). A Whitman.

--Brillstone Break-in. Rubin, Caroline, ed. LC 77-2220. (Pilot Bks). (Illus.). (gr. 4-8). 1977. 6.95g (ISBN 0-8075-0888-8). A Whitman.

--The Face at the Brillstone Window. Pucini, Kathy, ed. LC 78-15060. (Pilot Bks). (Illus.). (gr. 4-9). 1979. 6.95g (ISBN 0-8075-2216-3). A Whitman.

--A Monster Is Coming! a Monster Is Coming! (gr. k-3). 1980. 3.95 (ISBN 0-531-03449-6); PLB 6.45 (ISBN 0-531-04136-0). Watts.

--Mystery at Keyhole Carnival. Rubin, Caroline, ed. LC 76-45426. (Spotlight Club Mysteries & Pilot Bks). (Illus.). (gr. 3-8). 1976. 6.95g (ISBN 0-8075-5361-1). A Whitman.

--Mystery at Southport Cinema. Pacini, Kathy, ed. LC 78-1300. (Spotlight Club Mysteries & Pilot Bks.). (Illus.). (gr. 3-8). 1978. 6.95g (ISBN 0-8075-5363-8). A Whitman.

--The Mystery of the Bewitched Bookmobile. LC 75-6763. (Pilot Bks. - Spotlight Club Mysteries Ser.). (gr. 3-8). 1975. 6.95g (ISBN 0-8075-5375-1). A Whitman.

--Mystery of the Forgotten Island. Tucker, Kathleen, ed. LC 79-18367. (Spotlight Club Mysteries & Pilot Bks.). (Illus.). (gr. 3-8). 1980. 6.95g (ISBN 0-8075-5376-X). A Whitman.

--The Mystery of the Lonely Lantern. Rubin, Caroline, ed. LC 76-28537. (Spotlight Club Mysteries-Pilot Bks). (Illus.). 128p. 1976. 6.95g (ISBN 0-8075-5377-8). A Whitman.

--Mystery of the Melting Snowman. LC 74-16333. (Spotlight Club Mysteries & Pilot Books Ser.). (Illus.). 128p. (gr. 3-8). 1974. 6.95g (ISBN 0-8075-5378-6). A Whitman.

--Mystery of the Midnight Message. Rubin, Caroline, ed. LC 77-14382. (Spotlight Club Mysteries & Pilot Books Ser.). (Illus.). (gr. 3-8). 1977. 6.95g (ISBN 0-8075-5381-6). A Whitman.

--Mystery of the Mummy Mask. Pacini, Kathy, ed. LC 78-31728. (Spotlight Club Mysteries & Pilot Bks.). (Illus.). (gr. 3-8). 1979. 6.95g (ISBN 0-8075-5384-0). A Whitman.

--The Mystery of the Vanishing Visitor. Rubin, Caroline, ed. LC 75-33634. (Pilot Books-Spotlight Club Mysteries Ser.). (Illus.). 128p. (gr. 3-8). 1975. 6.95g (ISBN 0-8075-5388-3). A Whitman.

Heide, Florence P. & Van Clief, Sylvia. Hidden Box Mystery. LC 72-13351. (Pilot Bks. - Spotlight Club Mysteries Ser.). (Illus.). 128p. (gr. 3-6). 1973. 6.95g (ISBN 0-8075-3270-3). A Whitman.

--Mystery at Macadoo Zoo. LC 73-7316. (Pilot Bks. - Spotlight Club Mysteries Ser.). (Illus.). 128p. (gr. 3-7). 1973. 6.95g (ISBN 0-8075-5358-1). A Whitman.

--The Mystery of the Missing Suitcase. LC 72-83683. (Pilot Bks. - Spotlight Club Mysteries Ser.). (Illus.). 128p. (gr. 3-8). 1972. 6.95g (ISBN 0-8075-5382-4). A Whitman.

--Mystery of the Silver Tag. LC 75-188429. (Pilot Bks. - Spotlight Club Mysteries Ser.). (Illus.). 128p. (gr. 3-7). 1972. 6.95g (ISBN 0-8075-5387-5). A Whitman.

--Mystery of the Whispering Voice. LC 74-8511. (Pilot Bks. - Spotlight Club Mysteries Ser.). (Illus.). 128p. (gr. 3-7). 1974. 6.95g (ISBN 0-8075-5389-1). A Whitman.

Heide, Florence P., et al. Fear at Brillstone. LC 78-1307. (Pilot Bks.). (gr. 4-9). 1978. 6.95g (ISBN 0-8075-2304-6). A Whitman.

Heide, Fritz. Meteorites. Anders, Edward & DuFresne, Eugene, eds. (Illus.). 1964. 6.50x o.s.i. (ISBN 0-226-32338-2). U of Chicago Pr.

Heide, Roxanne, jt. auth. see Heide, Florence P.

Heidegger, Martin. Being & Time. LC 72-78334. 1962. 19.95 (ISBN 0-06-063850-8, HarpR). Har-Row.

--Piety of Thinking: Essays. Hart, James G. & Maraldo, John C., eds. LC 75-3889. (Studies in Phenomenology & Existential Philosophy). 224p. 1976. 10.95x (ISBN 0-253-34498-0). Ind U Pr.

Heidemann, R. Export Marketing German. 1978. pap. text ed. 7.95 (ISBN 0-582-35158-8); cassettes 30.00x (ISBN 0-582-37374-3). Longman.

Heidenheimer, Arnold J. & Elvander, Nile, eds. The Shaping of the Swedish Health System. LC 80-12410. 256p. 1980. write for info. (ISBN 0-312-71627-3). St Martin.

Heidenheimer, Arnold J., jt. ed. see Flora, Peter.

Heidenreich, Alfred. The Book of Revelation. 1977. 12.50 (ISBN 0-903540-03-7, Pub. by Floris Books); pap. 7.50 (ISBN 0-903540-04-5). St George Bk Serv.

--Growing Point. (Illus.). 15.75 (ISBN 0-903540-17-7, Pub. by Floris Books). St George Bk Serv.

--Healings in the Gospels. 1980. pap. 7.25 (ISBN 0-903540-36-3, Pub. Floris Books). St George Bk Serv.

Heidenreich, Steve & Dorr, Dave. Running Back. 1979. 11.95 (ISBN 0-8015-6494-8, Hawthorn). Dutton.

Heidensohn, K., jt. auth. see Farquhar, J. D.

Heidenstem, Oscar. Modern Health & Figure Culture. (Illus.). 1960. 6.50 (ISBN 0-571-03850-6, Pub. by Faber & Faber). Merrimack Bk Serv.

Heider, Karl G. Ethnographic Film. LC 76-10454. (Illus.). 1976. text ed. 6.95x (ISBN 0-292-72020-3); pap. text ed. 5.95x (ISBN 0-292-72025-4). U of Tex Pr.

Heider, M. W. Von see Von Heider, W. M.

Heider, W. M. Von see Von Heider, W. M.

Heiderich, Birgit. Mit Geschlossenen Augen: Ein Tagebuch. (Suhrkamp Taschenbuecher: No. 638). 144p. (Orig.). 1980. pap. text ed. 4.55 (ISBN 3-518-37138-X, Pub. by Insel Verlag Germany). Suhrkamp.

Heidi, Gloria. Winning the Age Game. 1977. pap. 6.95 (ISBN 0-89104-061-7). A & W Pubs.

Heidingsfield, Myron S. & Blankenship, Albert B. Marketing. 3rd ed. 1974. pap. 3.95 (ISBN 0-06-460157-9, CO 157, COS). Har-Row.

Heidish, Marcy M. Witnesses. 1981. lib. bdg. 13.95 (ISBN 0-8161-3159-7, Large Print Bks). G K Hall.

Heidmann, J. Relativistic Cosmology: An Introduction. (Illus.). 168p. 1980. pap. 24.80 (ISBN 0-387-10138-1). Springer-Verlag.

Heidolph, Karl E., jt. ed. see Bierwisch, Manfred.

Heidt, Patricia, jt. auth. see Borelli, Marianne.

Heidtmann, Frank, et al, eds. German Photographic Literature, Eighteen Thirty-Nine to Nineteen Seventy-Eight: Theory, Technology, Visual. A Classified Bibliography of German-Language Photographic Publications. 690p. 1980. 85.00 (ISBN 3-598-10026-4, Dist. by Gale Research Co.). K G Saur.

Heier, K. S., jt. auth. see Killeen, P. G.

Heifetz, Milton D. & Mangel, Charles. The Right to Die. pap. 1.95 o.p. (ISBN 0-425-03151-9). Berkley Pub.

Height, Frank, ed. Design for Passenger Transport. new ed. (Illus.). 1979. text ed. 32.00 (ISBN 0-08-023735-5). Pergamon.

Height, Frank, jt. ed. see Gorman, Michael.

Heikal, Mohamed. The Road to Ramadan. 1976. pap. 1.95 o.p. (ISBN 0-345-25351-5). Ballantine.

Heikkinen, Henry, jt. ed. see Gardner, Marjorie.

Heil, Anne R., jt. auth. see Marquis, Thomas B.

Heil, John. Logic & Language: An Introduction to Elementary Logic & the Theory of Linguistic Descriptions. 1978. pap. text ed. 16.75x (ISBN 0-8191-0396-9). U Pr of Amer.

Heilbron, Bertha L. The Thirty-Second State: A Pictorial History of Minnesota. LC 54-14431. (Illus.). 306p. 1978. pap. 7.50 (ISBN 0-87351-130-1). Minn Hist.

Heilbron, J. L. Electricity in the Seventeenth & Eighteenth Centuries: A Study of Early Modern Physics. 1979. 46.75x (ISBN 0-520-03478-3). U of Cal Pr.

Heilbron, J. L. & Wheaton, B. R. Literature on the General History of Physics in the First Half of the 20th Century. LC 80-51580. (Berkeley Papers in the History of Science: No. V). (Orig.). 1981. pap. write for info. (ISBN 0-918102-05-7). U Cal Hist Sci Tech.

Heilbron, J. L., jt. auth. see Shumaker, Wayne.

Heilbron, John L. H. G. J. Moseley: The Life & Letters of an English Physicist, 1887-1915. 1974. 25.00x (ISBN 0-520-02375-7). U of Cal Pr.

Heilbron, Louis H. The College & University Trustee. LC 72-5888. (Higher Education Ser). 288p. 1973. 14.95x o.p. (ISBN 0-87589-196-9). Jossey-Bass.

Heilbroner, R. & Thorou, L. Understanding Microeconomics. 5th ed. 1981. pap. 10.95 (ISBN 0-13-936567-2); pap. 7.95 study guide (ISBN 0-13-233296-5). P-H.

Heilbroner, R. L. & London, P. Corporate Social Policy: Selections from Business & Society Review. 1975. pap. 10.95 (ISBN 0-201-04360-2). A-W.

Heilbroner, Robert L. Beyond Boom & Crash. 1978. 6.95 (ISBN 0-393-05707-0); pap. 2.95x (ISBN 0-393-95003-4). Norton.

--The Great Ascent. LC 62-17086. 1963. 8.95 o.s.i. (ISBN 0-06-011810-5, HarpT). Har-Row.

--An Inquiry into the Human Prospect. 1979. 8.95 (ISBN 0-393-01256-5). Norton.

--The Making of Economic Society. 6th ed. (Illus.). 1980. pap. text ed. 11.95 (ISBN 0-13-545830-7). P-H.

Heilbroner, Robert L. & Thurow, Lester C. The Economic Problem. 5th rev. ed. (Illus.). 1978. ref. ed. 19.95 (ISBN 0-13-233338-4); student companion 8.95 (ISBN 0-13-233353-8). P-H.

--Understanding Macroeconomics. 6th ed. LC 77-28332. Orig. Title: The Economic Problem. 1978. pap. 10.95 ref. ed. (ISBN 0-13-936575-3). P-H.

--Understanding Microeconomics. 4th ed. LC 77-26296. 1978. pap. 10.95 ref. ed. (ISBN 0-13-936583-4). P-H.

Heilbrun, Alfred B., Jr. Human Sex-Role Behavior. (Pergamon General Psychology Ser.). 250p. 1981. 23.01 (ISBN 0-08-025974-X). Pergamon.

Heilbrun, Carolyn. Christopher Isherwood. LC 73-126543. (Columbia). (Orig.). 1970. pap. 2.00 (ISBN 0-231-03257-9, MW53). Columbia U Pr.

--Reinventing Womanhood. 248p. 1981. pap. 4.95 (ISBN 0-393-00997-1). Norton.

Heilbrun, James. Real Estate Taxes & Urban Housing. LC 66-20489. 1966. 15.00x (ISBN 0-231-02821-0). Columbia U Pr.

Heilbrunn, L. V. Viscosity of Protoplasm. (Protoplasmatologia: Vol. 2, Pt. C1). (Illus.). 1958. pap. 32.50 o.p. (ISBN 0-387-80485-4). Springer-Verlag.

Heilbrunn, Otto. The Soviet Secret Services. LC 80-27994. 216p. 1981. Repr. of 1956 ed. lib. bdg. 21.75x (ISBN 0-313-22892-2, HESSE). Greenwood.

Heiles, Carl E. Radioastronomy: Extremes of the Universe. 375p. pap. text ed. 12.00x (ISBN 0-935702-06-7). Univ Sci Bks.

Heiliger, Wilhelm S. Soviet and Chinese Personalities. LC 80-1383. 221p. 1980. lib. bdg. 17.75 (ISBN 0-8191-1213-5); pap. text ed. 9.50 (ISBN 0-8191-1214-3). U Pr of Amer.

Heilman. A Handbook for Differential Diagnosis of Neurologic Signs & Symptoms. (Illus.). 1977. pap. text ed. 12.95 (ISBN 0-8385-3617-4). ACC.

Heilman, ed. see Hull, Marion A.

Heilman, Arthur, ed. see Gilliland, Hap.

Heilman, Arthur, et al. Principles & Practices of Teaching Reading. 5th ed. (Illus.). 544p. 1981. text ed. 16.95 (ISBN 0-675-08150-5); instr's. manual 3.75 (ISBN 0-686-69498-8). Merrill.

Heilman, Arthur W. Phonics in Proper Perspective. 3rd ed. (Elementary Education Ser.). 144p. 1976. pap. text ed. 7.50x (ISBN 0-675-08681-7). Merrill.

--Principles & Practices of Teaching Reading. 4th ed. (Elementary Education Ser.). 1977. text ed. 17.95 (ISBN 0-675-08537-3). Merrill.

Heilman, Arthur W. & Holmes, Eliazbeth A. Smuggling Language into the Teaching of Reading. 2nd ed. (Elementary Education Ser.). 1978. pap. text ed. 8.95x (ISBN 0-675-08360-5). Merrill.

Heilman, Arthur W., ed. see Mangrum, Charles T. & Forgan, Harry W.

Heilman, Arthur W., ed. see Pflaum-Connor, Susanna.

Heilman, Arthur W., ed. see Shepherd, David L.

Heilman, Joan, jt. auth. see Eden, Alvin N.

Heilman, Joan R., jt. auth. see Eden, Alvin N.

Heilman, Robert B. Magic in the Web: Action and Language in Othello. LC 56-6993. 304p. 1969. pap. 4.50 o.p. (ISBN 0-8131-0122-0). U Pr of Ky.

Heilman, Robert L., jt. auth. see Ashby, Gordon P.

Heilmeyer, L., ed. see Begemann, H. & Rastetter, J.

Heilpern, John, ed. see Klein, William.

Heim, A. W. Appraisal of Intelligence. 1970. pap. text ed. 12.50x (ISBN 0-901225-62-2, NFER). Humanities.

Heim, Alice. Teaching & Learning in Higher Education. (General Ser.). (Orig.). 1976. pap. text ed. 13.25x (ISBN 0-85633-094-9, NFER). Humanities.

Heim, Michael H., tr. see Karlinsky, Simon.

Heim, Ralph D. Harmony of the Gospels. LC 47-2807. 228p. 1974. pap. 4.95 (ISBN 0-8006-1494-1, 1-1494). Fortress.

Heiman, Grover, Jr. Aerial Photography: The Story of Aerial Mapping & Reconnaissance. (U. S. Air Force Academy Ser.). (Illus.). 192p. 1972. 5.95 o.s.i. (ISBN 0-02-550770-2). Macmillan.

Heiman, J., et al. Becoming Orgasmic: A Sexual Growth Program for Women. 1976. text ed. 11.95 (ISBN 0-13-072652-4, Spec); pap. text ed. 5.95 (ISBN 0-13-072645-1). P-H.

Heimann, Jim, jt. auth. see Georges, Rip.

Heimann, Sue. Christopher Columbus. LC 72-10402. (Visual Biography Ser). (Illus.). 64p. (gr. 4-5). 1973. PLB 4.90 o.p. (ISBN 0-531-00971-8); pap. 1.95 o.p. (ISBN 0-531-02707-4). Watts.

Heimann, Susan, jt. auth. see Edison, Michael.

Heimann, Werner. Fundamentals of Food Chemistry. american ed. (Illus.). 1980. pap. text ed. 30.00 (ISBN 0-87055-356-9). AVI.

Heimer, Ralph T. & Trueblood, Cecil R. Strategies for Teaching Children Mathematics. LC 76-20030. 1977. text ed. 16.95 (ISBN 0-201-02882-4). A-W.

Heimer, Roger C. A Pioneer Family in Colonial Pennsylvania. 144p. 1979. 6.95 (ISBN 0-8059-2588-0). Dorrance.

Heimerdinger, J. Sumerian Literary Fragments from Nippur. (Occasional Pubns. of the Babylonian Fund Ser.: Vol. 4). 1980. 20.00 (ISBN 0-934718-31-8). Univ Mus of U PA.

Heimert, Alan & Miller, Perry, eds. The Great Awakening: Documents Illustrating the Crisis & Its Consequences. LC 66-23537. 1967. 24.50x (ISBN 0-672-50977-6). Irvington.

Heimert, Alan E. & Miller, Perry, eds. Great Awakening: Documents Illustrating the Crisis & Its Consequences. LC 66-23537. (Orig.). 1967. pap. 9.95 (ISBN 0-672-60044-7, AHS34). Bobbs.

Heimler, Eugene. Survival in Society. LC 74-12871. 159p. 1975. 11.95 o.p. (ISBN 0-470-36901-9). Halsted Pr.

Heimlich, Richard A., jt. auth. see Feldmann, Rodney M.

Heimovics, Rachel B. Chicago Jewish Source Book. 336p. 1981. pap. 6.95 (ISBN 0-695-81568-7). Follett.

Heimpel, H., et al, eds. Aplastic Anemia. (Illus.). 290p. 1980. pap. 36.50 (ISBN 0-387-09772-4). Springer-Verlag.

Heimstra, Norman W. Injury Control in Traffic Safety. 256p. 1970. 12.75 (ISBN 0-398-00823-X). C C Thomas.

Hein, Leonard. Quantitative Approach to Managerial Decisions. 1967. 17.95 o.p. (ISBN 0-13-746800-8). P-H.

Hein, Lucille. From Sea to Shining Sea. LC 75-11839. 32p. (gr. 4-8). 1975. 4.95 o.p. (ISBN 0-8170-0681-8). Judson.

Hein, Lucille E. Thank You, God. (Illus.). 32p. 1981. pap. 3.50 (ISBN 0-8170-0912-4). Judson.

Hein, Marvin. Like a Shock of Wheat. LC 80-22224. 192p. 1981. pap. 7.95 (ISBN 0-8361-1938-X). Herald Pr.

Hein, Morris. Foundations of College Chemistry: The Alternate Edition. LC 80-259. 1980. text ed. 12.95 (ISBN 0-8185-0402-1). Brooks-Cole.

Hein, Morris & Best, Leo. College Chemistry: An Introduction to Inorganic, Organic & Biochemistry. LC 80-257. 1980. text ed. 19.95 (ISBN 0-8185-0349-1). Brooks-Cole.

Hein, Morris, et al. Foundations of Chemistry in the Laboratory. 4th ed. (Orig.). 1977. pap. 10.95x (ISBN 0-8221-0206-4). Dickenson.

Hein, Ruth, tr. see Buchheim, Hans.

Hein, Ruth, tr. see Vandenberg, Philipp.

Heinberg, John D. The Transfer Cost of a Housing Allowance: Conceptual Issues & Benefit Patterns. 80p. 1971. pap. 2.50 o.p. (ISBN 0-87766-068-9, 30004). Urban Inst.

Heinberg, John D., jt. auth. see Carlson, David B.

Heindel, Ned D., et al, eds. The Chemistry of Radiopharmaceuticals. 3rd ed. LC 77-94827. (Cancer Management Ser.). (Illus.). 1978. 37.75 (ISBN 0-89352-019-5). Masson Pub.

Heine, Heinrich. Poems. Webber, Kathleen, ed. 1952. pap. 9.95x (ISBN 0-631-01550-7, Pub. by Basil Blackwell). Biblio Dist.

Heine, Helme. Merry-Go-Round. 26p. (gr. 1-6). 1980. 4.95 (ISBN 0-8120-5393-1). Barron.

--Mr. Miller the Dog. LC 80-81298. (Illus.). 64p. (gr. 1 up). 1980. 8.95 (ISBN 0-689-50174-9, McElderry). Atheneum.

Heine, Irwin M. The U. S. Maritime Industry in the National Interest: A Comprehensive History & Statistical Reference. 1981. pap. 11.95 (ISBN 0-87491-518-X). Acropolis.

Heine, John A., jt. auth. see Kolevzon, Edward R.

Heine, V. Group Theory in Quantum Mechanics. 1963. 30.00 (ISBN 0-08-009242-X). Pergamon.

Heinecken, Robert F. Heinecken. Enyeart, James L., ed. & pref. by. LC 80-69559. (Illus.). 160p. 1981. 75.00 (ISBN 0-933286-19-8). Friends Photography.

Heinegg, Peter, jt. auth. see Holl, Adolf.

Heinegg, Peter, tr. see Hasler, August B.

Heineke, J. Microeconomics for Business Decisions: Theory & Application. 1976. text ed. 16.95 (ISBN 0-13-581389-1). P-H.

Heinemaann, M. Edith, jt. auth. see Estes, Nada J.

Heineman, John. Human Nutrition the Value of Herbs. Date not set. cancelled (ISBN 0-89557-018-1). Bi World Indus.

Heineman, John L. Hitler's First Foreign Minister: Constantin Freiherr von Neurath. 1980. 30.00x (ISBN 0-520-03442-2). U of Cal Pr.

Heinemann, Edward H. & Rausa, Rosario. Ed Heinemann: Combat Aercraft Designer. LC 79-87869. (Illus.). 296p. 1980. 18.95 (ISBN 0-87021-264-8). Naval Inst Pr.

Heiner, Carol W. & Hendrix, Wayne R. People Create Technology. LC 79-53802. (Technology Séries). (Illus.). 256p. (gr. 5-9). 1980. text ed. 12.95 (ISBN 0-87192-109-X, 000-2); tchr's guide 10.60 (ISBN 0-87192-111-1); activity manual 4.95 (ISBN 0-87192-110-3). Davis Pubns.

Heinerman, John. The Science of Herbal Medicine. pap. 15.95 (ISBN 0-89557-044-0). Bi World Indus.

--The Treatment of Cancer with Herbs. 1980. 12.95 (ISBN 0-89557-047-5). Bi World Indus.

Heines, Donald S., ed. Times Four: The Short Story in Depth. (Orig.). 1968. pap. text ed. 9.95 (ISBN 0-13-921809-2). P-H.

Heiney, Donald. America in Modern Italian Literature. 278p. 1965. 15.50 (ISBN 0-8135-0471-6). Rutgers U Pr.

Heinig, Ruth B. & Stillwell, Lyda. Creative Dramatics for the Classroom Teacher. LC 73-21875. 240p. 1974. 13.95 (ISBN 0-13-189407-2). P-H.

Heiniger, Margot C. Neurophysiological Concepts of Patient Learning: The Tree of Learning. LC 80-25454. (Illus.). 350p. 1981. text ed. 23.00 (ISBN 0-8016-2203-4). Mosby.

Heinisch, K. F. Dictionary of Rubber. Lee, K. S. & Smith, D. A., eds. Ford-Smith, J., tr. from Ger. LC 74-932. 545p. 1974. 54.95 (ISBN 0-470-36897-7). Halsted Pr.

Heinl, Robert D., Jr. Victory at High Tide: The Inchon-Seoul Campaign. LC 79-90111. (Illus.). 307p. 1979. Repr. of 1968 ed. 17.95 (ISBN 0-933852-03-7). Nautical & Aviation.

Heinle, Erwin & Bacher, Max. Building in Visual Concrete. Berger, Joseph, et al, trs. from Ger. (Illus.). 1971. 25.00x (ISBN 0-291-39299-7). Intl Ideas.

Heinlein, Robert A. Assignment in Eternity. (RL 7). 1970. pap. 1.95 (ISBN 0-451-09360-7, J9360, Sig). NAL.

--Between Planets. (Del Rey Bk.). 1978. pap. 1.75 (ISBN 0-345-27796-1). Ballantine.

--Beyond This Horizon. (Science Fiction Ser.). 1981. PLB 14.95 (ISBN 0-8398-2672-9). Gregg.

--Citizen of the Galaxy. (Del Rey Bks.). 1978. pap. 1.75 o.p. (ISBN 0-345-26074-0). Ballantine.

--Expanded Universe. Baen, Jim, ed. 1980. pap. 8.95 (ISBN 0-441-21883-0). Ace Bks.

--Farmer in the Sky. 224p. 1975. pap. 1.75 (ISBN 0-345-27596-9). Ballantine.

--Farnham's Freehold. pap. 2.25 (ISBN 0-425-04856-X, Dist. by Putnam). Berkley Pub.

--The Green Hills of Earth. 176p. (RL 7). 1973. pap. 1.75 (ISBN 0-451-09264-3, E9264, Sig). NAL.

--The Number of the Beast. 1980. 6.95 (ISBN 0-449-90019-3, Columbine). Fawcett.

--The Puppet Masters. 176p. (RL 7). Date not set. pap. 1.50 (ISBN 0-451-07339-8, W7339, Sig). NAL.

--The Star Beast. (A Del Rey Bk.). 1977. pap. 1.75 (ISBN 0-345-27580-2). Ballantine.

--Time for the Stars. (Del Rey Bk.). Date not set. pap. 1.95 (ISBN 0-345-29389-4). Ballantine.

--Tunnel in the Sky. (A Del Rey Bk.). Date not set. pap. 1.75 (ISBN 0-345-28195-0). Ballantine.

Heinrich, Anthony P. The Dawning of Music in Kentucky, The Western Minstrel. LC 79-39732. (Earlier American Music Ser: Vol. 10). 297p. 1973. Repr. of 1820 ed. lib. bdg. 29.50 (ISBN 0-306-77310-4). Da Capo.

Heinrich, Bernd. Insect Thermoregulation. LC 80-19452. 312p. 1981. 27.50 (ISBN 0-471-05144-6, Pub. by Wiley-Interscience). Wiley.

Heinrich, Herbert W., et al. Industrial Accident Prevention: A Safety Management Approach. 5th rev. ed. (Illus.). 1980. text ed. 23.95 (ISBN 0-07-028061-4); instructor's manual 10.95 (ISBN 0-07-028062-2). McGraw.

Heinrich, Janet, jt. auth. see Freeman, Ruth B.

Heinrich, Kurt F. Electron Beam X-Ray Microanalysis. 608p. 1980. text ed. 42.50 (ISBN 0-442-23286-1). Van Nos Reinhold.

Heinrichs, Waldo H., Jr. American Ambassador: Joseph C. Grew & the Development of the United States Diplomatic Tradition. Freidel, Frank, ed. LC 78-66536. (The History of the United States Ser.: Vol. 7). 474p. 1979. lib. bdg. 35.00 (ISBN 0-8240-9705-X). Garland Pub.

Heinritz, Fred. J., jt. auth. see Dougherty, Richard M.

Heinritz, Stuart F. & Farrell, Paul V. Purchasing: Principles & Applications. 5th ed. (Business Management Ser). (Illus.). 1971. ref. ed. 18.95 (ISBN 0-13-742148-6). P-H.

Heins, Maurice. Complex Function Theory. (Pure & Applied Mathematics Ser.: Vol. 28). 1968. text ed. 24.95 (ISBN 0-12-337950-4). Acad Pr.

Heins, Paul, ed. Crosscurrents of Criticism: Horn Book Essays, 1968-1977. LC 77-24256. 1977. 14.50 (ISBN 0-87675-034-X). Horn Bk.

Heins, Paul, tr. see Brothers Grimm.

Heins, Richard M., jt. auth. see Williams, C. Arthur, Jr.

Heinsohn, A. G., Jr. Cousin Mercedes & the White Russian. LC 74-18736. 1974. 4.00 (ISBN 0-88279-231-8). Western Islands.

Heinsohn, G. E. Ecology & Reproduction of the Tasmanian Bandicoots (Perameles gunni & Isodon obesulus) (U. C. Publ. in Zoology: Vol. 80). 1966. pap. 7.00x (ISBN 0-520-09337-2). U of Cal Pr.

Heintz, Ruth. Mathematics for Elementary Teachers: A Content Approach. LC 79-18727. (Illus.). 512p. 1980. text ed. 17.95 (ISBN 0-201-03227-9); instructor's manual 2.50 (ISBN 0-201-03228-7). A-W.

Heintze, Ingeborg. Organization of the Small Public Library. 1963. pap. 2.50 (ISBN 92-3-100523-5, U442, UNESCO). Unipub.

Heintzelman, Donald S. Autumn Hawk Flights: The Migrations in Eastern North America. (Illus.). 500p. 1975. 20.00 o.p. (ISBN 0-8135-0777-4). Rutgers U Pr.

--The Illustrated Bird Watcher's Dictionary. 1980. 11.95 (ISBN 0-87691-314-1). Winchester Pr.

Heintzelman, John. The Complete Handbook of Maintenance Management. 336p. pap. 9.95 (ISBN 0-13-160986-6, Reward). P-H.

Heintzelman, Oliver K. & Highsmith, R. M., Jr. World Regional Geography. 4th ed. (Illus.). 1973. text ed. 20.95 (ISBN 0-13-969006-9). P-H.

Heinz & Donnay. Lumumba. pap. 1.45 (ISBN 0-394-17185-3, B272, BC). Grove.

Heinz, Cecilia & Straw Dog. Improvising Blues Guitar: A Programmed Manual of Instruction. LC 70-143775. (Contemporary Guitar Styles Ser.). (Illus.). 84p. (Prog. Bk.). 1970. pap. 6.95 (ISBN 0-912910-01-1). Green Note Music.

Heinz, Grete, tr. see Kehr, Eckart.

Heinz, Heinz A. Germany's Hitler. (Illus.). 1976. pap. 4.00x (ISBN 0-911038-46-9). Noontide.

Heinze, Evelyn B., jt. auth. see Macdonald, Eleanor J.

Heinze, R. M. The Proclamations of Tudor Kings. LC 27-22983. 320p. 1976. 49.50 (ISBN 0-521-20938-2). Cambridge U Pr.

Heinze, Thomas F. Creation Vs. Evolution Handbook. (Direction Books). 1973. pap. 2.25 (ISBN 0-8010-4002-7). Baker Bk.

Heinzelman, Kurt. The Economics of the Imagination. LC 79-4019. 1980. lib. bdg. 18.50x (ISBN 0-87023-274-6). U of Mass Pr.

Heinzen, Richard H. & Clemons, Neil L. Breaking Through: Photography & Poetry Celebrating the Many Shades of Earthly Joys. (Illus.). 80p. (Orig.). 1980. pap. 10.95 (ISBN 0-686-28881-5, 880). Sunshine Arts WA.

Heinzkill, Richard. Film Criticism: An Index to Critics' Anthologies. LC 75-20159. 1975. 10.00 (ISBN 0-8108-0840-4). Scarecrow.

Heirich, Max. Beginning: Berkeley, 1964. LC 77-125074. (Illus.). 1971. 17.50x (ISBN 0-231-03467-9). Columbia U Pr.

--The Spiral of Conflict: Berkeley, 1964. LC 73-125073. (Illus.). 502p. 1973. 22.50x (ISBN 0-231-03243-9); pap. 7.50x (ISBN 0-231-08325-4). Columbia U Pr.

Heironimus, Terring W., 3rd & Bageant, Robert A. Mechanical Artificial Ventilation: A Manual for Students & Practitioners. 3rd ed. (Amer. Lec. in Anesthesiology Ser.). (Illus.). 560p. 1977. 33.50 (ISBN 0-398-03541-5). C C Thomas.

Heise, David R. Causal Analysis. LC 75-20465. 301p. 1975. 24.95 (ISBN 0-471-36898-9, Pub. by Wiley-Interscience). Wiley.

--Understanding Events. LC 78-24177. (ASA Rose Monograph). (Illus.). 1979. 19.95 (ISBN 0-521-22539-6); pap. 6.95x (ISBN 0-521-29544-0). Cambridge U Pr.

Heise, Jon O., ed. The Travel Books: Guide to the Travel Guides. (Popular Bks.). 304p. 1981. pap. 24.95 (ISBN 0-8352-1337-4). Bowker.

Heisel, Dorelle. Biofeedback Strategies for Interpersonal Relationships. 1981. write for info. Gordon.

Heisenberg, Werner. Physical Principles of the Quantum Theory. 1930. pap. text ed. 3.00 (ISBN 0-486-60113-7). Dover.

--Physics & Beyond. (World Perspectives Ser.). pap. 5.50x (ISBN 0-06-131622-9, TB1622, Torch). Har-Row.

Heiser, Charles B., Jr. Nightshades: The Paradoxical Plants. LC 70-85798. (Biology Ser.). (Illus.). 1969. text ed. 9.95x (ISBN 0-7167-0672-5). W H Freeman.

--Seed to Civilization: The Story of Food. 2nd ed. LC 80-18208. (Illus.). 1981. text ed. 19.95x (ISBN 0-7167-1264-4); pap. text ed. 9.95x (ISBN 0-7167-1265-2). W H Freeman.

--Seed to Civilization: The Story of Man's Food. LC 73-2949. (Biology Ser.). (Illus.). 1973. pap. text ed. 9.95x (ISBN 0-7167-0594-X). W H Freeman.

--The Sunflower. LC 74-15906. (Illus.). 198p. 1981. pap. 5.95 (ISBN 0-8061-1743-5). U of Okla Pr.

Heiser, F. A., jt. auth. see Colangelo, Vito J.

Heiser, Herman C. Budgeting: Principles & Practice. (Illus.). 1959. 24.95 (ISBN 0-8260-4040-3). Ronald Pr.

Heiserman, Arthur. The Novel Before the Novel. LC 76-8102. 1977. lib. bdg. 17.50x o.s.i. (ISBN 0-226-32572-5). U of Chicago Pr.

Heiserman, D. Handbook of Digital IC Applications. 1980. 22.95 (ISBN 0-13-372698-3). P-H.

Heiserman, David L. Beginner's Handbook of IC Projects. (Illus.). 272p. 1981. 18.95 (ISBN 0-13-074229-5). P-H.

--Build Your Own Working Robot. LC 75-41725. 238p. 1976. 9.95 (ISBN 0-8306-6841-1); pap. 5.95 (ISBN 0-8306-5841-6, 841). TAB Bks.

--Handbook of Small Appliance Troubleshooting & Repair. LC 73-14989. (Illus.). 320p. 1974. 16.95x o.p. (ISBN 0-13-381749-0). P-H.

--Pascal. (Illus.). 350p. (Orig.). 1980. 15.95 (ISBN 0-8306-9934-1); pap. 9.95 (ISBN 0-8306-1205-X, 1205). Tab Bks.

Heisey, John, et al, eds. A Checklist of American Coverlet Weavers. LC 77-15968. 1980. Repr. of 1978 ed. 15.00x (ISBN 0-87935-048-2). U Pr of Va.

Heisig, James W., tr. see Waldenfels, Hans.

Heisinger, Brent. Comprehensive Musicianship Through Band Performance: Zone 4, Book B. (University of Hawaii Music Project). (gr. 7-8). 1976. 10.24 o.p. (ISBN 0-201-00849-1). A-W.

Heisler, Martin O., jt. ed. see Lawrence, Robert M.

Heiss, ed. see Schmutzler, et al.

Heiss, Aloiss. Description Generale Des Monnaies Des Rois Wisigoths d'Espagne. (Illus.). iv, 185p. (Fr.). 1980. Repr. 30.00 (ISBN 0-916710-64-5). Obol Intl.

Heiss, Ann M. Challenges to Graduate Schools. LC 73-129770. (Higher Education Ser). 1970. 14.95x o.p. (ISBN 0-87589-072-5). Jossey-Bass.

Heiss, Jerold. The Case of the Black Family: A Sociological Inquiry. new ed. LC 74-34418. 288p. 1975. 17.50x (ISBN 0-231-03782-1). Columbia U Pr.

Heiss, Kreuzer. Quantification of Myocardial Ischemia. (Advances in Clinical Cardiology: Vol. 1). 656p. 1980. pap. 36.00x (ISBN 0-933682-00-X). G Witzstrock Pub Hse.

Heiss, Robert. Hegel Kierkegaard Marx. 1975. 12.50 o.s.i. (ISBN 0-440-03526-0, Sey Lawr). Delacorte.

Heisserer, A. J. Alexander the Great & the Greeks: The Epigraphic Evidence. LC 79-6712. (Illus.). 350p. 1980. 29.95x (ISBN 0-8061-1612-9). U of Okla Pr.

Heissig, Walther. The Religions of Mongolia. Samuel, Geoffrey, tr. from Ger. 1980. 17.50x (ISBN 0-520-03857-6). U of Cal Pr.

Heist, Paul, ed. The Creative College Student: An Unmet Challenge. LC 68-21316. (Higher Education Ser.). 1968. 13.95x o.p. (ISBN 0-87589-015-6). Jossey-Bass.

Heitger, Lester E. & Matulich, Serge. Managerial Accounting. 1980. text ed. 18.95 (ISBN 0-07-027941-1); study guide 6.95 (ISBN 0-07-027942-X); job costing packet (ISBN 0-07-027943-8); profit planning packet (ISBN 0-07-027946-2); solutions manual 25.00 (ISBN 0-07-027944-6); examination questions 15.00 (ISBN 0-07-027945-4); overhead transparencies 325.00 (ISBN 0-07-074792-X). McGraw.

Heitler, Walter. Elementary Wave Mechanics: With Applications to Quantum Chemistry. 2nd ed. 1956. 8.00x o.p. (ISBN 0-19-851103-5); pap. 8.50x (ISBN 0-19-851115-9). Oxford U Pr.

Heitner, Jack. The Search for the Real Self: Humanistic Psychology & Literature. LC 78-62174. 1978. pap. text ed. 8.75 (ISBN 0-8191-0474-4). U Pr of Amer.

Heitzman & Mueller. Statistics for Business & Economics. 1980. text ed. 19.95 (ISBN 0-205-06753-0, 106753-2); solutions manual 7.95 (ISBN 0-205-06754-9, 1067540); study guide 6.95 (ISBN 0-205-06756-5, 1067567). Allyn.

Heizer, Robert F. California Indians Two. Horr, David A., ed. (American Indian Ethnohistory Ser.). 1978. lib. bdg. 42.00 (ISBN 0-8240-0772-7). Garland Pub.

--California Indians Vs the U. S. A. (Ballena Press Publications in Archaeology, Ethnology & History Ser.: No. 12). 1979. pap. 5.95 o.p. (ISBN 0-87919-080-9). Ballena Pr.

Heizer, Robert F. & Baumhoff, Martin A. Prehistoric Rock Art of Nevada & California. (California Library Reprint). (Illus.). 430p. 1976. Repr. 36.50x (ISBN 0-520-02911-9). U of Cal Pr.

Heizer, Robert F. & Sturtevant, William C., eds. Handbook of North American Indians: California, Vol. 8. LC 77-17162. (Illus.). 800p. 13.50 (ISBN 0-87474-188-2). Smithsonian.

Heizer, Robert F., et al. Archaeology: A Bibliographical Guide to the Basic Literature. LC 77-83376. 400p. 1980. lib. bdg. 38.00 (ISBN 0-8240-9826-9). Garland Pub.

Hejduk, John, jt. auth. see Eisenman, Peter.

Hela, Ilmo & Laevastu, Taivo. Fisheries Oceanography. (Illus.). 254p. 22.00 (ISBN 0-85238-009-7, FN). Unipub.

Helal, Basil, jt. auth. see Benjamin, Alexander.

Helander, Martin. Human Factors-Ergonomics for Building & Construction. (Construction Management & Engineering Ser.). 400p. 1981. 35.00 (ISBN 0-471-05075-X, Pub. by Wiley-Interscience). Wiley.

Helber, Larry E., jt. auth. see Kaiser, Charles, Jr.

Helberg, Kristen & Lewis, Daniel. The Victorian House Coloring Book. (Pictorial Archive Ser.). (Illus.). 1980. pap. 2.00 (ISBN 0-486-23908-X). Dover.

Helbing, Wolfgang & Burkart, Adolf. Chemical Tables for Laboratory & Industry. LC 79-26137. 1980. 19.95x (ISBN 0-470-26910-3). Halsted Pr.

Helburn, et al. Economics in Society Series. Incl. Concepts & Institutions. text ed. 10.93 softbound (ISBN 0-201-02856-5); tchr's guide 8.32 (ISBN 0-201-02902-2); Industry Performance. text ed. softbound o.p. (ISBN 0-201-02857-3); tchrs' guide o.p. (ISBN 0-201-02903-0). (gr. 9-12). 1974 (Sch Div). A-W.

Helcke, G. The Energy Saving Guide: Tables for Assessing the Profitability of Energy Saving Measures with Explanatory Notes and Worked Examples. Published for the Commission of the European Communities. LC 80-41528. 230p. 1981. 45.00 (ISBN 0-08-026738-6); pap. 15.50 (ISBN 0-08-026739-4). Pergamon.

Held, A., ed. General Relativity & Gravitation: One Hundred Years After the Birth of Albert Einstein, 2 vols. (Illus.). 1980. Set. 99.50 (ISBN 0-686-58609-3, Plenum Pr); 57.50 ea. Vol. 1 (ISBN 0-306-40265-3). Vol. 2 (ISBN 0-306-40266-1). Plenum Pub.

Held, Burnell, jt. auth. see Clawson, Marion.

Held, David. Introduction to Critical Theory: Horkheimer to Habermas. 497p. 1980. 32.50x (ISBN 0-520-04121-6); pap. 12.75x (ISBN 0-520-04175-5, CAMPUS 261). U of Cal Pr.

Held, Felix E., tr. see Andrea, Johann V.

Held, Joseph, ed. The Modernization of Agriculture: Rural Transformation in Hungary, 1848-1975. (East European Monographs: 3no. 67). 1980. 25.00x (ISBN 0-914710-60-5, Dist. by Columbia U Pr). East Eur Quarterly.

Held, Julius & Posner, Donald. Seventeenth & Eighteenth Century Art: Baroque Painting, Sculpture & Architecture. Janson, H., ed. (Illus.). 492p. 1972. text ed. 21.95 (ISBN 0-13-807339-2). P-H.

Held, R. E. Public Libraries in California, 1849-1878. (U. C. Publ. in Librarianship: Vol. 4). 1963. pap. 8.00x (ISBN 0-520-09207-4). U of Cal Pr.

Held, Richard, intro. by. Image, Object, & Illusion: Readings from Scientific American. LC 74-11012. (Illus.). 1974. pap. text ed. 7.95x (ISBN 0-7167-0504-4). W H Freeman.

Held, Richard & Richards, Whitmanintro. by. Perception: Mechanisms & Models: Readings from Scientific American. LC 70-190437. (Illus.). 1972. text ed. 19.95x (ISBN 0-7167-0853-1); pap. text ed. 9.95x (ISBN 0-7167-0852-3). W H Freeman.

Held, Robert, ed. Arms & Armor Annual, Vol. I. 320p. 1973. pap. 9.95 (ISBN 0-695-80407-3). Arma Pr.

Held, Virginia. Property, Profits & Economic Justice. 256p. 1979. pap. text ed. 8.95x (ISBN 0-534-00819-4). Wadsworth Pub.

Held, Virginia, et al, eds. Philosophy & Political Action. 288p. 1972. pap. text ed. 4.95x (ISBN 0-19-501503-7). Oxford U Pr.

Heldman, D. R. Food Process Engineering. (Illus.). 1975. text ed. 32.00 o.p. (ISBN 0-87055-174-4); pap. text ed. 20.00 o.p. (ISBN 0-87055-298-8). AVI.

Heldman, D. R. & Singh, R. P. Food Process Engineering. (Illus.). 1981. pap. text ed. 24.00 (ISBN 0-686-69097-4). AVI.

Heldman, Dan C. American Labor Unions: Political Values & Financial Structure. 1977. 10.00 (ISBN 0-685-85740-9). Coun Am Affairs.

--Trade Unions & Labor Relations in the USSR. 1977. pap. 10.00 (ISBN 0-685-85742-5). Coun Am Affairs.

Heldman, E., et al, eds. Neurobiology of Cholinergic & Adrenergic Transmitters. (Monographs in Neural Sciences: Vol. 7). (Illus.). xvi, 200p. 1980. pap. 53.60 (ISBN 3-8055-0828-X). S Karger.

Heldman, Gladys, ed. see Gonzales, Pancho.

Helen, Mary. Sibyl's Dream. 1980. deluxe ed. 14.95 autographed (ISBN 0-912492-18-X). Pyquag.

--A Sybil's Dreams, Autographed. 1980. deluxe ed. 14.95 (ISBN 0-912492-15-5). Pyquag.

Helena, Ann. I'm Running Away. LC 77-19138. (Moods & Emotions Ser.). (Illus.). (gr. k-3). 1978. PLB 8.95 (ISBN 0-8172-1154-3). Raintree Pubs.

--The Lie. LC 77-23395. (Moods & Emotions Ser.). (Illus.). (gr. k-3). 1977. PLB 8.95 (ISBN 0-8172-0958-1). Raintree Pubs.

Helfand, Arthur E. Clinical Podogeriatrics. (Illus.). 248p. 1981. write for info. (3951-2). Williams & Wilkins.

Helfant, Richard H. Bellet's Essentials of Cardiac Arrhythmias. 2nd ed. (Illus.). 450p. 1980. text ed. 24.50 (ISBN 0-7216-4626-3). Saunders.

Helfer, Ray E., jt. auth. see Kempe, C. Henry.

Helfer, Ray E. & Kempe, C. Henry, eds. Child Abuse & Neglect: The Family & the Community. LC 76-8891. 1976. 25.00 (ISBN 0-88410-217-3); pap. text ed. 9.95 (ISBN 0-88410-240-8). Ballinger Pub.

Helfer, Toni R. The Gentle Jungle. LC 80-10275. (Illus.). 336p. 1980. 9.95 (ISBN 0-8425-1790-1). Brigham.

Helfert, Erich A., ed. Techniques of Financial Analysis. 4th ed. 1977. pap. text ed. 10.95 (ISBN 0-256-01916-9). Irwin.

Helfet, Arthur J., et al. Disorders of the Foot. 1980. text ed. 27.50 (ISBN 0-397-50430-6). Lippincott.

Helfgot, Joseph H. Professional Reforming: Mobilization for Youth & the Failure of Social Science. 240p. 1981. 23.95 (ISBN 0-669-04100-9). Lexington Bks.

Helfgott, Roy B. Labor Economics. 2nd ed. 674p. 1981. text ed. 19.95 (ISBN 0-394-32325-4). Random.

Helfman, Elizabeth. Blissymbolics: Speaking Without Speech. (Illus.). 144p. 1981. 10.95 (ISBN 0-525-66678-8). Elsevier-Nelson.

Helfman, Elizabeth, jt. auth. see Helfman, Harry.

Helfman, Elizabeth S. Signs & Symbols of the Sun. LC 73-20121. (Illus.). (gr. 4-7). 1974. 8.95 (ISBN 0-395-28860-6, Clarion). HM.

Helfman, Harry. Creating Things That Move, Fun with Kinetic Art. LC 75-11719. (Illus.). 48p. (gr. 4-6). 1975. PLB 6.48 (ISBN 0-688-32038-4). Morrow.

--Tricks with Your Fingers. (Illus.). (gr. 3-7). 1967. PLB 6.48 (ISBN 0-688-31583-6). Morrow.

Helfman, Harry & Helfman, Elizabeth. Strings on Your Fingers: How to Make String Figures. (Illus.). (gr. 3-7). 1965. PLB 6.48 (ISBN 0-688-31582-8). Morrow.

Helfreich, W. & Heppke, G. Liquid Crystals of One- & Two-Dimensional Order: Proceedings. (Springer Series in Chemical Physics: Vol. 11). (Illus.). 416p. 1981. 39.50 (ISBN 0-387-10399-6). Springer-Verlag.

Helgeland, G. Archery World's Complete Guide to Bow Hunting. 1975. 8.95 o.p. (ISBN 0-13-044024-8); pap. 3.95 (ISBN 0-13-044016-7). P-H.

Helgerson, Richard. The Elizabethan Prodigals. 1977. 14.50x (ISBN 0-520-03264-0). U of Cal Pr.

Helgesen, Sally. Wildeaters. LC 79-7867. 168p. 1981. 9.95 (ISBN 0-385-14637-X). Doubleday.
Helgeson, J. P., jt. auth. see Ingram, D. S.
Helick, R. Martin. Fugue for an October Age. 340p. 1980. pap. 6.95 (ISBN 0-912710-09-8). Regent Graphic Serv.
Heline, Corinne. Beethoven's Nine Symphonies, & the Nine Lesser Mysteries. 4.50 (ISBN 0-87613-000-7). New Age.
--The Cosmic Harp: For Musicologist & Astrologer. 4.95 o.p. (ISBN 0-87613-005-8). New Age.
Helitzer, Morrie. The Cold War. (gr. 7 up). 1977. lib. bdg. 6.45 s&l (ISBN 0-531-02464-4). Watts.
Helium Study Committee. Helium: A Public Policy Program. 1978. pap. 10.50 (ISBN 0-309-02742-X). Natl Acad Pr.
Helke, Michael. The Grammar of English Reflexives. Hankamer, Jorge, ed. LC 78-66542. (Outstanding Dissertations in Linguistics Ser.). 1979. lib. bdg. 22.00 (ISBN 0-8240-9684-3). Garland Pub.
Hellbing, L. Alasia Problems. (Studies in Mediterranean Archaeology: No. 57). 1979. pap. text ed. 35.00x (ISBN 9-1850-5890-4). Humanities.
Helldorfer, Martin. The Work Trap. LC 80-53205. (Illus.). 140p. 1981. pap. 4.95 (ISBN 0-88489-127-5). St Mary's.
Helleberg, Marilyn. Beyond T.M. A Practical Guide to the Lost Tradition of Christian Meditation. LC 80-82811. 144p. (Orig.). 1981. pap. 6.95 (ISBN 0-8091-2325-8). Paulist Pr.
Helleberg, Marilyn M. Your Hearing Loss: How to Break the Sound Barrier. LC 78-8663. 1979. 13.95 (ISBN 0-88229-341-9). Nelson-Hall.
Hellebust, J. A. & Craigie, J. S. Handbook of Phycological Methods. LC 73-79496. (Illus.). 1978. 39.95 (ISBN 0-521-21855-1). Cambridge U Pr.
Helleiner, G. H., et al, eds. Protectionism or Industrial Adjustment. (Atlantic Papers Ser.: No. 39). 72p. 1980. write for info. (ISBN 0-916672-79-4). Allanheld.
Helleiner, G. K., ed. A World Divided. LC 75-16606. (Perspectives on Development Ser.: No. 5). 1976. 47.50 (ISBN 0-521-20948-X); pap. 15.95x (ISBN 0-521-29006-6). Cambridge U Pr.
Helleiner, Gerald K. Intra - Firm Trade & the Developing Countries. 1981. 25.00 (ISBN 0-312-42538-4). St Martin.
Hellekson, Terry. Popular Fly Patterns. LC 76-49452. (Illus.). 1975. 15.95 o.p. (ISBN 0-87905-066-7); pap. 10.95 (ISBN 0-87905-065-9). Peregrine Smith.
Helleman-Elgersma, W. Soul Sisters: A/Commentary on Enneads IV 3(27), 1-8 of Plotinus. 485p. 1980. pap. text ed. 51.50x (ISBN 90-6203-931-6, Pub. by Rodopi Holland). Humanities.
Heller, Agnes. Renaissance Man. LC 80-6192. 490p. 1981. pap. 9.95 (ISBN 0-8052-0674-4). Schocken.
--Renaissance Man. Allen, Richard E., tr. 1978. 45.00x (ISBN 0-7100-8881-7). Routledge & Kegan.
--Theory of Feelings. (Dialectic & Society Ser.: No. 6). 1979. pap. text ed. 23.50x (ISBN 90-232-1699-7). Humanities.
--The Theory of Need in Marx. (Allison & Busby Motive Ser.). 136p. 1981. pap. 7.95 (ISBN 0-8052-8075-8, Pub. by Allison & Busby England). Schocken.
Heller, Alfred, ed. The California Tomorrow Plan. LC 72-85217. (Illus.). 120p. 1972. 5.95 (ISBN 0-913232-01-7). W Kaufmann.
Heller, Alfred L. Your Body, His Temple. 192p. 1981. pap. 4.95 (ISBN 0-8407-5769-7). Nelson.
Heller, Celia. On the Edge of Destruction: Jews in Poland 1918-39. LC 76-22646. (Illus.). 1977. 20.00x (ISBN 0-231-03819-4). Columbia U Pr.
Heller, Charles F., et al. Population Patterns of Southwestern Michigan. 1974. 5.00 (ISBN 0-932826-10-5). New Issues MI.
Heller, David. Vortex. 1978. pap. 1.95 (ISBN 0-380-42762-1, 42762). Avon.
Heller, Erich. The Poet's Self & the Poem: Essays on Goethe, Nietzsche & Thomas Mann. 1976. text ed. 12.50x (ISBN 0-485-11164-0, Athlone Pr). Humanities.
Heller, Francis H. Sixth Amendment to the Constitution of the United States: A Study in Constitutional Development. LC 69-13931. 1969. Repr. of 1951 ed. lib. bdg. 15.00x (ISBN 0-8371-0471-8, HESI). Greenwood.
Heller, Frank A. Competence & Power in Managerial Decision-Making. Wilpert, Bernhard, ed. 256p. 1981. 34.50 (ISBN 0-471-27837-8, Pub. by Wiley-Interscience). Wiley.
Heller, Gerhardt B., ed. Thermophysics & Temperature Control of Spacecraft & Entry Vehicles. (Progress in Astronautics & Aeronautics: Vol. 18). 1966. 27.00 (ISBN 0-12-535118-6). Acad Pr.
Heller, H., jt. ed. see Von Euler, U. S.
Heller, H. Robert. International Monetary Economics. (Illus.). 256p. 1974. ref. ed. 17.95 (ISBN 0-13-473140-9). P-H.
Heller, Jack. Typing for Individual Achievement. Rubin, Audrey, ed. LC 80-26244. (Illus.). 192p. 1981. text ed. 13.80 (ISBN 0-686-69551-8). McGraw.
Heller, Janet R., ed. Primavera, I: Women Writers & Artists Anthology. (Illus.). 90p. 1975. pap. 4.00 (ISBN 0-916980-00-6). Primavera.
Heller, Janet R., et al, eds. Primavera, II. LC 76-647540. (Illus., Orig.). 1976. pap. 4.00 (ISBN 0-916980-02-2). Primavera.
--Primavera, III. LC 76-647540. (Illus.). 1977. pap. 4.00 (ISBN 0-916980-03-0). Primavera.
Heller, Janet R., et al, eds. see Cotich, Felicia, et al.
Heller, Janet R., et al, eds. see Mueller, Lisel, et al.
Heller, Janet R., et al, eds. see Susskind, Harriet, et al.
Heller, Joseph. British Policy Towards the Ottoman Empire Nineteen Hundred Eight - Nineteen Fourteen. 1980. 26.00x (ISBN 0-7146-3127-2, F Cass Co). Biblio Dist.
--Catch Twenty-Two. 1976. pap. 2.95 (ISBN 0-440-11120-X). Dell.
Heller, Kenneth & Monahan, John. Psychology & Community Change. 1977. 17.50x (ISBN 0-256-01941-X). Dorsey.
Heller, Linda. Lily at the Table. LC 79-11415. (Illus.). (ps-2). 1979. 8.95 (ISBN 0-02-743530-X). Macmillan.
--Trouble at Goodewoode Manor. LC 80-27417. (Illus.). 32p. (gr. k-3). 1981. PLB 8.95 (ISBN 0-02-743570-9). Macmillan.
Heller, Lois J. & Mohrman, David E. Cardiovascular Physiology. Mixter, Richard W., ed. (Illus.). 176p. 1980. pap. text ed. 9.95 (ISBN 0-07-027973-X). McGraw.
Heller, Lynne E. Ann Radcliffe's Gothic Landscape of Fiction & the Various Influences Upon It. Varma, Devendra P., ed. LC 79-8452. (Gothic Studies & Dissertations Ser.). (Illus.). 1980. lib. bdg. 40.00x (ISBN 0-405-12666-2). Arno.
Heller, Marjorie K. Legal P's & Q's in the Doctor's Office. (Orig.). 1981. pap. 12.50 (ISBN 0-686-59766-4). Monarch Pr.
Heller, R. International Trade: Theory & Empirical Evidence. 2nd ed. 1973. 17.95 (ISBN 0-13-473918-3). P-H.
Heller, Reinhold. The Art of Wilhelm Lehmbruck. (Illus.). 200p. 1972. 17.50 o.s.i. (ISBN 0-02-550800-8). Macmillan.
Heller, Robert. The Common Millionaire. 384p. 1974. 8.95 o.p. (ISBN 0-440-03353-5). Delacorte.
--The Naked Investor. 1977. 8.95 o.p. (ISBN 0-440-06257-8). Delacorte.
Heller, Robert, jt. auth. see Salvadori, Mario G.
Heller, Ruth. Butterflies. (Creative Coloring Activity Pandabacks). (Illus.). 32p. 1981. pap. 1.25 (ISBN 0-448-49624-0). G&D.
--Cats. (Creative Coloring Activity Pandabacks). (Illus.). 32p. 1981. pap. 1.25 (ISBN 0-448-49626-7). G&D.
--Delux Designs for Coloring Transfers. Incl. Bk. 1. (Illus.). 48p. pap. 2.95 (ISBN 0-448-14759-9); Bk. 2. (Illus.). 48p. pap. 2.95 (ISBN 0-448-14760-2). 1981. G&D.
--Designs. (Creative Coloring Activity Pandabacks). (Illus.). 32p. 1981. pap. 1.25 (ISBN 0-448-49621-6). G&D.
--Flowers. (Creative Coloring Activity Pandabacks). (Illus.). 32p. 1981. pap. 1.25 (ISBN 0-448-49623-2). G&D.
--More Designs. (Creative Coloring Activity Pandabacks). (Illus.). 32p. 1981. pap. 1.25 (ISBN 0-448-49622-4). G&D.
--Snowflakes. (Creative Coloring Activity Pandabacks). (Illus.). 32p. 1981. pap. 1.25 (ISBN 0-448-49625-9). G&D.
Heller, Samuel. Multispeed & Standard Squirrel Cage Motors. Vol. 1 Standard (Single Sped) Motors Only: Testing, Rewinding, Reconnecting, & Redesigning. LC 75-36709. (Illus.). 704p. 1976. pap. 35.00 (ISBN 0-911740-07-4). Datarule.
Heller, Steven, et al. The Empire State Building Book. (Illus.). 96p. 1980. 14.95 (ISBN 0-312-24456-8); pap. 7.95 (ISBN 0-686-65894-9). St Martin.
Heller, Susan & Wallin, Douglas. Volcano. (Orig.). 1981. pap. 3.25 (ISBN 0-440-19319-2). Dell.
Heller, Suzanne. Misery in Four Languages. LC 80-15416. (Illus.). 96p. 1981. 4.95 (ISBN 0-8397-5803-0). Eriksson.
Heller, Walter. New Dimensions of Political Economy. 1967. pap. 3.95x (ISBN 0-393-09755-2). Norton.
Heller, Walter W. New Dimensions of Political Economy. LC 66-23467. (Godkin Lectures Ser.: 1966). 1966. 10.00x (ISBN 0-674-61100-4). Harvard U Pr.
Heller, Wendy. My Name Is Nabil. (Illus.). 59p. (gr. 3-6). 1981. price not set (ISBN 0-933770-17-0). Kalimat.
Heller, William. Mr. President... 260p. 1980. 10.00 (ISBN 0-8059-2753-0). Dorrance.
Hellerman, Leon, et al, eds. China: Selected Readings on the Middle Kingdom. (Illus.). 1971. pap. 1.25 o.s.i. (ISBN 0-671-48111-8). WSP.
Hellerstein, Erna O., et al, eds. Victorian Women: A Documentary Account of Women's Lives in Nineteenth-Century England, France, & the United States. LC 79-67770. 544p. 1981. 27.50x (ISBN 0-8047-1088-0); pap. 11.95x (ISBN 0-8047-1096-1). Stanford U Pr.
Hellerstein, H. K., jt. auth. see Wenger, Nanette K.
Hellerstein, Jerome R. & Hellerstein, Walter. Cases & Materials on State & Local Taxation. 4th ed. LC 78-2418. (American Casebook Ser.). 1041p. 1978. text ed. 21.95 (ISBN 0-8299-2000-5). West Pub.
Hellerstein, Walter, jt. auth. see Hellerstein, Jerome R.
Hellgren, Ludmila. Dialogue's in Turgenev's Novels: Speech Introductory Devices. (Stockholm Studies in Russian Literature: No. 12). 148p. 1980. pap. 15.00x (ISBN 91-22-00369-X). Humanities.
Hellicar, Eileen. Prime Ministers of Britain. LC 77-85014. 1978. 14.95 (ISBN 0-7153-7486-9). David & Charles.
Hellier, Marjorie. How to Develop a Better Speaking Voice. pap. 3.00 (ISBN 0-87980-056-9). Wilshire.
Hellinger, Douglas A., jt. auth. see Hellinger, Stephen H.
Hellinger, Ernst & Toeplitz, Otto. Integralgleichungen. LC 54-2866. (Ger). 14.95 (ISBN 0-8284-0089-X). Chelsea Pub.
Hellinger, Stephen H. & Hellinger, Douglas A. Unemployment & the Multinationals: A Strategy for Technological Change in Latin America. 1976. 13.95 (ISBN 0-8046-9126-6, National University Pub). Kennikat.
Helliwell, P. R., ed. Urban Storm Drainage. LC 78-18235. 1978. 64.95 (ISBN 0-470-26461-6). Halsted Pr.
Helliwell, P. R. & Bossanji, J., eds. Pollution Criteria for Estuaries. LC 74-26695. 1975. 44.95 (ISBN 0-470-36920-5). Halsted Pr.
Hellman, Charles S. & Tiritilli, Robert A. OlympiX: A Spoof on the Games. (Illus.). 1980. 4.95x (ISBN 0-935938-01-X). Hit Ent.
Hellman, Donald C., jt. auth. see Commission on Critical Choices.
Hellman, Hal. Biology in the World of the Future. LC 70-12218. (World of the Future Ser.). (Illus.). 192p. (gr. 7 up). 1971. 6.95 (ISBN 0-87131-104-6). M Evans.
--Deadly Bugs & Killer Insects. LC 78-17403. 192p. (gr. 5 up). 1978. 6.95 (ISBN 0-87131-269-7). M Evans.
Hellman, Hal, jt. auth. see Klass, Morton.
Hellman, Hal, jt. auth. see Kowalski, Ludwik.
Hellman, John. Emmanuel Mounier & the New Catholic Left, 1930 to 1950. 276p. 1981. 35.00x (ISBN 0-8020-2399-1). U of Toronto Pr.
Hellman, Lillian. Little Foxes & Another Part of the Forest. (Plays Ser). 1976. pap. 2.95 o.p. (ISBN 0-14-048132-X). Penguin.
--Pentimento. pap. 4.95 (ISBN 0-452-25107-9, ZS107, Plume). NAL.
--Six Plays by Lillian Hellman: The Children's Hour, Days to Come, the Little Foxes, Watch on the Rhine, Another Part of the Forest, the Autumn Garden. LC 79-2160. 1979. pap. 3.95 (ISBN 0-394-74112-9, Vin). Random.
Hellman, Peter. Avenue of the Righteous. (Illus.). 1980. 11.95 (ISBN 0-689-11109-6). Atheneum.
Hellman, Rainer. Gold Dollars, & the European Currency System: The Seven Year Monetary War. (Praeger Special Studies). 1979. 24.95 (ISBN 0-03-041611-6). Praeger.
--Transnational Control of Multinational Corporations. LC 77-7342. (Praeger Special Studies). 1977. text ed. 21.95 (ISBN 0-03-021941-8). Praeger.
Hellmann, John. Fables of Fact: The New Journalism As New Fiction. LC 80-23881. 175p. 1981. 11.95 (ISBN 0-252-00847-2). U of Ill Pr.
Hellmann, Kurt, ed. see Stanford Cade Memorial Symposium, Royal Institute, London, Sept. 1976.
Hellmuth, Charles F. Manic: Anatomy of a Mental Illness. 1977. 7.95 o.p. (ISBN 0-8059-2417-5). Dorrance.
Hellmuth, James G. Finding Money: A Businessman's Guide to Sources of Financing. 227p. 1980. 50.00 (ISBN 0-932648-12-6). Boardroom.
Hellmuth, Jerome, ed. George Washington & the Wolves. LC 77-20798. (Illus.). 1977. pap. 3.95 (ISBN 0-914842-23-4). Madrona Pubs.
Hellriegel, Don & Slocum, John. Organizational Behavior. 2nd ed. (Management Ser.). (Illus.). 1979. text ed. 19.50 (ISBN 0-8299-0195-7); instrs.' manual avail. (ISBN 0-8299-0487-5). West Pub.
Hellriegel, Don & Slocum, John W., Jr. Management: Contingency Approaches. 2nd ed. LC 77-76177. 1978. text ed. 17.95 (ISBN 0-201-02854-9). A-W.
--Management in the World Today: A Book of Readings. 400p. 1975. pap. text ed. 8.95 (ISBN 0-201-02833-6). A-W.
Hellstrom, Pontus & Langballe, Hans. The Rock Drawings, 2 pts. Save-Soderbergh, Torgny, ed. (Scandinavian Joint Expedition to Sudanese Nubia). (Illus.). 1970. Set. text ed. 55.00x (ISBN 0-8419-8800-5). Holmes & Meier.
Hellstrom, Sten-Gunnar, et al. Rendez-Vous en France. 1972. pap. text ed. 4.25 (ISBN 0-912022-28-0); exercise bk 3.50 (ISBN 0-912022-29-9). EMC.
Hellwege, K. H., jt. ed. see Fischer, H.
Hellwig, Jessica. Introduction to Computers & Programming. LC 71-85919. 1969. 15.00x (ISBN 0-231-03263-3). Columbia U Pr.
Hellwig, Monika K. Unnderstanding Catholicism. 192p. (Orig.). 1981. pap. 3.50 (ISBN 0-8091-2384-3). Paulist Pr.
--What Are They Saying About Death & Christian Hope? LC 78-61726. 1978. pap. 2.45 (ISBN 0-8091-2165-4). Paulist Pr.
Helly, Walter. Urban Systems Models. 1975. 25.00 (ISBN 0-12-339450-3). Acad Pr.
Hellyer, Barbara. Sewing Magic. Zieman, Nancy L. & Buttel, Paula W., eds. LC 79-92573. (Illus.). 56p. 1979. pap. 3.80 (ISBN 0-933956-04-5); 3.04. Sew-Fit.
Hellyer, Clement D. Making Money with Words. (Illus.). 256p. 1981. 10.95 (ISBN 0-13-547414-0, Spec); pap. 5.95 (ISBN 0-13-547406-X). P-H.
Helm, Christine, ed. see Helm, Mike.
Helm, F. G. Van Der see Van Der Helm, F. G.
Helm, June. Indians of the Subarctic: A Critical Bibliography. LC 76-12373. (Newberry Library Center for the History of the American Indian Bibliographical Ser.). 104p. 1976. pap. 3.95x (ISBN 0-253-33004-1). Ind U Pr.
Helm, Mackinley. John Marin. LC 75-87484. (Library of American Art Ser.). (Illus.). 1970. Repr. of 1948 ed. lib. bdg. 29.50 (ISBN 0-306-71489-2). Da Capo.
Helm, Mike. Eugene, Oregon--a Guide: America's Most Livable City. LC 79-63656. (Illus.). 1979. 5.95 (ISBN 0-931742-01-3). Rainy Day Oreg.
--Ghosts, Monsters, & Wild Men: Legends of the Oregon Country. (Illus.). 1981. write for info. (ISBN 0-931742-03-X). Rainy Day Oreg.
--A Guide to Eating & Drinking in Eugene. new ed. Helm, Christine, ed. LC 79-65123. (Illus.). 1979. 3.25 (ISBN 0-931742-02-1). Rainy Day Oreg.
--How I Did My Own Legal Work for Our Adoption Book. 1978. 4.00 (ISBN 0-931742-00-5). Rainy Day Oreg.
Helm, Mike, ed. see Lockley, Fred.
Helm, P. J. England Under the Yorkists & Tudors 1471 - 1603. (Illus.). 1968. text ed. 9.50x (ISBN 0-7135-0541-9); pap. text ed. 9.75x (ISBN 0-7135-0542-7). Humanities.
--Exploring Prehistoric England. (Illus.). 8.50 (ISBN 0-912728-13-2). Newbury Bks Inc.
Helm, Paul, ed. Divine Commands & Morality. (Readings in Philosophy Ser.). 192p. 1981. pap. 11.50 (ISBN 0-19-875049-8). Oxford U Pr.
Helm, Robert M., jt. auth. see Angell, J. William.
Helm, Sanford M. Catalog of Chamber Music for Wind Instruments. rev. ed. LC 70-86597. (Music Reprint Ser). 1969. Repr. of 1952 ed. lib. bdg. 14.50 (ISBN 0-306-71490-6). Da Capo.
Helman, Edith F & Arjona, Doris K., eds. Narradores De Hoy. 1966. 7.95x (ISBN 0-393-09693-9, NortonC); tapes o.p. 50.00 (ISBN 0-685-18949-X). Norton.
Helman, Edith F., jt. ed. see Arjona, Doris K.
Helman, Patricia K. At Home in the World. 120p. (Orig.). 1980. pap. 4.95 (ISBN 0-87178-065-8). Brethren.
Helmantoler, Michael C., ed. Mass Media College Catalog. rev. ed. 132p. 1980. pap. 15.00 (ISBN 0-87117-048-5). Am Assn Comm Jr Coll.
Helmbold, F. Wilbur. Tracing Your Ancestry: A Step-by-Step Guide to Researching Your Family History. LC 76-14109. (Illus.). 1976. 9.95 (ISBN 0-8487-0415-0); logbook o.p. 3.95 (ISBN 0-8487-0414-2). Oxmoor Hse.
--Tracing Your Ancestry Logbook. LC 76-14113. (Illus.). 256p. 1978. pap. 4.95 (ISBN 0-8487-0414-2). Oxmoor Hse.
Helmbold, W. C., tr. see Plato.
Helmer, Barbara. Better Baby Food Cookbook. LC 80-22314. (Orig.). 1980. pap. 4.95 spiral bdg. (ISBN 0-87123-018-6, 210018). Bethany Fell.
Helmer, John & Eddington, Neil A., eds. Urbanman: The Psychology of Urban Survival. LC 71-190152. 1973. 14.95 (ISBN 0-02-914480-9); pap. 3.95 (ISBN 0-02-914630-5). Free Pr.

Helmer, M. Jane. African Violets & Other Gesneriads for Modern Living. (Modern Living Ser.). (Illus.). 80p. (Orig.). 1978. pap. 2.95 (ISBN 0-89484-006-1, 10108). Merchants Pub Co.
--Hanging Plants for Modern Living. (Modern Living Ser.). (Illus.). 80p. (Orig.). 1975. pap. 2.95 (ISBN 0-89484-001-0, 10102). Merchants Pub Co.
--Pictorial Library of Landscape Plants. 2nd ed. Threlkeld, John L., ed. (Illus.). 352p. 1979. 60.00 (ISBN 0-89484-008-8, 11101). Merchants Pub Co.
Helmering, Doris W. I Have Two Families. LC 80-22392. 48p. (gr. 1-3). 1981. 8.95g (ISBN 0-687-18507-6). Abingdon.
Helmers, Dow. Historic Alpine Tunnel. (Illus.). 208p. 1978. 15.00 (ISBN 0-937080-02-0); pap. 8.50 (ISBN 0-937080-03-9). Century One.
Helmes, Winifred G., ed. Notable Maryland Women. LC 77-966. 1977. 12.50 (ISBN 0-87033-236-8, Pub. by Tidewater); pap. 8.00 (ISBN 0-685-80908-0). Cornell Maritime.
Helmholz, R. H. Marriage Litigation in Medieval England. LC 73-93395. (Studies in English Legal History). 272p. 1975. 36.00 (ISBN 0-521-20411-9). Cambridge U Pr.
Helmkamp, George K. & Johnson, Harry, Jr. Selected Experiments in Organic Chemistry. 2nd ed. (Illus.). 1968. lab manual 9.95x (ISBN 0-7167-0138-3); teacher's manual avail. (ISBN 0-685-00895-9); indiv. experiments 0.50 ea. W H Freeman.
Helmken, Charles M. Creative Newsletter Graphics. 1976. 40.00 (ISBN 0-89964-014-1). CASE.
Helmlinger, Trudy. After You've Said Goodbye: How to Recover After Ending a Relationship. 1977. 8.95 (ISBN 0-8467-0214-2, Pub. by Two Continents). Hippocrene Bks.
Helmore, G. A. Piaget: A Practical Consideration. LC 75-94933. 1970. pap. 6.05 o.p. (ISBN 0-08-006893-6). Pergamon.
Helmore, Leonard M. Corrupt & Illegal Practices: A General Survey & a Case Study of an Election Petition. (Library of Political Studies). (Orig.). 1967. text ed. 4.25x (ISBN 0-7100-5124-7); pap. text ed. 2.25x (ISBN 0-7100-5113-1). Humanities.
Helmrath, M. O. & Bartlett, J. L. Bobby Bear & the Bees. LC 68-56806. (Bobby Bear Ser). (Illus.). (ps-1). 1970. PLB 7.99 prebound (ISBN 0-87783-003-7); pap. 2.75 deluxe ed (ISBN 0-87783-080-0); cassette 5.95 (ISBN 0-685-04642-7). Oddo.
--Bobby Bear Finds Maple Sugar. LC 68-56805. (Bobby Bear Ser). (ps-1). 1970. PLB 7.99 prebound (ISBN 0-87783-005-3); pap. 2.75 deluxe ed (ISBN 0-87783-081-9); cassette 5.95 (ISBN 0-685-04643-5). Oddo.
--Bobby Bear Goes Fishing. LC 68-56807. (Bobby Bear Ser). (Illus.). (ps-1). 1970. PLB 7.99 prebound (ISBN 0-87783-006-1); pap. 2.75 deluxe ed. (ISBN 0-87783-082-7); cassette 5.95 (ISBN 0-685-04644-3). Oddo.
--Bobby Bear in the Spring. LC 68-56810. (Bobby Bear Ser). (Illus.). (ps-1). 1970. PLB 7.99 prebound (ISBN 0-87783-007-X); pap. 2.75 (ISBN 0-87783-083-5); cassette 5.95 (ISBN 0-685-04645-1). Oddo.
--Bobby Bear Series, 10 bks. (Two titles by Marilue). (ps-1). Set. lib. bdg. 81.90 (ISBN 0-685-28655-X); Set. pap. 27.50 deluxe ed (ISBN 0-685-28656-8); (10) cassettes 59.50 (ISBN 0-685-28657-6). Oddo.
--Bobby Bear's Halloween. LC 68-56808. (Bobby Bear Ser). (Illus.). (ps-1). 1970. PLB 7.99 prebound (ISBN 0-87783-004-5); pap. 2.75 deluxe ed (ISBN 0-87783-084-3); cassettes 5.95 (ISBN 0-685-04646-X). Oddo.
--Bobby Bear's Rocket Ride. LC 68-56809. (Bobby Bear Ser). (Illus.). (ps-1). 1970. PLB 7.99 prebound (ISBN 0-87783-008-X); pap. 2.75 deluxe ed (ISBN 0-87783-087-8); cassette 5.95 (ISBN 0-685-04647-8). Oddo.
Helmreich, E. C., jt. auth. see Black, C. E.
Helmreich, Ernst. The German Churches Under Hitler: Background, Struggle & Epilogue. LC 78-17737. 1978. 30.00 (ISBN 0-8143-1603-4). Wayne St U Pr.
Helmreich, Ernst C. History at a Glance: A Chronological Chart of European Civilization. LC 63-16881. (Orig.). (gr. 9 up). 1974. pap. text ed. 1.95 o.p. (ISBN 0-8120-0074-9). Barron.
--Religious Education in German Schools: An Historical Approach. LC 59-11509. 1959. 17.50x (ISBN 0-674-75850-1). Harvard U Pr.
Helmreich, Robert L., jt. auth. see Spence, Janet T.
Helmrich, Ernst, ed. Church & State in Europe. LC 78-68021. (Problems in Civilization Ser.). 1979. pap. 3.95 (ISBN 0-88273-405-9). Forum Pr MO.
Helms, Christine M. The Cohesion of Saudi Arabia: Evolution of Political Identity. LC 80-8026. (Illus.). 320p. 1981. text ed. 28.00x (ISBN 0-8018-2475-3). Johns Hopkins.
Helms, Christopher L. & DenDooven, Gweneth R., eds. The Sonoran Desert. LC 80-82918. (Illus.). 1980. 8.95 (ISBN 0-916122-72-7); pap. 3.75 (ISBN 0-916122-71-9). K C Pubns.
Helms, Cynthia. An Ambassador's Wife in Iran. LC 80-25090. (Illus.). 284p. 1981. 9.95 (ISBN 0-396-07881-8). Dodd.
Helms, Harry L., jt. auth. see Bennett, Hank.
Helms, R. Illumination Engineering for Energy Efficient Luminous Environments. 1980. 28.95 (ISBN 0-13-450809-2). P-H.
Helms, Randel. Tolkien & the Silmarils. 128p. 1981. 10.95 (ISBN 0-395-29469-X). HM.
Helms, Robert, ed. International Supply of Medicines: Implications of U. S. Regulatory Reform. 1980. 14.25 (ISBN 0-8447-2190-5); pap. 6.25 (ISBN 0-8447-2191-3). Am Enterprise.
Helms, Tom. Against All Odds. LC 78-3302. 1978. 10.95- (ISBN 0-690-01763-4, TYC-T). T Y Crowell.
Helmstrom, C. W. Statistical Theory of Signal Detection. 2nd ed. 1968. 26.00 (ISBN 0-08-013265-0). Pergamon.
Helnig, Floy. Clinical Simulations in Pediatrics. (Clinical Simulation Ser.). 218p. 1979. pap. 33.50x (ISBN 0-8385-1173-2). ACC.
Heloise. Help! from Heloise. LC 80-70543. (Illus.). 500p. 1981. 12.95 (ISBN 0-87795-318-X). Arbor Hse.
Helprin, Ben & PhotoGraphic Magazine Editors. Photo Lighting Techniques. LC 73-82538. (PhotoGraphic's Basic Ser.). (Illus.). 80p. (Orig.). 1973. pap. 3.95 o.p. (ISBN 0-8227-0022-0). Petersen Pub.
Helprin, Mark. A Dove of the East. 1981. pap. 5.95 (ISBN 0-440-52151-3, Delta). Dell.
Helps, Arthur. The Claims of Labour. 288p. 1971. Repr. of 1845 ed. 21.00x (ISBN 0-686-28329-5, Pub. by Irish Academic Pr). Biblio Dist.
Helterman, Jeffrey. The Blue Frogs. (Orig.). 1980. pap. 1.95 (ISBN 0-532-23197-X). Manor Bks.
--Symbolic Action in the Plays of the Wakefield Master. LC 80-18273. (South Atlantic Modern Language Association Award Study). 216p. 1981. lib. bdg. 17.50x (ISBN 0-8203-0534-0). U of Ga Pr.
Helterman, Jeffrey, ed. American Novelists Since World War Two. LC 77-82804. (Dictionary of Literary Biography: Vol. 2). (Illus.). 1978. 54.00 (ISBN 0-8103-0914-9, Bruccoli Clark Book). Gale.
Heltne, Paul, ed. see Institute for Laboratory Animal Resources.
Helton, Tinsley, ed. see Symposium on the Renaissance, University of Wisconsin, 1959.
Helveston, Eugene M. Atlas of Strabismus Surgery. 2nd ed. LC 77-3542. (Illus.). 1977. text ed. 41.50 (ISBN 0-8016-2138-0). Mosby.
Helveston, Eugene M. & Ellis, Forrest D. Pediatric Opthalmology Practice. LC 79-18469. 1979. text ed. 49.50 (ISBN 0-8016-2129-1). Mosby.
Helvetius, Claude. The Child of Nature, 1774, 2 vols. in 1. Shugrue, Michael F., ed. (The Flowering of the Novel, 1740-1775 Ser: Vol. 105). 1974. lib. bdg. 50.00 (ISBN 0-8240-1204-6). Garland Pub.
Helvie, Carl O. Self-Assessment of Current Knowledge in Community Health Nursing. 1975. spiral bdg. 9.50 (ISBN 0-87488-285-0). Med Exam.
Helweg, Arthur W. Sikhs in England: The Development of a Migrant Community. (Illus.). 190p. 1979. text ed. 10.95x (ISBN 0-19-561150-0). Oxford U Pr.
Helweg, Hans. Farm Animals. LC 79-27483. (Picturebacks Ser.). (Illus.). 32p. (ps-3). 1980. PLB 3.99 (ISBN 0-394-93733-3); pap. 1.25 (ISBN 0-394-83733-9). Random.
Helweg, Marianne, tr. see Lilius, Irmelin S.
Helwig, E. B., jt. auth. see Ten Seldam, R. E.
Hemans, Felicia D. The Domestic Affections, & Other Poems. 1812. Reiman, Donald H., ed. LC 75-31214. (Romantic Context Ser.: Poetry 1789-1830). 1978. lib. bdg. 47.00 (ISBN 0-8240-2164-9). Garland Pub.
--Records of Women: With Other Poems. Reiman, Donald H., ed. LC 75-31218. (Romantic Context Ser.: Poetry 1789-1930 Ser.). 1978. lib. bdg. 47.00 (ISBN 0-8240-2168-1). Garland Pub.
--The Siege of Valencia...the Last Constantine & Other Poems. 1823. Reiman, Donald H., ed. LC 75-31216. (Romantic Context Ser.: Poetry 1789-1830). 1978. lib. bdg. 47.00 (ISBN 0-8240-2166-5). Garland Pub.
--Tales & Historic Scenes, in Verse. 1819. Reiman, Donald H., ed. LC 75-31215. (Romantic Context Ser.: Poetry 1789-1830). 1978. lib. bdg. 47.00 (ISBN 0-8240-2165-7). Garland Pub.
--The Vespers of Palermo, 1823; The Forest Sanctuary; & Other Poems, 1825. Reiman, Donald H., ed. LC 75-31217. (Romantic Context Ser.: Poetry 1789-1930). 1978. lib. bdg. 47.00 (ISBN 0-8240-2167-3). Garland Pub.
Hembree, Charles R., tr. Fruto Do Espirito. (Portuguese Bks.). 1979. 1.50 (ISBN 0-8297-0652-6). Life Pubs Intl.
Hembree, Ron. The Shepherd Psalm. (Direction Bks). 64p. 1981. pap. text ed. 1.75 (ISBN 0-8010-4249-6). Baker Bk.
--You & Your Money: A Guide from God's Word. (Orig.). 1981. pap. 4.95 (ISBN 0-8010-4252-6). Baker Bk.
Hemdahl, Reuel. Cologne & Stockholm: Urban Planning & Land-Use Controls. LC 77-167645. 1971. 12.00 (ISBN 0-8108-0421-2). Scarecrow.
Hemenway, Jack E. RA Sixty-Eight Hundred ML: An M-Sixty Eight Hundred Relocatable Macro Assembler. 184p. (Orig.). 1979. pap. 25.00 (ISBN 0-07-028056-8, BYTE Bks); instructor's manual 6.95 (ISBN 0-07-007036-9). McGraw.
Hemenway, Jack E., jt. auth. see Grappel, Robert D.
Hemenway, Robert E. Zora Neale Hurston: A Literary Biography. LC 77-9605. (Illus.). 1977. 15.00 (ISBN 0-252-00652-6); pap. 8.95 (ISBN 0-252-00807-3). U of Ill Pr.
Hemenway, Steven. The Novel of India, 2 vols. Incl. Vol. 1. The Anglo-Indian Novel. flexible cloth 8.00 (ISBN 0-89253-667-5); Vol. 2. The Indo-Anglian Novel. 15.00 (ISBN 0-89253-668-3); flexible cloth 8.00 (ISBN 0-89253-669-1). Ind-US Inc.
Hemingway, Allan. Measurement of Airway Resistance with the Body Plethysmograph. (Illus.). 116p. 1973. 13.50 (ISBN 0-398-02633-5). C C Thomas.
Hemingway, Ernest. Across the River & into the Trees. LC 75-100353. 1950. lib. rep. ed. 15.00x (ISBN 0-684-15313-0, ScribT); pap. 4.95 (ISBN 0-684-71795-6, SL 202). Scribner.
--By-Line: Ernest Hemingway. White, William, ed. LC 67-15483. 1967. pap. 6.95 (ISBN 0-684-13685-6, SL501, ScribT). Scribner.
--Death in the Afternoon. (Illus.). 1932. lib. rep. ed. 27.50x (ISBN 0-684-15750-0, ScribT); pap. 6.95 (ISBN 0-684-71796-4, SL175, ScribT). Scribner.
--The Fable of the Good Lion. 28p. 1981. 4.95 (ISBN 0-8120-5276-5). Barron.
--Farewell to Arms. LC 67-13157. 1929. lib. rep. ed. 17.50x (ISBN 0-684-15562-1, ScribT); pap. 3.95 (ISBN 0-684-71797-2, SL61, ScribT). Scribner.
--Fifth Column & Four Stories of the Spanish Civil War. LC 70-182369. 1969. pap. 3.45 (ISBN 0-684-12723-7, SL329, ScribT); Hudson River Edition. 12.50x (ISBN 0-684-15815-9). Scribner.
--For Whom the Bell Tolls. 1940. 17.50x (ISBN 0-684-15316-5, ScribT); pap. 5.95 (ISBN 0-684-71798-0, SL4, ScribT). Scribner.
--Green Hills of Africa. 1935. Hudson River Edition. 17.50x (ISBN 0-684-16481-7); pap. 4.95 (ISBN 0-684-71799-9, SL50, ScribT). Scribner.
--Hemingway Reader. 1953. lib. rep. ed. 25.00x (ISBN 0-684-15164-2, ScribT); pap. 7.95 o.p. (ISBN 0-684-71872-3, SL119, ScribT). Scribner.
--In Our Time. 1930. Hudson River Edition. 15.00x (ISBN 0-684-16480-9); pap. 2.95 (ISBN 0-684-71802-2, SL56, ScribT). Scribner.
--Islands in the Stream. LC 71-123834. 1970. Hudson River Edition. 20.00x (ISBN 0-684-16499-X); pap. 4.95 (ISBN 0-684-14642-8, ScribT). Scribner.
--Old Man & the Sea. (Hudson River Edition). 1952. 12.50x (ISBN 0-684-15363-7, ScribT); pap. 3.25 (ISBN 0-684-71805-7, SL104); text ed. 4.80 (ISBN 0-684-51528-8); pap. text ed. 2.44 (ISBN 0-684-51529-6, SSP6, ScribC); pap. 2.25 (ISBN 0-684-16326-8, SL885, ScribC). Scribner.
--Short Stories of Ernest Hemingway. 1938. lib. rep. ed. 25.00x (ISBN 0-684-15155-3, ScribT); pap. 5.95 (ISBN 0-684-71806-5, SL141, ScribT). Scribner.
--Snows of Kilimanjaro & Other Stories. 1961. 6.95 o.p. (ISBN 0-684-10249-8, ScribT); Hudson River Edition. pap. 2.95 (ISBN 0-684-71807-3, SL32, ScribT); 15.00x (ISBN 0-684-16479-5). Scribner.
--The Sun Also Rises. (Arabic.). pap. 7.95x (ISBN 0-686-63550-7). Intl Bk Ctr.
--To Have & Have Not. 1937. 17.50x (ISBN 0-684-15328-9, ScribT); pap. 3.95 (ISBN 0-684-71809-X, SL132, ScribT). Scribner.
Hemingway, G. S. Introduction to Business Finance. 1975. 19.95x (ISBN 0-434-90730-8); pap. 12.95x (ISBN 0-434-90731-6). Intl Ideas.
Hemingway, Joan & Maricich, Connie. The Picnic Gourmet. (Illus.). 1978. pap. 6.95 (ISBN 0-394-72164-0, Vin). Random.
Hemingway, John. Conflict & Democracy: Studies in Trade Union Government. 1978. 16.95x o.p. (ISBN 0-19-827418-1). Oxford U Pr.
Hemingway, Muffet & Armstrong, Russ. Dining in-Sun Valley. (Dining in Ser.). 1981. pap. 7.95 (ISBN 0-89716-078-9). Peanut Butter.
Hemingway, Pamela. Direct Marketing Market Place 1981. 375p. 1981. pap. 40.00 (ISBN 0-934464-02-2). Hilary House Pubs.
Hemley, Cecil. Dimensions of Midnight: Poetry & Prose. Gottlieb, E., ed. LC 66-25957. xv, 233p. 1966. 10.95 (ISBN 0-8214-0023-1). Ohio U Pr.
Hemlon, Joyce see Burney, Fanny.
Hemlow, Joyce. History of Fanny Burney. 1958. 37.50x (ISBN 0-19-811549-0). Oxford U Pr.
Hemlow, Joyce see Burney, Fanny.
Hemlow, Joyce, et al see Burney, Fanny.
Hemmaplardh, Brecharr, jt. auth. see Shuffstall, Richard M.
Hemmer, Joseph J., Jr. Communication Under Law: Vol. I, Free Speech. LC 79-19166. 307p. 1979. 16.50 (ISBN 0-8108-1248-7). Scarecrow.
Hemmerling, Edwin M. Fundamentals of College Geometry. 2nd ed. (Illus.). 1970. text ed. 20.95x (ISBN 0-471-37034-7). Wiley.
Hemming, Doris, tr. see Siegfried, Andre.
Hemming, H. H., tr. see Siegfried, Andre.
Hemming, James. The Betrayal of Youth: Secondary Education Must Be Changed. LC 79-56484. (Ideas in Progress Ser.). 160p. 1980. 12.00 (ISBN 0-7145-2692-4, Pub. by M Boyars); pap. 6.95 (ISBN 0-7145-2693-2). Merrimack Bk Serv.
Hemming, John. Machu Picchu. Bayrd, Edwin, ed. LC 80-82066. (Illus.). 1981. 16.95 (ISBN 0-88225-302-6). Newsweek.
--Red Gold: The Conquest of the Brazilian Indians, 1500-1760. LC 77-22863. 1978. 20.00 (ISBN 0-674-75107-8). Harvard U Pr.
Hemmings, D. W. Culture & Society in France: Eighteen Forty-Eight to Eighteen Ninety-Eight. 1971. 40.00 (ISBN 0-7134-1522-3, Pub. by Batsford England). David & Charles.
Hemmings, F. W. Alexandre Dumas: The King of Romance. (Illus.). 1980. 12.95 (ISBN 0-684-16391-8, ScribT). Scribner.
--The Life & Times of Emile Zola. LC 77-73899. (Illus.). 1977. encore ed. 4.95 o.p. (ISBN 0-684-16356-X, ScribT). Scribner.
Hemmings, F. W., ed. The Age of Realism. 1978. Repr. of 1974 ed. text ed. 27.50x (ISBN 0-391-00817-X). Humanities.
Hemmings, J. A. G. & White, A., eds. Drag Reduction by Additives: Review & Bibliography. 1976. pap. 50.00 (ISBN 0-900983-58-2, Dist. by Air Science Co.). BHRA Fluid.
Hemmings, W. A., ed. Materno Foetal Transmission of Immunoglobulins. LC 75-2721. (Clinical & Experimental Immunoreproduction: No. 2). (Illus.). 400p. 1975. 57.50 (ISBN 0-521-20747-9). Cambridge U Pr.
Hemmings, W. A., ed. see Brambell Symposium 2nd, Wales, July 1978.
Hemmingway. Men at War: The Best War Stories of All Time. Date not set. 5.98 (ISBN 0-517-02084-X). Bonanza.
Hempel & Solem. Introduction to Data Processing for the New Age: Syllabus. 1977. pap. text ed. 7.95 (ISBN 0-89420-034-8, 223020); cassette recordings 139.65 (ISBN 0-89420-138-7, 223000). Natl Book.
Hempel, Carl. Philosophy of Natural Science. (Orig.). 1966. pap. 7.95x ref. ed. (ISBN 0-13-663823-6). P-H.
Hempel, Carl G. Aspects of Scientific Explanation. LC 65-15441. 1970. pap. text ed. 9.95 (ISBN 0-02-914340-3). Free Pr.
Hempel, Goerge, jt. auth. see Crosse, Howard.
Hempel, Gotthilf. Early Life History of Marine Fish: The Egg Stage. LC 79-14549. (Washington Sea Grant). 86p. 1980. pap. 7.50 (ISBN 0-295-95672-0). U of Wash Pr.
Hempel, Marvin W. Introductory Accounting: Part One, Syllabus. 1972. pap. text ed. 9.95 (ISBN 0-89420-024-0, 351004); cassette recordings 201.10 (ISBN 0-89420-154-9, 351100). Natl Book.
--Introductory Accounting: Part Two Syllabus. (gr. 8-12). 1973. pap. text ed. 10.75 (ISBN 0-89420-027-5, 351006); cassette recordings 248.15 (ISBN 0-89420-155-7, 351125). Natl Book.
--Record Keeping for Business: Syllabus. 1977. pap. text ed. 8.75 (ISBN 0-89420-018-6, 359090); cassette recordings 138.60 (ISBN 0-89420-180-8, 359000). Natl Book.
--Record Keeping for Personal Finance: Syllabus. 1976. pap. text ed. 7.95 (ISBN 0-89420-005-4, 358080); cassette recordings 123.25 (ISBN 0-89420-181-6, 358000). Natl Book.
--Ten-Key Adding Machine: Student Guide. 1970. pap. text ed. 5.55 (ISBN 0-89420-056-9, 126600); cassette recordings 142.40 (ISBN 0-89420-187-5, 156700). Natl Book.
Hemphill, Charles. Business Communications with Writing Improvement Exercises. 256p. 1981. pap. text ed. 11.95 (ISBN 0-13-093880-7). P-H.
Hemphill, Charles F., jt. auth. see Hemphill, Phyllis D.
Hemphill, Elizabeth. The Least of These: Miki Sawada & Her Children. 176p. 1981. 12.50 (ISBN 0-8348-0155-8, Pub. by John Weatherhill Inc Japan). C E Tuttle.
Hemphill, Gary B. Blasting Operations. (Illus.). 1980. 21.50 (ISBN 0-07-028093-2). McGraw.

Hemphill, Grace F. The Political, Economic & Labor Climate in Colombia. 1980. pap. 15.00 (ISBN 0-89546-025-4). Indus Res Unit-Wharton.

Hemphill, Paul. The Nashville Sound. (Mockingbird Bks). 224p. 1975. pap. 1.50 o.p. (ISBN 0-345-24521-0). Ballantine.

--Too Old to Cry. LC 80-51776. 288p. 1981. 11.95 (ISBN 0-670-72017-8). Viking Pr.

Hemphill, Phyllis D. & Hemphill, Charles F. A Practical Guide to Real Estate Law. (Illus.). 272p. 1980. text ed. 14.95 (ISBN 0-13-691022-X, Spec); pap. text ed. 7.95 (ISBN 0-13-691014-9). P-H.

Hems, Jack, jt. auth. see Hervey, George F.

Hemschemeyer, Judith. I Remember the Room Was Filled with Light. LC 72-11055. (Wesleyan Poetry Program: Vol. 66). 72p. 1973. pap. 4.95 (ISBN 0-8195-1066-1, Pub. by Wesleyan U Pr). Columbia U Pr.

--Very Close & Very Slow. LC 74-20951. (Wesleyan Poetry Program: Vol. 76). 69p. 1975. pap. 10.00x (ISBN 0-8195-2076-4, Pub. by Wesleyan U Pr); pap. 4.95 (ISBN 0-8195-1076-9). Columbia U Pr.

Hemsing, Esther D., ed. Good & Inexpensive Books for Children. rev. ed. LC 72-75054. (Illus.). 1972. pap. 2.00x o.p. (ISBN 0-87173-022-7). ACEI.

Hemstock, H. F. & Costelloe, J. Modern Business Arithmetic. 3rd ed. 1974. pap. text ed. 11.95x (ISBN 0-17-741005-1). Intl Ideas.

Henak, Richard M. Lesson Planning for Meaningful Variety in Teaching. 110p. 1980. 6.25 (ISBN 0-8106-1515-0). NEA.

Hencken, Hugh. The Earliest European Helmets: Bronze Age or Early Iron Age. LC 78-152525. (ASPR Bulletin: No. 28). 1971. pap. text ed. 17.00 (ISBN 0-87365-530-3). Peabody Harvard.

--Mecklenburg Collection, Pt. II: The Iron Age Cemetary of Magdalenska gora in Slovenia. Condon, Lorna, ed. LC 78-52401. (American School of Prehistoric Research Bulletin Ser.: No. 32). 1978. pap. text ed. 30.00 (ISBN 0-87365-539-7). Peabody Harvard.

--Tarquinia, Villanovans & Early Etruscans. LC 67-24729. (ASPR Bulletin: No. 23). 1968. pap. text ed. 50.00 (ISBN 0-87365-524-9). Peabody Harvard.

Hencken, Hugh, ed. Mecklenburg Collection: Part I. LC 68-22588. (ASPR Bulletin: No. 25). 1968. pap. text ed. 12.00 (ISBN 0-87365-526-5). Peabody Harvard.

Hencley, Stephan P. & Yates, James R. Futurism in Education: Methodologies. LC 73-20853. 1974. 20.50x (ISBN 0-8211-0753-4); text ed. 18.50x (ISBN 0-685-42634-3). McCutchan.

Hendee, W. R. Radioactive Isotopes in Biological Research. LC 73-8966. 27.50 (ISBN 0-471-37043-6, Pub. by Wiley-Interscience). Wiley.

Hendel, Charles W., ed. see Hume, David.

Hendel, Samuel & Bishop, Hillman. Basic Issues of American Democracy. 8th ed. 1975. pap. 9.95 (ISBN 0-13-062521-3). P-H.

Hendel, Samuel, ed. The Politics of Confrontation. LC 75-148865. 1971. pap. text ed. 6.95x (ISBN 0-89197-893-3). Irvington.

Henderlite, Rachel. Exploring the New Testament. (Orig.). (gr. 6 up). 1946. pap. 4.95 (ISBN 0-8042-0240-0). John Knox.

--Exploring the Old Testament. (Orig.). (gr. 6 up). 1945. pap. 4.95 (ISBN 0-8042-0120-X). John Knox.

Hendershot, Anna I. Duplicate Partners. 1975. pap. text ed. 2.25 (ISBN 0-911832-08-4). Hendershot.

Hendershot, Carl H. Programmed Learning: A Bibliography of Programs & Presentation Devices. 4th ed. LC 67-16988. (Incl. suppl. 1-6). 1971. 45.00 (ISBN 0-911832-04-1). Hendershot.

Hendershot, Carl H., compiled by. Programmed Learning: A Bibliography of Programs & Presentation Devices. 2nd ed. 1963. 15.00 (ISBN 0-911832-12-2). Hendershot.

--Programmed Learning: A Bibliography of Programs & Presentation Devices. 3rd ed. LC 64-11824. (Illus.). 1965. 30.00 (ISBN 0-911832-11-4). Hendershot.

--Programmed Learning & Individually Paced Instruction Bibliography. 5th ed. LC 73-77783. 1973. 45.00 (ISBN 0-911832-05-X); basic bibl. & suppls. 1-5 95.00 (ISBN 0-911832-14-9); basic bibl. & suppls. 1-4 o.p. 70.00 (ISBN 0-911832-07-6); basic bibl. & suppls. 1 & 2 o.p. 58.00 (ISBN 0-911832-06-8); suppl. 5 25.00 (ISBN 0-911832-13-0); suppl. 6 27.75 (ISBN 0-911832-06-8) (ISBN 0-911832-16-5). Hendershot.

Hendershot, Gerry E. Predicting Fertility. Placek, Paul J., ed. LC 79-9686. 352p. 1981. 23.95x (ISBN 0-669-03618-8). Lexington Bks.

Hendershott, Patric H., et al. Understanding Capital Markets, 2 vols. Incl. Vol. 1. A Flow of Funds Financial Model. LC 76-55112 (ISBN 0-669-01006-5). 29.50 (ISBN 0-686-67901-6); Vol. 2. The Financial Environment & the Flow of Funds in the Next Decade. LC 76-55113. 22.00 (ISBN 0-669-01007-3). 1977. Lexington Bks.

Henderson, A. The Twenty-Seven Lines Upon the Cubic Surface. (Cambridge Tracts in Mathematics & Mathematical Physics Ser.: No. 13). (Illus.). 1969. Repr. of 1911 ed. 7.50 o.s.i. (ISBN 0-02-845930-X). Hafner.

Henderson, A. Corbin. Brothers of Light: The Penitentes of the Southwest. LC 77-88835. 1977. Repr. of 1937 ed. 13.50 (ISBN 0-88307-534-2); pap. 3.95 o.p. (ISBN 0-88307-535-0). Gannon.

Henderson, Alexander, tr. see Bauer, Arnold.

Henderson, Algo D. The Innovative Spirit. LC 78-128698. (Higher Education Ser.). 1970. 14.95x o.p. (ISBN 0-87589-073-3). Jossey-Bass.

Henderson, Andrew. Scottish Proverbs. LC 70-75962. 1969. Repr. of 1881 ed. 18.00 (ISBN 0-8103-3894-7). Gale.

Henderson, Archibald. George Bernard Shaw, 2 vols. LC 79-87485. (Illus.). 1078p. 1972. Repr. of 1956 ed. Set. lib. bdg. 55.00 (ISBN 0-306-71491-4). Da Capo.

Henderson, Archibald, Jr., tr. see Mauron, Charles.

Henderson, B. & Wertz, J. E. Defects in the Alkaline Earth Oxides: With Applications to Radiation Damage & Catalysis. LC 77-23366. 1977. 27.95 (ISBN 0-470-99205-0). Halsted Pr.

Henderson, Betty, jt. auth. see Vaughan-Wrobel, Beth C.

Henderson, Bill. His Son: A Child of the Fifties. 1981. 12.95 (ISBN 0-393-01439-8). Norton.

--How to Run Your Own Rock & Roll Band. (Orig.). 1977. pap. 1.50 o.p. (ISBN 0-445-04043-2). Popular Lib.

Henderson, Bill, ed. The Pushcart Prize: Best of the Small Presses. LC 75-40812. 1976. pap. 5.95 (ISBN 0-916366-01-4). Pushcart Pr.

--Pushcart Prize II. 1978. pap. 5.95 (ISBN 0-380-01895-0, 37275). Avon.

--The Pushcart Prize Six: Best of the Small Presses. 1981. 19.50 (ISBN 0-916366-12-X). Pushcart Pr.

--Pushcart Prize VI. 600p. 1980. pap. 7.95 (ISBN 0-380-48827-2, 48827). Avon.

Henderson, Brian. Critique of Film Theory. 224p. 1980. 15.95 (ISBN 0-525-08740-0); pap. 8.95 (ISBN 0-525-47526-5). Dutton.

Henderson, D. see Eyring, H., et al.

Henderson, Davd. The Low East. 80p. 1980. 30.00 (ISBN 0-913028-73-8); pap. 4.95 (ISBN 0-913028-72-X). North Atlantic.

Henderson, David. Jimi Hendrix: Voodoo Child of the Aquarian Age. LC 76-56299. 1978. 13.95 (ISBN 0-385-07357-7). Doubleday.

Henderson, David & Gillespie, R. D. Textbook of Psychiatry for Students & Practitioners. 10th ed. Batchelor, Ivor R., ed. 1969. 16.95x o.p. (ISBN 0-19-264412-2); pap. 10.95x (ISBN 0-19-264413-0). Oxford U Pr.

Henderson, David, intro. by. Joe Overstreet. LC 72-85404. (Illus.). 1972. pap. 2.25 (ISBN 0-914412-02-7). Inst for the Arts.

Henderson, Davis & Steffel, Victor L. McCracken's Removable Partial Prosthodontics. 6th ed. (Illus.). 516p. 1981. text ed. 28.75 (ISBN 0-8016-2146-1). Mosby.

Henderson, Diane. Guide to Basic Reference Materials for Canadian Libraries. 6th ed. 1980. looseleaf 16.50x (ISBN 0-8020-2410-6). U of Toronto Pr.

Henderson, Dion. Algonquin. (gr. 3 up). 1979. pap. 1.25 (ISBN 0-307-21618-7, Golden Pr). Western Pub.

Henderson, Donald, et al, eds. Effects of Noise on Hearing. LC 75-14576. 1976. 43.50 (ISBN 0-89004-012-5). Raven.

Henderson, Douglas, ed. Theoretical Chemistry: Theory of Scattering-Papers in Honor of Henry Eyring, Vol. 6a. (Serial Publication). 1981. write for info. (ISBN 0-12-681906-8). Acad Pr.

--Theoretical Chemistry: Theory of Scattering: Papers in Honor of Henry Eyring, Vol. 6B. (Serial Publications). 1981. price not set (ISBN 0-12-681907-6). Acad Pr.

Henderson, E. J. & Asher, R. Towards a History of Phonetics. 256p. 1980. 32.50x (ISBN 0-85224-374-X, Pub. by Edinburgh U Pr Scotland). Columbia U Pr.

Henderson, Edith G. Foundations of English Administrative Law: Certiorari & Mandamus in the Seventeenth Century. LC 63-11421. (Ames Foundation Publications Ser). 1963. 10.00x (ISBN 0-674-31351-8). Harvard U Pr.

Henderson, Elizabeth, tr. see Bauer, Arnold.

Henderson, Ernest F., ed. Select Historical Documents of the Middle Ages. LC 65-15247. 1892. 10.50x (ISBN 0-8196-0149-7). Biblo.

Henderson, G. E. Planning for an Individual Water System. 7.95 (ISBN 0-914452-45-2). Green Hill.

Henderson, G. G. Geology of Tom Green County. (Illus.). 116p. 1928. 0.50 (BULL 2807). Bur Econ Geology.

Henderson, G. P. & Henderson, S. P., eds. Directory of British Associations & Associations in Ireland. 6th ed. 1980. 125.00 (ISBN 0-900246-34-0, Pub. by CBD Research). Gale.

Henderson, George. Thhe Celtic Dragon Myth. (Newcastle Mythology Library: Vol. 4). 160p. 1981. Repr. lib. bdg. 12.95 (ISBN 0-89370-648-5). Borgo Pr.

--Human Relations: From Theory to Practice. LC 73-19387. (Illus.). 450p. 1981. pap. 9.95 (ISBN 0-8061-1709-5). U of Okla Pr.

--Introduction to American Education: A Human Relations Approach. LC 77-18609. 1979. 13.95 (ISBN 0-8061-1458-4). U of Okla Pr.

Henderson, George, jt. auth. see Campbell, J. F.

Henderson, Glenn V., jt. auth. see Wert, James E.

Henderson, H. J. Party Politics in the Continental Congress. 1974. text ed. 17.50 o.p. (ISBN 0-07-028143-2, P&RB). McGraw.

Henderson, Harry, jt. auth. see Bearden, Romare.

Henderson, Hazel. Politics of the Solar Age: The Alternative to Economics. LC 80-1723. (Illus.). 312p. 1981. pap. 5.95 (ISBN 0-385-17150-1, Anchor Pr); pap. 5.95 (ISBN 0-385-17151-X). Doubleday.

Henderson, Hubert. Supply & Demand. (Cambridge Economic Handbook Ser). 1958. pap. 8.95x (ISBN 0-521-08760-0). Cambridge U Pr.

Henderson, I. W., jt. ed. see Chester-Jones, I.

Henderson, Ian. Rudolf Bultmann. Nineham, D. E. & Robertson, E. H., eds. LC 66-11071. (Makers of Contemporary Theology Ser). 1966. pap. 3.45 (ISBN 0-8042-0698-8). John Knox.

Henderson, J., ed. Aristophanes: Essays in Interpretation. LC 80-40042. (Yale Classical Studies: No. 26). 248p. Date not set. 35.00 (ISBN 0-521-23120-5). Cambridge U Pr.

Henderson, J. Frank & Paterson, A. R. Nucleotide Metabolism. 1973. 33.50 (ISBN 0-12-340550-5). Acad Pr.

Henderson, J. L. Education for World Understanding. 1969. 12.25 (ISBN 0-08-013217-0); pap. 5.75 (ISBN 0-08-013216-2). Pergamon.

Henderson, J. Lloyd. Fluid Milk Industry. 3rd ed. LC 75-137709. Orig. Title: The Market Milk Industry. (Illus.). 1971. 39.50 (ISBN 0-87055-090-X). AVI.

Henderson, J. Welles, jt. ed. see Stewart, Harris B., Jr.

Henderson, James D. & Henderson, Linda R. Ten Notable Women of Latin America. LC 78-15253. (Illus.). 1978. 17.95 (ISBN 0-88229-426-1); pap. 8.95 (ISBN 0-88229-596-9). Nelson-Hall.

Henderson, Janice A. Don't Worry. 250p. 1981. 8.95 (ISBN 0-396-07901-6). Dodd.

Henderson, Joe. Jog, Run, Race. LC 77-73651. (Illus.). 204p. 1977. pap. 3.95 (ISBN 0-89037-122-9); handbk. 4.95 (ISBN 0-89037-121-0). Anderson World.

--Long Run. LC 75-20958. (Illus.). 1976. pap. 3.95 (ISBN 0-89037-101-6); handbk. 5.95 (ISBN 0-89037-102-4). Anderson World.

Henderson, John W. Orbital Tumors. LC 72-90722. (Illus.). 705p. 1973. text ed. 45.00 (ISBN 0-7216-4633-6). Saunders.

Henderson, Joseph L. Thresholds of Initiation. LC 67-24110. 1979. pap. 9.00 (ISBN 0-8195-6061-8, Pub. by Wesleyan U Pr). Columbia U Pr.

Henderson, Joseph L. & Oakes, Maud. Wisdom of the Serpent. 1971. pap. 1.95 o.s.i. (ISBN 0-02-065370-0, Collier). Macmillan.

Henderson, Lawrence J. Fitness of the Environment: An Inquiry into the Biological Significance of the Properties of Matter. 8.00 (ISBN 0-8446-0691-X). Peter Smith.

Henderson, Lawrence W. Angola: Five Centuries of Conflict. LC 79-5089. (Africa in the Modern World Ser.). (Illus.). 1979. 17.50x (ISBN 0-8014-1247-1). Cornell U Pr.

Henderson, Linda R., jt. auth. see Henderson, James D.

Henderson, Lois T. Abigail. LC 80-65429. 256p. 1980. 8.95 (ISBN 0-915684-62-4). Christian Herald.

--Lydia: A Novel. LC 79-50946. 1981. pap. 5.95 (ISBN 0-915684-88-8). Christian Herald.

Henderson, M. A. Essential Surgery for Nurses. (Illus.). 240p. 1980. pap. text ed. 12.00 (ISBN 0-443-01737-9). Churchill.

--The Survival Resource Book. (Illus.). 180p. 1981. pap. 8.95 (ISBN 0-312-77951-8). St Martin.

Henderson, M. D., jt. auth. see Wilson, Malcolm.

Henderson, M. Sturge. George Meredith. 324p. 1980. Repr. of 1907 ed. lib. bdg. 30.00. Darby Bks.

Henderson, Marina, jt. auth. see Mucha, Jiri.

Henderson, Marjorie & Wilkinson, Elizabeth. Naturally Powered Old Time Toys: How to Make Sun Yachts, Sail Cars, a Monkey on a String, & Other Moving Toys. LC 78-8556. (Illus.). 1978. 12.95 o.p. (ISBN 0-397-01308-6); pap. 6.95 o.p. (ISBN 0-397-01316-7). Lippincott.

Henderson, Martha & Paladin Press, eds. Great Survival Resource Book. (Illus.). 188p. 1981. 19.95 (ISBN 0-87364-199-X). Paladin Ent.

Henderson, Mary. Famous Personalities of Flight Cookbook. LC 80-20331. (Illus.). 136p. 1981. pap. 4.95 (ISBN 0-87474-515-2). Smithsonian.

Henderson, Michael D. Experiment with Untruth: India Under Emergency. 1978. 12.50x (ISBN 0-8364-0128-X). South Asia Bks.

Henderson, Nancy & Dewey, Jane. Circle of Life: The Miccosukee Indian Way. LC 73-19325. (Illus.). (gr. 3-6). 1974. PLB 5.29 o.p. (ISBN 0-671-32658-9). Messner.

Henderson, Paul & Thomas, David N. Skills in Neighbourhood Work. (National Institute Social Services Library: No. 39). (Illus.). 280p. 1981. text ed. 27.50x (ISBN 0-04-361042-0, 2554); pap. text ed. 12.95x (ISBN 0-04-361043-9, 2555). Allen Unwin.

Henderson, Paul, jt. ed. see Thomas, David N.

Henderson, Paul, et al, eds. Boundaries of Change in Community Work. (National Institute Social Services Library: No. 37). (Illus.). 256p. 1980. text ed. 27.50x (ISBN 0-04-361038-2); pap. text ed. 12.50x (ISBN 0-04-361039-0). Allen Unwin.

Henderson, Peter. Disability in Childhood & Youth. 208p. 1974. pap. text ed. 6.95x o.p. (ISBN 0-19-264168-9). Oxford U Pr.

--Functional Programming. (Ser. in Computer Science). (Illus.). 1980. text ed. 33.95 (ISBN 0-13-331579-7). P-H.

Henderson, Peter M. A Nut Between Two Blades: The Novels of Charles Robert Maturin. Varma, Devendra P., ed. LC 79-8457. (Gothic Studies & Dissertations Ser.). 1980. lib. bdg. 25.00x (ISBN 0-405-12672-7). Arno.

Henderson, Peter V. Felix Diaz, the Porfirians, & the Mexican Revolution. LC 80-13934. xiv, 239p. 1981. 18.50x (ISBN 0-8032-2312-9). U of Nebr Pr.

Henderson, Philip. Christopher Marlowe. Dobree, Bonamy, et al, eds. Bd. with Ben Jonson. Bamborough, J. B; John Webster. Scott-Kilvert, Ian; John Ford. Leech, Clifford. LC 63-63096. (British Writers & Their Work Ser: Vol. 11). 1966. pap. 3.25x (ISBN 0-8032-5661-2, BB 460, Bison). U of Nebr Pr.

--The Life of Laurence Oliphant: Traveller, Diplomat & Mystic. 281p. 1981. Repr. of 1956 ed. lib. bdg. 30.00 (ISBN 0-8495-2364-8). Arden Lib.

--Swinburne: Portrait of a Poet. LC 74-478. (Illus.). 312p. 1974. 10.95 o.s.i. (ISBN 0-02-550960-8). Macmillan.

--Tennyson: Poet & Prophet. (Illus.). 1978. 20.00x (ISBN 0-7100-8776-4). Routledge & Kegan.

Henderson, Philip see Doughty, Oswald.

Henderson, R. A. The Location of Immigrant Industry Within a U. K. Assisted Area: The Scottish Experience. (Progress in Planning Ser.: Vol. 14, Part 2). (Illus.). 121p. 1980. pap. 13.50 (ISBN 0-08-026807-2). Pergamon.

Henderson, Richard. East to the Azores: A Guide to Offshore Passage-Making. LC 77-91878. (Illus.). 1978. 12.50 (ISBN 0-87742-097-1). Intl Marine.

Henderson, Richard B. Maury Maverick: A Political Biography. (Illus.). 1970. 17.95 (ISBN 0-292-70090-3). U of Tex Pr.

Henderson, Richard I., jt. auth. see Suojanen, Waino.

Henderson, Richard I., et al. Job Pay for Job Worth: Designing & Managing an Equitable Job Classification & Pay System. (Research Monograph: No. 86). 320p. 1981. pap. 24.00 (ISBN 0-88406-130-2). Ga St U Busn Pub.

Henderson, Robert D. The Esophagus: Reflex & Primary Motor Disorders. 2nd ed. (Illus.). 312p. 1980. lib. bdg. 39.00 (ISBN 0-683-03948-2). Williams & Wilkins.

Henderson, Robert M. D. W. Griffith: The Years at Biograph. (Illus.). 1970. pap. 2.95 (ISBN 0-374-50958-1). FS&G.

Henderson, Robert T. Joy to the World: An Introduction to Kingdom Evangelism. LC 80-14597. 207p. (Orig.). 1980. pap. 6.95 (ISBN 0-8042-2096-4, 2096-4). John Knox.

Henderson, Robert W. Ball, Bat & Bishop: The Origin of Ball Games. LC 73-10389. (Illus.). 221p. 1974. Repr. of 1947 ed. 18.00 (ISBN 0-8103-3877-7). Gale.

Henderson, Ronald W. & Bergan, John R. The Cultural Context of Childhood. new ed. 1976. text ed. 17.95 (ISBN 0-675-08599-3); instructor's manual 3.95 (ISBN 0-686-67315-8). Merrill.

Henderson, Ronald W., ed. Parent-Child Interaction: Theory, Research & Projects. LC 80-2336. (Educational Psychology Ser.). 1981. write for info. (ISBN 0-12-340620-X). Acad Pr.

Henderson, S. M. & Perry, R. L. Agricultural Process Engineering. 3rd ed. (Illus.). 1976. pap. text ed. 20.50 (ISBN 0-87055-300-3). AVI.

Henderson, S. P., jt. ed. see Henderson, G. P.

Henderson, S. T. Daylight & Its Spectrum. 2nd ed. LC 77-88254. 1978. 36.95 (ISBN 0-470-99328-6). Halsted Pr.

Henderson, S. T. & Marsden, A. M., eds. Lamps & Lighting. 2nd ed. LC 72-83310. 600p. 1972. 42.50x (ISBN 0-8448-0063-5). Crane-Russak Co.

Henderson, Sally & Landau, Robert. Billboard Art. LC 79-24115. (Illus.). 112p. (Orig.). 1980. pap. 9.95 (ISBN 0-87701-167-2, Prism Edns). Chronicle Bks.

Henderson, Scott D. Pathology in Computed Tomography of the Brain. (Illus.). 216p. 1978. 22.50 (ISBN 0-398-03749-3). C C Thomas.

Henderson, Stephen E., jt. auth. see Cook, Mercer.

Henderson, T. F., ed. see Scott, Walter.

Henderson, Thomas A. & Foster, John L. Urban Policy Game: A Simulation of Urban Politics. LC 78-17118. 1978. pap. text ed. 9.95x (ISBN 0-471-03398-7); tchr's manual avail. (ISBN 0-471-04219-6). Wiley.

Henderson, Thomas E., jt. auth. see Moore, Ballard J.

Henderson, Thomas F. Scottish Vernacular Literature: A Succinct History. 3rd. ed. LC 70-75473. 1969. Repr. of 1910 ed. 22.00 (ISBN 0-8103-3884-X). Gale.

Henderson, Virginia. Nursing Studies Index, 4 vols. Yale University Index Staff, ed. Incl. Vol. 1. 1900-1929. 900p. 35.00 o.p. (ISBN 0-397-54125-2); Vol. 2. 1930-1949. 1037p. 28.00 o.p. (ISBN 0-397-54104-X); Vol. 3. 1950-1956. 653p. 25.00 o.p. (ISBN 0-397-54053-1); Vol. 4. 1957-1959. 280p. 15.00 o.p. (ISBN 0-685-22858-4). Lippincott.

Henderson, W. J. The Art of Singing. LC 78-4953. (Music Reprint 1978 Ser.). 1978. Repr. of 1938 ed. lib. bdg. 35.00 (ISBN 0-306-77593-X). Da Capo.

Henderson, W. L. & Ledebur, L. C. Economic Disparity. LC 79-96833. 1970. 10.95 (ISBN 0-02-914440-X); pap. text ed. 10.95 (ISBN 0-02-914400-0). Free Pr.

Henderson, W. O. Life of Friedrich Engels, 2 vols. Incl. Vol. 1. Young Revolutionary; Vol. 2. Marx's Alter Ego. (Illus.). 1974. 65.00x set (ISBN 0-7146-3065-9, F Cass Co). Biblio Dist.

--The Rise of German Industrial Power, 1834-1914. LC 75-17293. 1976. 22.50x (ISBN 0-520-03073-7); pap. 5.95x (ISBN 0-520-03120-2). U of Cal Pr.

Henderson, William D. Gilded Age City: Politics, Life, & Labor in Petersburg, Virginia, 1874-1889. LC 80-1385. (Illus.). 603p. 1980. lib. bdg. 25.50 (ISBN 0-8191-1294-1); pap. text ed. 17.50 (ISBN 0-8191-1295-X). U Pr of Amer.

Henderson, William O. J. C. Fischer & His Diary of Industrial England, 1815-1841. LC 66-55759. (Illus.). 1966. 19.50x (ISBN 0-678-05059-7). Kelley.

--Studies in the Economic Policy of Frederick the Great. LC 64-39262. 1963. 22.50x (ISBN 0-678-05176-3). Kelley.

Henderson, William O., ed. Industrial Britain Under the Regency. LC 67-30258. (Illus.). 1968. 19.50x (ISBN 0-678-05058-9). Kelley.

Henderson, Zenna. Pilgrimage. 1973. pap. 1.50 (ISBN 0-380-01507-2, 36681). Avon.

Hendin, David. Death As a Fact of Life. 224p. 1974. pap. 2.25 o.s.i. (ISBN 0-446-92241-2). Warner Bks.

Hendler, Munice. Ready-to-Use Dollhouse Floor Coverings: Eight Full-Color Patterns to Decorate 8 Rooms. (Illus.). 1978. pap. 3.00 (ISBN 0-486-23666-8). Dover.

Hendler, Nelson, ed. Diagnosis & Nonsurgical Management of Chronic Pain. LC 78-51277. 1980. 25.00 (ISBN 0-89004-289-6). Raven.

Hendler, Nelson H., ed. Pain: A Comprehensive View. 250p. 1981. 24.00 (ISBN 0-88416-287-7, 287). PSG Pub.

Hendon, William S. Analyzing an Art Museum. LC 79-10753. 27.95 (ISBN 0-03-050386-8). Praeger.

Hendren, Bob. Chosen for Riches. LC 77-25775. (Journey Bks.). 1978. 2.35 (ISBN 0-8344-0096-0). Sweet.

--Life Without End. LC 80-54164. (Journey Bks.). 144p. (Orig.). 1981. pap. 2.35 (ISBN 0-8344-0118-5). Sweet.

Hendrich, Paula. The Birds Are in Your Hands. (Illus.). 160p. (gr. 5 up). Date not set. 8.95 (ISBN 0-688-00417-2); PLB 8.59 (ISBN 0-688-00418-0). Morrow. Postponed.

--Who Says So? LC 73-177318. (Illus.). 128p. (gr. 4 up). 1972. PLB 6.96 o.p. (ISBN 0-688-51481-2). Lothrop.

Hendrick. Total Learning for the Whole Child. LC 79-20624. 1980. 16.95 (ISBN 0-8016-2150-X). Mosby.

--The Whole Child: New Trends in Early Education. 2nd ed. LC 79-9135. 1980. 18.95 (ISBN 0-8016-2145-3). Mosby.

Hendrick, Burton J see Johnson, Allen & Nevins, Allan.

Hendrick, Clyde & Jones, Russell A. Nature of Theory & Research in Social Psychology. 1972. text ed. 17.95 (ISBN 0-12-340750-8). Acad Pr.

Hendrick, George. Katherine Anne Porter. (U. S. Authors Ser.: No. 90). 1965. lib. bdg. 9.95 (ISBN 0-8057-0592-9). Twayne.

Hendrick, George, jt. auth. see Gerstenberger, Donna.

Hendrick, Gladys W. My First Three Hundred Babies. LC 78-50853. 1978. 5.95 (ISBN 0-88449-030-0). Vision Hse.

Hendrick, John R. Opening the Door of Faith: The Why, When & Where of Evangelism. LC 76-12404. 1977. pap. 4.50 (ISBN 0-8042-0675-9). John Knox.

Hendrick, Leo T., jt. auth. see Amend, Victor E.

Hendrick, Leo T., jt. ed. see Amend, Victor E.

Hendrick, Thomas, jt. auth. see Moore, Franklin G.

Hendrick, Thomas E., jt. auth. see Johnson, George A.

Hendricks, Albert C., jt. auth. see Buikema, Arthur L., Jr.

Hendricks, C. & Leavenworth, C. Living: The Adult Centering Book. 1978. 8.95 (ISBN 0-13-538512-1); pap. 3.95 (ISBN 0-13-538504-0). P-H.

Hendricks, C. G. & Wills, Russell. The Centering Book: Awareness Activities for Children, Parents & Teachers. (Transpersonal Bks.). (Illus.). 192p. 1975. 11.95 (ISBN 0-13-122192-2, Spec); pap. 4.95 (ISBN 0-13-122184-1, Spec). P-H.

Hendricks, C. Gaylord & Fadiman, James. Transpersonal Education: A Curriculum for Feeling & Being. 1976. pap. text ed. 4.95x (ISBN 0-13-930461-4, Spec). P-H.

Hendricks, C. H., jt. auth. see Elder, M. G.

Hendricks, Davis, jt. auth. see Hendricks, Jan.

Hendricks, G. & Roberts, T. The Second Centering Book: More Awareness Activites for Children, Parents, & Teachers. 1977. 11.95 (ISBN 0-13-797332-2, Spec); pap. 5.95 (ISBN 0-13-797324-1, Spec). P-H.

Hendricks, Gay. The Centered Teacher: Awareness Activities for Teachers & Their Students. (Transformation Ser.). 192p. 1981. 9.95 (ISBN 0-13-122234-1, Spec); pap. 4.95 (ISBN 0-13-122226-0). P-H.

Hendricks, George D. Mirrors, Mice, & Mustaches. 110p. 1981. pap. 4.95 (ISBN 0-87074-075-X). SMU Press.

--Roosters, Rhymes, & Railroad Tracks. 200p. 1980. pap. 6.95 (ISBN 0-87074-177-2). SMU Press.

Hendricks, Glenn. The Dominican Diaspora: From the Dominican Republic to New York City, Villagers in Transition. LC 74-4203. 1974. text ed. 10.50x (ISBN 0-8077-2426-2); pap. text ed. 7.95x (ISBN 0-8077-2459-9). Tchrs Coll.

Hendricks, Howard & Hendricks, Jeanne. Footprints: Walking Through the Passages of Life. LC 80-25868. (Illus.). 96p. 1981. pap. 8.95 (ISBN 0-930014-55-3). Multnomah.

Hendricks, Howard G. Heaven Help the Home! LC 73-78689. 1974. pap. 3.95 (ISBN 0-88207-240-4). Victor Bks.

--Say It with Love. 143p. 1972. pap. 3.95 (ISBN 0-88207-050-9). Victor Bks.

Hendricks, Jan & Hendricks, Davis. Aging in Mass Society. 420p. 1981. ref. ed. 15.95 (ISBN 0-87626-017-2). Winthrop.

Hendricks, Jeanne. A Woman for All Seasons. LC 77-23045. 1977. pap. 3.95 (ISBN 0-8407-5630-5). Nelson.

Hendricks, Jeanne, jt. auth. see Hendricks, Howard.

Hendricks, Kenneth C. Shadow of His Hand. (Orig.). 1967. kivar 3.95 o.p. (ISBN 0-8272-3402-3). Bethany Pr.

Hendricks, Rhoda A. Latin Made Simple. LC 62-12101. pap. 3.50 (ISBN 0-385-01756-1, Made). Doubleday.

--Mythologies of the World: A Concise Encyclopedia. Shapiro, Max S., ed. 240p. 1981. pap. 4.95 (ISBN 0-07-056421-3). McGraw.

Hendricks, William. Bible Jumble Word Puzzles. 1978. pap. 2.50 (ISBN 0-310-37192-9). Zondervan.

Hendricks, William & Noord, Glenn Van. Bible Word Chain Puzzles. (Quiz & Puzzle Bks.). 96p. (Orig.). 1981. pap. 2.95 (ISBN 0-8010-4238-0). Baker Bk.

Hendricks, William C. Under God. 1966. 5.50 o.p. (ISBN 0-8028-3108-7). Eerdmans.

Hendricks, William S. America's Health Care Crisis. LC 80-66321. 1980. 9.95 (ISBN 0-686-28081-4). Ducky Ent.

Hendricksen, W., tr. see Bavinck, Herman.

Hendrickson, E. S. & Budge, B. P. Contemporary Accounting Theory. LC 73-81294. 1973. pap. 9.95 (ISBN 0-8221-0116-5). CBI Pub.

Hendrickson, Gayle A. Promoting Continuing Education Programs. 80p. (Orig.). 1980. pap. 10.50 (ISBN 0-89964-169-5). CASE.

Hendrickson, J. B., et al. Organic Chemistry. 1970. text ed. 26.00 o.p. (ISBN 0-07-028150-5, C). McGraw.

Hendrickson, James M. & LaBarca, Angela. Spice of Life. 180p. 1979. pap. text ed. 6.95 (ISBN 0-15-583251-4, HC). HarBraceJ.

Hendrickson, Linnea, jt. auth. see Renford, Beverly.

Hendrickson, Robert. The Berry Book: The Illustrated Home Gardener's Guide to Growing & Using Over 50 Kinds & 300 Varieties of Berries from Strawberries, Blueberries & Raspberries to Currants, Dewberries, & Gooseberries. LC 78-22326. (Illus.). 192p. 1981. 9.95 (ISBN 0-385-13589-0). Doubleday.

--The Grand Emporiums: The Illustrated History of America's Great Department Stores. LC 78-7555. (Illus.). 616p. 1980. pap. 9.95 (ISBN 0-8128-6092-6). Stein & Day.

--The Great American Chewing Gum Book. LC 79-6055. (Illus.). 254p. 1980. 6.95 (ISBN 0-8128-6050-0). Stein & Day.

Hendrickson, William see Summerlin, Lee R.

Hendriksen, Eldon S. Accounting Theory. 3rd. ed. 1977. text ed. 19.95 (ISBN 0-256-01901-0). Irwin.

Hendriksen, V. Christmas in Norway. (Tanum of Norway Tokens Ser). pap. 7.50x (ISBN 82-518-1375-1, N501). Vanous.

Hendriksen, William. Bible on the Life Hereafter. (Direction Books). 1971. pap. 3.45 (ISBN 0-8010-4189-9). Baker Bk.

--Romans, Vol. 1. 336p. 1980. 14.95 (ISBN 0-8010-4236-4). Baker Bk.

Hendriks-Jansen, Horst, jt. auth. see Sandhu, J. Singh.

Hendrikson, William. Galatians & Ephesians. (New Testament Commentary). 290p. 1979. 15.95 (ISBN 0-8010-4211-9). Baker Bk.

Hendrix, Robert C. Investigation of Violent & Sudden Death: A Manual for Medical Examiners. (Illus.). 104p. 1972. 9.75 (ISBN 0-398-02474-X). C C Thomas.

Hendrix, Scott H. Luther & the Papacy: Stages in a Reformation Conflict. LC 80-2393. 224p. 1981. 14.95 (ISBN 0-8006-0658-2, 1-658). Fortress.

Hendrix, Sue. Dwight D. Eisenhower. LC 74-19176. (Illus.). 40p. (gr. 4-8). 1975. PLB 5.95 (ISBN 0-87191-409-3). Creative Ed.

Hendrix, T. G. & LaFevor, C. S. Mathematics for Auto Mechanics. LC 77-72431. 1978. pap. text ed. 9.04 (ISBN 0-8273-1630-5); instructor's guide 1.60 (ISBN 0-8273-1631-3). Delmar.

Hendrix, Wayne R., jt. auth. see Heiner, Carol W.

Hendrix, William. Beginning French. 5th ed. LC 77-93107. (Illus.). 1978. pap. text ed. 15.75 (ISBN 0-395-25739-5); wkbk. 6.60 (ISBN 0-395-25740-9); tapes 207.28 (ISBN 0-395-25741-7). HM.

Hendry, Fay L. Outdoor Sculpture in Grand Rapids. LC 80-7500. (Illus.). 145p. (Orig.). 1980. pap. 3.50 (ISBN 0-936412-00-3). Iota Pr.

Hendry, Maurice D. Cadillac, Standard of the World: The Complete History. 3rd ed. LC 72-85846. 1979. 29.95 (ISBN 0-915038-10-2). Princeton Pub.

Hendry, R. Preston. Isle of Man Railway Album. LC 75-28. (Illus.). 96p. 1976. 13.50 (ISBN 0-7153-6828-1). David & Charles.

Hendy, Bruce. Membrane Physiology & Cell Excitation. 160p. 1980. 30.00x (Pub. by Croom Helm England). State Mutual Bk.

Heneage, Simon & Ford, Henry. Sidney Sime: Master of the Mysterious. 1980. pap. 8.95 (ISBN 0-500-27154-2). Thames Hudson.

Henegan, J. M. Pulse. 1980. 11.95 (ISBN 0-7145-3667-9); pap. 6.95 (ISBN 0-7145-3618-0). Riverrun NY.

Henege, Thomas. Death of a Shipowner. LC 80-26917. 224p. 1981. 8.95 (ISBN 0-396-07952-0). Dodd.

Heneman, Herbert G. & Schwab, Donald P., eds. Perspectives on Personnel - Human Resource Management. 1978. pap. text ed. 11.95x (ISBN 0-256-02071-X). Irwin.

Heneman, Herbert G., III, et al. Managing Personnel & Human Resources: Strategies & Programs. 350p. 1981. 15.95 (ISBN 0-87094-234-4). Dow Jones-Irwin.

Heneman, Herbert G., Jr., et al. Personnel-Human Resource Management. 1980. 18.95x (ISBN 0-256-02279-8). Irwin.

Henerson, Marlene E., et al. How to Measure Attitudes. LC 78-57010. (Program Evaluation Kit: Vol. 5). 1978. pap. 7.95x (ISBN 0-8039-1070-3). Sage.

Henes, Donna. Dressing Our Wounds in Warm Clothes. LC 81-65197. (Illus.). 72p. (Orig.). 1981. pap. 9.00 (ISBN 0-937122-02-5). Astro Artz.

Henfrey, Colin & Bernardo, Sorj, eds. Chilean Voices: Activists Describe Their Experiences of the Popular Unity Period. (Marxist Theory & Contemporary Capitalism). (Illus.). 1977. text ed. 13.00x (ISBN 0-391-00697-5); pap. text ed. 9.25x (ISBN 0-391-00698-3). Humanities.

Henfrey, J., tr. see Leal, V. N.

Henfrey, Norman, ed. see Santayana, George.

Hengel, Martin. Acts & the History of Earliest Christianity. LC 79-8893. 160p. 1980. 8.95 (ISBN 0-8006-0630-2, 1-630). Fortress.

--The Atonememt: The Origins of the Doctrine in the New Testament. Bowden, John, tr. from Ger. LC 80-2384. 128p. 1981. pap. 6.95 (ISBN 0-8006-1446-1, 1-1446). Fortress.

--Christ & Power. Kalin, Everett R., tr. from Ger. LC 76-62608. 96p. (Orig.). 1977. pap. 3.25 (ISBN 0-8006-1256-6, 1-1256). Fortress.

--Judaism & Hellenism: Studies in Their Encounter in Palestine During the Early Hellenistic Period. Bowden, John, tr. from Ger. 672p. 1981. Set. 19.95 (ISBN 0-8006-1495-X, 1-1495). Fortress.

--Property & Riches in the Early Church: Aspects of a Social History of Early Christianity. Bowden, John, tr. from Ger. LC 75-305658. 104p. 1974. pap. 4.50 (ISBN 0-8006-1201-9, 1-1201). Fortress.

Henglein, F. A. Chemical Technology. 1969. 105.00 (ISBN 0-08-011848-8). Pergamon.

Hengstenberg, E. W. Commentary on the Gospel of John, 2 vols. Date not set. Set. 34.95 (ISBN 0-86524-047-7). Klock & Klock.

Henifin, M. S., jt. ed. see Morse, L. E.

Henig, S. & Pinder, J., eds. European Political Parties. (Political & Economic Planning Ser.). 1970. text ed. 32.50x o.p. (ISBN 0-04-327030-1). Allen Unwin.

Henige, David P. The Chronology of Oral Tradition: Quest for a Chimera. (Oxford Studies in African Affairs). (Illus.). 266p. 1974. 27.00x (ISBN 0-19-821694-7). Oxford U Pr.

--Colonial Governors from the Fifteenth Century to the Present. LC 73-81320. 1970. 50.00x (ISBN 0-299-05440-3). U of Wis Pr.

Henin, Claude G. & Ryan, Peter J. Options: Theory & Practice. LC 77-2687. 1977. 21.95 (ISBN 0-669-01623-3). Lexington Bks.

Henin, F., jt. auth. see Ter-Haar, D.

Heninger, S. K., Jr., ed. English Prose, Prose Fiction, & Criticism to 1660: A Guide to Information Sources. LC 73-16980. (American Literature, English Literature, & World Literatures in English Information Guide Ser.: Vol. 2). 350p. 1975. 30.00 (ISBN 0-8103-1233-6). Gale.

Henisch, B. A. & Henisch, H. K. Chipmunk Portrait. LC 78-88029. (Illus.). 98p. 1970. 11.95 (ISBN 0-87601-003-6). Carnation.

Henisch, H. K. & Roy, R. Silicon Carbide-1968. 1969. 28.00 (ISBN 0-08-006768-9). Pergamon.

Henisch, H. K., jt. auth. see Henisch, B. A.

Henisch, H. K., et al, eds. Phase Transitions & Their Applications in Materials Science. LC 73-14411. 300p. 1974. text ed. 38.00 (ISBN 0-08-017955-X). Pergamon.

Henisch, Peter. Hamlet, Fables & Other Poems. Salinger, Herman, tr. LC 78-64434. 7.50 (ISBN 0-685-39467-0). Charioteer.

Henisz-Dostert, Bozena, et al. Machine Translation. (Trends in Linguistics, Studies, & Monographs: No. 16). 1979. text ed. 44.25x (ISBN 90-279-7836-0). Mouton.

Henke, Dan. California Law Guide. LC 76-19950. 1976. 50.00 (ISBN 0-911110-21-6); 1980 suppl. incl. Parker & Son.

Henke, Dan F., jt. ed. see Schwartz, Mortimer D.

Henke, Emerson O. Introduction to Nonprofit Organization Accounting. 464p. 1979. text ed. 19.95x (ISBN 0-534-00742-2). Wadsworth Pub.

Henke, Jack. Lawyers & the Law in New York State: A Short History & Guide. (Illus.). 187p. 1979. 11.95 (ISBN 0-89062-066-0, Pub. by Hughes Press); pap. 6.95 (ISBN 0-89062-065-2). Pub Ctr Cult Res.

Henke, James T. & Dean, John. The Ego King, 2 vols. in 1. Incl. An Archetype Approach to Elizabethan Political Thought & Shakespeare's Henry VII Plays; Shakespeare's Romances & Herodotus' Histories. (Salzburg Studies in English Literature: Jacobean Drama Studies: No. 74). 1977. pap. text ed. 25.00x (ISBN 0-391-01405-6). Humanities.

Henke, R. W. Introduction to Fluid Mechanics. 1966. 15.95 (ISBN 0-201-02809-3). A-W.

Henkel, Barbara O., et al. Foundations of Health Science. 3rd ed. 1977. text ed. 17.95 (ISBN 0-205-05739-X). Allyn.

Henkel, James G., jt. auth. see Abdel-Monem, Mahmoud M.

Henkels, Stan V., ed. see Bradford, Thomas L.

Henkin, Alan B. & Liem Thanh Nguyen. Between Two Cultures: The Vietnamese in America. LC 80-69333. 125p. 1981. perfect bdg. 7.95 (ISBN 0-86548-039-7). Century Twenty One.
Henkin, Bill. The Rocky Horror Picture Show Book. LC 79-63619. (Illus., Orig.). 1979. pap. 8.95 (ISBN 0-8015-6436-0, Hawthorn). Dutton.
Henkin, Harmon. Complete Fisherman's Catalog: A Source Book of Information About Tackle & Accessories. LC 76-56200. 1977. 14.95 o.s.i. (ISBN 0-397-01186-5); pap. 8.95 (ISBN 0-397-01205-5). Lippincott.
--Fly Tackle: A Guide to the Tools of the Trade. LC 75-18644. (Illus.). 1976. 9.95 o.p. (ISBN 0-397-01072-9). Lippincott.
Henkin, L., ed. see Symposia in Pure Mathematics, University of Calif. Berkeley June 1971.
Henkin, Louis. How Nations Behave. 2nd ed. LC 79-1015. 1979. 25.00x (ISBN 0-231-04756-8); pap. 10.00x (ISBN 0-231-04757-6). Columbia U Pr.
--The Rights of Man Today. LC 78-6722. 1978. lib. bdg. 17.50x (ISBN 0-89158-174-X). Westview.
Henkin, Louis, et al. Cases & Materials on International Law. 2nd ed. LC 80-17731. (American Casebook Ser.). 1210p. 1980. text ed. 22.95 (ISBN 0-8299-2099-4). West Pub.
Henkin, William A. Energy-Saving Projects for the Home. Ortho Books Editorial Staff, ed. LC 80-66348. (Illus.). 112p. (Orig.). 1981. pap. 5.95 (ISBN 0-917102-86-X, Ortho Bks). Chevron Chem.
Henle, Michael. A Combinatorial Introduction to Topology. LC 78-14874. (Mathematical Sciences Ser.). (Illus.). 1979. text ed. 22.95x (ISBN 0-7167-0083-2). W H Freeman.
Henle, Theda O. Death Files for Congress. LC 72-134670. 1970. 6.95 (ISBN 0-8149-0687-7). Vanguard.
Henley, Catherine, jt. auth. see Costello, D. P.
Henley, E. Reliability Engineering & Risk Assessment. 1980. 39.00 (ISBN 0-13-772251-6). P-H.
Henley, E. J. & Kouts, H. H., eds. Advances in Nuclear Science & Technology, Vol. 8. (Serial Publication). 1975. 48.00 (ISBN 0-12-029308-0). Acad Pr.
Henley, Ernest J. & Seader, J. D. Equilibrium-Stage Separation Operations in Chemical Engineering. LC 80-13293. 816p. 1981. text ed. 27.95 (ISBN 0-471-37108-4, Pub by Wiley-Interscience). Wiley.
Henley, Ernest M., jt. auth. see Frauenfelder, Hans.
Henley, Marshall. Positive Salvation. Date not set. 6.95 (ISBN 0-533-04861-3). Vantage.
Henley, Martin. Orienteering. rev ed. (EP Sport Ser.). (Illus.). 119p. 1978. 12.95 (ISBN 0-8069-9136-4, Pub. by EP Publishing England); pap. 6.95 (ISBN 0-8069-9138-0). Sterling.
Henley, Nancy M. Body Politics: Power, Sex, & Nonverbal Communication. (Patterns of Social Behavior Ser.). (Illus.). 1977. 12.95 (ISBN 0-13-079640-9, Spec); pap. 3.95 (ISBN 0-13-079632-8). P-H.
Henley, W. E., jt. auth. see Farmer, John S.
Henley, Wallace. White House Mystique. 1977. pap. 1.50 (ISBN 0-89129-253-5). Jove Pubns.
Henn, Henry. Death Switch. (Orig.). 1980. pap. 2.25 (ISBN 0-532-23221-6). Manor Bks.
Henn, T. R. Five Arches with 'philoctetes' & Other Poems. 1980. pap. text ed. 24.75x (ISBN 0-901072-92-3). Humanities.
--Five Arches with Philoctetes & Other Poems. 1980. text ed. 24.75x (ISBN 0-391-02105-2). Humanities.
Henn, Thomas R. The Apple & the Spectroscope. 1966. pap. 3.95x (ISBN 0-393-09703-X, NortonC). Norton.
--Last Essays. 1978. text ed. 14.50x (ISBN 0-901072-03-6). Humanities.
Henneberry, Mrs. Janet, jt. auth. see McCarty, Diane.
Hennebo, D. & Hoffman, A. Geschichte der deutschen Gartenkunst, 3 vols. (Illus.). 930p. 1980. Repr. of 1962 ed. Set. lib. bdg. 187.00x (ISBN 3-87429-176-6). Lubrecht & Cramer.
Hennell, Thomas. Lady Filmy Fern: Or the Voyage of the Window Box. (Illus.). 1981. 12.95 (ISBN 0-241-10468-8, Pub. by Hamish Hamilton England). David & Charles.
Hennen, J. F., jt. auth. see Buritica, P.
Hennes, James D., jt. auth. see Stahl, Sidney M.
Hennessee, Don, jt. auth. see Hixon, Don L.
Hennessee, Don A., jt. auth. see Hixon, Don L.
Hennessen, W. & Huygelen, C., eds. Immunization: Benefit Versus Risk Factors. (Developments in Biological Standardization: Vol. 43). (Illus.). 1979. pap. 60.00 (ISBN 3-8055-2816-7). S Karger.
Hennessen, W. & Van Wezel, A. L., eds. Reassessment of Inactivated Poliomyelitis Vaccine. (Developmentsin Biological Standardization Ser.: Vol. 47). (Illus.). 1981. soft cover 45.00 (ISBN 3-8055-1820-X). S Karger.
Hennessy, Bernard C. Public Opinion. 4th ed. LC 80-27733. 350p. (Orig.). 1981. pap. text ed. 12.95 (ISBN 0-8185-0449-8). Brooks-Cole.
Hennessy, Charles A. The Federal Republic in Spain: Pi y Margall & the Federal Republican Movement, 1868-74. LC 80-13187. xiv, 299p. 1980. Repr. of 1962 ed. lib. bdg. 26.75x (ISBN 0-313-22458-7, HEFP). Greenwood.
Hennessy, John F. Hypothyroidism. (Discussions in Patient Management Ser.). 1978. spiral 10.00 (ISBN 0-87488-898-0). Med Exam.
Hennessy, Thomas, ed. Value & Moral Development. LC 76-18053. (Exploration Book). 1976. pap. 7.95 (ISBN 0-8091-1972-2). Paulist Pr.
--Value Moral Education. LC 78-70814. 1979. pap. 9.95 (ISBN 0-8091-2150-6). Paulist Pr.
Henni, Mustapha. Dictionaire Des Termes Economiques et Commerciaux: Francais-Arabe. 20.00x. Intl Bk Ctr.
Hennie, Fred. Introduction to Computability. LC 76-12796. (Illus.). 1977. text ed. 24.95 (ISBN 0-201-02848-4). A-W.
Hennig, Andreas. My Friend the Ski Pro. 1981. 8.95 (ISBN 0-8062-1617-4). Carlton.
Hennig, Margaret & Jardim, Anne. The Managerial Woman. 221p. 1981. pap. 5.95 (ISBN 0-385-02291-3, Anch). Doubleday.
Hennig, Willi. Insect Phylogeny. 528p. 1981. price not set (ISBN 0-471-27848-3, Pub. by Wiley-Interscience). Wiley.
Henniker, Florence. In Scarlet & Grey. Fletcher, Ian & Stokes, John, eds. LC 76-20067. (Decadent Consciousness Ser.). 1977. lib. bdg. 38.00 (ISBN 0-8240-2762-0). Garland Pub.
Henning, Basil D., ed. see Dering, Edward.
Henning, Charles, et al. Financial Markets & the Economy. 2nd ed. (Illus.). 1978. ref. 19.95 (ISBN 0-13-316083-1). P-H.
Henning, Charles N., et al. International Financial Management. (Illus.). 1978. text ed. 20.50x (ISBN 0-07-028175-0, C); instructor's manual 4.95 (ISBN 0-07-028176-9). McGraw.
Henning, D. R. & Vincent, J. R. Graphic Teaching Aids in Basic Anthropometry. LC 71-635321. (Museum Brief: No. 6). (Illus.). i, 57p. 1971. pap. 2.60x (ISBN 0-913134-05-8). Mus Anthro Mo.
Henning, Edward B. Fifty Years of Modern Art 1916-1966. LC 66-21228. (Illus.). 220p. 1966. 17.50x (ISBN 0-910386-06-4, Pub. by Cleveland Mus Art). Ind U Pr.
--Spirit of Surrealism. LC 79-63387. (Illus.). 228p. 1979. 29.95x (ISBN 0-910386-52-8, Pub. by Cleveland Mus Art). Ind U Pr.
Henning, Standish, ed. see Middleton, Thomas.
Hennings, Dorothy G. Words, Sounds & Thoughts: More Activities to Enrich Children's Communication Skills. LC 76-57242. 352p. 1977. text ed. 11.95 (ISBN 0-590-07522-5, Citation); pap. 5.95 (ISBN 0-590-09616-8). Schol Bk Serv.
Hennings, Dorothy G., jt. auth. see Grant, Barbara M.
Hennings, Dorothy G., ed. see Russell, David H. & Russell, Elizabeth F.
Henningsen, Gustav. The Witches' Advocate: Basque Witchcraft & the Spanish Inquisition, 1609-1614. LC 79-23102. (Basque Book Ser.). (Illus.). xxxii, 607p. 1980. 24.00 (ISBN 0-87417-056-7). U of Nev Pr.
Henretta, James A. The Evolution of American Society, 1700-1815. (Civilization & Society Ser). 1973. pap. text ed. 6.95x (ISBN 0-669-84608-2). Heath.
Henri, Andrian. Total Art: Environments, Happenings, & Performances. (World of Art Ser.). (Illus.). 1974. pap. 9.95 (ISBN 0-19-519934-0). Oxford U Pr.
Henri, Florette & Stillman, Richard. Bitter Victory: A History of Black Soldiers in World War I. 1970. 4.95 o.p. (ISBN 0-385-05193-X); pap. 2.50 o.p. (ISBN 0-385-05194-8). Doubleday.
Henri, Robert. Art Spirit. Ryerson, Margery A., ed. LC 39-4273. (Illus.). 1960. pap. 4.95 (ISBN 0-397-00121-5, KB18, Key). Lippincott.
Henrichsen, Lynn, jt. auth. see Pack, Alice.
Henrichsen, Lynn, jt. auth. see Pack, Alice C.
Henrichsen, Margaret K. Seven Steeples. LC 78-26203. 1978. lib. bdg. 11.50 o.p. (ISBN 0-89621-023-5); pap. 4.95x (ISBN 0-89621-022-7). Thorndike Pr.
Henrichsen, Walter A. Disciples Are Made-Not Born. LC 74-79162. 160p. 1974. pap. 2.95 (ISBN 0-88207-706-6). Victor Bks.
--Entendamos. Cook, David A., tr. from Eng. 112p. (Orig., Span.). 1979. pap. 2.75 (ISBN 0-89922-131-9). Edit Caribe.
--How to Disciple Your Children. 120p. 1981. pap. 3.95 (ISBN 0-88207-260-9). Victor Bks.
--A Layman's Guide to Interpreting the Bible. 1979. pap. 5.95 (ISBN 0-310-37701-3). Zondervan.
Henrici, Henry. Applied & Computational Complex Analysis: Power Series, Integration-Conformal Mapping-Location of Zeroes. LC 73-19723. (Pure & Applied Mathematics Ser.: Vol. 1). 704p. 1974. 45.95 (ISBN 0-471-37244-7, Pub. by Wiley-Interscience). Wiley.
Henrici, Peter. Applied & Computational Complex Analysis: Special Functions-Integral Transforms-Asymptotics-Continued Fractions, Vol. 2. LC 73-19723. 1977. 45.95 (ISBN 0-471-01525-3, Pub. by Wiley-Interscience). Wiley.
--Discrete Variable Methods in Ordinary Differential Equations. LC 61-17359. 1962. 27.50 (ISBN 0-471-37224-2, Pub. by Wiley-Interscience). Wiley.
Henrici, Peter K. Elements of Numerical Analysis. LC 64-23840. 1964. 23.95 (ISBN 0-471-37241-2). Wiley.
Henrickson, Charles & Byrd, Larry. Chemistry for the Health Professions. (Illus.). 798p. 1980. text ed. 21.95 (ISBN 0-442-23258-6); instr's. manual 3.50 (ISBN 0-442-26252-3); Student Self Study Guide by John R. Wilson 7.95. D Van Nostrand.
Henrickson, Robert L. Meat, Poultry & Seafood Technology. LC 77-25350. (Illus.). 1978. ref. ed. 17.95 (ISBN 0-13-568600-8). P-H.
Henrie. Cats. (gr. 2-5). 1980. PLB 5.90 (ISBN 0-531-04119-0, E18). Watts.
--Gerbils. (gr. 2-5). 1980. PLB 5.90 (ISBN 0-531-04121-2, E40). Watts.
Henrie, Fiona. Rabbits. (gr. 2-5). 1980. PLB 5.90 (ISBN 0-531-04122-0, G10). Watts.
Henrie, Fiora. Dogs. (gr. 2-5). 1980. PLB 5.90 (ISBN 0-531-04120-4, E30). Watts.
Henriksen, C., tr. see Pedersen, Holger.
Henriksen, Erik K. Jig & Fixture Design Manual. (Illus.). 308p. 1973. 35.00 (ISBN 0-8311-1098-8). Indus Pr.
Henriksen, P., tr. see Pedersen, Holger.
Henriksen, Thomas H., jt. ed. see Weinstein, Warren.
Henriod, Lorraine. Ancestor Hunting. LC 79-10767. (Illus.). 64p. (gr. 3-5). 1979. PLB 7.29 (ISBN 0-671-32998-7). Messner.
Henriques, Fernando. Children of Conflict: A Study of Interracial Sex & Marriage. 224p. 1975. 8.95 (ISBN 0-525-07996-3); pap. 3.95 o.p. Dutton.
--Family & Colour in Jamaica. 2nd ed. 1968. text ed. 9.00x (ISBN 0-261-62000-2). Humanities.
Henriques, Maria H. Unioes Legais e Consensuais: Incidencia e Fecundidade na America Latina. (Port.). 1980. pap. text ed. 2.00 (ISBN 0-89383-069-0). Intl Program Labs.
Henroid, Lorraine. Special Olympics & Paralympics. (First Bks.). (Illus.). (gr. 4 up). 1979. PLB 6.45 s&l (ISBN 0-531-02263-3). Watts.
Henry & Symonds. Energy Management. 352p. 1980. 23.50. Dekker.
Henry, et al. Online Searching: An Introduction. LC 80-40242. 1980. 31.95 (ISBN 0-408-10696-4). Butterworths.
Henry, Alexander. Travels & Adventures in Canada & the Indian Territories Between the Years 1760 & 1776. LC 75-7053. (Indian Captivities Ser.: Vol. 31). 1976. Repr. of 1809 ed. lib. bdg. 44.00 (ISBN 0-8240-1655-6). Garland Pub.
Henry, Avril, ed. Biblia Pauperum. (Illus.). 112p. 1981. 55.00x (ISBN 0-85967-542-4, Pub. by Scolar Pr England). Biblio Dist.
Henry, Bamman A., ed. see Belden, Bernard R.
Henry, Brian, ed. see Rowley, J. C.
Henry, C. D., jt. ed. see Walton, A. W.
Henry, Clement M. Politics & International Relations in the Middle East: An Annotated Bibliography. 114p. (Orig.). 1980. pap. 4.00 (ISBN 0-932098-18-5). Ctr for NE & North Aafrican Stud.
--Politics & International Relations in the Middle East: An Annotated Bibliography. 114p. (Orig.). 1980. pap. text ed. 8.00 (ISBN 0-932098-18-5). Ctr for NE & North African Stud.
Henry, D. P. Medieval Logic & Metaphysics: A Modern Introduction. (Orig.). 1972. text ed. 7.50x (ISBN 0-09-110830-6, Hutchinson U Lib); pap. text ed. 6.75x (ISBN 0-09-110831-4, Hutchinson U Lib). Humanities.
Henry, Dennis C. & Nelson, Edward B. Experiments in Light, Electricity, & Modern Physics, Laboratory Manual. 1978. pap. text ed. 7.50 (ISBN 0-8403-1889-8). Kendall-Hunt.
Henry, Eric. Chinese Amusement: The Lively Plays of Li Yu. 1980. 23.50 (ISBN 0-208-01837-9, Archon). Shoe String.
Henry, Francoise. Irish Art in the Romanesque Period (1020-1170 A.D) LC 76-82117. (Illus.). 386p. 1969. 30.00x (ISBN 0-8014-0526-2). Cornell U Pr.
Henry, G. M. A Guide to the Birds of Ceylon. 2nd ed. (Illus.). 1971. 37.50x (ISBN 0-19-217629-3). Oxford U Pr.
Henry, George W. Society & the Sex Variant. (Orig.). 1965. pap. 0.95 o.s.i. (ISBN 0-02-095900-1, Collier). Macmillan.
Henry, Joanne L. Marie Curie: Discoverer of Radium. (gr. 4-6). 1968. 8.95 (ISBN 0-02-743680-2). Macmillan.
Henry, John B. & Giegel, Joseph L. Quality Control in Laboratory Medicine. LC 77-78559. (Illus.). 250p. 1977. 35.00 (ISBN 0-89352-008-X). Masson Pub.
Henry, Kenneth. Social Problems: Institutional & Interpersonal Perspectives. 1978. pap. 8.95x (ISBN 0-673-15101-8). Scott F.
Henry, L. D. The Border Lion. (Orig.). 1980. pap. 1.95 (ISBN 0-532-23207-0). Manor Bks.
Henry, Laurin L. Presidential Transitions. 1960. 13.95 (ISBN 0-8157-3576-6). Brookings.
Henry, Leigh. Doctor John Bull 1562-1628. LC 68-15589. (Music Ser). (Illus.). 1968. Repr. of 1937 ed. lib. bdg. 29.50 (ISBN 0-306-70982-1). Da Capo.
Henry, Lewis C., ed. Best Quotations for All Occasions. rev ed. 1977. pap. 2.25 (ISBN 0-449-30824-3, Prem). Fawcett.
Henry, M. Daniel, jt. auth. see Morell, R. W.
Henry, Marguerite. Cinnabar, the One O'Clock Fox. LC 56-11343. (Illus.). 1956. pap. 2.95 (ISBN 0-528-87768-2). Rand.
--Five O'Clock Charlie. LC 62-11987. (Illus.). (gr. 2-4). 1962. 4.95 (ISBN 0-528-82618-2); pap. 2.95 (ISBN 0-528-87006-8). Rand.
--King of the Wind. LC 48-8773. (Illus.). (gr. 2-9). 1948. 5.95 (ISBN 0-528-82265-9); deluxe ed. 10.00 slipcased (ISBN 0-528-82267-5); PLB 5.97 o.p. (ISBN 0-528-80174-0); pap. 2.95 (ISBN 0-528-87686-4). Rand.
--Marguerite Henry's All About Horses. (gr. 4-8). 1967. deluxe ed. 4.95 (ISBN 0-394-81699-4, BYR); PLB 6.99 (ISBN 0-394-91699-9). Random.
--Misty of Chincoteague. LC 47-11404. (Illus.). (gr. 2-9). 1947. 6.95 (ISBN 0-528-82315-9); pap. 2.95 (ISBN 0-528-87685-6). Rand.
--Stormy: Misty's Foal. LC 63-13334. (Illus.). (gr. 4-9). 1963. 5.95 o.s.i. (ISBN 0-528-82083-4); pap. 2.95 (ISBN 0-528-87690-2). Rand.
Henry, Marilyn & DeSourdis, Ron. The Films of Alan Ladd. (Illus.). 256p. 1981. 16.95 (ISBN 0-8065-0736-5). Citadel Pr.
Henry, Marvin A., jt. auth. see Henson, Kenneth T.
Henry, Matthew. Acts-Revelation. (A Commentary on the Whole Bible Ser: Vol. 6). 1192p. 12.00 (ISBN 0-8007-0202-6). Revell.
--Genesis-Deuteronomy. (A Commentary on the Whole Bible Ser: Vol. 1). 12.00 (ISBN 0-8007-0197-6). Revell.
--Isaiah-Malachi. (A Commentary on the Whole Bible Ser: Vol. 4). 12.00 (ISBN 0-8007-0200-X). Revell.
--Job to Song of Solomon. (A Commentary on the Whole Bible Ser: Vol. 3). 12.00 (ISBN 0-8007-0199-2). Revell.
--Joshua-Esther. (A Commentary on the Whole Bible Ser: Vol. 2). 12.00 (ISBN 0-8007-0198-4). Revell.
--Matthew Henry's Commentary on the Whole Bible. Church, Leslie F., ed. 1966. 24.95 (ISBN 0-310-26010-8). Zondervan.
--Matthew-John. (A Commentary on the Whole Bible Ser: Vol. 5). 12.00 (ISBN 0-8007-0201-8). Revell.
--The Secret of Communion with God. LC 79-93431. (Shepperd Classics Ser.). 144p. 1981. pap. 5.95 (ISBN 0-87983-245-2). Keats.
Henry, Matthew & Scott, Thomas. Concise Commentary on the Whole Bible. 18.95 (ISBN 0-8024-5190-X). Moody.
Henry, O. The Best of O. Henry. LC 78-14841. 1978. lib. bdg. 12.90 (ISBN 0-89471-047-8); pap. 4.95 (ISBN 0-89471-046-X). Running Pr.
--Complete Works of O. Henry. LC 53-6098. 1953. 14.95 (ISBN 0-385-00961-5). Doubleday.
--The Gift of the Magi. LC 78-55660. (Illus.). 1978. Repr. 7.95 (ISBN 0-672-52296-9). Bobbs.
--The Gift of the Magi. (Creative's Classics Ser.). 32p. (gr. 4-9). 1980. PLB 6.95 (ISBN 0-87191-775-0). Creative Ed.
--The Last Leaf. (Creative's Classics Ser.). (Illus.). 32p. (gr. 4-9). 1980. PLB 6.95 (ISBN 0-87191-774-2). Creative Ed.
--The Ransom of Red Chief. (Creative's Classics Ser.). (Illus.). 40p. (gr. 4-9). 1980. PLB 6.95 (ISBN 0-87191-776-9). Creative Ed.
Henry, O., et al. The Gifts & Other Stories. (Oxford Progressive English Readers Ser.). (Illus.). (gr. 3up). 1974. pap. text ed. 2.95x (ISBN 0-19-580574-7). Oxford U Pr.
Henry, P. & Henry, P., eds. Konstantin Paustovskii: Selected Stories. 1967. pap. 6.25 (ISBN 0-08-011859-3). Pergamon.
Henry, P., ed. see Plotinus.
Henry, Patricia, jt. auth. see Miller, Richard.
Henry, Porter J., jt. auth. see Barry, John W.
Henry, Ralph L. St. Croix Boyhood. LC 72-84771. (Illus.). 107p. 1972. 4.95 (ISBN 0-685-26839-X). Minn Hist.
Henry, Ralph L. & Salisbury, Rachel. Current Thinking & Writing. (Seventh Ser.). 1976. pap. 9.95 (ISBN 0-13-195693-0). P-H.

Henry, Rene A., Jr. How to Profitably Buy & Sell Land. LC 76-22522. (Real Estate for Professional Practitioners: a Wiley Ser.). 1977. 19.95 (ISBN 0-471-37291-9, Pub by Wiley-Interscience). Wiley.

Henry, Robert E. The Jazz Ensemble. (Illus.). 144p. 1981. 15.95 (ISBN 0-13-509992-7, Spec); pap. 7.95 (ISBN 0-13-509984-6). P-H.

Henry, Robert G. & Miller, Richards T. Sailing Yacht Design: An Appreciation of a Fine Art. LC 65-18207. (Illus.). 1965. 6.00 (ISBN 0-87033-093-4). Cornell Maritime.

Henry, S. Mark, ed. Symbiosis: Its Physiological & Biochemical Significance, 2 vols. Incl. Vol. 1. Association of Microorganisms, Plants & Marine Organisms. 1966. 49.25 (ISBN 0-12-341101-7); Vol. 2. Association of Invertebrates, Birds, Ruminants & Other Biota. 1967. 49.25 (ISBN 0-12-341102-5). Set. 80.00 (ISBN 0-685-23224-7). Acad Pr.

Henry, Stuart. The Hidden Economy: The Context & Control of Borderline Crime. 194p. 1978. 29.50x (ISBN 0-85520-240-8, Pub by Martin Robertson England); pap. 8.95x (ISBN 0-85520-353-6). Biblio Dist.

Henry, Stuart, jt. auth. see Robinson, David.

Henry, Sue. Group Skills in Social Work: A Four Dimensional Approach. LC 80-83378. 416p. 1981. text ed. 12.50 (ISBN 0-87581-268-6). Peacock Pubs.

Henry, Victor. La Magie dans L'Inde Antique: Paris, 1904. LC 78-74261. (Oriental Religions Ser.: Vol. 5). 325p. 1980. lib. bdg. 33.00 (ISBN 0-8240-3903-3). Garland Pub.

Henry, Will. The Bear Paw Horses. 224p. 1980. pap. 1.75 (ISBN 0-553-14236-4). Bantam.

--Chiricahua. LC 78-38941. (YA) 1972. 6.95 (ISBN 0-397-00887-2). Lippincott.

--The Gates of the Mountains. (Western Fiction Ser.). 1980. lib. bdg. 13.95 (ISBN 0-8398-2689-3). Gregg.

--I, Tom Horn. LC 74-23407. 1975. 7.95 o.s.i. (ISBN 0-397-01073-7). Lippincott.

--The Summer of the Gun. 1978. 9.95 (ISBN 0-397-01309-4). Lippincott.

Henry, William E., et al. The Fifth Profession: Becoming a Psychotherapist. LC 71-148655. (Social & Behavioral Science Ser.). 1971. 14.95x o.p. (ISBN 0-87589-088-1). Jossey-Bass.

Henry, William R. & Haynes, Warren W. Managerial Economics: Analysis and Cases. 4th ed. 1978. 19.95x (ISBN 0-256-02079-5). Business Pubns.

Henschel, George. Musings & Memories of a Musician. (Music Reprint Ser.). 1979. Repr. of 1919 ed. lib. bdg. 32.50 (ISBN 0-306-79540-X). Da Capo.

Henschel, Stan. How to Raise & Train a Chesapeake Bay Retriever. (Orig.). 1965. pap. 2.00 (ISBN 0-87666-265-3, DS1069). TFH Pubns.

--How to Raise & Train a Coonhound. (Orig.). pap. 2.00 (ISBN 0-87666-274-2, DS1057). TFH Pubns.

--How to Raise & Train a Labrador Retriever. (Illus.). pap. 2.00 (ISBN 0-87666-330-7, DS1095). TFH Pubns.

Hensel, John. The Book of Ornamental Knots. (Encore Edition). (Illus.). 1978. pap. 2.95 (ISBN 0-684-16900-2, ScribT); 12.50 (ISBN 0-684-13409-8). Scribner.

Hensel, John, jt. auth. see Graumont, Raoul.

Hensel, Kurt & Landsberg, G. Algebraische Funktionen. LC 65-11624. (Ger). 1965. 29.50 (ISBN 0-8284-0179-9). Chelsea Pub.

Hensel, Mary D., jt. auth. see Lipson, Stephen H.

Henshall, Don, jt. auth. see Mumford, Enid.

Henshaw, Paul & Weemshall, H. Family Worship. 84p. 1981. pap. 2.25x (ISBN 0-8358-0421-6). Upper Room.

Henshaw, Richard. The Encyclopedia of World Soccer. LC 78-26570. (Illus.). 1979. 25.00 o.p. (ISBN 0-915220-34-2). New Republic.

Henshaw, Richard C. & Jackson, James R. Executive Game. 3rd ed. 1978. pap. text ed. 9.95 (ISBN 0-256-02034-5). Irwin.

Henshaw, William. The Orderly Books of Colonel William Henshaw: October 1, 1775, Through October 3, 1776. 1948. pap. 4.00x (ISBN 0-912296-29-1, Dist. by U Pr of Va). Am Antiquarian.

Henshel, Anne-Marie. The Forgotten Ones: A Sociological Study of Anglo & Chicano Retardates. 338p. 1973. 15.00x (ISBN 0-292-72403-9). U of Tex Pr.

Henshel, Richard L. On the Future of Social Prediction. LC 75-26745. 1975. pap. 2.55 (ISBN 0-672-61334-4). Bobbs.

Henshel, Richard L. & Silverman, Robert A. Perception in Criminology. LC 74-23621. 384p. 1975. 25.00x (ISBN 0-231-03760-0); pap. 9.00x (ISBN 0-231-03761-9). Columbia U Pr.

Hensher, D. A., ed. Urban Transport Economics. LC 76-11061. (Illus.). 1977. 45.00 (ISBN 0-521-21128-X); pap. 14.95x (ISBN 0-521-29140-2). Cambridge U Pr.

Hensher, David & Dalvi, Quasin. Determinants of Travel Choice. LC 78-58818. 1978. 37.95 (ISBN 0-03-046236-3). Praeger.

Hensher, David A. Applied Discrete-Choice Modelling. Johnson, Lester W., ed. LC 80-23517. 468p. 1980. 29.95 (ISBN 0-470-27078-0). Halsted Pr.

Henshu-sha, Century E., tr. see Asano, Osamu & Ishiwata, Mutsuko.

Hensinger, Robert N. Neonatal Orthapeadics. (Neonatology Ser.). 1981. write for info. (ISBN 0-8089-1355-7). Grune.

Hensley, Dana & Prentice, Diana. Mastering Competitive Debate. 1977. lib. bdg. 6.000 (ISBN 0-931054-05-2). Clark Pub.

Hensley, Joe L. A Killing in Gold. LC 76-56300. 1978. 7.95 o.p. (ISBN 0-385-12854-1). Doubleday.

--Outcasts. LC 80-705. (Crime Club Ser.). 192p. 1981. 9.95 (ISBN 0-385-15820-3). Doubleday.

Hensley, Thomas R. The Kent State Incident: Impact of Judicial Process on Public Attitudes. LC 80-1712. (Contributions in Political Science Ser.: No. 56). 224p. 1981. lib. bdg. 27.50 (ISBN 0-313-21220-1, HKS/). Greenwood.

Henslin, James M. Down to Earth Sociology. 2nd ed. LC 75-36108. 1976. pap. text ed. 6.95 (ISBN 0-02-914620-8). Free Pr.

--Introducing Sociology. LC 74-12595. (Illus.). 1975. text ed. 12.95 (ISBN 0-02-914430-2); student's guide 3.95 (ISBN 0-02-914300-4). Free Pr.

Henslin, James M. & Reynolds, Larry T. Social Problems in American Society. 3rd ed. 1979. pap. text ed. 12.95 (ISBN 0-205-06575-9, 8165750). Allyn.

Henslin, James M., ed. Down to Earth Sociology: Society, Structure, & Everyday Life. 3rd ed. LC 80-2315. 1981. pap. text ed. 9.95 (ISBN 0-02-914660-7). Free Pr.

--Introducing Sociology: Selected Readings. LC 74-16903. 1975. pap. text ed. 4.95 (ISBN 0-02-914650-X). Free Pr.

Henslow, G. The Plants of the Bible. 294p. 1981. Repr. of 1900 ed. lib. bdg. 75.00 (ISBN 0-8495-2375-3). Arden Lib.

Henslowe, Philip. Diary. Foakes, R. A. & Rickert, R. T., eds. 1961. 80.00 (ISBN 0-521-05244-0). Cambridge U Pr.

--The Henslowe Papers, 2 vols. facsimile ed. Repr. of 1977 ed. Set. 220.00x o.p. (ISBN 0-85967-355-3, Pub. by Scolar Pr England). Biblio Dist.

Hensman, Bertha. The Shares of Fletcher, Field & Massinger in Twelve Plays of the Beaumont & Fletcher Canon, 2 vols. (Salzburg Studies in English Literature, Jacobean Drama Studies: No.6). 1974. Set. pap. text ed. 50.25x (ISBN 0-391-01406-4). Humanities.

Henson Associates. Muppet Madness. LC 79-5269. (Illus., Orig.). (gr. 2-6). 1980. pap. 3.95 (ISBN 0-394-84393-2). Random.

Henson, Curtis, jt. auth. see Culbertson, Jack A.

Henson, Josiah. Father Henson's Story of His Own Life. 1962. pap. 1.50 o.s.i. (ISBN 0-87091-017-5, AE). Corinth Bks.

Henson, Kenneth T. Secondary Teaching Methods. 384p. 1980. text ed. 14.95 (ISBN 0-669-03316-2). Heath.

Henson, Kenneth T. & Henry, Marvin A. Becoming Involved in Teaching. LC 75-46377. 1976. 8.95 o.p. (ISBN 0-916768-01-5); pap. 5.95 o.p. (ISBN 0-685-89710-9). Sycamore Pr.

Henson, Kenneth T. & Higgins, James E. Personalizing Teaching in the Elementary School. 1978. text ed. 13.95 (ISBN 0-675-08427-X). Merrill.

Henson, Mike. Ransack. LC 80-53807. (Illus.). 151p. (Orig.). 1980. pap. 3.00 (ISBN 0-931122-18-X). West End.

Henson, Ray D. Handbook on Secured Transactions Under the Uniform Commercial Code. 2nd ed. LC 78-26098. (Hornbook Ser). 504p. 1979. text ed. 17.95 (ISBN 0-8299-2023-4). West Pub.

Henson, Robert. Transports & Disgraces. LC 80-19131. (Illinois Short Fiction Ser.). 140p. 1980. 10.00 (ISBN 0-252-00840-5); pap. 3.95 (ISBN 0-252-00841-3). U of Ill Pr.

Henstell, Bruce. Los Angeles: An Illustrated History. LC 80-7642. (Illus.). 224p. 1980. 25.00 (ISBN 0-394-50941-2). Knopf.

Henstock, M. & Bever, M. B., eds. New & Better Uses of Secondary Resources: Proceedings of the Second Recycling World Congress, Philippine International Conventional Center, Manila, March 1979. 278p. 1980. pap. 40.00 (ISBN 0-08-026245-7). Pergamon.

Henstock, M. E. Recycling & Disposal of Solid Waste. LC 75-4235. 223p. 1975. pap. 34.00 (ISBN 0-08-019685-3). Pergamon.

Henthorn, Taesoon, jt. auth. see Thorlin, Eldora.

Henthorn, William E. History of Korea. LC 75-143511. 1971. 14.95 (ISBN 0-02-914460-4); pap. text ed. 7.95 (ISBN 0-02-914610-0). Free Pr.

Hentoff, Nat. Does This School Have Capital Punishment? LC 80-68733. 160p. (YA) (gr. 8-12). 1981. 8.95 (ISBN 0-440-02051-4). Delacorte.

--The Jazz Life. LC 74-23383. (The Roots of Jazz Ser.). 1978. lib. bdg. 22.50 (ISBN 0-306-70681-4); pap. 5.95 (ISBN 0-306-80088-8). Da Capo.

Hentoff, Nat & McCarthy, Albert. Jazz: New Perspectives on the History of Jazz. (Music Reprint Ser.). 1974. Repr. of 1959 ed. lib. bdg. 25.00 (ISBN 0-306-70592-3). Da Capo.

Henton, Richard W. Quick-Sketch: A New Technique in Interior Design Graphics. 144p. 1980. pap. text ed. 8.95 (ISBN 0-8403-2233-X). Kendall-Hunt.

Hentschke, Guilbert C. Management Operations in Education. LC 75-9168. (Illus.). 280p. 1976. 20.00x (ISBN 0-8211-0757-7); text ed. 18.00x (ISBN 0-685-61057-8). McCutchan.

Henvey, Thom, jt. auth. see Davis, Kenneth.

Heny, Frank, jt. auth. see Akmajian, Adrian.

Heny, Frank W., jt. auth. see Akmajian, Adrian.

Henyey, Frank, jt. ed. see Frazer, William.

Henze, Paul B. Ethiopian Journeys: Travels in Ethiopia 1969-72. (Illus.). 1978. lib. bdg. 39.50 o.p. (ISBN 0-510-44220-X). Westview.

Henzl, Elizabeth M. Visual Aural Discriminations: A Self-Instructional Workbook for Initial Two-Letter Blends, 5 bks. reusable ed. (gr. 1-12). 1973. wkbk. 5.00 ea.; Bk. 1. (ISBN 0-89039-035-5); Bk. 2. (ISBN 0-89039-037-1); Bk. 3. (ISBN 0-89039-039-8); Bk. 4. (ISBN 0-89039-041-X); Bk. 5. (ISBN 0-89039-043-6). Ann Arbor Pubs.

Hepburn, A. C., ed. Conflict of Nationality in Modern Ireland. 1980. 19.95 (ISBN 0-312-16231-6). St Martin.

Hepburn, James. Arnold Bennett: The Critical Heritage. (The Critical Heritage Ser.). 576p. 1981. pap. 48.50 (ISBN 0-7100-0512-1). Routledge & Kegan.

Hepburn, Lawrence R. State Government in Georgia. 200p. (Orig.). (gr. 8-12). 1981. pap. text ed. 10.00 (ISBN 0-89854-067-4). U of GA Inst Govt.

Hepburn, Mary A., et al. City Government in Georgia. LC 79-24128. 150p. (Orig.). (gr. 8-12). 1980. pap. 7.50 (ISBN 0-89854-052-6). U of GA Inst Govt.

Hepburn, Ronald W. Christianity & Paradox: Critical Studies in Twentieth-Century Theology. LC 68-17550. 1968. pap. 3.50 (ISBN 0-672-63723-5). Bobbs.

Hepburne, Melissa. Passion's Wicked Torment. (Orig.). 1981. pap. 2.75 (ISBN 0-523-41004-2). Pinnacle Bks.

Hepher, Dalfour & Pruginin, Yoel. Commercial Fish Farming: With Special Reference to Fish Culture in Israel. 250p. 1981. 25.00 (ISBN 0-686-69368-X, Pub. by Wiley-Interscience). Wiley.

Hephner, Thomas, jt. auth. see Koeninger, Jimmy.

Hepler, Cedric L., ed. see Wieman, Henry N.

Hepler, Don, jt. auth. see Wallach, Paul.

Hepler, Molly L., ed. see Van Duyne, Carl.

Hepler, Opal. Manual of Clinical Laboratory Methods. 4th ed. (Illus.). 416p. 1977. pap. 22.50 spiral (ISBN 0-398-03057-X). C C Thomas.

Hepner, Harry W. Psychology Applied to Life & Work. 6th ed. LC 78-11923. (Illus.). 1979. text ed. 17.95 (ISBN 0-13-732461-8). P-H.

Hepner, J. O. Case Studies in Health Administration, 2 vols. Incl. Vol. 1. Health Planning for Emergency Multi-Hospital Systems. LC 77-17008. (Illus.). 1978. pap. text ed. 15.95 (ISBN 0-8016-2156-9); Vol. 2. Hospital Administrator-Physician Relationships. LC 80-16073. 1980. pap. text ed. 21.95 (ISBN 0-8016-2158-5). Mosby.

Hepp, Ferenc, tr. see Rajki, Bela.

Heppel, R. T. Seacook. 1979. 12.95x (ISBN 0-8464-0066-9). Beekman Pubs.

Heppell, Muriel, tr. see Cosic, Dobrica.

Heppenheimer, T. A. Colonies in Space. (Illus.). 1978. pap. 2.75 (ISBN 0-446-95559-0). Warner Bks.

--Toward Distant Suns. (Illus.). 256p. 1979. 19.95 (ISBN 0-8117-1578-7). Stackpole.

--Towards Distant Suns. (Illus.). 1980. pap. 8.95 (ISBN 0-449-90035-5, Columbine). Fawcett.

Heppenstall, Margit S. Deborah. new ed. LC 67-19497. (Crown Ser.). (gr. 5-8). 1977. pap. 4.50 (ISBN 0-8127-0169-0). Southern Pub.

Heppenstall, R. Bruce, ed. Fracture Treatment & Healing. LC 77-79395. (Illus.). 1087p. 1980. text ed. 75.00 (ISBN 0-7216-4638-7). Saunders.

Heppenstall, Rayner. Raymond Roussel. 1967. 16.50x (ISBN 0-520-00554-6). U of Cal Pr.

--The Wood Shed. 1980. pap. 4.95 (ISBN 0-7145-0616-8). Riverrun NY.

--Woodshed. 1967. pap. 4.95 (ISBN 0-214-15817-9). Dufour.

Heppke, G., jt. auth. see Helfreich, W.

Hepple, P., ed. Lead in the Environment. 1972. 18.60x (ISBN 0-85334-485-X). Intl Ideas.

Hepple, Peter, ed. Outlook for Natural Gas: A Quality Fuel. LC 73-661. 268p. 1973. 29.95 (ISBN 0-470-37303-2). Halsted Pr.

Heptner, Angelo M. & Steinburg, Sheldon. Multivista Cultural. (Orig.). (gr. 11-12). 1975. text ed. 15.60 (ISBN 0-205-04593-6, 4245938); tchrs'. guide 4.96 (ISBN 0-205-04594-4, 4245946); cassettes 172.00 (ISBN 0-205-04851-X, 4248511); dupl. masters wkbk. 32.00 (ISBN 0-205-04852-8, 424852X). Allyn.

Hepworth, Andrew & Osbaldeston, Michael. The Way We Work. 1979. text ed. 26.50x (ISBN 0-566-00212-4, Pub. by Gower Pub Co England). Renouf.

Hepworth, Barbara. A Pictorial Autobiography. rev. ed. Adams, A., ed. (Illus.). 1978. text ed. 10.00x o.p. (ISBN 0-239-00179-6). Humanities.

Hepworth, Brian. Robert Lowth. (English Authors Ser.: No. 224). 1978. lib. bdg. 12.50 (ISBN 0-8057-6695-2). Twayne.

Hepworth, H. How to Find Out in History. (How to Find Out Series). (Illus.). 1966. 16.00 (ISBN 0-08-011482-2). Pergamon.

Hepworth, Martyn. Amateur Drama: Production & Management. (Illus.). 120p. 1980. 16.95 (ISBN 0-7134-0937-1, Pub. by Batsford England). David & Charles.

Hepworth, Mike. Blackmail: Publicity & Secrecy in Everyday Life. 192p. 1975. 14.95x (ISBN 0-7100-8235-5); pap. 6.95 (ISBN 0-7100-8236-3). Routledge & Kegan.

Hepworth, N. P. Finance of Local Government. 6th rev. ed. (New Local Government Ser.: No. 6). 328p. 1981. pap. text ed. 15.95x (ISBN 0-04-352087-1, 2405). Allen Unwin.

Hepworth, Philip. Victorian & Edwardian Norfolk. 1972. 22.50 (ISBN 0-7134-0124-9, Pub. by Batsford England). David & Charles.

Her Majesty's Stationary Office. Catalog Translators Library, Vols. 1-4. 1976. Set. 9.00 (ISBN 0-379-00651-0). Oceana.

Heraclitus. Cosmic Fragments. Kirk, G. S., ed. 1954. 62.00 (ISBN 0-521-05245-9). Cambridge U Pr.

Heraclitus of Ephesius & Diogenes, the Cynic. Herakleitos & Diogenes. Davenport, Guy, tr. from Gr. LC 78-17310. 1979. 10.00 (ISBN 0-912516-35-6); pap. 4.00 (ISBN 0-912516-36-4). Grey Fox.

Heraclius. Here Begynneth the Boke Intituled Eracles & Also Godefrey of Boloyne. Caxton, William, tr. LC 73-6140. (English Experience Ser.: No. 604). 1973. Repr. of 1481 ed. 52.00 (ISBN 90-221-0604-7). Walter J Johnson.

Heradstveit, Daniel. The Arab-Israeli Conflict: Psychological Obstacles to Peace. 1979. pap. 23.50x (ISBN 82-00-01822-9, Dist. by Columbia U Pr.). Universitet.

Herald. Shining Stranger. 3.95 (ISBN 0-916438-29-5). Univ of Trees.

Herald, F. A., ed. Occurrence of Oil & Gas in West Texas. (Illus.). 456p. 1957. 9.00 (PUB 5716). Bur Econ Geology.

Heras, F. G. de las see De las Heras, F. G. & Vega, S.

Heraud, B. J. Sociology & Social Work. LC 79-119894. 1971. 18.00 (ISBN 0-08-015855-2); pap. 8.50 (ISBN 0-08-015854-4). Pergamon.

Herb Society of America, ed. Herbs for Use & for Delight: An Anthology from The Herbarist. LC 74-80287. (Illus.). 352p. 1974. pap. 4.50 (ISBN 0-486-23104-6). Dover.

Herbach, L., jt. auth. see Barra, Jean-Rene.

Herbart, J. F. Science of Education. Bd. with Education of Man. (Contributions to the History of Psychology Ser.). 1978. Repr. of 1902 ed. 30.00 (ISBN 0-89093-161-5). U Pubns Amer.

Herbart, Johann F. Textbook of Psychology. Smith, Margaret K., tr. Bd. with Study of Psychology; Outlines of Psychology. (Contributions to the History of Psychology Ser., Vol. VI, Pt. A: Orientations). 1978. Repr. of 1891 ed. 30.00 (ISBN 0-89093-155-0). U Pubns Amer.

Herber, Bernard P. Modern Public Finance. 4th ed. 1979. text ed. 18.50 (ISBN 0-256-02159-7). Irwin.

Herber, Harold L. Teaching Reading in Content Areas. 2nd ed. (Illus.). 1978. ref. ed. 16.95 (ISBN 0-13-894170-X). P-H.

Herber, Reginald. Palestine, a Prize Poem, Recited in the Theatre, Oxford, June 15, 1803, Repr. Of 1803. Bd. with Europe: Lines on the Present War. Repr. of 1809 ed; Palestine...to Which Is Added, the Passage of the Red Sea, a Fragment. Repr. of 1809 ed. LC 75-31211. (Romantic Context Ser.: Poetry 1789-1830: Vol. 62). 1978. lib. bdg. 47.00 (ISBN 0-8240-2161-4). Garland Pub.

Herberg, Will. Protestant-Catholic-Jew: An Essay in American Religious Sociology. rev. ed. LC 60-5931. 1955. pap. 2.50 (ISBN 0-385-09438-8, A195, Anch). Doubleday.

Herberg, Will, ed. see Buber, Martin.

Herberman, Ronald B. Natural Cell-Mediated Immunity Against Tumors. 1980. 65.00 (ISBN 0-12-341350-8). Acad Pr.

Herbert, A. J. The Structure of Technical English. 1975. pap. text ed. 5.00x (ISBN 0-582-52523-3). Longman.

Herbert, A. S., ed. Historical Catalogue of Printed Editions of the English Bible 1525-1961. rev. ed. 1968. 10.50 (ISBN 0-564-00130-9, 17066). United Bible.

Herbert, Alan P. Mr. Gay's London. LC 75-25258. (Illus.). 136p. 1975. Repr. of 1948 ed. lib. bdg. 13.50x (ISBN 0-8371-4805-7, HEGL). Greenwood.

Herbert, Charlotte H. Charlotte Hughes Herbert's Cookery for Special Occasions. (Illus.). 1980. pap. 7.85 (ISBN 0-9604928-0-1). Sullivan Prod.

Herbert, Cheryl. Night Chase. LC 77-71006. (Crown Ser.). 1977. pap. 4.50 (ISBN 0-8127-0135-6). Southern Pub.

Herbert, Cindy. I See a Child: Learning About Learning. LC 72-96280. 112p. 1974. pap. 2.95 (ISBN 0-385-04158-6, Anch). Doubleday.

Herbert, D. T. & Johnston, R. J. Geography & the Urban Environment: Progress in Research & Applications, 3 vols. LC 77-13555. 1979. Vol. 1. 44.50 (ISBN 0-471-99575-4, Pub. by Wiley-Interscience); Vol. 2. 44.50 (ISBN 0-471-99725-0); Vol. 3. 51.95 (ISBN 0-471-27632-4). Wiley.

Herbert, David, ed. The Operas of Benjamin Britten. LC 79-2052. (Illus.). 1979. 65.00 (ISBN 0-231-04868-8). Columbia U Pr.

Herbert, Frank. Children of Dune. (YA) 1976. 2.50 (ISBN 0-425-04383-5, Dist. by Putnam). Berkley Pub.

--Destination: Void. 1978. pap. 2.25 (ISBN 0-425-04366-5, Dist. by Putnam). Berkley Pub.

--The Dosadi Experiment. LC 77-3653. (YA) 1977. 2.25 (ISBN 0-425-03834-3, Dist. by Putnam). Berkley Pub.

--The Dragon in the Sea. (Science Fiction Ser.). 1980. lib. bdg. 13.95 (ISBN 0-8398-2646-X). Gregg.

--God Emperor of Dune. 432p. 1981. 12.95 (ISBN 0-399-12593-0). Putnam.

--The Green Brain. (Science Fiction Ser.). 1981. PLB 13.95 (ISBN 0-8398-2667-2). Gregg.

--The Heaven Makers. (A Del Rey Bk.). 1977. pap. 1.50 o.p. (ISBN 0-345-25304-3). Ballantine.

--The Santaroga Barrier. LC 77-49. (YA) 1977. 1.95 (ISBN 0-425-04334-7, Dist. by Putnam). Berkley Pub.

--Whipping Star. (Science Fiction Ser.). 1980. pap. 13.95 (ISBN 0-8398-2648-6). Gregg.

Herbert, Frank & Barnard, Max. Without Me You're Nothing: The Essential Guide to Home Computers. 1981. 12.95 (ISBN 0-671-41287-6). S&S.

Herbert, Frank & Ransom, Bill. The Jesus Incident. 1979. 10.95 o.p. (ISBN 0-399-12268-0). Berkley Pub.

Herbert, Frank, ed. Nebula Winners Fifteen. LC 78-645226. 256p. 1981. 12.95 (ISBN 0-06-014830-6, HarpT). Har-Row.

Herbert, G. W., jt. auth. see Wilson, Harriet.

Herbert, George. Bodleian Manuscript of George Herbert's "the Temple". Date not set. write for info. Schol Facsimiles.

--The English Poems of George Herbert. Patrides, C. A., ed. (Rowman & Littlefield University Library). 247p. 1974. 10.00x (ISBN 0-87471-551-2); pap. 4.50x (ISBN 0-87471-552-0). Rowman.

Herbert, George see Thomas, R. S.

Herbert, George, ed. The Latin Poetry of George Herbert: A Bilingual Edition. Murphy, Paul R. & McCloskey, Mark, trs. from Latin & Eng. LC 64-22888. vii, 181p. 1965. 10.95x (ISBN 0-8214-0007-X). Ohio U Pr.

Herbert, Harry J. The Population Dynamics of the Waterbuck, Kobus ellipsiprymnus (Ogilby, 1833), in the Sabi-Sand Wildtuin. (Mammalia Depicta Ser.). (Illus.). 68p. (Orig.). 1972. pap. text ed. 20.00. Parey Sci Pubs.

Herbert, Ian, ed. Who's Who in the Theatre, 2 vols. 17th ed. 1500p. 1981. Set. 150.00 (ISBN 0-8103-0234-9). Gale.

Herbert, James. The Survivor. 1977. pap. 1.95 (ISBN 0-451-08369-5, J8369, Sig). NAL.

Herbert, Janice S. Oriental Rugs: The Illustrated Guide. 1978. 19.95 (ISBN 0-02-551120-3). Macmillan.

Herbert, John. Creating Your Own Restaurant. (Herman's Foodservice Guide Ser.). (Illus., Prof. ed.). 1981. price not set (ISBN 0-89047-040-5). Herman Pub.

--Fortune & Men's Eyes. LC 67-31624. (Photos). 1968. pap. 4.95 (ISBN 0-394-17357-0, E457, Ever). Grove.

Herbert, John, ed. see Christie's.

Herbert, John D. Urban Development in the Third World: Policy Guidelines. LC 78-19769. (Praeger Special Studies). 1979. 24.95 (ISBN 0-03-045731-9). Praeger.

Herbert, M. V. The Hickmans of Oldswinford. 196p. 1980. 37.50x (ISBN 0-7050-0061-3, Pub. by Skilton & Shaw England). State Mutual Bk.

Herbert, Martin. Conduct Disorders of Childhood & Adolescence: A Behavioral Approach to Assessment & Treatment. LC 77-9633. 1978. 36.50 (ISBN 0-471-99509-6, Pub. by Wiley-Interscience). Wiley.

Herbert, Miranda, jt. auth. see McNeil, Barbara.

Herbert, Miranda C. & McNeil, Barbara, eds. Biographical Dictionaries Master Index: First & Second Supplements 1979-80. LC 79-22270. 1979. Set. pap. 90.00 (ISBN 0-8103-1082-1). Gale.

--Biography & Geneology Master Index, 8 vols. 2nd ed. (Gale Biographical Index Ser.: No. 1). 1980. Set. 575.00 (ISBN 0-8103-1094-5). Gale.

Herbert, Miranda C., jt. ed. see McNeil, Barbara.

Herbert, Mollie, jt. auth. see Cunningham-Smith, Judy.

Herbert, N. M., ed. A History of the County of Gloucester, Vol 7. (Victoria History of the Counties of England Ser.). (Illus.). 250p. 1980. 149.00 (ISBN 0-19-722755-4). Oxford U Pr.

--The Victoria History of the Counties of England: A History of Gloucester, Vol.11. (Illus.). 1976. 65.00x o.p. (ISBN 0-19-722745-7). Oxford U Pr.

Herbert, Paul D. The Sincerest Form of Flattery. LC 80-67699. (Sherlock Holmes Reference Ser.). 128p. 1981. 14.95 (ISBN 0-934468-04-4). Gaslight.

Herbert, R. T. Paradox & Identity in Theology. LC 78-20784. 1979. 15.00x (ISBN 0-8014-1222-6). Cornell U Pr.

Herbert, Richard A., jt. auth. see D'Albert, Joseph L.

Herbert, Sandra, ed. The Red Notebook of Charles Darwin. LC 78-74215. (Illus.). 1980. 19.50x (ISBN 0-8014-1226-9). Cornell U Pr.

Herbert, Susan H., ed. see Hollander, Mary K.

Herbert, T. Walter, Jr. Moby-Dick & Calvinism: A World Dismantled. 1977. 14.00 (ISBN 0-8135-0829-0). Rutgers U Pr.

Herbert, Sir Thomas. A Relation of Some Yeares Travaile Begunne Anno 1626, into Afrique & the Greater Asia. LC 76-25706. (English Experience Ser.: No. 349). 1971. Repr. of 1634 ed. 42.00 (ISBN 90-221-0349-8). Walter J Johnson.

Herbert, W. L. & Jarvis, F. J. Marriage Counselling in the Community. 1970. 8.25 (ISBN 0-08-006911-8); pap. 5.25 o.p. (ISBN 0-08-006910-X). Pergamon.

Herbert, Wally. Polar Deserts. LC 73-153825. (International Library). (Illus.). (gr. 7 up). 1971. PLB 6.90 o.p. (ISBN 0-531-02101-7). Watts.

Herbert, Xavier. Dream Road. 108p. 1980. 20.95x (ISBN 0-00-221593-4, Pub. by W Collins Australia). Intl Schol Bk Serv.

--Poor Fellow My Country. 1466p. 1980. 17.95 (ISBN 0-312-63015-8). St Martin.

Herberts, Peter, et al, eds. The Control of the Upper-Extremity Prostheses & Orthoses. (Illus.). 276p. 1974. 25.50 (ISBN 0-398-02869-9). C C Thomas.

Herbert-Sturtridge. Simulations. (ELT Guide Ser.: No. 2). 1979. pap. text ed. 14.50x (ISBN 0-85633-192-9, NFER). Humanities.

Herbic, Herbert J., jt. auth. see Cahill, Robert B.

Herbig, George H., ed. Spectroscopic Astrophysics: An Assessment of the Contributions of Otto Struve. LC 69-15939. 1970. 32.50x (ISBN 0-520-01410-3). U of Cal Pr.

Herbruck, Christine. Breaking the Cycle of Child Abuse. 1979. 8.95 o.p. (ISBN 0-03-052691-4); pap. 5.95 (ISBN 0-03-045691-6). Winston Pr.

Herbst, et al. Grimm's Grandchildren: Current Topics in German Linguistics. (Longman Linguistics Library). (Illus.). 1980. text ed. 27.00 (ISBN 0-582-55487-X); pap. text ed. 15.95 (ISBN 0-582-55489-6). Longman.

Herbst, J. F., ed. see IFAC Symposium, Pretoria, Republic of South Africa 15-19 September 1980.

Herbst, Josephine. New Green World. (American Procession Ser.). (Illus.). 1954. 7.95 (ISBN 0-8038-5001-8). Hastings.

Herbst, Jurgen, compiled by. The History of American Education. LC 76-178293. (Goldentree Bibliographies in American History Ser.). 172p. (Orig.). 1973. pap. 6.95x (ISBN 0-88295-531-4). AHM Pub.

Herbst, R. Dictionary of Commercial, Financial & Legal Terms, 3 Vols. (Eng, Fr. & Ger.). 93.50 ea. Adler.

Herd, E. Don, Jr. The South Carolina Upcountry, Fifteen Forty to Nineteen Eighty: Historical & Biographical Sketches, Vol. 1. 1981. pap. 11.95 (ISBN 0-87921-062-1). Attic Pr.

Herd, J. Alan. Cardiovascular Diseases & Therapy, 6 vols. 2nd ed. Incl. Bk. 1. The Circulatory System & Blood Pressure Control. pap. text ed. 13.50 (ISBN 0-89147-041-7); Bk. 2. Hypertension & Anti-Hypertensive Agents. pap. text ed. 16.50 (ISBN 0-89147-042-5); Bk. 3. Beta-Adrenergic Blocking Agents. pap. text ed. 16.50 (ISBN 0-89147-043-3); Bk. 4. Electrolyte Balance & Diffusion of Body Fluids. pap. text ed. 13.50 (ISBN 0-89147-044-1); Bk. 5. Kidney Structure & Function. pap. text ed. 13.50 (ISBN 0-89147-045-X); Bk. 6. Diuretics. (Illus.). pap. text ed. 13.50 (ISBN 0-89147-046-8). 1976. Set. pap. text ed. 75.00 (ISBN 0-89147-040-9). CAS.

Herda, D. J. Free Spirit: Evonne Goolagong. LC 76-16197. (Sports Profiles Ser.). (Illus.). 48p. (gr. 4-11). 1976. PLB 8.50 (ISBN 0-8172-0146-7). Raintree Pubs.

--Growing Trees Indoors. LC 78-37164. 1979. 14.95 (ISBN 0-88229-346-X); pap. 7.95 (ISBN 0-686-66163-X). Nelson-Hall.

--Photography: Close-up. LC 76-45947. (Photography Ser.). (Illus.). (gr. 4-6). 1977. PLB 8.65 (ISBN 0-8172-0019-3). Raintree Pubs.

--Photography: Picture Perfect. LC 76-46369. (Photography Ser.). (Illus.). (gr. 3-5). 1977. PLB 8.65 (ISBN 0-8172-0017-7). Raintree Pubs.

--Photography: Take A Look. LC 76-46367. (Photography Ser.). (Illus.). (gr. k-3). 1977. 8.65 (ISBN 0-8172-0015-0). Raintree Pubs.

--Photography: Through the Lens. LC 76-45778. (Photography Ser.). (Illus.). (gr. 4-7). 1977. PLB 8.65 (ISBN 0-8172-0003-7). Raintree Pubs.

--Roller Skating. (First Bks.). (Illus.). (gr. 4 up). 1979. PLB 6.45 s&l (ISBN 0-531-02262-5). Watts.

Herda, D. J. & Herda, Judy B. Carpentry for Kids. LC 79-26793. (Illus.). 96p. (gr. 4 up). 1980. PLB 7.29 (ISBN 0-671-33042-X). Messner.

Herda, Judy B., jt. auth. see Herda, D. J.

Herdan, Innes. Introduction to China. 1979. pap. 3.95 (ISBN 0-8351-0643-8). China Bks.

Herdeck, Donald E., ed. African Authors: A Companion to Black African Writing 1300-1973, Vol. 1. LC 73-172338. (Illus.). 605p. 1973. 48.00 (ISBN 0-685-53608-4, Pub. by Black Orpheus Press). Gale.

Herdeg, Walter, ed. Archigraphia. (Illus.). 1978. 39.50 (ISBN 0-8038-0470-9). Hastings.

--Film & TV Graphics, 2. (Visual Communication Bks.). (Illus.). 1976. 39.50 (ISBN 0-8038-2322-3). Hastings.

--Graphics Annual, 1980-1981: International Annual of Advertising & Editorial Graphics. (Visual Communications Bks.). (Illus.). 247p. 1980. 59.50 (ISBN 0-8038-2709-1). Hastings.

--Graphics Posters '81: The International Annual of Poster Art. (Visual Communications Bks.). (Illus.). 204p. 1981. 59.50 (ISBN 0-8038-2714-8). Hastings.

--Photographis '81: The International Annual of Advertising, Editorial & Television Photography. (Illus.). 264p. 1981. 59.50 (ISBN 0-8038-5893-0, Visual Communication). Hastings.

Herder, Johann G. Journal Meiner Reise Im Jahr, 1769. 2nd, rev. ed. Gillies, A., ed. (Blackwell's German Text Ser.). 1969. pap. 6.50x o.p. (ISBN 0-631-01830-1, Pub. by Basil Blackwell). Biblio Dist.

Herdt, Gilbert H. Guardians of the Flutes: Idioms of Masculinity. (Illus.). 1980. 17.95 (ISBN 0-07-028315-X). McGraw.

Heredia. Les Trophees. Ince, W. N., ed. (French Poets Ser.). 1979. text ed. 25.00x (ISBN 0-485-14709-2, Athlone Pr); pap. text ed. 11.25x (ISBN 0-485-12709-1). Humanities.

Heren, Louis. Alas, Alas for England: What Went Wrong with Britain. 192p. 1981. 22.50 (ISBN 0-241-10538-2, Pub. by Hamish Hamilton England). David & Charles.

Heren, Louis & Fitzgerald, C. P. China's Three Thousand Years: The Story of a Great Civilisation. LC 73-12638. (Illus.). 240p. 1974. pap. 3.95 o.s.i. (ISBN 0-02-032200-3, Collier). Macmillan.

Heren, Louis, et al. China's Three Thousand Years: The Story of a Great Civilization. (Illus.). 240p. 1974. 8.95 o.s.i. (ISBN 0-02-550080-5). Macmillan.

Heresbach, Conrad. Foure Bookes of Husbandry, Newely Englished & Increased by B. Googe. LC 72-205. (English Experience Ser.: No. 323). 1971. Repr. of 1577 ed. 49.00 (ISBN 90-221-0323-4). Walter J Johnson.

Herford, C. H., et al, eds. see Jonson, Ben.

Herford, Julius, jt. ed. see Decker, Harold A.

Hergenhahn, B. R. An Introduction to the Theories of Personality. (Illus.). 1980. 18.95 (ISBN 0-13-498766-7). P-H.

--An Introduction to Theories of Learning. (Illus.). 352p. 1976. 18.95 (ISBN 0-13-498733-0). P-H.

Herget, C., jt. auth. see Michel, A.

Herhold, Robert M., ed. see Sittler, Joseph A.

Heriam, J. L. Engineering Mechanics, 2 vols. Incl. Vol. 1. Statics: SI Version. text ed. 18.95 (ISBN 0-471-05558-1); Arabic ed. (ISBN 0-471-06312-6); Vol. 2. Dynamics: SI Version. text ed. 17.95 (ISBN 0-471-05559-X); Arabic ed. (ISBN 0-471-06311-8). LC 79-11173. 1980. Wiley.

--Engineering Mechanics, 2 vols. Incl. Vol. 1. Statics. text ed. 18.95x (ISBN 0-471-59460-1); Vol. 2. Dynamics. text ed. 19.95x (ISBN 0-471-59461-X). LC 77-24716. 1978. Wiley.

Hericourt, Jenny P. A Woman's Philosophy of Woman: Or, Woman Affranchised. an Answer to Michelet, Proudhon, Girardin, Legouve, Comte, & Other Modern Innovators. LC 79-2940. 317p. 1981. Repr. of 1864 ed. 23.50 (ISBN 0-8305-0105-3). Hyperion Conn.

Heriman, J. L. ARA Engineering Mechanics, 2 vols. Incl. Vol. 1. SI Statics (ISBN 0-471-06312-6); Vol. 2. SI Dynamics (ISBN 0-471-06311-8). 1980. 18.95 ea. Wiley.

Hering, Ewald. Outlines of a Theory of the Light Sense. LC 64-11130. (Illus.). 1964. 16.50x (ISBN 0-674-64900-1). Harvard U Pr.

Hering, H. Robert Leroy Platzman Memorial. 428p. 1976. pap. text ed. 71.00 (ISBN 0-08-019957-7). Pergamon.

Hering, Richard. Hering's Dictionary of Classical & Modern Cookery. rev. ed. Bickel, Walter, tr. from Ger. (Illus.). 1977. text ed. 29.95 (ISBN 0-685-01584-X). Radio City.

Herington, C. John, tr. see Aeschylus.

Heriot, Angus. The Castrati in Opera. LC 74-1332. (Music Ser.). 243p. 1974. Repr. of 1956 ed. lib. bdg. 22.50 (ISBN 0-306-70650-4). Da Capo.

Heriot, Celia. Handbook for Cat People. 1978. pap. 1.95 (ISBN 0-441-31596-8). Charter Bks.

Heritage, Bill. Ponds & Water Gardens. (Illus.). 176p. 1981. 12.95 (ISBN 0-7137-1015-2, Pub. by Blandford Pr England); pap. 6.95 (ISBN 0-7137-1141-8). Sterling.

Heritage Home Plans, Inc. Luxury Home Plans. LC 79-2769. (Illus.). 1980. pap. 7.95 (ISBN 0-15-654309-5, Harv). HarBraceJ.

Heritage, P., et al, eds. Machining for Toolmaking & Experimental Work, 3 vols. 2nd ed. (Engineering Craftsmen: No. H1). (Illus.). 1977. Set. spiral bdg. 36.50x (ISBN 0-85083-024-9). Intl Ideas.

Heriteau, Jacqueline. The Complete Book of Beans. LC 77-92314. 1978. 8.95 (ISBN 0-8015-1474-6, Hawthorn); pap. 5.95 (ISBN 0-8015-1475-4, Hawthorn). Dutton.

Heriteau, Jacqueline & Erath, Thalia. Preserving & Pickling: Putting Foods by in Small Batches. (Illus.). 1976. pap. 2.95 (ISBN 0-307-42019-1, Golden Pr). Western Pub.

Heritte-Viardot, Louise. Memories & Adventures. LC 77-22220. (Music Reprint Ser.). (Illus.). 1977. Repr. of 1913 ed. lib. bdg. 25.00 (ISBN 0-306-77515-8). Da Capo.

Herity, Michael & Eogan, George. Ireland in Prehistory. (Illus.). 1976. 30.00 (ISBN 0-7100-8413-7). Routledge & Kegan.

Herken, Gregg F. The Winning Weapon: The Atomic Bomb in the Cold War Nineteen Forty-Five to Nineteen Fifty. LC 80-7643. 416p. 1981. 15.00 (ISBN 0-394-50394-5). Knopf.

Herkimer, Allen G. Understanding Hospital Financial Management. LC 78-12182. 1978. text ed. 25.95 (ISBN 0-89443-047-5). Aspen Systems.

Herkimer, L. R. & Hollander, Phyllis, eds. The Complete Book of Cheerleading. LC 73-81436. 288p. 1975. 9.95 (ISBN 0-385-08057-3); pap. 4.95 (ISBN 0-385-08059-X). Doubleday.

Herklots, G. A., tr. see Sharif, Ja'Far.

Herklots, G. A. C. Vegetables in South-East Asia. (Illus.). 1972. text ed. 20.00x (ISBN 0-04-635008-X). Allen Unwin.

Herlick, Stanford D. California Workers' Compensation Law Handbook, 2 vols. 1981. Set. incl. 1979 suppl. 92.00 (ISBN 0-911110-25-9). Parker & Son.

Herlihy, David. History of Feudalism. (Documentary History of Western Civilization Ser). 1971. 15.00x o.s.i. (ISBN 0-8027-2024-2). Walker & Co.

Herlihy, David, ed. Medieval Culture & Society. LC 68-13326. (Documentary History of Western Civilization Ser). 1968. 15.00x o.s.i. (ISBN 0-8027-2013-7). Walker & Co.

Herlin, Hans. Commemorations. 320p. 1976. pap. 1.95 o.p. (ISBN 0-345-25223-3). Ballantine.

--Which Way the Wind. Winston, Richard & Winston, Clara, trs. from Ger. LC 78-4013. 1978. 10.00 o.p. (ISBN 0-312-86709-3). St Martin.

Herman. Our Snowman Had Olive Eyes. (gr. 4-5). 1980. pap. 1.25 (ISBN 0-590-30253-1, Schol Pap). Schol Bk Serv.

Herman, A. G., jt. ed. see Boeynaems, J. M.

Herman, A. L. The Bhagavad Gita: A Translation & Critical Commentary. (Illus.). 200p. 1973. 11.75 (ISBN 0-398-02772-2). C C Thomas.

--Introduction to Indian Thought. (Illus.). 375p. 1976. pap. text ed. 11.95 (ISBN 0-13-484477-7). P-H.

Herman, A. L. & Blackwood, R. T., eds. Problems in Philosophy: West & East. 544p. 1975. 17.95 (ISBN 0-13-719708-X). P-H.

Herman, Ben. The Rhapsody in Blue of Mickey Klein. 144p. (gr. 7 up). 1981. 8.95 (ISBN 0-916144-68-2). Stemmer Hse.

Herman, Charles F., ed. International Crises. LC 74-165102. 1973. 19.95 (ISBN 0-02-914560-0). Free Pr.

Herman, Charlotte. My Mother Didn't Kiss Me Goodnight. LC 80-190. (Illus.). 32p. (ps-3). 1980. PLB 7.95 (ISBN 0-525-35495-6). Dutton.

--On the Way to the Movies. LC 79-19015. (Illus.). 32p. (gr. k-3). 1980. PLB 7.95 (ISBN 0-525-36400-5). Dutton.

Herman, Daniel J. The Philosophy of Henri Bergson. LC 80-5044. 117p. 1979. text ed. 16.75 (ISBN 0-8191-1029-9); pap. text ed. 7.50 (ISBN 0-8191-1030-2). U Pr of Amer.

Herman, E. Edward. Collective Bargaining & Labor Relations. (Illus.). 576p. 1981. text ed. 19.95 (ISBN 0-13-140558-6). P-H.

Herman, Edward S. Corporate Control, Corporate Power. LC 80-29447. (Illus.). 336p. 1981. 17.95 (ISBN 0-521-23996-6). Cambridge U Pr.

Herman, Esther, jt. ed. see Wasserman, Paul.

Herman, G. The Who. 1972. 5.95 o.s.i. (ISBN 0-02-551180-7). Macmillan.

--The Who. 1972. pap. 1.95 o.s.i. (ISBN 0-02-060730-X, Collier). Macmillan.

Herman, G. T. & Natterer, F., eds. Mathematical Aspects of Computerized Tomography: Proceedings. (Lecture Notes in Medical Information Ser.: Vol. 8). 309p. 1981. pap. 28.10 (ISBN 0-387-10277-9). Springer-Verlag.

Herman, Gabor H. Image Reconstruction from Projections: The Fundamentals of Computerized Tomography. LC 79-6785. (Computer Science & Applied Mathematics Ser.). 1980. 29.50 (ISBN 0-12-342050-4). Acad Pr.

Herman, George, ed. R. D. Mindlin & Applied Mechanics: A Collection of Studies in the Development of Applied Mechanics Dedicated to Prof. R. D. Mindlin by His Former Students. LC 73-22346. 1974. text ed. 46.00 (ISBN 0-08-017710-7). Pergamon.

Herman, H. A. & Madden, F. A. Artificial Insemination of Dairy & Beef Cattle. 6th ed. 1980. 13.95x (ISBN 0-87543-109-7). Lucas.

Herman, Harold & McKay, Mary E. Community Health Services. 2nd ed. LC 61-15342. (Municipal Management Ser). 1969. 20.00 (ISBN 0-87326-007-4). Intl City Mgt.

Herman, Harry A. Artificial Insemination of Dairy Goat. Date not set. 2.50 (ISBN 0-686-26684-6). Dairy Goat.

--Improving Cattle by the Millions: NAAB & the Development & Worldwide Application of Artificial Insemination. LC 80-25899. 352p. 1981. text ed. 30.00x (ISBN 0-8262-0320-5). U of Mo Pr.

Herman, Ira. Dark Horses Leaping into Flames. 1979. 10.95 (ISBN 0-89002-122-8); pap. 3.50 (ISBN 0-89002-121-X). Northwoods Pr.

Herman, J. B. Grandmother's House. (Orig.). 1980. pap. 1.75 (ISBN 0-532-23136-8). Manor Bks.

Herman, Jill H., jt. auth. see Rossand, Colette.

Herman, John R. & Goldberg, Richard A. Sun, Weather, & Climate. LC 79-22363. (Illus.). 1980. Repr. of 1978 ed. 30.00 (ISBN 0-8103-1018-X). Gale.

Herman, Judith M., tr. see Shalom ben-Chorin.

Herman, Lewis, jt. auth. see Herman, Marguerite S.

Herman, Linda & Stiel, Beth. Corpus Delicti of Mystery Fiction: A Guide to the Body of the Case. LC 74-16319. 1974. 10.00 (ISBN 0-8108-0770-X). Scarecrow.

Herman, Lloyd. American Porcelain. (Illus.). 150p. 1980. pap. 14.95 (ISBN 0-917304-60-8, Pub. by Timber Pr). Intl Schol Bk Serv.

Herman, Marguerite S. & Herman, Lewis. Foreign Dialects. LC 58-10332. 1943. 12.95 (ISBN 0-87830-048-1). Theatre Arts.

Herman, Marian A., ed. Semiconductor Optoelectronics: Proceedings. 1981. 44.00 (ISBN 0-471-27589-1, Pub. by Wiley-Interscience). Wiley.

Herman, Melvin. Administrative Justice & Supplementary Benefits. 68p. 1972. pap. text ed. 5.00x (ISBN 0-7135-1711-5, Pub. by Bedford England). Renouf.

Herman, Melvin & Freeman, Lucy. The Pursuit of Mental Health: For the Individual, the Community & the Nation. LC 74-9774. 256p. 1974. 6.95 o.s.i. (ISBN 0-02-551190-4). Macmillan.

Herman, Paul E. & Ihde, Sheila H. Let's Communicate: Using Grammar Effectively. 235p. (Orig.). (gr. 4-6). 1979. pap. text ed. 5.25x (ISBN 0-88334-123-9). Ind Sch Pr.

Herman, Robert. Algebro - Geometric & Lie Theoretic Tecniques in Systems Theory: Part A. (Interdisciplinary Mathematics Ser.: No. 13). 1977. 22.00 (ISBN 0-915692-17-1). Math Sci Pr.

Herman, Robert D. Gamblers & Gambling. (Illus.). 1976. 16.95 (ISBN 0-669-00963-6). Lexington Bks.

Herman, Robert H., et al, eds. Neural Control of Locomotion. LC 76-18949. (Advances in Behavioral Biology: Vol. 18). 822p. 1976. 55.00 (ISBN 0-306-37918-X, Plenum Pr). Plenum Pub.

--Principles of Metabolic Control in Mammalian Systems. (Illus.). 690p. 1980. 35.00 (ISBN 0-306-40261-0, Plenum Pr). Plenum Pub.

Herman, Ron, jt. auth. see Treib, Marc.

Herman, Scheffauer, tr. see Mayreder, Rosa.

Herman, V. & Van Schendelen, M. P. The European Parliament & the National Parliaments. 1978. text ed. 26.50x (ISBN 0-566-00251-5, Pub. by Gower Pub Co England). Renouf.

Herman, Valentine & Hagger, Mark. The Legislation of Direct Elections to the European Parliament. 1979. text ed. 36.00 (ISBN 0-566-00247-7, Pub. by Gower Pub Co England). Renouf.

Hermann, B. P. A Multidisciplinary Handbook of Epilepsy. (Illus.). 388p. 1980. 34.50 (ISBN 0-398-04070-2); pap. 26.75 (ISBN 0-398-04069-9). C C Thomas.

Hermann, Charles F. see East, Maurice A., et al.

Hermann, E. R., et al, eds. Piaget: Dictionary of Terms. 1973. text ed. 26.00 (ISBN 0-08-017039-0). Pergamon.

Hermann, Evelyn. Shinichi Suzuki: The Man & His Philosophy. LC 80-67542. 1980. write for info (ISBN 0-918194-07-5). Accura.

Hermann, Henry R. Social Insects, Vol. 2. 1981. write for info. (ISBN 0-12-342202-7). Acad Pr.

Hermann, Janet S. The Pursuit of a Dream. (Illus.). 288p. 1981. 17.50 (ISBN 0-19-502887-2). Oxford U Pr.

Hermann, John P. & Burke, John J., Jr. Signs & Symbols in Chaucer's Poetry. 272p. 1981. 16.75 (ISBN 0-8173-0038-4); pap. 8.95 (ISBN 0-8173-0042-2). U of Ala Pr.

Hermann, Judith M., tr. see Gmelin, Otto.

Hermann, Margaret G. & Milburn, Thomas W., eds. A Psychological Examination of Political Leaders. LC 75-32366. 1977. 19.95 (ISBN 0-02-914590-2). Free Pr.

Hermann, Michele G. Search & Seizure Checklists. LC 79-9734. 1979. pap. 11.50 spiral (ISBN 0-87632-110-4). Boardman.

Hermann, Michele G. & Haft, Marilyn G. Prisoners' Rights Sourcebook: Theory-Litigation-Practice. LC 73-82906. 1973. 40.00 (ISBN 0-87632-100-7). Boardman.

Hermann, Michele G., ed. Federal Rules of Criminal Procedure. 2nd ed. LC 80-10646. 1980. looseleaf with 1978 rev. pages 35.00 (ISBN 0-87632-106-6). Boardman.

Hermann, Philip. Better Settlements Through Leverage. 1965. 19.50x o.p. (ISBN 0-686-00450-7). Lawyers Co-Op.

Hermann, Philip J. Do You Need a Lawyer? (Illus.). 160p. 1980. 12.95 (ISBN 0-13-216721-2, Spec); pap. 4.95 (ISBN 0-13-216713-1). P-H.

Hermann, R., jt. auth. see Hurt, Norman.

Hermann, Robert. Cartanian Geometry, Nonlinear Waves, & Control Theory, Pt. B. Ackerman, Michael, tr. (Interdisciplinary Mathematics Ser.: Vol. 21). 585p. 1980. text ed. 60.00x (ISBN 0-915692-29-5, QA649.H46). Math Sci Pr.

--Diffferential Geometry and the Calculus of Variations. 2nd ed. LC 68-14664. (Intermath Ser.: No. 17). 1977. 42.00 (ISBN 0-915692-24-4). Math Sci Pr.

--Energy Momentum Tensors. (Interdisciplinary Mathematics Ser: No. 4). 153p. 1973. 11.00 (ISBN 0-915692-03-1). Math Sci Pr.

--Gauge Fields, & Cartan-Enresmann Connections: Part a. LC 75-12199. (Interdisciplinary Mathematics: No. 10). 500p. 1975. 35.00 (ISBN 0-915692-09-0). Math Sci Pr.

--General Algebraic Ideas. (Interdisciplinary Mathematics Ser: No. 1). 205p. 1973. 10.00 (ISBN 0-915692-00-7). Math Sci Pr.

--Geometric Structure of Systems Control Theory & Physics: Part B. LC 74-30856. (Interdisciplinary Mathematics Ser.: No. 11). 1976. 40.00 (ISBN 0-915692-14-7). Math Sci Pr.

--Geometric Structure of Theory & Physics: Part A. LC 74-30856. (Interdisciplinary Mathematics Ser: No. 9). 450p. 1974. 35.00 (ISBN 0-915692-08-2). Math Sci Pr.

--Geometric Theory of Non-Linear Differential Equations, Backlund Transformations, Solitons: Part A. LC 76-17201. (Interdisciplinary Mathematics Ser.: No. 12). 1976. 30.00 (ISBN 0-915692-16-3). Math Sci Pr.

--Linear & Tensor Algebra. (Interdisciplinary Mathematics Ser: No. 2). 163p. 1973. 9.00 (ISBN 0-915692-01-5). Math Sci Pr.

--Linear Systems Theory and Introductory Algebraic Geometry. (Interdisciplinary Mathematics Ser: No. 8). 282p. 1974. 24.00 (ISBN 0-915692-07-4). Math Sci Pr.

--Quantum & Fermion Differential Geometry, Pt. A. (Interdisciplinary Mathematics Ser.: No. 16). 1977. 18.00 (ISBN 0-915692-22-8). Math Sci Pr.

--Spinors, Clifford, and Cayley Algebras. (Interdisciplinary Mathematics Ser: No. 7). 276p. 1974. 20.00 (ISBN 0-915692-06-6). Math Sci Pr.

--Toda Lattices, Cosymplectic Manifolds, Baecklund Transformations & Kinks, Pt. B. (Interdisciplinary Mathematics Ser.: No. 18). 1979. 15.00 (ISBN 0-915692-24-4). Math Sci Pr.

--Topics in General Relativity. (Interdisciplinary Mathematics Ser: No. 5). 171p. 1973. 12.00 (ISBN 0-915692-04-X). Math Sci Pr.

--Topics in the Mathematics of Quantum Mechanics. (Interdisciplinary Mathematics Ser: No. 6). 250p. 1973. 16.00 (ISBN 0-915692-05-8). Math Sci Pr.

Hermann, Robert & Ackerman, M. Sophus Lie's Eighteen Eighty Transformation Group Paper. LC 75-43189. (Lie Groups: History Frontiers & Applications Ser.: No. 3). 1976. 26.00 (ISBN 0-915692-13-9). Math Sci Pr.

Hermann, Robert, jt. auth. see Ackerman, M.

Hermann, Robert, ed. The Nineteen Seventy Six Ames Research Center (NASA) Conference on Geometric Nonlinear Wave Theory. (Lie Groups; History, Frontiers & Applications: Vol. 6). 1977. pap. 13.00x (ISBN 0-915692-19-8). Math Sci Pr.

Hermann, Robert, et al. Counsel for the Poor: Criminal Defense in Urban America. LC 77-9151. 1977. 17.95 (ISBN 0-669-01810-4). Lexington Bks.

Hermannsson, Halldor, ed. Catalogue of the Icelandic Collection: Additions 1913-1926. (University Library Publications). 1960. soft cover 25.00x (ISBN 0-8014-9817-1). Cornell U Pr.

--Catalogue of the Icelandic Collection: Additions 1927-1942. (University Library Publications). 1960. soft cover 25.00x (ISBN 0-8014-9818-X). Cornell U Pr.

--Catalogue of the Icelandic Collection Bequeathed by Willard Fiske. (University Library Publications). 1960. soft cover 35.00x (ISBN 0-8014-9816-3). Cornell U Pr.

--Holar Cato. 91p. 1958. 12.50x (ISBN 0-8014-0202-6); soft cover 9.50x (ISBN 0-8014-9822-8). Cornell U Pr.

Hermans, Hubert J. Value Areas & Their Development: Theory & Method of Self-Confrontation. Spiekerman, Joseph A., tr. from Dutch. 306p. 1975. text ed. 49.95 (ISBN 90-265-0225-7, Pub. by Swets Pub Serv Holland). Swets North Am.

Hermanson, Roger H., et al. Accounting Principles. 1980. 18.95x (ISBN 0-256-02258-5); study guide 6.95x (ISBN 0-256-02262-3); working papers, bk. 5.95x (ISBN 0-256-02263-1); working papers, bk. 2 avail. (ISBN 0-256-02264-X); practice set no. 1 avail. (ISBN 0-256-02305-0); practice set no. 2 avail. (ISBN 0-256-02306-9); practice set no. 3 avail. (ISBN 0-256-02383-2). Business Pubns.

--Auditing Theory & Practice. rev. ed. 1980. 19.95x (ISBN 0-256-02330-1). Irwin.

--Auditing Theory & Practice. 1976. text ed. 16.95x o.p. (ISBN 0-256-01445-0). Irwin.

Hermassi, Elbaki. Leadership & National Development in North Africa: A Comparative Study. LC 70-182279. 250p. 1973. pap. 6.95x (ISBN 0-520-02894-5). U of Cal Pr.

--The Third World Reassessed. 1980. 16.50x (ISBN 0-520-03764-2). U of Cal Pr.

Hermassi, Karen. Polity & Theatre in Historical Perspective. 1977. 16.50x (ISBN 0-520-03294-2). U of Cal Pr.

Hermelin, B. & O'Connor, N. Psychological Experiments with Autistic Children. 1970. 27.00 (ISBN 0-08-016088-3). Pergamon.

Hermes, Eberhard, ed. see Alfonsi, Petrus.

Hermes, Hans-Joachim. Liefer in Anomyman Englischen Drama, 1580-1603. (Salzburg Studies in English Literature, Elizabethan & Renaissance Studies: No. 40). (Illus.). 323p. 1974. pap. text ed. 25.00x (ISBN 0-391-01407-2). Humanities.

Hermes, Margaret. The Phoenix Nest. 1981. 8.95 (ISBN 0-8092-5905-2). Contemp Bks.

Hermet, Guy. The Communists in Spain. 1974. 22.95 (ISBN 0-347-01032-6, 93492-5, Pub. by Saxon Hse England). Lexington Bks.

Hermet, Guy, et al, eds. Elections Without Choice. LC 77-16116. 1978. 17.95 (ISBN 0-470-99292-1). Halsted Pr.

Hermey, Carl W., ed. see Chedid, Andree.

Hermission, Hans-Jurgen & Lohse, Eduard. Faith. Stott, Douglas, tr. LC 80-22542. (Biblical Encounter Ser.). 176p. 1981. pap. 6.95 (ISBN 0-687-12520-0). Abingdon.

Hermitage Staff. The Hermitage. 315p. 1980. 75.00 (ISBN 0-569-08426-1, Pub. by Collets Holdings England). Intl Schol Bk Serv.

Hern, Nicholas. Peter Handke. LC 76-190349. (Modern Literature Ser.). 1972. 10.95 (ISBN 0-8044-2380-6). Ungar.

Hernadi, Paul. Beyond Genre: New Directions in Literary Classification. (Illus.). 224p. 1972. 19.50x o.p. (ISBN 0-8014-0732-X). Cornell U Pr.

Hernadi, Paul, ed. What is Literature? LC 77-23640. 288p. 1978. 12.50x (ISBN 0-253-36505-8). Ind U Pr.

Hernandez, Carrol A., et al. Chicanos: Social & Psychological Perspectives. 2nd ed. LC 75-37769. (Illus.). 376p. 1976. pap. 12.00 (ISBN 0-8016-5316-9). Mosby.

Hernandez, J. A., jt. auth. see Guillermo, E.

Hernandez, Jose. The Gaucho Martin Fierro. Carrino, Frank G., et al, trs. LC 74-12185. (Unesco Collection of Representative Works, Latin American Ser.). 192p. (Eng. & Span.). 1974. Repr. of 1872 ed. 20.00x (ISBN 0-8201-1133-3). Schol Facsimiles.

Hernandez, Jose C., ed. see Statt, David A.

Hernandez, Miguel. Songbook of Absences. Jones, Tom, tr. LC 72-91778. 1980. 7.50 (ISBN 0-685-25407-0). Charioteer.

Hernandez Aquino, Luis. Nuestra Aventura Literaria: Los Ismos En la Poesia Puertorriquena, 1913-1940. 2nd, rev. ed. pap. 3.10 o.p. (ISBN 0-8477-3134-0). U of PR Pr.

Herndl, George C. The High Design: English Renaissance Tragedy & the Natural Law. LC 78-111511. 352p. 1970. 14.00x (ISBN 0-8131-1217-6). U Pr of Ky.

Herndon, James F., jt. ed. see Bernd, Joseph L.

Herndon, Marcia. Native American Music. new ed. 233p. 1980. lib. bdg. 20.00 (ISBN 0-8482-4475-3). Norwood Edns.

Herne, Brian. Ugandi Safaris. 1980. 12.95 (ISBN 0-87691-316-8). Winchester Pr.

Herner & Co. Staff. EIS Cumulative: 1978. LC 79-640191. 1979. text ed. 75.00 (ISBN 0-87815-025-0). Info Resources.

Hernes, Helga, ed. The Multinational Corporation: A Guide to Information Sources. LC 73-17509. (International Relations Information Guide Series: Vol. 4). 1977. 30.00 (ISBN 0-8103-1327-8). Gale.

Hernon, Peter, et al. Library & Library Related Publications: A Directory of Publishing Opportunities in Journals, Serials & Annuals. LC 73-84183. 180p. 1973. lib. bdg. 10.00 o.p. (ISBN 0-87287-068-5). Libs Unl.

Hernton, Calvin C., jt. auth. see Berke, Joseph.

Hero, Alfred O., Jr., jt. ed. see Beigie, Carl E.

Herodotus. Herodotus, Book 6: Erato. Shuckburgh, E. S., ed. text ed. 9.95x (ISBN 0-521-05248-3). Cambridge U Pr.

--Historiae, 2 Vols. 3rd ed. Hude, Karl, ed. (Oxford Classical Texts Ser). 1927. Vol. 1. 18.95x (ISBN 0-19-814526-8); Vol. 2. 18.95x (ISBN 0-19-814527-6). Oxford U Pr.

Herold, A. Ferdinand. Life of Buddha: According to the Legend of Ancient India. LC 55-12748. 1954. pap. 5.95 (ISBN 0-8048-0382-X). C E Tuttle.

Herold, Earl. Living Fishes of the World. LC 61-6384. 1975. 19.95 o.p. (ISBN 0-385-00988-7). Doubleday.

Herold, J. Christopher. The Mind of Napoleon: A Selection of His Written & Spoken Words. LC 55-9068. 1955. pap. 6.95 (ISBN 0-231-08523-0). Columbia U Pr.

Herold, J. Christopher & Horizon Magazine Editors. Horizon Book of the Age of Napoleon. (Illus.). 1963. 30.00 o.s.i. (ISBN 0-06-011835-0, HarpT). Har-Row.

Herold, J. Christopher & Wright, Gordon. Battle of Waterloo. LC 67-15416. (Horizon Caravel Bks). (Illus.). 153p. (gr. 6 up). 1967. 9.95 (ISBN 0-06-022307-3, Dist. by Har-Row); PLB 6.89 o.p. (ISBN 0-06-022308-1). Am Heritage.

Heroldt, Johann. Heydenweldt und Ihrer Gotter: The Renaissance & the Gods. Orgel, Stephen, ed. LC 78-68202. (The Philosophy of Images Ser.). 1980. lib. bdg. 66.00 (ISBN 0-8240-3676-X). Garland Pub.

Heron, Alasdair I. A Century of Protestant Theology. LC 80-17409. (Orig.). 1980. pap. write for info. (ISBN 0-664-24346-0). Westminster.

Heron, David W., ed. A Unifying Influence: Essays of Raynard Coe Swank. LC 80-28595. 237p. 1981. 13.50 (ISBN 0-8108-1407-2). Scarecrow.

Heron, Inez. When Trees Were Green: The Story of Robin Heron. LC 78-53879. 1978. 10.00 o.p. (ISBN 0-312-86673-9). St Martin.

Heron, Michael, tr. see Lindgren, Astrid.

Heron, S. D., jt. auth. see Schlaifer, R.

Herondas. The Mimes of Herondas. Davenport, Guy, ed. & tr. from Greek. 100p. 1981. 12.00 (ISBN 0-912516-63-1); pap. 4.95 (ISBN 0-912516-64-X). Grey Fox.

Heroux, Richard L. & Wallace, William A. Financial Analysis & the New Community Development Process. LC 72-92458. (Special Studies in U.S. Economic, Social, & Political Issues). 1973. 28.50x (ISBN 0-275-28646-0). Irvington.

Herpel, George & Collins, Richard. Specialty Advertising in Marketing. LC 78-165355. (Illus.). 1972. 9.95 o.p. (ISBN 0-87094-002-3). Dow Jones-Irwin.

Herpy, Miklos. Analog Integrated Circuits: Operational Amplifiers & Analog Multipliers. 479p. 1980. 58.95 (ISBN 0-471-99604-1, Pub. by Wiley-Interscience). Wiley.

Herr, Edward, jt. auth. see Evans, Rupert.

Herr, Edwin L. & Moore, Roberta. Your Working Life: A Guide to Getting & Holding a Job. LC 79-28360. Orig. Title: Career Education. (Illus.). 464p. 1980. 13.28 (ISBN 0-07-028342-7, G); tchrs. manual 3.00 (ISBN 0-07-028344-3); student wkbk. 5.00 (ISBN 0-07-028343-5). McGraw.

Herr, Larry G. The Scripts of Ancient Northwest Semitic Seals. LC 78-18933. (Harvard Semitic Museum. Harvard Semitic Monographs: No. 18). (Illus.). 1978. 9.00 (ISBN 0-89130-237-9, 040018). Scholars Pr Ca.

Herr, Michael. Dispatches. 288p. 1980. pap. 2.50 (ISBN 0-380-01976-0, 52639). Avon.

Herr, Richard. An Historical Essay on Modern Spain. 1974. pap. 6.50x (ISBN 0-520-02534-2). U of Cal Pr.

--Spain. LC 70-126814. (Modern Nations in Historical Perspective Ser). (Illus.). 1971. pap. 12.95 o.p. (ISBN 0-13-824094-9). P-H.

Herr, Selma E. Diagnostic & Corrective Procedure in Teaching Reading. spiral bdg. 2.95x (ISBN 0-87543-507-6). Lucas.

Herreid, Clyde F. Biology. (Illus.). 1977. text ed. 20.95 (ISBN 0-686-65372-6). Macmillan.

Herrel, Stephen & Schonbach, Michael. Steve's Ice Cream Book. LC 79-56530. (Illus.). 224p. (Orig.). 1981. pap. 5.95 (ISBN 0-89480-080-9). Workman Pub. Postponed.

Herrera, Barbara H. Funky. LC 77-80685. (Destiny Ser.). 1978. pap. 4.95 (ISBN 0-8163-0001-1, 06829-6). Pacific Pr Pub Assn.

Herrera, Jesus V., ed. see Gitman, Lawrence J.

Herrera, Juan F. Akrilica: Poemas 1978-1980. Alarcon, Francisco X., ed. LC 80-83765. (Hand-Size Poetry Ser.: No. 1). (Illus.). 48p. (Orig.). 1981. pap. cancelled (ISBN 0-938254-00-6). Poetasumanos.

Herrera, R. A. Anselm's Proslogion: An Introduction. LC 79-66421. 1979. pap. text ed. 8.75 (ISBN 0-8191-0825-1). U Pr of Amer.

Herreshoff, L. F. Capt. Nat Herreshoff: The Wizard of Bristol. LC 80-28519. (Illus.). 350p. 1981. Repr. of 1953 ed. 17.50 (ISBN 0-911378-32-4). Sheridan.

Herreshoff, L. Francis. The Compleat Cruiser. (Illus.). 372p. 1980. Repr. 14.50 (ISBN 0-911378-05-7). Sheridan.

--An Introduction to Yachting. LC 61-18278. (Illus.). 1980. Repr. of 1963 ed. 30.00 (ISBN 0-911378-14-6). Sheridan.

--An L. Francis Hereshoff Reader. LC 77-85403. 1978. 17.50 (ISBN 0-87742-091-2). Intl Marine.

Herrick, Clyde & Howery, Gerry. Electronic Assembly. 176p. 1980. text ed. 14.95 o.p. (ISBN 0-8359-1639-1); pap. text ed. 10.95 o.p. (ISBN 0-8359-1638-3). Reston.

Herrick, Clyde N. Audio Systems. LC 74-9696. 1974. 17.95 (ISBN 0-87909-049-9). Reston.

--Radio: Theory & Servicing. (Illus.). 288p. 1975. 16.95 (ISBN 0-87909-697-7). Reston.

--Television Troubleshooting. (Illus.). 240p. 1975. 17.50 o.p. (ISBN 0-87909-830-9). Reston.

Herrick, Joy F. & Schraffenberger, Nancy. Something's Got to Help - & Yoga Can. LC 73-80177. (Illus.). 128p. 1974. 5.95 (ISBN 0-87131-126-7). M Evans.

Herrick, Lee, jt. auth. see La Roe, Marlene S.

Herrick, Marvin T. The Poetics of Aristotle in England. LC 76-12455. 1976. Repr. of 1930 ed. 9.00x (ISBN 0-87753-061-0, Phaeton). Gordian.

Herrick, Neal Q., jt. auth. see Sheppard, Harold L.

Herrick, Robert. The Common Lot. 395p. 1980. Repr. of 1904 ed. lib. bdg. 25.00x (ISBN 0-89968-187-5). Lightyear.

--The Master of the Inn. 274p. 1980. Repr. of 1908 ed. lib. bdg. 12.95x (ISBN 0-89968-188-3). Lightyear.

--Poetical Works. Martin, L. C., ed. (Oxford English Texts). 1956. 55.00x o.p. (ISBN 0-19-811813-9). Oxford U Pr.

--The Web of Life. 321p. 1980. Repr. of 1900 ed. lib. bdg. 15.95x (ISBN 0-89968-189-1). Lightyear.

Herrick, William. Love & Terror. LC 80-25140. 256p. 1981. 12.95 (ISBN 0-8112-0791-9). New Directions.

Herrigel, Gustie L. Zen in the Art of Flower Arrangement: An Introduction to the Spirit of the Japanese Art of Flower Arrangement. 1974. 10.00 (ISBN 0-7100-7941-9); pap. 6.00 (ISBN 0-7100-7942-7). Routledge & Kegan.

Herrin, Lamar. American Baroque. 336p. 1981. pap. 3.50 (ISBN 0-380-77362-7, 77362, Bard). Avon.

Herring, Ann, tr. see Otsuka, Yuzo.

Herring, Clyde L. When God & I Talk. (gr. 7-12). 1981. pap. 3.50 (ISBN 0-8054-5334-2). Broadman.

Herring, George C. Aid to Russia: Nineteen Forty-One to Nineteen Forty-Six. LC 72-10545. (Contemporary American History Ser). 1976. pap. 9.00x (ISBN 0-231-08348-3). Columbia U Pr.

--America's Longest War: The U. S. & Vietnam 1950 to 1975. LC 79-16408. (America in Crisis Ser.). 1979. text ed. 14.95 o.p. (ISBN 0-471-01546-6); pap. text ed. 7.95 (ISBN 0-471-01547-4). Wiley.

Herring, George C., Jr. Aid to Russia, Nineteen Forty-One to Nineteen Forty-Six: Strategy, Diplomacy, the Origins of the Cold War. 364p. 1973. 22.50x (ISBN 0-231-03336-2). Columbia U Pr.

Herring, James E. Teaching Library Skills in Schools. (General Ser.). 1979. pap. text ed. 11.75x (ISBN 0-85633-171-6, NFER). Humanities.

Herring, Robert. Hub. 1981. 12.95 (ISBN 0-670-38552-2). Viking Pr.

Herriot, James. All Creatures Great & Small. LC 72-79632. 1972. 10.95 (ISBN 0-312-01960-2, A20000). St Martin.

--All Things Bright & Beautiful. LC 73-87407. 400p. 1974. 10.95 (ISBN 0-312-02030-9). St Martin.

--All Things Wise & Wonderful. LC 77-76640. 1977. 10.95 (ISBN 0-312-02031-7). St Martin.

--James Herriot's Yorkshire. 1979. 16.95 (ISBN 0-312-43970-9). St Martin.

--James Herriot's Yorkshire. (Illus.). 224p. 1981. pap. 9.95 (ISBN 0-312-43971-7). St Martin.

--The Lord God Made Them All. 320p. 1981. 12.95 (ISBN 0-312-49834-9). St Martin.

Herriot, James, et al. Animals Tame & Wild. Phelps, Gilbert & Phelps, John, eds. LC 78-57781. (Illus.). 1979. 16.95 (ISBN 0-8069-3098-5); lib. bdg. 14.99 (ISBN 0-8069-3099-3). Sterling.

Herriott, James. Illustrated Textbook of Dog Diseases. (Illus.). 284p. 1980. 7.95 (ISBN 0-87666-733-7, PS-770). TFH Pubns.

Herriott, Robert E. & Gross, Neal, eds. The Dynamics of Planned Educational Change: Case Studies & Analyses. LC 78-61456. 1979. 17.00 (ISBN 0-8211-0761-5); text ed. 15.25 ten or more copies (ISBN 0-685-59768-7). McCutchan.

Herrmann, Arthur R. Designs Upon the Trestleboard. 1980. Repr. softcover 6.00 (ISBN 0-686-68267-X). Macoy Pub.

Herrmann, Charles F., III. The Trick Book. McCarthy, Pat, ed. (Pal Paperbacks Kit B Ser.). (Illus., Orig.). (gr. 7-12). 1974. pap. text ed. 1.25 (ISBN 0-8374-3514-5). Xerox Ed Pubns.

Herrmann, Elizabeth R. & Spitz, Edna H., eds. German Women Writers of the Twentieth Century. LC 78-40139. 1978. text ed. 25.00 (ISBN 0-08-021827-X); pap. text ed. 14.00 (ISBN 0-08-021828-8). Pergamon.

Herrmann, Frank. Sotheby's: Portrait of an Auction House. (Illus.). 1981. 29.95 (ISBN 0-393-01424-X). Norton.

Herrmann, Fred. Tricks & Games on the Pool Table. Orig. Title: Fun on the Pool Table, Illustrated. pap. 1.75 (ISBN 0-486-21814-7). Dover.

Herrmann, G. & Perrone, N., eds. The Dynamic Response of Structures. 1972. 51.00 (ISBN 0-08-016850-7). Pergamon.

Herrmann, Luke. Ruskin & Turner. 1968. 17.95 o.p. (ISBN 0-571-08497-4, Pub. by Faber & Faber). Merrimack Bk Serv.

Herrmann, Robert O., jt. auth. see Jelley, Herbert M.

Herrmann, Roland, jt. auth. see Alkemade, Cornelis T.

Herrmann, Siegfried. A History of Israel in Old Testament Times. Bowden, John, tr. from Ger. LC 74-24918. 384p. 1975. 15.50x (ISBN 0-8006-0405-9, 1-405). Fortress.

--Time & History. Belvins, James L., tr. LC 80-25323. (Biblical Encounter Ser.). 208p. (Orig.). 1981. pap. 7.95 (ISBN 0-687-42100-4). Abingdon.

Herrnstein, Richard J. & Boring, Edwin G., eds. Source Book in the History of Psychology. (Source Books in the History of the Sciences Ser). (Illus.). 1965. 20.00x (ISBN 0-674-82410-5); pap. 7.95 (ISBN 0-674-82411-3). Harvard U Pr.

Herron, Bill, ed. see Moser, Norman.

Herron, Caroline R., ed. see Poets & Writers, Inc.

Herron, Dudley. Understanding Chemistry. Incl. Kean, Elizabeth. wkbk. 6.95 (ISBN 0-394-32423-4); Copes, Jane. lab manual 6.95 (ISBN 0-394-32437-4). 515p. 1981. text ed. 16.95 (ISBN 0-394-32087-5). Random.

Herron, Edward A. Cobra in the Sky: The Supersonic Transport. LC 68-22123. (World in the Making Ser). (Illus.). (gr. 7-10). 1968. 3.95g o.s.i. (ISBN 0-02-743690-X, CCPr). Macmillan.

Herron, J. Dudley, et al. A Summary of Research in Science Education, 1974. (A Supplement Volume of Science Education Ser.). 1976. pap. 8.95 (ISBN 0-471-05189-6, Pub. by Wiley-Interscience). Wiley.

Herron, Jim, jt. auth. see Chrisman, Harrys E.

Herron, Orley. Who Controls Your Child? 176p. 1980. pap. 8.95 (ISBN 0-8407-5221-0). Nelson.

Herron, Robin & Sutton-Smith, Brian, eds. Childs Play: Collected Readings on the Biology, Ecology, Psychology & Sociology of Play. LC 73-136714. 1971. 25.50 (ISBN 0-471-37330-3). Wiley.

Herrtage, Sidney J., ed. The English Charlemagne Romances. Incl. Pt. 1. Sir Ferumbras. 1879. 14.95x (ISBN 0-19-722569-1); Pt. 6. The Tail of Rauf Coilyear, with the Fragments of Roland & Vernagu & Otuel. Herrtage, Sidney J., ed. 164p. 1882. 12.95x (ISBN 0-19-722513-6). Oxford U Pr.

Herschy, R. W. Hydrometry: Principles & Practices. LC 78-4101. 1978. 81.00 (ISBN 0-471-99649-1, Pub. by Wiley-Interscience). Wiley.

Hersen, Michel & Barlow, David H. Single Case Experimental Designs: Strategies for Studying Behavior Change. Goldstein, A. P. & Krasner, L., eds. 1975. text ed. 40.00 (ISBN 0-08-019512-1); pap. text ed. 14.75 (ISBN 0-08-019511-3). Pergamon.

Hersen, Michel & Bellack, Alan, eds. Behavioral Assessment: A Practical Handbook. 2nd ed. (Pergamon General Psychology Ser.: No. 98). (Illus.). 500p. 1981. 42.50 (ISBN 0-08-025956-1); pap. 19.50 (ISBN 0-08-025955-3). Pergamon.

Hersen, Michel & Bellack, Alan S., eds. Behavioral Assessment: A Practical Handbook. 2nd ed. (Pergamon General Psychology Ser.). 500p. Date not set. price not set (ISBN 0-08-025956-1); pap. price not set (ISBN 0-08-020531-3). Pergamon.

Hersen, Michel, et al, eds. Progress in Behavior Modification, Vol. 10. 1980. 27.00 (ISBN 0-12-535610-2); 35.00 (ISBN 0-12-535692-7); microfiche ed. 19.00 (ISBN 0-12-535693-5). Acad Pr.

--Progress in Behavior Modification, Vol. 11. 1981. write for info. (ISBN 0-12-535611-0); lib. bdg. write for info. (ISBN 0-12-535694-3); price not set microfiche (ISBN 0-12-535695-1). Acad Pr.

Hersey, John. Bell for Adano. (Literature Ser). (gr. 9-12). 1970. pap. text ed. 3.92 (ISBN 0-87720-749-6). AMSCO Sch.

--Writer's Craft. 1973. 10.95 (ISBN 0-394-31799-8). Random.

Hersey, Paul & Blanchard, Ken. Family Game: A Situational Approach to Effective Parenting. LC 77-92163. 1978. 9.95 o.p. (ISBN 0-201-03068-3); pap. 5.95 o.p. (ISBN 0-201-03069-1). A-W.

--Management of Organizational Behavior: Utilizing Human Resources. 3rd ed. LC 76-28443. (Illus.). 1977. ref. ed. 15.95x (ISBN 0-13-548875-3); pap. 10.95x (ISBN 0-13-548867-2). P-H.

Hersh, Evan M., et al. Immunotherapy of Cancer in Man: Scientific Basis & Current Status. (Illus.). 152p. 1973. 13.75 (ISBN 0-398-02678-5). C C Thomas.

Hersh, Evan M., et al, eds. Augmenting Agents in Cancer Therapy. (Progress in Cancer Research & Therapy Ser.). 585p. 1981. text ed. 49.00 (ISBN 0-89004-525-9). Raven.

Hersh, Leroy, ed. New Developments in Clinical Instrumentation. 192p. 1981. 49.95 (ISBN 0-8493-5305-X). CRC Pr.

Hersh, Richard & Miller, John. Models of Moral Education. 1979. pap. text ed. 7.95 (ISBN 0-582-28123-7). Longman.

Hersh, Richard H., et al. Promoting Moral Growth: From Piaget to Kohlberg. LC 78-19945. 256p. 1979. pap. text ed. write for info. Longman.

Hersh, Seymour M. My Lai Four: A Report on the Massacre & Its Aftermath. 1970. 10.95 o.p. (ISBN 0-394-43737-3). Random.

Hershauer, James C., jt. auth. see Adam, Everett E., Jr.

Hershbell, Jackson P. Pseudo-Plato, Axiochus. Hershbell, Jackson P., tr. LC 79-20127. (Society of Biblical Literature, Text & Translations: 21). Date not set. price not set (ISBN 0-89130-353-7, 060221); pap. price not set (ISBN 0-89130-354-5). Scholars Pr CA.

Hershberg, Theodore, ed. Philadelphia: Work, Space, Family & Group Experience in the Nineteenth Century. Essays Toward an Interdisciplinary History of the City. (Illus.). 608p. 1981. 29.95 (ISBN 0-19-502752-3). Oxford U Pr.

--Philadelphia: Work, Space, Family & Group Experience in the Nineteenth Century. Essays Toward an Interdisciplinary History of the City. (Illus.). 608p. 1981. pap. 8.95 (ISBN 0-19-502753-1, 619, GB). Oxford U Pr.

Hershberger, C. Sugarbush, an Aristocat. 4.50 o.p. (ISBN 0-8062-1100-8). Carlton.

Hershberger, Guy F. War, Peace & Nonresistance. rev. ed. LC 53-7586. 1969. 12.95 (ISBN 0-8361-1449-3). Herald Pr.

Hershey, Daniel. Lifespan - & Factors Affecting It: Aging Theories in Gerontology. (Illus.). 165p. 1974. pap. 11.25 o.p. (ISBN 0-398-03041-3). C C Thomas.

Hershey, Nathan & Miller, Robert D. Human Experimentation & the Law. LC 76-2179. 1976. 27.50 (ISBN 0-912862-19-X). Aspen Systems.

Hershey, Nathan, et al. Cases in Medical Staff Administration. 350p. 1981. text ed. price not set (ISBN 0-89443-282-6). Aspen Systems.

Hershey, Ronald A. Physical Therapy Examination Review Book Clinical Application, Vol. 2. 2nd ed. 1973. pap. 9.50 (ISBN 0-87488-482-9). Med Exam.

--Physical Therapy Examination Review Book: Vol. 1, Basic Sciences. 3rd ed. Seibert, Helen K., ed. 1976. pap. 9.50 (ISBN 0-87488-481-0). Med Exam.

Hershey, Virginia S. Those Southern Milners: A Collection of Record Abstracts for the Southern States Between 1606 & 1850 with Biographical & Historical Sketches, Family Records, & Genealogies up to 1900. (Illus.). 426p. 1980. 40.00x (ISBN 0-9605320-0-5, TX-578-128). Hershey.

Hershfield, William, ed. see Houston, Albert.

Hershhorn, Bernard. Active Years for Your Aging Dog. LC 78-52966. (Illus.). 1978. 12.50 (ISBN 0-8015-4599-4, Hawthorn). Dutton.

Hershinow, Sheldon J. Bernard Malamud. LC 79-4877. (Modern Literature Ser.). 160p. 1980. 10.95 (ISBN 0-8044-2377-6). Ungar.

Hershkowitz, Leo. Tweed's New York-Another Look. LC 76-5338. (Illus.). 1977. 12.50 o.p. (ISBN 0-385-07656-8). Doubleday.

Hershkowitz, Leo & Klein, Milton M., eds. Courts & Law in Early New York: Selected Essays. (National University Pubns., Multi-Disciplinary Series in the Law). 1978. 12.50 (ISBN 0-8046-9206-8). Kennikat.

Hershman, Jerome M., ed. Management of Endocrine Disorders. LC 80-10850. (Illus.). 259p. 1980. pap. 13.50 (ISBN 0-8121-0715-2). Lea & Febiger.

Hershman, Jerome M. & Bray, G. A., eds. The Thyroid: Physiology & Treatment of Disease. 1979. text ed. 60.00 (ISBN 0-08-023202-7). Pergamon.

Hershman, Jerome M. & Bray, George A., eds. The Thyroid: Physiology & Treatment of Disease. (International Encyclopedia of Pharmacology & Therapeutics: Vol. 101). (Illus.). 1979. 140.00 (ISBN 0-08-017685-2). Pergamon.

Hershowitz, Mickey, jt. auth. see Tierney, Gene.

Hersker, Barry J. & Stroh, Thomas F. Purchasing Agent's Guide to the Naked Salesman. LC 75-17522. 1975. 15.95 (ISBN 0-8436-1308-4). CBI Pub.

Herskovits, Melville J. Acculturation: The Study of Culture Contact. 7.00 (ISBN 0-8446-1235-9). Peter Smith.

--Background of African Art. lim. ed. LC 67-18433. (Cooke-Daniels Lecture Ser., Denver Art Museum). (Illus.). 1945. 10.50x (ISBN 0-8196-0201-9). Biblo.

Herskowitz, Mickey, jt. auth. see Rather, Dan.

Herskowitz, Mickey, jt. auth. see Spitz, Mark.

Herskowitz, Mickey, jt. auth. see Uecker, Bob.

Hersom, A. C. & Hulland, E. D. Baumgartner's Canned Foods. 7th ed. (Illus.). 400p. 1980. text ed. 35.00 (ISBN 0-443-02122-8). Churchill.

--Canned Foods. 1981. text ed. 35.00 (ISBN 0-8206-0288-4). Chem Pub.

Hersov, L., et al, eds. Aggression & Anti-Social Behaviour in Childhood & Adolescence. 1977. pap. text ed. 11.25 (ISBN 0-08-021810-5). Pergamon.

Hersov, L. A., et al, eds. Language & Language Disorders in Childhood. 1980. 21.00 (ISBN 0-08-025206-0); pap. 9.00 (ISBN 0-08-025205-2). Pergamon.

Hersov, Lionel & Berg, Ian, eds. Out of School: Modern Perspectives in Truancy & School Refusal. LC 79-41725. (Studies in Child Psychiatry Ser.). 320p. 1980. 45.50 (ISBN 0-471-27743-6, Pub. by Wiley-Interscience). Wiley.

Herspring, Dale R. & Volgyes, Ivan, eds. Civil-Military Relations in Communist Systems. 1978. lib. bdg. 28.50x (ISBN 0-89158-165-0, Dawson). Westview.

Herst, Herman, Jr. Fun & Profit in Stamp Collecting. (gr. 9 up). 1975. pap. 3.95 (ISBN 0-8015-2851-8, Hawthorn). Dutton.

Herst, Roger E. Ghost Sub. 384p. 1980. pap. 2.50 (ISBN 0-89083-655-8). Zebra.

Herstein, Sheila & Robbins, Naomi. United States of America. (World Bibliographical Ser.: No. 16). 1981. write for info. (ISBN 0-903450-29-1). Abc-Clio.

Hertmann, A. I., et al, eds. New Developments with Human & Veterinary Vaccines. Kohn, A. LC 80-19130. (Progress in Clinical & Biological Research: Vol. 47). 444p. 1980. 36.00 (ISBN 0-8451-0047-5). A R Liss.

Herttell, Thomas. The Demurrer; or, Proofs of Error in the Decision of the Supreme Court of the State of New York Requiring Faith in a Particular Religious Doctrine As a Legal Qualification of Witnesses. LC 70-122160. (Civil Liberties in American History Ser). 154p. 1972. Repr. of 1828 ed. lib. bdg. 15.00 (ISBN 0-306-71971-1). Da Capo.

Hertz, Eric & Sherman, Jerry. Woman Power in Textile & Apparel Sales. LC 78-61155. 1979. 8.95 (ISBN 0-87005-199-7). Fairchild.

Hertz, Frederick. The Economic Problem of the Danubian States: A Study in Economic Nationalism. LC 68-9662. 1970. 13.50 (ISBN 0-86527-054-6). Fertig.

Hertz, H. G. Electrochemistry: A Reformaulation of the Basic Principles. (Lecture Notes in Chemistry: Vol. 17). (Illus.). 254p. 1980. pap. 24.80 (ISBN 0-387-10008-3). Springer-Verlag.

Hertz, Hamilton & Hertz, Joan. How to Raise & Train a Standard Schnauzer. (Orig.). pap. 2.00 (ISBN 0-87666-400-1, DS1124). TFH Pubns.

Hertz, Joan, jt. auth. see Hertz, Hamilton.

Hertz, Joseph H. Authorized Daily Prayer Book. (Eng. & Heb.). 1948. 17.50x (ISBN 0-8197-0094-0). Bloch.

Hertz, L., jt. ed. see Federoff, S.

Hertz, L., jt. ed. see Fedoroff, S.

Hertz, Leif, jt. ed. see Fedoroff, S.

Hertz, Roy. Choriocarcinoma & Related Gestational Trophoblastic Tumors in Women. LC 75-31481. 1978. 19.50 (ISBN 0-89004-086-9). Raven.

Hertzano, Ephraim. The Official Rummikub Book: Including Rules, Strategy & Tactics for Winning. LC 77-93321. (Illus.). 1978. 6.95 (ISBN 0-8069-4944-9); lib. bdg. 6.69 (ISBN 0-8069-4945-7); pap. 2.95 (ISBN 0-8069-4946-5). Sterling.

Hertzberg, Arthur. French Enlightenment & the Jews. LC 68-18996. 1968. 22.50x (ISBN 0-231-03049-5). Columbia U Pr.

Hertzberg, Arthur, ed. Judaism. LC 61-15498. (Great Religions of Modern Man Ser). 8.95 o.s.i. (ISBN 0-8076-0163-2). Braziller.

Hertzberg, Robert. The Modern Handgun. 1977. 4.95 o.p. (ISBN 0-668-01464-4); pap. 2.50 o.p. (ISBN 0-668-04074-2). Arco.

--So You Want to Be a Ham. 8th ed. LC 79-63820. 1979. pap. 6.95 (ISBN 0-672-21600-0). Sams.

Hertzel, Bob. The Big Red Machine. LC 75-45010. (Illus.). 1976. 7.95 o.p. (ISBN 0-13-076190-7). P-H.

Hertzfelt, Bruce D. An Investigation into the Powers of the Conscious, the Subconscious & of the Unconscious. (Illus.). 1980. 37.55 (ISBN 0-89920-005-2). Am Inst Psych.

Hertzler, Arthur E. Horse & Buggy Doctor. LC 78-105646. (Illus.). 1970. 10.95x (ISBN 0-8032-0769-7); pap. 3.95 (ISBN 0-8032-5717-1, BB 517, Bison). U of Nebr Pr.

Hertzler, Daniel. From Germantown to Steinbach. 248p. 1981. pap. 7.95 (ISBN 0-8361-1949-5). Herald Pr.

Hertzler, Joyce O. History of Utopian Thought. LC 65-22443. 321p. 1965. Repr. of 1923 ed. 28.50x (ISBN 0-8154-0113-2). Cooper Sq.

Hertzog, Ed. Slowly Strangle All Political Rapists: The Story of the Voters' Vendetta. LC 80-83137. 1981. 15.00 (ISBN 0-937894-00-1); pap. 10.00 (ISBN 0-937894-01-X). Life Arts.

Hertzson, David. Hotel-Motel Marketing. LC 76-142509. 1971. text ed. 14.50 (ISBN 0-672-96083-4); tchr's manual 5.90 (ISBN 0-672-96085-0); wkbk. 6.95 (ISBN 0-672-96084-2). Bobbs.

Hertzson, Seymour. Hospitality Industry Cooperative Training. LC 75-142506. 1971. pap. text ed. 13.95 (ISBN 0-672-96098-2); tchr's manual 6.67 (ISBN 0-672-96099-0). Bobbs.

Hertzstein, Robert. The Nazis. Time-Life Bks, ed. (World War II Ser.). (Illus.). 208p. 1980. 13.95 (ISBN 0-8094-2534-3). Time-Life.

Herubin, Charles & Marotta, Theodore. Basic Construction Materials. 2nd ed. 1981. text ed. 17.50 (ISBN 0-8359-0362-1); solutions manual avail. (ISBN 0-8359-0363-X). Reston.

Herubin, Charles A. Principles of Surveying. 2nd ed. (Illus.). 1978. text ed. 16.95 (ISBN 0-87909-620-9); instrs's. manual avail. Reston.

Herum, John, jt. ed. see Cummings, Donald W.

Herver & Co. Staff. EIS Cumulative 1979. LC 79-640191. 459p. 1979. 75.00 (ISBN 0-87815-029-3). Info Resources.

Hervey, G. F. Your Book of Patience. (Your Book Ser.). 1966. 6.95 (ISBN 0-571-06560-0, Pub. by Faber & Faber). Merrimack Bk Serv.

Hervey, George. The Complete Illustrated Book of Card Games. LC 73-78145. 242p. 1973. 7.95 o.p. (ISBN 0-385-03251-X). Doubleday.

Hervey, George F. & Hems, Jack. The Goldfish. rev. ed. (Illus.). 284p. 1981. pap. 9.50 (ISBN 0-571-11611-6, Pub. by Faber & Faber). Merrimack Bk Serv.

Hervey, Sandor G. Axiomatic Semantics: A Linguistic Theory. 320p. 1980. 20.00x (ISBN 0-7073-0222-6, Pub. by Scottish Academic Pr). Columbia U Pr.

Herwig, Rob. One Hundred & Twenty Eight Garden Plants You Can Grow. (Illus.). 60p. 1976. pap. 1.95 o.s.i. (ISBN 0-02-063070-0, Collier). Macmillan.

--One Hundred & Twenty Eight Houseplants You Can Grow. 1972. pap. 1.95 o.s.i. (ISBN 0-02-063090-5, Collier). Macmillan.

--One Hundred Twenty-Eight Bulbs You Can Grow. (Illus.). 60p. 1975. pap. 1.95 o.s.i. (ISBN 0-02-065390-5, Collier); pap. 39.00 pre-pack o.s.i. (ISBN 0-02-065410-3). Macmillan.

Herwig, Rob & Schubert, Margot. The Treasury of Houseplants. LC 75-34283. (Illus.). 368p. 1976. 12.95 o.s.i. (ISBN 0-02-551171-8). Macmillan.

Herwitz, David R. Materials on Accounting for Lawyers. LC 80-18163. (University Casebook Ser.). 636p. 1980. text ed. write for info. (ISBN 0-88277-014-4). Foundation Pr.

Herz, Irene. Hey, Don't Do That! LC 77-27054. (Illus.). 32p. 1978. 7.95 (ISBN 0-13-387365-X). P-H.

Herz, John H. International Politics in the Atomic Age. LC 59-6901. 1959. pap. 9.00x (ISBN 0-231-08534-6, 34). Columbia U Pr.

Herz, Martin F. How the Cold War Is Taught: Six American History Textbooks Examined. 82p. 1978. pap. 3.00 (ISBN 0-89633-009-5). Ethics & Public Policy.

Herz, Martin F., ed. Decline of the West? George Kennan & His Critics. 189p. 1978. 9.50 (ISBN 0-89633-036-2); pap. 5.00 (ISBN 0-89633-018-4). Ethics & Public Policy.

Herz, Michael J., jt. ed. see Peeke, Harmon V.

Herz, Peggy. All About Rhoda. (Illus.). (gr. 7-12). 1975. pap. 1.25 o.p. (ISBN 0-590-10113-7, Schol Pap). Schol Bk Serv.

--TV Time Seventy-Nine. (gr. 4-6). 1979. pap. 1.25 o.p. (ISBN 0-590-12105-7, Schol Pap). Schol Bk Serv.

--TV's Fabulous Faces. (gr. 4-6). 1977. pap. 1.25 o.p. (ISBN 0-590-10428-4, Schol Pap). Schol Bk Serv.

Herz, R. H. Photographic Action of Ionizing Radiation in Dosimetry & Medical, Industrial, Neutron, Auto & Microradiography. 629p. 1969. text ed. 29.50 o.p. (ISBN 0-471-37430-X, Pub. by Wiley). Krieger.

Herz, Rudolf, ed. see Neufert, Ernst.

Herz, Stephanie M., T.O.C.D. My Words Are Spirit & Life: Meeting Christ Through Daily Meditation. LC 78-4790. 1979. pap. 3.95 (ISBN 0-385-14258-7, Im). Doubleday.

Herz, W., et al, eds. Progress in the Chemistry of Organic Natural Products, Vols. 21-31. Incl. Vol. 21. 1963. 56.70 (ISBN 0-387-80638-5); Vol. 22. 1964. 67.30 (ISBN 0-387-80678-4); Vol. 23. 1965. 70.30 (ISBN 0-387-80716-0); Vol. 24. 1966. 83.80 (ISBN 0-387-80757-8); Vol. 25. 1967. 57.90 (ISBN 0-387-80811-6); Vol. 26. 1968. 93.30 (ISBN 0-387-80864-7); Vol. 27. 1969. 83.80 (ISBN 0-387-80909-0); Vol. 28. 1970. 91.50 (ISBN 0-387-80975-9); Vol. 29. 1972. 106.80 (ISBN 0-387-81024-2); Vol. 30. 1973. 132.80 (ISBN 0-387-81062-5); Vol. 31. 1974. 136.30 (ISBN 0-387-81172-9). Springer-Verlag.

--Progress in the Chemistry of Organic Natural Products, Vol. 38. (Illus.). 450p. 1980. 115.10 (ISBN 0-387-81529-5). Springer-Verlag.

Herzberg, Frederick. The Managerial Choice: To Be Efficient & to Be Human. 1976. pap. 11.95 (ISBN 0-256-01882-0). Irwin.

--Work & the Nature of Man. (Illus.). 224p. 1973. pap. 1.50 o.p. (ISBN 0-451-61239-6, MW1239, Ment). NAL.

--Work & the Nature of Man. LC 65-27422. 1966. 9.95 (ISBN 0-690-00371-4, TYC-T). T Y Crowell.

Herzberg, Frederick, et al. Motivation to Work. 2nd ed. 1959. 15.95 (ISBN 0-471-37389-3, Pub. by Wiley-Interscience). Wiley.

Herzberg, Gerhard. Atomic Spectra & Atomic Structure. 2nd ed. Spinks, J. W., tr. (Illus.). 1944. pap. text ed. 3.50 (ISBN 0-486-60115-3). Dover.

Herzberg, Max J., ed. see O'Neill, Eugene.

Herzberg, Max J., et al. Reader's Encyclopedia of American Literature. LC 62-16546. (Illus.). 1962. 15.00 o.s.i. (ISBN 0-690-67341-8, TYC-T). T Y Crowell.

Herzberg, R. J., jt. auth. see Thorner, Marvin E.

Herzele, Margarethe. Carinthian Love Songs. Kuhner, Herbert, tr. LC 78-56886. (Bilingual Poetry Ser.: No. 2). (Illus., Ger.). 1978. 10.00x (ISBN 0-89304-025-8, CCC113); signed ed. o.p. 10.50x (ISBN 0-89304-040-1); special signed ed. o.p. 25.00 (ISBN 0-89304-027-4); pap. 4.50x (ISBN 0-89304-026-6); pap. 6.50x signed ed. o.p. (ISBN 0-89304-041-X). Cross Cult.

Herzfeld, Hans. Berlin in der Weltpolitik 1945-1970. (Veroeffentlichungen der Historischen Kommission zu Berlin, Vol. 38). xxii, 666p. (Ger.). 1973. 72.95 (ISBN 3-11-003890-0). De Gruyter.

Herzig, Alison C. & Mali, Jane L. Oh Boy! Babies! (Illus.). 144p. (gr. 5 up). 1980. 9.95g (ISBN 0-316-35896-7); pap. 5.95 (ISBN 0-316-35897-5). Little.

Herzlinger, Regina E., jt. auth. see Anthony, Robert.

Herzlinger, Regina E., jt. auth. see Anthony, Robert N.

Herzog, Barbara R., ed. Aging & Income: Programs & Prospects for the Elderly. LC 78-2510. 1978. 24.95 (ISBN 0-87705-369-3). Human Sci Pr.

Herzog, David A. Collecting Today for Tomorrow. LC 79-18557. (Illus.). 192p. 1981. pap. 4.95 (ISBN 0-668-04883-2, 4883). Arco.

--Collecting Today for Tomorrow. LC 79-18557. (Illus.). 1981. 10.00 (ISBN 0-668-04717-8). Arco.

--A Guide to Big Water Canoeing. LC 77-91195. 1978. 8.95 o.p. (ISBN 0-8092-7689-5); pap. 4.95 o.p. (ISBN 0-8092-7688-7). Contemp Bks.

Herzog, George, ed. see Cox, John Harrington.

Herzog, H., ed. Asthma. (Progress in Respiration Research Ser.: Vol. 14). (Illus.). x, 314p. 1980. pap. 54.00 (ISBN 3-8055-0991-X). S Karger.

--Ketotifen in the Prophylactic Treatment of Bronchial Asthma. (Journal: Respiration: Vol. 39). (Illus.). 54p. 1980. pap. 24.00 (ISBN 3-8055-1171-X). S Karger.

Herzog, Werner. Of Walking in Ice. Greenberg, Alan, tr. from Ger. 96p. 1980. 9.95 (ISBN 0-934378-14-2); pap. 4.95 (ISBN 0-934378-01-0). Tanam Pr.

--Screenplays. Greenberg, Alan, tr. from Ger. 208p. 1980. 10.95 (ISBN 0-934378-02-9); pap. 5.95 (ISBN 0-934378-03-7). Tanam Pr.

Herzstein, Robert E. Western Civilization, 2 vols. Incl. Vol. 1. From the Origins Through the Seventeenth Century. 11.95 (ISBN 0-395-19370-2); Vol. 2. From the Seventeenth Century to the Present. 11.95 (ISBN 0-395-19371-0); instructor's manual pap. 2.50 (ISBN 0-395-14043-9). 1975. Set. 20.50 (ISBN 0-395-14042-0). HM.

Hesburgh, Theodore. The Hesburgh Papers: Higher Values in Higher Education. 1979. 12.95 o.p. (ISBN 0-8362-5908-4). Andrews & McMeel.

Heschel, Abraham J. The Earth Is the Lord's. 109p. 1978. 7.50 o.p. (ISBN 0-374-50958-1). FS&G.

--Man's Quest for God: Studies in Prayer & Symbolism. LC 54-10371. (Hudson River Edition Ser.). 1981. 15.00x (ISBN 0-684-16829-4, ScribT). Scribner.

--Man's Quest for God: Studies in Prayer & Symbolism. LC 54-10371. 1954. 5.95 o.p. (ISBN 0-684-13582-5, ScribT). Scribner.

Heshusius, Lous. Meaning in Life As Experienced by Persons Labeled Retarded in a Group Home: Their Quest to Be. (Illus.). 176p. 1980. 19.50 (ISBN 0-398-04064-8); pap. 15.75 (ISBN 0-398-04079-6). C C Thomas.

Hesiod. Theogony. Brown, Norman O., tr. LC 53-4359. 1953. pap. 2.50 (ISBN 0-672-60202-4, LLA36). Bobbs.

Heske, Franz. German Forestry. 1938. 47.50x (ISBN 0-686-51394-0). Elliots Bks.

Heskes, Deborah. Supportive Services for Disadvantaged Workers & Trainees. (Key Issues Ser.: No. 12). 1973. pap. 2.00 (ISBN 0-87546-225-1). NY Sch Indus Rel.

Hesketh, John D. & Jones, J. W. Predicting Photosynthesis for Ecosystem Models, 2 vols. 1980. Vol. 2, 304p. 69.95 (ISBN 0-8493-5337-8); Vol. 2. (ISBN 0-8493-5336-X). CRC Pr.

Heskett, J. L., et al. Business Logistics: Physical Distribution & Materials Management. 2nd ed. (Illus.). 789p. 1973. 26.95 (ISBN 0-8260-4071-3); instr's manual avail. (ISBN 0-471-07468-3). Wiley.

--Case Problems in Business Logistics. 1973. 16.95x (ISBN 0-8260-4072-1). Wiley.

Heskett, John. Industrial Design. (World of Art Ser.). (Illus.). 300p. 1980. 17.95 (ISBN 0-19-520217-1); pap. 9.95 (ISBN 0-19-520218-X). Oxford U Pr.

Heslep, Robert D., jt. ed. see Blackstone, William T.

Hesler, L. R. Mushrooms of the Great Smokies: A Field Guide to Some Mushrooms & Their Relatives. LC 60-12221. (Illus.). 1960. 9.95 (ISBN 0-87049-028-1). U of Tenn Pr.

Heslin, Jo-Ann & Natow, Annette B. No-Nonsense Nutrition for Your Baby's First Year. LC 78-12359. 1978. pap. 8.95 (ISBN 0-8436-2134-6). CBI Pub.

Heslin, Jo Ann, et al. No-Nonsense Nutrition for Your Baby's First Year. 288p. 1980. pap. 2.95 (ISBN 0-553-13725-5). Bantam.

Heslin, William H., Jr., jt. auth. see Handelsman, Michael H.

Heslinga, M. R. The Irish Border As a Cultural Divide: A Contribution of the Study of Regionalism in the British Isles. 1980. pap. text ed. 18.75x (ISBN 90-232-0864-1). Humanities.

Heslop, Alan. The World Capital Shortage. (Key Issues Lecture Ser). 1978. 8.50 (ISBN 0-672-97208-5); pap. 5.50 (ISBN 0-686-68026-X). Bobbs.

Heslop, R. B. Numerical Aspects of Inorganic Chemistry. (Illus.). 1970. text ed. 18.60x (ISBN 0-444-20060-6). Intl Ideas.

Heslop-Harrison, J. see Jackson, B. D., et al.

Hesoid. The Georgicks of Hesoid. Chapman, G., tr. LC 74-26251. (English Experience Ser.: No. 324). 1971. Repr. of 1618 ed. 8.00 (ISBN 90-221-0324-2). Walter J Johnson.

Hess, Amy M., jt. auth. see Gouldman, W. Clyde.

Hess, Clinton W. & Kerschner, Paul A. The Silver Lobby: A Guide to Advocacy for Older Persons. LC 78-61804. 1978. pap. 2.50 (ISBN 0-88474-075-7). USC Andrus Geron.

Hess, Donald T., jt. auth. see Clarke, Kenneth K.

Hess, Eckhard H. & Petrovich, S. B., eds. Imprinting. (Benchmark Papers in Animal Behavior: Vol. 5). 1977. 37.00 (ISBN 0-12-786658-2). Acad Pr.

Hess, Fred C. Chemistry Made Simple. 1955. pap. 3.50 (ISBN 0-385-01207-1, Made). Doubleday.

Hess, Gary R. Sam Higginbottom of Allahabad. LC 67-17631. 1967. 7.95x (ISBN 0-8139-0118-9). U Pr of Va.

Hess, George H. Living at Your Best with Multiple Sclerosis. rev. ed. (Illus.). 128p. 1972. pap. 11.75 photocopy ed., spiral (ISBN 0-398-02621-1). C C Thomas.

Hess, Hans. How Pictures Mean. LC 74-26195. (Illus.). 1975. pap. 5.95 (ISBN 0-394-73057-7). Pantheon.

Hess, Hans-Jurgen, ed. Annual Reports in Medicinal Chemistry, Vol. 15. 1980. 22.50 (ISBN 0-12-040515-6). Acad Pr.

Hess, Harley. Corey's Revenge. (Orig.). 1980. pap. 1.75 (ISBN 0-532-23231-3). Manor Bks.

--Grass War. (Orig.). 1979. pap. 1.75 (ISBN 0-532-23180-5). Manor Bks.

Hess, Herbert J. & Tucker, Charles O. Talking About Relationships. 2nd ed. 80p. 1980. pap. text ed. 2.95x (ISBN 0-917974-47-6). Waveland Pr.

Hess, J. Daniel. From the Other's Point of View. LC 79-22405. 1980. pap. 7.95 (ISBN 0-8361-1912-6). Herald Pr.

Hess, Jeffrey A. Alexander Harkin: Dealer in Dry Goods & Groceries. LC 77-23425. (Minnesota Historic Sites Pamphlet Ser.: No. 14). (Illus.). 1977. pap. 2.00 (ISBN 0-87351-115-8). Minn Hist.

Hess, John M., jt. auth. see Cateora, Philip R.

Hess, Karen, ed. Martha Washington's Book of Cookery. LC 80-18257. 464p. 1981. 19.95 (ISBN 0-231-04930-7). Columbia U Pr.

Hess, Karen M., jt. auth. see Bennett, Wayne W.

Hess, Karen M., jt. auth. see Wrobleski, Henry M.

Hess, Karen M., et al. Developing Reading Efficiency. LC 74-26850. 288p. 1975. text ed. 10.50x (ISBN 0-471-37452-0). Wiley.

Hess, Karl. Community Technology. LC 78-15828. 1979. pap. 3.50x (ISBN 0-06-090689-8, TB 1958, Torch). Har-Row.

--Community Technology. LC 78-15828. 1979. 7.95 o.p. (ISBN 0-06-011874-1, HarpT). Har-Row.

Hess, L. Y. Reprocessing & Disposal of Waste Petreoum Oils. LC 79-20213. (Pollution Technology Review No. 64; Chemical Technology Review: No. 140). (Illus.). 1980. 42.00 (ISBN 0-8155-0775-5). Noyes.

Hess, Lee R., jt. auth. see Sperry, Len.

Hess, Lilo. The Amazing Earthworm. (Illus.). 48p. (gr. 2-7). 1979. 7.95 (ISBN 0-684-16079-X). Scribner.

--Bird Companions. (Illus.). 32p. (gr. 4-7). 1981. 9.95 (ISBN 0-684-16874-X). Scribner.

Hess, Lucille & Bahr, Robert. What Every Family Should Know About Strokes. (Appleton Consumer Health Guides). 128p. 1981. 12.95 (ISBN 0-8385-9717-3); pap. 5.95 (ISBN 0-8385-9716-5). ACC.

Hess, Margaret. Esther: Courage in Crisis. 1980. pap. 2.50 (ISBN 0-88207-216-1). Victor Bks.

--Love Knows No Barriers. 1979. pap. 2.50 (ISBN 0-88207-780-5). Victor Bks.

Hess, Mary A., jt. auth. see Middleton, Katherine.

Hess, Nancy R. The Home Buyer's Guide. (Illus.). 224p. 1981. pap. 5.95 (ISBN 0-13-392647-8, Spec). P-H.

Hess, Newton T. Before-After All Alone. new ed. 80p. 1980. looseleaf bdg. 7.50x (ISBN 0-9605232-0-0). Bala Pub Div.
Hess, Patricia & Day, Candra. Understanding the Aging Patient. LC 77-2596. 1977. 13.95 (ISBN 0-87618-733-5). R J Brady.
Hess, Patricia, jt. auth. see Ebersole, Priscilla.
Hess, R. D. Speaking of Early Childhood Education. (Distinguished Scholars Ser.). 1974. 32.50 o.p. (ISBN 0-07-079432-4, P&RB). McGraw.
Hess, Robert & Croft, Doreen J. Teachers of Young Children. 3rd ed. LC 80-81928. (Illus.). 528p. 1981. text ed. 17.50 (ISBN 0-395-29172-0); instr's. manual 0.70 (ISBN 0-395-29173-9). HM.
Hess, Robert D. & Croft, Robert J. Teachers of Young Children. 2nd ed. 1975. text ed. 16.75 (ISBN 0-395-18711-7); instructor's manual pap. 1.50 (ISBN 0-395-18779-6). HM.
Hess, Robert D., jt. auth. see Croft, Doreen.
Hess, Robert L. Ethiopia: The Modernization of Autocracy. Carter, Gwendolen M., ed. LC 79-120290. (Africa in the Modern World Ser). (Illus.). 294p. 1971. pap. 6.95x (ISBN 0-8014-9107-X, CP107). Cornell U Pr.
Hess, S. & Kaplan, M. The Ungentlemanly Art. 1968. 14.95 o.s.i. (ISBN 0-02-551280-3). Macmillan.
Hess, Stephen. Organizing the Presidency. 1976. 11.95 (ISBN 0-8157-3588-X); pap. 4.95 (ISBN 0-8157-3587-1). Brookings.
--The Presidential Campaign. rev. ed. 1978. pap. 3.95 (ISBN 0-8157-3591-X). Brookings.
--The Washington Reporters. LC 80-70077. 275p. 1981. 17.95 (ISBN 0-8157-3594-4); pap. 6.95 (ISBN 0-8157-3593-6). Brookings.
Hess, Stephen & Kaplan, Milton. The Ungentlemanly Art: A History of American Political Cartoons. (Illus.). 252p. 1975. 12.95 o.s.i. (ISBN 0-02-551320-6). Macmillan.
Hess, T. B. & Baker, E. C. Art & Sexual Politics. 1973. 5.95 o.s.i. (ISBN 0-02-551260-9). Macmillan.
Hess, Thomas B. & Feldman, Morton. Six Painters: Mondrian, DeKooning, Guston, Kline, Pollock, Rothko. LC 67-30452. (Illus.). 1968. pap. 3.00 (ISBN 0-914412-22-1). Inst for the Arts.
Hess, W. M., jt. auth. see Weber, Darrell J.
Hess, Wilford. Science & Religion: Toward a More Useful Dialogue, Vol. 1. 1979. perfect bdg. 7.95 (ISBN 0-88252-089-X). Paladin Hse.
Hess, William. P-Forty-Seven Thunderbolt at War. (Illus.). 176p. 1980. 17.50 (ISBN 0-684-16656-9, ScribT). Scribner.
--A Twenty Havoc at War. (Illus.). 1980. 17.50 (ISBN 0-684-16453-1, ScribT). Scribner.
Hess, William N. Thunderbolt. 1975. pap. 1.95 (ISBN 0-345-28307-4). Ballantine.
Hessayon, D. G. Be Your Own Gardening Expert. 36p. 1977. pap. 1.95 (ISBN 0-8119-0355-9). Fell.
--Be Your Own House Plant Expert. 1976. pap. 1.95 (ISBN 0-8119-0356-7). Fell.
--Be Your Own House Plant Spotter. 1977. 1.95 (ISBN 0-8119-0357-5). Fell.
Hessayon, D. G. & Wheatcroft, Harry. Be Your Own Rose Expert. 36p. 1977. pap. 1.95 (ISBN 0-8119-0358-3). Fell.
Hesse, Eva. Method & Madness. Date not set. 20.00 (ISBN 0-89396-024-1). Urizen Bks. Postponed.
Hesse, Eva, ed. New Approaches to Ezra Pound: A Co-ordinated Investigation of Pound's Poetry & Ideas. LC 76-78928. 1969. 16.50x (ISBN 0-520-01439-1). U of Cal Pr.
Hesse, Everett W. Calderon de la Barca. (World Authors Ser.: Spain: No. 30). 1968. lib. bdg. 10.95 (ISBN 0-8057-2100-2). Twayne.
Hesse, Hermann. Beneath the Wheel. Roloff, Michael, tr. from Ger. 192p. 1968. pap. 3.95 (ISBN 0-374-50748-1, N360). FS&G.
--Hermann Hesse: A Pictorial Autobiography. Ziolkowski, Theodore & Ziolkowski, Yetta, trs. 240p. 1975. 10.00 (ISBN 0-374-16988-8). FS&G.
--Klingsor's Last Summer. Winston, Richard & Winston, Clara, trs. from Ger. 217p. 1970. 6.50 (ISBN 0-374-18166-7). FS&G.
--Rosshalde. (Suhrkamp Taschenbuecher: No. 312). 192p. 1980. pap. text ed. 3.90 (ISBN 0-686-64718-1, Pub. by Insel Verlag Germany). Suhrkamp.
Hesse, M. B., jt. ed. see Cohen, L. J.
Hesse, Manfred. Alkaloid Chemistry. 384p. 1981. 22.50 (ISBN 0-471-07973-1, Pub. by Wiley-Interscience). Wiley.
Hesse, Mary. Revolutions & Reconstructions in the Philosophy of Science. LC 80-7819. 224p. 1980. 22.50x (ISBN 0-253-33381-4). Ind U Pr.
--Structure of Scientific Inference. 1974. 22.50x (ISBN 0-520-02582-2). U of Cal Pr.
Hesse, Mary B. Forces & Fields. 320p. 1962. 10.00 (ISBN 0-8022-0712-X). Philos Lib.
Hesse, Susan, jt. auth. see Kwanten, Luc.
Hesse, Walter H. & McDonald, Robert L. The Earth & Its Environment. 1974. text ed. 18.95x (ISBN 0-8221-0115-7). Dickenson.
Hessel, Alfred. History of Libraries. LC 57-2485. 1955. 10.00 (ISBN 0-8108-0058-6). Scarecrow.
Hessel, Bertil, ed. Theses: Resolutions & Manifestos of the First Four Congresses of the Third International. (Rus.). 1980. text ed. 45.50x (ISBN 0-391-01875-2). Humanities.
Hessel, Dieter & Hissel, Dieter, eds. The Agricultural Mission of Churches & Land-Grant Universities: Papers. 1979. pap. text ed. 7.50 (ISBN 0-8138-0920-7). Iowa St U Pr.
Hessel, Dieter T., ed. Energy Ethics: A Christian Response. (Orig.). 1979. pap. 4.25 (ISBN 0-377-00094-9). Friend Pr.
Hesselgrave, David & Hesselgrave, Ronald. What in the World Has Gotten into the Church? 128p. 1981. pap. 3.95 (ISBN 0-8024-9386-6). Moody.
Hesselgrave, David J. Planting Churches Cross-Culturally. 1980. pap. 12.95 (ISBN 0-8010-4219-4). Baker Bk.
Hesselgrave, Ronald, jt. auth. see Hesselgrave, David.
Hesselgrave, Ruth A. Lady Miller & Batheaston Literary Circle. 1927. Limited Ed. 27.50x (ISBN 0-685-69826-2). Elliots Bks.
Hesseling, Dirk C. On the Origin & Formation of Creoles: A Miscellany of Articles by Dirk Christiaan Hesseling. Markey, T. L. & Roberge, Paul T., eds. (Linguistica Extranea Ser.: Studia 4). 120p. 1979. lib. bdg. 7.50 (ISBN 0-89720-005-5); pap. 4.50 (ISBN 0-89720-006-3). Karoma.
Hessen, Robert. In Defense of the Corporation. LC 78-24743. (Publications 207 Ser.). 1979. 7.95 (ISBN 0-8179-7071-1). Hoover Inst Pr.
--Steel Titan: The Life of Charles M. Schwab. (Illus.). 352p. 1975. 19.95x (ISBN 0-19-501937-7). Oxford U Pr.
Hesser, James E., ed. see Eighty-Fifth Symposium of the International Astronomical Union, Victoria, B. C., Canada, August 27-30, 1979.
Hession, Roy. Not I but Christ. 1980. pap. 2.95. Chr Lit.
Hessler, Richard M., jt. auth. see Twaddle, Andrew C.
Hessler, Robert R. The Desmosomatidae (Isopoda: Asellota) of the Gay Head Bermuda Transect. (Bulletin of the Scripps Institution of Oceanography: Vol. 15). 1970. pap. 10.00x (ISBN 0-520-09320-8). U of Cal Pr.
Hesslink, G. K. Black Neighbors: Negroes in a Northern Rural Community. 2nd ed. LC 73-8915. 345p. 1974. 8.95 (ISBN 0-672-51522-9); pap. text ed. 5.25 o.p. (ISBN 0-672-61237-2). Bobbs.
Hes-Swartenberg, Hindle S. Jewish Physicians in the Netherlands Sixteen Hundred to Nineteen-Forty. (Illus.). 1980. pap. text ed. 17.75x (ISBN 90-237-1743-0). Humanities.
Hestenes, Magnus R. Calculus of Variations & Optimal Control Theory. LC 79-25451. 418p. 1980. Repr. of 1966 ed. lib. bdg. 25.50 (ISBN 0-89874-092-4). Krieger.
Hestenes, Marshall & Hill, Richard. Algebra & Trigonometry with Calculators. (Illus.). 512p. 1981. text ed. 17.95 (ISBN 0-13-021857-X). P-H.
Hestenes, Susan. Marionettes. 1975. 3.50x (ISBN 0-686-17212-4). Sandollar Pr.
Hester, H. I. The Heart of Hebrew History. 1980. Repr. of 1949 ed. 8.95 (ISBN 0-8054-1217-4). Broadman.
--The Heart of the New Testament. 1980. Repr. of 1950 ed. 8.95 (ISBN 0-8054-1386-3). Broadman.
--Introduccion Al Estudio Del Nuevo Testamento. Benlliure, Felix, tr. from Eng. Orig. Title: The Heart of the New Testament. 366p. (Span.). 1980. pap. 6.60 (ISBN 0-311-04330-5). Casa Bautista.
Hester, Thomas R. Digging into South Texas Prehistory. (Illus.). 202p. 1980. 14.00 (ISBN 0-931722-05-5); pap. 8.95 (ISBN 0-931722-04-7). Corona Pub.
Heston, Charlton. The Actors Life: Journals, 1956-1976. 1978. 12.95 o.p. (ISBN 0-525-05030-2, Henry Robbins Book). Dutton.
Hestwood, Diana & Huseby, Edward. Crossnumber Puzzle Books, 2 bks. 1972. Bk. 1. pap. 4.95 wkbk. (ISBN 0-88488-013-3); Bk. 2. pap. 4.95 wkbk. (ISBN 0-88488-014-1). Creative Pubns.
Hetherington, Alma. The River of the Long Water. LC 79-92112. (Illus.). 1980. 17.95 (ISBN 0-913122-09-2). Mickler Hse.
Hetherington, E. Mavis, ed. Review of Child Development Research, 9 chapters, Vol. 5. Incl. Chap. 1. Your Ancients Revisited: A History of Child Development. Sears, Robert S. 80p. pap. 2.50x (ISBN 0-226-33154-7); Chap. 2. Ecological Psychology & Children. Gump, Paul V. 64p. pap. 2.25x (ISBN 0-226-33156-3); Chap. 3. Children's Cooperation & Helping Behaviors. Bryan, James H. 64p. 2.25x (ISBN 0-226-33157-1); Chap. 4. Impact of Television on Children & Youth. Stein, Aletha H. & Friedrich, Lynette K. 80p. pap. 3.00x (ISBN 0-226-33159-8); Chap. 5. The Development of Social Cognition. Shantz, Carolyn U. 72p. pap. 3.25x (ISBN 0-226-33160-1); Chap. 6. Children's Attention: The Development of Selectivity. Pick, Anne D., et al. 72p. pap. 2.25x (ISBN 0-226-33162-8); Chap. 7. Problems & Prospects in the Study of Learning Disabilities. Torgeson, Joseph. 64p. pap. 2.25x (ISBN 0-226-33163-6); Chap. 9. An Interdisciplinary Analysis. Parke, Ross D. & Collmer, Candace W. 88p. pap. 3.25x (ISBN 0-226-33165-2). LC 64-20472. **(Review of Child Development Research Ser). 608p. 1976. PLB 20.00x (ISBN 0-226-33155-5); pap. in indiv. chapters avail. (ISBN 0-685-63976-2). U of Chicago Pr.**
Hetherington, John. Melba. (Illus.). 1968. 7.50 o.p. (ISBN 0-374-20560-4). FS&G.
--Melba. (Illus., Orig.). 1973. pap. 5.95 (ISBN 0-571-10286-7, Pub. by Faber & Faber). Merrimack Bk Serv.
--The Morning Was Shining. 1971. 8.95 (ISBN 0-571-09569-0, Pub. by Faber & Faber). Merrimack Bk Serv.
Hetherington, Keith. Patrick. 1979. pap. 1.95 (ISBN 0-380-48363-7, 48363). Avon.
Hetherington-Parke. Contemporary Readings in Child Psychology. 2nd ed. Nave, Patricia S., ed. 448p. 1981. pap. text ed. 11.97 (ISBN 0-07-028426-1, C). McGraw.
Hetland, Philip R. Physics Experiments for Laboratory & Life. 1978. pap. text ed. 8.95 (ISBN 0-8403-1907-X). Kendall-Hunt.
Hetrick, Patrick, ed. see Silverman, Ruth D.
Hettlinger, Richard F. Living with Sex: The Students' Dilemma. 1966. pap. 3.95 (ISBN 0-8164-2043-2, SP32). Crossroad NY.
Hetzel, Howard R., jt. auth. see Ward, Jack A.
Hetzel, Nancy K. Environmental Cooperation Among Industrialized Countries: The Role of Regional Organizations. LC 79-5438. 1980. pap. text ed. 12.75 (ISBN 0-8191-0886-3). U Pr of Amer.
Hetzer, Linda. Creative Crafts. LC 77-28864. (Illustrated Crafts for Beginners). (Illus.). (gr. 3-7). Date not set. PLB cancelled (ISBN 0-8172-1194-2). Raintree Pubs.
--Decorative Crafts. LC 77-28702. (Illustrated Crafts for Beginners). (Illus.). (gr. 3-7). 1978. PLB 9.95 (ISBN 0-8172-1178-0). Raintree Pubs.
--Designer Crafts. LC 77-28784. (Illustrated Crafts for Beginners). (Illus.). (gr. 3-7). PLB 9.95 (ISBN 0-8172-1188-8). Raintree Pubs.
--Hobby Crafts. LC 77-28949. (Illustrated Crafts for Beginners). (Illus.). (gr. 3-7). 1978. PLB 9.95 (ISBN 0-8172-1180-2). Raintree Pubs.
--Paper Crafts. LC 77-28796. (Illustrated Crafts for Beginners). (Illus.). (gr. 3-7). 1978. PLB 9.95 (ISBN 0-8172-1186-1). Raintree Pubs.
--Playtime Crafts. LC 77-28790. (Illustrated Crafts for Beginners). (Illus.). (gr. 3-7). 1978. PLB 9.95 (ISBN 0-8172-1182-9). Raintree Pubs.
--Traditional Crafts. LC 77-28740. (Illustrated Crafts for Beginners). (Illus.). (gr. 3-7). 1978. PLB 9.95 (ISBN 0-8172-1190-X). Raintree Pubs.
--Workshop Crafts. LC 77-28707. (Illustrated Crafts for Beginners). (Illus.). (gr. 3-7). 1978. PLB 9.95 (ISBN 0-8172-1184-5). Raintree Pubs.
--Yarn Crafts. LC 77-29052. (Illustrated Crafts for Beginners). (Illus.). (gr. 3-7). 1978. PLB 9.95 (ISBN 0-8172-1176-4). Raintree Pubs.
Hetzron, Robert. The Verbal System of Southern Agaw. (U. C. Publ. in Near Eastern Studies: Vol. 12). 1969. pap. 8.50x (ISBN 0-520-09306-2). U of Cal Pr.
Heubach, Paul. Make It Plain! LC 80-13864. (Orion Ser.). 128p. 1980. pap. 2.50 (ISBN 0-8127-0295-6). Southern Pub.
Heuer, John. Innocent Thoughts, Harmless Intentions. Date not set. pap. 2.50 (ISBN 0-686-69001-X). Dramatists Play.
Heuer, Kenneth. Rainbows. Halos, & Other Wonders. LC 77-16865. (gr. 5 up). 1978. 5.95 (ISBN 0-396-07557-6). Dodd.
Heuer, Richards J., Jr. Quantitative Approaches to Political Intelligence: The CIA Experience. (A Westview Special Study). 1978. lib. bdg. 23.50x (ISBN 0-89158-096-4). Westview.
Heuman, Gad J. Between Black & White: Race, Politics, & the Free Coloreds in Jamaica, 1792-1865. LC 80-661. (Contributions in Comparative Colonial Studies: No. 5). (Illus.). 240p. 1981. lib. bdg. 35.00 (ISBN 0-313-20984-7, HBW/). Greenwood.
Heun, Linda & Heun, Richard. Developing Skills for Human Interaction. 2nd ed. (Speech & Drama Ser.). 1978. pap. text ed. 13.50x (ISBN 0-675-08396-6); instructor's manual 3.95 (ISBN 0-686-67976-8). Merrill.
Heun, Linda, jt. auth. see Heun, Richard.
Heun, Richard & Heun, Linda. Public Speaking: A New Speech Book. (Illus.). 1979. pap. text ed. 11.50 (ISBN 0-8299-0239-2); instrs.' manual avail. (ISBN 0-8299-0488-3). West Pub.
Heun, Richard, jt. auth. see Heun, Linda.
Heurck, Jan Van see Von Der Grun, Max.
Heurgon, Jacques. The Rise of Rome. LC 70-126762. 1973. 21.50x (ISBN 0-520-01795-1). U of Cal Pr.
Heuscher, Julius E. A Psychiatric Study of Myths & Fairy Tales: Their Origins, Meaning & Usefulness. 2nd ed. (Illus.). 440p. 1974. 21.50 (ISBN 0-398-02851-6). C C Thomas.
Heusinger, Lutz. Michelangelo: The Complete Works. (Illus., Orig.). 1978. pap. 7.95 o.p. (ISBN 0-8467-0469-2, Pub. by Two Continents). Hippocrene Bks.
Heuson, John C., et al, eds. Breast Cancer: Trends in Research & Treatment. LC 76-22910. (European Organization for Research on Treatment of Cancer Monograph: Vol. 2). 1976. 32.00 (ISBN 0-89004-096-6). Raven.
Heussler, Robert. British Rule in Malaya: The Malayan Civil Service & Its Predecessors, Eighteen Sixty-Seven to Nineteen Forty-Two. LC 80-658. (Contributions in Comparative Colonial Studies: No. 6). (Illus.). xx, 356p. 1981. lib. bdg. 37.50 (ISBN 0-313-22243-6, HBM/). Greenwood.
Hevener, Fillmer, Jr. Successful Student Teaching: A Handbook for Elementary & Secondary Student Teachers. LC 80-69332. 125p. 1981. perfect bdg. 8.95 (ISBN 0-86548-040-0). Century Twenty One.
Hevener, Natalie K., ed. Dynamics of Human Rights in U. S. Foreign Policy. 305p. 1981. 19.95 (ISBN 0-87855-347-9). Transaction Bks.
Heverly, Judith. Fratonizing in the Office: The Book the Boss Should Never Have. 1981. 8.95 (ISBN 0-87949-177-9). Ashley Bks.
Hevesi, Alan G. Legislative Politics in New York State: A Comparative Analysis. LC 74-6864. (Special Studies). 265p. 1975. text ed. 24.95 (ISBN 0-275-05520-5). Praeger.
Hew, Dan. Heere Beginneth a Mery Jest of Dan Hew, Munk of Leicester. LC 74-80186. (English Experience Ser.: No. 666). 1974. Repr. 3.50 (ISBN 90-221-0666-7). Walter J Johnson.
Heward, William L. & Orlansky, Michael D. Exceptional Children: An Introductory Survey to Special Education. (Special Education Ser.). 480p. 1980. text ed. 17.95 (ISBN 0-675-08179-3); instructor's manual 3.95 (ISBN 0-686-63187-0). Merrill.
Heward, William L., jt. auth. see Dardig, Jill C.
Heward, William L., jt. auth. see Orlansky, Michael D.
Hewer & Senecki. Practical Herb Growing. 12.50x (ISBN 0-392-05980-0, LTB). Soccer.
Hewes, Henry, ed. The Best Plays of 1963-1964, Vol. 3. (The Burns Mantle Yearbook of the Theater Ser.). 15.00 o.p. (ISBN 0-396-05074-3). Dodd.
Hewes, Jeremy J. Worksteads. LC 80-941. 1981. pap. 9.95 (ISBN 0-385-15995-1, Dolp). Doubleday.
Hewett & Taylor. The Emmotionally Disturbed Child in the Classroom. 2nd ed. 416p. 1980. text ed. 17.95 (ISBN 0-205-06725-5, 2467259). Allyn.
Hewett, C. A., jt. auth. see Martin, M. C.
Hewett, E. A. Foreign Trade Prices in the Council for Mutual Economic Assistance. LC 73-86045. (Soviet & East European Studies). (Illus.). 212p. 1974. 35.50 (ISBN 0-521-20377-5). Cambridge U Pr.
Hewett, Edgar L. Ancient Andean Life. LC 67-29547. (Illus.). 1968. Repr. of 1939 ed. 15.00x (ISBN 0-8196-0204-3). Biblo.
--Ancient Life in Mexico & Central America. LC 67-29546. (Illus.). 1968. Repr. of 1936 ed. 15.00x (ISBN 0-8196-0205-1). Biblo.
--Ancient Life in the American Southwest. LC 67-29548. (Illus.). 1968. Repr. of 1930 ed. 15.00x (ISBN 0-8196-0203-5). Biblo.
Hewett, Edgar L., jt. auth. see Bandelier, Adolph F.
Hewett, Frank M. Emotionally Disturbed Child in the Classroom. 2nd ed. text ed. 16.95x o.s.i. (ISBN 0-205-06725-5). Allyn.
Hewett, Frank M. & Forness, Steven R. Education of Exceptional Learners. 2nd ed. 1977. text ed. 18.50 (ISBN 0-205-05729-2); instr's manual avail. (ISBN 0-205-05783-7). Allyn.
Hewett, H. P. The Fairest Hunting. (Illus.). 3.25 o.p. (ISBN 0-85131-065-6, Dist. by Sporting Book Center). J A Allen.
Hewett, Joan. Fly Away Free. LC 80-50449. (Illus.). 32p. (gr. 2-5). 1981. 8.95 (ISBN 0-8027-6402-9); PLB 9.85 (ISBN 0-8027-6403-7). Walker & Co.

Hewett, Robert B., ed. Political Changes & the Economic Future of East Asia. 208p. 1981. pap. write for info. (ISBN 0-8248-0750-2). U Pr of Hawaii.

Hewins, Caroline M. Mid-Century Child & Her Books. LC 69-16070. 1969. Repr. of 1926 ed. 15.00 (ISBN 0-8103-3857-2). Gale.

Hewish, Mark. The Young Scientist Book of Jets. LC 78-17507. (Young Scientist Ser.). (Illus.). (gr. 4-5). 1978. text ed. 6.95 (ISBN 0-88436-527-1). EMC.

Hewison, Christian H. Shedmaster to Railway Inspectorate. LC 80-68694. (Illus.). 192p. 1981. 19.95 (ISBN 0-7153-8074-5). David & Charles.

Hewison, Robert. In Anger: British Culture in the Cold War, 1945-60. (Illus.). 212p. 1981. 19.95 (ISBN 0-19-520238-4). Oxford U Pr.

Hewitson, J. N. Grammar School Tradition in a Comprehensive World. 1969. text ed. 6.50x (ISBN 0-7100-6392-X). Humanities.

Hewitt. Conceptual Physics: A New Introduction to Your Environment. 4th ed. 1981. text ed. 16.95 (ISBN 0-316-35969-6); tchrs'. manual free (ISBN 0-316-35971-8); test bank avail. Little.

Hewitt, Abram. Sire Lines. 26.25 (ISBN 0-936032-09-X). Thoroughbred Own and Breed.

Hewitt, David. Scott on Himself. 288p. 1981. 15.00x (ISBN 0-7073-0283-8, Pub. by Scottish Academic Pr Scotland). Columbia U Pr.

Hewitt, Elinor, tr. see Shestov, Lev.

Hewitt, Emily C. & Hiatt, Suzanne R. Women Priests: Yes or No? LC 72-81027. 128p. 1973. pap. 2.95 (ISBN 0-8164-2076-9, SP77). Crossroad NY.

Hewitt, G. F., jt. auth. see Butterworth, D.

Hewitt, Geoffrey F., et al, eds. Multiphase Science & Technology, Vol. 1. (Multiphase Science & Technology Ser.). (Illus.). 400p. 1981. text ed. 49.75 (ISBN 0-89116-222-4). Hemisphere Pub.

Hewitt, Graily. Lettering. (Illus.). 336p. 1981. pap. 9.95 (ISBN 0-8008-4728-8, 76-26844). Taplinger.

--Lettering. (Illus.). 336p. 1981. 10.00 (ISBN 0-8008-4726-1, Pentalic); pap. 9.95 (ISBN 0-8008-4728-8). Taplinger.

Hewitt, Helen, ed. Petrucci's Harmnica Musices Odhecation-A. LC 77-25989. (Music Reprint Ser., 1978). 1978. Repr. of 1942 ed. lib. bdg. 42.50 (ISBN 0-306-77562-X). Da Capo.

Hewitt, James R. Andre Malraux. LC 70-15661. (Modern Literature Ser.). 1978. 10.95 (ISBN 0-8044-2379-2). Ungar.

--Marcel Proust. LC 74-76127. (Modern Literature Ser.). 136p. 1975. 10.95 (ISBN 0-8044-2382-2). Ungar.

Hewitt, John P. Self & Society: A Symbolic Interactionist Social Psychology. 312p. 1976. text ed. 11.95x o.s.i. (ISBN 0-205-05471-4); pap. text ed. 6.95x o.s.i. (ISBN 0-685-63061-7). Allyn.

Hewitt, Joseph, jt. auth. see Mather, Maurice W.

Hewitt, K. & Hare, F. K. Man & Environment. LC 72-90876. (CCG Resource Papers Ser.: No. 20). (Illus.). 1973. pap. text ed. 4.00 (ISBN 0-89291-067-4). Assn Am Geographers.

Hewitt, Karen & Roomet, Louise. Educational Toys in America: Eighteen Hundred to the Present. (Illus.). 151p. (Orig.). 1979. pap. 10.00 (ISBN 0-87451-988-8). U Pr of New Eng.

Hewitt, Paul G., jt. auth. see Epstein, Lewis C.

Hewitt, Robert L. Workhorse of the Western Front: The Story of the 30th Infantry Division. LC 80-68981. (Divisional Ser.: No. 16). (Illus.). 404p. 1980. Repr. of 1946 ed. 25.00 (ISBN 0-89839-036-2). Battery Pr.

Hewitt, Shirley. Individualized Typing Series, Pt. II, Intermediate. 1973. student guide 6.55 (ISBN 0-89420-036-4, 118100); pap. text ed. 234.85 cassette recordings (ISBN 0-89420-151-4, 118000). Natl Book.

--Individualized Typing Series, Pt. III, Advanced. 1972. student guide 7.55 (ISBN 0-89420-088-7, 119100); cassette recordings 240.90 (ISBN 0-89420-152-2, 119000). Natl Book.

--Individualized Typing Series: Pt. I, Beginning. 1972. student guide 6.05 (ISBN 0-89420-048-8, 117100); cassette recordings 234.60 (ISBN 0-89420-150-6, 117000). Natl Book.

Hewlett-Packard. Optoelectronics-Fiber-Optics Applications Manual. 2nd ed. (Illus.). 448p. 1981. 27.50 (ISBN 0-07-028606-X, P&RB). McGraw.

Hewson, Anthony M. Giles of Rome and the Medieval Theory of Conception. (University of London Historical Ser: No. 38). 280p. 1975. text ed. 47.50x (ISBN 0-485-13138-2, Athlone Pr). Humanities.

Hewson, John. Liquidity Creation & Distribution in the Eurocurrency Markets. LC 75-2804. 208p. 1975. 19.50 (ISBN 0-669-99556-8). Lexington Bks.

Hewson, P. E. Process Instrumentation Manifolds: Their Selection & Application. 350p. 1980. text ed. 35.00 (ISBN 0-87664-447-7). Instru Soc.

Hexham, Irving. The Irony of Apartheid: The Struggle for National Independence of Afrikaner Calvinism Against British Imperialism. (Texts & Studies in Religion: Vol. 8). 1981. soft cover 24.95x (ISBN 0-88946-904-0). E Mellen.

Hexter, J. H., tr. see Seyssel, Claude De.

Hexter, W. & Yost, H. T. The Science of Genetics. (Illus.). 592p. 1976. 21.95 (ISBN 0-13-794750-X). P-H.

Hey, jt. auth. see Peterson.

Hey, David G. An English Rural Community: Myddle Under the Tudors & Stuarts. (Illus.). 260p. 1974. text ed. 17.50x (ISBN 0-7185-1115-8, Leicester). Humanities.

Hey, J. S. The Radio Universe. 2nd ed. 256p. 1975. text ed. 28.00 (ISBN 0-08-018760-9); pap. text ed. 13.25 (ISBN 0-08-018761-7). Pergamon.

Hey, Richard D., jt. auth. see O'Riordan, Timothy.

Heydebrand, Wolf. Comparative Organizations. (General Sociology Ser.). (Illus.). 608p. 1973. text ed. 22.95 (ISBN 0-13-153932-9). P-H.

Heyden, Doris, jt. auth. see Gendrop, Paul.

Heyden, Doris, tr. see Duran, Fr. Diego.

Heyden, Francoise, tr. see Nolte, Dietrich.

Heyden, Fransois, tr. see Petzoldt, Rudiger.

Heyden, Fransosis, tr. see Schrage, Rainer.

Heyden, Siegfried. Keep Your Heart in Shape. 96p. (Orig.). 1981. pap. 1.95 (ISBN 0-8326-2249-4, 7446). Delair.

Heyden, Siegfried & Pittillo, Elen S. Sensible Talk About Cancer: A Physician's Program for Prevention. 128p. (Orig.). 1981. pap. 3.95 (ISBN 0-8326-2247-8, 7440). Delair.

Heydron, Vicki A., jt. auth. see Garrett, Randall.

Heyel, Carl & Naidich, Arnold. Encyclopedia on How to Cut Overhead. 1980. 89.95. Busn Res Pubns.

Heyen, William. American Poets in Nineteen Seventy-Six. LC 75-37522. (Illus.). 517p. 1976. 12.05 (ISBN 0-672-52174-1); pap. 10.50 (ISBN 0-672-61349-2). Bobbs.

--The City Parables. 43p. 1980. 10.95 (ISBN 0-912348-06-2). Croissant & Cot.

--Long Island Light. LC 78-68733. 1979. 10.00 (ISBN 0-8149-0811-X); pap. 7.95 (ISBN 0-8149-0817-9); ltd. ed. 20.00 (ISBN 0-8149-0818-7). Vanguard.

--Lord Dragonfly: Five Sequences. 64p. (Orig.). 1981. 30.00 (ISBN 0-8149-0853-5); pap. 8.95 (ISBN 0-8149-0839-X). Vanguard.

--Noise in the Trees. 152p. 1974. 5.95 o.s.i. (ISBN 0-8149-0739-3). Vanguard.

--The Swastika Poems. LC 76-39729. 1977. 7.95 (ISBN 0-8149-0780-6). Vanguard.

Heyer, Friedrich. Die Kirche Aethiopiens: Eine Bestandsaufnahme. (Theologische Bibliothek Toepelmann 22). 360p. 1971. 32.25 (ISBN 3-11-001850-0). De Gruyter.

Heyer, George S., Jr. Signs of Our Times: Theological Essays on Art in the Twentieth Century. 1980. 15.95 (ISBN 0-8028-3543-0). Eerdmans.

Heyer, Georgette. April Lady. 288p. 1981. pap. 2.50 (ISBN 0-515-06004-6). Jove Pubns.

--Barren Corn. 1976. Repr. of 1930 ed. lib. bdg. 13.35x (ISBN 0-89966-123-8). Buccaneer Bks.

--Bath Tangle. (Regency Romance Ser.). 320p. 1981. pap. 1.95 (ISBN 0-515-05760-6). Jove Pubns.

--Cousin Kate. 288p. 1978. pap. 2.25 (ISBN 0-449-23723-0, Crest). Fawcett.

--False Colours. 1977. pap. 1.50 o.p. (ISBN 0-449-23169-0, Crest). Fawcett.

--Footsteps in the Dark. 1976. Repr. of 1932 ed. lib. bdg. 14.75x (ISBN 0-89966-122-X). Buccaneer Bks.

--The Grand Sophy. 320p. 1981. pap. 1.95 (ISBN 0-515-05928-5). Jove Pubns.

--The Great Roxhythe. 1976. Repr. of 1922 ed. lib. bdg. 17.55x (ISBN 0-89966-117-3). Buccaneer Bks.

--Helen. 1976. Repr. of 1928 ed. lib. bdg. 14.65x (ISBN 0-89966-120-3). Buccaneer Bks.

--Infamous Army. 1977. pap. 1.75 o.p. (ISBN 0-449-23263-8, Crest). Fawcett.

--Instead of the Thorn. 1976. Repr. of 1923 ed. lib. bdg. 15.50x (ISBN 0-89966-119-X). Buccaneer Bks.

--The Masqueraders. 1979. pap. 2.25 (ISBN 0-449-23253-0, Crest). Fawcett.

--The Nonesuch. 1978. pap. 2.25 (ISBN 0-449-23716-8, Crest). Fawcett.

--Pastel. 1976. Repr. of 1929 ed. lib. bdg. 15.25x (ISBN 0-89966-121-1). Buccaneer Bks.

--Simon the Coldheart. 1976. Repr. of 1925 ed. lib. bdg. 16.20x (ISBN 0-89966-118-1). Buccaneer Bks.

--The Talisman Ring. 1978. pap. 2.25 (ISBN 0-449-23675-7, Crest). Fawcett.

--Venetia. 320p. 1981. pap. 1.95 (ISBN 0-515-05728-2). Jove Pubns.

Heyer, Georgette, jt. auth. see Raine, Harmony.

Heyerdahl, Thor. The Tigris Expedition: In Search of Our Beginnings. LC 80-1862. 360p. 1981. 17.95 (ISBN 0-385-17357-1). Doubleday.

Heygate, William E. William Blake; or, the English Farmer, 1848. Wolff, Robert L., ed. LC 75-473. (Victorian Fiction Ser.). 1975. lib. bdg. 66.00 (ISBN 0-8240-1551-7). Garland Pub.

Heyl, Edgar. I Didn't Know That: An Exhibition of First Happenings in Maryland. LC 73-85764. (Illus.). 1973. 3.00 (ISBN 0-938420-07-0). Md Hist.

Heylyn, Peter. Microcosmus, or a Little Description of the Great World. LC 74-28863. (English Experience Ser.: No. 743). 1975. Repr. of 1621 ed. 31.00 (ISBN 90-221-0743-4). Walter J Johnson.

Heym, Stefan. Collin. 12.95 (ISBN 0-8184-0300-4). Lyle Stuart.

Heyman, J. Beams & Framed Structures. 2nd ed. LC 74-2234. 160p. 1974. text ed. 18.75 (ISBN 0-08-017945-2); pap. text ed. 9.25 (ISBN 0-08-017946-0). Pergamon.

Heyman, J., jt. auth. see Baker, John.

Heyman, Jacques. Coulomb's Memoir on Statics: An Essay in the History of Civil Engineering. (Illus.). 240p. 1972. 44.50 (ISBN 0-521-08395-8). Cambridge U Pr.

--The Equilibrium of Shell Structures. (Oxford Engineering Science Ser.). (Illus.). 1977. text ed. 24.95x (ISBN 0-19-856139-3). Oxford U Pr.

Heymann, C. David. American Aristocracy: The Lives & Times of James Russell, Amy, & Robert Lowell. LC 79-9351. (Illus.). 1980. 17.95 (ISBN 0-396-07608-4). Dodd.

--Ezra Pound: The Last Rower. (Seaver-Grove Bk.). 1980. pap. 6.95 o.p. (ISBN 0-394-17748-7). Grove.

--Ezra Pound: The Last Rower. a Political Profile. LC 80-52073. 320p. 1980. pap. 6.95 (ISBN 0-394-17748-7). Seaver Bks.

Heymann, M. M. Reptiles & Amphibians of the American Southwest. LC 74-81405. (Illus.). Date not set. pap. 6.95 (ISBN 0-9603270-1-0). Doubleshoe.

Heyn, Ernest V., et al. Fire of Genius: Inventors of the Past Century. LC 75-21227. 12.95 o.p. (ISBN 0-385-03776-7). Doubleday.

Heyne & Van Winkle. Art for Young America. 1979. text ed. 15.96 (ISBN 0-87002-294-6). Bennett IL.

Heyne, Paul. Economic Way of Thinking. 3rd ed. 400p. 1980. pap. text ed. 12.95 (ISBN 0-574-19295-6, 13-2295); instr's. guide avail. (ISBN 0-574-19296-4, 13-2296); study guide 3.95 (ISBN 0-574-19297-2, 13-2297). SRA.

Heyne, Paul & Johnson, Thomas. Toward Understanding Macroeconomics. LC 76-22501. 1976. pap. text ed. 10.95 (ISBN 0-574-19275-1, 13-2275); instr's guide avail. (ISBN 0-574-19256-5, 13-2256). SRA.

--Toward Understanding Microeconomics. LC 76-22434. 1976. pap. text ed. 10.95 (ISBN 0-574-19270-0, 13-2270); instr's guide avail. (ISBN 0-574-19256-5, 13-2256). SRA.

Heyne, Paul T. & Johnson, Thomas. Toward Economic Understanding. LC 75-31554. (Illus.). 720p. 1976. text ed. 17.95 (ISBN 0-574-19255-7, 13-2255); instr's guide avail. (ISBN 0-574-19256-5, 13-2256); study guide 6.95 (ISBN 0-574-19257-3, 13-2257). SRA.

Heyneman, Stephen P. Conflict Over What Is to Be Learned in Schools: A History of Curriculum Politics in Africa. (Foreign & Comparative Studies-Eastern African Ser.: No. 2). 113p. 1971. pap. 4.50x (ISBN 0-915984-01-6). Syracuse U Foreign Comp.

Heyneman, Stephen P. & Currie, Janice K. Schooling, Academic Performance & Occupational Attainment in a Non-Industrialized Society. LC 79-63564. 1979. pap. text ed. 8.00 (ISBN 0-8191-0729-8). U Pr of Amer.

Heynen, James. The Man Who Kept Cigars in His Cap. LC 77-95332. Orig. Title: The Boys. (Illus.). 1978. 10.00 (ISBN 0-915308-18-5); pap. text ed. 5.00 (ISBN 0-915308-17-7). Graywolf.

Heyningen, C. Van see Manson, H. W.

Heys, H. L. New Organic Chemistry. 2nd ed. (Illus.). 1973. 17.95x (ISBN 0-245-50693-4). Intl Ideas.

--Physical Chemistry. 5th ed. (Illus.). 1975. pap. text ed. 16.95x (ISBN 0-245-52675-7). Intl Ideas.

Heyward, Carter. A Priest Forever. LC 75-38932. (Illus.). 160p. 1976. 6.95 o.p. (ISBN 0-06-063893-1, HarpR). Har-Row.

Heyward, Edna Earle. The Rehabilitation of the Severely Mentally Retarded Trainable Child. 1978. 10.00 o.p. (ISBN 0-682-49044-X). Exposition.

Heywood, Arthur. Elementary Algebra: Lecture-Lab. 2nd ed. 1977. pap. text ed. 14.95x o.p. (ISBN 0-8221-0190-4). Dickenson.

Heywood, Harry & MacNaghten, Patrick. Your Book About the Way a Car Works. 2nd ed. (Your Book Ser.). (Illus.). 1971. 5.95 (ISBN 0-571-04749-1, Pub. by Faber & Faber). Merrimack Bk Serv.

Heywood, J. S. & Allen, B. K. Financial Help in Social Work: A Study of Preventive Work with Families Under the Children & Young Persons Act, 1963. 102p. 1971. 21.00x (ISBN 0-7190-0487-X, Pub. by Manchester U Pr England). State Mutual Bk.

Heywood, John. Assessment in Higher Education. LC 76-12786. 1977. 39.75 (ISBN 0-471-99404-9, Pub. by Wiley-Interscience). Wiley.

--A Play of Love. La Rosa, Frank E., ed. LC 78-66855. (Renaissance Experience Ser.). 1979. lib. bdg. 33.00 (ISBN 0-8240-9743-2). Garland Pub.

--Play of the Weather & Other Tudor Comedies. Hussey, Maurice & Agarwala, Surendra, eds. LC 68-18403. 1968. 1.15x (ISBN 0-87830-101-1). Theatre Arts.

Heywood, R. B. Photoelasticity for Designers. (International Series in Mechanical Engineering: Vol. 2). 1969. 24.00 o.p. (ISBN 0-08-013005-4). Pergamon.

Heywood, Rosalind. Beyond the Reach of Sense. 1974. pap. 3.45 o.p. (ISBN 0-525-47381-5). Dutton.

Heywood, Thomas. An Apology for Actors. Bd. with A Refutation of the 'Apology for Actors' Greene, Iohn. LC 74-170415. (The English Stage Ser.: Vol. 12). lib. bdg. 50.00 (ISBN 0-8240-0595-3). Garland Pub.

--Fair Maid of the West, Parts I & II. Turner, Robert K., Jr., ed. LC 67-15069. (Regents Renaissance Drama Ser.). 1967. pap. 3.25x (ISBN 0-8032-5263-3, BB 226, Bison). U of Nebr Pr.

--The Fair Maid of the West: Pt.I, a Critical Edition. Salomon, Brownell, ed. (Salzburg Studies in English Literature, Jacobean Drama Studies Ser.: No. 36). 209p. 1976. pap. text ed. 25.00x (ISBN 0-391-01408-0). Humanities.

--The Late Lancashire Witches. Barber, Laird H. & Orgel, Stephen, eds. LC 78-66751. (Renaissance Drama Ser.). 1979. 41.00 (ISBN 0-8240-9752-1). Garland Pub.

Heywood, V. H., ed. Botanical Systematics, Vol. 1. 1976. 61.00 (ISBN 0-12-346901-5). Acad Pr.

Heywood Broun, May, tr. see Valle-Inclan, Ramon.

Hiatt, H. H., et al, eds. see Cold Spring Harbor Conferences on Cell Proliferation.

Hiatt, Mary P. Artful Balance: The Parallel Structures of Style. LC 75-11673. 192p. 1975. text ed. 13.60x (ISBN 0-8077-2487-4); pap. text ed. 7.50x (ISBN 0-8077-2486-6). Tchrs Coll.

--The Way Women Write: Sex & Style in Contemporary Prose. LC 77-14122. 1977. pap. 7.75x (ISBN 0-8077-2542-0). Tchrs Coll.

Hiatt, Suzanne R., jt. auth. see Hewitt, Emily C.

Hiatt, Thomas A. & Gerzon, Mark F., eds. The Young Internationalists. LC 70-188981. 224p. 1973. 12.00x (ISBN 0-8248-0218-7, Eastwest Ctr). U Pr of Hawaii.

Hibbard, Addison & Frenz, Horst, eds. Writers of the Western World. 2nd ed. LC 67-6008. 1967. text ed. 21.50 (ISBN 0-395-04601-7, 3-24495). HM.

Hibbard, G. R. The Making of Shakespeare's Dramatic Poetry. 184p. 1981. 17.50x (ISBN 0-8020-2400-9); pap. 7.50 (ISBN 0-8020-6424-8). U. of Toronto Pr.

Hibbard, G. R., ed. Elizabethan Theatre Seven. 220p. 1980. 18.50 (ISBN 0-208-01815-8, Archon). Shoe String.

--Elizabethan Theatre Six. (Elizabethan Theatre Ser.). 1978. 15.00 (ISBN 0-208-01636-8, Archon). Shoe String.

Hibbard, Howard. Bernini. (Illus., Orig.). 1966. pap. 5.95 (ISBN 0-14-020701-5, Pelican). Penguin.

--The Metropolitan Museum of Art. (Illus.). 600p. 1980. 50.00 (ISBN 0-06-011887-3, HarpT). Har-Row.

--Michelangelo. LC 74-6576. (Icon Editions). (Illus.). 348p. 1975. 16.95 (ISBN 0-06-433323-X, HarpT); pap. 6.95 (ISBN 0-06-430056-0, IN-56, HarpT). Har-Row.

Hibbard, Jack. Karate Breaking Techniques: With Practical Applications to Self-Defense. LC 80-50893. (Illus.). 1981. 23.50 (ISBN 0-8048-1225-X). C E Tuttle.

Hibbard, Jack & Fried, Bryan A. Weaponless Defense: A Law Enforcement Guide to Non-Violent Control. (Illus.). 184p. 1980. pap. text ed. 15.75 spiral vinyl bdg. (ISBN 0-398-03936-4). C C Thomas.

Hibbard, Lester T. Infections in Obstetrics & Gynecology. LC 80-18670. (Discussions in Patient Management Ser.). 1980. pap. 8.00 (ISBN 0-87488-896-4). Med Exam.

Hibbard, Whitney & Worring, Raymond. Forensic Hypnosis: The Practical Application of Hypnosis in Criminal Investigations. (Illus.). 400p. 1980. text ed. 34.75 (ISBN 0-398-04098-2). C C Thomas.

Hibben, Frank C. Kiva Art of the Anasazi at Pottery Mound, N.M. DenDooven, Gweneth R., ed. LC 75-19742. (Illus.). 1975. 35.00 (ISBN 0-916122-16-6); signed, limited ed. 100.00 (ISBN 0-685-60911-1). K C Pubns.
--Lost Americans. (Apollo Eds.). pap. 2.95 (ISBN 0-8152-0003-X, A3, TYC-T). T Y Crowell.
--Prehistoric Man in Europe. (Illus.). 1958. 13.95x (ISBN 0-8061-0415-5). U of Okla Pr.
Hibberd, J. Salomon Gessner. LC 76-7139. (Anglica Germanica Ser.: No. 2). (Illus.). 1977. 33.00 (ISBN 0-521-21234-0). Cambridge U Pr.
Hibbert, Christopher. Agincourt. 1978. 22.50 (ISBN 0-7134-1150-3, Pub. by Batsford England). David & Charles.
--George the Fourth: Regent & King, 1811-1830, Vol. 2. LC 72-9122. (Illus.). 352p. 1974. 15.00 o.s.i. (ISBN 0-06-011886-5, HarpT). Har-Row.
--The Great Mutiny: India, Eighteen Fifty-Seven. 472p. 1980. pap. 6.95 (ISBN 0-14-004752-2). Penguin.
--The House of Medici: Its Rise & Fall. LC 74-15763. (Illus.). 352p. 1975. 12.50 o.p. (ISBN 0-688-00339-7); pap. 6.95 (ISBN 0-688-05339-4). Morrow.
--Personal History of Samuel Johnson. Repr. of 1970 ed. 10.95 (ISBN 0-911660-26-7). Yankee Peddler.
--The Roots of Evil: A Social History of Crime & Punishment. LC 77-18940. 1978. Repr. of 1963 ed. lib. bdg. 32.75x (ISBN 0-313-20198-6, HIRE). Greenwood.
--The Royal Victorians: King Edward VII His Family & Friends. LC 75-46507. (Illus.). 1976. 12.95 o.p. (ISBN 0-397-01111-3). Lippincott.
Hibbert, Christopher & Thomas, Charles. Search for King Arthur. LC 77-91594. (Horizon Caravel Bks). (Illus.). 153p. (gr. 6 up). 1969. 9.95 (ISBN 0-06-022313-8, Dist. by Har-Row); PLB 12.89 (ISBN 0-06-022314-6, Dist. by Har-Row). Am Heritage.
Hibbet, Howard, tr. see Kawabata, Yasunari.
Hibbett, Howard. The Floating World in Japanese Fiction. LC 75-28976. (Illus.). 1974. pap. 5.95 (ISBN 0-8048-1154-X). C E Tuttle.
Hibbett, Howard, tr. see Kawabata, Yasunari.
Hibbett, Howard, tr. see Tanizaki, Junichiro.
Hibbin, Sally, ed. Politics, Ideology & the State: Papers from the Communist University of London. 1978. pap. text ed. 6.50x (ISBN 0-85315-462-7). Humanities.
Hibble, S. W., ed. see Clare, John.
Hibner, Dixie, jt. auth. see Cromwell, Liz.
Hibschman, Harry J. see Janney, Abel.
Hichens, Robert. Green Carnation. Weintraub, Stanley, ed. LC 74-93105. 1970. pap. 2.45 (ISBN 0-8032-5703-1, BB 507, Bison). U of Nebr Pr.
Hichens, Robert S. An Imaginative Man. LC 76-24387. (The Decadent Consciousness Ser.: Vol. 15). 1977. Repr. of 1895 ed. lib. bdg. 38.00 (ISBN 0-8240-2763-9). Garland Pub.
--The Londoners: An Absurdity. Fletcher, Ian & Stokes, John, eds. LC 76-24388. (Decadent Consciousness Ser.: Vol. 16). 1977. Repr. of 1898 ed. lib. bdg. 38.00 (ISBN 0-8240-2764-7). Garland Pub.
Hick, John. Classical & Contemporary Readings in the Philosophy of Religion. 2nd ed. LC 75-98092. (Philosophy Ser). 1969. text ed. 18.95 (ISBN 0-13-135269-5). P-H.
--God Has Many Names. 108p. 1981. text ed. 20.00x (ISBN 0-333-27747-3, Pub. by Macmillan, England); pap. text ed. 7.50 (ISBN 0-333-27758-9). Humanities.
--Philosophy of Religion. 2nd ed. LC 72-5429. (Foundations of Philosophy). 144p. 1973. pap. 7.95x ref. ed. (ISBN 0-13-663948-8). P-H.
Hick, John & Hebblethwaite, Brian, eds. Christianity & Other Religions: Selected Readings. LC 80-2383. 256p. 1981. pap. 6.95 (ISBN 0-8006-1444-5, 1-1444). Fortress.
Hick, John, ed. see Nielsen, Kai.
Hick, John, ed. see Smart, Ninian.
Hick, John H. Death & Eternal Life. LC 76-9965. 496p. 1980. pap. text ed. 9.95 (ISBN 0-06-063904-0, RD 332, HarpR). Har-Row.
--Death & Eternal Life. LC 76-9965. 1977. 15.00 o.p. (ISBN 0-06-063901-6, HarpR). Har-Row.
--Existence of God. 1964. pap. 3.95 (ISBN 0-02-085450-1). Macmillan.
Hick, John H. & McGill, Arthur C., eds. Many-Faced Argument: Recent Studies in the Ontological Argument for the Existence of God. (Orig.). 1967. 8.95 (ISBN 0-02-551360-5); pap. 11.95 (ISBN 0-02-085440-4). Macmillan.
Hickerson, Harold. Chippewa Indians II: Ethnohistory of Mississippi Bands, & Pillager & Winnibigoshish Bands of Chippewa. (American Indian Ethnohistory Ser: North Central & Northeastern Indians). (Illus.). lib. bdg. 42.00 (ISBN 0-8240-0809-X). Garland Pub.
--Chippewa Indians III. Horr, David A., ed. (American Indian Ethnohistory Ser.). 1978. lib. bdg. 42.00 (ISBN 0-8240-0810-3). Garland Pub.
--Chippewa Indians IV: Ethnohistory of Chippewa in Central Minnesota. (American Indian Ethnohistory Ser: North Central & Northeastern Indians). (Illus.). lib. bdg. 42.00 (ISBN 0-8240-0811-1). Garland Pub.
--Sioux Indians, Vol. One: Mdewakanton Band of Sioux Indians. (American Indian Ethnohistory Ser: Plains Indians). (Illus.). lib. bdg. 42.00 (ISBN 0-8240-0794-8). Garland Pub.
Hickerson, J. Mel. How I Made the Sale That Did the Most for Me: Fifty Great Sales Stories by Fifty Great Salespeople. 400p. 1981. 10.95 (ISBN 0-471-07769-0, Pub. by Wiley-Interscience). Wiley.
Hickey, Albert E., ed. Simulation & Training Technology for Nuclear Power Plant Safety. 350p. 1981. pap. 40.00 (ISBN 0-89785-975-8). AIR Systems.
Hickey, Dave, et al, eds. Michelangelo Pistoletto. (Illus.). 1980. pap. 5.00. Inst for the Arts.
Hickey, Denis & Doherty, James. Dictionary of Irish History Since 1800. 615p. 1980. 38.50x (ISBN 0-389-20160-X). B&N.
Hickey, Judson C. & Zarb, George A. Boucher's Prosthodontic Treatment for Edentulous Patients. LC 80-11234. (Illus.). 1980. text ed. 34.50 (ISBN 0-8016-0725-6). Mosby.
Hickey, M. & King, C. One Hundred Families of Flowering Plants. LC 79-42670. (Illus.). 220p. Date not set. 66.00 (ISBN 0-521-23283-X); pap. 19.95 (ISBN 0-521-29891-1). Cambridge U Pr.
Hickey, Tom. Health & Aging. LC 79-25033. (Social Gerontology Ser.). 1980. pap. text ed. 7.95 (ISBN 0-8185-0374-2). Brooks-Cole.
Hickford, Jessie. I Never Walked Alone. LC 76-10556. 1977. 6.95 o.p. (ISBN 0-312-40250-3). St Martin.
Hickie, W. J. Greek-English Lexicon of the New Testament. (Direction Bks.). 1977. pap. 2.95 (ISBN 0-8010-4164-3). Baker Bk.
Hickin, Norman. Irish Nature: The Book of Plant & Animal Life. (Illus.). 224p. 1981. 29.50x (ISBN 0-8476-6291-8). Rowman.
Hickler, Holly & May, C. Lowell. Creative Writing: From Thought to Action. 1979. pap. text ed. 5.32 (ISBN 0-205-06187-7, 4961870); wkbk. 5.36 (ISBN 0-685-99030-3). Allyn.
--Expository Writing: From Thought to Action. 1979. pap. text ed. 5.32 (ISBN 0-205-06190-7, 4961900); wkbk. 5.36 (ISBN 0-205-06191-5, 4961919); tchrs.' guide 3.20 (4961927). Allyn.
Hickling, C. F. Water As a Productive Environment. 250p. 1980. 29.00x (ISBN 0-85664-062-X, Pub. by Croom Helm England). State Mutual Bk.
Hickling, C. F. & Brown, Peter Lancaster. The Seas & the Oceans in Color. LC 73-18511. (Color Ser). (Illus.). 192p. 1974. 9.95 (ISBN 0-02-551380-X). Macmillan.
Hickman, B., ed. Japanese Crafts: Materials & Their Applications. (Illus.). 1978. 18.00 (ISBN 0-87773-749-5). Great Eastern.
Hickman, C. Addison. J. M. Clark. (Essays on the Great Economists). 112p. 1975. 12.50x (ISBN 0-231-03187-4); pap. 5.00x (ISBN 0-231-03918-2). Columbia U Pr.
Hickman, Cleveland P. Biology of the Invertebrates. 2nd ed. LC 72-83970. (Illus.). 720p. 1973. text ed. 18.95 (ISBN 0-8016-2170-4). Mosby.
Hickman, Cleveland P., et al. Biology of Animals. 2nd ed. LC 77-10766. (Illus.). 1978. text ed. 19.50 (ISBN 0-8016-2166-6). Mosby.
--Integrated Principles of Zoology. 6th ed. LC 78-27064. (Illus.). 1979. text ed. 21.95 (ISBN 0-8016-2172-0). Mosby.
Hickman, Cleveland P., Sr., jt. auth. see Andrew, Warren.
Hickman, Douglas. Warwickshire: A Shell Guide. (Illus.). 1979. 15.95 (ISBN 0-571-10831-8, Pub. by Faber & Faber). Merrimack Bk Serv.
Hickman, Frances M. Laboratory Studies in Integrated Zoology. 5th ed. (Illus.). 1979. pap. text ed. 11.95 (ISBN 0-8016-2177-1). Mosby.
Hickman, Hal. The Bachelor Party. 1978. pap. 1.75 o.p. (ISBN 0-685-54625-X, 04767-8). Jove Pubns.
--The Bachelor Party. LC 77-4842. 1977. 7.95 o.p. (ISBN 0-397-01236-5). Lippincott.
Hickman, J. Farriery. (Illus.). 1976. 29.75 (ISBN 0-85131-228-4, Dist. by Sporting Book Center). J A Allen.
Hickman, Janet. The Stones. LC 76-11037. (gr. 3-6). 1976. 8.95 (ISBN 0-02-743760-4, 74376). Macmillan.
--The Valley of the Shadow. LC 73-10691. (Illus.). 288p. (gr. 4-8). 1974. 8.95 (ISBN 0-02-743750-7). Macmillan.
--Zoar Blue. LC 78-3828. (gr. 6 up). 1978. 8.95 (ISBN 0-02-743740-X, 74374). Macmillan.
Hickman, Larry & Al-Hibri, Azizah. Technology & Human Affairs. 650p. 1980. text ed. 16.95 (ISBN 0-8016-2164-X). Mosby.
Hickman, Mae & Guy, Maxine. Care of the Wild Feathered & Furred: A Guide to Wildlife Handling & Care. LC 73-76970. (Illus.). 175p. (Orig.). 1973. 8.95 o.p. (ISBN 0-913300-29-2); pap. 5.95 (ISBN 0-913300-26-8). Unity Pr.
Hickman, Martha W. The Growing Season. LC 80-68983. 128p. (Orig.). 1980. pap. write for info. (ISBN 0-8358-0411-9). Upper Room.
--My Friend William Moved Away. LC 78-24319. (Illus.). (gr. k-3). 1979. 7.95g (ISBN 0-687-27540-7). Abingdon.
--The Reason I'm Not Quite Finished Tying My Shoes. LC 80-22237. 32p. (gr. k-3). 1981. 8.95g (ISBN 0-687-35595-8). Abingdon.
Hickman, Martin. Military & American Society. (Studies in Contemporary Issues). 1971. pap. text ed. 4.95x (ISBN 0-02-474790-4, 47479). Macmillan.
--Problems of American Foreign Policy. Krinsky, Fred & Boskin, Joseph, eds. (Insight Series: Studies in Contemporary Issues). (Illus.). 128p. 1968. pap. text ed. 4.95x o.p. (ISBN 0-02-474800-5, 47480). Macmillan.
Hickman, Martin B. Problems in American Foreign Policy. 2nd ed. 1975. pap. text ed. 4.95x (ISBN 0-02-474270-8, 47427). Macmillan.
Hickman, Peggy. Jane Austen Household Book. LC 77-89377. 1978. 10.50 (ISBN 0-7153-7324-2). David & Charles.
Hickock, L. A. The Story of Helen Keller. 1980. pap. 1.50 (ISBN 0-448-17149-X, Tempo). G&D.
Hickok, Lorena. Eleanor Roosevelt: Reluctant First Lady. LC 79-26769. (Illus.). 176p. 1980. 8.95 (ISBN 0-396-07836-2). Dodd.
Hickok, Robert. Exploring Music. 3rd ed. LC 78-62545. (Illus.). 1979. text ed. 15.95 (ISBN 0-201-02929-4); instructor's manual 3.00 (ISBN 0-201-02932-4); student's wkbk. 4.95 (ISBN 0-201-02933-2); record 21.95 (ISBN 0-201-02934-0). A-W.
Hicks. Alvin Fernald: Superweasel. (gr. 4-6). pap. 1.25 o.s.i. (ISBN 0-686-68474-5, 29844). Archway.
Hicks, Benjamin E. Plots & Characters in Classic French Fiction. (Plots & Characters Ser.). 1981. 27.50 (ISBN 0-208-01703-8, Archon). Shoe String.
Hicks, Bernice E. All the World Is Kin. (Illus.). 212p. 1981. lib. bdg. 9.95 (ISBN 0-87961-116-2); pap. 5.95 (ISBN 0-87961-117-0). Naturegraph.
Hicks, C. S. Man & Natural Resources: An Agricultural Perspective. 250p. 1980. 29.00x (Pub. by Croom Helm England). State Mutual Bk.
Hicks, Clifford B. Alvin Fernald, Foreign Trader. (gr. 4-6). 1979. pap. 1.50 (ISBN 0-671-29941-7). PB.
Hicks, Darryl E., jt. auth. see Lewis, David A.
Hicks, Dave. Solutions to CB Problems. (Illus.). 1977. pap. cancelled (ISBN 0-672-21441-5). Sams.
Hicks, David. Calling All Beginners - a Basic Course in English for Arabic Speaking People. 1976. 14.00x (ISBN 0-917062-01-9). Intl Bk Ctr.
--David Hicks on Living with Taste. 1969. 12.95 o.s.i. (ISBN 0-02-551370-2). Macmillan.
Hicks, David L., jt. auth. see Parkinson, Dan.
Hicks, Diana, et al. A Case for English Student's Book. (Cambridge English Language Learning Ser.). 112p. 1980. pap. 5.95x (ISBN 0-521-22291-5); cassette 13.95x (ISBN 0-521-22527-2); tchr's bk. 8.95x (ISBN 0-521-22526-4, 84 PAGES). Cambridge U Pr.
Hicks, Dorothy J. Patient Care Techniques. LC 74-18673. (Allied Health Ser). 1975. pap. 7.05 (ISBN 0-672-61394-8). Bobbs.
Hicks, E. & Teasdale, A. Accounting for the Distrubutive Trades. 2nd ed. 1975. pap. text ed. 16.50x (ISBN 0-685-83680-0). Intl Ideas.
Hicks, Elizabeth see Janney, Abel.
Hicks, Frederick C. Men & Books Famous in the Law. LC 72-81454. (Illus.). vi, 259p. 1972. Repr. of 1921 ed. 20.00x (ISBN 0-8377-2230-6). Rothman.
Hicks, George L. & McNicoll, Geoffrey. The Indonesian Economy, Nineteen Fifty to Nineteen Sixty-Five: A Bibliography. (Bibliography: No. 9). x, 248p. 1967. 4.25 o.p. (ISBN 0-686-63733-X). Yale U Pr.
--The Indonesian Economy, Nineteen Fifty to Nineteen Sixty-Seven: Bibliographic Supplement. (Bibliography: No. 10). xii, 211p. 1968. 5.25 o.p. (ISBN 0-686-63732-1). Yale U Pr.
Hicks, Granville. Granville Hicks in the 'New Masses' Robbins, Jack A., ed. LC 73-83265. (National University Pubns.). 1974. 22.50 (ISBN 0-8046-9042-1). Kennikat.
Hicks, Herbert G. & Gullett, C. Ray. The Management of Organizations. 4th ed. (Illus.). 656p. 1981. text ed. 16.95 (ISBN 0-07-028773-2, C); instr's manual 5.95 (ISBN 0-07-028774-0); study guide 5.95 (ISBN 0-07-028777-5). McGraw.
Hicks, J. L. A Closer Look at Arctic Lands. LC 76-27971. (Closer Look at Ser.). (Illus.). (gr. 4-7). 1977. 2.95 (ISBN 0-531-02477-6); PLB 6.90 s&l (ISBN 0-531-00367-1). Watts.
Hicks, James. The Empire Builders. (The Emergence of Man Ser.). (Illus.). 1974. 9.95 (ISBN 0-8094-1320-5); lib. bdg. avail. (ISBN 0-685-48126-3). Time-Life.
Hicks, James O., Jr. & Leininger, Wayne E. Accounting Information Systems. 500p. 1981. text ed. 15.96 (ISBN 0-8299-0384-4). West Pub.
Hicks, Jim. A Closer Look at Birds. (A Closer Look at Ser.). (Illus.). 32p. (gr. 5-8). 1976. 2.95 (ISBN 0-531-02433-4); PLB 6.90 (ISBN 0-531-01189-5). Watts.
--The Empire Builders. LC 74-75832. (The Emergence of Man Ser). 160p. (gr. 6 up). 1974. lib. bdg. 9.63 o.p. (ISBN 0-8094-1321-3, Pub. by Time-Life). Silver.
--The Persians. (Emergence of Man Ser.). (Illus.). 1975. 9.95 (ISBN 0-8094-1297-7). Time-Life.
--The Persians. LC 75-10727. (Emergence of Man Ser.). (gr. 6 up). 1975. PLB 9.63 o.p. (ISBN 0-8094-1298-5, Pub. by Time-Life). Silver.
Hicks, John. Capital & Growth. 352p. 1972. pap. 5.95 (ISBN 0-19-877001-4, GB375, GB). Oxford U Pr.
Hicks, John & Hicks, Regina. Cannery Row. (A Pictorial History: No. 1). (Illus.). 48p. 1972. pap. 2.95 (ISBN 0-914606-01-8). Creative Bks.
--Conceptography. (Illus.). 52p. 1972. pap. 3.95 (ISBN 0-914606-00-X). Creative Bks.
--Monterey. (A Pictorial History: No. 2). (Illus.). 64p. 1973. pap. 3.95 (ISBN 0-914606-02-6). Creative Bks.
Hicks, John D. Populist Revolt: A History of the Farmers' Alliance & the People's Party. LC 61-7237. 1961. pap. 2.75x (ISBN 0-8032-5085-1, BB 111, Bison). U of Nebr Pr.
--Rehearsal for Disaster: The Boom & Collapse of 1919-1920. LC 61-12136. 1961. 4.00 (ISBN 0-8130-0110-2). U Presses Fla.
Hicks, John G. Welded Joint Design. LC 78-32047. 82p. 1979. 19.95 (ISBN 0-470-26686-4). Halsted Pr.
Hicks, John R. Capital & Growth. (Illus.). 1965. 22.50x (ISBN 0-19-828150-1). Oxford U Pr.
--Capital & Time: A Neo-Austrian Theory. (Illus.). 226p. 1973. text ed. 22.50x (ISBN 0-19-828179-X). Oxford U Pr.
--Contribution to the Theory of the Trade Cycle. (Illus.). 1950. 11.50x (ISBN 0-19-828112-9). Oxford U Pr.
Hicks, Sir John. Economic Perspectives. 1977. text ed. 19.50x (ISBN 0-19-828407-1). Oxford U Pr.
Hicks, M. Robert, et al, eds. Laboratory Instrumentation. (Illus.). 240p. 1980. pap. text ed. 17.50 (ISBN 0-06-141191-4). Har-Row.
Hicks, Mack R., et al. Parent, Child, & Community. LC 79-13816. (Illus.). 1979. 14.95 (ISBN 0-88229-231-5). Nelson-Hall.
Hicks, Mary W., jt. auth. see Sporakowski, Michael.
Hicks, Michael. False Fleeting Perjur'd Clarence. (Illus.). 272p. 1980. text ed. 22.00x (ISBN 0-904387-44-5). Humanities.
Hicks, Olan, jt. auth. see Connally, Andrew M.
Hicks, Philip, jt. auth. see Nilsson, W. D.
Hicks, R. D. Undercover Operations & Persuasion. (Illus.). 104p. 1973. 8.75 (ISBN 0-398-02807-9). C C Thomas.
Hicks, Regina, jt. auth. see Hicks, John.
Hicks, Richard, jt. ed. see Christian, Portia.
Hicks, Ron. Understanding Cancer. 141p. (Orig.). 1980. pap. 4.75 (ISBN 0-7022-1425-6). U of Queensland Pr.
Hicks, Stanley E., ed. Exhibits Directory: 1981. 92p. (Orig.). 1981. pap. 20.00 (ISBN 0-933636-01-6). AAP.
Hicks, Tony, jt. auth. see Granger, Colin.
Hicks, Tyler G. Business Borrowers Complete Success Kit. 2nd ed. 596p. 1981. pap. 99.50 (ISBN 0-914306-44-8). Intl Wealth.
--Business Capital Sources. 2nd ed. 150p. 1981. pap. 15.00 (ISBN 0-914306-47-2). Intl Wealth.
--Directory of High-Discount Merchandise & Product Sources for Distributors & Mail-Order Wealth Builders. 2nd ed. 150p. 1981. pap. 17.50 (ISBN 0-914306-58-8). Intl Wealth.
--Fast Financing of Your Real Estate Fortune Success Kit. 2nd ed. 523p. 1981. pap. 99.50 (ISBN 0-914306-46-4). Intl Wealth.
--Financial Broker-Finder-Business Broker-Consultant Success Kit. 2nd ed. 485p. 1981. pap. 99.50 (ISBN 0-686-69033-8). Intl Wealth.
--Franchise Riches Success Kit. 2nd ed. 876p. 1981. pap. 99.50 (ISBN 0-914306-40-5). Intl Wealth.
--Go Where the Money Is: Mideast & North African Banks & Financial Institutions. 2nd ed. 150p. 1981. pap. 15.00 (ISBN 0-914306-56-1). Intl Wealth.
--How to Borrow Your Way to Real Estate Riches Using Government Money. 2nd ed. 150p. 1981. pap. 15.00 (ISBN 0-914306-52-9). Intl Wealth.
--How to Make a Fortune Through Export Mail-Order Riches. 2nd ed. 150p. 1981. pap. 17.50 (ISBN 0-914306-57-X). Intl Wealth.

--How to Prepare & Process Export-Import Documents: A Fully Illustrated Guide. 2nd ed. 320p. 1981. pap. 25.00 (ISBN 0-914306-51-0). Intl Wealth.

--Mail Order Riches Success Kit. 2nd ed. 927p. 1981. pap. 99.50 (ISBN 0-914306-41-3). Intl Wealth.

--Raising Money from Grants & Other Sources Success Kit. 2nd ed. 496p. 1981. pap. 99.50 (ISBN 0-914306-45-6). Intl Wealth.

--Real Estate Riches Success Kit. 2nd ed. 466p. 1981. pap. 99.50 (ISBN 0-914306-43-X). Intl Wealth.

--Sixty Day Fully Financed Fortune. 2nd ed. 150p. 1981. pap. 29.50 (ISBN 0-914306-54-5). Intl Wealth.

--Small Business Investment Company Directory & Handbook. 2nd ed. 150p. 1981. pap. 15.00 (ISBN 0-914306-48-0). Intl Wealth.

--Starting Millionaire Success Kit. 2nd ed. 361p. 1981. pap. 99.50 (ISBN 0-914306-39-1). Intl Wealth.

--Worldwide Riches Opportunites, Vol. 1. 150p. 1981. pap. 25.00 (ISBN 0-914306-49-9). Intl Wealth.

--Worldwide Riches Opportunities, Vol. 2. 2rd ed. 150p. 1981. pap. 25.00 (ISBN 0-914306-50-2). Intl Wealth.

--Zero Cash Success Techniques Kit. 2nd ed. 876p. 1981. pap. 99.50 (ISBN 0-914306-42-1). Intl Wealth.

Hicks, Ursula K. Development from Below: Local Government & Finance in Developing Countries of the Commonwealth. 1961. 24.95x o.p. (ISBN 0-19-828139-0). Oxford U Pr.

--Public Finance. new ed. (Cambridge Economic Handbook Ser). 1968. 10.95x (ISBN 0-521-08762-7). Cambridge U Pr.

Hickson, D. C. & Taylor, F. R. Enthalpy-Entropy Diagram for Steam. 1964. pap. 3.95x (ISBN 0-631-97470-9, Pub. by Basil Blackwell England). Biblio Dist.

--Pressure-Enthalpy Diagram for Ammonia. 1978. pap. 3.95x (ISBN 0-631-94210-6, Pub. by Basil Blackwell England). Biblio Dist.

--Pressure-Enthalpy Diagram for Refrigerant 12. 1977. pap. 3.95x (ISBN 0-631-94220-3, Pub. by Basil Blackwell England). Biblio Dist.

Hickson, D. J., jt. auth. see Pugh, D. S.

Hidalgo, D. Diccionario General de Bibliografia Espanola, 7 vols. Repr. of 1881 ed. Set. 279.50 (ISBN 3-4870-4678-4). Adler.

Hidalgo-Gato, Cary. Bedeviled. LC 79-66162. 446p. 1980. 11.95 (ISBN 0-533-04364-6). Vantage.

Hidayatullah, M. South-West Africa Case. 1968. 7.25x (ISBN 0-210-27194-9). Asia.

Hiddleston, J. A. Essai sur Laforgue et les Derniers Vers suivi de Laforgue et Baudelaire. LC 80-66331. (French Forum Monographs: No. 23). 132p. (Orig., Fr.). 1980. pap. 9.50 (ISBN 0-917058-22-4). French Forum.

Hiddleston, J. A., ed. Poems: Jules Laforgue. (Blackwell's French Text Ser.). 1975. pap. 7.00x o.p. (ISBN 0-631-15940-1, Pub. by Basil Blackwell). Biblio Dist.

Hiden, John. Germany & Europe, 1919-1939. LC 77-3299. 1978. text ed. 15.00x (ISBN 0-582-48489-8); pap. text ed. 8.50x (ISBN 0-582-48490-1). Longman.

Hiden, John, tr. see Broszat, Martin.

Hides, Margaret. Holland. LC 74-29023. 1976. 12.95 o.p. (ISBN 0-684-14188-4, ScribT). Scribner.

Hidy, Vernon S. & Sports Illustrated Editors. Sports Illustrated Fly Fishing. rev. ed. LC 74-38908. (Illus.). (YA) 1972. 5.95 (ISBN 0-397-00859-7); pap. 2.95 (ISBN 0-397-00858-9, LP-63). Lippincott.

Hieatt, Constance. Sword & the Grail. LC 78-139097. (Illus.). (gr. 5-8). 1972. 8.95 (ISBN 0-690-79873-3, TYC-J); PLB 6.49 o.p. (ISBN 0-690-79874-1). T Y Crowell.

Hieatt, Constance B., tr. Beowulf & Other Old English Poems. LC 67-25645. (Orig.). (gr. 9-12). 1967. pap. 3.95 (ISBN 0-672-63012-5). Odyssey Pr.

Hieb, Elizabeth, ed. Communications Institute, Palm Springs Calif. April,12-15, 1977: Proceedings. 1977. spiral bdg. 7.00 (ISBN 0-89154-059-8). Intl Found Employ.

--Institute for Fund Advisors, Denver, May 10-12,1978: Proceedings. 1978. pap. 10.50 (ISBN 0-89154-083-0). Intl Found Employ.

--Institute for Fund Advisors, Lake Tahoe, June, 1977: Proceedings. 1977. spiral bdg. 10.50 (ISBN 0-89154-067-9). Intl Found Employ.

--Institute for Fund Advisors, Tahoe, Nevada, June 24-27, 1979: Proceedings. 97p. (Orig.). 1980. pap. text ed. 10.50 (ISBN 0-89154-115-2). Intl Found Employ.

Hieb, Elizabeth A., ed. Investmensts Institute, Miami, April 1978: Proceedings. 1978. pap. 7.50 (ISBN 0-89154-079-2). Intl Found Employ.

--Proceedings: Proceedings. 1978. spiral 8.75 (ISBN 0-89154-075-X). Intl Found Employ.

Hiebert, D. Edmond. Thessalonian Epsitles. 1971. 11.95 (ISBN 0-8024-8640-1). Moody.

Hiebert, Ray, et al. Informing the People: A Public Information Handbook. (Longman Public Communication Ser.). (Illus.). 512p. 1981. 24.95 (ISBN 0-582-28200-4). Longman.

Hiebert, Ray E. Courtier to the Crowd. (Illus.). 1966. 8.95 o.p. (ISBN 0-8138-0355-1). Iowa St U Pr.

Hiebert, Ray E. & Hiebert, Roslyn. Stock Market Crash, 1929. LC 73-115411. (Focus Bks). (Illus.). (gr. 7 up). 1970. PLB 4.47 o.p. (ISBN 0-531-01015-5); pap. 1.25 o.p. (ISBN 0-531-02330-3). Watts.

Hiebert, Ray E., jt. auth. see Hiebert, Roslyn.

Hiebert, Roslyn & Hiebert, Ray E. Franklin Delano Roosevelt, President for the People. LC 68-15570. (Biography Ser). (Illus.). (gr. 6 up). 1968. PLB 5.90 o.p. (ISBN 0-531-00920-3). Watts.

Hiebert, Roslyn, jt. auth. see Hiebert, Ray E.

Hiebert, William, jt. auth. see Stahmann, Robert F.

Hieftje, Gary, et al, eds. Lasers in Chemical Analysis. LC 80-84082. (Contemporary Instrumentation & Analysis). (Illus.). 352p. 1981. price not set (ISBN 0-89603-027-X). Humana.

Hienton, Louise J. Prince George's Heritage. LC 72-86376. (Illus.). 1972. 12.50 (ISBN 0-938420-13-5). Md Hist.

Hiernaux, Jean. The People of Africa. LC 74-26003. (Peoples of the World Ser.). 1975. 12.50 o.p. (ISBN 0-684-14040-3, ScribT); pap. 4.95 o.p. (ISBN 0-684-14043-8, SL565, ScribT). Scribner.

Hieronymi, Otto, ed. The New Economic Nationalism. 300p. 1980. 29.95 (ISBN 0-03-056676-2). Praeger.

Hieronymussen, Paul. Orders, Medals & Decorations of Britain & Europe in Color. (Illus.). 256p. 1980. 11.95 (ISBN 0-7137-0445-4, Pub. by Blandford Pr England). Sterling.

Hiers, John T., et al. Today's Language: A Vocabulary Workbook. 272p. 1980. pap. text ed. 7.95 (ISBN 0-669-03078-3); cancelled (ISBN 0-669-03080-5). Heath.

Hiers, Richard H., jt. auth. see Riegert, Eduard.

Hiers, Richard H., tr. see Weiss, Johannes.

Hiesberger, Jean M., ed. Healing Family Hurts. LC 79-90991. (Paths of Life Ser.). 124p. (Orig.). 1979. pap. 2.45 (ISBN 0-8091-2266-9). Paulist Pr.

--Marriage Enrichment Manual. (Paths of Life Ser.). 1980. cancelled (ISBN 0-8091-9187-3). Paulist Pr.

Hiesey, William M., et al. Biosystematics, Genetics, & Physiological Ecology of the Erythranthe Section of Mimulus. LC 40-14859. (Experimental Studies on the Nature of Species: Vol. 5). (Illus.). 219p. 1971. 13.75 (ISBN 0-87279-639-6, 628). Carnegie Inst.

Hiesinger, Ulrich W. & Percy, Ann, eds. A Scholar Collects: Selections from the Anthony Morris Clark Bequest. LC 80-82234. (Illus.). 171p. (Orig.). 1980. pap. 14.95 (ISBN 0-87633-036-7). Phila Mus Art.

Hiestand, Dale L. Changing Careers After Thirty-Five: New Horizons Through Professional & Graduate Study. LC 73-142890. 1971. 17.50x (ISBN 0-231-03482-2). Columbia U Pr.

Hiestand, Dale L. & Morse, Dean W. Comparative Metropolitan Employment Complexes: New York, Chicago, Los Angeles, Houston, Atlanta. LC 77-84456. (Conservation of Human Resources Ser.: No. 7). 141p. 1979. text ed. 21.50x (ISBN 0-916672-82-4). Allanheld.

Hiett, Harry L. Fifty-Seven How-To-Do-It Charts. 1980. pap. 5.00 (ISBN 0-911380-48-5). Signs of Times.

Hieu, Nguyen-Trung, ed. Practical English-Vietnamese Idioms for Teachers & Students. 1981. 6.50 (ISBN 0-533-04431-6). Vantage.

Higa, H. String Ensemble Performance, Zone 3, Book A. (University of Hawaii Music Project). (gr. 4-6). 1975. pap. write for info o.p.; tchr's ed. 7.84 o.p. (ISBN 0-201-00816-5). A-W.

Higashi, Shinbu, tr. see Asano, Osamu & Ishiwata, Mutsuko.

Higashi, Sumiko. Virgins, Vamps & Flappers: The American Silent Movie Heroine. LC 78-74106. 1979. 17.95 (ISBN 0-88831-028-5). EPWP.

Higashimura, T., jt. ed. see Imahori, K.

Higbee, Kenneth. Your Memory: How It Works & How to Improve It. 1977. 13.95 (ISBN 0-13-980144-8, Spec); pap. 3.95 (ISBN 0-13-980136-7). P-H.

Higby, Roy C. A Man from the Past. 2nd ed. (Illus.). (gr. 5-12). Date not set. pap. 4.25 (ISBN 0-914692-02-X). Big Moose.

Higdon & Stiles. Engineering Mechanics: Statics, Vol. 1. (Civil Engineering & Engineering Mechanic Ser.). (Illus.). 400p. 1976. 17.95x o.p. (ISBN 0-13-279398-9). P-H.

Higdon, A. & Stiles. Engineering Mechanics, 2 vols. 2nd ed. Incl. Vol. I. Statics (ISBN 0-13-279398-9); Vol. II. Dynamics (ISBN 0-13-279406-3). (Civil Engineering & Engineering Mechanic Ser.). (Illus.). 928p. 1976. 27.95x (ISBN 0-13-279380-6). P-H.

Higdon, A., et al. Engineering Mechanics. 3rd ed. Incl. Vol. 1. Statics. 21.95 (ISBN 0-13-279273-7); Vol. 2. Dynamics. 21.95 (ISBN 0-13-279281-8). 1968. 27.95 set (ISBN 0-13-279299-0). P-H.

Higdon, Archie, et al. Engineering Mechanics: Second Vector Edition, 2 vols. Incl. Vol. 1. Statics, SI Version (ISBN 0-13-279018-1); Vol. 2. Dynamics, SI Version (ISBN 0-13-279026-2). (Illus.). 1979. 18.95 ea. o.p. P-H.

--Mechanics of Materials. 3rd ed. LC 75-28453. 1976. text ed. 24.95x (ISBN 0-471-38812-2); instr's manual avail. (ISBN 0-471-01679-9). Wiley.

--Mechanics of Materials: SI Version. 3rd ed. LC 77-7069. 1978. text ed. 26.95 (ISBN 0-471-02379-5); solutions manual 10.00 (ISBN 0-471-03683-8). Wiley.

Higdon, Barbara M. Good News for Today. 1981. pap. write for info. (ISBN 0-8309-0298-8). Herald Hse.

Higdon, Hal. Beginner's Running Guide. LC 78-369. (Illus.). 340p. 1978. 10.00 (ISBN 0-89037-130-X). Anderson World.

Higdon, Hal, jt. auth. see Cantu, Robert C.

Higelin, S., et al. Svenska Fur Er, Part 1. (Illus.). Set. pap. text ed. 27.50 exercise, wordlist (ISBN 9-1522-1363-3, SW174); 8 tapes 75.00x (ISBN 0-686-05370-2, SW174T); cassettes 75.00x (ISBN 0-686-05371-0, SW174C); lecture outline 6.00 (ISBN 91-522-1395-1); o.p. (ISBN 91-522-1363-3); o.p. (ISBN 91-522-1376-5); o.p. (ISBN 91-522-1381-1). Vanous.

--Svenska Fur Er, Part 2. (Illus.). 1971. Set. pap. text ed. 27.50x exercise wordlist (ISBN 0-686-05373-7, SW175); 4 tapes 75.00x (ISBN 0-686-05374-5, SW175T); 3 cassettes 75.00 (ISBN 0-686-05375-3, SW175C); lecture outline 7.50 (ISBN 0-686-05376-1); o.p. (ISBN 91-522-1424-9); o.p. (ISBN 91-522-1425-7); o.p. (ISBN 91-522-1503-2). Vanous.

Higgenbotham, Pearl, jt. auth. see Pinkham, Mary E.

Higginbotham, Don. Guide to Virginia. LC 80-53941. 1981. pap. 7.95 (ISBN 0-528-84540-3). Rand.

--War of American Independence: Military Attitudes, Policies & Practice,1763-1789. LC 77-74433. (Wars of the United States Ser.). (Illus.). 524p. 1977. pap. 6.95x (ISBN 0-253-28910-6). Ind U Pr.

Higginbotham, Jay. Old Mobile: Fort Louis De la Louisiana, 1702-1711. LC 77-89698. (Illus., Orig.). 1977. 50.00 (ISBN 0-914334-04-2); pap. 25.00 (ISBN 0-914334-03-4). Museum Mobile.

Higginbotham, Jay, jt. ed. see Escoffier, Francis.

Higginbotham, Jay, tr. see Escoffier, Francis & Higginbotham, Jay.

Higginbotham, John, tr. & annotations by. Cicero on Moral Obligation: A New Translation of Cicero's De Officiis. 1967. 16.50x (ISBN 0-520-00556-2). U of Cal Pr.

Higginbotham, Sanford W. The Keystone in the Democratic Arch: Pennsylvania Politics, 1800-1816. LC 52-14646. (Orig.). 1952. 8.00 (ISBN 0-911124-27-6). Pa Hist & Mus.

Higginbotham, Virginia. Luis Bunuel. (Theatrical Arts Ser.). 1979. lib. bdg. 12.50 (ISBN 0-8057-9261-9). Twayne.

Higgingbotham, Bill. Living Country Characters: Step-by-Step Instructions for Eighteen Projects. (Illus., Orig.). 1981. pap. price not set (ISBN 0-486-24135-1). Dover.

Higgins. Die Fabelhafte Getraume Von Taifun Willi. pap. write for info. (ISBN 0-914162-57-8). Knowles.

--Of Celebration of Morning. write for info. (ISBN 0-914162-45-4); signed & numbered ed. avail. (ISBN 0-914162-46-2). Knowles.

--Organizational Policy: Strat Mgmt. 1979. 21.95 (ISBN 0-03-022186-2). Dryden Pr.

--Piano Album. pap. write for info. (ISBN 0-914162-42-X). Knowles.

--Ten Ways of Looking at a Bird. pap. write for info. (ISBN 0-914162-55-1). Knowles.

--Twenty Six Mountains for Viewing the Sunset from. pap. write for info. (ISBN 0-914162-54-3). Knowles.

Higgins, A. J. The Son of Man in the Teaching of Jesus. LC 79-42824. (Society for New Testament Studies Monographs: No. 40). 186p. Date not set. 24.50 (ISBN 0-521-22363-6). Cambridge U Pr.

Higgins, Afred. Common-Sense Guide to Refinishing Antiques. rev. ed. LC 76-8913. (Funk & W Bk.). (Illus.). 288p. 1976. 9.95 (ISBN 0-308-10252-5, TYC-T). T Y Crowell.

Higgins, Aidan. Asylum. 1980. 12.95 (ISBN 0-7145-0229-4); pap. 5.95 (ISBN 0-7145-0230-8). Riverrun NY.

--Balcony of Europe. LC 72-10772. 1973. 8.95 o.p. (ISBN 0-440-00654-6, Sey Lawr). Delacorte.

--Images of Africa. 1980. pap. 3.95 (ISBN 0-7145-0775-X). Riverrun NY.

--Langrische Go Down. 1980. 10.95 (ISBN 0-7145-0328-2); pap. 6.95 (ISBN 0-7145-0329-0). Riverrun NY.

--Scenes from a Receding Past. 1979. 9.95 (ISBN 0-7145-3556-7); pap. 5.95 (ISBN 0-7145-3753-5). Riverrun NY.

Higgins, Benjamin. Economic Development. rev. ed. (Illus.). 1968. 17.95x (ISBN 0-393-09714-5, NortonC). Norton.

Higgins, Benjamin & Higgins, Jean D. Economic Development of a Small Planet. (Illus.). 1979. 14.95 (ISBN 0-393-05697-X); pap. text ed. 8.95x (ISBN 0-393-09084-1). Norton.

Higgins, D. S., ed. The Private Diaries of Sir H. Rider Haggard, Nineteen Fourteen to Nineteen Twenty-Five. LC 80-5496. 326p. 1980. 19.95 (ISBN 0-8128-2738-4). Stein & Day.

Higgins, David. Portrait of Emily Dickinson: The Poet & Her Prose. LC 67-28132. (Orig.). 1967. 15.00 (ISBN 0-8135-0542-9); pap. 3.95 (ISBN 0-8135-0798-7). Rutgers U Pr.

Higgins, Dick. The Colors: I Colori. Niccolai, Giulia, tr. from Eng. Reggio Emilia. (Illus., It.). 1981. pap. 10.00 (ISBN 0-914162-32-2). Printed Edns.

Higgins, Don. Catlin. 1980. 9.95 (ISBN 0-312-12471-6). St Martin.

Higgins, Dorothy. Ring of Hades. LC 79-77795. (Illus.). 160p. (gr. 3-7). 1969. 5.95 o.s.i. (ISBN 0-8193-0297-X, Four Winds); PLB 5.41 o.s.i. (ISBN 0-8193-0298-8). Schol Bk Serv.

Higgins, E. Tory, et al, eds. Social Cognition: The Ontario Symposium, Vol. 1. 512p. 1981. 30.00 (ISBN 0-89859-049-3). L Erlbaum Assocs.

Higgins, F. R. The Pseudo-Cleft Construction in English. Hankamer, Jorge, ed. LC 78-66547. (Outstanding Dissertations in Linguistics Ser.). 1979. lib. bdg. 44.00 (ISBN 0-8240-9683-5). Garland Pub.

Higgins, George V. The Digger's Game. 176p. 1981. pap. 2.25 (ISBN 0-345-28970-6). Ballantine.

--The Digger's Game. 224p. 1974. pap. 1.75 o.p. (ISBN 0-445-08256-9). Popular Lib.

--The Friends of Eddie Coyle. 176p. 1981. pap. 2.50 (ISBN 0-345-28635-9). Ballantine.

--The Friends of Richard Nixon. 1976. pap. 1.95 o.p. (ISBN 0-345-25226-8). Ballantine.

--Kennedy for the Defense. 224p. 1981. pap. 2.75 (ISBN 0-345-29315-0). Ballantine.

--The Rat on Fire. LC 80-22713. 192p. 1981. 10.95 (ISBN 0-394-42409-3). Knopf.

Higgins, Ian. Francis Ponge. (Athlone French Poets Ser.). 1979. text ed. 23.50x (ISBN 0-485-14612-6, Athlone Pr); pap. text ed. 10.00x (ISBN 0-485-12212-X, Anthlone Pr). Humanities.

Higgins, Ian, ed. see Ponge, Francis.

Higgins, J., ed. Cesar Vallejo: An Anthology of Poetry. 1970. 22.00 (ISBN 0-08-015762-9); pap. 10.75 (ISBN 0-08-015761-0). Pergamon.

Higgins, J. C. Information Systems for Panning & Control: Concepts & Cases. 1976. 29.95x (ISBN 0-7131-3375-9); pap. 15.95x (ISBN 0-7131-3376-7). Intl Ideas.

Higgins, J. R. Completeness & Basis Properties of Sets of Special Functions. LC 76-19630. (Cambridge Tracts in Mathematics Ser.: No. 72). (Illus.). 1977. 47.50 (ISBN 0-521-21376-2). Cambridge U Pr.

Higgins, Jack. Hell Is Too Crowded. 160p. 1977. pap. 1.95 (ISBN 0-449-14274-4, GM). Fawcett.

--In the Hour Before Midnight. 1978. pap. 2.25 (ISBN 0-449-13954-9, GM). Fawcett.

--The Iron Tiger. 1979. pap. 2.25 (ISBN 0-449-14225-6, GM). Fawcett.

--Keys of Hell. 160p. 1976. pap. 1.95 (ISBN 0-449-14298-1, GM). Fawcett.

--The Last Place God Made. 1978. pap. 1.75 o.p. (ISBN 0-449-23468-1, Crest). Fawcett.

--Passage by Night. 1978. pap. 1.95 (ISBN 0-449-13891-7, GM). Fawcett.

--Savage Day. 1979. pap. 1.75 o.p. (ISBN 0-449-23982-9, Crest). Fawcett.

--Solo. (Large Print Bks.). 1980. lib. bdg. 11.95 (ISBN 0-8161-3120-1). G K Hall.

--Toll for the Brave. 1979. pap. 1.75 o.p. (ISBN 0-449-14105-5, GM). Fawcett.

--Wrath of the Lion. 192p. 1977. pap. 1.95 (ISBN 0-449-13739-2, GM). Fawcett.

Higgins, James, jt. auth. see Matles, James J.

Higgins, James E. Beyond Words: Mystical Fancy in Children's Literature. LC 71-96760. 1970. pap. 4.25x (ISBN 0-8077-1517-4). Tchrs Coll.

Higgins, James E., jt. auth. see Henson, Kenneth T.

Higgins, Jean C. Lindy. LC 70-91245. 1970. pap. 1.50 o.p. (ISBN 0-8170-0461-0). Judson.

Higgins, Jean D., jt. auth. see Higgins, Benjamin.

Higgins, Joan M. The Poverty Business: Britain & America. (Aspects of Social Policy Ser.). 1978. 22.00x (ISBN 0-631-16260-7, Pub. by Basil Blackwell). Biblio Dist.

Higgins, Judith H. Energy: A Multimedia Guide for Children & Young Adults. LC 78-15611. (Selection Guide Ser.: No. 2). 195p. 1979. text ed. 16.50 (ISBN 0-87436-266-0, Co-Pub. by Neal-Schuman). ABC-Clio.

Higgins, Lois L. Policewoman's Manual. (Illus.). 196p. 1972. 11.75 (ISBN 0-398-00836-1). C C Thomas.

Higgins, Loretta P., jt. auth. see Hawkins, Joellen W.

Higgins, M. F. Security Regulations in Hong Kong, Nineteen Seventy-Two to Nineteen Seventy-Seven. 192p. 1978. 25.00x (ISBN 90-286-0948-2). Sijthoff & Noordhoff.

Higgins, P. J. An Introduction to Topological Groups. LC 74-82222. (London Mathematical Society Lecture Note Ser.: No. 15). 100p. 1974. 12.95 (ISBN 0-521-20527-1). Cambridge U Pr.

Higgins, Paul C. Outsiders in a Hearing World: A Sociology of Deafness. LC 80-12150. (Sociological Observations: Vol. 10). (Illus.). 205p. 1980. 18.95 (ISBN 0-8039-1421-0); pap. 8.95 (ISBN 0-8039-1422-9). Sage.

Higgins, R. A. Properties of Engineering Materials. LC 77-22284. 448p. 1978. pap. 14.50 (ISBN 0-88275-575-7). Krieger.

Higgins, Reynold. Minoan & Mycehaean Art. (World of Art Ser.). (Illus.). 1967. pap. 9.95 (ISBN 0-19-519918-9). Oxford U Pr.

--Minoan & Mycenaean Art. rev. ed. (World of Art Ser.). (Illus.). 288p. 1981. 17.95 (ISBN 0-19-520256-2); pap. 9.95 (ISBN 0-19-520257-0). Oxford U Pr.

Higgins, Robert C. Financial Management: Theory & Applications. LC 76-25053. 600p. 1977. text ed. 19.50 (ISBN 0-574-19240-9, 13-2240); instr's guide avail. (ISBN 0-574-19241-7, 13-2241). SRA.

Higgins, Rosalyn. United Nations Peacekeeping, 1946-1967: Documents & Commentary, Africa, Vol. 3 Africa. 486p. 1980. 87.00x (ISBN 0-19-218321-4). Oxford U Pr.

--United Nations Peacekeeping, 1946-1967: Documents & Commentary Vol. 1: The Middle East. 1969. 34.95x o.p. (ISBN 0-19-214975-X). Oxford U Pr.

Higgins, Thomas, ed. Chopin, Preludes, Opus 28. (Illus.). 101p. 1974. 7.95x (ISBN 0-393-02161-0); pap. 4.95x (ISBN 0-393-09699-8). Norton.

Higgins, Thomas, ed. see Chopin, Frederick F.

Higgins, Thomas J. Judicial Review Unmasked. 1981. 14.95 (ISBN 0-8158-0405-9). Chris Mass.

Higgins, Vera. Cactus Growing for Beginners. (Illus.). 1964. 4.95 (ISBN 0-7137-0128-5, Pub by Blandford Pr England). Sterling.

Higginson, Mary T., ed. see Higginson, Thomas W.

Higginson, T. W., tr. see Epictetus.

Higginson, Thomas W. Army Life in a Black Regiment. 1962. pap. 0.95 o.s.i. (ISBN 0-02-033260-2, Collier). Macmillan.

--Letters & Journals of Thomas Wentworth Higginson, 1846-1906. Higginson, Mary T., ed. LC 73-87489. (American Public Figures Ser). 1969. Repr. of 1921 ed. lib. bdg. 37.50 (ISBN 0-306-71495-7). Da Capo.

--Margaret Fuller Ossoli. LC 80-24233. (American Men & Women of Letters Ser.). 324p. 1981. pap. 4.95 (ISBN 0-87754-159-0). Chelsea Hse.

--Tales of Atlantis & the Enchanted Islands. LC 80-19670. (Newcastle Mythology Library Ser.: Vol. 3). 259p. 1980. Repr. of 1977 ed. lib. bdg. 10.95x (ISBN 0-89370-642-6). Borgo Pr.

Higginson, William J. Death Is, & Approaches to the Edge. (Xtras Ser.: No. 9). (Orig.). 1980. pap. 2.00 (ISBN 0-89120-019-3). From Here.

--Paterson Pieces: Poems, 1969-1979. (Illus.). 80p. (Orig.). 1981. pap. 3.95 (ISBN 0-89120-018-5, Old Plate). From Here.

Higginson, William J. & Harter, Penny, eds. Between Two Rivers: Poems by Ten North Jersey Poets. 48p. (Orig.). 1981. pap. 3.95 (ISBN 0-89120-015-0). From Here.

Higginson, William J., jt. ed. see Harter, Penny.

Higgs, D., jt. auth. see Callahan, W. J.

Higgs, E. S., ed. Palaeoeconomy. LC 74-76576. (Illus.). 330p. 1975. 42.50 (ISBN 0-521-20449-6). Cambridge U Pr.

--Papers in Economic Prehistory. LC 78-180019. (Illus.). 250p. 1972. 37.50 (ISBN 0-521-08452-0). Cambridge U Pr.

Higgs, Jim, jt. auth. see Milligan, Charles.

Higgs, R. Competition & Coercion: Blacks in the American Economy, 1865-1914. LC 76-9178. (Illus.). 1977. 29.95 (ISBN 0-521-21120-4). Cambridge U Pr.

Higgs, Ralph, tr. El Espiritu Mismo. (Spanish Bks.). 1979. 1.90 (ISBN 0-8297-0551-1). Life Pubs Intl.

Higgs, Robert J. Laurel and Thorn: The Athlete in American Literature. LC 80-51014. 1981. price not set (ISBN 0-8131-1412-8). U Pr of Ky.

Higgs, Roger, et al. Agricultural Mathematics. 2nd ed. 1981. 9.25 (ISBN 0-8134-2130-6); pap. 5.95x; ans. bk. 1.00x (ISBN 0-8134-2131-4, 2131). Interstate.

--Agricultural Mathematics. 1981. 10.50 o.p. (ISBN 0-685-40545-1); pap. 6.95x o.p. (ISBN 0-8134-2130-6); ans. bk. 1.00x o.p. (ISBN 0-8134-2131-4, 2131). Interstate.

High, Monique R. The Four Winds of Heaven. 695p. 1980. 10.95 (ISBN 0-440-02573-7). Delacorte.

--The Four Winds of Heaven. 1981. pap. 3.25 o.s.i. (ISBN 0-440-12566-9). Dell.

High Times Magazine Editors, ed. The High Times Encyclopedia of Recreational Drugs. (Illus.). 1978. 19.95 (ISBN 0-88373-081-2); pap. 10.95 (ISBN 0-88373-082-0). Stonehill Pub Co.

Higham, Charles. Earliest Farmers & the First Cities. LC 78-179166. (Cambridge Introduction to the History of Mankind). 1972. 3.95 (ISBN 0-521-08440-7). Cambridge U Pr.

--Errol Flynn: The Untold Story. 1981. pap. 3.50 (ISBN 0-440-12307-0). Dell.

--Life in the Old Stone Age. 2nd ed. (Introduction to the History of Mankind Ser). (Illus.). (gr. 4-9). 1971. 3.95 (ISBN 0-521-21869-1). Cambridge U Pr.

Higham, Charles & Greenberg, Joel. Hollywood in the Forty's. 192p. 1981. pap. 5.95 (ISBN 0-498-06928-1). A S Barnes.

Higham, Charles, jt. auth. see Wallis, Hal.

Higham, John. Strangers in the Land: Patterns of American Nativism, 1860 to 1925. LC 80-22204. (Illus.). xiv, 431p. 1981. Repr. of 1963 ed. lib. bdg. 35.50x (ISBN 0-313-22459-5, HISL). Greenwood.

Higham, R. & Kipp, Jacob, eds. Soviet Aviation & Air Power: A Historical Review. LC 76-30815. (Illus.). 1978. lib. bdg. 35.00x (ISBN 0-89158-116-2). Westview.

Higham, Robert A. Impact of Product Substitution & New Technologies on the Pulp, Paper & Board Industry. (Illus.). 1977. 400.00 o.p. (ISBN 0-87930-100-7). Miller Freeman.

Higham, Robin, jt. auth. see Zook, David H., Jr.

Higham, Robin, ed. Civil Wars in the Twentieth Century. LC 78-160044. 272p. 1972. 12.00x (ISBN 0-8131-1261-3). U Pr of Ky.

--A Guide to the Sources of British Military History. LC 74-104108. 1971. 38.50x (ISBN 0-520-01674-2). U of Cal Pr.

--Guide to the Sources of U. S. Military History: Supplement. 1981. 37.50 (ISBN 0-208-01750-X, Archon). Shoe String.

--Intervention or Abstention: The Dilemma of American Foreign Policy. LC 74-18934. 232p. 1975. 15.50x (ISBN 0-8131-1317-2). U Pr of Ky.

Highberger, Ruth & Schramm, Carol. Child Development for Day Care Workers. LC 75-31008. (Illus.). 288p. 1976. text ed. 14.50 (ISBN 0-395-20631-6); resource manual 1.50 (ISBN 0-395-20632-4). HM.

Highdon, A., et al. Engineering Mechanics, 2nd Vector Ed., Vol. 2: Dynamics. (Civil Engr. & Engr. Mechanics Ser). 1976. 21.95 (ISBN 0-13-279406-3). P-H.

Highet, Gilbert. Man's Unconquerable Mind. LC 54-6133. 1954. 11.00x (ISBN 0-231-02016-3); pap. 3.95 (ISBN 0-231-08501-X). Columbia U Pr.

--Powers of Poetry. 1960. 19.95 (ISBN 0-19-500573-2). Oxford U Pr.

Highet, Gilbert, tr. see Jaeger, Werner.

Highfield, Arnold, jt. ed. see Valdman, Albert.

Highfield, Arnold R. The French Dialect of St. Thomas U.S. Virgin Islands: A Descriptive Grammar with Texts & Glossary. 350p. 1979. pap. 10.50 (ISBN 0-89720-026-8). Karoma.

Highfield, Arnold R. & Valdman, Albert, eds. Historicity & Variation in Creole Studies. 210p. 1981. 14.50 (ISBN 0-89720-036-5); pap. 10.50 (ISBN 0-89720-037-3). Karoma.

Highfield, Beryl S. & Hale, John, eds. Europe in the Late Middle Ages. (Illus., Orig.). 1970. pap. 7.95 (ISBN 0-571-09413-9, Pub. by Faber & Faber). Merrimack Bk Serv.

Highfield, J. R., ed. see McFarlane, K. B.

Highfill, Byron. Mexican Gunhawk. 176p. (Orig.). 1980. pap. 1.95 (ISBN 0-89083-650-7). Zebra.

Highfill, Philip H., Jr., et al. A Biographical Dictionary of Actors, Actresses, Musicians, Dancers, Managers, & Other Stage Personnel in London, 1660-1800, 6 vols. Incl. Vol. 1. Abago to Belfille. 462p. 1973 (ISBN 0-8093-0517-8); Vol. 2. Belfort to Byzand. 494p. 1973 (ISBN 0-8093-0518-6); Vol. 3. Cabanel to Cory. 544p. 1975 (ISBN 0-8093-0692-1); Vol. 4. Coryne to Dvnion. 576p. 1975 (ISBN 0-8093-0693-X); Vol. 5. Eagan to Garrett. 504p. 1978 (ISBN 0-8093-0832-0); Vol. 6. Garrick to Gyngell. 512p. 1978 (ISBN 0-8093-0833-9). LC 71-157068. (Biographical Dictionary of Actors Ser.). (Illus.). 40.00x ea. S Ill U Pr.

Highland, Esther H. Business Mathematics. 2nd ed. (Illus.). 512p. 1981. text ed. 15.95 (ISBN 0-8359-0585-3); instr's manual free (ISBN 0-8359-0586-1). Reston.

Highman, Arthur & De Limur, Charles. The Highman - de Limur Hypotheses. LC 79-28660. (Illus.). 196p. 1980. 14.95 (ISBN 0-88229-702-3). Nelson-Hall.

Highmore, Anthony, jt. auth. see Brydall, John.

Highmore, Anthony, Jr., jt. auth. see Coke, Edward.

Highsmith, David. Poison in the System. 1979. pap. 5.00. Black Stone.

Highsmith, Patricia. The Boy Who Followed Ripley. 1980. 10.95 (ISBN 0-690-01911-4). Lippincott & Crowell.

--Plotting & Writing Suspense Fiction. rev. ed. 1972. 8.95 o.p. (ISBN 0-87116-072-2). Writer.

--Plotting & Writing Suspense Fiction. rev. ed. 1981. 10.95 (ISBN 0-87116-125-7). Writer.

Highsmith, Patricia, ed. Plotting & Writing Suspense Fiction. 1981. 10.95 (ISBN 0-87116-125-7). Writer.

Highsmith, R. M., Jr., jt. auth. see Heintzelman, Oliver K.

Hight, Donald W. A Concept of Limits. 2nd ed. LC 77-80029. 1978. pap. text ed. 3.25 (ISBN 0-486-63543-0). Dover.

Hightower, Beverly. The Pence. 1981. 4.95 (ISBN 0-8062-1447-3). Carlton.

Hightower, James R., ed. see T'Ao Ch'Ien.

Hightower, Jim, et al. Hard Tomatoes, Hard Times: The Hightower Report. (Orig.). 1978. pap. 5.95 (ISBN 0-8467-0516-8, Pub. by Two Continents). Hippocrene Bks.

Highwater, Jamake. ANPAO: An American Indian Odyssey. LC 77-9264. (gr. 5-9). 1977. 10.95 (ISBN 0-397-31750-6); pap. 3.95. Lippincott.

--Song from the Earth: American Indian Painting. LC 75-37201. (Illus.). 1980. pap. 12.95 (ISBN 0-8212-1091-2, 804061). NYGS.

--The Sweet Grass Lives on: Fifty Contemporary North American Indian Artists. LC 80-7776. (Illus.). 192p. 1980. 35.00 (ISBN 0-690-01925-4). Lippincott & Crowell.

Higley, John, et al. Elite Structure & Ideology: A Theory with Applications to Norway. 377p. 1976. 20.00x (ISBN 0-231-04068-7). Columbia U Pr.

Higman, B. W. Slave Population & the Economy of Jamaica: 1807-1834. LC 75-28627. (Illus.). 1977. 47.50 (ISBN 0-521-21053-4); pap. 11.50 (ISBN 0-521-29569-6). Cambridge U Pr.

Higman, F. M., ed. see Calvin, Jean.

Hignett, Charles. Xerxes' Invasion of Greece. 1963. 29.00x o.p. (ISBN 0-19-814247-1). Oxford U Pr.

Higonnet-Schnopper, Janet, tr. Tales from Atop a Russian Stove. LC 70-188430. (Folklore Ser). (Illus.). 160p. (gr. 3 up). 1973. 5.95g o.p. (ISBN 0-8075-7755-3). A Whitman.

Higson, John W., Jr. A Historical Guide to Florence. LC 72-91632. (Illus.). 1977. pap. 5.95 (ISBN 0-87663-951-1). Universe.

Hihara, Koho, et al. Ikebana in Quick & Easy Series. (Illus., Orig.). 1978. pap. 3.95 (ISBN 0-8048-1335-3, Pub. by Shufunotomo Co Ltd Japan). C E Tuttle.

Hijiya, Yukihito. Ishikawa Takuboku. (World Authors Ser.: No. 539). 1979. lib. bdg. 14.95 (ISBN 0-8057-6381-3). Twayne.

Hikmet, Nazim. Things I Didn't Know I Loved: Selected Poems of Nazim Hikmet. Blasing, Randy & Konuk, Mutlu, trs. LC 75-10789. 96p. 7.95 (ISBN 0-89255-000-7); pap. 4.95 (ISBN 0-89255-001-5). Persea Bks.

Hilado, Carlos J., ed. Bedding & Furniture Materials, Vol. 14. LC 73-82115. (Fire & Flammability Ser.). (Illus.). 1976. pap. 20.00x (ISBN 0-87762-174-8). Technomic.

--Smoke & Products of Combustion, Part 2, Vol. 15. LC 73-82115. (Fire & Flammability Ser.). (Illus.). 1976. pap. 25.00 (ISBN 0-87762-175-6). Technomic.

Hilberman, Elaine. The Rape Victim. 112p. 1976. 7.95 (ISBN 0-685-77446-5, P243-0, Basic); pap. 5.00 (ISBN 0-685-77447-3). Am Psychiatric.

Hilberry, Conrad. Encounter on Burrows Hill & Other Poems. LC 69-10511. 1968. 4.50 o.p. (ISBN 0-8214-0041-X). Ohio U Pr.

--Rust. LC 73-92903. 61p. 1974. 6.95 (ISBN 0-8214-0153-X). Ohio U Pr.

Hilberry, Conrad, ed. see Collop, John.

Hilberry, Conrad, et al, eds. Third Coast: Contemporary Michigan Poetry. Tipton, James. LC 76-49581. 1977. 8.95 (ISBN 0-8143-1567-4); pap. 3.95 (ISBN 0-8143-1568-2). Wayne St U Pr.

Hilbert, D., jt. auth. see Courant, R.

Hilbert, D., et al. Hilbert's Papers on Invariant Theory. LC 78-17596. (LIE Groups: History Frontiers & Applications Ser.: No. 8). 1978. 35.00 (ISBN 0-915692-26-0). Math Sci Pr.

Hilbert, David. Gesammelte Abhandlungen, 3 Vols. 3rd ed. LC 65-21834. (Ger). 1981. Set. 49.95 (ISBN 0-8284-0195-0). Chelsea Pub.

Hilbert, David & Ackermann, W. Principles of Mathematical Logic. LC 50-4784. 9.50 (ISBN 0-8284-0069-5). Chelsea Pub.

Hilbert, David & Cohn-Vossen, Stephan. Geometry & the Imagination. LC 52-2894. (gr. 9 up). 1952. text ed. 14.95 (ISBN 0-8284-0087-3). Chelsea Pub.

Hilborn, Nat & Hilborn, Sam. Battleground of Freedom: South Carolina in the Revolution. LC 70-143042. (Illus.). 256p. 1970. 12.95 o.s.i. (ISBN 0-87844-000-3). Sandlapper Store.

Hilborn, Sam, jt. auth. see Hilborn, Nat.

Hilburn, J. L. & Julich, P. Microcomputers - Microprocessors: Hardware, Software & Applications. 1976. text ed. 24.95 (ISBN 0-13-580969-X). P-H.

Hild, Walter J., ed. see Sobotta, Johannes.

Hilde, Reuben. Rod VS the M&M's. (Dimension Ser.). 1976. pap. 5.95 (ISBN 0-8163-0221-9, 18340-0). Pacific Pr Pub Assn.

--Your Remarkable Mind. LC 76-7851. (Dimension Ser.). 1976. pap. 5.95 (ISBN 0-8163-0275-8, 24517-5). Pacific Pr Pub Assn.

Hilde, Rueben. In the Manner of Jesus. LC 76-14727. (Dimension Ser.). 1976. pap. 5.95 (ISBN 0-8163-0259-6, 09415-1). Pacific Pr Pub Assn.

Hildebidle, John. The Old Chore. LC 80-70828. 72p. (Orig.). 1981. pap. 4.95 (ISBN 0-914086-34-0). Alicejamesbooks.

Hildebrand, Adolf. The Problem of Form in Painting and Sculpture. Freedberg, Sydney J., ed. LC 77-19375. (Connoisseurship & Art History Ser.: Vol. 11). (Illus.). 141p. 1979. lib. bdg. 20.00 (ISBN 0-8240-3269-1). Garland Pub.

Hildebrand, D. Von see Von Hildebrand, D.

Hildebrand, David K., et al. Prediction Analysis of Cross Classifications. LC 76-25575. (Probability & Mathematical Statistics Ser.). 1977. 30.95 (ISBN 0-471-39575-7, Pub. by Wiley-Interscience). Wiley.

Hildebrand, Francis B. Advanced Calculus for Applications. 2nd ed. (Illus.). 816p. 1976. 26.95 (ISBN 0-13-011189-9). P-H.

--Methods of Applied Mathematics. 2nd ed. 1965. ref. ed. 24.95 (ISBN 0-13-579201-0). P-H.

Hildebrand, George. The Golden Age of the Luxury Car: An Anthology of Articles & Photographs from Autobody, 1927-1931. (Illus., Orig.). 1980. pap. 6.00 (ISBN 0-486-23984-5). Dover.

Hildebrand, George H. Growth & Structure in the Economy of Modern Italy. LC 65-24450. 1965. 20.00x (ISBN 0-674-36450-3). Harvard U Pr.

Hildebrand, Grant. Designing for Industry: The Architecture of Albert Kahn. 224p. 1974. pap. 8.95x (ISBN 0-262-58040-3). MIT Pr.

Hildebrand, J., ed. Lesions of the Nervous System in Cancer Patients. LC 78-3000. (European Organization for Research on Treatment of Cancer Monograph: Vol. 5). 1978. 20.00 (ISBN 0-89004-269-1). Raven.

Hildebrand, James K. Maintenance Turns to the Computer. LC 75-109095. 1972. 11.95 (ISBN 0-8436-0808-0). CBI Pub.

Hildebrand, Klaus. The Foreign Policy of the Third Reich. 1974. 15.75x (ISBN 0-520-01965-2); pap. 5.50x (ISBN 0-520-02528-8). U of Cal Pr.

Hildebrand, Milton. Analysis of Vertebrate Structure. LC 73-11486. (Illus.). 704p. 1974. text ed. 26.50x (ISBN 0-471-39580-3). Wiley.

--Anatomical Preparations. 1968. 15.75x (ISBN 0-520-00558-9); pap. 4.75 o.p. (ISBN 0-520-00559-7). U of Cal Pr.

Hildebrand, Ron. Projects for the Home. Ortho Books Editorial Staff, ed. LC 80-66343. (Illus.). 96p. (Orig.). 1981. pap. 4.95 (ISBN 0-917102-85-1, Ortho Bks). Chevron Chem.

--Wood Projects for the Home. Ortho Books Editorial Staff, ed. LC 80-66343. (Illus.). 96p. (Orig.). 1981. pap. 4.95 (ISBN 0-917102-85-1). Ortho.

Hildebrand, Samuel F. & Schroeder, William C. The Fishes of the Chesapeake Bay. LC 72-5565. (Illus.). 388p. 1972. Repr. of 1928 ed. 8.00x. Smithsonian.

Hildebrand, Verna. Parenting & Teaching Young Children. Newman, Carol, ed. (Illus.). 432p. (gr. 10-12). 1980. text ed. 15.92 (ISBN 0-07-028775-9, W); tchrs. manual avail. (ISBN 0-07-051305-8). McGraw.

Hildebrand, William H. Shelley's Polar Paradise: A Reading of Prometheus Unbound. (Salzburg Studies in English Literature, Romantic Reassessment: No.18). 1974. pap. text ed. 25.00x (ISBN 0-391-01409-9). Humanities.

Hildeman, Beite. Swedish Basic Grammar. 3rd ed. 1976. text ed. 18.50x (ISBN 9-1210-1551-1, SW145). Vanous.

Hildeman, N., et al. Lar Er Svenska. (gr. 9 up). 1971. pap. text ed. 16.00x (ISBN 9-1210-2141-4, SW158); exercise bk. (ISBN 0-686-66880-4, SW158E). key 3.00x 14.00x (ISBN 0-686-66880-4, SW158E). key to exercise bk 3.00x (ISBN 0-686-66881-2, SW158K); 7 45 rpm records 70.00x (ISBN 0-686-66882-0, SW158R); 3 tapes 95.00x (ISBN 0-686-66883-9, SW158T); 3 cassettes 100.00x (ISBN 0-686-66884-7, SW158C); wordlist 7.00 (ISBN 9-1200-0645-4, SW158W). Vanous.

--Swedish, Learn: Reader for Beginners. (Swedish Language Ser.). 1975. text ed. 18.50x (ISBN 9-1210-3042-1, SW143); 5 45 rpm records 90.00x (ISBN 91-21-90171-6, SW143R); 5 tapes 90.00x (ISBN 91-21-90332-8, SW143T); 2 cassettes 90.00x (ISBN 91-21-90089-2, SW143C). Vanous.

Hildeman, N. H., et al. Swedish Practice. 1975. text ed. 8.50x (ISBN 9-1210-2423-5, SW144); key to exercise book 6.00x (SW144K). Vanous.

Hilder, Brett. The Voyage of Torres: The Discovery of the Southern Coastline of New Guinea & Torres Strait by Captain Luis Baez De Torres in 1606. (Illus.). 194p. 1981. 21.75x (ISBN 0-7022-1275-X). U of Queensland Pr.

Hildesheimer, Wolfgang. Mozart. (Suhrkamp Taschenbuecher: No. 598). 432p. 1980. pap. text ed. 6.50 (ISBN 3-518-37098-7, Pub. by Insel Verlag Germany). Suhrkamp.

--Mozart. Faber, Marion, tr. from Ger. (Illus.). 1981. 20.00 (ISBN 0-374-21483-2). FS&G.

Hildesheimer, Wolfgang see Otten, Anna.

Hildesley, Angela, jt. auth. see Cooper, Christine.

Hildick, E. W. The Case of the Bashful Bank Robber. LC 80-27422. (McGurk Mystery Ser.). (Illus.). 128p. (gr. 3-6). 1981. PLB 8.95 (ISBN 0-02-743870-8). Macmillan.

--The Case of the Condemned Cat: A McGurk Mystery. LC 75-14196. (Illus.). 112p. (gr. 3-6). 1975. 6.95 o.s.i. (ISBN 0-02-743810-4, 74381). Macmillan.

--The Case of the Condemned Cat: A McGurk Mystery, No. 2. (gr. 3-5). 1978. pap. 1.75 (ISBN 0-671-41404-6). Archway.

--Case of the Invisible Dog: A McGurk Mystery, No. 5. (gr. 3-5). 1978. pap. 1.75 (ISBN 0-671-41406-2). PB.

--The Case of the Invisible Dog: A McGurk Mystery. LC 77-4466. (A "McGurk Mystery" Ser.). (Illus.). (gr. 3-6). 1977. 8.95 (ISBN 0-02-743830-9, 74383). Macmillan.

--The Case of the Nervous Newsboy: A McGurk Mystery. LC 75-35873. (Illus.). 112p. (gr. 4-6). 1976. 7.95 (ISBN 0-02-743790-6, 74379). Macmillan.

--The Case of the Nervous Newsboy: A McGurk Mystery, No. 3. (gr. 3-5). 1978. pap. 1.75 (ISBN 0-671-41405-4). Archway.

--Case of the Nervous Newsboy: A McGurk Mystery, No. 3. (Illus.). (gr. 3-5). 1978. pap. 1.75 (ISBN 0-671-41405-4). PB.

--The Case of the Phantom Frog. LC 78-10836. (McGurk Mystery Ser.). (Illus.). (gr. 3-6). 1979. 7.95 (ISBN 0-02-743840-6). Macmillan.

--The Case of the Secret Scribbler. LC 78-2340. (McGurk Mystery Ser.). (Illus.). (gr. 3-6). 1978. 7.95 (ISBN 0-02-743780-9). Macmillan.

--Case of the Secret Scribbler: A McGurk Mystery, No. 6. (Illus.). (gr. 3-5). 1979. pap. 1.75 (ISBN 0-671-43293-1). PB.

--The Case of the Treetop Treasure: A McGurk Mystery No. 8. (A McGurk Mystery Bk.: No. 8). 1981. pap. write for info. (ISBN 0-671-41868-8). Archway.

--A Cat Called Amnesia. (Illus.). (gr. 5-7). 1977. pap. 1.50 (ISBN 0-671-56003-4). PB.

--A Cat Called Amnesia. (gr. 5-7). 1977. pap. 1.75 (ISBN 0-671-42132-8). Archway.

--Deadline for McGurk. LC 74-20616. (Illus.). 112p. (gr. 4-6). 1975. 5.95g o.s.i. (ISBN 0-02-743800-7). Macmillan.

--Deadline for McGurk: A McGurk Mystery, No. 1. (Illus.). (gr. 3-5). 1978. pap. 1.50 (ISBN 0-671-56107-3). PB.

--Great Rabbit Rip-off. (A McGurk Mystery Ser.: No. 4). (Illus.). (gr. 3-5). 1978. pap. 1.75 (ISBN 0-671-41106-3). PB.

--The Great Rabbit Rip-off: A McGurk Mystery, No. 4. (gr. 3-5). 1978. pap. 1.75 (ISBN 0-671-41454-2). Archway.

--Manhattan Is Missing. (gr. 3). 1973. pap. 1.95 (ISBN 0-380-01488-2, 55012, Camelot). Avon.

Hildick, E. W. & Schweitzer, Iris. The Top-Flight Fully-Automated Junior High School Girl Detective. pap. write for info. (ISBN 0-671-29911-5). PB.

Hildick, E. Wallace. The Doughnut Dropout. LC 70-180081. (gr. 4-7). 1972. PLB 4.50 o.p. (ISBN 0-385-09113-3). Doubleday.

Hildick, Wallace. Word for Word: The Rewriting of Fiction. 1966. pap. 2.95x (ISBN 0-393-09674-2, NortonC). Norton.

Hildreth, R. J., ed. Readings in Agricultural Policy. LC 68-12705. 1968. pap. 3.95x o.p. (ISBN 0-8032-5087-8, 380, Bison). U of Nebr Pr.

Hileman, Josephine & Colman, Bruce. Coming to America. (Newbury House Readers Ser.: Stage 3 - Intermediate). 48p. (Orig.). (gr. 7-12). 1981. pap. text ed. 1.95 (ISBN 0-88377-196-9). Newbury Hse.

Hileman, Sam, tr. see Fuentes, Carlos.

Hileman, Sam, tr. see Rodrigues, Jose H.

Hiler, Craig. Monkey Mountain. 1979. pap. 2.25 (ISBN 0-505-51403-6). Tower Bks.

Hiler, Hilaire. The Painter's Pocket Book of Methods & Materials. 3rd ed. 1970. 8.95 o.p. (ISBN 0-686-28562-X, Pub. by Faber & Faber); pap. 6.95 (ISBN 0-571-04696-7). Merrimack Bk Serv.

Hilf, Russell, jt. auth. see Kellen, John A.

Hilf, Russell, jt. ed. see Bianchi, C. Paul.

Hilfer, Anthony C. The Ethics of Intensity in American Fiction. 264p. 1981. text ed. 19.95x (ISBN 0-292-72029-7). U of Tex Pr.

Hilferding, Rudolf. Finance Capital: A Study of the Latest Phase of Capitalist Development. Bottomore, Tom, tr. from Ger. 500p. 1981. 60.00 (ISBN 0-7100-0618-7). Routledge & Kegan.

Hilgard, Ernest J., jt. auth. see Bower, Gordon H.

Hilgard, Ernest R. Divided Consciousness: Multiple Controls in Human Thought & Action. LC 77-7925. (Wiley Ser. in Behavior). 1977. 24.95 (ISBN 0-471-39602-8, Pub. by Wiley-Interscience). Wiley.

Hilgard, Ernest R. & Bower, Gordon H. Theories of Learning. 4th ed. 1975. text ed. 20.95x (ISBN 0-13-914457-9). P-H.

Hilgard, Henry R., jt. auth. see Singer, Sam.

Hilgartner. Hemophilia in the Child. Date not set. price not set. Masson Pub. Postponed.

Hilgemann, Werner, jt. auth. see Kinder, Herman.

Hilgers, Thomas & Horan, Dennis J., eds. Abortion & Social Justice. LC 72-6690. (Illus.). 320p. 1973. pap. 3.95 o.p. (ISBN 0-8362-0542-1). Andrews & McMeel.

Hilgert, Raymond L., jt. auth. see Schoen, Sterling H.

Hilgert, Raymond L., et al. Cases & Policies in Human Resources Management. 3rd ed. LC 77-72903. (Illus.). 1977. pap. text ed. 10.95 (ISBN 0-395-25070-6); inst. manual 0.75 (ISBN 0-395-25071-4). HM.

Hilken, Thomas J. Engineering at Cambridge University, 1783-1965. 1967. 26.95 (ISBN 0-521-05256-4). Cambridge U Pr.

Hill. Principless of Learning. 1981. 7.95 (ISBN 0-88284-123-8). Alfred Pub.

--Where's Spot? 6.95 (ISBN 0-399-20758-9). Putnam.

Hill, A. W. see Jackson, B. D., et al.

Hill, A. W., et al. Handbook to BS 5337, 1976: The Structural Use of Concrete for Retaining Aqueous Liquids. (Viewpoint Publication Ser.). (Illus.). 60p. 1979. pap. text ed. 25.00x (ISBN 0-7210-1078-4, Pub. by C&CA London). Scholium Intl.

Hill, Adrian. Drawing & Painting Faces & Figures. (Illus.). 79p. 1973. 6.50 (ISBN 0-7137-0026-2). Transatlantic.

Hill, Albert F. The North Avenue Irregulars. 1979. pap. 1.95 o.p. (ISBN 0-425-04085-2). Berkley Pub.

Hill, Albert F. & Hill, David C. Invader. 304p. (Orig.). 1981. pap. 2.75 (ISBN 0-515-05415-1). Jove Pubns.

Hill, Alexis. Passion's Slave. (Orig.). 1979. pap. 2.50 (ISBN 0-515-04862-3). Jove Pubns.

--The Untamed Heart. 416p. (Orig.). 1980. pap. 2.75 (ISBN 0-515-04863-1). Jove Pubns.

Hill, Andrew E., compiled by. Baker's Handbook of Bible Lists. 288p. (Orig.). 1981. pap. 6.95 (ISBN 0-8010-4242-9). Baker Bk.

Hill, Ann & Hill, Daryl. The Sultanate of Oman: A Heritage. LC 76-49444. (Illus.). 1977. text ed. 42.00x (ISBN 0-582-78050-0). Longman.

Hill, Ann, ed. A Visual Dictionary of Art. LC 73-76181. (Illus.). 1980. pap. 14.95 (ISBN 0-8212-1094-7, 903825PB). NYGS.

Hill, Arthur C. & Lubin, Isador. The British Attack on Unemployment. xiv, 325p. 1980. Repr. of 1934 ed. lib. bdg. 19.50x (ISBN 0-87991-087-9). Porcupine Pr.

Hill, Barbara. Cooking the British Way. (Easy Menu Ethnic Cookbooks). (Illus.). (YA) (gr. 5 up). 1981. PLB 4.95g (ISBN 0-8225-0903-2). Lerner Pubns.

--Graphology. (Illus.). 143p. 1981. 9.95 (ISBN 0-686-69111-3). St Martin.

Hill, Beth & Youngberg, Norma. Dixie. LC 67-28841. 1967. pap. 4.50 o.p. (ISBN 0-8163-0094-1, 04375-2). Pacific Pr Pub Assn.

Hill, Brennan & Newland, Mary R., eds. Theologians & Catechists in Dialogue: The Albany Forum. 64p. (Orig.). 1977. pap. 2.25 (ISBN 0-697-01671-4). Wm C Brown.

--Why Be a Catholic? 108p. (Orig.). 1979. pap. 2.00 (ISBN 0-697-01713-3). Wm C Brown.

Hill, Brian V. Education & the Endangered Individual: A Critique of Ten Modern Thinkers. LC 73-82283. 322p. 1974. pap. text ed. 7.00x (ISBN 0-8077-2432-7). Tchrs Coll.

Hill, C. J. Transfer at Eleven. 1972. pap. text ed. 3.75x (ISBN 0-901225-99-1, NFER). Humanities.

Hill, Carol. Jeremiah, Eight Twenty. 1970. 8.95 o.p. (ISBN 0-394-43119-7). Random.

--Let's Fall in Love. 256p. 1975. pap. 1.95 o.p. (ISBN 0-345-24425-7). Ballantine.

Hill, Carol, ed. see Hoffman, William.

Hill, Carole E., jt. auth. see Dickens, Roy S.

Hill, Charles C. Royal Canadian Academy, Eighteen Hundred to Nineteen Thirteen. (Illus.). 225p. 1980. write for info. (ISBN 0-88884-429-8, 56496-7, Pub. by Natl Mus Canada). U of Chicago Pr.

Hill, Christine M., ed. see Garnier, Robert.

Hill, Christopher. Antichrist in Seventeenth Century England. 1971. 9.95x (ISBN 0-19-713911-6). Oxford U Pr.

--Change & Continuity in Seventeenth-Century England. LC 74-12878. 1975. 16.50x (ISBN 0-674-10765-9). Harvard U Pr.

--Lenin & the Russian Revolution. 1978. pap. 2.95 (ISBN 0-14-021297-3). Penguin.

Hill, Claude. Bertolt Brecht. (World Authors Ser.: Germany: No. 331). 1975. lib. bdg. 12.50 (ISBN 0-8057-2179-7). Twayne.

Hill, D. A. Fibre Optics. 176p. 1977. text ed. 29.50x (ISBN 0-220-66333-5, Pub. by Busn Bks England). Renouf.

Hill, D. Fleet, jt. auth. see Forman, George E.

Hill, D. S. Agricultural Insect Pests of the Tropics. (Illus.). 584p. 1975. 60.00 (ISBN 0-521-20261-2); pap. 19.95 (ISBN 0-521-29441-X). Cambridge U Pr.

Hill, D. W. Electronic Techniques in Anesthesia & Surgery. 2nd ed. (Illus.). 448p. 1973. 39.95 (ISBN 0-407-16401-4). Butterworths.

--Physics Applied to Anaesthesia. 3rd ed. 320p. 1976. 39.95 (ISBN 0-407-00039-9). Butterworths.

--Physics Applied to Anesthesia. 4th ed. LC 80-40011. (Illus.). 420p. 1980. text ed. 52.95 (ISBN 0-407-00188-3). Butterworths.

Hill, D. W., jt. auth. see Payne, J. P.

Hill, Daryl, jt. auth. see Hill, Ann.

Hill, Dave. El Nino que Regalo Su Merienda. Villalobos, Fernando, tr. from Eng. (Illus.). 32p. (Orig., Span.). (gr. 1-3). 1977. pap. 0.95 (ISBN 0-89922-146-7). Edit Caribe.

--El Rey Mas Maravilloso. Ross, Ronald, tr. from Eng. (Libros Arco). (Illus.). 32p. (Span.). (gr. 1-3). 1972. pap. 0.95 o.s.i. (ISBN 0-89922-046-0). Edit Caribe.

Hill, David C., jt. auth. see Hill, Albert F.

Hill, Dilys M. Democratic Theory & Local Government. (New Local Government Ser.). 1974. pap. text ed. 9.95x (ISBN 0-04-352053-7). Allen Unwin.

Hill, Donna. Mr. Peeknuff's Tiny People. LC 80-12271. 32p. (ps-2). 1981. PLB 9.95 (ISBN 0-689-30778-0). Atheneum.

Hill, Douglas. Deathwing Over Veynaa. LC 80-20262. (Illus.). 132p. (gr. 7 up). 1981. 7.95 (ISBN 0-689-50192-7, McElderry Book). Atheneum.

Hill, Douglas & Williams, Pat. Supernatural. pap. 6.95 o.p. (ISBN 0-452-25094-3, Z5094, Plume). NAL.

--Supernatural. pap. 1.95 (ISBN 0-451-09265-1, J9265, Sig). NAL.

Hill, E. Joy. Core Skills for the Health Occupations. LC 71-176181. 320p. 1981. 24.50 (ISBN 0-87527-108-1). Green.

Hill, E. Leon. Miguel Angel Asturias, Lo Ancestral En Su Obra Literaria. 1972. 11.95 (ISBN 0-88303-007-1); pap. 9.95 (ISBN 0-685-73211-8). E Torres & Sons.

Hill, E. P. Rev. A. A. Lindsley. 6p. Repr. of 1902 ed. pap. 0.50 (ISBN 0-8466-0059-5, SJS59). Shorey.

Hill, Earle. Quietly Crush the Lizard. LC 79-155668. 1972. 6.95 (ISBN 0-8149-0698-2). Vanguard.

Hill, Edward B. Modern French Music. LC 71-87491. (Music Reprint Ser). 1969. Repr. of 1924 ed. lib. bdg. 27.50 (ISBN 0-306-71497-3). Da Capo.

Hill, Eldon C. George Bernard Shaw. (English Authors Ser.: No. 236). 1978. lib. bdg. 9.95 (ISBN 0-8057-6709-6). Twayne.

Hill, Elliott M., ed. see Jones, Thomas.

Hill, Emily, tr. see Karasowski, Maurycy.

Hill, Evan & Stekl, William. The Connecticut River. LC 72-3727. (Illus.). 144p. 1972. 15.00x (ISBN 0-8195-4051-X, Pub. by Wesleyan U Pr); pap. 7.95 o.p. (ISBN 0-8195-6042-1). Columbia U Pr.

Hill, F. S., Jr., jt. auth. see Glorioso, Robert M.

Hill, Faith F., jt. auth. see Stollberg, Robert.

Hill, Fiona. The Autumn Rose. LC 78-7615. 1978. 9.95 o.p. (ISBN 0-399-12280-X). Berkley Pub.

--The Autumn Rose. 1979. pap. 2.25 o.p. (ISBN 0-425-04224-3). Berkley Pub.

--The Love Child. 1979. pap. 1.95 o.p. (ISBN 0-425-04102-6). Berkley Pub.

--The Love Child. LC 77-82863. (YA) 1977. 8.95 o.p. (ISBN 0-399-12061-0, Dist. by Putnam). Berkley Pub.

--The Stanbroke Girls. 256p. 1981. 10.95 (ISBN 0-312-75570-8). St Martin.

--Sweet's Folly. LC 76-22717. (YA) 1977. 8.95 o.p. (ISBN 0-399-11877-2, Dist. by Putnam). Berkley Pub.

Hill, Frank W. English Springer Spaniels. Foyle, Christina, ed. (Foyle's Handbks). 1973. 3.95 (ISBN 0-685-55817-7). Palmetto Pub.

Hill, Fred. Grassroots: An Illustrated History of Bluegrass & Mountain Music. LC 80-67106. (Illus.). 160p. (Orig.). 1980. 15.00 (ISBN 0-914960-26-1); pap. 8.95 (ISBN 0-914960-25-3). Academy Bks.

Hill, Frederick J. & Peterson, Gerald R. Digital Systems: Hardware Organization & Design. 2nd ed. LC 78-7209. 1978. text ed. 29.95 (ISBN 0-471-39608-7); tchrs. ed. avail. (ISBN 0-471-03694-3). Wiley.

--Introduction to Switching Theory & Logical Design. 3rd ed. LC 80-20333. 640p. 1981. text ed. 27.95 (ISBN 0-471-04273-0). Wiley.

Hill, G. F. Becker the Counterfeiter. 111p. 1979. 20.00 (ISBN 0-916710-52-1). Obol Intl.

Hill, Gene. Hill Country: Stories About Hunting & Fishing & Dogs & Guns & Such. 1978. 11.95 (ISBN 0-87690-297-2). Dutton.

--A Hunter's Fireside Book: Tales of Dogs, Ducks, Birds & Guns. (Illus.). 1972. 11.95 (ISBN 0-87691-076-2). Winchester Pr.

--Mostly Tailfeathers. 192p. 1975. 11.95 (ISBN 0-87691-167-X). Winchester Pr.

Hill, George E. Management & Improvement of Guidance. 2nd ed. 1974. text ed. 20.95 (ISBN 0-13-548453-7). P-H.

Hill, Grace L. All Through the Night. 1980. pap. cancelled. Bantam.

--Amorelle. 320p. Repr. of 1934 ed. lib. bdg. 13.30x (ISBN 0-89190-055-1). Am Repr-Rivercity Pr.

--Amorelle, No. 4. 224p. 1980. pap. 1.95 (ISBN 0-553-13726-3). Bantam.

--April Gold, No. 27. 224p. 1980. pap. 1.95 (ISBN 0-553-14170-8). Bantam.

--Ariel Custer. 192p. 1981. pap. 1.95 (ISBN 0-553-14520-7). Bantam.

--Astra, No. 59. 240p. 1980. pap. 1.95 (ISBN 0-553-13819-7). Bantam.

--The Best Man No. 7. 176p. 1981. pap. 1.95 (ISBN 0-553-14505-3). Bantam.

--Blue Ruin, No. 41. 288p. 1981. pap. 1.95 (ISBN 0-553-14533-9). Bantam.

--By the Way of the Silverthorns. 1980. pap. cancelled. Bantam.

--Crimson Roses, No. 10. 192p. 1981. pap. 1.95 (ISBN 0-553-14510-X). Bantam.

--The Girl of the Woods. 192p. 1981. pap. 1.95 (ISBN 0-553-14599-1). Bantam.

--Miranda, No. 60. 224p. 1981. pap. 2.25 (ISBN 0-553-14270-4). Bantam.

--Mystery Flowers, No. 61. 256p. 1981. pap. 2.25 (ISBN 0-553-14655-6). Bantam.

--The Patch of Blue. (Grace Hill Ser.: No. 34). 176p. 1980. pap. 1.95 (ISBN 0-553-14172-4). Bantam.

--The Short Stories of Grace Livingston Hill. Clauss, J. E., ed. 1976. lib. bdg. 8.20 (ISBN 0-89190-101-9). Am Repr-Rivercity Pr.

--Sunrise: No. 25. 208p. 1980. pap. 1.95 (ISBN 0-553-14169-4). Bantam.

Hill, Graham L. Ileostomy: Surgery, Physiology & Management. LC 75-44116. (Illus.). 208p. 1976. 25.50 (ISBN 0-8089-0928-2). Grune.

--Ileostomy, Surgery, Physiology, & Management. 1976. 25.50 (ISBN 0-8089-0928-2). Grune.

Hill, Gregory C. I'm O. K. - You're a Jerk. 144p. 1980. 9.95 (ISBN 0-917224-08-6). Gregory Pubns.

Hill, Hamilton & Bucknell. Evolution of Fashion: Pattern & Cut from 1066-1930. 25.00x (ISBN 0-7134-0851-0). Drama Bk.

Hill, Hamlin. Mark Twain: God's Fool. 320p. 1975. pap. 3.95 o.p. (ISBN 0-06-090391-0, CN391, CN). Har-Row.

Hill, Hamlin, ed. see Twain, Mark.

Hill, Harold. How to Live in High Victory. 1978. 1.90 (ISBN 0-8297-0863-4). Life Pubs Intl.

--How to Live Like a King's Kid. LC 73-93002. 1974. pap. 2.95 (ISBN 0-88270-083-9). Logos.

Hill, Harold & Harrell, Irene. How to Be a Winner. LC 76-12035. 1976. 5.95 o.p. (ISBN 0-88270-178-9); pap. 2.95 (ISBN 0-88270-179-7). Logos.

Hill, Harold & Harrell, Irene B. How to Live the Bible Like a King's Kid. 1980. pap. 3.95 (ISBN 0-8007-5051-9). Revell.

Hill, Harold, tr. Comment Vaincre. (French Bks.). (Fr.). 1979. 1.75 (ISBN 0-8297-0814-6). Life Pubs Intl.

--Como Ser un Triunfador. (Spanish Bks.). (Span.). 1977. 1.90 (ISBN 0-8297-0750-6). Life Pubs Intl.

--Como Servencedor. (Portuguese Bks.). 1979. 1.40 (ISBN 0-8297-0824-3). Life Pubs Intl.

--Como Vivir Como un Hijo Del Rey. (Spanish Bks.). (Span.). 1978. 1.90 (ISBN 0-8297-0517-1). Life Pubs Intl.

--Diez Pasos Para Alcanzar la Victoria. (Spanish Bks.). (Span.). 1978. 1.90 (ISBN 0-8297-0864-2). Life Pubs Intl.

--Homme Ou Singe, Mr. Darwin? (French Bks.). (Fr.). 1979. 1.75 (ISBN 0-8297-0840-5). Life Pubs Intl.

--Las Monerias De Darwin. (Spanish Bks.). (Span.). 1977. 1.60 (ISBN 0-8297-0771-9). Life Pubs Intl.

--Pleine Victoire. (French Bks.). (Fr.). 1979. 1.95 (ISBN 0-8297-0942-8). Life Pubs Intl.

--Supreme Victorie. (French Bks.). (Fr.). 1979. 1.95 (ISBN 0-8297-0942-8). Life Pubs Intl.

Hill, Harold E. NAEB History, Vol. 1. 85p. 1954. pap. 4.00 (Pub Telecomm). NAEB.

Hill, Harry G. Automotive Service & Repair Tools. LC 73-907400. 288p. 1975. pap. 10.36 (ISBN 0-8273-1035-8); instructor's guide 1.60 (ISBN 0-8273-1036-6). Delmar.

--Interpreting Automotive Systems. LC 75-19527. 1977. pap. 10.36 (ISBN 0-8273-1057-9); instructor's guide 1.60 (ISBN 0-8273-1058-7). Delmar.
Hill, Heather. Green Paradise. 192p. 1981. pap. 1.50 (ISBN 0-671-57060-9). S&S.
Hill, Henry B., tr. Political Testament of Cardinal Richelieu: The Significant Chapters & Supporting Selections. (Illus.). 1961. 15.00x (ISBN 0-299-02420-2); pap. 5.95 (ISBN 0-299-02424-5). U of Wis Pr.
Hill, Herbert, ed. Anger, & Beyond: The Negro Writer in the United States. 1966. 10.00 o.p. (ISBN 0-06-011892-X, HarpT). Har-Row.
Hill, Herminie W. Pekingese. Foyle, Christina, ed. (Foyles Handbks). 1973. 3.95 (ISBN 0-685-55813-4). Palmetto Pub.
Hill, Howard E. Introduction to Lecithin. 1976. pap. 1.25 o.s.i. (ISBN 0-515-04219-6). Jove Pubns.
Hill, I. C. First Teeline Workbook. 1977. pap. text ed. 4.00x (ISBN 0-435-45341-6). Heinemann Ed.
--Teeline. 1977. pap. text ed. 9.95x o.p. (ISBN 0-435-45329-7). Heinemann Ed.
Hill, I. C. & Hill, James. Advanced Teeline. 1972. pap. text ed. 5.50x o.p. (ISBN 0-435-45334-3); practical exercises 3.25x o.p. (ISBN 0-435-45337-8). Heinemann Ed.
Hill, I. C., jt. auth. see Hill, James.
Hill, I. D. & Meek, B. L. Programming Language Standardisation: Computer & Their Applications. LC 80-41092. 261p. 1980. 65.00 (ISBN 0-470-27077-2). Halsted Pr.
Hill, J. L. End of the Cattle Trail. LC 73-94430. (Illus.). 1969. 8.95 (ISBN 0-8363-0030-0). Jenkins.
Hill, J. W. F. Victorian Lincoln. LC 73-82661. (Illus.). 350p. 1974. 48.00 (ISBN 0-521-20334-1). Cambridge U Pr.
Hill, Jack. The Complete Practical Book of Country Crafts. LC 79-51091. (Illus.). 1979. 22.50 (ISBN 0-7153-7706-X). David & Charles.
Hill, James & Hill, I. C. Basic Teeline. 1969. pap. text ed. 4.95x o.p. (ISBN 0-435-45331-9); tchr's ed 1.75x o.p. (ISBN 0-435-45335-1). Heinemann Ed.
Hill, James, jt. auth. see Hill, I. C.
Hill, James E. & Kedar, Ervin Y. Ecology-Environment Handbook. LC 78-57574. 1978. pap. text ed. 6.75 (ISBN 0-8191-0525-2). U Pr of Amer.
Hill, James H., tr. see Marcion Of Sinope.
Hill, Janet. Children Are People: The Librarian in the Community. LC 73-16277. (Illus.). 1974. 8.95 o.s.i. (ISBN 0-690-00475-3, TYC-T). T Y Crowell.
Hill, Jeanne. Secrets of Prayer Joy. 64p. 1981. pap. 2.95 (ISBN 0-8170-0910-8). Judson.
Hill, Jeanne F. Great Horned Owl. 1980. 2.50 (ISBN 0-934834-02-4). White Pine.
Hill, Jill, jt. auth. see Hill, Robert.
Hill, Jim D. The Civil War Sketchbook of Charles Ellery Stedman, Surgeon, United States Navy. LC 76-4164. (Illus.). 217p. 1976. 24.95 o.p. (ISBN 0-89141-001-5). Presidio Pr.
Hill, John. The Adventures of Mr. George Edwards, a Creole, 1751. Shugrue, Michael F., ed. (The Flowering of the Novel, 1740-1775 Ser: Vol. 34). 1974. lib. bdg. 50.00 (ISBN 0-8240-1133-3). Garland Pub.
--The Ethics of G.E. Moore: A New Interpretation. 156p. 1976. Repr. text ed. 16.75x o.p. (ISBN 0-685-66836-3). Humanities.
Hill, John & Hill, Laurita. Raymond Fourth, Count of Toulouse. LC 62-14120. 1962. 12.00x o.p. (ISBN 0-8156-0026-7). Syracuse U Pr.
Hill, John G., Jr., jt. auth. see O'Hara, William T.
Hill, John H. & Hill, Laurita L. Raymond IV, Count of Toulouse. LC 80-11116. (Illus.). viii, 177p. 1980. Repr. of 1962 ed. lib. bdg. 19.50x (ISBN 0-313-22362-9, HIRA). Greenwood.
Hill, John W., jt. auth. see Zaborowski, Leon M.
Hill, Jonathan. Cat's Whisker: Fifty Years of Wireless Design. LC 78-52365. (Art Bks). (Illus.). 1978. 15.95 (ISBN 0-8467-0477-3, Pub. by Two Continents); pap. 9.95 (ISBN 0-8467-0478-1). Hippocrene Bks.
Hill, Jonathan S., jt. auth. see Wasserman, Tamara E.
Hill, Kathleen K. Rosalia De Castro. (World Authors Ser.: No. 446). lib. bdg. 12.50 (ISBN 0-8057-6282-5). Twayne.
Hill, Kenneth C., ed. see Bickerton, Derek, et al.
Hill, Kim Q., jt. auth. see Carter, Ronald L.
Hill, L. A. Contextualized Vocabulary Tests. 1975. Bk. 1. pap. text ed. 3.50x o.p. (ISBN 0-19-432564-4); Bk. 2. pap. text ed. 3.50x o.p. (ISBN 0-19-432565-2). Oxford U Pr.
--Elementary Anecdotes in American English. (Anecdotes in American English Ser.). (Illus.). 72p. 1980. 2.50x (ISBN 0-19-502601-2). Oxford U Pr.
--Intermediate Anecdotes in American English. (Anecdotes in American English Ser.). (Illus.). 80p. 1980. pap. 2.50x (ISBN 0-19-502602-0). Oxford U Pr.
Hill, L. M., ed. The Ancient State, Authorite & Proceedings of the Court of Requests by Julius Caesar. LC 73-93399. (Studies in English Legal History). 308p. 1975. 49.00 (ISBN 0-521-20386-4). Cambridge U Pr.
Hill, L. R., ed. see Cowan, S. T.
Hill, Laurita, jt. auth. see Hill, John.
Hill, Laurita L., jt. auth. see Hill, John H.
Hill, Lawrence F. Jose De Escandon & the Founding of Nuevo Santander: A Study in Spanish Colonization. (Perspectives in Latin American History Ser.). (Illus.). v, 149p. 1980. Repr. of 1926 ed. lib. bdg. 15.00x (ISBN 0-87991-086-0). Porcupine Pr.
Hill, Leslie & Popkin, P. R. A First Crossword Puzzle Book. 64p. 1968. pap. text ed. 2.95x (ISBN 0-19-432551-2). Oxford U Pr.
--A Fourth Crossword Puzzle Book. 62p. 1971. pap. text ed. 2.95x (ISBN 0-19-432550-4). Oxford U Pr.
--A Second Crossword Puzzle Book. 62p. 1969. pap. text ed. 2.95x (ISBN 0-19-432552-0). Oxford U Pr.
--A Third Crossword Puzzle Book. 64p. 1970. pap. text ed. 2.95x (ISBN 0-19-432553-9). Oxford U Pr.
Hill, Leslie A. Advanced Stories for Reproduction. 62p. 1965. pap. 2.50x (ISBN 0-19-432543-1). Oxford U Pr.
--Elementary Stories for Reproduction. 64p. 1965. pap. 2.50x (ISBN 0-19-432541-5). Oxford U Pr.
--Intermediate Stories for Reproduction. 68p. 1965. pap. 2.50x (ISBN 0-19-432542-3). Oxford U Pr.
Hill, Lewis. Pruning Simplified: A Complete Guide to Pruning Trees, Shrubs, Bushes, Hedges, Vines, Flowers, Garden Plants, Houseplants & Bonsai. Yepsen, Roger B., ed. (Illus.). 224p. 1981. pap. 9.95 (ISBN 0-87857-249-X). Rodale Pr Inc.
--Successful Cold Climate Gardening. 288p. (Orig.). 1981. 14.95 (ISBN 0-8289-0421-9). Greene.
Hill, Louis A., Jr. Structured Programming in FORTRAN. (Illus.). 512p. 1981. text ed. 13.95 (ISBN 0-13-854612-6). P-H.
Hill, M. N. The Sea: Vol. 1 Physical Oceanography. 2nd ed. 880p. 1981. Repr. of 1962 ed. lib. bdg. write for info. (ISBN 0-89874-097-5). Krieger. Postponed.
Hill, M. N., ed. The Sea: Vol. 2, Composition of Sea Water. 570p. 1981. Repr. of 1963 ed. lib. bdg. write for info. (ISBN 0-89874-098-3). Krieger. Postponed.
--The Sea: Vol. 3 the Earth Beneath the Sea; History. LC 80-248. 980p. 1981. Repr. of 1963 ed. lib. bdg. write for info. (ISBN 0-89874-099-1). Krieger.
Hill, M. R. The Export Marketing of Capital Goods to the Socialist Countries of Eastern Europe. 200p. 1978. text ed. 45.75x (ISBN 0-566-03004-7, Pub. by Gower Pub Co England). Renouf.
Hill, Malcolm. Forecast. 1980. pap. 1.25 (ISBN 0-440-42607-3, YB). Dell.
Hill, Marnesba & Schleifer, Herbert B. Puerto Rican Authors: A Biobibliographic Handbook. LC 73-15604. 1974. 10.00 (ISBN 0-8108-0681-9). Scarecrow.
Hill, Mary. Geology of the Sierra Nevada. LC 73-93053. (California Natural History Guides Ser.). (Illus.). 1975. 12.95x (ISBN 0-520-02801-5); pap. 5.95 (ISBN 0-520-02698-5). U of Cal Pr.
Hill, Mary Ann, ed. BMDP User's Digest. (BMDP Statistical Software Ser.). 115p. 1979. text ed. 5.00 (ISBN 0-935386-00-9). UCLA Dept Biomath.
Hill, Michael. Understanding Social Policy. (Aspects of Social Policy Ser.). 272p. 1981. pap. 10.00x (ISBN 0-631-18180-6, Pub. by Basil Blackwell England). Biblio Dist.
--Understanding Social Policy. (Aspects of Social Policy Ser.). 1980. 27.50x (ISBN 0-631-08190-9, Pub. by Basil Blackwell). Biblio Dist.
Hill, Michael & Laing, Peter. Social Work & Money. (Studies in the Personal Social Ser.). (Orig.). 1979. text ed. 17.95x (ISBN 0-04-360051-4); pap. text ed. 7.95x (ISBN 0-04-360052-2). Allen Unwin.
Hill, Morgan. Boot Hill Brother. (Orig.). 1981. pap. 1.95 (ISBN 0-440-10794-6). Dell.
--Dead Man's Noose. (Orig.). 1980. pap. 1.95 (ISBN 0-440-12073-X). Dell.
--The Quick & the Deadly. (Orig.). 1981. pap. 1.95 (ISBN 0-440-17173-3). Dell.
Hill, Myron G., et al. Smith's Review of Agency & Partnership: For Law School, Bar & College Examinations. 3rd ed. LC 79-7186. (Legal Gem Ser.). 264p. 1979. pap. text ed. 8.95 (ISBN 0-8299-2033-1). West Pub.
--Smith's Review of Labor Law & Employment Discrimination, for Law School, Bar & College Examinations. 2nd ed. LC 79-23934. (Legal Gem Ser.). 235p. 1980. pap. text ed. 8.95 (ISBN 0-8299-2069-2). West Pub.
Hill, Myron G., Jr., et al. Smith's Review of Family Law. 2nd ed. (Smith's Review Ser.). 140p. 1981. pap. text ed. 10.95 (ISBN 0-8299-0515-4). West Pub.
Hill, N. The Think & Grow Rich Action Pack. 1966. pap. 4.95 (ISBN 0-8015-7560-5, Hawthorn). Dutton.
Hill, Napoleon. Laws of Success. 1977. 19.95 (ISBN 0-685-74304-7). Success Unltd.
--Master-Key to Riches. 1978. pap. 2.25 (ISBN 0-449-23953-5, Crest). Fawcett.
Hill, Norman C. Increasing Managerial Effectiveness: Keys to Management & Motivation. LC 78-62547. 1979. pap. text ed. 8.95 (ISBN 0-201-02888-3). A-W.
Hill, Norman L. Claims to Territory in International Law & Relations. LC 75-25488. (Illus.). 248p. 1976. Repr. of 1945 ed. lib. bdg. 20.25x (ISBN 0-8371-8430-4, HICT). Greenwood.
Hill, Olivia R., ed. see Hill, Richard T. & Anthony, William E.
Hill, Pamela. The Green Salamander. 1978. pap. 1.95 o.p. (ISBN 0-449-23642-0, Crest). Fawcett.
--Norah. 1978. pap. 1.95 o.p. (ISBN 0-449-23482-7, Crest). Fawcett.
--Place of Ravens. 224p. 1981. 9.95 (ISBN 0-312-61373-3). St Martin.
--Strangers' Forest. 1979. pap. 1.95 o.p. (ISBN 0-449-23907-1, Crest). Fawcett.
Hill, Pati. Impossible Dreams. LC 76-4419. 142p. 1976. pap. 4.95 (ISBN 0-914086-13-8). Alicejamesbooks.
Hill, Paul, jt. auth. see Cooper, Thomas.
Hill, Percy H., et al. Making Decisions: A Multi-Disciplinary Introduction. 2nd. ed. 1980. pap. text ed. 14.50 (ISBN 0-201-03103-5). A-W.
Hill, Peter. The Fanatics. LC 78-53482. 1978. 7.95 o.p. (ISBN 0-684-15821-3, ScribT). Scribner.
Hill, Peter J., jt. auth. see Anderson, Terry L.
Hill, Philip G. & Peterson, C. R. Mechanics & Thermodynamics of Propulsion. 1965. 28.95 (ISBN 0-201-02838-7). A-W.
Hill, Polly. Migrant Cocoa Farmers of Southern Ghana. 42.95 (ISBN 0-521-05264-5). Cambridge U Pr.
--Studies in Rural Capitalism in West Africa. LC 77-96093. (Cambridge African Studies: No. 2). (Illus.). 27.95 (ISBN 0-521-07622-6). Cambridge U Pr.
Hill, R. Principles of Dynamics. 1964. 22.00 (ISBN 0-08-010571-8); pap. 7.50 o.p. (ISBN 0-08-013540-4). Pergamon.
Hill, R., jt. auth. see Halstead, L. B.
Hill, R. W., jt. auth. see Hanks, R. J.
Hill, Ralph N. Lake Champlain: Key to Liberty. 296p. 1978. 14.95 (ISBN 0-936896-01-9). VT Life Mag.
Hill, Ray. Unsung Heroes of Pro Basketball. (Illus.). (gr. 5 up). 1973. 2.50 o.p. (ISBN 0-394-82415-6, BYR); PLB 3.69 (ISBN 0-394-92415-0). Random.
Hill, Ray & White, B. Joseph, eds. Matrix Organization & Project Management: Theory & Practice. (Michigan Business Papers Ser.: No. 64). (Illus.). 1979. pap. 12.95 (ISBN 0-87712-196-6). U Mich Busn Div Res.
Hill, Reginald. A Killing Kindness. 1981. 10.95 (ISBN 0-394-51910-8). Pantheon.
--The Spy's Wife. 1980. 9.95 (ISBN 0-394-51402-5). Pantheon.
Hill, Reuben L., jt. auth. see Duvall, Evelyn M.
Hill, Richard, jt. auth. see Hestenes, Marshall.
Hill, Richard, jt. ed. see Santi, Paul.
Hill, Richard F., ed. Energy Technology: Expanding Energy Supplies, Vol. VII. LC 80-66431. (Illus.). 1400p. 1980. pap. text ed. 45.00 (ISBN 0-86587-006-3). Gov Insts.
Hill, Richard F., et al, eds. Synfuels Industry Opportunities. Boardman, Elliot B. & Heavner, Martin L. LC 80-84730. 256p. 1981. 32.50 (ISBN 0-86587-088-8). Gov Insts.
Hill, Richard M., et al. Industrial Marketing. 4th ed. 1975. text ed. 19.50 (ISBN 0-256-00010-7). Irwin.
Hill, Richard T. & Anthony, William E. Confederate Longarms & Pistols: A Pictorial Study. Hill, Olivia R., ed. (Illus.). 304p. 1978. 29.95 (ISBN 0-87833-309-6); lib. bdg. 26.95 (ISBN 0-686-28758-4). Confed Arms.
Hill, Robert. The Pathway to Prayer & Pietie. LC 74-28864. (English Experience Ser.: No. 744). 1975. Repr. of 1613 ed. 26.50 (ISBN 90-221-0744-2). Walter J Johnson.
Hill, Robert & Hill, Jill. Stained Glass: Music for the Eye. LC 79-65725. (Illus.). 108p. (Orig.). 1979. pap. 9.95 (ISBN 0-295-95699-2). U of Wash Pr.
Hill, Robert A., ed. see Harding, Vincent.
Hill, Robert A., ed. see Nettleford, Rex.
Hill, Robert A., ed. see Tolbert, Emory J.
Hill, Robert Allen. Your Children: The Victims of Public Education. pap. 2.95 (ISBN 0-89728-004-0). Omega Pubns OR.
Hill, Robert H., jt. auth. see Frasca, Albert J.
Hill, Robert L., jt. auth. see Neurath, Hans.
Hill, Robert W. What the Moon Astronauts Do. LC 75-143416. (Illus.). (gr. 3 up). 1971. PLB 7.89 (ISBN 0-381-99795-2, A87120, JD-J). John Day.
Hill, Ron, jt. auth. see Wasley, John.
Hill, Ronald. Soviet Politics: Political Science & Reform. LC 79-55751. 256p. 1980. lib. bdg. 27.50 (ISBN 0-87332-156-1). M E Sharpe.
Hill, Ronald C. Union Pacific Eight Thousand, Four Hundred Forty-Four. (Illus.). 1978. pap. 9.00 (ISBN 0-918654-28-9). CO RR Mus.
Hill, Ruth B. Hanta Yo: An American Saga. 1980. 9.95 (ISBN 0-446-96298-8); pap. 3.50 (ISBN 0-446-97857-4). Warner Bks.
Hill, Ruth L. This Side of Tomorrow. 230p. (gr. 7-12). 1973. pap. 2.25 (ISBN 0-310-26062-0). Zondervan.
Hill, S. R. The Distributive System. 1966. 15.00 (ISBN 0-08-011738-4); pap. 7.00 (ISBN 0-08-011737-6). Pergamon.
Hill, Samuel E., jt. auth. see Norgren, Paul H.
Hill, Scott, jt. auth. see Playfair, Guy L.
Hill, Sheelagh, jt. auth. see Curtis, Audrey.
Hill, Sondra. Fun Astrology. Orig. Title: All About Astrology. (Illus.). 96p. (gr. 4-7). 1981. PLB price not set (ISBN 0-671-41629-4). Messner.
Hill, Susan, jt. auth. see Chicago, Judy.
Hill, Terrell L. Introduction to Statistical Thermodynamics. 1960. 22.95 (ISBN 0-201-02840-9). A-W.
--Thermodynamics for Chemists & Biologists. (Chemistry Ser). 1968. text ed. 16.95 (ISBN 0-201-02841-7). A-W.
Hill, Terry, jt. auth. see Naysmith, Brian.
Hill, Thomas. The Art of Gardening. LC 79-84117. (English Experience Ser.: No. 936). 276p. 1979. Repr. of 1608 ed. lib. bdg. 26.00. Walter J Johnson.
Hill, Thomas A. Country Music. (First Bks.). (Illus.). (gr. 4-6). 1978. PLB 6.45 (ISBN 0-531-01405-3). Watts.
--The Drum: An Introduction to the Instrument. LC 74-10694. (Keynote Bks). (Illus.). 28p. (gr. 6 up). 1975. PLB 5.90 (ISBN 0-531-02789-9). Watts.
--The Guitar: An Introduction to the Instrument. LC 73-4532. (Keynote Bks.). (gr. 5 up). 1973. PLB 4.90 o.p. (ISBN 0-531-02635-3). Watts.
Hill, Tomas. Rios De Tinta: Historia y Ministerio De la Casa Bautista De Publicaciones. Smith, Josie, tr. from Eng. Orig. Title: Rivers of Ink. 64p. 1980. pap. 1.25 (ISBN 0-311-29009-4). Casa Bautista.
Hill, W. Aber. Ten Million Photoplay Plots. Kupelnick, Bruce S., ed. LC 76-52108. (Classics of Film Literature Ser.). 1978. lib. bdg. 15.00 (ISBN 0-8240-2879-1). Garland Pub.
Hill, W. W. Ethnography of Santa Clara Pueblo. Lange, Charles H., ed. (Illus.). 550p. 1981. 35.00x (ISBN 0-8263-0555-5). U of NM Pr.
Hill, Walter R. Secondary School Reading: Process-Program-Procedure. 1978. text ed. 17.95 (ISBN 0-205-06129-X, 2361299). Allyn.
Hill, Wanda J. We Remember, Elvis! LC 78-59596. (Illus.). 1978. 17.50 (ISBN 0-89430-028-8). Morgan-Pacific.
Hill, Weldon. The Iceman. LC 76-15607. 320p. 1976. 8.95 o.p. (ISBN 0-688-03071-8). Morrow.
Hill, West T., Jr. Theatre in Early Kentucky, 1790-1820. LC 73-132829. (Illus.). 246p. 1971. 12.00x (ISBN 0-8131-1240-0). U Pr of Ky.
Hill, Winfield, jt. auth. see Horowitz, Paul.
Hill, Winfred, jt. ed. see Bishop, Gale B.
Hill, Wm. F. Learning Thru Discussion. rev., 2nd ed. LC 78-87064. 1977. 2.95x (ISBN 0-8039-0711-7). Sage.
Hillard, A. E., jt. auth. see North, M. A.
Hillard, Denise, jt. ed. see Rinet, Jacqueline.
Hillard, James M. Where to Find More: A Handbook to Reference Service. LC 77-6406. 1977. 10.00 (ISBN 0-8108-1039-5). Scarecrow.
--Where to Find What: A Handbook to Reference Service. LC 75-6723. 281p. 1975. 12.00 (ISBN 0-8108-0813-7). Scarecrow.
Hillary, Anne. Compromised Love. (Candlelight Romance Ser.). (Orig.). 1981. pap. 1.50 (ISBN 0-440-11351-2). Dell.
Hillary, Clarence F. Basic Architectural Drawing. (A Promotion of the Arts Library Bk.). (Illus.). 141p. 1981. 37.45 (ISBN 0-930582-98-5). Gloucester Art.
Hillary, George. A Research Odyssey: Developing & Testing a Community Theory. 158p. 1981. 15.95 (ISBN 0-87855-400-9); text ed. 15.95 (ISBN 0-686-68061-8). Transaction Bks.
Hillas, A. M. Cosmic Rays. 306p. 1972. text ed. 23.00 (ISBN 0-08-016724-1). Pergamon.
Hillcourt, William. Official Boy Scout Handbook. 9th ed. LC 78-72563. (Illus.). (gr. 6-12). 1979. 3.45x (ISBN 0-8395-3227-X). BSA.

Hilldrup, Robert P. To Die for a Golden Leaf. (Orig.). 1980. pap. 1.95 (ISBN 0-532-23217-8). Manor Bks.

Hille, Einar. Analytic Function Theory, 2 vols. 2nd ed. LC 73-647. 308p. 1973. 12.95. Vol. 1 (ISBN 0-8284-0269-8). Vol. 2 (ISBN 0-8284-0270-1). Chelsea Pub.

--Ordinary Differential Equations in the Complex Domain. LC 75-44231. (Pure & Applied Mathematics Ser.). 432p. 1976. 43.95 (ISBN 0-471-39964-7, Pub. by Wiley-Interscience). Wiley.

Hille, Einar, jt. auth. see Salas, Saturnino L.

Hilleborg, Arno. Strip Method of Design. 2nd ed. (C & CA Viewpoint Publication Ser.). (Illus.). 1976. pap. text ed. 22.50 (ISBN 0-7210-1012-1). Scholium Intl.

Hillegas, Mark R. The Future As Nightmare: H. G. Wells & the Anti-Utopians. LC 74-4084. (Arcturus Books Paperbacks Ser.). 212p. 1974. lib. bdg. 12.95x (ISBN 0-8093-0680-8); pap. 6.95 (ISBN 0-8093-0676-X). S Ill U Pr.

Hillegas, Mark R., ed. Shadows of Imagination: The Fantasies of C. S. Lewis, J. R. R. Tolkien, & Charles Williams. 2nd ed. LC 78-13983. (Crosscurrents Modern Critiques Ser.). 210p. 1979. 12.95 (ISBN 0-8093-0897-5). S Ill U Pr.

--Shadows of Imagination: The Fantasies of C. S. Lewis, J. R. R. Tolkien, & Charles Williams. 2nd ed. LC 78-13983. (Arcturus Books Paperbacks). 210p. 1979. pap. 6.95 (ISBN 0-8093-0908-4). S Ill U Pr.

Hillel, Daniel. Soil & Water: Physical Principles & Processes. (Physiological Ecology Ser). 1971. 29.50 (ISBN 0-12-348550-9). Acad Pr.

Hillenbrand, Martin J., ed. The Future of Berlin. LC 79-55003. (Atlantic Institute for International Affairs Research Ser.: Vol. 3). (Illus.). 313p. 1981. text ed. 27.50 (ISBN 0-916672-46-8). Allanheld.

Hillenkamp, F., et al, eds. Lasers in Biology & Medicine. (NATO Advanced Study Institute Ser.-Series A-Life Sciences: Vol. 34). 450p. 1981. 49.50 (ISBN 0-306-40470-2, Plenum Pr). Plenum Pub.

Hiller, Catherine. Abracatabby. (Illus.). 64p. (gr. 6-9). 1981. PLB 6.99 (ISBN 0-698-30727-5). Coward.

Hiller, James & Neary, Peter, eds. Newfoundland in the Nineteenth & Twentieth Centuries. 1980. 20.00x (ISBN 0-8020-5486-2); pap. 7.50 (ISBN 0-8020-6391-8). U of Toronto Pr.

Hiller, Marc D. Medical Ethics & the Law. Date not set. write for info. (ISBN 0-88410-707-8). Ballinger Pub. Postponed.

Hillerbrand, Hans J. The World of the Reformation. (Twin Brooks Ser.). 229p. 1981. pap. 6.95 (ISBN 0-8010-4248-8). Baker Bk.

Hillerbrand, Hans J. & Lehmann, Helmut T., eds. Luther's Works: Sermons II, Vol. 52. LC 55-9893. 416p. 1974. 15.95 (ISBN 0-8006-0352-4, 1-352). Fortress.

Hillerich, Robert L. Pacemaker Core Vocabularies, One & Two. LC 79-54762. (gr. 7-12). 1980. pap. 4.60 (ISBN 0-8224-5225-1). Pitman Learning.

--Reading Fundamentals for Preschool and Primary Children. (Elementary Education Ser.). 1977. pap. text ed. 9.95 (ISBN 0-675-08543-8). Merrill.

Hillerman, Tony. Blessing Way. LC 73-96009. (Harper Novel of Suspense). 1970. 10.00 o.p. (ISBN 0-06-011896-2, HarpT). Har-Row.

--Dance Hall of the Dead. 1975. pap. 1.75 (ISBN 0-380-49494-9, 49494). Avon.

Hillert. It's Halloween, Dear Dragon. Date not set. lib. bdg. 4.39 (ISBN 0-695-41361-9). Follett.

Hillert, Margaret. The Ball Book. (Just Beginning-to-Read Ser.). (Illus.). 32p. (gr. 1-6). 1981. PLB 4.39 (ISBN 0-695-41553-0); pap. 1.50 (ISBN 0-695-31553-6). Follett.

--The Boy & the Goats. (Just Beginning-to-Read Ser.). (Illus.). 32p. (gr. 1-6). 1981. PLB 4.39 (ISBN 0-695-41545-X). Follett.

--City Fun. (Just Beginning-to-Read Ser.). 32p. 1980. PLB 4.39 (ISBN 0-695-41457-7); pap. 1.50 (ISBN 0-695-31457-2). Follett.

--Fun Days. (Just Beginning-to-Read Ser.). (Illus.). (gr. 1-6). 1981. PLB 4.39 (ISBN 0-695-41546-8); pap. 1.50 (ISBN 0-695-31546-3). Follett.

--The Funny Ride. (Just Beginning-to-Read Ser.). (Illus.). 32p. (gr. 1-6). 1981. PLB 4.39 (ISBN 0-686-68656-X); pap. 1.50 (ISBN 0-695-31552-8). Follett.

--House for Little Red. new ed. LC 75-85953. (Just Beginning-To-Read Ser). (Illus.). (ps). 1970. 2.50 o.p. (ISBN 0-695-80082-5); PLB 3.39 o.p. (ISBN 0-695-40082-7). Follett.

--I Like Things. (Just Beginning-to-Read Ser.). (Illus.). (gr. 1-6). 1981. 4.39 (ISBN 0-695-41554-9); pap. 1.50 (ISBN 0-695-31554-4). Follett.

--Let's Have a Play. (Just Beginning-to-Read Ser.). (Illus.). 32p. (gr. 1-6). 1981. PLB 4.39 (ISBN 0-695-41544-1); pap. 1.50 (ISBN 0-695-31544-7). Follett.

--Little Red Riding Hood. (Just Beginning-to-Read Ser.). (Illus.). 32p. (gr. 1-6). 1981. PLB 4.39 (ISBN 0-695-41543-3); pap. 1.50 (ISBN 0-695-31543-9). Follett.

--The Magic Nutcracker. (Just-Beginning-to-Read Ser.). 1980. PLB 4.39 (ISBN 0-695-41456-9); pap. 1.50 (ISBN 0-695-31456-4). Follett.

--Pinocchio. (Just Beginning-to-Read Ser.). (Illus.). 32p. (gr. 1-6). 1981. PLB 4.39 (ISBN 0-695-41551-4); pap. 1.50 (ISBN 0-695-31551-X). Follett.

--Tom Thumb. (Just Beginning-to-Read Ser.). (Illus.). 32p. (gr. 1-6). 1981. PLB 4.39 (ISBN 0-695-41542-5); pap. 1.50 (ISBN 0-695-31542-0). Follett.

--Up, Up, & Away. (Just Beginning-to-Read Ser.). (Illus.). 32p. (gr. 1-6). 1981. PLB 4.39 (ISBN 0-695-41541-7); pap. 1.50 (ISBN 0-695-31541-2). Follett.

--Who Comes to Your House? (Illus.). (ps-2). 1973. PLB 4.57 o.p. (ISBN 0-307-60575-2, Golden Pr). Western Pub.

--Who Goes to School? (Just Beginning-to-Read Ser.). 1980. PLB 4.39 (ISBN 0-695-41458-5); pap. 1.50 (ISBN 0-695-31458-0). Follett.

--Why We Have Thanksgiving. (Just Beginning-to-Read Ser.). (Illus.). 32p. (gr. 1-6). 1981. PLB 4.39 o.p. (ISBN 0-695-41550-6); pap. 1.50 o.p. (ISBN 0-695-31550-1). Follett.

--The Witch Who Went for a Walk. (Illus.). (gr. 1-6). 1981. PLB 4.39 (ISBN 0-695-41549-2); pap. 1.50 (ISBN 0-695-31549-8). Follett.

Hillery, D., ed. see Verlaine.

Hilles, Frederick W. Literary Career of Sir Joshua Reynolds. 1967. Repr. of 1936 ed. 15.00 o.p. (ISBN 0-208-00418-1, Archon). Shoe String.

Hilles, Richard J., jt. auth. see Golembiewski, Robert T.

Hillesheim, James W. & Merrill, George D., eds. Theory & Practice in the History of American Education: A Book of Readings. LC 79-3735. 439p. 1980. Repr. of 1971 ed. 10.50 (ISBN 0-8191-0929-0). U Pr of Amer.

Hillgarth, J. N. Ramon Lull & Lullism in Fourteenth-Century France. (Oxford-Warburg Ser.). 1971. 59.00x (ISBN 0-19-824348-0). Oxford U Pr.

--Spanish Kingdoms Twelve Fifty to Fiften Sixteen, Vol. II: Castilian Hegemony, 1410-1516. 1978. 49.50x (ISBN 0-19-822531-8). Oxford U Pr.

--The Spanish Kingdoms, 1250-1516, Vol. 1: 250-1410 Precarious Balance. 1976. 49.50x (ISBN 0-19-822530-X). Oxford U Pr.

Hillgruber, Andreas. Germany & the Two World Wars. Kirby, William C., tr. LC 80-27036. 144p. 1981. text ed. 14.50 (ISBN 0-674-35321-8). Harvard U Pr.

Hillhouse, Marion S. & Mansfield, E. A. Dress Design: Draping & Flat Pattern Making. LC 48-7554. 1948. text ed. 19.50 (ISBN 0-395-04627-0, 3-25310). HM.

Hilliard, John N., ed. see Downs, T. Nelson.

Hilliard, Sam B. Hog Meat & Hoecake: Food Supply in the Old South, 1840-1860. LC 75-156778. 309p. 1972. 17.95x (ISBN 0-8093-0512-7). S Ill U Pr.

Hillier, Bevis, ed. Fougasse. (Illus.). 1978. 15.95 (ISBN 0-241-89462-X, Pub. by Hamish Hamilton England). David & Charles.

Hillier, Frederick S. & Lieberman, Gerald J. Introduction to Operations Research. 3rd ed. 848p. 1980. text ed. 28.95 (ISBN 0-8162-3867-7); solutions manual 7.50 (ISBN 0-8162-3868-5). Holden-Day.

--Operations Research. 2nd ed. LC 73-94383. 816p. 1974. text ed. 27.95x (ISBN 0-8162-3856-1); solutions manual o.p. 7.50 (ISBN 0-8162-3866-9). Holden-Day.

Hillier, Jack. The Art of Hokusai in Book-Illustration. 1980. 95.00 (ISBN 0-520-04137-2). U of Cal Pr.

Hilling, John B. Snowdonia & Northern Wales. (Illus.). 192p. 1980. 27.00 (ISBN 0-7134-3793-6, Pub. by Batsford England). David & Charles.

--Wales: South & West. 1976. 17.95 (ISBN 0-7134-3057-5, Pub. by Batsford England). David & Charles.

Hillis, David, et al. Manual of Clinical Problems in Cardiology: With Annotated Key References. 1980. 12.95 (ISBN 0-316-36400-2). Little.

Hillis, Dick & Hillis, Don. The Spirit Speaks: Are You Listening? LC 80-50260. 96p. 1980. pap. 2.50 (ISBN 0-8307-0752-2, 5016606). Regal.

Hillis, Don, jt. auth. see Hillis, Dick.

Hillis, Don H. John. (Teach Yourself The Bible Ser). 1962. pap. 1.75 (ISBN 0-8024-4306-0). Moody.

Hillis, Don W. Live Happily with Yourself. 1978. pap. 1.75 (ISBN 0-88207-507-1). Victor Bks.

Hillis, James. Pari Mutuel Betting. (Gambler's Book Shelf). (Illus.). 122p. 1972. pap. 2.95 (ISBN 0-89650-527-8). Gamblers.

Hillis, W. E. & Brown, A. G. Eucalypts for Wood Production. 1980. 50.00x (ISBN 0-643-02245-7, Pub. by CSIRO Australia). State Mutual Bk.

Hillison, John & Crunkilton, John. Human Relations in Agribusiness: Career Preparation for Agriculture-Agribusiness. Moore, R., ed. (Illus.). 128p. (gr. 9-12). 1980. pap. text ed. 5.00 (ISBN 0-07-028904-2); activity guide 3.00 (ISBN 0-686-64659-2); tchrs. manual & key 3.70 (ISBN 0-07-028906-9). McGraw.

Hillman, et al. Facing the Gods. Hillman, James, ed. 171p. (Orig.). 1980. pap. text ed. 8.50 (ISBN 0-88214-312-3). Spring Pubns.

--Spring 'seventy-Six: An Annual of Archetypal Psychology & Jungian Thought. Hillman, James, ed. 218p. (Orig.). 1976. pap. text ed. 12.00 (ISBN 0-88214-011-6). Spring Pubns.

Hillman, Anthony, jt. auth. see Shourds, Harry V.

Hillman, Bill W. Teaching with Confidence: How to Get off the Classroom Wall. (Illus.). 284p. 1981. 19.50 (ISBN 0-398-04103-2). C C Thomas.

Hillman, Harold H. Certainty & Uncertainty in Biochemical Techniques. 1972. 22.50x (ISBN 0-903384-00-0). Intl Ideas.

Hillman, Howard. Art of Winning Corporate Grants. LC 79-64398. (Art of Winning Grants Ser.). 1980. 8.95 (ISBN 0-8149-0822-5). Vanguard.

--The Art of Winning Government Grants. LC 77-75582. 1977. 8.95 (ISBN 0-8149-0784-9). Vanguard.

--The Art of Writing Business Reports & Proposals. (Illus.). 256p. 1981. 12.50 (ISBN 0-8149-0850-0). Vanguard.

--The Diner's Guide to Wine. LC 77-70119. Orig. Title: Art of Serving Wine with Food. (Illus.). 1978. pap. 5.95 o.p. (ISBN 0-8015-0416-3). Dutton.

--Hawaii at-a-Glance. LC 76-185131. (At-a-Glance Guides Ser). 1972. pap. 1.95 o.p. (ISBN 0-679-50132-0). McKay.

--New York at-a-Glance. 1971. pap. 2.50 o.p. (ISBN 0-679-50133-9). McKay.

Hillman, Howard & Abarbanel, Karin. The Art of Winning Foundation Grants. LC 75-387. 192p. 1975. 8.95 (ISBN 0-8149-0759-8). Vanguard.

Hillman, J. R., ed. Isolation of Plant Growth Substances. LC 77-83997. (Society for Experimental Biology Seminar Ser.: No. 4). (Illus.). 1978. 39.50 (ISBN 0-521-21866-7); pap. 13.95x (ISBN 0-521-29297-2). Cambridge U Pr.

Hillman, James. The Dream & the Underworld. LC 78-4733. 1979. 10.95 o.p. (ISBN 0-06-011902-0, HarpT). Har-Row.

--Insearch. (Jungian Classics). 1979. pap. 7.50 (ISBN 0-88214-501-0). Spring Pubns.

--Loose Ends: Primary Papers in Archetypal Psychology. 212p. 1975. pap. 8.50 (ISBN 0-88214-308-5). Spring Pubns.

--The Myth of Analysis. 1978. pap. 5.95 (ISBN 0-06-090600-6, CN 600, CN). Har-Row.

Hillman, James, jt. auth. see Von Franz, Marie-Louise.

Hillman, James, ed. An Annual of Archetypal Psychology & Jungian Thought. annual 304p. 1975. pap. 12.00 (ISBN 0-88214-010-8). Spring Pubns.

--Spring, Nineteen Seventy-Seven: An Annual of Archetypal Psychology & Jungian Thought. 1977. pap. 12.00 (ISBN 0-88214-012-4). Spring Pubns.

--Spring, Nineteen Seventy-Three: An Annual of Archetypal Psychology & Jungian Thought. annual 1973. pap. 12.00 o.p. (ISBN 0-88214-008-6). Spring Pubns.

Hillman, James, ed. see Christou, Evangelos.

Hillman, James, ed. see Corbin, et al.

Hillman, James, ed. see Guggenbuhl-Craig, Adolf.

Hillman, James, ed. see Hillman, et al.

Hillman, James, ed. see Kluger, Rivkah S.

Hillman, James, jt. ed. see Roscher, Wilhelm.

Hillman, James, ed. see Von Franz, M-L.

Hillman, James, ed. see Von Franz, Marie-Louise.

Hillman, James, ed. see Von Franz, Mary-Louise.

Hillman, James, et al. Puer Papers. (Dunquin Ser.). (Orig.). 1979. pap. 11.00 (ISBN 0-88214-310-7). Spring Pubns.

--Spring 1979: An Annual of Archetypal Psychology & Jungian Thought. 1979. pap. 10.00 (ISBN 0-88214-014-0). Spring Pubns.

Hillman, Jimmye S. & Schmitz, Andrew, eds. International Trade & Agriculture: Theory & Policy. (Special Studies in International Economics & Business). 1979. lib. bdg. 28.50 (ISBN 0-89158-498-6). Westview.

Hillman, Priscilla. A Merry-Mouse Book of Nursery Rhymes. LC 80-2053. (Illus.). 32p. (gr. k-1). 1981. 4.95a (ISBN 0-385-17102-1); PLB (ISBN 0-385-17103-X). Doubleday.

Hillman, Robin A. Multiple-Choice Questions in O Level Chemistry. 1971. pap. text ed. 3.95x o.p. (ISBN 0-435-64320-7); pap. text ed. 4.95x with ans. o.p. (ISBN 0-435-64321-5). Heinemann Ed.

Hillman, Robin A. & Cane, Michael C. Structured Questions in O Level Chemistry. 1973. pap. text ed. 3.95x o.p. (ISBN 0-435-64322-3). Heinemann Ed.

Hillman, Ruth E. Pieces of Christmas. (Illus.). 96p. (Orig.). 1975. pap. 0.75 (ISBN 0-8272-2923-2). Bethany Pr.

Hillmann, Michael C. Unity in the Ghazals of Hafez. LC 74-27614. (Studies in Middle Eastern Literatures: No. 6). 1976. 20.00x (ISBN 0-88297-010-0). Bibliotheca.

Hillmar, Ellis D., jt. auth. see Beck, Arthur C.

Hillmar, Ellis D., jt. auth. see Beck, Arthur C., Jr.

Hillner, K. P. Learning: A Conceptual Approach. 1977. text ed. 33.00 (ISBN 0-08-017864-2); pap. text ed. 13.25 (ISBN 0-08-017865-0). Pergamon.

Hillock, Wilfred M. Involved. LC 77-78102. (Anvil Ser.). 1977. pap. 7.95 (ISBN 0-8127-0140-2). Southern Pub.

Hillquit, Morris. Loose Leaves from a Busy Life. LC 78-146160. (Civil Liberties in American History Ser). 1971. Repr. of 1934 ed. lib. bdg. 35.00 (ISBN 0-306-70102-2). Da Capo.

Hills, A. Swedish-English-Swedish Pocket Dictionary. 1978. 7.50x (ISBN 0-89918-134-1, SW134). Vanous.

Hills, B. A. Decompression Sickness: The Biophysical Basis of Prevention & Treatment, Vol. 1. LC 76-55806. 1977. 49.00 (ISBN 0-471-99457-X, Pub. by Wiley-Interscience). Wiley.

--Gas Transfer in the Lung. (Monographs in Experimental Biology: No. 19). (Illus.). 200p. 1974. 38.50 (ISBN 0-521-20167-5). Cambridge U Pr.

Hills, C., ed. The Secrets of Spirulina. LC 80-22087. 1980. 6.95 (ISBN 0-916438-38-4). Univ of Trees.

Hills, C. A. The Fascist Dictatorships. 1979. 16.95 (ISBN 0-7134-0979-7, Pub. by Batsford England). David & Charles.

--The Hitler File. (Leaders Ser.). (Illus.). 96p. (gr. 9-12). 1980. 14.95 (ISBN 0-7134-1919-9, Pub. by Batsford England). David & Charles.

Hills, Car. The Danube. LC 78-62988. (Rivers of the World Ser.). (Illus.). 1978. lib. bdg. 7.95 (ISBN 0-686-50005-9). Silver.

--The Rhine. LC 78-62989. (Rivers of the World Ser.). (Illus.). 1978. lib. bdg. 7.95 (ISBN 0-686-50006-7). Silver.

Hills, Christopher. The Christ Book: What Did He Really Say? Hills, Norah, ed. LC 80-5865. (Illus.). 204p. 1980. text ed. 10.95 (ISBN 0-916438-37-6). Univ of Trees.

--Creative Conflict: Learning to Love with Total Honesty. Rozman, Deborah & Ray, Ann, eds. LC 80-5562. (Illus.). 324p. (Orig.). 1980. pap. 5.95 (ISBN 0-916438-36-8). Univ of Trees.

Hills, Christopher, ed. see Beasley, Victor.

Hills, D. A. Heat Transfer & Vulcanisation of Rubber. (Illus.). 1971. text ed. 22.30x (ISBN 0-444-20075-4, Pub. by Applied Science). Burgess-Intl Ideas.

Hills, Desmond B. Light for My Life. Van Dolson, Bobbie J., ed. 384p. (gr. 3-8). 1981. price not set (ISBN 0-8280-0041-7). Review & Herald.

Hills, G. S. Managing Corporate Meetings: A Legal & Procedural Guide. LC 75-35288. 1976. 42.95 (ISBN 0-8260-4121-3). Ronald Pr.

Hills, Gerald E., jt. auth. see Cravens, David W.

Hills, Ida. Shalom, My Love. (Orig.). 1981. pap. 1.50 (ISBN 0-440-17928-9). Dell.

Hills, John R. Measurement & Evaluation. 2nd ed. (Illus.). 480p. 1981. pap. text ed. 14.95 (ISBN 0-675-08044-4); instr's. manual 3.95 (ISBN 0-686-69495-3). Merrill.

--Measurement & Evaluation in Schools. (Illus.). 352p. 1976. pap. text ed. 13.95x (ISBN 0-675-08632-9); instructor's manual 3.95 (ISBN 0-686-67250-X). Merrill.

Hills, L. Rust & Hills, Penny C. How We Live. 1968. 12.50 o.s.i. (ISBN 0-02-551570-5). Macmillan.

Hills, Lawrence D. Comfrey: Fodder, Food & Remedy. LC 75-33485. (Illus.). 254p. 1976. 12.50x o.p. (ISBN 0-87663-273-8); pap. 5.95 (ISBN 0-87663-932-5). Universe.

--Comfrey Report. Rateaver, Bargyla & Rateaver, Gylver, eds. Bd. with Comfrey, the Herbal Healer. LC 75-23178. (Conservation Gardening & Farming Ser: Ser. C). 1975. pap. 6.00 (ISBN 0-9600698-9-5). Rateavers.

--Grow Your Own Fruit & Vegetables. 1974. 14.00 (ISBN 0-571-04830-7). Transatlantic.

Hills, M. T. & Eisenhart, E. J., eds. Ready Reference History of the English Bible. 6th ed. 1979. pap. 0.95 o.p. (ISBN 0-686-23172-4, 16228). United Bible.

Hills, Mathilda M. Time, Space & Structure in King Lear. (Salzburg Studies in English Literature, Jacobean Drama Studies: No. 64). (Orig.). 1976. pap. text ed. 25.00x (ISBN 0-391-01410-2). Humanities.

Hills, Michael. Statistics for Comparative Studies. LC 74-14542. 194p. 1974. pap. 10.95 o.p. (ISBN 0-470-39960-0). Halsted Pr.

Hills, Michael T. Telecommunications Switching Principles. (Illus.). 1979. text ed. 25.00x (ISBN 0-262-08092-3). MIT Pr.
Hills, Norah, ed. see Hills, Christopher.
Hills, P. J. The Self-Teaching Process in Higher Education. LC 75-44716. 1976. 15.95 (ISBN 0-470-15024-6). Halsted Pr.
Hills, P. J., ed. Aspects of Educational Technology XI: The Spread of Educational Technology. Gilbert, J. 1977. 32.50x (ISBN 0-85038-093-6, Pub by Kogan Pg). Nichols Pub.
Hills, Patricia. The Genre Painting of Eastman Johnson: The Sources & Development of His Styles & Themes. LC 76-23627. (Outstanding Dissertations in the Fine Arts - American). (Illus.). 1977. Repr. of 1973 ed. lib. bdg. 48.00 (ISBN 0-8240-2697-7). Garland Pub.
Hills, Patricia & Tarbell, Roberta K. The Figurative Tradition & the Whitney Museum of American Art: Paintings & Sculpture from the Permanent Collection. LC 80-12650. 192p. 1980. 25.00 (ISBN 0-87413-184-7). U Delaware Pr.
Hills, Penny C., jt. auth. see Hills, L. Rust.
Hills, Philip, ed. The Future of the Printed Word. LC 80-1716. 172p. 1980. lib. bdg. 25.00 (ISBN 0-313-22693-8, HIP/). Greenwood.
Hills, Phillip J. Teaching & Learning As a Communication Process. LC 79-1060. 1979. 15.95x (ISBN 0-470-26700-3). Halsted Pr.
Hills, Rust, ed. Writers Choice: Twenty American Authors Introduce Their Own Best Story. LC 74-82985. 416p. 1974. pap. text ed. 7.95x (ISBN 0-582-28132-6). Longman.
Hills, Sarah Jane, jt. auth. see Hills, Theo L.
Hills, Theo L. & Hills, Sarah Jane. Canada. rev. ed. LC 77-80448. (American Neighbors Ser.). (Illus.). 224p. (gr. 5 up). 1979. text ed. 9.95 1-4 copies, 5 or more copies 7.96 (ISBN 0-88296-090-3); tchrs'. guide 6.96 (ISBN 0-88296-353-8). Fideler.
Hills, Tynette, jt. auth. see Ross, Floyd H.
Hillway, Tyrus. Herman Melville. rev. ed. (United States Authors Ser.: No. 37). 1979. lib. bdg. 9.95 (ISBN 0-8057-7256-1). Twayne.
--Herman Melville. LC 78-11937. (Twayne's U. S. Authors Ser.). 177p. 1979. pap. text ed. 4.95 (ISBN 0-672-61504-5). Bobbs.
Hillyer, Norman, ed. see Spurgeon, Charles H.
Hillyer, Robert. First Principles of Verse. 1950. text ed. 8.95 (ISBN 0-87116-032-3). Writer.
Hillyer, Robert S. In Pursuit of Poetry. 1971. pap. 2.95 o.p. (ISBN 0-07-028923-9, SP). McGraw.
Hilowitz, Beverley, jt. ed. see Horizon Magazine.
Hilowitz, Beverly, ed. see Horizon Magazine Editors.
Hilpinen, Risto, ed. Scientific Rationality: Studies in the Foundations of Science & Ethics. (Philosophical Studies in Philosophy: No. 21). 247p. 1980. lib. bdg. 44.75 (ISBN 90-277-1112-7, Pub. by D. Reidel). Kluwer Boston.
Hilsum, S. & Cane, B. S. The Teacher's Day. (Research Report Ser.). 312p. 1971. text ed. 20.75x (ISBN 0-901225-78-9, NFER). Humanities.
Hilsum, S. & Strong, C. R. The Secondary Teacher's Day. (Research Report). (Illus.). 1978. pap. text ed. 25.50x (ISBN 0-85633-139-2, NFER). Humanities.
Hilsum, Sidney. The Teacher at Work. (Exploring Education Ser). 64p. (Orig.). 1972. pap. text ed. 3.75x (ISBN 0-901225-94-0, NFER). Humanities.
Hilsum, Sidney & Start, K. B. Promotion & Careers in Teaching. (Research Reports Ser.). 312p. 1974. text ed. 22.00x (ISBN 0-85633-043-4, NFER). Humanities.
Hilt, Douglas. Ten Against Napoleon. LC 75-9724. (Illus.). 224p. 1975. 13.95 (ISBN 0-88229-253-6). Nelson-Hall.
Hilt, Nancy E. & Cogburn, Shirley B. Manual of Orthopedics. LC 79-31732. (Illus.). 1979. text ed. 36.50 (ISBN 0-8016-2198-4). Mosby.
Hilt, Nancy E. & Schmitt, E. William, Jr. Pediatric Orthopedic Nursing. LC 74-13222. (Illus.). 1975. text ed. 16.95 (ISBN 0-8016-2188-7). Mosby.
Hilt, Robert. Die Varieties of Early United States Coins. 208p. 1980. 75.00x (ISBN 0-934904-08-1). J & L Lee.
Hiltebeitel, Alf. The Ritual of Battle: Krishna in the Mahabharata. LC 75-18496. 1975. 25.00x (ISBN 0-8014-0970-5). Cornell U Pr.
Hiltner, Seward, ed. Toward a Theology of Aging: A Special Issue of Pastoral Psychology. LC 74-19593. 1975. 12.95 (ISBN 0-87705-278-6); pap. 6.95 (ISBN 0-87705-287-5). Human Sci Pr.
Hilton, Anthony. Employee Reports: How to Communicate Financial Information to Employees. (Illus.). 200p. 1980. 29.95 (ISBN 0-85941-057-9). Herman Pub.
Hilton, Bruce. Highly Irregular: Biafran Relief Story. 1969. 5.95 o.s.i. (ISBN 0-02-551670-1); pap. 1.95 o.s.i. (ISBN 0-02-085490-0). Macmillan.
Hilton, Dale K., jt. auth. see Johnson, Margaret K.
Hilton, George W. The Ma & Pa. 2nd rev. ed. LC 80-19531. (Illus.). 210p. 1980. 12.95 (ISBN 0-8310-7127-3). Howell-North.
--Monon Route. LC 78-52512. (Illus.). 468p. 1978. Repr. of 1978 ed. 30.00 (ISBN 0-8310-7115-X). Howell-North.
Hilton, Gordon. Intermediate Politometrics. LC 74-43733. 336p. 1976. 17.00x (ISBN 0-231-03783-X). Columbia U Pr.
Hilton, Ian, tr. see Kohlschmidt, Werner.
Hilton, Jack. Quest for Carp. (Illus.). 188p. 1972. 14.00 (ISBN 0-7207-0582-7). Transatlantic.
Hilton, James. Lost Horizon. (Illus.). 1936. Repr. of 1922 ed. 10.95 (ISBN 0-688-02007-0). Morrow.
--Was It Murder? LC 75-44984. (Crime Fiction Ser). 1976. Repr. of 1935 ed. lib. bdg. 17.50 (ISBN 0-8240-2376-5). Garland Pub.
Hilton, Jennifer, jt. auth. see Hunt, Sonja.
Hilton, John. Catch That Catch Can. LC 75-87492. (Music Ser). 1970. Repr. of 1652 ed. lib. bdg. 17.50 (ISBN 0-306-71498-1). Da Capo.
Hilton, John B. Playground of Death. 224p. 1981. 9.95 (ISBN 0-312-61559-0). St Martin.
--Some Run Crooked. LC 77-10182. 1978. 7.95 o.p. (ISBN 0-312-74355-6). St Martin.
Hilton, Lewis B. Learning to Teach Through Playing: A Woodwind Method. (Music Ser). (Orig.). 1970. pap. text ed. 17.95 (ISBN 0-201-02850-6). A-W.
Hilton, P. J. Differential Calculus. (Library of Mathematics). 1968. pap. 5.00 (ISBN 0-7100-4341-4). Routledge & Kegan.
--Partial Derivatives. (Library of Mathematics). 1973. pap. 5.00 (ISBN 0-7100-4347-3). Routledge & Kegan.
Hilton, Peter. Lectures in Homological Algebra. LC 70-152504. (CBMS Regional Conference Series in Mathematics: No. 8). 1971. pap. 5.20 o.p. (ISBN 0-8218-1657-8, CBMS-8). Am Math.
Hilton, Peter & Wu, Yel-Chiang. A Course in Modern Algebra. LC 73-18043. (Pure & Applied Mathematics Ser). 272p. 1974. 29.95 (ISBN 0-471-39967-1, Pub. by Wiley-Interscience). Wiley.
Hilton, Peter J. General Cohomology Theory & K. Theory. (London Mathematics Society Lecture Note Ser.: No. 1). 1970. text ed. 11.95 (ISBN 0-521-07976-4). Cambridge U Pr.
--Introduction to Homotopy Theory. (Cambridge Tracts in Mathematics & Mathematical Physics: No. 43). 1953. 21.50 (ISBN 0-521-05265-3). Cambridge U Pr.
Hilton, Peter J. & Wylie, Shaun. Homology Theory. 1961. 59.50 (ISBN 0-521-05266-1); pap. 20.50x (ISBN 0-521-09422-4, 422). Cambridge U Pr.
Hilton, R. H. Peasants, Knights & Heretics. LC 76-1137. (Past & Present Publications Ser.). 320p. 1976. 29.95 (ISBN 0-521-21276-6). Cambridge U Pr.
Hilton, Stanley E. Brazil & the Great Powers, 1930-1939: The Politics of Trade Rivalry. (Latin American Monographs Ser.: No. 38). 304p. 1975. 12.95x (ISBN 0-292-70713-4). U of Tex Pr.
Hilton, Timothy. Picasso. (World of Art Ser.). (Illus.). 1975. pap. 9.95 (ISBN 0-19-519935-9). Oxford U Pr.
--Pre-Raphaelites. (World of Art Ser.). (Illus.). 1977. pap. 9.95 (ISBN 0-19-519929-4). Oxford U Pr.
Hilton, W. S. Industrial Relations in Construction. 1969. 22.00 (ISBN 0-08-013040-2); pap. 10.75 (ISBN 0-08-013039-9). Pergamon.
Hilton, Wendy. Dance of Court & Theatre: The French Noble Style 1690-1725. LC 78-70248. (Illus.). 1981. 35.00 (ISBN 0-916622-09-6). Princeton Bk Co.
Hilts, Len. The Home Electrician's Bible. (Illus.). 160p. 1976. pap. 2.95 o.p. (ISBN 0-385-11234-3). Doubleday.
Hiltz, Starr R. Creating Community Services for Widows: A Pilot Project. LC 76-18292. 1977. 12.95 (ISBN 0-8046-9157-6). Kennikat.
Hiltz, Starr R. & Turoff, Murray. Network Nation: Human Communication Via Computer. 1978. text ed. 34.50 (ISBN 0-201-03140-X, Adv Bk Prog); pap. text ed. 22.50 (ISBN 0-201-03141-8). A-W.
Him, G., jt. auth. see Ward, Dennis.
Himber, Jane A., jt. auth. see Robins, Alan.
Himden, Michael. Byrd Thou Never Wert: The Collected Poems & Post Cards of Emmett Byrd. LC 80-65365. 1980. pap. 4.95 (ISBN 0-89815-023-X). Ten Speed Pr.
Hime, Malcolm. Handbook of Diseases of Laboratory Animals. 1979. pap. text ed. 32.00 (ISBN 0-433-14723-7). Intl Ideas.
Himes, Chester. If He Hollers, Let Him Go. 1971. pap. 0.95 (ISBN 0-451-04846-6, Q4846, Sig). NAL.
Himes, Ellvert H. Growing in the Priesthood: Messages of Inspiration & Motivation with Personal Records of Fulfillment. LC 75-17103. (Illus.). 128p. 1975. 5.95 (ISBN 0-88290-052-8). Horizon Utah.
Himes, Joseph S. Conflict & Conflict Management. LC 78-32164. 342p. 1980. 23.00x (ISBN 0-8203-0473-5); pap. 9.00 (ISBN 0-8203-0509-X). U of Ga Pr.
Himmelblau, David M. Basic Principles & Calculations in Chemical Engineering. 3rd ed. (P-H Int'l Series in Physical & Chemical Engineering Sciences). (Illus.). 544p. 1974. ref. ed. 27.95 (ISBN 0-13-066472-3). P-H.
--Process Analysis & Simulation: Deterministic Systems. (Illus.). 333p. 1980. pap. text ed. 29.95 (ISBN 0-88408-132-X). Sterling Swift.
--Process Analysis by Statistical Methods. (Illus.). 471p. 1981. pap. text ed. 29.95 (ISBN 0-88408-140-0). Sterling Swift.
Himmelfarb, Gertrude, ed. see Mill, John S.
Himmelfarb, Milton & Baras, Victor, eds. Zero Population Growth--For Whom? Differential Fertility & Minority Group Survival. LC 77-87966. (Contributions in Sociology: No. 30). (Illus.). 1978. lib. bdg. 22.50x (ISBN 0-313-20041-6, AJC/). Greenwood.
Himmelheber, Georg. Biedermeier Furniture. LC 74-29024. 1975. 30.00 o.p. (ISBN 0-684-14132-9, ScribT). Scribner.
--Biedermeier Furniture. 1974. 48.00 (ISBN 0-571-08719-1, Pub. by Faber & Faber). Merrimack Bk Serv.
Himmelstein, Jack, jt. auth. see Dvorkin, Elizabeth.
Himstreet & Baty. Plaid for Business Communications. 1976. pap. 5.50 (ISBN 0-256-01769-7, 12-1175-00). Learning Syst.
--Plaid for Business Communications. rev. ed. 1981. price not set (ISBN 0-256-02720-X, 12-1175-02). Learning Syst. Postponed.
Himstreet, William C. & Baty, Wayne M. Business Communications: Principles & Methods. 5th ed. 1977. 18.95x (ISBN 0-534-00476-8). Wadsworth Pub.
Himsworth, Daniel C., jt. ed. see McNeil, William J.
Hinchcliffe, A. J., jt. auth. see Cradock, S.
Hinchcliffe, Arnold P. Harold Pinter. (English Authors Ser.: No. 51). lib. bdg. 9.95 (ISBN 0-8057-1448-0). Twayne.
Hinchcliffe, Mary K., et al. The Melancholy Marriage: Depression in Marriage & Psychosocial Approaches to Therapy. LC 78-4526. 1978. 23.95 (ISBN 0-471-99650-5, Pub. by Wiley-Interscience). Wiley.
Hinchey, F. A. Vectors & Tensors for Engineers & Scientists. LC 76-21725. 1976. 13.95 (ISBN 0-470-15194-3). Halsted Pr.
Hinchey, Fred A. Introduction to Applicable Mathematics: Elementary Analysis, Vol. 1. LC 80-18569. 290p. 1981. 19.95 (ISBN 0-470-27041-1). Halsted Pr.
Hinchiffe, A. P., ed. see Eliot, T. S.
Hinchliffe, Arnold P. Harold Pinter. rev. ed. (English Authors Ser.: No. 51). 1981. lib. bdg. 9.95 (ISBN 0-8057-6784-3). Twayne.
Hinchliffe, Arnold P., jt. ed. see Cox, C. B.
Hinchman, Lydia S., compiled by. The Early Settlers of Nantucket: Sixteen Fifty-Nine to Eighteen Fifty. LC 80-54078. (Illus.). 346p. 1981. Repr. of 1926 ed. 35.00 (ISBN 0-8048-1354-X). C E Tuttle.
Hinck, Henry W. Three Studies on Charles Robert Maturin. Varma, Devendra P., ed. LC 79-8458. (Gothic Studies & Dissertations Ser.). 1980. lib. bdg. 19.00x (ISBN 0-405-12647-6). Arno.
Hinckle, Warren & Turner, William. The Fish Is Red: The Story of the Secret War Against Castro. 288p. 1981. 12.95 (ISBN 0-8129-0908-9). Times Bks.
Hinckley, Barbara. Outline of American Government: The Continuing Experiment. (Illus.). 288p. 1981. pap. 7.95 (ISBN 0-13-645200-0). P-H.
Hinckley, Gordon B. Truth Restored. 168p. 1979. pap. 1.50 (ISBN 0-87747-765-5). Deseret Bk.
Hinckley, Helen. The Land & People of Iran. rev. ed. LC 70-37733. (Portraits of the Nations Series). (Illus.). 1973. 8.79 (ISBN 0-397-31202-4). Lippincott.
Hinckley, Thomas K. Transcontinental Rails. LC 71-43562. (Wild & Woolly West Ser., No. 12). (Illus., Orig.). 1969. 7.00 (ISBN 0-910584-92-3); pap. 2.00 (ISBN 0-910584-13-3). Filter.
Hind, Arthur M. Catalogue of Rembrandt's Etchings 2 Vols. 2nd ed. LC 67-27456. (Graphic Art Ser). 1967. Repr. of 1923 ed. lib. bdg. 35.00 (ISBN 0-306-70977-5). Da Capo.
--History of Engraving & Etching: From the Fifteenth Century to the Year 1914. 3rd ed. (Illus.). 1923. pap. text ed. 6.00 (ISBN 0-486-20954-7). Dover.
Hind, J. Anthony. Stability & Trim of Fishing Vessels. (Illus.). 120p. 9.50 (FN). Unipub.
Hinde, Cecilia H. Floury Fingers. (Illus.). 1962. 5.95 (ISBN 0-571-04522-7, Pub. by Faber & Faber); pap. 1.95 o.p. (ISBN 0-571-09075-3). Merrimack Bk Serv.
--Time for Tea. (Illus., Orig.). 1973. pap. 5.95 (ISBN 0-686-24627-6, Pub. by Faber & Faber). Merrimack Bk Serv.
--Your Book of Breadmaking. (Your Book Ser.). (Illus.). 1977. 6.95 (ISBN 0-571-10641-2, Pub. by Faber & Faber). Merrimack Bk Serv.
Hinde, R. A., ed. Bird Vocalizations: Their Relation to Current Problems in Biology & Psychology. (Illus.). 1969. 72.00 (ISBN 0-521-07409-6). Cambridge U Pr.
--Non-Verbal Communication. LC 75-171675. (Illus.). 464p. 1972. 47.50 (ISBN 0-521-08370-2); pap. 14.95x (ISBN 0-521-29012-0). Cambridge U Pr.
Hinde, R. A., jt. ed. see Bateson, P. P.
Hinde, R. A., jt. ed. see Horn, G.
Hinde, Thomas. Games of Chance. LC 66-29207. (Two complete novels). 1966. 8.95 (ISBN 0-8149-0119-0). Vanguard.
--Our Father. LC 75-43649. 351p. (Orig.). 1976. 8.95 o.p. (ISBN 0-8076-0821-1). Braziller.
Hindell, Keith, jt. auth. see Simms, Madeleine.
Hindemith, Paul. A Composer's World: Horizons & Limitations. 7.50 (ISBN 0-8446-0697-9). Peter Smith.
Hinderschiedt, Ingeborg. Zur Helian Dmetrick: Das Verhaltnis Von Rhythmus und Satzewicht Im Altsachsischen. (German Language & Literature Monographs: No. 8). 143p. 1980. text ed. 20.00x (ISBN 90-272-4001-9). Humanities.
Hindess, Barry & Hirst, Paul. Pre-Capitalist Modes of Production. 1975. 28.00x (ISBN 0-7100-8168-5). Routledge & Kegan.
Hindess, Barry & Hirst, Paul Q. Pre-Capitalist Modes of Production. 1977. pap. 11.00 (ISBN 0-7100-8169-3). Routledge & Kegan.
Hindle, Brooke. Emulation & Invention. (The Anson G. Phelps Lectureship Ser. on Early American History). (Illus.). 224p. 1981. text ed. 19.50x (ISBN 0-8147-3409-X). NYU Pr.
Hindle, John H., jt. auth. see Feldman, Harold.
Hindle, John J., jt. ed. see Young, Thomas D.
Hindley, Charles. History of the Catnach Press. LC 67-27867. 1969. Repr. of 1887 ed. 20.00 (ISBN 0-8103-3259-0). Gale.
--History of the Cries of London. LC 67-23948. 1969. Repr. of 1884 ed. 15.00 (ISBN 0-8103-0156-3). Gale.
--Life & Times of James Catnach, Late of Seven Dials, Ballad Monger. LC 68-20122. 1968. Repr. of 1878 ed. 24.00 (ISBN 0-8103-3412-7). Gale.
Hindley, Donald. The Communist Party of Indonesia, 1951-1963. 1964. 24.50x (ISBN 0-520-00561-9). U of Cal Pr.
Hindley, Judy & Rumbelow, Donald. The Know How Book of Detection. LC 78-59661. (Know How Books). (gr. 4-5). 1978. text ed. 6.95 (ISBN 0-88436-532-8). EMC.
Hindley, Patricia, et al. The Tangled Net: Basic Issues in Canadian Communications. LC 78-311500. 198p. 1980. pap. 7.95 (ISBN 0-295-95773-5, Pub. by Douglas & McIntyre Canada). U of Wash Pr.
Hindman, Darwin A. Eighteen-Hundred Riddles, Enigmas & Conundrums. (Orig.). (gr. 4 up). 1963. pap. 2.50 (ISBN 0-486-21059-6). Dover.
Hindmarsh, J. Electrical Machines & Their Applications. LC 79-20595. (Illus.). 800p. (Arabic.). 1981. pap. 20.00 (ISBN 0-08-026158-2). Pergamon.
Hinds, Lennox S. Illusions of Justice. LC 79-19318. 432p. (Orig.). 1979. pap. 6.50 (ISBN 0-934936-00-5). U of Iowa Sch Soc Wk.
Hinds, Marjorie M. How to Make Money Writing Short Articles & Fillers. 1967. 6.95 o.s.i. (ISBN 0-8119-0097-5). Fell.
Hinds, Shirley, jt. auth. see Bolian, Polly.
Hindus, Michael S. Prison & Plantation: Crime, Justice, & Authority in Massachusetts & South Carolina, 1767-1878. LC 79-19493. (Studies in Legal History). (Illus.). 1980. 20.00x (ISBN 0-8078-1417-2). U of NC Pr.
Hindus, Michael S., et al. The Files of the Massachusetts Superior Court, 1859-1959: An Analysis & a Plan for Action. (Reference Publications Ser.). 1980. lib. bdg. 50.00 (ISBN 0-8161-9037-2). G K Hall.
Hindus, Milton, ed. Walt Whitman: The Critical Heritage. 1971. 27.00x (ISBN 0-7100-7087-X). Routledge & Kegan.
Hine, Al, ed. This Land Is Mine: An Anthology of American Verse. LC 65-13437. (Illus.). (gr. 7-9). 1965. 8.95 o.p. (ISBN 0-397-30840-X). Lippincott.
Hine, Daryl. Selected Poems. LC 80-68135. 144p. 1981. 10.95 (ISBN 0-689-11117-7); pap. 6.95 (ISBN 0-689-11118-5). Atheneum.
Hine, J. & Wetherill, G. B. A Programmed Text in Statistics. Incl. Bk. 1. Summarizing Data. 95p. pap. text ed. 10.95x o.p. (ISBN 0-412-13590-6); Bk. 3. The t-Test & Goodness of Fit. 53p. pap. text ed. 10.95x o.p. (ISBN 0-412-13740-2); Bk. 4. Tests on Variance & Regression. 69p. pap. text ed. 10.95x o.p. (ISBN 0-412-13750-X). (Orig.). 1975 (Pub. by Chapman & Hall). Methuen Inc.

--A Programmed Text in Statistics. Incl. Bk 1. Summarizing Data. 104p. pap. text ed. 8.95x o.p. (ISBN 0-470-40040-4); Bk. 2. Basic Theory. 116p. pap. text ed. o.p. (ISBN 0-470-40041-2); Bk 3. The T-Test & Goodness of Fit. 56p. pap. text ed. 7.50 o.p. (ISBN 0-470-40042-0); Bk. 4. Tests on Variance & Regression. 76p. pap. text ed. 8.95x o.p. (ISBN 0-686-10589-3). (Orig.). 1975. Halsted Pr.

Hine, James R. Will We Meet Each Other's Needs? 1979. pap. text ed. 7.50 (ISBN 0-8134-2052-0, 2052). Interstate.

Hine, Lewis. Women at Work: One Hundred Fifty Photographs by Lewis Hine. (Illus.). 128p. (Orig.). 1981. pap. price not set (ISBN 0-486-24154-8). Dover.

Hine, Maynard K. & Phillips, Ralph W. Review of Dentistry: Questions & Answers. 7th ed. LC 78-15590. 1979. pap. text ed. 19.95 (ISBN 0-8016-2197-6). Mosby.

Hine, Robert V. Community on the American Frontier: Separate but Not Alone. LC 80-5238. (Illus.). 300p. 1980. 12.50 (ISBN 0-8061-1678-1). U of Okla Pr.

Hine, Virginia H., jt. auth. see Gerlach, Luther P.

Hines, A. G. On the Reappraisal of Keynesian Economics. 85p. 1972. pap. 7.95x (ISBN 0-85520-004-9, Pub. by Martin Robertson England). Biblio Dist.

Hines, Barry & Stronach, Allan. Kes: A Play of the Novel. 1976. pap. text ed. 2.95x (ISBN 0-435-23500-1). Heinemann Ed.

Hines, Benjamin M. Hines & Allied Families. LC 80-67479. 360p. 1981. 25.00 (ISBN 0-8059-2748-4). Dorrance.

Hines, Henry & Morgenstern, Carol. Quick Tennis: The Professional's Method for Quickness, Mobility, & Court Control--the Secret Ingredient in Winning Tennis. LC 77-3402. 1977. pap. 4.95 o.p. (ISBN 0-525-04275-X). Dutton.

Hines, Jeanne. The Keys to Queenscourt. 1976. pap. 1.75 o.p. (ISBN 0-445-08508-8). Popular Lib.

--The Legend of Witchwynd. 256p. 1976. pap. 1.25 o.p. (ISBN 0-445-00420-7). Popular Lib.

Hines, Mary A. Principles & Practices of Real Estate. 1976. text ed. 17.95 (ISBN 0-256-01845-6); student workbook 5.25 (ISBN 0-256-01855-3). Irwin.

--Real Estate Finance. LC 77-13003. (Illus.). 1978. ref. 18.95 (ISBN 0-13-762724-6). P-H.

Hines, Millie, ed. Crafty Ideas for the Home. (Illus.). 96p. (Orig.). 1980. pap. 2.00 (ISBN 0-918178-20-7). Simplicity.

--Easy Ways to Decorate Your Kitchen. (Illus.). 96p. (Orig.). 1981. pap. 2.00 (ISBN 0-918178-24-X). Simplicity.

Hines, Neal O. Denny's Knoll: A History of the Metropolitan Tract of the University of Washington. LC 79-6760. (Illus.). 480p. 1980. 14.95 (ISBN 0-295-95718-2). U of Wash Pr.

Hines, R. D., jt. auth. see Jensen, C. H.

Hines, Robert S., jt. auth. see Trubitt, Allen R.

Hines, Theodore C., jt. auth. see Regazzi, John J.

Hines, William W. & Montgomery, Douglas C. Introduction to Probability & Statistics in Engineering & Management Science. 2nd ed. LC 79-26257. 1980. text ed. 22.95 (ISBN 0-471-04759-7); write for info. solutions manual (ISBN 0-471-05006-7). Wiley.

Hing, Ester. Characteristics of Nursing Home Residents Health Status, & Care Received: National Nursing Home Survey, May-December 1977. Cox, Klaudia, ed. 60p. 1981. pap. 1.95 (ISBN 0-8406-0212-X). Natl Ctr Health Stats.

Hingley, Marjorie. Field-Work Projects in Biology. (Illus.). 176p. 1980. 11.95 o.p. (ISBN 0-7137-0964-2, Pub by Blandford Pr England). Sterling.

Hingley, Ronald, ed. & tr. see Chekhov, Anton.

Hingley, Ronald, ed. see Chekhov, Anton.

Hingley, Ronald, tr. see Chekhov, Anton.

Hingorani, A. T., ed. see Gandhi, Mohandas K.

Hingorani, Anand T., ed. see Gandhi, Mohandas K.

Hingorani, Anand T., ed. see Ghandhi, Mohandas K.

Hingorani, R. C. Indian Extradition Law. 10.00x (ISBN 0-210-98127-X). Asia.

Hingson, Ralph, et al. In Sickness & in Health: Social Dimensions of Medical Care. 300p. 1981. pap. text ed. 12.50 (ISBN 0-8016-4411-9). Mosby.

Hinich, Melvin J. & Staelin, Richard. Consumer Protection Legislation & the Food Industry. (Policy Studies). 1980. text ed. 16.25 (ISBN 0-08-025093-9). Pergamon.

Hinkemeyer, Michael. Harbinger. (Orig.). 1980. pap. write for info. (ISBN 0-671-82179-2). PB.

Hinkemeyer, Michael T. Summer Solstice. (Orig.). 1980. pap. 2.50 o.p. (ISBN 0-425-04706-7). Berkley Pub.

--Summer Solstice. LC 75-33587. (YA) 1976. 7.95 o.p. (ISBN 0-399-11645-1, Dist. by Putnam). Berkley Pub.

Hinkle, Bliss M., ed. see McGlashan, Charles F.

Hinkle, George H., ed. see McGlashan, Charles F.

Hinkle, Lawrence E., Jr., jt. ed. see Nelson, Norton.

Hinkle, Vernon. Music to Murder by. 1978. pap. 1.75 (ISBN 0-505-51262-9). Tower Bks.

Hinkley, D. H., jt. ed. see Fienberg, S. E.

Hinkley, James W. The Book of Vampires. (Easy-Read Fact Bks.). (Illus.). (gr. 2-4). 1979. PLB 6.45 s&l (ISBN 0-531-02276-5). Watts.

Hinman, Bob. The Duck Hunter's Handbook. 1974. 11.95 (ISBN 0-87691-146-7). Winchester Pr.

Hinman, Charlton, ed. see Shakespeare, William.

Hinman, Frank, Jr. Hydrodynamics of Micturition. (Illus.). 436p. 1971. 36.25 (ISBN 0-398-00839-6). C C Thomas.

Hinman, P. G. Recursion-Theoretic Hierarchies. (Perspectives in Mathematical Logic). 1977. 46.20 (ISBN 0-387-07904-1). Springer-Verlag.

Hinman, Sukit & Bolton, Brian. Factor Analytic Studies: 1941-1975, 5 vols. Set. 32.50 (ISBN 0-686-64136-1). Whitston Pub.

Hinmon, Nelson E. An Answer to Humanistic Psychology. LC 80-81890. 144p. 1980. pap. text ed. 3.95 (ISBN 0-89081-259-4). Harvest Hse.

Hinnant, Charles H. Thomas Hobbes. (English Authors Ser.: No. 215). 1977. lib. bdg. 9.95 (ISBN 0-8057-6684-7). Twayne.

Hinnebusch, Paul. Community in the Lord. LC 75-14741. 240p. 1975. pap. 3.50 o.p. (ISBN 0-87793-099-6). Ave Maria.

--St. Matthew's Earthquake: Judgement & Discipleship in the Gospel of Matthew. 154p. (Orig.). 1980. pap. 3.95 (ISBN 0-89283-093-X). Servant.

Hinnebusch, Thomas J & Mirza, Sarah M. Swahili: A Foundation for Speaking, Reading & Writing. LC 78-65430. (Illus., English & Swahili). 1978. pap. 10.50 (ISBN 0-8191-0659-3). U Pr of Amer.

Hinnels, J. R., ed. Mithraic Studies, 2 vols. (Illus.). 1975. Set. 52.50x o.p. (ISBN 0-87471-557-1). Rowman.

Hinojosa, Rolando. Estampas del Valle. new ed. 1978. 7.50 (ISBN 0-915808-26-9); pap. 4.50 (ISBN 0-685-87637-3). Editorial Justa.

Hinojosa, Santiago N., jt. auth. see Hardgrave, Robert L., Jr.

Hinrichs, Roy S. Measuring. LC 80-67036. (Industrial Arts Ser.). 96p. 1981. pap. 4.60 (ISBN 0-8273-1916-9). Delmar.

Hinrup, Hans J. An Index to 'Chinese Literature' (Scandinavian Institute of Asian Studies Monographs: No. 38). 1978. pap. text ed. 15.75x (ISBN 0-7007-0122-2). Humanities.

Hinshaw. Domestic Goals in an Interdependent World: The Frankfurt Dialogue. Date not set. 25.00 (ISBN 0-8247-6999-6). Dekker.

Hinshaw, H. Corwin & Murray, Johhn F. Diseases of the Chest. 4th ed. LC 77-16975. (Illus.). 1044p. 1980. text ed. 46.00 (ISBN 0-7216-4697-2). Saunders.

Hinshaw, Robert, ed. Currents in Anthropology: Essays in Honor of Sol Tax. 1979. text ed. 88.25x (ISBN 90-279-7758-5). Mouton.

Hinshelwood, R. D. & Manning, Nick, eds. Therapeutic Communities. 1979. 26.00x (ISBN 0-7100-0109-6); pap. 14.00 (ISBN 0-7100-0108-8). Routledge & Kegan.

Hinsley, Charles M., Jr. Savages & Scientists: The Smithsonian Institution & the Development of American Anthropology, 1846-1910. (Illus.). 225p. 1980. text ed. 15.00x (ISBN 0-87474-518-7). Smithsonian.

Hinsley, Curtis M., Jr. Savages & Scientists: The Smithsonian Institution & the Development of American Anthropology 1846-1910. (Illus.). 326p. 1981. text ed. 17.50x (ISBN 0-87474-518-7). Smithsonian.

Hinsley, F. H., ed. British Foreign Policy Under Sir Edward Grey. LC 76-19631. 1977. 93.00 (ISBN 0-521-21347-9). Cambridge U Pr.

Hinsley, F. H., et al. British Intelligence in the Second World War: Its Influence on Strategy & Operations, Vol. I. LC 79-87703. 1979. 29.95 (ISBN 0-521-22940-5). Cambridge U Pr.

Hinsley, Francis H. Power & the Pursuit of Peace. (Orig.). 1968. 31.50 (ISBN 0-521-05274-2); pap. 13.95x (ISBN 0-521-09448-8). Cambridge U Pr.

Hinson, Dolores A. A Second Quilter's Companion. LC 80-17912. (Illus.). 288p. 1980. 12.95 (ISBN 0-668-04924-3, 4924-3). Arco.

Hinson, E. Glenn, ed. Doubleday Devotional Classics, Vol. 1. LC 77-16923. 1978. pap. 4.95 o.p. (ISBN 0-385-13424-X, Galilee). Doubleday.

--Doubleday Devotional Classics, Vol. 2. LC 77-16923. 1978. pap. 5.95 o.p. (ISBN 0-385-13425-8). Doubleday.

--Doubleday Devotional Classics, Vol. 3. LC 77-16923. 1978. pap. 3.95 o.p. (ISBN 0-385-13426-6, Galilee). Doubleday.

Hinson, Marilyn M. Kinesiology. 2nd ed. 336p. 1981. text ed. write for info. (ISBN 0-697-07173-1). Wm C Brown.

Hinson, Maurice. Piano in Chamber Ensemble: An Annotated Guide. LC 77-9862. 1978. 19.50x (ISBN 0-253-34493-X). Ind U Pr.

Hinton, Charles H. Speculations on the Fourth Dimension: Selected Writings of C. H. Hinton. Rucker, Rudolf V., ed. (Illus.). 1980. pap. 4.00 (ISBN 0-486-23916-0). Dover.

Hinton, David A. A Catalogue of the Anglo-Saxon Ornamental Metalwork 700-1100 in the Department of Antiquities, Ashmolean Museum. (Illus.). 140p. 1974. 30.50x o.p. (ISBN 0-19-813187-9). Oxford U Pr.

Hinton, David B. The Films of Leni Riefenstahl. LC 78-7036. 1978. 10.00 (ISBN 0-8108-1141-3). Scarecrow.

Hinton, Edward M. Ireland Through Tudor Eyes. 111p. 1980. Repr. of 1935 ed. lib. bdg. 22.50 (ISBN 0-89987-362-6). Darby Bks.

Hinton, H. E. Biology of Insect Eggs, 3 vols. LC 77-30390. (Illus.). 1500p. 1980. Set. 350.00 (ISBN 0-08-021539-4). Pergamon.

Hinton, Harold C. The People's Republic of China: A Handbook. (Illus.). 1979. lib. bdg. 30.00x (ISBN 0-89158-419-6, Dawson). Westview.

--Three & A Half Powers: The New Balance in Asia. LC 74-17565. (Midland Bks.: No. 184). 320p. 1975. 15.00x (ISBN 0-253-36013-7); pap. 3.95x (ISBN 0-253-20184-5). Ind U Pr.

Hinton, Harold C., ed. The People's Republic of China, Nineteen Forty-Nine to Nineteen Seventy-Nine: A Documentary Survey, 5 vols. LC 80-5228. 3000p. 1980. Set. lib. bdg. 295.00 (ISBN 0-8420-2166-3). Scholarly Res Inc.

Hinton, John. Dying. rev. ed. (Orig.). 1967. pap. 2.95 o.p. (ISBN 0-14-020866-6, Pelican). Penguin.

Hinton, Nigel. Collision Course. (YA) 1980. pap. 1.50 (ISBN 0-440-91367-5, LFL). Dell.

Hinton, Thomas B. & Weigand, Phil C., eds. Themes of Indigenous Acculturation in Northwest Mexico. (Anthropological Papers: No. 38). 1981. pap. text ed. 7.95x (ISBN 0-8165-0324-9). U of Ariz Pr.

Hinton, W. Elmer, Jr. A Manual of Arms, a Practical Guide to the Heraldic Art. LC 79-55379. (Illus., Orig.). Date not set. pap. 4.99 (ISBN 0-935426-00-0). Gamesmasters.

Hinton Of Bankside, Lord. Development of Heavy Current Electricity in the United Kingdom. 1978. text ed. 15.00 (ISBN 0-08-023246-9); pap. text ed. 7.00 (ISBN 0-08-023247-7). Pergamon.

Hintz, Martin. Circus Workin's. LC 80-19784. (Illus.). 96p. (gr. 4-6). 1980. PLB 7.79 (ISBN 0-671-34006-9). Messner.

Hintz, Martin, jt. auth. see Hintz, Sandy.

Hintz, O. S. Fisherman's Paradise. LC 75-322904. 1979. 9.95 (ISBN 0-370-10486-2, Pub. by Chatto Bodley Jonathan). Merrimack Bk Serv.

Hintz, Sandy & Hintz, Martin. We Can't Afford It. LC 76-46433. (Interaction 2 Ser). (Illus.). (gr. k-3). 1977. PLB 7.95 o.p. (ISBN 0-8172-0066-5, Raintree Editions). Raintree Pubs.

Hintzman, Douglas L. The Psychology of Learning & Memory. LC 77-16295. (Psychology Ser.). (Illus.). 1978. text ed. 18.95x (ISBN 0-7167-0035-2). W H Freeman.

Hinwood, Tony. Advertising Art. 16.95 (ISBN 0-7153-5694-1). David & Charles.

Hinz, Earl. Sail Before Sunset. (Illus.). 244p. 1979. 12.95 (ISBN 0-679-51350-7). Western Marine Ent.

Hinz, Earl R. Landfalls of Paradise: The Guide to Pacific Islands. LC 79-17600. (Illus.). 384p. 1980. 29.95 (ISBN 0-930030-13-3). Western Marine Ent.

Hinz, Evelyn, ed. A Woman Speaks: The Lectures, Seminars, & Interviews of Anais Nin. LC 75-15111. 270p. 1975. 13.95x (ISBN 0-8040-0693-8); pap. 6.95x (ISBN 0-8040-0694-6). Swallow.

Hinz, Evelyn J. The Mirror & the Garden: Realism & Reality in the Writings of Anais Nin. LC 73-4979. 127p. 1973. pap. 2.45 o.p. (ISBN 0-15-660500-7, HB259, Harv). HarBraceJ.

Hioki, Kojiro, jt. auth. see Seiler, Hansjakob.

Hionides, Harry T. Paisius Ligarides. (World Authors Ser.: Greece: No. 240). lib. bdg. 10.95 (ISBN 0-8057-2536-9). Twayne.

--Yannis Manglis. LC 74-31099. (World Authors Ser.: Greece: No. 350). 1975. lib. bdg 10.95 (ISBN 0-8057-2578-4). Twayne.

Hiorns. Demographic Patterns in Developed Societies. (Symposia Ser.: Vol. 12). 216p. 1980. text ed. 26.00x (ISBN 0-85066-173-0). Humanities.

Hip Society. The Hip Society: The Hip, 8 vols. Incl. Vol. 1. 1973. text ed. 25.00 (ISBN 0-8016-0019-7); Vol. 2. 1974. text ed. 35.00 (ISBN 0-8016-0020-0); Vol. 3. 332p. 1975. text ed. 39.50 (ISBN 0-8016-0035-9); Vol. 4. Evarts, C. M., ed. 1976. text ed. 32.50 (ISBN 0-8016-0036-7); Vol. 5. 1977. text ed. 34.50 (ISBN 0-8016-0038-3); Vol. 6. 1978. text ed. 34.50 (ISBN 0-8016-0041-3); Vol. 7. 1979. text ed. 39.50 (ISBN 0-8016-0033-2); Vol. 8. 336p. 1980. text ed. 44.50 (ISBN 0-8016-0049-9). LC 73-7515. (Illus.). Mosby.

Hipona, Florencio A. X-Ray Case Studies. 1974. spiral bdg. 13.75 (ISBN 0-87488-026-2). Med Exam.

Hipona, Florencio A., jt. auth. see Shapiro, Jerome H.

Hippchen, Leonard. Holistic Approaches to Offender Rehabilitation. 400p. 1981. price not set (ISBN 0-398-04448-1). C C Thomas.

Hippel, Arndt Von see Von Hippel, Arndt.

Hipple, John & Cimbolic, Peter. The Counselor & Suicidal Crisis: Diagnosis & Intervention. 136p. 1979. text ed. 11.50 (ISBN 0-398-03872-4). C C Thomas.

Hipple, Theodore W., ed. Stories from Around the World. (Literature Ser.). (gr. 7-12). 1979. pap. text ed. 5.88 (ISBN 0-205-06418-3, 4964187); tchrs'. guide 2.96 (ISBN 0-205-06419-1, 4964195). Allyn.

Hipple, Theodore W. & Wright, Robert G., eds. The Worlds of Science Fiction. (Literature Ser.). (gr. 7-12). 1979. pap. text ed. 5.88 (ISBN 0-205-06416-7, 4964160); tchrs'. ed. 2.96 (ISBN 0-685-63615-1). Allyn.

Hippler, Arthur E. & Wood, John R. The Subarctic Athabascans: A Selected Bibliography. LC 74-620010. (Joint Institute of Social & Economic Research, Univ. of Alaska Publ. Ser.: No. 39). 360p. 1974. pap. 15.00 (ISBN 0-295-95362-4). U of Wash Pr.

Hipsher, Edward E. American Opera & Its Composers. LC 77-25413. (Music Reprint Ser., 1978). (Illus.). 1978. Repr. of 1927 ed. lib. bdg. 35.00 (ISBN 0-306-77516-6). Da Capo.

Hirai, Tomio. Zen & the Mind: A Scientific Approach to Zen Practice. (Illus., Orig.). 1978. 9.95 (ISBN 0-87040-391-5). Japan Pubns.

Hirano, Asao. A Guide to Neuropathology. LC 80-83980. (Illus.). 1981. 60.00. Igaku-Shoin.

Hirano, Asao, jt. auth. see Malamud, Nathan.

Hirano, Asao, jt. auth. see Matsui, Takayoshi.

Hirano, Asao, et al. Color Atlas of Pathology of the Nervous System. LC 80-81620. (Illus.). 222p. 1980. 74.00 (ISBN 0-89640-045-X). Igaku Shoin.

Hirayama, T., ed. see Yashiro, Nobutaka.

Hirchter, Gertrude, tr. see Friedman, Alexander Z.

Hird. Introduction to Photo-Offset Lithography. 1981. text ed. price not set (ISBN 0-87002-336-5). Bennett Co.

Hird, Gladys. Swedish. 2nd ed. LC 78-74534. 1980. 18.95x (ISBN 0-521-22644-9). Cambridge U Pr.

Hire. Managing a Real Estate Team. 1980. 18.95 (ISBN 0-03-056788-2). Dryden Pr.

Hiriart, Rosario. Las Alusiones Literarias En la Obra Narrativa De Francisco Ayala. 1972. 10.50 (ISBN 0-88303-016-0); pap. 7.50 (ISBN 0-685-73218-5). E Torres & Sons.

Hirn, jt. auth. see Bumagin.

Hirnschall, Helmut. Eyes on the Wilderness. 175p. 1975. text ed. 5.95 (ISBN 0-919654-39-8). Hancock Hse.

Hiro, Dilip. Black British, White British. LC 72-92026. 384p. 1973. 8.95 o.p. (ISBN 0-85345-270-9, CL2709); pap. 3.95 (ISBN 0-85345-304-7, PB3047). Monthly Rev.

--To Anchor a Cloud. (Writers Workshop Bluebird Ser.). 96p. 1975. 15.00 (ISBN 0-88253-662-1); pap. text ed. 6.75 (ISBN 0-88253-661-3). Ind-US Inc.

--Untouchables of India. (Minority Rights Group: No. 26). 1975. pap. 2.50 (ISBN 0-89192-112-5). Interbk Inc.

Hiromi, Keitaro. Kinetics of Fast Enzyme Reactions: Theory & Practice. LC 79-19391. 346p. 1980. 49.95x (ISBN 0-470-26866-2). Halsted Pr.

Hiroshige, Ando. A Shoal of Fishes. LC 80-5170. 1980. 16.95 (ISBN 0-670-37262-5, Studio). Viking Pr.

Hirsch, Alison, ed. see Museum Staff.

Hirsch, Andrew von see Gross, Hyman & Von Hirsch, Andrew.

Hirsch, Andrew Von see Von Hirsch, Andrew.

Hirsch, Bernard A. see Cherry, Richard L., et al.

Hirsch, C. Cervical Pain. Zotterman, Y., ed. 232p. 1972. text ed. 50.00 (ISBN 0-08-016875-2). Pergamon.

Hirsch, Charles P., et al. Handbook of Legal Medicine. 5th ed. LC 79-16053. (Illus.). 1979. pap. text ed. 19.95 (ISBN 0-8016-3509-8). Mosby.

Hirsch, David. Alpha Moonbase Technical Notebook. (Illus.). (gr. 4 up). 1977. 9.95 (ISBN 0-931064-02-3). Starlog.

Hirsch, E. D., Jr. Innocence & Experience: An Introduction to Blake. LC 74-22905. (Midway Reprint Ser). xvi, 336p. 1975. pap. 12.00x (ISBN 0-226-34238-7). U of Chicago Pr.

--The Philosophy of Composition. LC 77-4944. xiv, 200p. 1981. pap. 4.95 (ISBN 0-226-34243-3). U of Chicago Pr.

Hirsch, Edward. For the Sleepwalker. LC 80-2726. (Knopf Poetry Ser.: No. 6). 1981. 10.95 (ISBN 0-394-51474-2); pap. 5.95 (ISBN 0-394-74908-1). Knopf.

Hirsch, Felice L., jt. auth. see Hall, Sandra P.

Hirsch, Foster. George Kelly. LC 75-2086. (U. S. Authors Ser.: No. 259). 1975. lib. bdg. 10.95 (ISBN 0-8057-7158-1). Twayne.

--Joseph Losey. (Theater Arts Ser.). 1980. lib. bdg. 12.95 (ISBN 0-8057-9257-0). Twayne.

--Laurence Olivier. (Theatrical Arts Ser.). 1979. lib. bdg. 12.50 (ISBN 0-8057-9260-0). Twayne.

--A Portrait of the Artist: The Plays of Tennessee Williams. (National Univ. Pubns. Literary Criticism Ser.). 1979. 10.00 (ISBN 0-8046-9230-0). Kennikat.

Hirsch, G. P., jt. auth. see Maunder, A. H.

Hirsch, H. & Hancock, M. Comparative Legislative Systems. LC 78-136612. 1971. 14.95 (ISBN 0-02-914720-4). Free Pr.

Hirsch, H. J., tr. see Begemann, H. & Rastetter, J.

Hirsch, H. J., tr. see Grewe, Horst-Eberhard & Kremer, Karl.

Hirsch, H. N. The Enigma of Felix Frankfurter. LC 80-68184. 320p. 1981. 14.95 (ISBN 0-465-01979-X). Basic.

Hirsch, Herbert. The Right of the People: An Introduction to American Politics. LC 79-47987. 531p. 1980. text ed. 22.50 (ISBN 0-8191-0990-8); pap. text ed. 12.75 (ISBN 0-8191-0991-6). U Pr of Amer.

Hirsch, Jerry A. Concepts in Theoretical Organic Chemistry. 320p. 1974. text ed. 24.95x o.p. (ISBN 0-205-03999-5). Allyn.

Hirsch, John D. The Complete Book of Car Maintenance & Repair. LC 77-3252. (Illus.). 1977. 14.95 o.p. (ISBN 0-684-14900-1, ScribT). Scribner.

Hirsch, Julia. Family Photographs: Content, Meaning & Effect. LC 80-25591. (Illus.). 160p. 1981. 12.95 (ISBN 0-19-502889-9). Oxford U Pr.

Hirsch, Karen. Becky. LC 80-27619. (Illus.). 40p. (gr. k-3). 1981. PLB 4.95 (ISBN 0-87614-144-0). Carolrhoda Bks.

Hirsch, Katrine De see De Hirsch, Katrine, et al.

Hirsch, Miriam F. Women & Violence. 416p. 1980. text ed. 17.95. Van Nos Reinhold.

Hirsch, Morris & Smale, Stephen. Differential Equations, Dynamical Systems & Linear Algebra. 1974. text ed. 21.95 (ISBN 0-12-349550-4). Acad Pr.

Hirsch, P. B. The Physics of Metals, Vol. 2: Defects. LC 74-14439. (Illus.). 304p. 1976. 68.50 (ISBN 0-521-20077-6). Cambridge U Pr.

Hirsch, Paul, jt. ed. see Janowitz, Morris.

Hirsch, Paul M., et al, eds. Strategies for Communication Research. LC 77-88630. (Sage Annual Reviews of Communication Research: Vol. 6). 1977. 20.00x (ISBN 0-8039-0891-1); pap. 9.95x (ISBN 0-8039-0892-X). Sage.

Hirsch, Phil. One Hundred One Shark Jokes. (Orig.). 1976. pap. 0.95 o.s.i. (ISBN 0-515-04075-4). Jove Pubns.

Hirsch, Phil, ed. Vampire Jokes & Cartoons: A Comedy of Terrors. 1974. pap. 0.95 o.s.i. (ISBN 0-515-03498-3, N3498). Jove Pubns.

Hirsch, Richard, jt. auth. see Tyler, Christopher.

Hirsch, Richard G. There Shall Be No Poor. 1965. pap. 0.50 (ISBN 0-8074-0092-0, 707930). UAHC.

--Thy Most Precious Gift: Peace in Jewish Tradition. (Issues of Conscience Ser.). 128p. (Orig.). 1974. pap. 0.50 (ISBN 0-8074-0093-9, 180203). UAHC.

--The Way of the Upright: A Jewish View of Economic Justice. (Issues of Conscience Ser.). 128p. (Orig.). 1973. pap. 0.50 (ISBN 0-8074-0094-7, 180205). UAHC.

Hirsch, Richard S. & Orgel, Stephen, eds. A Pleasant Commodie Called Looke About You. LC 79-54343. (Renaissance Drama Second Ser.). 130p. 1980. lib. bdg. 16.50 (ISBN 0-8240-4460-6). Garland Pub.

Hirsch, Roland F., ed. Statistics. LC 78-10508. (Eastern Analytical Symposiam Ser.). 1978. pap. 24.00 (ISBN 0-89168-017-9). Franklin Inst.

Hirsch, Rudolf. The Printed Word: Its Impact & Diffusion (Primarily in the 15th & 16th Centuries) 338p. 1980. 70.00x (ISBN 0-86078-026-0, Pub. by Variorum England). State Mutual Bk.

Hirsch, S. Carl. He & She: How Males & Females Behave. LC 75-15983. (Illus.). 160p. (gr. 5-8). 1975. 8.95 o.p. (ISBN 0-397-31633-X). Lippincott.

--Stilts. (Illus.). 48p. (gr. 4-6). 1972. PLB 4.75 o.p. (ISBN 0-670-67053-7). Viking Pr.

Hirsch, S. R., jt. ed. see Farmer, R. D.

Hirsch, Samson. The Pentateuch. 4257p. (Eng. & Hebrew.). 1962. 60.00 (ISBN 0-910818-12-6). Judaica Pr.

Hirsch, Seev. Location of Industry & International Competitiveness. 1967. 22.00x (ISBN 0-19-828236-2). Oxford U Pr.

Hirsch, Seymour. BASIC: A Programmed Text. LC 75-6806. 496p. 1975. text ed. 15.95 (ISBN 0-471-40045-9). Wiley.

Hirsch, Seymour C. BASIC Programming: Self-Taught. (Illus.). 1980. pap. text ed. 11.95 (ISBN 0-8359-0432-6). Reston.

--Cobol: A Simplified Approach. LC 73-13879. (Illus.). 160p. 1974. 8.95 (ISBN 0-87909-128-2). Reston.

Hirsch, Steven, jt. ed. see Farmer, Richard.

Hirsch, Susan E. Roots of the American Working Class: The Industrialization of Crafts in Newark, 1800-1860. LC 78-51784. (Illus.). 1978. 15.00 (ISBN 0-8122-7747-3). U of Pa Pr.

Hirsch, Sylvia. Art of Table Setting & Flower Arrangement. rev. ed. (Illus.). 1967. 9.95 (ISBN 0-690-10325-5, TYC-T). T Y Crowell.

Hirsch, W., jt. auth. see Zollschan, G. K.

Hirsch, W. Z. Urban Life & Form. 1963. 7.50 o.p. (ISBN 0-03-026525-8). HR&W.

Hirsch, Werner Z., et al. Local Government Program Budgeting Theory & Practice: With Special Reference to Los Angeles. LC 74-5746. 236p. 1974. text ed. 19.50 o.p. (ISBN 0-275-28859-5). Praeger.

Hirschberg, Stuart. Myth in the Poetry of Ted Hughes. 1980. 22.50x. B&N.

Hirschel, Joseph D. Fourth Amendment Rights. LC 78-57161. (Illus.). 1979. 17.95 (ISBN 0-669-02361-2). Lexington Bks.

Hirschfeld, Al. Hirschfeld by Hirschfeld. LC 79-17023. 1979. 15.00 (ISBN 0-396-07777-3). Dodd.

Hirschfeld, Burt. Cindy on Fire. 1971. pap. 2.50 (ISBN 0-380-00267-1, 49270). Avon.

--Fire Island. (Orig.). 1970. pap. 2.50 (ISBN 0-380-00232-9, 50427). Avon.

--Women of Dallas. (Dallas Ser.: Vol. 2). 288p. (Orig.). 1981. pap. 2.75 (ISBN 0-553-14497-9). Bantam.

Hirschfelder, Joseph O., ed. Intermolecular Forces, Vol. 12. 648p. 1967. 32.50 (ISBN 0-470-40067-6). Krieger.

Hirschfield, Ira S. & Lambert, Theresa N. Audio Visual Aids: Uses & Resources in Gerontology. LC 78-59262. 1978. pap. 4.50 (ISBN 0-88474-047-1). USC Andrus Geron.

Hirschfield, Robert S. Selection-Election, 1980. 264p. 1981. text ed. price not set. Aldine Pub.

Hirschfield, Robert S., ed. The Power of the Presidency. 2nd ed. 464p. 1981. 24.95 (ISBN 0-202-24159-9); pap. text ed. 14.95 (ISBN 0-202-24160-2). Aldine Pub.

--The Power of the Presidency: Concepts & Controversy. 2nd ed. LC 71-169513. 350p. 1973. text ed. 23.95x (ISBN 0-202-24137-8); pap. text ed. 12.95x (ISBN 0-202-24138-6). Aldine Pub.

Hirschhorn, Howard. All About Mice. (Illus.). 96p. (Orig.). 1974. pap. 2.50 (ISBN 0-87666-210-6, M-542). TFH Pubns.

--All About Rabbits. (Illus.). 96p. (Orig.). 1974. pap. 2.50 (ISBN 0-87666-214-9, M-543). TFH Pubns.

--All About Rats. (Illus.). 96p. (Orig.). 1974. pap. 2.50 (ISBN 0-87666-217-3, M-544). TFH Pubns.

Hirschhorn, Howard H. Spanish-English - English-Spanish Medical Guide. (gr. 11 up). 1968. pap. text ed. 1.95 (ISBN 0-88345-157-3, 17429). Regents Pub.

--Technical & Scientific Reader in English. (gr. 9-12). 1970. pap. text ed. 3.95 (ISBN 0-88345-158-1, 17430). Regents Pub.

Hirschhorn, Norbert, et al. Quality of Care Assessment & Assurance: An Annotated Bibliography with a Point of View. (Medical Bks.). 1979. lib. bdg. 15.95 (ISBN 0-8161-2123-0, Hall Medical). G K Hall.

Hirschhorn, Richard. Target Mayflower. 1978. pap. 1.75 o.s.i. (ISBN 0-515-04079-7). Jove Pubns.

Hirschi, Travis. Causes of Delinquency. 1969. 18.50x (ISBN 0-520-01487-1); pap. 4.95x (ISBN 0-520-01901-6, CAMPUS47). U of Cal Pr.

Hirschi, Travis & Selvin, Hanan C. Principles of Survey Analysis. LC 67-15058. Orig. Title: Delinquency Research. 1973. pap. text ed. 5.95 (ISBN 0-02-914740-9). Free Pr.

Hirschman, Albert O. Development Projects Observed. 1967. 11.95 (ISBN 0-8157-3650-9); pap. 4.95 (ISBN 0-8157-3649-5). Brookings.

--Exit, Voice, & Loyalty: Responses to Decline in Firms, Organizations, & States. LC 77-99517. 1970. 8.95x (ISBN 0-674-27650-7); pap. 2.50 (ISBN 0-674-27660-4). Harvard U Pr.

--National Power & the Structure of Foreign Trade. (California Library Reprint Ser.: No. 105). 1980. 45.50 (ISBN 0-520-04084-8); pap. 4.95 (ISBN 0-520-04082-1, CAMPUS 254). U of Cal Pr.

Hirschman, I. I. Decomposition of Walsh & Fourier Series. LC 52-42839. (Memoirs: No. 15). 1980. pap. 4.40 (ISBN 0-8218-1215-7, MEMO-15). Am Math.

Hirschman, Jack. Kameas. Date not set. 4.00 (ISBN 0-686-13974-7). Tree Bks. Postponed.

Hirschman, Jack, tr. see Elaezer Of Worms.

Hirschmann, Edwin. The White Mutiny. 1980. 24.00x (ISBN 0-8364-0639-7). South Asia Bks.

Hirschmann, Ira A. Life Line to a Promised Land. (Return to Zion Ser.). (Illus.). xvi, 214p. 1980. Repr. of 1946 ed. lib. bdg. 15.00x (ISBN 0-87991-120-4). Porcupine Pr.

Hirschmann, Linda. In a Lick of a Flick of a Tongue. LC 80-12632. (Illus.). 48p. (gr. 1-4). 1980. PLB 6.95 (ISBN 0-396-07833-8). Dodd.

Hirschmann, Maria A., tr. Hansi. (Portuguese Bks.). 1979. write for info. (ISBN 0-8297-0825-1). Life Pubs Intl.

--Hansi. (Spanish Bks.). (Span.). 1979. 1.90 (ISBN 0-8297-0563-5). Life Pubs Intl.

Hirschmeier, Johannes. Origins of Entrepreneurship in Meiji Japan. LC 64-20973. (East Asian Ser: No. 17). 1964. 16.50x (ISBN 0-674-64475-1). Harvard U Pr.

Hirschmeier, Johannes & Yui, Tsunehiko. The Development of Japanese Business, 1600-1973. LC 74-82190. 350p. 1975. 16.50x (ISBN 0-674-20045-4). Harvard U Pr.

Hirsch-Reich, Beatrice, jt. auth. see Reeves, Marjorie.

Hirsh, Diana. World of Turner. (Library of Art). (Illus.). 1969. 15.95 (ISBN 0-8094-0250-5). Time-Life.

--World of Turner. LC 73-78989. (Library of Art Ser.). (Illus.). (gr. 6 up). 1969. 12.96 (ISBN 0-8094-0279-3, Pub. by Time-Life). Silver.

Hirsh, Foster. The Dark Side of the Screen: Film Noir. LC 80-28955. (Illus.). 192p. 1981. 14.95 (ISBN 0-498-02234-X). A S Barnes.

--Love, Sex, Death, & the Meaning of Life: Woody Allen's Comedy. (McGraw-Hill Paperbacks Ser.). (Illus.). 192p. (Orig.). 1981. pap. 5.95 (ISBN 0-07-029054-7, GB). McGraw.

Hirsh, Marilyn. Could Anything Be Worse. LC 73-17364. (Illus.). 32p. (gr. k-3). 1974. reinforced bdg. 8.95 (ISBN 0-8234-0239-8). Holiday.

--The Rabbi & the Twenty-Nine Witches. LC 75-30710. (Illus.). 32p. (gr. k-3). 1981. PLB 7.95 (ISBN 0-8234-0270-3). Holiday.

Hirsh, Marilyn, illus. The Tower of Babel. LC 80-21196. (Illus.). 32p. (ps-2). 1981. PLB 6.95 (ISBN 0-8234-0380-7). Holiday.

Hirshberg, Al, jt. auth. see Green, Ted.

Hirshberg, Edgar W. George Henry Lewes. (English Authors Ser.: No. 100). lib. bdg. 10.95 (ISBN 0-8057-1332-8). Twayne.

Hirshberg, Jack. Portrait of "All the President's Men". 1976. pap. 6.95 o.s.i. (ISBN 0-446-87105-2). Warner Bks.

Hirshey, David, jt. auth. see Messing, Shep.

Hirshfield, Daniel S. Lost Reform: The Campaign for Compulsory Health Insurance in the United States from 1932 to 1943. LC 71-115187. (Commonwealth Fund Publications Ser). 1970. 11.00x (ISBN 0-674-53917-6). Harvard U Pr.

Hirshi, Travis & Gottfredson, Michael, eds. Understanding Crime: Current Theory & Research. LC 80-19376. (Sage Research Progress Ser. in Criminology: Vol. 18). (Illus.). 144p. 1980. 12.95 (ISBN 0-8039-1517-9); pap. 6.50 (ISBN 0-8039-1518-7). Sage.

Hirshleifer, Jack. Investment, Interest, & Capital. (Finance Ser). 1970. text ed. 16.95x (ISBN 0-13-502955-4). P-H.

--Price Theory & Applications. 2nd ed. (Illus.). 1980. text ed. 19.95 (ISBN 0-13-699710-4). P-H.

Hirshman, Jack, tr. see Barron, Stephanie, et al.

Hirshman, S., jt. auth. see Simpson, Colleen E.

Hirson, Roger O. & Schwartz, Stephen. Pippin. 1977. pap. 2.25 (ISBN 0-380-01635-4, 45740, Bard). Avon.

Hirst, D. The Representative of the People? LC 75-9283. 320p. 1975. 35.50 (ISBN 0-521-20810-6). Cambridge U Pr.

Hirst, Michael. Sebastiano Del Piombo. (Studies in the History of Art & Architecture). (Illus.). 288p. 1981. 98.00 (ISBN 0-19-817308-3). Oxford U Pr.

Hirst, Michael, ed. see Wilde, Johannes.

Hirst, Paul. On Law & Ideology. 1979. text ed. 20.00x (ISBN 0-391-00970-2); pap. 10.25x (ISBN 0-391-01009-3). Humanities.

Hirst, Paul, jt. auth. see Hindess, Barry.

Hirst, Paul H. Knowledge & the Curriculum: A Collection of Philosophical Papers. (International Library of the Philosophy of Education). 1975. 12.50x (ISBN 0-7100-7929-X); pap. 8.95 (ISBN 0-7100-7930-3). Routledge & Kegan.

Hirst, Paul Q. Durkheim, Bernard & Epistemology. 1975. 18.50 (ISBN 0-7100-8071-9). Routledge & Kegan.

Hirst, Paul Q., jt. auth. see Hindess, Barry.

Hirst, R. J. Problems of Perception. (Muirhead Library of Philosophy). 1978. Repr. of 1959 ed. text ed. 15.00x (ISBN 0-391-00566-9). Humanities.

Hirst, R. J., ed. Philosophy: An Outline for the Intending Student. (Outlines Ser). 1968. cased 15.00x (ISBN 0-7100-2038-4); pap. 6.95 (ISBN 0-7100-6099-8). Routledge & Kegan.

Hirstein, Sandra J., jt. auth. see Tully, Mary Jo.

Hirszowicz, Maria, ed. The Bureaucratic Leviathan: A Study in the Sociology of Communism. 224p. 1980. text ed. 27.50x (ISBN 0-8147-3406-5). NYU Pr.

Hirt, Geoffrey A., jt. auth. see Block, Stanley B.

Hirtz, Jean L. Fate of Drugs in the Organism: A Bibliographic Survey, Vol. 4. 1979. 82.50 (ISBN 0-8247-6587-7). Dekker.

Hirtz, Jean L. & Garrett, E. R., eds. Drug Fate & Metabolism, Vol. 2. 1978. 49.50 (ISBN 0-8247-6603-2). Dekker.

Hisamatsu, Sen'Ichi. Biographical Dictionary of Japanese Literature. LC 75-14730. (Illus.). 437p. 1976. 35.00x (ISBN 0-87011-253-8). Kodansha.

Hisatake, Masayuki. Scientific Karatedo: Spiritual Development of Individuality in Mind and Body. (Illus.). 256p. 1976. 25.00 (ISBN 0-87040-362-1). Japan Pubns.

Hiscock, Eric. Cruising Under Sail. rev. ed. (Illus.). 544p. 1981. 35.00 (ISBN 0-19-217599-8). Oxford U Pr.

Hiscock, W. G. John Evelyn & His Family Circle. 256p. 1980. Repr. of 1955 ed. lib. bdg. 35.00 (ISBN 0-8495-2374-5). Arden Lib.

Hise, Richard T. Effective Salesmanship. 480p. 1980. text ed. 17.95 (ISBN 0-03-054676-1). Dryden Pr.

Hiser, Berniece T. Quare Do's in Appalachia: Thirty Legends & Memorates of Eastern Kentucky. LC 78-56593. 1978. pap. 6.00 (ISBN 0-933302-32-0). Pikeville Coll.

Hisis, Richard H. Jesus & the Future: Unsolved Questions on Eschatology. LC 80-82189. 1981. 16.50 (ISBN 0-8042-0341-5); pap. 9.95 (ISBN 0-8042-0340-7). John Knox.

Hiskett, M. & Awad, Sheikh M. Story of the Arabs. (Illus.). 1963. pap. text ed. 2.50x o.p. (ISBN 0-582-60244-0). Humanities.

Hislop, Alexander. Proverbs of Scotland. LC 68-21774. 1968. Repr. of 1868 ed. 20.00 (ISBN 0-8103-3201-9). Gale.

--Two Babylons. 1932. 6.95 (ISBN 0-87213-330-3). Loizeaux.

Hislop, Codman. Eliphalet Nott. LC 71-161696. (Illus.). 1971. 27.50x (ISBN 0-8195-4037-4, Pub. by Wesleyan U Pr). Columbia U Pr.

Hislop, D. H. Our Heritage in Public Worship. LC 36-2187. 350p. 7.50. Attic Pr.

Hislop, J. From Start to Finish. (Illus.). 1978. 24.35 (ISBN 0-85131-265-9, Dist. by Sporting Book Center). J A Allen.

Hisrich, Robert D., jt. auth. see Peters, Michael P.

Hiss, Alger. In the Court of Public Opinion. 448p. 1972. pap. 3.95x o.p. (ISBN 0-06-090293-0, CN293, CN). Har-Row.

Hiss, Stephen S. Understanding Radiography. (Illus.). 392p. 1980. 29.50 (ISBN 0-398-03685-3). C C Thomas.

Hissel, Dieter, jt. ed. see Hessel, Dieter.

Historic House Association of America. Historic Property Owner's Handbook. 2nd ed. (Illus.). 96p. (Orig.). 1981. pap. 7.95 (ISBN 0-89133-094-1). Preservation Pr.

Historic Restoration Project. Historic Buildings of Centre County, Pennsylvania. Ramsey, Gregory, ed. LC 79-29737. (Keystone Bks.). (Illus.). 256p. 1980. 15.00 (ISBN 0-271-00258-1). Pa St U Pr.

Historic Santa Fe Foundation. Old Santa Fe Today. 3rd, enl. ed. (Illus.). 128p. 1981. pap. price not set (ISBN 0-8263-0562-8). U of NM Pr.

Historical Association, London. Social Life in Early England: Historical Association Essays. Barraclough, Geoffrey, ed. LC 79-16998. (Illus.). xi, 264p. 1980. Repr. of 1960 ed. lib. bdg. 34.50x (ISBN 0-313-21298-8, HASL). Greenwood.

History Task Force, Centro De Estudios Puertorriquenos. Labor Migration Under Capitalism: The Puerto Rican Experience. LC 78-13918. (Modern Reader Paperback Ser.). (Illus.). 287p. 1980. pap. 6.50 (ISBN 0-85345-494-9). Monthly Rev.

Hitch, Charles J., ed. Energy Conservation & Economic Growth. (AAAS Selected Symposium: No. 22). (Illus.). 1978. lib. bdg. 20.00x (ISBN 0-89158-354-8). Westview.

Hitchcock, Alfred. Alfred Hitchcock Presents: Sixteen Skeletons from My Closet. 1976. pap. 1.25 o.s.i. (ISBN 0-440-18011-2). Dell.

--Alfred Hitchcock Presents Slay Ride. 1977. pap. 1.50 o.s.i. (ISBN 0-440-13641-5). Dell.

--Alfred Hitchcock's Spellbinders in Suspense. (Illus.). (gr. 7-11). 1967. 4.95 o.s.i. (ISBN 0-394-81665-X, BYR); PLB 6.99 o.s.i. (ISBN 0-394-91665-4). Random.

--Behind the Death Ball. 1979. pap. 1.50 o.s.i. (ISBN 0-440-13497-8). Dell.

--I Want My Mummy. 1981. pap. 2.25 o.s.i. (ISBN 0-440-13985-6). Dell.
--Murder Go Round. 1981. pap. 2.25 (ISBN 0-440-15607-6). Dell.
--Murder Racquet. 1980. pap. 2.25 (ISBN 0-440-15931-8). Dell.
--Scream Along with Me. 1981. pap. 2.25 (ISBN 0-440-13633-4). Dell.
--Slay Ride. 1981. pap. 2.95 (ISBN 0-440-13641-5). Dell.
--Speak of the Devil. 1980. pap. 2.25 (ISBN 0-440-17654-9). Dell.
--Stories to Be Read with the Door Locked. 1981. pap. 2.25 (ISBN 0-440-10138-7). Dell.
Hitchcock, Alfred, ed. Alfred Hitchcock & the Three Investigators in the Mystery of the Laughing Shadow. (Three Investigators Ser.: No. 12). (Illus.). (gr. 4-7). 1969. 2.95 (ISBN 0-394-81492-4, BYR); PLB 5.39 (ISBN 0-394-91492-9); pap. 1.95 (ISBN 0-394-83775-4). Random.
--Alfred Hitchcock Presents Scream Along with Me. 1977. pap. 1.25 o.s.i. (ISBN 0-440-13633-4). Dell.
--Alfred Hitchcock Presents: The Master's Choice. 1979. 10.00 (ISBN 0-394-50419-4, BYR). Random.
--Alfred Hitchcock's Monster Museum. (gr. 6-11). 1965. 4.95 (ISBN 0-394-81230-1, BYR); PLB 6.99 (ISBN 0-394-91230-6). Random.
--Alfred Hitchcock's Solve-Them-Yourself Mysteries. (Illus.). (gr. 6-9). 1963. 5.95 (ISBN 0-394-81242-5, BYR); PLB 6.99 (ISBN 0-394-91242-X). Random.
--My Favorites in Suspense. (YA) 1959. 10.00 o.p. (ISBN 0-394-41223-0, BYR). Random.
Hitchcock, Alfred, ed. see Arden, William.
Hitchcock, Alfred, ed. see Arthur, Robert.
Hitchcock, Alfred, ed. see Carey, M. V.
Hitchcock, Bert. Richard Malcolm Johnston. (United States Authors Ser.: No. 314). 1978. 12.50 (ISBN 0-8057-7238-3). Twayne.
Hitchcock, E., et al. Psychosurgery. (Illus.). 456p. 1972. 33.75 (ISBN 0-398-02314-X). C C Thomas.
Hitchcock, Edward & Massan, Alastair. Management of the Unconscious Patient. 1st ed. (Illus.). 96p. 1970. 3.50 (ISBN 0-632-07860-X, Blackwell Scientific). Mosby.
Hitchcock, Ethan A. Remarks Upon Alchemy & the Alchemists. LC 79-8614. Repr. of 1857 ed. 30.00 (ISBN 0-404-18478-2). AMS Pr.
Hitchcock, George. The Collected Poems, Stories, & Collages: George Hitchcock. (Illus.). 340p. 1981. 12.95 (ISBN 0-937310-04-2); pap. 7.95 (ISBN 0-937310-05-0). Jazz Pr.
--Five Plays. 330p. (Orig.). 1981. pap. 7.95 (ISBN 0-937310-10-7). Jazz Pr.
--Ship of Bells. (Illus.). 1968. pap. 1.50 o.p. (ISBN 0-87711-022-0). Kayak.
Hitchcock, H. Wiley. Marc-Antoine Charpentier's Pestis Mediolanensis: (the Plague of Milan) LC 79-320. (Early Musical Masterworks-Critical Editions & Commentaries Ser.). 1979. 19.00x (ISBN 0-8078-1365-6). U of NC Pr.
Hitchcock, H. Wiley, ed. The Phonograph & Our Musical Life: Proceedings of a Centennial Conference. LC 80-82409. (I. S.A.M Monograph: No. 14). 1980. pap. 7.50 (ISBN 0-914678-14-0). Inst Am Music.
Hitchcock, H. Wiley, ed. see Belcher, Supply.
Hitchcock, H. Wiley, ed. see Foster, Stephen.
Hitchcock, H. Wiley, ed. & intro. by see Riley, Edward.
Hitchcock, Henry R. American Architectural Books: A List of Books, Portfolios, and Pamphlets on Architecture and Related Subjects Published in America Before 1895. LC 75-25672. (Architectural and Decorative Arts Ser.). xii, 130p. 1975. Repr. of 1962 ed. lib. bdg. 19.50 (ISBN 0-306-70742-X). Da Capo.
Hitchcock, Henry-Russell. Early Victorian Architecture in Britain, 2 vols. LC 72-151765. (Architecture & Decorative Art Ser.). 658p. 1972. Repr. of 1954 ed. Set. lib. bdg. 65.00 (ISBN 0-306-70195-2). Da Capo.
--In the Nature of Materials: The Buildings of Frank Lloyd Wright, 1887-1941. LC 72-75322. (Architecture & Decorative Arts Ser). 1973. Repr. of 1942 ed. lib. bdg. 29.50 (ISBN 0-306-71283-0). Da Capo.
--Rhode Island Architecture. 2nd ed. LC 68-27725. (Architecture & Decorative Art Ser.: Vol. 19). (Illus.). 1968. Repr. of 1939 ed. lib. bdg. 29.50 (ISBN 0-306-71037-4). Da Capo.
Hitchcock, J. Gareth. Profiles in Innocence by Quentin K. Y. Huang: With an Introduction by Himself. 64p. 1980. 8.00 o.p. (ISBN 0-682-49669-3). Exposition.
Hitchcock, James. Catholicism & Modernity: Confrontation or Capitulation? 1979. 13.95 (ISBN 0-8164-0427-5). Crossroad NY.
--The Recovery of the Sacred. LC 73-17899. 1974. 6.95 (ISBN 0-8164-1150-6). Crossroad NY.
Hitchcock, James & Bednarski, Gloriana. Charismatics. (Catholic Perspectives Ser.). 104p. (Orig.). 1980. pap. 3.95 (ISBN 0-88347-114-0). Thomas More.
Hitchcock, Thomas H., ed. Monogram Close-up: Mess Bf-109k. (Close-up Ser.: No. 16). Date not set. pap. 5.95 (ISBN 0-914144-16-2, Pub. by Monogram). Aviation.
--Monogram Close-up: Taifun. (Close-up Ser.: No. 5). (Illus.). Date not set. pap. 5.95 (ISBN 0-914144-05-7, Pub. by Mombgram). Aviation.
Hitchener, Elizabeth see Booth, David.
Hitchman, M. L., jt. auth. see Albery, W. J.
Hitchman, Michael L. Measurement of Dissolved Oxygen. LC 77-26710. (Monographs on Analytical Chemistry & Its Applications: Vol. 49). 1978. 28.00 (ISBN 0-471-03885-7, Pub. by Wiley-Interscience). Wiley.
Hitchner, Dell G. & Levine, Carol. Comparative Government & Politics. 2nd ed. 270p. 1980. pap. 11.50 scp (ISBN 0-06-042828-7, HarpC). Har-Row.
Hite, James C. Room & Situation: The Political Economy of Land-Use Policy. LC 79-11691. 1979. 19.95 (ISBN 0-88229-479-2); pap. 10.95 (ISBN 0-88229-700-7). Nelson-Hall.
Hite, Jordan F., et al. Readings, Cases, Materials in Canon Law: A Textbook for Ministerial Students. (Orig.). 1980. pap. text ed. 8.50 (ISBN 0-8146-1081-1). Liturgical Pr.
Hite, Shere. The Hite Report. Date not set. pap. price not set (ISBN 0-440-13690-3). Dell.
--The Hite Report on Male Sexuality. LC 80-2709. 1981. 17.95 (ISBN 0-394-41392-X). Knopf.
Hitler, Adolf. The Testament of Adolf Hitler. (Illus.). 1978. pap. 3.00x (ISBN 0-911038-44-2). Noontide.
Hitler, Adolph, jt. auth. see People's Court, Munich.
Hitner, Henry & Nagle, Barbara T. Basic Pharmacology for Health Occupations. (Health Occupations Ser.). 1980. pap. 12.95 (ISBN 0-672-61437-5); tchrs. manual 6.67 (ISBN 0-672-61438-3). Bobbs.
Hitt, Michael A., jt. auth. see Middlemist, R. Dennis.
Hitt, Michael A., et al. Effective Management. (Management Ser). (Illus.). 1979. text ed. 18.50 (ISBN 0-8299-0196-5); pap. study guide 6.95 (ISBN 0-686-67442-1); instrs.' manual avail. (ISBN 0-8299-0489-1); transparency masters avail. (ISBN 0-8299-0490-5); study guide 6.95 (ISBN 0-8299-0246-5). West Pub.
Hitt, Russell T. How Christians Grow. 1979. 8.95 (ISBN 0-19-502558-X). Oxford U Pr.
--Jungle Pilot. 320p. 1973. pap. 3.50 (ISBN 0-310-26082-5). Zondervan.
Hitti, Jusuf. Medical English, Arabic Dictionary. (Illus.). 1973. 35.00x (ISBN 0-685-72051-9). Intl Bk Ctr.
Hittleman, Richard L. Be Young with Yoga. 240p. 1973. pap. 1.95 o.s.i. (ISBN 0-446-89432-X). Warner Bks.
--Yoga for Personal Living. (Illus.). 1972. pap. 2.50 o.s.i. (ISBN 0-446-91186-0). Warner Bks.
Hively, Wells, jt. auth. see Reynolds, Maynard.
Hix, Charles & Taylor, Michael. Male Model. (Illus.). 192p. 1980. pap. 7.95 (ISBN 0-312-50938-3). St Martin.
Hixon, Don L. & Hennessee, Don. Women in Music: A Biobibliography. LC 75-23075. 358p. 1975. 15.00 (ISBN 0-8108-0869-2). Scarecrow.
Hixon, Don L. & Hennessee, Don A. Nineteenth Century American Drama: A Finding Guide. LC 77-12057. 1977. 24.00 (ISBN 0-8108-1083-2). Scarecrow.
Hixon, Lex. Coming Home: The Experience of Enlightenment in Sacred Traditions. LC 77-77656. 1978. pap. 2.95 (ISBN 0-385-12907-6, Anch). Doubleday.
Hixon, Thomas J., et al. Introduction to Communication Disorders. (Illus.). 1979. text ed. 18.95 (ISBN 0-13-480186-5). P-H.
Hixson, Richard F. Isaac Collins: A Quaker Printer in 18th Century America. (Illus.). 1968. 16.00 (ISBN 0-8135-0570-4). Rutgers U Pr.
Hjelle, Larry A. & Ziegler, Daniel J. Personality Theories. 2nd, rev. ed. (Illus.). 512p. 1981. text ed. 17.95 (ISBN 0-07-029063-6, C); write for info instrs.' manual (ISBN 0-07-029064-4). McGraw.
Hjelmslev, Louis. Prolegomena to a Theory of Language. rev. ed. Whitfield, Francis J., tr. 1961. 15.00x (ISBN 0-299-02470-9). U of Wis Pr.
--Resume of a Theory of Language. Whitfield, Francis J., tr. 1976. 25.00x (ISBN 0-299-07040-9). U of Wis Pr.
Hjul, Peter, ed. The Stern Trawler. (Illus.). 228p. 22.50 (ISBN 0-85238-025-9, FN). Unipub.
Hlawiczka, P. Introduction to Quantum Electronics. 1972. 38.50 (ISBN 0-12-349950-X). Acad Pr.
Hlawitscka, Eduard. Franken, Alemannen, Bayern und Burgunder in Oberitalien, 774-962. LC 80-2025. 1981. Repr. of 1960 ed. 38.50 (ISBN 0-404-18569-X). AMS Pr.
Hlibok, Albert J., jt. auth. see Edgerton, William H.
Hlongwane, Themba. The Light of Dark. 1978. 4.00 o.p. (ISBN 0-682-49074-1). Exposition.
Hlope, Stephen S. Class, Ethnicity & Politics in Liberia: Analysis of Power Struggles in the Tubman & Tolbert Administrations from 1944-1975. LC 79-63261. 1979. pap. text ed. 11.25 (ISBN 0-8191-0721-2). U Pr of Amer.
Hnatek, Eugene R. A User's Handbook of D-A & A-D Converters. LC 75-14341. 496p. 1976. 35.00 (ISBN 0-471-40109-9, Pub. by Wiley-Interscience). Wiley.
--A User's Handbook of Semiconductor Memories. LC 77-362. 1977. 40.00 (ISBN 0-471-40112-9, Pub. by Wiley-Interscience). Wiley.
Ho, Betty Y. How to Stay Healthy a Lifetime Without Medicines. LC 77-86248. 1979. pap. 10.00 (ISBN 0-9600148-3-7). Juvenescent.
--Living Function of Sleep, Life & Aging. LC 79-13810. (Illus., Orig.). 1967. pap. 3.50 (ISBN 0-9600148-0-2). Juvenescent.
--Origin of Variation of Races of Mankind & the Cause of Evolution. LC 68-57933. (Illus., Orig.). 1969. pap. 4.00 (ISBN 0-9600148-1-0). Juvenescent.
--Scientific Guide to Peaceful Living. LC 77-142457. (Illus., Orig.). 1973. pap. 7.50 (ISBN 0-9600148-2-9). Juvenescent.
Ho, C. Y., jt. auth. see Touloukian, U. S.
Ho, C. Y., jt. auth. see Touloukian, Y. S.
Ho, Eugene H., jt. auth. see Kong, Bucksam.
Ho, Lucy C., ed. Exhibition Catalogue Manual in Use in the Library of the Metropolitan Museum of Art. (Illus.). 40p. 1974. 2.50 (ISBN 0-87099-099-3). Metro Mus Art.
Ho, Ping-Ti. Studies on the Population of China, 1368-1953. LC 59-12970. (East Asian Ser: No. 4). 1959. 17.50x (ISBN 0-674-85245-1). Harvard U Pr.
Ho, Van H. Moving Meditation: Enlightenment of the Mind & Total Fitness. LC 79-88748. (Illus.). 214p. 1979. pap. 12.00 (ISBN 0-9602904-1-9). V H Ho.
Ho, Y. C., jt. auth. see Bryson, A. E.
Ho, Yu-Chi, jt. auth. see Bryson, A. E.
Hoadley, Irene B. & Clark, Alice S., eds. Quantitative Methods in Librarianship: Standards, Research, Management. LC 73-149962. (Contributions in Librarianship & Information Science: No. 4). 256p. 1972. lib. bdg. 17.95 (ISBN 0-8371-6061-8, HOQ/). Greenwood.
Hoadley, M. C. & Hooker, M. B. Introduction to Javanese Law. LC 80-26636. (Monographs of the Association for Asian Studies: No. XXXVII). 1981. text ed. 9.95x (ISBN 0-8165-0727-9). U of Ariz Pr.
Hoadley, R. Bruce. Understanding Wood. (Illus.). 1979. 14.95 o.p. (ISBN 0-918804-05-1, ScribT); pap. 9.95 o.p. (ISBN 0-918804-06-X). Scribner.
--Understanding Wood: A Craftsman's Guide to Wood Technology. LC 78-65177. (Illus.). 1980. 17.95 (ISBN 0-918804-05-1, Dist. by Van Nostrand Reinhold). Taunton.
Hoag, jt. auth. see Pawlak, Elizabeth A.
Hoag, Albert L., jt. auth. see McNeese, Donald G.
Hoag, David. The Robber's Cook. 1st ed. 50p. 1973. pap. 1.95x o.p. (ISBN 0-686-05510-1). SF Arts & Letters.
Hoag, Edwin. American Houses: Colonial, Classic, Contemporary. LC 64-19042. (Illus.). (gr. 7-9). 1964. 12.95 (ISBN 0-397-30721-7). Lippincott.
Hoag, Ernest B. & Williams, Edward H. Crime, Abnormal Minds & the Law. (Historical Foundations of Forensic Psychiatry & Psychology Ser.). 405p. 1980. Repr. of 1923 ed. lib. bdg. 35.00 (ISBN 0-306-76060-6). Da Capo.
Hoag, John D. Western Islamic Architecture. LC 63-7516. (Great Ages of World Architecture Ser). (Illus.). 1963. 7.95 o.s.i. (ISBN 0-8076-0212-4); pap. 5.95 o.s.i. (ISBN 0-8076-0341-4). Braziller.
Hoagland, Clayton. Pleasures of Sketching Outdoors. rev. ed. (Illus.). 1970. pap. 4.50 (ISBN 0-486-22229-2). Dover.
Hoagland, Edward. African Calliope. 256p. 1981. pap. 4.95 (ISBN 0-14-005806-0). Penguin.
Hoagland, Henry E., et al. Real Estate Finance. 6th ed. 1977. text ed. 18.95 (ISBN 0-256-01930-4). Irwin.
Hoagland, Kathleen, ed. One Thousand Years of Irish Poetry. 832p. 1981. 12.95 (ISBN 0-517-34295-2). Devin.
Hoagland, Victoria, jt. auth. see Casto, Helen.
Hoak, D. E. The King's Council in the Reign of Edward VI. LC 75-9286. (Illus.). 394p. 1975. 51.50 (ISBN 0-521-20866-1). Cambridge U Pr.
Hoar, William S. General & Comparative Physiology. 2nd ed. (Illus.). 896p. 1975. 24.95 (ISBN 0-13-350272-4); lab. companion 7.95 (ISBN 0-13-347724-X). P-H.
Hoard, Samuel L. Almost a Layman. 1981. price not set. Drake's Ptg & Pub.
Hoare, A., ed. Short Italian Dictionary, 2 vol. in 1. 59.50 (ISBN 0-521-05279-3). Cambridge U Pr.
Hoare, C. A. & Perrott, R. H., eds. Operating Systems Techniques. (Automatic Programming Information Centre Studies in Data Processing: No. 9). 1973. 55.00 (ISBN 0-12-350650-6). Acad Pr.
Hoare, John. Tumult in the Clouds. 1976. 10.95 o.p. (ISBN 0-7181-1410-8, Pub. by Michael Joseph). Merrimack Bk Serv.
Hoare, R. J., jt. auth. see Harrison, P. M.
Hoare, Robert. When the West Was Wild. (Junior Reference Ser.). (Illus.). 64p. (gr. 7 up). 1976. 7.95 (ISBN 0-7136-1619-9). Dufour.
Hoare, Sophy. Japan. LC 75-44864. (Macdonald Countries). (Illus.). (gr. 7 up). 1976. PLB 7.95 (ISBN 0-382-06106-3, Pub. by Macdonald Ed). Silver.
Hoath, David C., jt. auth. see Smith, Chris.
Hoatland, Irene F. Copper Red Filly & Her Enemy. 1981. 3.95 (ISBN 0-8062-0854-6). Carlton.
Hoban, Lillian. No, No, Sammy Crow. LC 80-15299. (Illus.). 32p. (gr. k-3). 1981. 7.95 (ISBN 0-688-80297-4); PLB 7.63 (ISBN 0-688-84297-6). Greenwillow.
Hoban, Lillian, jt. auth. see Hoban, Russell.
Hoban, Lillian, ed. Here Come Raccoons. LC 76-25205. (Illus.). (gr. k-4). 6.95 (ISBN 0-03-017781-2); pap. 2.25 (ISBN 0-03-048951-2). HR&W.
Hoban, Russell. Arthur's New Power. LC 77-11550. (Illus.). (gr. 1-5). 1978. 6.95 (ISBN 0-690-01370-1, TYC-J); PLB 7.89 (ISBN 0-690-01371-X). T Y Crowell.
--Arthur's New Power. (gr. k-6). 1980. pap. 1.50 (ISBN 0-440-40183-6, YB). Dell.
--Bread & Jam for Frances. (Illus.). (gr. k-3). 1969. pap. 1.50 (ISBN 0-590-02566-X, Schol Pap); pap. 3.50 bk. & record (ISBN 0-590-04414-1). Schol Bk Serv.
--La Corona & the Tin Frog. (Illus.). 30p. (gr. k-3). 1981. 8.95 (ISBN 0-224-01397-1, Pub. by Chatto-Bodley-Jonathan). Merrimack Bk Serv.
--The Dancing Tigers. (Illus.). 32p. (gr. k-3). 1981. 8.95 (ISBN 0-224-01374-2, Pub. by Chatto-Bodley-Jonathan). Merrimack Bk Serv.
--Dinner at Alberta's. LC 73-94796. (Illus.). 40p. (gr. 1-3). 1975. 8.95 (ISBN 0-690-23992-0, TYC-J); PLB 8.79 (ISBN 0-690-23993-9). T Y Crowell.
--Emmet Otter's Jug-Band Christmas. LC 76-117560. (Illus.). 48p. (ps-3). 1978. Repr. of 1971 ed. 4.95 (ISBN 0-590-17707-9, Four Winds); lib. bdg. 4.95 (ISBN 0-590-07707-4). Schol Bk Serv.
--Harvey's Hideout. LC 80-15292. (Illus.). 48p. (ps-3). 1980. Repr. of 1969 ed. 8.95 (ISBN 0-590-07767-8, Four Winds). Schol Bk Serv.
--Little Brute Family. (Illus.). (gr. k-2). 1966. 6.95 (ISBN 0-02-744110-5). Macmillan.
--The Little Brute Family. (Illus.). (gr. k-2). 1972. pap. 1.95 o.s.i. (ISBN 0-02-043650-5, Collier). Macmillan.
--The Little Brute Family. (Snuggle & Read Ser.). (Illus.). 32p. (ps-2). 1980. pap. 1.95 (ISBN 0-380-51151-7, 51151, Camelot). Avon.
--The Mole Family's Christmas. LC 80-17068. (Illus.). 48p. (ps-3). 1980. Repr. of 1969 ed. 8.95 (ISBN 0-590-07774-0, Four Winds). Schol Bk Serv.
--The Mouse & His Child. 1975. pap. 1.50 (ISBN 0-380-00910-2, 31765, Camelot). Avon.
--Riddley Walker. 1981. 12.95 (ISBN 0-671-42147-6). Summit Bks.
--Stone Doll of Sister Brute. LC 68-12089. (ps-3). 1968. 5.95 (ISBN 0-02-744080-X). Macmillan.
--The Stone Doll of Sister Brute. (Snuggle & Read Ser.). (Illus.). 32p. (ps-2). 1980. pap. 1.95 (ISBN 0-380-51169-X, 51169, Camelot). Avon.
--Ugly Bird. LC 69-11301. (Illus.). (gr. k-2). 1969. 3.95 o.s.i. (ISBN 0-02-744100-8). Macmillan.
Hoban, Russell & Hoban, Lillian. Charlie the Tramp. (gr. 2-3). 1970. pap. 1.50 (ISBN 0-590-02254-7, Schol Pap); pap. 3.50 bk. & record (ISBN 0-590-04392-7). Schol Bk Serv.
Hoban, Russell & McCully, Emily Arnold. The Twenty-Elephant Restaurant. LC 77-1056. (gr. k-5). 1978. 9.95 (ISBN 0-689-30593-1). Atheneum.
Hoban, Tana. Big Ones, Little Ones. LC 75-34440. (Illus.). 32p. (gr. k-3). 1976. 7.25 (ISBN 0-688-80040-8); PLB 6.67 (ISBN 0-688-84040-X). Greenwillow.
--Circles, Triangles & Squares. LC 72-93305. (Illus.). 32p. (ps-2). 1974. 8.95 (ISBN 0-02-744830-4, 74483). Macmillan.
--Count & See. LC 72-175597. (Illus.). 40p. (ps-2). 1972. 8.95 (ISBN 0-02-744800-2). Macmillan.
--Dig, Drill, Dump, Fill. LC 75-11987. (Illus.). 32p. (ps-3). 1975. PLB 6.96 (ISBN 0-688-84016-7). Greenwillow.

--Is It Red? Is It Yellow? Is It Blue? LC 78-2549. (Illus.). (gr. k-3). 1978. 7.95 (ISBN 0-688-80171-4); PLB 7.63 (ISBN 0-688-84171-6). Greenwillow.
--Look Again. LC 72-127469. (Illus.). (gr. k-2). 1971. 8.95 (ISBN 0-02-744050-8). Macmillan.
--One Little Kitten. LC 78-31862. (Illus.). (gr. k-3). 1979. 6.95 (ISBN 0-688-80222-2); PLB 6.67 (ISBN 0-688-84222-4). Greenwillow.
--Over, Under & Through & Other Spatial Concepts. LC 72-81055. (Illus.). 32p. (ps-2). 1973. 8.95 (ISBN 0-02-744820-7). Macmillan.
--Push Pull, Empty Full: A Book of Opposites. LC 72-175597. (Illus.). (ps-2). 1972. 8.95 (ISBN 0-02-744810-X). Macmillan.
--Take Another Look. LC 80-21342. (Illus.). 32p. (ps-3). 1981. 7.95 (ISBN 0-688-80298-2); PLB 7.63 (ISBN 0-688-84298-4). Greenwillow.
--Where Is It? LC 73-8573. (Illus.). 32p. (ps-2). 1974. 7.95 (ISBN 0-02-744070-2). Macmillan.
Hoban, Tana, illus. Shapes & Things. (Illus.). (ps-3). 1970. 8.95 (ISBN 0-02-744060-5). Macmillan.
Hobart, F. W. Pictorial History of the Sub-Machine Gun. LC 74-19683. 1975. 14.95 o.p. (ISBN 0-684-14186-8, ScribT). Scribner.
Hobbes, Thomas. Leviathan, 2 Pts. Schneider, Herbert W., ed. LC 58-9957. 1958. Set. pap. 6.50 (ISBN 0-672-60246-6, LLA69). Bobbs.
--Leviathan. 1953. 6.00x (ISBN 0-460-00691-6, Evman); pap. 5.95 (ISBN 0-460-01691-1). Dutton.
Hobbie, Barbara. Oil Company Divestiture & the Press: Economic Vs. Journalistic Perceptions. LC 77-10627. (Praeger Special Studies). 1977. 24.95 (ISBN 0-03-022841-7). Praeger.
Hobbie, Holly. Holly Hobbie's Jumbo Activity Book. (Illus.). (gr. 1-5). 1980. 3.95 (ISBN 0-525-69526-5, Gingerbread). Dutton.
Hobbis, Charles I. Pencil Drawing for the Architect. (gr. 10-12). 1954. 5.95 (ISBN 0-85458-100-6); pap. 3.95 (ISBN 0-85458-101-4). Transatlantic.
Hobbs, jt. auth. see Constantine.
Hobbs, B. A., ed. A Special Issue Surveying Electromagnetic Induction in the Earth & Moon. 185p. pap. 23.50 (ISBN 90-277-9041-8, Pub. by D. Reidel). Kluwer Boston.
Hobbs, Betty C. & Christian, J. H., eds. The Microbiological Safety of Foods. 1974. 67.00 (ISBN 0-12-350750-2). Acad Pr.
Hobbs, Charles, jt. auth. see Reagan, Ronald.
Hobbs, Charles R. Power of Teaching with New Techniques. rev. ed. LC 72-92037. 357p. 1979. 6.95 (ISBN 0-87747-805-8). Deseret Bk.
Hobbs, Deborah, jt. auth. see Hobbs, Fredric.
Hobbs, Donald A. & Blank, Stuart J. Sociology & the Human Experience. 2nd ed. LC 77-16060. 1978. pap. text ed. 15.95x (ISBN 0-471-03108-9); tchr's manual avail. (ISBN 0-471-04071-1); tests avail. (ISBN 0-471-04078-9). Wiley.
Hobbs, F. D. Traffic Planning & Engineering. 2nd, rev. ed. 1975. text ed. 29.70 o.p. (ISBN 0-08-017926-6); pap. text ed. 17.00 o.p. (ISBN 0-08-017927-4). Pergamon.
--Traffic Planning & Engineering. 3rd ed. (Pergamon International Library, Civil Engineering Series). (Illus.). 1979. 82.00 (ISBN 0-08-022696-5); pap. 28.00 (ISBN 0-08-022697-3). Pergamon.
Hobbs, F. D. & Doling, J. F. Planning for Engineers & Surveyors. LC 80-41553. (Illus.). 230p. 1980. 30.00 (ISBN 0-08-025459-4); pap. 15.00 (ISBN 0-08-025458-6). Pergamon.
Hobbs, Fredric. Eat Your House: Art Eco Guide to Self Sufficiency. (Illus.). 120p. (Orig.). 1980. pap. 9.95 (ISBN 0-686-28070-9). VA City Rest.
Hobbs, Fredric & Hobbs, Deborah. American Paradise: Four Hundred Years on the Monterey Coast. Larrick, Gail, ed. LC 80-66581. (Illus.). 224p. (Orig.). Date not set. pap. 9.95 (ISBN 0-89395-044-0). Cal Living Bks.
Hobbs, Graham, tr. see Sollertinsky, Dmitri & Sollertinsky, Ludmilla.
Hobbs, Harry J. Veneering Simplified. (Illus.). 126p. 1976. 6.95 o.p. (ISBN 0-684-14544-8, ScribT). Scribner.
Hobbs, Herschel H. An Expostion of the Four Gospels. 1977. pap. 19.95 (ISBN 0-8054-1370-7); Matthew, John, Mark, & Luke. Broadman.
--Fundamentals of Our Faith. LC 60-5200. (Orig.). 1960. pap. 4.95 (ISBN 0-8054-1702-8). Broadman.
Hobbs, Jack. Installing & Servicing Home Audio Systems. LC 75-94452. (Orig. Ils Ser.). 1969. pap. 5.95 o.p. (ISBN 0-8306-8505-7, 505). TAB Bks.
Hobbs, Jack A. Art in Context. 2nd ed. 320p. 1980. text ed. 12.95 (ISBN 0-686-64964-8, HC). HarBraceJ.
Hobbs, Jackie, et al. The Egg Cookbook. (Illus.). 136p. (Orig.). 1979. pap. 6.75 (ISBN 0-589-01220-7, Pub. by Reed Books Australia). C E Tuttle.
Hobbs, James. Wild Life in the Far West...Comprising Hunting & Trapping Adventures with Kit Carson & Others: Captivity & Life Among the Comanches. LC 75-7113. (Indian Captivities Ser.: Vol. 87). 1977. Repr. of 1872 ed. 44.00 (ISBN 0-8240-1711-0). Garland Pub.
Hobbs, John. Applied Climatology. LC 79-5287. (Westview Studies in Physical Geography). (Illus.). 224p. 1980. lib. bdg. 30.00x (ISBN 0-89158-697-0). Westview.
Hobbs, Laura. Cars. (Easy-Read Fact Books). (Illus.). (gr. 2-4). 1977. PLB 6.45 s&l (ISBN 0-531-00375-2). Watts.
Hobbs, M. J., jt. auth. see Young, John Z.
Hobbs, Marvin. Modern CB Radio Servicing. 1979. pap. 7.75 (ISBN 0-8104-0865-1). Hayden.
Hobbs, Michael. The Great Opens. LC 76-23536. (Illus.). 1977. 8.95 o.p. (ISBN 0-498-02035-5). A S Barnes.
Hobbs, Michael, ed. Golf for the Connoisseur: A Golfing Anthology. (Illus.). 256p. 1980. 30.00 (ISBN 0-7134-1397-2, Pub. by Batsford England). David & Charles.
Hobbs, Nancy. Imaginative Canvas Embroidery. (Imaginative Craft Ser.). (Illus.). 1977. 12.95x o.p. (ISBN 0-8464-0500-8). Beekman Pubs.
Hobbs, Nicholas, ed. Issues in the Classification of Children: A Sourcebook on Categories, Labels, & Their Consequences. LC 73-20966. (Social & Behavioral Science Ser.). 1104p. 1974. Set. 37.50x (ISBN 0-87589-426-7); Vol. 1. (ISBN 0-87589-244-2); Vol. 2. (ISBN 0-87589-245-0). Jossey-Bass.
Hobbs, Peter, jt. auth. see Wallace, John M.
Hobbs, Peter V. Ice Physics. (Illus.). 782p. 1975. 105.00x (ISBN 0-19-851936-2). Oxford U Pr.
Hobbs, Richard. The Myth of Victory: What Is Victory in War? (Special Studies in Peace, Conflict & Conflict Resolution). 1979. lib. bdg. 32.50x (ISBN 0-89158-388-2). Westview.
Hobbs, Susan. Whistler Peacock Room. rev. ed. LC 80-20516. (Illus.). 1980. pap. 1.50 (ISBN 0-934686-34-3). Freer.
Hobby, Charles R., jt. auth. see Peterson, Thurman S.
Hobcraft, John & Rees, Philip, eds. Regional Demographic Development. (Illus.). 287p. 1977. 36.00x (ISBN 0-7099-0245-X, Pub. by Croom Helm Ltd England). Biblio Dist.
Hobday, Victor C. Sparks at the Grassroots: Municipal Distribution of TVA Electricity in Tennessee. LC 70-77845. (Illus.). 1969. 14.50x (ISBN 0-87049-099-0). U of Tenn Pr.
Hobden, Eileen. Fun with Weaving. (Learning with Fun Ser.). (Illus.). 64p. (gr. 5 up). text ed. 11.50x (ISBN 0-7182-1317-3, SpS). Soccer.
Hobe, Laura. Try God. 1978. pap. 1.95 o.s.i. (ISBN 0-446-89708-6). Warner Bks.
Hobe, Phyllis, compiled by. Fragile Moments. 1980. 14.95 (ISBN 0-8007-1176-9). Revell.
Hoben, Brent. Drug & Alcohol Emergencies. 1980. pap. 4.95. Hazelden.
Hoben, James E., jt. ed. see Black, J. Thomas.
Hoberman, John, tr. see Alfven, Hannes.
Hoberman, Mary Ann. Yellow Butter Purple Jelly Red Jam Black Bread. (Illus.). 64p. (ps-3). 1981. 8.95 (ISBN 0-670-79382-5). Viking Pr.
Hobhouse, Caroline, ed. Winter's Tales. 1980. 9.95 (ISBN 0-312-88375-7). St Martin.
Hobhouse, John C. John Cam Hobhouse (Seventeen Eighty-Six to Eighteen Sixty-Nine) Reiman, Donald H., ed. LC 75-31220. (Romantic Context Ser.: Poetry 1789-1830). 1977. lib. bdg. 42.00 (ISBN 0-8240-2170-3). Garland Pub.
Hobkirk, Ronald. Steroid Biochemistry: Selected Topics in Biosynthesis & Metabolism, 2 vols. 1979. 53.50 ea.; Vol. 1, 176p. (ISBN 0-8493-5193-6); Vol. 2, 208p. (ISBN 0-8493-5194-4). CRC Pr.
Hobrook, Jay M. Shipton Quebec Canada Eighteen Twenty Five Census. LC 76-364055. 1976. pap. 7.50 (ISBN 0-931248-07-8). Holbrook Res.
Hobsbaum, Philip. Tradition & Experiment in English Poetry. 343p. 1979. 22.50x (ISBN 0-8476-6128-8). Rowman.
Hobsbaum, Phillip. A Reader's Guide to D. H. Lawrence. 160p. 1981. 17.95 (ISBN 0-500-14023-5); pap. 9.95 (ISBN 0-500-15017-6). Thames Hudson.
Hobsbawm, E. J. Bandits. (Illus.). 1981. pap. 3.95 (ISBN 0-394-74850-6). Pantheon.
Hobsbawm, Eric & Rude, George. Captain Swing: A Social History of the Great English Agricultural Uprising of 1830. (Illus.). 384p. 1975. pap. 5.95 (ISBN 0-393-00793-6, Norton Lib). Norton.
Hobsbawm, Eric J., ed. see Marx, Karl.
Hobsbawn, Eric J. Bandits. (Pageant of History Ser). (Illus.). 1969. 4.50 o.s.i. (ISBN 0-440-00420-9). Delacorte.
Hobsley, M. Arbeitsdiagnose - Neve Wege der Chirusischen Diagnose und Therapie. Seemann, Caroline, tr. from Eng. Orig. Title: Pathways in Surgical Management. 480p. (Ger.). 1981. pap. 58.75 (ISBN 3-8055-0747-X). S Karger.
Hobson, Andrew & Hobson, Mark. Film Animation As a Hobby. LC 75-14523. 60p. 1975. 6.95 o.p. (ISBN 0-8069-5330-6); PLB 6.69 o.p. (ISBN 0-8069-5331-4). Sterling.
Hobson, Burton. Getting Started in Stamp Collecting. rev. ed. LC 62-18631. (Illus.). (gr. 4 up). 7.95 (ISBN 0-8069-6010-8); PLB 7.49 (ISBN 0-8069-6011-6). Sterling.
Hobson, Burton & Reinfeld, Fred. Coin Collecting for Beginners. pap. 3.00 (ISBN 0-87980-022-4). Wilshire.
Hobson, Burton, jt. auth. see Reinfeld, Fred.
Hobson, Burton H. Coin Collecting As a Hobby. rev. ed. LC 67-27759. (Illus.). (gr. 6 up). 1980. 7.95 (ISBN 0-8069-6018-3); PLB 7.49 (ISBN 0-8069-6019-1). Sterling.
--Coin Collecting As a Hobby. LC 67-27759. (Illus.). (gr. 3 up). 1977. 7.95 (ISBN 0-8069-6018-3); lib. bdg. 7.49 (ISBN 0-8069-6019-1). Sterling.
--Coins of the Americas: A Catalogue of North, South, & Central American Coins Since 1525 & Their Valuations. LC 80-52323. (Illus.). 384p. 1980. cancelled o.p. (ISBN 0-8069-6072-8); lib. bdg. cancelled o.p. (ISBN 0-8069-6073-6). Sterling.
Hobson, Burton H., jt. auth. see Reinfeld, Fred.
Hobson, Charles F., jt. ed. see Rutland, Robert A.
Hobson, Dale. Second Growth. (Illus.). 36p. (Orig.). 1980. pap. 3.00 (ISBN 0-918092-09-4). Tamarack Edns.
Hobson, Derek & Holmes, King K., eds. Nongonococcal Urethritis & Related Infections. LC 77-24329. 1977. 14.00 (ISBN 0-914826-12-3). Am Soc Microbio.
Hobson, Ernest W. Spherical & Ellipsoidal Harmonics. LC 55-233. 1955. 14.95 (ISBN 0-8284-0104-7). Chelsea Pub.
Hobson, G. D., ed. Advances in Organic Geochemistry, 1969: Proceedings. 1970. 82.00 (ISBN 0-08-012758-4). Pergamon.
--Developments in Petroleum Geology, Vol. 1. (Illus.). 1977. 77.70x (ISBN 0-85334-745-X, Pub. by Applied Science). Burgess-Intl Ideas.
--Developments in Petroleum Geology - Two. (Illus.). 345p. 1980. 70.00x (ISBN 0-85334-907-X). Burgess-Intl Ideas.
Hobson, G. S. Charge Transfer Devices. LC 78-40587. (Contemporary Electrical Engineering Ser.). 1978. 42.95 (ISBN 0-470-26458-6). Halsted Pr.
--The Gunn Effect. (Monographs in Electrical & Electronic Engineering). (Illus.). 142p. 1974. 27.00x (ISBN 0-19-859318-X). Oxford U Pr.
Hobson, Geary, ed. The Remembered Earth: An Anthology of Contemporary Native American Literature. (Illus.). 1978. pap. text ed. 6.95 o.p. (ISBN 0-918434-03-3). Red Earth.
Hobson, George, jt. auth. see Hobson, Sam B.
Hobson, Harold. French Theatre Since Eighteen Thirty. 1979. 17.95 (ISBN 0-7145-3650-4). Riverrun NY.
Hobson, J. A. The War in South Africa: Its Causes & Effects. LC 68-9620. 1970. Repr. of 1900 ed. 16.50 (ISBN 0-86527-208-5). Fertig.
Hobson, J. Allan & Brazier, Mary A., eds. The Reticular Formation. (International Brain Research Organization Monograph: Vol. 6). 1979. text ed. 53.50 (ISBN 0-89004-379-5). Raven.
Hobson, John A. Imperialism. 1965. pap. 5.95 (ISBN 0-472-06103-8, 103, AA). U of Mich Pr.
--Incentives in the New Industrial Order. LC 79-51860. 1981. Repr. of 1922 ed. 16.00 (ISBN 0-88355-953-6). Hyperion Conn.
--Towards International Government. LC 70-147581. (Library of War & Peace; Int'l. Organization, Arbitration & Law). lib. bdg. 38.00 (ISBN 0-8240-0345-4). Garland Pub.
--War in South Africa: Its Causes & Effects. Bd. with War & Its Causes. Gooch, George P. (Library of War & Peace; The Political Economy of War). lib. bdg. 38.00 (ISBN 0-8240-0290-3). Garland Pub.
Hobson, Mark, jt. auth. see Hobson, Andrew.
Hobson, P. N. & Robertson, A. M. Waste Treatment in Agriculture. (Illus.). 1977. 43.50x (ISBN 0-85334-736-0, Pub. by Applied Science). Burgess-Intl Ideas.
Hobson, Robert W., II, ed. Venous Trauma & Its Management. Date not set. price not set (ISBN 0-87993-155-8). Futura Pub.
Hobson, Sam B. & Hobson, George. The Lion of the Kalahari. Linfield, Esther, tr. from Afrikaans. LC 76-3432. (Eng.). (gr. 5-9). 1976. 7.75 o.p. (ISBN 0-688-80049-1); PLB 7.44 o.p. (ISBN 0-688-84049-3). Greenwillow.
Hobson, Sarah. Belts for All Occasions. (Illus.). 64p. (Orig.). 1976. 6.95 (ISBN 0-263-05599-X). Transatlantic.
Hobson, Wilder. American Jazz Music. LC 76-22565. (Roots of Jazz Ser.). 1976. Repr. of 1939 ed. lib. bdg. 19.50 (ISBN 0-306-70816-7). Da Capo.
Hobusch, Erich. Fair Game: A History of Hunting, Shooting & Animal Conservation. Michaelis-Jena, Ruth & Murray, Patrick, trs. from Ger. LC 80-19008. (Illus.). 280p. 1981. 29.95 (ISBN 0-668-05101-9, 5101). Arco.
Hoby, Otto, ed. see D'Espanha, Guiraut.
Hobzek, Mildred. We Came a-Marching... One, Two, Three. LC 78-7793. (Illus.). 40p. (ps-3). 1978. PLB 5.95 (ISBN 0-590-07720-1, Four Winds). Schol Bk Serv.
Hoch, Edward D. Best Detective Stories of the Year: Thirty-Fifth Annual Collection. 224p. 1981. 10.95 (ISBN 0-525-06440-0). Dutton.
Hoch, Elisabeth, tr. see Antalffy, Gyula.
Hoch, Elisabeth, tr. see Boskovits, Miklos.
Hoch, Elisabeth, tr. see Szigethi, Agnes.
Hoch, Frederick L. Energy Transformations in Mammals: Regulatory Mechanisms. LC 74-135326. (Illus.). 1971. 10.00 o.p. (ISBN 0-7216-4700-6). Saunders.
Hoch, Paul. The Newspaper Game. LC 74-192811. 1979. 10.95 (ISBN 0-7145-0857-8, Pub. by M Boyars); pap. 5.95 (ISBN 0-7145-1125-0, Pub. by M Boyars). Merrimack Bk Serv.
--Rip off the Big Game: The Exploitation of Sports by the Power Elite. LC 72-76230. 200p. 1972. pap. 2.50 o.p. (ISBN 0-385-04960-9, Anch). Doubleday.
Hochachka, P. W., ed. Biochemistry at Depth. 203p. 1976. text ed. 37.00 (ISBN 0-08-019960-7). Pergamon.
Hochbaum, H. Albert. Canvasback on a Prairie Marsh. LC 80-22699. (Illus.). xx, 208p. 1981. 15.95x (ISBN 0-8032-2300-5); pap. 5.95 (ISBN 0-8032-7200-6, BB 681, Bison). U of Nebr Pr.
Hochberg, Bette. Handspinner's Handbook. 3rd rev. ed. LC 76-12949. 1978. 5.95 o.p. (ISBN 0-9600990-1-8). B&B Hochberg.
--Handspinner's Handbook. rev. ed. LC 76-12949. (Illus.). 68p. 1980. pap. 5.95 (ISBN 0-9600990-5-0). B&B Hochberg.
Hochberg, Howard, jt. auth. see Lauersen, Neils H.
Hochberg, Irving. Interpretation of Audiometric Results. LC 72-85146. (Studies in Communicative Disorders Ser). 45p. 1973. pap. text ed. 2.50 (ISBN 0-672-61285-2). Bobbs.
Hochberg, Julian. Perception. 2nd ed. LC 77-27274. (Foundations of Modern Psychology Ser.). (Illus.). 1978. 12.95 o.p. (ISBN 0-13-657106-9); pap. text ed. 10.95 (ISBN 0-13-657098-4). P-H.
Hochberg, Matthew. Sweet Gogarty: A Darkly Comic Novel. LC 80-28358. 224p. 1981. 10.95 (ISBN 0-8253-0048-7). Beaufort Bks NY.
Hochberg, Phillip R., jt. auth. see Blackman, Martin E.
Hochheimer, Laura. A Sequential Sourcebook for Elementary School Music. 2nd ed. 1980. pap. 12.95 (ISBN 0-918812-12-7). Magnamusic.
Hochman, Harold M. & Peterson, George E. Redistribution Through Public Choice. 1974. 20.00x (ISBN 0-231-03775-9). Columbia U Pr.
Hochman, Sandra. Endangered Species. 1978. pap. 2.25 (ISBN 0-380-42366-9, 42366). Avon.
--Happiness Is Too Much Trouble. 1977. pap. 1.75 o.p. (ISBN 0-345-25509-7). Ballantine.
--Playing Tahoe. 1981. 13.95 (ISBN 0-671-25358-1, Wyndham Bks). S&S.
Hochman, Shel. How to Save Money on Car Repairs. LC 76-6960. (Illus.). 1976. 5.95 (ISBN 0-396-07322-0). Dodd.
Hochman, Stanley. Dictionary of Recent American History. LC 79-12265. 1979. 19.95 (ISBN 0-07-029103-9, P&RB). McGraw.
--Yesterday & Today: A Dictionary of Recent American History. LC 79-12265. (Illus.). 407p. 1979. 21.95 (ISBN 0-07-029103-9). McGraw.
Hochman, Stanley, ed. From Quasimodo to Scarlett O'Hara: A National Board of Review Anthology. LC 80-53695. (Ungar Film Library). 400p. 1981. 25.00 (ISBN 0-8044-2381-4); pap. 10.95 (ISBN 0-8044-6274-7). Ungar.
Hochschild, Arlie R. The Unexpected Community: Portrait of an Old Age Subculture. 1978. 18.50x (ISBN 0-520-03663-8); pap. 3.95 (ISBN 0-520-03624-7). U of Cal Pr.
Hochschild, Harold K. Adirondack Railroads, Real & Phantom. (Illus.). 20p. 1962. pap. 3.00 (ISBN 0-8156-8020-1, Pub. by Adirondack Museum). Syracuse U Pr.
--Doctor Durant & His Iron Horse. (Illus.). 15p. 1962. pap. 3.50 (ISBN 0-8156-8019-8, Pub. by Adirondack Museum). Syracuse U Pr.
Hochstadt, Harry. Differential Equations: A Modern Approach. LC 75-2569. (Illus.). 320p. 1975. pap. text ed. 5.00 (ISBN 0-486-61941-9). Dover.
--Functions of Mathematical Physics. LC 78-141199. (Pure & Applied Mathematics Ser.: Vol. 28). 1971. 32.95 (ISBN 0-471-40170-6, Pub. by Wiley-Interscience). Wiley.
Hochstein, Rolaine, jt. auth. see Sugarman, Daniel A.

Hochwalder, Fritz. The Public Prosecutor & Other Plays. LC 78-8814. 1980. 16.50 (ISBN 0-8044-2391-1). Ungar.
Hock, Saw S. Population Control for Zero Growth in Singapore. 250p. 1981. 29.95 (ISBN 0-19-580430-9). Oxford U Pr.
Hock, Tan K. & Brown, Ewen D. Geographical Interpretation Through Photographs (& Interpretation of Statistics) 1972. pap. text ed. 4.95x (ISBN 0-04-910048-3). Allen Unwin.
Hocker, Harold W., Jr. Introduction to Forest Biology. LC 78-26878. 1979. text ed. 25.95 (ISBN 0-471-01978-X). Wiley.
Hockert, Valerie. The Whole Body Tone-up Book. LC 80-53499. (Orig.). 1980. pap. 5.95 (ISBN 0-935698-01-9). Tasa Pub Co.
Hockett, Charles F. Man's Place in Nature. (Illus.). 736p. 1973. text ed. 17.95 o.p. (ISBN 0-07-029120-9, C); instructor's manual 3.95 o.p. (ISBN 0-07-029133-0). McGraw.
Hockett, H. C. Western Influences on Political Parties to 1825. LC 75-87650. (American Scene Ser.). 1970. Repr. of 1917 ed. lib. bdg. 19.50 (ISBN 0-306-71777-8). Da Capo.
Hockett, Shirley. Barron's How to Prepare for Advanced Placement in Mathematics. rev. ed. (gr. 10-12). 1981. pap. text ed. 8.50 (ISBN 0-8120-2071-5). Barron.
--Basic Mathematics: What Every College Student Should Know. (Illus.). 1977. pap. 14.95 (ISBN 0-13-063446-8). P-H.
Hockett, Shirley O. How to Prepare for Advanced Placement Examinations: Mathematics. rev. ed. LC 77-149360. (gr. 11-12). 1977. pap. text ed. 8.50 (ISBN 0-8120-0354-3). Barron.
Hockey, Lisbeth, ed. Current Issues in Nursing. (Recent Advances in Nursing Ser.). 200p. 1981. pap. text ed. 14.00 (ISBN 0-443-02186-4). Churchill.
Hockey, Robert V. Physical Fitness: The Pathway to Healthful Living. (Illus.). 195p. 1981. pap. text ed. 8.95 (ISBN 0-8016-2216-6). Mosby.
Hockey, S. F. Quarr Abbey & Its Lands, 1132-1631. 1970. text ed. 12.00x (ISBN 0-7185-1087-9, Leicester). Humanities.
Hockey, S. W. Introduction to Calculus. 1970. 8.50 (ISBN 0-08-012579-4). Pergamon.
Hockin, T. Apex of Power: The Prime Minister & Political Leadership in Canada. 2nd ed. 1977. pap. 11.25 (ISBN 0-13-038653-7). P-H.
Hocking, John G. & Young, G. S. Topology. 1961. 17.95 o.p. (ISBN 0-201-02855-7). A-W.
Hocking, William E. Freedom of the Press. LC 77-39587. (Civil Liberties in American History Ser). 240p. 1972. Repr. of 1947 ed. lib. bdg. 22.50 (ISBN 0-306-70231-2). Da Capo.
Hockings, Paul. Sex & Disease in a Mountain Community. 1980. 14.00x (ISBN 0-8364-0625-7, Pub. by Vikas). South Asia Bks.
Hockings, Paul, ed. Ancient Hindu Refugees: Badaga Social History 1550-1975. (Studies in Anthropology). 1980. text ed. 23.50x (ISBN 90-279-7798-4). Mouton.
Hockley, Graham. Public Finance: An Introduction. (Illus.). 1979. 32.00 (ISBN 0-7100-0148-7); pap. 15.00 (ISBN 0-7100-0149-5). Routledge & Kegan.
Hockley, William B. Pandurang Hari: Or, Memoirs of a Hindoo (A Novel, 3 vols. LC 80-2484. 1981. Repr. of 1826 ed. Set. 149.50 (ISBN 0-404-19140-1). AMS Pr.
Hockney, David. Paper Pools. Stangos, Nikos, ed. (Illus.). 100p. 1980. 22.50 (ISBN 0-686-62704-0, 1461-1); pap. 14.95 (ISBN 0-686-62705-9, 2229-0). Abrams.
Hockney, Monica. Meals in Minutes. 3.95 (ISBN 0-685-44121-0). Transatlantic.
Hockridge, Derek, tr. see Goscinny & Uderzo.
Hocks, Richard A., ed. see James, Henry.
Hockstein, Peter & Hoffman, Sandy. Up from Seltzer. LC 80-54617. (Illus.). 96p. 1981. pap. 3.95 (ISBN 0-89480-145-7). Workman Pub.
Hockwin, O. Bonn, ed. Growth Control, Differentiation, & Aging of the Eye Lens. (Journal: Ophthalmic Research, Vol. 11, No. 5-6, 1979). (Illus.). 242p. 1979. softcover 29.50 (ISBN 3-8055-0862-X). S Karger.
Hocutt, Charles H. & Stauffer, Jay R., Jr., eds. Biological Monitoring of Fish. LC 79-3049. 432p. 1980. 31.95x (ISBN 0-669-03309-X). Lexington Bks.
Hocutt, Charles H., et al. Power Plants: Effects on Fish & Shellfish Behavior. 1980. 25.00 (ISBN 0-12-350950-5). Acad Pr.
Hocutt, Max. First Philosophy: An Introduction to Philosophical Issues. 272p. 1980. pap. text ed. 9.95x (ISBN 0-534-00790-2). Wadsworth Pub.
Hodder, E. The Life & Work of the Seventh Earl of Shaftesbury, 3 vols. 2150p. 1971. Repr. of 1886 ed. 110.00x (ISBN 0-686-20140-X, Pub. by Irish Academic Pr Ireland). Biblio Dist.
Hodder, I. & Orton, C. Spatial Analysis in Archaeology. LC 75-44582. (New Studies in Archaeology Ser.). (Illus.). 1976. 35.00x (ISBN 0-521-21080-1). Cambridge U Pr.
--Spatial Analysis in Archaeology. LC 75-44582. (New Studies in Archaeology). (Illus.). 260p. 1980. pap. 14.50 (ISBN 0-521-29738-9). Cambridge U Pr.
Hodder, I., ed. Simulation Studies. LC 78-51670. (Illus.). 1979. 24.95 (ISBN 0-521-22025-4). Cambridge U Pr.
Hodder, I., et al. Pattern of the Past. LC 79-8497. (Illus.). 424p. Date not set. 49.50 (ISBN 0-521-22763-1). Cambridge U Pr.
Hoddinott, R. F. The Thracians. (Ancient Peoples & Places Ser.). (Illus.). 192p. 1981. 19.95 (ISBN 0-500-02099-X). Thames Hudson.
Hoddinott, Ralph. Bulgaria in Antiquity. LC 74-77766. 1975. 25.00 (ISBN 0-312-10780-3). St Martin.
Hodeir, Andre. Jazz: Its Evolution & Essence. Noakes, David, tr. from Fr. LC 74-23387. (Roots of Jazz Ser). ix, 295p. 1975. Repr. of 1956 ed. lib. bdg. 22.50 (ISBN 0-306-70682-2). Da Capo.
--Jazz: Its Evolution & Essence. rev. ed. Noakes, David, tr. from French. LC 79-52101. (Illus.). 1980. pap. 3.95 (ISBN 0-394-17525-5, B436, BC). Grove.
--Since Debussy: A View of Contemporary Music. Burch, Noel, tr. LC 74-28310. (Illus.). 256p. 1975. Repr. of 1961 ed. lib. bdg. 22.50 (ISBN 0-306-70662-8). Da Capo.
--Toward Jazz. LC 76-7568. (The Roots of Jazz Ser.). 1976. Repr. of 1962 ed. lib. bdg. 22.50 (ISBN 0-306-70810-8). Da Capo.
Hodenfield, G. K., jt. auth. see Diehl, Kathryn.
Hodes, Art & Hansen, Chadwick, eds. Selections from the Gutter: Portraits from the Jazz Record. LC 75-7193. 1977. 15.95x (ISBN 0-520-02999-2); pap. 5.95 (ISBN 0-520-03719-7). U of Cal Pr.
Hodes, R. Aims & Methods of Scientific Research. (No. 9). 1.00 (ISBN 0-89977-011-8). Am Inst Marxist.
Hodgart, Alan. The Economics of European Imperialism. (Foundations of Modern History Ser.). 1978. 7.95 (ISBN 0-393-05667-8); pap. 4.95x (ISBN 0-393-09061-2). Norton.
Hodgart, Matthew. James Joyce: A Student's Guide. 1978. 16.00x (ISBN 0-7100-8817-5); pap. 7.95 (ISBN 0-7100-8943-0). Routledge & Kegan.
Hodgart, Matthew, ed. The Faber Book of Ballads. 1965. 11.95 o.p. (ISBN 0-571-06236-9, Pub. by Faber & Faber). Merrimack Bk Serv.
Hodge, A. A. Confession of Faith. 1978. 12.95 (ISBN 0-85151-275-5). Banner of Truth.
--Evangelical Theology. 1976. pap. 5.45 (ISBN 0-85151-236-4). Banner of Truth.
--Outlines of Theology. 580p. 1972. text ed. 12.95 (ISBN 0-310-26200-3). Zondervan.
Hodge, A. Trevor. Woodwork of Greek Roofs. (Cambridge Classical Studies). 1960. 17.95 (ISBN 0-521-05280-7). Cambridge U Pr.
Hodge, Alan, ed. Varieties of Travel. LC 79-351286. (Selections from History Today Ser.: No. 8). (Illus.). 1969. 5.00 (ISBN 0-05-001535-4); pap. 3.95 (ISBN 0-685-09206-2). Dufour.
Hodge, Ben. Football. LC 75-6822. (Target Bks.). (Illus.). (gr. 4-6). 1977. PLB 6.45 s&l (ISBN 0-531-00768-5). Watts.
Hodge, Carleton. Spoken Serbo-Croatian. Incl. Bk. 1, Units 1-12. viii, 254p. pap. 9.00x (ISBN 0-87950-210-X); Bk. 2, Units 13-30. 432p. 1973. pap. 10.00x (ISBN 0-87950-211-8); Records, Six 12-Inch lp (33.3 rpm) 55.00x (ISBN 0-87950-213-4); Record Course-Bk 1 & Records. pap. 55.00x (ISBN 0-87950-214-2); Cassettes, Six Dual Track. 60.00x (ISBN 0-87950-215-0); Cassette Course-Bk. 1 & Cassettes. pap. text ed. 65.00x (ISBN 0-87950-216-9). LC 74-150403. (Spoken Language Ser). (Prog. Bk.). 1976. Spoken Lang Serv.
Hodge, Charles. Corinthians 1 & 2. (Geneva Commentaries Ser.). 1978. 11.95 (ISBN 0-85151-185-6). Banner of Truth.
--Princeton Sermons. 1979. 11.95 (ISBN 0-85151-285-2). Banner of Truth.
--Romans. (Geneva Commentaries Ser.). 1975. 11.95 (ISBN 0-85151-213-5). Banner of Truth.
--Way of Life. 1978. pap. 3.95 (ISBN 0-85151-273-9). Banner of Truth.
Hodge, Francis. Play Directing: Analysis, Communication & Style. LC 75-143030. (Theatre & Drama Ser). 1971. ref. ed. 15.95 (ISBN 0-13-682815-9). P-H.
Hodge, Frederick W. & Lewis, Theodore H., eds. Spanish Explorers in the Southern United States, 1528-1543. (Original Narratives). (Illus.). 1977. Repr. of 1907 ed. 15.00x (ISBN 0-06-480372-4). B&N.
Hodge, J. C. Brickwork for Apprentices. 3rd ed. (Illus.). 1971. pap. 13.95x (ISBN 0-7131-3250-7). Intl Ideas.
Hodge, James R. Practical Psychiatry for the Primary Physician. LC 75-9857. 368p. 1975. 19.95 (ISBN 0-88229-157-2). Nelson Hall.
Hodge, Jane A. Greek Wedding. 320p. 1977. pap. 1.75 o.p. (ISBN 0-449-23216-6, Crest). Fawcett.
--Here Comes a Candle. 1978. pap. 1.95 o.p. (ISBN 0-449-23600-5, Crest). Fawcett.
--Last Act. 256p. 1981. pap. 2.50 (ISBN 0-449-24379-6, Crest). Fawcett.
--Marry in Haste. 1976. pap. 1.50 o.p. (ISBN 0-449-23068-6, Crest). Fawcett.
--Maulever Hall. 1977. pap. 1.50 o.s.i. (ISBN 0-515-04332-X). Jove Pubns.
--Runaway Bride. 1978. pap. 1.75 o.p. (ISBN 0-449-23591-2, Crest). Fawcett.
--Shadow of a Lady. 1977. pap. 1.75 o.p. (ISBN 0-449-23117-8, Crest). Fawcett.
--The Winding Stair. 1978. pap. 2.25 (ISBN 0-449-23590-4, Crest). Fawcett.
Hodge, Jeannine G. History of Holliday, Texas. 7.95 (ISBN 0-685-48799-7). Nortex Pr.
Hodge, M. J., jt. auth. see Cantor, G. N.
Hodge, Marshall Bryant. Your Fear of Love. LC 67-15960. 1969. pap. 2.50 (ISBN 0-385-04372-4, C483, Dolp). Doubleday.
Hodge, Melville H. Medical Information Systems: A New Resource for Hospitals. LC 77-12739. 1977. 25.75 (ISBN 0-912862-47-5). Aspen Systems.
Hodge, Paul W. Atlas of the Andromeda Galaxy. (Illus.). 80p. 1981. 50.00 (ISBN 0-295-95795-6). U of Wash Pr.
Hodge, Peter. Aspects of Roman Life: Folder 1. (Illus.). 1977. folder 12.85x (ISBN 0-582-31416-X). Longman.
--Roman Army. (Aspects of Roman Life). (Illus.). 1978. pap. text ed. 2.95x (ISBN 0-582-31414-3). Longman.
--Roman House. (Aspects of Roman Life Ser.). (Illus.). 1976. pap. text ed. 2.95x (ISBN 0-582-20300-7). Longman.
--Roman Towns. (Aspects of Roman Life). (Illus.). 1977. pap. text ed. 2.95x (ISBN 0-582-20301-5). Longman.
--Roman Trade & Travel. (Aspects of Roman Life Ser). (Illus.). 1978. pap. text ed. 2.95x (ISBN 0-582-31413-5). Longman.
Hodge, R. I., ed. see Milton, John.
Hodge, Robert, jt. auth. see Kress, Gunther.
Hodge, S. E. & Seed, M. L. Statistics & Probability. 2nd ed. (Illus.). 1977. pap. text ed. 12.95x (ISBN 0-216-90450-1). Intl Ideas.
Hodge, Virginia. Personality & Second Language Learning. (Language in Education Ser.: No. 12). 1978. pap. 2.95 (ISBN 0-87281-086-0). Ctr Appl Ling.
Hodgen, Margaret T. Early Anthropology in the Sixteenth & Seventeenth Centuries. LC 62-11265. (Illus.). 1971. pap. text ed. 6.95x (ISBN 0-8122-1014-X, Pa Paperbks). U of Pa Pr.
Hodges, Allan. Psychological Counseling in General Medical Practice. 1977. 14.95 (ISBN 0-669-01039-1). Lexington Bks.
Hodges, Allan & Hodges, Carol. Washington on Foot. 2nd ed. LC 80-15844. (Illus.). 202p. 1980. pap. 4.25 (ISBN 0-87474-527-6). Smithsonian.
Hodges, Allan A. & Hodges, Carol, eds. Washington on Foot: A City Planner's Guide to the Nation's Capital. 2nd. ed. LC 76-1355. (Illus.). 208p. 1980. pap. 4.25 o.p. (ISBN 0-87474-525-X). Smithsonian.
Hodges, Carol, jt. auth. see Hodges, Allan.
Hodges, Carol, jt. ed. see Hodges, Allan A.
Hodges, D. R., ed. Recent Analytical Developments in the Petroleum Industry. LC 74-23137. 337p. 1974. 44.95 (ISBN 0-470-40208-3). Halsted Pr.
Hodges, David A., ed. Semiconductor Memories. LC 72-86206. 1972. 8.95 o.p. (ISBN 0-87942-013-8). Inst Electrical.
Hodges, Donald C. The Bureaucratization of Socialism. LC 80-23253. 240p. 1981. lib. bdg. 15.00x (ISBN 0-87023-138-3). U of Mass Pr.
Hodges, George. Short History of the Episcopal Church. 1967. 1.10 (ISBN 0-686-28793-2). Forward Movement.
Hodges, Henry. Artifacts: An Introduction to Early Materials & Technology. rev. ed. (Illus., Orig.). 1976. pap. text ed. 11.75x (ISBN 0-212-35918-5). Humanities.
Hodges, Herbert A. Wilhelm Dilthey: An Introduction. 1969. Repr. of 1944 ed. 13.00 (ISBN 0-86527-211-5). Fertig.
Hodges, Hollis. Don't Tell Your Name. 192p. 1981. pap. 2.25 (ISBN 0-380-53751-6, 53751). Avon.
--Why Would I Lie? 1980. pap. 2.25 (ISBN 0-686-69259-4, 50732). Avon.
Hodges, Lewis H. How to Build Your Own Fine Doll Houses & Furnishings. (Illus.). 1979. 14.95 (ISBN 0-8306-9853-1); pap. 9.95 (ISBN 0-8306-1102-9, 1102). TAB Bks.
Hodges, Margaret. Sing Out Charley. 96p. 1968. 3.50 (ISBN 0-374-36930-5). FS&G.
Hodges, Margaret, jt. auth. see Smith, Elva S.
Hodges, Margaret, ed. Constellation: A Shakespeare Anthology. LC 68-13677. (Index). (gr. 7 up). 1968. 4.95 o.p. (ISBN 0-374-31485-3). FS&G.
Hodges, Melvin, tr. Como Fundar Iglesias. (Spanish Bks.). (Span.). 1978. 1.50 (ISBN 0-8297-0560-0). Life Pubs Intl.
--Crecimiento De la Iglesia. (Spanish Bks.). (Span.). 1979. 1.50 (ISBN 0-8297-0905-3). Life Pubs Intl.
--Desarrollo Del Varon De Dios. (Spanish Bks.). (Span.). 1978. 0.80 (ISBN 0-8297-0528-7). Life Pubs Intl.
--Edificare My Iglesia. (Spanish Bks.). 1979. 1.50 (ISBN 0-8297-0544-9); wkbk. 0.80 (ISBN 0-8297-0545-7). Life Pubs Intl.
--Um Guia Para Fundacao De Igrejas. (Portuguese Bks.). 1979. 1.10 (ISBN 0-686-28807-6). Vida Pub.
Hodges, Michael. Multinational Corporations & National Governments: A Case Study of the United Kingdom's Experience, 1964-1970. 1974. 21.95 (ISBN 0-347-01034-2, 93500-X, Pub. by Saxon Hse England). Lexington Bks.
Hodges, Paul, ed. Then & Now. 1979. 10.95 (ISBN 0-89002-153-8); pap. 3.50 (ISBN 0-89002-152-X). Northwoods Pr.
Hodges, Pauline. A Resource Book for Teaching Reading in the Content Areas. 96p. 1980. pap. text ed. 6.95 (ISBN 0-8403-2263-1). Kendall-Hunt.
Hodges, R. E. & Rudorf, E. Hugh. Language & Learning to Read: What Teachers Should Know About Language. LC 70-175170. 1972. pap. text ed. 10.95 (ISBN 0-395-12639-8, 3-25626). HM.
Hodges, Raymond W. High School Equivalency Test Guide. LC 75-2181. 95p. (Orig.). (gr. 9-12). 1975. pap. text ed. 5.00 (ISBN 0-913310-13-1). Par Inc.
Hodges, Raymond W., et al. Reading & Word Skills. Smith, Barry M., ed. LC 73-80232. (Basic Studies Program). (Illus.). 282p. 1973. pap. text ed. 11.25 (ISBN 0-913310-19-0). PAR Inc.
--Understanding Mathematics. Smith, Barry M., ed. LC 73-80234. (Basic Studies Program). (Illus.). 166p. 1973. pap. text ed. 7.65 (ISBN 0-913310-30-1). PAR Inc.
--College Word Study. LC 74-12551. (Illus.). 197p. 1980. pap. text ed. 10.15 (ISBN 0-913310-10-7). PAR Inc.
--Writing, Speaking & Listening. Smith, Barry M., ed. LC 73-80233. (Basic Studies Program). 184p. 1973. pap. text ed. 7.65 (ISBN 0-913310-34-4). PAR Inc.
Hodges, Susan, jt. ed. see Bryant, M. Darrol.
Hodges, Tony. Jehovah's Witnesses in Central Africa. (Minority Rights Group Ser.: No. 29). 16p. (Orig.). 1976. pap. 2.50 (ISBN 0-89192-120-6). Interbk Inc.
Hodges, Walter, et al. School Psychology & Early Childhood Education. LC 68-52341. 1977. pap. 6.95 (ISBN 0-87705-326-X). Human Sci Pr.
Hodges, Wilfrid. Logic. 1980. 3.95 (ISBN 0-14-021985-4). Penguin.
Hodgetts. Business Enterprise. 1977. 11.95 (ISBN 0-7216-4709-X). Dryden Pr.
--Organizational Behavior. 1979. 19.95 (ISBN 0-7216-4713-8). Dryden Pr.
Hodgetts, Blake. Dream of the Dinosaurs. LC 77-82949. (gr. k-3). 1978. PLB 6.95 (ISBN 0-385-12139-3). Doubleday.
Hodgetts, Colin. We Will Suffer & Die If We Have To. 1971. pap. 1.95 o.p. (ISBN 0-8170-0527-7). Judson.
Hodgetts, J. E. Canadian Public Service: A Physiology of Government, 1867-1970. LC 72-90738. 400p. 1973. pap. 8.50 (ISBN 0-8020-6260-1). U of Toronto Pr.
Hodgetts, J. Frederick. Olden England, 2 vols. 413p. 1981. Repr. of 1884 ed. Set. lib. bdg. 200.00 (ISBN 0-89987-364-2). Darby Bks.
Hodgetts, Richard M. Introduction to Business. 2nd ed. LC 76-12797. 1981. text ed. write for info. (ISBN 0-201-02897-2); write for info. resource guide; write for info. study guide (ISBN 0-201-03896-X). A-W.
--Introduction to Business. 2nd ed. LC 80-21284. (Business Ser.). (Illus.). 600p. 1981. text ed. 15.95 (ISBN 0-201-03894-3). A-W.
--Management Fundamentals. LC 80-65800. 464p. 1981. text ed. 17.95 (ISBN 0-03-058104-4). Dryden Pr.
--Modern Human Relations. 512p. 1980. text ed. 18.95 (ISBN 0-03-054276-6). Dryden Pr.
Hodgetts, Richard M. & Wortman, Max S. Administrative Policy: Text & Cases in Strategic Management. 2nd ed. LC 78-24528. (Management Ser.). 712p. 1979. text ed. 22.95 (ISBN 0-471-03605-6); case notes avail. (ISBN 0-471-05041-5). Wiley.
Hodgetts, Victoria, jt. auth. see Quigley, Pax.
Hodgins, Bruce W. & Page, Robert J. D. Canadian History Since Confederation. 2nd ed. 1979. pap. text ed. 12.50x (ISBN 0-256-02137-6). Dorsey.
Hodgins, Gordon W. The Broadway Musical: A Complete LP Discography. LC 80-18911. 188p. 1980. 10.00 (ISBN 0-8108-1343-2). Scarecrow.
Hodgkin, Alan, et al. The Pursuit of Nature. LC 76-58844. (Illus.). 1979. pap. 8.50 (ISBN 0-521-29617-X). Cambridge U Pr.

--The Pursuit of Nature. LC 76-58844. (Illus.). 1977. 35.50 (ISBN 0-521-21505-6). Cambridge U Pr.
Hodgkin, Joan & Hodgkin, Norman. What a Way to See. (Illus.). (gr. k-2). 1974. 2.25x (ISBN 0-933892-12-8). Child Focus Co.
Hodgkin, Norman, jt. auth. see Hodgkin, Joan.
Hodgkin, Robin. Born Curious: New Perspectives in Educational Theory. LC 75-16340. 1976. 22.95 (ISBN 0-471-40220-6, Pub. by Wiley-Interscience). Wiley.
Hodgkins, John, jt. auth. see Love, John.
Hodgkins, W. R., jt. ed. see Ockendon, J. R.
Hodgkinson, Alan, ed. AJ Handbook of Building Structure. 2nd ed. LC 75-301801. (Illus.). 360p. 1980. 32.50x (ISBN 0-85139-273-3). Intl Pubns Serv.
Hodgkinson, Allan. A J Handbook of Building Structure. 2nd ed. (Illus.). 428p. (Orig.). 1980. pap. 37.50x (ISBN 0-85139-273-3). Intl Pubns Serv.
Hodgkinson, Edith. Season's Edge. 1980. pap. 2.00 (ISBN 0-914610-22-8). Hanging Loose.
Hodgkinson, Harold L. & Bloy, Myron B., Jr., eds. Identity Crisis in Higher Education. LC 78-110644. (Higher Education Ser.). 1971. 11.95x o.p. (ISBN 0-87589-085-7). Jossey-Bass.
Hodgman, Francis. Land Surveying. 1976. Repr. of 1913 ed. 15.00 (ISBN 0-686-18868-3, 609). CARBEN Survey.
Hodgson, D., jt. ed. see Marden, P. G.
Hodgson, David. All About Action Photography. (Illus.). 1976. 18.00 (ISBN 0-7207-0888-5). Transatlantic.
Hodgson, Francis. International Medical Who's Who, 2 vols. 1300p. 1980. Set. text ed. 180.00x (ISBN 0-582-90107-3). Churchill.
--Lady Jane Gray: With Miscellaneous Poems in English & Latin. 1809. Reiman, Donald H., ed. LC 75-31221. (Romantic Context Ser.: Poetry 1789-1830). 1978. lib. bdg. 47.00 (ISBN 0-8240-2171-1). Garland Pub.
--Medical Research Index, 2 vols. 2nd ed. 1360p. 1980. text ed. 150.00x (ISBN 0-582-90005-0). Churchill.
--Sir Edgar. 1810. Reiman, Donald H., ed. LC 75-31222. (Romantic Context Ser.: Poetry 1789-1810). 1977. lib. bdg. 47.00 (ISBN 0-8240-2172-X). Garland Pub.
Hodgson, Godfrey. All Things to All Men. 1980. 12.95 (ISBN 0-671-24782-4). S&S.
Hodgson, J. M. Soil Sampling & Soil Description. (Monographs on Soil Survey). (Illus.). 1978. 29.95x (ISBN 0-19-854511-8). Oxford U Pr.
Hodgson, Jane E. Abortion & Sterilization: Medical & Social Aspects. 1981. write for info. (ISBN 0-8089-1344-1). Grune.
Hodgson, Joan. Angels & Indians. (Illus.). (gr. 2-7). 1974. 6.95 (ISBN 0-85487-033-4). De Vorss.
--Hullo Sun. (Illus.). (ps-3). 1972. 6.95 (ISBN 0-85487-019-9). De Vorss.
--Reincarnation Through the Zodiac. LC 79-444. (Illus.). 1979. pap. 4.95 (ISBN 0-916360-11-3). CRCS Pubns NV.
--Why on Earth. rev. ed. 144p. 1979. pap. 4.95 (ISBN 0-85487-043-1). De Vorss.
Hodgson, John A. Wordsworth's Philosophical Poetry, 1797-1814. LC 79-24921. xxii, 216p. 1980. 17.50x (ISBN 0-8032-2310-2). U of Nebr Pr.
Hodgson, John H. Earthquakes & Earth Structure. (Illus.). 1964. text ed. 10.95 (ISBN 0-13-222455-0). P-H.
Hodgson, Marshall G. The Venture of Islam, 3 vols. Incl. Vol. 1. The Classical Age of Islam. pap. 9.50 (ISBN 0-226-34683-8, P716); Vol. 2. The Expansion of Islam in the Middle Period. pap. 9.50 (ISBN 0-226-34684-6, P717); Vol. 3. The Gunpowder Empire & Modern Times. pap. 9.50 (ISBN 0-226-34685-4, P718). LC 73-87243. (Illus.). 1977 (Phoen). U of Chicago Pr.
Hodgson, Mary Anne & Paine, Josephine Ruth. Fast & Easy Needlepoint. LC 76-56302. (gr. 3-7). 1978. PLB 5.95 (ISBN 0-385-12432-5). Doubleday.
Hodgson, Myra, ed. An American Response to the Foreign Industrial Challenge in High Technology Industries. 175p. (Orig.). 1980. pap. 95.00 (ISBN 0-686-69372-8). W Fraser Pubs.
Hodgson, P. E. Growth Points in Nuclear Physics, Vol. 1. (Illus.). 1980. 21.00 (ISBN 0-08-023080-6); pap. 9.50 (ISBN 0-08-023079-2). Pergamon.
--Growth Points in Nuclear Physics, Vol, 2. (Illus.). 1980. 21.00 (ISBN 0-08-023082-2); pap. text ed. 9.50 (ISBN 0-08-023081-4). Pergamon.
--Nuclear Heavy-Ion Reactions. (Oxford Studies in Nuclear Physics). (Illus.). 598p. 1978. text ed. 55.00x (ISBN 0-19-851514-6). Oxford U Pr.
Hodgson, Pat. Growing up with the North American Indians. (Illus.). 72p. (gr. 6-10). 1980. 16.95 (ISBN 0-7134-2732-9, Pub. by Batsford England). David & Charles.
Hodgson, Peter C., tr. see Hegel, Georg W.
Hodgson, Shadworth H. & Nathanson, Maurice. The Metaphysic of Experience, 4 vols. LC 78-66730. (Phenomenology Ser.). 858p. 1980. lib. bdg. 193.00 (ISBN 0-8240-9564-2). Garland Pub.
Hodgson, Thomas A. Social & Economic Implications of Cancer in the United States. Cox, Klaudia, ed. (Ser. 3, No. 20). 50p. 1980. pap. text ed. 1.50 (ISBN 0-8406-0203-0). Natl Ctr Health Stats.
Hodgson, W. H. The Ghost Pirates. 276p. 1980. Repr. of 1909 ed. lib. bdg. 13.95x (ISBN 0-89968-209-X). Lightyear.
--House on the Borderland. 1976. lib. bdg. 12.95x (ISBN 0-89968-178-6). Lightyear.
--The Night Land. 1976. lib. bdg. 12.95x (ISBN 0-89968-179-4). Lightyear.
Hodgson, W. R. & Skinner, Paul. Hearing Aid Assessment & Use in Audiologic Rehabilitation. 2nd ed. (Illus.). 343p. 1981. write for info. (ISBN 0-683-04092-8). Williams & Wilkins.
Hodin, J. P. Edvard Munch. (World of Art Ser.). (Illus.). 1972. pap. text ed. 9.95 (ISBN 0-19-519936-7). Oxford U Pr.
Hodkinson, H. M. An Outline of Geriatrics. 1975. 11.50 (ISBN 0-12-351450-9). Acad Pr.
Hodkinson, L. J., jt. auth. see Roaf, R.
Hodkinson, M. A. Nursing the Elderly. 1967. 18.00 (ISBN 0-08-011987-5); pap. 7.00 (ISBN 0-686-66515-5). Pergamon.
Hodnett, Edward. English Woodcuts: Fourteen Eighty to Fifteen Thirty-Five. (Illus.). 611p. 1973. 45.00x o.p. (ISBN 0-19-721728-1). Oxford U Pr.
--Francis Barlow: First Master of English Book Illustration. 1978. 42.50x (ISBN 0-520-03409-0). U of Cal Pr.
Hodnett, Grey. Leadership in Soviet National Republics. 409p. (Orig.). 1978. pap. text ed. 45.00 (ISBN 0-686-61282-5, Pub. by K G Saur). Gale.
Hodnett, Grey see McNeal, Robert H.
Hodson, Alexander C., jt. auth. see Eddy, Samuel.
Hodson, Alfred. The Fishing Cadet's Handbook. (Illus.). 108p. 7.50 (ISBN 0-85238-011-9, FN). Unipub.
Hodson, C. J., et al. The Pathogenesis of Reflux Nephropathy. Maling, T. M. & McManamon, P. J., eds. 1980. 10.00x (Pub. by Brit Inst Radiology). State Mutual Bk.
Hodson, F. R., ed. The Place of Astronomy in the Ancient World: A Joint Symposium of the Royal Society & the British Academy. (Illus.). 280p. 1974. 69.00x (ISBN 0-19-725944-8). Oxford U Pr.
Hodson, G. Fairies at Work & Play. pap. 5.95 (ISBN 0-7229-5232-5). Theos Pub Hse.
Hodson, Geoffrey. The Hidden Wisdom in the Holy Bible, Vol. 3. 1971. 7.95 (ISBN 0-8356-7493-2). Theos Pub Hse.
--The Hidden Wisdom in the Holy Bible, Vol. 4. LC 67-8724. 375p. (Orig.). 1981. pap. 5.95 (ISBN 0-8356-0548-5, Quest). Theos Pub Hse.
--The Miracle of Birth. rev. ed. LC 80-53950. (Illus.). 100p. 1981. pap. 3.95 (ISBN 0-8356-0545-0). Theos Pub Hse.
--Seven Human Temperaments. 6th ed. 1977. 3.25 (ISBN 0-8356-7222-0). Theos Pub Hse.
Hodson, H. V., ed. The International Foundation Directory. 2nd ed. LC 73-90303. 1980. 65.00 (ISBN 0-8103-2018-5, Europa Publication). Gale.
Hodson, H. V. & Engel, M., eds. The Business Who's Who, 1974-5. LC 73-91903. 30.00x (ISBN 0-900537-21-3, H-316, Dist. by Hippocrene Books Inc.). Leviathan Hse.
Hodson, Harry V., jt. ed. see Corson, John J.
Hodson, J. H. The Administration of Archives. LC 72-163642. 224p. 1972. 42.00 (ISBN 0-08-016676-8). Pergamon.
Hodson, John C. & Kincaid-Smith, Priscilla, eds. Reflux Nephropathy. LC 79-84477. (Illus.). 366p. 1979. text ed. 43.50 (ISBN 0-89352-044-6). Masson Pub.
Hodson, Violet. Charlie Churchmouse. (Illus.). 40p. (gr. k-4). 1976. pap. 1.95 o.p. (ISBN 0-87239-104-3, 2761). Standard Pub.
Hodza, Aaron C. & Fortune, George, eds. Shona Praise Poetry. (Oxford Library of African Literature). (Illus.). 1979. 49.50x (ISBN 0-19-815144-6). Oxford U Pr.
Hoebel, E. Adamson. Plains Indians: A Critical Bibliography. LC 77-6914. (Newberry Library Center for the History of the American Indian Bibl. Ser.). 88p. 1977. pap. 3.95x (ISBN 0-253-34509-X). Ind U Pr.
Hoeber, Amoretta M., jt. auth. see Douglass, Joseph D., Jr.
Hoeber, Daniel R. & Kasden, Lawrence N. Basic Writing: Essays for Teachers, Researchers, & Administrators. LC 80-14634. 185p. (Orig.). 1980. pap. 9.50 (ISBN 0-8141-0268-9). NCTE.
Hoeber, Francis P. How Little Is Enough? SALT & Security in the Long Run. (NSIC Strategy Paper Ser.: No. 35). 96p. 1981. pap. text ed. 5.95x (ISBN 0-8448-1383-4). Crane-Russak Co.
Hoeber, Frank. Slow to Take Offense: Bombers, Cruise Missiles, & Prudent Deterrence. LC 80-80662. (CSIS Monograph). 137p. 1980. pap. text ed. 6.95. CSI Studies.
Hoeber, Ralph, et al. Contemporary Business Law: Principles & Cases. Severance, Gordon, ed. (Illus.). 1980. text ed. 19.95 (ISBN 0-07-029160-8); instr's manual 6.95 (ISBN 0-07-029161-6); test bank 13.95 (ISBN 0-07-029163-2); study guide 6.95 (ISBN 0-07-029162-4); student CPA examination suppl. 1.50 (ISBN 0-07-029164-0). McGraw.
Hoeber, Thomas R., et al, eds. California Government & Politics Annual, 1980-81. (Illus.). 128p. (Orig.). 1980. pap. text ed. 3.95x (ISBN 0-930302-24-9). Cal Journal.
Hoefer, George, jt. auth. see Smith, Willie.
Hoefer, Hans. Stoned Images. 1979. pap. 7.95 o.p. (ISBN 0-525-47510-9). Dutton.
Hoefler, Richard C. The Divine Trap: Background on the Parables, Ser. A. 168p. (Orig.). 1980. pap. 5.70 (ISBN 0-89536-445-X). CSS Pub.
--I Knew You'd Come! The Miracles of Jesus, Ser. A. 80p. (Orig.). 1980. pap. text ed. 4.65 (ISBN 0-89536-444-1). CSS Pub.
--A Sign in the Straw. 128p. (Orig.). 1980. pap. text ed. 6.25 (ISBN 0-89536-465-4). CSS Pub.
Hoefnagels, Mario. Repression & Repressive Violence. (Publications of the Ppolemological Centre of the Free University of Brussels: Vol. 7). 200p. 1977. pap. text ed. 20.50 (ISBN 90-265-0256-7, Pub. by Swets Pub Serv Holland). Swets North Am.
Hoefs, J. Stable Isotope Geochemistry. LC 73-75422. (Minerals, Rocks & Inorganic Materials Ser.: Vol. 9). (Illus.). ix, 140p. 1973. 22.70 o.p. (ISBN 0-387-06176-2). Springer-Verlag.
Hoegner, W. & Richter, N. Isophotometric Atlas of Comets, 2 pts. (Illus.). 1979. Pt. 1. 72.60 (ISBN 0-387-09171-8); Pt. 2. 52.00 (ISBN 0-387-09172-6). Springer-Verlag.
Hoeher, Siegfried. Birds' Eggs & Nesting Habits. (Color Ser.). (Illus.). 1974. 9.95 (ISBN 0-7137-0609-0, Pub by Blandford Pr England). Sterling.
Hoehler, G., ed. Springer Tracts in Modern Physics, Vol. 37. (Illus.). iv, 180p. (Eng. & Ger.). 1965. 34.30 (ISBN 0-387-03404-8). Springer-Verlag.
--Springer Tracts in Modern Physics, Vol. 38. (Illus.). iv, 188p. (Eng. & Ger.). 1965. 34.30 (ISBN 0-387-03405-6). Springer-Verlag.
--Springer Tracts in Modern Physics, Vol. 40. (Illus., Eng. & Ger.). 1966. 34.30 (ISBN 0-387-03669-5). Springer-Verlag.
--Springer Tracts in Modern Physics, Vol. 46. (Illus.). iv, 132p. (Eng. & Ger.). 1968. 34.90 (ISBN 0-387-04340-3). Springer-Verlag.
--Springer Tracts in Modern Physics, Vol. 47. (Illus.). v, 225p. (Eng. & Ger.). 1968. 50.80 (ISBN 0-387-04341-1). Springer-Verlag.
--Springer Tracts in Modern Physics, Vol. 49. (Illus.). iii, 146p. 1969. 34.30 (ISBN 0-387-04712-3). Springer-Verlag.
--Springer Tracts in Modern Physics, Vol. 51. LC 25-9130. (Illus.). 1969. 29.00 (ISBN 0-387-04714-X). Springer-Verlag.
--Springer Tracts in Modern Physics, Vol. 53. (Illus.). 1970. 29.00 (ISBN 0-387-05016-7). Springer-Verlag.
--Springer Tracts in Modern Physics, Vol. 54. LC 25-9130. (Illus.). 1970. 43.70 (ISBN 0-387-05017-5). Springer-Verlag.
--Springer Tracts in Modern Physics, Vol. 58. (Illus.). 1971. 56.70 (ISBN 0-387-05383-2). Springer-Verlag.
--Springer Tracts in Modern Physics, Vol. 60. LC 25-9130. (Illus.). iv, 233p. 1972. 56.70 (ISBN 0-387-05653-X). Springer-Verlag.
--Springer Tracts in Modern Physics, Vol. 65. LC 25-9130. (Illus.). 148p. 1972. 37.80 (ISBN 0-387-05876-1). Springer-Verlag.
Hoehling, A. A. & Hoehling, Mary. Day Richmond Died. (Illus.). 272p. 1981. 12.95 (ISBN 0-498-02313-3). A S Barnes.
Hoehling, Mary, jt. auth. see Hoehling, A. A.
Hoehn, Robert G. Playing Slow Pitch Softball. LC 78-66319. (Illus.). 1979. 8.95 (ISBN 0-8069-4136-7); lib. bdg. 8.29 (ISBN 0-8069-4137-5). Sterling.
Hoehn-Saric, Rudolph, jt. auth. see Frank, Jerome D.
Hoek, E. & Imperial College of Science & Technology, Rock Mechanics Section. KWIC Index of Rock Mechanics Literature: Pt. 1, 1870-1968. 1977. pap. text ed. 165.00 (ISBN 0-08-022063-0). Pergamon.
Hoekelman, Robert, jt. auth. see Friedman, Stanford.
Hoekelman, Robert A. Principles of Pediatrics: Pretest Self-Assessment & Review. (Illus.). 248p. 1980. 25.00 (ISBN 0-07-079159-7, HP). McGraw.
Hoekema, Anthony A. Tongues & Spirit-Baptism. 264p. 1981. pap. 6.95 (ISBN 0-8010-4243-7). Baker Bk.
Hoeksema, Herman. Reformed Dogmatics. LC 66-24047. 1966. 12.95 (ISBN 0-8254-2806-8). Kregel.
--Triple Knowledge: Heidelberg Catechism, 3 Vols. LC 71-129740. 1972. Set. 29.95 (ISBN 0-8254-2813-0). Kregel.
--When I Survey. LC 76-57122. 1977. 9.95 (ISBN 0-8254-2817-3). Kregel.
--Whosoever Will. LC 77-189070. 1973. pap. 2.95 (ISBN 0-8254-2819-X). Kregel.
Hoeksma, Homer C. Voice of Our Fathers. LC 80-8082. 1980. 18.95 (ISBN 0-8254-2841-6). Kregel.
Hoekstra, Ray & Wagner, Walter. God's Prison Gang. 1977. 6.95 o.p. (ISBN 0-8007-0840-7). Revell.
Hoel, Paul, et al. Introduction to Probability Theory. LC 74-136173. 1971. text ed. 19.50 (ISBN 0-395-04636-X, 3-25650). HM.
--Introduction to Statistical Theory. LC 70-136172. 1971. text ed. 19.75 (ISBN 0-395-04637-8, 3-25652). HM.
--Introduction to Stochastic Processes. LC 79-105035. (Illus.). 1972. text ed. 19.75 (ISBN 0-395-12076-4, 3-25656). HM.
Hoel, Paul G. Elementary Statistics. 4th ed. LC 75-33400. (Probability & Mathematical Statistics Ser). 400p. (Arabic Translation available). 1976. text ed. 19.95 (ISBN 0-471-40302-4); instr's manual avail. (ISBN 0-471-40269-9); wkbk. 7.95 (ISBN 0-471-01613-6). Wiley.
--Finite Mathematics & Calculus with Applications to Business. LC 73-19505. 464p. 1974. text ed. 18.50x (ISBN 0-471-40430-6); tchr's manual avail. (ISBN 0-471-40432-2). Wiley.
Hoel, Paul G. & Jessen, Raymond J. Basic Statistics for Business & Economics. 2nd ed. LC 76-54504. (Management & Administration Ser.). 1977. 22.95x (ISBN 0-471-40268-0); study guide 6.95 (ISBN 0-471-01697-7). Wiley.
Hoelderlin, Friedrich. Hyperion. (Insel-Bibliothek). 228p. 1980. leather bnd 46.80 (ISBN 3-458-04942-8, Pub. by Insel Verlag Germany); text ed. 18.20 (ISBN 3-458-04935-5). Suhrkamp.
Hoeldtke, Clyde, jt. auth. see Richards, Lawrence O.
Hoelker, Klaus, jt. ed. see Burghardt, Wolfgang.
Hoeller, Stephan H. The Royal Road. LC 75-4244. (Illus.). 119p. (Orig.). 1975. pap. 4.75 (ISBN 0-8356-0465-9, Quest). Theos Pub Hse.
Hoelscher, R. P., et al. Graphics for Engineers: Visualizations, Communication & Design. LC 67-29722. 1968. text ed. 28.95x (ISBN 0-471-40558-2). Wiley.
Hoemann, H. Psychology of Deafness. Date not set. cancelled (ISBN 0-685-32504-0). Univ Park.
Hoemann, Harry W. & Lucafo, Rosemarie. I Want to Talk: A Child Model of American Sign Language. 189p. 1981. pap. text ed. 7.95x (ISBN 0-913072-41-9). Natl Assn Deaf.
Hoenig, Stuart A. How to Build & Use Electronic Devices Without Frustration, Panic, Mountains of Money, or an Engineering Degree. 2nd ed. 1980. pap. 12.95 (ISBN 0-316-36808-3). Little.
Hoenig, Stuart A. & Scott, Daphne H. Medical Instrumentation & Electrical Safety: The View from the Nursing Station. LC 77-5878. 1977. 15.95 (ISBN 0-471-40566-3, Pub. by Wiley Medical). Wiley.
Hoenigswald, Henry. Spoken Hindustani. Incl. Bk. 1, Units 1-12. viii, 169p. pap. 9.00x (ISBN 0-87950-110-3); Bk. 2, Units 13-30. pap. 9.00x (ISBN 0-87950-111-1); Cassettes, Six Dual Track. 60.00x (ISBN 0-87950-115-4); Cassette Course-Bk. 1 & Cassettes. 65.00x (ISBN 0-685-73298-3). LC 74-175966. (Spoken Language Ser). (Prog. Bk.). 1976. Spoken Lang Serv.
Hoeper, Claus-Juergen, et al. Awareness Games: Personal Growth Through Group Interaction. Davies, Hilary, tr. 160p. 1976. pap. 4.95 (ISBN 0-312-06300-8). St Martin.
Hoepli, Nancy, ed. West Africa Today. (Reference Shelf Ser.). 1970. 6.25 (ISBN 0-8242-0414-X). Wilson.
Hoepli, Nancy L., ed. The Aftermath of Colonialism. 206p. 1973. 6.25 (ISBN 0-8242-0470-0). Wilson.
--Common Market. (Reference Shelf Ser: Vol. 46, No. 5). 1975. 6.25 (ISBN 0-8242-0525-1). Wilson.

Hoercker, Bernard L. & Stadtman, Earl R., eds. Current Topics in Cellular Regulation, 016 vols. Incl. Vol. 1. 1969. 41.00 (ISBN 0-12-152801-4); Vol. 2. 1970. 41.00 (ISBN 0-12-152802-2); Vol. 3. 1971. 41.00 (ISBN 0-12-152803-0); Vol. 4. 1971. 41.00 (ISBN 0-12-152804-9); Vol. 5. 1972. 41.00 (ISBN 0-12-152805-7); Vol. 6. 1973. 41.00 (ISBN 0-12-152806-5); Vol. 7. 1973. 37.50 (ISBN 0-12-152807-3); Vol. 8. 1974. 48.00 (ISBN 0-12-152808-1); Vol. 9. 1976. 41.00 (ISBN 0-12-152811-1); lib ed. 52.50 (ISBN 0-12-152878-2); microfiche 29.50 (ISBN 0-686-66776-X); Vol. 10. 1974. 48.00 (ISBN 0-12-152810-3); lib ed. 59.50 (ISBN 0-12-152876-6); 36.50 (ISBN 0-12-152877-4); Vol. 11. 1974. 44.50 (ISBN 0-12-152811-1); Vol. 12. 1977. 44.00 (ISBN 0-12-152812-X); lib. ed. 56.00 (ISBN 0-12-152880-4); microfiche 33.00 (ISBN 0-12-152881-2); Vol. 13. 1978. 40.00 (ISBN 0-12-152813-8); lib ed. 51.00 (ISBN 0-12-152882-0); microfiche 29.00 (ISBN 0-12-152883-9); Vol. 14. 1978. 37.00 (ISBN 0-12-152814-6); lib ed. 47.50 (ISBN 0-12-152884-7); microfiche 27.00 **(ISBN 0-12-152885-5); Vol. 15. 1979. 36.50 (ISBN 0-12-152815-4); lib. bdg. 43.50 (ISBN 0-12-152886-3); microfiche 23.50 (ISBN 0-12-152887-1); Vol. 16. 1980. 36.00 (ISBN 0-12-152816-2); lib. bdg. 44.00 (ISBN 0-12-152888-X); microfiche 24.00 (ISBN 0-12-152889-8); Vol. 17. 1980. 35.00 (ISBN 0-12-152817-0); lib. bdg. 45.50 (ISBN 0-12-152890-1); microfiche 24.50 (ISBN 0-12-152891-X). Acad Pr.**

Hoerder, Dick, ed. Protest, Direct Action, Repression: Dissent in American Society from Colonial Times to the Present. 434p. 1977. text ed. 48.00 (ISBN 3-7940-7009-7, Pub. by K G Saur). Gale.

Hoerl, Bryan G., jt. auth. see Boyd, Robert R.

Hoerlein, B. F. Canine Neurology: Diagnosis & Treatment. 3rd ed. LC 77-72825. (Illus.). 1978. text ed. 39.00 (ISBN 0-7216-4712-X). Saunders.

Hoermann, H. Psycholinguistics: An Introduction to Research & Theory. Stern, H. H., tr. (Illus.). 1970. 25.20 o.p. (ISBN 0-387-05159-7); pap. 14.00 o.p. (ISBN 0-387-05665-3). Springer-Verlag.

Hoerner, Earl F., jt. ed. see Vinger, Paul F.

Hoerschelmann, Fred Von see Otten, Anna.

Hoerz, Herbert, et al. Philosophical Problems in Physical Science. rev. ed. Marquit, Erwin, ed. Genin, Salomea, tr. from Ger. (Studies in Marxism: Vol. 7). Orig. Title: Philosophische Probleme der Physik. 1980. 15.95 (ISBN 0-930656-14-8); pap. 8.50 (ISBN 0-930656-13-X). Marxist Educ.

Hoesen, Karl Van see Van Hoesen, Karl.

Hoest, Bill. Agatha Crumm. (Orig.). 1980. pap. 1.50 (ISBN 0-451-09422-0, W9422, Sig). NAL.

--Bumper Snickers. 128p. pap. 0.95 o.p. (ISBN 0-451-07128-X, Q7128, Sig). NAL.

--I See You Burned the Cold Cuts Again. (Lockhorns No. 5). (Orig.). 1981. pap. 1.50 (ISBN 0-451-09711-4, J9711, Sig). NAL.

Hoest, R. Laplanders. (Illus.). 20.00x o.p. (ISBN 0-686-17926-9, N385). Vanous.

Hoest, William. Taste of Carrot. (Illus.). (gr. 1 up). 1967. pap. 1.95 (ISBN 0-689-20168-0). Atheneum.

Hoetink, Harry. Two Variants in Caribbean Race Relations: A Contribution to the Sociology of Segmented Societies. Hooykaa, Eva M., tr. 1967. 7.00x o.p. (ISBN 0-19-218164-5). Oxford U Pr.

Hoeveler, Diane L., jt. ed. see Wilson, Harris W.

Hoeveler, J. David, Jr. James McCosh & the Scottish Intellectual Tradition: From Glasgow to Princeton. (Illus.). 384p. 1981. 25.00x (ISBN 0-691-04670-0). Princeton U Pr.

--The New Humanism: A Critique of Modern America, 1900-1940. LC 76-25168. 1977. 13.95x (ISBN 0-8139-0658-X). U Pr of Va.

Hoeven, Johan Van Der. Karl Marx: The Roots of His Thought. (Bidragen Tot De Filosophie: No. 8). (Orig.). 1976. pap. text ed. 14.00x (ISBN 90-232-1388-2). Humanities.

Hoeven, Johan Van Der see Van Der Hoeven, Johan.

Hoexter, Corinne K. From Canton to California: The Epic of Chinese Immigration. LC 76-14504. (Illus.). 320p. (gr. 7 up). 1976. 9.95 (ISBN 0-590-07344-3, Four Winds). Schol Bk Serv.

Hoey, Allen. Cedar Light. 10.00 (ISBN 0-686-65776-4); pap. 2.00 (ISBN 0-935252-16-9). Street Pr.

Hoey, Mary. Journey South: Discovering the Americas. (gr. 4-6). 1980. pap. 3.50 (ISBN 0-377-00099-X). Friend Pr.

Hoey, Robert F. Experimental Liturgy Book. 1969. pap. 4.95 (ISBN 0-8164-1029-1). Crossroad NY.

Hof, Larry & Miller, William. Marriage Enrichment: Philosophy Process & Program. (Illus.). 192p. 1980. text ed. 14.95 (ISBN 0-87619-717-9). R J Brady.

Hofacker, Erich P. Christian Morgenstern. (World Authors Ser.: No. 508 (Germany)). 1978. 12.50 (ISBN 0-8057-6349-X). Twayne.

Hofacker, Ursula A. Chemical Experimentation: An Integrated Course in Inorganic, Analytical & Physical Chemistry. (Illus.). 1972. lab. manual 10.95x (ISBN 0-7167-0166-9). W H Freeman.

Hofdstadter, Richard, et al. The United States: Brief Edition. (Illus.). 1979. pap. text ed. 13.95 (ISBN 0-13-938860-5). P-H.

Hofeditz, Calvin A. Computers & Data Processing Made Simple. LC 78-22635. (Made Simple Books). (Illus.). 1979. pap. 3.50 (ISBN 0-385-14945-X, Made). Doubleday.

Hofeldt, Fred D. Preventing Reactive Hypoglycemia. 300p. 1981. 27.50 (ISBN 0-87527-214-2). Green.

Hofer, Charles W., et al. A Casebook in Business Policy & Planning. 150p. Date not set. price not set instr's. manual (ISBN 0-8299-0614-2). West Pub.

Hofer, Myron. The Roots of Human Behavior: An Introduction to the Psychobiology of Early Development. LC 80-28377. (Psychology Ser.). (Illus.). 1981. text ed. price not set (ISBN 0-7167-1277-6); pap. text ed. price not set (ISBN 0-7167-1278-4). W H Freeman.

Hofer, T & Fel, E. Hungarian Folk Art. (Illus.). 1979. 35.00 (ISBN 0-19-211448-4). Oxford U Pr.

Hoff, Benjamin, tr. The Way of Life at the Heart of the Tao Te Ching. 1980. 16.95 (ISBN 0-8348-0156-6, Pub. by John Weatherhill Inc Japan). C E Tuttle.

Hoff, Ebbe C. Alcoholism: The Hidden Addiction. LC 74-13014. 1975. 7.95 (ISBN 0-8164-0248-5). Crossroad NY.

Hoff, Hebbel E., et al, trs. see Bernard, Claude.

Hoff, Johan E. & Janick, Julesintro. by. Food: Readings from Scientific American. LC 73-3138. (Illus.). 1973. text ed. 17.95x (ISBN 0-7167-0876-0); pap. text ed. 9.95x (ISBN 0-7167-0875-2). W H Freeman.

Hoff, Lee A. People in Crisis: Understanding & Helping. LC 77-79466. 1978. 11.95 (ISBN 0-201-02939-1, M&N Div). A-W.

Hoff, Marilyn G., jt. auth. see McFadyen, Barbara.

Hoff, Nicholas J. Analysis of Structures: Based on the Minimal Principles & the Principle of Virtual Displacement. LC 56-6503. 1956. 30.00 (ISBN 0-471-40590-6, Pub. by Wiley-Interscience). Wiley.

Hoff, Pablo, tr. El Pentateuco. (Spanish Bks.). 1979. 2.95 (ISBN 0-8297-0876-6). Life Pubs Intl.

Hoff, Syd. Amy's Dinosaur. LC 80-14082. (Illus.). 48p. (ps-2). 1980. pap. 3.95 (ISBN 0-671-41338-4, Pub. by Windmill). S&S.

--The Art of Cartooning. LC 72-12659. (Illus.). 224p. 1973. 11.95 (ISBN 0-87396-072-6). Stravon.

--Dinosaur Do's & Don't's. LC 80-13729. (Illus.). 48p. (ps-2). 1980. pap. 2.95 (ISBN 0-671-41200-0, Pub. by Windmill). S&S.

--Editorial & Political Cartooning. LC 75-45314. (Illus.). 1976. 14.95 (ISBN 0-87396-078-5). Stravon.

--Henrietta, Circus Star. (Illus.). 48p. (ps-2). 1981. pap. 1.95 (ISBN 0-671-42661-3, Pub. by Windmill). S&S.

--Henrietta the Early Bird. (Illus.). 48p. (ps-2). 1981. pap. 1.95 (ISBN 0-671-42659-1, Pub. by Windmill). S&S.

--The Littlest Leaguer. LC 75-25782. (Illus.). 48p. (ps-2). 1981. pap. 1.95 (ISBN 0-671-42580-3, Pub. by Windmill). S&S.

--Slugger Sal's Slump. LC 78-26338. (Illus.). 48p. (ps-2). 1981. pap. 1.95 (ISBN 0-671-42581-1, Pub. by Windmill). S&S.

--Soft Skull Sam. LC 80-23104. (A Let Me Read Bk.). (Illus.). 32p. (ps-3). 1981. pap. 2.95 (ISBN 0-15-277063-1, VoyB). HarBraceJ.

--Soft Skull Sam. LC 80-24590. (A Let Me Read Bk.). (Illus.). 32p. (gr. 4-6). 1981. 6.95 (ISBN 0-15-277062-3, HJ). HarBraceJ.

--Syd Hoff's How to Draw Dinosaurs. (Illus.). 64p. (gr. 3 up). 1981. pap. 3.95 (ISBN 0-671-42553-6). Windmill Bks.

Hoff, Trygve J. Economic Calculation in the Socialist Society. LC 79-51861. 1981. Repr. of 1949 ed. 21.50 (ISBN 0-88355-954-4). Hyperion Conn.

Hoff, Ursula. National Gallery of Victoria. (Illus.). 216p. 1974. 18.00 (ISBN 0-500-18139-X); pap. 6.95 (ISBN 0-500-20133-1). Transatlantic.

Hoffecker, Carol E. Delaware, a Bicentennial History. (States & the Nation Ser.). (Illus.). 1977. 12.95 (ISBN 0-393-05620-1). Norton.

--Wilmington: A Pictorial History. Friedman, Donna R., ed. (Illus.). 208p. 1981. pap. write for info. (ISBN 0-89865-057-7). Donning Co.

Hoffecker, W. Andrew. Piety & the Princeton Theologians. (Orig.). 1981. pap. 5.95 (ISBN 0-8010-4253-4). Baker Bk.

Hoffenberg, Jack. A Raging Talent. 1972. pap. 1.95 o.p. (ISBN 0-380-00836-X, 31021). Avon.

--Reap in Tears. 1969. pap. 1.95 (ISBN 0-380-00477-1, 26401). Avon.

--Thunder at Dawn. 1969. pap. 1.95 (ISBN 0-380-01583-8, 37226). Avon.

--A Time for Pagans. 1971. pap. 1.95 (ISBN 0-380-00876-9, 31435). Avon.

Hoffer, Abram & Walker, Morton. Nutrients to Age Without Senility. LC 79-93428. 265p. 1980. 10.50 (ISBN 0-87983-217-7); pap. 2.95 (ISBN 0-87983-218-5). Keats.

Hoffer, Alice. Gretchen's World. LC 80-83354. (Illus.). 48p. (gr. k-3). 1981. 5.95 (ISBN 0-448-16560-0); PLB 11.85 (ISBN 0-448-13491-8). G&D.

Hoffer, Charles. A Concise Introduction to Music Listening. 2nd. ed. 1979. pap. 12.95x (ISBN 0-534-00627-2); study guide 6.95x (ISBN 0-534-00705-8); records 16.95x (ISBN 0-534-00692-2). Wadsworth Pub.

Hoffer, Charles & Hoffer, Marjorie. Basic Musicianship for Classroom Teachers. 1976. pap. text ed. 12.95x (ISBN 0-534-00394-X). Wadsworth Pub.

Hoffer, Charles R. Understanding of Music. 3rd ed. 1976. 15.95x (ISBN 0-534-00443-1); study guide 5.95x (ISBN 0-534-00458-X); enrichment record album 16.95x (ISBN 0-534-00457-1). Wadsworth Pub.

Hoffer, Eric. In Our Time. LC 75-23887. 128p. 1976. 8.95 o.s.i. (ISBN 0-06-011922-5, HarpT). Har-Row.

Hoffer, Jay. Radio Production Techniques. LC 73-89814. 1974. 16.95 (ISBN 0-8306-3661-7, 661). TAB Bks.

Hoffer, Marjorie, jt. auth. see Hoffer, Charles.

Hoffer, Paul B., et al. Gallium-67 Imaging. LC 77-13125. (Diagnostic & Therapeutic Radiology Ser.). 1978. 32.50 (ISBN 0-471-02601-8, Pub. by Wiley Medical). Wiley.

Hoffer, Peter C. & Hull, N. E. Murdering Mothers: Infanticide in England & New England, 1558-1803. (NYU School of Law Ser. in Anglo-American Legal History). 208p. 1981. text ed. 22.50x (ISBN 0-8147-3412-X). NYU Pr.

Hoffer, Peter T. Klaus Mann. (World Authors Ser.: No. 435). 1978. lib. bdg. 12.50 (ISBN 0-8057-6309-0). Twayne.

Hoffer, Willi. Early Development & Education of the Child. LC 76-5230. 196p. 1980. 10.00 (ISBN 0-686-64206-6). Aronson.

Hofferber, Connie & Hofferber, Terry. Portland Super Shopper. LC 80-51868. (Illus.). 128p. 1980. pap. 3.50 (ISBN 0-916076-40-7). Writing.

Hofferber, Terry, jt. auth. see Hofferber, Connie.

Hofferbert, Richard I. The Study of Public Policy. LC 73-9826. (Policy Analysis Ser). 1974. 11.95 (ISBN 0-672-51475-3); pap. text ed. 10.50 (ISBN 0-672-61062-0). Bobbs.

Hoffman. Baccarat: Fair & Foul. (Gambler's Book Shelf Ser.). 1977. pap. 2.95 (ISBN 0-89650-578-2). Gamblers.

--Federal Taxation: Corporations, Partnerships, Estates & Trusts. 420p. 1979. write for info. (ISBN 0-8299-0491-3); solutions manual avail. West Pub.

--How Many Zen Buddhists Does It Take to Screw in a Light Bulb? (Illus.). 96p. 1980. pap. 3.95 (ISBN 0-312-39527-2); prepack 39.50 (ISBN 0-312-39528-0). St Martin.

Hoffman, et al. Movement for Developing Children. 344p. 1980. 16.95 (ISBN 0-205-06953-3); tchrs'. manual free. Allyn.

Hoffman, A., jt. auth. see Hennebo, D.

Hoffman, A. C., jt. auth. see Cornell, F. M.

Hoffman, Abbie. Soon to Be a Major Motion Picture. 1980. 13.95 (ISBN 0-686-68806-6, Perigee); pap. 6.95 (ISBN 0-686-68807-4). Putnam.

Hoffman, Adeline M. Clothing for the Handicapped, the Aged & Other People with Special Needs. (Illus.). 212p. 1979. text ed. 14.75 (ISBN 0-398-03860-0). C C Thomas.

--Daily Needs & Interests of Older People. (Illus.). 528p. 1976. 24.75 (ISBN 0-398-00852-3). C C Thomas.

Hoffman, Alice. The Drowning Season. 1980. pap. 2.50 (ISBN 0-449-24352-4, Crest). Fawcett.

--Property of. 1977. 8.95 o.p. (ISBN 0-374-23828-6). FS&G.

Hoffman, Ann. Majorca. (Island Ser.). 1978. 14.95 (ISBN 0-7153-7492-3). David & Charles.

Hoffman, Arthur S., ed. Japan & the Pacific Basin. (Atlantic Papers Ser.: No. 40). 68p. 1980. write for info. (ISBN 0-86598-042-X). Allanheld.

Hoffman, Banesh. The Tyranny of Testing. LC 77-26028. 1978. Repr. of 1962 ed. lib. bdg. 18.75x (ISBN 0-313-20097-1, HOTT). Greenwood.

Hoffman, Banesh, jt. auth. see Dukas, Helen.

Hoffman, Brian F. Brief Reviews from Circulation Research, 1978. (AHA Monograph: No. 62). pap. 6.00 (ISBN 0-686-59599-8, 73-048-A). Am Heart.

--Brief Reviews from Circulation Research, 1978. (AHA Monograph: No. 64). pap. 6.00 (ISBN 0-686-59600-5, 73-049A). Am Heart.

Hoffman, Byrd see Hoffmann, William M.

Hoffman, Carolyn. Fifty Hikes in Eastern Pennsylvania. (Illus., Orig.). 1981. pap. price not set (ISBN 0-89725-018-4). NH Pub Co.

Hoffman, Charles H. How to Improve Collections Without Really Trying. 1977. pap. 2.75 (ISBN 0-934914-07-9). NACM.

Hoffman, Daniel. The Center of Attention. 96p. Date not set. pap. 1.95 (ISBN 0-394-71988-3, Vin). Random.

Hoffman, Daniel G. Poetry of Stephen Crane. LC 57-11017. 1957. 20.00x (ISBN 0-231-02195-X); pap. 7.50x (ISBN 0-231-08662-8). Columbia U Pr.

Hoffman, Daniel G. & Hynes, Samuel, eds. English Literary Criticism: Romantic & Victorian. 334p. 1980. Repr. of 1963 ed. text ed. 20.00x (ISBN 0-8290-0125-5); pap. text ed. 8.95x (ISBN 0-8290-0455-6). Irvington.

Hoffman, Daniel N., jt. auth. see Halperin, Morton H.

Hoffman, Dietrich, jt. ed. see Wynder, Ernest L.

Hoffman, Dona. Yes, Lord. LC 74-30867. 1974. pap. 4.50 (ISBN 0-570-03195-8, 12-2596). Concordia.

Hoffman, Donald, et al, eds. Lifelong Learning in the Visual Arts: A Book of Readings. 160p. 1980. 9.25 (ISBN 0-686-27494-6). Natl Art Ed.

Hoffman, E. Practical Problems in Mathematics for Machinists. LC 78-74432. (Mathematics Ser.). (gr. 8). 1980. 6.60 (ISBN 0-8273-1281-4); instr's guide 1.75 (ISBN 0-8273-1282-2). Delmar.

Hoffman, E. T. Best Tales of Hoffman. Bleiler, E. F., ed. & intro. by. 8.00 (ISBN 0-8446-2262-1). Peter Smith.

--The Devil's Elixirs. 1980. 10.95 (ISBN 0-7145-0194-8). Riverrun NY.

--Prinzessin Brambilla. Raraty, M., ed. (Blackwell's German Text Ser.). 1972. pap. 9.95x (ISBN 0-631-01880-8, Pub. by Basil Blackwell). Biblio Dist.

Hoffman, Edward, jt. auth. see Mann, W. Edward.

Hoffman, Edward G. Jig & Fixture Design, Vol.1. LC 78-55901. 330p. pap. 8.00 (ISBN 0-8273-1694-1); instructor's guide 1.60 (ISBN 0-686-67378-6). Delmar.

Hoffman, Elizabeth. Visions of the Future: Palm Reading. LC 77-22207. (Myth, Magic & Superstition Ser.). (Illus.). (gr. 4-5). 1977. PLB 9.65 (ISBN 0-8172-1029-6). Raintree Pubs.

Hoffman, Elizabeth P. This House Is Haunted! LC 77-10981. (Myth, Magic & Superstition Ser.). (Illus.). (gr. 4-5). 1977. PLB 9.65 (ISBN 0-8172-1033-4). Raintree Pubs.

Hoffman, Erik P. & Fleron, Frederick J., Jr., eds. The Conduct of Soviet Foreign Policy. 2nd ed. LC 80-68483. 1980. 34.95 (ISBN 0-202-24155-6); pap. 14.95 (ISBN 0-202-24156-4). Aldine Pub.

Hoffman, F. G., jt. ed. see Root, W. S.

Hoffman, Felix. The Wolf & the Seven Little Kids. LC 59-16357. (Illus.). 32p. (ps-3). 1959. 6.95 (ISBN 0-15-299108-5, HJ). HarBraceJ.

Hoffman, Felix, ed. & illus. King Thrushbeard. LC 74-123890. (Illus.). (gr. k-3). 1970. 5.95 o.p. (ISBN 0-15-242940-9, HJ). HarBraceJ.

Hoffman, Felix, ed. Seven Ravens. LC 63-2506. (Illus.). (gr. k-3). 1963. 6.95 (ISBN 0-15-272920-8, HJ). HarBraceJ.

Hoffman, Frederick J. Twenties: American Writing in the Postwar Decade. 1965. pap. text ed. 6.95 (ISBN 0-02-914780-8). Free Pr.

--William Faulkner. (U. S. Authors Ser.: No. 1). lib. bdg. 9.95 (ISBN 0-8057-0244-X). Twayne.

Hoffman, Gale, tr. see Bragadin, Marc'Antonio.

Hoffman, George W., ed. Federalism & Regional Development: Case Studies on the Experience in the United States & the Federal Republic of Germany. (Illus.). 784p. 1981. text ed. 40.00x (ISBN 0-292-73825-0). U of Tex Pr.

Hoffman, George W., et al, eds. A Geography of Europe. 4th ed. LC 77-75128. (Illus.). 671p. 1977. 24.95 (ISBN 0-8260-4176-0). Wiley.

Hoffman, Gerald N., jt. auth. see Lombardi, Tarky, Jr.

Hoffman, Glenn L. Parasites of North American Freshwater Fishes. 1967. 30.00x (ISBN 0-520-00565-1). U of Cal Pr.

Hoffman, Gregg, jt. auth. see Spitzer, R. R.

Hoffman, Heinrich see Lear, Edward.

Hoffman, Herbert H. Alphanumeric Filing Rules for Business Documents. 118p. 1977. pap. 4.00x (ISBN 0-89537-001-8). Headway Pubns.

--Bibliography Without Footnotes. 2nd. ed. 93p. 1978. pap. 4.00x (ISBN 0-89537-013-1). Headway Pubns.

--Descriptive Cataloging in a New Light: Polemical Chapters for Librarians. LC 76-380445. 171p. 1976. pap. 6.00x (ISBN 0-89537-000-X). Headway Pubns.

--WORKMAC: A Bibliographic Format for Works in Analytic On-Line Library Union Catalogs. 1980. pap. 5.00x (ISBN 0-89537-016-6). Headway Pubns.

Hoffman, Herbert H. & Ludwig, Rita T. Spoken World Poetry Index, Vol. 1. (Reference Aids Ser.). 1981. 45.00x (ISBN 0-89537-012-3) (ISBN 0-89537-012-3). Headway Pubns.

Hoffman, Herbert H., jt. auth. see Srikantaiah, Taverekere.

Hoffman, Herbert H., compiled by. Cuento Mexicano Index. LC 79-127156. (Humanitas Books). 600p. 1978. 22.00x (ISBN 0-89537-007-7). Headway Pubns.

Hoffman, Hilde. Green Grass Grows All Around. LC 68-10032. (gr. k-2). 1968. 7.95g (ISBN 0-02-744180-6). Macmillan.

Hoffman, Howard, jt. ed. see Reiss, David.

Hoffman, Hy & Pagano, Jules. ABE Staff Training. 58p. 1971. 4.00 (ISBN 0-685-63816-2). Adult Ed.

Hoffman, Irwin, et al. Spatial Analysis of the Eletrocardiogram: A Program. (Illus.). 150p. 1975. pap. text.ed. 8.25 o.p. (ISBN 0-8016-3124-6). Mosby.

Hoffman, Jacquie. Musings for a Mellow Mood. (Illus.). 65p. (Orig.). 1979. pap. 4.95 (ISBN 0-9604082-0-7). I J Hoffman.

Hoffman, Jay, et al. Study in Regional Taste: The May Show 1919-1975. LC 77-78145. (Themes in Art Ser.). (Illus.). 72p. 1977. pap. 4.95x (ISBN 0-910386-36-6, Pub. by Cleveland Mus Art). Ind U Pr.

Hoffman, Jeanne, jt. auth. see Prizzi, Elaine.

Hoffman, Jim. Rodale Plans: Solar Food Dryer. Wolf, Ray, ed. (Illus.). 64p. (Orig.). 1981. pap. 12.95 (ISBN 0-87857-333-X). Rodale Pr Inc.

Hoffman, Joe D., jt. auth. see Zucrow, Maurice J.

Hoffman, John P. Introduction to Electronics for Technologists. LC 77-74381. (Illus.). 1978. text ed. 17.95 (ISBN 0-395-25115-X); solutions manual 1.25 (ISBN 0-395-25819-7). HM.

Hoffman, Joseph F., ed. Membrane Transport Processes, Vol. 1. LC 76-19934. 1978. 43.50 (ISBN 0-89004-170-9). Raven.

Hoffman, K. Analysis of Euclidian Space. 1975. text ed. 23.95 (ISBN 0-13-032656-9). P-H.

Hoffman, Kenneth & Kunze, Ray. Linear Algebra. 2nd ed. LC 75-142120. (Illus.). 1971. ref. ed. 20.95 (ISBN 0-13-536797-2). P-H.

Hoffman, Kenneth E. Rx for Us-a Revitalized Constitution: Increased Democracy. LC 78-66119. 1979. pap. text ed. 8.75 (ISBN 0-8191-0686-0). U Pr of Amer.

Hoffman, L., jt. auth. see Graves, Harold F.

Hoffman, L. J. Security & Privacy in Computer Systems. LC 73-6744. 1973. 35.50 (ISBN 0-471-40611-2, Pub. by Wiley-Interscience). Wiley.

Hoffman, L. Richard. Group Problem Solving Process: Studies of a Valence Model. LC 79-12578. 256p. 1979. 24.95 (ISBN 0-03-047636-4). Praeger.

Hoffman, Lance J. Modern Methods for Computer Security & Privacy. LC 76-49896. (Illus.). 1977. 23.95x (ISBN 0-13-595207-7). P-H.

Hoffman, Lawrence, ed. Gates of Understanding. LC 77-23488. 1977. text ed. 6.95 o.p. (ISBN 0-685-87866-X, 142686); pap. text ed. 4.95 (ISBN 0-8074-0009-2, 142689). UAHC.

Hoffman, Lee. The Land Killer. LC 78-406. 1978. 7.95 o.p. (ISBN 0-385-13379-0). Doubleday.

Hoffman, Leon. The Evaluation & Care of Severely Disturbed Children & Their Families. 1981. text ed. write for info. (ISBN 0-89335-129-6). Spectrum Pub.

Hoffman, Leon-Francois. La Pratique du Francais Parle. LC 72-7530. 93p. 1973. pap. text ed. 6.50 (ISBN 0-684-13208-7); cassettes 4.95 (ISBN 0-684-13696-1). Scribner.

--Travaux Pratiques. 2nd ed. LC 73-8687. 1973. pap. text ed. 7.95 (ISBN 0-684-13577-9). Scribner.

Hoffman, Lynn. Foundations of Family Therapy. LC 80-68956. 416p. 1981. 25.00x (ISBN 0-465-02498-X). Basic.

Hoffman, M., et al. Polymer Analytics. Stahlberg, H., tr. from Ger. (MMI Press Polymer Monographs). 623p. 1981. 124.00 (ISBN 3-7186-0024-2). Harwood Academic.

Hoffman, Mable. Chocolate Cookery. LC 78-61007. (Illus.). 1978. pap. 5.95 (ISBN 0-89586-017-1). H P Bks.

--Crepe Cookery. LC 76-3230. (Illus.). 1976. pap. 5.95 (ISBN 0-912656-50-6). H P Bks.

--Crockery Cookery. LC 74-30823. 192p. 1975. pap. 5.95 (ISBN 0-912656-43-3). H P Bks.

--Mini Deep-Fry Cookery. LC 77-83277. (Illus.). 1977. 7.95 (ISBN 0-912656-81-6); pap. 5.95 (ISBN 0-912656-80-8). H P Bks.

Hoffman, Margaret A. & Fischer, Gerald C. Credit Department Management. LC 80-65026. (Illus.). 264p. 1980. 23.00 (ISBN 0-936742-00-3). R Morris Assocs.

Hoffman, Marian, ed. Newcomer's Guide to Metropolitan Washington. 4th ed. LC 78-54447. (Illus.). 168p. (Orig.). 1978. pap. 2.75 (ISBN 0-915168-27-8). Washingtonian.

Hoffman, Michael J. Gertrude Stein. (U. S. Authors Ser.: No. 268). 1976. lib. bdg. 10.95 (ISBN 0-8057-7168-9). Twayne.

Hoffman, Nancy. Woman's "True" Profession: Voices from the History of Teaching. (Women's Lives - Women's Work Ser.). (Illus.). 352p. (Orig.). (gr. 11-12). 1981. 17.95 (ISBN 0-912670-93-2); pap. 6.95 (ISBN 0-912670-72-X). Feminist Pr.

Hoffman, Nancy & Howe, Florence, eds. Women Working: An Anthology of Stories & Poems. (Women's Lives-Women's Work Ser). (Illus.). 1979. pap. 5.95 (ISBN 0-912670-57-6, Co-Pub. by McGraw). Feminist Pr.

Hoffman, Paul. Courthouse. 1979. 12.50 (ISBN 0-8015-1790-7, Hawthorn). Dutton.

Hoffman, Paul & Pecznick, Ira. To Drop a Dime. 1977. pap. 1.95 o.s.i. (ISBN 0-515-04424-5). Jove Pubns.

Hoffman, Peter. The Forever Fuel: The Story of Hydrogen. 250p. 1981. 16.00x (ISBN 0-89158-581-8). Westview.

Hoffman, R. News of the Nation. 1975. kit 83.61 o.p. (ISBN 0-13-620609-3). P-H.

Hoffman, Raymond A. & Gunders, Henry. Inventories: Control, Costing, & Effect Upon Income & Taxes. 2nd ed. LC 75-128350. 420p. 1970. 29.95 (ISBN 0-8260-4205-8, 49781). Ronald Pr.

Hoffman, Richard L. Ovid & the Canterbury Tales. LC 67-17174. 1967. 7.50x o.p. (ISBN 0-8122-7553-5). U of Pa Pr.

Hoffman, Robert & Cantlay, Jed. Running Together: The Family Book of Jogging. LC 79-92135. (West Point Sports Fitness Ser.: Vol. 5). (Illus.). 1980. pap. text ed. 4.95 (ISBN 0-918438-18-7). Leisure Pr.

Hoffman, Robert, ed. see Mother Earth News Staff.

Hoffman, Robert L. More Than a Trial: The Struggle Over Captain Dreyfus. LC 80-642. (Illus.). 1980. 14.95 (ISBN 0-02-914770-0). Free Pr.

Hoffman, Robert R., jt. ed. see Honeck, Richard P.

Hoffman, Ronald & Albert, Peter J., eds. Diplomacy & Revolution: The Franco-American Alliance of 1778. LC 80-13931. 1981. write for info. (ISBN 0-8139-0864-7). U Pr of Va.

Hoffman, Roslyn. Phoenix: A Pictorial History. Friedman, Donna R., ed. (Illus.). 208p. 1981. pap. write for info. (ISBN 0-89865-090-9). Donning Co.

Hoffman, Sandy, jt. auth. see Hockstein, Peter.

Hoffman, Stanley. Duties Beyond Borders: On the Limits & Possibilities of Ethical International Politics. 288p. 1981. 18.00 (ISBN 0-8156-0167-0); pap. 9.95 (ISBN 0-8156-0168-9). Syracuse U Pr.

Hoffman, Stephen, jt. auth. see Willerding, Margaret F.

Hoffman, Susan, jt. auth. see Mainardi, Patricia.

Hoffman, W. Michael. Kant's Theory of Freedom: A Metaphysical Inquiry. LC 78-70860. 1978. pap. text ed. 7.50 (ISBN 0-8191-0651-8). U Pr of Amer.

Hoffman, W. Michael, ed. Proceedings of the Second National Conference on Business Ethics. LC 79-64514. 1979. pap. text ed. 16.50 (ISBN 0-8191-0762-X). U Pr of Amer.

Hoffman, W. Michael & Wyly, Thomas J., eds. The Work Ethic in Business: Proceedings of the Third National Conference on Business Ethics. LC 80-22708. (Ethics Resource Center Ser.). 320p. 1981. lib. bdg. 22.50 (ISBN 0-89946-068-2). Oelgeschlager.

Hoffman, Wayne. Letters to the Modern Church. LC 79-88401. 1979. pap. 2.75 (ISBN 0-933350-23-6). Morse Pr.

Hoffman, Wayne L. The Earned Income Tax Credit: Welfare Reform or Tax Relief? an Analysis of Alternative Proposals. (Welfare Reform Policy Analysis Ser.: No. 5). 52p. 1978. pap. 3.50 (ISBN 0-87766-235-5, 23300). Urban Inst.

Hoffman, William. Queen Juliana: The Richest Woman in the World. Hill, Carol, ed. LC 79-1827. 1979. 11.95 (ISBN 0-15-146531-2). HarBraceJ.

Hoffman, William G. How to Make Better Speeches. LC 48-6985. (Funk & W Bk.). 1976. pap. 3.00 o.s.i. (ISBN 0-308-10251-7, TYC-T). T Y Crowell.

Hoffman, William H., jt. auth. see Phillips, Lawrence C.

Hoffman, William H., ed. Gay Plays: First Collection. 1978. pap. 3.95 (ISBN 0-380-42788-5, 77263, Bard). Avon.

Hoffman, William M; see Hoffmann, William M.

Hoffman-Axthelm, Walter A. History of Dentistry. (Illus.). 400p. 1981. 46.00. Quint Pub Co.

Hoffmann, Ann. Lives of the Tudor Age, 1485 to 1603. LC 76-15685. (Lives of the...Age Ser.). (Illus.). 1977. text ed. 25.00x (ISBN 0-06-494331-3). B&N.

Hoffmann, Banesh. Strange Story of the Quantum. 1959. pap. text ed. 3.00 (ISBN 0-486-20518-5). Dover.

Hoffmann, Charles G. Ford Madox Ford. (English Authors Ser.: No. 55). lib. bdg. 10.95 (ISBN 0-8057-1200-3). Twayne.

Hoffmann, Christa F. Getting Ready for AACR2: The Cataloger's Guide. LC 80-15168. (Professional Librarian Ser.). 225p. 1980. pap. 24.50 (ISBN 0-914236-64-4). Knowledge Indus.

Hoffmann, E. T. Das Fraeulein Von Scuderi. (Insel Taschenbuecher: It 410). (Illus.). 126p. (Ger.). 1980. pap. text ed. 3.25 (ISBN 3-458-32110-1, Pub. by Insel Verlag Germany). Suhrkamp.

--Der Goldene Topf ein Marchen Aus der Neuen Zeit. Mainland, W. F., ed. (Blackwell's German Text Ser.). 1967. pap. 9.95x (ISBN 0-631-01310-5, Pub. by Basil Blackwell). Biblio Dist.

--The King's Bride. 1980. pap. 3.95 (ISBN 0-7145-0326-6). Riverrun NY.

Hoffmann, Felix, ed. & illus. see Grimm Brothers.

Hoffmann, Gretl. Doors: Excellence in International Design. (Illus.). 144p. 1977. 35.00x (ISBN 0-8230-7135-9). Intl Ideas.

Hoffmann, Hans W. Die Intention der Verkuendigung Jesajas. LC 74-80632. (Beiheft 136 zur Zeitschrift fuer die alttestamentliche Wissenschaft). 125p. 1974. 37.10 (ISBN 3-11-004672-5). De Gruyter.

Hoffmann, Heinrich. Adolf Hitler: Faces of a Dictator. LC 68-24392. 1969. 9.50 (ISBN 0-15-103551-2). HarBraceJ.

Hoffmann, Heinrich, ed. Hitler Was My Friend. Stevens, R. H., tr. from Ger. 1978. pap. 4.50x (ISBN 0-911038-36-1). Noontide.

Hoffmann, Herbert. Sexual & Asexual Pursuit. (Occasional Papers Ser.: No. 34). 1977. pap. text ed. 8.00x (ISBN 0-391-01111-1). Humanities.

Hoffmann, Joseph E. Classical Mathematics. 4.75 o.p. (ISBN 0-685-28345-3). Philos Lib.

Hoffmann, Karlheinz. Verliebtheit und Rollenspiel in Shakespeare's Verkleidungskomodien. (Salzburg Studies in English Literature: Elizabethan & Renaissance Studies: No. 73). 1978. pap. text ed. 25.00x (ISBN 0-391-01411-0). Humanities.

Hoffmann, Kurt, et al. Designing Architectural Facades: An Ideas File for Architects. (Illus.). 168p. 1975. 29.95x (ISBN 0-7114-3408-5). Intl Ideas.

Hoffmann, Peter. History of German Resistance, Nineteen Thirty-Three to Nineteen Forty-Five. Barry, Richard, tr. from Ger. 1979. 25.00 (ISBN 0-262-08088-5); pap. 9.95 (ISBN 0-262-58038-1). MIT Pr.

Hoffmann, R., jt. auth. see Woodward, R. B.

Hoffmann, Thomas R. & Johnson, Brian. The World Energy Triangle: A Strategy for Cooperation. 1981. 20.00 (ISBN 0-905347-15-3). Ballinger Pub.

Hoffmann, William M., ed. New American Plays, Vol. 3. Incl. The Electronic Nigger. Bullins, Ed; The Poet's Papers. Starkweather, David; Always with Love. Harris, Tom; Thank You, Miss Victoria. Hoffman, William M; The Golden Circle. Patrick, Robert; An American Playground Sampler. Estrin, Marc; The King of Spain. Hoffman, Byrd. (Illus.). 288p. (Orig.). 1969. 5.95 (ISBN 0-8090-7252-1, Mermaid, Mermaid). Hill & Wang.

Hoffman-Ostenhof, O., et al, eds. Affinity Chromatography: Proceedings of an International Symposium Held in Vienna, 1977. LC 78-40289. 1978. text ed. 60.00 (ISBN 0-08-022632-9). Pergamon.

Hoffmaster, Henry R. Financial Statements: How to Read & Interpret Them for Success in the Stock Market. (Illus.). 1980. deluxe ed. 49.45 (ISBN 0-918968-62-3). Inst Econ Finan.

Hoffmeister, August W. Die Blume in der Dichtung der Englischen Romantik. (Salzburg Studies in English Literature Romantic Reassessment Ser.: No. 76). 1978. pap. text ed. 25.00x (ISBN 0-391-01412-9). Humanities.

Hoffmeister, Donald F. Zoo Animals. Zim, Herbert S. & Fichter, George S., eds. (Golden Guide Ser). (Illus.). (gr. k-4). 1967. PLB 9.15 (ISBN 0-307-63538-4, Golden Pr); pap. 1.95 o.p. (ISBN 0-307-24019-3). Western Pub.

Hoffmeister, Elizabeth R., jt. auth. see Goehlert, Robert.

Hoffmeister, Werner G., jt. auth. see Weimar, Karl S.

Hoffner, Harry A., Jr. & Guterbock, Hans G., eds. The Hittite Dictionary of the Oriental Institute of the University of Chicago, Vol. 3, Fasc. 1, L. LC 79-53554. 1980. pap. 9.00x (ISBN 0-918986-27-3). Oriental Inst.

Hofland, Barbara H. The Stolen Boy: A Story Founded on Facts, Repr. Of 1828 Ed. Bd. with Seizure of the Ship Industry, by a Conspiracy, & the Consequent Sufferings of Capt. James Fox & His Companions: Their Captivity Among the Esquimaux Indians in North America; & the Miraculous Escape of the Captain. Repr. of 1830 ed; St. Maur: Or, the Captive Babes Recovered, Pub. by Emory & Waugh for the Tract Society of the Methodist Epescopal Church, New York. Repr. of 1830 ed. LC 75-7066. (Indian Captivities Ser.: Vol. 44). 1976. lib. bdg. 44.00 (ISBN 0-8240-1668-8). Garland Pub.

Hofling, Charles K. Custer & the Little Big Horn: A Psychobiographical Inquiry. 152p. 1981. 15.95 (ISBN 0-8143-1668-9). Wayne St U Pr.

Hofling, Charles K., jt. auth. see Kyes, Joan J.

Hofling, Charles K., ed. Law & Ethics in the Practice of Psychiatry. LC 80-22091. 280p. 1980. 20.00 (ISBN 0-87630-250-9). Brunner-Mazel.

Hofman, David. God & His Messengers. (Illus.). 1978. pap. 4.50 o.s.i. (ISBN 0-85398-049-7, 7-52-43, Pub. by G Ronald England). Baha'i.

--The Renewal of Civilization. rev. ed. 1969. 2.95 (ISBN 0-87743-009-8, 7-31-31); pap. 1.50 o.s.i. (ISBN 0-87743-057-8, 7-31-32). Baha'i.

Hofman, David, ed. see Blomfield, Lady.

Hofman, Helenmarie & Ricker, Kenneth S., eds. Sourcebook, Science Education & the Physically Handicapped. (Orig.). 1979. pap. 6.00 (ISBN 0-87355-014-5). Natl Sci Tchrs.

Hofman, Jaroslav. Ornamental Shrubs. (Concise Guides Ser.). (Illus.). 1979. 7.95 (ISBN 0-600-38246-X). Transatlantic.

Hofmann, A. W., et al. Geochemical Transport & Kinetics. 1974. 27.00 (ISBN 0-87279-644-2, 634). Carnegie Inst.

Hofmann, Adele D., et al. The Hospitalized Adolescent: A Guide to Managing the Ill & Injured Youth. LC 76-1698. 1976. 17.95 (ISBN 0-02-914790-5). Free Pr.

Hofmann, Albert, jt. auth. see Schultes, Richard E.

Hofmann, Charles. Sounds for Silents. LC 74-107465. (Illus.). 1969. 10.00 (ISBN 0-910482-14-4); record incl. (ISBN 0-89676-035-9). Drama Bk.

Hofmann, E. & Pfeil, E., eds. Protein: Structure, Function & Industrial Applicatons. (Federation of European Biochemical Society Ser.: Vol. 52). (Illus.). 1979. text ed. 60.00 (ISBN 0-08-023176-4). Pergamon.

Hofmann, Herbert. Ten Centuries That Shaped the West: Greek & Roman Art in Texas Collections. LC 71-131999. (Illus.). 1970. 18.00 (ISBN 0-914412-18-3); pap. 12.00 (ISBN 0-914412-01-9). Inst for the Arts.

Hofmann, J. E. Leibniz in Paris, 1672-1676. LC 73-80469. (Illus.). 230p. 1974. 65.00 (ISBN 0-521-20258-2). Cambridge U Pr.

Hofmann, Werner, intro. by. Max Ernst-Exhibition Catalog: Inside the Sight. (Illus.). 164p. 1973. pap. 6.00 (ISBN 0-914412-06-X). Interbk Inc.

Hofmann, Werner, et al. Max Ernst: Inside the Sight. LC 77-125283. (Illus.). 1973. pap. 6.00 (ISBN 0-914412-06-X). Inst for the Arts.

Hofmannsthal, Hugo Von. Selected Essays. Gilbert, Mary E., ed. (Blackwell's German Text Ser.). 1955. pap. 5.00x o.p. (ISBN 0-631-01600-7, Pub. by Basil Blackwell). Biblio Dist.

Hofmannsthal, Hugo Von see Strauss, Richard & Von Hofmannsthal, Hugo.

Hofmannsthal, Hugo Von see Von Hofmannsthal, Hugo.

Hofsinde, Robert. The Indian & His Horse. (Illus.). (gr. 3-7). 1960. PLB 6.48 (ISBN 0-688-31421-X). Morrow.

--The Indian & the Buffalo. (Illus.). (gr. 3-7). 1961. PLB 6.67 (ISBN 0-688-31420-1). Morrow.

--Indian Arts. LC 73-137100. (Illus.). (gr. 3-7). 1971. PLB 6.48 (ISBN 0-688-31617-4). Morrow.

--Indian Beadwork. (Illus.). (gr. 5-9). 1958. PLB 6.48 (ISBN 0-688-31575-5). Morrow.

--Indian Costumes. LC 68-11895. (Illus.). (gr. 3-7). 1968. PLB 6.48 (ISBN 0-688-31614-X). Morrow.

--Indian Fishing & Camping. (Illus.). (gr. 4-7). 1963. PLB 6.48 (ISBN 0-688-31797-9). Morrow.

--Indian Games & Crafts. (Illus.). (gr. 5-9). 1957. PLB 6.67 (ISBN 0-688-21607-2). Morrow.

--Indian Hunting. (Illus.). (gr. 4-7). 1962. PLB 6.48 (ISBN 0-688-31608-5). Morrow.

--The Indian Medicine Man. (Illus.). (gr. 3-7). 1966. PLB 6.48 (ISBN 0-688-31618-2). Morrow.

--Indian Music Makers. (Illus.). (gr. 3-7). 1967. PLB 6.48 (ISBN 0-688-31616-6). Morrow.

--Indian Picture Writing. (Illus.). (gr. 5-9). 1959. PLB 6.48 (ISBN 0-688-31609-3). Morrow.

--Indian Sign Language. (Illus.). (gr. 5 up). 1956. PLB 6.48 (ISBN 0-688-31610-7). Morrow.

--Indian Warriors & Their Weapons. (Illus.). (gr. 4-7). 1965. PLB 6.48 (ISBN 0-688-31613-1). Morrow.

--Indians at Home. (Illus.). (gr. 3-7). 1964. PLB 6.48 (ISBN 0-688-31611-5). Morrow.
--Indians on the Move. (Illus.). (gr. 3-7). 1970. PLB 6.48 (ISBN 0-688-31615-8). Morrow.
Hofstader & Miller. United States. 4th ed. 464p. 1976. Pt. 1. pap. 13.95 (ISBN 0-13-938639-4); Pt. 2. pap. 13.95 (ISBN 0-13-938647-5); combined ed. 17.95 (ISBN 0-13-938654-8). P-H.
Hofstadster, jt. auth. see Ver Steeg.
Hofstadter, Albert. Truth & Art. LC 65-12521. (Illus.). 1965. 15.00x (ISBN 0-231-02794-X). Columbia U Pr.
Hofstadter, Richard. Academic Freedom in the Age of the College. LC 61-2329. 1955. pap. 7.00 (ISBN 0-231-08511-7). Columbia U Pr.
--The Age of Reform: From Bryan to F. D. R. 328p. Date not set. pap. 3.95 (ISBN 0-394-70095-3, Vin). Random.
--American Political Tradition. LC 73-20353. 1954. pap. 3.95 (ISBN 0-394-70009-0, Vin). Random.
--The Idea of a Party System: The Rise of Legitimate Opposition in the United States, 1780-1840. LC 76-82377. (Jefferson Memorial Lectures). 1969. 15.75x (ISBN 0-520-01389-1); pap. 3.95 (ISBN 0-520-01754-4, CAL196). U of Cal Pr.
--Progressive Historians. LC 68-23944. 1970. pap. 3.95 (ISBN 0-394-70591-2, Vin). Random.
--Social Darwinism in American Thought. rev. ed. LC 59-9543. 1959. 7.95 o.p. (ISBN 0-8076-0079-2). Braziller.
Hofstadter, Richard & Hardy, C. De Witt. Development & Scope of Higher Education in the United States. LC 52-14741. 1952. 20.00x (ISBN 0-231-01956-4). Columbia U Pr.
Hofstadter, Richard & Wallace, Michael, eds. American Violence: A Documentary History. LC 73-111238. 1971. pap. 4.95 (ISBN 0-394-71686-8, Vin). Random.
Hofstatter, Ellen, jt. auth. see Nortman, Dorothy.
Hofstatter, Hans H. Gustav Klimt: Erotic Drawings. (Illus.). 88p. 1980. 145.00 (ISBN 0-686-62690-7, 1203-1). Abrams.
Hofstead, Jolyon. Ceramics, Step by Step. (Step by Step Craft Ser). 1974. PLB 9.15 o.p. (ISBN 0-307-62001-8, Golden Pr); pap. 2.95 o.p. (ISBN 0-307-42001-9). Western Pub.
Hofstede, Geert. Culture's Consequences: International Differences in Work-Related Values. LC 80-16327. (Sage Ser. on Cross-Cultural Research & Methodology: Vol. 5). (Illus.). 475p. 1980. 29.95 (ISBN 0-8039-1444-X). Sage.
Hogaboom, George B., jt. auth. see Blum, William.
Hogalin, jt. auth. see Velleman.
Hogan, Ben. Modern Fundamentals of Golf. 128p. 1962. pap. 3.95 (ISBN 0-346-12326-7). Cornerstone.
Hogan, Cecily. Best of All! (A Young Reader Ser.). (Illus.). (gr. k-3). 1979. PLB 5.00 (ISBN 0-307-60170-6, Golden Pr). Western Pub.
--Lassie & Her Friends. (ps-1). PLB 5.38 (ISBN 0-307-68950-6, Golden Pr). Western Pub.
--Tweety & Sylvester at the Farm. (Tell-a-Tale Readers). (gr. k-3). 1978. PLB 4.77 (ISBN 0-307-68642-6, Whitman). Western Pub.
Hogan, Charles B. London Stage, 1776-1800: A Critical Introduction. LC 60-6539. (Arcturus Books Paperbacks). (Illus.). 230p. 1968. pap. 6.95 (ISBN 0-8093-0340-X). S Ill U Pr.
Hogan, David J. Who's Who of Horrors. LC 79-17606. 1980. 19.95 (ISBN 0-498-02475-X). A S Barnes.
Hogan, Desmond. Diamonds at the Bottom of the Sea & Other Stories. 1980. 8.95 (ISBN 0-8076-0934-X). Braziller.
--The Leaves on Grey. large print ed. LC 80-25146. 213p. 1980. Repr. 8.95 (ISBN 0-89621-258-0). Thorndike Pr.
--The Leaves on Grey. 8.95 (ISBN 0-8076-0948-X). Braziller.
Hogan, Edward J., et al, eds. The Aspect Anthology. (Illus.). 250p. (Orig.). 1981. pap. 3.95 (ISBN 0-939010-01-1). Zephyr.
Hogan, Elizabeth. The Curse of King Tut. Uhlich, Richard, ed. (Bluejeans Paperbacks Ser.). (Illus., Orig.). (gr. 7-12). 1978. pap. text ed. 1.25 (ISBN 0-8374-5007-1). Xerox Ed Pubns.
Hogan, Elizabeth, jt. auth. see Curtis, Richard.
Hogan, James. Giants' Star. 320p. (Orig.). 1981. pap. 2.50 (ISBN 0-345-28771-1, Del Rey). Ballantine.
Hogan, James C. A Guide to the Iliad. LC 78-58757. 1979. pap. 4.95 (ISBN 0-385-14519-5, Anch). Doubleday.
Hogan, James P. Inherit the Stars. (A Del Rey Bk.). 1978. pap. 1.95 (ISBN 0-345-28907-2). Ballantine.
Hogan, John C. The Schools, the Courts & the Public Interest. LC 73-1005. (Politics of Education Ser.). 320p. 1974. 17.95 (ISBN 0-669-86892-2). Lexington Bks.
Hogan, Kirk, jt. auth. see Hogan, Paula Z.
Hogan, Paula Z. The Black Swan. LC 78-27416. (Life Cycles Ser.). (Illus.). (gr. k-3). 1979. PLB 9.95 (ISBN 0-8172-1254-X). Raintree Pubs.
--The Butterfly. LC 78-26827. (Life Cycles Ser.). (Illus.). (gr. k-3). 1979. PLB 9.95 (ISBN 0-8172-1252-3). Raintree Pubs.
--The Dandelion. LC 78-21155. (Life Cycles Ser.). (Illus.). (gr. k-3). 1979. PLB 9.95 (ISBN 0-8172-1250-7). Raintree Pubs.
--The Frog. LC 78-21240. (Life Cycles Ser.). (Illus.). (gr. k-3). 1979. PLB 9.95 (ISBN 0-8172-1253-1). Raintree Pubs.
--The Honeybee. LC 78-21165. (Life Cycles Ser.). (Illus.). (gr. k-3). 1979. PLB 9.95 (ISBN 0-8172-1256-6). Raintree Pubs.
--I Hate Boys - I Hate Girls. LC 79-24056. (Life & Living from a Child's Point of View Ser.). (Illus.). (gr. k-5). 1980. PLB 9.65 (ISBN 0-8172-1358-9). Raintree Child.
--The Oak Tree. LC 78-21183. (Life Cycles Ser.). (Illus.). (gr. k-3). 1979. PLB 9.95 (ISBN 0-8172-1251-5). Raintree Pubs.
--The Penguin. LC 78-21225. (Life Cycles Ser.). (Illus.). (gr. k-3). 1979. PLB 9.95 (ISBN 0-8172-1257-4). Raintree Pubs.
--The Salmon. LC 78-21178. (Life Cycles Ser.). (Illus.). (gr. k-3). 1979. PLB 9.95 (ISBN 0-8172-1255-8). Raintree Pubs.
--Sometimes I Don't Like School. LC 79-24055. (Life & Living from a Child's Point of View Ser.). (Illus.). (gr. k-5). 1980. PLB 9.65 (ISBN 0-8172-1357-0). Raintree Child.
--Sometimes I Get So Mad. LC 79-24057. (Life & Living from a Child's Point of View Ser.). (Illus.). (gr. k-5). 1980. PLB 9.65 (ISBN 0-8172-1359-7). Raintree Child.
--Will Dad Ever Move Back Home? LC 79-24058. (Life & Living from a Child's Point of View Ser.). (Illus.). (gr. k-5). 1980. PLB 9.65 (ISBN 0-8172-1356-2). Raintree Child.
Hogan, Paula Z. & Hogan, Kirk. The Hospital Scares Me. LC 79-23886. (Life & Living from a Child's Point of View Ser.). (Illus.). (gr. k-5). 1980. PLB 9.65 (ISBN 0-8172-1351-1). Raintree Child.
Hogan, Ray. The Doomsday Bullet. LC 80-2839. 192p. 1981. 9.95 (ISBN 0-385-17554-X). Doubleday.
--The Hell Raiser. 1980. pap. 1.75 (ISBN 0-451-09489-1, E9489, Sig). NAL.
--The Iron Jehu. LC 76-10518. 1976. 5.95 o.p. (ISBN 0-385-12409-0). Doubleday.
--Omaha Crossing. 1977. pap. 1.75 (ISBN 0-441-62341-7). Ace Bks.
--Outlaw's Pledge. (Orig.). 1981. pap. 1.95 (ISBN 0-451-09778-5, 9778, Sig). NAL.
--Pilgrim. 1981. pap. 1.75 (ISBN 0-451-09576-6, E9576, Sig). NAL.
--The Proving Gun. LC 75-9224. 192p. 1975. 5.95 o.p. (ISBN 0-385-11177-0). Doubleday.
--The Proving Gun. 1980. lib. bdg. 10.95 (ISBN 0-8161-3172-4, Large Print Bks). G K Hall.
Hogan, Robert & Burnham, R. The Art of the Amateur Nineteen Sixteen to Nineteen Twenty: The Modern Irish Drama V. (Irish Theatre Ser.: No. 11). 400p. 1980. text ed. 35.50x (ISBN 0-391-02153-2). Humanities.
Hogan, Robert & Kilroy, James. The Modern Irish Drama, No. 3: The Abbey Theatre, the Years of Synge 1905-1909. (Irish Theatre Ser.: No. 8). 1978. text ed. 30.00x (ISBN 0-391-00754-8, Dolmen Pr). Humanities.
--Modern Irish Drama, Vol. 2: Laying the Foundations, 1902-1904. (Irish Theatre Ser: No. 7). 164p. 1976. text ed. 16.00x (ISBN 0-391-00609-6, Dolmen Pr). Humanities.
--The Modern Irish Drama 1: The Irish Literary Theater 1899-1901. (The Irish Theatre Ser.: No. 6). 160p. (Orig.). 1975. text ed. 12.00x (ISBN 0-391-00377-1, Dolmen Pr); pap. text ed. 7.50x (ISBN 0-391-00378-X). Humanities.
Hogan, Robert, et al. Modern Irish Drama IV: The Rise of the Realists. 1979. text ed. 45.00x (ISBN 0-391-01118-9, Dolmen Pr). Humanities.
Hogan, Rosemarie. Human Sexuality: A Nursing Perspective. 768p. 1980. pap. text ed. 13.95 (ISBN 0-8385-3955-6). ACC.
Hogan, Terrence P., jt. auth. see Erickson, Gerald D.
Hogan, Thom. CP-M User's Guide. 350p. (Orig.). 1981. pap. 12.99 (ISBN 0-931988-44-6). Osborne-McGraw.
Hogan, Thomas, jt. auth. see Fenichel, Carol.
Hogan, William J. Complete Book of Bacon. (Illus.). 1978. 22.50x (ISBN 0-7198-2627-6). Intl Ideas.
Hogan, William R. Texas Republic: A Social & Economic History. rev. ed. LC 68-59357. (Texas History Paperback Ser: No. 3). 1969. pap. 7.95 (ISBN 0-292-78423-6). U of Tex Pr.
Hogarth, C. J., tr. see Dostoyevsky, Fedor.
Hogarth, C. J., tr. see Goncharov, Ivan.
Hogarth, David G. Arabia. LC 79-2862. 139p. 1981. Repr. of 1922 ed. 15.00 (ISBN 0-8305-0036-7). Hyperion Conn.
--The Penetration of Arabia: A Record of the Development of Western Knowledge Concerning the Arabian Peninsula. LC 79-2863. (Illus.). 359p. 1981. Repr. of 1904 ed. 35.00 (ISBN 0-8305-0037-5). Hyperion Conn.
Hogarth, G. Memoirs of the Opera, 2 vols. LC 71-166101. (Music Ser.). 1972. Repr. of 1851 ed. Set. lib. bdg. 49.50 (ISBN 0-306-70256-8). Da Capo.
Hogarth, George. Musical History, Biography, & Criticism. LC 69-12685. (Music Reprint Ser). 1969. Repr. of 1848 ed. lib. bdg. 22.50 (ISBN 0-306-71234-2). Da Capo.
Hogarth, Grace. A Sister for Helen. LC 79-64313. (Illus.). (gr. 4-7). 1980. 8.95 (ISBN 0-233-96817-2). Andre Deutsch.
Hogarth, James, tr. see Belenitsky, Alexandr.
Hogarth, P. J. Biology of Reproduction. LC 78-4620. (Tertiary Level Biology Ser.). 1978. text ed. 18.95 (ISBN 0-470-26314-8). Halsted Pr.
Hogarth, Paul. Creative Pencil Drawing. (Illus.). 1964. 14.95 o.p. (ISBN 0-8230-1100-3); pap. 9.95 o.p. (ISBN 0-8230-1101-1). Watson-Guptill.
--Paul Hogarth's Walking Tour of Old Boston. (Illus.). 1978. pap. 7.95 (ISBN 0-87690-295-6). Dutton.
--Paul Hogarth's Walking Tours of Old Washington. 1979. 14.95 o.p. (ISBN 0-87690-347-2); pap. 7.95 o.p. (ISBN 0-87690-326-X). Dutton.
Hogarth, Peter & Clery, Val. Dragons. LC 79-4530. (Illus.). 1979. 16.95 o.p. (ISBN 0-670-28176-X, Studio). Viking Pr.
Hogarth, Robin M. Judgement & Choice: Strategies for Decisions. LC 79-42822. 250p. 1980. 23.95 (ISBN 0-471-27744-4, Pub. by Wiley-Interscience). Wiley.
Hogarth, W. D., tr. see Momigliano, Arnaldo.
Hogarth, William. The Artistic & Psychological Analysis of Beauty. (Illus.). 127p. 1981. 31.45 (ISBN 0-930582-90-X). Gloucester Art.
Hogben, Carol, ed. The Art of Bernard Leach. (Illus.). 1978. 32.50 o.p. (ISBN 0-8230-0263-2). Watson-Guptill.
Hoge, Cecil C., Sr. Mail Order Moonlighting. LC 78-61866. 1978. 10.95 (ISBN 0-913668-95-8); pap. 7.95 (ISBN 0-913668-94-X). Ten Speed Pr.
Hoge, Dean R. & Roozen, David A., eds. Understanding Church Growth & Decline, 1950-78. LC 79-4166. (Illus.). 1979. pap. 9.95 (ISBN 0-8298-0358-0). Pilgrim NY.
Hoge, James O. & James O., eds. Lady Tennyson's Journal. LC 80-21387. 1981. price not set (ISBN 0-8139-0876-0). U Pr of Va.
Hoge, James O. & West, James L., eds. Review: Vol. 2. 1981. 20.00x (ISBN 0-8139-0865-5). U Pr of Va.
Hogeboom, Amy. Familiar Animals & How to Draw Them. (gr. 1-4). 3.95 o.s.i. (ISBN 0-8149-0323-1). Vanguard.
Hogendorn, J. S. Nigerian Groundnut Exports: Origins & Early Developments. (Illus.). 1979. 29.95x (ISBN 0-19-575443-3). Oxford U Pr.
Hogendorn, Jan S. & Brown, Wilson H. New International Economics. LC 78-67953. (Economics Ser.). (Illus.). 1979. text ed. 17.95 (ISBN 0-201-02824-7). A-W.
Hogenmiller, Peter U. The West German Mark & the New Monetary World Leadership. (Illus.). 1980. deluxe ed. 59.75 (ISBN 0-930008-56-1). Inst Econ Pol.
Hogg, A. H. Hill-Forts of Britain. 1979. 29.95x (ISBN 0-8464-0100-2). Beekman Pubs.
Hogg, Anthony. Guide to Visiting Vineyards. (Illus.). 1978. 12.50 o.p. (ISBN 0-7181-1560-0). Transatlantic.
--The Winetaster's Guide to Europe: How to Visit Over 300 Vineyards & Cellars on Your European Vacation. (Illus.). 1980. 17.50 (ISBN 0-525-93071-X); pap. 8.95 (ISBN 0-525-93084-1). Dutton.
Hogg, C. F. & Vine, W. E. Epistles of Paul the Apostle to the Thessalonians. 5.95 (ISBN 0-89315-040-1). Lambert Bk.
Hogg, Gary. Batsford Book of the Cotswolds. 1979. pap. 11.95 (ISBN 0-7134-2449-4, Pub. by Batsford England). David & Charles.
--Batsford Colour Book of Shakespeare's Country. 1976. 10.50 (ISBN 0-7134-3151-2, Pub. by Batsford England). David & Charles.
Hogg, Ian. Artillery in Color: Nineteen Twenty to Nineteen Sixty-Three. LC 80-379. (Illus.). 192p. 1980. 11.95 (ISBN 0-668-04939-1); pap. 7.95 (ISBN 0-668-04941-3). Arco.
--The Encyclopedia of Infantry Weapons of World War II. LC 76-51525. Orig. Title: Infantry Weapons of World War II by Sidney Mayer. (Illus.). 1977. 15.95 o.p. (ISBN 0-690-01447-3, TYC-T). T Y Crowell.
Hogg, Ian V. Coast Defences of England & Wales: 1856-1956. 1974. 8.95 (ISBN 0-7153-6353-0). David & Charles.
Hogg, Ivan V. & Weeks, John. The Illustrated Encyclopedia of Military Vehicles. LC 80-8006. 1980. 30.00 (ISBN 0-13-450817-3). P-H.
Hogg, James. Dryden As Propagandist: Absalom & Architophel & Its Background. (Salzburger Studien Anglistik & Amerikanistik). 1979. pap. text ed. 25.00x (ISBN 0-391-01426-9). Humanities.
--Jacobean Miscellany. (Jacobean Drama Ser.: No. 95). 1980. pap. text ed. 25.00x (ISBN 0-391-02144-3). Humanities.
--The Leysin Version of James Elroy Flecker's Hassan. (Salzburg Studies in English Literature: Poetic Drama & Poetic Theory: No. 30). 142p. 1976. pap. text ed. 25.00x (ISBN 0-391-01417-X). Humanities.
--The Rewyll of Seynt Sauioure, Vol. 1. (Salzburger Studien zur Anglistik und Amerikanistik). 1980. pap. text ed. 31.25x (ISBN 0-391-01195-2). Humanities.
--The Rewyll of Seynt Sauioure & Other Middle English Brigittine Legislative, Vol. 2. (Salzburger Studien Zur Anglistik und Amerikanistik: No. 6). 1978. pap. text ed. 38.75x (ISBN 0-391-01415-3). Humanities.
--Richard Whytford's the Pype or Tonne of the Lyfe of Perfection, Vol. 2, Pt. 1. (Elizabethan Studies: No. 89). (Orig.). 1979. pap. text ed. 25.00x (ISBN 0-391-01693-8). Humanities.
--Richard Whytford's the Pype or Tonne of the Lyfe of Perfection, Vol. 3, Pt. 2. (Elizabethan Studies: No. 89). (Orig.). 1979. pap. text ed. 25.00x (ISBN 0-391-01692-X). Humanities.
--Richard Whytford's the Pype or Tonne of the Lyfe of Perfection, Vol. 4, Pt. 3. (Elizabethan & Renaissance Studies: No. 89). 1979. pap. text ed. 25.00 (ISBN 0-391-01689-X). Humanities.
--Robert Browning & Other Victorian Theatre Vol. 2: Acting Versions of Strafford, a Blot on the Scutcheon & Colombe's Birthday. (Salzburger Studien Zur Anglistik und Amerikanistik: No. 4). 1977. pap. text ed. 34.75x (ISBN 0-391-01414-5). Humanities.
--The Yorkshire Cistercian Heritage: Vol. 2, Rievaulx, Jervaulx, Byland. (Salzburg Studien Zur Anglistik und Amerikanistik: 8). (Illus.). 1979. pap. 45.00x (ISBN 0-391-01429-3). Humanities.
--The Yorkshire Cistercian Heritage: Vol. 3, Fountains, Kirkstall, Meaux. (Salzburg Studien zur Anglistik und Amerikanistik: 8). (Illus.). 1979. pap. 45.00x (ISBN 0-391-01430-7). Humanities.
--The Yorkshire Cisterician Heritage: Vol. 4, Roche, Salley. (Salzurg Studien Zur Anglistik und Amerikanistik 8). (Illus.). 1979. pap. 45.00x (ISBN 0-391-01431-5). Humanities.
Hogg, James & Clancy, Charles J. Salzburg Studies in English Literature & the Critics: Review of Don Juan Criticism, 1900 to 1973. (Salzburg Studies in English Literature, Romantic Reassessment: No. 40). 1974. pap. text ed. 25.00x (ISBN 0-391-01413-7). Humanities.
Hogg, James & Mitgutsch, Waltraud. Ted Hughes & the Drama: Zur Lyrik Von Ted Hughes, eine Interpretation Nach Leitmotiven. (Salzburg Studies in English Literature, Poetic Drama & Poetic Theory: No. 22). 282p. 1974. pap. text ed. 25.00x (ISBN 0-391-01418-8). Humanities.
Hogg, James & Muller, Robert. The Nineteen Fifty-Three Production of "Venice Preserv'd". Bd. with Zur Rezeption Von Otway's "Venice Preserv'd" in der Restaurationszeit. Hogg, James; Nahum Tate's "Richard II" & Censorship During Theexclusion Bill Crisis. Muller, Robert; James Elroy Flecker's "Hassan: a Near East Masterpiece?". Muller, Robert. (Salzburg Studies in English Literature, Poetic Drama & Poetry Theory Ser.: No. 26). 121p. 1976. pap. text ed. 25.00x (ISBN 0-391-01416-1). Humanities.
Hogg, James, jt. auth. see Mayr, Roswitha.
Hogg, James, ed. Elizabethan Miscellany No. Two. (Salzburg Studies in English Literature, Elizabethan & Renaissance Studies: No. 71). 1978. pap. text ed. 25.00x (ISBN 0-391-01420-X). Humanities.
--Essays in Honour of Professor Erwin Sturzl on His 60th Birthday, 2 vols. (Salzburger Studien: No. 10). 1980. pap. text ed. 34.75x ea. Vol. 1 (ISBN 0-391-01923-6). Vol. 2 (ISBN 0-391-01924-4). Humanities.
--Richard Whytford: A Dayly Exercyse of Dethe. (Salzburg Institute for English Literature: Elizabethan Studies: No. 89: Pt. 5). (Orig.). 1979. pap. text ed. 25.00x (ISBN 0-391-01709-8). Humanities.
--Romantic Reassessmeent: Studies in Nineteenth Century Literature. (Salzberg Studies in English Literature: 87-2). 144p. 1981. pap. text ed. 25.00x (ISBN 0-391-02245-8, Pub. by Salzburg, Austria). Humanities.
--Studies in Nineteenth Century Literature. (SSEL: Salzburg Studies in English Literature: No. 87). 264p. 1980. text ed. 25.00x (ISBN 0-391-01782-9). Humanities.

--Studies in the Romantics. (SSEL: Salzburg Studies in English Literature: No. 81). 129p. 1980. text ed. 25.00x (ISBN 0-391-01781-0). Humanities.

Hogg, James, et al. New Light on Byron. (Salzburg Studies in English Literature: Romantic Reassessment: No. 74). 1978. pap. text ed. 25.00x (ISBN 0-391-01419-6). Humanities.

Hogg, John. Success in Swimming. (Success Sportbooks Ser.). (Illus.). 1977. 9.95 (ISBN 0-7195-3376-7). Transatlantic.

Hogg, Margaret E. Man in Society. (Biology of Man Ser.). 1968. pap. text ed. 7.95x o.p. (ISBN 0-435-60427-9). Heinemann Ed.

--Man the Animal. (Biology of Man Ser.). 1966. pap. text ed. 11.50x o.p. (ISBN 0-435-60426-0). Heinemann Ed.

Hogg, Robert V., ed. Modern Statistics: Methods & Applications. (Proceedings of Symposia in Applied Mathematics: Vol. 23). 1980. 12.00 (ISBN 0-8218-0023-X, PSAPMS-23). Am Math.

Hoggard, Kevin, ed. Summer Theatre Directory: 1980. 1980. pap. 3.50, ATA members 3.00 (ISBN 0-686-18919-1). Am Theatre Assoc.

Hoggart, Keith. Geography & Local Administration: A Bibliography. (Public Administration Ser.: Bibliography P-530). 84p. 1980. pap. 9.00. Vance Biblios.

Hoggart, Richard see Bradbrook, M. C.

Hoggarth, Pauline, jt. auth. see Gifford, Douglas.

Hoggett, J. G., et al. Nitration & Aromatic Reactivity. LC 76-138374. (Illus.). 1971. 42.50 (ISBN 0-521-08029-0). Cambridge U Pr.

Hogins, Burl & Bryant, Gerald. The Generation Gap. 1970. pap. text ed. 3.95x (ISBN 0-02-474970-2, 47497). Macmillan.

Hogins, Burl & Bryant, Gerald, Jr. Alienation. 1970. pap. text ed. 3.95x (ISBN 0-02-474950-8, 47495). Macmillan.

--Drugs & Dissent. 1970. pap. text ed. 3.95x (ISBN 0-02-474960-5, 47496). Macmillan.

Hogins, J. Burl & Bryant, Gerald A. Reading for Insight: A Perceptual Approach to College English. 2nd ed. LC 73-7371. (Illus.). 416p. 1974. pap. text ed. 9.95 (ISBN 0-02-474880-3, 47488). Macmillan.

Hogins, J. Burl & Bryant, Gerald A., Jr. A Perceptual Approach to College English: Experiments in Composition. 1970. pap. text ed. 6.95x o.p. (ISBN 0-02-474860-9, 47486). Glencoe.

--Reading for Insight: A Perceptual Approach to College English. LC 70-101716. 1970. text ed. 6.95x o.p. (ISBN 0-02-474850-1, 47485). Glencoe.

Hogins, James B. Literature: Fiction. LC 73-90125. (Illus.). 368p. 1974. pap. text ed. 5.25 (ISBN 0-574-19130-5, 13-2130). SRA.

Hogins, James B. & Bryant, Gerald R., Jr. Juxtaposition, Encore! LC 74-15169. (Illus.). 304p. 1975. pap. text ed. 11.95 (ISBN 0-574-17000-6, 13-5000); instr's guide avail. (ISBN 0-574-17001-4, 13-5001). SRA.

Hogins, James B. & Yarber, Robert E. Phase Blue. rev. ed. LC 73-87858. (Illus.). 464p. 1974. pap. text ed. 8.95 (ISBN 0-574-18370-1, 13-1370); instr's guide avail. (ISBN 0-574-18371-X, 13-1371); student guide 3.95 (ISBN 0-574-18395-7, 13-1395); instructor's guide 2.50 (ISBN 0-574-18372-8, 13-1372). SRA.

--Reading, Writing, & Rhetoric. 4th ed. LC 78-13940. 1979. pap. text ed. 9.95 (ISBN 0-574-22045-3, 13-5045); instr's guide avail. (ISBN 0-574-22046-1, 13-5046). SRA.

--Theme & Rhetoric. LC 76-28344. 1977. pap. text ed. 8.95 (ISBN 0-574-22025-9, 13-5025); instr's guide avail. (ISBN 0-574-22026-7, 13-5026). SRA.

Hogner, Dorothy C. Endangered Plants. LC 77-2310. (Illus.). (gr. 3-7). 1977. 8.95 (ISBN 0-690-01362-0, TYC-J). T Y Crowell.

--Frogs & Polliwogs. LC 56-7795. (Illus.). (gr. 2-5). 1956. 6.95 o.p. (ISBN 0-690-31769-7, TYC-J). T Y Crowell.

--Good Bugs & Bad Bugs in Your Garden: Backyard Ecology. LC 74-6235. (Illus.). 96p. (gr. 3-7). 1974. PLB 7.89 (ISBN 0-690-00120-7, TYC-J). T Y Crowell.

--Grasshoppers & Crickets. LC 60-9219. (Illus.). (gr. 2-5). 1960. 7.95 (ISBN 0-690-35035-X, TYC-J); pap. 7.89 (ISBN 0-690-35036-8). T Y Crowell.

Hogrogian, Nonny. Apples. LC 71-146626. (ps-2). 1972. 4.95 o.s.i. (ISBN 0-02-744010-9). Macmillan.

--Carrot Cake. LC 76-17628. (Illus.). (ps-3). 1977. 7.50 (ISBN 0-688-80061-0); PLB 7.63 (ISBN 0-688-84061-2). Greenwillow.

--The Contest. LC 75-40389. (Illus.). (gr. k-3). 1976. 8.95 (ISBN 0-688-80042-4); PLB 8.59 (ISBN 0-688-84042-6). Greenwillow.

--One Fine Day. LC 75-119834. (Illus.). (gr. k-3). 1971. 8.95 (ISBN 0-02-744000-1). Macmillan.

--Rooster Brother. LC 73-8090. (Illus.). 32p. (gr. 1-4). 1974. 5.95g o.s.i. (ISBN 0-02-743990-9). Macmillan.

Hogrogian, Rachel. Armenian Cookbook. LC 76-139312. (Illus.). 1975. pap. 4.95 (ISBN 0-689-70518-2, 208). Atheneum.

Hogstel, Mildred O. Nursing Care of the Older Adult. 650p. 1981. 16.95 (ISBN 0-471-06022-4, Pub. by Wiley Med). Wiley.

Hogstrom, Daphne. My Little Book of Farm Animals. (Tell-a-Tale Reader). 24p. (ps-3). 1980. PLB 4.77 (ISBN 0-307-68490-3, Golden Pr). Western Pub.

Hogue, Charles L. The Net-Winged Midges or Blephariceridae of California. (Bulletin of the California Insect Survey: Vol. 15). 1973. pap. 7.00x (ISBN 0-520-09454-9). U of Cal Pr.

Hogue, Charles L., jt. auth. see Powell, Jerry A.

Hogue, L. L. Public Health & the Law: Issues & Trends. LC 80-15041. 427p. 1980. text ed. 29.95 (ISBN 0-89443-289-3). Aspen Systems.

Hogue, Richard. The Jesus Touch. LC 72-79168. 128p. 1972. pap. 2.50 (ISBN 0-8054-5524-8, 42-5524). Broadman.

Hogue, W. Dickerson, jt. auth. see Farmer, Richard N.

Hogwood, Brian. Government Policy & Shipbuilding. 1979. text ed. 28.25x (ISBN 0-566-00233-7, Pub. by Gower Pub Co England). Renouf.

Hohenberg, John. Free Press - Free People: The Best Cause. LC 70-133912. 1971. 20.00x o.p. (ISBN 0-231-03315-X). Columbia U Pr.

--Free Press, Free People: The Best Cause. LC 70-133912. 1973. pap. 3.95 o.s.i. (ISBN 0-02-914800-6). Free Pr.

--Pulitzer Prize Story. LC 59-7702. 1959. pap. 7.00x (ISBN 0-231-08663-6). Columbia U Pr.

--The Pulitzer Prizes. 1974. 20.00x (ISBN 0-231-03771-6). Columbia U Pr.

Hohenemser, Kurt. Elastokinetik. LC 50-2567. (Ger). 9.95 (ISBN 0-8284-0055-5). Chelsea Pub.

Hohenstein, C. Louis. Computer Peripherals for Minicomputers, Microprocessors & Personal Computers. (Illus.). 320p. 1980. 19.50 (ISBN 0-07-029451-8, P&RB). McGraw.

Hohenstein, Charles L., Jr., jt. auth. see Banks, Jerry.

Hohenstein, Mary, compiled by. Games. 160p. (Orig.). 1980. pap. 5.95 (ISBN 0-87123-191-3, 210191). Bethany Fell.

Hohl, Ludwig. Das Wort Fasst Nicht Jeden. (Bibliothek Suhrkamp: 675). 133p. text ed. 8.30 (ISBN 3-518-01675-X, Pub. by Insel Verlag Germany). Suhrkamp.

Hohman, Edward J. & Leary, Norma E. The Greeting Card Handbook. (Barnes & Noble Everyday Handbook). (Illus.). 160p. (Orig.). 1981. pap. 4.95 (ISBN 0-06-463532-5, EH532, BN). Har-Row.

Hohman, Jo. Focus on Nurse Credentialing. LC 80-17049. 96p. (Orig.). 1980. 10.00 (ISBN 0-87258-303-1, 1460). Am Hospital.

Hohmann, Hans-Hermann, et al, eds. The New Economic Systems of Eastern Europe. LC 74-76386. 1975. 36.50x (ISBN 0-520-02732-9). U of Cal Pr.

Hohn, Max T., ed. Stories in Verse. rev. ed. LC 61-3198. 1961. pap. 5.50 o.p. (ISBN 0-672-73234-3). Odyssey Pr.

Hohweiler, Daryl, jt. ed. see Cummins, D. Duane.

Hoiberg, P. The Older Deaf Child: Pedagogical, Methodical & Didactical Aspects. (Modern Approaches to the Diagnosis & Instructionsof Multi-Handicapped Children: Vol. 12). 64p. 1973. text ed. 15.00 (ISBN 90-237-4112-9, Pub. by Swets Pub Serv Holland). Swets North Am.

Hoig, Stan. The Battle of the Washita: The Sheridan-Custer Indian Campaign of 1867-1869. LC 79-14844. 1979. 15.75x (ISBN 0-8032-2307-2); pap. 4.95 (ISBN 0-8032-7204-9, BB 720, Bison). U of Nebr Pr.

--Humor of the American Cowboy. LC 58-5328. (Illus.). 1970. pap. 2.45 (ISBN 0-8032-5719-8, BB 520, Bison). U of Nebr Pr.

Hoigne, J., jt. ed. see Gaumann, T.

Hoijer, Harry. Tonkawa Texts. (U. C. Publ. in Linguistics: Vol. 73). 1973. pap. 8.00x (ISBN 0-520-09451-4). U of Cal Pr.

Hoitash, Charles. Achieving Success in Manufacturing Management. LC 80-51544. (Manufacturing Update Ser.). (Illus.). 260p. 1980. 29.00 (ISBN 0-87263-055-2). SME.

Hojer, Gerhard, jt. auth. see Jervis, Simon.

Hokanson, Jack E. The Physiological Bases of Motivation. 192p. 1981. pap. write for info. (ISBN 0-89874-187-4). Krieger.

Hoke, H. & Pitt, V. Fleas. LC 73-12147. (First Bks). 4.47 o.p. (ISBN 0-531-00815-0). Watts.

Hoke, Helen. Big Book of Jokes. LC 78-161837. (Big Bks). (Illus.). (gr. 4-6). 1971. PLB 6.90 (ISBN 0-531-01990-X). Watts.

--Devils, Devils, Devils. LC 75-38035. (Terrific Triple Titles Ser). (Illus.). 224p. (gr. 4 up). 1976. PLB 6.90 o.p. (ISBN 0-531-01140-2). Watts.

--Etiquette, Your Ticket to Good Times. LC 70-93223. (First Bks). (Illus.). (gr. 4-6). 1970. PLB 4.90 o.p. (ISBN 0-531-00686-7). Watts.

--First Book of Ants. LC 74-98668. (First Bks). (Illus.). (gr. k-3). 1970. PLB 4.90 o.p. (ISBN 0-531-00700-6). Watts.

--Ghost & Ghastlies. (Illus.). 192p. (gr. 4-6). 1976. PLB 7.90 (ISBN 0-531-01210-7). Watts.

--Haunts, Haunts, Haunts. (Terrific Triple Titles Ser.). (Illus.). (gr. 4 up). 1977. PLB 7.90 s&l (ISBN 0-531-00098-2). Watts.

--Hoke's Jokes Cartoons & Funny Things. LC 74-7459. (Illus.). (gr. 1-4). 1975. PLB 4.90 o.p. (ISBN 0-531-02682-5). Watts.

--Horrors, Horrors, Horrors. LC 78-2350. (Terrific Triple Titles Ser.). (Illus.). 1978. lib. bdg. 7.90 s&l (ISBN 0-531-02211-0). Watts.

--Jokes & Fun. LC 72-2403. (Illus.). 48p. (gr. 1-4). 1973. PLB 3.90 o.p. (ISBN 0-531-02616-7). Watts.

--Jokes, Giggles & Guffaws. LC 75-6047. 160p. (gr. 3 up). 1975. 6.90 (ISBN 0-531-02844-5). Watts.

--Monsters, Monsters, Monsters. LC 75-6045. (Terrific Triple Titles Ser). 187p. (gr. 7 up). 1975. PLB 6.90 o.p. (ISBN 0-531-02846-1). Watts.

--More Riddles, Riddles, Riddles. LC 10-696. (Illus.). (gr. 4 up). 1976. PLB 7.90 (ISBN 0-531-00351-5). Watts.

--Riddle Giggles. LC 74-26364. (Illus.). 48p. (gr. k-4). 1975. PLB 4.90 o.p. (ISBN 0-531-02096-7). Watts.

Hoke, Helen & Pitt, Valerie. Owls. LC 74-23981. (Illus.). 64p. (gr. 3-7). 1975. PLB 4.47 o.p. (ISBN 0-531-00832-0). Watts.

--Whales. LC 72-11769. (First Bks). (Illus.). 72p. (gr. 4 up). 1973. PLB 6.45 (ISBN 0-531-00779-0). Watts.

Hoke, Helen, ed. Creepies, Creepies, Creepies. (Terrific Triple Titles Ser.). (Illus.). (gr. 7 up). 1977. s&l 7.90 (ISBN 0-531-01323-5). Watts.

--Dragons, Dragons, Dragons. LC 74-182300. (Terrific Triple Titles Ser). (Illus.). 256p. (gr. 1 up). 1972. PLB 6.90 o.p. (ISBN 0-531-02036-3). Watts.

--Jokes, Jokes, Jokes. (Terrific Triple Titles Ser). (Illus.). (gr. 4-6). 1963. PLB 7.90 (ISBN 0-531-01704-4). Watts.

--More Jokes, Jokes, Jokes. (Illus.). (gr. 4-6). 1965. PLB 7.90 (ISBN 0-531-01736-2). Watts.

--Sinister, Strange & Supernatural. (gr. 6 up). 1981. 9.95 (ISBN 0-525-66703-2). Elsevier-Nelson.

--Spooks, Spooks, Spooks. LC 66-10138. (Terrific Triple Titles Ser). (Illus.). (gr. 7 up). 1956. PLB 7.90 (ISBN 0-531-01797-4). Watts.

--Weirdies, Weirdies, Weirdies. LC 73-14010. (Terrific Triple Titles Ser). (Illus.). 244p. (gr. 6 up). 1975. PLB 7.90 (ISBN 0-531-02683-3). Watts.

Hoke, John. Discovering the World of the Three-Toed Sloth. (Illus.). 96p. (gr. 4 up). 1976. PLB 4.33 o.p. (ISBN 0-531-00339-6). Watts.

--Ecology. rev. ed. (First Books Ser.). (Illus.). 96p. (gr. 4-6). 1977. PLB 6.45 (ISBN 0-531-00745-6). Watts.

--First Book of Snakes. rev. ed. (First Bks). (Illus.). (gr. 4-6). 1956. PLB 4.90 o.p. (ISBN 0-531-00631-X). Watts.

--First Book of Solar Energy. LC 68-10336. (First Bks). (Illus.). (gr. 4-6). 1968. PLB 4.90 o.p. (ISBN 0-531-00634-4). Watts.

--First Book of Turtles & Their Care. LC 78-98669. (First Bks). (Illus.). (gr. 7 up). 1970. PLB 4.90 o.p. (ISBN 0-531-00696-4). Watts.

--Solar Energy. rev. ed. (Impact Bks.). (Illus.). (gr. 7 up). 1978. PLB 6.90 s&l (ISBN 0-531-01329-4). Watts.

--Terrariums. LC 70-189761. (First Bks). (Illus.). 96p. (gr. 4-6). 1972. PLB 4.90 o.p. (ISBN 0-531-00777-4). Watts.

Hokelman, Robert A., jt. auth. see Smith, David H.

Hoklin, Lonn, jt. auth. see Oran, Dan.

Holahan, C. J. Environment & Behavior: A Dynamical Perspective. LC 77-25400. (Plenum Social Ecology Ser.). (Illus.). 206p. 1977. 14.95 (ISBN 0-306-31086-4, Plenum Pr). Plenum Pub.

Holahan, John. Financing Health Care for the Poor. LC 74-25273. (Illus.). 1975. 17.95 (ISBN 0-669-97634-2). Lexington Bks.

--Physician Supply, Peer Review, & Use of Health Services in Medicaid. (An Institute Paper). 70p. 1976. pap. 3.50 (ISBN 0-87766-159-6, 13800). Urban Inst.

Holahan, John & Scanlon, William. Price Controls, Physician Fees, & Physician Incomes from Medicare & Medicaid. (An Institute Paper). 110p. 1978. pap. 4.50 (ISBN 0-87766-219-3, 21800). Urban Inst.

Holahan, John & Stuart, Bruce. Controlling Medicaid Utilization Patterns. (Medicaid Cost Containment Ser.). 127p. 1977. pap. 4.00 (ISBN 0-87766-196-0, 17900). Urban Inst.

Holahan, John, jt. auth. see Feder, Judith.

Holahan, John, jt. auth. see Wilensky, Gail R.

Holahan, John, et al. Altering Medicaid Provider Reimbursement Methods. (Medicaid Cost Containment Ser.). 215p. 1977. pap. 8.50 (ISBN 0-685-99509-7, 17800). Urban Inst.

--Restructuring Federal Medicaid Controls & Incentives. (Medicaid Cost Containment Ser.). 96p. 1977. pap. 2.00 (ISBN 0-87766-198-7, 18100). Urban Inst.

Holahan, William L., jt. auth. see Call, Steven T.

Holand, Hjalmar R. Norwegians in America. LC 78-55075. (Illus.). 1978. pap. 8.95 (ISBN 0-931170-07-9). Ctr Western Studies.

Holashan, John, jt. auth. see Spitz, Bruce.

Holaves, Sharon. ABC Around the House. (Little Golden Reader Ser.). (Illus.). (gr. k-3). 1979. PLB 5.00 (ISBN 0-307-60176-5, Golden Pr). Western Pub.

--Where Will All the Animals Go? (Illus.). (gr. k-2). 1978. PLB 5.00 (ISBN 0-307-60175-7, Golden Pr). Western Pub.

Holbach, Paul-Henri Thiry. Ethocratie Ou le Gouvernement Fonde Sur la Morale. (Fr.). 1977. lib. bdg. 33.00x o.p. (ISBN 0-8287-0441-4); pap. text ed. 23.00x o.p. (ISBN 0-685-77009-5). Clearwater Pub.

Holberg, Ludwig. A Journey to the World Underground, 1742. Shugrue, Michael F., ed. LC 74-18234. (Novel in England 1700-1775). 1974. lib. bdg. 50.00 (ISBN 0-8240-1105-8). Garland Pub.

Holbert, Al, jt. auth. see Holbert, Bob.

Holbert, Bob & Holbert, Al. Driving to Win. (Illus.). 1981. pap. 7.95 (ISBN 0-89404-024-3). Aztex.

Holbik, Karel & Myers, Henry Allen. West German Foreign Aid, 1956-1966. LC 68-58498. 1968. 7.95x (ISBN 0-8419-8716-5, Pub. by Boston U Pr). Holmes & Meier.

Holborn, Louise W. Refugees: a Problem of Our Time: The Work of the United Nations High Commissioner for Refugees; 1951-1972, 2 vols. LC 74-19471. (Illus.). 1975. Set. 55.00 (ISBN 0-8108-0746-7). Scarecrow.

Holborne, Anthony. Complete Works, 2 vols. Kanazawa, Masakata, ed. Incl. Vol. 1. Music for Lute & Bandora. (Illus.). 1967. pap. 17.50x (ISBN 0-674-15500-9); Vol. 2. Music for Cittern. 1974. pap. 15.95x (ISBN 0-674-15512-2). LC 67-14341. (Publications in Music Ser: No. 1, 5). Harvard U Pr.

Holborow, E. J. & Reeves, W. G., eds. Immunology in Medicine: A Comprehensive Guide to Clinical Immunology. 1977. 57.00 (ISBN 0-8089-1028-0). Grune.

Holbrook, Charles & Holbrook, Linda. Run-a-Day Logbook. Groninger, Vicki, ed. (Illus.). 420p. (Orig.). 1980. pap. 8.95 (ISBN 0-9604998-0-6). DCT Ent.

Holbrook, D. & Postan, E. The Apple Tree: Christmas Music from the Cambridge Hymnal. LC 76-12916. 1976. 14.95 (ISBN 0-521-21479-3); pap. 5.75 (ISBN 0-521-29116-X). Cambridge U Pr.

Holbrook, David. Children's Writing. 1967. 22.50 (ISBN 0-521-05284-X); pap. 7.95x (ISBN 0-521-09434-8, 434). Cambridge U Pr.

--Dylan Thomas: The Code of Night. 1972. text ed. 25.00x (ISBN 0-391-00261-9, Athlone Pr). Humanities.

--English for Maturity. 2nd ed. 1967. 25.95 (ISBN 0-521-05286-6); pap. 9.95x (ISBN 0-521-09134-9, 134). Cambridge U Pr.

--English for Meaning. 241p. 1980. pap. text ed. 16.25x (ISBN 0-85633-184-8, NFER). Humanities.

--English for the Rejected. (Orig.). 1964. pap. 9.95x (ISBN 0-521-09215-9). Cambridge U Pr.

--English in Australia Now. LC 76-183224. 250p. 1973. 26.50 (ISBN 0-521-08469-5); pap. text ed. 9.95x (ISBN 0-521-09706-1). Cambridge U Pr.

--Exploring Word. (Orig.). 1967. 26.50 (ISBN 0-521-05288-2); pap. 9.95x (ISBN 0-521-09425-9). Cambridge U Pr.

--Human Hope & the Death Instinct: An Exploration of Psychoanalytical Theories of Human Nature & Their Implications for Culture & Education. 1976. Repr. of 1971 ed. 26.00 (ISBN 0-08-015798-X). Pergamon.

--The Masks of Hate: The Problem of False Solutions in the Culture of an Acquisitive Society. 276p. 1976. Repr. of 1972 ed. 26.00 (ISBN 0-08-015799-8). Pergamon.

Holbrook, David, ed. The Case Against Pornography. LC 72-5279. 294p. 1973. 17.50 (ISBN 0-912050-28-4, Library Pr); pap. 5.95. Open Court.

Holbrook, J. G. Laplace Transforms for Electronic Engineers. 2nd ed. 1966. 25.00 (ISBN 0-08-011411-3). Pergamon.

Holbrook, Jay M. Ascott Quebec Canada Eighteen Twenty Five Census. LC 80-117991. 1976. pap. 7.50 (ISBN 0-931248-06-X). Holbrook Res.

--Connecticut Sixteen Hundred-Seventy Census. LC 77-152342. 1977. pap. 15.00 (ISBN 0-931248-04-3). Holbrook Res.

--New Hampshire Seventeen Hundred & Seventy-Six Census. LC 76-151110. 1976. pap. 20.00 (ISBN 0-931248-02-7). Holbrook Res.

--Vermont's First Settlers. LC 76-151555. 1976. pap. 15.00 (ISBN 0-931248-03-5). Holbrook Res.

Holbrook, John H. Physical Diagnosis Review. LC 79-88046. 1979. pap. 8.50 (ISBN 0-87488-135-8). Med Exam.

Holbrook, Linda, jt. auth. see Holbrook, Charles.

Holbrook, Martin L. Hygiene of the Brain & Nerves & the Cure of Nervousness. LC 78-72799. Repr. of 1878 ed. 27.50 (ISBN 0-404-60862-0, RC351). AMS Pr.

Holbrook, Mary, ed. & tr. see Daumas, Maurice.

Holbrook, Stewart. Davy Crockett. (Landmark Ser.: No. 57). (Illus.). (gr. 4-6). 1955. 2.95 o.p. (ISBN 0-685-19688-7, BYR); PLB 5.99 (ISBN 0-394-90357-9). Random.

Holbrook, Stewart H. Dreamers of the American Dream. LC 57-11424. 6.95 o.p. (ISBN 0-385-04889-0). Doubleday.

Holbrook, Wallace W. Contemporary Lamps. (gr. 9 up). 1968. text ed. 13.28 (ISBN 0-87345-029-9). McKnight.

Holcenberg, John C. & Roberts, Joseph. Enzymes As Drugs. LC 80-20641. 450p. 1981. 55.00 (ISBN 0-471-05061-X, Pub. by Wiley-Interscience). Wiley.

Holck, Manfred, Jr. Making It on a Pastor's Pay. LC 73-18105. 1974. 4.95 o.p. (ISBN 0-687-23034-9). Abingdon.

Holcomb, Adele M., jt. ed. see Sherman, Claire R.

Holcomb Research Institute. Environmental Modeling & Decision Making: The United States Experience. LC 76-28798. 1976. text ed. 20.95 (ISBN 0-275-24190-4). Praeger.

Holcomb, Richard L. Police & the Public. (Illus.). 1975. pap. 4.25 (ISBN 0-398-00857-4). C C Thomas.

--Police Patrol. (Amer. Lec. Public Protection Ser). (Illus.). 128p. 1971. 6.75 (ISBN 0-398-00856-6). C C Thomas.

Holcombe, A. D., jt. auth. see Pisano, Beverly.

Holcombe, Arthur N. The Chinese Revolution: A Phase in the Regeneration of a World Power. LC 76-80557. xii, 401p. 1974. Repr. of 1930 ed. 19.00 (ISBN 0-86527-024-4). Fertig.

--Our More Perfect Union: From Eighteenth-Century Principles to Twentieth-Century Practice. 1950. 20.00x (ISBN 0-674-64650-9). Harvard U Pr.

Holcombe, Henry. Patent Medicine Tax Stamps: A History of the Firms Using U.S. Private Die Proprietary Medicine Tax Stamps. LC 76-51546. 1979. 100.00x (ISBN 0-88000-098-8). Quarterman.

Holcombe, Marya & Stein, Judith. Writing for Decision Makers. LC 80-24900. 260p. 1980. text ed. 14.95 leaders manual (ISBN 0-534-97980-7). Lifetime Learn.

Holcroft, Thomas. Memoirs of Bryan Perdue, 3 vols. Paulson, Ronald, ed. LC 78-60851. (Novel 1720-1805 Ser.: Vol. 15). 1979. Set. lib. bdg. 93.00 (ISBN 0-8240-3664-6); lib. bdg. 31.00 ea. Garland Pub.

--Road to Ruin. Aldrich, Ruth I., ed. LC 68-18245. 1968. 8.95x (ISBN 0-8032-0074-9); pap. 1.65x o.p. (ISBN 0-8032-5090-8). U of Nebr Pr.

Hold, William T. & Todd, Jerry D. Foundations of Life & Health Insurance. (Studies in Insurance & Actuarial Science: No. 2). (Orig.). 1971. pap. 3.50 o.p. (ISBN 0-87755-068-9). U of Tex Busn Res.

Holdanowicz, M. J. Metalwork: A Course for Schools & Colleges. 1971. pap. text ed. 3.95x o.p. (ISBN 0-435-75395-9). Heinemann Ed.

Holdaway, Simon, ed. The British Police. LC 80-7573. (Illus.). 188p. 1980. 18.50 (ISBN 0-8039-1464-4); pap. 8.95 (ISBN 0-8039-1465-2). Sage.

Holdcraft, Paul E. One Hundred One Snappy Sermonettes for the Children's Church. 1951. pap. 2.50 (ISBN 0-687-29015-5). Abingdon.

--Snappy Sentences for Church Bulletin Boards. pap. 0.75 o.p. (ISBN 0-687-38803-1). Abingdon.

--Snappy Sermon Starters. 1940. pap. 3.95 (ISBN 0-687-38828-7). Abingdon.

--Snappy Squibs for the Church Calendar. 1940. pap. 3.95 (ISBN 0-687-38878-3). Abingdon.

Holdcroft, Anita. Body Temperature Control: In Relation to Anaesthesia, Surgery & Intensive Care. 1980. text ed. 29.95 (ISBN 0-02-858050-8). Macmillan.

Holde, Kensal E. Van see Halvorson, Harlyn O. & Van Holde, Kensal E.

Holden, Alan. Bonds Between Atoms. (Illus.). 1971. pap. text ed. 3.95x (ISBN 0-19-501498-7). Oxford U Pr.

--Nature of Atoms. (Illus.). 1971. pap. text ed. 3.95x (ISBN 0-19-501499-5). Oxford U Pr.

--The Nature of Solids. LC 65-22156. (Illus.). 1968. 20.00x (ISBN 0-231-02785-0); pap. 7.50x (ISBN 0-231-08591-5). Columbia U Pr.

--Shapes, Space, & Symmetry. LC 71-158459. (Illus.). 1971. 17.50x (ISBN 0-231-03549-7); pap. 7.50 (ISBN 0-231-08323-8). Columbia U Pr.

--Stationary States. (Illus.). 1971. pap. text ed. 3.95x (ISBN 0-19-501497-9). Oxford U Pr.

Holden, Alan & Singer, Phyllis. Crystals & Crystal Growing. LC 60-5932. pap. 2.95 (ISBN 0-385-09430-2, S7, Anch). Doubleday.

Holden, Anton. Prince Valium. LC 80-6148. 256p. 1981. 12.95 (ISBN 0-8128-2795-3). Stein & Day.

Holden, Donald. Whistler Landscapes & Seascapes. (Illus.). 1976. pap. 8.95 o.p. (ISBN 0-8230-5726-7). Watson-Guptill.

Holden, E. Michael, jt. auth. see Janov, Arthur.

Holden, Edith. The Country Diary of an Edwardian Lady. LC 77-71359. (Illus.). 1977. 16.95 (ISBN 0-03-021026-7). HR&W.

Holden, Edward S. A Primer of Heraldry for Americans. LC 73-2815. (Illus.). 129p. 1973. Repr. of 1898 ed. 15.00 (ISBN 0-8103-3271-X). Gale.

Holden, George. On Loving. LC 75-2425. (Personal Guidance & Social Adjustment Ser.). 190p. (gr. 7-12). 1975. PLB 5.97 o.p. (ISBN 0-8239-0324-9). Rosen Pr.

Holden, George, tr. see Zola, Emile.

Holden, Jonathan. Rhetoric of the Contemporary Lyric. LC 79-3383. 160p. 1980. 12.95x (ISBN 0-253-15667-X). Ind U Pr.

Holden, K., jt. auth. see Wynn, R. F.

Holden, Matthew, ed. Varieties of Political Conservatism. LC 74-78561. (Sage Contemporary Social Science Issues: No. 16). 1974. 4.95x (ISBN 0-8039-0441-X). Sage.

Holden, Michael & Reed, William. West African Freshwater Fish. LC 74-170516. (West African Nature Handbooks). (Illus.). 68p. (Orig.). 1972. pap. 5.00x (ISBN 0-582-60426-5). Intl Pubns Serv.

Holden, Ursula. The Cloud Catchers. 224p. 1981. pap. 2.25 (ISBN 0-523-41272-X). Pinnacle Bks.

--Fallen Angels: Endless Race. 192p. 1981. pap. 1.95 (ISBN 0-523-41273-8). Pinnacle Bks.

Holden, William C. Espuela Land & Cattle Company: The Study of a Foreign-Owned Ranch in Texas. LC 70-84084. (Illus.). 1970. 9.00 (ISBN 0-87611-023-5). Tex St Hist Assn.

--Teresita. LC 78-2321. (Illus.). 1978. 14.95 (ISBN 0-916144-24-0); pap. 8.95 (ISBN 0-916144-25-9). Stemmer Hse.

Holder, Alan. A. R. Ammons. (United States Authors Ser.: No. 303). 1978. lib. bdg. 12.50 (ISBN 0-8057-7208-1). Twayne.

--The Imagined Past. LC 78-75202. 298p. 1980. 22.50 (ISBN 0-8387-2319-5). Bucknell U Pr.

--Three Voyagers in Search of Europe. LC 64-24513. 1966. 9.75x o.p. (ISBN 0-8122-7486-5). U of Pa Pr.

Holder, Angela R. Legal Issues in Pediatrics & Adolescent Medicine. LC 76-41385. 1977. 35.95 (ISBN 0-471-40612-0, Pub. by Wiley-Medical). Wiley.

--Medical Malpractice Law. 2nd ed. LC 77-27288. 1978. 36.50 (ISBN 0-471-03882-2, Pub. by Wiley Medical). Wiley.

Holder, C. & Manning, W. H. South Wales. 1967. 3.95x o.p. (ISBN 0-435-32963-4). Heinemann Ed.

Holder, Leonard. Primer for Calculus. 1978. text ed. 18.95x (ISBN 0-534-00554-3); solutions manual 6.95x (ISBN 0-534-00590-X). Wadsworth Pub.

Holder, Maryse. Give Sorrow Words: Maryse Holder's Letters from Mexico. 336p. (Orig.). 1980. pap. 2.50 (ISBN 0-380-51466-4, 51466). Avon.

Holder, Preston. The Hoe & the Horse on the Plains: A Study of Cultural Development Among North American Indians. LC 70-98474. (Illus.). xiv, 176p. 1970. 9.95x (ISBN 0-8032-0730-1); pap. 3.75x (ISBN 0-8032-5809-7, BB 594, Bison). U of Nebr Pr.

Holder, Robert. You Can Analyze Handwriting. pap. 2.00 o.p. (ISBN 0-87980-176-X). Wilshire.

Holderbaum, James. The Sculptor Giovanni Bologna. LC 76-23626. (Outstanding Dissertations in the Fine Arts Ser.). 1978. lib. bdg. 56.00x (ISBN 0-8240-2696-9). Garland Pub.

Holder-Bryant, Lenora Foreword by see Shepherd-Moore, Marie.

Holderness, A. Ordinary Level Revision Notes in Chemistry. 1971. pap. text ed. 4.95x o.p. (ISBN 0-435-64423-8). Heinemann Ed.

--Revision Notes in Advanced Level Chemistry: Organic Chemistry. 1975. pap. text ed. 7.50x o.p. (ISBN 0-435-65433-0). Heinemann Ed.

Holderness, A. & Lambert, J. A Class Book of Problems in "A" Level Chemistry. 3rd ed. 1971. pap. text ed. 3.95x o.p. (ISBN 0-435-65431-4). Heinemann Ed.

--The Essentials of Qualitative Analysis. 1974. pap. text ed. 3.95x (ISBN 0-435-65535-3). Heinemann Ed.

--Graded Problems in Chemistry to Ordinary Level. 1979. pap. text ed. 3.95x o.p. (ISBN 0-435-64427-0). Heinemann Ed.

--Problems & Worked Examples in Chemistry to Advanced Level. 3rd ed. 1978. pap. text ed. 4.95x o.p. (ISBN 0-435-65438-1). Heinemann Ed.

--Worked Examples & Problems in Ordinary Chemistry. 1971. pap. text ed. 3.95x o.p. (ISBN 0-435-64422-X). Heinemann Ed.

Holderness, A., et al. A New Certificate Chemistry. 5th, rev. ed. (Illus.). 1977. pap. text ed. 9.50x o.p. (ISBN 0-435-64424-6). Heinemann Ed.

Holderness, Esther. Peasant Chic. (Illus.). 1977. pap. 7.95 o.p. (ISBN 0-8015-5811-5). Dutton.

Holderness, Ginny W. The Exuberant Years: A Guide for Junior High Leaders. LC 75-13458. 128p. 1976. pap. 6.50 (ISBN 0-8042-1225-2). John Knox.

--Youth Ministry: The New Team Approach. LC 80-82186. (Illus.). 160p. (Orig.). 1981. pap. 9.95 (ISBN 0-8042-1410-7). John Knox.

Holderness, Lawson, jt. auth. see Callicott, Catherine D.

Holdgate, M. W. A Perspective of Environmental Pollution. LC 78-8394. (Illus.). 288p. 1981. pap. 13.95 (ISBN 0-521-29972-1). Cambridge U Pr.

--A Perspective of Environmental Pollution. LC 78-8394. (Illus.). 1979. 42.50 (ISBN 0-521-22197-8). Cambridge U Pr.

Holding, Audrey. The Art of Royal Icing. (Illus.). xviii, 176p. 1980. pap. 16.25x (ISBN 0-85334-860-X, Pub. by Applied Science). Burgess-Intl Ideas.

Holding, David. A History of British Bus Services: The North East. LC 79-52370. 1979. 17.95 (ISBN 0-7153-7813-9). David & Charles.

Holding, Dennis H. Human Skills. (Studies in Human Performance Ser.). 304p. 1981. 39.95 (ISBN 0-471-27838-6, Pub. by Wiley-Interscience). Wiley.

Holding, James. Mystery of Dolphin Inlet. (gr. 5-8). 1968. 4.95g o.s.i. (ISBN 0-02-744190-3). Macmillan.

Holdom, Lynne. Capsule Reviews. LC 80-20445. 51p. 1980. Repr. of 1977 ed. lib. bdg. 9.95 (ISBN 0-89370-056-8). Borgo Pr.

Holdridge, L. R., et al. Forest Environments in Tropical Life Zones: A Pilot Study. LC 75-129847. 1971. 165.00 (ISBN 0-08-016340-8). Pergamon.

Holdridge, Larry. Symphony in B Minor: The Passion of Peter Ilitch Tchaikovsky. LC 78-2284. (Illus.). 1978. 10.95 (ISBN 0-916144-26-7); pap. 3.95 (ISBN 0-916144-27-5). Stemmer Hse.

Holdstock, Robert & Edwards, Malcolm. Tour of the Universe. (Illus.). 144p. 17.95 (ISBN 0-8317-8797-X); pap. 11.95 (ISBN 0-8317-8798-8). Mayflower Bks.

Holdsworth. Digital Logic Design. 1981. text ed. price not set (ISBN 0-408-00404-5); pap. text ed. price not set (ISBN 0-408-00566-1). Butterworth.

Holdsworth, Eugene I., jt. auth. see Swenson, Christian N.

Hole, Christina. Witchcraft in England. 1966. pap. 1.50 o.s.i. (ISBN 0-02-028860-3, Collier). Macmillan.

Hole, Francis D. Soils of Wisconsin. LC 75-12209. 264p. 1976. 30.00 (ISBN 0-299-06830-7). U of Wis Pr.

Hole, Francis D., jt. auth. see Harpstead, Milo I.

Hole, John W., Jr. Human Anatomy & Physiology. 2nd ed. 880p. 1981. text ed. 21.60 (ISBN 0-697-04597-8); write for info. instr's. manual (ISBN 0-697-04647-8); write for info. transparencies; study guide avail. (ISBN 0-697-04640-0). Wm C Brown.

Holeman, Jack R. Condominium Management. (Illus.). 1980. text ed. 18.95 (ISBN 0-13-167155-3). P-H.

Holenstein, Elmar. Von der Hintergehbarkeit der Sprache. (Suhrkamp Taschenbuecher Wissenschaft: No. 316). 216p. (Orig.). 1980. pap. text ed. 7.15 (ISBN 3-518-07916-6, Pub. by Insel Verlag Germany). Suhrkamp.

Holford, Ingrid. Interpreting the Weather: A Practical Guide for Householders, Gardners, Motorist and Sportsmen. (Illus.). 1973. 13.50 (ISBN 0-7153-5800-6). David & Charles.

Holiday & Hunt. Intermediate Chemistry: Organic Chemistry. 1981. text ed. price not set (ISBN 0-408-70915-4). Butterworth.

Holiday, Billie & Dufty, William. Lady Sings the Blues. 1979. pap. 2.50 (ISBN 0-380-00491-7, 53173). Avon.

Holiday Editors. Holiday Guide to Ireland. 1976. pap. 2.95 o.p. (ISBN 0-394-73195-6). Random.

--Holiday Guide to Italy. 1976. pap. 2.95 o.p. (ISBN 0-394-73197-2). Random.

Holiday Editors, ed. Holiday Guide to Britain. 1976. pap. 2.95 o.p. (ISBN 0-394-73190-5). Random.

--Holiday Guide to Caribbean. 1976. pap. 2.95 o.p. (ISBN 0-394-73191-3). Random.

--Holiday Guide to France. 1976. pap. 2.95 o.p. (ISBN 0-394-73192-1). Random.

--Holiday Guide to Greece & the Aegean Islands. 1976. pap. 2.95 o.p. (ISBN 0-394-73193-X). Random.

--Holiday Guide to Hawaii. 1976. pap. 2.95 o.p. (ISBN 0-394-73194-8). Random.

--Holiday Guide to Israel. 1976. pap. 2.95 o.p. (ISBN 0-394-73196-4). Random.

--Holiday Guide to London. 1976. pap. 2.95 o.p. (ISBN 0-394-73198-0). Random.

--Holiday Guide to Mexico. 1976. pap. 2.95 o.p. (ISBN 0-394-73199-9). Random.

--Holiday Guide to Paris. 1976. pap. 2.95 o.p. (ISBN 0-394-73200-6). Random.

--Holiday Guide to Rome. 1976. pap. 2.95 o.p. (ISBN 0-394-73201-4). Random.

--Holiday Guide to Scandinavia. 1976. pap. 2.95 o.p. (ISBN 0-394-73202-2). Random.

--Holiday Guide to Spain. 1976. pap. 2.95 o.p. (ISBN 0-394-73203-0). Random.

--Holiday Guide to West Germany. 1976. pap. 2.95 o.p. (ISBN 0-394-73204-9). Random.

Holiday, Ensor. Altair Design. (Illus.). (gr. 1 up). 1973. pap. 3.95 (ISBN 0-394-82548-9). Pantheon.

--Altair Design 3. (Illus.). 1976. pap. 3.95 (ISBN 0-394-83329-5). Pantheon.

--Altair Design 4. LC 77-17417. (gr. 1 up). 1978. pap. 3.95 (ISBN 0-394-83794-0). Pantheon.

Holiner, Richard. Collectible Locks. (Illus.). 1979. pap. 5.95 (ISBN 0-89145-115-3). Collector Bks.

Holinshed. Irish Chronicle Fifteen Seventy-Seven: The Historie of Ireland from the First Inhabitation Thereof, Unto the Years 1509. LC 78-12424. (Dolemen Edition: No. XXVIII). 1979. Repr. of 1577 ed. text ed. 96.75x (ISBN 0-391-00562-6, Dolmen Pr). Humanities.

Holister, G. S. Experimental Stress Analysis. (Cambridge Engineering Pubns.). 1967. 47.95 (ISBN 0-521-05312-9). Cambridge U Pr.

Holister, G. S., ed. Developments in Composite Materials, Vol. 1. (Illus.). 1977. 43.50x (ISBN 0-85334-740-9, Pub. by Applied Science). Burgess-Intl Ideas.

--Developments in Stress Analysis, Vol. 1. (Illus.). 1979. 41.40x (ISBN 0-85334-812-X, Pub. by Applied Science). Burgess-Intl Ideas.

Holl, Adelaide. Colors Are Nice. (Illus.). (gr. k-2). 1962. PLB 5.00 (ISBN 0-307-60496-9, Golden Pr). Western Pub.

--Have You Seen My Puppy. (Early Bird Bks). (Illus.). (ps-1). 1968. 2.50 o.p. (ISBN 0-394-81249-2, BYR); PLB 3.69 (ISBN 0-394-91249-7). Random.

--My Weekly Reader Picture Word Book. (Illus.). 128p. (ps-k). Date not set. pap. 5.95 (ISBN 0-671-42542-0, Little Simon). S&S.

--New Friends for the Saggy Baggy Elephant. (Illus.). (gr. k-3). 1976. PLB 5.00 (ISBN 0-307-60131-5, Golden Pr). Western Pub.

--Poky Little Puppy Follows His Nose Home. (Illus.). (gr. k-3). 1977. PLB 5.00 (ISBN 0-307-60030-0, Golden Pr). Western Pub.

Holl, Adolf. Death & the Devil. 1976. 9.95 (ISBN 0-8164-0313-9). Crossroad NY.

Holl, Adolf & Heinegg, Peter. The Last Christian: A Biography of Francis Assisi. LC 79-7868. 288p. 1980. 12.95 (ISBN 0-385-15499-2). Doubleday.

Holl, Dio L., et al. Introduction to the Laplace Transform. LC 59-7720. (Century Mathematics Ser.). (Illus.). 1959. 28.50 (ISBN 0-89197-247-1). Irvington.

Holl, Karl. The Distinctive Elements in Christianity. Hope, Norman V., tr. LC 38-24885. 79p. pap. text ed. 3.50. Attic Pr.

Holladay, Carl R. Theios Aner in Hellenistic-Judaism: A Critique of the Use of This Category in New Testament Christology. LC 77-20712. (Society of Biblical Literature. Dissertation Ser.: No. 40). 1977. pap. 7.50 (ISBN 0-89130-205-0, 060140). Scholars Pr Ca.

Holladay, Sylvia & Brown, Thomas. Options in Rhetoric: Writing & Reading. (Illus.). 416p. 1981. pap. text ed. 8.95 (ISBN 0-13-638254-1). P-H.

Holladay, William L. Jeremiah: Spokesman Out of Time. LC 74-7052. 160p. 1974. pap. 3.95 (ISBN 0-8298-0283-5). Pilgrim NY.

Hollaender, Alexander, jt. ed. see Setlow, Jane K.

Hollahan, John R. & Bell, Alexis T., eds. Techniques & Applications of Plasma Chemistry. LC 74-5122. 416p. 1974. 35.00 (ISBN 0-471-40628-7, Pub. by Wiley-Interscience). Wiley.

Hollan, S. R., et al. Genetics, Structure & Function of Blood Cells: Proceedings of the 28th International Congress of Physiological Sciences, Budapest, 1980. LC 80-41876. (Advances in Physiological Sciences: Vol. 6). (Illus.). 310p. 1981. 40.00 (ISBN 0-08-026818-8). Pergamon.

Holland. Britain & the Commonwealth Alliance 1918-1939. 1979. text ed. 52.00x (ISBN 0-333-27295-1). Humanities.

Holland, A. J. Ships of British Oak: The Rise & Decline of Wooden Shipbuilding in Hampshire. (Illus.). 192p. 1972. 5.95 o.p. (ISBN 0-7153-5344-6). David & Charles.

Holland, Ada M., jt. auth. see White, C. C.

Holland, Andy. Switchbacks. Mallory, Cynthia, ed. LC 80-25407. (Illus.). 144p. (Orig.). 1980. pap. 6.95 (ISBN 0-916890-99-6). Mountaineers.

Holland, Barbara. The Pony Problem. (gr. 4-7). 1977. PLB 6.95 (ISBN 0-525-37345-4). Dutton.
Holland, Brad. The Human Scandals. LC 76-57759. (Illus.). 1977. 12.95 o.s.i. (ISBN 0-690-01466-X, TYC-T). T Y Crowell.
Holland, C. Fundamentals & Modeling of Separation Processes: Absorption, Distillation, Evaporation & Extraction. (International Ser. in Physical & Chemical Engineering Science). (Illus.). 464p. 1975. 29.95 (ISBN 0-13-344390-6). P-H.
Holland, Cecelia. City of God. 320p. 1981. pap. 2.50 (ISBN 0-446-91517-3). Warner Bks.
--Floating Worlds. 1976. 10.95 o.p. (ISBN 0-394-49330-3). Knopf.
--Great Maria. 1974. 8.95 o.p. (ISBN 0-394-48509-2). Knopf.
--Home Ground. LC 80-2710. 384p. 1981. 13.95 (ISBN 0-394-50405-4). Knopf.
Holland, Charles D. & Anthony, Raymond G. Fundamentals of Chemical Reaction Engineering. (International Ser. in the Physical & Chemical Engineering Sciences). (Illus.). 1979. text ed. 26.95 (ISBN 0-13-335596-9). P-H.
Holland, Charles H., ed. Geology of Ireland. 400p. 1980. 40.00x (ISBN 0-7073-0269-2, Pub. by Scottish Academic Pr). Columbia U Pr.
Holland, Clifton L. The Religious Dimension in Hispanic Los Angeles: A Protestant Case Study. LC 74-5123. 542p. (Orig.). 1974. pap. 10.95 (ISBN 0-87808-309-X). William Carey Lib.
Holland, D. K., jt. auth. see Wentzell, Melinda.
Holland, Dan. Upland Game Hunter's Bible. LC 61-7604. pap. 3.50 o.p. (ISBN 0-385-01171-7). Doubleday.
Holland, Daniel M., ed. Assessment of Land Value: Proceedings. (Publication No. 5 of the Committee on Taxation Resources & Economic Development). 1970. 25.00 (ISBN 0-299-05621-X). U of Wis Pr.
Holland, Daniel W., et al. Using Nonbroadcast Video in the Church. 128p. 1980. pap. 5.95 (ISBN 0-8170-0895-0). Judson.
Holland, Dave. Secret of the Old Church. LC 39-1109. (Bro-Kee Ser.). (gr. 5-10). 1978. pap. 3.50 (ISBN 0-570-07763-X, 39-1109). Concordia.
Holland, David L., tr. see Weiss, Johannes.
Holland, DeWitte T. The Preaching Tradition: A Brief History. LC 80-16339. (Abingdon Preacher's Library). 128p. (Orig.). 1980. pap. 4.95 (ISBN 0-687-33875-1). Abingdon.
Holland, Florence. Summer in Sodom with Kitchen Privileges. 1977. 6.50 o.p. (ISBN 0-682-48968-9). Exposition.
Holland, Francis R., Jr. America's Lighthouses. rev. ed. (Illus.). 240p. 1981. pap. 19.95 (ISBN 0-8289-0441-3). Greene.
--America's Lighthouses: Their Illustrated History Since 1716. LC 74-170080. 1972. 17.50 o.p. (ISBN 0-8289-0148-1). Greene.
Holland, H., tr. see Calvin, Jean.
Holland, Henry. Chapters on Mental Physiology. Bd. with On Man's Power Over Himself to Prevent or Control Insanity. Barlow, John. (Contributions to the History of Psychology Ser., Vol. VI, Pt. C: Medical Psychology). 1980. Repr. of 1858 ed. 30.00 (ISBN 0-89093-321-9). U Pubns Amer.
Holland, Isabelle. Alan & the Animal Kingdom. (YA) 1980. pap. 1.50 (ISBN 0-440-90382-3, LFL). Dell.
--Alan the Animal Kingdom. LC 76-55371. 1977. 9.95 (ISBN 0-397-31745-X). Lippincott.
--Amanda's Choice. LC 71-101901. (gr. 4-6). 1970. 9.95 (ISBN 0-397-31112-5). Lippincott.
--Counter Point. large print ed. LC 80-27954. 1981. Repr. of 1980 ed. 11.95 (ISBN 0-89621-262-9). Thorndike Pr.
--Darcourt. 1977. pap. 1.75 o.p. (ISBN 0-449-23224-7, Crest). Fawcett.
--Dinah & the Fat Green Kingdom. LC 78-8612. (gr. 5-12). 1978. 8.95 (ISBN 0-397-31818-9). Lippincott.
--Dinah & the Green Kingdom. (gr. 7 up). 1981. pap. 1.75 (ISBN 0-440-91918-5, LE). Dell.
--Grenelle. LC 80-24329. 357p. 1980. Repr. of 1976 ed. large print ed. 9.95 (ISBN 0-89621-252-1). Thorndike Pr.
--Heads You Win, Tails I Lose. LC 73-5811. 160p. (gr. 7-10). 1973. 9.95 (ISBN 0-397-31380-2). Lippincott.
--Hitchhike. (YA) 1979. pap. 1.50 (ISBN 0-440-93663-2, LFL). Dell.
--Hitchhike. LC 77-7931. (gr. 5-9). 1977. 9.95 (ISBN 0-397-31751-4). Lippincott.
--The Man Without a Face. (gr. 6-12). 1980. pap. 1.50 (ISBN 0-440-96097-5, LFL). Dell.
--The Man Without a Face. LC 71-37736. (gr. 7 up). 1972. 9.95 (ISBN 0-397-31211-3, LSC-9). Lippincott.
--Of Love & Death & Other Journeys. LC 74-30012. (gr. 7 up). 1975. 9.95 (ISBN 0-397-31566-X). Lippincott.
Holland, J. L. College Degrees Through Independent Studies: An Alternative Approach. LC 78-67669. 1978. 5.98x (ISBN 0-932700-00-4). Centaur Pubn VA.
Holland, Jack. Too Long a Sacrifice: Life & Death in Northern Ireland Since Nineteen Sixty-Nine. LC 80-27267. (Illus.). 240p. 1981. 8.95 (ISBN 0-686-69573-9). Dodd.
Holland, James. Percussion. (The Yehudi Menuhin Music Guides Ser.). (Illus.). 1981. 12.95 (ISBN 0-02-871600-0); pap. 6.95 (ISBN 0-02-871610-8). Schirmer Bks.
Holland, Janet & Steuer, M. D. Mathematical Sociology: A Selective Annotated Bibliography. LC 72-97255. 1970. 8.50x (ISBN 0-8052-3336-9). Schocken.
Holland, John. Bird Spotting. (Illus.). 292p. 1981. pap. 6.95 (ISBN 0-7137-1148-5, Pub. by Blandford Pr England). Sterling.
Holland, John, ed. Way It Is. LC 69-11495. (Curriculum Related Bks). (Illus.). (gr. 7 up). 1969. 6.75 o.p. (ISBN 0-15-294830-9, HJ). HarBraceJ.
Holland, John L. Making Vocational Choices: A Theory of Careers. LC 73-4847. (Counseling & Human Development Ser). (Illus.). 192p. 1973. pap. text ed. 10.95 (ISBN 0-13-547810-3). P-H.
Holland, Margaret. The Phaidon Guide to Silver. (Illus., Orig.). 1979. pap. 5.95 o.p. (ISBN 0-8467-0538-9, Pub. by Two Continents). Hippocrene Bks.
Holland, Marion. Secret Horse. (gr. 4-6). 1976. pap. 1.50 (ISBN 0-590-03845-1, Schol Pap). Schol Bk Serv.
Holland, Morris K. Introductory Psychology. 688p. 1981. text ed. 17.95 (ISBN 0-669-03347-2); instr's. guide with test avail. (ISBN 0-669-03346-4); student guide 5.95 (ISBN 0-669-03347-2). Heath.
--Psychology: An Introduction to Human Behavior. 2nd ed. 1978. text ed. 16.95x (ISBN 0-669-00994-6); inst. manual free (ISBN 0-669-00998-9); wkbk. 5.95x (ISBN 0-669-00995-4); indiv. prog. 6.95x (ISBN 0-669-00996-2); test item file to adopters free (ISBN 0-669-00997-0); tests for indiv. prog. free (ISBN 0-669-01161-4). Heath.
Holland, Muhtar, tr. Al Ghazali: On the Duties of Brotherhood. LC 76-8057. 96p. 1979. pap. 5.95 (ISBN 0-87951-083-8). Overlook Pr.
Holland, Muhtar, tr. see Muzaffer, Sheikh.
Holland, Norman N. Shakespearean Imagination: A Critical Introduction. LC 63-15685. (Midland Bks.: No. 114). (Illus.). 1968. pap. 3.95x o.p. (ISBN 0-253-20114-4). Ind U Pr.
Holland, P. The Ornament of Action. LC 78-1157. (Illus.). 1979. 42.00 (ISBN 0-521-22048-3). Cambridge U Pr.
--The Plays of William Wycherley. (Plays by Renaissance & Restoration Dramatists). (Illus.). 400p. Date not set. price not set (ISBN 0-521-23250-3); pap. price not set (ISBN 0-521-29880-6). Cambridge U Pr.
Holland, Philemon, tr. see Pliny.
Holland, Ruth. Mill Child. LC 75-92072. (Illus.). (gr. 5-9). 1970. 7.95 (ISBN 0-02-744260-8, CCPr). Macmillan.
--The Room. LC 73-6240. 192p. (gr. 5-9). 1973. 5.95 o.s.i. (ISBN 0-440-07541-6). Delacorte.
Holland, Seamas. Rutland Street: The Story of an Educational Experiment for Disadvantaged Children in Dublin. (Illus.). 1979. 17.75 (ISBN 0-685-97185-6). Pergamon.
Holland, Stuart. Capital Versus the Regions. LC 77-70277. 1977. 17.95x (ISBN 0-312-11945-3). St Martin.
Holland, Stuart, ed. Beyond Capitalist Planning. LC 78-19586. 1979. 19.95 (ISBN 0-312-07778-5). St Martin.
Hollander, jt. auth. see Duncan.
Hollander, A. Den see Den Hollander, A.
Hollander, A. N. & Skard, Sigmund. American Civilization: An Introduction. 1970. Repr. of 1968 ed. text ed. 13.25x (ISBN 0-582-48226-7). Humanities.
Hollander, Anne. Seeing Through Clothes. 528p. 1980. pap. 8.95 (ISBN 0-380-48777-2, 48777-2). Avon.
Hollander, Annette. How to Help Your Child Have a Spiritual Life: Inner Development with or Withoout Organized Religion. LC 79-28074. (Illus.). 224p. 1980. 12.95 (ISBN 0-89479-061-7). A & W Pubs.
Hollander, Bernard. The Psychology of Misconduct, Vice, & Crime. (Historical Foundations of Forensic Psychiatry & Psychology Ser.). 220p. 1980. Repr. lib. bdg. 25.00 (ISBN 0-306-76063-0). Da Capo.
Hollander, C. den see Den Hollander, C.
Hollander, Carlton. How to Build a Hot Tub. (Illus.). 128p. 1980. 12.95 (ISBN 0-8069-0212-4); lib. bdg. 11.69 (ISBN 0-8069-0213-2); pap. 6.95 (ISBN 0-8069-8948-3). Sterling.
Hollander, Edwin P. Leadership Dynamics: A Practical Guide to Effective Relationships. LC 77-15884. 1978. 14.95 (ISBN 0-02-914820-0). Free Pr.
--Principles & Methods of Social Psychology. 4th ed. (Illus.). 548p. 1981. text ed. 18.95x (ISBN 0-19-502822-8). Oxford U Pr.
Hollander, Gayle D. Soviet Political Indoctrination: Developments in Mass Media & Propaganda Since Stalin. LC 70-163927. (Special Studies in International Politics & Government). 1972. 27.00x (ISBN 0-275-28202-3). Irvington.
Hollander, Jack M., et al, eds. Annual Review of Energy, Vol. 5. (Illus.). 1980. text ed. 20.00 (ISBN 0-8243-2305-X). Annual Reviews.
Hollander, Jacob H. Economic Library of Jacob H. Hollander. Marsh, Elsie A., ed. LC 67-14032. 1966. Repr. of 1937 ed. 18.00 (ISBN 0-8103-3103-9). Gale.
Hollander, John. Spectral Emanations: New & Selected Poems. LC 77-20645. 1978. pap. 7.95 (ISBN 0-689-10878-8). Atheneum.
--Vision & Resonance: Two Senses of Poetic Form. 325p. 1975. 16.95 (ISBN 0-19-501898-2). Oxford U Pr.
Hollander, John, ed. Modern Poetry: Essays in Criticism. (Orig.). (YA) (gr. 9 up). 1968. pap. 6.95 (ISBN 0-19-500757-3, GB). Oxford U Pr.
--Poems of Our Moment: Contemporary Poets of the English Language. LC 67-25507. (Orig.). 1968. pap. 6.55 o.p. (ISBN 0-672-63575-5). Pegasus.
Hollander, Lawrence J., ed. see Apfelbaum, H. Jack & Ottesen, Walter O.
Hollander, Lawrence J., ed. see Lyons, John S. & Dublin, Stanley W.
Hollander, Lee M., tr. see Sturluson, Snorri.
Hollander, Leslie. The Exhibit. 384p. (Orig.). 1981. pap. 2.75 (ISBN 0-523-41479-X). Pinnacle Bks.
Hollander, Lewis, jt. auth. see Ingram, Patricia.
Hollander, Mary K. Chicken Favorites. Herbert, Susan H., ed. (Illus.). 64p. (Orig.). 1981. pap. 2.50 (ISBN 0-915942-18-6). Owlswood Prods.
Hollander, Neil & Mertes, Harald. The Yachtsman's Emergency Handbook. (Illus.). 320p. 1980. 14.95 (ISBN 0-87851-803-7). Hearst Bks.
Hollander, Nicole. That Woman Must Be on Drugs. (Illus.). 128p. 1981. pap. 3.95 (ISBN 0-312-79510-6). St Martin.
Hollander, Patricia A. Legal Handbook for Educators. LC 77-26092. 1978. lib. bdg. 22.50x (ISBN 0-89158-420-X); pap. text ed. 13.75x (ISBN 0-86531-073-4). Westview.
Hollander, Phyllis, jt. ed. see Herkimer, L. R.
Hollander, Rene & Percy, Bernard. Everyone's Guide to Saving Gas. (Illus., Orig.). 1979. pap. 2.95 (ISBN 0-9603194-0-9). Old Oaktree.
Hollander, Robert. Boccaccio's Two Venuses. LC 77-5144. 1977. 20.00x (ISBN 0-231-04224-8). Columbia U Pr.
Hollander, Xaviera. Xaviera Goes Wild. 368p. (Orig.). 1974. pap. 2.95 (ISBN 0-446-93657-X). Warner Bks.
--Xaviera: Her Continuing Adventures by the Author of the Happy Hooker. (Orig.). 1973. pap. 2.95 (ISBN 0-446-93660-X). Warner Bks.
--Xaviera's Supersex: Her Personal Techniques for Total Lovemaking. 1978. pap. 2.25 o.p. (ISBN 0-451-08384-9, E8384, Sig). NAL.
Hollander, Xaviera & Chambers, Marilyn. Xaviera Meets Marilyn Chambers. (Orig.). 1976. pap. 2.95 (ISBN 0-446-93979-X). Warner Bks.
Hollander, Xaviera, ed. Letters to the Happy Hooker. (Orig.). 1973. pap. 2.50 (ISBN 0-446-91491-6). Warner Bks.
Hollander, Zander. Complete Handbook of Baseball, 1980 Edition. (Orig.). (RL 7). 1980. pap. 2.50 (ISBN 0-451-09129-9, E9129, Sig). NAL.
--The Complete Handbook of the Winter Olympic Games, Nineteen Eighty. (Illus., Orig.). 1979. pap. cancelled o.p. (ISBN 0-451-08904-9, E8904, Sig). NAL.
Hollander, Zander, ed. The Complete Handbook of Baseball - 1981 Edition. (Orig.). 1981. pap. 2.95 (ISBN 0-451-09682-7, Sig). NAL.
--Complete Handbook of College Basketball, 1981. 1980. pap. 2.75 (ISBN 0-451-09497-2, E9487, Sig). NAL.
--The Complete Handbook of College Basketball: 1980 Edition. (Illus.). (RL 7). 1979. pap. 2.50 (ISBN 0-451-08936-7, E8936, Sig). NAL.
--The Complete Handbook of Pro Football: 1980. (Illus.). 275p. (Orig.). (YA) (RL 7). 1980. pap. 2.75 (ISBN 0-451-09359-3, E9359, Sig). NAL.
--The Complete Handbook of Pro Hockey, 1981. 1980. pap. 2.75 (ISBN 0-451-09470-0, E9470, Sig). NAL.
--Pro Basketball: Its Superstars & History. (gr. 9 up). 1971. pap. 1.50 (ISBN 0-590-09157-3, Schol Pap). Schol Bk Serv.
--Strange But True Football Stories. (NFL Punt, Pass & Kick Library: No. 8). (Illus.). (gr. 5-9). 1967. 2.95 (ISBN 0-394-80198-9, BYR); PLB 4.39 (ISBN 0-394-90198-3); pap. 0.95 o.p. (ISBN 0-394-82202-1). Random.
Holland-Moritz, jt. auth. see Siesler.
Hollaran, Carolyn. Meet the Stars of Country Music, Vol. 2. 1978. 4.95 o.s.i. (ISBN 0-87695-212-0). Aurora Pubs.
Hollas, Dave, jt. auth. see Ballas, George C.
Hollatz, Tom. White Earth Snowshoe Guidebook. LC 72-89554. (Illus.). 128p. 1973. 5.00 (ISBN 0-87839-014-6); pap. 3.50 (ISBN 0-87839-010-3). North Star.
Holle, Britta. Motor Development in Children Normal & Retarded. 1977. pap. 24.00 (ISBN 0-397-60509-9, Pub by Blackwell Scientific). Mosby.
Holle, F. & Holle, G. E., eds. Vagotomy & Pyloroplasty: Latest Advances, 1975-1980. (Illus.). 160p. 1980. pap. 58.00 (ISBN 0-387-10083-0). Springer-Verlag.
Holle, G. E., jt. ed. see Holle, F.
Holleman, Thomas J., jt. auth. see Nawrocki, Dennis A.
Hollen, Norma R. Pattern Making by the Flat Pattern Method. 5th ed. 1981. 12.95 (ISBN 0-8087-3173-4). Burgess.
Hollenbeck, Leon. Dynamics of Canine Gait. (Other Dog Bk.). (Illus.). 240p. 1981. write for info. (ISBN 0-87714-081-2). Denlingers.
Hollender, Betty R. Bible Stories for Little Children, 3 bks. (Illus.). (gr. k-3). text ed. 4.00 ea. o.p. UAHC.
Hollender, Louis F. & Marrie, Alain. Highly Selective Vagotomy. LC 78-61475. (Illus.). 144p. 1979. 22.50 (ISBN 0-89352-026-8). Masson Pub.
Hollender, M. H., jt. auth. see Ban, T. A.
Holler, Frederick L. The Information Sources of Political Science, 5 vols. 2nd, rev. ed. LC 74-80344. 440p. 1975. Set. text ed. 12.00 (ISBN 0-87436-190-7); text ed. 8.75 ea.; Set. pap. text ed. 21.75 (ISBN 0-685-93193-5); pap. text ed. 1.75 ea.; Vol. 1. pap. text ed. (ISBN 0-87436-181-8); Vol. 2. pap. text ed. (ISBN 0-87436-183-4); Vol. 3. pap. text ed. (ISBN 0-87436-185-0); Vol. 4. pap. text ed. (ISBN 0-87436-187-7); Vol. 5. pap. text ed. (ISBN 0-87436-189-3). ABC-Clio.
--The Information Sources of Political Science. 3rd, rev. ed. 288p. 1980. 65.00 (ISBN 0-87436-179-6). ABC-Clio.
Holler, Ronald F. & DeLong, George M. Human Services Technology. LC 73-1441. 1973. text ed. 11.75 o.p. (ISBN 0-8016-2227-1). Mosby.
Hollerman, Charles E. Pediatric Nephrology. (Medical Outline Ser.). 1979. pap. 18.00 (ISBN 0-87488-590-6). Med Exam.
Hollerman, Leon. Japan's Dependence on World Economy: An Approach Toward Economic Liberalization. 1967. 17.00x o.p. (ISBN 0-691-05625-0). Princeton U Pr.
Hollerman, Leon, ed. Japan & the United States: Economic & Political Adversaries. LC 79-18646. (Westview Special Studies in International Economics & Business). (Illus.). 245p. 1980. 23.50x (ISBN 0-89158-582-6). Westview.
Holles, Robert. Spawn. 1980. pap. 2.50 (ISBN 0-425-04570-6). Berkley Pub.
--Spawn. 1979. pap. cancelled o.s.i. (ISBN 0-515-05182-9). Jove Pubns.
Holley, B. & Skelton, V. Economics Education Fourteen to Sixteen. 250p. 1981. pap. text ed. 15.25x (ISBN 0-85633-215-1, NFER). Humanities.
Holley, Frederick S., ed. Los Angeles Times Stylebook: A Manual for Writers, Editors, Journalists & Students. 1981. pap. 6.95 (ISBN 0-452-00552-3, F552, Mer). NAL.
Holley, Horace. Religion for Mankind. 1956. 8.95 (ISBN 0-87743-028-4, 7-31-29); pap. 2.95 (ISBN 0-85398-000-4, 7-31-30, Pub. by George Ronald England). Baha'i.
Holley, Raymond. Religious Education & Religious Understanding: An Introduction to the Philosophy of Religious Education. 1978. 19.50x (ISBN 0-7100-8995-3). Routledge & Kegan.
Holley, W., et al. Plantation South. LC 78-166955. (FDR & the Era of the New Deal Ser). 1971. Repr. of 1940 ed. lib. bdg. 15.00 (ISBN 0-306-70354-8). Da Capo.
Holley, William H., Jr. & Jennings, Ken. The Labor Relations Process: Form & Content. 600p. 1980. text ed. 21.95 (ISBN 0-03-046556-7). Dryden Pr.
Holli, Melvin G., jt. ed. see Jones, Peter D.
Hollick, Ann L. U.S. Foreign Policy & the Law of the Sea. LC 80-8554. 456p. 1981. 27.50x (ISBN 0-691-09387-3); pap. 12.50x (ISBN 0-686-69179-2). Princeton U Pr.
Holliday, A. K. & Massey, A. G. Inorganic Chemistry in Nonaqueous Solvents. 1965. 16.50 (ISBN 0-08-011335-4); pap. 7.25 (ISBN 0-08-011334-6). Pergamon.
Holliday, Bob. Motorcycle Panorama: A Pictorial Review of Motorcycle Development. LC 74-14052. (Illus.). 224p. 1975. 7.95 o.p. (ISBN 0-668-03647-8). Arco.
--Racing Round the Island. 5.95 (ISBN 0-7153-7205-X, Pub. by Batsford England). David & Charles.
Holliday, C. B., jt. auth. see Le Rossignol, J. N.

Holliday, Carl. Wit & Humor of Colonial Days 1607-1800. LC 71-148586. 1970. Repr. of 1912 ed. 15.00 (ISBN 0-8103-3592-1). Gale.
--Woman's Life in Colonial Days. LC 72-140408. 1970. Repr. of 1922 ed. 18.00 (ISBN 0-8103-3593-X). Gale.
Holliday, George D. Technology Transfer to the U. S. S. R., Nineteen Twenty-Eight to Nineteen Thirty-Seven & Nineteen Sixty-Six to Nineteen Seventy-Five: The Role of Western Development in Soviet Economic Development. (A Westview Replica Edition Ser.). 1979. lib. bdg. 24.50x (ISBN 0-89158-189-8). Westview.
Holliday, J., ed. City Centre Redevelopment. LC 73-17764. (Illus.). 1973. 27.95 (ISBN 0-470-40644-5). Halsted Pr.
Holliday, L., ed. Ionic Polymers. LC 74-11509. 416p. 1975. 53.95 (ISBN 0-470-40640-2). Halsted Pr.
Holliday, Paul. Fungus Diseases of Tropical Crops. LC 79-41602. (Illus.). 500p. 1980. 125.00 (ISBN 0-521-22529-9). Cambridge U Pr.
Holliday, Robin. The Science of Human Progress. 112p. 1981. 21.00 (ISBN 0-19-854711-0). Oxford U Pr.
Hollindale, Peter. Choosing Books for Children. 1974. 9.95 o.p. (ISBN 0-236-15482-6, Pub. by Paul Elek). Merrimack Bk Serv.
Holling, C. S., ed. Adaptive Environmental Assessment & Management. LC 78-8523. (IIASA International Series on Applied Systems Analysis). 1978. 24.75 (ISBN 0-471-99632-7, Pub. by Wiley-Interscience). Wiley.
Holling, Fred, jt. ed. see Shevelov, George Y.
Hollingdale, R. J. Nietzsche. (Author Guides Ser). 238p. 1973. 17.50x (ISBN 0-7100-7562-6); pap. 8.95 (ISBN 0-7100-7563-4). Routledge & Kegan.
--Thomas Mann: a Critical Study. LC 79-161509. 204p. 1971. 12.00 (ISBN 0-8387-1004-2). Bucknell U Pr.
--Western Philosophy: An Introduction. 1966. text ed. 5.00x (ISBN 0-900707-02-X). Humanities.
Hollinger, David A. Morris R. Cohen & the Scientific Ideal. 288p. 1980. pap. 5.95 (ISBN 0-262-58041-1). MIT Pr.
--Morris R. Cohen & the Scientific Ideal. LC 75-12850. 384p. 1975. text ed. 20.00x (ISBN 0-262-08084-2). MIT Pr.
Hollings, C. S., jt. ed. see Norton, G. A.
Hollingshead, A. B. & Redlich, F. C. Social Class & Mental Illness: A Community Study. LC 58-6076. 1958. pap. 16.95 (ISBN 0-471-40685-6). Wiley.
Hollingsworth. Guide to Small Business Management. 1979. 10.95. Dryden Pr.
--Readings in Basic Management. 2nd ed. 1979. pap. 10.95 (ISBN 0-7216-4753-7). Dryden Pr.
Hollingsworth, Brian. Festiniog Adventure: The Festiniog Railway's Deviation Project. LC 80-68683. (Illus.). 160p. 1981. 16.95 (ISBN 0-7153-7956-9). David & Charles.
Hollingsworth, Dorothy & Morse, Elisabeth, eds. People & Food Tomorrow: The Scientific, Economic, Political, & Social Factors Affecting Food Supplies in the Last Quarter of the 20th Century. 1976. 40.90x (ISBN 0-85334-701-8). Intl Ideas.
Hollingsworth, Paul, jt. auth. see Hoover, Kenneth.
Hollington, Michael. Gunter Grass: The Writer in a Pluralist Society. LC 79-56840. 192p. 1980. 15.00 (ISBN 0-7145-2678-9, Pub. by M Boyars). Merrimack Bk Serv.
Hollingworth, Brian, ed. Songs of the People: Lancashire Dialect Poetry of the Industrial Revolution. 1977. text ed. 10.25x (ISBN 0-7190-0612-0). Humanities.
Hollingworth, June. Collecting Decanters. (The Christies International Collectors Ser.). (Illus.). 128p. 1980. 14.95 (ISBN 0-8317-2161-8). Mayflower Bks.
Hollingworth, Leta S. The Psychology of the Adolescent. 256p. 1980. Repr. lib. bdg. 30.00 (ISBN 0-89984-294-1). Century Bookbindery.
Hollins, R. J. Production & Planning Applied to Building. 2nd ed. 1971. 16.50x (ISBN 0-7121-4606-7). Intl Ideas.
Hollins, T. H., ed. Aims in Education. 1966. text ed. 14.50x (ISBN 0-7190-0038-6). Humanities.
Hollinshead, W. Henry. Anatomia Humana. 1000p. 1981. pap. text ed. 26.00 (ISBN 0-06-313375-X, Pub. by by HarlA Mexico). Har-Row.
Hollinson, Harry. Background to the New Testament. 4.00x (ISBN 0-392-07650-0, SpS). Soccer.
Hollis, A. S., ed. see Ovid.
Hollis, Christopher. Parliament & Its Sovereignty. 189p. 1973. 10.00 o.p. (ISBN 0-370-01358-1). Transatlantic.
Hollis, F. & Woods, M. E. Casework: A Psychological Therapy. 3rd ed. 552p. 1981. text ed. 16.95 (ISBN 0-394-32368-8). Random.
Hollis, H. F. Perspective Drawing. (Teach Yourself Ser.). 1974. pap. 2.95 o.p. (ISBN 0-679-10405-4). McKay.
Hollis, J. Another Eden: a New Paradise: A Story of the Regeneration of Mankind, an Epic Poem. LC 79-53813. (Illus.). 68p. 1980. pap. 10.00 (ISBN 0-933486-18-9). Am Poetry Pr.
--A Planet Probable: A One-Act Poetic Play. (Orig.). 1981. pap. 2.95 (ISBN 0-933486-20-0). Am Poetry Pr.
Hollis, Jocelyn. Modern Religious Lyrics. LC 80-80565. (Contemporary American Traditional Poetry Ser.: Vol. 2, No. 1). 28p. (Orig.). 1980. pap. 2.95 (ISBN 0-933486-19-7). Am Poetry Pr.
--Sex Songs. LC 78-75357. (Contemporary American Traditional Poetry Ser.: Vol. 1, No. 4). 60p. 1980. pap. cancelled (ISBN 0-933486-00-6). Am Poetry Pr.
--Sonnets of Jocelyn Hollis. LC 81-90002. 62p. 1981. pap. 3.95 (ISBN 0-933486-21-9). Am Poetry Pr.
--Vietnam War Poems. LC 80-65621. 48p. 1981. pap. 3.95 (ISBN 0-933486-14-6). Am Poetry Pr.
Hollis, M. The Light of Reason. 1973. pap. 2.95 o.p. (ISBN 0-531-06046-2, Fontana Pap). Watts.
--Models on Man. LC 76-49902. (Illus.). 1977. 32.95 (ISBN 0-521-21546-3); pap. 8.95x (ISBN 0-521-29181-X). Cambridge U Pr.
Hollis, Martin. Tantalizers: A Book of Original Logical Puzzles. 1975. 7.95 o.p. (ISBN 0-04-793023-3). Allen Unwin.
Hollis, Martin I. & Nell, Edward J. Rational Economic Man. (Illus.). 288p. 1975. 32.95x (ISBN 0-521-20408-9). Cambridge U Pr.
Hollis, Patrica, ed. see Lowery, Robert.
Hollis, Patricia. Women in Public: The Women's Movement 1850-1900. 1979. text ed. 25.00x (ISBN 0-04-900033-0). Allen Unwin.
Hollis, Patricia, ed. Class & Conflict in Nineteenth-Century England, 1815-1850. (Birth of Modern Britain Ser). 402p. 1973. 20.00x (ISBN 0-7100-7419-0); pap. 10.00 (ISBN 0-7100-7420-4). Routledge & Kegan.
Hollister, C. W. see Smith, Lacey B.
Hollister, C. Warren. Odysseus to Columbus: A Synopsis of Classical & Medieval History. LC 74-2428. 352p. 1974. pap. text ed. 10.95 (ISBN 0-471-40689-9). Wiley.
Hollister, C. Warren, ed. Landmarks of the Western Heritage, 2 vols. 2nd ed. Incl. Vol. 1. The Ancient Near East to 1789. 544p. pap. text ed. 14.95x (ISBN 0-471-40700-3); Vol. 2. 1715 to Present. 416p. pap. text ed. 14.95x (ISBN 0-471-40704-6). LC 72-7315. (Illus.). 1973. Wiley.
Hollister, C. Warren, et al. River Through Time: The Course of Western Civilization. LC 74-14972. 576p. 1975. pap. 14.95x (ISBN 0-471-40695-3). Wiley.
Hollister, Charles D., jt. auth. see Heezen, Bruce C.
Hollister, Leo E. Chemical Psychoses: LSD & Related Drugs. (Amer. Lec. Living Chemistry Ser). (Illus.). 200p. 1972. 11.75 (ISBN 0-398-00860-4). C C Thomas.
--Clinical Use of Psychotherapeutic Drugs. 200p. 1977. 12.75 (ISBN 0-398-02749-8). C C Thomas.
Hollister, Paul & Lanmon, Dwight P. Paperweights: Flowers Which Clothe the Meadows. (Illus.). 167p. 1981. pap. price not set. Dover.
Hollman, Kenneth W., jt. auth. see Davidge, William F.
Hollo, Anselm, tr. see Arsan, Emmanuelle.
Hollo, Anselm, tr. see Barkan, Stanley H.
Hollo, Anselm, tr. see Harding, Gunnar & Barkan, Stanley H.
Hollo, Reuven & Fifadara, Haresh. TI-Fifty-Nine Reservoir Engineering Manual. 264p. 1980. 50.00 (ISBN 0-87814-134-0). Pennwell Pub.
Hollon, Jennifer K. Solar Energy for California's Residential Sector: Progress, Problems, & Prospects. LC 80-29096. (IGS Research Report: No. 80-3). 71p. 1980. pap. text ed. 4.50 (ISBN 0-87772-279-X). Inst Gov Stud Berk.
Hollon, S. D., jt. ed. see Kendall, P. C.
Hollon, W. Eugene. Frontier Violence. 1974. 14.95 (ISBN 0-19-501750-1). Oxford U Pr.
--Frontier Violence: Another Look. LC 73-87617. (Illus.). 288p. 1976. pap. 4.95 (ISBN 0-19-502098-7, 475, GB). Oxford U Pr.
--The Great American Desert Then & Now. LC 75-5512. (Illus.). xxviii, 284p. 1975. pap. 3.95 (ISBN 0-8032-5806-2, BB 592, Bison). U of Nebr Pr.
--Southwest: Old & New. LC 61-9232. (Illus.). 1968. pap. 5.75 (ISBN 0-8032-5091-6, BB 353, Bison). U of Nebr Pr.
Holloran, Carolyn. Meet the Stars of Country Music, Vol. 1. 1977. 4.95 o.s.i. (ISBN 0-87695-204-X). Aurora Pubs.
Hollos, Marida. Growing up in Flathill: Social Environment & Cognitive Development. 165p. 1974. 20.50x (ISBN 8-200-08944-4, Dist. by Columbia U Pr). Universitet.
Holloway, A. H., et al. Information Work with Unpublished Reports. LC 76-43366. (Institute of Information Scientists Monograph Ser.). (Illus.). 1978. lib. bdg. 28.50x (ISBN 0-89158-717-9). Westview.
Holloway, David. Derby Day. (Folio Miniature Ser.). 1975. 4.95 (ISBN 0-7181-1303-9, Pub. by Michael Joseph). Merrimack Bk Serv.
Holloway, Emory. Whitman: An Interpretation in Narrative. LC 70-79953. (Illus.). 1969. Repr. of 1926 ed. 16.00x (ISBN 0-8196-0236-1). Biblo.
Holloway, G. E. Introduction to the Child's Conception of Geometry. (Illus.). 1967. pap. text ed. 1.50x (ISBN 0-7100-1543-7). Humanities.
Holloway, Gordon F. & Berkey, Gordon. Elementary Physics of Sound for Speech Pathology & Audiology. LC 73-571. (Illus.). 244p. 1981. 14.50 (ISBN 0-87527-190-1). Green. Postponed.
Holloway, Gordon F., jt. ed. see Wingo, John W.
Holloway, John. Narrative & Structure: Exploratory Essays. LC 78-20826. 1979. 19.95 (ISBN 0-521-22574-4). Cambridge U Pr.
--Social Policy Harmonisation in the European Communities. 1980. text ed. 27.00x (ISBN 0-566-00196-9, Pub. by Gower Pub Co England). Renouf.
Holloway, John & Black, Joan. Later English Broadside Ballads, Vol. 2. (Illus.). 1979. 40.00x (ISBN 0-7100-0282-3). Routledge & Kegan.
Holloway, John, ed. see Dickens, Charles.
Holloway, Mark. Heavens on Earth: Utopian Communities in America 1680-1880. rev. ed. 1966. pap. 4.00 (ISBN 0-486-21593-8). Dover.
Holloway, Maurice R., jt. auth. see Klubertanz, George P.
Holloway, Nancy M. Nursing the Critically Ill Adult. LC 78-21153. 1979. 20.95 (ISBN 0-201-02948-0, 02948, M&N Div). A-W.
Holloway, R. Ross. Satrianum: The Archaeological Investigations Conducted by Brown University in 1966 & 1967. LC 76-91654. (Illus.). 150p. 1970. 25.00x (ISBN 0-87057-118-4, Pub. by Brown U Pr). Univ Pr of New England.
--A View of Greek Art. LC 72-187947. (Illus.). 213p. 1973. 15.00 (ISBN 0-87057-133-8, Pub. by Brown U Pr). Univ Pr of New England.
Holloway, Sally. The London Zoo. (Folio Miniature Ser.). 1976. 4.95 (ISBN 0-7181-1475-2, Pub. by Michael Joseph). Merrimack Bk Serv.
Holloway Staff. Dutch. (Harper Phrase Books for the Traveler Ser.). (Orig.). 1977. pap. 1.00 o.p. (ISBN 0-8467-0308-4, Pub. by Two Continents). Hippocrene Bks.
--French. (Harper Phrase Books for the Traveler Ser.). (Orig.). 1977. pap. 1.00 (ISBN 0-8467-0309-2, Pub. by Two Continents). Hippocrene Bks.
--German. (Harper Phrase Books for the Traveler Ser.). (Orig.). 1977. pap. 1.00 (ISBN 0-8467-0310-6, Pub. by Two Continents). Hippocrene Bks.
--Italian. (Harper Phrase Books for the Traveler Ser.). (Orig.). 1977. pap. 1.00 (ISBN 0-8467-0312-2, Pub. by Two Continents). Hippocrene Bks.
--Portuguese. (Harper Phrase Books for the Traveler Ser.). (Orig.). 1977. pap. 1.00 o.p. (ISBN 0-8467-0313-0, Pub. by Two Continents). Hippocrene Bks.
--Scandinavian. (Harper Phrase Books for the Traveler Ser.). (Orig.). 1977. pap. 1.00 o.p. (ISBN 0-8467-0315-7, Pub. by Two Continents). Hippocrene Bks.
--Spanish. (Harper Phrase Books for the Traveler Ser.). (Orig.). 1977. pap. 1.00 (ISBN 0-8467-0316-5, Pub. by Two Continents). Hippocrene Bks.
--Yugoslavian. (Harper Phrase Books for the Traveler Ser.). (Orig.). 1977. pap. text ed. 1.00 o.p. (ISBN 0-8467-0317-3, Pub. by Two Continents). Hippocrene Bks.
Holloway, Stephen, jt. auth. see Brager, George.
Holloway, William J., ed. Infectious Disease Reviews, Vol VI. LC 78-50693. (Illus.). 192p. 1981. monograph 23.75 (ISBN 0-87993-151-5). Futura Pub.
Holloway-Calthrop, H. C. Petrarch His Life & Times. 319p. 1980. Repr. of 1907 ed. lib. bdg. 45.00 (ISBN 0-89984-274-7). Century Bookbindery.
Hollowell, Mary L. The Cable-Broadband Communications Book, 1980-1981, Vol. 2. (Video Bookshelf Ser.). 300p. 1980. text ed. 29.95x (ISBN 0-914236-79-2). Knowledge Indus.
Hollowell, Mary L., ed. The Cable Broadband Communications Book, 1977-1978, Vol. 1. LC 77-81692. 1977. pap. 15.50x (ISBN 0-89461-027-9). Comm Pr Inc.
--The Cable Broadband Communications Book, 1980-1981, Vol. 2. LC 77-81692. 1980. 19.50x (ISBN 0-89461-031-7). Comm Pr Inc.
Hollreiser, Len. The Sports Fan's Nineteen Seventy-Nine Calender: 365 Great Moments in Sports History. (Illus.). 1978. 3.95 o.p. (ISBN 0-690-01225-X, TYC-T). T Y Crowell.
Hollstein, M., jt. ed. see Morgenthaler, G. W.
Hollway-Calthrop, H. C. Petrarch: His Life & Times. LC 75-187413. (Illus.). xi, 319p. 1972. Repr. of 1907 ed. lib. bdg. 13.75x (ISBN 0-8154-0406-9). Cooper Sq.
Holly, Brian P. & Harvey, Milton E. Themes in Geographic Thought. 224p. 1980. write for info. St Martin.
Holly, David. A Complete Categorized Greek-English New Testament Vocabulary. 1980. pap. 6.95 (ISBN 0-8010-4224-0). Baker Bk.
Holly, Henry H. Church Architecture. 1980. lib. bdg. 75.00 (ISBN 0-8490-3141-9). Gordon Pr.
Holly, J. Hunter. Mind Traders. (YA) 5.95 (ISBN 0-685-07448-X, Avalon). Bouregy.
Hollyfield, J. P., jt. auth. see Tindell-Hopwood, A.
Holm, Bill. Northwest Coast Indian Art: An Analysis of Form. LC 65-10818. (Thomas Burke Memorial Washington State Museum Monograph: No. 1). (Illus.). 133p. 1965. 12.95 (ISBN 0-295-73855-3); pap. 7.95 (ISBN 0-295-95102-8). U of Wash Pr.
Holm, Hans-Henrik, jt. ed. see Rudeng, Erik.
Holm, Jean. The Study of Religions. LC 76-15426. 1977. pap. 3.95 (ISBN 0-8164-1227-8). Crossroad NY.
Holm, John D., et al. A Comparative Study of Political Involvement in Three African States: Botswana, Ghana & Kenya. LC 78-14731. (Foreign & Comparative Studies-African Ser.: No. XXX). 139p. 1979. pap. 6.50x (ISBN 0-915984-52-0). Syracuse U Foreign Comp.
Holm, Leroy, et al. A Geographical Atlas of World Weeds. LC 78-24280. 1979. 37.50 (ISBN 0-471-04393-1, Pub. by Wiley-Interscience). Wiley.
Holm, Wayne, jt. auth. see Rosier, Paul.
Holman, Alfred L., ed. see Ryerson, Albert W.
Holman, Bob. Kids at the Door: A Preventative Project on a Council Estate. (Practical of Social Work Ser.: No. 8). 208p. 1981. 25.00x (ISBN 0-631-12586-8, Pub. by Basil Blackwell England); pap. 12.50x (ISBN 0-631-12587-6). Biblio Dist.
Holman, C. Hugh. A Handbook to Literature. 4th ed. LC 79-10061. 1980. 12.95 (ISBN 0-672-61477-4); pap. 8.95 (ISBN 0-672-61441-3). Bobbs.
--The Immoderate Past. LC 76-28927. 118p. 1977. 8.00x (ISBN 0-8203-0419-0). U of Ga Pr.
Holman, Donna, ed. Rhineland: Winter in a Missouri Rivertown. (Illus.). 191p. (Orig.). 1979. pap. text ed. 8.00 (ISBN 0-930552-02-4). Tech Ed Serv.
Holman, Edward R. Commodity Futures Trading & the Secrets to Make a Success of It. (The International Council for Excellence in Management Library). (Illus.). 107p. 1980. plastic spiral bdg. 28.95 (ISBN 0-89266-252-2). Am Classical Coll Pr.
Holman, Felice. Blackmail Machine. LC 68-11002. (gr. 3-7). 1968. 8.95g (ISBN 0-02-744140-7). Macmillan.
--Elisabeth & the Marsh Mystery. (Illus.). (gr. k-3). 1966. 4.95g o.s.i. (ISBN 0-02-744090-7). Macmillan.
--Elisabeth the Bird Watcher. (Illus.). (gr. k-3). 1963. 5.95 (ISBN 0-02-744250-0). Macmillan.
--Elisabeth the Treasure Hunter. (gr. k-3). 1964. 4.95g o.s.i. (ISBN 0-02-744300-0). Macmillan.
Holman, Halsted R., jt. auth. see Fries, James F.
Holman, J. Allan & Gringhuis, Dirk. Mystery Mammals of the Ice Age-Great Lakes Region. LC 72-90919. (Illus.). 45p. (Orig.). (gr. 5-8). 1972. pap. 1.75 (ISBN 0-910726-74-4). Hillsdale Educ.
Holman, J. P. Heat Transfer. 5th ed. (Illus.). 672p. 1981. text ed. 27.95x (ISBN 0-07-029618-9, C); solutions manual 8.95 (ISBN 0-07-029619-7). McGraw.
Holman, L. Bruce. Puppet Animation in the Cinema: History & Technique. LC 73-10523. (Illus.). 192p. 1975. 9.95 o.p. (ISBN 0-498-01385-5). A S Barnes.
Holman, Mary A., jt. auth. see Watson, Donald S.
Holman, Michael. Cats. (Easy-Read Fact Book Ser.). (Illus.). 48p. (gr. 2-4). 1976. PLB 6.45 (ISBN 0-531-01220-4). Watts.
--Dogs. LC 76-13877. (Easy-Read Fact Book Ser.). (Illus.). 48p. (gr. 2-4). 1976. PLB 6.45 (ISBN 0-531-01213-1). Watts.
Holman, R. T., ed. Progress in Lipid Research, Vol. 17. 396p. 1980. 68.75 (ISBN 0-08-023797-5). Pergamon.
Holman, Ralph T., ed. New Concepts in Lipid Research in Honor of Stina & Einar Stenhagen, Vol. 16. new ed. (Progress in the Chemistry of Fats & Other Lipids). 1978. text ed. 71.00 (ISBN 0-08-022663-9). Pergamon.

Holmberg, Bengt. Paul & Power: The Structure of Authority in the Primitive Church Reflected in the Pauline Epistles. LC 79-8905. 240p. 1980. 14.95 (ISBN 0-8006-0634-5, 1-634). Fortress.

Holme, Anthea & Maizels, Joan. Social Workers & Volunteers. 1978. text ed. 25.00x (ISBN 0-04-361031-5); pap. text ed. 9.95x (ISBN 0-04-361032-3). Allen Unwin.

Holme, Bryan. Creatures of Paradise: Pictures to Grow Up With. (Illus.). 96p. (gr. 4 up). 1980. 12.95 (ISBN 0-19-520205-8). Oxford U Pr.

Holme, Bryan & Simpson, Jeffery. A Book of Favorite Games. (Illus.). 1979. cancelled (ISBN 0-670-17942-6, Studio). Viking Pr.

Holme, Bryan, ed. The Kate Greenaway Book: A Collection of Illustration, Verse, & Text. LC 76-7904. (Illus.). 144p. 1976. 8.95 o.p. (ISBN 0-670-41183-3, Studio). Viking Pr.

Holme, C. Geoffrey, ed. see James, Philip.

Holme, Geoffrey. Caricature of Today. LC 73-20081. (Illus.). 136p. 1974. Repr. of 1928 ed. 18.00 (ISBN 0-8103-3969-2). Gale.

Holme, Geoffrey, ed. see Salaman, Malcolm C.

Holme, T., et al. The Travellers' Guide to Sardinia. rev. ed. (Travellers' Guide Ser.). (Illus.). 1979. 9.95 (ISBN 0-224-01283-5, Pub. by Chatto Bodley Jonathan). Merrimack Bk Serv.

Holmes, A. L., jt. auth. see Harding, Robert T.

Holmes, A. S. Belinda, or, the Rivals. (Found Books: No. 2). 122p. (Orig.). 1975. pap. 3.95 (ISBN 0-88784-333-6, Pub. by Hse Anansi Pr Canada). U of Toronto Pr.

Holmes, Arthur & Holmes, Doris L. Holmes Principles of Physical Geology. 3rd ed. 1978. 27.95 (ISBN 0-471-07251-6). Halsted Pr.

Holmes, Arthur W. & Burns, David C. Audit Problem: Crafters, Inc. 1980. pap. 12.95x (ISBN 0-256-02162-7). Irwin.

--Auditing: Standards & Procedures. 9th ed. 1979. text ed. 19.95 (ISBN 0-256-02161-9). Irwin.

Holmes, Arthur W. & Overmyer, Wayne S. Basic Auditing Principles. 5th ed. (Illus.). 1976. text ed. 17.95x (ISBN 0-256-01778-6). Irwin.

Holmes, Beth. The Whipping Boy. 1979. pap. 2.50 (ISBN 0-515-04698-1). Jove Pubns.

Holmes, Bill. Home Workshop Guns for Defense & Resistance: The Handgun, Vol. II. Christensen, Devon, ed. (Illus.). 144p. (Orig.). 1979. pap. 6.00 (ISBN 0-87364-154-X). Paladin Ent.

Holmes, Brian. Comparative Education: Some Considerations of Method. (Unwin Education Bks.). (Illus.). 1981. text ed. 22.50 (ISBN 0-04-370101-9, 2624/5); pap. text ed. 9.50 (ISBN 0-04-370102-7). Allen Unwin.

Holmes, Brian, ed. Diversity & Unity in Education. 176p. 1980. text ed. 25.00 (ISBN 0-04-370094-2). Allen Unwin.

--Educational Policy & the Mission Schools: Case Studies from the British Empire. 1967. text ed. 16.75x (ISBN 0-7100-6002-5). Humanities.

Holmes, Bruce E. Manual of Comparative Anatomy: A Laboratory Guide & Brief Text. 416p. 1980. pap. text ed. 12.95 (ISBN 0-8403-2254-2). Kendall-Hunt.

Holmes, Burnham. Basic Training: A Portrait of Today's Army. LC 78-22128. (Illus.). 128p. (gr. 7 up). 1979. 8.95 (ISBN 0-590-07528-4, Four Winds). Schol Bk Serv.

--Early Morning Rounds: A Portrait of a Hospital. LC 80-69995. (Illus.). 128p. (gr. 7 up). 1981. 9.95 (ISBN 0-590-07611-6, Four Winds). Schol Bk Serv.

--The First Seeing Eye Dogs. LC 78-14804. (Famous Firsts Ser.). (Illus.). 1978. lib. bdg. 7.35 (ISBN 0-686-51104-2). Silver.

--Nefertiti: The Mystery Queen. LC 77-10445. (Great Unsolved Mysteries Ser.). (Illus.). (gr. 4-5). 1977. PLB 9.65 (ISBN 0-8172-1056-3). Raintree Pubs.

--The World's First Baseball Game. LC 78-14581. (Famous Firsts Ser.). (Illus.). 1978. lib. bdg. 7.35 (ISBN 0-686-51115-8). Silver.

Holmes, C. The Eastern Association in the English Civil War. LC 73-91616. (Illus.). 320p. 1974. 35.50 (ISBN 0-521-20400-3). Cambridge U Pr.

Holmes, C. Raymond. Stranger in My Home. LC 73-9253. (Crown Ser.). 128p. 1974. pap. 4.50 (ISBN 0-8127-0075-9). Southern Pub.

Holmes, Carolyn, jt. auth. see McClintock, Dalene.

Holmes, Charles S. The Clocks of Columbus: The Literary Career of James Thurber. LC 72-78287. (Illus.). 1978. pap. 6.95 (ISBN 0-689-70574-3, 242). Atheneum.

Holmes, D. The Papacy in the Modern World. 288p. 1981. 14.95 (ISBN 0-8245-0047-4). Crossroad NY.

Holmes, D. R. & Rahmel, A., eds. Materials & Coatings to Resist High Temperature Corrosion. (Illus.). 1978. text ed. 91.10x (ISBN 0-85334-784-0). Intl Ideas.

Holmes, Deb, jt. auth. see Christie, Tom.

Holmes, Deborah A. Family Ties. LC 77-82171. 1979. pap. 2.25 o.p. (ISBN 0-87216-426-8). Playboy Pbks.

--Survival Prayers for Young Mothers. LC 76-12390. 1976. 4.95 (ISBN 0-8042-2195-2). John Knox.

Holmes, Derek, ed. see Newman, John H.

Holmes, Donald J. The Adolescent in Psychotherapy. 337p. 1964. 15.95 (ISBN 0-316-37060-6). Little.

Holmes, Doris L., jt. auth. see Holmes, Arthur.

Holmes, Douglas, jt. ed. see Holmes, Monica B.

Holmes, Edward. An Age of Cameras. 1978. 24.95 o.p. (ISBN 0-85242-346-2, Pub. by Fountain). Morgan.

--The Life of Mozart. (Music Reprint Ser.). 1979. Repr. of 1845 ed. lib. bdg. 29.50 (ISBN 0-306-79560-4). Da Capo.

--Ramble Among the Musicians of Germany. 2nd ed. LC 68-16239. 1969. Repr. of 1828 ed. lib. bdg. 29.50 (ISBN 0-306-71086-2). Da Capo.

Holmes, Eliazbeth A., jt. auth. see Heilman, Arthur W.

Holmes, Ernest. The Basic Ideas of Science of Mind. 1957. pap. 3.50 (ISBN 0-911336-23-0). Sci of Mind.

--Creative Ideas. 1964. pap. 3.50 (ISBN 0-911336-00-1). Sci of Mind.

--Creative Living. Kinnear, Willis, ed. 96p. 1975. pap. 4.50 (ISBN 0-911336-63-X). Sci of Mind.

--Discover a Richer Life. 1961. pap. 3.50 (ISBN 0-911336-27-3). Sci of Mind.

--Effective Prayer. 1966. pap. 2.50 (ISBN 0-911336-02-8). Sci of Mind.

--Freedom from Stress. 1964. pap. 3.50 (ISBN 0-911336-30-3). Sci of Mind.

--Freedom to Live. 1969. pap. 3.50 (ISBN 0-911336-35-4). Sci of Mind.

--Gateway to Life. Kinnear, Willis, ed. 96p. (Orig.). 1974. pap. 4.50 (ISBN 0-911336-59-1). Sci of Mind.

--It Can Happen to You. Kinnear, Willis, ed. 1959. pap. 3.50 (ISBN 0-911336-25-7). Sci of Mind.

--It's up to You. 95p. 1968. pap. 3.50 (ISBN 0-911336-34-6). Sci of Mind.

--Journey into Life. 1967. pap. 4.50 (ISBN 0-911336-05-2). Sci of Mind.

--Keys to Wisdom. 1965. pap. 4.50 (ISBN 0-911336-06-0). Sci of Mind.

--Living Without Fear. 1962. pap. 3.50 (ISBN 0-911336-28-1). Sci of Mind.

--New Horizons. Kinnear, Willis, ed. 96p. (Orig.). 1973. pap. 4.50 (ISBN 0-911336-52-4). Sci of Mind.

--Observations. 1968. pap. 4.50 (ISBN 0-911336-12-5). Sci of Mind.

--The Philosophy of Jesus. Kinnear, Willis, ed. 96p. (Orig.). 1973. pap. 3.50 (ISBN 0-911336-51-6). Sci of Mind.

--The Power of an Idea. 1965. pap. 3.50 (ISBN 0-911336-31-1). Sci of Mind.

--Power of Belief. Kinnear, Willis H., ed. 1970. pap. 4.50 (ISBN 0-911336-13-3). Sci of Mind.

--Sermon by the Sea. 1967. pap. 2.50 o.p. (ISBN 0-911336-17-6). Sci of Mind.

--Spiritual Awareness. Kinnear, Willis, ed. 95p. 1972. pap. 4.50 (ISBN 0-911336-41-9). Sci of Mind.

--The Spiritual Universe & You. Kinnear, Willis H., ed. 1971. pap. 3.50 (ISBN 0-911336-37-0). Sci of Mind.

--Ten Ideas That Make a Difference. 1966. pap. 3.50 (ISBN 0-911336-32-X). Sci of Mind.

--Think Your Troubles Away. 1963. pap. 3.50 (ISBN 0-911336-29-X). Sci of Mind.

Holmes, Ernest & Barker, Raymond C. Richer Living. 366p. 1973. pap. 7.95 (ISBN 0-911336-48-6). Sci of Mind.

Holmes, Ernest & Holmes, Fenwicke. The Voice Celestial. (Illus.). 1978. pap. 8.95 (ISBN 0-911336-71-0). Sci of Mind.

Holmes, Ernest & Hornaday, William H. Help for Today. 1969. pap. 6.50 (ISBN 0-911336-04-4). Sci of Mind.

Holmes, Ernest & Kinnear, Willis. Know Yourself. (Orig.). 1970. pap. 3.50 (ISBN 0-911336-36-2). Sci of Mind.

--The Magic of the Mind. 1960. pap. 3.50 (ISBN 0-911336-26-5). Sci of Mind.

--A New Design for Living. 1959. pap. 5.95 (ISBN 0-911336-11-7). Sci of Mind.

--Practical Application of Science of Mind. 1958. pap. 3.50 (ISBN 0-911336-24-9). Sci of Mind.

--Thoughts Are Things. 1967. pap. 3.50 (ISBN 0-911336-33-8). Sci of Mind.

Holmes, Ernest & Kinnear, Willis H. The Larger Life. 1969. pap. 4.50 (ISBN 0-911336-07-9). Sci of Mind.

Holmes, Ernest, et al. Light. Kinnear, Willis, ed. 93p. 1971. pap. 4.50 (ISBN 0-911336-09-5). Sci of Mind.

Holmes, Fenwicke, jt. auth. see Holmes, Ernest.

Holmes, Francis S., jt. auth. see Tuomey, Michael.

Holmes, Frederick L. Claude Bernard & Animal Chemistry. LC 73-88497. (Commonwealth Fund Publications Ser). 640p. 1974. text ed. 25.00x (ISBN 0-674-13485-0). Harvard U Pr.

Holmes, George. The Good Parliament. 210p. 1975. 29.95x (ISBN 0-19-822446-X). Oxford U Pr.

--He Is Lord. LC 76-20891. (Radiant Life Ser.). 1977. pap. 1.25 (ISBN 0-88243-902-2, 02-0902); teacher's ed 2.50 (ISBN 0-88243-172-2, 32-0172). Gospel Pub.

Holmes, George A. The Estates of the Higher Nobility in Fourteenth-Century England. LC 80-2024. 1981. Repr. of 1957 ed. 25.00 (ISBN 0-404-18570-3). AMS Pr.

Holmes, Geraldine C., jt. auth. see Bergin, James J.

Holmes, Gordon. Selected Letters of Gordon Holmes. Phillips, C. G., ed. (Illus.). 500p. 1979. text ed. 53.00 (ISBN 0-19-920105-6). Oxford U Pr.

Holmes, Hamilton see Hazelton.

Holmes, Helen B., et al. Birth Control & Controlling Birth: Women-Centered Perspectives. LC 80-82173. (Contempory Issues in Biomedicine, Ethics, & Society Ser.). 352p. 1980. 14.95 (ISBN 0-89603-022-9); pap. 7.95 (ISBN 0-89603-023-7). Humana.

Holmes, Helen B., et al, eds. The Custom-Made Child? Women-Centered Perspectives. (Contemporary Issues in Biomedicine, Ethics, & Society Ser.). 384p. 1981. 14.95 (ISBN 0-89603-024-5); pap. 7.95 (ISBN 0-89603-025-3). Humana.

Holmes, Irvin. The Christian Path of Intuitive Wisdom. 80p. (Orig.). 1981. pap. 3.50 (ISBN 0-87516-408-0). De Vorss.

Holmes, J. Derek, ed. see Newman, John H.

Holmes, J. W., jt. auth. see Marshall, T. J.

Holmes, Jack K. Coherent Communication with Applications to Pseudo-Noise Spread Spectrum Synchronization. 850p. 1981. 50.00 (ISBN 0-471-03301-4, Pub. by Wiley-Interscience). Wiley.

Holmes, James D. Official Indicators & the Prediction of the Economic & Stock Market Future. (Illus.). 1980. deluxe ed. 37.75 (ISBN 0-918968-61-5). Inst Econ Finan.

Holmes, James S., et al, trs. see Van de Warsenburg, Hans.

Holmes, Jean & Sharman, Campbell. The Australian Federal System. LC 77-78552. 1978. pap. text ed. 8.50x (ISBN 0-86861-080-1). Allen Unwin.

Holmes, John C. Visitor: Jack Kerouac in Old Saybrook. 1980. limited edition, numbered & signed by the author 8.00 (ISBN 0-934660-04-2). TUVOTI.

Holmes, John H., jt. ed. see Lonsdale, Richard E.

Holmes, John R. Refuse Recycling & Recovery: A Review of the State of the Art. 168p. 1981. 38.00 (ISBN 0-471-27902-1, Pub. by Wiley-Interscience); pap. 14.00 (ISBN 0-471-27903-X). Wiley.

Holmes, John W. The Shaping of Peace, Vol. I: Canada & the Search for World Order 1943-57. 1979. 25.00 (ISBN 0-8020-5461-7). U of Toronto Pr.

Holmes, Kenneth. Basic Shapes...Plus. (Illus.). 24p. (gr. k-3). 1980. pap. 3.95 (ISBN 0-933358-63-6). Enrich.

Holmes, King, jt. auth. see Wear, Jennifer.

Holmes, King K., jt. ed. see Hobson, Derek.

Holmes, L. P. Flame of Sunset. 1979. pap. 1.75 o.p. (ISBN 0-445-04161-7). Popular Lib.

--High Starlight. 1976. pap. 0.95 o.p. (ISBN 0-445-00708-7). Popular Lib.

--Night Marshal. 1981. pap. 1.75 (ISBN 0-445-00701-X). Popular Lib.

--Summer Range. 1981. pap. 1.75 (ISBN 0-445-00697-8). Popular Lib.

Holmes, Lawrence B., ed. see Gas Dynamics Symposium - 7th Biennial - 1968.

Holmes, Lowell E. & Parris, Wayne. Anthropology, an Introduction. 3rd ed. LC 80-22138. 450p. 1981. text ed. 14.95 (ISBN 0-471-08107-8). Wiley.

Holmes, M. R. Nutrition of the Oilseed Rape Crop. (Illus.). xii, 148p. 1980. 25.00x (ISBN 0-85334-900-2). Burgess-Intl Ideas.

Holmes, Malcolm H. Conducting an Amateur Orchestra. LC 51-10271. 1951. 6.95x (ISBN 0-674-16000-2). Harvard U Pr.

Holmes, Margaret. Every Person's Guide to Good Self-Esteem. (Illus.). 1980. pap. 12.95 o.p. (ISBN 0-930490-17-7). Future Shop.

Holmes, Marguerite C. & Gottlieb, Marvine I. Anatomy & Physiology. 3rd ed. (Nursing Examination Review Bk: Vol. 5). 1975. pap. 6.00 (ISBN 0-87488-505-1). Med Exam.

Holmes, Marguerite C. & Levine, Harriet, eds. Medical Surgical Nursing. 3rd ed. (Nursing Examination Review Books Vol. 1). 1972. spiral bdg. 6.00 (ISBN 0-87488-501-9). Med Exam.

Holmes, Marguerite C., et al. Practical Nursing Examination Review Book Vol. 1. 3rd ed. 1973. spiral bdg. 6.00 (ISBN 0-87488-711-9). Med Exam.

Holmes, Marjorie. God & Vitamins. LC 80-911. 360p. 1980. 10.95 (ISBN 0-385-15249-3, Galilee). Doubleday.

--I've Got to Talk to Somebody, God. LC 69-10938. 1969. 6.95 (ISBN 0-385-05209-X). Doubleday.

--Lord, Let Me Love. 288p. 1981. pap. 2.75 (ISBN 0-553-14915-6). Bantam.

--Lord, Let Me Love: A Marjorie Holmes Treasury. LC 77-26516. 1978. 8.95 (ISBN 0-385-14093-2, Galilee). Doubleday.

--Writing the Creative Article. rev ed. 1976. 8.95 (ISBN 0-87116-100-1). Writer.

Holmes, Martin. Shakespeare & Burbage: The Sound of Shakespeare As Devised to Suit the Voice & Talents of His Principal Player. 209p. 1978. 19.50x (ISBN 0-8476-6070-2). Rowman.

--Shakespeare & His Players. LC 72-2773. (Illus.). 1979. pap. 3.95 o.p. (ISBN 0-684-15971-6). Scribner.

Holmes, Maureen. The Wheaten Years: The History of Ireland's Soft Coated Wheaten Terrier. LC 77-88422. 14.95. B P Reynolds.

Holmes, Monica B. & Holmes, Douglas, eds. Handbook for Human Services for Older People. LC 78-27668. 1979. text ed. 19.95 (ISBN 0-87705-381-2). Human Sci Pr.

Holmes, Oakley, Jr. The Complete Annotated Resource Guide to Black American Art. LC 78-112785. 275p. 1978. pap. text ed. 12.00 (ISBN 0-9604026-4-0). O N Holmes.

--The Complete Annotated Resource Guide to Black American Art. (Orig.). pap. 12.00 (ISBN 0-686-27594-2, 0960426). O N Holmes.

Holmes, Oliver W. Ralph Waldo Emerson. LC 67-23884. 1967. Repr. of 1885 ed. 20.00 (ISBN 0-8103-3039-3). Gale.

--Ralph Waldo Emerson. LC 80-23687. (American Men & Women of Letters Ser.). 330p. 1981. pap. 5.95 (ISBN 0-87754-157-4). Chelsea Hse.

Holmes, Oliver W., Jr. Collected Legal Papers. 8.50 (ISBN 0-8446-1241-3). Peter Smith.

--The Common Law. 1964. 15.00 (ISBN 0-316-37131-9); pap. 4.95. Little.

--Representative Opinions of Mr. Justice Holmes. Lief, Alfred, compiled by. LC 76-156194. 319p. 1972. Repr. of 1931 ed. lib. bdg. 22.50x (ISBN 0-8371-6143-6, HORO). Greenwood.

Holmes, Oliver Wendell. Holmes-Sheehan Correspondence: The Letters of Justice Oliver W. Holmes, Jr. & Canon Patrick Augustine Sheehan. Burton, David H., ed. 1976. 8.95 (ISBN 0-8046-9164-9, National University Pub). Kennikat.

Holmes, Paul C. Phonics Guidelines: An Introduction. 320p. 1980. pap. text ed. 12.95 (ISBN 0-8403-2225-9). Kendall-Hunt.

Holmes, Paul C. & Souza, Harry E. The Touch of a Poet. 1976. pap. text ed. 10.50 scp o.p. (ISBN 0-06-042869-4, HarpC). Har-Row.

Holmes, R. L. & Ball, J. N. The Pituitary Gland. LC 73-75856. (Biological Structure & Function Ser.: No. 4). (Illus.). 300p. 1974. 79.00 (ISBN 0-521-20247-7). Cambridge U Pr.

Holmes, R. L., jt. ed. see Harrison, R. J.

Holmes, Reed M. The Forerunners. 1981. pap. price not set (ISBN 0-8309-0315-1). Herald Hse.

Holmes, Richard. Communities in Transition: Bedford & Lincoln, Massachusetts, Seventeen Twenty-Nine to Eighteen Fifty. Berkhofer, Robert, ed. (Studies in American History & Culture III). 285p. 1980. 27.95 (ISBN 0-8357-1098-X, Pub by UMI Res Pr). Univ Microfilms.

Holmes, Robert R. Pentacoordinated Phosphorus. Incl. Structure & Spectroscopy. (No. 175). Vol. I. 92.00 (ISBN 0-8412-0458-6); Reaction Mechanisms. (176). Vol. II. 52.00 (ISBN 0-8412-0528-0); Set. 144.00 (ISBN 0-8412-0529-9). LC 80-26302. (Acs Monograph). 1980. Am Chemical.

--Pentacoordinated Phosphorus. Incl. Vol. 1, Structure & Spectroscopy. (No. 175). 92.00 (ISBN 0-8412-0458-6); Vol. 2, Reaction Mechanisms. (No. 176). 52.00 (ISBN 0-8412-0528-0). (ACS Monograph). 1980. Set. 144.00 (ISBN 0-8412-0529-9). Am Chemical.

Holmes, Ronald. Witchcraft in History. 1977. pap. 5.95 (ISBN 0-8065-0575-3). Citadel Pr.

Holmes, Roy. Easy Magic: Good Tricks & How to Present Them. (Illus.). 144p. pap. 2.25 o.p. (ISBN 0-06-463412-4, 412, EH). Har-Row.

Holmes, Sandra. Henderson's Dictionary of Biological Terms. 9th ed. 521p. text ed. 29.95 (ISBN 0-442-24865-2). Van Nos Reinhold.

Holmes, Timothy. Vile Florentines. 196p. 1981. 10.95 (ISBN 0-312-84677-0). St Martin.

Holmes, Urban. Medieval Man: His Understanding of Himself, His Society, & the World: Illustrated from His Own Literature. (Studies in the Romance Languages & Literatures). 1980. pap. 16.00x o.p. (ISBN 0-8078-9212-2). U of NC Pr.

--The Priest in Community: Exploring the Roots of Ministry. LC 78-17645. 1978. 8.95 (ISBN 0-8164-0400-3). Crossroad NY.

Holmes, Urban T. Future Shape of Ministry. pap. 5.95 (ISBN 0-8164-2025-4). Crossroad NY.

--Introduction to the History of Christian Spirituality. 176p. 1980. 8.95 (ISBN 0-8164-0141-1). Crossroad NY.

--Ministry & Imagination. 1976. 10.95 (ISBN 0-8164-0292-2). Crossroad NY.

--Praying with the Family of God. 1979. pap. 7.50 (ISBN 0-03-043931-0); 3.95 (ISBN 0-03-049551-2). Winston Pr.
--Praying with the Family of God: Leader Guide. 1980. pap. 3.95 (ISBN 0-03-049551-2). Winston Pr.
--Young Children & the Eucharist. pap. 2.95 (ISBN 0-8164-5700-X). Crossroad NY.
Holmes, Urban T., jt. auth. see Barnhouse, Ruth T.
Holmes, Urban T., jt. auth. see Terwilliger, Robert E.
Holmes, Urban T., jt. ed. see Cabeen, David C.
Holmes, Urban T., Jr. Daily Living in the Twelfth Century: Based on the Observations of Alexander Neckam in London & Paris. (Illus.). 1952. pap. 7.95x (ISBN 0-299-00854-1). U of Wis Pr.
--Daily Living in the Twelfth Century: Based on the Observations of Alexander Neckam in London & Paris. LC 80-19991. (Illus.). ix, 337p. 1980. Repr. of 1973 ed. lib. bdg. 29.50x (ISBN 0-313-22796-9, HODL). Greenwood.
Holmes, Urban T., 3rd. The Confirmation Issue: Celebrations of Maturity in Christ. 112p. (Orig.). 1975. pap. 3.95 (ISBN 0-8164-2589-2). Crossroad NY.
--To Speak of God: Theology for Beginners. 1974. 6.95 (ISBN 0-8164-1169-7). Crossroad NY.
Holmes, Urban T., 3rd, jt. ed. see Stough, Furman C.
Holmes, W. D., jt. auth. see Waltham, J. E.
Holmes, W. J. Double-Edged Secrets. 1981. pap. 2.95 (ISBN 0-425-04714-8). Berkley Pub.
--Underseas Victory I. (Zebra World at War Ser.: No. 10). 352p. 1980. pap. 2.50 (ISBN 0-89083-613-2). Zebra.
Holmes-Walker, W. A. Polymer Conversion. LC 74-11510. 286p. 1975. 41.95 (ISBN 0-470-40767-0). Halsted Pr.
Holmgren, John H. Purchasing for the Health Care Facility. (Illus.). 288p. 1975. 28.75 (ISBN 0-398-03399-4). C C Thomas.
Holmgren, Rod & Norton, William. The Mass Media Book. 416p. 1972. pap. text ed. 10.95 (ISBN 0-13-559781-1). P-H.
Holmquist, ed. Life Sciences & Space Research XVIII: Committee on Space Research. 1980. 53.00 (ISBN 0-08-024436-X). Pergamon.
Holmquist, Ingrid. From Society to Nature: A Study of Doris Lessing's "Children of Violence". (Gothenburg Studies in English: No. 46). 1980. pap. 19.75x (ISBN 91-7346-083-4). Humanities.
Holmquist, R., ed. Life Sciences & Space Research. LC 63-6132. 1977. text ed. 53.00 (ISBN 0-08-021635-8). Pergamon.
--Life Sciences & Space Research XVII. (Illus.). 1979. text ed. 53.00 (ISBN 0-08-023416-X). Pergamon.
Holms, R., jt. auth. see Beck, L.
Holmstedt, B., jt. ed. see Costa, E.
Holmstrom, Lakshmi. The Novels of R. K. Narayan. (Writers Workshop Greybird Ser.). 130p. 1975. 15.00 (ISBN 0-88253-584-6); pap. text ed. 8.00 (ISBN 0-88253-583-8). Ind-US Inc.
Holmstrom, Lynda L. & Burgess, Ann W. The Victim of Rape: Institutional Reactions. LC 77-27074. 1978. 18.95 (ISBN 0-471-40785-2, Pub. by Wiley-Interscience). Wiley.
Holmstrom, Lynda L., jt. auth. see Burgess, Ann W.
Holoien, Renee A., jt. ed. see Patton, Peter C.
Holorenshaw, Henry. Levellers & the English Revolution. LC 73-80559. 1971. Repr. 12.50 (ISBN 0-86527-116-X). Fertig.
Holoway Staff. Greek. (Harper Phrase Books for the Traveler Ser.). (Orig.). 1977. pap. 1.00 (ISBN 0-8467-0311-4, Holloway). Hippocrene Bks.
Holquist, Michael, ed. see Bakhtin, M. M.
Holroyd, Howard B. Quest for Valid Economics. 1981. 12.95 (ISBN 0-533-04830-3). Vantage.
Holroyd, Sam V., jt. auth. see Requa-Clark, Barbara.
Holroyd, Sam V., ed. Clinical Pharmacology in Dental Practice. 2nd ed. LC 77-22265. (Illus.). 1978. pap. text ed. 19.95 (ISBN 0-8016-2241-7). Mosby.
Holscher, Harry H. Simplified Statistical Analysis: Handbook of Methods, Examples & Tables. LC 78-132672. (Illus.). 1971. 19.95 (ISBN 0-8436-0305-4). CBI Pub.
Holsinger, James W., ed. Self-Assessment of Current Knowledge in Internal Medicine. 4th ed. LC 79-91971. 1980. pap. 16.50 (ISBN 0-87488-257-5). Med Exam.
Holsinger, James W., Jr. & Miscia, Vincent F. Cardiology Specialty Board Review. 1975. spiral bdg. 16.50 (ISBN 0-87488-314-8). Med Exam.
Holst, Art. Sunday Zebras. 1980. 10.00 (ISBN 0-9605118-0-6). Forest Pub.
Holst, Hermann E. von see Von Holst, Hermann E.
Holst, Imogen. A B C of Music: A Short Practical Guide to the Basic Essentials of Rudiments, Harmony, & Form. (Orig.). 1963. 8.95x (ISBN 0-19-317103-1). Oxford U Pr.
--Britten. (The Great Composer Ser.). (gr. 9 up). 1980. 10.95 (ISBN 0-571-18000-0, Pub. by Faber & Faber). Merrimack Bk Serv.
--Byrd. (Great Composers Ser.). (Illus.). 1972. 7.95 o.p. (ISBN 0-571-09813-4, Pub. by Faber & Faber). Merrimack Bk Serv.
--Holst. (Great Composers Ser.). (Illus.). 1974. 7.95 o.p. (ISBN 0-571-09967-X, Pub. by Faber & Faber). Merrimack Bk Serv.
--Your Book of Music. (Your Book Ser.). (Illus.). 1964. 4.95 o.p. (ISBN 0-571-05917-1, Pub. by Faber & Faber). Merrimack Bk Serv.
Holst, J. J. & Schneider, W., Jr., eds. Why A B M? Policy Issues in the Missile Defense Controversy. 1969. 12.75 (ISBN 0-08-015625-8). Pergamon.
Holst, Per. Computer Simulation, 1951-1976: An Index to the Literature. 1979. 49.50 (ISBN 0-7201-0734-2, Pub. by Mansell England). Merrimack Bk Serv.
Holstein, G., tr. see Paalman, Anthony.
Holstein, J. E., jt. auth. see Williams, Frederick.
Holstein, Jonathon. Pieced Quilt: An American Design Tradition. LC 73-79991. (Illus.). 1975. pap. 12.95 (ISBN 0-8212-0686-9, 707317). NYGS.
Holstein, Philip M., jt. ed. see Erdman, Donnelley.
Holsti, Kalvei J. International Politics: A Framework for Analysis. 3rd ed. (Illus.). 1977. 17.95 (ISBN 0-13-473371-1). P-H.
Holsti, O. R. Content Analysis for the Social Sciences & Humanities. (Orig.). 1969. pap. text ed. 10.95 (ISBN 0-201-02940-5). A-W.
Holsti, Ole R., et al, eds. Change in the International System. 460p. 1980. lib. bdg. 27.50x (ISBN 0-89158-846-9); pap. text ed. 12.50x (ISBN 0-89158-895-7). Westview.
Holsworth, Robert D. Public Interest Liberalism & the Crisis of Affluence: Reflections on Nader, Environmentalism, & the Politics of a Sustainable Society. (Reference Bks.). 1980. lib. bdg. 17.50 (ISBN 0-8161-9032-1). G K Hall.
Holt, Alfred H. American Place Names. LC 68-26574. 1969. Repr. of 1938 ed. 15.00 (ISBN 0-8103-3235-3). Gale.
--Phrase & Word Origins: A Study of Familiar Expressions. 2nd ed. Orig. Title: Phrase Origins. 1961. pap. 4.00 (ISBN 0-486-20758-7). Dover.
Holt, Arthur G. Handwriting in Psychological Interpretations. (Illus.). 276p. 1974. text ed. 21.75 (ISBN 0-398-00864-7). C C Thomas.
Holt, Charles A. Electronic Circuits: Digital & Analog. LC 77-11654. 1978. 26.95x (ISBN 0-471-02313-2); tchr's manual avail. (ISBN 0-471-03044-9). Wiley.
Holt, Charles C., et al. Unemployment-Inflation Dilemma: A Manpower Solution. 1970. pap. 2.95 o.p. (ISBN 0-87766-009-3, 60003). Urban Inst.
Holt, Claire, tr. see Lubis, Mochtar.
Holt, D. B., et al, eds. Quantitative Scanning Electron Microscopy. 1975. 79.00 (ISBN 0-12-353850-5). Acad Pr.
Holt, Dave & Holt, Pat. How Not to Raise Cain. 1978. pap. 1.95 (ISBN 0-88207-515-2). Victor Bks.
Holt, David B. & Haneman, Dan. Defects & Surfaces in Semiconducting Materials & Devices. (International Series in the Science of the Solid State: Vol. 12). Date not set. cancelled (ISBN 0-08-020620-4). Pergamon.
Holt, Edgar A. Claiborne County. Dunn, Joy B. & Crawford, Charles W., eds. (Tennessee County History Ser.: No. 13). (Illus.). 144p. 1981. 12.50x (ISBN 0-87870-101-X). Memphis St Univ.
Holt, Elizabeth G. The Art of All Nations, 1850-1873: A Continuation of the Triumph of Art for the Public. LC 80-1666. (Illus.). 640p. (Orig.). 1981. pap. 8.95 (ISBN 0-385-14879-8, Anch). Doubleday.
Holt, Elizabeth G., ed. A Documentary History of Art, Vol. 1. pap. 3.50 ea. (Anch); Vol. 1. pap. (ISBN 0-385-09320-9); Vol. 2. pap. (ISBN 0-385-09366-7). Doubleday.
Holt, Elizabeth Gilmore, ed. Triumph of Art for the Public: The Emerging Role of Exhibitions & Critics. LC 77-27708. 1979. pap. 5.95 (ISBN 0-385-13511-4, Anch). Doubleday.
Holt, Emily S. Ye Olden Time: English Customs in the Middle Ages. LC 72-164343. 1971. Repr. of 1884 ed. 15.00 (ISBN 0-8103-3798-3). Gale.
Holt, Francis L. The Law of Libel, in Which Is Contained a General History of This Law in the Ancient Codes, & of Its Introduction, & Successive Alterations in the Law of England, Comprehending a Digest of All the Leading Cases Upon Libels. Berkowitz, David & Thorne, Samuel, eds. LC 77-89192. (Classics of English Legal History in the Modern Era Ser.: Vol. 115). 1979. Repr. of 1812 ed. lib. bdg. 55.00 (ISBN 0-8240-3152-0). Garland Pub.
Holt, G. O. A Regional History of the Railways of Great Britain: The North West, Vol. 10. 1978. 19.95 (ISBN 0-7153-7521-0). David & Charles.
Holt, George C. The Concurrent Jurisdiction of the Federal & State Courts. xxvi, 237p. 1980. Repr. of 1888 ed. lib. bdg. 24.00x (ISBN 0-8377-0630-0). Rothman.
Holt, Glen & Pacyga, Dominic A. Chicago: A Historical Guide to Neighborhoods. 1980. pap. 8.95 (ISBN 0-686-65047-6, 10413-3). U of Chicago Pr.
Holt, Glen E. & Pacyga, Dominic A. Chicago: a Historical Guide to the Neighborhoods: Vol. I: the Loop & South Side, Vol. 1. LC 78-60184. (Illus.). 174p. 1979. pap. 8.95 (ISBN 0-913820-07-5). Chicago Hist.
Holt, Helen. One Love Lost. (Aston Hall Romances Ser.). 192p. 1981. pap. 1.75 (ISBN 0-523-41130-8). Pinnacle Bks.
Holt, Herbert. Free to Be Good or Bad. 1977. pap. 2.50 o.p. (ISBN 0-06-464005-1, BN). Har-Row.
Holt, Jerry. Making for the Falcon: Studies in Recent Film. 1976. pap. text ed. 7.25x (ISBN 0-8191-0017-X). U Pr of Amer.
Holt, John. Escape from Childhood: The Needs & Rights of Children. LC 73-18060. 1974. 7.95 o.p. (ISBN 0-525-09955-7). Dutton.
--How Children Fail. pap. text ed. 1.95 (ISBN 0-440-33869-7). Dell.
Holt, John D. Monarchy in Hawaii. rev., 2nd ed. 1971. pap. 3.50 (ISBN 0-686-63589-2). Topgallant.
Holt, John G. Supplement to the Index Bergeyana. 387p. 1981. write for info. (4106-1). Williams & Wilkins.
Holt, Kare. The Race. (YA) 1976. 8.95 o.s.i. (ISBN 0-440-07198-4, Sey Lawr). Delacorte.
Holt, Kenneth S. Developmental Pediatrics. (Postgraduate Pediatric Ser.). 304p. 1977. 14.95 (ISBN 0-407-00065-8). Butterworths.
Holt, Lockie. Once Upon a Mouse. LC 79-1868. (Illus.). (ps-2). 1979. 1.95 (ISBN 0-525-69006-9, Gingerbread Bks); DLLB 5.95 (ISBN 0-525-69007-7). Dutton.
Holt, Marion P. The Contemporary Spanish Theater, 1949-1972. (World Authors Ser.: Spain: No. 336). 1975. lib. bdg. 12.50 (ISBN 0-8057-2243-2). Twayne.
Holt, Marion P., ed. Modern Spanish Stage for Plays. LC 78-106966. 388p. 1970. pap. 6.95 (ISBN 0-8090-0746-0). Hill & Wang.
Holt, Maurice. The Common Curriculum: Its Structure & Style in the Comprehensive School. (Education Bks.). 1978. 16.00x (ISBN 0-7100-8895-7). Routledge & Kegan.
Holt, Maurice, ed. Basic Developments in Fluid Dynamics, 2 Vols. Vol. 1. 1965. 55.25 (ISBN 0-12-354001-1); Vol. 2, 1968. 36.50 (ISBN 0-12-354002-X). Acad Pr.
Holt, Michael. Maps, Tracks, & the Bridges of Konigsberg: A Book About Networks. LC 74-31176. (Young Math Ser.). (Illus.). 40p. (gr. k-3). 1975. 7.95 (ISBN 0-690-00746-9, TYC-J); PLB 7.89 (ISBN 0-690-00753-1). T Y Crowell.
--More Math Puzzles & Games. LC 77-75319. 1978. 7.95 o.s.i. (ISBN 0-8027-0561-8); pap. 3.95 (ISBN 0-8027-7114-9). Walker & Co.
Holt, Michael F. Political Crisis of the 1850's. LC 77-13564. (Critical Episodes in American Politics Ser.). 1978. text ed. 11.95 o.p. (ISBN 0-471-40840-9); pap. text ed. 8.95 (ISBN 0-471-40841-7). Wiley.
Holt, Nancy. Ransacked Aunt Ethel: An Ending. LC 79-92752. 1980. pap. 5.00 (ISBN 0-930378-11-3). Printed Matter.
Holt, P. M. & Lambton, Ann, eds. Cambridge History of Islam: Central Islamic Lands from Pre Islamic Times to the First World War, Vol. 1A. (Illus.). 1977. 59.00 (ISBN 0-521-21946-9); pap. 19.95 (ISBN 0-521-29135-6). Cambridge U Pr.
--Cambridge History of Islam: Central Islamic Lands Since 1918, Vol. 1B. 1977. 42.00 (ISBN 0-521-21947-7); pap. 14.95 (ISBN 0-521-29136-4). Cambridge U Pr.
Holt, P. M., et al, eds. The Cambridge History of Islam: Islamic Society & Civilisation, Vol. 2B. LC 73-77291. (Illus.). 1978. 59.00 (ISBN 0-521-21949-3); pap. 21.95 (ISBN 0-521-29138-0). Cambridge U Pr.
--The Cambridge History of Islam: The Indian Sub-Continent, South-East Asia, Africa & the Muslim West, Vol. 2A. (Illus.). 1978. 48.00 (ISBN 0-521-21948-5); pap. 18.50 (ISBN 0-521-29137-2). Cambridge U Pr.
--Cambridge History of Islam. Incl. Vol. 1A. Central Islamic Lands from Pre-Islamic Times to the First World War. 59.00 (ISBN 0-521-21946-9); pap. 19.95 (ISBN 0-521-29135-6); Vol. 1B. Central Islamic Lands Since 1918. 42.00 (ISBN 0-521-21947-7); pap. 14.95 (ISBN 0-521-29136-4); Vol. 2A. The Indian Subcontinent, Southeast Asia, Africa & the Muslim West. 48.00 (ISBN 0-521-21948-5); pap. 18.50 (ISBN 0-521-29137-2); Vol. 2B. Islamic Society & Civilization. 59.00 (ISBN 0-521-21949-3); pap. 21.95 (ISBN 0-521-29138-0). 1977-78. Set. 178.00 (ISBN 0-521-22310-5); Set. pap. 62.00 (ISBN 0-521-08755-4). Cambridge U Pr.
Holt, Pat, jt. auth. see Holt, Dave.
Holt, Pat M. United States Policy in Foreign Affairs. (Studies in Political Science). (Orig.). (gr. 10-12). 1971. pap. text ed. 3.60 o.p. (ISBN 0-205-02871-3, 7628714). Allyn.
--War Powers Resolution: The Role of Congress in U. S. Armed Intervention. 1978. pap. 4.25 (ISBN 0-8447-3299-0). Am Enterprise.
Holt, Perry C., et al, eds. The Distributional History of the Biota of the Southern Appalachians, 3 vols. Incl. Pt. 1. Invertebrates. 1969. pap. 4.95x (ISBN 0-8139-0538-9); Pt 2. Flora. 1970. pap. 5.95x (ISBN 0-8139-0539-7); Pt 3. Vertebrates. 1971. pap. 5.95x o.p. (ISBN 0-8139-0540-0); Pt. 4, Algae & Fungi. Parker, Bruce C. & Roane, Martha K., eds. LC 75-636021. 1977. 20.00x (ISBN 0-8139-0660-1). Set, Pt. I-III. 15.00x o.p. (ISBN 0-685-56113-5). U Pr of Va.
Holt, Peter M. Egypt & the Fertile Crescent, 1516-1922: A Political History. LC 66-18429. 1969. pap. 6.95 (ISBN 0-8014-9079-0, CP79). Cornell U Pr.
Holt, R. C. & Hume, J. N. Fundamentals of Structured Programming Using FORTRAN with SF-K & WATFIV-S. (Illus.). 1977. pap. text ed. 12.95 (ISBN 0-87909-302-1); case ed. 14.95 (ISBN 0-8359-7131-7). Reston.
Holt, R. C., jt. auth. see Hume, J. N.
Holt, Rackham. George Washington Carver: An American Biography. LC 62-11430. 1963. 7.95 (ISBN 0-385-03045-2). Doubleday.
Holt, Richard. Sport & Society in Modern France. 1980. 25.00 (ISBN 0-208-01887-5, Archon). Shoe String.
Holt, Richard C., et al. Structured Concurrent Programming with Operating Systems Applications. 1978. pap. text ed. 10.95 (ISBN 0-201-02937-5). A-W.
Holt, Robert. Straight Teeth: Orthodontics & Dental Care for Everyone. LC 80-10562. (Illus.). 224p. 1980. 13.95 (ISBN 0-688-03625-2); pap. 7.95 (ISBN 0-688-08625-X). Morrow.
Holt, Robert L. Bonds: How to Double Your Money Quickly & Safely. LC 80-66576. 1980. 10.00x (ISBN 0-930926-03-X). Calif Health.
--How Women Stay Slim. LC 80-92693. 1980. 12.95x (ISBN 0-930926-04-8); pap. 7.95x (ISBN 0-930926-05-6). Calif Health.
Holt, Robert T. & Turner, John E., eds. The Methodology of Comparative Political Research. LC 70-80471. 1972. 10.95 (ISBN 0-02-914850-2); pap. text ed. 5.95 (ISBN 0-02-914840-5). Free Pr.
Holt, Rochelle, tr. see Carrington, Leonora.
Holt, Smith, et al, eds. Solid State Chemistry: A Contemporary Overview. LC 80-17185. (Advances in Chemistry Ser.: No. 186). 1980. 59.50 (ISBN 0-8412-0472-1). Am Chemical.
Holt, Thomas J. Total Investing. 1976. 8.95 o.p. (ISBN 0-87000-357-7). Arlington Hse.
Holt, Victoria. Bride of Pendorric. LC 63-12964. 10.95 (ISBN 0-385-01523-2). Doubleday.
--Bride of Pendorric. 272p. 1981. pap. 2.50 (ISBN 0-449-23280-8, Crest). Fawcett.
--Bride of Pendorric. 1978. pap. 1.95 o.p. (ISBN 0-449-23280-8, Crest). Fawcett.
--The Curse of the Kings. 1978. pap. 2.50 (ISBN 0-449-23284-0, Crest). Fawcett.
--The House of a Thousand Lanterns. 384p. 1978. pap. 2.25 (ISBN 0-449-23685-4, Crest). Fawcett.
--King of the Castle. 1978. pap. 2.25 (ISBN 0-449-23587-4, Crest). Fawcett.
--Kirkland Revels. LC 62-7646. 1962. 10.95 (ISBN 0-385-00061-8). Doubleday.
--Kirkland Revels. 1978. pap. 2.25 (ISBN 0-449-23920-9, Crest). Fawcett.
--Legend of the Seventh Virgin. 1978. pap. 1.95 o.p. (ISBN 0-449-23281-6, Crest). Fawcett.
--Legend of the Seventh Virgin. 288p. 1981. pap. 2.50 (ISBN 0-449-23281-6, Crest). Fawcett.
--Lord of the Far Island. 320p. 1978. pap. 2.25 (ISBN 0-449-22874-6, Crest). Fawcett.
--The Mask of the Enchantress. 1980. lib. bdg. 16.95 (ISBN 0-8161-3142-2, Large Print Bks). G K Hall.
--Mistress of Mellyn. 240p. 1978. pap. 2.25 (ISBN 0-449-23924-1, Crest). Fawcett.
--On the Night of the Seventh Moon. 1978. pap. 1.95 (ISBN 0-449-23568-8, Crest). Fawcett.
--The Secret Woman. 352p. 1981. pap. 2.50 (ISBN 0-449-23283-2, Crest). Fawcett.
--Shadow of the Lynx. LC 72-144273. 1971. 11.95 (ISBN 0-385-05427-0). Doubleday.

--The Shadow of the Lynx. 320p. 1981. pap. 2.50 (ISBN 0-449-23278-6, Crest). Fawcett.
--The Shivering Sands. 1978. pap. 1.95 o.p. (ISBN 0-449-23282-4, Crest). Fawcett.
--The Shivering Sands. 288p. 1981. pap. 2.50 (ISBN 0-449-23282-4, Crest). Fawcett.
Holt, Virginia, tr. see Muir, John.
Holtan, O. I. Introduction to Theatre: A Mirror to Nature. (Theatre & Drama Ser.). (Illus.). 240p. 1976. ref. ed. 14.95 (ISBN 0-13-498741-1). P-H.
Holtbecker, H., jt. auth. see Coen, V.
Holte, Susan & Wynar, Bohdan S., eds. Best Reference Books, 1970-1980: Titles of Lasting Value Selected from American Reference Books Annual. 450p. 1981. lib. bdg. 30.00x (ISBN 0-87287-255-6). Libs Unl.
Holtham, Gerald & Hazelwood, Arthur. Aid & Inequality in Kenya: British Development Assistance to Kenya. 1976. text ed. 25.00x o.p. (ISBN 0-8419-5508-5). Holmes & Meier.
Holtje, Herbert, jt. ed. see Stockwell, John.
Holt-Jensen, Arild. The Norwegian Wilderness: National Parks & Protected Areas. LC 79-321366. (Tokens of Norway Ser.). (Illus.). 78p. (Orig.). 1978. pap. 10.50x (ISBN 82-518-0719-0). Intl Pubns Serv.
Holtman, Robert B. Napoleonic Revolution. LC 67-11308. (Critical Periods of History Ser). (Illus.). 1967. pap. 4.50 o.p. (ISBN 0-397-47134-3). Lippincott.
Holtom, Pat, jt. auth. see Sutton, Ann.
Holton, Frances. Home from Hawaii. (YA) 5.95 (ISBN 0-685-19058-7, Avalon). Bouregy.
Holton, G. The Scientific Imagination. LC 76-47196. (Illus.). 1978. 39.95 (ISBN 0-521-21700-8); pap. 10.95 (ISBN 0-521-29237-9). Cambridge U Pr.
Holton, G. E. Guatemala-Indios De Guatemala. (Illus.). 10.00 o.p. (ISBN 0-911268-08-1). Rogers Bk.
Holton, George S. Metamorphosis of a Poet. 1981. 7.95 (ISBN 0-533-04886-9). Vantage.
Holton, Gerald, jt. ed. see Graubard, Stephen R.
Holton, Gerald J. Introduction to Concepts & Theories in Physical Science. 2nd ed. LC 72-2787. 1973. text ed. 19.95 (ISBN 0-201-02971-5). A-W.
Holton, J., et al. Spanish Review Grammar: Theory & Practice. 1977. 14.95 (ISBN 0-13-824409-X). P-H.
Holton, Pamela & Emmelin, N., eds. Pharmacology of Gastrointestinal Secretion. 700p. 1974. Set. 125.00 (ISBN 0-08-016552-4). Pergamon.
Holton, Richard H., jt. ed. see Sethi, S. Prakash.
Holton, S. Fantastic Worlds. 1978. pap. 7.95 (ISBN 0-931064-03-1). Starlog Pr.
Holton, Scot, jt. auth. see Skotak, Robert.
Holtrop, ed. see Newell, Adnah C.
Holtrop, Wm., jt. auth. see Cunningham, Beryl M.
Holtsmark, Erling B. Tarzan & Tradition: Classical Myth in Popular Literature. LC 80-1023. (Contributions to the Study of Popular Culture: No. 1). (Illus.). 216p. 1981. lib. bdg. 22.50 (ISBN 0-313-22530-3, HOT/). Greenwood.
Holty, Carl, jt. auth. see Bearden, Romare.
Holtz, Herman R. & Schmidt, Terry D. The Winning Proposal: How to Write It. (Business Communication Ser.). (Illus.). 384p. 1981. text ed. 18.95x (ISBN 0-07-029649-9). McGraw.
Holtz, R., jt. auth. see Kovaco, W.
Holtz, Robert D., jt. auth. see Kovacs, William D.
Holtz, William V. Image & Immortality: A Study of Tristram Shandy. LC 79-118582. (Illus.). 175p. 1970. 8.00x (ISBN 0-87057-121-4, Pub. by Brown U Pr). Univ Pr of New England.
Holtzclaw, Robert F. The Saints Go Marching in. LC 78-71499. (Illus.). 216p. 1980. 12.50 (ISBN 0-933144-00-8). Keeble Pr.
--William Henry Holtzclaw: Scholar in Ebony. LC 76-29278. (Illus.). 252p. 1977. 8.92 (ISBN 0-913228-19-2). Keeble Pr.
Holtzman, Abraham. American Government: Ideals & Reality. (Illus.). 1980. pap. text ed. 12.50 (ISBN 0-13-027151-9). P-H.
Holtzman, Jerome, jt. auth. see Gorman, Tom.
Holtzman, Jerry. Fielder's Choice: An Anthology of Baseball Fiction. 1979. 12.95 o.p. (ISBN 0-15-130681-8). HarBraceJ.
Holtzman, W. H., jt. auth. see Moore, Bernice M.
Holtzmann, Adolf. Uber den Umlaut: Zwei Abhandlungen & Uber den Ablaut. (Amsterdam Classics in Linguistics 1800-1925: No. 12). 1979. text ed. 27.50x (ISBN 90-272-0871-9). Humanities.
Holum, Dianne. World of Speed Skating. (Illus.). 320p. 1981. 17.50 (ISBN 0-89490-051-X). Enslow Pubs.
Holum, John R. Fundamentals of General, Organic, & Biological Chemistry. LC 77-10418. 1978. text ed. 23.95x (ISBN 0-471-40873-5); study guide 7.50 (ISBN 0-471-02454-6); tchr's manual avail. (ISBN 0-471-03669-2). Wiley.
--Organic & Biological Chemistry. LC 78-634. 1978. text ed. 19.95x (ISBN 0-471-40872-7). Wiley.
--Organic Chemistry: A Brief Course. LC 74-20773. (Illus.). 528p. 1975. text ed. 19.95x (ISBN 0-471-40849-2); solutions manual 5.50 (ISBN 0-471-40861-1); instructors' manual avail. (ISBN 0-471-51716-X). Wiley.
--Topics & Terms in Environmental Problems. LC 77-12805. 1977. 31.00 (ISBN 0-471-01982-8, Pub. by Wiley-Interscience). Wiley.
Holway, John. Voices from the Great Black Baseball Leagues. LC 75-11931. (Illus.). 384p. 1975. 9.95 (ISBN 0-396-07124-4). Dodd.
Holweck, Frederick G. Biographical Dictionary of the Saints. LC 68-30625. 1969. Repr. of 1924 ed. 40.00 (ISBN 0-8103-3158-6). Gale.
Holy, M. Erosion & Environment. (Environmental Sciences & Applications: Vol. 9). (Illus.). 266p. 1980. 58.00 (ISBN 0-08-024466-1). Pergamon.
Holy Transfiguration Monastery, ed. & tr. see Mother Martha.
Holy Transfiguration Monastery, tr. from Rus. Seraphim's Seraphim: The Life of Pelagia Ivanovna Serebrenikova, Fool for Christ's Sake of the Seraphim-Diveyevo Convent. LC 79-90720. (Illus.). 184p. (Orig.). 1980. pap. 4.50 (ISBN 0-913026-08-5). St Nectarios.
Holyoake, Janet. Your Book of Keeping Ponies. 2nd ed. (Your Book Ser.). (Illus.). 1968. 6.95 (ISBN 0-571-04604-5, Pub. by Faber & Faber). Merrimack Bk Serv.
Holz, Arno. Deutsches Dichterjubilaum: A Facsimile in Color & Halftone of the Special Hand-Colored Edition of 1923. 1977. 15.00 (ISBN 0-88233-279-1). Kylix Pr.
Holz, Loretta. The Christmas Spider: A Puppet Play from Poland & Other Traditional Games, Crafts & Activities. (gr. 3-7). 5.95 (ISBN 0-399-20754-6); lib. bdg. 5.99g (ISBN 0-399-61164-9). Philomel.
Holz, R. K., et al. Mendes I. Hall, E. S. & Bothmer, B. V., eds. (Illus.). 83p. 45.00 (ISBN 0-936770-02-3). Am Res Ctr Egypt.
Holz, Robert K., ed. Surveillant Sceince: Remote Sensing of the Environment. LC 72-7922. (Illus.). 300p. (Orig.). 1973. pap. text ed. 15.25 (ISBN 0-395-14041-2, 3-25711). HM.
Holzbecher, Z., et al. Organic Reagents in Inorganic Analysis. LC 75-34459. (Ser. in Analytical Chemistry). 734p. 1976. 85.95 (ISBN 0-470-01396-6). Halsted Pr.
Holzer, E., ed. see Wilcockson, John.
Holzer, H. & Tschesche, J., eds. Biological Functions of Proteinases. (Colloquium Mosbach: Vol. 30). (Illus.). 1980. 42.90 (ISBN 0-387-09683-3). Springer-Verlag.
Holzer, Hans. Beyond Medicine. 192p. 1974. pap. 1.95 (ISBN 0-345-28001-6). Ballantine.
--Demonic Possession. (Orig.). 1980. pap. 2.25 (ISBN 0-532-23128-7). Manor Bks.
--In Search of Ghosts. (Orig.). 1979. pap. 2.25 (ISBN 0-532-23272-0). Manor Bks.
--Inside Witchcraft. (Orig.). 1980. pap. 2.25 (ISBN 0-532-23220-8). Manor Bks.
--More Than One Life. (Orig.). 1980. pap. 2.25 (ISBN 0-532-23127-9). Manor Bks.
--The Power of Hypnosis. LC 72-7841. 1973. 5.95 o.p. (ISBN 0-672-51584-9). Bobbs.
--Psychic Healing. (Orig.). 1979. pap. 2.25 (ISBN 0-532-23123-6). Manor Bks.
--The Ufonauts. 304p. (Orig.). 1978. pap. 1.75 o.p. (ISBN 0-449-13569-1, GM). Fawcett.
--Westghosts: The Psychic World of California. LC 77-88693. 253p. 1980. pap. 5.95 (ISBN 0-8040-0759-4). Swallow.
--Yankee Ghosts. LC 66-16029. 1966. 5.00 o.p. (ISBN 0-672-50856-7). Bobbs.
Holzman, Carl & Holzman, Phoebe. How to Select & Use Photographic Gadgets. (Illus.). 1980. pap. 7.95 (ISBN 0-89586-043-0). H P Bks.
--Photographic Gadgets. (Illus.). 160p. 1980. pap. 7.95 (ISBN 0-89586-043-0). H P Bks.
Holzman, Phoebe, jt. auth. see Holzman, Carl.
Holzman, Robert S. Business Tax Traps & How to Avoid Them. LC 80-23343. 1980. 50.00 (ISBN 0-686-51196-4). Boardroom.
--Dun & Bradstreet's Handbook of Executive Tax Management. 512p. 1974. 25.00 o.p. (ISBN 0-690-00309-9, TYC-T). T Y Crowell.
--Encyclopedia of Estate Planning. LC 80-19441. 312p. 1980. 50.00 (ISBN 0-932648-15-0). Boardroom.
--Take It Off! One Thousand Four Hundred & Fourteen Tax Deductions Most People Overlook: One Thousand Four Hundred & Fourteen Tax Deductions Most Poeple Overlook. 6th, annual ed. LC 79-18542. 1979. 10.95 o.p. (ISBN 0-690-01843-6, TYC-T); pap. 5.95 o.p. (ISBN 0-690-01844-4, TYC-T). T Y Crowell.
--Take It off! One Thousand Six Hundred Ninety-Five Tax Deductions Most People Overlook. rev. ed. 336p. 1980. 10.95 (ISBN 0-690-01931-9); pap. 5.95 (ISBN 0-690-01933-5). Lippincott & Crowell.
--Tax-Free Reorganizations (After the Pension Reform Act of 1974) LC 75-7574. 350p. 1967. 24.95 (ISBN 0-910580-09-X). Farnswth Pub.
Holzner, Burkart & Marx, John H. Knowledge Application: The Knowledge System in Society. 1978. text ed. 20.95 (ISBN 0-205-06516-3). Allyn.
Homan, Theo, ed. Skidarima: An Inquiry into the Written & Printed Texts, References & Commentaries. (Amsterdamer Publikationen Zur Sprache und Literatur: No. 20). 430p. (Orig.). 1975. pap. text ed. 85.50x (ISBN 90-6203-079-3). Humanities.
Homans, George C. Sentiments & Activities. LC 62-10590. 1962. 9.95 o.s.i. (ISBN 0-02-914890-1). Free Pr.
Homans, George C. & Curtis, Charles P., Jr. An Introduction to Pareto: His Sociology. LC 68-9664. 1970. Repr. 17.00 (ISBN 0-86527-106-2). Fertig.
Homans, Margaret. Women Writers & Poetic Identity: Dorothy Wordsworth, Emily Bronte & Emily Dickinson. LC 80-7527. 244p. 1980. 14.75x (ISBN 0-691-06440-7). Princeton U Pr.
Homans, Peter. Theology After Freud: An Interpretive Inquiry. LC 76-84162. 1970. 18.50x (ISBN 0-672-51245-9); pap. text ed. 5.95x (ISBN 0-672-60802-2). Irvington.
Homburger, Wolfgang S., jt. auth. see Carter, Everett.
Home Economics Ducation Association. Test Item Construction in the Cognitive Domain. 1979. pap. 2.00 o.p. (ISBN 0-686-28360-0, A261-8442). Home Econ Educ.
Home, Lord. Reflections on Field & Stream. (Illus.). 112p. 1980. 12.50 (ISBN 0-316-37196-3). Little.
Homelsky, Geri & Kaufman, Herb. Calligraphy in the Copperplate Style. (Illus.). 50p. (Orig.). 1981. pap. 1.75 (ISBN 0-486-24037-1). Dover.
Homer. The Iliad. LC 80-15669. (Raintree Short Classics). (Illus.). 48p. (gr. 4 up). 1981. PLB 9.95 (ISBN 0-8172-1663-4). Raintree Pubs.
--The Iliad of Homer. Rees, Ennis, tr. LC 76-56428. (Library of Liberal Arts Ser.). 1977. pap. text ed. 7.95 (ISBN 0-672-61414-6). Bobbs.
--La Iliada. (Span.). 7.95 (ISBN 84-241-5415-0). E Torres & Sons.
--The Illustrated Odyssey: Translated from Homer. Tieu, E. V., tr. from Greek. (Illus.). 256p. 1981. 17.95 (ISBN 0-89479-076-5). A & W Pubs.
--Odyssey. Rouse, W. H., tr. 1971. pap. 1.75 (ISBN 0-451-61824-6, ME1824, Ment). NAL.
--Odyssey. LC 61-8886. 1961. 12.50 o.p. (ISBN 0-385-09553-8). Doubleday.
--Odyssey. Andrew, S. O., tr. 1953. 5.00x o.p. (ISBN 0-460-00454-9, Evman). Dutton.
--The Odyssey. Shewring, Walter, tr. (The World's Classics Ser.). 384p. 1981. pap. 4.95x (ISBN 0-19-281542-3). Oxford U Pr.
--Odyssey, Bks. 6 & 7. Edwards, Gerald M., ed. (Gr.). 1915. text ed. 5.75x (ISBN 0-521-05322-6). Cambridge U Pr.
--Odyssey: Critical Ed. Cook, Albert, ed. & tr. 1974. 10.00 (ISBN 0-393-04161-1); pap. 4.95x (ISBN 0-393-09971-7). Norton.
--The Odyssey of Homer. Rees, Ennis, tr. LC 76-55800. (Library of Liberal Arts: 225). 1977. pap. 6.50 (ISBN 0-672-61415-4). Bobbs.
--Opera, 5 vols. Monro, D. B. & Allen, T. W., eds. Incl. Vol. 1. Iliad 1-12. 3rd ed. 1920. 14.95x o.p. (ISBN 0-19-814528-4); Vol. 2. Iliad 13-24. 3rd ed. 1920. 14.95x o.p. (ISBN 0-19-814529-2); Vol. 3. Odyssey, 1-12. 2nd ed. 1917. 14.95x o.p. (ISBN 0-19-814531-4); Vol. 4. Odyssey, 13-24. 2nd ed. 1919. 13.95x o.p. (ISBN 0-19-814532-2); Vol. 5. Hymns, Etc. 1911. 16.95x o.p. (ISBN 0-19-814534-9). (Oxford Classical Texts Ser.). Oxford U Pr.
--Selections from Homer's Iliad. Benner, Allen R., ed. (Gr.). 1976. Repr. of 1931 ed. text ed. 16.95x (ISBN 0-89197-636-1). Irvington.
Homer, F., jt. auth. see Curtiss, Harriete.
Homer, Sidney. My Wife & I: The Story of Louise & Sidney Homer. LC 77-10561. (Music Reprint Ser.). (Illus.). 1978. Repr. of 1939 ed. lib. bdg. 27.50 (ISBN 0-306-77526-3). Da Capo.
Homer, William I. Alfred Stieglitz & the American Avant-Garde. LC 76-50068. (Illus.). 1977. 17.50 (ISBN 0-8212-0676-1, 031917); pap. 9.95 o.p. (ISBN 0-8212-0755-5). NYGS.
Homero. La Iliada. 5th ed. (Biblioteca Basica De Cultura Ser.). (Span.). pap. 6.25 (ISBN 0-8477-0708-3). U of PR Pr.
Homet, Roland. Politics, Cultures & Communications: European Vs. American Approaches to Communications Policy Making. LC 79-53594. (Praeger Special Studies Ser.). 1979. 19.95 (ISBN 0-03-049786-8). Praeger.
Homewood, C. A., jt. auth. see Neame, K. D.
Homewood, Harry. Thavis Is Here. 1978. pap. 1.75 o.p. (ISBN 0-449-13991-3, GM). Fawcett.
Homewood, Inez V. Music in Further Education. (Student's Music Library Ser). 1958. 6.95 (ISBN 0-234-77217-4). Dufour.
Hommes, E. A. & Van Den Berg, C. J., eds. Normal & Pathological Development of Energy Metabolism. 1976. 34.00 (ISBN 0-12-354560-9). Acad Pr.
Homonoff, Richard B. & Mullins, David W., Jr. Cash Management. LC 74-23318. (Illus.). 1975. 13.00 o.p. (ISBN 0-669-97485-4). Lexington Bks.
Homsher, Lola M., ed. see Chisholm, James.
Hon, David C. Trade-Offs: For the Person Who Can't Have Everything. (Illus.). 150p. 1981. text ed. 14.95 (ISBN 0-89384-048-3). Learning Concepts.
Honadle, George & Klaus, Rudi, eds. International Development Administration: Implementation Analysis for Development Projects. LC 79-65182. (Praeger Special Studies). 236p. 1979. 23.95 (ISBN 0-03-051041-4). Praeger.
Honda, H. H. Manyoshu: A New & Complete Translation. 45.00 o.p. (ISBN 0-89346-075-3, Pub. by Hokuseido Pr). Heian Intl.
Honda, Isao. The World of Origami. abr. ed. LC 65-27101. (Illus.). 200p. 1976. pap. 11.00 (ISBN 0-87040-383-4). Japan Pubns.
Honda, Nobuo. Exploring Kittens. (Illus., Orig.). 1980. pap. 5.95 (ISBN 0-89346-142-3). Heian Intl.
Honderich, Ted, ed. Essays on Freedom of Action. 1978. pap. 7.95 (ISBN 0-7100-8883-3). Routledge & Kegan.
--Social Ends & Political Means. 1976. 20.00x (ISBN 0-7100-8370-X). Routledge & Kegan.
Hone, Elizabeth B., et al. A Sourcebook for Elementary Science. 2nd ed. (Teaching Science Ser.). 475p. 1971. text ed. 14.95 (ISBN 0-15-582855-X, HC). HarBraceJ.
Hone, Harry. Back from the Dead. (Illus.). 1978. pap. text ed. write for info o.p. (ISBN 0-9601168-2-6); pap. text ed. write for info o.p. (ISBN 0-9601168-3-4). Am Biog Ctr.
--The Light at the End of the Tunnel. (Illus.). 1980. pap. text ed. 10.00 (ISBN 0-9601168-4-2). Am Biog Ctr.
Hone, Joseph, ed. Irish Ghost Stories. 1978. 17.95 (ISBN 0-241-89680-0, Pub. by Hamish Hamilton England). David & Charles.
Hone, Ralph E. Dorothy L. Sayers: A Literary Biography. LC 79-9783. (Illus.). 1979. 15.00x (ISBN 0-87338-228-5); pap. 7.00 (ISBN 0-87338-253-6). Kent St U Pr.
Hone, William. Ancient Mysteries Described. LC 67-23905. (Illus.). 1969. Repr. of 1823 ed. 15.00 (ISBN 0-8103-3444-5). Gale.
--Every-Day Book, 2 Vols. LC 67-12945. 1967. Repr. of 1827 ed. Set. 76.00 (ISBN 0-8103-3005-9). Gale.
--The Year Book of Daily Recreation & Information. LC 67-12947. 1967. Repr. of 1832 ed. 30.00 (ISBN 0-8103-3007-5). Gale.
Honeck, Richard P. & Hoffman, Robert R., eds. Cognition & Figurative Language. LC 80-17225. 448p. 1980. text ed. 29.95 (ISBN 0-89859-047-7). L Erlbaum Assocs.
Honecker, Erich. From My Life. LC 80-41162. (Leaders of the World Ser.: Vol. 3). (Illus.). 500p. 1980. 24.00 (ISBN 0-08-024532-3). Pergamon.
Honer, Stanley M. & Hunt, Thomas C. Invitation to Philosophy. 3rd ed. 1978. pap. 9.95x (ISBN 0-534-00564-0). Wadsworth Pub.
Honess, Brian C. Structured Business Problem Solving with Fortran. 300p. 1981. text ed. 13.95 (ISBN 0-205-07332-8); free (ISBN 0-205-07328-X). Allyn.
Honess, C. Brian, jt. auth. see Fleck, Robert.
Honey, W. B. Old English Porcelain: A Handbook for Collectors. rev. 3rd ed. (Illus.). 1978. 35.00 o.p. (ISBN 0-571-04902-8, Pub. by Faber & Faber). Merrimack Bk Serv.
Honey, W. B., jt. auth. see Cushion, J. P.
Honey, William B. French Porcelain of the Eighteenth Century. 2nd ed. 1972. 24.95 o.p. (ISBN 0-571-04741-6, Pub. by Faber & Faber). Merrimack Bk Serv.
Honeyman, Arthur. Sam & His Cart. LC 80-36714. (Illus.). 64p. (gr. 2-6). 1980. Repr. of 1977 ed. 6.95 (ISBN 0-88436-793-2). EMC.
Hong, Alfred. Marketing Economics Guide 1976-77: Current Market Dimensions for 1500 Cities, All 3100 Countie S, All Metro Areas. new ed. LC 76-647896. (Illus.). 280p. 1976. 20.00 (ISBN 0-914078-21-6). Marketing Econs.
Hong, Alfred, ed. Marketing Economics Guide Nineteen Seventy-Nine to Nineteen Eighty: Current Market Dimensions for 1500 Cities, All 3100 Counties All Metro Areas. LC 73-647896. (Illus.). 1979. 20.00 (ISBN 0-914078-33-X). Marketing Econs.
--Marketing Economics Guide 1973-74: Current Market Dimensions for 1500 Cities, All 3100 Counties, All Metro Areas. new ed. (Illus.). 264p. 1973. 20.00 (ISBN 0-914078-09-7). Marketing Econs.
--Marketing Economics Guide 1974-75: Current Market Dimensions for 1500 Cities, All 3100 Counties, All Metro Areas. (Illus.). 280p. 1974. 20.00 (ISBN 0-914078-10-0). Marketing Econs.

Hopkins, Ernest J. Our Lawless Police. LC 74-168829. (Civil Liberties in American History Ser.). 379p. 1972. Repr. of 1931 ed. lib. bdg. 32.50 (ISBN 0-306-70213-4). Da Capo.
--What Happened in the Mooney Case. LC 73-107411. (Civil Liberties in American History Ser). 1970. Repr. of 1932 ed. lib. bdg. 27.50 (ISBN 0-306-71891-X). Da Capo.
Hopkins, Fred W., Jr. Tom Boyle, Master Privateer. LC 76-6026. (Illus.). 1976. pap. 4.00 (ISBN 0-87033-218-X, Pub. by Tidewater). Cornell Maritime.
Hopkins, George D., Jr. Urban Ecology Through the Adaptive Use of Existing Buildings: A Selected Bibliography, Revising A-22 of Oct. 1978. (Architecture Ser.: Bibliography a-281). 78p. 1980. pap. 8.50. Vance Biblios.
Hopkins, George E. Airline Pilots: A Study in Elite Unionization. LC 71-152699. (Illus.). 1971. 11.00x (ISBN 0-674-01275-5). Harvard U Pr.
Hopkins, Gerard, tr. see Mauriac, Francois.
Hopkins, Gerard, tr. see Maurois, Andre.
Hopkins, Gerard M. All My Eyes See. Thornton, R. K., ed. 148p. 1980. pap. 12.95x (ISBN 0-904461-06-8, Pub. by Geolfrith Pr England). Intl Schol Bk Serv.
--Further Letters of Gerard Manley Hopkins, Including His Correspondence with Coventry Patmore. 2nd ed. Abbott, C. C., ed. 1956. 45.00x (ISBN 0-19-212116-2). Oxford U Pr.
--Gerard Manley Hopkins: Selected Prose. Roberts, Gerald, ed. (Standard Authors Ser.). 288p. 1981. 19.50x (ISBN 0-19-254173-0); pap. 8.95x (ISBN 0-19-281272-6). Oxford U Pr.
Hopkins, Glenn see Foster, Rick.
Hopkins, H. G. & Sewell, M. J., eds. Mechanics of Solids: The Rodney Hill 60th Anniversary Volume. (Illus.). 720p. Date not set. 101.00 (ISBN 0-08-025443-8). Pergamon.
Hopkins, H. H., jt. auth. see Gow, J. G.
Hopkins, Hugh E. Charles Simeon of Cambridge. 1977. 7.95 o.p. (ISBN 0-8028-3498-1). Eerdmans.
Hopkins, J. F. McEckr'n. 1980. 9.95 (ISBN 0-312-52365-3). St Martin.
Hopkins, J. F., jt. auth. see Levtzion, N.
Hopkins, James F., ed. see Clay, Henry.
Hopkins, James F., jt. ed. see Hargreaves, Mary W.
Hopkins, James K. A Woman to Deliver Her People: Joanna Southcott & English Millenarianism in an Era of Revolution. (Illus.). 320p. 1981. text ed. 22.50x (ISBN 0-292-79017-1). U of Tex Pr.
Hopkins, Jasper. A Concise Introduction to the Philosophy of Nicholas of Cusa. 2nd ed. xii, 185p. 1980. 20.00x (ISBN 0-8166-1016-9). U of Minn Pr.
--Nicholas of Cusa on Learned Ignorance: A Translation & an Appraisal of De Docta Ignorantia. (Texts & Studies in Religion: Vol. 9). 256p. 1981. cancelled (ISBN 0-88946-978-4); cancelled soft cover (ISBN 0-88946-980-6). E Mellen.
--Nicholas of Cusa on Learned Ignorance: A Translation & an Appraisal of De Docta Ignorantia. LC 80-82907. (Illus.). 216p. text ed. 27.00x (ISBN 0-938060-23-6). Banning Pr.
--Nicholas of Cusa's Debate with John Wenck: A Translation & Appraisal of De Ignota Litteratura & Apologia Doctae Ignorantiae. (Texts & Studies in Religion: Vol. 10). 128p. 1981. cancelled (ISBN 0-88946-979-2); cancelled (ISBN 0-88946-981-4). E Mellen.
--Nicholas of Cusa's Debate with John Wenck: A Translation & an Appraisal of De Ignota Litteratura & Apologia Doctae Ignorantiae. LC 80-82908. 1981. 23.00x (ISBN 0-938060-24-4). Banning Pr.
Hopkins, Jasper, ed. see Anselm Of Canterbury.
Hopkins, Jeanne, ed. Glossary of Astronomy & Astrophysics. rev. ed. LC 80-5226. 224p. 1980. lib. bdg. 17.50x (ISBN 0-226-35171-8). U of Chicago Pr.
Hopkins, Jeannette, jt. auth. see Clark, Kenneth B.
Hopkins, Jeffrey, tr. see Nagarjuna.
Hopkins, Jerry. Elvis. (Illus.). 480p. 1972. pap. 2.50 o.s.i. (ISBN 0-446-81665-5). Warner Bks.
Hopkins, Jerry & Sugarman, Daniel. No One Here Gets Out Alive. 1980. pap. 7.95 (ISBN 0-446-97133-2); pap. 2.95 (ISBN 0-446-93921-8). Warner Bks.
Hopkins, Jerry & Sugerman, Danny. No One Here Gets Out Alive. 400p. (Orig.). 1981. pap. 2.95 (ISBN 0-446-93921-8). Warner Bks.
Hopkins, John A. Changing Technology & Employment in Agriculture. LC 73-174470. (FDR & the Era of the New Deal Ser.). 242p. 1973. Repr. of 1941 ed. lib. bdg. 20.00 (ISBN 0-306-70380-7). Da Capo.
Hopkins, K. Conquerors & Slaves. LC 77-90209. (Illus.). 272p. 1981. pap. 12.50 (ISBN 0-521-28181-4). Cambridge U Pr.
--Conquerors & Slaves: Sociological Studies in Roman History, Vol. 1. LC 77-90209. (Illus.). 1978. 32.50 (ISBN 0-521-21945-0). Cambridge U Pr.
Hopkins, Kenneth & Stanley, Julian. Educational & Psychological Measurement & Evaluation. 5th ed. (Illus.). 528p. 1972. ref. ed. 19.95 (ISBN 0-13-236281-3). P-H.
Hopkins, Kenneth D. & Glass, Gene V. Basic Statistics for the Behavioral Sciences. LC 77-10877. (Educational, Measurement, Research & Statistics Ser.). (Illus.). 1978. pap. text ed. 18.95 (ISBN 0-13-069377-4). P-H.
Hopkins, Lee B. Elves, Fairies & Gnomes. LC 79-19753. (Illus.). (ps-2). Date not set. 5.95 (ISBN 0-394-84351-7); PLB 5.99 (ISBN 0-394-94351-1). Knopf.
--A Haunting We Will Go: Ghostly Stories & Poems. Rubin, Caroline, ed. LC 76-45449. (Anthology). (Illus.). 128p. (gr. 3-6). 1977. 7.75 (ISBN 0-8075-0006-2). A Whitman.
--Important Dates in Afro-American History. LC 73-83648. (Illus.). (gr. 4-6). 1969. PLB 5.90 (ISBN 0-531-01897-0). Watts.
--Wonder Wheels. (YA) (gr. 7-12). 1980. pap. 1.50 (ISBN 0-440-99511-6, LFL). Dell.
Hopkins, Lee B., compiled By. By Myself. LC 79-7830. (Illus.). 40p. (ps-3). 1980. 7.95 (ISBN 0-690-04070-9); lib. bdg. 7.89 (ISBN 0-690-04071-7). T y Crowell.
Hopkins, Lee B., ed. City Spreads Its Wings. LC 73-117179. (gr. k-3). 1970. PLB 4.90 o.p. (ISBN 0-531-01942-X). Watts.
--Girls Can Too. LC 72-887. (Illus.). 48p. (gr. k-3). 1972. PLB 4.90 o.p. (ISBN 0-531-02587-X). Watts.
--Me: A Book of Poems. LC 72-115782. (Illus.). (gr. k-3). 1970. 7.95 (ISBN 0-395-28815-0, Clarion). HM.
--Merely Players: An Anthology of Life Poems. LC 79-12474. 1979. 7.95 (ISBN 0-525-66645-1). Elsevier-Nelson.
--Sing Hey for Christmas Day! LC 75-6612. (Illus.). 32p. (gr. 1-5). 1975. 4.75 (ISBN 0-15-274960-8, HJ). HarBraceJ.
--To Look at Any Thing. LC 77-88962. (Illus.). (gr. 1 up). 1978. 6.95 (ISBN 0-15-289083-1, HJ). HarBraceJ.
Hopkins, Lee Bennett & Arenstein, Misha. Do You Know What Day Tomorrow Is? A Teacher's Almanac. LC 75-23145. 240p. 1975. pap. text ed. 4.75 (ISBN 0-590-09604-4, Citation). Schol Bk Serv.
Hopkins, Margaret. Corfu. 1977. 22.50 (ISBN 0-7134-0880-4). David & Charles.
Hopkins, Marjorie. A Gift for Tolum. LC 72-272. (Illus.). 48p. (gr. k-3). 1972. 5.95 o.s.i. (ISBN 0-8193-0588-X, Four Winds); PLB 5.41 o.s.i. (ISBN 0-8193-0589-8). Schol Bk Serv.
Hopkins, Phil, jt. auth. see Peters, Barbara H.
Hopkins, Richard L. Freedom & Education: The Beginnings of a New Philosophy. LC 79-66475. 1979. text ed. 14.50 (ISBN 0-8191-0836-7); pap. text ed. 7.75 (ISBN 0-8191-0837-5). U Pr of Amer.
Hopkins, Robert A. Living Without Gasoline. LC 76-19477. 1979. 10.95 (ISBN 0-917240-06-5). Am Metric.
Hopkins, S. J. Principal Drugs: An Alphabetical Guide. 6th ed. 176p. 1980. pap. 5.50 (ISBN 0-571-18006-X, Pub. by Faber & Faber). Merrimack Bk Serv.
Hopkins, S. J., ed. Principal Drugs: An Alphabetical Guide. rev. 5th ed. 1977. pap. 3.95 o.p. (ISBN 0-571-04938-9, Pub. by Faber & Faber). Merrimack Bk Serv.
Hopkins, Terence K. & Wallerstein, Immanuel, eds. Processes of the World-System. LC 79-27385. (Political Economy of the World-System Annuals: Vol. 3). (Illus.). 320p. 1980. pap. 20.00x (ISBN 0-8039-1378-8); pap. 9.95 (ISBN 0-8039-1379-6). Sage.
Hopkins, Thomas. The Hindu Religious Tradition. (The Religious Life of Man Ser). 1971. pap. text ed. 7.95x (ISBN 0-8221-0022-3). Dickenson.
Hopkins, Thomas M. see Wakefield, Sarah.
Hopkins, Vivian C. Spires of Forms: A Study of Emerson's Aesthetic Theory. LC 80-2537. 1981. Repr. of 1951 ed. 33.50 (ISBN 0-404-19263-7). AMS Pr.
Hopkinson, Anthony. Papermaking at Home. 1979. pap. 3.95 o.s.i. (ISBN 0-7225-0483-7). Newcastle Pub.
Hopkinson, Michael, jt. auth. see Daniel, Peter.
Hopkinson, R. G. & Kay, J. D. The Lighting of Building. 1972. 16.95 (ISBN 0-571-04770-X, Pub. by Faber & Faber); pap. 7.95 (ISBN 0-571-09933-5). Merrimack Bk Serv.
Hopkinson, Shirley L. Instructional Materials for Teaching the Use of the Library. 1975. pap. 4.50x (ISBN 0-913860-03-4). Claremont House.
Hopkirk, Peter. Foreign Devils on the Silk Road: The Search for the Lost Cities & Treasures of Chinese Central Asia. (Illus.). 264p. 1981. lib. bdg. 27.50x (ISBN 0-87023-234-7). U of Mass Pr.
Hopko, T., et al. God & Charity: Images of Eastern Orthodox Theology, Spirituality & Practice. Costa, Francis D., ed. LC 79-3027. (Pan-Am Books). 103p. (Orig.). 1979. pap. text ed. 3.95 (ISBN 0-916586-34-0). Holy Cross Orthodox.
Hopley, Catherine C. Life in the South, from the Commencement of the War: Being a Social History of Those Who Took Part in the Battles, from a Personal Acquaintance with Them in Their Own Homes, 2 vols. LC 68-16240. (American Scene Ser.). 831p. 1974. Repr. of 1863 ed. Set. lib. bdg. 65.00 (ISBN 0-306-71015-3). Da Capo.
Hopman, Harry. Better Tennis. (Better Ser.). (Illus.). (gr. 7 up). 1976. 14.50x (ISBN 0-7182-0486-7, SpS). Soccer.
Hoppe, Donald J. How to Invest in Gold Coins. LC 70-115342. (Dollar Growth Lib.). (Illus.). 1970. 8.95 o.p. (ISBN 0-87000-076-4). Arlington Hse.
Hoppe, H. Whittling & Wood Carving. LC 69-19488. (Little Craft Book Ser). (gr. 4 up). 1969. 5.95 (ISBN 0-8069-5126-5); PLB 6.69 (ISBN 0-8069-5127-3). Sterling.
Hoppe, Willie. Billards As It Should Be Played. 7.95 o.p. (ISBN 0-8092-8837-0). Contemp Bks.
Hoppenfeld. Physical Examination of the Spine & Extremities: Slide Package. (Illus.). 621p. 1976. 19.50 (ISBN 0-8385-7853-5); 35 mm b-w slides 385.00 (ISBN 0-8385-7854-3). ACC.
Hopper, Arthur F. & Hart, Nathan H. Foundations of Animal Development. (Illus.). 1979. text ed. 21.95x (ISBN 0-19-502569-5). Oxford U Pr.
Hopper, C. Edmund & Allen, William A. Sex Education for Physically Handicapped Youth. (Illus.). 154p. 1980. pap. text ed. 9.75 (ISBN 0-398-03935-6). C C Thomas.
Hopper, Earl. Readings in the Theory of Educational Systems. 1971. text ed. 10.25x (ISBN 0-09-109230-2, Hutchinson U Lib). Humanities.
Hopper, Maurice. Spaniel Training: For Modern Shooters. (Illus.). 120p. 1974. 14.95 (ISBN 0-7153-6446-4). David & Charles.
Hopper, R. J. Acropolis. LC 76-134880. (Illus.). 1971. 10.00 o.s.i. (ISBN 0-02-553980-9). Macmillan.
Hopper, Ted. Guide to Bees & Honey. (Illus.). 260p. 1981. 12.50 (ISBN 0-7137-0782-8, Pub. by Blandford Pr England). Sterling.
Hopper, Vincent F. Barron's Simplified Approach to Goethe's Faust 1 & 2. (YA) 1964. pap. text ed. 1.50 o.p. (ISBN 0-8120-0173-7). Barron.
--Medieval Number Symbolism: Its Sources, Meaning & Influence on Thought & Expression. LC 70-85372. 241p. 1969. Repr. of 1938 ed. 22.50x (ISBN 0-8154-0305-4). Cooper Sq.
Hopper, Vincent F. & Lahey, Gerald B., eds. Medieval Mysteries, Moralities & Interludes. LC 61-18362. (gr. 10 up). 1962. pap. text ed. 3.95 (ISBN 0-8120-0135-4). Barron.
Hopper, Vincent F., ed. see Chaucer, Geoffrey.
Hopper, Vincent F., ed. see Farquhar, George.
Hopper, Vincent F., ed. see Goldsmith, Oliver.
Hopper, Vincent F., ed. see Webster, John.
Hopper, Vincent F., et al. Essentials of English. rev. ed. LC 67-20430. 224p. (gr. 9 up). 1973. text ed. 5.95 (ISBN 0-8120-5031-2); pap. 3.95 (ISBN 0-8120-0059-5). Barron.
Hoppin, Richard H. Medieval Music. (Introduction to Music History Ser.). (Illus.). 1978. 14.95x (ISBN 0-393-09090-6). Norton.
Hopple, Gerald W. & Kuhlman, James A. Expert-Generated Data: Applications in International Affairs. (Westview Replica Edition Ser.). 225p. 1981. lib. bdg. 22.50x (ISBN 0-89158-870-1). Westview.
Hoppmann-Liecty, Susanne, jt. auth. see Mueller, Klaus A.
Hopson, B. & Hayes, J. The Theory & Practice of Vocational Guidance. 1969. 34.00 (ISBN 0-08-013284-7); pap. 15.00 (ISBN 0-08-013391-6). Pergamon.
Hopson, D., Jr., et al. Juvenile Offender & the Law: A Symposium. LC 79-146557. (Symposia on Law & Society Ser). 1968. Repr. lib. bdg. 22.50 (ISBN 0-306-70095-6). Da Capo.
Hopson, William. Apache Kill. 256p. (YA) 1974. 5.95 (ISBN 0-685-40095-6, Avalon). Bouregy.
--Border Raider. 1979. pap. 1.25 (ISBN 0-505-51420-6). Tower Bks.
--Cry Viva! 1978. pap. 1.25 (ISBN 0-505-51256-4). Tower Bks.
--Gunfighters Pay. (YA) 1973. 5.95 (ISBN 0-685-31776-5, Avalon). Bouregy.
--Hangtree Range. 1978. pap. 1.25 (ISBN 0-505-51249-1). Tower Bks.
--The Last Apaches. 256p. (YA) 1975. 5.95 (ISBN 0-685-50530-8, Avalon). Bouregy.
Hopson, William L. The Laughing Vaquero. 1978. pap. 1.25 (ISBN 0-505-51245-9). Tower Bks.
Hopwood, D. A., jt. ed. see Glover, S. W.
Hopwood, Jim. Death Rides the Rails. (Orig.). 1980. pap. 1.95 (ISBN 0-532-23126-0). Manor Bks.
Hopwood, Robert F., ed. Germany: People & Politics. LC 68-134435. (Selections from History Today Ser.: No. 12). (Illus.). 1969. 3.95 (ISBN 0-05-001656-3). Dufour.
Hoque, Richard. Sex, Satan, & Jesus. LC 73-86668. 4.95 (ISBN 0-8054-5319-9); pap. 3.50 (ISBN 0-8054-5320-2). Broadman.
Hora, Bayard, ed. Oxford Encyclopedia of Trees of the World. (Illus.). 1981. write for info. Oxford U Pr.
Hora, Heinrich. Physics of Laser Driven Plasmas. 325p. 1981. 30.00 (ISBN 0-471-07880-8, Pub. by Wiley-Interscience). Wiley.
Hora, Thomas. Dialogues in Metapsychiatry. LC 77-8268. 1977. 12.95 (ISBN 0-8164-0352-X). Crossroad NY.
--Existential Metapsychiatry. 12.95 (ISBN 0-8164-0337-6). Crossroad NY.
Horace. Opera. 2nd ed. Wickham, E. C. & Garrod, H. W., eds. (Oxford Classical Texts Ser). 1912. 14.95 (ISBN 0-19-814618-3). Oxford U Pr.
--Satires & Epistles. Bovie, Smith P., tr. LC 59-16413. 1959. pap. 6.50 (ISBN 0-226-06777-7, P39, Phoen). U of Chicago Pr.
Horacek, J., jt. auth. see Borchardt, D. H.
Horadam, A. F. A Guide to Undergraduate Projective Geometry. LC 71-110243. 1970. 27.00 (ISBN 0-08-017479-5). Pergamon.
--Outline Course of Pure Mathematics. 1969. 23.00 (ISBN 0-08-012593-X). Pergamon.
Horak, Stephan. Poland's International Affairs 1919-1960. LC 64-63009. (Russian & East European Ser.: Vol. 31). 268p. 1964. pap. 7.50x (ISBN 0-253-39031-1). Ind U Pr.
Horak, V., jt. auth. see Ma, T. S.
Horan, Dennis J. & Mall, David, eds. Death, Dying, & Euthanasia. 1977. 24.00 (ISBN 0-89093-139-9); pap. 10.00 (ISBN 0-89093-140-2). U Pubns Amer.
Horan, Dennis J., jt. ed. see Hilgers, Thomas.
Horan, James F. & Taylor, G. Thomas, Jr. Experiments in Metropolitan Government. LC 77-7816. (Praeger Special Studies). 1978. 27.95 (ISBN 0-03-022336-9). Praeger.
Horatius Flaccus, Quintus. Horace His Arte of Poetrie, Pistles, & Satyrs Englished (1567) Drant, Thomas H., tr. from Lat. LC 73-173753. 296p. 1972. Repr. of 1567 ed. 30.00x (ISBN 0-8201-1099-X). Schol Facsimiles.
Horblit, Marcus & Nielsen, Kaj L. Plane Geometry Problems with Solutions. (Orig.). 1947. pap. 3.89 (ISBN 0-06-460063-7, CO 63, COS). Har-Row.
Horcasitas, Fernando, tr. see Duran, Fr. Diego.
Hord, R. Michael. The Illiac IV: The First Super Computer. (Illus.). 1981. text ed. price not set (ISBN 0-914894-71-4). Computer Sci.
Horder, Mervyn, ed. On Christmas Day: First Carols to Play & Sing. LC 69-11103. (Illus.). (gr. 1-7). 1969. 5.95 o.s.i. (ISBN 0-02-744400-7). Macmillan.
--Ronald Firbank-Memoirs & Critiques: Memoir by I. Kyrle Fletcher Included. 228p. 1977. 28.00x (ISBN 0-7156-0763-4, Pub. by Duckworth England). Biblio Dist.
Hordern, A. Legal Abortion: The English Experience. 1971. 30.00 (ISBN 0-08-016567-2). Pergamon.
Hordern, William. Introduction. (New Directios in Theology Today: Vol. 1). 1966. pap. 4.95 (ISBN 0-664-24706-7). Westminster.
Hordern, William & Otwell, John. Lent. LC 74-24901. (Proclamation 1: Aids for Interpreting the Lessons of the Church Year Ser. B). 64p. 1974. pap. 1.95 (ISBN 0-8006-4073-X, 1-4073). Fortress.
Hordeski, Michael. Illustrated Dictionary of Terminology Microcomputer. (Illus.). 1978. 12.95 (ISBN 0-8306-9875-2); pap. 8.95 (ISBN 0-8306-1088-X, 1088). TAB Bks.
Hore, B. D. Alcohol Dependence. (Postgraduate Psychiatry Ser). 1976. 17.95 (ISBN 0-407-00082-8). Butterworths.
Hore, Brian, ed. Alcohol Problems in Employment. 200p. 1980. 35.00x (Pub. by Croom Helm England). State Mutual Bk.
Hore, Brian & Plant, Michael, eds. Alcohol Problems in Employment. 200p. 1981. 35.00x (ISBN 0-7099-1202-1, Pub. by Croom Helm LTD England). Biblio Dist.
Horecker, Bernard & Estabrook, Ronald, eds. Current Topics in Cellular Regulation: Biological Cycles, Vol. 18. (Serial Publication Ser.). 1981. write for info. (ISBN 0-12-152818-9); lib ed. (ISBN 0-12-152892-8); microfiche ed. (ISBN 0-12-152893-6). Acad Pr.
Horejsi, Charles R., et al. Social Work Practice with Parents of Children in Foster Care: A Handbook. write for info. (ISBN 0-398-04471-6). C C Thomas.
Horemis, Spyros. Geometrical Design Coloring Book. 1973. pap. 1.75 (ISBN 0-486-20180-5). Dover.
Horgan, Gertrude M., ed. see Berry, James.
Horgan, Paul. A Distant Trumpet. 1960. 12.95 o.p. (ISBN 0-374-14089-8). FS&G.
--Josiah Gregg & His Vision of the Early West. 116p. 1979. 8.95 (ISBN 0-374-18017-2). FS&G.
--Lamy of Santa Fe: His Life & Times. 1980. 25.00 (ISBN 0-374-18301-5); Limited Ed. 150.00 (ISBN 0-374-18301-5); pap. 12.95 (ISBN 0-374-51588-3). FS&G.

--Memories of the Future. 21... (ISBN 0-374-20756-9). FS&G.
--Whitewater. 1971. pap. 1.50 o.s.i. (ISBN 0-446-68625-5). Warner Bks.
Horgen, P. A., jt. ed. see O'Day, D. H.
Hori, J. Spectral Properties of Disordered Chains & Lattices. 1968. 34.00 (ISBN 0-08-012359-7). Pergamon.
Horikawa, K. Coastal Engineering: An Introduction to Ocean Engineering. 1978. 42.95 (ISBN 0-470-26449-7). Halsted Pr.
Horioka, Yasuko. Life of Kakuzo. 1963. 5.50 o.p. (ISBN 0-89346-074-5, Pub. by Hokuseido Pr). Heian Intl.
Horiuchi, Yoshitaka, et al. Afro-Asian, Japanese, & Euro-American Contributions to Mankind & Civilization Yestermorrow, Vol. 1. 1981. 9.50 (ISBN 0-533-04486-3). Vantage.
Horizon Magazine & Hilowitz, Beverley, eds. A Horizon Guide: Great Historic Places of Europe. LC 74-10941. (Illus.). 384p. 1974. 10.00 (ISBN 0-8281-0275-9, Dist. by Scribner). Am Heritage.
Horizon Magazine Editors. Great Historic Places of Europe: A Horizon Guide. Hilowitz, Beverly, ed. LC 74-10941. (Illus.). 384p. 1974. 10.00 (ISBN 0-686-65706-3, 23073, Pub. by Am Heritage). S&S.
--The Horizon Book of the Arts of China. Froncek, Thomas, ed. LC 69-15082. (Illus.). 383p. 1969. deluxe ed. 23.00 (ISBN 0-8281-0025-X, BO27D). Am Heritage.
Horizon Magazine Editors, jt. auth. see Herold, J. Christopher.
Horkheimer, Max. Critical Theory. O'Connell, Matthew J., et al, trs. from Ger. LC 72-5309. 300p. 1972. pap. 3.50 (ISBN 0-8164-9226-3); o.p. (ISBN 0-8164-9272-7, Continuum). Continuum.
Horkheimer, Max, et al. Critique of Instrumental Reason. LC 74-8450. 160p. 1974. 7.95 (ISBN 0-8164-9221-2); pap. 4.95 (ISBN 0-8164-9336-7). Continuum.
Horlock, Carole. Initial Consonants. (Illus.). 44p. (gr. 1-3). 1980. pap. 5.95 (ISBN 0-933358-60-1). Enrich.
--Initial Vowels. (Illus.). 24p. (gr. 1-3). 1980. pap. 3.95 (ISBN 0-933358-61-X). Enrich.
Hormachea, Marion, jt. auth. see Reynolds, Jesse A.
Horman, William. Vulgaria Uiri Doctissimi Guil. Hormani Caesarisburgensis. LC 74-28865. (English Experience Ser.: No. 745). 1975. Repr. of 1519 ed. 46.00 (ISBN 90-221-0745-0). Walter J Johnson.
Horn, Berthold K., jt. auth. see Winston, Patrick H.
Horn, Beth. Pacific Coast Wildflowers. Shangle, Robert D., ed. LC 80-15350. (Illus.). 48p. 1980. pap. 8.95 (ISBN 0-89802-099-9). Beautiful Am.
Horn, Carin & Poirot, James. Computer Literacy: Problem-Solving with Computers. (Illus.). 215p. (Orig.). (gr. 7 up). 1981. pap. 10.95 (ISBN 0-88408-133-8). Sterling Swift.
Horn, Carl E. Van see Van Horn, Carl E.
Horn, David. Literature of American Music in Books & Folk Mmusic Collections: A Fully Annotated Bibliography. LC 76-13160. 1977. 24.00 (ISBN 0-8108-0996-6). Scarecrow.
Horn, Delton T. Electronic Music Synthesizers. (Illus.). 168p. 1980. 10.95 (ISBN 0-8306-9722-5); pap. 5.95 (ISBN 0-8306-1167-3, 1167). TAB Bks.
Horn, Elizabeth. Wildflowers 1, the Cascades. (Illus.). 1977. pap. 8.95 (ISBN 0-911518-07-X). Touchstone Pr Ore.
Horn, G. & Hinde, R. A., eds. Short-Term Changes in Neural Activity & Behaviour. LC 71-121367. (Illus.). 1970. 92.00 (ISBN 0-521-07942-X). Cambridge U Pr.
Horn, Geoffrey & Cavanaugh, Arthur, eds. Bible Stories for Children. (Illus.). 1980. 12.95 (ISBN 0-686-64566-9). Macmillan.
Horn, Harold R. Practical Considerations for Successful Crown and Bridge Therapy: Biologic Considerations- Psychologic Considerations-Preventive Factors. LC 76-8577. (Illus.). 1976. text ed. 29.00 (ISBN 0-7216-4783-9). Saunders.
Horn, Huston. The Pioneers. (The Old West Ser.). (Illus.). 1974. 12.95 (ISBN 0-8094-1475-9). Time-Life.
--The Pioneers. LC 73-94242. (The Old West). (Illus.). (gr. 5 up). 1974. kivar 12.96 (ISBN 0-8094-1477-5, Pub. by Time-Life). Silver.
Horn, Lister W., jt. auth. see Gleason, Gary N.
Horn, Marilyn J. The Second Skin. 2nd ed. 1975. text ed. 19.50 (ISBN 0-395-18552-1); instructor's manual pap. 2.00 (ISBN 0-395-18780-X). HM.
Horn, Marilyn J. & Gurel, Lois M. The Second Skin: An Interdisciplinary Study of Clothing. 3rd ed. LC 80-81918. (Illus.). 480p. 1981. text ed. write for info. (ISBN 0-395-28974-2); instr's. manual 1.60 (ISBN 0-395-28963-7). HM.

...Mary. Children & Plastics: Stages 1 & 2 & ...nd. LC 77-83010. (Science 5-13 ... pap. text ed. 9.30 (ISBN 0-356-... Raintree Child.
Horn, ...ce. Comics of the American West. (Illus.). 1978. pap. 7.95 o.p. (ISBN 0-695-80954-7). Follett.
--Women in the Comics. LC 77-24317. (Illus.). 240p. 1981. pap. 9.95 (ISBN 0-87754-205-8). Chelsea Hse.
Horn, Maurice, ed. The World Encyclopedia of Comics. 1977. pap. 10.00 (ISBN 0-380-01735-0, 34249). Avon.
Horn, Maurice & Marschall, Richard E., eds. The World Encyclopedia of Cartoons, 6 vols. LC 79-26071. (Illus.). 1981. pap. 70.00 (ISBN 0-87754-121-3). Chelsea Hse.
Horn, Max. Intercollegiate Socialist Society, Nineteen Hundred Five to Nineteen Twenty-One: Origins of the Modern American Student Movement. LC 79-9404. (A Westview Replica Edition Ser.). (Illus.). 1979. lib. bdg. 24.00x (ISBN 0-89158-584-2). Westview.
Horn, Michiel. The League for Social Reconstruction: Intellectual Origins of the Democratic Left in Canada, 1930-1942. 1980. 20.00 (ISBN 0-8020-5487-0). U of Toronto Pr.
Horn, Pamela. The Rural World: Social Change in the English Counryside 1780-1850. 1981. 25.00 (ISBN 0-312-69606-X). St Martin.
Horn, Richard. Designs. 350p. 1980. 10.95 (ISBN 0-87131-329-4). M Evans.
Horn, Richard J., ed. Studies in the Management of Government Enterprise. (Social Dimensions of Economics Ser.: Vol. 1). 1981. lib. bdg. price not set (ISBN 0-89838-052-9, Pub. by Martinus Nijhoff). Kluwer Boston.
Horn, Robert M. Go Free! The Meaning of Justification. LC 76-4736. 128p. (Orig.). 1976. pap. 2.25 o.p. (ISBN 0-87784-644-8). Inter-Varsity.
Horn, Stephen. Unused Power: The Work of the Senate Committee on Appropriations. 1970. 11.95 (ISBN 0-8157-3730-0). Brookings.
Horn, Stephen, jt. auth. see Beard, Edmund.
Horn, Tom. Life of Tom Horn, Government Scout & Interpreter, Written by Himself, Together with His Letters & Statements by His Friends: A Vindication. (Western Frontier Library: No. 26). 1964. pap. 4.95 (ISBN 0-8061-1044-9). U of Okla Pr.
--Shallow Grass. 1968. 5.95 o.s.i. (ISBN 0-02-554100-5). Macmillan.
Hornaday, William H. & Ware, Harlan. Your Aladdin's Lamp. 1978. pap. 7.95 (ISBN 0-911336-75-3). Sci of Mind.
Hornaday, William H., jt. auth. see Holmes, Ernest.
Hornback, Bert G. Metaphor of Chance: Vision & Technique in the Works of Thomas Hardy. LC 77-122099. viii, 177p. 1971. 12.00x (ISBN 0-8214-0077-0). Ohio U Pr.
Hornback, Ned B. Self-Assessment of Current Knowledge in Therapeutic Radiology. 2nd ed. 1979. spiral bdg. 16.50 (ISBN 0-87488-286-9). Med Exam.
Hornbein, Thomas F. Everest: The West Ridge. LC 80-16088. (Illus.). 224p. 1980. Repr. of 1965 ed. 17.50 (ISBN 0-916890-90-2). Mountaineers.
Hornblass, Albert. Tumors of the Ocular Adnexa & Orbit. LC 79-11089. (Illus.). 1979. text ed. 49.50 (ISBN 0-8016-2246-8). Mosby.
Hornbrook, John F. Glimpse of Perfection. 178p. (Orig.). 1979. pap. 3.95 (ISBN 0-89841-004-5). Zoe Pubns.
Hornbrook, John F. & Wolf, Allan C. You Are Somebody Special. 148p. (Orig.). 1980. pap. 3.95 (ISBN 0-89841-005-3). Zoe Pubns.
Hornby, A. S. Guide to Patterns & Usage in English. 2nd ed. 256p. 1975. pap. text ed. 4.95x (ISBN 0-19-431318-2). Oxford U Pr.
Hornby, A. S., compiled by. Oxford Student's Dictionary of Current English. 1978. pap. text ed. 6.95x (ISBN 0-19-431114-7). Oxford U Pr.
Hornby, A. S. & Parnwell, E. C., eds. The Progressive English Dictionary. 2nd ed. 352p. 1972. pap. 2.50x (ISBN 0-19-431120-1). Oxford U Pr.
Hornby, Albert S. & Parnwell, E. C., eds. English-Reader's Dictionary. 2nd ed. 1969. pap. 5.95x (ISBN 0-19-431116-3). Oxford U Pr.
Hornby, George, ed. Poems for Children & Other People. rev. & expanded ed. (Illus.). 1980. 6.95 (ISBN 0-517-52588-7). Crown.
Hornby, James A. Introduction to Company Law. (Repr. of 1957 ed). 1970. text ed. 5.75 (ISBN 0-09-020713-0, Hutchinson U Lib); pap. text ed. 3.75 (ISBN 0-09-020714-9, Hutchinson U Lib). Humanities.
Hornby, W. F. & Jones, M. An Introduction to Population Geography. LC 78-74536. (Illus.). 1980. pap. 11.50 (ISBN 0-521-21395-9). Cambridge U Pr.
Horne, A. D., ed. The Wounded Generation: America After Vietnam. (A Washington Post Bk.). 160p. 1981. 10.95 (ISBN 0-13-969154-5); pap. 5.95 (ISBN 0-13-969147-2). P-H.

Horne, Alistair. The Fall of Paris: The Siege & the Commune 1870-71. 464p. 1981. pap. 2.95 (ISBN 0-14-005210-0). Penguin.
Horne, Caroline. Crochet: Pretty & Practical. (Illus.). 120p. 1975. 11.50 (ISBN 0-263-05151-X). Transatlantic.
Horne, D. F. Lens Mechanism Technology. LC 75-21733. (Illus.). 150p. 1975. 79.50x (ISBN 0-8448-0770-2). Crane-Russak Co.
Horne, Dennis. Trampolining: A Complete Handbook. rev. 2nd ed. (Illus.). 1978. 11.95 o.p. (ISBN 0-571-04868-4, Pub. by Faber & Faber); pap. 6.95 (ISBN 0-571-04945-1). Merrimack Bk Serv.
Horne, Herbert P., et al, eds. Nero & Other Plays. Ellis, Havelock & Symons, Arthur. Verity, Arthur & Wilson, A., trs. 488p. 1980. Repr. of 1888 ed. lib. bdg. 17.50 (ISBN 0-89760-333-8). Telegraph Bks.
Horne, James C. Van see Van Horne, James C.
Horne, M. R. Plastic Theory of Structures: In SI-Metric Units. 2nd ed. 1979. text ed. 19.50 (ISBN 0-08-022737-6); pap. text ed. 23.00 (ISBN 0-08-022738-4). Pergamon.
Horne, P. Women in Law Enforcement. 2nd ed. (Illus.). 288p. 1980. 15.50 (ISBN 0-398-04029-X); pap. 10.50 (ISBN 0-398-04030-3). C C Thomas.
Horne, R. A. The Chemistry of Our Environment. LC 77-1156. 1978. 37.50 (ISBN 0-471-40944-8, Pub. by Wiley-Interscience). Wiley.
Horne, Richard H. Memoirs of a London Doll. new ed. Fisher, Margery, ed. LC 68-18475. (Illus.). (gr. 3-5). 1968. 4.50g o.s.i. (ISBN 0-02-744540-2). Macmillan.
Horne, Thomas A. The Social Thought of Bernard Mandeville: Virtue & Commerce in Early Eighteenth Century England. LC 77-13573. 1978. 15.00x (ISBN 0-231-04274-4). Columbia U Pr.
Horne, Virginia L. Stunts & Tumbling for Girls: A Textbook for Schools & Colleges. (Illus.). (gr. 9 up). 1943. 13.95 (ISBN 0-8260-4385-2). Ronald Pr.
Hornemann, Grace V. Basic Nursing Procedures. LC 77-94835. (Illus.). 272p. 1980. pap. 9.80 (ISBN 0-8273-1320-9); instructors's guide 1.50 (ISBN 0-8273-1321-7). Delmar.
Horner, Deborah R. The Time & Space Theatre. (Illus.). 24p. (gr. 3-7). 1978. pap. 7.95 o.p. (ISBN 0-684-15546-X, ScribJ). Scribner.
Horner, Lance. Rogue Roman. 1978. pap. 2.25 (ISBN 0-449-13968-9, GM). Fawcett.
Horner, Lance, jt. auth. see Onstott, Kyle.
Horner, Thetus W., jt. auth. see Lyle, William H., Jr.
Horner, Tom. All About the Bull Terrier. 1973. 9.95 (ISBN 0-7207-0691-2, Pub. by Michael Joseph). Merrimack Bk Serv.
--Take Them Round, Please: The Art of Judging Dogs. LC 74-19782. (Illus.). 160p. 1975. 13.50 (ISBN 0-7153-6880-X). David & Charles.
Horner, Winifred B., ed. Historical Rhetoric: An Annotated Bibliography of Selected Sources in English. 1980. lib. bdg. 35.00 (ISBN 0-8161-8191-8). G K Hall.
Horney, Karen. The Adolescent Diaries of Karen Horney. LC 80-50552. (Illus.). 271p. 1980. 12.95 (ISBN 0-465-00055-X). Basic.
--Neurotic Personality of Our Times. 1937. 6.75 (ISBN 0-393-01012-0, Norton Lib); pap. 3.95 (ISBN 0-393-00742-1). Norton.
--Self-Analysis. 1942 6.50 (ISBN 0-393-01025-2); pap. 3.95, 1968 (ISBN 0-393-00134-2). Norton.
Horngren, C. Introduction to Financial Accounting. 1981. 21.00 (ISBN 0-13-483743-6); practice set 6.95, (ISBN 0-13-483701-0); working papers 6.95 (ISBN 0-13-483727-4); student guide 6.95 (ISBN 0-13-483750-9). P-H.
Horngren, C., et al. Prentice-Hall CPA Review Course. 1979. 43.95 (ISBN 0-13-695510-X). P-H.
Horngren, Charles T. Cost Accounting: A Managerial Emphasis. 4th ed. LC 76-45816. (Illus.). 992p. 1977. pap. text ed. 22.95 (ISBN 0-13-179739-5); study guide 8.95 (ISBN 0-13-179705-0). P-H.
--Introduction to Financial Accounting. 5th ed. (Ser. in Accounting). 672p. 1981. text ed. 21.95 (ISBN 0-686-69276-4). P-H.
--Introduction to Management Accounting. 5th ed. (Ser. in Accounting). (Illus.). 848p. 1981. text ed. 21.00 (ISBN 0-13-487652-0); wkbk. by Dudley W. Curry 8.95 (ISBN 0-13-487785-3). P-H.
--Introduction to Management Accounting. 4th ed. LC 77-14973. 1978. ref. ed. 19.95 (ISBN 0-13-487595-8). P-H.
Horngren, Charles T. & Leer, J. Arthur. CPA Problems & Approaches to Solutions, Vol. 2. 5th ed. 1979. 14.95 o.p. (ISBN 0-13-187906-5); text ed. 11.20 o.p. (ISBN 0-686-67265-8). P-H.
Hornick, William F., jt. auth. see Enk, Gordon A.

Hornidge, Marilis. That Yankee Cat: The Maine Coon. LC 80-67660. (Illus., Orig.). 1981. 14.95 (ISBN 0-911764-22-4). Durrell.
Horning, D. S., jt. auth. see Bohart, R. M.
Hornsey, et al. Mechanics of Materials: An Individualized Approach. LC 76-18470. (Illus.). 1977. pap. 18.95 incl. ref. manual & study guide (ISBN 0-395-24993-7); solutions manual 2.15 (ISBN 0-395-24994-5). HM.
Hornsey, A. W., ed. see Borchert, Wolfgang.
Hornstein, H. A., et al. Social Intervention. LC 77-143509. 1971. text ed. 17.95 (ISBN 0-02-914960-6). Free Pr.
Hornung, Clarence. Antique Automoblies. (Illus.). 1978. pap. 1.75 (ISBN 0-486-22742-1). Dover.
--Background Patterns, Textures & Tints. (Pictorial Archive Ser.). (Illus.). 112p. (Orig.). 1976. pap. 5.00 (ISBN 0-486-23260-3). Dover.
Hornung, Clarence P. A Source Book of Antiques & Jewelry Designs. LC 68-16512. (Illus.). 1968. 12.50 o.s.i. (ISBN 0-8076-0439-9). Braziller.
--Treasury of American Antiques. concise ed. LC 76-49914. (Illus.). 1977. 17.50 (ISBN 0-8109-1670-3); pap. 8.95 o.p. (ISBN 0-8109-2060-3). Abrams.
Hornung, Ernest W. Raffles: The Amateur Cracksman. LC 75-38587. (Illus.). 1976. pap. 3.25 (ISBN 0-8032-5836-4, BB 616, Bison). U of Nebr Pr.
Hornung, W. Raffles. 302p. 1980. lib. bdg. 14.50x (ISBN 0-89968-186-7). Lightyear.
Hornung, William J. Builder's Vestpocket Reference Book. 1956. 6.95 (ISBN 0-13-085951-6). P-H.
Hornus, Jean-Michel. It Is Not Lawful for Me to Fight. LC 79-26846. 376p. 1980. pap. 13.95 (ISBN 0-8361-1911-8). Herald Pr.
Horny, J. Differential Diagnostisches Kompendium. 2nd ed. (Illus.). xvi, 260p. 1980. pap. text ed. 17.00 (ISBN 3-8055-0585-X). S Karger.
Hornyak, W. F. see Marton, L.
Horobin, G. W., ed. Experience with Abortion. LC 73-77171. (Illus.). 280p. 1973. 69.50 (ISBN 0-521-20240-X). Cambridge U Pr.
Horodniceanu, Michael & Cantilli, Edmund J. Transportation-System Safety. LC 78-7126. (Illus.). 1979. 21.00 (ISBN 0-669-02467-8). Lexington Bks.
Horos, Carol. Prepared Childbirth. Date not set. pap. 2.25 (ISBN 0-440-07087-2). Dell.
Horosz, William. Religion & Human Purpose. LC 73-176179. 500p. Date not set. 16.50 (ISBN 0-87527-109-X). Green. Postponed.
Horoszowski, Pawel. Economic Special-Opportunity Conduct & Crime. LC 78-24829. 222p. 1980. 24.95x (ISBN 0-669-02849-5). Lexington Bks.
Horowitz. Image Formation & Cognition. 2nd ed. (Illus.). 1978. 24.50 (ISBN 0-8385-4274-3). ACC.
Horowitz & Karst. Law, Lawyers & Social Change. 1969. 16.50 (ISBN 0-672-81003-4, Bobbs-Merrill Law); 1978 suppl. by Warren S. Bracy 6.00 (ISBN 0-672-83545-2). Michie.
Horowitz, Al. Chess for Beginners: A Picture Guide. (Illus.). 1959. pap. 3.50 (ISBN 0-06-463223-7, EH 223, EH). Har-Row.
--Chess Self-Teacher. (Orig.). 1961. pap. 2.95 (ISBN 0-06-463257-1, EH 257, EH). Har-Row.
--The World Chess Championship - a History. (Illus.). 288p. 1973. 9.95 o.s.i. (ISBN 0-02-554150-1). Macmillan.
Horowitz, Dan, jt. auth. see Luttwak, Edward.
Horowitz, David. The Enigma of Economic Growth: A Case Study of Israel. LC 77-184338. (Special Studies in International Economics & Development). 1972. 27.50x (ISBN 0-275-28272-4). Irvington.
--Fight Back: & Don't Get Ripped off. LC 78-19498. 304p. 1981. pap. 2.95 (ISBN 0-06-250392-8, P 5001, PL). Har-Row.
Horowitz, Donald L. The Courts & Social Policy. LC 76-48944. 1977. 14.95 (ISBN 0-8157-3734-3); pap. 5.95 (ISBN 0-8157-3733-5). Brookings.
--The Jurocracy: Government Lawyers, Agency Programs, & Judicial Decisions. LC 76-27921. 1977. 16.95 (ISBN 0-669-00986-5). Lexington Bks.
Horowitz, Frances D., ed. Early Developmental Hazards: Predictors & Precautions. LC 78-352. (AAAS Selected Symposium Ser.: No. 19). 1978. lib. bdg. 16.00x (ISBN 0-89158-084-0). Westview.
Horowitz, Gene. The Ladies of Levittown. 352p. 1981. pap. 2.95 (ISBN 0-449-24401-6, Crest). Fawcett.
Horowitz, Gideon. Sadistic Statistics: An Introduction to Statistics for the Behavioral Sciences. 1979. pap. text ed. 9.95 (ISBN 0-89529-091-X). Avery Pub.
Horowitz, Helen L. Culture & the City: Cultural Philanthropy in Chicago from the 1880's to 1917. LC 75-3546. 302p. 1976. 17.50x (ISBN 0-8131-1344-X). U Pr of Ky.

Horowitz, I. A. All About Chess. 1971. pap. 2.95 o.s.i. (ISBN 0-02-028880-8, Collier). Macmillan.
--All About Chess. 1971. 6.95 o.s.i. (ISBN 0-02-554110-2). Macmillan.
--Winning Chess Tactics. LC 73-81634. (Illus.). 3.95 o.s.i. (ISBN 0-88365-060-6). Brown Bk.
Horowitz, I. A. & Reinfeld, Fred. First Book of Chess. 1953. pap. 2.95 (ISBN 0-06-463241-5, EH 241, EH). Har-Row.
--First Book of Chess. (Illus.). 1966. pap. 3.50 o.p. (ISBN 0-571-06731-X, Pub. by Faber & Faber). Merrimack Bk Serv.
--How to Think Ahead in Chess. (Illus., Orig.). 1972. pap. 3.50 o.p. (ISBN 0-571-09912-2, Pub. by Faber & Faber). Merrimack Bk Serv.
--Macmillan Handbook of Chess. (Illus.). 1956. 10.95 (ISBN 0-02-554140-4). Macmillan.
Horowitz, I. L. Sociological Self-Images. 1970. 26.00 (ISBN 0-08-016400-5). Pergamon.
Horowitz, Ira. Introduction to Quantitative Business Analysis. 2nd ed. (Illus.). 352p. 1972. text ed. 19.95 (ISBN 0-07-030398-3); solutions to problems 2.75 (ISBN 0-07-030399-1). McGraw.
Horowitz, Ira, jt. auth. see Spulber, Nicolas.
Horowitz, Irving L. Contemporary Earth Science. (Orig.). (gr. 10). 1976. pap. text ed. 6.00 (ISBN 0-87720-150-1). AMSCO Sch.
--Cuban Communism. 550p. 1981. pap. 9.95 (ISBN 0-87855-838-1). Transaction Bks.
--Earth Science Investigations. (gr. 9-12). 1973. pap. text ed. 7.08 (ISBN 0-87720-155-2). AMSCO Sch.
--Ideology & Utopia in the United States, 1956-1976. 1977. pap. text ed. 7.95 (ISBN 0-19-502107-X, 477, GB). Oxford U Pr.
--Israeli Ecstacies - Jewish Agonies. 240p. 1974. 12.95 (ISBN 0-19-501747-1). Oxford U Pr.
--Philosophy, Science & the Sociology of Knowledge. LC 76-27756. 1976. Repr. of 1961 ed. lib. bdg. 16.75x (ISBN 0-8371-9051-7, HOPS). Greenwood.
--Professing Sociology: Studies in the Life Cycle of Social Science. abr. ed. LC 75-15534. (Arcturus Books Paperbacks). 238p. 1976. pap. 6.95 (ISBN 0-8093-0741-3). S Ill U Pr.
--Radicalism & the Revolt Against Reason. 1961. text ed. 8.75x (ISBN 0-391-02031-5). Humanities.
--Radicalism & the Revolt Against Reason: The Social Theories of Georges Sorel. LC 68-25562. (Arcturus Books Paperbacks). 287p. 1968. pap. 7.95 (ISBN 0-8093-0323-X). S Ill U Pr.
--War & Peace in Contemporary Social & Philosophical Theory. Orig. Title: Idea of War & Peace in Contemporary Philosophy. 218p. 1973. Repr. of 1957 ed. text ed. 9.50x (ISBN 0-391-00284-8). Humanities.
Horowitz, Irving L. & Katz, James E. Social Science & Public Policy in the United States. LC 74-33034. (Illus.). 206p. 1975. text ed. 24.95 (ISBN 0-275-05310-5); pap. text ed. 11.95 (ISBN 0-275-89160-7). Praeger.
Horowitz, Irving L. & Lipset, Seymour M. Dialogues on American Politics. 1978. 12.95 (ISBN 0-19-502449-4). Oxford U Pr.
Horowitz, Irving L., ed. Constructing Policy: Dialogues with Social Scientists in the National Political Arena. 1979. 25.95 (ISBN 0-03-046696-2). Praeger.
--Equity, Income, & Policy: Comparative Studies in Three Worlds of Development. LC 76-2904. (Special Studies). 1977. text ed. 32.95 (ISBN 0-275-56570-X). Praeger.
--Masses in Latin America. LC 73-83045. 1970. 19.95 (ISBN 0-19-500586-4). Oxford U Pr.
--Masses in Latin America. LC 73-83045. 1970. pap. 7.95 (ISBN 0-19-500795-6, 297, GB). Oxford U Pr.
--New Sociology: Essays in Social Science & Social Theory in Honor of C. Wright Mills. 1964. 19.95 (ISBN 0-19-500587-2). Oxford U Pr.
--New Sociology: Essays in Social Science & Social Theory in Honor of C. Wright Mills. (YA) (gr. 9 up). 1965. pap. 6.95 (ISBN 0-19-500722-0, GB). Oxford U Pr.
--Science, Sin & Scholarship: The Politics of Reverend Moon & the Unification Church. 312p. 1980. 12.50 (ISBN 0-262-08100-8); pap. 6.95 (ISBN 0-262-58042-X). MIT Pr.
Horowitz, Irving L., ed. see Mills, C. Wright.
Horowitz, Isaac M. Synthesis of Feedback Systems. 1963. text ed. 24.95 (ISBN 0-12-355950-2). Acad Pr.
Horowitz, Israel A. & Rothenberg, P. L. Complete Book of Chess. Orig. Title: Personality of Chess. (Illus.). 1969. pap. 2.95 o.s.i. (ISBN 0-02-028870-0, Collier). Macmillan.
Horowitz, Laurence J., jt. auth. see Daniels, Victor.
Horowitz, Mannie. Citizen Band Transceivers: Installation & Troubleshooting. (Illus.). 1978. ref. 17.95 (ISBN 0-87909-102-9). Reston.
Horowitz, Michael M. Mo[illegible] Village in Martiniqu[illegible] Spindler, Louise, eds[illegible] ultural Anthropology). 128p. [illegible] .95x (ISBN 0-8290-0309-6). Irving[illegible]
Horowitz, Morris A., jt. auth. see Goldstein, Harold M.
Horowitz, Norman H. & Hutchings, Edward, Jr., eds. Genes, Cells, & Behavior: A View of Biology Fifty Years Later. LC 80-18744. (Biology Ser.). (Illus.). 1980. text ed. 12.95x (ISBN 0-7167-1217-2). W H Freeman.
Horowitz, Paul & Hill, Winfield. The Art of Electronics. LC 79-27170. (Illus.). 544p. 1980. 24.95 (ISBN 0-521-23151-5). Cambridge U Pr.
Horowitz, Robert E. The Great Impeacher. (Brooklyn College Studies on Society in Change Ser.). 1979. 20.00 (ISBN 0-930888-03-0). Brooklyn Coll Pr.
Horowitz, S. H. Protective Relaying for Power Systems. 560p. 1980. 39.95 (ISBN 0-471-08968-0, Pub. by Wiley-Interscience); pap. 26.00 (ISBN 0-471-08967-2). Wiley.
Horowitz, Shirley, ed. see Burch, Monte.
Horowitz, Shirley, ed. see Derven, Ronald & Nichols, Carol.
Horowitz, Shirley, ed. see Schram, Joseph.
Horowitz, Shirley M., ed. see Burch, Monte.
Horowitz, Shirley M., ed. see Cornell, Jane.
Horowitz, Shirley M., ed. see Hedden, Jay.
Horowitz, Shirley M., ed. see Hughes, Herb.
Horowitz, Shirley M., ed. see Jones, Robert E. & Burch, Monte.
Horowitz, Shirley M., ed. see Meyers, Donald L.
Horowitz, Shirley M., ed. see Nunn, Richard V.
Horowitz, Shirley M., ed. see Philbin, Tom.
Horowitz, Shirley M., ed. see Russell, James E.
Horowitz, Shirley M., ed. see Schram, Joseph.
Horowitz, Shirley M., ed. see Shapiro, Cecile, et al.
Horowitz, Steve & Offen, Neil. Calling Dr. Horowitz. 1978. pap. 1.95 o.s.i. (ISBN 0-515-04509-8). Jove Pubns.
Horowitz, Sylvia. The Find of a Lifetime: Sir Arthur Evans & the Discovery of Knossos. LC 80-36851. (Illus.). 288p. 1981. 14.95 (ISBN 0-670-13575-5). Viking Pr.
Horowitz, Z. P. Angiotensin Converting Enzyme Inhibitors: Mechanisms of Action & Clinical Implications. 1981. text ed. price not set (ISBN 0-8067-0821-2). Urban & S.
Horr, David A., ed. American Indian Ethnohistory, 118 vols. (Illus.). lib. bdg. 2400.00 set (ISBN 0-685-37527-7); lib. bdg. 42.00 ea. Garland Pub.
--Indians of Ohio, Indiana, Illinois, Southern Michigan & Southern Wisconsin: Findings of Fact & Opinion, 3 vols. (North Central & Northeastern Indians - American Indian Ethnohistory Ser.). 1974. Set. lib. bdg. 99.00 (ISBN 0-8240-0807-3); lib. bdg. 42.00 ea. Garland Pub.
--Kiowa-Commanche Indians, 2 vols. (American Indian Ethnohistory Ser.: Plains Indians). 1974. Set. lib. bdg. 76.00 (ISBN 0-8240-0724-7); lib. bdg. 42.00 ea. Garland Pub.
--Piankashaw & Kaskaskia Indians. Incl. An Anthropological Report on the Piankashaw Indians. Libby, Dorothy; Report on the Piankashaw & Kaskaskia & the Treaty of Greene Ville. Stout, David B. (American Indian Ethnohistory Ser: North Central & Northeastern Indians). (Illus.). lib. bdg. 42.00 (ISBN 0-8240-0760-3). Garland Pub.
Horr, David A., ed. see Basehart, Harry W.
Horr, David A., ed. see Beals, Ralph L.
Horr, David A., ed. see Bell, Robert E.
Horr, David A., ed. see Bender, Averam B., et al.
Horr, David A., ed. see Bender, Averam B.
Horr, David A., ed. see Chapman, Berlin B.
Horr, David A., ed. see Cline, Howard F.
Horr, David A., ed. see Doster, James F.
Horr, David A., ed. see Driver, Harold E., et al.
Horr, David A., ed. see Ewers, John C.
Horr, David A., ed. see Fairbanks, Charles H.
Horr, David A., ed. see Gordon, B. L., et al.
Horr, David A., ed. see Gussow, Zachary, et al.
Horr, David A., ed. see Heizer, Robert F.
Horr, David A., ed. see Hickerson, Harold.
Horr, David A., ed. see Jablow, Joseph.
Horr, David A., ed. see Jicarilla Apache Tribe.
Horr, David A., ed. see Kroeber, Alfred L.
Horr, David A., ed. see Manners, Robert A., et al.
Horr, David A., ed. see Neuman, Robert W.
Horr, David A., ed. see Ray, Verne F., et al.
Horr, David A., ed. see Schroeder, Albert H.
Horr, David A., ed. see Smith, G. Hubert.
Horr, David A., ed. see Tanner, Helen H.
Horr, David A., ed. see Thomas, Alfred B., et al.
Horr, David A., ed. see Wheeler-Voegelin, Erminie, et al.
Horr, David A., ed. see Wheeler-Voegelin, Erminie.
Horr, David A., ed. see Williams, Stephen.
Horrell, Benjamin C. Broken Chains. 1972. pap. 2.25 (ISBN 0-87148-106-5). Pathway Pr.
Horrell, C. William & Steffes, Robert A. Introductory & Publications Photography. 3rd ed. 1976. 5.50x (ISBN 0-9603876-0-9). Kenilworth.
Horrell, Muriel, ed. Bantu Education to 1968. LC 76-484665. 176p. 1968. 5.00x (ISBN 0-8002-0521-9). Intl Pubns Serv.
Horribin, David F., ed. see Flodin, Nestor W.
Horridge, G. A., ed. The Compound Eye & Vision of Insects. (Illus.). 614p. 1975. 74.00x (ISBN 0-19-857375-8). Oxford U Pr.
Horridge, G. Adrian, jt. auth. see Bullock, Theodore H.
Horrobin, D., ed. see Oparil, Suzanne & Katholi, Richard.
Horrobin, D., ed. see Ziegler, Thomas W.
Horrobin, D. F., ed. see Brain, Paul F.
Horrobin, D. F., ed. see Damjanov, Ivan.
Horrobin, D. F., ed. see Flodin, N. W.
Horrobin, D. F., ed. see Fulkerson, W. J.
Horrobin, D. F., ed. see Hamblin, T. J.
Horrobin, D. F., ed. see Hume, Wilfred I.
Horrobin, D. F., ed. see Hume, Wilfrid I.
Horrobin, D. F., ed. see Hutchinson, J. S.
Horrobin, D. F., ed. see McQuillan, Mary T.
Horrobin, D. F., ed. see Oparil, Suzanne, et al.
Horrobin, D. F., ed. see Reiter, Russel J.
Horrobin, D. F., ed. see Rix, Keith B.
Horrobin, D. F., ed. see Skrabanek, Petr & Powell, David.
Horrobin, D. F., ed. see Smith, Cedric.
Horrobin, D. F., ed. see Taylor, Clive R.
Horrobin, D. F., ed. see Taylor, Cliver R.
Horrobin, David. Medical Hubris: A Reply to Ivan Illich. LC 80-66836. 146p. 1980. 9.95 (ISBN 0-88831-080-3); pap. 6.95 (ISBN 0-88831-086-2). Eden Med Res.
--Prostaglandins: Physiology, Pharmacology & Clinical Signifiance. 1978. 21.60 (ISBN 0-88831-032-3). Eden Med Res.
Horrobin, David F. Medical Hubris: A Reply to Ivan Illich. 1977. 9.00 o.p. (ISBN 0-88831-001-3). Eden Med Res.
--Prolactin, Vol. 2. (Annual Research Reviews Ser.). 1974. 19.20 (ISBN 0-85200-120-7). Eden Med Res.
--Prolactin, Vol. 4. (Annual Research Reviews Ser.). 1976. 24.00 (ISBN 0-904406-47-4). Eden Med Res.
--Prolactin, Vol. 5. LC 77-369577. (Annual Research Reviews Ser.). 1977. 24.00 (ISBN 0-88831-009-9). Eden Med Res.
--Prolactin, Vol. 6. (Annual Research Reviews Ser.). 1979. 21.60 (ISBN 0-88831-041-2). Eden Med Res.
--Prolactin, Vol. 7. LC 77-369577. (Annual Research Reviews Ser.). 126p. 1980. 18.00 (ISBN 0-88831-069-2). Eden Med Res.
--Prolactin, Vol. 8. (Annual Research Reviews Ser.). 152p. 1981. 24.00 (ISBN 0-88831-093-5). Eden Med Res.
Horrobin, David F., ed. see Augusteyn, R. C. & Collin, H. B.
Horrobin, David F., ed. see Lamberts, Steven W. & MacLeod, Robert M.
Horrobin, David F., ed. see Watkins, Wayne B.
Horrobin, Peter. Constructional Mathematics, Vol. 1. 1969. pap. 7.00 (ISBN 0-08-006890-1). Pergamon.
Horrocks, Brian, et al. Corps Commander. LC 77-7921. (Illus.). 1978. 14.95 o.p. (ISBN 0-684-15324-6, ScribT). Scribner.
Horrow, Richard B. Sports Violence: The Interaction Between Private Lawmaking & the Criminal Law. LC 80-65053. (Scholarly Monographs). 286p. 1980. 27.50 (ISBN 0-8408-0500-4); pap. 17.50 (ISBN 0-686-63392-X). Carrollton Pr.
Horry, Peter. Parson Weem's Life of Francis Marion. LC 76-21439. 1976. 10.00 (ISBN 0-937684-04-X). Tradd St Pr.
Horsburgh, David B. & Heath, James P. Atlas of Cat Anatomy. 3rd ed. (Illus.). 1950. pap. 2.00x o.p. (ISBN 0-8047-0357-4). Stanford U Pr.
Horsely, Joanne. Structured Preoperative Teaching: Using Research to Improve Clinical Practice. 1980. 9.50 (ISBN 0-8089-1311-5). Grune.
Horsfall, Frank L. & Tamm, Igor. Viral & Rickettsial Infections of Man. 4th ed. (Illus., Span. & Ital. eds. avail). 1965. 15.50 o.p. (ISBN 0-397-52024-7). Lippincott.
Horsfall, James G. & Cowling, Ellis B., eds. Plant Disease: An Advanced Treatise, Vol. 3: How Plants Suffer from Disease. 1979. 48.50 (ISBN 0-12-356403-4); by subscription 42.00 (ISBN 0-686-66289-X). Acad Pr.
Horsfield, John. The Art of Leadership in War: The Royal Navy from the Age of Nelson to the End of World War II. LC 79-54059. (Contributions in Military History: No. 21). (Illus.). xiv, 240p. 1980. lib. bdg. 25.00 (ISBN 0-313-20919-7, HLE/). Greenwood.
Horsley, J. E. & Carlova, J. Testifying in Court. 1972. 8.95 (ISBN 0-87489-039-X). Med Economics.
--Your Family & the Law. 1975. 9.95 (ISBN 0-87489-096-9). Med Economics.
Horsley, John. Tools of the Maritime Trades. LC 78-51829. (Illus.). 1978. 15.00 o.p. (ISBN 0-87742-101-3). Intl Marine.
Horsman, Alan, ed. see Dickens, Charles.
Horsman, Reginald. The Frontier in the Formative Years, 1783-1815. LC 76-94404. (Histories of the American Frontier Ser). (Illus.). 253p. 1979. pap. 6.50x (ISBN 0-8263-0313-7). U of NM pr.
Horst, Brian Van Der see Van Der Horst, Brian.
Horst, Irvin B. The Radical Brethren: Anabaptism & the English Reformation to 1558. (Bibliotheca Humanistica & Reformatorica: No. 2). 1972. text ed. 37.25x (ISBN 90-6004-292-1). Humanities.
Horst, Pamela, et al. Evaluation Planning at the National Institute of Mental Health: A Case History. 166p. 1974. pap. 5.00 o.p. (ISBN 0-87766-097-2, 27000). Urban Inst.
Horst, Paul. Personality: Measurement of Dimensions. LC 68-54939. (Social & Behavioral Science Ser.). 1968. 14.95x o.p. (ISBN 0-87589-020-2). Jossey-Bass.
Horst, Robert ter see Ter Horst, Robert.
Horstadius, Sven. Experimental Embryology of Echinoderms. (Illus.). 201p. 1973. 29.95x (ISBN 0-19-857373-1). Oxford U Pr.
Horsting, Al G. The Complete Book on Hatching Egg Care & Sanitation. 1981. write for info. Franklin Inst Pr.
Horstman, Thomas. The Kessler Alliance. 1980. pap. 2.25 (ISBN 0-505-51463-X). Tower Bks.
Hort, N. D., jt. auth. see Wright, R. C.
Horton. Plaid for Social Problems. 1975. pap. 5.50 (ISBN 0-256-01483-3, 17-1036-00). Learning Syst.
Horton, Andrew S. & Magretta, Joan, eds. Modern European Filmmakers & the Art of Adaption. LC 79-48073. (Ungar Film Library). (Illus.). 400p. 1981. 14.95 (ISBN 0-8044-2403-9); pap. 6.95 (ISBN 0-8044-6277-1). Ungar.
Horton, Arthur M., Jr., ed. Psychotherapeutic Treatment Approaches for the Aging. 320p. 1981. 24.95 (ISBN 0-89789-007-8). J F Bergin.
Horton, Catherine. A Closer Look at Grasslands. (Closer Look at Ser.). (Illus.). (gr. 4 up). 1979. PLB 6.90 s&l (ISBN 0-531-03411-9). Watts.
Horton, Claude A. Money Counts: A Handbook on Local Church Finance. 88p. 1980. pap. 4.95 (ISBN 0-89367-051-0). Light & Life.
Horton, D., jt. auth. see Pigman, W.
Horton, David L. & Turnage, Thomas W. Human Learning. (P-H Series in Experimental Psychology). (Illus.). 464p. 1976. Ref. Ed. 19.95 (ISBN 0-13-445312-3). P-H.
Horton, Dereck & Tipson, R. Stuart. Advances in Carbohydrate Chemistry & Biochemistry, Vol. 38. 1981. write for info. (ISBN 0-12-007238-6); lib. bdg. write for info. (ISBN 0-12-007288-2); write for info. microfiche (ISBN 0-12-007289-0). Acad Pr.
Horton, Derek see Pigman, Ward & Wolfrom, Melville L.
Horton, Derek, jt. ed. see Tipson, R. Stuart.
Horton, F. L. The Melchizedek Tradition. LC 75-32479. (Society for New Testament Studies Monographs: No. 30). 220p. 1976. 36.00 (ISBN 0-521-21014-3). Cambridge U Pr.
Horton, Frank E., jt. auth. see Berry, Brian J.
Horton, H. Mack, tr. see Hashimoto, Fumio.
Horton, H. Mack, tr. see Takeda, Tsuneo.
Horton, Harold, tr. Os Dons Do Espirito Santo. (Portuguese Bks.). 1979. 1.35 (ISBN 0-8297-0837-5). Life Pubs Intl.
Horton, Holbrook L. Mathematics at Work. 2nd ed. (Illus.). 1957. 16.00 (ISBN 0-8311-1047-3). Indus Pr.
Horton, John E., et al, eds. Mechanisms of Localized Bone Loss. (Illus.). 1978. pap. 18.00 (ISBN 0-917000-03-X). Info Retrieval.
Horton, John J. Yugoslavia. (World Bibliography Ser.: No. 1). 194p. 1978. text ed. 25.25 (ISBN 0-903450-09-7). ABC-Clio.
Horton, John T. James Kent: A Study in Conservatism, 1763-1847. LC 76-84189. (American Scene, Comments & Commentators Ser). 1969. Repr. of 1939 ed. lib. bdg. 35.00 (ISBN 0-306-71502-3). Da Capo.
Horton, Louise. Careers in Office Work. (Career Concise Guides Ser.). (Illus.). (gr. 7 up). 1977. PLB 6.45 s&l (ISBN 0-531-01308-1). Watts.
--Careers in Theatre, Music & Dance. (Career Concise Guides Ser.). (Illus.). 72p. (gr. 7 up). 1976. PLB 6.45 (ISBN 0-531-01205-0). Watts.
Horton, Louise, ed. Art Careers. LC 75-12785. (Career Concise Guide Ser). (Illus.). 72p. (gr. 5 up). 1975. PLB 6.45 (ISBN 0-531-02841-0). Watts.
Horton, Patricia M., jt. auth. see Magarian, Judith A.
Horton, Paul B. & Horton, Robert L. Plaid for Introductory Sociology. 1977. pap. 5.50 (ISBN 0-256-01987-8, 17-0302-02). Learning Syst.
Horton, Paul B. & Leslie, Gerald R. The Sociology of Social Problems. 7th ed. (Illus.). 672p. 1981. text ed. 18.95 (ISBN 0-13-821702-5). P-H.

--The Sociology of Social Problems. 6th ed. LC 77-14610. (Illus.). 1978. text ed. 17.95 (ISBN 0-13-821637-1); study guide & wkbk. 4.95 (ISBN 0-13-821611-8). P-H.
Horton, Philip C., ed. The Third World & Press Freedom. LC 78-17072. (Praeger Special Studies). 1978. 25.95 (ISBN 0-03-045551-0). Praeger.
Horton, Raymond D. & Brecher, Charles, eds. Setting Municipal Priorities, Nineteen Eighty. LC 79-88261. 224p. 1979. text ed. 24.00 (ISBN 0-916672-37-9). Allanheld.
--Setting Municipal Priorities, 1980. LC 79-88261. 224p. Date not set. price not set o.s.i. Allanheld & Schram.
Horton, Raymond D., jt. ed. see Brecher, Charles.
Horton, Robert L., jt. auth. see Horton, Paul B.
Horton, Rod W. & Edwards, Herbert W. Backgrounds of American Literary Thought. 3rd ed. 1974. pap. 12.95 (ISBN 0-13-056291-2). P-H.
Horton, Ronald A. The Unity of "The Faerie Queene". LC 77-15793. 240p. 1978. 15.00x (ISBN 0-8203-0440-9). U of Ga Pr.
Horton, Russell M. Lincoln Steffens. LC 74-3089. (World Leaders Ser: No. 35). 168p. 1974. lib. bdg. 9.95 (ISBN 0-8057-3721-9). Twayne.
Horton, Stanley. Ready Always. LC 74-76802. (Radiant Life Ser). 1974. pap. 1.25 (ISBN 0-88243-575-2, 02-0575); teacher's ed 2.50 (ISBN 0-88243-182-X, 32-0182). Gospel Pub.
Horton, Stanley M. The Book of Acts: A Radiant Commentary on the New Testament. LC 80-65892. 304p. 1981. 10.95 (ISBN 0-88243-317-2, 02-0317). Gospel Pub.
Horton, Susan R. The Reader in the Dickens World. LC 80-53031. 215p. 1981. 29.95 (ISBN 0-8229-1140-X). U of Pittsburgh Pr.
Horton, T. R. The Reading Standards of Children in Wales. (Illus.). 156p. 1973. pap. text ed. 11.25x (ISBN 0-85633-009-4, NFER). Humanities.
Horton, Wade H. Evangel Sermons. LC 76-57860. 1977. pap. 2.95 (ISBN 0-87148-287-8). Pathway Pr.
--Sound Scriptual Sermon Outlines, No. 2. 1974. 5.95 (ISBN 0-87148-769-1); pap. 4.95 (ISBN 0-87148-770-5). Pathway Pr.
--Sound Scriptual Sermons. 1973. 5.95 (ISBN 0-87148-775-6); pap. 4.95 (ISBN 0-87148-776-4). Pathway Pr.
--Sound Scriptural Outlines: No. 3. 1977. 5.95 (ISBN 0-87148-781-0); pap. 4.95 (ISBN 0-87148-780-2). Pathway Pr.
--Trinitarian Concept of God. 1964. pap. 1.50 (ISBN 0-87148-833-7). Pathway Pr.
Horvasse, R. see Satir, P.
Horvat, Branko. An Essay on Yugoslav Society. Mins, Henry F., tr. from Yug. LC 79-77456. 1969. 15.00 o.p. (ISBN 0-87332-009-3). M E Sharpe.
--The Yugoslav Economic System: The First Labor-Managed Economy in the Making. LC 75-46111. 1976. 20.00 o.p. (ISBN 0-87332-074-3); pap. 7.95 (ISBN 0-87332-175-8). M E Sharpe.
Horvat, Branko, et al, eds. Self-Governing Socialism: A Reader, 2 vols. Incl. Vol. 1. 491p. text ed. 25.50 (ISBN 0-87332-050-6); pap. 10.95 (ISBN 0-87332-060-3); Vol. 2. 329p. text ed. 22.50 (ISBN 0-87332-061-1); pap. 9.95 (ISBN 0-87332-062-X). LC 73-92805. 1975. Set (ISBN 0-87332-048-4). M E Sharpe.
Horvath, Betty. Jasper & the Hero Business. (Easy-Read Storybook Ser.). (Illus.). (gr. k-3). 1977. lib. bdg. 4.90 s&l o.p. (ISBN 0-531-01317-0). Watts.
Horvath, Csaba, ed. High Performance Liquid Chromatography: Advances & Perspectives, Vol. 2. 1980. lib ed 39.50 (ISBN 0-12-312202-3). Acad Pr.
Horville, R. Don Juan De Moliere: Une Dramaturgie De Rupture. (La Collection Themes & Textes Ser.). 288p. (Orig., Fr.). 1972. pap. 6.75 (ISBN 2-03-035011-7, 2690). Larousse.
Horvitz, Diana F., jt. auth. see Sloane, R. Bruce.
Horvitz, Leslie & Gerhard, H. Harris. The Compton Effect. 1980. pap. 2.25 (ISBN 0-451-09299-6, E9299, Sig). NAL.
Horvitz, P. Monetary Policy & the Financial System. 4th ed. 1979. 18.95 (ISBN 0-13-599944-8). P-H.
Horwath, Ernest B., et al. Hotel Accounting. 4th ed. LC 77-79169. 1978. 26.95 (ISBN 0-471-07247-8, Pub. by Wiley-Interscience). Wiley.
Horwich, R. H. The Ontogeny of Social Behavior in the Gray Squirrel (Sciurus carolinensis) (Advances in Ethology Ser.: Vol. 8). (Illus.). 103p. (Orig.). 1972. pap. text ed. 23.50. Parey Sci Pubs.
Horwill, Herbert W. Dictionary of Modern American Usage. 2nd ed. 1944. 19.50x (ISBN 0-19-869109-2). Oxford U Pr.
Horwitz, Eleanor, ed. Ways of Wildlife. LC 77-2208. 172p. 1977. text ed. 7.95 (ISBN 0-590-07527-6, Citations); pap. 2.95 (ISBN 0-590-09617-6). Schol Bk Serv.
Horwitz, Eleanor & Wildlife Society Elementary Education Committee, eds. Ways of Wildlife. LC 77-2208. (Illus.). 159p. (gr. 1-6). 1977. 7.95 (ISBN 0-590-07527-6, Citation); pap. 2.95 (ISBN 0-590-09617-6). Schol Bk Serv.
Horwitz, Elinor. Soothsayer's Handbook: A Guide to Bad Signs & Good Vibrations. LC 76-172143. (Illus.). (gr. 9 up). 1972. 7.95 o.p. (ISBN 0-397-31538-4). Lippincott.
Horwitz, Elinor L. On the Land: The Evolution of American Agriculture. LC 79-3545. (gr. 7 up). 1980. 8.95 (ISBN 0-689-50165-X, McElderry Bk). Atheneum.
--Sometimes It Happens. LC 79-2687. (Illus.). 40p. (gr. 1-4). 1981. 7.95 (ISBN 0-06-022596-3, HarpJ); PLB 7.89 (ISBN 0-06-022597-1). Har-Row.
--When the Sky Is Like Lace. LC 75-9664. 32p. (gr. k-2). 1975. 8.95 (ISBN 0-397-31550-3). Lippincott.
Horwitz, G. & Fusco, P. La Causa. 1970. 7.95 o.s.i. (ISBN 0-02-554120-X). Macmillan.
--La Causa. 1970. pap. 3.95 o.s.i. (ISBN 0-02-073560-X, Collier). Macmillan.
Horwitz, Gene. I Remain, Your Uncle Ambrogio. 1977. pap. 1.50 o.p. (ISBN 0-445-03197-2). Popular Lib.
Horwitz, Henry. Welding: Principles & Practice. LC 77-76341. (Illus.). 1978. text ed. 19.50 (ISBN 0-395-24473-0); instr's. manual 1.15 (ISBN 0-395-24474-9). HM.
Horwitz, James. They Went Thataway. 1978. pap. 1.95 o.p. (ISBN 0-345-27126-2). Ballantine.
Horwitz, John J. Team Practice & the Specialist: An Introduction to Interdisciplinary Teamwork. 172p. 1970. text ed. 12.75 (ISBN 0-398-00873-6). C C Thomas.
Horwitz, Julius. The Best Days. LC 80-12649. 216p. 1980. 10.95 (ISBN 0-03-056051-9). HR&W.
Horwitz, Michael B. Guide to Smoke-Free Dining: National Directory of Restaurants Catering to Non-Smokers. LC 80-66634. 112p. 1980. pap. 5.00 (ISBN 0-936960-01-9). Environ Pr.
Horwitz, Morton J. The Transformation of American Law, 1790-1860. (Studies in Legal History). 1977. 18.50x (ISBN 0-674-90370-6). Harvard U Pr.
Horwitz, Richard. Anthropology Toward History: Culture & Work in a 19th-Century Maine Town. LC 77-74560. (Illus.). 1978. lib. bdg. 17.50x (ISBN 0-8195-5014-0, Pub. by Wesleyan U Pr). Columbia U Pr.
Horwitz, Tem, ed. see Lynch, Jane S., et al.
Horwood, William. Duncton Wood. 736p. 1981. pap. 3.50 (ISBN 0-345-29113-1). Ballantine.
Hosburgh, David. Thirteen Poems. (Writers Workshop Redbird Ser.). 1975. 8.00 (ISBN 0-88253-658-3); pap. text ed. 4.00 (ISBN 0-88253-657-5). Ind-US Inc.
Hosek, William R. Macroeconomic Theory. 1975. text ed. 17.50x (ISBN 0-256-01669-0). Irwin.
Hoselitz, Bert F., tr. see Menger, Carl.
Hoselitz, Bert F., et al, eds. Theories of Economic Growth. LC 60-10898. 1965. pap. text ed. 5.95 (ISBN 0-02-915220-8). Free Pr.
Hoselitz, Berthold F., ed. Economics & the Idea of Mankind. LC 65-12109. 1965. 20.00x (ISBN 0-231-02750-8). Columbia U Pr.
Hosen, Ron. Who Would You Like to Be. 200p. (Orig.). 1980. pap. 4.95 (ISBN 0-89260-195-7). Hwong Pub.
Hosh, Koi, jt. auth. see Coffer, William E.
Hoshii, Iwao, jt. auth. see Adams, T. F. M.
Hoshiko, Patsy Rose, jt. auth. see Kilpatrick, Thomas L.
Hoshino, H., jt. auth. see Kato, Genchi.
Hosie, Alexander. Manchuria: Its People, Resources & Recent History, London, 1904. LC 78-74311. (The Modern Chinese Economy Ser.: Vol. 24). 326p. 1980. lib. bdg. 38.00 (ISBN 0-8240-4272-7). Garland Pub.
Hosier, Helen K. How to Know When God Speaks. LC 79-84721. 160p. (Orig.). pap. 4.95 (ISBN 0-89081-197-0). Harvest Hse.
--Joyfully Expectant. 1977. pap. 1.50 o.p. (ISBN 0-8007-8296-8, Spire Bks). Revell.
--Profiles: People Who Are Helping to Change the World. 1977. 6.95 o.p. (ISBN 0-8015-6082-9). Dutton.
Hoskin, M. A., ed. see Newton, Isaac.
Hoskin, Marilyn, jt. auth. see Sigel, Roberta S.
Hosking, Eric, jt. auth. see Reade, Winwood.
Hoskins, Halford. Atlantic Pact. 5.00 (ISBN 0-8183-0229-1). Pub Aff Pr.
Hoskins, J. M. Virological Procedures. 1967. 19.95 (ISBN 0-407-79000-4). Butterworths.
Hoskins, Katherine B. Anderson County. LC 79-126928. (Tennessee County History Ser.). (Illus.). 1979. 12.50x (ISBN 0-87870-061-7). Memphis St Univ.
Hoskins, R. F. Generalised Functions. (Mathematics & Its Applications Ser.). 1980. pap. 43.95 (ISBN 0-470-26608-2). Halsted Pr.
Hoskins, Robert. Prisoner, Cell Block H: Number 4, The Frustrations of Vera. 224p. (Orig.). 1981. pap. 2.25 (ISBN 0-523-41215-0). Pinnacle Bks.
--To Escape the Stars. 1978. pap. 1.75 o.p. (ISBN 0-345-25856-8, Del Rey Bks). Ballantine.
Hoskins, Robert L. Black Administrators in Higher Education: Conditions & Perceptions. LC 78-19740. 1978. 24.95 (ISBN 0-03-046611-3). Praeger.
Hoskins, W. G. The Age of Plunder. LC 75-43647. (Social & Economic History of England Ser.). (Illus.). 1976. pap. text ed. 9.95x (ISBN 0-582-48544-4). Longman.
--Devon. (Illus.). 624p. 1972. 25.00 (ISBN 0-7153-5577-5). David & Charles.
--Leicestershire: A Shell Guide. 1970. 9.95 (ISBN 0-571-09467-8, Pub. by Faber & Faber). Merrimack Bk Serv.
Hoskins, W. G., ed. History from the Farm. (Illus.). 1970. 6.95 o.p. (ISBN 0-571-09437-6, Pub. by Faber & Faber). Merrimack Bk Serv.
Hoskyns, Edwyn C., tr. see Barth, Karl.
Hosler, Virginia, jt. auth. see Fadely, Jack L.
Hosler, Virginia N., jt. auth. see Fadely, Jack L.
Hosmer, Charles B., Jr. Presence of the Past: A History of the Preservation Movement in the United States Before Williamsburg. LC 65-13292. (Illus.). 386p. 1965. text ed. 12.95 (ISBN 0-89133-085-2). Preservation Pr.
--Preservation Comes of Age: From Williamsburg to the National Trust, 1926-1949, 2 vols. 1981. Set. 37.50x (ISBN 0-8139-0712-8). U Pr of Va.
Hosmer, G. L., jt. auth. see Breed, C. B.
Hosmer, James K. The Life of Thomas Hutchinson: Royal Governor of the Province of Massachusetts Bay. LC 70-124926. (American Scene Ser). (Illus.). 454p. 1972. Repr. of 1896 ed. lib. bdg. 42.50 (ISBN 0-306-71038-2). Da Capo.
--Samuel Adams. LC 80-23753. (American Statesmen Ser.). 445p. 1980. pap. 6.95 (ISBN 0-87754-195-7). Chelsea Hse.
Hosmer, Larue T., et al. Entrepreneurial Function: Text & Cases on Smaller Firms. LC 76-50928. (Illus.). 1977. text ed. 21.95 (ISBN 0-13-283093-0). P-H.
Hosmer, Margaret K. The Child Captives: A True Tale of Life Among the Indians of the West. LC 75-7109. (Indian Captivities Ser.: Vol. 83). 1976. Repr. of 1870 ed. lib. bdg. 44.00 (ISBN 0-8240-1707-2). Garland Pub.
Hosono, Masanobu. Nagasaki Prints & Early Copperplates. Craighill, Lloyd R., tr. LC 77-75972. (Japanese Arts Library: Vol. 6). (Illus.). 150p. 1978. 16.95 (ISBN 0-87011-311-9). Kodansha.
Hospers, John. Introduction to Philosophical Analysis. 2nd ed. 1967. lib. bdg. 17.95 (ISBN 0-13-491688-3). P-H.
--Introductory Readings in Aesthetics. LC 69-15921. 1969. pap. text ed. 8.95 (ISBN 0-02-915260-7). Free Pr.
Hospers, John, ed. Artistic Expression. LC 71-142225. (Century Philosophy Ser). (Illus., Orig.). 1971. 28.50x (ISBN 0-89197-035-5); pap. text ed. 9.50x (ISBN 0-89197-036-3). Irvington.
Hospers, John, jt. ed. see Sellars, Wilfrid.
Hospital Financial Management Association. Cost Effectiveness Notebook: Nineteen Eighty Update. 1980. write for info. (ISBN 0-930228-14-6). Hospital Finan.
--Cost Effectiveness Notebook: Nineteen Seventy-Nine Update. 1979. looseleaf 4.00 (ISBN 0-930228-12-X). Hospital Finan.
--Departmental Method Handbook. LC 79-88945. 70p. 1979. pap. 10.00 (ISBN 0-930228-11-1, 14411). Hospital Finan.
Hospital Research & Educational Trust of the AHA. Being a Food Service Worker. (Illus.). 1967. pap. 9.95 (ISBN 0-87618-046-2). R J Brady.
--Training the Food Service Worker. (Illus.). 1967. pap. 9.95 (ISBN 0-87618-047-0). R J Brady.
--Training the Housekeeping Aide. (Illus.). 1968. pap. 9.95 (ISBN 0-87618-049-7). R J Brady.
--Training the Ward Clerk. (Illus.). 1967. pap. 9.95 (ISBN 0-87618-053-5). R J Brady.
Hossain, Kamal, ed. Legal Aspects of the New International Economic Order. 300p. 1980. 32.50x (ISBN 0-89397-088-3). Nichols Pub.
Host. Danish Pocket Dictionary. (English-Danish-English., Dan). 1978. pap. text ed. 7.00x (ISBN 8-7146-1178-3, D711). Vanous.
Hostage, Jacqueline. Jackie's Book of Household Charts. LC 80-68361. (Illus.). 112p. (Orig.). 1981. plastic comb bdg. 5.95 (ISBN 0-932620-04-3). Betterway Pubns.
--Jackie's Indoor-Outdoor Gardening Charts. (Illus.). 128p. (Orig.). 1981. pap. 5.95 plastic comb bdg. (ISBN 0-932620-07-8). Betterway Pubns.
--Living...Without Milk. 3rd ed. LC 78-72504. (Illus.). 128p. (Orig.). 1981. text ed. 7.95 (ISBN 0-932620-06-X); pap. 3.95 (ISBN 0-932620-05-1). Betterway Pubns.
Hostetler, Lester & Yoder, Walter E., eds. Mennonite Hymnal. LC 69-18131. 1969. 6.95x (ISBN 0-87303-515-1). Faith & Life.
Hostetler, Robert P., jt. auth. see Larson, Roland E.
Hostetter, B. Charles. How to Grow in the Christian Life. 1960. pap. 0.95 (ISBN 0-8024-3603-X). Moody.
--Keep Yourself Pure. 1957. pap. 0.95 deluxe ed. (ISBN 0-8024-4521-7). Moody.
Hostrop, Richard W. Programmed Learning Aid for Orientation to the Two-Year College. 217p. 1970. lib. bdg. 5.95 o.p. (ISBN 0-256-01259-8, 22-0296-01). Learning Syst.
Hot Rod Magazine Editorial Staff. Big Book of Kit Cars. (Illus.). 192p. (Orig.). 1980. pap. 8.95 (ISBN 0-8227-5062-7). Petersen Pub.
Hot Rod Magazine Editors, ed. Bolt-on Performance. (Hot Rod Shop Ser.). (Illus.). 1981. pap. 8.95 (ISBN 0-8227-6013-4). Petersen Pub.
--Engine Swapping. 5th, rev. ed. (Hot Rod Shop Ser.). 192p. 1981. pap. 8.95 (ISBN 0-8227-6014-2). Petersen Pub.
Hotchkiss, Bill. The Medicine Calf. 1981. 13.95 (ISBN 0-393-01389-8). Norton.
--To Christ, Dionysus, Odin. 1969. 6.00 o.p. (ISBN 0-912950-06-4); pap. 4.00 o.p. (ISBN 0-912950-05-6). Blue Oak.
Hotchkiss, J. Art Glass Handbook & Price Guide. 1972. pap. 3.95 (ISBN 0-8015-0360-4, Hawthorn). Dutton.
Hotchkiss, Jeanette K. African-Asian Reading Guide for Children & Young Adults. LC 74-37530. 1976. 10.00 o.p. (ISBN 0-8108-0886-2). Scarecrow.
--American Historical Fiction & Biography for Children & Young People. LC 73-13715. 1973. 10.00 (ISBN 0-8108-0650-9). Scarecrow.
--European Historical Fiction & Biography for Children & Young People. 2nd ed. LC 72-1599. 1972. 10.00 (ISBN 0-8108-0515-4). Scarecrow.
Hotchkiss, John. Hummel Art & Hummel Art Price Guide & Supplement. (Illus.). 22.90 o.p. (ISBN 0-87069-298-4). Wallace-Homestead.
Hotchkiss, John F. Cut Glass Handbook & Price Guide. LC 76-131428. (Illus.). 1970. pap. 4.75 o.p. (ISBN 0-8015-1878-4, Pub. by Hotchkiss House). Dutton.
—Hummel Art. (Illus.). 1978. 17.95 o.p. (ISBN 0-87069-184-8); softbound o.p. 13.95 o.p. (ISBN 0-87069-249-6). Wallace-Homestead.
Hotchkiss, Robert V. A Pseudo-Epiphanius Testimony Book. LC 74-15203. (Society of Biblical Literature. Texts & Translation-Early Christian Literature Ser.). 1974. pap. 4.50 (ISBN 0-88414-043-1, 060204). Scholars Pr Ca.
Hotchner, A. E. King of the Hill. LC 72-77751. (YA) 1972. 10.00 o.p. (ISBN 0-06-011964-0, HarpT). Har-Row.
Hotham, David. Turkey. LC 77-70192. (Countries Ser.). (Illus.). 1977. lib. bdg. 7.95 (ISBN 0-686-51153-0). Silver.
Hotson, Leslie. Shakespeare by Hilliard. 1977. 18.50x (ISBN 0-520-03313-2). U of Cal Pr.
Hottenstein, M. P., jt. auth. see Greenlaw, P. S.
Hottinger, Arnold. Spain in Transition: Franco's Regime. LC 74-21523. (Policy Papers: The Washington Papers, No. 18). 1975. 3.50x (ISBN 0-8039-0204-2). Sage.
--Spain in Transition: Prospects & Policies. LC 74-21523. (Policy Papers: The Washington Papers, No. 19). 1975. 3.50x (ISBN 0-8039-0205-0). Sage.
Hottois, James W. & Milner, Neal. The Sex-Education Controversy. LC 72-469. (Politics of Education Ser.). 1975. 18.95 (ISBN 0-669-83634-6). Lexington Bks.
Hotton, Nicholas. The Evidence of Evolution. LC 68-24491. (Illus.). 160p. 1968. 4.95 (ISBN 0-8281-0341-0, JO42-0, Co-Pub. by Smithsonian). Am Heritage.
Hotton, Peter. Coal Comfort: An Alternative Way to Heat Your House. (Illus.). 128p. (Orig.). 1980. pap. 7.95 (ISBN 0-316-37388-5). Little.
Hou, Chi-Ming & Yu, Tzong-shian, eds. Modern Chinese Economic History: Proceedings of the Conference on Modern Chinese Economic History, Academia Sinica. LC 79-4926. 694p. 1980. pap. 25.00 (ISBN 0-295-95675-5, Pub. by Coun Econ Planning Taiwan). U of Wash Pr.
Houart, Victor. Buttons: A Collector's Guide. LC 77-79904. (Encore Edition). (Illus.). 1977. 3.95 o.p. (ISBN 0-684-16196-6, ScribT). Scribner.
Houba, Vaclav, ed. Immunological Investigation of Tropical Parasitic Disease. (Practical Methods in Clinical Immunology Ser.: Vol. 2). (Illus.). 225p. 1980. text ed. 40.00x (ISBN 0-443-01900-2). Churchill.
Houben, Milton & Kropf, William. Dr. Harmful Food Additives: The Eat-Safe Guide. 8.95 (ISBN 0-87949-161-2). Ashley Bks.
Houchin, Thomas D. Sounds of American English. (Orig.). 1976. pap. text ed. 3.83 (ISBN 0-87720-974-X). AMSCO Sch.

Houck, Carter. Warm As Wool, Cool As Cotton: The Story of Natural Fibers & Fabrics & How to Work with Them. LC 74-18089. (Illus.). 96p. (gr. 3-6). 1975. 6.95 (ISBN 0-395-28861-4, Clarion). HM.

Houck, Carter & Miller, Myron. American Quilts & How to Make Them. LC 75-5541. 1975. pap. 12.95 (ISBN 0-684-16272-5, ScribT). Scribner.

--The Big Bag Book: How to Make All Kinds of Carry-Alls. (Encore Edition). (Illus.). 1977. pap. 2.95 (ISBN 0-684-16903-7). Scribner.

--The Boat Buff's Book of Embroidery: Needlepoint, Crewel, Applique. (Encore Edition). (Illus.). 1979. pap. 8.95 (ISBN 0-684-16052-8); pap. 4.95 (ISBN 0-684-16904-5). Scribner.

Houck, Lewis D., Jr. A Practical Guide to Budgetary & Management Control Systems. LC 78-14716. 272p. 1979. 22.95 (ISBN 0-669-02705-7). Lexington Bks.

Houdas, Y. & Guieu, J. D., eds. New Trends in Thermal Physiology. 212p. 1978. pap. 30.00 (ISBN 2-225-49874-1). Masson Pub.

Houde, Frank, jt. auth. see Cohen, Stan B.

Houdini, Harry. Houdini on Magic. Gibson, Walter & Young, Morris, eds. (Illus.). 1954. pap. 3.95 (ISBN 0-486-20384-0). Dover.

--Miracle Mongers & Their Methods: A Complete Expose. LC 80-84404. (Skeptic's Bookshelf Ser.). 240p. 1981. Repr. of 1920 ed. 13.95 (ISBN 0-87975-143-6). Prometheus Bks.

Houdriaan, J., jt. auth. see DeWit, C. T.

Houfe, Simon, ed. Dictionary of British Book Illustrators & Caricaturists, Eighteen Hundred to Nineteen Fourteen. (Illus.). 520p. 1978. 94.00 (ISBN 0-902028-73-1, Pub. by Antique Collectors Club England). Gale.

Hougen, O. A., et al. Chemical Process Principles, 3 pts. Incl. Pt. 1. Material & Energy Balances. 2nd ed. 525p. 1954. 33.50x (ISBN 0-471-41283-X); Pt. 2. Thermodynamics. 2nd ed. 624p. 1959. 33.50x (ISBN 0-471-41382-8); Pt. 3. Kinetics & Catalysis. 303p. 1947. o.p. (ISBN 0-471-41415-8). LC 54-13512. Wiley.

Hougen, Richard T. Look No Further. 1958. 8.95 (ISBN 0-687-22622-8). Abingdon.

Hough, B. K. Basic Soils Engineering. 2nd ed. LC 69-14671. (Illus.). 635p. 1969. 23.95 (ISBN 0-8260-4445-X); tchrs. manual avail. (ISBN 0-471-07502-7). Wiley.

Hough, C. A., et al, eds. Developments in Sweeteners, Vol. 1. (Illus.). 1979. 38.90x (ISBN 0-85334-820-0, Pub. by Applied Science). Burgess-Intl Ideas.

Hough, Charles M. Reports of Cases in the Vice Admiralty of the Province of New York & in the Courts of Admiralty of the State of New York, 1715-1788. (Yale Historical Pubs., Manuscripts & Edited Texts Ser.: No. VIII). 1925. 65.00x (ISBN 0-685-89777-X). Elliots Bks.

Hough, Douglas E. The Market for Human Blood. LC 77-3856. 1978. 17.95 (ISBN 0-669-01729-9). Lexington Bks.

Hough, Emerson. Fifty-Four-Forty or Fight. 1976. lib. bdg. 17.75x (ISBN 0-89968-043-7). Lightyear.

--The Girl at the Half-Way House. 1976. lib. bdg. 16.75x (ISBN 0-89968-044-5). Lightyear.

--Heart's Desire. 1976. lib. bdg. 16.25x (ISBN 0-89968-045-3). Lightyear.

--The Mississippi Bubble. 1976. lib. bdg. 19.25x (ISBN 0-89968-042-9). Lightyear.

--The Passing of the Frontier. 1976. lib. bdg. 10.95x (ISBN 0-89968-046-1). Lightyear.

--The Singing Mouse Stories. 1976. lib. bdg. 12.50x (ISBN 0-89968-047-X). Lightyear.

--The Way Out: A Story of the Cumberland Today. 1976. lib. bdg. 14.75x (ISBN 0-89968-048-8). Lightyear.

--The Young Alaskans. 1976. lib. bdg. 14.25x (ISBN 0-89968-049-6). Lightyear.

--The Young Alaskans in the Rockies. 1976. lib. bdg. 15.25x (ISBN 0-89968-050-X). Lightyear.

Hough, Franklin B. The Seige of Savannah: Era of the American Revolution Ser. LC 77-165683. 187p. 1974. Repr. of 1866 ed. lib. bdg. 20.00 (ISBN 0-306-70619-9). Da Capo.

Hough, G. Selected Essays. LC 77-85692. 1978. 32.50 (ISBN 0-521-21901-9). Cambridge U Pr.

Hough, George A. News Writing. 1975. text ed. 13.95 o.p. (ISBN 0-395-18593-9); instructor's manual pap. 2.00 o.p. (ISBN 0-395-18788-5); wkbk. 7.25 o.p. (ISBN 0-395-18597-1). HM.

--News Writing. 2nd ed. LC 79-91631. (Illus.). 1980. text ed. 14.50 (ISBN 0-395-28636-0); inst. man. 0.75 (ISBN 0-395-28638-7). HM.

Hough, George A., 3rd. Practice Exercises in News Writing. 2nd ed. 1980. pap. text ed. 7.95 (ISBN 0-395-28637-9); instrs'. manual .75 avail. (ISBN 0-395-28638-7). HM.

Hough, George P., jt. auth. see Raudsepp, Eugene.

Hough, Graham. The Last Romantics. 284p. 1961. pap. 5.75x (ISBN 0-686-63944-8). B&N.

Hough, Graham, ed. see Wood, Michael.

Hough, Henry B. Country Editor. 1980. pap. 3.95 (ISBN 0-85699-091-4). Devin.

--Martha's Vineyard. (Large Format Ser.). (Illus.). 1979. pap. 5.95 o.s.i. (ISBN 0-14-005165-1). Penguin.

Hough, J. M., jt. ed. see Clarke, R. V. G.

Hough, Jerry F. Soviet Leadership in Transition. LC 80-67873. 175p. 1980. 11.95 (ISBN 0-8157-3742-4); pap. 4.95 (ISBN 0-8157-3741-6). Brookings.

--Soviet Prefects: The Local Party Organs in Industrial Decision-Making. LC 69-18033. (Russian Research Center Studies: No. 58). 1969. 18.50x (ISBN 0-674-82785-6). Harvard U Pr.

Hough, John B. & Duncan, James K. Teaching: Description & Analysis. (Education Ser). 1970. text ed. 14.95 (ISBN 0-201-02987-1). A-W.

Hough, John B., jt. auth. see Amidon, Edmund J.

Hough, R. Admiral of the Fleet. LC 72-77970. (Illus.). 1970. 8.95 o.s.i. (ISBN 0-02-554480-2). Macmillan.

Hough, Richard. Battle of Britain: The Triumph of R.A.F. Fighter Pilots. LC 73-138029. (Battle Bks). (Illus.). (gr. 5-8). 1971. 5.95 o.s.i. (ISBN 0-02-744590-9). Macmillan.

--Battle of Midway: Victory in the Pacific. LC 70-89588. (Battle Bks). (gr. 5-8). 1970. 4.50g o.s.i. (ISBN 0-02-744600-X). Macmillan.

--Fight of the Few. Date not set. pap. 2.50 (ISBN 0-440-12771-8). Dell.

--The Last Voyage of Captain James Cook. LC 79-63210. (Illus.). 1979. 10.95 (ISBN 0-688-03413-6). Morrow.

--Mountbatten. 1981. 15.00 (ISBN 0-394-51162-X). Random.

--Wings Against the Sky. 1981. pap. 2.50 (ISBN 0-440-19591-8). Dell.

--Wings of Victory. LC 80-24111. Orig. Title: Fight to the Finish. 224p. 1980. 8.95 (ISBN 0-688-03758-5). Morrow.

Hough, Richard & Frostick, M. History of the World's Racing Cars. (Illus.). 1965. 15.00 o.s.i. (ISBN 0-06-002700-2, HarpT). Har-Row.

Houghtby, Natalie. The Music of Szymanowski. LC 80-51747. 120p. 1981. 11.95 (ISBN 0-8008-7539-7, Crescendo). Taplinger.

Houghton, Bryan. Mitre & Crook. LC 80-52682. 1981. pap. write for info. o.p. (ISBN 0-89555-160-8). Tan Bks Pubs.

Houghton, E. L. & Carruthers, N. B. Wind Forces on Buildings & Structures: An Introduction. 1976. 22.95 (ISBN 0-470-15147-1). Halsted Pr.

Houghton, Eric. A Giant Can Do Anything. LC 80-65669. (Illus.). 32p. (ps-2). 1980. 8.95 (ISBN 0-233-96237-9). Andre Deutsch.

--The Mouse & the Magician. LC 79-64187. (Illus.). (gr. k-4). 1979. 8.95 (ISBN 0-233-96777-X). Andre Deutsch.

Houghton, Frank. Amy Carmichael of Dohnavur. 7.95 (ISBN 0-87508-063-4); pap. 5.95 (ISBN 0-87508-084-7). Chr Lit.

Houghton, J. T. The Physics of Atmospheres. LC 76-26373. (Illus.). 1977. 32.95 (ISBN 0-521-21443-2). Cambridge U Pr.

--The Physics of Atmospheres. LC 76-26373. (Illus.). 1979. pap. 10.95x (ISBN 0-521-29656-0). Cambridge U Pr.

Houghton, Leighton. Guide to the British Cathedrals. (Illus.). 128p. 1974. pap. 5.95 (ISBN 0-212-97007-0). Transatlantic.

Houghton, P. S. Ball & Roller Bearings. (Illus.). 1976. 104.40x (ISBN 0-85334-598-8, Pub. by Applied Science). Burgess-Intl Ideas.

Houghton, R. P. Metal Complexes in Organic Chemistry. LC 78-51685. (Cambridge Texts in Chemistry & Biochemistry). 1979. 59.50 (ISBN 0-521-21992-2); pap. 18.50x (ISBN 0-521-29331-6). Cambridge U Pr.

Houghton, Walter E. Victorian Frame of Mind, 1830-1870. 1963. pap. 6.45x (ISBN 0-300-00122-3, Y99). Yale U Pr.

Houghton, Walter E. & Stange, G. Robert. Victorian Poetry & Poetics. 2nd ed. LC 74-370. 1968. text ed. 21.50 (ISBN 0-395-04646-7, 3-26316). HM.

Houghton, Walter E., ed. Wellesley Index to Victorian Periodicals, 1824-1900, 3 vols. Incl. Vol. 1. 1966. 115.00x (ISBN 0-8020-1393-7); Vol. 2. 1972. 125.00x (ISBN 0-8020-1910-2); Vol. 3. 1978. 125.00x (ISBN 0-8020-2253-7). LC 66-5405. Set. 300.00x (ISBN 0-8020-2343-6). U of Toronto Pr.

Houk, Annelle S. & Bogart, Carlotta L. Understanding the Short Story. LC 68-55259. (Orig.). (gr. 9-12). 1969. pap. 6.50 (ISBN 0-672-63132-6). Odyssey Pr.

Houlbrooke, Ralph. Church Courts & the People During the English Reformation Fifteen-Twenty to Fifteen Seventy. (Oxford Historical Monographs). 1979. 29.95x (ISBN 0-19-821876-1). Oxford U Pr.

Houldcroft, P. T. Welding Processes. (Engineering Design Guides). (Illus.). 30p. 1975. pap. 9.95x (ISBN 0-19-859137-3). Oxford U Pr.

Houldcroft, Peter Thomas. Welding Process Technology. LC 76-47408. (Illus.). 1977. 35.50 (ISBN 0-521-21530-7). Cambridge U Pr.

Houlehen, Robert J. & Hall, Elvajean. The Battle for Sales. LC 73-6962. (Illus.). 160p. (gr. 7 up). 1973. 5.95 o.p. (ISBN 0-397-31249-0). Lippincott.

Houlihan, William J. The Chemistry of Heterocyclic Compounds: Indoles. LC 76-154323. (Chemistry of Heterocyclic Compounds: Monographs: Vol. 25, Pt. 3). 1979. 93.50 (ISBN 0-471-05132-2, Pub. by Wiley-Interscience). Wiley.

Hoult, Thomas F. Sociology for a New Day. 384p. 1974. pap. text ed. 7.95 o.p. (ISBN 0-394-31736-X). Random.

--Sociology for a New Day: Reader. 2nd ed. 1979. pap. text ed. 6.95x (ISBN 0-394-32243-6). Random.

Hounshell, Paul B. & Trollinger, Ira R. Games for the Science Classroom: An Annotated Bibliography. 1977. pap. 3.75 (ISBN 0-87355-006-4). Natl Sci Tchrs.

Hounslow Press, ed. Canada in Colour. (Illus.). 1973. pap. 7.95 o.p. (ISBN 0-684-16372-1, SL694, ScribT). Scribner.

Houp, Kenneth W. & Pearsall, Thomas E. Reporting Technical Information. 3rd ed. 1977. pap. text ed. 9.95 (ISBN 0-02-475430-7). Macmillan.

Houpis, Constantine, jt. auth. see D'Azzo, John.

Houppert, J. W., ed. see Lodge, Thomas.

Houppert, Joseph W. John Lyly. LC 74-20932. (English Authors Ser.: No. 177). 1975. lib. bdg. 10.95 (ISBN 0-8057-1349-2). Twayne.

Houpt, Katherine A. & Wolski, Thomas R. Domestic Animal Behavior for Veterinarians & Animal Scientists. text ed. 16.50 (ISBN 0-8138-1060-4). Iowa St U Pr.

Houpt, Katherine A., jt. auth. see Pond, Wilson G.

Hourani, Albert. Europe & the Middle East. 1980. 20.00x (ISBN 0-520-03742-1). U of Cal Pr.

Hourani, H. Syria & Lebanon. (Arab Background Ser.). 1968. 14.00x (ISBN 0-685-77096-6). Intl Bk Ctr.

Hourigan, Patrick W. A Manual of Seamanship for the Officer of the Deck, Ship Under Sail Alone: The 1903 Edition. LC 79-93029. 148p. 1980. 7.50 (ISBN 0-87021-361-X). Naval Inst Pr.

Housby, Trevor. Fishing for Food. pap. 2.95 (ISBN 0-7153-7546-6, Pub. by Batsford England). David & Charles.

House & Garden, ed. Twentieth Century Decorating Architecture & Gardens. LC 80-12593. (Illus.). 320p. 1980. 34.95 (ISBN 0-03-047581-3); pre-Jan. 29.95. HR&W.

House & Garden Editors, ed. House & Garden's Book of Remodeling. (Illus.). 1979. 35.00 o.p. (ISBN 0-670-37974-3, Studio). Viking Pr.

House, Arthur H. The U.N. in the Congo: The Political & Civilian Efforts. LC 78-56052. 1978. pap. text ed. 14.25 (ISBN 0-8191-0516-3). U Pr of Amer.

House, C. R. Water Transport in Cells & Tissue. 562p. 1974. 39.75 o.p. (ISBN 0-685-90285-4, Pub. by W & W). Krieger.

House, Charles Van see Van House, Charles & Hammond, Rogers.

House, David. The Biogas Handbook. LC 80-8998. Orig. Title: The Compleat Biogas Handbook. (Illus.). 224p. 1981. pap. 10.95 (ISBN 0-915238-47-0). Peace Pr.

House, Ernest R. Evaluating with Validity. LC 80-14695. (Illus.). 295p. 1980. 20.00 (ISBN 0-8039-1438-5); pap. 9.95 (ISBN 0-8039-1439-3). Sage.

--The Politics of Educational Innovation. LC 74-12822. 324p. 1974. 17.90x (ISBN 0-8211-0754-2); text ed. 16.20x (ISBN 0-685-57222-6). McCutchan.

House, Ernest R. & Lapan, Stephen D. Survival in the Classroom: Negotiating with Kids, Colleagues & Bosses. 1978. pap. text ed. 18.95x (ISBN 0-205-06082-X); tchr's ed. 14.95x (ISBN 0-685-89341-3). Allyn.

House, Ernest R., ed. School Evaluation: Politics & Process. LC 72-91622. 370p. 1973. 17.90x (ISBN 0-8211-0750-X); text ed. 16.20x (ISBN 0-685-28806-4). McCutchan.

House, H., jt. auth. see Harman, Susan E.

House, Herbert O. Modern Synthetic Reactions. 2nd ed. LC 78-173958. 1972. text ed. 27.95 (ISBN 0-8053-4501-9). Benjamin-Cummings.

House, Homer D. Wild Flowers. (Illus.). 626p. 1974. 19.95 (ISBN 0-02-554560-4). Macmillan.

House, Humphrey. Coleridge: The Clark Lectures, Nineteen Fifty-One to Nineteen Fifty-Two. 1979. 14.95x (ISBN 0-8464-0086-3). Beekman Pubs.

House, J. D. Contemporary Entrepreneurs: The Sociology of Residential Real Estate Agents. LC 76-52329. (Contributions in Sociology: No. 25). 1977. lib. bdg. 15.95x (ISBN 0-8371-9533-0, HCE/). Greenwood.

House, Jack. Portrait of the Clyde. LC 79-448420. (Portrait Bks.). (Illus.). 1969. 10.50x (ISBN 0-7091-4994-8). Intl Pubns Serv.

--Pride of Perth: The Story of Arthur Bell & Sons Ltd. Scotch Whiskey Distillers. (Illus.). 1976. text ed. 9.25x (ISBN 0-09-127320-X). Humanities.

House, James S. Work Stress & Social Support. LC 80-22234. 200p. 1981. pap. text ed. cancelled (ISBN 0-201-03101-9). A-W.

House, Madeline, et al, eds. see Dickens, Charles.

House, Marilyn G. Ice Skating Fundamentals. (Illus.). 1978. pap. text ed. 4.25 (ISBN 0-8403-1285-7, 40128502). Kendall-Hunt.

House of Collectibles. Official Price Guide to Paper Collectibles. (Collector Ser.). (Illus.). 400p. 1980. pap. 9.95 (ISBN 0-87637-114-4, 114-04). Hse of Collectibles.

House, Peter W. Trading-off Environment, Economics, & Energy. LC 76-50435. (Illus.). 1977. 17.95 (ISBN 0-669-01284-X). Lexington Bks.

House, Peter W. & Jones, David W., Jr. Getting It off the Shelf: A Methodology for Implementing Federal Research. LC 77-3918. (Special Studies in Public Systems Management Ser.). (Illus.). 1977. lib. bdg. 27.50x (ISBN 0-89158-347-5). Westview.

House, Peter W. & Ryan, Gerard R. The Future Indefinite: Decision-Making in a Transition Economy. LC 79-2723. 192p. 1979. 19.95 (ISBN 0-669-03231-X). Lexington Bks.

House, Peter W. & Williams, Edward R. The Carrying Capacity of a Nation: Growth & the Quality of Life. LC 75-16623. 1976. 22.95 (ISBN 0-669-00056-6). Lexington Bks.

--Planning & Conservation: The Emergence of the Frugal Society. LC 77-7584. (Praeger Special Studies). 1977. text ed. 28.95 (ISBN 0-03-021946-9); pap. 9.95 (ISBN 0-03-022281-8). Praeger.

House, Robert W. Administration in Music Education. LC 72-4564. (Contemporary Perspective in Music Education Ser). (Illus.). 192p. 1973. pap. text ed. 9.95 (ISBN 0-13-005132-2). P-H.

House, William C., ed. Business Simulation for Decision Making. LC 77-24080. (Illus.). 1977. text ed. 22.95 (ISBN 0-89433-005-5); pap. text ed. 17.50 (ISBN 0-89433-017-9). Petrocelli.

--Laser Beam Information Systems. 1978. text ed. 17.50 (ISBN 0-89433-049-7). Petrocelli.

Household, Geoffrey. The Cats to Come. (Greenwich Ed.). 1975. 5.95 o.p. (ISBN 0-7181-1347-0, Pub. by Michael Joseph). Merrimack Bk Serv.

--Escape into Daylight. (gr. 5-7). 1977. pap. 1.25 o.s.i. (ISBN 0-671-29845-3). Archway.

--The Sending. 192p. 1981. pap. 2.95 (ISBN 0-14-005780-3). Penguin.

Householder, Alston S. The Theory of Matrices in Numerical Analysis. LC 74-83763. 288p. 1975. pap. text ed. 4.00 (ISBN 0-486-61781-5). Dover.

Householder, Fred W. Linguistics Speculations. LC 78-145601. (Illus.). 1971. 39.95 (ISBN 0-521-07986-1). Cambridge U Pr.

Houseman, Gerald L. G. D. H. Cole. (English Authors Ser.: No. 255). 1979. lib. bdg. 14.50 (ISBN 0-8057-6746-0). Twayne.

Houseman, John. Front & Center. 1981. pap. 6.95 (ISBN 0-671-41391-0, Touchstone Bks). S&S.

--Run-Through. 1981. pap. 6.95 (ISBN 0-671-41391-0, Touchstone Bks). S&S.

Houser, Caroline. Greek Monumental Bronze Sculpture of the Fifth & Fourth Centuries B.C. LC 76-23628. (Outstanding Dissertations in the Fine Arts Ser.). 1978. lib. bdg. 52.00x (ISBN 0-8240-2698-5). Garland Pub.

Houser, L. & Schrader, Alvin M. The Search for a Scientific Profession: Library Science Education in the U.S. & Canada. LC 77-17563. 1978. 10.00 (ISBN 0-8108-1062-X). Scarecrow.

Houser, Roy. Catalogue of Chamber Music for Woodwind Instruments. LC 76-166093. (Music Ser). 1973. Repr. of 1960 ed. lib. bdg. 17.00 (ISBN 0-306-70257-6). Da Capo.

Housh, Barbara. Brashki: A Gypsy Fantasy. 1980. pap. 6.95 o.p. (ISBN 0-8362-6109-7). Andrews & McMeel.

Housley, Charles E. Hospital Materiel Management. LC 78-14526. (Illus.). 1978. text ed. 32.95 (ISBN 0-89443-046-7). Aspen Systems.

Housley, Trevor. Data Communications & Teleprocessing Systems. (P-H Data Processing Management Ser.). (Illus.). 1979. text ed. 25.95 (ISBN 0-13-197368-1). P-H.

Housman, A. E. A Shropshire Lad. 100p. 1981. Repr. lib. bdg. 9.95x (ISBN 0-89966-285-4). Buccaneer Bks.

Houssiadas, L., jt. ed. see Welford, A. T.

Houston, ed. see Schiff, S. O. & Griffith, D. A.

Houston, Albert. Big Dummy's Guide to CB Radio. Hershfield, William, ed. (Illus.). 1976. 4.00 (ISBN 0-913990-04-3). Book Pub Co.

Houston, Beverle, jt. auth. see Kinder, Marsha.

Houston, D. Heroes. 1980. pap. 3.95. Starlog Pr.

--Villains. 1980. pap. 3.95 (ISBN 0-931064-21-X). Starlog Pr.

Houston, George, jt. auth. see Bryden, John.

Houston, J., ed. see Mitchell, Colin.

Houston, J. C., et al. Short Textbook of Medicine. 6th ed. (Illus., Orig.). 1980. pap. 14.75 (ISBN 0-397-58266-8). Lippincott.

--Short Textbook of Medicine. 5th ed. (Illus., Orig.). 1975. pap. 14.75 o.p. (ISBN 0-397-58159-9). Lippincott.

Houston, J. G. Questions in Physics. 3rd ed. 1971. pap. text ed. 5.50x o.p. (ISBN 0-435-67425-0). Heinemann Ed.

Houston, J. G., et al. Multiple-Choice Questions for Assessment in Physics. 1971. pap. text ed. 5.95 with answers o.p. (ISBN 0-435-67424-2). Heinemann Ed.

Houston, James. Eagle Mask: A West Coast Indian Tale. LC 66-10074. (Illus.). (gr. 2-6). 1966. 5.50 (ISBN 0-15-224444-1, HJ); pap. 5.50 o.p. (ISBN 0-15-224445-X). HarBraceJ.

--Frozen Fire. (gr. 7 up). pap. 2.95 (ISBN 0-689-70489-5, A-116, Aladdin). Atheneum.

--River Runners: A Tale of Hardship & Bravery. LC 79-14337. (Illus.). (gr. 7 up). 1979. 8.95 (ISBN 0-689-50151-X, McElderry Bk). Atheneum.

--Tikta'liktak: An Eskimo Legend. LC 65-21696. (Illus.). (gr. 2-4). 1965. 6.25 (ISBN 0-15-287745-2, HJ). HarBraceJ.

--The White Archer: An Eskimo Legend. LC 67-17154. (gr. 8-12). 1979. Repr. of 1967 ed. 2.95 (ISBN 0-15-696224-1, HJ). HarBraceJ.

--White Dawn: A Eskimo Saga. LC 72-134575. 1971. 8.50 o.p. (ISBN 0-15-196115-8, HJ). HarBraceJ.

Houston, James D. Gasoline: The Automotive Adventures of Charles Bates. (A Noel Young Bk). 128p. 1980. 8.95 (ISBN 0-88496-144-3). Capra Pr.

--An Occurance at Norman's Burger Castle. (Capra Chapbook Ser.: No. 2). (Orig.). 1972. pap. 2.50 o.p. (ISBN 0-912264-41-1). Capra Pr.

Houston, Jean. Lifeforce. 1980. 12.95 (ISBN 0-440-05011-1). Delacorte.

Houston, John. The Pursuit of Happiness. 1981. pap. text ed. 7.95x (ISBN 0-673-15421-1). Scott F.

Houston, John A. Latin America in the United Nations. LC 78-2805. (Carnegie Endowment for International Peace, United Nations Studies: No. 8). 1978. Repr. of 1956 ed. lib. bdg. 27.00x (ISBN 0-313-20335-0, HOLU). Greenwood.

Houston, John P. Fundamentals of Learning. 1976. text ed. 16.95 (ISBN 0-12-356850-1); instrs' manual 3.00 (ISBN 0-12-356852-8). Acad Pr.

--Victor Hugo. LC 74-8729. (World Authors Ser.: France: No. 312). 1974. lib. bdg. 9.95 (ISBN 0-8057-2443-5). Twayne.

Houston, John P. & Benassi, Victor. Invitation to Psychology. 741p. 1979. text ed. 17.95 (ISBN 0-12-356860-9); instrs'. manual 2.00 (ISBN 0-12-356862-5); study guide 6.95 (ISBN 0-12-356864-1); test blank 1.00 (ISBN 0-12-356861-7); test bklt. 2.00 (ISBN 0-12-356863-3); test tape bank (ISBN 0-12-356865-X). Acad Pr.

Houston, John P. & Houston, Mona T., trs. French Symbolist Poetry: An Anthology. LC 79-3381. 288p. 1980. 25.00x (ISBN 0-253-16725-6); pap. 10.95x (ISBN 0-253-20250-7). Ind U Pr.

Houston, Lloyd. The New Approach for the Understanding & Interpretation of Financial Statements. (Illus.). 1978. 51.85 (ISBN 0-918968-05-4). Inst Econ Finan.

Houston, Mona T., jt. tr. see Houston, John P.

Houston, Peyton. Arguments of Idea. 1980. pap. 8.50 (ISBN 0-912330-45-7). Jargon Soc.

Houston, Ralph. Talk Does Not Cook the Rice: The Teachings of Agni Yoga. Phillips, Amelia, ed. 416p. 1981. pap. 7.95 (ISBN 0-87728-530-6). Weiser.

Houston, Robert. Summer Story. 1978. pap. 1.75 o.p. (ISBN 0-449-14019-9, GM). Fawcett.

Houston, Robert W. Exploring Competency Based Education. LC 74-76532. 1974. 17.00x (ISBN 0-8211-0752-6); text ed. 15.25x (ISBN 0-685-42635-1). McCutchan.

Houston, Sam. Battle of San Jacinto. wrappers 4.50 (ISBN 0-8363-0010-6). Jenkins.

Houston, Samuel. The Autobiography of Sam Houston. Day, Donald & Ullom, Harry H., eds. LC 80-18864. (Illus.). xviii, 298p. 1980. Repr. of 1954 ed. lib. bdg. 29.95x (ISBN 0-313-22704-7, HOAUS). Greenwood.

Houtchens, Carolyn Washburn & Houtchens, Lawrence Huston, eds. The English Romantic Poets & Essayists: A Review of Research & Criticism. rev. ed. LC 66-12599. 1966. 17.50x (ISBN 0-8147-0205-8). NYU Pr.

Houtchens, Lawrence Huston, jt. ed. see Houtchens, Carolyn Washburn.

Houten, Ron Van see Van Houten, Ron.

Houtmann, ed. Six Days: An Anthology of Canadian Christian Poetry. 1973. pap. 2.50 o.p. (ISBN 0-686-11983-5). Wedge Pub.

Houts, Mary D. Lesson Plans for Using the Outdoors in Teaching. LC 75-22544. 1976. pap. text ed. 2.95x o.p. (ISBN 0-685-73368-8, 1760). Interstate.

Hovanessian, S. A. Computational Mathematics in Engineering. 1976. 31.50 (ISBN 0-669-00733-1). Lexington Bks.

Hovannisian, Richard G. Armenia on the Road to Independence, 1918. (Near Eastern Center, UCLA). 1967. 18.75x (ISBN 0-520-00574-0). U of Cal Pr.

--The Republic of Armenia, Vol. 1: the First Year, 1918-1919. LC 72-129613. (Illus.). 1971. 24.50x (ISBN 0-520-01984-9). U of Cal Pr.

Hovasse, R. see Dangeard, P.

Hovater, Shea J. Hardships of a Woman Plant Worker. LC 79-66795. 71p. 1980. 5.95 (ISBN 0-533-04404-9). Vantage.

Hovenkamp, Herbert. Science & Religion in America, 1800-1860. LC 78-53332. 1978. 18.00x (ISBN 0-8122-7748-1). U of Pa Pr.

Hover, Craig R. Beyond the Valley of the Dollar. (Illus.). 224p. Date not set. 10.95 (ISBN 0-89913-004-6). Entity Pub Co. Postponed.

Hover, Margot K. & Breidenbach, Monica E. Chrisitan Family Almanac. 128p. (Orig.). 1980. pap. 9.95 (ISBN 0-697-01740-0). Wm C Brown.

Hover, Margot K. & Breidenbarn, Monica E. Christian Family Almanac. 128p. 1980. pap. 9.95 (ISBN 0-697-01740-0). Wm C Brown.

Hovet, Thomas, Jr. Africa in the United Nations. (African Studies Ser.: No. 10). (Illus.). 1963. 14.95x o.s.i. (ISBN 0-8101-0124-6). Northwestern U Pr.

Hovey, Allen B. The Hidden Thoreau. LC 80-2450. 1981. Repr. of 1966 ed. 22.75 (ISBN 0-404-19056-1). AMS Pr.

Hovey, Alvah. Memoir of the Life & Times of the Reverend Isaac Backus. LC 73-148598. (Era of the American Revolution Ser.). 367p. 1972. Repr. of 1858 ed. lib. bdg. 37.50 (ISBN 0-306-70415-3). Da Capo.

Hovey, Alvah, ed. An American Commentary on the New Testament, 7 vols. Incl. Matthew. Broadus, John A., ed (ISBN 0-8170-0002-X); Mark & Luke. Clark, William N. & Bliss, George R., eds. (ISBN 0-8170-0003-8); John. Hovey, Alvah, ed (ISBN 0-8170-0004-6); Acts & Romans (ISBN 0-8170-0005-4); Corinthians-Thessalonians. Gould, Ezra P., ed (ISBN 0-8170-0006-2); Timothy-Peter (ISBN 0-8170-0007-0); John, Jude, & Revelation (ISBN 0-8170-0008-9). Set. 70.00 (ISBN 0-8170-0001-1); 10.95 ea. Judson.

Hovey, Eddy. Shark Gourmet Seafood of the Future. Sharp, George, ed. LC 80-52109. (Illus.). 111p. pap. 6.95 (ISBN 0-937496-00-6). Sea Harvest.

Hovey, Richard. Along the Trail. LC 76-108772. 1970. Repr. of 1903 ed. 14.50 (ISBN 0-685-05680-5). AMS Pr.

Hovey, Wendy R., jt. auth. see Wilson, Christine C.

Hovgaard, William. Modern History of Warships. 516p. 1980. 44.50x (ISBN 0-85177-040-1, Pub. by Cornell England). State Mutual Bk.

Hovland, Carl I., jt. auth. see Sherif, Muzafer.

How, Louis, tr. see Baroja, Pio.

How, W. W., ed. see Cicero.

How, Walter W. & Wells, Joseph, eds. Commentary on Herodotus, 2 Vols. 1928. Vol. 1. 28.50x (ISBN 0-19-814128-9); Vol. 2. 23.50x (ISBN 0-19-814129-7). Oxford U Pr.

Howar, Barbara. Laughing All the Way. 1977. pap. 2.50 (ISBN 0-449-23145-3, Crest). Fawcett.

Howard, A. D. Road from Runnymede: Magna Carta & Constitutionalism in America. LC 68-15941. (Virginia Legal Studies Series). (Illus.). 492p. 1968. 20.00x (ISBN 0-8139-0122-7). U Pr of Va.

Howard, Alan. Learning to Be Rotuman: Enculturation in the South Pacific. LC 77-122746. (Illus.). 1970. text ed. 11.00x (ISBN 0-8077-1520-4). Tchrs Coll.

--Nativity Stories. LC 79-20746. (Illus.). 96p. (gr. 5 up). 1980. 9.95 (ISBN 0-89742-027-6). Dawne-Leigh.

--Sex in the Light of Reincarnation & Freedom. 1980. pap. 4.95 (ISBN 0-916786-48-X). St George Bk Serv.

Howard, Alan, illus. David & Goliath. (Illus.). 1977. 5.95 (ISBN 0-571-08413-3, Pub. by Faber & Faber). Merrimack Bk Serv.

Howard, Albert. An Agricultural Testament. (Illus.). 253p. 1973. 7.95 (ISBN 0-87857-060-8). Rodale Pr Inc.

Howard, Anne. Welfare Rights- the Local Authorities Role. 52p. 1978. pap. text ed. 4.40x (ISBN 0-7199-0946-5, Pub. by Bedford England). Renouf.

Howard, Anne see Long, Catherine.

Howard, Barbara, ed. Children: Of Such Is the Kingdom of God. LC 79-7102. 1979. pap. 8.00 (ISBN 0-8309-0243-0). Herald Hse.

Howard, C., jt. auth. see Summers, Robert S.

Howard, C., et al. Contact: A Textbook in Applied Communications. 3rd ed. 1979. pap. 9.95 (ISBN 0-13-169052-3). P-H.

Howard, C. Jeriel, jt. auth. see Brock, Dee.

Howard, Christopher. Britain & the Casus Belli 1822-1902: A Study of Britain's International Position from Canning to Salisbury. 204p. 1974. text ed. 21.00x (ISBN 0-485-11149-7, Athlone Pr). Humanities.

Howard, Claire. Beach Club. (Orig.). 1980. pap. 2.50 (ISBN 0-446-91616-1). Warner Bks.

Howard, Clark. The Hunters. 1978. pap. 1.95 o.s.i. (ISBN 0-515-04710-4). Jove Pubns.

--Six Against the Rock. 1978. pap. 2.25 (ISBN 0-515-04709-0). Jove Pubns.

--Traces of Mercury. (Orig.). 1979. pap. 1.95 o.s.i. (ISBN 0-515-04339-7). Jove Pubns.

--Zebra. 1980. pap. 2.75 (ISBN 0-425-04635-4). Berkley Pub.

Howard, Colin R., ed. see Symposium Held by European Group for Rapid Virus Diagnosis, London, Jan. 1978.

Howard, Constance. The Constance Howard Book of Stitches. (Illus.). 1979. 15.50 o.s.i. (ISBN 0-7134-1005-1, Pub. by Batsford). Hippocrene Bks.

--The Constance Howard Book of Stitches. (Illus.). 144p. 1980. 13.75 (ISBN 0-7134-1005-1). Branford.

--Inspiration for Embroidery. 240p. 1967. 15.50 (ISBN 0-8231-4017-2). Branford.

Howard, Coral, jt. auth. see Frost, Anne.

Howard, David H. The Disequilibrium Model in a Controlled Economy. LC 78-24828. (Illus.). 128p. 1979. 14.95 (ISBN 0-669-02851-7). Lexington Bks.

Howard, David M. Student Power in World Missions. 2nd ed. LC 79-122918. (Orig.). 1979. pap. 2.25 (ISBN 0-87784-493-3). Inter-Varsity.

Howard, David M., jt. auth. see Owen, Robert.

Howard, David S. Chinese Armorial Porcelain. 1974. 185.00 (ISBN 0-571-09811-8, Pub. by Faber & Faber). Merrimack Bk Serv.

Howard, Deborah. The Architectural History of Venice. LC 80-24856. (Illus.). 260p. 1981. pap. text ed. 22.50x (ISBN 0-8419-0681-5). Holmes & Meier.

--Jacopo Sansovino: Architecture & Patronage in Renaissance Venice. LC 75-8441. 208p. 1975. 30.00x (ISBN 0-300-01891-6). Yale U Pr.

Howard, Dennis. Kaleidoscope of Motor Cycling. (Old Motor Kaleidoscopes Ser.). (Illus.). 1978. 12.50 o.p. (ISBN 0-906116-00-7, Pub. by Old Motor Magazine England). Motorbooks Intl.

Howard, Dick, ed. see Luxemburg, Rosa.

Howard, Dick, ed. see Mallet, Serge.

Howard, Dick, tr. see Mallet, Serge.

Howard, Donald. Christians Grieve Too. 1980. pap. 1.45 (ISBN 0-85151-315-8). Banner of Truth.

Howard, Donald R. The Idea of the Canterbury Tales. LC 74-81433. 400p. 1976. 20.00x (ISBN 0-520-02816-3); pap. 5.95 (ISBN 0-520-03492-9). U of Cal Pr.

--Writers & Pilgrims: Medieval Pilgrimage Narratives & Their Posterity. (A Quantum Bk.). 100p. 1980. 10.95 (ISBN 0-520-03926-2). U of Cal Pr.

Howard, Donald S. The WPA & the Federal Relief Policy. LC 72-2374. (FDR & the Era of the New Deal Ser). 888p. 1973. Repr. of 1943 ed. lib. bdg. 75.00 (ISBN 0-306-70489-7). Da Capo.

Howard, Edward G., jt. auth. see Filby, P. W.

Howard, Edwin J. Geoffrey Chaucer. (English Authors Ser.: No. 1). 1964. lib. bdg. 9.95 (ISBN 0-8057-1088-4). Twayne.

Howard, Elizabeth. Out of Step with the Dancers. LC 77-25928. (gr. 7 up). 1978. 8.95 (ISBN 0-688-22141-6); PLB 8.59 (ISBN 0-688-32141-0). Morrow.

--Wilderness Venture. LC 72-12945. (gr. 7 up). 1973. 6.75 o.p. (ISBN 0-688-20074-5). Morrow.

--Winter on Her Own. LC 68-16625. (gr. 7 up). 1968. 7.75 (ISBN 0-688-21710-9). Morrow.

Howard, G. Paul: Crisis in Galatia. LC 77-82498. (Society for New Testament Studies Monographs: No. 35). 1979. 17.95 (ISBN 0-521-21709-1). Cambridge U Pr.

Howard, George P., ed. Airport Economic Planning. 688p. 1974. 23.00x (ISBN 0-262-08072-9) MIT Pr.

Howard, Godfrey. Getting Through: How to Make Words Work for You. LC 80-66087. 176p. 1980. 11.95 (ISBN 0-7153-7821-X). David & Charles.

Howard, Harry N. The King-Crane Commission. (Return to Zion Ser.). (Illus.). xiv, 369p. 1980. Repr. of 1963 ed. lib. bdg. 25.00x (ISBN 0-87991-121-2). Porcupine Pr.

Howard, Helen A. American Indian Poetry. (United States Authors Ser.: No. 334). 1979. lib. bdg. 13.50 (ISBN 0-8057-7271-5). Twayne.

Howard, Herbert H., jt. auth. see Zeigler, Sherilyn K.

Howard, J. Grant. Knowing God's Will - & Doing It. 128p. 1976. o. p. 4.95 (ISBN 0-310-26280-1); pap. 2.50 (ISBN 0-310-26282-8). Zondervan.

Howard, J. Woodford, Jr. Courts of Appeals in the Federal Judicial System: A Study of the Second, Fifth, & District of Columbia. LC 80-7529. 408p. 1981. 32.50 (ISBN 0-691-07623-5); pap. 12.50 (ISBN 0-691-10100-0). Princeton U Pr.

Howard, James H. Shawnee: The Ceremonialism of a Native American Tribe & Its Cultural Background. LC 80-23752. (Illus.). xvi, 434p. 1981. 24.95 (ISBN 0-8214-0417-2); pap. 11.95 (ISBN 0-8214-0614-0). Ohio U Pr.

Howard, James H., Jr., jt. auth. see Getty, David J.

Howard, Jane. Families. 1980. pap. 2.75 (ISBN 0-425-04486-6). Berkley Pub.

Howard, Jean G. Of Mice & Mice. LC 78-50486. (Illus., Ltd. ed. 1000 trade, 35 deluxe). (ps-3). 1978. 10.50 (ISBN 0-930954-03-3); deluxe ed. 50.00 (ISBN 0-930954-04-1). Tidal Pr.

Howard, Jessica. Savage Embrace. (Orig.). 1978. pap. 2.25 o.s.i. (ISBN 0-446-82322-8). Warner Bks.

--Traitor's Bride. (Orig.). 1979. pap. 2.25 (ISBN 0-515-04728-7). Jove Pubns.

Howard, Jimmy L., et al, eds. Current Veterinary Therapy: Food Animal Practice. (Illus.). 800p. 1981. text ed. write for info. (ISBN 0-7216-4778-2). Saunders.

Howard, John, jt. auth. see Sturholm, Larry.

Howard, John A. Marketing: Executive & Buyer Behavior. LC 63-10525. 1963. 20.00x (ISBN 0-231-01979-3). Columbia U Pr.

--Marketing Management: Analysis & Planning. 3rd ed. 1973. text ed. 15.50x o.p. (ISBN 0-256-00227-4). Irwin.

Howard, John M. The Movie Murder Mystery Quiz Book. (Illus.). 160p. 1980. pap. 9.95 (ISBN 0-498-02522-5). A S Barnes.

Howard, John R. Fourteen Decisions for Undeclared War. LC 78-62668. (Illus.). 1978. pap. text ed. 9.00 (ISBN 0-8191-0585-6). U Pr of Amer.

Howard, John T. The World's Great Operas. LC 80-2278. 1981. Repr. of 1948 ed. 49.50 (ISBN 0-404-18848-6). AMS Pr.

Howard, John W. Easy Company & the Big Medicine. (Easy Company Ser.: No. 6). (Orig.). 1981. pap. 1.95 (ISBN 0-515-05947-1). Jove Pubns.

--Easy Company & the Green Arrows. (Easy Company Ser.: No. 3). 192p. (Orig.). 1981. pap. 1.95 (ISBN 0-515-05887-4). Jove Pubns.

--Easy Company & the Longhorns. (Easy Company Ser.: No. 5). (Orig.). 1981. pap. 1.95 (ISBN 0-515-05946-3). Jove Pubns.

--Easy Company & the Medicine Gun. (Easy Company Ser.: No. 2). 240p. (Orig.). 1981. pap. 1.95 (ISBN 0-515-05804-1). Jove Pubns.

--Easy Company & the Suicide Boys. (Easy Company Ser.: No. 1). 224p. (Orig.). 1981. pap. 1.95 (ISBN 0-515-05761-4). Jove Pubns.

--Easy Company & the White Man's Path. (Easy Company Ser.: No. 4). 192p. (Orig.). 1981. pap. 1.95 (ISBN 0-515-05945-5). Jove Pubns.

Howard, Katherine. Jeanne. 1979. pap. 1.95 (ISBN 0-505-51331-5). Tower Bks.

Howard, Kenneth I., jt. auth. see Orlinsky, David O.

Howard, Lauren D. Principles of Biology Laboratory Manual. (Illus.). 1980. pap. 12.50 (ISBN 0-87055-354-2). AVI.

Howard, Lee. How to Publish Your Own Book Successfully. 80p. 1980. pap. 10.00 (ISBN 0-912584-00-9). Selective.

Howard, Leslie R. Auditing. 6th ed. 320p. (Orig.). 1978. pap. text ed. 11.95x (ISBN 0-7121-0169-1, Pub. by Macdonald & Evans England). Intl Ideas.

Howard, Linda. Sons for King Yah. LC 75-7480. 1975. pap. 2.25 o.p. (ISBN 0-88270-120-7). Logos.

Howard, Lowell B. Business Law: An Introduction. rev. ed. 608p. 1981. pap. text ed. 6.50 (ISBN 0-8120-2260-2). Barron.

Howard, M. Skyblazer. (Illus.). (gr. 7-9). 1966. 2.95 (ISBN 0-394-81642-0, BYR); PLB 5.69 (ISBN 0-394-91642-5). Random.

Howard, Marion. Did I Have a Good Time? Teenage Drinking. 192p. 1980. 10.95 (ISBN 0-8264-0017-5). Continuum.

--Those Fascinating Paper Dolls: An Illustrated Handbook for Collectors. (Illus.). 320p. 1981. pap. 6.95 (ISBN 0-486-24055-X). Dover.

Howard, Matthew V. Blink, the Patchwork Bunny. (Kindergarten Read-to Bks.). (Illus.). (gr. k-2). PLB 5.95 o.p. (ISBN 0-513-00302-9). Denison.

Howard, Maureen. Not a Word About Nightingales. 196p. 1980. pap. 4.50 (ISBN 0-14-005596-7). Penguin.

Howard, Michael. The Franco-Prussian War: The German Invasion of France 1870-71. 1979. Repr. of 1961 ed. text ed. 26.00x (ISBN 0-246-63587-8). Humanities.

--War & the Liberal Conscience. 1978. 9.50 (ISBN 0-8135-0866-5). Rutgers U Pr.

Howard, Michael & King, John. The Political Economy of Marx. (Modern Economics Ser.). (Illus.). 376p. 1976. text ed. 17.95x (ISBN 0-582-44610-4); pap. text ed. 10.95 (ISBN 0-582-44611-2). Longman.

Howard, Michael, ed. Restraints on War: Studies in the Limitation of Armed Conflict. 1979. 24.00x (ISBN 0-19-822545-8). Oxford U Pr.

Howard, Michael, ed. see Von Clausewitz, Carl.

Howard, Neale E. The Telescope Handbook & Star Atlas. rev. ed. LC 75-6601. (Illus.). 226p. 1975. 16.95 (ISBN 0-690-00686-1, TYC-T). T Y Crowell.

Howard, Nina. Barber, Barber, Shave a Pig. 16p. (ps-k). 1981. tchr's ed. 4.95 (ISBN 0-917206-13-4). Children Learn Ctr.

--Do Your Own Thing. (Illus.). 96p. (ps-6). 1980. 9.90 (ISBN 0-917206-12-6). Children Learn Ctr.

Howard, Oliver O. My Life & Experiences Among Our Hostile Indians. LC 76-87436. (The American Scente Ser.). Repr. of 1907 ed. lib. bdg. 37.50 (ISBN 0-306-71506-6). Da Capo.

--Nez Perce Joseph. LC 70-39379. (Law, Politics, & History Ser). (Illus.). 274p. 1972. Repr. of 1881 ed. lib. bdg. 37.50 (ISBN 0-306-70461-7). Da Capo.

Howard, Pat, jt. auth. see Black, Maggie.

Howard, Patricia. C. W. von Gluck: Orfeo. (Cambridge Opera Handbooks Ser.). (Illus.). 200p. Date not set. price not set (ISBN 0-521-22827-1); pap. price not set (ISBN 0-521-29664-1). Cambridge U Pr.

Howard, Philip. Words Fail Me. 1981. 13.95 (ISBN 0-19-520237-6). Oxford U Pr.

Howard, Phillip L. & Trainer, Thomas D. Radionuclides in Clinical Chemistry. 1980. text ed. 22.50 (ISBN 0-316-37470-9). Little.

Howard Press. C. Wright Mills. (World Leaders Ser.). 1978. lib. bdg. 12.50 (ISBN 0-8057-7708-3). Twayne.

Howard, Richard. Alone with America. enlarged ed. LC 79-64718. 1980. 25.00 (ISBN 0-689-11000-6); pap. 12.95 (ISBN 0-689-70594-8, 177). Atheneum.

--The Damages. LC 67-24112. (Wesleyan Poetry Program: Vol. 35). (Orig.). 1967. 10.00x (ISBN 0-8195-2035-7, Pub. by Wesleyan U Pr); pap. 4.95x (ISBN 0-8195-1035-1). Columbia U Pr.

--Quantities. LC 62-18342. (Wesleyan Poetry Program: Vol. 16). (Orig.). 1962. 10.00x (ISBN 0-8195-2016-0, Pub. by Wesleyan U Pr); pap. 4.95 (ISBN 0-8195-1016-5). Columbia U Pr.

--The War of Eighteen Twelve. (Jackdaw Ser: No. C25). 1972. 5.95 o.s.i. (ISBN 0-670-74967-2, Grossman). Viking Pr.

Howard, Richard, tr. see Barthes, Roland.

Howard, Richard, tr. see Bathes, Roland.

Howard, Richard, tr. see De Brunhoff, Laurent.

Howard, Richard, tr. see Mauriac, Claude.

Howard, Richard, tr. see Moniere, Denis.

Howard, Richard, tr. see Simon, Claude.

Howard, Richard C., jt. ed. see Boorman, Howard L.

Howard, Robert. Performance in a World of Change: Perspective on Learning Environments. LC 79-65294. 1979. pap. text ed. 8.75 (ISBN 0-8191-0785-9); lib. bdg. 17.75 (ISBN 0-8191-1275-5). U Pr of Amer.

Howard, Robert E. Conan the Conqueror, No. 9. Sprague de Camp, L., ed. 1977. pap. 2.25 (ISBN 0-441-11638-8). Ace Bks.

--Conan the Warrior, No. 7. Sprague de Camp, L., ed. 1977. pap. 2.25 (ISBN 0-441-11636-1). Ace Bks.

--Red Nails. 1979. 2.25 (ISBN 0-425-04360-6). Berkley Pub.

--The Road of Azrael. 192p. 1980. pap. 2.25 (ISBN 0-553-13326-8). Bantam.

--Son of the White Wolf. LC 77-73604. 1977. 12.95 (ISBN 0-913960-09-8). Fax Collect.

--Sword of Shahrazar. LC 76-16707. 1976. 12.95 (ISBN 0-913960-08-X). Fax Collect.

--The Vultures. (Illus.). 1973. 8.50 (ISBN 0-87707-115-2). Fictioneer Bks.

Howard, Robert E. & Lupoff, Richard. The Return of Skull-Face. LC 77-89158. 1977. 9.95 (ISBN 0-913960-17-9). Fax Collect.

Howard, Robert E. & Sprague de Camp, L. Conan the Adventurer, No. 5. 1977. pap. 2.25 (ISBN 0-441-11634-5). Ace Bks.

--Conan the Freebooter: No. 3. 1977. pap. 2.25 (ISBN 0-441-11632-9). Ace Bks.

--Conan the Usurper, No. 8. 1977. pap. 2.25 (ISBN 0-441-11637-X). Ace Bks.

Howard, Robert E., et al. Conan: No. 1. 1977. pap. 2.25 (ISBN 0-441-11630-2). Ace Bks.

--Conan of Cimmeria: No. 2. 1977. pap. 2.25 (ISBN 0-441-11631-0). Ace Bks.

--Conan the Wanderer: No. 4. 1977. pap. 2.25 (ISBN 0-441-11633-7). Ace Bks.

--Pathophysiology PreTest Self-Assessment & Review. (Illus.). 200p. (Orig.). 1980. pap. 9.95 (ISBN 0-07-051575-1). McGraw Pretest.

Howard, Ronald L. A Social History of American Family Sociology, 1865-1940. Mogey, John H. & Van Leeuwen, Louis Th., eds. LC 80-1790. (Contributions in Family Studies Ser.: No. 4). 168p. 1981. lib. bdg. 22.50 (ISBN 0-313-22767-5, MOA/). Greenwood.

Howard, Ronald L., et al. A Social History of American Family Sociology, 1865-1940. Mogey, John H. & Van Leeuwen, Louis T., eds. LC 80-1790. (Contributions in Family Studies: No. 4). 168p. 1981. lib. bdg. 22.50 (ISBN 0-313-22767-5, MOA/). Greenwood.

Howard, Ronnalie R. The Dark Glass: Vision & Technique in the Poetry of Dante Gabriel Rossetti. LC 70-158176. xiii, 218p. 1972. 12.00x (ISBN 0-8214-0099-1). Ohio U Pr.

Howard, Ted, jt. auth. see Rifkin, Jeremy.

Howard, Thomas. The Achievement of C. S. Lewis: A Reading of His Fiction. LC 80-14188. (Wheaton Literary Ser.). 200p. 1980. pap. 5.95 (ISBN 0-87788-004-2). Shaw Pubs.

Howard, Thomas, jt. auth. see Hagerty, Robert.

Howard, Thomas W., ed. The North Dakota Political Tradition. 192p. 1981. 8.95 (ISBN 0-8138-0520-1). Iowa St U Pr.

Howard, Vechel. Tall in the West. 1978. pap. 1.25 o.p. (ISBN 0-449-13898-4, GM). Fawcett.

Howard, Velma S., tr. see Lagerlof, Selma.

Howard, Vernon. The Esoteric Encyclopedia of Eternal Knowledge. LC 80-6203. 256p. 1981. 9.95 (ISBN 0-8128-2797-X); pap. 6.95 (ISBN 0-8128-6117-5). Stein & Day.

--Esoteric Mind Power. 196p. 1980. pap. 5.50 (ISBN 0-87516-401-3). De Vorss.

--Mystic Path to Cosmic Power. 1969. pap. 2.50 (ISBN 0-446-91831-8). Warner Bks.

--Pantomimes, Charades & Skits. rev. ed. LC 59-12983. (Illus.). 124p. (gr. 4 up). 1974. 6.95 (ISBN 0-8069-7004-9); PLB 6.69 (ISBN 0-8069-7005-7). Sterling.

Howard, Vernon, ed. Complete Book of Children's Theater. LC 69-10951. 1969. 9.95 o.p. (ISBN 0-385-03682-5). Doubleday.

Howard, Veronica. Rebel in Love. (Orig.). 1981. pap. 1.50 (ISBN 0-440-17423-6). Dell.

Howard W. Sams Editorial Staff. Color TV Training Manual. 4th ed. LC 77-76538. (Illus.). 1977. pap. 12.95 (ISBN 0-672-21412-1). Sams.

Howard W. Sams Engineering Staff. Photofact Television Course. 5th ed. LC 80-50060. (Illus.). 1980. pap. 8.95 (ISBN 0-672-21630-2). SAMS.

--Semiconductor General Purpose Replacements. 3rd ed. 1980. pap. 17.95 (ISBN 0-672-21730-9). Sams.

--Semiconductor General Purpose Replacements. 2nd ed. LC 78-64982. 1979. pap. 14.95 o.p. (ISBN 0-672-21576-4). Sams.

--Tube Substitution Handbook. 21st ed. LC 80-13842. 1980. pap. 3.95 (ISBN 0-672-21746-5). Sams.

--Tube Substitution Handbook. 20th ed. LC 76-42880. 1977. pap. 2.95 o.p. (ISBN 0-672-21405-9, 21405). Sams.

Howard, Wayne, jt. auth. see Abersold, John.

Howard, Will. Cyclone, South by Southwest. LC 79-52113. 247p. 1979. 9.95 (ISBN 0-686-69222-5). Red Feather.

--H. C. The Secret Menopause of H. C. Douglas. Parnell, Joy, ed. LC 80-52018. 400p. 1980. 12.95 (ISBN 0-936430-77-X). Red Feather.

Howard, William. Caligula. (Illus., Orig.). 1979. pap. 2.50 (ISBN 0-446-91799-0). Warner Bks.

Howard, William J., ed. Editor, Author, & Publisher. (Conference on Editorial Problems Ser.). 1976. lib. bdg. 16.50 (ISBN 0-8240-2403-6). Garland Pub.

Howard, William W. Atlas of Operative Dentistry. 3rd ed. (Illus.). 295p. 1981. spiral bdg. 19.95 (ISBN 0-8016-2282-4). Mosby.

--Mosby's Comprehensive Review Series: Review of Operative Dentistry. LC 72-12874. 1973. pap. text ed. 9.95 o.p. (ISBN 0-8016-2279-4). Mosby.

Howard, Winston. Money Is Not Enough. 1980. 8.95 (ISBN 0-914244-05-1). Epic Pubns.

Howard-Hall, T. H. British Bibliography & Textual Criticism: A Bibliography. (Index to British Literary Bibliography Ser.: Vols. IV & V). 1254p. 1979. Set. 115.00x (ISBN 0-19-818163-9). Oxford U Pr.

Howard-Hill, T. H. Literary Concordances: A Complete Handbook for the Preparation of Manual & Computer Concordances. 1979. text ed. 15.00 (ISBN 0-08-023021-0). Pergamon.

Howard-Williams, Jeremy. Offshore Crew. LC 79-65613. (Illus.). 190p. 1980. 12.95 (ISBN 0-396-07779-X). Dodd.

--Sails. rev. ed. LC 68-19075. (Illus.). 1972. 15.00 (ISBN 0-8286-0054-6). De Graff.

Howard-Williams, Jeremy, tr. see Damour, Jacques.

Howarth, D. Men-of-War. Time-Life Books, ed. (The Seafarers). (Illus.). 1979. 13.95 (ISBN 0-8094-2666-8). Time-Life.

Howarth, David. Desert King: The Life of Ibn Saud. 14.00 (ISBN 0-685-89875-X). Intl Bk Ctr.

--Ten Sixty Six: The Year of the Conquest. 1978. 10.95 (ISBN 0-670-69601-3). Viking Pr.

Howarth, David A. Sledge Patrol. (Illus.). 1957. 5.50 o.s.i. (ISBN 0-02-555040-3). Macmillan.

Howarth, David P. The Dreadnoughts. (The Seafarers Ser.). (Illus.). 1979. lib. bdg. 11.97 (ISBN 0-8094-2712-5); kivar bdg. 9.93 (ISBN 0-8094-2713-3). Silver.

--The Men of War. (The Seafarers Ser.). (Illus.). 1978. lib. bdg. 11.97 (ISBN 0-686-50987-0). Silver.

Howarth, Edward G. & Wilson, Mona. West Ham: A Study in Social & Industrial Problems, London, 1907. LC 79-56958. (The English Working Class Ser.). 1980. lib. bdg. 35.00 (ISBN 0-8240-0111-7). Garland Pub.

Howarth, O. W. Theory of Spectroscopy: Elementary Introduction. LC 73-35. 214p. 1973. pap. text ed. 11.95 (ISBN 0-470-41667-X). Halsted Pr.

Howarth, Patrick. Undercover: The Men & Women of the Special Operations Executive. 224p. 1980. 18.95 (ISBN 0-7100-0573-3). Routledge & Kegan.

Howarth, R. Building Craft Foremanship: A Manual for the Trainee Building Supervisor. (Illus.). pap. 5.50 o.p. (ISBN 0-7153-5667-4). David & Charles.

Howarth, T. Charles Rennie Mackintosh & the Modern Movement. 1977. 60.00 (ISBN 0-7100-8538-9). Routledge & Kegan.

Howarth, Thomas. Charles Rennie Mackintosh & the Modern Movement. LC 76-17782. (Aesthetic Movement & the Arts & Crafts Movement Ser.: Vol. 38). (Illus.). 1977. Repr. of 1932 ed. lib. bdg. 44.00 (ISBN 0-8240-2487-7). Garland Pub.

Howarth, W. D. & Thomas, J. Merlin, eds. Moliere: Stage & Study. 1973. 29.95x (ISBN 0-19-815712-6). Oxford U Pr.

Howarth, W. D., ed. see Moliere.

Howarth, William L., ed. The John McPhee Reader. 1977. pap. 2.50 o.p. (ISBN 0-394-72113-6, Vin). Random.

--Twentieth Century Interpretations of Poe's Tales. LC 69-15337. (Twentieth Century Interpretations Ser). 1971. 8.95 (ISBN 0-13-684654-8, Spec). P-H.

Howarth-Williams, Martin. R.D. Laing: His Work & Its Relevance to Sociology. (Direct Editions Ser.). (Orig.). 1977. pap. 14.50 (ISBN 0-7100-8624-5). Routledge & Kegan.

Howat, G. R., jt. ed. see Sinclair, H. M.

Howat, Gerald. Village Cricket. LC 79-56048. (Illus.). 1980. 17.95 (ISBN 0-7153-7727-2). David & Charles.

Howatch, Susan. The Dark Shore. 192p. 1978. pap. 2.25 (ISBN 0-449-24241-2, Q2845, Crest). Fawcett.

--Penmarric. 704p. 1978. pap. 2.75 (ISBN 0-449-24090-8, Crest). Fawcett.

--The Shrouded Walls. 1978. pap. 2.25 (ISBN 0-449-23385-5, Crest). Fawcett.

Howath, C. I. & Gillham, W. E., eds. The Structure of Psychology: An Introductory Text. (Illus.). 792p. 1981. text ed. 57.50x (ISBN 0-04-150071-7, 2492); pap. text ed. 19.95x (ISBN 0-04-150072-5, 2493). Allen Unwin.

Howay, Frederic William. A List of Trading Vessels in the Maritime Fur Trade, 1785-1825. (Materials for the Study of Alaska History Ser.: No. 2). 1973. pap. 8.50x (ISBN 0-919642-51-9). Limestone Pr.

Howe, Bea. Antiques from the Victorian Home. 1973. 45.00 (ISBN 0-7134-0730-1, Pub. by Batsford England). David & Charles.

Howe, Bruce. The Palaeolithic of Tangier, Morroco. (American School of Prehistoric Research Bulletin Ser.: No. 22). (Orig.). 1967. pap. text ed. 10.00 (ISBN 0-87365-523-0). Peabody Harvard.

Howe, Carrol B. Ancient Tribes of the Klamath Country. LC 68-28922. (Illus.). 1972. 7.50 o.p. (ISBN 0-8323-0131-0); pap. 4.95 o.p. (ISBN 0-8323-0279-1). Binford.

Howe, Charles W. Natural Resource Economics: Issues Analysis & Policy. LC 78-24174. 1979. text ed. 24.95x (ISBN 0-471-04527-6). Wiley.

Howe, Christopher. Employment & Economic Growth in Urban China, 1949-57. LC 76-152641. (Contemporary China Institute Publications). (Illus.). 1971. 34.95 (ISBN 0-521-08172-6). Cambridge U Pr.

--Shanghai. LC 79-41616. (Contemporary China Institute Publications). (Illus.). 456p. Date not set. 69.50 (ISBN 0-521-23198-1). Cambridge U Pr.

--Wage Patterns & Wage Policy in Modern China, 1919-1972. (Studies in Chinese History, Literature & Institutions). (Illus.). 180p. 1973. 39.95 (ISBN 0-521-20199-3). Cambridge U Pr.

Howe, Claude L., Jr. Glimpses of Baptist Heritage. 1981. pap. 5.75 (ISBN 0-8054-6559-6). Broadman.

Howe, Daniel W., ed. Victorian America. LC 76-20155. 1976. 12.95 (ISBN 0-8122-7713-9); pap. 5.95x (ISBN 0-8122-1090-5). U of Pa Pr.

Howe, De M. Wolfe see Howe, M. De Wolfe.

Howe, Deborah & Howe, James. Bunnicula: A Rabbit-Tale of Mystery. (gr. 3-7). 1980. pap. 1.95 (ISBN 0-380-51094-4, 51094, Camelot). Avon.

--Teddy Bear's Scrapbook. LC 79-22794. (Illus.). (gr. 2-5). 1980. 7.95 (ISBN 0-689-30746-2). Atheneum.

Howe, Eric G. War Dance: A Study of the Psychology of War. LC 74-147471. (Library of War & Peace; the Character & Causes of War). lib. bdg. 38.00 (ISBN 0-8240-0263-6). Garland Pub.

Howe, Eunice D. The Hospital of Santo Spirito & Pope Sixtus IV. (Outstanding Dissertations in the Fine Arts Ser.). (Illus.). 1978. lib. bdg. 43.00x (ISBN 0-8240-3230-6). Garland Pub.

Howe, Fanny. First Marriage. 1977. pap. 1.75 (ISBN 0-380-01850-0, 36475). Avon.

--Poem from a Single Pallet. 1980. 4.50 (ISBN 0-932716-10-5). Kelsey St Pr.

Howe, Florence, ed. Female Studies, Two. 165p. 1970. pap. 5.00x o.p. (ISBN 0-912786-02-7). Know Inc.

Howe, Florence & Bass, Ellen, eds. No More Masks: An Anthology of Poems by Women. LC 72-89675. 432p. 1973. pap. 4.50 (ISBN 0-385-02553-X, Anch). Doubleday.

Howe, Florence & Rothermich, John A., eds. Household & Kin: Families in Flux. (Women's Lives - Women's Work Ser.). 208p. (Orig.). Date not set. pap. text ed. 4.71 (ISBN 0-07-020427-6). Webster-McGraw.

--Las Mujeres: Conversations from a Hispanic Community. (Women's Lives - Women's Work Ser.). 192p. (Orig.). 1980. pap. text ed. 4.23 (ISBN 0-07-020445-4). Webster-McGraw.

--The Sex-Role Cycle: Socialization from Infancy to Old Age. (Women's Lives - Women's Work Ser.). 192p. (Orig.). 1980. pap. text ed. 4.23. Webster-McGraw.

--With These Hands: Women Working on the Land. (Women's Lives - Women's Work). (Orig.). pap. text ed. 6.45 (ISBN 0-07-020441-1). Webster-McGraw.

--Women Have Always Worked: An Historical Overview. (Women's Always - Women's Work Ser.). 208p. (Orig.). 1980. pap. text ed. 4.71 (ISBN 0-07-020435-7). Webster-McGraw.

--Women's "True" Profession: Voices from the History of Teaching. (Women's Lives-Women's Work Ser.). 352p. (Orig.). 1981. pap. text ed. 6.45 (ISBN 0-07-020437-3). McGraw.

Howe, Florence, jt. ed. see Hoffman, Nancy.

Howe, Frederic C. City: The Hope of Democracy. LC 68-1361. (American Library Ser: No. 1). 350p. 1967. Repr. of 1905 ed. 11.50 (ISBN 0-295-97858-9). U of Wash Pr.

Howe, Frederick. Why War? LC 70-147497. (Library of War & Peace; the Political Economy of War). lib. bdg. 38.00 (ISBN 0-8240-0291-1). Garland Pub.

Howe, George. Call It Treason. LC 80-15043. (Great Classic Stories of World War II Ser.). 1980. 8.95 (ISBN 0-396-07870-2); pap. 5.95 (ISBN 0-396-07871-0). Dodd.

Howe, George & Harrer, G. A. Handbook of Classical Mythology. LC 77-121209. 1970. Repr. of 1947 ed. 15.00 (ISBN 0-8103-3290-6). Gale.

Howe, Herbert E., Jr. & Howe, Herbert E., eds. Nebraska Symposium on Motivation, 1978: Human Emotion. LC 53-11655. (Nebraska Symposia on Motivation Ser.: Vol. 26). 1979. 17.95x (ISBN 0-8032-2306-4); pap. 8.95x (ISBN 0-8032-7203-0). U of Nebr Pr.

Howe, Herbert E., Jr., ed. see Nebraska Symposium on Motivation, 1979.

Howe, Herbert M, jt. ed. see MacKendrick, Paul L.

Howe, Hubert S., Jr. TRS-80 Assembly Language. (Illus.). 192p. 1981. text ed. 15.95 (ISBN 0-13-931139-4, Spec); pap. text ed. 6.95 (ISBN 0-13-931121-1, Spec). P-H.

Howe, I. & Widick, B. J. The UAW & Walter Reuther. LC 72-2375. (FDR & the Era of the New Deal Ser.). 324p. 1973. Repr. of 1949 ed. lib. bdg. 29.50 (ISBN 0-306-70485-4). Da Capo.

Howe, Irving. Celebrations & Attacks. LC 80-14048. 1980. pap. 4.95 (ISBN 0-15-616248-2, Harv). HarBraceJ.

--World of Our Fathers. 1981. pap. 3.95 (ISBN 0-553-13810-3). Bantam.

Howe, Irving & Coser, Lewis. The American Communist Party: A Critical History. LC 73-22072. (FDR & the Era of the New Deal Ser.). x, 612p. 1974. Repr. of 1962 ed. lib. bdg. 39.50 (ISBN 0-306-70636-9). Da Capo.

Howe, Irving & Libo, Kenneth. How We Lived: A Documentary History of Immigrant Jews in America, Eighteen Eighty-Nineteen Thirty. 1981. pap. 6.95 (ISBN 0-452-25269-5, Z5269, Plume Bks). NAL.

Howe, Irving & Greenberg, Eliezer, eds. Yiddish Stories Old & New. LC 74-8116. 128p. (gr. 7 up). 1974. 6.95 (ISBN 0-8234-0246-0). Holiday.

Howe, Irving & Wisse, Ruth, eds. The Best of Sholem Aleichem. 1980. pap. 5.95 (ISBN 0-671-41092-X, Touchstone). S&S.

Howe, J. From the Revolution Through the Age of Jackson. 1973. pap. text ed. 10.95 (ISBN 0-13-331348-4). P-H.

Howe, James, jt. auth. see Howe, Deborah.

Howe, James R. Marlowe, Tamburlaine, & Magic. LC 75-36978. x, 220p. 1976. 12.95x (ISBN 0-8214-0200-5). Ohio U Pr.

Howe, James W. & Overseas Development Council Staff. The U. S. & the Developing World: Agenda for Action, 1974. LC 74-4234. (Agenda Ser.). 228p. 1974. pap. 3.95 (ISBN 0-686-28670-7). Overseas Dev Council.

--The U. S. & World Development: Agenda for Action, 1975. LC 75-11641. (Agenda Ser.). 288p. 1975. pap. 4.95 (ISBN 0-275-89310-3). Overseas Dev Council.

Howe, Jemima see Humphreys, David.

Howe, John, tr. see Eudes, Dominique.

Howe, John G. Skiing Mechanics. 1981. 16.95 (ISBN 0-686-28916-1). Poudre Pub Co.

Howe, Joseph. Poems & Essays. LC 73-78943. (Literature of Canada Ser.). 1973. pap. 4.95 (ISBN 0-8020-6208-3). U of Toronto Pr.

--Western & Eastern Rambles: Travel Sketches of Nova Scotia. Parks, M. G., ed. LC 72-97424. (Illus.). 1973. pap. 4.50 (ISBN 0-8020-6183-4). U of Toronto Pr.

Howe, Louise K., ed. White Majority: Between Poverty & Affluence. 1971. pap. 1.95 o.p. (ISBN 0-394-71666-3, V666, Vin). Random.

Howe, M., ed. Readings in American Legal History. LC 70-155924. (American Constitutional & Legal History Ser). 1971. Repr. of 1949 ed. lib. bdg. 49.50 (ISBN 0-306-70159-6). Da Capo.

Howe, M. De Wolfe. The Boston Symphony Orchestra: 1881-1931. rev. ed. Burk, John N., ed. LC 77-16532. (Music Reprint Ser.: 1978). (Illus.). 1978. Repr. of 1931 ed. lib. bdg. 29.50 (ISBN 0-306-77533-6). Da Capo.

Howe, Mark D. Justice Oliver Wendell Holmes, 2 vols. Incl. Vol. 1. The Shaping Years, 1841-1870. (Illus.). 330p. 1957 (ISBN 0-674-49500-4); Vol. 2. The Proving Years, 1870-1882. (Illus.). 1963 (ISBN 0-674-49501-2). 16.50x ea. (Belknap Pr). Harvard U Pr.

--Touched with Fire Civil War Letters & Diary of Oliver Wendell Holmes. LC 73-96218. (American Scene Ser). 1967. Repr. of 1947 ed. lib. bdg. 32.50 (ISBN 0-306-71825-1). Da Capo.

Howe, Mark D., ed. see Bancroft, George.

Howe, Michael J. A. Adult Learning: Psychological Research & Applications. LC 76-44226. 256p. 1977. 35.75 (ISBN 0-471-99458-8, Pub. by Wiley-Interscience). Wiley.

Howe, Phyllis. Basic Nutrition in Health & Disease: Including Selection & Care of Food. 7th ed. 450p. 1981. pap. text ed. price not set (ISBN 0-7216-4796-0). Saunders.

Howe, Randolph, jt. auth. see Fogel, Danny.

Howe, Reuel L. Creative Years. (Orig.). pap. 3.95 (ISBN 0-8164-2012-2, SP8). Crossroad NY.

--Man's Need & God's Action. 1953. pap. 4.95 (ISBN 0-8164-2046-7, SP7). Crossroad NY.

--Miracle of Dialogue. 1963. pap. 3.95 (ISBN 0-8164-2047-5, SP9). Crossroad NY.

--Partners in Preaching. 1967. 6.95 (ISBN 0-8164-0175-6). Crossroad NY.

--Survival Plus. LC 76-148143. 1974. pap. 2.95 (ISBN 0-8164-2088-2). Crossroad NY.

Howe, Robin. French Cookery. 4.50x (ISBN 0-392-06255-0, Ltcb). Soccer.

--Rice Cooking. 276p. 1973. 10.00 (ISBN 0-233-96364-2). Transatlantic.

Howe, Robin, jt. auth. see Simon, Andre L.

Howe, Roger J. Building Profits Through Organizational Change. 272p. 1981. 17.95 (ISBN 0-8144-5681-2). Am Mgmt.

Howe, Russell W. Weapons: The International Game of Arms, Money & Diplomacy. LC 79-7494. 1980. 19.95 (ISBN 0-385-12809-6). Doubleday.

Howe, Susannah. Fever Moon. (Orig.). 1978. pap. 1.95 (ISBN 0-515-04550-0). Jove Pubns.

Howe, Tom. Myself in the Rain. 64p. 1980. pap. 5.95 (ISBN 0-88894-243-5, Pub. by Douglas & McIntyre Canada). Intl Schol Bk Serv.

Howe, W. Asquith. Intermediate Accounting. (Illus.). 288p. (Orig.). 1974. pap. 4.50 (ISBN 0-06-460143-9, CO 143, COS). Har-Row.

Howe, Walter J. Professional Gunsmithing. (Illus.). 518p. 1946. 24.95 (ISBN 0-8117-1375-X). Stackpole.

Howe, William W. Studies in the Civil Law, & Its Relations to the Law of England & America. xv, 340p. 1980. Repr. of 1896 ed. lib. bdg. 27.50x (ISBN 0-8377-0631-9). Rothman.

Howell, et al. Business Law. 1978. 20.95 (ISBN 0-03-016711-6). Dryden Pr.

Howell, A. A., jt. auth. see Fletcher, H.

Howell, Almonte C., Jr., ed. see Lully, Jean B.

Howell, Clinton T., ed. Better Than Gold. LC 70-131117. (Illus.). 1970. 9.95 (ISBN 0-8407-5000-5); deluxe ed. 14.95 (ISBN 0-8407-5001-3). Nelson.

Howell, Clinton T., compiled by. Seasons of Inspiration. LC 74-14556. (Illus.). 160p. 1974. gift ed. 8.95 o.p. (ISBN 0-8407-5050-1). Nelson.

Howell, D. Your Solar Energy Home: Including Wind & Methane Applications. new ed. 1979. text ed. 37.00 (ISBN 0-08-022685-X); pap. text ed. 11.25 (ISBN 0-08-022686-8). Pergamon.

Howell, D. A. A Bibliography of Educational Administration in the United Kingdom. (General Ser.). 1980. pap. text ed. 11.00x (ISBN 0-85633-151-1, NFER). Humanities.

Howell, D. A., jt. auth. see Baron, George.

Howell, David. Aftershock. 192p. (Orig.). 1981. pap. 2.50 (ISBN 0-515-05454-2). Jove Pubns.

--British Social Democracy: A Study in Development & Decay. 2nd ed. 340p. 1980. 28.50 (ISBN 0-312-10536-3). St Martin.

Howell, David W. Land & People in Nineteenth-Century Wales. (Studies in Economic History). (Illus.). 1978. 22.00 (ISBN 0-7100-8673-3). Routledge & Kegan.

Howell, Denis. Soccer Refereeing. 1978. 10.95 (ISBN 0-7207-1003-0, Pub. by Michael Joseph). Merrimack Bk Serv.

Howell, Elsworth S. & Dangerfield, Stanley, eds. The International Encyclopedia of Dogs. 2nd ed. LC 74-19842. 1971. 24.95 (ISBN 0-87605-623-0). Howell Bk.

Howell, Elsworth S., et al. Howell Book of Dog Care & Training. 2nd ed. LC 63-14239. (Illus.). 1963. 5.95 o.p. (ISBN 0-87605-574-9). Howell Bk.

Howell, F. Clark. Early Man. rev. ed. LC 65-20165. (Life Nature Library). (Illus.). (gr. 5 up). 1973. PLB 8.97 o.p. (ISBN 0-8094-0636-5, Pub. by Time-Life). Silver.

--Early Man. (Young Readers Library). (Illus.). 1977. lib. bdg. 7.95 (ISBN 0-686-51087-9). Silver.

Howell, Frank, et al. The Craft of Pottery. LC 74-15859. (Illus.). 176p. 1975. 14.95 o.p. (ISBN 0-06-011966-7, HarpT); pap. 6.95 o.p. (ISBN 0-06-011959-4, TD-218, HarpT). Har-Row.

Howell, G. & Perez Y Sabido, J. Spanish-English Handbook. 1977. pap. 9.95 (ISBN 0-87489-073-X). Med Economics.

Howell, Helen, jt. auth. see Cushenbery, Donald C.

Howell, J. B., jt. ed. see Peebles, Margaret.

Howell, J. Emory, jt. auth. see Bedenbaugh, John H.

Howell, James E. & Teichroew, Daniel. Mathematical Analysis for Business Decisions. rev. ed. 1971. text ed. 14.95x o.p. (ISBN 0-256-00197-9). Irwin.

Howell, James M. & Stamm, Charles F. Urban Fiscal Stress: A Comparative Analysis of 66 U. S. Cities. LC 79-3083. 176p. 1979. 19.95 (ISBN 0-669-03372-3). Lexington Bks.

Howell, John C. The Complete Guide to Business Contracts. 160p. 1980. pap. 5.95 (Spec). P-H.

--Corporate Executive's Legal Handbook. 144p. 1980. pap. 5.95 (Spec). P-H.

--Estate Planning for the Small Business Owner. 176p. 1980. pap. 5.95 (Spec). P-H.

--Form Your Own Corporation. 128p. 1980. pap. 5.95 (Spec). P-H.

--Prepare Your Own Partnership Agreements. 144p. 1980. pap. 5.95 (Spec). P-H.

Howell, John R., jt. auth. see Siegel, Robert.

Howell, John T. Marin Flora: Manual of the Flowering Plants & Ferns of Marin County, California. 2nd ed. LC 71-100608. (Supplement). 1970. 16.75 (ISBN 0-520-00578-3). U of Cal Pr.

Howell, Joseph T. Hard Living on Clay Street. LC 73-79736. 440p. 1973. pap. 4.50 (ISBN 0-385-05317-7, Anch). Doubleday.

Howell, Kenneth W., et al. Handbook for Diagnosing Basic Skills: A Handbook for Deciding What to Teach. (Special Education Ser.). 393p. 1980. pap. text ed. 17.50 (ISBN 0-675-08130-0). Merrill.

Howell, Mary. Healing at Home: A Guide to Health Care for Children. LC 77-88329. (Illus.). 1979. 12.95 o.p. (ISBN 0-8070-2368-X); pap. 5.95 (ISBN 0-8070-2369-8, BP573). Beacon Pr.

Howell, Michael & Ford, Peter. The True History of the Elephant Man. 1980. pap. 2.95 (ISBN 0-14-005622-X). Penguin.

Howell, Neil. Allocating the Home Help Services. 110p. 1979. pap. text ed. 11.25x (ISBN 0-7199-1026-9, Pub. by Bedford England). Renouf.

Howell, P. A. The Judicial Committee of the Privy Council: 1833-1876. LC 78-54326. (Cambridge Studies in English Legal History). (Illus.). 1979. 35.50 (ISBN 0-521-22146-3). Cambridge U Pr.

Howell, Patricia L., jt. auth. see Howell, Robert G., Jr.

Howell, Paul P. Manual of Nuer Law: Being an Account of Customary Law, Its Evolution & Development in the Courts Established by the Sudan Government. LC 73-106840. (Illus.). Repr. of 1954 ed. 15.00x (ISBN 0-8371-3462-5). Negro U Pr.

Howell, Peter. A Commentary on Book One of the Epigrams of Martial. 369p. 1980. text ed. 65.00x (Athlone Pr). Humanities.

Howell, Peter S., jt. auth. see Kilburn, Robert E.

Howell, R. Rodney & Simon, Frank A. Patient Management Problems: Pediatrics. LC 80-18503. (Illus.). 160p. 1981. pap. text ed. 9.00 (ISBN 0-668-04780-1, 4780). Arco.

Howell, Rate A., et al. Business Law: Text & Cases. 2nd ed. LC 80-65801. 1104p. 1981. text ed. 21.95 (ISBN 0-03-058111-7). Dryden Pr.

Howell, Robert G., Jr. & Howell, Patricia L. Discipline in the Classroom: Solving the Teaching Puzzle. (Illus.). 1980. text ed. 13.95 (ISBN 0-8359-1344-9). Reston.

Howell, Roger, ed. see Prescott, William H.

Howell, Sandra C. Designing for Aging: Patterns of Use. (Illus.). 345p. 1980. text ed. 25.00x (ISBN 0-262-08107-5). MIT Pr.

Howell, Thoams R. Breeding Biology of the Egyptian Plover, Pluvianus aegyptius. (U. C. Publications in Zoology Ser.: Vol. 113). 1980. pap. 11.50 (ISBN 0-520-09603-7). U of Cal Pr.

Howell, Thomas R., et al. Breeding Biology of the Gray Gull, Larus Modestus. (Publications in Zoology: Vol. 104). 1975. pap. 6.50x (ISBN 0-520-09516-2). U of Cal Pr.

Howell, William C. Essentials of Industrial & Organizational Psychology. 1976. pap. 9.95x (ISBN 0-256-01806-5). Dorsey.

Howell, William C. & Fleishman, Edwin A., eds. Information Processing & Decision Making. (Human Performance & Productivity Ser.: Vol. 2). 1981. professional ref. text 19.95 (ISBN 0-89859-090-6). L Erlbaum Assocs.

Howell, William S., jt. auth. see Brembeck, Winston L.

Howell, Yvonne & Miller, Harry. Selling the Solar Home: California Edition. 93p. 1981. pap. 10.00 (ISBN 0-89934-081-4). Solar Energy Info.

Howells, Coral A. Love, Mystery & Misery: Feeling in Gothic Fiction. 1978. text ed. 28.50x (ISBN 0-485-11181-0, Athlone Pr). Humanities.

Howells, Harvey. Dowsing for Everyone. LC 78-26713. (Illus.). 1979. 8.95 o.p. (ISBN 0-8289-0341-7); pap. 5.95 (ISBN 0-8289-0342-5). Greene.

Howells, John G. Advances in Family Psychiatry, Vol. 2. LC 101. 1980. text ed. 29.95 (ISBN 0-8236-0101-3). Intl Univs Pr.

Howells, John G., ed. Modern Perspectives in the Psychiatry of Middle Age. LC 74-78715. 375p. 1981. 30.00 (ISBN 0-87630-245-2). Brunner-Mazel.

Howells, W. D. Hazard of New Fortunes. Nordloh, David J., ed. LC 73-75402. (A Selected Edition of W. D. Howells: Center for Editions of American Authors: Vol. 16). (Illus.). 592p. 1975. 20.00x (ISBN 0-253-32708-3). Ind U Pr.

--Leatherwood God. LC 74-189640. (Selected Edition of W. D. Howells: Center for Editions of American Authors: Vol. 27). 288p. 1976. 18.50x (ISBN 0-253-33285-0). Ind U Pr.

--Minister's Charge; Or, The Apprenticeship of Lemuel Barker. LC 77-22213. (A Selected Edition of W. D. Howells: Center for Editions of American Authors: Vol. 14). (Illus.). 1978. 20.00x (ISBN 0-253-33855-7). Ind U Pr.

--Quality of Mercy. LC 78-20655. (Center for Editions of American Authors, a Selected Edition of W. D. Howells Ser.: Vol. 18). (Illus.). 472p. 1979. 20.00x (ISBN 0-253-35789-6). Ind U Pr.

--Rise of Silas Lapham. LC 70-92321. (A Selected Edition of W.D. Howells: Center for Editions of American Authors: Vol. 12). 434p. 1971. 17.50x (ISBN 0-253-35016-6). Ind U Pr.

--Selected Letters of W. D. Howells: 1852-1872, Vol. 1. Arms, George, et al, eds. (Critical Editions Programs Ser.). 1979. lib. bdg. 30.00 (ISBN 0-8057-8527-2). Twayne.

--Shadow of a Dream & An Imperative Duty. LC 71-79475. (A Selected Edition of W. D. Howells: Center for Editions of American Authors: Vol. 17). 272p. 1969. 15.00x (ISBN 0-253-35190-1). Ind U Pr.

--Son of Royal Langbrith. LC 75-79476. (A Selected Edition of W.D. Howells: Center for Editions of American Authors: Vol. 26). (Illus.). 344p. 1970. 17.50x (ISBN 0-253-35393-9). Ind U Pr.

Howells, W. W. Cranial Variation in Man: A Study by Multivariate Analysis. LC 73-77203. (Peabody Museum Papers: Vol. 67). 1973. pap. text ed. 17.00 (ISBN 0-87365-189-8). Peabody Harvard.

Howells, W. W. & Bleibtreu, Hermann K. Hutterite Age Differences in Body Measurements. LC 78-115048. (Museum Papers 57, No. 2). (Orig.). 1970. pap. text ed. 10.00 (ISBN 0-87365-168-5). Peabody Harvard.

Howells, W. W. & Crichton, J. M. Craniometry & Multivariate Analysis. LC 66-4603. (Peabody Museum Papers Ser.: Vol. 57, No. 1). 1966. pap. text ed. 8.00 (ISBN 0-87365-167-7). Peabody Harvard.

Howells, William D. Rise of Silas Lapham. (Literature Ser). (gr. 10-12). 1970. pap. text ed. 3.67 (ISBN 0-87720-737-2). AMSCO Sch.

--Rise of Silas Lapham. (RL 9). pap. 1.95 (ISBN 0-451-51400-9, CJ1400, Sig Classics). NAL.

--The Rise of Silas Lapham. rev. ed. Dixson, Robert J., ed. (American Classics Ser.: No. 8). 1974. pap. text ed. 2.75 (ISBN 0-88345-204-9, 18127); cassettes 40.00 (ISBN 0-685-38925-1); tapes 40.00 (ISBN 0-685-38926-X). Regents Pub.

Howells, William D., jt. auth. see Twain, Mark.

Hower, Alfred & Preto-Rodas, Richard A., eds. Cronicas Brasileiras: A Portuguese Reader. LC 77-634081. 1971. pap. 7.00x (ISBN 0-8130-0325-3). U Presses Fla.

Hower, Edward. The New Life Hotel. 1980. pap. 2.95 (ISBN 0-686-69254-3, 76372, Bard). Avon.

Howerton, Paul W., jt. auth. see Enger, Norman L.

Howery, Gerry, jt. auth. see Herrick, Clyde.

Howes, Alan B., jt. auth. see Dunning, Stephen.

Howes, Alan B., ed. Sterne: The Critical Heritage. (Critical Heritage Ser). 1974. 40.00x (ISBN 0-7100-7788-2). Routledge & Kegan.

Howes, Barbara. The Blue Garden. LC 72-3697. (Wesleyan Poetry Program: Vol. 62). (Orig.). 1972. 10.00x (ISBN 0-8195-2062-4, Pub. by Wesleyan U Pr); pap. 4.95 (ISBN 0-8195-1062-9). Columbia U Pr.

--Light & Dark. LC 59-12478. (Wesleyan Poetry Program: Vol. 1). (Orig.). 1959. 10.00x (ISBN 0-8195-2001-2, Pub. by Wesleyan U Pr); pap. 4.95 (ISBN 0-8195-1001-7). Columbia U Pr.

Howes, Barbara & Smith, Gregory J., eds. Sea-Green Horse: A Collection of Short Stories. LC 73-89589. (gr. 7-12). 1970. 5.95g o.s.i. (ISBN 0-02-744610-7). Macmillan.

Howes, Connie B. Rand McNally Recreational Vehicle Handbook. LC 78-54622. (Illus.). 1979. pap. 2.95 o.s.i. (ISBN 0-528-84113-0). Rand.

Howes, F. A. Boundary-Interior Layer Interactions in Nonlinear Singular Perturbation Theory. LC 78-8693. 1978. 7.60 (ISBN 0-8218-2203-9, MEMO-203). Am Math.

Howes, F. N. Dictionary of Useful & Everyday Plants & Their Common Names. LC 73-91701. 300p. 1974. 32.95 (ISBN 0-521-08520-9). Cambridge U Pr.

Howes, Frank. The Music of William Walton. 2nd ed. (Illus.). 1973. 24.00x (ISBN 0-19-315431-5). Oxford U Pr.

Howes, M. J. & Morgan, D. V. Optical Fibre Communications: Devices, Circuits & Systems. LC 79-40512. (Wiley Series in Solid State Devices & Circuits). 1980. 46.75 (ISBN 0-471-27611-1, Pub. by Wiley-Interscience). Wiley.

Howes, M. J. & Morgan, D. V., eds. Microwave Devices: Device Circuit Interaction. LC 75-15387. (Solid State Devices & Circuits Ser.). 426p. 1976. 55.00 (ISBN 0-471-41729-7, Pub. by Wiley-Interscience). Wiley.

Howes, Robert C., tr. The Tale of the Campaign of Igor. 1974. pap. text ed. 2.95x (ISBN 0-393-09310-7). Norton.

Howes, Vernon E. Essentials of Mathematics: Precalculus- a Programmed Text, 3 bks. LC 75-9733. 1975. Bk. 1: Algebra I. text ed. 18.95x (ISBN 0-471-41736-X); Bk. 2: Algebra II. text ed. o.p. (ISBN 0-471-41737-8); Bk. 3: Trigonometric Functions & Applications. text ed. 18.95x (ISBN 0-471-41738-6); instr's manual avail. (ISBN 0-471-41739-4). Wiley.

Howes, William. Quest for Barbel. pap. 3.50x o.p. (ISBN 0-392-06529-0, SpS). Soccer.

Howett, J. Basic Skills with Decimals & Percents. 128p. 1980. pap. text ed. 3.00 (ISBN 0-8428-2118-X). Cambridge Bk.

--Basic Skills with Fractions. 128p. 1980. pap. text ed. 3.00 (ISBN 0-8428-2117-1). Cambridge Bk.

--Basic Skills with Whole Numbers. 128p. 1980. pap. text ed. 3.00 (ISBN 0-8428-2116-3). Cambridge Bk.

Howey, Kenneth R., jt. ed. see Corrigan, Dean C.

Howgego, James. Victorian & Edwardian City of London. 1977. 14.95 (ISBN 0-7134-0598-8, Pub. by Batsford England). David & Charles.

Howick, William H. Philosophies of Education. 2nd ed. 150p. 1980. pap. 8.95x (ISBN 0-8134-2146-2). Interstate.

Howie, Carl G. The Date & Composition of Ezekiel. (Society of Biblical Literature, Monographs). 1950. pap. 7.50 (ISBN 0-89130-174-7, 060004). Scholars Pr Ca.

Howie, J. G. Research in General Practice. 193p. 1979. 30.00x (ISBN 0-85664-506-0, Pub. by Croom Helm Ltd England). Biblio Dist.

Howie, J. M. Acoustical Studies of Mandarin Vowels & Tones. LC 74-19529. (Princeton-Cambridge Studies in Chinese Linguistics: No. 6). (Illus.). 281p. 1976. 64.00 (ISBN 0-521-20732-0). Cambridge U Pr.

Howie, John. Perspectives for Moral Decisions. LC 80-6102. 192p. 1981. lib. bdg. 17.50 (ISBN 0-8191-1375-1); pap. text ed. 9.00 (ISBN 0-8191-1376-X). U Pr of Amer.

Howie, John & Rouner, Leroy, eds. The Wisdom of William Earnest Hocking. LC 78-61397. 1978. pap. text ed. 6.75 (ISBN 0-8191-0595-3). U Pr of Amer.

Howie, Will. Trade Unions & the Professional Engineer. 80p. 1980. 15.00x (ISBN 0-7277-0044-8, Pub. by Telford England). State Mutual Bk.

Howie-Willis, Ian. A Thousand Graduates: Conflict in University Development in Papua New Guinea, 1961-1976. Fisk, E. K., ed. (Pacific Research Series Monograph: No. 3). 362p. 1980. pap. text ed. 12.95 (ISBN 0-909150-01-X, 0014). Bks Australia.

Howington, Jon. Laboratory Manual for Introductory Criminal Investigation. pap. text ed. 8.50x (ISBN 0-8191-0070-6). U Pr of Amer.

Howink, Eda. They Lived Their Lives (As Best They Could) 1981. 5.50 (ISBN 0-8233-0329-2). Golden Quill.

--The We & the Other. 1980. 5.50 (ISBN 0-8233-0315-2). Golden Quill.

Howitt, Alfred W., jt. auth. see Fison, Lorimer.

Howitt, M., tr. see Bremer, Fredrika.

Howitt, William. The Rural Life of England. 615p. Repr. of 1844 ed. 31.00x (ISBN 0-686-28330-9, Pub. by Irish Academic Pr). Biblio Dist.

--Woodburn Grange. Wolff, Robert L., ed. LC 75-1511. (Victorian Fiction Ser.). 1975. Repr. of 1867 ed. lib. bdg. 66.00 (ISBN 0-8240-1585-1). Garland Pub.

Howkes. Twentieth Century Interpretations of Macbeth. 1977. 7.95 (ISBN 0-13-541458-X, Spec); pap. 2.45 (ISBN 0-13-541441-5, Spec). P-H.

Howl, Barbara. Simplified Physics for Radiology Students. (Illus.). 96p. 1971. 8.75 (ISBN 0-398-02184-8). C C Thomas.

Howland. Plaid for Principles of Salesmanship. rev. ed. 1978. 5.50 (ISBN 0-256-02102-3, 09-0303-02). Learning Syst.

Howland, Charles P. Survey of American Foreign Relations: 1928, 1929, 1930, 1931. Ea. 47.50x (ISBN 0-686-50174-8). Elliots Bks.

Howland, Gerald. You're in the Driver's Seat. 128p. (Orig.). 1980. pap. write for info. (ISBN 0-8289-0418-9). Greene.

Howland, Harold see Johnson, Allen & Nevins, Allan.

Howland, Joseph E. How to Select & Care for Shrubs & Hedges. Ortho Books Staff, ed. LC 80-66346. (Illus.). 96p. (Orig.). 1980. pap. 4.95 (ISBN 0-917102-88-6). Ortho.

--How to Select & Care for Shrubs & Hedges. Ortho Books Editorial Staff, ed. LC 80-66346. (Illus.). 96p. (Orig.). 1981. pap. 4.95 (Ortho Bks). Chevron Chem.

Howland, Marguerite S., jt. auth. see Poulton, Helen J.

Howle, Harriet, jt. auth. see Coates, Felicia.

Howlett, Charles F. Troubled Philosopher: John Dewey & the Struggle for World Peace. 1977. 15.00 (ISBN 0-8046-9153-3). Kennikat.

Howlett, Duncan. The Critical Way in Religion. LC 80-7460. 360p. 1980. 14.95 (ISBN 0-87975-133-9). Prometheus Bks.

Howlett, Noel. Hidden Worlds: An Asian Journey. Amber Crest Bks. Staff, ed. LC 77-94417. (Hidden World Ser.: Vol. 1). (Illus.). 320p. 1980. 14.50 (ISBN 0-86533-001-8). Amber Crest.

Howman, K. C. Pheasants: Their Breeding & Management. (Illus.). 126p. 1980. 9.95 (ISBN 0-903264-35-8, 4903-0, Pub. by K & R Bks England). Arco.

Howorth, Muriel. Atomic Transmutation: Memoirs of Fred Soddy. 1953. 7.50 o.p. (ISBN 0-911268-01-4). Rogers Bk.

Howse, P. E. Termites: A Study in Social Behavior. 1970. pap. text ed. 5.50x (ISBN 0-09-100841-7, Hutchinson U Lib). Humanities.

Howson, A. G. A Handbook of Terms Used in Algebra & Analysis. LC 71-178281. (Illus.). 260p. 1972. 32.95 (ISBN 0-521-08434-2); pap. 11.50 (ISBN 0-521-09695-2). Cambridge U Pr.

Howson, A. G., jt. auth. see Griffiths, H. B.

Howson, A. G., ed. Developments in Mathematical Education. (Illus.). 250p. 1973. 35.50 (ISBN 0-521-20190-X); pap. 13.95 (ISBN 0-521-09803-3). Cambridge U Pr.

Howson, A. G., et al. Curriculum Development in Mathematics. 200p. Date not set. price not set (ISBN 0-521-23767-X). Cambridge U Pr.

Howson, C., ed. Method & Appraisal in the Physical Sciences. LC 75-44580. 280p. 1976. 44.50 (ISBN 0-521-21110-7). Cambridge U Pr.

Howson, D. P. Mathematics for Electronic Technology. 280p. 1976. text ed. 29.00 (ISBN 0-08-018219-4); pap. text ed. 17.00 (ISBN 0-08-018218-6). Pergamon.

Howson, Geoffrey, ed. Children at School: Primary Education in Britain Today. LC 75-106645. (Illus.). 1970. pap. text ed. 6.50x (ISBN 0-8077-1523-9). Tchrs Coll.

Howson, S. & Winch, D. The Economic Advisory Council 1930-1939. LC 75-38187. (Illus.). 1977. 68.50 (ISBN 0-521-21138-7). Cambridge U Pr.

Howton, F. William. Functionaries. 1969. 6.95; pap. 2.95 (ISBN 0-531-06454-9). Watts.

Hoy, Cyrus. Introductions, Notes & Commentaries to Texts in the Dramatic Works of Thomas Dekker, 2 vols. Bowers, Fredson, ed. LC 77-80838. 1980. 57.50 ea. Vol. 1 (ISBN 0-521-21786-5). Vol. 2 (ISBN 0-521-21894-2). Set. 97.50 (ISBN 0-521-23647-9). Cambridge U Pr.

Hoy, Cyrus, ed. see Massinger, Phillip.

Hoy, Cyrus, ed. see Shakespeare, William.

Hoy, David C. The Critical Circle: Literature & History in Contemporary Hermeneutics. 1978. 15.75x (ISBN 0-520-03434-1). U of Cal Pr.

Hoy, John C., ed. Higher Education & the New England Economy in the Nineteen Eighties. 160p. 1981. 10.00x (ISBN 0-87451-197-6). U Pr of New Eng.

Hoy, Ray. AMC Service-Repair Handbook: Pacer, Gremlin, Hornet-1971-1979. Robinson, Jeff, ed. (Illus.). 1977. pap. 10.95 (ISBN 0-89287-139-3, A129). Clymer Pubns.

--Dodge Service - Repair Handbook: Colt; 1971-1979. Robinson, Jeff, ed. (Illus.). 1978. pap. 10.95 (ISBN 0-89287-162-8, A154). Clymer Pubns.

--Ford Pickups: 1969-1979 Shop Manual. Jorgensen, Eric, ed. (Illus.). 368p. (Orig.). 1979. pap. text ed. 10.95 (ISBN 0-89287-303-5, A248). Clymer Pubns.

--Ford Tune-up Maintenance: All Models/1969-1979. Robinson, Jeff, ed. 1977. pap. 7.95 (ISBN 0-89287-135-0, A-170). Clymer Pubns.

--Ford Vans: 1969-1979 Shop Manual. Jorgensen, Eric, ed. (Illus.). 360p. (Orig.). 1979. pap. text ed. 10.95 (ISBN 0-89287-302-7, A249). Clymer Pubns.

--Honda ATC-Seventy & ATC Ninety Singles: Service, Repair, Performance, 1970-79. Jorgensen, Eric, ed. (Illus.). 1978. pap. 3.95 (ISBN 0-89287-214-4, M311). Clymer Pubns.

--Honda 125-200cc Twins, 1964-1977: Service, Repair, Performance. Jorgensen, Eric, ed. (Illus.). 1978. pap. 9.95 (ISBN 0-89287-208-X, M321). Clymer Pubns.

--Honda 250 & 350cc Twins, 1964-1974: Service-Repair-Performance. Jorgensen, Eric, ed. 1978. pap. 9.95 (ISBN 0-89287-209-8, M322). Clymer Pubns.

--Honda 250 & 360cc Twins, 1974-1977: Service-Repair-Performance. Jorgensen, Eric, ed. (Illus.). 1978. pap. 9.95 (ISBN 0-89287-210-1, M323). Clymer Pubns.

--Opel Service Repair Handbook: All Models, 1966-1979. Jorgensen, Eric, ed. (Illus.). 1977. pap. 10.95 (ISBN 0-89287-171-7, A175). Clymer Pubns.

--Porsche: Nine Twenty-Four Series, 1976-1978. Service Repair Handbook. Jorgensen, Eric, ed. (Illus.). 1978. pap. 10.95 (ISBN 0-89287-204-7, A182). Clymer Pubns.

--Saab Service Repair Handbook 95, 96, 99, & Sonett 1967-1979. Robinson, Jeff, ed. (Illus.). 1976. pap. 10.95 (ISBN 0-89287-121-0, A185). Clymer Pubns.

--Subaru Service Repair Handbook: All Models, 1972-1979. Jorgensen, Eric, ed. (Illus.). 1977. pap. 10.95 (ISBN 0-89287-146-6, A186). Clymer Pubns.

--Suzuki Service-Repair Handbook 125-500cc Twins: 1964-1976. 3rd rev. ed. Robinson, Jeff, ed. (Illus.). 1977. pap. 9.95 (ISBN 0-89287-132-6, M-366). Clymer Pubns.

--Volvo: 240 Series 1975-1979--Service, Repair Handbook. Jorgensen, Eric, ed. (Illus.). 1978. pap. 10.95 (ISBN 0-89287-278-0, A223). Clymer Pubns.

Hoyem, George A. History of the Development of Small Arms Ammunition, Vol. I: Martial Long Arms, Flintlock Through Rimfire. LC 80-67532. (Illus.). 240p. 1981. 27.50x (ISBN 0-9604982-8-1). Armory Pubns.

Hoyem, T. & Kvale, O., eds. Physical, Chemical & Biological Changes in Food Caused by Thermal Processing. (Illus.). 1977. 104.40x (ISBN 0-85334-729-8). Intl Ideas.

Hoyer, George W. & Roth, Wolfgang. Pentecost 2. LC 73-88347. (Proclamation 1: Aids for Interpreting the Lessons of the Church Year, Ser. C). 64p. 1974. pap. 1.95 (ISBN 0-8006-4057-8, 1-4057). Fortress.

Hoyer, Robert. Seventy Times Seven. LC 75-30668. 112p. 1976. pap. 3.25 o.p. (ISBN 0-687-38199-1). Abingdon.

Hoyle, Brian & Pinder, David, eds. Spatial Analysis & Planning Strategies Cityport Industrialization, 15-18 Nov. 1978: Spatial Analysis & Planning Strategies Cityport Industrialization,15-18 Nov. 1978, Univ. Ofsouthampton. LC 80-40837. (Urban & Regional Planning Ser.). (Illus.). 350p. 1981. 60.00 (ISBN 0-08-025815-8); prepub. 50.00 (ISBN 0-08-025816-6). Pergamon.

Hoyle, Brian S. Spatial Aspects of Development. LC 73-2785. 372p. 1974. 36.50 (ISBN 0-471-41753-X). Wiley.

Hoyle, Edmund. Hoyle's Card Games. 1979. pap. 6.95 (ISBN 0-7100-0115-0). Routledge & Kegan.

--Hoyle's Games. 20th. rev ed. 1967. Repr. of 1950 ed. 14.00 (ISBN 0-7100-1566-6). Routledge & Kegan.

Hoyle, Eric. Role of the Teacher. (Students Library of Education). 1969. text ed. 6.75x (ISBN 0-7100-6435-7); pap. text ed. 2.75x (ISBN 0-7100-6436-5). Humanities.

Hoyle, Fred. Astronomy & Cosmology: A Modern Course. LC 74-28441. (Illus.). 1975. text ed. 24.95x (ISBN 0-7167-0351-3). W H Freeman.

--Frontiers of Astronomy. LC 55-6582. (Illus.). 1955. 12.50 o.s.i. (ISBN 0-06-002760-6, HarpT). Har-Row.

--Highlights in Astronomy. LC 75-1300. (Illus.). 1975. pap. text ed. 9.95x (ISBN 0-7167-0354-8). W H Freeman.

--Man in the Universe. LC 66-17067. 1966. 12.00x (ISBN 0-231-02941-1). Columbia U Pr.

--Nature of the Universe. rev. ed. LC 60-13436. (Illus.). 1960. 8.95 o.s.i. (ISBN 0-06-002820-3, HarpT). Har-Row.

--October the First Is Too Late. LC 66-20764. 1966. 7.95 o.s.i. (ISBN 0-06-002845-9, HarpT). Har-Row.

--Of Men & Galaxies. LC 64-25266. (Jessie & John Danz Lecture Ser). 83p. 1964. 6.95 (ISBN 0-295-73859-6). U of Wash Pr.

--On Stonehenge. LC 76-49469. (Illus.). 1977. pap. text ed. 8.95x (ISBN 0-7167-0363-7). W H Freeman.

--Ten Faces of the Universe. LC 76-44336. (Illus.). 1977. text ed. 19.95x (ISBN 0-7167-0384-X); pap. text ed. 9.95x (ISBN 0-7167-0383-1). W H Freeman.

Hoyle, Fred & Hoyle, Geoffrey. Commonsense in Nuclear Energy. LC 80-11811. (Illus.). 1980. text ed. 8.95x (ISBN 0-7167-1247-4); pap. text ed. 4.95x (ISBN 0-7167-1237-7). W H Freeman.

--The Incandescent Ones. LC 76-47254. 1977. 8.95 o.s.i. (ISBN 0-06-011956-X, HarpT). Har-Row.

Hoyle, Fred & Narlikar, J. V. Action at a Distance in Physics & Cosmology. LC 74-4158. (Astronomy & Astrophysics Ser.). (Illus.). 1974. text ed. 31.95x (ISBN 0-7167-0346-7). W H Freeman.

Hoyle, Fred & Narlikar, Jayant V. The Physics-Astronomy Frontier. LC 80-11708. (Illus.). 1980. text ed. 21.95x (ISBN 0-7167-1160-5). W H Freeman.

Hoyle, Geoffrey. Two Thousand & Ten: Living in the Future. LC 73-12832. (Finding-Out Books for Science & Social Studies, Grades 1-4). (Illus.). 64p. (gr. 2-4). 1974. PLB 6.95 (ISBN 0-8193-0708-4, Pub. by Parents). Enslow Pubs.

Hoyle, Geoffrey, jt. auth. see Hoyle, Fred.

Hoyt, Charles A. Witchcraft. 1981. price not set (ISBN 0-8093-0964-5); pap. price not set (ISBN 0-8093-1015-5). S Ill U Pr.

Hoyt, Charles A., ed. Minor American Novelists. LC 70-86184. (Crosscurrents-Modern Critiques Ser.). 160p. 1970. 8.95 (ISBN 0-8093-0447-3). S Ill U Pr.

Hoyt, Edwin P. Guadalcanal. LC 80-5433. 320p. 1981. 14.95 (ISBN 0-8128-2735-X). Stein & Day.

--The Mutiny on the Globe. LC 75-5779. 224p. 1975. 7.95 o.p. (ISBN 0-394-49365-6). Random.

--To the Marianas: War in the Central Pacific: 1944. 192p. 1980. deluxe ed. 12.95 (ISBN 0-442-26105-5). Van Nos Reinhold.

Hoyt, Edwin P., jt. auth. see Hoyt, Olga G.

Hoyt, Erich. The Whale Called Killer. (Illus.). 28p. 1981. 15.95 (ISBN 0-525-22970-1). Dutton.

Hoyt, J. H. Field Guide to Beaches. (Earth Science Curriculum Project Pamphlet Ser). 1971. pap. 3.20 (ISBN 0-395-02621-0, 2-14607). HM.

Hoyt, Kenneth. Career Education: Where It Is & Where It's Going. 280p. 1981. text ed. price not set (ISBN 0-913420-92-1). Olympus Pub Co.

Hoyt, Kenneth B., et al. Career Education & the Elementary School Teacher. LC 73-78952. 200p. 1973. pap. 5.95 o.p. (ISBN 0-913420-06-9). Olympus Pub Co.

Hoyt, Nelly S., tr. see Diderot, Denis.

Hoyt, Olga. Exorcism. (Illus.). (gr. 7 up). 1978. 7.45 (ISBN 0-531-01480-0). Watts.

Hoyt, Olga G. & Hoyt, Edwin P. Censorship in America. LC 73-125833. (gr. 6 up). 1970. 6.95 o.p. (ISBN 0-8164-3013-6, Clarion). HM.

--Freedom of the News Media. LC 72-93809. 192p. (gr. 6 up). 1973. 6.95 (ISBN 0-395-28910-6, Clarion). HM.

Hoyt, Patricia. How to Get Started When You Dont Know Where to Begin. LC 79-3762. (Illus.). 224p. (gr. 10 up). 1980. 8.95 (ISBN 0-15-232263-9, HJ). HarBraceJ.

Hoyt, Robert. Issues That Divide the Church. 1968. 4.95 o.p. (ISBN 0-02-555190-6); pap. 1.45 (ISBN 0-02-085500-1). Macmillan.

Hoyt, Samuel L. Men of Metals. 1979. 18.00 (ISBN 0-87170-059-X). ASM.

Hoyt, William G. Planets X & Pluto. LC 79-15665. 1980. 17.95x o.s.i. (ISBN 0-8165-0684-1); pap. 9.50 (ISBN 0-8165-0664-7). U of Ariz Pr.

Hoyt, William Henry. The Mecklenburg Declaration of Independence. LC 76-166330. (Era of the American Revolution Ser). 284p. 1972. Repr. of 1907 ed. lib. bdg. 32.50 (ISBN 0-306-70248-7). Da Capo.

Hraba, Joseph. American Ethnicity. LC 78-61877. 1979. text ed. 12.95 (ISBN 0-87581-236-8). Peacock Pubs.

Hrabal, Bohmil. Closely Watched Trains. (Writers from the Other Europe Ser.). 1981. pap. 3.95 (ISBN 0-14-005808-7). Penguin.

Hralick, R. M. & Simon, J. C., eds. Issues in Digital Image Processing. LC 80-50682. (NATO Advanced Study Institute Ser.: No. 34). 356p. 1980. 40.75x (ISBN 90-286-0460-X). Sijthoff & Noordhoff.

Hranitz, John R. & Noakes, Ann M., eds. Working with the Young Child: A Text of Readings-II. LC 78-56266. 1978. pap. text ed. 18.75 (ISBN 0-8191-0520-1). U Pr of Amer.

Hrapchak, Barbara B., jt. auth. see Sheehan, Denza C.

Hrebenar, Ronald J., jt. auth. see Scott, Ruth K.

Hren, John J., jt. auth. see Guy, Albert G.

Hresko, Wayne, jt. auth. see Reid, Kim.

Hrsch, Giselle & Mann, Peggy. Giselle, Save the Children. LC 79-51194. 288p. 1980. 12.95 (ISBN 0-89696-054-4). Everest Hse.

Hrubesh, Lawrence W., jt. auth. see Varma, Ravi.

Hruby, Peter. Fools & Heroes: The Changing Role of Communist Intellectuals in Czechoslovakia. 1980. 35.00 (ISBN 0-08-024276-6). Pergamon.

Hryciw, Carol A. John Hawkes: An Annotated Bibliography. LC 77-700. (Author Bibliographies Ser.: No. 32). 1977. 10.00 (ISBN 0-8108-1024-7). Scarecrow.

Hsia, Adrian. The Chinese Cultural Revolution. LC 72-3940. 1972. 8.95 o.p. (ISBN 0-8164-9107-0); pap. 3.95 o.p. (ISBN 0-8164-9213-1). Continuum.

Hsia, Chih-Tsing & Lau, Joseph S., eds. Twentieth Century Chinese Stories. LC 72-173986. 250p. 1972. 17.50x (ISBN 0-231-03589-6); pap. 5.00x (ISBN 0-231-03590-X). Columbia U Pr.

Hsia, Ching-Lin. Studies in Chinese Diplomatic History. 226p. 1977. Repr. of 1925 ed. 17.00 (ISBN 0-89093-088-0). U Pubns Amer.

Hsia, Ching-Lin see Chang, Yu-Kon, et al.

Hsia, Tien C. System Identification: Least Squares Method. LC 75-3515. (Illus.). 1977. 27.95 (ISBN 0-669-99630-0). Lexington Bks.

Hsia Chih-Tsing. Classic Chinese Novel: A Critical Introduction. LC 68-18997. (Companions to Asian Studies). 1968. 20.00x o.p. (ISBN 0-231-03109-2); pap. 7.50 o.p. (ISBN 0-231-08669-5). Columbia U Pr.

Hsiang, W., et al, eds. The Chern Symposium Nineteen Seventy Nine. (Illus.). 259p. 1981. 29.50 (ISBN 0-387-90537-5). Springer-Verlag.

Hsiao, Gene T. Foreign Trade of China: Policy, Law, & Practice. LC 76-7768. 1977. 27.50x (ISBN 0-520-03257-8). U of Cal Pr.

Hsiao, Gene T., ed. Sino-American Detente & Its Policy Implications. LC 73-13346. (Special Studies). (Illus.). 352p. 1974. text ed. 23.95 o.p. (ISBN 0-275-28787-4); pap. text ed. 9.95 o.p. (ISBN 0-275-88810-X). Praeger.

Hsiao, Katherine H. Money & Monetary Policy in Communist China. LC 77-158341. (Illus.). 1971. 20.00 (ISBN 0-231-03510-1). Columbia U Pr.

Hsiao, Kung-Chuan. Compromise in Imperial China. 68p. 1979. pap. 3.00 (ISBN 0-295-95726-3). U of Wash Pr.

--A Modern China & a New World: K'ang Yu-Wei, Reformer & Utopian, 1858-1927. LC 74-28166. (Publications on Asia of School of International Studies: No. 25). 680p. 1975. 26.50 (ISBN 0-295-95385-3). U of Wash Pr.

Hsiao, T. C., ed. Computer Dissertations: First Supplement 1976-1978. LC 78-59418. 400p. 1981. 25.00x (ISBN 0-686-60280-3). Sci & Tech Pr.

--Computer Dissertations Nineteen Fifty to Nineteen Seventy-Five. LC 78-59418. 450p. 1980. 35.00x (ISBN 0-686-09239-2). Sci & Tech Pr.

--Computer Dissertations: Second Supplement, 1979-1980. LC 78-59418. 300p. 1981. 25.00 (ISBN 0-686-28922-6). Sci & Tech Pr.

--Computer Faculty Directory (U. S. Edition) 350p. 1981. 35.00 (ISBN 0-686-28923-4). Sci & Tech Pr.

--Who's Who in Computer Education & Research: International Edition. LC 75-16506. 300p. cancelled (ISBN 0-686-11153-2). Sci & Tech Pr.

Hsiao, T. C., tr. Directory of Computer Education & Research. 1100p. 1981. 120.00. Sci & Tech Pr.

Hsiao, Tso-liang. Land Revolution in China, 1930-34: A Study of Documents. LC 69-14205. (Publications on Asia of the School of International Studies: No. 18). 374p. 1969. 16.00 (ISBN 0-295-73857-X). U of Wash Pr.
--Power Relations Within the Chinese Communist Movement, 1930-34: Vol. 1-a Study of Documents. (Publications on Asia of the School of International Studies: No. 9). 416p. 1961. 11.50 (ISBN 0-295-73891-X). U of Wash Pr.
Hsiao Hung. Field of Life & Death. Goldblatt, Howard & Yeung, Ellen, trs. Bd. with Tales of Hulan River. LC 78-19549. (Chinese Literature in Translation Ser.). 320p. 1979. 14.95x (ISBN 0-253-15821-4). Ind U Pr.
Hsie, Abraham W., et al, eds. Mammalian Cell Mutagenesis: The Maturation of Test Systems. LC 79-21186. (Banbury Report Ser.: No. 2). (Illus.). 504p. 1979. 45.00x (ISBN 0-87969-201-4). Cold Spring Harbor.
Hsieh, Yuan-Yu. Elementary Steel Structures. (Civil Engineering & Engineering Mechanics Ser). (Illus.). 192p. 1973. ref. ed. 24.95 (ISBN 0-13-260158-3). P-H.
Hsieh Pingying. Girl Rebel: The Autobiography of Hsieh Pingying with Extracts from Her "New War Diaries". Lin, Adet & Lin, Anor, trs. from Chinese. LC 74-34583. (China in the 20th Century Ser). (Illus.). xviii, 270p. 1975. Repr. of 1940 ed. lib. bdg. 25.00 (ISBN 0-306-70691-1). Da Capo.
Hsieh Yuan-Yu. Elementary Theory of Structures. (Civil Engineering Ser). 1970. ref. ed. 25.95 (ISBN 0-13-261552-5). P-H.
Hsi-en Chen, Theodore. Chinese Education Since the Revolution: Development, Modernization or Revolutionary Communism. (Pergamon Policy Studies). Date not set. 25.01 (ISBN 0-08-023861-0). Pergamon.
Hsien-Chi Teng. The Hoyt Collection Catalogue, Vol. 1. 1964. 20.00 (ISBN 0-87846-022-5). Mus Fine Arts Boston.
Hsiung, Chuan-Chih. A First Course in Differential Geometry. LC 80-22112. (Pure & Applied Mathematics Ser.). 375p. 1981. 24.00 (ISBN 0-471-07953-7, Pub. by Wiley-Interscience). Wiley.
Hsiung, Gueh-Djen. Recent Advances in Clinical Virology. 128p. 1981. 19.95 (ISBN 0-03-059013-2); pap. 8.95 (ISBN 0-03-059014-0). Praeger.
Hsiung, Gueh-Djen & Green, Robert H. Handbook in Clinical Laboratory Science, CRC: Section H-Virology & Rickettsiology, 2 pts, Vol. 1. (Clinical Laboratory Science Ser.). (Illus.). 1979. Pt. 1, 488p. 62.95 (ISBN 0-8493-7061-2); Pt. 2, 448p. 62.95 (ISBN 0-8493-7062-0). CRC Pr.
Hsiung, James C., ed. The Logic of "Maoism". Critiques & Explication. LC 74-3515. 300p. 1974. text ed. 32.50 (ISBN 0-275-09070-1). Praeger.
Hsiung, James C. & Kim, Samuel S., eds. China in the Global Community. 288p. 1980. 27.95 (ISBN 0-03-057009-3). Praeger.
Hsiung, James Chieh. Law & Policy in China's Foreign Relations: A Study of Attitudes & Practices. LC 75-180045. (East Asian Institute Ser.). 448p. 17.50x (ISBN 0-231-03552-7). Columbia U Pr.
Hsiung, S. I. Lady Precious Stream: Retold by L. W. Taylor. (Oxford Progressive English Readers Ser.). (Illus.). (gr. k-6). 1971. pap. text ed. 2.95 (ISBN 0-19-638235-1). Oxford U Pr.
--Romance of the Western Chamber. LC 68-22412. (Translations from the Oriental Classics Series). (Illus.). 1968. 20.00x (ISBN 0-231-02996-9); pap. 7.50x (ISBN 0-231-08615-6). Columbia U Pr.
Hsu, Cho-yun. Han Agriculture: The Formation of the Early Chinese Agrarian Economy. Dull, Jack, ed. LC 79-4920. (Illus.). 404p. (Includes material translated from Chinese). 1980. 20.00 (ISBN 0-295-95676-3). U of Wash Pr.
Hsu, D. F. Cyclic Neofields & Combinatorial Designs. (Lecture Notes in Mathematics Ser.: Vol. 824). (Illus.). 230p. 1981. pap. 14.00 (ISBN 0-387-10243-4). Springer-Verlag.
Hsu, Donald K., et al. Spectral Atlas of Nitrogen Dioxide: 5530a to 6480a. 1978. 48.50 (ISBN 0-12-357950-3). Acad Pr.
Hsu, Hsien-Wen, jt. auth. see Weissberger, Arnold.
Hsu, John, ed. see Marais, Marin.
Hsu, John C., tr. see Xu Liangying & Fan Dianian.
Hsu, Kai-Yu, ed. Literature of the People's Republic of China. LC 78-24807. (Chinese Literature in Translation Ser.). 1000p. 1980. 37.50x (ISBN 0-253-16015-4). Ind U Pr.
Hsu, L. Shihlien. The Political Philosophy of Confucianism: An Interpretation of the Social & Political Ideas of Confucius, His Forerunners & His Early Disciples. (Illus.). 1975. text ed. 11.75x (ISBN 0-7007-0079-X). Humanities.
Hsu, Shu-Hsi. Essays on the Manchurian Problem. (Studies in Chinese History & Civilization). 349p. 1977. 22.00 (ISBN 0-89093-093-7). U Pubns Amer.
Hsu, T. C., ed. Cytogenetic Testing of Environmental Mutagens. LC 79-88262. 430p. 1981. text ed. 35.00 (ISBN 0-916672-56-5). Allanheld.
Hsueh, Chun-Tu, ed. Dimensions of China's Foreign Relations. LC 76-24354. 1977. text ed. 32.50 (ISBN 0-275-56780-X). Praeger.
Hsun Lu. Three Stories. Kratochvil, P., ed. LC 69-19378. (Cambridge Readers in Modern Chinese Ser). 1970. text ed. 9.95x (ISBN 0-521-09589-1). Cambridge U Pr.
Htin Aung, M., ed. Burmese Monk's Tales. LC 66-10871. 1966. 15.00x (ISBN 0-231-02878-4). Columbia U Pr.
Hu, C. T. & Beach, Beatrice. Russian - Chinese - English Glossary of Education. LC 73-108419. 1970. text ed. 9.25x (ISBN 0-8077-1529-8). Tchrs Coll.
Hu, C. T., ed. Aspects of Chinese Education. LC 73-95245. 1969. pap. 5.00x (ISBN 0-8077-1528-X). Tchrs Coll.
--Chinese Education Under Communism. 2nd ed. LC 62-20698. 1974. text ed. 9.75 (ISBN 0-8077-2462-9); pap. text ed. 4.25x (ISBN 0-8077-2461-0). Tchrs Coll.
Hu, Herman. Barron's How to Prepare for the Dental Admission Test (DAT) 256p. 1981. pap. text ed. 4.95 (ISBN 0-8120-2162-2). Barron.
Hu, John Y. Ts'Ao Yu. (World Authors Ser.: China: No. 201). lib. bdg. 10.95 (ISBN 0-8057-2894-5). Twayne.
Hu, Sheng. Imperialism & Chinese Politics. (Studies in Chinese Government & Law). 308p. 1977. Repr. of 1955 ed. 19.50 (ISBN 0-89093-054-6). U Pubns Amer.
Hu, Shih & Lin, Yu-T'Ang. China's Own Critics. LC 79-2829. 166p. 1981. Repr. of 1931 ed. 16.00 (ISBN 0-8305-0006-5). Hyperion Conn.
Hu, Sze-Tsen. Mathematical Theory of Switching Circuits & Automata. LC 68-18370. (Illus.). 1968. 24.50x (ISBN 0-520-00581-3). U of Cal Pr.
Hu, T. C. Integer Programming & Network Flows. (Mathematics Ser). 1969. text ed. 19.95 (ISBN 0-201-03003-9). A-W.
Hua, Ellen K. Wisdom from the East: Meditations, Reflections, Proverbs & Chants. LC 73-21886. (Illus.). 128p. (Orig.). 1974. pap. 2.25 (ISBN 0-87407-202-6, FP2). Thor.
Hua, Ellen K., adapted by. Kung Fu Meditations & Chinese Proverbial Wisdom. LC 73-7731. (Illus.). 1973. 3.95 (ISBN 0-87407-511-4); pap. 2.50 (ISBN 0-87407-200-X, FPI). Thor.
Hua, Ellen Kei see Hua, Ellen K.
Hua, L. K. Harmonic Analysis of Functions of Several Complex Variable in the Classical Domains. rev. ed. LC 63-16769. 1979. 19.60 (ISBN 0-8218-1556-3, MMONO-6). Am Math.
Hua, L. K., jt. auth. see Dieudonne, Jean.
Huaain, Ashfaque. The Spirit of Islam: A Summary of the Commentary of Maulana Abul Kalam Azad on A-Fateha, the First Chapter of the Quran. 3rd ed. 95p. 1980. text ed. 12.00 (ISBN 0-8426-1664-0). Verry.
Hua-Ching, jt. auth. see Ni Hua-Ching, Master.
Huang, Chieh-Shan, jt. auth. see Wolf, Arthur P.
Huang, Dorothy. Dorothy Huang's Chinese Cooking. Harju, Lorry B., ed. 200p. 1980. 12.95. Pinewood.
Huang, Kee-Chang. Outline of Pharmacology. (Illus.). 420p. 1974. pap. 21.75 (ISBN 0-398-02717-X). C C Thomas.
Huang, Lien-Fu, jt. auth. see Lee, Byung S.
Huang, Parker P., et al. Twenty Lectures on Chinese Culture: An Intermediary Chinese Textbook. 1967. 0.p. 13.00 (ISBN 0-300-00579-2); pap. text ed. 8.50x (ISBN 0-300-00127-4). Yale U Pr.
Huang, Parker Po-fei. Twenty Lectures on Chinese Culture: Exercise Book. LC 66-21520. 1967. pap. text ed. 8.50x (ISBN 0-300-00128-2). Yale U Pr.
Huang, Paul C. Illustrated Step-by-Step Beginner's Cookbook. LC 79-18829. (Illus.). 96p. (gr. 3 up). 1980. 9.95 (ISBN 0-590-07476-8, Four Winds). Schol Bk Serv.
Huang, Philip C., ed. The Development of Underdevelopment in China: A Symposium. LC 80-51203. 1980. text ed. 15.00 (ISBN 0-87332-164-2). M E Sharpe.
Huang Po. The Zen Teaching of Huang Po: On the Transmission of the Mind. Blofeld, John, tr. 1959. pap. 4.95 (ISBN 0-394-17217-5, E171, Ever). Grove.
Huang, R. Taxation & Governmental Finance in 16th Century Ming China. LC 73-79311. (Studies in Chinese History, Literature & Institutions). (Illus.). 420p. 1975. 55.00 (ISBN 0-521-20283-3). Cambridge U Pr.
Huang, Ray. Fifteen-Eighty-Seven, a Year of No Significance: The Mingdynasty in Decline. LC 80-5392. (Illus.). 396p. 1981. 19.95x (ISBN 0-300-02518-1). Yale U Pr.
Huang, Stanley. Investment Analysis & Management. (Illus.). 500p. 1981. text ed. 19.95 (ISBN 0-87626-453-4). Winthrop.
Huang, T. C. Engineering Mechanics, 2 vols. Incl. Vol. 1. Statics (ISBN 0-201-03005-5); Vol. 2. Dynamics (ISBN 0-201-03006-3). 1967. 16.95 ea.; 24.95 set (ISBN 0-201-03007-1). A-W.
Huang, T. S. Picture Processing & Digital Filtering. LC 75-5770. (Illus.). 270p. 1975. 39.60 o.p. (ISBN 0-387-07202-0). Springer-Verlag.
Huang, T. S., ed. Two-Dimensional Digital Signal Processing I: Linear Filters. (Topids in Applied Physics Ser.: Vol. 42). (Illus.). 1981. 46.60 (ISBN 0-686-69432-5). Springer-Verlag.
--Two-Dimensional Digital Signal Processing II: Transforms & Median Filters. (Topics in Applied Physics Ser.: Vol. 43). (Illus.). 260p. 1981. 46.60 (ISBN 0-686-69433-3). Springer-Verlag.
Huang, Tsokan. The Magazine Reviews of Keats's Lamia Volume (1820) (Salzburg Studies in English Literature, Romantic Reassessment: No. 26). 123p. 1973. pap. text ed. 25.00x (ISBN 0-391-01424-2). Humanities.
Huang, Y. P., jt. auth. see Salamon, G.
Huang Hung, Josephine. Classical Chinese Plays. rev. ed. 288p. 1980. 7.95x (ISBN 0-89955-152-1, Pub. by Mei Ya China); pap. 6.95x (ISBN 0-89955-186-6). Intl Schol Bk Serv.
Huang Jiemin. China. 83p. Date not set. 50.00 (ISBN 0-07-056830-8). McGraw.
Huang Shou-Fu & T'An Chung-Yo. Mount Omei Illustrated Guide. Phelps, Dryden L., tr. from Chinese. (Illus.). 472p. 1981. pap. 15.00 (ISBN 0-85656-113-4). Great Eastern.
Huard, Pierre & Wong, Ming. Oriental Methods of Mental & Physical Fitness: The Complete Book of Meditation, Kinesitherapy & Martial Arts in China, India & Japan. LC 76-23163. (Funk & W Bk.). (Illus.). 1977. 16.95 o.s.i. (ISBN 0-308-10271-1, TYC-T); pap. 9.95 o.s.i. (ISBN 0-308-10277-0, TYC-T). T Y Crowell.
Huart, Clement. Ancient Persia & Iranian Civilization. (History of Civilization Ser.). (Illus.). 1972. 25.00x (ISBN 0-7100-7242-2). Routledge & Kegan.
Huarte Navarro, Juan de Dios. Examen De Ingenios, the Examination of Mens Wits. Carew, R., tr. LC 75-26368. (English Experience Ser.: No. 126). 1969. Repr. of 1594 ed. 28.50 (ISBN 90-221-0126-6). Walter J Johnson.
Hub, D. R., jt. ed. see Probert, S. D.
Hubala, Erich. Baroque & Rococo Art. LC 73-88459. (History of Art Ser). (Illus.). 196p. 1976. 8.95x (ISBN 0-87663-195-2). Universe.
Hubank, Roger. North Wall. 1978. 8.95 o.p. (ISBN 0-670-51551-5). Viking Pr.
Hubbard, jt. auth. see Hailes.
Hubbard, Bela. Memorials of a Half-Century in Michigan & the Lake Region. LC 75-23322. (Illus.). 1978. Repr. of 1888 ed. 22.00 (ISBN 0-8103-4268-5). Gale.
Hubbard, Benjamin J. The Matthean Redaction of a Primitive Apostolic Commissioning: An Exegesis of Matthew 28: 16-20. LC 74-16566. (Society of Biblical Literature. Dissertation Ser.). 1974. pap. 7.50 (ISBN 0-89130-219-0, 060119). Scholars Pr Ca.
Hubbard, Charles L., jt. auth. see Grawoig, Dennis E.
Hubbard, David A. Pictures of the New Kingdom. 110p. (Orig.). 1981. pap. 2.95 (ISBN 0-87784-471-2). Inter-Varsity.
--Right Living in a World Gone Wrong. 128p. (Orig.). 1981. pap. 3.25 (ISBN 0-87784-470-4). Inter Varsity.
--Themes from the Minor Prophets. LC 74-17861. 1978. pap. 2.25 (ISBN 0-8307-0498-1, S323-1-09). Regal.
--They Met Jesus. 1976. pap. 1.25 (ISBN 0-89129-184-9). Jove Pubns.
Hubbard, David G. Skyjacker: His Flights of Fancy. Alexandre, Clement, ed. 1971. 5.95 o.p. (ISBN 0-02-555290-2); pap. 1.95 (ISBN 0-02-095920-6). Macmillan.
Hubbard, Don. The Complete Book of Inflatable Boats. LC 79-27460. (Illus.). 256p. (Orig.). 1980. pap. 7.95 (ISBN 0-930030-15-X). Western Marine Ent.
Hubbard, Earl. The Creative Intention. 192p. 1974. 8.75 o.p. (ISBN 0-913456-67-5); pap. 3.95 (ISBN 0-913456-68-3). Interbk Inc.
--The Search Is on. 1969. pap. 2.00 o.p. (ISBN 0-89192-081-1). Interbk Inc.
Hubbard, Freeman & Farley, Leonard. Great Days of the Circus. (American Heritage Junior Library). (Illus.). 153p. (gr. 5 up). 1962. 9.95 (ISBN 0-8281-0394-1, J010-0). Am Heritage.
Hubbard, Freeman, jt. auth. see Knapke, William F.
Hubbard, G. Art for Elementary Classrooms. Date not set. 14.95 (ISBN 0-13-047274-3). P-H.
Hubbard, Harlan. Payne Hollow: Life on the Fringe of Society. LC 75-34720. (Illus.). 168p. 1976. 6.95 o.s.i. (ISBN 0-690-01023-0, TYC-T); pap. 3.95 (ISBN 0-690-01024-9, TYC-T). T Y Crowell.
Hubbard, Helen I. Modigliani & the Painters of Montparnasse. (Illus.). 1975. Repr. 5.95 o.p. (ISBN 0-88308-008-7). Lamplight Pub.
Hubbard, Irene & Soderstrom, Lori. Primarily Me. (gr. k-3). 1976. 9.50 (ISBN 0-916456-09-9, GA65). Good Apple.
Hubbard, John. Greenberg's Operating & Repair Manual for Lionel Trains: 1906-1942. Greenberg, Bruce C., ed. (Illus.). 1981. 9.95 (ISBN 0-89778-071-X). Greenberg Pub Co.
Hubbard, John I. Biological Basis of Mental Activity. 224p. 1975. text ed. 8.95 (ISBN 0-201-03086-1). A-W.
Hubbard, L. Ron. Fear--Typewriter in the Sky. 1977. pap. 1.50 o.p. (ISBN 0-445-04006-8). Popular Lib.
Hubbard, Lincoln B., jt. auth. see Stefani, S.
Hubbard, Margaret. Propertius: Classical Life & Letters. LC 75-11481. (Illus.). 182p. 1976. 10.00 o.p. (ISBN 0-684-14464-6, ScribT). Scribner.
Hubbard, Margaret, jt. auth. see Nisbet, Robin G.
Hubbard, P. M. The Quiet River. LC 77-27709. 1978. 7.95 o.p. (ISBN 0-385-14244-7). Doubleday.
Hubbard, Ray. Majestic. 432p. (Orig.). 1981. pap. 2.75 (ISBN 0-553-13218-0). Bantam.
Hubbard, Stanley. Nietzche und Emerson. LC 80-2538. 1981. Repr. of 1958 ed. 25.50 (ISBN 0-404-19264-5). AMS Pr.
Hubbard, Thomas D., et al. Readings & Cases in Auditing. rev. ed. LC 79-52071. 550p. (Orig.). 1980. pap. text ed. 10.95x (ISBN 0-931920-22-1). Dame Pubns.
--Readings & Cases in Auditing, Vol. 1. LC 79-52071. (Illus.). 543p. (Orig.). 1979. pap. text ed. 10.95x o.p. (ISBN 0-931920-12-4). Dame Pubns.
Hubbard, W. P. & Harris, Peggy. Notorious Grizzly Bears. LC 60-14583. (Illus.). 205p. 1960. pap. 4.95 (ISBN 0-8040-0617-2, Sage). Swallow.
Hubbard, William Q. Complicity & Conviction: An Architecture of Convention. (Illus.). 1980. text ed. 12.50 (ISBN 0-262-08106-7). MIT Pr.
Hubbell, George S. Writing Term Papers & Reports. 4th ed. (Orig.). 1969. pap. 2.50 (ISBN 0-06-460037-8, CO 37, COS). Har-Row.
Hubbell, Lindley W. Seventy Poems. LC 65-16528. 96p. 1965. 6.95 (ISBN 0-8040-0272-X). Swallow.
Hubbell, Ned. Adventures of Creighton Holmes. 1979. pap. 1.95 o.p. (ISBN 0-445-04350-4). Popular Lib.
Hubbell, Robert D. Children's Language Disorders: An Integrated Approach. (Illus.). 432p. 1981. text ed. 18.95 (ISBN 0-13-132001-7). P-H.
Hubbell, Ruth. Foster Care & Families: Conflicting Values & Policies. (Family Impact Seminar Ser.). 200p. 1981. 15.00x (ISBN 0-87722-206-1). Temple U Pr.
Hubbert, William T., et al, eds. Diseases Transmitted from Animals to Man. 6th ed. (Illus.). 1236p. 1975. text ed. 79.75 (ISBN 0-398-03056-1). C C Thomas.
Hubbs, D. L., et al. External & Internal Characters, Horizontal & Vertical Distribution, Luminescence, & Food of the Dwarf Pelagic Shark, Euproomicrus bispinatus. (Bulletin of the Scripps Institution of Oceanography: Vol. 10). 1967. pap. 6.50x (ISBN 0-520-09314-3). U of Cal Pr.
Huber, Barbara, jt. auth. see Smith, Elizabeth.
Huber, Charlotte, et al. After the Sun Sets. (Wonder-Story Books Ser). (gr. 3). text ed. 10.28 (ISBN 0-06-517503-4, SchDept). Har-Row.
--Brave & Bold. (Wonder-Story Books Ser). Orig. Title: They Were Brave & Bold. (gr. 5). text ed. 11.84 (ISBN 0-06-517505-0, SchDept). Har-Row.
--I Know a Story. (Wonder-Story Books Ser). (gr. 1). text ed. 7.60 (ISBN 0-06-517501-8, SchDept). Har-Row.
--It Happened One Day. (Wonder-Story Books Ser). (gr. 2). text ed. 8.76 (ISBN 0-06-517502-6, SchDept). Har-Row.
--It Must Be Magic. (Wonder-Story Books Ser). (gr. 4). text ed. 5.16 (ISBN 0-06-517504-2, SchDept). Har-Row.
--Once Upon a Time. (Wonder-Story Books Ser). (primer). text ed. 7.16 (ISBN 0-06-517500-X, SchDept). Har-Row.
--The Tales They Tell. (Wonder-Story Books Ser). Orig. Title: These Are the Tales They Tell. (gr. 6). text ed. 11.84 (ISBN 0-06-517506-9, SchDept). Har-Row.
Huber, Fred. Apple Crunch. 230p. 1981. 10.95 (ISBN 0-87223-687-0). Seaview Bks.
Huber, Helen, et al. Homemaker-Home Health Aide. LC 78-66616. 1980. pap. 8.80 (ISBN 0-8273-1704-2); instr's. guide 1.50 (ISBN 0-8273-1705-0). Delmar.
Huber, J. Parker. Thoreau's Travels in Maine. (Illus.). 200p. 1981. pap. 8.95 (ISBN 0-686-69095-8). Appalach Mtn.

Huber, J. T. Upgrading Residues & by-Products for Animals. 160p. 1981. 44.95 (ISBN 0-8493-5445-5). CRC Pr.
Huber, Jack T. & Millman, Howard L. Goals & Behavior in Psychotherapy & Counseling: Readings & Questions. LC 73-190060. 384p. 1972. pap. text ed. 12.95 (ISBN 0-675-09092-X). Merrill.
Huber, Joan & Form, William H. Income & Ideology: An Analysis of the American Political Formula. LC 73-2128. (Illus.). 1973. 12.95 (ISBN 0-02-915330-1). Free Pr.
Huber, Joan E., ed. Directory of U.S. & Canadian Marketing Surveys & Services. 3rd ed. 1979. loose-leaf 125.00 (ISBN 0-917148-75-4). Kline.
Huber, John E., ed. Kline Guide to the Paper Industry. 4th ed. (Illus.). 343p. 1980. pap. 110.00 (ISBN 0-685-99099-0). Kline.
Huber, John P., ed. Directory of Vermont Foundations. rev. 2nd ed. 24p. 1975. pap. 3.00 o.p. (ISBN 0-915884-07-0). Eastern CT St Coll Fdn.
Huber, K. A. Morphologisch und Entwicklungsgeschichtliche Untersuchungen an Blueten und Bluetenstaenden Von Solannaceen und Von Nolana Paradoxa Lindl: Nolanaceae. (Dissertationes Botanicae: No. 55). (Illus.). 486p. (Ger.). 1980. pap. text ed. 50.00x (ISBN 3-7682-1268-8). Lubrecht & Cramer.
Huber, Leonard & Wilson, Samuel, Jr. Baroness Pontalba's Buildings. 1973. pap. 3.95 (ISBN 0-911116-40-0). Pelican.
Huber, P., jt. auth. see Frauenfelder, P.
Huber, Peter J. Robust Statistics. LC 80-18627. (Wiley Ser. on Probability & Math Statistics). 300p. 1981. 22.95 (ISBN 0-471-41805-6, Pub. by Wiley-Interscience). Wiley.
Huber, Phillip C., jt. auth. see Gobbel, A. Roger.
Huber, Robert B., jt. auth. see Burgess, John A.
Huber, Roger, ed. Where My Money Is Going: Income & Expense Budget. (Orig.). 1980. pap. 10.00x (ISBN 0-918300-00-2); wkbk. 10.00. Lankey.
Huber, Thomas M. The Revolutionary Origins of Modern Japan. LC 79-64214. (Illus.). 288p. 1981. 18.50x (ISBN 0-8047-1048-1). Stanford U Pr.
Huberman, A. M., jt. auth. see Havelock, Ronald G.
Huberman, Alice, jt. auth. see Adasko, Laura.
Huberman, Edward & Huberman, Elizabeth, eds. War: An Anthology. (Orig.). 1969. pap. 1.50 o.s.i. (ISBN 0-671-48109-6). WSP.
Huberman, Elizabeth, jt. ed. see Huberman, Edward.
Huberman, Jack, jt. auth. see Gopnik, Adam.
Huberman, Leo. Labor Spy Racket. LC 77-139201. (Civil Liberties in American History Ser). (Illus.). 1971. Repr. of 1937 ed. lib. bdg. 22.50 (ISBN 0-306-70080-8). Da Capo.
Huberman, Leo & Sweezy, Paul M., eds. Regis Debray & the Latin American Revolution. LC 68-8077. 5.00 o.p. (ISBN 0-85345-077-3, CL-0773). Monthly Rev.
Huberman, Leo, et al. Vietnam: The Endless War. LC 77-127927. 1971. 5.95 o.p. (ISBN 0-85345-147-8, CL-1478); pap. 2.25 (ISBN 0-85345-196-6, PB-1966). Monthly Rev.
Hubert, Henri H. Rise of the Celts. LC 66-23521. (Illus.). 1934. 15.00x (ISBN 0-8196-0183-7). Biblo.
Hubert, J. D. Moliere & the Comedy of Intellect. (California Library Reprint). 1974. 18.50x (ISBN 0-520-02520-2). U of Cal Pr.
Hubert, J. J. & Carter. Biostatistics: 1064 Answers. 64p. 1980. pap. text ed. 3.95 saddle stitched (ISBN 0-8403-2288-7). Kendall-Hunt.
--Biostatistics: 1064 Questions. LC 80-82899. 160p. 1980. pap. text ed. 6.95 (ISBN 0-8403-2287-9). Kendall-Hunt.
Hubin, Vincent. New Jersey Supplement for Real Estate Principles and Practices. (Business and Economics Ser.). 112p. 1976. 4.95 (ISBN 0-675-08561-6). Merrill.
Hubin, Wilbert N. Basic Programming for Scientists & Engineers. LC 77-21343. (Illus.). 1978. pap. 13.95 ref. ed. (ISBN 0-13-066480-4). P-H.
Hubka, Betty. Where Is the Bear? (A Young Reader Ser.). (gr. k-3). 1979. PLB 5.00 (ISBN 0-307-60204-4, Golden Pr). Western Pub.
Hublow, Karl. The Working of Christ in Man: The Thousand-Year Old Frescoes in the Church of St. George on the Island of Reichenau. 1979. 15.75 (ISBN 0-903540-28-2, Pub. by Floris Books). St George Bk Serv.
Hubmann-Uhlich, Inge. Colloquial German. rev. ed. (Colloquial Ser.). 1980. pap. 7.50 (ISBN 0-7100-8032-8). Routledge & Kegan.
Hubner, Carol K. The Haunted Shul. (Judaica Youth Series: Devorah Doresh Mysteries). (gr. 3-8). 1979. 5.95 (ISBN 0-910818-14-2); pap. 4.95 (ISBN 0-686-64803-X). Judaica Pr.
--The Tattered Tallis. (Judaica Youth Series: Devorah Doresh Mysteries). (Illus.). 128p. (gr. 3-8). 1979. 5.95 (ISBN 0-910818-19-3); pap. 4.95. Judaica Pr.
--The Whispering Mezuzah. (Judaica Youth Series: Devorah Doresh Mysteries). (Illus.). 1979. 5.95 (ISBN 0-910818-18-5); pap. 4.95 (ISBN 0-686-64802-1). Judaica Pr.
Hubschman, Thomas. Alpha-II. (Orig.). 1979. pap. 1.95 (ISBN 0-532-23266-6). Manor Bks.
Huby, Pamela. Plato & Modern Morality. 135p. 1972. text ed. 6.25x (ISBN 0-333-12053-1). Humanities.
Huch, Albert, et al, eds. Continous Transcutaneous Blood Gas Monitorin. LC 79-2586. (Alan R. Liss Ser.: Vol. 15, No. 4). 1979. 68.00 (ISBN 0-8451-1027-6). March of Dimes.
Huch, Ricarda. Der Letzte Sommer. Cunz, Dieter, ed. (Ger). 1963. pap. 2.95x (ISBN 0-393-09603-3, NortonC). Norton.
Huchingson, Dale. New Horizons for Human Factors in Design. (Illus.). 512p. Date not set. text ed. 22.95 (ISBN 0-07-030815-2, C). McGraw.
Huck, Arthur. Security of China. LC 72-113406. 1970. 15.00x (ISBN 0-231-03410-5); pap. 5.00x (ISBN 0-231-08636-9). Columbia U Pr.
Huck, Gabe. A Book of Family Prayer. 1979. 12.50 (ISBN 0-8164-0415-1). Crossroad NY.
Huck, Virginia & Andersen, Ann H., eds. Minnesota Centennial Cookbook: One Hundred Years of Good Cooking. 7th print. ed. LC 58-12061. 191p. 1958. pap. 3.00 (ISBN 0-87351-014-3). Minn Hist.
Huckabay, Loucine, jt. auth. see Arndt, Clara.
Huckabay, Loucine M. The Conditions of Learning & Instruction in Nursing: Modularized. LC 79-17015. 1979. text ed. 18.95 (ISBN 0-8016-2304-9). Mosby.
Huckabay, Loucine M., jt. auth. see Arndt, Clara.
Huckabee, Harlow. Lawyers, Psychiatrists & Criminal Law: Cooperation or Chaos? 220p. 1980. 16.75 (ISBN 0-398-04084-2). C C Thomas.
Hucker, Charles O. China to Eighteen Fifty: A Short History. LC 77-79998. 1978. 8.50x (ISBN 0-8047-0957-2); pap. 2.95x (ISBN 0-8047-0958-0). Stanford U Pr.
Hucker, Charles O., ed. Chinese Government in Ming Times: Seven Studies. LC 69-14265. (Oriental Culture Ser.: No. 2). 1969. 20.00x (ISBN 0-231-03172-6). Columbia U Pr.
Huckett, H. C. The Anthomyiidae of California, Exclusive of Subfamily Scatophaginae (Diptera) (Bulletin of the California Insect Survey: Vol. 12). 1971. pap. 8.00x (ISBN 0-520-09355-0). U of Cal Pr.
--The Muscidae of California, Exclusive of Subfamily Scatophaginae (Diptera) (Bulletin of the California Insect Survey: Vol. 12). 1974. pap. 13.50x (ISBN 0-520-09508-1). U of Cal Pr.
Huckins, Wesley C., jt. auth. see Bernard, Harold W.
Huckle, John. The Gospel According to St. John Vols. 1, 2, & 3, the New Testament for Spiritual Reading Vols. 7, 8, & 9. 1978. 6.00 ea. Crossroad NY.
Huckleberry, Alan W. & Strother, Edward. Speech Education for the Elementary Teacher. 2nd ed. 1972. text ed. 13.95x o.p. (ISBN 0-205-03320-2, 4833201). Allyn.
Huckleberry, Alan W., jt. auth. see Strother, Edward S.
Huckshorn, Robert. American Political Parties. LC 79-9328. 1980. text ed. 13.95 (ISBN 0-87872-235-1). Duxbury Pr.
Hudak, Julia S. Handbook for Technologists of Nuclear Medicine. (Illus.). 168p. 1971. 12.75 (ISBN 0-398-02178-3). C C Thomas.
Hudak, Leona M. Early American Women Printers & Publishers, 1639-1820. LC 78-825. 1978. 35.00 (ISBN 0-8108-1119-7). Scarecrow.
Huddart, D. see Bowen, D. Q.
Huddart, Henry. Comparative Structure & Function of Muscle. 1975. text ed. 56.00 (ISBN 0-08-017845-6). Pergamon.
Huddart, Henry & Hunt, Stephen. Visceral Muscle: Its Structure & Function. LC 75-42464. (Tertiary Level Biology Ser.). 1975. 18.95 (ISBN 0-470-15221-4). Halsted Pr.
Huddleston, Eugene L. & Noverr, Douglas A., eds. The Relationship of Painting & Literature: A Guide to Information Sources. LC 78-53436. (American Studies Information Guide Ser.: Vol. 4). 1978. 30.00 (ISBN 0-8103-1394-4). Gale.
Huddleston, John. The Earth Is but One Country. (Illus.). 1978. 15.00 (ISBN 0-900125-31-4, 7-32-31, Pub. by British Baha'i Pub Trust). Baha'i.
Huddleston, Rodney. An Introduction to English Transformational Syntax. (English Language Ser.). (Illus.). 304p. 1975. text ed. 19.95x (ISBN 0-582-55061-0); pap. text ed. 13.50x (ISBN 0-582-55062-9). Longman.
Huddleston, Rodney D. Sentence in Written English: A Syntactic Study Based on an Analysis of Scientific Texts. LC 76-139714. (Cambridge Studies in Linguistics). 1971. 49.50 (ISBN 0-521-08062-2). Cambridge U Pr.
Huddy, Delia. Time Piper. LC 78-24339. (gr. 7 up). 1979. 8.50 (ISBN 0-688-80212-5); PLB 8.16 (ISBN 0-688-84212-7). Greenwillow.
Hude, Karl, ed. see Herodotus.
Hudec, Robert E. The GATT Legal System & World Trade Diplomacy. LC 75-23972. 416p. 1975. text ed. 28.95 o.p. (ISBN 0-275-01320-0). Praeger.
Hudgeons. Hewitt-Donln Catalog of U. S. Small Size Paper Money. 14th ed. (Collector Ser.). (Illus.). 192p. 1981. pap. 3.50 (ISBN 0-87637-112-8, 112-08). Hse of Collectibles.
--The Official Guide to Detecting Altered Counterfeit Coins & Currency. (Collector Ser.). (Illus.). 160p. (Orig.). 1981. pap. 4.95 (ISBN 0-87637-169-1, 169-01). Hse of Collectibles.
--The Official Investors Guide to Buying & Selling Gold, Silver & Diamonds. (Collector Ser.). (Illus.). 160p. (Orig.). 1981. pap. 4.95 (ISBN 0-87637-171-3, 171-03). Hse of Collectibles.
--The Official Price Guide to Mint Errors & Varieties. 3rd ed. (Collector Ser). (Illus.). 182p. 1981. pap. 4.95 (167-05). Hse of Collectibles.
Hudiburg, Everett, ed. see IFSTA Committee.
Hudiburg, Everett, ed. see Ifsta Committee.
Hudiburg, Everett, ed. see IFSTA Committee.
Hudis, Morris. Dental Laboratory Prosthodontics. LC 76-8578. (Illus.). 1977. text ed. 25.00 (ISBN 0-7216-4794-4). Saunders.
Hudlicka, O. Circulation of Skeletal Muscle. 1968. 27.50 o.p. (ISBN 0-08-012466-6). Pergamon.
Hudlicky, Milos. Chemistry of Organic Fluorine Compounds. LC 73-14377. 903p. 1976. text ed. 145.95 (ISBN 0-470-41835-4). Halsted Pr.
Hudman, Lloyd E. Tourism: A Shrinking World. LC 79-22325. 1980. pap. text ed. 16.95 (ISBN 0-88244-208-2). Grid Pub.
Hudnut, Robert K. Church Growth Is Not the Point. LC 74-25692. 160p. 1975. 7.95 o.p. (ISBN 0-06-064062-6, HarpR). Har-Row.
Hudson & Weaver. Reading, Writing & Speaking: Here & Now. (Illus.). 1980. pap. 2.95x (ISBN 0-88323-160-3, 248). Richards Pub.
Hudson, Anne, ed. Selections from English Wycliffite Writings. LC 77-1506. 1978. 38.50 (ISBN 0-521-21667-2). Cambridge U Pr.
Hudson, Arthur P. Songs of the Carolina Charter Colonists, 1663-1763. 1962. pap. 0.50 o.p. (ISBN 0-86526-104-0). NC Archives.
Hudson, Betty J. Off Key. (Orig.). 1979. pap. 1.75 (ISBN 0-532-23150-3). Manor Bks.
Hudson, C. S., jt. auth. see Rash, J. E.
Hudson, C. S. see Pigman, Ward & Wolfrom, Melville L.
Hudson, C. S., et al see Pigman, Ward & Wolfrom, Melville L.
Hudson, C. Wayne. The Marxist Philosophy of Ernest Bloch. Date not set. price not set (ISBN 0-312-51860-9). St Martin.
Hudson, Charles. The Southeastern Indians. LC 75-30729. (Illus.). 1976. 25.00 (ISBN 0-87049-187-3); pap. 9.50x (ISBN 0-87049-248-9). U of Tenn Pr.
Hudson, D. C. Your Book of Golf. (Your Book Ser.). (Illus.). 1967. 6.95 (ISBN 0-571-08123-1, Pub. by Faber & Faber). Merrimack Bk Serv.
Hudson, D. F. Teach Yourself Bengali. (Teach Yourself Ser). 1965. pap. 2.95 o.p. (ISBN 0-679-10207-8). McKay.
Hudson, Donald. A Century of Moral Philosophy. 1980. 18.95 (ISBN 0-312-12777-4). St Martin.
Hudson, F. S. North America. 4th ed. (Illus.). 464p. 1978. pap. 14.95x (ISBN 0-7121-1410-6, Pub. by Macdonald & Evans England). Intl Ideas.
Hudson, Gladys W. Paradise Lost: A Concordance. LC 74-127413. 1971. 28.00 (ISBN 0-8103-1002-3). Gale.
Hudson, Gladys W., ed. Elizabeth Barrett Browning Concordance, 4 vols. LC 73-5735. 1973. Set. 125.00 (ISBN 0-8103-1003-1). Gale.
Hudson, Hamilton C., jt. auth. see Galaway, Burton.
Hudson Institute. The U. K. in 1980: The Hudson Report. LC 74-25234. 127p. 1974. 17.95 (ISBN 0-470-41855-9). Halsted Pr.
Hudson, J. A. The Excitation & Propagation of Elastic Waves. LC 79-4505. (Monographs on Mechanics & Applied Mathematics Ser.). (Illus.). 1980. 38.50 (ISBN 0-521-22777-1). Cambridge U Pr.
Hudson, J. A., jt. auth. see Wolfskill, G.
Hudson, J. E. Adaptive Arrays. (IEE Electromagnetic Waves Ser.). 1981. price not set (Pub. by Peregrinus England). Inst Electrical.
Hudson, J. W. The History of Adult Education. (Social History of Education Ser.: First Series, No. 5). 238p. 1980. Repr. of 1851 ed. 17.50x (ISBN 0-7130-0006-6, Woburn Pr England). Biblio Dist.
Hudson, James, jt. auth. see Rivers, Gayle.
Hudson, James F., et al. Pollution-Pricing: Industrial Response to Wastewater Charges. LC 80-8363. 1981. price not set (ISBN 0-669-04033-9). Lexington Bks.
Hudson, James T. The Epistle to the Hebrews: Its Meaning & Message. 78p. Repr. of 1937 ed. 3.50 (ISBN 0-567-02144-0). Attic Pr.
--Pauline Epistles: Their Meaning & Message. 1958. 6.00 (ISBN 0-227-67558-4). Attic Pr.
Hudson, Jean B. Rivers of Time. 1978. pap. 1.95 (ISBN 0-380-40444-3, 40444). Avon.
Hudson, Joe & Galaway, Burton. Considering the Victim: Readings in Restitution & Victim Compensation. 496p. 1975. 37.50 (ISBN 0-398-03216-5). C C Thomas.
Hudson, Joe & Galaway, Burt, eds. Restitution in Criminal Justice: A Critical Assessment of Sanctions. LC 76-43614. 1977. 18.95 (ISBN 0-669-00991-1). Lexington Bks.
--Victims, Offenders, & Alternative Sanctions. LC 80-7578. 1980. 21.95x (ISBN 0-669-03758-3). Lexington Bks.
Hudson, Joe, jt. ed. see Fogel, David.
Hudson, Joe, jt. ed. see Galaway, Burt.
Hudson, K. Social History of Archaeology. 1980. text ed. 37.50x (ISBN 0-333-25679-4). Humanities.
--World Industrial Archaeology. LC 77-94225. (New Studies in Archaeology). 1979. 49.50 (ISBN 0-521-21991-4); pap. 14.50x (ISBN 0-521-29330-8). Cambridge U Pr.
Hudson, Kenneth. The Archaeology of Industry. LC 75-38404. (Encore Edition). 1976. 3.95 o.p. (ISBN 0-684-15719-5, ScribT). Scribner.
--The Businessman in Public. LC 75-40414. 153p. 1976. 24.95 (ISBN 0-470-01377-X). Halsted Pr.
--A Dictionary of Diseased English. LC 77-11529. 1978. 12.95 o.p. (ISBN 0-06-011955-1, HarpT). Har-Row.
--The Language of Modern Politics. 1978. text ed. 20.75x (ISBN 0-333-21438-2). Humanities.
--Museums for the Nineteen Hundred & Eighties: A Survey of World Trends. LC 77-24930. 1978. text ed. 49.50x (ISBN 0-8419-0327-1). Holmes & Meier.
--Pleasures & People of Bath. (Folio Miniature Ser.). (Illus.). 1978. 6.95 (ISBN 0-7181-1588-0, Pub. by Michael Joseph). Merrimack Bk Serv.
--Where We Used to Work. 1980. text ed. 20.75x (ISBN 0-212-97025-9). Humanities.
Hudson, Kenneth & Nicholl, Ann. Directory of World Museums. 900p. 1981. 75.00 (ISBN 0-87196-468-6). Facts on File.
Hudson, Leslie & Hay, Frank C. Practical Immunology. (Blackwell Scientific Pubns.). (Illus.). 1976. softcover 16.25 (ISBN 0-632-00353-7). Mosby.
Hudson, Marc. Island. 1977. 2.50 (ISBN 0-918116-07-4). Jawbone Pr.
Hudson, Margaret W. & Weaver, Ann A. Young American Series, 5 bks. Incl. Bk. 1. In Your Family. 1973 (ISBN 0-8224-7025-X); Bk. 2. In Your Community. 1973 (ISBN 0-8224-7026-8); Bk. 3. In Your State. 1973 (ISBN 0-8224-7027-6); Bk. 4. In Your Country. 1973 (ISBN 0-8224-7028-4); Bk. 5. Know Your Rights. LC 65-158878. 1971 (ISBN 0-8224-7029-2). (Illus.). (gr. 4-12). 1973. pap. 2.00 ea.; tchrs' manual free (ISBN 0-8224-7652-5). Pitman Learning.
Hudson, Michael. Canada in the New Monetary Order: Borrow? Devalue? Restructure! 117p. 1978. pap. text ed. 6.95x (ISBN 0-920380-06-9, Pub. by Inst Res Pub Canada). Renouf.
--Economics & Technology in Nineteenth Century American Thought: The Neglected American Economists. (The Neglected American Economists Ser.). 1974. lib. bdg. 50.00 (ISBN 0-8240-1037-X). Garland Pub.
Hudson, Michael, jt. auth. see Panati, Charles.
Hudson, Michael, ed. see Carey, Mathew.
Hudson, Michael, ed. see Everett, Alexander.
Hudson, Michael, ed. see Jarvis, William C.
Hudson, Michael C. Arab Politics: The Search for Legitimacy. LC 77-75379. 1977. 27.50x (ISBN 0-300-02043-0); pap. 8.95 (ISBN 0-300-02411-8). Yale U Pr.
Hudson, Michael C., jt. auth. see Taylor, Charles L.
Hudson, Norman. Field Engineering for Agricultural Development. (Oxford Tropical Handbooks). (Illus.). 160p. 1975. 29.95x (ISBN 0-19-859442-9). Oxford U Pr.
Hudson, Norman W. Soil Conservation. pap. 21.50 o.p. (ISBN 0-7134-0562-7, Pub. by Batsford England). David & Charles.
Hudson, P. S., tr. see Domsch, K. H. & Gams, W.
Hudson, R. A. Sociolinguistics. LC 79-51824. (Cambridge Textbooks in Linguistics Ser.). (Illus.). 1980. 37.50 (ISBN 0-521-22833-6); pap. 10.95x (ISBN 0-521-29668-4). Cambridge U Pr.
Hudson, Ralph G. Engineers' Manual. 2nd ed. 1939. 17.50 (ISBN 0-471-41844-7, Pub. by Wiley-Interscience). Wiley.

--Table of Integrals. 1917. pap. text ed. 8.50 (ISBN 0-471-41877-3, Pub. by Wiley-Interscience). Wiley.
Hudson, Randolph, ed. Technology, Culture & Language: Selected Essays. (Uses of English Ser.). 1966. pap. 2.95x o.p. (ISBN 0-669-21014-5). Heath.
Hudson, Ray, jt. auth. see Pocock, Douglas.
Hudson, Ronald, jt. ed. see Kelley, Philip.
Hudson, Theodore R. From Leroi Jones to Amiri Baraka: The Literary Works. LC 72-97096. 256p. 1973. 12.75 (ISBN 0-8223-0296-9); pap. 6.75 (ISBN 0-8223-0454-6). Duke.
Hudson, Toni, et al. Racquetball for Women. pap. 3.00 (ISBN 0-87980-384-3). Wilshire.
Hudson, Travis, et al. Tomol: Chumash Watercraft. (Ballena Press Anthropological Papers: No. 9). (Illus.). 1978. pap. 8.95 o.p. (ISBN 0-87919-069-8). Ballena Pr.
Hudson, Virginia C. O Ye Jigs & Juleps. 1962. 6.95 (ISBN 0-02-555340-2). Macmillan.
Hudson, W. H. Far Away & Long Ago. 350p. 1981. 14.95 (ISBN 0-8180-0251-4). Horizon.
Hudson, W. J., ed. Australia & the League of Nations. 224p. 1980. 20.00x (ISBN 0-424-00084-9, Pub. by Sydney U Pr Australia). Intl Schol Bk Serv.
--Australia in World Affairs: Nineteen Seventy to Seventy Five. 466p. 1981. text ed. 29.50x (ISBN 0-86861-369-X, 2565). Allen Unwin.
Hudson, William H. Green Mansions. (Literature Ser). (gr. 9-12). 1970. pap. text ed. 3.42 (ISBN 0-87720-726-7). AMSCO Sch.
Hudson, Wilson M., ed. see Adams, Andy.
Hudson, Winthrop S. Baptist Convictions. pap. 0.85 ea. (ISBN 0-8170-0295-2). pap. 8.50 doz. Judson.
--The Cambridge Connection & the Elizabethan Settlement of Fifteen Fifty-Nine. LC 79-56513. x, 158p. 1980. 14.75 (ISBN 0-8223-0440-6). Duke.
--Religion in America. 2nd ed. 1973. pap. text ed. 9.95x (ISBN 0-684-13873-5, ScribC). Scribner.
Hudson-Evans, Richard. Competing with Production Cars. (Illus.). 1978. 10.95 o.s.i. (ISBN 0-7134-0132-X). Hippocrene Bks.
Hudspeth, Robert N. Ellery Channing. (U. S. Authors Ser.: No. 223). 1973. lib. bdg. 10.95 (ISBN 0-8057-0131-1). Twayne.
Huebener, Theodore. How to Teach Foreign Languages Effectively. rev. ed. LC 65-13880. 1965. 10.00x (ISBN 0-8147-0209-0). NYU Pr.
Huebner, A. & Black, K. Life Insurance. 10th ed. 1981. 22.95 (ISBN 0-13-535799-3). P-H.
Huebner, Kenneth H. Finite Element Method for Engineers. LC 74-17452. 448p. 1975. 35.00 (ISBN 0-471-41950-8, Pub. by Wiley-Interscience). Wiley.
Huebner, S. S. & Black, K. Life Insurance. 9th ed. (Illus.). 608p. 1976. 20.95 (ISBN 0-13-535781-0). P-H.
Huebner, S. S., et al. Property & Liability Insurance. 2nd ed. (Risk & Insurance Ser.). 1976. 19.95 (ISBN 0-13-730960-0). P-H.
Huebner, Theodore. Special Education Careers: Training the Handicapped Child. (Career Concise Guides Ser.). (Illus.). (gr. 7up). 1977. lib. bdg. 6.45 (ISBN 0-531-01311-1). Watts.
Huegel, F. J. Bone of His Bone. (Christian Classic Ser.). 96p. 1980. pap. 2.95 (ISBN 0-310-26321-2). Zondervan.
--Cross of Christ, the Throne of God. 1965. pap. 2.50 (ISBN 0-87123-068-2, 210068). Bethany Fell.
--Cross Through the Scriptures. LC 65-25948. 1969. pap. 3.50 (ISBN 0-87123-069-0, 210069). Bethany Fell.
--Forever Triumphant. 96p. 1967. pap. 1.50 (ISBN 0-87123-155-7, 200155). Bethany Fell.
--Ministry of Intercession. LC 76-15861. (Orig.). 1971. pap. 1.75 (ISBN 0-87123-365-7, 200365). Bethany Fell.
--Reigning with Christ. 1969. pap. 1.50 (ISBN 0-87123-480-7, 200480). Bethany Fell.
--Successful Praying. 1967. pap. 1.95 (ISBN 0-87123-453-X, 200453). Bethany Fell.
--Why Jesus? 1970. pap. 1.50 (ISBN 0-87123-635-4, 200635). Bethany Fell.
Huelsberg, Enid L. Michigan Programmed Spelling Series, Basic Word List Level 1: Reusable Edition. (gr. 1). 1974. wkbk. 7.00 (ISBN 0-89039-085-1). Ann Arbor Pubs.
--Michigan Programmed Spelling Series, Basic Word List, Level 3: Reusable Edition. (gr. 3). 1974. wkbk. 7.00 (ISBN 0-89039-089-4). Ann Arbor Pubs.
--Michigan Programmed Spelling Series, High School & College, Level 7: Reusable Edition. (gr. 7-9). 1975. wkbk. 7.00 (ISBN 0-89039-137-8). Ann Arbor Pubs.
--Michigan Programmed Spelling Series,Basic Work List,Level 2: Reusable Edition. (gr. 2). 1974. 7.00 (ISBN 0-89039-087-8). Ann Arbor Pubs.
--Michigan Programmed Spelling Series,High School & College, Level 8: Reusable Edition. (gr. 10-12). 1975. wkbk. 7.00 (ISBN 0-89039-138-6). Ann Arbor Pubs.
--Michigan Programmed Spelling Series,Use Frequency Based Words, Level 4: Reusable Edition. (gr. 4). 1975. wkbk. 7.00 (ISBN 0-89039-091-6). Ann Arbor Pubs.
--Michigan Programmed Spelling Series,Use Frequency Based Words,Level 5: Reusable Edition. (gr. 5). 1975. wkbk. 7.00 (ISBN 0-89039-093-2). Ann Arbor Pubs.
--Michigan Programmed Spelling Series,Use Frequency Based Words,Level 6: Reusable Edition. (gr. 6). 1975. wkbk. 7.00 (ISBN 0-89039-095-9). Ann Arbor Pubs.
Huelsbergd, Enid L. Crossword Puzzle Mastery, Level 1. (Michigan Progrrammed Spelling Ser.). (gr. 1-3). 1975. wkbk. 2.50 (ISBN 0-89039-090-8). Ann Arbor Pubs.
Huelsberrg, Enid L. Crossword Puzzle Mastery: Level 2. (gr. 4-7). 1975. wkbk. 2.50 (ISBN 0-89039-092-4). Ann Arbor Pubs.
Huelsman, L. P. Basic Circuit Theory with Digital Computations. (Illus.). 1972. ref. ed. 27.95 (ISBN 0-13-057430-9). P-H.
Huenefeld, John & Wiley, Virginia. Planning & Control Guides & Forms for Small Book Publishers. LC 80-21051. 72p. 1980. 44.00 (ISBN 0-931932-01-7). Huenefeld Co.
Hueneke, K., jt. auth. see Mortlock, A. J.
Huenemann, Ruth L., et al. Teenage Nutrition & Physique. (Illus.). 256p. 1974. 13.75 (ISBN 0-398-03135-5). C C Thomas.
Huer, Jon H. Ideology & Social Character. LC 78-56917. 1978. pap. write for info. (ISBN 0-8191-0522-8). U Pr of Amer.
--Society & Social Science. LC 79-63563. 1979. pap. text ed. 9.50 o.p. (ISBN 0-8191-0730-1). U Pr of Amer.
Huet, Marcel. Textbook of Fish Culture: Breeding & Cultivation of Fish. (Illus.). 454p. 41.25 (ISBN 0-85238-020-8, FN). Unipub.
Huett, Leonard, et al. The Path to Illumination. LC 75-34746. softcover 4.95 o.p. (ISBN 0-912216-14-X). Angel Pr.
Huettich, H. G. Theater in the Planned Society: Contemporary Drama in the German Democratic Republic in Its Historical, Political & Cultural Context. (Studies in the Germanic Languages & Literatures). 1978. 11.50x (ISBN 0-8078-8088-4). U of NC Pr.
Huey, F. B., Jr. Exodus: A Study Guide Commentary. 1977. pap. 3.50 (ISBN 0-310-36053-6). Zondervan.
--Jeremiah: A Study Guide Commentary. (Study Guide Commentary Ser.). 144p. (Orig.). 1981. pap. 3.95 (ISBN 0-310-36063-3). Zondervan.
Huey, Talbott H. see Solomon, Richard H.
Huff, C. Ronald, jt. auth. see Conner, Ross F.
Huff, C. Ronald, ed. Issues in Contemporary Corrections: Social Control & Conflict. LC 77-81150. (Sage Research Progress Series in Criminology: Vol. 3). 1977. 12.95x (ISBN 0-8039-0914-4); pap. 6.50x (ISBN 0-8039-0909-8). Sage.
Huff, Charles & Marinacci, Barbara. Commodity Speculation for Beginners: A Guide to the Futures Market. (Illus.). 224p. 1980. 11.95 (ISBN 0-02-555450-6). Macmillan.
Huff, Darrell & Huff, Frances. Complete Book of Home Improvement. (Illus.). 1971. 14.95 o.s.i. (ISBN 0-06-011983-7, HarpT). Har-Row.
Huff, Douglas & Prewett, Omer, eds. The Nature of the Physical Universe: 1976 Nobel Conference. LC 78-14788. 1979. 22.95 (ISBN 0-471-03190-9, Pub. by Wiley-Interscience). Wiley.
Huff, Elizabeth, ed. see Fang, Chaoying.
Huff, Frances, jt. auth. see Huff, Darrell.
Huff, Theodore. An Index to the Films of Charles Chaplin. (Gordon Press Film Ser.). 1980. lib. bdg. 59.95 (ISBN 0-8490-3090-0). Gordon Pr.
Huff, Toby E., ed. see Nelson, Benjamin.
Huffaker, Clair. Nobody Loves a Drunken Indian. 1980. pap. write for info. (ISBN 0-671-83058-9). PB.
Huffer, Virginia, et al. The Sweetness of the Fig: The Australian Aboriginal Woman As a Transitional Figure. LC 80-21658. (Illus.). 244p. 1981. 15.00 o.p. (ISBN 0-295-95790-5). U of Wash Pr.
--The Sweetness of the Pig: Aboriginal Women in Transition. LC 80-21658. (Illus.). 244p. 1981. 15.00 (ISBN 0-295-95790-5). U of Wash Pr.
Huffman & Bruce. How to Debug Your Personal Computer. 175p. 1980. pap. 7.95 (ISBN 0-8359-2924-8). Reston.
Huffman, Franklin E., et al. Modern Spoken Cambodian. LC 71-104615. 1970. text ed. 30.00x (ISBN 0-300-01315-9); pap. text ed. 12.00x (ISBN 0-300-01316-7). Yale U Pr.
Huffman, Harry. Programmed Business Mathematics, Bk. 2. 4th, rev. ed. (Illus.). 256p. 1980. pap. text ed. 8.75 (ISBN 0-07-030902-7); test bklet 4.95 (ISBN 0-07-030905-1). McGraw.
--Programmed Business Mathematics, Bk. 3. 4th rev. ed. (Illus.). 192p. 1980. pap. 8.70 (ISBN 0-07-030903-5, G). McGraw.
Huffman, Harry & Stewart, Jeffrey R. General Recordkeeping, Bk. 1. 8th ed. (Illus.). 224p. (gr. 9-11). 1980. 13.96 (ISBN 0-07-031040-8, G); tchrs. ed. 7.50 (ISBN 0-07-031043-2); activity guide & working papers 4.72 (ISBN 0-07-031041-6); tchrs. ed. for activity guide & working papers 5.25 (ISBN 0-07-031043-2). McGraw.
Huffman, Jim. Personal Computing. (Illus.). 1979. text ed. 15.95 (ISBN 0-8359-5516-8); pap. 11.95 (ISBN 0-8359-5515-X). Reston.
Huffman, John A., Jr. Forgive Us Our Prayers. 1980. pap. 1.95 (ISBN 0-88207-519-5). Victor Bks.
--Wholly Living. 132p. 1981. pap. 3.95 (ISBN 0-89693-005-X). Victor Bks.
Huffman, Virginia, jt. auth. see Kutie, Rita.
Hufford, Susan. Cove's End. 1977. pap. 1.50 o.p. (ISBN 0-445-04066-1). Popular Lib.
--Devil's Sonata. 256p. 1976. pap. 1.25 o.p. (ISBN 0-445-00340-5). Popular Lib.
Huffsey, R. R., jt. ed. see De Vore, R. William.
Hufnagl, Ernst. Libyan Mammals. (Illus.). 16.00 (ISBN 0-902675-08-7). Oleander Pr.
Hufner, Klaus & Naumann, Jens. The United Nations System International Bibliography, Vol. 3B. new ed. (Monographs & Articles in Collective Vols. 1971-75). 692p. 1979. 78.00 (ISBN 0-686-52995-2, Pub. by K G Saur). Gale.
Hufner, Klaus, ed. United Nations System: International Bibliography. Naumann, Jens. 286p. 1977. 58.00 (ISBN 3-7940-2251-3, Dist. by Gale Research Co). K G Saur.
--United Nations System; International Bibliography: Vol. 1, Learned Journals & Monographs Nineteen Forty-Five to Nineteen Sixty-Five. Naumann, Jens. 520p. 1976. 65.00 (ISBN 3-7940-2250-5, Dist. by Gale Research Co). K G Saur.
Hufner, Klaus & Naumann, Jens, eds. United Nations System; Internaional Bibliography: Vol. 2B, Learned Journals Nineteen Seventy-One to Nineteen Seventy-Five. 436p. 1977. 68.00 (ISBN 3-7940-2252-1, Dist. by Gale Research Co). K G Saur.
--United Nations System; International Bibliography: Vol. 3A, Monographs & Articles in Collective Volumes Nineteen Sixty-Five to Nineteen Seventy. 492p. 1978. 68.00 (ISBN 3-7940-2253-X, Dist. by Gale Research Co). K G Saur.
Hufstader, Alice A. Sisters of the Quill. LC 78-2642. (Illus.). 1978. 15.00 (ISBN 0-396-07544-4). Dodd.
Hufton, Olwen H. Bayeux in the Late Eighteenth Century. 1967. 33.00x (ISBN 0-19-821462-6). Oxford U Pr.
--Europe: Privilege & Protest Seventeen Thirty to Seventeen Eighty-Nine. LC 80-66911. (History of Europe Ser.; Cornell Paperbacks Ser.). 398p. 1980. pap. 5.95 (ISBN 0-8014-9208-4). Cornell U Pr.
Hugard, Jean & Braue, Frederick. Royal Road to Card Magic. 1949. 9.50 (ISBN 0-571-11399-0, Pub. by Faber & Faber). Merrimack Bk Serv.
Huggett, Frank. Farming in Great Britain. (Junior Reference Ser.). (Illus.). 64p. (gr. 7 up). 1970. 7.95 (ISBN 0-7136-1527-3). Dufour.
--The Newspapers. (Liberal Studies). 1972. pap. text ed. 2.50x o.p. (ISBN 0-435-46542-2). Heinemann Ed.
Huggett, Frank E. A Day in the Life of a Victorian Factory Worker. (Victorian Day Ser.). 1973. pap. text ed. 5.95x (ISBN 0-04-942113-1). Allen Unwin.
--A Day in the Life of a Victorian Farm Worker. (Victorian Day Ser.). (Illus.). 1972. text ed. 12.50x (ISBN 0-04-942099-2); pap. text ed. 5.95x (ISBN 0-04-942100-X). Allen Unwin.
--Life Below Stairs: Domestic Servants in England from Victorian Times. LC 77-83231. (Illus.). 1978. 12.00 o.p. (ISBN 0-684-15513-3, ScribT). Scribner.
Huggett, Richard, jt. auth. see Meyer, Iain.
Huggins, Eli L. Kodiak & Afognak Life, 1868-1870. Pierce, Richard A., ed. (Materials for the Study of Alaska History Ser.: No. 20). (Illus.). 1981. 16.50x (ISBN 0-919642-96-9). Limestone Pr.
Huggins, Hal A. Why Raise Ugly Kids? How You Can Fulfill Your Child's Health & Happiness Potential. (Illus.). 256p. 1981. 12.95 (ISBN 0-87000-507-3). Arlington Hse.
Huggins, Nathan I. Slave & Citizen: The Life of Frederick Douglas. (Library of American Biography). 1980. 9.95 (ISBN 0-316-38001-6); pap. 4.95 (ISBN 0-316-38000-8). Little.
Huggins, Robert A., et al, eds. Annual Review of Materials Science, Vol. 10. LC 75-172108. (Illus.). 1980. text ed. 20.00 (ISBN 0-8243-1710-6). Annual Reviews.
Hughes, et al. REACH. (gr. 4-9). 1974. pap. text ed. 3.99 student's text (ISBN 0-87892-864-2); tchr's handbook 3.99 (ISBN 0-87892-870-7); tapes 159.60 (ISBN 0-87892-868-5). Economy Co.
Hughes, A. E., et al. Real Solids & Radiation. LC 74-32348. (Wykeham Science Ser.: No. 35). 1975. 8.60x (ISBN 0-8448-1162-9). Crane-Russak Co.
Hughes, A. I., ed. Lead Nineteen Sixty-Eight: Proceedings, International Conference on Lead - 3rd - Venice - 1968. LC 66-18688. 1970. 69.00 (ISBN 0-08-015644-4). Pergamon.
Hughes, Allan. Henry Irving, Shakespearean. LC 79-54019. (Illus.). 304p. Date not set. 44.50 (ISBN 0-521-22192-7). Cambridge U Pr.
Hughes, Alton. Pecos: A History of the Pioneer West, Vol. 2. (Illus.). 232p. 1981. 16.95 (ISBN 0-933512-34-1). Pioneer Bk Tx.
Hughes, Andrew. Medieval Manuscripts for Mass & Office: A Guide to Their Organization & Terminology. 496p. 1981. 45.00x (ISBN 0-8020-5467-6). U of Toronto Pr.
--Medieval Music: The Sixth Liberal Art. 2nd ed. (Toronto Medieval Bibliographies Ser.). 1980. 25.00x (ISBN 0-8020-2358-4). U of Toronto Pr.
Hughes, Ann, ed. Seventeenth-Century England: A Changing Culture, Primary Sources, Vol. 1. 1981. 28.50x (ISBN 0-389-20168-5). B&N.
Hughes, Ann J. & Grawoig, Dennis E. Linear Programming: An Emphasis on Decision Making. LC 72-1938. 1973. text ed. 19.95 (ISBN 0-201-03024-1). A-W.
Hughes, Anne E. A Book of Sounds: A, B, C. LC 78-62981. (Learn-a-Sound). (Illus.). (gr. 1-3). 1979. PLB 9.95 (ISBN 0-8393-0188-X). Raintree Child.
--A Book of Sounds: Blends & Ends. LC 79-62984. (Learn-a-Sound). (Illus.). (gr. 1-3). 1979. PLB 9.95 (ISBN 0-8393-0191-X). Raintree Child.
--A Book of Sounds: ee, oo, ai. LC 79-62983. (Learn-a-Sound). (Illus.). (gr. 1-3). 1979. PLB 9.95 (ISBN 0-8393-0190-1). Raintree Child.
--A Book of Sounds: sl, ch, pr. LC 79-62982. (Learn-a-Sound). (Illus.). (gr. 1-3). 1979. PLB 9.95 (ISBN 0-8393-0189-8). Raintree Child.
Hughes, Anne E. & Hart, Hazel C. Developmental Reading Ser, One, Two, Three. Incl. Forward in Reading. (gr. 7). o.p. (ISBN 0-672-70573-7); Onward in Reading. (gr. 8) (ISBN 0-672-70575-3); Upward in Reading. (gr. 9) (ISBN 0-672-70577-X). (gr. 7-9). 1970. text ed. 3.48 ea.; annot. tehr's ed. 3.48 ea. Bobbs.
Hughes, B. P. Limit State Theory for Reinforced Concrete Design. 2nd ed. (Illus.). 1977. 24.95x (ISBN 0-8464-0572-5); pap. text ed. 17.50x (ISBN 0-8464-0573-3). Beekman Pubs.
Hughes, B. R. Modern Handmade Knives. Date not set. price not set (ISBN 0-913150-44-4). Pioneer Pr.
Hughes, Barnabas, tr. Regiomontanus: On Triangles. (Illus.). 1967. 25.00x (ISBN 0-299-04210-3). U of Wis Pr.
Hughes, Barnabas E., ed. Jordanus De Nemore, De Numeris Datis: A Critical Edition & Translation. (Publications of the Center for Medieval & Renaissance Studies, UCLA). 200p. 1981. 40.00x (ISBN 0-520-04283-2). U of Cal Pr.
Hughes, Barry B. The Domestic Context of American Foreign Policy. LC 77-17472. (Illus.). 1978. text ed. 18.95x (ISBN 0-7167-0040-9); pap. text ed. 9.95x (ISBN 0-7167-0039-5). W H Freeman.
Hughes, Beryl & Bunkle, Phillida, eds. Women in New Zealand Society. 304p. 1980. text ed. 21.00x (ISBN 0-86861-026-7, 2521); pap. text ed. 11.50x (ISBN 0-86861-034-8, 2522). Allen Unwin.
Hughes, Billy G., Jr. You Can Make Horseman Clocks. 52p. 1980. pap. 4.00 (ISBN 0-914208-08-X). Longhorn Pr.
Hughes, Catharine R., ed. American Theatre Annual, 1978-1979. (Illus.). 1980. 35.00 (ISBN 0-8103-0418-X, Incorporates New York Theatre Annual). Gale.
--American Theatre Annual, 1979-80. (Illus.). 200p. 1981. 35.00 (ISBN 0-8103-0419-8). Gale.
--New York Theatre Annual: Nineteen Seventy-Seven to Seventy Eight. LC 78-50757. (Illus.). 1978. 35.00 (ISBN 0-8103-0417-1). Gale.
--New York Theatre Annual: 1976-77. LC 78-50757. (Illus.). 1978. 35.00 (ISBN 0-8103-0416-3). Gale.
Hughes, Catherine A., ed. Economic Education: A Guide to Information Sources. LC 73-17576. (Economics Information Guide Ser.: Vol. 6). 1977. 30.00 (ISBN 0-8103-1290-5). Gale.
Hughes, Charles C. Eskimo Boyhood: An Autobiography in Psychosocial Perspective. LC 73-80465. (Illus.). 440p. 1974. 17.50x (ISBN 0-8131-1301-6). U Pr of Ky.
Hughes, Charles E. The Autobiographical Notes of Charles Evans Hughes. Danelski, David J. & Tulchin, Joseph S., eds. LC 72-88130. (Studies in Legal History). 1973. 17.50x (ISBN 0-674-05325-7). Harvard U Pr.
--Supreme Court of the United States. LC 66-2855. 1928. pap. 9.50x (ISBN 0-231-08567-2, 67). Columbia U Pr.

Hughes, Charles E., et al, eds. Advanced Programming Techniques: A Second Course in Programming Using Fortran. 287p. 1978. text ed. 19.95 (ISBN 0-471-02611-5). Wiley.

Hughes, Charles L. Goal Setting. LC 65-26864. 1965. 12.95 (ISBN 0-8144-5116-0). Am Mgmt.

Hughes, Charles W. Human Side of Music. LC 70-107871. (Music Ser). 1970. Repr. of 1948 ed. lib. bdg. 32.50 (ISBN 0-306-71895-2). Da Capo.

Hughes, Christopher, tr. see Switzerland. Constitution.

Hughes, Clarence R., et al, eds. Collective Negotiations in Higher Education: A Reader. 226p. (Orig.). 1973. pap. 5.95 o.p. (ISBN 0-686-02465-6). Blackburn Coll.

Hughes, Cledwyn. Batsford Colour Book of Wales. 1975. 8.95 (ISBN 0-7134-3003-6, Pub. by Batsford England). Dayid & Charles.

Hughes, Colin A. The Government of Queensland. (Governments of the Australian States & Territories Ser.). (Illus.). 322p. 1981. text ed. 36.25x (ISBN 0-7022-1515-5); pap. text ed. 19.25x (ISBN 0-7022-1516-3). U of Queensland Pr.

Hughes, D. E. & Rose, eds. Microbes & Biological Productivity. (Illus.). 1971. 42.50 (ISBN 0-521-08112-2). Cambridge U Pr.

Hughes, D. J. Science & Starvation. 1969. 14.50 (ISBN 0-08-012327-9); pap. 10.75 (ISBN 0-08-012326-0). Pergamon.

Hughes, D. T. & Marshall, P. T. Tropical Health Science. 2nd ed. LC 73-84315. (Illus.). 160p. 1974. pap. text ed. 8.50x (ISBN 0-521-20304-X). Cambridge U Pr.

Hughes, Daniel J. Homicide: Investigative Techniques. (Illus.). 376p. 1974. 22.50 (ISBN 0-398-02952-0). C C Thomas.

Hughes, Dave, ed. Radio Control Soaring. rev. ed. (Illus.). 270p. (Orig.). 1977. pap. 13.50x (ISBN 0-8002-2260-1). Intl Pubns Serv.

Hughes, David. Flowers. (Illus.). (ps). 1979. 1.25 (ISBN 0-370-10728-4, Pub. by Chatto Bodley Jonathan). Merrimack Bk Serv.

--Fruit. (Illus.). (ps). 1979. 1.25 (ISBN 0-370-02040-5, Pub. by Chatto Bodley Jonathan). Merrimack Bk Serv.

Hughes, David, ed. see Wells, H. G.

Hughes, David G., ed. Instrumental Music: A Conference, at Isham Memorial Library, Harvard University. LC 70-166094. 152p. 1972. Repr. of 1959 ed. lib. bdg. 14.50 (ISBN 0-306-70273-8). Da Capo.

Hughes, David T. & Marshall, P. T. Human Health, Biology & Hygiene. LC 79-128501. (Illus.). 1970. text ed. 8.50x (ISBN 0-521-07731-1). Cambridge U Pr.

Hughes, Dean. As Wide As the River. LC 80-14646. 150p. 1980. 6.95 (ISBN 0-87747-820-1). Deseret Bk.

--Nutty for President. LC 80-36719. 144p. (gr. 4-6). 1981. PLB 8.95 (ISBN 0-689-30812-4). Atheneum.

Hughes, Dom A. see Abraham, Gerald.

Hughes, Dom Anselm see Abraham, Gerald, et al.

Hughes, Donald. In the House of Stone & Light. LC 77-93502. 137p. 1978. pap. 7.50 (ISBN 0-938216-00-7). GCNHA.

Hughes, E., ed. Jobson's Mining Year Book, 1979. LC 66-2200. 305p. 1979. 50.00x (ISBN 0-8002-2224-5). Intl Pubns Serv.

Hughes, E. J., jt. auth. see Reynolds, P. A.

Hughes, Eden. The Wiltons. (Orig.). 1980. pap. 2.95 (ISBN 0-451-09520-0, E9520, Sig). NAL.

Hughes, Emmet J. Ordeal of Power: A Political Memoir of the Eisenhower Years. LC 63-12783. 1975. pap. text ed. 5.95x (ISBN 0-689-70523-9, 213). Atheneum.

Hughes, Eric L. Gymnastics for Men: A Competitive Approach for Teacher & Coach. (Illus.). 1966. 15.95 (ISBN 0-8260-4460-3). Wiley.

Hughes, Eugene, jt. auth. see Musselman, Vernon A.

Hughes, Eugene H., jt. auth. see Musselman, Vernon L.

Hughes, Everett C. Men & Their Work. LC 80-29143. 184p. 1981. Repr. of 1958 ed. lib. bdg. 17.50x (ISBN 0-313-22791-8, HUMW). Greenwood.

Hughes, Everett C. & Hughes, Helen M. Where Peoples Meet: Racial & Ethnic Frontiers. LC 80-27901. 204p. 1981. Repr. of 1952 ed. lib. bdg. 19.75x (ISBN 0-313-22785-3, HUWP). Greenwood.

Hughes, F. Quentin. Seaport: Architecture & Townscape of Liverpool. 16.00 (ISBN 0-685-20625-4). Transatlantic.

Hughes, Francis, jt. auth. see Forney, Robert.

Hughes, Frank. Everyday Heroes. 1981. pap. 2.50 (ISBN 0-8439-0885-8, Leisure Bks). Nordon Pubns.

Hughes, Frederick W. OP AMP Handbook. (Illus.). 304p. 1981. text ed. 21.95 (ISBN 0-13-637298-8). P-H.

Hughes, G. Hebrews & Hermeneutics. LC 77-84806. (Society for New Testament Studies Monographs: No. 36). 1980. 22.50 (ISBN 0-521-21858-6). Cambridge U Pr.

Hughes, G. A. & Heal, G. M. Public Policy & the Tax System. (Illus.). 224p. 1980. text ed. 29.50 (ISBN 0-04-336067-X, 2575). Allen Unwin.

Hughes, G. Bernard. Antique Sheffield Plate. 1970. 40.50 o.p. (ISBN 0-686-63852-2, Pub. by Batsford England). David & Charles.

--The Country Life Collector's Pocket Book. 1976. 16.95 (ISBN 0-600-43055-3). Transatlantic.

Hughes, G. David. Demand Analysis for Marketing Decisions. 1973. text ed. 18.95x (ISBN 0-256-01479-5). Irwin.

--Marketing Management: A Planning Approach. LC 77-83036. 1978. text ed. 17.95 (ISBN 0-201-03057-8); instr's resource manual o. p. 6.95 (ISBN 0-201-03056-X). A-W.

Hughes, G. M., jt. auth. see Marshall, P. T.

Hughes, G. R., jt. ed. see Jarman, A. O.

Hughes, G. T., ed. Gregynog: A History of the House. 1977. 40.00 (ISBN 0-7083-0634-9). Verry.

Hughes, Gerald & Travis, Stephen. Harper's Introduction to the Bible. LC 80-8607. (Illus.). 144p. (Orig.). 1981. pap. 9.95 (ISBN 0-06-064078-2). Har-Row.

Hughes, Glenn. Imagism & Imagists: A Study in Modern Poetry. 1973. Repr. of 1931 ed. 15.00x (ISBN 0-8196-0282-5). Biblo.

Hughes, Glyn. Best of Neighbors. 64p. 1980. signed ed. 14.95x (ISBN 0-686-68860-0, Pub. by Geolfrith Pr England); pap. 7.50x (ISBN 0-904461-57-2). Intl Schol Bk Serv.

Hughes, Graham, ed. Law, Reason, & Justice: Essays in Legal Philosophy. LC 69-19264. (Studies in Peaceful Change: Vol. 3). 269p. 1969. 15.00x (ISBN 0-8147-0212-0). NYU Pr.

Hughes, H. Stuart. Contemporary Europe: A History. 4th ed. (Illus.). 656p. 1976. Ref. Ed. 18.95 (ISBN 0-13-170019-7). P-H.

Hughes, Harold & Schneider, Dick. The Man from Ida Grove. 346p. 1979. 10.95 (ISBN 0-912376-38-4). Chosen Bks Pub.

Hughes, Harold K. A Dictionary of Abbreviations in Medicine & the Health Sciences. 1977. 25.95 (ISBN 0-669-00688-2). Lexington Bks.

Hughes, Helen & Seng, You-Poh, eds. Foreign Investment & Industrialisation in Singapore. LC 69-14301. 1969. 21.50 (ISBN 0-299-05420-9). U of Wis Pr.

Hughes, Helen M. Inquiries in Sociology. rev. ed. (Sociological Resources for the Social Studies). (gr. 9-12). 1978. text ed. 15.36 (ISBN 0-205-05866-3, 8158665); tchr's guide 13.20 (ISBN 0-205-05867-1, 8158673). Allyn.

Hughes, Helen M., jt. auth. see Hughes, Everett C.

Hughes, Herb. Home Remodeling Design & Plans. Horowitz, Shirley M., ed. LC 79-23347. (Illus.). 144p. (Orig.). 1979. 12.95 (ISBN 0-932944-11-6); pap. 4.95 (ISBN 0-932944-12-4). Creative Homeowner.

Hughes, Hugh P. A History of the Issues & Problems Surrounding Goodwill in Accounting. (Research Monograph: No. 80). 1981. pap. 15.00 postponed (ISBN 0-88406-119-1). Ga St U Busn Pub.

Hughes, Irene F. ESPecially Irene: A Guide to Psychic Awareness. LC 70-189997. 160p. 1972. pap. 1.95 (ISBN 0-8334-1730-4). Steinerbks.

Hughes, J. Donald, ed. see Earthday X Colloquium, University of Denver, April 21-24, 1980.

Hughes, J. K. Structured Programming Using PL-C. 512p. 1981. text ed. 14.95 (ISBN 0-471-04969-7). Wiley.

Hughes, J. R. Social Control in the Colonial Economy. LC 75-17630. 1976. 13.95x (ISBN 0-8139-0623-7). U Pr of Va.

--The Storage & Handling of Petroleum Liquids. 332p. 1978. 85.00x (ISBN 0-85264-251-2, Pub. by Griffin England). State Mutual Bk.

Hughes, Jack T. Caddoan Indians Three: Prehistory of the Caddoan - Speaking Tribes. (American Indian Ethnohistory Ser.: Plains Indians). (Illus.). lib. bdg. 42.00 (ISBN 0-8240-0815-4). Garland Pub.

Hughes, James G. Guide to the Automobile Mechanics Certification Examination. (Illus.). 1978. ref. ed. 15.95; pap. 10.50 (ISBN 0-8359-2618-4). Reston.

--Synopsis of Pediatrics. 5th ed. LC 79-14927. 1979. pap. text ed. 26.50 (ISBN 0-8016-2309-X). Mosby.

Hughes, James W., jt. auth. see Drummond, Harold D.

Hughes, Jill. Aztecs. (Gloucester Press Ser.). (gr. 4-8). 1980. PLB 6.90 (ISBN 0-531-03414-3). Watts.

--Eskimos. (Civilization Library). (Illus.). (gr. 5-8). 1978. PLB 6.90 s&l (ISBN 0-531-01427-4). Watts.

Hughes, Joan. Programming the IBM 1130. LC 69-16045. 1969. 24.95x (ISBN 0-471-42040-9). Wiley.

Hughes, Joan, jt. ed. see Krieger, Dorothy T.

Hughes, Joan K. PL-One Structured Programming. 2nd ed. LC 78-15665. 1979. text ed. 21.95 (ISBN 0-471-01908-9); tchrs. manual avail. (ISBN 0-471-03051-1). Wiley.

Hughes, John & Breckinridge, John. Discussion on Civil & Religious Liberty. LC 76-122167. (Civil Liberties in American History Ser). 1970. Repr. of 1836 ed. lib. bdg. 55.00 (ISBN 0-306-71979-7). Da Capo.

Hughes, John D., jt. auth. see Streilein, Wayne J.

Hughes, Jonathan. The Vital Few: American Economic Progress & Its Protagonists. LC 65-23202. 520p. 1973. pap. 6.95 (ISBN 0-19-519743-7, GB393, GB). Oxford U Pr.

Hughes, K. Scott, jt. auth. see Dickmeyer, Nathan.

Hughes, Kathleen. Celtic Britain in the Early Middle Ages: Studies in Scottish & Welsh Sources. Dumville, David, ed. (Studies in Celtic History). 123p. 1980. 35.00x (ISBN 0-8476-6771-5). Rowman.

Hughes, Kathleen, jt. ed. see Clemoes, Peter.

Hughes, Kendall S., jt. auth. see Hughes, Thomas.

Hughes, Kenneth. Slavery. (Greek & Roman Topics Ser.). 1975. pap. text ed. 3.95x (ISBN 0-04-930004-0). Allen Unwin.

Hughes, Kent H. Trade, Taxes, & Transnational. LC 79-13795. (Praeger Special Studies Ser.). 271p. 1979. 24.95 (ISBN 0-03-051111-9). Praeger.

Hughes, Langston. First Book of Africa. rev ed. (First Bks). (Illus.). (gr. 4-6). 1965. PLB 4.90 o.p. (ISBN 0-531-00452-X). Watts.

--The First Book of Jazz. rev. ed. (First Bks. Ser.). (Illus.). 72p. (gr. 7-9). 1976. PLB 4.90 o.p. (ISBN 0-531-00565-8). Watts.

--The Langston Hughes Reader. LC 58-7871. 1958. 10.00 o.p. (ISBN 0-8076-0057-1). Braziller.

Hughes, Larry W. & Ubben, Gerald C. The Elementary Principal's Handbook: A Guide to Effective Action. abr. ed. 1978. text ed. 17.95 (ISBN 0-205-06080-3). Allyn.

--The Secondary Principal's Handbook: A Guide to Executive Action. 350p. 1980. text ed. 18.95 (ISBN 0-205-06875-8). Allyn.

Hughes, Leo, ed. see Wycherley, William.

Hughes, Lynn, ed. Monkeys. LC 80-57619. (Illus.). 56p. 1980. 4.95 (ISBN 0-89480-098-1). Workman Pub.

Hughes, M. G., ed. Secondary School Administration: A Management Approach. 2nd ed. LC 74-4453. 1974. text ed. 16.50 (ISBN 0-08-018010-8); pap. text ed. 8.50 (ISBN 0-08-018011-6). Pergamon.

Hughes, M. N. The Inorganic Chemistry of Biological Processes. 2nd ed. 336p. 1981. pap. 24.50 (ISBN 0-471-27815-7, Pub. by Wiley-Interscience). Wiley.

Hughes, M. T., ed. Stochastic Processes in Control Systems. (Iee Control Engineering Ser.). (Illus.). 408p. 1981. write for info. (Pub. by Peregrinus London). Inst Elect Eng.

Hughes, M. Vivian. A London Child of the 1870's. (Oxford Paperbacks Ser.: No. 383). 146p. 1977. pap. text ed. 3.95x (ISBN 0-19-281216-5); pap. 3.95 o.p. (ISBN 0-686-68023-5). Oxford U Pr.

--A London Girl of the Eighteen Eighties. 254p. (Orig.). 1978. pap. 4.95x (ISBN 0-19-281243-2). Oxford U Pr.

Hughes, Marija M. The Sexual Barrier: Legal, Medical, Economic & Social Aspects of Sex Discrimination. LC 77-83214. 1977. 60.00 (ISBN 0-912560-04-5). Hughes Pr.

Hughes, Mary G. The Calling: Stories. LC 80-20981. (Illinois Short Fiction Ser.). 130p. 1980. 10.00 (ISBN 0-252-00842-1); pap. 3.95 (ISBN 0-252-00843-X). U of Ill Pr.

Hughes, Mary Margaret, ed. Successful Retail Security. LC 73-91244. 320p. 1974. 15.95 (ISBN 0-913708-15-1). Butterworths.

Hughes, Maysie J. & Barnes, Charles D., eds. Neural Control of Circulation. LC 79-6784. (Research Topics in Physiology Ser.). 1980. 24.00 (ISBN 0-12-360850-3). Acad Pr.

Hughes, Meredydd, ed. Administering Education: International Challenge. (Illus.). 320p. 1975. pap. text ed. 20.75x (ISBN 0-485-12026-7, Athlone Pr). Humanities.

Hughes, Merritt Y., ed. A Variorum Commentary on the Poems of John Milton, Vol. 1, LC 70-129962. 30.00x (ISBN 0-231-08879-5). Columbia U Pr.

--A Variorum Commentary on the Poems of John Milton, Vol. 2, 3 Pts. LC 70-129962. 1972. 30.00x ea. Pt. 1 (ISBN 0-231-08880-9). Pt. 2 (ISBN 0-231-08881-7). Pt. 3 (ISBN 0-231-08882-5). Columbia U Pr.

Hughes, Merritt Y., ed. see Milton, John.

Hughes, Michael, jt. auth. see Callaway, Bob.

Hughes, Monica. Beyond the Dark River. LC 80-36726. 168p. (gr. 5-8). 1981. PLB 7.95 (ISBN 0-689-30811-6). Atheneum.

Hughes, N. F. Paleobiology of Angiosperm Origins. LC 75-3855. (Illus.). 216p. 1976. 40.50 (ISBN 0-521-20809-2). Cambridge U Pr.

Hughes, O. R., jt. ed. see Slocum, D. W.

Hughes, Olga R. The Poetic World of Boris Pasternak. LC 73-2467. (Princeton Essays in Literature). 196p. 1974. text ed. 12.50 (ISBN 0-691-06262-5). Princeton U Pr.

Hughes, Patti. Sunday Supplement for Kids. (Illus.). 63p. (Orig.). (gr. 3-6). 1980. pap. 3.95 (ISBN 0-87747-848-1). Deseret Bk.

Hughes, Paul & Varley, Mike. Reproduction in the Pig. LC 80-40241. 254p. 1980. text ed. 39.95 (ISBN 0-408-70946-4); pap. text ed. 23.95 (ISBN 0-408-70921-9). Butterworths.

Hughes, Paul L., jt. ed. see Larkin, James F.

Hughes, R. C. Membrane Glycoproteins. 1976. 64.95 (ISBN 0-408-70705-4). Butterworths.

Hughes, Ray H. The Order of Future Events. 1970. pap. 2.25 (ISBN 0-87148-650-4). Pathway Pr.

Hughes, Richard. Wooden Shepherdess: The Human Predicament, 2. LC 76-181656. 400p. 1973. 10.00 o.s.i. (ISBN 0-06-011986-1, HarpT). Har-Row.

Hughes, Richard & Brewin, Robert. Tranquilizing of America. 1980. pap. 2.95 (ISBN 0-446-93638-3). Warner Bks.

Hughes, Richard & Serig, Joseph A., eds. Evangelism: The Ministry of the Church. 1981. pap. 12.00 (ISBN 0-8309-0304-6). Herald Hse.

Hughes, Richard A. The Wonder-Dog. LC 77-1977. (gr. 3up). 1977. 9.25 (ISBN 0-688-80099-8); PLB 8.88 (ISBN 0-688-84099-X). Greenwillow.

Hughes, Richard E. & Duhamel, P. A. Rhetoric: Principles & Usage. 2nd ed. 1967. text ed. 12.95 (ISBN 0-13-780718-X). P-H.

Hughes, Riley. How to Write Creatively. (gr. 7 up). 1980. PLB 6.45 (ISBN 0-531-04128-X). Watts.

Hughes, Robert. The Shock of the New: Art & the Century of Change. 423p. 1981. pap. text ed. 15.95 (ISBN 0-394-32800-0). Knopf.

--The Shock of the New: The Life & Death of Modern Art. LC 80-7631. (Illus.). 400p. 1981. 29.95 (ISBN 0-394-51378-9). Knopf.

Hughes, Rupert, ed. Songs by Thirty Americans for High Voice. LC 77-1948. (Music Reprint Series). 1977. Repr. of 1904 ed. lib. bdg. 25.00 (ISBN 0-306-70824-8). Da Capo.

Hughes, Rupert, et al. Music Lovers' Encyclopedia. LC 55-368. 1957. 7.95 o.p. (ISBN 0-385-00124-X). Doubleday.

Hughes, Serge, tr. see Catherine Of Genoa.

Hughes, Shirley. Clothes. (Illus.). (ps). 1979. 1.25 (ISBN 0-370-02039-1, Pub. by Chatto Bodley Jonathan). Merrimack Bk Serv.

--George the Babysitter. LC 77-4833. Orig. Title: Helpers. (Illus.). (ps-2). 1978. PLB 8.95 (ISBN 0-13-352682-8); pap. 2.95 (ISBN 0-13-352674-7). P-H.

--Sally's Secret. 32p. (ps-1). 1980. 6.50 (ISBN 0-370-02010-3, Pub. Chatto Bodley Jonathan). Merrimack Bk Serv.

Hughes, Spike. Glyndebourne: A History of the Festival Opera. LC 80-70705. (Illus.). 400p. 1981. 27.50 (ISBN 0-7153-7891-0). David & Charles.

Hughes, Sukey. Washi: The World of Japanese Paper. LC 78-55094. (Illus.). 1978. 50.00 (ISBN 0-87011-318-6); deluxe ed. 250.00 (ISBN 0-87011-350-X). Kodansha.

Hughes, T. J., jt. auth. see Denton, G. H.

Hughes, Ted. The Hawk in the Rain. 1968. pap. 4.95 (ISBN 0-571-08614-4, Pub. by Faber & Faber). Merrimack Bk Serv.

--Lupercal. 1960. 4.95 o.p. (ISBN 0-571-07035-3, Pub. by Faber & Faber). Merrimack Bk Serv.

--Lupercal. 1970. pap. 4.95 (ISBN 0-571-09246-2, Pub. by Faber & Faber). Merrimack Bk Serv.

--Poetry in the Making. 1967. pap. 4.95 (ISBN 0-571-09076-1, Pub. by Faber & Faber). Merrimack Bk Serv.

--Under the North Star. LC 80-17894. (Illus.). 48p. 1981. 14.95 (ISBN 0-670-73942-1, Studio). Viking Pr.

--Wodwo. LC 67-28808. 1967. 6.95 o.p. (ISBN 0-06-011992-6, HarpT). Har-Row.

--Wodwo. 1971. pap. 5.95 (ISBN 0-571-09714-6, Pub. by Faber & Faber). Merrimack Bk Serv.

Hughes, Ted, jt. auth. see Gunn, Thom.

Hughes, Ted, ed. see Shakespeare, William.

Hughes, Ted, tr. see Pilinszky, Janos.

Hughes, Therle. Introduction to Antiques. (Illus.). 1978. 12.00 (ISBN 0-600-30346-2). Transatlantic.

Hughes, Thomas & Hughes, Kendall S. Casebook for Special Education & Elementary Education. LC 76-57115. 1977. pap. 7.50x (ISBN 0-8134-1905-0, 1905). Interstate.

Hughes, Thomas L. The Fate of Facts in a World of Men: Foreign Policy & Intelligence Making. (Headline Ser.: 233). 1976. pap. 2.00 (ISBN 0-87124-038-6, 76-45580). Foreign Policy.

Hughes, Thomas P. A Dictionary of Islam. 1976. Repr. 35.00x (ISBN 0-8364-0395-9). South Asia Bks.

Hughes, Tom. Chemistry: Ideas to Interpret Your Changing Environment. 1975. text ed. 19.95x (ISBN 0-8221-0138-6). Dickenson.

Hughes, V. E., jt. auth. see Kaminsky, Max.

Hughes, Vernon & Wu, C. S., eds. Muon Physics. Incl. Vol. 1. 47.00 (ISBN 0-12-360601-2); Vol. 2. Weak Interactions. 81.00 (ISBN 0-12-360602-0); Vol. 3. Chemistry & Solids. 58.00 (ISBN 0-12-360603-9). 1975. 150.50 set (ISBN 0-685-72444-1). Acad Pr.

Hughes, Vernon W. see Marton, L.

Hughes, W. H. & Stewart, H. C. Concise Antibiotic Treatment. 2nd ed. 148p. 1973. text ed. 12.40 (ISBN 0-407-13881-1). Butterworths.

Hughes, W. J. Building the Allchin. (Illus., Orig.). 1979. pap. 17.50x (ISBN 0-85242-635-6). Intl Pubns Serv.

--Rebellious Ranger: Rip Ford & the Old Southwest. (Illus.). 300p. 1964. pap. 6.95 o.p. (ISBN 0-8061-1084-8). U of Okla Pr.

Hughes, Walter T. & Buescher, E. Stephen. Pediatric Procedures. 2nd ed. (Illus.). 400p. 1980. text ed. 24.95 (ISBN 0-7216-4826-6). Saunders.

Hughes, William. Aspects of Biophysics. LC 78-8992. 1979. text ed. 25.95 (ISBN 0-471-01990-9). Wiley.

Hughes, William, jt. auth. see Burton, Leon.

Hughes, William, jt. auth. see Settlemire, C. Thomas.

Hughes, William F. Introduction to Viscous Flow. LC 78-14471. (Illus.). 1979. text ed. 24.95 (ISBN 0-07-031130-7, C). McGraw.

Hughes, Winifred. The Maniac in the Cellar: Sensation Novels of the Eighteen Sixties. LC 80-7530. 232p. 1980. 15.00x (ISBN 0-691-06441-5). Princeton U Pr.

Hughes, Zach. For Texas & Zed. 256p. (Orig.). 1976. pap. 1.25 o.p. (ISBN 0-445-00370-7). Popular Lib.

--Pressure Man. (Orig.). 1980. pap. 1.95 (ISBN 0-451-09498-0, J9498, Sig). NAL.

--The St. Francis Effect. pap. 1.75 o.p. (ISBN 0-425-03111-X). Berkley Pub.

Hughes-Evans, ed. Environmental Education - Key Issues of the Future: Proceedings of the Conference Held at the College of Technology, Farnborough, England. LC 77-827. 1977. pap. text ed. 12.00 (ISBN 0-08-021490-8). Pergamon.

Hugh-Jones, Christine. From the Milk River. LC 76-73126. (Cambridge Studies in Social Anthropology: No. 26). (Illus.). 1980. 24.95 (ISBN 0-521-22544-2). Cambridge U Pr.

Hugh-Jones, S. The Palm & the Pleiades. LC 78-5533. (Studies in Social Anthropology: No. 24). (Illus.). 1979. 24.95 (ISBN 0-521-21952-3). Cambridge U Pr.

Hugh-Jones, Stephens. Amazonian Indians. (Civilization Library). (Illus.). (gr. 5-8). 1979. PLB 6.90 s&l (ISBN 0-531-01448-7). Watts.

Hughson, E. A., jt. auth. see Brown, R. I.

Hughson, Lois. Thresholds of Reality: George Santayana & Modernist Poetics. (Literary Criticism Ser.). 1976. 15.00 (ISBN 0-8046-9154-1, National University Pub). Kennikat.

Hughston, George, jt. auth. see Keller, James F.

Hugh The Chantor, pseud. The History of the Church of York, 1066-1127. Johnson, Charles, tr. from Lat. & intro. by. LC 80-2227. 1981. Repr. of 1961 ed. 34.50 (ISBN 0-404-18764-1). AMS Pr.

Hugman, Bruce. Act Natural. 95p. 1977. text ed. 9.90x (ISBN 0-7199-0933-3, Pub. by Bedford England). Renouf.

Hugo, Grant. Appearance & Reality in International Relations. LC 72-137420. 207p. 1970. 15.00x (ISBN 0-231-03468-7). Columbia U Pr.

--Britain in Tomorrow's World. LC 78-84062. 1969. 20.00x (ISBN 0-231-03330-3). Columbia U Pr.

Hugo, I. S. Marketing & the Computer. 1967. 25.00 (ISBN 0-08-012606-5); pap. 13.25 (ISBN 0-08-012605-7). Pergamon.

Hugo, Richard. Death & the Good Life. 192p. 1981. 10.95 (ISBN 0-312-18588-X). St Martin.

Hugo, Thomas. Bewick Collector, 2 Vols. LC 67-24353. (Illus.). 1968. Repr. of 1866 ed. Set Incl. Suppl. 34.00 (ISBN 0-8103-3491-7). Gale.

Hugo, Victor. Chatiments. Yarrow, P. J., ed. (French Poets Ser). 312p. 1975. text ed. 22.50x (ISBN 0-485-14707-6, Athlone Pr); pap. text ed. 9.00x (ISBN 0-485-12707-5). Humanities.

--Les Feuilles D'Automne. Bisson, L., ed. (French Texts Ser.). 1964. pap. text ed. 4.50x o.p. (ISBN 0-631-00420-3, Pub. by Basil Blackwell). Biblio Dist.

--The Hunchback of Notre Dame. 1953. 17.95x (ISBN 0-460-00422-0, Evman). Dutton.

--The Hunchback of Notre Dame. (Arabic.). pap. 7.95x (ISBN 0-686-63547-7). Intl Bk Ctr.

--Last Day of a Condemmed. Eugenia, De B., tr. LC 76-25870. 1977. Repr. of 1894 ed. 15.50 (ISBN 0-86527-269-7). Fertig.

--La Legende des Siecles. Hunt, H. J., ed. (French Texts Ser.). 1968. pap. text ed. 4.50x o.p. (ISBN 0-631-00490-4, Pub. by Basil Blackwell). Biblio Dist.

--Les Miserables. (Literature Ser). (gr. 10-12). 1970. pap. text ed. 6.33 (ISBN 0-87720-732-1). AMSCO Sch.

--Les Miserables, 2 vols. Denny, Norman, tr. from Fr. (Penguin Classics). 1160p. 1980. pap. 4.95 ea. (ISBN 0-14-044403-3). Vol. 1. Vol. 2 (ISBN 0-14-044404-1). Penguin.

--Les Miserables. (Arabic.). pap. 8.95x (ISBN 0-686-63556-6). Intl Bk Ctr.

--Notre-Dame de Paris. (Documentation thematique). pap. 2.95 (ISBN 0-685-14001-6, 127). Larousse.

Hugon, Paul D. The Modern Word-Finder: A Living Guide to Modern Usage, Spelling, Synonyms, Pronunciation, Grammar, Word Origins, & Authorship. LC 73-20139. 420p. 1974. Repr. of 1934 ed. 26.00 (ISBN 0-8103-3970-6). Gale.

Hugonnier, Rene & Clayette-Hugonnier, Suzanne. Strabismus, Heterophoria, Ocular Motor Paralysis (Clinical Ocular Muscle Imbalance) 2nd ed. Veronneau-Troutman, Suzanne, tr. LC 78-8814. (Illus.). 1969. 49.50 o.p. (ISBN 0-8016-2312-X). Mosby.

Huguenin, Jean-Rene. The Other Side of the Summer. LC 61-12953. 1961. 4.00 o.s.i. (ISBN 0-8076-0150-0). Braziller.

Huguenin, Kathleen, et al. Narrowing the Gap Between Intent & Practice: A Report to Policy-Makers on Community Organizations & School Decisionmaking. 118p. (Orig.). 1979. pap. 5.00 (ISBN 0-917754-13-1). Inst Responsive.

Huhm, Halla Pai. Kut: Korean Shamanist Rituals. 102p. 1980. 12.50 (ISBN 0-930878-18-3). Hollym Intl.

Huidekoper, Virginia. Early Days in Jackson Hole. LC 78-60201. (Illus.). 1979. 19.50 (ISBN 0-87081-118-5); pap. 8.95 (ISBN 0-87081-119-3). Colo Assoc.

Huie, William B. In the Hours of Night. 352p. 1975. 8.95 o.p. (ISBN 0-440-04367-0). Delacorte.

Huilgol, R. R. Continuum Mechanics of Viscoelastic Liquids. LC 73-14413. (Illus.). 675p. 1975. 34.50 o.p. (ISBN 0-470-42043-X). Halsted Pr.

Huish, Ian. Horvath: A Study. 105p. 1980. 11.50x (ISBN 0-8476-6269-1). Rowman.

Huisman, jt. auth. see Schreeder.

Huitema, Bradley E. The Analysis of Convariance & Alternatives. LC 80-11319. 1980. 27.50 (ISBN 0-471-42044-1, Pub. by Wiley-Interscience). Wiley.

Huizing, Peter & Basset, Williams, eds. The Future of Religious Life. (Concillium Ser.: Vol. 97). pap. 4.95 (ISBN 0-8164-2094-7). Crossroad NY.

Huizing, Peter & Bassett, William, eds. Experience of the Spirit. (Concilium Ser.: Religion in the Seventies: Vol. 99). 1976. pap. 4.95 (ISBN 0-8164-2096-3). Crossroad NY.

Huizing, Peter & Walf, Knut, eds. Electing Our Own Bishops, Concilium 137. (New Concilium 1980). 128p. 1980. pap. 5.95 (ISBN 0-8245-0116-0). Crossroad NY.

--The Roman Curia & the Communion of Churches. (The New Concilium: Vol. 127). 120p. (Orig.). 1980. pap. 4.95 (ISBN 0-8164-2042-4). Crossroad NY.

Huizing, Peter, jt. ed. see Bassett, William.

Huizing, Peter J., jt. ed. see Basset, William W.

Huizing, Peter J., jt. ed. see Bassett, William W.

Huizinga, J. In the Shadow of Tomorrow. 6.50 (ISBN 0-8446-0717-7). Peter Smith.

--Waning of the Middle Ages. LC 54-4529. pap. 3.95 (ISBN 0-385-09288-1, A42, Anch). Doubleday.

Huizinga, J., jt. ed. see Weiner, J. S.

Huizinga, Jehan. Homo Ludens: A Study of the Play Element in Culture. 256p. 1980. Repr. of 1949 ed. 18.50x (ISBN 0-7100-0578-4). Routledge & Kegan.

Hulanicki, Adam & Glab, Stanislaw, eds. Redox Indicators: Characteristics & Applications. 1978. pap. text ed. 10.00 (ISBN 0-08-022383-4). Pergamon.

Hulbert, Anne. Making Gifts. 1975. 14.95 (ISBN 0-7134-2948-8, Pub. by Batsford England). David & Charles.

Hulbert, James R., jt. ed. see Craigie, William A.

Huldebrand, Nicholas, jt. auth. see Deroche, Andre.

Hulett, Malcolm. Unit Load Handling. 351p. 1970. 39.95 (ISBN 0-7161-0035-5). CBI Pub.

Hulick, Nancy. Little Golden Picture Dictionary. (gr. k-1). 1959. PLB 5.00 (ISBN 0-307-60369-5, Golden Pr). Western Pub.

Hulicka, Irene M. & Whitbourne, Susan K. Teaching Undergraduate Courses in Adult Development & Aging. LC 79-83690. 1979. text ed. 9.95 (ISBN 0-933786-02-6); pap. text ed. 5.95 (ISBN 0-933786-01-8). Beech Hill.

Hull, jt. auth. see Schuler.

Hull, Anthony H. Charles III & the Revival of Spain. LC 80-491. (Illus.). 416p. 1980. text ed. 22.00 (ISBN 0-8191-1021-3); pap. text ed. 14.00 (ISBN 0-8191-1022-1). U Pr of Amer.

Hull, Barbara S. St. Simons: Enchanted Island. LC 80-80048. (Illus.). 136p. 1980. 7.95 (ISBN 0-87797-049-1). Cherokee.

Hull, C., jt. auth. see Rhodes, R. A.

Hull, C. Hadlai & Nie, Norman H. SPSS-Eleven: The SPSS Batch System for the DEC PDP-11. 265p. 1980. pap. text ed. 6.95 (ISBN 0-07-046537-1, C). McGraw.

Hull, Clark L. Hypnosis & Suggestibility: An Experimental Approach. LC 33-30268. (Century Psychology Ser.). (Illus.). 1933. pap. text ed. 12.95x (ISBN 0-89197-223-4). Irvington.

Hull, David. Recent Advances in Paediatrics, No. 6. (Recent Advances Ser.). (Illus.). 300p. 1981. lib. bdg. 42.50 (ISBN 0-443-02208-9). Churchill.

Hull, David L. Philosophy of Biological Science. LC 73-12981. (Foundations of Philosophy Ser). (Illus.). 192p. 1974. ref. ed. o.p. 11.95 (ISBN 0-13-663617-9); pap. text ed. 7.95x (ISBN 0-13-663609-8). P-H.

Hull, David S. Film in the Third Reich: A Study of the German Cinema, 1933-1945. 1969. 17.50 (ISBN 0-520-01489-8). U of Cal Pr.

Hull, Denison B., tr. from Medieval Greek. Digenis Akritas: The Two Blood Border Lord. LC 79-141384. (Illus.). xlviii, 148p. 1972. 10.00x (ISBN 0-8214-0097-5). Ohio U Pr.

Hull, Derek. Introduction to Dislocations. 2nd ed. 280p. 1976. text ed. 27.00 (ISBN 0-08-018129-5); pap. text ed. 14.00 (ISBN 0-08-018128-7). Pergamon.

Hull, E. M. The Sheik. (Barbara Cartland's Library of Love: Vol. 1). 216p. 1980. 12.95x (ISBN 0-7156-1377-4, Pub. by Duckworth England). Biblio Dist.

--The Sons of the Sheik. (Barbara Cartland's Library of Love: Vol. 11). 213p. 1980. 12.95x (ISBN 0-7156-1472-X, Pub. by Duckworth England). Biblio Dist.

Hull, J. C. The Evaluation of Risk in Business Investment. LC 80-40136. (Illus.). 192p. 1980. 27.00 (ISBN 0-08-024075-5); pap. 15.00 (ISBN 0-08-024074-7). Pergamon.

Hull, John, et al. Model Building Techniques for Management. (Illus.). 1977. 19.95 (ISBN 0-566-00149-7, 00719-6, Pub. by Saxon Hse). Lexington Bks.

Hull, Katharine & Whitlock, Pamela. Far Distant Oxus. abr. ed. LC 69-11300. (gr. 5-8). 1969. 4.95g o.s.i. (ISBN 0-02-745760-5). Macmillan.

Hull, Marion. Phonics for the Teacher of Reading. 3rd ed. (Illus.). 144p. 1981. pap. text ed. 5.95 (ISBN 0-675-08074-6). Merrill.

Hull, Marion A. Phonics for the Teacher of Reading. 2nd ed. Heilman, ed. (Elementary Education Ser.). 128p. 1976. pap. text ed. 7.95x (ISBN 0-675-08655-8). Merrill.

Hull, N. E., jt. auth. see Hoffer, Peter C.

Hull, R. Modern Africa: Change & Continuity. 1980. pap. 11.95 (ISBN 0-13-586305-8). P-H.

Hull, R. A., jt. auth. see Martin, J. W.

Hull, R. A., jt. auth. see Southworth, H. N.

Hull, R. F., ed. see Jung, Carl G.

Hull, R. F., tr. see Campbell, Joseph.

Hull, R. F., tr. see Jung, C. G.

Hull, R. F., tr. see Jung, Carl G.

Hull, Raymona E. Nathaniel Hawthorne: The English Experience 1853-1864. LC 79-26616. (Illus.). 1980. 21.95 (ISBN 0-8229-3418-3). U of Pittsburgh Pr.

Hull, Raymond. How to Get What You Want. 1973. pap. 6.50 (ISBN 0-8015-3780-0, Hawthorn). Dutton.

Hull, Raymond & Larden, Ida C. The Off-Wheel Pottery Book. (Encore Edition). (Illus.). 1977. 3.95 o.p. (ISBN 0-684-14980-X, ScribT). Scribner.

Hull, Raymond & Sleight, Jack. Home Book of Smoke-Cooking Meat, Fish & Game. LC 76-162445. (Illus.). 160p. 1971. 10.95 (ISBN 0-8117-0803-9). Stackpole.

Hull, Raymond, jt. auth. see Anderson, Stanley F.

Hull, Raymond, jt. auth. see Peter, Laurence J.

Hull, Raymond, jt. auth. see Sleight, Jack.

Hull, Richard W. African Cities & Towns Before the European Conquest. LC 76-16038. (Illus.). 1976. 10.95x (ISBN 0-393-05581-7); pap. 4.95x (ISBN 0-393-09166-X). Norton.

--Southern Africa: Civilizations in Turmoil. (Illus.). 240p. 1981. text ed. 17.50x (ISBN 0-8147-3410-3); pap. text ed. 9.00x (ISBN 0-8147-3411-1). NYU Pr.

Hull, Robert. September Champions: The Story of America's Air Racing Pioneers. (Illus.). 224p. 1979. 21.95 (ISBN 0-8117-1519-1); pap. 14.95 (ISBN 0-8117-2096-9). Stackpole.

Hull, Ronald E. & Mohan, Madan, eds. Individualized Instruction & Learning. LC 73-89605. 1974. 19.95 (ISBN 0-88229-113-0). Nelson-Hall.

Hull, Suzanne W. Chaste, Silent & Obedient: English Books for Women, 1475-1640. (Illus.). 1980. write for info. (ISBN 0-87328-115-2). Huntington Lib.

Hull, T. E. & Day, D. D. Computers & Problem Solving. 1969. pap. 8.95 o.p. (ISBN 0-201-03017-9). A-W.

Hull, W. Frank, IV. Foreign Students in the United States of America: Coping Behavior Within the Educational Environment. LC 78-19741. 1978. 23.95 (ISBN 0-03-046151-0). Praeger.

Hull, W. Frank, IV, jt. auth. see Klineberg, Otto.

Hull, William. Collected Poems, 1942-1968. 20.00 (ISBN 0-89253-473-7); flexible cloth 10.00 (ISBN 0-89253-474-5). Ind-US Inc.

--Visions of Handy Hopper, 7 vols. 1975. Set. 100.00 (ISBN 0-88253-813-6); Set. pap. 50.00 (ISBN 0-88253-812-8). Ind-US Inc.

Hull, William, tr. see Catullus.

Hull, William I. Two Hague Conferences & Their Contributions to International Law. LC 73-147582. (Library of War & Peace; Int'l. Organization, Arbitration & Law). lib. bdg. 38.00 (ISBN 0-8240-0346-2). Garland Pub.

Hullaad, E. D., jt. auth. see Hersom, A. C.

Hulley, Clarence C. Alaska: Past & Present. 3rd ed. LC 80-25274. (Illus.). 477p. 1981. Repr. of 1970 ed. lib. bdg. 39.75x (ISBN 0-313-22845-0, HUAL). Greenwood.

Hulley, O. S., jt. auth. see Ritchey, John A.

Hullinger, Robert & Grosch, Robert. Move Yourself, & Save! 1980. pap. 3.50 (ISBN 0-915644-15-0). Clayton Pub Hse.

Hulliung, Mark. Montesquieu & the Old Regime. 1977. 18.50x (ISBN 0-520-03108-3). U of Cal Pr.

Hullmandel, Charles J. The Art of Drawing on Stone, Giving a Full Explanation of the Various Styles of the Different Methods to Be Employed to Ensure Success, & of the Modes of Correcting, As Well As of the Several Causes of Failure. LC 78-74392. (Nineteenth-Century Book Arts & Printing History Ser.: Vol. 7). 1980. lib. bdg. 22.00 (ISBN 0-8240-3881-9). Garland Pub.

Hullum, Everett, jt. auth. see Loucks, Celeste.

Hullum, Everett, ed. see Furlow, Elaine.

Hulme, F. Edward. The Birth & Development of Ornament. LC 79-78173. (Illus.). xii, 340p. 1974. Repr. of 1893 ed. 21.00 (ISBN 0-8103-4026-7). Gale.

--History, Principles, & Practice of Symbolism in Christian Art. LC 68-18027. 1969. Repr. of 1891 ed. 20.00 (ISBN 0-8103-3214-0). Gale.

Hulme, Francis. Directory of Buyers. 2nd ed. 1981. pap. 7.95x (ISBN 0-936588-01-2). Buyer's Directory.

Hulme, H. R. & Collieu, A. Nuclear Fusion. (Wykeham Science Ser.: No. 4). 1969. 8.75x (ISBN 0-8448-1106-8). Crane-Russak Co.

Hulme, Hilda M. Explorations in Shakespeare's Language: Some Problems of Word Meaning in the Dramatic Text. LC 77-4361. 1977. pap. text ed. 10.95x (ISBN 0-582-48726-9). Longman.

Hulme, T. E., tr. see Bergson, Henri.

Hulme, William E. Am I Losing My Faith? LC 71-133035. (Pocket Counsel Bks.). 56p. (Orig.). 1971. pap. 1.75 (ISBN 0-8006-0154-8, 1-154). Fortress.

--How to Start Counseling. (Abingdon Reprint Library). 1971. pap. 2.95 (ISBN 0-687-17940-8). Abingdon.

Hulme, William E., ed. see Jackson, Edgar N.

Hulme, William E., ed. see Keller, John E.

Hulme, William E., ed. see Vayhinger, John M.

Hulse, Stewart, jt. auth. see Renouf, Jane.

Hulsius, Levinus, ed. see Asher, A.

Hulsizer, Allan L. Animal Friends. LC 79-66936. (Illus.). 63p. 1980. 5.95 (ISBN 0-533-04421-9). Vantage.

Hulsizer, R. I. & Lazarus, D. The World of Physics. rev ed. (gr. 11-12). 1977. text ed. 14.92 o.p. (ISBN 0-201-02967-7, Sch Div). A-W.

Hulsker, Jan. The Complete Van Gogh: Paintings, Drawings, Graphic Sketches. (Illus.). 496p. 1980. 95.00 (ISBN 0-686-62711-3, 1701-7). Abrams.

Hulten, K. G. Jean Tinguely "Meta". LC 73-80231. (Illus.). 364p. 1976. signed limited ed. 100.00 (ISBN 0-8212-0547-1, 459054). NYGS.

Hulteng, Hung L. Messenger's Motive: Ethical Problems of the News Media. 250p. 1976. pap. 8.95 (ISBN 0-13-577460-8). P-H.

Hulteng, John L. The News Media: What Makes Them Tick? (Topics in Mass Communications Ser.). 1979. ref. 9.95 (ISBN 0-13-621094-5); pap. 7.95 (ISBN 0-13-621086-4). P-H.

Hultkrantz, Ake. The Religions of the American Indians. (Hermeneutics--Studies in the History of Religions: Vol. 7). 1979. 14.95 (ISBN 0-520-02653-5); pap. 5.95 (ISBN 0-520-04239-5, CAL 463). U of Cal Pr.

Hultman, Kenneth E. The Path of Least Resistance. LC 79-11178. 1979. text ed. 15.95 (ISBN 0-89384-046-7). Learning Concepts.

Hultquist, Lee. They Followed the Piper. pap. 2.95 o.p. (ISBN 0-88270-195-9, P195-8). Logos.

Hultsch, David F. & Deutsch, Francine. Adult Development & Aging. (Illus.). 448p. 1980. 18.95 (ISBN 0-07-031156-0, C); instr's manual 4.95 (ISBN 0-07-031157-9). McGraw.

Hultsch, F. Die Polemaischen Munz-und Rechnungswerte. 66p. (Ger.). 15.00 (ISBN 0-916710-81-5). Obol Intl.

Hultstrand, Bonnie, jt. auth. see Grinfelds, Vesma.

Hultstrand, Donald M. The Praying Church. LC 77-8337. 1977. pap. 3.95 (ISBN 0-8164-2159-5). Crossroad NY.

Human Resource Development Press. The Complete Guide to Packaged Training Programs. Nadler, Leonard, ed. 250p. (Orig.). 1981. book with periodic supplements 65.00x (ISBN 0-914234-52-8). Human Res Dev.

Humason, Gretchen L. Animal Tissue Techniques. 4th ed. LC 78-17459. (Illus.). 1979. text ed. 24.95x (ISBN 0-7167-0299-1). W H Freeman.

Humayun, Kabir. Science, Democracy, and Islam: And Other Essays. LC 80-2195. 1981. Repr. of 1955 ed. 20.00 (ISBN 0-404-18967-9). AMS Pr.

Humbaraci & Mucnik. Portugal's African Wars. LC 72-93676. 1974. 10.00 (ISBN 0-89388-072-8). Okpaku Communications.

Humbard, Rex. To Tell the World: The Driving Passion of Rex Humbard & the Cathedral of Tomorrow. LC 75-19273. (Illus.). 224p. 1975. 7.95 o.p. (ISBN 0-13-923094-7). P-H.

Humbertson, Albert O., Jr., jt. auth. see Hall, James L.

Humbertson, James E. Evangelical Sunday School Lesson Commentary 1978-79. 1979. 5.50 o.p. (ISBN 0-87148-290-8). Pathway Pr.

Humbertson, James E., ed. Evangelical Sunday School Lesson Commentary, 1979-80. 448p. 1979. 5.95 (ISBN 0-87148-291-6). Pathway Pr.

Humble, John & Humble, John W. The Effective Computer: A Management by Objectives Approach. LC 73-79243. 160p. 1974. 14.95 (ISBN 0-8144-5334-1). AM Mgmt.

Humble, John W. How to Manage by Objectives. (AMACOM Executive Bks). 1978. pap. 5.95 (ISBN 0-8144-7508-6). Am Mgmt.

Humble, John W., jt. auth. see Humble, John.

Humble, Lance & Cooper, Carl. The World's Greatest Blackjack Book. LC 79-8930. (Illus.). 432p. 1980. 12.95 (ISBN 0-385-15370-8). Doubleday.

Humble, R. The Explorers. new ed. (Seafarers Ser.). (Illus.). 1978. 13.95 (ISBN 0-8094-2658-7). Time-Life.

Humble, Richard. The Explorers. LC 78-1292. (The Seafarers Ser.). (Illus.). 1978. lib. bdg. 11.97 (ISBN 0-686-50984-6). Silver.

--The Saxon Kings. (Illus.). 223p. 1980. 17.00x (ISBN 0-297-77784-X, Pub. by Weidenfeld & Nicolson England). Biblio Dist.

Hume, Abraham. Learned Societies & Printing Clubs of the United Kingdom. LC 66-16418. 1966. Repr. of 1853 ed. 18.00 (ISBN 0-8103-3081-4). Gale.

Hume, Charles. Raise & Train Skunks. pap. 2.50 (ISBN 0-87666-223-8, M527). TFH Pubns.

Hume, David. Dialogues Concerning Natural Religion. Smith, Norman K., ed. 1947. pap. 5.95 (ISBN 0-672-60404-3, LLA174). Bobbs.

--Dialogues Concerning Natural Religion: Text & Critical Essays. Pike, Nelson, ed. LC 77-132933. (Text & Critical Essays Ser). (Orig.). 1970. pap. 6.50 (ISBN 0-672-61119-8, TC6). Bobbs.

--Enquiries Concerning the Human Understanding. 2nd ed. Selby-Bigge, L. A., ed. Bd. with Concerning the Principles of Morals. LC 80-13382. xl, 371p. 1980. Repr. of 1902 ed. 30.00x (ISBN 0-313-22462-5, HUEH). Greenwood.

--Inquiry Concerning Human Understanding: An Abstract of a Treatise of Human Nature. Hendel, Charles W., ed. LC 59-11685. 1955. pap. 5.50 (ISBN 0-672-60218-0, LLA49). Bobbs.

--Inquiry Concerning the Principles of Morals: With a Supplement, a Dialogue. Hendel, Charles W., ed. 1957. pap. 4.95 (ISBN 0-672-60236-9, LLA62). Bobbs.

--Moral & Political Philosophy. Aiken, Henry D., ed. (Library of Classics Ser.: No. 3). 1975. pap. text ed. 6.95 (ISBN 0-02-846170-3). Hafner.

--The Natural History of Religion & Dialogues Concerning Natural Religion. Colver, A. Wayne & Price, Vladimir, eds. 1976. 34.95x (ISBN 0-19-824379-0). Oxford U Pr.

--Of the Standard of Taste & Other Essays. Lenz, John W., ed. LC 64-66070. 1965. pap. 6.50 (ISBN 0-672-60269-5). Bobbs.

--A Treatise of Human Nature. Selby-Bigge, L. A. & Nidditch, P. H., eds. 1978. text ed. 19.95x (ISBN 0-19-824587-4); pap. text ed. 5.50x (ISBN 0-19-824588-2). Oxford U Pr.

Hume, J. N. & Holt, R. C. Programming FORTRAN Seventy-Seven. (Illus.). 1979. pap. text ed. 12.95 (ISBN 0-8359-5671-7). Reston.

Hume, J. N. & Ivey, D. G. Physics: Relativity, Electromagnatism, & Quantum Physics, Vol. 2. 1974. 24.95x (ISBN 0-471-07173-0). Wiley.

Hume, J. N., jt. auth. see Holt, R. C.

Hume, J. N. P., jt. auth. see Ivey, D. G.

Hume, John R. & Johnston, Colin. Glasgow Stations. 1979. 19.95 (ISBN 0-7153-7569-5). David & Charles.

Hume, John R. & Moss, Michael S. Beardmore: The History of a Scottish Industrial Giant. 1980. text ed. 34.95 o.p. (ISBN 0-435-32589-2). Heinemann Ed.

Hume, Lotta C. Favorite Children's Stories from China & Tibet. LC 61-6219. (Illus.). (gr. 1-4). 1962. bds. 13.50 (ISBN 0-8048-0179-7). C E Tuttle.

Hume, Michael, et al. Venous Thrombosis & Pulmonary Embolism. LC 70-122215. (Commonwealth Fund Publications Ser). 1970. 20.00x (ISBN 0-674-93320-6). Harvard U Pr.

Hume, Pat. Dick Whittington & His Amazing Cat. (Orig.). 1980. playscript 2.00 (ISBN 0-87602-230-1). Anchorage.

Hume, Paul, jt. auth. see Weaver, William.

Hume, Robert D., ed. The London Theatre World, Sixteen Sixty to Eighteen Hundred. LC 79-20410. (Illus.). 416p. 1980. 24.95x (ISBN 0-8093-0926-2). S Ill U Pr.

Hume, Robert E. World's Living Religions. rev. ed. LC 58-12515. 1959. pap. text ed. 5.95x (ISBN 0-684-15611-3). Scribner.

Hume, Roberto E. Las Religiones Vivas. Beltroy, Manuel, tr. from Eng. Orig. Title: Living Religions of the World. 320p. (Span.). 1980. pap. 4.50 (ISBN 0-311-05758-6, Edit Mundo). Casa Bautista.

Hume, Sandy. Western Man: Photographs from the National Western Stock Show. 1980. 18.95 (ISBN 0-933472-48-X); pap. 12.95 (ISBN 0-933472-49-8). Johnson Colo.

Hume, Wilfred I. Biofeedback, Vol. II. Horrobin, D. F., ed. (Biofeedback Research Review Ser.). 75p. 1980. Repr. of 1977 ed. 9.95x (ISBN 0-87705-966-7). Human Sci Pr.

Hume, Wilfrid I. Biofeedback, Vol. 1. Horrobin, D. F., ed. (Biofeedback Research Review Ser.). 126p. 1980. Repr. of 1977 ed. 9.95 (ISBN 0-87705-965-9). Human Sci Pr.

--Biofeedback Therapy, Vol. 1. 1976. 10.00 o.p. (ISBN 0-904406-46-6). Human Sci Pr.

Humern, jt. ed. see Rowlands.

Humes, James C. How to Get Invited to the White House & Other Tricky Maneuvers. 1977. 7.95 o.s.i. (ISBN 0-690-01658-1, TYC-T). T Y Crowell.

Humez, Alexander & Humez, Nicholas. From Alpha to Omega. (Illus.). 256p. 1980. write for info. (ISBN 0-87923-386-9). Godine.

Humez, Nicholas, jt. auth. see Humez, Alexander.

Humfrey, Belinda, ed. Recollections of the Powys Brothers. 1980. text ed. 26.00x (ISBN 0-7206-0547-4). Humanities.

Hum-Ishu-Ma. Co-Ge-We-a, the Half-Blood: A Depiction of the Great Montana Cattle Range. xviii, 320p. 1981. pap. 6.25 (ISBN 0-8032-8110-2, BB 754, Bison). U of Nebr Pr.

--Coge-we-a, the Half-Blood: A Depiction of the Great Montana Cattle Range. xvii, 320p. 1981. 17.95x (ISBN 0-8032-3069-9, BB 754, Bison); pap. 6.25 (ISBN 0-8032-8110-2). U of Nebr Pr.

Humiston, Fred. Blue Water Men & Women. 4.95 (ISBN 0-686-15976-4). G Gannett.

Humiston, G., jt. auth. see Brady, J. E.

Humiston, Gerard E., jt. auth. see Brady, James E.

Humm, Harold J. & Wicks, Susanne B. Introduction & Guide to the Marine Bluegreen Algae. LC 79-24488. 1980. 23.50 (ISBN 0-471-05217-5, Pub. by Wiley Interscience). Wiley.

Hummel & Seebeck. Mathematics of Finance. 3rd ed. 1970. text ed. 16.50 (ISBN 0-07-031161-7, C). McGraw.

Hummel, Berta. The Hummel. (Illus.). 78p. 1972. 11.00 (ISBN 0-686-68935-6). Heinman.

Hummel, Horace. The Word Becoming Flesh. 1979. 20.95 (ISBN 0-570-03273-3, 15-2718). Concordia.

Hummel, Konrad. Biostatistical Opinion of Parentage, Based on the Results of Blood Group Tests, 2 vols. LC 72-175560. 1973. Set. 135.00x (ISBN 0-8002-1284-3). Vol. 1 (ISBN 3-437-10246-X). Vol. 2 (ISBN 3-437-10310-5). Intl Pubns Serv.

Hummel, Ralph P. & Isaak, Robert. Politics for Human Beings. 2nd ed. (Illus.). 1980. pap. text ed. 10.95 (ISBN 0-87872-229-7). Duxbury Pr.

Hummel, Raymond C. & Nagle, John N. Urban Education in America: Problems & Prospects. (Illus.). 350p. 1973. 15.95 (ISBN 0-19-501656-4); pap. 5.95x (ISBN 0-19-501655-6). Oxford U Pr.

Hummel, Robert P., Jr. Clinical Burn Therapy: A Complete Guide for Physicians & Surgeons in a Community Hospital Setting. 500p. 1981. 49.00 (ISBN 0-88416-284-2). PSG Pub.

Hummel, Thomas J., jt. ed. see Collier, Raymond O., Jr.

Hummelinck, M. W., jt. auth. see Dieren, W. V.

Hummell, Ruth S. Wonderfully Made. LC 67-24878. (Concordia Sex Education Ser). (gr. 4-6). 1967. 4.50 (ISBN 0-570-06602-6, 14-1502); color film & 33 1 10.00 (ISBN 0-685-08655-0, 79-3101). Concordia.

Hummert, Paul A. Bernard Shaw's Marxian Romance. LC 75-144815. 1973. 13.95x (ISBN 0-8032-0774-3). U of Nebr Pr.

Humphrey, Caroline, ed. see Vainshtein, Sevyan.

Humphrey, David C. From King's College to Columbia, 1746-1800. (Illus.). 328p. 1976. 22.50x (ISBN 0-231-03942-5). Columbia U Pr.

Humphrey, Deirdre, jt. auth. see Humphrey, Henry.

Humphrey, Donald R., jt. ed. see Talbott, Richard E.

Humphrey, Edward, ed. Encyclopedia International, 20 vols. LC 80-84815. (Illus.). 1981. write for info. (ISBN 0-7172-0712-9). Grolier Ed Corp.

--Encyclopedia International, 20 vols. LC 79-67180. (Illus.). 1980. write for info o.p. (ISBN 0-7172-0711-0). Grolier Ed Corp.

Humphrey, Edward & Churchill, James E., eds. Americana Annual, 1980. LC 23-10041. (Illus.). 1980. write for info. o.p. (ISBN 0-7172-0211-9). Grolier Ed Corp.

--Americana Annual, 1981. LC 23-10041. (Illus.). 1981. write for info. (ISBN 0-7172-0212-7). Grolier Ed Corp.

Humphrey, G. A., ed. see Graphic Arts Trade Journal Intl Inc.

Humphrey, Grace. Stories of the World's Holidays. LC 74-3023. 1974. Repr. of 1923 ed. 22.00 (ISBN 0-8103-3660-X). Gale.

Humphrey, Henry. The Farm. LC 76-23768. (gr. 1-3). 1978. 6.95a (ISBN 0-385-01388-4); PLB (ISBN 0-385-03447-4). Doubleday.

Humphrey, Henry & Humphrey, Deirdre. When Is Now: Experiments with Time & Timekeeping Devices. (Illus.). 80p. (gr. 6-7). 1981. 7.95a (ISBN 0-385-13215-8); PLB (ISBN 0-385-13216-6). Doubleday.

Humphrey, J. H. Child Development Through Physical Education. (Illus.). 200p. 1980. 15.75 (ISBN 0-398-03981-X). C C Thomas.

Humphrey, J. H. & Humphrey, J. N. Sports Skills for Boys & Girls. (Illus.). 128p. 1980. pap. 9.75 (ISBN 0-398-04027-3). C C Thomas.

Humphrey, J. H. & Sullivan, Dorothy D. Teaching Slow Learners Through Active Games. 192p. 1973. 12.75 (ISBN 0-398-00886-8). C C Thomas.

Humphrey, J. H., jt. ed. see Taliaferro, W. H.

Humphrey, J. H. see Taliaferro, W. H. & Humphrey, J. H.

Humphrey, J. N., jt. auth. see Humphrey, J. H.

Humphrey, James & Humphrey, Joy. Help Your Child Learn the Three R's Through Active Play. 184p. 1980. 13.75 (ISBN 0-398-04106-7). C C Thomas.

Humphrey, James H. Education of Children Through Motor Activity. 220p. 1975. 16.75 (ISBN 0-398-03471-0). C C Thomas.

--Improving Learning Ability Through Compensatory Physical Education. (Illus.). 160p. 1976. 14.75 (ISBN 0-398-03561-X). C C Thomas.

--Physical Education As a Career: A Text for the Introductory Course. (Illus.). 216p. 1978. 16.75 (ISBN 0-398-03801-5); pap. 12.25 (ISBN 0-398-03802-3). C C Thomas.

--Teaching Elementary School Science Through Motor Learning. 144p. 1975. 11.75 (ISBN 0-398-03252-1). C C Thomas.

Humphrey, James H., jt. auth. see Sullivan, Dorothy D.

Humphrey, James H., et al. Health Teaching in Elementary Schools. (Illus.). 356p. 1975. 18.75 (ISBN 0-398-03356-0). C C Thomas.

--Principles & Techniques of Supervision in Physical Education. 3rd ed. LC 79-92383. 272p. 1980. Repr. of 1972 ed. text ed. 15.00x (ISBN 0-916622-14-2). Princeton Bk Co.

Humphrey, Joy, jt. auth. see Humphrey, James.

Humphrey, Michael. Hostage Seekers: A Study of Childless & Adopting Couples. (Studies in Child Development). (Orig.). 1969. pap. text ed. 4.50x (ISBN 0-582-32438-6). Humanities.

Humphrey, N., et al. The Future of Cincinnati's Capital Plant. (America's Urban Capital Stock Ser.: Vol. 3). 66p. (Orig.). 1980. pap. 4.00 (ISBN 0-87766-264-9, 27400). Urban Inst.

--The Future of Cleveland's Capital Plant. (America's Urban Capital Stock Ser.: Vol. 2). 77p. (Orig.). 1979. pap. text ed. 4.00 (ISBN 0-87766-264-9, 26900). Urban Inst.

Humphrey, Robert E. Children of Fantasy: The First Rebels of Greenwich Village. LC 77-28242. 1978. 19.95 (ISBN 0-471-42100-6, Pub. by Wiley-Interscience). Wiley.

Humphrey, Sylvia W. Matter of Taste. 1965. 6.95 o.s.i. (ISBN 0-02-557120-6). Macmillan.

Humphrey, Thomas J. Basic Programming for the Financial Executive. LC 78-5670. 1978. 29.95 (ISBN 0-471-03020-1, Pub. by Wiley-Interscience). Wiley.

Humphreys, Alice L. Heaven in My Hand. LC 50-3332. 1950. deluxe ed. 4.95 (ISBN 0-8042-2352-1). John Knox.

Humphreys, Christmas. Buddhist Way of Life. (Unwin Paperback Ser.). 224p. (Orig.). 1980. pap. 6.50x (ISBN 0-04-294111-3, 9066). Allen Unwin.

--Karma & Rebirth. (Wisdom of the East Ser). 6.50 (ISBN 0-7195-0684-0). Paragon.

--Teach Yourself Zen, a Way of Life. (Orig.). 1980. pap. cancelled o.p. (ISBN 0-679-12625-2). McKay.

Humphreys, Christmas, ed. The Wisdom of Buddhism. new ed. 1979. text ed. 13.50x (ISBN 0-391-00950-8). Humanities.

Humphreys, Christmas, ed. see Suzuki, D. T.

Humphreys, David. An Essay on the Life of the Honorable Major-General Israel Putnam, Repr. Of 1788 Ed. Bd. with A Genuine & Correct Account of the Captivity, Sufferings & Deliverance of Mrs. Jemima Howe. Howe, Jemima. Repr. of 1792 ed; The Affecting History of Mrs. Howe. Repr. of 1815 ed. LC 75-7040. (Indian Captivities Ser.: Vol. 19). 1977. lib. bdg. 44.00 (ISBN 0-8240-1643-2). Garland Pub.

--Miscellaneous Works. LC 68-24210. 1968. Repr. of 1804 ed. 42.00x (ISBN 0-8201-1028-0). Schol Facsimiles.

Humphreys, David, tr. see De Montfaucon, Bernard.

Humphreys, David, tr. see Montfaucon, Bernard de.

Humphreys, Mrs. Desmond. Sheba: A Story of Girlhood. Wolff, Robert L., ed. LC 75-1535. (Victorian Fiction Ser.). 1975. lib. bdg. 66.00 (ISBN 0-8240-1607-6). Garland Pub.

Humphreys, G. S. Letter Writer. (Teach Yourself Ser.). 1975. pap. 3.50 (ISBN 0-679-10475-5). McKay.

Humphreys, H. I., jt. auth. see Nelkon, M.

Humphreys, J. E. Arithmetics Groups. (Lecture Notes in Mathematics: Vol. 789). 158p. 1980. pap. 11.80 (ISBN 0-387-09972-7). Springer-Verlag.

--Introduction to Lie Algebras & Representation Theory. LC 72-85951. (Graduate Texts in Mathematics: Vol. 9). (Illus.). 170p. 1978. 18.80 (ISBN 0-387-90053-5). Springer-Verlag.

Humphreys, J. R. Subway to Samarkand. 1979. pap. 2.25 o.p. (ISBN 0-425-03938-2). Berkley Pub.

Humphreys, Joe. Joe Humphreys's Trout Tactics. (Illus.). 192p. (Orig.). 1981. pap. 12.95 (ISBN 0-8117-2079-9). Stackpole.

Humphreys, John. The Sportsman Head to Toe. (Illus.). 96p. (Orig.). 1980. pap. 8.50 (ISBN 0-85242-733-6). Intl Pubns Serv.

Humphreys, Martha, tr. see Langen, Dietrich.

Humphreys, Robert A. Tradition & Revolt in Latin America: & Other Essays. LC 69-12966. 1969. 17.50x (ISBN 0-231-03238-2). Columbia U Pr.

Humphreys, Robert E., et al, eds. Pharmacology. 2nd ed. LC 79-83721. (Basic Sciences PreTest Self-Assessment & Review Ser.). (Illus.). 1980. 9.95 (ISBN 0-07-050965-4). McGraw-Pretest.

Humphreys, W. J., jt. auth. see Bentley, W. A.

Humphries, Christmas. Concentration & Meditation. 343p. 1981. pap. 10.00 (ISBN 0-89540-068-5). Sun Pub.

--Zen: A Way of Life. 6.95 o.s.i. (ISBN 0-87523-154-3). Emerson.

Humphries, David A., jt. auth. see Bennett, Donald P.

Humphries, Jackie. All the Things You Aren't...Yet. LC 77-92468. 1980. cancelled (ISBN 0-8499-0071-9, 0071-9); pap. 5.95 (ISBN 0-8499-2891-5). Word Bks.

Humphries, Martha, tr. see Haid, Helmut.

Humphries, Rolfe. Aeneid of Virgil. 1951. pap. 4.95 (ISBN 0-684-71816-2, SL6, ScribT). Scribner.

Humphries, Winifred, jt. auth. see Getty, Kathleen.

Humphry. X-Ray Sermons. pap. 3.50 o.p. (ISBN 0-686-13328-5). Schmul Pub Co.

Humula, Robert R. The Planets & Cataclysm. LC 79-67520. 1980. 7.95 (ISBN 0-533-04469-3). Vantage.

Huncke, Herbert E. The Evening Sun Turned Crimson. LC 79-2555. 1980. 15.00x o.p. (ISBN 0-916156-45-1); pap. 5.00x (ISBN 0-916156-43-5); signed & numbered ed. 25.00x (ISBN 0-916156-44-3). Cherry Valley.

Hunczak, Taras, ed. Russian Imperialism: From Ivan the Great to the Revolution. (Illus.). 415p. 1974. 27.50 (ISBN 0-8135-0737-5). Rutgers U Pr.

Hundell, C. L., jt. auth. see Bold, Harold C.

Hunderfund, Richard. Magic, Myths & Medicine. (Illus.). 1980. write for info. (ISBN 0-89863-036-3). Star Pub CA.

Hundley, Margaret. Australia Bombshell. 1981. 5.75 (ISBN 0-8062-1645-X). Carlton.

Hundley, Norris, Jr. Dividing the Waters: A Century of Controversy Between the United States & Mexico. 1966. 18.50x (ISBN 0-520-00586-4). U of Cal Pr.

--Water & the West: The Colorado River Compact & the Politics of Water in the American West. (Illus.). 432p. 1975. 30.00x (ISBN 0-520-02700-0). U of Cal Pr.

Hundley, Norris, Jr., ed. The American Indian: Essays from the Pacific Historical Review. LC 74-76443. 151p. 1975. 11.80 (ISBN 0-87436-139-7); pap. text ed. 5.20 (ISBN 0-87436-140-0). ABC-Clio.
--The Chicano: Essays from the Pacific Historical Review. LC 75-2354. 168p. 1975. 11.80 (ISBN 0-87436-212-1); pap. 5.20 (ISBN 0-87436-213-X). ABC-Clio.
Hundsalz, A. & Fachinger, B. Schulschwierigkeiten bei Kindern. (Psycholgische Praxis Ser.: Vol. 53). (Illus.). 1980. pap. 21.95 (ISBN 3-8055-0148-X). S Karger.
Huneker, James G. Chopin: Man & His Music. Weinstock, Herbert, ed. (Illus.). 1966. pap. 3.50 (ISBN 0-486-21687-X). Dover.
Huneycutt, James. Introduction to Probability. LC 72-97005. (gr. 9-12). 1973. text ed. 16.95 (ISBN 0-675-08960-3). Merrill.
Hunez, Jean M., ed. Gifts of Power: The Writings of Rebecca Jackson, Black Visionary, Shaker Eldress. (Illus.). 370p. 1981. lib. bdg. 20.00x (ISBN 0-87023-299-1). U of Mass Pr.
Hung, G. Nguyen. Economic Development of Socialist Vietnam 1955-80. LC 77-11149. (Praeger Special Studies). 1977. 23.95 (ISBN 0-275-24080-0). Praeger.
Hung, Wellington, et al. Pediatric Endocrinology. (Medical Outline Ser.). 1978. pap. 16.50 (ISBN 0-87488-674-0). Med Exam.
Hung, William S. Outlines of Modern Chinese Law. (Studies in Chinese Government & Law). 317p. 1977. Repr. of 1934 ed. 23.50 (ISBN 0-89093-057-0). U Pubns Amer.
Hungarian Historical Research Society. Records, Notes, Reports Connected with the Removal to Germany in the Year 1945. LC 77-95243. 120p. 1980. pap. 6.50 (ISBN 0-935484-07-8). Universe Pub Co.
--Secrete Correspondences of the Leaders of Governments in the Year Nineteen Forty-Four & Earlier Years. LC 80-65046. Orig. Title: Allamvezetok Titkos Levelei Az 1944 Ev Elotti Es Az 1944 Evbol. 110p. 1980. pap. 7.95 (ISBN 0-935484-04-3). Universe Pub Co.
Hungarian Pharmacological Society, 3rd Congress, Budapest, 1979. Modulation of Neurochemical Transmission: Proceedings. Knoll, J. & Vizi, E. S., eds. LC 80-41281. (Advances in Pharmacological Research & Practice Ser.: Vol. II). (Illus.). 450p. 1981. 84.00 (ISBN 0-08-026387-9). Pergamon.
Hungate, Lois A. & Sherman, Ralph W. Food & Economics. (Illus.). 1979. pap. text ed. 13.50 (ISBN 0-87055-229-5). AVI.
Hungerford, Mary J. Childbirth Education. (Illus.). 344p. 1972. pap. text ed. 17.50 (ISBN 0-398-02321-2). C C Thomas.
Hungerford, T. W. Algebra. (Graduate Texts in Mathematics: Vol. 73). 526p. 1981. 24.00 (ISBN 0-387-90518-9). Springer-Verlag.
Hungness, Carl, et al. Indianapolis Five Hundred Yearbook: 1980. (Illus.). 224p. 1980. lib. bdg. 13.95 (ISBN 0-915088-24-X); pap. 7.95 (ISBN 0-915088-23-1). C Hungness.
--USAC Sprint History: Twenty-Five Years of United States Sprint Car Racing. Mahoney, John & Cadou, Jep, eds. (Illus.). 208p. 1981. pap. 14.95 (ISBN 0-915088-26-6). C Hungness.
Hung-po Chao. Economies with Exhaustible Resourses. LC 78-74998. (Outstanding Dissertations on Energy Ser.). 1979. lib. bdg. 15.50 (ISBN 0-8240-3980-7). Garland Pub.
Hunisak, John M. The Sculptor Jules Dalou: Studies in His Style & Imagery. LC 76-23629. (Outstanding Dissertations in the Fine Arts - 19th Century). (Illus.). 1977. Repr. of 1976 ed. lib. bdg. 60.00 (ISBN 0-8240-2699-3). Garland Pub.
Hunius, Gerry, jt. auth. see Gustavson, Bjorn.
Hunkins, Dalton R. & Pirnot, Thomas L. Mathematics: Tools & Models. LC 76-15462. (Illus.). 1977. text ed. 17.95 (ISBN 0-201-03046-2); instr's man 2.00 (ISBN 0-201-03047-0). A-W.
Hunkins, Francis P. Curriculum Development: Program Planning & Improvement. (Elementary Education Ser.: No. C22). 410p. 1980. text ed. 16.95 (ISBN 0-675-08177-7). Merrill.
--Questioning Strategies & Techniques. (Illus.). 1972. text ed. 8.95x o.p. (ISBN 0-205-03406-3, 2234068). Allyn.
Hunner, Robert J., ed. Exploring the Relationship Between Child Abuse & Deliquency. LC 79-5178. 320p. 1981. text ed. 19.50 (ISBN 0-916672-31-X). Allanheld.
Hunnisett, Basil. Steel-Engraved Book Illustration in England. LC 79-92108. (Illus.). 288p. 1980. 40.00 (ISBN 0-87923-322-2). Godine.
Hunsacker, Philip & Alessandra, Anthony. The Art of Managing People. (Illus.). 1980. 15.95 (ISBN 0-13-047472-X, Spec); pap. 7.95 (ISBN 0-13-047464-9, Spec). P-H.
Hunsaker, David M., jt. auth. see Smith, Craig R.
Hunsaker, Jerome C. Aeronautics at the Mid-Century. 1952. 24.50x (ISBN 0-685-89732-X). Elliots Bks.
Hunsberger, Arn, jt. auth. see May, Eydie.
Hunsberger, Donald. The Remington Warm-up Studies for Trombone. LC 80-67541. (Illus.). 1980. 8.95 (ISBN 0-918194-10-5). Accura.
Hunsberger, Mabel, jt. auth. see Tackett, Jo J.
Hunsberger, Willard D. Clarence Darrow: A Bibliography. LC 80-26317. viii, 215p. 1981. 12.50 (ISBN 0-8108-1384-X). Scarecrow.
Hunsinger, Carlos L. The Art of Argument. LC 79-15660. Date not set. 10.95 (ISBN 0-87949-154-X). Ashley Bks.
Hunt. Encyclopedia of American Architecture. 100p. Date not set. 35.00 (ISBN 0-07-031299-0). McGraw.
Hunt, jt. auth. see Holiday.
Hunt, Alan. Marxism & Democracy. 1980. text ed. 20.75x (ISBN 0-391-01879-5). Humanities.
Hunt, Alan see Fryer, Bob, et al.
Hunt, Alan, ed. Class & Class Structure. 1977. pap. text ed. 7.75x (ISBN 0-85315-402-3). Humanities.
Hunt, Alfred. Management Consultant. LC 76-49741. 1977. 14.95 (ISBN 0-8260-4557-X). Ronald Pr.
Hunt, Alfred L. Corporate Cash Management: Including Electronic Funds Transfer. LC 78-16648. 1978. 19.95 (ISBN 0-8144-5464-X). Am Mgmt.
Hunt, Alice. Archeology of the Death Valley Salt Pan. (Illus.). xvi, 313p. 1960. Repr. 25.50 (ISBN 0-384-24920-5). Johnson Repr.
Hunt, Arnold D. & Grotty, Robert B. Ethics of World Religions. (Illus.). (gr. 9-12). 1978. lib. bdg. 8.95 (ISBN 0-912616-74-1); pap. 3.95 (ISBN 0-912616-73-3). Greenhaven.
Hunt, B. American Indian Beadwork. 1971. pap. 4.95 (ISBN 0-02-011700-0, Collier). Macmillan.
Hunt, B. R., jt. auth. see Andrews, Harry C.
Hunt, Bernice. Great Bread: The Easiest Possible Way to Make Almost a Hundred Kinds. (Illus.). 124p. 1980. pap. 5.95 (ISBN 0-14-046472-7). Penguin.
--Great Bread! The Easiest Possible Way to Make Almost 100 Kinds. (Illus.). (gr. 6 up). 1977. 8.95 o.p. (ISBN 0-670-34861-9). Viking Pr.
Hunt, Bernice K. Apples: A Bushel of Fun & Facts. LC 75-17911. (Finding-Out Books for Science & Social Studies, Grades 1-4). (Illus.). 64p. (gr. 2-4). 1976. PLB 6.95 (ISBN 0-8193-0838-2, Pub by Parents). Enslow Pubs.
--Your Ant Is a Which: Fun with Homophones. LC 75-37582. (Let Me Read Ser.). (Illus.). 32p. (gr. 1-5). 1976. 4.95 o.p. (ISBN 0-15-299880-2, HJ). HarBraceJ.
Hunt, Bruce, jt. auth. see Blair, William.
Hunt, Carl M. Oyotunji Village: The Yoruba Movement in America. LC 79-51467. (Illus.). 1979. pap. text ed. 7.50 (ISBN 0-8191-0748-4). U Pr of Amer.
Hunt, Carleton, ed. see May, George O.
Hunt, Cecily. How to Get Work & Make Money in Commercials & Modeling. 1981. pap. 12.95 (ISBN 0-938814-02-8). Barrington.
Hunt, Charles B. Death Valley: Geology, Ecology, Archaeology. LC 74-2460. 256p. 1975. 14.95 (ISBN 0-520-02460-5); CAL 315. pap. 7.95 (ISBN 0-520-03013-3). U of Cal Pr.
--Geology of Soils: Their Evolution, Classification, & Uses. LC 71-158739. (Geology Ser.). (Illus.). 1972. text ed. 28.95x (ISBN 0-7167-0253-3). W H Freeman.
--Natural Regions of the United States & Canada. LC 73-12030. (Geology Ser.). (Illus.). 1974. text ed. 23.95x (ISBN 0-7167-0255-X); tchr's manual avail. W H Freeman.
Hunt, Christopher, jt. auth. see Curtis, Seng-gye T.
Hunt, Dave. On the Brink. LC 72-76590. Orig. Title: Confessions of a Heretic. 1975. pap. 1.95 o.p. (ISBN 0-88270-099-5). Logos.
--A Study Guide for the Cult Explosion. 128p. (Orig.). 1981. pap. 2.95 (ISBN 0-89081-280-2). Harvest Hse.
Hunt, Dave, jt. auth. see Frandon, Ramona.
Hunt, David C. Guide to Oklahoma Museums. LC 80-5939. (Illus.). 250p. 1981. 17.50 (ISBN 0-8061-1567-X); pap. 9.95 (ISBN 0-8061-1752-4). U of Okla Pr.
Hunt, Dennis D. Common Sense Industrial Relations. LC 77-89384. 1978. 14.95 (ISBN 0-7153-7453-2). David & Charles.
--Employment Dismissal Without Fear. LC 78-6692. 1979. 14.95 (ISBN 0-7153-7700-0). David & Charles.
Hunt, Derald D. California Criminal Law Manual. 5th ed. 240p. 1980. pap. 12.95 (ISBN 0-8087-3178-5). Burgess.
Hunt, E. H. Regional Wage Variations in Britain 1850-1914. (Illus.). 398p. 1973. 23.50x o.p. (ISBN 0-19-828262-1). Oxford U Pr.
Hunt, E. Howard. Counterfeit Kill. 160p. 1975. pap. 1.25 o.p. (ISBN 0-523-00589-X). Pinnacle Bks.
--The Gaza Intercept. LC 80-6171. 256p. 1981. 12.95 (ISBN 0-8128-2804-6). Stein & Day.
--Give Us This Day. 240p. 1974. pap. 1.25 o.p. (ISBN 0-445-00212-3). Popular Lib.
Hunt, E. K. History of Economic Thought: A Critical Perspective. 1979. pap. text ed. 19.95x (ISBN 0-534-00581-0). Wadsworth Pub.
Hunt, Earl B. Concept Learning: An Information Processing Problem. LC 73-92140. 296p. 1974. Repr. of 1962 ed. 14.50 o.p. (ISBN 0-88275-152-2). Krieger.
Hunt, Earl G., Jr. I Have Believed: A Bishop Talks About His Faith. LC 80-50240. 175p. 1980. 6.95 (ISBN 0-8358-0401-1); pap. 4.50x (ISBN 0-8358-0403-8). Upper Room.
Hunt, Edward L., jt. auth. see Kimeldorf, Donald J.
Hunt, Effie H. How to Have a Perfect Wedding. rev. ed. LC 69-20380. 1980. pap. 4.95 (ISBN 0-8119-0353-2). Fell.
Hunt, Florine E., ed. Public Utilities Information Sources. LC 65-24658. (Management Information Guide Ser.: No. 7). 1965. 30.00 (ISBN 0-8103-0807-X). Gale.
Hunt, Forrest S. Shakespeare Explained. 191p. 1980. Repr. of 1915 ed. lib. bdg. 25.00 (ISBN 0-8495-3255-8). Arden Lib.
Hunt, Frazier. Frazier Hunt's Story of General Custer. (Monograph: No. 5). (Orig.). 1979. pap. 2.50x (ISBN 0-686-27215-3). Monroe County Lib.
Hunt, Gaillard. Israel Elihu & Cadwallader Washburn. LC 71-87440. (American Scene Ser). 1969. Repr. of 1925 ed. lib. bdg. 39.50 (ISBN 0-306-71510-4). Da Capo.
--Life in America One Hundred Years Ago. LC 74-6223. (Illus.). xiv, 298p. 1976. Repr. of 1914 ed. 15.00 (ISBN 0-8103-4017-8). Gale.
Hunt, Gary. Public Speaking. (Illus.). 386p. 1981. text ed. 12.95 (ISBN 0-13-738807-1). P-H.
Hunt, Gary T. Communication Skills in the Organization. (Illus.). 1980. text ed. 16.95 (ISBN 0-13-153296-0). P-H.
Hunt, George. John Updike & the Three Great Secret Things: Sex, Religion, & Art. 176p. 1980. 13.95 (ISBN 0-8028-3539-2). Eerdmans.
Hunt, George T. Wars of the Iroquois: A Study in Intertribal Trade Relations. 1960. pap. 7.95x (ISBN 0-299-00164-4). U of Wis Pr.
Hunt, Gladys. Esa Soy Yo. Roberts, Grace S., tr. from Eng. LC 77-83671. 172p. (Orig., Span.). 1977. pap. 2.25 (ISBN 0-89922-094-0). Edit Caribe.
--Gladys Hunt's "How to" Handbook. LC 73-169168. 1971. pap. 1.95 (ISBN 0-87788-396-3). Shaw Pubs.
--Honey for a Child's Heart. 1969. o. p. 6.95 (ISBN 0-310-26380-8); pap. 4.95 (ISBN 0-310-26381-6). Zondervan.
--Romans: Made Righteous by Faith. (Fisherman Bible Studyguide Ser.). 94p. (Orig.). 1981. saddle stitch 2.25 (ISBN 0-87788-733-0). Shaw Pubs.
Hunt, Gladys M. The God Who Understands Me: Studies in the Sermon on the Mount. LC 75-181992. (Fisherman Bible Study Guide). 1971. pap. 1.95 (ISBN 0-87788-316-5). Shaw Pubs.
Hunt, Greg. Dewitt's Strike. 1980. pap. 1.95 (ISBN 0-440-12024-1). Dell.
--The Haven's Raid. (Orig.). 1980. pap. 1.95 o.s.i. (ISBN 0-440-13557-5). Dell.
Hunt, H. Allan. Inflation Protection for Workers' Compensation Claimants in Michigan: A Simulation Study. LC 80-28834. 125p. (Orig.). 1981. pap. text ed. write for info. (ISBN 0-911558-77-2). Upjohn Inst.
Hunt, H. J., ed. see Hugo, Victor.
Hunt, Harrison J. North to the Horizon. Thompson, Ruth H., ed. LC 80-69081. (Illus.). 135p. 1981. 11.95 (ISBN 0-89272-080-8). Down East.
Hunt, Henry. Lapidary Carving for Creative Jewelry. LC 80-67509. (Illus.). 144p. (Orig.). 1981. 17.95 (ISBN 0-937764-01-9); pap. 12.95 (ISBN 0-937764-02-7). Desert Pr.
Hunt, Henry T. Case of Thomas J. Mooney & Warren K. Billings. LC 72-122166. (Civil Liberties in American History Ser). (Illus.). 1970. Repr. of 1929 ed. lib. bdg. 42.50 (ISBN 0-306-71976-2). Da Capo.
Hunt, Herbert J. Balzac's Comedie Humaine. 1959. pap. text ed. 13.00x (ISBN 0-485-12008-9, Athlone Pr). Humanities.
Hunt, Herbert J., tr. see Balzac, Honore de.
Hunt, Hugh. Old Vic Prefaces: Shakespeare & the Producer. LC 72-6197. (Illus.). 193p. 1973. Repr. of 1954 ed. lib. bdg. 22.75x (ISBN 0-8371-6460-5, HUOV). Greenwood.
--Sean O'Casey. (Gillis Irish Lives Ser.). 153p. 1980. 20.00 (ISBN 0-7171-1080-X, Pub. by Gill & Macmillan Ireland); pap. 6.50 (ISBN 0-7171-1034-6). Irish Bk Ctr.
Hunt, Hugh, jt. auth. see O'Connor, Frank.
Hunt, Irene. Across Five Aprils. 192p. 1981. pap. 1.95 (ISBN 0-448-17032-9, Tempo). G&D.
--Claws of a Young Century. LC 80-10571. (gr. 7 up). 1980. 9.95 (ISBN 0-686-59963-2). Scribner.
--No Promises in the Wind. 224p. (gr. 5 up). 1981. pap. 1.95 (ISBN 0-448-17271-2, Tempo). G&D.
--Up a Road Slowly. 192p. (YA) (gr. 8-12). 1980. pap. 1.95 (ISBN 0-448-16496-5, Tempo). G&D.
Hunt, J. M. Intelligence & Experience. (Illus.). 1961. 17.50 (ISBN 0-8260-4535-9). Wiley.
Hunt, J. N. No Higher Calling. (Horizon Ser.). 96p. 1981. pap. price not set (ISBN 0-8280-0064-6). Review & Herald.
Hunt, James. Stammering & Stuttering: Their Nature & Treatment. 1967. Repr. of 1861 ed. 13.00 o.s.i. (ISBN 0-02-846200-9). Hafner.
Hunt, James, jt. auth. see Young, Eoin.
Hunt, James G. & Larson, Lars L., eds. Crosscurrents in Leadership. LC 79-13576. (Southern Illinois Leadership Symposium Ser.). 316p. 1979. 18.95x (ISBN 0-8093-0932-7). S Ill U Pr.
Hunt, John D., ed. Pope: The Rape of the Lock. (Casebook Ser.). 1970. 2.50 o.s.i. (ISBN 0-87695-045-4). Aurora Pubs.
Hunt, John D., ed. see Pope, Alexander.
Hunt, John M. Petroleum Geochemistry & Geology. LC 79-1281. (Illus.). 1979. text ed. 32.95x (ISBN 0-7167-1005-6). W H Freeman.
Hunt, Joyce, jt. auth. see Selsam, Millicent.
Hunt, Joyce, jt. auth. see Selsam, Millicent E.
Hunt, Joyce, ed. see Selsam, Millicent E.
Hunt, Judith, tr. see Fulton, Mary.
Hunt, Kari & Carlson, Bernice W. Masks & Mask Makers. (Illus.). (gr. 4 up). 1961. 5.95 (ISBN 0-687-23705-X). Abingdon.
Hunt, Kenneth E., jt. ed. see Dams, Theodor.
Hunt, Leigh, jt. auth. see Byron.
Hunt, Leon G. Assessment of Local Drug Abuse Problems. LC 76-42694. 1977. 19.95 (ISBN 0-669-01053-7). Lexington Bks.
Hunt, Lesley. Inside Tennis for Women. LC 77-91157. 1978. 8.95 o.p. (ISBN 0-8092-7715-8); pap. 4.95 (ISBN 0-8092-7713-1). Contemp Bks.
Hunt, Leslie. Veteran & Vintage Aircraft. LC 74-29025. 1975. pap. 12.50 o.p. (ISBN 0-684-14895-1, SL 695, ScribT). Scribner.
Hunt, Mabel L. Miss Jellytot's Visit. (Illus.). (gr. 4-6). 1955. PLB 7.89 o.p. (ISBN 0-397-30305-X). Lippincott.
Hunt, Margaret, tr. see Grimm, Jakob L.
Hunt, N. Jane, ed. Brevet's Nebraska Historical Markers- Sites. LC 74-79979. (Historical Markers-Sites Ser). (Illus.). 228p. (Orig.). 1974. 10.95 o.p. (ISBN 0-88498-020-0); text ed. 8.06 o.p. (ISBN 0-685-50458-1); pap. 6.95 (ISBN 0-88498-021-9); pap. text ed. 4.46 o.p. (ISBN 0-685-50459-X). Brevet Pr.
--Brevet's South Dakota Historical Markers. LC 73-86007. (Historical Markers-Sites Ser). (Illus.). 285p. 1974. 10.95 (ISBN 0-88498-013-8); pap. 6.95 (ISBN 0-88498-014-6); text ed. 4.45 o.p. (ISBN 0-685-46502-0); map 1.95 (ISBN 0-685-46503-9). Brevet Pr.
--Brevet's Wisconsin Historical Markers & Sites. LC 74-79980. (Historical Markers-Sites Ser). (Illus.). 254p. 1974. 10.95 (ISBN 0-88498-015-4); text ed. 8.05 o.p. (ISBN 0-685-46505-5); pap. 6.95 (ISBN 0-88498-016-2); pap. text ed. 4.45 o.p. (ISBN 0-685-46506-3). Brevet Pr.
Hunt, N. Jane, ed. see Sneve, Virginia.
Hunt, Nan T. Behold These Hills. (Illus.). Date not set. cancelled (ISBN 0-89482-050-8). pap. 6.50 (ISBN 0-89482-045-1). Stevenson Pr.
Hunt, P. J. History of the Bible. (Ladybird Ser.). 1975. pap. 1.49 (ISBN 0-87508-839-2). Chr Lit.
Hunt, Patricia. Koalas. LC 80-13717. (A Skylight Bk.). (Illus.). 48p. (gr. 2-5). 1980. PLB 4.95 (ISBN 0-396-07849-4). Dodd.
--Tigers. LC 80-2785. (A Skylight Bk.). (Illus.). 64p. (gr. 2-5). 1981. PLB 5.95 (ISBN 0-396-07932-6). Dodd.
Hunt, Pauline. Gender & Class Consciousness. LC 79-22107. 1980. text ed. 36.50x (ISBN 0-8419-0580-0). Holmes & Meier.
Hunt, Pearson, jt. auth. see Andrews, Victor L.
Hunt, Pearson, et al. Basic Business Finance: Text & Cases. 4th ed. 1971. text ed. 19.95x (ISBN 0-256-00209-6). Irwin.
--Basic Business Finance: Text. 1974. text ed. 17.95x (ISBN 0-256-01553-8). Irwin.
Hunt, R. Multiplication & Division. LC 78-730962. 1978. pap. text ed. 99.00 (ISBN 0-89290-093-8, A509-SATC). Soc for Visual.
Hunt, R. Kevin, ed. Current Topics in Developmental Biology: Emergence of Specificity in Neural Histogenesis, Vol. 15. LC 66-28604. (Serial Publication). 1980. 34.00 (ISBN 0-12-153115-5). Acad Pr.
--Current Topics in Developmental Biology: Vol. 16, Neural Development in Model Systems. LC 66-28604. 1980. 34.00 (ISBN 0-12-153116-3). Acad Pr.
Hunt, R. W. Collected Papers on the History of Grammar in the Middle Ages. Bursill-Hall, G., ed. (Studies in the History of Linguistics: No. 5). 1980. text ed. 31.50x (ISBN 0-391-01667-9). Humanities.
--The Reproduction of Colour in Photography, Printing & Television. 3rd ed. LC 76-6096. 1976. 19.95 (ISBN 0-470-15085-8). Halsted Pr.

Hunt, Raymond G. Interpersonal Strategies for Systems Management. LC 73-85594. (Behavior Science in Industry Ser.). (Orig.). 1974. pap. text ed. 6.95 o.p. (ISBN 0-8185-0099-9). Brooks-Cole.

Hunt, Robert. Glu the Emperor Penguin. LC 72-736442. (Adventures of Wild Animals Book). (Illus.). 16p. (gr. 2-5). 1978. pap. 21.00 10 bks. & one cassette (ISBN 0-89290-027-X). Soc for Visual.

--Jamboo the African Elephant. LC 72-736441. (Adventures of Wild Animals Book). (Illus.). (gr. 2-5). 1978. 10 bks. & one cassette 21.00 (ISBN 0-89290-026-1). Soc for Visual.

--Koolah: The White Koala. LC 74-735895. (Wildlife Stories Book). (Illus.). (gr. 2-5). 1978. 10 bks. & one cassette 21.00 (ISBN 0-89290-036-9). Soc for Visual.

Hunt, Roland. The Seven Keys to Colour Healing. 124p. 1971. 7.25x (ISBN 0-8464-1063-X). Beekman Pubs.

Hunt, Rosemary. Get to Know Spain. 1979. pap. text ed. 7.50 (ISBN 0-435-39003-1). Heinemann Ed.

Hunt, Ruth. Sparrow on the House Top. 1976. 5.95 o.p. (ISBN 0-8007-0814-8). Revell.

Hunt, S. Polysaccharide-Protein Complexes in Invertebrates. 1970. 44.00 (ISBN 0-12-362050-3). Acad Pr.

Hunt, S. E. Fission, Fusion, & the Energy Crisis. LC 74-9926. 1974. text ed. 19.50 o.p. (ISBN 0-08-018102-3); pap. text ed. 10.50 o.p. (ISBN 0-08-018079-5). Pergamon.

--Fission, Fusion & the Energy Crisis. 2nd ed. (Illus.). 180p. 1980. 23.00 (ISBN 0-08-024734-2); pap. 11.00 (ISBN 0-08-024733-4). Pergamon.

Hunt, Sara M., et al. Nutrition: Principles & Clinical Practice. LC 79-25899. 1980. text ed. 20.95 (ISBN 0-471-03149-6). Wiley.

Hunt, Sarah E. Games & Sports the World Around. 3rd ed. (Illus.). (gr. 9-12). 1964. 13.95 (ISBN 0-8260-4565-0). Ronald Pr.

Hunt, Shelby D. Marketing Theory: Conceptual Foundations of Research in Marketing. LC 75-26013. (Marketing Ser.). 1976. text ed. 16.95 o.p. (ISBN 0-88244-097-7). Grid Pub.

Hunt, Sonja & Hilton, Jennifer. Individual Development & Social Experience. (Illus.). 296p. 1981. pap. text ed. 12.50x (ISBN 0-04-150077-6, 2623). Allen Unwin.

Hunt, Stephen, jt. auth. see Huddart, Henry.

Hunt, Tamara & Renfro, Nancy. Puppetry & Early Childhood Education: Preschool & Primary. Scwalb, Ann W., ed. (Puppetry in Education Ser.). (Illus.). 200p. (Orig.). Date not set. pap. 10.95 (ISBN 0-931044-04-9). Renfro Studios.

Hunt, Thomas C., jt. auth. see Honer, Stanley M.

Hunt, Thomas K., ed. Wound Healing & Wound Infection: Theory & Surgical Practice. 303p. 1980. 18.95x (ISBN 0-8385-9836-6). ACC.

Hunt, Thomas K. & Englebert, J., eds. Fundamentals of Wound Management. (Illus.). 612p. 1979. 29.50 (ISBN 0-8385-2837-6). ACC.

Hunt, Tim. Kerouacs Crooked Road: Development of a Fiction. 288p. 1981. 19.50 (ISBN 0-208-01871-9, Archon). Shoe String.

Hunt, V. Daniel. Windpower: Handbook of Wind Energy Conversion. 640p. 1981. text ed. 39.50 (ISBN 0-442-27389-4). Van Nos Reinhold.

Hunt, Valerie. Nannie's Niece's Notes. (Illus.). 32p. 1980. 5.00 (ISBN 0-934750-07-6). Jalamap.

Hunt, Valerie V. Recreation for the Handicapped. 1955. text ed. 15.95 (ISBN 0-13-767640-9). P-H.

Hunt, Violet. The Wife of Rossetti. 338p. 1980. Repr. of 1932 ed. lib. bdg. 30.00 (ISBN 0-8492-5283-0). R West.

Hunt, W. Ben. Ben Hunt's Big Book of Whittling. 1970. 11.95 (ISBN 0-02-557430-2). Macmillan.

--How to Build & Furnish a Log Cabin: The Easy-Natural Way Using Only 12 Hand Tools & the Woods Around You. (Illus.). 160p. 1974. 8.95 o.s.i. (ISBN 0-02-557440-X). Macmillan.

Hunt, W. F., jt. auth. see Kraus, Edward H.

Hunt-Wesson Kitchens. The Cooking Lite Feeling Right Cookbook. 1980. 2.99 (ISBN 0-671-41778-9, Fireside). S&S.

Hunt, William R. North of 53 Degrees: The Wild Days of the Alaska-Yukon Mining Frontier 1870-1914. LC 74-12404. (Illus.). 416p. 1975. 12.95 o.s.i. (ISBN 0-02-557510-4). Macmillan.

--To Stand at the Pole: The Dr. Cook-Admiral Peary North Pole Controversy. LC 80-6156. 272p. 1981. 14.95 (ISBN 0-8128-2773-2). Stein & Day.

Hunte, George. The Bahamas. 1974. 24.00 (ISBN 0-7134-2992-5, Pub. by Batsford England). David & Charles.

--Barbados. (Batsford Countries Ser). Date not set. 9.95 (ISBN 0-8038-0755-4). Hastings.

Hunter & Jacobus. Modern Art from Post Impressionisms to the Present. LC 76-14611. (Illus.). 1977. 45.00 o.p. (ISBN 0-8109-1616-9). Abrams.

Hunter, A. M. Christ & the Kingdom: What Scripture Says About Living in the Kingdom of God. 120p. 1980. pap. 3.95 (ISBN 0-89283-092-1). Servant.

Hunter, Alan. Gently in the Highlands. LC 74-18254. 174p. 1975. 5.95 o.s.i. (ISBN 0-02-557550-3, 55755). Macmillan.

--Gently Through the Woods. LC 75-15852. 191p. 1975. Repr. 5.95 o.s.i. (ISBN 0-02-557560-0, 55756). Macmillan.

--Gently with the Innocents. 183p. 1974. 5.95 o.s.i. (ISBN 0-02-557530-9). Macmillan.

--Gently with the Ladies. LC 74-477. 186p. 1974. 5.95 o.s.i. (ISBN 0-02-557540-6). Macmillan.

--Gently with the Painters. LC 75-43639. 208p. 1976. 6.95 o.s.i. (ISBN 0-02-557570-8, 55757). Macmillan.

--The Honfleur Decision. 1981. 9.95 (ISBN 0-8027-5437-6). Walker & Co.

--Landed Gently. (Illus.). 1976. 6.95 o.s.i. (ISBN 0-02-557580-5). Macmillan.

Hunter, Albert S., ed. Advances in Agronomy: Vol. 32, Cumulative Index for Volumes 1-30. 1980. 18.50 (ISBN 0-12-000732-0); lib ed. 24.00 (ISBN 0-12-000784-3); microfiche ed. 13.00 (ISBN 0-12-000785-1). Acad Pr.

Hunter, Archibald M. Jesus, Lord & Savior. 1978. pap. 3.95 o.p. (ISBN 0-8028-1755-6). Eerdmans.

Hunter, Beatrice T. Beatrice Trum Hunter's Whole-Grain Baking Sampler. LC 74-190457. 320p. 1974. pap. 2.25 (ISBN 0-87983-078-6). Keats.

--How Safe Is the Food in Your Kitchen. 96p. 1981. 5.95 (ISBN 0-684-16752-2, ScribT). Scribner.

--The Mirage of Safety: Food Additives & Federal Policy. LC 75-20299. 192p. 1976. 9.95 o.p. (ISBN 0-684-14426-3, ScribJ). Scribner.

--The Natural Foods Cookbook. 1972. pap. 2.75 o.p. (ISBN 0-515-05691-X, V2850). Jove Pubns.

Hunter, C. Bruce. A Guide to Ancient Maya Ruins. LC 74-5956. (Illus.). 300p. 1974. 14.95 (ISBN 0-8061-1214-X); pap. 6.95 (ISBN 0-8061-1215-8). U of Okla Pr.

Hunter, Catherine A. The Square Meal Cookbook. 206p. (Orig.). 1980. pap. write for info. Ref Guides.

Hunter, Charles. The Book Book. 1979. wire coil bdg. 4.50 (ISBN 0-88252-082-2). Paladin Hse.

--Follow Me! 1975. pap. 1.95 (ISBN 0-917726-35-9). Hunter Bks.

Hunter, Charles & Hunter, Frances. Angels on Assignment. 1979. pap. 3.50 (ISBN 0-917726-33-2). Hunter Bks.

--Nuggets of Truth. 1975. pap. 1.95 (ISBN 0-917726-01-4). Hunter Bks.

--The Two Sides of a Coin. 1973. pap. 1.95 (ISBN 0-917726-36-7). Hunter Bks.

Hunter, Charles, jt. auth. see Hunter, Frances.

Hunter, Christine. Gladys Aylward. 1970. pap. 1.95 (ISBN 0-8024-2986-6). Moody.

Hunter, Claud, jt. auth. see Weathers, Thomas.

Hunter, Claud, jt. auth. see Weathers, Tom.

Hunter, Dard. Paper Making in Pioneer America. LC 78-74388. (Nineteenth Century Book Arts & Printing History Ser.: Vol. 3). 1980. lib. bdg. 22.00 (ISBN 0-8240-3877-0). Garland Pub.

Hunter, David M. Supervisory Management: Skill Building Techniques. 300p. 1981. text ed. 16.95 (ISBN 0-8359-7155-4); pap. text ed. 12.95 (ISBN 0-8359-7156-2); instr's. manual free (ISBN 0-8359-7157-0). Reston.

Hunter, Don & Dahinden, Rene. Sasquatch. 208p. (RL 9). Date not set. pap. 1.95 (ISBN 0-451-09186-8, J9186, Sig). NAL.

Hunter, Edgar H., jt. auth. see Hunter, Margaret K.

Hunter, Edna & Nice, Stephen D. Military Families: Adaptation to Change. LC 78-13067. (Praeger Special Studies). 1978. 27.95 (ISBN 0-03-043106-9). Praeger.

Hunter, Edwin R. Shakespeare & Commun Sense. 1954. 4.00 o.p. (ISBN 0-8158-0119-X). Chris Mass.

Hunter, Elena Mellado De see Mellado De Hunter, Elena.

Hunter, Elizabeth. Bride of the Sun. 192p. (Orig.). 1980. pap. 1.50 (ISBN 0-671-57051-X). S&S.

--The Lion's Shadow. (Silhouette Ser.: No. 18). pap. 1.50 (ISBN 0-686-68327-7). PB.

--The Lion's Shadow. 192p. (Orig.). 1980. pap. 1.50 (ISBN 0-671-57018-8). S&S.

--A Touch of Magic. 192p. 1981. pap. 1.50 (ISBN 0-671-57065-X). S&S.

Hunter, Emily. Como Ser Encantadora (Para Alumna) Mendoza De Mann, Wilma & Mariotti, F. A., trs. Orig. Title: Christian Charm Notebook. (Illus.). 56p. (Span.). Date not set. pap. price not set (ISBN 0-311-46054-2). Casa Bautista.

Hunter, Eric J. & Fox, Nicholas J. Examples Illustrating AACR2. 192p. 1980. pap. 12.50 (ISBN 0-8389-3249-5). ALA.

Hunter, Evan. The Blackboard Jungle. LC 73-183139. 320p. 1971. Repr. of 1954 ed. lib. bdg. 12.50x (ISBN 0-8376-0404-4). Bentley.

--The Chisholms: A Novel of the Journey West. LC 75-25086. 288p. (YA) 1976. 8.95 o.s.i. (ISBN 0-06-012013-4, HarpT). Har-Row.

Hunter, F. M. Account of the British Settlement of Aden in Arabia. 232p. 1968. 28.50x (ISBN 0-7146-1986-8, F Cass Co). Biblio Dist.

Hunter, Floyd. Community Power Succession. LC 79-305. 220p. 1980. 15.00x o.p. (ISBN 0-8078-1314-1); pap. 9.00x o.p. (ISBN 0-8078-4067-X). U of NC Pr.

--Community Power Succession: Atlanta's Policy Makers Revisited. 220p. 1980. 15.00x (ISBN 0-8078-1314-1); pap. 9.00x (ISBN 0-8078-4067-X). U of NC Pr.

Hunter, Frances. Come Alive. 1975. pap. 2.95 (ISBN 0-917726-34-0). Hunter Bks.

--A Confession a Day Keeps the Devil Away. 1980. pap. 3.95 (ISBN 0-917726-37-5). Hunter Bks.

--Hot Line to Heaven. 1978. pap. 1.95 (ISBN 0-87162-117-7). Hunter Bks.

--Skinnie Minnie Recipe Book. 1976. pap. 2.95 (ISBN 0-917726-06-5). Hunter Bks.

Hunter, Frances & Hunter, Charles. Since Jesus Passed by. 1973. pap. 1.95 (ISBN 0-917726-38-3). Hunter Bks.

Hunter, Frances, jt. auth. see Hunter, Charles.

Hunter, Frances G. P.T.L.A. 1972. pap. 1.25 o.s.i. (ISBN 0-89129-074-5). Jove Pubns.

Hunter, G. K. Lyle. Incl. Peele. Hunter, G. K. pap. 2.95 (ISBN 0-8277-6206-2, WTW206). British Bk Ctr.

--Paradise Lost. (Unwin Critical Library). 232p. 1980. text ed. 15.95x (ISBN 0-04-800004-3, 2384). Allen Unwin.

Hunter, G. K., ed. see Marston, John.

Hunter, Geoffrey. Metalogic: An Introduction to the Metatheory of Standard First Order Logic. LC 71-131195. 1971. 18.50x (ISBN 0-520-01822-2); pap. 6.95x (ISBN 0-520-02356-0). U of Cal Pr.

Hunter, Gladys H. Assignment: Tokyo. 234p. (Orig.). 1980. 9.95 (ISBN 0-931290-33-3). Nettleton Hse.

Hunter, Graham M. Solar Heating for the Home. LC 79-52372. (Illus.). 1979. 11.95 (ISBN 0-7153-7726-4). David & Charles.

Hunter, Guy, et al, eds. Policy & Practice in Rural Development. LC 76-15078. 526p. text ed. 19.50 (ISBN 0-86598-002-0). Allanheld.

Hunter, Hilda. Grammar of Music. (Student's Music Library Ser). 1952. 6.95 (ISBN 0-234-77208-5). Dufour.

Hunter, Holland, ed. The Future of the Soviet Economy: 1978-1985. (Westview Special Studies on the Soviet Union & Eastern Europe Ser.). 1978. lib. bdg. 22.50x (ISBN 0-89158-097-2). Westview.

Hunter, Ian. Malcolm Muggeridge: A Life. 1980. 13.95 (ISBN 0-8407-4084-0). Nelson.

--Reflections of a Rock Star. LC 75-45514. (Illus.). 196p. (Orig.). 1976. pap. 3.95 o.p. (ISBN 0-8256-3905-0, Quick Fox). Music Sales.

Hunter, J. Paul, ed. Norton Introduction to Literature: Poetry. 600p. 1973. pap. text ed. 10.95x (ISBN 0-393-09380-8); teachers guide to poetry 1.25x (ISBN 0-393-09333-6). Norton.

Hunter, James. Coping with Uncertainty Policy & Politics in the National Health Service. 320p. 1981. write for info. (ISBN 0-471-27906-4, Pub. by Wiley-Interscience). Wiley.

Hunter, James M., et al. Rehabilitation of the Hand. LC 78-59659. 1978. text ed. 74.50 (ISBN 0-8016-2317-0). Mosby.

Hunter, Jim. Modern Poets Five. 160p. 1981. pap. 8.95 (ISBN 0-571-11567-5, Pub. by Faber & Faber). Merrimack Bk Serv.

Hunter, Jim, ed. Modern Poetry Four. 2nd ed. 1979. 5.95 o.p. (ISBN 0-571-08862-7, Pub. by Faber & Faber); pap. 4.95 (ISBN 0-571-04977-X). Merrimack Bk Serv.

Hunter, John. Limiting God. 160p. 1972. pap. 2.95 (ISBN 0-310-26462-6). Zondervan.

--Milton's Samson Agonistes & Lycidas. 92p. 1980. Repr. of 1872 ed. text ed. 17.50 (ISBN 0-8492-5271-7). R West.

Hunter, John, jt. auth. see Pace, David.

Hunter, John D. Manners & Customs of Several Indian Tribes Located West of the Mississippi... to Which Is Prefixed the History of the Author's Life During a Residence of Several Years Among Them. LC 75-7061. (Indian Captivities Ser.: Vol. 39). 1976. Repr. of 1823 ed. lib. bdg. 44.00 (ISBN 0-8240-1663-7). Garland Pub.

Hunter, John M. & Foley, James W. Economic Problems of Latin America. 1975. text ed. 20.95 (ISBN 0-395-18941-1). HM.

Hunter, John M. see Knowles, Nathaniel.

Hunter, Julius. Absurd Alphabedtime Stories. (Illus.). (gr. k-4). 1976. 1.50 (ISBN 0-8272-0012-9). Bethany Pr.

Hunter, Julius & Gross, Lynne S. Broadcast News: The Inside Out. LC 79-2441. (Illus.). 1980. 14.95 (ISBN 0-8016-2319-7). Mosby.

Hunter, Kristin. The Lakestown Rebellion. LC 78-1085. 1978. 8.95 o.p. (ISBN 0-684-15572-9, ScribT). Scribner.

--Soul Brothers & Sister Lou. (YA) (gr. 7 up). 1975. pap. 1.50 (ISBN 0-380-00686-3, 42143). Avon.

Hunter, L. The Production & Properties of Staple-Fibre Yarns Made by Recently Developed Techniques. 168p. 1978. 70.00x (ISBN 0-686-27733-3). State Mutual Bk.

Hunter, Linell P. Eating What Comes Naturally: A Guide to Vegetarian Restaurants in New York City. (Illus.). 130p. (Orig.). 1980. pap. 4.95 (ISBN 0-934700-00-1). Old Mill.

Hunter, Margaret K. & Hunter, Edgar H. The Indoor Garden: Design, Construction & Furnishing. LC 77-20942. 1978. 24.50 (ISBN 0-471-03016-3, Pub. by Wiley-Interscience). Wiley.

Hunter, Mary Vann see Vann Hunter, Mary.

Hunter, Merrily F., jt. auth. see Suitor, Carol W.

Hunter, Michael. Science & Society in Restoration England. LC 80-41071. 224p. Date not set. 37.50 (ISBN 0-521-22866-2); pap. 12.95 (ISBN 0-521-29685-4). Cambridge U Pr.

Hunter, Monica. Reaction to Conquest: Effects of Contact with Europeans on the Pondo of South Africa. abr. ed. (Illus.). 439p. 1979. pap. 14.00x (ISBN 0-8476-3112-5). Rowman.

Hunter, Norman. The Wizard Book of Magic. LC 78-52333. (gr. 4-8). 1978. 6.95 (ISBN 0-8069-4586-9); PLB 6.69 (ISBN 0-8069-4587-7). Sterling.

Hunter, Peter. General Microbiology: The Students' Textbook. LC 76-28532. (Illus.). 500p. 1977. pap. text ed. 12.50 (ISBN 0-8016-2313-8). Mosby.

Hunter, R. H. & Brown, T. C. Battle Coast: An Illustrated History of D-Day. (Illus.). 142p. 1974. 14.50 (ISBN 0-902875-24-8). Transatlantic.

Hunter, Rich, jt. auth. see Broccoletti, Pete.

Hunter, Richard J., Jr. Not-for-Profit Business: Readings, Legal Documents & Commentary. 273p. 1980. pap. text ed. 12.95 (ISBN 0-89651-509-5). Icarus.

Hunter, Richard S. The Measurement of Appearance. LC 75-20429. 348p. 1975. 31.50 (ISBN 0-471-42141-3, Pub. by Wiley-Interscience). Wiley.

Hunter, Rob, jt. auth. see Brown, Terry.

Hunter, Robert E. & Overseas Development Council Staff. The United States & the Developing World: Agenda for Action, 1973. LC 73-76292. (Agenda Ser.). 172p. 1973. pap. 2.50 (ISBN 0-686-28671-5). Overseas Dev Council.

Hunter, Robert G. Shakespeare & the Comedy of Forgiveness. LC 65-15096. 1965. 17.50x (ISBN 0-231-02757-5). Columbia U Pr.

--Shakespeare & the Mystery of God's Judgments. LC 75-11449. 208p. 1976. 12.50x (ISBN 0-8203-0388-7). U of Ga Pr.

Hunter, Robert S. Federal Trial Handbook. LC 74-15928. 1974. 50.00 (ISBN 0-686-14509-7). Lawyers Co-Op.

--Invitation to Flying. (Illus.). 1978. 12.95 (ISBN 0-87165-032-0, Flying-Zd). Ziff-Davis Pub.

Hunter, Rodello. Wyoming Wife. (YA) 1969. 7.95 o.p. (ISBN 0-394-45290-9). Knopf.

Hunter, S. C. Mechanics of Continuous Media. LC 76-7923. (Mathematics & Its Applications Ser.). 567p. 1977. text ed. 66.95 (ISBN 0-470-15092-0). Halsted Pr.

--Mechanics of Continuous Media Paper. 567p. 1980. pap. 34.00 (ISBN 0-470-27015-2, Pub. by Halsted Pr). Wiley.

Hunter, S. H., jt. ed. see Levandowsky, M.

Hunter, S. Leslie. The Scottish Educational System. 2nd rev. ed. 296p. 1972. text ed. 17.25 (ISBN 0-08-016667-9); pap. text ed. 7.75 (ISBN 0-08-016668-7). Pergamon.

Hunter, Sam. Larry Rivers. LC 69-12483. (Contemporary Art & Artists Ser). (Illus.). 1969. 65.00 o.p. (ISBN 0-8109-0451-9). Abrams.

--Masters of 20th Century Art. LC 79-56348. (Illus.). 106p. 1980. pap. 14.95 (ISBN 0-89659-088-7). Abbeville Pr.

--Rivers. (Abrams-Meridian Modern Painters Ser). (Illus.). pap. 3.95 o.p. (ISBN 0-452-00357-1, FM357, Mer). NAL.

--Twentieth Century Painting. (Abbeville Library of Art: No. 8). (Illus.). 112p. 1980. pap. 4.95 (ISBN 0-89659-123-9). Abbeville Pr.

Hunter, Sam & Jacobus, John. American Art of the Twentieth Century. (Illus.). 580p. 1974. text ed. 20.95 (ISBN 0-13-024075-3). P-H.

Hunter, Stephen. The Master Sniper. 304p. 1981. pap. 2.95 (ISBN 0-425-04800-4). Berkley Pub.

Hunter, Susan. A Family Guide to Amusement Centers: From Disneyland to Jungle Habitat. (Illus.). 1975. 9.95 o.s.i. (ISBN 0-8027-0451-4); pap. 5.95 (ISBN 0-8027-7092-4). Walker & Co.

Hunter, Tim, jt. auth. see Haas, Charlie.

Hunter, W. F. & La Follette, P. Learning Skills Series: Arithmetic. 1969. 5.20 o.p. (ISBN 0-07-031314-8, W); 7.68x o.p. (ISBN 0-07-031315-6). McGraw.

Hunter, W. F., et al. Acquiring Arithmetic Skills. 2nd ed. (gr. 8-12). 1976. 5.80 (ISBN 0-07-031321-0, W); tchr's manual 6.64 (ISBN 0-07-031325-3). McGraw.

--Building Arithmetic Skills. 2nd ed. (gr. 8-12). 1976. 5.60 (ISBN 0-07-031322-9, W); tchr's manual 6.64 (ISBN 0-07-031325-3). McGraw.

--Directing Arithmetic Skills. 2nd ed. (gr. 8-12). 1976. 5.60 (ISBN 0-07-031324-5, W); tchr's manual 6.64 (ISBN 0-07-031325-3). McGraw.

Hunter, W. J. & Smeets, G. P., eds. The Evaluation of Toxicological Data for the Protection of Public Health: Proceedings of an International Colloquium, Luxemburg, 1976. 1977. pap. text ed. 57.00 (ISBN 0-08-021998-5). Pergamon.

Hunter, William. CMOS Databook. (Illus.). 1978. 9.95 (ISBN 0-8306-7984-7); pap. 8.95 (ISBN 0-8306-6984-1, 984). TAB Bks.

--Digital-Logic Electronics Handbook. LC 75-29681. (Illus.). 308p. 1975. 9.95 o.p. (ISBN 0-8306-5774-6); pap. 6.95 (ISBN 0-8306-4774-0, 774). TAB Bks.

--Master Handbook of Digital Logic Applications. LC 76-24788. (Illus.). 1976. 12.95 o.p. (ISBN 0-8306-6874-8); pap. 7.95 (ISBN 0-8306-5874-2). TAB Bks.

Hunter, William F., et al. Continuing Language Skills. (Learning Skills Ser: Language Arts). (Illus.). 1978. pap. text ed. 4.52 (ISBN 0-07-031333-4, W); tchr's manual 6.32 (ISBN 0-07-031335-0). McGraw.

--Directing Language Skills. (Learning Skill Ser: Lanugage Arts). (Illus.). 1978. pap. text ed. 4.52 (ISBN 0-07-031334-2, W); tchr's manual 6.32 (ISBN 0-07-031335-0). McGraw.

--Building Language Skills. (Learning Skills Ser: Language Arts). (Illus.). (gr. 7-12). 1978. pap. text ed. 4.92 (ISBN 0-07-031332-6, W); tchr's manual 6.32 (ISBN 0-07-031335-0). McGraw.

Hunter, William W. Statistical Account of Assam, 2 vols. new ed. LC 75-903409. 1975. Repr. Set. 37.50x o.p. (ISBN 0-88386-078-3). South Asia Bks.

Hunting, Constance, ed. see Sarton, May.

Hunting, Constance, ed. see Slade, Ruth.

Hunting, Constance, ed. see Young, Douglas.

Hunting Magazine Eds., ed. Hunting Annual 1981. (Illus.). 320p. 1980. pap. 6.95 (ISBN 0-8227-3016-2). Petersen Pub.

Hunting, Robert. Jonathan Swift. (English Authors Ser.: No. 42). 1966. lib. bdg. 10.95 (ISBN 0-8057-1520-7). Twayne.

Hunting, Warren B. The Obligation of Contracts Clause of the United States Constitution. LC 75-31433. (Johns Hopkins Univ Studies in Hist & Pol. Science, Ser.: No. 37, Pt.4). 1976. Repr. of 1919 ed. lib. bdg. 13.75x (ISBN 0-8371-8524-6, HUOC). Greenwood.

Huntingford, Peter J., et al, eds. Perinatal Medicine. 1970. 32.00 (ISBN 0-12-362550-5). Acad Pr.

Huntington, Ellsworth. Season of Birth: Its Relation to Human Abilities. 1938. 27.50 (ISBN 0-686-51307-X). Elliots Bks.

Huntington, Gale. Vineyard Tales. LC 80-52793. 250p. (Orig.). (gr. 1-6). 1980. pap. 7.95 (ISBN 0-932384-13-7). Tashmoo.

Huntington, J. F., tr. see Jouvenel, Bertrand de.

Huntington, R. & Metcalf, P. Celebrations of Death. LC 79-478. (Illus.). 1979. 27.50 (ISBN 0-521-22531-0); pap. 7.95x (ISBN 0-521-29540-8). Cambridge U Pr.

Huntington, Samuel P. Common Defense: Strategic Programs in National Politics. LC 61-18197. 1961. 22.50x (ISBN 0-231-02518-1); pap. 7.50x (ISBN 0-231-08566-4). Columbia U Pr.

--Soldier & the State: The Theory & Politics of Civil Military Relations. LC 57-6349. 1957. 25.00x (ISBN 0-674-81735-4, Belknap Pr). Harvard U Pr.

Huntington, Samuel P., ed. Changing Patterns of Military Politics. LC 61-18255. 1962. 9.95 o.s.i. (ISBN 0-02-915530-4). Free Pr.

Huntington, Whitney C. & Mickadeit, Robert E. Building Construction: Materials & Types of Construction. 5th ed. LC 79-24467. 1981. text ed. 19.95 (ISBN 0-471-05354-6). Wiley.

Huntley, Frank L. Essays in Persuasion: On Seventeenth-Century English Literature. LC 80-14477. 1981. 14.00x (ISBN 0-226-36088-1). U of Chicago Pr.

Huntley, H. E. Divine Proportion: A Study in Mathematical Beauty. LC 70-93195. (Orig.). 1970. pap. text ed. 3.00 (ISBN 0-486-22254-3). Dover.

Hunton, Richard E. Formula for Fitness. 1973. pap. 1.95 o.p. (ISBN 0-8054-5218-4). Broadman.

Huntoon, Maxwell C., Jr. PUD: A Better Way for the Suburbs. LC 70-18755. (Special Report Ser.). (Illus.). 1971. pap. 9.75 (ISBN 0-87420-909-9). Urban Land.

Huntsberger & Billingsley. Elements of Statistical Inference. 5th ed. 416p. 1981. text ed. 15.95 (ISBN 0-205-07305-0, 5673054); free tchr's ed. (ISBN 0-205-07306-9); free student's guide (ISBN 0-205-07307-7). Allyn.

Huntsberger, et al. Statistical Inference for Management & Economics. 2nd ed. 640p. 1980. text ed. 18.95 (ISBN 0-205-06803-0, 1068032). Allyn.

Huntsberger, David V. & Billingsley, Patrick. Elements of Statistical Inference. 4th ed. 1977. text ed. 18.95x (ISBN 0-205-05734-9); instructors manual avail. (ISBN 0-205-05735-7); student supplement 6.95 (ISBN 0-205-05736-5). Allyn.

Huntsberger, David V., jt. auth. see Lynch, D.

Huntsberger, David V., et al. Statistical Inference for Management & Economics. 1975. text ed. 15.95x o.p. (ISBN 0-205-04654-1, 1646540); instr's manual free o.p. (ISBN 0-205-04655-X, 1646559); sol. manual 2.95 o.p. (ISBN 0-205-04748-3, 1647482). Allyn.

Huntsinger, Dave, jt. auth. see Rambo, Dottie.

Huntsman, Ann & Binger, Jane. Communicating Effectively. LC 80-83694. (Management Anthology Ser.). 200p. 1981. pap. text ed. 10.95 (ISBN 0-913654-67-1). Nursing Res.

Hupka, Robert, jt. auth. see Antek, Samuel.

Huq, Muhammad S. Education, Manpower, & Development in South & Southeast Asia. LC 74-19336. (Special Studies). (Illus.). 240p. 1975. 18.95 (ISBN 0-275-09120-1). Praeger.

Huray, P. Le see Le Huray, P.

Huray, Peter Le see Le Huray, Peter & Day, James.

Huray, Peter Le see Le Huray, Peter, et al.

Hurd, C. M. Electrons in Metals. LC 80-11429. 344p. 1980. Repr. of 1975 ed. lib. bdg. write for info. (ISBN 0-89874-157-2). Krieger.

Hurd, Colin M. The Hall Effect in Metals & Alloys. LC 76-157936. (International Cryogenics Monographs). 400p. 1972. 39.50 (ISBN 0-306-30530-5, Plenum Pr). Plenum Pub.

Hurd, David. Home to My Island. (Illus.). 192p. 1981. 9.50 (ISBN 0-682-49727-4). Exposition.

Hurd, Florence. Shadows of the Heart. 400p. 1980. pap. 2.50 (ISBN 0-380-76406-7, 76406). Avon.

--Voyage of the Secret Duchess. (Orig.). 1975. pap. 0.95 o.s.i. (ISBN 0-380-00353-8, 24554). Avon.

Hurd, Frank J. & Hurd, Rosalie. Ten Talents Cookbook: Vegetarian Natural Foods. 1968. 9.95 (ISBN 0-9603532-0-8). Ten Talents.

Hurd, Geoffrey. Human Societies: An Introduction to Sociology. 228p. 1973. cased 18.50x (ISBN 0-7100-7611-8); pap. 8.95 (ISBN 0-7100-7612-6). Routledge & Kegan.

Hurd, John. Pyramid. 1977. 3.00 (ISBN 0-918116-05-8). Jawbone Pr.

Hurd, M. K. Formwork for Concrete. 1979. 39.25 (ISBN 0-685-85098-6, SP-4) (ISBN 0-685-85099-4). ACI.

Hurd, P. D., Jr. & Moure, J. S. A Classification of the Large Carpenter Bees (Hylocopini) (Hymenoptera: Apoidea) (U. C. Publ. in Entomology: Vol. 29). 1963. pap. 12.00x (ISBN 0-520-09096-9). U of Cal Pr.

Hurd, Paul D., Jr. & Linsley, E. Gorton. A Classification of the Squash & Gourd Bees Peponapis & Xenoglossa (Hymenoptera: Apoidea) (U. C. Publ. in Entomology: Vol. 62). 1970. pap. 6.00x (ISBN 0-520-09356-9). U of Cal Pr.

Hurd, Peter. Sketch Book. LC 70-150951. (Illus.). 121p. 1971. 45.00 (ISBN 0-8040-0531-1, SB). Swallow.

Hurd, Rollin Carlos. A Treatise on the Right of Personal Liberty & on Writ of Habeas Corpus. LC 77-37767. (American Constitutional & Legal History Ser). 670p. 1972. Repr. of 1876 ed. lib. bdg. 59.50 (ISBN 0-306-70431-5). Da Capo.

Hurd, Rosalie, jt. auth. see Hurd, Frank J.

Hurd, Thacher. The Old Chair. LC 77-1581. (Illus.). (gr. k-3). 1978. 5.95 (ISBN 0-688-80104-8); PLB 5.71 (ISBN 0-688-84104-X). Greenwillow.

--The Quiet Evening. LC 78-2797. (Illus.). (gr. k-3). 1978. 6.95 (ISBN 0-688-80166-8); PLB 6.67 (ISBN 0-688-84166-X). Greenwillow.

Hurdy, John M., ed. see Cooper, James F.

Hureau, Jean. Mecca Today. (J. A. Editions: Today Ser.). (Illus.). 240p. 1980. cancelled (ISBN 0-88254-538-8, Pub. by J. A. Editions France). Hippocrene Bks.

Hurford, J. R. The Linguistic Theory of Numerals. LC 74-25652. (Studies in Linguistics: No. 16). 260p. 1975. 42.50 (ISBN 0-521-20735-5). Cambridge U Pr.

Hurh, Won M. & Kim, Hei C. Assimilation Patterns of Immigrants in the United States: A Case Study of Korean Immigrants in the Chicago Area. LC 78-59860. (Illus.). 1978. pap. text ed. 7.75 (ISBN 0-8191-0553-8). U Pr of Amer.

Hurlburt, Delpha. Spelling: Syllabus. 2nd ed. (gr. 7-12). 1980. pap. text ed. 6.95 student syllabus (ISBN 0-89420-053-4, 187898); cassette recordings 133.40 (ISBN 0-89420-185-9, 187900). Natl Book.

Hurlbut, C. S., jt. auth. see Dana, E. S.

Hurlbut, Cornelius, Jr. Minerals & Man. (Illus.). 1975. 20.00 o.p. (ISBN 0-394-43625-3). Random.

Hurlbut, Cornelius S., Jr. & Klein, Cornelis. Manual of Mineralogy After J. D. Dana. 19th ed. LC 77-1131. 1977. 27.95 (ISBN 0-471-42226-6). Wiley.

Hurlbut, Cornelius S., Jr. & Switzer, George S. Geomology. LC 78-13262. 1979. 25.50 (ISBN 0-471-42224-X, Pub. by Wiley-Interscience). Wiley.

Hurlbut, Hermine, ed. see Kulvinskas, Viktoras.

Hurlbut, Jesse L. Hurlbut's Story of the Bible. pap. 1.95 o.s.i. (ISBN 0-89129-116-4). Jove Pubns.

--Story of the Christian Church. rev. ed. 1970. 8.95 (ISBN 0-310-26510-X). Zondervan.

Hurlbut, Lyman & Flower, J. R. History of the Christian Church. 1979. 3.35 (ISBN 0-8297-0575-9); pap. 2.35 (ISBN 0-8297-0574-0). Life Pubs Intl.

Hurlbut, Lyman, tr. Historia Da Igraja. (Portuguese Bks.). 1979. write for info. (ISBN 0-8297-0667-4). Life Pubs Intl.

Hurley. Personal Money Management: A Consumer Guide. 1976. 16.95 (ISBN 0-13-657650-8); instr. manual o.p. free (ISBN 0-685-78800-8). P-H.

Hurley, F. Jack. Russell Lee: Photographer. LC 78-61494. 1979. o.p. (ISBN 0-87100-151-9, 2151); pap. 15.95 (ISBN 0-87100-150-0, 2150). Morgan.

Hurley, Frank, jt. auth. see Ponting, Herbert.

Hurley, Jack F. Industry & the Photographic Image: One Hundred & Sixty Five Great Prints from 1845 to the Present. (Illus.). 160p. 1980. pap. 7.95 (ISBN 0-486-23980-2). Dover.

Hurley, James P. & Garrod, Claude. Principles of Physics. LC 77-75475. (Illus.). 1978. text ed. 23.95 (ISBN 0-395-25036-6); sol. manual 0.35 (ISBN 0-395-25037-4). HM.

Hurley, John. Assassination American Style. 209p. (Orig.). 1980. pap. cancelled (ISBN 0-933990-03-0). Canterbury Pr.

Hurley, L. S., tr. see Tuchmann-Duplessis, H., et al.

Hurley, Lucille. Developmental Nutrition. (Illus.). 1979. text ed. 16.95 (ISBN 0-13-207639-X). P-H.

Hurley, Pat. The Magic Bubble. 1978. pap. 3.50 (ISBN 0-88207-181-5). Victor Bks.

--Penetrating the Magic Bubble. 1978. pap. 3.50 (ISBN 0-88207-183-1). Victor Bks.

--The Penetrators. 1978. pap. 3.50 (ISBN 0-88207-184-X). Victor Bks.

Hurley, Patrick M. How Old Is the Earth. LC 59-11599. 1959. pap. 1.45 (ISBN 0-385-09431-0, S5, Anch). Doubleday.

Hurley, Robert, tr. see Clastres, Pierre.

Hurley, William M. Prehistoric Cordage: Identification of Impressions on Pottery. (Manuals on Archaeology Ser.: No. 3). (Illus.). xii, 154p. 1979. 18.00x (ISBN 0-9602822-0-3). Taraxacum.

Hurlimann, Ruth. The Proud White Cat. (Illus.). (ps-3). 1977. 8.25 (ISBN 0-688-22095-9); PLB 7.92 (ISBN 0-688-32095-3). Morrow.

Hurling, Joan. Boomers. LC 78-63640. 1979. 8.95 (ISBN 0-8149-0814-4). Vanguard.

--The Ledger. 256p. 1981. 10.95 (ISBN 0-8149-0847-0). Vanguard.

Hurlington, Vincent J. Great Art Madonnas Classed According to Their Significance As Types of Impressive Motherhood. (The Great Art Masters Library Bk.). (Illus.). 143p. 1981. 37.45 (ISBN 0-930582-97-7). Gloucester Art.

Hurll, Estelle M. Life of Our Lord in Art: With Some Account of the Artistic Treatment of the Life of St. John the Baptist. LC 76-89272. 1969. Repr. of 1898 ed. 18.00 (ISBN 0-8103-3137-3). Gale.

Hurman, Ann. A Charter for Choice: A Study of Options Schemes. (General Ser.). 1979. pap. text ed. 25.00x (ISBN 0-85633-161-9, NFER). Humanities.

Hurme, R. & Pesonen, M. Finnish Deluxe Dictionary: English-Finnish. 2nd ed. 1978. 85.00x (ISBN 9-5100-5699-5, F-565). Vanous.

Hurn, Christopher J. The Limits & Possibilities of Schooling: An Introduction to the Sociology of Education. 1978. text ed. 15.95 (ISBN 0-205-05969-4). Allyn.

Hurn, Russ. Not for the Boys Only. LC 80-51432. 154p. 1980. 8.95 (ISBN 0-533-04695-5). Vantage.

Hurrell, Elaine. The Common Dormouse. (Mammel Society Ser.). (Illus.). 50p. 1980. 6.95 (ISBN 0-7137-0985-5, Pub. by Blandford Pr England). Sterling.

Hurrell, George. The Hurrell Style. Stine, Whitney, ed. LC 76-15396. (John Day Bk.). (Illus.). 1976. 16.95 o.s.i. (ISBN 0-381-98293-9, TYC-T); pap. 9.95 o.s.i. (ISBN 0-381-98299-8, TYC-T). T Y Crowell.

Hurrle, Karl, et al. Technical Dictionary of Vacuum Physics & Vacuum Technology (English, French, German, Russian) 1973. text ed. 37.00 (ISBN 0-08-016957-0). Pergamon.

Hursch, Carolyn J. The Trouble with Rape: A Psychologist's Report on the Legal, Medical, Social, & Psychological Problems. LC 76-28757. (Illus.). 1977. 12.95 (ISBN 0-88229-323-0); pap. 6.95 (ISBN 0-88229-470-9). Nelson-Hall.

Hursch-Cesar, Gerald, jt. auth. see Backstrom, Charles H.

Hursh, Robert D. & Bailey, Henry J. American Law of Products Liability, 6 vols. 2nd ed. LC 73-88585. 1976. 255.00 (ISBN 0-686-14536-4). Lawyers Co-Op.

Hursh-Cesar, Gerald & Roy, Prodipto, eds. Third World Surveys: Survey Research in Developing Countries. 1976. 11.00x o.p. (ISBN 0-333-90099-5). South Asia Bks.

Hurst, A. E. & Goodier, J. M. Painting & Decorating. 620p. 1980. 75.00x (ISBN 0-85264-243-1, Pub. by Griffin England). State Mutual Bk.

Hurst, Charles. The Anatomy of Social Inequality. LC 78-31587. (Illus.). 1979. text ed. 16.95 (ISBN 0-8016-2314-6). Mosby.

Hurst, D. V., tr. E Ele Concedeu Uns Para Mestres. (Portuguese Bks.). 1979. 2.35 (ISBN 0-8297-0838-3). Life Pubs Intl.

Hurst, G. Cameron. Insei: Abdicated Sovereigns in the Politics of Late Heian Japan, 1086-1185. 368p. 1976. 22.50x (ISBN 0-231-03932-8). Columbia U Pr.

Hurst, G. S. & Turner, J. E. Elementary Radiation Physics. LC 70-949221. 166p. 1970. 15.95 o.p. (ISBN 0-471-42472-2, Pub. by Wiley). Krieger.

--Elementary Radiation Physics. 180p. 1981. Repr. of 1970 ed. text ed. 15.50 (ISBN 0-89874-249-8). Krieger.

Hurst, Hugo. A Search for Meaning in Love, Sex, & Marriage. rev. ed. LC 75-9961. 232p. (gr. 11-12). 1975. pap. text ed. 4.60x (ISBN 0-88489-063-5); tchr's ed. 2.60x (ISBN 0-88489-119-4). St. Marys.

Hurst, J. Willard. Law & the Conditions of Freedom in the Nineteenth-Century United States. 1956. pap. 5.45 (ISBN 0-299-01363-4). U of Wis Pr.

Hurst, J. Willis. The Heart. (Update Ser.: No. 5). (Illus.). 352p. 1981. text ed. 30.00 (ISBN 0-07-031495-0, HP). McGraw.

--Update IV: The Heart. (Updates Ser.). (Illus.). 224p. 1980. text ed. 30.00 (ISBN 0-07-031493-4, HP). McGraw.

Hurst, James C., jt. ed. see Morrill, Weston H.

Hurst, James W. Law & Social Process in United States History. LC 74-173669. (American Constitutional & Legal History Ser.). 359p. 1971. Repr. of 1960 ed. lib. bdg. 35.00 (ISBN 0-306-70409-9). Da Capo.

Hurst, Joseph, jt. auth. see Massialas, Byron G.

Hurst, M. Dale, ed. see Cohen, David.

Hurst, Michael C. Maria Edgeworth & the Public Scene. LC 70-88024. 1969. 10.95x o.p. (ISBN 0-87024-135-4). U of Miami Pr.

Hurst, Richard M. Republic Studios: Between Poverty Row & the Majors. LC 79-19844. 1979. 14.50 (ISBN 0-8108-1254-1). Scarecrow.

Hurst, Ronald, ed. Pilot Error: A Professional Study of Contributory Factors. (Illus.). Date not set. 14.95 o.p. (ISBN 0-258-97072-3, ScribT). Scribner. Postponed.

Hurstfield, Joel. Freedom, Corruption, & Government in Elizabethan England. LC 73-76380. 368p. 1973. pap. text ed. 16.50x (ISBN 0-674-31925-7). Harvard U Pr.

--The Historian As Moralist: Reflections on the Study of Tudor England. (John Coffin Memorial Lectures 1974 Ser.). 37p. 1975. pap. text ed. 2.50x (ISBN 0-485-16209-1, Athlone Pr). Humanities.

--The Illusion of Power in Tudor Politics. (Creighton Lectures in History 1978 Ser.). (Orig.). 1979. pap. text ed. 4.75x (ISBN 0-485-14123-X, Athlone Pr). Humanities.

Hurstfield, Joel, ed. see Brock, Michael.

Hurston, Zora N. Jonah's Gourd Vine. LC 70-166496. 1971. 5.95 o.p. (ISBN 0-397-00754-X); pap. 2.95 o.p. (ISBN 0-397-00723-X, LP-45). Lippincott.

--Tell My Horse. (New World Writing Ser). (Illus.). 296p. 1981. 17.95 (ISBN 0-913666-31-9); pap. 8.95 (ISBN 0-913666-31-9). Turtle Isl Foun.

Hurt, H. R., Jr. Aerodynamics for Naval Aviators. 2nd ed. (Pilot Training Ser.). (Illus.). 416p. 1975. pap. 9.95 (ISBN 0-89100-182-4, E*A-182-4). Aviation Maintenance.

Hurt, H. Thomas, et al. Communication in the Classroom. LC 77-73960. (Education Ser.). (Illus.). 1978. pap. text ed. 7.95 (ISBN 0-201-03048-9). A-W.

Hurt, Harry, III. Texas Rich: The Hunt Dynasty from the Early Oil Days Through the Silver Crash. 1981. 16.95 (ISBN 0-393-01391-X). Norton.

Hurt, J. Focus on Film & Theatre. 1974. pap. 2.95 (ISBN 0-13-314658-8, Spec). P-H.

Hurt, Norman & Hermann, R. Quantum Statistical Mechanics & Lie Group Harmonic Analysis, Pt. A. (Lie Groups; History, Frontiers & Applications: Vol. X). 1980. text ed. 30.00x (ISBN 0-915692-30-9, QC174.8.H87). Math Sci Pr.

Hurt, Peyton. Bibliography & Footnotes: A Style Manual for Students & Writers. 3rd ed. (Illus., Rev. & enl. ed.). 1968. pap. 5.75x (ISBN 0-520-00589-9, CAL150). U of Cal Pr.

Hurt, W. Glenn. Textbook Study Guide of Gynecology. 2nd ed. (Medical Examination Review Book: Vol. 4A). 1976. pap. 8.50 (ISBN 0-87488-152-8). Med Exam.

Hurt, Wesley R. Sioux Indians, Vol. Two: Dakota Sioux Indians. (American Indian Ethnohistory Ser: Plains Indians). (Illus.). lib. bdg. 42.00 (ISBN 0-8240-0795-6). Garland Pub.

Hurt, William C. Current Therapy in Dentistry, Vol. 7. LC 78-31587. (Current Therapy Ser.). 1980. text ed. 47.50 (ISBN 0-8016-1189-X). Mosby.

--Periodontics in General Practice. (American Lectures in Dentistry Ser.). (Illus.). 528p. 1976. 42.75 (ISBN 0-398-03495-8). C C Thomas.

Hurtado, Hernan, jt. auth. see Watson, Diana C.

Hurtado, Larry. Text-Critical Methodology & the Pre-Caesarean Text. 112p. (Orig.). 1981. pap. 13.00 (ISBN 0-8028-1872-2). Eerdmans.

Hurtado, Mario, jt. auth. see Rivera, Francisco P.

Hurtado, Osvaldo. Political Power in Ecuador. Mills, Nick D., Jr., tr. LC 79-56822. (Illus.). 328p. 1980. 25.00x (ISBN 0-8263-0533-4). U of NM Pr.

Hurtekant, Barbara. How to Teach Your Child to Spell: A Guide for Parents. LC 80-24308. 1980. pap. 7.95 (ISBN 0-937838-40-3); tchr's ed. 7.95 (ISBN 0-937838-41-1). Open Roads.

Hurter, Bill. Money-Making Photography. LC 80-81784. (Petersen's Photographic Libray). (Illus.). 160p. (Orig.). (gr. 8-12). pap. 8.95 (ISBN 0-8227-4040-0). Petersen Pub.

Hurtgen, Andre O., jt. auth. see Boucher, John G.

Hurtgen, Andre O., ed. Poemes Pour le Cours Avance Nineteen Eighty to Nineteen Eighty-Three. (Illus.). 65p. (Orig.). 1979. pap. text ed. 4.95x (ISBN 0-88334-117-4). Ind Sch Pr.

Hurtig, Judith W. Armored Gisant Before Fourteen Hundred. LC 78-74368. (Outstanding Dissertations in the Fine Arts, Fourth Ser.). 1979. lib. bdg. 52.00 (ISBN 0-8240-3956-4). Garland Pub.

Hurtik, Emil & Yarber, Robert, eds. Introduction to Short Fiction & Criticism. LC 73-138096. (Orig.). 1971. pap. text ed. 12.95 (ISBN 0-471-00273-9). Wiley.

Hurtt, Jane, et al. Comprehensive Review of Orthoptics & Ocular Motility: Theory, Therapy & Surgery. 2nd ed. LC 77-8830. (Illus.). 1977. 26.50 o.p. (ISBN 0-8016-2316-2). Mosby.

Hurtubise. Solid Surface Luminescence Analysis. 288p. Date not set. 37.50. Dekker.

Hurty, Walter C. & Rubinstein, M. F. Dynamics of Structures. (Illus.). 1964. ref. ed. 27.95 (ISBN 0-13-222075-X). P-H.

Hurvich, Leo M. Color Vision. LC 80-19077. (Illus.). 280p. 1981. text ed. 37.50 (ISBN 0-87893-336-0); pap. text ed. 25.00 (ISBN 0-87893-337-9). Sinauer Assoc.

Hurvitz, Leon, tr. from Chin & Sanskrit. Scripture of the Lotus Blossom of the Fine Dharma. LC 75-45381. 1976. 20.00x (ISBN 0-231-03789-9); pap. 10.00x (ISBN 0-231-03920-4). Columbia U Pr.

Hurwicz, L., jt. ed. see Arrow, K. J.

Hurwitz, Abraham, jt. auth. see Sternlict, Manny.

Hurwitz, Abraham B., et al. More Number Games: Mathematics Made Easy Through Play. LC 74-23849. (Funk & W Bk.). (gr. 5 up). 1976. 9.95 o.s.i. (ISBN 0-308-10255-X, TYC-T). T Y Crowell.

Hurwitz, Al & Madeja, Stanley. The Joyous Vision: A Sourcebook for Elementary Art Appreciation. (Illus.). 320p. 1977. text ed. 16.95 (ISBN 0-13-511600-7). P-H.

Hurwitz, Hohanna. Nora & Brs. Mind Your Own Business. (gr. k-6). Date not set. pap. price not set (ISBN 0-440-45668-1, YB). Dell.

Hurwitz, Johanna. Aldo Ice Cream. LC 80-24371. (Illus.). 128p. (gr. 4-6). 1981. 6.95 (ISBN 0-688-00375-3); PLB 6.67 (ISBN 0-688-00376-1). Morrow.

--Busybody Nora. LC 75-25921. (Illus.). 64p. (gr. 1-5). 1976. PLB 6.00 (ISBN 0-688-32057-0). Morrow.

--The Law of Gravity. LC 77-13656. (Illus.). (gr. 3-7). 1978. 7.50 o.p. (ISBN 0-688-22142-4); PLB 7.63 (ISBN 0-688-32142-9). Morrow.

--Much Ado About Aldo. (Illus.). (gr. 4-6). 1978. 7.95 (ISBN 0-688-22160-2); PLB 7.62 (ISBN 0-688-32160-7). Morrow.

--New Neighbors for Nora. LC 78-12631. (Illus.). (gr. k-3). 1979. 6.50 (ISBN 0-688-22173-4); PLB 6.24 (ISBN 0-688-32173-9). Morrow.

--Nora & Mrs. Mind-Your-Own-Business. (Illus.). (gr. 1-5). 1977. PLB 6.00 (ISBN 0-688-32097-X). Morrow.

--Once I Was a Plum Tree. LC 79-23518. (Illus.). 160p. (gr. 4-6). 1980. 7.50 (ISBN 0-688-22223-4); PLB 7.20 (ISBN 0-688-32223-9). Morrow.

--Superduper Teddy. LC 80-12962. (Illus.). 80p. (gr. k-3). 1980. 6.95 (ISBN 0-688-22234-X); PLB 6.67 (ISBN 0-688-32234-4). Morrow.

Hurwitz, Leon. An Introduction to Political Science. LC 79-11293. (Illus.). 1979. text ed. 16.95 (ISBN 0-88229-321-4); pap. text ed. 8.95 (ISBN 0-88229-677-9). Nelson-Hall.

--The State As Defendant: Governmental Accountability & the Redress of Individual Grievances. LC 80-657. (Contributions in Political Science: No. 51). (Illus.). 224p. 1981. lib. bdg. 27.50 (ISBN 0-313-21257-0, HSD/). Greenwood.

Hurwitz, Leon, ed. Contemporary Perspectives on European Integration: Attitudes, Nongovernmental Behavior & Collective Decision Making. LC 79-6573. (Contributions in Political Science: No. 45). (Illus.). xx, 292p. 1980. lib. bdg. 27.50 (ISBN 0-313-21357-7, HEI/). Greenwood.

Hurwitz, Sidney. Clinical Pediatric Dermatology. (Illus.). 656p. 1980. write for info. (ISBN 0-7216-4872-X). Saunders.

Hurwitz, Stephan & Christiansen, Karl O. Criminology. LC 74-7977. (Illus.). 400p. 1981. 30.00 (ISBN 0-8386-1477-9). Fairleigh Dickinson.

Hurwood & Dipego. Born Innocent. 1975. pap. 1.95 (ISBN 0-441-07122-8). Ace Bks.

Hurwood, Bernhardt. By Blood Alone. 1979. pap. 1.95 (ISBN 0-441-08990-9). Charter Bks.

Hurwood, Bernhardt J. Vampires. (Illus.). 160p. 1981. pap. 7.95 (ISBN 0-8256-3202-1, Quick Fox). Music Sales.

Husain, Javed. What Must Humanity Do? 39p. 1980. 3.95 (ISBN 0-8059-2729-8). Dorrance.

Husain, Majid. Agricultural Geography. (Illus.). 1980. text ed. 17.50x (ISBN 0-391-01931-7). Humanities.

Husain, S. S. Implications in Indian Agriculture. 1980. text ed. write for info. (ISBN 0-391-01836-1). Humanities.

Husain, Taqdir. Introduction to Topological Groups. 230p. 1981. Repr. of 1966 ed. lib. bdg. write for info. (ISBN 0-89874-193-9). Krieger.

Husain, Yusuf, ed. Selected Documents from the Aligarh Archives. 1967. 10.00x o.p. (ISBN 0-210-98101-6). Asia.

Husain, Zakir. Dynamic University. 1965. 5.00x o.p. (ISBN 0-210-27053-5). Asia.

Husaini, Khwaza K. Ma'asir-I-Jahanjiri: A Contemporary Account of Jahangir. Nizami, Azra, ed. & tr. 537p. (Persian & Eng.). 1978. lib. bdg. 35.00x (ISBN 0-210-40566-X). Asia.

Husaini, M. A., tr. see Ruswa, Mirza.

Husar, R. B., et al, eds. see International Symposium, Dubrovnik, Yugoslavia, 7-14 Sept. 1977.

Husband, M. F. Dictionary of the Characters in the Waverley Novels of Sir Walter Scott. 1962. Repr. of 1910 ed. text ed. 15.00x (ISBN 0-391-00626-6). Humanities.

Husband, William H. & Dockeray, James C. Modern Corporation Finance. 7th ed. 1972. text ed. 17.95x (ISBN 0-256-00221-5). Irwin.

Husch, Bertram, et al. Forest Mensuration. 2nd ed. (Illus.). 1972. 21.95 (ISBN 0-8260-4595-2). Wiley.

Huse, Dennis & Watson, Geralyn. Speak Lord, I'm Listening. LC 80-70851. 176p. 1981. pap. 7.95 perfect bnd. (ISBN 0-87793-220-4). Ave Maria.

Huse, Edgar F. The Modern Manager. (Illus.). 1979. text ed. 18.95 (ISBN 0-8299-0197-3); pap. study guide 7.50 (ISBN 0-686-67406-5); study guide 7.50 (ISBN 0-8299-0253-8). instrs.' manual avail. (ISBN 0-8299-0492-1); transparency masters avail. (ISBN 0-8299-0493-X). West Pub.

Huse, Edgar F. & Bowditch, James L. Behavior in Organizations: A Systems Approach to Managing. 2nd ed. LC 76-9329. (Illus.). 1977. text ed. 18.95 (ISBN 0-201-02965-0). A-W.

Huse, Edgar F., jt. auth. see Schuler, Randall S.

Huseboe, Arthur R. Sir John Vanbrugh. (English Authors Ser: No. 191). 1976. lib. bdg. 12.50 (ISBN 0-8057-6665-0). Twayne.

Huseby, Edward, jt. auth. see Hestwood, Diana.

Husek, Jiri, ed. see Equipment Guide-Book Co.

Huseman, Richard B., et al. Business Communication. LC 80-65802. 448p. 1981. text ed. 16.95 (ISBN 0-03-050946-7). Dryden Pr.

--Readings in Business Communication. 1981. pap. text ed. 8.95 (ISBN 0-03-058206-7). Dryden Pr.

Huseman, Richard C., ed. see Academy of Management, 40th Annual Meeting, 1980.

Huseman, Richard C., et al. Readings in Interpersonal & Organizational Communication. 3rd ed. 1977. text ed. 12.95 (ISBN 0-205-05900-7, 485777-1). Allyn.

--Interpersonal Communication in Organizations. 1975. text ed. 15.95 (ISBN 0-205-04897-8, 484897-7). Allyn.

Husen, Torstein. The School in Question: A Comparative Study of School & Its Future in Western Societies. (Illus.). 1979. 22.00x (ISBN 0-19-874085-9); pap. 11.95x (ISBN 0-19-874086-7). Oxford U Pr.

Husen, Torsten, ed. International Study of Achievement in Mathematics, Vol. 1 & 2. (Orig.). 1967. 10.95 ea. o.p. (Pub. by Wiley). Vol. 1, 304 Pgs. Vol. 2, 368 Pgs. Wiley.

Huser, H. J. Atlas of Comparative Primate Hematology. 1970. 54.00 (ISBN 0-12-362750-8). Acad Pr.

Huseyin, K. Vibrations & Stability of Multiple Parameter System. (Mechanics of Elastic Stability: No. 3). 228p. 1978. 37.50x (ISBN 90-286-0136-8). Sijthoff & Noordhoff.

Husford, Bob, jt. auth. see Husford, Sharon.

Husford, Sharon & Husford, Bob. Collector's Encyclopedia of Roseville Pottery. (2nd Ser.). (Illus.). 1980. 19.95 (ISBN 0-89145-139-0). Collector Bks.

Husher, R. W. & Welch, W. W. A Study of Simon Willard's Clocks. LC 80-65021. (Illus.). 292p. 1980. 35.00x (ISBN 0-9603944-0-0). Husher & Welch.

Hu Shiu-Ying. An Enumeration of Chinese Materia Medica. 200p. 1981. 21.50 (ISBN 0-295-95744-1, Pub by Chinese Univ Hong Kong). U of Wash Pr.

Husk, William H. Songs of the Nativity. 205p. 1980. Repr. of 1868 ed. lib. bdg. 17.50 (ISBN 0-8414-2094-7). Folcroft.

Huskey, Hyrum H., Jr. Counseling Skills for Church Leadership. 1980. pap. 5.75 (ISBN 0-8309-0295-3). Herald Hse.

Husmann, Siegfried, ed. see Proceedings, Schlitz, September 1975.

Huss, Barbara, jt. auth. see Lubowe, Irwin I.

Huss, Richard E. Dr. Church's "Hoax". LC 75-44946. (Illus.). 1976. 12.00 (ISBN 0-9605622-0-6). Graphic Crafts.

Huss, Roy & Silverstein, Norman. Film Experience. LC 67-28833. (Illus.). 1968. 8.95 o.p. (ISBN 0-06-032967-X, HarpT). Har-Row.

Hussain, Fakhir, tr. see Sharar, Abdul H.

Hussein, Mahmoud. Class Conflict in Egypt, 1945-1970. Ehrenfeld, Alfred, et al, trs. from Fr. LC 72-81767. (Illus.). 416p. 1973. 13.95 o.p. (ISBN 0-85345-233-4, CL2334). Monthly Rev.

Hussein, Taha. An Egyptian Childhood. (Arab Writers Series). 200p. (Orig.). 1980. 10.00x (ISBN 0-89410-210-9); pap. 5.00x (ISBN 0-89410-211-7). Three Continents.

Husseiny. Icebergs. 350p. Date not set. text ed. price not set (ISBN 0-08-023911-0). Pergamon.

Husseiny, compiled by. Toward a New Strategy for Development. LC 79-9861. 1979. 25.00 (ISBN 0-08-023913-7); pap. 8.95 (ISBN 0-08-023912-9). Pergamon.

Husseiny, A. A., ed. see International Iceberg Utilization Conference, 1st Ames, Iowa.

Husselbee, William. Automatic Transmission Service: A Text-Workbook. (Orig.). 1981. pap. 9.95 (ISBN 0-8359-0266-8). Reston.

Husselbee, William K. Automatic Transmission Fundamentals. (Illus.). 1980. text ed. 17.95 (ISBN 0-8359-0257-9). Reston.

Hussell, C. G. & Laing, A. F. Biological & Psychological Background to Education. 1967. 14.50 (ISBN 0-08-012195-0); pap. 9.75 (ISBN 0-08-012194-2). Pergamon.

Husserl, Edmund. Logical Investigations, 2 vols. Findlay, J. N., tr. (International Library of Philosophy & Scientific Method). 1970. Set. 52.00x (ISBN 0-391-00053-5). Humanities.

--Phenomenology & the Crisis of Philosophy. Lauer, Quentin, tr. (Orig.). pap. 4.95x (ISBN 0-06-131170-7, TB1170, Torch). Har-Row.

--Phenomenology & the Foundations of the Sciences. Klein, Ted & Pohl, William, trs. (Edmund Husserl, Collected Works: Vol. 1). 152p. 1980. lib. bdg. 29.00 (ISBN 90-247-2093-1). Kluwer Boston.

Hussey, Anne. Baddeck & Other Poems. LC 78-9337. (Wesleyan Poetry Program: Vol. 92). 1978. pap. 10.00x (ISBN 0-8195-2092-6, Pub. by Wesleyan U Pr); pap. 4.95 (ISBN 0-8195-1092-0). Columbia U Pr.

Hussey, D. E. Introducing Corporate Planning. 2nd ed. (Pergamon International Library). 1979. 27.00 (ISBN 0-08-022491-1); pap. 17.75 (ISBN 0-08-022485-7). Pergamon.

Hussey, David. Inflation & Business Policy. LC 76-7065. (Business Strategy & Planning Ser.). (Illus.). 1976. text ed. 22.00x (ISBN 0-582-45073-X). Longman.

Hussey, David & Langham, M. J. Corporate Planning: The Human Factor. 1978. text ed. 45.00 (ISBN 0-08-022464-4); pap. text ed. 19.50 (ISBN 0-08-022475-X). Pergamon.

Hussey, David, ed. The Corporate Planners' Yearbook 1978-9. (Illus.). 1979. 36.00 (ISBN 0-08-022255-2). Pergamon.

Hussey, David, jt. ed. see Taylor, Bernard.

Hussey, David E. Corporate Planning: Theory & Practice. LC 73-17304. 400p. 1974. text ed. 37.00 (ISBN 0-08-017748-4). Pergamon.

--Introducing Corporate Planning. 220p. 1976. text ed. 7.15 o.p. (ISBN 0-08-017793-X). Pergamon.

Hussey, David E., ed. The Corporate Planner's Yearbook, 1974. 1974. text ed. 17.05 o.p. (ISBN 0-08-017817-0). Pergamon.

Hussey, Dyneley. Eurydice: Or, the Nature of Opera. LC 80-2283. 1981. Repr. of 1929 ed. 17.50 (ISBN 0-404-18849-4). AMS Pr.

Hussey, Edward. The Presocratics. (Classical Life & Letters Ser.). 1972. 40.50x (ISBN 0-7156-0630-1, 477, Pub. by Duckworth England); pap. 13.50x (ISBN 0-7156-0824-X, 478, Pub. by Duckworth England). Biblio Dist.

Hussey, J. M., tr. see Cabasilas, Nicholas.

Hussey, Lois J. & Pessino, Catherine. Collecting for the City Naturalist. LC 73-17293. (Illus.). 96p. (gr. 5 up). 1975. 7.95 (ISBN 0-690-00317-X, TYC-J). T Y Crowell.

--Collecting Small Fossils. LC 77-101932. (Illus.). (gr. 4-7). 1971. 7.95 (ISBN 0-690-19733-0, TYC-J). T Y Crowell.

Hussey, M., ed. see Chaucer, Geoffrey.

Hussey, M., et al, eds. see Chaucer, Geoffrey.

Hussey, Maurice, ed. Chester Mystery Plays. pap. 3.25x (ISBN 0-87830-572-6). Theatre Arts.

Hussey, Maurice, ed. see Heywood, John.

Hussey, Maurice, ed. & frwd. by see Shire, Helena.

Hussey, W. D. British Empire & Commonwealth, Fifteen Hundred - Nineteen Sixty-One. 1963. text ed. 11.95x (ISBN 0-521-05351-X). Cambridge U Pr.

--British History, Eighteen Fifteen to Nineteen Thirty-Nine. LC 79-149429. (Illus.). 1972. 11.50 (ISBN 0-521-07985-3). Cambridge U Pr.

--Discovery, Expansion & Empire. text ed. 4.95x (ISBN 0-521-05352-8). Cambridge U Pr.

Husted, Darrell. A Country Girl. 1978. pap. 1.75 o.p. (ISBN 0-445-04186-2). Popular Lib.

Husted, Virginia, jt. auth. see Foreman, Ken.

Hustedt, Friedrich. Bacillariophyta: Diatomeae. (Suesswasserflora Mitteleuropas Ser.: Vol. 10). (Illus.). 466p. (Ger.). 1976. 71.75x (ISBN 3-87429-111-1). Lubrecht & Cramer.

Huston, Fred. Those S. O. B.'s at Tarryall & Other Tales of the Rockies. 1st ed. (Mesquite Collector Ser.: No. 5). (Illus.). 102p. 1974. 6.95 (ISBN 0-89015-061-3). Nortex Pr.

Huston, J. Dennis. Shakespeare's Comedies of Play. LC 80-21366. 150p. 1981. text ed. 15.00x (ISBN 0-231-05142-5). Columbia U Pr.

Huston, John. The Income Tax Treaty Between the U. S. & Japan. (Asian Law Ser: 8). 1981. price not set o.p. U of Wash Pr.

Huston, Paul, pref. by see Siegler, Miriam & Osmond, Humphry.

Huston, Perdita. Third World Women Speak Out: Interviews in Six Countries on Change, Development, & Basic Needs. LC 78-32180. 172p. 1979. pap. 4.95 (ISBN 0-686-28701-0). Overseas Dev Council.

--Third World Women Speakout. LC 78-32180. (Praeger Special Studies Ser.). 1979. 20.95 (ISBN 0-03-052116-5); student edition 4.95 (ISBN 0-03-052121-1). Praeger.

Huston, Rose A., tr. see Li, Jeanette.

Huston, Theodore, ed. Foundations of Interpersonal Attraction. 1974. 28.00 (ISBN 0-12-362950-0). Acad Pr.

Hustrulid, William A., jt. ed. see Crawford, John T., III.

Hustrulid, William A., ed. see Rapid Excavation & Tunneling Conference, 1979.

Hustuedt, Sigurd B., tr. see Munch, Peter A. & Olsen, Magnus.

Huszar, Robert S. Emergency Cardiac Care. 2nd ed. (Illus.). 350p. 1981. pap. text ed. 14.95 (ISBN 0-87619-863-9). R J Brady.

Hutas, I. & Debreczeni, L. A., eds. Respiration: Proceedings of the 28th International Congress of Physiological Sciences, Budapest 1980. (Advances in Physiological Sciences: Vol. 10). (Illus.). 665p. 1981. 70.00 (ISBN 0-08-026823-4). Pergamon.

Hutcheon, Wallace S., Jr. Robert Fulton: Pioneer of Undersea Warfare. 192p. 1981. 15.95 (ISBN 0-87021-547-7). Naval Inst Pr.

Hutcheson, Francis. Essay on the Nature & Conduct of the Passions & Affections, 1742. 3rd ed. LC 76-81361. (History of Psychology Ser). 1969. Repr. of 1742 ed. 38.00x (ISBN 0-8201-1058-2). Schol Facsimiles.

--Illustrations on the Moral Sense. Peach, Bernard, ed. LC 71-135545. 1971. 10.00x (ISBN 0-674-44326-8, Belknap Pr). Harvard U Pr.

Hutcheson, George. John. (Geneva Commentaries Ser.). 8.95 o.p. (ISBN 0-686-12457-X). Banner of Truth.

Hutcheson, Gladys. The Flower Book. 96p. 1980. 19.75x (ISBN 0-7050-0071-0, Pub. by Skilton & Shaw England). State Mutual Bk.

Hutcheson, Harold. Tench Coxe: A Study in American Economic Development. LC 77-98690. (American Scene Ser.). 1969. Repr. of 1938 ed. lib. bdg. 25.00 (ISBN 0-306-71511-2). Da Capo.
Hutcheson, John D., Jr. & Shevin, Jann. Citizen Groups in Local Politics: A Bibliographic Review. LC 76-23441. 275p. 1976. text ed. 8.75 (ISBN 0-87436-231-8). ABC-Clio.
Hutcheson, Robert H., jt. auth. see Von Raffler-Engel, Walburga.
Hutchesson, P. G., jt. auth. see Wraith, R. E.
Hutchings, jt. auth. see Feirer.
Hutchings, Arthur. Companion to Mozart's Piano Concertos. 2nd ed. 1950. 14.95x (ISBN 0-19-318404-4). Oxford U Pr.
Hutchings, Arthur, jt. auth. see Ottaway, Hugh.
Hutchings, D., ed. Late Seventeenth Century Scientists. 1969. 19.50 (ISBN 0-08-013359-2); pap. 10.50 (ISBN 0-08-013358-4). Pergamon.
Hutchings, Edward, Jr., jt. ed. see Horowitz, Norman H.
Hutchings, Ernest A. Survey of Printing Processes. 2nd ed. (Illus.). 1978. pap. 13.95x (ISBN 0-434-90801-0). Intl Ideas.
Hutchings, Gilbert, jt. auth. see Feirer, John.
Hutchings, Gilbert R., jt. auth. see Feirer, John.
Hutchings, James M. Seeking the Elephant, Eighteen Forty-Nine: James Mason Hutchings' Journal of His Overland Trek to California. Sargent, Shirley, ed. LC 80-67777. (American Trail Ser.: No. XII). (Illus.). 210p. 1981. 30.00 (ISBN 0-87062-136-X). A H Clark.
Hutchings, Margaret. Button-Box Book. (Make & Play Ser.). (Illus.). 48p. 1976. pap. 1.50 (ISBN 0-685-69138-1). Transatlantic.
--Making New Testament Toys. 1975. pap. 3.95 o.p. (ISBN 0-8015-4802-0). Dutton.
--Making Old Testament Toys. 1975. pap. 3.95 o.p. (ISBN 0-8015-4804-7). Dutton.
--Wool-Bag Book. (Make & Play Ser.). (Illus.). 48p. (gr. 5-6). 1976. pap. 1.50 (ISBN 0-263-05911-1). Transatlantic.
Hutchings, Raymond. Soviet Economic Development. 1971. 36.00x (ISBN 0-631-12830-1, Pub. by Basil Blackwell); pap. 14.00x (ISBN 0-631-13560-X, Pub. by Basil Blackwell). Biblio Dist.
Hutchins, B. L. Women in Modern Industry: London Nineteen Fifteen. LC 79-56959. (The English Working Class Ser.). 1980. lib. bdg. 28.00 (ISBN 0-8240-0112-5). Garland Pub.
Hutchins, C. R., jt. auth. see Martin, W. C.
Hutchins, Carleen M., ed. Musical Acoustics: Violin Family Functions, 2 pts. (Benchmark Papers in Acoustics Ser.: No. 5). 1975-76. Pt. 1. 48.50 (ISBN 0-12-786691-4); Pt. 2. 48.50 (ISBN 0-12-786692-2); Set. 85.00. Acad Pr.
Hutchins, Carleen M., intro. by. The Physics of Music: Readings from Scientific American. LC 77-28461. (Illus.). 1978. pap. 7.95x (ISBN 0-7167-0095-6). W H Freeman.
Hutchins, Edwin. Culture & Inference: A Trobriand Case Study. LC 80-13280. (Cognitive Science Ser.: No. 2). 1980. text ed. 14.00x (ISBN 0-674-17970-6). Harvard U Pr.
Hutchins, Elizabeth L. & Harrison, Amy. A History of Factory Legislation. 3rd ed. LC 66-5599. 1981. Repr. of 1926 ed. lib. bdg. 25.00x (ISBN 0-678-05173-9). Kelley.
Hutchins, Francis G. India's Revolution: Gandhi & the Quit India Movement. LC 72-96630. 384p. 1973. 17.50x (ISBN 0-674-45025-6). Harvard U Pr.
Hutchins, James S. Boots & Saddles at the Little Big Horn. LC 76-17375. (Source Custeriana Ser.: No. 7). (Illus.). pap. 4.50 o.p. (ISBN 0-88342-237-9). Old Army.
Hutchins, John G. B. Transportation & the Environment. Rose, J. & Weidner, Edward W., eds. LC 77-2350. (Environmental Studies: Vol. 5). 1977. lib. bdg. 18.00x (ISBN 0-89158-738-1). Westview.
Hutchins, Maude. Victorine. 191p. 1959. 7.95 (ISBN 0-8040-0311-4); pap. 3.95 (ISBN 0-8040-0312-2, 37). Swallow.
Hutchins, Nigel. Restoring Old Houses. 240p. 1980. 29.95 (ISBN 0-442-29625-8). Van Nos Reinhold.
Hutchins, P. J., jt. auth. see Frank, Marjorie S.
Hutchins, Pat. Clocks & More Clocks. (Illus.). (gr. k-3). 1970. 8.95 (ISBN 0-02-745860-1). Macmillan.
--Don't Forget the Bacon! LC 75-17935. (Illus.). 32p. (gr. k-3). 1976. 8.25 (ISBN 0-688-80019-X); PLB 7.92 (ISBN 0-688-84019-1). Greenwillow.
--Follow That Bus! LC 76-21822. (Illus.). (gr. 2-5). 1977. PLB 7.92 (ISBN 0-688-84068-X). Greenwillow.
--Good-Night Owl. LC 72-186355. (Illus.). (ps-2). 1972. 8.95 (ISBN 0-02-745900-4). Macmillan.
--Good-Night, Owl! LC 74-20794. (Illus.). 32p. (ps-2). 1976. pap. 1.95 o.s.i. (ISBN 0-02-043730-7, 04373, Collier). Macmillan.
--Happy Birthday, Sam. LC 78-1295. (Illus.). (gr. k-3). 1978. 7.95 (ISBN 0-688-80160-9); PLB 7.63 (ISBN 0-688-84160-0). Greenwillow.
--The House That Sailed Away. LC 74-9823. (Illus.). 192p. (gr. 2-6). 1975. PLB 7.92 (ISBN 0-688-84013-2). Greenwillow.
--The Mona Lisa Mystery. LC 79-20263. (Illus.). 192p. (gr. 3-5). 1981. 8.95 (ISBN 0-688-80243-5); PLB 8.59 (ISBN 0-688-84243-7). Greenwillow.
--One-Eyed Jake. LC 78-18346. (Illus.). (gr. k-3). 1979. 7.95 (ISBN 0-688-80183-8); PLB 7.63 (ISBN 0-688-84183-X). Greenwillow.
--Rosie's Walk. (Illus.). (gr. k-2). 1968. 8.95 (ISBN 0-02-745850-4). Macmillan.
--The Silver Christmas Tree. LC 73-19052. (Illus.). 32p. (gr. k-3). 1974. 6.95 o.s.i. (ISBN 0-02-745920-9). Macmillan.
--Surprise Party. LC 69-18239. (Illus.). (gr. k-2). 1969. 8.95 (ISBN 0-02-745830-X). Macmillan.
--Surprise Party. LC 69-18239. (Illus.). 32p. (gr. k-3). 1972. pap. 0.95 o.s.i. (ISBN 0-02-043760-9, Collier). Macmillan.
--The Tale of Thomas Mead. (Greenwillow Read-Alone Bks.). (Illus.). 32p. (gr. 1-4). 1980. 5.95 (ISBN 0-688-80282-6); PLB 5.71 (ISBN 0-688-84282-8). Greenwillow.
--Titch. LC 77-146622. (Illus.). (gr. k-3). 1971. 8.95g (ISBN 0-02-745880-6). Macmillan.
--Tom & Sam. LC 68-24104. (Illus.). (gr. k-2). 1968. 5.95g o.s.i. (ISBN 0-02-745840-7). Macmillan.
--Wind Blew. LC 73-11691. (Illus.). 32p. (ps-2). 1974. 10.95 (ISBN 0-02-745910-1). Macmillan.
Hutchins, R., jt. auth. see Martin, W. C.
Hutchins, Ross E. Nature Invented It First. LC 79-23791. (Illus.). (gr. 5 up). 1980. 5.95g (ISBN 0-396-07788-9). Dodd.
--Scaly Wings: A Book About Moths & Their Caterpillars. LC 78-131257. (Finding-Out Book). (Illus.). 64p. (gr. 2-3). 1971. PLB 6.45 o.s.i. (ISBN 0-8193-0440-9). Enslow Pubs.
--Trails to Nature's Mysteries. LC 76-50554. (gr. 7 up). 1977. 6.95 (ISBN 0-396-07401-4). Dodd.
Hutchins, Ross E., ed. Insects. 336p. 1966. pap. 3.50 o.p. (ISBN 0-13-467423-5). P-H.
Hutchins, Sheila. Pates & Terrines. 1979. 17.95 (ISBN 0-241-89892-7, Pub. by Hamish Hamilton England). David & Charles.
Hutchins, Thomas. Historical Narrative & Topographical Description of Louisiana & West Florida. Tregle, J. G., Jr., ed. LC 68-21657. (Floridiana Facsimile & Reprint Ser). 1968. Repr. of 1784 ed. 7.75 (ISBN 0-8130-0119-6). U Presses Fla.
Hutchinson. Guinea Pigs: Their Care & Breeding. (Illus.). 104p. 1981. 3.95 (ISBN 0-903264-21-8, 5213-9, Pub. by K & R Bks England). Arco.
Hutchinson, Ann. Labanotation: The System of Analyzing & Recording Movement. rev. ed. LC 69-11446. 1970. pap. 8.95 (ISBN 0-87830-527-0, 18). Theatre Arts.
Hutchinson, C. Alan, tr. see Figueroa, Jose.
Hutchinson, C. R., jt. ed. see Trost, Barry M.
Hutchinson, Derek. Sea Canoeing. 2nd ed. (Illus.). 204p. 1980. 24.00 (ISBN 0-7136-2005-6). Transatlantic.
Hutchinson, E. C. & Acheson, E. J. Strokes: Natural History, Pathology & Surgical Treatment. LC 74-28100. (Major Problems in Neurology: Vol. 4). (Illus.). 283p. 1975. text ed. 28.00 (ISBN 0-7216-4870-3). Saunders.
Hutchinson, Edward, jt. auth. see Hutchinson, Enid.
Hutchinson, Enid & Hutchinson, Edward. Learning Later: Fresh Horizons in English Adult Education. 1978. 21.00x (ISBN 0-7100-8952-X). Routledge & Kegan.
Hutchinson, G. Evelyn. A Treatise on Liminology, 3 vols. Incl. Vol. 1, 2 pts. 1975. Set. 29.95 (ISBN 0-471-42567-2); Pt. 1. Geography & Physics of Lakes. 672p. 17.95 (ISBN 0-471-42567-2); Pt. 2. Chemistry of Lakes. 474p. 16.50 (ISBN 0-471-42569-9); Vol. 2. Introduction to Lake Biology & the Limnoplankton. 1957. 79.50 (ISBN 0-471-42572-9); Vol. 3. Limnological Biology. 704p. 1975. 43.50 (ISBN 0-471-42574-5). LC 57-8888 (Pub. by Wiley-Interscience). Wiley.
Hutchinson, G. Evelyn & Wollack, Anne. Biological Accumulators of Aluminum. 1943. pap. 24.50x (ISBN 0-686-50040-7). Elliots Bks.
Hutchinson, George. The Last Edwardian at Number Ten: An Impression of Harold Macmillian. (Illus.). 160p. 1980. 12.95 (ISBN 0-7043-2232-3, Pub. by Quartet England). Horizon.
Hutchinson, Harry D. Economics & Social Goals: An Introduction. LC 72-93643. (Illus.). 514p. 1973. pap. text ed. 11.95 (ISBN 0-574-17975-5, 13-0975); instr's guide avail. (ISBN 0-574-17976-3, 13-0976). SRA.
Hutchinson, Henry N. Marriage Customs in Many Lands. LC 73-5520. (Illus.). xii, 348p. 1975. Repr. of 1897 ed. 28.00 (ISBN 0-8103-3971-4). Gale.
Hutchinson, J. The Genera of Flowering Plants: Angiospermae, 2 vols. 1200p. 1980. Repr. of 1964 ed. Set. lib. bdg. 129.60x (ISBN 0-686-28721-5); Vol. I. lib. bdg. 64.80x (ISBN 3-87429-177-4); Vol. 2. lib. bdg. 64.80x (ISBN 3-87429-178-2). Lubrecht & Cramer.
Hutchinson, J. M. & Mann, W. B., eds. Metrology Needs in the Measurement of Environmental Radioactivity: Seminar Sponsered by the International Committee for Radionuclide Metrology. (Illus.). 1980. pap. 35.00 (ISBN 0-08-022943-3). Pergamon.
Hutchinson, J. S. The Hypothalamo-Pituitary Control of the Ovary. Horrobin, D. F., ed. (Annual Research Reviews Ser.: Vol. 2). 215p. 1980. 28.00 (ISBN 0-88831-091-9). Eden Med Res.
Hutchinson, James C. Hypertension: A Practitioner's Guide to Therapy. 1975. spiral bdg. 13.00 (ISBN 0-87488-709-7). Med Exam.
Hutchinson, John. Edinburgh in Colour. (Illus.). 96p. 1980. 17.95 (ISBN 0-7134-1998-9, Pub. by Batsford England). David & Charles.
--The Genera of Flowering Plants: Dicotyledones. 1964-67. Vol. 1. 43.50x o.p. (ISBN 0-19-854351-4); Vol. 2. 41.00x o.p. (ISBN 0-19-854361-1). Oxford U Pr.
Hutchinson, Joseph. The Challenge of the Third World. (Eddington Memorial Lecture Ser.: No. 2). 80p. 1975. 12.50 (ISBN 0-521-20853-X); pap. 4.50 (ISBN 0-521-09996-X). Cambridge U Pr.
Hutchinson, Joyce. Voix d'Afrique. 4.95x (ISBN 0-521-05356-0). Cambridge U Pr.
Hutchinson, Joyce A., ed. see Laye, Camara.
Hutchinson, K. M. Memoir of Abijah Hutchinson: A Soldier of the Revolution, Repr. Of 1843 Ed. Bd. with Narrative of the Massacre at Chicago, August 15, 1812, & of Some Preceding Events. Kinzie, Juliette A. Repr. of 1844 ed; A History of the Cooper Mines & Newgate Prison... Also, of the Captivity of Daniel Hayes... by the Indians in 1707. Phelps, Noah A. Repr. of 1845 ed; A Long Journey. the Story of Daniel Hayes. Repr. of 1876 ed; The Bible Boy Taken Captive by the Indians. Cope, Herman. Repr. of 1845 ed. LC 75-7082. (Indian Captivities Ser.: Vol. 59). 1977. lib. bdg. 44.00 (ISBN 0-8240-1683-1). Garland Pub.
Hutchinson, Louise D. Out of Africa: From West African Kingdoms to Colonization. LC 78-22469. (Illus.). 223p. 1979. 25.00x o.p. (ISBN 0-87474-534-9). Smithsonian.
Hutchinson, Margaret. The Elementary Functions. new ed. LC 73-89294. (Mathematics Ser). 352p. 1974. text ed. 14.95x o.p. (ISBN 0-675-08855-0); instructor's manual 3.95 o.p. (ISBN 0-686-66942-8). Merrill.
Hutchinson, Margaret R. Geometry: An Intuitive Approach. LC 79-171538. 352p. 1972. 13.95x o.p. (ISBN 0-675-09427-5); instructor's manual 3.95 o.p. (ISBN 0-686-66709-3). Merrill.
Hutchinson, Martha C. Revolutionary Terrorism: The FLN in Algeria, 1954-1962. LC 78-59130. (Publications 196 Ser.). 1978. 10.95 (ISBN 0-8179-6961-6). Hoover Inst Pr.
Hutchinson, Peter. Literary Presentations of Divided Germany. LC 76-51414. (Anglica Germanica Ser.: No. 2). 1977. 28.50 (ISBN 0-521-21609-5). Cambridge U Pr.
Hutchinson, Ron. Says I, Says He. (Phoenix Theatre Ser.). pap. 2.95 (ISBN 0-912262-69-9). Proscenium.
Hutchinson, T. W. On Revolutions & Progress in Economic Knowledge. LC 77-82498. 1978. 44.50 (ISBN 0-521-21805-5). Cambridge U Pr.
Hutchinson, Thomas, ed. see Shelley, Percy Bysshe.
Hutchinson, Thomas, ed. see Wordsworth, William.
Hutchinson, W. H. & Mullins, R. N. Whiskey Jim & a Kid Named Billie. 5.00 o.p. (ISBN 0-685-48822-5). Nortex Pr.
Hutchinson, Warner A., ed. see Guyon, Madame.
Hutchinson, William. A Treatise on Naval Architecture. 303p. 1980. 49.95x (ISBN 0-85177-002-9, Pub. by Conway Maritime England). State Mutual Bk.
--A Treatise on Practical Seamanship. (Scolar Maritime Library). (Illus.). 240p. 1979. Repr. of 1777 ed. 60.00x (ISBN 0-85967-566-1, Pub. by Scolar Pr England). Biblio Dist.
Hutchinson, William A. Plant Propagation & Cultivation. (Illus.). 1980. pap. text ed. 18.00 (ISBN 0-87055-340-2). AVI.
Hutchinson, William K. History of Economic Analysis. LC 73-17578. (Economics Information Guide Ser.: Vol. 3). 1976. 30.00 (ISBN 0-8103-1295-6). Gale.
Hutchinson, William K., ed. American Economic History: A Guide to Information Sources. LC 73-17577. (Economic Information Guide Ser.: Vol. 16). 250p. 1980. 30.00 (ISBN 0-8103-1287-5). Gale.
Hutchinson, William T. Cyrus Hall Maccormick, 2 Vols. 2nd ed. LC 68-8127. (American Scene Ser). 1969. Repr. of 1935 ed. lib. bdg. 69.50 (ISBN 0-306-71162-1). Da Capo.
Hutchison, Alan. China's African Revolution. LC 75-45233. 1976. 21.50x (ISBN 0-89158-025-5). Westview.
Hutchison, Charles S. Laboratory Handbook of Petrographic Techniques. LC 73-17336. 544p. 1974. 35.00 (ISBN 0-471-42550-8, Pub. by Wiley-Interscience). Wiley.
Hutchison, D. Special Effects, Vol. I. 1979. pap. 6.95 (ISBN 0-931064-07-4). Starlog Pr.
Hutchison, David. Special Effects, Vol. I. LC 79-63384. 1979. pap. 6.95 (ISBN 0-931064-07-4). Starlog.
--Special Effects, Vol. II. 1980. pap. 7.95 (ISBN 0-931064-22-8). O'Quinn Studio.
Hutchison, Frances. Gardening for Beginners. Steffek, Edwin, ed. (Illus.). 152p. 1976. pap. 5.95 o.s.i. (ISBN 0-02-063250-9, Collier). Macmillan.
Hutchison, J. B., ed. Biological Determinants of Sexual Behavior. LC 76-57753. 1978. 88.95 (ISBN 0-471-99490-1, Pub by Wiley-Interscience). Wiley.
Hutchison, John A. Paths of Faith. 3rd ed. (Illus.). 608p. Date not set. text ed. 18.95 (ISBN 0-07-031532-9, C). McGraw.
Hutchison, Terence W. Positive Economics & Policy Objectives. LC 64-55440. 1964. 10.00x (ISBN 0-674-69300-0). Harvard U Pr.
Huth, H. & Pugh, W., eds. Talleyrand in America As a Financial Promoter, 1794-96. LC 76-75323. (American Scene Ser). 1971. Repr. of 1942 ed. lib. bdg. 22.50 (ISBN 0-306-71286-5). Da Capo.
Huth, Hans. Nature & the American: Three Centuries of Changing Attitudes. LC 57-12393. (Illus.). 250p. 1972. 13.95x (ISBN 0-8032-0926-6); pap. 3.95x (ISBN 0-8032-5761-9, BB 554, Bison). U of Nebr Pr.
Huth, Mark W. Basic Construction Blueprint Reading. 144p. 1980. 9.95 (ISBN 0-442-23874-6). Van Nos Reinhold.
--Basic Construction Blueprint Reading. LC 79-50919. (gr. 9). 1980. pap. text ed. 7.20 (ISBN 0-8273-1865-0); instructor's guide 1.45 (ISBN 0-8273-1866-9). Delmar.
--Introduction to Construction. LC 78-60838. (Construction Ser.). (YA) (gr. 9-12). 1980. pap. text ed. 14.52 (ISBN 0-8273-1737-9); instr's manual 2.00 (ISBN 0-8273-1738-7). Delmar.
Huth, Mary J. The Urban Habitat: Past, Present & Future. LC 77-7273. (Illus.). 1978. text ed. 17.95 (ISBN 0-88229-333-8). Nelson-Hall.
Hutheesing, Krishina N., jt. auth. see Anand, Mulk Raj.
Hutheesing, Raja, ed. The Great Peace: An Asian's Candid Report on Red China. LC 74-28428. (China in the 20th Century Ser). 246p. 1975. Repr. of 1953 ed. lib. bdg. 22.50 (ISBN 0-306-70694-6). Da Capo.
Hutin, Serge. Casting Spells. 1978. 9.50 o.p. (ISBN 0-214-20522-3, 8064, Dist. by Arco). Barrie & Jenkins.
Hutka, Ed F. Boom or Busted: Family Dollars & Sense. 1979. 2.95 (ISBN 0-88270-452-4). Logos.
Hutmacher, William F. Wynkyn De Worde & Chaucer's Canterbury Tales: A Transcription & Collation of the 1498 Edition with Caxton from the General Proloque Through the Knights Tale. (Costerus, New Ser.: No. 10). 1978. pap. text ed. 23.00x (ISBN 90-6203-502-7). Humanities.
Hutner, S. H. & Lwoff, Andre, eds. Biochemistry & Physiology of Protozoa, 3 vols. Incl. Vol. 1. 1951. 36.00 o.p. (ISBN 0-12-363001-0); Vol. 2. 1955. 36.00 o.p. (ISBN 0-12-363002-9); Vol. 3. 1964. 48.00 o.p. (ISBN 0-12-363003-7). Acad Pr.
Hutner, S. H., ed. see International Congress of Protozoology, 5th.
Hutner, S. H., jt. ed. see Levandowsky, Michael.
Hutnick, M. B. Criminal Law & Court Procedures. 176p. 1974. pap. 8.00 o.p. (ISBN 0-8273-1429-9); instructor's guide 1.45 o.p. (ISBN 0-8273-1430-2). Delmar.
Hutschnecker, Arnold A. The Drive for Power. LC 74-79982. 360p. 1974. 9.95 (ISBN 0-87131-165-8). M Evans.
--Hope: The Dynamics of Self-Fulfillment. 320p. 1981. 11.95 (ISBN 0-399-12589-2). Putnam.
Hutson, Alice. From Chalk to Bronze: A Biography of Waldine Tauch. 1978. 6.95 (ISBN 0-88319-037-0). Shoal Creek Pub.
Hutson, D. H. & Roberts, T. R. Progress in Pesticide Biochemistry, Vol. 1. 360p. 1981. 71.95 (ISBN 0-471-27920-X, Pub. by Wiley-Interscience). Wiley.
Hutson, James H. John Adams & the Diplomacy of the American Revolution. LC 79-57575. 208p. 1980. 13.00x (ISBN 0-8131-1404-7). U Pr of Ky.
Hutson, James H., jt. ed. see Kurtz, Stephen G.
Hutson, Joan. I Think...I Know: A Poster Book About God. (Illus.). 32p. (Orig.). (gr. 2-4). 1979. pap. 1.95 (ISBN 0-87793-186-0). Ave Maria.
Hutson, Sandy. Return to Sender. (Orig.). 1981. price not set (ISBN 0-451-09808-0, Signet Bks). NAL.

Hutson, Tony. Your Book of Tall Ships. (Your Book Ser.). (Illus.). 1978. 7.95 (ISBN 0-571-10889-X, Pub. by Faber & Faber). Merrimack Bk Serv.
Hutt, A. T. A Relational Data Base Management System. 208p. 1979. 27.00 (ISBN 0-471-27612-X, Pub. by Wiley-Interscience). Wiley.
Hutt, C., jt. auth. see Hutt, S. J.
Hutt, Corrine, jt. auth. see Hutt, S. J.
Hutt, Frederick B. Animal Genetics. (Illus.). 1964. 21.95 (ISBN 0-8260-4625-8). Wiley.
--Genetics for Dog Breeders. LC 79-15169. (Illus.). 1979. text ed. 17.95x (ISBN 0-7167-1069-2). W H Freeman.
Hutt, Michael D. & Speh, Thomas W. Industrial Marketing Management. LC 80-65803. 576p. 1981. text ed. 18.95 (ISBN 0-03-052656-6). Dryden Pr.
Hutt, Michael D., jt. auth. see Moyer, Reed.
Hutt, Peter B., jt. auth. see Merrill, Richard A.
Hutt, S. J. & Hutt, C. Behaviour Studies in Psychiatry. 1970. 17.25 (ISBN 0-08-015780-7). Pergamon.
Hutt, S. J. & Hutt, Corrine. Direct Observation & Measurement of Behavior. (American Lecture Living Chemistry Ser). (Illus.). 240p. 1978. 18.50 (ISBN 0-398-00892-2). C C Thomas.
Hutt, W. H. A Rehabilitation of Say's Law. LC 74-82499. xiii, 150p. 1974. 10.95x (ISBN 0-8214-0164-5). Ohio U Pr.
--The Theory of Collective Bargaining Nineteen Thirty to Nineteen Seventy-Five. LC 80-36792. (Cato Papers Ser.: No. 14). 160p. 1980. pap. 5.00 (ISBN 0-932790-20-8). Cato Inst.
--Theory of Collective Bargaining 1930-1975. (Hobart Paperbacks Special Ser.: No. 8). 1976. pap. 7.50 (ISBN 0-255-36072-X). Transatlantic.
Hutten, Joan M. Short-Term Contracts in Social Work. (Library of Social Work Ser.). 1977. 15.00x (ISBN 0-7100-8584-2); pap. 7.95 (ISBN 0-7100-8585-0). Routledge & Kegan.
Huttenlocker, Keith. Love Makes the World Go Round. 1976. pap. 1.50 (ISBN 0-89129-181-4). Jove Pubns.
Hutter, Heribert. Styles in Art. LC 73-88460. (Universe History of Art Ser.). (Illus.). 192p. (Orig.). 1981. pap. 6.95 (ISBN 0-87663-558-3). Universe.
--Styles in Art: An Historical Survey. LC 73-88460. (Illus.). 189p. 1978. 8.95x (ISBN 0-87663-205-3). Universe.
Hutter, Mark. The Family & Social Change: Comparative Perspectives. 500p. 1981. text ed. 16.95 (ISBN 0-471-08394-1). Wiley.
Hutterer, Karl L., ed. Economic Exchange & Social Interaction in Southeast Asia: Perspectives from Prehistory, History, & Ethnography. LC 77-95147. (Michigan Papers on South & Southeast Asia: No. 13). (Illus.). 300p. 1977. pap. 7.50x (ISBN 0-89148-013-7). Ctr S&SE Asian.
Huttig, Jack. Nineteen Twenty-Seven: Summer of Eagles. (Illus.). 1980. 22.95 (ISBN 0-88229-525-X); pap. 11.95 (ISBN 0-88229-723-6). Nelson-Hall.
--Psycho-Sales-Analysis: The New Art of Self-Taught Sales Success. LC 73-154979. (Illus.). 1971. 14.95 (ISBN 0-911012-09-5). Nelson-Hall.
Huttman, Barbara. The Patient's Advocate. 416p. 1981. pap. 8.95 (ISBN 0-14-046492-1). Penguin.
Huttman, Elizabeth D. Housing & Social Services for the Elderly: Social Policy Trends. LC 75-44932. (Special Studies). 1977. text ed. 29.95 (ISBN 0-275-23830-X). Praeger.
--Introduction to Social Policy. Black, Nelson W., ed. (Illus.). 368p. 1980. text ed. 14.95x (ISBN 0-07-031548-5). McGraw.
Huttmann, Barbara. The Patient's Advocate, the Complete Handbook of Patient's Rights' How to Get Them & How to Use Them to Save Your Time, Your Money, & Your Life. LC 80-52005. 400p. 1981. 16.95 (ISBN 0-670-54273-3). Viking Pr.
Hutton. General Chemistry Lab Text with Quantitative Analysis. 1968. text ed. 10.95 (ISBN 0-675-09629-4). Merrill.
Hutton, Darryl. Ventriloquism: How to Put on an Act, Use the Power of Suggestion, Write a Clever Accompanying Patter, & Make Your Own Dummy. LC 75-14508. (Illus.). 96p. 1975. 7.95 (ISBN 0-8069-7022-7); lib. bdg. 7.49 (ISBN 0-8069-7023-5). Sterling.
Hutton, David V. Applied Mechanical Vibrations. (Mechanical Engineering Ser.). (Illus.). 416p. 1980. text ed. 23.95x (ISBN 0-07-031549-3, C); solutions manual avail. (ISBN 0-07-031550-7). McGraw.
Hutton, Geoffrey & Rostron, Michael. Computer Programs for the Building Industry 1979: International Directory for the Building Industry. 2nd ed. 312p. (Orig.). 1979. pap. 65.00x (ISBN 0-85139-312-8). Intl Pubns Serv.
Hutton, Harold. Doc Middleton: Life & Legends of the Notorious Plains Outlaw. LC 67-14260. (Illus.). 290p. 1980. 14.95 (ISBN 0-8040-0532-X, SB). Swallow.
--Vigilante Days: Frontier Justice Along the Niobrara. LC 76-17742. (Illus.). 365p. 1978. 17.95 (ISBN 0-8040-0738-1, SB). Swallow.
Hutton, Jessie & Cunningham, Gladys. Singer Sewing Book. (Illus.). 1976. 14.95 (ISBN 0-307-09870-2, Golden Pr); pap. 9.95 (ISBN 0-307-09871-0). Western Pub.
Hutton, John. The Mystery of Wealth: Political Economy, Its Development & Impact on World Events. LC 78-13743. 1979. 24.95 (ISBN 0-470-26515-9). Halsted Pr.
Hutton, Luara, tr. see Van Der Hoop, J. H.
Hutton, Richard. The Cosmic Chase. 1981. pap. 3.50 (ISBN 0-451-61925-0, ME1925, Ment). NAL.
Hutton, W. H. A Disciple's Religion. (Scholar As Preacher Ser.). 246p. Repr. of 1911 ed. 7.75 (ISBN 0-567-04410-6). Attic Pr.
Hutton, Warwick. The Nose Tree. LC 79-23247. (Illus.). 32p. Date not set. price not set (ISBN 0-689-50166-8, McElderry Bk). Atheneum. Postponed.
Hutzler, Laurie H. Attorney's Malpractice Prevention Manual. 4th ed. (Illus.). 1979. 29.95x (ISBN 0-937542-00-8); pap. 15.00x (ISBN 0-937542-01-6). Legal Mgmt Serv.
--A Financing Survival Manual for Small Business. (Illus.). 1981. pap. 15.00 (ISBN 0-937542-05-9). Legal Mgmt Serv.
--The Regulatory & Paperwork Maze. Incl. A Guide for Association Executives. pap. (ISBN 0-937542-03-2); A Guide for Government Personnel. pap. (ISBN 0-937542-04-0); A Guide for Small Business. pap. (ISBN 0-937542-02-4). (Illus.). 1980. pap. 10.00 ea. Legal Mgmt Serv.
--The Regulatory & Paperwork Maze: A Guide for Small Business, New 1981 "Reagan" Edition. 2nd ed. (Illus.). 1981. pap. 15.00 (ISBN 0-937542-06-7). Legal Mgmt Serv.
Huwayyik, Yusaf. Gibran in Paris. Mossa, Matti, tr. & intro. by. (Gideon Detective Ser.). 192p. 1976. pap. 1.75 o.p. (ISBN 0-445-08425-1). Popular Lib.
Huxford, Bob, jt. auth. see Huxford, Sharon.
Huxford, Sharon & Huxford, Bob. Collector's Encyclopedia of Fiesta. 4th rev. ed. (Illus.). 1981. pap. 8.95 (ISBN 0-89145-168-4). Collector Bks.
Huxham, Mona. All About the Chihuahua. (Illus.). 1976. 9.95 (ISBN 0-7207-0891-5, Pub. by Michael Joseph). Merrimack Bk Serv.
--All About the Jack Russell Terrier. 1975. 8.95 (ISBN 0-7207-0825-7, Pub. by Michael Joseph). Merrimack Bk Serv.
--All About the Yorkshire Terrier. 1971. 9.95 (ISBN 0-7207-0333-6, Pub. by Michael Joseph). Merrimack Bk Serv.
Huxhold, Harry N. Power for the Church in the Midst of Chaos. LC 73-82078. 1973. pap. 2.25 (ISBN 0-570-03160-5, 12-2557). Concordia.
Huxhold, Harry N., ed. Adventures with God. LC 66-15551. 1966. pap. 5.50 (ISBN 0-570-03736-0, 12-2640). Concordia.
Huxley, jt. auth. see Volk.
Huxley, Aldous. Art of Seeing. (Illus.). 1975. pap. 4.95 (ISBN 0-685-52953-3, Pub. by Montana Bks). Madrona Pubs.
--Brave New World Revisited. 1965. pap. 1.95 (ISBN 0-06-080023-2, P23, PL). Har-Row.
--The Devils of Loudun. 1979. pap. 5.95 (ISBN 0-06-090210-8, CN-210, CN). Har-Row.
--Letters of Aldous Huxley. Smith, Grover, ed. LC 69-15263. 1970. 15.00 o.s.i. (ISBN 0-06-013937-4, HarpT). Har-Row.
--Perennial Philosophy. 1970. pap. 4.95 (ISBN 0-06-090191-8, CN191, CN). Har-Row.
Huxley, Alyson. Herbs for Better Body Beauty. (The Living with Herbs Ser: Vol. 5). Date not set. pap. 2.50 (ISBN 0-87983-177-4). Keats. Postponed.
Huxley, Andrew. Reflections on Muscle. LC 79-5480. (Illus.). 120p. 1980. 15.95x (ISBN 0-691-08255-3). Princeton U Pr.
Huxley, Ann. Four Against the Bank of England. LC 80-82216. 224p. 1980. pap. 2.50 (ISBN 0-87216-750-X). Playboy Pbks.
Huxley, Anthony. Deciduous Garden Trees and Shrubs: A Macmillan Color-Identification Guide. Toogood, Alan R. & Hardwicke, Denis, trs. from Danish. (Illus.). 192p. 1973. 7.95 o.s.i. (ISBN 0-02-557970-3). Macmillan.
--Evergreen Garden Trees & Shrubs: A Macmillan Color Indentification Guide. LC 73-8709. (Illus.). 192p. 1973. 7.95 o.s.i. (ISBN 0-02-557960-6). Macmillan.
--Garden Flowers in Color, Vol. 1: Annuals & Bulbs. Spilsbury, W. J., tr. (Pocket Encyclopedias of Flowers Ser). (Illus.). 1971. 8.95 o.s.i. (ISBN 0-02-562950-6). Macmillan.
--Garden Flowers in Color, Vol. 2: Garden Perennials & Water Plants. (Pocket Encyclopedias of Flowers Ser). 1971. 5.95 o.s.i. (ISBN 0-02-562960-3). Macmillan.
Huxley, Anthony & Taylor, William. Flowers of Greece & the Aegean. (Illus.). 1977. 24.00 (ISBN 0-7011-2190-4). Transatlantic.
Huxley, Anthony, jt. auth. see Edlin, Herbert L.
Huxley, Anthony, jt. auth. see Polunin, Oleg.
Huxley, Elspeth. The African Poison Murders. LC 80-8717. 288p. 1981. pap. 2.25 (ISBN 0-06-080540-4, P/540, PL). Har-Row.
Huxley, Elspeth, ed. see Grant, Nellie.
Huxley, Francis. Peoples of the World in Color. LC 70-77361. (Illus.). 1970. 7.50 (ISBN 0-8023-1215-2). Dufour.
Huxley, G. L. Early Ionians. 1966. pap. text ed. 8.50x (ISBN 0-7165-2065-6). Humanities.
--Early Sparta. 164p. 1970. Repr. of 1962 ed. 17.00x (ISBN 0-7165-0596-7, Pub. by Irish Academic Pr Ireland). Biblio Dist.
Huxley, Julian. Essays of a Biologist. 304p. 1980. Repr. of 1929 ed. lib. bdg. 25.00 (ISBN 0-8495-2274-9). Arden Lib.
--Problems of Relative Growth. 312p. 1972. pap. 3.50 o.p. (ISBN 0-486-61114-0). Dover.
Huxley, Laura Archera. Between Heaven & Earth: Recipes for Living & Loving. 1975. 8.95 o.p. (ISBN 0-374-11234-7). FS&G.
Huxley, M. N. The Distribution of Prime Numbers: Large Sieves & Zero-Density Theorems. (Oxford Mathematical Monographs). (Illus.). 145p. 1972. text ed. 37.50x (ISBN 0-19-853518-X). Oxford U Pr.
Huxley, T. H; see Magendie, Francois.
Huxley, Thomas H. Huxley: Selections from the Essays. Castell, Alburey, ed. LC 48-5544. (Crofts Classics Ser.). 1948. pap. text ed. 2.95x (ISBN 0-88295-043-6). AHM Pub.
Huxley, Thomas H., jt. auth. see Darwin, Charles.
Huxtable, Ada Louise. Pier Luigi Nervi. LC 60-6076. (Masters of World Architecture Ser). (Illus.). 7.95 o.s.i. (ISBN 0-8076-0106-3); pap. 3.95 o.s.i. (ISBN 0-8076-0223-X). Braziller.
Huxtable, Ryan & Barbeau, Andre, eds. Taurine. LC 75-14577. 416p. 1976. 41.50 (ISBN 0-89004-064-8). Raven.
Huxtable, Ryan, jt. ed. see Barbeau, Andre.
Huyck, W., et al. American Graffiti. LC 73-17640. 1979. pap. 1.95 (ISBN 0-345-28408-9). Ballantine.
Huygelen, C., jt. ed. see Hennessen, W.
Huyghe, Rene. Watteau. LC 75-97899. (Great Draughtsmen Ser.). 1970. 7.95 o.p. (ISBN 0-8076-0545-X). Braziller.
Huyre. Los Deportes En Puerto Rico. 1968. 19.95 (ISBN 0-87751-013-X, Pub by Troutman Press). E Torres & Sons.
Huysmans, Joris K. En Route. Paul, C. Kegan, tr. from Fr. LC 76-15215. xi, 313p. 1976. Repr. of 1918 ed. 17.50 (ISBN 0-86527-243-3). Fertig.
--The Oblate. Perceval, Edward, tr. from Fr. LC 77-11670. 1978. Repr. of 1924 ed. 17.50 (ISBN 0-86527-284-0). Fertig.
Huyssen, Chester & Huyssen, Lucille, eds. Visions of Jesus. 1977. pap. 2.95 (ISBN 0-88270-223-8). Logos.
Huyssen, Lucille, jt. ed. see Huyssen, Chester.
Huzan, E., jt. auth. see Carter, L. R.
Hvass, Hans. Reptiles & Amphibians in Color. (European Ecology Ser.). (Illus.). 1972. 9.95 (ISBN 0-7137-0743-7, Pub by Blandford Pr England). Sterling.
Hveem, Helge. The Political Economy of Producer Assoeiations. 1978. pap. 19.00x (ISBN 82-00-01671-4, Dist. by Columbia U Pr). Universitet.
Hwang, Kai. Computer Arithmetic: Principles, Architecture & Design. LC 78-18922. 1979. text ed. 27.95 (ISBN 0-471-03496-7); solutions manual (ISBN 0-471-05200-0). Wiley.
Hwang, N. H. & Gross, D. R., eds. Biorheology: Physics of Biological Tissues. (NATO Advanced Study Institute Ser.: Applied Science). 382p. 1980. 42.50x (ISBN 90-286-0950-4). Sijthoff & Noordhoff.
Hwang, Ned H. Fundamentals of Hydraulic Systems. (P-H Ser. in Environmental Sciences). (Illus.). 352p. 1981. text ed. 28.95 (ISBN 0-13-340000-X). P-H.
Hwang, S. T. see Weissberger, A.
Hwang, W., jt. auth. see Kao, K. C.
Hyams, Barry, ed. Theatre, Vol. 2. (Orig.). 1965. pap. 1.95 o.p. (ISBN 0-8090-0602-2, Drama). Hill & Wang.
Hyams, Edward. Animals in the Service of Man. LC 78-147890. (Illus.). 1972. 7.75 o.p. (ISBN 0-397-00780-9). Lippincott.
--Capability Brown & Humphry Repton. LC 71-123850. (Illus.). 1971. 12.95x o.p. (ISBN 0-912158-83-2). Hennessey.
--Plants in the Service of Man. LC 71-147891. (Illus.). 1972. 7.75 o.p. (ISBN 0-397-00781-7). Lippincott.
--Soil & Civilization. 312p. 1980. 15.00x (ISBN 0-7195-3311-2, Pub. by Murray Pubs England). State Mutual Bk.
Hyams, Joe. Bogart & Bacall. (Illus.). 1976. pap. 2.50 (ISBN 0-446-91228-X). Warner Bks.
Hyams, Paul R. King, Lords, & Peasants in Medieval England: The Common Law of Villeinage in the Twelfth & Thirteenth Centuries. (Oxford Historical Monograph). 350p. 1980. 49.50 (ISBN 0-19-821880-X). Oxford U Pr.
Hyams, Vincent J., et al. Pathology of the Ear. (Atlases of the Pathology of the Head & Neck). 1976. 80.00 (ISBN 0-89189-095-5, 15-1-017-00); microfiche ed. 22.00 (ISBN 0-686-67784-6, 17-1-017-00). Am Soc Clinical.
Hyamson, Albert M. Dictionary of English Phrases: Phraseological Allusions, Catchwords, Stereotyped Modes of Speech & Metaphors, Nicknames, Sobriquets, Derivations from Personal Names. LC 66-22673. 1970. Repr. of 1922 ed. 20.00 (ISBN 0-8103-3852-1). Gale.
--A Dictionary of Universal Biography of All Ages & of All People. 2nd ed. 1976. Repr. of 1916 ed. 46.00 (ISBN 0-7100-1580-1). Routledge & Kegan.
Hyatt, Betty H. Fandora's Story. LC 81-80089. (The House of Lancien Ser.). 192p. (Orig.). 1981. pap. 1.95 (ISBN 0-87216-790-9). Playboy Pbks.
--The Jade Pagoda. LC 79-8433. (Romantic Suspense Ser.). 1980. 8.95 (ISBN 0-385-15746-0). Doubleday.
Hyatt, Carole. Woman's Selling Game: How to Sell Yourself & Anything Else. 1980. pap. 4.95 (ISBN 0-446-97195-2). Warner Bks.
--Women & Work: Honest Answers to Real Questions. 400p. 1980. 14.95 (ISBN 0-87131-324-3). M Evans.
Hyatt, E. C. & White, J. M. Respirators & Protective Clothing. (Safety Ser.: No. 22). 1967. pap. 5.00 (ISBN 92-0-123367-1, IAEA). Unipub.
Hyatt, Herman R., et al. Arithmetic with Pushbutton Accuracy. LC 76-4558. 1977. text ed. 17.95 (ISBN 0-471-22308-5); tchrs. manual 5.00 (ISBN 0-471-02395-7). Wiley.
--Introduction to Technical Mathematics: A Calculator Approach. LC 78-17016. 1979. text ed. 17.95x (ISBN 0-471-22240-2); tchrs. manual avail. (ISBN 0-471-04053-3). Wiley.
Hyatt, J. P. Commentary on Exodus. Clements, Ronald E., ed. (New Century Bible Commentary Ser.). 1980. pap. 7.95 (ISBN 0-8028-1844-7). Eerdmans.
Hyatt, Ralph & Rolnick, Norma, eds. Teaching the Mentally Handicapped Child. LC 74-2323. 352p. 1974. text ed. 19.95 (ISBN 0-87705-158-5). Human Sci Pr.
Hyatt, Ralph I. Before You Love Again. (Paperbacks Ser.). 192p. 1980. pap. 3.95 (ISBN 0-07-031555-8, GB). McGraw.
Hyatt, Ronald W. Intramural Sports: Organization & Administration. LC 76-29694. (Illus.). 1977. pap. text ed. 10.95 (ISBN 0-8016-2320-0). Mosby.
Hybels, Bill & Caress, Jay. Caution: Christians Under Construction. 1978. pap. 2.50 (ISBN 0-88207-759-7). Victor Bks.
Hyde, Albert C. & Shafritz, Jay, eds. Program Evaluation in the Public Sector. LC 78-19742. (Praeger Special Studies). 325p. 1979. 29.95 (ISBN 0-03-042976-5). Praeger.
Hyde, Arnout, Jr. West Virginia. LC 80-82049. (Illus.). 128p. 1980. 25.00 (ISBN 0-9604590-0-6); lea. bdg. 125.00 (ISBN 0-9604590-1-4). A Hyde.
Hyde, Bryden B. Bermuda's Antique Furniture & Silver. LC 76-157116. (Illus.). 1971. 15.00x (ISBN 0-938420-03-8). Md Hist.
Hyde, Christopher. The Wave. LC 81-80090. 272p. 1981. pap. 2.95 (ISBN 0-87216-848-4). Playboy Pbks.
--A Week Down in Devon: A History of the Devon Horse Show. LC 76-3102. (Illus.). 160p. 1976. 15.00 o.p. (ISBN 0-685-62924-4). Chilton.
Hyde, Dayton. Cranes in My Corral. LC 70-153737. (Illus.). (gr. 4-6). 4.95 (ISBN 0-8037-1550-1); PLB 4.58 (ISBN 0-8037-1551-X). Dial.
Hyde, Dayton O. Yamsi. 352p. 1974. pap. 1.95 o.p. (ISBN 0-345-24286-6). Ballantine.
Hyde, Douglas. Beside the Fire. 254p. Date not set. Repr. of 1910 ed. 11.00x (ISBN 0-7165-2073-7, Pub by Irish Academic Pr). Biblio Dist.
--Irish Poetry: An Essay in Irish with Translation in English. LC 77-94587. 1979. Repr. of 1902 ed. lib. bdg. cancelled o.p. (ISBN 0-89341-189-2). Longwood Pr.
Hyde, Douglas, ed. & tr. The Stone of Truth & Other Irish Folk Tales. 126p. 1979. 10.00x (ISBN 0-8476-6232-2). Rowman.
Hyde, E., jt. ed. see Ash, J.
Hyde, Earl K., et al. Nuclear Properties of Heavy Elements, 3 vols. rev. ed. LC 70-153894. (Orig.). 1971. Repr. text ed. 15.00 ea. Vol. I (ISBN 0-486-62805-1). Vol. II (ISBN 0-486-62806-X). Vol. III (ISBN 0-486-62807-8). Dover.
Hyde, Francis E. Far Eastern Trade Eighteen-Sixty to Nineteen-Fourteen. (Merchant Adventurers Ser.). 1979. text ed. 9.75x (ISBN 0-7136-1345-9). Humanities.
--Liverpool & the Mersey: An Economic History of a Port 1700-1970. (Illus.). 256p. 1971. 13.50x o.p. (ISBN 0-87471-337-4). Rowman.
Hyde, Frank W. Radio Astronomy for Amateurs. (Illus.). 1963. 5.00 o.p. (ISBN 0-393-06331-3). Norton.

Hyde, George. Vladimir Nabokov: America's Russian Novelist. (Critical Appraisals Ser.). 1977. text ed. 18.25x (ISBN 0-391-00763-7). Humanities.

Hyde, George E. Indians of the Woodlands: From Prehistoric Times to 1725. (Civilization of the American Indian Ser.: No. 64). (Illus.). 1962. pap. 6.95 (ISBN 0-8061-1058-9). U of Okla Pr.

--Life of George Bent: Written from His Letters. Lottinville, Savoie, ed. (Illus.). 1968. 14.50 o.p. (ISBN 0-8061-0769-3). U of Okla Pr.

--A Sioux Chronicle. (Civilization of the American Indian Ser.: Vol. 45). 334p. 1956. 15.95 (ISBN 0-8061-0358-2). U of Okla Pr.

--Spotted Tail's Folk: A History of the Brule Sioux. LC 61-6497. (Civilization of the American Indian Ser.: Vol. 57). (Illus.). 361p. 1961. 15.95 (ISBN 0-8061-0484-8); pap. 7.95 (ISBN 0-8061-1380-4). U of Okla Pr.

Hyde, George E., jt. auth. see Will, George F.

Hyde, George E., ed. Life of George Bent: Written from His Letters. (Illus.). 1979. pap. 6.95 o.p. (ISBN 0-8061-1577-7). U of Okla Pr.

Hyde, Gordon. Rags to Righteousness. LC 77-80684. (Dimension Ser.). 1978. pap. 5.95 (ISBN 0-8163-0296-0, 18031-5). Pacific Pr Pub Assn.

Hyde, H. Montgomery. The Atom Bomb Spies. LC 80-65998. (Illus.). 1980. 14.95 (ISBN 0-689-11075-8). Atheneum.

--The Londonderrys: Portrait of a Noble Family. (Illus.). 1979. 30.00 (ISBN 0-241-10153-0, Pub. by Hamish Hamilton England). David & Charles.

--The Trials of Oscar Wilde. (Illus.). 8.50 (ISBN 0-8446-5049-8). Peter Smith.

Hyde, Janet & Rosenberg, B. G. Half the Human Experience. 2nd ed. 1980. pap. text ed. 9.95x (ISBN 0-669-02500-3); instrs'. manual (ISBN 0-669-02502-X). Heath.

Hyde, Judy. Nail Biter's Handbook. (Illus.). 24p. (Orig.). 1980. pap. 2.95 (ISBN 0-930380-11-8). Quail Run.

Hyde, Margaret & Forsyth, Elizabeth. Know Your Feelings. LC 74-12119. 128p. (gr. 7 up). 1975. PLB 5.90 o.p. (ISBN 0-531-02797-X). Watts.

Hyde, Margaret O. Crime & Justice in Our Time. (gr. 7 up). 1980. PLB 7.90 (ISBN 0-531-04116-6, A34). Watts.

--Energy: The New Look. 128p. (gr. 7-9). 1981. 7.95 (ISBN 0-07-031552-3). McGraw.

--Is the Cat Dreaming Your Dream. LC 79-22684. (gr. 7-9). 1980. 7.95 (ISBN 0-07-031594-9). McGraw.

--Juvenile Justice & Injustice. (gr. 7 up). 1977. lib. bdg. 7.90 s&l (ISBN 0-531-00122-9). Watts.

--The New Genetics: Promises & Perils. LC 74-916. (Illus.). (gr. 9 up). 1974. PLB 6.88 o.p. (ISBN 0-531-02672-8). Watts.

Hyde, Martha B., jt. auth. see Jordaan, Jean-Pierre.

Hyde, Mary. The Impossible Friendship: Boswell & Mrs. Thrale. LC 72-88127. (Illus.). 200p. 1972. 10.00x (ISBN 0-674-44541-4). Harvard U Pr.

--The Thrales of Streatham Park. (Illus.). 1977. 16.50x (ISBN 0-674-88746-8). Harvard U Pr.

Hyde, R. M. & Patnode, Robert. Immunology. (Illus.). 1978. text ed. 11.95 (ISBN 0-87909-385-4); pap. text ed. 10.95 (ISBN 0-8359-3853-0); instrs'. manual avail. Reston.

Hyde, Sarah & Engle. The Potomac Program. 439p. 1977. 34.95 (ISBN 0-86575-037-8). Dormac.

Hyde, Stuart W. Television & Radio Announcing. 3rd ed. LC 78-69615. (Illus.). 1979. text ed. 17.95 (ISBN 0-395-27108-8). HM.

Hyde, Tracy E. The Single Grandmother. LC 73-88510. 250p. 1974. 11.95 (ISBN 0-88229-128-9). Nelson-Hall.

Hyde, Walter W. Greek Religion & Its Survivals. LC 63-10268. (Our Debt to Greece & Rome Ser). 1963. Repr. of 1930 ed. 7.50x (ISBN 0-8154-0117-5). Cooper Sq.

Hyde, Wendell, jt. auth. see Eisberg, Robert.

Hyde, William. The Epicurean Pursuit of Pleasure. (Illus.). 1980. Repr. of 1904 ed. deluxe ed. 47.95 (ISBN 0-89901-009-1). Found Class Reprints.

Hyde, William F. Timber Supply, Land Allocation, & Economic Efficiency. LC 80-8021. (Illus.). 248p. 1980. text ed. 19.00x (ISBN 0-8018-2489-3). Johns Hopkins.

Hyden, Goran. Beyond Ujamaa in Tanzania: Underdevelopment & an Uncaptured Peasantry. 1980. 20.00 (ISBN 0-520-03997-1); pap. 7.95 (ISBN 0-520-04017-1). U of Cal Pr.

Hyden, Goran, et al. Development Administration: The Kenyon Experience. (Illus.). 384p. 1970. text ed. 12.95x. Oxford U Pr.

Hyder, Clyde K., ed. Swinburne: The Critical Heritage. 1970. 24.00x (ISBN 0-7100-6656-2). Routledge & Kegan.

Hyer, Paul, jt. auth. see Jagchid, Sechin.

Hyginus, et al. Fabularum Liber. LC 75-27848. (Renaissance & the Gods Ser.: Vol. 6). 1976. Repr. of 1535 ed. lib. bdg. 73.00 (ISBN 0-8240-2055-3). Garland Pub.

Hyland, Ann. Foal to Five Years. LC 80-11310. 128p. 1980. 12.95 (ISBN 0-668-04952-9, 4952-9). Arco.

Hyland, Fay & Steinmetz, Ferdinand H. Trees & Other Woody Plants of Maine. LC 78-18706. 1978. lib. bdg. 7.50x o.p. (ISBN 0-89621-019-7); pap. 3.50x o.p. (ISBN 0-89621-018-9). Thorndike Pr.

Hyland, Francis, jt. auth. see St. John Williams, Guy.

Hyland, J. The Trainer's Guide to Time Management. 1981. write for info. (ISBN 0-201-03109-4). A-W.

Hyland, Patricia A., jt. auth. see Saxton, Dolores F.

Hyland, Peter. Disguise & Role-Playing in Ben Jonson's Drama. (Salzburg Studies in English Literature, Jacobean Drama Studies: No. 69). (Orig.). 1977. pap. text ed. 25.00x (ISBN 0-391-01432-3). Humanities.

Hyland, Wende & Haynes, Roberta. How to Make It in Hollywood. LC 75-17523. 250p. 1975. 13.95 (ISBN 0-88229-239-0). Nelson Hall.

Hylander, Clarence J. Animals in Fur. (Illus.). (gr. 7 up). 1956. 8.95g (ISBN 0-02-746200-5). Macmillan.

--World of Plant Life. 2nd ed. (Illus.). 1956. 19.95 (ISBN 0-02-558050-7). Macmillan.

Hylen, Arnold. Bunker Hill: A Los Angeles Landmark. (L.A. Miscellany Ser.: No. 7). (Illus.). 1976. 22.50 o.p. (ISBN 0-87093-172-5). Dawsons.

Hylton, John. Reintegrating the Offender: Assessing the Impact of Community Corrections. LC 80-5730. 334p. 1981. lib. bdg. 20.75 (ISBN 0-8191-1387-5); pap. text ed. 11.75 (ISBN 0-8191-1388-3). U Pr of Amer.

Hylton, William, ed. The Rodale Herb Book: How to Use, Grow & Buy Nature's Miracle Plants. LC 73-18902. (Illus.). 658p. 1974. 13.95 (ISBN 0-87857-076-4); deluxe ed. 15.95 (ISBN 0-87857-196-5). Rodale Pr Inc.

Hylton, William H., ed. Build Your Harvest Kitchen. (Illus.). 640p. 1980. 24.95 (ISBN 0-87857-316-X). Rodale Pr Inc.

Hyman, A. A., jt. auth. see Brandstatter, A. F.

Hyman, Allen & Johnson, M. Bruce, eds. Advertising & Free Speech. LC 77-5272. 1977. 14.95 (ISBN 0-669-01604-7). Lexington Bks.

Hyman, Andrew A. & Sainer, Elliot A., eds. Who's Who in Health Care. LC 77-79993. 1977. text ed. 60.00 (ISBN 0-89443-074-2). Aspen Systems.

Hyman, Arthur, jt. ed. see Lieberman, Saul.

Hyman, Dick. Cockeyed Americana. LC 72-81526. 1972. 6.95 (ISBN 0-8289-0170-8). Greene.

--Potomac Wind & Wisdom: Jokes, Lies & True Stories About America's Politics & Politicians. LC 80-13482. (Illus.). 1980. 6.95 (ISBN 0-8289-0372-7). Greene.

--The Trenton Pickle Ordinance & Other Bonehead Legislation. LC 75-41874. (Illus.). 132p. 1976. 6.95 (ISBN 0-8289-0278-X). Greene.

Hyman, Eric, et al. The Theory & Practice of Environmental Quality Analysis: Water Resources Management, Land Suitability Analysis, Economics & Aesthetics, No. 27. 103p. 1980. pap. 15.00 (ISBN 0-86602-027-6). CPL Biblios.

Hyman, Harold & Nevins, Allan, eds. Heard 'round the World. (Impact of the Civil War Ser, Vol. 3). 1969. 7.95 o.p. (ISBN 0-394-42802-1). Knopf.

Hyman, Harold, ed. see McPherson, Edward.

Hyman, Harold M., jt. auth. see Thomas, Benjamin P.

Hyman, Harold M., ed. The New American State Papers: Labor & Slavery Subject Set, 7 vols. LC 72-95577. 1973. Set. 425.00 o.p. (ISBN 0-8420-1505-1). Scholarly Res Inc.

Hyman, Harold T. Differential Diagnosis: An Integrated Handbook. 1965. 14.00 o.p. (ISBN 0-397-50136-6). Lippincott.

Hyman, Herbert H. Health Planning: A Systematic Approach. LC 75-37405. 460p. 1976. text ed. 27.50 (ISBN 0-912862-17-3). Aspen Systems.

--Health Regulation: Certificate of Need & 1122. LC 76-45524. 1977. 22.00 (ISBN 0-912862-34-3). Aspen Systems.

--Secondary Analysis of Sample Surveys: Principles, Procedures & Potentialities. LC 72-251. 347p. 1972. 18.50 (ISBN 0-471-42605-9, Pub. by Wiley). Krieger.

--Survey Design & Analysis. 1955. text ed. 10.95 o.s.i. (ISBN 0-02-915770-6). Free Pr.

Hyman, Herbert H. & Singer, Eleanor D., eds. Readings in Reference Group Theory & Research. LC 68-10366. 1968. 17.95 (ISBN 0-02-915700-5). Free Pr.

Hyman, Herbert Harvey, jt. auth. see Spiegel, Allen D.

Hyman, Isabelle. Fifteenth Century Florentine Studies: The Palazzo Medici & a Ledger for the Church of San Lorenzo. LC 76-23631. (Outstanding Dissertations in the Fine Arts - Fifteenth Century). (Illus.). 1977. Repr. of 1968 ed. lib. bdg. 70.00 (ISBN 0-8240-2700-0). Garland Pub.

Hyman, J. D., et al. Toward Equal Opportunity in Employment, the Role of State & Local Government: Proceedings. LC 74-15228. (Symposia on Law and Society Ser). 1971. Repr. of 1964 ed. lib. bdg. 17.50 (ISBN 0-306-70120-0). Da Capo.

Hyman, June. Deafness. (gr. 4 up). 1980. PLB 6.45 (ISBN 0-531-02940-9). Watts.

Hyman, Lawrence. The Quarrel Within: Art & Morality in Milton's Poetry. LC 76-189559. 1972. 11.00 (ISBN 0-8046-9018-9, Natl U). Kennikat.

Hyman, Louis. The Jews of Ireland. 422p. 1972. 15.00x (ISBN 0-7165-2082-6, Pub. by Irish Academic Pr Ireland). Biblio Dist.

Hyman, Mary, tr. see LeNotre, Gaston.

Hyman, Merv, jt. auth. see White, Gordon.

Hyman, Philip, tr. see LeNotre, Gaston.

Hyman, R. Disputes Procedure in Action. 1972. text ed. 6.95x o.p. (ISBN 0-435-85320-1). Heinemann Ed.

--Strikes. pap. 1.95 o.p. (ISBN 0-531-06033-0, Fontana Pap). Watts.

Hyman, Richard. Ceramics Handbook. (Illus.). 1977. 4.95 o.p. (ISBN 0-668-00347-2); pap. 2.50 o.p. (ISBN 0-668-04066-1). Arco.

--Shelf Classification Research. (Occasional Papers: No. 146). 1980. pap. 3.00. U of Ill Lib Sci.

Hyman, Richard & Brough, Ian. Social Values & Industrial Relations: A Study of Fairness & Inequality. 1975. 20.00x (ISBN 0-631-16640-8, Pub. by Basil Blackwell); pap. 14.00x (ISBN 0-631-16610-6, Pub. by Basil Blackwell). Biblio Dist.

Hyman, Robin. Quotation Dictionary. 1965. 10.95 (ISBN 0-02-558060-4). Macmillan.

Hyman, Ronald. Improving Discussion Leadership. 154p. (Orig.). 1980. pap. 9.95x (ISBN 0-8077-2610-9). Tchrs Coll.

Hyman, Ronald T. Simulation Gaming for Values Education: The Prisoner's Dilemma. LC 77-93726. 1978. pap. text ed. 8.50x o.p. (ISBN 0-8191-0428-0). U Pr of Amer.

--Strategic Questioning. LC 79-783. (Illus.). 1979. pap. text ed. 9.95 (ISBN 0-13-851055-5). P-H.

Hyman, Ronald T., jt. ed. see Baily, Samuel L.

Hyman, Ruth L. Gustav Landauer: Philosopher of Utopia. LC 76-49585. 1977. 25.00 (ISBN 0-915144-27-1). Hackett Pub.

Hyman, Stanley. Associations & Consultants. 1970. 15.00x o.p. (ISBN 0-8464-0158-4). Beekman Pubs.

Hyman, Stanley, ed. William Troy: Selected Essays. 1967. 19.00 (ISBN 0-8135-0553-4). Rutgers U Pr.

Hyman, Trina S. A Little Alphabet. (Illus.). 32p. 1980. 4.95 (ISBN 0-316-38705-3). Little.

--Self-Portrait: Trina Schart Hyman. LC 80-26662. (Self-Portrait Collection Ser.). (Illus.). 32p. (gr. 1-9). 1981. PLB 8.95 (ISBN 0-201-09308-1, A-W Childrens). A-W.

Hyman, Vernon T. Giant Killer. 352p. 1981. 12.95 (ISBN 0-399-90099-3). Marek.

Hymen, Mervin D. & White, Gordon S., Jr. Big Ten Football: Its Life & Times, Great Coaches, Players & Games. (Illus.). 1977. 12.95 o.s.i. (ISBN 0-02-558070-1). Macmillan.

Hymer, Dian D. Sew, Recycle, & Save: Practical Solutions to the Challenges of the 80's. (Urban Life Ser.). (Illus.). 96p. (Orig.). 1981. pap. 4.95 (ISBN 0-87701-179-6). Chronicle Bks.

Hymer, S. The Multinational Corporation. Cohen, R. B., et al, eds. LC 79-52327. (Illus.). 1979. 39.50 (ISBN 0-521-22695-3). Cambridge U Pr.

Hymer, S. see Kay, Geoffrey.

Hymers, R. L. Encounters of the Fourth Kind. Orig. Title: UFO's & Bible Prophecy. pap. 1.95 (ISBN 0-89728-028-8, 698609). Omega Pubns OR.

--Holocaust II. 1978. pap. 1.95 (ISBN 0-89728-005-9, 711269). Omega Pubns OR.

--UFO's & Bible Prophecy. pap. 1.95 (ISBN 0-89728-061-X, 665117). Omega Pubns OR.

Hymers, R. L., jt. auth. see Philpott, Kent.

Hymes, Dell. Foundations in Sociolinguistics: An Ethnographic Approach. LC 73-89288. (Conduct & Communication Ser.). 1974. 15.00x (ISBN 0-8122-7675-2); pap. 7.95x (ISBN 0-8122-1065-4, Pa Paperbks). U of Pa Pr.

--Pidginization & Creolization of Languages: Proceedings. LC 77-123672. 1971. 42.50 (ISBN 0-521-07833-4); pap. 14.95x (ISBN 0-521-09888-2). Cambridge U Pr.

Hymes, James L. Teaching the Child Under Six. 3rd ed. (Illus.). 224p. Date not set. pap. text ed. 7.95 (ISBN 0-675-08063-0). Merrill.

Hymes, James L., Jr. Teaching the Child Under Six. 2nd ed. LC 73-84784. (Education - Elementary Ser.). 192p. 1974. pap. text ed. 8.95x (ISBN 0-675-08891-7). Merrill.

Hymes, Jesild, Jr. Child Under Six. 1963. 9.95 (ISBN 0-13-132209-5). P-H.

Hynd, Noel. The Sandler Inquiry. 1979. pap. 2.50 o.s.i. (ISBN 0-440-17958-0). Dell.

Hyndman, D. E. Analog & Hybrid Computing. LC 75-120691. 1970. 25.00 (ISBN 0-08-015573-1); pap. 13.25 (ISBN 0-08-015572-3). Pergamon.

Hyndman, Michael. Schools & Schooling in England & Wales (1800-1977) A Documentary History. 1978. 16.95 o.p. (ISBN 0-06-318077-4, IntlDept); pap. text ed. 11.90 (ISBN 0-06-318078-2, IntlDept). Har-Row.

Hynds, Ernest C. American Newspapers in the Nineteen Seventies. (Studies in Media Management). 1975. 13.50 o.p. (ISBN 0-8038-0375-3); pap. text ed. 7.95x o.p. (ISBN 0-8038-0383-4). Hastings.

Hynek, J. Allen & Vallee, Jacques. The Edge of Reality: A Progress Report on Unidentified Flying Objects. LC 75-13226. (Illus.). 288p. 1976. 14.95 o.p. (ISBN 0-8092-8209-7); pap. 5.95 o.p. (ISBN 0-8092-8150-3). Contemp Bks.

Hyneman, Charles S. The Study of Politics. LC 59-10554. 1959. 12.00 (ISBN 0-252-72671-5). U of Ill Pr.

--The Supreme Court on Trial. LC 73-20501. 308p. 1974. Repr. of 1963 ed. lib. bdg. 21.75x (ISBN 0-8371-7326-4, HYSC). Greenwood.

Hyneman, Charles S. & Carey, George W., eds. Second Federalist: Congress Creates a Government. LC 66-27380. (Orig.). 1966. pap. text ed. 6.95x (ISBN 0-89197-510-1). Irvington.

Hynes, Arleen. Passover Meal. LC 76-187207. 1972. pap. 1.95 (ISBN 0-8091-1653-7). Paulist Pr.

Hynes, J. Dennis. Agency & Partnership, Cases, Materials & Problems. (Contemporary Legal Eucation Ser.). 1975. 20.00 (ISBN 0-672-81769-1, Bobbs-Merrill Law). Michie.

Hynes, R. & Fox, C. Fred, eds. Tumor Cell Surfaces & Malignancy: Proceedings. LC 80-7798. (Progress in Clinical & Biological Research Ser.: Vol. 41). 214p. 1980. 130.00 (ISBN 0-8451-0041-6). A R Liss.

Hynes, Samuel. Edwardian Occasions. 250p. 1972. 14.95 (ISBN 0-19-519709-7). Oxford U Pr.

Hynes, Samuel, ed. see Bennett, Arnold.

Hynes, Samuel, jt. ed. see Hoffman, Daniel G.

Hynes, V. Barbara. Orthopedic & Rehabilitation Nursing Continuing Education Review. 1976. sprial bdg. 9.50 (ISBN 0-87488-397-0). Med Exam.

Hynes, William G. The Economics of Empire: Britain, Africa & the New Imperialism, 1870-1895. (Illus.). 1979. text ed. 22.00 (ISBN 0-582-64234-5). Longman.

Hyslop, Francis E., ed. see Baudelaire, Charles P.

Hyslop, Lois B. Henry Becque. (World Authors Ser.: France: No. 180). pap. 10.95 (ISBN 0-8057-2128-2). Twayne.

Hyslop, Lois B., ed. see Baudelaire, Charles P.

Hyslop, N., ed. see Eighth International Biometeorological Congress 9-15 September 1979.

Hyslop, N. St. G., jt. ed. see Zemel, Z.

Hyslop, Theophilus B. Great Abnormals. LC 79-162514. xxviii, 289p. 1971. Repr. of 1925 ed. 20.00 (ISBN 0-8103-3797-5). Gale.

Hysom, J., jt. auth. see Norcross, C.

Hytier, Jean. Questions De Litterature. LC 68-4151. 1967. 20.00x (ISBN 0-231-03123-8). Columbia U Pr.

Hyvaerinen, L. P. Information Theory for Systems Engineers. rev ed. (Lecture Notes in Operations Research & Mathematical Systems: Vol. 5). 1968. pap. 14.70 o.p. (ISBN 0-387-04254-7). Springer-Verlag.

--Mathematical Modeling for Industrial Processes. LC 70-111899. (Lecture Notes in Operations Research & Mathematical Systems: Vol. 19). (Illus.). 1970. pap. 10.70 o.p. (ISBN 0-387-04943-6). Springer-Verlag.

I

I Ching. I Ching: The Book of Changes. Legge, James, tr. (Sacred Books of the East Ser.). 8.75 (ISBN 0-8446-2291-5). Peter Smith.

I, Jalal Huma, ed. see Ghazali.

I. O. T. T. S. Group. International Oil Tanker & Terminal Safety Guide. 2nd ed. LC 75-2371. 185p. 1975. 19.95 (ISBN 0-470-42807-4). Halsted Pr.

I. P. A. New York. Government in Metropolitan Calcutta. 6.50x o.p. (ISBN 0-210-22663-3). Asia.

I. P. R. A. Proceedings of the Third General Conference, Vol. 3. 1970. pap. text ed. 59.00x (ISBN 90-232-0839-0). Humanities.

I U B - I U B S Joint Symposium - 1st - Stockholm - 1960. Biological Structure & Function: Proceedings, 2 Vols. Goodwin, T. W. & Lindberg, Olov, eds. 1961. Vol. 1. 50.00 (ISBN 0-12-289851-6). Acad Pr.

Iacobelli, Stefano & Dimarco, A., eds. Role of Medroxyprogesterone in Endocrine-Related Tumors. (Progress in Cancer Research & Therapy Ser.: Vol. 15). 168p. 1980. text ed. 15.00 (ISBN 0-89004-512-7). Raven.

Iacobelli, Stefano, et al, eds. Hormones & Cancer. (Progress in Cancer Research & Therapy Ser.). 589p. 1980. text ed. 49.00 (ISBN 0-89004-486-4). Raven.

Iacopi, Robert, ed. Earthquake Country: California. LC 78-163736. (Illus.). 160p. 1971. pap. 5.95 (ISBN 0-376-06144-8, Sunset Bks.). Sunset-Lane.

IAEA. Origin & Fate of Chemical Residues in Food, Agriculture & Fisheries: Proceedings. (Illus.). 189p. 1976. pap. 17.75 (ISBN 92-0-111375-7, ISP399, IAEA). Unipub.

IAEA-NEA Symposium, Julich, Oct. 13-17, 1975. Gas-Cooled Reactors with Emphasis on Advanced Systems Vol. 2, 1976: Proceedings. (Proceedings Ser.). (Illus., Orig.). 1976. pap. 44.00 (ISBN 92-0-050176-1, IAEA). Unipub.

Iagolnitzer, D., ed. Complex Analysis, Microbial Calculus & Relativistic Quantum Theory. (Lecture Notes in Physics: Vol. 126). 502p. 1980. pap. 33.60 (ISBN 0-387-09996-4). Springer-Verlag.

Ianacio, Del Rio see Del Rio, Ignacio.

Ianacone, Evonne. Changing More Than the Channel: How to Form a Media Access Group. pap. 6.00 (ISBN 0-9603466-2-7). NCCB.

Iannaccone, Laurence, jt. ed. see Lutz, Frank W.

Iannacconne, Laurence, jt. auth. see Lutz, Frank W.

Ianni, Francis A., et al. Conflict & Change in Education. 470p. 1975. pap. 9.95x (ISBN 0-673-07750-0). Scott F.

Iannone, N. Supervision of Police Personnel. 3rd ed. 1980. 15.95 (ISBN 0-13-876987-7). P-H.

I.A.U Symposium No. 78, Kiev, USSR, May 23-28, 1977, et al. Nutation & the Earth's Rotation: Proceedings. Smith, M. L. & Bender, P. L., eds. 284p. 1980. lib. bdg. 34.00 (ISBN 90-277-1113-5); pap. 21.00 (ISBN 90-277-1114-3). Kluwer Boston.

Iavanainen, Matti. A Study on the Origins of Mental Rehabilitation. (Clinics in Developmental Medicine Ser.: Vol. 51). 173p. 1974. 23.00 (ISBN 0-685-59045-3). Lippincott.

IAVSD-Symposium Held at the Technical University Berlin, 6th, September 1979. The Dynamics of Vehicles on Roads & on Tracks: Proceedings. Willumeit, H. P., ed. 522p. 1980. pap. text ed. 46.00 (ISBN 90-265-0327-X, Pub. by Swets Pub Serv Holland). Swets North Am.

Ibanez, Carmen, jt. auth. see Shaw, Lawrence.

Ibbetson, J., jt. auth. see Whitmore, D. A.

Ibele, Oscar. Political Science: An Introduction. LC 72-103933. 546p. 1971. text ed. 20.50 scp o.p. (ISBN 0-685-03947-1, HarpC); inst. manual free o.p. (ISBN 0-06-363175-X). Har-Row.

Ibele, Warren E., ed. Modern Developments in Heat Transfer. 1963. 55.50 (ISBN 0-12-369550-3). Acad Pr.

Ibingira, Grace S. African Upheavals Since Independence. (Westview Special Studies on Africa). 1980. lib. bdg. 25.00x (ISBN 0-89158-585-0). Westview.

Ibish, Yusuf & Wilson, Peter L., eds. Traditional Modes of Contemplation & Action. 1978. 25.00 (ISBN 0-87773-729-0). Great Eastern.

Ibn Al-Tiqtaqa. Al-Fakhri: On the Systems of Government & the Moslem Dynasties. Whitting, C. E., tr. LC 79-2869. 326p. 1981. Repr. of 1947 ed. 26.50 (ISBN 0-8305-0041-3). Hyperion Conn.

Ibn Al-Titaka. Al-Fakhr: On the Systems of Government and the Moslem Dynasties. Whitting, C. E., tr. LC 80-2201. 1981. Repr. of 1947 ed. 35.00 (ISBN 0-404-18968-7). AMS Pr.

Ibn Aslam, Abukamil Shuja see Shuja Ibn Aslam, Abukamil.

Ibp Research & Editorial Staff. Life Insurance Desk Book. 4th ed. 1976. 32.50 o.p. (ISBN 0-685-73750-0). P-H.

Ibrahim, Hilmi M. & Martin, Fred, eds. Leisure: An Introduction. 2nd ed. LC 77-89694. 1978. pap. text ed. 8.95x (ISBN 0-89260-085-3). Hwong Pub.

Ibrahim, I., et al. Readings in Managerial Economics. LC 75-4618. 1976. text ed. 41.00 (ISBN 0-08-019605-5); pap. text ed. 18.00 (ISBN 0-08-019604-7). Pergamon.

Ibrahim, M. Z. Glycogen & Its Related Enzymes of Metabolism in the Central Nervous System. (Advances in Anatomy, Embryology & Cell Biology: Vol. 52, Pt. 1). (Illus.). 90p. 1976. pap. 33.10 (ISBN 0-387-07454-6). Springer-Verlag.

Ibrahim, Sonallah. The Smell of It. Johnson-Davies, Denys, tr. from Arabic. 118p. (Orig.). 1971. pap. 5.00 (ISBN 0-89410-194-3); pap. 5.00 (ISBN 0-89410-195-1). Three Continents.

IBRO Symposium, Italy, September 1978. Reflex Control of Posture & Movement: Proceedings. Granit, R. & Pompeiano, O., eds. (Progress in Brain Research Ser.: Vol. 50). 1980. 122.00 (ISBN 0-444-80099-9, North Holland). Elsevier.

Ibsen, Hendrik. Brand. 1961. 5.00x o.p. (ISBN 0-460-00716-5, Evman). Dutton.

Ibsen, Henrik. Doll's House & Other Plays. Watts, Peter, tr. Incl. League of Youth; Lady from the Sea. (Classics Ser.). 1965. pap. 2.95 (ISBN 0-14-044146-8). Penguin.

--A Doll's House, The Wild Duck & Lady from the Sea. 1979. 7.00x (ISBN 0-460-00494-8, Evman); pap. 3.75 (ISBN 0-460-01494-3, Evman). Dutton.

--Ghosts. 1979. 7.95x (ISBN 0-8464-0091-X). Beekman Pubs.

--Ghosts & Three Other Plays. LC 66-11746. 1966. pap. 2.95 (ISBN 0-385-02147-X, A215E, Anch). Doubleday.

--Hedda Gabler & Other Plays. LeGallienne, Eva & Ginsbury, Norman, trs. (Illus.). 1976. pap. 2.95 (ISBN 0-460-01111-1, Evman). Dutton.

--John Gabriel Borkman. 1979. 7.95x (ISBN 0-8464-0092-8). Beekman Pubs.

--The Lady from the Sea. 1979. 7.95x (ISBN 0-8464-0093-6). Beekman Pubs.

--The Master Builder. 1979. 7.95x (ISBN 0-8464-0095-2). Beekman Pubs.

--The Oxford Ibsen. McFarlane, James W., ed. Incl. Vol. 2. The Vikings at Helgeland; Love's Comedy; The Pretenders. Arup, Jens, tr. 1962. 24.00x (ISBN 0-19-211334-8); Vol. 4. The League of Youth; Emperor Galilean. McFarlane, James W. & Orton, Graham, trs. 1963. 32.00x (ISBN 0-19-211338-0); Vol. 5. Pillars of Society, a Doll's House, Ghosts. McFarlane, James W., tr. 1961. 18.50x (ISBN 0-19-211326-7); Vol. 7. The Lady from the Sea; Hedda Gabler; The Master Builder. Arup, Jens & McFarland, James W., trs. 1966. 32.00x (ISBN 0-19-211342-9); Vol. 3. Brand, Peer Gynt. Kirkup, James & Fry, Christopher, trs. 1972. 24.00x (ISBN 0-19-211360-7); Vol. 1. Early Plays. Orton, Graham, tr. 1970. 45.00x (ISBN 0-19-211357-7). Oxford U Pr.

--Peer Gynt. rev. ed. Fjelde, Rolf, tr. from Norwegian. (Vol. 2). 260p. 1981. 15.00x (ISBN 0-8166-0912-8); pap. 5.95 (ISBN 0-8166-0915-2). U of Minn Pr.

--Peer Gynt. Farquharson, R., tr. 1956. 7.95x (ISBN 0-460-00747-5, Evman). Dutton.

--The Pillars of Society. 1979. 7.95x (ISBN 0-8464-0096-0). Beekman Pubs.

--Wild Duck. Jurgensen, Kai & Schenkkan, Robert, eds. Jurgensen, Kai & Schenkkan, Robert, trs. LC 66-21588. 1966. pap. text ed. 2.95x (ISBN 0-88295-046-0). AHM Pub.

--Wild Duck. Christiani, Dounia B., ed. (Critcal Editions). (gr. 9-12). 1969. 5.00 (ISBN 0-393-04187-5, NortonC); pap. text ed. 5.00 (ISBN 0-393-09825-7). Norton.

--The Wild Duck. Hampton, Christopher, tr. 120p. 1981. pap. 7.50 (ISBN 0-571-11601-9, Pub. by Faber & Faber). Merrimack Bk Serv.

Ibsen, Henrik see Caputi, Anthony.

Ibsen, Henrik see Watson, E. Bradlee & Pressey, Benfield.

Ibuse, Masuji. Lieutenant Lookest & Other Stories. Bester, John, tr. from Jap. LC 71-135143. 308p. 1971. 8.95 (ISBN 0-87011-147-7). Kodansha.

Icaza, Jorge. The Villagers (Huasipungo) A Novel. Dulsey, Bernard M., tr. from Span. LC 73-9551. (Arcturus Books Paperbacks). 238p. 1973. pap. 6.95 (ISBN 0-8093-0653-0). S Ill U Pr.

Ice Skating Institute of America Staff. Olympic Alpine Skiing. LC 79-19029. (Olympic Bks.). (Illus.). (gr. 4 up). 1979. lib. bdg. 7.95 (ISBN 0-516-02551-1); pap. 1.95 (ISBN 0-516-42551-X). Childrens.

--Olympic Bobsledding. LC 79-18842. (Olympic Bks.). (Illus.). (gr. 4 up). 1979. lib. bdg. 7.95 (ISBN 0-516-02552-X); pap. 1.95 (ISBN 0-516-42552-8). Childrens.

--Olympic Figure Skating. LC 79-16948. (Olympic Bks.). (Illus.). (gr. 4 up). 1979. lib. bdg. 7.95 (ISBN 0-516-02553-8); pap. 1.95 (ISBN 0-516-42553-6). Childrens.

--Olympic Ice Hockey. LC 79-16382. (Olympic Bks.). (Illus.). (gr. 4 up). 1979. lib. bdg. 7.95 (ISBN 0-516-02554-6); pap. 1.95 (ISBN 0-516-42554-4). Childrens.

--Olympic Nordic Skiing. LC 79-18626. (Olympic Bks.). (Illus.). (gr. 4 up). 1979. lib. bdg. 7.95 (ISBN 0-516-02555-4); pap. 1.95 (ISBN 0-516-42555-2). Childrens.

--Olympic Speed Skating. LC 79-16969. (Olympic Bks.). (Illus.). (gr. 4 up). 1979. lib. bdg. 7.95 (ISBN 0-516-02556-2); pap. 1.95 (ISBN 0-516-42556-0). Childrens.

Icenhower, Joseph B. First Book of the Antarctic. (First Bks). (Illus.). (gr. 4-6). 1971. PLB 4.90 o.p. (ISBN 0-531-00468-6). Watts.

--Panay Incident, December 12, 1937: The Sinking of an American Gunboat Worsens U. S. - Japanese Relations. LC 70-161832. (Focus Bks). (Illus.). (gr. 7 up). 1971. PLB 4.90 o.p. (ISBN 0-531-00992-0). Watts.

--Perry & the Open Door to Japan, July, 1853: An American Commander Ends Centuries of Japanese Isolation. LC 72-10423. (World Focus Bks). (Illus.). 72p. (gr. 7 up). 1973. PLB 4.47 o.p. (ISBN 0-531-02167-X). Watts.

--Tecumseh & the Indian Confederation: The Indian Nations East of the Mississippi Are Defeated. (Focus Bks). (Illus.). 96p. (gr. 8 up). 1975. PLB 4.90 o.p. (ISBN 0-531-02780-5). Watts.

Icerman, Larry J., jt. auth. see Morgan, Robert P.

Ichheiser, Gustav. Appearances & Realities: Misunderstanding in Human Relations. LC 70-110631. (Social & Behavioral Science Ser.). 1970. 15.95x o.p. (ISBN 0-87589-060-1). Jossey-Bass.

Ichikawa, M., jt. auth. see Tamaru, K.

Ichikawa, Satomi. A Child's Book of Seasons. LC 74-31047. (Illus.). (gr. k-3). 1976. 5.95 o.s.i. (ISBN 0-8193-0795-5, Four Winds); PLB 5.41 o.s.i. (ISBN 0-8193-0796-3). Schol Bk Serv.

--Friends. LC 76-46146. (Illus.). (ps-2). 1977. 5.95 o.s.i. (ISBN 0-8193-0870-6, Four Winds); PLB 5.41 o.s.i. (ISBN 0-8193-0871-4). Schol Bk Serv.

--Suzanne & Nicholas at the Market. (Illus.). (gr. k-3). 1978. PLB 6.90 s&l o.p. (ISBN 0-531-01357-X). Watts.

--Suzanne & Nicholas in the Garden. (Illus.). (gr. k-3). 1978. PLB 6.90 s&l o.p. (ISBN 0-531-01358-8). Watts.

Ichioka, Yuji, et al, eds. A Buried Past: An Annotated Bibliography of the Japanese American Research Project Collection. 1974. 18.50x (ISBN 0-520-02541-5). U of Cal Pr.

Ickes, Harold L. Back to Work. LC 72-7426. (FDR & the Era of the New Deal Ser.). (Illus.). 276p. Repr. of 1935 ed. lib. bdg. 29.50 (ISBN 0-306-70527-3). Da Capo.

Ickie, John, jt. auth. see Elliot, R. S.

Ickis, Marguerite. Weaving As a Hobby. (Illus.). (gr. 9 up). 1968. 6.95 o.p. (ISBN 0-8069-5110-9); PLB 6.69 o.p. (ISBN 0-8069-5111-7). Sterling.

ICN-UCLA Conference, Squaw Valley, Calif., March 2-7, 1975. Cell Surface Receptors: Proceedings. Nicolson, Garth L., et al, eds. LC 76-8160. (Progress in Clinical & Biological Research: Vol. 8). 1976. 49.00x (ISBN 0-8451-0008-4). A R Liss.

ICN-UCLA Symposia on Molecular & Cellular Biology. Human Cytogenetics, Vol. 7. Sparkes, Robert S., et al, eds. (ICN-UCLA Symposia on Molecular & Cellular Biology Ser.). 1977. 26.00 (ISBN 0-12-656350-0). Acad Pr.

ICN-UCLA Symposia on Molecular & Cellular Biology, 1979. T & B Lymphocytes: Recognition & Function: Symposium, Vol. XVI. Bach, Fritz H., et al, eds. LC 79-26438. 1979. 39.50 (ISBN 0-12-069850-1). Acad Pr.

ICN-UCLA Symposium, Keystone, Colo., February 1979. Biological Recognition & Assembly: Proceedings. Lake, J. & Fox, C. Fred, eds. LC 80-7797. (Progress in Clinical & Biological Research Ser.: Vol. 40). 362p. 1980. 52.00x (ISBN 0-8451-0040-8). A R Liss.

ICN-UCLA Symposium on Transmembrane Signaling, Keystone, Colorado, February, 1978. Transmembrane Signaling: Proceedings. Bitensky, M., et al, eds. LC 79-5061. (Progress in Clinical & Biological Research Ser.: Vol. 31). 1979. 78.00x (ISBN 0-8451-0031-9). A R Liss.

Idaikkadar, N. M. Agricultural Statistics: A Handbook for Developing Countries. (Illus.). 1979. text ed. 28.00 (ISBN 0-08-023388-0); pap. text ed. 11.50 (ISBN 0-08-023387-2). Pergamon.

Ide, Arthur F. Woman in Ancient Greece. LC 79-19011. (Woman in History Ser.: Vol. 7). (Illus.). 51p. 1980. 9.00 (ISBN 0-86663-012-0); pap. 6.00 (ISBN 0-86663-013-9). Ide Hse.

--Woman in Biblical Israel. LC 79-19011. (Woman in History Ser.: Vol. 5). (Illus.). 50p. 1980. 9.00 (ISBN 0-86663-008-2); pap. 6.00 (ISBN 0-86663-009-0). Ide Hse.

--Woman in Early Christianity & Christian Society. LC 79-19011. (Woman in History Ser.: Vol. 9). (Illus.). 53p. 1980. 9.00 (ISBN 0-86663-016-3); pap. 6.95 (ISBN 0-86663-017-1). Ide Hse.

--Woman in the American Colonial South. LC 79-19011. (Woman in History Ser.: Vol. 30). 88p. (Orig.). 1980. 12.00 (ISBN 0-86663-018-X); pap. 8.00 (ISBN 0-86663-019-8). Ide Hse.

--Woman in the Civilization of the Ancient Near East. LC 79-19011. (Woman in History Ser.: Vol. 2). (Illus.). 82p. (Orig.). 1981. 8.00 (ISBN 0-86663-006-6); pap. 6.00 (ISBN 0-86663-007-4). Ide Hse.

Ide, Arthur F. & Ide, Charles A. To Live Happily Ever After: A Guide to a Lasting Relationship. 60p. (Orig.). 1981. 12.95 (ISBN 0-86663-998-5); pap. 7.50 (ISBN 0-86663-999-3). Ide Hse.

--Woman in the Age of Christian Martyrs. LC 79-19011. (Woman in History Ser.: Vol. 10). (Illus.). ix, 98p. 1980. 9.00 (ISBN 0-86663-000-7); pap. 8.00 (ISBN 0-86663-001-5). Ide Hse.

Ide, Arthur F., ed. see Bayless, Gordon E.

Ide, Arthur F., ed. see Blade, Melinda K.

Ide, Arthur F., ed. see Frazier, A. Eugene.

Ide, Arthur F., ed. see Frazier, Alton E.

Ide, Arthur F., ed. see Nelson, Robert V.

Ide, Arthur F., ed. & illus. see Nelson, Robert V.

Ide, Arthur F., ed. see Nelson, Robert V. & Nelson, Rosalie K.

Ide, Arthur F., ed. see SorBello, Marisa.

Ide, Arthur F., ed. see Struggs, Callie F.

Ide, Arthur F., ed. see Tempelton, Darlene.

Ide, Charles A., jt. auth. see Ide, Arthur F.

Ide, Charles A., jt. auth. see Ide, Frederick A.

Ide, Frederick. Woman in Ancient Rome. LC 79-19011. (Woman in History Ser.: Vol. 6). (Illus.). 54p. 1980. 9.00 (ISBN 0-86663-010-4); pap. 7.00 (ISBN 0-86663-011-2). Ide Hse.

Ide, Frederick A. & Ide, Charles A. Prehistoric Woman. LC 79-19011. (Woman in History Ser.: Vol. 1). (Illus.). 49p. (Orig.). 1980. 8.00 (ISBN 0-86663-002-3); pap. 5.00 (ISBN 0-86663-003-1). Ide Hse.

Idle, Christopher. Stories of Our Favorite Hymns. (Illus.). 80p. 1980. 10.95 (ISBN 0-8028-3535-X). Eerdmans.

Idleman, H. K. & McKitrick, M. O. Transportation. (Contemporary Consumer Ser.). 1974. text ed. 4.24 (ISBN 0-07-031691-0, G); tchr's. manual & key 4.95 (ISBN 0-07-031692-9). McGraw.

Idleman, H. K. & Stanton, E. N. Food & Clothing. (Contemporary Consumer Ser.). 1976. text ed. 4.24 (ISBN 0-07-031689-9, G); tchr's manual & key 4.95 (ISBN 0-07-031690-2). McGraw.

Idler, Ellen, jt. auth. see Levin, Lowell.

Idt, G. Le Mur de Jean-Paul Sarte: Techniques et contexte d'une provocation. new ed. (Collection themes et textes). 224p. (Orig., Fr.). 1972. pap. 6.75 (ISBN 2-03-035013-3, 2659). Larousse.

Idung Of Prufening. Cistercians & Cluniacs: The Case for Citeaux. O'Sullivan, Jeremiah F. & Leahey, Joseph, trs. LC 77-9289. 1977. 12.95 (ISBN 0-87907-633-X). Cistercian Pubns.

Idyll, C. P. The Sea Against Hunger. new, rev. ed. LC 77-2655. (Apollo Eds.). (Illus.). 1978. pap. 6.95 o.s.i. (ISBN 0-8152-0422-1, A-422, TYC-T). T Y Crowell.

Idzerda, Stanley J., et al, eds. Lafayette in the Age of the American Revolution: Selected Letters & Papers, 1776-1790 Vol. III: April 27, 1780-March 29, 1781. LC 76-50268. (The Lafayette Papers). (Illus.). 584p. 1981. 35.00x (ISBN 0-8014-1335-4). Cornell U Pr.

--Lafayette in the Age of the American Revolution, Selected Letters & Papers, 1776-1790: April 1, 1781-December 23, 1781, Vol. IV. LC 76-50268. (The Lafayette Papers Ser.). (Illus.). 1981. 38.50 (ISBN 0-8014-1335-4). Cornell U Pr.

--Lafayette in the Age of the American Revolution, Vol. II, Selected Letters & Papers 1776-1790. LC 76-50268. (Illus.). 1979. 22.50x (ISBN 0-8014-1246-3). Cornell U Pr.

Idziak, Janine Marie. Divine Command Morality: Historical & Contemporary Readings. (Texts & Studies in Religion: Vol. 5). 1980. soft cover 24.95x (ISBN 0-88946-969-5). E Mellen.

IEA, jt. auth. see Organization for Economic Cooperation & Development.

IEA, jt. ed. see OECD.

Iefremov, Serhii O. Korotka Istoriia Ukrains'koho Pys'mentsva. (Ukra.). 1972. 18.00 (ISBN 0-918884-22-5). Slavia Lib.

Iersel, B. Van see Murphy, R. & Van Iersel, B.

Iersel, B. Van see Schillebeeckx, E. & Van Iersel, B.

Iersel, Van B., jt. ed. see Schillebeeck, Edward.

Ietswaart, J. H. Taxonomic Review of the Genus Origanum (Labiatae) (Leiden Botanical Ser.: No. 4). (Illus.). 1980. pap. 31.60 (ISBN 90-6021-463-3). Kluwer Boston.

IFAC Conference, Cairo, A.R.E., November 1977. Systems Approach for Development: Proceedings. (International Federation of Automatic Control(IFAC). Proceedings). 1979. text ed. 125.00 (ISBN 0-08-022017-7). Pergamon.

IFAC-IFIP Symposium on Software for Computer Control, 2nd, Prague, Czechoslovakia, 11-15, June 1979. Software for Computer Control: Proceedings. Novak, M., ed. (IFAC Proceedings). (Illus.). 430p. 1979. 84.00 (ISBN 0-08-024448-3). Pergamon.

IFAC - IFIP Workshop, Leibnitz, Austria, April 1980. Real Time Programming, 1980: Proceedings. Haase, V. H., ed. LC 80-49720. (IFAC Proceedings Ser.). 150p. 1980. 40.00 (ISBN 0-08-027305-X). Pergamon.

IFAC-IFIP Workshop, Mariehamn-Aland, Finland, 1978. Real Time Programming Nineteen Seventy-Eight: Proceedings. Cronhjort, B., ed. (IFAC Proceedings). (Illus.). 96p. 1979. 26.00 (ISBN 0-08-024492-0). Pergamon.

IFAC Symposium, Pretoria, Republic of South Africa 15-19 September 1980. Automatic Control in Power Generation, Distribution & Protection: Proceedings. Herbst, J. F., ed. LC 80-40912. 550p. Date not set. 105.00 (ISBN 0-686-63497-7). Pergamon.

IFAC Symposium, Zurich, Switzerland, 29-31 Aug. 1979. Computer Aided Design of Control Systems: Proceedings. Cuenod, M. A., ed. LC 79-42655. (IFAC Proceedings Ser.). (Illus.). 702p. 1980. 145.00 (ISBN 0-08-024488-2). Pergamon.

IFAC Symposium, 8th, Oxford, England, 2-6 July 1979. Automatic Control in Space: Proceedings. Munday, C. W., ed. (IFAC Proceedings Ser.). 492p. 1980. 105.00 (ISBN 0-08-024449-1). Pergamon.

IFAC Workshop, Kyoto Japan, Aug. 1978, jt. auth. see Hasegawa, T.

Ife, Barry, jt. auth. see Quevedo, Francisco De.

Ifft, James B. & Roberts, Julian L. Frantz-Malm's Essentials of Chemistry in the Laboratory. 3rd ed. (Illus.). 1975. 9.95x (ISBN 0-7167-0175-8); individual experiments 0.50 ea.; tchr's manual avail. W H Freeman.

Ifft, James B. & Roberts, Julian L., Jr. Frantz - Malm's Chemistry in the Laboratory. (Illus.). 1981. 8.95x (ISBN 0-7167-1238-5); tchrs. manual avail.; individual exercises 0.50 ea. W H Freeman.

Ifft, James B., jt. auth. see Hearst, John E.

Ifft, James B., jt. auth. see Roberts, Julian L., Jr.

Ifft, James B. & Hearst, John E.intro. by. General Chemistry: Readings from Scientific American. LC 73-13624. (Illus.). 1974. text ed. 19.00x o.p. (ISBN 0-7167-0886-8); pap. text ed. 8.75x o.p. (ISBN 0-7167-0885-X). W H Freeman.

Iffy, Leslie & Langer, Alvin. Perinatology Case Studies. 1978. pap. 18.75 (ISBN 0-87488-043-2). Med Exam.

IFIP Workshop on Methodology in Computer Graphics, France, May 1976. Methodology in Computer Graphics: Proceedings. Guedj, R. A. & Tucker, H., eds. 1979. 29.50 (ISBN 0-444-85301-4, North Holland). Elsevier.

IFLA Council Meeting, 44th, Strbske, Pleso, et al. IFLA Annual 1978: Proceedings. Koops, Willem R. & Harvard-Williams, Peter, eds. 197p. Date not set. text ed. 30.00 (ISBN 0-89664-112-0). K G Saur.

IFSTA Committee. Essentials of Fire Fighting, IFSTA 200. Peige, John D., et al, eds. LC 77-75408. (Illus.). 1977. pap. text ed. 15.00 (ISBN 0-87939-000-X). Intl Fire Serv.

--Fire Apparatus Practices. 6th ed. Carlson, Gene & Orton, Charles, eds. LC 80-82822. (IFSTA Ser.: No. 106). 1980. pap. text ed. 7.00 (ISBN 0-87939-040-9). Intl Fire Serv.

--Fire Apparatus Practices: 106. Hudiburg, Everett, ed. (Illus.). 1970. pap. text ed. 6.00 o.p. (ISBN 0-87939-006-9). Intl Fire Serv.

--The Fire Department Company Officer. Carlson, Gene & Orton, Charles, eds. LC 80-85349. (Orig.). 1981. pap. text ed. 7.00 (ISBN 0-87939-043-3). Intl Fire Serv.

--The Fire Department Officer: 301. Hudiburg, Everett, ed. (Illus.). 1967. pap. text ed. 3.50 o.p. (ISBN 0-87939-018-2). Intl Fire Serv.

--Fire Service Instructor Training: 303. Hudiburg, Everett, ed. (Illus.). 1970. pap. text ed. 6.00 o.p. (ISBN 0-87939-020-4). Intl Fire Serv.

--Fire Service Rescue Practices. 5th ed. Carlson, Gene, ed. (IFSTA Ser.: No. 108). 1981. pap. 7.00 (ISBN 0-87939-044-1). Intl Fire Serv.

--Fire Stream Practices. 6th ed. Carlson, Gene & Orton, Charles, eds. LC 80-80447. (IFSTA: No. 105). (Illus.). 206p. 1980. pap. text ed. 7.00 (ISBN 0-87939-041-7). Intl Fire Serv.

--Fire Ventilation Practices. 6th ed. Carlson, Gene & Orton, Charles, eds. LC 80-84149. (IFSTA Ser.: No. 107). 1981. pap. text ed. 70.00 (ISBN 0-87939-039-5). Intl Fire Serv.

--Fire Ventilation Practices: 107. Hudiburg, Everett & McCoy, Carl, eds. (Illus.). 1970. pap. text ed. 6.00 o.p. (ISBN 0-87939-007-7). Intl Fire Serv.

--Firefighters Occupational Safety: 209. 1st ed. Laughlin, Jerry & Osterhout, Connie, eds. LC 79-83647. 1979. pap. text ed. 7.00 (ISBN 0-87939-028-X). Intl Fire Serv.

--Forcible Entry, Rope & Portable Extinguisher Practices, No. 101. Peige, John, et al, eds. LC 77-94425. (Illus.). 1978. pap. text ed. 7.00 (ISBN 0-87939-032-8). Intl Fire Serv.

--Private Fire Protection & Detection Systems, No. 210. Carlson, Gene P., ed. LC 79-55670. (Illus., Orig.). 1979. pap. 7.00 (ISBN 0-87939-036-0). Intl Fire Serv.

--Public Fire Education: IFSTA 606. Osterhout, Connie, et al, eds. LC 79-89165. (Illus., Orig.). 1979. pap. 7.00 (ISBN 0-87939-034-4). Intl Fire Serv.

--Water Supplies for Fire Protection. Laughlin, Jerry & Williams, Connie E., eds. LC 78-58881. (IFSTA Ser.: No. 205). (Illus.). 1978. pap. text ed. 7.00 (ISBN 0-87939-029-8). Intl Fire Serv.

IFSTA Committee & Walker, Lorrin. Self-Instruction for IFSTA 200: Essentials of Fire Fighting, SI-200. 1st ed. Carlson, Gene & Orton, Charles, eds. LC 77-75408. (Illus.). 204p. (Orig.). 1980. pap. text ed. 7.00 (ISBN 0-87939-042-5). Intl Fire Serv.

Igel & Calloway. American Health & Safety Series. (gr. 8-12). 1972. pap. text ed. 6.00 incl. 6 texts, tchrs' manuals, & tests (ISBN 0-8449-1100-3). Learning Line.

Igfabe, Philip A. Benin Under British Administration,1897-1938: The Impact of Colonial Rule on an African Kingdom. (Ibadan History Ser.). 1978. text ed. 36.50x (ISBN 0-391-00564-2). Humanities.

Iggers, Georg G. The German Conception of History: The National Tradition of Historical Thought from Herder to the Present. LC 68-17147. 1968. 20.00x (ISBN 0-8195-3088-3, Pub. by Wesleyan U Pr). Columbia U Pr.

--New Directions in European Historiography. LC 75-12665. 240p. 1975. 20.00x (ISBN 0-8195-4084-6, Pub. by Wesleyan U Pr). Columbia U Pr.

Iggers, Georg G., ed. see Von Ranke, Leopold.

Iggers, Jeremy & Bovbjerg, Dana. The Joy of Cheesecake. (Illus.). 1980. 11.95 (ISBN 0-8120-5350-8). Barron.

Iggers, Wilma, tr. see Von Ranke, Leopold.

Igglesden, Charles. Those Superstitions. LC 73-12798. 1974. Repr. of 1932 ed. 18.00 (ISBN 0-8103-3621-9). Gale.

Iglehardt, Anne. Radio Dog. LC 79-1949. (Illus.). (ps-2). 1979. 1.95 (ISBN 0-525-69016-6, Gingerbread Bks); PLB 5.95 (ISBN 0-525-69017-4). Dutton.

Iglehart, Alfreda P. Married Women & Work: Nineteen Fifty-Seven & Nineteen Seventy-Six. LC 78-75320. (Illus.). 128p. 1979. 13.95 (ISBN 0-669-02838-X). Lexington Bks.

Iglehart, Susan & Schweizer, Barbara, eds. The Quickpoint Book. LC 77-71371. (Illus.). 1977. 10.95 o.p. (ISBN 0-685-81541-2); pap. 5.95 o.p. (ISBN 0-03-016896-1). HR&W.

Iglesia, Ramon. Columbus, Cortes, & Other Essays. Simpson, Lesley B., tr. LC 69-13727. 1969. 18.50x (ISBN 0-520-01469-3). U of Cal Pr.

Iglesias, Jose L., jt. auth. see Andujar, Maria D.

Iglitzin, Lynne B. & Ross, Ruth, eds. Women in the World: A Comparative Study. new ed. LC 74-14197. (Studies in International & Comparative Politics: No. 6). 427p. 1976. text ed. 26.50 (ISBN 0-87436-200-8); pap. text ed. 8.25 (ISBN 0-87436-201-6). ABC-Clio.

Ignarro, Louis, ed. see International Conference on Cyclic Nucleotide, 3rd, New Orleans, la., July 1977.

Ignas, Edward & Corsini, Raymond J. Alternative Educational Systems. LC 78-61883. 1979. text ed. 10.95 (ISBN 0-87581-246-5); pap. text ed. 7.95 o.p. (ISBN 0-87581-242-2). Peacock Pubs.

Ignas, Edward & Corsini, Raymond J., eds. Comparative Educational Systems. LC 80-52449. 450p. 1981. text ed. 12.50 (ISBN 0-87581-260-0). Peacock Pubs.

Ignatieff, Michael. A Just Measure of Pain: The Penitentiary in the Industrial Revolution, 1750-1850. (Morningside Bks.). 272p. 1980. pap. 6.50x (ISBN 0-231-05057-7, Pub. by Morningside). Columbia U Pr.

Ignatius Of Loyola, St. The Constitutions of the Society of Jesus. Ganss, George E., tr. & commentary by. LC 72-108258. (Jesuit Primary Sources in English Translation Ser.: No. 1). 432p. 1970. 11.00 (ISBN 0-912422-03-3); smyth sewn o.s.i. 6.00 (ISBN 0-912422-20-3); pap. 5.00 (ISBN 0-912422-06-8). Inst Jesuit.

Ignatov, Il'Ia Nikolaevich. Entsiklopediia Russkikh Pisatelei. LC 75-561569. (Illus., Rus.). 1972. 37.00 (ISBN 0-918884-12-8). Slavia Lib.

Ignatow, David. Poems, Nineteen Thirty-Four to Nineteen Sixty-Nine. LC 79-105500. 1979. pap. 8.95 (ISBN 0-8195-6059-6, Pub. by Wesleyan U Pr). Columbia U Pr.

--Rescue the Dead. LC 68-16005. (Wesleyan Poetry Program: Vol. 37). (Orig.). 1968. pap. text ed. 10.00x (ISBN 0-8195-2037-3, Pub. by Wesleyan U Pr). Columbia U Pr.

--Say Pardon. LC 61-6973. (Wesleyan Poetry Program: Vol. 10). (Orig.). 1961. 10.00x (ISBN 0-8195-2010-1, Pub. by Wesleyan U Pr); pap. 2.45 o.p. (ISBN 0-8195-1010-6). Columbia U Pr.

Ignatow, Yaedi. Plans. 80p. 1981. pap. 4.95 (ISBN 0-935296-19-0). Sheep Meadow.

Ignatowsky, W. Von see Von Ignatowsky, W.

Ignition Manufacturers Institute. Automotive Emission Control & Tune-Up Procedures,1976. pap. 11.95 (ISBN 0-13-054809-X). P-H.

--Automotive Emission Control & Tune-up Procedures. 3rd ed. (Illus.). 1980. text ed. 17.95 (ISBN 0-13-054791-3); pap. text ed. 13.95 (ISBN 0-13-054783-2). P-H.

Ignizio, James P. Goal Programming & Extensions. LC 75-12089. (Illus.). 192p. 1976. 21.95 (ISBN 0-669-00021-3). Lexington Bks.

Ignizio, James P., et al. Operations Research in Decision Making. LC 74-12829. 360p. 1975. 22.50x (ISBN 0-8448-0670-6); pap. 9.50x (ISBN 0-8448-0671-4). Crane-Russak Co.

Ignoffo, Robert, jt. auth. see See-Lasley, Kay.

Ihara, Toni, jt. auth. see Warner, Ralph.

Ihde, Sheila H., jt. auth. see Herman, Paul E.

Ihnatiienko, Varfolomii Adrianovych. Biblohrafiia Ukrains'koi Presy, 1816-1916. LC 74-220297. (Bibliohrafiia I Bibliotekoznavstvo). (Ukra.). 1968. 25.00 o.p. (ISBN 0-685-89029-5). Slavia Lib.

Iida, Miyuki & Iida, Tomoko. The Art of Handmade Flowers. LC 77-128687. (Illus.). 124p. 1971. 14.95 (ISBN 0-87011-136-1). Kodansha.

--The Art of Handmade Flowers. LC 77-128687. (Illus.). 124p. 1980. pap. 9.95 (ISBN 0-87011-419-0). Kodansha.

Iida, Tomoko, jt. auth. see Iida, Miyuki.

Iijima, Kanjitsu. Buddhist Yoga. (Illus.). 184p. 1975. pap. 8.95 (ISBN 0-87040-349-4). Japan Pubns.

Iijima, Nobuku. Pollution Japan: Historical Chronology. 401p. 1980. 64.00 (ISBN 0-08-026242-2). Pergamon.

Iitaka, Y., jt. auth. see Motte, G. A.

Iivanainen, Matti. Study on the Origins of Mental Retardation. 1974. 18.95x (ISBN 0-433-16300-3). Intl Ideas.

Ijiri, Yuji. The Foundations of Accounting Measurement. LC 67-15629. 1978. Repr. of 1967 ed. text ed. 13.00 (ISBN 0-914348-22-1). Scholars Bk.

Ijiri, Yuji, jt. auth. see Cooper, W. W.

Ikaunieks, Ya Y., jt. auth. see Alksne, Z. K.

Ike, Jane. The Birthday Book. (ps-1). 1975. PLB 4.60 o.p. (ISBN 0-307-68963-8, Golden Pr). Western Pub.

Ike, Nobutaka. A Theory of Japanese Democracy. LC 77-8279. (Westview Special Studies on China & East Asia). (Illus.). 178p. 1980. lib. bdg. 16.50x o.p. (ISBN 0-89158-066-2); pap. text ed. 8.50x (ISBN 0-89158-932-5). Westview.

Ike, Nobutake. Japan: The New Superstate, a Portable Stanford. pap. text ed. 4.95x (ISBN 0-393-95011-5). Norton.

Ikeda, Daisaku. Buddhism: The First Millennium. Watson, Burton, tr. LC 77-84915. 1978. cancelled (ISBN 0-87011-321-6). Kodansha.

--The Human Revolution. rev. ed. Gage, Richard L., tr. from Japanese. LC 72-79121. (The Human Revolution Ser: Vol. 2). (Illus.). 272p. 1974. 9.50 (ISBN 0-8348-0087-X). Weatherhill.

Ikeda, Daisaku & Inoue, Yasushi. Letters of Four Seasons. Gage, Richard L., tr. LC 79-91521. 112p. 1980. 10.95 (ISBN 0-87011-413-1). Kodansha.

Ikeda, Joanne. For Teenagers Only, Change Your Habits to Change Your Shape. LC 78-12697. 1978. pap. 5.95 (ISBN 0-915950-23-5). Bull Pub.

Ikeda, Kyoko, jt. auth. see Tsujita, Mariko.

Ikeda, Masuo. My Imagination Map. (Illus.). 200p. Date not set. price not set cancelled (ISBN 0-87011-243-0). Kodansha. Postponed.

Ikeda, Yutaka, jt. auth. see Sivam, Avraham J.

Ikeda, Yutakada, jt. ed. see Sivan, Avraham J.

Ikehara, Akira J., jt. auth. see Mount, Tom.

Ikemoto, Takashi, jt. ed. see Stryk, Lucien.

Ikemoto, Takashi, tr. see Stryk, Lucien & Ikemoto, Takashi.

Ikenberry, Stanley O. & Friedman, Renee C. Beyond Academic Departments: The Story of Institutes & Centers. LC 72-6045. (Higher Education Ser.). 1972. 10.95x o.p. (ISBN 0-87589-144-6). Jossey-Bass.

Ikime, Obaro, ed. Leadership in Nineteenth Century Africa. (Illus.). 208p. (Orig.). 1974. pap. text ed. 7.00x (ISBN 0-391-00357-7). Humanities.

Ikoku, Chi. Natural Gas Engineering. 776p. 1980. 45.00 (ISBN 0-87814-141-3). Pennwell Pub.

Ikram, Khalid. Egypt: Economic Management in a Period of Transition. LC 80-552. (World Bank Country Economic Report). (Illus.). 464p. 1981. text ed. 32.50x (ISBN 0-8018-2418-4); pap. text ed. 10.50x (ISBN 0-8018-2419-2). Johns Hopkins.

Ikram, S. M. Muslim Civilization in India. Embree, A. T., ed. LC 64-14656. (Illus.). 1964. 17.50x (ISBN 0-231-02580-7). Columbia U Pr.

Ilardi, Frank A. Computer Circuit Analysis: Theory & Application. (Illus.). 416p. 1976. 21.95 (ISBN 0-13-165357-1). P-H.

Ilardi, Vincent, ed. Dispatches with Related Documents of Milanese Ambassadors in France, (Mar. 11- June 29 1466, Vol. 3. Fata, Frank J., tr. LC 68-20933. 444p. 1980. 35.00 (ISBN 0-87580-069-6). N Ill U Pr.

Ilardi, Vincent, jt. ed. see Kendall, Paul M.

Ilardo, Joseph A., jt. auth. see Eisenberg, Abne M.

Ilchman, Warren F. & Uphoff, Norman T. The Political Economy of Change. LC 71-81743. 1969. 17.50x (ISBN 0-520-01390-5); pap. 4.95x (ISBN 0-520-02033-2, CAMPUS58). U of Cal Pr.

Ilchman, Warren F., jt. ed. see Uphoff, Norman T.

Iles, T. D., jt. auth. see Fryer, G.

Ileto, Reynaldo C. Pasyon & Revolution: Popular Movements in the Philippines, 1840-1910. (Illus.). 345p. 1980. 18.75x (ISBN 0-686-28640-5); pap. 13.75x (ISBN 0-686-28641-3). Cellar.

Ilg, jt. auth. see Ames.

Ilg, Frances L., jt. auth. see Ames, Louise B.

Ilg, Frances L., et al. Child Behavior. rev. ed. LC 80-8371. (Illus.). 1981. 14.95 (ISBN 0-06-014829-2, HarpT). Har-Row.

Ilian, Martin. Bay Area Sports & Recreation Directory. 224p. (Orig.). 1981. pap. 7.95 (ISBN 0-87701-164-8). Chronicle Bks.

Ilie, A. V., jt. auth. see Baiulescu, G. E.

Ilie, Paul. Literature & the Inner Exile: Authoritarian Spain, 1939-1975. LC 80-18281. 208p. 1981. text ed. 14.50x (ISBN 0-8018-2424-9). Johns Hopkins.

Iliffe, J. A Modern History of Tanganyika. LC 77-95445. (African Studies Ser.: No. 25). 1979. 79.50 (ISBN 0-521-22024-6); pap. 19.95x (ISBN 0-521-29611-0). Cambridge U Pr.

Illich, Ivan. Church, Change & Development. 4.95 o.p. (ISBN 0-8164-1010-0); pap. 2.45 (ISBN 0-8164-2505-1). Crossroad NY.

--De-Schooling Society. Anshen, Ruth N., ed. LC 74-138738. (World Perspectives). 1971. 8.95 o.s.i. (ISBN 0-06-012139-4, HarpT). Har-Row.

--Shadow Work. 160p. 1981. 15.00 (ISBN 0-7145-2710-6, Pub. by M. Boyars); pap. 5.95 (ISBN 0-7145-2711-4). Merrimack Bk Serv.

--Tools for Conviviality. LC 72-9125. (World Perspectives Ser). 142p. 1973. 8.95 o.p. (ISBN 0-06-012138-6, HarpT). Har-Row.

--Toward a History of Needs. (Bantam New Age Bk.). 192p. 1980. pap. 2.95 (ISBN 0-553-12276-2). Bantam.

Illich, Ivan, et al. Disabling Professions. (Ideas in Progress Ser.). 1978. 11.95 (ISBN 0-7145-2509-X, Pub. by M Boyars); pap. 5.95 (ISBN 0-7145-2510-3). Merrimack Bk Serv.

Illich, Ivan D. Celebration of Awareness. LC 71-113986. 1971. pap. 1.95 (ISBN 0-385-07386-0, Anch). Doubleday.

Illick, Joseph E., ed. America & England, 1558-1776. LC 70-11183. 1970. pap. text ed. 5.95x (ISBN 0-89197-006-1). Irvington.

Illies, Joachim, ed. Limnofauna Europaea: A Checklist of the Animals Inhabiting European Inland Waters, with Accounts of Their Distribution & Ecology (Except Protozoa) 532p. 1978. text ed. 120.00 (ISBN 90-265-0275-3, Pub. by Swets Pub Serv Holland). Swets North Am.

Illingworth, J. H. Further Offshore. (Illus.). 1979. 30.00 o.p. (ISBN 0-229-63890-2). Scribner.

Illingworth, Ronald. Your Child's Development in the First Five Years. (Churchill Livingstone Patient Handbook Ser.). (Illus.). 96p. 1981. pap. text ed. 3.00 (ISBN 0-686-28941-2). Churchill.

Illingworth, Valerie. The Anchor Dictionary of Astronomy. LC 79-6538. (Illus.). 448p. (Orig.). 1980. pap. 6.95 (ISBN 0-385-15936-6, Anch). Doubleday.

Illot, Anna, jt. auth. see Jeffries, Leila.

Illsley, Charles P. see Meredith, Grace E.

ILO International Labour Office, ed. Employment, Growth & Basic Needs: A One-World Problem. LC 77-70278. 256p. 1977. pap. 3.95 (ISBN 0-686-28705-3). Overseas Dev Council.

Ilon. The Supremacy of God. LC 80-66408. 1980. pap. 3.00 (ISBN 0-9600958-6-1). Birth Day.

Ilowite, Sheldon. Centerman from Quebec. (Illus.). 128p. (gr. 4-7). 1972. 5.95g (ISBN 0-8038-1174-8). Hastings.

--Fury on Ice: A Canadian-American Hockey Story. LC 72-124617. 128p. (gr. 6-9). 1970. 4.95g o.s.i. (ISBN 0-8038-2284-7). Hastings.

--Hockey Defenseman. (Illus.). (gr. 4-7). 1971. 4.95g o.s.i. (ISBN 0-8038-3018-1). Hastings.

--On the Wing: Rod Gilbert. LC 76-12547. (Sports Profiles Ser.). (Illus.). 48p. (gr. 4-11). 1976. PLB 8.50 (ISBN 0-8172-0134-3). Raintree Pubs.

--Penalty Killer: A Hockey Story. (Illus.). (gr. 4-6). 1974. 5.95g (ISBN 0-8038-5799-3). Hastings.

Ilsley, Paul & Niemi, John A. Recruiting & Training Volunteers. (Adult Education Association Professional Development Ser.). (Illus.). 176p. 1980. text ed. 12.95x (ISBN 0-07-000556-7, C). McGraw.
Ilyin, Donna, jt. auth. see Doherty, Cecelia.
Ilyushin, A. A. & Lenskii, V. S. Strength of Materials. Redshaw, L. C., ed. Loshor, J. K., tr. 1967. 75.00 (ISBN 0-08-011461-X). Pergamon.
Imahori, K. & Higashimura, T., eds. Progress in Polymer Science, Japan, Vol. 8. LC 72-7446. 244p. 1975. 38.95 (ISBN 0-470-65727-8). Halsted Pr.
Imahori, K. & Murahashi, S., eds. Progress in Polymer Science, Japan, Vol. 5. LC 72-5794. 308p. 1973. 22.95 (ISBN 0-470-42661-6). Halsted Pr.
Imai, Ryukichi & Rowen, Henry S. Nuclear Energy & Nuclear Proliferation: Japanese & American Views. LC 79-16589. (Special Studies in International Relations). 1979. lib. bdg. 18.50x (ISBN 0-89158-667-9). Westview.
Imai, Ryukichi & Barton, John, eds. Arms Control II: A New Approach to International Security. LC 80-22700. 352p. 1981. lib. bdg. 25.00 (ISBN 0-89946-069-0). Oelgeschlager.
Imakita, Junichi. A Techno-Economic Analysis of the Port Transport System. 1978. 29.95 (ISBN 0-03-046241-X). Praeger.
Imam, Zafar, ed. Muslims in India. LC 75-905301. 1975. 12.50x o.p. (ISBN 0-88386-077-5, Orient Longman). South Asia Bks.
Imber, Steve, ed. Readings in Emotional & Behavioral Disorders. rev. ed. (Special Education Ser.). (Illus.). 224p. pap. text ed. 9.95 (ISBN 0-89568-294-X). Spec Learn Corp.
Imbert, Enrique Anderson see Anderson Imbert, Enrique.
Imbiorski, W. Adventure Together: Teacher's Manual. 60p. 1974. pap. 3.00. Buckley Pubns.
Imbo, M. Mi Guia Telefonica. Mann, Philip, ed. Kreps, Georgian, tr. from Eng. (Shape Board Play Book). Orig. Title: My Telephone Book. (Illus.). 14p. (Span.). (ps-3). 1981. bds. 3.50 plastic come bdg. (5009SP). Tuffy Bks.
--Mi Querido Reloj. Mann, Philip, ed. Kreps, Georgian, tr. from Eng. (Shape Board Lay Book). Orig. Title: The Happy Clock Book. (Illus.). 14p. (Span.). (ps-3). 1981. bds. 3.50 plastic comb bdg (ISBN 0-89828-204-7, 5008SP). Tuffy Bks.
Imboden, Nicolas & OECD. Managing Information for Rural Development Projects. (Illus.). 87p. (Orig.). 1980. pap. 6.50 (ISBN 92-64-12039-4, 41-80-03-1). OECD.
Imershein, Allen W., jt. ed. see Liebert, Roland J.
Imhoof-Blumer, F. Mallos, Megarsos, Antioche du Pyramos. 37p. (Fr.). 1979. pap. 5.00 (ISBN 0-916710-58-0). Obol Intl.
Immegart, Glenn L. & Pilecki, Francis J. An Introduction to Systems for the Educational Administrator. LC 72-1939. 1973. text ed. 13.95 (ISBN 0-201-03175-2). A-W.
Immegart, Glenn L. & Boyd, William L., eds. Problem-Finding in Educational Administration: Trends in Research & Theory. LC 78-19912. 320p. 1979. 23.95 (ISBN 0-669-02438-4). Lexington Bks.
Immergut, E. H., jt. ed. see Brandrup, Johannes.
Immerman, Richard H., jt. auth. see Ambrose, Stephen E.
Immone, David, commentary by. Art of the Pacific: Conversations by James Neneish. (Illus.). 1980. 29.95 (ISBN 0-8109-0686-4). Abrams.
Immroth, J. Philip & Daily, Jay E. Library Cataloging: A Guide for a Basic Course. LC 72-147066. 1971. 10.00 (ISBN 0-8108-0396-8). Scarecrow.
Immroth, J. Philip, compiled by. Ronald Brunlees McKerrow: A Selection of His Essays. LC 73-19882. (Great Bibliographers Ser.: No. 1). (Illus.). 1974. 10.00 (ISBN 0-8108-0690-8). Scarecrow.
Immroth, John P. & Mai Chan, Lois. Immroth's Guide to the Library of Congress Classification. 3rd ed. LC 80-16981. (Library Science Text Ser.). 1980. lib. bdg. 25.00x (ISBN 0-87287-224-6); pap. text ed. 14.50 (ISBN 0-87287-235-1). Libs Unl.
Impe, Jack Van & Campbell, Roger F. Israel's Final Holocaust. 1980. pap. 3.95 (ISBN 0-8407-9400-2). Nelson.
Impe, Jack Van see Van Impe, Jack & Campbell, Roger F.
Impeachment Inquiry Staff of the House Judiciary Committee. Constitutional Grounds for Impeachment. 1.00 (ISBN 0-8183-0129-5). Pub Aff Pr.
Imperato, P. J. Treatment & Control of Infectious Diseases in Man. (Illus.). 760p. 1974. 46.75 (ISBN 0-398-02979-2). C C Thomas.
Imperato, Pascal J., ed. Historical Dictionary of Mali. LC 76-55775. (African Historical Dictionaries Ser: No. 11). (Illus.). 1977. 12.00 (ISBN 0-8108-1004-2). Scarecrow.
Imperial College of Science & Technology, Rock Mechanics Section, jt. auth. see Hoek, E.
Imre, Samu, jt. ed. see Benko, Lorand.
Imrie, B. W., jt. auth. see Clift, J. C.
Imwinkelried, Edward J., et al. Criminal Evidence. (Criminal Justice Ser.). 1979. pap. text ed. 16.95 (ISBN 0-8299-0221-X); tchrs.' manual avail. (ISBN 0-8299-0591-X). West Pub.
Inada, Hogitaro, jt. auth. see Koop, Albert J.
Inalcik, Halil. The Ottoman Empire: Conquest, Organization & Economy. 362p. 1980. 60.00x (ISBN 0-86078-032-5, Pub. by Variorum England). State Mutual Bk.
Inamdar, F. A. Image & Symbol in Joseph Conrad's Novels. 1980. text ed. 15.50x (ISBN 0-391-01916-3). Humanities.
Inam-Ur-Rahman, jt. auth. see Shieh, Paulinus S.
Inayat-Khan, Fazal. Old Thinking, New Thinking: A Sufi Prism. LC 77-7831. 1979. pap. 5.95 (ISBN 0-06-064086-3, RD 239, HarpR). Har-Row.
Inbar, Michael & Stoll, Clarice. Simulation & Gaming in Social Science. LC 74-143527. 1972. 17.95 (ISBN 0-02-915750-1). Free Pr.
Inbau, Fred E., et al. Cases & Comments on Criminal Procedure. 2nd ed. LC 80-17843. (University Casebooks Ser.). 1598p. text ed. write for info. (ISBN 0-88277-011-X). Foundation Pr.
Inbucon Consultants. Managing Human Resources. LC 76-39984. 1976. 14.95 (ISBN 0-470-98954-8). Halsted Pr.
Ince, Edward L. Ordinary Differential Equations. (Illus.). 1953. pap. text ed. 6.00 (ISBN 0-486-60349-0). Dover.
Ince, Laurence P. Behavior Modification in Rehabilitation Medicine. (Illus.). 316p. 1976. 29.50 (ISBN 0-398-03532-6). C C Thomas.
--The Rehabilitation Medicine Services. (Illus.). 592p. 1974. 32.50 (ISBN 0-398-02852-4). C C Thomas.
Ince, Richard. England's High Chancellor: Francis Bacon-a Romance. 324p. 1980. Repr. of 1935 ed. lib. bdg. 35.00 (ISBN 0-89984-297-6). Century Bookbindery.
Ince, W. N. Heredia. (French Poets Ser.). 1979. text ed. 25.00x (ISBN 0-485-14607-X, Athlone Pr); pap. text ed. 11.25x (ISBN 0-485-12207-3). Humanities.
Ince, W. N., ed. see Heredia.
Inch, Morris A. & Bullock, C. Hassell, eds. The Literature & Meaning of Scripture. 360p. 1981. 14.95 (ISBN 0-8010-5032-4). Baker Bk.
Inciardi, James A., ed. Radical Criminology: The Coming Crises. LC 80-14408. (Sage Focus Editions: Vol. 23). (Illus.). 320p. 1980. 18.95 (ISBN 0-8039-1489-X); pap. 9.95 (ISBN 0-8039-1490-3). Sage.
Inciardi, James A. & Faupel, Charles E., eds. History & Crime: Implications for Criminal Justice Policy. LC 80-19532. (Focus Editions Ser.: Vol. 27). (Illus.). 288p. 1980. 18.95 (ISBN 0-8039-1410-5); pap. 9.95 (ISBN 0-8039-1411-3). Sage.
Inciardi, James A. & Pottieger, Anne E., eds. Violent Crime: Historical & Contemporary Issues. LC 78-14944. (Sage Research Progress Series in Criminology: Vol. 5). 1978. 12.95x (ISBN 0-8039-1107-6); pap. 6.50x (ISBN 0-8039-1108-4). Sage.
Inciardi, James A., et al. Legal & Illicit Drug Use: Acute Reactions of Emergency Room Populations. LC 78-19743. 1978. 25.95 (ISBN 0-03-046701-2). Praeger.
Inclan, Josefina. Carmen Conde y el Mar - Carmen Conde & the Sea. Santayana, Manuel J., tr. LC 80-69623. (Coleccion Polymita). 81p. (Orig., Span. & Eng.). 1980. pap. 8.95 (ISBN 0-89729-277-4). Ediciones.
Incropera, Frank P. Fundamentals of Heat Transfer. DeWitt, David P., ed. LC 80-17209. 656p. 1981. text ed. 23.95 (ISBN 0-471-42711-X). Wiley.
Inczedy, J. Analytical Applications of Complex Equilibria. LC 75-25687. (Ser. in Analytical Chemistry). 415p. 1976. 78.95 (ISBN 0-470-42713-2). Halsted Pr.
Inden, Ronald B. Marriage & Rank in Bengali Culture: A History of Caste & Clan in Middle-Period Bengal. LC 73-85789. 176p. 1976. 17.50x (ISBN 0-520-02569-5). U of Cal Pr.
Inderwick, Sheila. Lungeing the Horse & Rider. LC 77-76095. 1977. 15.95 (ISBN 0-7153-7370-6). David & Charles.
Indian Claims Commission. Chippewa Indians VII: Findings of Fact, & Opinion. (American Indian Ethnohistory Ser: North Central & Northeastern Indians). (Illus.). lib. bdg. 42.00 (ISBN 0-8240-0814-6). Garland Pub.
--Coast Salish & Western Washington Indians, Vol. 5: Findings of Fact, & Opinion. (American Indian Ethnohistory Ser: Indians of the Northwest). (Illus.). lib. bdg. 42.00 (ISBN 0-8240-0787-5). Garland Pub.
--Osage Indians, Vol. Five: Findings of Fact, & Opinion. (American Indian Ethnohistory Ser: Plains Indians). (Illus.). lib. bdg. 42.00 (ISBN 0-8240-0751-4). Garland Pub.
--Paiute Indians, Vol. Five: Findings of Fact, & Opinion. (American Indian Ethnohistory Ser: California & Basin - Plateau Indians). (Illus.). lib. bdg. 42.00 (ISBN 0-8240-0744-1). Garland Pub.
--Puebla Indians, Vol. Five: Findings of Fact, & Opinion. (American Indian Ethnohistory Ser: Indians of the Southwest). (Illus.). lib. bdg. 42.00 (ISBN 0-8240-0729-8). Garland Pub.
--Sac, Fox & Iowa Indians, Vol. 3: Findings of Fact, & Opinion. (American Indian Ethnohistory Ser: North Central & Northeastern Indians). (Illus.). lib. bdg. 42.00 (ISBN 0-8240-0791-3). Garland Pub.
--Sioux Indians, Vol. Four: Findings of Fact, & Opinion. (American Indian Ethnohistory Ser: Plains Indians). (Illus.). lib. bdg. 42.00 (ISBN 0-8240-0797-2). Garland Pub.
Indian Claims Commission see Jablow, Joseph.
Indian Council For Cultural Relations. Studies in Asian History: Proceedings of the Asian History Congress 1961. 15.00x o.p. (ISBN 0-210-22748-6). Asia.
Indian Law Institute. Indian Legal System. 1979. 28.00 (ISBN 0-379-20368-5). Oceana.
Indian Ocean Fishery Commission. Report of the Sixth Joint Meeting of the Indian Ocean Fishery Commission, Committee on Management of Indian Ocean Tuna. 18p. 1980. pap. 6.00 (ISBN 92-5-100939-2, F2045, FAO). Unipub.
Indian Society of Theoretical & Applied Mechanics, 20th Congress, India, 1975. Dynamics of Rotors: Selected Papers. Rao, J. S., ed. 1977. pap. text ed. 29.00 (ISBN 0-08-022124-6). Pergamon.
Indiana Judges Association. Indiana Pattern Jury Instructions - Criminal. 250p. 1980. 50.00 (ISBN 0-87215-353-3). Michie.
Indiana University & Charnego, Michael. General Biology Laboratory Manual. 2nd ed. 1978. 8.50 (ISBN 0-8403-2268-2). Kendall-Hunt.
Indiana University School of Medicine Faculty Women's Club. Cocktail Party Cookbook & Guide. Mealey, Barbara, ed. LC 76-12382. (Illus.). 256p. 1977. 7.95x (ISBN 0-253-11235-4). Ind U Pr.
Indich, William M. Consciousness in Advaita Vedanta. 1980. 14.00x (ISBN 0-8364-0607-9). South Asia Bks.
Industrial Accident Commission, ed. see Thurber, Packard.
Industrial Arts Curriculum Project Staff. The World of Construction. (gr. 7-9). text ed. 14.64 (ISBN 0-87345-462-6); tchrs' guide 32.00 (ISBN 0-87345-465-0); lab. manual 5.28 (ISBN 0-87345-463-4); big builder game 14.00 (ISBN 0-685-28871-4); filmstrip set 90.00 (ISBN 0-685-28872-2); transparency set 390.00 (ISBN 0-685-28873-0). McKnight.
Industrial Democracy in Europe (IDE) International Research Group, ed. European Industrial Relations. (Illus.). 256p. 1981. 45.00 (ISBN 0-19-827254-5). Oxford U Pr.
Industrial Design Magazine. Designer's Choice: The Best Products, Graphics & Environments of 1980. Finley, George, ed. 120p. 1980. pap. 7.95 (ISBN 0-07-031710-0, P&RB). McGraw.
Industrial Heating Equipment Assn. The Directory of Industrial Heat Processing & Combustion Equipment: U. S. Manufacturers, 1981-1982. 3rd biennial ed. 224p. (Orig.). 1981. pap. write for info. (ISBN 0-931634-05-9). Info Clearing House.
Ineson, Frank A., jt. auth. see Read, William R.
Iness, Lowell, intro. by. M'kee & Bros. Victorian Glass: Five Complete Glass Catalogues from 1859 - 60, 71. (Illus.). 160p. 1981. pap. price not set (ISBN 0-486-24121-1). Dover.
Inez, Colette. Alive & Taking Names. LC 77-86351. 74p. 1977. 8.95 (ISBN 0-8214-0377-X); pap. 4.95 (ISBN 0-8214-0393-1). Ohio U Pr.
Infanger, jt. auth. see Casavant.
Infante, Jaime T. The Political, Economic, & Labor Climate in the Philippines. LC 80-53988. (Multinational Industrial Relations Ser.: No. 8a). (Illus.). 147p. 1980. pap. 15.00 (ISBN 0-89546-024-6). Indus Res Unit-Wharton.
Infante, Mary S. The Clinical Laboratory in Nursing Education. LC 74-12454. 112p. 1975. text ed. 13.50 (ISBN 0-471-42715-2, Pub. by Wiley Medical). Wiley.
Infeld, Leopold. Quest: An Autobiography. viii, 361p. 1980. 14.95. Chelsea Pub.
--Quest: An Autobiography. 2nd ed. LC 79-55510. Orig. Title: Quest: the Evolution of a Scientist. 1979. text ed. 17.50 o.p. (ISBN 0-8284-0309-0). Chelsea Pub.
Infield, Glenn. Disaster at Bari. (Illus.). 1971. 7.95 o.s.i. (ISBN 0-02-558150-3). Macmillan.
--The Poltava Affair: A Russian Warning - an American Tragedy. LC 72-93628. 256p. 1973. 7.95 o.s.i. (ISBN 0-02-558140-6). Macmillan.
--Skorzeny: Hitler's Commando. (Illus.). 304p. 1981. 15.95 (ISBN 0-312-72777-1). St Martin.
Infield, Glenn B. Leni Riefenstahl: The Fallen Film Goddess. LC 76-7084. (Illus.). 1976. 9.95 o.s.i. (ISBN 0-690-01167-9, TYC-T). T Y Crowell.
--Secrets of the SS. LC 80-5434. 304p. 1981. 14.95 (ISBN 0-8128-2790-2). Stein & Day.
Informatik Symposium, 4th, IBM Germany, Wildbad, Sept. 25-27, 1974. Programming Methodology: Proceedings. Hackl, C. E., ed. (Lecture Notes in Computer Science Ser.: Vol. 23). (Illus.). vi, 501p. 1975. pap. 20.40 o.p. (ISBN 0-387-07131-8). Springer-Verlag.
Informational Advertising Association. Controversy Advertising: How Advertisers Present Points of View in Public Affairs. (Illus.). 1977. pap. 9.50 (ISBN 0-8038-1215-9). Hastings.
Ing, Catherine & Pond, Grace. Champion Cats of the World. LC 70-188397. (Illus.). 1978. 17.50 o.p. (ISBN 0-312-12846-0). St Martin.
Ing, Nancy, ed. New Voices: Stories & Poems by Young Chinese Writers. rev. 2nd ed. (Asian Library Ser.: No. 15). Orig. Title: New Voices: Fiction & Poetry by Young Chinese Writers. 212p. 1980. pap. 5.00 (ISBN 0-89644-580-1). Chinese Materials.
Ing, Nancy, tr. see Chen, Jo-hsi.
Ingalese, Isabella. Occult Philosophy. LC 80-23861. 321p. 1980. Repr. lib. bdg. 12.95x (ISBN 0-89370-649-3). Borgo Pr.
--Occult Philosophy. 1980. pap. 5.95 (ISBN 0-87877-049-6). Newcastle Pub.
Ingalese, Richard. The History & Power of Mind. LC 80-19897. 332p. 1980. Repr. of 1976 ed. lib. bdg. 11.95x (ISBN 0-89370-637-X). Borgo Pr.
Ingalls, A. Joy & Salerno, M. Constance. Maternal & Child Health Nursing. 4th ed. LC 78-32131. (Illus.). 1979. text ed. 17.95 (ISBN 0-8016-2326-X). Mosby.
Ingalls, Jeremy, tr. & intro. by see Yao Hsin-Nung.
Ingalls, Robert P. Mental Retardation: The Changing Outlook. LC 77-23359. 1978. text ed. 21.95x (ISBN 0-471-42716-0). Wiley.
Ingamells, Lynn & Porter, Standish. Variedades del Espanol Actual. (Illus.). 384p. (Span., Prog. Bk.). 1975. pap. text ed. 13.95x (ISBN 0-582-35026-3); tapes 45.00x (ISBN 0-582-37394-8); tapescript 4.00x (ISBN 0-582-35027-1). Longman.
Ingbar, S. H., ed. The Year in Endocrinology, 1975 to 1976. 327p. 1977. 29.50 (ISBN 0-306-32101-7, Plenum Pr). Plenum Pub.
Ingber-Irvin, Beth. Knifemakers Guild Directory. (Illus.). 200p. 1981. pap. 12.95 (ISBN 0-917714-32-6). Beinfeld Pub.
Inge, M. Thomas, jt. auth. see Young, Thomas D.
Inge, M. Thomas, ed. Agrarianism in American Literature. LC 68-31706. (Prospectives in American Literature Ser). 1969. pap. 8.95 (ISBN 0-672-63005-2). Odyssey Pr.
Inge, M. Thomas, et al, eds. Black American Writers: Bibliographic Essays, 2 vols. LC 75-38033. 200p. 1978. text ed. 15.95 ea.; Vol. 1. text ed. (ISBN 0-312-08260-6); Vol. 2. (ISBN 0-312-08295-9). St Martin.
Inge, William. Summer Brave. Orig. Title: Picnic. pap. 2.50 (ISBN 0-686-62807-1). Dramatists Play.
Inge, William see Watson, E. Bradlee & Pressey, Benfield.
Ingebritsen, Karl J. Reston Home Owners Association: A Case Study in New Community Management. Ader-Brin, Dianne, ed. 1977. pap. text ed. 11.50 (ISBN 0-912104-26-0). Inst Real Estate.
Ingells, Douglas J. The McDonnell Douglas Story. LC 79-54064. 1979. 17.95 (ISBN 0-8168-4995-1). Aero.
Ingelow, Jean. Allerton & Dreux; or, the War of Opinion, 1851. Wolff, Robert L., ed. LC 75-475. (Victorian Fiction Ser.). 1975. lib. bdg. 66.00 (ISBN 0-8240-1553-3). Garland Pub.
--Mopsa the Fairy. LC 75-32172. (Classics of Children's Literature, 1621-1932: Vol. 35). (Illus.). 1976. Repr. of 1869 ed. PLB 38.00 (ISBN 0-8240-2284-X). Garland Pub.
Ingels, Jack E. Landscaping: Principles & Practices. LC 76-51686. 1978. pap. text ed. 11.24 (ISBN 0-8273-1634-8); instructor's guide 1.60 (ISBN 0-8273-1635-6). Delmar.
Ingen, J. Van see Van Ingen, J.
Ingenkamp, Karlheinz. Educational Assessment. (Council of Europe European Trend Reports on Educational Research: No. 3). (Orig.). 1977. pap. text ed. 15.00x (ISBN 0-85633-130-9, NFER). Humanities.
Ingerman, Peter Z. Syntax Oriented Translator. 1966. text ed. 10.95 (ISBN 0-12-370850-8). Acad Pr.
Ingersoll, et al. New Mexico One Hundred Years Ago. (Sun Historical Ser.). (Illus.). pap. 3.50 (ISBN 0-89540-057-X). Sun Pub.
Ingersoll, Daniel, et al, eds. Experimental Archeology. LC 77-4250. 1977. 27.50x (ISBN 0-231-03658-2). Columbia U Pr.
Ingersoll, Ernest. Birds in Legend, Fable & Folklore. LC 68-26576. 1968. Repr. of 1923 ed. 18.00 (ISBN 0-8103-3548-4). Gale.

Ingersoll, Lurton D. Life of Horace Greeley: Founder of the N. Y. Tribune. (American Newspapermen 1790-1933 Ser.). (Illus.). 688p. 1974. Repr. 26.50x (ISBN 0-8464-0018-9). Beekman Pubs.
Ingersoll, R. H., jt. auth. see Jopp, Harold D.
Ingersoll, Robert G. Atheist Truth Vs. Religion's Ghosts. 1980. pap. 3.29. Am Atheist.
--A Few Reasons for Doubting the Inspiration of the Bible. 1976. pap. 3.00. Am Atheist.
Ingersoll, William B., jt. auth. see Bloch, Stuart M.
Ingham, Barbara. Tropical Exports & Economic Development. Date not set. 22.50 (ISBN 0-312-81918-8). St Martin.
Ingham, Geoffrey. Strikes & Industrial Conflict: Britain & Scandinavia. (Studies in Sociology). 95p. (Orig.). 1974. pap. 3.25x (ISBN 0-333-13435-4). Humanities.
Ingham, Henry L., Jr. The United States: The Destiny of a Democracy, 2 vols. 1978. Vol. 1. pap. text ed. 14.00 (ISBN 0-8191-0384-5); Vol. 2. pap. text ed. 15.00 (ISBN 0-8191-0385-3). U Pr of Amer.
Ingle, Annie. Alph & Ralph. (Illus.). (gr. 1-4). 1980. 3.95 (ISBN 0-525-69304-1, Gingerbread); PLB 5.95 (ISBN 0-525-69305-X). Dutton.
--Brenda the Brat. (Illus.). (gr. 1-4). 1980. 3.95 (ISBN 0-525-69306-8, Gingerbread); PLB 5.95 (ISBN 0-525-69307-6). Dutton.
--Nosy Norman. (Illus.). (ps-3). 1980. 3.95 (ISBN 0-525-69453-6, Gingerbread); PLB 5.95 (ISBN 0-525-69457-9). Dutton.
Ingle, E. Local Institutions of Virginia. 1973. Repr. of 1885 ed. pap. 11.00 (ISBN 0-384-25741-0). Johnson Repr.
Ingle, Harold N. Nesselrode & the Russian Rapprochement with Britain, 1836-1843. LC 74-79764. 1976. 18.50x (ISBN 0-520-02795-7). U. of Cal Pr.
Ingle, Lydia R. Edades: Kites & Visions. (Illus.). 103p. 1980. pap. 7.50x (ISBN 0-686-28646-4). Cellar.
Ingle, Robert, jt. auth. see Gephart, William.
Ingleby, Clement M. Shakespeare's Bones. 48p. 1980. Repr. of 1883 ed. lib. bdg. 10.00 (ISBN 0-89987-400-2). Darby Bks.
Ingleby, David, ed. Critical Psychiatry: The Politics of Mental Health. 1980. 11.95 (ISBN 0-394-42622-3); pap. 5.95 (ISBN 0-394-73560-9). Pantheon.
Ingleby, Helen & Gershon-Cohen, Jacob. Comparative Anatomy, Pathology, & Roentgenology of the Breast. LC 59-8457. 1960. 10.00 o.p. (ISBN 0-8122-7279-X). U of Pa Pr.
Ingleby, Terry, jt. auth. see Taylor, Jenny.
Ingledew, Roberto, tr. see Collins, Gary.
Ingledew, Roberto, tr. see Lewis, C. S.
Inglehart, Ronald, jt. auth. see Rabier, Jacques-Rene.
Ingles, Lloyd G. Mammals of the Pacific States: California, Oregon, Washington. (Illus.). 1965. 14.95 (ISBN 0-8047-0297-7); text ed. 11.20 (ISBN 0-8047-0298-5). Stanford U Pr.
Ingleson, John. Road to Exile: Indonesian Nationalist Movement. 1979. text ed. 28.95x o.p. (ISBN 0-686-65416-1); pap. text ed. 12.50x (ISBN 0-686-65417-X, 00130). Heinemann Ed.
Inglett, George E. Corn: Culture, Processing, Products. LC 77-126335. (Illus.). 1970. 29.50 (ISBN 0-87055-088-8). AVI.
--Seed Proteins Symposium. (Illus.). 1972. text ed. 28.00 (ISBN 0-87055-117-5). AVI.
--Symposium: Processing Agricultural & Municipal Wastes. (Illus.). 1973. text ed. 23.50 (ISBN 0-87055-139-6). AVI.
--Wheat: Production & Utilization. (Illus.). 1974. text ed. 35.00 (ISBN 0-87055-154-X). AVI.
Inglett, George E., ed. Fabricated Foods. (Illus.). 395p. 1975. lib. bdg. 25.00 (ISBN 0-87055-179-5). AVI.
--Symposium: Sweeteners: Proceedings. (Illus.). 1974. 24.50 (ISBN 0-87055-153-1). AVI.
Ingley, James M., jt. auth. see Smith, B. J.
Inglin, Meinrad. Begraebnis Eines Schirmflicker. 260p. (Ger.). 1980. text ed. 16.25 (ISBN 3-288-03326-7, Pub. by Insel Verlag Germany). Suhrkamp.
Inglis, Brian. The Forbidden Game: A Social History of Drugs. LC 75-12382. 1975. 8.95 o.p. (ISBN 0-684-14428-X, ScribT). Scribner.
--Men of Conscience. LC 76-116780. (Illus.). 1971. 10.00 o.s.i. (ISBN 0-02-558190-2). Macmillan.
Inglis, David R. Nuclear Energy: Its Physics & Its Social Challenge. LC 78-186840. 1973. pap. text ed. 10.95 (ISBN 0-201-03199-X). A-W.
--Wind Power & Other Energy Options. LC 78-9102. (Illus.). 1978. 16.00 (ISBN 0-472-09303-7); pap. 8.50 (ISBN 0-472-06303-0). U of Mich Pr.
Inglis, F. Ideology & Imagination. LC 74-82220. 240p. 1975. 27.50 (ISBN 0-521-20540-9); pap. 8.95x (ISBN 0-521-09886-6). Cambridge U Pr.
--The Promise of Happiness. LC 80-49986. 250p. Date not set. 39.50 (ISBN 0-521-23142-6). Cambridge U Pr.
Inglis, J. K. Laboratory Animal Technology. 1980. 48.00 (ISBN 0-08-023772-X); pap. 23.00 (ISBN 0-08-023771-1). Pergamon.
--A Textbook of Human Biology. 2nd rev. ed. LC 73-21696. 1974. text ed. 14.50 (ISBN 0-08-017846-4); pap. text ed. 6.75 (ISBN 0-08-017847-2). Pergamon.
Inglis, J. K., jt. auth. see Lee, C. M.
Inglis, K. A., ed. Energy: From Surplus to Scarcity? LC 73-22112. (Illus.). 242p. 1974. 29.95 (ISBN 0-470-42731-0). Halsted Pr.
Inglis, Stuart J. Planets, Stars, & Galaxies. 4th ed. LC 75-31542. 352p. 1976. pap. text ed. 18.95x (ISBN 0-471-42738-1). Wiley.
Ingmanson, Dale E. & Wallace, William J. Oceanography: An Introduction. 2nd ed. 1979. text ed. 19.95x (ISBN 0-534-00538-1); lab manual 8.95x (ISBN 0-534-00624-8). Wadsworth Pub.
Ingoglia, Gina. Joe Camp's Benji: Fastest Dog in the West. (A Big Picture Bk.). (Illus.). (ps-k). 1979. 1.95 (ISBN 0-307-10826-0, Golden Pr); PLB 7.62 (ISBN 0-307-60826-3). Western Pub.
Ingoglie, Gina. Benji, Fastest Dog in the West. (A Big Picture Book Ser.). (Illus.). (gr. k-3). 1979. PLB 7.62 (ISBN 0-307-10826-0, Golden Pr). Western Pub.
Ingold, Cecil T. Biology of Fungi. 3rd rev. ed. (Hutchinson Biology Monographs). (Illus., Orig.). 1973. pap. text ed. 10.50x (ISBN 0-09-105120-7, Hutchinson U Lib). Humanities.
Ingold, Gerard. The Art of the Paperweight: Saint Louis. L. H. Selman Ltd., ed. (Illus.). 1981. price not set (ISBN 0-933756-01-1). Paperweight Pr.
Ingold, Tim. Hunters, Pastoralists & Ranchers. LC 78-73243. (Cambridge Studies in Social Anthropology: No. 28). (Illus.). 1980. 27.50 (ISBN 0-521-22588-4). Cambridge U Pr.
Ingraham. Slavery in the United States. LC 68-27402. (First Bks). (Illus.). (gr. 4-6). 6.45 (ISBN 0-531-02317-6). Watts.
Ingraham, Barton. Political Crime in Europe: A Comparative Study of France, Germany, & England. 1979. 25.00 (ISBN 0-520-03562-3). U of Cal Pr.
Ingraham, Claire R., jt. auth. see Ingraham, Leonard W.
Ingraham, Erick, tr. see Foster, Catharine O.
Ingraham, F. & Anderson, Eric. Prince of the House of David. Orig. Title: Three Years in the Holy City. 363p. 1980. Repr. text ed. 9.95 (ISBN 0-89841-003-7). Zoe Pubns.
Ingraham, Leonard. Album of Colonial America. LC 71-75721. (Picture Albums Ser). (Illus.). (gr. 4-6). 1969. PLB 5.90 o.p. (ISBN 0-531-01507-6). Watts.
Ingraham, Leonard W. First Book of Slavery in the United States. LC 68-27402. (First Bks). (Illus.). (gr. 4-6). 1968. PLB 6.45 (ISBN 0-531-00630-1). Watts.
Ingraham, Leonard W. & Ingraham, Claire R. An Album of Women in American History. LC 72-6138. (Picture Albums Ser.). (Illus.). 96p. (gr. 4 up). 1972. PLB 5.90 o.p. (ISBN 0-531-01515-7). Watts.
Ingram, A. W., jt. auth. see Avery, J. H.
Ingram, Allan. Boswell's Creative Gloom: A Study of Imagery & Melancholy in the Writings of James Boswell. 1981. 28.50x (ISBN 0-389-20157-X). B&N.
Ingram, Arthur. Off Highway & Construction Trucks. (Illus.). 160p. 1980. 17.50 (ISBN 0-7137-0960-X, Pub. by Blandford Pr England). Sterling.
Ingram, Arthur & Bishop, Denis. Fire Engines in Color. (Illus.). 235p. 1980. 9.95 (ISBN 0-7137-0627-9, Pub. by Blandford Fr England). Sterling.
Ingram, Arthur, ed. Trucks of the World Highways. (Illus.). 1979. 17.50 (ISBN 0-7137-0994-4, Pub by Blandford Pr England). Sterling.
Ingram, D. The Commonwealth at Work. 1969. 12.25 (ISBN 0-08-013869-1); pap. 4.40 (ISBN 0-08-013868-3). Pergamon.
Ingram, D. G., jt. auth. see Bylanski, P.
Ingram, D. J. Radiation & Quantum Physics. (Oxford Physics Ser.). (Illus.). 112p. 1974. pap. text ed. 6.95x (ISBN 0-19-851814-5). Oxford U Pr.
Ingram, D. S. & Helgeson, J. P. Tissue Culture Methods for Plant Pathologists: Organized by the British Plant Pathologists, Vol. 2. 250p. 1981. 47.50 (ISBN 0-470-27048-9). Halsted Pr.
Ingram, David, et al, eds. Proceedings of the First International Congress for the Study of Child Language. LC 80-7952. 668p. 1980. lib. bdg. 32.75 (ISBN 0-8191-1084-1). U Pr of Amer.
Ingram, David J., jt. ed. see Lieshout, Cornelis F.
Ingram, Edward. The Beginning of the Great Game in Asia 1828-1834. (Illus.). 1979. 39.50x (ISBN 0-19-822470-2). Oxford U Pr.
Ingram, Grace. Gilded Spurs. 1979. pap. 1.95 o.p. (ISBN 0-449-23910-1, Crest). Fawcett.
Ingram, Helen M. & Mann, Dean E., eds. Why Policies Succeed or Fail. LC 79-26317. (Sage Yearbooks in Politics & Public Policy: Vol. 8). (Illus.). 312p. 1980. 20.00 (ISBN 0-8039-1416-4); pap. 9.95 (ISBN 0-8039-1417-2). Sage.
Ingram, I. M., et al. Notes on Psychiatry. 4th ed. LC 75-17741. (Illus.). 128p. 1976. pap. text ed. 5.75 (ISBN 0-443-01334-9). Churchill.
Ingram, J. A. Fellcraft. 12.50x (ISBN 0-392-07812-0, SpS). Soccer.
Ingram, J. B. Curriculum Integration & Lifelong Education. (Advances in Lifelong Education: Vol 6). 1979. 15.00 (ISBN 0-08-024301-0); pap. 9.00 (ISBN 0-08-024300-2). Pergamon.
Ingram, James C. International Economic Problems. 3rd ed. LC 77-11139. (Wiley Introduction to Economic Ser.). 1978. pap. text ed. 9.50 (ISBN 0-471-02182-2). Wiley.
Ingram, John A. Introductory Statistics. LC 73-90820. 1974. text ed. 18.95 (ISBN 0-8465-2640-9). Benjamin-Cummings.
Ingram, Patricia & Hollander, Lewis. Successful Endurance Riding: The Ultimate Test of Horsemanship. 192p. 1981. 11.95 (ISBN 0-8289-0423-5). Greene.
Ingram, Paul O. The Dharma of Faith: An Introduction to Classical Pure Land Buddhism. 1978. pap. text ed. 7.75x (ISBN 0-8191-0373-X). U Pr of Amer.
Ingram, R. E., ed. see Hamilton, William R.
Ingram, R. W. John Marston. (English Authors Ser.: No. 216). 1978. 12.50 (ISBN 0-8057-6725-8). Twayne.
Ingram, Reginald W., ed. Coventry. (Records of Early English Drama Ser.). 700p. 1981. 47.50x (ISBN 0-8020-5542-7). U of Toronto Pr.
Ingram, T. T., et al. Living with Cerebral Palsy. (Clinics in Developmental Medicine Ser. No. 14). 105p. 1964. 5.00 o.p. (ISBN 0-685-24717-1). Lippincott.
Ingram, Terrence. A Matter of Taste. 152p. 1980. 20.95x (ISBN 0-00-211444-5, Pub. by W Collins Australia). Intl Schol Bk Serv.
Ingram, Terry. A Question of Polish: The Antique Market in Australia. 176p. 1980. 27.95x (ISBN 0-00-216412-4, Pub. by W Collins Australia). Intl Schol Bk Serv.
Ingram, William & Swain, Kathleen M., eds. Concordance to Milton's English Poetry. 1972. 98.00x (ISBN 0-19-811138-X). Oxford U Pr.
Ingstad, Anne. Norse Discovery of America, Vol. 1. 1977. 40.00x (ISBN 82-00-01513-0, Dist. by Columbia U Pr). Universitet.
Ingstad, H. Vinland the Good. (Tanum of Norway Tokens Ser). pap. 12.00x o.p. (ISBN 0-686-66670-4, N475). Vanous.
Ingwall, Joanne, jt. auth. see Jacobus, William E.
Ingwersen, Faith & Ingwersen, Neils. Martin A. Hansen. (World Authors Ser.: No. 419). 1976. lib. bdg. 11.95 (ISBN 0-8057-6259-0). Twayne.
Ingwersen, Neils, jt. auth. see Ingwersen, Faith.
Ingwersen, Ulla. Respiratory Physical Therapy & Pulmonary Care. LC 76-27094. 1976. 20.95 (ISBN 0-471-02473-2, Pub. by Wiley Medical). Wiley.
Ingwersen, Will. Alpine Garden Plants in Color. (Illus.). 168p. 1981. 12.95 (ISBN 0-7137-0968-5, Pub. by Blandford Pr England); pap. 6.95 (ISBN 0-7137-1143-4). Sterling.
Inhaber, Herbert. Environmental Indices. LC 75-34290. (Environmental Science & Technology Ser). 176p. 1976. 26.00 (ISBN 0-471-42796-9, Pub. by Wiley-Interscience). Wiley.
Inhelder, Barbel & Piaget, Jean. Early Growth of Logic in the Child: Classification & Seriation. Orig. Title: Genesedes Structures Logiques Elementaires. 1970. text ed. 16.25x (ISBN 0-391-00124-8). Humanities.
Inkeles, Alex & Smith, David H. Becoming Modern: Individual Change in Six Developing Countries. LC 73-92534. 416p. 1974. text ed. 18.50x (ISBN 0-674-06375-9); pap. 7.95 (ISBN 0-674-06376-7). Harvard U Pr.
Inkeles, Alex, et al, eds. Annual Review of Sociology, Vol. 1. LC 75-648500. (Illus.). 1975. text ed. 17.00 (ISBN 0-8243-2201-0). Annual Reviews.
--Annual Review of Sociology, Vol. 6. LC 75-648500. (Illus.). 1980. text ed. 20.00 (ISBN 0-8243-2206-1). Annual Reviews.
Inkiow, Dimiter. Me & Clara & Baldwin the Pony. McGuire, Paul, tr. from Ger. LC 79-21820. (A Me-&-Clara Storybook). (Illus.). 96p. (gr. k-4). 1980. 3.95 (ISBN 0-394-84434-3); PLB 4.99 (ISBN 0-394-94434-8). Pantheon.
Inman, Billie A. Walter Pater's Reading: A Bibliography of His Library Borrowings & Literary References, 1858 to 1873. LC 78-68284. 390p. 1981. lib. bdg. 40.00 (ISBN 0-8240-9790-4). Garland Pub.
Inman, Clarence. What to Do with Your Pictures. (Orig.). 1980. pap. cancelled (ISBN 0-89586-058-9). H P Bks.
Inman, Don. Introduction to TRS-Eighty Graphics. LC 78-24835. 175p. 1979. pap. 9.95 (ISBN 0-918398-18-5). Dilithium Pr.
--More TRS-80 Basic. (Self-Teaching Guide Ser.). 300p. 1981. pap. text ed. 8.95 (ISBN 0-471-08010-1). Wiley.
Inman, Don & Inman, Kurt. Introduction to T-Bug. LC 79-67461. 1979. pap. 7.95 (ISBN 0-918398-33-9). Dilithium Pr.
Inman, Don, et al. Real Time BASIC for the TRS-Eighty. Date not set. pap. 9.95 (ISBN 0-918398-05-3). Dilithium Pr.
--Introduction to TI BASIC. 300p. (gr. 10-12). 1980. pap. 10.95 (ISBN 0-8104-5185-9). Hayden.
Inman, Douglas & Lovering, David G., eds. Ionic Liquids. 445p. 1981. 49.50 (ISBN 0-306-40412-5, Plenum Pr). Plenum Pub.
Inman, Kurt, jt. auth. see Inman, Don.
Inman, Marianne. Foreign Languages, English As a Second & Foreign Language, & the U. S. Multinational Corporation. (Language in Education Ser.: No. 16). (Orig.). 1979. pap. text ed. 4.95x (ISBN 0-87281-102-6). Ctr Appl Ling.
Inman, V. Kerry. Prophets of Doom in an Age of Optimism. (Orig.). 1981. pap. 4.95 (ISBN 0-934688-02-8). Great Comm Pubns.
Inman, Virginia, ed. Cumulative Index to Nursing & Allied Health Literature, Vol. 23. LC 78-643434. 1978. 50.00 (ISBN 0-910478-14-7). Glendale Advent Med.
Inmon, Marvin, jt. auth. see Wright, Norman.
Inmon, Marvin N., jt. auth. see Wright, Norman H.
Inmon, William. Effective Data Base Design. (P-H Ser. in Data Processing Management). (Illus.). 240p. 1981. text ed. 24.95 (ISBN 0-13-241489-9). P-H.
Inner London Education Assn. You in the Seventies: Families. 1976. 11.95x o.p. (ISBN 0-435-46560-0). Heinemann Ed.
--You in the Seventies: Individual & Society. 1977. 11.95x o.p. (ISBN 0-435-46561-9). Heinemann Ed.
Innes, C. D. Erwin Piscator's Political Theatre: The Development of Modern German Drama. LC 72-183223. (Illus.). 256p. 1972. 42.50 (ISBN 0-521-08456-3); pap. 10.50x (ISBN 0-521-29196-8). Cambridge U Pr.
Innes, Christopher. Modern German Drama: A Study in Form. LC 78-26597. 1979. 56.00 (ISBN 0-521-22576-0); pap. 13.95 (ISBN 0-521-29560-2). Cambridge U Pr.
Innes, Chritoper. Holy Theatre: Ritual & the Avant Garde. (Illus.). 280p. Date not set. price not set (ISBN 0-521-22542-6). Cambridge U Pr.
Innes, G. S., ed. The Production & Hazards of a Hyperbaric Oxygen Environment: Proceedings. 1970. 19.50 (ISBN 0-08-006767-0). Pergamon.
Innes, Hammond. Campbell's Kingdom. 1979. pap. 1.95 o.p. (ISBN 0-345-27413-X). Ballantine.
--Levkas Man. (YA) 1971. 6.95 o.p. (ISBN 0-394-44240-7). Knopf.
--North Star. 1979. pap. 1.95 o.p. (ISBN 0-345-25194-6). Ballantine.
--Solomons Seal. LC 80-7632. 352p. 1980. 11.95 (ISBN 0-394-51326-6). Knopf.
Innes, J. H. Plumbing. (Teach Yourself Ser.). 1975. pap. 3.95 o.p. (ISBN 0-679-10484-4). McKay.
Innes, Michael. The Daffodil Affair. LC 75-44986. (Crime Fiction Ser). 1976. Repr. of 1942 ed. lib. bdg. 17.50 (ISBN 0-8240-2378-1). Garland Pub.
--The Gay Phoenix. LC 79-28521. 1977. 6.95 (ISBN 0-396-07442-1). Dodd.
Innes, Stephen, jt. auth. see Breen, T. H.
Inness, George, Jr. Life, Art, & Letters of George Inness. LC 76-87444. (Library of American Art Ser). 1969. Repr. of 1917 ed. lib. bdg. 32.50 (ISBN 0-306-71515-5). Da Capo.
Innis, Harold A. Bias of Communication. 2nd ed. LC 65-97355. 1964. 12.50x o.p. (ISBN 0-8020-1040-7); pap. 6.50 (ISBN 0-8020-6027-7). U of Toronto Pr.
Innis, Mary Q., ed. Nursing Education in a Changing Society. LC 70-498725. 1970. pap. 3.00 (ISBN 0-8020-6112-5). U of Toronto Pr.
Innocent, C. F. The Development of English Building Construction (1916) (Illus.). 320p. 1971. 32.00 (ISBN 0-7153-5299-7). David & Charles.
Inoue, K., ed. see Hasegawa, T. & IFAC Workshop, Kyoto Japan, Aug. 1978.
Inoue, S. & Stephens, R. E., eds. Molecules & Cell Movement. LC 75-16666. (Society of General Physiologists Ser.: Vol. 30). 350p. 1975. 36.00 (ISBN 0-89004-041-9). Raven.
Inoue, Yasushi. The Hunting Gun. LC 61-8740. 1977. pap. 3.95 (ISBN 0-8048-0257-2). C E Tuttle.
Inoue, Yasushi, jt. auth. see Ikeda, Daisaku.
Inouye, Carol. It's Easy to Sew with Scraps & Remnants. LC 76-2784. (gr. 8-9). 1977. 6.95a (ISBN 0-385-11052-9); PLB Doubleday.
Inouye, Masayori. Bacterial Outer Membranes: Biogenesis & Functions. LC 79-13999. 1980. 57.50 (ISBN 0-471-04676-0, Pub. by Wiley-Interscience). Wiley.

Inrig, Gary. Quality Friendship. 192p. (Orig.). 1981. pap. 2.95 (ISBN 0-8024-2891-6). Moody.
Insall, A. J., tr. see Coppens de Houthulst, Willy.
Inscho, Frederick R., jt. ed. see Milbrath, Lester W.
Insdorf, Annette. Francois Truffaut. (Theatrical Arts Ser.). 1978. lib. bdg. 9.95 (ISBN 0-8057-9253-8). Twayne.
Insel, Paul M. & Jacobson, Lenore F. What Do You Expect? An Inquiry into Self-Fulfilling Prophecies. LC 75-2529. (Education Ser.). 246p. 1975. pap. text ed. 8.95 (ISBN 0-8465-2670-0, 52670). Benjamin-Cummings.
Insel, Paul M., ed. Environmental Variables & the Prevention of Mental Illness. LC 79-3521. 240p. 1980. 25.95x (ISBN 0-669-03457-6). Lexington Bks.
Insko, Chester A. Theories of Attitude Change. (Century Psychology Ser.). (Illus.). 1980. Repr. of 1967 ed. text ed. 24.50x (ISBN 0-8290-0068-2). Irvington.
Insko, Chester A. & Schoeninger, Douglas A. Introductory Statistics for Psychology. 2nd ed. 1977. text ed. 19.95 (ISBN 0-205-05514-1); test manual free (ISBN 0-685-71781-X); student guide avail. (ISBN 0-205-05516-8). Allyn.
Insley, Gerald S. Practical Guidelines for the Teaching of Physical Education. LC 71-186841. 1973. pap. text ed. 7.50 (ISBN 0-201-03155-8). A-W.
In-Sob, Zong, ed. & tr. Folk Tales from Korea. LC 53-12953. 1979. 6.95 (ISBN 0-394-17096-2, E738, Ever). Grove.
Inst. of Real Estate Management. Income-Expense Analysis: Apartments. Anderson, Kenneth, ed. (Orig.). 1980. lib. bdg. 49.00 (ISBN 0-912104-48-1). Inst Real Estate.
Inst. Real Estate & U. S. Department of Energy. Conserving Energy in Multifamily Housing: Alternatives to Master Metering. Kirk, Nancye J., ed. 100p. (Orig.). pap. text ed. write for info. (ISBN 0-912104-50-3). Inst Real Estate.
Institut De Droit International, ed. Session d'athenes Nineteen Seventy-Nine. (Institut de Droit international Annuaire: Vol. 58, Tome II). vii, 260p. 1980. 141.50 (ISBN 3-8055-3076-5). S Karger.
--Session D'Athens Nineteen Seventy-Nine: Travaux Preparatoires, 2 vols. 600p. 1980. Set. 320.00 (ISBN 3-8055-0070-X). S Karger.
Institut du Petrole Francaise, ed. Drilling Data Handbook. (Illus.). 420p. 1980. 39.95x (ISBN 0-87201-204-2). Gulf Pub.
Institut Francais De Pertrole. Manual of Economic Analysis of Chemical Processes. Miller, Ryle & Miller, Ethel B., trs. (Illus.). 1980. 37.95 (ISBN 0-07-031745-3). McGraw.
Institut National De la Statistique et Des Etudes Economiques. Annuaire Statistique De la France 1979. 84th ed. LC 79-39079. (Illus.). 920p. (Fr.). 1979. 80.00x (ISBN 0-8002-2274-1). Intl Pubns Serv.
Institut National De Recherche Chimique Appliguee. Pollution by the Food Processing Industries in the EEC. 193p. 1977. 33.00x (ISBN 0-86010-074-X, Pub. by Graham & Trotman England). State Mutual Bk.
Institute for Information Studies. Rehabilitation Engineering Sourcebook Supplement. Vash, Carolyn, et al, eds. LC 79-24747. (Illus.). 85p. 1981. pap. write for info. (ISBN 0-935294-05-8). Inst Info Stud.
Institute for Information Studies, et al. Financial Resources for Disabled Individuals. Vash, Carolyn & Crane, Marjorie Boyer, eds. LC 80-84166. 70p. 1980. pap. write for info. (ISBN 0-935294-06-6). Inst Info Stud.
Institute for Laboratory Animal Resources. Animals for Research. 10th ed. 1979. pap. 6.25 (ISBN 0-309-02920-1). Natl Acad Pr.
--Neotropical Primates: Field Studies & Conservation. Thorington, Richard, Jr. & Heltne, Paul, eds. (Illus.). 1976. pap. 10.25 (ISBN 0-309-02442-0). Natl Acad Pr.
Institute For Law Librarians - 6th Biennial - 1963. Law Library - a Living Trust. (AALL Publications Ser: No. 7). 58p. (Orig.). 1964. pap. text ed. 8.50x (ISBN 0-8377-0105-8). Rothman.
Institute for Marine Studies see Mundt, J. Carl.
Institute for Paralegal Training. Introduction to Estates & Trusts. Stern, Steven & Laden, Caroline S., eds. LC 78-27574. (Paralegal Ser). 697p. 1979. text ed. 18.95 (ISBN 0-8299-2025-0). West Pub.
--Introduction to Real Estate Law. Bellavance, Russell C. & Laden, Caroline S., eds. LC 78-7930. (Paralegal Ser.). 466p. 1978. text ed. 17.95 (ISBN 0-8299-2006-4). West Pub.
Institute for Religious & Social Studies. Communication of Ideas. Bryson, Lyman, ed. (Religion & Civilization Ser). 1964. Repr. of 1948 ed. 28.50x (ISBN 0-8154-0035-7). Cooper Sq.
Institute for Research on Public Policy, Canada & Brookings. Conferences on Canadian-U. S. Economic Relations. 94p. 1978. pap. text ed. 3.00x (ISBN 0-920380-09-3, Pub. by Inst Res Pub Canada). Renouf.
Institute for Responsive Action Staff, jt. auth. see Walker, Ronald.
Institute for the Study of Conflict, ed. Annual of Power & Conflict Nineteen Seventy-Nine to Nineteen Eighty. 465p. 1980. 50.00x (ISBN 0-8448-1386-9). Crane-Russak Co.
Institute for the Study of the U. S. S. R. Who Was Who in the U. S. S. R. A Biographic Directory Containing Five Thousand & Fifteen Biographies of Prominent Soviet Historical Personalities. Schulz, Heinrich E., et al, eds. LC 70-161563. 1972. 50.00 (ISBN 0-8108-0441-7). Scarecrow.
Institute of Advanced Legal Studies, University of London. Catalogue of the Library of the Institute of Advanced Legal Studies, 6 vols. 1978. lib. bdg. 480.00 (ISBN 0-8161-0099-3). G K Hall.
Institute of Bankers, UK. The Banks & Their Competitors. 108p. 1980. 12.00x (ISBN 0-85297-057-9, Pub. by Woodhead-Faulkner England). State Mutual Bk.
Institute of Child Health Athens International Symposium 2-8, July 1978 Athens, Greece. The Child in the World of Tomorrow: a Window into the Future: Proceedings. Doxiadis, Spyros & Tyrwhitt, Jaqueline, eds. (Illus.). 1979. 45.00 (ISBN 0-686-67666-1). Pergamon.
Institute of Civil Engineers. Aircraft Pavement Design. 114p. 1980. 79.00x (ISBN 0-901948-04-7, Pub. by Telford England). State Mutual Bk.
--Airports for the Eighties. 220p. 1980. 80.00x (ISBN 0-901948-72-1, Pub. by Telford England). Sate Mutual Bk.
--Airports for the Future. 129p. 1980. 60.00x (ISBN 0-901948-36-5, Pub. by Telford England). State Mutual Bk.
--Behaviour of Piles. 244p. 1980. 75.00x (ISBN 0-901948-07-1, Pub. by Telford England). State Mutual Bk.
--Diaphragm Walls & Anchorages. 234p. 1980. 79.00x (ISBN 0-7277-0005-7, Pub. by Telford England). State Mutual Bk.
--ICE Yearbook 1980. 848p. 1980. pap. 69.00 (ISBN 0-7277-0081-2, Pub. by Telford England). State Mutual Bk.
--Numerical Methods in Offshore Piling. 224p. 1980. 69.00x (ISBN 0-7277-0086-3, Pub. by Telford England). State Mutual Bk.
--Piles in Weak Rock. 244p. 1980. 35.00x (ISBN 0-7277-0034-0, Pub. by Telford England). State Mutual Bk.
--Piling: Model Procedures & Specifications. 168p. 1980. pap. 40.00x (ISBN 0-7277-0036-7, Pub. by Telford England). State Mutual Bk.
--A Review of Diaphragm Walls. 158p. 1980. 35.00x (ISBN 0-7277-0045-6, Pub. by Telford England). State Mutual Bk.
Institute of Civil Engineers, ed. Large Bored Piles. 160p. 1980. 40.00x (ISBN 0-901948-67-5, Pub. by Telford England). State Mutual Bk.
Institute of Civil Engineers, UK. Advanced in Sewage Treatment. 88p. 1980. 60.00x (ISBN 0-901948-70-5, Pub. by Telford England). State Mutual Bk.
--Airports--- the Challenging Future. 256p. 1980. 79.00x (ISBN 0-7277-0017-0, Pub. by Telford England). State Mutual Bk.
--Concrete Afloat. 208p. 1980. 55.00x (ISBN 0-7277-0048-0, Pub. by Telford England). State Mutual Bk.
--Dredging. 124p. 1980. 70.00x (ISBN 0-901948-40-3, Pub. by Telford England). State Mutual Bk.
--Engineering Hydrology Today. 152p. 1980. 65.00x (ISBN 0-7277-0012-X, Pub. by Telford England). State Mutual Bk.
--Flood Studies Conference. 106p. 1980. 75.00x (ISBN 0-7277-0014-6, Pub. by Telford England). State Mutual Bk.
--Floods & Reservoir Safety: An Engineering Guide. 1980. pap. 25.00x (ISBN 0-7277-0033-2, By Telford England). State Mutual Bk.
--Highways & the Environment. 1980. pap. 15.00x (ISBN 0-7277-0065-0, Pub. by Telford England). State Mutual Bk.
--Management of National & Regional Water Resources. 98p. 1980. 60.00x (ISBN 0-901948-65-9, Pub. by Telford England). State Mutual Bk.
--Mechanization for Road & Bridge Construction. 54p. 1980. 55.00x (ISBN 0-901948-58-6, Pub. by Telford England). State Mutual Bk.
--Operational Aspects of the Drought of 1975-76. 142p. 1980. pap. 50.00x (ISBN 0-7277-0059-6, Pub. by Telford England). State Mutual Bk.
--Reservoir Flood Standards. 1980. pap. 20.00x (ISBN 0-7277-0023-5, Pub. by Telford England). State Mutual Bk.
--Safety in Sewers & at Sewage Works. 64p. 1980. pap. 12.00x (ISBN 0-901948-12-8, Pub. by Telford England). State Mutual Bk.
--Safety in Wells & Boreholes. 1980. pap. 12.00x (ISBN 0-901948-57-8, Pub. by Telford England). State Mutual Bk.
--Thames Barrier Design. 202p. 1980. 50.00x (ISBN 0-7277-0057-X, Pub. by Telford England). State Mutual Bk.
--Thames Groundwater Scheme. 242p. 1980. 60.00x (ISBN 0-7277-0060-X, Pub. by Telford England). State Mutual Bk.
--Traffic Data Collection. 178p. 1980. 40.00x (ISBN 0-7277-0061-8, Pub. by Telford England). State Mutual Bk.
--Transport for Society. 180p. 1980. 75.00x (ISBN 0-7277-0015-4, Pub. by Telford England). State Mutual Bk.
--Transport of Hazardous Materials. 160p. 1980. 39.00x (ISBN 0-7277-0058-8, Pub. by Telford England). State Mutual Bk.
--Transportation Engineering. 174p. 1980. 50.00x (Pub. by Telford England). State Mutual Bk.
Institute of Civil of Engineers. Recent Developments in the Design & Construction of Piles. 380p. 1980. 80.00x (ISBN 0-7277-0082-0, Pub. by Telford England). State Mutual Bk.
Institute of Criminology, University of Cambridge, England. The Library Catalogue of the Radzinowicz Library, 6 vols. Perry, R., ed. (Library Catalogs Bib.Guides). 1979. Set. lib. bdg. 475.00 (ISBN 0-8161-0242-2). G K Hall.
Institute of Graphic Designers. Graphic Design, San Francisco. LC 79-23535. (Illus.). 144p. 1980. 22.50 (ISBN 0-87701-160-5). Chronicle Bks.
Institute of Internal Auditors, Inc. Compendium: Questions & Suggested Solutions, Certified Internal Auditor Examinations, 1976 Through 1979. (Illus.). 152p. 1980. pap. text ed. 16.00 (ISBN 0-89413-083-8). Inst Inter Aud.
--Survey of Internal Auditing: 1979. Newman, Samuel, ed. (Illus.). 250p. 1980. pap. text ed. 20.00 (ISBN 0-89413-085-4). Inst Inter Aud.
Institute of International Education. Open Doors. 157p. 1980. pap. 15.00 o.p. (ISBN 0-87206-098-5). Inst Intl Educ.
Institute Of Laboratory Animal Research. Laboratory Animals in Gerontological Research. LC 68-60087. 1968. pap. 5.75 o.p. (ISBN 0-309-01591-X). Natl Acad Pr.
Institute of Laboratory Animal Resources. Amphibians: Guidelines for the Breeding, Care & Management of Laboratory Animals. (Illus.). 160p. 1974. pap. 10.75 (ISBN 0-309-02210-X). Natl Acad Pr.
--Animal Models for Biochemical Research, No. 2. 1969. 4.00 o.p. (ISBN 0-309-01736-X). Natl Acad Pr.
--Animal Models for Biomedical Research, No. 3. LC 76-607190. (Illus.). 1970. pap. 5.75 (ISBN 0-309-01854-4). Natl Acad Pr.
--Animal Models for Biomedical Research, No. 4. LC 76-607190. (Illus., Orig.). 1971. pap. text ed. 6.25 (ISBN 0-309-01918-4). Natl Acad Pr.
--Coturnix (Coturnix Coturnix Japonica) Standards & Guidelines for the Breeding, Care, & Management of Laboratory Animals. LC 73-601933. (Illus., Orig.). 1969. pap. 4.00 (ISBN 0-309-01703-3). Natl Acad Pr.
--Defining the Laboratory Animal. LC 72-609048. (Illus.). 1971. 19.25 (ISBN 0-309-01862-5). Natl Acad Pr.
--Dogs: Standards & Guidelines for the Breeding, Care, & Management of Laboratory Animals. (Illus.). 60p. 1973. pap. 3.75 (ISBN 0-309-02102-2). Natl Acad Pr.
--Fishes: Guidelines for the Breeding, Care, & Management of Laboratory Animals. LC 74-3462. (Illus.). 88p. 1974. pap. 5.00 o.p. (ISBN 0-309-02213-4). Natl Acad Pr.
--Guide to Infectious Diseases of Mice & Rats. LC 72-611182. (Orig.). 1971. pap. text ed. 4.25 (ISBN 0-309-01914-1). Natl Acad Pr.
Institute of Laboratory Animal Resources, National Research Council. Laboratory Animal Housing. 1979. pap. text ed. 12.00x (ISBN 0-309-02790-X). Natl Acad Pr.
Institute of Laboratory Animal Resources. Laboratory Animal Medical Subject Headings. LC 78-178256. 224p. 1972. pap. 8.00 (ISBN 0-309-01933-8). Natl Acad Pr.
--Research in Zoos & Aquariums. 1975. pap. 10.00 (ISBN 0-309-02319-X). Natl Acad Pr.
--Ruminants: Cattle, Sheep & Goats, Guidelines for Breeding, Care & Management of Laboratory Animals. (Illus.). 76p. 1974. pap. 5.50 (ISBN 0-309-02149-9). Natl Acad Pr.
Institute of Marine Engineering, jt. ed. see Royal Institution of Naval Architects.
Institute of Marine Engineers. Factors in the Selection of Marine Machinery & Plant with Particular Reference to Reliability, Maintenance & Cost. (Illus.). 104p. 1972. limp bdg. 15.00x (ISBN 0-900976-91-8, Pub. by Inst Marine Eng). Intl Schol Bk Serv.
--Glossary of Marine Technology Terms. 178p. 1980. pap. 15.00 (ISBN 0-434-90840-1). Sheridan.
Institute of Marine Engineers, International Marine & Shipping Conference, 1973. IMAS Seventy-Three: Proceedings. Incl. Boilers, Main Steam Turbines & Gearing. 76p. Group 1. 9.00 (ISBN 0-900976-16-0); Ship Operation & Management: Ship & Propulsion Systems. 60p. Group 2. 9.00 (ISBN 0-900976-17-9); Fuel, Lubrication & Fire. 22p. Group 3. 6.00 (ISBN 0-900976-18-7); Marine Pollution - Noise, Sewage & Oil. 66p. Group 4. 9.00 (ISBN 0-686-11943-6); Training & Manning. 30p. Group 5. 6.00 (ISBN 0-900976-20-9); Radio Communications & Navigational Aids. 34p. Group 6. 6.00 (ISBN 0-900976-21-7); Ocean Engineering. 16p. Group 7. 6.00 (ISBN 0-900976-22-5); Marine Diesel Engines. 66p. Group 8. 9.00 (ISBN 0-900976-23-3); Stern Gear, Shafting & Propellers. 70p. Group 9. 9.00 (ISBN 0-900976-24-1). 434p. 1973. Set Of Parts. 89.00 (ISBN 0-900976-25-X, Pub. by Inst Marine Eng); Bound Volume. 36.00 (ISBN 0-686-11942-8). Intl Schol Bk Serv.
Institute of Marine Engineers, Ministry of Defense. Lubrication - Successes & Failures. (Illus.). 70p. 1973. limp bdg. 10.55 (ISBN 0-900976-12-8, Pub. by Inst Marine Eng). Intl Schol Bk Serv.
Institute of Marketing, ed. Marketing in the Construction Industry. 1974. pap. 12.95x (ISBN 0-434-90845-2). Intl Ideas.
Institute of Medicine. Assessing Quality in Health Care. LC 77-74650. 1977. pap. 6.50 o.p. (ISBN 0-309-02611-3). Natl Acad Pr.
--Assessment of Medical Care for Children. (Contrasts in Health Status Ser.). (Illus.). 224p. 1974. 12.00 (ISBN 0-309-02145-6); pap. 8.50 (ISBN 0-686-66904-5). Natl Acad Pr.
--Beyond Malpractice: Compensation for Medical Injuries. LC 78-58382. 1978. pap. text ed. 6.50 (ISBN 0-309-02765-9). Natl Acad Pr.
--Controlling the Supply of Hospital Beds. LC 77-74651. 1977. pap. 6.00 (ISBN 0-309-02610-5). Natl Acad Pr.
--Controls on Health Care. 1975. pap. 7.25 (ISBN 0-309-02330-0). Natl Acad Pr.
--Ethics of Health Care. Tancredi, Laurence, ed. LC 74-28130. xi, 313p. 1974. pap. 8.25 (ISBN 0-309-02249-5). Natl Acad Pr.
--Health Services Research. 1979. pap. text ed. 5.50 (ISBN 0-309-02875-2). Natl Acad Pr.
--A Manpower Policy for Primary Health Care. LC 78-56907. 1978. 6.25 (ISBN 0-309-02764-0). Natl Acad Pr.
--Pharmaceuticals for Developing Countries. 1979. pap. 13.50 (ISBN 0-309-02891-4). Natl Acad Pr.
--Sleeping Pills, Insomnia, & Medical Practice. 1979. pap. text ed. 6.00 (ISBN 0-309-02881-7). Natl Acad Pr.
--A Strategy for Evaluating Health Services. (Contrasts in Health Status Ser. Vol. 2). (Illus.). 256p. 1973. pap. 8.50 (ISBN 0-309-02104-9). Natl Acad Pr.
Institute of Pacific Relations. Economic Trends & Problems in the Early Republican Period: 1931. LC 78-74312. (The Modern Chinese Economy Ser.: Vol. 25). 537p. 1980. lib. bdg. 55.00 (ISBN 0-8240-4273-5). Garland Pub.
Institute of Personnel Management's National Committee on Employee Relations. Trade Union Recognition. LC 77-372028. (Orig.). 1977. pap. 22.50x (ISBN 0-85292-148-9). Intl Pubns Serv.
Institute of Petroleum. Mechanical Systems for the Recovery of Oil Spilled on Water. (Illus.). 1975. 29.90x (ISBN 0-85334-451-5). Intl Ideas.
--Petroleum Measurement Manual: Tank Calibration Section - Liquid Calibration Methods, Pt. II, Pt. Ii. 1980. 22.00 (ISBN 0-85501-433-4). Heyden.
Institute of Petroleum Oil Pollution Analysis Committee, London. Marine Pollution by Oil. (Illus.). 1974. 40.90x (ISBN 0-85334-452-3). Intl Ideas.
Institute of Real Estate Management Staff. How To Write an Operations Manual: A Guide for Apartment Management. Kirk, Nancye J., ed. LC 78-61862. 1978. pap. text ed. 18.95 (ISBN 0-912104-35-X). Inst Real Estate.
Institute of Real Estate Management. Income-Expense Analysis: Suburban Office Buildings. Anderson, Kenneth A., ed. (Orig.). 1980. lib. bdg. 35.00 (ISBN 0-912104-47-3). Inst Real Estate.
Institute of Traffic Engineers. Transportation & Traffic Engineering Handbook. 1976. 35.95 (ISBN 0-13-930578-5). P-H.
Institute of Vertebrate Paleontology & Paleoanthropology of the Chinese Academy of Sciences. Atlas of Primitive Man in China. (Illus.). 200p. 1980. text ed. 52.50 (ISBN 0-442-20013-7, Pub. by Sci Pr China). Van Nos Reinhold.
Institutes of the Christian Religion, jt. ed. see McNeil, John T.
Institution of Electrical Engineers. Conference on Power Thyristors & Their Applications. LC 74-288481. (Illus.). 555p. 1970. pap. 50.00x (ISBN 0-85296-015-8). Intl Pubns Serv.

Instruction Advisory Board & Tennis Magazine Editors. Tennis: How to Play, How to Win. LC 77-92906. (Second Instructional Portfolio Ser.). (Illus.). 222p. 1978. 11.95 (ISBN 0-914178-19-9, 24172, Pub. by Tennis Mag). Golf Digest.

Instrumentation Laboratory Spring Symposium, Boston, Ma, April 1980. Erythrocyte Pathobiology: Proceedings. Wallach, Donald F., ed. (Progress in Clinical & Biological Research Ser.: No. 54). 250p. 1981. price not set (ISBN 0-8451-0054-8). A R Liss.

Instrumentation Technology Magazine Editors. Instrumentation & Control Systems Engineering Handbook. (Illus.). 1979. 22.95 (ISBN 0-8306-9867-1, 1035). TAB Bks.

Integrated Education Associates Editorial Staff, ed. Chinese Americans. LC 72-83395. pap. 2.70 (ISBN 0-912008-04-0). Integrated Ed Assoc.

--Desegregation Law: An Introduction. pap. 1.00 o.p. (ISBN 0-912008-05-9). Integrated Ed Assoc.

Inter-American Juridical Committee, Jul 25 - Aug 23 1972. Proceedings. (Inter-American Juridical Committee Ser). 102p. (Orig.). 1972. pap. 1.00 o.p. (ISBN 0-685-30409-4). OAS.

Inter-American Statistical Conference - 6th - Santiago, Chile - 1972. Final Act. (Eng, Fr, Port, & Span.). pap. 1.00 ea. o.p. OAS.

Inter-Varsity Staff. Grow Your Christian Life. pap. 3.50 (ISBN 0-87784-661-8). Inter-Varsity.

Interchurch World Movement. Report on the Steel Strike of 1919. LC 73-139200. (Civil Liberties in American History Ser). (Illus.). 1971. Repr. of 1920 ed. lib. bdg. 29.50 (ISBN 0-306-70081-6). Da Capo.

Interchurch World Movement, Commission of Inquiry. Public Opinion & the Steel Strike. LC 77-119052. (Civil Liberties in American History Ser). 1970. Repr. of 1921 ed. lib. bdg. 37.50 (ISBN 0-306-71938-X). Da Capo.

Intergovernmental Group on Oilseeds, Oils & Fats. Report on the Fourteenth Session of the Intergovernmental Group on Oilseeds, Oils & Fats. 14p. 1980. pap. 6.00 (ISBN 92-5-100937-6, F2044, FAO). Unipub.

Intergovernmental Group on Rice. Report of the Twenty-Third Session of the Intergovernmental Group on Rice to the Committee on Commodity Problems. 29p. 1980. pap. 6.00 (ISBN 92-5-100926-0, F2043, FAO). Unipub.

Intermed Communications, ed. Diagnostics. (Nurse's Reference Library). (Illus.). 1200p. 1981. text ed. 19.95 (ISBN 0-916730-29-8). Intermed Comm.

Internaional Associaion of Logopedics & Phoniatrics, 18th Congress, Washington, D.C., August 1980. Main Report. Fritzell, B., et al, eds. (Journal: Folia Phoniatricia: Vol. 32, No. 2). (Illus.). 72p. 1980. soft cover 19.75 (ISBN 3-8055-1235-X). S Karger.

Internaional Conference on Industrial Economics, 2nd. Industrial Development & Industrial Policy: Proceedings. Roman, Zoltan, ed. 1979. 43.00 (ISBN 0-9960016-3-8, Pub. by Kiado Hungary). Heyden.

Internaional Numismatic Symposium, Warsaw & Budapest, 1976. Proceedings. Niro-Sey, K. & Gedai, I., eds. (Illus.). 221p. 1980. 27.50x (ISBN 963-05-2055-9). Intl Pubns Serv.

Internal & External Protection of Pipes, 3rd International Conference. Proceedings, 2 vols. pap. 94.00 (ISBN 0-906085-18-7, Dist. by Air Science Co.). BHRA Fluid.

Internal Revenue Service, ed. Nineteen Seventy-Eight U. S. Income Tax Guide. rev. ed. (Illus.). 1977. pap. 1.95 (ISBN 0-89552-010-9). DMR Pubns.

Internation Institute of Strategic Studies. Strategic Survey 1979. (Illus.). 144p. 1980. lib. bdg. 12.50x (ISBN 0-86079-037-1, International Institute for Strategic Studies). Westview.

International Academy of Oral Pathology. Proceedings, Vol. 4. Cahn, L. R., ed. 1970. 49.50 (ISBN 0-677-62260-0). Gordon.

International Academy of Pathology see Yardley, John H. & Morson, Basil C.

International Advanced Course & Workshop on Thermal Effluent Disposal from Power Generation, Aug. 23-28, 1976, Dubrovnik, Yugoslavia. Thermal Effluent Disposal from Power Generation: Proceedings. new ed. Zaric, Z., ed. LC 77-28808. (Thermal & Fluids Engineering Ser.). (Illus.). 1978. text ed. 49.50 (ISBN 0-89116-093-0, Co-Pub. by McGraw Intl). Hemisphere Pub.

International Advanced Course & Workshop on Thermomechanics of Magnetic Fluids, Udine, Italy, Oct. 3-7, 1977. Thermomechanics of Magnetic Fluids: Theory & Applications, Proceedings. new ed. Berkovsky, Boris, ed. LC 78-15126. 1978. text ed. 45.00 (ISBN 0-89116-143-0, Co-Pub. by McGraw Intl). Hemisphere Pub.

International Agency for the Prevention of Blindness, jt. auth. see Wilson, John.

International Agricultural Machinery Workshop. Proceedings. 203p. 1978. pap. 16.00 (R036, IRRI). Unipub.

International AIRAPT Conference, Le Creuset, France, July 30-Aug. 3, 1979. High Pressure Science & Technology: Proceedings. Vodar, B. & Marteau, P., eds. (Illus.). 1200p. 1980. 230.00 (ISBN 0-08-024774-1). Pergamon.

International Association for Educational Assessment, Third Annual Conference Narrobi, May 23, 1977. Criteria for Awarding School Leaving Certificates, an International Discussion: Proceedings. Ottobre, Frances M., ed. 1979. 30.00 (ISBN 0-08-024685-0). Pergamon.

International Association for Philosophy of Law & Social Philosophy. Equality & Freedom, Vols. 1-3. 1977. Set. 35.00 (ISBN 0-379-00657-X). Oceana.

International Association for the Advancement of Appropriate Technology for Developing Countries, 1979 Symposium. New Dimensions of Appropriate Technology: Selected Proceedings. Edwards, Alfred L. & Wagner, Thomas, eds. Wagner, Thomas, tr. xii, 251p. (Orig.). 1980. pap. 5.00 (ISBN 0-87712-208-3). U Mich Busn Div Res.

International Association of Business Communicators. Inside Organizational Communication. (Longman Public Communication Ser.). 384p. (Orig.). 1981. text ed. 22.50 (ISBN 0-582-28235-7); pap. text ed. 12.50 (ISBN 0-582-28234-9). Longman.

International Association of Fish & Wildlife Agencies. Proceedings of the Sixty-Ninth Convention. Blouch, Ralph I., ed. (Orig.). 1980. 11.00 (ISBN 0-932108-04-0). IAFWA.

International Association Of Gerontology - 5th Congress. Medical & Clinical Aspects of Aging, Proceedings, Vol. 4. Blumenthal, H. T., ed. (Aging Around the World Ser.). 1962. 30.00x (ISBN 0-231-08952-X). Columbia U Pr.

--Social Welfare of the Aging, Proceedings, Vol. 2. Kaplan, Jerome & Aldridge, G. J., eds. (Aging Around the World Ser.). 1962. 20.00x (ISBN 0-231-08950-3). Columbia U Pr.

International Association of Logopedics & Phoniatrics, 18th Congress, Washington, D.C. August, 1980. Abstracts. Loebell, E., ed. (Journal: Folia Phoniatrica: Vol. 32, No. 3). 110p. 1980. soft cover 19.75 (ISBN 3-8055-1249-X). S Karger.

International Astronautical Congress, 27th, Anaheim, Ca., Oct. 1976, jt. auth. see Napolitano, Luigi G.

International Astronautical Congress, 28th, Prague, 1977, jt. auth. see Napolitano, Luigi G.

International Astronautical Congress, 29th, Dubrovnik, 1-8 October 1978. Astronautics for Peace & Human Progress: Proceedings. Napolitano, L. G., ed. LC 79-40049. (Illus.). 1979. 82.00 (ISBN 0-685-97183-X). Pergamon.

International Astronomical Union Symposium, 44th, Uppsala, Sweden, 1970. External Galaxies & Quasi-Stellar Objects: Proceedings. Evans, D. S., ed. LC 77-154736. (Illus.). 549p. 1972. 40.50 (ISBN 0-387-91092-1). Springer-Verlag.

International Atomic Energy Agency. INIS Reference Series, 16 vols. (Orig.). 1969-1974. pap. 72.25 (ISBN 0-685-02939-5, IAEA). Unipub.

--Programming & Ultilization of Research Reactors: Proceedings, 3 vols. Eklund, Sigvard, ed. (International Atomic Energy Agency Symposia). 1962. Vol. 1. 17.00 (ISBN 0-12-572501-9); Vol. 2, 1963. 17.00 (ISBN 0-12-572502-7); Vol. 3. 17.00 (ISBN 0-12-572503-5). Acad Pr.

International Atomic Energy Agency Seminar, Vienna Austria. Transport Packaging for Radioactive Materials: Proceedings. (Illus.). 1977. pap. 54.25 (ISBN 92-0-020576-3, ISP 437, IAEA). Unipub.

International Biological Program, National Research Council. Productivity of World Ecosystems. 1975. pap. 16.00 (ISBN 0-309-02317-3). Natl Acad Pr.

International Biometeorological Congress, 7th, College Park, MD 1975. Biometeorology: Proceedings, Vol. 6. Landsberg, H. E., ed. 380p. (Supplements to vol. 19 & 20 of the international journal of biometeorology). 1976. pap. text ed. 77.50 (ISBN 90-265-0241-9, Pub. by Swets Pub Serv Holland). Swets North Am.

International Business & Management Institute. Little Known Business Secrets & Shortcuts for Entrepreneurs & Managers. (Illus.). 110p. (Orig.). pap. 25.00 (ISBN 0-935402-03-9). Intl Comm Serv.

International Cancer Congress, 12th, Buenos Aires, 5-11 October 1978. Abstracts of the Proceedings of the Twelfth Cancer Congress, Buenos Aires, 1978. Estevez, O. & Chacon, R., eds. LC 79-40032. (Advances in Medical Oncology, Research & Education: Vol. 12). 1979. 205.00 (ISBN 0-08-024378-9). Pergamon.

--Basis for Cancer Therapy One, No. 1. LC 79-40485. (Advances in Medical Oncology, Research & Education: Vol. V). 1979. 68.00 (ISBN 0-08-024388-6). Pergamon.

International Cancer Congress, 12th, Buenos Aires, 5-11 October 1979. Basis for Cancer Therapy Two. LC 79-40064. (Advances in Medical Oncology Research & Education: Vol. VI). (Illus.). 1979. 68.00 (ISBN 0-08-024389-4). Pergamon.

International Cancer Congress, 12th, Buenos Aires, 5-11 October. Epidemiology. Birch, Jillian, ed. LC 79-40693. (Advances in Medical Oncology, Research & Education Ser.: Vol. III). (Illus.). 1979. 68.00 (ISBN 0-08-024386-X). Pergamon.

International Cancer Congress, 12th, Buenos Aires 5-11 Oct. 1978. Gynecological Cancer. Thatcher, N., ed. LC 79-40719. (Illus.). 1979. 68.00 (ISBN 0-08-024391-6). Pergamon.

International Center for Settlement of Investment Disputes. Investment Laws of the World, Binder 10. 1979. 75.00 (ISBN 0-379-00650-2). Oceana.

International Clean Air Congress, 2nd. Proceedings. Englund, Harold M. & Beery, W. T., eds. 1971. 128.00 (ISBN 0-12-239450-X). Acad Pr.

International Codata Conference, 6th Biennial, Santa Flavia, Italy, May 22-25, 1978. Proceedings. Dreyfus, Bertrand, ed. (Illus.). 400p. 1979. 145.00 (ISBN 0-08-023371-6). Pergamon.

International Colloquium on Irradiation Tests for Reactor Safety Programmes, Petten, Holland, June 1979 & Joint Research Center, Petten Establishment of the Commission of the European Communities. Aspects of Nuclear Reactor Safety: Proceedings. (European Applied Research Reports Special Topics Ser.). 600p. 1980. lib. bdg. 46.00 (ISBN 3-7186-0016-1). Harwood Academic.

International Colloquium on Science, Technology & Society, Vienna, 1979. Science, Technology & Society--Needs, Challenges & Limitations: Proceedings. Standke, Klaus-Heinrich, ed. (Pergamon Policy Studies on International Development). 656p. 1980. 100.00 (ISBN 0-08-025947-2). Pergamon.

International Commission on Irrigation & Drainage, New Delhi, India, ed. The Application of Systems Analysis to Problems of Irrigation, Drainage & Flood Control: A Manual for Engineers & Water Technologists. (Water Development, Supply & Management Ser.: Vol. 11). (Illus.). 1980. text ed. 48.00 (ISBN 0-08-023425-9); pap. text ed. 18.00 (ISBN 0-08-023431-3). Pergamon.

International Commission on Optics International Congress, 9th. Space Optics: Proceedings. Thompson, B. J. & Shannon, R. R., eds. (Illus.). 849p. 1974. 37.50 (ISBN 0-309-02144-8). Natl Acad Pr.

International Commission on Radiological Protection. Permissible Dose for Internal Radiation. (ICRP Publication Ser.: No. 2). 1960. pap. 10.45 (ISBN 0-08-009254-3). Pergamon.

--Radiation Protection - Recommendations of the ICRP. (ICRP Publication Ser.: No. 9). 1959. pap. 7.15 (ISBN 0-08-013160-3). Pergamon.

International Committee for Nomenclature & Nosology of Renal Disease. A Handbook of Kidney Nomenclature & Nosology. LC 73-17665. 400p. 1975. text ed. 19.95 (ISBN 0-316-41920-6). Little.

International Computer Music Conference, 1978. Proceedings, 2 vols. Roads, C., ed. 1979. Vol. 1. pap. 10.00 (ISBN 0-8101-0600-0); Vol. 2. pap. 10.00 (ISBN 0-8101-0601-9). Northwestern U Pr.

International Conference, Amsterdam, 1972. Parapsychology & the Sciences: Proceedings. Angoff, Allan & Shapin, Betty, eds. LC 73-92492. 1974. 8.50 (ISBN 0-912328-23-1). Parapsych Foun.

International Conference, France, 1970. Century of Psychical Research: The Continuing Doubts & Affirmations; Proceedings. LC 73-153407. 1971. 7.00 (ISBN 0-912328-19-3). Parapsych Foun.

International Conference, France, 1971. Parapsychology Today: A Geographic View; Proceedings. Angoff, Allan & Shapin, Betty, eds. LC 72-94940. 1973. 8.00 (ISBN 0-912328-21-5). Parapsych Foun.

International Conference, Geneva, 1974. Quantum Physics & Parapsychology: Proceedings. Oteri, Laura, ed. LC 75-14867. 1975. 13.50 (ISBN 0-912328-26-6). Parapsych Foun.

International Conference Held in Bangkok, Jan. 7-9, 1980 & Karasudhi, Pisidhi. Engineering for Protection from Natural Disasters: Proceedings. Kanok-Nukulchai, Worsak, ed. 1980. write for info. (ISBN 0-471-27895-5, Pub. by Wiley-Interscience). Wiley.

International Conference, Kent State U., April 4-5, 1975. Noncommutative Ring Theory: Papers. Cozzens, J. H., et al, eds. (Lecture Notes in Mathematics: Vol. 545). 1976. soft cover 13.00 (ISBN 0-387-07985-8). Springer-Verlag.

International Conference London, 1973. Parapsychology & Anthropology: Proceedings. Angoff, Allan & Barth, Diana, eds. LC 74-82959. 10.50 (ISBN 0-912328-24-X). Parapsych Foun.

International Conference, Montreal Canada, Aug. 24-25, 1978. Brain-Mind & Parapsychology: Proceedings. Shapin, Betty & Coly, Lisette, eds. LC 79-84820. 1979. 14.00 (ISBN 0-912328-31-2). Parapsych Foun.

International Conference of Selected Papers, 2nd, Kingston. Ont. August, 6-10, 1974. Applied Cross-Cultural Psychology: Proceedings. Berry, J. W. & Lonner, W., eds. 340p. (Orig.). 1975. pap. text ed. 19.50 (ISBN 0-686-27809-7, Pub. by Swets Pub Serv Holland). Swets North Am.

International Conference on Armenian Linguistics, 1st. Proceedings: Proceedings. LC 80-24203. 1980. 25.00 (ISBN 0-88206-044-9). Caravan Bks.

International Conference on Collective Phenomena, 3rd, et al. Proceedings, Vol. 337. new ed. Langer, James S., et al, eds. LC 80-17323. (N.Y. Academy of Sciences Annals: Vol. 337). 39.00x (ISBN 0-89766-074-9); pap. write for info. (ISBN 0-89766-075-7). NY Acad Sci.

International Conference on Computational Methods in Nonlinear Mechanics, 2nd, Univ. of Texas at Austin. Computational Methods in Nonlinear Mechanics: Selected Papers. Oden, J. T., ed. 160p. pap. 41.25 (ISBN 0-08-025068-8). Pergamon.

International Conference on Computing Methods in Optimization Problems - 2nd San Remo, Italy - 1968. Proceedings. Balakrishnan, A. V., ed. LC 78-94162. (Lecture Notes in Operations Research & Mathematical Economics: Vol. 14). (Orig.). 1969. pap. 10.70 o.p. (ISBN 0-387-04637-2). Springer-Verlag.

International Conference on Cyclic Amp, 2nd, July, 1974. Advances in Cyclic Nucleotide Research: Proceedings. Drummond, G. I., et al, eds. LC 74-24679. (Advances in Cyclic Nucleotide Research Ser.: Vol. 5). 1975. 67.00 (ISBN 0-89004-021-4). Raven.

International Conference on Cyclic Nucleotide, 3rd, New Orleans, la., July 1977. Advances in Cyclic Nucleotide Research: Proceedings, Vol. 9. George, William J. & Ignarro, Louis, eds. LC 77-84555. 1978. 72.50 (ISBN 0-89004-240-3). Raven.

International Conference on Drug Absorption, Edinburgh, 1979. Proceedings. Nimmo, W. S. & Prescott, L. F., eds. 355p. 1980. text ed. 45.00 (ISBN 0-909337-30-6). ADIS Pr.

International Conference on Environmental Carcinogensis, Amsterdam, May 1979. Environmental Carcinogenesis. Occurrence Risk Evaluation & Mechanisms: Proceedings. Emmelot, P. & Kriek, E., eds. 402p. 1979. 58.75 (ISBN 0-444-80158-8, North Holland). Elsevier.

International Conference on Environment Future, 2nd. Growth Without Ecodisasters: Proceedings. Polunin, Nicholas, ed. LC 78-26933. 1979. 49.95 (ISBN 0-470-26615-5). Halsted Pr.

International Conference on Fluid Sealing, 4th. Proceedings. 1969. 29.00 (ISBN 0-900983-04-3). BHRA Fluid.

International Conference on Fluid Sealing, 3rd. Proceedings. 1967. 47.00. BHRA Fluid.

International Conference on Fluid Sealing, 2nd. Proceedings. 1964. 45.00. BHRA Fluid.

International Conference on Fluid Sealing, 1st. Proceedings. 1961. 45.00. BHRA Fluid.

International Conference on Fluid Sealing, 6th. Proceedings. 1973. text ed. 52.00 (ISBN 0-900983-27-2, Dist. by Air Science Co.). BHRA Fluid.

International Conference on Historical Linguistics, 4th. Papers. Traugott, Elizabeth, ed. 500p. 1980. text ed. 54.25x (ISBN 90-272-3501-5). Humanities.

International Conference on Historical Linguistics, 3rd, Hamburg 22-26 August, 1977. Proceedings. (Current Issues in Linguistic Theory). 1980. text ed. 45.75x (ISBN 0-391-01653-9). Humanities.

International Conference on Hot Electrons in Semiconductors, Denton, TX, 6-8 Jul. 1977. Hot Electrons in Semiconductors. Dunlap, W. Crawford, ed. 1978. pap. text ed. 38.50 (ISBN 0-08-022692-2). Pergamon.

International Conference on Housing, Planning, Financing, Construction, 2-7 December, 1979, Miami Beach, Florida. Housing As Human Habitat: Proceedings. Ural, Oktay, ed. (Pergamon Policy Studies Ser.). 1200p. 1980. Vol. 1. 165.00 (ISBN 0-08-025592-2); Vol. 2. 125.00 (ISBN 0-08-025593-0). Pergamon.

International Conference on Hydraulics, Pneumatics & Fluidics in Control & Automation. Proceedings. 1977. text ed. 65.00 (ISBN 0-900983-53-1, Dist. by Air Science Co.). BHRA Fluid.

International Conference On Hyperbaric Medicine - 3rd - Durham - N. C. - 1965. Proceedings. Brown, Ivan W. & Cox, Barbara G., eds. 1966. 16.00 (ISBN 0-309-01404-2). Natl Acad Pr.

International Conference on Hypnosis, Drugs, Dreams, & Psi, France, 1967. Psi & Altered States of Consciousness: Proceedings. Cavanna, Roberto & Ullman, Montague, eds. LC 68-8909. 1968. 7.00 (ISBN 0-912328-11-8). Parapsych Foun.

International Conference on Infrared Physics, 2nd, (CIRP 2), Zurich, 1979. Papers. Kneubuhl, Fritz, ed. 264p. 1980. 40.00 (ISBN 0-08-025055-6). Pergamon.

International Conference on Internal & External Protection of Pipes, 1st. Proceedings. 1976. 60.00 (ISBN 0-900983-46-9). BHRA Fluid.

International Conference on Light Scattering in Solids, 3rd & Balkanski, M. Proceedings. 1976. 55.95 o.p. (ISBN 0-470-15034-3). Halsted Pr.

International Conference on Marketing Systems for Developing Countries. Agricultural Marketing for Developing Countries: Proceedings, Vol. 2. Izaeli, D. N. & Messner, F., eds. 1977. 39.95 (ISBN 0-470-15095-5). Halsted Pr.

--Marketing Systems for Developing Countries: Proceedings, Vol. 1. Izraeli, D. N. & Messner, F., eds. LC 76-8243. 1977. 34.95 (ISBN 0-470-15094-7). Halsted Pr.

International Conference on Mechanics in Medicine & Biology, 1st, Aachen, Germany, 1978. Perspectives in Biomechanics: Proceedings, Vol. 1. Reul, I. H., et al, eds. 1300p. 1980. lib. bdg. 205.00 (ISBN 3-7186-0006-4). Harwood Academic.

International Conference on Methodology in Psi Research, France, 1968. PSI Favorable States of Consciousness: Proceedings. Cavanna, Roberto, ed. LC 75-97821. 1970. 8.00 (ISBN 0-912328-17-7). Parapsych Foun.

International Conference on Parkinson's Disease, No. 6. The Extrapyramidal System & Its Disorders. Poirier, Louis J., et al, eds. LC 78-57817. (Advances in Neurology Ser.: Vol. 24). 1979. text ed. 53.00 (ISBN 0-89004-369-8). Raven.

International Conference on Plant Growth Substances, 7th, Canberra, 1970. Plant Growth Substances, 1970: Proceedings. Carr, D. J., ed. LC 72-80291. (Illus.). 849p. 1972. pap. 27.90 (ISBN 0-387-05850-8). Springer-Verlag.

International Conference on Plasma Physics & Controlled Nuclear Fusion. Plasma Physics & Controlled Nuclear Fusion Research: Nuclear Fusion, Supplement 1975. (Illus.). 186p. 1976. pap. 14.50 (ISBN 92-0-139075-0, IAEA). Unipub.

International Conference on Pressure Surges, 3rd. Proceedings, 2 vols. Hansan, J. A. & Stephens, H. S., eds. 600p. (Orig.). 1980. PLB 99.00 (ISBN 0-906085-24-1, Dist. by Air Science Co.). BHRA Fluid.

International Conference on Red Cell Metabolism & Function, 3rd, Ann Arbor, Michigan, Oct., 1974. Erythrocyte Structure & Function: Proceedings. Brewer, George, ed. LC 75-999. (Progress in Clinical & Biological Research: Vol. 1). 812p. 1975. 55.00x (ISBN 0-8451-0001-7). A R Liss.

International Conference on Social Welfare, 18th, San Juan, P.R. International Council of Social Welfare: The Struggle for Equal Opportunity: Proceedings. LC 77-5341. 1977. 20.00x (ISBN 0-231-04346-5). Columbia U Pr.

International Conference On Social Welfare. New Strategies for Social Development. LC 31-3460. 1971. 20.00x (ISBN 0-231-03580-2). Columbia U Pr.

International Conference on Submillimetre Waves & Their Applications, 3rd, 1978. Submillimetre Waves & Their Applications: Proceedings. LC 79-40065. (Illus.). 1979. 46.00 (ISBN 0-08-023817-3). Pergamon.

International Conference on the Hydraulic Transport of Solids in Pipes, 6th. Hydrotransport Six: Proceedings, 2 vols. Stephens, H. S., ed. 400p. 1979. Set. pap. 112.00 lib. ed. (ISBN 0-906085-21-7, Dist. by Air Science Co.). BHRA Fluid.

International Conference on the Mediterranean Monk Seal, 1st, Rhodes, Greece, 1978. The Mediterranean Monk Seal: Proceedings. Ronald, K. & Duguy, R., eds. LC 79-41227. (UNEP Technical Ser.: Vol. 1). (Illus.). 250p. 1979. 23.00 (ISBN 0-08-025654-6); pap. 17.25 (ISBN 0-08-025655-4). Pergamon.

International Conference on the Peaceful Uses of Atomic Energy, 4th, Geneva, 1971. Peaceful Uses of Atomic Energy: Proceedings, 15 vols. (Orig., Eng., Fr., Rus. & Span., Vols. 1, 4, 5, 6, 8, 10, 12 avail. only). 1972. pap. 15.00 ea. (IAEA); pap. 10.75 ea. discussion vols. in Fr., Rus. & Span. Unipub.

International Conference on the Physics & Chemistry on Semiconductor Heterjunctions & Layer Structures, Budapest, 1970. Proceedings, 5 vols. Szigeti, G., ed. (Illus.). 1317p. 1970. pap. 82.50 o.p. (ISBN 0-685-27544-2). Adler.

International Conference on the Properties of Steam, 9th, Munich, West Germany, Sep. 10-14, 1979. Water & Steam: Their Properties & Current Industrial Applications: Proceedings. (Illus.). 704p. 1980. 115.00 (ISBN 0-08-025431-4). Pergamon.

International Conference off the Synapse, Czechoslovakia, May, 1978. The Cholinergic Synapse: Proceedings. Tucek, S., et al, eds. LC 79-577. (Progress in Brain Research Ser.: Vol. 49). 1979. 92.75 (ISBN 0-444-80105-7, North Holland). Elsevier.

International Conference on the Theory of Groups, 1969. Proceedings. Neumann, B. H. & Kovacs, L. G., eds. 414p. 1969. 49.00 (ISBN 0-677-10780-3). Gordon.

International Conference on Thermal Analysis, 3rd, Davos, Switzerland, 23-28 August 1971. Proceedings, 3 vols. Wiedemann, H. G., ed. Incl. Vol. 1. Advances in Instrumentation. 65.00x (ISBN 3-7643-0636-X); Vol. 2. Inorganic Chemistry. 82.50x (ISBN 3-7643-0637-8); Vol. 3. Organic & Macromolecular Chemistry, Ceramics, Earth Sciences. 72.50x (ISBN 3-7643-0638-6). 1972. Intl Pubns Serv.

International Conference, St. Michielsgestel, Netherlands, August 25-29, 1968. Deaf-Blind Children & Their Education: Proceedings. (Modern Approaches to the Diagnosis & Instruction of Multi-Handicapped Children Ser.: Vol. 2). 150p. 1971. text ed. 21.50 (ISBN 90-237-4102-1, Pub. by Swets Pub Serv Holland). Swets North Am.

International Conference, 10th, Lyon, July 2-6, 1979. Solid State Nuclear Track Detectors: Proceedings. Francois, H., et al, eds. (Illus.). 1082p. 1980. 235.00 (ISBN 0-08-025029-7). Pergamon.

International Conference, 2nd, Tokyo, 1972. The Properties of Liquid Metals: Proceedings. Takeuchi, S. & Takeuchi, S., eds. LC 73-1286. 640p. 1973. 46.95 (ISBN 0-470-84414-0). Halsted Pr.

International Conference, 7th, Tel Aviv, June 23-28, 1974. General Relativity & Gravitation: Proceedings. Shaviv, G., ed. LC 75-33824. 1976. 54.95 (ISBN 0-470-77939-X). Halsted Pr.

International Congress for Analytical Psychology, 5th. Success & Failure in Analysis: Proceedings. Adler, Gerhard, ed. LC 73-76973. (Illus.). 231p. 1974. 15.00 o.p. (ISBN 0-913430-21-8). C G Jung Foun.

International Congress for Energy & the Ecosystem, University of North Dakota, 12-16 June 1978. Ecology & Coal Resource Development, 2 vols. Wali, Mohan K., ed. LC 78-26238. 1980. 140.00 (ISBN 0-08-023863-7). Pergamon.

International Congress for Suicide Prevention, 7th, Amstersdam, August 27-30, 1973, et al. Suicide Prevention: Proceedings. 677p. 1974. pap. text ed. 44.50 (ISBN 90-265-0186-2, Pub. by Swets Pub Serv Holland). Swets North Am.

International Congress of Allergology, 10th, Jerusalem, Israel, Nov. 1979. Advances in Allergology & Applied Immunology: Proceedings. Oehling, A., et al, eds. (Illus.). 680p. 1980. 145.00 (ISBN 0-08-025519-1). Pergamon.

International Congress Of Americanists - 29th. Civilizations of Ancient America. Tax, Sol, ed. (Illus.). 328p. 1952. Repr. 17.50x (ISBN 0-8154-0231-7). Cooper Sq.

International Congress of Botany, Edinburgh, 1964. Incompatability in Fungi: A Symposium. Raper, J. R. & Esser, K., eds. (Illus.). viii, 124p. 1965. pap. 25.80 (ISBN 0-387-03334-3). Springer Verlag.

International Congress of Chemotherapy, 11th & Interscience Conference on Antimicrobial Agents & Chemotherapy, 19th. Current Chemotherapy & Infectious Disease: Proceedings, 2 vols. Nelson, John D. & Grassi, Carlo, eds. (Illus.). 1980. Set. 75.00 (ISBN 0-914826-22-0). Am Soc Microbio.

International Congress of Game Biologists, Thirteenth, Atlanta, Ga., March 11-15, 1977. Proceedings. Peterle, Tony J., ed. (Illus.). 538p. (Orig.). 1978. pap. 10.00 (ISBN 0-933564-04-X). Wildlife Soc.

International Congress of Life Insurance, 13th, Madrid 1979. Annals of Life Insurance Medicine: Proceedings, Vol. 6. Tanner, E. & Hefti, M. L., eds. (Illus.). 270p. 1980. 37.80 (ISBN 0-387-10050-4). Springer-Verlag.

International Congress of Mathematicians, 1978, Helsinki. Proceedings. 1980. 70.00 (ISBN 951-41-0352-1). Am Math.

International Congress of Pediatrics, Fifteenth, New Delhi, India, Oct 23-29, 1977. Dictionary of Participants. 148p. 1980. pap. 15.00x (ISBN 0-89955-327-3, Pub. by Interprint India). Intl Schol Bk Serv.

International Congress of Pesticide Chemistry, 4th, Zurich, 1978. Advances in Pesticide Science: Proceedings, 3 vols. Geissbuehler, H., et al, eds. 1979. Set. text ed. 225.00 (ISBN 0-08-022349-4). Pergamon.

International Congress of Pesticides Chemistry, 4th, Zurich, July 1978. World Food Production--Environment--Pesticides: Plenary Lectures. Geissbuehler, H., et al, eds. (IUPAC Symposia). 1978. text ed. 30.00 (ISBN 0-08-022374-5); pap. text ed. 10.00 o.p. (ISBN 0-08-022375-3). Pergamon.

International Congress of Pharmacology, 7th, Reims, 1978. Satellite Symposium. Marihuana - Biological Effects, Analysis, Metabolism, Cellular Responses, Reproduction & Brain: Proceedings. Nahas, Gabriel G. & Paton, William D., eds. (Illus.). 1979. text ed. 80.00 (ISBN 0-08-023759-2). Pergamon.

International Congress of Phonetic Sciences, 9th, Copenhagen, 1979. Special Lectures. Fischer-Jorgensen, ed. (Journal: Phonetica: Vol. 37, No. 1-2). (Illus.). 108p. 1980. pap. 19.75 (ISBN 3-8055-1414-X). S Karger.

International Congress of Protozoology, 5th. Proceedings. Hutner, S. H., ed. (Illus.). 222p. 1979. pap. text ed. 19.00 (ISBN 0-935868-00-3). Allen Pr.

International Congress of Pure & Applied Chemistry, 27th, Helsinki, Finland, Aug. 27-31, 1979. International Congress of Pure & Applied Chemistry, 27th. Varmavuori, A., ed. LC 79-42639. 396p. 1980. 115.00 (ISBN 0-08-023936-6). Pergamon.

International Congress on Analytical Techniques in Environmental Chemistry, Barcelona, 27-30 November 1978. Analytical Techniques in Environmental Chemistry. Albaiges, J., ed. LC 79-41670. 1980. 98.00 (ISBN 0-08-023809-2). Pergamon.

International Congress on Archives, 8th. Proceedings, Archivum, Vol. Xxvi. International Council on Archives, ed. 207p. 1979. 35.00 (ISBN 0-89664-135-X, Pub. by K G Saur). Gale.

International Congress on Asian Pediatrics. Proceedings. Bose, S. K., ed. 31.50x o.p. (ISBN 0-210-26977-4). Asia.

International Congress on Biblical Studies. Studia Biblica Nineteen Seventy-Eight II: Papers on the Gospels. Livingston, E. A., ed. (Journal for the Study of the New Testament Supplement Ser.: No. 2). 350p. 1980. text ed. 21.95 (ISBN 0-905774-22-1, Pub. by JSOT Pr England). Eisenbrauns.

International Congress on Child Abuse & Neglect, 2nd, London 1978. Abstracts of the Second International Congress on Child Abuse & Neglect. Franklin, A. White, ed. LC 78-41195. 1979. 30.00 (ISBN 0-08-023438-0). Pergamon.

International Congress on Child Abuse & Neglect, 2nd, London, 1978. Selected Papers, Vol. 3. Kempe, C. H., et al, eds. 1100p. 1980. 125.00 (ISBN 0-08-023430-5). Pergamon.

International Congress on Hormonal Steroids, 5th, New Delhi, Oct.-Nov. 1978 & James, V. H. T. Hormonal Steroids: Proceedings. LC 79-40734. 950p. 1980. 160.00 (ISBN 0-08-023796-7). Pergamon.

International Congress on Twin Studies, 2nd. Twin Research: Proceedings, 3 vols. Nance, Walter E., et al, eds. Incl. Pt. A. Psychology & Methodology. 32.00 (ISBN 0-8451-0150-1); Pt. B. Biology & Epidemiology. 26.00 (ISBN 0-8451-0151-X); Pt. C. Clinical Studies. 35.00 (ISBN 0-8451-0152-8). LC 78-8480. (Progress in Clinical & Biological Research: Vols. 24A, 24B, 24C). 1978. Set. 93.00 (ISBN 0-8451-0024-6). A R Liss.

International Convocation on Immunology, 7th, Niagra Falls, N. Y., July 1980, et al. Immunobiology of the Major Histocompatibility Complex. Zaleski, M. B. & Kano, K., eds. (Illus.). xii, 390p. 1981. 90.00 (ISBN 3-8055-1896-X). S Karger.

International Cooperative Alliance. Agricultural Cooperative Credit in South East Asia. 7.25x (ISBN 0-210-33926-8). Asia.

--Cooperation in the European Market Economies. Watkins, W. P., ed. 1967. pap. 4.50x (ISBN 0-210-22555-6). Asia.

--Cooperative Leadership in South-East Asia. 1963. 6.00x (ISBN 0-210-34055-X). Asia.

International Council on Archives, ed. see International Congress on Archives, 8th.

International Council on Social Welfare. Development & Participation: Operational Implications for Social Welfare. 404p. 1975. 23.00x (ISBN 0-231-03972-7). Columbia U Pr.

International Course, Trieste, Jan. 16-April 10, 1974. Surface Science: Proceedings, 2 vols. (Illus.). 503p. 1976. Vol. 1. pap. 37.50 (ISBN 92-0-130375-0, IAEA); Vol. 2. pap. 22.50 (ISBN 0-685-62848-5). Unipub.

International Deep-Water Rice Workshop, 1977. Proceedings. 239p. 1977. pap. 14.50 (R028, IRRI). Unipub.

International Economic Association Conference, Tokyo. The Economics of Health & Medical Care: Proceedings. Perlman, Mark, ed. LC 73-20107. 1974. 39.95 (ISBN 0-470-68051-2). Halsted Pr.

International Economic Studies Institute & Stanley, Timothy W. Raw Materials & Foreign Policy. (Illus.). 1977. lib. bdg. 21.00x o.p. (ISBN 0-89158-340-8); pap. text ed. 11.50 o.p. (ISBN 0-89158-446-3). Westview.

International Expert Seminar of the International Management Association. Project Management: New Conceptions & Approaches, Proceedings. (Eng. & Ger.). 1979. pap. 25.00 o.p. (ISBN 0-89192-288-1, Pub. by Gottlieb Duttweiler Inst). Interbk Inc.

International Experts Discussion on Lead Occurrence, Fate & Pollution in the Marine Environment, Rovinj, Yugoslavia, 18-22 October 1977. Lead in the Marine Environment: Proceedings. Konrad, Z. & Branica, M., eds. LC 80-40023. (Illus.). 364p. 1980. pap. 69.00 (ISBN 0-08-022960-3). Pergamon.

International Federation of Automatic Control, 7th Triennial World Congress, Helsinki, Finland, June 1978. A Link Between Science & Applications of Automatic Control: Proceedings, 4 vols. Niemi, A., et al, eds. (International Federation of Automatic Control Ser.). 1979. Set. 680.00 (ISBN 0-08-022414-8). Pergamon.

International Fluidization Conference, 1975. Fluidization Technology: Proceedings, 2 vols. Keairns, Dale L., ed. LC 75-40106. (Thermal & Fluids Engineering Ser.). (Illus.). 1000p. 1976. Set. 119.50 (ISBN 0-89116-162-7, Co-Pub. by McGraw Intl). Hemisphere Pub.

International Galvanizing Conference Madrid 1976. Intergalva 76: Proceedings. Zinc Development Assoc., London, ed. (Illus.). 272p. (Orig.). 1978. pap. 32.50x (ISBN 0-8002-2228-8). Intl Pubns Serv.

International Gas Bearings Symposium, 5th. Proceedings. 1969. lib. bdg. 29.00. BHRA Fluid.

International Gas Bearings Symposium, 2nd. Proceedings. 1965. 26.00. BHRA Fluid.

International Gas Research Conference, 1st, 1980. Proceedings. LC 80-83454. 1016p. 1980. 43.50 (ISBN 0-86587-085-3). Gov Insts.

International Iceberg Utilization Conference, 1st Ames, Iowa. Iceberg Utilization: Proceedings. Husseiny, A. A., ed. LC 78-5119. (Illus.). 780p. 1978. 73.00 (ISBN 0-08-022916-6); pap. 49.00 (ISBN 0-08-022915-8). Pergamon.

International Institute for Environment & Development (I.I.E.D.) Human Settlements, an Annotated Bibliography. Anglemyer, Mary & Ottersen, Signe R., eds. LC 76-10832. 1976. pap. text ed. 37.00 (ISBN 0-686-67630-0). Pergamon.

International Institute for Strategic Studies. Military Balance Nineteen Eighty--Eighty-One. 119p. 1980. 17.95x (ISBN 0-87196-446-5). Facts on File.

International Institute for Strategic Studies, ed. The Military Balance, Nineteen Seventy-Nine to Nineteen Eighty. LC 76-617319. (Illus.). 120p. 1980. lib. bdg. 12.50x (ISBN 0-89158-920-1). Westview.

International Institute for Strategic Studies. The Military Balance, 1975-1976. 114p. 1976. 20.00x (ISBN 0-89158-522-2). Westview.

--The Military Balance, 1980-1981. 120p. 1980. lib. bdg. 15.00x (ISBN 0-86079-040-1). Westview.

--Strategic Survey 1975. LC 76-24927. 1976. 20.00x (ISBN 0-89158-545-1). Westview.

--Strategic Survey 1976. (Illus.). 1977. pap. text ed. 10.50 o.p. (ISBN 0-86079-006-1). Westview.

International Institute for Strategic Studies, ed. Strategic Survey 1978. LC 76-24927. 140p. 1980. pap. text ed. 11.50x (ISBN 0-86079-026-6). Westview.

International Institute for Temporary Work. Temporary Work in Modern Society, part 3. 1979. lib. bdg. 25.30 (ISBN 90-312-0088-3). Kluwer Boston.

International Institute for the Unification of Private Law. Digest of Legal Activities of International & Other Institutions, Release 1. 4th ed. 1980. 85.00 (ISBN 0-379-00545-X). Oceana.

International Institute of Public Finance, 35th Congress, 1979. Reforms of Tax Systems: Proceedings. Roskamp, Karl W., ed. 1981. 30.00 (ISBN 0-686-64651-7). Wayne St U Pr.

International Institute of Refrigeration. Heat Transfer-Current Application of Air Conditioning. Van Iherbeek, A., ed. 1971. 90.00 (ISBN 0-08-016597-4). Pergamon.

--Low Temperatures & Electric Power. Van Iherbeek, A., ed. 1971. 67.00 (ISBN 0-08-016370-X). Pergamon.

--The New International Dictionary of Refrigeration in English, French, Russian, German, Italian, Spanish, & Norwegian. 550p. 1975. text ed. 145.00 (ISBN 0-08-020368-X). Pergamon.

--Progress in Refrigeration Science & Technology, 11th Conference, 3 Vols. 1965. Set. 180.00 (ISBN 0-08-011439-3). Pergamon.

International Irrigation Information Center, Bet Dagan, Israel, ed. Irrigation Equipment Manufacturers Directory. 2nd ed. LC 79-42940. (IIIC Publications: No. 5). 312p. 1980. 58.00 (ISBN 0-08-025512-4). Pergamon.

International Irrigation Information Center Bet Dagan, Israel, ed. Irrigation: International Guide to Organizations & Institutions. LC 80-49935. 165p. 1980. 46.00 (ISBN 0-08-026363-1). Pergamon.

International ISBN Agency, ed. International ISBN Publishers' Directory. edition 1980 ed. 1433p. 1981. 95.00 (ISBN 3-88053-010-6). Bowker.

International Labour Office. Asian Regional Conference, Manila, December 1980, 9th Session: Problems of Rural Workers in Asia & the Pacific, Report III. ii, 104p. (Orig.). 1980. pap. 10.00 (ISBN 92-2-102500-4). Intl Labour Office.

--Contract Labour in the Clothing Industry: Second Tripartite Technical Meeting for the Clothing Industry, Geneva, 1980, Report II. ii, 75p. (Orig.). 1980. pap. 7.15 (ISBN 92-2-102432-6). Intl Labour Office.

--The Employment Effects on the Clothing Industry of Changes in International Trade: Second Tripartite Technical Meeting for the Clothing Industry, Geneve, 1980, Report III. ii, 49p. (Orig.). 1980. pap. 7.15 (ISBN 92-2-102433-4). Intl Labour Office.

--Employment, Growth, & Basic Needs: A One-World Problem. LC 77-70278. (Special Studies). 1977. text ed. 18.95 o.p. (ISBN 0-03-021601-X); pap. 3.95 o.p. (ISBN 0-03-021606-0). Praeger.

--Freedom of Association, Labour Relations & Development in Asia: Asian Regional Conference, Manila, December, 1980, Ninth Session, Report II. ii, 61p. (Orig.). 1980. pap. 7.15 (ISBN 92-2-102499-7). Intl Labour Office.

--General Report: Second Tripartite Technical Meeting for the Clothing Industry, Geneva, 1980. v, 154p. (Orig.). 1980. pap. 11.40 (ISBN 92-2-102431-8). Intl Labour Office.

--Man in His Working Environment. (Workers' Education Manual). (Illus.). 142p. 1979. pap. 7.15 (ISBN 92-2-102060-6). Intl Labour Office.

--New Forms of Work Organisation: German Democratic Republic, India, Italy, USSR, Economic Costs & Benefits, Vol.2. (Illus.). 1979. lib. bdg. 14.25 (ISBN 92-2-102110-6). Intl Labour Office.

--Ninth Asian Regional Conference, Manila, December, 1980: Report of the Director-General Asian Development in the 1980s-Growth, Employment & Working Conditions, Report I, Pt. 1. iii, 100p. (Orig.). 1980. pap. 10.00 (ISBN 92-2-102497-0). Intl Labour Office.

--Ninth Asian Regional Conference, Manila, December 1980: Report of the Director-General Application of ILO Standards, Report I, Pt. 2. iii, 45p. (Orig.). 1980. pap. text ed. 7.15 (ISBN 92-2-102498-9). Intl Labour Office.

--Programme of Industrial Activities Advisory Committee of Salaried Employees & Professional Workers, 8th Session, Geneva, 1981: The Effects of Technological & Structural Changes on the Employment & Working Conditions of Non-Manual Workers, Report II. iv, 117p. (Orig.). 1980. pap. 8.55 (ISBN 92-2-102557-8). Intl Labour Office.

--Safety & Health & the Working Environment: International Labour Conference, 1981, 67th Session. 68p. (Orig.). 1980. pap. 8.55 (ISBN 92-2-102407-5). Intl Labour Office.

--Tasks to Jobs: Developing a Modular System of Training for Hotel Occupations. (Hotel & Tourism Management Ser.: No. 3). 302p. 1979. text ed. 17.10 (ISBN 9-22-102148-3). Intl Labour Office.

--Wage Determination in Asia & the Pacific: The Views of Employers' Organisations-Reports & Documents Submitted to an ILO-DANIDA Regional Seminar (Singapore, October 8-12, 1979) (Labour-Management Relations Ser.: No. 58). ii, 169p. (Orig.). 1980. pap. 11.40 (ISBN 92-2-102492-X). Intl Labour Office.

International Labour Office, ed. Equal Opportunities & Equal Treatment for Men & Women Workers: Workers with Family Responsibilities, Report V (1) 84p. (Orig.). 1980. pap. 10.00 (ISBN 92-2-102405-9). Intl Labour Office.

International Labour Office, ed. see Fraser, T. M.

International Labour Office, ed. see Kujawa, D.

International Labour Office, Central Library, Geneva. International Labour Documentation: Cumulative Edition 1970-71, 2 vols. 1972. Set. lib. bdg. 210.00 (ISBN 0-685-24887-9). G K Hall.

International Labour Office, Geneva, ed. see Bell, Michael.

International Labour Office, Geneva, ed. see De Veen, J. J.

International Labour Office, Geneva, ed. see Woillet, M. J.

International Labour Office, Geneva. Audiovisual, Draughting, Office, Reproduction & Other Ancillary Equipment & Supplies: Equipment Planning Guide for Vocational & Technical Trading & Education Programmes. (No. 15). (Illus.). 279p. (Orig.). 1979. pap. 22.80 (ISBN 9-22-102112-2). Intl Labour Office.

--Building Work: A Compendium of Occupational Safety & Health. (Occupational Safety & Health Ser.: No. 42). (Illus.). 256p. (Orig.). 1980. pap. 14.25 (ISBN 92-2-101907-1). Intl Labour Office.

--Children at Work. Mendelievich, Elias, ed. (Illus.). 176p. 1979. 16.25 (ISBN 9-22-102165-3); pap. 11.25 (ISBN 9-22-102072-X). Intl Labour Office.

--Employment & Basic Needs in Portugal. (Illus.). 228p. 1979. 22.80 (ISBN 9-22-102202-1); pap. 17.10 (ISBN 9-22-102072-X). Intl Labour Office.

--Employment: Outlook & Insights. A Collection of Essays on Industrialised Market-Economy Countries. Freedman, David H., ed. (Illus.). 148p. (Orig.). 1979. 17.10 (ISBN 9-22-102155-6); pap. 11.40 (ISBN 0-686-65773-X). Intl Labour Office.

--Guide to Health & Hygiene in Agricultural Work. (Illus.). 317p. 1980. pap. 15.70 (ISBN 92-2-101974-8). Intl Labour Office.

--Guidelines for the Development of Employment & Manpower Information Programmes in Developing Countries: A Practical Manual. (Illus.). 87p. (Orig.). 1979. pap. 7.15 (ISBN 9-22-102176-9). Intl Labour Office.

--Labour Market Information in Asia: Present Issues & Tasks for the Future. Report on Two Workshops Conducted with the Support of the Federal Republic of Germany. 116p. (Orig.). 1979. pap. 5.70 (ISBN 9-22-102168-8). Intl Labour Office.

--Migrant Workers. 196p. (Orig.). 1980. pap. 14.25 (ISBN 92-2-102093-2). Intl Labour Office.

--Optimisation of the Working Environment: New Trends. 428p. (Orig.). 1980. pap. 22.80 (ISBN 92-2-001905-1). Intl Labour Office.

--Profiles of Rural Poverty. (Illus.). 50p. (Orig.). 1979. pap. 4.30 (ISBN 9-22-102142-4). Intl Labour Office.

--Standards & Policy Statements of Special Interest to Workers Adopted Under the Auspices of the International Labour Office. 132p. (Orig.). 1980. pap. 7.15 (ISBN 92-2-102441-5). Intl Labour Office.

--Technical Guide, Nineteen Eighty: Consumer Prices. Descriptions of Series Published in the Bulletin of Labour Statistics, Vol. 1. (Illus.). 300p. (Orig.). 1980. pap. 17.95 (ISBN 92-2-102285-4). Intl Labour Office.

--Technical Guide, 1980: Employment, Unemployment, Hours of Work, Wages, Vol. II. 432p. (Orig.). 1980. pap. 15.70 (ISBN 92-2-102286-2). Intl Labour Office.

--Ten Years of Training: Developments in France, Federal Republic of Germany & United Kingdom, 1968-1978. 263p. (Orig.). 1980. pap. 10.00 (ISBN 92-2-102254-4). Intl Labour Office.

--Tool & Die. (Equipment Planning Guide for Vocational & Technical Training & Education Programmes Ser.: No. 2). x, 214p. (Orig.). 1980. pap. 22.80 spiral (ISBN 92-2-101891-1). Intl Labour Office.

--Women in Rural Development: Critical Issues. (a WEP Study) x, 214p. (Orig.). 1980. pap. 7.15 (ISBN 92-2-102388-5). Intl Labour Office.

--Work & Family Life: The Role of the Social Infrastructure in Eastern European Countries. (Illus.). vi, 77p. (Orig.). 1980. pap. 8.55 (ISBN 92-2-102167-X). Intl Labour Office.

--World Employment Programme, Seventh Progress Report on Income Distribution & Employment: A Progress Report on WEP Research Undertaken Within the Framework of the Income Distribution & Employment Programme. 80p. (Orig.). 1979. pap. 5.70 (ISBN 9-22-102294-3). Intl Labour Office.

--Year Book of Labour Statistics,1979. 39th ed. (Illus.). 711p. 1980. 47.50 (ISBN 0-686-61301-5). Intl Labour Office.

International Maize & Wheat Improvement Center. Corn: A Bibliography of the World Literature, 3 vols. LC 78-154562. 1971. Set. 67.50 (ISBN 0-8108-0378-X). Scarecrow.

--Wheat: A Bibliography of the World Literature, 3 Vols. LC 71-154563. 1971. Set. 77.50 (ISBN 0-8108-0393-3). Scarecrow.

International Marine & Shipping Conference, 1969. Proceedings. (Illus.). 832p. 1970. 36.00 (ISBN 0-900976-93-4, Pub. by Inst Marine Eng). Intl Schol Bk Serv.

International Mass Media Research Center see Intl. Mass Media Research Ctr.

International Mass Media Research Center. Marxism & the Mass Media: Towards a Basic Bibliography, No. 4-5. (Illus.). 96p. (Orig.). 1976. pap. 6.00 (ISBN 0-88477-007-9). Intl General.

International Meeting on Solid Electrolytes, 2nd, University of St. Andrews, Sep. 20-22, 1978. Solid Electrolytes: Proceedings. Armstrong, R. D., ed. (Illus.). 68p. 1979. pap. 27.50 (ISBN 0-08-025267-2). Pergamon.

International Microsurgical Society, 5th, Germany, Oct. 1978. Microsurgery: Proceedings. Lie, T. S., ed. (International Congress Ser.: No. 465). 1979. 78.00 (ISBN 0-444-90077-2, Excerpta Medica). Elsevier.

International Mine Ventilation Congress, 2nd. Proceedings. Mousset-Jones, Pierre, ed. LC 80-52943. (Illus.). 864p. 1980. 34.00x (ISBN 0-89520-271-9). Soc Mining Eng.

International Ophthalmic Congress. Transactions of the International Ophthalmic Optical Congress, 1961. 1962. 19.25 o.s.i. (ISBN 0-02-846270-X). Hafner.

International Organization of Citrus Virologists, 5th Conference. Proceedings. Price, W. C., ed. LC 59-63553. 1972. 11.50 (ISBN 0-8130-0327-X). U Presses Fla.

International Pigment Cell Conference - 6th. Structure & Control of the Melanocyte: Proceedings. Della Porta, G. & Muehlbock, O., eds. (Illus.). 1966. 44.00 (ISBN 0-387-03676-8). Springer-Verlag.

International Planned Parenthood Federation. Handbook of Infertility. Kleinman, Ronald L. & Senayake, Pramilla, eds. (Illus.). 58p. (Orig.). 1979. pap. 6.50x (ISBN 0-86089-034-1). Intl Pubns Serv.

International Protoplast Symposium, 5th, July 1979, Szeged, Hungary. Advances in Protoplast Research: Proceedings. Ferenczy, L. & Farks, G. L., eds. LC 79-41251. 550p. 1980. 84.00 (ISBN 0-08-025528-0). Pergamon.

International Seaweed Symposium, 7th, Sappora, Japan, Aug. 1971. Proceedings. Science Council of Japan, ed. 607p. 1973. 53.95 (ISBN 0-470-77090-2). Halsted Pr.

International Seminar, Trieste. Control Theory & Topics in Functional Analysis: Proceedings, 2 vols. (Illus.). 1976. Vol. 2. pap. 26.75 (ISBN 92-0-130176-6, IAEA); Vol. 3. pap. 33.25 (ISBN 9-2013-0276-2). Unipub.

International Society For Cell Biology. Cytogenetics of Cells in Culture. Harris, R. J., ed. (Proceedings: Vol. 3). 1964. 49.00 (ISBN 0-12-611903-1). Acad Pr.

--Differentiation & Immunology. Warren, Katherine B., ed. (Proceedings: Vol. 7). 1969. 49.00 (ISBN 0-12-611907-4). Acad Pr.

--Formation & Fate of Cell Organelles. Warren, Katherine B., ed. (Proceedings: Vol. 6). 1968. 49.00 (ISBN 0-12-611906-6). Acad Pr.

--Intracellular Transport. Warren, Katherine B., ed. (Proceedings: Vol. 5). 1967. 49.00 (ISBN 0-12-611905-8). Acad Pr.

--Use of Radioautography in Investigating Protein Synthesis, Proceedings. Leblond, C. P. & Warren, K. B., eds. (Vol. 4). 1966. 49.00 (ISBN 0-12-611904-X). Acad Pr.

International Society for Education Through Art. Arts in Cultural Diversity. 292p. (Orig.). 1980. 21.95. Praeger.

International Society for Rock Mechanics, 3rd Congress. Advances in Rock Mechanics: Proceedings, Vol. 2, Pts. A & B. xxxii, 1505p. 1974. 33.75 (ISBN 0-309-02246-0). Natl Acad Pr.

International Solar Energy Society. International Solar Energy Congress: Proceedings Held May 28 to June 1,1979, Atlanta, Georgia. 1980. 360.00 (ISBN 0-08-025074-2); pap. 275.00 (ISBN 0-08-025075-0). Pergamon.

International Spores Conference, Michigan State University. Spores, 4 vols, Vols. 3-6. Gerhardt, Philipp, et al, eds. (Illus.). Vol. 3. 7.00 o.p. (ISBN 0-685-88612-3); Vol. 4. 7.00 (ISBN 0-685-88613-1); Vol. 5. 10.00 o.p. (ISBN 0-685-88614-X); Vol. 6. 1974 15.00 (ISBN 0-685-88615-8). Am Soc Microbio.

International Summer School on Mathematical Systems Theory & Economics, Varenna, Italy, 1967. Proceedings. Kuhn, H. W. & Szegoe, G. P., eds. LC 70-81409. (Lecture Notes in Operations Research and Mathematical Economics: Vols. 11 & 12). 1969. pap. 21.90 o.p. (ISBN 0-387-04635-6). Springer-Verlag.

International Summer School, University of Antwerp, 1972. Modular Functions of One Variable 2: Proceedings. Kuyk, W. & Deligne, P., eds. (Lecture Notes in Mathematics: Vol. 349). v, 598p. 1974. pap. 20.50 (ISBN 0-387-06558-X). Springer-Verlag.

International Symposium. Urgent Endoscopy of Digestive & Abdominal Diseases: New Fields of Gastrointestinal Endoscopy. (Illus.). 260p. 1972. 74.25 (ISBN 3-8055-1349-6). S Karger.

International Symposium Clausthal - Zellerfeld, 1968. Textures in Research & Practice: Proceedings. Grewen, J. & Wassermann, G., eds. (Illus.). 1969. 34.30 (ISBN 0-387-04733-6). Springer-Verlag.

International Symposium, Dubrovnik, Yugoslavia, 7-14 Sept. 1977. Sulphur in the Atmosphere: Proceedings. Husar, R. B., et al, eds. 1978. text ed. 75.00 (ISBN 0-08-022932-8). Pergamon.

International Symposium Held at St. Ode, Belgium, Oct. 1-3, 1979. Lateralisation of Language in the Child: Proceedings. Lebrun, Yvan & Zangwill, O., eds. 1981. text ed. write for info. (ISBN 90-265-0337-7, Pub. by Swets Pub Serv Holland). Swets North Am.

International Symposium in Chemical Synthesis of Nucleic Acids, Egestorf, West Germany, May 1980. Nucleic Acid Synthesis: Applications to Molecular Biology & Genetic Engineering. (Nucleic Acids Symposium Ser.: No. 7). 396p. 1980. 40.00 (ISBN 0-904147-26-6). Info Retrieval.

International Symposium of the American Society of Zoologists, Toronto, December 27-30, 1977. Animal Models of Comparative & Developmental Aspects of Immunity & Disease: Proceedings. Gershwin, M. Eric & Cooper, Edwin L., eds. LC 78-15022. 1978. text ed. 43.00 (ISBN 0-08-022648-5). Pergamon.

International Symposium on Analysis, Chemistry, & Biology, No. 2. Polynuclear Aromatic Hydrocarbons. Jones, Peter W. & Freudenthal, Ralph I., eds. LC 77-87456. (Carcinogenesis-A Comprehensive Survey Ser.: Vol. 3). 1978. 49.00 (ISBN 0-89004-241-1). Raven.

International Symposium on Carotenoids, Madison, 5th, U. S. A., July 23-28 1978. Carotenoids Five. Goodwin, T. W., ed. (IUPAC Symposium Ser.). (Illus.). 1979. 50.00 (ISBN 0-08-022359-1). Pergamon.

International Symposium on Cell Biology & Cytopharmacology, First. Advances in Cytopharmacology, Vol. 1. Clementi, F. & Ceccarelli, B., eds. LC 70-84115. (Illus.). 1971. 48.00 (ISBN 0-911216-09-X). Raven.

International Symposium on Chironomidae, 7th, Dublin, August 1979. Chironomidae-Ecology Systematics Cytology & Physiology: Proceedings. Murray, D. A., ed. (Illus.). 380p. 1980. 69.00 (ISBN 0-08-025889-1). Pergamon.

International Symposium on Cooling Systems. Proceedings. 1975. pap. 34.00 (ISBN 0-900983-41-8, Dist. by Air Science Co.). BHRA Fluid.

International Symposium on Diagnosis & Treatment of Cardiac Arrhythmias, Barcelona, Spain, 5-8 October 1977. Diagnosis & Treatment of Cardiac Arrhythmias: Proceedings. Bayes De Luna, A. J., ed. (Illus.). 1980. 220.00 (ISBN 0-08-024426-2). Pergamon.

International Symposium on Flow Visualization, Tokyo, Oct. 12-14, 1977. Flow Visualization: Proceedings. new ed. Asanuma, Tsuyoshi, ed. LC 79-12407. (Thermal & Fluids Engineering Ser.). (Illus.). 413p. 1979. text ed. 89.50 (ISBN 0-89116-155-4, Co-Pub. with McGraw Intl). Hemisphere Pub.

International Symposium on Function & Molecular Aspects of Biomembrane Transport, Italy, April 1979. Function & Molecular Aspects of Biomembrane Transport: Proceedings. Quagliariello, E., et al, eds. (Developments in Bioenergetics & Biomembranes Ser.: Vol. 3). 526p. 1979. 68.50 (ISBN 0-444-80149-9, North Holland). Elsevier.

International Symposium on Gas-Flow and Chemical Lasers, 2nd, Rhode-St-Genese, Belgium, Sept. 11-15, 1978. Gas-Flow & Chemical Lasers: Proceedings. new ed. Wendt, John F., ed. LC 79-12779. (Illus.). 608p. 1979. text ed. 49.50 (ISBN 0-89116-147-3). Hemisphere Pub.

International Symposium on Glycoconjugates, Fourth. Glycoconjugate Research: Proceedings, Vol. 1. Gregory, John D. & Jeanloz, Roger, eds. LC 79-15164. 1979. 35.00 (ISBN 0-12-301301-1). Acad Pr.

International Symposium on Hearing, Fifth, Noordwijkerhout, the Netherlands, April 8-12, 1980. Psychophysical Physiological & Behavioral Studies in Hearing: Proceedings. Van den Brink, G. & Bilsen, F. A., eds. 480p. 1980. 42.50x (ISBN 90-286-0780-3). Sijthoff & Noordhoff.

International Symposium on Hydrotransport of Solids in Pipes, 4th. Proceedings. 1977. 60.00 (ISBN 0-900983-56-6). BHRA Fluid.

International Symposium on Hydrotransport of Solids in Pipes, 3rd. Proceedings. 1974. 50.00 (ISBN 0-900983-38-8). BHRA Fluid.

International Symposium on Intracranial Pressure, 2nd. Intracranial Pressure Two: Proceedings. Lundberg, N. & Poten, U., eds. (Illus.). 560p. 1975. 37.50 (ISBN 0-387-07199-7). Springer-Verlag.

International Symposium on Macro Molecular Chemistry. Kinetics & Mechanism of Polyreactions: Symposium, 6 vols. Tuedoes, F., ed. Vols. 1-5. pap. 64.00 o.p. (ISBN 0-685-27541-8); Vol. 6. pap. 35.00 o.p. (ISBN 0-685-27542-6). Adler.

International Symposium on Malignant Lymphomas of the Nervous System. Proceedings. Jellinger, K. & Seitelberger, F., eds. (Acta Neuropathologica Ser: Suppl. 6). (Illus.). 320p. 1975. pap. 49.60 o.p. (ISBN 0-387-07208-X). Springer-Verlag.

International Symposium on Olfaction & Taste, 6th, Gif Sur Yvette, France, 1977. Olfaction & Taste VI: Proceedings. 500p. 25.00 (ISBN 0-904147-08-8). Info Retrieval.

International Symposium on Pneumotransport of Solids in Pipes, 3rd. Proceedings. 1977. 60.00 (ISBN 0-900983-52-3). BHRA Fluid.

International Symposium on Pneumotransport of Solids in Pipes, 1st. Proceedings. 1972. 37.00 (ISBN 0-900983-15-9). BHRA Fluid.

International Symposium On Poly-A-Amino Acids - 1st - University Of Wisconsin - 1961. Polyamino Acids, Polypeptides, & Proteins: Proceedings. Stahmann, Mark C., ed. (Illus.). 1962. 45.00 (ISBN 0-299-02620-5). U of Wis Pr.

International Symposium on Polymers in Concrete. Proceedings. 1978. 22.25 (SP-58); 17.50. ACI.

International Symposium on Quantum Biology & Quantum Pharmacology. Proceedings. (International Journal of Quantum Chemistry-Quantum Biology Symposium: No. 5). 472p. 1978. 40.50 (ISBN 0-471-05635-9). Wiley.

International Symposium on Radiopharmaceuticals, 2nd. Radiopharmaceuticals II: Proceedings. Sodd, et al, eds. LC 79-67730. (Illus.). 857p. (Orig.). 1979. pap. text ed. 42.50 (ISBN 0-932004-05-9). Soc Nuclear Med.

International Symposium on Recent Developments in Classical Wave Scattering, Ohio State Univ., Columbus, 1979. Recent Developments in Classical Wave Scattering: Focus on the T-Matrix Approach. Varadan, V. V. & Varadan, V. K., eds. (Illus.). 670p. 1980. 70.00 (ISBN 0-08-025096-3). Pergamon.

International Symposium on Science & Technology for Development, Singapore, 1979. Science, Technology & Global Problems: Issues of Development: Towards a New Role for Science & Technology. Goldsmith, Maurice & King, Alexander, eds. LC 79-40879. (Illus.). 200p. 1979. 48.00 (ISBN 0-08-024691-5). Pergamon.

International Symposium on Science & Technology for Development, Mexico City, 1979. Science, Technology & Global Problems: Science & Technology in Development Planning. Urquidi, Victor L., ed. LC 79-40912. 200p. 1979. 41.00 (ISBN 0-08-025227-3). Pergamon.

International Symposium on Superheavy Elements, March 9-11, 1978, Lubbock, Texas. Superheavy Elements: Proceedings. Lodhi, M. A., ed. 604p. 1979. 60.00 (ISBN 0-08-022946-8). Pergamon.

International Symposium on the Design & Operation of Siphons & Siphon Spillways. Proceedings. 1976. text ed. 52.00 (ISBN 0-900983-44-2, Dist. by Air Science Co.). BHRA Fluid.

International Symposium on the Transportation & Handling of Minerals, 3rd British Columbia, Canada, Oct. 1979. Minerals Transportion: Proceedings, Vol. 3. Argall, George O., Jr., ed. LC 76-189985. (A World Mining Bk.). 1980. pap. 50.00 (ISBN 0-87930-080-9). Miller Freeman.

International Symposium on the Use of Models in Fire Research - November 9-10, 1959. Proceedings. 1959. 6.00 o.p. (ISBN 0-309-00786-0). Natl Acad Pr.

International Symposium on Theory & Practice in Transport Economics, 8th, Istanbul, 24-28 Sept. 1979. Transport & the Challenge of Structural Change: Proceedings. (Illus.). 539p. (Orig.). 1980. pap. 20.00x (ISBN 92-821-1061-3). OECD.

International Symposium on Unsteady Flow in Open Channels. Proceedings. 1977. text ed. 68.00 (ISBN 0-900983-54-X, Dist. by Air Science Co.). BHRA Fluid.

International Symposium on Urban Storm Runoff, July 28-31, 1980. Proceedings. 1980. 33.50 (ISBN 0-89779-040-5). U of Ky OES Pubns.

International Teaching Systems Inc. International Code Training System. LC 62-21976. (Illus., Orig.). (YA) (gr. 8 up). 1963. pap. 12.50 with records o.p. (ISBN 0-672-20138-0, 20138); pap. 12.95 with tape cassette (ISBN 0-672-20812-1, 20812). Sams.

International Technical Communication Conference, 27th, Minneapolis, May 14-17, 1980. Technical Communication--the Bridge of Understanding: Proceedings. Society for Technical Communication, ed. 1058p. 1980. pap. text ed. 35.00x (ISBN 0-914548-32-8). Univelt Inc.

International Technical Conference on Slurry Transportation, 2nd. Proceedings. Linderman, Charles W., ed. LC 77-81416. (Illus.). 152p. 1977. pap. 40.00 (ISBN 0-932066-02-X). Slurry Transport.

International Technical Conference on Slurry Transportation, 3rd. Proceedings. LC 78-52717. (Illus.). 224p. 1978. pap. 50.00 (ISBN 0-932066-03-8). Slurry Transport.

International Telos Conference, 1st, Waterloo, Ont., Oct. 8-11, 1970. Towards a New Marxism: Proceedings. Piccone, Paul & Grahl, Bart, eds. LC 73-87129. 240p. 1973. 12.00 (ISBN 0-914386-03-4); pap. 3.95 (ISBN 0-914386-04-2). Telos Pr.

International Union Against Cancer - Committee on Professional Education - Geneva. Clinical Oncology: A Manual for Students & Doctors. Veronesi, U., et al, eds. (Illus.). xvii, 321p. 1973. pap. 14.10 o.p. (ISBN 0-387-05851-6). Springer Verlag.

International Union of Marine Insurance. Cargo Loss Prevention Recommendation. 3rd ed. 1980. pap. 2.00 (ISBN 0-685-64826-5). Helios.

International Union of Offical Travel Organisations. Aims, Activities & Fields of Competence of National Tourist Organisations, 3 pts. 2nd ed. 505p. 1974. Set. 35.00x o.p. (ISBN 0-8002-0324-0). Intl Pubns Serv.

International Union of Pure & Applied Chemistry. Stability Constants of Metal Complexes: Critical Survey of Stability Constants of EDTA Complexes. Anderegg, G., ed. 1977. text ed. 12.00 (ISBN 0-08-022009-6). Pergamon.

International Union of Theoretical & Applied Mechanics Colloquium, Madrid, 1955. Deformation & Flow of Solids: Proceedings. Grammel, Richard, ed. (Illus., Eng, Ger, Fr. & Span.). 1956. 34.30 (ISBN 0-387-02095-0). Springer-Verlag.

International Working Seminar on the Role of the History of Physics in Physics Education. History in the Teaching of Physics: Proceedings. Brush, Stephen G. & King, Allen L., eds. LC 71-188602. 128p. 1972. text ed. 7.50x (ISBN 0-87451-065-1). U Pr of New Eng.

International Workshop on Ergonomic Aspects of Visual Display Terminals, Milan, March 1980. Proceedings. Grandjean, Etienne & Vigliani, E., eds. (Illus.). 300p. 1980. 47.50x (ISBN 0-85066-211-7). Intl Pubns Serv.

International Workshop on Morphogenesis & Malformation, 4th, Grand Canyon, Ariz., 1977. Morphogenesis & Malformation of the Cardiovascular System: Proceedings. Rosenquist, Glenn C. & Bergsma, Daniel, eds. LC 78-14527. (Birth Defects Original Article Ser.: Vol. 14, No. 7). 452p. 1978. 53.00x (ISBN 0-8451-1023-3). A R Liss.

International Zentralinstitut Fur das Jugend und Bildung Fernsehen. Television & Socialization Processes in the Family. (Fernschen und Bildung Ser.). 192p. 1976. text ed. 14.80 (ISBN 3-7940-3368-X, Pub. by K G Saur). Shoe String.

Internationales Zentratinstitut Fundas Jugend-Und Bildungsfernsehen, ed. Perception, Development, Communication. 118p. 1978. pap. 13.00 (ISBN 0-89664-025-6, Pub. by K G Saur). Shoe String.

Internatonal Deep-Water Rice Workshop, 1978. Proceedings. 300p. 1979. pap. 15.50 (R037, IRRI). Unipub.

Interscience Conference on Antimicrobial Agents & Chemotherapy, 19th, jt. auth. see International Congress of Chemotherapy, 11th.

Intl City Management Assn. Effective Supervisory Practices. LC 77-28712. (Municipal Management Ser.). 1978. pap. text ed. 19.50 (ISBN 0-87326-019-8). Intl City Mgt.

Intl Labour Office, ed. see Loutfi, Martha F.

Intl. Mass Media Research Ctr., ed. Marxism & the Mass Media: Towards a Basic Bibliography, Nos. 1-2-3. rev. ed. International Mass Media Research Center. (Illus.). 106p. (Orig.). 1978. pap. 6.00 (ISBN 0-88477-009-5). Intl General.

Intl. Pubns. Serv. International Publications: An Annual Annotated Subject Bibliography 1980-1981. 4th ed. LC 72-626822. 256p. 1981. pap. 7.50x (ISBN 0-8002-0140-X). Intl Pubns Serv.

Intrator, Mira, tr. see Mornand, Pierre.

Intriligator, Michael D. Econometric Models, Techniques & Applications. (Illus.). 1978. pap. 22.95 ref. (ISBN 0-13-223255-3). P-H.

--Mathematical Optimization & Economic Theory. (Mathematical Economics Ser.). 1971. text ed. 22.95 (ISBN 0-13-561753-7). P-H.

Investors Chronicle. City Directory 1980-1981: An Investors Chronicle Guide to Financial & Professional Services Allied to the City of London. 376p. 1980. pap. 20.00 (ISBN 0-85941-083-8). Herman Pub.

Inwood, Robert & Bruyere, Christian. In Harmony with Nature. LC 80-54351. (Illus.). 224p. 1981. pap. 7.95 (ISBN 0-8069-7504-0). Sterling.

Inwood, Robert, jt. auth. see Bruyere, Christain.

Inwood, Robert, jt. auth. see Bruyere, Christian.

Inyart, Gene. Jenny. (gr. 3-5). 1970. pap. 1.50 (ISBN 0-671-29917-4). PB.

Ioachim, H. L., ed. Pathobiology Annual. LC 75-151816. 1978. 41.00 (ISBN 0-89004-277-2). Raven.

Ioachim, Harry L., ed. Pathobiology Annual, 1979. LC 75-151816. 1979. text ed. 38.00 (ISBN 0-89004-360-4). Raven.

--Pathobiology Annual, 1980. 336p. 1980. text ed. 32.00 (ISBN 0-89004-437-6). Raven.

Ionesco, Eugene. The Hermit. Seaver, Richard, tr. (Seaver-Grove Bk.). 1980. pap. 4.95 o.p. (ISBN 0-394-17746-0). Grove.

--The Hermit. LC 80-52072. 169p. 1980. pap. 4.95 (ISBN 0-394-17746-0). Seaver Bks.

--Le Roi se meurt. (Documentation thematique). (Illus., Fr.). pap. 2.95 (ISBN 0-685-14068-7, 245). Larousse.

--Victimes du Devoir. Lee, Vera G., ed. LC 72-4875. (Illus.). 178p. (Orig.). 1973. pap. text ed. 6.60 (ISBN 0-395-12745-9, 3-32658). HM.

Ionescu. Techniques in Extracorporeal Circulation. 2nd ed. 1981. text ed. price not set (ISBN 0-407-00173-5). Butterworth.

Ionescu, G., ed. Between Sovereignty & Integration. LC 73-19586. 192p. 1973. text ed. 17.95 (ISBN 0-470-42800-7). Halsted Pr.

Ionescu, M. I. Tissue Heart Values. 112p. 1979. text ed. 64.95 (ISBN 0-407-00139-5). Butterworths.

Ionescu, M. I., et al, eds. Biological Tissue in Heart Valve Replacement. (Illus.). 956p. 1971. 94.95 (ISBN 0-407-11730-X). Butterworths.

Ions, Edmund. Against Behaviouralism: A Critique of Behavioural Science. 165p. 1977. 22.50x (ISBN 0-87471-864-3). Rowman.

Iooss, G. & Joseph, D. Elementary Stability & Bifurcation Theory. (Undergraduate Texts in Mathematics Ser.). (Illus.). 286p. 1981. 22.00 (ISBN 0-387-90526-X). Springer-Verlag.

Iorio, Dominick A. Nicolas Malebranche: Dialogue Between a Christian Philosopher & a Chinese Philosopher on the Existence & Nature of God. LC 80-5045. 115p. 1980. text ed. 16.00 (ISBN 0-8191-1027-2); pap. text ed. 7.50 (ISBN 0-8191-1028-0). U Pr of Amer.

Iorio, John J., jt. auth. see Gould, James A.

Iorizzo, Luciano J. & Mondello, Salvatore. The Italian-Americans. (Immigrant Heritage of America Ser.). lib. bdg. 9.95 (ISBN 0-8057-3234-9). Twayne.

Iosifescu, Marius. Finite Markov Processes & Applications. LC 79-42726. 250p. 1980. 32.50 (ISBN 0-471-27677-4). Wiley.

Iotti, Oscar R., jt. auth. see Feinland, Alexander.

Iowa State University Research Foundation, jt. auth. see Rahman, Mushtaqur.

Iowa State University Research Foundation. Fundamentals of Engineering Review. LC 80-83440. 208p. 1980. pap. text ed. 14.95 (ISBN 0-8403-2305-0). Kendall-Hunt.

Ipcar. The Lobsterman. 1980. Repr. 2.95 (ISBN 0-89272-032-8). Down East.

Ipcar, Dahlov. Hard Scrabble Harvest. 32p. (gr. k-3). 1976. 6.95a (ISBN 0-385-00769-8); PLB (ISBN 0-385-00777-9). Doubleday.

--Lost & Found: A Hidden Animal Book. (gr. k-3). 1981. 8.95a (ISBN 0-385-15170-5); PLB (ISBN 0-385-15171-3). Doubleday.

Ippolito, D. S. The Budget & National Politics. LC 78-5102. (Illus.). 1978. text ed. 16.95x (ISBN 0-7167-0298-3); pap. text ed. 7.50x o.p. (ISBN 0-7167-0297-5). W H Freeman.

Ippolito, Dennis S. & Walker, Thomas G. Political Parties: Interest Groups & Public Policy: Group Influence in American Politics. 431p. 1980. text ed. 16.95 (ISBN 0-13-684357-3). P-H.

Iqbal, Muhammad. The Development of Metaphysics in Persia: A Contribution to the History of Philosophy. (Studies in Islamic History: No. 19). 195p. 1980. Repr. of 1908 ed. lib. bdg. 15.00x (ISBN 0-686-63157-9). Porcupine Pr.

Iranzo, Carmen. Juan Eugenio Hartzenbusch. (World Authors Ser.: No. 501 (Spain)). 1978. 12.95 (ISBN 0-8057-6342-2). Twayne.

Irby, David M., jt. auth. see Morgan, Margaret K.

Irby, James E., ed. see Borges, Jorge L.

Irby, William B. Facial Trauma & Concomitant Problems: Evaluation & Treatment. 2nd ed. LC 79-15473. 1979. text ed. 39.50 (ISBN 0-8016-2349-9). Mosby.

Irby, William B., ed. Current Advances in Oral Surgery, Vols. 2-3. LC 74-8602. (Illus.). Vol. 2, 1977. 49.95 (ISBN 0-8016-2341-3); Vol. 3, 1980. 49.95 (ISBN 0-8016-2342-1). Mosby.

--Facial Trauma & Concomitant Problems - Evaluation & Treatment. LC 74-524. 1974. text ed. 34.50 o.p. (ISBN 0-8016-2348-0). Mosby.

Iredale, David. Enjoying Archives: What They Are, Where to Find Them, How to Use Them. 1973. 14.95 (ISBN 0-7153-5669-0). David & Charles.

Ireland, Alexander. Book-Lover's Enchiridion. LC 78-76113. 1969. Repr. of 1888 ed. 18.00 (ISBN 0-8103-3895-5). Gale.

Ireland, Glen E. Automotive Fuel, Ignition, & Emission Control Systems. 1980. pap. 10.95 (ISBN 0-534-00866-6, Breton Pubs). Wadsworth Pub.

Ireland, John. Word Attack Skills. LC 77-82988. (Teaching 5 to 13 Reading Ser.). (Illus.). 1977. pap. text ed. 6.95 (ISBN 0-356-05055-6). Raintree Child.

Ireland, Karen. Kitty O'Neil: Daredevil Woman. LC 80-80604. (Starpeople Ser.). (Illus.). 78p. (gr. 4 up). 1980. lib. bdg. 5.79 (ISBN 0-8178-0004-2). Harvey.

Ireland, Patrick J. Drawing & Designing Children's & Teenage Fashions. LC 79-1265. 1979. 13.95x (ISBN 0-470-26592-2). Halsted Pr.

--Fashion Design Drawing. LC 73-134681. 1972. pap. 10.95 (ISBN 0-470-42837-6). Halsted Pr.

Ireland, Robert M. The County Courts in Antebellum Kentucky. LC 71-160045. 208p. 1972. 12.00x (ISBN 0-8131-1257-5). U Pr of Ky.

--Little Kingdoms: The Counties of Kentucky, 1850-1891. LC 76-24341. (Illus.). 200p. 1977. 13.00x (ISBN 0-8131-1351-2). U Pr of Ky.

Ireland, Thomas R. Monetarism: How the Financial Crisis Can Help You Make Money in the Stock Market. 1974. 7.95 o.p. (ISBN 0-87000-235-X). Arlington Hse.

Ireland, Timothy P. Creating the Entangling Alliance: The Origins of the North Atlantic Treaty Organization. LC 80-655. (Contributions in Political Science: No. 50). 264p. 1981. lib. bdg. 27.50 (ISBN 0-313-22094-8, IRC/). Greenwood.

Irele, F. A., ed. Selected Poems of Leopold Sedar Senghor. LC 76-16919. 1977. 23.95 (ISBN 0-521-21339-8); pap. 8.50x (ISBN 0-521-29111-9). Cambridge U Pr.

Iremonger, Lucille. My Sister, My Love. LC 80-21357. 320p. 1981. 11.95 (ISBN 0-688-00055-X). Morrow.

Iremonger, Valentin. Horan's Field & Other Reservations. 1972. pap. text ed. 4.25x (ISBN 0-85105-303-3, Dolmen Pr). Humanities.

Iremonger, Valentin, tr. see MacGowan, Michael.

Ireson, Amy G. & Lipscomb, Shirley F. Cooking for One or Two-or More. LC 77-75156. (Illus.). 1978. spiral 8.75 (ISBN 0-395-25823-5). HM.

--Foods for One or Two--or More. LC 77-75158. (Illus.). 1978. spiral bdg. o.p. 7.25 (ISBN 0-395-25823-5); text ed. 18.50 (ISBN 0-395-25820-0). HM.

Ireson, Barbara. The Faber Book of Nursery Verse. (gr. 4 up). 8.95 (ISBN 0-571-06335-7). Transatlantic.

Ireson, Barbara, ed. Faber Book of Nursery Stories. (gr. k-3). 1967. 8.95 (ISBN 0-571-06623-2). Transatlantic.

--Tales Out of Time. 224p. (gr. 10 up). 1981. 8.95 (ISBN 0-399-20786-4). Philomel.

--Verse That Is Fun. 1962. 6.95 (ISBN 0-571-05050-6, Pub. by Faber & Faber). Merrimack Bk Serv.

Ireson, William G. Reliability Handbook. 1966. 49.50 o.p. (ISBN 0-07-032040-3, P&RB). McGraw.

Ireys, Alice R. Small Gardens for City & Country: A Guide to Designing & Planting Your Own Property. (Illus.). 1978. 14.95 o.p. (ISBN 0-13-813063-9, Spec); pap. 8.95 (ISBN 0-13-813055-8, Spec). P-H.

Ireys, Katharine. Encyclopedia of Canvas Embroidery Stitch Patterns. rev. ed. LC 72-78267. (Illus.). 160p. 1977. 10.95 o.s.i. (ISBN 0-690-01665-4, TYC-T); pap. 6.95 (ISBN 0-690-01666-2, TYC-T). T Y Crowell.

Iri, M. Network Flow, Transportation & Scheduling: Theory & Algorithms. (Mathematics in Science & Engineering Ser., Vol. 57). 1969. 47.00 (ISBN 0-12-373850-4). Acad Pr.

Iribarne, Louis, tr. see Lem, Stanislaw.

Iribarne, Louis, tr. see Milosz, Czeslaw.

Iribe, Maybelle, jt. auth. see Wilder, Barbara.

Irigaray, Louis & Taylor, Theodore. A Shepherd Watches, a Shepherd Sings. LC 76-50772. 1977. 8.95 o.p. (ISBN 0-385-11652-7). Doubleday.

Irimie, Cornel & Focsa, Marcela. Romanian Icons Painted on Glass. (Illus.). 1971. 75.00x (ISBN 0-393-04309-6). Norton.

Irish, Bill. Championship Bowls. LC 78-74073. 1979. 8.95 (ISBN 0-7153-7469-9). David & Charles.

Irish, Marion D. & Frank, Elke. Introduction to Comparative Politics: Thirteen Nation States. 2nd ed. LC 77-22021. (Illus.). 1978. ref. ed. 17.95 (ISBN 0-13-500991-X). P-H.

Irish, Marion D., et al. Politics of American Democracy. 6th ed. (Illus.). 1977. text ed. 17.95 (ISBN 0-13-685453-2). P-H.

Irish, Richard K. Go Hire Yourself an Employer. rev. expanded ed. LC 77-15159. 1978. pap. 4.95 (ISBN 0-385-13638-2, Anch). Doubleday.

--How to Live Separately Together: A Guide for Working Couples. LC 78-22637. 264p. 1981. 11.95 (ISBN 0-385-14650-7, Anchor Pr). Doubleday.

Iriye, Akira. From Nationalism to Internationalism: US Foreign Policy Before 1917. (Foreign Policies of the Great Powers Ser.). 1977. 22.00 (ISBN 0-7100-8444-7). Routledge & Kegan.

Iriye, Akira, jt. ed. see Passin, Herbert.

Irizarry, Carmen. Spain. LC 75-44868. (Macdonald Countries). (Illus.). (gr. 6 up). 1976. PLB 7.95 (ISBN 0-382-06100-4, Pub. by Macdonald Ed). Silver.

Irizarry, Estelle. Francisco Ayala. (World Authors Ser.: No. 450). 1977. lib. bdg. 11.95 (ISBN 0-8057-6287-6). Twayne.

--Rafael Dieste. (World Authors Ser.: No. 554). 1979. lib. bdg. 14.50 (ISBN 0-8057-6396-1). Twayne.

Irland, Lloyd C. Wilderness Economics & Policy. LC 78-24791. 256p. 1979. 19.95 (ISBN 0-669-02821-5). Lexington Bks.

Irmiter, Theodore F., jt. auth. see Morr, Mary L.

Ironmonger, D. S. New Commodities & Consumer Behaviour. new ed. LC 75-163056. (Department of Applied Economics Monographs: No. 20). (Illus.). 1972. 36.00 (ISBN 0-521-08337-0). Cambridge U Pr.

Irons, Bruce & Ahmad, Sohrab. Techniques of Finite Elements. LC 79-40994. (Engineering Science Ser.: Civil Engineering). 529p. 1979. 87.95x (ISBN 0-470-26855-7). Halsted Pr.

Irons, Owen G. Back to Texas. (YA) 1978. 5.95 (ISBN 0-685-85776-X, Avalon). Bouregy.

--Blood on the Range. 1980. pap. 1.95 (ISBN 0-89083-686-8, Kable News Co). Zebra.

--Guns of the Hawk. (YA) 1976. 5.95 (ISBN 0-685-69050-4, Avalon). Bouregy.

--The Marshal from Texas. 192p. (YA) 1975. 5.95 (ISBN 0-685-53496-0, Avalon). Bouregy.

--The Mustangers. (YA) 1978. 5.95 (ISBN 0-685-87345-5, Avalon). Bouregy.

--Wilderness Track. 224p. (Orig.). 1980. pap. 1.95 (ISBN 0-89083-659-0). Zebra.

Ironside, H. A. Acts. 9.95 (ISBN 0-87213-351-6). Loizeaux.

--The Best of H. A. Ironside. (Best Ser.). 296p. (Orig.). 1981. pap. 4.95 (ISBN 0-8010-5033-2). Baker Bk.

--Complete Set of Commentaries, 28 vols. 170.00 (ISBN 0-87213-350-8). Loizeaux.

--Daniel the Prophet. Date not set. with chart 6.75 (ISBN 0-87213-357-5); chart only 0.15 (ISBN 0-87213-358-3). Loizeaux.

--Doctor Ironside's Bible. (Illus.). Date not set. pap. 2.50 (ISBN 0-87213-393-1). Loizeaux.

--Ezekiel: Notes. Date not set. 6.50 (ISBN 0-87213-359-1). Loizeaux.

--Gospel of John: Addresses: Date not set. 10.95 (ISBN 0-87213-373-7). Loizeaux.

--Gospel of Luke. Date not set. 8.75 (ISBN 0-87213-376-1). Loizeaux.

--Gospel of Mark. Date not set. 5.50 (ISBN 0-87213-377-X). Loizeaux.

--Gospel of Matthew. Date not set. 7.00 (ISBN 0-87213-378-8). Loizeaux.

--Hebrews & Titus. Date not set. 5.25 (ISBN 0-87213-363-X). Loizeaux.

--Holy Spirit: Mission of, & Praying in. Date not set. pap. 1.95 (ISBN 0-87213-366-4). Loizeaux.

--In the Heavenlies: Ephesians. 6.95 (ISBN 0-87213-367-2). Loizeaux.

--Jeremiah: Prophecy & Lamentations. Date not set. 6.50 (ISBN 0-87213-371-0). Loizeaux.

--Joshua. Date not set. 4.50 (ISBN 0-87213-374-5). Loizeaux.

--Philippians, Notes. Date not set. 4.95 (ISBN 0-87213-381-8). Loizeaux.

--Proverbs, Notes. Date not set. 8.25 (ISBN 0-87213-382-6). Loizeaux.

--Psalms, Studies on Book One. Date not set. 5.50 (ISBN 0-87213-383-4). Loizeaux.

--Revelation. Date not set. 6.75 (ISBN 0-87213-384-2); 0.15, chart only (ISBN 0-87213-385-0). Loizeaux.

--Romans. Date not set. 4.95 (ISBN 0-87213-386-9). Loizeaux.

--Sailing with Paul. Date not set. pap. 1.25 (ISBN 0-87213-387-7). Loizeaux.

--Song of Solomon. Date not set. 4.95 (ISBN 0-87213-389-3). Loizeaux.

--Timothy, Titus & Philemon. Date not set. 5.95 (ISBN 0-87213-391-5). Loizeaux.

Ironside, Harry A. Full Assurance. 1937. pap. 1.50 (ISBN 0-8024-2896-7). Moody.

Irsch, Ed. As It Was Told: A Play for Christmas. 16p. (Orig.). 1980. pap. text ed. 1.55 (ISBN 0-89536-439-5). CSS Pub.

Irschick, Eugene F. Politics & Social Conflict in South India: The Non-Brahman Movement & Tamil Separatism, 1916-1929. (Center for South & Southeast Asia Studies, UC Berkeley). (Illus.). 1969. 21.50x (ISBN 0-520-00596-1). U of Cal Pr.

Irvin, Eric. Gentleman George - King of Melodrama. (Illus.). 234p. 1981. text ed. 18.00x (ISBN 0-7022-1536-8). U of Queensland Pr.

Irvine. Engineering Technology Problem Solving. Date not set. price not set (ISBN 0-8247-1169-6). Dekker.

Irvine, Alexander R. & O'Malley, Conor. Advances in Vitreous Surgery. (Illus.). 736p. 1976. 66.75 (ISBN 0-398-03391-9). C C Thomas.

Irvine, Betty J. & Fry, P. Eileen. Slide Libraries: A Guide for Academic Institutions, Museums, & Special Collections. 2nd ed. LC 79-17354. (Illus.). 1979. lib. bdg. 22.50 (ISBN 0-87287-202-5). Libs Unl.

Irvine, Demar, jt. ed. see Moldenhauer, Hans.

Irvine, Doreen. Freed from Witchcraft. 192p. 1981. pap. 3.95 (ISBN 0-8407-5771-9). Nelson.

Irvine, Elizabeth E. Social Work & Human Problems: Casework, Consultation & Other Topics. (International Series in Social Work). 1979. 41.00 (ISBN 0-08-023128-4); pap. 19.25 (ISBN 0-08-023127-6). Pergamon.

Irvine, H. M. Cable Structures. (Illus.). 304p. 1981. text ed. 50.00x (ISBN 0-686-69224-1). MIT Pr.

Irvine, J. M. Heavy Nuclei, Superheavy Nuclei, & Neutron Stars. (Oxford Studies in Nuclear Physics). (Illus.). 200p. 1975. 34.95x (ISBN 0-19-851510-3). Oxford U Pr.

--Neutron Stars. (Oxford Studies in Physics). (Illus.). 150p. text ed. 32.00x (ISBN 0-19-851460-3). Oxford U Pr.

--Nuclear Structure Theory. 492p. 1972. text ed. 55.00 (ISBN 0-08-016401-3); pap. text ed. 27.00 (ISBN 0-08-018991-1). Pergamon.

Irvine, Keith, ed. see Ayensu, Edward S.

Irvine, Keith, ed. see Marquis, Thomas B.

Irvine, Lynn M., Jr. & Brelje, Terry B., eds. Law, Psychiatry & the Mentally Disordered Offender, Vol. 1. 164p. 1972. 13.75 (ISBN 0-398-02530-4). C C Thomas.

--Law, Psychiatry & the Mentally Disordered Offender, Vol. 2. 148p. 1973. 13.75 (ISBN 0-398-02645-9). C C Thomas.

Irvine, Peter. Victorian & Edwardian Dorset. 1977. pap. 8.50 o.p. (ISBN 0-7134-0149-4, Pub. by Batsford England). David & Charles.

Irvine, R. R. The Face Out Front. (Orig.). 1977. pap. 1.25 o.p. (ISBN 0-445-00449-5). Popular Lib.

--Freeze Frame. 192p. 1976. pap. 1.25 o.p. (ISBN 0-445-00351-0). Popular Lib.

Irvine, Robert G. Operational Amplifier Characteristics & Applications. (Illus.). 416p. 1981. text ed. 24.95 (ISBN 0-13-637751-3). P-H.

Irvine, S. H. & Sanders, J. T., eds. Cultural Adaptation Within Modern Africa. LC 79-171692. 1972. text ed. 9.25x (ISBN 0-8077-1550-6). Tchrs Coll.

Irvine, T. N., ed. Chromium: Its Physicochemical Behaviour & Petrologic Significance: Proceedings of the Carnegie Institute of Washington Conference, Geophysical Laboratory. LC 75-33383. 1977. text ed. 47.00 (ISBN 0-08-019954-2). Pergamon.

Irvine, Theodora U. How to Pronounce the Names in Shakespeare. LC 74-7114. 1974. Repr. of 1919 ed. 22.00 (ISBN 0-8103-3653-7). Gale.

Irvine, Thomas F., Jr. & Hartnett, James P. Steam & Air Tables, SI Units. new ed. LC 75-34007. (Illus.). 125p. (Orig.). 1976. pap. text ed. 9.95 (ISBN 0-89116-004-3, Co-Pub. by McGraw Intl); data for other substances incl. Hemisphere Pub.

Irvine, Thomas F., Jr. & Hartnett, James P., eds. Advances in Heat Transfer, 14 vols. Incl. Vol. 1. 1964. 51.00 (ISBN 0-12-020001-5); Vol. 2. 1965. 51.00 (ISBN 0-12-020002-3); Vol. 3. 1966. 51.00 (ISBN 0-12-020003-1); Vol. 4. 1967. 51.00 (ISBN 0-12-020004-X); Vol. 5. 1968. 55.25 (ISBN 0-12-020005-8); Vol. 6. 1970. 55.25 (ISBN 0-12-020006-6); Vol. 7. 1970. 51.00 (ISBN 0-12-020007-4); Vol. 8. 1972. 51.00 (ISBN 0-12-020008-2); Vol. 9. 1973. 51.00 (ISBN 0-12-020009-0); Vol. 10. 1974. 51.00 (ISBN 0-12-020010-4); Vol. 11. 1975. 59.00 (ISBN 0-12-020011-2); lib. bdg. 75.50 (ISBN 0-12-020074-0); microfiche 42.25 (ISBN 0-12-020075-9); Vol. 12. 1976. 49.00 (ISBN 0-12-020012-0); lib. bdg. 63.00 (ISBN 0-12-020076-7); microfiche 55.50 (ISBN 0-12-020077-5); Vol. 13. 1977. 49.00 (ISBN 0-12-020013-9); lib. bdg. 63.00 (ISBN 0-12-020078-3); microfiche 35.50 (ISBN 0-12-020079-1); Vol. 14. 1979. 43.00 (ISBN 0-12-020014-7); lib. bdg. 55.00 (ISBN 0-12-020080-5); microfiche 31.00 (ISBN 0-12-020081-3). Acad Pr.

Irvine, W. James, ed. Medical Immunology. (Illus.). 506p. 1980. pap. text ed. 25.00x (ISBN 0-07-032049-7, HP). McGraw.

Irvine, W. M., tr. see Sobolev, V. V.

Irvine, William. Army of the Indian Moghuls: Its Organization & Administration. 1962. 7.75x o.p. (ISBN 0-8426-0249-6). Verry.

Irvine, William C. Heresies Exposed. 1917. pap. 2.75 (ISBN 0-87213-401-6). Loizeaux.

Irving, Clifford. Battle of Jerusalem: The Six-Day War of June, 1967. LC 69-11302. (Battle Bks). (Illus.). (gr. 5-8). 1970. 8.95g (ISBN 0-02-747340-6). Macmillan.

--The Hoax. 380p. 1981. 14.95 (ISBN 0-932966-14-4). Permanent Pr.

Irving, Clifford & Buckholz, Herbert. The Death Freak. 1979. pap. 2.50 o.p. (ISBN 0-345-28155-1). Ballantine.

Irving, Clifford & Burkholz, Herbert. Spy: The Story of Modern Espionage. LC 77-78080. (Illus.). (gr. 7 up). 1969. 8.95g (ISBN 0-02-747330-9). Macmillan.

Irving, Clive. Axis. 1981. pap. 2.95 (ISBN 0-553-14590-8). Bantam.

Irving, David. The Trail of the Fox. 1978. pap. 2.50 (ISBN 0-380-40022-7, 40022). Avon.

--The War Between the Generals. (Illus.). 480p. 1981. 17.95 (ISBN 0-312-92920-X). St Martin.

--The War Between the Generals: Inside the Allied High Command. (Illus.). 384p. 1981. 17.95 (ISBN 0-312-92920-X). Congdon & Lattes.

Irving, H. M., ed. Guide to Trivial Names, Trade Names & Synonyms for Substances Used in Analytical Chemistry. 1978. pap. text ed. 10.00 (ISBN 0-08-022382-6). Pergamon.

Irving, Hancock & Zimmerman, Gary. Money Begets Money: A Guide to Personal Finance. LC 75-28508. 1975. pap. 5.00 (ISBN 0-916202-02-X). Zimmerman.

Irving, Howard I. Divorce Mediation. LC 80-54399. 216p. 1981. 11.95 (ISBN 0-87663-351-3). Universe.

Irving, Irene M., jt. auth. see Rickham, P. P.

Irving, J. & Searl, C. Knots, Ties & Splices: A Handbook for Seafarers, Travellers, & All Who Use Cordage. rev. ed. 1978. pap. 4.50 (ISBN 0-7100-8671-7). Routledge & Kegan.

Irving, Jack H., et al. Fundamentals of Personal Rapid Transit. 1978. 11.95 (ISBN 0-669-02520-8). Lexington Bks.

Irving, James T. Calcium & Phosphoros Metabolism. 1973. 37.50 (ISBN 0-12-374350-8). Acad Pr.

Irving, Joe. Training Spaniels. (Illus.). 230p. 1980. 19.95 (ISBN 0-7153-8008-7). David & Charles.

Irving, John. Setting Free the Bears. LC 68-28537. 1968. 8.95 o.p. (ISBN 0-394-44496-5). Random.

Irving, Mary B., jt. auth. see Robbins, Maurice.

Irving, Pierre M. The Life & Letters of Washington Irving, 4 vols. LC 67-23893. 1967. Repr. of 1863 ed. 50.00 set (ISBN 0-8103-3044-X). Gale.

Irving, R. E. Christian Democracy in France. 1973. text ed. 27.50x o.p. (ISBN 0-04-320085-0). Allen Unwin.

Irving, R. J. The North Eastern Railway 1870-1914: An Economic History. 1976. text ed. 28.75x (ISBN 0-7185-1141-7, Leicester). Humanities.

Irving, Robert H., Jr. & Draper, Verden R. Accounting Practices in the Petroleum Industry. 1958. 16.50 o.p. (ISBN 0-8260-4685-1). Ronald Pr.

Irving, W. Rip Van Winkle. (Peter Possum Paperbacks Ser). 1967. pap. 0.95 o.p. (ISBN 0-531-05127-7). Watts.

Irving, W. Ronald, jt. auth. see Jackson, Frank.

Irving, Washington. Legend of Sleepy Hollow & Other Stories. (Classics Ser). (gr. 6 up). 1964. pap. 1.25 (ISBN 0-8049-0050-7, CL-50). Airmont.

--Letters from Sunnyside & Spain. Williams, S. T., ed. 1928. 13.50x (ISBN 0-685-89761-3). Elliots Bks.

--Old Christmas - Bracebridge Hall. (Illus.). 528p. 1980. boxed set 22.00 (ISBN 0-912882-43-3). Sleepy Hollow.

--Rip Van Winkle & the Legend of Sleepy Hollow. (gr. 4-6). 4.95g o.s.i. (ISBN 0-02-747390-2). Macmillan.

--Washington Irving's Tales of the Supernatural. Wagenknecht, Edward, ed. (Illus.). 288p. 1981. 14.95 (ISBN 0-916144-64-X); pap. 7.95 (ISBN 0-916144-65-8). Stemmer Hse.

Irving, Washington, et al. A Landscape Book, by American Artists & American Authors. Weinberg, H. Barbara, ed. LC 75-28865. (Art Experience in Late 19th Century America Ser.: Vol. 1). (Illus.). 1977. Repr. of 1868 ed. lib. bdg. 44.00 (ISBN 0-8240-2225-4). Garland Pub.

Irwin, Ann. Successful Treatment of Stuttering. 1981. 9.95 (ISBN 0-8027-0671-1). Walker & Co.

Irwin, Ann, et al. Moon of the Red Strawberry. LC 72-85163. 1977. 4.95 o.s.i. (ISBN 0-87695-159-0). Aurora Pubs.

Irwin, Charles N. The Shoshoni Indians of Inyo County, California. (Ballena Press Publications in Archaeology, Ethnology & History: No. 15). (Illus.). 114p. (Orig.). 1980. pap. 6.95 (ISBN 0-87919-090-6). Ballena Pr.

Irwin, David. English Neoclassical Art. 1966. 19.95 o.p. (ISBN 0-571-06678-X, Pub. by Faber & Faber). Merrimack Bk Serv.

Irwin, David & Irwin, Francina. Scottish Painters. 1975. 78.00 (ISBN 0-571-08822-8, Pub. by Faber & Faber). Merrimack Bk Serv.

Irwin, Francina, jt. auth. see Irwin, David.

Irwin, Godfrey. American Tramp & Underworld Slang. LC 75-149783. 1971. Repr. of 1931 ed. 18.00 (ISBN 0-8103-3748-7). Gale.

Irwin, Grace. The Seventh Earl of Shaftesbury. 1976. 6.95 (ISBN 0-8028-6058-3). Eerdmans.

Irwin, Graham W., ed. Africans Abroad: A Documentary History of the Black Diaspora in Asia, Latin America, and the Caribbean in the Age of Slavery. LC 77-457. 1977. 25.00x (ISBN 0-231-03936-0); pap. 10.00 (ISBN 0-231-03937-9). Columbia U Pr.

Irwin, H. J. PSI & the Mind: An Information Processing Approach. LC 79-20587. 1979. 10.00 (ISBN 0-8108-1258-4). Scarecrow.

Irwin, Hadley. Moon & Me. LC 80-24053. 168p. (gr. 5-9). 1981. 8.95 (ISBN 0-689-50194-3, McElderry Bk). Atheneum.

--We Are Mesquakie, We Are One. 128p. (gr. 5 up). 1980. 7.95 (ISBN 0-912670-85-1). Feminist Pr.

Irwin, Inez. The Story of Alice Paul. 6.95 (ISBN 0-87714-058-8). Green Hill.

Irwin, J. & Marge, M. Principles of Childhood Language Disabilities. 1972. 19.95 (ISBN 0-13-708180-4). P-H.

Irwin, James B., Jr. & Emerson, W. A. Un Astronauta y la Lumbrera De la Noche. Date not set. Repr. of 1978 ed. 3.75 (ISBN 0-311-01066-0). Casa Bautista.

Irwin, John. Disorders of Articulation. LC 79-186626. (Studies in Communicative Disorders Ser). 1972. pap. 2.95 (ISBN 0-672-61278-X). Bobbs.

Irwin, John L. The Finns & the Lapps: How They Live & Work. 171p. 1973. text ed. 8.95 (ISBN 0-03-030206-4, HoltC). HR&W.

Irwin, John T. Doubling and Incest Repetition and Revenge: A Speculative Reading of Faulkner. LC 75-11341. 192p. 1975. 12.50x (ISBN 0-8018-1722-6); pap. text ed. 4.95 (ISBN 0-8018-2564-4). Johns Hopkins.

Irwin, Joseph J. M. G. Lewis. LC 76-26062. (English Author Ser.: No. 198). 1976. lib. bdg. 10.95 (ISBN 0-8057-6670-7). Twayne.

Irwin, Joyce L. Womanhood in Radical Protestantism: 1525-1675. (Studies in Women & Religion: Vol. 1). 1979. soft cover 24.95x (ISBN 0-88946-547-9). E Mellen.

Irwin, Michael. Picturing: Description & Illusion in the Nineteenth Century Novel. 1979. text ed. 22.50x (ISBN 0-04-801021-9). Allen Unwin.

Irwin, Orvis C. Communication Variables of Cerebral Palsied & Mentally Retarded Children. (Illus.). 400p. 1972. text ed. 29.75 (ISBN 0-398-02322-0). C C Thomas.

Irwin, Paul. Liptako Speaks: History from Oral Tradition in Africa. LC 80-7531. (Illus.). 250p. 1981. 16.00 (ISBN 0-691-05309-X). Princeton U Pr.

Irwin, Paul B. The Care & Counseling of Youth in the Church. Clinebell, Howard J. & Stone, Howard W., eds. LC 74-26334. (Creative Pastoral Care & Counseling Ser.). 96p. 1975. pap. 3.25 (ISBN 0-8006-0552-7, 1-552). Fortress.

Irwin, Robert. The One Hundred Thousand Dollar Decision: The Older American's Guide to Selling a Home & Choosing Retirement Housing. (Illus.). 192p. 1981. 14.95 (ISBN 0-07-032070-5, P&RB). McGraw.

--The Small Investor's Guide to Big Profits in Real Estate. (Illus.). 224p. 1980. 12.95 (ISBN 0-07-032062-4, C). McGraw.

Irwin, Robert, jt. auth. see Davis, Lloyd.

Irwin, Stevens. Dictionary of Hammond Organ Stops. 4th rev. ed. 1970. pap. 8.95 (ISBN 0-02-871110-6). Schirmer Bks.

--Dictionary of Pipe Organ Stops. rev. ed. 1965. pap. 10.95 (ISBN 0-02-871130-0). Schirmer Bks.

Irwin, Terence. Plato's Moral Theory: The Early & Middle Dialogues. 1979. pap. 13.50x (ISBN 0-19-824614-5). Oxford U Pr.

Irwin, Terence, tr. see Plato.

Irwin, Vincent & Spira, Michael. Basic Health Education. (Illus.). 1978. pap. text ed. 10.95x (ISBN 0-582-48829-X). Longman.

Irwin, Walter & Love, G. B., eds. The Best of Trek No. 3. 1981. pap. 1.95 (ISBN 0-451-09582-0, J9582, Sig). NAL.

Irwin, Yukiko & Wagenvoord, James. Shiatzu: Japanese Finger Pressure for Energy. (Illus.). 240p. 1976. 9.50 o.p. (ISBN 0-397-01054-0); pap. 7.95 (ISBN 0-397-01107-5). Lippincott.

Isaac, B. L., jt. ed. see Brady, I. A.

Isaac, Glynn, intro. by. Human Ancestors: Readings from Scientific American. LC 79-4486. (Illus.). 1979. text ed. 15.95x (ISBN 0-7167-1100-1); pap. text ed. 7.95x (ISBN 0-7167-1101-X). W H Freeman.

Isaac, Godfrey & Kleiner, Richard. I'll See You in Court. LC 79-51021. 1979. 9.95 o.p. (ISBN 0-8092-7399-3). Contemp Bks.

Isaac, Paul E. Prohibition & Politics: Turbulent Decades in Tennessee, 1885-1920. LC 65-17347. 1965. 14.50x (ISBN 0-87049-059-1). U of Tenn Pr.

Isaac, Rael J. Party & Politics in Israel: Three Visions of a Jewish State. (Professional Ser.). 256p. 1980. lib. bdg. 19.50 (ISBN 0-582-28196-2). Longman.

Isaac, Stephen. The Way of Discipleship to Christ. LC 76-57021. 1976. pap. 3.50 (ISBN 0-910378-12-6). Christward.

Isaac, Stephen & Michael, William B. Handbook in Research & Evaluation. LC 70-14612. pap. text ed. 8.95 (ISBN 0-912736-12-7). EDITS Pubs.

Isaacman, Allen. The Tradition of Resistance in Mozambique: The Zambesi Valley. 1977. 20.00x (ISBN 0-520-03065-6). U of Cal Pr.

Isaacs. Darwin to Double Helix: The Biological Theme in Science Fiction. 1977. 3.95 (ISBN 0-408-71302-X). Butterworths.

Isaacs, A. & Gray, H. J., eds. A New Dictionary of Physics. 2nd ed. LC 75-307635. Orig. Title: Dictionary of Physics. (Illus.). 640p. 1975. text ed. 42.00x (ISBN 0-582-32242-1). Longman.

Isaacs, Alan. Electrons & Gods. rev. ed. Date not set. cancelled (ISBN 0-89793-007-X). Hunter Hse.

Isaacs, Benno & Kobler, Jay. What It Takes to Feel Good: The Nickolaus Technique. (Illus.). 1978. 12.95 o.p. (ISBN 0-670-75824-8). Viking Pr.

Isaacs, Bernard, et al. Survival of the Unfittest: A Study of Geriatric Patients in Glasgow. 1972. 14.50 o.p. (ISBN 0-7100-7233-3). Routledge & Kegan.

Isaacs, Elizabeth. An Introduction to the Poetry of Yvor Winters. LC 80-17013. 240p. 1981. 15.00x (ISBN 0-8040-0353-X). Swallow.

Isaacs, H. D., ed. see Ghazali.

Isaacs, Harold R. Power & Identity: Tribalism in World Politics. LC 79-55304. (Headline Ser.: No. 246). (Orig.). 1979. pap. 2.00 (ISBN 0-87124-057-2). Foreign Policy.

Isaacs, Hope L., et al. Public Administration Ser.: Bibliographies, 2 vols. (Public Administration Ser.: Bibliography: P-638). 304p. 1981. pap. 20.00. Vance Biblios.

Isaacs, Neil. Reactive Intermediates in Organic Chemistry. LC 73-8194. 560p. 1974. 60.25 (ISBN 0-471-42861-2, Pub. by Wiley-Interscience); pap. 24.75 (ISBN 0-471-42859-0, Pub. by Wiley-Interscience). Wiley.

Isaacs, Neil, jt. auth. see Strine, Gerry.

Isaacs, Neil D. & Motta, Dick. Sports Illustrated Basketball. rev. ed. LC 80-7896. (Illus.). 160p. 1981. 8.95 (ISBN 0-690-01990-4, HarpT); pap. 5.95 (ISBN 0-690-01992-0). Har-Row.

--Sports Illustrated Basketball. rev. ed. LC 80-7896. (Illus.). 160p. 1981. pap. 5.95 (ISBN 0-690-01992-0, CN 865, CN). Har-Row.

Isaacs, Neil D., ed. & tr. Tolkien: New Critical Perspectives. LC 80-51015. 184p. 1981. 10.50 (ISBN 0-8131-1408-X). U Pr of Ky.

Isaacs, Neil S. Liquid Phase High Pressure Chemistry. 384p. 1981. 100.00 (ISBN 0-471-27849-1, Pub. by Wiley-Interscience). Wiley.

Isaacs, Susan. Compromising Positions. (Orig.). pap. 2.95 (ISBN 0-515-05976-5). Jove Pubns.

Isaacs, Susan & Keller, Marti. The Inner Parent: Raising Ourselves, Raising Our Children. 1979. 9.95 o.p. (ISBN 0-15-144423-4). HarBraceJ.

Isaacson, Ben. Dictionary of the Jewish Religion. Gross, David C., ed. 208p. 1980. 12.95 (ISBN 0-89961-002-1). SBS Pub.

Isaacson, Dean L. & Madsen, Richard W. Markov Chains: Theory & Applications. LC 75-30646. (Probability & Mathematical Statistics Ser.). 1976. 28.95 (ISBN 0-471-42862-0, Pub. by Wiley-Interscience). Wiley.

Isaacson, E. & Isaacson, M. Dimensional Methods in Physics: Reference Sets & Their Extensions. LC 75-8311. 1975. 27.95 (ISBN 0-470-42866-X). Halsted Pr.

Isaacson, Eugene & Keller, H. B. The Analysis of Numerical Methods. LC 66-17630. 1966. 30.95 (ISBN 0-471-42865-5). Wiley.

Isaacson, Harold J., tr. The Throat of the Peacock: Japanese Senryo on Filial Devotion. 4.45 (ISBN 0-87830-158-5); pap. 1.85 (ISBN 0-87830-557-2); ltd. ed 10.00 (ISBN 0-87830-158-5). Theatre Arts.

Isaacson, Knight. The Store. LC 73-93927. 256p. 1974. 6.95 o.s.i. (ISBN 0-8027-0454-9). Walker & Co.

Isaacson, Lee E. Career Information in Counseling & Teaching. 3rd ed. 1977. text ed. 18.95 (ISBN 0-205-05785-3). Allyn.

Isaacson, M., jt. auth. see Isaacson, E.

Isaacson, Robert L. & Pribram, Karl H., eds. The Hippocampus. Incl. Vol. 1. Structure & Development. 418p. 27.50 (ISBN 0-306-37535-4); Vol. 2. Neurophysiology & Behavior. 445p. 29.50 (ISBN 0-306-37536-2). (Illus.). 1975 (Plenum Pr). Plenum Pub.

Isaak. Individuals & World Politics. 265p. (Orig.). 1980. pap. text ed. 6.95 (ISBN 0-87872-274-2). Duxbury Pr.

Isaak, Alan C. Scope & Methods of Political Science: An Introduction to the Methodology of Political Inquiry. 3rd. rev. ed. 1980. pap. text ed. 10.95x (ISBN 0-256-02375-1). Dorsey.

Isaak, Robert, jt. auth. see Hummel, Ralph P.

Isaaksson, Olov & Hallgren, Soren. Frost & Fire. (Illus.). 1980. 27.50 (ISBN 0-906191-36-X, Pub. by Thule England). Intl Schol Bk Serv.

Isabel, Maderiaga de see De Madariaga, Isabel.

Isachsen, Arne. The Demand for Money in Norway. 1976. pap. text ed. 6.00x (ISBN 8-200-01569-6, Dist. by Columbia U Pr). Universitet.

Isacson, Peter. Public Health & Preventive Medicine Continuing Education Review. 1980. pap. 15.00 (ISBN 0-87488-348-2). Med Exam.

Isadora, Rachel. Ben's Trumpet. LC 78-12885. (Illus.). (gr. k-3). 1979. 7.50 (ISBN 0-688-80194-3). Greenwillow.

--Jesse & Abe. LC 80-15584. (Illus.). 32p. (gr. k-4). 1981. 7.95 (ISBN 0-688-80302-4); PLB 7.63 (ISBN 0-688-84302-6). Greenwillow.

--Max. LC 76-9088. (Illus.). 32p. (gr. k-3). 1976. 8.95 (ISBN 0-02-747450-X). Macmillan.

--No, Agatha. LC 79-26734. (Illus.). 32p. (ps-3). 1980. 7.95 (ISBN 0-688-80274-5); PLB 7.63 (ISBN 0-688-84274-7). Greenwillow.

--The Potters' Kitchen. LC 76-47666. (Illus.). (gr. 1-4). 1977. 7.25 (ISBN 0-688-80089-0); PLB 6.96 (ISBN 0-688-84089-2). Greenwillow.

--Willaby. LC 77-4469. (Illus.). (gr. k-3). 1977. 8.95 (ISBN 0-02-747460-7, 74746). Macmillan.

Isakson, Marne & Bradley, Lonnie. Reading with Race Cars. (gr. k-3). 1981. 26.80 (ISBN 0-8027-9079-8). Walker & Co.

Isaksson, Hans. Lars Gyllensten. (World Authors Ser.: No. 473). 1978. lib. bdg. 12.50 (ISBN 0-8057-6314-7). Twayne.

Isaku, Patia R. Mountain Storm, Pine Breeze: Folk Song in Japan. 1981. text ed. 12.95x (ISBN 0-8165-0564-0); pap. 6.50 (ISBN 0-8165-0722-8). U of Ariz Pr.

Isard, Walter. Ecologic Economic Analysis for Regional Development. LC 75-134313. 1972. 25.00 (ISBN 0-02-915810-9). Free Pr.

--Introduction to Regional Science. (Illus.). 544p. 1975. ref. ed. 21.95 (ISBN 0-13-493841-0). P-H.

Isbell, Charles D. Corpus of the Aramaic Incantation Bowls. LC 75-15949. (Society of Biblical Literature. Dissertation Ser.). xiv, 200p. 1975. pap. 7.50 (ISBN 0-89130-010-4, 060117). Scholars Pr Ca.

Isbister, Clair. Birth of a Family. LC 78-52878. (Illus.). 1978. 8.95 o.p. (ISBN 0-8015-0653-0). Dutton.

--Mommy, I Feel Sick. 1979. 7.95 o.p. (ISBN 0-8015-5116-1). Dutton.

Ise, John. Sod & Stubble: The Story of a Kansas Homestead. LC 37-10937. (Illus.). 1967. 13.50x (ISBN 0-8032-0207-5); pap. 3.50 (ISBN 0-8032-5098-3, BB 372, Bison). U of Nebr Pr.

Isely, M. D. Arkansas Valley Interurban. (Special Ser.: No. 19). (Illus.). 1977. pap. 6.00 (ISBN 0-916374-29-7). Interurban.

Iseminger, Gary. Introduction to Deductive Logic. LC 68-14984. (Century Philosophy Ser.). (Illus., Orig.). 1968. pap. text ed. 5.95x (ISBN 0-89197-239-0). Irvington.

Iseminger, Gary, ed. Logic & Philosophy: Selected Readings. (Century Philosophy Ser). 1980. text ed. 18.95x o. p. (ISBN 0-89197-829-1); pap. text ed. 8.95x (ISBN 0-89197-830-5). Irvington.

Isenberg, Henry, jt. auth. see Balows, Albert.

Isenberg, Irwin, ed. China: New Force in World Affairs, Vol. 44, No. 5. (Reference Shelf Ser.: Vol. 44, No. 5). 200p. 1972. 6.25 (ISBN 0-8242-0468-9). Wilson.

--The Death Penalty. (Reference Shelf Ser.). 1977. 6.25 (ISBN 0-8242-0604-5). Wilson.

--Developing Nations. (Reference Shelf Ser: Vol. 41, No. 1). 1968. 6.25 (ISBN 0-8242-0106-X). Wilson.

--Drive Against Illiteracy. (Reference Shelf Ser.: Vol. 36, No. 5). 1964. 6.25 (ISBN 0-8242-0082-9). Wilson.

--Ferment in Eastern Europe. (Reference Shelf Ser: Vol. 37, No. 1). 1965. 6.25 (ISBN 0-8242-0084-5). Wilson.

--France Under De Gaulle. (Reference Shelf Ser: Vol. 39, No. 1). 1967. 6.25 (ISBN 0-8242-0094-2). Wilson.

--The Nations of the Indian Subcontinent. (Reference Shelf Ser: Vol. 46, No. 1). 1974. 6.25 (ISBN 0-8242-0521-9). Wilson.

--Outlook for Western Europe. LC 79-95635. (Reference Shelf Ser: Vol. 42, No. 2). 1970. 6.25 (ISBN 0-8242-0410-7). Wilson.

--South America: Problems & Prospects. (Reference Shelf Ser: Vol. 47, No. 2). 1975. 6.25 (ISBN 0-8242-0570-7). Wilson.

Isenberg, J., ed. see Conference Sponsored by ASCE Construction Division, May 1980, San Francisco, CA.

Isenberg, Michael T. War on Films: The American Cinema & World War I, 1914-1941. LC 76-19835. 400p. 1981. 20.00 (ISBN 0-8386-2004-3). Fairleigh Dickinson.

Isenhour, et al. Introduction to Computer Programming for Chemists: BASIC Version. 16.95 o.p. (ISBN 0-205-04392-5, 6943926). Allyn.

Isenhour, Thomas L. & Jurs, Peter C. Introduction to Computer Programming for Chemists: Fortran. 2nd ed. 1979. text ed. 17.95 (ISBN 0-205-05897-3). Allyn.

Iser, Wolfgang. The Act of Reading: A Theory of Aesthetic Response. LC 78-58296. 1979. 15.00x o.p. (ISBN 0-8018-2101-0); pap. 5.95 (ISBN 0-8018-2371-4). Johns Hopkins.

--The Implied Reader: Patterns of Communication in Prose Fiction from Bunyan to Beckett. LC 73-20075. 1978. text ed. 16.00x o.p. (ISBN 0-8018-1569-X); pap. text ed. 5.95 (ISBN 0-8018-2150-9). Johns Hopkins.

Isermann, R. & Kaltenecker, H. Digital Computer Applications to Process Control: Proceedings of the Sixth IFAC-IFIP Conference, Dusseldorf, Federal Republic of Germany, 14-17 October 1980. LC 80-41343. (IFAC Proceedings). 550p. 1981. 100.00 (ISBN 0-08-026749-1). Pergamon.

Isermann, R., ed. Identification & System Parameter Estimation: Proceedings of the Fifth IFAC Symposium, Darmstadt, Federal Republic of Germany, 24-28 Sept. 1979, 2 vols. LC 79-42935. (IFAC Prodeedings Ser.). 1394p. 1980. Set. 225.00 (ISBN 0-08-024451-3). Pergamon.

Isham, C. J., et al, eds. Quantum Gravity: An Oxford Symposium. (Illus.). 600p. 1975. 49.95x (ISBN 0-19-851943-5). Oxford U Pr.

Isham, Norman M. Early American Houses & a Glossary of Colonial Architectural Terms, 2 vols. LC 67-27458. (Architecture & Decorative Art Ser). 1967. Repr. of 1939 ed. lib. bdg. 17.50 (ISBN 0-306-70973-2). Da Capo.

Isherwood, Christopher. Berlin Stories. LC 79-17316. 1979. Repr. of 1946 ed. lib. bdg. 12.50x (ISBN 0-8376-0449-4). Bentley.

--A Meeting by the River. 1978. pap. 1.95 (ISBN 0-380-01945-0, 37945, Bard). Avon.

--Memorial. LC 72-106718. Repr. of 1946 ed. lib. bdg. 22.50x (ISBN 0-8371-3544-3). Irvington.

--My Guru & His Disciple. 338p. 1980. 12.95 (ISBN 0-374-21702-5). FS&G.

--Ramakrishna & His Disciples. LC 65-17100. 384p. 1980. pap. 7.95 (ISBN 0-87481-037-X). Vedanta Pr.

Isherwood, Christopher, tr. see Baudelaire, Charles.

Isherwood, Christopher, jt. tr. see Prabhavananda, Swami.

Isherwood, Justin. Wisconsin. (Illus.). 128p. 1981. 27.50 (ISBN 0-912856-67-X). Graphic Arts Ctr.

Isherwood, Margaret. Lodestars for the Journey of Life. 91p. 1980. pap. text ed. 6.50 (ISBN 0-227-67840-0). Attic Pr.

Ishibashi, W. Chie, tr. see Mori, Hisashi.

Ishida, Mosaku, ed. Japanese Buddhist Prints. LC 63-22012. (Illus.). 1964. 85.00 (ISBN 0-87011-005-5). Kodansha.

Ishigai, Seiken, jt. ed. see Bergles, Arthur E.

Ishihara, Akira & Levy, Howard S. Tao of Sex. 2nd enl. ed. LC 68-30574. (Sino-Japanese Sexology Classics Ser., Vol. 1). 1969. 15.50x (ISBN 0-685-19350-0). Paragon.

Ishii, S., ed. Hormones, Adaptation & Evolution: International Symposium. 300p. 1980. 44.80 (ISBN 0-387-10033-4). Springer-Verlag.

Ishikowa, Kaorn. Guide to Quality Control. (Industrial Engineering & Technology Ser.). (Illus.). 1976. 20.75 (ISBN 92-833-1035-7, APO24, APO). Unipub.

Ishimaru, A. Single Scattering & Transport Theory. (Wave Propagation & Scattering in Random Media: Vol. 1). 1978. 31.00 (ISBN 0-12-374701-5). Acad Pr.

Ishiwata, Mutsuko, jt. ed. see Asano, Osamu.

Ish-Kishor, S. A Boy of Old Prague. (gr. 3-5). 1980. pap. 1.50 (ISBN 0-590-30381-3, Schol Pap). Schol Bk Serv.

Ish-Kishor, Sulamith. Our Eddie. (Windward Bks.). (gr. 7 up). 1969. pap. 0.75 o.p. (ISBN 0-394-82177-7, BYR). Random.

Ishumi, A. G. Kiziba: The Cultural Heritage of an Old African Kingdom. LC 80-19238. (African Ser.: Vol. 34). (Illus.). viii, 109p. (Orig.). 1980. pap. 7.00x (ISBN 0-915984-56-3). Syracuse U Foreign Comp.

Ishwaran, K. Shivapur: A South Indian Village. (International Library of Sociology & Social Reconstruction). (Illus.). 1968. text ed. 9.00x (ISBN 0-7100-3499-7). Humanities.

Ishwaran, K., ed. Change & Continuity in India's Villages. LC 79-110604. 1970. 17.50x (ISBN 0-231-03323-0). Columbia U Pr.

Isichei, Elizabeth. Entirely for God. (Cistercian Studies: No. 43). 132p. 1980. pap. 11.95 (ISBN 0-87907-943-6). Cistercian Pubns.

Isidore of Seville. Isidore of Seville's History of the Goths, Vandals, & Suevi. 2nd, rev. ed. Ford, Gordon B., Jr., tr. LC 70-509890. 1970. pap. 8.00 o.p. (ISBN 0-916760-00-6). Medieval Latin.

Iskander, Fazil. Sandro Iz Chegema: Sandro from Chegem. 1979. 20.00 (ISBN 0-88233-392-5); pap. 10.00 o.p. (ISBN 0-88233-394-1). Ardis Pubs.

Iskander, I. K. Modeling Wastewater Renovation Land Treatment. 343p. 1981. 20.00 (ISBN 0-471-08128-0, Pub. by Wiley-Interscience). Wiley.

Islam, A. Aminul. Victorious Victims: Political Transformation in a Traditional Society. 1981. pap. 7.95 (ISBN 0-87073-820-8). Schenkman.

Islam, A. S. Fundamentals of Genetics. 2nd ed. 520p. 1981. text ed. 27.50x (ISBN 0-7069-1238-1, Pub. by Vikas India). Advent Bk.

Islam, N., ed. Agricultural Policy in Developing Countries. LC 74-108. (International Economic Association Ser.). 1974. 40.95 (ISBN 0-470-42875-9). Halsted Pr.

Islam, Nural. Development Strategy of Bangladesh. 1977. text ed. 19.00 (ISBN 0-08-021840-7). Pergamon.

Isler, Hansruedi. Thomas Willis, 1621-1675: Doctor & Scientist. 1968. 13.75 o.s.i. (ISBN 0-02-846980-1). Hafner.

Isler, Morton L. Thinking About Housing: A Policy Research Agenda. 47p. 1970. pap. 1.25 o.p. (ISBN 0-87766-004-2, 60004). Urban Inst.

Isler, Werner, ed. Acute Hemiplegias & Hemisyndromes in Childhood. (Clinics in Developmental Medicine, Vol, 41-42). 1971. 25.50 (ISBN 0-685-27034-3). Lippincott.

Ismail. Motor Aptitude & Intellectual Performance. 1967. pap. text ed. 6.95 (ISBN 0-675-09680-4). Merrill.

Ismaili, Rashidah, et al. Womanrise (Anthology) Rivera, Louis R., ed. (Illus.). 128p. (Orig.). 1978. pap. 4.25 (ISBN 0-917886-05-4). Shamal Bks.

Isman, Warren E. Fire Service Pumps & Hydraulics. LC 76-3943. 1977. pap. 8.40 (ISBN 0-8273-0591-5). Delmar.

Ison, Joan S. The Moon in Five Disguises. LC 80-70081. (Illus.). 54p. (Orig.). 1981. pap. 4.95 (ISBN 0-938604-00-7). Foxmoor.

Ison, Terence G. Accident Compensation. 240p. 1981. 37.50x (ISBN 0-7099-0249-2, Pub. by Croom Helm Ltd England). Biblio Dist.

Israel, Abby. A Boy & a Boa. LC 80-25812. 64p. (gr. 3-6). 1981. 8.95 (ISBN 0-8037-0708-8); PLB 8.44 (ISBN 0-8037-0716-9). Dial.

Israel, Charles E. Five Ships West: The Story of Magellan. (gr. 4-6). 1966. 5.95g o.s.i. (ISBN 0-02-747410-0). Macmillan.

Israel, Elaine. The Hungry World. LC 77-24424. (Illus.). 64p. (gr. 3 up). 1977. PLB 6.97 (ISBN 0-671-32821-2). Messner.

--Up, Over, Under & Around: The New Explorers. LC 80-19618. (Illus.). 96p. (gr. 4 up). 1980. PLB 7.79 (ISBN 0-671-34002-6). Messner.

Israel, F. L., jt. auth. see Schlesinger, Arthur M., Jr.

Israel, Fred L., ed. Eighteen Ninety-Seven Sears Roebuck Catalogue. abr. ed. LC 80-69200. (Illus.). 320p. 1981. pap. 2.75 (ISBN 0-87754-138-8). Chelsea Hse.
--Major Peace Treaties of Modern History, 1967-1979. LC 67-27855. (Major Peace Treaties of Modern History, 1648-1979, Ser.: Vol. 5). 490p. 1981. pap. 19.95 (ISBN 0-87754-126-4). Chelsea Hse.
--Major Presidential Decisions. LC 80-22040. 850p. 1980. pap. 11.95 (ISBN 0-87754-218-X). Chelsea Hse.
--State of the Union Messages of the Presidents Seventeen Eighty-Nine to Nineteen Sixty-Six, 3 vols. LC 66-20309. (Illus.). 1981. pap. 42.50 (ISBN 0-87754-131-0). Chelsea Hse.
Israel, Fred L., jt. ed. see Friedman, Leon.
Israel, Fred L., jt. ed. see Schlesinger, Arthur M., Jr.
Israel, J. I. Race, Class & Politics in Colonial Mexico, 1610-1665. (Oxford Historical Monographs). 320p. 1975. text ed. 29.00x o.p. (ISBN 0-19-821860-5). Oxford U Pr.
Israel, Jacob S., jt. auth. see Barnes, Thomas A.
Israel, Jerold H. & LaFave, Wayne R. Criminal Procedure in a Nutshell: Constitutional Limitations. 3rd ed. LC 80-23164. (Nutshell Ser.). 438p. 1980. pap. text ed. 6.95 (ISBN 0-8299-2107-9). West Pub.
Israel, Jerold H., jt. auth. see Kerper, Hazel B.
Israel, Jerry, ed. Building the Organizational Society. LC 70-170872. 1972. 14.95 (ISBN 0-02-915780-3). Free Pr.
Israel, John & Klein, Donald. Rebels & Bureaucrats: China's December 9ers. LC 74-18757. 1976. 21.50x (ISBN 0-520-02861-9). U of Cal Pr.
Israel, Milton, ed. Pax Britannica. LC 68-113032. (Selections from History Today Ser.: No. 9). (Illus.). 1968. 5.00 (ISBN 0-05-001653-9); pap. 3.95 (ISBN 0-685-09189-9). Dufour.
Israel Ministry. What Is a Jew? 1975. 30.00 (ISBN 0-379-13904-9). Oceana.
Israel, Peter. The French Kiss. 1977. pap. 1.75 (ISBN 0-380-01827-6, 36178). Avon.
--The Stiff Upper Lip. 160p. 1979. pap. 1.95 (ISBN 0-380-46086-6, 46086). Avon.
Israel Program for Scientific Translations, tr. see Kurpel, N. S.
Israel, W., jt. ed. see Hawking, S. W.
Israeli Vacuum Congress, Fifth, Israel, April 1978. Advances in Vacuum Science & Technology: Proceedings. Yarwood, J. & Margoninski, Y., eds. 1979. pap. 13.00 (ISBN 0-08-024238-3). Pergamon.
Israels, M. G. & Delamore, I. W. Haematological Aspects of Systemic Disease. LC 76-26782. (Illus.). 1976. text ed. 30.00 (ISBN 0-7216-5047-3). Saunders.
Israelsen, Orson W. & Hansen, Vaughn E. Irrigation Principles & Practices. 3rd ed. LC 62-15179. 1962. 25.95 (ISBN 0-471-42999-6). Wiley.
Isreal, Lee. Kilgallen. 1980. pap. 2.95 o.s.i. (ISBN 0-440-14565-1). Dell.
Issa. The Year of My Life: A Translation of Issa's Oraga Haru. rev. ed. Yuasa, Nobuyuki, tr. LC 60-9651. (Illus.). 1973. 14.75x (ISBN 0-520-00598-8); pap. 2.45 (ISBN 0-520-02160-6, CAL35). U of Cal Pr.
Issari, M. Ali & Paul, Doris A. What Is Cinema Verite? LC 79-20110. 216p. 1979. 11.50 (ISBN 0-8108-1253-3). Scarecrow.
Issawi, Charles. The Economic History of Turkey, Eighteen Hundred to Nineteen Fourteen. LC 80-444. (Publications of the Center for Middle Eastern Studies: No. 13). 1981. lib. bdg. 20.00x (ISBN 0-226-38603-1). U of Chicago Pr.
--Oil, the Middle East & the World. LC 72-5301. (Policy Papers: The Washington Papers, No. 4). 1972. 3.50x (ISBN 0-8039-0278-6). Sage.
Isselbacher, Kurt J., et al. Harrison's Principles of Internal Medicine. 400p. 1981. text ed. 30.00 (ISBN 0-07-032131-0). McGraw.
Isselbacher, Kurt J., et al, eds. Harrison's Principles of Internal Medicine. 9th ed. (Illus.). 1980. text ed. 45.00 1 vol. ed. (ISBN 0-07-032068-3); text ed. 55.00 2 vol. ed. (ISBN 0-07-032069-1); medical review bk. 25.00 (ISBN 0-07-051657-X). McGraw Pretest.
Isselhard, Donald E., jt. auth. see Brand, Richard W.
ISTA Committee. Fire Service Instructor Training. 4th ed. Carlson, Gene, ed. (Illus.). 1981. pap. text ed. 7.00 (ISBN 0-87939-045-X, IFSTA 302). Intl Fire Serv.
Iswolsky, tr. see Elchaninov, Alexander.
Ita, Koko. Twenty One. (Gambler's Book Shelf). 64p. 1976. pap. 2.95 (ISBN 0-89650-563-4). Gamblers.

Italian National Institute of Higher Mathematics Conventions. Symposia Mathematica: Proceedings. Incl. Vol. 1. Group Theory. 1970. 59.50 (ISBN 0-12-612201-6); Vol. 2. Functional Analysis & Geometry. 1970. 56.50 (ISBN 0-12-612202-4); Vol. 3. Problems in the Evolution of the Solar System. 1970. 69.00 (ISBN 0-12-612203-2); Vol. 4. 1971. 60.50 (ISBN 0-12-612204-0); Vol. 5. 1971. 64.00 (ISBN 0-12-612205-9); Vol. 6. 1971. 54.50 (ISBN 0-12-612206-7); Vol. 7. 1972. 68.00 (ISBN 0-12-612207-5); Vol. 8. 1972. 38.50 (ISBN 0-12-612208-3); Vol. 9. 1972. 71.50 (ISBN 0-12-612209-1); Vol. 10. 1973. 56.00 (ISBN 0-12-612210-5); Vol. 18. 1977. 68.00 (ISBN 0-12-612218-0); Vol. 19. 1977. 52.50 (ISBN 0-12-612219-9). Acad Pr.
Itallie, Jean-Claude Van see Van Itallie, Jean-Claude.
Iterson, S. R. Van see Van Iterson, S. R.
Iterson, S. R. van see Van Iterson, S. R.
Iterson, S. R. Van see Van Iterson, S. R.
Itkin, Irving H., ed. Allergy Case Studies. 1973. spiral bdg. 14.00 (ISBN 0-87488-027-0). Med Exam.
Itkis, U. Control Systems of Variable Structure. LC 76-4870. 1976. 43.95 (ISBN 0-470-15072-6). Halsted Pr.
Ito, Dee, jt. auth. see Harihar Das, Swami.
Ito, Hirobumi. Commentaries on the Constitution of the Empire of Japan. (Studies in Japanese Law & Government). 310p. 1979. Repr. of 1906 ed. 25.00 (ISBN 0-89093-212-3). U Pubns Amer.
Ito, Kiyosi, ed. Proceedings of the International Symposium on Stochastic Differential Equations, Kyoto, 1976. LC 78-19655. 1978. 43.95 (ISBN 0-471-05375-9, Pub. by Wiley-Interscience). Wiley.
Ito, Masami, et al. Broadcasting in Japan. (Case Studies on Broadcasting Systems). (Orig.). 1978. pap. 14.00 (ISBN 0-7100-0043-X). Routledge & Kegan.
Ito, Robert & Dolney, Pam C. Mastering Women's Gymnastics. LC 77-23696. 1978. 9.95 (ISBN 0-8092-7744-1); pap. 6.95 (ISBN 0-8092-7743-3). Contemp Bks.
Ito, Teiji. The Japanese Garden. 2nd ed. LC 72-75196. (Illus.). 1978. 29.50 o.p. (ISBN 0-87040-441-5). Japan Pubns.
Ito, Toshiko. Tsujigahana: The Flower of Japanese Textile Art. Bethe, Monica, tr. LC 80-82525. (Illus.). 144p. 1981. 200.00 (ISBN 0-87011-397-6). Kodansha.
Ito, Y. Comparative Ecology. 2nd ed. Kikkawa, J., tr. LC 79-41581. (Illus.). 350p. Date not set. text ed. 54.00 (ISBN 0-521-22977-4); pap. text ed. 19.95 (ISBN 0-521-29845-8). Cambridge U Pr.
Itoh, Hiroshi, ed. & tr. Japanese Politics, an Inside View: Readings from Japan. LC 72-12407. (Illus.). 248p. 1973. 19.50x (ISBN 0-8014-0735-4); pap. 6.95 (ISBN 0-8014-9138-X, CP138). Cornell U Pr.
Itoh, Makoto. Value & Crisis: Essays on Marxian Economics in Japan. LC 80-8084. 192p. 1980. 13.50 (ISBN 0-85345-556-2); pap. 7.00 (ISBN 0-85345-557-0). Monthly Rev.
Itoh, Teiji. Kura: Design & Tradition of the Japanese Storehouse. LC 73-81112. (Illus.). 252p. 1973. 85.00 (ISBN 0-87011-217-1). Kodansha.
--Kura: Design & Tradition of the Japanese Storehouse. abr. ed. Terry, Charles S., tr. from Japanese. LC 80-21087. (Illus.). 192p. 1980. pap. 15.00 (ISBN 0-914842-53-6). Madrona Pubs.
--Space & Illusion in the Japanese Garden. (Illus.). 232p. 1980. pap. 9.95 (ISBN 0-8348-1522-2, Pub. by John Weatherhill Inc Japan). C E Tuttle.
Itrat-Husain. Mystical Element in the Metaphysical Poets of the Seventeenth Century. LC 66-23522. 1948. 12.00x (ISBN 0-8196-0177-2). Biblo.
ITT Educational Services Inc. This Is Electronics, 2 bks. Incl. Bk. 1. Basic Principles (ISBN 0-672-20740-0); Bk. 2. Circuits & Applications (ISBN 0-672-20741-9). LC 74-105093. 1978. text ed. 21.95 ea. Set. Bobbs.
Ittelson, William H., ed. Environment & Cognition. LC 72-7698. 1973. 23.00 o.p. (ISBN 0-12-785363-4). Acad Pr.
Itzhak, Benjamin Avi see Vardi, Joseph & Avi-Itzhak, Benjamin.
Itzin, Catherine, ed. British Alternative Theatre Directory 1979. (Orig.). 1979. pap. text ed. cancelled o.s.i. (ISBN 0-903931-19-2, Pub. by John Offord Pubns England). Drama Bk.
Itzin, Cathy, tr. see Drosdowski, Bohdan.
Itzkoff, Seymour W. Ernst Cassirer. (World Leaders Ser.: No. 60): 1977. lib. bdg. 12.50 (ISBN 0-8057-7712-1). Twayne.
Itzoe, Linda V. The Inconsistant Lady by Arthur Wilson: An Edition with Introduction and Notes. Orgel, Stephen, ed. LC 79-54345. (Renaissance Drama Second Ser.). 300p. 1980. lib. bdg. 33.00 (ISBN 0-8240-4462-2). Garland Pub.

IUA Symposium, College Park, Md., Aug. 7-10, 1979. Radio Physics of the Sun: Proceedings. Gergely, T. E. & Kundu, M. R., eds. (International Astronomical Union Symposium: No. 86). 472p. 1980. lib. bdg. 60.50 (ISBN 90-277-1120-8); pap. 28.95 (ISBN 90-277-1121-6). Kluwer Boston.
Iunes, Michael. Silence Observed. 160p. 1975. pap. 1.25 o.p. (ISBN 0-345-24627-6). Ballantine.
IUTAM Symposium Held at the Delft University of Technology, Department of Mechanical Engineering, Delft, August 1975. The Dynamics of Vehicles on Roads & on Railway Tracks: Proceedings. Pacejka, Hans B., ed. 586p. 1976. pap. text ed. 50.75 (ISBN 90-265-0234-6, Pub. by Swets Pub Serv Holland). Swets North Am.
I.U.T.A.M Symposium on Optical Methods in Mechanics of Solids. Optical Methods in Mechanics of Solids: Proceedings. Lagarde, Alexis, ed. 692p. 1980. 50.00x (ISBN 90-286-0860-5). Sijthoff & Noordhoff.
IUTAM Symposium 5th, VSD-2nd, Held at Technical University, Vienna, Austria, Sept. 19-23, 1977. The Dynamics of Vehicles on Roads & on Tracks: Proceedings. Slibar, A. & Springer, H., eds. 530p. 1978. pap. text ed. 46.00 (ISBN 90-265-0270-2, Pub. by Swets Pub Serv Holland). Swets North Am.
Ivancevich, John, jt. auth. see Matteson, Michael.
Ivancevich, John M. & Matteson, Michael T. Stress & Work: A Managerial Perspective. 1981. pap. text ed. 7.95x (ISBN 0-673-15381-9). Scott F.
Ivancevich, John M., et al. Business in a Dynamic Environment. (Illus.). 1979. text ed. 17.50 (ISBN 0-8299-0180-9); pap. study guide b Curtis G. Mason 6.95 (ISBN 0-8299-0257-0); instrs.' manual avail. (ISBN 0-8299-0494-8); transparency masters avail. (ISBN 0-8299-0495-6); study guide avail. (ISBN 0-8299-0257-0). West Pub.
--Managing for Perfomance. 1980. 18.95x (ISBN 0-256-02274-7); wkbk. 5.50x (ISBN 0-256-02356-5). Business Pubns.
Ivanov, E. K. Group Production Organization & Technology. Grayson, T. J., ed. Bishop, E., tr. (Illus.). 144p. 1968. 9.95x o.p. (ISBN 0-8464-0457-5). Beekman Pubs.
Ivashkin, V. M. Essentials of Nematodology: Camallanata of Animals & Man & Diseases Caused by Them, Vol. 22. 1977. 64.95 (ISBN 0-470-99321-9). Halsted Pr.
Ivask, Astrid. At the Fallow's Edge. Cedrins, Inara, tr. LC 79-114869. (Inklings Ser.: No. 3). (Latvian & Eng.). Date not set. 5.00 (ISBN 0-930012-33-X). Mudborn. Postponed.
Ivask, Ivar. Odysseus Elytis: Analogies of Light. LC 80-5240. (Illus.). 130p. 1980. 12.50 (ISBN 0-8061-1715-X); pap. 5.95 (ISBN 0-8061-1692-7). U of Okla Pr.
Ivask, Ivar, jt. auth. see Dunham, Lowell.
Ivenbaum, Elliott. Drawing People. (gr. 4 up). 1980. PLB 6.90 (ISBN 0-531-02283-8, A46). Watts.
Ivener, Martin H. & Rosefsky, Robert S. Telecourse Study Guide for Personal Finance & Money Management. 1978. pap. text ed. 8.95 (ISBN 0-471-03797-4); Set. 23.90 (ISBN 0-471-03796-6). Wiley.
Iversen, Edwin S. Farming the Edge of the Sea. 2nd ed. (Illus.). 440p. 37.50 (ISBN 0-85238-079-8, FN). Unipub.
Iversen, Gudmund R. & Norpoth, Helmut. Analysis of Variance. LC 76-25695. (University Papers: Quantitative Applications in the Social Sciences, No. 1). 1976. 3.50x (ISBN 0-8039-0650-1). Sage.
Iversen, Gudmund R., jt. auth. see Boyd, Lawrence H.
Iversen, J., jt. auth. see Faegri, Knut.
Iversen, Leslie L. Uptake & Storage of Noradrenaline in Sympathic Nerves. 1967. 35.50 (ISBN 0-521-05390-0). Cambridge U Pr.
Iversen, Leslie L., jt. auth. see Iversen, Susan D.
Iversen, Susan D. & Iversen, Leslie L. Behavioral Pharmacology. (Illus.). 275p. 1975. text ed. 19.95x (ISBN 0-19-501860-5). Oxford U Pr.
--Behavioral Pharmacology. 2nd ed. (Illus.). 288p. 1981. text ed. 17.95 (ISBN 0-19-502778-7); pap. text ed. 10.95 (ISBN 0-19-502779-5). Oxford U Pr.
Iverson, Genie. Louis Armstrong. LC 76-4975. (Biography Ser.). (Illus.). 40p. (gr. 1-4). 1976. PLB 7.89 (ISBN 0-690-01127-X, TYC-J). T Y Crowell.
--Margaret Bourke-White. (People to Remember Ser.). 32p. (gr. 4-12). 1980. PLB 5.95 (ISBN 0-87191-743-2). Creative Ed.
Iverson, Kenneth E., jt. auth. see Brooks, Frederick P.
Iverson, Peter. The Navajo Nation. LC 80-1024. (Contributions in Ethnic Studies: No. 3). (Illus.). 312p. 1981. lib. bdg. 25.00 (ISBN 0-313-22309-2, INN/). Greenwood.

--Navajos: A Critical Bibliography. LC 76-12374. (Newberry Library Center for the History of the American Indian Bibliographical Ser.). 80p. 1976. pap. 3.95x (ISBN 0-253-33986-3). Ind U Pr.
Iverstine, Joe C. & Kinard, Jerry. Cases in Production & Operations Management. 1977. pap. text ed. 12.95 (ISBN 0-675-08521-7). Merrill.
Ives, David G. & Janz, George J., eds. Reference Electrodes: Theory & Practice. 1969. pap. 33.00 (ISBN 0-12-376856-X). Acad Pr.
Ives, E. W., et al, eds. Wealth & Power in Tudor England: Essays Pressented to S. T. Bindoff. (Illus.). 1978. text ed. 43.00x (ISBN 0-485-11176-4, Athlone Pr). Humanities.
Ives, G. B., tr. see Sand, George.
Ives, Howard C. Portals to Freedom. 1937. 7.95 (ISBN 0-85398-012-8, 7-31-21, Pub. by George Ronald England); pap. 4.95 o.s.i. (ISBN 0-87743-056-X, 7-31-22, Pub. by George Ronald England). Baha'i.
Ives, Howard C. & Kissam, P. Seven-Place Natural Trigonometrical Functions. 1929. 19.50 (ISBN 0-471-43098-6, Pub. by Wiley-Interscience). Wiley.
Ives, J. Moss. Ark & the Dove: The Beginnings of Civil & Religious Liberties in America. LC 76-79200. (Illus.). 1969. Repr. of 1936 ed. 32.50x (ISBN 0-8154-0293-7). Cooper Sq.
Ives, Jack, ed. see Bradley, Raymond S.
Ives, John. Fear in a Handful of Dust. 1979. pap. 1.95 o.s.i. (ISBN 0-685-92516-1). Jove Pubns.
--The Marchand Woman. 1981. pap. 2.75 (ISBN 0-425-04731-8). Berkley Pub.
Ives, Joseph C. Report Upon the Colorado River of the West. LC 69-18459. (American Scene Ser). (Illus.). 1969. Repr. of 1861 ed. lib. bdg. 45.00 (ISBN 0-685-19443-4). Da Capo.
Ives, K. J., ed. The Scientific Basis of Flocculation. 375p. 1978. 36.00x (ISBN 90-286-0758-7). Sijthoff & Noordhoff.
Ives, Rich. Notes from the Water Journals. 1980. pap. 4.00 (ISBN 0-917652-20-7). Confluence Pr.
Ives, Suzy. Dolls for Children to Make. 1975. 14.95 (ISBN 0-7134-2991-7, Pub. by Batsford England). David & Charles.
--Ideas for Patchwork. (Illus.). 112p. 1974. 7.95 o.p. (ISBN 0-8231-5042-9). Branford.
--Making Felt Toys. (Illus.). 1971. 7.25 o.p. (ISBN 0-8231-5029-1). Branford.
--Patterns for Patchwork Quilts & Cushions. (Illus.). 63p. 1977. pap. 6.50 (ISBN 0-8231-5050-X). Branford.
Ives, Viveca. The Fox & His Vixen. 1977. pap. 1.95 o.p. (ISBN 0-345-27325-7). Ballantine.
Ivey, Allen E. Counseling & Psychotherapy: Skills, Theories & Practices. (Illus.). 1980. text ed. 18.95 (ISBN 0-13-183152-6). P-H.
Ivey, D. G. & Hume, J. N. P. Physics: Classical Mechanics & Introductory Statistical Mechanics, Vol. 1. 1974. 24.95x (ISBN 0-471-06756-3). Wiley.
Ivey, D. G., jt. auth. see Hume, J. N.
Ivey, Donald. Sound Pleasure: A Prelude to Active Listening. LC 75-30287. (Illus., Orig.). 1977. pap. text ed. 12.95 (ISBN 0-02-870900-4); record package 12.95 (ISBN 0-02-870870-9). Schirmer Bks.
Ivey, Elizabeth, jt. auth. see Dym, Clive L.
Ivey, Henry F. see Marton, L.
Ivey, Jean. The Prices Through the Years: A Model for Preparing Your Family Roots. White, Moseqelle, ed. 120p. 1980. pap. 9.95x (ISBN 0-936026-07-3). R&M Pub Co.
Ivey, P. M., et al. Alaska-Energy Lands: The Inside Story. LC 79-5457. 300p. 1980. 12.95 (ISBN 0-918270-06-5). That New Pub.
Ivimey, Joseph. John Milton, His Life & Times, Religious & Political Opinions. 397p. 1980. Repr. of 1833 ed. lib. bdg. 40.00 (ISBN 0-8495-2619-1). Arden Lib.
Ivimy, John. The Sphinx & the Megaliths. 1976. pap. 3.45 o.p. (ISBN 0-06-090533-6, CN533, CN). Har-Row.
Ivins, Dan. God's People in Transition. Date not set. 5.95 (ISBN 0-8054-6932-X). Broadman. Postponed.
Ivins, J., jt. ed. see Hebblethwaite, Paul.
Ivins, William M., Jr. Notes on Prints. LC 67-25544. (Graphic Art Ser). 1967. Repr. of 1930 ed. lib. bdg. 27.50 (ISBN 0-306-70957-0). Da Capo.
--Prints & Books. LC 76-75295. (Graphic Art Ser). 1969. Repr. of 1927 ed. lib. bdg. 32.50 (ISBN 0-306-71288-1). Da Capo.
--Prints & Visual Communication. LC 68-31583. (Graphic Art Ser). (Illus.). 1969. Repr. of 1953 ed. lib. bdg. 25.00 (ISBN 0-306-71159-1). Da Capo.
Ivison, Stuart & Rosser, Fred. Baptists in Upper & Lower Canada before 1820. LC 57-2798. (Illus.). 1956. 15.00x (ISBN 0-8020-5046-8). U of Toronto Pr.
Ivlev, V. S. Experimental Ecology & the Feeding of Fishes. 1961. 32.50x (ISBN 0-685-89751-6). Elliots Bks.

Ivory, James. Savages & Shakespeare Wallah. 1973. pap. 3.95 (ISBN 0-394-17799-1, E604, Ever). Grove.

Ivory, Thomas P., ed. see Archdiocese of Newark.

Iwanska, Alicja. Exile Governments. LC 76-40139. 192p. 1981. text ed. 13.25x (ISBN 0-87073-555-1); pap. text ed. 7.95x (ISBN 0-87073-553-5). Schenkman.

Iwasaki, Yoji, ed. Cadaveric Renal Transplantation. (Illus.). 1974. 40.00 (ISBN 0-89640-019-0). Igaku-Shoin.

Iwatsuki, Z., et al. Qwint Systems, Inc. 1976. 12.50 (ISBN 3-7682-1061-8). Qwint Systems.

Iwersen, Marguerite. Mind Matters. LC 80-67158. 123p. (Orig.). 1981. pap. 5.50 (ISBN 0-87516-421-8). De Vorss.

Iyanaga, Shokichi & Kawada, Yukiyosi, eds. Encyclopedic Dictionary of Mathematics, 2 vols. 1977. Set. text ed. 150.00 (ISBN 0-262-09016-3); pap. text ed. 40.00x (ISBN 0-262-59010-7). MIT Pr.

Iyayi, Festus. Violence. 316p. (Orig.). 1979. 9.00 (ISBN 0-89410-105-6); pap. 5.00 (ISBN 0-89410-104-8). Three Continents.

Iyengar, B. K. Light on Pranayama: The Yogic Art of Breathing. 320p. 1981. 12.95 (ISBN 0-8245-0048-2). Crossroad NY.

Iyengar, K. T. & Ramu, S. Anantha. Design Tables for Beams on Elastic Foundations & Related Structural Problems. (Illus.). 1979. 38.90x (ISBN 0-85334-841-3, Pub. by Applied Science). Burgess-Intl Ideas.

Iyer, K. A. Vakyapadiya of Bharthari-Chapter Three. 1974. 15.00 (ISBN 0-8426-0617-3). Orient Bk Dist.

Iyer, Raghavan. The Descent of the Gods: Mystical Writings of A. E. Raghavan Iyer & Nandini Iyer. (Collected Edition of the Writings of G.W. Russell III). 1980. text ed. write for info. (ISBN 0-391-01143-X). Humanities.

--Moral & Political Thought of Mahatma Gandhi. 400p. 1973. 17.95 (ISBN 0-19-501692-0). Oxford U Pr.

--Parapolitics: Toward the City of Man. (Illus.). 1979. 17.95 (ISBN 0-19-502596-2). Oxford U Pr.

Iyer, Raghavan N. The Moral & Political Thought of Mahatma Gandhi. LC 72-96613. 1978. pap. 6.95 (ISBN 0-19-502357-9, GB527, GB). Oxford U Pr.

Iz, Fahir, jt. ed. see Alderson, A. D.

Izaeli, D. N., ed. see International Conference on Marketing Systems for Developing Countries.

Izant, Edith. The Kerry Blue Terrier. LC 77-87764. (Other Dog Books). (Illus.). 1981. price not set (ISBN 0-87714-060-X). Denlingers.

Izard, Carroll E. Face of Emotion. (Century Psychology Ser.). (Illus.). 1981. Repr. of 1971 ed. text ed. 24.50x (ISBN 0-8290-0059-3). Irvington.

Izard, Ralph, jt. auth. see McCracken, Paul W.

Izatt, Reed M. & Christensen, James J. Progess in Macrocyclic Chemistry, Vol. 2. (Progress in Macrocyclic Chemistry Ser.). 384p. 1981. 35.00 (ISBN 0-471-05178-0, Pub. by Wiley-Interscience). Wiley.

--Progress in Macrocyclic Chemistry, Vol. 2. 300p. 1981. 35.00 (ISBN 0-471-05178-0, Pub. by Wiley-Interscience). Wiley.

Izawa, T. & Hijkata, S., illus. Hansel & Gretel. (Puppet Storybooks). (Illus.). 18p. (gr. k-2). 1981. 3.50 (ISBN 0-448-09754-0). G&D.

--Jack & the Beanstalk. (Puppet Storybooks). (Illus.). 18p. (gr. k-2). 1981. 3.50 (ISBN 0-448-09758-3). G&D.

--The Little Red Hen. (Puppet Storybooks). (Illus.). 18p. (gr. k-2). 1981. 3.50 (ISBN 0-448-09756-7). G&D.

--Peter Rabbit. (Puppet Storybooks). (Illus.). 18p. (gr. k-2). 1981. 3.50 (ISBN 0-448-09755-9). G&D.

--Snow White & the Seven Dwarfs. (Puppet Storybooks). (Illus.). 18p. (gr. k-2). 1981. 3.50 (ISBN 0-448-09757-5). G&D.

--What Time Is It? (Puppet Storybooks). (Illus.). 18p. (gr. k-2). 1981. 3.50 (ISBN 0-448-09753-2). G&D.

Izbicki, Thomas M. Protector of the Faith: Cardinal Johannes De Turrecremata & the Defense of the Institutional Church. 1981. price not set (ISBN 0-8132-0558-1). Cath U Pr.

Ize, A. F., ed. Functional Differential Equations & Bifurcations: Proceedings. (Lecture Notes in Mathematics: Vol. 799). 409p. 1980. pap. 24.50 (ISBN 0-387-09986-7). Springer-Verlag.

Izerghina, Antonina, jt. auth. see Barskaya, Anna.

Izraeli, D. & Zif, J. Societal Marketing Boards. LC 77-10606. 1978. 45.95 (ISBN 0-470-99308-1). Halsted Pr.

Izraeli, D. N., ed. see International Conference on Marketing Systems for Developing Countries.

Izumiya, Nobuo. Synthetic Aspects of Biologically Active Cyclic Peptides: Gramicidei S & Tyrocidres. LC 79-19998. 1979. 32.95x (ISBN 0-470-26863-8). Halsted Pr.

Izutsu, Toshihiko. Toward a Philosophy of Zen Buddhism. 1978. 12.50 o.p. (ISBN 0-87773-732-0). Great Eastern.

Izzo, Herbert J., ed. Italic & Romance: Studies in Historical & Descriptive Linguistics in Honor of Ernst Pulgram. (Current Issues in Linguistic Theory: Vol. 18). 400p. 1980. text ed. 42.75x (ISBN 90-272-3511-2, Pub. by Benjamins Holland). Humanities.

Izzo, Herbert J., jt. ed. see McCormack, William G.

J

J. & P. Coats Ltd. Fifty Needlepoint Stitches. (Illus.). 1977. pap. 2.95 (ISBN 0-684-14786-6, ScribT). Scribner.

J. K. Lasser Tax Institute. Financial Planning for Your Family. 1979. 10.95 (ISBN 0-671-96099-7); pap. 2.95 (ISBN 0-346-12410-7). Cornerstone.

J. M. Gelfand Library of School Mathematics. Method of Coordinates, Vol. 1. 1967. 7.50x (ISBN 0-262-07028-6). MIT Pr.

Jabay, Earl. God-Players. LC 69-11637. 1970. pap. 4.95 (ISBN 0-310-26541-X). Zondervan.

Jabber, Paul. Not by War Alone: Security & Arms Control in the Middle East. 200p. 1981. 12.50x (ISBN 0-520-04050-3). U of Cal Pr.

Jabbour, J. T., et al. Atlas of Computerized Tomography Scans in Pediatric Neurology. 1977. 36.00 o.p. (ISBN 0-87488-979-0). Med Exam.

Jabbour, J. T., et al, eds. Pediatric Neurology Handbook. 2nd ed. (Illus.). 1976. pap. 19.50 (ISBN 0-87488-636-8). Med Exam.

Jabenis, Elaine. The Fashion Director: What She Does & How to Be One. LC 72-768. 300p. 1972. text ed. 14.50x (ISBN 0-471-43125-7); pap. text ed. 9.75 (ISBN 0-471-43126-5). Wiley.

Jaber, William. Exploring the Sun. LC 80-10985. (Illus.). 96p. (gr. 4 up). 1980. PLB 7.29 (ISBN 0-671-32997-9). Messner.

Jaber, William, jt. ed. see Shapiro, Max S.

Jaberg, Gene & Wargo, Louis G., Jr. The Video Pencil: Cable Communications for Church & Community. LC 80-7951. 156p. 1980. lib. bdg. 15.50 (ISBN 0-8191-1085-X); pap. text ed. 7.75 (ISBN 0-8191-1086-8). U Pr of Amer.

Jabes, Edmond. The Book of Questions, Vol. 1. Waldrop, Rosmarie, tr. from Fr. LC 75-34058. 1976. text ed. 12.00 o.p. (ISBN 0-8195-4091-9, Pub. by Wesleyan U Pr); pap. 7.95 (ISBN 0-8195-6043-X). Columbia U Pr.

--The Book of Questions: The Book of Yukel & Return to the Book, Vols. 2 & 3. Waldrop, Rosmarie, tr. from Fr. LC 77-74561. 1977. 17.50 (ISBN 0-8195-5011-6, Pub. by Wesleyan U Pr); pap. 8.95 (ISBN 0-8195-6049-9). Columbia U Pr.

Jabes, Jak. Individual Processes in Organizational Behavior. MacKenzie, Kenneth D., ed. LC 77-86012. (Organizational Behavior Ser.). 1978. pap. text ed. 9.95x (ISBN 0-88295-450-4). AHM Pub.

Jabine, William. Case Histories in Construction Law: A Guide for Architects, Engineers, Contractors, Builders. LC 72-81985. 1973. 15.95 o.p. (ISBN 0-8436-0113-2). CBI Pub.

Jabir, Ibn H. The Works of Geber. LC 79-8615. Repr. of 1928 ed. 32.50 (ISBN 0-404-18479-0). AMS Pr.

Jablons, Beverly. Dance Time. 1981. pap. 2.25 (ISBN 0-425-04797-0). Berkley Pub.

Jablonski, David, ed. Behold the Mighty Dinosaur. 1981. 10.95 (ISBN 0-525-66704-0). Elsevier-Nelson.

Jablonski, Edward. Air War: One Volume Edition. LC 78-8213. 1979. 19.95 (ISBN 0-385-14279-X). Doubleday.

--Flying Fortress. LC 65-19886. 1965. 16.95 (ISBN 0-385-03855-0). Doubleday.

Jablonski, Edward & Stewart, Lawrence D. The Gershwin Years. rev. ed. LC 73-78334. 384p. 1973. 6.95 o.p. (ISBN 0-385-02847-4). Doubleday.

Jablonski, Ramona. The Chinese Cut-Out Design Coloring Book: Designs from the World of Nature. (The International Design Library). (Illus.). 48p. 1980. pap. 2.95 (ISBN 0-916144-55-0). Stemmer Hse.

--Folk Art Designs to Color or Cut. LC 78-13765. (International Design Library). (Illus.). 1978. pap. 2.95 (ISBN 0-916144-33-X). Stemmer Hse.

--The Paper Cut-Out Design Book. LC 76-2467. (Illus.). 1976. 15.95 (ISBN 0-916144-03-8); pap. 7.95 (ISBN 0-916144-04-6). Stemmer Hse.

--Traditional Designs of Armenia & the Near East to Color. LC 79-15212. (International Design Library). (Illus., Orig.). 1979. pap. 2.95 (ISBN 0-916144-41-0). Stemmer Hse.

Jablonsky, Stephen F., jt. auth. see Gross, Malvern J.

Jablow, Alta, jt. auth. see Hammond, Dorothy.

Jablow, Joseph. Indians of Illinois & Indiana: Illinois, Kickapoo & Potawatomi Indians. Horr, David A., ed. (American Indian Ethnohistory Ser.: North Central & Northeastern Indians). 1974. lib. bdg. 42.00 (ISBN 0-8240-0805-7). Garland Pub.

--Ponca Indians. Horr, David A., ed. Incl. Ethnology of the Ponca. Jablow, Joseph; Findings of Fact, & Opinion. Indian Claims Commission. (American Indian Ethnohistory Ser: Plains Indians). (Illus.). 1974. lib. bdg. 42.00 (ISBN 0-8240-0734-4). Garland Pub.

Jabusch, David M. & Littlejohn, Stephen. Elements of Speech Communication: Achieving Competency. LC 80-82760. (Illus.). 464p. 1981. pap. text ed. 11.50 (ISBN 0-395-29730-3); instrs' manual 0.75 (ISBN 0-395-29731-1). HM.

Jacauin, P. The Indian Nations of America. (Illus.). 1980. cancelled (ISBN 0-686-65197-9). Atheneum.

Jacaz, Jane W. African Policy Crossroads. (Illus.). 68p. (Orig.). 1979. pap. text ed. 3.00 (ISBN 0-89192-315-2). Interbk Inc.

Jachna, Joseph. Light Touching Silver: Photographs by Joseph Jachna. Klindt, Steven, ed. (Illus.). 48p. (Orig.). 1980. pap. 5.00 (ISBN 0-932026-05-2). Chicago Contemp Photo.

Jack, Adolphus A. Shelley: An Essay. LC 70-113337. 1970. Repr. of 1904 ed. 11.00 (ISBN 0-8046-1022-3). Kennikat.

--Shelley, an Essay. 127p. 1980. Repr. of 1904 ed. lib. bdg. 15.00 (ISBN 0-8492-1368-1). R West.

Jack, Donald. Me Bandy, You Cissie: The Journals of Bartholomew Bandy. 1979. 8.95 o.p. (ISBN 0-385-14396-6). Doubleday.

Jack, Ion, ed. see Bronte, Emily.

Jack, Jane, ed. see Bronte, Charlotte.

Jack, LaWant P. All Things in Their Time. pap. 5.95 (ISBN 0-89036-145-2). Hawkes Pub Inc.

Jack, Ronald, ed. Scottish Prose, Fifteen Fifty-Seventeen Hundred. (The Scottish Library Ser). 220p. 1971. text ed. 13.00x (ISBN 0-7145-0798-9). Humanities.

Jack, Susan S. & Ries, Peter W. Current Estimates from the Health Interview Survey: United States-1979. Cox, Klaudia, ed. (Ser. 10: No. 136). 55p. 1981. pap. text ed. 1.75 (ISBN 0-8406-0219-7). Natl Ctr Health Stats.

Jacka, Alan A. Adoption in Brief: Research & Other Literature in the United States, Canada & Great Britain 1966-72, an Annotated Bibliography. (General Ser.). 72p. 1973. pap. text ed. 6.25x (ISBN 0-85633-015-9, NFER). Humanities.

Jacka, Jerry, photos by. Pottery Treasures. LC 76-657. (Illus.). 96p. (Text by Spencer Gill). 1976. pap. 9.95 (ISBN 0-912856-28-9); 19.50 o.p. (ISBN 0-686-67419-7). Graphic Arts Ctr.

--Turquoise Treasures. LC 75-7141. (Illus.). 96p. (Text by Spencer Gill). 1975. 19.50 (ISBN 0-912856-21-1); pap. 9.95 o.p. (ISBN 0-912856-25-4). Graphic Arts Ctr.

Jackall, Robert. Workers in a Labyrinth: Jobs & Survival in a Bank Bureaucracy. LC 77-84347. 202p. 1978. text ed. 18.00x (ISBN 0-916672-09-3). Allanheld.

Jackendoff, Nathaniel. Money, Flow of Funds, & Economic Policy. LC 68-30892. (Illus.). 523p. 1968. 20.95 (ISBN 0-8260-4730-0) (ISBN 0-471-07469-1). Wiley.

Jacker, Corinne. Window on the Unknown: A History of the Microscope. LC 66-24490. (Illus.). (gr. 6 up). 1966. 5.95 o.p. (ISBN 0-684-20857-1, ScribJ). Scribner.

Jackins, Harvey. The Fundamentals of Co-Counseling Manual: Spanish Translation. Ramos-Diaz, Emma & Bacal, Azril, trs. from Eng. (Span.). 1981. pap. 5.00 (ISBN 0-911214-28-3). Rational Isl.

--The Human Side of Human Beings: Spanish Translation. Ramos-Diaz, Emma & Bacal, Azril, trs. from Eng. (Span.). 1980. pap. 3.00 (ISBN 0-911214-27-5). Rational Isl.

--Human Side of Human Beings: The Theory of Re-Evaluation Counseling. 1965. 3.00 o.p. (ISBN 0-911214-00-3); pap. 2.00 o.p. (ISBN 0-911214-01-1). Rational Isl.

Jackiw, Roman, jt. auth. see Treiman, Sam B.

Jackiw, Roman W., jt. auth. see Bethe, Hans A.

Jackle, Mary & Halligan, Marney. Cardiovascular Problems: A Critical Care Nursing Focus. (Illus.). 1980. pap. text ed. 19.95 (ISBN 0-87619-667-9). R J Brady.

Jackle, Mary & Rasmussen, Claire. Renal Problems: A Critical Care Nursing Focus. LC 79-9498. (Illus.). 356p. 1979. pap. text ed. 16.95 (ISBN 0-87619-408-0). R J Brady.

Jackle, Mary, jt. auth. see Snyder, Mariah.

Jacklin, Carol N., jt. auth. see Maccoby, Eleanor E.

Jackman, James L. Fifteenth Century Basse Dances. LC 79-7767. (Dance Ser.). (Illus.). 1980. Repr. of 1964 ed. lib. bdg. 14.00x (ISBN 0-8369-9295-4). Arno.

Jackman, L. M. & Sternhell, S. Applications of Nuclear Magnetic Resonance Spectroscopy in Organic Chemistry. 2nd ed. 1969. 50.00 (ISBN 0-08-012542-5). Pergamon.

Jackman, Raymond J. & Beahrs, Oliver H. Tumors of the Large Bowel. LC 28-23685. (Major Problems in Clinical Surgery Ser.: Vol. 8). (Illus.). 1968. 16.00 (ISBN 0-7216-5060-0). Saunders.

Jackman, Robert W. Politics & Social Equality: A Comparative Analysis. LC 74-24725. (Comparative Studies in Behavioral Science Ser). 256p. 1975. 23.95 (ISBN 0-471-43128-1, Pub. by Wiley-Interscience). Wiley.

Jackman, William T. Development of Transportation in Modern England. LC 67-40294. Repr. of 1916 ed. 30.00x (ISBN 0-678-05178-X). Kelley.

Jacks, L. P. Responsibility & Culture. 1924. 19.50x (ISBN 0-685-89778-8). Elliots Bks.

Jacks, Maurice Leonard. The Education of Good Men. LC 80-19910. 192p. 1980. Repr. of 1955 ed. lib. bdg. 19.50x (ISBN 0-313-22800-0, JAEG). Greenwood.

Jacks, Oliver. Autumn Heroes. 1979. pap. 1.95 o.p. (ISBN 0-425-04037-2). Berkley Pub.

Jackson, et al, eds. Student Activities in Secondary Schools: A Bibliography. Battiste. 92p. 1980. pap. 4.00 (ISBN 0-88210-109-9). Natl Assn Principals.

Jackson, Abraham. The Pious Prentice, or, the Prentices Piety. LC 74-28866. (English Experience Ser.: No. 746). 1975. Repr. of 1640 ed. 7.00 (ISBN 90-221-0746-9). Walter J Johnson.

Jackson, Al & Tardy, Gene. Drag Boat Racing: The National Championships. (Sports Action Ser). (Illus.). 48p. (gr. 3-12). 1973. PLB 5.51 (ISBN 0-914844-05-9); pap. 3.95 (ISBN 0-914844-06-7). J Alden.

Jackson, Al, jt. auth. see Tardy, Gene.

Jackson, Alan. London's Local Railways. LC 77-85017. 1978. 38.00 (ISBN 0-7153-7479-6). David & Charles.

Jackson, Albert & Day, David. The Modelmaker's Handbook. LC 80-2702. (Illus.). 352p. 1981. 19.95 (ISBN 0-394-50788-6). Knopf.

Jackson, Andrew S., jt. auth. see Baumgartner, Ted A.

Jackson, Anita. Specter Series. Incl. The Actor (ISBN 0-8224-6432-2); Dreams (ISBN 0-8224-6435-7); A Deadly Game (ISBN 0-8224-6434-9); The Ear (ISBN 0-8224-6436-5); Fifty-Seven T-Bird (ISBN 0-8224-6437-3); Homecoming (ISBN 0-8224-6438-1); No Rent to Pay (ISBN 0-8224-6439-X); ZB4 (ISBN 0-8224-6433-0). (gr. 6 up). 1979. pap. 3.56 ea.; Set. pap. 28.00 (ISBN 0-8224-6430-6). Pitman Learning.

Jackson, Arlene M. Illustration & the Novels of Thomas Hardy. (Illus.). 168p. 1981. 25.00x (ISBN 0-8476-6275-6). Rowman.

Jackson, B. D., jt. ed. see Hooker, J. D.

Jackson, B. D. see Jackson, B. D., et al.

Jackson, B. D., et al, eds. Index Kewensis Supplements. Incl. Vol. 1. 1866-1895. Durand, T. & Jackson, B. D., eds. 1901-06. 49.00x (ISBN 0-19-854310-7); Vol. 4. 1906-1910. Prain, D., ed. 1913. 49.00x (ISBN 0-19-854313-1); Vol. 6. 1916-1920. Hill, A. W., ed. 1926. 49.00x (ISBN 0-19-854315-8); Vol. 7. 1921-1925. Hill, A. W., ed. 1929. 49.00x (ISBN 0-19-854316-6); Vol. 8. 1926-1930. Hill, A. W., ed. 1933. 49.00x (ISBN 0-19-854317-4); Vol. 10. 1936-1940. Hill, A. W. & Salisbury, E. J., eds. 1947. 34.95x (ISBN 0-19-854319-0); Vol. 12. 1951-1955. Taylor, George, ed. 1959. 39.95x (ISBN 0-19-854321-2); Vol. 13. 1956-1960. Taylor, George, ed. 1966. 43.50x (ISBN 0-19-854354-9); Vol. 14. 1961-1965. Taylor, George, ed. 1970. 45.00x (ISBN 0-19-854370-0); Vol. 15. 1966-1970. Heslop-Harrison, J., compiled by. 156p. 1973. 45.00x (ISBN 0-19-854382-4); Vol. 16. 1971-1976. Brenan, J. P., ed. 250p. 1980. 42.00 (ISBN 0-19-854531-2). Oxford U Pr.

Jackson, B. E., jt. auth. see Berkeley, S. G.

Jackson, Barbara, jt. auth. see Blondis, Marion N.

Jackson, Barbara B. Computer Models in Management. 1979. 19.95 (ISBN 0-256-02225-9). Irwin.

Jackson, Berners, ed. see Shakespeare, William.

Jackson, Bernetta M., jt. auth. see Vivian, Charles H.

Jackson, Bob. Street Biking: How to Ride to Save Your Hide. 1980. pap. 5.95 (ISBN 0-89586-081-3). H P Bks.

Jackson, Brenda B. Model Making in Schools. 1971. 15.95 o.p. (ISBN 0-7134-2298-X, Pub. by Batsford England). David & Charles.

Jackson, Brian & Marsden, Dennis. Education & the Working Class. (Reports of the Institute of Community Studies). 1968. Repr. of 1962 ed. 19.50x (ISBN 0-7100-3916-6). Routledge & Kegan.

Jackson, Bruce. Killing Time: Life in the Arkansas Penitentary. 1977. 18.50 (ISBN 0-8014-1101-7); pap. 6.95 (ISBN 0-8014-9176-2). Cornell U Pr.

--Thief's Primer: Life of an American Character. 1969. 5.95 o.s.i. (ISBN 0-02-558280-1). Macmillan.

Jackson, Bruce & Christian, Diane. Death Row. LC 79-53752. (Illus.). 312p. 1981. pap. 6.95 (ISBN 0-8070-3203-4). Beacon Pr.
Jackson, Bruce, ed. see Jackson, Michael & Jackson, Jessica.
Jackson, Byron, jt. auth. see Jackson, Kathryn.
Jackson, C. I., ed. Human Settlements & Energy: A Seminar of the United Nations Economic Commission for Europe. 1978. text ed. 23.00 (ISBN 0-08-022427-X); pap. text ed. 11.25 (ISBN 0-08-022411-3). Pergamon.
Jackson, C. Paul. Fullback in the Large Fry League. (Illus.). (gr. 6-9). 1965. 4.95g o.p. (ISBN 0-8038-2261-8). Hastings.
--How to Play Better Basketball. LC 68-13584. (Illus.). (gr. 4 up). 1968. 8.95 o.p. (ISBN 0-690-41425-0, TYC-J). T Y Crowell.
--How to Play Better Football. LC 72-158707. (Illus.). (gr. 3-5). 1972. 8.79 (ISBN 0-690-41567-2, TYC-J). T Y Crowell.
--Little Major Leaguer. (Illus.). (gr. 3-6). 1963. 4.95 o.s.i. (ISBN 0-8038-4242-2). Hastings.
Jackson, Carlton. Zane Grey. (U. S. Authors Ser.: No. 218). 1973. lib. bdg. 10.95 (ISBN 0-8057-0338-1). Twayne.
Jackson, Carole. Color Me Beautiful. 216p. 1981. pap. 8.95 (ISBN 0-345-29015-1). Ballantine.
--Color Me Beautiful: The Engagement & Beauty Calender for 1981. 1980. pap. 6.95 o.p. (ISBN 0-87491-410-8). Acropolis.
Jackson, Charles J. English Goldsmiths & Their Marks. 22.50 (ISBN 0-486-21206-8). Dover.
Jackson, Charles T. Buffalo Wallow: A Prairie Boyhood. LC 52-14022. 1967. pap. 3.25 (ISBN 0-8032-5099-1, BB 373, Bison). U of Nebr Pr.
Jackson, Charles W., jt. auth. see Johnson, Charles O.
Jackson, Clara O. Bibliography of Afro-American & Other American Minorities Represented in Library & Library Related Listings. (Bibliographical Ser.: No. 9). 1972. 1.50 (ISBN 0-89977-013-4). Am Inst Marxist.
Jackson, Clyde O. Come Like the Benediction. (Illus.). 1981. 7.00 (ISBN 0-682-49723-1). Exposition.
Jackson, D. Unfair Dismissal. (Department of Applied Economics, Occasional Papers Ser.: No. 1). (Illus.). 200p. 1975. 18.95 (ISBN 0-521-20751-7); pap. 11.95x (ISBN 0-521-09942-0). Cambridge U Pr.
Jackson, D. & Wood, Peter. The Sierra Madre. (The American Wilderness Ser.). (Illus.). 184p. 1975. 12.95 (ISBN 0-8094-1342-6). Time-Life.
Jackson, D., jt. auth. see Lyons, M.
Jackson, D. D. & Wood, P. The Sierra Madre. LC 75-21613. (American Wilderness). (Illus.). (gr. 6 up). 1975. PLB 11.97 (ISBN 0-8094-1339-6, Pub. by Time-Life). Silver.
Jackson, D. L. Australian Agricultural Plants. Date not set. write for info. (ISBN 0-686-15350-2, Pub. by Sydney U Pr). Intl Schol Bk Serv. Postponed.
Jackson, Daphne F., jt. auth. see Barrett, Roger C.
Jackson, Darrell, jt. ed. see Epstein, T. Scarlett.
Jackson, Dave. Coming Together: All Those Communities & What They're up to. LC 78-16123. 1978. pap. 3.95 (ISBN 0-87123-087-9, 210087). Bethany Fell.
--Dial Nine One Nine. 160p. 1981. pap. text ed. 5.95 (ISBN 0-8361-1952-5). Herald Pr.
Jackson, David. Cell System of Production. 170p. 1978. text ed. 23.50x (ISBN 0-220-66345-9, Pub. by Busn Bks England). Renouf.
Jackson, David A. & Stitch, Stephen P. Recombinant DNA Battle. 1979. text ed. 25.95 (ISBN 0-13-767442-2). P-H.
Jackson, David J. & Borgatta, Edgar F., eds. Factor Analysis & Measurement in Sociological Research: A Multi-Dimensional Perspective. (Sage Studies in International Sociology: Vol. 21). 320p. 1981. 20.00 (ISBN 0-8039-9814-7) (ISBN 0-8039-9815-5). Sage.
Jackson, David J., jt. ed. see Borgatta, Edgar F.
Jackson, Dennis B. Exam Secret. pap. 3.00 (ISBN 0-87980-033-X). Wilshire.
Jackson, Don. Sagebrush Country. (The American Wilderness Ser). (Illus.). 184p. 1975. 12.95 (ISBN 0-8094-1217-9). Time-Life.
Jackson, Don D., jt. auth. see Lederer, William J.
Jackson, Donald. Custer's Gold: The United States Cavalry Expedition of 1874. LC 66-21521. (Illus.). 1972. pap. 2.25 (ISBN 0-8032-5750-3, BB 543, Bison). U of Nebr Pr.
--Form & Expression in Calligraphy. LC 78-20704. (Illus.). Date not set. pap. 3.95 (ISBN 0-8008-2683-3, Pentalic). Taplinger. Postponed.
--Sagebrush Country. LC 74-32622. (American Wilderness Ser.). (Illus.). 184p. (gr. 6 up). 1975. lib. bdg. 11.97 (ISBN 0-8094-1218-7). Silver.
--Thomas Jefferson & the Stony Mountains: Exploring the West from Monticello. LC 80-10546. (Illus.). 290p. 1981. 19.95 (ISBN 0-252-00823-5). U of Ill Pr.
Jackson, Donald, jt. ed. see Spence, Mary L.
Jackson, Donald, ed. see Washington, George.
Jackson, Donald D., jt. auth. see Time-Life Books Editors.
Jackson, Earl, ed. see Meketa, Charles & Meketa, Jacqueline.
Jackson, Edgar, et al. Tracking Down the Sickle Cell. (gr. 9-12). 1976. kit 212.00 (ISBN 0-205-05006-9, 7150067). Allyn.
Jackson, Edgar N. Telling a Child About Death. 1965. 4.95 o.p. (ISBN 0-8015-7488-9); pap. 2.95 (ISBN 0-8015-7494-3, Hawthorn). Dutton.
--When Someone Dies. Hulme, William E., ed. LC 76-154488. (Pocket Counsel Bks). 64p. (Orig.). 1971. pap. 1.75 (ISBN 0-8006-1103-9, 1-1103). Fortress.
--You & Your Grief. 1961. 3.95 (ISBN 0-8015-9036-1, Hawthorn). Dutton.
Jackson, Edwin L. Handbook for Georgia Legislators. 8th ed. 220p. 1980. pap. 10.00x (ISBN 0-89854-069-0). U. of GA Inst Govt.
Jackson, Eileen. Autumn Lace. 1976. 7.95 o.s.i. (ISBN 0-8027-0538-3). Walker & Co.
--Autumn Lace. 1977. pap. 1.50 o.p. (ISBN 0-449-23297-2, Crest). Fawcett.
--Lord Rivington's Lady. 1977. pap. 1.75 (ISBN 0-451-09408-5, E9408, Sig). NAL.
--Lord Rivington's Lady: A Regency Romance. LC 75-40762. 1976. 7.95 o.s.i. (ISBN 0-8027-0533-2). Walker & Co.
Jackson, Elinor & Dundon, H. Dwyer, eds. Occupational Therapy Examination Review Book, Vol. 1. 3rd ed. 1974. pap. 9.50 (ISBN 0-87488-475-6). Med Exam.
Jackson, Ellen. The Bear in the Bathtub. LC 80-26535. (Illus.). 32p. (ps-3). 1981. PLB 6.95 (ISBN 0-201-04701-2, A-W Childrens). A-W.
Jackson, Emily. The History of Hand Made Lace: Dealing with the Origin of Lace, the Growth of the Great Lace Centres, Etc. LC 70-136558. (Tower Bks.). (Illus.). xiv, 245p. 1972. Repr. of 1900 ed. 28.00 (ISBN 0-8103-3935-8). Gale.
Jackson, Eugene & Geiger, Adolph. German Made Simple. LC 65-10615. pap. 3.50 (ISBN 0-385-00129-0, Made). Doubleday.
Jackson, Eugene & LoPreato, Joseph. Italian Made Simple. 1960. pap. 3.50 (ISBN 0-385-00736-1, Made). Doubleday.
Jackson, Eugene & Rubio, Antonio. French Made Simple. LC 73-9033. pap. 3.50 (ISBN 0-385-08691-1, Made). Doubleday.
--Spanish Made Simple. pap. 3.50 (ISBN 0-385-01212-8, Made). Doubleday.
Jackson, Eugene B., ed. Special Librarianship: A New Reader. LC 80-11530. 773p. 1980. 27.50 (ISBN 0-8108-1295-9). Scarecrow.
Jackson, F. Perception: A Representative Theory. LC 76-30316. 1977. 26.95 (ISBN 0-521-21550-1). Cambridge U Pr.
Jackson, F. Scott & Lippman, William J., eds. Condominium & Cooperative Conversions 1980: Course Handbook. LC 80-81527. (Nineteen Seventy-Nine to Nineteen Eighty Real Estate Law & Practice Course Handbook Ser.). 549p. 1981. pap. 25.00 (ISBN 0-686-69166-0, N4-4352). PLI.
Jackson, Florence. Black Man in America, 1791-1861. LC 72-136833. (Black Man in America Ser: Vol. 2). (Illus.). (gr. 7 up). 1971. PLB 4.90 o.p. (ISBN 0-531-01965-9). Watts.
--The Black Man in America, 1861-1877. LC 71-183578. (Black Man in America Ser: Vol. 3). (Illus.). 96p. (gr. 4-6). 1971. PLB 4.90 o.p. (ISBN 0-531-02022-3). Watts.
--The Black Man in America, 1877-1905. LC 72-10406. (Black Man in America Ser: Vol. 4). (Illus.). 96p. (gr. 5 up). 1973. PLB 4.90 o.p. (ISBN 0-531-02611-6). Watts.
--Black Man in America, 1905-1932. LC 73-12931. (Black Man in America Ser: Vol. 5). (Illus.). 96p. (gr. 7 up). 1974. PLB 4.90 o.p. (ISBN 0-531-02667-1). Watts.
--The Black Man in America 1932-1954. LC 74-13440. (Black Man in America Ser: Vol. 6). (Illus.). (gr. 4-6). 1975. PLB 4.90 o.p. (ISBN 0-531-02799-6). Watts.
Jackson, Florence & Jackson, J. B. Black Man in America, 1619-1790. LC 73-101749. (Black Man in America Ser: Vol. 1). (Illus.). (gr. 7 up). PLB 4.90 o.p. (ISBN 0-531-01839-3). Watts.
Jackson, Frank. Woodworking. LC 68-121944. (Pegasus Books: No. 7). (Illus.). 1966. 10.50x (ISBN 0-234-77878-4). Intl Pubns Serv.
Jackson, Frank & Irving, W. Ronald. Border Terriers. (Foyle's Handbks). 1969. 3.95 (ISBN 0-685-55815-0). Palmetto Pub.
Jackson, G. N., jt. auth. see Hope, C. E.
Jackson, Sir Geoffrey. Surviving the Long Night: An Autobiographical Account of a Political Kidnapping. LC 74-83673. Orig. Title: People's Prison. 22p. 1974. 8.95 (ISBN 0-8149-0756-3). Vanguard.
Jackson, George. Blood in My Eye. (YA) 1972. 8.95 o.p. (ISBN 0-394-47981-5). Random.
--Sixty Years in Texas. (Illus.). 200p. 1975. Repr. 12.00 o.p. (ISBN 0-89015-105-9). Nortex Pr.
Jackson, George A. A Case Study: Mr. Paranoid. 64p. 1981. 4.00 (ISBN 0-682-49692-8). Exposition.
Jackson, George D., Jr. Comintern & Peasant in East Europe, 1919-1930. LC 66-15489. 1966. 20.00x (ISBN 0-231-02912-8). Columbia U Pr.
Jackson, George P. White & Negro Spirituals, Their Life Span & Kinship. (Music Reprint Ser). (Illus.). xii, 349p. 1975. Repr. of 1944 ed. lib. bdg. 32.50 (ISBN 0-306-70667-9). Da Capo.
Jackson, George P., ed. Down-East Spirituals & Others: Three Hundred Songs Supplementary to the Author's "Spiritual Folk-Songs of Early America". LC 74-34317. (Music Reprint Ser). (Illus.). 296p. 1975. Repr. of 1943 ed. lib. bdg. 27.50 (ISBN 0-306-70666-0). Da Capo.
--Spiritual Folk-Songs of Early America. 8.50 (ISBN 0-8446-2297-4). Peter Smith.
Jackson, Graham. The Haphazard Amorist. 127p. 1981. text ed. 12.00 (ISBN 0-7022-1497-3); pap. 6.00 (ISBN 0-7022-1498-1). U of Queensland Pr.
Jackson, H. A. Mr. Jackson's Mushrooms. Cazort, Mimi, intro. by. (Illus.). 1979. 35.00 (ISBN 0-88884-364-X, 56430-4, Pub. by Natl Gallery Canada). U of Chicago Pr.
Jackson, H. C. The Good 'uns: A Memoir of H.C. "Bud Jackson. (Illus.). 280p. 1980. 17.95 (ISBN 0-914330-38-1). Pioneer Pub Co.
Jackson, Harold. The Two Irelands. (Minority Rights Group: No. 2). 1972. pap. 2.50 (ISBN 0-89192-092-7). Interbk Inc.
Jackson, Hartley H. Mammals of Wisconsin. (Illus.). 1961. 22.50x (ISBN 0-299-02150-5). U of Wis Pr.
Jackson, Hartley H., jt. auth. see Young, Stanley P.
Jackson, Helen H. Century of Dishonor: The Early Crusade for Indian Reform. Rolle, ed. 8.00 (ISBN 0-8446-2298-2). Peter Smith.
--Mammy Tittleback & Her Family. 1976. lib. bdg. 8.50x (ISBN 0-89968-052-6). Lightyear.
--Ramona. (Illus.). (gr. 6 up). 1939. Repr. of 1884 ed. 8.95 (ISBN 0-316-45467-2). Little.
--Ramona. 1970. pap. 2.50 o.p. (ISBN 0-380-00383-X, 51680). Avon.
--Ramona. 1976. lib. bdg. 20.10x (ISBN 0-89968-051-8). Lightyear.
Jackson, Helen Hunt. Nelly's Silver Mine: A Story of Colorado Life. LC 75-32183. (Classics of Children's Literature, 1621-1932: Vol. 46). (Illus.). 1976. Repr. of 1878 ed. PLB 38.00 (ISBN 0-8240-2295-5). Garland Pub.
Jackson, Henry F. The FLN in Algeria: Party Development in a Revolutionary Society. LC 76-47889. (Contributions in Afro-American & African Studies: No. 30). (Illus.). 1977. lib. bdg. 19.95 (ISBN 0-8371-9401-6, JFA/). Greenwood.
Jackson, Herbert L. Basic Nuclear Physics for Medical Personnel. (Illus.). 164p. 1973. 13.75 (ISBN 0-398-02663-7). C C Thomas.
Jackson, Holbrook, ed. see Burton, Robert.
Jackson, Holdrook, ed. see Lear, Edward.
Jackson, Howard. Analyzing English: An Introduction to Descriptive Linguistics. (Pergamon Institute of English). (Illus.). 1980. pap. 11.95 (ISBN 0-08-024556-0). Pergamon.
Jackson, Howard, tr. see Zosimos Of Panopolis.
Jackson, Hulen. Sunshine Through the Shadows. 4.95 (ISBN 0-89315-283-8). Lambert Bk.
Jackson, I. J., ed. see Fails Management Institute.
Jackson, Ian J. Climate, Water and Agriculture in the Tropics. LC 76-53759. (Illus.). 1977. pap. text ed. 11.95x (ISBN 0-582-48529-0). Longman.
Jackson, Ian T., jt. auth. see Macallan, E. S.
Jackson, Ivor C., tr. see Friedman, Samy.
Jackson, J. & Morgan, C. Organization Theory: A Macro-Perspective for Management. 1978. 19.95 (ISBN 0-13-641407-9). P-H.
Jackson, J. B. The Necessity for Ruins, & Other Topics. LC 79-23212. 1980. lib. bdg. 10.00x (ISBN 0-87023-291-6); pap. 4.95 (ISBN 0-87023-292-4). U of Mass Pr.
Jackson, J. B., jt. auth. see Jackson, Florence.
Jackson, J. D. Classical Electrodynamics. 2nd ed. LC 75-9962. 864p. 1975. text ed. 29.50 (ISBN 0-471-43132-X). Wiley.
Jackson, J. D., et al, eds. Annual Review of Nuclear & Particle Science, Vol. 30. LC 53-995. (Annual Review of Nuclear Science Ser.: 1950-1977). (Illus.). 1980. text ed. 22.50 (ISBN 0-8243-1530-8). Annual Reviews.
Jackson, J. E. Sphere Spheroid & Projections for Surveyors: Aspects of Modern Land Surveying. LC 80-82507. 138p. 1980. 37.95 (ISBN 0-470-27044-6). Halsted Pr.
Jackson, J. H. A Short History of France from Early Times to 1972. 2nd ed. (Illus.). 260p. 1974. 34.95 (ISBN 0-521-20485-2); pap. 8.95x (ISBN 0-521-09864-5). Cambridge U Pr.
--A Story of Christian Activism: History of the National Baptist Convention U. S. A., Inc. LC 80-17408. (Illus.). 790p. 1980. 19.95 (ISBN 0-935990-01-1). Townsend Pr.
Jackson, J. R., ed. Coleridge: The Critical Heritage. 1970. 40.00x (ISBN 0-7100-6594-9). Routledge & Kegan.
Jackson, J. R., ed. see Coleridge, Samuel T.
Jackson, J. S. see De Vore, R. William.
Jackson, J. S., jt. ed. see De Vore, R. William.
Jackson, J. S., ed. see Third International Conference.
Jackson, J. W. Cardiothoracic Surgery. 3rd ed. (Operative Surgery Ser.). 1978. 135.00 (ISBN 0-407-00604-4). Butterworths.
Jackson, Jacquelyne J. Minorities & Aging. 272p. 1979. pap. text ed. 8.95x (ISBN 0-534-00779-1). Wadsworth Pub.
Jackson, James C., jt. auth. see Fryer, D. W.
Jackson, James R., jt. auth. see Henshaw, Richard C.
Jackson, Jane F. & Jackson, Joseph. Infant Culture. LC 78-4351. 1978. 9.95 o.s.i. (ISBN 0-690-01670-0, TYC-T). T Y Crowell.
Jackson, Janice E., jt. auth. see Schantz, William T.
Jackson, Jeremy C. No Other Foundation. LC 79-92017. 384p. 1979. pap. 12.95 (ISBN 0-89107-169-5, Cornerstone Bks). Good News.
Jackson, Jessica, jt. auth. see Jackson, Michael.
Jackson, Joan S., jt. ed. see De Ford, Miriam A.
Jackson, John A., ed. Professions & Professionalization. LC 75-123346. (Sociological Studies: No. 3). 1970. 30.50 (ISBN 0-521-07982-9). Cambridge U Pr.
Jackson, John G. Pagan Origins of the Christ Myth. 1980. pap. 3.00. Am Atheist.
Jackson, John H. & Bollinger, Lee C. Contract Law in Modern Society, Cases & Materials: Cases & Materials. 2nd ed. LC 80-15562. (American Casebook Ser.). 1478p. 1980. text ed. 23.95 (ISBN 0-8299-2098-6). West Pub.
Jackson, John H., jt. auth. see Mathis, Robert L.
Jackson, John J. Sport Administration. write for info. (ISBN 0-398-04440-6). C C Thomas.
Jackson, John M. & Shinn, Byron M. Fundamentals of Food Canning. (Illus.). 1979. text ed. 29.00 (ISBN 0-87055-257-0). AVI.
Jackson, John N. The Urban Future: A Choice Between Alternatives. (Urban & Regional Studies). 1972. text ed. 35.00x (ISBN 0-04-352034-0). Allen Unwin.
Jackson, John S., jt. ed. see De Vore, R. William.
Jackson, John W. Pennsylvania Navy, Seventeen Seventy-Five to Seventeen Eighty-One: The Defense of the Delaware. 2nd ed. (Illus.). 528p. 1974. 27.50 (ISBN 0-8135-0766-9). Rutgers U Pr.
Jackson, Joseph, jt. auth. see Jackson, Jane F.
Jackson, Joseph H. Bad Company: The Story of California's Legendary & Actual Stage-Robbers, Bandits, Highwaymen & Outlaws from the Fifties to the Eighties. LC 77-7300. (Illus.). 1977. 17.50x (ISBN 0-8032-0930-4); pap. 5.95 (ISBN 0-8032-5866-6, BB 649, Bison). U of Nebr Pr.
Jackson, Joseph H. & Baumert, John H. Pictorial Guide to the Planets. 3rd ed. LC 80-7897. (Illus.). 256p. 1981. 19.95 (ISBN 0-06-014869-1, HarpT). Har-Row.
Jackson, Joseph H., III. Pictorial Guide to the Planets. rev. & enl. ed. LC 72-7573. (Illus.). 256p. 1973. 13.95 o.s.i. (ISBN 0-690-62443-3, TYC-T). T Y Crowell.
Jackson, Judy. The Home Book of Jewish Cookery. 176p. 1981. 24.00 (ISBN 0-571-11697-3, Pub. by Faber & Faber); pap. 9.95 (ISBN 0-571-11737-6). Merrimack Bk Serv.
Jackson, K. G. & Feinberg, R. Dictionary of Electrical Engineering. 2nd ed. 1981. text ed. price not set (ISBN 0-408-00450-9, Newnes-Butterworth). Butterworth.
Jackson, Karl D. Traditional Authority, Islam, & Rebellion: A Study of Indonesian Political Behavior. 1980. 22.50x (ISBN 0-520-03769-3). U of Cal Pr.
Jackson, Kathryn. The Animals' Merry Christmas. (Illus.). 72p. (ps-3). 1950. PLB 9.15 (ISBN 0-307-63773-5, Golden Pr); pap. 2.95 (ISBN 0-307-13773-2). Western Pub.
--Around the World with Koa Koala. (Illus.). 144p. (ps-3). 1974. PLB 12.23 o.p. (ISBN 0-307-66817-7, Golden Pr). Western Pub.
--Golden Book of Three Hundred Sixty-Five Stories. 1955. 6.95 (ISBN 0-307-15557-9, Golden Pr); PLB 12.23 o.p. (ISBN 0-307-65575-X). Western Pub.
--Tawny, Scrawny Lion. (Illus.). (ps-3). 1952. PLB 5.00 (ISBN 0-307-60138-2, Golden Pr). Western Pub.
Jackson, Kathryn & Jackson, Byron. The Big Elephant. (Illus.). 32p. (ps-1). 1974. PLB 7.15 o.p. (ISBN 0-307-62064-6, Golden Pr). Western Pub.
--Saggy, Baggy Elephant. (Illus.). (ps-1). 1975. PLB 5.38 (ISBN 0-307-68908-5, Golden Pr). Western Pub.
Jackson, Kenneth T. Ku Klux Klan in the City, 1915-1930. (Urban Life in America Ser.). 1967. 17.95 (ISBN 0-19-500591-0); pap. text ed. 4.50x (ISBN 0-19-500918-5). Oxford U Pr.
Jackson, Laird G. & Schimke, R. Neil. Clinical Genetics: A Sourcebook for Physicians. LC 78-24414. 1979. 42.95 (ISBN 0-471-01943-7, Pub. by Wiley Medical). Wiley.

Jackson, Louise A. Grandpa Had a Windmill, Grandma Had a Churn. LC 77-23313. (Illus.). 40p. (gr. k-6). 1977. 6.25 o.s.i. (ISBN 0-8193-0872-2, Four Winds); PLB 5.71 o.s.i. (ISBN 0-8193-0873-0). Schol Bk Serv.

Jackson, M., et al. Vaginal Contraception. 1980. lib. bdg. 29.95 (ISBN 0-8161-2211-3, Medical Publications). G K Hall.

Jackson, M. D. Welding: Methods & Metallurgy. 422p. 1967. 37.50x (ISBN 0-85264-003-X, Pub. by Griffin England). State Mutual Bk.

Jackson, MacD. P. Studies in Attribution: Shakespeare & Middleton. (SSEL Jacobean Drama Studies: No. 79). (Orig.). 1979. pap. text ed. 25.00x (ISBN 0-391-01699-7). Humanities.

Jackson, Mahalia. Mahalia Jackson Cooks Soul. LC 74-114780. cancelled o.s.i. (ISBN 0-87695-014-4). Aurora Pubs.

Jackson, Margaret E., et al. General Chemistry Laboratory Manual. 1977. pap. text ed. 6.95 o.p. (ISBN 0-8403-1204-0). Kendall-Hunt.

Jackson, Martin, jt. auth. see Cassel, Don.

Jackson, Marvin. Mama Was a Preacher. 5.95 (ISBN 0-686-05781-3). Prod Hse.

Jackson, Mary H. Que divertido! (gr. 9-12). 1978. pap. text ed. 4.80 (ISBN 0-205-05881-7, 4258819). Allyn.

Jackson, Mason. Pictorial Press, Its Origin & Progress. LC 68-21776. (Illus.). 1968. Repr. of 1885 ed. 15.00 (ISBN 0-8103-3355-4). Gale.

Jackson, Melvin H. Privateers in Charleston, 1793 to 1796. (Illus.). 160p. 1969. 17.50x (ISBN 0-87474-158-0). Smithsonian.

Jackson, Michael & Jackson, Jessica. Your Father's Not Coming Home Anymore: Children Tell How They Survive Divorce. Jackson, Bruce, ed. 324p. 1981. 12.95 (ISBN 0-399-90109-4). Marek.

Jackson, Michael P. & Valencia, B. Michael. Financial Aid Through Social Work. (Library of Social Work Ser.). 1979. 17.00x (ISBN 0-7100-0176-2). Routledge & Kegan.

Jackson, Mildred. Blame the Teacher? LC 79-54107. 180p. 1979. 5.95 (ISBN 0-8059-2672-0). Dorrance.

Jackson, Nancy E., et al. Cognitive Development in Young Children. Goulet, Larry, ed. LC 77-1725. (Basic Concepts in Educational Psychology Ser.). 1977. pap. text ed. 5.95 o.p. (ISBN 0-8185-0225-8). Brooks-Cole.

Jackson, Neil. Civil Engineering Materials. LC 76-381536. (Illus.). 1977. pap. 17.50x (ISBN 0-333-19310-5). Scholium Intl.

Jackson, P. B. & Ribbinck, Tony. Mbunas, Malawi Cichlids. (Illus.). 128p. (Orig.). 1975. pap. 5.95 (ISBN 0-87666-454-0, PS-740). TFH Pubns.

Jackson, P. M., jt. auth. see Brown, C. V.

Jackson, P. M., jt. ed. see Cook, S. T.

Jackson, R., jt. ed. see Corbet, H.

Jackson, Raymond, jt. ed. see Boochever, Florence.

Jackson, Richard. Holistic Massage. rev. ed. LC 77-72393. (Illus.). 128p. 1980. pap. 5.95 (ISBN 0-8069-8382-5). Sterling.

Jackson, Richard H. Land Use in America. LC 80-20184. (Scripta Ser. in Geography). 224p. 1981. 29.95 (ISBN 0-470-27063-2). Halsted Pr.

Jackson, Richard L. Black Writers in Latin America. LC 78-21431. 1979. 12.50x (ISBN 0-8263-0501-6). U of NM Pr.

Jackson, Richard M. The Machinery of Justice in England. 7th ed. LC 77-4401. 1978. 74.50 (ISBN 0-521-21688-5); pap. 24.95 (ISBN 0-521-29231-X). Cambridge U Pr.

Jackson, Robert. Air War Over Korea. LC 74-19687. 1975. 9.95 o.p. (ISBN 0-684-14193-0, ScribT). Scribner.

--Dunkirk. LC 79-89323. (World War II Ser.). 1980. pap. 2.25 (ISBN 0-87216-597-3). Playboy Pbks.

--Fighter Pilots of World War II. 1977. pap. 1.50 (ISBN 0-505-51192-4). Tower Bks.

--Morphological Dermatology: A Study of the Living Gross Pathology of the Skin. (Illus.). 368p. 1979. text ed. 34.50 (ISBN 0-398-03849-X). C C Thomas.

--South Asian Crisis - India, Pakistan, & Bangladesh: A Political & Historical Analysis of the 1971 War. LC 74-8921. (Special Studies). (Illus.). 240p. 1975. text ed. 17.95 o.p. (ISBN 0-275-09560-6). Praeger.

--World Military Aircraft Since Nineteen Forty-Five. (Illus.). 1980. 10.95 (ISBN 0-684-16265-2, ScribT). Scribner.

Jackson, Robert J. & Atkinson, Michael M. The Canadian Legislative System: Politicians & Policy-Making. 1980. pap. 8.95x (ISBN 0-7705-0960-6, Pub. by Macmillan of Canada). NYU Pr.

Jackson, Robert L., ed. Twentieth Century Interpretations of Crime & Punishment. (Twentieth Century Interpretations Ser.). (Illus.). 128p. 1973. 8.95 (ISBN 0-13-193086-9, Spec). P-H.

Jackson, Robert W. Jonathan Swift: Dean & Pastor. 185p. 1980. Repr. of 1939 ed. lib. bdg. 20.00 (ISBN 0-8492-1279-0). R West.

Jackson, Robert Wyse see Wyse Jackson, Robert.

Jackson, Ronald V. & Teeples, Gary R. Index to South Carolina Land Grants, 1794-1800. LC 77-86082. (Illus.). Date not set. lib. bdg. price not set (ISBN 0-89593-134-6). Accelerated Index.

Jackson, Russell L. The Physicians of Essex County (Mass.) (Illus.). 152p. 1948. 10.00 o.p. (ISBN 0-88389-009-7). Essex Inst.

Jackson, Ruth. The Cervical Syndrome. 4th ed. (Amer. Lec. in Orthopaedic Surgery Ser.). (Illus.). 416p. 1978. 26.50 (ISBN 0-398-03696-9). C C Thomas.

--Combing the Coast. (Illus.). 160p. 1972. pap. 3.95 o.p. (ISBN 0-87701-014-5). Chronicle Bks.

Jackson, Ruth A. Combing the Coast: San Francisco to Santa Cruz. (Illus.). 116p. (Orig.). 1981. pap. 4.95 (ISBN 0-87701-140-0). Chronicle Bks.

Jackson, S. E. & Taylor, G. R. School Organization for the Mentally Retarded: Basic Guides. 2nd ed. (Illus.). 160p. 1973. 13.75 (ISBN 0-398-02742-0). C C Thomas.

Jackson, S. Trevena. Fanny Crosby's Story. (Christian Biography Ser.). 198p. 1981. pap. 2.95 (ISBN 0-8010-5127-4). Baker Bk.

Jackson, Samuel M., tr. see Zwingli, Ulrich.

Jackson, Sarah & Patterson, Mary Ann. A Children's History of Texas: Text & Coloring Book. (Illus.). (gr. 1-6). 2.50 (ISBN 0-685-48834-9). Nortex Pr.

Jackson, Sheila. Costumes for the Stage: A Complete Handbook for Every Kind of Play. (Illus.). 1978. 12.95 (ISBN 0-87690-298-0). Dutton.

Jackson, Sheldon G. A British Ranchero in Old California: The Life & Times of Henry Dalton & the Rancho Azusa. LC 77-79745. (Western Frontiersmen Ser.: Vol. 17). (Illus.). 1977. 22.50 o.p. (ISBN 0-87062-122-X). A H Clark.

Jackson, Shirley. Lottery. LC 79-24173. 1980. Repr. of 1949 ed. 12.50x (ISBN 0-8376-0455-9). Bentley.

--The Lottery. 224p. 1975. pap. 2.50 (ISBN 0-445-00300-6). Popular Lib.

--The Lottery or, The Adventures of James Harris. LC 79-24173. 1980. Repr. of 1949 ed. lib. bdg. 12.50x (ISBN 0-8376-0455-9). Bentley.

--We Have Always Lived in the Castle. 1974. pap. 2.25 (ISBN 0-445-08321-2). Popular Lib.

--Witchcraft of Salem Village. (gr. 4-6). 1956. 2.95 o.p. (ISBN 0-394-80369-8, BYR). Random.

Jackson, Stanley E., jt. auth. see Taylor, George R.

Jackson, T. H. Number Theory. (Library of Mathematics). 1975. pap. 5.00 (ISBN 0-7100-7998-2). Routledge & Kegan.

Jackson, Thomas, ed. Nuclear Waste Management: The Ocean Alternative- Edited Proceedings of a Public Policy Forum Sponsored by the Oceanic Society in the Georgetown University Law Center, DC, February 6, 1980. (Pergamon Policy Studies on Energy). (Illus.). 100p. 15.00 (ISBN 0-08-027204-5). Pergamon.

Jackson, Tom. Twenty-Eight Days to a Better Job. 1977. pap. 6.95 (ISBN 0-8015-8013-7, Hawthorn). Dutton.

Jackson, Valerie, jt. auth. see Flick, Pauline.

Jackson, W. A. Douglas see Creed, Virginia & Douglas Jackson, W. A.

Jackson, W. H. Rocky Mountain Railroad Album: Stream & Steel Cross the Great Divide. (Illus.). 79p. 195.00 (ISBN 0-913582-14-X). Sundance.

Jackson, W. P. Estimating Home Building Costs. 288p. (Orig.). 1981. pap. 14.00 (ISBN 0-910460-80-9). Craftsman.

Jackson, W. Turrentine. Wagon Roads West: A Study of Federal Road Surveys and Construction in the Trans-Mississippi West, 1846-1869. LC 79-13959. (Illus.). 1979. 19.95x (ISBN 0-8032-4405-3); pap. 6.50 (ISBN 0-8032-9402-6, BB 712, Bison). U of Nebr Pr.

Jackson, Wallace. Immediacy: The Development of a Critical Concept from Addison to Coleridge. LC 72-93571. 129p. (Orig.). 1973. pap. text ed. 14.25x (ISBN 0-391-01991-0). Humanities.

--The Probable & the Marvelous: Blake, Wordsworth, & the Eighteenth-Century Critical Tradition. LC 77-17807. 1978. 16.00x (ISBN 0-8203-0439-5). U of Ga Pr.

Jackson, Ward C. & Harvey, Denis E. English Gypsy Caravan. 1974. 16.95 (ISBN 0-7153-5680-1). David & Charles.

Jackson, Wes. New Roots for Agriculture. LC 79-56913. (Orig.). 1980. pap. 4.95 (ISBN 0-913890-38-3). Friends Earth.

Jackson, William. Overlord: Normandy, Nineteen Forty-Four. Frankland, Noble & Dowling, Christopher, eds. LC 79-52238. (The Politics & Strategy of the Second World War Ser.). 1979. 15.00 (ISBN 0-87413-161-8). U Delaware Pr.

Jackson, William, jt. auth. see Martin, Joseph H.

Jackson, William E. Reinmars Women: A Study of the Womans Song of Reinmar der Alte. (German Language & Literature Monographs: No. 9). 300p. 1980. text ed. 37.25x (ISBN 90-272-4002-7). Humanities.

Jackson, William J. Sai Krishna Lila. LC 80-67137. 1980. pap. 3.60 (ISBN 0-9600958-7-X). Birth Day.

Jackson, William T. Anatomy of Love: A Study of the Tristan of Gottfried Von Strassburg. LC 70-154859. 1971. 16.00x (ISBN 0-231-03504-7). Columbia U Pr.

--Literature of the Middle Ages. LC 60-13153. 1960. 20.00x (ISBN 0-231-02429-0). Columbia U Pr.

Jackson-Beeck, Marilyn see Bishop, George F., et al.

Jackson-Stevens, E. British Electric Tramways. (Illus.). 112p. 1971. 16.95 (ISBN 0-7153-5105-2). David & Charles.

Jackson-Stops, Gervase, ed. National Trust Studies Nineteen Seventy-Nine. (Illus.). 184p. 1978. 27.50x (ISBN 0-85667-051-0, Pub. by Sotheby Parke Bernet England). Biblio Dist.

--National Trust Studies, 1980. (Illus.). 175p. 1979. 27.50x (ISBN 0-85667-065-0, Pub. by Sotheby Parke Bernet England). Biblio Dist.

--National Trust Studies 1981. (Illus.). 160p. 1980. 32.50x (ISBN 0-85667-110-X, Pub. by Sotheby Parke Bernet England). Biblio Dist.

Jaco, William. Lectures on Three-Manifold Topology. LC 79-28488. (CBMS Regional Conference Series in Mathematics: No. 43). 1980. 9.60 (ISBN 0-8218-1693-4). Am Math.

Jacob, Anthony. White Man, Think Again. pap. 4.00x (ISBN 0-911038-09-4). Noontide.

Jacob, Archibald. Musical Handwriting. (Music Reprint Ser.). 1979. Repr. of 1947 ed. lib. bdg. 13.50 (ISBN 0-306-79578-7). Da Capo.

Jacob, E. F., ed. Italian Renaissance Studies. 1960. 24.95 o.p. (ISBN 0-571-06930-4, Pub. by Faber & Faber). Merrimack Bk Serv.

Jacob, E. F., jt. ed. see Crump, C. G.

Jacob, Ernest F. Fifteenth Century, Thirteen Ninety-Nine to Fourteen Eighty-Five. (Oxford History of England Ser.). 1961. 33.00x (ISBN 0-19-821714-5). Oxford U Pr.

Jacob, Gale S. Independent Reading Grades One Through Three: An Annotated Bibliography with Reading Levels. LC 78-26607. 1975. pap. 4.50 o.p. (ISBN 0-87272-064-0). Brodart.

Jacob, Giles see Hale, Sir Matthew.

Jacob, Giles, jt. auth. see Somers, John.

Jacob, Giles, et al. Laws of Liberty & Property. Berkowitz, David. S. & Thorne, Samuel E., eds. LC 77-89197. (Classics of English Legal History in the Modern Era Ser.: Vol. 56). 325p. 1979. lib. bdg. 40.00 (ISBN 0-8240-3156-3). Garland Pub.

Jacob, Gordon. The Elements of Orchestration. LC 76-15191. 1976. Repr. of 1962 ed. lib. bdg. 22.25x (ISBN 0-8371-8955-1, JAEO). Greenwood.

Jacob, Henry. An Attestation of Many Learned, Godly, & Famous Divines...Justifying...That the Church Government Ought to Bee Always with the Peoples Free Consent. LC 74-28868. (English Experience Ser.: No. 747). 1975. Repr. of 1613 ed. 16.00 (ISBN 90-221-0747-7). Walter J Johnson.

--To the Right High & Mightie Prince James...An Humble Supplication for Toleration & Libertie. LC 74-28869. (English Experience Ser.: No. 748). 1975. Repr. of 1609 ed. 5.00 (ISBN 90-221-0748-5). Walter J Johnson.

Jacob, John. Making Play. (Orig.). 1975. pap. 2.50x (ISBN 0-915316-21-8); pap. 3.00 ltd. signed ed. (ISBN 0-915316-22-6). Pentagram.

Jacob, Lucy M. Sri Lanka from Dominion to Republic. LC 73-906251. 243p. 1973. 11.50x o.p. (ISBN 0-88386-250-6). South Asia Bks.

Jacob, Margaret C. The Radical Enlightenment: Pantheists, Fremasons & Republicans. (Early Modern Europe Today Ser.). (Illus.). 352p. 1981. text ed. 29.50x (ISBN 0-04-901029-8, 2595). Allen Unwin.

Jacob, Max. The Dice Cup: Selected Prose Poems. Brownstein, Michael, ed. Ashbery, John, et al, trs. LC 79-26610. 122p. (Orig.). 1980. pap. 5.00 (ISBN 0-915342-32-4). SUN.

Jacob, Nancy L., jt. auth. see Sharpe, William F.

Jacob, Paul. Alter Sonnets. 8.00 (ISBN 0-89253-481-8); flexible cloth 4.00 (ISBN 0-89253-482-6). Ind-US Inc.

--Sonnets. 8.00 (ISBN 0-89253-553-9); flexible cloth 4.00 (ISBN 0-89253-554-7). Ind-US Inc.

--Swedish Exercises. (Writers Workshop Redbird Ser.). 1975. 8.00 (ISBN 0-88253-656-7); pap. text ed. 4.00 (ISBN 0-88253-655-9). Ind-US Inc.

Jacob, Paul E. Remy de Gourmont. 176p. 1980. Repr. of 1931 ed. lib. bdg. 25.00 (ISBN 0-89984-260-7). Century Bookbindery.

Jacobe, Dennis & Kendall, James N. How to Get the Money to by Your New Home. 200p. 1981. 10.95 (ISBN 0-87094-258-1). Dow Jones-Irwin.

Jacobi, Charles A. Textbook of Anatomy & Physiology in Radiologic Technology. 2nd ed. LC 74-20889. 1975. text ed. 18.95 (ISBN 0-8016-2390-1). Mosby.

Jacobi, Charles T. The Printers' Vocabulary. LC 68-30613. 1975. Repr. of 1888 ed. 15.00 (ISBN 0-8103-3309-0). Gale.

Jacobi, Ernst. Work at Writing: A Workbook to Accompany Writing at Work. 112p. 1980. pap. text ed. 5.50x (ISBN 0-8104-6117-X). Hayden.

--Writing at Work: Do's, Dont's & How To's. 1976. 12.90 (ISBN 0-8104-5730-X); pap. 9.50 (ISBN 0-8104-5729-6). Hayden.

Jacobi, Hermann, tr. Jaina Sutras, Part One: The Akaranga Sutra, the Kapla Sutra. (The Sacred Books of the East Ser.: Vol. 22). Date not set. 6.50 (ISBN 0-8446-0725-8). Peter Smith.

--Jaina Sutras, Part Two: The Uttaradyayana Sutra, the Sutrakritanga Sutra, Vol. 45. (The Sacred Books of the East Ser.). Date not set. 6.50 (ISBN 0-8446-0726-6). Peter Smith.

Jacobi, Jolande. Masks of the Soul. 1976. pap. text ed. 2.95 o.p. (ISBN 0-8028-1656-8). Eerdmans.

Jacobi, Jolande, ed. see Jung, Carl G.

Jacobi, Karl G. Gesammelte Werke, 8 vols. 2nd ed. LC 68-31427. (Illus., Ger., Includes Supplementband Vorlesugen Uber Dynamik). 1969. Vols. 1-7. 160.00 (ISBN 0-8284-0226-4); Vol. 8. 15.00 (ISBN 0-8284-0227-2). Chelsea Pub.

Jacobitti, Edmund D. Revolutionary Humanism & Historicism in Modern Italy. LC 80-5393. 240p. 1981. text ed. 18.00x (ISBN 0-300-02479-7). Yale U Pr.

Jacobowitz, Henry. Electricity Made Simple. pap. 3.50 (ISBN 0-385-00436-2, Made). Doubleday.

--Electronic Computers Made Simple. LC 62-7648. 1963. pap. 3.95 (ISBN 0-385-03225-0, Made). Doubleday.

--Electronics Made Simple. rev. ed. LC 64-20579. pap. 3.50 (ISBN 0-385-01227-6, Made). Doubleday.

Jacobs, Albert L. Patent & Trademark Forms, 4 vols. LC 67-26112. 1977. looseleaf with 1979 rev. pages 210.00 (ISBN 0-87632-217-8); Vols. 4 & 4A. 110.00; Vols. 4B & 4C. 111.00; Vols. 4, 4A, 4B, & 4C. 210.00. Boardman.

Jacobs, Angeline M., et al. Critical Behaviors in Psychiatric-Mental Health Nursing: Monograph, 2 vols. Incl. Vol. 1. A Survey of Mental Health Nursing Practices. 119p. pap. 4.00 (ISBN 0-89785-546-9); Vol. 3. Behavior of Attendants. 525p. pap. 8.50 (ISBN 0-89785-547-7). 1973. Am Inst Res.

Jacobs, Arnold S. The Impact of Rule 10b-5, 3 vols. LC 74-27270. 1974. looseleaf with 1979 rev. pages 165.00 (ISBN 0-87632-093-0). Boardman.

Jacobs, Arthur. Short History of Western Music. 16.95 (ISBN 0-7153-5743-3). David & Charles.

Jacobs, Arthur, ed. British Music Yearbook, 1980. 6th ed. 637p. 1980. pap. 24.50x (ISBN 0-8476-6255-1). Rowman.

Jacobs, Arthur, tr. see Gossett, et al.

Jacobs, B. E., jt. auth. see Baker, P. J.

Jacobs, Barry L. & Gelperin, Alan, eds. Serotonin Transmission & Behavior. 430p. 1981. text ed. 45.00x (ISBN 0-686-69226-8). MIT Pr.

Jacobs, Bert & Jacobs, Isabel. Home Pool Safety. LC 77-26215. (Illus.). 1978. 13.95 (ISBN 0-88229-392-3); pap. 7.95 (ISBN 0-88229-509-8). Nelson-Hall.

Jacobs, Betty E. Growing Herbs for the Kitchen. (Illus.). 1972. 6.95 (ISBN 0-910458-14-6). Select Bks.

Jacobs, C. M., tr. see Luther, Martin.

Jacobs, Charles, ed. see Fuenllana, Miguel De.

Jacobs, Clyde. Justice Frankfurter & Civil Liberties. LC 74-1331. (Civil Liberties in American History Ser.). 265p. 1974. Repr. of 1961 ed. lib. bdg. 25.00 (ISBN 0-306-70585-0). Da Capo.

Jacobs, Clyde E. Law Writers & the Courts. LC 73-251. (American Constitutional & Legal History Ser.). 234p. 1973. Repr. of 1954 ed. lib. bdg. 25.00 (ISBN 0-306-70570-2). Da Capo.

Jacobs, Dan N. & Paul, Ellen F., eds. Studies of the Third Wave: Recent Migration of Soviet Jews to the United States. (Replica Edition Ser.). 176p. 1981. lib. bdg. 20.00x (ISBN 0-86531-143-9). Westview.

Jacobs, Dan N., et al. Comparative Politics: Introduction to the Politics of Britain, France, Germany, & the Soviet Union. pap. 9.95 (ISBN 0-934540-05-5). Chatham Hse Pubs.

--Comparative Politics: Introduction to the Politics of Britain, the United Kingdom, France, Germany, & the Soviet Union. 320p. 1981. pap. text ed. 9.95x (ISBN 0-934540-05-5). Chatham Hse Pubs.

Jacobs, David & Forbes, Elliot. Beethoven. (Horizon Caravel Bks). (Illus.). 152p. (gr. 6 up). 1970. 9.95 (ISBN 0-8281-5026-5, J039-0); PLB 12.89 (ISBN 0-06-022797-4, Dist. by Har-Row). Am Heritage.

Jacobs, David & Mango, Cyril A. Constantinople, City on the Golden Horn. LC 78-81403. (Horizon Caravel Bks). (Illus.). 153p. (gr. 6 up). 1969. 9.95 (ISBN 0-8281-5003-6, J037-0); PLB 6.89 (ISBN 0-06-022799-0, Dist. by Har-Row). Am Heritage.

Jacobs, Dick. An MG Experience. (Illus.). 1976. 15.95 (ISBN 0-85184-013-2, Pub. by Transport Bookman Ltd. England). Motorbooks Intl.

Jacobs, Don. Happy Exercise: An Adventure into a Fit World. LC 80-23547. (Illus.). 48p. (Orig.). (ps-5). 1980. pap. 4.95 (ISBN 0-89037-170-9). Anderson World.

Jacobs, Don T. Getting Your Executives Fit. LC 79-64731. (Illus.). 256p. (Orig.). 1981. pap. 12.95 (ISBN 0-89037-176-8). Anderson World.

Jacobs, Donald P., et al. Financial Institutions. 5th ed. 1972. text ed. 17.50x o.p. (ISBN 0-256-00262-2). Irwin.

Jacobs, Erwin M. & DeNault, Phyllis M. Neurology for Nurses: Including Nursing Technics in Neurology. (Illus.). 208p. 1964. 13.75 (ISBN 0-398-00908-2). C C Thomas.

Jacobs, Eva, et al, eds. Woman & Society in Eighteenth Century France: Essays in Honour of John Stephenson Spink. 1979. text ed. 37.50x (ISBN 0-485-11184-5, Athlone Pr). Humanities.

Jacobs, Flora G. Dolls' Houses in America: Historic Preservation in Miniature. LC 73-1100. (Encore Edition). (Illus.). 1978. pap. 6.95 (ISBN 0-684-16905-3). Scribner.

--A History of Doll Houses. LC 65-24648. 1965. pap. 14.95 (ISBN 0-684-14538-3, SL630, ScribT). Scribner.

Jacobs, Francine. Barracuda: Tiger of the Sea. (Illus.). 48p. (gr. 1-4). 1981. 8.95 (ISBN 0-8027-6413-4); lib. bdg. 9.85 (ISBN 0-8027-6414-2). Walker & Co.

--Bermuda Petrel: The Bird That Would Not Die. LC 80-20466. (Illus.). 40p. (gr. k-3). 1981. 7.95 (ISBN 0-688-00240-4); PLB 7.63 (ISBN 0-688-00244-7). Morrow.

--Nature's Light: The Story of Bioluminescence. LC 73-18326. (Illus.). 96p. (gr. 3-7). 1974. 7.25 (ISBN 0-688-20115-6); PLB 6.96 (ISBN 0-688-30115-0). Morrow.

--The Red Sea. (Illus.). (gr. 4-6). 1978. 6.95 (ISBN 0-688-22150-5); PLB 6.67 (ISBN 0-688-32150-X). Morrow.

--The Sargasso Sea: An Ocean Desert. LC 74-30376. (Illus.). 96p. (gr. 3-7). 1975. PLB 6.48 o.p. (ISBN 0-688-32029-5). Morrow.

--Sea Turtles. LC 74-187717. (Illus.). 64p. (gr. 3-7). 1972. PLB 6.00 o.p. (ISBN 0-688-31937-8). Morrow.

--A Secret Language of Animals, Communication by Pheromones. LC 75-42409. (gr. 4-6). 1976. 6.25 (ISBN 0-688-22071-1); PLB 6.00 (ISBN 0-688-32071-6). Morrow.

--Sounds in the Sea. LC 77-345. (Illus.). (gr. 3-7). 1977. 6.25 (ISBN 0-688-22113-0); PLB 6.00 (ISBN 0-688-32113-5). Morrow.

Jacobs, Frank. Mad's Talking Stamps. (Mad Ser.). (Illus.). 192p. (Orig.). 1974. pap. 1.50 (ISBN 0-446-88752-8). Warner Bks.

Jacobs, Frank & Clarke, Bob. Mad Goes Wild. (Mad Ser.). (Illus., Orig.). 1981. pap. 1.75 (ISBN 0-446-94283-9). Warner Bks.

--More Mad About Sports. (Mad Ser.). (Illus., Orig.). 1977. pap. 1.75 (ISBN 0-446-94600-1). Warner Bks.

Jacobs, Fred E. Takeoffs & Touchdowns: My Sixty Years of Flying. LC 80-28865. (Illus.). 304p. 1981. 12.95 (ISBN 0-498-02540-3). A S Barnes.

Jacobs, G., jt. ed. see Gerstl, Joel.

Jacobs, Gabriel. When Children Think: Using Journals to Encourage Creative Thinking. LC 71-78837. 1970. pap. text ed. 4.75 (ISBN 0-8077-1558-1). Tchrs Coll.

Jacobs, H. S., jt. auth. see Foth, H.

Jacobs, Harold R. Elementary Algebra. LC 78-10744. (Illus.). 1979. text ed. 12.95x (ISBN 0-7167-1047-1); tchrs. guide 7.95x (ISBN 0-7167-1075-7); test masters 7.95x (ISBN 0-7167-1077-3); transparency masters 50.00x (ISBN 0-7167-1076-5). W H Freeman.

--Geometry. LC 73-20024. (Illus.). 1974. text ed. 12.95 (ISBN 0-7167-0456-0); tchr's guide 6.95x (ISBN 0-7167-0460-9); test masters 4.95x (ISBN 0-7167-0459-5); transparency masters 45.00x (ISBN 0-7167-0458-7). W H Freeman.

--Mathematics, a Human Endeavor: A Textbook for Those Who Think They Don't Like the Subject. LC 70-116898. (Illus.). 1970. text ed. 11.95x (ISBN 0-7167-0439-0); tchr's guide 6.95x (ISBN 0-7167-0446-3). W H Freeman.

Jacobs, Helen J., ed. see McCully, Ron.

Jacobs, Howard. Charlie the Mole & Other Droll Souls. LC 73-12219. (Illus.). 288p. 1973. 5.95 (ISBN 0-88289-001-8). Pelican.

Jacobs, Howard, ed. see Trosclair.

Jacobs, Isabel, jt. auth. see Jacobs, Bert.

Jacobs, J. A. The Earth's Core. (International Geophysics Ser.). 1976. 25.00 (ISBN 0-12-378950-8). Acad Pr.

--A Textbook on Geonomy. LC 74-9662. 328p. 1974. text ed. 28.95 (ISBN 0-470-43445-7). Halsted Pr.

Jacobs, Jack & Braum, Myron. The Films of Norma Shearer. LC 74-9286. (Illus.). 320p. 1976. 17.50 o.p. (ISBN 0-498-01552-1). A S Barnes.

Jacobs, Jane. Economy of Cities. LC 69-16413. 1969. 5.95 o.p. (ISBN 0-394-42296-1). Random.

--The Question of Separatism: Quebec & the Struggle Over Sovereignty. LC 80-5268. (Illus.). 160p. 1980. 8.95 (ISBN 0-394-50981-1). Random.

Jacobs, Jerome L. Interplay. 1979. 10.00 (ISBN 0-07-032146-9). Readers Digest Pr.

Jacobs, Jerry. Adolescent Suicide: With a New Preface. 1980. text ed. 18.00x o.p. (ISBN 0-8290-0113-1); pap. text ed. 8.95x (ISBN 0-8290-0114-X). Irvington.

--Mental Retardation: A Phenomenological Approach. (Illus.). 244p. 1980. 24.50 (ISBN 0-398-04062-1); pap. 16.75 (ISBN 0-398-04063-X). C C Thomas.

--Older Persons & Retirement Communities: Case Studies in Social Gerontology. 144p. 1975. 14.75 (ISBN 0-398-03445-1); pap. 9.75 (ISBN 0-398-03446-X). C C Thomas.

Jacobs, Joel H. The Myths & the Truth About Selecting a Marine Sextant. LC 75-4318. (Illus.). 1975. pap. 3.00 (ISBN 0-87033-203-1). Cornell Maritime.

Jacobs, John J., jt. auth. see Tobin, Charles E.

Jacobs, John K. Against All Odds. (gr. 7 up). 1967. 8.95g (ISBN 0-02-747580-8). Macmillan.

Jacobs, Joseph. Jack & the Beanstalk. Walser, David, tr. LC 77-23586. (The Jan Pienkowski Fairy Tale Lib.). (Illus.). (gr. 1 up). 1978. 2.95 o.p. (ISBN 0-690-03821-6, TYC-J). T Y Crowell.

--The Stars in the Sky. LC 78-11718. (Illus.). 32p. (ps-3). 1979. 6.95 (ISBN 0-374-37229-2). FS&G.

Jacobs, Joseph, ed. see Aesop.

Jacobs, Joseph, ed. see Painter, William.

Jacobs, Judy, jt. auth. see Enteen, Shellie.

Jacobs, Kenneth C., jt. ed. see Saslaw, William C.

Jacobs, Lawrence, et al. Computerized Tomography of the Orbit & Sella Turcica. 1980. text ed. 92.00 (ISBN 0-685-95340-8). Raven.

Jacobs, Leland B., ed. Using Literature with Young Children. LC 65-24617. (Illus., Orig.). 1965. pap. 4.75x (ISBN 0-8077-1557-3). Tchrs Coll.

Jacobs, Leo M. A Deaf Adult Speaks Out. 2nd, rev. ed. xiv, 192p. 1981. 7.95 (ISBN 0-913580-63-5); pap. 5.95 (ISBN 0-913580-71-6). Gallaudet Coll.

Jacobs, Lewis. Rise of the American Film: A Critical History with an Essay "Experimental Cinema in America 1921-1947". LC 68-25845. (Illus.). 1968. text ed. 21.50 (ISBN 0-8077-1556-5); pap. 14.95x (ISBN 0-8077-1555-7). Tchrs Coll.

Jacobs, Lewis, ed. Compound Cinema: The Film Writings of Harry Alan Potamkin. LC 76-55401. 1977. text ed. 26.50 (ISBN 0-8077-1559-X). Tchrs Coll.

Jacobs, Lou, Jr. Basic Guide to Photography. 2nd ed. Stensvold, Mike, ed. LC 73-79969. (Photography How-to Ser.). (Illus.). (gr. 8-12). 1980. pap. 5.95 (ISBN 0-8227-4038-9). Petersen Pub.

--The Konica Guide. rev. ed. (Illus.). 128p. 1980. 11.95 (ISBN 0-8174-4124-7); pap. 6.95 (ISBN 0-8174-4125-5). Amphoto.

Jacobs, Louis. Chain of Tradition Series, 5 vols. Incl. Vol. 1. Jewish Law. LC 68-27329. pap. text ed. 3.95x (ISBN 0-87441-211-0); Vol. 2. Jewish Ethics, Philosophy & Mysticism. LC 71-80005. pap. text ed. 3.95x (ISBN 0-87441-212-9); Vol. 3. Jewish Thought Today. LC 73-116679. (Illus.). 1974. pap. text ed. 3.95x (ISBN 0-87441-213-7); Vol. 4. Hasidic Thought. pap. text ed. o.p. (ISBN 0-87441-242-0); Vol. 5. Jewish Biblical Exegesis. pap. text ed. 4.50x o.p. (ISBN 0-685-63822-7). LC 78-1487. (Illus.). (gr. 8 up). 1974. Behrman.

Jacobs, M., ed. see Buchner, G.

Jacobs, Marcia, jt. auth. see Greenberg, Dan.

Jacobs, Marjorie K., ed. see Wine Advisory Board.

Jacobs, Milton C. Outline of Theatre Law. LC 72-5454. 148p. 1972. Repr. of 1949 ed. lib. bdg. 12.50x (ISBN 0-8371-6436-2, JATL). Greenwood.

Jacobs, Norman. Fab Fifties. LC 79-63383. 1979. pap. 1.95 (ISBN 0-931064-09-0). Starlog.

--Fab Fifties. 1980. pap. 2.25. O'Quinn Studio.

Jacobs, O. L. Introduction to Control Theory. 378p. 1974. 29.95x (ISBN 0-19-856108-3). Oxford U Pr.

Jacobs, Paul. Prelude to Riot: A View of Urban America from the Bottom. 1968. pap. 2.45 o.p. (ISBN 0-394-70433-9, Vin). Random.

Jacobs, Robert D., jt. ed. see Rubin, Louis D., Jr.

Jacobs, Roderick A., jt. auth. see Jacobs, Suzanne E.

Jacobs, Roderick A. & Rosenbaum, Peters S., eds. Readings in English Transformational Grammar. LC 76-88102. 277p. Repr. of 1970 ed. text ed. 12.50x (ISBN 0-87840-187-3). Georgetown U Pr.

Jacobs, Russell F. Problem Solving with the Calculator. (gr. 6-9). 1977. pap. text ed. 4.25 (ISBN 0-918272-00-9); tchr's guide with ans. key 0.75 (ISBN 0-918272-01-7); answer key 0.75 (ISBN 0-918272-02-5). Jacobs.

Jacobs, Stephen, et al, eds. Free-Electron Generators of Coherent Radiation. (Physics of Quantum Electronics: Vol. 7). 848p. 1980. text ed. cancelled (ISBN 0-201-05687-9). A-W.

--Adaptive Optics & Short Wavelength Sources. LC 78-17486. (Physics of Quantum Electronics: Vol. 6). (Illus.). text ed. cancelled o.s.i. (ISBN 0-201-05686-0, Adv Bk Prog). A-W.

Jacobs, Stephen F., et al, eds. Novel Sources of Coherent Radiation: Adaptive Optics. LC 78-3420. (Physics of Quantum Electronics: Vol. 5). (Illus.). text ed. cancelled o.s.i. (ISBN 0-201-05685-2, Adv Bk Prog). A-W.

--Physics of Quantum Electronics, 4 vols. Incl. Vol. 1. High Energy Lasers & Their Applications. cancelled o.s.i. (ISBN 0-201-05681-X); Vol. 2. Laser Applications to Optics & Spectroscopy. LC 75-1438. cancelled o.s.i. (ISBN 0-201-05682-8); Vol. 3. Laser Induced Fusion & X-Ray Studies. cancelled o.s.i. (ISBN 0-201-05683-6); Vol. 4. Laser Photochemistry, Tunable Lasers & Topics. LC 76-8326. cancelled o.s.i. (ISBN 0-201-05684-4). (Illus., Adv Bk Prog). A-W.

Jacobs, Stephen W. Wayne County: The Aesthetic Heritage of a Rural Area. LC 79-64132. (Architecture Worth Saving Ser.). (Illus.). 288p. 1979. 22.50 (ISBN 0-89062-044-X, Pub. by Wayne County Hist Soc); pap. 10.00 (ISBN 0-89062-041-5). Pub Ctr Cult Res.

Jacobs, Suzanne E. & Jacobs, Roderick A. The College Writer's Handbook. 2nd ed. LC 75-28036. 288p. 1976. pap. text ed. 9.50x (ISBN 0-471-43591-0). Wiley.

Jacobs, Sylvia M. The African Nexus: Black American Perspectives on the European Partitioning of Africa, 1880-1920. LC 80-660. (Contributions in Afro-American & African Studies: No. 55). (Illus.). 264p. 1981. lib. bdg. 27.50 (ISBN 0-313-22312-2, JEP/). Greenwood.

Jacobs, Vernon K. & Schoeneman, Charles W. The Taxpayers' Audit Survival Manual. 1981. 35.00 (ISBN 0-932496-08-3). Green Hill.

--Taxpayer's Audit Survival Manual. 256p. 1980. spiral bdg. 35.00 (ISBN 0-932496-08-3). Alexandria Hse.

Jacobs, W. J. Prince Henry the Navigator. (Visual Biography Ser). (Illus.). 64p. (gr. 4-5). 1973. PLB 4.90 o.p. (ISBN 0-531-00972-6). Watts.

Jacobs, Wilbur R. Wilderness Politics & Indian Gifts: The Northern Colonial Frontier, 1748-1763. LC 51-2149. Orig. Title: Anglo-French Rivalry Along the Ohio & Northwest Frontier-1748-1763. (Illus.). 1966. pap. 1.65 (ISBN 0-8032-5100-9, BB 351, Bison). U of Nebr Pr.

Jacobs, Wilbur R., et al. Turner, Bolton, & Webb: Three Historians of the American Frontier. (Illus.). 127p. (Orig.). 1979. pap. 4.95 (ISBN 0-295-95677-1). U of Wash Pr.

Jacobs, William. A Young Person's Book of Catholic Words. LC 80-2078. 128p. (gr. 6 up). 1981. pap. 2.75 (ISBN 0-385-17434-9, Im). Doubleday.

Jacobs, William J. Hernando Cortes. LC 73-9509. (Visual Biography Ser). (Illus.). 64p. (gr. 4-5). 1974. PLB 4.90 o.p. (ISBN 0-531-00974-2). Watts.

--Robert Cavelier De la Salle. LC 75-8598. (Visual Biography Ser). 64p. (gr. 4-6). 1975. PLB 4.90 o.p. (ISBN 0-531-02843-7). Watts.

--Roger Williams. LC 74-12280. (Visual Biography Ser). (Illus.). (gr. 4-6). 1975. PLB 4.90 o.p. (ISBN 0-531-02784-8). Watts.

--Samuel De Champlain. LC 73-14554. (Visual Biography Ser). (Illus.). 64p. (gr. 4-5). 1974. PLB 4.90 o.p. (ISBN 0-531-01275-1). Watts.

--William Bradford of Plymouth Colony. LC 74-870. (Visual Biography Ser.). (Illus.). 64p. (gr. 4-6). 1974. PLB 4.90 o.p. (ISBN 0-531-02724-4). Watts.

Jacobs, Wilma J. Any Love Notes Today? LC 76-48409. 143p. (Orig.). 1976. pap. 4.95 (ISBN 0-89146-002-0). Learn Pathways.

--Any Love Notes Today? 1976. 4.95 (ISBN 0-89146-002-0). J&J Dist.

Jacobs, Zeney, jt. auth. see French, Francis G.

Jacobs, Zeney P., et al. Computer Programming in the Basic Language. (gr. 9-12). 1978. pap. text ed. 11.60 (ISBN 0-205-05836-1, 2058367); tchrs.' guide 4.40 (ISBN 0-205-05837-X, 2058375). Allyn.

--Communicating with the Computer: Introductory Experiences, Fortran IV. (gr. 9-12). 1973. text ed. 11.40 (ISBN 0-205-03819-0, 2038196); tchrs'. guide 4.40 (ISBN 0-205-03820-4, 203820X). Allyn.

Jacobsen, C. J. Soviet Strategic Initiatives: Challenge & Response. LC 79-89850. 183p. 1979. 22.95 (ISBN 0-03-053216-7). Praeger.

Jacobsen, David, et al. Methods for Teaching: A Skills Approach. (Illus.). 304p. 1981. pap. text ed. 11.95 (ISBN 0-675-08079-7). Merrill.

Jacobsen, Gertrude A. William Blathwayt. (Yale Historical Studies, Miscellany: No. XXI). 1932. 47.50x (ISBN 0-685-69829-7). Elliots Bks.

Jacobsen, Gertrude A. & Lipman, Miriam H. Political Science. 2nd ed. (Illus.). 1979. pap. 3.95 (ISBN 0-06-460178-1, CO 178, COS). Har-Row.

--Political Science. rev. ed. (Orig.). 1965. pap. 3.50 o.p. (ISBN 0-06-460022-X, 22, COS). Har-Row.

Jacobsen, Henry. The Acts: Then & Now. LC 72-96738. 224p. 1973. pap. 3.95 (ISBN 0-88207-239-0). Victor Bks.

--The Good Life. LC 68-11556. 96p. 1968. pap. 2.95 (ISBN 0-88207-018-5). Victor Bks.

Jacobsen, Hermann. The Lexicon of Succulent Plants. (Illus.). 1974. 37.50 (ISBN 0-7137-0652-X, Pub by Blandford Pr England). Sterling.

Jacobsen, L., ed. Proceedings: 30th Annual Conference Preprint of Paper's Summaries. new ed. (Illus.). 1977. pap. 12.00 (ISBN 0-89208-090-6). Soc Photo Sci & Eng.

Jacobsen, Margret B. What Happens When Children Grow. 1977. pap. 2.50 o.p. (ISBN 0-88207-736-8). Victor Bks.

Jacobsen, Phebe R., jt. auth. see Stiverson, Gregory A.

Jacobsen, Thorkild. The Treasures of Darkness: A History of Mesopotamian Religon. LC 75-27576. (Illus.). 1976. 18.50x (ISBN 0-300-01844-4); pap. 4.95x (ISBN 0-300-02291-3). Yale U Pr.

Jacobsohn, Annette, tr. see Rauch, Georg von.

Jacobsohn, Peter, tr. see Rauch, Georg von.

Jacobson, Adrienne C., jt. auth. see Emery, Jared M.

Jacobson, Alan M. & Parmelee, Dean X., eds. Psychoanalysis: A Contemporary Appraisal. 250p. 1981. 20.00 (ISBN 0-87630-269-X). Brunner-Mazel.

Jacobson, Alma, jt. auth. see Jacobson, E. A.

Jacobson, Angeline. Contemporary Native American Literature: A Selected & Partially Annotated Bibliography. LC 77-56114. 1977. lib. bdg. 13.50 (ISBN 0-8108-1031-X). Scarecrow.

Jacobson, Bertil & Webster, John G. Medicine & Clinical Engineering. LC 76-13842. (Illus.). 1977. text ed. 28.95 (ISBN 0-13-572966-1). P-H.

Jacobson, Boyd, jt. auth. see Van Der Zee, John.

Jacobson, Clifford. Wilderness Canpeina & Campina. (Illus.). 1977. 13.95 (ISBN 0-87690-228-X); pap. 6.95 (ISBN 0-87690-229-8). Dutton.

Jacobson, Dale. Poems for Goya's Disparates. (Illus.). 48p. (Orig.). 1981. pap. 4.95 (ISBN 0-937310-00-X). Jazz Pr.

Jacobson, Dan. Rape of Tamar. Markel, Robert, ed. LC 78-119134. 1970. 5.95 o.s.i. (ISBN 0-02-558570-3). Macmillan.

--Through the Wilderness & Other Stories. 1968. 5.95 o.s.i. (ISBN 0-02-558550-9). Macmillan.

Jacobson, Daniel. The Gatherers. LC 76-9810. (Indians of North America Ser.). (Illus.). 96p. (gr. 7 up). 1977. PLB 5.90 (ISBN 0-531-00326-4). Watts.

--The Hunters. LC 74-963. (Indians of North America Ser.). 96p. (gr. 4-7). 1974. PLB 5.90 (ISBN 0-531-02725-2). Watts.

--The Language of the Revenger's Tragedy. (Salzburg Studies in English Literature, Jacobean Drama Studies: No. 38). 246p. 1974. pap. text ed. 25.00x (ISBN 0-391-01433-1). Humanities.

Jacobson, Daniel, ed. The Fisherman. LC 74-34264. (Indians of North America Ser). 96p. (gr. 4-7). 1975. PLB 4.90 o.p. (ISBN 0-531-02830-5). Watts.

Jacobson, David. Itinerant Townsmen: Friendship & Social Order in Urban Uganda. LC 72-89137. 160p. 1973. pap. 5.95 (ISBN 0-8465-3751-6). Benjamin-Cummings.

Jacobson, David B. Program for Revision: A Practical Guide. (Illus.). 352p. 1973. pap. text ed. 9.95 (ISBN 0-13-730671-7). P-H.

Jacobson, Doranne & Wadley, Susan. Women in India: Two Perspectives. 1977. 7.00x (ISBN 0-8364-0012-7); pap. text ed. 5.00x (ISBN 0-8364-0013-5). South Asia Bks.

Jacobson, E. A. & Jacobson, Alma. The Dental Assistant: Syllabus. 1978. pap. text ed. 9.75 (ISBN 0-89420-046-1, 198040); cassette recordings 228.60 (ISBN 0-89420-139-5, 198000). Natl Book.

Jacobson, Edmund. Biology of Emotions: New Understanding Derived from Biological Multidisciplinary Investigation; First Electrophysiological Measurements. (Illus.). 232p. 1967. pap. 9.75 spiral (ISBN 0-398-00909-0). C C Thomas.
--Modern Treatment of Tense Patients: Including the Neurotic & Depressed with Case Illustrations, Follow-Ups, & EMG Measurements. (Illus.). 484p. 1970. text ed. 45.50 photocopy ed. (ISBN 0-398-00910-4). C C Thomas.
Jacobson, Helen & Mischel, Florence. First Book of Letter Writing. (First Bks). (Illus.). (gr. 4-6). 1957. PLB 4.90 o.p. (ISBN 0-531-00569-0); pap. 1.25 (ISBN 0-685-21863-5). Watts.
Jacobson, Helen S., tr. see Kolupaev, Victor.
Jacobson, Howard. Racewalk to Fitness. 1980. 11.95 (ISBN 0-686-62860-8, 24938). S&S.
Jacobson, Howard B., ed. Mass Communications Dictionary: A Reference Work of Common Terminologies for Press, Print, Broadcast, Film, Advertising & Communications Research. Repr. of 1961 ed. lib. bdg. 25.00x (ISBN 0-8371-2124-8, JAMC). Greenwood.
Jacobson, Jay. El Mormonismo Refutado. (Modern Doctrines Collection). 1978. Repr. of 1972 ed. 0.55 (ISBN 0-311-05030-1). Casa Bautista.
Jacobson, K. I. & Jacobson, R. E. Imaging Systems: Mechanism & Applications of Established & New Photosensitive Processes. LC 76-23144. 1976. 34.95 (ISBN 0-470-98905-X). Halsted Pr.
Jacobson, K. K., jt. auth. see Milbauer, B.
Jacobson, Lenore F., jt. auth. see Insel, Paul M.
Jacobson, M., ed. Development of Sensory Systems. (Handbook of Sensory Physiology: Vol. 9). (Illus.). 1978. 120.80 (ISBN 0-387-08632-3). Springer-Verlag.
Jacobson, Michael F. Eater's Digest: The Consumer's Factbook of Food Additives. LC 75-186030. pap. 3.50 (ISBN 0-385-05341-X). Doubleday.
--How Sodium Nitrite Can Affect Your Health. rev. ed. 1979. pap. 2.00. Ctr Sci Public.
--Nutrition Scoreboard. 1975. pap. 2.25 (ISBN 0-380-00534-4, 44537). Avon.
Jacobson, Morris & Franz, David R. Wonders of Jellyfish. LC 77-92326. (Wonders Ser.). (Illus.). (gr. 5 up). 1978. 5.95 (ISBN 0-396-07560-6). Dodd.
Jacobson, Morris & Pang, Rosemary. Wonders of Sponges. LC 75-38363. (Wonder Ser.). 1976. 5.95 (ISBN 0-396-07300-X). Dodd.
Jacobson, Morris K. & Franz, David R. Wonders of Coral & Coral Reefs. LC 78-22437. (Wonder Ser.). (Illus.). (gr. 5 up). 1979. 5.95 (ISBN 0-396-07679-3). Dodd.
Jacobson, Myrtle S. Night & Day: The Interaction Between an Academic Institution & Its Evening College. 1970. 12.50 o.p. (ISBN 0-8108-0324-0). Scarecrow.
Jacobson, N. Lectures in Abstract Algebra, Vol. 3: Theory of Fields & Galois Theory. LC 75-15564. (Graduate Texts in Ma Thematics: Vol. 32). 330p. 1976. 28.00 (ISBN 0-387-90168-X). Springer-Verlag.
Jacobson, Nathan. Basic Algebra One. LC 73-22316. (Illus.). 1974. text ed. 23.95x (ISBN 0-7167-0453-6); solutions 2.50x (ISBN 0-7167-1030-7). W H Freeman.
--Basic Algebra Two. LC 73-22316. 1980. 29.95x (ISBN 0-7167-1079-X); answer bk. avail. W H Freeman.
Jacobson, Nils O. Life Without Death. 320p. 1974. 10.00 o.s.i. (ISBN 0-440-04801-X, Sey Lawr). Delacorte.
Jacobson, Nolan P. Buddhism: The Religion of Analysis. LC 66-71124. (Arcturus Books Paperbacks). 202p. 1970. pap. 5.95 (ISBN 0-8093-0463-5). S Ill U Pr.
Jacobson, Norman. Pride & Solace: The Functions & Limits of Political Theory. 1978. 12.95 (ISBN 0-520-03438-4). U of Cal Pr.
Jacobson, Paul B., et al. The Principalship: New Perspectives. 512p. 1973. ref. ed. 18.95 (ISBN 0-13-700856-2). P-H.
Jacobson, R. E., jt. auth. see Jacobson, K. I.
Jacobson, Robert E. Municipal Control of Cable Communications. LC 77-7815. (Praeger Special Studies). 1977. text ed. 22.95 (ISBN 0-03-021831-4). Praeger.
Jacobson, Scott, jt. auth. see Allison, Dorothy.
Jacobson, Sheldon A. Comparative Pathology of the Tumors of Bone. (Illus.). 500p. 1971. 39.75 (ISBN 0-398-02166-X). C C Thomas.
--The Man Who Moved the World. LC 80-83024. (Illus.). 298p. 1980. 10.95 (ISBN 0-9604800-0-5). Galley OR.
Jacobson, Willard & Bergman, Abby. Science for Children: A Book for Teachers. (Illus.). 1980. text ed. 18.95 (ISBN 0-13-794784-4). P-H.
Jacobson, Willard J. Modern Elementary School Science: A Recommended Sequence. LC 61-14667. (Orig.). (gr. 1-6). 1961. pap. text ed. 4.75x (ISBN 0-8077-1560-3). Tchrs Coll.
--Population Education: A Knowledge Base. LC 78-13398. 1979. text ed. 15.95 (ISBN 0-8077-2533-1). Tchrs Coll.
Jacobsson, Erin E. A Life for Sound Money: Per Jacobsson-His Biography. LC 78-41135. (Illus.). 1979. 49.50x (ISBN 0-19-828411-X). Oxford U Pr.
Jacobstein, J. Myron, jt. ed. see Mersky, Roy M.
Jacobsthal, P., jt. auth. see Jope, E. M.
Jacobus, jt. auth. see Hunter.
Jacobus, Charles. Texas Real Estate Law. 1979. ref. ed. 19.95; text ed. 15.95 (ISBN 0-8359-7569-X); instr's. manual avail. Reston.
--Texas Real Estate Law. 2nd ed. 1981. 19.95 (ISBN 0-8359-7571-1); text ed. 15.95 (ISBN 0-686-68878-3); instr's. manual free (ISBN 0-8359-7572-X). Reston.
Jacobus, John. Matisse. LC 72-6633. (Library of Great Painters). (Illus.). 160p. 1973. 35.00 (ISBN 0-8109-0277-X). Abrams.
Jacobus, John, jt. auth. see Hunter, Sam.
Jacobus, Lee. Longman Anthology of American Drama. (Illus.). 512p. 1981. pap. text ed. 14.95 (ISBN 0-582-28242-X). Longman.
Jacobus, Lee A. John Cleveland. (English Authors Ser.: No. 180). 1975. lib. bdg. 12.50 (ISBN 0-8057-1095-7). Twayne.
Jacobus, Verheiden. The History of the Moderne Protestant Divines, Containing Their Parents, Countries, Education, with Register of Their Writings. Lupton, D., tr. from Latin. LC 79-84142. (English Experience Ser.: No. 959). 400p. 1979. Repr. of 1637 ed. lib. bdg. 28.00 (ISBN 90-221-0959-3). Walter J Johnson.
Jacobus, William E. & Ingwall, Joanne. Heart Creatin Kinase. (Illus.). 216p. 1980. 39.00 (ISBN 0-683-04353-6). Williams & Wilkins.
Jacobus, X. Documents on Medical Anthropology: Untrodden Fields of Anthropology, 2 vols. LC 73-185239. 906p. 1972. Repr. of 1898 ed. 35.00 o.p. (ISBN 0-88275-028-3). Krieger.
Jacoby, Annalee, jt. auth. see White, Theodore H.
Jacoby, Beverly S., jt. ed. see Oberhuber, Konrad.
Jacoby, E. G., ed. & tr. see Tonnies, Ferdinand.
Jacoby, Florence G. Nursing Care of the Patient with Burns. 2nd ed. LC 75-15578. (Illus.). 176p. 1976. pap. 8.95 o.p. (ISBN 0-8016-2396-0). Mosby.
Jacoby, Helmut. Architectural Drawings: Nineteen Sixty-Eight to Nineteen Seventy-Six. Date not set. 22.95 (ISBN 0-8038-0016-9). Hastings.
Jacoby, Henry. The Bureaucratization of the World. LC 74-166224. 1973. 23.75x (ISBN 0-520-02083-9); pap. 4.95 (ISBN 0-520-03044-3). U of Cal Pr.
Jacoby, Henry D., jt. auth. see Brooman, Frederick.
Jacoby, Neil H. Corporate Power & Social Responsibility: A Blueprint for the Future. LC 72-14073. (Studies of the Modern Corporation). 1977. pap. text ed. 7.95 (ISBN 0-02-915950-4). Free Pr.
--Corporate Power & Social Responsibility. (Studies of the Modern Corporation Ser.). 1973. 15.00 (ISBN 0-02-915940-7). Macmillan.
--Multinational Oil: A Study in Industrial Dynamics. LC 74-22381. (Studies of the Modern Corporation Ser.). (Illus.). 304p. 1974. 17.95 (ISBN 0-02-915990-3); pap. 3.95 (ISBN 0-02-915980-6). Macmillan.
Jacoby, Oswald. How to Win at Gin Rummy. (Illus.). 1978. pap. 3.95 (ISBN 0-03-042886-6). HR&W.
--Oswald Jacoby on Poker. LC 80-70553. 192p. 1981. pap. 4.95 (ISBN 0-385-17590-6, Dolp). Doubleday.
--Oswald Jacoby on Poker. rev. ed. 1947. 7.95 o.p. (ISBN 0-385-04781-9). Doubleday.
--Penny Ante & up. LC 76-40882. 1979. pap. 3.95 (ISBN 0-385-11173-8, Dolp). Doubleday.
Jacoby, Samuel L. & Kowalik, Janusz S. Mathematical Modeling with Computers. (Illus.). 1980. text ed. 23.95 (ISBN 0-13-561555-0). P-H.
Jacoby, Stephen M. Architectural Sculpture in New York City. LC 74-15247. (Illus.). 128p. (Orig.). 1975. pap. text ed. 5.00 (ISBN 0-486-23120-8). Dover.
Jacoby, Susan. Inside Soviet Schools. 1974. 8.95 o.p. (ISBN 0-8090-5846-4). Hill & Wang.
--The Possible She. 160p. 1980. pap. 2.50 (ISBN 0-345-28735-5). Ballantine.
Jacoebee, W. Pierre. La Persuasion De la Charite: Themes, Formes et Structure Dans les Jornaux et Oeuvres Diverses De Marivaux. (Orig., Fr.). 1976. pap. text ed. 20.00x (ISBN 90-6203-239-7). Humanities.
Jacosen, Rolf. Twenty Poems of Rolf Jacobsen. Bly, Robert, ed. 1977. pap. 3.50 (ISBN 0-685-88845-2). Eighties Pr.
Jacot, Yves, jt. auth. see Low, Jacqueline.
Jacque, Laurent L. Management of Foreign Exchange Risk. LC 77-12281. (Illus.). 1978. 24.95 (ISBN 0-669-01954-2). Lexington Bks.
Jacquemard, Yves & Senecal, Jean-Michel. The Body Vanishes. Latta, Gordon, tr. from Fr. LC 80-17077. 224p. 1980. 8.95 (ISBN 0-396-07884-2). Dodd.
Jacquemin, Alex & De Jong, Henry W. European Industrial Organization. LC 76-58378. (Problems of Economic Integration Ser.). 1977. 22.95 (ISBN 0-470-99079-1). Halsted Pr.
Jacquemont, Victor. Letters from India, Describing a Journey in the British Dominions of India, Tibet, Lahore & Cashmere, During the Years 1828-31, 2 vols. (Oxford in Asia Historical Reprints). (Illus.). 1976. 39.95x (ISBN 0-19-577216-4). Oxford U Pr.
Jacques Cattell Press, ed. Library Journal Book Review 1980. LC 68-59515. 760p. 32.50 (ISBN 0-8352-1344-7). Bowker.
Jacques, Elliott. The Health Services. (Brunel Institute of Organization & Social Studies Ser.). 1978. text ed. 39.95x (ISBN 0-435-82474-0). Heinemann Ed.
Jacques, J., jt. auth. see Wilen, Sam.
Jacques, Michael. Images of Age. LC 80-69225. (Illus.). 146p. 1980. 30.00 (ISBN 0-89011-550-8). Abt Assoc.
Jacquet, Constant H., Jr., ed. Yearbook of American & Canadian Churches, 1981. 304p. (Orig.). 1981. pap. 14.95 (ISBN 0-687-46636-9). Abingdon.
Jacquez, John A. Computer Diagnosis & Diagnostic Methods: The Proceedings of the Second Conference on the Diagnostic Process, University of Michigan. (Illus.). 400p. 1972. 29.75 (ISBN 0-398-02521-5). C C Thomas.
Jacquillat, Bertrand, jt. auth. see Feiger, George.
Jacquin, Nicolaus J. Selectarum Stirpium Americanarum Historia. 1971. Repr. of 1763 ed. 77.00 o.s.i. (ISBN 0-02-847130-X). Hafner.
Jacqz, Jane W. The Absolute Poor. 54p. 1974. pap. 1.00 (ISBN 0-89192-073-0). Interbk Inc.
Jaedicke, Robert K. & Sprouse, Robert T. Accounting Flows: Income, Funds & Cash. (Orig.). 1965. pap. 9.95x ref. ed. (ISBN 0-13-002352-3). P-H.
Jaeger, C. Rock Mechanics & Engineering. 2nd ed. LC 77-85700. (Illus.). 1979. 90.00 (ISBN 0-521-21898-5). Cambridge U Pr.
Jaeger, Charles. Fluid Transients in Hydro-Electric Engineering Practice. (Illus.). 1977. 62.50x (ISBN 0-216-90225-8). Intl Ideas.
Jaeger, Doris, jt. ed. see Meiss, Harriet.
Jaeger, Edmund. The Biologists Handbook of Pronunciations. 336p. 1960. pap. 29.75 photocopy ed., spiral (ISBN 0-398-00915-5). C C Thomas.
Jaeger, Edmund C. The North American Deserts. (Illus.). 1957. 12.50 (ISBN 0-8047-0498-8). Stanford U Pr.
--A Source-Book of Biological Names & Terms. 3rd ed. (Illus.). 360p. 1978. 13.75 (ISBN 0-398-00916-3). C C Thomas.
Jaeger, Ellsworth. Nature Crafts. (Illus.). (gr. 9 up). 1950. 8.95 (ISBN 0-02-558770-6). Macmillan.
--Tracks & Trailcraft. (Illus.). 1948. 9.95 (ISBN 0-02-558830-3). Macmillan.
--Wildwood Wisdom. (Illus.). (gr. 7 up). 1966. 12.95 (ISBN 0-02-558890-7). Macmillan.
Jaeger, Herbert, ed. Kriminologie Im Strafprozess. (Suhrkamp Taschenbuecher Wissenschaft: No. 300). 208p. pap. text ed. 7.15 (ISBN 3-518-07909-3, Pub. by Insel Verlag Germany). Suhrkamp.
Jaeger, J. C., jt. auth. see Carslaw, Horatio S.
Jaeger, L. G. Cartesian Tensors in Engineering Science. 1966. 23.00 (ISBN 0-08-011222-6); pap. 11.25 (ISBN 0-08-011221-8). Pergamon.
--Elementary Theory of Elastic Plates. 1964. 16.50 (ISBN 0-08-010342-1); pap. 7.75 (ISBN 0-08-010341-3). Pergamon.
Jaeger, Richard & Title, Carol K., eds. Minimum Competency Achievement Testing. 487p. 18.25 (ISBN 0-8211-0909-X); institutional price 21.25. Am Educ Res.
Jaeger, Richard M. & Tittle, Carol K., eds. Minimum Competency Achievement Testing: Motives, Models, Measures & Consequences. LC 79-88823. 1980. 19.50 (ISBN 0-685-96790-5); in copies of 10 17.50 (ISBN 0-685-96791-3). McCutchan.
Jaeger, Sig, jt. auth. see Larssen, A. K.
Jaeger, W., ed. Biological Growth & Spread: Proceedings. (Lecture Notes in Biomathematics: Vol. 38). 511p. 1981. pap. 34.00 (ISBN 0-387-10257-4). Springer-Verlag.
Jaeger, Walter H. Williston on Contracts: 1957-1977, 22 vols. 3rd ed. LC 59-558. 1957. Vols. 1-16. 803.00 (ISBN 0-686-14488-0). Lawyers Co-Op.
Jaeger, Werner. Paideia: The Ideals of Greek Culture, Vol. 1. Archaic Greece & Mind Of Athens. Highet, Gilbert, tr. (YA) (gr. 9 up). 1965. pap. 7.95 (ISBN 0-19-500425-6, 144, GB). Oxford U Pr.
Jaeger, Werner, ed. see Aristotle.
Jaegers, Beverly C. Secrets of the Aura. 3.00 (ISBN 0-89861-014-1). Esoteric Pubns.
Jaenen, Cornelius J. Friend & Foe: Aspects of French-American Cultural Contact in the Sixteenth & Seventeenth Centuries. (Illus.). 1976. 15.00x (ISBN 0-231-04088-1). Columbia U Pr.
Jaenicke, Henry R., jt. auth. see Johnson, Kenneth P.
Jaffa, Alisa, tr. see Burckhardt, Titus.
Jaffa, Harry V. Thomism & Aristotelianism: A Study of the Commentary by Thomas Aquinas on the Nicomachean Ethics. LC 78-21520. 1979. Repr. of 1952 ed. lib. bdg. 21.75x (ISBN 0-313-21149-3, JATA). Greenwood.
Jaffa, Herbert C. Kenneth Slessor. (World Authors Ser.: Australia: No. 145). lib. bdg. 10.95 (ISBN 0-8057-2838-4). Twayne.
Jaffa, Herbert C., ed. Modern Australian Poetry: A Guide to Information Sources. LC 74-11535. (The American Literature, English Literature, & World Literatures in English Information Guide Ser.: Vol. 24). 1979. 30.00 (ISBN 0-8103-1242-5). Gale.
Jaffe. Property Management in Real Estate Investment Decision-Making. (Special Ser. in Real Estate & Urban Land Economics). (Illus.). 1979. 21.95 (ISBN 0-669-02453-8). Lexington Bks.
Jaffe, Abraham J., et al. Changing Demography of Spanish Americans. (Studies in Population Ser.). 1980. 31.00 (ISBN 0-12-379580-X). Acad Pr.
Jaffe, Aniela. Apparitions: An Archetypal Approach to Death, Dreams & Ghosts Jungian Classics. rev. ed. 1979. pap. text ed. 9.50 (ISBN 0-88214-500-2). Spring Pubns.
Jaffe, Aniela, ed. see Jung, C. G.
Jaffe, Austin J., jt. auth. see Sirmans, C. F.
Jaffe, Bernard. Crucibles: The Story of Chemistry from Ancient Alchemy to Nuclear Fission. (Illus.). 1976. pap. text ed. 5.00 (ISBN 0-486-23342-1). Dover.
--Crucibles: The Story of Chemistry from Ancient Alchemy to Nuclear Fission. 4th rev. ed. 9.00 (ISBN 0-8446-5486-8). Peter Smith.
Jaffe, Dan. Dan Freeman. LC 67-13150. (Illus.). 1967. pap. 1.65 (ISBN 0-8032-5101-7, BB 371, Bison). U of Nebr Pr.
Jaffe, Dennis T. & Clarke, Ted, eds. Worlds Apart: Young People & Drug Programs. 160p. (Orig.). 1974. pap. 1.95 o.p. (ISBN 0-394-71017-7, Vin). Random.
Jaffe, Dennis T., jt. ed. see Allman, Lawrence R.
Jaffe, Frederick S., et al. Abortion Politics: Private Morality & Public Policy. LC 80-17035. 224p. 1980. 14.95 (ISBN 0-07-032189-2, P&RB). McGraw.
Jaffe, Fredericks S., jt. auth. see Cutright, Phillips.
Jaffe, H. H., jt. auth. see Orchin, Milton.
Jaffe, Hans L. Mondrian. (Library of Great Painters Ser). (Illus.). 1970. 35.00 (ISBN 0-8109-0325-3). Abrams.
Jaffe, Hans L., ed. see Picasso, Pablo.
Jaffe, Jerome, et al. Addictions: Issues & Answers. (Life Cycle Ser.). 1979. pap. text ed. 4.95 scp (ISBN 0-06-384748-5, HarpC). Har-Row.
Jaffe, Julian F. Crusade Against Radicalism; New York During the Red Scare, Nineteen Fourteen to Nineteen Twenty Four. LC 75-189556. (National University Publications). 1972. 17.50 (ISBN 0-8046-9026-X). Kennikat.
Jaffe, Louis L. English & American Judges As Lawmakers. 1969. 16.95x (ISBN 0-19-825193-9). Oxford U Pr.
--Judicial Control of Administrative Action. 704p. 1966. pap. 12.50 o.s.i. (ISBN 0-316-45604-7). Little.
Jaffe, Nora C., jt. auth. see Skarda, Patricia L.
Jaffe, Norman S. Cateract Surgery & Its Complications. 3rd ed. LC 80-19355. (Illus.). 611p. 1980. text ed. 69.50 (ISBN 0-8016-2404-5). Mosby.
Jaffe, Norman S., et al. Pseudophakos. new ed. LC 77-27307. (Illus.). 1978. text ed. 44.50 (ISBN 0-8016-2401-0). Mosby.
Jaffe, Philip M. & Maglio, Rodolfo. Technical Mathematics. 1979. 16.95x (ISBN 0-673-15111-5). Scott F.
Jaffe, Rona. The Best of Everything. 1976. pap. 2.75 (ISBN 0-380-00581-6, 54221). Avon.
--The Best of Everything. 1976. Repr. of 1958 ed. lib. bdg. 18.95x (ISBN 0-89966-130-0). Buccaneer Bks.
--Class Reunion. 1980. pap. 2.75 o.s.i. (ISBN 0-440-11408-X). Dell.
--The Fame Game. 1976. Repr. of 1969 ed. lib. bdg. 12.25x (ISBN 0-89966-131-9). Buccaneer Bks.
Jaffe, Susanne. The Other Anne Fletcher. 1980. 9.95 (ISBN 0-453-00386-9, H386). NAL.
Jaffee, Al. Al Jaffee: Dead or Alive. 1980. pap. 1.75 (ISBN 0-451-09494-8, E9494, Sig). NAL.
--Al Jaffee Fowls His Nest. 1981. pap. 1.95 (ISBN 0-451-09741-6, J9741). NAL.
--Al Jaffee Hogs the Show. (Orig.). 1981. pap. price not set (ISBN 0-451-09908-7, Sig). NAL.

--Al Jaffee Sinks to a New Low. (Orig.). 1978. pap. 1.50 (ISBN 0-451-09009-8, W9009, Sig). NAL.
--Al Jaffee's Mad Book of Magic & Other Dirty Tricks. (Mad Ser.). (Illus.). 1976. pap. 1.75 (ISBN 0-446-94406-8). Warner Bks.
--Al Jaffee's Mad Inventions. (Mad Ser.). (Illus., Orig.). 1978. pap. 1.75 (ISBN 0-446-94407-6). Warner Bks.
--Good Lord! Not Another Book of Snappy Answers to Stupid Questions. (Mad Ser.). (Illus., Orig.). 1980. pap. 1.75 (ISBN 0-446-94450-5). Warner Bks.
--Mad's Snappy Answers to Stupid Questions. (Mad Ser.). (Illus.). 1975. pap. 1.75 (ISBN 0-446-94409-2). Warner Bks.
--More Mad's Snappy Answers to Stupid Questions. pap. 1.25 (ISBN 0-451-06740-1, Y6740, Sig). NAL.
--More Snappy Answers to Stupid Questions. (Mad Ser.). (Illus.). 1979. pap. 1.75 (ISBN 0-446-94410-6). Warner Bks.
--Still More Snappy Answers to Stupid Questions. (Mad Ser.). (Illus.). 192p. 1976. pap. 1.75 (ISBN 0-446-94411-4). Warner Bks.
Jaffee, Annette W. Adult Education. LC 80-84834. 220p. 1981. 12.95 (ISBN 0-86538-007-4). Ontario Rev. NJ.
Jaffee, Benson & Fanshel, David. How They Fared in Adoption. LC 79-132192. 1970. pap. 7.50 (ISBN 0-231-08642-3). Columbia U Pr.
Jaffee, Benson, jt. auth. see Kline, Draza.
Jaffee, Cabot. Reassessing & Developing Management Skills: Perception, Vol. 1. 204p. 1981. 3-ring special binder 19.95 (ISBN 0-8436-0791-2). CBI Pub.
Jaffee, Cabot J. & Burroughs, Wayne A. Manipulation People Like. LC 78-15278. 1978. 10.95 (ISBN 0-88229-347-8). Nelson-Hall.
Jaffke, Freya. Making Soft Toys. Gebert, Rosemary, tr. from Ger. LC 80-66665. Orig. Title: Spielzeug Von Eltern Selbstgemacht. (Illus.). 1981. pap. 6.95 (ISBN 0-89742-044-6). Dawne-Leigh.
Jaffray, G., jt. auth. see Gruenberger, F. J.
Jafri, Syed H. Origins & Early Development in Shi'a Islam. (Arab Background Ser). 1979. text ed. 28.00x (ISBN 0-582-78080-2). Longman.
Jagadananda, Swami, tr. see Saradananda, Swami.
Jagannath, S. Calculator Programs for the Hydrocarbon Processing Industries, Vol. 2. 1981. 19.95 (ISBN 0-87201-092-9). Gulf Pub.
Jagchid, Sechin & Hyer, Paul. Mongolia's Culture & Society. LC 79-1438. (Illus.). 461p. 1980. 35.00x (ISBN 0-89158-390-4). Westview.
Jagendorf, M. A. Folk Stories of the South. LC 70-134672. (Illus.). (gr. 3 up). 1969. 8.95 (ISBN 0-8149-0000-3). Vanguard.
--Stories & Lore of the Zodiac. LC 76-39724. 1978. 6.95 (ISBN 0-8149-0752-0). Vanguard.
Jagendorf, M. A. & Weng, Virginia. The Magic Boat & Other Chinese Folk Stories. LC 79-67814. (Illus.). (gr. 4-9). 1980. 8.95 (ISBN 0-8149-0823-3). Vanguard.
Jagendorf, Moritz. Folk Wines, Cordials & Brandies: How to Make Them, Along with the Pleasures of Their Lore. LC 63-21854. (Illus.). 1963. 12.50 (ISBN 0-8149-0125-5). Vanguard.
Jagendorf, Moritz A. Ghost of Peg-Leg Peter & Other Stories of Old New York. LC 65-17371. (Illus.). (gr. 3 up). 1965. 7.95 (ISBN 0-8149-0327-4). Vanguard.
--Noodlehead Stories from Around the World. LC 57-12266. (Illus.). (gr. 4-6). 7.95 (ISBN 0-8149-0329-0). Vanguard.
--Priceless Cats & Other Italian Folk Stories. LC 56-12039. (Illus.). (gr. 4-6). 7.95 (ISBN 0-8149-0330-4). Vanguard.
--Sand in the Bag & Other Stories of Ohio, Indiana & Illinois. LC 52-11125. (Illus.). (gr. 4-9). 7.95 (ISBN 0-8149-0332-0). Vanguard.
--Tales from the First Americans. LC 78-56057. (The World Folktale Library). (Illus.). 1979. lib. bdg. 7.65 (ISBN 0-686-51164-6). Silver.
--Tales of Mystery. LC 78-56056. (The World Folktale Library). (Illus.). 1979. lib. bdg. 7.65 (ISBN 0-686-51167-0). Silver.
Jagendorf, Moritz A. & Boggs, R. S. King of the Mountains: A Treasury of Latin-American Folk Stories. LC 60-15073. (Illus.). (gr. 4-8). 1960. 8.95 (ISBN 0-8149-0338-X). Vanguard.
Jager, C. De see Bilderberg Conference - Arnhem - Holland - 1968.
Jager, C. De see De Jager, C.
Jager, E. J. De see De Jager, E. J.
Jager, Susan G., jt. auth. see Fencl, Shirley.
Jagers, D. P. Branching Processes with Biological Applications. LC 74-32296. (Wiley Series in Probability & Mathematical Statistics). 276p. 1975. 52.50 (ISBN 0-471-43652-6). Wiley.
Jaggard, William. Catalogue of Such English Books As Lately Have Been, or Now Are, in Printing for Publication. LC 78-26323. (English Experience Ser.: No. 196). 1969. Repr. of 1618 ed. 7.00 (ISBN 90-221-0196-7). Walter J Johnson.
Jagger, B., ed. Basketball Coaching & Playing. 1971. 12.75 (ISBN 0-571-04743-2). Transatlantic.
Jagger, Brenda. Verity. 1981. pap. 2.95 (ISBN 0-451-09718-1, E9718, Sig). NAL.
Jaggi, O. P. History of Science & Technology in India, 5 vols. Incl. Vol. 1. Dawn of Indian Technology-Pre-&-Proto-Historic Period. text ed. 18.00x (ISBN 0-8426-0743-9); Vol. 2. Dawn of Indian Science-Vedic & Upanishadic Period. text ed. 12.00x (ISBN 0-8426-0744-7); Vol. 3. Folk Medicine (India) text ed. 18.00x (ISBN 0-8426-0745-5); Vol. 4. Indian System of Medicine. text ed. 24.00x (ISBN 0-8426-0746-3); Vol. 5. Yogic & Tantric Medicine. text ed. 18.00x (ISBN 0-8426-0747-1). (Illus.). 1975. Set. text ed. 77.50x set o.p. (ISBN 0-8426-1314-5). Verry.
Jagiello, Georgiana & Vogel, Henry J., eds. Bioregulators of Reproduction. (P&S Biomedical Sciences Ser.). 1981. price not set. Acad Pr.
Jagirdar, P. J. Studies in the Social Thought of Mahadeo Govind Ranade. 5.50x o.p. (ISBN 0-210-27033-0). Asia.
Jagtiani, Duru, ed. Fruit Preservation. 128p. 1980. text ed. 10.50 (ISBN 0-7069-1039-7, Pub. by Vikas India). Advent Bk.
Jahan, Rounaq. Pakistan: Failure in National Integration. LC 72-3771. 320p. 1972. 17.50x (ISBN 0-231-03625-6). Columbia U Pr.
Jahan, Rounaq & Papanek, H., eds. Women & Development: Perspectives from South & Southeast Asia. 439p. 1979. text ed. 27.00 (ISBN 0-8426-1657-8). Verry.
Jahan, Rounaq & Papanek, Hanna, eds. Women & Development: Perspectives from South & Southeast Asia. 1980. 16.00x (ISBN 0-8364-0596-X, Pub. by Bangladesh Inst Law India). South Asia Bks.
Jaher, Frederick C. Age of Industrialism in America. LC 68-14107. 1968. 10.95 o.s.i. (ISBN 0-02-915970-9). Free Pr.
Jahn, Egbert. Soviet Foreign Policy. (Allison & Busby's Motive Ser.). 160p. 1981. pap. 7.95 (ISBN 0-8052-8096-0, Pub. by Allison & Busby England). Schocken.
Jahn, Ernest, jt. auth. see Sachs, Margaret.
Jahn, Ernest T. The Clinging. 336p. (Orig.). 1981. pap. 2.50 cancelled (ISBN 0-89083-705-8). Zebra.
Jahn, Melvin E., tr. see Beringer, Johann B.
Jahn, Michael. Armada. 224p. (Orig.). 1981. pap. 2.25 (ISBN 0-449-14388-0, GM). Fawcett.
--Killer on the Heights. 1977. pap. 1.75 o.p. (ISBN 0-449-13906-9, GM). Fawcett.
--The Six Million Dollar Man, No. 1: Wine, Women & Wars. 1975. pap. 1.25 o.s.i. (ISBN 0-446-76833-2). Warner Bks.
Jahn, Mike. The Deadliest Game. (Rockford Ser.: No. 2). 192p. 1976. pap. 1.25 o.p. (ISBN 0-445-00354-5). Popular Lib.
--How to Make a Hit Record. LC 76-9939. 192p. 1976. 7.95 o.p. (ISBN 0-87888-106-9). Bradbury Pr.
--The Quark Maneuver. (Orig.). 1977. pap. 1.50 o.p. (ISBN 0-685-75029-9, 345-25171-7-150). Ballantine.
--Six Million Dollar Man: International Incidents, No. 2. 1977. pap. 1.25 o.p. (ISBN 0-425-03331-7). Berkley Pub.
--The Six Million Dollar Man: The Secret of Big Foot Pass. 1976. pap. 1.25 o.p. (ISBN 0-425-03307-4). Berkley Pub.
--Switch, No. 2. pap. 1.25 o.p. (ISBN 0-425-03252-3). Berkley Pub.
--Thunder, Mighty Stallion of the Hills, No. 1. 160p. (gr. 4 up) 1981. pap. 1.50 (ISBN 0-448-17275-5, Tempo). G&D.
Jahn, Penelope & Campbell, Charles. The Self-Help Guide to Divorce, Children & Welfare. 2nd rev. ed. 116p. 1979. pap. 4.95 (ISBN 0-88784-075-2, Pub. by Hse Anansi Pr Canada). U of Toronto Pr.
Jahn, R. G. The Role of Consciousness in the Physical World. (AAAS Selected Symposium: No. 57). 136p. 1981. lib. bdg. 15.00x (ISBN 0-89158-955-4). Westview.
Jahn, Rudiger, et al. Skiing Skills. (Illus.). 160p. 1980. 19.95 (ISBN 0-87691-330-3). Winchester Pr.
Jahner, Elaine A., ed. see Walker, James R.
Jahng, K., tr. see Fukuda, Tsuneari.
Jahnke, Eugene & Emde, Fritz. Tables of Functions with Formulae & Curves. 4th ed. (Ger & Eng). 1945. pap. text ed. 5.00 (ISBN 0-486-60133-1). Dover.
Jahns, Patricia. Violent Years. 6.95 (ISBN 0-8038-7726-9). Hastings.
Jahoda, Marie. Freud & the Dilemmas of Psychology. LC 80-17140. vi, 186p. 1981. pap. 4.50x (ISBN 0-8032-7553-6, BB 759, Bison). U of Nebr Pr.
--Race Relations & Mental Health. (Orig.). 1960. pap. 2.50 (ISBN 0-685-20792-7, U510, UNESCO). Unipub.
Jahss, Betty, jt. auth. see Jahss, Melvin.
Jahss, Melvin & Jahss, Betty. Inro & Other Miniature Forms of Japanese Lacquer Art. LC 76-109406. 75.00 (ISBN 0-8048-0263-7). C E Tuttle.
Jaimes, Rogelio. Borrasca de Pasiones. new ed. (Pimienta Collection Ser). 160p. 1974. pap. 1.00 o.p. (ISBN 0-88473-193-6). Fiesta Pub.
Jaimini. Karma Mimansa Sutras of Jaimini. 91p. 1980. pap. 5.50. KMS Pr CO.
Jain, Arvind K. Commodity Futures Markets & the Law of One Price. (Michigan International Business Studies: No. 16). (Illus.). 140p. 1980. pap. 6.00 (ISBN 0-87712-210-5). U Mich Busn Div Res.
Jain, B. B. Poetry of George Crabbe. (Salzburg Studies in English Literature, Romantic Reassessment Ser.: No. 37). 340p. 1976. pap. text ed. 25.00x (ISBN 0-391-01434-X). Humanities.
Jain, Chaman L. Contemporary Monetary Economics Theory & Policy. LC 79-55682. (Illus.). 266p. (Orig.). 1981. text ed. 21.50 (ISBN 0-932126-02-2); pap. text ed. 17.50x (ISBN 0-932126-03-0). Graceway.
Jain, Devaki. Indian Women. 312p. 1975. pap. 3.75x (ISBN 0-89253-538-5). Ind-US Inc.
Jain, Gian C. Design, Operation & Testing of Synchronous Machines. 1966. 20.00x o.p. (ISBN 0-210-33836-9). Asia.
Jain, H. Contemporary Issues in Canadian Personnel Administration. 1974. 14.95 o.p. (ISBN 0-13-170324-2); pap. 11.50 o.p. (ISBN 0-13-170316-1). P-H.
Jain, Hem C., ed. Worker Participation: Success & Problems. LC 80-57. (Praeger Special Studies). 1980. 24.95 (ISBN 0-03-052451-2). Praeger.
Jain, J. P. Soviet Policy Towards Pakistan & Bangladesh. LC 74-903227. 1974. 15.00x o.p. (ISBN 0-88386-482-7). South Asia Bks.
Jain, Jagdish P. After Mao What? LC 75-31534. 1976. 24.50x (ISBN 0-89158-528-1). Westview.
--China in World Politics. 2nd ed. 1980. text ed. 15.00x (ISBN 0-391-01691-1). Humanities.
Jain, M. K. Numerical Solution of Differential Equations. LC 78-26649. 1979. 21.95 (ISBN 0-470-26609-0). Halsted Pr.
Jain, Mahendra K. & Wagner, Roger C. Introduction to Biological Membranes. LC 79-16690. 1980. 32.50 (ISBN 0-471-03471-1, Pub. by Wiley-Interscience). Wiley.
Jain, N. K., ed. Muslims in India: A Biographical Dictionary, 1857-1976. 1980. 38.00x (ISBN 0-88386-886-5). South Asia Bks.
Jain, R. B., jt. ed. see Bain, J. S.
Jain, R. C., tr. see Castro, R. & De Cadenet, J. J.
Jain, R. K. China & Japan Nineteen Forty-Nine to Nineteen Seventy-Six. LC 77-70008. 1977. text ed. 17.50x (ISBN 0-391-00749-1). Humanities.
--China & the Politics of Disarmament, 1949 to 1980: A Documentary Study. 400p. 1980. text ed. 20.50x (ISBN 0-391-02118-4). Humanities.
--China & Yugoslavia, Nineteen Forty-Nine to Nineteen-Eighty. 400p. 1980. text ed. 20.50x (ISBN 0-391-02117-6). Humanities.
--Chinese Foreign Policy After Mao, Vol. 1. 450p. 1980. text ed. 25.75x (ISBN 0-391-02113-3). Humanities.
--Chinese Foreign Policy After Mao: Volume 3, 1979. 500p. 1980. text ed. 30.75x (ISBN 0-391-02115-X). Humanities.
--Chinese Foreign Policy After Mao: Volume 2, 1978. 500p. 1980. text ed. 30.75x (ISBN 0-391-02114-1). Humanities.
--Party Politics in China, Nineteen Forty-Five to Nineteen Eighty. 1000p. 1980. text ed. 41.00x (ISBN 0-391-02048-X). Humanities.
--Soviet South Asian Relations Nineteen Fourty-Seven to Nineteen Seventy-Eight: The Kashmir Question 1952-1964, 2 vols. Incl. Vol. 1. The Kutch Conflict Indo-Pak Conflict of 1965 Bangladesh Crisis & Indo-Pak War of 1971 India; Vol. 2. Pakistan, Bangladesh, Nepal. 1979. Set. 55.00x set (ISBN 0-391-00974-5). Humanities.
--State Politics in China, Nineteen Forty-Nine to Nineteen Eighty. 600p. 1980. text ed. 30.75 (ISBN 0-391-02108-7). Humanities.
--U. S. - South Asian Relations, Nineteen Forty-Seven to Nineteen Eighty, 2 vols. 1400p. 1981. text ed. 61.50x (ISBN 0-391-02119-2). Humanities.
Jain, Rajendra K., ed. China-South Asian Relations: 1949-1980, 2 vols. 1400p. 1980. Set. text ed. write for info. (ISBN 0-391-01896-5). Humanities.
Jain, Rakesh K. & Gullino, Pietro M., eds. Thermal Characteristics of Tumors: Applications in Detection & Treatment. LC 80-13379. (N.Y. Academy of Sciences Annals: Vol. 335). 542p. 1980. 95.00x (ISBN 0-89766-046-3). NY Acad Sci.
Jain, S. C., jt. ed. see Kalpakjian, S.
Jain, S. K. Fundamental Aspects of the Normality Rule & Their Role in Deriving Constitutive Laws of Soils. (Civil Engineering & Engineering Mechanics Ser.: No. 1). (Illus.). 178p. 1980. 23.50 (ISBN 0-9605004-0-5, 5004-0-5). Eng Pubns.
Jain, S. K., jt. auth. see Bhattacharya, P. B.
Jain, Sagar C., ed. Management Development in Population Programs. 200p. (Orig.). 1981. pap. 15.00 (ISBN 0-89055-307-6). U of NC Pr.
Jain, Subhash C. & Mathur, Iqbal. Cases in Marketing Management. LC 77-81539. (Marketing Ser.). 1978. text ed. 19.95 o.p. (ISBN 0-88244-129-9). Grid Pub.
Jaini, Jagmandar L. Outlines of Jainism. Thomas, F. W., ed. LC 78-14128. (Illus.). 1981. Repr. of 1940 ed. 19.00 (ISBN 0-88355-801-7). Hyperion Conn.
Jaini, Padmanabh S. The Jaina Path of Purification. LC 77-73496. 1979. 21.50x (ISBN 0-520-03459-7). U of Cal Pr.
Jairazbhoy, R. A. Ancient Egyptians & Chinese in America. (Old World Origins of American Civilization Ser). (Illus.). 110p. 1974. 13.50x o.p. (ISBN 0-87471-571-7). Rowman.
Jakes, John. The Asylum World. 1969. pap. 1.95 o.s.i. (ISBN 0-446-89720-5). Warner Bks.
--The Bastard, No. 1. (Kent Family Chronicles). 1978. pap. 2.95 (ISBN 0-515-05862-9). Jove Pubns.
--Excalibur. (Orig.). 1980. pap. 2.50 o.s.i. (ISBN 0-440-12291-0). Dell.
--The Furies. (Kent Family Chronicle: No. 4). (Orig.). 1976. pap. 2.95 (ISBN 0-515-05890-4). Jove Pubns.
--King's Crusader. 1977. pap. 1.95 o.p. (ISBN 0-685-78258-1). Pinnacle Bks.
--The Lawless: Kent Family Chronicle. 1978. pap. 2.95 (ISBN 0-515-05892-0). Jove Pubns.
--The Man from Cannae. 1977. pap. 1.95 o.p. (ISBN 0-523-40161-2). Pinnacle Bks.
--On Wheels. 1973. pap. 1.95 o.s.i. (ISBN 0-446-89932-1). Warner Bks.
--The Rebels, No. 2. (Kent Family Chronicle). (Orig.). 1979. pap. 2.95 (ISBN 0-515-05894-7). Jove Pubns.
--The Seekers, No. 3. (The Kent Family Chronicles). (Orig.). 1979. pap. 2.75 (ISBN 0-515-05712-6). Jove Pubns.
--Six Gun Planet. 1970. pap. 1.75 o.s.i. (ISBN 0-446-84721-6). Warner Bks.
--The Titans. (The Kent Family Chronicle: No. 3). (Orig.). 1976. pap. 2.95 (ISBN 0-515-05891-2). Jove Pubns.
--The Warriors. (Kent Family Chronicles: No. 6). (Orig.). 1977. pap. 2.95 (ISBN 0-515-05893-9). Jove Pubns.
Jakes, John, photos by. The Bastard Photostory. (Orig.). 1980. pap. 2.75 (ISBN 0-515-05433-X). Jove Pubns.
Jaki, Stanley L. The Milky Way: An Elusive Road for Science. 363p. 1975. pap. 8.95 o.p. (ISBN 0-88202-022-6, Sci Hist). N Watson.
--The Paradox of Olbers' Paradox: A Case History of Scientific Thought. LC 70-80053. 1969. lib. bdg. 15.00 o.p. (ISBN 0-685-52443-4). N Watson.
--Planets & Planetarians: A History of Theories of the Origin of Planetary Systems. LC 77-4200. 1978. 21.95 (ISBN 0-470-99149-6). Halsted Pr.
--The Road of Science & the Ways to God. LC 77-21667. viii, 478p. 1980. pap. 8.95 (ISBN 0-226-39145-0, P897). U of Chicago Pr.
Jaki, Stanley L., tr. see Bruno, Giordano.
Jakle, John A. Images of the Ohio Valley: A Historical Geography of Travel. (Illus.). 1977. text ed. 14.95 (ISBN 0-19-502240-8); pap. text ed. 6.95x (ISBN 0-19-502241-6). Oxford U Pr.
Jakle, John A. & Oliver, Virginia. Past Landscapes: A Bibliography for Historic Preservationists. rev. ed. (Architecture Ser.: Bibliography A-314). 68p. 1980. pap. 7.50. Vance Biblios.
Jakob, Max & Hawkins, G. A. Elements of Heat Transfer. 3rd ed. LC 57-12230. 1957. text ed. 25.95x (ISBN 0-471-43725-5). Wiley.
Jakobovits, L. A., jt. auth. see Steinberg, D. D.
Jakobson, R., ed. see Symposia in Applied Mathematics - New York - 1960.
Jakobson, Roman. Main Trends in the Science of Language. 1973. pap. 1.95x o.p. (ISBN 0-06-131809-4, TB1809, Torch). Har-Row.
--O Cheshskom Stikhe, Preimushchestvenno V Sopostavlenii S Russkim. LC 68-8623. (Slavic Reprint Ser.: No. 6). 125p. (Rus). 1969. pap. 3.00 (ISBN 0-87057-119-2, Pub. by Brown U Pr). Univ Pr of New England.
Jakobson, Roman & Waugh, Linda R. Sound Shape of Language. LC 78-19552. (Illus.). 352p. 1979. 17.50x (ISBN 0-253-16417-6). Ind U Pr.
Jakobson, Roman & Kawamoto, Shigeo, eds. Studies in General & Oriental Linguistics Presented to Shiro Hattori on the Occasion of His Sixtieth Birthday. 685p. 1970. 24.95x o.p. (ISBN 0-87774-500-5). Schoenhof.

Jakoby, William B. Enzymatic Basis of Detoxication, Vol. 2. LC 80-17350. (Biochemical Pharmacology & Toxicology Ser.). 1980. lib ed 38.50 (ISBN 0-12-380002-1). Acad Pr.

Jakoby, William B., ed. Enzymatic Basis of Detoxication, Vol. 1. (Biochemical Pharmacology & Toxicology Ser.). 1980. 43.00 (ISBN 0-12-380001-3). Acad Pr.

Jakubauskas, Edward B. & Palomba, Neil A. Manpower Economics. LC 79-186208. 1973. text ed. 15.95 (ISBN 0-201-03284-8). A-W.

Jakubke, H. D. & Jeschkeit, H. Amino Acids, Peptides & Proteins: An Introduction. 1st English ed. Cotterell, G. P. & Jones, J. H., trs. LC 77-23945. 1978. 27.95 (ISBN 0-470-99279-4). Halsted Pr.

Jakucs, Laszlo. The Morphogenesis of Karst Regions: Variants of Karst Evolution. LC 76-40003. 1977. 57.95 (ISBN 0-470-98952-1). Halsted Pr.

Jal, Augustin. Nouveau Glossaire Nautique, Lettre C: Revision De L'edition Publiee En 1848. (Fr.). 1978. pap. 57.00x (ISBN 90-279-7538-8). Mouton.

Jalan, Bimal. Essays in Development Policy. LC 75-904389. 1975. 9.00x o.p. (ISBN 0-88386-622-6). South Asia Bks.

Jalim, M. Psychiatric Nursing Objective Tests. 128p. 1981. pap. 5.95 (ISBN 0-571-11582-9, Pub. by Faber & Faber). Merrimack Bk Serv.

Jaluria, Y. Natural Convection Heat & Mass Transfer. LC 79-41176. (HMT Ser.). (Illus.). 400p. 1980. 59.00 (ISBN 0-08-025432-2). Pergamon.

Jamaspasa, Kaikhusroo M. Pursisniha: A Zoroastrian Catechism, 2 vols. LC 72-179885. 174p. 1971. Set. 42.50x (ISBN 3-447-01351-6). Intl Pubns Serv.

James. Stand Firm: The Teenager's Guide to Self-Defense. (gr. 7-12). 1980. pap. 1.25 (ISBN 0-590-30033-4, Schol Pap). Schol Bk Serv.

James, jt. auth. see Theander.

James, A. & Rudin, Marcia R. Prison or Paradise? The New Religious Cults. 1980. 8.95 (ISBN 0-529-05737-9, RB 5737, Pub. by Collins Pubs). Fortress.

James, A., jt. auth. see Dagg, A. I.

James, A., ed. Mathematical Models in Water Pollution Control. LC 77-7214. 1978. 55.50 (ISBN 0-471-99471-5, Pub. by Wiley-Interscience). Wiley.

James, A. Everette, jt. auth. see Fleischer, Arthur C.

James, A. M., jt. auth. see Davies, C. W.

James, Albert. Like & Unlike: Stages 1, 2, & 3. LC 77-83007. (Science 5-13 Ser.). (Illus.). 1977. pap. text ed. 8.25 (ISBN 0-356-04350-9). Raintree Child.

--Structures & Forces: Stage 3. LC 77-82991. (Science 5-13 Ser.). (Illus.). 1977. pap. text ed. 8.25 (ISBN 0-356-04107-7). Raintree Child.

--Structures & Forces: Stages 1 & 2. LC 77-82991. (Science 5-13 Ser.). (Illus.). 1977. pap. text ed. 8.25 (ISBN 0-356-04007-0). Raintree Child.

James, Anna. The Darker Side of Love. (Orig.). 1979. pap. 2.50 (ISBN 0-515-05096-2). Jove Pubns.

--Sweet Love, Bitter Love. 1978. pap. 2.25 (ISBN 0-515-04697-3, 04697-3). Jove Pubns.

James, Antony. Capital Punishment. 1977. pap. 1.75 (ISBN 0-505-51189-4). Tower Bks.

--Presley: Entertainer of the Century. 1976. pap. 1.95 (ISBN 0-505-51239-4). Tower Bks.

James, Arthur M. A Dictionary of Thermodynamics. LC 76-5472. 1976. 19.95 (ISBN 0-470-15035-1). Halsted Pr.

James, Barrie G. The Future of the Multinational Pharmaceutical Industries to 1990. LC 77-72268. 1977. 39.95 (ISBN 0-470-99130-5). Halsted Pr.

James, Barry. Man's Guide to Business & Social Success. 1969. 13.65 (ISBN 0-87350-151-9); instructor's manual 14.95 (ISBN 0-685-16768-2). Milady.

James, Bessie R. Anne Royall's U. S. A. 1972. 27.50 (ISBN 0-8135-0732-4). Rutgers U Pr.

James, Blakely St. Christinas Escape. LC 80-85112. (Christina Van Bell Ser.). 256p. (Orig.). 1981. pap. 2.50 (ISBN 0-87216-820-4). Playboy Pbks.

James, Bruno S., tr. see St. Bernard de Clairvaux.

James, C. D. Twentieth Century French Reader. 1966. 8.00 (ISBN 0-08-011232-3); pap. 6.70 (ISBN 0-08-011231-5). Pergamon.

James, C. L. Mariners, Renegades & Castaways. 2nd ed. xvi, 154p. 1978. pap. 3.00 (ISBN 0-935590-10-2). Bewick Edns.

--Modern Politics. pap. 4.00 (ISBN 0-685-20861-3). Univ Place.

--Modern Politics. 2nd ed. (Illus.). iv, 167p. 1973. pap. 3.00 (ISBN 0-935590-09-9). Bewick Edns.

James, C. L., et al. Facing Reality. (Illus.). 174p. 1974. pap. 3.00 (ISBN 0-935590-05-6). Bewick Edns.

James, C. L. R. The Future in the Present: Selected Writings of C. L. R. James. LC 77-73129. 228p. 1980. pap. 6.95 (ISBN 0-88208-125-X). Lawrence Hill.

James, C. V., ed. see Rozental, D. E.

James, Carl. Contrastive Analysis. (Applied Linguistics & Language Study). 1980. pap. text ed. 9.00 (ISBN 0-582-55370-9). Longman.

James, Charles F. Documentary History of the Struggle for Religious Liberty in Virginia. LC 70-121101. (Civil Liberties in American History Ser). 1971. Repr. of 1900 ed. lib. bdg. 27.50 (ISBN 0-306-71977-0). Da Capo.

James, Clifford L. Principles of Economics. rev. 9th ed. (Orig.). 1972. pap. 4.95 (ISBN 0-06-460008-4, CO 8, COS). Har-Row.

James, Clive. The Crystal Bucket. 192p. 1981. 11.95 (ISBN 0-224-01890-6, Pub. by Chatto-Bodley-Jonathan). Merrimack Bk Serv.

--Unreliable Memoirs. LC 80-24245. 176p. 1981. 10.00 (ISBN 0-394-51263-4). Knopf.

James, Dan. Gunsmoke Mesa. 256p. (YA) 1974. 5.95 (ISBN 0-685-49094-7, Avalon). Bouregy.

--Shadow Guns. (YA) 1972. 5.95 (ISBN 0-685-24999-9, Avalon). Bouregy.

--Trouble at Choctaw Bend. (YA) 1972. 5.95 (ISBN 0-685-28626-6, Avalon). Bouregy.

James, David G. Scepticism & Poetry: An Essay on the Poetic Imagination. LC 80-21749. 274p. 1980. Repr. of 1960 ed. lib. bdg. 25.00x (ISBN 0-313-22840-X, JASP). Greenwood.

James, Dilmus D., jt. ed. see Street, James H.

James, Dorothy. Poverty, Politics & Change. (Illus.). 224p. 1972. pap. text ed. 8.95 (ISBN 0-13-686584-4). P-H.

James, Dorothy B. The Contemporary Presidency. 2nd ed. LC 73-19657. 350p. 1974. 9.85 o.p. (ISBN 0-672-53716-8); pap. 7.95 (ISBN 0-672-63716-2). Pegasus.

James, E. Anthony. Daniel Defoe's Many Voices: A Rhetorical Study of Prose Style & Literary Method. 269p. (Orig.). 1972. pap. text ed. 27.50x (ISBN 9-0620-3317-2). Humanities.

James, Edgar C. Epistles of Peter. (Teach Yourself the Bible Ser.). 1964. pap. 1.75 (ISBN 0-8024-2355-8). Moody.

--Second Corinthians: Keys to Triumphant Living. (Teach Yourself the Bible Ser.). 1964. pap. 1.75 (ISBN 0-8024-7680-5). Moody.

James, Edward. America Against Poverty. (Library of Social Policy & Administration). 1970. 10.00x (ISBN 0-7100-6760-7). Routledge & Kegan.

James, Edwin C., et al. Thoracic and Cardiovascular Surgery Continuing Education Review. 1980. pap. 16.00 (ISBN 0-87488-439-X). Med Exam.

James, Elizabeth & Barkin, Carol. How to Keep a Secret. (gr. k-6). 1980. pap. 1.25 (ISBN 0-440-43483-1, YB). Dell.

--How to Write a Term Paper. LC 80-13734. 96p. (gr. 7 up). 1980. PLB 6.67 (ISBN 0-688-51951-2); pap. 3.95 (ISBN 0-688-45025-3). Lothrop.

--Managing Your Money. LC 76-48287. (Money Ser.). (Illus.). (gr. 4-6). 1977. PLB 8.65 (ISBN 0-8172-0279-X). Raintree Pubs.

--Understanding Money. LC 76-47030. (Money Ser.). (Illus.). (gr. 2-3). 1977. PLB 8.65 (ISBN 0-8172-0277-3). Raintree Pubs.

--What Is Money? LC 76-46589. (Money Ser.). (Illus.). (gr. k-1). 1977. PLB 8.65 (ISBN 0-8172-0275-7). Raintree Pubs.

James, Elizabeth, jt. auth. see Barkin, Carol.

James, Elizabeth, jt. auth. see Pennington, R. Corbin.

James, Felix. The American Addition: History of a Black Community. LC 78-65427. (Illus.). 1979. pap. 8.25 (ISBN 0-8191-0663-1). U Pr of Amer.

James Ford Bell Library, University of Minnesota & University of Minnesota. The James Ford Bell Library: An Annotated Catalog of Original Source Materials Relating to the History of European Expansion, 1400-1800. (Library Catalogs). Date not set. lib. bdg. 95.00 (ISBN 0-8161-0361-5). G K Hall.

James, Francis G. North Country Bishop: A Biography of William Nicolson. 1956. 42.50x (ISBN 0-686-51425-4). Elliots Bks.

James, G. Circulation of the Blood. 1978. 59.50 (ISBN 0-8391-1241-6). Univ Park.

James, G. V. Water Treatment: A Survey of Current Methods of Purifying Domestic Supplies & Treating Industrial Effluents & Sewage. 4th ed. (Illus.). 1971. 28.95x (ISBN 0-291-39360-8). Intl Ideas.

James, Gene G., jt. auth. see Simco, Nancy D.

James, Henry. Ambassadors. 1902. 11.95 o.s.i. (ISBN 0-06-012170-X, HarpT). Har-Row.

--The Ambassadors. 1957. 12.95x (ISBN 0-460-00987-7, Evman); pap. 2.95 (ISBN 0-460-01987-2). Dutton.

--The American. (Norton Critical Edition). 1978. 14.95. Norton.

--Art of the Novel. 1934. lib. rep. ed. 6.95x (ISBN 0-684-15531-1, ScribC); pap. text ed. 5.95x (ISBN 0-684-15050-6, SL10, ScribC). Scribner.

--The Bodley Head Henry James, 11 vols. Incl. Vol. 1. The Europeans & Washington Square. 392p. 1967. 10.50x (ISBN 0-87471-341-2); Vol. 2. The Awkward Age. 432p. 1967. 14.50x (ISBN 0-87471-342-0); Vol. 3. The Bostonians. 448p. 1967. o.p. (ISBN 0-87471-343-9); Vol. 4. The Spoils of Poynton. 208p. 1967. 10.00x (ISBN 0-87471-344-7); Vol. 5. The Portrait of a Lady. 640p. 1968. 16.50x (ISBN 0-87471-345-5); Vol. 6. What Mazie Knew. 288p. 1969. 12.50x (ISBN 0-87471-346-3); Vol. 7. The Wings of the Dove. 544p. 1969. 11.00x (ISBN 0-87471-347-1); Vol. 8. The Ambassadors. 468p. 1970. 11.00x (ISBN 0-87471-348-X); Vol. 9. The Golden Bowl. 608p. 1971. 11.50x (ISBN 0-87471-349-8); Vol. 10. Princess Casamassima. 600p. 1972. 14.50x (ISBN 0-87471-350-1); Vol. 11. Daisy Miller & the Turn of the Screw. 208p. 1974. 10.00x (ISBN 0-87471-573-3). Rowman.

--English Hours. 376p. 1980. cancelled (ISBN 0-8180-1129-7). Horizon.

--The Europeans. 176p. 1976. Repr. of 1878 ed. lib. bdg. 12.95x (ISBN 0-89244-018-X). Queens Hse.

--The Golden Bowl. (Illus.). 592p. 1973. pap. 1.50 o.p. (ISBN 0-445-08227-5). Popular Lib.

--Hawthorne. 145p. (YA) (gr. 9-12). 1956. pap. 12.50x o.p. (ISBN 0-8014-0203-4). Cornell U Pr.

--International Episodes. Date not set. pap. write for info. (ISBN 0-14-004641-0). Penguin. Postponed.

--Lady Barberina & Other Tales. Ruhm, Herbert, ed. LC 62-51791. 8.95 (ISBN 0-8149-0126-3). Vanguard.

--Notes on Novelists, with Some Other Notes. LC 68-56451. 1969. Repr. of 1914 ed. 16.00x (ISBN 0-8196-0233-7). Biblo.

--The Other House. 228p. 1976. Repr. of 1896 ed. lib. bdg. 12.95x (ISBN 0-89244-083-X). Queens Hse.

--The Outcry. LC 80-17012. xii, 261p. 1981. Repr. of 1911 ed. 20.00 (ISBN 0-86527-335-9). Fertig.

--The Portrait of a Lady. Bamberg, Robert D., ed. (Norton Critical Edition Ser.). 1975. pap. text ed. 5.95 (ISBN 0-393-09259-3). Norton.

--The Portrait of a Lady. rev. ed. Dixson, Robert J., ed. (American Classics Ser.: Bk. 7). (gr. 9 up). 1974. pap. text ed. 2.75 (ISBN 0-88345-203-0, 18126); cassettes 40.00 (ISBN 0-685-38927-8); tapes 40.00 (ISBN 0-685-38928-6). Regents Pub.

--The Princess Casamassima. (Apollo Eds.). 608p. 1976. pap. 5.95 o.s.i. (ISBN 0-8152-0395-0, A-395, TYC-T). T Y Crowell.

--Richard Olney & His Public Service. LC 70-87445. (American Scene Ser). (Illus.). 1971. Repr. of 1923 ed. lib. bdg. 32.50 (ISBN 0-306-71516-3). Da Capo.

--Roderick Hudson. 1981. pap. 3.95 (ISBN 0-14-002982-6). Penguin.

--Tales of Henry James: Vol. 1, 1864-1869. Aziz, Maqbool, ed. (Illus.). 528p. 1973. 45.00x (ISBN 0-19-812457-0). Oxford U Pr.

--The Tales of Henry James, Vol. 2: 1870-1874. Aziz, Madbool, ed. 1979. 49.00x (ISBN 0-19-812572-0). Oxford U Pr.

--Theory of Fiction: Henry James. Miller, James E., Jr., ed. LC 78-147168. 1972. pap. 6.50x (ISBN 0-8032-5747-3, BB 542, Bison). U of Nebr Pr.

--Transatlantic Sketches. 448p. 1981. cancelled (ISBN 0-8180-1177-7). Horizon.

--The Turn of the Screw. Incl. The Aspern Papers. 1957. 10.50x (ISBN 0-460-00912-5, Evman); pap. 2.95 (ISBN 0-460-01912-0). Dutton.

--Washington Square. (Literature Ser). (gr. 10-12). 1970. pap. text ed. 3.33 (ISBN 0-87720-743-7). AMSCO Sch.

--Washington Square. 1963. pap. 1.95 (ISBN 0-14-001920-0). Penguin.

--What Maisie Knew. pap. 2.50 o.p. (ISBN 0-385-09289-X, A43, Anch). Doubleday.

--William Wetmore Story & His Friends, 2 vols. in one. LC 69-18460. (Library of American Art Ser). 1969. Repr. of 1903 ed. lib. bdg. 49.50 (ISBN 0-306-71249-0). Da Capo.

--The Wing of the Dove. 1978. 17.50 (ISBN 0-393-04478-5). Norton.

--The Wings of the Dove. Crowley, J. Donald & Hocks, Richard A., eds. (Norton Critical Edition Ser.). 1978. 17.50x (ISBN 0-393-04478-5); pap. 7.95 (ISBN 0-393-09088-4). Norton.

James, Henry see Hawthorne, Nathaniel.

James, Henry, jt. ed. see Honig, Werner K.

James, Houston T. The Spud Book: One Hundred One Ways to Cook Potatoes. LC 80-50166. (Illus.). 134p. 1980. pap. 4.95 (ISBN 0-934726-01-9). Seven Seven Search.

James, Hubert M., jt. auth. see Svoboda, Antonin.

James, I. M. The Topology of Stiefel Manifolds. LC 76-9646. (London Mathematical Society Lecture Notes Ser.: No. 24). 1977. 14.50x (ISBN 0-521-21334-7). Cambridge U Pr.

James, Janet W., ed. Women in American Religion. LC 79-5261. 288p. 1980. 21.95x (ISBN 0-8122-7780-5); pap. 9.95x (ISBN 0-8122-1104-9). U of Pa Pr.

James, Janice. A Lady of Repute. LC 78-20079. 264p. 1980. 10.95 (ISBN 0-385-13507-6). Doubleday.

James, Jean M., tr. see She, Lao.

James, John. The Contractors of Chartres. (Illus.). 232p. 1980. 60.00 (ISBN 0-7099-0180-1, Pub. by Croom Held Ltd England). Biblio Dist.

--Flowers When You Want Them: A Grower's Guide to Out-of-Season Bloom. LC 77-70139. (Illus.). 1977. 10.95 o.p. (ISBN 0-8015-2679-5); pap. 5.95 o.p. (ISBN 0-8015-2680-9). Dutton.

--History of the Worsted Manufacture in England from the Earliest Times. LC 68-93903. Repr. of 1857 ed. 25.00x (ISBN 0-678-05179-8). Kelley.

James, John H., jt. auth. see Champion, John M.

James, Judson L. American Political Parties: Potential & Performance. LC 79-77133. (Studies in Contemporary American Politics Ser.). (Orig.). 1969. 7.65 o.p. (ISBN 0-672-53504-1); pap. 4.95 (ISBN 0-672-63504-6). Pegasus.

James, Kristen. Windswept. (Orig.). 1981. pap. 2.75 (ISBN 0-671-42773-3). PB.

James, Leigh F. Wings of the Hawk. (Colonization of America Ser.). 408p. (Orig.). 1981. pap. 2.95 (ISBN 0-553-14276-3). Bantam.

James, Leonard F. Following the Frontier: American Transportation in the Nineteenth Century. LC 68-13811. (Curriculum Related Bks). (Illus.). (gr. 5-8). 1968. 4.95 o.p. (ISBN 0-15-228827-9, HJ). HarBraceJ.

James, Lloyd, et al. Reform & Development of Higher Education: A European Symposium. (Council of Europe Ser.). 1978. pap. text ed. 27.00x (ISBN 0-85633-152-X, NFER). Humanities.

James, Louis. English Popular Literature: Eighteen Nineteen to Eighteen Fifty-One. 1976. 22.50x (ISBN 0-231-04140-3). Columbia U Pr.

James, M. & Jongeward, D. Winning with People for Health Care Professionals. 1980. pap. cancelled (ISBN 0-201-00451-8). A-W.

James, M. E. Family, Lineage & Civil Society: A Study of Society, Politics & Mentality in the Durham Region, 1500-1640. 240p. 1973. 33.00x (ISBN 0-19-822408-7). Oxford U Pr.

James, M. Lynn, et al. General, Organic, & Biological Chemistry: Chemistry for the Living System. 1980. text ed. 21.95 (ISBN 0-669-01329-3); lab. guide 8.95 (ISBN 0-669-01332-3); study guide 7.95 (ISBN 0-669-01331-5); instrs'. guide free (ISBN 0-669-01330-7). Heath.

James, Maurice T., jt. auth. see Merritt, Richard W.

James, Maynard. I Believe in the Holy Spirit. LC 23-9036. Orig. Title: I Believe in the Holy Ghost. 176p. 1965. pap. 1.95 (ISBN 0-87123-241-3, 200241). Bethany Fell.

James, Michael. The Quiltmaker's Handbook. LC 77-15592. (Creative Handcraft Ser.). (Illus.). 1978. 14.95 (ISBN 0-13-749416-5, Spec); pap. 7.95 (ISBN 0-13-749408-4, Spec). P-H.

--The Second Quiltmaker's Handbook. (Creative Handcrafts Ser.). 208p. 1981. 24.95 (ISBN 0-13-797795-6, Spec); pap. 10.95 (ISBN 0-13-797787-5). P-H.

James, Millicent. What You Want to Know About Childbirth. rev. ed. (Illus.). 1971. pap. 2.95 (ISBN 0-589-00619-3, Dist. by C E Tuttle). Reed.

James, Montague R., tr. Apocryphal New Testament. 1924. 27.00x (ISBN 0-19-826121-7). Oxford U Pr.

James, Muriel. Techniques in Transactional Analysis: For Psychotherapists & Counselors. LC 76-9325. (Psychology Ser.). text ed. 22.95 (ISBN 0-201-03256-2). A-W.

James, Muriel & Savary, Louis. The Heart of Friendship. LC 74-25702. 1978. pap. 4.95 (ISBN 0-06-064113-4, RD 254, HarpR). Har-Row.

James, Muriel, jt. auth. see Jongeward, Dorothy.

James, N. D. The Arboriculturalist's Companion. 1972. 17.25x (ISBN 0-631-14110-3, Pub. by Basil Blackwell). Biblio Dist.

--The Forester's Companion. 2nd ed. 1966. 12.50x (ISBN 0-631-09620-5, Pub. by Basil Blackwell); pap. 8.95x (ISBN 0-631-10811-4). Biblio Dist.

James, N. P. & Ginsburg, R. N. The Seaward Margin of Belize Barrier & Atoll Reefs. (Special Publication of the International Association of Sedimentologist Ser.: No. 3). 191p. 1980. pap. 29.95x (ISBN 0-470-26928-6). Halsted Pr.

James One of Scotland. The King's Quair. (Clarendon Medieval & Tudor Ser.). 130p. 1971. 6.50x o.p. (ISBN 0-19-871022-4). Oxford U Pr.

James, Otis. Dolly Parton: A Photo-Bio. (Orig.). pap. 1.95 (ISBN 0-515-05157-8). Jove Pubns.
James, P. D. The Black Tower. 1980. pap. 2.25 (ISBN 0-445-08499-5). Popular Lib.
--Death of an Expert Witness. 1980. pap. write for info. (ISBN 0-445-04301-6). Popular Lib.
--Innocent Blood. 352p. 1981. pap. 3.50 (ISBN 0-445-04630-9). Popular Lib.
--A Mind to Murder. 1976. pap. 2.25 (ISBN 0-445-03154-9). Popular Lib.
--Unnatural Causes. 256p. 1975. pap. 2.25 (ISBN 0-445-00308-1). Popular Lib.
--An Unsuitable Job for a Woman. 288p. 1975. pap. 2.25 (ISBN 0-445-00297-2). Popular Lib.
--An Unsuitable Job for a Woman. 1980. lib. bdg. 13.95 (ISBN 0-8161-6788-5, Large Print Bks). G K Hall.
James, Patricia, tr. see Arnauld, Antoine.
James, Peter. The Air Force Mafia. 1974. 9.95 o.p. (ISBN 0-87000-289-9). Arlington Hse.
James, Peter N. Soviet Conquest from Space. (Illus.). 1974. 8.95 o.p. (ISBN 0-87000-224-4). Arlington Hse.
James, Philip. Children's Books of Yesterday. Holme, C. Geoffrey, ed. LC 79-174059. (Illus.). 128p. 1976. Repr. of 1933 ed. 22.00 (ISBN 0-8103-4135-2). Gale.
James, Phillip H. The Reorganization of Secondary Education. 145p. 1980. pap. text ed. 19.25x (ISBN 0-85633-214-3, NFER). Humanities.
James, Preston E. & Martin, Geoffrey J. All Possible Worlds, a History of Geographical Ideas. 2nd ed. LC 80-25021. 650p. 1981. text ed. 19.95 (ISBN 0-471-06121-2). Wiley.
James, Preston E. & Webb, Kempton. One World Divided: A Geographer Looks at the Modern World. 3rd ed. LC 79-12136. 1980. text ed. 20.95 (ISBN 0-471-02687-5). Wiley.
James, R., et al. Lab Manual for Criminalistics. 1980. 10.95 (ISBN 0-13-519819-4). P-H.
James, Richard & Plant, Richard M. Study Guide to the Multiple Choice Examinations for Chief Mate & Master. LC 76-48096. (Illus.). 1976. 25.00x (ISBN 0-87033-232-5). Cornell Maritime.
--Study Guide to the Multiple Choice Examinations for Third & Second Mates. 3rd ed. LC 79-1735. 1979. pap. 20.00x (ISBN 0-87033-252-X). Cornell Maritime.
James, Richard H. Reality and Other Writings. 1977. 4.00 o.p. (ISBN 0-682-48917-4). Exposition.
James, Robert R., ed. Churchill Speaks: Winston S. Churchill in Peace & War Collected Speeches, 1897-1963. abr. ed. LC 80-21880. 1000p. 1980. pap. 25.00 (ISBN 0-87754-256-2). Chelsea Hse.
--Winston S. Churchill: His Complete Speeches, 1897-1963, 8 vols. LC 74-505. 1981. pap. 97.50 (ISBN 0-87754-128-0). Chelsea Hse.
James, Roger. The Super Powers. 1978. 14.95 (ISBN 0-7134-0081-1, Pub. by Batsford England). David & Charles.
James, Sally. Heir to Rowanlea. 224p. 1981. pap. 1.95 (ISBN 0-449-50175-2, Coventry). Fawcett.
James, Shirley M., jt. auth. see Lutgendorf, Philip.
James, Simon & Nobes, Christopher. The Economics of Taxation. 320p. 1978. 33.00x (ISBN 0-86003-507-7, Pub. by Allan Pubs England); pap. 16.50x (ISBN 0-86003-607-3). State Mutual Bk.
--Workbook for the Economics of Taxation. 72p. 1978. pap. 3.00x (ISBN 0-86003-608-1, Pub. by Allan Pubs England). State Mutual Bk.
James, Stuart. The Complete Beginner's Guide to Judo. LC 76-56306. (gr. 6-12). 1978. PLB 6.95 (ISBN 0-385-06041-6). Doubleday.
--Lacrosse for Beginners. (Illus.). 128p. (gr. 7 up). 1981. PLB price not set. Messner.
James, T., jt. auth. see Obolensky, A.
James, T. G. An Introduction to Ancient Egypt. (British Museum Bks.). 286p. 1979. 20.00 (ISBN 0-374-83343-5); pap. 8.95 (ISBN 0-374-84339-2). FS&G.
James, Terry, jt. auth. see Poulton, G. A.
James, V. H. & Pasqualini, J. R., eds. Hormonal Steroids: Proceedings of the Fourth International Congress. 1976. 160.00 (ISBN 0-08-019682-9). Pergamon.
James, V. H. T., jt. auth. see International Congress on Hormonal Steroids, 5th, New Delhi, Oct.-Nov. 1978.
James, Vivian H., ed. The Adrenal Gland. LC 77-85870. 1979. 34.50 (ISBN 0-89004-297-7). Raven.
James, Warren St. see St. James, Warren.
James, Wendy & Kedgley, Susan J. The Mistress. 208p. 1974. 10.00 (ISBN 0-200-72102-X). Transatlantic.
James, Will. Cow Country. LC 27-22183. (Illus.). xii, 242p. 1973. pap. 4.25 (ISBN 0-8032-5774-0, BB 557, Bison). U of Nebr Pr.
--Scorpion: A Good Bad Horse. LC 36-23527. (Illus.). vi, 312p. 1975. pap. 5.95 (ISBN 0-8032-5822-4, BB 604, Bison). U of Nebr Pr.
James, William. Essays in Radical Empiricism & Pluralistic Universe: Radical Empiricism. 1971. pap. 2.25 o.p. (ISBN 0-525-47256-8). Dutton.
--Meaning of Truth: A Sequel to Pragmatism. 1970. pap. 3.45 o.p. (ISBN 0-472-06162-3, 162, AA). U of Mich Pr.
--Pragmatism. Kuklick, Bruce, ed. (Philosophical Classics Ser.). 152p. 1980. lib. bdg. 13.50 (ISBN 0-915145-04-9); pap. text ed. 2.95 (ISBN 0-915145-05-7). Hackett Pub.
--Principles of Psychology, 2 Vols. 1890. Vol. 1. pap. text ed. 6.50 (ISBN 0-486-20381-6); Vol. 2. pap. text ed. 6.50 (ISBN 0-486-20382-4). Dover.
--Selected Papers on Philosophy. 1917. 5.00x o.p. (ISBN 0-460-00739-4, Evman). Dutton.
--Varieties of Religious Experience. pap. 2.50 (ISBN 0-451-61603-0, ME1875, Ment). NAL.
--The Varieties of Religious Experience. LC 77-76278. 1978. pap. 2.95 o.p. (ISBN 0-385-13267-0, Im). Doubleday.
James, William see Lynd, Staughton.
James, William M. Apache: Fast Living, No. 19. 160p. (Orig.). 1981. pap. 1.50 (ISBN 0-523-40696-7). Pinnacle Bks.
Jameson & Sternlicht. Yankee Racehorse: U. S. Frigate Constellation. 1981. 10.00 (ISBN 0-87233-013-3). Bauhan.
Jameson, Anna B. The History of Our Lord As Exemplified in Works of Art; with That of His Type; St. John the Baptist; & Other Persons of the Old & New Testament, 2 vols. LC 92-167006. (Illus.). 1976. Repr. of 1890 ed. Set. 35.00 (ISBN 0-8103-4304-5). Gale.
--Legends of the Madonna, As Represented in the Fine Arts. LC 70-89273. (Tower Bks). (Illus.). lxxvi, 344p. 1972. Repr. of 1890 ed. 24.00 (ISBN 0-8103-3114-4). Gale.
Jameson, Cynthia. The Flying Shoes. LC 72-8126. (Illus.). 48p. (gr. k-3). 1973. 5.95 o.s.i. (ISBN 0-8193-0642-8, Four Winds); PLB 5.41 o.s.i. (ISBN 0-8193-0643-6). Schol Bk Serv.
--One for the Price of Two. LC 72-705. (Illus.). 48p. (gr. k-3). 1972. 5.95 o.s.i. (ISBN 0-8193-0602-9, Four Winds); PLB 5.41 o.s.i. (ISBN 0-8193-0603-7). Schol Bk Serv.
Jameson, Dee Dee & Schwalb, Bobbie. Every Woman's Guide to Hysterectomy: Taking Charge of Your Own Body. LC 77-14339. (Illus.). 1978. 8.95 o.p. (ISBN 0-13-292821-3, Spec); pap. 3.95 o.p. (ISBN 0-13-292813-2, Spec). P-H.
Jameson, E. C. Thermal Machining Processes. LC 79-62917. (Manufacturing Update Ser.). (Illus.). 29.00x (ISBN 0-87263-049-8). SME.
Jameson, Edwin. Gynecology & Obstetrics. (Illus.). 1962. Repr. of 1936 ed. pap. 7.50 o.s.i. (ISBN 0-02-847150-4). Hafner.
Jameson, F. A. Against All Odds. McCarthy, Pat, ed. (Pal Paperbacks Ser., Kit B). (Illus., Orig.). (gr. 7-12). 1974. pap. text ed. 1.25 (ISBN 0-8374-3504-8). Xerox Ed Pubns.
Jameson, Fredric. Fables of Aggression: Wyndham Lewis, the Modernist As Fascist. 1979. 12.95x (ISBN 0-520-03792-8). U of Cal Pr.
--Fables of Aggression: Wyndham Lewis, the Modernist As Facist. 1981. pap. 5.95 (ISBN 0-520-04398-7, CAL 496). U of Cal Pr.
--The Political Unconscious: Narrative As a Socially Symbolic Act. 320p. 1981. 19.50 (ISBN 0-8014-1233-1). Cornell U Pr.
Jameson, J. The Picture Life of O. J. Simpson. 1978. pap. 1.75 (ISBN 0-380-01906-X, 51649, Camelot). Avon.
Jameson, J. Franklin. Dictionary of United States History: Alphabetical, Chronological, Statistical. rev. ed. McKinley, Albert E., ed. LC 68-30658. (Illus.). 1971. Repr. of 1931 ed. 34.00 (ISBN 0-8103-3332-5). Gale.
--Essays on the Constitutional History of the United States in the Formative Period, 1775-1789. LC 78-99473. (American Constitutional & Legal History Ser.). 1970. Repr. of 1889 ed. lib. bdg. 32.50 (ISBN 0-306-71856-1). Da Capo.
Jameson, Jean, ed. see Rado, Sandor.
Jameson, John A. Treatise on Constitutional Conventions Their History, Powers, & Modes of Proceeding. LC 73-166332. (American Constitutional & Legal History Ser). 1972. Repr. of 1887 ed. lib. bdg. 59.50 (ISBN 0-306-70243-6). Da Capo.
Jameson, Jon. Monsters of the Mountains. (Easy-Read Facts Bks.). (Illus.). (gr. 2-4). 1979. PLB 6.45 s&l (ISBN 0-531-02269-2). Watts.
--The Picture Life of O. J. Simpson. (Picture Life Bks.). (Illus.). (gr. 2 up). 1977. PLB 5.90 (ISBN 0-531-01270-0). Watts.
Jameson, Kenneth. You Can Draw. LC 79-92494. (Start to Paint Ser.). (Illus.). 1980. pap. 3.95 (ISBN 0-8008-8755-7, Pentalic). Taplinger.
Jameson, Kenneth P. & Wilber, Charles K., eds. Religious Values & Development. (Illus.). 154p. 1981. 34.50 (ISBN 0-08-026107-8). Pergamon.
Jameson, Mack & Nist, Al. The Last Good-Bye & Other Stories. Roderman, Winifred H., ed. (Read on - Write on Ser). (Illus.). 64p. (Orig.). (gr. 7-12). 1981. pap. text ed. 2.85 (ISBN 0-915510-55-3); tchrs. ed. free. Janus Bks.
--Time to Change & Other Stories. Roderman, Winifred H., ed. (Read on - Write on Ser.). (Illus.). (gr. 7-12). 1981. pap. text ed. 2.85 (ISBN 0-915510-56-1). Janus Bks.
Jameson, R. Monnaies Grecques Antiques et Romaines. 1007p. (Fr.). 1980. Repr. 295.00 (ISBN 0-916710-65-3). Obol Intl.
Jameson, Storm. Love in Winter. pap. 1.95 o.p. (ISBN 0-425-03207-8). Berkley Pub.
Jamgotch, Nish, Jr. Soviet-East European Dialogue: Relations of a New Type? LC 68-29991. (Studies: No. 21). 1968. 5.50 (ISBN 0-8179-3211-9); pap. 4.00 (ISBN 0-8179-3212-7). Hoover Inst Pr.
Jamgotch, Nish, Jr., ed. Thinking the Thinkable: Investment in Human Survival. LC 77-18592. 1978. pap. text ed. 11.50x (ISBN 0-8191-0402-7). U Pr of Amer.
Jamieson, Archibald. Introduction to Quality Control. 1981. text ed. 16.95 (ISBN 0-8359-3264-8); instr's. manual free (ISBN 0-8359-3265-6). Reston.
Jamieson, B. G. & Reynolds, J. F. Tropical Plant Types. 1967. 29.00 (ISBN 0-08-012119-5); pap. 17.00 (ISBN 0-08-012120-9). Pergamon.
Jamieson, G. A. & Robinson, D. M., eds. Mamalian Cell Membranes, 5 vols. (Illus.). 1977. text ed. 159.95 set (ISBN 0-686-25573-9). Butterworths.
Jamieson, G. A., ed. see American Red Cross Seventh Annual Scientific Symposium, Washington, D.C., May 1975.
Jamieson, K. G. A First Notebook of Head Injury. 2nd ed. (Illus.). 1971. 14.95 (ISBN 0-407-17350-1). Butterworths.
Jamieson, Monika, et al. Towards Integration: A Study of Blind & Partially Sighted Children in Ordinary Schools. (Orig.). 1977. pap. text ed. 22.00x (ISBN 0-85633-119-8, NFER). Humanities.
Jamieson, Pat. A Topsy-Turvy Tale. (Golden Look-Look Bks.). 24p. (ps-3). 1978. PLB 5.38 (ISBN 0-307-61850-1, Golden Pr); pap. 0.95 (ISBN 0-307-11850-9). Western Pub.
Jamieson, Paul. Adirondack Canoe Waters: North Flow. 2nd ed. LC 80-26774. (Illus.). 300p. (Orig.). 1981. pap. 8.95 (ISBN 0-935272-13-5). ADK Mtn Club.
Jamiluddin, K. The Tropic Sun: Kipling & the Raj. 5th ed. 1975. 10.00x o.p. (ISBN 0-88386-950-0). South Asia Bks.
Jamison, Andrew. Steam-Powered Automobile: An Answer to Air Pollution. LC 78-108211. 1970. 8.50x o.p. (ISBN 0-253-18400-2). Ind U Pr.
Jamison, Dean T. Cost Factors in Planning Educational Technology Systems. (Fundamentals of Educational Planning Ser: No. 24). 1978. pap. 4.75 (ISBN 92-803-1076-3, U774, UNESCO). Unipub.
Jamison, Dean T. & McAnany, Emile G. Radio for Education & Development. LC 77-28472. (People & Communication Ser.: Vol. 4). 1978. 20.00x (ISBN 0-8039-0865-2); pap. 9.95x (ISBN 0-8039-0866-0). Sage.
Jamison, Rex L. & Kriz, Wilhelm. Urinary Concentrating Mechanism: Structure & Function. (Illus.). 425p. 1981. text ed. 35.00x (ISBN 0-19-502801-5). Oxford U Pr.
Jamison, Robert V. Introduction to Computer Science Mathematics. LC 70-39901. (Illus.). 256p. 1972. text ed. 14.95 o.p. (ISBN 0-07-032276-7, G); answer key 1.50 o.p. (ISBN 0-07-032281-3). McGraw.
Jammer, Max. The Philosophy of Quantum Mechanics: The Interpretations of Quantum Mechanics in Historical Perspective. LC 74-13030. 672p. 1974. 32.95 (ISBN 0-471-43958-4, Pub. by Wiley-Interscience). Wiley.
Jammes, Andre. William H. Fox Talbot. 1974. pap. 5.95 o.s.i. (ISBN 0-02-000450-8, Collier). Macmillan.
--William H. Fox Talbot: Inventor of the Positive-Negative Process. Oberli-Turner, Maureen, tr. (Men & Movements Ser.: Vol. 2). (Illus.). 96p. 1974. 10.95 o.s.i. (ISBN 0-02-558900-8). Macmillan.
Jammet, H., jt. ed. see Duchene, A.
Jampolsky, Gerald. Love Is Letting Go of Fear. 144p. 1981. pap. 2.50 (ISBN 0-553-14651-3). Bantam.
Jan. And Kyroot Said: Contemporary Work Commentaries from a Sanguinary Cosmic Sage. 315p. 1980. 9.00 (ISBN 0-936380-04-7). Chan Shal Imi.
--The Death of Gurdjieff in the Foothills of Georgia: Secret Papers of an American Work Group. 316p. 1980. 9.00 (ISBN 0-936380-03-9). Chan Shal Imi.
--Dialogues of Gurdjieff: An Allegorical Work Adventure, Vol. 1. rev., enl. ed. 314p. 1980. 9.00 (ISBN 0-936380-02-0). Chan Shal Imi.
--Magnus Machina: The Great Machine, (Work Maps of the Inner Terrain of Modern Man) rev., enl. ed. 216p. 1980. 6.00 (ISBN 0-936380-05-5). Chan Shal Imi.
Jan, G. & Sordelli, F. Iconographie Generale Des Ophidens: 1860-61, 3vols. in 1. 1961. 100.00 o.p. (ISBN 3-7682-0044-2). Lubrecht & Cramer.
Janae, Melanie. A Treasury of Poetry. 1981. 4.50 (ISBN 0-8062-1687-5). Carlton.
Janardhan, Pandarinath. Physico Chemical Techniques of Analysis, 2 vols. Vol. 1. 15.00x (ISBN 0-210-26919-7); Vol. 2. 15.00x (ISBN 0-210-22530-0). Asia.
Janaro, Richard P. Philosophy: Something to Believe in. 1975. pap. text ed. 7.95x (ISBN 0-02-475800-0, 47580). Macmillan.
Jancel, R. Foundations of Classical & Quantum Statistical Mechanics. 1970. 50.00 (ISBN 0-08-012823-8). Pergamon.
Jancura, Elise G. & Boos, Robert V. Establishing Controls & Auditing the Computerized Accounting System. 224p. 1980. text ed. 19.95 (ISBN 0-442-80507-1). Van Nos Reinhold.
Janda, Kenneth. Comparative Political Parties Data, Nineteen Fifty to Nineteen Sixty-Two. LC 79-90467. 1980. 14.00 (ISBN 0-89138-966-0). ICPSR.
--Political Parties: A Cross-National Survey. LC 80-15430. (Illus.). 1980. 100.00 (ISBN 0-02-916120-7). Free Pr.
Janda, Louis & Klenke-Hamel, Karen. Exploring Human Sexuality. (Orig.). 1980. pap. 9.95 (ISBN 0-442-25869-0); instr's. manual 2.50 (ISBN 0-442-25732-5). D Van Nostrand.
Janda, Louis, jt. auth. see Derlega, Valerian J.
Janda, Louis H., jt. auth. see Derlega, Valerian.
Jane, Fred T., ed. All the World's Fighting Ships, Eighteen Ninety-Eight. LC 69-14519. (Illus.). Repr. of 1898 ed. 14.95x (ISBN 0-685-06494-8, Pub by Arco). Biblo.
--Jane's All in the World's Aircraft, Nineteen Nuneteen. LC 69-14964. (Illus.). Repr. 25.00x (ISBN 0-685-06493-X, Pub by Arco). Biblo.
--Jane's Fighting Ships, 1914. facs. ed. LC 69-14519. (Illus.). 1969. 19.95 o.p. (ISBN 0-668-01873-9). Arco.
--Jane's Fighting Ships, 1919. facsimile ed. LC 69-14519. (Illus.). 1970. lib. bdg. 25.00 o.p. (ISBN 0-668-02018-0). Arco.
Jane, Margoe. Nowhere Fast. Hastings, Craig H., ed. (Illus.). 64p. (Orig.). 1980. pap. 4.00 (ISBN 0-9602330-1-6). Margoe Jane.
--Resurrection. 1976. 4.00 (ISBN 0-686-14638-7). Margoe Jane.
Janecek, Gerald, ed. Andrey Bely: A Critical Review. LC 77-75449. 232p. 1978. 16.00x (ISBN 0-8131-1368-7). U Pr of Ky.
Janeczko, Paul B., ed. Postcard Poems: A Collection of Poetry for Sharing. LC 79-14192. (gr. 6 up). 1979. 9.95 (ISBN 0-87888-155-7). Bradbury Pr.
Janes. The Odd Lot Boys & the Tree Fort War. (gr. 3-5). pap. 1.25 o.p. (ISBN 0-590-05408-2, Schol Pap). Schol Bk Serv.
Janes, Burton K. A Russian Adventure. 1980. 5.95 (ISBN 0-533-04479-0). Vantage.
Janes, E. C. The First Book of Camping. rev. ed (First Bks.). (Illus.). 72p. (gr. 3-6). 1977. PLB 6.45 (ISBN 0-531-00494-5). Watts.
Janes, Edward C., jt. auth. see Bergman, Ray.
Janes, Margaret E. The Literary World of Ana Maria Mantute. LC 77-119813. (Studies in Romance Languages: No. 3). 160p. 1970. 10.00x (ISBN 0-8131-1228-1). U Pr of Ky.
Jane's Pocket Books. Jane's Pocket Book of Record Breaking Aircraft. Taylor, John W., ed. (Jane's Pocket Book Ser.). 1981. pap. 6.95 (ISBN 0-02-080630-2, 08063, Collier). Macmillan.
Janes, Regina. Gabriel Garcia Marquez: Revolution in Wonderland. 136p. 1981. text ed. 9.00x (ISBN 0-8262-0337-X). U of Mo Pr.
Janes, Robert. The Great Canadian Outback. (Illus.). 1979. 19.95 (ISBN 0-295-95678-X, Pub. by Douglas & McIntyre Canada). U of Wash Pr.
Janes, W. H., jt. ed. see Allport, D. C.
Jane's Yearbooks. Jane's Historical Aircraft from Nineteen Two to Nineteen Sixteen. 96p. 1973. 4.95 o.p. (ISBN 0-385-01314-0). Doubleday.
Janet, Pierre. The Major Symptoms of Hysteria. 345p. 1980. Repr. of 1920 ed. lib. bdg. 40.00 (ISBN 0-8492-1367-3). R West.
--Mental State of Hystericals. (Contributions to the History of Psychology Ser.: Pt. 2, Medical Psychology). 1978. Repr. of 1901 ed. 30.00 (ISBN 0-89093-166-6). U Pubns Amer.
--Principles of Psychotherapy. Guthrie, H. M. & Guthrie, E. R., trs. 322p. 1980. Repr. of 1924 ed. lib. bdg. 40.00 (ISBN 0-8495-2760-0). Arden Lib.
Janet, Stanley A. Lessons Learned: South Vietnam Conflict. 1981. 6.95 (ISBN 0-533-03712-3). Vantage.
Janeway, Eliott see Johnson, Allen & Nevins, Allan.
Janeway, Elizabeth. Early Days of Automobiles. (Landmark Ser). (Illus.). (gr. 4-6). 1956. PLB 5.99 (ISBN 0-394-90368-4, BYR). Random.

Janeway, James. A Token for Children, Being an Exact Account of the Conversion, Holy & Exemplary Lives & Joyful Deaths of Several Young Children, Repr. Of 1676 Ed. Bd. with The Holy Bible in Verse. Harris, Benjamin. Repr. of 1717 ed; History of the Holy Jesus. Repr. of 1746 ed; The School of Good Manners....Rules for Children's Behavior, at the Meeting-House, at Home, at the Table, in Company, in Discourse, at School, Etc. Repr. of 1754 ed; The Prodigal Daughter....Who Because Her Parents Would Not Support Her in All of Her Extravagance, Bargained with the Devil to Poison Them, Etc. Williams, Elizabeth, pref. by. Repr. of 1771 ed. LC 75-32134. (Classics of Children's Literature, 1621-1932: Vol. 2). 1976. PLB 38.00 (ISBN 0-8240-2251-3). Garland Pub.

Janice. Little Bear Learns to Read the Cookbook. LC 69-14315. (Illus.). (gr. k-3). 1969. 7.25 (ISBN 0-688-41072-3); PLB 6.96 (ISBN 0-688-51072-8). Lothrop.

Janick, Jules. Horticultural Reviews, Vol. 2. (Illus.). 1980. lib. bdg. 33.00 (ISBN 0-87055-352-6). AVI.

--Horticultural Science. 3rd ed. LC 78-13053. (Illus.). 1979. text ed. 21.95x (ISBN 0-7167-1031-5). W H Freeman.

Janick, Jules, ed. Horticultural Reviews, Vol. 1. 1979. lib. bdg. 33.00 (ISBN 0-87055-314-3). AVI.

--Horticultural Reviews, Vol 3. (Illus.). 1981. lib. bdg. 33.00 (ISBN 0-87055-383-6). AVI.

Janick, Jules see Hoff, Johan E.

Janick, Jules, et al. Plant Science: An Introduction to World Crops. 2nd ed. LC 73-13921. (Illus.). 1974. text ed. 23.95x (ISBN 0-7167-0713-6). W H Freeman.

Janis, Arthur, jt. auth. see Miller, Morris.

Janis, Irving L. & Mann, Leon. Decision Making: A Psychological Analysis of Conflict, Choice & Commitment. LC 76-19643. (Illus.). 1979. pap. text ed. 9.95 (ISBN 0-02-916190-8). Free Pr.

--Decision Making: A Psychological Analysis of Conflict, Choice, & Commitment. LC 76-19643. 1977. 17.95 (ISBN 0-02-916160-6). Free Pr.

Janis, J. Harold & Dressner, Howard R. Business Writing. rev. ed. (Orig.). 1972. pap. 3.95 (ISBN 0-06-460151-X, CO 151, COS). Har-Row.

Janis, Mark W. Sea Power & the Law of the Sea. LC 76-11973. (Lexington Books Studies of Marine Affairs). (Illus.). 1976. 15.95 (ISBN 0-669-00717-X). Lexington Bks.

Janitch, Valerie. Dolls for Sale. (Illus.). 1980. 15.95 (ISBN 0-571-11535-7, Pub. by Faber & Faber); pap. 6.95 (ISBN 0-571-11536-5, Pub. by Faber & Faber). Merrimack Bk Serv.

Jank, Joseph K. Spices: Their Botanical Origin, Their Chemical Composition, Their Commercial Use Including Seeds, Herbs & Leaves. 1980. lib. bdg. 49.95 (ISBN 0-8490-3111-7). Gordon Pr.

Janke, James A. Jermiah Bacon. (Orig.). 1980. pap. 1.95 (ISBN 0-440-15289-5). Dell.

Janke, Rolf. Architectural Models. Date not set. 29.95 (ISBN 0-8038-0012-6). Hastings.

Jankowski, James P. Egypt's Young Rebels: "Young Egypt", 1933-1952. LC 75-8654. (Publications Ser.: No.145). 1975. 7.00 (ISBN 0-8179-6451-7). Hoover Inst Pr.

Jankowski, Stanislaw & Rafalski, Piotr. Warsaw: A Portrait of the City. Lubon, Miroslan, tr. from Pol. LC 80-460054. Orig. Title: Warszawa - Portret Miasta. (Illus.). 1979. 25.00x (ISBN 0-8002-2289-X). Intl Pubns Serv.

Jannacone, Pasquale. Walt Whitman's Poetry & the Evolution of Rhythmic Forms & Walt Whitman's Thought & Art. Militineos, Peter, tr. LC 72-90791. 1973. 19.00 o.s.i. (ISBN 0-910972-31-1). IHS-PDS.

Janner, Greville. Janner's Compendium of Employment Law. 759p. 1979. text ed. 45.50x (ISBN 0-220-66363-7, Pub. by Busn Bks England). Renouf.

--Janner's Employment Forms. 397p. 1979. text ed. 61.25x (ISBN 0-220-67027-7, Pub. by Busn Bks England). Renouf.

--Janner's Product Liability. 405p. 1979. text ed. 36.75x (ISBN 0-220-67008-0, Pub. by Busn Bks England). Renouf.

Jannersten, Eric. Precision Bridge. LC 73-7165. 224p. 1973. pap. 3.45 o.p. (ISBN 0-684-13541-8, SL485, ScribT). Scribner.

Jannerston, Eric. The Only Chance. Kelsey, H. W., tr. (Illus.). 176p. 1981. 12.95 (ISBN 0-370-30266-4, Pub. by Chatto-Bodley-Jonathan). Merrimack Bk Serv.

Janney, Abel. Narrative of the Capture of Abel Janney by the Indians in 1782. from His Diary: In: Ohio State Arch. & Hist. Society Publications, Vol. 8, 465-73, Columbus, Repr. Of 1900 Ed. Bd. with The Shetek Pioneers & the Indians. Hibschman, Harry J. Repr. of 1901 ed; Captivity Among the Sioux, August 18 to September 26, 1862: In: Minnesota Historical Society Collections, Vol. 9, St. Paul, 1901, pp. 395-426. White, Mrs. N. D. (Illus.). Repr. of 1901 ed; Elizabeth Hicks, a True Romance of the American War of Independence, 1775 to 1783, Abridged from Her Own Manuscript by Her Daughter Fanny Bird, Completed & Ed. by Her Granddaughter Louisa J. Marriott. Hicks, Elizabeth. Repr. of 1902 ed; Scout Journals, 1757. Narrative of James Johnson, a Captive During French & Indian Wars. Repr. of 1902 ed. LC 75-7132. (Indian Captivities Ser.: Vol. 104). 1976. lib. bdg. 44.00 (ISBN 0-8240-1728-5). Garland Pub.

Jannis, C. Paul, et al. Managing & Accounting for Inventories: Control, Income Recognition, & Tax Strategy. 3rd ed. 1979. 34.50 (ISBN 0-471-05016-4, Pub by Ronald Pr). Wiley.

Jannuzi, F. Tomasson & Peach, James T. Agrarian Structure of Bangladesh: Impediments to Development. (Westview Special Studies on China & East Asia). 1980. lib. bdg. 20.00x (ISBN 0-89158-682-2). Westview.

Janos, Andrew C. & Slottman, William B., eds. Revolution in Perspective: Essays on the Hungarian Soviet Republic. LC 74-138510. 1971. 21.50x (ISBN 0-520-01920-2). U of Cal Pr.

Janosch. Hey Presto! You're a Bear! (Illus.). 28p. (gr. 1-3). 1980. 8.95g (ISBN 0-316-45765-5, Pub. by Atlantic-Little Brown). Little.

--The Trip to Panama. (Illus.). 48p. (ps-3). 1981. 8.95 (ISBN 0-316-45766-3, Atlantic). Little.

Janousek, Patsy. Search to Find Happiness. 1981. 5.95 (ISBN 0-8062-1613-1). Carlton.

Janov, Arthur. The Primal Scream. 448p. 1981. pap. 6.95 (ISBN 0-399-50537-7, Perigee). Putnam.

--Prisoners of Pain: Unlocking the Power of the Mind to End Suffering. LC 79-8501. 288p. 1980. 11.95 (ISBN 0-385-15791-6, Anchor Pr). Doubleday.

Janov, Arthur & Holden, E. Michael. Primal Man: The New Consciousness. LC 75-20416. (Illus.). 522p. 1976. 10.00 o.s.i. (ISBN 0-690-01015-X, TYC-T). T Y Crowell.

Janov, Carol, ed. see Chetverikov, Sergii.

Janovic, Florence, jt. auth. see Nierenberg, Judith.

Janovski, N. A. & Paramanandhan, T. L. Ovarian Tumors. LC 77-176208. (Major Problems in Obstetrics & Gynecology Ser.: Vol. 4). (Illus.). 220p. 1973. 24.00 (ISBN 0-7216-5115-1). Saunders.

Janovy, John, Jr. Keith County Journal. 1980. pap. 4.95 (ISBN 0-312-45124-5). St Martin.

Janowitz, M. B., jt. auth. see Bettelheim, Bruno.

Janowitz, M. F., jt. auth. see Blyth, T. S.

Janowitz, Morris. Community Press in an Urban Setting: The Social Elements of Urbanism. 2nd ed. LC 67-21391. 1967. 8.00x o.s.i. (ISBN 0-226-39312-7). U of Chicago Pr.

--Professional Soldier: A Social & Political Portrait. LC 60-7090. 1960. 12.95 (ISBN 0-02-916170-3); pap. 6.95 (ISBN 0-02-916180-0). Free Pr.

Janowitz, Morris & Hirsch, Paul, eds. Reader in Public Opinion & Mass Communication. 3rd ed. LC 80-2444. 448p. 1981. pap. text ed. 10.95 (ISBN 0-02-916020-0). Free Pr.

Janowitz, Morris, ed. see Park, Robert E. & Burgess, Ernest W.

Janowitz, Tama. American Dad. 256p. 1981. 11.95 (ISBN 0-399-12585-X). Putnam.

Janowski, et al. SJIS State of the Art, Nineteen Eighty. 500p. 1980. pap. 15.00 (ISBN 0-89656-047-3, F-006). Natl Ctr St Courts.

Janowsky, David S., et al. Psychopharmacology Case Studies. 1978. pap. 12.75 (ISBN 0-87488-052-1). Med Exam.

Jansen, C. J. Readings in the Sociology of Migration. LC 72-105954. 1970. 21.00 (ISBN 0-08-006915-0); pap. 11.25 (ISBN 0-08-006914-2). Pergamon.

Jansen, Elly, ed. The Therapeutic Community: Outside the Hospital. 392p. 1980. 31.50x (ISBN 0-85664-967-8, Pub. by Croom Helm Ltd England). Biblio Dist.

--The Theraputic Community. 320p. 1980. 35.00x (ISBN 0-85664-967-8, Pub. by Croom Helm England). State Mutual Bk.

Jansen, Ewa, tr. see Wojcicki, Ryszard.

Jansen, F. J. Ludvig Holberg. LC 74-2171. (World Authors Ser.: Denmark: No. 321). 136p. 1974. lib. bdg. 10.95 (ISBN 0-8057-2431-1). Twayne.

Jansen, Frances O. & Johns, Ruth. Management & Supervision of Small Jails. (Illus.). 360p. 1978. 23.75 (ISBN 0-398-03680-2). C C Thomas.

Jansen, Frank, ed. Studies on Fronting. 1978. pap. text ed. 10.25x (ISBN 90-316-0163-2). Humanities.

Jansen, G. R., et al, eds. New Developments in Modelling Travel Demand & Urban Systems. 1979. 40.25x (ISBN 0-566-00269-8, Pub. by Gower Pub Co England). Renouf.

Jansen, Marius B. Japan & Its World: Two Centuries of Change. LC 80-7532. (Illus.). 120p. 1980. 9.50 (ISBN 0-691-05310-3). Princeton U Pr.

Jansen, Robert B. The ABC's of Bureaucracy. LC 78-1840. 1978. 13.95 (ISBN 0-88229-331-1). Nelson-Hall.

Jansen, Virginia. Fourty-Four Pounds or Size & Piece. (Illus.). 1978. pap. 3.50 o.p. (ISBN 0-931212-00-6, Pub. by Jansen). Caroline Hse.

Jansky, Robert. Interpreting the Eclipses. 1979. pap. 5.95 (ISBN 0-917086-08-2, Pub. by Astro Comp Serv). Para Res.

Janson. History of Art. 2nd ed. 1977. 21.95 (ISBN 0-13-389296-4). P-H.

Janson, Anthony F., ed. see Janson, H. W. & Cauman, Samuel.

Janson, H. & Kerman, Joseph. History of Art & Music. 1969. pap. text ed. 12.95 (ISBN 0-13-389312-X). P-H.

Janson, H., ed. see Held, Julius & Posner, Donald.

Janson, H. W. Paris Salon De 1843. (Catalogues of the Paris Salon 1673 to 1881: Vol. 29). 1977. Repr. lib. bdg. 50.00 (ISBN 0-8240-1853-2). Garland Pub.

--Paris Salon De 1847. (Catalogues of the Paris Salon 1673 to 1881: Vol. 33). 1977. Repr. lib. bdg. 50.00 (ISBN 0-8240-1857-5). Garland Pub.

--Paris Salon De 1853. (Catalogues of the Paris Salon 1673 to 1881: Vol. 38). 1977. Repr. lib. bdg. 50.00 (ISBN 0-8240-1862-1). Garland Pub.

--Paris Salons De 1796, 1797. (Catalogues of the Paris Salon 1673 to 1881: Vol. 8). 1977. Repr. lib. bdg. 50.00 (ISBN 0-8240-1832-X). Garland Pub.

--Paris Salons De 1806, 1808. (Catalogues of the Paris Salon 1673 to 1881: Vol. 12). 1977. Repr. lib. bdg. 50.00 (ISBN 0-8240-1836-2). Garland Pub.

Janson, H. W. & Cauman, Samuel. History of Art for Young People. 2nd, rev., enl. ed. Janson, Anthony F., ed. (Illus.). 440p. 1980. 18.50 o.p. (ISBN 0-686-62689-3, 0700-3). Abrams.

Janson, H. W., ed. Paris Salon de 1827 with Societe Louvre de 1827. (Catalogues of the Paris Salon, 1673 to 1881). 1978. lib. bdg. 50.00 (ISBN 0-8240-1841-9). Garland Pub.

--Paris Salon de 1833. (Catalogues of the Paris Salon, 1673 to 1881). 1977. lib. bdg. 50.00 (ISBN 0-8240-1843-5). Garland Pub.

--Paris Salon de 1834. (Catalogues of the Paris Salon, 1673 to 1881). 1977. lib. bdg. 50.00 (ISBN 0-8240-1844-3). Garland Pub.

--Paris Salon de 1835. (Catalogues of the Paris Salon, 1673 to 1881). 1977. lib. bdg. 50.00 (ISBN 0-8240-1845-1). Garland Pub.

--Paris Salon de 1836. (Catalogues of the Paris Salon, 1673 to 1881). 1977. lib. bdg. 50.00 (ISBN 0-8240-1846-X). Garland Pub.

--Paris Salon de 1837. (Catalogues of the Paris Salon, 1673 to 1881). 1977. lib. bdg. 50.00 (ISBN 0-8240-1847-8). Garland Pub.

--Paris Salon de 1838. (Catalogues of the Paris Salon, 1673 to 1881). 1977. lib. bdg. 50.00 (ISBN 0-8240-1848-6). Garland Pub.

--Paris Salon de 1839. (Catalogues of the Paris Salon, 1673 to 1881). 1977. lib. bdg. 50.00 (ISBN 0-8240-1849-4). Garland Pub.

--Paris Salon de 1840. (Catalogues of the Paris Salon, 1673 to 1881). 1977. lib. bdg. 50.00 (ISBN 0-8240-1850-8). Garland Pub.

--Paris Salon de 1841. (Catalogues of the Paris Salon, 1673 to 1881). 1977. lib. bdg. 50.00 (ISBN 0-8240-1851-6). Garland Pub.

--Paris Salon de 1842. (Catalogues of the Paris Salon, 1673 to 1881). 1977. lib. bdg. 50.00 (ISBN 0-8240-1852-4). Garland Pub.

--Paris Salon de 1844. (Catalogues of the Paris Salon, 1673 to 1881). 1977. lib. bdg. 50.00 (ISBN 0-8240-1854-0). Garland Pub.

--Paris Salon de 1845. (Catalogues of the Paris Salon, 1673 to 1881). 1977. lib. bdg. 50.00 (ISBN 0-8240-1855-9). Garland Pub.

--Paris Salon de 1846. (Catalogues of the Paris Salon, 1673 to 1881). 1978. lib. bdg. 50.00 (ISBN 0-8240-1856-7). Garland Pub.

--Paris Salon de 1848. (Catalogues of the Paris Salon, 1673 to 1881). 1977. lib. bdg. 50.00 (ISBN 0-8240-1858-3). Garland Pub.

--Paris Salon de 1849. (Catalogues of the Paris Salon, 1673 to 1881). 1977. lib. bdg. 50.00 (ISBN 0-8240-1859-1). Garland Pub.

--Paris Salon de 1850. (Catalogues of the Paris Salon, 1673 to 1881). 1977. lib. bdg. 50.00 (ISBN 0-8240-1860-5). Garland Pub.

--Paris Salon de 1852. (Catalogues of the Paris Salon, 1673 to 1881). 1977. lib. bdg. 50.00 (ISBN 0-8240-1861-3). Garland Pub.

--Paris Salon de 1855. LC 77-24778. (Catalogues of the Paris Salon, 1673 to 1881: Vol. 39). 1977. lib. bdg. 50.00 (ISBN 0-8240-1863-X). Garland Pub.

--Paris Salon de 1857. LC 77-24778. (Catalogues of the Paris Salon, 1673 to 1881: Vol. 40). 1977. lib. bdg. 50.00 (ISBN 0-8240-1864-8). Garland Pub.

--Paris Salon de 1859. LC 77-24778. (Catalogues of the Paris Salon, 1673 to 1881: Vol. 41). 1978. lib. bdg. 50.00 (ISBN 0-8240-1865-6). Garland Pub.

--Paris Salon de 1861. LC 77-24778. (Catalogues of the Paris Salon, 1673 to 1881: Vol. 42). 1977. lib. bdg. 50.00 (ISBN 0-8240-1866-4). Garland Pub.

--Paris Salon de 1863. LC 77-24778. (Catalogues of the Paris Salon, 1673 to 1881: Vol. 43). 1977. lib. bdg. 50.00 (ISBN 0-8240-1867-2). Garland Pub.

--Paris Salon de 1864. LC 77-24778. (Catalogues of the Paris Salon, 1673 to 1881: Vol. 44). 1977. lib. bdg. 50.00 (ISBN 0-8240-1868-0). Garland Pub.

--Paris Salon de 1865. LC 77-24778. (Catalogues of the Paris Salon, 1673 to 1881: Vol. 45). 1977. lib. bdg. 50.00 (ISBN 0-8240-1869-9). Garland Pub.

--Paris Salon de 1866. LC 77-24778. (Catalogues of the Paris Salon, 1673 to 1881: Vol. 46). 1977. lib. bdg. 50.00 (ISBN 0-8240-1870-2). Garland Pub.

--Paris Salon de 1867. LC 77-24778. (Catalogues of the Paris Salon, 1673 to 1881: Vol. 47). 1978. lib. bdg. 50.00 (ISBN 0-8240-1871-0). Garland Pub.

--Paris Salon de 1868. LC 77-24778. (Catalogues of the Paris Salon, 1673 to 1881: Vol. 48). 1977. lib. bdg. 50.00 (ISBN 0-8240-1872-9). Garland Pub.

--Paris Salon de 1869. LC 77-24778. (Catalogues of the Paris Salon, 1673 to 1881: Vol. 49). 1977. lib. bdg. 50.00 (ISBN 0-8240-1873-7). Garland Pub.

--Paris Salon de 1870. LC 77-24778. (Catalogues of the Paris Salon, 1673 to 1881: Vol. 50). 1977. lib. bdg. 50.00 (ISBN 0-8240-1874-5). Garland Pub.

--Paris Salon de 1872. LC 77-24778. (Catalogues of the Paris Salon, 1673 to 1881: Vol. 51). 1977. lib. bdg. 50.00 (ISBN 0-8240-1875-3). Garland Pub.

--Paris Salon de 1873. LC 77-24778. (Catalogues of the Paris Salon, 1673 to 1881: Vol. 52). 1977. lib. bdg. 50.00 (ISBN 0-8240-1876-1). Garland Pub.

--Paris Salon de 1874. LC 77-24778. (Catalogues of the Paris Salon, 1673 to 1881: Vol. 53). 1978. lib. bdg. 50.00 (ISBN 0-8240-1877-X). Garland Pub.

--Paris Salon de 1875. LC 77-24778. (Catalogues of the Paris Salon, 1673 to 1881: Vol. 54). 1977. lib. bdg. 50.00 (ISBN 0-8240-1878-8). Garland Pub.

--Paris Salon de 1876. LC 77-24778. (Catalogues of the Paris Salon, 1673 to 1881: Vol. 55). 1977. lib. bdg. 50.00 (ISBN 0-8240-1879-6). Garland Pub.

--Paris Salon de 1877. LC 77-24778. (Catalogues of the Paris Salon, 1673 to 1881: Vol. 56). 1977. lib. bdg. 50.00 (ISBN 0-8240-1880-X). Garland Pub.

--Paris Salon de 1878. LC 77-24778. (Catalogues of the Paris Salon, 1673 to 1881: Vol. 57). 1977. lib. bdg. 50.00 (ISBN 0-8240-1881-8). Garland Pub.

--Paris Salon de 1879. LC 77-24778. (Catalogues of the Paris Salon, 1673 to 1881: Vol. 58). 1977. lib. bdg. 50.00 (ISBN 0-8240-1882-6). Garland Pub.

--Paris Salon de 1880. LC 77-24778. (Catalogues of the Paris Salon, 1673 to 1881: Vol. 59). 1977. lib. bdg. 50.00 (ISBN 0-8240-1883-4). Garland Pub.

--Paris Salon de 1881. LC 77-24778. (Catalogues of the Paris Salon, 1673 to 1881: Vol. 60). 1977. lib. bdg. 50.00 (ISBN 0-8240-1884-2). Garland Pub.

--Paris Salons De 1673-1881, Vols. 2-5. Incl. Vol. 2. 1737-1743, 1745-48 (ISBN 0-8240-1826-5); Vol. 3. 1751, 1755, 1757, 1759, 1761, 1763 (ISBN 0-8240-1827-3); Vol. 4. 1765, 1767, 1769, 1771, 1773 (ISBN 0-8240-1828-1); Vol. 5. 1775, 1777, 1779, 1781, 1783 (ISBN 0-8240-1829-X). 1976. Repr. lib. bdg. 50.00 ea. Garland Pub.

Janson, H. W., compiled by. Paris Salons De 1785, 1787, 1789, 1791. (Catalogues of the Paris Salon 1673 to 1881: Vol. 6). 1977. Repr. lib. bdg. 50.00 (ISBN 0-8240-1830-3). Garland Pub.

--Paris Salons De 1793, 1795. (Catalogues of the Paris Salon 1673 to 1881: Vol. 7). 1977. Repr. lib. bdg. 50.00 (ISBN 0-8240-1831-1). Garland Pub.

Janson, H. W., ed. Paris Salons de 1800, 1801. (Catalogues of the Paris Salon, 1673 to 1881). 1977. lib. bdg. 50.00 (ISBN 0-8240-1834-6). Garland Pub.

--Paris Salons de 1802, 1804. (Catalogues of the Paris Salon, 1673 to 1881). 1977. lib. bdg. 50.00 (ISBN 0-8240-1835-4). Garland Pub.
--Paris Salons de 1810, 1812. (Catalogues of the Paris Salon, 1673 to 1881). 1977. lib. bdg. 50.00 (ISBN 0-8240-1837-0). Garland Pub.
--Paris Salons de 1814, 1817. (Catalogues of the Paris Salon, 1673 to 1881). 1977. lib. bdg. 50.00 (ISBN 0-8240-1838-9). Garland Pub.
--Paris Salons de 1819, 1822. (Catalogues of the Paris Salon, 1673 to 1881). 1977. lib. bdg. 50.00 (ISBN 0-8240-1839-7). Garland Pub.
--Paris Salons de 1830, 1831. (Catalogues of the Paris Salon, 1673 to 1881). 1977. lib. bdg. 50.00 (ISBN 0-8240-1842-7). Garland Pub.

Janson, H. W., et al. A Basic History of Art. 2nd ed. (Illus.). 444p. 1981. pap. text ed. 15.95 (ISBN 0-686-69326-4). P-H.

Janson, Lone E. The Copper Spike. LC 75-16446. (Illus.). 160p. 1975. pap. 9.95 (ISBN 0-88240-066-5). Alaska Northwest.

Janssen, G. E., ed. Selections from Science & Sanity. 1972. Repr. of 1948 ed. 8.00x (ISBN 0-937298-02-6). Inst Gen Semantics.

Janssen, Horst, illus. Horst Janssen: Master Drawings. LC 79-92751. (Illus.). 50p. (Orig.). 1980. pap. 6.50 (ISBN 0-88397-026-0). Intl Exhibit Foun.

Janssen, Robert B., jt. auth. see Green, Janet C.

Janssen-Jurreit, Marielouise. Sexism: The Male Monopoly on History & Thought. Moberg, Verne, tr. from Ger. 384p. 1981. 19.95 (ISBN 0-374-26167-9). FS&G.

Jansson, B. & Winqvist, T. Planning of Subsurface Use. 1978. text ed. 42.00 (ISBN 0-08-022689-2). Pergamon.

Jansson, Tove. Comet in Moominland. (gr. 3-5). 1975. pap. 1.95 (ISBN 0-380-00436-4, 52100, Camelot). Avon.
--The Exploits of Moominpappa. 1978. pap. 1.50 (ISBN 0-380-41665-4, 41665, Camelot). Avon.
--Finn Family Moomintroll. 1975. pap. 1.95 (ISBN 0-380-00350-3, 51771, Camelot). Avon.
--Moominhsummer Madness. (ps-8). 1976. pap. 1.25 o.s.i. (ISBN 0-380-00633-2, 39768, Camelot). Avon.
--Moominland Midwinter. 1976. pap. 1.95 (ISBN 0-380-00748-7, 51789, Camelot). Avon.
--Moominstroll, 7 vols. Incl. Comet in Moominland. Vol. 1 (ISBN 0-380-00436-4, 39784); Finn Family Moomintroll. Vol. 2 (ISBN 0-380-00350-3, 39776); Moominland Midwinter. Vol. 3 (ISBN 0-380-00748-7, 30205); Moominpappa at Sea. Vol. 4 (ISBN 0-380-01726-1, 34157); Moomin's Summer Madness. Vol. 5 (39768); Moominvalley in November. Vol. 6 (ISBN 0-380-00765-7, 30544); Tales from Moominvalley. Vol. 8 (ISBN 0-380-00911-0, 30544). (gr. 6 up). 1978. pap. 1.25 ea. o.s.i. (Camelot); pap. 8.75 boxed set o.s.i. (ISBN 0-380-34926-4, 34926). Avon.

Jantsch, Erich. The Self-Organizing Universe: Scientific & Human Implications of the Emerging Paradigm of Evolution. (Systems Science & World Order Library). (Illus.). 1980. text ed. 52.00 (ISBN 0-08-024312-6); pap. text ed. 16.00 (ISBN 0-08-024311-8). Pergamon.

Jantsch, Erich, ed. The Evolutionary Vision: Toward a Unifying Paradigm of Physical, Biological, & Sociocultural Evolution. (AAAS Selected Symposium: No. 6). 200p. 1981. lib. bdg. 17.50x (ISBN 0-86531-140-4). Westview.

Jantsch, Erich & Waddington, Conrad H., eds. Evolution & Consciousness: Human Systems in Transition. (Illus.). 1976. 26.50 (ISBN 0-201-03438-7, Adv Bk Prog); pap. 14.50 (ISBN 0-201-03439-5). A-W.

Jantscher, Gerald R. Bread Upon the Waters: Federal Aids to the Maritime Industries. (Studies in the Regulation of Economic Activity). 164p. 1975. 10.95 (ISBN 0-8157-4574-5). Brookings.
--Trusts & Estate Taxation. (Studies of Government Finance). 11.95 (ISBN 0-8157-4576-1); pap. 4.95 (ISBN 0-8157-4575-3). Brookings.

Jantz, Ursula. Targets of Satire in the Comedies of Etherege, Wycherley & Congreve. (Salzburg Studies in English Literature: Poetic Drama & Poetic Theory Ser.: No. 42). 1978. pap. text ed. 25.00x (ISBN 0-391-01435-8). Humanities.

Jantzen, Steven L. Winning Ideas in the Social Studies. LC 77-9530. (Illus.). 1977. pap. text ed. 5.50x (ISBN 0-8077-2541-2). Tchrs Coll.

Janus. Man Ray. (Illus.). 160p. 1981. 19.95 (ISBN 0-8120-5374-5). Barron.

Janus, Christopher G. & Brashler, William. The Search for the Peking Man. (Illus.). 208p. 1975. 11.95 o.s.i. (ISBN 0-02-558990-3). Macmillan.

Janvier, Ludovic. The Bathing Girl. Mathew, John, tr. 1980. 8.95 (ISBN 0-7145-3519-2). Riverrun NY.

Janz, D., et al, eds. Epilepsy, Pregnancy, & Child. 1981. text ed. price not set (ISBN 0-89004-654-9). Raven.

Janz, George J. & Tompkins, R. P. T. Non-Aqueous Electrolytes Handbook, 2 vols. Vol. 1, 1972. 88.00 (ISBN 0-12-380401-9); Vol. 2, 1974. 88.00 (ISBN 0-12-380402-7); Set. 142.00 (ISBN 0-685-36102-0). Acad Pr.

Janz, George J., jt. ed. see Ives, David G.

Janzen, Curtis, jt. ed. see Harris, Oliver.

Janzen, John M. The Quest for Therapy in Lower Zaire. (Comparative Studies of Health Systems & Medical Care). 1978. 23.75x (ISBN 0-520-03295-0). U of Cal Pr.

Janzen, Peter A. How to Operate & Maintain Your Car & Save Thousands of Dollars. 120p. (Orig.). 1981. pap. 4.95 (ISBN 0-9604458-0-3). P A Janzen.

Janzen, Reinhild. Albrecht Altdorfer: Four Centuries of Criticism. Kuspit, Donald B., ed. (Studies in Fine Arts: Criticism). 208p. 1980. 24.95 (ISBN 0-8357-1120-X, Pub. by UMI Res Pr). Univ Microfilms.

Janzen, Waldemar, tr. see Wolff, Hans W., Jr.

Jao, Y. C. Banking & Currency in Hong Kong: A Study of Postwar Financial Development. 350p. 1975. 37.50x (ISBN 0-8419-5002-4). Holmes & Meier.

Japan Broadcasting Corporation, ed. Unforgettable Fire: Pictures Drawn by Atomic Bomb Survivors. (Illus.). 1981. 15.95 (ISBN 0-394-51585-4); pap. 7.95 (ISBN 0-394-74823-9). Pantheon.

Japan External Trade Organization & Press International, Ltd. (Tokyo) China: A Business Guide. (Illus.). 216p. (Orig.). 1979. pap. 30.00x (ISBN 0-8002-2235-0). Intl Pubns Serv.

Japan Institute of International Affairs, ed. White Papers of Japan: Annual Abstract of Official Reports & Statistics of the Japanese Government 1978-79. LC 72-620531. (Illus.). 228p. (Orig.). 1980. pap. 37.50x (ISBN 0-8002-2734-4). Intl Pubns Serv.

Japan National Committee for Theoretical & Applied Mechanics, ed. Theoretical & Applied Mechanics, Vol. 28. 579p. 1980. 89.50x (ISBN 0-86008-264-4, Pub. by Univ Tokyo Pr Japan). Intl Schol Bk Serv.

Japan National Preparatory Committee. A Call from Hibakusha of Hiroshima & Nagasaki: Proceedings of the International Symposium on the Damage & After-Effects of the Atomic Bombing of Hiroshima & Nagasaki, 21 July - 9 August 1977, Tokyo, Hiroshima & Nagasaki. (Illus.). 1979. pap. 37.00 (ISBN 0-08-024306-1). Pergamon.

Japan Photographers Association. A Century of Japanese Photography. (Illus.). 1981. 45.00 (ISBN 0-394-51232-4). Pantheon. Postponed.

Japan Textile Color Design Center. Textile Designs of Japan, Vol. I: Free-Style Designs. LC 79-89347. (Textile Designs of Japan Ser.). (Illus.). 440p. 1980. 150.00 (ISBN 0-87011-396-8). Kodansha.
--Textiles Designs of Japan, Vol. III: Okinawan, Ainu, & Foreign Designs. LC 79-89347. (Illus.). 400p. 1981. 150.00 (ISBN 0-87011-404-2). Kodansha.

Japan-U.S. Conference on Libraries & Information Science in Higher Education, 3rd, Kyoto, Japan, Oct. 28-31, 1975. Japanese & U.S. Research Libraries at the Turning Point: Proceedings. Stevens, Robert D., et al, eds. LC 77-2535. 1977. 12.00 (ISBN 0-8108-1028-X). Scarecrow.

Japanese Culture Institute. A Hundred Things Japanese. (Illus.). 216p. 1976. 15.00 (ISBN 0-87040-364-8). Japan Pubns.

Japikse, Carl, jt. auth. see Leichtman, Robert R.

Japp, Alexander H. Three Great Teachers of Our Own Time. 255p. 1980. Repr. of 1865 ed. lib. bdg. 30.00 (ISBN 0-8492-1281-2). R West.

Japrisot, Sebastien. Trap for Cinderella. (Crime Monthly Ser). 1979. pap. 2.50 (ISBN 0-14-005364-6). Penguin.

Jaques Cattell Press, ed. American Book Trade Directory 1979. LC 15-23627. 1026p. 1979. 49.95 o.p. (ISBN 0-8352-1137-1). Bowker.
--American Book Trade Directory 1980. 26th ed. LC 15-23627. 1090p. 1980. 54.95 o.p. (ISBN 0-8352-1252-1). Bowker.
--American Library Directory 1979. 32nd ed. LC 23-3581. 1979. 49.95 o.p. (ISBN 0-8352-1139-8). Bowker.
--American Library Directory 1980. 33rd ed. LC 23-3581. 1700p. 1980. 54.95 (ISBN 0-8352-1251-3). Bowker.
--American Society of Composers, Authors & Publishers Biographical Dictionary. 4th ed. 560p. 1980. 43.95 (ISBN 0-8352-1283-1). Bowker.
--Association of Executive Recruiting Consultants. 256p. 1980. 38.50 (ISBN 0-8352-1256-4). Bowker.
--Association of Executive Recruiting Consultants. 2nd ed. 300p. 1981. 38.50 (ISBN 0-8352-1355-2). Bowker.
--Biographical Directory of the American Academy of Pediatrics. 1604p. 1980. 95.00 (ISBN 0-8352-1282-3). Bowker.
--Energy Research Programs. 450p. 1981. 75.00 (ISBN 0-8352-1352-8). Bowker.
--Energy Research Programs Directory. 944p. 1980. 75.00 (ISBN 0-8352-1242-4). Bowker.
--The Librarians Phone Book 1981. 2nd ed. 445p. 1980. pap. 9.95 (ISBN 0-8352-1321-8). Bowker.
--Library Journal Book Review, 1979. LC 68-59515. 769p. 1980. 28.95 (ISBN 0-8352-1272-6). Bowker.
--Research Programs in the Medical Sciences. 816p. 1980. 79.95 (ISBN 0-8352-1293-9). Bowker.

Jaques, E. A General Theory of Bureaucracy. LC 76-7380. 1976. 24.95 (ISBN 0-470-15097-1). Halsted Pr.
--Measurement of Responsibility: A Study of Work, Payment & Individual Capacity. LC 72-5856. 144p. 1972. 12.95 (ISBN 0-470-44020-1). Halsted Pr.

Jaques, Faith. Tilly's Rescue. LC 80-14419. (Illus.). 32p. (ps-4). 1981. 9.95 (ISBN 0-689-50175-7, McElderry Bk). Atheneum.

Jaques, H. E. Plants We Eat & Wear. LC 74-12656. (Illus.). 192p. 1975. pap. 2.50 o.p. (ISBN 0-486-22563-1). Dover.

Jaques, Harry E., jt. auth. see Wilkinson, R. E.

Jaquette, Jane S., ed. Women in Politics. LC 74-1037. 384p. 1974. 26.50 (ISBN 0-471-44022-1, Pub. by Wiley-Interscience). Wiley.

Jaquish, M. P. Personal Resume Preparation. LC 68-20098. (Wiley Series on Human Communication). 1968. 15.95 (ISBN 0-471-44025-6, Pub. by Wiley-Interscience). Wiley.

Jaquith, Priscilla. Bo Rabbit Smart for True: Folktales from the Gullah. (Illus.). 64p. (gr. 6-12). 1981. 8.95 (ISBN 0-399-20793-7); PLB 8.99 (ISBN 0-686-28869-6). Philomel.

Jarabak, Joseph R. & Fizzell, James A. Technique & Treatment with Light-Wire Edgewise Appliances, 2 vols. 2nd ed. LC 72-91624. (Illus.). 1300p. 1972. 62.50 (ISBN 0-8016-2429-0); Vol. 1. 62.50 (ISBN 0-8016-2430-4, 2430); Vol. 2. 62.50 (ISBN 0-8016-2431-2, 2431). Mosby.

Jarass, L., et al. Wind Energy. (Illus.). 230p. 1981. 43.70 (ISBN 0-387-10362-7). Springer-Verlag.

Jarchow, Willard R. Computer Programming Assembler Language. 1970. pap. text ed. 13.30 o.p. (ISBN 0-672-96100-8); tchrs'. manual 5.00 o.p. (ISBN 0-672-26101-4). Bobbs.
--Computer Programming-RPG. 2nd ed. LC 70-96931. 1969. pap. text ed. 15.50 (ISBN 0-672-96025-7); tchrs'. manual 6.67 (ISBN 0-672-96026-5). Bobbs.

Jardim, Anne, jt. auth. see Hennig, Margaret.

Jardin, Pascal. Vichy Boyhood. 1975. 7.95 o.p. (ISBN 0-571-10739-7, Pub. by Faber & Faber). Merrimack Bk Serv.

Jardin, Rosamond see Du Jardin, Rosamond.

Jardin, Rosamond Du see Du Jardin, Rosamond.

Jardine, A. K. Operational Research in Maintenance. 242p. 1970. 45.00x (ISBN 0-7190-0389-X, Pub. by Manchester U Pr England). State Mutual Bk.

Jardine, Alice, tr. see Kristeva, Julia.

Jardine, Jim. Nat Phil. Yrs. 3 & 4, 1974. text ed. 11.00x combined ed. o.p. (ISBN 0-435-67494-3); Yr. 5, 1973. text ed. 10.95x o.p. (ISBN 0-435-68220-2); Yr. 3, 1970. wkbk. 4.95 o.p. (ISBN 0-435-67491-9); Yr. 4, 1971. wkbk. 4.25x o.p. (ISBN 0-435-67492-7); wkbk. 4.25 o.p. (ISBN 0-435-67493-5). Heinemann Ed.
--Physics Is Fun, 4 bks. 1972. Bk. 1. text ed. 5.50x o.p. (ISBN 0-435-67470-6); Bk. 2. pap. text ed. 6.50x o.p. (ISBN 0-435-67496-X); Bk. 3. text ed. 9.50x o.p. (ISBN 0-435-67474-9); Bk. 4. text ed. 9.50x o.p. (ISBN 0-435-67476-5); tchr's guide to bks. 1 & 2 5.50x o.p. (ISBN 0-435-67480-3); tchr's guide to bk.3 3.95x o.p. (ISBN 0-435-67481-1); tchr's guide to bk.4 3.95x o.p. (ISBN 0-435-67482-X). Heinemann Ed.
--Physics Workbook, 3 bks. 1970. pap. text ed. 4.25x ea. o.p.; Yr. 3. pap. text ed. (ISBN 0-435-67485-4); Yr. 4. pap. text ed. (ISBN 0-435-67486-2); Yr. 5. pap. text ed. (ISBN 0-435-67487-0). Heinemann Ed.

Jardine, Lisa. Francis Bacon: Discovery & the Art of Discourse. (Illus.). 304p. 1975. 32.95 (ISBN 0-521-20494-1). Cambridge U Pr.

Jardine, N. & Sibson, R. Mathematical Taxonomy. LC 70-149578. 1971. 38.50 (ISBN 0-471-44050-7, Pub. by Wiley-Interscience). Wiley.

Jaremko, Matt E. Cognitive-Behavioral Reflections on Some Dimensions of Personality. LC 79-6602. 1980. pap. text ed. 9.50 (ISBN 0-8191-0924-X). U Pr of Amer.

Jaress, Michael F. Congratulations, You Made It... Again. (Illus.). 288p. (Orig.). 1981. pap. 6.95 (ISBN 0-938320-04-1). Comm Consultants.

Jarett, D. England in the Age of Hogarth. (Illus.). 256p. 1980. text ed. 13.75x (ISBN 0-246-64064-2). Humanities.

Jarett, Leonard, jt. auth. see Sonnenwirth, Alex C.

Jarir & Farazdag. Al Naqaid. Wormhoudt, Arthur, tr. from Arabic. (Arab Translation Ser.: No. 7). 1974. pap. 6.50 (ISBN 0-916358-57-7). Wormhoudt.

Jarman, A. O. & Hughes, G. R., eds. A Guide to Welsh Literature, Vol. 1. 1976. text ed. 15.50x (ISBN 0-7154-0124-6). Humanities.
--A Guide to Welsh Literature, Vol. 2. 1980. text ed. 23.50x (ISBN 0-7154-0457-1). Humanities.

Jarman, Christopher. The Development of Handwriting Skills: A Book of Resources for Teachers. 150p. 1980. 17.95x (ISBN 0-631-19240-9, Pub. by Basil Blackwell); pap. 9.95x (ISBN 0-631-19230-1). Biblio Dist.
--Teach Your Children Woodwork. LC 74-11762. (Illus.). 96p. 1975. 7.95 (ISBN 0-87749-722-2). Sterling.

Jarman, Colin. Buying a Boat. LC 80-68904. (Illus.). 160p. 1981. 19.95 (ISBN 0-7153-7960-7). David & Charles.

Jarman, Colin & Beavis, Bill. Modern Rope Seamanship. LC 76-20290. (Illus.). 1979. 15.00 (ISBN 0-87742-074-2). Intl Marine.

Jarman, Douglas. The Music of Alban Berg. 1978. 45.00x (ISBN 0-520-03485-6). U of Cal Pr.

Jarman, John. Junior Soccer. (Illus.). 1976. 7.95 (ISBN 0-571-10846-6, Pub. by Faber & Faber); pap. 3.95 (ISBN 0-571-10847-4). Merrimack Bk Serv.

Jarman, Lytton P. & Barraclough, Robin I. The Bullnose & Flatnose Morris. LC 75-42598. (Illus.). 264p. 1976. 21.00 (ISBN 0-7153-6665-3). David & Charles.

Jarman, Martha V. Impala Social Behavior: Territory, Hierarchy, Mating, & the Use of Space. (Advances in Ethology Ser.: Vol. 21). (Illus.). 96p. (Orig.). 1979. pap. text ed. 33.00 (ISBN 3-489-60936-0). Parey Sci Pubs.

Jarman, Ray C. & Benson, Carmen. The Grace & the Glory of God: Deliverance from Cults. 98p. 1968. pap. 2.95 o.p. (ISBN 0-912106-71-9). Logos.

Jarman, Ronald F. & Das, J. P. Issues in Developmental Disabilities. LC 80-12931. 136p. (Orig.). 1980. pap. 11.50 (ISBN 0-8357-0524-2, SS-00136). Univ Microfilms.

Jarman, T. L. Democracy & World Conflict, 1868-1965: A History of Modern Britain. (History of England Ser). 1968. text ed. 5.50x o.p. (ISBN 0-7137-0315-6). Humanities.
--Landmarks in the History of Education. 1973. pap. 8.95 (ISBN 0-7195-0710-3). Transatlantic.
--The Rise & Fall of Nazi Germany. LC 56-9548. 388p. 1956. 15.00x, usa (ISBN 0-8147-0217-1). NYU Pr.

Jarnow, Jeannette A. Inside the Fashion Business: Text & Readings. 3rd ed. 450p. 1981. text ed. 20.95 (ISBN 0-471-06038-0). Wiley.

Jarnstrom, Edward G. Recueil De Chansons Pieuses Du XIIIe Siecle. LC 80-2162. 1981. Repr. of 1910 ed. 29.50 (ISBN 0-404-19024-3). AMS Pr.

Jaroch, F. A., et al. Washout at Liberty Valley. (Adventures of the Sneeky Sneekers Ser.). (Illus.). 32p. (gr. 1-4). 1978. PLB 7.95 (ISBN 0-516-03407-3). Childrens.

Jarrard, Leonard E., ed. Cognitive Processes of Nonhuman Primates. 1971. 26.50 (ISBN 0-12-380850-2). Acad Pr.

Jarrell, Randall. A Bat Is Born. LC 76-52725. (ps-3). 1978. 5.95a o.p. (ISBN 0-385-12223-3); PLB (ISBN 0-385-12224-1). Doubleday.
--Bat-Poet. (Illus.). (gr. 4-6). 1964. 8.95g (ISBN 0-02-747640-5). Macmillan.
--The Complete Poems. 507p. 1969. 20.00 (ISBN 0-374-12716-6); pap. 10.95 (ISBN 0-374-51305-8). FS&G.
--Kipling, Auden & Co. Essays & Reviews, 1935-1964. 1980. 17.50 (ISBN 0-374-18153-5). FS&G.
--Lost World. 1965. 3.95 o.s.i. (ISBN 0-02-558980-6). Macmillan.
--Pictures from an Institution. 1980. pap. 2.95 (ISBN 0-686-69257-8, 49650, Bard). Avon.

Jarrell, Randall, tr. see Grimm Brothers.

Jarrell, Randall, tr. see Grimm, Jacob & Grimm, Wilhelm.

Jarrett. Britain: Sixteen Eighty-Eight to Eighteen Fifteen. 1976. pap. 9.95 (ISBN 0-312-09695-X). St Martin.

Jarrett, A., ed. The Physiology & Pathophysiology of the Skin, 3 vols. Incl. Vol. 1. The Epidermis. 1973. 51.00 (ISBN 0-12-380601-1); Vol. 2. The Nerves & Blood Vessels. 1973. 64.50 (ISBN 0-12-380602-X); Vol. 3. 64.50 (ISBN 0-12-380603-8). 150.50 set (ISBN 0-686-66931-2). Acad Pr.

Jarrett, Bella. Aloha Love. 1979. pap. 1.25 o.s.i. (ISBN 0-440-10697-4). Dell.

Jarrett, David. Witherwing. (Orig.). 1979. pap. 1.95 o.s.i. (ISBN 0-446-90115-6). Warner Bks.

Jarrett, Derek. England in the Age of Hogarth. 1979. 14.95x (ISBN 0-8464-0101-0). Beekman Pubs.

Jarrett, H. R. Africa. 5th ed. (Illus.). 624p. (Orig.). 1979. pap. text ed. 24.00x (ISBN 0-7121-0153-5, Pub by MacDonald & Evans England). Intl Ideas.

Jarrett, James L., ed. Educational Theories of the Sophists. LC 71-108882. 1969. text ed. 8.25 (ISBN 0-8077-1565-4); pap. text ed. 4.00 (ISBN 0-8077-1564-6). Tchrs Coll.

Jarrett, John, jt. auth. see Keen, Harry.

Jarrod, Keith. Night Riders. 1980. pap. 1.95 (ISBN 0-440-16368-4). Dell.

Jarry, Alfred. The Ubu Plays. Connolly, Cyril & Taylor, Simon W., trs. Incl. Ubu Rex; Ubu Cuckolded; Ubu Enchained. 1969. pap. 4.95 (ISBN 0-394-17485-2, E496, Ever). Grove.

Jarver, Jess, ed. Middle Distances: Contemporary Theory, Technique, & Training. (Illus., Orig.). 1979. pap. text ed. 7.50 (ISBN 0-911520-87-2). Tafnews.

--Throws: Contemporary Theory, Technique & Training. 2nd ed. (Illus.). 1980. pap. 7.50 (ISBN 0-911520-98-8). Tafnews.

Jarves, James J. Art Thoughts: the Experiences & Observations of an American Amateur in Europe. Weinberg, H. Barbara, ed. LC 75-28866. (Art Experience in Late 19th Century America Ser.: Vol. 2). (Illus.). 1976. Repr. of 1869 ed. lib. bdg. 37.50x (ISBN 0-8240-2226-2). Garland Pub.

Jarvesoo, Elmar, jt. ed. see Parming, Tonu.

Jarvie, I. C. Concepts & Society. (International Library of Sociology). 230p. 1972. 20.00x (ISBN 0-7100-7265-1). Routledge & Kegan.

--Functionalism. LC 72-97621. (Basic Concepts in Anthropology Ser.). 1973. pap. text ed. 2.95 o.p. (ISBN 0-8087-1018-4). Burgess.

--Movies As Social Criticism: Aspects of Their Social Psychology. LC 77-26778. 1978. 12.00 (ISBN 0-8108-1106-5). Scarecrow.

Jarvie, I. C., ed. see Gellner, Ernest.

Jarvik, L. F., et al, eds. Clinical Pharmacology & the Aged Patient. (Aging Ser.: Vol. 16). 256p. 1981. text ed. 25.00 (ISBN 0-89004-340-X). Raven.

--Clinical Pharmacology & the Aged Patient. (Aging Ser.). 1980. 25.00 (ISBN 0-89004-340-X, 349). Raven.

Jarvinen. Finite & Infinite Dimensional Linear Spaces. 185p. 1981. price not set. Dekker. Postponed.

Jarvis, A. C. & Gregory, C. Advanced Level Physics Questions. 1974. pap. text ed. 4.95x o.p. (ISBN 0-435-68230-X). Heinemann Ed.

Jarvis, A. C. & Gregory, C. R. Modern Revision Questions in Physics. 1975. pap. text ed. 5.50x o.p. (ISBN 0-435-67540-0). Heinemann Ed.

Jarvis, Ana C. & Lebredo, Raquel. Basic Spanish Grammar. (Orig.). Date not set. pap. text ed. 8.95 (ISBN 0-669-03086-4); Business & Finance wkbk. 6.95 (ISBN 0-669-03089-9); spanish for communication wkbk. 6.95 (ISBN 0-669-03592-0); wkbk. for Medical Personnel 6.95 (ISBN 0-669-03090-2); wkbk. for Law Enforcement Personnel 6.95 (ISBN 0-669-03593-9); Social Sciences wkbk. (ISBN 0-699-03593-9) 6.95, inst. guide free to adopters (ISBN 0-686-65955-4); business cassettes 35.00 (ISBN 0-669-03465-7); medical cassettes 35.00 (ISBN 0-669-03466-5); social sciences cassettes (isbn 0-669-03464 9) 35.00, spanish for communications cassettes, 35.00 (ISBN 0-669-03634-X). Heath.

Jarvis, Ana C., et al. Como Se Dice. 1976. text ed. 16.95x (ISBN 0-669-00192-9); instructor's manual free (ISBN 0-669-00357-3); wkbk. 5.95x (ISBN 0-669-00189-9); reels 70.00 (ISBN 0-669-00191-0); cassettes 70.00 (ISBN 0-669-00358-1). Heath.

Jarvis, B., jt. ed. see Stephens, H. S.

Jarvis, D. C. Folk Medicine. 1978. pap. 2.50 (ISBN 0-449-24161-0, Crest). Fawcett.

Jarvis, F. J., jt. auth. see Herbert, W. L.

Jarvis, F. Washington. Come & Follow. pap. 3.95 (ISBN 0-8164-2072-6). Crossroad NY.

--Prophets, Poets, Priests, & Kings: The Old Testament Story. 288p. 1975. pap. 5.95 (ISBN 0-8164-2089-0). Crossroad NY.

Jarvis, Gilbert A. & Adams, Shirley J. Evaluating a Second Language Program. (Language in Education Ser.: No. 19). 1979. pap. 2.95 (ISBN 0-87281-105-0). Ctr Appl Ling.

Jarvis, John J., jt. auth. see Bazaraa, Mokhtar S.

Jarvis, Lance P., jt. auth. see Mayo, Edward J.

Jarvis, Linda L. Community Health Nursing: Keeping the Public Healthy. LC 80-16953. (Illus.). 896p. 1980. 22.00 (ISBN 0-8036-4925-8). Davis Co.

Jarvis, Margaret. Your Book of Swimming. 3rd ed. (gr. 4 up). 1979. 6.95 (ISBN 0-571-04971-0, Pub. by Faber & Faber). Merrimack Bk Serv.

Jarvis, Margaret A. Your Book of Survival Swimming & Lifesaving. (gr. 6 up). 9.50 (ISBN 0-571-06438-8). Transatlantic.

Jarvis, N. L. Woman's Guide to Wall Street. 195p. 1981. 28.50 (ISBN 0-686-68312-9). Porter.

Jarvis, P. R. Practical Weaving Course. 6.00 o.p. (ISBN 0-87245-157-7). Textile Bk.

Jarvis, R. C. & Craig, R. Liverpool Registry of Merchant Ships. 278p. 1967. 33.00x (ISBN 0-686-63740-2, Pub. by Manchester U Pr England). State Mutual Bk.

Jarvis, Suzan. Emerald. (Orig.). 1980. pap. 1.95 (ISBN 0-532-23120-1). Manor Bks.

Jarvis, William C. The Republican or, a Series of Essays on the Principles & Policy of Free States. Hudson, Michael, ed. (The Neglected American Economists Ser.). 1974. lib. bdg. 50.00 (ISBN 0-8240-1001-9). Garland Pub.

Jarzebski, Z. M. Oxide Semiconductors. LC 73-6971. 304p. 1974. 42.00 (ISBN 0-08-016968-6). Pergamon.

Jasek, Jan. Disco Text: The Complete Book of Disco Dance Instruction. LC 78-70439. (Illus.). 1978. pap. 4.95 o.p. (ISBN 0-932846-01-7). And Bks.

Jasen, David A. P. G. Wodehouse: Portrait of a Master. (Illus.). 352p. 1981. 17.50 (ISBN 0-8264-0046-9); pap. 8.95 (ISBN 0-8264-0033-7). Continuum.

Jasen, David A., ed. see Jerome, Jerome K.

Jasen, David A., ed. see McCutcheon, George B.

Jaske, Carl E., et al. Corrosion Fatigue of Metals in Marine Environments. (Metals & Ceramics Information Center Ser.). (Illus.). 160p. 1981. 45.00 (ISBN 0-935470-07-7). Battelle.

Jasmin, G., ed. Cell Markers. (Methods & Achievements in Experimental Pathology: Vol. 10). (Illus.). vi, 294p. 1981. 90.00 (ISBN 3-8055-1736-X). S Karger.

Jasmin, Sylvia & Trygstad-Durland, Louise. Behavioral Concepts & the Nursing Process. LC 78-26960. (Illus.). 1979. pap. text ed. 8.50 (ISBN 0-8016-2435-5). Mosby.

Jasner, W. K. Which Is the Witch? LC 78-11757. (I Am Reading Bks.). (Illus.). (gr. 2-4). 1979. 4.95 (ISBN 0-394-83978-1); PLB 5.99 (ISBN 0-394-93978-6). Pantheon.

Jasny, Naum. Soviet Economists of the Twenties: Names to Be Remembered. Kaser, M., ed. LC 77-168894. (Soviet & East European Studies). 1972. 29.95 (ISBN 0-521-08302-8). Cambridge U Pr.

Jason, Heda & Segal, Dimitri, eds. Patterns in Oral Literature. (World Anthropology Ser.). 1977. text ed. 33.00x (ISBN 90-279-7969-3). Mouton.

Jason, Leonard, jt. ed. see Glenwick, David.

Jason, Philip K., ed. Anais Nin Reader. LC 72-91913. 316p. 1972. 10.00 o.p. (ISBN 0-8040-0595-8); pap. 7.95 (ISBN 0-8040-0596-6). Swallow.

Jason, Stuart. Butcher, Number Thirty: Coffin Corner. 192p. (Orig.). 1981. pap. 1.95 (ISBN 0-523-41260-6). Pinnacle Bks.

--Kill Quick or Die. (Butcher Ser.: No. 1). 1979. pap. 1.75 (ISBN 0-523-40678-9). Pinnacle Bks.

Jasper, Tony, ed. The Illustrated Family Hymn Book. (Illus.). 192p. 1980. 19.50 (ISBN 0-8164-0143-8); pap. 9.95 (ISBN 0-8164-2051-3). Seabury.

Jaspers, Karl. Philosophy of Existence. Grabau, Richard F., tr. LC 79-133203. 1971. 10.00x (ISBN 0-8122-7629-9); pap. 4.95x (ISBN 0-8122-1010-7, Pa Paperbks). U of Pa Pr.

--Socrates, Buddha, Confucius & Jesus: Taken from Vol. 1 of the Great Philosophers. Manheim, Ralph, tr. Orig. Title: Great Philosophers, Vol. 1 (Pt. 1) 1966. pap. 2.50 (ISBN 0-15-683580-0, HB99, Harv). HarBraceJ.

Jaspersohn, William. A Day in the Life of a Television News Reporter. (Illus.). 96p. (gr. 5 up). 1981. 9.95 (ISBN 0-316-45813-9). Little.

Jassey, William, ed. French: Three Thousand One Hundred Steps to Master Vocabulary. LC 67-18801. (Prog. Bk.). 1969. pap. 2.95 (ISBN 0-668-01680-9). Arc Bks.

Jassy, Marie-France P. Basic Community in the African Churches. Lyons, Sr. Jeanne M., tr. from Fr. LC 72-93342. Orig. Title: La Communaute De Base Dans les Eglises Africaines. 195p. 1973. pap. 4.95x o.p. (ISBN 0-88344-025-3). Orbis Bks.

Jastak, J. Theodore & Yagiela, John A. Regional Anesthesia of the Oral Cavity. 1st ed. (Illus.). 200p. 1981. text ed. 20.00 (ISBN 0-8016-2434-7). Mosby.

Jastak, Joseph F. & MacPhee, Halsey M. Mental Retardation, Its Nature & Incidence: A Population Survey of the State of Delaware. LC 62-19658. 184p. 10.00 (ISBN 0-87413-103-0). U Delaware Pr.

Jastram, Roy W. Silver: The Restless Metal. 225p. 1981. 23.95 (ISBN 0-471-03912-8, Pub. by Wiley-Interscience). Wiley.

Jastrow, Robert. God & the Astronomers. 1980. pap. 4.95 (ISBN 0-446-97350-5). Warner Bks.

--Red Giants & White Dwarfs. 1980. pap. 7.95 (ISBN 0-446-97349-1). Warner Bks.

--Until the Sun Dies. 1980. pap. 4.95 (ISBN 0-446-97348-3). Warner Bks.

Jastrow, Robert & Thompson, Malcolm H. Astronomy: Fundamentals & Frontiers. 3rd ed. LC 76-46622. 1977. text ed. 22.95x (ISBN 0-471-01845-7); tchr's manual avail. (ISBN 0-471-02728-6); study guide 8.95 (ISBN 0-471-03035-X). Wiley.

Jastrzebski, Zbigniew D. The Nature & Properties of Engineering Materials. 2nd ed. LC 75-20431. 656p. 1975. text ed. 28.95x (ISBN 0-471-44089-2). Wiley.

--The Nature & Properties of Engineering Materials: SI Version. 2nd ed. LC 77-83735. 1977. text ed. 27.95 (ISBN 0-471-02859-2); solns. manual avail. (ISBN 0-471-03671-4). Wiley.

Jasudowicz, Dennis see Corrigan, Robert W.

Jaswon, M. A. & Symm, G. T. Integral Equation Methods in Potential Theory & Elastostatics. 1978. 39.50 (ISBN 0-12-381050-7). Acad Pr.

Jaszi, Oscar. Revolution & Counter-Revolution in Hungary. LC 68-9595. 1969. Repr. of 1924 ed. 15.50 (ISBN 0-86527-168-2). Fertig.

Jauch, J. M. & Rohrlich, F. The Theory of Photons & Electrons: Second Corrected Printing. 2nd rev. ed. LC 75-8890. (Texts & Monographs in Physics). (Illus.). 533p. 1980. 19.80 (ISBN 0-387-07295-0). Springer-Verlag.

Javarek, Vera, ed. Serbo-Croatian Prose & Verse. 1958. text ed. 13.25x (ISBN 0-485-17506-1, Athlone Pr). Humanities.

Javid, M., jt. auth. see Brenner, Egon.

Javits, Jacob K. & Steinberg, Rafael. Javits: The Autobiography of a Public Man. (Illus.). 1981. 16.95 (ISBN 0-395-29912-8). HM.

Javitz, Alex E., ed. Materials Science & Technology for Design Engineers. (Materials for Electrical & Electronics Design Ser.). (Illus.). 560p. 1972. 27.55 o.p. (ISBN 0-8104-5640-0). Hayden.

Javor, George. The Challange of Cancer. LC 79-29674. (Orion Ser.). 96p. 1980. pap. 2.50 (ISBN 0-8127-0275-1). Southern Pub.

--Once Upon a Molecule. LC 78-27359. (Flame Ser.). 1979. pap. 0.95 (ISBN 0-8127-0227-1). Southern Pub.

Jawdat, Nameer A., ed. Selected Documents of the International Petroleum Industry: 1967. 1968. 32.50x (ISBN 0-8002-0003-9). Intl Pubns Serv.

Jawin, P. B., jt. auth. see Casady, R. B.

Jaworski, Irene D. & Joseph, Alexander. Atomic Energy: The Story of Nuclear Science. LC 60-13702. (Illus.). (gr. 9 up). 1961. 4.95 o.p. (ISBN 0-15-204438-8, HJ). HarBraceJ.

Jay, Elisabeth. The Religion of the Heart: Anglican Evangelicalism & the Nineteenth-Century Novel. 1979. write for info. (ISBN 0-19-812092-3). Oxford U Pr.

Jay, Eric G. The Church: Its Changing Image Through Twenty Centuries. LC 79-92070. 1980. 18.00 (ISBN 0-8042-0877-8); pap. 9.95 (ISBN 0-8042-0878-6). John Knox.

Jay, Jon C., ed. Basic Ignition & Electrical Systems. 5th rev. ed. LC 73-79968. (Basic Repair & Maintenance Manuals Ser.). (Illus.). (gr. 9-12). 1977. pap. 6.95 (ISBN 0-8227-5014-7). Petersen Pub.

Jay, Karla & Young, Allen. Lavender Culture. (Orig.). 1979. pap. 2.50 (ISBN 0-515-04462-8). Jove Pubns.

--Out of the Closets, Voices of Gay Liberation. 1977. pap. 1.95 (ISBN 0-515-04497-0). Jove Pubns.

--We Are Everywhere: A Celebration of Lavender Culture. (Orig.). 1978. pap. 1.95 o.p. (ISBN 0-685-87092-8). Jove Pubns.

Jay, L. J. Geography Teaching with a Little Latitude. (Classroom Close-Ups Ser.: No. 7). (Illus.). 160p. 1981. text ed. 17.95x (ISBN 0-04-371077-8, 2606); pap. text ed. 8.95x (ISBN 0-04-371078-6, AU 461). Allen Unwin.

Jay, Madeline, tr. see Klein, Robert.

Jay, Michael. Gay Love Signs. (Orig.). 1980. pap. 6.95 (ISBN 0-345-28774-6). Ballantine.

Jay, P. see Jones, M. S.

Jay, Stephen J. & Stonehill, Robert B. A Manual of Pulmonary Procedures. (Blue Book Ser.). (Illus.). 224p. 1980. 19.95 (ISBN 0-7216-8607-9). Saunders.

Jay, Tony A. Time Study. (Illus.). 1981. 17.50 (ISBN 0-7137-1085-3, Pub. by Blandford Pr England); pap. 9.95 (ISBN 0-7137-1126-4). Sterling.

Jay, William. Autobiography of William Jay. 1974. 10.95 (ISBN 0-85151-177-5). Banner of Truth.

Jayadeva. Gita Govinda. Keyt, G., tr. 1974. 10.00 (ISBN 0-88253-488-2). Ind-US Inc.

Jayatilaka, Ayal De S. Fracture of Engineering Brittle Materials. (Illus.). 1979. 64.60x (ISBN 0-85334-825-1, Pub. by Applied Science). Burgess-Intl Ideas.

Jaycock, M. J. & Parfitt, G. D. Chemistry of Interfaces. LC 80-40387. (Physical Chemistry Ser.). 370p. Date not set. 90.00 (ISBN 0-470-27013-6, Pub. by Halsted Pr). Wiley.

Jayewardene, C. H. Penalty of Death: The Canadian Experiment. LC 77-167. (Illus.). 1977. 15.95 (ISBN 0-669-01464-8). Lexington Bks.

Jayne, A. G., tr. see Bojer, Johan.

Jayne, Fred E. How to Survive Hard Times. pap. 1.95 (ISBN 0-89036-146-0). Hawkes Pub Inc.

Jayne, Sears R. John Colet & Marsilio Ficino. LC 80-17262. (Illus.). 172p. 1980. Repr. of 1963 ed. lib. bdg. 18.75x (ISBN 0-313-22606-7, JACF). Greenwood.

Jaynes, Thomas L. The Organ: A Guide for Student & Teacher. 27p. 1979. pap. 7.00 (ISBN 0-935514-00-7). T L Jaynes.

Jazani, Bizhan. Capitalism & Revolution in Iran: Selected Writings. 1981. 17.00 (ISBN 0-905762-82-7, Pub. by Zed Pr); pap. 7.95 (ISBN 0-905762-57-6). Lawrence Hill.

Jazayery, Mohammad A., et al, eds. Linguistic & Literary Studies in Honor of Archibald A. Hill: General & Theoretical Linguistics, 4 vols, Vol. 1. (Illus., Orig.). 1976. pap. text ed. 45.75x (ISBN 90-3160-108-X). Humanities.

Jazbi, Basharat, ed. Pediatric Otorhinolaryngology: A Review of Ear, Nose, & Throat Problems in Children. 320p. 1980. 24.50x (ISBN 0-8385-7799-7). ACC.

Jeaffreson, J. Cordy. Novels & Novelists: From Elizabeth to Victorian, 2 vols. 405p. 1980. Repr. of 1858 ed. Set. lib. bdg. 85.00 (ISBN 0-8414-5416-7). Folcroft.

Jeal, Tim. A Marriage of Convenience. 1981. pap. price not set. PB.

--Until the Colors Fade. 1976. 10.00 o.s.i. (ISBN 0-440-09299-X). Delacorte.

Jean, Georges, ed. see Goupil, Armand.

Jean-Aubry, Georges. Une Amitie Exemplaire: Villiers De L'isle-Adam et Stephane Mallarme. LC 80-205. (Symbolists Ser.). (Illus.). 228p. (Fr.). 1980. Repr. of 1942 ed. 18.50 (ISBN 0-404-16300-9). AMS Pr.

Jeanloz, Roger, ed. see International Symposium on Glycoconjugates, Fourth.

Jeanneret, Charles E., pseud. Etude Sur Le Mouvement D'art Decoratif En Allemagne. LC 68-26652. (Architecture & Decorative Art Ser). (Fr). 1968. Repr. of 1912 ed. lib. bdg. 22.50 (ISBN 0-306-71147-8). Da Capo.

Jeanneret, Georges. Paris Pendant la Commune Revolutionnaire De 1871. (The Paris Commune Ser.). (Fr.). 1976. lib. bdg. 22.00x o.p. (ISBN 0-8287-0463-5); pap. text ed. 12.00x o.p. (ISBN 0-685-74532-5). Clearwater Pub.

Jeans, James. Physics & Philosophy. 232p. 1981. pap. price not set (ISBN 0-486-24117-3). Dover.

Jeavons, P. M. & Bower, B. D. Infantile Spasms. (Clinics in Developmental Medicine Ser. No. 15). 82p. 1964. 4.50 o.p. (ISBN 0-685-24736-8). Lippincott.

Jebb, ed. see Sophocles.

Jebb, Richard C., tr. see Sophocles.

Jebe, E. H., jt. auth. see Little, R. E.

Jedamus, Paul & Frame, R. Business Decision Theory. LC 69-13609. (Illus.). 1969. text ed. 19.95 (ISBN 0-07-032307-0, C); instructor's manual 4.95 (ISBN 0-07-032311-9). McGraw.

Jedamus, Paul, et al. Statistical Analysis for Business Decisions. new ed. (Illus.). 1976. text ed. 18.50 (ISBN 0-07-032302-X, C); inst. manual 5.95 (ISBN 0-07-032306-2). McGraw.

--Improving Academic Management: A Handbook of Planning & Institutional Research. LC 80-8009. (Higher Education Ser.). 1980. text ed. 29.95x (ISBN 0-87589-477-1). Jossey-Bass.

Jedick, Peter. Cleveland: Where the East Coast Meets the Midwest. (Illus.). 105p. (Orig.). 1980. pap. 11.95 (ISBN 0-9605508-1-X). Jedick Ent.

Jedin, Hubert & Dolan, John P., eds. The Church Between Revolution & Restoration. (History of the Church: Vol. 7). 1980. 37.50 (ISBN 0-8245-0446-1). Crossroad NY.

--The Church in the Age of Absolutism & Enlightenment. (History of the Church: Vol. 6). 1981. 37.50 (ISBN 0-8245-0445-3). Crossroad NY.

--The Church in the Age of Feudalism. (History of the Church: Vol. 3). 1980. 37.50 (ISBN 0-8164-1039-9). Crossroad NY.

--The Church in the Age of Liberalism. (History of the Church: Vol. 8). 1981. 37.50 (ISBN 0-8245-0447-X). Crossroad NY.

--The Church in the Industrial Age. (History of the Church: Vol. 9). 1981. 37.50 (ISBN 0-8245-0448-8). Crossroad NY.

--The Church in the Modern Age. (History of the Church: Vol. 10). 1980. 37.50 (ISBN 0-8245-0452-6). Crossroad NY.

--From the Apostolic Community to Constantine. (History of the Church: Vol. 1). 1980. 37.50 (ISBN 0-8164-1038-0). Crossroad NY.

--From the High Middle Ages to the Eve of the Reformation. (History of the Church: Vol. 4). 1980. 37.50 (ISBN 0-8164-1040-2). Crossroad NY.

--The History of the Church, Vol. 5: Reformation & Counter-Reformation. 920p. 1980. 37.50 (ISBN 0-8164-0449-6). Crossroad NY.

--The Imperial Church from Constantine to the Early Middle Ages. (History of the Church: Vol. 2). 1980. 37.50 (ISBN 0-8164-0444-5). Crossroad NY.

Jedlicka, Allen D. Organization for Rural Development: Risk Taking & Appropriate Technology. LC 77-10757. (Praeger Special Studies). 1977. 22.95 (ISBN 0-03-022341-5). Praeger.

Jedrzejewicz, Waclaw, ed. Diplomat in Berlin, 1933-1939: Papers & Memoris of Jozef Lipski, Ambassador of Poland. LC 67-25871. (Illus.). 1968. 22.50x (ISBN 0-231-03070-3). Columbia U Pr.

--Diplomat in Paris, 1936-1939: Memoirs of Juliusz Lukasiewicz, Ambassador of Poland. LC 79-83535. 1969. 22.50x (ISBN 0-231-03308-7). Columbia U Pr.

Jeejeebhoy, Khursheed N. Gastrointestinal Diseases: Focus on Clinical Diagnosis. 1979. pap. 19.50 (ISBN 0-87488-831-X). Med Exam.

Jeep, Elizabeth. Classroom Creativity: An Idea Book for Religion Teachers. LC 77-24719. 1977. pap. 4.95 (ISBN 0-8164-2160-9). Crossroad NY.

Jeeves, Alan, ed. see Phillips, Lionel.

Jeeves, Malcolm, ed. Psychology Survey, No. 3. 208p. (Orig.). 1980. text ed. 25.00x (ISBN 0-04-150073-3, 2311); pap. text ed. 11.50 (ISBN 0-04-150074-1, 2312). Allen Unwin.

Jeffares, A. Norman. Politics, Society & Nationhood, Vol. 1. (Collected Edition of the Writings of G. W. Russell Ser.: VI-1). 1980. text ed. write for info. (ISBN 0-391-01185-5). Humanities.

--Politics, Society & Nationhood, Vol. 2. (Collected Edition of the Writings of G. W. Russell Ser.: VI-2). 1980. text ed. write for info. (ISBN 0-391-01183-9). Humanities.

--Yeats, Sligo & Ireland. 1981. text ed. 23.50x (ISBN 0-86140-041-0). Humanities.

Jeffares, A. Norman, ed. W.B. Yeats: The Critical Heritage. (The Critical Heritage Ser.). 1977. 34.00 (ISBN 0-7100-8480-3). Routledge & Kegan.

--Yeats, Sligo & Ireland: Essays to Mark the 21st Yeats International Summer School. (Irish Literary Studies: No. 6). 267p. 1980. 24.75x (ISBN 0-389-20095-6). B&N.

Jeffares, Bo. The Artist in Nineteenth Century Fiction. 195p. 1979. text ed. 23.75x (ISBN 0-391-00976-1). Humanities.

Jeffcoate, N. Principles of Gynecology. 4th ed. 1975. 67.50 (ISBN 0-407-00000-3). Butterworths.

Jeffcott, H. A., Jr., jt. auth. see Brown, A. E.

Jeffcott, L. B., jt. ed. see Archer, R. K.

Jefferies, Greg. Volcanoes. (Jackdaw Ser: No. 76). 1970. 5.95 o.p. (ISBN 0-670-74762-9, Grossman). Viking Pr.

Jefferies, R. L., ed. Ecological Processes in Coastal Environments: Nineteenth Symposium of the British Ecological Society. 684p. 1979. 87.95x (ISBN 0-470-26741-0). Halsted Pr.

Jefferies, Richard. Amaryllis at the Fair. 192p. 1980. pap. 3.95 (ISBN 0-686-68572-5, Pub. by Quartet England). Horizon.

--Hodge & His Masters. 310p. 1980. pap. 4.95 (ISBN 0-7043-3259-0, Pub. by Quartet England). Horizon.

Jeffers, Coleman R., jt. ed. see Dobrian, Walter A.

Jeffers, Janet & Barley, Margaret. Look, Now Hear This: Combined Auditory Training & Speechreading Instruction. (Illus.). 230p. 1979. text ed. 17.75 (ISBN 0-398-03830-9). C C Thomas.

Jeffers, P. E., jt. auth. see Svec, J. J.

Jeffers, Robinson. The Alpine Christ & Other Poems. Everson, William, ed. 1974. 15.00 (ISBN 0-9600372-4-1). Cayuco's.

--Cawdor & Medea. LC 76-103374. 1970. pap. 5.95 (ISBN 0-8112-0073-6, NDP293). New Directions.

--The Women at Point Sur. 1975. 12.00 o.p. (ISBN 0-912950-23-4). Blue Oak.

Jeffers, Susan. All the Pretty Horses. LC 73-19053. (Illus.). 32p. (gr. k-3). 1974. 6.95g o.s.i. (ISBN 0-02-747680-4). Macmillan.

Jeffers, Susan, illus. Three Jovial Huntsmen: A Mother Goose Rhyme. LC 70-122739. (Illus.). 32p. (gr. k-2). 1973. 9.95 (ISBN 0-87888-023-2). Bradbury Pr.

Jefferson. Minister As Shepherd. (Orig.). 1970. pap. 1.75 (ISBN 0-87508-290-4). Chr Lit.

Jefferson, Alan. Delius. (Master Musicians Ser). (Illus.). 189p. 1972. 7.95x (ISBN 0-460-03131-7, Pub. by J. M. Dent England). Biblio Dist.

Jefferson, Ann. The Nouveau Roman & the Poetics of Fiction. LC 79-41507. 225p. 1980. 29.50 (ISBN 0-521-22239-7). Cambridge U Pr.

Jefferson, D. T., jt. auth. see Jefferson, Ted B.

Jefferson, D. T., jt. ed. see Jefferson, T. B.

Jefferson, G. & Smith-Burnett, G. C. The College Library: A Collection of Essays. 1978. 12.50 (ISBN 0-208-01665-1, Linnet). Shoe String.

Jefferson, Michael, et al. Inflation. 1979. 11.95 (ISBN 0-7145-3539-7); pap. 4.95 (ISBN 0-7145-3547-8). Riverrun NY.

Jefferson, Rees. Clinical Cardiac Radiology. 2nd ed. LC 79-40913. (Illus.). 1980. text ed. 75.95 (ISBN 0-407-13576-6). Butterworths.

Jefferson, T. B. The Oxyacetylene Weldor's Handbook. 7th ed. (Monticello Bks). 320p. 1972. 5.00 (ISBN 0-686-12005-1). Jefferson Pubns.

Jefferson, T. B. & Jefferson, D. T., eds. Welding Encyclopedia. 18th ed. (Monticello Bks). 1981. 20.00 (ISBN 0-686-28906-4). Jefferson Pubns.

Jefferson, Ted B. & Jefferson, D. T. Jefferson's Gas Welding Manual. 4th ed. (Monticello Bks). 140p. 1980. pap. 5.00. Jefferson Pubns.

Jefferson, Thomas. Complete Annals of Thomas Jefferson. Sawvel, Franklin R., ed. LC 70-75272. (Amer. Public Figures Ser.). 1970. Repr. of 1903 ed. lib. bdg. 32.50 (ISBN 0-306-71311-X). Da Capo.

--Correspondence Between Thomas Jefferson & Pierre Samuel Du Pont De Nemours, 1798-1817. Malone, Dumas, ed. Lehmann, Linwood, tr. LC 78-75282. (American Public Figures Ser). 1970. Repr. of 1930 ed. lib. bdg. 37.50 (ISBN 0-306-71301-2). Da Capo.

--Papers of Thomas Jefferson, 60 vols. Boyd, J. P., et al, eds. Incl. Vol. 1. 1760-1776. 1950 (ISBN 0-691-04533-X); Vol. 2. 1777-1779. 1950 (ISBN 0-691-04534-8); Vol. 3. 1779-1780. 1951 (ISBN 0-691-04535-6); Vol. 4. 1780-1781. 1951 (ISBN 0-691-04536-4); Vol. 5. 1781. 1952 (ISBN 0-691-04537-2); Vol. 6. 1781-1784. 1952 (ISBN 0-691-04538-0); Vol. 7. 1784-1785. 1953 (ISBN 0-691-04539-9); Vol. 8. 1785. 1953 (ISBN 0-691-04540-2); Vol. 9. 1785-1786. 1954 (ISBN 0-691-04541-0); Vol. 10. 1786-1787. 1954 (ISBN 0-691-04542-9); Vol. 11. 1787. 1955 (ISBN 0-691-04543-7); Vol. 12. 1787-1788. 1955 (ISBN 0-691-04544-5); Vol. 13. Mar.-Oct. 1788. 1956 (ISBN 0-691-04545-3); Vol. 14. Oct. 1788-Mar. 1789. 1958 (ISBN 0-691-04546-1); Vol. 15. Mar.-Nov. 1789. 1958 (ISBN 0-691-04547-X); Vol. 16. Nov. 1789-Aug. 1790. 1961 (ISBN 0-691-04548-8); Vol. 17. July to Dec. 1790. 1965 (ISBN 0-691-04549-6); Vol. 18. Nov. 1790-Jan. 1791. 1971 (ISBN 0-691-04582-8); Vol. 19. Jan. 24-March 10, 1791 (ISBN 0-691-04583-6). Vols. 1-19. 30.00 ea.; Index To Vols. 1-6. 7.50x (ISBN 0-691-04531-3); Index To Vols. 7-12. 7.50x (ISBN 0-691-04532-1); Index To Vols. 13-18. 7.50x (ISBN 0-691-04618-2). Princeton U Pr.

--Thomas Jefferson: A Biography in His Own Words. Newsweek Books Editors, ed. LC 72-92143. (The Founding Fathers Ser.). (Illus.). 416p. (YA) 1974. 15.00 o.s.i. (ISBN 0-06-011148-8, HarpT). Har-Row.

Jefferson-Brown, M. J. Enjoying Your Garden. 1970. 4.75 o.p. (ISBN 0-8231-6034-3). Branford.

--Small Garden Design. 1969. 6.25 o.p. (ISBN 0-8231-6032-7). Branford.

Jeffery, Arthur. The Qur'an As Scripture. LC 80-1924. 1981. Repr. of 1952 ed. 18.00 (ISBN 0-404-18970-9). AMS Pr.

Jeffery, L. H. Archaic Greece. LC 75-10758. (Illus.). 300p. 1976. 22.50 (ISBN 0-312-04760-6). St Martin.

Jeffery, P. G. Chemical Methods of Rock Analysis. 2nd ed. Belcher, R. & Freiser, H., eds. LC 74-16500. 526p. 1975. text ed. 75.00 (ISBN 0-08-013076-0). Pergamon.

Jefferys, J. G. A Wicked Way to Die. (Jeremy Sturrock Ser). 256p. 1973. 5.95 o.s.i. (ISBN 0-8027-5284-5). Walker & Co.

Jeffrey, A., jt. auth. see Coulson, C. A.

Jeffrey, Adi-Kent T. Ghosts in the Valley. LC 75-4658. 96p. 1971. pap. 1.50 o.p. (ISBN 0-915460-00-9). New Hope.

Jeffrey, Arthur, ed. Islam: Muhammad & His Religion. LC 58-9958. 1958. pap. 5.75 (ISBN 0-672-60348-9, LLA137). Bobbs.

Jeffrey, E. J. Brewing Theory & Practice. 25.00x (ISBN 0-392-03817-0, LTB). Soccer.

Jeffrey, Harry R. Wood Finishing. (gr. 9-12). 1957. pap. text ed. 6.56 (ISBN 0-87002-012-9). Bennett IL.

Jeffrey, Lloyd N. Shelley's Knowledge & Use of Natural History. (Salzburg Studies: Romantic Reassessment Ser.: No. 48). 1976. pap. text ed. 25.00x (ISBN 0-391-01436-6). Humanities.

--Thomas Hood. (English Authors Ser.: No. 137). lib. bdg. 10.95 (ISBN 0-8057-1268-2). Twayne.

Jeffrey, R., jt. auth. see Boolos, G. S.

Jeffrey, R. C., jt. auth. see Boolos, G. S.

Jeffrey, Richard C. Formal Logic: Its Scope & Limits. 2nd ed. (Illus.). 256p. 1981. text ed. 17.95 (ISBN 0-07-032321-6, C); instr's manual 5.95 (ISBN 0-07-032322-4). McGraw.

Jeffrey, Richard C., ed. Studies in Inductive Logic & Probability, Vol. II. 312p. 1980. 20.00x (ISBN 0-520-03826-6). U of Cal Pr.

Jeffrey, Richard C., jt. ed. see Carnap, Rudolf.

Jeffrey, Rosalind. Chess in the Mirror: A Study of Theatrical Cubism in Francis Warner's Requiem & Its Maquettes. 1981. text ed. 13.00 (ISBN 0-85455-020-8). Humanities.

Jeffrey, William, Jr., jt. auth. see Crosskey, W. W.

Jeffrey, William, Jr., jt. auth. see Crosskey, William W.

Jeffreys. A Conspiracy of Poisons. 1977. 6.95 o.s.i. (ISBN 0-8027-5359-0). Walker & Co.

Jeffreys, Alan E. Michael Faraday: A List of His Lectures & Published Writings. 1961. 25.00 (ISBN 0-12-383050-8). Acad Pr.

Jeffreys, Bertha S., jt. auth. see Jeffreys, Harold.

Jeffreys, G. V., jt. ed. see Jenson, V. G.

Jeffreys, Harold. Cartesian Tensors. (Orig.). 1931-1962. 17.95 (ISBN 0-521-05423-0); pap. 6.95x (ISBN 0-521-09191-8, 191). Cambridge U Pr.

--The Earth. 6th ed. LC 74-19527. (Illus.). 600p. 1976. 83.50 (ISBN 0-521-20648-0). Cambridge U Pr.

--Scientific Inference. 3rd ed. LC 71-179159. (Illus.). 280p. 1973. 42.50 (ISBN 0-521-08446-6). Cambridge U Pr.

Jeffreys, Harold & Jeffreys, Bertha S. Methods of Mathematical Physics. 3rd ed. (Illus.). 1956. pap. 22.95x (ISBN 0-521-09723-1). Cambridge U Pr.

Jeffreys-Jones, Rhodri. American Espionage: From Secret Service to C.I.A. LC 77-74854. (Illus.). 1977. 14.95 (ISBN 0-02-916360-9). Free Pr.

Jeffri, Joan. The Emerging Arts: Management, Survival, & Growth. LC 80-18784. 301p. 1980. 22.59 (ISBN 0-03-056707-6). Praeger.

Jeffries & Ransford. Social Stratification: A Multiple Hierarchy Approach. 640p. 1980. text ed. 19.95 (ISBN 0-205-06858-8, 816858X). Allyn.

Jeffries, Leila & Illot, Anna. Working with Photography. 1980. 16.95 (ISBN 0-7134-3311-6). David & Charles.

Jeffries, N. P., jt. auth. see Shell, R. L.

Jeffries, Paul, jt. auth. see Liebers, Arthur.

Jeffries, Richard. The Story of My Heart: My Autobiography. 144p. 1980. pap. 3.95 (ISBN 0-7043-3257-4, Pub. by Quartet England). Horizon.

Jeffries, Roderic. Just Deserts. 208p. 1981. 9.95 (ISBN 0-312-44942-9). St Martin.

Jeffries, Wendy. That's Incredible, Vol. 1. (That's Incredible TV Show Ser.). 192p. (Orig.). 1981. pap. 2.25 (ISBN 0-515-05807-6). Jove Pubns.

--That's Incredible, Vol. 2. (That's Incredible TV Show Ser.). 192p. (Orig.). 1981. pap. 2.25 (ISBN 0-515-05870-X). Jove Pubns.

--That's Incredible, Vol. 3. (That's Incredible TV Show Ser.). 192p. (Orig.). 1981. pap. 2.25 (ISBN 0-515-05986-2). Jove Pubns.

Jeffrys, J. G. Suicide Most Foul. 192p. 1981. 9.95 (ISBN 0-8027-5430-9). Walker & Co.

Jeffs, Angela, ed. Creative Crafts. (Illus.). 1977. 35.00 (ISBN 0-8069-5378-0); lib. bdg. 32.99 (ISBN 0-8069-5379-9). Sterling.

Jeffus, Larry. Safety for Welders. LC 78-73579. (Metalworking Ser.). (gr. 8). 1980. pap. text ed. 3.20 (ISBN 0-8273-1684-4); instructor's guide 1.50 (ISBN 0-8273-1685-2). Delmar.

Jefkins, F. W. Marketing & PR Media Planning. LC 74-618347. 1974. text ed. 28.00 (ISBN 0-08-018086-8); pap. text ed. 13.25 (ISBN 0-08-018085-X). Pergamon.

Jefkins, Frank. Advertising Today. 2nd ed. 1977. text ed. 27.50x (ISBN 0-7002-0263-3); pap. text ed. 16.95x (ISBN 0-7002-0265-X). Intl Ideas.

--Dictionary of Marketing & Communication. 1973. text ed. 16.50x (ISBN 0-7002-0218-8). Intl Ideas.

--Planned Press & Public Relations. 1977. text ed. 29.95x (ISBN 0-7002-0264-1); pap. text ed. 17.95x (ISBN 0-7002-0272-2). Intl Ideas.

--Public Relations. 232p. 1980. pap. text ed. 11.95x (ISBN 0-7121-1698-2). Intl Ideas.

Jegen, Mary E. & Wilbur, Charles K., eds. Growth with Equity: Strategies for Meeting Human Needs. LC 78-70818. 242p. (Orig.). 1979. pap. 4.95. Paulist Pr.

Jeger, Max. Transformation Geometry. (Mathematical Studies Ser.). 1971. text ed. 6.50x o.p. (ISBN 0-04-513002-7). Allen Unwin.

Jehlen, Myra. Class & Character in Faulkners South. LC 76-3519. 176p. 1976. 12.50x (ISBN 0-231-04011-3). Columbia U Pr.

Jehoram, Herman C., ed. see Spoor, J. H., et al.

Jehu, Derek, et al. Behaviour Modification in Social Work. LC 70-37111. 192p. 1972. 20.25 (ISBN 0-471-44140-6, Pub. by Wiley-Interscience). Wiley.

Jekel, James F., jt. auth. see Klerman, Lorraine V.

Jelavich, Barbara. Ottoman Empire, the Great Powers, & the Straits Question: 1870-1887. LC 72-88631. 224p. 1973. 10.00x (ISBN 0-253-34276-7). Ind U Pr.

Jelinek, Mariann. Institutionalizing Innovation: A Study of Organizational Learning Systems. (Praeger Special Studies). 1979. 23.95 (ISBN 0-03-047031-5). Praeger.

Jelinek, Mariann, ed. Career Management for the Organization: The Individual. 1979. pap. text ed. 12.50 (ISBN 0-914292-18-8); teacher's manual avail. (ISBN 0-471-06292-8). Wiley.

Jelinek, Z. K. Particle Size Analysis. Bryce, W. A., tr. LC 73-14415. (Ser. in Analytical Chemistry). (Illus.). 178p. 1974. 34.95 (ISBN 0-470-44148-8). Halsted Pr.

Jellema, William W. From Red to Black? The Financial Status of Private Colleges & Universities. LC 73-7155. (Higher Education Ser.). 208p. 1973. 11.95x o.p. (ISBN 0-87589-188-8). Jossey-Bass.

Jelley, Herbert M. & Herrmann, Robert O. The American Consumer: Issues & Decisions. 2nd ed. (gr. 11-12). 1978. pap. text ed. 12.20 (ISBN 0-07-032341-0, G); student activity guide 5.32 (ISBN 0-07-032342-9); tchrs. manual & key 6.00 (ISBN 0-07-032343-7). McGraw.

Jellicoe, Ann. The Sport of My Mad Mother. 1964. pap. 3.95 o.p. (ISBN 0-571-05935-X, Pub. by Faber & Faber). Merrimack Bk Serv.

Jellicoe, Ann & Mayne, Roger. Devon: A Shell Guide. (Shell Guide Ser.). (Illus.). 1975. 12.95 (ISBN 0-571-04836-6, Pub. by Faber & Faber). Merrimack Bk Serv.

Jelliffe, D. B. & Stanfield, J. Paget. Diseases of Children in the Subtropics & Tropics. 3rd ed. (Illus.). 1978. 80.00x (ISBN 0-7131-4277-4). Intl Ideas.

Jelliffe, D. B. & Jelliffe, E. F., eds. Advances in International Maternal & Child Health, Vol. 1. 250p. 1981. text ed. 45.00x (ISBN 0-19-261281-6). Oxford U Pr.

Jelliffe, E. F., jt. ed. see Jelliffe, D. B.

Jellinck, P. H. Biochemistry. (Teach Yourself Ser.). 1973. pap. 2.95 o.p. (ISBN 0-679-10387-2). McKay.

Jellinek, Frank. The Civil War in Spain. 1969. Repr. of 1938 ed. 23.50 (ISBN 0-86527-028-7). Fertig.

Jellinek, Frank, tr. see Chevalier, Louis.

Jellinek, Frank, tr. see Chevalier, Luois.

Jellinek, J. Stephan. The Use of Fragrance in Consumer Products. LC 75-2106. 219p. 1975. 27.50 (ISBN 0-471-44151-1, Pub. by Wiley-Interscience). Wiley.

Jellinger, K., ed. see International Symposium on Malignant Lymphomas of the Nervous System.

Jemenez, J., jt. ed. see Florit, E.

Jemie, Onwuchekwa. Langston Hughes: An Introduction to Poetry. LC 76-18219. (Columbia Introductions to Twentieth Century American Poetry Ser.). 1977. 15.00x (ISBN 0-231-03780-5). Columbia U Pr.

Jenaro-Maclennan, L. The Trecento Commentaries on the Divina Commedia & the Epistle to Cangrande. (Oxford Modern Languages & Literature Monographs). 164p. 1974. 29.95x (ISBN 0-19-815519-0). Oxford U Pr.

Jenck, John E., jt. ed. see Fussler, Herman H.

Jenckes, Norma, ed. see Shaw, George B.

Jencks, Beate. Your Body - Biofeedback at Its Best. LC 77-24618. (Illus.). 1978. 15.95 (ISBN 0-88229-351-6); pap. 8.95 (ISBN 0-88229-508-X). Nelson-Hall.

Jencks, Charles. Modern Movements in Architecture. 432p. 1973. pap. 7.95 (ISBN 0-385-02554-8, Anch). Doubleday.

Jencks, Tina. In Good Taste. 150p. (Orig.). 1980. pap. 4.95 (ISBN 0-89581-020-4). Lancaster-Miller.

Jendrick, Barbara W., ed. Antique Advertising Paper Dolls. (Illus.). 64p. (Orig.). 1981. pap. write for info. (ISBN 0-486-24045-2). Dover.

Jenison, Don P. Ambush Range. 224p. (Orig.). 1980. pap. 1.95 (ISBN 0-89083-696-5). Zebra.

Jenkin, Leonard. Monarch Notes on Dickens' Great Expectations. (Orig.). pap. 1.75 (ISBN 0-671-00610-X). Monarch Pr.

Jenkin, P. M. Animal Hormones, Pt. 2: Control of Growth & Metamorphosis. LC 60-8977. 1970. 42.00 (ISBN 0-08-015648-7). Pergamon.

Jenkin, Robyn. The New Zealand Ghost Book. (Illus.). 1980. 13.50 (ISBN 0-589-01118-9, Pub. by Reed Books Australia). C E Tuttle.

Jenkins, A. D., jt. ed. see Stannett, V.

Jenkins, A. L., ed. see American College of Emergency Physicians.

Jenkins, Alan. The Thirties. LC 75-45511. (Illus.). 1976. 35.95x (ISBN 0-8128-1829-6). Stein & Day.

Jenkins, Alan C. World of Ghosts. (Illus.). 1978. 6.95 (ISBN 0-7011-5087-4, Pub. by Chatto Bodley Jonathan). Merrimack Bk Serv.

Jenkins, Annibel. Nicholas Rowe. (English Authors Ser.: No. 200). 1977. lib. bdg. 10.95 (ISBN 0-8057-6663-4). Twayne.

Jenkins, Betty. Bulletin Board Book No. 1. (gr. k-3). 5.95 (ISBN 0-916456-15-3, GA72). Good Apple.

--Bulletin Board Book No. 2. (gr. k-3). 5.95 (ISBN 0-916456-14-5). Good Apple.

Jenkins, Brian. Britain & the War for the Union, Vol. 2. 480p. 1980. 26.50 (ISBN 0-7735-0354-4). McGill-Queens U Pr.

Jenkins, C. & Mortimer, J. E. British Trade Unions Today. 1965. 13.75 (ISBN 0-08-011169-6); pap. 6.25 (ISBN 0-08-011168-8). Pergamon.

Jenkins, Cecil. Practical Chemistry for Schools. 1958. text ed. 5.95x (ISBN 0-521-05427-3). Cambridge U Pr.
Jenkins, Clive & Sherman, Barrie. Collective Bargaining: What You Always Wanted to Know About Trade Unions & Never Dared to Ask. 1977. 16.00 (ISBN 0-7100-8690-3); pap. 6.95 (ISBN 0-7100-8691-1). Routledge & Kegan.
Jenkins, Clive & Sherman, Barry. White-Collar Unionism: The Rebellious Salariat. 1979. 20.00x (ISBN 0-7100-0216-5); pap. 8.75 (ISBN 0-7100-0237-8). Routledge & Kegan.
Jenkins, D. & Owen, M. E., eds. The Welsh Law of Women: Studies Presented to Professor Daniel A. Binchy-1980. 1980. write for info. (ISBN 0-7083-0771-X). Verry.
Jenkins, D. A., et al. A Manual of Spinal Surgery. 1981. text ed. price not set. Butterworth.
Jenkins, D. L., tr. see Desoutter, D. M.
Jenkins, Dave. The Dinghy-Owner's Handbook. (Illus.). 224p. 1976. 14.00 (ISBN 0-370-10243-6); pap. 9.95 (ISBN 0-370-10346-7). Transatlantic.
--Peripherals & Interconnects. 300p. 1982. text ed. 12.95 (ISBN 0-8359-5501-X). Reston.
Jenkins, David. What Is Man? LC 79-132998. 1971. pap. 1.95 o.p. (ISBN 0-8170-0516-1). Judson.
Jenkins, David & Visocchi, Mark. Mendelssohn in Scotland. 1979. 17.95 (ISBN 0-903443-18-X, Pub. by Hamish Hamilton England). David & Charles.
--Portraits in Music I. 66p. 1980. 6.00 (ISBN 0-19-321400-8). Oxford U Pr.
Jenkins, David, jt. auth. see Snoeyink, Vernon L.
Jenkins, David, et al. Lex Terrae. Berkowitz, David S. & Thorne, Samuel E., eds. LC 77-89226. (Classics of English Legal History in the Modern Era Ser.: Vol. 70). 313p. 1979. lib. bdg. 40.00 (ISBN 0-8240-3169-5). Garland Pub.
Jenkins, Dorothy. Woman's Day Book of Antique Collectibles. (Illus.). 240p. 1981. 19.95 (ISBN 0-312-88647-0). St Martin.
Jenkins, Dorothy H., jt. auth. see Gaines, Edith.
Jenkins, Edward S., et al. American Black Scientists & Inventors. 1975. pap. 2.50 (ISBN 0-87355-003-X). Natl Sci Tchrs.
Jenkins, Emyl. Gregg Walker, News Photographer. LC 78-91739. (Illus.). (gr. 5-8). 1978. 5.95g o.p. (ISBN 0-8075-3041-7). A Whitman.
Jenkins, G. Curtis & Newton, R. The First Year of Life. (Library of General Practice). (Illus.). 260p. 1981. pap. text ed. 18.00 (ISBN 0-443-01717-4). Churchill.
Jenkins, G. Neil. The Physiology of the Mouth. 4th ed. (Illus.). 508p. 1970. 42.50 (ISBN 0-632-00138-0, Blackwell). Mosby.
--Preventing Dental Caries. 1981. write for info (ISBN 0-87527-217-7). Green.
Jenkins, Geraint H. Literature, Religion & Society in Wales, 1660-1730. (Studies in Welsh History Ser.: Vol. 2). 1978. text ed. 40.00x (ISBN 0-7083-0669-1). Verry.
Jenkins, Gilbert. Oil Economists' Handbook. 1977. 68.30x (ISBN 0-85334-728-X). Intl Ideas.
Jenkins, Gwilym, jt. auth. see Box, George E.
Jenkins, Gwilym M. & Watts, Donald G. Spectral Analysis & Its Applications. LC 67-13840. 1968. pap. 36.95x (ISBN 0-8162-4464-2). Holden-Day.
Jenkins, Hugh. Rank & File. 181p. 1980. 25.00x (ISBN 0-7099-0331-6, Pub by Croom Helm Ltd England). Biblio Dist.
Jenkins, J. C. Self-Propelled in the Southern Sierra, Vol. 1. Winnett, Thomas, ed. LC 74-27689. (Illus., Orig.). 1978. pap. 9.95 (ISBN 0-911824-39-1). Wilderness.
--Self-Propelled in the Southern Sierra, Vol. 2. Winnett, Thomas, ed. (Illus., Orig.). 1979. pap. 9.95 (ISBN 0-911824-77-4). Wilderness.
Jenkins, J. Geraint. The English Farm Wagon: Origins & Structure. (Illus.). 264p. 1981. 22.50 (ISBN 0-7153-8119-9). David & Charles.
--Traditional Country Craftsmen. (Illus.). 1968. Repr. of 1965 ed. 20.00 (ISBN 0-7100-1610-7). Routledge & Kegan.
Jenkins, J. P. & Brown, E. T., eds. KWIC Index of Rock Mechanics Literature: Pt. 2, 1969-1976. LC 79-40980. 742p. 1979. 142.00 (ISBN 0-08-022065-7). Pergamon.
Jenkins, Jeffrey. Twist of Sand. (Keith Jennison Large Type Bks). 8.95 (ISBN 0-531-00299-3). Watts.
Jenkins, Jerry. Light on the Heavy. 1978. pap. 2.50 (ISBN 0-88207-769-4). Victor Bks.
--Paige. (Margo Ser.). 128p. 1981. pap. 2.50 (ISBN 0-8024-4314-1). Moody.
Jenkins, Jerry, jt. auth. see Tippit, Sammy.
Jenkins, John. Early American Imprints, 2 vols. (Illus.). Date not set. Vol. 1. 15.00 (ISBN 0-8363-0158-7). Vol. 2 (ISBN 0-8363-0163-3). Jenkins.
Jenkins, John B. Genetics. 2nd ed. LC 78-69608. (Illus.). 1979. text ed. 21.95 (ISBN 0-395-26502-9); inst. manual 0.65 (ISBN 0-395-26501-0). HM.
Jenkins, John B., jt. auth. see Corwin, Harry O.
Jenkins, John D., jt. auth. see Dennis, Erwin A.
Jenkins, John H. Audubon & Other Capers: Confessions of a Texas Bookmaker. LC 76-2347. (Illus.). 1976. 12.50 (ISBN 0-8363-0139-0). Jenkins.
--Neither the Fanatics nor the Fainthearted: The Tour Leading to President Kennedy's Death & the Two Speeches He Could Not Give. 25.00 (ISBN 0-685-13277-3); pap. 4.50 wrappers (ISBN 0-685-13278-1). Jenkins.
--Works of Genius: A Catalogue & a Commentary, Pt. 1, A-c. (Illus.). 9.50 (ISBN 0-8363-0151-X). Jenkins.
Jenkins, John H., jt. auth. see Frost, H. Gordon.
Jenkins, John H., ed. Papers of the Texas Revolution, 10 vols. Set. 145.00 (ISBN 0-685-83961-3, Pub. by Presidential Press). Jenkins.
Jenkins, Lee C. Faulkner & Black-White Relations: A Psychoanalytic Approach. LC 80-21937. 288p. 1981. 20.00x (ISBN 0-231-04744-4). Columbia U Pr.
Jenkins, Leonard C. General Anesthesia & the Central Nervous System. LC 74-81839. 554p. 1969. 22.50 o.p. (ISBN 0-88275-120-4). Krieger.
Jenkins, Linda W., jt. auth. see Chinoy, Helen K.
Jenkins, Loa T., jt. auth. see Eliason, Claudia.
Jenkins, Marie M. The Curious Mollusks. LC 72-75597. (Illus.). (gr. 7 up). 1972. 7.95 o.p. (ISBN 0-8234-0209-6). Holiday.
--Embryos & How They Develop. LC 74-23547. (Illus.). 192p. (gr. 7 up). 1975. 7.95 (ISBN 0-8234-0254-1). Holiday.
--Kangaroos, Opossums, & Other Marsupials. LC 75-10798. (Illus.). 160p. (gr. 5 up). 1975. 7.95 o.p. (ISBN 0-8234-0264-9). Holiday.
Jenkins, Michael D. Starting a Business in California. 185p. 1980. pap. 25.00 (ISBN 0-916378-12-8). Oasis Pr.
Jenkins, Mick. The General Strike of Eighteen Forty-Two. (Illus.). 300p. 1980. text ed. 24.75x (ISBN 0-85315-488-0). Humanities.
Jenkins, Newell & Brook, Barry S., eds. Burnetti Gaetano Seventeen Forty-Four to Seventeen Ninety-Eight: Nine Symphonies. LC 79-9531. (The Symphony 1720-1840 Ser.: Ser. A, Vol. V). 635p. 1980. lib. bdg. 60.00 (ISBN 0-8240-3801-0). Garland Pub.
Jenkins, Peggy D. Art for the Fun of It: A Guide for Teaching Young Children. (Illus.). 208p. 1980. 13.95 (ISBN 0-13-047241-7, Spec); pap. 6.95 (ISBN 0-13-047233-6). P-H.
--Art for the Fun of It: A Guide for Teaching Young Children. (Illus.). 224p. 1980. 13.95 (Spec); pap. 6.95. P-H.
Jenkins, Peter. School Grounds: Some Ecological Enquiries. Wright, D. F., ed. 1973. pap. text ed. 3.95x o.p. (ISBN 0-435-59450-8). Heinemann Ed.
Jenkins, Philip. Focal Guide to Movie Tilting. (Focal Guide Ser.). (Illus.). 160p. 1981. pap. 7.95 (ISBN 0-240-51011-9). Focal Pr.
--The Focalguide to Movie Titling. (Focalguide Ser.). (Illus.). 1980. pap. 7.95 o.p. (ISBN 0-240-51011-9). Focal Pr.
Jenkins, R., et al. Properties of Polymers. (Advances in Polymer Sciences: Vol. 36). (Illus.). 150p. 1980. 40.20 (ISBN 0-387-10204-3). Springer-Verlag.
Jenkins, Rhys O. Dependent Industrialization in Latin America: The Automotive Industry in Argentina, Chile, & Mexico. LC 76-25352. (Illus.). 1976. text ed. 29.95 (ISBN 0-275-23220-4). Praeger.
Jenkins, Richard L. Behavior Disorders of Childhood & Adolescence. (Illus.). 148p. 1973. text ed. 9.75 (ISBN 0-398-02786-2). C C Thomas.
Jenkins, Robin. The Cone-Gathers: A Novel. LC 80-25757. 223p. 1981. 9.95 (ISBN 0-8008-1808-3). Taplinger.
Jenkins, Romilly J. Studies on Byzantine History of the 9th & 10th Centuries. 386p. 1980. 50.00x (ISBN 0-902089-07-2, Pub. by Variorum England). State Mutual Bk.
Jenkins, Ruth, et al. Four Great Southern Cooks. LC 80-68989. (Illus.). 200p. (Orig.). 1980. pap. 7.95 (ISBN 0-938072-00-5). DuBose Pub.
Jenkins, S. C., jt. auth. see Quayle, H. I.
Jenkins, S. H. Mediterranean Pollution: Proceedings of a Conference Held in Palma, Mallorca, Sept. 1979. (Progress in Water Technology Ser.: Vol. 12, Nos. 1 & 4). 850p. 1980. 100.00 (ISBN 0-08-026058-6). Pergamon.
--Treatment of Domestic & Industrial Wastewaters in Large Plants: Proceedings of a Workshop Held in Vienna, Austria, Sept. 1979. (Progress in Water Technology: Vol. 12, Nos. 3 & 5). 550p. 1980. 90.00 (ISBN 0-08-026033-0). Pergamon.
Jenkins, S. H., ed. Eutrophication of Deep Lakes: Proceedings of Seminar Held in Oslo, Norway June 1978. (Progress in Water Technology Ser.: Vol. 12, No. 2). (Illus.). 208p. 1980. pap. 47.00 (ISBN 0-08-026024-1). Pergamon.
Jenkins, Sheila, et al. Polka Dotted Pals, Pt. 1. 100p. (gr. k-1). 1980. pap. write for info (ISBN 0-932970-13-3). Prinit Pr.
Jenkins, Shirley. Comparative Recreation Needs & Services in New York Neighborhoods. 1963. 4.00 (ISBN 0-86671-000-0). Comm Coun Great NY.
--The Ethnic Dilemma in Social Services. LC 80-2155. (Illus.). 1981. 14.95 (ISBN 0-02-916400-1). Free Pr.
--Social Security in International Perspective: Essays in Honor of Eveline M. Burns. LC 71-94628. (Social Work & Social Issues Ser). 1969. 17.50x (ISBN 0-231-03294-3). Columbia U Pr.
Jenkins, Shirley & Norman, Elaine. Filial Deprivation & Foster Care. LC 72-3564. 320p. 1972. 16.00x (ISBN 0-231-03575-6). Columbia U Pr.
Jenkins, Shirley, jt. auth. see Kogan, Leonard S.
Jenkins, T. M., jt. ed. see Nelson, Walter R.
Jenkins, Ulysses D. Ancient African Religion & the African American Church. LC 78-65794. (Illus.). 1978. 10.00 (ISBN 0-933184-00-X); pap. 5.95 (ISBN 0-933184-10-7). Flame Intl.
Jenkins-Murphy, Andrew. Readings in English: Leisure. (Readings in English Ser.). (gr. 9-12). 1981. pap. text ed. write for info. (ISBN 0-88345-417-3, 18882). Regents Pub.
Jenkinson, Denis. Porsche 356. (AutoHistory Ser.). (Illus.). 128p. 1980. 12.95 (ISBN 0-85045-363-1, Pub. by Osprey England). Motorbooks Intl.
Jenkinson, Denis & Verstappen, Peter. The Schlumpf Obsession. LC 78-50878. 1978. 8.95 (ISBN 0-385-14409-1). Doubleday.
Jenkinson, Dennis. Batsford Guide to Racing Cars. 1979. 14.95 (ISBN 0-7134-1273-9, Pub. by Batsford England). David & Charles.
Jenkinson, Edward B. Censors in the Classroom: The Mind Benders. LC 79-17417. 206p. 1979. 13.95 (ISBN 0-8093-0929-7). S Ill U Pr.
Jenkinson, Edward B., jt. ed. see Auer, J. Jeffery.
Jenks, Alan W. The Elohist & North Israelite Traditions. LC 76-40189. (Society of Biblical Literature. Monograph). 1977. 9.00 (ISBN 0-89130-088-0, 060022); pap. 7.50 (ISBN 0-89130-145-3). Scholars Pr Ca.
Jenks, James M., ed. see Alexander Hamilton Institiue, Inc.
Jenks, James M., ed. see Alexander Hamilton Institute, Inc.
Jenks, James M., ed. see Alexander Hamilton Institute, Nc.
Jenks, Jamess M., ed. see Alexander Institute, Inc.
Jenks, Jjames M., ed. see Alexander Hamilton Institute, Inc.
Jenks, Stephen, jt. auth. see Steele, Fritz.
Jenks, Wilfred C. Social Justice in the Law of Nations: The ILO Impact After Fifty Years. (Royal Institute of International Affairs Ser.). 1970. pap. 2.50x o.p. (ISBN 0-19-285044-X). Oxford U Pr.
Jenkyn, J. F. & Plumb, R. T. Strategies for the Control of Cereal Disease: Organized by the British Plant Pathologist, Vol. 2. 250p. 1981. 47.50 (ISBN 0-470-27049-7). Halsted Pr.
Jenkyns, Chris, jt. auth. see Diska, Pat.
Jenkyns, Chris, jt. auth. see McGrath, Thomas.
Jenner, Bruce & Abraham, Marc. Bruce Jenner's Guide to the Olympics. (Illus.). 1979. 12.95 o.p. (ISBN 0-8362-6702-8); pap. 6.95 o.p. (ISBN 0-8362-6700-1). Andrews & McMeel.
Jenner, Charles. The Placid Man; or, Memoirs of Sir Charles Beville, 1770, 2 vols. in 1. Shugrue, Michael F., ed. (The Flowering of the Novel, 1740-1775 Ser: Vol. 91). 1974. lib. bdg. 50.00 (ISBN 0-8240-1190-2). Garland Pub.
Jenner, Chrystie. I Am Chrystie. LC 77-77949. (Illus.). 1977. pap. 4.95 o.p. (ISBN 0-89087-925-7). Les Femmes Pub.
Jenner, P. & Testa, B. Concepts in Drug Metabolism, Vol. 1. (Drugs & the Pharmaceutical Sciences: Vol. 10). 424p. 1980. 49.50 (ISBN 0-8247-6906-6). Dekker.
Jenner, Paul. Your Business Problems Solved. LC 79-51089. 1979. 17.95 (ISBN 0-7153-7646-2). David & Charles.
Jeness, Aylette. The Bakery Factory. LC 77-8094. (Illus.). (gr. 3-7). 1978. 5.95 (ISBN 0-690-03805-4, TYC-J); PLB 7.89 (ISBN 0-690-01338-8). T Y Crowell.
--Dwellers of the Tundra: Life in an Alaskan Eskimo Village. LC 74-93716. (gr. 7 up). 1970. 9.95 o.s.i. (ISBN 0-02-747720-7, CCPr). Macmillan.
Jennett, Bryan & Teasdale, Graham. Management of Head Injuries. LC 80-16785. (Contemporary Neurology Ser.: Vol. 20). (Illus.). 361p. 1980. text ed. 35.00 (ISBN 0-8036-5017-5). Davis Co.
Jennett, Sean. Cork & Kerry. (Batsford Travel Ser.). (Illus.). 1977. 9.50 o.s.i. (ISBN 0-7134-0437-X). Hippocrene Bks.
--The Making of Books. 5th ed. 1974. 24.00 o.p. (ISBN 0-571-04786-6, Pub. by Faber & Faber). Merrimack Bk Serv.
Jenney, Charles & Scudder, Rogers. First Year Latin. (New Jenney Latin Series). (gr. 10). 1975. text ed. 14.40 (ISBN 0-205-04595-2, 3945952); tchr's. guide 3.60 (ISBN 0-205-04596-0, 3945960); wkbk 5.40 (ISBN 0-205-02482-3, 3924823); tchrs'. guide to wkbk. 3.60 (ISBN 0-205-02483-1, 3924831); tests 4.12 (ISBN 0-205-02484-X, 392484X); tchrs'. ed. 4.12 (ISBN 0-205-02485-8, 3924858). Allyn.
Jenney, Charles, Jr. & Scudder, Robers V. Third Year Latin. (Latin Program Ser.). (gr. 9-12). 1980. text ed. 15.24 (ISBN 0-205-06811-1, 3968111); tchrs.' guide 2.40 (ISBN 0-205-00541-1, 3905411). Allyn.
Jenney, Charles, Jr. & Scudder, Rogers V. First Year Latin. rev. ed. 1979. text ed. 14.40 (ISBN 0-205-06177-X, 396177X); wkbk. 5.40 (ISBN 0-205-06178-8, 3961796); tchrs.' guide 3.60 (3961788). Allyn.
Jenney, Charles, Jr., et al. Second Year Latin. rev. ed. (gr. 7-12). 1979. text ed. 14.80 (ISBN 0-205-06182-6, 3961826); 4.96 (ISBN 0-205-02488-2, 3924882); tchrs'. guide 3.60 (ISBN 0-205-02489-0, 3924890); tests 3.60 (ISBN 0-205-02490-4, 3924904); tchrs'. ed. 3.60 (ISBN 0-205-02491-2, 3924912). Allyn.
Jennings. Applications of Glass Capilary Gas Chromatography. Date not set. price not set (ISBN 0-8247-1223-4). Dekker.
Jennings, Alan. Matrix Computation for Engineers & Scientists. LC 76-21079. 330p. 1980. pap. 16.50 (ISBN 0-471-27832-7, Pub. by Wiley Interscience). Wiley.
--Matrix Computation for Engineers & Scientists. LC 76-21079. 1977. 41.25 (ISBN 0-471-99421-9, Pub. by Wiley-Interscience). Wiley.
Jennings, B. R. & Morris, V. J. Atoms in Contact. (Oxford Paperbacks Ser). (Illus.). 112p. 1974. text ed. 16.95x (ISBN 0-19-851809-9); pap. text ed. 4.95x o.p. (ISBN 0-19-851804-8). Oxford U Pr.
Jennings, Charles, jt. auth. see Tager, Mark.
Jennings, Charles B., et al. Consider Your Words. 3rd ed. 1980. pap. text ed. 10.50 scp (ISBN 0-06-043292-6, HarpC); instructor's manual free. Har-Row.
Jennings, Dana C. Free Ice Water: The Story of the Wall Drug. rev. ed. LC 76-92836. (Illus.). 96p. 1975. pap. 2.95 (ISBN 0-87970-139-0). North Plains.
Jennings, Don J. Arise & Evangelize. 1975. pap. 1.25 (ISBN 0-87398-024-7, Pub. by Bibl Evang Pr). Sword of Lord.
Jennings, E., jt. auth. see Ward, J., Jr.
Jennings, Edward H., jt. auth. see Stevenson, Richard A.
Jennings, Elizabeth. Growing Points. 94p. 1975. 7.50 o.p. (ISBN 0-8023-1262-4). Dufour.
Jennings, Eugene E. Executive Success: Stresses, Problems, & Adjustment. LC 67-27560. 1967. 18.95x (ISBN 0-89197-156-4); pap. text ed. 6.95x (ISBN 0-89197-157-2). Irvington.
Jennings, F. C. Isaiah. rev. ed. LC 55-41748. 1935. 9.50 (ISBN 0-87213-420-2). Loizeaux.
Jennings, Gary. Aztec. (Illus.). 1980. 15.95 (ISBN 0-689-11045-6). Atheneum.
--Killer Storms: Hurricanes, Typhoons, & Tornadoes. LC 78-101899. (Illus.). (gr. 7-9). 1970. 7.89 (ISBN 0-397-31128-1). Lippincott.
--The Rope in the Jungle. LC 76-14466. (gr. 5-7). 1976. 7.95 o.p. (ISBN 0-397-31267-9). Lippincott.
Jennings, H. S; see Haeckel, Ernst.
Jennings, Ivor. Parliament. 1969. 53.95 (ISBN 0-521-07056-2); pap. 11.95x (ISBN 0-521-09532-8). Cambridge U Pr.
Jennings, J. G., ed. Vedantic Buddhism of the Buddha: A Collection of Historical Texts. 679p. 1975. text ed. 19.50x o.p. (ISBN 0-8426-0683-1). Verry.
Jennings, Jerry, ed. The Northeast. rev. ed. LC 78-54254. (United States Ser.). (Illus.). 320p. (gr. 5 up). 1979. text ed. 9.93 ea. 1-4 copies (ISBN 0-88296-057-1); text ed. 7.94 ea. 5 or more copies; tchrs.' annotated ed. 13.68 (ISBN 0-88296-347-3). Fideler.
Jennings, Jerry E. The West. rev ed. LC 78-54256. (United States Ser). (Illus.). (gr. 5 up). 1979. text ed. 9.93 1-4 copies & 5 or more 7.94 (ISBN 0-88296-077-6); tchrs' annotated ed. 13.68 (ISBN 0-88296-347-3). Fideler.
Jennings, Jerry E. & Smith, Marion H. The South. rev. ed. LC 78-70052. (United States Ser). (Illus.). 288p. (gr. 5 up). 1979. text ed. 9.93 ea. 1-4 copies (ISBN 0-88296-064-4); 5 or more copies 7.94 ea.; tchrs' annotated ed. 13.68 (ISBN 0-88296-347-3). Fideler.
Jennings, Jerry E., ed. The United States. LC 78-62083. (Illus.). (gr. 4 up). 1979. text ed. 13.68 1-4 copies, 5 or more 10.94 o.p. (ISBN 0-88296-477-1); tchr's annotated ed. 13.68 o.p. (ISBN 0-686-66762-X). Fideler.

Jennings, Jesse D., ed. Ancient Native Americans. LC 78-7989. (Illus.). 1978. pap. text ed. 21.95x (ISBN 0-7167-0074-3). W H Freeman.

Jennings, Jesse D., et al. Cowboy Cave. (University of Utah Anthropological Papers: No. 104). (Illus.). 220p. (Orig.). 1981. pap. 20.00 (ISBN 0-87480-182-6). U of Utah Pr.

--Sudden Shelter. (University of Utah Anthropological Papers: No. 103). (Illus., Orig.). 1980. pap. 15.00x (ISBN 0-87480-166-4). U of Utah Pr.

Jennings, K. R. & Cundall, R. B., eds. Progress in Reaction Kinetics: Vol. 9 Complete. 368p. 1980. 76.00 (ISBN 0-08-020343-4). Pergamon.

Jennings, Ken, jt. auth. see Holley, William H., Jr.

Jennings, Kenneth M., Jr., et al. Labor Relations in a Public Service Industry: Unions, Management, & the Public Interest in Mass Transit. LC 77-13717. (Praeger Special Studies). 1978. 32.95 (ISBN 0-03-040866-0). Praeger.

Jennings, Lawrence C. France & Europe in Eighteen Forty-Eight: A Study of French Foreign Affairs in Time of Crisis. 1973. 28.50x (ISBN 0-19-822514-8). Oxford U Pr.

Jennings, Lee B. Justinus Kerners Weg Nach Weinsberg 1809-1819: Die Entpolitisierung eines Romantikers. LC 80-69125. (Studies in German Literature, Linsuitics, & Culture: Vol. 3). (Illus.). 160p. 1981. text ed. 17.00x (ISBN 0-938100-00-9). Camden Hse.

Jennings, Louis B. The Function of Religion: An Introduction. LC 79-53368. 1979. pap. text ed. 12.00 (ISBN 0-8191-0789-1). U Pr of Amer.

Jennings, M. K. High School Seniors Cohort Study, Nineteen Sixty-Five & Nineteen Seventy-Three. 1980. 14.00 (ISBN 0-89138-964-4). ICPSR.

Jennings, M. Kent & Niemi, Richard G. Generations & Politics: A Panel Study of Young Adults & Their Parents. LC 80-8555. (Illus.). 408p. 1981. 25.00x (ISBN 0-691-07626-X); pap. 6.95x (ISBN 0-691-02201-1). Princeton U Pr.

Jennings, Paul. The Great Jelly of London. (Illus.). (ps-5). 1967. 6.95 (ISBN 0-571-08546-6, Pub. by Faber & Faber); pap. 2.95 (ISBN 0-571-10844-X). Merrimack Bk Serv.

Jennings, R. Y. & Brownlie, Ian. The British Year Book of International Law 1979, Vol. 50. 464p. 1981. 98.00 (ISBN 0-19-825360-5). Oxford U Pr.

Jennings, R. Y. & Brownlie, Ian, eds. The British Year Book of International Law 1978, Vol. XLIX. (British Year Book of International Law). (Illus.). 1980. 89.00x (ISBN 0-19-818178-7). Oxford U Pr.

Jennings, R. Y. see Royal Institute of International Affairs.

Jennings, Richard W. & Buxbaum, Richard M. Cases & Materials on Corporations. 5th ed. LC 79-9237. (American Casebook Ser.). 1397p. 1979. text ed. 23.95 (ISBN 0-8299-2054-4). West Pub.

Jennings, Robert E. Education & Politics. 1976. 32.00 (ISBN 0-7134-0474-4, Pub. by Batsford England); pap. 15.95 (ISBN 0-7134-0475-2). David & Charles.

--Education & Politics. 1978. 14.50x o.s.i. (ISBN 0-7134-0474-4). Hippocrene Bks.

Jennings, Robert E., jt. auth. see Milstein, Mike M.

Jennings, Royalston F. Gas & A.C. Arc Welding & Cutting. 3rd ed. (gr. 7 up). 1956. pap. text ed. 5.00 (ISBN 0-87345-119-8). McKnight.

Jennings, Sue. Remedial Drama. LC 74-77191. 1978. pap. 5.85 (ISBN 0-87830-563-7). Theatre Arts.

Jennings, T. Studying Birds in the Garden. 1976. 7.80 (ISBN 0-08-017802-2). Pergamon.

Jennings, T. J. Collecting from Nature. (gr. 3 up). 1976. 8.10 o.p. (ISBN 0-08-016046-8). Pergamon.

Jennings, Terry. Your Book of Prehistoric Animals. (Illus.). 64p. (gr. 5-8). 1980. 8.95 (ISBN 0-571-11455-5, Pub. by Faber & Faber). Merrimack Bk Serv.

Jennings, Thelma. The Nashville Convention: Southern Movement for Unity, Eighteen Forty-Nine to Eighteen Fifty. LC 80-12917. 1980. 16.95x (ISBN 0-87870-097-8). Memphis St Univ.

Jennings, Tony, jt. auth. see Sharp, Clifford.

Jennings, Walter & Shibamoto, Takayuki. Qualitative Analysis of Flavor & Fragrance Volatiles by Glass Capillary Gas Chromtography. LC 79-26034. 1980. 39.00 (ISBN 0-12-384250-6). Acad Pr.

Jennings, William I. & Tambiah, Henry W. Dominion of Ceylon, the Development of Its Laws & Constitution. Repr. of 1952 ed. lib. bdg. 19.75x (ISBN 0-8371-3023-9, JEDC). Greenwood.

Jennison, Keith. New England in the Off-Color Season. LC 80-67659. (Illus., Orig.). 1980. pap. 5.95 (ISBN 0-911764-23-2). Durrell.

Jenny, H. The Soil Resource: Origin & Behavior. (Ecological Studies: Vol. 37). (Illus.). 377p. 1981. 29.80 (ISBN 0-387-90543-X). Springer-Verlag.

Jensema, Carl J., jt. auth. see Corbett, Edward E.

Jensen. Principles of Physiology. 2nd ed. (Illus.). 1980. text ed. 29.50 (ISBN 0-8385-7931-0). ACC.

Jensen, Alfred D., jt. auth. see Dew, Donald.

Jensen, Alfred E. & Chenoweth, H. Applied Engineering Mechanics. 3rd ed. 1971. 16.95 (ISBN 0-07-032480-8, G); problem answers 1.50 (ISBN 0-07-032481-6). McGraw.

Jensen, Ann & Watkins, Mary L. Franz Anton Mesmer: Physician Extraordinaire. LC 66-28499. 7.50 o.p. (ISBN 0-912326-19-0). Garrett-Helix

Jensen, Arthur R. Educability & Group Differences. LC 72-9126. (Illus.). 416p. 1973. 10.95 o.s.i. (ISBN 0-06-012194-7, HarpT). Har-Row.

--Genetics & Education. LC 72-86636. 384p. 1973. 10.95 o.s.i. (ISBN 0-06-012192-0, HarpT). Har-Row.

--Straight Talk About Mental Tests. LC 80-83714. (Illus.). 1981. 12.95 (ISBN 0-02-916440-0). Free Pr.

Jensen, Bernard. Ciencia y Practica de la Iridologia. Orig. Title: The Science & Practice of Iridology. (Spanish.). 18.50 o.s.i. (ISBN 0-89557-027-0). Bi World Indus.

Jensen, C. H. Engineering Drawing & Design. 1968. text ed. 18.95 o.p. (ISBN 0-07-094866-6, G). McGraw.

--Interpreting Engineering Drawings. LC 70-92052. 256p. 1972. 10.40 (ISBN 0-8273-0061-1); instructor's guide 1.60 (ISBN 0-8273-0062-X). Delmar.

Jensen, C. H. & Hines, R. D. Interpreting Engineering Drawings: Metric Edition. LC 77-78175. 1979. pap. text ed. 10.60 (ISBN 0-8273-1061-7); instructor's guide 1.60 (ISBN 0-8273-1062-5). Delmar.

Jensen, C. Russell. Preliminary Survey of the French Collection. (Finding Aids to the Microfilmed Manuscript Collection of the Genealogical Society of Utah). (Orig.). 1981. pap. 20.00x (ISBN 0-87480-171-0). U of Utah Pr.

Jensen, C. W. & Fisher, Eugene. The I E E E Four Eighty-Eight Interface Parts Handbook. 280p. (Orig.). 1980. pap. 6.99 (ISBN 0-931988-50-0). Osborne-McGraw.

Jensen, C. William, jt. auth. see Fisher, Eugene.

Jensen, Clarence W., jt. auth. see Cramer, Gail L.

Jensen, David. The Human Nervous System. 416p. 1980. pap. text ed. 14.95x (ISBN 0-8385-3944-0). ACC.

Jensen, De Lamar. Reformation Europe: Age of Reform & Revolution. 480p. 1981. pap. text ed. 10.95 (ISBN 0-669-03626-9). Heath.

--Renaissance Europe: Age of Recovery & Reconciliation. 416p. 1980. pap. text ed. 10.95 (ISBN 0-669-51722-4). Heath.

Jensen, Ejner J. John Marston, Dramtist. (Salzburg Institute for English Literature Jacobean Drama Studies). (Orig.). 1980. pap. text ed. 25.00x (ISBN 0-391-01717-9). Humanities.

Jensen, Erik. The Iban & Their Religion. (Oxford Monographs on Social Anthropology). (Illus.). 220p. 1975. 29.95x (ISBN 0-19-823179-2). Oxford U Pr.

Jensen, Gale E. Problems & Principles of Human Organization in Educational Systems. (Educational Ser.). 239p. 1969. pap. text ed. 5.00 o.p. (ISBN 0-89039-005-3). Ann Arbor FL.

Jensen, Gale E. & Medlin, William K. Readings on the Role of Education in Community & National Development in Problems in Education & Nation Building. 82p. 1969. pap. text ed. 3.50x o.p. (ISBN 0-89039-004-5). Ann Arbor Pubs.

Jensen, Gale E., ed. Dynamics of Instructional Groups. LC 60-1494. (National Society for the Study of Education Yearbooks Ser: No. 59, Pt. 2). 1960. 6.00x o.s.i. (ISBN 0-226-60057-2). U of Chicago Pr.

Jensen, Gary F. & Rojek, Dean G. Readings in Juvenile Delinquency. 448p. 1981. pap. text ed. 9.95 (ISBN 0-669-03763-X). Heath.

Jensen, Gordon D. Youth & Sex: Pleasure & Responsibility. LC 72-77121. (Illus.). 1973. 11.95 (ISBN 0-911012-99-0); pap. 6.95 (ISBN 0-88229-499-7). Nelson-Hall.

Jensen, Harlan E. Steroscopic Atlas of Ophthalmic Surgery of Domestic Animals. (Illus.). 1973. text ed. 61.50 o.p. (ISBN 0-8016-2493-2). Mosby.

Jensen, Harlan E., jt. auth. see Doering, George G.

Jensen, Howard G., jt. auth. see Schattke, Rudolph W.

Jensen, Irving. Haggai, Zechariah & Malachi. (Bible Self Study Guide Ser.). 1976. pap. 2.25 (ISBN 0-8024-1037-5). Moody.

--Second Corinthians. (Bible Self-Study Ser). (Illus.). 108p. 1972. pap. 2.25 (ISBN 0-8024-1047-2). Moody.

--Timothy & Titus. pap. 2.25 (ISBN 0-8024-1054-5). Moody.

Jensen, Irving L. Acts. (Bible Self-Study Ser). 1970. pap. 2.25 (ISBN 0-8024-1044-8). Moody.

--Ecclesiastes & the Song of Solomon. (Bible Self Study Guide Ser.). 1974. pap. 2.25 (ISBN 0-8024-1021-9). Moody.

--Ephesians. (Bible Self-Study Ser). 1973. pap. 2.25 (ISBN 0-8024-1049-9). Moody.

--Exodus. (Bible Self-Study Ser). 1970. pap. 2.95 (ISBN 0-8024-1002-2). Moody.

--Ezekial Daniel. 1970. pap. 2.25 (ISBN 0-8024-1026-X). Moody.

--Ezra - Esther. (Bible Self-Study Ser). 1970. pap. 2.25 (ISBN 0-8024-1015-4). Moody.

--First & Second Peter. (Bible Self-Study Ser). 1971. pap. 2.25 (ISBN 0-8024-1060-X). Moody.

--First & Second Samuel. (Bible Self-Study Ser.). 1970. pap. 2.25 (ISBN 0-8024-1009-X). Moody.

--First & Second Thessalonians. (Bible Self-Study Ser.). 112p. 1974. pap. 2.25 (ISBN 0-8024-1053-7). Moody.

--First & Second Timothy & Titus. (Bible Self-Study Ser.). 1973. pap. 2.25 (ISBN 0-8024-1054-5). Moody.

--Galatians. (Bible Self Study Ser). 1973. pap. 2.25 (ISBN 0-8024-1048-0). Moody.

--Hebrews. (Bible Self-Study Ser). 1970. pap. 2.25 (ISBN 0-8024-1058-8). Moody.

--James. (Bible Self-Study Ser). (Illus.). 1972. pap. 2.25 (ISBN 0-8024-1059-6). Moody.

--Jensen's Bible Study Charts. 128p. 1981. pap. 19.95 (ISBN 0-8024-4296-X). Moody.

--Jensen's Survey of the New Testament. 608p. 1981. text ed. 14.95 (ISBN 0-8024-4308-7). Moody.

--Jensen's Survey of the Old Testament. 1978. text ed. 12.95 (ISBN 0-8024-4307-9). Moody.

--Job. (Bible Self Study Guide Ser.). 1975. pap. 2.25 (ISBN 0-8024-1018-9). Moody.

--John. (Bible Self-Study Guide). 1970. pap. 2.25 (ISBN 0-8024-1043-X). Moody.

--Leviticus. (Bible Self Study Ser.). 1970. pap. 2.25 (ISBN 0-8024-1003-0). Moody.

--Luke. (Bible Self Study Ser.). 1970. pap. 2.25 (ISBN 0-8024-1042-1). Moody.

--Mark. (Bible Self-Study Ser). (Illus.). 1972. pap. 2.25 (ISBN 0-8024-1041-3). Moody.

--Matthew. (Bible Self Study Ser). 1974. pap. 2.25 (ISBN 0-8024-1040-5). Moody.

--Minor Prophets of Israel. (Bible Self-Study Guides Ser.). 112p. (Orig.). 1975. pap. 2.25 (ISBN 0-8024-1028-6). Moody.

--Minor Prophets of Judah. (Bible Self-Study Guide Ser.). 112p. 1976. pap. 2.25 (ISBN 0-8024-1029-4). Moody.

--Numbers, Deuteronomy. (Bible Self Study Ser.). 1970. pap. 2.25 (ISBN 0-8024-1004-9). Moody.

--Philippians. (Bible Self-Study Ser). 80p. 1973. pap. 2.25 (ISBN 0-8024-1051-0). Moody.

--Psalms. (Bible Self-Study Ser). 1970. pap. 2.25 (ISBN 0-8024-1019-7). Moody.

--Revelation. (Bible Self-Study Ser.). 124p. (Orig.). 1971. pap. 2.25 (ISBN 0-8024-1066-9). Moody.

Jensen, Irving L., ed. First Kings & Chronicles. rev.ed ed. (Bible Self-Study Ser). (Illus.). 1968. pap. 2.25 (ISBN 0-8024-1011-1). Moody.

--Genesis. (Bible Self-Study Ser.). 1967. pap. 2.25 (ISBN 0-8024-1001-4). Moody.

--Isaiah - Jeremiah. rev. ed. (Bible Self-Study Ser). (Illus., Orig.). 1968. pap. 2.25 (ISBN 0-8024-1023-5). Moody.

--Joshua. rev. ed. (Bible Self-Study Ser). (Illus.). 80p. 1967. pap. 2.25 (ISBN 0-8024-1006-5). Moody.

--Judges, Ruth. rev. ed. (Bible Self-Study Ser). (Illus.). 96p. 1967. pap. 2.25 (ISBN 0-8024-1007-3). Moody.

--Second Kings with Chronicles. rev. ed. (Bible Self-Study Ser). (Illus., Orig.). 1968. pap. 2.25 (ISBN 0-8024-1012-X). Moody.

Jensen, Irving R. Life of Christ. (Bible Self Study Ser.). pap. 2.25 (ISBN 0-8024-1067-7). Moody.

Jensen, Jay R. Six Years in Hell: A Returned POW Views Captivity, Country & the Nation's Future. 1979. 7.95 o.p. (ISBN 0-88290-043-9). Horizon Utah.

Jensen, Joan M. With These Hands: Women Working on the Land. (Women's Lives - Women's Work Ser.). (Illus.). 336p. 1981. 17.95 (ISBN 0-912670-90-8); pap. 6.95 (ISBN 0-912670-71-1). Feminist Pr.

Jensen, Johannes. Energy Storage. (Illus.). 1979. text ed. 19.95 (ISBN 0-408-00390-1). Butterworths.

Jensen, John, compiled by. The Human Development Program for Institutionalized Teenagers. 1974. 9.95 (ISBN 0-86584-034-2). Human Dev Train.

Jensen, L. E., et al. Automotive Science. LC 76-3940. 1977. pap. 6.60 (ISBN 0-8273-1302-0); instructor's guide 1.60 (ISBN 0-8273-1303-9). Delmar.

Jensen, Larry C., jt. auth. see Boyce, William D.

Jensen, Lloyd B. Poisoning Misadventures: Narrative Excerpts on Food-Borne Diseases & Poisoning for the Physician, Microbiologist, Attorney & Nutritionist. 212p. 1970. 15.75 (ISBN 0-398-00927-9). C C Thomas.

Jensen, M. L. & Bateman, A. M. Economic Mineral Deposits. 3rd rev. ed. 608p. 1981. text ed. 24.95 (ISBN 0-471-09043-3). Wiley.

--Economic Mineral Deposits. 3rd ed. LC 78-9852. 1979. text ed. 25.95 (ISBN 0-471-01769-8). Wiley.

Jensen, Malcolm C. Francisco Coronado. LC 73-12087. (Visual Biography Ser). (Illus.). 64p. (gr. 4-5). 1974. PLB 4.90 o.p. (ISBN 0-531-00973-4). Watts.

--Leif Erikson the Lucky. (Visual Biographies). (Illus.). (gr. 4 up). 1979. PLB 6.90 s&l (ISBN 0-531-02297-8). Watts.

Jensen, Margaret & Bobak, Irene. Handbook of Maternity Care: A Guide for Nursing Practice. LC 79-18163. 1980. pap. text ed. 9.95 (ISBN 0-8016-2490-8). Mosby.

Jensen, Margaret D., et al. Maternity Care: The Nurse & the Family. 2nd ed. LC 80-20723. (Illus.). 966p. 1981. text ed. 24.95 (ISBN 0-8016-2492-4). Mosby.

Jensen, Margie C., ed. Blue Ribbon Breads. (Blue Ribbon Cookbks: No. 6). (Illus.). 1978. pap. 3.95 o.p. (ISBN 0-695-80896-6). Follett.

--Blue Ribbon Cakes. (Blue Ribbon Cookbks: No. 6). (Illus.). 1978. pap. 3.95 o.p. (ISBN 0-695-80947-4). Follett.

--Blue Ribbon Candies. (Blue Ribbon Cookbks: No. 6). (Illus.). 1978. pap. 3.95 o.p. (ISBN 0-695-80950-4). Follett.

--Blue Ribbon Cookies. (Blue Ribbon Cookbks: No. 6). (Illus.). 1978. pap. 3.95 o.p. (ISBN 0-695-80948-2). Follett.

--Blue Ribbon Jams & Jellies, Pickles & Relishes. (Blue Ribbon Cookbks: No. 6). (Illus.). 1978. pap. 3.95 o.p. (ISBN 0-695-80894-X). Follett.

--Blue Ribbon Pies. (Blue Ribbon Cookbks: No. 6). (Illus.). 1978. pap. 3.95 o.p. (ISBN 0-695-80949-0). Follett.

Jensen, Marilyn. Phillis Wheatley: Negro Slave. 288p. 1981. PLB 8.95 (ISBN 0-87460-326-9). Lion.

--Phillis Wheatley, Negro Slave of John Wheatley. pap. 9.95. Lion.

Jensen, Merill. Articles of Confederation: An Interpretation of the Social Constitutional History of the American Revolution, 1774-1781. 1940. pap. 7.95x (ISBN 0-299-00204-7). U of Wis Pr.

Jensen, Merrill. The American Revolution Within America. LC 74-11113. 224p. 1974. 12.00x (ISBN 0-8147-4154-1). NYU Pr.

--The New Nation: A History of the United States During the Confederation 1781-1789. 446p. 1981. text ed. 19.95 (ISBN 0-930350-15-4); pap. text ed. 9.95 (ISBN 0-930350-14-6). NE U Pr.

Jensen, Merrill, ed. Regionalism in America. 1965. pap. 9.95 (ISBN 0-299-00794-4). U of Wis Pr.

--Tracts of the American Revolution, 1763-1776. LC 66-26805. (Orig.). 1967. 10.95 (ISBN 0-672-60046-3, AHS35). Bobbs.

Jensen, Merrill & Becker, Robert A., eds. A Documentary History of the First Federal Elections, Vol. 1. LC 74-5903. 800p. 1976. 50.00x (ISBN 0-299-06690-8). U of Wis Pr.

Jensen, Oliver. America's Yesterdays: Images of Our Lost Past Discovered in the Photographic Archives of the Library of Congress. (Illus.). 352p. 1978. 12.95 (ISBN 0-8281-3074-4, Dist. by Scribner). Am Heritage.

--America's Yesterdays: Images of Our Lost Past Discovered in the Photographic Archives of the Library of Congress. LC 78-18426. (Illus.). 352p. 1978. deluxe ed. 39.95 slipcased (ISBN 0-8281-3073-6). Am Heritage.

Jensen, Oliver, intro. by. Great Stories of American Businessmen from American Heritage. LC 72-80701. (Illus.). 382p. 1972. 15.00 (ISBN 0-8281-0327-5, B071). Am Heritage.

Jensen, Oliver, ed. Picturesque America: The Mountains, Rivers, Lakes, Forests, Waterfalls, Shores, Canyons, Valleys, Cities, & Other Picturesque Features of Our Country by Eminent American Artists. facsimile ed. LC 73-21908. (Illus.). 1974. 25.00 (ISBN 0-8281-0337-2, M013). Am Heritage.

Jensen, Oliver, ed. see Catton, Bruce.

Jensen, Paul J., jt. auth. see Dew, Donald.

Jensen, Paul M. Boris Karloff & His Films. LC 72-9940. (International Film Guide Ser.). (Illus.). 208p. 1975. 10.00 o.p. (ISBN 0-498-01324-3). A S Barnes.

Jensen, Peter. Die Kosmologie der Babylonier: Studien und Materialien. Mit einem mythologischen Anhang. 546p. 1974. Repr. of 1890 ed. 102.35x (ISBN 3-11-003425-5). De Gruyter.

Jensen, Randall W. & Watkins, Bruce O. Network Analysis: Theory & Computer Methods. (Illus.). 544p. 1974. ref. ed. 26.95 (ISBN 0-13-611061-4). P-H.

Jensen, Richard J. Illinois: A History. (States & the Nation Ser.). (Illus.). 1978. 12.95 (ISBN 0-393-05596-5, Co-Pub by AASLH). Norton.

Jensen, Richard J., et al. Rhetorical Perspectives on Communication and Mass Madia. 176p. 1980. pap. text ed. 9.95 (ISBN 0-8403-1902-9). Kendall-Hunt.

Jensen, Richard N. Microteaching: Planning & Implementing a Competency-Based Training Program. (Illus.). 92p. 1974. text ed. 9.75 (ISBN 0-398-02930-X). C C Thomas.

Jensen, Robert G., jt. auth. see Patton, Stuart.

Jensen, Rolf. Cities of Vision. (Illus.). 1974. 40.90x (ISBN 0-85334-569-4, Pub. by Applied Science). Burgess-Intl Ideas.

Jensen, Rolf, ed. Fire Protection for the Design Professional. LC 75-9508. 198p. 1975. 29.95 (ISBN 0-8436-0152-3). CBI Pub.

Jensen, Ronald & Cherrington, David J. The Business Management Laboratory: Participants' Manual. rev. ed. 1977. pap. 9.95x (ISBN 0-256-01953-3). Business Pubns.

Jensen, Steven A. Paramedic Emergency Handbook. (Illus.). 128p. Date not set. text ed. 7.95 (ISBN 0-8016-2495-9). Mosby. Postponed.

Jensen, T. R., jt. auth. see Wright, R. T.

Jensen, Thomas R., jt. auth. see Wright, R. Thomas.

Jensen, Vernon. Argumentation: Reasoning in Communication. 1980. text ed. 15.95 (ISBN 0-442-25396-6); instr's. manual 2.00 (ISBN 0-442-24213-1). D Van Nostrand.

Jensen, Virginia A. Sara & the Door. LC 76-28987. (Illus.). (gr. k-1). 1977. 5.95 (ISBN 0-201-03446-8, 3446, A-W Childrens). A-W.

Jensen, Virginia A., tr. see Olsen, Ib S.

Jensen, William A. Plant Cell. 2nd ed. 1970. pap. 7.95x (ISBN 0-534-00273-0). Wadsworth Pub.

Jensen, William A., et al. Biology. 1979. text ed. 21.95x (ISBN 0-534-00621-3); study guide 5.95x (ISBN 0-534-00721-X). Wadsworth Pub.

Jensen, William E. & Winters, Donna. Keep Healthy Keep Active. 1979. pap. 1.95 (ISBN 0-910286-73-6). Boxwood.

Jensen-Worth, Veryl M. Early Days on the Upper Willamette. 2nd, rev ed. (Illus.). 142p. 1981. 17.50; pap. 9.95. Worth Co.

Jenson, Irving L. Epistles of John & Jude. (Bible Self-Study Ser). 128p. (Orig.). 1971. pap. 2.25 (ISBN 0-8024-1062-6). Moody.

Jenson, Robert, jt. auth. see Cotman, Carl W.

Jenson, Robert W., jt. auth. see Gritsch, Eric W.

Jenson, V. G. & Jeffreys, G. V., eds. Mathematical Methods in Chemical Engineering. 2nd ed. 1978. text ed. 32.00 (ISBN 0-12-384456-8). Acad Pr.

Jenyns, Soame. A Free Enquiry into the Nature & Origin of Evil. 2nd ed. Wellek, Rene, ed. LC 75-11226. (British Philosophers & Theologians of the 17th & 18th Centuries: Vol. 28). 1976. Repr. of 1757 ed. lib. bdg. 42.00 (ISBN 0-8240-1780-3). Garland Pub.

--Japanese Porcelain. (Illus.). 1965. 65.00 (ISBN 0-571-06446-9, Pub. by Faber & Faber). Merrimack Bk Serv.

--Japanese Pottery. 1971. 65.00 (ISBN 0-571-08709-4, Pub. by Faber & Faber). Merrimack Bk Serv.

--Later Chinese Porcelain. 4th ed. (Illus.). 1971. 43.00 (ISBN 0-571-04761-0, Pub. by Faber & Faber). Merrimack Bk Serv.

Jeon, K. see Bourne, G. H. & Danielli, J. F.

Jephcott, Edmund, tr. see Elias, Norbert.

Jeppesen, Knud. Counterpoint: The Polyphonic Vocal Style of the Sixteenth Century. Haydon, G., tr. 1939. ref. ed. 19.95 (ISBN 0-13-183608-0). P-H.

Jeppesen Sanderson. Airline Transport Pilot Course: Mach IV. (Illus.). 390p. 1977. write for info. 3-ring binder (ISBN 0-88487-003-0, JE304913). Jeppesen Sanderson.

--Aviation-Aerospace Fundamentals Instructors Guide. (Illus.). 1979. text ed. 31.80 3-ring binder ed. (ISBN 0-88487-031-6, SA418077). Jeppesen Sanderson.

Jeppson, J. O. The Last Immortal. 256p. 1981. pap. 2.25 (ISBN 0-449-24385-0, Crest). Fawcett.

Jeppson, Lee R., et al. Mites Injurious to Economic Plants. LC 72-93523. (Illus.). 1975. 46.00x (ISBN 0-520-02381-1). U of Cal Pr.

Jepson, jt. auth. see Finney.

Jepson, J. W. What You Should Know About the Holy Spirit. pap. 2.95 (ISBN 0-89728-062-8, 669313). Omega Pubns OR.

Jepson, Maud. Illustrated Biology, 2 pts. Incl. Pt. 1. Plants (ISBN 0-7195-0735-9); Pt. 2. Animals (ISBN 0-7195-0734-0). (Illus.). (gr. 8-12). 6.95x ea. Transatlantic.

Jepson, R. W. Express Yourself. (Teach Yourself Ser.). 1974. pap. 2.95 o.p. (ISBN 0-679-10427-5). McKay.

Jepson, W. L. Flora of California, Vols. 1,2 & Vol. 3, Pts. 1 & 2. (Illus.). 1722p. 1979. Set. pap. 40.00x (ISBN 0-935628-00-2). Jepson Herbarium.

Jepson, Willis L. A Manual of the Flowering Plants of California. (Illus.). 1925. 40.00x (ISBN 0-520-00606-2). U of Cal Pr.

Jepsson, Lennart. Aspects of Late Silurian Conodonts. (Fossils & Strata Ser: No. 6). 1975. pap. text ed. 13.00x (ISBN 8-200-09373-5, Dist. by Columbia U Pr). Universitet.

Jerabek, Esther A., compiled by. Bibliography of Minnesota Territorial Documents. LC 36-28069. 157p. 1936. pap. 3.00 (ISBN 0-87351-005-4). Minn Hist.

Jeremiah, James T. God's Answers to Our Anxieties. (Direction Books Ser.). 1979. pap. 1.45 (ISBN 0-8010-5083-9). Baker Bk.

Jeremiah, Maryalyce. Coaching Basketball: Ten Winning Concepts. LC 78-12292. 1979. text ed. 18.50 (ISBN 0-471-04090-8). Wiley.

Jeremias, Joachim. Jerusalem in the Time of Jesus: An Investigation into Economic & Social Conditions During the New Testament Period. Cave, F. H. & Cave, C. H., trs. from Ger. LC 77-81530. 434p. 1975. pap. 5.95 (ISBN 0-8006-1136-5, 1-1136). Fortress.

--New Testament Theology. LC 70-143936. lib. rep. ed. 20.00x (ISBN 0-684-15157-X, ScribT). Scribner.

--The Prayers of Jesus. Bowden, John, et al, trs. from Ger. LC 77-10427. 132p. 1978. pap. 3.75 (ISBN 0-8006-1322-8, 1-1322). Fortress.

--Problem of the Historical Jesus. Reumann, John, ed. Perrin, Norman, tr. from Ger. LC 64-23064. (Facet Bks.). 1964. pap. 1.95 (ISBN 0-8006-3015-7, 1-3015). Fortress.

Jeremy, David J. Origins of the Industrial Revolution in the U.S. (Illus.). 544p. 1981. text ed. 32.50x (ISBN 0-262-10022-3). MIT Pr.

Jeresaty, Robert M. Mitral Valve Prolapse. LC 78-66350. 1979. 27.00 (ISBN 0-89004-230-6). Raven.

Jerger, James, ed. Modern Development in Audiology. 2nd ed. 1973. 24.50 (ISBN 0-12-385156-4). Acad Pr.

Jerison, M., jt. auth. see Gillman, L.

Jerman, Max E. & Beardslee, Edward C. Elementary Mathematics Method. (Illus.). 1978. text ed. 16.50 (ISBN 0-07-032531-6, C); 3.95 (ISBN 0-07-032532-4). McGraw.

Jern, Helen Z. Hormone Therapy of the Menopause & Aging. (Illus.). 196p. 1973. text ed. 15.75 (ISBN 0-398-02744-7). C C Thomas.

Jernick, Ruth. Housewife. 1981. 10.95 (ISBN 0-698-11081-1). Coward.

Jernigan, Anna K. & Ross, Lynne N. Food Service Equipment. 2nd ed. (Illus.). 122p. 1980. pap. text ed. 6.75 (ISBN 0-8138-0550-3). Iowa St U Pr.

Jernigan, Anna K., et al. Food Service Management: Study Course. 1977. pap. text ed. 6.95 (ISBN 0-8138-0790-5). Iowa St U Pr.

Jernigan, E. Jay. Henry Demarest Lloyd. LC 76-17104. (U.S. Authors Ser: No. 277). 1976. lib. bdg. 12.50 (ISBN 0-8057-7177-8). Twayne.

Jernigan, E. Wesley. Jewelry of the Prehistoric Southwest. LC 77-89436. (Southwestern Indian Arts Ser). (Illus.). 1978. 30.00x (ISBN 0-8263-0459-1). U of NM Pr.

Jerome, Carl, jt. auth. see Beard, James.

Jerome, Jerome K. Three Men in a Boat. Jasen, David A., ed. (A Continuum Classic of Humor Ser.). 208p. 1980. 11.95 (ISBN 0-8264-0018-3). Continuum.

Jerome, John. The Sweet Spot in Time. LC 80-15793. 348p. 1980. 13.95 (ISBN 0-671-40039-8). Summit Bks.

Jerome, John, jt. auth. see Sports Illustrated Editors.

Jerome, Judson. The Poet & the Poem. rev ed. LC 79-10828. 330p. 1979. 11.95x (ISBN 0-911654-70-4). Writers Digest.

--The Poet's Handbook. LC 80-17270. 88p. 1980. 10.95 (ISBN 0-89879-021-2). Writers Digest.

Jerome, K. Three Men in a Boat. Incl. Three Men on the Bummell. 1957. 5.00x (ISBN 0-460-00118-3, Evman); pap. 8.95 (ISBN 0-460-01118-9, Evman). Dutton.

Jerome, Saint. Vitas Patrum: The Lyff of the Olde Auncyent Fathers Hermytes. Caxton, W., tr. LC 77-7409. (English Experience Ser.: No. 874). 1977. Repr. of 1495 ed. lib. bdg. 99.00 (ISBN 90-221-0874-0). Walter J Johnson.

Jerrehian, Aram. Oriental Rug Primer. (Illus.). 1980. 12.95 (ISBN 0-87196-494-5). Facts on File.

Jerrehian, Aram K. Oriental Rug Primer: Buying & Understanding New Oriental Rugs. LC 79-19724. (Illus.). 1980. lib. bdg. 12.90 (ISBN 0-89471-078-8); pap. 7.95 (ISBN 0-89471-077-X). Running Pr.

Jerrell, Jeanette M., jt. ed. see Schulberg, Herbert C.

Jerrett, Robert & Barocci, Thomas A. Public Works, Government Spending & Job Creation: The Job Opportunities Program. (Praeger Special Studies). 352p. 1979. 29.95 (ISBN 0-03-051336-7). Praeger.

Jerrold, Blanchard. Life of Gustave Dore. LC 69-17492. (Illus.). 1969. Repr. of 1891 ed. 24.00 (ISBN 0-8103-3532-8). Gale.

Jerrold, Walter, ed. see Hood, Thomas.

Jerrold, Walter C. A Book of Famous Wits. LC 77-155086. 1971. Repr. of 1912 ed. 22.00 (ISBN 0-8103-3757-6). Gale.

--A Descriptive Index to Shakespeare's Characters, in Shakespeare's Words. LC 74-23634. xvi, 176p. 1975. Repr. of 1905 ed. 25.00 (ISBN 0-8103-4097-6). Gale.

Jerrold, Walter C. & Leonard, R. M. Century of Parody & Imitation. LC 68-30585. 1968. Repr. of 1913 ed. 20.00 (ISBN 0-8103-3215-9). Gale.

Jerrome, Edward G. Tales of Explorers. (Pacemaker True Adventures Ser.). (Illus., Orig.). 1973. pap. 2.36 (ISBN 0-8224-9182-6); tchrs'. manual free (ISBN 0-8224-5208-1). Pitman Learning.

--Tales of Invention. (Pacemaker True Adventures Ser.). (Illus., Orig.). 1973. pap. 2.36 (ISBN 0-8224-9186-9); tchrs' manual free (ISBN 0-8224-5208-1). Pitman Learning.

--Tales of Pirates. (Pacemaker True Adventures Ser.). (Illus., Orig.). 1973. pap. 2.36 (ISBN 0-8224-9189-3); tchrs' manual free (ISBN 0-8224-5208-1). Pitman Learning.

--Tales of Railroads. (Pacemaker True Adventure Ser.). (Illus., Orig.). 1972. pap. 2.36 (ISBN 0-8224-9188-5); tchrs' manual free (ISBN 0-8224-5208-1). Pitman Learning.

--Tales of Rescue. (Pacemaker True Adventure Ser). (Illus., Orig.). 1972. pap. 2.36 (ISBN 0-8224-9190-7); tchrs' manual free (ISBN 0-8224-5208-1). Pitman Learning.

--Tales of Shipwreck. (Pacemaker True Adventure Ser). (Illus., Orig.). 1970. pap. 2.36 (ISBN 0-8224-9187-7); tchrs' manual free (ISBN 0-8224-5208-1). Pitman Learning.

--Tales of Speed. (Pacemaker True Adventures Ser.). (Illus., Orig.). 1973. pap. 2.36 (ISBN 0-8224-9194-X); tchrs' manual free (ISBN 0-685-30383-7). Pitman Learning.

--Tales of Spies. (Pacemaker True Adventure Ser.). (Illus., Orig.). 1972. pap. 2.36 (ISBN 0-8224-9195-8); tchrs' manual free (ISBN 0-8224-5208-1). Pitman Learning.

Jerschow, Peter. Das Wunderpferdchen. (It 490). (Orig., Ger.). 1980. pap. text ed. 6.50 (ISBN 3-458-32190-X, Pub. by Insel Verlag Germany). Suhrkamp.

Jersild, Arthur T. When Teachers Face Themselves. LC 55-12176. (Horace Mann Lincoln Institute Ser). 1955. pap. text ed. 6.95x (ISBN 0-8077-1575-1). Tchrs Coll.

Jersild, Arthur T., et al. Child Psychology. 7th ed. LC 74-20723. (Illus.). 640p. 1975. text ed. 18.95 (ISBN 0-13-130971-4). P-H.

Jerusalem Conference on Impaired Vision in Childhood, May 1977. Impaired Vision in Childhood: Proceedings. Nawratzki, I. & Merin, S., eds. (Illus.). 1979. text ed. 82.50 (ISBN 0-08-024416-5). Pergamon.

Jervell, Jacob. God's Christ & His People. 1977. pap. 31.00x (ISBN 82-00-01628-5, Dist. by Columbia U Pr). Universitet.

Jervey, Theodore D. Robert Y. Hayne & His Times. LC 73-104330. (American Scene Ser). (Illus.). 1970. Repr. of 1909 ed. lib. bdg. 49.50 (ISBN 0-306-71870-7). Da Capo.

Jervis, F. R. Bosses in British Business. 1974. 16.00 (ISBN 0-7100-7803-X). Routledge & Kegan.

Jervis, Margaret E., jt. auth. see Rees, B. R.

Jervis, Simon & Hojer, Gerhard. Designs for the Dream King: The Castles & Palaces of Ludwig II of Bavaria. (Illus.). 1979. 17.50 o.p. (ISBN 0-670-26892-5, Debrett's Peerage, Ltd.). Viking Pr.

Jeschke, Susan. Perfect the Pig. LC 80-39998. (Illus.). 48p. (gr. k-3). 1981. 9.95 (ISBN 0-03-058622-4). HR&W.

Jeschkeit, H., jt. auth. see Jakubke, H. D.

Jeske, Richard L. Understanding & Teaching the Bible. Rast, Harold W., ed. LC 80-69756. (A Lead Book). 128p. (Orig.). 1981. pap. 3.25 (ISBN 0-8006-1601-4, 1-1601). Fortress.

Jeske, Richard L. & Barr, Browne. Holy Week. Achtemeier, Elizabeth, et al, eds. LC 79-7377. (Proclamation 2: Aids for Interpreting the Lessons of the Church Year, Ser. A). 64p. (Orig.). 1980. pap. 2.50 (ISBN 0-8006-4094-2, 1-4094). Fortress.

Jespersen, Otto. How to Teach a Foreign Language. 1904. text ed. 13.50x o.p. (ISBN 0-04-407001-2). Allen Unwin.

--The Philosophy of Grammar. 1924. text ed. 25.00x (ISBN 0-04-400009-X). Allen Unwin.

Jesse, F. Tennyson. The Lacquer Lady. (Virago Modern Classics Ser.). 1981. pap. 5.96. Dial.

Jesse, John. Explosive Muscular Power for Championship Football. LC 68-58253. pap. 4.95 (ISBN 0-87095-032-0). Athletic.

--Wrestling Physical Conditioning Encyclopedia. LC 74-5197. pap. 8.95 (ISBN 0-87095-043-6). Athletic.

Jessee, Dean C. Letters of Brigham Young to His Sons. LC 74-80041. (Mormon Heritage Ser., Vol. 1). 1974. 10.95 o.p. (ISBN 0-87747-522-9). Deseret Bk.

Jessee, Michael A. & Seelig, Steven A. Bank Holding Companies & the Public Interest. LC 76-8744. 1977. 21.50- (ISBN 0-669-00689-0). Lexington Bks.

Jessen, Ellen. Peruvian Designs for Cross-Stitch. 64p. 1980. pap. 6.95 (ISBN 0-442-21926-1). Van Nos Reinhold.

Jessen, Peter. Masterpieces of Calligraphy: Two Hundred & Sixty-One Examples, 1500-1800. (Illus.). 1981. pap. price not set (ISBN 0-486-24100-9). Dover.

Jessen, Raymond J., jt. auth. see Hoel, Paul G.

Jessop, H. T. & Harris, F. C. Photoelasticity: Principles & Methods. (Illus.). 1950. pap. text ed. 3.00 (ISBN 0-486-60720-8). Dover.

Jessup, Claudia. The Woman's Guide to Starting a Business. LC 75-21463. 1976. 8.95 o.p. (ISBN 0-03-014606-2); pap. 4.95 o.p. (ISBN 0-03-017611-5). HR&W.

Jessup, Josephine L. Faith of Our Feminists. LC 65-23482. 1950. 9.00x (ISBN 0-8196-0158-6). Biblo.

Jessup, L. F. Law of Retirement, Vol. 48. 2nd ed. 1979. 5.95 (ISBN 0-379-11124-1). Oceana.

Jessup, M. K. The Case for the UFO. 1973. pap. 32.50 (ISBN 0-685-37599-4). Saucerian.

Jessup, Myrtle S. Gems of Truth. 64p. 1981. 5.00 (ISBN 0-682-49688-X). Exposition.

Jessup, P. C. The Use of International Law. LC 79-173670. 164p. 1972. Repr. of 1959 ed. lib. bdg. 22.50 (ISBN 0-306-70407-2). Da Capo.

Jessup, Paul F. Modern Bank Management: A Casebook. 1978. text ed. 15.95 (ISBN 0-8299-0207-4); instrs.' maual avail. (ISBN 0-8299-0496-4). West Pub.

--Theory & Practice of Nonpar Banking. 1967. 7.95x- o.s.i. (ISBN 0-8101-0128-9). Northwestern U Pr.

Jessup, Philip C. Price of International Justice. LC 76-158460. (Jacob Blaustein Lectures in International Affairs Ser.: No. 2). 1971. 17.50x (ISBN 0-231-03545-4). Columbia U Pr.

--Transnational Law. 1956. 24.50x (ISBN 0-685-89792-3). Elliots Bks.

--United States & the World Court. Incl. What's Wrong with International Law? Friedman, Wolfgang; Foreign Policy of a Free Democracy. Jessup, Philip C; Fallacy of a "Preventive" War. Jessup, Philip C; Legal Process & International Order. Kelsen, Hans. LC 70-147750. (Library of War & Peace; International Law). lib. bdg. 38.00 (ISBN 0-8240-0490-6). Garland Pub.

Jessup, Phillip C. Birth of Nations. LC 73-15515. (Illus.). 1974. 17.50x (ISBN 0-231-03721-X). Columbia U Pr.

Jessup, Richard. Threat. LC 80-52001. 288p. 1981. 12.95 (ISBN 0-670-70618-3). Viking Pr.

Jester, Pat. Burger Cookery. LC 77-95176. (Illus.). 1978. 7.95 o.p. (ISBN 0-89586-002-3); pap. 4.95 o.p. (ISBN 0-89586-001-5). H P Bks.

--Easy Suppers. (Orig.). 1980. pap. 5.95 (ISBN 0-89586-064-3). H P Bks.

Jeter, Hugh, tr. Para Ses Meurtrissures. (French Bks.). (Fr.). 1979. 2.50 (ISBN 0-8297-0928-2). Vida Pub.

Jeter, Hugo, tr. Por Su Llaga. (Spanish Bks.). (Span.). 1978. 2.50 (ISBN 0-8297-0858-8). Life Pubs Intl.

Jeter, Jacky. The Cat & the Fiddler. LC 68-11654. (Illus.). (ps-3). 1968. 5.95 o.s.i. (ISBN 0-8193-0203-1, Four Winds); PLB 5.41 o.s.i. (ISBN 0-8193-0204-X). Schol Bk Serv.

Jeter, Jan, ed. Approaches to Individualized Education. LC 80-67363. 83p. (Orig.). 1980. pap. 4.75 (ISBN 0-87120-101-1, 611-80204). Assn Supervision.

Jett, Stephen C. & Spencer, Virginia E. Navajo Architecture: Forms, History, Distributions. 1981. text ed. 24.50x (ISBN 0-8165-0688-4); pap. text ed. 12.50x (ISBN 0-8165-0723-6). U of Ariz Pr.

Jetzinger, Franz. Hitler's Youth. Wilson, Lawrence, tr. from German. LC 75-36096. (Illus.). 1976. Repr. of 1958 ed. lib. bdg. 18.00x (ISBN 0-8371-8617-X, JEHY). Greenwood.

Jeunesse, Steftung P., ed. What Do TV Producers Know About Their Young Viewers. 1979. text ed. 12.00 (ISBN 3-598-10092-2). K G Saur.

Jevnikar, Jana M. Video Service Profiles. 60p. (Orig.). 1981. pap. price not set (ISBN 0-935654-02-X, Pub. by Ctr for Arts Info). Pub Ctr Cult Res.

Jewell, A. P., et al, eds. Island Survivors: The Ecology of the Soay Sheep of St. Kilda. (Illus.). 400p. 1974. text ed. 40.00x (ISBN 0-485-11141-1, Athlone Pr). Humanities.

Jewell, Aurelia M. Loundoun County, Virginia: Marriage Records to 1891. 100p. 1975. 12.50 (ISBN 0-685-65071-5). Va Bk.

Jewell, Brian. Collecting for Tomorrow. (Illus.). 1979. 9.95 (ISBN 0-7137-0937-5, Pub by Blandford Pr England). Sterling.
--Conquest & Overlord. (Illus.). 96p. 1981. 25.00 (ISBN 0-686-69381-7, 5209). Arco.
--Veteran Scales & Balances. 1979. pap. 7.50 (ISBN 0-85936-081-4, Pub. by Midas Bks England). Intl Schol Bk Serv.
Jewell, Don. Public Assembly Facilities: Planning & Management. LC 77-16524. 1978. 22.50 (ISBN 0-471-02437-6, Pub. by Wiley-Interscience). Wiley.
Jewell, Donald V. Southern Pacific Motive Power Annual 1977-1980. LC 80-66138. (Illus.). 88p. 1981. 15.00 (ISBN 0-89685-009-9). Chatham Pub CA.
Jewell, Malcolm E. Kentucky Votes: U. S. House Primary & Genral Elections, 1920-1960. LC 63-12390. 104p. 1963. pap. 2.25x (ISBN 0-8131-0083-6). U Pr of Ky.
Jewell, Malcolm E. & Olson, David M. American State Political Parties & Elections. 1978. pap. text ed. 11.50 (ISBN 0-256-02053-1). Dorsey.
Jewell, Nancy. Time for Uncle Joe. LC 79-2695. (Illus.). 48p. (gr. k-3). 1981. 8.95 (ISBN 0-06-022843-1, HarpJ); PLB 8.79g (ISBN 0-06-022844-X). Har-Row.
Jewell, Willis A. Change Your Life. 1977. 17.95 o.p. (ISBN 0-686-22159-1). W A Jewell.
--Learn to Relax. 1980. pap. 9.95. W a Jewell.
Jewett, Dick. Sex Is Not to Lose Sleep Over. LC 78-70729. (Redwood Ser.). 1979. pap. 3.95 (ISBN 0-8163-0246-4). Pacific Pr Pub Assn.
--Why Do I Shout at My Wife? (Uplook Ser.). 1978. pap. 0.75 (ISBN 0-8163-0300-2, 23617-4). Pacific Pr Pub Assn.
Jewett, Don L. & McCarroll, H. Relton, Jr. Nerve Repair & Regeneration: Its Clinical & Experimental Basis. LC 79-19276. 1979. pap. text ed. 52.50 (ISBN 0-8016-2507-6). Mosby.
Jewett, Frank I., jt. auth. see Ruprecht, Theodore K.
Jewett, Iran B. Edward Fitzgerald. (English Authors Ser.: No. 205). 1977. lib. bdg. 9.95 (ISBN 0-8057-6675-8). Twayne.
Jewett, P. Emil Brunner. LC 61-10788. pap. 0.95 o.p. (ISBN 0-87784-425-9). Inter-Varsity.
Jewett, Paul K. El Hombre como Varon y Hembra. Vilela, Ernesto S., tr. from Eng. 205p. (Orig., Span.). 1979. pap. 4.95 (ISBN 0-89922-132-7). Edit Caribe.
--The Ordination of Women. LC 80-15644. 160p. (Orig.). 1980. pap. 5.95 (ISBN 0-8028-1850-1). Eerdmans.
Jewett, Robert. Letter to Pilgrims. 244p. (Orig.). 1981. pap. 7.95 (ISBN 0-8298-0425-0). Pilgrim NY.
Jewett, Sarah O. Country By-Ways. 249p. 1980. Repr. of 1881 ed. lib. bdg. 20.00 (ISBN 0-89987-428-2). Darby Bks.
--Country of the Pointed Firs. (Keith Jennison Large Type Bks). (gr. 7 up). PLB 7.95 o.p. (ISBN 0-531-00177-6). Watts.
--Sarah O. Jewett: Letters. rev. & enl. ed. Cary, Richard, ed. 1967. 7.50 o.p. (ISBN 0-910394-06-7). Colby.
--Yankee Ranger. Orig. Title: Tory Lover. 1975. pap. 1.50 o.p. (ISBN 0-685-57555-1, LB300DK, Leisure Bks). Nordon Pubns.
Jewsbury, Geraldine E. Zoe: The History of Two Lives 1845. Wolff, Robert L., ed. LC 75-1518. (Victorian Fiction Ser.). 1975. lib. bdg. 66.00 (ISBN 0-8240-1591-6). Garland Pub.
Jha, Akhileshwar. The Imprisoned Mind: Guru Shisya Tradition in Indian Culture. 1980. 18.50x (ISBN 0-8364-0665-6, Pub. by Ambika India). South Asia Bks.
Jha, Ganganath. Foreign Policy of Thailand, 1954-1971. 1979. text ed. 14.50x (ISBN 0-391-01012-3). Humanities.
Jha, Prem S. India: A Political Economy of Stagnation. (Illus.). 330p. 1980. 13.95x (ISBN 0-19-561153-5). Oxford U Pr.
Jha, Shree Nagesh. Leadership & Local Politics: A Study of Meerut District District in Uttar Pradesh (India) 1923-73. 175p. 1979. text ed. 14.50 (ISBN 0-8426-1640-3). Verry.
Jhabvala, Ruth P. How I Became a Holy Mother & Other Stories. LC 76-9206. 224p. (YA) 1976. 9.95 o.s.i. (ISBN 0-06-012198-X, HarpT). Har-Row.
--How I Became a Holy Mother: And Other Short Stories. LC 76-9206. (Orig.). 1979. pap. 2.50 (ISBN 0-06-080474-2, P 474, PL). Har-Row.
--Travelers. LC 72-9765. 256p. (YA) 1973. 8.95 o.p. (ISBN 0-06-012193-9, HarpT). Har-Row.
Jhaveri, S., et al. Abstracts of Methods Used to Assess Fish Quality. (Marine Technical Report Ser.: No. 69). 3.00 (ISBN 0-938412-00-0). URI MAS.
Jhingan, M. L. Micro-Economic Theory. 1979. text ed. 25.00x (ISBN 0-7069-0569-5, Pub. by Vikas India). Advent Bk.
Jicarilla Apache Tribe. Apache Indians VII. Horr, David A., ed. (American Indian Ethnohistory Ser.). 1978. lib. bdg. 42.00 (ISBN 0-8240-0709-3). Garland Pub.
Jick, Leon A. The Americanization of the Synagogue, 1820-1870. LC 75-18213. (Illus.). 260p. 1976. text ed. 15.00x (ISBN 0-87451-119-4). U Pr of New Eng.
Jicks, John M. & Morton, Bruce L. Woman's Role in the Church. pap. 2.95 (ISBN 0-89315-362-1). Lambert Bk.
Jiggins, Janice. Caste & Family in the Politics of the Sinhalese. LC 78-54715. (Illus.). 1979. 24.95 (ISBN 0-521-22069-6). Cambridge U Pr.
Jim, Strange De see De Jim, Strange.
Jimenez, Jacques, jt. auth. see O'Connor, Daniel.
Jimenez, Sherry L. Childbearing: A Guide for Pregnant Parents. (Illus.). 176p. 1980. 12.95 (Spec); pap. 5.95. P-H.
Jimenez de Arechaga, Eduardo. Voting & the Handling of Disputes in the Security Council. LC 78-3780. (Carnegie Endowment for International Peace, United Nations: No. 5). 1978. Repr. of 1950 ed. lib. bdg. 17.75x (ISBN 0-313-20332-6, ARVH). Greenwood.
Jimenez de Asua, L., ed. Control Mechanisms in Animal Cells: Specific Growth Factors. 400p. 1980. text ed. 36.50 (ISBN 0-89004-509-7). Raven.
Jimenez-Fajardo, Salvador. Claude Simon. LC 74-30154. (World Authors Ser.: France: No. 346). 1975. lib. bdg. 12.50 (ISBN 0-8057-2828-7). Twayne.
--Luis Cernuda. (World Authors Ser.: No. 455). 1978. lib. bdg. 11.95 (ISBN 0-8057-6292-2). Twayne.
Jinarajadasa, C. Seven Veils Over Consciousness. 2.50 (ISBN 0-8356-7231-X). Theos Pub Hse.
Jinks, J. L., jt. auth. see Mather, K.
Jinks, Roy G. History of Smith & Wesson. (Illus.). 290p. 1977. 15.95 (ISBN 0-917714-14-8). Beinfeld Pub.
Jinks, William. The Celluloid Literature: Film in the Humanities. 2nd ed. LC 73-7361. (Illus.). 208p. 1974. pap. text ed. 6.95x (ISBN 0-02-474910-9, 47490). Macmillan.
Jippensha, Ikku. Shank's Mare. LC 60-14370. (Illus.). 1960. pap. 8.25 (ISBN 0-8048-0524-5). C E Tuttle.
JK Lasser Tax Inst. How to Avoid a Tax Audit. 1979. pap. 2.95 (ISBN 0-346-12363-1). Cornerstone.
Joachim, Harold, jt. auth. see Art Institute of Chicago.
Joad, C. E. The Highbrows. 256p. 1980. Repr. of 1922 ed. lib. bdg. 20.00 (ISBN 0-89987-449-5). Darby Bks.
Joalson, Robert F., jt. auth. see Rodney, Lynn S.
Joans, Ted. A Black Manifesto in Jazz Poetry & Prose. LC 79-869997. 1979. 9.95 (ISBN 0-7145-0713-X, Pub. by M Boyars); pap. 5.95 (ISBN 0-7145-0714-8). Merrimack Bk Serv.
Job, J. C. Pediatric Endocrinology. 700p. 1981. 75.00 (ISBN 0-471-05257-4, Pub. by Wiley Med). Wiley.
Jobbins, Allan, ed. see Webster, Robert.
Jobes, Gertrude. Dictionary of Mythology, Folklore & Symbols, 2 Vols. LC 61-860. 1961. Set. 50.00 (ISBN 0-8108-0034-9). Scarecrow.
Jobling, David. The Sense of Biblical Narrative: Three Structural Analyses in the Old Testament. (JSOT Supplement Ser.: No. 7). 104p. 1978. text ed. 25.95x (ISBN 0-905774-06-X, Pub. by JSOT Pr England); pap. text ed. 12.95x (ISBN 0-905774-12-4, Pub. by JSOT Pr England). Eisenbrauns.
Jobling, Megan. Helping the Handicapped Child, No. 1: In the Family. (Illus.). 40p. 1975. pap. text ed. 2.50x (ISBN 0-85633-058-2, NFER). Humanities.
Jobson, jt. auth. see Walshaw.
Jobson, Hamilton. Waiting for Thursday. LC 77-10284. 1978. 7.95 o.p. (ISBN 0-312-85426-9). St Martin.
Joby, R. S. Forgotten Railways: East Anglia. LC 76-48824. (Forgotten Railways Ser.). (Illus.). 1977. 14.95 (ISBN 0-7153-7312-9). David & Charles.
Jocelyn, John. Meditation on the Signs of the Zodiac. LC 79-3594. (Harper Library of Spiritual Wisdom). 288p. 1980. pap. 5.95 (ISBN 0-06-064140-1, RD 403). Har-Row.
Jocelyn, S., jt. auth. see Nichols, E.
Jocher, Willy. Live Foods for Aquarium & Terrarium Animals. Vevers, Gwynne, tr. (Illus.). 1973. pap. 5.95 (ISBN 0-87666-097-9, PS-309). TFH Pubns.
--Spawning Problem Fishes. Incl. Book 1 (ISBN 0-87666-146-0, PS-302); Book 2 (ISBN 0-87666-147-9, PS-303). (Illus.). 1972. pap. 2.95 ea. (ISBN 0-685-32894-5). TFH Pubns.
Jochim, Michael. Strategies for Survival: Cultural Behavior in an Ecological Context. 1981. price not set (ISBN 0-12-385460-1). Acad Pr.
Jochle, Wolfgang & Lamond, Ross. Control of Reproductive Functions in Domestic Animals. (Current Topics in Veterinary Medicine & Animal Science Ser.: No. 7). (Illus.). 1981. PLB 39.50 (ISBN 90-247-2400-7, Pub. by Martinus Nijhoff). Kluwer Boston.
Jochmans, Joey R. Rolling Thunder: The Coming Earth Changes. (Illus.). 240p. (Orig.). 1980. pap. 7.50 (ISBN 0-89540-058-8). Sun Pub.
Jochnowitz, Carol. Careers in Medicine for the New Woman. (Choosing Careers & Life-Styles Ser.). (Illus.). (gr. 7 up). 1978. PLB 7.90 s&l (ISBN 0-531-01444-4). Watts.
Jochum, Helen P. Alaskan Journey. LC 80-51526. (Illus.). 153p. 1980. 10.00. Jochum.
Jocz, Jakob. The Jewish People & Jesus Christ After Auschwitz. 172p. (Orig.). 1981. pap. 6.95 (ISBN 0-8010-5123-1). Baker Bk.
Jody, Ruth & Lindner, Vicki. Facelift Without Surgery: A Four Point Program to Maintain a Youthful Face. LC 78-21474. 1979. 9.95 (ISBN 0-397-01313-2). Lippincott.
Jody, Ruth, jt. auth. see Cohen, Robert D.
Joel, David & Schapira, Karl. The Book of Coffee & Tea: A Guide to the Appreciation of Fine Coffees, Teas & Herbal Beverages. LC 73-90585. (Illus.). 1977. pap. 6.95 (ISBN 0-312-08821-3). St Martin.
Joens, Clifford J. Technical Drafting, 4 bks. LC 77-12932. 686p. 1977. Set. pap. text ed. 19.95 (ISBN 0-87618-891-9). R J Brady.
Joerg, Ernest A. & Polito, Nat A. Electronic Experimentation in Semiconductor & Vacuous Media. 1979. pap. text ed. 9.50 (ISBN 0-89669-038-5). Collegium Bk Pubs.
Joerns, Consuelo. The Foggy Rescue. LC 80-11375. (Illus.). 40p. (gr. k-3). 1980. 7.95 (ISBN 0-590-07744-9, Four Winds). Schol Bk Serv.
--The Forgotten Bear. LC 78-1546. (Illus.). (gr. k-3). 1978. 5.95 (ISBN 0-590-07560-8, Four Winds). Schol Bk Serv.
Joes, Anthony J. Fascism in the Contemporary World: Ideology, Evolution, Resurgence. LC 77-14141. (A Westview Special Study Ser.). 1978. pap. text ed. 9.50x (ISBN 0-89158-159-6). Westview.
Jofen, Jean, jt. auth. see Mok, Ellie M.
Joffe, Carole E. Friendly Intruders: Childcare Professionals & Family Life. 1977. 14.95x (ISBN 0-520-02925-9); pap. 3.95 (ISBN 0-520-03934-3). U of Cal Pr.
Joffe, Gerardo. How You Too Can Make at Least One Million Dollars (But Probably Much More) in the Mail-Order Business. LC 77-92067. 1979. 19.95 (ISBN 0-930992-02-4, HarpT). Har-Row.
Joffe, Irwin L. Opportunity for Skillful Reading. 3rd ed. 496p. 1979. pap. text ed. 9.95x (ISBN 0-534-00774-0). Wadsworth Pub.
--Reading Skills for Successful Living. 1979. pap. text ed. 8.95x (ISBN 0-534-00618-3). Wadsworth Pub.
Joffe, Jacob S. Pedology. 1949. 40.00 (ISBN 0-8135-0103-2). Rutgers U Pr.
Joffe, Judah A., tr. see Sabaneyeff, Leonid.
Joffe, Justin M., ed. Prevention Through Political Action & Social Change. (Primary Prevention of Psychopathology Ser.: No. 5). 330p. 1981. 20.00 (ISBN 0-87451-187-9). U Pr of New Eng.
Joffe, Justin M., jt. ed. see Albee, George W.
Joffo, Joseph. A Bag of Marbles. LC 74-11132. 304p. 1974. 6.95 o.p. (ISBN 0-395-19392-3). HM.
Jogues, Isaac see Summers, Thomas O.
Johann Gottfried Herder Institute. Alphabetischer Katalog der Bibliothek Des Johann Gottfried Herder - Instituts: Second Supplement. (Library Catalogs-Supplements Ser.). 1981. lib. bdg. 350.00 (ISBN 0-8161-0277-5). G K Hall.
Johannes, R. E. Words of the Lagoon: Fishing & Marine Lore in the Palau District of Micronesia. (Illus.). 320p. 1981. 14.95x (ISBN 0-520-03929-7). U of Cal Pr.
Johannes, Walter & Stein. Man & His Place in History. 1980. pap. 4.25x (ISBN 0-906492-35-1, Pub. by Kolisko Archives). St George Bk Serv.
Johannesen, Richard L. Ethics in Human Communication. LC 74-24780. 176p. pap. text ed. 5.95x (ISBN 0-917974-58-1). Waveland Pr.
Johannessen, Jan V., jt. ed. see Lapis, Karoly.
Johannessen, Jans V. Electron Microscopy in Human Medicine: Vol. 9, Urogenital System & Breast. (Illus.). 396p. 1980. text ed. 74.00 (ISBN 0-07-032508-1, HP). McGraw.
Johannessen, Svein, et al, eds. Antiepileptic Therapy: Advances in Drug Monitoring. 1980. text ed. 42.00 (ISBN 0-89004-407-4). Raven.
Johannesson, Eric O. The Novels of August Strindberg: A Study in Theme & Structure. LC 68-29156. 1968. 18.75x (ISBN 0-520-00607-0). U of Cal Pr.
Johannesson, Sigrid. Some Silent Shore. 178p. 1980. 10.95 (ISBN 0-86629-020-6). Sunrise MO.
Johannides, David F. Cost Containment Through Systems Engineering: A Guide for Hospitals. LC 79-15217. 1979. text ed. 31.00 (ISBN 0-89443-098-X). Aspen Systems.
Johannis, Theodore B., Jr. & Bull, Neil, eds. Sociology of Leisure. LC 73-87853. (Sage Contemporary Social Science Issues: No. 1). 1974. 4.95x (ISBN 0-8039-0318-9). Sage.
Johannsen, H. Management Glossary: (English-Arabic) 15.00 (ISBN 0-685-89878-4). Intl Bk Ctr.
Johannsen, Oskar A. Aquatic Diptera. LC 78-7782. (Illus.). 370p. 1969. Repr. of 1937 ed. 17.50 (ISBN 0-911836-01-2); pap. 8.95 o.p. (ISBN 0-911836-03-9). Entomological Repr.
Johannsen, Robert W. Reconstruction: 1865-1877. LC 74-91691. (Orig.). 1970. pap. text ed. 4.95 (ISBN 0-02-916540-7). Free Pr.
Johannsen, Robert W., ed. Union in Crisis, Eighteen Fifty-Eighteen Seventy-Seven. LC 65-11899. (Orig.). 1965. pap. text ed. 3.50 o.s.i. (ISBN 0-02-916500-8). Free Pr.
Johannson, K. Homotopy Equivalence of Three-Manifolds with Boundaries. (Lecture Notes in Mathematics: Vol. 761). 303p. 1979. pap. 18.00 (ISBN 0-387-09714-7). Springer-Verlag.
Johansen, Erling & Taves, Donald R., eds. Continuing Evaluation of the Use of Fluorides. (AAAS Selected Symposium Ser.: No. 11). (Illus.). 1979. lib. bdg. 27.50x (ISBN 0-89158-439-0). Westview.
Johansen, H. William, ed. Coralline Algae: A First Synthesis. 272p. 1981. 74.95 (ISBN 0-8493-5261-4). CRC Pr.
Johanson, Brenda C., et al. Standards for Critical Care. LC 80-15476. (Illus.). 536p. 1980. pap. text ed. 15.95 (ISBN 0-8016-2527-0). Mosby.
Johanson, Donald C. & Edey, Maitland A. Lucy: The Beginnings of Human Evolution. (Illus.). 1981. 13.95 (ISBN 0-671-25036-1). S&S.
Johansson, Bunn, jt. auth. see Gardell, Bertil.
Johansson, E. R., jt. auth. see Singleton, W. R.
Johansson, Gunn, jt. auth. see Gardell, Bertil.
Johansson, Rune. The Psychology of Nirvana. 1969. text ed. 4.95x o.p. (ISBN 0-04-150026-1). Allen Unwin.
Johany, Ali D. The Myth of the OPEC Cartel: The Role of Saudi Arabia. 191p. 1981. 34.00 (ISBN 0-471-27864-5, Pub. by Wiley-Interscience). Wiley.
Johari, O., jt. auth. see Becker, R. P.
Johari, Om. Scanning Electron Microscopy 1980, Pt. I. LC 72-626068. (Illus.). xvi, 608p. 1980. 50.00 (ISBN 0-931288-11-8). Scanning Electron.
Johari, Om, jt. auth. see Becker, Robert P.
Johari, Om & Becker, R. P., eds. Scanning Electron Microscopy 1980, No. III. LC 72-62608. (Illus.). xx, 670p. 50.00 (ISBN 0-931288-13-4). Scanning Electron.
Johl, S. S. & De Clerq, C. Irrigation & Agricultural Development. LC 80-40435. (Illus.). 386p. 1980. 58.00 (ISBN 0-08-025675-9). Pergamon.
John. Incomplete Block Design. 112p. 1980. 17.75 (ISBN 0-8247-6995-3). Dekker.
John, Angela. By the Sweat of Their Brow: Women Workers at Victorian Coal Mines. (Illus.). 245p. 1980. 29.00x (ISBN 0-85664-748-9, Pub. by Croom Helm Ltd England). Biblio Dist.
John, B. & Lewis, K. R. Chromosome Complement. (Protoplasmatologia: Vol. 6, Pt. A). (Illus.). 1968. pap. 57.90 o.p. (ISBN 0-387-80881-7). Springer-Verlag.
--Chromosome Cycle. (Protoplasmatologia: Vol. 6, Pt. B). (Illus.). 1969. 42.50 o.p. (ISBN 0-387-80918-X). Springer-Verlag.
--Meiotic System. (Protoplasmatologia: Vol. 6, Pt. F1). (Illus.). 1965. pap. 93.30 o.p. (ISBN 0-387-80733-0). Springer-Verlag.
John, B. S., jt. auth. see Sugden, D. E.
John, Brian. Pembrokeshire. (Illus.). 192p. 1976. 14.95 (ISBN 0-7153-7171-1). David & Charles.
--The Winters of the World: Earth Under the Ice Ages. 256p. 1979. 24.95x (ISBN 0-470-26844-1). Halsted Pr.
John Carter Brown Library. Bibliotheca Americana: Catalogue of the John Carter Brown Library in Brown University, Short-Title List of Additions, Books Printed 1471-1700. 67p. 1973. 10.00x (ISBN 0-87057-141-9). Univ Pr of New England.
--Bibliotheca Americana: Catalogue of the John Carter Brown Library in Brown University, Books Printed 1675-1700. 484p. 1973. 50.00x (ISBN 0-87057-140-0, Pub. by Brown U Pr). Univ Pr of New England.
John Crerar Library. List of Books on the History of Industry & the Industrial Arts. LC 67-14030. 1966. Repr. of 1915 ed. 22.00 (ISBN 0-8103-3104-7). Gale.
John, D. A., ed. Virgil's Georgics: Selections. (Illus., Orig.). 1973. pap. 4.50 (ISBN 0-571-09731-6, Pub. by Faber & Faber). Merrimack Bk Serv.
John, David St. see Wright, Charles & St. John, David.
John, E. Roy. Mechanisms of Memory. 1967. text ed. 21.95 (ISBN 0-12-385850-X). Acad Pr.
John, Errol. Moon on a Rainbow Shawl. 1958. pap. 4.95 (ISBN 0-571-05403-X, Pub. by Faber & Faber). Merrimack Bk Serv.
John, F. Partial Differential Equations. 2nd ed. LC 74-26827. (Applied Mathematical Sciences Ser.: Vol. 1). (Illus.). ix, 250p. 1975. pap. 9.50 o.p. (ISBN 0-387-90111-6). Springer-Verlag.
John, Fritz, jt. auth. see Courant, Richard.
John, J. & Haberman, W. Introduction to Fluid Mechanics. 2nd ed. 1980. 25.95 (ISBN 0-13-483941-2). P-H.

John, James E. Gas Dynamics. 1969. text ed. 25.95x (ISBN 0-205-02262-6, 3222624). Allyn.

John, James E. & Haberman, William L. Engineering Thermodynamics. 1979. text ed. 23.50 (ISBN 0-205-06570-8); solutions man. avail. (ISBN 0-205-06571-6). Allyn.

John, Martha T., jt. auth. see Chase, W. Linwood.

John, Michael St. see St. John, Michael.

John, Nancy. Prisoner of Passion. 192p. 1981. pap. 1.50 (ISBN 0-671-57057-9). S&S.

--The Spanish House. 192p. (Orig.). 1980. pap. 1.50 (ISBN 0-671-57034-X). S&S.

--Tormenting Flame. (Silhouette Ser.: No. 17). pap. 1.50 (ISBN 0-686-68326-9). PB.

--Tormenting Flame. 192p. (Orig.). 1980. pap. 1.50 (ISBN 0-671-57017-X). S&S.

John, Naomi. Roadrunner. LC 80-10213. (Illus.). 32p. (gr. k-3). 1980. PLB 8.95 (ISBN 0-525-38485-5). Dutton.

John, Nicholas, ed. English National Opera Guides: Caida, Generentola, Fidelio, Magic Flute, Vol. I. 1981. 25.00. Riverrun NY.

John, Nicole St. see St. John, Nicole.

John Of Salisbury. Metalogicon of John of Salisbury. McGarry, Daniel, tr. 8.50 (ISBN 0-8446-0159-4). Peter Smith.

John Offord Pubns & British Theatre Institute, eds. British Theatre Directory 1979. 1979. text ed. cancelled o.s.i. (ISBN 0-903931-20-6, Pub. by John Offord Pubns England). Drama Bk.

John, Patricia St. see St. John, Patricia.

John, Robert W. & Douglas, Charles N. Playing Social & Recreational Instruments. (Illus.). 144p. 1972. pap. text ed. 9.95 (ISBN 0-13-683680-1). P-H.

John, Robin, tr. see Bermann, Richard A.

John, Wylly F. St. see St. John, Wylly F.

John, Yvonne A. Guyanese Seed of Soul: How to Prepare West Indian Food. Nichols, Mosezelle, ed. (Orig.). 1980. pap. text ed. 8.95x (ISBN 0-936026-04-9). R&M Pub Co.

John Chrysostom, St. Homilies, 48-88. (Fathers of the Church Ser.: Vol. 41). 25.00 (ISBN 0-8132-0041-5). Cath U Pr.

John de St. Jorre. The Guards. 1981. 25.00 (ISBN 0-517-54376-1). Crown.

Johndro, L. Edward. The Earth in the Heavens. 1979. pap. 6.95 (ISBN 0-87728-486-5). Weiser.

--The Stars. 1979. pap. 6.95 (ISBN 0-87728-485-7). Weiser.

Johnes, Carl. Friends & Betrayers. (Orig.). Date not set. pap. 2.50 (ISBN 0-440-12570-7). Dell.

John Of The Cross. Spiritual Canticle. 1975. pap. 2.95 (ISBN 0-385-08919-8, Im). Doubleday.

John Of The Cross, St. Ascent of Mount Carmel. 480p. 1973. pap. 2.95 o.p. (ISBN 0-385-01111-3, Im). Doubleday.

John Paul, Pope, II. Faith According to St. John of the Cross. Aumann, Jordan, tr. LC 80-82265. Orig. Title: Doctrina de Fide apud S. Joannem a Cruce. 376p. (Orig.). 1981. price not set (ISBN 0-89870-010-8); pap. price not set (ISBN 0-89870-005-1). Ignatius Pr.

John Paul, Pope Toward a Philosophy of Praxis. Bloch, Alfred & Czuczka, George T., eds. 160p. Date not set. 10.95 (ISBN 0-8245-0463-1). Crossroad NY.

Johnpoll, Bernard K., compiled By. The League for Industrial Democracy: A Documentary History, 3 vols. LC 80-537. (Documentary Reference Ser.). (Illus.). xiii, 2587p. 1980. Set. lib. bdg. 225.00 (ISBN 0-313-22084-0, YIN/). Greenwood.

Johnpoll, Bernard K., ed. see Thomas, Norman.

Johns, Bud. Ombibulous Mister Mencken. LC 68-8421. (Illus.). 1968. bds. 3.95 (ISBN 0-912184-01-9). Synergistic Pr.

Johns, D. J. Thermal Stress Analysis. 1965. 16.00 (ISBN 0-08-011153-X); pap. 7.75 (ISBN 0-08-011152-1). Pergamon.

Johns, E. A. The Social Structure of Modern Britain. 3rd ed. 1978. text ed. 30.00 (ISBN 0-08-023343-0); pap. 12.00 (ISBN 0-08-023342-2). Pergamon.

--The Sociology of Organizational Change. LC 73-8972. 182p. 1974. text ed. 25.00 (ISBN 0-08-017601-1); pap. text ed. 12.75 (ISBN 0-08-017602-X). Pergamon.

Johns, E. A., jt. auth. see Green, B. S.

Johns, Eric. Dames of the Theatre. (Illus.). 1975. 8.95 o.p. (ISBN 0-87000-310-0). Arlington Hse.

Johns, Francis A. A Bibliography of Arthur Waley. LC 67-20388. 1968. 12.50 (ISBN 0-910294-17-8). Brown Bk.

Johns, H. E., jt. auth. see Bruce, W. R.

Johns, Harold E. & Cunningham, John R. The Physics of Radiology. 3rd ed. (Illus.). 816p. 1980. 30.75 (ISBN 0-398-03007-3). C C Thomas.

Johns, Jerry L. Basic Reading Inventory. (Kendall-Hunt Reading Ser.). (pre-primer-8). 1978. pap. text ed. 5.95 (ISBN 0-8403-2315-8). Kendall-Hunt.

--A Secondary Reading Inventory. 100p. (gr. 7 up). 1981. write for info. wire coil (ISBN 0-697-06058-6). Wm C Brown.

Johns, Leland. California Damages, Law & Proof. 2nd ed. LC 77-89697. 1977. 49.50 (ISBN 0-911110-24-0); 1980 suppl. incl. Parker & Son.

Johns, Richard S. German Shorthaired Pointers. (Illus.). 128p. 1974. pap. cancelled o.p. (ISBN 0-87666-302-1, HS-1046). TFH Pubns.

Johns, Roe L. & Morphet, Edgar L. The Economics & Financing of Education: A Systems Approach. 3rd ed. LC 74-30213. (Illus.). 496p. 1975. ref. ed. 19.95 (ISBN 0-13-229898-8). P-H.

Johns, Roger D. Man in the World: The Political Theology of Johannes Baptist Metz. LC 76-26491. (American Academy of Religion. Dissertation Ser.). 1976. pap. 7.50 (ISBN 0-89130-079-1, 010116). Scholars Pr Ca.

Johns, Ruth, jt. auth. see Jansen, Frances O.

Johns, S., jt. ed. see Sideri, S.

Johns, William D., tr. see Engelhardt, W. V., et al.

Johns, Yohani. Dishes from Indonesia. (Illus.). 1978. 17.95 (ISBN 0-241-89943-5, Pub. by Hamish Hamilton England). David & Charles.

Johnsen, Arne O. & King, Peter, eds. The Tax Book of the Cisterian Order. 1980. pap. 14.00x (ISBN 82-00-12653-6, Dist. by Columbia U. Pr.). Universitet.

Johnsen, Arne Odd & Tonnessen, Joh. N. The History of Modern Whaling. 1980. 45.00 (ISBN 0-520-03973-4). U of Cal Pr.

Johnsen, Frederick. B-Twenty-Nine Book. (Illus.). 1978. pap. 3.95 (ISBN 0-911721-40-1, Pub. by Bomber). Aviation.

Johnsen, Frederick A. Bombers in Blue: PB4Y-2 Privateers & PB4Y-1 Liberators. (Illus.). 1979. pap. 3.95 (ISBN 0-911721-53-3, Pub. by Bomber). Aviation.

--Thundering Peacemaker: The B-36 Story. (Illus.). 1978. pap. 3.95 (ISBN 0-911721-31-2, Pub. by Bomber). Aviation.

Johnsgard, Paul A. Guide to North American Waterfowl. LC 78-20612. (Illus.). 288p. 1979. 15.95x (ISBN 0-253-12789-0). Ind U Pr.

--North American Game Birds of Upland & Shoreline. LC 74-15274. (Illus.). xxx, 229p. 1975 (ISBN 0-8032-5811-9). pap. 7.95 (ISBN 0-8032-5811-9, BB 597, Bison). U of Nebr Pr.

Johnsich, John R. Real Estate Mathematics Study Manual & Reference Book. rev. ed. (Illus.). 131p. 1980. pap. 9.95 (ISBN 0-914256-13-0). Real Estate Pub.

Johnson. Christy. (gr. 7-12). 1980. pap. 1.50 (ISBN 0-590-31261-8, Schol Pap). Schol Bk Serv.

--Communication: The Process of Organizing. 1977. text ed. 17.95 (ISBN 0-205-05786-1); instructor's manual avail. (ISBN 0-205-05788-8). Allyn.

--Education & Society in England, 1780-1870. (Studies in Economic & Social History). 1980. pap. text ed. 11.50x (ISBN 0-391-01131-6). Humanities.

--An Essay on West African Therapeutics. (Traditional Healing Ser.: No. 7). 1981. 15.00 (ISBN 0-932426-09-3, Trado-Medic Bks); pap. 7.50 (ISBN 0-932426-10-7, Trado-Medic Bks). Conch Mag.

--Manufacturing Process. 1979. text ed. 23.72 (ISBN 0-87002-299-7); study guide 5.28 (ISBN 0-87002-044-7). Bennett IL.

--MORT Safety Assurance Systems. (Occupational Safety & Health Ser.: Vol. 4). 544p. 1980. 35.00 (ISBN 0-8247-6897-3). Dekker.

--Sixteen Can Be Sweet. (gr. 7-12). pap. 1.25 (ISBN 0-590-03860-5, Schol Pap). Schol Bk Serv.

--Technical Metals. (gr. 9-12). 1980. text ed. 20.20 (ISBN 0-87002-313-6). Bennett IL.

Johnson & Morasky. Learning Disabilities. 2nd ed. 450p. text ed. 17.95 (ISBN 0-205-06898-7, 2468980). Allyn.

Johnson & Swanson. SG Elementary Statistics for Business. (Illus.). 1980. write for info. Duxbury Pr.

Johnson, jt. auth. see Altheide.

Johnson, jt. auth. see Boone.

Johnson, A. D., et al, eds. Testis. Vol. 1 1970. 72.50 (ISBN 0-12-386601-4); Vol. 2 1970. 68.50 (ISBN 0-12-386602-2); Vol. 3 1971. 69.00 (ISBN 0-12-386603-0); Vol. 4 1977. 62.50 (ISBN 0-12-386604-9); Set. 222.75 (ISBN 0-685-02412-1). Acad Pr.

Johnson, A. F., jt. auth. see Berry, Turner W.

Johnson, A. H. The Disappearance of the Small Landowner. LC 79-14625. (Illus.). xiii, 164p. 1979. Repr. of 1909 ed. lib. bdg. 13.50x (ISBN 0-678-08077-1). Kelley.

Johnson, A. S. Marketing & Financial Control. 1967. 23.00 (ISBN 0-08-012614-6); pap. text ed. 11.25 (ISBN 0-08-012613-8). Pergamon.

Johnson, Alan. Freedom Letter. 1979. 4.95 (ISBN 0-8024-2874-6). Moody.

Johnson, Alan F., jt. ed. see Gundry, Stanley N.

Johnson, Alan P. Auditing Judgement: A Book of Cases. 1980. 19.95x (ISBN 0-256-02382-4). Irwin.

Johnson, Albert. Shakespeare Vignettes: Adaptations for Acting. LC 79-88273. 1970. 7.95 o.p. (ISBN 0-498-06768-8). A S Barnes.

Johnson, Albert & Johnson, Bertha. Drama for Classroom & Stage. LC 68-27249. (Illus.). 1969. 12.00 o.p. (ISBN 0-498-06711-4). A S Barnes.

Johnson, Alexander B. Treatise on Language. Rynin, David, ed. LC 68-25841. 1969. pap. text ed. 4.00 (ISBN 0-486-22019-2). Dover.

Johnson, Alexandra W. Jerusalem Fifteen Hundred. (Illus.). 1981. 12.95 (ISBN 0-930720-66-0). Liberator Pr.

Johnson, Alfred M., Jr., ed. & tr. The New Testament & Structuralism: A Collection of Essays. LC 76-25447. (Pittsburgh Theological Monographs: No. 11). 1976. pap. text ed. 7.95 (ISBN 0-915138-13-1). Pickwick.

Johnson, Alfred M., Jr., tr. see Marin, Louis & Chabrol, Claude.

Johnson, Allen. Stephen A. Douglas: A Study in American Politics. LC 77-98690. (American Scene Ser). 1970. Repr. of 1908 ed. lib. bdg. 39.50 (ISBN 0-306-71836-7). Da Capo.

Johnson, Allen & Nevins, Allan, eds. Chronicles of America, 27 vols, Vols. 30-56. Incl. Vol. 30. The Day of the Confederacy. Stephenson, Nathaniel W (ISBN 0-911548-29-7); Vol. 31. Captains of the Civil War. Wood, William (ISBN 0-911548-30-0); Vol. 32. The Sequel of Appomattox. Fleming, Walter L (ISBN 0-911548-31-9); Vol. 33. The American Spirit in Education. Slosson, Edwin E (ISBN 0-911548-32-7); Vol. 34. The American Spirit in Literature. Perry, Bliss (ISBN 0-911548-33-5); Vol. 35. Our Foreigners. Orth, Samuel P (ISBN 0-911548-34-3); Vol. 36. The Old Merchant Marine. Paine, Ralph D (ISBN 0-911548-35-1); Vol. 37. The Age of Invention. Thompson, Holland (ISBN 0-911548-36-X); Vol. 38. The Railroad Builders. Moody, John (ISBN 0-911548-37-8); Vol. 39. The Age of Big Business. Hendrick, Burton J (ISBN 0-911548-38-6); Vol. 40. The Armies of Labour. Orth, Samuel P (ISBN 0-911548-39-4); Vol. 41. The Masters of Capital. Moody, John (ISBN 0-911548-40-8); Vol. 42. The New South. Thompson, Holland (ISBN 0-911548-41-6); **Vol. 43. The Boss & the Machine. Orth, Samuel P (ISBN 0-911548-42-4); Vol. 44. The Cleveland Era. Ford, Henry J (ISBN 0-911548-43-2); Vol. 45. The Agrarian Crusade. Buck, Solon J (ISBN 0-911548-44-0); Vol. 46. The Path of Empire. Fish, Carl R (ISBN 0-911548-45-9); Vol. 47. Theodore Roosevelt & His Times. Howland, Harold (ISBN 0-911548-46-7); Vol. 48. Woodrow Wilson & the World War. Seymour, Charles (ISBN 0-911548-47-5); Vol. 49. The Canadian Dominion. Skelton, Oscar D (ISBN 0-911548-48-3); Vol. 50. Hispanic Nations of the New World. Shepherd, William R (ISBN 0-911548-49-1); Vol. 51. From Versailles to the New Deal. Faulkner, Harold U (ISBN 0-911548-50-5); Vol. 52. Era of Franklin D. Roosevelt. Brogan, Denis W (ISBN 0-911548-51-3); Vol. 53. The Struggle for Survival. Janeway, Eliott (ISBN 0-911548-52-1); Vol. 54. War for the World. Pratt, Fletcher (ISBN 0-911548-53-X); Vol. 55. The United States in a Chaotic World. Nevins, Allan (ISBN 0-911548-54-8); Vol. 56. The New Deal & World Affairs. Nevins, Allan (ISBN 0-911548-55-6). 8.95 ea.; 56 vols. 445.00 set (ISBN 0-911548-71-8). US Pubs.**

Johnson, Alvin D. The Work of the Usher. (Orig.). pap. 2.75 (ISBN 0-8170-0356-8). Judson.

Johnson, Alvin W. & Yost, Frank H. Separation of Church & State in the United States. Repr. of 1948 ed. lib. bdg. 15.75x (ISBN 0-8371-2436-0, JOCS). Greenwood.

Johnson & Johnson. Your Toddler. 1980. 16.95 (ISBN 0-02-559550-4); pap. 10.95 (ISBN 0-02-043920-2). Macmillan.

Johnson & Johnson Baby Products Company. The First Wondrous Year: You & Your Baby. (Illus.). 1979. 16.95 (ISBN 0-02-559530-X); pap. 10.95 (ISBN 0-02-077100-2). Macmillan.

Johnson, Andrew. Trial of Andrew Johnson. LC 69-11326. (Law, Politics, & History Ser). 1970. Repr. of 1868 ed. lib. bdg. 95.00 (ISBN 0-306-71184-2). Da Capo.

Johnson, Ann D. The Value of Adventure: The Story of Sacajawea. LC 80-17623. (Value Tales Ser.). (Illus.). 66p. (gr. k-5). 1980. 6.95 (ISBN 0-916392-59-7, Dist. by Oak Tree Pubns). Value Comm.

--The Value of Creativity: The Story of Thomas Edison. (Valuetales Ser.). (Illus.). 64p. (gr. k-6). 1981. 6.95 (ISBN 0-916392-72-4). Oak Tree Pubns.

--Value of Foresight: The Story of Thomas Jefferson. LC 79-19548. (Illus.). (gr. k-6). 1979. 6.95 (ISBN 0-916392-42-2, Dist. by Oak Tree Pubns.). Value Comm.

--The Value of Friendship: The Story of Jane Addams. LC 79-21643. (Value Tales Ser.). (Illus.). 1979. 6.95 (ISBN 0-916392-45-7). Value Comm.

--The Value of Giving: The Story of Beethoven. LC 78-31545. (ValueTales Ser.). (Illus.). (gr. k-6). 1979. 6.95 (ISBN 0-916392-34-1, Dist. by Oak Tree Pubns). Value Comm.

--The Value of Helping: The Story of Harriet Tubman. LC 79-21652. (Illus.). (gr. k-6). 1979. PLB 6.95g (ISBN 0-916392-41-4, Dist. by Oak Tree Pubns). Value Comm.

--The Value of Love: The Story of Johnny Appleseed. LC 79-31873. (ValueTales Ser.). (Illus.). (gr. k-6). 1979. 6.95 (ISBN 0-916392-35-X, Dist. by Oak Tree Pubns). Value Comm.

Johnson, Annabel & Johnson, Edgar. Finders, Keepers. LC 80-69994. 192p. (gr. 7 up). 1981. 7.95 (ISBN 0-590-07790-2, Four Winds). Schol Bk Serv.

Johnson, Anne. Mosses of Singapore & Malaysia. 126p. 1980. pap. 7.50 (ISBN 0-8214-0547-0). Swallow.

Johnson, Anne & Johnson, Russ. Ghost Town of Bodie. LC 67-31002. 3.45 (ISBN 0-912494-19-0); pap. 3.45 (ISBN 0-912494-02-6). Chalfant Pr.

Johnson, Arnold & Peterson, Martin, eds. Encyclopedia of Food Technology. (Technologic Food Encyclopedia). (Illus.). 1974. 75.00 (ISBN 0-87055-157-4). AVI.

Johnson, Arnold H., jt. auth. see Peterson, Martin S.

Johnson, Arthur. Manual of Bookbinding. (Illus.). 1978. 15.95 o.p. (ISBN 0-684-15332-7, ScribT). Scribner.

Johnson, Arthur M., ed. The American Economy: An Historical Introduction to the Problem's of the 1970's. LC 74-2652. (Urgent Issues in American Society Ser). 1974. 10.00 o.s.i. (ISBN 0-02-916580-6). Free Pr.

--The American Economy: An Historical Introduction to the Problems of the 1970's. LC 74-2652. (Urgent Issues in American Society Ser). 1975. pap. text ed. 6.95 (ISBN 0-02-916590-3). Free Pr.

Johnson, Ashley S. The Great Controversy. 7.50 o.p. (ISBN 0-89225-096-8). Gospel Advocate.

Johnson, Aubrey R. Sacral Kingship in Ancient Israel. rev. ed. 1967. 18.00 (ISBN 0-7083-0344-7). Verry.

--Vitality of the Individual in the Thought of Ancient Israel. 2nd ed. 1964. 12.50x (ISBN 0-7083-0349-8). Verry.

Johnson, Audrey. Dressing Dolls. (Illus.). 1969. 16.95 (ISBN 0-8231-3025-8). Branford.

--Furnishing Dolls' Houses. LC 72-75079. (Illus.). 284p. 1972. 23.00 (ISBN 0-8231-3029-0). Branford.

--How to Make Dolls' Houses. (Illus.). 1975. pap. 5.50 (ISBN 0-8231-7008-X). Branford.

--How to Repair & Dress Old Dolls. 128p. 1967. pap. 6.95 o.p. (ISBN 0-8231-3026-6). Branford.

Johnson, Audrey P. Hush, Winifred Is Dead. 192p. (YA) 1976. 4.95 o.p. (ISBN 0-685-67082-1, Avalon). Bouregy.

--Nurse of the Thousand Islands. (YA) 1978. 5.95 (ISBN 0-685-85780-8, Avalon). Bouregy.

Johnson, B. C. The Atheist Debater's Handbook: The/Skeptics Bookshelf. 100p. 1981. 15.95 (ISBN 0-87975-152-5); pap. 9.95 (ISBN 0-87975-154-1). Prometheus Bks.

Johnson, B. L. Pakistan. LC 79-10749. 1980. text ed. 19.95 (ISBN 0-435-35484-1). Heinemann Ed.

Johnson, Barbara. The Critical Difference: Essays in the Contemporary Rhetoric of Reading. LC 80-21533. 176p. 1981. text ed. 12.00x (ISBN 0-8018-2458-3). Johns Hopkins.

--Where Does a Mother Go to Resign? LC 79-12686. 1979. pap. 3.50 (ISBN 0-87123-606-0, 210606). Bethany Fell.

Johnson, Barbara F. The Heirs of Love. 1980. 2.95 (ISBN 0-380-75739-7, 75739, 75739). Avon.

--Homeward Winds the River. 1980. pap. 2.50 (ISBN 0-686-69242-X, 42952). Avon.

Johnson, Barbara L. Book Scouting: How to Turn Your Love for Books in Print. (Illus.). 192p. 1981. 10.95 (Spec); pap. 4.95. P-H.

Johnson, Ben, jt. auth. see Stevick, Daniel B.

Johnson, Ben, tr. see Svevo, Italo.

Johnson, Bertha, jt. auth. see Johnson, Albert.

Johnson, Beverly. Beverly Johnson's Guide to a Life of Beauty. 1980. 12.50 o.p. (ISBN 0-8129-0911-9). Times Bks.

Johnson, Bobby J. Poems from the Asylum. 34p. 1978. 2.95 (ISBN 0-8059-2496-5). Dorrance.

Johnson, Bradley T. Reports of Cases Decided by Chief Justice Chase in the Circuit Court of the United States for the Fourth Circuit: 1865-1869. facsimile ed. LC 75-75292. (American Constitutional & Legal History Ser.). 1972. Repr. of 1876 ed. lib. bdg. 59.50 (ISBN 0-306-71291-1). Da Capo.

Johnson, Brian, jt. auth. see Hoffmann, Thomas R.

Johnson, Brian, jt. auth. see Stein, Robert E.

Johnson, Brian F., ed. Transition Metal Clusters. 1980. 96.50 (ISBN 0-471-27817-3, Pub. by Wiley-Interscience). Wiley.

Johnson, Broderick A., ed. see Callaway, Sydney M. & Witherspoon, Gary.

Johnson, Bruce C. Basic Handtools for the Aviation Technician. (Aviation Technician Training Ser.). (Orig.). 1980. pap. write for info. (ISBN 0-89100-204-9). Aviation Maintenance.

Johnson, Bruce G., et al. Basic Steel Design. 2nd ed. 1980. text ed. 24.95 (ISBN 0-13-069344-8). P-H.

Johnson, C. Practical Arithmetic: The Third "R". (Illus.). 1977. pap. 14.95 (ISBN 0-13-689273-6). P-H.

Johnson, C. D. The Hammet Equation. LC 79-42670. (Cambridge Texts in Chemistry & Biochemistry). (Illus.). 196p. 1980. pap. 12.95 (ISBN 0-521-29970-5). Cambridge U Pr.

--The Hammett Equation. LC 72-93140. (Chemistry Texts Ser). (Illus.). 180p. 1973. 28.95 (ISBN 0-521-20138-1). Cambridge U Pr.

Johnson, C. E., jt. auth. see Sparks, J. E.

Johnson, C. W., et al. Basic Psychotherapeutics: A Programmed Text. 605p. 1980. soft bound 14.95 (ISBN 0-89335-128-8). Spectrum Pub.

Johnson, Carl. Field Athletics. (Ep Sport Ser). (Illus.). 113p. 1978. 12.95 (ISBN 0-8069-9114-3, Pub by EP Publishing England). Sterling.

--Success in Athletics. (Success Sportbooks Ser.). (Illus.). 1977. 9.95 (ISBN 0-7195-3375-9). Transatlantic.

Johnson, Carl, jt. auth. see Pasto, Daniel.

Johnson, Carl E., jt. auth. see Sparks, J. E.

Johnson, Carl G. Fifty-Two Story Telling Programs. (Paperback Prog. Ser.). (Orig.). 1964. pap. 2.50 o.p. (ISBN 0-8010-5004-9). Baker Bk.

--My Favorite Illustration. (Preaching Helps Ser.). 1972. pap. 1.95 o.p. (ISBN 0-8010-5016-2). Baker Bk.

Johnson, Carol & Johnstone, Ann. Golf: A Positive Approach. LC 74-24619. 1975. pap. text ed. 6.75 (ISBN 0-201-03416-6). A-W.

Johnson, Carol R., jt. auth. see Pasto, Daniel J.

Johnson, Carole L., et al. Burn Management. 130p. 1981. 12.50 (ISBN 0-89004-320-5, 466). Raven.

Johnson, Carrie E. Medical Spelling Guide: A Reference Aid. 560p. 1966. 14.75 (ISBN 0-398-00931-7). C C Thomas.

Johnson, Carroll B. Matias de los Reyes & the Craft of Fiction. (U. C. Publ. in Modern Philology: Vol. 101). 1973. pap. 13.75x (ISBN 0-520-09386-0). U of Cal Pr.

Johnson, Catherine E. TV Guide Twenty-Five Year Index: Nineteen Fifty-Three to Nineteen Seventy-Seven. LC 79-67725. 506p. 1980. text ed. 77.50 (ISBN 0-9603684-0-X). Triangle Pubns.

Johnson, Cecelia D. Her Life for His Friends: A Biography of Terry McHugh. LC 80-25996. 1980. pap. 7.95 (ISBN 0-8190-0640-8). Fides Claretian.

Johnson, Cecil. Communist China & Latin America. LC 76-129054. 1970. 20.00x (ISBN 0-231-03309-5). Columbia U Pr.

Johnson, Chalmers. Autopsy on People's War. (A Quantum Book). 1974. 11.50x (ISBN 0-520-02516-4); pap. 2.85 (ISBN 0-520-02518-0). U of Cal Pr.

--Conspiracy at Matsukawa. LC 73-161998. (Illus.). 1972. 25.00x (ISBN 0-520-02063-4). U of Cal Pr.

Johnson, Chalmers A. Peasant Nationalism & Communist Power: The Emergence of Revolutionary China, 1937-1945. 1962. 12.50x (ISBN 0-8047-0073-7); pap. 4.95 (ISBN 0-8047-0074-5). Stanford U Pr.

Johnson, Charles. A General History of the Robberies & Murders of the Most Notorious Pyrates. LC 71-170563. (Foundations of the Novel Ser.: Vol. 44). lib. bdg. 50.00 (ISBN 0-8240-0556-2). Garland Pub.

Johnson, Charles, tr. from Lat. see Hugh The Chantor.

Johnson, Charles B. Harrap's New German Grammar. 1971. pap. text ed. 13.50x (ISBN 0-245-52989-6). Intl Ideas.

Johnson, Charles O. & Jackson, Charles W. City Behind a Fence: Oak Ridge, Tennessee, 1942-1946. LC 80-15897. (Illus.). 272p. 1981. 18.50 (ISBN 0-87049-303-5); pap. 9.50 (ISBN 0-87049-309-4). U of Tenn Pr.

Johnson, Charles S. & Pedersen, L. G. Problems & Solutions in Quantum Chemistry. 1974. pap. text ed. 13.95 (ISBN 0-201-03415-8). A-W.

Johnson, Charles W. The Nature of Vermont: Introduction & Guide to a New England Environment. LC 79-56774. (Illus.). 250p. 1980. text ed. 15.00x (ISBN 0-87451-182-8); pap. 7.50 (ISBN 0-87451-183-6). U Pr of New Eng.

Johnson, Christiane, jt. ed. see Johnson, Ira D.

Johnson, Christopher B. Physiological Processes Limiting Plant Productivity. 1981. text ed. price not set (ISBN 0-408-10649-2). Butterworth.

Johnson, Clarence D. The Biosystematics of the Arizona, California & Oregon Species of the Genus Acanthoscelides Schilsky (Coleoptera: Bruchidae) (U. C. Publ. in Entomology: Vol. 59). 1970. pap. 8.50x (ISBN 0-520-09132-9). U of Cal Pr.

Johnson, Clark. The Diagnosis of Learning Disabilities. 400p. 1981. text ed. 15.00x (ISBN 0-87108-236-5). Pruett.

Johnson, Clive, ed. Vedanta: An Anthology of Hindu Scripture, Commentary, & Poetry. LC 75-126033. 1971. 2.50 o.p. (ISBN 0-685-57296-X). Weiser.

Johnson, Colton, ed. see Yeats, W. B.

Johnson, Corinne B. & Johnson, Eric W. Love & Sex & Growing up. LC 77-22462. 1977. 6.95 o.p. (ISBN 0-397-31768-9). Lippincott.

Johnson, Crockett. Harold & the Purple Crayon. LC 55-7683. (Trophy Picture Bks.). (Illus.). 64p. (ps-3). 1981. pap. 1.95 (ISBN 0-06-443022-7, Trophy). Har-Row.

--Harold's ABC. LC 63-14444. (Trophy Picture Bks.). (Illus.). 64p. (ps-3). 1981. pap. 1.95 (ISBN 0-06-443023-5, Trophy). Har-Row.

--Harold's Circus. LC 59-5318. (Trophy Picture Bks.). (Illus.). 64p. (ps-3). 1981. pap. 1.95 (ISBN 0-06-443024-3, Trophy). Har-Row.

--Harold's Trip to the Sky. LC 57-9262. (Trophy Picture Bks.). (Illus.). 64p. (ps-3). 1981. pap. 1.95 (ISBN 0-06-443025-1, Trophy). Har-Row.

--A Picture for Harold's Room. (Illus.). (gr. k-3). 1974. pap. 1.25 (ISBN 0-590-02396-9, Schol Pap); pap. 3.50 (ISBN 0-590-20795-4). Schol Bk Serv.

Johnson, Curtis D. Process Control Instrumentation Technology. LC 76-26543. 1977. text ed. 21.95 (ISBN 0-471-44614-9). Wiley.

Johnson, D. French Society & the Revolution. LC 76-1136. (Past and Present Publications Ser.). 300p. 1976. 26.95 (ISBN 0-521-21275-8). Cambridge U Pr.

Johnson, D. & Johnson, J. Introductory Electric Circuit Analysis. 1981. 21.00 (ISBN 0-13-500835-2). P-H.

Johnson, D., jt. auth. see Teitelbaum, M. J.

Johnson, D. A. Some Thermodynamic Aspects of Inorganic Chemistry. LC 68-29118. (Cambridge Chemistry Texts Ser). (Orig.). 1968. pap. 12.50x (ISBN 0-521-09544-1). Cambridge U Pr.

Johnson, D. C., jt. auth. see Bishop, R. E.

Johnson, D. G. Medieval Chinese Oligarchy. LC 76-44875. (Westview Special Studies on China & East Asia & Studies of the East Asian Institute, Columbia University). 1977. lib. bdg. 25.00x (ISBN 0-89158-140-5). Westview.

Johnson, D. J. Topics in the Theory of Group Presentations. (London Mathematical Society Lecture Note Ser.: No. 42). (Illus.). 230p. (Orig.). 1980. pap. 29.95x (ISBN 0-521-23108-6). Cambridge U Pr.

Johnson, Dale. The Sociology of Change & Reaction in Latin America. LC 73-7794. (Studies in Sociology Ser). 1973. pap. text ed. 3.50 (ISBN 0-672-61238-0). Bobbs.

Johnson, Daniel M., jt. auth. see Dart, John O.

Johnson, David. American Law Enforcement: A History. LC 80-68814. (Orig.). 1981. text ed. 15.95x (ISBN 0-88273-271-4). Forum Pr MO.

--The Anglo-Boer War. (Jackdaw Ser: No. 68). (Illus.). 1969. 5.95 o.p. (ISBN 0-670-12618-7, Grossman). Viking Pr.

--Home Decorating. LC 78-74079. (Penny Pinchers Ser). 1979. 2.95 (ISBN 0-7153-7751-5). David & Charles.

--The London Blitz: The City Ablaze, December 29, 1940. LC 80-6199. 224p. 1981. 13.95 (ISBN 0-8128-2799-6). Stein & Day.

--Presentations of Groups. LC 74-31803. (London Mathematical Society Lecture Note Ser.: No. 22) 140p. 1976. 18.95x (ISBN 0-521-20829-7). Cambridge U Pr.

--Shooter, Fighter, Wild Horse Rider. LC 79-90843. (Illus.). 72p. (Orig.). 1981. pap. 4.95 (ISBN 0-935342-05-2). Jalapeno Pr.

Johnson, David A. & Graybill, Michael. The Tufted Puffin. (Life Forms of the Oregon Coast: Vol. I). (Illus.). 22p. (Orig.). (gr. 6 up). 1979. pap. 2.75 (ISBN 0-932368-07-7). Bandon Hist.

Johnson, David E. Introduction to Filter Theory. (Illus.). 336p. 1976. 24.95 (ISBN 0-13-483776-2). P-H.

--Toward a Theory of Rationally Based Grammar. Hankamer, Jorge, ed. LC 78-66553. (Outstanding Dissertations in Linguistics Ser.). 1979. lib. bdg. 21.00 (ISBN 0-8240-9682-7). Garland Pub.

Johnson, David E. & Johnson, Johnny R. Graph Theory: With Engineering Applications. 350p. 1972. 32.50x (ISBN 0-8260-4775-0, Pub. by Wiley-Interscience). Wiley.

Johnson, David E. & Postal, Paul M. Arc Pair Grammar. LC 80-7533. (Illus.). 700p. 1980. 35.00x (ISBN 0-691-08270-7). Princeton U Pr.

Johnson, David E., et al. Basic Electric Circuit Analysis. LC 77-24210. (Illus.). 1978. ref. 27.95x (ISBN 0-13-060137-3). P-H.

--Digital Circuits & Microcomputers. LC 78-13244. (Illus.). 1979. ref. ed. 23.95 (ISBN 0-13-214015-2). P-H.

--A Handbook of Active Filters. (Illus.). 1980. text ed. 21.95 (ISBN 0-13-372409-3). P-H.

Johnson, David J. Southwark & the City. 1969. 10.25x o.p. (ISBN 0-19-711630-2). Oxford U Pr.

Johnson, David P. Heraldry: The Armiger's News, 1979-1980. LC 80-70043. (Illus.). 55p. 1980. pap. 9.95 (ISBN 0-9605668-0-5). Am Coll Heraldry.

Johnson, David S., jt. auth. see Garey, Michael R.

Johnson, David W. Educational Psychology. (Illus.). 1979. pap. 17.95 ref. ed. (ISBN 0-13-236760-2). P-H.

--Human Relations & Your Career: A Guide to Interpersonal Skills. (Illus.). 1978. 13.95 (ISBN 0-13-445601-7). P-H.

--Reaching Out: Interpersonal Effectiveness & Self Actualization. (Illus.). 272p. 1972. ref. ed. 13.95 (ISBN 0-13-753277-6); pap. text ed. 10.95 ref. ed. (ISBN 0-13-753269-5). P-H.

--Reaching Out: Interpersonal Effectiveness & Self-Actualization. 2nd ed. (Illus.). 320p. 1981. text ed. 14.95 (ISBN 0-13-753327-6); pap. text ed. 10.95 (ISBN 0-13-753319-5). P-H.

Johnson, David W. & Johnson, Frank P. Joining Together: Group Theory & Group Skills. LC 74-23698. (Illus.). 480p. 1975. pap. 12.95 (ISBN 0-13-510370-3). P-H.

Johnson, David W. & Johnson, Roger T. Learning Together & Alone: Cooperation, Competition, & Individualization. (Illus.). 224p. 1975. pap. text ed. 10.95 (ISBN 0-13-527945-3). P-H.

Johnson, Dean L. & Stratton, Russell J. Fundamentals of Removable Prosthodontics. (Illus.). 500p. 1980. 46.00 (ISBN 0-931386-10-1). Quint Pub Co.

Johnson, Deborah. A Blooming Success. (Illus.). 1978. pap. 7.95 (ISBN 0-88453-019-1). Barrington.

Johnson, Deborah K., ed. see Attitude Research Conference, October, 1974, San Francisco.

Johnson, Derek E. Collector's Guide to Militaria. (Illus.). 1977. 8.95 o.p. (ISBN 0-8069-0110-1); lib. bdg. 8.29 o.p. (ISBN 0-8069-0111-X). Sterling.

Johnson, Diane. Edwin Broun Fred: Scientist, Administrator, Gentleman. 1974. 20.00 (ISBN 0-299-06580-4). U of Wis Pr.

Johnson, Donald. Canberra & Walter Burley Griffin: A Bibliography of Eighteen Seventy-Six to Nineteen Seventy-Six & a Guide to Published Sources. (Illus.). 128p. (Orig.). 1980. pap. 6.50x (ISBN 0-19-554203-7). Oxford U Pr.

Johnson, Donald L., ed. Australian Architecture, 1901 to 1951: Sources of Modernism. 240p. 1980. 35.00x (ISBN 0-424-00071-7, Pub. by Sydney U Pr Australia). Intl Schol Bk Serv.

Johnson, Donald R., jt. auth. see Larrison, Earl J.

Johnson, Donna K. Brighteyes. LC 78-4353. (Illus.). (gr. 1 up). 1978. 5.95 o.p. (ISBN 0-03-044651-1). HR&W.

Johnson, Donovan A. & Glenn, William H. Exploring Mathematics on Your Own. Incl. No. 1. Invitation to Mathematics. pap. o.p. (ISBN 0-685-30036-6); No. 2. The World of Measurement. pap. o.p. (ISBN 0-7195-1659-5); No. 3. Number Patterns (ISBN 0-7195-1661-7); No. 4. The Theorem of Pythagoras. pap. o.p. (ISBN 0-7195-1663-3); No. 5. The World of Statistics. pap. o.p. (ISBN 0-7195-1665-X); No. 6. Sets, Sentences & Operations (ISBN 0-7195-1667-6); No. 7. Fun with Mathematics. pap. o.p. (ISBN 0-7195-1669-2); No. 8. Understanding Numeration Systems (ISBN 0-7195-1671-4); No. 9. Short Cuts in Calculating. pap. o.p. (ISBN 0-7195-1673-0); No. 10. Graphs. pap. o.p. (ISBN 0-7195-1675-7); No. 11. Calculating Devices. pap. o.p. (ISBN 0-685-30037-4); No. 12. Topology (ISBN 0-7195-1679-X); No. 13. Logic & Reasoning in Mathematics. pap. o.p. (ISBN 0-685-30038-2); No. 14. Curves. pap. o.p. (ISBN 0-7195-1683-8); No. 15. Probability & Chance. pap. o.p. (ISBN 0-7195-1685-4); No. 16. Basic Concepts of Vectors. pap. o.p. (ISBN 0-7195-1687-0); **No. 17. Finite Mathematical Systems. o.p. (ISBN 0-7195-1689-7); No. 18. Computer Programming (ISBN 0-7195-1881-4); No. 19. Matrices (ISBN 0-7195-2013-4); No. 20. Infinite Numbers (ISBN 0-7195-3097-0); No. 21. Permutations & Groups (ISBN 0-7195-2909-3); No. 22. Numbers: Their Personalities & Properties. (gr. 10-12). 1973. Nos. 1-18. pap. 5.95 ea. (ISBN 0-685-30033-1); No. 19. pap. 5.95x (ISBN 0-685-30034-X); Nos.20-22. pap. 5.95 (ISBN 0-685-30035-8). Transatlantic.**

Johnson, Donovan A. & Rising, Gerald R. Guidelines for Teaching Mathematics. 2nd ed. 560p. 1972. 17.95x (ISBN 0-534-00189-0). Wadsworth Pub.

Johnson, Dora E., jt. auth. see Smith, Robert E.

Johnson, Dorothy. To Find a Blessing. 59p. 1980. 3.95 (ISBN 0-8059-2745-X). Dorrance.

Johnson, Dorothy E. & Vestermark, Mary J. Barriers & Hazards in Counseling. LC 73-14990. (Orig.). 1970. pap. text ed. 9.50 (ISBN 0-395-04694-7, 3-28202). HM.

Johnson, Dorothy M. All the Buffalo Returning. LC 78-22425. 1979. 6.95 (ISBN 0-396-07668-8). Dodd.

--Buffalo Woman. LC 76-53436. (gr. 5-10). 1977. 6.95 (ISBN 0-396-07423-5). Dodd.

--The Hanging Tree. 1977. pap. 1.95 (ISBN 0-345-28621-9). Ballantine.

--The Hanging Tree. (Western Fiction Ser.). 1980. lib. bdg. 9.95 (ISBN 0-8398-2616-8). Gregg.

Johnson, Douglas. France. LC 75-78381. (Nations & Peoples Library). 1969. 8.50x o.s.i. (ISBN 0-8027-2105-2). Walker & Co.

Johnson, Douglas & Bedarida, Francois, eds. Britain & France: Ten Centuries. 250p. 1980. cancelled (ISBN 0-87480-189-3). U of Utah Pr.

Johnson, Douglas E. Testicular Tumors. 2nd ed. 1976. 30.00 o.p. (ISBN 0-87488-743-7). Med Exam.

Johnson, Douglas E. & Samuels, Melvin L., eds. Cancer of the Genitourinary Tract. LC 79-2070. 1979. text ed. 34.50 (ISBN 0-89004-383-3). Raven.

Johnson, Douglas P. Beethoven's Early Sketches in the 'fischhof Miscellany' Berlin Autograph 28, 2 vols. Buelow, George, ed. (Studies in Musicology). 887p. 1980. Set. 59.95 (ISBN 0-8357-1137-4, Pub. by UMI Res Pr); Vol. 1. (ISBN 0-8357-1138-2); Vol. 2. (ISBN 0-8357-1139-0). Univ Microfilms.

Johnson, Douglas W. & Cornell, George W. Punctured Preconceptions: What North American Christians Think About the Church. 128p. (Orig.). 1974. pap. 1.95 o.p. (ISBN 0-685-27369-5). Friend Pr.

Johnson, Doyle P. Sociological Theory: Classical Founders & Contemporary Perspectives. 600p. 1981. text ed. 16.95 (ISBN 0-471-02915-7); tchrs.' ed. avail. (ISBN 0-471-08958-3). Wiley.

Johnson, Edgar, jt. auth. see Johnson, Annabel.

Johnson, Edith, ed. see Meldman, Monte J.

Johnson, Edna, et al. Anthology of Children's Literature. 5th ed. 1977. text ed. 21.95 (ISBN 0-395-24554-0). HM.

Johnson, Elden, ed. Aspects of Upper Great Lakes Anthropology: Papers in Honor of Lloyd A. Wilford. LC 74-17003. (Prehistoric Archaeology Ser: No. 11). (Illus.). 190p. 1974. pap. 9.50 (ISBN 0-87351-087-9). Minn Hist.

Johnson, Elmer D. Communication: An Introduction to the History of Writing, Printing, Books & Libraries. 4th ed. LC 73-83. 1973. 11.00 (ISBN 0-8108-0588-X). Scarecrow.

Johnson, Elmer D. & Harris, Michael H. History of Libraries in the Western World. 3rd ed. LC 76-25422. 1976. 12.00 (ISBN 0-8108-0949-4). Scarecrow.

Johnson, Elmer H. Crime, Correction, & Society. 4th ed. 1978. text ed. 17.95x (ISBN 0-256-02063-9). Dorsey.

--Natural Regions of Texas. (Research Monograph: No. 8). 1933. pap. 5.00 (ISBN 0-87755-005-0). U of Tex Busn Res.

--Social Problems of Urban Man. 1973. text ed. 17.50x (ISBN 0-256-01124-9). Dorsey.

Johnson, Elsie M. The Man of Geneva. 1977. pap. 3.45 (ISBN 0-85151-254-2). Banner of Truth.

Johnson, Eric, tr. see Alfven, Hannes & Alfven, Kerstin.

Johnson, Eric W. How to Live Through Jr. High School. new ed. LC 75-829. 288p. 1975. 9.95 (ISBN 0-397-01076-1). Lippincott.

--Improve Your Own Spelling. (gr. 6-9). 1977. pap. text ed. 2.95 (ISBN 0-88334-093-3). Ind Sch Pr.

--Love & Sex in Plain Language. 3rd ed. LC 77-5705. (Illus.). (YA) 1977. 8.95 (ISBN 0-397-01231-4). Lippincott.

--Sex: Telling It Straight. LC 79-124545. 1979. 8.95 (ISBN 0-397-01323-X). Lippincott.

--V. D. Venereal Disease and What You Should Do About It. new, rev ed. LC 78-8666. (Illus.). (YA) (gr. 5-12). 1978. 7.95 (ISBN 0-397-31811-1). Lippincott.

Johnson, Eric W., jt. auth. see Calderone, Mary S.

Johnson, Eric W., jt. auth. see Johnson, Corinne B.

Johnson, Eugene M., jt. auth. see Dunn, Albert H.

Johnson, Eyvind. Days of His Grace. LC 77-134666. 1970. 10.00 (ISBN 0-8149-0681-8). Vanguard.

Johnson, F. Swahili-English Dictionary. 15.00 (ISBN 0-685-20193-7). Saphrograph.

Johnson, F., et al. Investigations in Southwest Yukon, Vol. 6. 1964. 12.50 (ISBN 0-686-21691-1). Northland Pubns WA.

Johnson, F. B. Hour of Redemption. 1978. pap. 2.50 (ISBN 0-532-25000-1). Manor Bks.

Johnson, F. Ernest, ed. Foundations of Democracy. (Religion & Civilization Series of the Institute for Religious & Social Studies). 1964. Repr. of 1947 ed. 27.50x (ISBN 0-8154-0120-5). Cooper Sq.

--Wellsprings of the American Spirit. (Religion & Civilization Series of the Institute for Religious & Social Studies). 1964. Repr. of 1948 ed. 22.50x (ISBN 0-8154-0121-3). Cooper Sq.
Johnson, F. N. Lithium Research & Therapy. 1975. 77.50 (ISBN 0-12-386550-6). Acad Pr.
Johnson, F. Roy. Before the Rebel Flag Fell. 1968. 4.95 (ISBN 0-930230-03-5). Johnson NC.
--Fabled Doctor Jim Jordan. 1968. 4.95 (ISBN 0-930230-08-6). Johnson NC.
--In the Old South with Brer Rabbit & His Neighbors. 1977. 4.95 (ISBN 0-930230-35-3). Johnson NC.
--Tales from Old Carolina. LC 65-8878. (Illus.). 1980. Repr. of 1965 ed. 7.50 (ISBN 0-930230-38-8). Johnson NC.
--Tales of Country Folks Down Carolina Way. (Illus.). 1978. 9.50 (ISBN 0-930230-36-1). Johnson NC.
--Witches & Demons in History & Folklore. (Illus.). 1978. Repr. 8.50 (ISBN 0-930230-31-0). Johnson NC.
Johnson, Francis, jt. auth. see Ainsworth, Henry.
Johnson, Frank A., ed. Alienation: Concept, Term, & Meaning. LC 72-7702. 1973. 25.00 (ISBN 0-12-785381-2). Acad Pr.
Johnson, Frank E. The Professional Wine Reference. (Illus.). 354p. 1978. leather gold-gilded cover 19.95 (ISBN 0-9602566-1-X); pap. 8.95 (ISBN 0-9602566-0-1). Beverage Media.
Johnson, Frank P., jt. auth. see Johnson, David W.
Johnson, Franklin. The Development of State Legislation Concerning the Free Negro. LC 78-118. 1979. Repr. of 1919 ed. lib. bdg. 19.25x (ISBN 0-8371-5844-3, JOD&). Greenwood.
Johnson, Franklyn. Defence by Ministry. LC 79-28587. 234p. 1980. text ed. 42.50x (ISBN 0-8419-0598-3). Holmes & Meier.
Johnson, Fred. The Big Bears. Bourne, Russell & Lawrence, Bonnie S., eds. LC 73-83783. (Ranger Rick's Best Friends Ser.). (Illus.). 32p. (gr. 1-6). 1973. 2.50 o.p. (ISBN 0-912186-05-4). Natl Wildlife.
--Turtles & Tortoises. Bourne, Russell & Rifkin, Natalie, eds. LC 73-91357. (Ranger Rick's Best Friends Ser.: No. 2). (Illus.). 32p. (gr. 1-6). 1974. 2.50 o.p. (ISBN 0-912186-10-0). Natl Wildlife.
Johnson, Fred H. The Anatomy of Hallucinations. LC 77-22711. 1978. 18.95x (ISBN 0-88229-155-6). Nelson-Hall.
Johnson, G. Provincial Politics & Indian Nationalism. (South Asian Studies: No. 14). 300p. 1973. 29.95 (ISBN 0-521-20259-0). Cambridge U Pr.
Johnson, G. & Gentry, J. Finney & Miller's Principles of Accounting, Introductory. 8th ed. 1980. 19.95 (ISBN 0-13-317370-4); Pt. 1. working papers 5.95 (ISBN 0-13-317594-4); Part 2. working papers 5.95 (ISBN 0-13-317602-9); practice set 7.95 (ISBN 0-13-317636-3); student guide 6.95 (ISBN 0-13-317628-2). P-H.
Johnson, G., jt. ed. see Gentry, J.
Johnson, G. G., ed. see United States National Resources Planning Board, Public Works Committee.
Johnson, G. Orville, jt. auth. see Cruickshank, William M.
Johnson, Gail C. High Level Manpower in Iran: From Hidden Conflict to Crisis. LC 79-21419. (Praeger Special Studies Ser.). 136p. 1980. 24.50 (ISBN 0-03-053366-X). Praeger.
Johnson, Gary L. Come Songbook. 1980. pap. 1.95 (ISBN 0-87123-777-6, 280777). Bethany Fell.
--Son Songs for Christian Folk, 2 vols. Incl. Vol. I. pap. 1.25 (ISBN 0-87123-509-9, 280509); Vol. II. pap. 1.50 (ISBN 0-87123-532-3, 280532). 1975. Bethany Fell.
--Thanks Songbook. 1980. pap. 1.95 (ISBN 0-87123-776-8, 280776). Bethany Fell.
Johnson, Gayle, jt. ed. see Gordon, Chad.
Johnson, George. The Story of the Church. LC 80-51329. 521p. (gr. 9). 1980. pap. 10.00 (ISBN 0-89555-156-X). Tan Bks Pubs.
Johnson, George & Tanner, Don. The Bible & the Bermuda Triangle. 1977. pap. 2.95 (ISBN 0-88270-321-8). Logos.
Johnson, George A. & Hendrick, Thomas E. Computer Oriented Production Exercise: An Experience in Understanding the Controlling the Behavior of a Productive System. 54p. 1977. 4.00 (ISBN 0-686-64181-7). U CO Busn Res Div.
Johnson, George E., II. The Nebraskan. 240p. 1981. write for info. (ISBN 0-89305-036-9). Anna Pub.
Johnson, Gerald W. America Grows Up: A History for Peter. (Illus.). (gr. 5 up). 1960. 8.75 (ISBN 0-688-21015-5). Morrow.
--America Is Born: A History for Peter. (Illus.). (gr. 5 up). 1959. 8.75 (ISBN 0-688-21071-6). Morrow.
--America-Watching: Perspectives in the Course of an Incredible Century. LC 76-12459. 368p. 1976. 12.95 (ISBN 0-916144-05-4). Stemmer Hse.
--The Cabinet. (Illus.). (gr. 7 up). 1966. PLB 7.44 (ISBN 0-688-31136-9). Morrow.
--The Congress. (Illus.). (gr. 5-9). 1963. PLB 7.44 (ISBN 0-688-31182-2). Morrow.
--The Presidency. (Illus.). (gr. 5-9). 1962. 7.75 (ISBN 0-688-21465-7). Morrow.
Johnson, Gil, ed. see Demura, Funio.
Johnson, Gilbert, ed. see Lee, Chong.
Johnson, Gilbert, et al, eds. see Chun, Richard.
Johnson, Gordon E. Basics of Circuit Analysis for Practicing Engineers. LC 71-150505. 1971. 10.95 (ISBN 0-8436-0320-8); pap. 4.95 o.p. (ISBN 0-8436-0321-6). CBI Pub.
Johnson, Guy B. Folk Culture on St. Helena Island, South Carolina. LC 68-5945. xxiv, 183p. Repr. of 1930 ed. 15.00 (ISBN 0-8103-5015-7). Gale.
Johnson, H. Patterns of Pulmonary Interstitial Disease. (Illus.). 320p. 1981. 15.00 (ISBN 0-87527-218-5). Green. Postponed.
Johnson, H. D. Progress in Animal Biometeorology: The Effects of Weather & Climate on Animals; Vol 1 Period 1963-1973, 2 pts. Incl. Pt. 1. Effects of Temperature on Animals: Including Effects of Humidity, Radiation & Wind. 624p. 1976. text ed. 115.00 (ISBN 90-265-0196-X); Effect of Light, High Actitude, Noise, Electric, Magnetic & Electro-Magnetic Fields, Ionization, Gravity & Air Pollutions on Animals. 322p. 1976. text ed. 57.00 (ISBN 90-265-0235-4). (Progress in Biometeorology). 1976 (Pub. by Swets Pub Serv Holland). Swets North Am.
Johnson, H. Earle. Symphony Hall, Boston. (Music Reprint Ser.). 1979. Repr. of 1950 ed. lib. bdg. 32.50 (ISBN 0-306-79518-3). Da Capo.
Johnson, H. Wayne, ed. Rural Human Services: A Book of Readings. LC 79-91102. 228p. 1980. pap. text ed. 7.95 (ISBN 0-87581-248-1). Peacock Pubs.
Johnson, H. Webster & Savage, William G. Administrative Office Management. 1968. 16.95 (ISBN 0-201-03325-9). A-W.
Johnson, Harold L. Cities of the Blue Distance. (Illus.). 104p. 1980. 10.50x (ISBN 0-937308-01-3); pap. 7.25 (ISBN 0-937308-02-1). Hearthstone.
--Disclosure of Corporate Social Performance: Survey, Evaluation, & Prospects. LC 78-10594. (Praeger Special Studies). 1979. 20.95 (ISBN 0-03-047206-7). Praeger.
Johnson, Harold V. General-Industrial Machine Shop. 1979. text ed. 17.00 (ISBN 0-87002-293-8); student guide 2.96 (ISBN 0-87002-295-4); visual masters 13.40 (ISBN 0-87002-054-4). Bennett IL.
--Technical Metals. rev. ed. (gr. 10-12). 1973. text ed. 19.96 (ISBN 0-87002-139-7); wrbk. 6.40 (ISBN 0-87002-147-8). Bennett IL.
Johnson, Harold V., ed. see Ray, J. Edgar.
Johnson, Harriet. Honolulu Zoo Riddles. (Illus.). 1974. pap. 1.25 (ISBN 0-686-63590-6). Topgallant.
Johnson, Harry & Lightfoot, Frederick. Maritime New York in Nineteenth Century Photographs. (Illus.). 160p. (Orig.). 1980. pap. 7.95 (ISBN 0-486-23963-2). Dover.
Johnson, Harry G. Macroeconomics & Monetary Theory. 214p. 1972. 14.95x (ISBN 0-202-06053-5). Aldine Pub.
--The Theory of Income Distribution. 1973. 18.00x o.p. (ISBN 0-85641-006-3, Pub. by Basil Blackwell England). Biblio Dist.
Johnson, Harry G., jt. auth. see Frenkel, Jacob A.
Johnson, Harry, Jr., jt. auth. see Helmkamp, George K.
Johnson, Harry L., ed. State & Local Tax Problems. LC 69-10113. 1969. 12.50x (ISBN 0-87049-089-3). U of Tenn Pr.
Johnson, Haynes. Bay of Pigs. (Illus.). 1964. 10.50 o.p. (ISBN 0-393-04263-4). Norton.
Johnson, Helgi & Smith, Bennett L., eds. The Megatectonics of Continents & Oceans. LC 69-13555. 1970. 20.00x (ISBN 0-8135-0625-5). Rutgers U Pr.
Johnson, Henry C., Jr. The Public School & Moral Education. (The Education of the Public & the Public School Ser.). 96p. (Orig.). 1981. pap. 3.95 (ISBN 0-8298-0420-X). Pilgrim NY.
Johnson, Hildegard B. Order Upon the Land: The U. S. Rectangular Land Survey & the Upper Mississippi Country. (The Andrew H. Clark Ser in the Historical Geography of North America). (Illus.). 350p. 1976. text ed. 12.95x (ISBN 0-19-501912-1); pap. text ed. 6.95x (ISBN 0-19-501913-X). Oxford U Pr.
Johnson, Howard. Home in the Woods: Pioneer Life in Indiana. LC 77-74426. (Illus.). 104p. 1978. Repr. of 1951 ed. 8.95x (ISBN 0-253-32842-X). Ind U Pr.
Johnson, Hubert R. Who Then Is Paul? Chevy Chase Manuscripts, ed. LC 80-1406. 272p. 1981. lib. bdg. 19.75 (ISBN 0-8191-1364-6); pap. text ed. 10.75 (ISBN 0-8191-1365-4). U Pr of Amer.
Johnson, Ira D. Glenway Wescott: The Paradox of Voice. LC 74-138301. 1971. 11.95 (ISBN 0-8046-0572-6, Natl U). Kennikat.
Johnson, Ira D. & Johnson, Christiane, eds. Les Americanistes: New French Criticism on Modern American Fiction. LC 76-58512. (National University Publications Literary Criticism Ser.). (Illus.). 1977. 12.95 o.p. (ISBN 0-8046-9176-2). Kennikat.
Johnson, Irene. Life & Letters of Paul. (Find-a-Word Puzzles Ser.). 48p. (Orig.). (gr. 6 up). 1981. pap. 1.25 (ISBN 0-87239-448-4, 2838). Standard Pub.
Johnson, Irvin E. Instant Mortgage-Equity: Extended Tables of Overall Rates. LC 80-7729. (Lexington Books Real Estate & Urban Land Economics Special Ser.). 464p. 1980. 23.95 (ISBN 0-669-03808-3). Lexington Bks.
--The Instant Mortgage Equity Technique. LC 72-6464. (Special Ser. in Real Estate & Urban Land Economics). 400p. 1972. 17.95 (ISBN 0-669-84749-6). Lexington Bks.
--Selling Real Estate by Mortgage Equity Analysis. LC 74-15543. (Special Ser. in Real Estate & Urban Land Economics). (Illus.). 352p. 1976. 18.95 (ISBN 0-669-95588-4). Lexington Bks.
Johnson, Isabel, jt. auth. see Ridenour, Nina.
Johnson, J., jt. auth. see Johnson, D.
Johnson, J. Alan & Anderson, Ralph R., eds. The Renin-Angiotensin System. (Advances in Experimental Medicine & Biology Ser.: Vol. 130). 315p. 1980. 37.50 (ISBN 0-306-40469-9, Plenum Pr). Plenum Pub.
Johnson, J. C., ed. Sustained Release Medications. LC 80-23455. (Chemical Technology Review: No. 177). (Illus.). 412p. 1981. 54.00 (ISBN 0-8155-0826-3). Noyes.
Johnson, J. Donald, ed. Disinfection Chemistry & Biology. LC 79-55143. Date not set. 39.95 (ISBN 0-250-40267-X). Ann Arbor Science. Postponed.
Johnson, J. Douglas. Advertising Today. LC 78-15897. 416p. 1978. pap. text ed. 15.95 (ISBN 0-574-19355-3, 13-2355); instr's guide avail. (ISBN 0-574-19356-1, 13-2356). SRA.
Johnson, J. Douglas, jt. auth. see Zeigler, Sherilyn.
Johnson, J. E. Full Circle. (War Book Ser.). 288p. 1980. pap. 2.50 (ISBN 0-553-13568-6). Bantam.
Johnson, J. G., et al. Pridolian & Early Gedinnian Age Brachiopods from the Roberts Mountains Formation of Central Nevada. (U. C. Publ. in Geological Sciences: Vol. 100). 1973. pap. 11.00x (ISBN 0-520-09447-6). U of Cal Pr.
--Wenlockian & Ludlovian Ages Brachiopods from the Roberts Mountain Formation of Central Nevada. (Publications in Geological Sciences: Vol. 115). 1976. pap. 13.75x (ISBN 0-520-09542-1). U of Cal Pr.
Johnson, J. H. Suburban Growth: Geographical Processes at the Edge of the Western City. LC 73-8195. 272p. 1974. 31.75 (ISBN 0-471-44390-5, Pub. by Wiley-Interscience). Wiley.
--Urban Geography. 2nd ed. 217p. 1973. text ed. 17.25 (ISBN 0-08-016927-9); pap. text ed. 7.00 (ISBN 0-08-016928-7). Pergamon.
Johnson, J. H., jt. auth. see Cooke, R. V.
Johnson, J. M., jt. ed. see Douglas, J. D.
Johnson, J. P. Nature & Treatment of Articulation Disorders. (Illus.). 304p. 1980. 19.75 (ISBN 0-398-03983-6). C C Thomas.
Johnson, J. Richard. How to Troubleshoot a Color TV Receiver. 1978. pap. 9.50 (ISBN 0-8104-0820-1). Hayden.
Johnson, J. Stewart. Eileen Gray: Designer. LC 79-33188. (Illus.). 1979. pap. 7.95 (ISBN 0-87070-308-0). Museum Mod Art.
Johnson, Jack. Jack Johnson in the Ring & Out. LC 72-162515. (Illus.). ix, 259p. 1975. Repr. of 1927 ed. 15.00 (ISBN 0-8103-4047-X). Gale.
Johnson, James. Profits, Power & Piety: An Inside Look at What Goes on Behind the Velvet Curtains of Christian Business. LC 72-83881. 1980. pap. 2.50 (ISBN 0-89081-240-3). Harvest Hse.
Johnson, James A., et al. Foundation of American Education: Readings. 4th ed. 1979. pap. 9.85x (ISBN 0-205-06565-1). Allyn.
--Introduction to the Foundations of American Education. 3rd ed. 560p. 1976. text ed. 13.95x o.s.i. (ISBN 0-205-05018-2); instr's manual free o.s.i. (ISBN 0-205-05019-0). Allyn.
--Introduction to the Foundations of American Education. 4th ed. 1979. text ed. 16.95 (ISBN 0-205-06566-X); instr's man. avail. (ISBN 0-205-06567-8). Allyn.
Johnson, James B. Daughter & Shadow. (Science Fiction Ser.). 1981. pap. 1.95 (ISBN 0-87997-605-5, UJ1605). DAW Bks.
--Daystar & Shadow. (Science Fiction Ser.). 1981. pap. 1.95 (ISBN 0-87997-605-5, UJ1605, Daw Bks). DAW Bks.
Johnson, James C., jt. auth. see Wood, Donald F.
Johnson, James E. Freedom from Depression. (Orig.). 1981. pap. 2.95 (ISBN 0-88270-494-X). Logos.
Johnson, James E. & Balsiger, David W. Beyond Defeat. 224p. 1980. pap. cancelled (ISBN 0-553-12651-2). Bantam.
Johnson, James H., jt. auth. see Schwartz, Steven.
Johnson, James H., jt. auth. see Williams, Thomas A.
Johnson, James L. All the King's Men. nd ed. LC 80-83842. 328p. 1981. pap. 3.25 (ISBN 0-89081-267-5). Harvest Hse.
--Code Name Sebastian. 1978. pap. 2.95 (ISBN 0-310-37402-2). Zondervan.
--How to Enjoy Life & Not Feel Guilty. LC 79-85748. 176p. 1980. pap. 4.95 (ISBN 0-89081-121-0). Harvest Hse.
--Kinetics of Coal Gasification. LC 79-10439. 1979. 27.50 (ISBN 0-471-05575-1, Pub. by Wiley-Interscience). Wiley.
--The Last Train from Canton. (Sebastian Suspense Ser.). 288p. (Orig.). 1981. pap. 6.95 (ISBN 0-310-26631-9). Zondervan.
--Sepastian Agente Secreto. Lievano, Francisco, tr. 1977. pap. 2.50 (ISBN 0-311-37021-7). Casa Bautista.
Johnson, James R. Managing for Productivity in Data Processing. 1980. pap. text ed. 21.50 (ISBN 0-89435-041-2). QED Info Sci.
Johnson, James R., jt. auth. see Milhollen, Hirst D.
Johnson, James W. Along This Way: The Autobiography of James Weldon Johnson. LC 72-8404. (Civil Liberties in American History). (Illus.). 450p. 1973. Repr. of 1933 ed. lib. bdg. 39.50 (ISBN 0-306-70539-7). Da Capo.
--God's Trombones. (Poets Ser). 1976. pap. 3.50 (ISBN 0-14-042217-X). Penguin.
--Utopian Literature: A Selection. 1968. pap. text ed. 1.95 (ISBN 0-394-30996-0, RanC). Random.
Johnson, Jane. Maroni De Chypre. (Studies in Mediterranean Archaeology Ser.: LIX). 1980. text ed. 42.00x (ISBN 91-85058-94-7). Humanities.
Johnson, Janeen A. Games to Improve Perceptual Skills of Pre-Schoolers: Ideas for Parents & Teachers. 1978. pap. text ed. 0.25 (ISBN 0-8134-2049-0, 2049); for 25 copies 4.38; for 100 copies 14.75. Interstate.
Johnson, Jeffrey, jt. auth. see Childs, David.
Johnson, Jerry W. & Boxx, W. Randy. Formalized Planning for Institutions of Higher Learning. 1978. 4.00 (ISBN 0-938004-04-2). U MS Bus Econ.
Johnson, Jesse J. Black Armed Forces Officers, 1736-1971: A Documented Pictorial History. LC 75-178014. (Illus.). 170p. 8.95 (ISBN 0-915044-10-2). Carver Pub.
--The Black Soldier. 1976. 3.95 (ISBN 0-915044-04-8); pap. 1.50 rev. ed. (ISBN 0-915044-05-6); pap. 1.10 pocketbook (ISBN 0-915044-06-4). Carver Pub.
--Ebony Brass. 1976. 8.00 (ISBN 0-915044-01-3); pap. 2.00 (ISBN 0-915044-02-1); pap. 1.50 pocketbook (ISBN 0-915044-03-X). Carver Pub.
--A Pictorial History of Black Servicemen: Air Force, Army, Navy, Marines. LC 70-130752. (Illus.). 10.00 (ISBN 0-915044-09-9). Carver Pub.
--A Pictorial History of the Black Soldier in the United States (1619-1969) in Peace & War. 1976. 10.00 (ISBN 0-915044-08-0); pap. 3.00 (ISBN 0-915044-07-2). Carver Pub.
--Roots of Two Black Marine Sergeant Majors. LC 78-55171. (Illus.). 1978. 10.00 (ISBN 0-915044-13-7); pap. 2.25 (ISBN 0-915044-14-5). Carver Pub.
Johnson, Jim. Lasers. LC 80-17871. (A Look Inside Ser.). (Illus.). 48p. (gr. 4-12). 1981. PLB 10.25 (ISBN 0-8172-1400-3). Raintree Child.
Johnson, Joan D. & Xanthos, Paul. Tennis. 4th ed. (Pysical Education Activities Ser.). 1981. pap. text ed. 3.25x (ISBN 0-697-07174-X). Wm C Brown.
Johnson, Joanna. Working at Home for Profit. 243p. 1980. 25.00x (ISBN 0-631-12771-2, Pub. by Basil Blackwell); pap. 9.95x (ISBN 0-631-12583-3). Biblio Dist.
Johnson, Joe, jt. auth. see Racina, Thom.
Johnson, John E. The Sky Is Blue, the Grass Is Green. (Cloth Bks.). (Illus.). 8p. (ps). pap. 2.50 (ISBN 0-394-84403-3, BYR). Random.
Johnson, John E., illus. This Is My House. (Golden Sturdy Shape Bk.). (Illus.). 14p. (ps). 1981. 2.95 (ISBN 0-307-12251-4, Golden Pr). Western Pub.
Johnson, John J. The Military & Society in Latin America. 1964. 15.00x (ISBN 0-8047-0198-9); pap. 4.50 o.p. (ISBN 0-8047-0199-7). Stanford U Pr.

Johnson, John J., ed. The Role of the Military in Underdeveloped Countries: Papers of a Conference Sponsored by the Rand Corp. at Santa Monica, Calif. in August 1959. LC 80-25808. viii, 423p. 1981. Repr. of 1967 ed. lib. bdg. 39.75x (ISBN 0-313-22784-5, JORM). Greenwood.
--The Role of the Military in Underdeveloped Countries: Papers of a Conference Sponsored by the Rand Corp. at Santa Monica, Calif. in August 1959. LC 80-25808. viii, 423p. 1981. Repr. of 1962 ed. lib. bdg. 39.75x (ISBN 0-313-22784-5, JORM). Greenwood.
Johnson, John M. Doing Field Research. LC 74-27599. 1975. 12.95 (ISBN 0-02-916600-4). Free Pr.
--Doing Field Research. LC 74-27599. 1978. pap. text ed. 7.95 (ISBN 0-02-916610-1). Free Pr.
Johnson, John S. The Rosary in Action. LC 54-8388. 1977. pap. 4.00 (ISBN 0-89555-023-7, 185). TAN Bks Pubs.
Johnson, John W. American Legal Culture, 1908-1940. LC 80-1027. (Contributions in Legal Studies: No. 16). 192p. 1981. lib. bdg. 23.95 (ISBN 0-313-22337-8, JAM/). Greenwood.
Johnson, Johnny R., jt. auth. see Johnson, David E.
Johnson, Josephine W., jt. auth. see Stock, Dennis.
Johnson, Joy & Johnson, Marvin. Tell Me Papa. 1980. pap. 6.95 boards (ISBN 0-930194-02-0). Highly Specialized.
Johnson, Judith K., ed. see Newcomb, Charles K.
Johnson, Judith M. Victorian House-Keeping: A Combined Study of Restoration & Photography. Smith, Linda H., ed. 1978. pap. 3.95 (ISBN 0-936386-05-3). Creative Learning.
Johnson, K., jt. auth. see Morrow, K.
Johnson, Karen, jt. auth. see Korn, Errol R.
Johnson, Karl R., Jr. The Written Spirit: Thematic & Rhetorical Structure in Wordsworth's the Prelude. (Salzburg Studies in English Literature, Romantic Reassessment: No. 72). 1978. pap. text ed. 25.00x (ISBN 0-391-01437-4). Humanities.
Johnson, Kathryn A. see Kane, Lucile M.
Johnson, Keene. The Public Papers of Governor Keen Johnson, Nineteen Thirty-Nine to Nineteen Forty-Three. Sexton, Robert F., ed. LC 79-57562. (The Public Papers of the Governors of Kentucky Ser.). 1981. 28.00x (ISBN 0-8131-0605-2). U Pr of Ky.
Johnson, Keith. The Art of Trumpet Playing. 168p. 1981. 11.95. Iowa St U Pr.
Johnson, Kenneth. Mexican Democracy: A Critical View. rev ed. LC 77-83473. (Praeger Special Studies). 1978. 25.95 (ISBN 0-03-027711-6); pap. 10.95 (ISBN 0-03-028151-2). Praeger.
Johnson, Kenneth F. & Ogle, Nina M. Illegal Mexican Aliens in the United States: A Teaching Manual on Impact Dimensions & Alternative Futures. LC 78-62177. 1978. pap. text ed. 9.25 (ISBN 0-8191-0575-9). U Pr of Amer.
Johnson, Kenneth G., et al. Nothing Never Happens: Exercises to Trigger Group Discussion & Promote Self-Discovery with Selected Readings. LC 72-91270. 352p. 1974. pap. text ed. 10.95x (ISBN 0-02-475140-5); tchr's ed. 10.95x (ISBN 0-02-475130-8). Macmillan.
Johnson, Kenneth P. & Jaenicke, Henry R. Evaluating Internal Control: Concepts, Guidelines, Procedures, Documentation. LC 79-23172. 1980. 39.95 (ISBN 0-471-05620-0, Ronald). Wiley.
Johnson, Kenneth R. The Succubus. (Orig.). 1980. pap. 2.50 (ISBN 0-440-17716-2). Dell.
Johnson, Kenneth W. & Walker, Willard C. The Science of Hi-Fidelity. LC 77-79557. (Illus.). 1981. pap. text ed. 16.95 (ISBN 0-8403-2297-6). Kendall-Hunt.
--Understanding Audio. (Illus.). 256p. 1980. pap. text ed. 5.75 (ISBN 0-8403-2216-X). Kendall-Hunt.
Johnson, L. D. Moments of Reflection. LC 80-67779. 1980. pap. 3.95 (ISBN 0-8054-5287-7). Broadman.
Johnson, L. M., jt. auth. see Steffensen, Arnold J.
Johnson, L. Murphy, jt. auth. see Steffensen, Arnold R.
Johnson, Lady Bird. Texas: A Roadside View. (Illus.). 51p. 1980. 12.00 (ISBN 0-911536-89-2). Trinity U Pr.
Johnson, Lanny L. The Comprehensive Arthroscopic Examination of the Knee. LC 77-21646. (Illus.). 1977. 47.50 (ISBN 0-8016-2534-3). Mosby.
Johnson, Larry. Fix Your Volkswagen. 1980. 6.00 (ISBN 0-87006-297-2). Goodheart.
Johnson, Larry, jt. auth. see Toboldt, William K.
Johnson, Leander F. & Curl, Elroy. Methods for Research on the Ecology of Soil-Borne Plant Pathogens. LC 77-176196. 1972. text ed. 24.95 (ISBN 0-8087-1016-8). Burgess.
Johnson, Lee, ed. The Painting of Eugene Delacroix: A Critical Catalogue, Vols. 1 & 2: 1816-1831. (Illus.). 556p. 1981. Set. 195.00 (ISBN 0-19-817314-8). Oxford U Pr.
Johnson, Lee M. The Metaphor of Painting: Essays on Baudelaire, Ruskin, Proust & Pater. Kuspit, Donald B., ed. (Studies in Fine Arts: Criticism). 249p. 1980. 24.95 (ISBN 0-8357-1092-0, Pub. by UMI Res Pr). Univ Microfilms.
Johnson, Lee W. & Riess, R. Dean. Introduction to Linear Algebra. LC 80-19984. (Mathematics Ser.). (Illus.). 352p. 1981. text ed. 16.95 (ISBN 0-201-03392-5). A-W.
--Numerical Analysis. LC 76-14658. (Illus.). 1977. text ed. 18.95 (ISBN 0-201-03442-5). A-W.
Johnson, Leonard, et al, eds. Physiology of the Gastrointestinal Tract, 2 vols. 1600p. 1981. 130.00 (ISBN 0-89004-440-6). Raven.
Johnson, Leonard R. Gastrointestinal Physiology. 2nd ed. LC 80-23381. (Illus.). 160p. 1981. text ed. 13.95 (ISBN 0-8016-2532-7). Mosby.
Johnson, Lester W., ed. see Hensher, David A.
Johnson, Lois. Christmas Stories Round the World. (Illus.). (gr. 3-7). 1970. pap. 2.95 o.s.i. (ISBN 0-528-87032-7). Rand.
Johnson, Lois G., et al. College English: Effective Usage Through Linguistics. rev. ed. LC 73-94293. (Illus.). 213p. 1980. pap. text ed. 10.15 (ISBN 0-913310-07-7). PAR Inc.
Johnson, Lois H. Cornflakes. (Illus.). 80p. 1981. 6.00 (ISBN 0-682-49695-2). Exposition.
Johnson, Louise. Outpost Encounters. LC 79-92927. (gr. 4 up). 1980. 12.95 (ISBN 0-89002-082-5); pap. 4.95 (ISBN 0-89002-081-7). Northwoods Pr.
Johnson, Lucile P. Miracles & Parables of the Bible. (Quiz & Puzzle Bks). 1971. pap. 2.95 (ISBN 0-8010-5007-3). Baker Bk.
Johnson, Luke T. The Literary Function of Possession in Luke-Acts. LC 77-21055. (Society of Biblical Literature. Dissertation Ser.: No. 39). 1977. pap. 7.50 (ISBN 0-89130-200-X, 060139). Scholars Pr Ca.
--Sharing Possessions: Mandate & Symbol of Faith, No. 9. Brueggemann, Walter & Donahue, John R., eds. LC 80-2390. (Overtures to Biblical Theology Ser.). 176p. (Orig.). 1981. pap. 8.95 (ISBN 0-8006-1534-4, 1-1534). Fortress.
Johnson, M. & Liebert. Statistics: Tool of the Behavioral Sciences. 1977. 16.95 (ISBN 0-13-844704-7). P-H.
Johnson, M., jt. auth. see Denne, L.
Johnson, M., jt. auth. see Harvey, J.
Johnson, M., jt. ed. see Taylor, P.
Johnson, M. Bruce, ed. Resolving the Housing Crisis. (Pacific Institute on Public Policy Research Ser.). 1981. price not set professional reference (ISBN 0-88410-381-1). Ballinger Pub.
Johnson, M. Bruce, jt. ed. see Hyman, Allen.
Johnson, M. E. I Heard the Trumpet. 5.95 o.p. (ISBN 0-8062-0940-2). Carlton.
Johnson, M. H., jt. ed. see Edinin, M.
Johnson, M. H., jt. ed. see Edwards, R. G.
Johnson, M. L., jt. auth. see Graham, Jerry.
Johnson, Manly. Patrick White. LC 76-15652. (Modern Literature Ser.). Date not set. 10.95 (ISBN 0-686-64253-8). Ungar. Postponed.
--Virginia Woolf. LC 72-79944. (Modern Literature Ser.). 1973. 10.95 (ISBN 0-8044-2424-1). Ungar.
Johnson, Margaret, jt. auth. see Hawes, Carolyn.
Johnson, Margaret, tr. Dezoito, Nao Ha Tempo Que Perder. (Portuguese Bks.). 1979. 1.30 (ISBN 0-8297-0656-9). Life Pubs Intl.
--Dieciocho, No Hay Tiempo Que Perder. (Spanish Bks.). (Span.). 1978. 1.65 (ISBN 0-8297-0533-3). Life Pubs Intl.
Johnson, Margaret K. & Hilton, Dale K. Japanese Prints Today: Tradition with Innovation. (Illus.). 256p. (Orig.). 1980. pap. 9.95 (ISBN 0-8048-1345-0, Pub. by Shufunotomo Co Ltd Japan). C E Tuttle.
Johnson, Marilyn L. Images of Women in the Works of Thomas Heywood. (Salzburg Studies in English Literature, Jacobean Drama Studies: No. 42). 178p. 1974. pap. text ed. 25.00x (ISBN 0-391-01438-2). Humanities.
Johnson, Marion. Functional Administration in Physical & Health Education. LC 76-13089. (Illus.). 1977. text ed. 17.75 (ISBN 0-395-20635-9); inst. manual 1.25 (ISBN 0-395-20636-7); study guide 8.25 (ISBN 0-395-20637-5). HM.
Johnson, Marta K., ed. & tr. from Czech. Recycling the Prague Linguistic Circle. (Linguistica Extranea Ser.: Studia 6). 103p. 1978. pap. 5.50 (ISBN 0-89720-010-1). Karoma.
Johnson, Martha S., jt. auth. see Lahey, Benjamin B.
Johnson, Martin. Safari: A Saga of the African Blue. LC 72-170251. (Tower Bks). (Illus.). x, 294p. 1972. Repr. of 1928 ed. 18.00 (ISBN 0-8103-3934-X). Gale.
Johnson, Martin W. The Palinurid & Scyllarid Lobster Larvae of the Tropical Eastern Pacific & Their Distribution As Related to the Prevailing Hydrography. (Bulletin of the Scripps Institution of Oceanography: Vol. 19). 1971. pap. 6.00x (ISBN 0-520-09388-7). U of Cal Pr.
Johnson, Marvin, jt. auth. see Johnson, Joy.
Johnson, Mary O. Burma Diary Nineteen Thirty-Eight to Nineteen Forty-Two. 1981. 5.75 (ISBN 0-8062-1697-2). Carlton.
Johnson, Marylou. Celebrated Thoughts. 60p. 1980. 3.95 (ISBN 0-8059-2737-9). Dorrance.
Johnson, Maurice O. Fielding's Art of Fiction. LC 61-5547. 1961. 7.50x o.p. (ISBN 0-8122-7260-9). U of Pa Pr.
Johnson, Mendal W. Let's Go Play at the Adams. 288p. 1980. pap. 2.50 (ISBN 0-553-14139-2). Bantam.
Johnson, Michael R., ed. Kenneth Callahan: Universal Voyage. LC 73-96. (Index of Art in the Pacific Northwest Ser: No. 6). (Illus.). 80p. 1973. 15.00 (ISBN 0-295-95270-9); pap. 7.50 (ISBN 0-295-95271-7). U of Wash Pr.
Johnson, Mildred E., tr. Swan, Cygnets, & Owl: An Anthology of Modernist Poetry in Spanish America. LC 56-12576. 1956. 15.00x o.p. (ISBN 0-8262-0599-2). U of Mo Pr.
Johnson, Miriam M., jt. auth. see Stockard, Jean.
Johnson, Moulton K. The Hand Book. (Illus.). 130p. 1973. 12.50 (ISBN 0-398-02595-9). C C Thomas.
Johnson, Myrtle E. & Snook, H. J. Seashore Animals of the Pacific Coast. (Illus.). 12.50 (ISBN 0-8446-2336-9). Peter Smith.
Johnson, N. L. & Kotz, S. I. Discrete Distributions: Distributions in Statistics. (Wiley Series in Math & Statistics). 1970. 31.95 (ISBN 0-471-44360-3, Pub. by Wiley-Interscience). Wiley.
Johnson, N. L., jt. auth. see Elderton, W. P.
Johnson, Nancy E., ed. The Diary of Gathorne Hardy, Later Lord Cranbook, 1866-1892: Political Selections. 650p. 1981. 144.00 (ISBN 0-19-822622-5). Oxford U Pr.
Johnson, Nancy P. Sources of Compiled Legislative Histories: Bibliography of Government Documents, Periodical Articles & Books, 1st Congress - 94th Congress. (AALL Publications Ser.: No. 14). 146p. 1979. loose-leaf in vinyl, 3-ring binder 22.50x (ISBN 0-8377-0112-0). Rothman.
Johnson, Ned K. Character Variation & Evolution of Sibling Species in the Empidonax Difficilis-Flavescens Complex (Aves: Tyrannidae) (University of California Publications in Zoology: Vol. 112). 1980. monograph 10.50x (ISBN 0-520-09599-5). U of Cal Pr.
Johnson, Nevil. Government in the Federal Republic of Germany: The Executive at Work. LC 73-12759. 232p. 1974. text ed. 16.50 (ISBN 0-08-017699-2). Pergamon.
--In Search of the Constitution: Reflections on State & Society in Britain. LC 76-43316. 1977. text ed. 23.00 (ISBN 0-08-021379-0). Pergamon.
Johnson, Nicholas L. Handbook of Soviet Lunar & Planetary Exploration. (Science & Technology Ser.: Vol. 47). 276p. 1979. lib. bdg. 35.00 (ISBN 0-87703-130-4); pap. text ed. 25.00 (ISBN 0-87703-131-2). Univelt Inc.
Johnson, Norman. The Complete Puppy & Dog Book. rev. ed. LC 77-5685. (Illus.). 1977. 16.95 (ISBN 0-689-10808-7). Atheneum.
Johnson, Norman & Kotz, Samuel. Urn Models & Their Application: An Approach to Modern Discrete Probability Theory. LC 76-58846. (Wiley Series in Probability & Mathematical Statistics). 1977. 31.50 (ISBN 0-471-44630-0, Pub. by Wiley-Interscience). Wiley.
Johnson, Norman, ed. see Landscape Architecture Magazine.
Johnson, Norman L. & Kotz, Samuel. Distributions in Statistics: Continuous Multivariate Distributions. LC 72-1342. (Probability & Statistics Ser.). 368p. 1972. 33.95 (ISBN 0-471-44370-0, Pub. by Wiley-Interscience). Wiley.
Johnson, Norman L. & Kotz, Samuel I. Continuous Univariate Distribution: Distributions in Statistics, 2 vols. (Wiley Series in Probability & Mathematical Statistics-Applied Probability & Statistics Section). 1970. Vol. 1. 31.95 (ISBN 0-471-44626-2, Pub. by Wiley-Interscience); Vol. 2. 31.95 (ISBN 0-471-44627-0). Wiley.
Johnson, Norman L., jt. auth. see Elandt-Johnson, Regina C.
Johnson, Norman L., jt. auth. see Ketz, Samuel.
Johnson, O. An Essay on West African Therapeutics. Singer, Philip & Titus, Elizabeth A., eds. 1981. 17.50 (ISBN 0-932426-09-3). Trado-Medic.
Johnson, Olaf A. Fluid Power for Industrial Use: Hydraulics, Vol. 2. 224p. 1981. lib. bdg. 12.50 (ISBN 0-89874-048-7). Krieger.
Johnson, Oliver A. Skepticism & Cognitivism: A Study in the Foundations of Knowledge. LC 77-91743. 1979. 16.50x (ISBN 0-520-03620-4). U of Cal Pr.
Johnson, Overton. Route Across the Rocky Mountains. Winter, William H., ed. LC 77-87648. (The American Scene Ser). (Illus.). 200p. 1972. Repr. of 1932 ed. lib. bdg. 25.00 (ISBN 0-306-71780-8). Da Capo.
Johnson, Owen. Stover at Yale. LC 68-22128. 1968. pap. 1.50 o.s.i. (ISBN 0-02-021780-3, Collier). Macmillan.
Johnson, P. S. The Economics of Invention & Innovation: With a Case Study of the Development of the Hovercraft. 329p. 1975. 36.00x (ISBN 0-85520-078-2, Pub by Martin Robertson England). Biblio Dist.
Johnson, Pamela H. A Bonfire. 192p. 1981. 10.95 (ISBN 0-684-16853-7, ScribT). Scribner.
--Too Dear for My Possessing. LC 72-2007. 319p. 1973. 7.95 o.p. (ISBN 0-684-13052-1, ScribT). Scribner.
--The Unspeakable Skipton. 249p. 1981. 10.95 (ISBN 0-684-16336-5, ScribT). Scribner.
Johnson, Patricia J., jt. auth. see Burns, Kenneth R.
Johnson, Paul. The Recovery of Freedom. 232p. 1980. 19.95x (ISBN 0-631-12562-0, Pub. by Basil Blackwell England). Biblio Dist.
Johnson, Paul, jt. auth. see Richards, Larry.
Johnson, Paul B. From Sticks & Stones: Personal Adventures in Mathematics. LC 74-23322. (Illus.). 552p. 1975. text ed. 16.95 (ISBN 0-574-19115-1, 13-6005); instr's guide avail. (ISBN 0-574-19116-X, 13-6006). SRA.
Johnson, Paul C. Peripheral Circulation. LC 77-26858. 1978. 41.50 (ISBN 0-471-44637-8, Pub. by Wiley Medical). Wiley.
--Sierra Album: A Pictorial History. LC 73-144276. 1971. 4.95 o.p. (ISBN 0-385-04832-7). Doubleday.
Johnson, Paul E. The Middle Years. LC 70-154489. (Pocket Counsel Bks). (Orig.). 1971. pap. 1.75x o.p. (ISBN 0-8006-1105-5, 1-1105). Fortress.
--A Shopkeeper's Millennium: Society & Revivals in Rochester, N. Y. 1815 to 1837. 1979. 10.95 (ISBN 0-8090-8654-9, AmCen); pap. 5.95 (ISBN 0-8090-0136-5). Hill & Wang.
Johnson, Pauline. Creating with Paper. LC 58-6007. (Illus.). 224p. (gr. 3 up). 1975. 12.50 (ISBN 0-295-95408-6). U of Wash Pr.
--Creative Bookbinding. LC 63-10798. (Illus.). 275p. 1973. pap. 12.95 (ISBN 0-295-95267-9). U of Wash Pr.
Johnson, Peter. Boating Facts & Feats. LC 76-1163. (Illus.). 256p. (YA) 1976. 17.95 (ISBN 0-8069-0094-6); PLB 15.99 (ISBN 0-8069-0095-4). Sterling.
--Boating Facts & Feats. LC 76-1163. (Illus.). 1979. pap. 7.95 (ISBN 0-8069-8860-6). Sterling.
Johnson, Philip & Burgee, John. Philip Johnson & John Burgee: Architecture. LC 79-4786. 1979. 40.00 (ISBN 0-394-50744-4). Random.
Johnson, Philip C. Architecture: 1949 to 1965. (Illus.). 1966. 15.00 o.p. (ISBN 0-03-057960-0). HR&W.
Johnson, Philip C. see O'Neal, William B.
Johnson, Philip M. How to Maximize Your Advertising Investment. LC 80-10997. 224p. 1980. 18.95 (ISBN 0-8436-0769-6). CBI Pub.
Johnson, Phillip A. & Thornberg, Samual T. The Complete Handbook of Electronics Principles & Applications. 1980. 29.95 o.p. (ISBN 0-932812-03-1). Bradley CPA.
Johnson, Phillip E. Criminal Law, Cases, Materials & Text on the Substantive Criminal Law in Its Procedural Context. 2nd ed. LC 80-14283. (American Casebook Ser.). 993p. 1980. text ed. 21.95 (ISBN 0-8299-2093-5). West Pub.
--Elements of Criminal Due Process. (Criminal Justice Ser.). 1975. pap. text ed. 11.95 (ISBN 0-685-99579-8); pap. text ed. write for info (ISBN 0-8299-0620-7). West Pub.
Johnson, R. & Cox, R. Electrical Wiring: Design & Construction. 1981. Repr. 19.95 (ISBN 0-13-247650-9). P-H.
Johnson, R., jt. auth. see Comyn, J.
Johnson, R., et al. Critical Issues in Modern Religion. 1973. pap. 12.95 (ISBN 0-13-193979-3). P-H.
Johnson, R. C., jt. auth. see Basolo, F.
Johnson, R. Charles & Sherman, Charles E. Don't Sit in the Draft. 240p. (Orig.). 1980. pap. 6.95 (ISBN 0-917316-32-0). Nolo Pr.
Johnson, R. E. Existential Man: The Challenge of Psychotherapy. 1971. 9.50 (ISBN 0-08-016325-4). Pergamon.
--Juvenile Delinquency & Its Origins. LC 78-67263. (ASA Rose Monograph). (Illus.). 1979. 19.95 (ISBN 0-521-22477-2); pap. 6.95 (ISBN 0-521-29516-5). Cambridge U Pr.
Johnson, R. M. & Siddiqi, I. W. The Determination of Organic Peroxides. LC 75-104884. 1970. 22.00 (ISBN 0-08-015586-3). Pergamon.
Johnson, Ralph H., jt. ed. see Blair, J. Antony.

Johnson, Ralph W. & Brown, Gardner M. Cleaning Up Europe's Waters: Economics, Management, Policies. LC 76-23193. 1976. 35.00 (ISBN 0-275-56930-6). Praeger.

Johnson, Ramon E., jt. auth. see Brigham, Eugene F.

Johnson, Randal & Stam, Robert. Brazilian Cinema. LC 80-66323. (Illus.). 260p. 1981. 20.00 (ISBN 0-8386-3078-2). Fairleigh Dickinson.

Johnson, Ray C. Optimum Design of Mechanical Elements. 2nd ed. LC 79-14363. 1979. 34.50 (ISBN 0-471-03894-6, Pub. by Wiley-Interscience). Wiley.

Johnson, Raymond B., jt. ed. see Lukash, William M.

Johnson, Rex. At Home with Sex. 1979. pap. 3.95 (ISBN 0-88207-639-6). Victor Bks.

Johnson, Rex E., jt. auth. see Reed, Bobbie.

Johnson, Richard, ed. Directory of Evaluation Consultants. LC 80-67499. (Orig.). 1981. pap. 8.95 (ISBN 0-87954-035-4). Foundation Ctr.

Johnson, Richard, et al. Algebra One: A Two Part Course. (gr. 9-12). 1977. First Book. text ed. 12.56 (ISBN 0-201-14300-3, Sch Div); Second Book. text ed. 12.56 (ISBN 0-201-14302-X); Course A. tchr's guide 16.32 (ISBN 0-201-14301-1); Course B. tchr's guide 16.32 (ISBN 0-201-14303-8). A-W.

Johnson, Richard A., et al. Production & Operations Management: A systems Concept. 2nd ed. 500p. 1974. text ed. 22.95 (ISBN 0-395-18029-5); instructor's manual 3.50 (ISBN 0-395-18028-7). HM.

Johnson, Richard B., et al. Town Meeting Time: A Handbook of Parliamentary Law. 1962. 8.95 (ISBN 0-316-46736-7). Little.

Johnson, Richard C., jt. ed. see Stahl, William H.

Johnson, Richard E. Elementary Algebra. 1980. 16.95 (ISBN 0-8053-5052-7). Benjamin-Cummings.

Johnson, Richard R. Adjustment to Empire: The New England Colonies in the Era of the Glorious Revolution, 1675-1715. (Illus.). 448p. 1981. 29.50 (ISBN 0-8135-0907-6). Rutgers U Pr.

Johnson, Rita B. & Johnson, Stuart R. Assuring Learning With Self-Instructional Packages, or Up the Up Staircase. 1973. pap. text ed. 9.95 (ISBN 0-201-03327-5). A-W.

--Toward Individualized Learning: A Developer's Guide to Self-Instruction. LC 74-19692. 1975. text ed. 12.95 (ISBN 0-201-03420-4). A-W.

Johnson, Rita B., jt. auth. see Johnson, Stuart R.

Johnson, Robert. Elementary Statistics. 3rd ed. LC 79-17146. 1980. text ed. 16.95 (ISBN 0-87872-232-7). Duxbury Pr.

--The New Life of Virginea: Being the Second Part of Nova Britannia. LC 73-17167. (English Experience Ser.: No. 332). 52p. 1971. Repr. of 1612 ed. 8.00 (ISBN 90-221-0332-3). Walter J Johnson.

Johnson, Robert A. Religious Assortative Mariage in the United States. LC 80-978. (Studies in Population). 1980. 25.00 (ISBN 0-12-386580-8). Acad Pr.

Johnson, Robert A., et al, eds. The Practice of Cardiology. 1980. text ed. 59.95 (ISBN 0-316-46945-9). Little.

Johnson, Robert C. Electrical Wiring: Design & Construction. 1971. ref. ed. 19.95 (ISBN 0-13-247635-5). P-H.

Johnson, Robert C., ed. see Preston, Thomas.

Johnson, Robert E. Rear Admiral John Rodgers: 1812-1882. LC 79-6110. (Navies & Men Ser.). (Illus.). 1980. Repr. of 1967 ed. lib. bdg. 35.00x (ISBN 0-405-13039-2). Arno.

--Thence Round Cape Horn. LC 79-6111. (Navies & Men Ser.). (Illus.). 1980. Repr. of 1963 ed. lib. bdg. 25.00x (ISBN 0-405-13040-6). Arno.

Johnson, Robert K. Francis Ford Coppola. (Theatrical Arts Ser.). 1977. lib. bdg. 10.95 (ISBN 0-8057-9252-X). Twayne.

Johnson, Robert L. Letter of Paul to the Galatians. Ferguson, Everett, et al, eds. LC 76-95018. (Living Word New Testament Commentary Ser: Vol. 10). 1969. 7.95 (ISBN 0-8344-0013-8). Sweet.

Johnson, Robert O. An Index to Literature in the New Yorker, 1925-194, Vols. 1-15. LC 71-7740. 1969. 20.50 (ISBN 0-8108-0272-4). Scarecrow.

--An Index to Literature in the New Yorker, 1940-195, Vol. 16-30. 1970. 13.50 (ISBN 0-8108-0314-3). Scarecrow.

--An Index to Literature in the New Yorker, 1955-1970, Vols. 31-45. LC 71-7740. 1971. 20.50 (ISBN 0-8108-0413-1). Scarecrow.

--An Index to Literature in the New Yorker, 1970-75, Vol. 46-50. LC 71-7740. 1976. 10.00 (ISBN 0-8108-0905-2). Scarecrow.

--An Index to Profiles in the New Yorker. LC 71-186947. 1972. 10.00 (ISBN 0-8108-0473-5). Scarecrow.

Johnson, Robert W. Financial Management. 4th ed. 1971. text ed. 20.95x (ISBN 0-205-03231-1, 1032313); tchrs. manual o.p. 2.00 (ISBN 0-685-00328-0). Allyn.

Johnson, Robert W., jt. auth. see Robinson, Roland I.

Johnson, Roberta. Carmen Laforet. (World Authors Ser: No. 601). 1981. lib. bdg. 14.50 (ISBN 0-8057-6443-7). Twayne.

Johnson, Roberta A. Puerto Rico: Commonwealth or Colony? LC 80-16879. 218p. 1980. 21.95 (ISBN 0-03-053576-X); text ed. 9.95 (ISBN 0-03-053581-6). Praeger.

Johnson, Rodney D. & Siskin, Bernard R. Quantitative Techniques for Business Decisions. (Illus.). 544p. 1976. 21.00 (ISBN 0-13-746990-X). P-H.

Johnson, Roger, commentary by. Scores: An Anthology of New Music. LC 80-53302. (Illus.). 450p. 1981. pap. text ed. 12.95 (ISBN 0-02-871190-4). Schirmer Bks.

Johnson, Roger T., jt. auth. see Johnson, David W.

Johnson, Ron. The Early Sculpture of Picasso, 1901-1914. LC 75-23795. (Outstanding Dissertations in the Fine Arts - 20th Century). (Illus.). 1976. lib. bdg. 41.00 (ISBN 0-8240-1990-3). Garland Pub.

Johnson, Ronald. Ark: The Foundations One to Thirty Three. 88p. 1980. 12.50 (ISBN 0-86547-011-1); pap. 6.00 (ISBN 0-86547-012-X). N Point Pr.

Johnson, Ronald C. George Gascoigne. (English Authors Ser.: No. 133). lib. bdg. 10.95 (ISBN 0-8057-1212-7). Twayne.

Johnson, Ronald C. & Medinnus, Gene R. Child Psychology: Behavior & Development. 3rd ed. LC 73-22298. 576p. 1974. text ed. 21.95x (ISBN 0-471-44624-6). Wiley.

Johnson, Ronald C., jt. auth. see Day, R. A., Jr.

Johnson, Ronald C., jt. auth. see Dixon, Linda K.

Johnson, Ross H. & Winn, Paul R. Quantitative Methods for Management. LC 75-25239. (Illus.). 448p. 1976. text ed. 19.95 (ISBN 0-395-20634-2); inst. manual with solutions 2.00 (ISBN 0-395-20634-0). HM.

Johnson, Rossiter, ed. A Dictionary of Biographies of Authors Represented in the Authors Digest Series: With a Supplemental List of Later Titles & a Supplementary Biographical Section. LC 71-167011. 476p. 1974. Repr. of 1927 ed. 28.00 (ISBN 0-8103-3876-9). Gale.

--A Dictionary of Famous Names in Fiction, Drama, Poetry, History & Art. LC 75-167012. 1974. Repr. of 1908 ed. 28.00 (ISBN 0-8103-3875-0). Gale.

Johnson, Rubellite K. & Mahelona, John. Na Inoa Hoku: A Catalogue of Hawaiian & Pacific Star Names. LC 75-23889. 1975. pap. 4.95 (ISBN 0-914916-09-2). Topgallant.

Johnson, Rubellite K., ed. Kukini 'aha 'ilono: Over a Century of Native Hawaiian Life & Thought from Hawaiian Newpapers, 1834-1948. (Illus.). 1976. pap. text ed. 20.00 (ISBN 0-914916-27-0). Topgallant.

Johnson, Rudolph, Jr. Opium. (Novel - Adventure Ser.). 232p. 1981. 11.95 (ISBN 0-938952-00-5). Mona Pub.

Johnson, Russ, jt. auth. see Johnson, Anne.

Johnson, Ruth I. Devotions for Early Teens, Vol. 4. 128p. (gr. 7-12). 1974. pap. 1.50 (ISBN 0-8024-2184-9). Moody.

--Joy Spartan & the Money Mix-Up. (gr. 5-8). 1960. pap. 1.50 (ISBN 0-8024-4403-2). Moody.

--Joy Spartan of Parsonage Hill. (gr. 5-8). 1958. pap. 1.50 (ISBN 0-8024-4401-6). Moody.

--Joy Sparton & Her Problem Twin. (gr. 5-8). 1963. pap. 1.50 (ISBN 0-8024-4404-0). Moody.

--Joy Sparton & the Mystery in Room Seven. (Preteen Ser). 128p. (Orig.). (gr. 5-8). 1974. pap. 1.50 (ISBN 0-8024-4405-9). Moody.

--Joy Sparton & the Vacation Mix-Up. (gr. 5-8). 1959. pap. 1.50 (ISBN 0-8024-4402-4). Moody.

Johnson, S. K. see Livy.

Johnson, S. O. Better Discipline. 142p. 1980. 11.50 (ISBN 0-398-03985-2). C C Thomas.

Johnson, Samuel. The Autobiography of Samuel Johnson. 1956. 4.50 o.p. (ISBN 0-8040-0078-6). Swallow.

--A Dictionary of the English Language, 2 vols. 4th ed. 1980. 230.00 (ISBN 0-686-63570-1). Intl Bk Ctr.

--Dictionary of the English Language: In Which the Words Are Deduced from Their Originals & Illustrated in Their Different Significations by Examples from the Best Writers, 2 Vols. 1968. Repr. of 1755 ed. Set. 283.25 (ISBN 3-4870-1935-3). Adler.

--The History of the Yorubas: From the Earliest Times to the Beginning of the British Protectorate. 1969. Repr. of 1921 ed. 32.50 (ISBN 0-7100-1615-8). Routledge & Kegan.

--The Literary Magazine: Or, Universal Review. Nos. 1-27. 1756-1758, 3 vols. Eddy, Donald D., ed. (Samuel Johnson & Periodical Literature Ser.: Vol. 5). 1979. lib. bdg. 58.50 (ISBN 0-8240-3430-9). Garland Pub.

--Lives of English Poets. 1977. 8.00x (ISBN 0-460-00770-X, Evman); pap. 5.95 (ISBN 0-460-01770-5). Dutton.

--Lives of the English Poets, 2 Vols. (World's Classics Ser.). Vol. 1. 11.95 (ISBN 0-19-250083-X); Vol. 2. 8.95 (ISBN 0-19-250084-8). Oxford U Pr.

--London: A Poem... 1738 & 48. Incl. The Vanity of Human Wishes - 1749 & 55. 1976. 17.95x o.p. (ISBN 0-8277-3876-5); pap. 9.50x o.p. (ISBN 0-685-62021-2). British Bk Ctr.

--The Prince of Abissinia: A Tale, 1759, 2 vols. in 1. Bd. with Candide; or, All for the Best, 1759. Voltaire, Francois M. LC 74-17303. (Novel in England, 1700-1775 Ser). 1974. lib. bdg. 50.00 (ISBN 0-8240-1150-3). Garland Pub.

--Religious Education Press, Inc. 323p. 1979. Repr. of 1888 ed. lib. bdg. 32.50 (ISBN 0-8482-1396-3). Norwood Edns.

--Samuel Johnson's Literary Criticism. Stock, R. D., ed. LC 73-91398. (Regents Critics Ser). xvi, 286p. 1974. 12.50x (ISBN 0-8032-0469-8); pap. 3.50x (ISBN 0-8032-5467-9, BB 415, Bison). U of Nebr Pr.

--Sayings of Doctor Johnson. (Little Treasury Ser). 1969. 1.75 o.p. (ISBN 0-212-99827-7). Dufour.

Johnson, Samuel A. Essentials of Comparative Government. rev. ed. LC 63-16873. (gr. 9-12). 1973. pap. text ed. 3.50 (ISBN 0-8120-0052-8). Barron.

--Essentials of Political Science. LC 65-25692. (Orig.). (gr. 10 up). 1971. pap. text ed. 3.95 (ISBN 0-8120-0146-X). Barron.

Johnson, Sheila K. Idle Haven: Community Building Among the Working-Class Retired. LC 72-145786. (California Studies in Urbanization & Environmental Studies). 1971. 17.50x (ISBN 0-520-01909-1). U of Cal Pr.

Johnson, Sherman E. Belonging: An Introduction to the Christian Church. 1978. 1.65 (ISBN 0-686-28773-8). Forward Movement.

Johnson, Shildes, jt. auth. see Bjornstad, James.

Johnson, Simon, jt. auth. see Sherman, Theodore A.

Johnson, Siskin. Elementary Statistics for Business. LC 78-13691. (Illus.). 1979. text ed. 17.95 (ISBN 0-87872-188-6); study guide 7.95 (ISBN 0-686-65910-4). Duxbury Pr.

Johnson, Spencer. Precious Present. LC 80-46478. (Illus.). 80p. 1981. 7.95 (ISBN 0-89087-286-4). Celestial Arts.

--The Value of Fantasy: The Story of Hans Christian Andersen. LC 79-18237. (ValueTales Ser.). (Illus.). (gr. k-6). 1979. 6.95 (ISBN 0-916392-43-0, Dist. by Oak Tree Pubns). Value Comm.

--The Value of Honesty: The Story of Confucius. LC 78-4351. (ValueTales Ser.). (Illus.). (gr. k-6). 1979. 6.95 (ISBN 0-916392-36-8, Dist. by Oak Tree Pubns). Value Comm.

--The Value of Understanding: The Story of Margaret Mead. LC 79-9800. (ValueTales Ser.). (Illus.). (gr. k-6). 1979. 6.95 (ISBN 0-916392-37-6, Dist. by Oak Tree Pubns). Value Comm.

Johnson, Stanley, et al, eds. Play & the Reader. alt. ed. (English Ser). 1971. pap. text ed. 9.50 (ISBN 0-13-682286-X). P-H.

Johnson, Stanley P. The Pollution Control Policy of the EEC. 224p. 1979. 26.00x (ISBN 0-86010-136-3, Pub. by Graham & Trotman England). State Mutual Bk.

Johnson, Stanley W. Arithmetic & Learning Disabilities: Guidelines for Identification & Remediation. 1979. pap. text ed. 10.95x (ISBN 0-205-06504-X). Allyn.

Johnson, Stephen, jt. auth. see Delpit, George.

Johnson, Stephen M. First Person Singular: Living the Good Life Alone. LC 76-51353. 1977. 10.00 o.p. (ISBN 0-397-01162-8). Lippincott.

Johnson, Stuart E. The Military Equation in Northeast Asia. (Studies in Defense Policy). 1979. pap. 3.95 (ISBN 0-8157-4689-X). Brookings.

Johnson, Stuart R. & Johnson, Rita B. Developing Individualized Instructional Material. 1970. text ed. 4.44 (ISBN 0-88250-403-7). Westinghouse Learn.

Johnson, Stuart R., jt. auth. see Johnson, Rita B.

Johnson, Susan M. Lovestorm. LC 80-85106. 352p. (Orig.). 1981. pap. 2.95 (ISBN 0-87216-833-6). Playboy Pbks.

Johnson, Sylvia A. Penguins. LC 80-2880. (Lerner Natural Science Bks.). (gr. 4-10). 1981. PLB 7.95 (ISBN 0-8225-1453-2). Lerner Pubns.

Johnson, T. A Precision Approach to Voice Disorders. Date not set. price not set (ISBN 0-685-32516-4). Univ Park.

Johnson, Thomas. Arriving at the Nadir. (Illus., Orig.). 1975. pap. 2.50 (ISBN 0-914278-06-1). Copper Beech.

Johnson, Thomas, jt. auth. see Heyne, Paul.

Johnson, Thomas, jt. auth. see Heyne, Paul T.

Johnson, Thomas C. The Life of Robert Lewis Dabney. 1977. 13.95 (ISBN 0-85151-253-4). Banner of Truth.

Johnson, Thomas H. Genitourinary Radiology Case Studies. 1980. pap. 16.75 (ISBN 0-87488-090-4). Med Exam.

Johnson, Thomas H., jt. ed. see Miller, Perry.

Johnson, Thomas H., ed. see Taylor, Edward.

Johnson, Thomas M. Collecting the Edged Weapons of the Third Reich, Vol. 4. Bradach, Wilfrid, tr. LC 75-15486. (Illus.). 1981. 25.00 (ISBN 0-686-69390-6). T M Johnson.

Johnson, Thomas P. When Nature Runs Wild. LC 67-31553. (Illus.). (gr. 5-9). 1969. PLB 7.50 o.p. (ISBN 0-87191-005-5). Creative Ed.

Johnson, Thomas W. & Stinson, John E. Managing Today & Tomorrow. LC 77-76123. (Illus.). 1978. text ed. 15.95 (ISBN 0-201-03487-5); instr's man. 3.95 (ISBN 0-201-03488-3). A-W.

Johnson, Timothy E. Investment Principles. LC 77-13345. (Illus.). 1978. ref. 18.95 (ISBN 0-13-504506-1). P-H.

Johnson, Timothy W., et al. Crime Fiction Criticism: An Annotated Bibliography. LC 80-8497. 450p. 1981. lib. bdg. 40.00 (ISBN 0-8240-9490-5). Garland Pub.

Johnson, Tom. Imaginary Music. 1974. pap. 5.95 (ISBN 0-938690-00-0). Two Eighteen.

--Private Pieces. LC 76-14367. 1976. pap. 2.95 (ISBN 0-938690-01-9). Two Eighteen.

Johnson, Trevor. Thomas Hardy. LC 78-123553. (Literary Critiques Ser). (Illus.). 1970. lib. bdg. 4.95 o.p. (ISBN 0-668-02362-7). Arco.

Johnson, U. Alexis & Packard, George R., eds. The Common Security Interests of Japan, the United States, & NATO. 200p. 1981. professional reference 19.50x. Ballinger Pub.

Johnson, Uwe. Begleitumstaende: Frankfurter Vorlesungen. (Edition Suhrkamp. Neue Folge: No. 19). 300p. (Orig., Ger.). 1980. pap. 7.80 (ISBN 3-518-11019-5, Pub. by Insel Verlag Germany). Suhrkamp.

--Third Book About Achim. LC 67-12273. (Helen & Kurt Wolff Bk). 1967. 5.75 (ISBN 0-15-189901-0). HarBraceJ.

Johnson, V. A. Karl Lark-Horovitz, Pioneer in Solid State Physics. LC 77-91464. (Men of Physics Ser.). 1970. 22.00 (ISBN 0-08-006581-3); pap. 10.75 (ISBN 0-08-006580-5). Pergamon.

Johnson, Vance. Heaven's Tableland: The Dust Bowl Story. LC 73-20453. (FDR & the Era of the New Deal Ser.). (Illus.). 288p. 1974. Repr. of 1947 ed. lib. bdg. 29.50 (ISBN 0-306-70606-7). Da Capo.

Johnson, Vernon E. I'll Quit Tomorrow. rev. ed. LC 79-3759. 192p. 1980. 9.95 (ISBN 0-06-250430-4, HarpR). Har-Row.

Johnson, Victor, ed. see Goodman, Robert B. & Spicer, Robert A.

Johnson, Vivian A. see Marton, L.

Johnson, W. Focus on the Science Fiction Film. 1972. 5.95 o.p. (ISBN 0-13-795161-2); pap. 2.95 o.p. (ISBN 0-13-795179-5). P-H.

--The Forty-Niners. (The Old West Ser.). (Illus.). 240p. 1974. 12.95 (ISBN 0-8094-1470-8). Time-Life.

--Science Fiction Film: Focus on. 1972. pap. 2.95 (ISBN 0-13-795161-2). P-H.

Johnson, W., ed. Safety Assurance Systems. (Occupational Safety & Health Ser.). 1980. 35.00 (ISBN 0-8247-6897-3). Dekker.

Johnson, W. B., et al. Symmetric Structures in Banach Spaces. (Memoirs Ser.: No. 217). 1979. write for info. o.p. (ISBN 0-8218-2217-9). Am Math.

Johnson, W. McAllister, jt. auth. see Graham, Victor E.

Johnson, W. R. Darkness Visible: A Study of Vergil's Aeneid. LC 74-82845. 1976. 16.60x (ISBN 0-520-02942-9); pap. 5.95x (ISBN 0-520-03848-7). U of Cal Pr.

--Sex Education & Counseling of Special Groups. 224p. 1975. 16.75 (ISBN 0-398-03197-5). C C Thomas.

Johnson, W. W. The Spanish West. LC 76-1423. (The Old West). (Illus.). (gr. 5 up). 1976. kivar 12.96 (ISBN 0-8094-1535-6, Pub. by Time-Life). Silver.

Johnson, Walter. August Strindberg. LC 76-17910. (World Authors Ser: No. 410). 1976. lib. bdg. 12.50 (ISBN 0-8057-6250-7). Twayne.

--The Battle Against Isolation. LC 72-3376. (FDR & the Era of the New Deal Ser.). 270p. 1974. Repr. of 1944 ed. lib. bdg. 29.50 (ISBN 0-306-70480-3). Da Capo.

--William Allen White's America. Freidel, Frank, ed. LC 78-66541. (The History of the United States Ser.: Vol. 10). 630p. 1979. lib. bdg. 50.00 (ISBN 0-8240-9702-5). Garland Pub.

Johnson, Walter, tr. see Strindberg, August.

Johnson, Walter S. Maxims of the Civil Law: Essays in the Evolution of Law. LC 74-26294. 252p. 1973. Repr. of 1929 ed. lib. bdg. 22.50x (ISBN 0-912004-10-X). W W Gaunt.

Johnson, Warren, jt. auth. see Glimcher, Sumner.

Johnson, Warren A. Muddling Toward Frugality. LC 79-5172. 1979. Repr. of 1978 ed. pap. 3.95 (ISBN 0-394-73835-7). Shambhala Pubns.

Johnson, Warren R. So Desperate the Fight: An Innovative Approach to Chronic Illness. LC 78-71009. 1981. pap. 6.95 (ISBN 0-917476-16-6). Rational Living.

Johnson, Warren R. & Buskirk, E. R., eds. Structural & Physiological Aspects of Exercise & Sport. LC 79-91733. (Illus.). 291p. 1980. text ed. 19.50x (ISBN 0-916622-16-9). Princeton Bk Co.
Johnson, Warren T. & Lyon, H. H. Insects That Feed on Trees & Shrubs: An Illustrated Practical Guide. (Illus.). 464p. 1976. 38.50x (ISBN 0-8014-0956-X). Comstock.
Johnson, Wayne. Helicopter Theory. LC 79-83995. 1000p. 1980. 95.00x (ISBN 0-691-07971-4). Princeton U Pr.
Johnson, Wayne L. Ray Bradbury. LC 79-4825. (Recognitions Ser.). 1980. 10.95 (ISBN 0-8044-2426-8); pap. 4.95 (ISBN 0-8044-6318-2). Ungar.
Johnson, Wendell. Your Most Enchanted Listener. LC 55-10696. 1956. 6.95 o.s.i. (ISBN 0-06-012230-7, HarpT). Har-Row.
Johnson, Wendell S. Living in Sin: The Victorian Sexual Revolution. LC 78-26845. 1979. 14.95 (ISBN 0-88229-445-8); pap. 7.95 (ISBN 0-88229-649-3). Nelson-Hall.
Johnson, Wendell S., jt. ed. see Danziger, Marlies K.
Johnson, Wesley M. & Maxwell, John A. Rock & Mineral Analysis. 584p. 1981. 40.00 (ISBN 0-471-02743-X, Pub. by Wiley-Interscience). Wiley.
Johnson, Willard, Jr. Poetry & Speculation of the Rg Veda. 175p. 1981. 25.00 (ISBN 0-520-02560-1). U of Cal Pr.
Johnson, William. Baja California. LC 72-85157. (American Wilderness Ser). (Illus.). (gr. 6 up). 1972. lib. bdg. 11.97 (ISBN 0-8094-1161-X, Pub. by Time-Life). Silver.
--Dinosaur Fun Book. (Illus.). 48p. (gr. k-12). 1979. pap. 2.25 (ISBN 0-89844-007-6, 007-6). Troubador Pr.
--Famous Monster Funbooks. (Illus.). 48p. (Orig.). 1981. pap. 2.50 (ISBN 0-89844-030-0). Troubador Pr.
--Sketches of the Life & Correspondences of Nathanael Green, 2 vols. LC 78-119063. 516p. 1974. Repr. of 1822 ed. lib. bdg. 65.00 (ISBN 0-306-71953-3). Da Capo.
Johnson, William A. Steel Industry of India. LC 66-23471. (Rand Corporation Research Studies). 1966. 16.50x (ISBN 0-674-83715-0). Harvard U Pr.
Johnson, William D. Jack & the Beanstalk. (gr. 1-3). 1976. 6.95 (ISBN 0-316-46941-6). Little.
Johnson, William G. & Stalonas, Peter. Weight No Longer. 188p. 1981. 19.95 (ISBN 0-88289-261-4). Pelican.
Johnson, William R., jt. auth. see Browning, Edgar K.
Johnson, William S., commentary by. W. Eugene Smith: Master of the Photographic Essay. LC 80-68723. (Illus.). 1981. 35.00 (ISBN 0-89381-070-3). Aperture.
Johnson, William W. Baja California. (The American Wilderness Ser.). (Illus.). 1972. 12.95 (ISBN 0-8094-1160-1). Time-Life.
--The Forty-Niners. LC 73-88997. (The Old West). (Illus.). (gr. 5 up). 1974. kivar 12.96 (ISBN 0-8094-1472-4, Pub. by Time-Life). Silver.
--The Great Chiefs. (The Old West Ser.). (Illus.). 240p. 1975. 12.95 (ISBN 0-8094-1492-9). Time-Life.
--Kelly Blue. LC 60-8875. 263p. 1974. pap. 2.95 (ISBN 0-8032-5795-3, BB 583, Bison). U of Nebr Pr.
--The Spanish West. (Old West Ser.). (Illus.). 1976. 12.95 (ISBN 0-8094-1533-X). Time-Life.
--The Story of Sea Otters. (Illus.). (gr. 4-7). 1973. PLB 5.99 (ISBN 0-394-92403-7, BYR). Random.
Johnsonbaugh & Pfaffenberger, eds. Foundations of Mathematical Analysis. 1981. 24.50 (ISBN 0-8247-6919-8). Dekker.
Johnson-Davies, D., tr. see Johnson-Davies, Denys.
Johnson-Davies, D., tr. see Tewfik Al, Hakim.
Johnson-Davies, Denys, ed. Egyptian Plays. (Arab Writers Series). 220p. (Orig.). 1981. 10.00 (ISBN 0-89410-236-2); pap. 5.00 (ISBN 0-89410-237-0). Three Continents.
--Modern Arabic Short Stories. Johnson-Davies, D., tr. from Arabic. (Orig.). 1976. 9.00x (ISBN 0-914478-75-3, Co-Pub by Heinemann Educ. Bks); pap. 5.00x (ISBN 0-435-99403-4). Three Continents.
Johnson-Davies, Denys, tr. from Arabic. Egyptian Short Stories. 1978. 9.00 (ISBN 0-89410-038-6); pap. 5.00 (ISBN 0-89410-039-4). Three Continents.
Johnson-Davies, Denys, tr. see Al-Hakim, Tewfik.
Johnson-Davies, Denys, tr. see Darwish, Mahmoud.
Johnson-Davies, Denys, tr. see Ibrahim, Sonallah.
Johnson-Davies, Denys, tr. see Salih, Tayeb.
Johnson-Laird, P. N., jt. auth. see Wason, P. C.
Johnson-Laird, P. N. & Wason, P. C., eds. Thinking: Readings in Cognitive Science. LC 77-78887. (Illus.). 1978. 49.50 (ISBN 0-521-21756-3); pap. 13.95x (ISBN 0-521-29267-0). Cambridge U Pr.
Johnsson, William. Religion in Overalls. LC 77-22464. (Anvil Ser.). 1977. pap. 7.95 (ISBN 0-8127-0143-7). Southern Pub.
Johnsson, William G. Clean: The Meaning of Christian Baptism. LC 80-15681. (Horizon Ser.). 96p. 1980. pap. write for info. (ISBN 0-8127-0293-X). Southern Pub.
--Hebrews. LC 79-92068. (Knox Preaching Guides Ser.). 98p. (Orig., John Hayes series editor). 1980. pap. 4.50 (ISBN 0-686-60242-0). John Knox.
--In Absolute Confidence. LC 79-1387. (Anvil Ser.). 1979. pap. 5.95 (ISBN 0-8127-0225-5). Southern Pub.
Johnstad, Jack & Johnstad, Lois. Attaining Financial Peace of Mind: A Practical Guide for the Thinking Person. LC 80-67104. (Illus.). 320p. 1980. pap. 8.95 (ISBN 0-937346-00-4). Bright Spirit.
Johnstad, Lois, jt. auth. see Johnstad, Jack.
Johnstad, Trygve, jt. ed. see European Institute.
Johnston. King Arthur: His Knights & Their Ladies. (gr. 7-12). 1980. pap. 1.50 (ISBN 0-590-30007-5, Schol Pap). Schol Bk Serv.
--My Diary. (gr. 7-12). pap. 1.50 (ISBN 0-590-02642-9, Schol Pap). Schol Bk Serv.
--They Led the Way: Fourteen American Women. (gr. 3-5). pap. 1.50 (ISBN 0-590-11908-7, Schol Pap). Schol Bk Serv.
Johnston & Bacon. Great Britain, Road Atlas. (Illus.). 372p. 1978. pap. 11.95 (ISBN 0-7179-4239-2). Bradt Ent.
Johnston, Annie F. The Little Colonel. new ed. (Illus.). 1974. 5.95 (ISBN 0-88289-050-6). Pelican.
Johnston, Annie F. see Page, Thomas N.
Johnston, Arthur. World Evangelism & the Word of God. LC 74-13788. 304p. 1974. pap. 3.95 (ISBN 0-87123-600-1, 210600). Bethany Fell.
Johnston, Avin H. The Forty Footers. (Orig.). 1980. pap. 1.95 (ISBN 0-532-23215-1). Manor Bks.
Johnston, Barry V. Russian American Social Mobility: An Analysis of the Achievement Syndrome. LC 80-65609. 145p. 1981. perfect bdg. 10.95 (ISBN 0-86548-041-9). Century Twenty One.
Johnston, Basil H. Ojibway Heritage. (Illus.). 1976. 14.00x (ISBN 0-231-04168-3). Columbia U Pr.
Johnston, Beverly, jt. auth. see Dukes, Ona B.
Johnston, Bruce G. Guide to Stability Design Criteria for Metal Structures. 3rd ed. LC 75-40155. 1976. 45.00 (ISBN 0-471-44629-7, Pub. by Wiley-Interscience). Wiley.
Johnston, Carol. Plane Trigonometry: A New Approach. 2nd ed. LC 77-16841. 1978. text ed. 16.95 (ISBN 0-13-677666-3). P-H.
Johnston, Carol L. & Willis, Alden T. Essential Algebra. 2nd ed. 1978. pap. text ed. 16.95x (ISBN 0-534-00579-9). Wadsworth Pub.
--Essential Arithmetic. 2nd ed. 1977. 15.95x (ISBN 0-534-00513-6). Wadsworth Pub.
--Intermediate Algebra. 2nd ed. 1979. pap. text ed. 16.95x (ISBN 0-534-00595-0). Wadsworth Pub.
Johnston, Charles & Giles, Lionel, trs. Selections from the Upanishads & The Tao Te King. 142p. 1951. Repr. of 1897 ed. 3.00 (ISBN 0-938998-15-3). Cunningham Pr.
Johnston, Charles M. McMaster University, Vol. 2: The Early Years in Hamilton, 1930-1957. 329p. 1981. 25.00x (ISBN 0-8020-3372-5). U of Toronto Pr.
Johnston, Claire & Willemen, Paul. Frank Tashlin. (EIFF Ser.). 1978. pap. 4.00 (ISBN 0-918432-13-8). NY Zoetrope.
Johnston, Claire, ed. Edinburgh Seventy-Seven: History-Production-Memory. (EIFF Ser.). 1978. pap. 6.00 (ISBN 0-918432-17-0). NY Zoetrope.
--Edinburgh Seventy-Six: Psychoanalysis, Cinema, Avante-Garde. (EIFF Ser.). 1978. pap. 5.00 (ISBN 0-918432-16-2). NY Zoetrope.
Johnston, Colin, jt. auth. see Hume, John R.
Johnston, Corinne. Wild Gypsy Love. (Orig.). 1976. pap. 1.75 o.s.i. (ISBN 0-515-04014-2). Jove Pubns.
Johnston, Corrinne. The Texan Women. 1977. pap. 2.25 o.s.i. (ISBN 0-515-04395-8). Jove Pubns.
Johnston, D., ed. see Driscoll, P., et al.
Johnston, D., ed. see Sullivan, George E. & Cox, Warren.
Johnston, D. E. The Saxon Shore. 92p. 1980. pap. 20.95x (ISBN 0-900312-43-2, Pub. by Coun Brit Arch England). Intl Schol Bk.
Johnston, David. The Craft of Furniture Making. 1979. 19.95 (ISBN 0-7134-1546-0, Pub. by Batsford England). David & Charles.
Johnston, Denis. The Brazen Horn. (Dolmen Editions: No. 22). (Illus.). 272p. 1976. text ed. 43.75x (ISBN 0-85105-259-2, Dolmen Pr). Humanities.
--The Dramatic Works of Denis Johnston, 2 vols. Incl. Vol. 1. 1977. text ed. 35.00x (ISBN 0-685-51837-X); Vol. 2. 1978. text ed. 36.50x (ISBN 0-901072-53-2). Humanities.
Johnston, Dorothy F. & Hood, Gail H. Total Patient Care: Foundations & Practice. 4th ed. LC 75-15563. 1976. pap. text ed. 14.95 (ISBN 0-8016-2573-4). Mosby.
Johnston, Douglas M., jt. auth. see Barros, James.
Johnston, E. Russell, Jr., jt. auth. see Beer, Ferdinand P.
Johnston, Edith M. Ireland in the Eighteenth Century. (Gill History of Ireland: Vol. 8). 224p. 1974. pap. 6.95 (ISBN 0-7171-0565-2). Irish Bk Ctr.
Johnston, Eliza G. Texas Wild Flowers. LC 72-77252. (Illus.). 240p. 1972. collectors ed. 100.00 (ISBN 0-88319-006-0). Shoal Creek Pub.
Johnston, F. E., et al, eds. Human Physical Growth & Maturation: Methodologies & Factors. (NATO Advanced Study Institute Series, Series A: Life Sciences: Vol. 30). 375p. 1980. 42.50 (ISBN 0-306-40420-6, Plenum Pr). Plenum Pub.
Johnston, Francis. Fatima. (The Great Sign). 1980. Repr. of 1979 ed. write for info. Tan Bks Pubs.
--Fatima: The Great Sign. 1980. 3.50 (ISBN 0-911988-37-8, Co-Pub by Augustine Pr England). AMI Pr.
Johnston, Francis E. Microevolution of Human Populations. (Illus.). 160p. 1973. pap. 9.95 ref. ed. (ISBN 0-13-581512-6). P-H.
Johnston, Francis S., jt. ed. see Green, Lawrence S.
Johnston, G. B., ed. see McCorvey, Thomas C.
Johnston, George, tr. Saga of Gisli the Outlaw. LC 67-207. (Illus.). 1963. pap. 5.50 (ISBN 0-8020-6219-9). U of Toronto Pr.
Johnston, Gordon J. Smooth Nonparametric Regression Analysis. 88p. 1979. pap. 2.80 (1253). U of NC Pr.
Johnston, H. P. Storming of Stony Point on the Hudson, Midnight, July 15, 1779. LC 70-146150. (Era of the American Revolution Ser). 1971. Repr. of 1900 ed. lib. bdg. 22.50 (ISBN 0-306-70141-3). Da Capo.
--Yorktown Campaign & the Surrender of Cornwallis, 1781. LC 75-146149. (Era of the American Revolution Ser). 1971. Repr. of 1881 ed. lib. bdg. 22.50 (ISBN 0-306-70142-1). Da Capo.
Johnston, H. P., ed. Correspondence & Public Papers of John Jay, 1763-1781. LC 69-16639. (American Public Figures Ser). 1971. Repr. of 1890 ed. lib. bdg. 65.00 (ISBN 0-306-71124-9). Da Capo.
Johnston, Harriet. Quality Quantity Cuisine, I. LC 75-38975. 350p. 1976. 21.50 (ISBN 0-8436-2079-X). CBI Pub.
--Quality Quantity Cuisine II. LC 75-38975. 1976. 21.50 (ISBN 0-8436-2119-2). CBI Pub.
Johnston, Hiram, et al. The Learning Center Ideabook: Activities for the Elementary & Middle Grades. new ed. 1978. pap. text ed. 18.95 (ISBN 0-205-05894-9). Allyn.
Johnston, Ivan A., jt. auth. see Walker, William F.
Johnston, J. M. Brainchild. (Orig.). 1979. pap. 1.95 (ISBN 0-532-23141-4). Manor Bks.
Johnston, James M. Behavior Research & Technology in Higher Education. (Illus.). 536p. 1975. 27.50 (ISBN 0-398-03315-3). C C Thomas.
Johnston, James M. & Pennypacker, H. S. Strategies & Tactics of Human Behavioral Research. LC 80-22612. 496p. 1980. text ed. 19.95 (ISBN 0-89859-030-2). L Erlbaum Assocs.
Johnston, James O. & Spatz, Chris. Study Guide for Basic Statistics: Tales of Distributions. 2nd ed. 150p. (Orig.). 1981. pap. text ed. 6.95 (ISBN 0-8185-0454-4). Brooks-Cole.
Johnston, James O., jt. auth. see Spatz, Chris.
Johnston, Johanna. Connecticut Colony. LC 69-19576. (Forge of Freedom Ser). (Illus.). (gr. 5-8). 1969. 8.95 (ISBN 0-02-747710-X, CCPr). Macmillan.
--The Fabulous Fox: An Anthology of Fact & Fiction. LC 78-21031. (Illus.). (gr. 5 up). 1979. 5.95 (ISBN 0-396-07652-1). Dodd.
--The Indians & the Strangers. LC 72-1447. (Illus.). (gr. 2 up). 1972. 5.95 (ISBN 0-396-06610-0). Dodd.
Johnston, John K., et al. Wrestling: Coaching to Win. (Illus.). 1979. pap. 5.95 (ISBN 0-8015-8933-9, Hawthorn). Dutton.
Johnston, Joseph E., jt. auth. see Feuer, Morton.
Johnston, Lloyd. Drugs & American Youth. LC 71-190022. 287p. 1973. cloth 10.00 (ISBN 0-87944-133-X); pap. 6.50 (ISBN 0-87944-120-8). U of Mich Soc Res.
Johnston, Louisa & Bristle, Mable C. A Monkey in the Family. LC 73-188431. (Illus.). 128p. (gr. 3-7). 1972. 5.95g o.p. (ISBN 0-8075-5256-9). A Whitman.
Johnston, Madeline. Channels Worth Watching. Van Dolson, Bobbie J., ed. 64p. 1981. pap. write for info. (ISBN 0-8280-0030-1). Review & Herald.
Johnston, Marliss. The Whole Garden Catalog. (Illus.). 1980. lib. bdg. 17.50 (ISBN 0-933474-13-X, Gabriel Bks); pap. 12.95 (ISBN 0-933474-17-2, Gabriel Bks). Minn Scholarly.
Johnston, Mary. Audrey. 1976. lib. bdg. 11.95 (ISBN 0-89968-150-6). Lightyear.
--To Have & to Hold. 1976. lib. bdg. 11.95x (ISBN 0-89968-149-2). Lightyear.
Johnston, Mary K. Great Danes. rev. ed. (Illus.). 126p. 1973. pap. 2.95 o.p. (ISBN 0-87666-309-9, HS-1052). TFH Pubns.
Johnston, Meda P. & Kaufman, Glen. Design on Fabrics. 2nd ed. 188p. 1981. 14.95 (ISBN 0-442-26339-2); pap. 9.95 (ISBN 0-442-23145-8). Van Nos Reinhold.
Johnston, Moira. The Last Nine Minutes: The Story of Flight 981. 1977. pap. 1.95 (ISBN 0-380-01808-X, 35642). Avon.
Johnston, Norma. Myself & I. LC 80-21855. 216p. (gr. 6 up). 1981. PLB 9.95 (ISBN 0-689-30814-0). Atheneum.
Johnston, Norman, jt. auth. see Savitz, Leonard D.
Johnston, O. R. Who Needs the Family? LC 80-7780. 152p. (Orig.). 1980. pap. 5.95 (ISBN 0-87784-588-3). Inter-Varsity.
Johnston, O. R., tr. see Luther, Martin.
Johnston, P. & Roots, B. Nerve Membranes: A Study of the Biological & Chemical Aspects of Neuron Glia Relationships. 279p. 1972. text ed. 55.00 (ISBN 0-08-013222-7). Pergamon.
Johnston, P. M. & Liebowitz, M. Basic Sheet Metal Skills. LC 76-14085. 1977. pap. text ed. 10.40 (ISBN 0-8273-1237-7); instructor's guide 3.00 (ISBN 0-8273-1238-5). Delmar.
Johnston, R. & Gummett, P. Directory Technology. 240p. 1980. 30.00x (ISBN 0-85664-740-3, Pub. by Croom Helm England). State Mutual Bk.
Johnston, R. C., ed. Jordan Fantosme's Chronicle. 256p. 1980. 60.00 (ISBN 0-19-815758-4). Oxford U Pr.
Johnston, R. J. Multivariate Statistical Analysis in Geography: A Primer of the General Linear Model. (Illus.). 1980. pap. text ed. 10.95 (ISBN 0-582-30034-7). Longman.
--The New Zealanders: How They Live & Work. LC 75-34976. 168p. 1976. text ed. 8.95 (HoltC). HR&W.
--Political, Electoral, & Spatial Systems. (Contemporary Problems in Geography Ser.). (Illus.). 1979. 29.95x (ISBN 0-19-874071-9); pap. 11.95x (ISBN 0-19-874072-7). Oxford U Pr.
Johnston, R. J., jt. auth. see Herbert, D. T.
Johnston, Ray E., ed. The Politics of Division, Partition, & Unification. LC 75-23973. (Special Studies). (Illus.). 1976. text ed. 21.95 (ISBN 0-275-55660-3). Praeger.
Johnston, Reginald F. Confucianism & Modern China. LC 79-2830. (Illus.). 272p. 1981. Repr. of 1934 ed. 23.50 (ISBN 0-8305-0007-3). Hyperion Conn.
Johnston, Richard E. Effect of Judicial Review on Federal-State Relations in Australia, Canada, & the United States. LC 70-80045. 1969. 20.00x (ISBN 0-8071-0901-0). La State U Pr.
Johnston, Richard F., et al, eds. Annual Review of Ecology & Systematics, Vol. 11. LC 71-135616. (Illus.). 1980. text ed. 20.00 (ISBN 0-8243-1411-5). Annual Reviews.
Johnston, Robert M. The Napoleonic Empire in Southern Italy & the Rise of the Secret Societies, 2 vols. LC 77-156852. (Europe 1815-1945 Ser). 640p. 1973. Repr. of 1904 ed. lib. bdg. 49.50 (ISBN 0-306-70558-3). Da Capo.
Johnston, Ronald J. Governments & the Geography of Federal Spending in the U.S.A. 208p. 1981. write for info. (ISBN 0-471-27865-3, Pub. by Wiley-Interscience). Wiley.
Johnston, Russ. God Can Make It Happen. 144p. 1976. pap. 3.50 (ISBN 0-88207-741-4). Victor Bks.
Johnston, Sarah H. Golden Anni-Verse-Ary. 1981. 5.95 (ISBN 0-533-04805-2). Vantage.
Johnston, Susan. Tangram ABC Kit. 1979. pap. 1.75 (ISBN 0-486-23853-9). Dover.
Johnston, Velda. The People from the Sea. 208p. 1980. pap. 2.25 (ISBN 0-553-13915-0). Bantam.
--A Presence in an Empty Room. LC 79-25431. 256p. 1980. 8.95 (ISBN 0-396-07796-X). Dodd.
--A Presence in an Empty Room. 1981. lib. bdg. 12.95 (ISBN 0-8161-3158-9, Large Print Bks). G K Hall.
--A Room with Dark Mirrors. 1976. pap. 1.50 o.p. (ISBN 0-451-07143-3, W7143, Sig). NAL.
--The Stone Maiden. LC 80-16109. 224p. 1980. 8.95 (ISBN 0-396-07882-6). Dodd.
Johnston, Wiliam. The Inner Eye of Love: Mysticism & Religion. LC 78-4428. 1978. 9.95 (ISBN 0-06-064195-9, HarpR). Har-Row.

Johnston, William. Bugs Bunny Party Pest. (Tell-a-Tale Readers). (Illus.). (gr. k-3). 1978. PLB 4.77 (ISBN 0-307-68607-8, Whitman). Western Pub.
--Christian Zen. 1974. pap. 3.95 o.p. (ISBN 0-06-090368-6, CN368, CN). Har Row.
--Christian Zen: A Way of Meditation. 2nd ed. LC 80-8430. (Illus.). 144p. 1981. pap. 4.95 (ISBN 0-06-064198-3, RD 343, HarpR). Har-Row.
--Echoes of a Summer. 1976. pap. 1.50 o.p. (ISBN 0-345-25633-6). Ballantine.
--England As It Is: Political, Social & Industrial in the Middle of the Nineteenth Century, 2 vols. (The Development of Industrial Society Ser.). 721p. 1980. 60.00x (ISBN 0-7165-1774-4, Pub. by Irish Academic Pr). Biblio Dist.
--The Mirror Mind: Spirituality & Transformation. LC 80-8350. 192p. 1981. 10.95 (ISBN 0-06-064197-5, HarpR). Har-Row.
Johnston, William M. The Austrian Mind: An Intellectual & Social History. (California Library Reprint Ser.). 1976. 35.00x (ISBN 0-520-03182-2). U of Cal Pr.
Johnston, William, S.J., ed. The Cloud of Unknowing & the Book of Privy Counselling. LC 73-79737. 200p. 1973. pap. 2.95 (ISBN 0-385-03097-5, Im). Doubleday.
Johnston, William W. & Frable, William J. Diagnostic Respiratory Cytopathology. LC 79-84478. (Masson Monographs in Diagnostic Cytopathology). 328p. 1979. 41.25 (ISBN 0-89352-047-0). Masson Pub.
Johnstone, A. H. & Duncan, I. M. Chemistry Check-up. 1974. pap. text ed. 3.95x o.p. (ISBN 0-435-64183-2). Heinemann Ed.
Johnstone, A. H. & Morrison, T. I. Chemistry Takes Shape. Incl. Book 1. 1964. pap. text ed. 4.50x o.p. (ISBN 0-435-64482-3); tchrs guide 2.50x o.p. (ISBN 0-435-64484-X); Book 2. 1965. pap. text ed. 4.50x o.p. (ISBN 0-435-64486-6); Book 3. 1966. pap. text ed. 5.50x o.p. (ISBN 0-435-64490-4); Book 4. pap. text ed. 5.50x o.p. (ISBN 0-435-64494-7); tchrs guide 2.50x o.p. (ISBN 0-435-64495-5); Book 5. 1970. pap. text ed. 6.50x o.p. (ISBN 0-435-64497-1); tchrs. ed. 2.50x o.p. (ISBN 0-435-64498-X). Heinemann Ed.
Johnstone, A. H., et al. Test Your Chemistry. 1968. pap. text ed. 2.95x o.p. (ISBN 0-435-64481-5). Heinemann Ed.
Johnstone, Ann, jt. auth. see Johnson, Carol.
Johnstone, B. Kenneth, jt. auth. see Birch, Jack W.
Johnstone, Charles. Chrysal, or the Adventures of a Guinea, 4 vols. Paulson, Ronald, ed. LC 78-60839. (Novel 1720-1805 Ser.: Vol. 5). 1979. Set. lib. bdg. 124.00 (ISBN 0-8240-3654-9). Garland Pub.
--The History of Arsaces, Prince of Betlis, 1774, 2 vols. in 1. Shugrue, Michael F., ed. (The Flowering of the Novel, 1740-1775 Ser: Vol. 106). 1974. lib. bdg. 50.00 (ISBN 0-8240-1205-4). Garland Pub.
--The Pilgrim; or, a Picture of Life, 1775, 2 vols. in 1. LC 74-16216. (Novel in England, 1700-1775 Ser). 1974. lib. bdg. 50.00 (ISBN 0-8240-1208-9). Garland Pub.
--The Reverie; or, a Flight to the Paradise of Fools, 1763, 2 vols. in 1. LC 74-16307. (Novel in England, 1700-1775 Ser). 1974. lib. bdg. 50.00 (ISBN 0-8240-1162-7). Garland Pub.
Johnstone, I. A Probabilistic Study of Linear Elliptic-Parabolic Equations of Second Order. (Notes on Pure Mathematics Ser.: No. 12). 217p. (Orig.). 1980. pap. text ed. 14.95 (ISBN 0-908160-32-1, 0564). Bks Australia.
Johnstone, K. R., tr. see Zakythinos, D. A.
Johnstone, Mildred T. Brother Wolf. LC 79-20422. (Illus.). 1980. 6.95 o.p. (ISBN 0-916820-13-0). Center Pubns.
Johnstone, P. T. Topos Theory. 1978. 50.50 (ISBN 0-12-387850-0). Acad Pr.
Johnstone, Parker L. Religion & Science Examine God. LC 80-83297. 212p. 1980. 7.95 (ISBN 0-917802-04-7). Theoscience Found.
--San Francisco Begins, Seventeen Seventy-Six. (gr. 4-5). 1979. 7.95 (ISBN 0-912748-01-X). Mission Dolores.
Johnstone, R. A. Mass Spectrometry for Organic Chemists. (Illus.). 1972. 32.50 (ISBN 0-521-08381-8); pap. 11.95x (ISBN 0-521-09685-5). Cambridge U Pr.
Johnstone, Robert. James. (Geneva Commentaries Ser.). 1977. 12.95 (ISBN 0-85151-257-7). Banner of Truth.
--Lectures on the Book of Philippians. 1977. 16.50 (ISBN 0-686-12969-5). Klock & Klock.
--Lectures on the Epistle of James. 1977. 14.00 (ISBN 0-686-12968-7). Klock & Klock.
--The Lost World Does It Exist? 1978. text ed. 13.00x (ISBN 0-901072-75-3). Humanities.
Johnstone, Robert E. Anesthesiology Continuing Education Review. 1975. spiral bdg. 14.00 (ISBN 0-87488-353-9). Med Exam.
Johnstone, Robert E. & Thring, Meredith W. Pilot Plants, Models, & Scale-up Methods in Chemical Engineering. (Chemical Engineering Ser.). (Illus.). 1957. 39.50 o.p. (ISBN 0-07-032693-2, P&RB). McGraw.
Johnstone, Robert H. Study Guide for Introduction to Statistics. 280p. (Orig.). 1980. pap. text ed. 7.95 (ISBN 0-8185-0410-2). Brooks-Cole.
Johnstone, Ronald L. Religion & Society in Interaction: The Sociology of Religion. 368p. 1975. text ed. 17.95 (ISBN 0-13-773085-3). P-H.
Johnston-Jones, D. R. The Deathless Train: The Life & Work of Robert Smith Surtees. (Salzburg Studies in English Literature, Romantic Reassessment: No. 36). 183p. 1974. pap. text ed. 25.00x (ISBN 0-391-01439-0). Humanities.
John The Scot. Periphyseon: On the Division of Nature. Uhlfelder, Myra, ed. & tr. LC 75-16475. (LLA Ser: No. 157). 408p. 1975. pap. 7.95 (ISBN 0-672-60377-2). Bobbs.
John Thomas, David St. see St. John Thomas, David.
John Van Leuv, De see American College of Emergency Physicians.
Johri, K. N. Macro & Semi-Micro Chemical Analysis Without H2S. 2nd rev. ed. pap. 3.00x o.p. (ISBN 0-210-31239-4). Asia.
Joiner, Jasper N. Foliage Plant Production. (Illus.). 608p. 1981. text ed. 24.95 (ISBN 0-13-322867-3). P-H.
Joiner, William L. Wanting, Becoming, Believing. 152p. 1981. pap. 5.95 (ISBN 0-8170-0884-5). Judson.
Joint Association of Classical Teachers. Greek Vocabulary. 1980. pap. 5.95 (ISBN 0-521-23277-5). Cambridge U Pr.
Joint Association of Classical Teachers-Greek Course. The Intellectual Revolution: Selections from Euripides, Thucydides & Plato. LC 79-16754. (Illus.). 160p. 1980. pap. 9.95x (ISBN 0-521-22461-6). Cambridge U Pr.
Joint Association of Classical Teachers. Reading Greek: Grammar, Vocabulary & Exercises. LC 77-91090. 1978. 10.95x (ISBN 0-521-21977-9). Cambridge U Pr.
Joint Association of Classical Teachers' Greek Course. A World of Heroes: Selections from Homer, Herodotus & Sophocles. LC 79-10740. (Illus.). 1979. pap. 9.95x (ISBN 0-521-22462-4). Cambridge U Pr.
Joint Bank-Fund Library, Washington, D.C. Economics & Finance: Index to Periodical Articles, Nineteen Forty-Seven to Nineteen Seventy-One. Second Supplement. (Library Catalogs-Bib. Guides). 1979. lib. bdg. 95.00 (ISBN 0-8161-0302-X). G K Hall.
Joint Bank-Fund Library (Washington, D. C.) Economics, Finance & Development: Subject Headings Used in the Main Catalog of the Joint Bank-Fund Library. 1979. lib. bdg. 88.00 (ISBN 0-8161-0276-7). G K Hall.
Joint Commission on Mental Health of Children. Adolescence: A Report. Josselyn, Irene M., ed. LC 78-127300. 1971. 12.50 o.p. (ISBN 0-06-012231-5, HarpT). Har-Row.
--Mental Health from Infancy Through Adolescence. LC 78-123939. (Illus.). 512p. 1973. 15.00x o.s.i. (ISBN 0-06-012228-5, HarpT). Har-Row.
Joint Committee of the American Psychiatric Association & the American Hospital Association. Psychiatric Emergencies & the General Hospital. 1965. pap. 1.25 o.p. (ISBN 0-685-24846-1, 159). Am Psychiatric.
Joint Committee on Junior & Senior Colleges. Guidelines for Improving Articulation Between Junior & Senior Colleges. 1966. pap. 2.50 10 copies o.p. (ISBN 0-685-32623-3). ACE.
Joint Committee on Standards for Educational Evaluation. Standards for Evaluations of Educational Programs, Projects & Materials. LC 80-12192. 224p. 1980. 8.95 (ISBN 0-07-032725-4). McGraw.
Joint FAO-IAEA Division of Atomic Energy in Food & Agriculture, Vienna, December 2-6, 1974. Tracer Techniques for Plant Breeding: Proceedings. (Illus.). 1976. pap. 9.75 (ISBN 92-0-111675-6, IAEA). Unipub.
Joint ISMAR-AMPERE International Conference on Magnetic Resonance. Proceedings. Smidt, J., ed. 1981. 60.00. Franklin Inst Pr.
Joint Publications Research Service. Modern Communist Chinese Usage: Chinese English Dictionary. 2nd ed. pap. 56.00 (ISBN 0-686-23791-9, JPRS 20904). Natl Tech Info.
Joint Research Center, Petten Establishment of the Commission of the European Communities, jt. auth. see International Colloquium on Irradiation Tests for Reactor Safety Programmes, Petten, Holland, June 1979.
Joint Research Centre, Workshop, Karlslruhe Establishment (European Inst. for Transuranium Elements), Germany, October 1978. Fission Gas Behaviour in Nuclear Fuels: Proceedings. Ronchi, C., et al, eds. (European Applied Research Reports Special Topics Ser.). 350p. 1979. pap. text ed. 82.00 (ISBN 3-7186-0010-2). Harwood Academic.
Joint Steering Group on Uranium Resources of the OECD Nuclear Energy Agency & the International Atomic Energy Agency. World Uranium Geology & Resource Potential. LC 80-81724. (Illus.). 524p. 1980. pap. 50.00 (ISBN 0-87930-085-X). Miller Freeman.
Joint Tax Program OAS IDB. Tax Systems of Latin America: Honduras & Nicaragua. 1967. pap. 1.00 ea. o.p. OAS.
Joinville, Jean De see De Villehardouin, Geoffrey & De Joinville, Jean.
Jokl, Ernst. The Clinical Physiology of Physical Fitness & Rehabilitation. (American Lecture Sportsmedicine Ser). (Illus.). 208p. 1971. photocopy ed., spiral 19.75 (ISBN 0-398-02198-8). C C Thomas.
--Physiology of Exercise. (American Lecture Sportsmedicine Ser). (Illus.). 156p. 1971. photocopy ed. 14.75 (ISBN 0-398-02152-X). C C Thomas.
Joklik, Wolfgang K. Principles of Animal Virology. 320p. 1980. text ed. 21.95x (ISBN 0-8385-7920-5). ACC.
Jolas, Maria, tr. see Sarraute, Nathalie.
Jolicoeur, Pamela M., jt. auth. see Rich, Harvey E.
Jolivet, A., jt. auth. see Pinloche, A.
Joll, Caroline, jt. auth. see George, K. D.
Joll, James. The Second International 1889-1914. 2nd ed. 1975. 21.50x (ISBN 0-7100-7966-4). Routledge & Kean.
Jolles, Isaac. Catalogue for the Qualitative Interpretation of the House-Tree-Person (H-T-P) rev. ed. LC 79-57217. 1971. pap. 7.50x (ISBN 0-87424-001-8). Western Psych.
Jolles, Isaac & Southwick, Selma I. Clinical Approach to Training the Educable Mentally Retarded: A Handbook. LC 70-95255. (Professional Handbook Ser.). (Illus.). 31p. 1971. pap. 7.00x (ISBN 0-87424-113-8). Western Psych.
Jolley, E. H. Telecommunications. Moore, Patrick, ed. (Young Engineer Ser). (Illus.). (gr. 7 up). 1963. 4.25 o.p. (ISBN 0-298-16439-6). Dufour.
Jolley, Miesje. A Crack in Time. (Illus.). 48p. (Orig.). 1980. pap. 6.00 (ISBN 0-931122-20-1). West End.
Jolley, Robert L., et al, eds. Water Chlorination: Environmental Impact & Health Effects, Vol. 3. LC 77-92588. (Illus.). 1200p. 1980. 37.50 (ISBN 0-250-40342-0). Ann Arbor Science.
Jolliffe, F. R. Commonsense Statistics for Economists & Others. (Students Library of Economics Ser.). 1974. 10.00x (ISBN 0-7100-7952-4); pap. 6.95 (ISBN 0-7100-7953-2). Routledge & Kegan.
Jolly, tr. see Mueller, F. Max.
Jolly, Elizabeth. The Invisible Chain: Diseases Passed on by Inheritance. LC 72-80166. 1972. 12.95 (ISBN 0-911012-26-5). Nelson-Hall.
Jolly, Hugh. Diseases of Children. 3rd ed. (Illus.). 1976. 21.75 (ISBN 0-632-00396-0, Blackwell). Mosby.
Jolly, P. W. & Wilke, G. The Organic Chemistry of Nickel, 2 vols. (Organometallic Chemistry Ser.). Vol. 1, 1974. 80.00 (ISBN 0-12-388401-2); Vol. 2, 1975. 66.50 (ISBN 0-12-388402-0). Acad Pr.
Jolly, Richard, ed. Disarmament & World Development. new ed. 1978. text ed. 23.00 (ISBN 0-08-023019-9); pap. text ed. 8.50 (ISBN 0-08-023018-0). Pergamon.
Jolly, Tony. Introducing Handbuilt Pottery. (Illus.). 96p. 1974. 9.95 o.p. (ISBN 0-8230-6194-9). Watson-Guptill.
Jolly, W. Synthesis & Characterization of Inorganic Compounds. 1970. 23.95 (ISBN 0-13-879932-6). P-H.
Jolowics, H. F. Historical Introduction to the Study of Roman Law. 3rd ed. Nicholas, B., ed. LC 74-164452. 624p. 1972. 79.00 (ISBN 0-521-08253-6). Cambridge U Pr.
Joly, Charles J., ed. see Hamilton, William R.
Jomini, Henri. Art of War. Repr. of 1862 ed. lib. bdg. 28.50x (ISBN 0-8371-5014-0, JOAW). Greenwood.
Jonas, David, jt. auth. see Jonas, Doris.
Jonas, Doris & Jonas, David. Primeval Mechanisms. Date not set. 14.95 (ISBN 0-89793-006-1). Hunter Hse.
--Sex & Status. LC 74-23275. 214p. (Orig.). 1980. pap. 6.95 (ISBN 0-8128-6069-1). Stein & Day.
Jonas, George & Amiel, Barbara. By Persons Unknown. 1978. pap. 2.25 o.p. (ISBN 0-440-00893-X, D0893, Dist. by Dell). Grove.
Jonas, Gerald. Stuttering: The Disorder of Many Theories. 64p. 1977. 5.95 (ISBN 0-374-27118-6); pap. 2.95 (ISBN 0-374-51429-1). FS&G.
Jonas, Hans. Philosophical Essays: From Ancient Creed to Technological Man. 14.00 (ISBN 0-226-40591-5, Phoen). U of Chicago Pr.
Jonas, Ilsedore B., jt. ed. see Jonas, Klaus W.
Jonas, Klaus W., ed. The World of Somerset Maugham: An Anthology. LC 73-156196. 200p. 1972. Repr. of 1959 ed. lib. bdg. 18.75x (ISBN 0-8371-6147-9, JOSM). Greenwood.
Jonas, Klaus W. & Jonas, Ilsedore B., eds. Thomas Mann Studies, Vol. 2. LC 66-12543. 1967. 15.00x o.p. (ISBN 0-8122-7527-6). U of Pa Pr.
Jonas, Nita. Wild & Woolly Animal Book. (Illus.). (gr. k-2). 1961. PLB 3.69 o.p. (ISBN 0-394-90688-8, BYR). Random.
Jonas, Oswald, ed. see Schenker, Heinrich.
Jonas, Paul. Taxation of Multinationals in Communist Countries. LC 77-13886. (Praeger Special Studies). 1978. 21.95 (ISBN 0-03-040676-5). Praeger.
Jonas, Steven. Health Care Delivery in the United States. 2nd ed. 512p. 1981. text ed. price not set (ISBN 0-8261-2072-5); pap. text ed. price not set (ISBN 0-8261-2073-3). Springer Pub.
Jonas, Susanne, jt. ed. see Dixon, Marlene.
Jonchay, Yvan du see Du Jonchay, Yvan.
Jonchere, E. L. De La see De La Jonchere, E. L.
Joncich, Geraldine. The Sane Positivist: A Biography of Edward L. Thorndike. LC 68-27542. (Illus.). 1968. 32.50x (ISBN 0-8195-3093-X, Pub. by Wesleyan U Pr). Columbia U Pr.
Jondorf, Gillian. Robert Garnier & the Themes of Political Tragedy. LC 69-11027. 1969. 36.00 (ISBN 0-521-07386-3). Cambridge U Pr.
Jone, Bryan J., et al see Weissberger, A.
Jones. Adolescents with Behavior Problems: Strategies for Teaching, Counseling & Parent Involvement. abr. ed. 1980. text ed. 10.50 (ISBN 0-205-06824-3). Allyn.
--North American Radio T. V. Station Guide. 14th ed. pap. 7.95 (ISBN 0-686-64616-9). Bobbs.
Jones, jt. auth. see Caves.
Jones, jt. auth. see Moncrief.
Jones, A. & Weinstock, H. Computer-Based Science Instruction. 376p. 1978. 37.50x (ISBN 90-286-0248-8). Sijthoff & Noordhoff.
Jones, A. H. The Decline of the Ancient World. (General History of Europe Ser.). 1975. pap. text ed. 11.95x (ISBN 0-582-48309-3). Longman.
--The Greek City from Alexander to Justinian. 404p. (Orig.). 1979. pap. text ed. 22.00x (ISBN 0-19-814842-9). Oxford U Pr.
--The Roman Economy: Studies in Ancient Economic & Administrative History. Brunt, P. A., ed. 450p. 1974. 27.50x o.p. (ISBN 0-87471-194-0). Rowman.
--Were Ancient Heresies Disguised Social Movements? Lee, Clarence L., ed. LC 66-11534. (Facet Bks.). 1966. pap. 1.00 (ISBN 0-8006-3023-8, 1-3023). Fortress.
Jones, A. H., ed. History of Rome Through the Fifth Century, Vols. 1 & 2. LC 68-13332. (Documentary History of Western Civilization Ser). 1969. 12.50x ea. o.s.i. Vol. 1 (ISBN 0-8027-2010-2). Vol. 2 (ISBN 0-8027-2011-0). Walker & Co.
Jones, A. J. & Barlow, N. Twenty-Four Worked Engineering Drawing Examples. 1966. pap. text ed. 4.20 (ISBN 0-08-012080-6). Pergamon.
Jones, A. J., jt. auth. see El-Agra, A. M.
Jones, A. R. The Ciliates. (Illus.). 1973. pap. text ed. 6.00x (ISBN 0-09-117301-9, Hutchinson U Lib). Humanities.
Jones, A. W. Introduction to Parasitology. 1967. 19.95 (ISBN 0-201-03365-8). A-W.
Jones, Abel J. In Search of Truth. 207p. 1980. Repr. of 1946 ed. lib. bdg. 25.00 (ISBN 0-89984-259-3). Century Bookbindery.
Jones, Alan W. Journey into Christ. 1977. pap. 4.95 (ISBN 0-8164-0338-4). Crossroad NY.
Jones, Alexander, ed. New Testament of the Jerusalem Bible: Reader's Edition. LC 69-11018. (Illus.). 1969. pap. 2.95 (ISBN 0-385-06569-8, D253, Im). Doubleday.
Jones, Alexander (General Editor) Psalms of the Jerusalem Bible. 1970. pap. 2.95 (ISBN 0-385-02525-4, Im). Doubleday.
Jones, Alfred H. Roosevelt's Image Brokers: Poets, Playwrights & the Use of the Lincoln Symbol. LC 74-77651. 129p. 1974. 12.95 (ISBN 0-8046-9079-0, Natl U). Kennikat.
Jones, Alick R. The Ciliates. LC 73-87077. (Illus.). 160p. 1974. 16.95 (ISBN 0-312-13860-1). St Martin.
Jones, Allen. World Protein Resources. LC 74-11219. 1974. 24.95 (ISBN 0-470-44935-7). Halsted Pr.
Jones, Alun & Bodmer, Walter F. Our Future Inheritance; Choice or Chance? A Study by a British Association Working Party. (Illus.). 156p. 1974. pap. 4.95x o.p. (ISBN 0-19-857390-1). Oxford U Pr.
Jones, Alwyn. Rural Housing. 76p. 1975. pap. text ed. 5.00x (ISBN 0-7135-1887-1, Pub. by Bedford England). Renouf.

Jones, Amanda T. A Psychic Autobiography. Baxter, Annette K., ed. LC 79-8798. (Signal Lives Ser.). (Illus.). 1980. Repr. of 1910 ed. lib. bdg. 42.00x (ISBN 0-405-12845-2). Arno.

Jones, Andrew. Flight Seaward. LC 78-6735. 1978. 8.95 o.p. (ISBN 0-688-03359-8). Morrow.

Jones, Andrew & Rutman, Leonard. In the Children's Aid: J. J. Kelso & Child Welfare in Ontario. 256p. 1981. 17.50 (ISBN 0-8020-5491-9). U of Toronto Pr.

Jones, Andrew N. & Cooper, Cary L. Combating Managerial Obsolescence. LC 80-16307. 192p. 1980. lib. bdg. 19.95 (ISBN 0-86003-509-3, JCO/). Greenwood.

Jones, Anthony S., et al. Strategies for Teaching. LC 79-20596. 249p. 1979. 13.50 (ISBN 0-8108-1257-6). Scarecrow.

Jones, Archer, jt. ed. see Bernd, Joseph L.

Jones, Arnold H. Later Roman Empire, Two Eighty-Four to Six Hundred Two: A Social, Economic, & Administrative Survey, 2 Vols. (Illus.). 1966. Repr. of 1964 ed. Set. 49.50 (ISBN 0-8061-0624-7). U of Okla Pr.

Jones, Arnold H. & Monroe, Elizabeth. History of Ethiopia. 1955. 14.95x (ISBN 0-19-821609-2). Oxford U Pr.

Jones, Arthur. Malcolm Forbes: Peripatetic Millionaire. LC 77-6885. (Illus.). 1977. 10.00 o.s.i. (ISBN 0-06-012204-8, HarpT). Har-Row.

Jones, Arthur F. The Art of Paul Sawyier. LC 75-41988. (Illus.). 208p. Date not set. pap. cancelled (ISBN 0-8131-0145-X). U Pr of Ky. Postponed.

Jones, Arthur J., et al. Principles of Unit Construction. 232p. 1980. Repr. of 1939 ed. lib. bdg. 20.00 (ISBN 0-89984-261-5). Century Bookbindery.

Jones, Aubrey. Mathematical Astronomy with a Pocket Calculator. LC 78-12075. 1979. 16.95 (ISBN 0-470-26552-3). Halsted Pr.

Jones, Aubrey, ed. Economics & Equality. 176p. 1976. 27.00x (ISBN 0-86003-010-5, Pub. by Allan Pubs England). State Mutual Bk.

Jones, Barbara S. Movement Themes: Topics for Early Childhood Learning Through Creative Movement. LC 80-65608. 115p. 1981. perfect bdg. 8.50 (ISBN 0-86548-042-7). Century Twenty One.

--Mrs. Jones, -----on You: Day-by-Day in an Inner City Preschool. 1977. pap. 7.95 (ISBN 0-8224-4531-X). Pitman Learning.

Jones, Bernard E. The Complete Woodworker. LC 80-634. (Illus.). 1980. pap. 7.95 (ISBN 0-89815-022-1). Ten Speed Pr.

Jones, Betty, jt. auth. see Jones, J. P.

Jones, Betty M. Nancy Lieberman, Basketball's Magic Lady. LC 80-82004. (Starpeople Ser.). (Illus.). 75p. (gr. 4-9). 1980. PLB 5.79 (ISBN 0-8178-0009-3). Harvey.

--Wonder Women of Sports. LC 80-20232. (Step-up Book Ser.: No. 33). (Illus.). 72p. (gr. 2-5). 1981. PLB 4.99 (ISBN 0-394-94475-5); pap. 3.95 boards (ISBN 0-394-84475-0). Random.

Jones, Bill & Kavanagh, Dennis, eds. British Politics Today. LC 78-21048. 1979. text ed. 13.50x (ISBN 0-8419-0473-1); pap. text ed. 6.00 o.p. (ISBN 0-8419-0475-8). Holmes & Meier.

Jones, Billy M., ed. The Heroes of Tennessee. LC 79-124288. (The Tennessee Ser.: No. 1). (Illus.). 1979. 11.95 (ISBN 0-87870-051-X). Memphis St Univ.

Jones, Bonzo. Train Your Human: A Manual for Caring Dogs. LC 79-52365. (Illus.). 1979. 10.50 (ISBN 0-7153-7678-0). David & Charles.

Jones, Brian. Circuit Electronics. 1974. text ed. 18.95 (ISBN 0-201-03374-7). A-W.

Jones, Brian, et al. New Methods for Delivering Human Services. Walz, Garry R. & Benjamin, Libby, eds. LC 77-1746. (New Vistas in Counseling: Vol. 2). 1977. 14.95 (ISBN 0-87705-309-X). Human Sci Pr.

Jones, Brian N. Car Values: 1981 Edition. 4th ed. (Illus.). 272p. (Orig.). 1981. pap. 12.95 (ISBN 0-528-88138-8). Rand.

Jones, Burton W. Linear Algebra. LC 72-83244. 1973. text ed. 19.95x (ISBN 0-8162-4544-4). Holden-Day.

Jones, C., ed. see Bowden, M. L., et al.

Jones, C. A. see Bowden, M. L. & Feller, I.

Jones, C. A., ed. Lope de Vega: El Castigo sin Venganza. 1966. 6.10 (ISBN 0-08-011775-9); pap. 4.80 (ISBN 0-08-011774-0). Pergamon.

Jones, C. B., jt. ed. see Bellringer, A. W.

Jones, C. David. The Pastoral Mentor. LC 80-51494. 1980. 16.95 (ISBN 0-931804-05-1). Skipworth Pr.

Jones, C. M. Bowls: How to Become a Champion. (Illus., Orig.). 1976. pap. 3.95 (ISBN 0-571-10708-7, Pub. by Faber & Faber). Merrimack Bk Serv.

--Match-Winning Tennis: Tactics, Temperament & Training. (Illus.). 1971. 9.95 (ISBN 0-571-09289-6). Transatlantic.

--Tennis: How to Become a Champion. (gr. 9 up). 1968. 12.00 (ISBN 0-571-04714-9); pap. 6.50 (ISBN 0-571-09415-5). Transatlantic.

--Tennis: How to Become a Champion. (Illus., Orig.). 1970. pap. 4.95 (ISBN 0-571-09415-5, Pub. by Faber & Faber). Merrimack Bk Serv.

--Your Book of Tennis. (gr. 4 up). 1970. 7.95 (ISBN 0-571-08767-1). Transatlantic.

Jones, C. M. & Harring, Mike. Improving Your Tennis: Strokes & Techniques. (Illus.). 132p. 1973. 7.50 o.p. (ISBN 0-571-10148-8). Transatlantic.

Jones, Candy. Candy Jones' Complete Book of Beauty & Fashion. LC 73-4095. (Illus.). 256p. (YA) 1976. 11.95 o.s.i. (ISBN 0-06-012223-4, HarpT). Har-Row.

--Modeling & Other Glamour Careers. LC 68-28204. (Illus.). 1969. 8.95 o.p. (ISBN 0-06-110901-0, HarpT). Har-Row.

Jones, Caroline M., jt. auth. see Scott, Natalie V.

Jones, Catherine. Immigration & Social Policy in Britain. 275p. 1977. pap. 9.95 (ISBN 0-422-74680-0, 6363). Methuen Inc.

Jones, Charles. Boat Maintenance: Ideas & Practice. 192p. 1980. 12.00x (ISBN 0-245-52347-2, Pub. by Nautical England). State Mutual Bk.

--Glass Fibre Yachts: Improvement & Repair. 128p. 1980. 12.00x (Pub. by Nautical England). State Mutual Bk.

Jones, Charles C., Jr. Negro Myths from the Georgia Coast. LC 68-21779. 1969. Repr. of 1888 ed. 18.00 (ISBN 0-8103-3836-X). Gale.

Jones, Charles E. Guide to the Study of the Holiness Movement. LC 74-659. (ATLA Bibliography Ser.: No. 1). 1974. 35.00 (ISBN 0-8108-0703-3). Scarecrow.

--Perfectionist Persuasion: The Holiness Movement & American Methodism, 1867-1936. LC 74-1376. (ATLA Monograph: No. 5). (Illus.). 1974. 10.00 (ISBN 0-8108-0747-5). Scarecrow.

Jones, Charles H. A Short Life of Charles Dickens with Selections from His Letters. 260p. 1980. Repr. of 1900 ed. lib. bdg. 30.00 (ISBN 0-8414-5406-X). Folcroft.

Jones, Charles L., jt. auth. see Coxon, Anthony P.

Jones, Charles O. Every Second Year: Congressional Behavior & the Two-Year Term. 1967. 9.95 (ISBN 0-8157-4712-8); pap. 3.95 (ISBN 0-8157-4711-X). Brookings.

Jones, Charles S. From the Rio Grande to the Arctic: Story of the Richfield Oil Corporation. LC 70-160504. (Illus.). 1972. 17.50 (ISBN 0-8061-0976-9); pap. 6.95 (ISBN 0-8061-1155-0). U of Okla Pr.

Jones, Charles W. The Saint-Nicholas Liturgy & Its Literary Relationship (10th-12th Centuries) (U. C. Publ. in English Studies: Vol. 27). 1963. pap. 7.00x (ISBN 0-520-09068-3). U of Cal Pr.

Jones, Charlie. Life Is Tremendous. 1981. pap. 2.25 (ISBN 0-8423-2184-5). Tyndale.

Jones, Cheslyn & Wainwright, Geoffrey, eds. The Study of Liturgy. 1978. 23.95 (ISBN 0-19-520075-6); pap. 9.95 (ISBN 0-19-520076-4). Oxford U Pr.

Jones, Chris. Y Ahora, Que Hago, Senor? Cabeza, Susana, tr. from Eng. 107p. (Orig., Span.). (gr. 6-9). 1978. pap. 2.50 (ISBN 0-89922-123-8). Edit Caribe.

Jones, Christina. Friends in Palestine. 1981. write for info. (ISBN 0-913408-62-X). Friends United.

Jones, Claire. Sailboat Racing. LC 80-12846. (Superwheels & Thrill Sports Bks.). (Illus.). (YA) (gr. 4 up). 1981. PLB 6.95g (ISBN 0-8225-0434-0). Lerner Pubns.

Jones, Claire, et al. Pollution: The Air We Breathe. LC 70-156364. (Real World of Pollution Ser). (Illus.). 100p. (gr. 5-11). 1971. PLB 4.95 o.p. (ISBN 0-8225-0628-9). Lerner Pubns.

--Pollution: The Dangerous Atom. LC 75-165322. (Real World of Pollution Ser). (Illus.). (gr. 5-12). 1972. PLB 4.95 o.p. (ISBN 0-8225-0630-0). Lerner Pubns.

Jones, Clinton R. Understanding Gay Relatives & Friends. 1978. pap. 3.95 (ISBN 0-8164-2179-X). Crossroad NY.

Jones, Cordelia. Cat Called Camouflage. LC 79-166339. (Illus.). (gr. 7 up). 1971. 9.95 (ISBN 0-87599-189-0). S G Phillips.

Jones, Craig. Blood Secrets. LC 78-4743. 1978. 8.95 o.s.i. (ISBN 0-06-012264-1, HarpT). Har-Row.

Jones, Curtis A. Your Second Mind. 1979. 5.75 (ISBN 0-8062-1285-3). Carlton.

Jones, D. The Phoneme: Its Nature & Use. 3rd ed. LC 70-377868. 1976. Repr. of 1976 ed. 29.50 (ISBN 0-521-21351-7). Cambridge U Pr.

Jones, D. & Ward, Dennis. Phonetics of Russian. 1969. text ed. 58.00 (ISBN 0-521-06736-7). Cambridge U Pr.

Jones, D. F. Colossus. pap. 1.95 (ISBN 0-425-04329-0). Berkley Pub.

Jones, D. G. Butterfly on Rock: A Study of Themes & Images in Canadian Literature. LC 75-133438. 1970. pap. 5.75 (ISBN 0-8020-6186-9). U of Toronto Pr.

--Synapses & Synaptosomes. LC 74-26646. 258p. 1975. text ed. 54.50x o.p. (ISBN 0-412-11270-1, Pub. by Chapman & Hall). Methuen Inc.

--Synapses & Synaptosomes: Morphological Aspects. LC 74-26646. 1975. 54.50 o.p. (ISBN 0-470-44942-X). Halsted Pr.

Jones, D. Gareth. Our Fragile Brains. (Illus.). 300p. 1980. pap. 8.95 (ISBN 0-87784-792-4). Inter-Varsity.

Jones, D. Llanwyn, ed. see Bliokh, P. V., et al.

Jones, D. Parry. Welsh Country Parson. 1975. 19.95 (ISBN 0-7134-2916-X, Pub. by Batsford England). David & Charles.

Jones, D. R., jt. auth. see Ashby, M. F.

Jones, D. S. Electrical & Mechanical Oscillations. (Library of Mathematics). 1968. pap. 5.00 (ISBN 0-7100-4346-5). Routledge & Kegan.

--Methods in Electromagnetic Wave Propagation. (Engineering Science Ser.). (Illus.). 1979. 74.00x (ISBN 0-19-856131-8). Oxford U Pr.

Jones, Daisy M. Curriculum Targets in the Elementary School. 1977. text ed. 17.95 (ISBN 0-13-196337-6). P-H.

Jones, Dan E. The Savannah Game. LC 80-68111. (Illus.). 106p. (Orig.). (gr. 5 up). 1980. pap. 9.95 (ISBN 0-9604808-0-3). Halfrubber.

Jones, Daniel. My Friend Dylan Thomas. (Illus.). 1978. 8.95 o.p. (ISBN 0-684-15917-1, ScribT). Scribner.

Jones, Daniel M. An American Epic: Virgil - A Story of Love. 73p. 1981. 6.95 (ISBN 0-533-01646-0). Vantage.

Jones, David. The Anathemata. (Orig.). 1972. pap. 8.95 o.p. (ISBN 0-571-10127-5, Pub. by Faber & Faber). Merrimack Bk Serv.

--Epoch & Artist. 1973. pap. 6.95 (ISBN 0-571-10152-6, Pub. by Faber & Faber). Merrimack Bk Serv.

--In Parenthesis. 1972. pap. 8.95 (ISBN 0-571-10127-5, Pub. by Faber & Faber). Merrimack Bk Serv.

--Your Book of Money. (gr. 7 up). 1971. 6.50 (ISBN 0-571-09341-8). Transatlantic.

--Your Book of Roman Britain. (Your Book Ser.). (Illus.). 1978. 7.95 (ISBN 0-571-09903-3, Pub. by Faber & Faber). Merrimack Bk Serv.

Jones, David & Crane, Dale, eds. Aviation Maintenance Handbook & Standard Hardware Digest. 2nd ed. 1981. pap. write for info. (ISBN 0-89100-151-4). Aviation Maintenance.

Jones, David, ed. see Cohen, David.

Jones, David A. Crime & Criminal Responsibility. LC 77-25906. (Nelson-Hall Law Enforcement Ser.). 1978. 20.95 (ISBN 0-911012-84-2). Nelson-Hall.

--Crime Without Punishment. LC 78-19538. 1979. 22.95 (ISBN 0-669-02512-7). Lexington Bks.

--The Health Risks of Imprisonment. LC 76-5620. (Illus.). 1976. 21.50 (ISBN 0-669-00651-3). Lexington Bks.

--The Law of Criminal Procedure: An Analysis & Critique. 600p. 1981. text ed. 17.95 (ISBN 0-316-47283-2); tchrs'. manual free (ISBN 0-316-47284-0). Little.

Jones, David A. & Wilkins, Dennis A. Variation & Adaptation in Plant Species. 2nd ed. 1971. pap. text ed. 5.50x o.p. (ISBN 0-435-61480-0). Heinemann Ed.

Jones, David G., ed. see Willis, John T.

Jones, David P. Peking. (The Great Cities Ser.). (Illus.). 1978. lib. bdg. 14.94 (ISBN 0-686-51005-4). Silver.

Jones, David R., ed. The Military-Naval Encyclopedia of Russia & the Soviet Union: MERSU, Vol. 1 1978. 31.50 (ISBN 0-87569-028-9). Academic Intl.

--Military-Naval Encyclopedia of Russia & the Soviet Union: MERSU, Vol. 2. 31.50 (ISBN 0-87569-033-5). Academic Intl.

--Military-Naval Encyclopedia of Russia & the Soviet Union: Mersu, Vol. 3. 1981. write for info. (ISBN 0-87569-041-6). Academic Intl.

--Soviet Armed Forces Review Annual: Safra, Vol. 4. 1981. 45.00 (ISBN 0-87569-037-8). Academic Intl.

Jones, David R., ed. & tr. see Zaionchkovsky, P. A.

Jones, David W., Jr., jt. auth. see House, Peter W.

Jones, Davis, tr. see Piltz, Anders.

Jones, Deborah, et al. Ambulatory Health Care in the City of Boston. (Abt Health-Medical Reports). 1974. pap. 43.00x o.p. (ISBN 0-89011-472-2, HMD-101). Abt Assoc.

Jones, Delmos J., jt. auth. see King, William S.

Jones, Diana. Patterns for Canvas Embroidery. 1977. 17.95 (ISBN 0-7134-3285-3). David & Charles.

Jones, Diana W. Charmed Life. LC 77-18414. (gr. 5-9). 1978. 7.95 (ISBN 0-688-80138-2); PLB 7.73 (ISBN 0-688-84138-4). Greenwillow.

--Dogsbody. LC 76-28715. (gr. 5-9). 1977. 8.25 (ISBN 0-688-80074-2); PLB 7.92 (ISBN 0-688-84074-4). Greenwillow.

--Power of Three. LC 77-3028. (gr. 5-9). 1977. 8.25 (ISBN 0-688-80106-4); PLB 7.92 (ISBN 0-688-84106-6). Greenwillow.

--The Spellcoats. 1980. pap. write for info. (ISBN 0-671-83599-8). PB.

Jones, Diane. When You Least Expect Love. (YA) 1978. 5.95 (ISBN 0-685-84750-0, Avalon). Bouregy.

Jones, Don. Miss Liberty Meet Crazyhorse. LC 74-18916. 62p. 1972. 5.00 o.p. (ISBN 0-8040-0584-2); pap. 3.25 (ISBN 0-8040-0585-0). Swallow.

Jones, Donald G. The Sectional Crisis & Northern Methodism: A Study in Piety, Political Ethics & Civil Religion. LC 78-9978. 1979. lib. bdg. 16.50 (ISBN 0-8108-1175-8). Scarecrow.

Jones, Dorothy K. A Century of Servitude: Pribilof Aleuts Under U. S. Rule. LC 80-1407. 198p. 1980. lib. bdg. 17.75 (ISBN 0-8191-1348-4); pap. text ed. 9.00 (ISBN 0-8191-1349-2). U Pr of Amer.

Jones, Dorothy M. & Wood, John R. An Aleut Bibliography. LC 74-620054. 192p. 1976. pap. 15.00 (ISBN 0-295-95529-5). U of Wash Pr.

Jones, Douglas. Arrest Sitting Bull. 1978. pap. 2.50 o.s.i. (ISBN 0-446-81474-1). Warner Bks.

Jones, Douglas C. The Court-Martial of George Armstrong Custer. 1977. pap. 2.25 o.s.i. (ISBN 0-446-82333-3). Warner Bks.

--A Creek Called Wounded Knee. LC 78-16660. 1978. 8.95 o.p. (ISBN 0-684-15822-1, ScribT). Scribner.

--A Creek Called Wounded Knee. 1979. pap. 2.50 (ISBN 0-446-91121-6). Warner Bks.

--Elkhorn Tavern. large print ed. 1981. Repr. of 1980 ed. 12.95 (ISBN 0-89621-273-4). Thorndike Pr.

--Treaty of Medicine Lodge. LC 66-22709. (Illus.). 237p. 1966. 12.95 o.p. (ISBN 0-8061-0712-X); pap. 5.95 (ISBN 0-8061-1165-8). U of Okla Pr.

Jones, Douglas E., jt. auth. see Thurmond, John T.

Jones, Douglas L. Village & Seaport: Migration & Society in Eighteenth-Century Massachusetts. LC 80-54469. (Illus.). 240p. 1981. 15.00x (ISBN 0-87451-200-X). U Pr of New Eng.

Jones, Douglas L., jt. ed. see Levy, Leonard W.

Jones, E. & Sinclair, D. J. Atlas of London. 1969. 205.00 (ISBN 0-08-013255-3). Pergamon.

Jones, E. J. Production Engineering: Jig & Tool Design. 8th ed. 288p. 1973. 35.00x (ISBN 0-408-70308-3); pap. 25.00x (ISBN 0-408-00079-1). Transatlantic.

Jones, E. L. Agriculture & the Industrial Revolution. LC 74-2400. 1974. 19.95 (ISBN 0-470-44870-9). Halsted Pr.

--The European Miracle: Environments, Economies & Geopolitics in the History of Europe & Asia. 274p. Date not set. text ed. price not set (ISBN 0-521-23588-X); pap. text ed. price not set (ISBN 0-521-28055-9). Cambridge U Pr.

Jones, E. Stanley. The Christ of the Mount. (Festival Ser.). 336p. 1981. pap. 2.45 (ISBN 0-687-06925-4). Abingdon.

--Cristo y el Comunismo. Gattinoni, C. T., tr. from Eng. Orig. Title: Christ's Alternative to Communism. 96p. (Span.). Date not set. pap. price not set (ISBN 0-311-05040-9, Edit Mundo). Casa Bautista.

--Divine Yes. 1976. pap. 1.50 (ISBN 0-89129-154-7). Jove Pubns.

--Growing Spiritually. 1953. 4.95 (ISBN 0-687-15967-9). Abingdon.

--How to Pray. (Mini-Libraries Ser.). 1975. pap. 1.25 (ISBN 0-687-17922-X). Abingdon.

--Victory Through Surrender: Self-Realization Through Self-Surrender. (Festival Ser.). 128p. 1980. pap. 1.50 (ISBN 0-687-43750-4). Abingdon.

Jones, Edith W. Excerpts from the Curry County Echoes, Vol. II. (Illus.). 110p. (Orig.). 1981. pap. 47.00 (ISBN 0-932368-08-5). Curry County.

Jones, Edward D. Economic Crises. LC 79-51862. 1981. Repr. of 1900 ed. 21.50 (ISBN 0-88355-955-2). Hyperion Conn.

Jones, Edward E. Ingratiation: A Social Psychological Analysis. LC 64-25812. (Century Psychology Ser.). 1964. 22.50x (ISBN 0-89197-230-7); pap. text ed. 9.50x (ISBN 0-89197-795-3). Irvington.

Jones, Edward G., jt. auth. see Berman, Alvin.

Jones, Edward T. L. P. Hartley. (English Author Ser.: No. 232). 1978. 12.50 (ISBN 0-8057-6703-7). Twayne.

Jones, Edwin R., jt. auth. see Childers, Richard L.

Jones, Eldred D. Wole Soyinka. (World Authors Ser.: Nigeria: No. 256). 1971. lib. bdg. 10.95 (ISBN 0-8057-2852-X). Twayne.

Jones, Eldred D., ed. African Literature Today: Myth, History & the Contemporary Writer, Vol. 11. LC 72-75254. 240p. 1980. text ed. 33.50x (ISBN 0-8419-0577-0, Africana); pap. text ed. 18.00x (ISBN 0-8419-0652-1). Holmes & Meier.

Jones, Elinor J. Tamara. 1980. pap. 2.75 (ISBN 0-451-09450-6, E9450, Sig). NAL.

Jones, Elizabeth, ed. Declassified Documents Reference System. (Nineteen Eighty Annual Collection). 1980. 685.00 (ISBN 0-8408-0330-3). Carrollton Pr.

--Declassified Documents Reference System: 1979 Annual Collection. 1979. 685.00 (ISBN 0-8408-0329-X). Carrollton Pr.

Jones, Elizabeth B., jt. auth. see Jones, William C.

Jones, Elizabeth G., ed. Ranger Rick's Holiday Book. LC 80-81621. (Illus.). 96p. (gr. 2-7). 1980. 8.95 (ISBN 0-912186-38-0). Natl Wildlife.

Jones, Elizabeth O. Big Susan. (Illus.). (gr. k-3). 1967. 3.95g o.s.i. (ISBN 0-02-747740-1). Macmillan.

Jones, Elwyn. Barlow Exposed. LC 76-28040. 1977. 7.95 o.p. (ISBN 0-312-06685-6). St Martin.

Jones, Emrys. Towns & Cities. LC 80-24687. (Illus.). viii, 152p. 1981. Repr. of 1966 ed. lib. bdg. 19.50x (ISBN 0-313-22724-1, JOTC). Greenwood.

Jones, Emrys & Eyles, John. An Introduction to Social Geography. 1977. text ed. 29.95x (ISBN 0-19-874062-X); pap. 8.95x (ISBN 0-19-874063-8). Oxford U Pr.

Jones, Emrys, ed. Readings in Social Geography. (Illus.). 360p. 1975. pap. 8.95x (ISBN 0-19-874060-3). Oxford U Pr.

Jones, Eric. Make-up for School Plays. 1969. 16.95 (ISBN 0-7134-2063-4, Pub. by Batsford England). David & Charles.

Jones, Ernest, tr. see Ferenczi, Sandor.

Jones, Esther L. Feelings. 1981. 4.95 (ISBN 0-8062-1651-4). Carlton.

Jones, Eugene W., et al. Practicing Texas Politics. 4th ed. LC 79-88888. 1980. pap. text ed. 9.95 (ISBN 0-395-28257-8); instrs' manual 1.25 (ISBN 0-395-28258-6); student guide 6.25 (ISBN 0-395-28259-4). HM.

Jones, Eva. Evalore. 1979. pap. 1.95 o.p. (ISBN 0-449-23912-8, Crest). Fawcett.

Jones, Evelyn, ed. see Jones, Ted.

Jones, Evelyn J., jt. auth. see Jones, Terri.

Jones, Everett, jt. ed. see Durham, Philip.

Jones, Sir F. Avery, et al. Clinical Gastroenterology. 2nd ed. (Illus.). 900p. 1968. 21.50 (ISBN 0-397-60057-7, Dist. by Mosby). Lippincott.

Jones, F. C. Extraterritoriality in Japan & the Diplomatic Relations Resulting in Its Abolition, Eighteen Fifty-Three to Eighteen Ninety-Nine. 1931. 18.50x (ISBN 0-686-51384-3). Elliots Bks.

--The Far East: A Concise History. 1966. 11.25 (ISBN 0-08-011642-6); pap. 5.75 (ISBN 0-08-011641-8). Pergamon.

Jones, F. L., jt. auth. see Lindeman, Joyce.

Jones, F. O., ed. Handbook of American Music & Musicians. LC 76-155355. (Music Ser). 1971. Repr. of 1886 ed. lib. bdg. 19.50 (ISBN 0-306-70163-4). Da Capo.

Jones, F. W. Arboreal Man. 1964. Repr. of 1917 ed. 10.75 o.s.i. (ISBN 0-02-847300-0). Hafner.

Jones, Franklin, ed. The Heart of the Ribhu Gita with a Story by Sri Ramana Maharshi. LC 73-88178. (Illus.). 1973. pap. 2.50 o.p. (ISBN 0-913922-03-X). Dawn Horse Pr.

Jones, Franklin D. Machine Shop Training Course, 2 Vols. 5th ed. (Illus.). (gr. 11-12). 1964. 14.00 ea. Vol. 1 (ISBN 0-8311-1039-2). Vol. 2 (ISBN 0-8311-1040-6). Indus Pr.

Jones, Franklin D. & Amiss, John M. Use of Handbook Tables & Formulas. 21st ed. (Illus.). 216p. (gr. 11-12). 1975. 8.00 (ISBN 0-8311-1080-5). Indus Pr.

Jones, Franklin D. & Ryffell, Henry. Gear Design Simplified. 3rd ed. (Illus.). 1961. text ed. 17.00 (ISBN 0-8311-1022-8). Indus Pr.

Jones, Franklin D., jt. auth. see Amiss, John M.

Jones, Franklin D., et al. Ingenious Mechanisms for Designers & Inventors, Vols. 1-4, 1930-67. (Illus.). Set. 70.00 (ISBN 0-685-12543-2); Vol. 1. 20.00 (ISBN 0-8311-1029-5); Vol. 2. 20.00 (ISBN 0-8311-1030-9); Vol. 3. 20.00 (ISBN 0-8311-1031-7); Vol. 4. 20.00 (ISBN 0-8311-1032-5). Indus Pr.

Jones, Fred R. Farm Gas Engines & Tractors. 4th ed. 1963. text ed. 18.50 o.p. (ISBN 0-07-032780-7, C). McGraw.

Jones, Frederick L., ed. see Gisborne, Maria & Williams, Edward E.

Jones, G. Vegetation Productivity. LC 78-40985. (Topics in Applied Geography Ser.). (Illus.). 1979. pap. text ed. 10.95 (ISBN 0-582-48577-0). Longman.

Jones, G., jt. auth. see Williams, D. A.

Jones, G. A. The Properties of Nuclei. (Oxford Physics Ser.). (Illus.). 1976. 21.00x (ISBN 0-19-851828-5). Oxford U Pr.

Jones, G. L. Financial Measurement for Managers. 1976. pap. text ed. 13.95x (ISBN 0-7131-3367-8). Intl Ideas.

Jones, Gareth. The Gentry & the Elizabethan State. (A New History of Wales). (Illus.). 1977. text ed. 7.75x (ISBN 0-7154-0303-6). Humanities.

Jones, Gareth H. History of the Law of Charity, 1532-1827. (Cambridge Studies in English Legal History). 1969. 45.00 (ISBN 0-521-07347-2). Cambridge U Pr.

Jones, George. In a Herb Garden. (Illus.). 98p. 1977. 12.95 (ISBN 0-85475-049-5). Dufour.

Jones, George, ed. New Approaches to the Study of Central-Local Government Relationships. 200p. 1980. text ed. 38.00x (ISBN 0-566-00332-5, Pub. by Gower Pr England). Renouf.

Jones, George F. Oswald Von Wolkenstein. (World Authors Ser.: Germany: No. 236). 1973. lib. bdg. 10.95 (ISBN 0-8057-2992-5). Twayne.

Jones, George F., ed. Foreign Language Teaching: Ideals & Practices. Incl. Foreign Languages in Colleges & Universities. Hadlich, Roger L; Foreign Languages in Elementary School. Schmitt, Conrad J; Foreign Languages in the Secondary School. Hahn, Milton R. 62p. 1964. pap. 7.95x (ISBN 0-915432-64-1). NE Conf Teach Foreign.

Jones, George F. & Wilson, Renate, eds. Detailed Reports on the Salzburger Emigrants Who Settled in America, Vol. 6. LC 67-27137. (Wormsloe Foundation Publication Ser.: No. 15). 360p. 1981. 20.00 (ISBN 0-8203-0512-X). U of Ga Pr.

Jones, George T. Music Theory. (Illus.). 288p. (Orig.). 1974. pap. 3.95 (ISBN 0-06-460137-4, CO 137, COS). Har-Row.

Jones, Georgeanna S., jt. auth. see Jones, Howard, Jr.

Jones, Gordon W., ed. see Mather, Cotton.

Jones, Grace. The Political Structure. 2nd ed. LC 76-7409. (Aspects of Modern Sociology). (Illus.). 1977. pap. text ed. 7.50x (ISBN 0-582-48193-7). Longman.

Jones, Greta. Social Darwinism & English Thought: The Interaction Between Biololgical & Social Theory. (Harvester Studies in Philosophy: No. 20). 1980. text ed. 30.00x (ISBN 0-391-01799-3). Humanities.

Jones, Gwendolyn, ed. Packaging Information Sources. LC 67-18370. (Management Information Guide Ser.: No. 10). 1967. 30.00 (ISBN 0-8103-0811-8). Gale.

Jones, H., jt. auth. see Hall, G.

Jones, H., jt. auth. see Mott, Nevill F.

Jones, H. B. & Jones, Helen C. Sensual Drugs. LC 76-8154. (Illus.). 1977. 29.50 (ISBN 0-521-21247-2); pap. 7.95 (ISBN 0-521-29077-5). Cambridge U Pr.

Jones, H. G., jt. auth. see Mitchell, B. R.

Jones, H. Gordon, ed. see Bridges, John H.

Jones, H. Kay. Butterworths: History of a Publishing House. 296p. 1980. text ed. 27.00 (ISBN 0-406-17606-X). Butterworths.

Jones, H. R. Population Geography. 1981. text ed. 25.85 (ISBN 0-06-318188-6, Pub. by Har-Row Ltd England); pap. text ed. 13.10 (ISBN 0-06-318189-4). Har-Row.

Jones, H. W., ed. see Thucydides.

Jones, Hardy E. Kant's Principle of Personality. LC 70-157393. 1971. 17.50x (ISBN 0-299-06020-9). U of Wis Pr.

Jones, Harold K. & Wakefield, Connie L. Sweetie Feetie. LC 74-19966. (Picture Bk). (Illus.). 32p. (ps-3). 1975. 5.95 o.p. (ISBN 0-695-80546-0); lib. ed. 5.97 o.p. (ISBN 0-695-40546-2). Follett.

Jones, Harry V. Spenser Handbook. (Illus.). 1930. 28.00x (ISBN 0-89197-423-7); pap. text ed. 14.50 (ISBN 0-89197-632-9). Irvington.

Jones, Harry W., et al. Cases & Text Materials on Legal Method: Successor Edition. LC 80-13230. (University Casebook Ser.). Orig. Title: Materials for Legal Method. 817p. 1980. text ed. write for info. (ISBN 0-88277-004-7). Foundation Pr.

Jones, Harvey L. Mathews: Masterpieces of the California Decorative Style. (Illus.). 116p. 1980. 24.95 (ISBN 0-87905-075-6). Peregrine Smith.

Jones, Helen C., jt. auth. see Jones, H. B.

Jones, Henry A; see Salerno, Henry F.

Jones, Henry J. The Egotistical Sublime: A History of Wordsworth's Imagination. LC 78-2460. ix, 212p. 1979. Repr. of 1954 ed. lib. bdg. 19.25x (ISBN 0-313-20307-5). Greenwood.

Jones, Hettie. How to Eat Your ABC's: A Book About Vitamins. LC 75-41442. (Illus.). 96p. (gr. 2-5). 1976. 7.95 (ISBN 0-686-67313-1, Four Winds). Schol Bk Serv.

--In Search of the Castaways. (gr. 5-7). pap. 1.50 o.s.i. (ISBN 0-671-81936-4). Archway.

Jones, Howard. The Residential Community. (Library of Social Work). 1979. 17.00x (ISBN 0-7100-0122-3); pap. 8.95 (ISBN 0-7100-0123-1). Routledge & Kegan.

--Uncle Tom's Cabin. LC 74-92333. (gr. 6-8). 1969. pap. text ed. 3.50x (ISBN 0-675-09414-3). Merrill.

Jones, Howard & Cornes, Paul. Open Prisons. (International Library of Social Policy). (Illus.). 1977. 25.00x (ISBN 0-7100-8602-4). Routledge & Kegan.

Jones, Howard, ed. Towards a New Social Work. (Library of Social Work). 1975. 15.00 (ISBN 0-7100-8045-X); pap. 7.95 (ISBN 0-685-52096-X). Routledge & Kegan.

Jones, Howard, Jr. & Jones, Georgeanna S. Novak's Textbook of Gynecology. 3rd, student ed. (Illus.). 450p. 1981. write for info. softcover (4467-2). Williams & Wilkins.

Jones, Howard M. Howard Mumford Jones: An Autobiography. LC 78-65013. 1979. 21.50 (ISBN 0-299-07770-5). U of Wis Pr.

--Jeffersonianism & the American Novel. LC 66-28267. (Orig.). 1966. text ed. 6.50x (ISBN 0-8077-1593-X); pap. text ed. 4.50x (ISBN 0-8077-1590-5). Tchrs Coll.

Jones, Howard M., ed. Emerson on Education: Selections. LC 66-11655. (Orig.). text ed. 9.50 (ISBN 0-8077-1587-5); pap. text ed. 4.00x (ISBN 0-8077-1584-0). Tchrs Coll.

Jones, Howard M., jt. ed. see Hayakawa, S. I.

Jones, Howard M., frwd. by see Tyler, Moses C.

Jones, I. S. The Effect of Vehicle Characteristics on Road Accidents. 200p. 1976. text ed. 34.00 (ISBN 0-08-018963-6). Pergamon.

Jones, Ivor W. Shipwrecks of North Wales. (Regional Shipwreck Ser.). (Illus.). 1973. pap. 8.95 (ISBN 0-7153-5787-5). David & Charles.

Jones, J. Private Army. 1969. pap. 1.95 o.s.i. (ISBN 0-02-073600-2, Collier). Macmillan.

Jones, J. B., et al. Techniques of Chemistry: Vol. 10 Applications of Biochemical Systems in Organic Chemistry, 2 pts. 522p. 1976. Pt. 1. 50.00 (ISBN 0-471-93267-1); Pt. 2, 575pp. 55.00 (ISBN 0-471-93270-1); Set. 80.95 (ISBN 0-471-02279-9). Wiley.

Jones, J. Christopher. Design Methods: Seeds of Human Factors. LC 77-122347. 1971. 25.75 (ISBN 0-471-44790-0, Pub. by Wiley-Interscience). Wiley.

--Design Methods: Seeds of Human Futures 1980 Edition a Review of New Topics. 440p. 1981. 22.50 (Pub. by Wiley Interscience). Wiley.

Jones, J. Farragut. Pearl Harbor Periscopes. (Orig.). 1981. pap. 2.95 (ISBN 0-440-16711-6). Dell.

--The Scourge of Scapa Flow. (Orig.). 1981. pap. 2.75 (ISBN 0-440-17701-4). Dell.

--Tracking the Wolfpack. (The Silent Service Ser.: No. 5). (Orig.). 1981. pap. 2.75 (ISBN 0-440-18589-0). Dell.

--Waters Dark & Deep. (Orig.). 1981. pap. 2.75 (ISBN 0-440-19470-9). Dell.

Jones, J. G., ed. The Biological Efficiency of Protein Production. LC 72-93672. (Illus.). 400p. 1973. 57.50 (ISBN 0-521-20179-9). Cambridge U Pr.

Jones, J. H., tr. see Jakubke, H. D. & Jeschkeit, H.

Jones, J. Knox, Jr., jt. ed. see Anderson, Sydney.

Jones, J. Morgan. Introduction to Decision Theory. 1977. 20.95 (ISBN 0-256-01950-9). Irwin.

Jones, J. P. & Jones, Betty. Of Smoke & Ash - Mt. St. Helens. (Illus., Orig.). 1980. pap. write for info. (ISBN 0-9604838-0-2). G & BJ's Serv.

Jones, J. R. Britain & the World, Sixteen Forty-Nine to Eighteen Fifteen. (Fontana History of England Ser.: No. 6). 1980. text ed. 31.50x (ISBN 0-391-01776-4). Humanities.

--The Ionisation of Carbon Acids. 1974. 32.00 (ISBN 0-12-389750-5). Acad Pr.

Jones, J. S. Bike & Hike. (Illus.). 225p. 1977. pap. 5.95 o.p. (ISBN 0-902280-45-7). Bradt Ent.

Jones, J. Sydney. Bike & Hike: Sixty Tours Around Great Britain & Ireland. (Illus., Orig.). 1978. pap. 3.95 (ISBN 0-8467-0439-0, Pub. by Two Continents). Hippocrene Bks.

Jones, J. W., jt. auth. see Hesketh, John D.

Jones, J. William. Budget - Finance Campaigns. 1977. pap. 9.50 (ISBN 0-87545-010-5). Natl Sch Pr.

--Building Public Confidence in Your Schools: Ideas That Work. 1978. pap. 13.95 (ISBN 0-87545-012-1). Natl Sch Pr.

--Communicating During Negotiations Strokes. 1976. pap. 5.75 o.p. (ISBN 0-87545-007-5). Natl Sch Pr.

Jones, J. William & National School Public Relations Association. Discipline Crisis in Schools: The Problem, Causes, & the Search for Solutions. 1973. 5.75 o.p. (ISBN 0-685-36732-0, 411-13445). Natl Sch PR.

Jones, Jacqueline. Soldiers of Light & Love: Northern Teachers & the Georgia Blacks, 1865-1873. 330p. 1980. 17.50 o.p. (ISBN 0-8078-1435-0). U of NC Pr.

Jones, James. Thin Red Line. 1962. lib. rep. ed. 20.00x (ISBN 0-684-15555-9, ScribT). Scribner.

--Viet Journal. 272p. 1974. 7.95 o.s.i. (ISBN 0-440-08764-3). Delacorte.

--Whistle. 1979. pap. 2.75 o.s.i. (ISBN 0-440-19262-5). Dell.

Jones, James B. & Hawkins, George A. Engineering Thermodynamics: An Introductory Textbook. LC 60-10316. (Illus.). 1960. text ed. 28.95x (ISBN 0-471-44946-6). Wiley.

Jones, James E. Saying Is Believing: Developing Credential Speeches. 1979. pap. text ed. 10.95 (ISBN 0-8403-2076-0). Kendall-Hunt.

Jones, James H. Bad Blood: The Tuskegee Syphilis Experiment. LC 80-69281. (Illus.). 1981. 12.95 (ISBN 0-02-916670-5). Free Pr.

Jones, James M. Prejudice & Racism. 1972. pap. text ed. 6.95 (ISBN 0-201-03376-3). A-W.

Jones, James P. Black Jack, John A. Logan & Southern Illinois in the Civil War Era. LC 67-64456. 1967. 8.95 o.p. (ISBN 0-8130-0485-3). U Presses Fla.

Jones, James W. The Texture of Knowledge: An Essay on Religion & Science. LC 80-69036. 112p. 1981. lib. bdg. 15.75 (ISBN 0-8191-1360-3); pap. text ed. 6.75 (ISBN 0-8191-1361-1). U Pr of Amer.

Jones, Jayne C. Greeks in America. rev. ed. LC 68-31504. (In America Bks.). (Illus.). (gr. 5-11). 1977. PLB 5.95 (ISBN 0-8225-0215-1). Lerner Pubns.

Jones, Jean C., ed. see APA Library.

Jones, Jeanne. Diet for a Happy Heart: A Low-Cholesterol, Low-Saturated Fat, Low Calorie Cookbook. rev. ed. (Illus.). 192p. 1981. pap. 6.95 (ISBN 0-89286-183-5). One Hurd One Prods.

--Jeanne Jones Party Planner & Entertaining Diary. (Illus.). 1979. 4.95 (ISBN 0-89286-156-8). One Hund One Prods.

--More Calculated Cooking: Practical Recipies for Diabetics & Dieters. 192p. (Orig.). 1981. 10.95 (ISBN 0-89286-185-1); pap. 6.95 (ISBN 0-89286-184-3). One Hurd One Prods.

Jones, Jeanne & Kientzler, Kharma. Fitness First-a-Fourteen-Day Diet & Exercise Program. LC 80-11320. (Illus.). 154p. (Orig.). 1980. 9.95 o.p. (ISBN 0-89286-168-1); pap. 6.95 (ISBN 0-89286-162-2). One Hund One Prods.

Jones, Jeff. Yesterday's Lily. (Illus.). 80p. 1980. pap. 8.95 (ISBN 0-8256-9552-X, Quick Fox). Music Sales.

Jones, Jerry, compiled by. First Person, Singular. 175p. 1981. pap. 4.95 (14018P). Impact Tenn.

Jones, Jerry L. & Radding, Shirley B., eds. Thermal Conversion of Solid Waste & Biomass. LC 80-14754. (ACS Symposium Ser.: No. 130). 1980. 57.50 (ISBN 0-8412-0565-5). Am Chemical.

Jones, Jesse H. Fifty Billion Dollars: My Thirteen Years with the RFC (1932-1945) LC 74-31415. (FDR & the Era of the New Deal Ser.). (Illus.). xvi, 631p. 1975. Repr. of 1951 ed. lib. bdg. 55.00 (ISBN 0-306-70715-2). Da Capo.

Jones, Jo, et al. Paintings & Drawings of the Gypsies of Granada. LC 78-8842. (Illus.). 1969. 18.00 (ISBN 0-8103-5003-3). Gale.

Jones, John. On Aristotle & Greek Tragedy. LC 80-50895. 288p. 1980. 16.50x (ISBN 0-8047-1092-9); pap. 6.95 (ISBN 0-8047-1093-7, SP11). Stanford U Pr.

Jones, John C. Lab Workbook for Introductory Cell Biology with Fundamentals of Biological Physics & Chemistry. 1976. wire coil bdg. 5.95 o.p. (ISBN 0-88252-052-0). Paladin Hse.

Jones, John D., tr. Pseudo-Dionysius Aeropagite: The Divine Names & Mystical Theology. (Translation Ser.: No. 21). 320p. 24.95 (ISBN 0-87462-221-2). Marquette.

Jones, John E. & Pfeiffer, J. William. Annual Handbook for Group Facilitators, 1977. LC 73-92841. (Series in Human Relations Training). 288p. 1977. pap. 20.00 (ISBN 0-88390-091-2); looseleaf ntbk. 44.50 (ISBN 0-88390-090-4). Univ Assocs.

Jones, John E., jt. auth. see Pfeiffer, J. William.

Jones, John E. & Pfeiffer, J. William, eds. Annual Handbook for Group Facilitators, 1973. LC 73-92841. (Series in Human Relations Training). 290p. 1973. pap. 20.00 (ISBN 0-88390-081-5); pap. 44.50 looseleaf ntbk. (ISBN 0-88390-073-4). Univ Assocs.

--The Annual Handbook for Group Facilitators, 1979. LC 73-92841. (Human Relations Training Ser.). 296p. 1979. pap. 20.00 (ISBN 0-88390-095-5); looseleaf notebook 44.50 (ISBN 0-88390-093-9). Univ Assocs.

--The Annual Handbook for Group Facilitators 1981. (Ser. in Human Relations Training). 290p. (Orig.). 1981. pap. 20.00 (ISBN 0-686-69076-1). Univ Assocs.

--Annual Handbook for Group Facilitators,1975. LC 73-92841. (Series in Human Relations Training). 290p. 1975. pap. 20.00 (ISBN 0-88390-079-3); looseleaf 44.50 (ISBN 0-88390-078-5). Univ Assocs.

Jones, John E., jt. ed. see Pfeiffer, J. William.

Jones, John F., jt. auth. see Gibbons, Don C.

Jones, John F., ed. Building China: Studies in Integrated Development. 158p. 1981. 14.95 (ISBN 0-295-95821-9, Pub. by Chinese Univ Hong Kong). U of Wash Pr.

Jones, John P. Gathering & Writing the News: A Reporter's Complete Guide to Techniques & Ethics of News Reporting. LC 75-33642. 304p. 1976. 16.95 (ISBN 0-88229-243-9); pap. 8.95x (ISBN 0-88229-583-7). Nelson-Hall.

Jones, John Paul. Memoirs of Rear-Admiral Paul Jones. LC 77-166333. (Era of the American Revolution Ser.). (Illus.). 1972. Repr. of 1830 ed. lib. bdg. 45.00 (ISBN 0-306-70247-9). Da Capo.

Jones, John W. Historical Introduction to the Theory of Law. Repr. of 1940 ed. lib. bdg. 17.50x (ISBN 0-8371-2810-2, JOTL). Greenwood.

Jones, Jonah. A Tree May Fall. 213p. 1981. 10.95 (ISBN 0-370-30320-2, Pub. by Chatto-Bodley-Jonathan). Merrimack Bk Serv.

Jones, Jonathan H. A Condensed History of the Apache & Comanche Indian Tribes. LC 75-7129. (Indian Captivities Ser.: Vol. 102). 1976. Repr. of 1899 ed. lib. bdg. 44.00 (ISBN 0-8240-1726-9). Garland Pub.

Jones, Joseph R. Antonio De Guevara. LC 75-4572. (World Authors Ser.: Spain: No. 360). 1975. lib. bdg. 10.95 (ISBN 0-8057-2409-5). Twayne.

Jones, Joseph R., ed. see De Cervantes, Miguel.

Jones, Joyce M. Jungian Psychology in Literary Analysis: A Demonstration Using T. S. Eliot's Poetry. LC 79-66227. 1979. pap. text ed. 5.75 (ISBN 0-8191-0810-3). U Pr of Amer.

Jones, Judith & Nance, Guinevera. Philip Roth. LC 80-53701. (Modern Literature Ser.). 160p. 1981. 9.95 (ISBN 0-8044-2438-1); pap. 4.95 (ISBN 0-8044-6320-4). Ungar.

Jones, Judith P. Thomas More. (English Authors Ser.: No. 247). 1979. lib. bdg. 9.95 (ISBN 0-8057-6711-8). Twayne.

Jones, Julie, tr. see Alas, Leopoldo.

Jones, K. The Chemistry of Nitrogen. (Pergamon Texts in Inorganic Chemistry: Vol. 11). 242p. 1975. text ed. 37.00 (ISBN 0-08-018796-X); pap. text ed. 22.00 (ISBN 0-08-018795-1). Pergamon.

Jones, Kathleen. A History of the Mental Health Services. (International Library of Social Policy). 422p. 1972. 30.00x (ISBN 0-7100-7452-2). Routledge & Kegan.

--The Teaching of Social Studies in British Universities. 87p. 1964. pap. text ed. 3.75x (Pub. by Bedford England). Renouf.

Jones, Kathleen, ed. Living the Faith: A Call to the Church. 192p. 1980. text ed. 16.95x (ISBN 0-19-213233-4). Oxford U Pr.

Jones, Kathleen, et al. Issues in Social Policy. 1978. 16.00 (ISBN 0-7100-8972-4); pap. 10.00 (ISBN 0-7100-8973-2). Routledge & Kegan.

Jones, Ken. Simulations: A Handbook for Teachers. 180p. 1980. 25.00x (ISBN 0-89397-090-5). Nichols Pub.

Jones, Ken & Chamberlain, Peter. Lee & Grant. (Illus.). 1977. 13.85 o.p. (ISBN 0-85059-269-0). Aztex.

Jones, Ken D., et al. Character People. LC 74-30972. (Illus.). 256p. 1976. 17.50 o.p. (ISBN 0-498-01697-8). A S Barnes.

Jones, Kenneth, et al. Drugs: Substance Abuse. 2nd ed. LC 75-1400. Orig. Title: Drugs, Alcohol & Tobacco. 196p. 1975. pap. text ed. 6.50 scp o.p. (ISBN 0-06-384361-7, HarpC). Har-Row.

Jones, Kenneth C. & Gaudin, Anthony J. Introductory Biology. LC 76-45648. 1977. text ed. 20.95x (ISBN 0-471-44875-3); instr's manual avail. (ISBN 0-471-02381-7); study guide avail. Wiley.

Jones, Kenneth G., ed. Webb Society Deep-Sky Obverser's Handbook: Galaxies, Vol. 4. 296p. 1981. pap. 14.95 (ISBN 0-89490-050-1). Enslow Pubs.

Jones, Kenneth G., ed. see Webb Society.

Jones, Kenneth L., et al, eds. Foods, Diet & Nutrition. 2nd ed. 141p. 1975. pap. text ed. 6.50 scp (ISBN 0-06-384341-2, HarpC). Har-Row.

Jones, Kenneth M. War with the Seminoles, 1835-1842: The Florida Indians Fight for Their Freedom & Homeland. LC 74-8811. (Focus Bks). (Illus.). 96p. (gr. 8 up). 1975. PLB 4.47 o.p. (ISBN 0-531-02781-3). Watts.

Jones, Kenneth W. Arya Dharm: Hindu Consciousness in Nineteenth-Century Punjab. LC 74-27290. 350p. 1976. 21.50x (ISBN 0-520-02919-4). U of Cal Pr.

Jones, Kirby, jt. ed. see Mankiewicz, Frank.

Jones, Langdon. The Eye of the Lens. (Illus.). 173p. 1973. pap. 1.25 o.s.i. (ISBN 0-02-021800-1, Collier). Macmillan.

Jones, Leon. From Brown to Boston: Desegregation in Education -- 1954-1974, 2 vols. LC 78-8312. 1979. Set. 72.50 (ISBN 0-8108-1147-2). Scarecrow.

Jones, LeRoi see Baraka, Imamu A., pseud.

Jones, Lewis. The Ocean. (Newbury Hse Raders Ser.: Stage 4 - Intermediate). (Illus.). 80p. (Orig.). (gr. 7-12). 1981. pap. text ed. 2.95 (ISBN 0-88377-197-7). Newbury Hse.

Jones, Lewis, adapted by. Darkness by the River & Other Stories. (Readers Ser.: Stage 2). 1981. pap. text ed. 1.95 (ISBN 0-88377-142-X). Newbury Hse.

Jones, Lewis, ed. The Tiger with the Bright Blue Eyes & Other Stories. (Readers Ser.: Stage 2). 1981. pap. text ed. 1.95 (ISBN 0-88377-137-3). Newbury Hse.

Jones, Linda K. Theme in English Expository Discourse. rev. 2nd ed. LC 78-100090. (Edward Sapir Monograph Series in Language, Culture, & Cognition: No. 2). xiv, 241p. 1980. pap. 8.00x (ISBN 0-933104-10-3). Jupiter Pr.

Jones, Lloyd. U. S. Bombers. 3rd ed. LC 80-66808. 272p. 1980. 14.95 (ISBN 0-8168-9128-1). Aero.

Jones, Lorella M. An Introduction to Mathematical Methods of Physics. LC 78-57377. 1979. text ed. 21.95 (ISBN 0-8053-5130-2). Benjamin-Cummings.

Jones, Lucile. Hop, Skip, & Jump. Van Dolson, Bobbie J., ed. 32p. 1981. pap. price not set (ISBN 0-8280-0038-7). Review & Herald.

--Tony's Tummy. Van Dolson, Bobbie J., ed. 32p. 1981. pap. price not set (ISBN 0-8280-0039-5). Review & Herald.

Jones, Lucille. History of Mineola. 7.95 (ISBN 0-685-48804-7). Nortex Pr.

Jones, M. Australian Local Government: Organizational & Social Planning. 1978. pap. text ed. 14.95x (ISBN 0-686-65324-6, 00512). Heinemann Ed.

Jones, M., jt. auth. see Hornby, W. F.

Jones, M., ed. New Essays on Tolstoy. LC 78-1158. (Illus.). 1979. 34.00 (ISBN 0-521-22091-2). Cambridge U Pr.

Jones, M. H. A Practical Introduction to Electric Circuits. LC 76-11083. (Illus.). 1977. 38.50 (ISBN 0-521-21291-X); pap. 13.95x (ISBN 0-521-29087-2). Cambridge U Pr.

Jones, M. J. A Guide to Metrication. 1969. pap. 7.00 (ISBN 0-08-006539-2). Pergamon.

Jones, M. S., ed. An Approach to Occupational Therapy. 3rd ed. Jay, P. 1977. 44.95 (ISBN 0-407-00053-4). Butterworths.

Jones, Mablen, jt. auth. see Adzema, Robert.

Jones, Mack M. Shopwork on the Farm. 2nd ed. (Test Ed.). 1955. text ed. 17.32x (ISBN 0-07-032868-4, W); text-films o.p. (ISBN 0-685-14477-1). McGraw.

Jones, Madeline. Churchill. (Leaders Ser.). (Illus.). 96p. (gr. 9-12). 1980. 14.95 (ISBN 0-7134-1922-9, Pub. by Batsford England). David & Charles.

--Growing up in Regency England. LC 79-56451. (Growing up Ser.). (Illus.). 72p. (gr. 7 up). 1980. text ed. 14.95 (ISBN 0-7134-3368-X, Pub. by Batsford England). David & Charles.

--Growing up in Stuart Times. (Growing Up Ser.). 1979. 16.95 (ISBN 0-7134-0771-9, Pub. by Batsford England). David & Charles.

--Stuart People. 1978. 16.95 (ISBN 0-7134-0617-8, Pub. by Batsford England). David & Charles.

Jones, Maitland & Moss, Robert A. Reactive Intermediates, Vol. II. (A Serial Publication Ser.). 380p. 1981. 35.00 (ISBN 0-471-01875-9, Pub. by Wiley-Interscience). Wiley.

Jones, Maitland, Jr., jt. auth. see Moss, Robert A.

Jones, Maitland, Jr. & Moss, Robert A., eds. Carbenes, Vol. 1. LC 80-11836. 364p. 1981. Repr. of 1973 ed. lib. bdg. write for info. (ISBN 0-89874-216-1). Krieger.

Jones, Major J. Black Awareness: A Theology of Hope. (Orig.). 1971. pap. 5.95 o.p. (ISBN 0-687-03585-6). Abingdon.

Jones, Malcolm. Music Librarianship. 370p. 1979. 12.00 (ISBN 0-89664-417-0, Pub. by K G Saur). Shoe String.

Jones, Malcolm, jt. auth. see Kiernan, Chris.

Jones, Marc E. Astrology: How & Why It Works. LC 76-84580. 1974. 13.50 o.p. (ISBN 0-87878-005-X, Sabian). Great Eastern.

--The Counseling Manual in Astrology. 200p. 1980. 13.50 o.p. (ISBN 0-87878-017-3, Sabian). Great Eastern.

--Essentials of Astrological Analysis. LC 60-15588. 1974. 16.50 o.p. (ISBN 0-87878-011-4, Sabian). Great Eastern.

--Fundamentals of Number Significance. LC 78-69854. 1978. 16.50 o.p. (ISBN 0-87878-015-7, Sabian). Great Eastern.

--The Guide to Horoscope Interpretation. LC 41-26719. 1972. 10.50 o.p. (ISBN 0-87878-003-3, Sabian). Great Eastern.

--Horary Astrology: Problem Solving. LC 78-149643. 1971. 13.50 o.p. (ISBN 0-87878-004-1, Sabian). Great Eastern.

--How to Learn Astrology. LC 76-55119. (Illus.). 1977. pap. 3.95 (ISBN 0-394-73342-8). Shambhala Pubns.

--How to Learn Astrology. LC 69-19864. 1969. 10.50 o.p. (ISBN 0-87878-002-5, Sabian). Great Eastern.

--Man, Magic & Fantasy. LC 78-63049. 1979. 13.50 o.p. (ISBN 0-87878-016-5, Sabian). Great Eastern.

--Mundane Perspectives in Astrology. LC 75-14608. 1975. 16.50 o.p. (ISBN 0-87878-014-9, Sabian). Great Eastern.

--Occult Philosophy. LC 48-5791. 1971. 13.50 o.p. (ISBN 0-87878-006-8, Sabian). Great Eastern.

--The Sabian Book: Letters of Insight. LC 73-76920. 1973. 13.50 o.p. (ISBN 0-87878-013-0, Sabian). Great Eastern.

--The Sabian Manual. LC 57-11471. 1957. 10.50 o.p. (ISBN 0-87878-010-6, Sabian). Great Eastern.

--The Sabian Symbols in Astrology. LC 72-91460. 1972. 13.50 o.p. (ISBN 0-87878-009-2, Sabian). Great Eastern.

--Scope of Astrological Prediction. LC 69-19863. 1973. 16.50 o.p. (ISBN 0-87878-012-2, Sabian). Great Eastern.

Jones, Margaret. The Confucius Enigma. 224p. 1981. 10.95 (ISBN 0-312-16238-3). St Martin.

Jones, Margaret B., jt. auth. see Nessel, Denise D.

Jones, Margaret E. Dolores Medio. (World Authors Ser.: Spain: No. 281). 1974. lib. bdg. 10.95 (ISBN 0-8057-2610-1). Twayne.

Jones, Margaret H., jt. auth. see Carterette, Edward C.

Jones, Marilyn. Exploring Careers in Special Education. (Careers in Depth Ser.). (Illus.). 128p. 1981. lib. bdg. 5.97 (ISBN 0-8239-0539-X). Rosen Pr.

Jones, Marilyn H., jt. ed. see Swanson, Edward.

Jones, Marshall R., ed. Nebraska Symposium on Motivation, 1955. LC 53-11655. (Nebraska Symposia on Motivation Ser: Vol. 3). 1955. pap. 4.95x (ISBN 0-8032-5602-7). U of Nebr Pr.

Jones, Martin. How to Organize Meetings: A Handbook for Better Workshop, Seminar and Conference Management. LC 80-28310. 138p. 1981. pap. 5.95 (ISBN 0-8253-0011-8). Beaufort Bks NY.

Jones, Mary A. His Name Was Jesus. (Illus.). 1950. pap. 2.50 o.p. (ISBN 0-528-87763-1). Rand.

--Tell Me About God. rev. ed. LC 67-15727. (ps-3). 1967. pap. 3.95 (ISBN 0-528-87656-2). Rand.

Jones, Mary G. & Gardner, David M. Consumerism: A New Force in Society. LC 76-10106. (Illus.). 1976. 18.95 (ISBN 0-669-00705-6). Lexington Bks.

Jones, Mary J. Congregational Commonwealth: Connecticut, Sixteen Thirty-Six to Sixteen Sixty-Two. LC 68-27543. (Illus.). 1968. 20.00x (ISBN 0-8195-3095-6, Pub. by Wesleyan U Pr). Columbia U Pr.

Jones, Mary V. First Songs: The Young Child Sings. LC 76-45936. 1977. pap. 4.95 (ISBN 0-8091-2000-3); record 6.98 (ISBN 0-8091-7625-4). Paulist Pr.

Jones, Mervyn. A Short Time to Live. 294p. 1981. 12.95 (ISBN 0-312-72221-4). St Martin.

Jones, Mervyn, tr. see Karol, K. S.

Jones, Michael, ed. Prayers & Graces. 1980. 5.50 (ISBN 0-903540-33-9, Pub. by Flores Books). St George Bk Serv.

Jones, Michael O. The Hand Made Object & Its Maker. LC 73-93055. (Illus.). 288p. 1975. 18.50 (ISBN 0-520-02697-7). U of Cal Pr.

Jones, Michael O., jt. auth. see Georges, Robert A.

Jones, Michael W. The Derby: A Celebration of the World's Most Famous Horse Race. (Illus.). 204p. 1980. 21.00x (ISBN 0-85664-884-1, Pub. by Croom Helm Ltd England). Biblio Dist.

--The World One Hundred Years Ago. 1980. cancelled o.p. McKay.

--The World One Hundred Years Ago. 1976. 4.98 o.p. (ISBN 0-679-50699-3). McKay.

Jones, Morris & Thomas, A. R. The Welsh Language: Studies in Its Syntax & Semantics. 1978. pap. text ed. 32.50x (ISBN 0-7083-0671-3). Verry.

Jones, Morris V. Language Development: The Key to Learning. 336p. 1972. pap. 31.75 photocopy ed., spiral (ISBN 0-398-02324-7). C C Thomas.

--Speech & Language Problems: An Overview. (Am. Lec. Special Education Ser.). (Illus.). 420p. 1979. 22.75 (ISBN 0-398-03790-6). C C Thomas.

Jones, N. D., ed. Semantics-Directed Compiler Generation: Proceedings. (Lecture Notes in Computer Science Ser.: Vol. 94). 489p. 1981. pap. 27.00 (ISBN 0-387-10250-7). Springer-Verlag.

Jones, Neil D., jt. auth. see Muchnick, Steven S.

Jones, Nita A. I Have Been Thinking About You. Date not set. 4.95 (ISBN 0-533-04784-6). Vantage.

Jones, O. A. & Endean, R., eds. Biology & Geology of Coral Reefs, 4 vols. Incl. Vol. 1. Geology. 1973. 48.50 (ISBN 0-12-389601-0); Vol. 2. Biology - One. 1974. 59.00 (ISBN 0-12-389602-9); Vol. 3. Biology - Two. 1975. 67.00 (ISBN 0-12-389603-7); Vol. 4. 1977. 51.50 (ISBN 0-12-389604-5). Set. 194.50. Acad Pr.

Jones, O. Garfield. Parliamentary Procedure at a Glance. (gr. 9 up). 1971. pap. 3.50 o.p. (ISBN 0-8015-5766-6). Dutton.

Jones, Owen C., ed. Nuclear Reactor Safety Heat Transfer: Proceedings of the International Centre for Heat & Mass Transfer. (International Centre for Heat & Mass Trans Transfer Ser.). (Illus.). 1981. text ed. 99.00 (ISBN 0-89116-224-0). Hemisphere Pub.

Jones, P., jt. auth. see Bowan, John T.

Jones, P. A., jt. auth. see Jones, R. K.

Jones, P. J. The Malatesta of Rimini & the Papal State. LC 72-87178. (Illus.). 360p. 1974. 49.95 (ISBN 0-521-20042-3). Cambridge U Pr.

Jones, P. M., jt. ed. see Lucas, St. John.

Jones, P. V., jt. auth. see Stace, C.

Jones, Pamela. Under the City Streets. (Illus.). 1979. 12.95 o.p. (ISBN 0-03-021596-X). HR&W.

Jones, Paul W. & Keene, Michael L. Writing Scientific Papers-Reports. 8th ed. 365p. 1981. pap. text ed. write for info. (ISBN 0-697-03773-8). Wm C Brown.

Jones, Peggy, jt. auth. see Brace, Pam.

Jones, Penelope. Holding Together. 160p. (gr. 3-5). 1981. 7.95 (ISBN 0-87888-177-8). Bradbury Pr.

--I Didn't Want to Be Nice. LC 76-57907. (Illus.). (ps-2). 1977. 7.95 (ISBN 0-87888-111-5). Bradbury Pr.

--I'm Not Moving. LC 79-13062. (Illus.). (ps-2). 1980. 8.95 (ISBN 0-87888-156-5). Bradbury Pr.

Jones, Peter. The Garden End. (Illus.). 116p. 1981. 15.00 (ISBN 0-933806-09-4). Black Swan CT.

--Handyman's Guide to Home Weather Proofing. 1981. 14.95 (ISBN 0-8359-2078-X); pap. text ed. 7.95 (ISBN 0-8359-2077-1). Reston.

--Home Renovation. Lawson, K., ed. (Home Environment "HELP" Ser.). (Illus.). 144p. pap. cancelled (ISBN 0-88421-154-1). Butterick Pub.

--Homeowner's Guide to Plumbing, Heating & Air Conditioning. (Illus.). 1980. text ed. 13.95 (ISBN 0-8359-2845-4). Reston.

--A Reader's Guide to Fifty American Poets. (A Reader's Guide Ser.). 386p. 1980. 16.50x (ISBN 0-389-20140-5). B&N.

--Skylights & Windows You Can Install. Lawson, K., ed. (Home Environment "HELP" Ser.). (Illus.). 144p. (Orig.). pap. cancelled (ISBN 0-88421-155-X). Butterick Pub.

--Start-to-Finish Cabinetmaking. 1980. pap. 7.95 (ISBN 0-8359-7062-0). Reston.

Jones, Peter, ed. The International Yearbook of Foreign Policy Analysis, Vol. 2. LC 75-21728. 256p. 1976. 17.50x (ISBN 0-8448-0762-1). Crane-Russak Co.

Jones, Peter, jt. ed. see Freudenthal, Ralph I.

Jones, Peter B. Hans Scharoun-A Monograph. LC 79-307585. 1979. 30.50 (ISBN 0-900406-57-7, Pub by G Fraser). Intl Schol Bk Serv.

Jones, Peter D. & Holli, Melvin G., eds. Ethnic Chicago. 336p. (Orig.). 1981. pap. 12.95 (ISBN 0-8028-1821-8). Eerdmans.

Jones, Peter d'A. The U.S.A, 2 vols. 1976. pap. text ed. 11.95x ea. Vol. 1 - A History Of It's People & Society To 1877 (ISBN 0-256-01801-4). Vol. 2 - A History Of It's People & Society Since 1865 (ISBN 0-256-01802-2). Dorsey.

Jones, Peter W., ed. see International Symposium on Analysis, Chemistry, & Biology, No. 2.

Jones, Philip. Racial Hybridity. (Illus.). 241p. (Orig.). 1979. pap. 5.50x (ISBN 0-911038-77-9, Uriel Pubns). Noontide.

Jones, Philip, compiled by. Britain & Palestine, Nineteen Seventy-Four to Nineteen Forty-Eight: Archival Sources for the History of the British Mandate. (British Academy Ser.). 256p. 1979. text ed. 55.00x (ISBN 0-19-725985-5). Oxford U Pr.

Jones, Phillip S., jt. auth. see Bunt, Lucas N. H.

Jones, Phyllis M., ed. English Critical Essays: Twentieth Century. (World's Classics Ser.). 7.95 (ISBN 0-19-250405-3). Oxford U Pr.

Jones, Preston. A Texas Trilogy. 338p. 1976. pap. 6.95 (ISBN 0-8090-1236-7, Mermaid). Hill & Wang.

Jones, R. Construction Estimating. 216p. 1967. pap. 14.00 (ISBN 0-8273-0108-1); instructor's guide 3.45 (ISBN 0-8273-0109-X). Delmar.

--Framing, Sheathing & Insulation. LC 73-1847. 235p. 1973. pap. 7.00 (ISBN 0-8273-0096-4); answer book 1.60 (ISBN 0-8273-0097-2). Delmar.

--Templet Development for the Pipe Trades. LC 63-22021. (Illus.). 175p. 1963. pap. 8.00 (ISBN 0-8273-0077-8); instructor's guide 1.45 (ISBN 0-8273-0078-6). Delmar.

Jones, R., jt. auth. see Dewar, M. J.

Jones, R., ed. Readings from Futures. 1980. pap. text ed. 40.00. Butterworths.

Jones, R., ed. see Nikolskii, G. V.

Jones, R. Ben. The Making of Contemporary Europe. 225p. 1981. text ed. 38.50x (ISBN 0-8419-0668-8); pap. text ed. 19.50x (ISBN 0-8419-0669-6). Holmes & Meier.

Jones, R. Duncan see Duncan-Jones, R.

Jones, R. K. & Jones, P. A. Sociology in Medicine. LC 75-11723. 1976. 15.95 (ISBN 0-470-44936-5). Halsted Pr.

Jones, R. N. see Bourne, G. H. & Danielli, J. F.

Jones, R. Page. The Man Who Killed Hitler. 256p. (Orig.). 1980. pap. 2.25 (ISBN 0-515-04855-0). Jove Pubns.

--Wine of the Generals. 1978. pap. 1.95 o.s.i. (ISBN 0-515-04547-0). Jove Pubns.

Jones, R. T. George Eliot. LC 75-114602. (British Authors Ser). 1971. 22.00 (ISBN 0-521-07832-6); pap. 6.95x (ISBN 0-521-09613-8). Cambridge U Pr.

Jones, R. T., ed. Sir Gawain & the Grene Gnome. 1972. text ed. 3.75x o.p. (ISBN 0-435-14511-8). Heinemann Ed.

Jones, Randall L. & Spolsky, Bernard, eds. Testing Language Proficiency. LC 75-13740. 1975. pap. text ed. 8.95x (ISBN 0-87281-040-2). Ctr Appl Ling.

Jones, Ray. Nineteenth Century Foreign Office: An Administrative History. (London School of Economics Research Monographs Ser: No. 9). 1971. bds. 14.00x (ISBN 0-297-00299-6). Humanities.

Jones, Ray & Pritchard, Colin. Social Work with Adolescents. (Library of Social Work). 260p. 1981. 16.95 (ISBN 0-7100-0632-2); pap. write for info. (ISBN 0-7100-0633-0). Routledge & Kegan.

Jones, Ray G. & Dudley, Dean. Essentials of Finance. (Illus.). 1978. 19.95 (ISBN 0-13-286088-0). P-H.

Jones, Rees L. & Rando, Guy L. Golf Course Developments. LC 73-86554. (Technical Bulletin Ser.: No. 70). (Illus.). 112p. 1974. pap. 12.00 (ISBN 0-87420-070-9). Urban Land.

Jones, Reginald L. Problems & Issues in the Education of Exceptional Children. LC 74-142329. 1971. pap. text ed. 11.95 (ISBN 0-395-11228-1, 3-28340). HM.

Jones, Rhodri. Conflict. pap. text ed. 2.95x o.p. (ISBN 0-435-14482-0); tchr's ed. 1.50 o.p. (ISBN 0-435-14486-3). Heinemann Ed.

--Families. 1971. pap. text ed. 2.50x o.p. (ISBN 0-435-14500-2). Heinemann Ed.

--Five Senses. 1971. pap. text ed. 2.50x o.p. (ISBN 0-435-14506-1). Heinemann Ed.

--Imagination. pap. text ed. 2.95x o.p. (ISBN 0-435-14481-2); tchr's ed 1.50x o.p. (ISBN 0-435-14485-5). Heinemann Ed.

--Men & Beasts. (Themes Ser.). pap. text ed. 1.95x o.p. (ISBN 0-435-14480-4); tchr's ed. 2.95x o.p. (ISBN 0-435-14484-7). Heinemann Ed.

--A New English Course. 2nd ed. 1976. pap. text ed. 8.50x o.p. (ISBN 0-435-10493-4). Heinemann Ed.

--New English First. (Illus.). 1977. pap. text ed. 5.95x o.p. (ISBN 0-435-10494-2). Heinemann Ed.

--New English Second. 1978. pap. text ed. 5.95 o.p. (ISBN 0-435-10495-0). Heinemann Ed.

--New English Third. 1979. pap. text ed. 5.95x o.p. (ISBN 0-435-10496-9). Heinemann Ed.

--Town & Country. pap. text ed. 2.95x o.p. (ISBN 0-435-14492-8); tchr's ed. 1.50x o.p. (ISBN 0-435-14493-6). Heinemann Ed.

--Weathers. 1971. pap. text ed. 2.50x o.p. (ISBN 0-435-14504-5). Heinemann Ed.

--Work & Play. 1971. pap. text ed. 2.50x o.p. (ISBN 0-435-14502-9). Heinemann Ed.

Jones, Rhodri, ed. Generations. (Themes Ser.: Bk. 4). 1969. pap. text ed. 2.95x o.p. (ISBN 0-435-14483-9); tchr's ed. 1.50x o.p. (ISBN 0-435-14487-1). Heinemann Ed.

Jones, Richard. Supply in a Market Economy. (Studies in Economics Ser.). 1976. text ed. 17.95x (ISBN 0-04-330270-X); pap. text ed. 8.95x (ISBN 0-04-330271-8). Allen Unwin.

Jones, Richard E. David Wynne. (Composers of Wales Ser.: No. 3). 1979. pap. text ed. 6.00 (ISBN 0-7083-0714-0). Verry.

Jones, Richard M. Fantasy & Feeling in Education. LC 68-29430. 1968. 15.00x (ISBN 0-8147-0220-1). NYU Pr.

Jones, Richard O. & Harwood, Bruce. Colorado Real Estate: An Introduction to the Profession. LC 79-939. (Illus.). 1979. text ed. 15.95 (ISBN 0-8359-0883-6). Reston.

Jones, Robert. George Washington. (World Leaders Ser.: No. 80). 1979. lib. bdg. 13.50 (ISBN 0-8057-7726-1). Twayne.

Jones, Robert & Seligman, Gustav L. The Sweep of American History, Vol. 1. 400p. 1981. pap. text ed. 8.95 (ISBN 0-471-07898-0). Wiley.

--The Sweep of American History, Vol. 2. 400p. 1981. pap. text ed. 8.95 (ISBN 0-471-07897-2). Wiley.

Jones, Robert C. Two Feet Between the Rails: The Early Years, Vol. 1. Collman, Russ, ed. (Illus.). 1979. 40.00 (ISBN 0-913582-17-4). Sundance.

--Two Feet Between the Rails: The Mature Years, Vol. II. (Illus.). 1980. 40.00 (ISBN 0-913582-18-2). Sundance.

Jones, Robert C., jt. auth. see Eilers, Robert D.

Jones, Robert E. Dramatic Imagination. 1941. 5.95 (ISBN 0-87830-035-X). Theatre Arts.

Jones, Robert E. & Burch, Monte. Fireplaces. Horowitz, Shirley M., ed. LC 80-67153. (Illus.). 144p. (Orig.). 1980. 12.95 (ISBN 0-932944-25-6); pap. 5.95 (ISBN 0-932944-26-4). Creative Homeowner.

Jones, Robert Kenneth. The Shudder Pulps. LC 74-82614. 1975. 11.95 (ISBN 0-913960-04-7). Fax Collect.

Jones, Robert L. History of Agriculture in Ontario 1613-1880. LC 47-27166. 1946. pap. 7.95 (ISBN 0-8020-6304-7). U of Toronto Pr.

Jones, Robin F., jt. ed. see Grunmann-Gaudet, Minnette.

Jones, Rochelle. The Other Generation: The New Power of Older People. LC 77-22306. 1977. 10.95 (ISBN 0-13-643064-3, Spec); pap. 4.95 (ISBN 0-13-643056-2, Spec). P-H.

Jones, Rodney W. Urban Politics in India: Area, Power, & Policy in a Penetrated System. 1974. 30.00x (ISBN 0-520-02545-8). U of Cal Pr.

Jones, Roger, jt. auth. see Winner, Ken.

Jones, Roger M. The Platonism of Plutarch & Selected Papers. Taran, Leonardo, ed. LC 78-66589. (Ancient Philosophy Ser.). 250p. 1980. lib. bdg. 24.00 (ISBN 0-8240-9593-6). Garland Pub.

Jones, Ron. No Substitute for Madness: The Collected Stories of Ron Jones. 280p. 1981. pap. 8.00 (ISBN 0-933280-06-8). Island CA.

Jones, Ronald E. Focus on Photography. Kirchem, Ronald, ed. (Illus.). 256p. (gr. 9-12). 1980. text ed. 13.28 (ISBN 0-07-033020-4, W). McGraw.

Jones, Rosemary D. Francesco Vettori: Florentine Citizen & Medici Servant. (University of London Historical Studies: No. 34). 366p. 1972. text ed. 39.00x (ISBN 0-485-13134-X, Athlone Pr). Humanities.

Jones, Roy. Primary School Management. 160p. 1980. 14.95 (ISBN 0-7153-7843-0). David & Charles.

Jones, Roy E. Analysing Foreign Policy: An Introduction to Some Conceptual Problems. 1970. 8.95x o.p. (ISBN 0-7100-6810-7). Routledge & Kegan.

--Functional Analysis of Politics: An Introductory Discussion. (Orig.). 1967. text ed. 5.75x (ISBN 0-7100-5131-X); pap. text ed. 2.75x (ISBN 0-7100-5120-4). Humanities.

--Nuclear Deterrence: A Short Political Analysis. (Library of Political Studies). 1968. text ed. 6.25x (ISBN 0-7100-6537-X). Humanities.

Jones, Rufus M. The Faith & Practice of the Quakers. 181p. 1980. pap. 3.95 (ISBN 0-913408-57-3). Friends United.

Jones, Russell A. Self-Fulfilling Prophecies: Social. Psychological, & Physiological Effects of Expectancies. 1977. 14.95 o.p. (ISBN 0-470-99301-4). Halsted Pr.

Jones, Russell A., jt. auth. see Hendrick, Clyde.

Jones, Samuel A. Pertaining to Thoreau. 171p. 1980. Repr. of 1901 ed. text ed. 20.00 (ISBN 0-8492-1280-4). R West.

Jones, Samuel A., ed. Pertaining to Thoreau. LC 80-2509. 1981. Repr. of 1901 ed. 26.00 (ISBN 0-404-19057-X). AMS Pr.

Jones, Samuel A., ed. see Thoreau, Henry D.

Jones, Samuel B. Property & Liability Insurance Investment Management. 1971. text ed. 7.95x o.p. (ISBN 0-256-00263-0). Irwin.

Jones, Sandra, jt. auth. see Bushman, John H.

Jones, Seaborn. Drowning from the Inside Out. LC 80-20642. 88p. 1981. 9.50x (ISBN 0-916156-53-2); pap. 4.00x (ISBN 0-916156-52-4). Cherry Valley.

Jones, Stan. Stan Jones' Cooking with Bacardi Rum. LC 80-68071. (Illus.). 192p. 1980. pap. 14.95 (ISBN 0-918338-03-4). Bar Guide.

Jones, Stanley E., et al. The Dynamics of Discussion: Communication in Small Groups. 2nd ed. (Illus.). 1980. pap. text ed. 10.95 scp (ISBN 0-06-380438-7, HarpC). Har-Row.

Jones, Stephen. Drifting. LC 75-122294. (Illus.). 1971. 12.50 o.s.i. (ISBN 0-02-559830-9). Macmillan.

--Harbor of Refuge. (Illus.). 1981. 16.95 (ISBN 0-393-01417-7). Norton.

--Turpin. 1968. 5.95 o.s.i. (ISBN 0-02-559820-1). Macmillan.

Jones, Susan L. Family Therapy: A Comparison of Approaches. new ed. LC 80-10161. (Illus.). 1980. text ed. 14.95 (ISBN 0-87619-625-3). R J Brady.

Jones, Susan S. The Main Ingredients: Positive Thinking, Exercise & Diet. 1978. 12.50 o.s.i. (ISBN 0-89557-029-7). Bi World Indus.

Jones, Swiftwater. Jake Claus, Santa's Brother. LC 79-56509. 1980. 5.95 (ISBN 0-533-04534-7). Vantage.

Jones, Sydney, jt. auth. see Ditchfield, P. H.

Jones, T. Mason. Old Trinity, a Story of Real Life. (Nineteenth Century Fiction Ser.: Ireland: Vol. 64). 900p. 1979. lib. bdg. 46.00 (ISBN 0-8240-3513-5). Garland Pub.

Jones, T. P. Creative Learning in Perspective. LC 72-8705. 112p. 1972. 7.95 o.p. (ISBN 0-470-44885-7). Halsted Pr.

Jones, Ted. Direct Silkscreen Printing & Painting: New Directions - Versatile Approaches. Jones, Evelyn, ed. (Illus.). 1980. pap. write for info. (ISBN 0-916928-05-5). New Dimen Studio.

--The Dogwatch. (Illus.). 1981. 14.95 (ISBN 0-393-03252-3). Norton.

Jones, Terri & Jones, Evelyn J. Green Felt & Funny-Money: A Complete Guide to Throwing a Home Casino Party. Piper, Sue, ed. (Illus.). 1980. pap. text ed. 6.95 (ISBN 0-686-28734-7). Univ Marketing.

Jones, Terry, jt. auth. see Palin, Michael.

Jones, Theodoric, ed. Great Story Poems. rev ed. LC 65-24688. (Illus.). 160p. (YA) 1972. PLB 6.99 (ISBN 0-87460-204-1); pap. 2.95 (ISBN 0-87460-205-X). Lion.

Jones, Thomas. The Tragedy of Nero. Hill, Elliott M. & Orgel, Stephen, eds. LC 78-66763. (Renaissance Drama Ser.). 1979. lib. bdg. 33.00 (ISBN 0-8240-9745-9). Garland Pub.

Jones, Thomas C., ed. The Halls of Fame. LC 77-70330. (Illus.). 1977. 29.95 o.s.i. (ISBN 0-690-01397-3, TYC-T). T Y Crowell.

Jones, Thomas E. Light on the Horizon: The Quaker Pilgrimage of Tom Jones. LC 74-14286. 200p. 1973. 3.95 (ISBN 0-913408-13-1). Friends United.

Jones, Thomas E., jt. auth. see Titus, Charles W.

Jones, Thomas H. How to Build Greenhouses, Garden Shelters & Sheds. LC 75-29779. (Popular Science Bk.). (Illus.). 1978. 11.95 o.s.i. (ISBN 0-06-012218-8, HarpT). Har-Row.

Jones, Thomas M. Ward of the Generations: The Revolt of 1173-4. LC 80-18411. (Sponsor Ser.). 242p. (Orig.). 1980. pap. 18.50 (ISBN 0-8357-0528-5, SS-00141). Univ Microfilms.

Jones, Thomas M., jt. auth. see Galbraith, Ronald E.

Jones, Thora B. & De Bear, Nicol. Neo-Classical Dramatic Criticism: 1560-1771. LC 75-16873. 172p. 1976. 32.50 (ISBN 0-521-20857-2). Cambridge U Pr.

Jones, Tom, tr. see Hernandez, Miguel.

Jones, Tom B. From the Tigris to the Tiber. rev. ed. 1978. pap. text ed. 10.50x (ISBN 0-256-01992-4). Dorsey.

--Paths to the Ancient Past. LC 67-12515. 1967. pap. text ed. 6.95 (ISBN 0-02-916630-6). Free Pr.

Jones, Tony. Encyclopedia of Pet Mice. (Illus.). 224p. 1979. 9.95 (ISBN 0-87666-910-0, H-973). TFH Pubns.

Jones, Tristan. Dutch Treat. 1979. 9.95 o.p. (ISBN 0-8362-6107-0). Andrews & McMeel.

--Ice. 1980. pap. 2.75 (ISBN 0-686-69264-0, 50757). Avon.

--The Incredible Voyage. 1980. pap. 2.95 (ISBN 0-380-49999-1, 49999). Avon.

--Saga of a Wayward Sailor. 1979. 9.95 o.p. (ISBN 0-8362-6303-0). Andrews & McMeel.

--Saga of a Wayward Sailor. 272p. (Orig.). 1980. pap. 2.75 (ISBN 0-380-52985-8, 52985). Avon.

Jones, Ulysses S. Fertilizers & Soil Fertility. (Illus.). 1979. text ed. 16.95 (ISBN 0-8359-1960-9); instrs'. manual avail. (ISBN 0-8359-1961-7). Reston.

Jones, Vane A. North American Radio-T.V. Station Guide: TV Station Guide. 14th ed. 1980. pap. 7.95 (ISBN 0-672-21725-2). Sams.

--North American Radio-TV Station Guide: TV Station Guide. 13th ed. LC 79-62993. 1979. pap. 6.95 o.p. (ISBN 0-672-21577-2). Sams.

Jones, Vaughan. Actions of Finite Groups on the Hyperfinite Type II (to the First Power) Factor. LC 80-22560. (Memoirs Ser.: No. 237). 4.40 (ISBN 0-8218-2237-3, MEMO-237). Am Math.

Jones, Vernon F. Adolescents with Behavior Problems: Strategies for Teaching, Counseling & Parent Involvement. 353p. 1979. 16.95 (ISBN 0-205-06801-4). Allyn.

Jones, Victor, ed. see Waldo, C. Dwight.

Jones, Victor H., jt. auth. see Lazarus, A. L.

Jones, Vincent. East Anglian Pubs. (Illus.). 1965. 3.50 o.p. (ISBN 0-8038-1874-2). Hastings.

Jones, W. & March, N. H. Theoretical Solid State Physics, 2 vols. Incl. Vol. 1. Perfect Lattices in Equilibrium. 107.95 (ISBN 0-471-44900-8); Vol. 2. Non-Equilibrium & Disorder. 92.00 (ISBN 0-471-44901-6). LC 70-165953. 1973 (Pub. by Wiley-Interscience). Wiley.

Jones, W., tr. see Lipsius, Justus.

Jones, W. E. & Laver, J., eds. Phonetics in Linguistics: A Book of Readings. (Linguistics Library, No. 12). 355p. 1973. text ed. 16.95x (ISBN 0-582-52451-2). Longman.

Jones, W. Glyn. William Heinesen. (World Authors Ser.: Denmark: No. 282). 1974. lib. bdg. 12.50 (ISBN 0-8057-2418-4). Twayne.

Jones, W. Landis, ed. see Ford, Wendell H.

Jones, W. M., ed. Chief Justice John Marshall: A Reappraisal. LC 70-152688. (American Constitutional & Legal History Ser). 1971. Repr. of 1956 ed. lib. bdg. 22.50 (ISBN 0-306-70132-4). Da Capo.

Jones, W. P. The Province Beyond the River: A Protestant's Days in a Trappist Monastery. 144p. (Orig.). 1981. pap. 5.95 (ISBN 0-8091-2363-0). Paulist Pr.

Jones, W. T. The Sciences & the Humanities: Conflict & Reconciliation. 1965. 15.75x (ISBN 0-520-00610-0); pap. 2.25 (ISBN 0-520-00611-9, CAL144). U of Cal Pr.

Jones, Warren, jt. auth. see Duffield, Mary R.

Jones, Warren H., jt. auth. see Zusne, Leonard.

Jones, Warren W. & Solnit, Albert. What Do I Do Next? A Manual for People Just Entering Government Service. LC 80-67754. (Illus.). 116p. (Orig.). 1980. pap. 9.95 (ISBN 0-918286-20-4). Planners Pr.

Jones, William. Credulities Past & Present. LC 67-24355. 1968. Repr. of 1880 ed. 22.00 (ISBN 0-8103-3447-X). Gale.

--Crowns & Coronations, a History of Regalia. LC 67-24356. (Illus.). 1968. Repr. of 1902 ed. 26.00 (ISBN 0-8103-3448-8). Gale.

--Denver: A Pictorial History. (Illus., Orig.). Date not set. pap. 10.95 (ISBN 0-87108-575-5). Pruett.

--Finger-Ring Lore. LC 67-24357. 1968. Repr. of 1890 ed. 25.00 (ISBN 0-8103-3449-6). Gale.

--History & Mystery of Precious Stones. LC 68-22031. 1968. Repr. of 1880 ed. 18.00 (ISBN 0-8103-3450-X). Gale.

Jones, William, jt. auth. see Wilson, Richard.

Jones, William B. & Thron, W. J. Continued Fractions: Analytic Theory & Applications. (Encyclopedia of Mathematics & Applications Ser.: Vol. II). (Illus.). 450p. 1980. cancelled (ISBN 0-201-13510-8). A-W.

Jones, William C. & Jones, Elizabeth B. William Henry Jackson's Colorado. (Illus.). 192p. 1976. 27.95 (ISBN 0-87108-092-3); deluxe limited edition o.p. 76.00 (ISBN 0-87108-093-1). Pruett.

Jones, William E. Monumental Silver: Selections from the Gilbert Collection. LC 76-57976. (Illus.). 1977. pap. text ed. 5.50 o.p. (ISBN 0-87587-077-5). LA CO Art Mus.

Jones, William E. & Bogart, Ralph. Genetics of the Horse. (Illus.). 21.00 o.p. (ISBN 0-85131-226-8, Dist. by Sporting Book Center). J A Allen.

Jones, William P. James Joyce & the Common Reader. rev. ed. LC 55-9624. 1970. 9.95x (ISBN 0-8061-0324-8); pap. 4.95 (ISBN 0-8061-0930-0). U of Okla Pr.

Jones, William R. Yosemite: The Story Behind the Scenery. rev. ed. LC 80-82917. (Illus.). 1980. 7.95 (ISBN 0-916122-33-6); pap. 3.00 (ISBN 0-916122-08-5). K C Pubns.

Jones, William R., ed. see Albright, Horace M. & Taylor, Frank J.

Jones, William R., ed. see Bishop, William H.

Jones, William R., ed. see Muir, John.

Jones, William R., ed. see Robertson, Walter J.

Jones, William R., ed. see Thornton, J. Quinn.

Jones, William R., ed. see Twain, Mark.

Jones, William S., jt. auth. see Finkle, Robert B.

Jones, Sir William. An Essay on the Law of Bailments. Berkowitz, David S., ed. Thorne, Samuel E. LC 77-86562. (Classics of English Legal History in the Modern Era Ser.: Vol. 14). 132p. 1979. lib. bdg. 40.00 (ISBN 0-8240-3063-X). Garland Pub.

Jones, Willis K., tr. see Aguilera Malta, Demetrio.

Jones, Wilmer L. Learning to Compute, 2 bks. 1978. Bk. 1. pap. text ed. 3.31 (ISBN 0-15-550402-9, HC); Bk. 2. pap. text ed. 3.31 (ISBN 0-15-550403-7); tchr's. manual avail. (ISBN 0-15-550404-5). HarBraceJ.

Jong, Anthony. Dental Public Health & Community Dentistry. (Illus.). 300p. Date not set. pap. text ed. 12.95 (ISBN 0-8016-2575-0). Mosby.

Jong, David C. De see De Jong, David C.

Jong, Dola De see De Jong, Dola.

Jong, Erica. Fanny. 1981. pap. 6.95 (ISBN 0-452-25273-3, Z5273, Plume). NAL.

--Fruits & Vegetables. LC 74-138876. 1971. 5.95 o.p. (ISBN 0-03-085998-0); pap. 3.95 (ISBN 0-03-085999-9). HR&W.

Jong, Frits J. De see De Jong, Frits J., et al.

Jong, Gerald F. De see De Jong, Gerald F.

Jong, Gordon F. De see De Jong, Gordon F.

Jong, H. G. Bungenberg De see Booij, H. L. & Bungenberg De Jong, H. G.

Jong, Kees A. De see De Jong, Kees A. & Scholten, Robert.

Jong, Marvin L. De see De Jong, Marvin L.

Jong, Tine H. Amse De see Amse-De Jong, Tine H.

Jonge, M. de see De Jonge, M.

Jonge, Marinus De see De Jonge, Marinus.

Jongeward, D., jt. auth. see James, M.

Jongeward, Dorothy & James, Muriel. Winning Ways in Health Care: Transactional Analysis for Effective Communication. 1981. pap. text ed. 7.95 (ISBN 0-201-00451-8). A-W.

Jongh, R. C., jt. auth. see Naerssen, F. H.

Jongkees, L. B. Iatrogenic Problems in Otorlaryngology. 1981. text ed. write for info. (ISBN 0-443-08050-X). Churchill.

Jongmans, D. G. & Gutkind, Peter C. Anthropologists in the Field. 1967. text ed. 25.50x (ISBN 90-232-0079-9). Humanities.
Jonklaas, Rodney. Collecting Marine Tropicals. 1975. 17.50 o.p. (ISBN 0-87666-119-3, PS728). TFH Pubns.
Jonland, Einar & Fitzgerald, Jim. Inside Ice Skating. 1978. 9.95 o.p. (ISBN 0-8092-7659-3); pap. 5.95 (ISBN 0-8092-7658-5). Contemp Bks.
Jonnes, J. Merryn. Organisational Aspects of Police Behaviour. 192p. 1980. 34.25x (ISBN 0-566-00402-X, Pub. by Gower Pub Co England). Renouf.
Jons, Rhodri. Men at Work. (Themes Ser.). pap. text ed. 2.95x o.p. (ISBN 0-435-14490-1); tchr's ed. 0.95x o.p. (ISBN 0-435-14491-X). Heinemann Ed.
Jonscher, A. K. Solid State Semi-Conductors. (Studies in Solid State Physics). 1965. pap. 16.50 (ISBN 0-7100-4384-8). Routledge & Kegan.
Jonsen, George. Favorite Tales of Monsters & Trolls. LC 76-24182. (Pictureback Library Editions). (ps-2). 1978. PLB 4.99 (ISBN 0-394-93477-6, BYR). Random.
Jonson, et al. Book of Masques. 1967. 68.00 (ISBN 0-521-05455-9). Cambridge U Pr.
Jonson, Ben. Alchemist. McCollum, John I., Jr., ed. 1965. 5.75 (ISBN 0-8120-5001-0); pap. 1.95 (ISBN 0-8120-0019-6). Barron.
--Alchemist. 1967 ed. Steane, J. B., ed. text ed. 5.95x (ISBN 0-521-06945-9). Cambridge U Pr.
--Bartholomew Fair. Partridge, Edward, ed. LC 63-14700. (Regents Renaissance Drama Ser). xx, 187p. 1964. 2.95x (ISBN 0-8032-5264-1, BB 202, Bison). U of Nebr Pr.
--The Case Is Altered. Selin, W. E., ed. 1917. pap. 34.50x (ISBN 0-685-89739-7). Elliots Bks.
--Epicoene; or, the Silent Woman. Beaurline, L., ed. LC 65-23327. (Regents Renaissance Drama Ser). 1966. 9.95x (ISBN 0-8032-0266-0); pap. 2.95x (ISBN 0-8032-5266-8, BB 216, Bison). U of Nebr Pr.
--Plays, 2 vols. 1953. Vol. 1. 6.00x ea. (ISBN 0-460-00489-1, Evman); Vol. 2. 6.00x (ISBN 0-460-00490-5). Dutton.
--Score for Lovers Made Men, a Masque by Ben Jonson. Sabol, Andrew J., ed. LC 63-8400. 93p. 1963. pap. 5.00 (ISBN 0-87057-073-0, Pub. by Brown U Pr). Univ Pr of New England.
--Work of Ben Jonson. Herford, C. H., et al, eds. Incl. Vol. 1. 42.00x (ISBN 0-19-811352-8); Vol. 2. 42.00x (ISBN 0-19-811353-6); Vol. 5. 46.50x (ISBN 0-19-811356-0); Vol. 7. 49.00x (ISBN 0-19-811358-7); Vol. 8. 49.00x (ISBN 0-19-811359-5); Vol. 10. 49.00x (ISBN 0-19-811361-7); Vol. 11. 49.00x (ISBN 0-19-811362-5). 1925-52. Oxford U Pr.
--The Workes. facsimile ed. 1976. Repr. of 1616 ed. 110.00x o.p. (ISBN 0-85967-240-9, Pub. by Scolar Pr England). Biblio Dist.
Jonsson, Bengt R. & Danielson, Eva. The Types of the Scandinavian Medieval Ballad. 1978. 23.00x (ISBN 82-00-01654-4, Dist. by Columbia U Pr). Universitet.
Jonsson, Christer. Soviet Bargaining Behavior. 1979. 14.50x (ISBN 0-231-04606-5). Columbia U Pr.
Joo, F., jt. ed. see Feher, O.
Joo Bang Lee. Hwa Rang Do II, No. 134. 1980. pap. 6.95 (ISBN 0-89750-066-0). Ohara Pubns.
Joo Ok Koo, see Dudewicz, Edward J. & Koo, Joo Ok.
Joos, Martin. Five Clocks. LC 62-62715. 1967. pap. 3.50 (ISBN 0-15-631380-4, H058, Hbgr). HarBraceJ.
Jope, Charlene A. Cellular & Molecular Laboratory Manual. 64p. 1981. pap. text ed. 5.95 (ISBN 0-8403-2353-0). Kendall-Hunt.
--Organismic & Environmental Laboratory Manual. 144p. 1981. pap. text ed. 6.95 (ISBN 0-8403-2322-0). Kendall-Hunt.
Jope, E. M. & Jacobsthal, P. Early Celtic Art in the British Isles, 2 vols. (Illus.). 392p. 1980. text ed. 99.00x (ISBN 0-19-817318-0). Oxford U Pr.
Jopling, W. H. Handbook of Leprosy. 2nd ed. (Illus.). 1978. pap. 13.50x (ISBN 0-433-17566-4). Intl Ideas.
Jopp, Harold D. & Ingersoll, R. H. Shoremen: An Anthology of Eastern Shore Prose & Verse. LC 74-7497. 1974. pap. 6.00 (ISBN 0-87033-186-8, Pub. by Tidewater). Cornell Maritime.
Joray. Vasarely Four. 1980. 195.95 (ISBN 0-8120-5394-X). Barron.
Jordaan, Jean-Pierre & Hyde, Martha B. Vocational Maturity During the High School Years. LC 78-23973. 1979. text ed. 22.50 (ISBN 0-8077-2453-X). Tchrs Coll.
Jordak, Francis E. A Bibliographical Survey for a Foundation in Philosophy. LC 78-64564. 1978. pap. text ed. 14.50 (ISBN 0-8191-0635-6). U Pr of Amer.
Jordan & LeMaster. Making Sense of Grammer. LC 79-24986. 1980. pap. 6.95x (ISBN 0-8077-2577-3). Tchrs Coll.
Jordan, jt. auth. see Fetterman, Elsie.
Jordan, A. C. Towards an African Literature: The Emergence of Literary Form in Xhosa. (Perspectives on Southern Africa: No. 6). 1973. 15.75x (ISBN 0-520-02079-0). U of Cal Pr.
Jordan, A. C., retold by. Tales from Southern Africa. (Perspectives on Southern Africa: No. 4). (Illus.). 1973. 18.50x (ISBN 0-520-01911-3); pap. 3.95 (ISBN 0-520-03638-7). U of Cal Pr.
Jordan, A. G., jt. auth. see Richardson, J. J.
Jordan, Alexander, tr. see Pertek, Jerzy.
Jordan, Alice M. From Rollo to Tom Sawyer & Other Papers. 160p. 1948. pap. 6.50 (ISBN 0-87675-058-7). Horn Bk.
Jordan, Alton, ed. see Barber, Phyllis.
Jordan, Alton, ed. see Burke, Suzanne.
Jordan, Alton, ed. see Reese, Bob.
Jordan, Alton, ed. see Reese, Bob, et al.
Jordan, Alton, ed. see Reese, Bob.
Jordan, Alton, ed. see Reese, Nancy.
Jordan, Alton, ed. see Reese, Ron.
Jordan, Alton, ed. see Selman, LaRue.
Jordan, Alton, ed. see Shebar, Sharon & Schoder, Judy.
Jordan, Alton, ed. see Smith, Glenna C.
Jordan, Alton, ed. see Stoddard, Darrell.
Jordan, Alton, ed. see Willoughby, Alan.
Jordan, Alton, ed. see Willoughby, Alana.
Jordan, Alton, ed. see Winder, Jack.
Jordan, Amos, et al. Facing the International Energy Problem, 1900 to 2000. 20.95 (ISBN 0-03-056162-0). Praeger.
Jordan, Amos A. & Kilmarx, Robert A. Strategic Mineral Dependence: The Stockile Dilemma. LC 79-66890. (The Washington Papers: No. 70). 89p. 1979. pap. 3.50 (ISBN 0-8039-1397-4). Sage.
Jordan, Anne. The Plains Woman. (Orig.). 1980. pap. 1.75 (ISBN 0-505-51545-8). Tower Bks.
Jordan, Anne H. & Jordan, Melbourne, eds. Cannons' Bibliography of Library Economy, 1876-1920: An Author Index with Citations. LC 76-3711. 481p. 1976. 22.50 (ISBN 0-8108-0918-4). Scarecrow.
Jordan, Bernice C. Acts: 14 Lessons, Vol. 1. (Footsteps of Faith Ser.). (gr. 3-9). 1954. pap. text ed. 1.95 (ISBN 0-86508-039-9); figures 7.95 (ISBN 0-86508-040-2). BCM Inc.
--Acts: 15 Lessons, Vol. 2. (Footsteps of Faith Ser.). (gr. 3-9). 1954. pap. text ed. 1.95 (ISBN 0-86508-041-0); figures 7.95 (ISBN 0-86508-042-9). BCM Inc.
--El Almacen De Dios: Exodo, 16 Lecciones, Vol. 2. (Pasos De Fe Ser.). (Span.). tchrs'. manual 2.25 (ISBN 0-86508-403-3); figuras 7.95 (ISBN 0-86508-404-1). BCM Inc.
--En las Huellas de los Heroes: 14 Lecciones, Tomo 4. (Pasos De Fe Ser.). (Span.). pap. text ed. 2.25 (ISBN 0-86508-407-6); figuras 7.95 (ISBN 0-86508-408-4). BCM Inc.
--Los Evangelios-Para que vino Jesus? 14 Lecciones, Tomo 2. (Pasos De Fe Ser.). (Span.). pap. text ed. 2.25 (ISBN 0-86508-411-4); figuras 7.95 (ISBN 0-86508-412-2). BCM Inc.
--Los Evangelios-Quien es Jesus? 14 Lecciones, Tomo 1. (Pasos De Fe Ser.). (Span.). pap. text ed. 2.25 (ISBN 0-86508-409-2); figuras 7.95 (ISBN 0-86508-410-6). BCM Inc.
--Fighting Giants: Joshua-Solomon 14 Lessons, Vol. 3. (Footsteps of Faith Ser.). (gr. 3-9). 1957. pap. text ed. 1.95 (ISBN 0-86508-031-3); figures 7.95 (ISBN 0-86508-032-1). BCM Inc.
--Genesis: Fifteen Lessons, Vol. 1. (Footsteps of Faith Ser.). (gr. 3-9) 1960. pap. text ed. 1.95 (ISBN 0-86508-027-5); figures 7.95 (ISBN 0-86508-028-3). BCM Inc.
--Genesis: Quinze Lecciones, Tomo 1. (Pasos De Fe Ser.). (Span.). pap. text ed. 2.25 (ISBN 0-86508-401-7); figuras 7.95 (ISBN 0-86508-402-5). BCM Inc.
--Los Gigantes en Canaan: 14 Lecciones, Tomo 3. (Pasos de Fe Ser.). (Span.). pap. text ed. 2.25 (ISBN 0-86508-405-X); figuras 7.95 (ISBN 0-86508-406-8). BCM Inc.
--God's Storehouse: Exodus 16 Lessons, Vol. 2. (Old Testament Ser.). (gr. 3-9). 1961. pap. text ed. 1.95 (ISBN 0-86508-029-1); figures 7.95 (ISBN 0-86508-030-5). BCM Inc.
--Gospels: 14 Lessons, Vol. 1, (New Testament Ser.). (gr. 3-9). 1955. pap. text ed. 1.95 (ISBN 0-86508-035-6); figures 7.95 (ISBN 0-86508-036-4). BCM Inc.
--Gospels: 14 Lessons, Vol. 2. (Footsteps of Faith Ser.). (gr. 3-9). 1956. pap. text ed. 1.95 (ISBN 0-86508-037-2); figures 7.95 (ISBN 0-86508-038-0). BCM Inc.
--Los Hechos Epistolas-El Mar De la Vida: 14 Lecciones. (Pasos De Fe Ser.). (Span.). pap. text ed. 2.25 (ISBN 0-86508-415-7); figuras 7.95 (ISBN 0-86508-416-5). BCM Inc.
--Los Hechos Epistolas-Vosotros sois Edificio de Dios: 14 Lecciones, Tomo 1. (Pasos De Fe Ser.). (Span.). pap. text ed. 2.25 (ISBN 0-86508-413-0); figuras 7.95 (ISBN 0-86508-414-9). BCM Inc.
Jordan, Bill. Automatic Poverty: The Ricardo Phenomenon. 208p. 1981. price not set (ISBN 0-7100-0824-4); pap. price not set (ISBN 0-7100-0825-2). Routledge & Kegan.
--Freedom & the Welfare State. 1978. pap. 6.95 (ISBN 0-7100-8910-4). Routledge & Kegan.
--Helping in Social Work. 1979. 14.95x (ISBN 0-7100-0126-6); pap. 8.95 (ISBN 0-7100-0127-4). Routledge & Kegan.
--Paupers: The Making of the New Claiming Class. 1973. 9.00x (ISBN 0-7100-7547-2); pap. 3.95 (ISBN 0-7100-7548-0). Routledge & Kegan.
--Poor Parents: Social Policy & the Cycle of Deprivation. 1974. 15.00 (ISBN 0-7100-7852-8); pap. 8.95 (ISBN 0-7100-7853-6). Routledge & Kegan.
Jordan, Bill, jt. ed. see Brandon, David.
Jordan, Brenda, jt. auth. see Leech, Kenneth.
Jordan, Brigitte. Birth in Four Cultures: A Cross-Cultural Investigation of Childbirth in Yucatan, Holland, Sweden & the United States. 2nd ed. (Illus.). 128p. 1980. pap. 6.95 (ISBN 0-920792-05-7). EPWP.
--Birth in Four Cultures: A Cross-Cultural Investigation of Childbirth in Yucatan, Holland, Sweden & the United States. (Illus.). 1978. 14.95 o.p. (ISBN 0-88831-024-2). EPWP.
Jordan, Carol. Tales from Third Street. (Illus.). 100p. 1980. pap. 3.50 (ISBN 0-9605360-0-0). C Jordan.
Jordan, Charles. Calculus of Finite Differences. 3rd ed. LC 65-29977. 22.50 (ISBN 0-8284-0033-4). Chelsea Pub.
Jordan, Clarence. Sermon on the Mount. 1970. pap. 2.50 (ISBN 0-8170-0501-3). Judson.
Jordan, D., tr. see Schmidt, R. F., et al.
Jordan, D. W. & Smith, P. Nonlinear Ordinary Differential Equations. (Oxford Applied Mathematics & Computing Science Ser.). (Illus.). 1977. pap. 17.95x (ISBN 0-19-859621-9). Oxford U Pr.
Jordan, Dale R. Dyslexia in the Classroom. 2nd ed. (Elementary Education Ser.). 1977. pap. text ed. 9.95 (ISBN 0-675-08466-0). Merrill.
Jordan, Daniel C. The Meaning of Deepening: Gaining a Clearer Apprehension of the Purpose of God for Man. LC 72-84824. (Comprehensive Deepening Program Ser.). 1973. pap. text ed. 4.00 (ISBN 0-87743-046-2, 7-64-01). Baha'i.
Jordan, David. Guide to the Romanization of Chinese. 78p. 1980. 3.95 (ISBN 0-89955-156-4, Pub. by Mei Ya Pub Taiwan). Intl Schol Bk Serv.
Jordan, David C. Spain, the Monarchy & the Atlantic Community. LC 79-65887. (Foreign Policy Reports Ser.). 55p. 1979. 5.00 (ISBN 0-89549-010-2). Inst Foreign Policy Anal.
Jordan, David K., jt. auth. see Swartz, Marc J.
Jordan, David P. The King's Trial: Louis XVI Vs. the French Revolution. 1981. pap. 5.95 (ISBN 0-520-04399-5, CAL 497). U of Cal Pr.
Jordan, David S. War & Waste: A Series of Discussions of War & War Accessories. LC 71-147473. (Library of War & Peace; the Character & Causes of War). lib. bdg. 38.00 (ISBN 0-8240-0265-2). Garland Pub.
Jordan, Derek, tr. see Reich, Wilhelm.
Jordan, Donald G. Chemical Process Development, 2 pts. 2nd ed. LC 78-23432. 1979. Repr. of 1968 ed. Pt. 1 428p. lib. bdg. 39.50 (ISBN 0-89874-064-9); Pt. 2 628p. lib. bdg. 45.50 (ISBN 0-88275-806-3); Set 1056p. lib. bdg. 76.50 (ISBN 0-89874-064-9). Krieger.
Jordan, Edward C. & Balmain, K. G. Electromagnetic Waves & Radiating Systems. 2nd ed. 1968. ref. ed. 27.95 (ISBN 0-13-249995-9). P-H.
Jordan, Gerald, ed. Naval Warfare in the Twentieth Century: A Festschrift in Honour of Professor Arthur J. Marder. LC 76-28613. 1977. 24.50x (ISBN 0-8448-1001-0). Crane-Russak Co.
Jordan, Gilbert, tr. see Von Schiller, Friedrich.
Jordan, Grace. Home Below Hell's Canyon. LC 54-6332. (Illus.). 1962. 11.95x (ISBN 0-8032-0946-0); pap. 4.95 (ISBN 0-8032-5107-6, BB 143, Bison). U of Nebr Pr.
Jordan, Helene J. How a Seed Grows. LC 60-11541. (A Let's-Read-&-Find-Out Science Bk). (Illus.). (gr. k-3). 1960. PLB 7.89 (ISBN 0-690-40645-2, TYC-J). T Y Crowell.
--Seeds by Wind & Water. LC 62-12820. (A Let's-Read-&-Find-Out Science Bk). (Illus.). (gr. k-3). 1962. bds. 7.95 (ISBN 0-690-72452-7, TYC-J); PLB 7.89 (ISBN 0-690-72453-5). T Y Crowell.
Jordan, Henry, et al. Eating Is Okay: A Radical Approach to Weight Loss. Gelman, Steve, ed. 1978. pap. 1.75 (ISBN 0-451-09305-4, E9305, Sig). NAL.
Jordan, Henry A. & Berland, Theodore. The Doctor's Calories-Plus Diet: The New Food IQ Way to Weight Loss. 1981. 10.95 (ISBN 0-8092-5939-7). Contemp Bks.
Jordan, Hoover H. Bolt Upright: The Life of Thomas Moore, 2 vols. (Salzburg Studies in English Literature, Romantic Reassessment Ser.: No. 38). (Illus.). 666p. 1975. Set. pap. text ed. 50.25x (ISBN 0-391-01440-4). Humanities.
Jordan, Hope D. Haunted Summer. (gr. 7-9). 1969. pap. 1.75 (ISBN 0-671-42063-1). Archway.
--Haunted Summer. (YA) (gr. 7-9). 1967. pap. 1.50 (ISBN 0-671-29963-8). PB.
Jordan, I., tr. see Schmidt, R. F., et al.
Jordan, Inge, tr. see Reich, Wilhelm.
Jordan, James M. & Alcorn, George T., eds. The Wildfowler's Heritage. LC 80-85152. (Illus.). 120p. 1981. 46.50 (ISBN 0-938694-03-0); deluxe ed. 125.00; deluxe ed. with remarque 175.00. Jordan & Co.
Jordan, Jerry M. Another Brown Bag. LC 80-36849. (Illus.). 1980. pap. 5.95 (ISBN 0-8298-0406-4). Pilgrim NY.
--The Brown Bag: A Bag Full of Sermons for Children. (Illus.). 117p. 1981. pap. 5.95 (ISBN 0-8298-0411-0). Pilgrim NY.
Jordan, Jim M. & Goldwater, Robert. The Paintings of Arshile Gorky: A Critical Catalogue. LC 79-2248. (Illus.). 480p. 1981. 60.00x (ISBN 0-8147-4160-6). NYU Pr.
Jordan, John E. Why the Lyrical Ballads? LC 75-27926. 1976. 15.75x (ISBN 0-520-03124-5). U of Cal Pr.
Jordan, Joseph A. & Singer, Albert, eds. The Cervix. LC 76-8579. (Illus.). 529p. 1976. text ed. 32.00 (ISBN 0-7216-5227-1). Saunders.
Jordan, June. Civil Wars. LC 80-68164. 192p. 1981. 12.95 (ISBN 0-8070-3232-8). Beacon Pr.
--Fannie Lou Hamer. LC 70-184982. (Biography Ser.). (Illus.). (gr. 1-5). 1972. 6.95 o.p. (ISBN 0-690-28893-X, TYC-J); PLB 7.89 (ISBN 0-690-28894-8). T Y Crowell.
--Things That I Do in the Dark: Selected Poems. LC 80-68165. 224p. 1981. pap. 6.95 (ISBN 0-8070-3235-2, BP 615). Beacon Pr.
--Things That I Do in the Dark: Selected Poems. 1977. 7.95 o.p. (ISBN 0-394-40937-X); pap. 4.95 (ISBN 0-394-73327-4). Random.
Jordan, June B. & Grossi, John A., eds. An Administrator's Handbook on Designing Programs for the Gifted & Talented. LC 80-68984. 144p. 1980. pap. 9.75 (ISBN 0-86586-112-9). Coun Exc Child.
Jordan, June Meyer, ed. Soulscript. LC 77-84390. 1970. pap. 2.50 (ISBN 0-385-07325-9, Zenith). Doubleday.
Jordan, K. Forbis, ed. see Seventeenth National Conference on School Finance.
Jordan, Leonard. Cabby. 1980. pap. 1.95 (ISBN 0-505-51466-4). Tower Bks.
Jordan, M., jt. auth. see Prenowitz, Walter.
Jordan, Melbourne, jt. ed. see Jordan, Anne H.
Jordan, Myra J. & Grant, Roy E. Floppy Rabbit: An Easter Musical. (Illus.). 30p. (Orig.). (ps-1). 1980. pap. 4.50. Merriam-Eddy.
--Santa's Problem. (Illus.). 30p. (Orig.). (ps-1). 1980. pap. 4.50 (ISBN 0-914562-08-8). Merriam-Eddy.
Jordan, Nehemiah. The Wisdom of Plato: An Attempt at an Outline, 2 vols. LC 80-1409. (Orig.). 1981. Set. lib. bdg. 47.50 (ISBN 0-8191-1408-1); Set. pap. text ed. 33.00 (ISBN 0-8191-1409-X). Vol. I, 544p. Vol. 2, 536p. U Pr of Amer.
Jordan, Neil. The Past. 1980. 8.95 (ISBN 0-8076-0982-X). Braziller.
Jordan, Pascual. The Expanding Earth. Beer, Arthur, ed. 224p. 1971. 34.00 (ISBN 0-08-015827-7). Pergamon.
Jordan, Pat. Broken Patterns. LC 76-48056. 1977. 7.95 (ISBN 0-396-07387-5). Dodd.
--Chase the Game. LC 78-31848. (Illus.). 1979. 8.95 (ISBN 0-396-07632-7). Dodd.
--A False Spring. LC 74-31082. 288p. 1975. 7.95 (ISBN 0-396-07078-7). Dodd.
Jordan, Payton & Spencer, Bud. Champions in the Making: Quality Training for Track & Field. LC 68-28877. 1968. text ed. 14.95 (ISBN 0-13-125401-4). P-H.
Jordan, Peter, jt. auth. see Bluestone, Barry.
Jordan, Philip, jt. auth. see Fairhall, David.
Jordan, Philip D. Fiddlefoot Jones of the North Woods. LC 57-7687. (Illus.). (gr. 4-7). 6.95 (ISBN 0-8149-0340-1). Vanguard.
--The People's Health: A History of Public Health in Minnesota to 1948. LC 53-38147. 524p. 1953. 5.00 (ISBN 0-87351-010-0). Minn Hist.
Jordan, Raimon. Le Troubadour Raimon Jordan Vicomte De Saint-Antonin. LC 80-2189. Repr. of 1922 ed. 25.00 (ISBN 0-404-19017-0). AMS Pr.
Jordan, Renee. Parents Love Your Children. 1977. pap. 2.95 (ISBN 0-89728-049-0, 670041). Omega Pubns OR.
Jordan, Richard D. The Temple of Eternity: Thomas Traherne's Philosophy of Time. LC 70-189560. (National University Publications). 1972. 11.00 (ISBN 0-8046-9019-7). Kennikat.
Jordan, Robert S. Political Leadership in NATO: A Study in Multilateral Diplomacy. 1979. lib. bdg. 27.50 (ISBN 0-89158-355-6). Westview.

Jordan, Robert S., jt. auth. see Weiss, Thomas G.

Jordan, Robert S., ed. International Administration: Its Evolution & Contemporary Applications. 1971. pap. 6.95x (ISBN 0-19-501462-6). Oxford U Pr.

Jordan, Robert S., jt. ed. see Graham, Norman A.

Jordan, Rudolf. The Autobiography of Rudolf Jordan. LC 80-70948. (Illus.). 227p. 1981. 10.95 (ISBN 0-8119-0415-6). Fell.

Jordan, Ruth. Daughter of the Waves: Memories of Growing up in Pre-War Palestine. LC 80-39526. 224p. 1981. 10.95 (ISBN 0-8008-2120-3). Taplinger.

Jordan, S., et al. Handbook of Technical Writing Practices, 2 vols. 1971. Set. 83.50 (ISBN 0-471-45062-6); Vol. 1. 40.00 (ISBN 0-471-45060-X); Vol. 2. 43.50 (ISBN 0-471-45059-6). Wiley.

Jordan, Terry G. German Seed in Texas Soil: Immigrant Farmers in Nineteenth Century Texas. 1966. pap. 5.95 (ISBN 0-292-72707-0). U of Tex Pr.

--Trails to Texas: Southern Roots of Western Cattle Ranching. LC 80-14169. (Illus.). xviii, 225p. 1981. 15.95 (ISBN 0-8032-2554-7). U of Nebr Pr.

Jordan, Terry G., et al. Log Cabin Village: A History & Guide. (Illus.). 1980. 15.00; pap. 6.95 (ISBN 0-87611-050-2). Tex St Hist Assn.

Jordan, Tina. A Visit to the Eagles' Nest. (Illus.). 20p. (gr. 3-5). 1980. PLB 1.85 (ISBN 0-938574-00-0). Cherubim.

Jordan, Tom. The Pahlavi Conjugation. LC 78-15981. Date not set. 10.95 (ISBN 0-87949-135-3). Ashley Bks.

Jordan, Virginia. Love in the Skies. 80p. 1981. 5.50 (ISBN 0-682-49684-7). Exposition.

Jordan, Walter H., jt. auth. see Glasstone, Samuel.

Jordan, Weymouth T., ed. Contributions to Science. (Illus.). 1954. pap. 2.00 o.p. (ISBN 0-8130-0461-6). U Presses Fla.

--Herbs, Hoecakes & Husbandry: The Daybook of a Planter of the Old South. LC 60-63360. (Florida State Univ. Studies). 1960. 8.00 o.p. (ISBN 0-8130-0496-9). U Presses Fla.

Jordan, William. Client-Worker Transactions. (Library of Social Work). 1970. 8.95 (ISBN 0-7100-6836-0). Routledge & Kegan.

Jordan, William C. Louis the Ninth: The Challenge of the Crusade. LC 79-83996. (Illus.). 1979. 17.50 (ISBN 0-691-05285-9). Princeton U Pr.

Jordan, Winthrop D. White Man's Burden: Historical Origins of Racism in the United States. 1974. pap. 4.95 (ISBN 0-19-501743-9, GB402, GB). Oxford U Pr.

Jordans. Dayananda Sarasvati: His Life & Ideas. 1979. 15.50x (ISBN 0-19-560995-6). Oxford U Pr.

Jorde, Emma M., jt. auth. see Landry, Lenore L.

Jorden, Eleanor H. & Chaplin, Hamako I. Beginning Japanese, Pt. 1. (Illus.). 1962. 27.50x o.p. (ISBN 0-300-00609-8); pap. text ed. 7.95x (ISBN 0-300-00135-5). Yale U Pr.

--Beginning Japanese, Pt. 2. (Linguistic Ser). (Illus.). 1963. text ed. 27.50x (ISBN 0-300-00610-1); pap. text ed. 7.95x (ISBN 0-300-00136-3). Yale U Pr.

Jordon, jt. auth. see Fetterman, Elsie.

Jordon, Alton, ed. see Reese, Bob, et al.

Jordon, Diana. Childhood & Movement. (gr. 9 up). 1972. 8.50x o.p. (ISBN 0-392-02545-0, SpS). Soccer.

Jordon, Ken W. The Economics of Stock Market Action. (New Stock Market Library). (Illus.). 1979. deluxe ed. 39.85 (ISBN 0-918968-33-X). Inst Econ Finan.

Jordy, Sarah S. see Keller, Mark.

Jordy, Sarah S., et al see Keller, Mark.

Jores, William R. Ten Trail Trips in Yosemite National Park. (Illus.). 1980. pap. 3.95 (ISBN 0-89646-064-9). Outbooks.

Joreskog, Karl G. & Sorbom, Dag. Advances in Factor Analysis & Structural Equation Models. LC 79-52433. 1979. 25.00 (ISBN 0-89011-535-4). Abt Assoc.

--Lisrel Four: Analysis of Linear Structural Relationships by the Method of Maximum Likelihood. pap. 10.00 (ISBN 0-89498-004-1). Natl Ed Res.

Jorgens, Elise B. The Well Tun'd Word: Musical Interpretations of English Poetry, 1597-1651. (Illus.). 320p. 1981. 25.00x (ISBN 0-8166-1029-0). U of Minn Pr.

Jorgensen. Tuning the Historical Temperments by Ear. LC 77-70993. 1977. 30.00 o.p. (ISBN 0-918616-00-X). Northern Mich.

Jorgensen, Eric. Audi Service-Repair Handbook: Fox--1973-1977. Robinson, Jeff, ed. (Illus.). 1977. pap. 10.95 (ISBN 0-89287-155-5, A132). Clymer Pubns.

--Chevette Service Repair Handbook: All Models 1976-1978. Robinson, Jeff, ed. (Illus.). 1978. pap. 11.95 (ISBN 0-89287-145-8, A290). Clymer Pubns.

--Corvette Service-Repair Handbook: All Models, 1966-1979. Robinson, Jeff, ed. (Illus.). 1976. pap. text ed. 10.95 (ISBN 0-89287-082-6, A146). Clymer Pubns.

--Fix Your Bicycle: All Speeds, All Major Makes, Simplified, Step by Step. 2nd ed. Robinson, Jeff, ed. (Illus.). 192p. 1975. pap. text ed. 7.00 (ISBN 0-89287-035-4, X901). Clymer Pubns.

--Honda: Four Fifty & Five Hundred cc Twins 1965-1977--Service, Repair, Performance. 7th ed. Robinson, Jeff, ed. (Illus.). 1978. pap. 9.95 (ISBN 0-89287-242-X, M333). Clymer Pubns.

--Honda: G L-One Thousand Fours, 1975-1979--Service, Repair, Performance. 2nd ed. Robinson, Jeff, ed. (Illus.). 1978. pap. 9.95 (ISBN 0-89287-238-1, M340). Clymer Pubns.

--Honda Service Repair Handbook: 350-550cc Fours,1972-1978. Robinson, Jeff, ed. (Illus.). 1978. pap. 9.95 (ISBN 0-89287-287-X, M332). Clymer Pubns.

--Porsche Nine-Fourteen Series. 1970-1976: Service, Repair Handbook: 914 Series, 1970-1976--Service, Repair Handbook. 3rd ed. Robinson, Jeff, ed. (Illus.). 1978. pap. 10.95 (ISBN 0-89287-203-9, A184). Clymer Pubns.

--Porsche Service-Repair Handbook: 911 & 912 Series, 1965-1978. Robinson, Jeff, ed. (Illus.). 1978. pap. text ed. 10.95 (ISBN 0-89287-060-5, A183). Clymer Pubns.

--Powerboat Maintenance. Robinson, Jeff, ed. (Illus.). 288p. 1975. pap. text ed. 9.00 (ISBN 0-89287-069-9, B620). Clymer Pubns.

--Volkswagen Performance Tuning: 1200-2000cc Engines, All Years. 2nd ed. Robinson, Jeff, ed. (Illus.). 200p. 1978. pap. text ed. 10.95 (ISBN 0-89287-223-3, A128). Clymer Pubns.

--Volkswagen Service - Repair Handbook: 411 & 412, 1968-1974. 2nd ed. Robinson, Jeff, ed. (Illus.). 248p. 1975. pap. text ed. 10.95 (ISBN 0-89287-041-9, A125). Clymer Pubns.

--Volkswagen Service--Repair Handbook: Beetle, Super Beetle, Karmann Ghia, 1961-1979. Robinson, Jeff, ed. (Illus.). 1977. pap. 11.95 (ISBN 0-89287-144-X, A104). Clymer Pubns.

--Volkswagen Service--Repair Handbook: Dasher, 1974-1980. Robinson, Jeff, ed. (Illus.). 1977. pap. 10.95 (ISBN 0-89287-154-7, A121). Clymer Pubns.

--Volkswagen Service--Repair Handbook: Rabbit, Scirocco-1975-1979. Robinson, Jeff, ed. (Illus.). 1978. pap. 10.95 (ISBN 0-89287-157-1, A122). Clymer Pubns.

--Volkswagen Service-Repair Handbook: Squareback & Fastback, 1962-1973. Robinson, Jeff, ed. (Illus.). 304p. 1974. pap. text ed. 10.95 (ISBN 0-89287-039-7, A120). Clymer Pubns.

--Volkswagen Transporter: 1961-1979, Service, Repair Handbk. Robinson, Jeff, ed. (Illus.). 1978. pap. 10.95 (ISBN 0-89287-277-2, A110). Clymer Pubns.

--Volvo Service Repair Handbook: 140 Series, 1967-1974. Robinson, Jeff, ed. (Illus.). 1978. pap. 10.95 (ISBN 0-89287-227-6, A222). Clymer Pubns.

Jorgensen, Eric, ed. Harley-Davidson Service, Repair Handbook: All 74 Cu. in. Models, 1959-1979. 3rd ed. (Illus.). 1977. pap. 9.95 (ISBN 0-89287-190-3, M420). Clymer Pubns.

--Honda Express: 1977-1980 Service-Repair-Performance. (Illus.). 128p. (Orig.). 1979. pap. text ed. 9.95 (ISBN 0-89287-194-6, M314). Clymer Pubns.

--Honda: One Hundred-Three Fifty cc Four-Stroke Singles 1970-1978--Service, Repair Performance. 5th ed. (Illus.). 1979. pap. 9.95 (ISBN 0-89287-184-9, M315). Clymer Pubns.

--Honda Service, Repair Handbook: 50-90cc Singles, 1963-1978. (Illus.). 1978. pap. 9.95 (ISBN 0-89287-187-3, M310). Clymer Pubns.

--Honda Three-Fifty - Five-Fifty cc Fours 1972-1978 Service Repair Performance. (Illus.). 208p. (Orig.). 1978. pap. text ed. 9.95 (ISBN 0-89287-27-X, M332). Clymer Pubns.

--Kawasaki K2650 Fours Nineteen Seventy-Six to Nineteen Eighty Service, Repair, Performance. (Illus.). 1979. pap. 9.95 (ISBN 0-89287-296-9, M358). Clymer Pubns.

--Kawasaki: 250-750cc Triples 1969-1979--Service, Repair, Maintenance Handbook. 4th ed. (Illus.). 1978. pap. 9.95 (ISBN 0-89287-192-X, M353). Clymer Pubns.

--Suzuki: 125-400cc Singles, 1964-1979 Service, Repair, Performance. 3rd ed. (Illus.). 1978. pap. 9.95 (ISBN 0-89287-280-2, M369). Clymer Pubns.

--Yamaha: XS360 & XS-400 Twins, 1976-78, Service, Repair, Maintenance. (Illus.). 1978. pap. 9.95 (ISBN 0-89287-170-9, M402). Clymer Pubns.

--Yamaha: 50-100cc Rotary Valve Singles, 1963-1976--Service, Repair, Maintenance. 3rd ed. (Illus.). 1979. pap. 9.95 (ISBN 0-89287-220-9, M389). Clymer Pubns.

--Yamaha: 650cc Twins, 1970-79, Service, Repair, Performance. (Illus.). 1978. pap. 9.95 (ISBN 0-89287-233-0, M403). Clymer Pubns.

Jorgensen, Eric, ed. see Ahlstrand, Alan.

Jorgensen, Eric, ed. see Bishop, Mike.

Jorgensen, Eric, ed. see Clymer Publications.

Jorgensen, Eric, ed. see Combs, Jim.

Jorgensen, Eric, ed. see Hoy, Ray.

Jorgensen, Eric, ed. see Price, Brick.

Jorgensen, Eric, ed. see Sales, David.

Jorgensen, Eric, ed. see Scott, Ed.

Jorgensen, Eric, ed. see Scott, Edward.

Jorgensen, Eric, ed. see Tabler, Dave.

Jorgensen, Eric, ed. see Vesely, Anton.

Jorgensen, Gunhild. Techniques of China Painting. 112p. 1980. pap. 7.95 (ISBN 0-442-20176-1). Van Nos Reinhold.

Jorgensen, Ivar. Ten Deadly Men. 192p. 1976. pap. 1.25 o.p. (ISBN 0-523-22817-1). Pinnacle Bks.

Jorgensen, James. The Graying of America: Retirement & Why You Can't Afford It. 245p. 1980. 10.95 (ISBN 0-8037-2913-8). Dial.

Jorgensen, James & Fautsko, Timothy. Quid: How to Make the Best Decisions of Your Life. LC 78-58623. 1978. 8.95 (ISBN 0-8027-0615-0); pap. 4.95 (ISBN 0-8027-7139-4). Walker & Co.

Jorgensen, James D., et al. Solving Problems in Meetings. LC 79-21782. 112p. 1981. 8.95 (ISBN 0-88229-521-7). Nelson-Hall.

Jorgensen, Johannes. Saint Francis of Assisi. pap. 2.95 (ISBN 0-385-02875-X, D22, Im). Doubleday.

Jorgensen, Joseph G., intro. by. Biology & Culture in Modern Perspective: Readings from Scientific American. LC 72-4237. (Illus.). 1972. text ed. 20.95x (ISBN 0-7167-0862-0); pap. text ed. 10.95x (ISBN 0-7167-0861-2). W H Freeman.

Jorgensen, Niels B. & Hayden, Jess. Sedation, Local & General Anesthesia in Dentistry. 3rd ed. LC 79-20549. (Illus.). 299p. 1980. text ed. 27.50 (ISBN 0-8121-0684-9). Lea & Febiger.

Jorgensen, Paul A. Our Naked Frailties: Sensational Art & Meaning in Macbeth. LC 70-145788. 1971. 14.50x (ISBN 0-520-01915-6). U of Cal Pr.

--Shakespeare's Military World. (California Library Reprint). 1974. 24.50x (ISBN 0-520-02519-9). U of Cal Pr.

Jorgensen, Paul A., ed. see Shakespeare, William.

Jorgensen, Poul. Salmon Flies: Their Character, Style, & Dressing. LC 78-17941. (Illus.). 192p. 1978. 19.95 (ISBN 0-8117-1426-8). Stackpole.

Jorgensen, Richard, jt. auth. see Murphey, Wayne K.

Jorgensen, Roy. Energy Philosophy: A System of Self-Mastery & Increased Personal Energy. LC 80-83506. (Illus.). 260p. (Orig.). 1980. pap. 7.95 (ISBN 0-938226-01-0). Pacific Edns.

Jorgensen, S. E. State-of-the-Art of Ecological Modelling: Proceedings of the Conference on Ecological Modelling, Copenhagen, 28 August - 2 September 1978. LC 78-41208. (Environmental Sciences & Applications Ser.: Vol. 7). 1979. 125.00 (ISBN 0-08-023443-7). Pergamon.

Jorgensen, S. E., ed. Handbook of Environmental Data & Ecological Parameters. rev. ed. LC 78-41207. (Enviromental Sciences & Applications Ser.: Vol. 6). (Illus.). 1100p. 1979. 225.00 (ISBN 0-08-023436-4). Pergamon.

--Industrial Waste Water Management. (Studies in Environmental Science: Vol. 5). 388p. 1979. 46.50 (ISBN 0-686-62655-9). Elsevier.

Jorgensen, S. E, ed. Lake Management. (Water Development, Supply & Management). 1980. 42.00 (ISBN 0-08-022432-6). Pergamon.

Jorgenson, Eric, ed. see Sales, David.

Jorgenson, Finn. The Complete Handbook of Magnetic Recording. (Illus.). 448p. (Orig.). 1980. 15.95 (ISBN 0-8306-9940-6); pap. text ed. 10.95 (ISBN 0-8306-1059-6, 1059). Tab Bks.

Jorgenson, Ronald, jt. ed. see Melnick, Michael.

Jorgenson, Ronald J., jt. ed. see Salinas, Carlos F.

Jorgesen, Eric, ed. see Scott, Ed.

Jorpes, T. E. & Mutt, V., eds. Secretin, Cholecystokinin - Pancreozymin & Gastrin. (Handbook of Experimental Pharmacology: Vol. 34). (Illus.). 350p. 1973. 106.20 (ISBN 0-387-05952-0). Springer-Verlag.

Jorstad, J. & Ugelstad, E. Schizophrenia 75. 1976. text ed. 31.00x (ISBN 8-200-02372-9, Dist. by Columbia U Pr). Universitet.

Jortner, J., jt. auth. see Levine, R. D.

Jortner, Joshua, et al, eds. Photoselective Chemistry, Pt. 1. (Advances in Chemical Physics Ser.). 736p. 1981. 49.50 (ISBN 0-471-06275-8, Pub. by Wiley-Interscience). Wiley.

--Photoselective Chemistry, Pt. 2. (Advances in Chemical Physics Ser.). 550p. 1981. 50.00 (ISBN 0-471-06274-X, Pub. by Wiley-Interscience). Wiley.

Joscelyn, Archie. Gunman. 256p. (YA) 1975. 5.95 (ISBN 0-685-51236-3, Avalon). Bouregy.

--Kiowa Pass. 192p. (YA) 1976. 5.95 (ISBN 0-685-66480-5, Avalon). Bouregy.

--The Lost Herd. (YA) 1978. 5.95 (ISBN 0-685-86409-X, Avalon). Bouregy.

--Lost River Canyon. 192p. (YA) 1976. 5.95 (ISBN 0-685-62024-7, Avalon). Bouregy.

--Ride to Blizzard. 256p. (YA) 1973. 5.95 (ISBN 0-685-30372-1, Avalon). Bouregy.

--The Trail to Dismal River. 192p. (YA) 1975. 5.95 (ISBN 0-685-53494-4, Avalon). Bouregy.

--The Trail to Lost Horse Ranch. (YA) 1977. 4.95 o.p. (ISBN 0-685-73810-8, Avalon). Bouregy.

Jose, Francisco & Cardona, Maria E., eds. Author Index to the Handbook of Latin American Studies: No. 1-28, 1936-1966. LC 36-32633. 1968. 32.50x (ISBN 0-8130-0265-6). U Presses Fla.

Jose, Nicholas. The Possession of Amber. 285p. 1981. text ed. 13.25 (ISBN 0-7022-1537-6); pap. 7.25 (ISBN 0-7022-1538-4). U of Queensland Pr.

Josefowitz, Natash. Paths to Power: A Working Woman's Guide from First Job to Top Executive. 1980. 11.95 (ISBN 0-201-03485-9); pap. 6.95 (ISBN 0-201-03486-7); instr's manual 2.50 (ISBN 0-201-03479-4). A-W.

Josefson, Ingela. Die Bezeichnungen fuer Gross-Klein, "Lang-Kurz" im Altschwedischen. (Nordistica Gothoburgensia: 9). (Ger.). 1976. pap. text ed. 10.00x (ISBN 91-7346-025-7). Humanities.

Joseloff, Samuel H., ed. A Time to Seek: An Anthology of Contemporary Jewish American Poets. 1975. 5.00 (ISBN 0-8074-0199-4, 168000); tchrs'. guide 5.00 (ISBN 0-685-55043-5, 208001). UAHC.

Joseph, Alaine, et al. Best of Pandora. new ed. Wickstrom, Lois, ed. (Illus., Orig.). Date not set. pap. price not set (ISBN 0-916176-09-6). Sproing.

Joseph, Alexander, jt. auth. see Jaworski, Irene D.

Joseph, Alexander, et al. Physics for Engineering Technology. 2nd ed. LC 76-55696. 1978. 21.95 (ISBN 0-471-45075-8); solutions manual avail. (ISBN 0-471-025364). Wiley.

Joseph, Bernard. British Rule in Palestine. (Return to Zion Ser.). vii, 279p. 1980. Repr. of 1949 ed. lib. bdg. 20.00x (ISBN 0-87991-136-0). Porcupine Pr.

--Nationality: Its Nature & Problems. 1923. 37.50x (ISBN 0-686-51422-X). Elliots Bks.

Joseph, Bertram. A Shakespeare Workbook, 2 vols. 1980. pap. 10.45 ea. Vol. 1 Tragedies (ISBN 0-87830-566-1). Vol. 2 Comedies & Histories (ISBN 0-87830-571-8). Theatre Arts.

Joseph, Carmen, jt. auth. see Buono, Dello.

Joseph, D., jt. auth. see Iooss, G.

Joseph, Dayle, jt. auth. see Hames, Carolyn C.

Joseph, Gerda. Follett Instant German Conversation Guide. (Illus., Orig.). 1966. 2.50 (ISBN 0-695-84197-1). Follett.

Joseph, Gloria & Lewis, Jill. Common Differences. LC 79-6885. 240p. 1981. pap. 7.95 (ISBN 0-385-14271-4, Anch). Doubleday.

Joseph, Harrison O. Collected Poems of Elizabeth Barger Joseph. 64p. 1981. 10.00 (ISBN 0-682-49674-X). Exposition.

Joseph, Jack. Follett Instant Spanish Conversation Guide. (Illus., Orig.). 2.50 (ISBN 0-695-84199-8). Follett.

Joseph, James, et al. Tuna & Billfish: Fish Without a Country. 2nd ed. LC 80-81889. (Illus.). 53p. (Orig.). (gr. 7-12). 1980. pap. 7.95 (ISBN 0-686-65904-X). Inter-Am Tropical.

Joseph, Joan. Black African Empires. LC 73-14555. (First Bks). (Illus.). 72p. (gr. 5-7). 1974. PLB 4.90 o.p. (ISBN 0-531-00811-8). Watts.

--Folk Toys Around the World & How to Make Them. LC 72-1127. (Illus.). 96p. (gr. 5 up). 1972. 5.95 o.s.i. (ISBN 0-686-66677-1, Four Winds); PLB 5.41 o.s.i. (ISBN 0-8193-0599-5). Schol Bk Serv.

--Folk Toys Around the World & How to Make Them. LC 72-1127. (Illus.). (gr. 3 up). 1972. 3.50 (ISBN 0-935738-01-0, 5016). US Comm UNICEF.

--Henry Hudson. LC 73-14704. (Visual Biography Ser). (Illus.). 64p. (gr. 4-5). 1974. PLB 4.90 o.p. (ISBN 0-531-02776-X). Watts.

--Pet Birds. LC 75-11902. (Career Concise Guides Ser.). (Illus.). 72p. (gr. 8 up). 1975. PLB 4.90 o.p. (ISBN 0-531-02837-2). Watts.

Joseph, Joan E., jt. ed. see Dahl, A. M.

Joseph, K. P. Notes on the Era & Other Poems. (Writers Workshop Redbird Ser.). 1975. 12.00 (ISBN 0-88253-590-0); pap. text ed. 4.80 (ISBN 0-88253-589-7). Ind-US Inc.

Joseph, Lou & Cucco, Ulisse. A Doctor Discusses Prepared Childbirth. 1980. pap. 2.50 (ISBN 0-910304-21-1). Budlong.

Joseph, Lou & Lynch, John J. A Doctor Discusses Diabetes. (Illus.). 1980. pap. 2.50 (ISBN 0-685-46339-7). Budlong.

Joseph, Lou & Mills, Alice S. A Doctor Discusses Allergy Fact & Fallacies. (Illus., Orig.). 1980. pap. 2.50 (ISBN 0-685-35676-0). Budlong.

Joseph, Lou & Novick, Oscar. Doctor Discusses Children's Colds. (Illus.). 1979. pap. 2.50 (ISBN 0-686-65549-4). Budlong.

Joseph, Marjory & Gieseking, Audrey. Illustrated Guide to Textiles. 2nd ed. (Illus.). 1972. pap. 7.50x (ISBN 0-916434-02-8). Plycon Pr.

Joseph, Marjory & Gieseking, Audrey G. Illustrated Guide to Textiles. 2nd ed. 1981. 8.95 (ISBN 0-8087-3400-8). Burgess.
Joseph, Rebecca. Simplified Indian Cookery. 1970. pap. 3.00 (ISBN 0-88253-144-1). Ind-US Inc.
Joseph, Richard A. Radical Nationalism in Cameroun: Social Origins of the U.P.C. Rebellion. 1977. 49.50x (ISBN 0-19-822706-X). Oxford U Pr.
Joseph, Ronald S. The Glory. 464p. (Orig.). 1980. pap. 2.75 (ISBN 0-446-85469-7). Warner Bks.
--The Kingdom. 480p. (Orig.). 1978. pap. 2.75 (ISBN 0-446-85699-1). Warner Bks.
Joseph, Stephen. Children in Fear. LC 72-91587. 224p. 1974. 6.95 o.p. (ISBN 0-03-007711-7). HR&W.
Joseph, Stephen M., ed. The Me Nobody Knows: Children's Voices from the Ghetto. 1969. pap. 1.75 (ISBN 0-380-01339-8, 48934, Discus). Avon.
Josephs, Ernest H., Jr., jt. auth. see Wicks, Robert J.
Josephs, M. Technology & the Future of Stockbroking. 61p. 1980. 57.50 (ISBN 0-85012-228-7). Intl Pubns Serv.
Josephs, Rebecca. Early Disorder. 1980. 10.95 (ISBN 0-374-14579-2). FS&G.
Josephson, B. D. & Ramachandran, V. S. Consciousness & the Physical World: Proceedings of an Interdisciplinary Symposium on Consciousness Held at the University of Cambridge, Jan. 1978. 1979. 25.00 (ISBN 0-08-024695-8). Pergamon.
Josephson, Emanuel. Breathe Deeply & Avoid Colds. (Natural Health Ser.). 127p. (Orig.). 1957. pap. 5.00 (Pub. by Chedney). Alpine Ent.
--The Federal Reserve Conspiracy & the Rockefellers: Their Gold Corner. LC 68-29455. (Blacked-Out History Ser.). 374p. 1968. 12.50 (Pub. by Chedney); pap. 8.00. Alpine Ent.
--Glaucoma & Its Medical Treatment with Cortin: Myopia Its Cause & Prevention. (Natural Health Ser.). 92p. (Orig.). 1937. pap. text ed. 6.95 (Pub. by Chedney). Alpine Ent.
--The Strange Death of Franklin Roosevelt: A History of the Roosevelt-Delano Dynasty: America's Royal Family. (Blacked-Out History Ser.). 284p. 11.00 (Pub. by Chedney); pap. 4.95. Alpine Ent.
--The Thymus Manganese, & Myasthenia Gravis. (Natural Health Ser.). 124p. 12.00 (Pub. by Chedney); pap. 6.00. Alpine Ent.
Josephson, Emanuel M., ed. see Brother Nectario M.
Josephson, Martin M. & Porter, Robert T. Clinician's Handbook of Childhood Psychopathology. 30.00x (ISBN 0-87668-359-6). Aronson.
Josephus. Jerusalem & Rome: The Writings of Josephus. Glatzer, Nahum N., ed. 8.00 (ISBN 0-8446-2341-5). Peter Smith.
Josephus, Flavius. Complete Works of Flavius Josephus. Whiston, William, tr. LC 60-15405. (Orig.). 1974. 17.95 (ISBN 0-8254-2951-X); kivar 12.95 (ISBN 0-8254-2952-8). Kregel.
--Jewish War. Williamson, Geoffrey A., tr. (Classics Ser.). (Orig.). 1959. pap. 3.95 (ISBN 0-14-044090-9). Penguin.
Josephy, Alvin M., Jr., ed. see Boahen, A. Adu, et al.
Josephy, Alvin M., Jr., ed. see Lavender, David.
Josephy, Alvin M., Jr., ed. see Severin, Timothy.
Josette, Frank, ed. see Barrie.
Josey, E. J. What Black Librarians Are Saying. LC 72-5372. 1972. 10.00 (ISBN 0-8108-0530-8). Scarecrow.
Josey, E. J. & Peeples, Kenneth E., Jr. Opportunities for Minorities in Librarianship. LC 77-375. 1977. 10.00 (ISBN 0-8108-1022-0). Scarecrow.
Josey, E. J., ed. & intro. by. Black Librarian in America. LC 79-17850. 1970. 10.00 (ISBN 0-8108-0362-3). Scarecrow.
Josey, E. J., ed. Libraries in the Political Process. (Neal-Schuman Professional Books Ser.). 1980. lib. bdg. 18.95x (ISBN 0-912700-25-4). Oryx Pr.
Josey, E. J. & Shockley, A. A., eds. Handbook of Black Librarianship. LC 77-21817. 1977. lib. bdg. 25.00x (ISBN 0-87287-179-7). Libs Unl.
Joshi, A. W. Elements of Group Therapy for Physicists. 2nd ed. LC 76-51385. 1977. 12.95 (ISBN 0-470-99062-7). Halsted Pr.
--Matrices & Tensors in Physics. LC 75-26772. 251p. 1976. 8.95 (ISBN 0-470-45086-X). Halsted Pr.
Joshi, Aravind, et al. Elements of Discourse Understanding. LC 80-29393. (Illus.). 352p. Date not set. price not set (ISBN 0-521-23327-5). Cambridge U Pr.
Joshi, Arun. The Foreigner. (Orient Paperback Ser). 244p. 1972. pap. 3.25 (ISBN 0-88253-106-9). Ind-US Inc.
--Foreigner: A Novel. 1969. 6.00x (ISBN 0-210-98113-X). Asia.
--Strange Case of Billy Biswas. 1971. 6.00x (ISBN 0-210-22385-5). Asia.
--The Strange Case of Billy Biswas. 1974. pap. 3.50 (ISBN 0-88253-387-8). Ind-US Inc.
Joshi, J. M. Theory of Value, Distribution & Welfare Economics. 1980. text ed. 20.00x (ISBN 0-7069-0689-6, Pub. by Vikas India). Advent Bk.
Joshi, K. S. Yoga in Daily Life. 163p. 1971. pap. 2.00 (ISBN 0-88253-044-5). Ind-US Inc.
Joshi, S. T. H. P. Lovecraft & Lovecraft Criticism: An Annotated Bibliography. LC 80-84662. (Serif Ser.: No. 38). 1981. 27.50x (ISBN 0-87338-248-X). Kent St U Pr.
Joshi, S. T., ed. H. P. Lovecraft: Four Decades of Criticism. LC 80-11535. xvi, 247p. 1980. 15.00 (ISBN 0-8214-0442-3, 0442E). Ohio U Pr.
Joshi, Shiv K. He Never Slept So Long. (Writers Workshop Bluebird Book Ser.). 49p. 1975. 14.00 (ISBN 0-88253-556-0); pap. text ed. 4.80 (ISBN 0-88253-555-2). Ind-US Inc.
Joshua, Joan, jt. auth. see White, Kay.
Joshua, Wynfred & Hahn, Walter F. Nuclear Politics: America, France, & Britain. LC 73-83411. (The Washington Papers: No. 9). 1973. 3.50x (ISBN 0-8039-0282-4). Sage.
Josimovich, John B., jt. auth. see Gold, Jay J.
Joslin. What Do You Say, Dear? (ps-3). 1980. pap. 1.50 (ISBN 0-590-01625-3, Schol Pap). Schol Bk Serv.
Joslin, Sesyle. Spy Lady & the Muffin Man. LC 74-137757. (Illus.). (gr. 4-6). 1971. 4.75 o.p. (ISBN 0-15-278182-X, HJ). HarBraceJ.
Joslin, Sesyle & Weisgard, Leonard. Brave Baby Elephant. LC 60-10245. (Illus.). (ps-1). 1960. 4.95 o.p. (ISBN 0-15-211598-6, HJ). HarBraceJ.
Josling, Timothy E., jt. ed. see McCalla, Alix F.
Joslyn, M. A., jt. auth. see Tressler, Donald K.
Joslyn, Maynard A. & Heid, J. L. Food Processing Operations, 3 Vols. 1963-64. 25.50 ea. o.p. Vol. 1 (ISBN 0-87055-015-2). Vol. 2 (ISBN 0-87055-016-0). Vol. 3 (ISBN 0-87055-017-9). AVI.
Joslyn, Maynard A., jt. auth. see Heid, John L.
Joslyn-Scherer, Marcia S. Communication in the Human Services: A Guide to Therapeutic Journalism. LC 79-28653. (Sage Human Services Guides: Vol. 13). 175p. 1980. pap. 8.00 (ISBN 0-8039-1418-0). Sage.
Jospe, Michael, et al. Psychological Factors in Health Care: A Practitioner's Manual. Cohen, Barry D., ed. LC 77-11395. 496p. 1980. 29.95x (ISBN 0-669-02076-1). Lexington Bks.
Jospe, Michael L. The Placebo Effect in Healing. LC 77-6582. 1978. 18.95 (ISBN 0-669-01611-X). Lexington Bks.
Joss, John, ed. Soaramerica. (Illus.). 216p. 1976. 9.95 o.p. (ISBN 0-930514-04-1, Pub. by Soaring); pap. 6.95 (ISBN 0-930514-06-8). Aviation.
Jossan, C. S. Stories of Buddha's Births: A Jataka Reader. LC 76-30762. (Foreign & Comparative Studies-South Asian Special Publications Ser.: No. 1). 1976. pap. text ed. 3.50x (ISBN 0-915984-77-6). Syracuse U Foreign Comp.
Josselin, Ralph. The Diary of Ralph Josselin, 1616-1683. Macffarlane, Alan, ed. (British Academy Ser.). (Illus.). 1976. 95.00x (ISBN 0-19-725955-3). Oxford U Pr.
Josselyn, Irene M., ed. see Joint Commission on Mental Health of Children.
Josserand, Frank B. Richard Wagner: Patriot & Politician. LC 80-5638. 351p. (Orig.). 1981. lib. bdg. 20.50 (ISBN 0-8191-1418-9); pap. text ed. 11.75 (ISBN 0-8191-1419-7). U Pr of Amer.
Josso, Nathalie, ed. The Intersex Child. (Pediatric & Adolescent Endocrinology Ser.: Vol. 8). 300p. 1980. soft cover 54.00 (ISBN 3-8055-0909-X). S Karger.
Jossua, J. P. & Metz, J. B. Doing Theology in New Places. (Concilium Ser.: Religion in the Seventies Vol. 115). 1979. pap. 4.95 (ISBN 0-8164-2611-2). Crossroad NY.
Jossua, J. P., jt. auth. see Metz, J. B.
Jossua, J. P., jt. ed. see Metz, J. B.
Jossua, Jean-Pierre, jt. ed. see Geffre, Claude.
Jost, Francois. Introduction to Comparative Literature. LC 73-19849. 1974. 14.95 (ISBN 0-672-63657-3). Pegasus.
Jost, Lee F. & Sutherland, C. Bruce. Guide to Professional Benefit Plan Management & Administration. 405p. (Orig.). 1980. pap. 35.00 (ISBN 0-89154-096-2). Intl Found Employ.
Jost, W. see Eyring, H., et al.
Jottrand, R., ed. Chemical Reaction Engineering: Proceedings of the Fourth International Symposium. 1971. 105.00 (ISBN 0-08-013182-4). Pergamon.
Joughin, Louis & Morgan, Edmund M. The Legacy of Sacco & Vanzetti. LC 77-92101. 596p. 30.00x (ISBN 0-691-04656-5); pap. 5.95 (ISBN 0-691-00588-5). Princeton U Pr.
Jouklova, Z. Technical Dictionary: English, Czech, English. 510p. (Czech.). 1970. 12.00x (ISBN 0-89918-301-8). Vanous.
Joule, James, jt. ed. see Smith, Michael H.
Jourdain, Rose. Those the Sun Has Loved: An American Family Saga. LC 77-82952. 1978. 10.95 o.p. (ISBN 0-385-13028-7). Doubleday.
Jourdan, Eveline. Butterflies & Moths Around the World. LC 80-20086. (Nature & Man Books). (Illus.). (gr. 5 up). 1981. PLB 7.95g (ISBN 0-686-59986-1). Lerner Pubns.
Jourlet, Marie de see De Jourlet, Marie.
Jourlet, Marie De see De Jourlet, Marie.
Journal of Nursing Administration, Staff, ed. Fundamental Issues in Nursing. LC 75-14685. 96p. 1975. pap. text ed. 7.95 o.s.i. (ISBN 0-913654-12-4). Nursing Res.
Journal of Nursing Administration Staff, ed. Staff Development, Vol. 1. LC 75-35067. 1975. pap. text ed. 8.95 (ISBN 0-913654-08-6). Nursing Res.
--Staffing Three. LC 75-43268. 48p. 1976. pap. text ed. 4.95 (ISBN 0-913654-21-3). Nursing Res.
--Staffing Two. LC 75-16751. 1975. pap. text ed. 4.95 (ISBN 0-913654-06-X). Nursing Res.
Journal of Nursing Administration, Staff, ed. The Techniques of Nursing Management, Vol. 1. LC 75-1674. 1975. pap. text ed. 4.95 o.s.i. (ISBN 0-913654-07-8). Nursing Res.
Journal of Nursing Administration Staff, ed. The Techniques of Nursing Management, Vol. 2. LC 75-1674. 1976. pap. 4.95 o.s.i. (ISBN 0-913654-32-9). Nursing Res.
Jousseaume, Andre. Progressive Dressage. Vigneron, Jeanette, tr. from Fr. pap. 8.75 (ISBN 0-85131-231-4). J A Allen.
Jouve, Nicole W. Baudelaire: A Fire to Conquer Darkness. LC 79-14978. 1980. 22.50 (ISBN 0-312-07005-5). St Martin.
Jouve, Pierre J. Idiom of Night. Bosley, Keith, tr. (Poetry Europe Ser.: No. 9). 80p. 1969. 6.95 (ISBN 0-8040-0150-2). Swallow.
Jouvency, Joseph de see Gautruche, Pierre.
Jouvenel, Bertrand de. On Power: Its Nature & the History of Its Growth. Huntington, J. F., tr. from Fr. LC 80-24721. xix, 421p. 1981. Repr. of 1949 ed. lib. bdg. 39.75x (ISBN 0-313-22515-X, JOOP). Greenwood.
Jovanovic, Uros J. Psychomotor Epilepsy: A Polydimensional Study. (American Lectures in Living Chemistry Ser.). (Illus.). 544p. 1974. 42.75 (ISBN 0-398-02691-2). C C Thomas.
Jowell, Frances S. Thore-Buerger & the Art of the Past. LC 76-23632. (Outstanding Dissertations in the Fine Arts - 19th Century). (Illus.). 1977. Repr. of 1971 ed. lib. bdg. 63.00 (ISBN 0-8240-2701-9). Garland Pub.
Jowell, J. L., jt. ed. see Partington, Martin.
Jowett, B., tr. see Plato.
Jowett, Benjamin, tr. see Plato.
Jowett, Benjamin E., tr. see Plato.
Jowett, C. E. Application of Engineering in Microelectronic Industries. 184p. 1975. text ed. 22.00x (ISBN 0-220-66278-9, Pub. by Busn Bks England). Renouf.
--Compatibility & Testing of Electronic Components. LC 72-7039. 345p. 1972. 32.95 (ISBN 0-470-45170-X). Halsted Pr.
Jowett, Garth & Linton, James M. Movies As Mass Communication. LC 80-13508. (The Sage Comtext Ser.: Vol. 4). (Illus.). 149p. 1980. 12.50 (ISBN 0-8039-1090-8); pap. 5.95 (ISBN 0-8039-1091-6). Sage.
Jowett, J. H. Epistles of St. Peter. LC 78-94111. 1970. 6.95 o.p. (ISBN 0-8254-2950-1). Kregel.
Jowett, John H. The Best of John H. Jowett. (Best Ser.). 256p. (Orig.). 1981. pap. 3.95 (ISBN 0-8010-5142-8). Baker Bk.
--Springs of Living Water. (Summit Bks). Orig. Title: My Daily Meditations. 1977. pap. text ed. 2.95 o.p. (ISBN 0-8010-5073-1). Baker Bk.
Jowitt, D. Dance Beat: Selected Views & Reviews Nineteen Sixty-Seven to Nineteen Seventy-Six. 1977. 9.95 o.p. (ISBN 0-8247-6506-0). Dekker.
Jowitt, Kenneth. Revolutionary Breakthroughs & National Development: The Case of Romania, 1944-1965. 1971. 25.00x (ISBN 0-520-01762-5). U of Cal Pr.
Jowitt, R., ed. Hygenic Design & Operation of Food Plant. (Illus., American edition). 1980. pap. text ed. 22.50 (ISBN 0-87055-345-3). AVI.
Jowsey, Jenifer. Metabolic Diseases of Bone. LC 76-50149. (Monographs in Clinical Orthopaedics Ser.: Vol. 1). (Illus.). 1977. text ed. 29.00 (ISBN 0-7216-5224-7). Saunders.
Joy, David. A Regional History of the Railways of Great Britain: South & West Yorkshire, Vol. 8. LC 74-20464. (Illus.). 288p. 1975. 19.95 (ISBN 0-7153-6883-4). David & Charles.
Joy, Edward. Connoisseur Illustrated Guide: Furniture. (Illus.). 1975. pap. 5.95 o.s.i. (ISBN 0-380-01112-3, 26161). Avon.
Joy, Edward T. English Furniture Eighteen Hundred to Eighteen Fifty-One. (Illus.). 318p. 1977. 60.00 (ISBN 0-85667-031-6, Pub. by Sotheby Parke Bernet England). Biblio Dist.
Joy, O. Maurice. Introduction to Financial Management. rev. ed. 1980. 19.95x (ISBN 0-256-02340-9). Irwin.
--Introduction to Financial Management. 1977. 17.50x o.p. (ISBN 0-256-01880-4). Irwin.
Joy, Robert O., jt. auth. see Pack, Alice C.
Joy, W. Brugh. Joy's Way: A Map for the Transformational Journey & an Introduction to the Potentials for Healing with Body Energies. LC 78-62795. (Illus.). 1979. 11.95 o.p. (ISBN 0-312-90644-7); pap. 6.95 o.p. (ISBN 0-312-90645-5). St Martin.
Joyce, Barbara. All About Dogs. (Illus.). 3.50x (ISBN 0-392-06370-0, SpS). Soccer.
Joyce, Bruce & Weil, Marsha. Models of Teaching. (Illus.). 368p. 1972. ref. ed. 17.95 (ISBN 0-13-586065-2). P-H.
Joyce, Bruce, jt. auth. see Weil, Marsha.
Joyce, C. R. see Hammond, Kenneth R.
Joyce, Ernest. Encyclopedia of Furniture Making. LC 76-49087. (Illus.). 1979. 17.50 (ISBN 0-8069-8302-7); PLB 14.99 (ISBN 0-8069-8303-5). Sterling.
Joyce, F. E. Metropolitan Development & Change: The West Midlands: a Policy Review. (Illus.). 1977. 27.95 (ISBN 0-566-00193-4, 01793-0, Pub. by Saxon Hse England). Lexington Bks.
Joyce, Gayle & Gallimore, Laurene. The Visual Language Cookbook. new ed. (Illus.). 60p. (gr. 6-12). 1979. 14.95 (ISBN 0-917002-41-5). Joyce Media.
Joyce, Irma. Never Talk to Strangers. (gr. 4 up). 1970. 1.95 (ISBN 0-307-10876-7, Golden Pr); PLB 7.62 (ISBN 0-307-60876-X). Western Pub.
Joyce, James. Dubliners: A Facsimile of Drafts & Manuscripts. Groden, Michael, ed. LC 78-16029. (The James Joyce Archive Ser.). 1978. lib. bdg. 73.00 (ISBN 0-8240-2803-1). Garland Pub.
--Dubliners: A Facsimile of Proofs for the 1910 Edition. Groden, Michael, ed. LC 77-22832. (James Joyce Archive Ser.). 1977. lib. bdg. 73.00 (ISBN 0-8240-2804-X). Garland Pub.
--Dubliners: A Facsimile of Proofs for the 1914 Edition. Groden, Michael, ed. LC 77-22835. (James Joyce Archive Ser.). 1977. lib. bdg. 73.00 (ISBN 0-8240-2805-8). Garland Pub.
--Exiles: A Facsimile of Notes, Manuscripts & Galley Proofs. Groden, Michael, ed. LC 77-18397. (James Joyce Archive Ser.). 1978. lib. bdg. 104.00 (ISBN 0-8240-2810-4). Garland Pub.
--Finnegans Wake: A Facsimile of Buffalo Notebooks VI.B.1 - VI.B.4. Groden, Michael, ed. LC 77-11978. (James Joyce Archive Ser.). 1978. lib. bdg. 104.00 (ISBN 0-8240-2828-7). Garland Pub.
--Finnegans Wake: A Facsimile of Buffalo Notebooks VI.B.5 - VI.B.8. Groden, Michael, ed. LC 77-12610. (James Joyce Archive Ser.). 1978. lib. bdg. 104.00 (ISBN 0-8240-2829-5). Garland Pub.
--Finnegans Wake: A Facsimile of Buffalo Notebooks VI.B.9 - VI.B.12. Groden, Michael, ed. LC 77-14619. (James Joyce Archive Ser.). 1978. lib. bdg. 104.00 (ISBN 0-8240-2830-9). Garland Pub.
--Finnegans Wake: A Facsimile of Buffalo Notebooks VI.B.33 - VI.B.36. Groden, Michael, ed. LC 78-1112. (James Joyce Archive Ser.). 1978. lib. bdg. 104.00 (ISBN 0-8240-2836-8). Garland Pub.
--Finnegans Wake: A Facsimile of Buffalo Notebooks VI.B.37 - VI.B.40. Groden, Michael, ed. LC 78-1109. (James Joyce Archive Ser.). 1978. lib. bdg. 104.00 (ISBN 0-8240-2837-6). Garland Pub.
--Finnegans Wake: A Facsimile of Buffalo Notebook VI. A. Groden, Michael, ed. LC 78-1113. (James Joyce Archive Ser.). 1978. lib. bdg. 104.00 (ISBN 0-8240-2827-9). Garland Pub.
--Finnegans Wake: A Facsimile of Buffalo Notebooks VI. B. 17-20. Groden, Michael, ed. LC 78-17967. (James Joyce Archive Ser.: Vol. 33). lib. bdg. 104.00 (ISBN 0-8240-2832-5). Garland Pub.
--Finnegans Wake: A Facsimile of Buffalo Notebooks VI. B. 13-16. Groden, Michael, ed. LC 78-9769. (James Joyce Archive Ser.). 1978. lib. bdg. 104.00 (ISBN 0-8240-2831-7). Garland Pub.
--Finnegans Wake: A Facsimile of Buffalo Notebooks VI. B. 29-32. Groden, Michael, ed. LC 78-4178. (James Joyce Archive Ser.: Vol. 36). lib. bdg. 104.00 (ISBN 0-8240-2835-X). Garland Pub.
--Finnegans Wake: A Facsimile of Buffalo Notebooks VI. B. 25-28. Groden, Michael, ed. LC 78-4135. (James Joyce Archive Ser.). 1978. lib. bdg. 104.00 (ISBN 0-8240-2834-1). Garland Pub.
--Finnegans Wake: A Facsimile of Buffalo Notebooks VI. B. 21-24. Groden, Michael, ed. LC 78-17966. (James Joyce Archive Ser.: Vol. 34). 1978. lib. bdg. 104.00 (ISBN 0-8240-2833-3). Garland Pub.
--Finnegans Wake: A Facsimile of Buffalo Notebooks VI. C. 1,2,3,4,5,7. Groden, Michael, ed. LC 78-1114. (James Joyce Archive Ser.). 1978. lib. bdg. 104.00 (ISBN 0-8240-2840-6). Garland Pub.

--Finnegans Wake: A Facsimile of Buffalo Notebooks VI. C. 12,13,14,17,11,18. Groden, Michael, ed. LC 78-51001. (James Joyce Archive Ser.). 1978. lib. bdg. 104.00 (ISBN 0-8240-2842-2). Garland Pub.
--Finnegans Wake: A Facsimile of Buffalo Notebooks VI. C. 6,8,9,10,15,16. Groden, Michael, ed. LC 78-51002. (James Joyce Archive Ser.). 1978. lib. bdg. 104.00 (ISBN 0-8240-2841-4). Garland Pub.
--Finnegans Wake: A Facsimile of Buffalo Notebooks VI.B. 41-44. LC 78-4174. (James Joyce Archive Ser.). 1978. lib. bdg. 104.00 (ISBN 0-8240-2838-4). Garland Pub.
--Finnegans Wake: Book I: A Facsimile of the Galley Proofs Volume II. Groden, Michael, ed. LC 77-23060. (James Joyce Archive Ser.). 1978. lib. bdg. 104.00 (ISBN 0-8240-2846-5). Garland Pub.
--Finnegans Wake: Book I: A Facsimile of the Galley Proofs Volume I. Groden, Michael, ed. LC 77-23060. (James Joyce Archive Ser.). 1978. lib. bdg. 104.00 (ISBN 0-8240-2845-7). Garland Pub.
--Finnegans Wake: Book I, Chapter I: A Facsimile of Drafts, Typescripts & Proofs. Groden, James, ed. LC 78-896. (James Joyce Archive Ser.). 1978. lib. bdg. 104.00 (ISBN 0-8240-2843-0). Garland Pub.
--Finnegans Wake: Book I, Chapter 8: a Facsimile of Drafts, Typescripts, & Proofs. Groden, Michael, ed. LC 78-4039. (James Joyce Archive Ser.). 1978. lib. bdg. 104.00 (ISBN 0-8240-2862-7). Garland Pub.
--Finnegans Wake: Book I, Chapters 2-3: a Facsimile of Drafts, Typescripts, & Proofs. Groden, Michael, ed. LC 78-4140. (James Joyce Archive Ser.). 1978. lib. bdg. 104.00 (ISBN 0-8240-2844-9). Garland Pub.
--Finnegans Wake: Book I, Chapters 4-5: a Facsimile of Drafts, Typescripts, & Proofs. Groden, Michael, ed. LC 78-4138. (James Joyce Archive Ser.). 1978. lib. bdg. 104.00 (ISBN 0-8240-2860-0). Garland Pub.
--Finnegans Wake: Book I, Chapters 6-7: a Facsimile of Drafts, Typescripts, & Proofs. Groden, Michael, ed. LC 78-8959. (James Joyce Archive Ser.: Vol. 62). 1978. lib. bdg. 104.00 (ISBN 0-8240-2861-9). Garland Pub.
--Finnegans Wake: Book II, Chapter I: A Facsimile of Drafts, Typescripts, & Proofs. Groden, Michael, ed. LC 77-11681. (James Joyce Archive Ser.). 1978. lib. bdg. 104.00 (ISBN 0-8240-2849-X). Garland Pub.
--Finnegans Wake: Book II, Chapter 2: A Facsimile of Drafts, Typescripts, & Proofs, Vol. 1. Groden, Michael, ed. LC 77-18399. (James Joyce Archive Ser.). 1978. lib. bdg. 104.00 (ISBN 0-8240-2853-8). Garland Pub.
--Finnegans Wake: Book II, Chapter 2: A Facsimile of Drafts, Typescripts, & Proofs, Vol. II. Groden, Michael, ed. LC 77-18399. (James Joyce Archive Ser.). 1978. lib. bdg. 104.00 (ISBN 0-8240-2854-6). Garland Pub.
--Finnegans Wake: Book II, Chapter 3: a Facsimile of Drafts, Typescripts, & Proofs, Vol. 1. Groden, Michael, ed. LC 77-10573. (James Joyce Archive Ser.). 1978. lib. bdg. 104.00 (ISBN 0-8240-2850-3). Garland Pub.
--Finnegans Wake: Book II, Chapter 3: A Facsimile of Drafts, Typescripts, & Proofs, Vol. II. Groden, Michael, ed. LC 77-10573. (James Joyce Archive Ser.). 1978. lib. bdg. 104.00 (ISBN 0-8240-2851-1). Garland Pub.
--Finnegans Wake: Book II, Chapter 4: A Facsimile of Drafts, Typescripts, & Proofs. Groden, Michael, ed. LC 77-84971. (James Joyce Archive Ser.). 1978. lib. bdg. 104.00 (ISBN 0-8240-2852-X). Garland Pub.
--Finnegans Wake: Book III: A Facsimile of the Galley Proofs. Groden, Michael, ed. LC 77-22951. (James Joyce Archive Ser.). 1978. lib. bdg. 104.00 (ISBN 0-8240-2847-3). Garland Pub.
--Finnegans Wake: Book III, Chapter 3: A Facsimile of Drafts, Typescripts, & Proofs, Vol. 1. Groden, Michael, ed. LC 78-899. (James Joyce Archive Ser.). 1978. lib. bdg. 104.00 (ISBN 0-8240-2856-2). Garland Pub.
--Finnegans Wake: Book III, Chapter 3: A Facsimile of Drafts, Typescripts, & Proofs, Vol. II. Groden, Michael, ed. LC 78-899. (James Joyce Archive Ser.). 1978. lib. bdg. 104.00 (ISBN 0-8240-2857-0). Garland Pub.
--Finnegans Wake: Book III, Chapter 4: A Facsimile of Drafts, Typescripts, & Proofs. Groden, Michael, ed. LC 78-4465. (James Joyce Archive Ser.). 1978. lib. bdg. 104.00 (ISBN 0-8240-2858-9). Garland Pub.
--Finnegans Wake: Book III, Chapters 1 & 2: A Facsimile of Drafts, Typescripts, & Proofs. Groden, Michael, ed. LC 78-898. (James Joyce Archive Ser.). 1978. lib. bdg. 104.00 (ISBN 0-8240-2855-4). Garland Pub.
--Finnegans Wake: Book III, Chapters 1-4: a Facsimile of Transition Pages. Groden, Michael, ed. LC 78-17968. (James Joyce Archive Ser.). 1978. lib. bdg. 104.00 (ISBN 0-8240-2859-7). Garland Pub.
--Finnegans Wake: Book IV: A Facsimile of Drafts, Typescripts, & Proofs. Groden, Michael, ed. LC 77-22867. (James Joyce Archive Ser.). 1978. lib. bdg. 104.00 (ISBN 0-8240-2848-1). Garland Pub.
--A Portrait of the Artist As a Young Man: A Facsimile of the Manuscript Fragments of Stephen Hero. Groden, Michael, ed. LC 78-12105. (James Joyce Archive Ser.: Vol. 7-10). 1979. lib. bdg. 415.00 (ISBN 0-8240-2807-4). Garland Pub.
--Stephen Hero. rev. ed. LC 63-14454. (Illus.). 1969. pap. 4.95 (ISBN 0-8112-0074-4, NDP133). New Directions.
--Ulysses: "Aeolus" "Lestrygonians," & "Scylla & Charybdis" a Facsimile of Page Proofs for Episodes 7-9. Groden, Michael, ed. LC 77-14621. (James Joyce Archive Ser.). 1978. lib. bdg. 104.00 (ISBN 0-8240-2817-1). Garland Pub.
--Ulysses: "Aeolus," "Lestrygonians," "Scylla & Charybdis," & "Wandering Rocks": A Facsimile of Placards for Pisodes 7-10. Groden, Michael, ed. LC 78-16031. (James Joyce Archive Ser.: Vol. 13). 1978. lib. bdg. 104.00 (ISBN 0-8240-2812-0). Garland Pub.
--Ulysses: "Circe": A Facsimile of Page Proofs for Episode 15. Groden, Michael, ed. LC 77-14656. (James Joyce Archive Ser.). 1978. lib. bdg. 104.00 (ISBN 0-8240-2820-1). Garland Pub.
--Ulysses: "Circe" & "Eumaeus": A Facsimile of Manuscripts & Typescripts for Episodes 15 (Part II) & 16. Groden, Michael, ed. LC 77-11971. (James Joyce Archive Ser.). 1978. lib. bdg. 104.00 (ISBN 0-8240-2825-2). Garland Pub.
--Ulysses: "Cyclops" & "Nausicaa", & "Oxen of the Sun": a Facsimile of Page Proofs of Episode 12-14. Groden, Michael, ed. LC 77-14655. (James Joyce Archive Ser.). 1978. lib. bdg. 104.00 (ISBN 0-8240-2819-8). Garland Pub.
--Ulysses: "Eumaeus," "Ithaca," & "Penelope": A Facsimile of Page Proofs for Chapters 16-18. Groden, Michael, ed. LC 77-14657. (James Joyce Archive Ser.), 1978. lib. bdg. 104.00 (ISBN 0-8240-2821-X). Garland Pub.
--Ulysses: Notes & "Telemachus" - "Scylla" & "Charybdis": A Facsimile of Notes for the Book & Mauscripts for Episodes 1-9. Groden, Michael, ed. LC 78-16032. (James Joyce Archive Ser.). 1978. lib. bdg. 104.00 (ISBN 0-8240-2822-8). Garland Pub.
--Ulysses: "Oxen of the Sun," & "Circe": A Facsimile of Drafts, Manuscripts, & Typescripts 14 & 15 (Part 1) Groden, Michael, ed. LC 77-22764. (James Joyce Archive Ser.). 1978. lib. bdg. 104.00 (ISBN 0-8240-2824-4). Garland Pub.
--Ulysses: "Telemachus," "Nestor," "Proteus" Calypso" "Lotus Eaters," & "Hades": a Facsimile of Placards for Episodes 1-6. Groden, Michael, ed. LC 78-16032. (James Joyce Archive Ser.: Vol. 17). 1978. lib. bdg. 104.00 (ISBN 0-8240-2811-2). Garland Pub.
--Ulysses: "Wandering Rocks" & "Sirens" A Facsimile of Page Proofs for Episodes 10-11. Groden, Michael, ed. LC 77-14654. (James Joyce Archive Ser.). 1978. lib. bdg. 104.00 (ISBN 0-8240-2818-X). Garland Pub.

Joyce, James, et al. Holograph Manuscript: "a Portrait of the Artist As a Young Man". Groden, Michael, ed. LC 77-6230. (James Joyce Archive Ser.: Vols. 9 & 10). (Illus.). 1977. Repr. Vol. 9. lib. bdg. 104.00 (ISBN 0-8240-2808-2); Vol. 10. lib. bdg. 94.38 (ISBN 0-8240-2809-0). Garland Pub.
Joyce, James E. The Federal Government Is Run by Idiots: Political Commentary. (Illus.). 1980. 3.50 (ISBN 0-932212-19-0). Avery Color.
Joyce, Jean, ed. see Frederick, J. George.
Joyce, Mary. First Steps in Teaching Creative Dancing. LC 72-97841. (Illus.). 192p. 1973. text ed. 9.95 o.p. (ISBN 0-87484-268-9). Mayfield Pub.
--First Steps in Teaching Creative Dance to Children. 2nd ed. LC 79-91834. (Illus.). 226p. 1980. pap. text ed. 7.95 (ISBN 0-87484-510-6). Mayfield Pub.
Joyce, Michael, et al, eds. see Plato.
Joyce, Nancy, jt. auth. see Rogers, Mary.
Joyce, P. W. Old Celtic Romances. 3rd ed. (Sackville Library Reprint Ser.). 1978. Repr. of 1907 ed. 25.00 o.p. (ISBN 0-7171-0940-2). Irish Bk Ctr.
Joyce, Patrick. Work, Society & Politics: The Factory North of England in the Second Half of the Nineteenth Century. 1980. text ed. write for info. (ISBN 0-391-02215-6). Humanities.
Joyce, Patrick W. English As We Speak It in Ireland. LC 68-26579. 1971. Repr. of 1910 ed. 24.00 (ISBN 0-8103-3356-2). Gale.
Joyce, R. D. Encounters in Organizational Behavior: Problem Situations. 1972. text ed. 18.50 (ISBN 0-08-017013-7); pap. text ed. 9.25 (ISBN 0-08-017116-8). Pergamon.
Joyce, Robert E. Human Sexual Ecology. LC 79-6727. 421p. 1981. lib. bdg. 22.75 (ISBN 0-8191-1359-X); pap. text ed. 12.00 (ISBN 0-8191-0937-1). U Pr of Amer.
Joyce, William. Twilight Over England. 1978. pap. 4.50x (ISBN 0-911038-37-X). Noontide.
Joyce, William L. Manuscript Collection of the American Antiquarian Society. 30p. 1980. pap. 3.00x (ISBN 0-912296-43-7, Dist. by U Pr of Va). Am Antiquarian.
Joyce, William W. & Banks, James A., eds. Teaching the Language Arts to Culturally Different Children. LC 78-136123. (Education Ser). 1971. pap. 6.95 (ISBN 0-201-03403-4). A-W.
Joyce, William W., jt. ed. see Banks, James A.
Joyner, Jerry, jt. auth. see Charlip, Remy.
Joyner, Nelson T., Jr. & Durham, Jackie, eds. Joyner's Guide to Official Washington for Doing Business Overseas. LC 79-20957. (Pergamon Policy Studies). 400p. 1980. 99.50 (ISBN 0-08-025108-0). Pergamon.
Joyner, S. M., jt. auth. see Crompton, D. W.
Joynes, Leger M., et al. The Insiders' Guide to the Outer Banks of North Carolina. rev. ed. (Insiders' Guides). (Illus.). 1981. pap. 3.95 (ISBN 0-932338-01-1). Insiders Pub.
Joynes, St. Leger, et al. The Insiders' Guide to Southeastern Virginia. rev. ed. (Insiders' Guides Ser.). (Illus.). 1981. pap. 3.95 (ISBN 0-932338-00-3). Insiders Pub.
Joynes, St. Leger M. & Du'Arte, Jack. Insiders' Guide to New Orleans. (Insiders' Guides Ser.). (Illus., Orig.). 1981. pap. 4.95 (ISBN 0-932338-03-8). Insiders Pub.
Joynes, St. Leger M., et al. Insiders' Guide to Ocean City Maryland. rev. ed. (Insiders' Guides Ser.). (Illus., Orig.). 1981. pap. 3.95 (ISBN 0-932338-02-X). Insiders Pub.
Joynson, R. B. Psychology & Common Sense. 1974. 8.95x (ISBN 0-7100-7827-7); pap. 6.95 (ISBN 0-7100-7899-4). Routledge & Kegan.
Joynt, Robert R., jt. auth. see Blackwell, Robert B.
Joynt, Robert R., jt. ed. see Blackwell, Robert B.
Joynt, W. D. Saving the Channel Ports. (Illus.). 233p. 1976. 19.95 (ISBN 0-85885-202-0). David & Charles.
Jo Young-Hawn, ed. Political Participation of Asian-Americans- Problems and Strategies. LC 80-25074. (Occasional Papers Ser.: No. 6). (Orig.). 1980. pap. 12.00 (ISBN 0-934584-14-1). Pacific-Asian.
Jreisat, Jamil E. Images & Policies in Senate Debates on Middle Eastern Issues. 1976. pap. 3.00 (ISBN 0-934484-07-4). Inst Mid East & North Africa.
Juayl, B. N. Integrated Economic Planning. 1980. text ed. write for info. (ISBN 0-391-01837-X). Humanities.
Jucius, Michael J. Personnel Management. 9th ed. 1979. text ed. 18.50x (ISBN 0-256-01644-5). Irwin.
Jud, Gustav D. Inflation & the Use of Indexing in Developing Countries. LC 76-12859. (Praeger Special Studies). 1978. 25.95 (ISBN 0-275-23840-7). Praeger.
Juda, Lawrence. Ocean Space Rights: Developing U.S. Policy. LC 74-1732. (Special Studies). 318p. 1975. text ed. 33.95 (ISBN 0-275-09240-2). Praeger.
Judd, Cameron. Bad Night at Dry Creek. 1981. pap. 1.75 (ISBN 0-8439-0894-7, Leisure Bks). Nordon Pubns.
--Beggar's Gulch. (Orig.). 1980. pap. 1.75 (ISBN 0-8439-0733-9, Leisure Bks). Nordon Pubns.
Judd, Deane B. & Wyszecki, Gunter. Color in Business, Science, & Industry. 3rd ed. LC 75-6590. (Pure & Applied Optics Ser). 553p. 1975. 42.95 (ISBN 0-471-45212-2, Pub. by Wiley-Interscience). Wiley.
Judd, Denis. Adventures of Long John Silver. (YA) 1978. pap. 1.75 (ISBN 0-380-42275-1, 42275). Avon.
--Prince Philip, Duke of Edinburgh. LC 80-22691. 1981. 16.95 (ISBN 0-689-11131-2). Atheneum.
Judd, Donald. Donald Judd: Complete Writings 1959-1975. LC 75-13761. (Nova Scotia Ser.). (Illus.). 229p. 1975. 25.00x, c (ISBN 0-8147-4155-X); pap. 14.95, c (ISBN 0-8147-4156-8). NYU Pr.
--Donald Judd: Drawings 1956-1976. LC 76-11429. (Nova Scotia Ser.). (Illus.). 110p. 1976. 20.00x, C (ISBN 0-8147-4157-6); pap. 12.95, c (ISBN 0-8147-4158-4). NYU Pr.
Judd, Frances K. The Mansion of Secrets. (Skylark Ser.). 176p. (gr. 4-9). 1980. pap. 1.75 (ISBN 0-553-15070-7). Bantam.
Judd, H. Stanley, et al. Think Rich. 1978. 8.95 o.s.i. (ISBN 0-440-08732-5). Delacorte.
Judd, Mary T. Love & Lifestyles. LC 80-54285. (Illus.). 200p. (Orig.). (gr. 12). 1981. pap. text ed. 5.25 (ISBN 0-88489-132-1). St Mary's.
Judd, Peter H., tr. see Giraudoux, Jean.
Judd, Rue & Worley, Ann. It's a Long Way to Guacamole: The Tex-Mex Cookbook. (Illus.). 106p. (Orig.). 1978. pap. 6.00 (ISBN 0-9604842-0-5). J&W Tex-Mex.
Judd, Stan. Inshore Fishing: Its Skills, Risks, Rewards. (Illus.). 144p. 10.00 (ISBN 0-85238-096-8, FN). Unipub.
Judd, Wallace. Dogfight & More Games Calculators Play. 1977. pap. 1.75 o.s.i. (ISBN 0-446-84398-9). Warner Bks.
Judd, Wallace P. Math Mat Activities. (Illus.). 80p. (Orig.). (gr. k-12). 1974. wkbk. 3.50 o.p. (ISBN 0-88488-011-7). Creative Pubns.
Judd, Wayne. Breaking up. (Uplook Ser.). 1978. pap. 0.75 (ISBN 0-8163-0194-8, 12466). Pacific Pr Pub Assn.
--Healing: Faith or Fraud. (Uplook Ser.). 1978. pap. 0.75 (ISBN 0-8163-0199-9, 08303-0). Pacific Pr Pub Assn.
--How to Wait for Jesus. LC 78-13975. (Nugget Ser.). 32p. 1979. pap. 0.65 (ISBN 0-8127-0206-9). Southern Pub.
--Kissing, Hugging, &... LC 79-20362. (Nugget Ser.). 1979. pap. 0.65 (ISBN 0-8127-0249-2). Southern Pub.
--Thirsty? (Uplook Ser.). 1975. pap. 0.75 (ISBN 0-8163-0177-8, 20728-2). Pacific Pr Pub Assn.
--Uneasy Breather. (Uplook Ser.). 1975. pap. 0.75 (ISBN 0-8163-0179-4, 20728-2). Pacific Pr Pub Assn.
Juddery, Bruce. White Collar Power: A History of the ACOA. 320p. 1981. text ed. 27.50x (ISBN 0-86861-138-7, 2519); pap. text ed. 12.50x (ISBN 0-86861-146-8, 2520). Allen Unwin.
Judet, R., jt. auth. see Letournel, E.
Judge, Arthur W. Car Maintenance & Repair. 6th ed. LC 67-31004. (Motor Manuals Ser.: Vol. 4). text ed. 10.95x o.p. (ISBN 0-8376-0067-7). Bentley.
--Modern Electrical Equipment for Automobiles. LC 68-31549. (Motor Manuals Ser.: Vol. 6). text ed. 10.95x o.p. (ISBN 0-8376-0002-2). Bentley.
Judge, George G., et al. The Theory & Practice of Econometrics. LC 80-150. (Applied Statistics Ser.). 1980. text ed. 26.95 (ISBN 0-471-05938-2). Wiley.
Judge, Ken & Matthews, James. Charging for Social Care. (National Institute Social Services Library: No. 39). (Illus.). 168p. (Orig.). 1980. text ed. 27.50x (ISBN 0-04-361040-4, 2528); pap. text ed. 12.95x (ISBN 0-04-361041-2, 2529). Allen Unwin.
Judge, William Q. Letters That Have Helped Me. new ed. Niemand, Jasper, ed. & intro. by. (Illus.). x, 300p. 1946. 6.00 (ISBN 0-938998-08-0). Theosophy.
--The Ocean of Theosophy. (Illus.). 153p. 1915. Repr. of 1893 ed. 5.00 (ISBN 0-938998-07-2). Theosophy.
--Practical Occultism. LC 78-63320. 1979. 10.00 (ISBN 0-911500-29-4); softcover 6.00 (ISBN 0-911500-30-8). Theos U Pr.
Judge, William Q. & Crosbie, Robert. Notes on the Bhagavad-Gita. 237p. 1918. Repr. 4.00 (ISBN 0-938998-10-2). Theosophy.
Judge, William Q., ed. Bhagavad-Gita: Recension with Essays. LC 70-92964. 1969. 6.00 (ISBN 0-911500-27-8); softcover 3.50 (ISBN 0-911500-28-6). Theos U Pr.
Judge, William Q., tr. from Sanskrit. & intro. by. The Bhagavad-Gita: The Book of Devotion Dialogue Between Krishna, Lord of Devotion, & Arjuna, Prince of India. xviii, 133p. 1930. Repr. of 1891 ed. 3.50 (ISBN 0-938998-09-9). Theosophy.
Judge, William Q., tr. & pref. by. The Yoga Aphorisms of Patanjali. xxi, 74p. 1930. Repr. of 1889 ed. 3.00 (ISBN 0-938998-11-0). Theosophy.
Judkins, Henry F. & Keener, H. A. Milk Production & Processing. LC 60-10317. 1960. 20.95 (ISBN 0-471-45276-9). Wiley.
Judkins, Winthrop. Fluctuant Representation in Synthetic Cubism: Picasso, Braque, Gris, 1910-1920. LC 75-23796. (Outstanding Dissertations in the Fine Arts - 20th Century). (Illus.). 1976. lib. bdg. 53.00 (ISBN 0-8240-1991-1). Garland Pub.
Judson, Clara I. George Washington. (Beginning-to-Read Bks). (Illus.). (gr. 3). 1.50 o.p. (ISBN 0-695-33350-X). Follett.
Judson, David M. Ghar Parau. (Illus.). 208p. 1973. 10.00 o.s.i. (ISBN 0-02-560320-5). Macmillan.
Judson, Harry P. Caesar's Army: A Study of the Military Art of the Romans in the Last Days of the Republic. LC 61-12877. (Illus.). 127p. (gr. 7 up). 1888. 8.50x (ISBN 0-8196-0113-6). Biblo.
Judson, Jeanne. Legacy of Redfern. (YA) 5.95 (ISBN 0-685-07441-2, Avalon). Bouregy.
--Treasure of Wycliffe House. (YA) 5.95 (ISBN 0-685-07462-5, Avalon). Bouregy.
Judson, John. North of Athens. LC 80-53396. 64p. 1980. pap. 3.95 (ISBN 0-933180-20-9). Spoon Riv Poetry.
--Routes from the Onion's Dark. 2nd ed. (Orig.). 1978. pap. 3.00x (ISBN 0-685-69451-8); ltd. signed ed. 7.50x (ISBN 0-685-69452-6). Pentagram.

Judson, John, ed. Voyages to the Inland Sea, Vol 3. McGrath, Thomas & Dana, Robert. LC 73-78705. 83p. 1973. 6.00x (ISBN 0-917540-03-4); pap. 3.50x (ISBN 0-917540-12-3). Ctr Cont Poetry.
Judson, Philips. Death As the Curtain Rises. 192p. 1981. 8.95 (ISBN 0-396-07954-7). Dodd.
Judson, S., et al. Physical Geology. (Illus.). 592p. 1976. text ed. 19.95 (ISBN 0-13-669655-4); study guide 5.95 (ISBN 0-13-669630-9). P-H.
Judson, Sheldon, jt. ed. see Fischer, Alfred G.
Judson, Stephanie, ed. A Manual on Nonviolence & Children. (Illus.). 115p. (Orig.). 1977. pap. 5.00 (ISBN 0-9605062-1-7). Friends Peace Comm.
Judt, T. Socialism in Provence Eighteen Seventy-One to Nineteen Fourteen. LC 78-16419. (Illus.). 1979. 42.50 (ISBN 0-521-22172-2); pap. 14.95x (ISBN 0-521-29598-X). Cambridge U Pr.
Judy, Harriet, jt. auth. see Tuch, Barbara.
Judy, Stephen, jt. auth. see Judy, Susan.
Judy, Stephen N. & Judy, Susan J. An Introduction to the Teaching of Writing. 225p. 1981. pap. text ed. 10.95 (ISBN 0-471-06222-7). Wiley.
Judy, Susan & Judy, Stephen. Gifts of Writing: Decorative Projects with Words & Art. LC 80-10360. (Illus.). (gr. 5-7). 1980. 8.95 (ISBN 0-684-16522-8). Scribner.
Judy, Susan J., jt. auth. see Judy, Stephen N.
Juel, Donald. Messiah & Temple: The Trial of Jesus in the Gospel of Mark. LC 76-46397. (Society of Biblical Literature. Dissertation Ser.). 1977. pap. 7.50 (ISBN 0-89130-120-8, 060131). Scholars Pr Ca.
Juel, Donald, et al. An Introduction to New Testament Literature. LC 77-18036. (Illus.). 1978. 13.95 (ISBN 0-687-01360-7); pap. 9.50 (ISBN 0-687-01361-5). Abingdon.
Juel, Donald H. & Buttrick, David. Pentecost 2. Achtemeier, Elizabeth, et al, eds. LC 79-7377. (Proclamation 2: Aids for Interpreting the Lessons of the Church Year, Ser. C). 64p. 1980. pap. 2.50 (ISBN 0-8006-4083-7, 1-4083). Fortress.
Juenger, Friedrich G. The Perfection of Technology. LC 79-92076. 192p. 1980. pap. cancelled (ISBN 0-89526-896-5). Regnery-Gateway.
Jue-Obermeyer, Pauline M., jt. auth. see Obermeyer, William G., Jr.
Juergens, Bonnie, ed. see Library & Information Technology Association.
Juergens, John L., et al. Allen-Barker-Hines Peripheral Vascular Diseases. 5th ed. LC 78-65379. (Illus.). 981p. 1980. text ed. 60.00 (ISBN 0-7216-5229-8). Saunders.
Juergensen, Hans. Journey Toward the Roots. LC 76-14366. (Illus.). 48p. 1976. 5.00 o.p. (ISBN 0-912760-23-0); pap. 2.50 (ISBN 0-685-67386-3). Valkyrie Pr.
--Major General George H. Thomas: A Summary in Perspective. (Illus.). 50p. (Orig.). 1980. pap. 3.00 (ISBN 0-934996-08-3). Am Stud Pr.
Juergensen, Ilse. I Don't Want a Thunderbird Anymore: And New Poems. 2nd ed. 60p. 1980. pap. 5.00 (ISBN 0-934996-10-5). Am Stud Pr.
Juergensmeyer, Mark & Barrier, Gerald, eds. Sikh Studies: Comparative Perspectives of a Changing Tradition. 1980. 16.00 (ISBN 0-89581-100-6). Lancaster-Miller.
Juergenson, E. M., jt. auth. see Baker, J. K.
Juergenson, E. M., jt. auth. see Scheer, Arnold H.
Juergenson, E. M., jt. auth. see Ulmer, Donald E.
Juergenson, Edward M., ed. Approved Practices in Beef Cattle Production. 5th ed. (Illus.). (gr. 9-12). 1980. 14.00 (ISBN 0-8134-2093-8, 2093); text ed. 10.50x (ISBN 0-686-60695-7). Interstate.
Juergenson, Elwood M. Approved Practices in Sheep Production. 4th ed. (Illus.). (gr. 9-12). 1981. 13.00 (ISBN 0-8134-2163-2, 2163); text ed. 9.75x. Interstate.
--Approved Practices in Sheep Production. 3rd ed. (Illus.). (gr. 9-12). 1981. 14.00 o.p. (ISBN 0-8134-2163-2, 2163); text ed. 10.50x o.p. (ISBN 0-685-03870-X). Interstate.
Juergenson, Elwood M. & Mortenson, William P. Approved Practices in Dairying. 4th ed. LC 77-74120. (Illus.). (gr. 9-12). 1977. 14.00 (ISBN 0-8134-1954-9, 1954); text ed. 10.50x (ISBN 0-685-03866-1). Interstate.
Juergenson, Elwood M., jt. auth. see Cassard, Daniel W.
Juffe, Mel. Flash. LC 73-2336. 256p. 1974. 7.95 o.p. (ISBN 0-670-31743-8). Viking Pr.
Juge, O. & Donath, A., eds. Neuronuclear Medicine. (Progress in Nuclear Medicine Ser.: Vol. 7). (Illus.). vii, 240p. 1981. 90.00 (ISBN 3-8055-2319-X). S Karger.
Jugenheimer, Donald W. & Turk, Peter B. Advertising Media. LC 79-23007. (Grid Ser. in Advertising-Journalism). 1980. text ed. 17.95 (ISBN 0-88244-210-4). Grid Pub.
Jugenheimer, Donald W. & White, Gordon E. Basic Advertising. LC 79-12108. (Grid Series in Advertising & Journalism). 1980. text ed. 20.50 (ISBN 0-88244-181-7). Grid Pub.
Jugenheimer, Donald W., jt. auth. see Michman, Ronald D.
Jugenheimer, Robert W. Corn: Improvement, Seed Production, & Uses. LC 75-32414. 1976. 49.95 (ISBN 0-471-45315-3, Pub. by Wiley-Interscience). Wiley.
Juhasz, Gyula. Hungarian Foreign Policy, 1919-1945. rev. ed. Simon, Sandor, tr. from Hungarian. LC 80-468278. Orig. Title: Magyarorszag Kulpolitikaja, 1919-1945. 356p. 1979. 30.00x (ISBN 963-05-1882-1). Intl Pubns Serv.
Juhasz, Leslie. Monarch Notes on Dostoyevsky's Notes from the Underground. (Orig.). pap. 1.95 (ISBN 0-671-00558-8). Monarch Pr.
Juhl, John H. Paul & Juhl's Essentials of Roentgen Interpretation. 4th ed. (Illus.). 1184p. 1981. text ed. price not set (ISBN 0-06-142143-X, Harper Medical). Har-Row.
Juhl, P. D. Interpretation: An Essay in the Philosophy of Literary Criticism. LC 80-7534. 276p. 1980. 20.00 (ISBN 0-691-07242-6). Princeton U Pr.
Juillard, E., ed. Recent Orientations of Regional Analysis in French Geography. 1976. pap. text ed. 28.00 (ISBN 0-08-019970-4). Pergamon.
Jukes, Thomas H. Molecules & Evolution. (Illus.). 1968. Repr. of 1966 ed. 18.00x (ISBN 0-231-08614-8). Columbia U Pr.
Jul, Mogens & Zeuthen, Peter. Quality of Pig Meat: Progress of Food & Nutrition Science. (Vol. 4, No. 6). 80p. 1981. 20.00 (ISBN 0-08-026831-5). Pergamon.
Julia, D. Dictionnaire philosophie. (Illus., Fr.). pap. 8.50 (ISBN 0-685-13881-X). Larousse.
Julian, Alfred C. & Lowenstein, Janet, eds. Open Doors Nineteen Seventy-Seven to Seventy-Eight: Report on International Educational Exchange. rev. ed. LC 55-4594. 1979. pap. text ed. 7.50 o.p. (ISBN 0-87206-093-4). Inst Intl Educ.
Julian, Desmond, jt. ed. see Resnekov, Leon.
Julian, Joseph. Social Problems. 3rd ed. (P-H Ser. in Sociology). (Illus.). 1980. text ed. 17.95 (ISBN 0-13-816777-X); wkbk & study guide 5.95 (ISBN 0-13-816801-6). P-H.
Julian, Joseph, jt. auth. see Bates, Alan P.
Julian, O. A. Materia Medica of New Homoeopathic Remedies. 637p. 1980. 60.00x (Pub. by Beaconsfield England). State Mutual Bk.
Julian, W. G., jt. auth. see Smith, P. R.
Juliano, R. L., ed. Drug Delivery Systems: Characteristics & Biomedical Applications. (Illus.). 336p. 1980. text ed. 27.50x (ISBN 0-19-502700-0). Oxford U Pr.
Julich, Louise. Roster of Revolutionary Soldiers & Patriots in Alabama. (Alabama Society Daughters of the American Revolution). 1979. 25.00 (ISBN 0-88428-045-4). Parchment Pr.
Julich, P., jt. auth. see Hilburn, J. L.
Julien, Claude. The Suicide of the Democracies. 1980. 13.95 (ISBN 0-7145-1061-0). Riverrun NY.
Julien, H. L., jt. ed. see Erickson, V. L.
Julien, Robert M. A Primer of Drug Action. 2nd ed. LC 77-13824. (Psychology Ser.). (Illus.). 1978. text ed. 16.50x o.p. (ISBN 0-7167-0053-0); pap. text ed. 8.95x (ISBN 0-7167-0052-2). W H Freeman.
Julio, C., tr. see Cho, Paul Y.
Jull, E. V. Aperture Antennas & Diffraction Theory. 1981. pap. price not set. Inst Electrical.
Julme, Willam E., ed. see Becker, Russell J.
July, Robert W. A History of the African People. 3rd ed. LC 73-1348. 1980. 22.50 o.p. (ISBN 0-684-16291-1, ScribT). Scribner.
--A History of the African People. 3rd ed. 832p. 1980. 22.50 (ISBN 0-684-16291-1); pap. text ed. 10.95 (ISBN 0-684-16411-6). Scribner.
Jumber, Joseph. An Altas of Overdentures & Precision Attachments. (Illus.). 256p. 1981. 60.00. Quint Pub Co.
Jumikis, Alfred R. Thermal Geotechnics. 1977. 42.00 (ISBN 0-8135-0824-X). Rutgers U Pr.
Jump, John, ed. see Marlowe, Christopher.
Jump, John, ed. see Shakespeare, William.
Jump, John D. Byron. (Routledge Author Guides). 1972. 16.50x (ISBN 0-7100-7334-8); pap. 6.95 (ISBN 0-7100-7393-3). Routledge & Kegan.
--Tennyson: The Critical Heritage. 1967. 30.00x (ISBN 0-7100-2941-1). Routledge & Kegan.
Jump, John D., ed. see Marlowe, Christopher.
Jumper, Andrew A. Chosen to Serve: The Deacon. LC 61-18257. (Orig.). 1961. pap. 3.00 (ISBN 0-8042-3912-6). John Knox.
--The Noble Task: The Elder. rev. ed. LC 65-14420. 1965. pap. 3.00 (ISBN 0-8042-3992-4). John Knox.
Jumper, S., et al. Economic Growth & Disparities: A World View. 1980. 20.95 (ISBN 0-13-225680-0). P-H.
Jundt, Dwight W. Buying & Selling Farmland: A Guide to Profitable Investment. LC 80-67887. (Illus.). 309p. 1980. 14.95; pap. text ed. 9.95 (ISBN 0-932250-10-6). Doane Agricultural.
Juneja, Renu, et al. Recent Research on Ben Jonson. (Salzburg Studies in English Literature, Jacobean Drama Studies: No.76). 1978. pap. text ed. 25.00x (ISBN 0-391-01441-2). Humanities.
Junemann, Joseph. The Mass of the Roman Rite. 25.00 (ISBN 0-87061-054-6). Chr Classics.
Jung, C. G. The Archetypes & the Collective Unconscious: Bollingen Ser. Hull, R. F., tr. from Ger. LC 75-156. (Xx: 9,I). (Illus.). 560p. 1980. 30.00x (ISBN 0-691-09761-5); pap. 9.95 (ISBN 0-691-01833-2). Princeton U Pr.
--Memories, Dreams, Reflections. rev. ed. Jaffe, Aniela, ed. Winston, Richard & Winston, Clara, trs. LC 62-14264. 1963. 17.50 (ISBN 0-394-43580-X). Pantheon.
--Mysterium Coniunctionis. 1977. pap. 9.95 (ISBN 0-691-01816-2). Princeton U Pr.
Jung, Carl G. Collected Works of Carl G. Jung, Vols. 1-20. Adler, G., et al, eds. Hull, R. F., tr. Incl. Vol. 1. Psychiatric Studies. 2nd ed. 1970. 13.00 (ISBN 0-691-09768-2); Vol. 2. Experimental Researches. 1972. 21.00 (ISBN 0-691-09764-X); Vol. 3. Psychogenesis of Mental Disease. 1960. 16.00 (ISBN 0-691-09769-0); Vol. 4. Freud & Psychoanalysis. 1961. 18.00 (ISBN 0-691-09765-8); Vol. 5. Symbols of Transformation. 2nd ed. 1967. 24.00 (ISBN 0-691-09775-5); Vol. 6. Psychological Types. 25.00 (ISBN 0-691-09770-4); pap. 8.95; Vol. 7. Two Essays on Analytical Psychology. 1972. 16.00 (ISBN 0-691-09776-3); Vol. 8. Structure & Dynamics of the Psyche. 2nd ed. 1970. 21.00 (ISBN 0-691-09774-7); Vol. 9, Pt. 1. Archetypes & the Collective Unconscious. 2nd ed. 1969. 30.00 (ISBN 0-691-09761-5); Vol. 9, Pt. 2. Aion: Researches into the Phenomonology of the Self. 2nd ed. 1968. 18.00 (ISBN 0-691-09759-3); Vol. 10. Civilization in Transition. 2nd ed. 1964. 21.00 (ISBN 0-691-09762-3); Vol. 11. Psychology & **Religion: East & West. 1970. 21.00 (ISBN 0-691-09772-0); Vol. 12. Psychology & Alchemy. 2nd ed. 1968. 24.00 (ISBN 0-691-09771-2); Vol. 13. Alchemical Studies. 1968. 20.00 (ISBN 0-691-09760-7); Vol. 14. Mysterium Coinunctionis. 2nd ed. 1970. 35.00 (ISBN 0-691-09766-6); Vol. 15. Spirit in Man, Art & Literature. 1971. 9.50 (ISBN 0-691-09773-9); Vol. 16. Practice of Psychotherapy. 2nd ed. 1966. 25.00 (ISBN 0-691-09767-4); Vol. 17. Development of Personality. 1954. 12.00 (ISBN 0-691-09763-1); Vol. 18. The Symbolic Life: Miscellaneous Writings. 1976. 30.00 (ISBN 0-691-09892-1); Vol. 19. General Bibliography. 1979. 17.50x (ISBN 0-691-09893-X); Vol.20. General Index. 1979. 25.00 (ISBN 0-691-09867-0). (Bollingen Ser.: No. 20). Princeton U Pr.**
--Man & His Symbols. LC 64-18631. 1969. Repr. of 1964 ed. 10.95 (ISBN 0-385-05221-9). Doubleday.
--Psyche & Symbol: A Selection from the Writings of C. G. Jung. LC 58-6627. 1958. pap. 3.50 (ISBN 0-385-09349-7, A136, Anch). Doubleday.
--Psychological Reflections: A New Anthology of His Writings, 1905-1961. Jacobi, Jolande & Hull, R. F., eds. (Bollingen Ser.: Vol. 31). 332p. 1970. 18.00 (ISBN 0-691-09862-X); pap. 4.95 (ISBN 0-691-01786-7). Princeton U Pr.
--The Visions Seminars. 1976. pap. 25.00 set (ISBN 0-88214-111-2). Spring Pubns.
Jung, Carl G. & Kerenyi, Carl. Essays on a Science of Mythology: The Myths of the Divine Child & the Mysteries of Eleusis. rev. ed. (Bollingen Ser.: Vol. 22). 1969. 12.50 (ISBN 0-691-09851-4); pap. 3.95 (ISBN 0-691-01756-5). Princeton U Pr.
Jung, Emma. Animus & Anima. Baynes, Cary F. & Nagel, Hildegard, trs. 94p. 1969. pap. text ed. 6.50 (ISBN 0-88214-301-8). Spring Pubns.
Jung, John & Bailey, Joan H. Contemporary Psychology Experiments: Adaptations for Laboratory. 2nd ed. LC 76-7896. 1976. text ed. 13.95x (ISBN 0-471-45327-7). Wiley.
Jung, Leo. The Jewish Library. Incl. Vol. 1. Faith. 9.50x (ISBN 0-685-23058-9); Vol. 2. Folk. 9.50x (ISBN 0-685-23059-7); Vol. 3. Women. 8.00x (ISBN 0-685-23060-0); Vol. 4. Judaism in a Changing World. 9.50x (ISBN 0-685-23061-9); Vol. 5. Panorama of Judaism: Part 1. 9.50x (ISBN 0-685-23062-7); Vol. 6. Panorama of Judaism: Part 2. 9.50x (ISBN 0-685-23063-5). Bloch.
Jung, Ralph C., jt. ed. see Balchum, Oscar J.
Jung, Walter G. Converter Cookbook. LC 78-54453. 1978. pap. 13.95 (ISBN 0-672-21527-6). Sams.
--IC Array Cookbook. 208p. 1980. pap. 8.85 (ISBN 0-8104-0762-0). Hayden.
--IC Op-Amp Cookbook. 2nd ed. LC 73-90289. (Illus.). 1980. pap. 14.95 (ISBN 0-672-21695-7). Sams.
Junge, Douglas. Nerve & Muscle Excitation. LC 75-30151. 1976. pap. text ed. 8.95x o.p. (ISBN 0-87893-408-1). Sinauer Assoc.
--Nerve & Muscle Excitation. 2nd ed. LC 80-18158. (Illus.). 230p. 1981. pap. text ed. 12.95x (ISBN 0-87893-410-3). Sinauer Assoc.
Jungel, Eberhard. La Doctrina de la Trinidad. Canclini, Arnoldo, tr. from Eng. 152p. (Orig., Span.). 1980. pap. 3.95 (ISBN 0-89922-153-X). Edit Caribe.
Junger, Ernst. The Storm of Steel. Creighton, B., tr. from Ger. LC 75-22372. xiii, 319p. 1975. Repr. of 1929 ed. 19.00 (ISBN 0-86527-310-3). Fertig.
Jungherr, E. L., jt. ed. see Brandly, C. A.
Jungius, Harmut. The Biology & Behavior of the Reedbuck (Redunca arundium Boddaert 1785) in the Kruger National Park. (Illus.). 106p. (Orig.). 1971. pap. text ed. 20.00 (ISBN 3-490-02818-X). Parey Sci Pubs.
Jungk, Robert. The New Tyranny: How Nuclear Power Enslaves Us. 1979. pap. 2.50 (ISBN 0-446-91351-0). Warner Bks.
Jungk, Robert & Galtung, Johan, eds. Mankind Two Thousand. 2nd ed. (Future Research Monographs from Institute for Fredsforskning: No. 1). 1969. pap. 22.00x (ISBN 8-200-04584-6, Dist. by Columbia U Pr). Universitet.
Jungk, Robert, et al. China & the West: Mankind Evolving. (Teilhard Study Library). 1970. text ed. 6.25x (ISBN 0-391-00023-3). Humanities.
Jungmann, Josef. Christian Prayer Through the Centuries. LC 78-61729. Orig. Title: Christliches Beten. 1978. pap. 2.95 (ISBN 0-8091-2167-0). Paulist Pr.
Jungmann, Josef A. Early Liturgy, to the Time of Gregory the Great. Brunner, Francis A., tr. (Liturgical Studies Ser.: No. 7). 1959. 10.95 (ISBN 0-268-00083-2). U of Notre Dame Pr.
Jungst, Dale, jt. auth. see Behr, Marlyn J.
Junior League of New Orleans. The Plantation Cookbook. LC 72-84921. 256p. 1972. 11.95 (ISBN 0-385-01157-1). Doubleday.
Junior League of New Orleans Inc. Jambalaya. (Illus.). 256p. (Orig.). 1980. pap. 7.95 (ISBN 0-9604774-0-3). Jr League New Orleans.
Junior League of Rochester, Inc. Applehood & Motherpie. Kessler, Tracy K., ed. 330p. 1981. 12.95 (ISBN 0-9605612-0-X). Jr League Rochester.
Junior League of Shreveport, Inc. A Cook's Tour of Shreveport. 9th ed. (Illus.). 336p. 1964. pap. 6.95x (ISBN 0-686-62767-9). Jr League Shreveport.
--Revel. LC 79-89035. (Illus.). 416p. 1980. 8.95 (ISBN 0-9602246-1-0); stacon 5.37 (ISBN 0-686-58146-6). Jr League Shreveport.
Junior League of Tulsa, Inc. Tulsa Art Deco: An Architectural Era Nineteen Twenty-Five to Nineteen Forty-Two. 204p. 1980. 40.00 (ISBN 0-9604368-1-2); pap. 15.95 (ISBN 0-9604368-2-0). Jr League Tulsa.
Junior Liaison Organization Annual Conference, London, 1974. Have You Got the Energy? Proceedings. 130p. 1975. pap. text ed. 23.00 (ISBN 0-08-019651-9). Pergamon.
Juniper, Dean F. Decision-Making for Schools & Colleges. 324p. 1976. text ed. 41.00 (ISBN 0-08-019885-6); pap. text ed. 17.25 (ISBN 0-08-019884-8). Pergamon.
Juniper, Kerrison, Jr., jt. auth. see Reimann, Hobart A.
Junk, Ray & Pancoast, Harry M. Handbook of Sugars: For Processors, Chemists & Technologists. (Illus.). 304p. 1973. 26.50 o.p. (ISBN 0-87055-133-7). AVI.
Junk, W. Ray, jt. auth. see Pancoast, Harry M.
Junker, John M. Standards Relating to Juvenile Delinquency & Sanctions. (Juvenile Justice Standards Project Ser.). 1980. softcover 5.95 (ISBN 0-88410-829-5); casebound 12.50 (ISBN 0-88410-235-1). Ballinger Pub.
--Standards Relating to Juvenile Delinquency and Sanctions. LC 76-27864. (Juvenile Justice Standards Project Ser.). 1976. soft cover 5.95 o.p. (ISBN 0-88410-774-4); 12.50, casebound o.p. Ballinger Pub.
Junker, Louis J., ed. The Political Economy of Food & Energy. (Michigan Business Papers: No. 62). 1977. pap. 6.00 o.p. (ISBN 0-87712-177-X). U Mich Busn Div Res.
Junod, Alain F. & DeHaller, Rodolphe, eds. Lung Metabolism: Proteolysis & Antiproteolysis, Biochemical Pharmacology, Handling of Bioactive Substances. 1976. 40.00 (ISBN 0-12-392250-X). Acad Pr.
Junod, Mae A. The W-O-T Position or Self-Actualization for Women. 280p. 12.95 (ISBN 0-938968-00-9). Impact MI.
Junqueira, Luis C. & Carneiro, Jose. Basic Histology. 3rd rev. ed. LC 80-81941. (Illus.). 504p. 1980. lexotone cover 15.50 (ISBN 0-87041-202-7). Lange.
Jupo, Frank. Christmas Here, There & Everywhere. LC 77-3893. (gr. 1 up). 1977. 5.95 (ISBN 0-396-07462-6). Dodd.
--The Thanksgiving Book. LC 79-12201. (Illus.). 32p. (gr. 1-4). 1980. PLB 6.95 (ISBN 0-396-07703-X). Dodd.

--To Carry & to Keep: The Story of Containers. LC 75-5543. 1976. 5.95 (ISBN 0-396-07178-3). Dodd.

Jupp, James. British Radical Left Nineteen Thirty One - Nineteen Forty One. 423p. 1981. 27.50x (ISBN 0-7146-3123-X, F Cass Co). Biblio Dist.

Jupp, Kenneth. Echo. 228p. 1981. 10.95 (ISBN 0-316-47703-6). Little.

Jupp, T. C. see Milne, John.

Juptner, Joseph. U. S. Civil Aircraft, Vol. 8. 351p. 1980. 13.95 (ISBN 0-8168-9178-8). Aero.

Jurd, Ron. Wooden Boat Construction. (Questions & Answers Ser.). (Illus.). 92p. (Orig.). 1979. pap. 7.50 (ISBN 0-408-00315-4). Transatlantic.

Jureidini, Paul & McLaurin, R. D. Beyond Camp David: Emerging Alignments & Leaders in the Middle East. LC 80-27406. (Contemporary Issues in the Middle East Ser.). 232p. 1981. text ed. 18.00x (ISBN 0-8156-2235-X); pap. text ed. 8.95x (ISBN 0-8156-2236-8). Syracuse U Pr.

Jurek, Mary B., jt. ed. see Waters, Brent G.

Juretic, Miro, et al, eds. Herpetic Infections of Man. LC 77-75516. (Illus.). 1980. text ed. 13.50x (ISBN 0-87451-151-8). U Pr of New Eng.

Jurgens, Marshall H. Animal Feeding & Nutrition. 4th ed. 1978. wire coil bdg. 11.95 (ISBN 0-8403-0600-8). Kendall Hunt.

Jurgens, Mary R. Confrontation Between the Young Deaf-Blind Child & the Outer World: How to Make the World Surveyable by Organized Structure? 58p. 1977. text ed. 11.50 (ISBN 90-265-0261-3, Pub. by Swets Pub Serv Holland). Swets North Am.

Jurgensen, Kai, ed. see Ibsen, Henrik.

Jurgensen, Kai, tr. see Ibsen, Henrik.

Jurika, Stephen, Jr., ed. From Pearl Harbor to Vietnam: The Memoirs of Admiral Arthur W. Radford. LC 78-59466. (Publications 221 Ser.). (Illus.). 488p. 1980. 15.00 (ISBN 0-8179-7211-0). Hoover Inst Pr.

Juris, Hervey A. & Feuille, Peter. Police Unionism: Power & Impact in Public-Sector Bargaining. LC 73-1565. (Illus.). 208p. 1973. 19.95 (ISBN 0-669-86801-9). Lexington Bks.

Juris, Hervey A. & Roomkin, Myron, eds. The Shrinking Perimeter: Unionism & Labor Relations in the Manufacturing Sector. LC 79-1864. 240p. 1980. 22.95 (ISBN 0-669-02939-4). Lexington Bks.

Jurjani, A. Kitab al-Ta Rifat (Book of Definitions) Arabic-Arabic Dictionary. 1969. 15.00x (ISBN 0-685-54029-4). Intl Bk Ctr.

Jurmain, et al. Physical Anthropology & Archaeology. (Illus.). 1981. pap. text ed. 11.96 (ISBN 0-8299-0388-7). West Pub.

Jurmain, Robert, jt. auth. see Nelson, Harry.

Juroe, David J. Money: How to Spend Less & Have More. 1981. pap. 4.95 (ISBN 0-8007-5056-X). Revell.

Jurras, Lee E., jt. auth. see Nonte, George C., Jr.

Jurras, Lee F., ed. see Nonte, George C., Jr.

Jurries, Ginger & Mulder, Karen. Fun Ideas for Family Devotions (with Activity Pages) (Illus.). 176p. (Orig.). 1981. pap. 5.95 (ISBN 0-87239-415-8, 2968). Standard Pub.

Jurs, Justin. The Princess of Thunder. 1980. pap. 2.50 (ISBN 0-686-69251-9, 75861). Avon.

Jurs, Peter C., jt. auth. see Isenhour, Thomas L.

Jury, Mark. Playtime! Americans at Leisure. LC 77-73123. (Illus.). 1977. pap. 5.95 o.p. (ISBN 0-15-672037-X, Harv). HarBraceJ.

Jusczyk, Peter W. & Klein, Raymond M., eds. The Nature of Thought: Essays in Honor of D. O. Hebb. LC 80-18697. (Illus.). 336p. 1980. text ed. 24.95 (ISBN 0-89859-034-5). L Erlbaum Assocs.

Jussawalla, Meheroo, jt. auth. see Middleton, Karen P.

Jussieu-Pontcarral, Pierre De see De Jussieu-Pontcarral, Pierre.

Jussim, Estelle. Slave to Beauty: The Eccentric Life & Singular Achievements of F. Holland Day Photographer, Publisher, Aesthete. LC 80-66460. (Illus.). 288p. 1981. 30.00 (ISBN 0-87923-346-X). Godine.

Just, jt. ed. see Mengden, V.

Just, Marion, et al. Coping in a Troubled Society. LC 74-13719. (Illus.). 1974. 14.95 (ISBN 0-669-95851-4). Lexington Bks.

Just, Ward. Military Men. LC 76-123428. 1971. 6.95 o.p. (ISBN 0-394-43617-2). Knopf.

--Nicholson at Large. 256p. 1976. pap. 1.95 o.p. (ISBN 0-345-25151-2). Ballantine.

Juster, T., ed. see Carnegie Commission on Higher Education.

Justice, Blair & Justice, Rita. The Broken Taboo: Sex in the Family. LC 78-23720. 1979. 14.95 (ISBN 0-87705-389-8). Human Sci Pr.

--Broken Taboo: Sex in the Family. 304p. 1981. pap. 6.95 (ISBN 0-87705-482-7). Human Sci Pr.

--Stress: In the Eye of the Beholder the Key to Competent Coping. 193p. (Orig.). 1980. pap. cancelled (ISBN 0-915190-29-X). Jalmar Pr.

Justice, Blair, jt. auth. see Justice, Rita.

Justice, Donald. Selected Poems. LC 79-52416. 1979. 10.95 (ISBN 0-689-11016-2); pap. 6.95 (ISBN 0-689-11020-0). Atheneum.

--The Summer Anniversaries. LC 60-7256. (Wesleyan Poetry Program: Vol. 6). (Orig.). 1960. 10.00x (ISBN 0-8195-2006-3, Pub. by Wesleyan U Pr). Columbia U Pr.

Justice, Donald, ed. see Kees, Weldon.

Justice, Jennifer. The Tiger. (First Look at Nature Bks.). (Illus.). (gr. 2-4). 1979. 2.50 (ISBN 0-531-09143-0); PLB 6.45 s&l (ISBN 0-531-09154-6). Watts.

Justice, Rita & Justice, Blair. The Abusing Family. LC 76-6478. 1976. text ed. 19.95 (ISBN 0-87705-294-8); pap. 8.95 (ISBN 0-87705-315-4). Human Sci Pr.

Justice, Rita, jt. auth. see Justice, Blair.

Justis, Robert T. Managing Your Small Business. (Illus.). 288p. 1981. text ed. 18.95 (ISBN 0-686-68607-1). P-H.

Justus, May. Fun for Hunkydory. (Illus.). 24p. (gr. k-3). 1976. PLB 5.00 (ISBN 0-307-60521-3, Golden Pr). Western Pub.

Juszli, Frank L. & Rodgers, Charles A. Elementary Technical Mathematics. 3rd ed. (Illus.). 1980. text ed. 17.95 (ISBN 0-13-260869-3). P-H.

--Elementary Technical Mathematics with Calculus. LC 72-75381. (Illus.). 1971. text ed. 19.95x (ISBN 0-13-272724-2). P-H.

Juszli, Frank L. & Rodgers, Charles A., Jr. Elementary Technical Mathematics. 2nd ed. 1969. text ed. 16.95 o.p. (ISBN 0-13-260786-7). P-H.

Jutisz, Marian & McKerns, Kenneth W., eds. Synthesis & Release of Adenohypophyseal Hormones. (Biochemical Endocrinology Ser.). (Illus.). 780p. 1980. 69.50 (ISBN 0-306-40247-5, Plenum Pr). Plenum Pub.

Jutte, Rudiger. The Future of International Organization. 1981. 22.50 (ISBN 0-312-31476-0). St Martin.

Juvenal. Satires. Duff, James D., ed. (Pitt Ser). 1971. text ed. 16.95x (ISBN 0-521-07370-7). Cambridge U Pr.

Juvenal, jt. auth. see Persius.

Juviler, Peter H. Revolutionary Law & Order: Politics & Social Change in the USSR. LC 76-12832. 1976. 17.95 (ISBN 0-02-916800-7). Free Pr.

Jwing-Ming, Yang. Shaolin Long Fist. (Illus.). 250p. (Orig.). 1981. pap. 7.95 (ISBN 0-86568-020-5). Unique Pubns.

Jyoti, Amar. Retreat into Eternity. LC 80-54236. (Illus.). 128p. (Orig.). 1980. pap. 10.95 (ISBN 0-933572-03-4). Truth Consciousness.

K

Kaak, H. Otto, jt. auth. see Fosson, Abe R.

Kaal, Hans, tr. see Frege, Gottlob.

Kaas, H. K. Von see Von Kaas, H. K.

Kaase, Max & Von Beyme, Klaus, eds. Elections & Parties. LC 78-63119. (German Political Studies: Vol. 3). 1979. 20.00x (ISBN 0-8039-9888-0); pap. 9.95x (ISBN 0-8039-9889-9). Sage.

Kaatz, Evelyn. Soccer! How One Player Made the Pros. (Illus.). 128p. (gr. 3 up). 1981. 7.95 (ISBN 0-316-47752-4). Little.

Kabailo, A. P., jt. auth. see Hall, A.

Kabat, Geoffrey C. Ideology & Imagination. 1978. 15.50x (ISBN 0-231-04422-4). Columbia U Pr.

Kabat, Herman. Low Back & Leg Pain from Herniated Cervical Disk. 164p. 1980. 14.50 (ISBN 0-87527-246-0). Green.

Kabata, Z. Parasitic Copepoda of British Fishes. (Illus.). 670p. 1979. 72.00x (ISBN 0-903874-05-9, Pub. by Brit Mus Nat Hist England). Sabbot-Natural Hist Bks.

Kabbe, Frederick & Kabbe, Lois. Chemistry, Energy, & Human Ecology. LC 75-27126. (Illus.). 464p. 1976. pap. text ed. 16.95 (ISBN 0-395-19833-X); instr. manual 1.00 (ISBN 0-395-19831-3); slides o.p. 11.25 (ISBN 0-395-19832-1). HM.

Kabbe, Lois, jt. auth. see Kabbe, Frederick.

Kabdebo, Thomas. Hungary. (World Bibliographical Ser.: No. 15). 236p. 1980. 31.50 (ISBN 0-903450-28-3). ABC-Clio.

Kabir. The Fish in the Sea Is Not Thirsty. (Translated from Hindi). 8.00 (ISBN 0-89253-602-0); flexible cloth 4.00 (ISBN 0-89253-603-9). Ind-US Inc.

--Try to Live to See This! Bly, Robert, tr. 1976. pap. 2.00 (ISBN 0-915408-12-0). Ally Pr.

Kabir, Hasan. Doing Business in Saudi Arabia. 350p. 1980. 49.95 (ISBN 0-89260-187-6). Hwong Pub.

Kabir, Humayuh. Indian Philosophy of Education. 1971. pap. 6.00x (ISBN 0-685-06519-7, 210-33880-6). Asia.

Kabir, Humayun. Indian Heritage. 3rd ed. 1970. pap. 4.50x (ISBN 0-210-33672-2). Asia.

Kabir, Mohammad G. Minority Politics in Bangladesh. LC 80-900147. 1980. text ed. 17.50x (ISBN 0-7069-1034-6, Pub. by Vikas India). Advent Bk.

Kabra, Pokar & Marton, Laurence J., eds. Liquid Chromotography in Clinical Analysis. LC 80-84083. (Biological Methods Ser.). 352p. 1981. 49.50 (ISBN 0-89603-026-1). Humana.

Kac, Arthur W. The Messiahship of Jesus. 350p. 1980. pap. 9.95 (ISBN 0-8024-5421-6). Moody.

Kac, Mark. Probability & Related Topics in Physical Sciences. LC 59-10443. (Lectures in Applied Mathematics Ser.: Vol. 1A). 1980. Repr. of 1977 ed. 24.00 (ISBN 0-8218-0047-7, LAM-1.1). Am Math.

Kachru, Yamuna, ed. Aspects of Hindi Grammar. 1980. 12.50x (ISBN 0-8364-0666-4, Pub. by Manohar India). South Asia Bks.

Kaczkowski, Henry & Patterson, C. H. Counseling & Psychology in Elementary Schools. (Illus.). 384p. 1975. photocopy ed., spiral 37.50 (ISBN 0-398-03218-1). C C Thomas.

Kadambi, V. & Prasad, Manchar. An Introduction to Energy Conversion, 3 vols. Incl. Vol. 1. Basic Thermodynamics. 1976. o.p. (ISBN 0-470-50925-2); Vol. 2. Energy Conversion Cycles. 1974 (ISBN 0-470-50926-0); Vol. 3. Principles of Turbomachinery. 1978 (ISBN 0-470-99157-7). LC 74-13881. 13.95 ea. Halsted Pr.

Kadarkay, Arpad, tr. see Farkas, Sandor B.

Kadel, Thomas E., ed. Growth in Ministry. LC 79-8902. 180p. 1980. pap. 5.95 (ISBN 0-8006-1383-X, 1-1383). Fortress.

Kadel, William H. Prayers for Every Need. LC 57-11747. 1957. 3.85 (ISBN 0-8042-2496-X). John Knox.

Kadir, Djelal. Juan Carlos Onetti. (World Authors Ser.: Peru: No. 469). 1977. lib. bdg. 12.50 (ISBN 0-8057-6310-4). Twayne.

Kadis, Averil J., ed. see Dameron, J. Lasley.

Kadish, Ferne & Kirtland, Katheleen. London on Five Hundred Dollars a Day. (Illus.). 190p. 1975. 7.95 o.s.i. (ISBN 0-02-560510-0). Macmillan.

Kadish, Ferne & Kirtland, Kathleen. Los Angeles on Five Hundred Dollars a Day: Tax & Gratuities Not Included. 256p. 1976. pap. 4.95 (ISBN 0-02-097770-0, Collier). Macmillan.

--Los Angeles on Five Hundred Dollars a Day: Tax & Gratuities Not Included. 256p. 1976. 8.95 o.s.i. (ISBN 0-02-560520-8). Macmillan.

Kadison, R. V., ed. C-Algebras & Applications to Physics: Proceedings Second Japan-USA Seminar, Los Angeles, April 18 - 22, 1977. (Lecture Notes in Mathematics: Vol. 650). 1978. pap. 9.40 (ISBN 0-387-08762-1). Springer-Verlag.

Kadloubovsky, Palmer, tr. see Chariton, Igumen.

Kadloubowsky, E. Writings from the Philokalia. Palmer, G. E., tr. (Illus.). 1951. 18.95 (ISBN 0-571-07062-0, Pub. by Faber & Faber). Merrimack Bk Serv.

Kadow, H., jt. auth. see Lammich, G.

Kaduck, John, jt. auth. see Kaduck, Margaret.

Kaduck, Margaret & Kaduck, John. Rare & Expensive Postcards: Book Two. (Illus.). pap. 8.95 (ISBN 0-87069-267-4). Wallace-Homestead.

Kadushin, Alfred. Adopting Older Children. LC 71-125918. 1970. 16.00x (ISBN 0-231-03322-2). Columbia U Pr.

--Consultation in Social Work. LC 77-24345. 1977. 16.00x (ISBN 0-231-04124-1). Columbia U Pr.

--Supervision in Social Work. 496p. 1976. 17.50x (ISBN 0-231-03657-4). Columbia U Pr.

Kadushin, Alfred & Martin, Judith A. Child Abuse: An Interactional Event. (Illus.). 360p. 1981. 25.00x (ISBN 0-231-04774-6). Columbia U Pr.

Kaegi, C. E., tr. see Rosenzweig, Mark R. & Brown, T. A.

Kael, Pauline. Deeper into Movies. 1980. pap. 2.95 (ISBN 0-446-93525-5). Warner Bks.

--Reeling. 1977. pap. 2.95 o.s.i. (ISBN 0-446-83420-3). Warner Bks.

Kaelble, Emmett F. Handbook of X-Rays. LC 63-23535. 1120p. 1967. 54.50 o.p. (ISBN 0-686-65349-1). Krieger.

Kaelble, Hartmut. Berliner Unternehmer waehrend der fruehen Industrialisierung: Herkunft, sozialer Status und politischer Einfluss. (Veroeffentlichungen der Historischen Kommission zu Berlin 40). xii, 302p. (Ger.). 1972. 42.00x (ISBN 3-11-003873-0). De Gruyter.

--Historical Research on Social Mobility. Noakes, Ingrid, tr. 1981. text ed. 22.50x (ISBN 0-231-05274-X). Columbia U Pr.

Kaempfer, H. M. & Sickinghe, Jhr. W., eds. The Fascinating World of the Japanese Artist: A Collection of Essays on Japanese Art. 1979. text ed. 20.00x (ISBN 0-87093-156-3). Humanities.

Kaempffer, F. A. Concepts in Quantum Mechanics. (Pure & Applied Physics: Vol. 18). 1964. 33.00 (ISBN 0-12-394150-4). Acad Pr.

Kaeppel, Al. The Cat Testrophy. LC 79-91599. (Illus., Orig.). 1981. 3.95 (ISBN 0-89896-000-2). Larksdale.

Kaeppler, Adrienne L. Artificial Curiosities: An Exposition of Native Manufactures Collected on the Three Pacific Voyages of Captain James Cook, R.N. LC 77-91442. (Bernia P. Bishop Museum Special Publications: No. 65). (Illus.). 310p. 1980. pap. 27.50 (ISBN 0-295-95727-1). U of Wash Pr.

Kaeppler, Adrienne L., ed. Cook Voyage Artifacts in Leningrad, Berne, & Florence Museums. LC 77-84835. (Bernice P. Bishop Museum Special Publications: No. 66). (Illus.). 196p. 1978. pap. 15.00 (ISBN 0-295-95728-X). U of Wash Pr.

Kaerre, Karl K., jt. auth. see Santesson, R.

Kaessman, et al. My Maryland. (Illus.). 1971. 4.50x (ISBN 0-938420-12-7). Md Hist.

Kaestle, C. F. & Vinovskis, M. A. Education & Social Change in Nineteenth Century Massachusetts. LC 78-32130. (Illus.). 1980. 27.50 (ISBN 0-521-22191-9). Cambridge U Pr.

Kaestle, Carl F. Joseph Lancaster & the Monitorial School Movement: A Documentary History. LC 72-97206. 200p. 1973. text ed. 12.00 (ISBN 0-8077-2375-4); pap. text ed. 5.50x (ISBN 0-8077-2380-0). Tchrs Coll.

Kaestner. Drei Manner Im Schnee. (Easy Reader, C). pap. 3.75 (ISBN 0-88436-038-5, GEA201051). EMC.

--Mein Onkel Franz. (Easy Reader, A). pap. 2.90 (ISBN 0-88436-037-7, GEA10051). EMC.

Kaestner, Dorothy. Bargello Antics. (Illus.). 1980. 14.95 o.p. (ISBN 0-684-15995-3, ScribT); pap. 8.95 (ISBN 0-684-15996-1, ScribT). Scribner.

--Four Way Bargello. rev. ed. LC 73-14400. (Illus.). 1972. encore ed. 4.95 (ISBN 0-684-16198-2, ScribT); pap. 8.95 (ISBN 0-684-15142-1, SL 733, ScribT). Scribner.

Kaestner, Erich. Verschwundene Miniatur. new ed. Schinnerer, Otto P., ed. (Illus.). 1962. text ed. 6.95x o.p. (ISBN 0-669-29488-8). Heath.

Kaff, Frank. Monster for a Day: Or, the Monster in Gregory's Pajamas. LC 79-1866. (Illus.). (ps-3). 1979. 1.95 (ISBN 0-525-69002-6, Gingerbread Bks); PLB 5.95 (ISBN 0-525-69003-4). Dutton.

Kafka, Francis J., jt. auth. see Eisenberg, James.

Kafkafi, U., ed. see Soil Chemistry, Soil Fertility & Soil Clay Mineralogy Commissions of the International Society of Soil Science, 13-18 July 1976, Jerusalem.

Kafton, Amy M., jt. auth. see Hammerstrom, Gary.

Kagan, A. M., et al. Characterization Problems in Mathematical Statistics. Ramachandran, B., tr. LC 73-9643. (Ser. in Probability & Mathematical Statistics Ser.). 499p. 1973. 37.95 (ISBN 0-471-45421-4). Wiley.

Kagan, A. Robert, jt. ed. see Gilbert, Harvey A.

Kagan, Benjamin M. Antimicrobial Therapy. 3rd ed. LC 80-50252. (Illus.). 542p. 1980. text ed. 35.00 (ISBN 0-7216-5234-4). Saunders.

Kagan, Dan, jt. auth. see Summers, Ian.

Kagan, Donald. Outbreak of the Peloponnesian War. LC 69-18212. 438p. 1969. 25.00 (ISBN 0-8014-0501-7). Cornell U Pr.

Kagan, Henri. Organic Stereochemistry. Whiting, M. C. & Whiting, U. H., trs. LC 79-11500. 166p. 1979. pap. text ed. 16.95x (ISBN 0-470-26725-9). Halsted Pr.

Kagan, Jerome. The Growth of the Child: Reflections on Human Development. (Illus.). 1978 12.95 (ISBN 0-393-01173-9); pap. 5.95x, 1979 (ISBN 0-393-95084-0). Norton.

Kagan, Jerome & Havemann, Ernest. Psychology: An Introduction. 4th ed. 647p. 1980. text ed. 16.95 (ISBN 0-15-572625-0, HC); instructor's manual avail.; write for info. study guide; test items avail. HarBraceJ.

Kagan, Richard L. Lawsuits & Litigants in Castile, 1500-1700. LC 80-17565. 304p. 1981. 23.00x (ISBN 0-8078-1457-1). U of NC Pr.

Kagan, Robert A., jt. auth. see Gilbert, Harvey A.

Kaganoff, Nathan M., ed. Guide to America-Holy Land Studies: Vol. 1, American Presence. LC 79-8575. (Illus.). 1980. lib. bdg. 20.00x (ISBN 0-405-12755-3). Arno.

--Solidarity & Kinship: Essays on American Zionism. (Illus.). 1980. 5.00. Am Jewish Hist Soc.

Kagen, Lawrence J. Myoglobin: Biochemical, Physiological & Clinical Aspects. LC 73-5658. (Molecular Biology Ser.). 144p. 1973. text ed. 17.50x (ISBN 0-231-03421-0). Columbia U Pr.

Kagin, Donald H. Private Gold Coins & Patterns of the United States. LC 79-21041. (Illus.). 400p. 1980. lib. bdg. 24.95 (ISBN 0-668-04830-1). Arco.

Kagle, Stephen. American Diary Literature. (United States Author Ser.: No. 342). 1979. lib. bdg. 13.50 (ISBN 0-8057-7280-4). Twayne.

Kagle, Steven. America: Travel & Exploration. LC 78-71883. 1979. 11.95 (ISBN 0-87972-134-0); pap. 6.95 (ISBN 0-87972-171-5). Bowling Green Univ.

Kagler, S. H. Spectroscopic & Chromatographic Analysis of Mineral Oil, 3 vols. LC 72-4105. 559p. 1973. Set. 79.95 (ISBN 0-470-45425-3). Halsted Pr.

Kagwa, Benjamin N. H. A Ugandan: Defiant & Triumphant. (Illus.). 1978. 10.00 o.p. (ISBN 0-682-49032-6). Exposition.

Kagy, Frederick D. Graphic Arts. LC 78-5456. (Illus.). 1978. text ed. 4.80 (ISBN 0-87006-252-2). Goodheart.

Kahan, Arcadius & Ruble, Blair A. Industrial Labor in the USSR. (Pergamon Policy Studies). 1979. 42.00 (ISBN 0-08-023701-0); pap. 13.00 (ISBN 0-08-023899-8). Pergamon.

Kahan, Barbara. Growing up in Care: Ten People Talking. (Practice of Social Work Ser.: Vol. 2). 201p. 1980. 29.00x (ISBN 0-631-12171-4, Pub. by Basil Blackwell); pap. 11.50x (ISBN 0-631-12161-7). Biblio Dist.

Kahan, Jane & Stone, Marie K. Writing the Expository Essay. LC 78-730063. (Illus.). 1977. pap. text ed. 99.00 (ISBN 0-89290-123-3, A322). Soc for Visual.

Kahan, Jane & Trotter, Gwendolyn. Reading Comprehension Skills. LC 78-730058. (Illus.). 1979. pap. text ed. 99.00 (ISBN 0-89290-104-7, A330-SATC). Soc for Visual.

Kahan, Jane M., et al. Understanding Your Sexuality. (Illus.). 1980. pap. text ed. 104.00 (ISBN 0-89290-100-4, A793-SATC). Soc for Visual.

Kahan, Jerome H. Security in the Nuclear Age: Developing U.S. Strategic Arms Policy. 351p. 1975. 16.95 (ISBN 0-8157-4818-3); pap. 7.95 (ISBN 0-8157-4817-5). Brookings.

Kahan, Michael. Energy. 1981. 16.95 (ISBN 0-936278-00-5). Green Hill.

Kahan, Mitchell D. American Paintings of the Sixties & Seventies: Selections from the Whitney Museum of American Art. LC 80-80977. (Illus.). 88p. 1980. pap. 8.00 (ISBN 0-89280-015-1). Montgomery Mus.

--Roger Brown. LC 80-24063. (Illus.). 96p. (Orig.). 1980. pap. 10.00 (ISBN 0-89280-042-9). Montgomery Mus.

Kahane, Henry, et al. Spoken Greek. Incl. Bk. 1, Units 1-12. xi, 279p. pap. 9.00x (ISBN 0-87950-100-6); Bk. 2, Units 13-30. 645p. pap. 12.00x (ISBN 0-87950-101-4); Records, Six 12-Inch LP (33.3 rpm) o.p. (ISBN 0-87950-103-0); Record Course-Bk. 1 & Records. pap. o.p. (ISBN 0-87950-104-9); Cassettes 1, Six Dual Track. 60.00x (ISBN 0-87950-105-7); Cassette Course 1-Bk. 1 & Cassettes 1. 65.00x (ISBN 0-87950-106-5); Cassettes 2, Six Dual Track. 60.00x (ISBN 0-87950-107-3); Cassette Course 2 - Bk. 2 & Cassettes 2. 65.00x (ISBN 0-87950-108-1); Combine Cassette Course-Bks. 1 & 2 & Cassettes 1 & 2. 110.00x (ISBN 0-87950-109-X). LC 74-150404. (Spoken Language Ser.). (Prog. Bk.). 1974. Spoken Lang Serv.

Kahane, Howard. Logic & Contemporary Rhetoric. 3rd ed. 288p. 1980. pap. text ed. 9.95x (ISBN 0-534-00850-X). Wadsworth Pub.

--Logic & Contemporary Rhetoric: The Use of Reason in Everyday Life. 2nd ed. 1976. pap. 7.95x o.p. (ISBN 0-534-00449-0). Wadsworth Pub.

--Logic & Philosophy. 3rd ed. 1978. text ed. 17.95x (ISBN 0-534-00555-1). Wadsworth Pub.

Kahaner, Larry. Audio & Video Interference Cures. 128p. 1979. pap. 6.10 (ISBN 0-8104-0895-3). Hayden.

Kahin, George M. Major Governments of Asia. 2nd ed. LC 63-15940. (Illus.). 1963. 24.50x o.p. (ISBN 0-8014-0218-2). Cornell U Pr.

Kahl, Kurt, jt. auth. see Dahmer, Sondra.

Kahl, Russell, ed. Selected Writings. LC 73-8385. 1973. 9.95 (ISBN 0-8195-4039-0, Pub. by Wesleyan U Pr); pap. 5.95 (ISBN 0-913372-10-2). Columbia U Pr.

Kahl, Virginia. Gunhilde & the Halloween Spell. (Illus.). 32p. (gr. k-3). pap. 2.95 (ISBN 0-689-70490-9, A-117, Aladdin). Atheneum.

--Whose Cat Is That? (Illus.). 32p. (gr. k-2). 1979. 7.95 (ISBN 0-684-16097-8). Scribner.

Kahl, Virginia, jt. auth. see Vacheron, Edith.

Kahl, William F. The Development of the London Livery Companies. (Kress Library of Business & Economics: No. 15). (Illus.). 1960. pap. 5.00x (ISBN 0-678-09910-3, Baker Lib). Kelley.

Kahlenberg, Mary H. Book of Grass Crafts. (Illus.). 1981. 18.95 (ISBN 0-525-06983-6); pap. 12.95 (ISBN 0-525-47630-X). Dutton.

Kahler, Martin. The So Called Historical Jesus & the Historic Biblical Christ. Braaten, Carl E., tr. from Ger. LC 64-12994. 168p. 1964. pap. 3.75 (ISBN 0-8006-1960-9, 1-1960). Fortress.

Kahn, jt. auth. see Marshall Kaplan, Gans.

Kahn, Albert E. Days with Ulanova. LC 79-7770. (Dance Ser.). (Illus.). 1980. Repr. of 1962 ed. lib. bdg. 43.00x (ISBN 0-8369-9297-0). Arno.

Kahn, Alfred J. Issues in American Social Work. LC 59-6701. 1959. 20.00x (ISBN 0-231-02239-5). Columbia U Pr.

--Planning Community Services for Children in Trouble. LC 63-10417. (Illus.). 1963. 22.50x (ISBN 0-231-02611-0). Columbia U Pr.

--Shaping the New Social Work. LC 73-4189. (Social Work & Social Issues Ser). 224p. 1973. 17.50x (ISBN 0-231-03605-1); pap. 6.00x (ISBN 0-231-08356-4). Columbia U Pr.

--Social Policy & Social Services. 1973. pap. text ed. 4.50 o.p. (ISBN 0-394-31388-7). Random.

Kahn, Alfred J., jt. auth. see Kamerman, Sheila B.

Kahn, Alfred J., jt. ed. see Kamerman, Sheila B.

Kahn, Charles H. & Hanna, J. Bradley. Money Makes Sense. 2nd ed. (Illus., Orig.). 1972. pap. 3.96 (ISBN 0-8224-4515-8); tchrs' manual free (ISBN 0-8224-5210-3). Pitman Learning.

--Working Makes Sense. 1973. pap. 3.96 (ISBN 0-8224-7490-5); tchrs. manual free (ISBN 0-8224-5212-X). Pitman Learning.

Kahn, Charles H., et al. Going Places with Your Personality: A Guide to Successful Living. (Special Education Ser for slow learners). (gr. 4-12,RL 2.7). 1971. pap. 2.56 (ISBN 0-8224-3495-4); tchrs' manual free (ISBN 0-8224-3496-2). Pitman Learning.

--Measure Up. LC 67-31749. (Illus., Special Education Ser. for slow learners). (gr. 4-12). 1968. pap. 2.72 (ISBN 0-8224-4460-7); tchrs' manual free (ISBN 0-8224-4461-5). Pitman Learning.

Kahn, Coppelia. Man's Estate: Masculine Identity in Shakespeare. 200p. 1981. 16.00x (ISBN 0-520-03899-1). U of Cal Pr.

Kahn, Daniel. Syllable-Based Generalizations in English Phonology. Hankamer, Jorge, ed. LC 79-55852. (Outstanding Dissertations in Linguistics Ser.). 218p. 1980. lib. bdg. 26.50 (ISBN 0-8240-4554-8). Garland Pub.

Kahn, David. Codebreakers. 1967. 29.95 (ISBN 0-02-560460-0). Macmillan.

--Hitler's Spies: German Military Intelligence in World War II. (Illus.). 1978. 19.95 (ISBN 0-02-560610-7). Macmillan.

Kahn, Donald W. Introduction to Global Analysis: Pure & Applied Mathematics Ser. LC 79-8858. 1980. 34.50 (ISBN 0-12-394050-8). Acad Pr.

Kahn, Douglas A. Basic Corporate Taxation. 3rd ed. LC 80-27245. 531p. 1980. pap. text ed. 18.95 (ISBN 0-8299-2114-1). West Pub.

Kahn, Douglas A. & Gann, Pamela B. Corporate Taxation & Taxation of Partnerships & Partners. LC 78-26612. (American Casebook Ser.). 1979. text ed. 23.95 (ISBN 0-8299-2026-9). West Pub.

Kahn, Douglas A. & Waggoner, Lawrence W. Federal Taxation of Gifts, Trusts & Estates. 1980. 1980 suppl. 6.95 (ISBN 0-316-48201-3). Little.

Kahn, Edgar A. Journal of a Neurosurgeon. (Illus.). 182p. 1972. 12.75 (ISBN 0-398-02325-5). C C Thomas.

Kahn, Emil. Conducting Guide to Selected Scores. 2nd ed. LC 75-30288. (Illus.). 1976. pap. text ed. 12.95 (ISBN 0-02-871030-4). Schirmer Bks.

--Elements of Conducting. 2nd ed. LC 75-4317. (Illus.). 1975. pap. text ed. 12.95 (ISBN 0-02-871050-9). Schirmer Bks.

Kahn, Eugen, jt. auth. see Dodge, Raymond.

Kahn, Evelyn. The Wayward Winds. (Orig.). 1980. pap. write for info. (ISBN 0-671-83128-3). PB.

Kahn, F., ed. Documents of American Broadcasting. 3rd ed. 1978. 19.50 (ISBN 0-13-217067-1). P-H.

Kahn, Gilbert, jt. auth. see Mulkerne, Donald, J.D.

Kahn, Guinter, ed. see Rassner, Gernot.

Kahn, Hannah D., tr. see Mosca, Gaetano.

Kahn, Harold L., jt. auth. see Loeb, James R.

Kahn, Hazrat I. Nature Meditations. LC 80-50829. (Collected Works of Hazrat Inayat Khan Ser.). (Illus.). 128p. (Orig.). 1980. pap. 5.00 (ISBN 0-930872-12-6). Sufi Order Pubns.

Kahn, Herman. World Economic Development. 1979. lib. bdg. 27.50 (ISBN 0-89158-392-0). Westview.

Kahn, Herman & Passin, Herbert. The Japanese Challenge: The Success & Failure of Economic Success. LC 78-69520. 1979. 10.95 (ISBN 0-690-01784-7, TYC-T). T Y Crowell.

Kahn, Herman & Pepper, Thomas. Will She Be Right? The Future of Australia. (Illus.). 199p. 1981. text ed. 18.75 (ISBN 0-7022-1568-6); pap. 7.25 (ISBN 0-7022-1569-4). U of Queensland Pr.

Kahn, J. H. Human Growth & the Development of Personality. 2nd ed. 264p. 1972. text ed. 21.00 (ISBN 0-08-015818-8); pap. text ed. 9.75 (ISBN 0-08-015817-X). Pergamon.

--Job's Illness: Loss, Grief & Integration; a Psychological Interpretation. 284p. 1975. text ed. 27.00 (ISBN 0-08-018087-6). Pergamon.

Kahn, J. H. & Nursten, J. P. Unwillingly to School. 2nd ed. 1964. 12.25 (ISBN 0-08-013304-5); pap. 6.50 (ISBN 0-08-013295-2). Pergamon.

Kahn, J. H., jt. auth. see Thompson, S.

Kahn, J. H., ed. see Morrice, J. K.

Kahn, Jack & Wright, Susan. Human Growth & the Development of Personality. 3rd ed. (Pergamon International Library, Mental Health & Social Medicine Division). Date not set. 36.00 (ISBN 0-08-023383-X); pap. 15.50 (ISBN 0-08-023382-1). Pergamon.

Kahn, Jack H., et al. Unwillingly to School: School Phobia or School Refusal - a Psycho-Social Problem. 3rd ed. 250p. 1980. 29.00 (ISBN 0-08-025229-X); pap. 12.00 (ISBN 0-08-025230-3). Pergamon.

Kahn, Joan, ed. Some Things Dark & Dangerous. 1970. pap. 1.50 (ISBN 0-380-01556-0, 36038). Avon.

--Some Things Strange & Sinister. 1974. pap. 1.50 (ISBN 0-686-68409-5, 36046). Avon.

Kahn, Joel & Llobera, Josep, eds. The Anthropology of Pre-Capitalist Societies. 1980. text ed. write for info. (ISBN 0-391-01943-0); pap. text ed. price not set. Humanities.

Kahn, Joel S. Minangkabau Social Formations: Indonesian Peasants & the World Economy. LC 79-7650. (Cambridge Studies in Social Anthropology: No. 30). (Illus.). 260p. 1981. 37.50 (ISBN 0-521-22993-6). Cambridge U Pr.

Kahn, Judd. Imperial San Francisco: Politics & Planning in an American City, 1897-1906. LC 79-9096. (Illus.). xiv, 263p. 1980. 17.95x (ISBN 0-8032-2702-7). U of Nebr Pr.

Kahn, L., jt. auth. see Hook, D. C.

Kahn, Lawrence E. When Couples Part: How the Legal System Can Work for You. 192p. 1981. 10.95 (ISBN 0-531-09944-X). Watts.

Kahn, Lloyd, ed. Shelter II. (Illus.). 224p. (Orig.). 1978. 15.00 (ISBN 0-394-50219-1); pap. 9.50 (ISBN 0-394-73611-7). Shelter Pubns.

Kahn, Lloyd, Jr., ed. Shelter. LC 73-5415. (Illus.). 1973. 20.00 (ISBN 0-394-48829-6); pap. 6.00 (ISBN 0-394-70991-8). Random.

Kahn, Lothar, ed. God: What People Have Said About Him. 320p. 1980. 9.95 (ISBN 0-8246-0251-X). Jonathan David.

Kahn, Marvin W. Basic Methods for Mental Health Practitioners. 350p. Date not set. ref. ed. 15.95. Winthrop.

Kahn, Michel. My Everyday Spanish Word Book. (Illus.). 46p. (gr. 3-9). 1981. 7.95 (ISBN 0-8120-5431-8). Barron.

Kahn, Michele. My Everyday French Word Book. 44p. (gr. 1-6). 1980. 7.95 (ISBN 0-8120-5344-3). Barron.

Kahn, Norma. More Learning in Less Time. 80p. 1979. pap. 3.90 (ISBN 0-8104-6043-2). Hayden.

Kahn, P. M., ed. Computational Probability. LC 80-15014. 1980. 21.00 (ISBN 0-12-394680-8). Acad Pr.

Kahn, R. L. & Cannell, C. F. Dynamics of Interviewing: Theory, Technique & Cases. 1957. 24.95 (ISBN 0-471-45441-9). Wiley.

Kahn, Richard. Selected Essays on Employment & Growth. LC 78-187079. 240p. 1972. 35.50 (ISBN 0-521-08493-8). Cambridge U Pr.

Kahn, Robert L., jt. auth. see Katz, Daniel.

Kahn, Roger. Boys of Summer. LC 76-144179. 13.95 o.s.i. (ISBN 0-06-012239-0, HarpT). Har-Row.

Kahn, Sanders A. & Case, Frederick E. Real Estate Appraisal & Investment. 2nd ed. LC 76-22316. 1977. 24.50 (ISBN 0-8260-4836-6, Pub. by Wiley-Hamilton). Wiley.

Kahn, Sandra & Davis, Jean. Sexual Preferences. 256p. 1981. 9.95 (ISBN 0-312-71351-7). St Martin.

Kahn, Sholem J., ed. Whole Loaf: Stories from Israel. 1962. 7.95 o.s.i. (ISBN 0-8149-0559-5). Vanguard.

Kahn, T. C., et al. Methods & Evaluation in Clinical & Counseling Psychology. 375p. 1975. text ed. 23.00 (ISBN 0-08-017862-6); pap. text ed. 16.00 (ISBN 0-08-017863-4). Pergamon.

Kahn-Freund, Otto, et al. A Source-Book on French Law: System, Methods, Outlines of Contract. 2nd ed. 1979. pap. 27.00 (ISBN 0-19-825349-4). Oxford U Pr.

Kahng, D., ed. Advances in Applied Solid State Science, Supplement, 2A: Silicon Integrated Circuits. (Serial Publication). 1981. price not set (ISBN 0-12-002954-5); price not set lib. ed. (ISBN 0-12-002955-3); price not set microfiche ed. (ISBN 0-12-002956-1). Acad Pr.

Kahng, Dawon, ed. Advances in Solid State Science, Supplement 2B: Silicon Integrated Circuits. (Serial Publication). 1981. price not set (ISBN 0-12-002957-X); price not set lib. ed. (ISBN 0-12-002958-8); microfiche ed. (ISBN 0-12-002959-6). Acad Pr.

Kahrl, George M., jt. auth. see Stone, George W., Jr.

Kahrs, Robert F. Viral Diseases of Cattle. (Illus.). 224p. 1981. text ed. 15.00 (ISBN 0-8138-0860-X). Iowa St U Pr.

Kaibara, Ekiken. Way of Contentment. Bd. with Greater Learning for Women. (Studies in Japanese History & Civilization). 1979. Repr. of 1913 ed. 19.00 (ISBN 0-89093-253-0). U Pubns Amer.

Kaid, Lynda L., et al. Political Campaign Communication: A Bibliography & Guide to the Literature. LC 73-22492. 1974. 10.00 (ISBN 0-8108-0704-1). Scarecrow.

Kaikini, P. R. Some of My Years. (Writers Workshop Redbird Ser.). 1975. 9.00 (ISBN 0-88253-638-9); pap. text ed. 4.80 (ISBN 0-88253-637-0). Ind-US Inc.

Kaiko, Ken. Into a Black Sun. Seigle, Cecilia S., tr. from Japan. LC 80-50500. 216p. 1980. 9.95 (ISBN 0-87011-428-X). Kodansha.

Kaiko, Takeshi. Darkness in Summer. Seigle, Cecilia S., tr. from Japanese. 212p. 1972. pap. 5.75 (ISBN 0-8048-1375-2). C E Tuttle.

Kail, Robert. The Development of Memory in Children. LC 79-12262. (Psychology Ser.). (Illus.). 1979. text ed. 14.95x (ISBN 0-7167-1097-8); pap. text ed. 7.95x (ISBN 0-7167-1098-6). W H Freeman.

Kailath, T. Lectures on Linear Least-Squares Estimation. (CISM International Centre for Mechanical Sciences: Vol. 140). (Illus.). 1979. pap. 14.80 o.p. (ISBN 0-387-81386-1). Springer-Verlag.

Kailath, Thomas. Linear Systems. (Information & Systems Sciences Ser.). (Illus.). 1980. text ed. 28.95 (ISBN 0-13-536961-4). P-H.

Kaim-Caudle, Peter, ed. Social Policy in the Irish Republic. 1967. text ed. 3.75x (ISBN 0-7100-4023-7). Humanities.

Kain, Richard. Automata Theory: Machines & Languages. (Computer Science Ser). (Illus.). 320p. 1972. text ed. 24.95 o.p. (ISBN 0-07-033195-2, C). McGraw.

Kain, Robert C. In the Valley of the Little Big Horn. rev. ed. (Illus.). 117p. 1978. 7.95 (ISBN 0-917714-16-4). Beinfeld Pub.

Kain, Roger. Planning for Conservation: An International Perspective. 1980. 30.00 (ISBN 0-312-61400-4). St Martin.

Kain, Roger & Prince, Hugh. The Tithe Surveys of England & Wales. (Studies in Historical Geography). (Illus.). Date not set. cancelled (ISBN 0-208-01726-7, Archon). Shoe String. Postponed.

Kainer, Gordon. Faith, Hope & Clarity. LC 77-72499. (Redwood Ser.). 1977. pap. 3.95 (ISBN 0-8163-0314-2, 06022-8). Pacific Pr Pub Assn.

Kaiser, Artur. Motivation Techniques. Peppe, G. & Birker, D., trs. from Ger. LC 79-89938. Orig. Title: Druck erzeugt Gegendruck. (Orig.). Date not set. pap. cancelled (ISBN 0-89793-013-4). Hunter Hse.

Kaiser, Charles, Jr. & Helber, Larry E. Tourism Planning & Development. LC 77-14474. 1978. 14.95 (ISBN 0-8436-2128-1); student ed. 10.95 (ISBN 0-8436-2169-9). CBI Pub.

Kaiser, David E. Economic Diplomacy & the Origins of the Second World War: Germany, Britain, France, & Eastern Europe, 1930-1939. LC 80-7536. 352p. 1980. 25.00 (ISBN 0-691-05312-X); pap. 12.50 (ISBN 0-691-10101-9). Princeton U Pr.

Kaiser, Edward J., jt. auth. see Chapin, F. Stuart, Jr.

Kaiser, Ernest, jt. auth. see Halliburton, Warren J.

Kaiser, Georg. Georg Kaiser Plays, Vol. 1. Kenworthy, B. J., tr. 1980. pap. 6.95 (ISBN 0-7145-0242-1). Riverrun NY.

Kaiser, Gerard A., et al. Thoracic Surgery Case Studies. 1979. pap. 15.75 (ISBN 0-87488-056-4). Med Exam.

Kaiser, Gerhard, ed. see Wentzlaff-Eggebert, Friedrich-Wilhelm.

Kaiser, Gerhard W. The Substance of Greek & Shakespearean Tragedy. (Salzburg Studies in English Literature: Elizabethan & Renaissance Studies: No. 67). 1977. pap. text ed. 25.00x (ISBN 0-391-01442-0). Humanities.

Kaiser, Hans E. Neoplasms - Comparative Pathology of Growth in Animals, Plants & Man. (Illus.). 820p. 1980. lib. bdg. write for info. (ISBN 0-683-04503-2). Williams & Wilkins.

Kaiser, Harvey. The Great Camps of the Adirondacks. LC 79-90360. (Illus.). Date not set. 40.00 (ISBN 0-87923-308-7); limited edition 140.00 (ISBN 0-87923-392-3). Godine. Postponed.

Kaiser, Karl. Europe & the United States: The Future of the Relationship. LC 73-75612. 146p. 1973. 3.95 o.p. (ISBN 0-910416-18-4, F70037); pap. 2.50 o.p. (ISBN 0-685-31761-7, F70038). Columbia Bks.

Kaiser, Karl & Schwartz, Hans-Peter, eds. America & Western Europe: Problems & Prospects of European-American Relations. LC 78-19242. 1979. 14.95 (ISBN 0-669-02450-3). Lexington Bks.

Kaiser, Leo, ed. The Seven Against Thebes. Thoreau, Henry D. LC 80-2522. (Emerson Society Quarterly No. Seventeen Nineteen Fifty Nine,1-30). 1981. Repr. of 1959 ed. 14.00 (ISBN 0-404-19070-7). AMS Pr.

Kaiser, Otto & Lohse, Eduard. Death & Life. Steely, John E., tr. LC 80-21265. (Biblical Encounter Ser.). 176p. 1981. pap. 6.95 (ISBN 0-687-10332-0). Abingdon.

Kaiser, Richard. Overing Discouragement. LC 79-84746. 128p. 1981. pap. 2.50 (ISBN 0-89081-269-1). Harvest Hse.

Kaiser, Robert G. Russia. (gr. 10 up). 1980. pap. 3.95 (ISBN 0-671-43285-0). PB.

Kaiser, Robert L., jt. ed. see Clark, David W.

Kaiser, Walter C., Jr. Classical Evangelical Essays in Old Testament Interpretation. 1972. pap. 6.95 (ISBN 0-8010-5314-5). Baker Bk.

--Toward an Exegetical Theology. 224p. 1981. 9.95 (ISBN 0-8010-5425-7). Baker Bk.

Kaisergruber, D., et al. Phedre De Racine: Pour une Semiotique De la Representation Classique. new ed. (Collection L Ser.). 288p. (Orig., Fr.). 1972. pap. 13.95 (ISBN 2-03-036001-5). Larousse.

Kak, Siddharth. Looking in Looking Out. (Redbird Bk.). 1976. lib. bdg. 8.00 (ISBN 0-89253-116-9); flexible bdg. 4.80 (ISBN 0-89253-134-7). Ind-US Inc.

Kak, Subhas. Conductor of the Dead. (Writers Workshop Redbird Ser.). 36p. 1975. 8.00 (ISBN 0-88253-516-1); pap. text ed. 4.80 (ISBN 0-88253-515-3). Ind-US Inc.

Kakabadse, George, ed. Chemistry of Effluent Treatment. (Illus.). 1979. 36.30x (ISBN 0-85334-840-5, Pub. by Applied Science). Burgess-Intl Ideas.

Kakac, S., ed. see Two-Phase Flow & Heat Transfer Workshop, Ft. Lauderdale, Oct. 1976.

Kakac, S., et al, eds. see NATO Advanced Study Institute on Two-Phase Flows & Heat Transfer, Istanbul, Aug. 1976.

Kakac, Sadik & Spalding, D. Brian, eds. Turbulent Forced Convection in Channels & Bundles: Theory & Applications to Heat Exchangers & Nuclear Reactors, 2 vols. LC 79-12842. 1132p. 1979. Set. 92.50 (ISBN 0-89116-148-1). Hemisphere Pub.

Kakac, Sadik, et al, eds. Heat Exchanges - Thermohydraulic Fundamentals & Design, 2 vols. (Illus.). 1000p. 1981. Set. text ed. 95.00 (ISBN 0-89116-225-9). Hemisphere Pub.

Kakalik, James & Wildhorn, Sorrel. The Private Police: Security & Danger. LC 76-10072. 500p. 1977. 37.50x (ISBN 0-8448-0365-0). Crane-Russak Co.

Kakar, Sudhir. The Inner World: A Psycho-Analytic Study of Hindu Childhood & Society. (Illus.). 1978. 12.95x (ISBN 0-19-560888-7). Oxford U Pr.

Kakkar, Vijay V., jt. auth. see Scully, Michael F.

Kakn, Jane & Trotter, Gwendolyn. Reading in the Content Areas. LC 78-730059. (Illus.). 1978. pap. text ed. 99.00 (ISBN 0-89290-102-0, A328-SATC). Soc for Visual.

Kakonis, Tom E. & Scally, John, eds. We Have but Faith. LC 74-20434. 152p. 1975. 6.95 (ISBN 0-88498-023-5); text ed. 6.25 o.p. (ISBN 0-685-52606-2). Brevet Pr.

Kakshmikantham, V. Nonlinear Differential Equations in Abstract Spaces. (I.S. Nonlinear Mathematics Series; Theory, Methods and Applications: Vol. 2). 272p. 1981. 45.00 (ISBN 0-08-025038-6). Pergamon.

Kakwani, Nanak. Income Inequality & Poverty: Methods of Estimation & Policy Applications. (World Bank Research Publications). (Illus.). 1980. 19.95x (ISBN 0-19-520126-4); pap. 8.95x (ISBN 0-19-520227-9). Oxford U Pr.

Kalafatich. Approaches to the Care of Adolescents. 1975. 15.50 o.p. (ISBN 0-8385-0289-X). ACC.

Kalakaua. The Legends & Myths of Hawaii: The Fables & Folk-Lore of a Strange People. Daggett, R. M., ed. & illus. LC 72-77519. (Illus.). (gr. 9 up). 1972. pap. 7.75 (ISBN 0-8048-1032-X). C E Tuttle.

Kalakian, Leonard H. & Goldman, Myra F. Introduction to Physical Education: A Humanistic Perspective. 224p. 1976. text ed. 15.95x (ISBN 0-205-05475-7). Allyn.

Kalan, Robert. Blue Sea. LC 78-18396. (Illus.). (gr. k-3). 1979. 7.50 (ISBN 0-688-80184-6); PLB 7.20 (ISBN 0-688-84184-8). Greenwillow.

--Rain. LC 77-25312. (Illus.). (gr. k-3). 1978. 7.95 (ISBN 0-688-80139-0); PLB 7.63 (ISBN 0-688-84139-2). Greenwillow.

Kalant, ed. Research Advances in Alcohol & Drug Problems: Volume 5, Drug Problems in Women. 730p. 1980. 55.00 (ISBN 0-306-40394-3, Plenum Pr). Plenum Pub.

Kalashnik, Ia. M., jt. ed. see Morozov, G. V.

Kalb, Jonah. The Easy Baseball Book. LC 75-44085. (Illus.). 64p. (gr. 2-5). 1976. 6.95 (ISBN 0-395-24385-8). HM.

Kalb, S. William. Your Future As a Physician. 2nd ed. LC 74-80997. (Career Guidance Ser.). 1974. pap. 2.95 o.p. (ISBN 0-668-02263-9). Arco.

Kalber, F. A., jt. ed. see Smith, F. Walton.

Kalbfleisch, J. G. Probability & Statistical Inference I. (Universitexts). (Illus.). 342p. 1980. pap. 15.00 (ISBN 0-387-90457-3). Springer-Verlag.

--Probability & Statistical Inference II. (Universitexts). (Illus.). 316p. 1980. pap. 15.00 (ISBN 0-387-90458-1). Springer-Verlag.

Kalchuri, Bhau. Let's Go to Meherabad. 100p. 1981. price not set. Meher Baba Info.

Kalck, Pierre. Historical Dictionary of the Central African Republic. O'Toole, Thomas, tr. LC 80-21199. (African Historical Dictionaries: No. 27). 194p. 1980. 10.00 (ISBN 0-8108-1360-2). Scarecrow.

Kaldor, George & DiBattista, William J., eds. Aging: Aging in Muscle, Vol. 6. LC 78-4356. 1978. 22.00 (ISBN 0-89004-097-4). Raven.

Kaldor, Mary & Eide, Ashborn. The World Military Order. LC 78-87885. 1979. 28.95 (ISBN 0-03-053371-6). Praeger.

Kaldor, Mary, et al, eds. Democratic Socialism & the Cost of Defence: The Report & Papers of the Labour Party Defence Study Group. Smith, Dan & Vines, Steve. 1979. 45.00x (ISBN 0-85664-886-8, Pub. by Croom Helm Ltd England). Biblio Dist.

Kaldor, Nicholas. Essays on Economic Policy I: Collected Essays, Vol. 3. LC 80-18155. 293p. 1980. text ed. 39.50x (ISBN 0-8419-0453-7). Holmes & Meier.

--Essays on Economic Policy II: Collected Economic Essays, Vol. 4. LC 80-18155. 320p. 1980. 39.50x (ISBN 0-8419-0454-5). Holmes & Meier.

--Essays on Economic Stability & Growth: Collected Economic Essays, Vol. 2. LC 80-18145. 302p. 1980. text ed. 39.50x (ISBN 0-8419-0452-9). Holmes & Meier.

--Essays on Value & Distribution. 1960. 12.95 (ISBN 0-02-916980-1). Free Pr.

--Reports on Taxation One. LC 78-31926. (Collected Economic Essays Ser.: Vol. 7). 1980. text ed. 39.50x (ISBN 0-8419-0296-8). Holmes & Meier.

--Reports on Taxation Two. LC 78-31926. (Collected Economics Essays Ser.: Vol. 8). 1980. text ed. 39.50x (ISBN 0-8419-0297-6). Holmes & Meier.

Kale, B. K., jt. auth. see Sinha, S. K.

Kale, Pramod, tr. see Madgulkar, Vyankatesh.

Kalechofsky, Roberta. George Orwell. LC 73-77054. (Modern Literature Ser.). 1973. 10.95 (ISBN 0-8044-2480-2). Ungar.

--Rejected Essays, & Other Matters. new ed. LC 80-83108. 256p. 1980. pap. 5.00 (ISBN 0-916288-08-0). Micah Pubns.

Kalecki, Michael. Selected Essays on the Economic Growth of the Socialist & Mixed Economy, Vol. 2. LC 73-179162. (Illus.). 188p. 1972. 29.50 (ISBN 0-521-08447-4). Cambridge U Pr.

Kaler, James B., jt. auth. see Wyatt, Stanley P.

Kalewold, Alaka I. Traditional Ethiopian Church Education. LC 70-93506. pap. text ed. 4.00x (ISBN 0-8077-1597-2). Tchrs Coll.

Kaley, G. & Altura, B. M. Microcirculation, 3 vols. (Illus.). 1978. Vol. I. 52.50 (ISBN 0-8391-0966-0); Vol. II. 52.50 (ISBN 0-8391-0980-6); Vol. III. 65.00 (ISBN 0-8391-1592-X). Univ Park.

Kalia, Mamta. Tribute to Papa & Other Poems. 8.00 (ISBN 0-89253-691-8); flexible cloth 4.80 (ISBN 0-89253-692-6). Ind-US Inc.

Kalich, Robert. The Handicapper. Michelman, Herbert, ed. 384p. 1981. 12.95 (ISBN 0-517-54024-X). Crown.

Kalidasa. Cloud Messenger: Translated from the Sanskrit Meghaduta. bilingual ed. Edgerton, Franklin & Edgerton, Eleanor, trs. (Sanskrit & Eng.). 1964. pap. 1.75 o.p. (ISBN 0-472-06087-2, 87, AA). U of Mich Pr.

--The Dynasty of Raghu. Antoine, Robert, tr. from Sanskrit. (Writers Workshop Saffronbird Book Ser.). 217p. 1975. 15.00 (ISBN 0-88253-532-3); pap. text ed. 6.75 (ISBN 0-88253-531-5). Ind-US Inc.

Kalin, Berkeley & Robinson, Clayton, eds. Myths & Realities: Conflicting Values in America. (Mississippi Valley Collection Bulletin, No. 5). 78p. 1972. pap. 5.95x (ISBN 0-87870-081-1). Memphis St Univ.

Kalin, Everett R., tr. see Braun, Herbert.

Kalin, Everett R., tr. see Hengel, Martin.

Kalin, Harold. The Indian Killer. 1976. pap. 1.25 o.p. (ISBN 0-685-74569-4, LB425ZK, Leisure Bks). Nordon Pubns.

Kalin, Martin G. The Utopian Flight from Unhappiness: Freud Against Marx on Social Progress. LC 73-80500. 1974. 14.95 (ISBN 0-911012-65-6). Nelson-Hall.

Kalina, Judith S. Creating in Cloth. LC 76-16601. (Illus.). 1976. pap. 4.95 o.p. (ISBN 0-915684-09-8). Christian Herald.

Kalina, Sigmund. The House That Nature Built. LC 72-177323. (Illus.). 64p. (gr. 2-7). 1972. PLB 6.48 o.p. (ISBN 0-688-41353-6); PLB 6.48 (ISBN 0-688-51353-0). Lothrop.

Kalinich, David P. & Postill, Frederick J. Principles of County Jail Administration Management. 1981. write for info (ISBN 0-398-04140-7). C C Thomas.

Kalir, Joseph. Introduction to Judaism. LC 79-6758. 170p. 1980. text ed. 17.50 (ISBN 0-8191-0948-7); pap. text ed. 8.50 (ISBN 0-8191-0949-5). U Pr of Amer.

Kalis, Murray. Love in Paris. 224p. 1981. pap. 1.95 (ISBN 0-449-14382-1, GM). Fawcett.

Kalisch, Beatrice J. Child Abuse & Neglect: An Annotated Bibliography. LC 78-3123. (Contemporary Problems of Childhood: No. 2). 1978. lib. bdg. 29.95 (ISBN 0-313-20376-8, KBA/). Greenwood.

Kalish, Donald, et al. Logic: Techniques of Formal Reasoning. 2nd ed. 520p. 1980. text ed. 7.95 (ISBN 0-686-64982-6, HC). HarBraceJ.

Kalish, Harry I. From Behavioral Science to Behavior Modification. (Illus.). 448p. 1980. 19.95 (ISBN 0-07-033245-2). McGraw.

Kalish, Richard, jt. auth. see Dangott, Lilliam.

Kalish, Richard A. Death, Grief & Caring Relationships. LC 80-18938. 350p. 1980. text ed. 13.95 (ISBN 0-8185-0417-X). Brooks-Cole.

Kalish, Richard A. & Collier, Kenneth W. Exploring Human Values: Psychological & Philosophical Considerations. LC 80-21875. 1980. pap. text ed. 9.95 (ISBN 0-8185-0331-9). Brooks-Cole.

Kalish, Richard A., ed. Perspectives on Death & Dying, 3 vols. Incl. Vol. 1. Death & Dying: Views from Many Cultures (ISBN 0-89503-012-8); Vol. 2. Caring Relationships (ISBN 0-89503-010-1); Vol. 15. Death, Dying, Transcending (ISBN 0-89503-011-X). 160p. soft cover 17.95x o.p. (ISBN 0-686-68243-2). Baywood Pub.

Kalish, Ruth A., ed. Therapy in Eucational Environments for Handicapped Children. 500p. 1981. 17.95 (ISBN 0-8036-5207-0). Davis Co.

Kaliski, Andrea, ed. see Cohn, Marjorie B. & Siegfried, Susan L.

Kaliski, Andrea, ed. see Simpson, Marianna S.

Kalita, Dwight K., jt. auth. see Philpott, William H.

Kalita, Dwight K., jt. ed. see Williams, Roger J.

Kalkman, Marion & Davis, Anne. New Dimensions in Mental Health - Psychiatric Nursing. rev. ed. Orig. Title: Psychiatric Nursing. (Illus.). 704p. 1974. text ed. 14.95 o.p. (ISBN 0-07-033242-8, HP). McGraw.

Kall, P. & Prekopa, A., eds. Recent Results in Stochastic Programming: Proceedings. (Lecture Notes in Economics & Mathematical Systems: Vol. 179). (Illus.). 256p. 1980. pap. 19.00 (ISBN 0-387-10013-X). Springer-Verlag.

Kallab, Valeriana, jt. ed. see Erb, Guy F.

Kallab, Valeriana, jt. ed. see Goulet, Denis.

Kalland, Arne. Shingu: A Japanese Fishing Community. (Scandanavian Institute of Asian Studies Monograph: No. 44). (Orig.). 1980. pap. text ed. 12.50x (ISBN 0-7007-0136-2). Humanities.

Kallberg, Sture. Off the Middle Way: Report from a Swedish Village. Gibbs, Angela, tr. LC 77-139709. 1972. 28.50x (ISBN 0-394-46853-8). Irvington.

Kallen. The Tanglewood Murder. 1980. 9.95 (ISBN 0-686-62898-5, 61018, Wyndham). S&S.

Kallen, Horace M. Cultural Pluralism & the American Idea: An Essay in Social Philosophy. LC 56-11801. 1956. 9.00x o.p. (ISBN 0-8122-7030-4). U of Pa Pr.

Kallen, Horace M., jt. auth. see Dewey, John.

Kallen, Lucille. Introducing C. B. Greenfield. LC 80-25043. 363p. Repr. of 1979 ed. large print ed. 11.95 (ISBN 0-89621-260-2). Thorndike Pr.

--The Tanglewood Murder. LC 80-25148. 325p. 1980. Repr. of 1980 ed. print ed. 10.95large (ISBN 0-89621-257-2). Thorndike Pr.

Kallenberg, Lawrence. Modeling in Wax for Jewelry & Sculpture. LC 80-70384. (Illus.). 288p. 1981. 18.50 (ISBN 0-686-69521-6); text ed. 18.50 (ISBN 0-686-69522-4). Chilton.

Kallfelz, J. M. & Karam, R. A., eds. Advanced Reactors: Physics, Design, & Economics: Proceedings, International Conference, Atlanta, Georgia, Sept. 1974. LC 75-4642. 864p. 1975. text ed. 46.00 (ISBN 0-08-019610-1). Pergamon.

Kallich, Martin, et al, eds. Book of the Sonnet: Poems & Criticism. LC 72-125263. 214p. 1972. text ed. 18.95x (ISBN 0-8290-0156-5); pap. text ed. 9.95x (ISBN 0-8290-0157-3). Irvington.

--Oedipus: Myth & Drama. LC 67-18744. 1968. pap. 7.95 (ISBN 0-672-63076-1). Odyssey Pr.

Kallman, Chester. Absent & Present. LC 63-8859. (Wesleyan Poetry Program: Vol. 17). (Orig.). 1963. 10.00x (ISBN 0-8195-2017-9, Pub. by Wesleyan U Pr); pap. 4.95x (ISBN 0-8195-1017-3). Columbia U Pr.

Kallman, Chester, jt. auth. see Auden, W. H.

Kallmann, Helmut, et al, eds. Encyclopedia of Music in Canada. 1504p. 1981. 45.00 (ISBN 0-8020-5509-5). U of Toronto Pr.

Kalman. Drug Assay. 2nd ed. 1981. price not set. Masson Pub.

Kalman, Bela. The World of Names: A Study in Hungarian Onomatology. LC 79-300962. 1978. 15.00x (ISBN 963-05-1399-4). Intl Pubns Serv.

Kalman, Bernard, jt. auth. see Anton, Howard.

Kalman, Sumner M. & Clark, Dennis R. Drug Assay: The Strategy of Therapeutic Drug Monitoring. LC 79-63201. 210p. 1979. 22.50 (ISBN 0-89352-053-5). Masson Pub.

Kalman, T. I., ed. see Medicinal Chemistry Symposium, 20th, New York, May 1979.

Kalman, Yvonne. Summer Rain. (Orig.). pap. 2.50 (ISBN 0-515-05702-9). Jove Pubns.

Kalmanson, Kenneth & Kenschaft, Patricia C. Calculus: A Practical Approach. 2nd ed. LC 77-81756. (Illus.). xiv, 335p. 1978. text ed. 16.95x (ISBN 0-87901-083-5). Worth.

--Mathematics: A Practical Approach. LC 77-81755. (Illus.). 1978. text ed. 18.95x (ISBN 0-87901-085-1). Worth.

Kalmus, Hans. Diagnosis & Genetics of Defective Color Vision. 1965. 25.00 (ISBN 0-08-011119-X). Pergamon.

Kalnay, Francis. It Happened in Chichipica. LC 74-158004. (Illus.). 127p. (gr. 4-6). 1971. 4.95 o.p. (ISBN 0-15-239340-4, HJ). HarBraceJ.

Kalnins, Mara, ed. D. H. Lawrence: Apocalypse & Other Writings on Revelation. (The Cambridge Edition of the Letters & Works of D. H. Lawrence Ser.). 200p. 1980. 27.50 (ISBN 0-521-22407-1); pap. cancelled (ISBN 0-521-29478-9). Cambridge U Pr.

Kalogerakis, Michael G., ed. The Emotionally Troubled Adolescent & the Family Physician. 144p. 1973. 11.50 (ISBN 0-398-02844-3). C C Thomas.

Kalokerinos, Archie. Every Second Child. LC 80-84435. 138p. 1981. pap. 2.95 (ISBN 0-87983-250-9). Keats.

Kalpakgian, Mitchell. The Marvellous in Fielding's Novels. LC 80-1411. 243p. 1981. lib. bdg. 18.75 (ISBN 0-8191-1505-3); pap. text ed. 9.75 (ISBN 0-8191-1506-1). U Pr of Amer.

Kalpakjian, S. & Jain, S. C., eds. Metalworking Lubrication. 259p. 1980. 40.00 (H00159). ASME.

Kals, William S. Practical Navigation. LC 72-76175. 312p. 1972. 9.95 o.p. (ISBN 0-385-00246-7). Doubleday.

Kalsbeek, L. Contours of a Christian Philosophy. 1975. 12.50x (ISBN 0-88906-000-2). Wedge Pub.

Kalshoven, Frits, et al, eds. Essays on the Development of the International Legal Order: In Memory of Haro F. van Panhuys. 240p. 1980. 50.00x (ISBN 90-286-0360-3). Sijthoff & Noordhoff.

Kalstersky, J., et al, eds. see Symposium on Aerobic Gram-Negative Bronchopneumonias, Brussels, Sep. 22, 1978.

Kalstone, David. Five Temperaments: Elizabeth Bishop, Robert Lowell, James Merrill, Adrienne Rich, John Ashbery. LC 76-42655. 1977. 13.95 (ISBN 0-19-502260-2). Oxford U Pr.

Kalt, Joseph P., jt. auth. see Arrow, Kenneth J.

Kalt, Nathan. Introduction to the Hospitality Industry. LC 71-142505. 1971. text ed. 13.50 (ISBN 0-672-96086-9); tchr's manual 5.90 (ISBN 0-672-96088-5); wkbk. 6.50 (ISBN 0-672-96087-7). Bobbs.

--Legal Aspects of Hotel, Motel, & Restaurant Operation. 1st ed. LC 78-142504. 1971. 19.95 (ISBN 0-672-96089-3); tchrs' manual 6.67 (ISBN 0-672-96091-5); wkbk. 9.95 (ISBN 0-672-96090-7). Bobbs.

Kalt, Neil C. & Zalkind, Sheldon S., eds. Urban Problems: Psychological Inquiries. (Illus.). 464p. 1976. text ed. 14.95x (ISBN 0-19-502056-1); pap. text ed. 9.95x (ISBN 0-19-502059-6). Oxford U Pr.

Kaltenbach, G. E. Dictionary of Pronunciation of Artists' Names. 2nd ed. 74p. 1935. pap. text ed. 0.75 (ISBN 0-86559-000-1). Art Inst Chi.

Kaltenecker, H., jt. auth. see Isermann, R.

Kalter, Joanmarie. Actors on Acting. LC 79-65062. (Illus.). 1981. pap. 7.95 (ISBN 0-8069-8976-9). Sterling.

--Actors on Acting: Performing in Theatre & Film Today. LC 79-65062. (Illus.). 1979. 12.95 (ISBN 0-8069-7026-X); lib. bdg. 11.69 (ISBN 0-8069-7027-8). Sterling.

Kalter, S. S. The Use of Nonhuman Primates in Cardiovascular Diseases. LC 79-91725. (Illus.). 476p. 1980. text ed. 35.00x (ISBN 0-292-78510-0). U of Tex Pr.

Kalthoff, Robert J. & Lee, Leonard S. Productivity & Records Automation. (Illus.). 400p. 1981. text ed. 24.95 (ISBN 0-13-725234-X). P-H.

Kaltsournis, T. Teaching Social Studies in the Elementary School: The Basics for Citizenship. 1979. 17.95 (ISBN 0-13-895631-6). P-H.

Kaluger. Profiles in Human Development. LC 75-37505. (Illus.). 320p. 1976. pap. 8.50 (ISBN 0-8016-2607-2). Mosby.

Kaluger, George & Kaluger, Merieum F. Human Development: The Span of Life. 2nd ed. LC 78-12022. (Illus.). 1979. 17.95 (ISBN 0-8016-2610-2). Mosby.

Kaluger, George & Kolson, Clifford. Reading & Learning Disabilities. 2nd ed. (Special Education Ser.). 1978. text ed. 18.50 (ISBN 0-675-08524-1). Merrill.

Kaluger, George, jt. auth. see Kolson, Clifford J.
Kaluger, Merieum F., jt. auth. see Kaluger, George.
Kalupahana, David J. Buddhist Philosophy: A Historical Analysis. LC 75-20040. 224p. 1976. text ed. 10.00x o.p. (ISBN 0-8248-0360-4, Eastwest Ctr); pap. 3.95x (ISBN 0-8248-0392-2). U Pr of Hawaii.
Kaluznin, Lev & Poschel, Reinhard. Funktionen und Relationenalgebren. (Mathematische Reihe: No. 67). (Illus., Ger.). 1979. Repr. 42.00 (ISBN 3-7643-1038-3). Birkhauser.
Kaluzny, Arnold D. & Veney, James E. Health Organizations: Research & Assessment of Health Services. LC 78-71810. (Health Care Ser.). 1979. 23.50 (ISBN 0-8211-1017-9); text ed. 21.00 ten or more copies (ISBN 0-685-63682-8). McCutchan.
Kaluzny, Arnold D., jt. auth. see Smith, David B.
Kaluzny, Eugene L. Pharmacy Law Digest: 1980-1981 Edition. rev. ed. LC 72-115322. 1980. loose-leaf 34.95 (ISBN 0-915712-10-5). Douglas-McKay.
Kalvaboer, Alexander. A Neurobehavioral Study in Preschool Children. (Clinics in Developmental Medicine Ser.: Vol. 54). 1975. 21.00 (ISBN 0-685-59120-4). Lippincott.
Kalven, H., Jr. & Clark, R.intro. by. Contempt: Transcript of the Contempt Citations, Sentences & Responses of the Chicago Conspiracy 10. LC 70-120687. 254p. (Orig.). 1970. 10.00 o.p. (ISBN 0-8040-0056-5); pap. 5.95 (ISBN 0-8040-0057-3). Swallow.
Kalven, Harry, Jr., jt. auth. see Blum, Walter J.
Kalvoda, Josef. Czechoslovakia's Role in Soviet Strategy. LC 77-18499. 1978. pap. text ed. 12.25x (ISBN 0-8191-0413-2). U Pr of Amer.
Kalvoda, Robert. Operational Amplifiers in Chemical Instrumentation. LC 75-8866. (Ser. in Analytical Chemistry). 1975. 29.95 (ISBN 0-470-45566-7). Halsted Pr.
Kalwies, Howard. Hugues Salel: His Life & Works. Parent, David J., ed. LC 79-27150. (Applied Literature Press Medieval Studies: Vol. 4). 286p. 1979. 22.00 (ISBN 0-8357-0500-5, IS-00104, Pub by Applied Lit Pr). Univ Microfilms.
Kalyanam, N. P. Common Insects of India. 1967. pap. 4.50x (ISBN 0-210-27166-3). Asia.
Kalyanaraman, A. Aryatarangini: The Saga of the Indo-Aryans, Vol. 2. 1970. 20.00x (ISBN 0-210-22305-7). Asia.
Kam, James Vander see Vander Kam, James.
Kamada, Annelise. Banner Red & Gold. 1980. pap. 2.75 (ISBN 0-446-95082-3). Warner Bks.
--A Love So Bold. (Orig.). 1978. pap. 2.50 o.s.i. (ISBN 0-446-81638-8). Warner Bks.
Kamara, Marjon V. & Plano, Jack C. United Nations Capital Development Fund: Poor & Rich Worlds in Collision. 1974. 5.00 (ISBN 0-932826-14-8). New Issues MI.
Kamarck, Lawrence. Informed Sources. Date not set. pap. 2.25 (ISBN 0-440-13750-0). Dell.
Kamath, P. M. Executive Privilege Vs. Democratic Accountability: The Special Assistant to the President for National Security Affairs, 1961-1969. 485p. 1980. text ed. 33.75x (ISBN 0-391-02173-7). Humanities.
Kambanis, M. L. Notes Sur le Classement Chronologique Des Monnaies D'athenes (Series Avec Noms De Magistrats) (Illus., Fr.). pap. 5.00 (ISBN 0-916710-78-5). Obol Intl.
Kambayashi, Yahiko. Database: A Bibliography of the Nineteen Seventy's, Vol. I. 1980. text ed. price not set o.p. (ISBN 0-914894-64-1). Computer Sci.
Kambe, H. & Garn, Paul D., eds. Thermal Analysis: Comparative Studies in Materials. LC 74-11511. 326p. 1975. 24.95 (ISBN 0-470-45567-5). Halsted Pr.
Kamei, Marlene. Stone Lantern Essays: Services for the Collapse of the Living Room Carpet. LC 79-91969. (Illus.). 75p. (Orig.). 1980. pap. 4.95 (ISBN 0-935684-02-6). Plumbers Ink.
Kamei, Marlene, ed. see Arreola, Allysia J.
Kamei, Marlene, ed. see Gomes, Teresa M.
Kamen, Martin D. Isotopic Tracers in Biology: An Introduction to Tracer Methodology. 3rd ed. (Organic & Biological Chemistry, Vol. 1). 1957. 40.50 (ISBN 0-12-394862-2). Acad Pr.
--Primary Processes in Photosynthesis. (Advanced Biochemistry Ser). (Orig.). 1964. pap. 10.00 (ISBN 0-12-394856-8). Acad Pr.
Kamenetez, Herman L. The Wheelchair Book: Mobility for the Disabled. (Illus.). 288p. 1969. pap. 18.75 photocopy ed., spiral (ISBN 0-398-00965-1). C C Thomas.
Kamenetsky, Ihor. Nationalism and Human Rights: Processes of Modernization in the USSR. LC 77-1257. (Series in Issues Studies (Ussr & East Europe): No. 1). 1977. lib. bdg. 18.50x (ISBN 0-87287-143-6). Libs Unl.
Kamenev, E. N., jt. auth. see Ravich, M. G.
Kamenka, Eugene. The Ethical Foundations of Marxism. rev. ed. 1972. 22.00x (ISBN 0-7100-7360-7). Routledge & Kegan.
Kamenka, Eugene & Krygier, Martin, eds. Bureaucracy: The Career of a Concept. 1979. 19.95x (ISBN 0-312-10803-6). St Martin.
Kamerman, Sheila B. Maternal & Parental Benefits & Leaves: An International Review. LC 80-69763. (Impact on Policy Monograph Ser.: No. 1). (Illus.). 80p. (Orig.). 1980. pap. text ed. 5.00 (ISBN 0-938436-00-7). Columbia U Ctr Soc Sci.
--Parenting in an Unresponsive Society: Managing Work & Family Life. LC 80-641. 1980. 15.95 (ISBN 0-02-916730-2). Free Pr.
Kamerman, Sheila B. & Kahn, Alfred J. Child Care, Family Benefits & Working Parents. (Illus.). 352p. 1981. text ed. 25.00x (ISBN 0-231-05170-0). Columbia U Pr.
Kamerman, Sheila B. & Kahn, Alfred J., eds. Family Policy. 1978. 27.50x (ISBN 0-231-04464-X); pap. 12.50x (ISBN 0-231-04465-8). Columbia U Pr.
Kamerman, Sylvia E., ed. Fifty Plays for Holidays. (gr. 3-6). 1975. Repr. 9.95 (ISBN 0-8238-0033-4). Plays.
Kameron, G., jt. auth. see Campbell, J. H.
Kamerschen, David R. & Vredeveld, George. Economics. (Cliffs Course Outlines Ser.). (Illus.). 186p. 1975. pap. text ed. 4.95 (ISBN 0-8220-1500-5). Cliffs.
Kames, Henry H. Essays on the Principles of Morality & Natural Religion. Wellek, Rene, ed. LC 75-11227. (British Philosophers & Theologians of the 17th & 18th Centuries: Vol. 29). 1976. Repr. of 1751 ed. lib. bdg. 42.00 (ISBN 0-8240-1781-1). Garland Pub.
Kamil, A. Abd-Al-Qadir. Islam & the Race Question. (Race Question & Modern Thought). (Orig.). 1970. pap. 2.50 (ISBN 92-3-100833-1, U342, UNESCO). Unipub.
Kamil, Jill. The Ancient Egyptians: How They Lived & Worked. 1977. 11.95 (ISBN 0-8023-1267-5). Dufour.
--Sakkara: A Guide to the Necropolis of Sakkara & the Site of Memphis. LC 77-27546. (Illus.). 1978. pap. text ed. 7.50x (ISBN 0-582-78069-1). Longman.
Kamin, Ira. Kid's Guide. Leonard, Jan, ed. LC 80-66586. (Savvy San Francisco Ser.). 64p. (Orig.). 1980. pap. 2.50 (ISBN 0-89395-046-7). Cal Living Bks.
Kaminska, I. My Life, My Theater. 1973. 12.95 o.s.i. (ISBN 0-02-560490-2). Macmillan.
Kaminska, Ruth T. I Don't Want to Be Brave Anymore. LC 78-17417. (Illus.). 1978. 10.95 o.p. (ISBN 0-915220-42-3). New Republic.
Kaminski, Gerald. Dominance Signals. LC 80-12997. 200p. Date not set. pap. price not set (ISBN 0-914974-25-4). Holmgangers. Postponed.
--Good Questions. (Illus.). 32p. (Orig.). (gr. k-3). 1980. pap. 3.75 (ISBN 0-931896-00-2). Cove View.
Kaminsky, A. R., jt. auth. see Kaminsky, J.
Kaminsky, Alice R. Chaucer's "Troilus & Criseyde" & the Critics. LC 79-27535. xiv, 245p. 1980. 15.00x (ISBN 0-8214-0428-8, 0428E). Ohio U Pr.
Kaminsky, Alice R., ed. see Lewes, George H.
Kaminsky, Daniel, et al. Microbiology. 3rd ed. (Nursing Examination Review Book: Vol. 7). 1974. spiral bdg. 6.00 (ISBN 0-87488-507-8). Med Exam.
Kaminsky, F. C., jt. auth. see Coleman, J. R.
Kaminsky, Howard. A History of the Hussite Revolution. 1967. 28.50x (ISBN 0-520-00625-9). U of Cal Pr.
Kaminsky, J. & Kaminsky, A. R. Logic: A Philosophical Introduction. 1974. 14.95 (ISBN 0-201-03576-6). A-W.
Kaminsky, Max & Hughes, V. E. Jazz Band: My Life in Jazz. (Da Capo Quality Paperbacks Ser.). (Illus.). 242p. 1981. pap. 6.95 (ISBN 0-306-80135-3). Da Capo.
Kaminsky, Stuart. Bullet for a Star. 1978. pap. 1.50 o.s.i. (ISBN 0-515-04625-6). Jove Pubns.
--Bullet for a Star. LC 76-62776. 144p. 1977. 7.95 o.p. (ISBN 0-312-10797-8). St Martin.
--Murder on the Yellow Brick Road. LC 77-15825. 1978. 7.95 o.p. (ISBN 0-312-55318-8). St Martin.
Kamisar, Yale. Police Interrogation & Confessions: Essays in Law & Policy. 1980. 17.50x (ISBN 0-472-09318-5). U of Mich Pr.
Kamisar, Yale, et al. Basic Criminal Procedure, Cases, Comments & Questions. 5th ed. LC 52-52950. (American Casebook Ser.). 920p. 1980. pap. text ed. 13.95 (ISBN 0-8299-2109-5). West Pub.
--Modern Criminal Procedure: Cases, Comments & Questions. 5th ed. LC 80-36680. (American Casebook Ser.). 1813p. 1980. text ed. 25.95 (ISBN 0-8299-2101-X). West Pub.
Kamiya, Joe, et al, eds. Biofeedback & Self-Control 1976-1977: An Aldine Annual on the Regulation of Bodily Processes & Consciousness. new ed. LC 77-81650. 1977. 34.95x (ISBN 0-202-25127-6). Aldine Pub.
Kamiya, N. Protoplasmic Streaming. (Protoplasmatologia: Vol. 8, Pt. 3a). (Illus.). 1959. pap. 57.90 o.p. (ISBN 0-387-80524-9). Springer-Verlag.
Kamke, Erich. Differentialgleichungen: Loesungsmethoden und Loesungen, Vol. 2: Partielle Differentialgleichungen Erster Ordnung Fuer eine Gesuchte Funktion. LC 49-5862. 243p. 1974. Repr. of 1967 ed. text ed. 11.95 (ISBN 0-8284-0277-9). Chelsea Pub.
--Differentialgleichungen, Vol. 1: Loesungsmethoden und Loesungen. LC 49-5862. (Ger). text ed. 24.95 (ISBN 0-8284-0044-X). Chelsea Pub.
Kamli, Constance & DeVries, Rheta. Physical Knowledge in Preschool Education: Implications of Piaget's Theory. (Illus.). 1978. ref. ed. 15.95 (ISBN 0-13-669804-2). P-H.
Kamm, Ernest, et al. Juvenile Law & Procedure in California. 2nd ed. (California Handbook Ser). 1971. pap. text ed. 7.95x (ISBN 0-02-474690-8, 47469). Macmillan.
Kamm, Josephine. Explorers into Africa. LC 72-116440. (Illus.). (gr. 7-10). 1970. 8.95 (ISBN 0-02-749380-6, CCPr). Macmillan.
--Indicative Past: A Hundred Years of the Girls' Public Day School Trust. 1971. text ed. 12.50x o.p. (ISBN 0-04-373002-7). Allen Unwin.
Kamman, Madeleine. The Making of a Cook. LC 75-162974. 1978. pap. 8.95 (ISBN 0-689-70559-X, 238). Atheneum.
Kammann, Richard, jt. auth. see Marks, David.
Kammen, Michael. Colonial New York: A History. (Illus.). 1978. pap. 6.95 (ISBN 0-527-18725-9, Pub. by Two Continents). Hippocrene Bks.
--Deputyes & Libertyes: The Origins of Representative Government in Colonial America. 1969. 6.95 o.p. (ISBN 0-394-42207-4). Knopf.
--People of Paradox: An Inquiry Concerning the Orignis of American Civilization. (Illus.). 368p. 1980. pap. 5.95 (ISBN 0-19-502803-1, GB 616). Oxford U Pr.
Kammer, Jerry. The Second Long Walk: The Navajo-Hopi Land Dispute. 1980. 14.95 (ISBN 0-8263-0549-0). U of NM Pr.
Kammer, Reinhard, ed. Zen & Confucius in the Art of Swordsmanship(the Tengu-Geijutsu-Ron of Chozan Shissai) Fitzgerald, Betty, tr. (Illus.). 1978. cased 16.00 (ISBN 0-7100-8737-3). Routledge & Kegan.
Kammerman, Mark. Sensory Isolation & Personality Change. (Illus.). 324p. 1977. 17.50 (ISBN 0-398-03581-4). C C Thomas.
Kammermeyer, K. see Weissberger, A.
Kammert, James L. International Commercial Banking Management. 336p. 1981. 19.95 (ISBN 0-8144-5680-4). Am Mgmt.
Kammeyer, Kenneth. Confronting the Issues: Sex Roles, Marriage & the Family. 2nd ed. 372p. 1980. pap. text ed. 10.45 (ISBN 0-205-06996-7, 816996-9). Allyn.
Kammeyer, Kenneth C. Confronting the Issues: Sex Roles, Marriage & the Family. 1975. pap. text ed. 7.95x o.p. (ISBN 0-205-04813-7, 8148139). Allyn.
Kamoroff, Bernard. Small Time Operator: How to Start Your Own Small Business, Keep Your Books, Pay Your Taxes, & Stay Out of Trouble. rev. ed. LC 76-29817. (Illus.). 192p. 1980. pap. 7.95 (ISBN 0-917510-00-3). Bell Springs Pub.
Kamp, Garth S. Van Der see Van Der Kamp, Garth S.
Kamp, Peter Van De see Van De Kamp, Peter.
Kampe, Livia. How to Learn Spanish the Easy Way. LC 79-6769. 192p. 1980. pap. text ed. 9.00 (ISBN 0-8191-0950-9). U Pr of Amer.
Kampen, Irene. Fear Without Childbirth. LC 77-19272. 1978. 8.95 o.p. (ISBN 0-397-01277-2). Lippincott.
Kampf, Avram. Contemporary Synagogue Art: Developments in the United States, 1945-1965. LC 65-25292. (Illus.). 1976. 15.00 o.p. (ISBN 0-8074-0085-8, 382630). UAHC.
Kampf, Louis & Lauter, Paul, eds. Politics of Literature: Dissenting Essays in the Teaching of English. 1972. 24.50x (ISBN 0-8290-0039-9). Irvington.
Kampine, John P., jt. auth. see Smith, James L.
Kampmann, Lothar. Creating with Puppets. Date not set. 9.95 (ISBN 0-8238-0248-5). Plays. Postponed.
--Picture Printing. 1970. 19.95 (ISBN 0-7134-2280-7, Pub. by Batsford England). David & Charles.
Kamrany, Nake, ed. The New Economics of the Less Developed Countries: Changing Perceptions in the North-South Dialogue. LC 77-14602. (Westview Special Studies in Social Political, & Economic Development Ser.). 1978. lib. bdg. 28.50x (ISBN 0-89158-449-8). Westview.
Kamrass, Murray, jt. ed. see Brounstein, Sidney H.
Kamshad, Hassan. Modern Persian Prose Literature. 1966. 48.00 (ISBN 0-521-05464-8). Cambridge U Pr.
--Modern Persian Prose Reader. LC 68-22663. (Persian). 1968. text ed. 48.00 (ISBN 0-521-07077-5). Cambridge U Pr.
Kan, Johnny & Leong, Charles L. Eight Immortal Flavors. rev. & expanded ed. Dahan, Bonnie, ed. LC 79-53192. 256p. 1980. 10.95 (ISBN 0-89395-032-7); pap. 6.95 (ISBN 0-89395-060-2). Cal Living Bks.
Kanable, Ann. Raising Rabbits. LC 77-23926. 1977. 8.95 (ISBN 0-87857-183-3); pap. 5.95 (ISBN 0-87857-314-3). Rodale Pr Inc.
Kanafani, Ghassan. Men in the Sun. Kilpatrik, Hilary, tr. from Arabic. 1978. 8.00 (ISBN 0-89410-021-1); pap. 5.00 (ISBN 0-89410-022-X). Three Continents.
Kanam, N. H., tr. Business Laws of Saudi Arabia. 500p. 1980. Set. 198.00x (ISBN 0-686-64698-3, Pub. by Graham & Trotman England); Vol. 1. (ISBN 0-86010-222-X); Vol. 2. (ISBN 0-86010-223-8). State Mutual Bk.
Kanazawa, Masakata, ed. see Holborne, Anthony.
Kanchi, M. B. Matrix Methods of Structural Analysis. LC 80-18442. 432p. 1981. 17.95 (ISBN 0-470-26945-6). Halsted Pr.
Kandel, Abraham & Lee, Samuel C. Fuzzy Switching & Automata: Theory & Applications. LC 76-29148. (Computer Systems Engineering Ser.). 1979. 34.50x (ISBN 0-8448-1020-7). Crane-Russak Co.
Kandel, Denise B., ed. Longitudinal Research in Drug Use: Empirical Findings & Methodological Issues. 1978. 22.50 (ISBN 0-470-26287-7). Halsted Pr.
Kandel, Eric R. Behavioral Biology of Aplysia. LC 78-18226. (Psychology Ser.). (Illus.). 1979. text ed. 48.00x (ISBN 0-7167-0021-2); pap. text ed. 24.95 (ISBN 0-7167-1070-6). W H Freeman.
--Cellular Basis of Behavior: An Introduction to Behavioral Neurobiology. LC 76-8277. (Psychology Ser.). (Illus.). 1976. text ed. 56.00x (ISBN 0-7167-0523-0); pap. text ed. 27.95x (ISBN 0-7167-0522-2). W H Freeman.
Kandel, Michael, ed. see Lem, Stanislaw.
Kandel, Michael, tr. see Lem, Stanislaw.
Kandel, Robert S. Earth & Cosmos. (Illus.). 1980. 35.00 (ISBN 0-08-025016-5); pap. 16.75 (ISBN 0-08-023086-5). Pergamon.
Kandias, Kostis. Revelations One: Noah's Flood Was a Result of Nuclear War. (Illus.). 256p. 1981. 10.00 (ISBN 0-682-49672-3). Exposition.
Kandinsky, Wassily. Concerning the Spiritual in Art. Sadler, M. T., tr. & intro. by. LC 76-23973. 160p. 1977. pap. text ed. 2.25 (ISBN 0-486-23411-8). Dover.
--Point & Line to Plane. LC 79-50616. (Illus.). 1979. pap. text ed. 3.50 (ISBN 0-486-23808-3). Dover.
--Sounds. Napier, Elizabeth R., tr. from Ger. LC 80-6211. (Illus.). 144p. 30.00 (ISBN 0-300-02510-6); pap. 11.95 (ISBN 0-300-02664-1). Yale U Pr.
Kando, Thomas. Sex Change: The Achievement of Gender Identity by Feminized Transsexuals. 172p. 1973. 10.75 (ISBN 0-398-02731-5). C C Thomas.
--Social Interaction. LC 76-26614. (Illus.). 1977. pap. text ed. 10.50 (ISBN 0-8016-2614-5). Mosby.
Kando, Thomas M. Leisure & Popular Culture in Transition. 2nd ed. LC 79-26032. (Illus.). 1980. text ed. 15.95 (ISBN 0-8016-2618-8). Mosby.
Kane, Basil, jt. auth. see Chinaglia, Giorgio.
Kane, C. Ambiguous Adventure. 1969. pap. 1.25 o.s.i. (ISBN 0-02-052410-2, Collier). Macmillan.
Kane, Elizabeth W. Twelve Mormon Homes. (Utah, the Mormons, & the West: No. 4). 1974. 12.00 (ISBN 0-87480-162-1, Tanner). U of Utah Pr.
Kane, G. Stanley. Anselm's Doctrine of Freedom & The Will. (Texts & Studies in Religion, Vol. 10). 1981. soft cover 24.95x (ISBN 0-88946-914-8). E Mellen.
Kane, George. Piers Plowman: The Evidence for Authorship. 1965. text ed. 23.50x (ISBN 0-485-11073-3, Athlone Pr). Humanities.
Kane, George & Donaldson, E. Talbot, eds. Piers Plowman: The B Version. (Piers Plowman: The Three Versions Ser). 681p. 1975. text ed. 72.50x (ISBN 0-485-13502-7, Athlone Pr). Humanities.
Kane, Gerry. The CRT Controller Handbook. 250p. (Orig.). 1980. pap. 6.99 (ISBN 0-931988-45-4). Osborne-McGraw.
Kane, Harnett. The Gallant Mrs. Stonewall. 320p. 1976. Repr. of 1957 ed. lib. bdg. 14.95x (ISBN 0-89244-075-9). Queens Hse.
Kane, Harnett T. Young Mark Twain & the Mississippi. (Landmark Ser.: No. 113). (Illus.). (gr. 4-6). 1966. PLB 4.39 o.p. (ISBN 0-394-90413-3, BYR). Random.

Kane, Harry, illus. Alfred Hitchcock & the Three Investigators, 4 bks. Incl. The Mystery of the Fiery Eye. Arthur, Robert. LC 77-28860; The Mystery of the Moaning Cave. Arden, William. LC 77-28731; The Mystery of the Silver Spider. Arthur, Robert. LC 77-19355; The Secret of Terror Castle. Arthur, Robert. LC 77-29129. (gr. 4-7). 1978. Boxed Set. pap. 6.00 (ISBN 0-394-84005-4, BYR). Random.

Kane, J. E., ed. Movement Studies & Physical Education: A Handbook for Teachers. 1978. 18.00 (ISBN 0-7100-8775-6); pap. 9.95 (ISBN 0-7100-8684-9). Routledge & Kegan.

--Psychological Aspects of Physical Education & Sport. 248p. 1975. pap. 7.75 (ISBN 0-7100-8299-1). Routledge & Kegan.

Kane, J. Herbert. The Christian World Mission: Today & Tomorrow. 240p. 1981. 9.95 (ISBN 0-8010-5426-5). Baker Bk.

--The Making of a Missionary. 160p. 1975. pap. 4.45 (ISBN 0-8010-5358-7). Baker Bk.

--Understanding Christian Missions. 10.95 (ISBN 0-8010-5344-7). Baker Bk.

Kane, Jack. Buzzard Bait. 192p. (YA) 1975. 5.95 (ISBN 0-685-54482-6, Avalon). Bouregy.

Kane, Jason, jt. auth. see Taylor, Charles G.

Kane, Jerry. The Eighty Eighty-Nine I-O Processor Handbook. 200p. (Orig.). 1980. pap. 6.99 (ISBN 0-931988-39-X). Osborne-McGraw.

Kane, Jerry, jt. auth. see Osborne, Adam.

Kane, Joanne E., ed. see Atwood, Beth, et al.

Kane, Joanne E., ed. see Mongillo, John F., et al.

Kane, John F. Pluralism & Truth in Religion. Dietrich, Wendell, ed. LC 80-20659. (American Academy of Religion Dissertation Ser.). 1981. write for info. (ISBN 0-89130-413-4); pap. write for info. (ISBN 0-89130-414-2). Scholars Pr CA.

Kane, Joseph A. Development Banking. LC 74-25071. 1975. 22.50 (ISBN 0-669-97402-1). Lexington Bks.

Kane, Joseph M. Facts About the Presidents. 4th ed. 1981. write for info. (ISBN 0-8242-0013-6). Wilson.

Kane, Joseph N. The American Counties. 3rd ed. LC 70-186010. 1972. 20.50 (ISBN 0-8108-0502-2). Scarecrow.

--Facts About the Presidents. 3rd ed. 1974. 15.00 o.p. (ISBN 0-8242-0538-3). Wilson.

Kane, Joseph N. & Alexander, Gerard L. Nicknames & Sobriquets of U. S. Cities, States, & Counties. 3rd ed. LC 79-20193. 445p. 1979. 19.00 (ISBN 0-8108-1255-X). Scarecrow.

Kane, Joseph N., ed. Famous First Facts. 4th ed. 1981. write for info. Wilson.

Kane, Joseph W. & Sternheim, Morton M. Physics, SI Version. LC 80-17205. 680p. 1980. text ed. 24.95 (ISBN 0-471-08036-5). Wiley.

Kane, Kay & Gold, Louise. Discover Denver: A Pennywise Survival Handbook. (Illus.). 184p. (Orig.). 1980. pap. 5.95 (ISBN 0-9604430-0-2). Gold-Kane Ent.

Kane, Lawrence, et al. Die Laughing. LC 79-7498. (Illus.). 1980. pap. 4.95 (ISBN 0-385-15071-7, Dolp). Doubleday.

Kane, Les A., ed. Process Control & Optimization Handbook. (Illus.). 160p. (Orig.). 1980. pap. 15.95 (ISBN 0-87201-144-5). Gulf Pub.

Kane, Lucile M. & Johnson, Kathryn A.compiled by. Manuscripts Collections of the Minnesota Historical Society, Guide No. 2. LC 35-27911. 212p. 1955. pap. 3.75 (ISBN 0-87351-011-9). Minn Hist.

Kane, Patricia E., jt. auth. see Battison, Edward A.

Kane, Robert J. The Industrial Resources of Ireland. 456p. Date not set. Repr. of 1845 ed. 31.00x (ISBN 0-686-28342-2, Pub. by Irish Academic Pr). Biblio Dist.

Kane, Robert L., et al. Geriatrics in the United States: Manpower Projections & Training Considerations. LC 80-8840. (Illus.). write for info. (ISBN 0-669-04386-9). Lexington Bks.

Kane, Robert M. & Vose, Allen D. Air Transportation. 7th ed. (Illus.). 1979. perfect bdg. 11.95 (ISBN 0-8403-2037-X). Kendall Hunt.

Kane, Robert S. Africa A to Z. LC 75-175386. 408p. 1972. 9.95 o.p. (ISBN 0-385-02679-X). Doubleday.

--Italy A to Z: A Grand Tour of the Classic Cities. LC 76-16247. 1977. 7.95 o.p. (ISBN 0-385-11623-3). Doubleday.

--London A to Z. LC 73-9035. pap. 3.95 (ISBN 0-385-08649-0, Dolp). Doubleday.

--Paris A to Z. LC 73-9036. 216p. 1974. 6.95 (ISBN 0-385-08650-4); pap. 3.95 Softbound (ISBN 0-385-08635-0). Doubleday.

Kane, Rosalyn & Wistreich, George. Biology for Survival: Text & Readings. LC 73-7358. (Illus.). 480p. 1974. pap. text ed. 8.95x (ISBN 0-02-475270-3). Macmillan.

Kane, Sharon, illus. Counting Rhymes. (Illus.). 24p. (ps-4). 1960. PLB 4.57 o.p. (ISBN 0-307-60361-X, Golden Pr). Western Pub.

Kane, T. Gregory. Consumers & the Regulators. 123p. 1980. pap. text ed. 10.95x (ISBN 0-920380-60-3, Pub. by Inst Res Pub Canada). Renouf.

Kane, Thomas A. Happy Are You Who Affirm. (Illus.). 144p. 1980. pap. 5.00 (ISBN 0-89571-010-2). Affirmation.

--The Healing Touch of Affirmation. LC 76-151154. 1976. 4.95 o.p. (ISBN 0-89571-001-3); pap. 2.95. Affirmation.

Kane, Thomas T., jt. auth. see Haupt, Arthur.

Kane, Wanden M. What Am I Doing Here? Dotson, Marlice, tr. (Illus.). 122p. (Orig.). 1979. pap. 4.50 (ISBN 0-910584-54-0). Filter.

Kane, William J., ed. see Murphy, Herta & Peck, Charles.

Kaneko, Akitomo. Olympic Gymnastics. LC 76-1171. (Illus.). 256p. 1980. pap. 7.95 (ISBN 0-8069-8926-2). Sterling.

Kaneko, J. J. & Cornelius, C. E., eds. Clinical Biochemistry of Domestic Animals, Vols. 1 & 2. 2nd ed. 1970. Set. 84.00 (ISBN 0-685-02413-X); Vol. 1. 52.50 (ISBN 0-12-396301-X); Vol. 2. 50.50 (ISBN 0-12-396302-8). Acad Pr.

Kaneko, Jiro J., ed. Clinical Biochemistry of Domestic Animals. 3rd ed. LC 79-8873. 1980. 60.00 (ISBN 0-12-396350-8). Acad Pr.

Kaneko, Takeo, et al, eds. Synthetic Production & Utilization of Amino Acids. LC 74-9924. 312p. 1974. 32.95 (ISBN 0-470-45590-X). Halsted Pr.

Kaner, N., tr. see Emanuel, N. M. & Evseenko, D. S.

Kaner, N., tr. see Ginzburg, S. I., et al.

Kaner, N., tr. see Kiselev, A. V. & Lygin, V. I.

Kaner, N., tr. see Kurtsin, I. T.

Kaner, N., tr. see Myasoedov, B. I., et al.

Kaner, N., tr. see Ravich, M. G. & Kamenev, E. N.

Kaner, N., tr. see Rogovin, Z. A.

Kaner, N., tr. see Vinogradov, A. P. & Udintsev, G. B.

Kanet, Roger E. Behavioral Revolution & Communist Studies: Applications of Behaviorally-Oriented Political Research on the Soviet Union & Eastern Europe. LC 73-116810. 1971. 10.95 o.s.i. (ISBN 0-02-916990-9). Free Pr.

--Soviet & East European Foreign Policy: A Bibliography of English- & Russian-Language Publications, 1967-1971. LC 74-76444. 208p. 1974. text ed. 9.95 (ISBN 0-87436-137-0). ABC-Clio.

Kanet, Roger E. & Simon, Maurice D. Background to Crisis: Policy & Politics in Gierek's Poland. (Westview Replica Edition). 1980. lib. bdg. 27.50x (ISBN 0-89158-393-9). Westview.

Kanetzke, Howard W. Airplanes & Balloons. LC 77-27532. (Read About Science Ser.). (Illus.). (gr. k-3). 1978. PLB 9.95 (ISBN 0-8393-0090-5). Raintree Child.

--Story of Cars. LC 77-27533. (Read About Science Ser.). (Illus.). (gr. k-3). 1978. PLB 9.95 (ISBN 0-8393-0086-7). Raintree Child.

--Trains & Railroads. LC 77-27599. (Read About Science Ser.). (Illus.). (gr. k-3). 1978. PLB 9.95 (ISBN 0-8393-0087-5). Raintree Child.

Kanfer, F. H. & Goldstein, A. P. Helping People Change. 1976. 18.50 o.p. (ISBN 0-08-018272-0); pap. 10.45 o.p. (ISBN 0-08-018271-2). Pergamon.

Kanfer, Frederick H. & Goldstein, Arnold P., eds. Helping People Change: A Textbook of Methods. 2nd ed. LC 79-17929. 560p. 1980. 39.50 (ISBN 0-08-025098-X); pap. 13.95 (ISBN 0-08-025097-1). Pergamon.

Kanfer, Frederick H., jt. ed. see Karoly, Paul.

Kanfer, Stefan. The Eighth Sin. 1979. pap. 2.50 o.p. (ISBN 0-425-04263-4). Berkley Pub.

Kangilaski, Jaan. Hands of Glory. 272p. (Orig.). 1981. pap. 2.25 (ISBN 0-345-28489-5, Del Rey). Ballantine.

--The Seeking Sword. 352p. (Orig.). 1981. pap. 2.25 (ISBN 0-345-29073-9, Del Rey). Ballantine.

Kang-I Sun Chang. The Evolution of Chinese Tz'u Poetry: From Late T'ang to Northern Sung. LC 79-3195. (Illus.). 1980. 17.50x (ISBN 0-691-06425-3). Princeton U Pr.

Kangro, Hans. Early History of Planck's Radiation Law. LC 76-40534. 1976. 39.50x (ISBN 0-8448-1029-0). Crane-Russak Co.

Kaniel, Michael. Judaism. (Illus.). 1979. 14.95 (ISBN 0-7137-0972-3, Pub by Blandford Pr England). Sterling.

Kaniki, M. H., ed. Tanzania Under Colonial Rule. (Illus.). 408p. 1980. pap. text ed. 9.95 (ISBN 0-582-64649-9). Longman.

Kanin, David B. A Political History of the Olympic Games. (Replica Edition Ser.). 160p. 1981. lib. bdg. 17.00x (ISBN 0-86531-109-9). Westview.

Kanin, Ruth. Write the Story of Your Life. 1981. 12.95 (ISBN 0-8015-3871-8, Hawthorn). Dutton.

Kanitkar, Helen & Kanitkar, Hemant. Asoka & Indian Civilization. Yapp, Malcolm, et al, eds. (World History Ser.). (Illus.). 32p. (gr. 10). 1980. Repr. lib. bdg. 5.95 (ISBN 0-89908-035-9); pap. text ed. 1.95 (ISBN 0-89908-010-3). Greenhaven.

Kanitkar, Hemant, jt. auth. see Kanitkar, Helen.

Kanizsa, Gaetano. Organization in Vision: Essays on Gestalt Perception. LC 79-11857. (Praeger Special Studies Ser.). 288p. 1979. 29.95 (ISBN 0-03-049071-5). Praeger.

Kann, Eduard A. The History of China's Internal Loan Issues: Shanghai, 1934. Bd. with China's Currency Reform, 1941. Lin Yu Shen. LC 78-74317. (The Modern Chinese Economy Ser.: Vol. 26). 288p. 1980. lib. bdg. 33.00 (ISBN 0-8240-4274-3). Garland Pub.

Kann, R. A., et al, eds. The Hapsburg Empire in World War I. (Monographs: No. 23). 1977. text ed. 14.00x o.p. (ISBN 0-914710-16-8, Dist. by Columbia U Pr). East Eur Quarterly.

Kann, Robert A. A History of the Habsburg Empire, 1526-1918. LC 72-97733. 1974. 36.50x (ISBN 0-520-02408-7). U of Cal Pr.

--A History of the Hapsburg Empire, 1526-1918. 2nd ed. 662p. 1981. pap. 10.95x (ISBN 0-520-04206-9, CAMPUS 265). U of Cal Pr.

--The Problem of Restoration: A Study in Comparative Political History. 1967. 28.50x (ISBN 0-520-00630-5). U of Cal Pr.

Kannan, Lakshmi. Impressions. flexible cloth 4.00 (ISBN 0-89253-504-0). Ind-US Inc.

Kannan, Narisimhan P. Energy, Economic Growth, & Equity in the U. S. LC 78-31204. (Praeger Special Studies). 1979. 23.95 (ISBN 0-03-046616-4). Praeger.

Kannenberg, Gary D. From Birth to Twelve: How to Be a Successful Parent to Infants & Children. LC 80-69331. 125p. 1981. 7.95 (ISBN 0-86548-043-5). Century Twenty One.

Kannenstine, Louis F. The Art of Djuna Barnes: Duality & Damnation. LC 76-55152. 1977. 12.00x (ISBN 0-8147-4564-4); pap. 5.00x (ISBN 0-8147-4565-2). NYU Pr.

Kanner, L. A History of the Care & Study of the Mentally Retarded. (Illus.). 160p. 1974. pap. 7.50 (ISBN 0-398-03038-3). C C Thomas.

Kanner, Leo. Child Psychiatry. 4th ed. (Illus.). 768p. 1979. 22.75 (ISBN 0-398-02199-6). C C Thomas.

--In Defense of Mothers: How to Bring up Children in Spite of the More Zealous Psychologists. (Illus.). 176p. 1962. pap. 16.75 photocopy ed., spiral (ISBN 0-398-00968-6). C C Thomas.

Kanno, C. K. & Glasscote, R. M. Private Psychiatric Hospitals - a National Survey. 1966. pap. 3.00 o.p. (ISBN 0-685-24855-0, 162). Am Psychiatric.

Kanno, C. K. & Scheidemandel, P. L. Psychiatric Treatment in the Community. 1974. 4.00 (ISBN 0-685-65572-5, 207). Am Psychiatric.

Kanno, C. K., jt. auth. see Glasscote, R. M.

Kanno, Charles & Scheidemandel, Patricia L. The Mentally Ill Offender: A Survey of Treatment Programs. 76p. 1969. pap. 3.00 (ISBN 0-685-24860-7, P244-0). Am Psychiatric.

Kanno, Charles K. & Scheidemandel, Patricia L. Salary Ranges of Personnel Employed in State Mental Hospitals & Community Mental Health Centers-1970. pap. 5.00 (ISBN 0-685-24871-2, P156-0). Am Psychiatric.

Kano, Chiaki. Origins of the Chavin Culture. LC 79-89241. (Studies in Pre-Columbian Art & Archaeology: No. 22). (Illus.). 87p. 1979. pap. 5.00 (ISBN 0-88402-092-4, Ctr Pre-Columbian). Dumbarton Oaks.

Kano, K., ed. see International Convocation on Immunology, 7th, Niagra Falls, N. Y., July 1980, et al.

Kano, Kanaan. Physical & Solid State Electronics. LC 77-145408. 1972. text ed. 22.95 (ISBN 0-201-03580-4). A-W.

Kanof, Abram. Jewish Ceremonial Art & Religious Observance. 32.50 (ISBN 0-8109-0178-1); pap. 12.50 (ISBN 0-8109-2215-0). Abrams.

Kanok-Nukulchai, Worsak, ed. see International Conference Held in Bangkok, Jan. 7-9, 1980 & Karasudhi, Pisidhi.

Kanovitz, Jacqueline R., jt. auth. see Klotter, John C.

Kanowitz, Leo. Sex Roles in Law & Society: Cases & Materials. LC 72-94656. 720p. 1973. 20.00x o.p. (ISBN 0-8263-0254-8); pap. 9.95x (ISBN 0-8263-0326-9). U of NM Pr.

Kansas City Star Staff. William Rockhill Nelson: A Story of a Man, a Newspaper, & a City. (American Newspapermen 1790-1933 Ser.). (Illus.). 274p. 1974. Repr. of 1915 ed. 17.50x o.s.i. (ISBN 0-8464-0017-0). Beekman Pubs.

Kansas State University, College of Home Economics, Dept. of Foods & Nutrition. Practical Cookery: A Compilation of Principles of Cookery & Recipes. 24th ed. LC 20-21946. 304p. 1975. text ed. 15.50 (ISBN 0-471-45641-1). Wiley.

Kansky, Karel J. Urbanization Under Socialism: The Case of Czechslovakia. LC 75-44934. (Special Studies). (Illus.). 350p. 1976. text ed. 32.50 (ISBN 0-275-56770-2). Praeger.

Kansler, Connie, jt. ed. see Green, Lawrence.

Kant, Immanuel. Critique of Practical Reason. Beck, Lewis W., tr. LC 56-2993. 1956. pap. 4.95 (ISBN 0-672-60223-7, LLA52). Bobbs.

--Critique of Practical Reason & Other Writings in Moral Philosophy. Beck, Lewis W., tr. LC 75-32038. (The Philosophy of Immanuel Kant Ser.: Vol. 1). 1977. Repr. of 1949 ed. lib. bdg. 35.00 (ISBN 0-8240-2325-0). Garland Pub.

--Critique of Pure Reason. pap. 3.95 (ISBN 0-385-07534-0, A551, Anch). Doubleday.

--Foundations of the Metaphysics of Morals. Beck, Lewis W., tr. Bd. with What Is Enlightenment. LC 59-11679. 1959. pap. 3.50 (ISBN 0-672-60312-8, LLA113). Bobbs.

--Foundations of the Metaphysics of Morals: Text & Critical Essays. Wolff, Robert P., ed. LC 68-9841. (Text & Critical Essays Ser.). 1969. pap. 6.95 (ISBN 0-672-61114-7, TC1). Bobbs.

--Fundamental Principles of the Metaphysics of Morals. Abbott, Thomas K., tr. 1949. pap. 2.95 (ISBN 0-672-60177-X, LLA16). Bobbs.

--Grounding for the Metaphysics of Morals. Ellington, James W., tr. from Ger. (HPC Philosophical Classics Ser.). 125p. 1981. lib. bdg. 12.50 (ISBN 0-915145-01-4); pap. text ed. 2.75 (ISBN 0-915145-00-6). Hackett Pub.

--Lectures on Philosophical Theology. Wood, Allen W. & Clark, Gertrude M., trs. LC 78-58034. 1978. 15.00 (ISBN 0-8014-1199-8). Cornell U Pr.

--Logic. Hartman, Robert S. & Schwarz, Wolfgang, trs. LC 72-10560. (LLA Ser). 279p. 1974. 5.50 o.p. (ISBN 0-672-61228-3). Bobbs.

--Metaphysical Elements of Justice: Part I of the Metaphysics of Morals. Ladd, John, tr. (Orig.). 1965. pap. 4.95 (ISBN 0-672-60250-4, LLA72). Bobbs.

--On History. Beck, Lewis W., ed. Beck, L. W., et al, trs. LC 62-22315. (Orig.). 1963. pap. 5.95 (ISBN 0-672-51070-7); pap. 3.95 (ISBN 0-672-60387-X, LLA162). Bobbs.

--On the Old Saw: That May Be Right in Theory but It Won't Work in Practice. Ashton, E. B., tr. from Ger. LC 73-83291. (Works in Continental Philosophy Ser.). 1974. 8.00x (ISBN 0-8122-7677-9); pap. 3.95x (ISBN 0-8122-1058-1, Pa Paperbks). U of Pa Pr.

--Perpetual Peace. Beck, Lewis W., tr. LC 57-3588. 1957. pap. 2.50 (ISBN 0-672-60227-X, LLA54). Bobbs.

--Prolegomena to Any Future Metaphysics. rev. ed. LC 51-10279. 1950. pap. 3.95 (ISBN 0-672-60187-7, LLA27). Bobbs.

Kantar, Edwin B. & Stanley, Jackson. Gamesman Bridge: Play Better with Kantar. (Illus.). 1972. 5.95 o.p. (ISBN 0-87140-543-1). Liveright.

Kantenwein, Louise. Henri & the Crocodile. (Illus.). 32p. (gr. 7 up). 1981. 5.00 (ISBN 0-682-49732-0). Exposition.

--Welcome Home, Charlie. (Illus.). 64p. 1981. 5.00 (ISBN 0-682-49681-2). Exposition.

Kanter, Muriel. Clinical Chemistry. LC 75-4050. (Allied Health Ser). 1975. pap. 8.35 (ISBN 0-672-61380-8). Bobbs.

Kanter, Rosabeth Moss, jt. ed. see Millman, Marcia.

Kanter, Shamai. Rabban Gamaliel II: The Legal Traditions. LC 80-12229. (Brown Judaic Studies: No. 8). 15.00x (ISBN 0-89130-403-7, 14 00 08); pap. 10.50x (ISBN 0-89130-404-5). Scholars Pr CA.

Kantor, Harvey A., jt. auth. see Klein, Maury.

Kantor, Mackinlay. The Children Sing. 1977. pap. 1.75 (ISBN 0-505-51108-8). Tower Bks.

--Gentle Annie. (Western Fiction Ser.). 1980. lib. bdg. 10.95 (ISBN 0-8398-2688-5). Gregg.

--Hamilton County. LC 70-101724. (Illus.). 1970. 9.95 o.s.i. (ISBN 0-02-560660-3). Macmillan.

--Valley Forge. 1976. pap. 1.95 o.p. (ISBN 0-345-25270-5). Ballantine.

--The Voice of Bugle Ann & the Daughter of Bugle Ann. 192p. 1980. pap. 1.95 (ISBN 0-515-05458-5). Jove Pubns.

Kantor, MacKinley. Andersonville. 1971. pap. 2.95 (ISBN 0-451-09279-1, E9279, Sig). NAL.

--Andersonville. LC 55-8257. 1955. 10.95 o.s.i. (ISBN 0-690-00329-3, TYC-T). T Y Crowell.

Kantor, Michael, jt. auth. see Earle, Olive L.

Kantor, Seth. The Ruby Cover Up. 1980. pap. 2.95 (ISBN 0-89083-680-9, Kable News Co). Zebra.

Kantorovich, L. V. & Akilov, G. P. Functional Analysis. 2nd ed. 800p. 1981. 100.00 (ISBN 0-08-023036-9); pap. 35.00 (ISBN 0-08-026486-7). Pergamon.

Kantorowicz, Ernest H. King's Two Bodies: A Study of Medieval Political Theology. 1957. 35.00x (ISBN 0-691-07120-9). Princeton U Pr.

Kantrowitz, Mildred. Good-Bye Kitchen. LC 76-174602. (gr. k-3). 1969. 5.95 o.s.i. (ISBN 0-8193-0542-1, Four Winds); PLB 5.41 o.s.i. (ISBN 0-8193-0543-X). Schol Bk Serv.
--Maxie. LC 80-15289. (Illus.). 36p. (ps-3). 1980. Repr. of 1970 ed. 8.95 (ISBN 0-590-07776-7, Four Winds). Schol Bk Serv.
--Willy Bear. LC 80-15295. (Illus.). 40p. (ps-1). 1980. Repr. of 1976 ed. 7.95 (ISBN 0-590-07781-3, Four Winds). Schol Bk Serv.
Kantrowitz, Nathan. Ethnic & Racial Segregation Patterns in the New York City Metropolis: Residential Patterns Among White Ethnic Groups, Blacks & Puerto Ricans. LC 72-86840. (Special Studies in U.S. Economic, Social & Political Issues). 1973. 29.50x (ISBN 0-275-06550-2). Irvington.
Kantzer, Kenneth. Evangelical Roots: A Tribute to Wilbur Smith. LC 77-17963. 1977. 8.95 o.p. (ISBN 0-8407-5120-6). Nelson.
Kanunga, R. N., jt. auth. see Dutta, S.
Kanya-Forstner, A. S., jt. auth. see Andrew, Christopher M.
Kanzaki, Noritake. Teapots. LC 78-71255. (Form & Function Ser.: Vol. 5). (Illus.). 80p. (Orig.). 1981. pap. 8.95 (ISBN 0-87011-392-5). Kodansha.
Kao, C. K. Optical Fiber Technology II. 304p. 1980. 24.00 (ISBN 0-471-09169-3, Pub. by Wiley-Interscience); pap. 15.75 (ISBN 0-471-09171-5). Wiley.
Kao, Charles H. Brain Drain. 178p. 1980. 10.50x (ISBN 0-89955-157-2, Pub. by Mei Ya Pub Taiwan); pap. 5.95x (ISBN 0-89955-188-2). Intl Schol Bk Serv.
Kao, Frederick F. & Kao, John J., eds. Chinese Medicine: New Medicine. (Illus.). 1977. 9.95 (ISBN 0-88202-174-5). N Watson.
Kao, George, ed. Two Writers & the Cultural Revolution: Lao She & Chen Jo-hsi. (Renditions Ser.). 170p. 1980. 19.50 (ISBN 0-295-95747-6, Pub by Chinese Univ Hong Kong). U of Wash Pr.
Kao, John J., jt. ed. see Kao, Frederick F.
Kao, K. C. & Hwang, W. Electrical Transport in Solids. (International Series in the Science of the Solid State: Vol. 14). 1981. 120.00 (ISBN 0-08-023973-0). Pergamon.
Kapany, N. S. & Burke, J. J. Optical Waveguides. (Quantum Electronics Ser). 1972. 48.00 (ISBN 0-12-396760-0). Acad Pr.
Kapela, May. A Time to Fantasize. LC 80-69294. (Illus.). 102p. (Orig.). 1980. pap. 4.50x (ISBN 0-9603118-7-4). Davenport.
Kapelle, William E. The Norman Conquest of the North: The Region & Its Transformation, 1000-1135. LC 79-10200. 1980. 19.00x (ISBN 0-8078-1371-0). U of NC Pr.
Kapelner, Alan. All the Naked Heroes. LC 60-5611. 1960. 4.00 o.s.i. (ISBN 0-8076-0102-0). Braziller.
Kapenzi, Geoffrey Z. The Clash of Cultures: Christian Missionaries & the Shona of Rhodesia. LC 78-68799. 1979. pap. text ed. 7.50 (ISBN 0-8191-0704-2). U Pr of Amer.
Kapitza, P. L. Collected Papers of P. L. Kapitza, 2 vols. Ter Haar, D., ed. Vol. 1. 1965. 42.35 o.p. (ISBN 0-08-010744-3); Vol. 2. 1965. o.p. (ISBN 0-08-010973-X). Pergamon.
Kapitza, S. P. & Melekhin, V. N. The Microtron. Rowe, Ednor, ed. Sviatoslavsky, I. N., tr. (Accelerators & Storage Rings: Vol. 1). 222p. 1979. lib. bdg. 24.50 (ISBN 0-906346-01-0). Harwood Academic.
Kaplan, A. R. Fundamentals of Pipe Flow. LC 79-23924. 1980. 39.95 (ISBN 0-471-03375-8, Pub. by Wiley-Interscience). Wiley.
Kaplan, Abraham, ed. Individuality & the New Society. LC 72-103294. (Washington Paperback Ser.: No. 59). 190p. 1970. 9.50 (ISBN 0-295-95057-9); pap. 2.95 (ISBN 0-295-95140-0). U of Wash Pr.
Kaplan, Albert S., ed. The Herpesviruses. 1974. 51.00 (ISBN 0-12-397050-4). Acad Pr.
Kaplan, Alexandra G., ed. Psychological Androgyny: Further Considerations. LC 79-1647. 1979. 7.95 (ISBN 0-87705-418-5). Human Sci Pr.
Kaplan, Andrew. The Hour of the Assassins. (Orig.). 1980. pap. 2.75 o.s.i. (ISBN 0-440-13530-3). Dell.
Kaplan, Ann. Women in Film Noir. (BFI Ser.). 1979. pap. 5.75 o.p. (ISBN 0-85170-083-7). NY Zoetrope.
Kaplan, Arthur. Basketball: How to Improve Your Technique. LC 73-14538. (Career Concise Guide Ser.). (Illus.). 72p. 1974. PLB 4.90 o.p. (ISBN 0-531-02674-4). Watts.
Kaplan, Arthur G. Official Price Guide to Antique Jewelry. (Collector Ser.). (Illus.). 400p. 1980. pap. 9.95 (ISBN 0-87637-341-4, 341-04). Hse of Collectibles.
Kaplan, Aryeh. The Handbook of Jewish Thought. 307p. 12.95 (ISBN 0-686-27547-0). Maznaim.
Kaplan, Aryeh, intro. by. see Magriso, Yitzchak.
Kaplan, Aryeh, tr. The Book of Esther. 268p. 7.95 (ISBN 0-686-27543-8); pap. 5.95 (ISBN 0-686-27544-6). Maznaim.
Kaplan, Aryeh, tr. & intro. by. The Meh'Am Lo'ez Haggadah. 216p. pap. 4.95 Ashkenazic (ISBN 0-686-27546-2). Maznaim.
Kaplan, Aryeh, tr. The Passover Haggadah. 288p. Sephardic 10.95 (ISBN 0-686-27545-4). Maznaim.
Kaplan, Aryeh, tr. see Culi, Yaakov.
Kaplan, Barbara. Home Furnishings. LC 74-19485. 1975. pap. text ed. 9.50 (ISBN 0-672-96412-0); tchr's manual 5.00 (ISBN 0-672-96832-0). Bobbs.
--Preparation of the Normal Karyotype. LC 78-720409. (Illus.). 1979. 55.00 (ISBN 0-89189-057-2, 21-9-015-00); student ed. 9.00 (ISBN 0-89189-071-8, 21-9-015-20). Am Soc Clinical.
Kaplan, Bert L. & Seitz, Martin. The Practical Guide to Foster Family Care. 112p. 1980. lexotone 9.75 (ISBN 0-398-04033-8). C C Thomas.
Kaplan, Boche, jt. auth. see Abisch, Roz.
Kaplan, C. A. see Katsh, Abraham I.
Kaplan, Colin, ed. Rabies - The Facts. (Illus.). 1977. text ed. 11.95x (ISBN 0-19-264918-3). Oxford U Pr.
Kaplan, David & Manners, Robert. Culture Theory. 224p. 1972. pap. 6.95 ref. ed. (ISBN 0-13-195511-X). P-H.
Kaplan, David, jt. auth. see Dickneider, William C., Jr.
Kaplan, Don. Video in the Classroom: A Guide to Creative Television. LC 79-18797. 161p. (Orig.). 1980. pap. 17.95 professional (ISBN 0-914236-46-6). Knowledge Indus.
Kaplan, Donald & Billink, Alan. Diners of the Northeast. (Illus., Orig.). Date not set. pap. 7.95 (ISBN 0-690-01880-0). Lippincott. Postponed.
Kaplan, Dorothy. The Comprehensive Diabetic Cookbook. 1977. pap. 5.95 (ISBN 0-8119-0360-5). Fell.
Kaplan, Emanuel B. Functional & Surgical Anatomy of the Hand. 2nd ed. 1965. 20.00 o.p. (ISBN 0-397-50137-4). Lippincott.
Kaplan, F. M. & Sobin, J. M. Encyclopedia of China Today. 352p. 1979. 37.50x (ISBN 90-286-0439-1). Sijthoff & Noordhoff.
Kaplan, Fred. Dubious Specter: A Skeptical Look at the Soviet Nuclear Threat. rev. ed. LC 80-50894. 93p. 1980. pap. 4.95 (ISBN 0-89758-023-0). Inst Policy Stud.
Kaplan, Frederic M., jt. auth. see Dekeijzer, Arne J.
Kaplan, Fredric, jt. auth. see Keijzer, Arne J. de.
Kaplan, George W., jt. auth. see Belman, A. Barry.
Kaplan, H. J., tr. see Queneau, Raymond.
Kaplan, Harold. Power & Order: Henry Adams & the Naturalist Tradition in American Fiction. LC 80-23414. 1981. lib. bdg. price not set (ISBN 0-226-42424-3). U of Chicago Pr.
--Urban Political Systems: A Functional Analysis of Metro Toronto. LC 67-29577. 1967. 20.00x (ISBN 0-231-02982-9). Columbia U Pr.
--Urban Renewal Politics: Slum Clearance in Newark. LC 63-19076. 1963. 20.00x (ISBN 0-231-02667-6). Columbia U Pr.
Kaplan, Harold I. & Sadock, Benjamin J. Comprehensive Group Psychotherapy. 1971. 38.00 o.p. (ISBN 0-683-04518-0). Williams & Wilkins.
Kaplan, Harold I., jt. auth. see Freedman, Alfred M.
Kaplan, Harold M. Anatomy & Physiology of Speech: Laboratory Textbook. LC 80-82927. (Illus.). 180p. 1981. text ed. 21.50 (ISBN 0-932126-04-9); pap. text ed. 16.50 (ISBN 0-932126-05-7). Graceway.
Kaplan, Harriet, jt. auth. see Lloyd, Lyle L.
Kaplan, Helen S. The New Sex Therapy: Active Treatment of Sexual Dysfunctions. LC 73-87724. 1974. 20.00 (ISBN 0-87630-083-2, Dist. by Quadrangle). Brunner-Mazel.
Kaplan, Henry S. & Tsuchitani, Patricia J., eds. Cancer in China. LC 78-14486. (Illus.). 240p. 1978. 32.00x (ISBN 0-8451-0202-8). A R Liss.
Kaplan, Herbert H. Russia & the Outbreak of the Seven Years' War. 1968. 17.50x (ISBN 0-520-00623-2). U of Cal Pr.
Kaplan, Howard. The Damascus Cover. 1978. pap. 1.75 o.p. (ISBN 0-449-23412-6, Crest). Fawcett.
Kaplan, Howard B. Deviant Behavior in Defense of Self. LC 79-6795. 1980. 22.00 (ISBN 0-12-396850-X). Acad Pr.
Kaplan, Irving. Nuclear Physics. 2nd ed. 1962. 24.95 (ISBN 0-201-03602-9). A-W.
Kaplan, J. G. The Molecular Basis of Immune Cell Function. 780p. 1979. 70.75 (ISBN 0-444-80168-5, North Holland). Elsevier.
Kaplan, Jerome, ed. see International Association Of Gerontology - 5th Congress.
Kaplan, Joanna O. The Piaroa People of the Orinoco Basin: A Study in Kinship & Marriage. (Illus.). 256p. 1975. 37.50x (ISBN 0-19-823189-X). Oxford U Pr.
Kaplan, Johanna. Other People's Lives. 1975. 6.95 o.p. (ISBN 0-394-47174-1). Knopf.
Kaplan, John. Marijuana: The New Prohibition. LC 75-7614. (Apollo Eds.). 400p. 1975. pap. 3.95 o.s.i. (ISBN 0-8152-0381-0, A-381, TYC-T). T Y Crowell.
--The Trial of the Kaohsiung Defendants. (Research Papers & Policy Studies: No. 2). 100p. 1981. pap. price not set (ISBN 0-912966-35-1). IEAS Ctr Chinese Stud.
Kaplan, John, jt. auth. see Louisell, David W.
Kaplan, Justin D. Walt Whitman: A Life. (Illus.). 1980. 15.00 (ISBN 0-671-22542-1). S&S.
Kaplan, Justin E., ed. see Plato.
Kaplan, L. Colonies into Nation. 1972. 14.95 (ISBN 0-02-560570-4). Macmillan.
Kaplan, Lawrence J. & Kessler, Dennis. An Economic Analysis of Crime: Selected Readings. (Illus.). 432p. 1976. 24.50 (ISBN 0-398-03407-9); pap. 17.75 (ISBN 0-398-03408-7). C C Thomas.
Kaplan, Lawrence S. & Clawson, Robert W. NATO After Thirty Years. LC 80-53885. 250p. 1981. lib. bdg. 19.95 (ISBN 0-8420-2172-8). Scholarly Res Inc.
Kaplan, Lawrence S., jt. auth. see Heald, Morrell.
Kaplan, Lisa. The Good Sign Cookbook. LC 80-67482. (Illus.). 80p. 1980. pap. 3.50 (ISBN 0-937730-00-9). Good Sign.
Kaplan, M., jt. auth. see Hess, S.
Kaplan, M. L., et al. The Structural Approach in Psychological Testing. LC 70-93755. 1970. 21.00 (ISBN 0-08-006867-7). Pergamon.
Kaplan, Marshall, jt. auth. see Eichler, Edward P.
Kaplan, Marshall H. Modern Spacecraft Dynamics & Control. LC 76-14859. 1976. text ed. 29.95 (ISBN 0-471-45703-5). Wiley.
Kaplan, Martin, ed. The Monday Morning Imagination: Report from the Boyer Workshop on State University Systems. (Special Studies). 1977. text ed. 23.95 (ISBN 0-03-021481-5). Praeger.
Kaplan, Milton, jt. auth. see Hess, Stephen.
Kaplan, Morton. Macropolitics: Essays on the Philosophy & Science of Politics. LC 68-8153. 1968. 20.00x (ISBN 0-89197-833-X). Irvington.
Kaplan, Morton & Kloss, Robert. The Unspoken Motive: A Guide to Psychoanalytic Literary Criticism. LC 79-163609. 1973. 10.00 o.s.i. (ISBN 0-02-916950-X). Free Pr.
Kaplan, Morton A. Alienation & Identification. LC 76-8146. 1976. 14.95 (ISBN 0-02-916790-6). Free Pr.
--Justice, Human Nature, & Political Obligation. LC 76-8145. 1976. 16.95 (ISBN 0-02-916890-2). Free Pr.
--The Life and Death of the Cold War: Selected Studies in Postwar Statecraft. LC 76-20539. 1976. 19.95 (ISBN 0-88229-335-4); pap. 10.95 (ISBN 0-88229-500-4). Nelson-Hall.
Kaplan, Morton A. & Mushakoji, Kinhide. Japan, America, & the Future World Order. LC 76-15063. 1976. 15.95 (ISBN 0-02-916910-0). Free Pr.
Kaplan, Morton A., ed. Great Issues of International Politics. 2nd ed. LC 73-84931. 576p. 1974. text ed. 24.95x (ISBN 0-202-24139-4); pap. text ed. 13.95x (ISBN 0-202-24140-8). Aldine Pub.
--Isolation or Interdependence? LC 74-32547. 1975. 15.95 (ISBN 0-02-916940-2). Free Pr.
--The Many Faces of Communism. LC 77-99096. 1978. 19.95 (ISBN 0-02-917230-6). Free Pr.
Kaplan, Nathan O. & Kennedy, Eugene P., eds. Current Aspects of Biochemical Energetics. 1967. 48.00 (ISBN 0-12-397350-3). Acad Pr.
Kaplan, Paul E., et al. Physical Medicine & Rehabilitation Continuing Education Review. 2nd ed. 1980. pap. 13.00x (ISBN 0-87488-335-0). Med Exam.
Kaplan, Richard. Great Linebackers of the NFL. (NFL Punt, Pass & Kick Library: No. 12). (Illus.). (gr. 5-9). 1970. 2.50 o.p. (ISBN 0-394-80152-0, BYR); PLB 3.69 (ISBN 0-394-90152-5). Random.
Kaplan, Roberta, ed. see Wider Opportunities for Women, Inc.
Kaplan, S. A. & Pikelner, S. B. Interstellar Medium. LC 70-85076. (Illus.). 1970. 22.50x (ISBN 0-674-46075-8). Harvard U Pr.
Kaplan, S. A. & Tsytovich, V. N. Plasma Astrophysics. LC 73-5785. 316p. 1974. text ed. 72.00 (ISBN 0-08-017190-7). Pergamon.
Kaplan, S. J. & Kivy-Rosenberg, E. Ecology & the Quality of Life. (Illus.). 308p. 1973. 23.75 (ISBN 0-398-02828-1). C C Thomas.
Kaplan, Stanley H. & Peters, Max. Mathematics. Incl. Ninth Year (Elementary Algebra) LC 58-33441. 1977. pap. 3.50 (ISBN 0-8120-0196-6); Tenth Year. pap. 3.95 (ISBN 0-8120-0204-0); Eleventh Year. LC 57-58722. 1977. pap. 3.95 (ISBN 0-8120-0112-5). (Regents Exams & Answers Ser.). (gr. 9-12). 1977. Barron.
Kaplan, Stanley H., ed. see Walsh, Michael J.
Kaplan, Stephen S. Diplomacy of Power: Soviet Armed Forces As a Political Instrument. 600p. 1980. 29.95 (ISBN 0-8157-4824-8); pap. 14.95 (ISBN 0-8157-4823-X). Brookings.
Kaplan, Stephen S., jt. auth. see Blechman, Barry M. C.
Kaplan, Stuart R. Tarot Classic Gift Set. (Illus.). 256p. 1972. card deck incl. 14.00 (ISBN 0-913866-55-5). US Games Syst.
Kaplan, Wilfred. Advanced Calculus. 2nd ed. LC 77-184161. 1973. text ed. 23.95 (ISBN 0-201-03611-8). A-W.
--Advanced Mathematics for Engineers. LC 80-19492. (Mathematics Ser.). (Illus.). 960p. 1981. text ed. 22.95 (ISBN 0-201-03773-4). A-W.
--Elements of Differential Equations. 1964. 16.95 (ISBN 0-201-03632-0). A-W.
--Operational Methods for Linear Systems. 1962. 24.95 (ISBN 0-201-03620-7). A-W.
--Ordinary Differential Equations. 1958. 20.95 (ISBN 0-201-03630-4). A-W.
Kaplansky, Irving. Algebraic & Analytic Aspects of Operator Algebras. LC 74-145635. (CBMS Regional Comference Series in Mathematics: Vol. 1). 1980. Repr. of 1970 ed. 6.40 (ISBN 0-8218-1650-0, CBMS-1). Am Math.
--Linear Algebra & Geometry: A Second Course. LC 74-2393. xiv, 143p. 1974. Repr. of 1969 ed. text ed. 9.50 (ISBN 0-8284-0279-5). Chelsea Pub.
Kaplinsky, Raphael, ed. Readings on the Multinational Corporation in Kenya. 326p. 1978. text ed. 24.95x (ISBN 0-19-572446-1). Oxford U Pr.
Kaploun, Uri, tr. see Zevin, Schlomo Y.
Kaplow, Julian, ed. see Hansen, Terrence L., et al.
Kapoor, Ashok, ed. International Business in the Middle East: Case Studies. (Special Studies in International Economics & Business). 1979. lib. bdg. 20.00x (ISBN 0-89158-257-6). Westview.
Kapoor, V. C. Taxonomic Approach to Insecta. 1980. text ed. 20.00x (ISBN 0-7069-0796-5, Pub. by Vikas India). Advent Bk.
--Taxonomic Approach to Insects. 500p. 1980. 25.00x (Pub. by Croom Helm England). State Mutual Bk.
Kapp, Ardeth G. Miracles in Pinafores & Bluejeans. LC 77-4268. 81p. pap. 1.50 (ISBN 0-87747-741-8). Deseret Bk.
Kapp, Colin. The Chaos Weapon. (Del Rey Bks.). (Orig.). 1977. pap. 1.50 o.p. (ISBN 0-345-27115-7). Ballantine.
--The Survival Game. 192p. 1976. pap. 1.50 o.p. (ISBN 0-345-25192-X). Ballantine.
Kappeler, Susanne. Writing & Reading in Henry James. LC 80-18181. 242p. 1981. 22.50x (ISBN 0-231-05198-0). Columbia U Pr.
Kapstein, Israel J., jt. tr. see Braude, William G.
Kaptchuk, Ted. Web That Has No Weaver. (Illus.). 304p. 1981. 15.00 (ISBN 0-312-92932-3). St Martin.
Kaptchuk, Ted J. The Web That Has No Weaver: Understanding Chinese Medicine. (Illus.). 304p. 1981. 15.00 (ISBN 0-312-92932-3). Congdon & Lattes.
Kapungu, Leonard. Rhodesia: The Struggle for Freedom. LC 74-76966. 160p. 1974. 5.95x o.p. (ISBN 0-88344-435-6). Orbis Bks.
Kapur, Ashde. International Nuclear Proliferation: Multilateral Diplomacy & Regional Aspects. LC 78-19744. (Praeger Special Studies). 1979. 29.95 (ISBN 0-03-046316-5). Praeger.
Kapur, Ashok. India's Nuclear Option: Atomic Diplomacy & Decision Making. LC 75-23974. (Illus.). 280p. 1976. text ed. 29.95 (ISBN 0-275-56100-3). Praeger.
Kapur, Gopal K. IBM 360 Assembler Language Programming. LC 76-12572. 1971. 23.50 (ISBN 0-471-45840-6). Wiley.
Kapur, Harish. Soviet Union & the Emerging Nations: A Case Study of Soviet Policy Towards India. 120p. (Orig.). 1972. pap. text ed. 12.00x (ISBN 0-391-00240-6). Humanities.
Kapur, K. C. & Lamberson, L. K. Reliability in Engineering Design. LC 76-1304. 1977. text ed. 30.95 (ISBN 0-471-51191-9). Wiley.
Kapur, Vijay. Virginia Woolf's Vision of Life & Her Search for Significant Form: A Study in the Shaping Vision. 195p. 1980. text ed. 15.50x (ISBN 0-391-01753-5). Humanities.
Kaput, James J., jt. auth. see Fleming, Daniel J.
Kaputa, Catherine, tr. see Takeda, Tsuneo.
Kar, Bijayananda. The Theories of Error in Indian Philosophy: An Analytical Study. 1980. text ed. cancelled o.p. (ISBN 0-391-01731-4). Humanities.
Kar, Chintamoni. Classical Indian Sculpture. (Illus.). 112p. 1974. pap. 6.95 (ISBN 0-685-50124-8). Transatlantic.
Kara, Ashok. Psychology of Buddhism. Date not set. pap. price not set (ISBN 0-89389-062-6). Himalayan Intl Inst.
Karabatsos, James. A Word-Index to a Week on the Concord & Merrimack Rivers. LC 80-2510. 1981. Repr. of 1971 ed. 18.50 (ISBN 0-404-19058-8). AMS Pr.
Karacan, I., jt. auth. see Williams, R. L.
Karageorghis, Vassos. Cyprus. (Archaeologia Mundi Ser.). (Illus.). 272p. 1968. 29.50 o.p. (ISBN 0-88254-149-8). Hippocrene Bks.
Karahan, Patricia, ed. see Kleefeld, Carolyn M.

Karalova, Z. K., jt. auth. see Nemodruk, A. A.

Karam, M. Learning Arabic Thru Phrases, 4 vols. pap. text ed. 22.00x o.p. (ISBN 0-686-63575-2). Intl Bk Ctr.

Karam, N. H., tr. Banking Laws of Kuwait. 275p. 1979. 22.00x (ISBN 0-86010-139-8, Pub.by Graham & Trotman England). State Mutual Bk.

Karam, R. A., jt. ed. see Kallfelz, J. M.

Karam, R. A., et al, eds. Environmental Impact of Nuclear Power Plants. LC 75-23351. 1977. text ed. 54.00 (ISBN 0-08-019956-9). Pergamon.

Karamcheti, Krishnamurty. Principles of Ideal-Fluid Aerodynamics. LC 79-26876. 654p. 1980. Repr. of 1966 ed. lib. bdg. 32.50 (ISBN 0-89874-113-0). Krieger.

Karamzin, N. M. Selected Prose of N. M. Karamzin. Nebel, Henry M., Jr., tr. (Publications of 18th Cent. Russ. Lit. Ser). 1969. 10.95x o.s.i. (ISBN 0-8101-0021-5). Northwestern U Pr.

Karan, Pradyumna P. Bhutan: A Physical & Cultural Geography. LC 67-17842. (Illus.). 112p. 1967. 21.50x (ISBN 0-8131-1137-4). U Pr of Ky.

--The Changing Face of Tibet: The Impact of Chinese Communist Ideology on the Landscape. LC 74-18935. (Illus.). 128p. 1976. 22.50x (ISBN 0-8131-1318-0). U Pr of Ky.

Karanjia, R. K. The Mind of a Monarch. (Illus.). 1977. 18.95 o.p. (ISBN 0-04-923069-7). Allen Unwin.

Karapet'Yants, M. Khand & Karapet'Yants, M. L. Handbook of Thermodynamic Constants of Inorganic & Organic Compounds. LC 72-122509. 1968. 39.95 (ISBN 0-470-45850-X). Halsted Pr.

Karapet'Yants, M. L., jt. auth. see Karapet'Yants, M. Khand.

Karas, Alex & Gluck, Herb. Even Big Guys Cry. LC 77-71376. 1977. 8.95 o.p. (ISBN 0-03-017371-X). HR&W.

Karas, Nicholas, jt. auth. see Missildine, Fred.

Karas, Nick, jt. auth. see Missildine, Fred.

Karas, Phyllis. A Life Worth Living. 392p. 1981. 12.95 (ISBN 0-312-48503-4). St Martin.

Karasik. Centrafugal Pump Clinic. 488p. 1981. 39.50 (ISBN 0-8247-1016-9). Dekker.

Karasik, V. M., et al. Slurry Hydrotransport of Minerals & Tailings. Cooley, W. C., ed. Peabody, A. L., tr. from Rus. LC 79-67434. (Illus., Eng.). 1979. 60.00x o.p. (ISBN 0-918990-05-X). Terraspace.

Karasowski, Maurycy. Frederic Chopin: His Life & Letters. Hill, Emily, tr. Repr. of 1938 ed. lib. bdg. 32.50x (ISBN 0-8371-3968-6, KAFC). Greenwood.

Karasudhi, Pisidhi, jt. auth. see International Conference Held in Bangkok, Jan. 7-9, 1980.

Karasz, Mariska. Adventures in Stitches. LC 59-10899. (Funk & W Bk.). (Illus.). 128p. 1975. pap. 5.95 o.s.i. (ISBN 0-308-10177-4, F-118, TYC-T). T Y Crowell.

--Adventures in Stitches & More Adventures, Fewer Stitches. (Funk & W Bk.). (Illus.). (gr. 7 up). 1959. 9.95 o.s.i. (ISBN 0-308-70181-X, TYC-T); pap. 5.95 o.s.i. (ISBN 0-308-10177-4). T y Crowell.

Karch, Amy M. Cardiac Care: A Guide for Patient Education. (The Patient Education Series). 1981. pap. 11.50 (ISBN 0-8385-1041-8). ACC.

Karch, Pat. Fifty-One Paper Craft Projects. LC 79-91249. (Illus.). 64p. (Orig.). 1979. pap. 3.50 (ISBN 0-87239-391-7, 2139). Standard Pub.

Karcher, Carolyn L. Shadow Over the Promised Land: Slavery, Race, & Violence in Melville's America. LC 79-14861. 1980. text ed. 25.00x (ISBN 0-8071-0565-1); pap. 8.95x (ISBN 0-8071-0595-3). La State U Pr.

Karcioglu, Z. A. & Sarper, R. M. Zinc & Copper in Medicine. (Illus.). 696p. 1980. 59.75 (ISBN 0-398-03977-1). C C Thomas.

Karcz, George, ed. see Wadekin, Karl-Eugen.

Karcz, Jerzy F., ed. Soviet & East European Agriculture. (Russian & East European Studies). 1967. 28.50x (ISBN 0-520-00631-3). U of Cal Pr.

Kardiner, Abram, et al. Psychological Frontiers of Society. 1945-1963. pap. 8.00x (ISBN 0-231-08548-6). Columbia U Pr.

Kardon, Janet. Masks Tents Vessels Talismans. LC 79-92164. (Illus.). 1979. pap. 5.00 (ISBN 0-88454-053-7). U of Pa Contemp Art.

--Robert Zakanitch. (Illus.). 1980. pap. 10.00 (ISBN 0-88454-025-1). U of Pa Contemp Art.

Kardon, Randy H., jt. auth. see Kessel, Richard G.

Kardos, Istvan, ed. Scientists Face to Face. (Illus.). 400p. (Orig.). 1978. pap. 5.00x (ISBN 963-13-0373-X). Intl Pubns Serv.

Kardos, L. T., et al. Waste & Water Renovation & Conservation. (Penn State Studies: No. 23). (Illus.). 72p. 1967. pap. 3.95x o.p. (ISBN 0-271-00272-7). Pa Hist & Mus.

Kardos, Lajos, ed. Attitudes, Interaction & Personality. Dajka, B., et al, trs. (Illus.). 149p. 1980. 10.50x (ISBN 963-05-2088-5). Intl Pubns Serv.

Kardos, Lajos & Pleh, Csaba, eds. Problems of the Regulations of Activity. (Illus.). 733p. 1980. write for info. (ISBN 963-05-2447-3). Intl Pubns Serv.

Kare, Morley R., jt. ed. see Cagan, Robert H.

Kareken, John H. & Wallace, Neil, eds. Models of Monetary Economies. 313p. (Orig., Avail. only from Publisher). 1980. pap. 5.00 (ISBN 0-9603936-0-9). Fed Res Bank MN.

Karel, Leonard. Dried Flowers from Antiquity to the Present: A History & Practical Guide to Flower Drying. LC 72-10909. 1973. 10.00 (ISBN 0-8108-0512-X). Scarecrow.

--Dried Grasses, Grains, Gourds, Pods & Cones. LC 74-31178. (Illus.). 1975. 10.00 (ISBN 0-8108-0792-0). Scarecrow.

Karelitz, Samuel. When Your Child Is Ill. rev. ed. LC 69-16463. 1969. 7.95 o.p. (ISBN 0-394-45168-6). Random.

Karen, Robert, jt. auth. see Rosenblum, Ralph.

Karen, Ruth. Feathered Serpent: The Rise & Fall of the Aztecs. LC 78-22129. (Illus.). 192p. 1979. 9.95 (ISBN 0-590-07413-X, Four Winds). Schol Bk Serv.

--Land & People of Central America. rev. ed. LC 71-37744. (Portraits of the Nations Ser.). (Illus.). (gr. 7-9). 1972. 8.79 (ISBN 0-397-31553-8). Lippincott.

Karen Van, Der Zee see Van Der Zee, Karen.

Karg, Franz. Modern Cabinetmaking in Solid Wood: Design for Handmade Furniture with Construction Details & Photographs. new ed. (Illus.). 136p. 1980. 29.95 (ISBN 0-8038-1276-0). Hastings.

Karger, Barry L., et al. Introduction to Separation Science. LC 73-4016. 586p. 1973. 32.50 (ISBN 0-471-45860-0, Pub. by Wiley-Interscience). Wiley.

Karger, Delmar W. How to Choose a Career. LC 78-6294. (Career Concise Guides Ser.). (Illus.). (gr. 7 up). 1978. PLB 6.45 s&l (ISBN 0-531-02836-4). Watts.

Karger, Delmar W & Bayha, Franklin H. Engineered Work Measurement. 3rd ed. LC 77-2626. (Illus.). 1977. 27.50 (ISBN 0-8311-1118-6). Indus Pr.

Karger, Delmar W. & Murdick, Robert G. Managing Engineering & Research. 2nd ed. (Illus.). 1969. 20.00 o.p. (ISBN 0-8311-1063-5). Indus Pr.

--Managing Engineering & Research. 3rd ed. (Illus.). 1980. 29.50 (ISBN 0-8311-1125-9). Indus Pr.

Kargere, Audrey. Color & Personality. pap. 3.95 (ISBN 0-686-69317-5). Weiser.

Karhu, Clifton. Kyoto Rediscovered: A Portfolio of Woodblock Prints. (Illus.). 216p. 1981. 125.00 (ISBN 0-8348-1521-4). Weatherhill.

Kari, James M. Navajo Verb Prefix Phonology. LC 75-25117. (American Indian Linguistics Ser.). 1976. lib. bdg. 42.00 (ISBN 0-8240-1968-7). Garland Pub.

Kariel, Henry S. Beyond Liberalism. LC 76-48302. 160p. 1977. 8.00 (ISBN 0-88316-526-0). Chandler & Sharp.

Kariel, Herbert G. & Kariel, Patricia E. Explorations in Social Geography. LC 71-173959. 1972. text ed. 15.95 (ISBN 0-201-03634-7). A-W.

Kariel, Patricia E., jt. auth. see Kariel, Herbert G.

Karier, Clarence J., ed. Shaping the American Educational State: 1900 to the Present. LC 74-4647. (Urgent Issues in American Society Ser). (Illus.). 1975. 10.95 o.s.i. (ISBN 0-02-917040-0); pap. text ed. 7.95 (ISBN 0-02-917030-3). Free Pr.

Karim, S. M. The Prostaglandins: Progress in Research. 372p. 1972. 18.95 (ISBN 0-471-45863-5). Wiley.

Karis, Thomas, et al, eds. From Protest to Challenge - a Documentary History of African Politics in South Africa, 1882-1964: Challenge & Violence 1953-1964, Vol. 3. LC 72-152423. (Publications Ser.: No. 123). 825p. 1977. 22.50 (ISBN 0-8179-6231-X). Hoover Inst Pr.

Kark, Pieter, et al, eds. The Inherited Ataxias: Biochemical, Viral, & Pathological Studies. LC 77-92490. (Advances in Neurology Ser.: Vol. 21). 1978. 45.50 (ISBN 0-89004-268-3). Raven.

Kark, Sidney L. The Practice of Community-Oriented Primary Health Care. 288p. 1980. pap. 13.50x (ISBN 0-8385-7865-9). ACC.

Karkhanis, Sharad. Indian Politics & the Role of the Press. 224p. 1981. text ed. 20.00x (ISBN 0-7069-1278-0, Pub. by Vikas India). Advent Bk.

--Indian Politics & the Role of the Press. 200p. 1980. write for info. (Pub. by Vikas India). Asia Bk Corp.

Karki, Chandra B., tr. see Verma, Bhawati C.

Karkoschka, Erhard. Notation in New Music: A Critical Guide to Interpretation & Realisation. Koenig, Rush, tr. from Ger. LC 75-134522. Orig. Title: Das Schriftbild der Neuen Musik. 1972. 31.25 (ISBN 0-900938-28-5, 50-26902). Eur-Am Music.

Karl, F. R., jt. ed. see Hamalian, Leo.

Karl, Frederick. C. P. Snow: The Politics of Conscience. LC 63-8905. (Arcturus Books Paperbacks). 175p. 1965. pap. 1.65 (ISBN 0-8093-0161-X). S Ill U Pr.

Karl, Frederick & Hamalian, Leo, eds. Existential Imagination. pap. 1.95 o.p. (ISBN 0-449-30779-4, C779, Prem). Fawcett.

Karl, Frederick R., jt. auth. see Hamalian, Leo.

Karl, Frederick R. & Hamalian, Leo, eds. Naked I: Fictions for the Seventies. 1975. pap. 1.75 o.p. (ISBN 0-449-30757-3, X757, Prem). Fawcett.

Karl, Jean. But We Are Not of Earth. LC 80-21849. (gr. 4-7). 1981. PLB 9.95 (ISBN 0-525-27342-5). Dutton.

--From Childhood to Childhood: Children's Books & Their Creators. (John Day Bk.). 1970. 8.95 (ISBN 0-381-98131-2, A29160, TYC-T). T Y Crowell.

Karl, Jean E. Beloved Benjamin Is Waiting. (gr. 7-12). 1980. pap. 1.50 (ISBN 0-440-90836-1, LFL). Dell.

Karl, S. W. Firepower. (Orig.). 1979. pap. 2.25 (ISBN 0-532-23182-1). Manor Bks.

--The Wine Merchants. (Orig.). 1979. pap. 1.95 (ISBN 0-532-23271-2). Manor Bks.

Karle, jt. auth. see Hauptman.

Karlekar, Bhalchandra V. & Desmond, Robert M. Engineering Heat Transfer. (Illus., Orig.). 1977. text ed. 24.50 (ISBN 0-8299-0054-3); solutions manual avail. (ISBN 0-8299-0497-2). West Pub.

Karlen, Arno. Sexuality & Homosexuality: A New View. 1971. 15.00 o.p. (ISBN 0-393-01087-2). Norton.

Karlen, Delmar. Citizen in Court: Litigant, Witness, Juror, Judge. LC 73-19739. (American Constitutional & Legal History Ser.). 211p. 1974. Repr. of 1964 ed. lib. bdg. 22.50 (ISBN 0-306-70614-8). Da Capo.

--Civil Litigation. 1978. text ed. 17.00 (ISBN 0-672-82898-7, Bobbs-Merrill Law). Michie.

Karlen, Harvey M. The Patterns of American Government. 2nd ed. 1975. pap. text ed. 7.95x (ISBN 0-02-475320-3, 47532); tchrs' manual free (ISBN 0-02-475330-0). Macmillan.

Karlesky, Joseph J., jt. auth. see Smith, Bruce L.

Karlin, Isaac W., et al. Development & Disorders of Speech in Childhood. (American Lecture Speech & Hearing Ser). (Illus.). 324p. 1977. 17.75 (ISBN 0-398-00973-2). C C Thomas.

Karlin, Nurit. No Comment. LC 78-16725. (Encore Edition). (Illus.). 1978. 2.95 (ISBN 0-684-16561-9, ScribT). Scribner.

Karlin, Robert. Teaching Elementary Reading: Principles & Strategies. 488p. 1980. 16.95 (ISBN 0-686-64993-1, HC). HarBraceJ.

--Teaching Reading in High School: Improving Reading in Content Areas. 3rd ed. LC 76-48523. 1977. 16.95 (ISBN 0-672-61402-2). Bobbs.

Karlin, Samuel. A First Course in Stochastic Processes. 2nd ed. 1975. text ed. 22.95 (ISBN 0-12-398552-8). Acad Pr.

Karlin, Samuel & Taylor, Howard M. A Second Course in Stochastic Processes. LC 80-533. 1980. 35.00 (ISBN 0-12-398650-8). Acad Pr.

Karlin, Sol. A. Introduction to the Living World. 1974. pap. text ed. 10.95 (ISBN 0-917962-33-8); lab manual 4.50 (ISBN 0-917962-29-X). Peek Pubns.

Karliner, Joel & Gregoratos, Gabriel, eds. Coronary Care. 1000p. 1980. text ed. 50.00x (ISBN 0-443-08061-5). Churchill.

Karling, J. S. The Simple Biflagellate Holocarpic Phycomycetes. 2nd ed. (Illus.). 1981. lib. bdg. 60.00x. Lubrecht & Cramer.

Karlins, Marvin. The Human Use of Human Resources. 1st ed. (Illus.). 208p. (Orig.). 11.95 (ISBN 0-07-033298-3); pap. text ed. 6.95 (ISBN 0-07-033297-5). McGraw.

--The Other Way to Better Grades. 168p. (Orig.). 1981. pap. 4.95 (ISBN 0-449-90046-0, Columbine). Fawcett.

Karlins, Marvin & Andrews, Lewis M. Biofeedback: Turning on the Power of Your Mind. LC 79-39759. (YA) 1972. 8.95 (ISBN 0-397-00855-4). Lippincott.

Karlinsky, Simon. Marina Cvetaeva: Her Life & Art. 1966. 20.00x (ISBN 0-520-00632-1). U of Cal Pr.

--The Sexual Labyrinth of Nikolai Gogol. 1976. 15.00x (ISBN 0-674-80281-0). Harvard U Pr.

Karlinsky, Simon, ed. Letters of Anton Chekhov. Heim, Michael H., tr. from Rus. (Illus.). 512p. 1973. 20.00 o.s.i. (ISBN 0-06-012263-3, HarpT). Har-Row.

--The Nabokov-Wilson Letters Nineteen Forty to Nineteen Seventy-One. LC 78-69627. 1980. pap. 6.95 (ISBN 0-06-090753-3, CN 753, CN). Har-Row.

Karlinsky, Simon, ed. see Poplavskii, Boris I.

Karlinsky, Simon, ed. see Zlobin, Vladimir.

Karlinsky, Simon, tr. see Nabokov, Vladimir.

Karlovich, T. A. Notes on a Social Theory: Twenty Six Annotations Related to Political Economy. LC 79-54249. 155p. 1979. 7.95 (ISBN 0-8059-2666-6). Dorrance.

Karlson, P. Introduction to Modern Biochemistry. 4th ed. Doering, Charles, tr. from Ger. 1975. 24.95 (ISBN 0-12-399764-X). Acad Pr.

Karlsson, John L. Inheritance of Creative Intelligence. LC 77-19297. 1978. text ed. 16.95 (ISBN 0-88229-391-5); pap. text ed. 8.95 (ISBN 0-88229-607-8). Nelson-Hall.

Karlweiss, Joseph R., ed. see Kierkegaard, Soren A.

Karmali, John. Birds of Africa. LC 80-5359. (Illus.). 192p. 1980. 25.00 (ISBN 0-670-16810-6, Studio). Viking Pr.

Karman, Theodore Von see Von Karman, Theodore.

Karman, Theodore Von see Von Mises, Richard & Von Karman, Theodore.

Karmas, E. Sausage Products Technology. LC 76-47276. (Food Technology Review Ser.: No. 39). (Illus.). 1977. 39.00 o.p. (ISBN 0-8155-0646-5). Noyes.

Karmas, Endel, jt. auth. see Harris, Robert S.

Karmel, Barbara. Point & Counterpoint in Organizational Behavior. 168p. 1980. pap. 8.95 (ISBN 0-03-054686-9). Dryden Pr.

Karmel, Marjorie. Thank You, Doctor Lamaze. pap. 1.95 (ISBN 0-385-03752-X, C458, Dolp). Doubleday.

--Thank You Dr. Lamaze. rev. ed. LC 80-8372. 192p. 1981. 10.95 (ISBN 0-06-014831-4, HarpT). Har-Row.

Karmel, Pepe, tr. see Apollinaire, Guillaume.

Karmi, Hasan. Al-Manar: An English-Arabic Dictionary. text ed. 12.00x (ISBN 0-685-77119-9). Intl Bk Ctr.

Karmi, Hasan, jt. auth. see Al-Manar.

Karmon, Yehuda. Ports Around the World. (Illus.). 1979. 15.95 (ISBN 0-517-53378-2). Crown.

Karn, Edwin D., jt. auth. see Sale, Randall D.

Karnani, Chetan. Nissim Ezekiel. (Indian Writers Ser.). 192p. 1975. 6.50 (ISBN 0-88253-699-0). Ind-US Inc.

Karnes, Frances A. & Collins, Emily C. Handbook of Instructional Resources & References for Teaching the Gifted. 1980. text ed. 16.95 (ISBN 0-205-06823-5, 246823-9). Allyn.

Karnes, Frances A. & Peddicord, Herschel, Jr. Programs, Leaders, Consultants & Other Resources in Gifted & Talented Education. 360p. 1980. 29.75 (ISBN 0-398-04099-0). C C Thomas.

Karnes, Merle B. & Lee, Richard C. Early Childhood. 1978. pap. text ed. 5.50 (ISBN 0-86586-023-8). Coun Exc Child.

Karnes, Thomas. Tropical Enterprise: Standard Fruit & Steamship Company in Latin America. LC 78-9641. 1979. 20.00x (ISBN 0-8071-0395-0). La State U Pr.

Karnes, Thomas L. William Gilpin: Western Nationalist. (Illus.). 1969. 19.95x (ISBN 0-292-70003-2). U of Tex Pr.

Karnig, Albert & Welch, Susan. Black Representation & Urban Policy. LC 80-16714. 1981. 20.00x (ISBN 0-226-42534-7). U of Chicago Pr.

Karnjanaprakorn, Choop, et al. Nida: A Case Study in Institution Development. 1974. pap. text ed. 3.00 (ISBN 0-89249-007-1). Intl Development.

Karnopp, Bruce H. Introduction to Dynamics. LC 73-3741. 1974. text ed. 22.95 (ISBN 0-201-03614-2). A-W.

Karnopp, Dean, et al. Bond Graph Techniques for Dynamic Systems in Engineering & Biology. 1979. pap. text ed. 28.00 (ISBN 0-08-025056-4). Pergamon.

Karnopp, Dean C. & Rosenberg, Ronald C. System Dynamics: A Unified Approach. LC 74-22466. 496p. 1975. 32.50 (ISBN 0-471-45940-2, Pub. by Wiley-Interscience). Wiley.

Karo, Nancy & Mickelson, Alvera. La Aventura de Morir. Flores, Jose, tr. from Eng. LC 77-15812. 197p. (Orig., Span.). 1977. pap. 3.50 (ISBN 0-89922-098-3). Edit Caribe.

Karo, Wolf, jt. auth. see Sandler, Stanley R.

Karol, Alexander. Sword of Vengence. 1977. pap. 1.50 (ISBN 0-505-51150-9). Tower Bks.

Karol, K. S. The Second Chinese Revolution. Jones, Mervyn, tr. 1975. 12.95 o.p. (ISBN 0-8090-8516-X). Hill & Wang.

Karolak, Tadeusz. John Paul II: The Pope from Poland. 2nd, enl. ed. Evans, David, tr. from Polish. LC 80-468695. (Illus.). 176p. 1979. 25.00x (ISBN 83-223-1845-6). Intl Pubns Serv.

Karolevitz, Robert F. Old Time Agriculture in the Ads. LC 77-122596. (Illus.). 96p. 1970. pap. 2.95 (ISBN 0-87970-116-1). North Plains.

Karoly, Gundel. Hungarian Cookery-Book: One Hundred Forty Hungarian Specialities. 10th rev. ed. (Illus.). 103p. 1980. 7.50x (ISBN 963-13-0949-5). Intl Pubns Serv.

Karoly, Paul & Steffen, John. Improving the Long-Term Effects of Psychotherapy. LC 79-18430. 1979. 27.95x (ISBN 0-470-26854-9). Halsted Pr.

Karoly, Paul & Kanfer, Frederick H., eds. Self-Management & Behavior Change: From Theory to Practice. (Pergamon General Psychology Ser.). 400p. Date not set. price not set (ISBN 0-08-025987-1); pap. price not set (ISBN 0-08-025986-3). Pergamon.

Karow, Juliette. The Necessary Diet. (Orig.). 1981. pap. 5.95 (ISBN 0-89865-085-2). Donning Co.

Karp, Ben. Ornamental Carpentry of Nineteenth-Century American Houses: One Hundred Sixty Five Photographs. rev. ed. Orig. Title: Wood Motifs in American Domestic Architecture. (Illus.). 96p. 1981. pap. price not set (ISBN 0-486-24144-0). Dover.

Karp, David A., et al. Being Urban: A Social Psychological View of City Life. 1976. pap. text ed. 7.95x (ISBN 0-669-95703-8). Heath.

Karp, Gerald & Berrill, N. J. Development. 2nd ed. (Illus.). 640p. 1981. text ed. 21.95 (ISBN 0-07-033340-8, C). McGraw.

Karp, Harry R., ed. see Electronics Magazine.

Karp, Ivan. Fields of Change Among the Iteso of Kenya. (International Library of Anthropology). 1978. 21.00x (ISBN 0-7100-8863-9). Routledge & Kegan.

Karp, Ivan & Bird, Charles S., eds. Explorations in African Systems of Thought. LC 80-7492. 352p. 1980. 22.50x (ISBN 0-253-19523-3). Ind U Pr.

Karp, Laurence E. Genetic Engineering: Threat or Promise? LC 76-3497. (Illus.). 320p. 1976. 17.95 (ISBN 0-88229-261-7); pap. 8.95 (ISBN 0-88229-460-1). Nelson-Hall.

Karp, Lila. Queen Is in the Garbage. LC 72-89665. 1969. 6.95 (ISBN 0-8149-0249-9). Vanguard.

Karp, Mark, ed. African Dimensions: Essays in Honor of William O. Brown. LC 74-84802. (African Studies Center Ser). 224p. 1975. text ed. 10.00x (ISBN 0-8419-8717-3, Africana). Holmes & Meier.

Karp, Walter & Burrow, J. W. Charles Darwin & the Origin of Species. LC 68-12439. (Horizon Caravel Bks). (Illus.). 153p. (gr. 7 up). 1968. 9.95 (ISBN 0-06-023094-0, Dist. by Har-Row); PLB 12.89 o.p. (ISBN 0-06-023095-9). Am Heritage.

Karpas, Alvin. On the Rock. (Illus.). 368p. 1981. 12.95 (ISBN 0-8253-0019-3). Beaufort Bks NY.

Karpat, K. H. The Gecekondu: Rural Migration & Urbanization in Turkey. LC 75-12159. (Illus.). 1976. 39.95 (ISBN 0-521-20954-4). Cambridge U Pr.

Karpati, G., jt. ed. see Aguayo, A. G.

Karpati, Janos. Bartok's String Quartets. 1978. 19.95 o.p. (ISBN 0-214-20469-3, 8060, Dist. by Arco). Barrie & Jenkins.

Karpel, Bernard, ed. Arts in America: A Bibliography, 4 vols. LC 79-15321. 2800p. 1979-1980. Set. 190.00x (ISBN 0-87474-578-0). Smithsonian.

Karpeles, Maud, jt. ed. see Sharp, Cecil.

Karpf, Elinor, jt. auth. see Karpf, Steve.

Karpf, Fay B. American Social Psychology: Its Origins, Development, & European Background. (Reprints in Sociology Ser). 1971. lib. bdg. 24.00x (ISBN 0-697-00216-0); pap. 8.95x (ISBN 0-89197-658-2). Irvington.

Karpf, Maurice J. The Scientific Basis of Social Work. 424p. 1981. Repr. of 1931 ed. lib. bdg. 35.00 (ISBN 0-8495-3049-0). Arden Lib.

Karpf, Steve & Karpf, Elinor. Atomica. (Orig.). 1981. pap. write for info. (ISBN 0-440-10384-3). Dell.

Karpinski, L. C. Maps of Famous Cartographers Depicting North America: An Historical Atlas of the Great Lakes & Michigan, with Bibliography of the Printed Maps of Michigan to 1880. 2nd ed. (Illus.). 1977. text ed. 82.75x (ISBN 90-6041-109-9). Humanities.

Karpinski, Leszek M. The Religious Life of Man: Guide to Basic Literature. LC 77-19338. 1978. 19.50 (ISBN 0-8108-1110-3). Scarecrow.

Karples, Maud & Shaw, Pat, eds. The Crystal Spring, 2 vols. 1975. Vol. 1. pap. 7.50 (ISBN 0-19-330516-X); Vol. 2. pap. 7.50 (ISBN 0-19-330517-8). Oxford U Pr.

Karplus, Elizabeth, jt. auth. see Lyon, Lorraine D.

Karplus, Robert. Introductory Physics: A Model Approach. 1969. 16.95 (ISBN 0-8053-5216-3). Benjamin-Cummings.

--Physics & Man. new ed. 1970. pap. 7.95 o.p. (ISBN 0-8053-5211-2). Benjamin-Cummings.

Karplus, Walter, jt. auth. see Vemuri, V.

Karpman, Harold L. & Locke, Sam. Your Second Life. 1977. pap. 1.75 o.s.i. (ISBN 0-515-04218-8). Jove Pubns.

Karpman, Itzhak, jt. ed. see Wigoder, Geoffrey.

Karpman, V. I. Non-Linear Waves in Dispersive Media. Cap, Ferdinand, tr. 1974. text ed. 30.00 (ISBN 0-08-017720-4). Pergamon.

Karpov, Anatoly & Roshal, A. Anatoly Karpov: Chess Is My Life. (Pergamon Chess Ser.). (Illus.). 1980. text ed. 35.00 (ISBN 0-08-023118-7); pap. text ed. 15.00 (ISBN 0-08-023119-5). Pergamon.

Karpovick, P., jt. auth. see Murray, J.

Karr, Clarence, Jr., ed. Analytical Methods for Coal & Coal Products, 2 vols. LC 78-4928. 58.00 ea. Vol. 1, 1978 (ISBN 0-12-399901-4). Vol. 2, 1979 (ISBN 0-12-399902-2). Set. 91.00. Acad Pr.

Karr, E. R. Rollicking Shore. 1960. 7.95 (ISBN 0-8392-1093-0). Astor-Honor.

Karr, Frederic H. Interest on Third Party Accounts: A Desk Top Primer. 160p. 1980. 18.95 (ISBN 0-03-058024-2). Praeger.

Karr, James. The Condominium Buyer's Guide: What to Look for - and Look Out for - in Resort, Residential & Commercial Condominiums. LC 72-97531. 1973. 9.95 (ISBN 0-8119-0219-6). Fell.

Karr, Jean. Grace Livingston Hill. 1976. lib. bdg. 8.20 (ISBN 0-89190-992-3). Am Repr-Rivercity Pr.

Karr, Lee. The Housesitter. 1980. pap. 2.25 (ISBN 0-686-69262-4, 76364). Avon.

Karran, S. J. Practical Nutritional Support. LC 79-56645. 351p. 1980. 27.95 (ISBN 0-471-08024-1, Pub. by Wiley Medical). Wiley.

Karran, Stephen. Controversies in Surgical Sepsis. 350p. 1980. 38.50. Praeger.

Karre, K. Swedish Karre Dictionary, Vol. 1: Svensk-Engelsk. 1976. 40.00x (ISBN 91-24-14308-1, SW132). Vanous.

--Swedish Karre Dictionary, Vol. 2: Engelsk-Svensk. 3rd ed. 1974. text ed. 60.00x (ISBN 91-24-19070-5, SW133). Vanous.

Karreman, George, ed. Cooperative Phenomena in Biology. LC 78-16572. 1980. 45.00 (ISBN 0-08-023186-1). Pergamon.

Karren, Keith, jt. auth. see Hafen, Brent.

Karren, Keith J., jt. auth. see Hafen, Brent Q.

Karrer, Rathe. Developmental Psychophysiology of Mental Retardation: Concepts & Studies. (Illus.). 528p. 1976. 35.50 (ISBN 0-398-03414-1). C C Thomas.

Karrer, W. Konstitution und Vorkommen der Organischen Pflanzenstoffe (Exklusive Alkaloide) Erganzungsband 2, 1. Teil. (LMW-C 25). 1980. write for info. (ISBN 3-7643-1154-1). Birkhauser.

Karris, Rev. Robert J. see Senior, Donald.

Karris, Robert. Romans: An Access Guide. 128p. (Orig.). 1981. pap. 4.95 (ISBN 0-8215-5926-5). Sadlier.

Karris, Robert J. Pastoral Epistles. Harrington, Wilfrid & Senior, Donald, eds. (New Testament Message Ser.: Vol. 17). 148p. 1979. 9.95 (ISBN 0-89453-139-5); pap. 4.95 (ISBN 0-89453-202-2). M Glazier.

--Pastoral Epistles. (New Testament Message Ser.). 9.95 (ISBN 0-89453-140-9); pap. 4.95 (ISBN 0-89453-205-7). M Glazier.

--What Are They Saying About Luke & Acts? A Theology of the Faithful God. LC 79-83899. (Orig.). 1979. pap. 2.45 (ISBN 0-8091-2191-3). Paulist Pr.

Karris, Robert J., tr. see Lohse, Eduard.

Karris, Robert J., Rev. Invitation to Luke: A Commentary on the Gospel of Luke with Complete Text from the Jerusalem Bible. LC 77-73331. 1977. pap. 3.50 (ISBN 0-385-12209-8, Im). Doubleday.

Karsavina, Tamara. Ballet Technique. LC 68-28084. (Illus.). 1956. 10.45 (ISBN 0-87830-011-2). Theatre Arts.

--Theatre Street. LC 79-7771. (Dance Ser.). (Illus.). 1980. Repr. of 1950 ed. lib. bdg. 21.00x (ISBN 0-8369-9298-9). Arno.

Karsch, Robert F. I'm from Missouri. (gr. 7-9). 1978. pap. text ed. 3.50x saddle stitched (ISBN 0-87543-107-0). Lucas.

Karselis, Terence C., jt. auth. see Griffin, James E.

Karsen, Sonja. Jaime Torres Bodet. (World Authors Ser.: Mexico: No. 157). lib. bdg. 10.95 (ISBN 0-8057-2156-8). Twayne.

Karsen, Sonja, tr. see Bodet, Jaime T.

Karsh, Bernard, jt. ed. see Okochi, Kazuo.

Karshan, Donald. Archipenko: The Sculpture & Graphic Art. LC 75-19245. (Illus.). 164p. 1976. 45.00 o.p. (ISBN 0-89158-500-1). Westview.

Karsk, Roger & Thomas, Bill. Working with Men's Groups, Vol. 1. new ed. 1979. pap. 6.50 (ISBN 0-686-25093-1). New Comm Pr.

Karsov, Nina, tr. see Szechter, Szymon.

Karssen, Gien. Her Name Is Woman, 2 bks. LC 77-81186. Bk. 1, 1975. pap. 3.95 (ISBN 0-89109-420-2, 14209); Bk. 2, 1977. pap. 3.95 (ISBN 0-89109-424-5, 14241). NavPress.

Karst, jt. auth. see Horowitz.

Karst, Kenneth L. & Rosen, Keith S. Law & Development in Latin America. LC 74-30525. 750p. 1976. 44.50x (ISBN 0-520-02955-0). U of Cal Pr.

Karsten, J., jt. ed. see Struhl, Paula R.

Karsten, Peter. The Naval Aristocracy. LC 76-136609. 1972. 15.95 (ISBN 0-02-917070-2). Free Pr.

Karsten, Rafael. Toba Indians of the Bolivian Gran Chaco. 1967. text ed. 6.75x (ISBN 90-6234-023-7). Humanities.

Kart & Manard. Aging in America. 2nd ed. 1981. 10.95 (ISBN 0-88284-121-1). Alfred Pub.

Kart, Cary S. Exploring Social Problems. LC 77-26096. 1978. pap. text ed. 8.50 (ISBN 0-88284-060-6). Alfred Pub.

Kart, Cary S., jt. auth. see Schwartz, Howard D.

Kart, Cary S. & Manard, Barbara, eds. Aging in America: Readings in Social Gerontology. LC 76-2051. 250p. 1976. pap. text ed. 10.95 (ISBN 0-88284-035-5). Alfred Pub.

Kart, Cary S., et al. Aging & Health: Biologic & Social Perspectives. LC 77-88690. 1978. 16.95 (ISBN 0-201-03600-2, M&N Div). A-W.

Kart Magazine. Complete Book of Karting. Day, Dick, ed. 1961. 14.95 (ISBN 0-13-157487-6). P-H.

Karta, Neturei. Judaism & Zionism: Principles & Definitions. 1980. lib. bdg. 59.95 (ISBN 0-686-68745-0). Revisionist Pr.

Kartesz, John T., jt. auth. see Duncan, Wilbur H.

Karttunen, Frances & Lockhart, James. Nahuatl in Middle Years: Language Contact Phenomena in Texts of the Colonial Period. (Publications in Linguistics Ser.: Vol. 85). 1977. pap. 10.75x (ISBN 0-520-09561-8). U of Cal Pr.

Karush, William. Crescent Dictionary of Mathematics. 1962. 7.50 o.s.i. (ISBN 0-02-560690-5). Macmillan.

Karve, D. D. & McDonald, Ellen E. The New Brahmans: Five Maharashtrian Families. 1963. 21.50x (ISBN 0-520-00635-6). U of Cal Pr.

Karve, D. G. & Ambekar, D. V., eds. Speeches & Writings of Gopal Krishna Gokhale. (Educational Series,: Vol. 3). 1968. 9.00x o.p. (ISBN 0-210-31207-6). Asia.

Karvel, George & Petry, Glenn H. Optimal City Size. 66p. 10.00 (ISBN 0-686-64197-3). U CO Busn Res Div.

Karvel, Roger. Profits from Real Estate Publicity. 225p. 1980. 21.95 (ISBN 0-88462-385-8). Real Estate Ed Co.

Kasahara, Kunihiko. Creative Origami. LC 67-87040. (Illus.). 1977. pap. 12.95 (ISBN 0-87040-411-3). Japan Pubns.

--Origami Made Easy. LC 73-83956. (Illus.). 128p. 1973. pap. 4.95 (ISBN 0-87040-253-6). Japan Pubns.

Kasahara, Kunihiko, jt. auth. see Gray, Alice.

Kasapor, Mary M. The Wondrous Cross. 1980. 6.95 (ISBN 0-533-04596-7). Vantage.

Kasavana, Michael L. Effective Front Office Operations. 352p. text ed. 16.95 (ISBN 0-8436-2200-8). CBI Pub.

--Hotel Information Systems: A Contemporary Approach to Front Office Procedures. LC 78-9310. 1978. text ed. 16.95 (ISBN 0-8436-2131-1). CBI Pub.

Kaschnitz, Mary L. Selected Later Poems of Marie Luise Kaschnitz. LC 80-7537. (Lockert Library of Poetry Translation). 128p. 1980. 9.95 (ISBN 0-691-06442-3); pap. 4.95 (ISBN 0-691-01374-8). Princeton U Pr.

Kasdan, Sara. Love & Knishes: An Irrepressible Guide to Jewish Cooking. LC 56-12031. (Illus.). 1956. 8.95 (ISBN 0-8149-0132-8). Vanguard.

--Mazel Toy, Y'all: A Bake Book for Happy Occasions. LC 68-8082. (Illus.). 1968. 8.95 (ISBN 0-8149-0131-X). Vanguard.

--So It Was Just a Simple Wedding. LC 61-13280. 8.95 (ISBN 0-8149-0133-6). Vanguard.

Kasden, Lawrence N., jt. auth. see Hoeber, Daniel R.

Kase, C. Robert, jt. ed. see Cornish, Roger.

Kase, Francis J., ed. Dictionary of Industrial Property, Legal & Related Terms: English, Spanish, French & German. 232p. 1980. 50.00x (ISBN 90-286-0619-X). Sijthoff & Noordhoff.

Kase, Kenneth R. & Nelson, Walter R. Concepts of Radiation Dosimetry. LC 78-5705. (Illus.). 232p. 1978. 25.00 (ISBN 0-08-023162-4); pap. 12.50 (ISBN 0-08-023161-6). Pergamon.

Kasell, Walter. Marcel Proust & the Strategy of Reading. (Purdue Univ. Monographs in Romance Languages: No. 4). 130p. 1980. text ed. 23.00x (ISBN 90-272-1714-9). Humanities.

Kasemann, Ernst. Commentary on Romans. Bromiley, Geoffrey W., tr. 1978. 22.50 (ISBN 0-8028-3499-X). Eerdmans.

--Jesus Means Freedom. Clarke, Frank, tr. from Ger. LC 75-94357. 168p. (Orig.). 1972. pap. 2.95 (ISBN 0-8006-1235-3, 1-1235). Fortress.

--New Testament Questions of Today. Montague, W. J., tr. from Ger. LC 70-81531. 320p. 1979. pap. 6.95 (ISBN 0-8006-1351-1, 1-1351). Fortress.

Kasendorf, E., jt. auth. see Hauser, Stuart T.

Kaser, M., ed. see Jasny, Naum.

Kaser, Michael, jt. ed. see Brown, Archie.

Kaserand, Michael & Zielinski, J. Planning in East Europe. 1971. 7.50 (ISBN 0-370-00397-7). Transatlantic.

Kasfir, Nelson. The Shrinking Political Arena: Participation & Ethnicity in African Politics, with a Case of Uganda. LC 73-85790. 320p. 1976. 33.75x (ISBN 0-520-02576-8). U of Cal Pr.

Kash, Don E., et al. Our Energy Future: The Role of Research, Development, & Demonstration in Reaching a National Consensus on Energy Supply. LC 76-46402. (Illus.). 1976. 24.95x (ISBN 0-8061-1400-2); pap. 9.95 (ISBN 0-8061-1408-8). U of Okla Pr.

Kash, Marilynn M. & Borich, Gary D. Teaacher Behavior & Pupil Self-Concept. LC 77-79452. (Education Ser.). (Illus.). 1978. text ed. 13.95 (ISBN 0-201-00843-2). A-W.

Kashap, S. Paul, ed. Studies in Spinoza: Critical & Interpretative Essays. 360p. 1973. 20.00x (ISBN 0-520-02142-8); pap. 6.50x (ISBN 0-520-02590-3). U of Cal Pr.

Kashdan, Isaac, ed. First Piatigorsky Cup. (Illus.). 224p. 1980. pap. 3.50 (ISBN 0-486-24066-5). Dover.

Kashima, Tetsuden. Buddhism in America: The Social Organization of an Ethnic Religious Institution. LC 76-57837. (Contributions in Sociology: No. 26). (Illus.). 1977. lib. bdg. 18.95 (ISBN 0-8371-9534-9, KSO/). Greenwood.

Kashyap, G. P., jt. auth. see Prasad, Amba.

Kashyap, L., jt. ed. see Dash, V.

Kashyap, Lalitesh, jt. auth. see Dash, Bhagan.

Kasimatis, A. N., et al. Wine Grape Varieties in the San Joaquin Valley. 1972. pap. 5.00x (ISBN 0-931876-23-0, 4009). Ag Sci Pubns.

Kasimow, Harold. Divine-Human Encounter: A Study of Abraham Joshua Heschel. LC 79-63562. 1979. pap. text ed. 7.75 (ISBN 0-8191-0731-X). U Pr of Amer.

Kasle, Myron J. & Langlais, Robert. Basic Principles of Oral Radiography. (Exercises in Dental Radiology Ser.: Vol. 4). (Illus.). 200p. 1981. text ed. price not set (ISBN 0-7216-5291-3). Saunders.

Kasper, Walker, jt. ed. see Kung, Hans.

Kasper, Walter. Introduction to Christian Faith. Smith, David, tr. from Ger. 224p. 1981. pap. 4.95 (ISBN 0-8091-2324-X). Paulist Pr.

--Theology of Christian Marriage. 112p. 1980. 7.95 (ISBN 0-8164-0209-4). Crossroad NY.

Kasper, Walter, jt. ed. see Kung, Hans.

Kasperson, R. E. & Breitbart, M. Participation, Decentralization & Advocacy Planning. LC 74-77537. (CCG Resource Papers Ser.: No. 25). 1974. pap. text ed. 4.00 (ISBN 0-89291-072-0). Assn Am Geographers.

Kaspin, A., tr. see Eikhenbaum, Boris.

Kasprisin, Christina A., jt. auth. see Kasprisin, Duke O.

Kasprisin, Duke O. & Kasprisin, Christina A. Introduction to Transfusion Therapy: A Programmed Text. LC 80-17972. 1980. pap. 10.50 (ISBN 0-87488-822-0). Med Exam.

Kass, Gerard A., jt. auth. see Geffner, Saul L.

Kass, Ilana. Soviet Involvement in the Middle East: Policy Formulation, 1966-1973. LC 77-8279. (Special Studies on the Soviet Union & Eastern Europe Ser.). 1978. lib. bdg. 26.50x (ISBN 0-89158-063-8). Westview.

Kass, Lawrence & Schnitzer, Bertram. Monocytes, Monocytosis & Monocytic Leukemia. (Illus.). 120p. 1973. 23.75 (ISBN 0-398-02883-4). C C Thomas.

--Refractory Anemia. (Illus.). 160p. 1975. 32.75 (ISBN 0-398-03341-2). C C Thomas.

Kass, Louis A. Civil Practice & Procedure: (N.Y.) 150p. 1980. 6.50 (ISBN 0-87526-093-4). Gould.

--Necessary Elements. 1979 ed. 59p. 1979. 4.50 (ISBN 0-87526-242-2). Gould.

Kass, N., jt. auth. see Spencer, T. D.

Kassalow, Everett M., ed. National Labor Movements in the Postwar World. 1963. 11.95x o.s.i. (ISBN 0-8101-0133-5). Northwestern U Pr.

Kassam, A. H., jt. auth. see Kowal, J. M.

Kassam, Shirin, et al. A Bibliography on Kenya. (Foreign & Comparative Studies-Eastern African Bibliographic Ser.: No. 2). 461p. 1967. pap. 8.00x. Syracuse U Foreign Comp.

Kassarjian, Harold & Robertson, Thomas. Perspectives in Consumer Behavior. 1981. pap. text ed. 10.95x (ISBN 0-673-15394-0). Scott F.

Kasschau, Patricia L. Aging & Social Policy: Leadership Planning. LC 78-15481. 1978. 29.95 (ISBN 0-03-046411-0). Praeger.

Kassel, Rudolf V., ed. see Aristotle.

Kassin, Saul J. The Light of the Law. LC 80-51979. 288p. 1981. 12.95 (ISBN 0-88400-069-9). Shengold.

Kassorla, Irene. Putting It All Together. 224p. 1976. pap. 2.50 (ISBN 0-446-91802-4). Warner Bks.

Kast, Fremont & Rosenzweig, James. Experiential Exercises & Cases in Management. (Illus.). 1976. text ed. 11.95 (ISBN 0-07-033343-2); instructor's manual 4.95 (ISBN 0-07-033344-0). McGraw.

--Organization & Management: A Systems & Contingency Approach. 3rd rev. ed. (Management Ser.). (Illus.). 1979. text ed. 22.50x (ISBN 0-07-033346-7, C); instructor's manual 7.50 (ISBN 0-07-033347-5). McGraw.

Kast, Fremont E. & Rosenzweig, James. Organization & Management: Experiential Exercises. 1976. text ed. 12.95x (ISBN 0-07-033346-7, C); instructor's manual 4.95 (ISBN 0-07-033347-5). McGraw.

Kastan, Harold G., jt. auth. see Ahner, Walter L.

Kasten, Ulla, ed. see Buchanan, Briggs.

Kastenbaum, Robert, ed. see Sherwood, Sylvia, et al.

Kastenbaum, Robert. Growing Old: Years of Fulfillment. (Life Cycle Ser.). 1979. pap. text ed. 4.95 scp (ISBN 0-06-384750-7, HarpC). Har-Row.

--Humans Developing: A Lifespan Perspective. 1979. text ed. 18.50x (ISBN 0-205-06513-9); instr's man. avail. (ISBN 0-205-06536-8); student guide avail. (ISBN 0-205-06535-X). Allyn.

--Old Age on the New Scene. (Springer Series on Adulthood & Aging: No. 9). 1981. pap. text ed. 19.95 (ISBN 0-8261-2361-9). Springer Pub.

Kastenbaum, Robert J., ed. Perspectives on Aging & Human Development, 3 vols. Incl. Vol. 1. Being & Becoming Old (ISBN 0-89503-014-4); Vol. 2. In the Country of the Old (ISBN 0-89503-015-2); Vol. 13. Institutionalization & Alternative Futures. 160p. softcover 17.95x o.p. (ISBN 0-686-68242-4). Baywood Pub.

Kastens, Merritt L. Long Range Planning for Your Business: An Operating Manual. (Illus.). 1976. 13.95 (ISBN 0-8144-5413-5). Am Mgmt.

Kastl, Albert J. & Kastl, Lena. Journey Back: Escaping the Drug Trap. LC 74-20711. 176p. 1975. 11.95 (ISBN 0-88229-123-8). Nelson-Hall.

Kastl, Lena, jt. auth. see Kastl, Albert J.

Kastle, Herbert. Cross-Country. 336p. 1975. 8.95 o.p. (ISBN 0-440-03383-7). Delacorte.

--Ellie. 1973. 7.95 o.p. (ISBN 0-440-02312-2). Delacorte.

--Sunset People. 384p. (Orig.). 1980. pap. 2.75 (ISBN 0-515-05488-7). Jove Pubns.

Kastner, Erich. Emil und die Detektive. (Easy Readers, B). 1979. pap. 3.75 (ISBN 0-88436-297-3). EMC.

--The Little Man. (Illus.). (gr. 5 up). 1980. pap. 1.95 (ISBN 0-380-51185-1, 51185, Camelot). Avon.

--The Little Man & the Big Thief. (Illus.). 176p. (gr. 5 up). 1981. pap. 1.95 (ISBN 0-380-53728-1, 53728, Camelot). Avon.

Kastner, John. Super Dan & the Dinosaurs. (Illus.). 32p. (gr. 1 up). 1980. PLB 6.95 (ISBN 0-201-03901-X, 3901, A-W Childrens); pap. 3.95 (ISBN 0-201-03910-9, 3910). A-W.

Kastner, Jonathan & Kastner, Marianna. Sleep: The Mysterious Third of Your Life. LC 67-22392. (Curriculum Related Bks). (Illus.). (gr. 7 up). 1968. 5.75 o.p. (ISBN 0-15-275911-5, HJ). HarBraceJ.

Kastner, Joseph. A Species of Eternity. 1978. pap. 8.95 o.p. (ISBN 0-525-47531-1). Dutton.

Kastner, Marianna, jt. auth. see Kastner, Jonathan.

Kastor, Frank S. Giles & Phineas Fletcher. (English Authors Ser.: No. 225). 1978. lib. bdg. 12.50 (ISBN 0-8057-6696-0). Twayne.

--Milton & the Literary Satan. LC 74-81305. 119p. (Orig.). 1976. pap. text ed. 11.50x (ISBN 90-6203-198-6). Humanities.

Kasulis, T. P. Zen Action-Zen Person. LC 80-27858. 192p. 1980. 12.95 (ISBN 0-8248-0702-2). U Pr of Hawaii.

Kaszniak, Alfred W. Developmental Psychology for the Health Care Professions: Young Adult Through Late Aging, Pt. II. (Behavioral Sciences for Health Care Professionals Ser.). 128p. (Orig.). 1981. lib. bdg. 15.00x (ISBN 0-86531-012-2); pap. text ed. 6.00x (ISBN 0-86531-013-0). Westview.

--An Introduction to the Biological Bases of Behavior for the Health Professions. (Behavioral Sciences for Health Care Professionals Ser.). 128p. (Orig.). 1981. lib. bdg. 15.00x (ISBN 0-86531-010-6); pap. text ed. 6.00x (ISBN 0-86531-011-4). Westview.

Kaszubski, Marek, jt. ed. see Wasserman, Paul.

Katan, L. L., jt. auth. see Briston, J. H.

Kataoka, Tetsuya. Resistance & Revolution in China: The Communists & the Second United Front. LC 73-84386. (Illus.). 1974. 25.00x (ISBN 0-520-02553-9). U of Cal Pr.

--Waiting for a "Pearl Harbor". Japan Debates Defense. (Publication Ser.: No. 232). 90p. (Orig.). 1981. pap. 7.95 (ISBN 0-8179-7322-2). Hoover Inst Pr.

Katch, Frank I. & McArdle, William D. Nutrition, Weight Control, & Exercise. LC 76-14695. (Illus.). 1977. pap. text ed. 12.25 (ISBN 0-395-24453-6). HM.

Katchadourian, Herant. The Biology of Adolescence. LC 76-44282. (Illus.). 1977. text ed. 18.95x (ISBN 0-7167-0376-9); pap. text ed. 10.95x (ISBN 0-7167-0375-0). W H Freeman.

--Human Sexuality: Sense & Nonsense. (Illus.). 160p. 1979. pap. text ed. 3.95x (ISBN 0-393-95017-4). Norton.

Kateman, G. & Pijpers, F. W. Quality Control in Analytical Chemistry. (Chemical Analysis Ser.). 320p. 1981. 28.50 (ISBN 0-471-46020-6, Pub. by Wiley-Interscience). Wiley.

Katen, Thomas E. Doing Philosophy. (Illus.). 368p. 1973. text ed. 15.95 (ISBN 0-13-217570-3). P-H.

Kates, Dan B. Restricting Handguns: The Liberal Sceptics Speak Out. 9.95 (ISBN 0-88427-033-5). Green Hill.

Kates, George. Chinese Household Furniture. (Illus.). 1948. pap. 3.50 (ISBN 0-486-20958-X). Dover.

Kates, Linda & Schein, Jerome. A Complete Guide to Communication with Deaf Blind Persons. (Illus.). 108p. 1981. pap. text ed. 3.95 (ISBN 0-913072-40-0). Natl Assn Deaf.

Kates, Robert W. Industrial Flood Losses: Damage Estimation in the Lehigh Valley. LC 65-22713. (Research Papers Ser.: No. 98). 76p. 1965. pap. 8.00 (ISBN 0-89065-011-X). U Chicago Dept Geog.

--Risk Assessment of Environmental Hazard: Scope Report 8. LC 77-12909. (Scientific Committee on Problems of the Environment). 1978. 15.75 (ISBN 0-471-99582-7, Pub. by Wiley-Interscience). Wiley.

Kates, Robert W., jt. auth. see Burton, Ian.

Kates, Robert W., jt. ed. see Berry, Leonard.

Kates, Steve. Encyclopedia of Cockatoos. (Illus.). 221p. 1980. 20.00 (ISBN 0-87666-896-1, H-1023). TFH Pubns.

Katholi, Richard, jt. auth. see Oparil, Suzanne.

Kathren, Ronald L. Health Physics: A Backward Glance. 1980. text ed. 28.00 (ISBN 0-08-021531-9). Pergamon.

Katkov, George. Russia Nineteen Hundred Seventeen. (Illus.). 240p. 1980. text ed. 22.50 (ISBN 0-582-49101-0). Longman.

Kato, Genchi & Hoshino, H. Kogoshui: Gleanings from Ancient Stories. (Records of Asian History). (Illus.). 1972. text ed. 8.00x (ISBN 0-7007-0022-6). Humanities.

Kato, S. & Roper, R. G. Electric Current & Atmospheric Motion. (Advances in Earth & Planetary Sciences Ser.: No. 7). 294p. 1980. 24.50x (ISBN 0-89955-314-1, Pub. by JSSP Japan). Intl Schol Bk Serv.

Kato, Shuichi. The Japan-China Phenomenon. Chibbett, David, tr. LC 75-11392. 103p. 1974. 8.75x (ISBN 0-87011-260-0). Kodansha.

Kato, Susumo, ed. Dynamics of the Upper Atmosphere. (Developments in Earth & Planetary Sciences Ser.: No. 1). 233p. 1980. PLB 29.95 (ISBN 90-277-1132-1, Pub. by D. Reidel). Kluwer Boston.

Kato, T. Perturbation Theory for Linear Operators. (Grundlehren der Mathematischen Wissenschaften: Vol. 132). 1966. 35.70 o.p. (ISBN 0-387-03526-5). Springer-Verlag.

--Perturbation Theory for Linear Operators. 2nd ed. (Grundlehren der Mathematischen Wissenschaften: Vol. 132). (Illus.). 619p. 1980. 72.00 (ISBN 0-387-07558-5). Springer-Verlag.

Katona, Anna B. Mihaly Vitez Csokonai. (World Authors Ser.: No. 579). 1980. lib. bdg. 13.95 (ISBN 0-8057-6421-6). Twayne.

Katona, George. Essays on Behavioral Economics. LC 80-15510. (Illus.). 108p. 1980. 10.50 (ISBN 0-87944-257-3). U of Mich Soc Res.

Katouzian, Homa. Ideology & Method in Economics. LC 79-3301. 1981. cUSA 22.50x (ISBN 0-8147-4574-1); pap. 12.50x cUSA (ISBN 0-8147-4575-X). NYU Pr.

--The Political Economy of Modern Iran: Despotism & Pseudo-Modernism, 1926-1979. 448p. 1981. 40.00x (ISBN 0-8147-4577-6); pap. 19.50x (ISBN 0-8147-4578-4). NYU Pr.

Katrak, K. D. Diversions by the Wayside. 23p. 1975. 8.00 (ISBN 0-88253-528-5); pap. text ed. 4.80 (ISBN 0-88253-527-7). Ind-US Inc.

--A Journal of the Way. 40p. 1975. 8.00 (ISBN 0-88253-570-6); pap. text ed. 4.80 (ISBN 0-88253-569-2). Ind-US Inc.

Katrak, K. D. & Katrak, Usha. Five Little Sermons. 9.00 (ISBN 0-89253-626-8); flexible cloth 4.80 (ISBN 0-89253-627-6). Ind-US Inc.

Katrak, Usha, jt. auth. see Katrak, K. D.

Katritzky, A. R., ed. Advances in Heterocyclic Chemistry, Vols. 1-16, 22-24. Incl. Vol. 1. 1963. 51.50 (ISBN 0-12-020601-3); Vol. 2. 1963. 51.50 (ISBN 0-12-020602-1); Vol. 3. 1964 (ISBN 0-12-020603-X); Vol. 4. 1965 (ISBN 0-12-020604-8); Vol. 5. 1965 (ISBN 0-12-020605-6); Vol. 6. Katritzky, A. R. & Boulton, A. J., eds. 1966 (ISBN 0-12-020606-4); Vol. 7. 1966. o.s.i. (ISBN 0-12-020607-2); Vol. 8. 1967 (ISBN 0-12-020608-0); Vol. 9. 1968 (ISBN 0-12-020609-9); Vol. 10. 1969. o.s.i. (ISBN 0-12-020610-2); Vol. 11. 1970 (ISBN 0-12-020611-0); Vol. 12. 1970 (ISBN 0-12-020612-9); Vol. 13. 1971. o.s.i. (ISBN 0-12-020613-7); Vol. 14. 1972 (ISBN 0-12-020614-5); Vol. 15. 1973 (ISBN 0-12-020615-3); Vol. 16. 1974 (ISBN 0-12-020616-1); Vol. 22. 1978. 48.00 (ISBN 0-12-020622-6); lib ed. 62.50 (ISBN 0-12-020682-X); microfiche 35.00 (ISBN 0-12-020683-8); Vol. 23. 52.50 (ISBN 0-12-020623-4); lib ed. 67.50 (ISBN 0-12-020684-6); microfiche 37.50 (ISBN 0-12-020685-4); Vol. 24. 1979. 51.00 (ISBN 0-12-020624-2); info. **lib ed. 65.50 (ISBN 0-12-020686-2); microfiche 33.50 (ISBN 0-12-020687-0). Vols. 1-16. 51.50 ea. Acad Pr.**

--Advances in Heterocyclic Chemistry, Vol. 28. (Serial Publication Ser.). 1981. write for info. (ISBN 0-12-020628-5); lib. ed. (ISBN 0-12-020730-3); microfiche ed. (ISBN 0-12-020731-1). Acad Pr.

Katritzky, A. R. & Boulton, A. J., eds. Advances in Heterocyclic Chemistry, Vol. 27. (Serial Publication). 1980. 49.50 (ISBN 0-12-020627-7); lib. bdg. 64.50 (ISBN 0-12-020728-1); microfiche ed. 34.50 (ISBN 0-12-020729-X). Acad Pr.

--Theoretical Chemistry: Advances & Perspectives, Vol. 5. LC 75-21963. 1980. 35.00 (ISBN 0-12-681905-X); lib ed. 45.50 (ISBN 0-12-681978-5); microfiche 24.50 (ISBN 0-12-681979-3). Acad Pr.

Katritzky, Alan R., ed. Advances in Heterocyclic Chemistry, Vol. 25. 1980. 41.00 (ISBN 0-12-020625-0); lib ed. 53.50 (ISBN 0-12-020689-7); microfiche 28.50 (ISBN 0-12-020690-0). Acad Pr.

Katritzky, Alan R. & Lagowski, J. M., eds. Principles of Heterocyclic Chemistry. 1968. 29.50 (ISBN 0-12-401150-0). Acad Pr.

Katsaros, Thomas & Schiro, George J. A Brief History of the Western World. LC 78-62178. 1978. pap. text ed. 13.25 (ISBN 0-8191-0466-3). U Pr of Amer.

Katsaros, Thomas & Teluk, John. Capitalism: A Cooperative Venture. LC 80-8163. 161p. 1981. lib. bdg. 17.50 (ISBN 0-8191-1484-7); pap. text ed. 8.50 (ISBN 0-8191-1485-5). U Pr of Amer.

Katsenelinboigen, Aron. Soviet Economic Thought & Political Power in the USSR. LC 78-17552. (Pergamon Policy Studies). 1980. 28.00 (ISBN 0-08-022467-9). Pergamon.

Katsh, Abraham I., ed. Bar Mitzvah Illustrated. 7th ed. LC 76-23713. (Illus.). 1976. 10.95 (ISBN 0-88400-048-6). Shengold.

--The Warsaw Diary of Chaim A. Kaplan. Kaplan, C. A. LC 72-90277. (Illus.). 400p. 1973. pap. 2.95 o.s.i. (ISBN 0-02-034000-1, Collier). Macmillan.

Katsh, Salem M., jt. auth. see Millstein, Ira M.

Katsuki, Yasuji & Sato, Masayasu. Brain Mechanisms of Sensation. 320p. 1981. 28.50 (ISBN 0-471-08148-5, Pub. by Wiley Med). Wiley.

Katsuyama, Allen, ed. see Food Processors Institute.

Katsuyama, Allen M., ed. see Food Processors Institute.

Kattan, Kenneth R. Trauma & No-Trauma of the Cervical Spine. (Illus.). 328p. 1975. 32.75 (ISBN 0-398-03371-4). C C Thomas.

Kattan-Zablah, Jorge, jt. auth. see Castro-Amaya, Rogelio A.

Kattell, Ted, jt. auth. see McCarty, Diane.

Katter, Reuben L. Creationism: Its Basis, Its Essence, & Its Interwoven Relation to All Life. Date not set. pap. price not set (ISBN 0-685-96812-X). Theotes.

--History of Creation & Origin of the Species: A Scientific Theological Viewpoint. 1967. 14.95 (ISBN 0-911806-01-6); pap. 9.95 (ISBN 0-911806-00-8). Theotes.

--Jesus Christ: The Divine Executive. 1981. price not set (ISBN 0-685-96808-1). Theotes.

Katz, Abraham. The Politics of Economic Reform in the Soviet Union. LC 74-180846. (Special Studies in International Economics & Development). 1972. 38.50x (ISBN 0-275-28260-0); pap. text ed. 18.50x (ISBN 0-89197-894-1). Irvington.

Katz, Adele T. Challenge to Musical Tradition. LC 79-180046. 408p. 1972. Repr. of 1945 ed. lib. bdg. 32.50 (ISBN 0-306-70428-5). Da Capo.

Katz, Alan. Child of an Oak. (Poetry Ser.). (Illus.). (gr. 9-12). 1971. pap. 3.00x o.p. (ISBN 0-89304-000-2, CCC099). Cross Cult.

Katz, Alfred. Government & Politics in Contemporary Israel, 1948 to Present. LC 79-5508. 1980. pap. text ed. 10.50 (ISBN 0-8191-0908-8). U Pr of Amer.

--Poland's Ghettos at War. LC 78-120535. 1978. text ed. 23.00x (ISBN 0-8290-0194-8); pap. text ed. 10.95x (ISBN 0-8290-0195-6). Irvington.

Katz, Alfred H. & Felton, J. S. Health & the Community. LC 65-10188. 1965. text ed. 19.75 (ISBN 0-02-917280-2). Free Pr.

Katz, Arnold M. Physiology of the Heart. LC 75-14580. 1977. 31.00 (ISBN 0-89004-053-2); pap. 15.95 (ISBN 0-686-67627-0). Raven.

Katz, Arthur M. Economic & Social Consequences of Nuclear Attacks on the United States. Date not set. write for info. (ISBN 0-88410-096-0). Ballinger Pub.

Katz, Bernard. Nerve, Muscle & Synapse. (New Biology Ser.). 1966. text ed. 10.95 o.p. (ISBN 0-07-033374-2, C); pap. text ed. 7.95 o.p. (ISBN 0-07-033383-1). McGraw.

Katz, Bill, ed. Library Literature Ten: The Best of 1979. LC 78-154842. 512p. 1980. 13.00 (ISBN 0-686-65869-8). Scarecrow.

Katz, Bobbi. One Thousand One Words. LC 75-6832. 96p. (gr. 4-8). 1975. 5.90 (ISBN 0-531-02849-6). Watts.

--Rod-&-Reel Trouble. LC 74-3314. (Springboard Sports Ser.). (Illus.). 64p. (gr. 3-5). 1974. 5.75g (ISBN 0-8075-7097-4). A Whitman.

--Snow Bunny. Rubin, Caroline, ed. LC 76-894. (Springboard Sports Ser.). (Illus.). 64p. (gr. 3-7). 1976. 5.75g (ISBN 0-8075-7518-6). A Whitman.

--Upside Down & Inside Out: Poems for All Your Pockets. LC 76-182294. (Illus.). 48p. (gr. 1-4). 1973. PLB 4.90 o.p. (ISBN 0-531-02621-3). Watts.

--Volleyball Jinx. Rubin, Caroline, ed. (Springboard Books Ser.). (Illus.). (gr. 3-7). 1977. 5.75g (ISBN 0-8075-8512-2). A Whitman.

Katz, Daniel & Kahn, Robert L. The Social Psychology of Organizations. 2nd ed. LC 77-18764. 1978. text ed. 24.95 (ISBN 0-471-02355-8). Wiley.

Katz, Daniel, et al. Public Opinion & Propaganda. 1954. 28.00x (ISBN 0-03-005965-8); pap. text ed. 14.50x (ISBN 0-89197-909-3). Irvington.

Katz, Daniel, et al, eds. The Study of Organizations: Findings from Field & Laboratory. LC 80-15488. (Social & Behavioral Science Ser.). 1980. text ed. 28.95x (ISBN 0-87589-464-X). Jossey-Bass.

Katz, E., jt. auth. see Lazarsfeld, P. F.

Katz, Elaine, ed. see Grebel, Rosemary & Pogrund, Phyllis.

Katz, Elias. The Retarded Adult in the Community. (Illus.). 292p. 1977. 17.50 (ISBN 0-398-00981-3). C C Thomas.

Katz, Elias, et al, eds. Mental Health Services for the Mentally Retarded. (Illus.). 292p. 1972. 17.50 (ISBN 0-398-02516-9). C C Thomas.

Katz, Elihu & Lazarsfeld, Paul. Personal Influence: The Part Played by People in the Flow of Mass Communications. LC 55-7334. 1964. pap. text ed. 6.95 (ISBN 0-02-917150-4). Free Pr.

Katz, Elihu, jt. auth. see Blumler, Jay G.

Katz, Elyse & Katz, Robert. Nautical No-No's. LC 80-50537. (Illus.). 160p. 1980. pap. 9.95 (ISBN 0-9604208-0-0). Shayna Ltd.

Katz, Fernando K., jt. ed. see Segre, Roberto.

Katz, Herbert M., ed. see Katz, Marjorie P.

Katz, Herbert M., ed. see Klein, Norma.

Katz, Herbert M., ed. see Mee, Charles L., Jr.

Katz, Herbert M., ed. see Van Lustbader, Eric.

Katz, Howard S. Honest Money Now! LC 78-75028. 1979. pap. 4.95 (ISBN 0-916728-22-6). Bks in Focus.

--The Paper Aristocracy. LC 76-467. (Illus.). 1976. 9.95 (ISBN 0-916728-01-3); pap. 5.95 (ISBN 0-916728-00-5). Bks in Focus.

--The Warmongers. Zarlenga, Stephen A., ed. LC 78-73738. (Illus.). 1979. 14.95 (ISBN 0-916728-06-4). Bks in Focus.

Katz, Irving. August Belmont: A Political Biography. LC 68-19751. (Illus.). 1968. 16.00x (ISBN 0-231-03112-2). Columbia U Pr.

Katz, Irving, ed. see Carosso, Vincent P.

Katz, Irwin. Stigma: A Social Psychological Analysis. LC 80-20765. 180p. 1981. ref. 16.50 (ISBN 0-89859-078-7). L Erlbaum Assocs.

Katz, J. Society, Schools & Progress in Canada. 1969. 16.50 (ISBN 0-08-006374-8); pap. 8.50 (ISBN 0-08-006373-X). Pergamon.

Katz, J., ed. Ozone & Chlorine Dioxide Technology for Disinfection of Drinking Water. LC 80-13134. (Pollution Tech. Review, No. 67; Chemical Tech. Review: No. 164). 659p. (Orig.). 1980. 36.00 (ISBN 0-8155-0809-3). Noyes.

Katz, J. J., jt. auth. see Fodor, Jerry.

Katz, Jacob. The Art of Electrostatic Precipitation. (Illus.). 350p. 1980. text ed. 45.00x (ISBN 0-9603986-1-9). Scholium Intl.

--Common Orthopedic Problems in Pediatric Practice. 250p. 1981. 16.50 (ISBN 0-89004-273-X, 298). Raven.

--Jews & Freemasons in Europe, 1723-1939. Oschry, Leonard, tr. from Heb. LC 71-115475. 1970. 16.00x (ISBN 0-674-47480-5). Harvard U Pr.
--Out of the Ghetto: The Social Background of Jewish Emancipation, 1770-1870. LC 72-86386. 1973. 15.00 (ISBN 0-674-64775-0). Harvard U Pr.
Katz, James E. Presidential Politics & Science Policy. LC 77-14024. (Praeger Special Studies). 1978. 28.95 (ISBN 0-03-040941-1). Praeger.
Katz, James E., jt. auth. see Horowitz, Irving L.
Katz, Jane. This Song Remembers: Self-Portraits of Native Americans in the Arts. (gr. 7 up). 1980. 8.95 (ISBN 0-395-29522-X). HM.
Katz, Jane & Bruning, Nancy P. Swimming for Total Fitness: A Progressive Aerobic Program. LC 80-708. (Illus.). 380p. 1981. pap. 10.95 (ISBN 0-385-15932-3, Dolp). Doubleday.
Katz, Jay & Capron, Alexander M. Catastrophic Diseases: Who Decides What? 273p. 1982. pap. 7.95 (ISBN 0-87855-686-9). Transaction Bks. Postponed.
Katz, Jay, et al. Psychoanalysis, Psychiatry & Law. LC 65-27757. 1967. text ed. 35.00 (ISBN 0-02-917200-4). Free Pr.
Katz, Jerrold J. Language & Other Abstract Objects. 1981. 25.00x (ISBN 0-8476-6912-2); pap. 9.95x (ISBN 0-8476-6913-0). Rowman.
Katz, Jonathan. Gay American History: Lesbians & Gay Men in the U.S.A., a Documentary. LC 76-2039. (Illus.). 1976. 19.95 o.p. (ISBN 0-690-01164-4, TYC-T); pap. 9.95 (ISBN 0-690-01165-2, TYC-T). T Y Crowell.
Katz, Jordan, et al. Anesthesia & Uncommon Diseases: Pathophysiologic & Clinical Correlations. 2nd ed. (Illus.). 600p. Date not set. text ed. price not set (ISBN 0-7216-5302-2). Saunders.
Katz, Joseph, ed. see Crane, Stephen.
Katz, Joseph, ed. see Marx, Karl & Engels, Friedrich.
Katz, Judy H. White Awareness: A Handbook for Anti-Racism Training. LC 77-18610. 1978. pap. 5.95 (ISBN 0-8061-1466-5). U of Okla Pr.
Katz, Laszlo. Art of Woodworking & Furniture Appreciation. 2nd ed. (Illus.). 1980. 37.50 (ISBN 0-686-00808-1). PFC.
Katz, Lilian G., ed. Current Topics in Early Childhood Education, Vol. 3. 304p. 1980. text ed. 17.50 (ISBN 0-89391-057-0); pap. 13.50 (ISBN 0-89391-066-X). Ablex Pub.
Katz, Louis N., et al. Introduction to the Interpretation of the Electrocardiogram. LC 52-14734. (Illus.). 1952. pap. 4.50x o.s.i. (ISBN 0-226-42590-8). U of Chicago Pr.
Katz, Marjorie P. Fingerprint Owls & Other Fantasies. Katz, Herbert M., ed. LC 72-85648. (Illus.). 54p. 1981. pap. 3.95 (ISBN 0-87131-341-3). M Evans.
--Fingerprint Owls & Other Fantasies. LC 72-85648. 64p. 1981. pap. cancelled (ISBN 0-87131-341-3). M Evans.
Katz, Martha E. The Complete Book of High Protein Baking. 1977. pap. 1.95 (ISBN 0-345-24186-X). Ballantine.
Katz, Menke. Rockrose. 4.50 (ISBN 0-912292-10-5). The Smith.
Katz, Michael. The Literary Ballad in Early Nineteenth-Century Russian Literature. (Oxford Modern Languages & Literature Monographs). 1976. 37.50x (ISBN 0-19-815528-X). Oxford U Pr.
Katz, Michael see Moskowitz, Milton, et al.
Katz, Michael B. & Mattingly, Paul H., eds. Education & Social Change: Themes from Ontario's Past. LC 74-21635. 324p. 1975. 15.00x (ISBN 0-8147-5372-8); pap. 6.00x (ISBN 0-8147-5422-8). NYU Pr.
Katz, Milton, jt. auth. see Bromberg, Murray.
Katz, Mort. Living Together: A Daily Workbook for Strengthening Relationships. (Illus.). 1981. pap. 5.95 (ISBN 0-87863-002-3). Farnswth Pub.
--Marriage Survival Kit. LC 75-536. 1974. 5.95 o.p. (ISBN 0-87863-080-5). Farnswth Pub.
Katz, Phyllis A., ed. Towards the Elimination of Racism. 1976. 32.00 (ISBN 0-08-018316-6); pap. 12.75 (ISBN 0-08-018317-4). Pergamon.
Katz, Richard. Preludes to Growth: An Experiential Approach. LC 72-94013. 1973. pap. text ed. 7.95 (ISBN 0-02-917190-3). Free Pr.
Katz, Richard N., et al, eds. An Inventory of the Records of the National Lawyers Guild, 1936-1976, & an Index to NIG Periodicals, 1936-1979. LC 80-81943. pap. 10.00 (ISBN 0-913876-12-7). Meiklejohn Civil Lib.
Katz, Richard S., jt. auth. see Mulcahy, Kevin V.
Katz, Richard W., jt. ed. see Murphy, Allan H.
Katz, Robert. Axiomatic Analysis. 1978. 25.00 (ISBN 0-685-60304-0). Mathco.
--The Cassandra Crossing. (Orig.). 1977. pap. 1.50 o.p. (ISBN 0-345-24283-1). Ballantine.
Katz, Robert, jt. auth. see Katz, Elyse.
Katz, Robert L. Cases & Concepts in Corporate Strategy. 1970. ref. ed 21.95 (ISBN 0-13-118422-9). P-H.
--Management of the Total Enterprise: Cases & Concepts in Business Policy. 1970. ref. ed. 20.95 (ISBN 0-13-548933-4). P-H.
Katz, Roger C. & Zlutnik, Steven, eds. Behavior Therapy & Health Care. LC 74-7331. 1975. 23.00; text ed. 19.80 o.p. (ISBN 0-08-017829-4); pap. text ed. 14.50 (ISBN 0-08-017828-6). Pergamon.
Katz, Ruth. Make It & Wear It. LC 80-54707. (Illus.). 48p. (gr. 5-9). 1981. 7.95 (ISBN 0-8027-6418-5); PLB 8.95 (ISBN 0-8027-6419-3). Walker & Co.
Katz, S. Stanley. External Assistance & Indian Economic Growth. 5.00x (ISBN 0-210-98137-7). Asia.
Katz, Samuel I., ed. U. S.-European Monetary Relations. 1979. 13.25 (ISBN 0-8447-2150-6); pap. 7.25 (ISBN 0-8447-2149-2). Am Enterprise.
Katz, Sedelle & Mazur, Mary Ann. Understanding the Rape Victim: A Synthesis of Research Findings. LC 78-25704. (Personality Processes Ser.). 1979. 25.95 (ISBN 0-471-03573-4, Pub. by Wiley-Interscience). Wiley.
Katz, Shlomo, ed. Negro & Jew: An Encounter in America. (Orig.). 1967. 4.95 o.s.i. (ISBN 0-02-560800-2); pap. 1.45 o.s.i. (ISBN 0-02-086180-X). Macmillan.
Katz, Shlomo, tr. see Amichai, Yehuda.
Katz, Sidney B., et al. Resources for Writing for Publication in Education. 1980. pap. text ed. 6.50x (ISBN 0-8077-2579-X). Tchrs Coll.
Katz, Sol, jt. auth. see Sulavik, Stephen.
Katz, Steven T. Mysticism & Philosophical Analysis. 1978. 15.95 (ISBN 0-19-520010-1); pap. 4.95 (ISBN 0-19-520011-X, GB 538). Oxford U Pr.
Katz, Susan. Frampton! 1978. pap. 1.75 o.s.i. (ISBN 0-515-04603-5). Jove Pubns.
Katz, W. L. Minorities in American History, 6 vols. Incl. Vol. 1 Early America: 1492-1812. LC 73-17282 (ISBN 0-531-02676-0, W39); Vol. 2. Slavery to the Civil War: 1812-1865. LC 73-17284 (ISBN 0-531-02677-9, W37); Vol. 3. Reconstruction & National Growth: 1865-1900. LC 73-22475 (ISBN 0-531-02715-5, O20); Vol. 4. From the Progressive Era to the Great Depression: 1900-1929. LC 73-23062 (ISBN 0-531-02716-3, O46); Vol. 5. Years of Strife: 1929-1956 (ISBN 0-531-02785-6, U27); Vol. 6. Modern America: 1957-Present (ISBN 0-531-02821-6). (gr. 6 up). 1974. 4.47 ea. o.p. Watts.
Katz, W. L. & Bernard, G. Constitutional Amendments. LC 73-14794. 6.45 (ISBN 0-531-00813-4). Watts.
Katz, William. An Album of the Depression. (Picture Albums Ser.). (Illus.). (gr. 5 up). 1978. PLB 7.90 s&l (ISBN 0-531-02914-X). Watts.
--North Star Crusade. 1977. pap. 1.95 o.s.i. (ISBN 0-515-04356-7). Jove Pubns.
Katz, William A. & Tarr, Andrea. Reference & Information Services: A Reader. LC 77-20698. 1978. 15.00 (ISBN 0-8108-1091-3). Scarecrow.
Katz, William A., ed. Library Literature Eight: The Best of 1977. LC 78-154842. 1978. lib. bdg. 13.00 (ISBN 0-8108-1125-1). Scarecrow.
--Library Literature Nine: The Best of 1978. LC 78-154842. 1979. 13.00 (ISBN 0-8108-1213-4). Scarecrow.
--Library Literature Seven: The Best of 1976. LC 78-154842. 1977. 13.00 (ISBN 0-8108-1017-4). Scarecrow.
--Library Literature Six: The Best of 1975. LC 78-154842. 1976. 13.00 (ISBN 0-8108-0923-0). Scarecrow.
--Library Literature Two: The Best of 1971. LC 78-154842. 1972. 13.00 (ISBN 0-8108-0519-7). Scarecrow.
Katz, William A. & Burgess, Robert, eds. Library Literature Five: The Best of 1974. LC 78-154842. 443p. 1975. 13.00 (ISBN 0-8108-0808-0). Scarecrow.
Katz, William A. & Gaherty, Sherry, eds. Library Literature Four: The Best of 1973. 1974. 13.00 (ISBN 0-8108-0702-5). Scarecrow.
Katz, William A. & Klaessig, Janet, eds. Library Literature Three: The Best of 1972. LC 78-15482. 1973. 13.00 (ISBN 0-8108-0613-4). Scarecrow.
Katz, William A. & Schwartz, Joel J., eds. Library Literature: The Best of 1970. LC 78-154842. 1971. 13.00 (ISBN 0-8108-0418-2). Scarecrow.
Katz, William L. An Album of Nazism. LC 78-12723. (Picture Album Ser.). (Illus.). (gr. 5 up). 1979. PLB 7.90 s&l (ISBN 0-531-01500-9). Watts.
--An Album of Reconstruction. LC 73-21933. (Picture Album Ser). (Illus.). 96p. (gr. 4-7). 1974. PLB 5.90 o.p. (ISBN 0-531-02701-5). Watts.
--An Album of the Civil War. LC 73-11031. (Picture Albums Ser.). (Illus.). 96p. (gr. 4-7). 1974. PLB 7.90 (ISBN 0-531-01518-1). Watts.
Katzan, Harry, Jr. Computer Data Management & Data Base Technology. 347p. 1980. pap. 10.95 (ISBN 0-442-23896-7). Van Nos Reinhold.
--An Introduction to Distributed Data Processing. LC 78-27323. (Illus.). 242p. 1979. text ed. 20.00 (ISBN 0-89433-061-6). Petrocelli.
--Invitation to Forth. (Illus.). 240p. 1981. 17.50 (ISBN 0-89433-173-6). Petrocelli.
--The Standard Data Encryption Algorithm. LC 77-13582. (Illus.). 1977. text ed. 14.00 (ISBN 0-89433-016-0). Petrocelli.
Katzeff, I. E. & Edwards, H. Angina Pectoris, Vol. 1. (Annual Research Reviews). 1978. 26.40 (ISBN 0-88831-023-4). Eden Med Res.
Katzeff, Paul. Full Moons. 1981. 12.95 (ISBN 0-8065-0737-3). Lyle Stuart.
Katzell, Raymond A., et al. Work, Productivity & Job Satisfaction: An Evaluation of Policy-Related Research. LC 75-21726. (Illus.). 445p. (Orig.). 1975. pap. text ed. 7.00 (ISBN 0-15-003082-7, Psych Corp). HarBraceJ.
Katzen, May. Mass Communication: Teaching & Studies at University. 278p. 1975. pap. text ed. 17.00 (ISBN 92-3-101158-8, U369, UNESCO). Unipub.
Katzenellenbogen, S. E. Railways & the Copper Mines in Katanga. (Oxford Studies in African Affairs). (Illus.). 165p. 1973. 12.00x o.p. (ISBN 0-19-821676-9). Oxford U Pr.
Katzenelson, Susan, jt. ed. see Szabo, Denis.
Katzenstein, Peter. Disjoined Partners: Austria & Germany Since 1815. LC 74-30526. 1976. 21.50x (ISBN 0-520-02945-3). U of Cal Pr.
Katzenstein, Peter J., ed. Between Power & Plenty: Foreign Economic Policies of Advanced Industrial States. LC 77-91053. 1978. 25.00 (ISBN 0-299-07560-5); pap. 8.95 (ISBN 0-299-07564-8). U of Wis Pr.
Katzer, J., tr. see Pisarev, Dimitri I.
Katzer, Jeffrey, et al. Evaluating Information: A Guide for Users of Social Science Research. LC 77-88057. (Sociology). (Illus.). 1978. pap. text ed. 7.95 (ISBN 0-201-00948-X). A-W.
Ka-Tzetnik. Phoenix Over the Galilee. 1977. pap. 1.75 o.s.i. (ISBN 0-515-04192-0). Jove Pubns.
Katzher, Louis. Man in Conflict. 1975. pap. text ed. 7.95x (ISBN 0-8221-0165-3). Dickenson.
Katzman, Natan. Program Decisions in Public Television. 72p. 1976. pap. 3.50 (Pub Telecomm). NAEB.
Katzman, Robert, ed. Congenital & Acquired Cognitive Disorders. LC 77-87458. (Association of Research in Nervous & Mental Disease Research Publication Ser.: Vol. 57). 1979. 29.00 (ISBN 0-89004-255-1). Raven.
Katzman, Robert, et al, eds. Alzheimer's Disease: Senile Dementia & Related Disorders. LC 77-84132. (Aging Ser.: Vol. 7). 1978. 49.00 o.p. (ISBN 0-89004-225-X). Raven.
Katznelson, Yitzhak. An Introduction to Harmonic Analysis. 264p. 1976. pap. text ed. 4.00 (ISBN 0-486-63331-4). Dover.
Katzner, Kenneth. Languages of the World. (Funk & W Bk.). 384p. 1974. 13.95 o.p. (ISBN 0-308-10120-0, TYC-T). T Y Crowell.
Kauchak, Donald P. & Eggen, Paul. Exploring Science in the Elementary Schools. 384p. 1980. pap. text ed. 11.50x (ISBN 0-528-61270-0); instr. manual free (ISBN 0-528-61271-9). Rand.
Kauder, Hugo. Counterpoint: An Introduction to Polyphonic Composition. (Music Reprint Ser.). 1979. Repr. of 1960 ed. lib. bdg. 19.50 (ISBN 0-306-79520-5). Da Capo.
Kauer, R., ed. see Terence.
Kaufelt, David A. Late Bloomer. pap. 2.50 (ISBN 0-440-15320-4). Dell.
--Midnight Movies: 1981. pap. 2.75 (ISBN 0-440-15728-5). Dell.
Kauffman, Christmas C. For One Moment. 1964. pap. 3.50 (ISBN 0-8024-3808-3). Moody.
--Lucy Winchester. 540p. 1974. pap. 5.50 (ISBN 0-8024-5040-7). Moody.
--Not Regina. (Giant Ser). (Illus.). 1971. pap. 2.95 (ISBN 0-8024-0072-8). Moody.
Kauffman, Christmas-Carol. Hidden Rainbow. 1963. pap. 3.50 (ISBN 0-8024-3807-5). Moody.
Kauffman, Christopher J. Ministry of Healing: The History of the Alexian Brothers from the French Revolution to the Present. 1978. 15.00 (ISBN 0-8164-0387-2). Crossroad NY.
--Tamers of Death: The History of the Alexian Brothers. 1977. 15.00 (ISBN 0-8164-0314-7). Crossroad NY.
Kauffman, George. Classics in Coordination Chemistry: The Selected Papers of Alfred Werner, Pt. I. (Illus.). 1974. pap. text ed. 2.50 (ISBN 0-486-61870-6). Dover.
Kauffman, George B., ed. Classics in Coordination Chemistry: Selected Papers (1798-1899, Pt. II. (Illus.). 1976. pap. text ed. 4.50 (ISBN 0-486-63343-8). Dover.
--Classics in Coordination Chemistry: Twentieth-Century Papers (1904-1935, Pt. III. LC 67-26870. (Classics of Science Ser.). (Illus.). 1978. pap. text ed. 6.00 (ISBN 0-486-63496-5). Dover.
Kauffman, Henry J. Pennsylvania Dutch American Folk Art. rev. & enl. ed. (Illus.). 10.00 (ISBN 0-8446-2354-7). Peter Smith.
--Pennsylvania Dutch American Folk Art. rev. & enl. ed. pap. 5.00 (ISBN 0-486-21205-X). Dover.
Kauffman, J., jt. auth. see Hallahan, D.
Kauffman, James M. Characteristics of Children's Behavior Disorders. 2nd ed. (Special Education Ser.). (Illus.). 352p. 1981. pap. text ed. 17.95 (ISBN 0-675-08055-X); write for info. instrs'. manual. Merrill.
Kauffman, James M., jt. auth. see Hallahan, Daniel P.
Kauffman, James M., jt. auth. see Wallace, Gerald M.
Kauffman, James M. & Payne, James S., eds. Mental Retardation: Introduction & Personal Perspectives. new ed. (Special Education Ser). 456p. 1975. text ed. 18.50x (ISBN 0-675-08728-7). Merrill.
Kauffman, Joseph F. At the Pleasure of the Board. 132p. 1980. 15.00 (ISBN 0-8268-1440-9). ACE.
Kauffman, Richard, jt. ed. see Brower, David.
Kauffman, Samuel H., jt. auth. see Reisman, Fredericka K.
Kauffmann, Stanley. Living Images: Film Comment & Criticism. LC 74-1822. 416p. (YA) 1975. 11.95 o.p. (ISBN 0-06-012269-2, HarpT); pap. 5.95 o.s.i. (ISBN 0-06-012268-4, TD 206, HarpT). Har-Row.
Kaufman, jt. auth. see Kiver.
Kaufman & Zimmerman, eds. Current Concepts in Ophthalmology, Vol. 5. LC 67-14718. (Illus.). 1976. 36.50 o.p. (ISBN 0-8016-2627-7). Mosby.
Kaufman, Aileen, tr. see Kloppenburg-Versteegh, J.
Kaufman, Alan S. Intelligent Testing with the WISC-R. LC 78-31174. (Personality Processes Ser.). 1979. 24.95 (ISBN 0-471-04971-9, Pub. by Wiley-Interscience). Wiley.
Kaufman, Arnold S., ed. see Edwards, Jonathan.
Kaufman, Barry N. A Miracle to Believe in. LC 80-942. 320p. 1981. 12.95 (ISBN 0-385-14991-3). Doubleday.
--Son-Rise. (Illus.). 1977. pap. 2.50 (ISBN 0-446-91828-8). Warner Bks.
Kaufman, Bel. Love Etc. 1981. pap. 2.75 (ISBN 0-380-53629-3, 53629). Avon.
--Up the Down Staircase. 1972. pap. 2.50 (ISBN 0-380-01598-6, 48421). Avon.
Kaufman, Bob. The Ancient Rain: Poems 1956-1978. Foye, Raymond, ed. 96p. 1981. 12.00 (ISBN 0-8112-0790-0); pap. 4.95 (ISBN 0-8112-0801-X). New Directions.
Kaufman, Burton I. The Oil Cartel Case: A Documentary Study of Antitrust Activity in the Cold War Era. LC 77-87963. (Contributions in American History: No. 72). (Illus.). 1978. lib. bdg. 17.95x (ISBN 0-313-20043-2, KOC/). Greenwood.
Kaufman, Charles H. Music in New Jersey, 1655-1860. LC 78-75180. 400p. 1981. 35.00 (ISBN 0-8386-2270-4). Fairleigh Dickinson.
Kaufman, Daniel. How to Get Out of Debt. 208p. (Orig.). 1981. pap. 2.50 (ISBN 0-523-41197-9). Pinnacle Bks.
Kaufman, David M. Clinical Neurology for Psychiatrists. 1981. write for info. (ISBN 0-8089-1321-2). Grune.
Kaufman, Doris, et al. Safe Within Yourself: A Woman's Guide to Rape Prevention & Self-Defense. LC 79-566334. (Illus.). 1980. pap. 7.95 (ISBN 0-916818-05-5). Visage Pr.
Kaufman, Felix. Methodology of the Social Sciences. 1978. Repr. of 1944 ed. text ed. 13.50x (ISBN 0-391-00931-1). Humanities.
Kaufman, Fredrick & Guckin, John P. The African Roots of Jazz. LC 78-8470. 148p. 1979. 14.95 (ISBN 0-88284-065-7); pap. 7.95 (ISBN 0-686-64874-9). Alfred Pub.
Kaufman, G. U. S. Financial Systems: The Money Markets & Institutions. 1980. 19.95 (ISBN 0-13-938084-1). P-H.
Kaufman, G. M., jt. auth. see Adelman, M. A.
Kaufman, George & Rosen, Kenneth T., eds. The Property Tax Revolt: The Case of Proposition 13. (Real Estate & Urban Economics Ser.). 1981. price not set prof. - refer. (ISBN 0-88410-693-4). Ballinger Pub.
Kaufman, Gershen. Shame: The Power of Caring. LC 80-17090. 160p. 1980. text ed. 13.25x (ISBN 0-87073-651-5); pap. text ed. 6.95x (ISBN 0-87073-652-3). Schenkman.
Kaufman, Glen, jt. auth. see Johnston, Meda P.
Kaufman, Gloria & Blakely, Mary K., eds. Pulling Our Own Strings: Feminist Humor & Satire. LC 79-3382. 192p. 1980. 20.00 (ISBN 0-253-13034-4); pap. 7.95 (ISBN 0-253-20251-5). Ind U Pr.
Kaufman, Gordon D. An Essay on Theological Method. LC 75-31656. (American Academy of Religion. Studies in Religion: No. 11). 1975. pap. 6.00 (ISBN 0-89130-307-3, 010011). Scholars Pr Ca.
Kaufman, Hal & Schroeter, Bob. Hocus-Focus. (Orig.). 1981. pap. 1.50 (ISBN 0-451-09781-5, J9781, Sig). NAL.
Kaufman, Helen A., ed. see Secchi, Nicolo.
Kaufman, Herb, jt. auth. see Homelsky, Geri.

Kaufman, Herbert. Administrative Feedback: Monitoring Subordinates' Behavior. 1973. 9.95 (ISBN 0-8157-4838-8); pap. 3.95 (ISBN 0-8157-4837-X). Brookings.

--Are Government Organizations Immortal? 1976. pap. 3.95 (ISBN 0-8157-4839-6). Brookings.

--Red Tape: Its Origins, Uses & Abuses. 1977. 9.95 (ISBN 0-8157-4842-6); pap. 3.95 (ISBN 0-8157-4841-8). Brookings.

Kaufman, Herbert, jt. auth. see Sayre, Wallace S.

Kaufman, Herbert J., ed. see Lefebvre, Jacques.

Kaufman, Jay, jt. auth. see Goldstein, Laurence.

Kaufman, Jerome E., jt. auth. see Devine, Donald F.

Kaufman, Joe. The Baseball Book. (A Golden Bk. for Early Childhood). (Illus.). 24p. (gr. k-2). 1976. PLB 5.38 (ISBN 0-307-68975-1, Golden Pr). Western Pub.

--Big & Little. (ps-1). 1967. PLB 7.62 (ISBN 0-307-60475-6, Golden Pr). Western Pub.

--The Toy Book. (Illus.). (ps-1). 1965. PLB 5.38 (ISBN 0-307-68915-8, Golden Pr). Western Pub.

Kaufman, John E., ed. IES Lighting Handbook-1981: Application Volume. 5th ed. (Illus.). 532p. 1981. 50.00 (ISBN 0-87995-008-0). Illum Eng.

--IES Lighting Handbook-1981: Reference Volume. 5th ed. (Illus.). 488p. 1981. 50.00 (ISBN 0-87995-007-2). Illum Eng.

Kaufman, Joseph. The Telephone Book. (Illus.). (ps-1). 1968. PLB 5.38 (ISBN 0-307-68938-7, Golden Pr). Western Pub.

Kaufman, Lloyd. Perception: The World Transformed. (Illus.). 1979. 22.50x (ISBN 0-19-502464-8); text ed. 15.95x (ISBN 0-19-502463-X). Oxford U Pr.

Kaufman, Milton. Radio Operator's License Q & A Manual. 9th, rev. ed. 1979. 15.85 (ISBN 0-8104-0651-9); pap. 9.95 (ISBN 0-8104-0650-0). Hayden.

Kaufman, Milton, jt. auth. see Duff, John R.

Kaufman, P. J. Technical Analysis in Commodities. LC 79-19513. 1980. 34.95 (ISBN 0-471-05627-8, Pub by Ronald Pr). Wiley.

Kaufman, Robert W., et al. Modernizing Calhoun County Government. 1975. 3.95 (ISBN 0-932826-08-3). New Issues MI.

Kaufman, Roger. Identifying & Solving Problems: A System Approach. 2nd ed. LC 76-5702. 134p. 1979. pap. 10.00 (ISBN 0-88390-050-5). Univ Assocs.

Kaufman, S. L. Investors Legal Guide. 2nd ed. 1979. 5.95 (ISBN 0-379-11126-8). Oceana.

Kaufman, Sherwin A. Sexual Sabotage: How to Enjoy Sex Inspite of Physical & Emotional Problems. 256p. 1981. 13.95 (ISBN 0-02-560740-5). Macmillan.

Kaufman, Ted, jt. auth. see Novich, Max.

Kaufman, W. I. Cholesterol Control Gram Counter. (Orig.). 1975. pap. 1.25 o.p. (ISBN 0-515-04936-0). Jove Pubns.

Kaufman, Wallace, jt. ed. see Rehder, Jessie.

Kaufman, Walter. Philosophic Classics, 2 vols. 2nd ed. Incl. Vol. 1. Thales to Ockham. text ed. 19.50 (ISBN 0-13-662403-0); Vol. 2. Bacon to Kant. text ed. 18.95 (ISBN 0-13-662411-1). LC 68-15350. 1968. text ed. (ISBN 0-685-73716-0). P-H.

Kaufman, Walter, ed. see Nietzsche, F.

Kaufman, William E. Journeys: An Introductory Guide to Jewish Mysticism. LC 80-69017. 1980. 12.50 (ISBN 0-8197-0482-2); pap. 7.95. Bloch.

Kaufman, William I. Brand Name Guide to Calories & Carbohydrates. (Orig.). 1973. pap. 2.25 o.p. (ISBN 0-515-05688-X, P3126). Jove Pubns.

--Calorie Counter for Six Quick-Loss Diets. 1973. pap. 1.25 o.p. (ISBN 0-515-04903-4, 9137). Jove Pubns.

--Calorie Guide to Brand Names. 1973. pap. 1.25 o.p. (ISBN 0-515-04905-0, 9177). Jove Pubns.

--Creative Crepe Cookery. (Orig.). pap. 1.50 o.s.i. (ISBN 0-515-04259-5). Jove Pubns.

--The Diet Diary. (Watch Your Diet Ser.). (Orig.). 1981. pap. 1.75 (ISBN 0-515-05915-3). Jove Pubns.

--Natural Foods & Health Foods Calorie Counter. (Orig.). 1973. pap. 1.25 o.s.i. (ISBN 0-515-04939-5, 9360). Jove Pubns.

--The New Low Carbohydrate Diet. 1973. pap. 1.25 o.p. (ISBN 0-515-04940-9, P101, Jove). BJ Pub Group.

--Pocket Encyclopedia of California Wine. Sullivan, Maurice T., ed. Titus, S., tr. 128p. (Orig.). 1980. 4.95 (ISBN 0-932664-09-1); pap. 3.95 (ISBN 0-932664-11-3). Wine Appreciation.

--Sugar-Free Cookbook. LC 64-15774. 1964. pap. 1.95 (ISBN 0-385-01549-6, C444, Dolp). Doubleday.

Kaufman, William I., jt. auth. see Reingold, Carmel B.

Kaufmann, B. P., jt. auth. see Demerec, M.

Kaufmann, Edgar, ed. see Wright, Frank L.

Kaufmann, Geir. Visual Imagery & Its Relations to Problem Solving. 1980. pap. 13.00x (ISBN 82-00-01788-5, Dist. by Columbia U Pr.). Universitet.

Kaufmann, Herbert, tr. see Birzle, Hermann, et al.

Kaufmann, Herbert J., ed. see Lefebvre, Jacques.

Kaufmann, Jerome E., jt. auth. see Devine, Donald F.

Kaufmann, John. Bats in the Dark. LC 72-158695. (A Let's Read & Find-Out Science Bk). (gr. k-3). 1972. 6.95 (ISBN 0-690-11780-9, TYC-J); PLB 7.89 (ISBN 0-690-11781-7). T Y Crowell.

--Birds in Flight. (Illus.). (gr. 5-9). 1970. PLB 6.96 (ISBN 0-688-31100-8). Morrow.

--Fish Hawk. (gr. 3-7). 1967. 6.75 (ISBN 0-688-21298-0); PLB 6.48 (ISBN 0-688-31298-5). Morrow.

--Flying Hand-Launched Gliders. LC 73-17236. (Illus.). 96p. (gr. 7 up). 1974. PLB 6.96 (ISBN 0-688-30108-8); pap. 2.50 o.p. (ISBN 0-688-25108-0). Morrow.

--Flying Reptiles, in the Age of Dinosaurs. LC 76-1919. (Illus.). 40p. (gr. 1-5). 1976. 5.75 o.p. (ISBN 0-688-22073-8); PLB 6.00 (ISBN 0-688-32073-2). Morrow.

--Insect Travelers. (Illus.). 128p. (gr. 7 up). 1972. 7.75 (ISBN 0-688-20036-2); PLB 7.44 (ISBN 0-688-30036-7). Morrow.

--Little Dinosaurs & Early Birds. LC 75-37575. (Let's Read & Find Out Science Book Ser.). (Illus.). (gr. k-3). 1977. PLB 7.89 (ISBN 0-690-01110-5, TYC-J). T Y Crowell.

--Robins Fly North, Robins Fly South. LC 70-109907. (Illus.). (gr. 2-5). 1970. PLB 7.89 (ISBN 0-690-70643-X, TYC-J). T Y Crowell.

--Streamlined. LC 74-2357. (A Let's-Read-&-Find-Out Science Bk). (gr. k-3). 1974. 6.95 o.p. (ISBN 0-690-00273-4, TYC-J); PLB 7.89 (ISBN 0-690-00565-2). T Y Crowell.

Kaufmann, John & Meng, Heinz. Falcons Return: Restoring an Endangered Species. (Illus.). 128p. (gr. 7 up). 1975. PLB 7.92 (ISBN 0-688-32027-9). Morrow.

Kaufmann, Sandra. The Cowboy Catalog. (Illus.). 192p. 1980. pap. 11.95 (ISBN 0-517-53950-0); pap. 10.95 (ISBN 0-517-54035-5). Potter.

Kaufmann, Thomas D. Variations on the Imperial Theme: Studies in Ceremonial Art & Collecting in the Age of Maximilian II & Rudolf II. LC 77-94699. (Outstanding Dissertations in the Fine Arts Ser.). 1978. lib. bdg. 24.00x (ISBN 0-8240-3231-4). Garland Pub.

Kaufmann, W. Nietzche: Philosopher, Psychologist, Architect. 4th ed. 1975. 25.00x (ISBN 0-691-07207-8); pap. 6.95 (ISBN 0-691-01983-5). Princeton U Pr.

Kaufmann, Walter. Critique of Religion & Philosophy. 1978. 17.50x (ISBN 0-691-07230-2); pap. 5.95 (ISBN 0-691-02001-9). Princeton U Pr.

--Discovering the Mind, Vol. 2: Nietzsche, Heidegger & Buber. LC 79-25209. (Discovering the Mind Ser.). 336p. 1980. 14.95 (ISBN 0-07-033312-2). McGraw.

--Hegel: Texts & Commentary. Incl. Who Thinks Abstractly. LC 65-13982. 1966. pap. 2.50 o.p. (ISBN 0-385-04058-X, A528B, Anch). Doubleday.

--Ragas of South India: A Catalogue of Scalar Material. LC 75-1941. (Oriental Ser.). 832p. 1976. 25.00x (ISBN 0-253-39508-9). Ind U Pr.

Kaufmann, Walter, ed. Religion from Tolstoy to Camus: Basic Writings on Religious Truth & Morals. pap. 8.95x (ISBN 0-06-130123-X, TB123, Torch). Har-Row.

Kaufmann, Walter A., ed. Existentialism from Dostoevsky to Sartre. 1958. 8.50 (ISBN 0-8446-2355-5). Peter Smith.

Kaufmann, William I. The Natural High Fiber Diet. 1976. pap. 1.25 o.p. (ISBN 0-515-04121-1, Jove). BJ Pub Group.

Kaufmann, William J., 3rd. Black Holes & Warped Spacetime. LC 79-18059. (Illus.). 1979. text ed. 14.00x o.p. (ISBN 0-7167-1152-4); pap. text ed. 8.95x (ISBN 0-7167-1153-2). W H Freeman.

--Galaxies & Quasars. LC 79-10570. (Illus.). 1979. text ed. 17.95x (ISBN 0-7167-1133-8); pap. text ed. 8.95x (ISBN 0-7167-1134-6). W H Freeman.

--Planets & Moons. LC 78-21156. (Illus.). 1979. text ed. 15.50x o.p. (ISBN 0-7167-1041-2); pap. text ed. 8.95x (ISBN 0-7167-1040-4). W H Freeman.

--Stars & Nebulas. LC 78-17544. (Illus.). 1978. text ed. 15.50x o.p. (ISBN 0-7167-0081-6); pap. text ed. 8.95x (ISBN 0-7167-0085-9). W H Freeman.

Kaufmann, William J., 3rd, intro. by. Particles & Fields: Readings from Scientific American. LC 80-10669. (Illus.). 1980. text ed. 15.95x (ISBN 0-7167-1233-4); pap. text ed. 7.95x (ISBN 0-7167-1234-2). W H Freeman.

Kaul, A. N. The American Vision: Actual & Ideal Society in Nineteenth-Century Fiction. LC 80-13606. (Yale Publications in American Studies: No. 7). xi, 340p. 1980. Repr. of 1963 ed. lib. bdg. 27.00x (ISBN 0-313-22427-7, KAAV). Greenwood.

Kaul, H. K. Travellers' India: An Anthology. 535p. 1980. 24.00x (ISBN 0-19-560654-X). Oxford U Pr.

Kaul, Lokesh. A Textbook on Educational Research. 432p. 1981. text ed. 22.50x (ISBN 0-7069-1186-5, Pub. by Vikas India). Advent Bk.

Kaul, Man M. The Philippines & Southeast Asia. 1978. text ed. 14.50x (ISBN 0-391-01010-7). Humanities.

Kaul, Mohini, et al. Human Histological Atlas. 200p. 1980. text ed. 50.00 (ISBN 0-7069-1055-9, Pub. by Vikas India). Advent Bk.

Kaul, Tej K., jt. auth. see Fox, Karl A.

Kaula, P. N., ed. Library Science Today. (Ranganathan Festschrift, Vol. 1). 1964. 30.00x (ISBN 0-210-34099-1). Asia.

Kaulins, Andis, jt. ed. see Kim, Kie-Taek.

Kaulla, K. N. Von see Von Kaulla, K. N. & Davidson, J. F.

Kaunda, Kenneth. The Riddle of Violence. LC 80-8348. 192p. 1981. 9.95 (ISBN 0-06-250450-9, HarpR, HarpR). Har-Row.

Kaung, Stephen, tr. see Nee, Watchman.

Kauper, P. G. Frontiers of Constitutional Liberty. LC 70-173668. (American Constitutional & Legal History Ser.). 252p. 1972. Repr. of 1956 ed. lib. bdg. 25.00 (ISBN 0-306-70408-0). Da Capo.

Kauper, P. G., et al. Article Five Convention Process: A Symposium. LC 70-150510. (Symposia on Law & Society Ser). 1971. Repr. lib. bdg. 25.00 (ISBN 0-306-70185-5). Da Capo.

Kauper, Paul G. Religion & the Constitution. LC 64-7898. (Edward Douglass White Lectures). 1964. 8.95 (ISBN 0-8071-0546-5); pap. text ed. 3.95x (ISBN 0-8071-0114-1). La State U Pr.

Kaur, Premka. Peace Lagoon. (Illus.). 1972. 8.95 o.p. (ISBN 0-913852-04-X); pap. 5.50 (ISBN 0-913852-03-1). Spiritual Comm.

Kaushik, R. P. Light of Exploration. LC 76-39622. 1977. 7.95 (ISBN 0-918038-01-4); pap. 3.95 (ISBN 0-918038-00-6). Journey Pubns.

Kautsky, John H. The Political Consequences of Modernization. LC 80-16087. 286p. 1980. Repr. lib. bdg. 11.50 (ISBN 0-89874-215-3). Krieger.

Kautsky, Karl. Thomas More & His Utopia. 258p. 1980. pap. text ed. 8.50x (ISBN 0-85315-493-7). Humanities.

Kautzky, Ted. Painting Trees & Landscapes in Watercolor. 1981. pap. 9.95 (ISBN 0-442-21918-0). Van Nos Reinhold.

Kauz, Herman. The Martial Spirit: An Introduction to the Origin, Philosophy & Psychology of the Martial Arts. LC 77-77808. (Illus.). 1978. 11.95 (ISBN 0-87951-067-6). Overlook Pr.

--Tai Chi Handbook: Exercise, Meditation, Self-Defense. LC 73-10552. 192p. 1974. pap. 5.50 (ISBN 0-385-09370-5, Dolp). Doubleday.

Kauz, Herman, tr. see Nakayama, M.

Kauzmann, Walter, jt. auth. see Eisenberg, David.

Kavadi, Naresh B. & Southworth, Franklin C. Spoken Marathi: Book One. rev. ed. LC 64-23368. 1968. text ed. 9.50x (ISBN 0-8122-7457-1). U of Pa Pr.

Kavaler, Lucy. Artificial World Around Us. LC 63-10233. (Illus.). (gr. 6-9). 1963. 7.95 (ISBN 0-381-99774-X, A05800, JD-J). John Day.

--Cold Against Disease. LC 69-10810. (Wonders of Cold Ser). (Illus.). (gr. 7-9). 1971. 8.95 (ISBN 0-381-99773-1, A14760, JD-J). John Day.

--Dangerous Air. LC 67-10819. (Illus.). (gr. 8 up). 1967. 8.95 (ISBN 0-381-99772-3, A17060, JD-J). John Day.

--The Dangers of Noise. LC 77-26588. (Illus.). (gr. 4-7). 1978. 8.95 (ISBN 0-690-03905-0, TYC-J); PLB 8.79 (ISBN 0-690-03906-9). T Y Crowell.

--A Matter of Degree: Heat Life & Death. LC 80-8789. 224p. 1981. 14.95 (ISBN 0-06-014854-3, HarpT). Har-Row.

--Noise: The New Menace. LC 74-9367. 224p. 1975. 9.95 (ISBN 0-381-98274-2, JD-J). John Day.

--Wonders of Fungi. LC 64-10450. (Illus.). (gr. 6-8). 1964. PLB 7.89 (ISBN 0-381-99770-7, A90800, JD-J). John Day.

Kavan, Anna. Asylum Piece. LC 79-28536. 1980. Repr. 11.95 (ISBN 0-935576-02-9). Unity Pr.

--Ice. 208p. 1974. pap. 0.95 o.p. (ISBN 0-445-00538-6). Popular Lib.

--Julia & the Bazooka. 1975. 6.95 o.p. (ISBN 0-394-49445-8). Knopf.

--Sleep Has His House. LC 79-26730. 1980. Repr. 11.95 (ISBN 0-935576-00-2). Unity Pr.

Kavanagh, Aidan, jt. auth. see Tiede, David L.

Kavanagh, Dennis, jt. auth. see Butler, David.

Kavanagh, Dennis, jt. ed. see Jones, Bill.

Kavanagh, P. J. People & Weather. 1980. pap. 5.95 (ISBN 0-7145-3666-0). Riverrun NY.

--People & Weather. 1980. pap. 5.95 (ISBN 0-686-68794-9). Riverrun NY.

Kavanagh, Patrick. Self Portrait: An Autobiographical Discourse. 2nd ed. 32p. 1975. pap. text ed. 2.25x (ISBN 0-85105-275-4, Dolmen Pr). Humanities.

Kavanagh, Peter. Garden of the Golden Apples: A Bibliography of Patrick Kavanagh. 1972. pap. 5.00 (ISBN 0-914612-05-0). Kavanagh.

--Sacred Keeper: A Biography of Patrick Kavanagh. (Illus.). 404p. 1980. text ed. 21.00x (ISBN 0-904984-48-6). Humanities.

Kavanagh, Terence. The Healthy Heart Program. 328p. 1981. pap. 6.95 (ISBN 0-442-29768-8). Van Nos Reinhold.

Kavanaugh, James. Celebrate the Sun. 1973. 6.95 (ISBN 0-87690-163-1). Dutton.

--Faces in the City. 1972. 6.95 (ISBN 0-87690-164-X). Dutton.

--Sunshine Days & Foggy Nights. (Illus.). 1975. 7.95 (ISBN 0-87690-167-4). Dutton.

--There Are Men Too Gentle. 1970. 5.95 (ISBN 0-87690-165-8). Dutton.

--Walk Easy on the Earth. (Illus.). 1979. 8.95 (ISBN 0-525-93078-7). Dutton.

--Will You Be My Friend? 1971. 6.95 (ISBN 0-87690-166-6). Dutton.

--Winter Has Lasted Too Long. 1977. 6.95 (ISBN 0-87690-248-4). Dutton.

Kavanaugh, Kieran & Rodriguez, Otilio, trs. The Collected Works of St. Teresa of Avila, Vol. 2. LC 75-31305. 560p. 1980. pap. 6.95x (ISBN 0-9600876-6-4). ICS Pubns.

Kavanaugh, Michael & Leckie, James O., eds. Particulates in Water: Characterization, Fate, Effects, & Removal. LC 80-19663. (Advances in Chemistry Ser.: No. 189). 1980. 59.50 (ISBN 0-8412-0499-3). Am Chemical.

Kavanaugh, Patrick & O'Connor, P. J. Tarry Flynn. Nemo, John, ed. (Abbey Theatre Ser.). pap. 2.50 (ISBN 0-912262-40-0). Proscenium.

Kavanaugh, Robert E. Facing Death. 1974. pap. 3.50 (ISBN 0-14-003812-4). Penguin.

Kavanaugh-Baran, Kathryn, jt. auth. see Adams, Bruce.

Kavasch, E. B. Introducing Eastern Wildflowers. (Northeast Color Ser.). (Illus.). 50p. 1981. pap. 3.95 (ISBN 0-88839-092-0). Hancock Hse.

Kavasch, E. Barrie. Wild Edibles of the Northeast. (Northeast Color Ser.). (Illus.). 64p. (Orig.). 1981. pap. 4.95 (ISBN 0-686-69148-2). Hancock Hse.

Kavenagh, W. Keith, ed. Foundations of Colonial America: A Documentary History, 3 vols. LC 72-80866. 2650p. 1981. Set. pap. 55.00 (ISBN 0-87754-208-2). Chelsea Hse.

Kavina, George, jt. auth. see Saville, Anthony.

Kaviratna, Harishchandra. Dhammapada, Wisdom of the Buddha. 1980. 8.50 (ISBN 0-911500-39-1); softcover 5.00 (ISBN 0-911500-40-5). Theos U Pr.

Kavrakoglu, Ibbrahim, ed. Mathematical Modeling of Energy Systems. (NATO Advanced Study Institute Ser.: Applied Science, No. 37). 490p. 1980. 55.00x (ISBN 90-286-0690-4). Sijthoff & Noordhoff.

Kavuma, Paulo. Crisis in Buganda 1953 to 1955: The Story of the Exile & Return of the Kaboka, Mutesa II. 112p. 1979. 12.50x (ISBN 0-8476-3280-6). Rowman.

Kaw, M. K. Look Closely at Om. 9.00 (ISBN 0-89253-768-X); flexible cloth 4.80 (ISBN 0-89253-769-8). Ind-US Inc.

--An Oasis of Solitude in the Sahara of Multitudes. (Writers Workshop Redbird Ser.). 72p. 1975. 14.00 (ISBN 0-88253-592-7); pap. text ed. 4.80 (ISBN 0-88253-591-9). Ind-US Inc.

Kawabata, Yasunari. Beauty & Sadness. Hibbett, Howard, tr. from Jap. 1975. 7.95 o.p. (ISBN 0-394-46055-3). Knopf.

--Beauty & Sadness. Hibbet, Howard, tr. from Jap. (Perigee Japanese Library). 224p. pap. 4.95 (ISBN 0-399-50529-6, Perigee). Putnam.

--Japan the Beautiful & Myself. Seidensticker, Edward G., tr. LC 75-90028. 1968. pap. 3.95 (ISBN 0-87011-088-8). Kodansha.

--The Lake. Tsukimura, Reiko, tr. from Japanese. LC 73-89699. 160p. 1980. pap. 3.95 (ISBN 0-87011-365-8). Kodansha.

--The Master of Go. Seidensticker, Edward G., tr. from Jap. (Perigee Japanese Library). 196p. 1981. pap. 4.95 (ISBN 0-399-50528-8, Perigee). Putnam.

--Snow Country. Seidensticker, Edward G., tr. from Jap. (Perigee Japanese Library). 192p. 1981. pap. 4.95 (ISBN 0-399-50525-3, Perigee). Putnam.

--The Sound of the Mountain. Seidensticker, Edward G., tr. from Jap. (Perigee Japanese Library). 288p. 1981. pap. 5.95 (ISBN 0-399-50527-X, Perigee). Putnam.

--Thousand Cranes. Seidensticker, Edward G., tr. from Jap. (Perigee Japanese Library). 160p. 1981. pap. 3.95 (ISBN 0-399-50526-1, Perigee). Putnam.

Kawada, Yukiyosi, jt. ed. see Iyanaga, Shokichi.

Kawamoto, Shigeo & Nishiwaki, Junzaburo, eds. The Kodansha English-Japanese Dictionary. Narita, Shigehisa & Shimizu, Mamoru, trs. 1557p. 1980. pap. 19.50 flexible soft-binding (ISBN 0-87011-420-4). Kodansha.

Kawamoto, Shigeo, jt. ed. see Jakobson, Roman.

Kawamoto, Shigeo, et al, eds. The Kodansha Japanese-English Dictionary. Shimizu, Hamoru & Harita, Shigehisa, trs. 1250p. 1980. flexible soft-binding 19.95 (ISBN 0-87011-421-2). Kodansha.

Kawamoto, Toshio. Saikei: Living Landscapes in Miniature. LC 67-26311. (Illus.). 132p. 1980. pap. 8.95 (ISBN 0-87011-418-2). Kodansha.

Kawamura, H., ed. see U. S.-Japan Seminar or Inelastic Light Scattering, Santa Monica, California. January 22-25, 1979.

Kawamura, K., jt. auth. see Brodal, A.

Kawase, Kozyun, ed. Das Sutra Vimalakirti. Fisher, Jakob & Yokota, Takezo, trs. (Ger.). 1969. 13.95 o.p. (ISBN 0-89346-060-5, Pub. by Hokuseido Pr). Heian Intl.

Kawashima, Masaaki. Men's Outerwear Design. LC 77-79658. (Illus.). 1978. text ed. 14.50 (ISBN 0-87005-196-2). Fairchild.

Kawharu, Ian H. Maori Land Tenure: Studies of a Changing Institution. 1977. 49.50x (ISBN 0-19-823177-6). Oxford U Pr.

Kawin, Ethel. Basic Concepts for Parents: Parenthood in a Free Nation, Vol. 1. (Illus.). 1969. pap. 2.00 (ISBN 0-931682-05-3). Purdue Univ Bks.

--Early & Middle Childhood: Parenthood in a Free Nation, Vol. 2. (Illus.). 1969. pap. 2.75 (ISBN 0-931682-06-1). Purdue Univ Bks.

--Later Childhood & Adolescence: Parenthood in a Free Nation, Vol. 3. (Illus.). 1969. pap. 3.00 (ISBN 0-931682-07-X). Purdue Univ Bks.

--Manual for Group Leaders & Participants: Parenthood in a Free Nation, Vol. 4. 1970. pap. 1.75 (ISBN 0-931682-08-8). Purdue Univ Bks.

Kay, Alan. Creative Art Through Photography. LC 72-8378. (Illus.). 128p. (gr. 5 up). 1973. 9.25 o.p. (ISBN 0-8231-1023-0). Branford.

Kay, Anthony & Rumble, Greville, eds. Distance Teaching. 350p. 1981. 37.50x (ISBN 0-89397-099-9). Nichols Pub.

Kay, Barbara A. & Vedder, Clyde B. Probation & Parole. 224p. 1980. 11.00 (ISBN 0-398-00986-4). C C Thomas.

Kay, Barbara A., jt. auth. see Vedder, Clyde B.

Kay, David. Poultry Keeping for Beginners. 1977. 11.95 (ISBN 0-7153-7395-1). David & Charles.

Kay, David A. New Nations in the United Nations. (International Organization Ser). (Illus.). 1970. 17.50x (ISBN 0-231-03350-8). Columbia U Pr.

Kay, David A., ed. The Changing United Nations: Options for the United States. LC 77-89037. (Praeger Special Studies). 1978. 24.95 (ISBN 0-03-043706-7). Praeger.

Kay, David A., jt. ed. see Goodrich, Leland M.

Kay, David A., et al. Environmental Protection: The International Dimension. 320p. 1981. text ed. 28.50 (ISBN 0-86598-034-9). Allanheld.

Kay, E. Legal Aspects of Business in Saudi Arabia. 160p. 1979. 40.00x (ISBN 0-86010-131-2, Pub. by Graham & Trotman England). State Mutual Bk.

--A Mathematical Model for Handling in a Warehouse. LC 68-21104. 1968. 22.00 (ISBN 0-08-012832-7); pap. 10.75 (ISBN 0-08-012831-9). Pergamon.

Kay, Eleanor. Clinic. LC 70-139486. (First Bks). (Illus.). (gr. 4-6). 1971. PLB 4.90 o.p. (ISBN 0-531-00721-9). Watts.

--First Book of the Emergency Room. LC 72-11774. (First Bks). (Illus.). (gr. 4-6). 1970. PLB 4.90 o.p. (ISBN 0-531-00712-X). Watts.

--Health Care Careers. LC 72-8881. (Career Concise Guides Ser.). (Illus.). 96p. (gr. 7 up). 1973. PLB 4.90 o.p. (ISBN 0-531-02607-8). Watts.

--Let's Find Out About Hospitals. LC 75-131145. (Let's Find Out Bks). 48p. (gr. k-3). 1971. PLB 4.47 o.p. (ISBN 0-531-00072-9). Watts.

--Sex & the Young Teen-Ager. LC 73-5861. (Career Concise Guides Ser.). (gr. 7-12). 1973. PLB 4.90 o.p. (ISBN 0-531-02641-8). Watts.

--Skydiving. LC 75-151885. (First Bks). (Illus.). (gr. 7-9). 1971. PLB 4.90 o.p. (ISBN 0-531-00750-2). Watts.

Kay, Elizabeth, jt. auth. see Fisher, Katherine.

Kay, Elster. Bel Canto. (Student's Music Library Ser). 1962. 6.95 (ISBN 0-234-77547-5). Dufour.

Kay, Ernest, ed. The World Who's Who of Women. 5th ed. (Illus.). 1167p. 1980. 65.00x (ISBN 0-900332-54-9, Pub. by Intl Biog). Biblio Dist.

Kay, Geoffrey, ed. Political Economy of Colonialism in Ghana: A Collection of Documents and Statistics, 1900-1960. Hymer, S. (Illus.). 1971. 47.50 (ISBN 0-521-07952-7). Cambridge U Pr.

Kay, George C. De see Ogle, Jane.

Kay, Helen. Apes. (Illus.). (gr. 5-8). 1970. 8.95g (ISBN 0-02-749490-X). Macmillan.

--Lincoln: A Big Man. (Illus.). (gr. 2-4). 1958. PLB 3.84 o.s.i. (ISBN 0-8038-4237-6). Hastings.

--A Pony for the Winter. (gr. 2-3). pap. 1.25 (ISBN 0-590-08082-2, Schol Pap). Schol Bk Serv.

Kay, J. D., jt. auth. see Hopkinson, R. G.

Kay, J. M. & Nedderman, R. M. An Introduction to Fluid Mechanics & Heat Transfer. 3rd. rev. ed. LC 74-77383. 300p. 1975. 44.50 (ISBN 0-521-20533-6); pap. 17.50x (ISBN 0-521-09880-7). Cambridge U Pr.

Kay, James T. Left-Handed Book. LC 66-23271. (Illus.). 64p. 1966. pap. 2.95 (ISBN 0-87131-156-9). M Evans.

--The Natural Superiority of the Left-Hander. LC 79-15824. (Illus.). 128p. 1979. pap. 3.95 (ISBN 0-87131-307-3). M Evans.

Kay, John. Plate Glass. limited ed. 1980. 2.00 (ISBN 0-917554-17-5). Maelstrom.

Kay, Joseph. The Social Condition & Education of the People in England & Europe, 2 vols. (The Development of Industrial Society Ser.). 1156p. 1980. Repr. 50.00x (ISBN 0-7165-1565-2, Pub. by Irish Academic Pr). Biblio Dist.

Kay, Marguerite, tr. see Degas, Edgar G.

Kay, Marguerite, et al, eds. Aging, Immunity & Arthritic Diseases. (Aging Ser.: Vol. 13). 275p. 1980. text ed. 27.00 (ISBN 0-89004-382-5). Raven.

Kay, Marshall & Colbert, E. H., eds. Stratigraphy & Life History. LC 64-20072. 1965. 23.95 (ISBN 0-471-46105-9). Wiley.

Kay, Norman. Shostakovitch. (Oxford Studies of Composers Ser). 72p. 1972. pap. 6.95x (ISBN 0-19-315422-6). Oxford U Pr.

Kay, Norman, ed. Complete Book of Duplicate Bridge. LC 78-89862. (Orig.). 1969. pap. 4.95 (ISBN 0-06-463262-8, EH 262, EH). Har-Row.

Kay, Ormonde De see De Kay, Ormonde, Jr.

Kay, Paul, jt. auth. see Berlin, Brent.

Kay, Robert E. Miniature Beer Bottles & Go-Withs: A Price Guide & Reference Manual for Miniature Beer Collectables. LC 80-81282. (Illus.). 166p. (Orig.). 1980. pap. 13.95 (ISBN 0-9604218-0-7). K & K Pubs.

Kay, Robert S. & Terry, Robert A., eds. How to Stay in College: A Learning Guide for Students. LC 78-61683. 1978. pap. text ed. 6.75 (ISBN 0-8191-0623-2). U Pr of Amer.

Kay, Ronald D. Farm & Ranch Management. Vastyan, James E., ed. (Agricultural Sciences Publications). (Illus.). 384p. Date not set. text ed. 15.95 (ISBN 0-07-033462-5, C). McGraw.

Kay, Shirley. The Bedouin. LC 77-88174. (This Changing World Ser.). 1978. 14.50x (ISBN 0-8448-1228-5). Crane-Russak Co.

Kay, Sophie & Consumer Guide Editors. The Chicken Cookbook. 160p. (Orig.). 1981. pap. 6.95 (ISBN 0-449-90049-5, Columbine). Fawcett.

Kay, Terry. After Eli. 288p. 1981. 10.95 (ISBN 0-395-30854-2). HM.

Kayal, Joseph M., jt. auth. see Kayal, Philip M.

Kayal, Philip M. & Kayal, Joseph M. The Syrian-Lebanese in America. (Immigrant Heritage of America Ser.). 1975. lib. bdg. 13.95 (ISBN 0-8057-8412-8). Twayne.

Kayber, Rudolf. Stendahl: The Life an Egoist. 278p. 1980. Repr. of 1930 ed. lib. bdg. 30.00 (ISBN 0-89760-427-X). Telegraph Bks.

Kayden, Xandra. Campaign Organization. 1978. pap. text ed. 5.95x (ISBN 0-669-01782-5). Heath.

Kaye, A. M. & Kaye, Myra, eds. The Development of Responsiveness to Steroid Hormones: Bat-Sheva Seminar on the Development of Responsiveness to Steroid Hormones Weizmann Institute of Science, Israel 18-26 Oct., 1978. LC 79-42938. (Advances in the Biosciences: Vol. 25). (Illus.). 494p. 1980. 68.00 (ISBN 0-08-024940-X). Pergamon.

Kaye, Anna & Mathan, Don C. Reflexology for Good Health. pap. 3.00 (ISBN 0-87980-383-5). Wilshire.

Kaye, Barrington. Participation in Learning. 1970. text ed. 17.95x o.p. (ISBN 0-04-370028-4). Allen Unwin.

Kaye, Brian H. Direct Characterization of Fine Particles. (Chemical Analysis Ser.). 500p. 1981. 50.00 (ISBN 0-471-46150-4, Pub. by Wiley-Interscience). Wiley.

Kaye, Dena. The Traveling Woman. 384p. 1981. pap. 2.95 (ISBN 0-553-14714-5). Bantam.

Kaye, Evelyn. Crosscurrents: Children, Families, & Religion. 224p. 1980. 11.95 (ISBN 0-517-53292-1). Potter.

Kaye, G., et al. Tables of Co-efficients for the Analysis of Triple Angular Correlations of Gamma-Rays from Aligned Nuclei. 1968. 42.00 (ISBN 0-08-012260-4). Pergamon.

Kaye, G. W. & Laby, T. H. Tables of Physical & Chemical Constants. 14th rev. ed. Bailey, A. E., et al, eds. LC 73-85205. (Illus.). 320p. 1973. text ed. 22.00x (ISBN 0-582-46326-2). Longman.

Kaye, Geraldine. The Day After Yesterday. (Illus.). 96p. (gr. 2-6). 1981. 8.95 (ISBN 0-233-97344-3). Andre Deutsch.

Kaye, Glen. Cape Cod: The Story Behind the Scenery. DenDooven, Gweneth R., ed. LC 80-81370. (Illus.). 1981. 7.95 (ISBN 0-916122-74-3); pap. 3.00 (ISBN 0-916122-73-5). K C Pubns.

--Hawaii Volcanoes: The Story Behind the Scenery. DenDooven, Gweneth R., ed. LC 76-23359. (Illus.). 1976. 7.95 (ISBN 0-916122-41-7); pap. 3.50 (ISBN 0-916122-18-2). K C Pubns.

Kaye, Jeremy J., jt. auth. see Freiberger, Robert H.

Kaye, M. M. Shadow of the Moon. 816p. 1980. pap. 3.95 (ISBN 0-553-13752-2). Bantam.

Kaye, Marvin. The Possession of Immanuel Wolf & Other Improbable Tales. LC 79-6865. 192p. 1981. 9.95 (ISBN 0-385-15862-9). Doubleday.

Kaye, Marvin, ed. Fiends & Creatures. 192p. 1975. pap. 1.25 o.p. (ISBN 0-445-00289-1). Popular Lib.

Kaye, Myra, jt. ed. see Kaye, A. M.

Kaye, Phyllis J., ed. National Playwrights Directory. LC 77-83135. (Illus.). 1977. 35.00 (ISBN 0-685-87023-5, O'Neill Theater Center). Gale.

Kaye, Seymour P. & Marsh, Arthur, eds. International Manual on Collective Bargaining for Public Employees. LC 71-130530. (Special Studies in International Economics & Development). 1973. 39.50x (ISBN 0-275-28074-8). Irvington.

Kaye, Sidney. Handbook of Emergency Toxicology. 3rd ed. 544p. 1977. 28.00 o.p. (ISBN 0-398-00987-2). C C Thomas.

--Handbook of Emergency Toxicology: A Guide for the Identification, Diagnosis, & Treatment of Poisoning. 4th ed. (American Lectures in Public Protection). (Illus.). 596p. 1980. 54.75 (ISBN 0-398-03960-7). C C Thomas.

Kayira, Legson. Jingala. 160p. (Orig.). (gr. 10up). 1979. pap. 5.00 (ISBN 0-582-64268-X, Drum Beat). Three Continents.

Kayira, Legsons. Looming Shadow. 1970. pap. 1.25 o.s.i. (ISBN 0-02-034010-9, Collier). Macmillan.

Kaylin, Arleen & Barnett, Laurie, eds. Update 1980. LC 80-21499. (The Great Contemporary Issues Ser.: Group Ii). (Illus.). 320p. 1980. 35.00 (ISBN 0-405-13781-8). Arno.

Kayne, Ronald C., ed. Drugs & the Elderly. rev. ed. LC 78-52886. 1978. 5.00 (ISBN 0-88474-045-5). USC Andrus Geron.

Kaynor, Richard S. & Schultz, Konrad F. Industrial Development: A Practical Handbook for Planning & Implementing Development Programs. LC 72-76450. (Special Studies in International Economics & Development). 1973. 29.50x (ISBN 0-275-28683-5). Irvington.

Kays, John M. Basic Animal Husbandry. 1958. text ed. 18.95x ref. ed. (ISBN 0-13-056598-9). P-H.

Kays, William M. & Crawford, Michael. Convective Heat & Mass Transfer. 2nd ed. (Mechanical Engineering Ser.). (Illus.). 1980. text ed. 27.95 (ISBN 0-07-033457-9); solutions manual 8.95 (ISBN 0-07-033458-7). McGraw.

Kaysar, Myrna, jt. auth. see Kysar, Robert.

Kaysen, Carl, ed. see Carnegie Commission on Higher Education.

Kaysen, Carl, ed. see Sloan Commission on Government & Higher Education.

Kayser-Jones, Jeanie S. Old, Alone, & Neglected: Care of the Aged in Scotland & in the United States. 160p. 1981. 14.95 (ISBN 0-520-04153-4). U of Cal Pr.

Kay-Shuttleworth, J. P. The Moral & Physical Condition of the Working Classes Employed in the Cotton Manufacture in Manchester. 76p. 1971. Repr. of 1832 ed. 15.00x (ISBN 0-7165-1772-8, Pub. by Irish Academic Pr Ireland). Biblio Dist.

Kaysing, Bill. Fell's Beginner's Guide to Motorcycling. LC 76-17052. 1976. pap. 4.95 (ISBN 0-8119-0365-6). Fell.

Kazamias, Andreas M. & Massialas, Byron G. Tradition & Change in Education: A Comparative Study. 1965. 9.95 (ISBN 0-13-925982-1). P-H.

Kazamias, Andreas M., ed. Herbert Spencer on Education. LC 66-17068. 1966. text ed. 9.75 (ISBN 0-8077-1602-2); pap. text ed. 4.25x (ISBN 0-8077-1599-9). Tchrs Coll.

Kazan, Elia. The Assassins. LC 70-16484. 312p. 1981. pap. 7.95 (ISBN 0-8128-6076-4). Stein & Day.

Kazanas & Klein. Technology of Industrial Materials. 1979. pap. 13.00 (ISBN 0-87002-301-2); lab manual 5.28 (ISBN 0-87002-170-2). Bennett IL.

Kazanas, Hercules. Readings in Career Education. 1981. pap. text ed. 10.96 (ISBN 0-87002-308-X). Bennett IL.

Kazanjian, Nuber. East & West. 1981. 8.95 (ISBN 0-533-04669-6). Vantage.

Kazantzaki. Zorba. (Arabic.). pap. 7.95x (ISBN 0-686-63551-5). Intl Bk Ctr.

Kazarian, E. A. Food Service Facilities Planning. (Illus.). 1975. text ed. 25.50 (ISBN 0-87055-168-X). AVI.

Kazarian, Edward A. Work Analysis & Design for Hotels, Restaurants & Institutions. 2nd ed. (Illus.). 1979. text ed. 19.50 (ISBN 0-87055-317-8). AVI.

Kazdin, Alan E. & Wilson, G. Terence. Evaluation of Behavior Therapy: Issues, Evidence & Research Strategies. LC 80-10311. xx, 230p. 1980. pap. 4.50x (ISBN 0-8032-7752-0, BB 745, Bison). U of Nebr Pr.

Kazemi, Farhad. Poverty & Revolution in Iran: The Migrant Poor, Urban Marginality & Politics. 180p. 1981. text ed. 17.50x (ISBN 0-8147-4576-8). NYU Pr.

Kazemzadeh, Firuz. The Baha'i Faith: A Summary Reprinted from the Encyclopedia Britannica. 1977. large type 0.60 (ISBN 0-87743-121-3, 7-40-79); 1976 ed. 0.50 (ISBN 0-87743-152-3, 7-40-80). Baha'i.

Kazic, Bozidar. The Chess Competitors Handbook. 1980. 22.50 (ISBN 0-7134-2035-9); pap. 14.50. David & Charles.

--International Championship Chess: A/Complete Record of Fide Events. 1974. 19.95 (ISBN 0-7134-2795-7). David & Charles.

Kazin, Alfred. Bright Book of Life: American Novelists & Storytellers from Hemingway to Mailer. LC 80-24576. 334p. 1980. pap. text ed. 6.95 (ISBN 0-268-00664-4). U of Notre Dame Pr.

--Contemporaries, from the Nineteenth Century to the Present. rev. ed. 500p. 1981. 17.95 (ISBN 0-8180-1131-9); pap. 9.95 (ISBN 0-8180-1132-7). Horizon.

Kazirmski. Arabe Francais Dictionnaire, 2 vols. 70.00x (ISBN 0-686-63571-X). Intl Bk Ctr.

Kazmer, Daniel R. & Kazmer, Vera, eds. Russian Economic History: A Guide to Information Sources. LC 73-17588. (Economics Information Guide Ser: Vol. 4). 550p. 1977. 30.00 (ISBN 0-8103-1304-9). Gale.

Kazmer, Vera, jt. ed. see Kazmer, Daniel R.

Kazmier, Leonard, jt. auth. see Philippakis, Andreas S.

Kazmier, Leonard J. Basic Statistics for Business & Economics. (Illus.). 1979. text ed. 16.95 (ISBN 0-07-033445-5, C); wkbk. 6.50 (ISBN 0-07-033446-3); instructor's manual 4.95 (ISBN 0-07-033447-1). McGraw.

--Statistical Analysis for Business & Economics. (Illus.). 1978. pap. text ed. 15.95 (ISBN 0-07-033439-0, C); instructors manual 5.95 (ISBN 0-07-033440-4). McGraw.

Kazmier, Leonard J., jt. auth. see Philippakis, Andreas S.

Kazovsky, L. G. Transmission of Information in the Optical Waveband. LC 77-28102. 1978. 24.95 (ISBN 0-470-26294-X). Halsted Pr.

Keach, Benjamin. Preaching from the Types & Metaphors of the Bible. LC 78-165059. (Kregel Reprint Library). 1975. 19.95 (ISBN 0-8254-3008-9). Kregel.

Keach, William. Elizabethan Erotic Narratives: Irony & Pathos in the Ovidian Poetry of Shakespeare, Marlowe, & Their Contemporaries. 1977. 19.50 (ISBN 0-8135-0830-4). Rutgers U Pr.

Keagan, Warren J. Mulitnational Marketing Management. 2nd ed. (Illus.). 1980. text ed. 21.00 (ISBN 0-13-605055-7). P-H.

Keairns, D. L. see Davidson, J. F.

Keairns, Dale L., ed. see International Fluidization Conference, 1975.

Kealey, Edward J. Medieval Medicus: A Social History of Anglo-Norman Medicine. LC 80-21870. (Illus.). 208p. 1981. text ed. 16.95x (ISBN 0-8018-2533-4). Johns Hopkins.

--Roger of Salisbury, Viceroy of England. (Illus.). 350p. 1972. 22.75x (ISBN 0-520-01985-7). U of Cal Pr.

Kealey, Greg, ed. Canada Investigates Industrialism: The Royal Commission on the Relations of Labour & Capital. LC 70-189604. (Social History of Canada Ser.). 1973. pap. 7.50 (ISBN 0-8020-6181-8). U of Toronto Pr.

Kealiinohomoku, Joann W., jt. ed. see Blacking, John.

Kean, Elizabeth see Herron, Dudley.

Kean, Mary-Louise, jt. ed. see Arnoff, Mark.

Kean, P. M. Chaucer & the Making of English Poetry, 2 vols. Incl. Vol. 1. Love Vision & Debate. 18.00 (ISBN 0-7100-7046-2); Vol. 2. The Art of Narrative. 18.00 (ISBN 0-7100-7250-3). (Illus.). 1972. Set. 35.00 (ISBN 0-685-25613-8). Routledge & Kegan.

Keane, A. H., ed. see Streeter, Edwin W.

Keane, Bil. For This I Went to College? (Family Circus Ser.). (Illus.). 1978. pap. 1.50 (ISBN 0-449-14069-5, GM). Fawcett.

--I Need a Hug. (Family Circus Ser.). (Illus., Orig.). 1978. pap. 1.50 (ISBN 0-449-14147-0, GM). Fawcett.

--I'm Taking a Nap. 1978. pap. 1.50 (ISBN 0-449-14144-6, GM). Fawcett.

--Look Who's Here. (Family Circus Ser.). (Illus.). (gr. 4 up). 1978. pap. 1.50 (ISBN 0-449-14207-8, GM). Fawcett.

--Smile! (Family Circus Ser.). (Illus.). 1979. pap. 1.50 (ISBN 0-449-14172-1, GM). Fawcett.
--Sunday with the Family Circus. (Illus., Orig.). pap. 1.75 (ISBN 0-8170-0364-9). Judson.
--When's Later, Daddy? (Family Circus Ser.). (Illus.). 1979. pap. 1.50 (ISBN 0-449-14124-1, GM). Fawcett.
--Where's PJ? (Family Circus Ser.). (Illus.). 1978. pap. 1.50 (ISBN 0-449-13982-4, GM). Fawcett.

Keane, Bil, jt. auth. see Bombeck, Erma.

Keane, Bill. Peace, Mommy, Peace. (Family Circus Ser.). (Illus.). 1978. pap. 1.50 (ISBN 0-449-14145-4, GM). Fawcett.

Keane, Claire. Management Essentials in Nursing. 1980. text ed. 15.95 (ISBN 0-8359-4220-1); pap. text ed. 12.95 (ISBN 0-8359-4202-3). Reston.

Keane, Jerryl. Book of Calendars. 700p. 1981. lib. bdg. 22.50 (ISBN 0-87196-467-8). Facts on File.

Keane, John. Sherlock Bones: Tracer of Missing Pets. 1979. 8.95 o.s.i. (ISBN 0-397-01335-3). Lippincott.

Keane, John B. Strong Tea. 1966. pap. 3.95 (ISBN 0-85342-255-9). Irish Bk Ctr.

Keane, Martin J. Classic Rods & Rodmakers. 1976. 17.95 (ISBN 0-87691-178-5). Winchester Pr.

Keane, Molly. Good Behavior. LC 80-8792. 288p. 1981. 10.95 (ISBN 0-394-51818-7). Knopf.

Kearin, Timothy. Year Around Conditioning for Army Football. LC 80-82965. (Illus.). 128p. (Orig.). 1980. pap. text ed. 4.95 (ISBN 0-918438-60-8). Leisure Pr.

Kearney, Elizabeth I. How to Write a Composition. (gr. 9-12). pap. text ed. 1.25x (ISBN 0-87543-535-1). Lucas.

Kearney, Jillian. Love's Claimant. 160p. (Orig.). 1981. pap. 1.75 (ISBN 0-446-94671-0). Warner Bks.

Kearney, P. C., ed. Ethylenethiourea. 14p. 1977. pap. text ed. 10.00 (ISBN 0-08-022026-6). Pergamon.

Kearney, Peter J., jt. auth. see Stuempfle, Herman G., Jr.

Kearney, Robert N. Trade Unions & Politics in Ceylon. LC 76-115495. (Center for South & Southeast Asia Studies, UC Berkeley). 1971. 21.50x (ISBN 0-520-01713-7). U of Cal Pr.

Kearney, Robert N., jt. ed. see Fernando, Tissa.

Kearney, Thomas H., et al. Arizona Flora. 2nd rev. ed. (Illus.). 1960. 26.50 (ISBN 0-520-00637-2). U of Cal Pr.

Kearns, George. Guide to Ezra Pound's Selected Cantos. 1980. text ed. 22.00x (ISBN 0-8135-0886-X); pap. 6.95 (ISBN 0-8135-0887-8). Rutgers U Pr.

Kearns, Graham. Arms for the Poor: President Carter's Polocies on Arms Transfers to the Third World. 136p. (Orig.). 1980. pap. text ed. 10.95 (ISBN 0-908160-57-7). Bks Australia.

Kearny, Edward. Dimensions of the Modern Presidency. LC 80-68461. (Orig.). 1981. pap. text ed. 7.95x (ISBN 0-88273-268-4). Forum Pr MO.

Kearny, Jillian. Agent of Love. 1979. pap. 1.75 (ISBN 0-446-94003-8). Warner Bks.

Kearsley, M. J., tr. see Nikitin, E. E.

Keary, Annie. Castle Daly: The Story of an Irish Home Thirty Years Ago. (Nineteenth Century Fiction Ser.: Ireland: Vol. 65). 1004p. 1979. lib. bdg. 46.00 (ISBN 0-8240-3514-3). Garland Pub.

Keasey, Charles B., Jr. & Keasey, Charles B., Jr., eds. Nebraska Symposium on Motivation, 1977: Social Cognitive Development. LC 53-11655. (Nebraska Symposia on Motivation: Vol. 25). 1978. 16.95x (ISBN 0-8032-2701-9); pap. 7.95x (ISBN 0-8032-7750-4). U of Nebr Pr.

Keasey, Merritt S. Gadsen's Silent Observers: An Introduction to Natural History of Southern Arizona. LC 75-103353. (Wild & Woolly West Ser.: No. 42). (Illus.). 56p. 1974. 7.00 (ISBN 0-910584-38-9); pap. 2.50 (ISBN 0-910584-68-0). Filter.

Keast, Allen & Morton, Eugene S., eds. Migrant Birds in the Neotropics: Ecology, Behavior, Distribution & Conservation. LC 80-607031. (Symposia of the National Zoological Park: No. 5). 576p. (Orig.). 1980. text ed. 35.00x (ISBN 0-87474-660-4); pap. text ed. 17.50x (ISBN 0-87474-661-2). Smithsonian.

Keat, Donald B. Fundamentals of Child Counseling. 300p. 1974. text ed. 19.50 (ISBN 0-395-17827-4); instructor's manual 2.50 (ISBN 0-395-17859-2). HM.

Keat, Donald B., II. Multimodal Therapy with Children. LC 78-7044. (Pergamon General Psychology Ser.: Vol. 73). 1979. 22.00 (ISBN 0-08-022236-6). Pergamon.

Keat, Russell & Urry, John. Social Theory As Science. 1975. 25.00x (ISBN 0-7100-8125-1); pap. 10.50 (ISBN 0-7100-8126-X). Routledge & Kegan.

Keates, J. S. Cartographic Design & Production. LC 72-9251. 240p. 1976. pap. 27.95 (ISBN 0-470-15106-4). Halsted Pr.

Keating, Bern. The Flamboyant Mr. Colt & His Deadly Six-Shooter. LC 78-8214. 1978. 9.95 o.p. (ISBN 0-385-12371-X). Doubleday.

Keating, Bridget. Why I Left the Convent. 1979. 4.50 o.p. (ISBN 0-8062-1062-1). Carlton.

Keating, Charles J. The Leadership Book. LC 77-99300. 1978. pap. 2.95 (ISBN 0-8091-2090-9). Paulist Pr.
--The Pastoral Planning Book. 96p. (Orig.). 1981. pap. 6.95 (ISBN 0-8091-2360-6). Paulist Pr.

Keating, Henry. Murder by Death. (Orig.). 1976. pap. 1.50 o.s.i. (ISBN 0-446-88161-9). Warner Bks.

Keating, James W. Competition & Playful Activities. LC 78-62741. 1978. pap. text ed. 8.75 (ISBN 0-8191-0589-9). U Pr of Amer.

Keating, L. Clark. Critic of Civilization: Georges Duhamel & His Writings. LC 65-12103. 288p. 1965. 11.00x (ISBN 0-8131-1104-8). U Pr of Ky.
--Etienne Pasquier. (World Authors Ser.: France: No. 241). lib. bdg. 10.95 (ISBN 0-8057-2674-8). Twayne.
--Joachim du Bellay. (World Authors Ser.: France: No. 162). lib. bdg. 10.95 (ISBN 0-8057-2132-0). Twayne.

Keating, L. Clark, ed. see Borges, Jorge L.

Keating, L. Clark, jt. ed. see Keller, John E.

Keating, L. Clark, tr. see Borges, Jorge L.

Keating, Lawrence A. & Nelson, Al P. The Deputy of San Riano. 1981. pap. 1.95 (ISBN 0-8439-0908-0, Leisure Bks). Nordon Pubns.

Keating, P. J. The Working Classes in Victorian Fiction. (Illus.). 1971. 22.50 (ISBN 0-7100-6991-X). Routledge & Kegan.
--The Working Classes in Victorian Fiction. (Illus.). 1979. pap. 8.95 (ISBN 0-7100-0196-7). Routledge & Kegan.

Keating, Thomas. The Heart of the World: An Introduction to Contemplative Christianity. 96p. 1981. 8.95 (ISBN 0-8245-0014-8). Crossroad NY.

Keatinge, Margaret C. Fighting Back: A Manual for Survival with Cancer. LC 79-67759. 146p. 1980. 8.95 (ISBN 0-533-04480-4). Vantage.

Keaton, Birchfield & Keaton, Henry F. Workbook for Short Term Planning. 58p. 1973. 15.00 (ISBN 0-686-68579-2, 14913). Hospital Finan.

Keaton, Henry F., jt. auth. see Keaton, Birchfield.

Keator, Glenn. Sierra Flower Finder: A Guide to Sierra Nevada Wildflowers. (Illus.). 1980. pap. 3.00 (ISBN 0-912550-09-0). Nature Study.

Keats, Ezra. The Trip. LC 77-24907. (Illus.). (gr. k-3). 1978. 8.95 (ISBN 0-688-80123-4); PLB 8.59 (ISBN 0-688-84123-6). Greenwillow.

Keats, Ezra J. Apartment Three. LC 78-123135. (Illus.). (gr. k-4). 1971. 8.95 o.s.i. (ISBN 0-02-749510-8). Macmillan.
--Dreams. LC 73-15857. (Illus.). 32p. (ps-2). 1974. 8.95g (ISBN 0-02-749610-4). Macmillan.
--Goggles. LC 70-78081. (Illus.). (gr. k-2). 1969. 8.95g o.p. (ISBN 0-02-749590-6). Macmillan.
--Hi, Cat. LC 71-102968. (Illus.). (gr. k-3). 1970. 8.95g (ISBN 0-02-749600-7). Macmillan.
--Kitten for a Day. LC 73-23057. (Illus.). 32p. (ps-2). 1974. PLB 4.95 o.p. (ISBN 0-531-02714-7). Watts.
--Little Drummer Boy. LC 68-25714. (Illus.). (gr. k-3). 1968. 8.95 (ISBN 0-02-749530-2). Macmillan.
--The Little Drummer Boy. LC 68-25714. (gr. k-3). 1972. pap. 2.50 (ISBN 0-02-044090-1, Collier); pre-pack 30.00 (ISBN 0-02-044080-4). Macmillan.
--Louie. LC 75-6766. (Illus.). 32p. (ps-3). 1975. 8.25 (ISBN 0-688-80002-5); PLB 7.92 (ISBN 0-688-84002-7). Greenwillow.
--Louie's Search. LC 80-10176. (Illus.). 32p. (gr. k-3). 1980. 9.95 (ISBN 0-590-07743-0, Four Winds). Schol Bk Serv.
--Pet Show! LC 73-156843. (Illus.). 32p. (gr. k-3). 1972. 7.95 (ISBN 0-02-749560-4). Macmillan.
--Pssst Doggie. LC 72-8642. (Illus.). 32p. (ps-1). 1973. PLB 4.95 o.p. (ISBN 0-531-02598-5). Watts.
--Skates. LC 73-6707. (Illus.). (ps-2). 1973. PLB 5.95 o.p. (ISBN 0-531-02652-3). Watts.
--Skates! LC 80-70119. (Illus.). 32p. (ps-3). 1981. Repr. of 1974 ed. 10.95 (ISBN 0-590-07812-7, Four Winds). Schol Bk Serv.
--The Snowy Day. (Illus.). (ps-1). 1962. PLB 7.95 (ISBN 0-670-65400-0). Viking Pr.
--Whistle for Willie. (Illus.). (ps-1). 1964. PLB 7.95 (ISBN 0-670-76240-7). Viking Pr.

Keats, John. Complete Poems & Selected Letters. Thorpe, Clarence D., ed. 1935. 13.95 (ISBN 0-672-63157-1). Odyssey Pr.
--Poems. Bullett, Gerald, ed. 1957. 12.95x (ISBN 0-460-00101-9, Evman); pap. 4.95 (ISBN 0-460-01101-4). Dutton.
--Poems. 336p. 1980. Repr. of 1897 ed. text ed. 15.75x (ISBN 0-8419-7301-6). Holmes & Meier.
--Poems of John Keats. Kunitz, Stanley, ed. LC 64-22174. (Poets Ser). (Illus.). (gr. 6 up). 1964. 8.95 (ISBN 0-690-63933-3, TYC-J). T Y Crowell.
--Poetical Works of John Keats. Garrod, H. W., ed. (Oxford Standard Authors). 1956. pap. 6.95x (ISBN 0-19-281067-7). Oxford U Pr.
--Poetical Works of John Keats. Garrod, Heathcote W., ed. (Oxford Standard Authors Ser.). 1956. 21.00x (ISBN 0-19-254132-3). Oxford U Pr.
--Poetical Works of John Keats. 2nd ed. Garrod, Heathcote W., ed. (Oxford English Texts Ser). 1958. 45.00x (ISBN 0-19-811815-5). Oxford U Pr.

Keats, Sidney. Cerebral Palsy. (Illus.). 384p. 1977. 18.75 (ISBN 0-398-00992-9). C C Thomas.
--Operative Orthopedics in Cerebral Palsy. (Illus.). 264p. 1970. photocopy ed. 19.75 (ISBN 0-398-00991-0). C C Thomas.

Keats, Theodore E., ed. Self-Assessment of Current Knowledge in Diagnostic Radiology. 2nd. ed. LC 80-81734. 1980. pap. 16.50 (ISBN 0-87488-278-8). Med Exam.

Keats, Warren A., jt. auth. see English, Frank P.

Keaveney, Sydney S. American Painting: A Guide to Information Sources. LC 73-17522. (Art & Architecture Information Guide Ser.: Vol. 1). 296p. 1974. 30.00 (ISBN 0-8103-1200-X). Gale.

Keavitt, Harold J. & Pondy, Louis R. Readings in Managerial Psychology. 3rd ed. LC 79-21587. xii, 732p. 1980. lib. bdg. 25.00x (ISBN 0-226-46986-7); pap. text ed. 12.95x (ISBN 0-226-46987-5). U of Chicago Pr.

Keavy, William T., tr. see Elbaz, Jean S. & Flageul, G.

Keay, F. Marketing & Sales Forecasting. 132p. 1972. text ed. 25.00 (ISBN 0-08-016737-3); pap. text ed. 12.75 (ISBN 0-08-016738-1). Pergamon.

Keay, F. & Wensley, G. F. Marketing Through Measurement. 1970. text ed. 27.00 (ISBN 0-08-015765-3); pap. 14.00 (ISBN 0-08-015764-5). Pergamon.

Keay, John. When Men & Mountains Meet: Explorers of the Western Himalayas 1820-75. (Illus.). 1978. 18.50 (ISBN 0-7195-3334-1). Transatlantic.

Keay, R.., jt. auth. see Garlick, J. P.

Kebabian, Paul B. & Lipke, William C., eds. Tools & Technologies: America's Wooden Age. (Illus.). 119p. (Orig.). 1979. pap. 10.00 (ISBN 0-87451-987-X). U Pr of New Eng.

Kebart, Richard C., et al. Self-Assessment of Current Knowledge in Radiologic Technology. 2nd ed. 1979. pap. 9.50 (ISBN 0-87488-274-5). Med Exam.

Kebart, Richard C., et al, eds. X-Ray Technology Examination Review Book, Vol. 3. 2nd ed. 1976. spiral bdg. 9.50 (ISBN 0-87488-443-8). Med Exam.

Kebbede, Girma. Basic Geographic Techniques in the Analysis of Public Policy. (Learning Packages in the Policy Sciences Ser.: No. 18). (Illus.). 46p. (Orig.). 1978. pap. text ed. 3.00 (ISBN 0-936826-07-X). Pol Stud Assocs.

Keble, John. The Christian Year: Thoughts in Verse for the Sundays & Holidays Throughout the Year. LC 70-167019. (Illus.). 291p. 1975. Repr. of 1896 ed. 20.00 (ISBN 0-8103-4095-X). Gale.

Keck, Caroline K. How to Take Care of Your Paintings: The Art Owner's Guide to Preservation & Restoration. (Illus.). 1978. pap. 5.95 (ISBN 0-684-15552-4, ScribT). Scribner.

Keck, Leander, jt. auth. see Craddock, Fred.

Keck, Leander E. & Martyn, J. Louis, eds. Studies in Luke-Acts. LC 79-8886. 324p. 1980. pap. 7.95 (ISBN 0-8006-1379-1, 1-1379). Fortress.

Keck, Leander E., ed. see Schleiermacher, Friedrich.

Keck, Leander E., ed. see Weiss, Johannes.

Keck, Leander E., tr. & intro. by see Strauss, David F.

Keck, Otto. Policy-Making in a Nuclear Program: The Case of the West German Fast-Breeder Reactor. LC 79-3831. 1981. write for info. (ISBN 0-669-03519-X). Lexington Bks.

Keckhut, John. The Dublin Pawn. 1977. 8.95 o.p. (ISBN 0-393-08761-1). Norton.

Kecskemeti, P. Insurgency As a Strategic Problem. 1977. pap. 4.00 o.p. (ISBN 0-87364-097-7). Paladin Ent.

Kecskemeti, Valeria & Knoll, J., eds. Prostanoids: Proceedings of the Third Congress of the Hungarian Pharmacological Society, Budapest, 1979. LC 80-41281. (Advances in Pharmacological Research & Practice Ser.: Vol. VI). 175p. 1981. 34.00 (ISBN 0-08-026391-7). Pergamon.

Kecskes, Bela, tr. see Shotski, V. P.

Kedar, Ervin Y., jt. auth. see Hill, James E.

Keddie, James & Cleghorn, William. Brewing in Developing Countries. 200p. 1980. pap. 11.50x (ISBN 0-7073-0250-1, Pub. by Scottish Academic Pr Scotland). Columbia U Pr.

Keddie, Kenneth M. Action with the Elderly: A Handbook for Relatives & Friends. 1978. text ed. 23.00 (ISBN 0-08-021442-8); pap. text ed. 9.75 (ISBN 0-08-021441-X). Pergamon.

Keddie, Nikki. The Middle East & Beyond. 1980. 29.50x (ISBN 0-7146-3151-5, F Cass Co). Biblio Dist.

Keddie, Nikki R. Iran: Religion, Politics & Society--Collected Essays. 243p. 1980. pap. 9.95x (ISBN 0-7146-4031-X, F Cass Co). Biblio Dist.
--Sayyid Jamal Ad-Din "Al-Afghani". A Political Biography. LC 74-159671. (Near Eastern Center, UCLA). 520p. 1972. 30.00x (ISBN 0-520-01986-5). U of Cal Pr.

Keddie, Nikki R., ed. Scholars, Saints & Sufis: Muslim Religious Institutions Since 1500. LC 77-153546. (Near Eastern Center, UCLA). 350p. 1972. 25.00 o.p. (ISBN 0-520-02027-8); pap. 7.95x (ISBN 0-520-03644-1). U of Cal Pr.

Keddie, William, ed. Cyclopaedia of Literary & Scientific Anecdote: Illustrative of the Characters, Habits, & Conversation of Men of Letters & Science. LC 74-156925. 1971. Repr. of 1859 ed. 26.00 (ISBN 0-8103-3730-4). Gale.

Keddington, Dorothy M. Return to Red Castle. 200p. 1981. 6.95 (ISBN 0-913420-93-X). Olympus Pub Co.

Kedgley, Susan J., jt. auth. see James, Wendy.

Kedourie, E. Nationalism. 3rd ed. 1979. pap. text ed. 6.50x (ISBN 0-391-02077-3, Hutchinson U Lib). Humanities.

Kedourie, Elie. Afghani & Abduh: An Essay on Religious Unbelief & Political Activism in Modern Islam. 1966. text ed. 7.50x (ISBN 0-391-01942-2). Humanities.
--Islam in the Modern World. 336p. 1981. 16.95 (ISBN 0-686-69288-8). HR&W.

Kedourie, Elie & Haim, Sylvia G., eds. Modern Egypt: Studies in Politics & Society. 136p. 1980. 25.00 (ISBN 0-7146-3168-X, F Cass Co). Biblio Dist.
--Palestine & Israel in the Nineteenth & Twentieth Centuries. 250p. 1981. 29.50x (ISBN 0-7146-3121-3, F Cass Co). Biblio Dist.
--Towards a Modern Iran: Studies in Thought, Politics & Society. 1980. 29.50x (ISBN 0-7146-3145-0, F Cass Co). Biblio Dist.

Kedrinsky, V. V., ed. English-Russian Dictionary of Petroleum Chemistry & Processing: Soviet Ed. 2nd rev. & enl. ed. 1978. text ed. 100.00 o.p. (ISBN 0-08-022945-X). Pergamon.

Kedron, Jane, tr. see Seidler, Babara.

Kedves. Paleogene Fossil Sporomorphus of the Bokony Mountains, Vol. I. 1973. 8.75 (ISBN 0-9960001-5-1, Pub. by Kaido Hungary). Heyden.
--Paleogene Fossil Sporomorphus of the Bokony Mountains, Vol. II. 1974. 8.00 (ISBN 0-9960001-6-X, Pub. by Kaido Hungary). Heyden.
--Paleogene Fossil Sporomorphus of the Bokony Mountains, Vol. III. 1979. 11.50 (ISBN 0-9960012-8-X, Pub. by Kaido Hungary). Heyden.

Kedward, H. R. Fascism in Western Europe Nineteen Hundred to Nineteen Forty-Five. LC 78-135658. 1971. 12.00x (ISBN 0-8147-4551-2). NYU Pr.
--Resistance in Vichy France. (Illus.). 1978. 29.95x (ISBN 0-19-822529-6). Oxford U Pr.

Kedzie, Daniel P., jt. auth. see Sommer, Armand.

Kee, Alistair, ed. The Scope of Political Theology. 1978. pap. text ed. 9.00x o.s.i. (ISBN 0-685-99193-8). Allenson.

Kee, Francis W. & Hong, Ee T. Education in Malaysia. 2nd ed. 1975. pap. text ed. 5.00 (ISBN 0-686-60350-8, 00101). Heinemann Ed.

Kee, Howard C. The Origins of Christianity: Sources & Documents. LC 73-4830. 320p. 1973. 9.95 (ISBN 0-13-642553-4). P-H.

Kee, Howard C. & Gomes, Peter J. Pentecost 1. Achtemeier, Elizabeth, et al, eds. LC 79-7377. (Proclamation 2: Aids for Interpreting the Lessons of the Church Year, Ser. C). 64p. 1980. pap. 2.50 (ISBN 0-8006-4081-0, 1-4081). Fortress.

Kee, Howard C., jt. auth. see Sloyan, Gerard S.

Kee, Howard C., et al. Understanding the New Testament. 3rd ed. (Illus.). 496p. 1973. 17.95 (ISBN 0-13-936104-9). P-H.

Kee, Kenneth, ed. see Chaucer, Geoffrey.

Keeble, T. W. Commercial Relations Between British Overseas Territories & South America, 1806-1914. (Institute of Latin American Studies Monographs: No. 3). 1970. text ed. 6.75x (ISBN 0-485-17703-X, Athlone Pr). Humanities.

Keeble, Ursula. Aids & Adaptations. 320p. 1979. pap. text ed. 14.90x (ISBN 0-7199-0963-5, Pub. by Bedford England). Renouf.

Keebler, Catherine M. & Reagan, James W., eds. A Manual of Cytotechnology. 5th rev ed. LC 77-9249. (Illus.). 1977. binder 45.00 (ISBN 0-89189-034-3, 45-3-001-00). Am Soc Clinical.

Keech, William R. The Impact of Negro Voting: The Role of the Vote in the Quest for Equality. LC 80-26518. (American Politics Research Series). ix, 113p. 1981. Repr. of 1968 ed. lib. bdg. 19.75x (ISBN 0-313-22774-8, KEIN). Greenwood.

--The Impact of Negro Voting: The Role of the Vote in the Quest for Equality. LC 80-26518. (American Politics Research Ser.). ix, 113p. 1981. Repr. of 1968 ed. lib. bdg. 19.75x (ISBN 0-313-22774-8, KEIN). Greenwood.

Keech, William R. & Matthews, Donald R. The Party's Choice with an Epilogue on the 1976 Nominations. (Studies in Presidential Selection). 1977. 14.95 (ISBN 0-8157-4852-3); pap. 5.95 (ISBN 0-8157-4851-5). Brookings.

Keedy, Mervin L. & Bittinger, Marvin L. Algebra, a Modern Introduction, 12 vols. Incl. Whole Numbers, Addition & Subtraction. 2.68 o.p. (ISBN 0-201-03635-5); Whole Numbers, Multiplication & Division. 2.68 o.p. (ISBN 0-201-03636-3); Operations of the Numbers of Arthmetic. 2.68 o.p. (ISBN 0-201-03637-1); Decimals & Percent. 2.68 o.p. (ISBN 0-201-03638-X); Measures, Ratio & Averages. 2.68 o.p. (ISBN 0-201-03639-8); The Numbers of Ordinary Arithmetic & Algebra. 2.68 o.p. (ISBN 0-201-03640-1); Rational Numbers, Albegra & Solving Equations. 2.68 o.p. (ISBN 0-201-03641-X); Polynomials. 2.68 o.p. (ISBN 0-201-03642-8); Functions & Basic Geometry. 2.68 o.p. (ISBN 0-201-03643-6); Linear Equations & Systems of Equations. 2.68 o.p. (ISBN 0-201-03644-4); Polynomials in Several Variables & Fractional Equations. 1.60 o.p. (ISBN 0-201-03645-2); Roots, Radicals & Quadratic Equations. 2.68 o.p. (ISBN 0-201-03646-0); tchrs' manual 4.04 o.p. (ISBN 0-201-03647-9). 1976. tchr's manual 4.04 o.p. (ISBN 0-201-03647-9). A-W.

--Algebra & Trigonometry: A Functions Approach. 2nd ed. LC 77-79461. (Illus.). 1978. pap. text ed. 16.95 (ISBN 0-201-03870-6); instructor's manual 5.95 (ISBN 0-201-03871-4); test booklet with answers 3.00 (ISBN 0-201-03872-2); dianostic test 0.35 (ISBN 0-201-03749-1). A-W.

--Arithmetic. 3rd ed. LC 78-18648. 1979. pap. text ed. 13.95 (ISBN 0-201-03791-2); avail. instructor's manual with tests (ISBN 0-201-03792-0); test book 9.95 (ISBN 0-201-03795-5); student's guide to margin exercises 3.95 (ISBN 0-201-03794-7). A-W.

--College Algebra: A Functions Approach. 2nd ed. LC 77-79464. 1978. pap. text ed. 15.95 (ISBN 0-201-03866-8); special supplement 0.50 (ISBN 0-201-03861-7). A-W.

--Essential Mathematics. 3rd ed. 1980. pap. text ed. 16.95 (ISBN 0-201-03837-4). A-W.

--Essential Mathematics: A Modern Approach. 2nd ed. LC 76-9337. (Illus.). 1977. pap. text ed. 14.95 o.p. (ISBN 0-201-03728-9); instr's manual 3.00 o.p. (ISBN 0-201-03742-4). A-W.

--Fundamental Algebra & Trigonometry. 2nd ed. (Mathematics-Remedial & Precalculus Ser.). (Illus.). 576p. 1981. text ed. 15.95 (ISBN 0-201-03839-0). A-W.

--Fundamental College Algebra. 2nd ed. (Mathematics-Remedial & Precalculus Ser.). 480p. 1981. text ed. 15.95 (ISBN 0-201-03847-1). A-W.

--Introductory Algebra. 3rd ed. LC 78-55821. (Illus.). 1979. pap. text ed. 14.95 (ISBN 0-201-03874-9); instr's man. 3.50 (ISBN 0-201-03875-7); answer book 3.50 (ISBN 0-201-03876-5); student sol. manual 3.50 (ISBN 0-201-03877-3). A-W.

--Trigonometry: Triangles & Functions. 2nd ed. 1978. pap. text ed. 13.95 (ISBN 0-201-03868-4). A-W.

Keedy, Mervin L. & Nelson, Charles W. Geometry: A Modern Introduction. 2nd ed. LC 79-178267. 1973. text ed. 13.95 (ISBN 0-201-03673-8). A-W.

Keefe, Joan, ed. & tr. Irish Poems, from Cromwell to the Famine: A Miscellany. LC 76-755. 1976. 12.00 (ISBN 0-8387-1887-6). Bucknell U Pr.

Keefe, John E. Aim for a Job As Electronic Technician. LC 67-11254. (Aim High Vocational Guidance Ser). (gr. 7up). 1978. PLB 5.97 (ISBN 0-8239-0451-2). Rosen Pr.

Keefe, John W. & Wise, Susan, eds. Selected Works of Eighteenth Century French Art in the Collections of the Art Institute of Chicago. LC 76-410. (Illus.). 219p. (Orig.). 1976. pap. 12.50 (ISBN 0-86559-019-2). Art Inst Chi.

Keefe, William F. Open Minds!: The Forgotten Side of Communication. LC 75-2412. 208p. 1975. 13.95 (ISBN 0-8144-5372-4). Am Mgmt.

--Successful Home Appliances: The 1980's Energy & Money Saving Guide. Case, Virginia, ed. (Successful Ser.). (Illus.). 1981. 18.95 (ISBN 0-89999-019-3); pap. 8.95 (ISBN 0-89999-020-7). Structures Pub.

Keefe, William F., jt. auth. see Drouillard, Anne.

Keefe, William J. Congress & the American People. (Illus.). 1980. pap. text ed. 8.50 (ISBN 0-13-167569-9). P-H.

Keefe, William J. & Ogul, Morris. The American Legislative Process: Congress & the States. 4th ed. (Illus.). 1977. text ed. 17.95 (ISBN 0-13-028100-X). P-H.

Keefe, William J. & Ogul, Morris S. The American Legislative Process. 5th ed. (Illus.). 544p. 1981. text ed. 17.95 (ISBN 0-13-028043-7). P-H.

Keefer, Anna. For Women Only. 112p. 1980. pap. 5.95 (ISBN 0-89305-037-7). Anna Pub.

Keefer, T. C. Philosophy of Railroads. LC 72-163835. (Social History of Canada Ser.). 1972. pap. 4.50 (ISBN 0-8020-6157-5). U of Toronto Pr.

Keefer, Truman F. Philip Wylie. (US. Authors Ser.). 1977. lib. bdg. 10.95 (ISBN 0-8057-7187-5). Twayne.

Keegan, B. F. & Ceidigh, P. O., eds. Biology of Benthic Organisms: 11th European Symposium on Marine Biology, Galway, Ireland. 1977. pap. text ed. 75.00 (ISBN 0-08-021378-2). Pergamon.

Keegan, Hugh L. Scorpions of Medical Importance. LC 80-16419. (Illus.). 1980. 22.50 (ISBN 0-87805-124-4). U Pr of Miss.

Keegan, John. Opening Moves: August, 1914. 160p. 1975. pap. 2.00 (ISBN 0-345-24339-0, 24339-0-200). Ballantine.

--Who Was Who in World War II. LC 77-95149. (Illus.). 1978. 14.95 o.p. (ISBN 0-690-01753-7, TYC-T). T Y Crowell.

--World Armies. 1980. 40.00 (ISBN 0-87196-407-4). Facts on File.

Keegan, John & Wheatcroft, Andrew. Who's Who in Military History. LC 76-13284. 1976. 25.00 o.p. (ISBN 0-688-02956-6). Morrow.

Keegan, Michele F. Of Clouds & Sunshine. 36p. 1981. 3.50 (ISBN 0-8059-2772-7). Dorrance.

Keehn, J. D. The Origins of Madness: The Psychopathology of Animal Life. (Illus.). 1979. text ed. 52.00 (ISBN 0-08-023725-8). Pergamon.

Keel, Bennie C. Cherokee Archaeology: A Study of the Appalachian Summit. LC 75-41444. (Illus.). 1976. 14.50x (ISBN 0-87049-189-X). U of Tenn Pr.

Keel, Charlene. Come Slowly, Eden. 1978. pap. 1.75 (ISBN 0-505-51322-6). Tower Bks.

Keel, John. The Eighth Tower. 1977. pap. 1.75 o.p. (ISBN 0-451-07460-2, E7460, Sig). NAL.

Keel, John A. Our Haunted Planet. 224p. 1977. pap. 1.50 o.p. (ISBN 0-449-13580-2, GM). Fawcett.

Keel, Othmar. The Symbolism of the Biblical World Ancient Near Eastern Iconography & the Book of Psalms. (Illus.). 1978. 24.50 (ISBN 0-8164-0353-8). Crossroad NY.

Keelan, Jim. Having Fun Being Yourself. 1975. Repr. 5.00 (ISBN 0-686-18725-3, Pub. by Professional Writers Group). Comm Unltd.

--Re-Entry into the Single Life. 1977. 5.00 (ISBN 0-686-18830-6, Pub. by Professional Writers Group). Comm Unltd.

Keele, Luqman & Pinkwater, Daniel. Java Jack. LC 79-7892. (Illus.). 160p. (gr. 5-12). 1980. 7.95 (ISBN 0-690-03995-6, TYC-J); PLB 7.89 (ISBN 0-690-03996-4). T Y Crowell.

Keele, Mary, ed. Florence Nightingale in Rome: Letters Written 1847 to 1848. 1981. 12.00 (ISBN 0-87169-143-4). Am Philos.

Keeler, Sr. Jerome, jt. auth. see Peters, Elizabeth.

Keeler, Mary F. Bibliography of British History: Stuart Period, Sixteen Hundred to Seventeen-Fourteen. 2nd ed. (Bibliography of British History Ser). 1970. 49.00x (ISBN 0-19-821371-9). Oxford U Pr.

Keeler, William F. Aboard the USS Florida: 1863-65. Daly, Robert W., ed. LC 79-6112. (Navies & Men Ser.). 1980. Repr. of 1968 ed. lib. bdg. 20.00x (ISBN 0-405-13041-4). Arno.

Keeley, Edmund, tr. see Elytis, Odysseus.

Keeley, Kim, jt. auth. see Solomon, Joel.

Keeley, Michael C. Labor Supply & Public Policy: A Critical Review. (Studies in Labor Economics Ser.). 1981. price not set (ISBN 0-12-403920-0). Acad Pr.

Keeley, Michael C., ed. Population, Public Policy, & Economic Development. LC 75-23975. (Praeger Special Studies). 24.95 (ISBN 0-275-55670-0). Praeger.

Keeley, Steve. The Complete Book of Racquetball. pap. 8.95 (ISBN 0-695-80651-3). Follett.

Keeling, D. F. British Library History, Nineteen Sixty-Nine to Nineteen Seventy-Two. (Bibliographic Ser.). 1975. pap. 13.50x (ISBN 0-85365-417-4, Pub. by Lib Assn England). Oryx Pr.

Keeling, D. F., ed. British Library History, Nineteen Seventy-Three to Nineteen Seventy-Six. (Bibliographic Ser.). pap. 15.50x (ISBN 0-85365-781-5, Pub. by Lib Assn England). Oryx Pr.

--British Library History, Nineteen Sixty-Two to Nineteen Sixty-Eight. (Bibliographic Ser.). 1971. pap. 13.50x (ISBN 0-85365-345-3, Pub. by Lib Assn England). Oryx Pr.

Keeling, Jill A. The Old English Sheepdog. Foyle, Christina, ed. (Foyle's Handbks). 1973. 3.95 (ISBN 0-685-55799-5). Palmetto Pub.

Keely, H. H. & Price, Christine. City of the Dagger. LC 70-161066. (Illus.). (gr. 3-6). 1971. 4.95 o.p. (ISBN 0-7232-6077-X). Warne.

Keely, John. Dolly Parton. (Rock 'n Pop Stars). (Illus.). (gr. 4-12). 1979. PLB 5.95 (ISBN 0-87191-695-9); pap. 2.95 (ISBN 0-89812-095-0). Creative Ed.

Keely, Stuart M., jt. auth. see Browne, M. Neil.

Keen, Benjamin. The Aztec Image in Western Thought. LC 74-163952. 1971. 40.00 (ISBN 0-8135-0698-0). Rutgers U Pr.

Keen, Benjamin & Wasserman, Mark. A Short History of Latin America. 1979. pap. text ed. 13.50 (ISBN 0-395-27838-4). HM.

Keen, Benjamin, ed. Latin American Civilization, 2 vols. 3rd ed. 1974. Vol. 1. pap. text ed. 11.50 (ISBN 0-395-17582-8); Vol. 2. pap. text ed. 11.50 (ISBN 0-395-17583-6). HM.

Keen, Benjamin, tr. see De Zorita, Alonso.

Keen, Ernest. Three Faces of Being: Toward an Existential Clinical Psychology. LC 78-128900. (Century Psychology Ser.). (Orig.). 1970. 22.50x (ISBN 0-89197-452-0); pap. text ed. 9.50x (ISBN 0-89197-453-9). Irvington.

Keen, Harry & Jarrett, John. Triumphs of Medicine. (Illus.). 1976. 19.95 o.p. (ISBN 0-236-30925-0, Pub. by Paul Elek). Merrimack Bk Serv.

Keen, Jeffrey S. Managing Systems Development. (Information Processing). 320p. 1981. 27.50 (ISBN 0-471-27839-4, Pub. by Wiley-Interscience). Wiley.

Keen, M. J. An Introduction to Marine Geology. 1968. 27.00 (ISBN 0-08-012506-9); pap. 9.25 (ISBN 0-08-012505-0). Pergamon.

Keen, Martin L. Lightning & Thunder. LC 69-12115. (Illus.). (gr. 4 up). 1969. PLB 4.29 o.p. (ISBN 0-671-32116-1). Messner.

Keen, Peter F. & Scott-Morton, Michael S. Decision Support Systems: An Organizational Perspective. 1978. text ed. 17.95 (ISBN 0-201-03667-3). A-W.

Keen, Sam. Apology for Wonder. LC 69-17017. 1969. pap. 4.95 (ISBN 0-06-064261-0, RD 158, HarpR). Har-Row.

--Gabriel Marcel. LC 67-11288. (Makers of Contemporary Theology Ser). 1967. pap. 3.45 (ISBN 0-8042-0584-1). John Knox.

Keenan, Brigid. The Women We Wanted to Look Like. LC 78-4014. (Illus.). 1978. 14.95 o.p. (ISBN 0-312-88783-3). St Martin.

Keenan, Charles, jt. auth. see Wood, Jesse H.

Keenan, E. L., ed. Formal Semantics of Natural Language. LC 74-25657. 456p. 1975. 59.50 (ISBN 0-521-20697-9). Cambridge U Pr.

Keenan, Edward P., jt. auth. see Dressler, Isidore.

Keenan, Jack. Cincinnati & Lake Erie. LC 74-23814. (Illus.). 224p. 1975. 21.95 o.p. (ISBN 0-87095-055-X). Golden West.

Keenan, Joseph H., et al. Steam Tables-Thermodynamic Properties of Water Including Vapor, Liquid & Solid Phases. LC 71-94916. 1969. Eng. units 22.95 (ISBN 0-471-46501-1, Pub by Wiley-Interscience). Wiley.

--Gas Tables: Thermodynamic Properties of Air Products of Combustion & Component Gases Compressible Flow Functions Including Those of Ascher H. Shapiro & Gilbert M. Edelman. 2nd ed. LC 79-15098. 1980. 22.50 (ISBN 0-471-02207-1, Pub. by Wiley-Interscience). Wiley.

--Steam Tables: Thermodynamic Properties of Water Including Vapor, Liquid, & Solid Phases. LC 77-28321. 1978. 22.95 (ISBN 0-471-04210-2, Pub. by Wiley-Interscience). Wiley.

Keenan, Joseph T. Plaid on the Constitution of the United States. 1975. pap. 4.95 (ISBN 0-256-01615-1, 06-1099-00). Learning Syst.

Keenan, Patricia A., jt. ed. see Haley, Harold B.

Keene & Edwards. Chess Players Bedside Book. 14.95 (Pub. by Batsford England); pap. 10.95. David & Charles.

Keene, Betsey D. History of Bourne, 1622-1937. LC 75-5093. (Illus.). 288p. 1975. Repr. of 1937 ed. 10.00x (ISBN 0-88492-006-2). W S Sullwold.

Keene, Carolyn. The Greek Symbol Mystery. Barish, Wendy, ed. (Nancy Drew Ser.). (Illus.). 192p. (gr. 3-7). 1981. 7.95 (ISBN 0-671-42297-9); pap. 1.95 (ISBN 0-671-42298-7). Wanderer Bks.

--Nancy Drew Book of Hidden Clues. 64p. (gr. 3-7). 1980. pap. 3.95 (ISBN 0-671-95713-9). Wanderer Bks.

--Nancy Drew: The Secret in the Old Lace. (Nancy Drew Mystery Stories). 192p. (gr. 3-7). 1980. PLB 7.95 (ISBN 0-671-41119-5); pap. 1.95 (ISBN 0-671-41114-4). Wanderer Bks.

Keene, Donald. Battles of Coxinga. (Cambridge Oriental Ser). 1951. 38.50 (ISBN 0-521-05469-9). Cambridge U Pr.

--Four Major Plays of Chikamatsu. LC 64-5372. 1961. 25.00x (ISBN 0-231-02490-8); pap. 6.00 (ISBN 0-231-08553-2). Columbia U Pr.

--Japanese Discovery of Europe, 1720-1830. rev. ed. LC 69-13180. (Illus.). 1969. 10.00x (ISBN 0-8047-0668-9); pap. 5.95 (ISBN 0-8047-0669-7). Stanford U Pr.

--Modern Japanese Novels & the West. (Illus.). 1961. 4.95x (ISBN 0-8139-0156-1). U Pr of Va.

Keene, Donald, ed. Anthology of Japanese Literature: Earliest Era to Mid-Nineteenth Century. 1955. pap. 7.95 (ISBN 0-394-17221-3, E216, Ever). Grove.

--Twenty Plays of the No Theatre. Tyler, et al, trs. from Jap. LC 74-121556. 1970. 22.50x (ISBN 0-231-03454-7); pap. 12.00x (ISBN 0-231-03455-5). Columbia U Pr.

Keene, Donald, jt. ed. see Birch, Cyril.

Keene, Donald, tr. from Japanese. Chushingura: The Treasury of Loyal Retainers. LC 78-142283. 1971. 17.50x (ISBN 0-231-03530-6); pap. 6.00x (ISBN 0-231-03531-4). Columbia U Pr.

Keene, Donald, tr. from Jap. see Dazai, Osamu.

Keene, Donald, tr. see Fischer, Sally.

Keene, Donald, tr. see Mishima, Yukio.

Keene, G. B., tr. see Blanche, R.

Keene, H. G. Hindustan Under Free Lances: Seventeen Seventy to Eighteen Twenty. (Illus.). 238p. 1972. Repr. of 1907 ed. 20.00x (ISBN 0-686-28319-8, Pub. by Irish Academic Pr). Biblio Dist.

Keene, J. Calvin. Western Heritage of Faith & Reason. LC 63-9052. 1963. 13.95 (ISBN 0-9603084-0-7). J Calvin Keene.

Keene, Michael L., jt. auth. see Jones, Paul W.

Keene, R. D. Becoming a Grandmaster. 1977. 13.95 (ISBN 0-7134-0830-8, Pub. by Batsford England). David & Charles.

--The Chess Combination from Philidor to Karpov. LC 77-4379. 1977. text ed. 12.25 (ISBN 0-08-019758-2); pap. text ed. 5.50 o.p. (ISBN 0-08-019757-4). Pergamon.

--Learn from the Grandmasters. 1975. pap. 9.95 (ISBN 0-7134-3043-5). David & Charles.

--Nimzowitsch Larsen Attack. 1977. pap. 13.95 (ISBN 0-7134-0245-8). David & Charles.

Keene, R. D. & Botterill, G. S. Modern Defence. 1979. 18.95 (ISBN 0-7134-0360-8). David & Charles.

Keene, R. D. & Levy, David. Chess Olympiad Skopje Nineteen Seventy-Two. 1973. 19.95 (ISBN 0-7134-0373-X). David & Charles.

--Chess Olympiad Skopje Nineteen Seventy-Two. 1975. 9.25 o.p. (ISBN 0-7134-3055-9). David & Charles.

Keene, R. D., jt. auth. see Hartston, W. R.

Keene, Raymond & Levy, David. An Opening Repertoire for the Attacking Player. (Clubplayers Library). (Illus.). 152p. (Orig.). 1980. 17.95 (ISBN 0-7134-1311-5, Pub. by Batsford England); pap. 10.50 (ISBN 0-7134-1312-3). David & Charles.

Keene, Raymond & Talbot, Shaun. French Defence: Tarrasch Variation. (Algebraic Chess Openings Ser.). (Illus.). 112p. 1981. pap. 11.95 (ISBN 0-7134-1898-2, Pub. by Batsford England). David & Charles.

Keener, Frederick M. English Dialogues of the Dead: A Critical History, an Anthology & a Check List. 300p. 1973. 18.50x (ISBN 0-231-03695-7). Columbia U Pr.

--An Essay on Pope. LC 74-1260. 192p. 1974. 20.00x (ISBN 0-231-03827-5). Columbia U Pr.

Keener, H. A., jt. auth. see Judkins, Henry F.

Keeney, Barnaby C. Judgment by Peers. LC 80-2023. 1981. Repr. of 1949 ed. 25.00 (ISBN 0-404-18571-1). AMS Pr.

Keeney, Ralph L. Siting Energy Facilities. LC 80-764. 1980. 32.00 (ISBN 0-12-403080-7). Acad Pr.

Keenlyside, Francis. Peaks & Pioneers. 1975. 23.95 o.p. (ISBN 0-236-31042-9, Pub. by Paul Elek). Merrimack Bk Serv.

Keep, J. L. Rise of Social Democracy in Russia. 1963. 29.95x (ISBN 0-19-827147-6). Oxford U Pr.

Keep, John L. H., ed. The Debate on Soviet Power: Minutes of the All-Russian Central Executive Committee of Soviets, October 1917-January 1918. 1979. 49.50x (ISBN 0-19-822554-7). Oxford U Pr.

Keep, Robert P., tr. see Autenrieth, Georg.

Keeping, Charles. The Nanny Goat & the Fierce Dog. LC 73-19598. (Illus.). 48p. (gr. k-3). 1974. 8.95 (ISBN 0-87599-201-3). S G Phillips.

--Willie's Fire Engine. (Illus.). 32p. (ps-3). 1980. 10.95 (ISBN 0-19-279728-X). Oxford U Pr.

Keer, L. M., jt. ed. see Cheng, H. S.

Keeran, Roger. Communist Party & the Auto Workers Unions. LC 79-2599. 352p. 1980. 22.50x (ISBN 0-253-15754-4). Ind U Pr.

Kees, Weldon. The Collected Poems of Weldon Kees. rev ed. Justice, Donald, ed. LC 75-3567. xviii, 180p. 1975. 11.50x (ISBN 0-8032-0864-2); pap. 3.95 (ISBN 0-8032-5828-3, BB 609, Bison). U of Nebr Pr.

Keese, Parton. The Measure of Greatness. LC 80-17027. (Illus.). 200p. 1981. 9.95 (ISBN 0-13-567800-5). P-H.

Keesey, Ray E. Modern Parliamentary Procedure. 208p. 1974. pap. text ed. 8.95 (ISBN 0-395-17015-X). HM.

Keesing's Publication Ltd. Africa Independent. LC 70-162750. (Keesing's Research Reports Ser.). 1971. 10.00 o.p. (ISBN 0-684-12532-3, ScribT). Scribner.

Keeton, G. W. & Schwarzenberger, G. Yearbook of World Affairs 1977. LC 47-29156. 1977. lib. bdg. 35.50x (ISBN 0-89158-814-0). Westview.

Keeton, George W. Social Change in the Law of Trusts. LC 73-9374. 128p. 1974. Repr. of 1958 ed. lib. bdg. 12.50x (ISBN 0-8371-7011-7, KELT). Greenwood.

Keeton, George W. & Scharzenberger, Georg, eds. The Yearbook of World Affairs, 1979. 1979. lib. bdg. 37.50x (ISBN 0-89158-551-6). Westview.

Keeton, George W. & Schwarzenberger, Georg, eds. Jeremy Bentham & the Law, a Symposium. Repr. of 1948 ed. lib. bdg. 15.00x (ISBN 0-8371-2832-3, KEJB). Greenwood.

--The Year Book of World Affairs, 1981. 285p. 1981. lib. bdg. 40.00x (ISBN 0-86531-150-1). Westview.

--The Yearbook of World Affairs, 1978. LC 47-29156. 1978. lib. bdg. 37.50x (ISBN 0-89158-824-8). Westview.

Keeton, Kenneth E., ed. Scherz und Ernst: A German Intermediate Oral Reader. LC 67-15832. (Orig., Ger.). 1967. pap. text ed. 5.95x (ISBN 0-89197-389-3). Irvington.

Keeton, William R. Equilibrium Credit Rationing. LC 78-75066. (Outstanding Dissertations in Economics). 1980. lib. bdg. 30.00 (ISBN 0-8240-4142-9). Garland Pub.

Keeton, William T. Biological Science. 3rd ed. (Illus.). 1980. text ed. 21.95x (ISBN 0-393-95021-2); pap. tchr's manual free (ISBN 0-393-95031-X); study guide 4.95x (ISBN 0-393-95028-X). Norton.

--Elements of Biological Science. 2nd ed. 1973. text ed. 17.95x (ISBN 0-393-09346-8). Norton.

Keever, Jack, jt. auth. see Crawford, Ann F.

Keeves, J. P., jt. ed. see Comber, L. C.

Keey, R. B. Drying: Principles & Practice. 1973. text ed. 67.00 (ISBN 0-08-016903-1). Pergamon.

--Introduction to Industrial Drying Operations. LC 77-30467. 396p. 1978. 52.00 (ISBN 0-08-020594-1); pap. 15.00 (ISBN 0-08-020593-3). Pergamon.

Kefford, J. F. see Mrak, E. M. & Stewart, G. F.

Kegan, Frank R. Instant Oracle. 1980. pap. 2.00 (ISBN 0-933646-07-0). Aries Pr.

Kegley, Charles W. & Kegley, Jacquelyn A. Introduction to Logic. (Philosophy Ser.). 1978. text ed. 15.95 (ISBN 0-675-08358-3); media pkg. 75.00 (ISBN 0-675-08357-5); instructor's manual 3.95 (ISBN 0-686-67979-2). Merrill.

Kegley, Charles W., Jr. & Wittkopf, Eugene R. American Foreign Policy: Pattern & Process. LC 78-65249. 1979. text ed. 16.95 (ISBN 0-312-02326-X); pap. text ed. 10.95x (ISBN 0-312-02327-8). St Martin.

Kegley, Jacquelyn A., jt. auth. see Kegley, Charles W.

Kegley, Jacquelyn A., et al. Person & Community in American Philosophy. Kolenda, Konstantin, ed. (Rice University Studies: Vol. 66, No. 4). (Orig.). 1981. pap. 5.50 (ISBN 0-89263-247-X). Rice Univ.

Kehl, James A. Boss Rule in the Gilded Age: Matt Quay of Pennsylvania. LC 80-5254. (Illus.). 315p. 1981. 24.95 (ISBN 0-8229-3426-4). U of Pittsburgh Pr.

--Ill Feeling in the Era of Good Feeling. LC 56-6425. 1956. 4.00 (ISBN 0-910294-25-9). Brown Bk.

Kehler, Dorothea & Dickinson, Fidelia. Problems in Literary Research: A Guide to Selected Reference Works. LC 75-16427. 169p. 1975. 10.00 (ISBN 0-8108-0841-2); tchrs. index incl. (ISBN 0-8108-0842-0). Scarecrow.

Kehoe, Andre J. His Irish Connection. (Illus.). 1980. 8.50 (ISBN 0-682-49575-1, Banner). Exposition.

Kehoe, Constance, jt. auth. see Kehoe, William.

Kehoe, Dalton, et al, eds. Public Land Ownership. LC 75-41925. 1976. 21.95 (ISBN 0-669-00486-3). Lexington Bks.

Kehoe, Michael. The Rock Quarry Book. LC 80-28165. (Illus.). 32p. (gr. k-3). 1981. PLB 5.95 (ISBN 0-87614-142-4). Carolrhoda Bks.

Kehoe, Monika, jt. auth. see Gillett, Margaret.

Kehoe, William & Kehoe, Constance. Enjoying Ireland. rev. ed. 288p. 1981. pap. 5.95 (ISBN 0-8159-5406-9). Devin.

Kehr, Eckart. Economic Interest, Militarism, & Foreign Policy: Essays on German History. Craig, Gordon A., ed. Heinz, Grete, tr. from Ger. 1977. 18.50x (ISBN 0-520-02880-5). U of Cal Pr.

Kehrer, James B. Oxygen Induced Lung Damage: The Chemistry of Oxygen Reduction. (Lectures in Toxicology: No. 4). (Illus.). 1981. 28.00 (ISBN 0-08-025706-2). Pergamon.

Keiburtz, Richard B. Structured Programming & Problem Solving with PL-One. (Illus.). 1977. 18.95 o.p. (ISBN 0-686-60837-2); pap. 13.95 (ISBN 0-13-854943-5). P-H.

Keidel, Eudene. African Fables, Bk. 2. (Illus.). 112p. 1981. pap. 3.25 (ISBN 0-8361-1945-2). Herald Pr.

Keiffer, Mildred & Smith, Harold. Pathways in Mathematics. Incl. Level One. rev. ed. (gr. 7). 1977. pap. text ed. 6.64 (ISBN 0-913688-31-2); tchr's guide 6.00 (ISBN 0-913688-33-9); Level Two. rev. ed. (gr. 8). 1977 (ISBN 0-913688-32-0). tchr's guide (ISBN 0-913688-34-7). pap. text ed. 6.64x ea.; tchr's guide 6.00x (ISBN 0-685-77480-5). Pawnee Pub.

Keiffer, Mildred, jt. auth. see Smith, Harold.

Keightley. The Fairy Mythology. LC 74-16410. 1975. Repr. of 1870 ed. 30.00 (ISBN 0-8103-3466-6). Gale.

Keightley, David, et al, eds. Early China, No. 5. 131p. 1980. pap. 7.00 (ISBN 0-912966-26-2). IEAS Ctr Chinese Stud.

Keightley, David N. Sources of Shang History: The Oracle-Bone Inscriptions of Bronze Age China. LC 74-29806. 1979. 30.00x (ISBN 0-520-02969-0). U of Cal Pr.

Keightley, Thomas. An Account of the Life, Opinions, & Writings of John Milton. 484p. 1980. Repr. of 1855 ed. lib. bdg. 50.00 (ISBN 0-8492-1495-5). R West.

Keighton, Robert L. & Sutton, Martin P. One Nation: An American Government Text with Readings. 512p. 1972. text ed. 12.95x o.p. (ISBN 0-669-61192-1); tchrs. guide free o.p. (ISBN 0-669-61200-6). Heath.

Keijzer, Arne J. de & Kaplan, Fredric. The China Guide Book: A Travel Guide to the People's Republic of China, 1979-80 Ed. 1979. 12.95 o.p. (ISBN 0-397-01358-2); pap. 8.95 (ISBN 0-397-01359-0). Lippincott.

Keil, A., jt. auth. see Schmidt, W. J.

Keil, Carl F. & Delitzsch, Franz. Old Testament Commentaries, 10 vols. Incl. Vol. 1. Pentateuch (ISBN 0-8028-8035-5); Vol. 2. Joshua - Second Samuel (ISBN 0-8028-8036-3); Vol. 3. First Kings - Esther (ISBN 0-685-25927-7); Vol. 4. Job (ISBN 0-8028-8038-X); Vol. 5. Psalms (ISBN 0-8028-8039-8); Vol. 6. Proverbs - Song of Solomon (ISBN 0-8028-8040-1); Vol. 7. Isaiah (ISBN 0-8028-8041-X); Vol. 8. Jeremiah-Lamentations (ISBN 0-8028-8042-8); Vol. 9. Ezekiel-Daniel (ISBN 0-8028-8043-6); Vol. 10. Minor Prophets (ISBN 0-8028-8044-4). 1971. Repr. Set. 149.50 o.p. (ISBN 0-8028-8034-7); 14.95 ea. o.p. Eerdmans.

Keil, Klaus & Gomes, Celso P. Brazilian Stone Meteorites. LC 80-5333. (Illus.). 192p. 1981. 20.00x (ISBN 0-8263-0543-1). U of NM Pr.

Keilin, David. History of Cell Respiration & Cytochrome. 1966. 59.50 (ISBN 0-521-05470-2). Cambridge U Pr.

Keilty, Ed. Interurbans Without Wires. Sebree, Mac, ed. LC 79-53961. (Special Ser.: No. 66). 1979. 23.95 (ISBN 0-916374-38-6). Interurban.

Keily, Danile. Programmed Basic Chemistry for Allied Health Students. LC 77-10774. (Illus.). 1978. pap. text ed. 12.95 (ISBN 0-8016-2637-4). Mosby.

Keinath, S., jt. ed. see Boyer, R.

Keiningham, C. W. Sermon Outlines for Funerals. (Sermon Outline Ser.). (Orig.). 1981. pap. 1.45 (ISBN 0-8010-5427-3). Baker Bk.

Keintz, Rita M., ed. Health Care Costs & Financing: A Guide to Information Sources. LC 80-23862. (Health Affairs Information Guide Ser.: Vol. 6). 400p. 1981. 30.00 (ISBN 0-8103-1482-7). Gale.

Keiper, Ralph L. The Power of Biblical Thinking. 1977. 5.95 o.p. (ISBN 0-8007-0862-8). Revell.

Keir, David L. & Lawson, Frederick H. Cases in Constitutional Law. 6th ed. Bentley, D. J., ed. 592p. 1979. text ed. 43.50x (ISBN 0-19-876065-5). Oxford U Pr.

Keir, Malcolm see Gabriel, Ralph H.

Keirsey, David & Bates, Marilyn. Please Understand Me: An Essay on Temperament Styles. 1978. write for info. Prometheus Nemesis.

Keiser & Lupul. Marketing Interaction. (Orig.). 1977. pap. 10.95 (ISBN 0-87814-029-8). Pennwell Pub.

Keiser, James. Principles & Practice of Management in the Hospitality Industry. LC 80-12866. 1980. text ed. 16.95 (ISBN 0-8436-2182-6). CBI Pub.

Keiser, S., jt. auth. see Haner, F.

Keith, Arthur B., ed. The Aitareya Aranyaka. 396p. 1969. Repr. of 1909 ed. text ed. 22.50x (ISBN 0-19-815442-9). Oxford U Pr.

Keith, Bruce E., jt. auth. see Lee, Eugene C.

Keith, Charles P. Chronicles of Pennsylvania, 3 Vols. LC 69-18291. (Keystone State Historical Publications Ser: No. 3). 1969. Repr. of 1917 ed. Set. 45.00x (ISBN 0-87198-503-9). Friedman.

Keith, David. Soccer Handbook. (Physical Education Ser.). (Illus.). 64p. (Orig.). 1980. pap. text ed. 5.95 (ISBN 0-88839-048-3). Hancock Hse.

Keith, Eros. In the Land of Enchantment: A Panorama of Fairy Tales. LC 75-654436. (Illus.). (ps-3). 1972. 7.95 (ISBN 0-87888-046-1). Bradbury Pr.

Keith, Harold. Komantcia. LC 65-14901. (gr. 7 up). 1965. 9.95 (ISBN 0-690-47744-9, TYC-J). T Y Crowell.

--The Obstinate Land. LC 77-1826. (gr. 5 up). 1977. 9.95 (ISBN 0-690-01319-1, TYC-J). T Y Crowell.

Keith, John D., jt. auth. see Kidd, B. S.

Keith, John D., et al. Heart Disease in Infancy & Childhood. 3rd ed. (Illus.). 1978. text ed. 58.00 (ISBN 0-02-362220-2). Macmillan.

Keith, Judith. I Haven't a Thing to Wear. LC 76-57886. (Illus.). 1980. 12.95 (ISBN 0-913024-11-2). Tandem Pr.

Keith, Pauline M. Four Generations of Verse. 1981. 5.95 (ISBN 0-930142-06-3). Merlin Pr.

Keith, Robert L. Graduated Language Training: For Patients with Aphasia & Children with Language Deficiencies. LC 79-91245. (Illus.). 320p. 1980. clinical test 24.95 (ISBN 0-933014-57-0). College-Hill.

--Speech & Language Rehabilitation: A Workbook for the Neurologically Impaired, Vol. 2. 1977. pap. text ed. 6.95x (ISBN 0-685-84999-6, 1949). Interstate.

Keith, Robert L. & Darley, Frederic L., eds. Laryngectomee Rehabilitation. LC 79-91246. (Illus.). 533p. 1980. text ed. 24.50 (ISBN 0-933014-56-2). College-Hill.

Keith, Robert W. Audiology for the Physician. (Illus.). 352p. 1980. 30.00 (ISBN 0-683-04551-2). Williams & Wilkins.

Keith, Robert W., ed. Central Auditory & Language Disorders in Children. (Illus.). 264p. 1981. text ed. 29.00 (ISBN 0-933014-61-9). College-Hill.

Keith, W. J. The Poetry of Nature: Rural Perspectives in Poetry from Wordsworth to the Present. 1980. 20.00x (ISBN 0-8020-5494-3). U of Toronto Pr.

Keith, W. J. & Shek, B. Z., eds. The Arts in Canada: The Last Fifty Years. 192p. 1980. 20.00x (ISBN 0-8020-2401-7); pap. 6.95 (ISBN 0-8020-6425-6). U of Toronto Pr.

Keith, W. J., ed. see Roberts, Charles G.

Keithley, Erwin & Thompson, Margaret H. English for Modern Business. 3rd ed. 1977. pap. text ed. 11.95 (ISBN 0-256-01852-9). Irwin.

Keith-Smith, B. Modern German Authors: Johannes Bobrowski. Last, R. W., tr. (Vol. 4). 8.95 (ISBN 0-85496-044-9). Dufour.

Keith-Smith, Brian, jt. ed. see Natan, Alex.

Keitner, Wendy. Ralph Gustafson. (World Authors Ser.: No. 531). 1979. lib. bdg. 14.95 (ISBN 0-8057-6373-2). Twayne.

Kekes, John. The Nature of Philosophy. (American Philosophical Quarterly Library of Philosophy). 226p. 1980. 24.50x (ISBN 0-8476-6247-0). Rowman.

Kekstadt, H. & Primrose, D. A. Mental Subnormality. (Modern Practical Nursing Ser: NO. 15). (Illus.). 1975. pap. text ed. 9.95x (ISBN 0-685-83644-4). Intl Ideas.

Kelber, Werner H. Mark's Story of Jesus. LC 78-14668. 96p. 1979. pap. 2.95 (ISBN 0-8006-1355-4, 1-1355). Fortress.

Kelber, Werner H., jt. auth. see Allison, C. Fitzsimons.

Kelch, Maxwell. Simple Celestial Navigation. (Illus.). 1975. pap. 5.95 o.p. (ISBN 0-87799-051-4). Aztex.

Kelch, Ray A. Newcastle: A Duke Without Money; Thomas Pelham-Holles, 1693-1768. 1974. 21.50x (ISBN 0-520-02537-7). U of Cal Pr.

Kelchner, Georgia D. Dreams in Old Norse Literature & Their Affinities in Folklore. 154p. 1980. Repr. of 1935 ed. lib. bdg. 30.00 (ISBN 0-8492-1496-3). R West.

Kelcy, Raymond C. Letters of Paul to the Thessalonians. Ferguson, Everett, et al, eds. LC 68-55947. (Living Word New Testament Commentary Ser.: Vol. 13). 1968. 7.95 (ISBN 0-8344-0017-0). Sweet.

--The Letters of Peter & Jude. Ferguson, Everett, ed. LC 78-179612. (The Living Word New Testament Commentary Ser.: Vol. 17). 1972. 7.95 (ISBN 0-8344-0073-1). Sweet.

Kelder, Diane. Aspects of "Official" Painting & Philosophic Art, 1789-1799. LC 75-23797. (Outstanding Dissertations in the Fine Arts - 18th Century). (Illus.). 1976. lib. bdg. 37.50 (ISBN 0-8240-1992-X). Garland Pub.

--French Impressionists. LC 79-57411. (Abbeville Library of Art: No. 2). (Illus.). 112p. 1980. pap. 4.95 (ISBN 0-89659-093-3). Abbeville Pr.

--The Great Book of French Impressionism. LC 80-66527. (Illus.). 448p. 1980. 100.00 (ISBN 0-89659-151-4). Abbeville Pr.

Kelder, James. How to Open a Swiss Bank Account. LC 75-34285. 324p. 1976. 9.95 o.s.i. (ISBN 0-690-01033-8, TYC-T). T Y Crowell.

Keleher, James F. Disputed Questions in Philosophy. LC 65-21757. 1966. 3.50 o.p. (ISBN 0-8022-0840-1). Philos Lib.

Kelejian, Harry H. & Oates, Wallace E. Introduction to Econometrics: Principles & Applications. 2nd ed. (Illus.). 384p. 1980. text ed. 10.50 scp (ISBN 0-06-043618-2, HarpC). Har-Row.

Keleman, Stanley. The Human Ground: Sexuality, Self & Survival. LC 75-12453. 1975. pap. 4.95 o.p. (ISBN 0-8314-0047-1). Sci & Behavior.

Kelemen, E. Physiopathology & Therapy of Human Blood Diseases. LC 68-18525. 1968. 90.00 (ISBN 0-08-012786-X). Pergamon.

Keleti. Mathematical Models of Metabolic Regulation. 1976. 17.00 (ISBN 0-9960001-2-7, Pub. by Kaido Hungary). Heyden.

Keliher, John G. The Negotiations on Mutual & Balanced Force Reductions: The Search for Arms Control in Central Europe. LC 80-16473. (Pergamon Policy Studies on International Politics). 240p. 1980. 25.00 (ISBN 0-08-025964-2). Pergamon.

Kelikian, H. Congenital Deformities of the Hand & Forearm. LC 73-89181. (Illus.). 1025p. 1974. text ed. 40.00 (ISBN 0-7216-5358-8). Saunders.

Kelkar, S. A. Occupational Exposure to Mercury. xi, 112p. 1980. text ed. 15.95x (ISBN 0-86590-001-9). Apt Bks.

Kell, Bill L. & Mueller, William J. Impact & Change: A Study of Counseling Relationships. (Orig.). 1966. pap. 8.95 (ISBN 0-13-451799-7). P-H.

Kell, Gulla & Moody, Ronald, trs. Amadu's Bundle. (African Writers Ser.). 1972. pap. text ed. 1.95 (ISBN 0-435-90118-4). Heinemann Ed.

Kell, J. Carroll. Southern Landscape & Garden Design. LC 80-473. (Illus.). 1980. pap. 3.95 (ISBN 0-88415-811-X). Pacesetter Pr.

Kell, J. Carroll, jt. auth. see Duble, Richard.

Kellagham, Thomas. The Evaluation of an Intervention Programme for Disadvantaged Children. (General Ser.). (Illus., Orig.). 1977. pap. text ed. 16.50x (ISBN 0-85633-124-4, NFER). Humanities.

Kellar, Elizabeth K., ed. Managing with Less. LC 79-26163. 1979. pap. 10.00 (ISBN 0-87326-995-0). Intl City Mgt.

Kellar, H. A., ed. Solon Robinson, Pioneer & Agriculturalist, 2 Vols. LC 68-16242. (American Scene Ser). (Illus.). 1968. Repr. of 1936 ed. lib. bdg. 75.00 (ISBN 0-306-71017-X). Da Capo.

Kellar, Jane C. & Miller, Ellen. Selected Receipts of a Van Rensselaer Family: 1785-1835. LC 77-85726. (Illus.). 110p. 1976. pap. 6.00 (ISBN 0-89062-026-1, Pub. by Historic Cherry). Pub Ctr Cult Res.

Kellar, Kenneth C. Seth Bullock: Frontier Marshall. LC 72-92726. 191p. 1972. 4.95 (ISBN 0-87970-126-9). North Plains.

Kellas, J. G. The Scottish Political System. 2nd ed. LC 75-2733. (Illus.). 1975. 33.95 (ISBN 0-521-20864-5); pap. 10.95x (ISBN 0-521-09972-2). Cambridge U Pr.

Kellas, James G. Modern Scotland. (Illus.). 208p. (Orig.). text ed. 22.50x (ISBN 0-04-941008-3); pap. text ed. 9.95x (ISBN 0-04-941009-1). Allen Unwin.

Kellaway, P. & Petersen, I., eds. Automation of Clinical Electroencephalography. LC 72-96334. (Illus.). 326p. 1973. 34.50 (ISBN 0-911216-45-6). Raven.

Kellaway, Peter & Petersen, Ingemar S., eds. Quantitative Analytic Studies in Epilepsy. LC 76-22912. 1976. 48.00 (ISBN 0-89004-133-4). Raven.

Kelleam, Joseph E. Hunters of Space. (YA) 5.95 (ISBN 0-685-07436-6, Avalon). Bouregy.

--When the Red King Woke. (YA) 4.95 o.p. (ISBN 0-685-07464-1, Avalon). Bouregy.

Kelleher, Catherine M. Germany, Nuclear Weapons & Alliance Relations: 1954-1966. 384p. 1975. 20.00x (ISBN 0-231-03960-3). Columbia U Pr.

Kelleher, Catherine M., ed. Political-Military Systems. LC 74-77094. (Sage Research Progress Ser. on War, Revolution & Peacekeeping: Vol. 4). 1974. 20.00x (ISBN 0-8039-0414-2); pap. 9.95x (ISBN 0-8039-0415-0). Sage.

Kelleher, John V. Too Small for Stove Wood, Too Big for Kindling. 1980. pap. text ed. 10.50x (ISBN 0-85105-312-2, Dolmen Pr). Humanities.

Kelleher, Stephen J. Divorce & Remarriage for Catholics. LC 75-17075. 160p. 1976. pap. 1.75 o.p. (ISBN 0-385-11371-4, Im). Doubleday.

Kellejian, Robert. Applied Electronic Communication: Circuits, Systems, Transmission. 608p. 1980. text ed. 23.95 (ISBN 0-574-21535-2, 13-4535); instr's. guide avail. (ISBN 0-574-21536-0, 13-4536). SRA.

Kellen, John A. & Hilf, Russell. Influences of Hormones in Tumor Development, 2 vols. 1979. Vol. 1, 192p. 51.99 (ISBN 0-8493-5351-3); Vol. 2, 224p. 54.95 (ISBN 0-8493-5352-1). CRC Pr.

Kellenberger, Hunter, ed. Foreign Language Teachers & Tests. Incl. Foreign Language Instruction in Elementary Schools. Selvi, Arthur S; Linguistic Aids. Walker, Richard H; The Qualifications of Foreign Language Teachers. Freeman, Stephen A; The Role of Foreign Languages in American Life. Andersson, Theodore; The Teaching of Literature. Torrey, Norman L; Tests: Listening Comprehension, Other Skills. 56p. 1954. pap. 7.95x (ISBN 0-915432-54-4). NE Conf Teach Foreign.

Keller. Electrical Methods of Geophysical Prospecting. 2nd ed. 400p. Date not set. text ed. price not set (ISBN 0-08-025979-0). Pergamon.

Keller & Mulbauer. Floating Zone Silicon. 256p. 1981. 39.75 (ISBN 0-8247-1167-X). Dekker.

Keller, A. G., jt. auth. see Sumner, Wm. G.

Keller, Abraham C., ed. see Atkinson, Geoffroy.

Keller, Albert G. Man's Rough Road. 1932. 37.50x (ISBN 0-685-69831-9). Elliots Bks.

--Reminiscences (Mainly Personal) of William Graham Sumner. 1933. 32.50x (ISBN 0-686-51300-2). Elliots Bks.

--Societal Evolution: A Study of the Evolutionary Basis of the Science of Society. 1931. 32.50x (ISBN 0-686-51315-0). Elliots Bks.

Keller, Allen, et al, trs. see Reyer, Eduard.

Keller, Beverly. Fiona's Flea. (Illus.). 64p. (gr. 7-10). 1981. PLB 6.99 (ISBN 0-698-30719-4). Coward.

--The Sea Watch. LC 80-70000. 128p. (gr. 3-7). 1981. 7.95 (ISBN 0-590-07703-1, Four Winds). Schol Bk Serv.

Keller, C. Silly Song Book. 1980. pap. 1.95 (ISBN 0-13-809954-5). P-H.

Keller, Charles. Ballpoint Bananas & Other Jokes for Kids. (Illus.). (gr. 3-7). 1973. pap. 1.95 (ISBN 0-13-055517-7). P-H.

--Giggle Puss: Pet Jokes for Kids. LC 76-44837. (Illus.). (gr. 1-4). 1977. 5.95 (ISBN 0-13-356295-6); pap. 1.95 (ISBN 0-13-356303-0). P-H.

Keller, Charles, compiled by. More Ballpoint Bananas. LC 77-5356. (Illus.). (gr. 1-4). 1977. 4.95 (ISBN 0-13-600767-8); pap. 1.95 (ISBN 0-13-600775-9). P-H.

--The Nutty Joke Book. (Illus.). (gr. 2-5). 1978. 6.95 (ISBN 0-13-627737-3). P-H.

--Daffynitions. LC 75-34280. (Illus.). (gr. 3 up). 1976. PLB 5.95 (ISBN 0-13-196584-0); pap. 1.95 (ISBN 0-13-196576-X). P-H.

Keller, Charles M. Montagu Cave in Prehistory: A Descriptive Analysis. (U. C. Publ. in Anthropological Records: Vol. 28). 1973. pap. 12.50x (ISBN 0-520-09401-8). U of Cal Pr.

Keller, Dean H. Index to Plays in Periodicals. rev. & expanded ed. LC 79-962. 836p. 1979. 37.50 (ISBN 0-8108-1208-8). Scarecrow.

Keller, Dean H., ed. see MacKaye, Steele & Tourgee, Albion W.

Keller, Dolores E. Sex & the Single Cell. LC 71-175220. (Science & Society Ser). 1972. pap. 4.50 (ISBN 0-672-63593-3). Pegasus.

Keller, Edward. Environmental Geology. 2nd ed. 1979. text ed. 19.95 (ISBN 0-675-08296-X). Merrill.

Keller, Fred S. The Definition of Psychology. 2nd ed. LC 72-94282. 128p. 1973. 8.95 (ISBN 0-13-197616-8). P-H.

--Learning: Reinforcement Theory. 2nd ed. (Psychology Studies). 1969. pap. text ed. 3.95x (ISBN 0-394-30898-0, RanC). Random.

Keller, Gail F. Jane Addams. LC 71-139098. (Biography Ser). (Illus.). (gr. 1-4). 1971. 7.95 (ISBN 0-690-45791-X, TYC-J). T Y Crowell.

Keller, Gary D., jt. ed. see Fishman, Joshua A.

Keller, Gottfried. Der Gruene Heinrich. (Insel-Bibliothek). 874p. (Ger.). 1980. 104.00 (ISBN 3-458-04821-9, Pub. by Insel Verlag Germany); text ed. 44.20 (ISBN 3-458-04937-1). Suhrkamp.

--Martin Salander. 1981. pap. 4.95 (ISBN 0-7145-0371-1). Riverrun NY.

Keller, Gunter. Discus. (Illus., Orig.). 1976. pap. 2.95 (ISBN 0-87666-457-5, PS-314). TFH Pubns.

Keller, H. B., jt. auth. see Isaacson, Eugene.

Keller, Helen R. Reader's Digest of Books. enl. ed. 1936. 9.95 o.s.i. (ISBN 0-02-561710-9). Macmillan.

Keller, Herbert B., ed. see Beam, R. M., et al.

Keller, Hermann. The Well-Tempered Clavier by Johann Sebastian Bach. Gerdine, Leigh, tr. 1977. 18.50 (ISBN 0-393-02187-4). Norton.

Keller, Horst. The Great Book of French Impressionism. Brown, Alexis, tr. from Ger. LC 80-13206. (Illus.). 272p. 1980. 50.00 (ISBN 0-933920-11-3). Hudson Hills.

Keller, Howard H. A German Word Family Dictionary: Together with English Equivalents. 1978. 14.95x (ISBN 0-520-03291-8). U of Cal Pr.

--New Perspectives on Teaching Vocabulary. (Language in Education Ser.: No. 8). 1978. pap. 2.95 (ISBN 0-87281-084-4). Ctr Appl Ling.

Keller, Irwin A., jt. auth. see Forsythe, Charles E.

Keller, J. B., ed. see Bucy, R. S., et al.

Keller, James F. & Hughston, George. Counseling the Elderly: A Systems Approach. (Illus.). 192p. 1980. scp 14.50 (ISBN 0-06-453511-8, HarpC). Har-Row.

Keller, John E. Drinking Problem. Hulme, William E., ed. LC 75-133036. (Pocket Counsel Bks.). 64p. 1971. pap. 1.95 (ISBN 0-8006-0155-6, 1-155). Fortress.

--Gonzalo de Berceo. (World Authors Ser.: Spain: No. 187). lib. bdg. 10.95 (ISBN 0-8057-2144-4). Twayne.

--Motif-Index of Mediaeval Spanish Exempla. 1949. pap. 5.00x o.p. (ISBN 0-87049-005-2). U of Tenn Pr.

--Pious Brief Narrative in Medieval Castilian & Galician Verse: From Berceo to Alfonso X. LC 77-84064. (Studies in Romance Languages: No. 21). 152p. 1979. 16.00x (ISBN 0-8131-1381-4). U Pr of Ky.

Keller, John E. & Keating, L. Clark, eds. The Book of Count Lucanor & Patronio: A Translation of Don Juan Manuel's "el Conde Lucanor". LC 76-24342. (Studies in Romance Languages: No. 16). 208p. 1977. 17.00x (ISBN 0-8131-1350-4). U Pr of Ky.

Keller, Julius. From Riva Ridge to Riva. 4.95 o.p. (ISBN 0-685-46465-2). Vantage.

Keller, Karl. The Only Kangaroo Among the Beauty: Emily Dickinson & America. LC 79-10462. 1980. text ed. 19.50x (ISBN 0-8018-2174-6); pap. text ed. 5.95 (ISBN 0-8018-2538-5). Johns Hopkins.

Keller, M. Wiles & Zant, James H. Basic Mathematics. 3rd ed. LC 78-69602. (Illus.). 1979. pap. text ed. 14.95 (ISBN 0-395-27050-2); inst. annot. ed. 15.95 (ISBN 0-395-27051-0). HM.

Keller, Marion W. Intermediate Algebra: A Text Workbook. LC 74-171526. pap. text ed. 12.25 (ISBN 0-395-12644-4, 3-29361); test ans. & prob. pap. 2.95 (ISBN 0-685-02020-7, 3-29362). HM.

Keller, Mark, ed. International Bibliography of Studies on Alcohol, 3 vols. Incl. Vol. 1. References, 1901-1950. Jordy, Sarah S., compiled by. 1966. 40.00x (ISBN 0-911290-34-6); Vol. 2. Indexes, 1901-1950. Efron, Vera & Jordy, Sarah S. 1968. 35.00x (ISBN 0-911290-35-4); Vol. 3. References, 1951-1960; Indexes, 1951-1960. Jordy, Sarah S., et al. 1980. 75.00x (ISBN 0-686-66592-9). LC 60-14437. Set Of Vols. 1 & 2. 65.00x (ISBN 0-911290-07-9). Rutgers Ctr Alcohol.

Keller, Marti, jt. auth. see Isaacs, Susan.

Keller, Morton. Affairs of State: Public Life in Late Nineteenth Century America. LC 76-21676. 1979. 20.00 (ISBN 0-674-00721-2, Belknap Pr); pap. 7.50 (ISBN 0-674-00710-7). Harvard U Pr.

--The Art & Politics of Thomas Nast. LC 68-19762. (Illus.). 365p. 1975. pap. 9.95 (ISBN 0-19-501929-6, GB437, GB). Oxford U Pr.

Keller, Paul F. Studies in Lutheran Doctrine. LC 60-15574. (YA) (gr. 7-8). 1959. pap. 5.50 (ISBN 0-570-03517-1, 14-1265); correction & profile chart 0.40 (ISBN 0-570-03526-0, 14-1267); tests 0.45 (ISBN 0-570-03525-2, 14-1266). Concordia.

Keller, Paul J. Hormonal Disorders in Gynecology. (Illus.). 113p. 1981. pap. 16.50 (ISBN 0-387-10341-4). Springer-Verlag.

Keller, Paul T., jt. auth. see Brown, Charles T.

Keller, Philip. A Shepherd Looks at the Good Shepherd & His Sheep. 1979. 7.95 (ISBN 0-310-26800-1); large print kivar 4.95 (ISBN 0-310-26807-9). Zondervan.

Keller, Phillip. La Vida En el Redil. Vargas, Carlos A., tr. from Eng. LC 76-14500. 141p. (Orig., Span.). 1976. pap. 2.50 (ISBN 0-89922-073-8). Edit Caribe.

Keller, Phillip, tr. Meditacoes De Um Leigo. (Portugese Bks.). (Port.). 1979. write for info. (ISBN 0-8297-0788-3). Life Pubs Intl.

Keller, Phillis, tr. Un Laico Examina el Padrenuestro. (Spanish Bks.). (Span.). 1978. 1.80 (ISBN 0-8297-0770-0). Life Pubs Intl.

Keller, Robert G. Warning Call. 1981. pap. 1.95 (ISBN 0-8439-0890-4, Leisure Bks). Nordon Pubns.

Keller, Rosemary, jt. auth. see Ruether, Rosemary.

Keller, Stephen L. Uprooting & Social Change: The Role of Refugees in Development. LC 75-900452. 1975. 15.00x o.p. (ISBN 0-88386-586-6). South Asia Bks.

Keller, Suzanne. Urban Neighborhood: A Sociological Perspective. (Orig.). 1968. pap. text ed. 4.50 (ISBN 0-394-30773-9, RanC). Random.

Keller, Suzanne, ed. Building for Women. LC 80-8783. 1981. price not set (ISBN 0-669-04368-0). Lexington Bks.

Keller, W. Philip. Layman Looks at the Lord's Prayer. study ed 4.95 (ISBN 0-8024-4647-7). Moody.

Keller, W. Phillip. A Child's Look at the Twenty-Third Psalm. LC 80-976. (Illus.). 96p. 1981. 7.95 (ISBN 0-385-15456-9, Galilee). Doubleday.

--Rabboni. 1981. pap. 5.95 (ISBN 0-8007-5053-5). Revell.

--Walking with God. 1980. 7.95 (ISBN 0-8007-1140-8). Revell.

Keller, Walter D. Principles of Chemical Weathering. rev ed. 1957. text ed. 3.50x spiral bdg. (ISBN 0-87543-033-3). Lucas.

Keller, Werner. The Bible As History. 2nd, rev. ed. Rehork, Joachim, ed. Neil, William & Rasmussen, B. H., trs. from Ger. LC 80-22218. Orig. Title: Und Die Bibel Hat Docht Recht. (Illus.). 448p. 1981. 16.95 (ISBN 0-688-03724-0). Morrow.

Kelleran, Marion & Krumm, John M. Denver Crossroads. 1979. 1.60 (ISBN 0-686-28775-4). Forward Movement.

Keller-Grimm, M., ed. see Grimm, George.

Kellerman, Henry. Sleep Disorders: Insomnia & Narcolepsy. 250p. 1981. 17.50 (ISBN 0-87630-264-9). Brunner-Mazel.

Kellerman, J. Psychological Aspects of Childhood Cancer. (Illus.). 336p. 1980. 32.50 (ISBN 0-398-03989-5). C C Thomas.

Kellerman, Jonathan. Helping the Fearful Child: A Guide to Everyday & Problem Anxieties. 1981. 13.95 (ISBN 0-393-01392-8). Norton.

Kellerman, Marcelle. The Forgotten Third Skill: Reading a Foreign Language. LC 80-41029. (Language Teaching Methodology Ser.). 96p. 1981. 11.95 (ISBN 0-08-024599-4); pap. 7.95 (ISBN 0-08-024598-6). Pergamon.

Kellermeyer, Robert, jt. auth. see Harris, John W.

Kellet, Alexander. A Pocket of Prose & Verse. Washburn, Wilcomb E., ed. LC 75-7031. (Narratives of North American Indian Captivities: Vol. 11). 1975. lib. bdg. 44.00 (ISBN 0-8240-1635-1). Garland Pub.

Kelley, Ann M., jt. auth. see Wang, Rosemary Y.

Kelley, C. Aron, jt. auth. see Powell, James D.

Kelley, Clifton G., jt. auth. see Sammet, George, Jr.

Kelley, Colleen. Assertion Training: A Facilitator's Guide. LC 78-69787. 382p. 1979. 18.50 (ISBN 0-88390-146-3). Univ Assocs.

Kelley, Dean M. Why Churches Should Not Pay Taxes. LC 76-62944. 1977. 6.95 o.p. (ISBN 0-06-064302-1, HarpR). Har-Row.

Kelley, Donald H., tr. see Seyssel, Claude De.

Kelley, Donald R. Foundations of Modern Historical Scholarship: Language, Law & History in the French Renaissance. LC 68-8875. 1970. 20.00x (ISBN 0-231-03141-6). Columbia U Pr.

Kelley, Donald R., ed. The Energy Crisis & the Environment: An International Perspective. LC 76-24355. (Praeger Special Studies). 1977. text ed. 29.95 (ISBN 0-275-23850-4). Praeger.

--Soviet Politics in the Brezhnev Era. LC 79-24741. (Praeger Special Studies). 282p. 1980. 22.95 (ISBN 0-03-046626-1); pap. 9.95 student edition (ISBN 0-03-046621-0). Praeger.

Kelley, Donald R., et al. The Economic Superpowers & the Environment: The U.S., the Soviet Union, & Japan. LC 76-1003. 1976. text ed. 22.95x (ISBN 0-7167-0720-9); pap. text ed. 10.95x (ISBN 0-7167-0721-7). W H Freeman.

Kelley, E. J., jt. ed. see Hood, D. W.

Kelley, Edgar A. School Climate. Koerner, Thomas F., ed. 80p. (Orig.). 1981. pap. text ed. 4.00 (ISBN 0-88210-115-3). Natl Assn Principals.

Kelley, Edward N. Practical Apartment Management. 2nd ed. Kirk, Nancye J., ed. 400p. 1980. write for info. (ISBN 0-912104-49-X). Inst Real Estate.

Kelley, Elmer. They Left Footprints. 3.50 o.p. (ISBN 0-685-48818-7). Nortex-Pr.

Kelley, Eugene J. Marketing Planning & Competitive Strategy. (Foundations of Marketing Ser). 1972. pap. 6.95 ref. ed. (ISBN 0-13-558304-7). P-H.

Kelley, Eugene J., jt. auth. see Lazer, William.

Kelley, Francis D., pref. by. Media & Catechetics Today: Towards the Year 2000. 3.00. Natl Cath Educ.

--The Vocation & Spirituality of the DRE: An NPCD Publication. 3.50. Natl Cath Educ.

Kelley, Harold H. & Thibaut, John W. Interpersonal Relations: A Theory of Interdependence. LC 78-164. 1978. 27.95 (ISBN 0-471-03473-8, Pub. by Wiley-Interscience). Wiley.

Kelley, J. C., jt. auth. see Townsend, P. D.

Kelley, J. L. General Topology. (Graduate Texts in Mathematics Ser.: Vol. 27). 310p. 1975. Repr. 19.80 (ISBN 0-387-90125-6). Springer-Verlag.

Kelley, Jain. Darkroom Two. (Illus., Orig.). 1979. pap. 17.50 (ISBN 0-912810-21-1). Lustrum Pr.

Kelley, Jan D. & Winship, Barbara J. I Am Worth It. LC 78-26111. 1979. 10.95 (ISBN 0-88229-291-9). Nelson-Hall.

Kelley, Joe. How Managers Manage. (Illus.). 1980. 14.95 (ISBN 0-13-423756-0, Spec); pap. 7.95 (ISBN 0-686-59488-6, Spec); study guide 5.95 (ISBN 0-13-423731-5). P-H.

Kelley, John H., jt. auth. see De Gravelles, William D.

Kelley, John H., jt. auth. see Degravelles, William D., Jr.

Kelley, John L. & Richert, Donald. Elementary Mathematics for Teachers. LC 70-11612. 1970. text ed. 18.95x (ISBN 0-8162-4654-8); sol. man 2.50x (ISBN 0-8162-4664-5). Holden-Day.

Kelley, Jonathan & Klein, Herbert S. Revolution & the Rebirth of Inequality: Stratification in Post-Revolutionary Bolivia. 1980. 14.95 (ISBN 0-520-04072-4). U of Cal Pr.

Kelley, Kitty. Jackie Oh! 1979. pap. 2.50 (ISBN 0-345-28327-9). Ballantine.

Kelley, Lane, jt. auth. see Whatley, Arthur.

Kelley, Leo P. Backward in Time. LC 79-51079. (Space Police Bks.). (Illus.). 64p. (gr. 4 up). 1980. PLB 7.95 (ISBN 0-516-02231-8). Childrens.

--Dead Moon. LC 78-68228. (Galaxy Five Ser.). (Illus.). 64p. (gr. 4 up). 1980. PLB 7.95 (ISBN 0-516-02251-2). Childrens.

--Death Sentence. LC 79-51081. (Space Police Bks.). (Illus.). 64p. (gr. 4 up). 1980. PLB 7.95 (ISBN 0-516-02232-6). Childrens.

--Earth Two. LC 79-51077. (Space Police Bks.). (Illus.). 64p. (gr. 4 up). 1980. PLB 7.95 (ISBN 0-516-02233-4). Childrens.

--Good-Bye to Earth. LC 78-68226. (Galaxy Five Ser.). (Illus.). 64p. (gr. 4 up). 1980. PLB 7.95 (ISBN 0-516-02252-0). Childrens.

--King of the Stars. LC 78-68231. (Galaxy Five Ser.). (Illus.). 64p. (gr. 4 up). 1980. PLB 7.95 (ISBN 0-516-02253-9). Childrens.

--On the Red World. LC 78-68227. (Galaxy Five Ser.). (Illus.). 64p. (gr. 4 up). 1980. PLB 7.95 (ISBN 0-516-02254-7). Childrens.

--Prison Satellite. LC 79-51075. (Space Police Bks.). (Illus.). 64p. (gr. 4 up). 1980. PLB 7.95 (ISBN 0-516-02234-2). Childrens.

--Sunworld. LC 79-51080. (Space Police Bks.). (Illus.). 64p. (gr. 4 up). 1980. PLB 7.95 (ISBN 0-516-02235-0). Childrens.

--Vacation in Space. LC 78-68232. (Galaxy Five Ser.). (Illus.). 64p. (gr. 4 up). 1980. PLB 7.95 (ISBN 0-516-02255-5). Childrens.

--Where No Sun Shines. LC 78-68229. (Galaxy Five Ser.). (Illus.). 64p. (gr. 4 up). 1980. PLB 7.95 (ISBN 0-516-02256-3). Childrens.

--Worlds Apart. LC 79-51079. (Space Police Bks.). (Illus.). 64p. (gr. 4 up). 1980. PLB 7.95 (ISBN 0-516-02236-9). Childrens.

Kelley, Mike. White-Collar Proletariat: The Industrial Behaviour of British Civil Servants. 208p. (Orig.). 1980. pap. 21.75 (ISBN 0-7100-0623-3). Routledge & Kegan.

Kelley, N. Edmund. The Contemporary Ecology of Arroyo Hondo, New Mexico. (Arroyo Hondo Archaeological Ser.: Vol. 1). (Illus., Orig.). 1979. pap. 6.25 (ISBN 0-933452-01-2). Schol Am Res.

Kelley, Nancy L., jt. auth. see Pollak, Otto.

Kelley, Nelson L. & Whatley, Arthur A. Personnel Management in Action, Skill Building Experiences. 2nd ed. (West Ser. in Management). 300p. 1981. pap. text ed. 13.95 (ISBN 0-8299-0389-5). West Pub.

Kelley, Patrick. Building Safe Driving Skills. rev ed. LC 75-186589. (Illus.). (gr. 9-12,RL 3). 1977. text ed. 10.00 (ISBN 0-8224-1104-0); tchrs' guide 2.80 (ISBN 0-8224-1107-5); duplicatable chapter tests 12.00 (ISBN 0-8224-1106-7); student wkbk. 3.96 (ISBN 0-8224-1105-9). Pitman Learning.

Kelley, Philip & Hudson, Ronald, eds. The Brownings Correspondence: A Checklist. LC 77-93932. (Illus.). 1978. 125.00x (ISBN 0-685-27179-X, Pub. by Browning Inst). Pub Ctr Cult Res.

--Diary by E. B. B. LC 68-18390. 1969. 17.50x (ISBN 0-8214-0047-9). Ohio U Pr.

Kelley, Red & Lader, Martin. Hockey: The Sport's Playbook. LC 75-40731. (Illus.). 144p. 1976. pap. 2.95 o.p. (ISBN 0-385-06045-9). Doubleday.

Kelley, Richard E., jt. auth. see Desmond, Glenn M.

Kelley, Richard N., jt. auth. see Billmeyer, Fred W.

Kelley, Robert. Introduction to Communication. Brooks, W. D. & Vogel, R. A., eds. LC 76-39748. (Ser. in Speech Communication). 1977. pap. text ed. 5.95 (ISBN 0-8465-7606-6). Benjamin-Cummings.

--The Sounds of Controversy: Crucial Arguments in the American Past. 640p. 1975. Vol. 1. pap. text ed. 10.95 (ISBN 0-13-823088-9). P-H.

Kelley, Shirley D. Love Is Not for Cowards: The Autobiography of Shirley Dyckes Kelley. LC 77-26211. 1978. 9.95 o.p. (ISBN 0-13-541029-0). P-H.

Kelley, Stanley, Jr. Political Campaigning: Problems in Creating an Informed Electorate. 1960. 9.95 (ISBN 0-8157-4878-7). Brookings.

Kelley, Thomas. I Found Cleopatra. LC 80-20507. 100p. 1980. Repr. of 1977 ed. lib. bdg. 11.95x (ISBN 0-89370-027-4). Borgo Pr.

Kelley, Thomas M., jt. auth. see Seitzinger, Jack M.

Kelley, Thomas P. I Found Cleopatra. LC 77-87563. 1977. 5.95 (ISBN 0-913960-18-7). Fax Collect.

Kelley, True. A Valentine for Fuzzboom. (gr. k-3). 1981. 5.95 (ISBN 0-395-30446-6). HM.

Kelley, Truman L. & Krey, A. C. Tests & Measurements in the Social Sciences. 635p. 1980. Repr. of 1934 ed. lib. bdg. 35.00 (ISBN 0-89987-452-5). Century Bookbindery.

Kelley, William Melvin. Different Drummer. LC 62-11453. 1969. pap. 2.50 (ISBN 0-385-01079-6, A678, Anch). Doubleday.

Kelley, William T. Genesis-Exodus: An Access Guide. 128p. (Orig.). 1981. pap. 4.95 (ISBN 0-8215-5927-3). Sadlier.

Kelling, George W. Language: Mirror, Tool & Weapon. LC 74-10511. 274p. 1974. 16.95 (ISBN 0-911012-85-0). Nelson-Hall.

Kelling, Harold D., jt. ed. see Frazer, Ray.

Kellington, S. H. & Mitchell, A. C. An Evaluation of New Science: Worksheets for Scottish Integrated Science. 1978. pap. text ed. 9.50x o.p. (ISBN 0-435-57500-7). Heinemann Ed.

Kellington, Stuart. Assessment Questions for Integrated Science: Questions 9 to 15, Bk. 2. 1979. pap. text ed. 3.95x o.p. (ISBN 0-435-57503-1); tchr's. ed. 9.95x o.p. (ISBN 0-435-57501-5). Heinemann Ed.

Kellison, Stephen G. Fundamentals of Numerical Analysis. LC 74-78157. 1974. text ed. 17.50x (ISBN 0-256-01612-7). Irwin.

--Theory of Interest. 1971. Repr. of 1970 ed. text ed. 14.50 (ISBN 0-256-00283-5). Irwin.

Kellman, Jerold L. A Writer's Guide to Chicago-Area Publishers & Other Freelance Markets. LC 79-90014. 320p. 1979. 8.95 (ISBN 0-914090-74-7). Gabriel Hse.

Kellman, Shelly, jt. auth. see Teplitz, Jerry.

Kellner, Bruce. Carl Van Vechten & the Irreverant Decades. (Illus.). 1968. 17.95 (ISBN 0-8061-0808-8). U of Okla Pr.

Kellner, Douglas, jt. ed. see Bronner, Stephen.

Kellner, Esther. Wild Animal Shelter. (gr. 4-6). 1978. pap. 1.25 (ISBN 0-590-11915-X, Schol Pap). Schol Bk Serv.

Kellner, Hugo M., tr. see Ekrutt, Joachim W.

Kellner, Leon. Restoring Shakespeare: A Critical Analysis of the Misreadings in Shakespeare's Works. LC 78-77027. (Illus.). 1969. Repr. of 1925 ed. 9.50x (ISBN 0-8196-0244-2). Biblo.

Kellock, Harold. Parson Weems of the Cherry-Tree. LC 75-107137. 1971. Repr. of 1928 ed. 15.00 (ISBN 0-8103-3785-1). Gale.

Kellogg, Carolyn J., jt. auth. see Peterson, Barbara H.

Kellogg, Carolyn J. & Sullivan, Barbara P., eds. Current Perspectives in Oncologic Nursing, Vol. II. LC 78-492. (Current Perspectives Ser.). (Illus.). 1978. 11.95 (ISBN 0-8016-3794-5); pap. 8.95 (ISBN 0-8016-3795-3). Mosby.

Kellogg, Charles E. Soils That Support Us. 1941. 6.95 o.s.i. (ISBN 0-02-561950-0). Macmillan.

Kellogg, Charlotte. Paderewski. 1956. 4.95 o.p. (ISBN 0-670-53416-1). Viking Pr.

Kellogg, Clara L. Memoirs of an American Prima Donna. LC 77-16534. (Music Reprint Ser., 1978). (Illus.). 1978. Repr. of 1913 ed. lib. bdg. 32.50 (ISBN 0-306-77527-1). Da Capo.

Kellogg Company. Design of Piping Systems. rev. 2nd ed. 1964. 37.50 (ISBN 0-471-46795-2, Pub. by Wiley-Interscience). Wiley.

Kellogg, Edward P. Roots of the American Indian. LC 79-91921. 1980. text ed. 14.95 (ISBN 0-9603914-0-1). EHUD.

Kellogg, L. A., jt. auth. see Kellogg, W. N.

Kellogg, L. P. American Colonial Charter. LC 71-75291. (Era of the American Revolution Ser). 1971. Repr. of 1904 ed. lib. bdg. 14.50 (ISBN 0-306-71292-X). Da Capo.

Kellogg, Louise P., ed. see Cole, Harry E.

Kellogg, Louise T. British Regime in Wisconsin & the Northwest. LC 74-124927. (American Scene Ser). (Illus.). 1970. Repr. of 1935 ed. lib. bdg. 35.00 (ISBN 0-306-71047-1). Da Capo.

Kellogg, Marjorie. Like the Lion's Tooth. (YA) (RL 10). 1973. pap. 1.25 (ISBN 0-451-05655-8, Y5655, Sig). NAL.

--Tell Me That You Love Me, Junie Moon. LC 68-24600. 1968. 7.95 (ISBN 0-374-27280-8). FS&G.

Kellogg, Oliver D. Foundations of Potential Theory. 1929. pap. text ed. 5.00 (ISBN 0-486-60144-7). Dover.

Kellogg, Orson. Every Pilot's Guide to Aviation Fuel Economy. (Illus.). 64p. (Orig.). 1980. pap. 4.95 (ISBN 0-935802-00-2). Taxlogs.

Kellogg, Robert, jt. auth. see Scholes, Robert.

Kellogg, Robert L., ed. see Spenser, Edmund.

Kellogg, Samuel H. The Book of Leviticus. 1978. 19.00 (ISBN 0-686-12941-5). Klock & Klock.

Kellogg, Steven. There Was an Old Woman. LC 80-15293. (Illus.). 48p. (ps-3). 1980. Repr. of 1974 ed. 8.95 (ISBN 0-590-07779-1, Four Winds). Schol Bk Serv.

Kellogg, W. N. & Kellogg, L. A. The Ape & the Child. 1967. 17.50 (ISBN 0-02-847590-9). Hafner.

Kellogg, Walter G. Conscientious Objector. LC 77-107412. (Civil Liberties in American History Ser). 1970. Repr. of 1919 ed. lib. bdg. 15.00 (ISBN 0-306-71893-6). Da Capo.

Kellogg, William O. Greece & the Aegean. 1975. pap. text ed. 4.95x (ISBN 0-88334-066-6). Ind Sch Pr.

--Out of the Past. (gr. 9-12). 1969. pap. text ed. 4.95x (ISBN 0-88334-022-4) (ISBN 0-685-39240-6). Ind Sch Pr.

Kellogg, William W. & Schware, Robert. Climate Change & Society: Consequences of Increasing Atmospheric Carbon Dioxide. (Special Study Ser.). 170p. (Orig.). 1981. lib. bdg. 15.00x (ISBN 0-86531-179-X); pap. 8.00x (ISBN 0-86531-180-3). Westview.

Kellogg, Winthrop N. Porpoises & Sonar. LC 61-11294. (Illus.). xiv, 178p. 1961. 8.00x o.s.i. (ISBN 0-226-43004-9). U of Chicago Pr.

Kells, H. R. Self-Study Processes: A Guide for Postsecondary Institutions. 132p. 1980. 15.00 (ISBN 0-8268-1442-5). ACE.

--Self-Study Processes: A Guide for Postsecondary Institutions. 1980. 15.00 o.p. (ISBN 0-686-65234-7). ACE.

Kells, Joe. Advanced Driver. LC 77-85033. (Illus.). 1978. 16.95 (ISBN 0-7153-7494-X). David & Charles.

Kells, Joseph. Learner Driver. LC 74-81073. (Illus.). 142p. 1975. 11.95 (ISBN 0-7153-6794-3). David & Charles.

Kellum, David F. American History Through Conflicting Interpretations. LC 68-54674. 1969. text ed. 6.00x (ISBN 0-8077-1604-9). Tchrs Coll.

--Social Studies. 1969. pap. 2.45 o.p. (ISBN 0-8362-0112-4). Andrews & McMeel.

Kelly & Landers. Today's Teen. rev. ed. (gr. 7-9). 1981. text ed. 14.60 (ISBN 0-87002-323-3). Bennett IL.

--Today's Teen. (YA) 1977. 12.40 (ISBN 0-87002-192-3); tchr's guide 6.60 (ISBN 0-87002-264-4); student guide 3.56 (ISBN 0-87002-268-7). Bennett IL.

Kelly, A. Strong Solids. 2nd ed. (Monographs on the Physics & Chemistry of Materials Ser.). (Illus.). 285p. 1973. 42.00x (ISBN 0-19-851350-X). Oxford U Pr.

Kelly, A. & Nicholson, R., eds. Strengthening Methods in Crystals. 627p. 1972. 54.95 (ISBN 0-470-46800-9). Halsted Pr.

Kelly, A. V. Curriculum Context. 1980. 18.50 (IntlDept). Har-Row.

--Mixed Ability Grouping: An Individualized Approach. 2nd ed. 1978. text ed. 15.70 (ISBN 0-06-318069-3, IntlDept); pap. text ed. 9.25 (ISBN 0-06-318070-7, IntlDept). Har-Row.

--Teaching Mixed Ability Classes: An Individualized Approach. 1975. pap. 4.00 o.p. (ISBN 0-06-318071-5, IntlDept). Har-Row.

Kelly, A. V. & Downey, Meriel. Moral Education: Theory & Practice. 1979. text ed. 15.70 (ISBN 0-06-318079-0, IntlDept); pap. text ed. 9.25 (ISBN 0-06-318080-4, IntlDept). Har-Row.

Kelly, A. V., jt. auth. see Blenkin, Geva.

Kelly, A. V., jt. auth. see Downey, M. E.

Kelly, Alfred. The Descent of Darwin: The Popularization of Darwinism in Germany, 1860-1914. LC 80-19445. 200p. 1981. 18.50x (ISBN 0-8078-1460-1). U of NC Pr.

Kelly, Annamaria. Kino Alla Conquista Dell 'America. LC 80-53508. (Illus.). 148p. (Orig.). 1980. pap. 6.50 (ISBN 0-915076-05-5). SW Mission.

Kelly, Anthony & Groves, G. W. Crystallography & Crystal Defects. (Engineering Ser). (Illus.). 1970. text ed. 25.95 (ISBN 0-201-03696-7). A-W.

Kelly, D. R. The Beginning of Ideology. 358p. Date not set. price not set (ISBN 0-521-23504-9). Cambridge U Pr.

Kelly, Dan H. & Welborn, Peggy. The Cover-Up: Neckwear for the Laryngectomee & Other Neck Breathers. LC 80-65470. (Illus.). 98p. 1980. pap. text ed. 14.95 (ISBN 0-933014-55-4). College-Hill.

Kelly, Dave. Instructions for Viewing a Solar Eclipse. LC 78-184365. (Wesleyan Poetry Program: Vol. 61). 72p. (Orig.). 1972. 10.00x (ISBN 0-8195-2061-6, Pub. by Wesleyan U Pr); pap. 4.95 (ISBN 0-8195-1061-0). Columbia U Pr.

Kelly, Dennis. Size Queen & Other Poems. (Illus.). 112p. (Orig.). 1981. ltd. ed. 30.00 (ISBN 0-917342-81-X); pap. 5.95 (ISBN 0-917342-82-8). Gay Sunshine.

Kelly, Don C. Thermodynamics & Statistical Physics. 1973. text ed. 22.95 (ISBN 0-12-404050-0). Acad Pr.

Kelly, Donna. ABC Play with Me. (A Golden Book for Early Childhood Ser.). (Illus.). (gr. k-3). 1979. PLB 5.38 (ISBN 0-307-68822-4, Golden Pr). Western Pub.

--Clock Book. (A Golden Book for Early Childhood Ser.). (Illus.). (gr. k-3). 1979. PLB 5.38 (ISBN 0-307-68962-X, Golden Pr). Western Pub.

--The Playground Book. (Illus.). (gr. k-2). 1978. PLB 5.38 (ISBN 0-307-68992-1, Golden Pr). Western Pub.

--Wizard of Oz. (Illus.). (gr. k-2). 1976. PLB 5.38 (ISBN 0-307-68906-9, Golden Pr). Western Pub.

Kelly, Douglas. Medieval Imagination: Rhetoric & the Poetry of Courtly Love. LC 78-3522. 1978. 32.50 (ISBN 0-299-07610-5). U of Wis Pr.

Kelly, Douglas, et al. The Westminster Confession of Faith: A New Edition. 102p. 1980. pap. 5.95 (ISBN 0-87921-060-5). Attic Pr.

Kelly, Earl. James, a Primer for Christian Living. 1973. kivar 3.95 o.p. (ISBN 0-934532-13-3). Presby & Reformed.

Kelly, Edward, ed. Moll Flanders. (Critical Editions Ser.). 500p. 1973. pap. text ed. 5.95x (ISBN 0-393-09412-X). Norton.

Kelly, Edward E. see Newman, John H.

Kelly, Eric P. The Land & People of Poland. rev. ed. Kostich, Dragos D., rev. by. LC 73-37924. (Portraits of the Nations Ser.). (Illus.). (gr. 6 up). 1972. 8.79 (ISBN 0-397-31313-6). Lippincott.

--Trumpeter of Krakow. new ed. (gr. 7 up). 1966. 8.95 (ISBN 0-02-750140-X). Macmillan.

Kelly, Eugene. Max Scheler. (Modern Masters Ser.: No. 55). 1977. lib. bdg. 12.50 (ISBN 0-8057-7707-5). Twayne.

Kelly, Eugene, jt. ed. see Navia, Luis E.

Kelly, Eugene W., Jr. Effective Interpersonal Communication: A Manual for Skill Development. 1977. pap. text ed. 7.50x (ISBN 0-8191-0125-7). U Pr of Amer.

Kelly, Eugene W., Jr., jt. auth. see Winecoff, H. Larry.

Kelly, F. M. Shakespearian Costume. 2nd rev. ed. Mansfield, A., ed. LC 76-123629. (Illus.). 1970. 14.95 o.s.i. (ISBN 0-87830-117-8). Theatre Arts.

Kelly, Fanny W. Narrative of My Captivity Among the Sioux Indians...with a Brief Account of General Sully's Indian Expedition in 1864, Bearing Upon Events Occurring in My Captivity. LC 75-7111. (Indian Captivities Ser.: Vol. 85). 1976. Repr. of 1871 ed. lib. bdg. 44.00 (ISBN 0-8240-1709-9). Garland Pub.

Kelly, G. V. The Old Gray Mayors of Denver. LC 73-94191. (Illus.). 1974. 9.95 o.p. (ISBN 0-87108-078-8). Pruett.

Kelly, Gail P., jt. ed. see Altbach, Philip G.

Kelly, Gary F., ed. Good Sex: The Healthy Man's Guide to Sexual Fulfillment. 1981. pap. 2.95 (ISBN 0-451-09572-3, Sig). NAL.

Kelly, George, ed. Human Sexuality in Our Time. 1979. 4.00 (ISBN 0-8198-0610-2); pap. 3.00 (ISBN 0-8198-0611-0). Dghtrs St Paul.

Kelly, George A. The Battle for the American Church. LC 80-22348. 528p. 1981. pap. 8.95 (ISBN 0-385-17433-0, Im). Doubleday.

Kelly, George V. & Farrar, Harry. Garden of Hope: Laradon Hall. (Illus.). 240p. 1980. 12.50 (ISBN 0-87108-561-5); pap. 7.50 (ISBN 0-87108-562-3). Pruett.

Kelly, George W. A Way to Beauty: Planting & Landscaping in the Rocky Mountains. (Illus.). 176p. 1976. pap. 2.95 o.p. (ISBN 0-87108-096-6). Pruett.

Kelly, George W., jt. auth. see Friar, John G.

Kelly, Gerard W. Metric System Simplified. LC 77-93317. 96p. (gr. 4 up). 1974. 5.95 (ISBN 0-8069-3058-6); PLB 5.89 (ISBN 0-8069-3059-4). Sterling.

Kelly, Harold C. Improving Your Clock Repairing Skills. (Illus.). 1976. pap. 5.50 o.p. (ISBN 0-8096-1907-5, Assn Pr). Follett.

Kelly, Henry A. The Matrimonial Trials of Henry VIII. LC 75-7483. xiv, 314p. 1976. 15.00x (ISBN 0-8047-0895-9). Stanford U Pr.

Kelly, Hugh. Memoirs of a Magdalen, or, the History of Louisa Mildmay, 1767, 2 vols. in 1. LC 74-16055. (Novel in England, 1700-1775 Ser). 1974. lib. bdg. 50.00 (ISBN 0-8240-1175-9). Garland Pub.

Kelly, Isabel. The Archaeology of the Autlan-Tuxcacuesco Area of Jalisco, II: The Tuxcacuesco-Zapotitlan Zone. (U. C. Publ. in Ibero-Americana: Vol. 27). 1949. pap. 9.00x (ISBN 0-520-09194-9). U of Cal Pr.

--Ceramic Sequence in Colima: Capacha, an Early Phase. (Anthropological Papers: No. 37). 1980. pap. text ed. 9.95x (ISBN 0-8165-0565-9). U of Ariz Pr.

Kelly, J. B. Eastern Arabian Frontiers. (Illus.). 1964. 5.95 o.p. (ISBN 0-571-06963-0, Pub. by Faber & Faber). Merrimack Bk Serv.

Kelly, J. F. Early Connecticut Meeting Houses, 2 Vols. (Illus.). 1948. Set. 75.00 (ISBN 0-685-02489-X). Kelly.

Kelly, J. M., tr. see Kunkel, Wolfgang.

Kelly, J. N. A Commentary of the Pastoral Epistles. (Thornapple Commentaries Ser.). 272p. 1981. pap. 6.95 (ISBN 0-8010-5428-1). Baker Bk.

--Early Christian Creeds. 3rd ed. 446p. 1979. text ed. 25.00x (ISBN 0-582-48931-8). Longman.

Kelly, J. W. Metachromatic Reaction. (Protoplasmatologia: Vol. 2, Pt. D2). (Illus.). 1956. pap. 32.50 o.p. (ISBN 0-387-80422-6). Springer-Verlag.

Kelly, J. W., jt. auth. see Davis, Raymond E.

Kelly, James E., jt. auth. see Harvey, Clair.

Kelly, James L. & Orr, Alan R. Self-Pacing Biology Experiences. (Illus.). 1980. 11.50 (ISBN 0-8138-1725-0). Iowa St U Pr.

Kelly, James W. The Faust Legend in Music. LC 74-75893. (Detroit Reprints in Music). 1976. 10.00 (ISBN 0-911772-81-2). Info Coord.

Kelly, Jeanne, tr. see Chi'en Chung-shu.

Kelly, Jim. Aquarium Guide. 6.98 o.p. (ISBN 0-385-01557-7). Doubleday.

Kelly, Joan, jt. auth. see Chamberlain, Valerie.

Kelly, Joan, jt. auth. see Chamberlain, Valerie M.

Kelly, Joe. Organizational Behavior. 3rd ed. 1980. 0.19.95x (ISBN 0-256-02284-4). Irwin.

--Organizational Behaviour. rev. ed. 1974. text ed. 16.95x o.p. (ISBN 0-256-01434-5). Irwin.

Kelly, John. The CIA in America. LC 78-24776. 256p. 1981. 14.95 (ISBN 0-88208-102-0); pap. 6.95 (ISBN 0-88208-103-9). Lawrence Hill.

Kelly, John, jt. auth. see Verny, Thomas.

Kelly, John, et al. Nursing Eighty Career Directory. 2nd, rev. ed. Gomez, June F., ed. (Illus.). 320p. 1980. pap. 10.00 (ISBN 0-916730-23-9). InterMed Comm.

Kelly, John B. Arabia, the Gulf, & the West: A Critical View of Arabs & Their Oil Policy. LC 80-80787. 530p. 1980. 25.00 (ISBN 0-465-00415-6). Basic.

Kelly, John C. Fifty Best of Baltimore & Ohio Railroad, Bk. 3. (Illus.). 1977. 12.00 (ISBN 0-934118-02-7). Barnard Robert.

Kelly, John F. Early Domestic Architecture of Connecticut. (Illus.). 13.50 (ISBN 0-8446-2363-6). Peter Smith.

Kelly, John R. Pedro Prado. (World Authors Ser.: Chile: No. 304). 1974. lib. bdg. 10.95 (ISBN 0-8057-2712-4). Twayne.

Kelly, Joyce. The Complete Visitor's Guide to Mesoamerican Ruins. (Illus.). 480p. 1981. 35.00 (ISBN 0-8061-1566-1). U of Okla Pr.

Kelly, K. B. Grains of Wheat. (Illus.). 128p. 1981. pap. 1.95 (ISBN 0-914544-32-2). Living Flame Pr.

Kelly, Kate. The Publicity Manual. LC 79-55946. 166p. 1980. 29.95 (ISBN 0-9603740-1-9). Visibility Ent.

Kelly, Kathleen W. Jean Anouilh: An Annotated Bibliography. LC 73-960. (Author Bibliographies Ser.: No. 10). 1973. 10.00 (ISBN 0-8108-0593-6). Scarecrow.

Kelly, L. G. Quaestiones Alberti De Modis Significandi by Pseudo-Albertus Magnus. (Studies in the History of Linguistics: No. 15). 1979. text ed. 37.25x (ISBN 0-391-01664-4). Humanities.

Kelly, Leo P. Luke Sutton Outlaw. LC 80-2322. 192p. 1981. 9.95 (ISBN 0-385-17254-0). Doubleday.

Kelly, Luther S. Yellowstone Kelly: The Memoirs of Luther S. Kelly. Quaife, M. M., ed. LC 26-9001. (Illus.). xiv, 268p. 1973. pap. 6.50 (ISBN 0-8032-5784-8, BB 571, Bison). U of Nebr Pr.

Kelly, Marguerite & Parsons, Elia S. The Mother's Almanac. LC 73-9166. 288p. 1975. softbound 6.95 (ISBN 0-385-01806-1). Doubleday.

Kelly, Mary P. Martin Scorsese: The First Decade. (Illus., Orig.). 1980. pap. 9.90 (ISBN 0-913178-67-5). Redgrave Pub Co.

Kelly, Michael. Music for Two Theatre Pieces: Pizarro (1799) & Love Laughs at Locksmiths (1803) (Music Reprint Ser.: 1979). 1979. Repr. of 1803 ed. lib. bdg. 18.50 (ISBN 0-306-79562-0). Da Capo.

--Reminiscences of Michael Kelly of the King's Theatre & Theatre Royal Drury Lane 2 Vols. 2nd ed. LC 68-16243. (Music Ser). 1968. Repr. of 1826 ed. lib. bdg. 45.00 (ISBN 0-306-71094-3). Da Capo.

Kelly, Michael B. The Fitness Factor: Practical Body Building for Health. LC 80-20432. (Illus.). 256p. 1981. 11.95 (ISBN 0-668-05115-9, 5115). Arco.

Kelly, Michael J. Legal Ethics & Legal Education. LC 80-10825. (The Teaching of Ethics Ser.). 69p. 1980. pap. 4.00 (ISBN 0-916558-06-1). Hastings Ctr Inst Soc.

Kelly, P., jt. auth. see Rudduck, J.

Kelly, Patricia M. Mighty Human Cell. LC 67-10823. (Illus.). (gr. 4-8). 1967. PLB 7.89 (ISBN 0-381-99768-5, A49000, JD-J). John Day.

Kelly, Patrick. Irish Family Names. LC 68-26580. 1975. Repr. of 1939 ed. 24.00 (ISBN 0-8103-4146-8). Gale.

Kelly, Paul J., jt. auth. see Busemann, Herbert.

Kelly, R. A. Use of English for Technical Students. 2nd ed. 1970. pap. text ed. 11.95x (ISBN 0-245-50843-0). Intl Ideas.

Kelly, Richard. Lewis Carroll. (English Authors Ser.: No. 212). 1977. lib. bdg. 10.95 (ISBN 0-8057-6681-2). Twayne.
Kelly, Richard, jt. ed. see Appelbaum, Stanley.
Kelly, Richard J. John Berryman: A Checklist. LC 72-6332. (Author Bibliographies Ser.: No. 8). 1972. 10.00 (ISBN 0-8108-0552-9). Scarecrow.
Kelly, Richard M. Douglas Jerrold. LC 79-187615. (English Authors Ser.: No. 146). lib. bdg. 10.95 (ISBN 0-8057-1292-5). Twayne.
Kelly, Richard M., ed. The Best of Mr. Punch: The Humorous Writings of Douglas Jerrold. LC 73-111045. (Illus.). 1970. 18.50x (ISBN 0-87049-116-4). U of Tenn Pr.
Kelly, Rita M. Community Control of Economic Development: The Boards of Directors of Community Development Corporations. LC 77-7814. (Praeger Special Studies). 1977. text ed. 23.95 (ISBN 0-03-022351-2). Praeger.
Kelly, Rita M. & Boutilier, Mary A. The Making of Political Women: A Study of Socialization & Role Conflict. LC 77-17081. 1978. text ed. 18.95 (ISBN 0-88229-290-0). Nelson-Hall.
Kelly, Robert. Baseball Trivia Puzzler, No. 1. (Orig.). 1981. pap. 1.95 (ISBN 0-440-00393-8). Dell.
--Kill the Messenger Who Brings Bad News. 242p. 1979. signed 20.00 (ISBN 0-87685-433-1); pap. 7.50 (ISBN 0-87685-432-3). Black Sparrow.
--Spiritual Exercises. 200p. (Orig.). 1981. signed ed. 20.00 (ISBN 0-87685-508-7); pap. 7.50 (ISBN 0-87685-507-9). Black Sparrow.
--Sports Trivia Puzzler, No. 4. (Orig.). 1981. pap. 1.95 (ISBN 0-440-07807-5). Dell.
Kelly, Rosalie. Addie's Year. LC 80-25566. 160p. (gr. 5 up). 1981. 7.95 (ISBN 0-8253-0028-2). Beaufort Bks NY.
Kelly, T. History of Public Libraries in Great Britain, 1845 to 1975. 2nd ed. 1977. 34.00x (ISBN 0-85365-239-2, Pub. by Lib Assn England). Oryx Pr.
Kelly, Terence F. & Schieber, George J. Factors Affecting Medical Services Utilization: A Behavioral Approach. 1972. pap. 3.50 o.p. (ISBN 0-87766-036-0, 21000). Urban Inst.
Kelly, Thaddeus E. Clinical Genetics & Genetics Counseling. (Illus.). 400p. 1980. 29.50 (ISBN 0-8151-5011-3). Year Bk Med.
Kelly, Thomas. The Eternal Promise. LC 77-71637. 1977. pap. 2.45 (ISBN 0-913408-30-1). Friends United.
Kelly, Walter K. Curiosities of Indo-European Tradition & Folk-Lore. LC 68-22032. 1969. Repr. of 1863 ed. 18.00 (ISBN 0-8103-3837-8). Gale.
Kelly, William. The Gospel of Luke. Date not set. 16.95 (ISBN 0-86524-046-9). Klock & Klock.
Kelly, William A., Jr. Macroeconomics. (Illus.). 496p. 1981. text ed. 17.95 (ISBN 0-13-542761-4). P-H.
Kelly, William J. Karl Rahner, S. J., Discoverer in Theology. 320p. 24.95 (ISBN 0-87462-521-1). Marquette.
Kelly-Bootle, Stan. The Devil's DP Dictionary. (Illus.). 160p. 1981. 5.95 (ISBN 0-07-034022-6, P&RB). McGraw.
Kelly-Crocker, Gay, et al. English Comprehensive, Three & Four Years. LC 56-35602. (High School Exams & Answer Ser). (gr. 11-12). 1977. pap. 3.50 (ISBN 0-8120-0197-4). Barron.
Kelly-Newton, Lauren. Accounting Policy Formation: The Role of Corporate Management. (A-W Paperback Accounting Ser.). 200p. 1980. pap. text ed. 4.95 (ISBN 0-201-05291-1). A-W.
Kelman, Arthur, ed. see American Phytopathological Society - Sourcebook Committee.
Kelman, G. R. Applied Cardiovascular Physiology. 2nd ed. 1977. 34.95 (ISBN 0-407-10881-5). Butterworths.
Kelman, Harold. Helping People: Karen Horney's Psychoanalytic Approach. LC 75-140098. 1971. 35.00x (ISBN 0-87668-039-2, 75-140098). Aronson.
Kelman, Herbert C., ed. International Behavior: A Social-Psychological Analysis. 1980. text ed. 38.50x (ISBN 0-8290-0027-5); pap. text ed. 18.50x (ISBN 0-8290-0028-3). Irvington.
Kelman, Steven. Improving Doctor Performance: A Study in the Use of Information & Organizational Change. LC 79-21211. 352p. 1980. 24.95x (ISBN 0-87705-444-4). Human Sci Pr.
--Regulating America, Regulating Sweden: A Comparative Study of Occupational Safety & Health Regulations. 320p. 1981. text ed. 19.95x (ISBN 0-262-11076-8). MIT Pr.
Kelnar, G. & Harvey, D. Intensive Care of the Newborn. (Illus.). 1980. pap. text ed. 17.95 (ISBN 0-02-858020-6). Macmillan.
Kelrich. Charades. 1979. pap. 2.50 (ISBN 0-441-10261-1). Ace Bks.
Kelsall, Charles. Horae Viaticae. LC 79-18052. 1979. Repr. of 1839 ed. 48.00 (ISBN 0-8201-1333-6). Schol Facsimiles.
Kelsall, H. M., jt. auth. see Kelsall, R. K.
Kelsall, Malcolm, ed. see Otway, Thomas.
Kelsall, R. K. Population. rev. ed. (Aspects of Modern Sociology, the Social Structure of Modern Britain Ser). 1967. text ed. 4.25x (ISBN 0-582-48771-4); pap. text ed. 3.00x (ISBN 0-582-48709-9). Humanities.
Kelsall, R. K. & Kelsall, H. M. The School Teacher in England & the United States. 1969. 22.00 (ISBN 0-08-006519-8); pap. 11.25 (ISBN 0-08-006518-X). Pergamon.
Kelsch, Mary L. & Kelsch, Thomas. Writing Effectively: A Practical Guide. 192p. 1981. 10.95 (ISBN 0-13-969832-9, Spec); pap. 4.95 (ISBN 0-13-969824-8, Spec). P-H.
Kelsch, Thomas, jt. auth. see Kelsch, Mary L.
Kelsen, Hans. Pure Theory of Law. Knight, Max, tr. from Ger. (Library Reprint Ser.: Vol. 94). 1978. 27.50x (ISBN 0-520-03692-1). U of Cal Pr.
Kelsen, Hans see Jessup, Philip C.
Kelsey, Alice G. Land of the Morning: Ten Stories from the Philippines. (gr. 5-9). 1968. teachers' guide 0.85 (ISBN 0-685-11651-4); pap. 1.75 o.p. (ISBN 0-685-11651-4). Friend Pr.
Kelsey, David H. Uses of Scripture in Recent Theology. LC 74-26344. 240p. 1975. pap. 6.95 (ISBN 0-8006-1374-0, 1-1374). Fortress.
Kelsey, George D. Social Ethics Among Southern Baptists, 1917-1969. (Atla Monograph: No. 2). 1973. 10.00 (ISBN 0-8108-0538-3). Scarecrow.
Kelsey, H. W. Advanced Play at Bridge. LC 68-87519. 1979. 11.95 (ISBN 0-571-08300-5, Pub. by Faber & Faber). Merrimack Bk Serv.
--Advanced Play at Bridge. 192p. 1981. pap. 6.95 (ISBN 0-571-11677-9, Pub. by Faber & Faber). Merrimack Bk Serv.
--How to Improve Your Bridge. (Illus.). 1971. 6.95 o.p. (ISBN 0-571-09726-X, Pub. by Faber & Faber). Merrimack Bk Serv.
--How to Improve Your Bridge. 1979. 6.95 o.p. (ISBN 0-571-09726-X, Pub. by Faber & Faber); pap. 4.95 (ISBN 0-571-11438-5). Merrimack Bk Serv.
--Killing Defence at Bridge. 1978. 8.95 o.p. (ISBN 0-571-06869-3, Pub. by Faber & Faber). Merrimack Bk Serv.
--Logical Bridge Play. 1976. 11.95 (ISBN 0-686-24615-2, Pub. by Faber & Faber). Merrimack Bk Serv.
--Match-Point Bridge. 1970. 6.95 o.p. (ISBN 0-571-09436-8, Pub. by Faber & Faber). Merrimack Bk Serv.
--More Killing Defence at Bridge. 1972. 8.95 o.p. (ISBN 0-571-10153-4, Pub. by Faber & Faber). Merrimack Bk Serv.
Kelsey, H. W., tr. see Jannerston, Eric.
Kelsey, J. H., jt. ed. see Schmoger, E.
Kelsey, Joe. Climbing & Hiking in the Wind River Mountains: Wyoming. LC 79-23882. (Illus.). 400p. (Totebook). 1980. pap. 8.95 (ISBN 0-87156-267-7). Sierra.
Kelsey, Morton. Dreams: A Way to Listen to God. LC 77-83583. 1978. pap. 2.95 (ISBN 0-8091-2046-1). Paulist Pr.
--Encounter with God: A Theology of Christian Experience. 288p. 1972. pap. 5.95 (ISBN 0-87123-123-9, 210123); study guide 1.25 (ISBN 0-87123-506-4, 210506). Bethany Fell.
--Myth, History & Faith: The Re-Mythologizing of Christianity. LC 73-94216. 1974. pap. 4.95 (ISBN 0-8091-1827-0). Paulist Pr.
Kelsey, Morton T. Caring: How Can We Love Each Other? 192p. (Orig.). 1981. pap. 6.95 (ISBN 0-8091-2366-5). Paulist Pr.
--The Cross. LC 80-82086. 118p. 1980. pap. 2.95 (ISBN 0-8091-2337-1). Paulist Pr.
--Transcend: A Guide to the Spiritual Quest. 240p. (Orig.). 1981. pap. 5.95 (ISBN 0-8245-0015-6). Crossroad NY.
Kelsey, Vera, et al. Four Keys to Guatemala. LC 77-2175. (Funk & W Bk.). (Illus.). 1978. 10.00 o.s.i. (ISBN 0-308-10293-2, TYC-T); pap. 5.95 o.s.i. (ISBN 0-308-10316-5, TYC-T). T Y Crowell.
Kelsey, W. Eric. Building Construction: An Illustrated Manual for Technicians, Estate Managers & Surveyors. (Illus.). 1974. 35.00 (ISBN 0-7153-6287-9). David & Charles.
--House Construction & Purchase: A Guide to Buying, Building & Living in Your Own House. (Illus.). 1973. 9.95 o.p. (ISBN 0-7153-5735-2). David & Charles.
Kelso, Linda. Mount St. Helens & Other Volcanoes of the West. Shangle, Robert D., ed. (Illus.). 144p. 1980. 27.50 (ISBN 0-89802-202-9). Beautiful Am.
--Mount St. Helens: Volcano. Shangle, Robert D., ed. (Illus.). 64p. 1980. pap. 7.95 (ISBN 0-89802-209-6). Beautiful Am.
Kelso, William M. Captain Jones's Wormslow: A Historical, Archaeological, & Architectural Study of an Eighteenth-Century Plantation Site Near Savannah, Georgia. LC 78-2288. (Wormsloe Foundations Publications Ser.: No. 13). (Illus.). 208p. 1979. 20.00x (ISBN 0-8203-0447-6). U of Ga Pr.
Kelting, Herman. Real Estate Investments. LC 78-6811. (Grid Series in Real Estate). 1980. 17.95 (ISBN 0-88244-171-X). Grid Pub.
Kelton, David, jt. auth. see Law, Averill M.
Kelton, Elmer. Captain's Rangers. 1981. pap. 1.95 (ISBN 0-553-14990-3). Bantam.
--The Day the Cowboys Quit. 1980. pap. 1.95 (ISBN 0-441-13907-8). Ace Bks.
Kelton, Nancy. The Finger Game Miracle. LC 76-46408. (When They Were Young Ser.). (Illus.). (gr. k-3). 1977. PLB 7.95 (ISBN 0-8172-0452-0). Raintree Pubs.
--Harry Four Eyes. LC 76-44244. (When They Were Young Ser.). (Illus.). (gr. k-3). 1977. PLB 7.95 (ISBN 0-8172-0453-9). Raintree Pubs.
--Rebel Slave. LC 76-46446. (When They Were Young Ser.). (Illus.). (gr. k-3). 1977. PLB 7.95 (ISBN 0-8172-0450-4). Raintree Pubs.
Kelz, Rochelle. Conversational Spanish for Medical Personnel. LC 76-55722. 1977. pap. text ed. 12.95 (ISBN 0-471-02154-7, Pub. by Wiley Medical). Wiley.
Kemal, Yashar. Seagull. 1981. 11.95 (ISBN 0-394-51856-X). Pantheon.
Kemali, D., ed. Advances in Biological Psychiatry, Vol. 6. (Illus.). 128p. 1981. pap. 48.00 (ISBN 3-8055-2420-X). S Karger.
Kemble, John Haskell. The Panama Route. LC 79-139195. (The American Scene Ser). (Illus.). 316p. 1972. Repr. of 1943 ed. lib. bdg. 29.50 (ISBN 0-306-70083-2). Da Capo.
Kemelman, Harry. Monday the Rabbi Took Off. (Rabbi Ser.). 288p. 1978. pap. 2.25 (ISBN 0-449-23872-5, Crest). Fawcett.
--Sunday the Rabbi Stayed Home. (Rabbi Ser.). 1979. pap. 2.25 (ISBN 0-449-24116-5, Crest). Fawcett.
Kemeny, John G., ed. The Accident at Three Mile Island: The Need for Change, the Legacy of TMI. (Illus.). 201p. 1981. 33.00 (ISBN 0-08-025949-9); pap. 25.00 (ISBN 0-08-025946-4). Pergamon.
Kemeny, John G., et al. Finite Mathematics with Business Applications. 2nd ed. (Quantitative Analysis for Business Ser). 1972. ref. ed. 19.95 (ISBN 0-13-317321-6). P-H.
Kemeny, Nancy see Rose, Louisa, et al.
Kemerer, Frank R. Understanding Faculty Unions & Collective Bargaining. 1976. pap. 6.50 (ISBN 0-934338-32-9). NAIS.
Kemerer, Frank R. & Satryb, Ronald P., eds. Facing Financial Exigency. LC 76-45606. (Illus.). 1977. 16.95 (ISBN 0-669-01114-2). Lexington Bks.
Kemmee, Douglas H., jt. auth. see Conte, Sylvester B.
Kemmer, N. Vector Analysis. LC 75-36025. (Illus.). 230p. 1977. 49.50 (ISBN 0-521-21158-1); pap. 15.95x (ISBN 0-521-29064-3). Cambridge U Pr.
Kemmer, Rick. A Guide to Paddle Adventure: How to Buy Canoes & Kayaks & Where to Travel. LC 75-386. 384p. 1975. 10.00 (ISBN 0-8149-0760-1); pap. 6.95 (ISBN 0-685-52406-X). Vanguard.
Kemmit, R., ed. The Chemistry of Manganese, Technetium & Rhenium. Peacock, R. (Pergamon Texts in Inorganic Chemistry: Vol. 22). 208p. 1975. text ed. 28.00 (ISBN 0-08-018870-2); pap. text ed. 17.50 (ISBN 0-08-018869-9). Pergamon.
Kemock, Nicholas. Ohio Supplement for Real Estate Principles & Practices. (Business & Economics Ser.). 80p. 1976. 4.95 (ISBN 0-675-08584-5). Merrill.
Kemp, Alasdair. Current Awareness Services. (Outlines of Modern Librarianship Ser.). 181p. 1979. text ed. 12.00 (ISBN 0-89664-420-0, Pub. by K G Saur). Shoe String.
Kemp, Anthony. The Maginot Line: Myth & Reality. LC 80-6260. 128p. 1981. 11.95 (ISBN 0-8128-2811-9). Stein & Day.
--The Unknown Battle: Metz 1944. LC 78-66240. (Illus.). 288p. 1980. 14.95 (ISBN 0-8128-2598-5). Stein & Day.
--Weapons & Equipment of the Marlborough Wars. (Illus.). 192p. 1981. 24.95 (ISBN 0-7137-1013-6, Pub. by Blandford Pr England). Sterling.
Kemp, Brian. English Church Monuments. 240p. 1980. 53.00 (ISBN 0-7134-1735-8, Pub. by Batsford England). David & Charles.
Kemp, C. Gratton. Perspectives on the Group Process: A Foundation for Counseling with Groups. 2nd ed. LC 64-346. 1970. text ed. 18.50 (ISBN 0-395-04723-4, 3-29410). HM.
--Small Groups & Self-Renewal. 1971. 7.95 (ISBN 0-8164-0191-8). Crossroad NY.
Kemp, Charles F. Pastoral Counseling Guidebook. (Orig.). 1971. pap. 6.50 o.p. (ISBN 0-687-30320-6). Abingdon.
--The World of Golf & the Game of Life. (Illus.). 1978. pap. 2.95 (ISBN 0-8272-4212-3). Bethany Pr.
Kemp, Charles F., jt. auth. see Bryant, Marcus D.
Kemp, Daniel S. & Vellaccio, Frank. Organic Chemistry. 1980. 26.95 (ISBN 0-87901-123-8); wkbk. & solutions manual 11.95 (ISBN 0-87901-124-6). Worth.
Kemp, Edward C. Manuscript Solicitation for Libraries, Special Collections, Museums & Archives. LC 77-29015. 1978. lib. bdg. 20.00x (ISBN 0-87287-183-5). Libs Unl.
Kemp, Gene. Christmas with Tamworth Pig. LC 78-300034. (Illus.). (gr. 8-12). 1979. 8.95 (ISBN 0-571-11117-3, Pub. by Faber & Faber). Merrimack Bk Serv.
--Dog Days & Cat Naps. (Illus.). 110p. (gr. 2-5). 1981. 11.95 (ISBN 0-571-11595-0, Pub. by Faber & Faber). Merrimack Bk Serv.
--Tamworth Pig Saves the Trees. (Fanfares Ser.). (Illus.). (ps-4). 1980. pap. 3.25 (ISBN 0-571-11493-8, Pub. by Faber & Faber). Merrimack Bk Serv.
Kemp, Gene, ed. Ducks & Dragons: Poems for Children. LC 80-670271. 128p. (gr. 2-5). 1980. 8.95 (ISBN 0-571-11523-3, Pub. by Faber & Faber). Merrimack Bk Serv.
Kemp, J. F. & Young, P. Notes on Cargo Work. 4th ed. (Kemp & Young Ser.). (Illus., Orig.). 1981. pap. text ed. 9.50x (ISBN 0-540-07332-6). Sheridan.
Kemp, Jack. An American Renaissance. 1981. pap. 2.50 (ISBN 0-425-04848-9). Berkley Pub.
Kemp, Jerrold E. Instructional Design. 2nd ed. LC 77-140897. 1977. pap. 4.95 (ISBN 0-8224-3920-4). Pitman Learning.
Kemp, Jonathon, ed. see Diderot, Denis.
Kemp, Jonathon, tr. see Diderot, Denis.
Kemp, Kenneth C. Laboratory Experiments to Chemistry: The Central Science. 2nd ed. 378p. 1981. wkbk. 10.95 (ISBN 0-13-128520-3). P-H.
Kemp, L., tr. see Domingo, Xavier.
Kemp, Michael A. Reduced Fare & Fare-Free Urban Transit Services: Some Case Studies. 37p. 1974. pap. 2.50 o.p. (ISBN 0-87766-122-7, 79000). Urban Inst.
--Transit Improvements in Atlanta-the Effects of Fare & Service Changes. 46p. 1974. pap. 2.50 o.p. (ISBN 0-87766-117-0, 71000). Urban Inst.
Kemp, Peter. The History of Ships. (Illus.). 1978. 19.95 o.p. (ISBN 0-8467-0499-4, Pub. by Two Continents). Hippocrene Bks.
Kemp, Robert. Irish Sea Cruising Guide. 1979. 47.95x (ISBN 0-8464-0076-6). Beekman Pubs.
Kemp, Roger. Cell Division & Heredity. 1971. text ed. 14.95 (ISBN 0-312-12635-2). St Martin.
Kemp, Roger L. Coping with Proposition Thirteen. LC 80-8188. 1980. 21.95x (ISBN 0-669-03974-8). Lexington Bks.
Kemp, Tom. Historical Patterns of Industrialization. LC 77-3574. (Illus.). 1978. text ed. 17.00x (ISBN 0-582-48922-9); pap. text ed. 8.95x (ISBN 0-582-48923-7). Longman.
--Industrialization in Nineteenth Century Europe. 1969. pap. text ed. 12.50x (ISBN 0-582-48025-6). Humanities.
Kemp, W. Organic Spectroscopy. LC 74-7675. 1975. text ed. 24.95 (ISBN 0-470-46842-4); pap. text ed. 14.95 (ISBN 0-470-99193-3). Halsted Pr.
Kemp, William. The Two Wonder of Women, or the Tragedy of Sophonisba. Orgel, Stephen, ed. LC 78-66805. (Renaissance Drama Ser.). 1979. lib. bdg. 24.00 (ISBN 0-8240-9744-0). Garland Pub.
Kempe, C. H., jt. auth. see Mrazek, Patricia B.
Kempe, C. H., et al, eds. see International Congress on Child Abuse & Neglect, 2nd, London, 1978.
Kempe, C. Henry & Helfer, Ray E. The Battered Child. 3rd rev. ed. LC 80-14329. (Illus.). 1980. 25.00 (ISBN 0-226-43038-3). U of Chicago Pr.
Kempe, C. Henry, jt. ed. see Helfer, Ray E.
Kempe, Helen. Pelican Guide to Old Homes of Mississippi, 2 vols. Incl. Vol. 1. Natchez & the South (ISBN 0-88289-134-0); Vol. 2. Columbus & the North (ISBN 0-88289-135-9). LC 76-20434. (Pelican Guide Ser.). (Illus.). 1977. pap. 3.95 ea. Pelican.
Kempe, L. G. Operative Neurosurgery, 2 vols. Incl. Vol. 1. Cranial, Cerebral & Intracranial Vascular Disease. (Illus.). xiii, 269p. 1968. 94.70 (ISBN 0-387-04208-3); Vol. 2. Posterior Fossa, Spinal Cord & Peripheral Nerve Disease. (Illus.). viii, 281p. 1970. 94.70 (ISBN 0-387-04890-1). Springer-Verlag.
Kempe, Margery B. Book of Margery Kempe. Meech, Sanford B., et al. (Early English Text Society Ser.). 1940. 24.95x (ISBN 0-19-722212-9). Oxford U Pr.
Kemper, A. Chemistry Experiments. (Science Experiments Ser). (Illus.). 1965. 17.50x (ISBN 0-222-69371-1). Intl Pubns Serv.
Kemper, Alfred M. Drawings by American Architects. LC 72-13428. 621p. 1973. 55.00 (ISBN 0-471-46845-2, Pub. by Wiley-Interscience). Wiley.
--Presentation Drawings by American Architects. LC 76-40891. 1977. 37.50 (ISBN 0-471-01369-2, Pub. by Wiley-Interscience). Wiley.

Kemper, Frederick & Bass, George M. You Are My Beloved Sermon Book. 1980. pap. 6.95 (ISBN 0-570-03821-9, 12-2761). Concordia.

Kemper, Frederick W., jt. auth. see Bauerle, Richard E.

Kemper, Robert C. An Elephant's Ballet. LC 77-22165. 1977. 6.95 (ISBN 0-8164-0373-2). Crossroad NY.

Kemper, Robert V. Migration & Adaptation: Tzintzuntzan Peasants in Mexico City. LC 77-2413. (Sage Library of Social Research: Vol. 43). 1977. 18.00x (ISBN 0-8039-0687-0); pap. 8.95x (ISBN 0-8039-0688-9). Sage.

Kemper, Robert V., jt. ed. see Cornelius, Wayne A.

Kemperman, Steve. Moonies. LC 80-54091. 192p. 1981. pap. 2.95 (ISBN 0-8307-0780-8). Regal.

Kempf, Albert F. New Math Made Simple. LC 66-12224. pap. 3.50 (ISBN 0-385-04174-8, Made). Doubleday.

Kempf, Albert F. & Richards, Thomas J. The Metric System Made Simple. LC 75-36631. 144p. 1977. 3.50 (ISBN 0-385-11032-4, Made). Doubleday.

Kempher, Ruth M. The Carnal Musings of Sylvia Savage. 1980. 2.00. Windless Orchard.

Kempis, Thomas A. The Imitation of Christ. 1976. 5.00x (ISBN 0-460-00484-0, Evman); pap. 2.95 (ISBN 0-460-01484-6). Dutton.

--Of the Imitation of Christ. 256p. 1981. pap. 2.50 (ISBN 0-88368-094-7). Whitaker Hse.

Kempis, Thomas A' see A'Kempis, Thomas.

Kempler, Walter. Experiential Psychotherapy Within Families. 320p. 1981. 20.00 (ISBN 0-87630-267-3). Brunner-Mazel.

Kempson, Ruth M. Presupposition & the Delinitation of Semantic. LC 74-25078. (Studies in Linguistics Monographs: No. 15). 260p. 1975. 39.95 (ISBN 0-521-20733-9); pap. 11.95x (ISBN 0-521-09938-2). Cambridge U Pr.

Kempton, Jean W. Living with Myasthenia Gravis: A Bright New Tomorrow. (Illus.). 112p. 1972. 9.75 (ISBN 0-398-02329-8). C C Thomas.

Kempton, Karl. Rune. (Illus.). 100p. 1981. 50.00 (ISBN 0-686-69461-9). Porter.

Kempton, Richard. French Literature: An Annotated Guide to Selected Bibliographies. LC 80-24230. (Selected Bibliographies in Language & Literature Ser.: No. 2). 56p. (Orig.). 1981. pap. 4.50x (ISBN 0-87352-951-0). Modern Lang.

Kemp-Welch, Alice, et al, trs. see De Pisan, Christine.

Kemsley, William, ed. The Whole Hiker's Handbook. LC 79-88627. (Illus.). 1979. 12.95 (ISBN 0-688-03476-4, Quill); pap. 9.95 (ISBN 0-688-08476-1). Morrow.

Kenaga, E. E. & Morgan, Robert W. Commercial & Experimental Organic Insecticides. 1978. 6.70 (ISBN 0-686-18862-4). Entomol Soc.

Kenan, Peter B. Essays in International Economics. (Princeton Series of Collected Essays). 432p. 1980. 22.50 (ISBN 0-691-04225-X); pap. 5.95 (ISBN 0-691-00364-5). Princeton U Pr.

Kenawell, William. Quest at Glastonbury: A Biographical Study of Frederick Bligh Bond. LC 65-18997. 1965. 8.50 o.p. (ISBN 0-912326-14-X). Garrett-Helix.

Kendal, Robert. Competitor's Handbook. 1978. 10.95 (ISBN 0-236-31083-6, Pub. by Paul Elek). Merrimack Bk Serv.

Kendall, Anne. Everyday Life of the Incas. 1978. pap. 14.95 (ISBN 0-7134-1072-8, Pub. by Batsford England). David & Charles.

Kendall, Arthur J., jt. auth. see Solomon, Daniel.

Kendall, Carol & Yao-wen, Li. Sweet & Sour: Tales from China. LC 78-24349. (Illus.). (gr. 3-6). 1979. 7.95 (ISBN 0-395-28958-0, Clarion). HM.

Kendall, D. G. & Harding, E. F. Stochastic Analysis. LC 72-8605. (Wiley Series in Probability & Mathematical Statistics: Probability & Mathematical Statistics Section). 1973. 62.95 (ISBN 0-471-46890-8, Pub. by Wiley-Interscience). Wiley.

Kendall, D. G., jt. ed. see Harding, E. F.

Kendall, E. J., ed. Transistors. LC 70-88307. 1969. 25.00 (ISBN 0-08-006511-2); pap. 12.75 (ISBN 0-08-006510-4). Pergamon.

Kendall, Edward C. Cortisone. LC 72-123853. 1971. 7.95 o.p. (ISBN 0-684-31062-7, ScribT). Scribner.

Kendall, Ingeborg U. School at Home, Teach Your Own Child. 1981. 6.95 (ISBN 0-914704-03-6). Intl Ctr Environment.

Kendall, James N., jt. auth. see Jacobe, Dennis.

Kendall, Lane C. The Business of Shipping. 3rd ed. LC 79-52466. (Illus.). 1979. text ed. 12.50x (ISBN 0-87033-253-8). Cornell Maritime.

Kendall, M. G. & Stuart, A. The Advanced Theory of Statistics, 3 vols. 3rd ed. Incl. Vol. 1. Distribution Theory. xii, 439p. 1969. o.p. (ISBN 0-02-847660-3); Vol. 2. Statistical Inference & Statistical Relationship. ix, 690p. 1974. 0.p. o.s.i. (ISBN 0-02-847670-0); Vol. 3. Design & Analysis, & Time-Series. (Illus.). x, 557p. 1976. 49.50 o.s.i. (ISBN 0-02-847640-9). Hafner.

--The Advanced Theory of Statistics, 3 vols. 4th ed. Incl. Vol. 1. Distribution Theory. 4th ed. 1977. 41.25 (ISBN 0-02-847630-1); Vol. 2. Statistical Inference & Statistical Relationship. th ed. 1979. 59.95 (ISBN 0-02-847820-7); Vol. 3. Design & Analysis, & Time Series. 3rd ed. (Illus.). 1976. 55.00 (ISBN 0-02-847640-9). Hafner.

Kendall, M. G., jt. ed. see Stuart, A.

Kendall, Martha B. Selected Problems in Yavapai Syntax: The Verde Valley Dialect. LC 75-25118. (American Indian Linguistics Ser.). 1976. lib. bdg. 42.00 (ISBN 0-8240-1969-5). Garland Pub.

Kendall, Maurice. Multivariate Analysis. LC 75-39882. (Griffin Statistical Monograph). 1976. 23.95 o.s.i. (ISBN 0-02-847790-1). Hafner.

--Multivariate Analysis. 2nd ed. (Griffin Statistical Monograph). 1980. 29.95 (ISBN 0-02-847570-4). Macmillan.

Kendall, P. C. & Hollon, S. D., eds. Assessment Strategies for Cognitive-Behavioral Intervention. 1980. 29.50 (ISBN 0-12-404460-3). Acad Pr.

Kendall, P. G., et al. Mathematics in the Archeological & Historical Sciences. 1972. 31.50 (ISBN 0-85224-213-1, Pub. by Edinburgh U Pr Scotland). Columbia U Pr.

Kendall, Paul M. The Story of Land Warfare. LC 74-3764. (Illus.). x, 194p. 1981. Repr. of 1957 ed. lib. bdg. 21.75x (ISBN 0-8371-7463-5, KELW). Greenwood.

Kendall, Paul M. & Ilardi, Vincent, eds. Dispatches, with Related Documents, of Milanese Ambassadors in France & Burgundy, 1450-1483. LC 68-20933. 1970. Vol. 1, lvi 390p. 15.00x (ISBN 0-8214-0067-3); Vol. 2, 486p. 15.00x (ISBN 0-8214-0082-7). Ohio U Pr.

Kendall, Sarita. Looking at Brazil. LC 73-19605. (gr. 4-6). 1974. 8.95 (ISBN 0-397-31527-9). Lippincott.

Kendall, Willmoore. Willmoore Kendall Contra Mundum. 1971. 11.95 o.s.i. (ISBN 0-87000-101-9). Arlington Hse.

Kendall, Willmoore, tr. see Rousseau, Jean-Jacques.

Kendeigh, S. C., jt. ed. see Pinowski, J.

Kendig, Joan, jt. auth. see Kendig, Keith.

Kendig, Keith & Kendig, Joan. Modern Vegetable Protein Cookery. LC 79-21127. 352p. 1980. 11.95 (ISBN 0-668-04617-1). Arco.

Kendig, Lane. Performance Zoning. LC 79-93346. (Illus.). 358p. 1980. 36.95 (ISBN 0-918286-18-2). Planners Pr.

Kendler, Howard H. Basic Psychology: Brief Version. 3rd ed. LC 76-20875. (Illus.). 1977. pap. text ed. 16.95 (ISBN 0-8053-5195-7); instr's guide 2.95 (ISBN 0-8053-5196-5). Benjamin-Cummings.

--Psychology: A Science in Conflict. (Illus.). 416p. 1981. text ed. 19.95x (ISBN 0-19-502900-3); pap. text ed. 9.95x (ISBN 0-19-502901-1). Oxford U Pr.

Kendrick, A. F. & Tattersall, C. E. Hand-Woven Carpets Oriental & European. LC 73-77381. (Illus.). 256p. 1973. Repr. of 1922 ed. 8.00 (ISBN 0-486-20385-9). Dover.

Kendrick, B., jt. auth. see Cole, G. T.

Kendrick, Bv. Ben. Battle for Yanga. LC 80-20643. 127p. 1980. pap. 3.95 (ISBN 0-87227-074-2). Reg Baptist.

Kendrick, D. G., jt. auth. see Edmunds, G.

Kendrick, David. Stochastic Control of Economic Models. (Economic Handbook Ser.). (Illus.). 288p. 1981. text ed. 39.50 (ISBN 0-07-033962-7, C). McGraw.

Kendrick, Rosalyn. Does God Have a Body? 1979. pap. 3.95 (ISBN 0-8192-1257-1). Morehouse.

Kendris. Dictionnaire De Two Hundred One Verbes Anglais Conjugues Completement a Tous les Temps et a Toutes les Personnes. Date not set. pap. 3.95 (ISBN 0-8120-0550-3). Barron.

Kendris, Christopher. Beginning to Write in French: A Workbook in French Composition. LC 65-25685. (gr. 7-12). 1971. pap. text ed. 3.50 (ISBN 0-8120-0234-2). Barron.

--Beginning to Write in French: A Workbook in French Composition. rev. ed. 1981. pap. text ed. 3.50 (ISBN 0-8120-2261-0). Barron.

--Beginning to Write in Spanish: A Workbook in Spanish Composition. LC 66-25379. (gr. 7-12). 1971. pap. text ed. 3.50 (ISBN 0-8120-0235-0). Barron.

--Beginning to Write in Spanish: A Workbook in Spanish Composition. rev ed. 1981. pap. text ed. 3.50 (ISBN 0-686-59969-1). Barron.

Kendris, Christopher, jt. auth. see Newmark, Maxim.

Kendris, Christopher, tr. see Grevisse, Maurice.

Keneally, Thomas. Blood Red, Sister Rose. 400p. 1976. pap. 1.95 o.p. (ISBN 0-345-24816-3). Ballantine.

--Ned Kelly & the City of the Bees. LC 80-66217. (Illus.). 128p. (gr. 4-8). 1980. 8.95g (ISBN 0-87923-338-9). Godine.

--Victim of the Aurora. 1978. pap. 1.75 o.p. (ISBN 0-685-54637-3, 04712-0). Jove Pubns.

Kenedi, R. M., ed. Advances in Biomedical Engineering. Incl. Vol. 1. 1971. 34.50 (ISBN 0-12-004901-5); Vol. 2. Brown, J. H. & Dickson, James F., 3rd, eds. 1972. 48.00 (ISBN 0-12-004902-3); Vol. 3. 1973. 48.00 (ISBN 0-12-004903-1). Acad Pr.

Kenefick, Madeleine. Positively Pregnant. (Illus.). 224p. 1981. pap. 2.75 (ISBN 0-523-41182-0). Pinnacle Bks.

Kenen, P. B., ed. International Trade & Finance. LC 75-2717. (Illus.). 580p. 1976. 32.50 (ISBN 0-521-20719-3). Cambridge U Pr.

Kenen, Peter B., jt. auth. see Allen, Polly R.

Kenen, Peter B. & Lawrence, Roger, eds. The Open Economy: Essays on International Trade & Finance. (Columbia Studies in Economics). xvi, 391p. 1968. 25.00x (ISBN 0-231-03009-6). Columbia U Pr.

Kenessey, Zoltan. Economic Planning. 1977. 22.50x (ISBN 0-231-03571-3). Columbia U Pr.

Kenez, Peter. Civil War in South Russia, 1918: The First Year of the Volunteer Army. LC 78-114339. 1971. 21.50c (ISBN 0-520-01709-9). U of Cal Pr.

Keng Keng. The Stuck-Up Kitty. (Illus.). 38p. (gr. 6-10). 1979. 3.95 o.p. (ISBN 0-8351-0693-4); pap. 1.75 o.p. (ISBN 0-8351-0694-2). China Bks.

Kenlay, G. & Harris, K. W. Manufacturing Technology, Vol. 1. (Illus.). 155p. 1979. pap. 12.95x (ISBN 0-7131-3401-1). Intl Ideas.

Kenmare, Dallas. Love the Unknown. 8.95 (ISBN 0-85307-067-9). Transatlantic.

Kennan, George. Campaigning in Cuba. LC 75-137918. (American History & Culture in the Nineteenth Century Ser). 1971. Repr. of 1899 ed. 15.00 o.p. (ISBN 0-8046-1484-9). Kennikat.

Kennan, George F. American Diplomacy: Nineteen Hundred to Nineteen Fifty. 1952. pap. 1.50 (ISBN 0-451-61168-3, MW1811, Ment). NAL.

--The Decline of Bismarck's European Order: Franco-Russian Relations, 1875-1890. LC 79-83997. (Illus.). 478p. (Orig.). 1981. pap. 6.95 (ISBN 0-691-00784-5). Princeton U Pr.

--The Decline of Bismarck's European Order: Franco-Russian Relations, 1875-1890. LC 79-83997. (Illus.). 1979. 25.00 (ISBN 0-691-05282-4); pap. 6.95 (ISBN 0-691-00784-5). Princeton U Pr.

--Russia & the West Under Lenin & Stalin. pap. 2.25 (ISBN 0-451-61861-0, ME1861, Ment). NAL.

Kennan, Kent. Counterpoint. 2nd ed. LC 73-168625. (Illus.). 1972. ref. ed. 19.50 (ISBN 0-13-184291-9); wkbk. 4.25 (ISBN 0-13-184309-5). P-H.

--Technique of Orchestration. 2nd ed. (Music Ser). (Illus.). 1970. 18.95 (ISBN 0-13-900316-9); wkbk. 2 9.50 (ISBN 0-13-900340-1); wkbk. 3.95 (ISBN 0-13-900332-0). P-H.

Kennard, Edward. Fieldmouse Goes to War. (Wild & Woolly West Ser.: No. 41). (Illus., Eng. & Hopi.). 1977. pap. 2.50 (ISBN 0-910584-47-8). Filter.

Kennard, Howard P. The Russian Peasant. LC 77-87519. (Anthro. Ser.). (Illus.). 336p. 1980. Repr. of 1908 ed. 28.50 (ISBN 0-404-16607-5). AMS Pr.

Kenneally, James J. Women & American Trade Unions. LC 77-9240. 1978. 17.95 (ISBN 0-88831-026-9). EPWP.

Kennedy, A. Six Dramatists in Search of a Language. LC 74-76572. 288p. 1975. 45.00 (ISBN 0-521-20492-5); pap. 10.95x (ISBN 0-521-09866-1). Cambridge U Pr.

Kennedy, Adam. Debt of Honor. 1981. 12.95 (ISBN 0-440-00012-2). Delacorte.

Kennedy, Adrienne see Harrison, Paul C.

Kennedy, Aileen, jt. auth. see Ross, Carole D.

Kennedy, Alan. The Protean Self: Dramatic Action in Contemporary Fiction. 240p. 1974. 17.50 (ISBN 0-231-03922-0). Columbia U Pr.

Kennedy, Alexander B., tr. see Reuleaux, Franz.

Kennedy, Mrs. Alexander, tr. see Mantegazza, Paolo.

Kennedy, Ann, jt. auth. see Shelton, William.

Kennedy, Beatrice B. Women Out of Bondage & in Love. 1978. 4.00 o.p. (ISBN 0-682-49152-7). Exposition.

Kennedy, C. R. Ecological Animal Parasitology. LC 75-5760. 1975. 13.95 o.p. (ISBN 0-470-46910-2). Halsted Pr.

Kennedy, Charles W., tr. Early English Christian Poetry. 1963. pap. 5.95 (ISBN 0-19-500246-6, GB94, GB). Oxford U Pr.

Kennedy, Charles W., tr. see Beowulf.

Kennedy, Cody, Jr. Warrior Flame. 1980. pap. 2.50 (ISBN 0-446-81676-0). Warner Bks.

Kennedy, D. & Kennedy, M. I., eds. Architects Year Book 14: The Inner City. LC 74-2429. 1974. 32.50 (ISBN 0-470-46904-8). Halsted Pr.

Kennedy, Daniel B. The Dysfunctional Alliance Emotion & Reason in Justice Administration. LC 77-73529. 1977. pap. text ed. 10.95 (ISBN 0-87084-483-0). Anderson Pub Co.

Kennedy, David. The American People in the Depression. new ed. LC 72-95873. (American People Ser.). (Illus.). 176p. (gr. 9-12). 1973. PLB 2.95 o.p. (ISBN 0-88301-091-7); pap. 2.50 (ISBN 0-88301-075-5). Pendulum Pr.

Kennedy, David M., jt. auth. see Bailey, Thomas A.

Kennedy, Donald, intro. by. Cellular & Organismal Biology: Readings from Scientific American. LC 74-775. (Illus.). 1974. text ed. 19.95x (ISBN 0-7167-0894-9); pap. text ed. 9.95x (ISBN 0-7167-0893-0). W H Freeman.

--From Cell to Organism: Readings from Scientific American. LC 66-30156. (Illus.). 1967. text ed. 15.95x (ISBN 0-7167-0963-5); pap. text ed. 7.95x (ISBN 0-7167-0962-7). W H Freeman.

Kennedy, Donald P. Minicomputers: Low-Cost Computer Power for Management. rev. ed. (Illus.). 1979. 15.95 (ISBN 0-8144-5484-4). Am Mgmt.

Kennedy, E. The Trouble Book. 1977. pap. 3.50 (ISBN 0-346-12287-2). Cornerstone.

Kennedy, E. C., ed. see Martial & Pliny.

Kennedy, E. C., ed. see Vergil.

Kennedy, E. S., ed. see Hashimi, Ali Ibn Sulayman al.

Kennedy, Eberhard C. Roman Poetry & Prose. 1957. text ed. 7.50x (ISBN 0-521-05880-5). Cambridge U Pr.

Kennedy, Eberhard C., ed. Four Latin Authors. 1940. text ed. 7.50x (ISBN 0-521-05881-3). Cambridge U Pr.

Kennedy, Eddie C. Classroom Approaches to Remedial Reading. 2nd ed. LC 76-53238. 1977. text ed. 14.95 (ISBN 0-87581-210-4, 210). Peacock Pubs.

Kennedy, Edward C. Methods in Teaching Developmental Reading. 2nd ed. LC 80-52445. 368p. 1981. pap. text ed. 9.95 (ISBN 0-87581-258-9). Peacock Pubs.

Kennedy, Elspeth, ed. Lancelot Du Lac: The Non-Cyclic Old French Prose Romance, 2 vols. 1152p. 1981. Set. 169.00 (ISBN 0-19-812064-8). Oxford U Pr.

Kennedy, Eugene. Crisis Counseling: The Essential Guide for Non-Professional Counselors. 208p. 1981. 12.95 (ISBN 0-8264-0038-8). Continuum.

--Father's Day: A Novel of Power, Passion & Conscience. LC 80-2566. 528p. 1981. 13.95 (ISBN 0-385-15415-1). Doubleday.

--On Becoming a Counselor: A Basic Guide for Non-Professional Counselors. 338p. 14.95 (ISBN 0-8164-0315-5); pap. 8.95 (ISBN 0-8264-0020-5). Continuum.

--Sexual Counseling. LC 76-30875. 1977. 9.95 o.p. (ISBN 0-8164-9312-X). Continuum.

--The Trouble Book. 1976. 10.95 (ISBN 0-88347-064-0). Thomas More.

Kennedy, Eugene C., M.M. In the Spirit, in the Flesh. LC 72-157604. 160p. 1972. pap. 1.45 o.p. (ISBN 0-385-02126-7, Im). Doubleday.

--The New Sexuality: Myths, Fables & Hang-Ups. LC 77-180907. 160p. 1973. pap. 2.45 (ISBN 0-385-06357-1, Im). Doubleday.

--The Pain of Being Human. LC 73-83645. 280p. 1974. pap. 3.50 (ISBN 0-385-06888-3, Im). Doubleday.

--A Sense of Life, a Sense of Sin. 200p. 1976. pap. 1.95 (ISBN 0-385-12070-2, Im). Doubleday.

--Time for Love. LC 75-121952. 1972. pap. 2.45 (ISBN 0-385-09481-7, Im). Doubleday.

Kennedy, Eugene P., jt. ed. see Kaplan, Nathan O.

Kennedy, Fern. Exploring Photography. rev. ed. (Illus.). 448p. 1980. 22.50 (ISBN 0-8174-2529-2); pap. 12.95 (ISBN 0-8174-2194-7). Amphoto.

Kennedy, Foster. The Disappearance of Mr. Allan. (gr. 4-6). 1977. pap. 1.50 o.p. (ISBN 0-590-11841-2, Schol Pap). Schol Bk Serv.

Kennedy, Gail, jt. ed. see Konvitz, Milton R.

Kennedy, Gavin. Economics of Defence. 1975. 17.95 o.p. (ISBN 0-571-10740-0, Pub. by Faber & Faber). Merrimack Bk Serv.

Kennedy, Gavin see Mackaness, George.

Kennedy, Gower A. Welding Technology Student's Manual. LC 77-4673. (gr. 11-12). 1977. pap. text ed. 7.50 (ISBN 0-672-97109-7); tchr's manual 6.67 (ISBN 0-672-97158-5). Bobbs.

Kennedy, Grace. Father Clement, 1823. Wolff, Robert L., ed. Bd. with Father Oswald 1842. LC 75-445. (Victorian Fiction Ser). 1975. lib. bdg. 66.00 (ISBN 0-8240-1525-8). Garland Pub.

Kennedy, Harold L. Ambulatory Electrocardiography: Including Holter Recording Technology. LC 80-26155. (Illus.). 300p. 1981. text ed. write for info. (ISBN 0-8121-0762-4). Lea & Febiger.

Kennedy, Helen. Systematics & Pollination of the "Closed Flowered" Species of Calathea (Mar-Antaceae) (Publications in Botany: No. 71). 1978. pap. 7.75x (ISBN 0-520-09572-3). U of Cal Pr.

Kennedy, Hubert C., tr. see Peano, Giuseppe.

Kennedy, Hugh. The Early Abbasid Caliphate: A Political History. 238p. 1981. 27.50x (ISBN 0-389-20018-2). B&N.

Kennedy, Hugh P. & Schrils, Rudolph, eds. Intermediate Structure in Nuclear Reactions. LC 67-29341. (Illus.). 232p. 1968. pap. 9.50x (ISBN 0-8131-1155-2). U Pr of Ky.

Kennedy, J. P., ed. Cationic Graft Copolymerization, No. 30. (Journal of Applied Polymer Science). 1977. pap. 22.95 (ISBN 0-471-04426-1, Pub. by Wiley-Interscience). Wiley.

Kennedy, James G. Herbert Spencer. (English Author Ser.: No. 219). 1978. 9.95 (ISBN 0-8057-6688-X). Twayne.

Kennedy, James W. Anglican Partners. 1978. 2.00 (ISBN 0-686-28772-X). Forward Movement.

Kennedy, James Y. South Seas Odyssey: An Escape. LC 79-904. (Illus.). 182p. (Orig.). 1979. pap. 5.95 (ISBN 0-9605088-0-5). Kennedy Pub.

Kennedy, Janet. The Mir iskusstva Group & Russian Art, 1898-1912. LC 76-23633. (Outstanding Dissertations in the Fine Arts - 20th Century). (Illus.). 1977. Repr. lib. bdg. 87.00 (ISBN 0-8240-2702-7). Garland Pub.

Kennedy, Jimmy. Teddy Bears' Picnic. (Dinosaur Ser.). (Illus.). (ps-1). 1978. pap. 1.45 ea. (ISBN 0-85122-067-3, Pub. by Dino Pub); pap. pack of 5 avail. Merrimack Bk Serv.

Kennedy, Joan. I Don't Want Much from Life - I Want More! 204p. 1980. 9.95 (ISBN 0-8119-0335-4). Fell.

Kennedy, John. Stem Dictionary of the English Language. LC 78-142547. 1971. Repr. of 1870 ed. 26.00 (ISBN 0-8103-3377-5). Gale.

Kennedy, John F. Profiles in Courage. (Memorial ed.). 1964. pap. 2.50 (ISBN 0-06-080001-1, PL). Har-Row.

--Sam Houston & the Senate. Smitherman, Larry, ed. LC 79-14422. 12.50 (ISBN 0-8363-0087-4). Jenkins.

--Strategy of Peace. Nevins, Allan, ed. LC 60-7530. 1960. 10.00 o.s.i. (ISBN 0-06-012325-7, HarpT). Har-Row.

--To Turn the Tide. Gardner, John W., ed. LC 61-12221. 1962. 10.00 o.p. (ISBN 0-06-012335-4, HarpT). Har-Row.

Kennedy, John G. The Tarahumara of the Sierra Madre: Beer, Ecology & Social Organization. LC 77-86044. (Worlds of Man Ser.). (Illus.). 1978. text ed. 12.00x (ISBN 0-88295-614-0); pap. text ed. 6.75x (ISBN 0-88295-615-9). AHM Pub.

Kennedy, John P. The Landon Experiments. 1976. pap. 1.75 o.p. (ISBN 0-8439-0371-6, Leisure Bks). Nordon Pubns.

--Slavery, the Mere Pretext for the Rebellion. 20p. 1967. Repr. of 1863 ed. pap. 3.65 (ISBN 0-910120-02-1). Americanist.

Kennedy, Joseph C. Color in a Cage: The Personal Journey of an American of Color. (Illus.). 1981. 9.95 (ISBN 0-933184-19-0); pap. 4.95 (ISBN 0-933184-20-4). Flame Intl.

Kennedy, Joseph P. & Marechal, Ernest. Carbocationic Polymerization. 675p. 1981. 65.00 (ISBN 0-471-01787-6, Pub. by Wiley-Interscience). Wiley.

Kennedy, Leonard M. Guiding Children to Mathematical Discovery. 3rd ed. 544p. 1979. text ed. 17.95x (ISBN 0-534-00757-0). Wadsworth Pub.

Kennedy, Ludovic. Railway Journeys. LC 80-14520. (Illus.). 256p. 1980. cancelled (ISBN 0-89256-135-1). Rawson Wade.

Kennedy, Ludovic, compiled by. A Book of Railway Journeys. (Illus.). 1980. 12.95 (ISBN 0-89256-135-1). Rawson Wade.

Kennedy, M. I., jt. ed. see Kennedy, D.

Kennedy, Malcolm D. The Estrangement of Great Britain & Japan, 1917-1935. LC 71-77517. (Illus.). 1969. 20.00x (ISBN 0-520-01431-6). U of Cal Pr.

Kennedy, Mary. The Glass Ring. LC 78-72143. (Illus.). (gr. 1-5). Date not set. price not set (ISBN 0-89799-106-0); pap. price not set (ISBN 0-89799-065-X). Dandelion Pr. Postponed.

--When the Owl Called. LC 78-73530. (Illus.). (gr. 2-5). Date not set. price not set (ISBN 0-89799-164-8); pap. price not set (ISBN 0-89799-082-X). Dandelion Pr. Postponed.

Kennedy, Maureen O. & Molnar, Gail. Current Practice, Issues, & Concepts: Nursing Care of the Ill Adult. LC 79-12298. (Current Practice Ser.). (Illus.). 1979. text ed. 12.50 (ISBN 0-8016-2646-3); pap. text ed. 9.50 (ISBN 0-8016-2635-8). Mosby.

Kennedy, Melville R. The Chaitanya Movement: 011calcutta & London, 1925. LC 78-74267. (Oriental Religions Ser.: Vol. 6). 283p. 1981. lib. bdg. 33.00 (ISBN 0-8240-3904-1). Garland Pub.

Kennedy, Michael. Britten. (The Master Musicians Ser.). (Illus.). 364p. 1981. 22.50x (ISBN 0-460-03175-9, Pub. by J. M. Dent England). Biblio Dist.

--Portrait of Manchester. LC 70-550611. (Portrait Bks.). 1970. 10.50x (ISBN 0-7091-1812-0). Intl Pubns Serv.

Kennedy, Michael & Solomon, Martin B. Structured PL-Zero PL-One. (Illus.). 1977. pap. 15.95 (ISBN 0-13-854901-X). P-H.

--Ten Statement Fortran Plus Fortran Four. 2nd ed. (Illus.). 400p. 1975. pap. text ed. 14.95 (ISBN 0-13-903385-8). P-H.

Kennedy, Michael, ed. The Concise Oxford Dictionary of Music. 3rd ed. (Out of Ser. K). (Illus.). 736p. 1981. 19.95 (ISBN 0-19-311315-5); pap. 9.95 (ISBN 0-19-311320-1). Oxford U Pr.

Kennedy, Michael L., jt. auth. see Payne, James F.

Kennedy, Monty. Checkering & Carving of Gunstocks. rev. ed. (Illus.). 352p. 1952. 21.95 (ISBN 0-8117-0630-3). Stackpole.

Kennedy, Pat, jt. auth. see Downie, Patricia A.

Kennedy, Patrick. Legendary Fictions of the Irish Celts. LC 68-25518. 1968. Repr. of 1866 ed. 18.00 (ISBN 0-8103-3467-4). Gale.

Kennedy, Paul. The Rise & Fall of British Naval Mastery. LC 75-34942. (Illus.). 405p. 1976. 15.00 o.p. (ISBN 0-684-14609-6, ScribT). Scribner.

Kennedy, Paul E. American Wild Flowers Coloring Book. (Illus.). 48p. 1971. pap. 1.75 (ISBN 0-486-20095-7). Dover.

Kennedy, Paul M. The Samoan Tangle: A Study in Anglo-German-American Relations 1878-1900. 325p. 1974. 30.00x (ISBN 0-686-28320-1, Pub. by Irish Academic Pr). Biblio Dist.

Kennedy, Peter E. Macroeconomics. 448p. 1975. 14.95x o.p. (ISBN 0-205-04282-1, 0942820). Allyn.

Kennedy, Raymond. Columbine. 1981. pap. 3.95 (ISBN 0-14-005882-6). Penguin.

Kennedy, Richard. Crazy in Love. (Illus.). (gr. 3-7). 1980. PLB 7.95 (ISBN 0-525-28364-1). Dutton.

--The Leprechaun's Story. LC 79-11410. (Illus.). (ps-3). 1979. PLB 8.95 (ISBN 0-525-33472-6, Unicorn Bk.). Dutton.

--Now That You're Saved. 1977. pap. 0.60 (ISBN 0-89265-046-X). Randall Hse.

Kennedy, Robert. Natural Body Building for Men & Women. LC 79-91395. (Illus.). 160p. 1980. 10.95 (ISBN 0-8069-4144-8); lib. bdg. 9.89 (ISBN 0-8069-4145-6); pap. 5.95 (ISBN 0-8069-8920-3). Sterling.

--Thirteen Days. (RL 8). pap. 1.95 (ISBN 0-451-09150-7, J9150, Sig). NAL.

Kennedy, Robert E., Jr. The Irish: Emigration, Marriage, & Fertility. LC 70-187740. 304p. 1973. 20.00x (ISBN 0-520-01987-3); pap. 4.95x (ISBN 0-520-02896-1). U of Cal Pr.

Kennedy, Robert F. Thirteen Days: A Memoir of the Cuban Missile Crisis. (Keith Jennison Large Type Bks). 8.95 o.p. (ISBN 0-531-00314-0). Watts.

Kennedy, Robert L., jt. auth. see Hardwick, Geraline B.

Kennedy, Sarah & Simon, John O., eds. A Raindrop Has to Do Her Work. 72p. (Orig.). (gr. k-12). 1979. pap. text ed. 4.00 (ISBN 0-917744-29-2). Aldebaran Rev.

Kennedy, Sherrel H., jt. auth. see Corkindale, David R.

Kennedy, Sherrie H. & Corkindale, David R. Managing the Advertising Process. LC 75-28612. (Illus.). 296p. 1976. 24.95 (ISBN 0-347-01109-8, 00205-4, Pub. by Saxon Hse). Lexington Bks.

Kennedy, Susan E. The Banking Crisis of 1933. LC 72-91666. 280p. 1973. 16.00x (ISBN 0-8131-1285-0). U Pr of Ky.

Kennedy, Terry. Heart-Organ: Part of My Body. 1981. pap. 3.50 (ISBN 0-915016-30-3). Second Coming.

Kennedy, Thomas C. The Hound of Conscience: A History of the No-Conscription Fellowship, 1914-1919. 304p. 1981. text ed. 22.00x (ISBN 0-938626-01-9). U of Mo Pr.

Kennedy, Thomas L. The Arms of Kiangnan: Modernization in the Chinese Ordnance Industry 1860-1895. 1978. lib. bdg. 24.50x (ISBN 0-89158-258-4). Westview.

Kennedy, Thomas L., jt. auth. see Mathias, Jim.

Kennedy, Tom & Simon, Charles E. An Examination of Questionable Payments & Practices. LC 78-14195. (Praeger Special Studies). 1978. 34.50 (ISBN 0-03-046321-1). Praeger.

Kennedy, William. English Taxation, Sixteen Forty to Seventeen Ninety-Nine. Repr. of 1913 ed. 22.50x (ISBN 0-678-05060-0). Kelley.

--Legs. 1976. pap. 1.75 o.s.i. (ISBN 0-446-84140-4). Warner Bks.

Kennedy, William F. Determinants of Large Bank Dividend Policy. Dufey, Gunter, ed. (Research for Business Decisions). 185p. 1980. 24.95 (ISBN 0-8357-1128-5, Pub. by UMI Res Pr). Univ Microfilms.

Kennedy, X. J. Did Adam Name the Vinegarron? (Illus.). 32p. 1980. 10.00 (ISBN 0-87923-389-3). Godine.

Kennedy, X. J., ed. The Tygers of Wrath: Poems of Hate, Anger, & Invective. LC 80-23212. 272p. 1981. 15.00 (ISBN 0-8203-0535-9). U of Ga Pr.

Kennedy-Brenner, C., jt. auth. see Organization for Economic Cooperation & Development.

Kenneke, Larry. Career Development Activities. 1973. pap. 6.00 o.p. (ISBN 0-672-97621-8). Bobbs.

Kennel, Charles F., jt. auth. see Abers, Ernest S.

Kennell, jt. auth. see Klaus.

Kennemore, Time. The Middle of the Sandwich. 112p. (gr. 3-7). 1981. 12.95 (ISBN 0-571-11678-7, Pub. by Faber & Faber). Merrimack Bk Serv.

Kenner, Cornelia V., et al. Critical Care Nursing: Body - Mind - Spirit. 1981. text ed. price not set (ISBN 0-316-48910-7). Little.

Kenner, Hugh. Bucky: A Guided Tour of Buckminster Fuller. LC 79-182966. (Illus.). 352p. 1973. pap. 3.25 o.p. (ISBN 0-688-05141-3). Morrow.

--Geodesic Math & How to Use It. LC 74-27292. 150p. 1976. 14.95x (ISBN 0-520-02924-0); pap. 5.95 (ISBN 0-520-03054-0, CAL 323). U of Cal Pr.

--Joyce's Voices. LC 76-38887. (Quantum Book Ser.). 1978. 8.95 (ISBN 0-520-03206-3, CAL 426); pap. 2.95 (ISBN 0-520-03935-1). U of Cal Pr.

--The Pound Era. LC 72-138349. 1971. 22.00x (ISBN 0-520-01860-5); pap. 6.95 (ISBN 0-520-02427-3). U of Cal Pr.

Kennet, Andrea. Beautiful Illinois. Shangle, Robert D., ed. LC 80-18774. (Illus.). 72p. 1980. 14.95 (ISBN 0-915796-73-2); pap. 7.95 (ISBN 0-915796-72-4). Beautiful Am.

--Beautiful Pittsburgh. Shangle, Robert D., ed. LC 79-20481. (Illus.). 80p. 1980. 14.95 (ISBN 0-89802-088-3); pap. 7.95 (ISBN 0-89802-087-5). Beautiful Am.

Kennet, W. The Futures of Europe. LC 76-9541. (Illus.). 1976. 27.50 (ISBN 0-521-21326-6). Cambridge U Pr.

Kenneth, Wallis F., jt. auth. see Stewart, Mark B.

Kennett, David. Victorian & Edwardian Horses from Historic Photographs. LC 79-56443. (Illus.). 120p. 1980. 19.95 (ISBN 0-7134-1569-X, Pub. by Batsford England). David & Charles.

Kennett, John, retold by. Twenty Thousand Leagues Under the Sea. 1977. pap. text ed. 2.95 o.p. (ISBN 0-8277-5383-7). British Bk Ctr.

Kennett, Lee & Anderson, James L. The Gun in America: The Origins of a National Dilemma. LC 74-5990. (Contributions in American History: No. 37). (Illus., Orig.). 1975. lib. bdg. 17.50 (ISBN 0-8371-7530-5, ARF/); pap. text ed. 3.95 (ISBN 0-8371-8715-X, ARF). Greenwood.

Kennett, Pat. M.A.N. (World Trucks: No. 4). (Illus.). 1979. 15.95 (ISBN 0-89404-015-4). Aztex.

--World Trucks: Berliet, No. 11. (Illus.). 88p. 1981. 19.95 (ISBN 0-85059-449-9). Aztex.

--World Trucks: International, No. 12. (Illus.). 88p. 1981. pap. 19.95 (ISBN 0-85059-503-7). Aztex.

Kennett, Roger H., et al, eds. Monoclonal Antibodies. (Illus.). 375p. 1980. 29.50 (ISBN 0-306-40408-7, Plenum Pr). Plenum Pub.

Kenneway, Eric. Making Pop-up Greeting Cards. (gr. 9-12). 8.95 (ISBN 0-263-05065-3). Transatlantic.

Kenney, Alice P. Access to the Past: Museum Programs & Handicapped Visitors. x, 131p. (Orig.). 1980. pap. 7.95 (ISBN 0-910050-45-7). AASLH.

Kenney, Anthony. Aquinas. 86p. 1980. 7.95 (ISBN 0-8090-2724-0); pap. 2.95 (ISBN 0-8090-1407-6). Hill & Wang.

Kenney, Charles L. A Memoir of Michael William Balfe. LC 77-13360. (Music Reprint Ser., 1978). (Illus.). 1978. Repr. of 1875 ed. lib. bdg. 25.00 (ISBN 0-306-77528-X). Da Capo.

Kenney, E. J., ed. see Ovid.

Kenney, Ed, ed. see Lucretius.

Kenney, Edward H. A Confucian Notebook. LC 79-2828. 89p. 1981. Repr. of 1950 ed. 12.00 (ISBN 0-8305-0008-1). Hyperion Conn.

Kenney, George B. An Analysis of the Energy Efficiency & Economic Viability of Expanded Magnesium Utilization. LC 78-75004. (Outstanding Dissertations on Energy Ser.). 1979. lib. bdg. 20.00 (ISBN 0-8240-3975-0). Garland Pub.

Kenney, John P. & More, Harry W., Jr. Principles of Investigation. (Criminal Justice Ser.). (Illus.). 1979. text ed. 17.95 (ISBN 0-8299-0284-8); wkbk. 5.50 (ISBN 0-686-67621-1); instrs. manual avail. (ISBN 0-8299-0592-8). West Pub.

Kenney, Lona B. The One Thing Worth Having. unpublished due to cancellation of publisher's rights.

Kenney, Maureen, ed. Circle Round the Zero: Play Chants & Singing Games of City Children. (Illus.). 1975. pap. 6.95 (ISBN 0-918812-08-9). Magnamusic.

Kenney, Shirley S., ed. see Steele, Richard.

Kennick, W. E., ed. Art & Philosophy: Readings in Aesthetics. 2nd ed. LC 78-65213. 1979. text ed. 14.95x (ISBN 0-312-05391-6). St Martin.

Kennihan, Marita, ed. see Fails Management Institute.

Kennon, Graham. Woodsy Owl & the Trail Bikers. (Illus.). 24p. (gr. k-3). 1976. PLB 5.00 (ISBN 0-307-60107-2, Golden Pr). Western Pub.

Kennon, Noel F. Patterns in Crystals. LC 78-4531. 1978. text ed. 31.95 (ISBN 0-471-99748-X); pap. text ed. 15.00 (ISBN 0-471-99652-1, Pub. by Wiley-Interscience). Wiley.

Kenny & Clemmens. Behavioral Pediatrics & Child Development. 240p. 1975. 16.95 o.p. (ISBN 0-683-04592-X). Williams & Wilkins.

Kenny, A. J., tr. see Wittgenstein, Ludwig.

Kenny, Anthony. Action Emotion & Will. 1963. pap. text ed. 8.50x (ISBN 0-391-00272-4). Humanities.

--Freewill & Responsibility: Four Lectures. 1978. 12.50x (ISBN 0-7100-8998-8). Routledge & Kegan.

--The God of the Philosophers. 1979. 16.50x (ISBN 0-19-824594-7). Oxford U Pr.

Kenny, Anthony J. The Computation of Style: An Introduction to Statistics for Students & Readers of Literature. Date not set. 30.01 (ISBN 0-08-024282-0); pap. 12.01 (ISBN 0-08-024281-2). Pergamon.

Kenny, David A. Correlation & Causality. LC 79-4855. 1979. 24.50 (ISBN 0-471-02439-2, Pub. by Wiley-Interscience). Wiley.

Kenny, Dick, jt. auth. see Banks, Bruce.

Kenny, Herbert A. Cape Ann: Cape America. LC 70-14190. 1971. 6.95 o.p. (ISBN 0-397-00694-2). Lippincott.

Kenny, Katherine, jt. auth. see Campbell, Julie.

Kenny, Kathryn. Mystery at Mead's Mountain. (Trixie Belden Mystery Stories). (gr. 4 up). 1978. PLB 5.52 (ISBN 0-307-61593-6, Golden Pr); pap. 1.25 (ISBN 0-307-21593-8). Western Pub.

--Mystery of the Castaway Children. (Trixie Belden Mystery Stories Ser.). (gr. 4 up). 1978. PLB 5.52 (ISBN 0-307-61592-8, Golden Pr); pap. 1.25 (ISBN 0-307-21592-X). Western Pub.

--Mystery off Old Telegraph Road. (Trixie Belden Mystery Stories Ser.). (gr. 4 up). 1978. PLB 5.52 (ISBN 0-307-61591-X, Golden Pr); pap. 1.25 (ISBN 0-307-21591-1). Western Pub.

--Trixie Belden Gift Set, 3 bks. (gr. 9 up). Date not set. pap. 3.75 boxed set (ISBN 0-307-13623-X, Golden Pr). Western Pub.

Kenny, Maurice, ed. From the Center: A Folio of Native American Art & Poetry. (Illus.). 30p. (Orig.). 1981. pap. 7.50 (ISBN 0-936574-03-8). Strawberry Pr NY.

Kenny, Robert W., ed. see Williams, John B.

Kenny, Thomas J. & Clemmens, Raymond L. Behavioral Pediatrics & Child Development: A Clinial Handbook. 2nd ed. (Illus.). 225p. 1980. lib. bdg. 23.95 (ISBN 0-683-04595-4). Williams & Wilkins.

Kenrick, Tony. The Eighty-First Site. 1980. 10.00 (ISBN 0-453-00379-6, H379). NAL.

--Eighty-First Site. 1981. pap. 2.75 (ISBN 0-451-09600-2, E9600, Sig). NAL.

--Two for the Price of One. 1981. pap. 2.50 (ISBN 0-451-09809-9, E9809, Signet Bks). NAL.

--Two Lucky People. 1981. pap. 2.50 (ISBN 0-451-09725-4, E9725, Sig). NAL.

Kenrick, Vivienne. Horses in Japan. (Illus.). 5.25 (ISBN 0-85131-084-2, Dist. by Sporting Book Center). J A Allen.

Kens, Paul, jt. auth. see Farrell, H. Clyde.

Kenschaft, Patricia C., jt. auth. see Kalmanson, Kenneth.

Kenseth, Arnold & Unsworth, Richard P. Prayers for Worship Leaders. LC 77-15249. 132p. (Orig.). 1978. pap. 3.95 (ISBN 0-8006-1331-7, 1-1331). Fortress.

Kent. Clotilda's Magic. (ps-3). 1980. pap. 1.50 (ISBN 0-590-31247-2, Schol Pap). Schol Bk Serv.

--Wizard & His Magic Spells. (Illus.). (gr. 2-3). 1980. pap. 3.50 incl. record (ISBN 0-590-24008-0, Schol Pap). Schol Bk Serv.

Kent, Alexander. Command a King's Ship. pap. 2.25 (ISBN 0-515-05498-4). Jove Pubns.

--Enemy in Sight. pap. 1.95 (ISBN 0-515-05375-9). Jove Pubns.

--The Flag Captain. 1979. pap. 1.95 o.p. (ISBN 0-425-04180-8). Berkley Pub.
--The Flag Captain. pap. 1.95 (ISBN 0-515-05349-X). Jove Pubns.
--Passage to Mutiny. 352p. 1980. pap. 1.95 (ISBN 0-515-05437-2). Jove Pubns.
--Signal - Close Action. pap. 2.25 (ISBN 0-515-05719-3). Jove Pubns.
--Sloop of War. 1979. pap. 1.95 (ISBN 0-515-05370-8). Jove Pubns.
--To Glory We Steer. pap. 2.25 (ISBN 0-515-05732-0). Jove Pubns.
Kent, Allen. Information Analysis & Retrieval. LC 70-155120. (Information Science Ser). 1971. 29.95 (ISBN 0-471-46995-5). Wiley.
Kent, B. Social Work Supervision in Practice. 1969. pap. 4.95 o.p. (ISBN 0-08-006363-2). Pergamon.
Kent, Barry C., et al, eds. Foundations of Pennsylvania Prehistory. LC 7-612349. (Pennsylvania Historical & Museum Commission Anthropological Ser.: No. 1). (Illus.). 1971. 13.00 (ISBN 0-911124-67-5). Pa Hist & Mus.
Kent, Bernard, jt. auth. see Freeston, Ewart Co.
Kent, C. Footnotes & Headlines. (Orig.). 1970. pap. 3.45 (ISBN 0-8164-2548-5). Crossroad NY.
Kent, Carol M. Aloe Vera. LC 78-74978. (Illus.). 1979. pap. 6.00 (ISBN 0-9604886-0-X). C M Kent.
Kent, Corita, jt. auth. see Gunther, Bernard.
Kent, Sr. Corita, jt. auth. see Pintauro, Joseph.
Kent, David L. Barbados & America. LC 80-80184. 1980. 25.00 (ISBN 0-9604886-1-8). C M Kent.
--Foreign Origins. LC 80-85008. 100p. 1981. softcover 10.00 (ISBN 0-9604886-3-4). C M Kent.
--Massachusetts Supplement for Modern Real Estate Practice. 2nd ed. 112p. (Orig.). 1979. pap. 7.95 (ISBN 0-88462-255-X). Real Estate Ed Co.
Kent, Donald H. Iroquois Indians, Vol. 1: History of Pennsylvania Purchases from the Indians. (American Indian Ethnohistory Ser: North Central & Northeastern Indians). (Illus.). lib. bdg. 42.00 (ISBN 0-8240-0768-9). Garland Pub.
Kent, Donald H., ed. see Simonett, Martha L.
Kent, Dorman B. Vermonters. 187p. 1937. 3.00x o.p. (ISBN 0-934720-05-3). VT Hist Soc.
Kent, Edward A., ed. Law & Philosophy: Readings in Legal Philosophy. 1970. text ed. 18.95 (ISBN 0-13-526459-6). P-H.
Kent, Ernest W. The Brains of Men & Machines. 1980. 15.95 (ISBN 0-07-034123-0, BYTE Bks); pap. 8.95 (ISBN 0-07-034122-2). McGraw.
Kent, Felix H. Legal & Business Problems of the Advertising Industry: 1980 Course Handbook. LC 80-80906. (Patents, Copyrights, Trademarks, & Literary Property Course Handbook Ser.). (Illus.). 465p. 1980. pap. text ed. 25.00 (ISBN 0-686-68827-9, G4-3672). PLI.
Kent, Frank R. The Story of Maryland Politics: An Outline History of the Big Political Battles of the State from 1864 to 1910, with Sketches & Incidents of the Men & Measures That Figured As Factors, & the Names of Most of Those Who Held Office in That Period. LC 68-31444. xiv, 439p. Repr. of 1911 ed. 18.00 (ISBN 0-8103-5035-1). Gale.
Kent, George. Anatomy of the Vertebrates: A Laboratory Guide. 3rd ed. LC 77-16049. (Illus.). 1978. pap. 8.50 lab manual (ISBN 0-8016-2644-7). Mosby.
--The Politics of Pacific Islands Fisheries. (Westview Replica Edition Ser.). 1980. lib. bdg. 22.00x (ISBN 0-89158-683-0). Westview.
Kent, George C. Comparative Anatomy of the Vertebrates. 4th ed. LC 77-13588. (Illus.). 1978. text ed. 21.95 (ISBN 0-8016-2650-1). Mosby.
Kent, George O. Bismarck & His Times. LC 78-2547. 192p. 1978. 12.50x (ISBN 0-8093-0858-4); pap. 5.95 (ISBN 0-8093-0859-2). S Ill U Pr.
Kent, H. S. War & Trade in the Northern Seas: Anglo-Scandinavian Economic Relations in the Mid-Eighteenth Century. LC 72-75304. (Studies in Economic History). (Illus.). 288p. 1973. 40.95 (ISBN 0-521-08579-9). Cambridge U Pr.
Kent, Homer A., Jr. Freedom of God's Sons: Studies in Galatians. (New Testament Studies). (Illus.). 144p. 1976. pap. 2.95 o.p. (ISBN 0-8010-5376-5). Baker Bk.
--Light in the Darkness: Studies in the Gospel of John. (Illus.). pap. 4.95 (ISBN 0-88469-055-5). BMH Bks.
--The Pastoral Epistles: Studies in I & II Timothy. 10.95 (ISBN 0-88469-075-X). BMH Bks.
Kent, Homer A., Sr. The Pastor & His Work. 8.95 o.p. (ISBN 0-88469-079-2). BMH Bks.
Kent, Homer, Jr. Pastoral Epistles. 1958. 9.95 (ISBN 0-8024-6356-8). Moody.
Kent, J. Commentaries on American Law, 4 Vols. LC 78-75290. (American Constitutional & Legal History Ser). 1971. Repr. of 1826 ed. Set. lib. bdg. 195.00 (ISBN 0-306-71293-8). Da Capo.
Kent, J. P. Roman Coins. LC 77-77534. (Illus.). 1978. 60.00 o.p. (ISBN 0-8109-1584-7). Abrams.
Kent, Jack. Blah. LC 73-93851. (Illus.). (gr. k-2). 1970. 5.95 o.s.i. (ISBN 0-8193-0394-1, Four Winds); PLB 5.41 o.s.i. (ISBN 0-8193-0395-X). Schol Bk Serv.
--Christmas Pinata. LC 74-30450. (Illus.). 40p. (gr. k-3). 1975. 5.95 o.s.i. (ISBN 0-8193-0815-3, Four Winds); PLB 5.41 o.s.i. (ISBN 0-8193-0816-1). Schol Bk Serv.
--Clotilda. LC 69-17438. (Illus.). (ps-2). 1978. 3.95 (ISBN 0-394-83911-0); PLB 4.99 (ISBN 0-394-93911-5). Random.
--Grown-up Day. LC 70-7782. (Illus.). (gr. k-2). 1969. 5.95 o.s.i. (ISBN 0-8193-0287-2, Four Winds); PLB 5.41 o.s.i. (ISBN 0-8193-0288-0). Schol Bk Serv.
--Jack Kent's Twelve Days of Christmas. LC 73-1823. (Illus.). 40p. (gr. 1 up). 1973. 5.95 o.s.i. (ISBN 0-8193-0696-7, Four Winds); PLB 5.41 o.s.i. (ISBN 0-8193-0697-5). Schol Bk Serv.
--Mr. Meebles. LC 70-117562. (Illus.). 48p. (gr. k-2). 1970. 5.95 o.s.i. (ISBN 0-8193-0408-5, Four Winds); PLB 5.41 o.s.i. (ISBN 0-8193-0409-3). Schol Bk Serv.
--More Fables of Aesop. LC 73-13635. (Illus.). 64p. (ps up). 1974. 5.95 o.s.i. (ISBN 0-8193-0750-5, Four Winds); PLB 5.41 o.s.i. (ISBN 0-8193-0751-3). Schol Bk Serv.
--Supermarket Magic. LC 78-55908. (Sniffy Bks.). (ps-2). 1978. 3.95 (ISBN 0-394-83921-8, BYR). Random.
--Wizard of Wallaby Wallow. LC 79-153785. (Illus.). (gr. k-3). 1971. 5.95 o.s.i. (ISBN 0-8193-0513-8, Four Winds); PLB 5.41 o.s.i. (ISBN 0-8193-0514-6). Schol Bk Serv.
Kent, Jack, illus. The Egg Book. LC 74-13662. (Illus.). 32p. (ps-1). 1975. 5.95g o.s.i. (ISBN 0-02-750200-7). Macmillan.
Kent, James. Memoirs & Letters of James Kent. Kent, William, ed. LC 78-99481. (American Public Figures Ser). 1970. Repr. of 1898 ed. lib. bdg. 32.50 (ISBN 0-306-71847-2). Da Capo.
Kent, K. V., tr. see Falco, Giorgio.
Kent, Katherine. Dreamtime. (Orig.). 1981. pap. 2.75 (ISBN 0-671-41783-5). PB.
--Falconer's Island. (Orig.). 1981. pap. write for info. (ISBN 0-671-41783-5). PB.
Kent, Kathryn. Druid's Retreat. 1979. pap. 1.75 o.p. (ISBN 0-523-40404-2). Pinnacle Bks.
Kent, Leona M., jt. auth. see Staub, George E.
Kent, M. Corita. Footnotes & Headlines: A Play-Pray Book. LC 67-27568. (Illus., Orig.). 1969. Repr. of 1967 ed. 6.00 (ISBN 0-8164-1032-1). Crossroad NY.
Kent, Maxwell. A Comparative Analysis of the Italians & the Jews: The Two People Who Contributed the Most to the Civilization of Mankind with Strange & Unexpected Conclusions. (Illus.). 1977. 47.75 (ISBN 0-89266-056-2). Am Classical Coll Pr.
Kent, N. L. Technology of Cereals. 2nd ed. LC 75-6654. 320p. 1975. text ed. 32.00 (ISBN 0-08-018175-9); pap. text ed. 14.00 (ISBN 0-08-018177-5). Pergamon.
Kent, P. W., ed. International Aspects of the Provision of Medical Care. 1976. 25.00 (ISBN 0-85362-160-8, Oriel). Routledge & Kegan.
--New Approaches to Genetics. 1978. 28.00 (ISBN 0-85362-169-1, Oriel). Routledge & Kegan.
Kent, Percy H. Passing of the Manchus. (Studies in Chinese History & Civilization). 1977. 24.00 (ISBN 0-89093-089-9). U Pubns Amer.
Kent, R. T. Mechanical Engineers' Handbook, 2 pts. 12th ed. Incl. Pt. 1. Design & Production. Carmichael, C., ed. 1611p (ISBN 0-471-46959-9); Pt. 2. Power. Salisbury, J. K., ed. 1409p (ISBN 0-471-46992-0). 1950. 39.95 ea. (Pub. by Wiley-Interscience). Wiley.
Kent, Robert B., jt. auth. see Scott, Austin W.
Kent, Robert W. & Corb, D. A. Practical Real Estate Brokerage. 1961. 12.95 o.p. (ISBN 0-13-693671-7). P-H.
Kent, Rockwell. It's Me, O Lord: The Autobiography of Rockwell Kent. LC 77-5590. (Graphic Arts Ser.). (Illus.). 1977. Repr. of 1955 ed. lib. bdg. 50.00 (ISBN 0-306-77412-7). Da Capo.
Kent, Roland G. Old Persian Grammar Texts Lexicon. 2nd rev. ed. (American Oriental Ser.: Vol. 33). 1953. 13.00x (ISBN 0-686-00016-1). Am Orient Soc.
Kent, Thomas H. General Pathology: A Programmed Text. 1975. pap. 16.95 (ISBN 0-316-48920-4). Little.
Kent, William, ed. see Kent, James.
Kent, William W. Hooked Rug. LC 78-172437. (Tower Bks). (Illus.). 1971. Repr. of 1941 ed. 18.00 (ISBN 0-8103-3914-5). Gale.
Kentner, Louis. The Piano. LC 76-329. (The Yehudi Menuhin Music Guide Ser). 1976. 12.95 (ISBN 0-02-871420-2); pap. 6.95 (ISBN 0-02-871370-2). Schirmer Bks.
Kenton, Warren. The Play Begins. 1971. 4.50 o.p. (ISBN 0-236-15401-X. Pub. by Paul Elek). Merrimack Bk Serv.
--Stage Properties & How to Make Them. (Illus.). 119p. pap. 11.50x (ISBN 0-273-43888-3, LTB). Soccer.
Kentwell, Richard G., jt. auth. see Barnes, Mildred J.
Kenward, M. Potential Energy. LC 75-36174. (Illus.). 256p. 1976. 35.50 (ISBN 0-521-21086-0); pap. 9.95x (ISBN 0-521-29056-2). Cambridge U Pr.
Kenward, Yvonne A. The Outsider. 96p. 1981. 6.95 (ISBN 0-8059-2760-3). Dorrance.
Kenworthy, B. J., tr. see Kaiser, Georg.
Kenworthy, Jack. Dog Training Guide. 6.98 o.p. (ISBN 0-385-01562-3) Doubleday.
Kenworthy, Leonard. Studying China. LC 74-23808. 1975. pap. text ed. 4.25x (ISBN 0-8077-2456-4). Tchrs Coll.
--Studying India. LC 74-23809. 1975. pap. text ed. 4.25x (ISBN 0-8077-2457-2). Tchrs Coll.
--Studying Japan. LC 74-23896. 1975. pap. text ed. 4.25x (ISBN 0-8077-2455-6). Tchrs Coll.
Kenworthy, Leonard S. Free & Inexpensive Materials on World Affairs. LC 68-56447. 1969. pap. text ed. 3.50x (ISBN 0-8077-1608-1). Tchrs Coll.
--Sixteen Quaker Leaders Speak. LC 79-50101. 1979. pap. 2.95 (ISBN 0-913408-49-2). Friends United.
--Social Studies for the Eighties: In Elementary & Middle Schools. 3rd ed. LC 80-19096. 480p. 1981. text ed. 12.95 (ISBN 0-471-05983-8). Wiley.
--Studying Africa in Elementary & Secondary Schools. rev. ed. LC 70-105869. (Illus.). 1970. pap. text ed. 3.50x (ISBN 0-8077-1606-5). Tchrs Coll.
--Studying South America in Elementary & Secondary Schools. rev. ed. LC 65-19211. (Illus.). 1965. pap. text ed. 3.50x (ISBN 0-8077-1614-6). Tchrs Coll.
--Studying the Middle East in Elementary & Secondary Schools. rev. ed. LC 65-19213. (Orig.). 1965. pap. text ed. 3.50x (ISBN 0-8077-1611-1). Tchrs Coll.
--Studying the U.S.S.R. in Elementary & Secondary Schools. LC 77-94510. 1970. pap. text ed. 3.50x (ISBN 0-8077-1615-4). Tchrs Coll.
Kenyon, Cecelia M., ed. The Antifederalists. LC 65-23008. (Orig.). 1966. pap. 9.10 o.p. (ISBN 0-672-60052-8, AHS38). Bobbs.
Kenyon, E. W. The Bible in the Light of Our Redemption. 320p. 1974. pap. 5.50 o.p. (ISBN 0-8007-0673-0). Revell.
Kenyon, F. G. The Text of the Greek Bible. 3rd ed. (Studies in Theology). 1975. 40.50x o.p. (ISBN 0-7156-0641-7, Pub. by Duckworth England). Biblio Dist.
Kenyon, F. W. The Duke's Mistress. 1978. pap. 1.95 (ISBN 0-505-51299-8). Tower Bks.
--Eugenie, That Spanish Woman. 1978. pap. 1.95 (ISBN 0-505-51301-3). Tower Bks.
--The Naked Sword. 1975. pap. 1.50 o.p. (ISBN 0-685-59191-3, LB308, Leisure Bks). Nordon Pubns.
--The Naked Sword. 1979. pap. 1.95 (ISBN 0-505-51341-2). Tower Bks.
Kenyon, J. D., jt. auth. see Whiiler, C. E.
Kenyon, J. R. Stuart England. 1978. pap. 3.50 (ISBN 0-14-022076-3, Pelican). Penguin.
Kenyon, Jane. From Room to Room. LC 78-60469. 68p. 1978. pap. 4.95 (ISBN 0-914086-24-3). Alicejamesbooks.
Kenyon, John P. Stuart Constitution, Sixteen Hundred Three to Sixteen Eighty Eight: Documents & Commentary. (Orig.). 1966. 62.00 (ISBN 0-521-05834-8); pap. 17.95x (ISBN 0-521-09370-8). Cambridge U Pr.
Kenyon, John S. & Knott, Thomas A. Pronouncing Dictionary of American English. 2nd ed. 1953. 7.95 (ISBN 0-87779-047-7). Merriam.
Kenyon, Mel & Christophus, Mike. Burned to Life. LC 76-1060. (Illus.). 1976. pap. 1.95 (ISBN 0-87123-044-5, 200044). Bethany Fell.
Kenyon, Richard A., jt. auth. see Bober, William.
Kenyon, Roger A. Existential Structures: An Analytic Enquiry. LC 76-4222. 1976. 6.00 (ISBN 0-8022-2181-5). Philos Lib.
--Existential Structures: An Analytic Inquiry. LC 76-4222. 1976. 6.00 o.p (ISBN 0-8022-2181-5). Philos Lib.
Kenyon, Ruth, tr. see Hasbach, Wilhelm.
Kenyon, Stewart. Hydroponics for the Home Gardener: An Easy to Follow Step-by-Step Guide for Growing Healthy Vegetables, Herbs & House Plants Without Soil. 158p. 1980. pap. 6.95 (ISBN 0-442-29702-5). Van Nos Reinhold.
Kenyon, Thedia C. New Hampshire's Covered Bridges. rev. ed. (Illus.). 1966. 5.00 o.p. (ISBN 0-87482-023-5). Wake-Brook.
Kenzie, Peggy, jt. ed. see Nemeth, Doris I.
Keogh, Conal P. Casebook of Self-Timed Exercises. (gr. 11-12). 1970. pap. text ed. 5.75x (ISBN 0-88334-025-9). Ind Sch Pr.
Keogh, D. To Light the Labyrinth. 7.95 o.p. (ISBN 0-8062-1136-9). Carlton.
Keough, Allen, jt. auth. see Lacey, Jim.
Keough, G. Arthur. Infinitely Happy. LC 78-21952. (Horizon Ser.). 1978. pap. 4.50 (ISBN 0-8127-0213-1). Southern Pub.
Keough, Lawrence, jt. auth. see Wicks, Robert G.
Kepert, D. L. & Vrieze, K. Compounds of the Transition Elements Involving Metal-Metal Bonds. (Pergamon Texts in Inorganic Chemistry: Vol. 27). 158p. 1975. text ed. 28.00 (ISBN 0-08-018880-X); pap. text ed. 17.50 (ISBN 0-08-018879-6). Pergamon.
Kepes. Histologic Variations of Meningiomas. 1981. price not set. Masson Pub.
Kepes, Gyorgy, ed. The Nature & Art of Motion. LC 65-10807. (Vision & Value Ser). 12.50 o.s.i. (ISBN 0-8076-0289-2). Braziller.
Kephart, Horace. Camping & Woodcraft. (Illus.). 1948. 10.95 (ISBN 0-02-562680-9). Macmillan.
--Our Southern Highlanders. LC 76-18903. (Illus.). 1976. 16.50x (ISBN 0-87049-197-0); pap. 6.95 (ISBN 0-87049-203-9). U of Tenn Pr.
Kephart, Newell. Slow Learner in the Classroom. 2nd ed. LC 77-158613. 1971. text ed. 17.95x (ISBN 0-675-09196-9). Merrill.
Kephart, Newell, jt. auth. see Roach, Eugene.
Kephart, William M. The Family, Society, & the Individual. 4th ed. LC 76-13094. (Illus.). 1977. text ed. 16.95 (ISBN 0-395-24247-9); inst. manual 1.00 (ISBN 0-395-24246-0). HM.
--The Family, Society, & the Individual. 5th ed. LC 80-81847. (Illus.). 624p. 1981. text ed. 16.95 (ISBN 0-395-29760-5); instr's. manual 0.75 (ISBN 0-395-29761-3). HM.
Kepler, Frank R., jt. auth. see Fryklund, Verne C.
Kepler, J. S. The Exchange of Christendom: The International Entrepot at Dover, 1622-1651. 200p. 1976. text ed. 17.25x (ISBN 0-7185-1144-1, Leicester). Humanities.
Kepler, James & Wolfe, Charles K., Jr. A Doctor Discusses How to Get a Good Nights Sleep. (A Doctor Discusses...Ser.). (Illus., Orig.). 1980. pap. 2.50 (ISBN 0-686-63406-3). Budlong.
Kepley, Ray R. Tails Up! LC 80-81060. (Illus.). 466p. 1980. 25.00 (ISBN 0-9604248-0-6). Kepley.
Keplicz, Krystyna, tr. see Osek, Andrzej & Skrodzki, Wojlciech.
Kepner, R. A. & Bainer, Roy. Principles of Farm Machinery. 3rd ed. (Illus.). 1978. text ed. 23.50 (ISBN 0-87055-252-X). AVI.
Keppel, Charlotte. Loving Sands, Deadly Sands. 1975. 7.95 o.p. (ISBN 0-440-05085-5). Delacorte.
Keppel, Geoffrey. Design & Analysis: A Researcher's Handbook. LC 72-6434. (Illus.). 640p. 1973. ref. ed. 21.95 (ISBN 0-13-200030-X). P-H.
Keppel, Geoffrey & Saufley, William H., Jr. Introduction to Design & Analysis: A Student's Handbook. LC 79-26166. (Psychology Ser.). (Illus.). 1980. text ed. 27.95x (ISBN 0-7167-1142-7); pap. text ed. 15.95x (ISBN 0-7167-1143-5). W H Freeman.
Keppel, Sonia. The Sovereign Lady: A Life of Elizabeth, Third Lady Holland, with Her Family. (Illus.). 1978. 22.50 (ISBN 0-241-02299-1, Pub. by Hamish Hamilton England). David & Charles.
Keppel-Jones, Arthur. South Africa: A Short History. 5th ed. 1975. pap. text ed. 8.75x (ISBN 0-09-042844-7, Hutchinson U Lib, Hutchinson U Lib). Humanities.
Keppes, Gyorgy, ed. Arts of the Environment. (Vision & Value Ser). (Illus.). 244p. 1972. 17.50 (ISBN 0-8076-0620-0). Braziller.
--Module, Proportion, Symmetry, Rhythm. LC 66-13044. (Vision & Value Ser). (Illus.). 1966. 17.50 (ISBN 0-8076-0363-5). Braziller.
Keppler, Victor. Your Future in Photography. 2nd ed. LC 71-114104. (Career Guidance Ser.). 1974. pap. 3.50 (ISBN 0-668-02262-0). Arco.
Ker, Neil R., ed. Facsimile of British Museum Ms. Harley 2253. (Early English Text Society Ser.). 1965. 29.50x o.p. (ISBN 0-19-722255-2). Oxford U Pr.
Kerber, Linda K. Daughters of Columbia: Women, Intellect, & Ideology in Revolutionary America. 320p. 1980. 19.50 o.p. (ISBN 0-8078-1440-7); pap. 9.00 o.p. (ISBN 0-8078-4065-3). U of NC Pr.
Kerboull, Jean. Voodoo & Magic Practices. 1978. 9.50 o.p. (ISBN 0-214-20524-X, 8063, Dist. by Arco). Barrie & Jenkins.
Kerbs, John G. Answers to Your People Problems. LC 68-25949. (Harvest Ser.). 1978. pap. 3.95 (ISBN 0-8163-0192-1, 01634-5). Pacific Pr Pub Assn.
Kerby, Robert L. Kirby Smith's Confederacy: The Trans-Mississippi South 1863-1865. LC 68-19752. 512p. 1972. 20.00x (ISBN 0-231-03585-3). Columbia U Pr.

Kerby, William F. A Proud Profession: Memoirs of a Wall Street Journal Reporter, Editor & Publisher. 200p. 1981. 12.95 (ISBN 0-87094-235-2). Dow Jones-Irwin.

Keren, David F. Immunology & Immunopathology of the Gastrointestinal Tract. LC 80-11922. (Illus.). 128p. 1980. pap. text ed. 18.00 (ISBN 0-89189-076-9, 45-1-001-00). Am Soc Clinical.

Keren, Gideon, ed. Statistical & Methodological Issues in Psychology & Social Sciences Research. LC 80-23720. 350p. 1981. text ed. 24.95 (ISBN 0-89859-062-0). L Erlbaum Assocs.

Kerensky, V. M., et al. Education II Revised. rev. ed. LC 74-156846. 1975. 14.25 o.s.i. (ISBN 0-87812-127-7). Pendell Pub.

Kerenyi, Carl. Archetypal Images in Greek Religion, 5 vols. Manheim, R., tr. Incl. Vol. 1. Prometheus: Archetypal Image of Human Existence. 1963. o.p. (ISBN 0-691-09705-4); Vol. 2. Dionysos: Archetypal Image of Industructible Life. 1976. 36.00x (ISBN 0-691-09863-8); Vol. 3. Asklepios: Archetypal Image of the Physician's Existence. 1959. 16.50 (ISBN 0-691-09703-8); Eleusis: Archetypal Image of Mother & Daughter. 1967. o.p. (ISBN 0-691-09704-6); Vol. 5. Zeus & Hera-Archetypal Image of Father, Husband & Wife. 1975. 18.00 (ISBN 0-691-09864-6). (Bollingen Ser.: Vol. 65). Princeton U Pr.

Kerenyi, Carl, jt. auth. see Jung, Carl G.

Kerenyi, Karl. Athene. Stein, Murray, tr. from Ger. (Orig.). 1978. pap. text ed. 7.00 (ISBN 0-88214-209-7). Spring Pubns.

--Goddesses of Sun & Moon: Circe, Aphrodite, Medea, Niobe, & Dunquin. (Dunquin Ser.). 1979. pap. text ed. 7.00 (ISBN 0-88214-211-9). Spring Pubns.

--Hermes - Guide of Souls. 100p. 1974. pap. 7.00 (ISBN 0-88214-207-0). Spring Pubns.

Keresztesi, Michael & Cocozzoli, Gary, eds. German American History & Life: A Guide to Information Sources. LC 79-24065. (Ethnic Studies Information Guide Ser.: Vol. 4). 1980. 30.00 (ISBN 0-8103-1459-2). Gale.

Kerfoot, H. F. Reglas Parlamentarias. Sanchez, Jose M., tr. 1980. Repr. of 1978 ed. 1.50 (ISBN 0-311-11012-6). Casa Bautista.

Kerfoot, John Barrett. American Pewter. LC 75-29215. (Illus.). xxii, 236p. 1976. Repr. of 1924 ed. 34.00 (ISBN 0-8103-4147-6). Gale.

Kerimov, Lyatif. Folk Designs from the Caucasus for Weaving & Needlework. (Illus.). 6.75 (ISBN 0-8446-5054-4). Peter Smith.

Kerin & Peterson. Perspectives on Strategic Marketing Management. 100p. 1980. text ed. 17.95 (ISBN 0-205-06722-0, 0867225). Allyn.

Kerin, Roger A. & Peterson, Robert A. Strategic Marketing Problems: Cases & Comments. 2nd ed. 1980. pap. text ed. 21.95 (ISBN 0-205-07329-8, 085980X); instr's man. o.p. avail. (ISBN 0-205-07330-1). Allyn.

Kerker, Ann E. & Murphy, Henry T., eds. Comparative & Veterinary Medicine: A Bibliography of Resource Literature. LC 72-7989. 224p. 1973. 29.50x (ISBN 0-299-06330-5). U of Wis Pr.

Kerker, Milton, ed. Colloid & Interface Science, Vols. 2-5. Incl. Vol. 2. Aerosols, Emulsions & Surfactants. 35.00 (ISBN 0-12-404502-2); Vol. 3. Adsorption, Catalysis, Solid Surfaces, Wetting, Surface Tension & Water. 37.50 (ISBN 0-12-404503-0); Vol. 4. Hydrosols & Rheology. 36.50 (ISBN 0-12-404504-9); Vol. 5. Biocolloids, Polymers, Monolayers, Membranes & General Papers. 36.50 (ISBN 0-12-404505-7). 1976. Set. 122.00. Acad Pr.

Kerkut, ed. see Matsuda, R.

Kerkut, G. A. Progress in Neurobiology, Vol. 12. (Illus.). 312p. 1980. pap. 103.00 (ISBN 0-08-024888-8). Pergamon.

Kerkut, G. A., ed. Laboratory Exercises in Comparative Biochemistry & Physiology. Incl. Vol. 1. 1968. 56.00 (ISBN 0-12-404650-9); Vol. 2. 1969. write for info. (ISBN 0-12-404652-5); Vol. 3. 1970. 69.00 (ISBN 0-12-404653-3); Vol. 4. 1971. 53.50 (ISBN 0-12-404654-1); Vol. 5. 1972. 47.50 (ISBN 0-12-404655-X); Vol. 6. 1972. 46.50 (ISBN 0-12-404656-8). Acad Pr.

--Progress in Neurobiology, Vol. 13, Complete. (Illus.). 440p. 1980. pap. 103.00 (ISBN 0-08-026039-X). Pergamon.

Kerkut, G. A. & Phillis, J. W., eds. Progress in Neurobiology, Vol. 11. 1979. 103.00 (ISBN 0-08-024857-8). Pergamon.

Kerkut, G. A., ed. see Threadgold, L. T.

Kerkvliet, Benedict J. The Huk Rebellion: A Study of Peasant Revolt in the Philippines. 1977. 22.00x (ISBN 0-520-03106-7). U of Cal Pr.

Kerley, Michael R. & Mother Earth News Staff, eds. The Mother Earth News Alcohol Fuel Handbook. 120p. (Orig.). 1980. pap. 12.95 (ISBN 0-938432-00-1). Mother Earth.

Kerman, Joseph. Listen. 3rd ed. 1980. 14.95x (ISBN 0-87901-127-0); single record 3.95; 10 record set 25.95. Worth.

--The Music of William Byrd, Volume 1: Latin Masses & Motets. (California Studies in Nineteenth-Century Music Ser.). 1980. 40.00x (ISBN 0-520-04033-3). U of Cal Pr.

Kerman, Joseph, jt. auth. see Janson, H.

Kerman, Joseph, ed. see Dahlhaus, Carl.

Kermode, D. G. Devolution at Work. 1979. text ed. 24.50x (ISBN 0-566-00237-X, Pub. by Gower Pub Co England). Renouf.

Kermode, Frank, ed. Selected Prose of T. S. Eliot. 320p. 1975. 10.95x (ISBN 0-15-180702-7, Co-Pub by FS&G); pap. 5.50 (ISBN 0-15-680654-1). HarBraceJ.

Kermode, Frank & Poirier, Richard, eds. Oxford Reader: Varieties of Contemporary Discourse. (Orig.). 1971. text ed. 12.95x (ISBN 0-19-501365-4); pap. 8.95x (ISBN 0-19-501366-2); pap. 6.95x shorter ed. (ISBN 0-19-501402-2). Oxford U Pr.

Kermode, Frank, et al. English Renaissance Literature: Introductory Lectures. 1974. 13.00x o.p. (ISBN 0-85641-022-5, Pub. by Basil Blackwell England); pap. 5.25x o.p. (ISBN 0-85641-023-3). Biblio Dist.

Kermode, Frank, et al, eds. The Oxford Anthology of English Literature. Incl. Vol. 1. Middle Ages Through the Eighteenth Century. 2406p. (ISBN 0-19-501659-9); pap. (ISBN 0-19-501657-2); Vol. 2. 1800 to the Present. 2270p. (ISBN 0-19-501660-2); pap. (ISBN 0-19-501658-0). (Illus.). 1973. 14.95x ea.; pap. 13.95x ea. Oxford U Pr.

Kern, Bernard D., jt. ed. see Davidson, J. P.

Kern, Gary, tr. see Kopelev, Lev.

Kern, Iso. Idee und Methode der Philosophie: Leitgedanken fuer eine Theorie der Vernunft. xiv, 441p. (Ger.). 1975. 54.10x (ISBN 3-11-004843-4). De Gruyter.

Kern, John Philip. Early Pliocene Marine Climate Environment of the Eastern Ventura Basin, Southern California. (U. C. Publ. in Geological Sciences: Vol. 96). pap. 10.00x (ISBN 0-520-09424-7). U of Cal Pr.

Kern, Ken. Owner-Built Pole Frame House. (Illus.). 192p. 1981. 14.95 (ISBN 0-684-16767-0, ScribT). Scribner.

Kern, Ken, et al. Stone Masonry. (Illus.). 1977. pap. 10.95 (ISBN 0-684-15288-6, SL747, ScribT). Scribner.

Kern, Kenneth R., ed. Corporate Diagrams & Administrative Personnel of the Chemical Industry, Nineteen Seventy Nine to Nineteen Eighty. rev. 14th ed. LC 58-1742. 1979. binder 150.00 (ISBN 0-912060-16-6); without binder 137.50 (ISBN 0-912060-17-4). Chem Econ.

Kern, Louis J. An Ordered Love: Sex Roles & Sexuality in Victorian Utopias--the Shakers, the Mormons, & the Oneida Community. LC 80-10763. xv, 430p. 1981. 24.00x (ISBN 0-8078-1443-1); pap. 12.50x (ISBN 0-8078-4074-2). U of NC Pr.

Kern, Roy F. & Suess, Manfred E. Steel Selection: A Guide for Improving Performance & Profit. LC 78-13610. 1979. 27.95 (ISBN 0-471-04287-0, Pub. by Wiley-Interscience). Wiley.

Kernan, Alvin B. Plot of Satire. LC 65-22327. 1965. 15.00x o.p. (ISBN 0-300-00621-7). Yale U Pr.

Kernan, D. Steps to English, Bks. 1-2. 1974. Bk. 1. text ed. 7.84x (ISBN 0-07-034151-6); Bk. 2. text ed. 7.84x (ISBN 0-07-034156-7). tchrs. eds. 8.76x ea.; ea. wkbks. 3.53 (ISBN 0-686-66128-1); cassettes 161.00 (ISBN 0-07-034153-2). McGraw.

Kernan, Doris, jt. auth. see Woodford, Protase E.

Kernan, Jerome B. & Sommers, Montrose S., eds. Perspectives in Marketing Theory. LC 68-19476. 1968. 24.50x (ISBN 0-89197-333-8); pap. text ed. 7.95x (ISBN 0-89197-334-6). Irvington.

Kernan, Roderick P. Cell Potassium. LC 80-133320. (Transport in the Life Sciences Ser.). 1980. 32.50 (ISBN 0-471-04806-2, Pub. by Wiley-Interscience). Wiley.

Kernberg, Otto. Borderline Conditions & Pathological Narcissism. LC 75-5606. 368p. 1975. 25.00x (ISBN 0-87668-205-0). Aronson.

Kernberg, Otto F. Object Relations Theory & Its Applications. LC 75-42548. 300p. 1981. 25.00x (ISBN 0-87668-247-6, 24760). Aronson.

Kernberger, David & Kernberger, Kathleen. Mark Strong's Napa Valley-1886-1924. new ed. (Illus.). 1978. spiral bd. leatherette 8.40 (ISBN 0-933206-00-3). Historic Photos.

Kernberger, Kathleen, jt. auth. see Kernberger, David.

Kerner, H. T. Foam Control Agents. LC 76-17942. (Chemical Technology Review: No. 75). (Illus.). 1977. 39.00 o.p. (ISBN 0-8155-0634-1). Noyes.

Kernicki, Jeanette & Weiler, Kathi. Electocardiography for Nurses: Physiological Correlates Electrical Disturbances of the Heart. 304p. 1981. 17.95 (ISBN 0-471-05752-5, Pub. by Wiley Med). Wiley.

Kernighan, Brian W. & Plauger, P. J. Software Tools. 286p. 1976. pap. text ed. 12.95 (ISBN 0-201-03669-X). A-W.

Kernochan, John M. The Legislative Process. abr. ed. 64p. 1980. pap. text ed. write for info. (ISBN 0-88277-023-3). Foundation Pr.

Kerns, D. M. & Beatty, R. W. Basic Theory of Waveguide Junctions & Introductory Microwave Network Analysis. 1967. text ed. 17.25 (ISBN 0-08-012064-4). Pergamon.

Kerns, Frances C. The Edges of Love. (Orig.). 1980. pap. 2.50 (ISBN 0-446-91093-7). Warner Bks.

--Savage. 576p. (Orig.). 1981. pap. 2.75 (ISBN 0-446-95603-1). Warner Bks.

Kerns, Robert L. Photojournalism: Photography with a Purpose. (Illus.). 1980. text ed. 16.95 (ISBN 0-13-665695-1). P-H.

Keros, John. Computers, Fortran IV, & Data-Processing Applications. 1972. text ed. 6.95x o.p. (ISBN 0-205-03280-X, 1732803). Allyn.

Kerouac, Jack. Dharma Bums. 1971. pap. 4.95 (ISBN 0-14-004252-0). Penguin.

--Mexico City Blues. 1959. pap. 3.95 (ISBN 0-394-17287-6, E552, Ever). Grove.

--On the Road. pap. 2.50 (ISBN 0-451-08198-6, E8973, Sig). NAL.

--On the Road. (Critical Library Ser.). 1979. 12.95 o.s.i. (ISBN 0-670-52513-8). Viking Pr.

--Scripture of Golden Eternity. new ed. 45p. 1970. pap. 4.00 (ISBN 0-87091-049-3). Corinth Bks.

Kerper, Hazel B. & Israel, Jerold H. Introduction to the Criminal Justice System. 2nd ed. (Criminal Justice Ser.). (Illus.). 1979. text ed. 15.95 (ISBN 0-8299-0276-7); pap. study guide 5.95 (ISBN 0-8299-0260-0); instrs.' manual avail. (ISBN 0-8299-0593-6). West Pub.

Kerper, Hazel B. & Kerper, Janeen. Legal Rights of the Convicted. (Criminal Justice Ser.). 1974. text ed. 16.95 (ISBN 0-8299-0622-3); pap. text ed. write for info. (ISBN 0-8299-0622-3). West Pub.

Kerper, Janeen, jt. auth. see Kerper, Hazel B.

Kerr, A. P., ed. see Tocqueville, Alexis de.

Kerr, Alex, ed. Resources & Development in the Indian Ocean Region. 256p. 1981. lib. bdg. 26.50x (ISBN 0-86531-123-4). Westview.

Kerr, Alexander. Fort Hare Nineteen Fifteen to Nineteen Forty-Eight: The Evolution of an African College. LC 68-22137. (Illus.). 1968. text ed. 8.50x (ISBN 0-903983-04-4). Humanities.

Kerr, Andrew, Jr. Subacute Bacterial Endocarditis. (Illus.). 344p. 1956. pap. 32.75 photocopy ed., spiral (ISBN 0-398-01008-0). C C Thomas.

Kerr, Arnold D. & Kornhauser, Alain L., eds. Productivity in Railroads: Proceedings of a Symposium Held at Princeton University, July, 1977. (Pergamon Policy Studies). 1980. 22.00 (ISBN 0-08-023871-8). Pergamon.

Kerr, Baine. Jumping off Place & Other Stories. LC 80-14023. 80p. 1981. text ed. 11.00x (ISBN 0-8262-0311-6). U of Mo Pr.

Kerr, Barbara. Bound to the Soil: A Social History of Dorset, 1750-1918. LC 67-30789. 1968. text ed. 11.50x (ISBN 0-391-01959-7). Humanities.

Kerr, Catherine, jt. auth. see Steltzer, Ulli.

Kerr, Clarence W. Love: Familystyle: How to Have a Happy Home. pap. 1.95 (ISBN 0-89107-142-3). Good News.

Kerr, Clark. Labor Markets & Wage Determination: The Balkanization of Labor Markets & Other Essays. LC 75-17291. 1977. 15.75x (ISBN 0-520-03070-2). U of Cal Pr.

Kerr, Clark, et al. Twelve Systems of Higher Education: Six Decisive Issues. 214p. (Orig.). 1978. pap. text ed. 8.00 (ISBN 0-89192-211-3). Interbk Inc.

Kerr, Cynthia B. L' Amour, L'Amitie et Laa Fourberie: Une Etude Des Premieres Comedies De Corneille. (Stanford French & Italian Studies: Vol. 20). 152p. (Fr.). 1980. pap. 20.00 (ISBN 0-915838-19-2). Anma Libri.

Kerr, David. Training Your Dog. 1978. 8.95 (ISBN 0-7153-7541-5). David & Charles.

Kerr, David, jt. auth. see Douglas, Adrian P.

Kerr, Don & Kerr, Vivian. Kerr's Country Kitchen. (Illus.). 164p. 1981. pap. 6.95 (ISBN 0-933614-08-X). Peregrine Pr.

Kerr, Donald A., et al. Oral Diagnosis. 5th ed. LC 77-10851. (Illus.). 1978. pap. text ed. 29.95 (ISBN 0-8016-2660-9). Mosby.

Kerr, Edwin F., ed. see Sullivan, Roger.

Kerr, George. Formosa Betrayed. LC 76-10805. (China in the 20th Century Ser.). 1976. Repr. of 1965 ed. lib. bdg. 45.00 (ISBN 0-306-70762-4). Da Capo.

Kerr, Graham. The New Seasoning. 1976. 7.95 o.p. (ISBN 0-8007-0804-0); pap. 1.95 o. p. o.p. (ISBN 0-8007-8333-6, Spire Bks). Revell.

Kerr, Graham, frwd. by. Cooking with Love. 1977. pap. 2.95 (ISBN 0-89728-023-7, 677547). Omega Pubns OR.

Kerr, Horace L. How to Minister to Senior Adults in Your Church. 1980. 4.95 (ISBN 0-8054-3222-1). Broadman.

Kerr, Jean. How I Got to Be Perfect. 1979. pap. 2.25 o.p. (ISBN 0-449-24039-8, Crest). Fawcett.

Kerr, John R. & Littlefield, James E. Marketing: An Environmental Approach. (Illus.). 672p. 1974. ref. ed. 18.95 (ISBN 0-13-557330-0). P-H.

Kerr, Judith. When Hitler Stole Pink Rabbit. (gr. 3 up). 1973. pap. 1.50 (ISBN 0-440-49017-0, YB). Dell.

--When Willy Went to the Wedding. LC 72-8027. (Illus.). (gr. k-3). 1973. 5.95 o.p. (ISBN 0-8193-0658-4, Four Winds); PLB 5.41 o.p. (ISBN 0-8193-0659-2). Schol Bk Serv.

Kerr, Kathleen W., et al. Cost Data for Landscape Construction: 1981 Edition. rev. ed. (Cost Data for Landscape Construction Ser.). (Illus.). 200p. 1981. pap. 24.95 (ISBN 0-937890-01-4). Kerr Assoc.

Kerr, Lois. How to Get the Most Out of Your Cruise to Alaska. 1978. pap. 4.95 (ISBN 0-88894-174-9, Pub. by Douglas & McIntyre). Madrona Pubs.

Kerr, Louise F. Love Me, Love My Doggerel. LC 70-107863. 1969. 3.00 (ISBN 0-937684-02-3). Tradd St Pr.

Kerr, M. E. Little Little. LC 80-8454. 160p. (YA) (gr. 7 up). 1981. 8.95 (ISBN 0-06-023184-X, HarpJ); PLB 8.79g (ISBN 0-06-023185-8). Har-Row.

Kerr, Pamela. Operation Apricot. LC 77-3792. (Harper Novel of Intrigue). 1978. 7.95 (ISBN 0-06-011707-9, HarpT). Har-Row.

Kerr, Robert B. Electrical Network Science. (Illus.). 1977. text ed. 23.95 (ISBN 0-13-247627-4). P-H.

Kerr, Roberta, jt. auth. see Richardson, Walter.

Kerr, Steven, ed. Organizational Behavior. LC 78-26718. (Grid Series in Management). 1979. text ed. 20.95 (ISBN 0-88244-182-5). Grid Pub.

Kerr, Sue F. Here Comes Weezie. LC 67-26516. (Illus.). (ps-2). 1967. 4.95g o.p. (ISBN 0-8075-3237-1). A Whitman.

Kerr, Thomas R., jt. auth. see Steffen, Roscoe T.

Kerr, Vivian, jt. auth. see Kerr, Don.

Kerr, W. G. Scottish Capital on the American Credit Frontier. LC 75-16575. (Illus.). xviii, 246p. 1976. 13.00 (ISBN 0-87611-035-9). Tex St Hist Assn.

Kerr, Walter. The Secret of Stalingrad. LC 79-52759. (World War II Ser.). 272p. 1981. pap. 2.25 (ISBN 0-87216-569-8). Playboy Pbks.

Kerri, James N. Unwilling Urbanites: The Life of Canadian Indians in a Prairie City. LC 78-63272. 1978. pap. text ed. 9.25 (ISBN 0-8191-0622-4). U Pr of Amer.

Kerridge, W. H., tr. see Wellesz, Egon.

Kerrigan, Anthony. At the Front Door of the Atlantic. 1969. 6.95 o.p. (ISBN 0-85105-008-5). Dufour.

Kerrigan, Anthony, ed. & intro. by see Borges, Jorge L.

Kerrigan, Anthony, ed. see Unamuno, Miguel De.

Kerrigan, Anthony, tr. see Chomei, Kano N.

Kerrigan, Anthony, tr. see Unamuno, Miguel De.

Kerrigan, Harry D., jt. auth. see Livingstone, J. L.

Kerrigan, John. The Phoenix Assault. (Orig.). 1980. pap. 2.50 (ISBN 0-451-09522-7, E9522, Sig). NAL.

Kerrigan, William. The Prophetic Milton. LC 74-6118. 1974. 13.95x (ISBN 0-8139-0512-5). U Pr of Va.

Kerrmode, Frank, ed. see Shakespeare, William.

Kerrod, Robin. Rocks & Minerals. (Modern Knowledge Library). (Illus.). (gr. 5 up). 1978. 3.95 o.p. (ISBN 0-531-09083-3); PLB 5.90 o.p. (ISBN 0-531-09058-2). Watts.

Kerr-Wilson, Marjorie, tr. see Lorenz, Konrad.

Kerry, J. F., Jr. The New Soldier. 1971. 7.95 o.s.i. (ISBN 0-02-562890-9). Macmillan.

Kerry, John F., Jr. & Vietnamese Veterans Against the War. New Soldier. Thorne, David & Butler, George, eds. (Illus.). 176p. 1971. pap. 3.95 o.s.i. (ISBN 0-02-073610-X, Collier). Macmillan.

Kersch, Mary E. How to Fight City Hall: Or, A Guide to Grassroots Politics. 1980. lib. bdg. 14.50 (ISBN 0-933474-15-6); pap. 5.95 (ISBN 0-933474-18-0). Minn Scholarly.

Kerschner, Paul A., jt. auth. see Hess, Clinton W.

Kerschner, Paul A., ed. Advocacy & Age: Issues, Experiences, Strategies. LC 76-22321. 1976. 4.50 (ISBN 0-88474-035-8). USC Andrus Geron.

Kersey, Shirley N. Classics in the Education of Girls & Women. LC 80-20711. 335p. 1981. 17.50 (ISBN 0-8108-1354-8). Scarecrow.

Kersh, Ronald C., jt. auth. see McGuire, Frederick L.

Kershaw, John D. Handicapped Children. 3rd ed. 1973. 17.50x (ISBN 0-433-18381-0). Intl Ideas.

--Microprocessor Technology. 1980. text ed. 18.95 (ISBN 0-534-00748-1, Breton Pubs). Wadsworth Pub.

Kershaw, Joseph A. Government Against Poverty. (Studies in Social Economics). 174p. 1970. 10.95 (ISBN 0-8157-4902-3). Brookings.

Kershner, Howard E. Dividing the Wealth. 1980. pap. 4.95 (ISBN 0-8159-5308-9). Devin.

Kershner, R. B. & Wilcox, L. R. The Anatomy of Mathematics. 2nd ed. 480p. 1974. 21.50x o.p. (ISBN 0-8260-4970-2). Wiley.

Kershner, William K. Advanced Pilot's Flight Manual. 4th ed. (Illus.). 246p. 1976. pap. 13.95 (ISBN 0-8138-1300-X). Iowa St U Pr.

--Flight Instructor's Manual. 2nd ed. (Illus.). 380p. 1980. pap. 15.95 (ISBN 0-8138-0635-6). Iowa St U Pr.

Kerslake, D. M. The Stress of Hot Environments. LC 74-168896. (Physiological Society Monographs: No. 29). (Illus.). 300p. 1972. 59.50 (ISBN 0-521-08343-5). Cambridge U Pr.

Kerslake, John. Early Georgian Portraits, 2 vols. (Illus.). 800p. Set. 160.00 (ISBN 0-312-22476-1). St. Martin.

Kersley, J. A. & Haworth, F. Training the Mind of Your Gun Dog. (Illus.). 1977. 15.95 (ISBN 0-7207-0948-2). Transatlantic.

Kerson, Toba S. Medical Social Work: The Pre-Professional Paradox. 320p. 1980. text ed. 19.50x (ISBN 0-8290-0237-5). Irvington.

Kerstein, Morris D., ed. Management of Surgical Infections. LC 80-16740. (Illus.). 224p. 1980. monograph 23.00 (ISBN 0-87993-067-5). Futura Pub.

Kersten, H. & Kersten, W. Inhibitors of Nucleic Acid Synthesis: Biophysical & Biochemical Aspects. (Molecular Biology Biochemistry & Biophysics Ser.: Vol. 18). (Illus.). ix, 184p. 1974. 33.70 (ISBN 0-387-06825-2). Springer-Verlag.

Kersten, W., jt. auth. see Kersten, H.

Kertesz, Andre. Andre Kertesz: Sixty Years of Photography. Ducrot, Nicolas, ed. (Large Format Ser). (Illus.). 1978. pap. 8.95 o.p. (ISBN 0-14-004744-1). Penguin.

--From My Window. 1981. 24.95 (ISBN 0-8212-1125-0). NYGS.

Kertesz, Andrew, jt. auth. see Buckingham, Hugh W.

Kertesz, Stephen D., ed. Task of Universities in a Changing World. LC 71-148191. 1971. 15.00x o.p. (ISBN 0-268-00444-7); pap. 6.95x o.p. (ISBN 0-268-00486-2). U of Notre Dame Pr.

Kerth, A. L. Successful Businesses for the Abandoned Service Station. (Illus.). 1981. 28.00x (ISBN 0-9601188-2-9). A L Kerth.

Kertzer, David I. Comrades & Christians. LC 79-15313. (Illus.). 1980. 29.95 (ISBN 0-521-22879-4); pap. 7.95x (ISBN 0-521-29700-1). Cambridge U Pr.

Kertzer, Morris N. What Is a Jew? 1978. pap. 2.95 (ISBN 0-02-086350-0, Collier). Macmillan.

Kervan, L. C. Bread's Biological Transmutations. De Langre, Jacques, ed. LC 78-56122. 1979. pap. 3.00 (ISBN 0-916508-06-4). Happiness Pr.

Kervran, C. L. Biological Transmutations. (Illus.). 180p. 1980. text ed. 14.95 (ISBN 0-8464-1069-9). Beekman Pubs.

Kerwood, John R., ed. The United States Capitol: An Annotated Bibliography. LC 72-870. 534p. 1973. 27.50x (ISBN 0-8061-1030-9); pap. 9.95x (ISBN 0-8061-1253-0). U of Okla Pr.

Kesaris, Paul, ed. see CIA.

Keshet, Harry F., jt. auth. see Rosenthal, Kristine M.

Kesich, Veselin. The Passion of Christ. 84p. pap. 1.95 (ISBN 0-913836-80-X). St Vladimirs.

Kesler, Harold. Comfort One Another with These Words. 1981. pap. 0.95 (ISBN 0-937396-11-7). Walterick Pubs.

Kesler, Jackson, ed. Theatrical Costume: A Guide to Information Sources. LC 79-22881. (Performing Arts Information Guide Ser.: Vol. 6). 1979. 30.00 (ISBN 0-8103-1455-X). Gale.

Kesler, Jay. The Strong Weak People. 1976. pap. 2.50 o.p. (ISBN 0-88207-739-2). Victor Bks.

--Too Big to Spank. LC 77-90580. 1978. pap. 4.95 (ISBN 0-8307-0623-2, 54-093-06). Regal.

Kesler, Jay & Stafford, Tim. Breakthrough! Questions for Youth About God. (Campus Life Bk.). 176p. (Orig.). 1981. pap. 4.95 (ISBN 0-310-43371-1). Zondervan.

Kesner, Raymond P., jt. ed. see Patterson, Michael M.

Kesner, Richard M. Automation, Machine-Readable Records & Archival Administration: An Annotated Bibliography. LC 79-92994. 72p. 1980. pap. 6.00 (ISBN 0-931828-22-8). Soc Am Archivists.

Kess, Joseph F. Psycholinguistics: Introductory Perspectives. 1976. 16.95 (ISBN 0-12-405250-9). Acad Pr.

Kessel, John H. Presidential Campaign Politics: Coalition Strategies & Citizen Response. 1980. pap. 9.95x (ISBN 0-256-02369-7). Dorsey.

--Presidential Campaign Politics: Coalition Strategies & Citizen Response. LC 79-56080. 1980. 14.95 o.p. (ISBN 0-87094-211-5). Dow Jones-Irwin.

Kessel, Joyce K. Halloween. LC 80-15890. (Carolrhoda on My Own Bks.). (Illus.). 48p. (gr. k-3). 1980. PLB 5.95g (ISBN 0-87614-132-7). Carolrhoda Bks.

Kessel, Richard G. & Kardon, Randy H. Tissues & Organs: A Text-Atlas of Scanning Electron Microscopy. LC 78-23886. (Illus.). 1979. text ed. 34.95x (ISBN 0-7167-0091-3); pap. text ed. 16.95x (ISBN 0-7167-0090-5); slides avail. (ISBN 0-7167-1231-8). W H Freeman.

Kessell, John L. The Missions of New Mexico Since 1776. LC 79-4934. (Illus.). 320p. 1980. 45.00x (ISBN 0-8263-0514-8). U of NM Pr.

Kesselman, Arthur. The Social Studies Student Investigates Foreign Policy. (gr. 7-12). 1977. PLB 7.97 o.p. (ISBN 0-8239-0377-X). Rosen Pr.

Kesselman, Judi R. & Peterson, Franklynn. I Can Use Tools. (Illus.). 32p. (gr. 1-4). 1981. 5.95 (ISBN 0-525-66725-3). Elsevier-Nelson.

Kesselman, Steven. The Modernization of American Reform: Structures & Perceptions. Freidel, Frank, ed. LC 78-62386. (Modern American History Ser.: Vol. 10). 550p. 1980. lib. bdg. 40.00 (ISBN 0-8240-3635-2). Garland Pub.

Kesselman, Wendy. Emma. LC 77-15161. (Illus.). 32p. (gr. k-3). 1980. 7.95a (ISBN 0-385-13461-4); PLB (ISBN 0-385-13462-2). Doubleday.

Kessels, A. H. Studies on the Dream in Greek Literature. 280p. 1980. pap. text ed. 34.25x (ISBN 90-6194-491-0). Humanities.

Kessen, W. The Child. LC 65-14253. (Perspectives in Psychology Ser.). 1965. pap. 11.50 (ISBN 0-471-47306-5, Pub. by Wiley-Interscience). Wiley.

Kessen, William, ed. Childhood in China. LC 75-8151. 320p. 1975. 15.00x (ISBN 0-300-01910-6); pap. 4.95x (ISBN 0-300-01917-3). Yale U Pr.

Kessing, Roger M. & Corris, Peter. Lighting Meets the West Wind: The Malaita Massacre. (Illus.). 236p. 1980. text ed. 28.00x (ISBN 0-19-554223-1). Oxford U Pr.

Kessinger, Tom G. Vilyatpur 1848-1968: Social & Economic Change in a North Indian Village. (Illus.). 1974. 20.00x (ISBN 0-520-02340-4). U of Cal Pr.

Kessler. What's Inside the Box? (gr. 2-3). 1980. pap. 3.50 incl. record (ISBN 0-590-24007-2, Schol Pap). Schol Bk Serv.

Kessler, intro. by. Was There a Resurrection? The Challenge to Reason & Belief. 1977. 6.95 o.p. (ISBN 0-533-02987-2). Vantage.

Kessler, Christel. The Carved Masonry Domes of Mediaeval Cairo. 1976. pap. 15.00x (ISBN 0-686-19945-6). Intl Learn Syst.

Kessler, Dennis, jt. auth. see Kaplan, Lawrence J.

Kessler, Ethel & Kessler, Leonard. All for Fall. LC 74-2249. (Illus.). 40p. (ps-3). 1974. 5.95 o.s.i. (ISBN 0-8193-0735-1, Four Winds); PLB 5.41 o.s.i. (ISBN 0-8193-0736-X). Schol Bk Serv.

--Big Red Bus. LC 57-8090. (gr. k up). 1964. PLB 7.95 (ISBN 0-385-07713-0). Doubleday.

--The Day Daddy Stayed Home. LC 59-5898. (gr. k-3). Softbound 1.95 (ISBN 0-385-01073-7, Zephyr). Doubleday.

--Night Story. LC 80-24626. (Ready-to-Read Ser.). (Illus.). 48p. (gr. 1-4). 1981. PLB 7.95 (ISBN 0-02-750220-1). Macmillan.

--Splish Splash. LC 72-8137. (Illus.). 48p. (ps-2). 1973. 5.95 o.s.i. (ISBN 0-8193-0654-1, Four Winds); PLB 5.41 o.s.i. (ISBN 0-8193-0655-X). Schol Bk Serv.

--Two, Four, Six, Eight: A Book About Legs. LC 80-12574. (Illus.). 48p. (ps-3). 1980. PLB 7.95 (ISBN 0-396-07842-7). Dodd.

--What Do You Play on a Summer Day? LC 76-18095. (Illus.). (ps-3). 1977. 5.95 o.s.i. (ISBN 0-8193-0866-8, Four Winds); PLB 5.41 o.s.i. (ISBN 0-8193-0867-6). Schol Bk Serv.

Kessler, Evelyn S. Anthropology: The Humanizing Process. 192p. 1974. text ed. 10.25x o.p. (ISBN 0-205-04415-8); pap. text ed. 6.95x o.p. (ISBN 0-205-04420-4). Allyn.

Kessler, Friedrich & Gilmore, Grant. Contracts: Cases & Materials. 2nd ed. 1396p. 1976. 27.50 o.p. (ISBN 0-316-49016-4). Little.

Kessler, Herman & Bay, Kenneth. Salt Water Flies: Popular Patterns & How to Tie Them. LC 72-6109. (Illus.). 1972. 8.95 o.s.i. (ISBN 0-397-00939-9). Lippincott.

Kessler, Hermann. Deutsch Fuer Auslaender: Grundstufe. Incl. Pt. 1. Leichter Anfang (Lehrbuch) pap. text ed. 9.10x (ISBN 0-685-47452-6); Pt. 1a. Leichte Aufgaben (Arbeitsheft) pap. text ed. 4.55x (ISBN 0-685-47453-4); Part 1 & Part 1a in One Volume. text ed. 8.50x (ISBN 0-685-47454-2); Pt. 1b. Leichte Erzaelungen (Leseband) pap. text ed. 3.60x (ISBN 0-685-47455-0); Pt. 1c. Sprachlaboruebungen. 4.25x (ISBN 0-685-47456-9); Tonbaender fuer das Sprachlabor. 11 tapes, 9.5 cm/s 260.00x (ISBN 0-685-47457-7); Tonband mit Lehrbuchtexten. tape, 9.5 cm/s 29.25 (ISBN 0-685-47458-5). Schoenhof.

--Deutsch Fuer Auslaender: Mittelstufe. Incl. Pt. 2. Schneller Fortgang (Lehrbuch) pap. text ed. 9.10x (ISBN 0-685-47459-3); Pt. 2a. Kurze Uebungen (Arbeitsheft) 4.55x (ISBN 0-685-47460-7); Part 2 & Part 2a in One Volume. text ed. 8.50x (ISBN 0-685-47461-5); Pt. 2b. Kurze Geschichten (Leseband) pap. text ed. 3.60x (ISBN 0-685-47462-3); Pt. 2c. Sprachlaboruebungen. 4.25x (ISBN 0-685-47463-1); Tonbaender fuer das Sprachlabor. 10 tapes, 9.5 cm/s 260.00x (ISBN 0-685-47464-X); Tonband mit Lehrbuchtexten. tape 29.25x (ISBN 0-685-47465-8). Schoenhof.

--Deutsch Fuer Auslaender: Oberstufe. Incl. Pt. 3. Deutschlandkunde (Lehrbuch) pap. text ed. 11.70 (ISBN 0-685-47466-6); Pt. 3b. Moderne Dichtungen (Leseband) pap. text ed. 4.25x (ISBN 0-685-47467-4); tonband 29.25x, tape, 9.5 cm/s (ISBN 0-685-47468-2); Pt. 3d. Dichter unserer Zeit. pap. text ed. 4.25x (ISBN 0-685-47469-0); tonband 29.25x, tape, 9.5 cm/s (ISBN 0-685-47470-4). Schoenhof.

Kessler, Hermann, jt. auth. see Kreh, Lefty.

Kessler, I. Cancer Control: Screening, Diagnosis, Therapy. 1980. 24.50 (ISBN 0-8391-1539-3). Univ Park.

Kessler, James B., ed. Empirical Studies of Indiana Politics. LC 79-85089. (Illus.). 320p. 1970. 13.95x (ISBN 0-253-31950-1). Ind U Pr.

Kessler, Jane W. Psychopathology of Childhood. (Illus.). 1966. text ed. 19.95 (ISBN 0-13-736751-1). P-H.

Kessler, Jascha, ed. American Poems: A Contemporary Collection. LC 64-10627. (Crosscurrents-Modern Critiques Ser.). 1964. 7.95 o.p. (ISBN 0-8093-0119-9). S Ill U Pr.

Kessler, Jean G., jt. auth. see Bisconti, Ann S.

Kessler, Julia. Getting Even with Getting Old. LC 80-11045. 228p. 1980. 15.95 (ISBN 0-88229-663-9); pap. 8.95 (ISBN 0-88229-754-6). Nelson-Hall.

Kessler, Leonard. Super Bowl. LC 80-10171. (Greenwillow Read-Alone Bks.). (Illus.). 56p. (gr. 1-4). 1980. 5.95 (ISBN 0-688-80270-2); PLB 5.71 (ISBN 0-688-84270-4). Greenwillow.

Kessler, Leonard, jt. auth. see Kessler, Ethel.

Kessler, P., jt. ed. see Cochard, G.

Kessler, Robert & Anderson, Rodney U. Handbook of Urologic Emergencies. 1976. spiral bdg. 11.00 (ISBN 0-87488-647-3). Med Exam.

Kessler, Ronald & Greenberg, David. Linear Panel Analysis: Quantitative Models of Change. (Quantitative Studies in Social Relations). 1981. price not set (ISBN 0-12-405750-0). Acad Pr.

Kessler, Sheila. The American Way of Divorce: Prescriptions for Change. LC 74-28078. 192p. 1975. 12.95 (ISBN 0-88229-234-X). Nelson-Hall.

Kessler, Suzanne & McKenna, Wendy. Gender, an Ethnomethodological Approach. LC 77-15957. 1978. 24.95 (ISBN 0-471-58445-2, Pub. by Wiley-Interscience). Wiley.

Kessler, Tracy K., ed. see Junior League of Rochester, Inc.

Kessler-Harris, Alice. Women Have Always Worked: An Historical Overview. (Women's Lives - Women's Work Ser.). (Illus.). 165p. (Orig.). (gr. 11-12). 1980. 14.95 (ISBN 0-912670-86-X); pap. 5.95 (ISBN 0-912670-67-3). Feminist Pr.

Kessner, Thomas. The Golden Door: Italian & Jewish Immigrant Mobility in New York City, 1880-1915. 1977. text ed. 14.95 (ISBN 0-19-502116-9); pap. 4.95 (ISBN 0-19-502161-4). Oxford U Pr.

Kessopulos, Gust. Dog Obedience Training. LC 73-10524. (Illus.). 160p. 1975. 7.95 o.p. (ISBN 0-498-01415-0). A S Barnes.

Kestenbaum, Jack. Clerical Techniques for a Business Career. (Orig.). (gr. 9-12). 1975. text ed. 13.20 (ISBN 0-205-04507-3, 1745077); tchrs'. guide 3.80 (ISBN 0-205-04508-1, 1745085); workbook 5.92 (ISBN 0-205-04509-X, 1745093). Allyn.

Kestenbaum, Victor. The Phenomenological Sense of John Dewey: Habit & Meaning. 1977. text ed. 8.50x (ISBN 0-391-00668-1). Humanities.

Kester, Dale E. & Hartmann, Hudson T. Plant Propagation: Principles & Practices. 3rd ed. (Illus.). 704p. 1975. ref. ed. 22.95 (ISBN 0-13-680991-X). P-H.

Kester, Paul. Tales of the Real Gypsy. LC 77-142004. 1971. Repr. of 1897 ed. 18.00 (ISBN 0-8103-3633-2). Gale.

Kester, T., jt. ed. see Camatini, E.

Kesterson, David B. Bill Nye. (United States Authors Ser: No. 403). 1981. lib. bdg. 11.95 (ISBN 0-8057-7332-0). Twayne.

--Josh Billings (Henry W. Shaw) (U. S. Authors Ser.: No. 229). 1974. lib. bdg. 10.95 (ISBN 0-8057-0058-7). Twayne.

Kestin, Joseph, ed. The Second Law of Thermodynamics. (Benchmark Papers on Energy: Vol. 5). 1976. 43.00 (ISBN 0-12-786839-9). Acad Pr.

Kestner, Joseph. Jane Austen: Spatial Structure of Thematic Variations. (Salzburg Studies in English Literature, Romantic Reassessment: No. 39). 145p. 1974. pap. text ed. 25.00x (ISBN 0-391-01443-9). Humanities.

Kestner, N., jt. auth. see Margenau, H.

Ketcham, Hank. Dennis the Menace: All American Kid. (Dennis the Menace Ser.). (Illus.). 1977. pap. 1.50 (ISBN 0-449-13779-1, GM). Fawcett.

--Dennis the Menace & His Pal Joey. (Dennis the Menace Ser.). (Illus.). 1978. pap. 1.50 (ISBN 0-449-13822-4, GM). Fawcett.

--Dennis the Menace & Poor Ol' Mr. Wilson. (Dennis the Menace Ser.). (Illus.). 1978. pap. 1.50 (ISBN 0-449-13837-2, GM). Fawcett.

--Dennis the Menace: Busy Body. (Dennis the Menace Ser.). (Illus.). 128p. 1977. pap. 1.50 (ISBN 0-449-13658-2, GM). Fawcett.

--Dennis the Menace: Happy Half-Pint. (Dennis the Menace Ser). (Illus.). 1977. pap. 1.50 (ISBN 0-449-13649-3, GM). Fawcett.

--Dennis the Menace: Here Comes Trouble. (Dennis the Menace Ser.). (Illus.). 1978. pap. 1.50 (ISBN 0-449-13634-5, GM). Fawcett.

--Dennis the Menace: Household Hurricane. (Dennis the Menace Ser.). (Illus.). 1977. pap. 1.50 (ISBN 0-449-13679-5, GM). Fawcett.

--Dennis the Menace: Little Man in a Big Hurry. (Dennis the Menace Ser.). (Illus.). 128p. 1978. pap. 1.50 (ISBN 0-449-13630-2, Gm). Fawcett.

--Dennis the Menace: Make-Believe Angel. (Dennis the Menace Ser.). (Illus.). 1977. pap. 1.50 (ISBN 0-449-13902-6, GM). Fawcett.

--Dennis the Menace: The Kid Next Door. (Dennis the Menace Ser.). (Illus.). 128p. 1977. pap. 1.50 (ISBN 0-449-13656-6, GM). Fawcett.

--Dennis the Menace to the Core. (Dennis the Menace Ser.). (Illus.). 128p. 1978. pap. 1.50 (ISBN 0-449-13873-9, GM). Fawcett.

--Dennis the Menace Versus Everybody. (Dennis the Menace Ser). (Illus.). 1978. pap. 1.50 (ISBN 0-449-13750-3, GM). Fawcett.

--Someone's in the Kitchen with Dennis. (Dennis the Menace Ser.). (Illus.). 1979. pap. 1.50 o.p. (ISBN 0-449-14253-1, GM). Fawcett.

Ketcham, Ralph, ed. Political Thought of Benjamin Franklin. LC 65-22344. 1965. pap. 8.95 (ISBN 0-672-60100-1, AHS64). Bobbs.

Ketcham, Robert T. I Shall Not Want. 1953. pap. 1.50 (ISBN 0-8024-0130-9). Moody.

Ketcher, Fritzi. Daisy. 1977. 4.00 o.p. (ISBN 0-682-48806-2). Exposition.

Ketcherside, Carl. Which Church. pap. 0.50. Reiner.

Ketchledge, E. H. Trees of the Adirondack High Peak Region. 2nd ed. LC 67-28444. (Illus.). pap. 2.50 (ISBN 0-935272-07-0). ADK Mtn Club.

Ketchum, Hank. Dennis the Menace: Good Intenshuns. 128p. 1981. pap. 1.50 (ISBN 0-449-14395-3, GM). Fawcett.

--Dennis the Menace: I Done It My Way. (Dennis the Menace Ser.). 1979. pap. 1.50 (ISBN 0-449-14095-4, GM). Fawcett.

Ketchum, Jack. Off Season. 1981. pap. 2.50 (ISBN 0-345-29427-0). Ballantine.

Ketchum, Milo S. Handbook of Standard Structural Details for Buildings. 1956. text ed. 18.95 (ISBN 0-13-381822-5). P-H.

Ketchum, Richard M. Will Rogers: His Life & Times. LC 73-8713. (Illus.). 416p. 1973. 15.00 (ISBN 0-8281-0262-7, Dist. by Scribner); deluxe ed. 17.50 slipcased (ISBN 0-8281-0263-5, Dist. by Scribner). Am Heritage.

Ketchum, Richard M., ed. see Lancaster, Bruce.

Ketchum, Richard M., ed. see Plumb, J. H.

Ketchum, William C. American Basketry & Woodenware: A Collector's Guide. LC 73-6486. (Illus.). 256p. 1974. 6.95 o.s.i. (ISBN 0-02-562970-0). Macmillan.

--Collecting American Craft Antiques. (Illus.). 160p. 1980. 12.95 (ISBN 0-525-93129-5); pap. 7.95 (ISBN 0-525-93130-9). Dutton.

Ketchum, William C., Jr. The Catalog of American Antiques. LC 77-1118. (Illus.). 1979. pap. 8.95 o.p. (ISBN 0-88332-109-2, 8147). Larousse.

--Hooked Rugs: A Historical Collector's Guide - How to Make Your Own. LC 76-13880. 1976. 14.95 o.p. (ISBN 0-15-142168-4). HarBraceJ.

--Western Memorabilia: Collectibles of the Old West. (Illus.). 256p. 1980. 30.00 (ISBN 0-8437-3357-8). Hammond Inc.

Ketefian, Shake, ed. see Stewart Conference on Research in Nursing, Sixteenth.

Ketels, Hank & McDowell, Jack. Sports Illustrated Scuba Diving. 1979. 8.95 (ISBN 0-397-01304-3); pap. 5.95 (ISBN 0-397-01305-1). Lippincott.

Ketner, Kenneth, et al, eds. see C. S. Peirce Bicentennial International Congress.

Ketner, Kenneth L. An Emendation of R. G. Collingwood's Doctrine of Absolute Presuppositions. (Graduate Studies: No. 4). 41p. (Orig.). 1973. pap. 2.00 (ISBN 0-89672-011-X). Tex Tech Pr.

Ketner, Kenneth L. & Cook, James E.compiled by. Charles Sanders Peirce: Contributions to the Nation Part One: 1869-1893. (Graduate Studies: No. 10). 1975. 15.00 (ISBN 0-89672-020-9); pap. 10.00 (ISBN 0-89672-019-5). Tex Tech Pr.

Keto, C. Tsehloane. America & the Aftermath of the Jamoson Raid. LC 80-65851. (Transactions Ser.: Vol. 70, Pt. 8). 1980. 6.00 (ISBN 0-87169-708-4). Am Philos.

Keto, David B. Law & Offshore Oil Development: The North Sea Experience. LC 78-19745. 1978. 20.95 (ISBN 0-03-046646-6). Praeger.

Kett, Joseph F. The Formation of the American Medical Profession: The Role of Institutions, 1780-1860. LC 80-14326. xi, 217p. 1980. Repr. of 1968 ed. lib. bdg. 22.00x (ISBN 0-313-22428-5, KEFO). Greenwood.

Kett, Merriellyn, jt. auth. see Underwood, Virginia.

Kettani, M. Ali. Direct Energy Conversion. (Electrical Engineering Ser). 1970. text ed. 25.95 (ISBN 0-201-03663-0). A-W.

Kettelkamp, Larry. Astrology, Wisdom of the Stars. (Illus.). 128p. (gr. 5-9). 1973. PLB 7.44 (ISBN 0-688-30085-5). Morrow.

--Dreams. (Illus.). (gr. 5-9). 1968. PLB 6.96 (ISBN 0-688-31245-4). Morrow.

--Drums, Rattles, & Bells. (Illus.). (gr. 3-7). 1960. PLB 7.44 (ISBN 0-688-31247-0). Morrow.

--Haunted Houses. (Illus.). (gr. 5-9). 1969. 7.25 (ISBN 0-688-21377-4); PLB 6.96 (ISBN 0-688-31377-9). Morrow.

--The Healing Arts. (gr. 4-6). 1978. 6.95 (ISBN 0-688-22161-0); PLB 6.67 (ISBN 0-688-32161-5). Morrow.

--Hypnosis: the Wakeful Sleep. LC 75-17605. (Illus.). 96p. (gr. 5-9). 1975. 7.25 (ISBN 0-688-22045-2); PLB 6.96 (ISBN 0-688-32045-7). Morrow.

--Investigating Psychics: Five Life Histories. (Illus.). (gr. 5-9). 1977. 7.25 (ISBN 0-688-22123-8); PLB 6.96 (ISBN 0-688-32123-2). Morrow.

--Investigating UFO's. LC 77-155993. (Illus.). (gr. 5-9). 1971. PLB 6.96 (ISBN 0-688-31768-5). Morrow.

--Kites. (Illus.). (gr. 3-7). 1959. PLB 7.44 (ISBN 0-688-31584-4). Morrow.

--Magic Made Easy. (Illus.). (gr. 3-7). 1954. PLB 6.67 (ISBN 0-688-31579-8). Morrow.

--Magic Made Easy. rev. ed. LC 80-22947. (Illus.). 96p. (gr. 4-6). 1981. pap. 6.95 (ISBN 0-688-00377-X); PLB 6.67 (ISBN 0-688-00458-X). Morrow.

--A Partnership of Mind & Body: Biofeedback. LC 76-24818. (Illus.). (gr. 5-9). 1976. 7.25 (ISBN 0-688-22088-6); PLB 6.96 (ISBN 0-688-32088-0). Morrow.

--Religions East & West. (Illus.). 128p. (gr. 5-9). 1972. PLB 6.96 (ISBN 0-688-31926-2). Morrow.

--Sixth Sense. (Illus.). (gr. 5-9). 1970. PLB 6.96 (ISBN 0-688-31463-5). Morrow.

--Song, Speech & Ventriloquism. (Illus.). (gr. 5-9). 1967. PLB 6.96 (ISBN 0-688-31799-5). Morrow.

--Spinning Tops. (Illus.). (gr. 3-7). 1966. 7.25 (ISBN 0-688-21585-8); PLB 6.96 (ISBN 0-688-31585-2). Morrow.

--Spooky Magic. (Illus.). (gr. 4-6). 1955. PLB 6.48 (ISBN 0-688-31581-X). Morrow.

--Tricks of Eye & Mind, the Story of Optical Illusion: The Story of Optical Illusion. LC 74-5935. (Illus.). 128p. (gr. 5-9). 1974. PLB 6.96 (ISBN 0-688-31829-0). Morrow.

--Your Marvelous Mind. LC 80-18614. (Illus.). (gr. 5-8). 9.95 (ISBN 0-664-32670-6). Westminster.

Kettell, Brian. The Finance of International Trade. LC 80-28878. (Illus.). xviii, 175p. 1981. lib. bdg. 40.00 (ISBN 0-89930-011-1, KFI/, Quorum Bks). Greenwood.

Kettell, Russell H. Pine Furniture of Early New England. 1929. 15.00 (ISBN 0-486-20145-7). Dover.

Kettelle, F. W. Filet Crochet. 1978. pap. 1.50 (ISBN 0-486-23745-1). Dover.

Ketterer, Wilson. How to Write & Sell a Book of Your Intimate Thoughts & of Your Personal Adventures. (Illus.). 1980. deluxe ed. 27.25 (ISBN 0-89266-233-6). Am Classical Coll Pr.

Ketterson, J. B., jt. ed. see Bennemann, Karl H.

Ketting, Kees & Peeters, Henk. Two Hundred Fishing Tips: Zander. (Illus.). 88p. (Orig.). 1980. pap. 5.00 (ISBN 0-85242-615-1). Intl Pubns Serv.

Kettl, Donald F. Managing Community Development & the New Federalism. LC 79-23504. 19.95 (ISBN 0-03-053311-2). Praeger.

Kettle, Arnold. Introduction to the English Novel, 2 vols. Incl. Vol. 1. Up to George Eliot. text ed. o.p. (ISBN 0-09-031603-7); pap. text ed. 9.00x (ISBN 0-09-031604-5); Vol. 2. Henry James to the Present. text ed. o.p. (ISBN 0-09-048543-2); pap. text ed. 8.50x (ISBN 0-09-048544-0). 1974 (Hutchinson U Lib). Humanities.

Kettle, Michael. Russia & the Allies Nineteen Seventeen to Nineteen Twenty, Vol. I: The Allies & the Russian Collapse; March 1917-1918. (Illus.). 300p. 1981. 27.50x (ISBN 0-8166-0981-0). U of Minn Pr.

Kettler, Robert, jt. auth. see Trimmer, Joseph.

Kettlewell, Bernard. The Evolution of Melanism: The Study of a Recurring Necessity, with Special Reference to Industrial Melanism in the Lepidoptera. (Illus.). 448p. 1973. 49.00x (ISBN 0-19-857370-7). Oxford U Pr.

Kettlewell, H. B. Your Book of Butterflies & Moths. (Your Book Ser.). (Illus.). 1963. 6.95 (ISBN 0-571-05576-1, Pub. by Faber & Faber). Merrimack Bk Serv.

Kettlewell, Mike, ed. Autocourse 1977-1978. (Ser. No.26). (Illus.). 1978. 26.95 o.p. (ISBN 0-905138-03-1). Motorbooks Intl.

Kettridge, J. O. French-English & English-French Dictionary of Commercial & Financial Terms, Phrases & Practice. 2nd ed. 1969. Repr. of 1968 ed. 30.00 (ISBN 0-7100-1671-9). Routledge & Kegan.

--French-English & English-French Dictionary of Financial & Mercantile Terms Phrases & Practice. 1971. Repr. of 1934 ed. 20.00 (ISBN 0-7100-1667-0). Routledge & Kegan.

--French-English & English-French Dictionary of Technical Terms & Phrases, 2 vols. Incl. Vol. 1. French-English. 40.00 (ISBN 0-7100-1672-7); Vol. 2. English-French. 40.00 (ISBN 0-7100-1673-5). 1970. Repr. of 1959 ed. Set. 70.00 (ISBN 0-685-25619-7). Routledge & Kegan.

--French for English Idioms & Figurative Phrases. 1966. Repr. of 1940 ed. 16.00 (ISBN 0-7100-1669-7). Routledge & Kegan.

--French Idioms & Figurative Phrases: With Many Quotations. 1970. Repr. of 1949 ed. 18.00 (ISBN 0-7100-1668-9). Routledge & Kegan.

--Travellers' Foreign Phrase Book. 1967. Repr. of 1960 ed. limp 5.00 (ISBN 0-7100-1674-3). Routledge & Kegan.

Kety, Seymour S., jt. auth. see Matthysse, Steven.

Ketz, Samuel & Johnson, Norman L. Encyclopedia of Statistical Sciences, 2 vols. 500p. 1981. Vol. 1. 82.50 (ISBN 0-471-05546-8, Pub. by Wiley-Interscience); Vol. 2. 82.50 (ISBN 0-471-05547-6). Wiley.

Keucher, William F. Main Street & the Mind of God. LC 74-2891. 128p. (Orig.). 1974. pap. 2.65 o.p. (ISBN 0-8170-0639-7). Judson.

Keup, Wolfram, ed. Drug Abuse: Current Concepts & Research. (Illus.). 496p. 1972. 27.50 (ISBN 0-398-02331-X). C C Thomas.

Keuren, Dolores Van see Siegel, Murray J. & Van Keuren, Dolores.

Kevan, Larry. Time Domain Electron Spin Resonance. Schwartz, Robert N., ed. LC 78-31128. 1979. 37.50 (ISBN 0-471-03814-8, Pub. by Wiley-Interscience). Wiley.

Kevan, Larry & Kispert, Lowell D. Electron Spin Double Resonance Spectroscopy. LC 75-44418. 380p. 1976. 37.50 (ISBN 0-471-47340-5, Pub. by Wiley-Interscience). Wiley.

Kevane, Eugene. Creed & Catechetics. 1978. lib. bdg. 12.50 o.p. (ISBN 0-87061-007-4); pap. text ed. 7.95 o.p. (ISBN 0-685-03667-7). Chr Classics.

Kevorkian, George. Business Mathematics. (Business and Economics Ser.). 288p. 1976. text ed. 14.95 (ISBN 0-675-08587-X); wkbk. 6.95 (ISBN 0-675-08586-1); instructor's manual 3.95 (ISBN 0-686-67425-1). Merrill.

Kevorkian, J. & Cole, J. D. Perturbation Methods in Applied Mathematics. (Applied Mathematical Sciences Ser.: Vol. 34). (Illus.). 512p. 1981. 42.00 (ISBN 0-387-90507-3). Springer-Verlag.

Kewley, T. H., ed. Australian Social Security Today. 248p. 1980. 22.50x (ISBN 0-424-00067-9, Pub. by Sydney U Pr Australia). Intl Schol Bk Serv.

Key, Alexander. Case of the Vanishing Boy. (gr. 5-7). 1979. pap. 1.75 (ISBN 0-671-56006-9). PB.

--Escape to Witch Mountain. (gr. 5-7). 1975. pap. 1.95 (ISBN 0-671-42453-X). Archway.

--Return from Witchmountain. (gr. 5-7). 1978. pap. 1.75 (ISBN 0-671-56073-5). PB.

Key, Bernard, jt. auth. see Ohkawa, Kazushi.

Key, Bernard, jt. ed. see Ohkawa, Kazushi.

Key, Betty M. Maryland Manual of Oral History. 1979. 2.00 (ISBN 0-938420-11-9). Md Hist.

Key, Della T. In the Cattle Country: History of Potter County, 1887-1966. 11.95 (ISBN 0-685-48805-5). Nortex Pr.

Key, Ellen. War, Peace, & the Future. LC 78-147728. (Library of War & Peace; the Character & Causes of War). lib. bdg. 38.00 (ISBN 0-8240-0507-4). Garland Pub.

Key, Eugene. Principles of Electricity for Students of Physics & Engineering. (Orig.). 1967. pap. 4.50 (ISBN 0-06-460118-8, CO 118, COS). Har-Row.

Key, Francis S. Star-Spangled Banner. LC 66-14940. (Illus.). (gr. 3 up). 1966. 7.95 o.p. (ISBN 0-690-77281-5, TYC-J). T Y Crowell.

Key, Mary R. Male-Female Language: With a Comprehensive Bibliography. LC 74-19105. (Illus.). 1975. 10.00 (ISBN 0-8108-0748-3). Scarecrow.

--Nonverbal Communication: A Research Guide & Bibliography. LC 76-53024. 1977. lib. bdg. 21.00 (ISBN 0-8108-1014-X). Scarecrow.

--Paralanguage & Kinesics: Nonverbal Communication with a Bibliography. LC 74-30217. 1975. 10.00 (ISBN 0-8108-0789-0). Scarecrow.

Key, Mary R., ed. The Relationship of Verbal & Non-Verbal Communication. (Contributions to the Sociology of Language: No. 25). 1980. text ed. 41.25x (ISBN 90-279-7878-6); pap. text ed. 12.50x (ISBN 90-279-7637-6). Mouton.

Key, Maude D. Grandmother's Amazing Housekeeping Secrets. 2nd ed. 91p. 1968. pap. 3.50 (ISBN 0-917420-01-2). Buck Hill.

Key, Ted. The Cat from Outer Space. (gr. 5-7). pap. 1.75 (ISBN 0-671-56106-5). Archway.

Key, Wilson B. The Clam Plate Orgy & Other Subliminal Techniques for Manipulating Your Behavior. (Illus.). 1981. pap. 2.95 (ISBN 0-686-69108-3, E9723, Sig). NAL.

Keydell, Rudolfus, ed. see Agathias.

Keyder, Caglar, jt. auth. see O'Brien, Patrick.

Keyes, Charles F., ed. Ethnic Change. LC 80-54426. (Publications on Ethnicity & Nationality of the School of International Studies: No. 2). 306p. 1981. 20.00 (ISBN 0-295-95812-X). U of Wash Pr.

Keyes, D. D. Four Types of Value Destruction: A Search for the Good Through an Ethical Analysis of Everyday Experience. 1978. pap. text ed. 7.00x (ISBN 0-8191-0395-0). U Pr of Amer.

Keyes, Daniel. Flowers for Algernon. LC 66-12366. 1966. 12.95 (ISBN 0-15-131510-8). HarBraceJ.

--Flowers for Algernon. (Amsco Literature Ser.). 1969. pap. text ed. 3.92 (ISBN 0-87720-751-8). AMSCO Sch.

Keyes, Fenton. Exploring Careers for the Gifted. (Careers in Depth Ser.). (Illus.). 160p. (gr. 7-12). 1981. lib. bdg. 5.97 (ISBN 0-8239-0533-0). Rosen Pr.

Keyes, Frances P. The Heritage. 1977. pap. 1.75 o.p. (ISBN 0-449-23236-0, Crest). Fawcett.

--Madame Castel's Lodger. 1977. pap. 1.95 o.p. (ISBN 0-449-23288-3, Crest). Fawcett.

Keyes, Jane. The Frozen Hors D'oeuvre Cookbook: You've Got It Made. (Illus.). 224p. 1980. 12.95 (ISBN 0-8038-8602-0). Hastings.

Keyes, Karl, ed. Pressworking: Stampings & Dies. LC 80-53009. (Manufacturing Update Ser.). (Illus.). 260p. 1980. 29.00 (ISBN 0-87263-061-7). SME.

Keyes, Ken, Jr. Prescriptions for Happiness. LC 80-84855. (Illus.). 132p. 1981. pap. 2.00 (ISBN 0-915972-02-6); pocketbook edition 0.95 (ISBN 0-915972-03-4). Living Love.

--Taming Your Mind. LC 75-4297. Orig. Title: How to Develop Your Thinking Ability. (Illus.). 264p. (Orig.). 1975. 5.95 (ISBN 0-9600688-7-2). Living Love.

Keyes, Ken, Jr. & Burkan, Bruce. How to Make Your Life Work. 1976. pap. 3.95 (ISBN 0-346-12226-0). Cornerstone.

Keyes, Ken, Jr. & Burkan, Bruce T. How to Make Your Life Work, or Why Aren't You Happy? LC 74-76803. (Illus.). 192p. 1974. pap. 2.00 (ISBN 0-9600688-5-6). Living Love.

Keyes, Kenneth S., Jr. How to Live Longer, Stronger, Slimmer. 1966. 7.95 o.p. (ISBN 0-8119-0093-2). Fell.

Keyes, Laurel E. Toning: The Creative Power of the Voice. rev. ed. LC 73-86021. 88p. 1973. pap. 3.95 (ISBN 0-87516-176-6). De Vorss.

Keyes, Lucille S. Regulatory Reform in Air Cargo Transportation. 1980. pap. 4.25 (ISBN 0-8447-3371-7). Am Enterprise.

Keyes, Margaret F. Inward Journey: Art As Therapy for You. LC 74-10070. (Illus.). 1974. pap. 4.95 o.p. (ISBN 0-912310-81-2). Celestial Arts.

Keyes, Nelson B. El Fascinante Mundo De la Biblia. Orig. Title: Story of the Bible World. (Illus.). 216p. (Span.). 1980. 15.95 (ISBN 0-311-03664-3, Edit Mundo); pap. 11.95 (ISBN 0-311-03665-1, Edit Mundo). Casa Bautista.

Keyes, R. J., ed. Optical & Infrared Detectors. 2nd ed. (Topics in Applied Physics Ser.: Vol. 19). (Illus.). 325p. 1981. pap. 24.80 (ISBN 0-387-10176-4). Springer-Verlag.

--Optical & Infrared Detectors. LC 77-7309. (Topics in Applied Physics Ser.: Vol. 19). (Illus.). 1977. 45.80 o.p. (ISBN 0-387-08209-3). Springer-Verlag.

Keyes, Roger & Kuwayama, George. The Bizarre Imagery of Yoshitoshi: The Herbert R. Cole Collection. LC 80-15938. (Illus.). 112p. (Orig.). 1980. pap. 10.00 (ISBN 0-87587-096-1). La Co Art Mus.

Keyes, Ruth & Cushman, Ronald. Essentials of Retailing. LC 76-55081. (Illus.). 1977. text ed. 13.95 (ISBN 0-87005-183-0). Fairchild.

Keyes, Sharrel, jt. auth. see Fromer, Margaret.

Keyfitz, Nathan. Applied Mathematical Demography. LC 77-1360. 1977. 28.95 (ISBN 0-471-47350-2, Pub. by Wiley-Interscience). Wiley.

Keyfitz, Nathan & Flieger, Wilhelm. Population: Facts & Methods of Demography. LC 70-141154. (Illus.). 1971. text ed. 33.95x (ISBN 0-7167-0931-7). W H Freeman.

Keyfitz, Nathan C. Introduction to the Mathematics of Population - with Revisions. LC 76-17718. 496p. 1977. 23.95 (ISBN 0-201-03649-5). A-W.

Keyishian, Harry. Michael Arlen. (English Author Ser.: No. 174). 1975. lib. bdg. 9.95 (ISBN 0-8057-1011-6). Twayne.

Keylin, Arleen & Cohen, Jonathan, eds. The Forties as Reported by the New York Times. LC 80-13897. (Illus.). 1980. lib. bdg. 9.98x (ISBN 0-405-12214-4). Arno.

Keylin, Arlene & Bowen, Douglas J., eds. The New York Times Book of the Civil War. LC 80-7799. (Illus.). 1980. lib. bdg. 12.98x (ISBN 0-405-13396-0). Arno.

Keynes, Darwin R., ed. The Beagle Record. LC 77-82500. (Illus.). 1979. 79.00 (ISBN 0-521-21822-5). Cambridge U Pr.

Keynes, Geoffrey. A Bibliography of George Berkeley, Bishop of Cloyne: His Work & His Critics in the Eighteenth Century. (Soho Bibliography Ser.). 1976. 25.00x (ISBN 0-19-818161-2). U of Pittsburgh Pr.

Keynes, Geoffrey, ed. Edward Gibbon's Library: A Catolgue. (Illus.). 288p. 1980. Repr. of 1940 ed. 30.00x (ISBN 0-906795-02-8). U Pr of Va.

--Hazlitt: Selected Essays. (The Nonesuch Library). 1978. 11.95 (ISBN 0-370-00511-2, Pub. by Chatto Bodley Jonathan). Merrimack Bk Serv.

Keynes, Geoffrey & Blake, William, eds. The Letters of William Blake with Related Documents. 3rd ed. (Illus.). 272p. 1980. 55.00x (ISBN 0-19-812654-9). Oxford U Pr.

Keynes, Geoffrey, ed. see Blake, William.

Keynes, John M. The Collected Writings, 23 vols. Incl. Vol. 1. Indian Currency & Finance. 184p. 1971. Repr. of 1913 ed (ISBN 0-521-22093-9); Vol. 2. The Economic Consequences of the Peace. LC 76-133449. 192p. 1971. Repr. of 1919 ed; Vol. 3. Revision of the Treaty. LC 76-133449. 158p. 1972 (ISBN 0-521-22095-5); Vol. 4. Tract on Monetary Reform. LC 76-133449. 172p. 1972 (ISBN 0-521-22096-3); Vol. 5. Pt. 1. Treatise on Money, the Pure Theory of Money. 336p. 1972 (ISBN 0-521-22097-1); Vol. 6, Pt.2. Treatise on Money, the Applied Theory of Money. 390p. 1972 (ISBN 0-521-22098-X); Vol. 7. The General Theory of Employment, Interest, & Money. 428p. 1973 (ISBN 0-521-22099-8). pap. 5.95 (ISBN 0-521-29382-0); Vol. 8. Treatise on Probability. 514p. 1972 (ISBN 0-312-31885-5); Vol. 9. Essays & Persuasions. 451p. 1972 (ISBN 0-312-26355-4); Vol. 10. Essays in Biography. 460p. 1972 (ISBN 0-521-22102-1); Vol. 13. The General Theory & After, Pt. One: Preparation. 653p. 1973 (ISBN 0-521-22103-X); Vol. 14. **The General Theory & After, Pt. Two: Defence & Development. 584p. 1973 (ISBN 0-521-22104-8); Vol. 15. Activities: Nineteen-Six to Nineteen-Fourteen: India & Cambridge. 312p. 1971 (ISBN 0-521-22105-6); Vol. 16. Activities, Nineteen-Fourteen to Nineteen-Nineteen: The Treasury & Versailles. 488p. 1971 (ISBN 0-521-22106-4); Vol. 17. Activities Nineteen Twenty to Twenty-Two: Treaty Revision & Reconstruction. 1978 (ISBN 0-521-21874-8); Vol. 18. Activities Nineteen Twenty-Two to Thirty-Two: The End of Reparations. 1978 (ISBN 0-521-21875-6); Vol. 19. Activities Nineteen Thirty-Nine to Forty-Five: Internal War Finance. 519p. 1978 (ISBN 0-521-21876-4); Vol. 20. Activities Nineteen Forty to Forty-Three: External War Finance. 330p. 1979 (ISBN 0-521-22016-5); Vol. 21. Activities Nineteen Forty-Four to Forty-Six: The Transition to Peace. 688p. 1979 (ISBN 0-521-22017-3); Vol. 22. Activities Nineteen Forty-Three to Forty-Six: Shaping the Post War World: the Clearing Union (ISBN 0-521-22018-1); Vol. 23. Activities Nineteen Forty-Three to Forty-Six: Shaping the Postwar World: Bretton Woods & Reparations. 368p. 1980 (ISBN 0-521-22934-0); Vol. 24. Activities Nineteen Forty to Forty-Six: Shaping the Post-War World: Employment & Commodities (ISBN 0-521-23074-8); General Theory & After: A Supplement. 309p. 1979 (ISBN 0-521-22949-9). 42.50 ea. Cambridge U Pr.**

--The Collected Writings of John Maynard Keynes: The General Theory & After - A Supplement, Vol. 29. Moggridge, D., ed. LC 76-13349. 1980. 42.50 (ISBN 0-521-22949-9). Cambridge U Pr.

--The Collected Writings of John Maynard Keynes, Vol. 25, Activities 1940-44: Shaping the Postwar World: The Clearing Union. Moggridge, D., ed. LC 76-13349. 360p. 1980. 42.50 (ISBN 0-521-22018-1). Cambridge U Pr.

--The Collected Writings of John Maynard Keynes, Vol. 27, Activities 1940-46: Shaping the Postwar World: Employment & Commodities. Moggridge, D., ed. LC 76-13349. 424p. 1980. 42.50 (ISBN 0-521-23074-8). Cambridge U Pr.

--The Collected Writings of John Maynard Keynes, Vol. 26, Activities 1943-46: Shaping the Postwar World: Bretton Woods & Reparations. Moggridge, D., ed. LC 76-13349. 1980. 42.50 (ISBN 0-521-22939-1). Cambridge U Pr.

Keynes, John M., et al. The Kress Library of Business & Economics. (Kress Library of Business & Economics: No. 1). 1939. pap. 5.00x (ISBN 0-678-09900-6, Baker Lib). Kelley.

Keynes, M., ed. Essays on John Maynard Keynes. LC 74-12975. (Illus.). 304p. 1975. 38.50 (ISBN 0-521-20534-4). Cambridge U Pr.

Keynes, Milo, ed. Essays on John Maynard Keynes. LC 74-12975. (Illus.). 1980. pap. 11.95 (ISBN 0-521-29696-X). Cambridge U Pr.

Keynes, Simon. The Diplomas of King Aethelred 'the Unready' 978 to 1016. LC 79-7651. (Studies in Medieval Life & Thought Ser.: No. 13). (Illus.). 1980. 42.50 (ISBN 0-521-22718-6). Cambridge U Pr.

Keyon, Rostam. Being & Alienation. LC 78-61109. 350p. 1981. 10.00 (ISBN 0-686-69333-7). Philos Lib.

Keys, Donald, jt. ed. see Laszlo, Ervin.

Keys, Ivor C. Texture of Music: From Purcell to Brahms. (Illus.). 1961. 6.95 (ISBN 0-234-77414-2). Dufour.

Keys, J. Bernard, jt. auth. see Scanlan, Burt.

Keys, Thomas E. Classics in Cardiology. 1981. Vol. 3. write for info. Krieger.

Keys, William J. & Cashman, Thomas J. Introduction to Computer Programming - Basic Fortran IV: A Practical Approach. (Illus.). 1972. pap. text ed. 10.95x (ISBN 0-88236-151-1). Anaheim Pub Co.

Keys, William J., jt. auth. see Cashman, Thomas J.

Keysell, Pat. Mime Themes & Motifs. (Illus.). 80p. 80. Repr. of 1975 ed. 9.95 (ISBN 0-8238-0245-0). Plays.

Keyser. Materials Science in Engineering. 3rd ed. (Engineering Ser.). 488p. 1980. text ed. 20.95 (ISBN 0-675-08182-3). Merrill.

Keyser, J. W. Human Plasma Proteins: Their Investigation in Pathological Conditions. LC 79-1089. 1979. 60.00 (ISBN 0-471-27598-0, Pub. by Wiley-Interscience). Wiley.

Keyser, Les. Hollywood in the Seventies. LC 78-75313. (Illus.). 172p. 1981. pap. 5.95 (ISBN 0-498-02545-4). A S Barnes.

Keyserling, Leon H. Liberal & Conservative National Economic Policies & Their Consequences, 1919-79. (Illus.). 1979. 3.00. Conf Econ Prog.

Keyserling, Leon H. & Conference of Economic Staff. Money, Credit, & Interest Rates: Their Gross Mismanagement by the Federal Reserve System. (Illus.). 1980. 3.00. Conf Econ Prog.

Keyserlingk, Robert H. Media Manipulation: A Study of the Press & Bismarck in Imperial Germany. 1977. pap. text ed. 8.00x o.p. (ISBN 0-685-87413-3). Renouf.

Keysor, Charles W. Come Clean. 128p. 1976. pap. 1.75 o.p. (ISBN 0-88207-732-5). Victor Bks.

--Forgiveness Is a Two-Way Street. 132p. 1981. pap. 3.95 (ISBN 0-88207-338-9). Victor Bks.

Keysor, Charles W., ed. What You Should Know About Homosexuality. pap. 6.95 (ISBN 0-310-38231-9). Zondervan.

Keysser, Christian. A People Reborn. Allin, Alfred & Kuder, John, trs. from Ger. LC 79-23623. 306p. (Orig.). 1980. pap. 9.95x (ISBN 0-87808-174-7). William Carey Lib.

Keyt, G., tr. see Jayadeva.

Keyt, George, tr. Song of Love. Orig. Title: Gita Govinda. 123p. 1969. pap. 2.00 (ISBN 0-88253-048-8). Ind-US Inc.

Keyzer, P., jt. auth. see Voogel, E.

Kezdi, P., ed. Baroreceptors & Hypertension. 1967. 67.00 (ISBN 0-08-012488-7). Pergamon.

Kezer, Glenn. The Queen Is Dead. (Orig.). 1979. pap. 1.75 o.s.i. (ISBN 0-515-04856-9). Jove Pubns.

Kezys, A., ed. A Lithuanian Cemetery. LC 75-21496. 1977. 19.95 (ISBN 0-8294-0279-9). Loyola.

Khabarova, A. Y. The Afferent Innervation of the Heart. LC 62-15548. 175p. 1963. 25.00 (ISBN 0-306-10656-6, Consultants). Plenum Pub.

Khabaza, I. M. Numerical Analysis. 1965. text ed. 25.00 (ISBN 0-08-010776-1); pap. text ed. 12.75 (ISBN 0-08-010775-3). Pergamon.

Khachaturov, T. S., ed. Methods of Long Term Planning & Forecasting. (International Economic Association Ser). 1976. 69.95 (ISBN 0-470-47368-1). Halsted Pr.

Khadduri, Majid. Independent Iraq, Nineteen Thirty-Two to Nineteen Fifty-Eight: A Study in Iraqi Politics. 2nd ed. LC 80-1919. 1981. Repr. of 1960 ed. 41.50 (ISBN 0-404-18972-5). AMS Pr.

--Law of War & Peace in Islam: A Study of Moslem International Law. LC 76-147599. (Library of War & Peace; International Law). lib. bdg. 38.00 (ISBN 0-8240-0360-8). Garland Pub.

--Republican Iraq: A Study in Iraqi Politics Since the Revolution of 1958. LC 80-1923. 1981. Repr. of 1969 ed. 37.00 (ISBN 0-404-18973-3). AMS Pr.

Khadduri, Majid & Liebesny, Herbert J., eds. Law in the Middle East: Origin & Development of Islamic Law, Vol. 1. LC 80-1921. 1981. Repr. of 1955 ed. 41.50 (ISBN 0-404-18974-1). AMS Pr.

Khailany, A. Business Programming in FORTRAN VI & ANSI FORTRAN: A Structured Approach. 1981. pap. 12.95 (ISBN 0-13-107607-8). P-H.

Khailany, Asad & Duplissey, Claude. Cobol for Small & Medium Sized Computers. LC 75-23647. (Illus.). 400p. 1976. pap. text ed. 15.25 (ISBN 0-395-18921-7). HM.

Khaing, Mi Mi. Cook & Entertain the Burmese Way. 12.95 (ISBN 0-89720-017-9). Green Hill.

Khairallah. This Is Lebanon. 5.95 (ISBN 0-686-65476-5). Intl Bk Ctr.

Khairallah, Shereen. Lebanon. (World Bibliographical Ser.: No. 2). 154p. 1979. 25.25 (ISBN 0-903450-10-0). ABC-Clio.

Khalatnikov, I. M. Physics Reviews Vol.III. (Soviet Scientific Reviews Ser.). 484p. 1980. 98.00 (ISBN 0-686-69597-6). Harwood Academic.

Khalatnikov, I. M., ed. Soviet Scientific Reviews: Physics Reviews, Vol. 1, Section A. 322p. 1979. lib. bdg. 67.75 (ISBN 3-7186-0004-8). Harwood Academic.

--Soviet Scientific Reviews: Physics Reviews, Vol. 2, Section A. 400p. 1980. lib. bdg. 98.00 (ISBN 0-686-65836-1). Harwood Academic.

Khalifa, Ali M. The United Arab Emirates: Unity in Fragmentation. (Special Studies on the Middle East). 1979. lib. bdg. 26.00x (ISBN 0-89158-394-7). Westview.

Khalil, ed. Flow, Mixing & Heat Transfer in Furnaces. 1978. 45.00 (ISBN 0-08-022695-7). Pergamon.

Khan, Arfa. Oblique Tomography. 1981. write for info. (ISBN 0-87527-219-3). Green.

Khan, Hazrat I. Gayan, Vadan, Nirtan. LC 80-52801. (The Collected Works of Hazrat Inayat Khan Ser.). 304p. 1980. 10.00 (ISBN 0-930872-21-5, 1006H); pap. 5.95 (ISBN 0-930872-16-9, 1006P). Sufi Order Pubns.

--Mastery Through Accomplishment. LC 79-101639. (The Collected Works of Hazrat Inayat Khan Ser.). 320p. 1978. 8.95 (ISBN 0-930872-06-1); pap. 5.95 (ISBN 0-930872-07-X). Sufi Order Pubns.

--The Soul Whence & Whither. LC 77-15697. (The Collected Works of Hazrat Inayat Khan Ser.). 190p. 1977. 6.95 o.p. (ISBN 0-930872-00-2); pap. 4.95 (ISBN 0-930872-01-0). Sufi Order Pubns.

--Tales Told by Hazrat Inayat Khan. LC 80-52548. (The Collected Works of Hazrat Inayat Khan). (Illus.). 288p. (Orig.). 1980. pap. 7.95 (ISBN 0-930872-15-0). Sufi Order Pubns.

--The Unity of Religious Ideals. (The Collected Works of Hazrat Inayat Khan Ser.). 264p. 1979. 8.95 (ISBN 0-930872-09-6); pap. 5.95 (ISBN 0-930872-10-X). Sufi Order Pubns.

Khan, Inayat. The Alchemy of Happiness. (Sufi Message of Hazrat Inayat Khan Ser.: Vol. 6). 1979. 6.95 (ISBN 90-6077-953-3, Pub. by Servire BV Netherlands). Hunter Hse.

--The Art of Personality. (Sufi Message of Hazrat Inayat Khan Ser.: Vol. 3). 1979. 6.95 (ISBN 90-6077-570-8, Pub. by Servire BV Netherlands). Hunter Hse.

--The Complete Sayings of Hazrat Inayat Khan. LC 77-94684. (The Collected Works of Hazrat Inayat Khan Ser.). 299p. 1978. 7.95 (ISBN 0-930872-02-9). Sufi Order Pubns.

--Healing & the Mind World. (Sufi Message of Hazrat Inayat Khan Ser.: Vol. 4). 1979. 6.95 (ISBN 90-6077-952-5, Pub. by Servire BV Netherlands). Hunter Hse.

--In an Eastern Rose Garden. (Sufi Message of Hazrat Inayat Khan Ser.: Vol. 7). 1979. 6.95 (ISBN 90-6325-096-7, Pub. by Servire BV Netherlands). Hunter Hse.

--The Inner Life. (Sufi Message of Hazrat Inayat Khan Ser.: Vol. 1). 1979. 6.95 (ISBN 90-6325-094-0, Pub. by Servire BV Netherlands). Hunter Hse.

--The Mysticism of Sound. (Sufi Message of Hazrat Inayat Khan Ser.: Vol. 2). 1979. 6.95 (ISBN 90-6077-569-4, Pub. by Servire BV Netherlands). Hunter Hse.

--The Path of Initiation. (Sufi Message of Hazrat Inayat Khan Ser.: Vol. 10). 1979. 6.95 (ISBN 90-6325-098-3, Pub. by Servire BV Netherlands). Hunter Hse.

--Philosophy, Psychology & Mysticism. (Sufi Message of Hazrat Inayat Khan Ser.: Vol. 11). 1979. 6.95 (ISBN 90-6325-099-1, Pub. by Servire BV Netherlands). Hunter Hse.

--Spiritual Liberty. (Sufi Message of Hazrat Inayat Khan Ser.: Vol. 5). 1979. 6.95 (ISBN 90-6325-095-9, Pub. by Servire BV Netherlands). Hunter Hse.

--Sufi Teachings. (Sufi Message of Hazrat Inayat Khan Ser.: Vol. 8). 1979. 6.95 (ISBN 90-6077-954-1, Pub. by Servire BV Netherlands). Hunter Hse.

--The Unity of Religious Ideals. (Sufi Message of Hazrat Inayat Khan Ser.: Vol. 9). 1979. 6.95 (ISBN 90-6325-097-5, Pub. by Servire BV Netherlands). Hunter Hse.

--The Vision of God & Man. (Sufi Message of Hazrat Inayat Khan Ser.: Vol. 12). 1979. 6.95 (ISBN 90-6325-100-9, Pub. by Servire BV Netherlands). Hunter Hse.

Khan, M. A. Sociological Aspects of Child Development: A Study of Rural Karnataka. 212p. 1980. text ed. 15.75x (ISBN 0-391-02127-3). Humanities.

Khan, M. A. & Matthews, B. Global Geology. LC 75-38616. (Wykeham Science Ser.: No. 41). 1976. 8.60x (ISBN 0-8448-1168-8). Crane Russak Co.

Khan, M. A., jt. auth. see Advanced Study Institute on Toxicity of Pesticides Used on Livestock, Lethbridge, 13-21 July, 1970.

Khan, M. E. & Prasad, C. V. Fertility Control in India. 1980. 14.00x (ISBN 0-8364-0628-1, Pub. by Manohar India). South Asia Bks.

--People's Perception About Family Planning: A Study of Andhra Pradesh & Bihar. 156p. 1980. text ed. 10.00x (ISBN 0-391-02131-1). Humanities.

Khan, M. M. & Martell, Arthur E. Homogeneous Catalysis by Metal Complexes, 2 vols. Incl. Vol. 1. Activation of Small Inorganic Molecules. 58.50 (ISBN 0-12-406101-X); Vol. 2. Activation of Alkenes & Alkynes. 38.00 (ISBN 0-12-406102-8). 1974. 78.50 set (ISBN 0-685-72440-9). Acad Pr.

Khan, M. Y. Indian Financial System. LC 80-904855. 464p. 1980. text ed. 27.50x (ISBN 0-7069-1101-6, Pub. by Vikas India). Advent Bk.

Khan, Mahmood H. The Economics of the Green Revolution in Pakistan. LC 75-19796. (Special Studies). (Illus.). 320p. 1975. text ed. 26.95 (ISBN 0-275-55680-8). Praeger.

--Underdevelopment & Agrarian Structure in Pakistan. (Replica Edition Ser.). 275p. 1981. lib. bdg. 20.00x (ISBN 0-86531-134-X). Westview.

Khan, Muhammad Z. Muhammad: Seal of the Prophets. 400p. 1980. pap. 12.50 (ISBN 0-7100-0610-1). Routledge & Kegan.

Khan, Noor I. Twenty Jataka Tales. (Illus.). 1978. 8.95; pap. 5.95 (ISBN 0-87773-747-9). Great Eastern.

Khan, Pir V. Toward the One. (Orig.). 1974. pap. 10.00 o.p. (ISBN 0-06-090352-X, CN352, CN). Har-Row.

Khan, Rais A., et al. An Introduction to Political Science. rev. ed. 1977. text ed. 14.95x (ISBN 0-256-01785-9). Dorsey.

Khan, S. U., jt. auth. see Backris, J. O'M.

Khanin, Ya, jt. auth. see Fain, V. M.

Khanna, J. L. Brain Damage & Mental Retardation: A Psychological Evaluation. 2nd ed. (Illus.). 232p. 1973. 12.75 (ISBN 0-398-02631-9). C C Thomas.

Khanna, J. L. & Khanna, Prabha. Sensitivity Training for Educators: An Evaluation. 1981. 7.95 (ISBN 0-533-04031-0). Vantage.

Khanna, J. L., ed. New Treatment Approaches to Juvenile Delinquency. (Illus.). 164p. 1975. 15.75 (ISBN 0-398-03184-3). C C Thomas.

Khanna, K. M. Statistical Mechanics. 15.00x (ISBN 0-210-27151-5). Asia.

Khanna, N. Miracle of Democracy in India. 124p. 1980. 4.50x (ISBN 0-89955-319-2, Pub. by Interprint India). Intl Schol Bk Serv.

Khanna, Prabha, jt. auth. see Khanna, J. L.

Khanna, V. K., jt. auth. see Zameeruddin, Qazi.

Khanolkar, Nishi. Dwasuparna: A Novel in Two Parts, 2 vols, Vol. 1. (Greenbird Bk.). 1976. Set. text ed. 24.00 (ISBN 0-89253-120-7); flexible bdg. 13.50 (ISBN 0-89253-136-3). Ind-US Inc.

Khantrouni, Dicran, jt. auth. see Koushakdjian, Mardiros.

Kharasch, Norman, ed. Trace Metals in Health & Disease: Conference Proceedings, Santa Monica, California, Nov-Dec., 1978. 1979. 32.00 (ISBN 0-89004-389-2). Raven.

Kharasch, Robert N. Institutional Imperative. LC 72-95169. 1979. pap. 7.95x (ISBN 0-582-28106-7). Longman.

--The Institutional Imperative. LC 72-95169. 1973. pap. 7.95x o.p. (ISBN 0-88327-039-0, Pub by McKay). Longman.

Kharkevich, D. A., ed. Pharmacology of Ganglionic Transmission. LC 79-9406. (Handbook of Experimental Pharmacology: Vol. 53). (Illus.). 1980. 134.75 (ISBN 0-387-09592-6). Springer-Verlag.

Khatchadourian, Haig. The Concept of Art. LC 70-145512. 1971. 17.50x (ISBN 0-8147-4553-9). NYU Pr.

Khatib, A. English-Arabic Dictionary of Petroleum Terms & the Oil Industry. (Illus.). 1975. 40.00x (ISBN 0-685-72036-5). Intl Bk Ctr.

--English-Arabic Dictionary of Scientific & Technical Terms. (Illus.). 1974. 40.00x (ISBN 0-685-82821-2). Intl Bk Ctr.

Khatib, A., ed. see Chihabi.

Khatib, Ahmad. Arabic-English Dictionary of Agricultural Terms. pap. 10.00x (ISBN 0-685-89876-8). Intl Bk Ctr.

--Chihabi's Dictionary of Agricultural & Forestry Terms: English-Arabic. 1978. 40.00x. Intl Bk Ctr.

--Dictionary of the Natural Environment: English-Arabic. 1979. pap. 5.95. Intl Bk Ctr.

Khatkhate, Deena R., Jr., jt. ed. see Coats, Warren L.

Khattab, Ezzat A. The Critical Reception of Browning's The Ring & the Book, 1868-89,1951-68. (Salzburg Studies in English Literature: Romantic Reassessment Ser.: No. 66). (Orig.). 1977. pap. text ed. 25.00x (ISBN 0-391-01444-7). Humanities.

Khayat, Marie. Food from the Arab World. pap. 5.00x (ISBN 0-686-63568-X). Intl Bk Ctr.

--Lebanon, Land of the Cedars. 8.50x (ISBN 0-686-65475-7). Intl Bk Ctr.

Khayyam, Omar. Rubaiyat of Omar Khayyam. Fitzgerald, Edward, tr. (Illus.). 1930. pap. 2.50 (ISBN 0-385-09499-X, C28, Dolp). Doubleday.

--Rubaiyat of Omar Khayyam. Fitzgerald, Edward, tr. (Illus.). pap. 2.00 (ISBN 0-8283-1452-7, 12, IPL). Branden.

Khera, Sucha S. Management & Control in Public Enterprise. 1972. pap. 4.95 o.p. (ISBN 0-210-27109-4). Asia.

Kherdian, David. Any Day of Your Life. LC 75-4381. 64p. 1975. 10.00 (ISBN 0-87951-034-X); ltd. ed. 15.00 (ISBN 0-685-53416-2). Overlook Pr.

--Any Day of Your Life. LC 75-4381. 1977. pap. 5.95 (ISBN 0-87951-062-5). Overlook Pr.

--The Farm. LC 79-64355. 1979. 6.95 (ISBN 0-89756-026-4). Two Rivers.

--Finding Home. LC 80-22805. 256p. (gr. 7 up). 1981. 8.95 (ISBN 0-688-00400-8); PLB 8.59 (ISBN 0-688-00401-6). Greenwillow.

--I Remember Root River. LC 77-80201. 72p. Date not set. pap. 6.95 (ISBN 0-87951-127-3). Overlook Pr.

--I Remember Root River. LC 77-80201. 72p. 1978. 10.00 (ISBN 0-87951-065-X). Overlook Pr.

--The Nonny Poems. LC 73-11832. 64p. 1974. 4.95 o.s.i. (ISBN 0-02-562990-5). Macmillan.

--Road from Home: The Story of an Armenian Childhood. LC 78-72511. (gr. 7 up). 1979. 9.50 (ISBN 0-688-80205-2); PLB 9.12 (ISBN 0-688-84205-4). Greenwillow.

--Taking the Soundings on Third Avenue. LC 80-14276. 64p. 1980. 10.00 (ISBN 0-87951-116-8); limited & signed deluxe ed. 35.00 (ISBN 0-87951-119-2). Overlook Pr.

Kherdian, David, ed. I Sing the Song of Myself: An Anthology of Autobiographical Poems. LC 78-5807. (gr. 7-9). 1978. 8.95 (ISBN 0-688-80172-2); PLB 8.59 (ISBN 0-688-84172-4). Greenwillow.

--If Dragon Flies Made Honey: Poems. LC 77-3730. (Illus.). (gr. 1-5). 1977. 8.25 (ISBN 0-688-80101-3); PLB 7.92 (ISBN 0-688-84101-5). Greenwillow.

--Settling America: The Ethnic Expression of Fourteen Contemporary Poets. LC 73-19066. 144p. (gr. 7 up). 1974. 8.95 (ISBN 0-02-750240-6). Macmillan.

--Traveling America with Today's Poets. LC 76-47535. (gr. 7 up). 1977. 9.95 (ISBN 0-02-750260-0, 75026). Macmillan.

--Visions of America: By the Poets of Our Time. LC 72-81067. (Illus.). 96p. (gr. 7 up). 1973. 8.95 (ISBN 0-02-750250-3). Macmillan.

Khin, Yvonne M. The Collector's Dicionary of Quilt Names & Patterns. 1980. 29.50 (ISBN 0-87491-408-6); pap. 16.95 (ISBN 0-87491-409-4). Acropolis.

Khinchin, Alexander I. Mathematical Foundations of Information Theory. 1957. pap. text ed. 2.50 (ISBN 0-486-60434-9). Dover.

--Mathematical Foundations of Statistical Mechanics. Gamow, George, tr. 1949. pap. text ed. 3.00 (ISBN 0-486-60147-1). Dover.

Khinchin, Alexander Y., jt. auth. see Gnedenko, Boris V.

Khleif, Bud B. Language, Ethnicity, & Education in Wales. (Contributions to the Sociology of Language Ser.: No. 28). 1979. text ed. 50.00x (ISBN 90-279-7898-0). Mouton.

Khodasevich, Vladislav. Iz Evreskikh Poetov. (Rus.). 1981. 10.50 (ISBN 0-88233-412-3); pap. 3.50 (ISBN 0-686-66059-5). Ardis Pubs.

--Stat'i O Literature. 124p. (Rus.). 1981. 11.50 (ISBN 0-88233-408-5); pap. 3.75 (ISBN 0-88233-409-3). Ardis Pubs.

--Tiazhelia Lira. 1975. pap. 10.00 (ISBN 0-88233-192-2). Ardis Pubs.
Khodorovich, T., ed. The Case of Leonid Plyushch. LC 76-6094. 1976. 18.50x (ISBN 0-89158-600-8). Westview.
Khokar, Mohan. Traditions of Indian Classical Dance. (Illus.). 1980. text ed. 23.25x (ISBN 0-7206-0574-1). Humanities.
Khomiakov, Aleksiei S. L' Eglise Latine et le Protestantisme, Au Point De Vue De l'Eglise d'Orient. LC 80-2362. 1981. Repr. of 1872 ed. 49.00 (ISBN 0-404-18908-3). AMS Pr.
Khomskaia. Brain & Activation. (National Library of Medicine Ser.). 380p. Date not set. text ed. 18.50 (ISBN 0-08-025993-6). Pergamon.
Khopkar, M. B., compiled by. Dictionary of Political Terminology. 1970. pap. 2.75 (ISBN 0-88253-149-2). Ind-US Inc.
Khoshkish, A. The Socio-Political Complex. 1979. 55.00 (ISBN 0-08-023391-0). Pergamon.
Khosla, G. D. Horoscope Cannot Lie & Other Stories. 4.50x o.p. (ISBN 0-210-33991-8). Asia.
--The Last Mughal. 376p. 1969. pap. 2.40 o.p. (ISBN 0-88253-050-X). Ind-US Inc.
--The Murder of the Mahatma & Other Cases from a Judge's Notebook. 276p. 1965. pap. 2.50 (ISBN 0-88253-051-8). Ind-US Inc.
--Never the Twain: A Novel. 177p. 1981. text ed. 15.00x (ISBN 0-7069-1270-5, Pub by Vikas India). Advent Bk.
Khouri, Fred J. Arab-Israeli Dilemma. 2nd ed. LC 68-20483. 1976. pap. 6.95x (ISBN 0-8156-2178-7). Syracuse U Pr.
Khouri, Mounah A. & Algar, Hamid, eds. An Anthology of Modern Arabic Poetry. Khouri, Mounah A. & Algar, Hamid, trs. 1974. 18.50x (ISBN 0-520-02234-3); pap. 3.95 (ISBN 0-520-02898-8). U of Cal Pr.
Khouri, Mounah A., tr. see Khouri, Mounah A. & Algar, Hamid.
Khoury, Sarkis J. Transnational Mergers & Acquisitions in the United States. 1980. 27.95 (ISBN 0-669-03960-8). Lexington Bks.
Khrenov, L. S. Six-Figure Tables of Trigonometric Functions. 1965. 33.00 o.p. (ISBN 0-08-010101-1). Pergamon.
Khul, Djwhal, jt. auth. see Bailey, Alice A.
Khullar, Ajit. In the Mirror. 8.00 (ISBN 0-89253-693-4); flexible cloth 4.80 (ISBN 0-89253-694-2). Ind-US Inc.
Khuri, Fuad I. Tribe & State in Bahrain: The Transformation of Social & Political Authority in an Arab State. LC 80-13528. (Publications of the Center for Middle Eastern Studies: No. 14). (Illus.). 1981. lib. bdg. 16.00x (ISBN 0-226-43473-7). U of Chicago Pr.
Khwaja, I., jt. auth. see Wilby, C. B.
Kiaer, Eigil. Garden Shrubs & Trees in Color. (Color Ser.). (Illus.). 1959. 9.95 (ISBN 0-7137-0649-X, Pub by Blandford Pr England). Sterling.
Kiang. Waste Energy Utilization Technology. 264p. 1981. 29.75 (ISBN 0-8247-1173-4). Dekker.
Kibbe, Doris E; see Bishop, G. Reginald, Jr.
Kibbe, Richard R., et al. Machine Tool Practices. LC 78-18533. 1979. text ed. 25.95x (ISBN 0-471-04331-1); tchrs. manual avail. (ISBN 0-471-05120-9). Wiley.
Kibbie, Dan, jt. auth. see Baker, Jerry.
Kibble, T. W. Classical Mechanics. 2nd ed. LC 73-8910. 254p. 1973. text ed. 19.95 (ISBN 0-470-47395-9). Halsted Pr.
Kibildis, Ralph. Turning Road. 112p. 1981. 1.95 (ISBN 0-914544-34-9). Living Flame Pr.
Kibler, Robert, et al. Objectives for Instruction & Evaluation. 225p. 1980. pap. text ed. 8.95 o.p. (ISBN 0-686-64464-6, 247174-4). Allyn.
Kibler, Robert J., jt. ed. see Barker, Larry L.
Kibler, Robert J, et al. Objectives for Instruction & Evaluation. 228p. 1974. text ed. 11.95x o.p. (ISBN 0-205-04402-6, 2244020); pap. text ed. 6.95x o.s.i. (ISBN 0-205-04399-2). Allyn.
Kibrick, Anne, ed. see Wechsler, Henry.
Kichenside, G. M. Farewell to the Westerns. LC 75-2915. 1975. 13.50 (ISBN 0-7153-7069-3). David & Charles.
Kichenside, Geoffrey. British Rail in Action. 1977. 8.95 (ISBN 0-7153-7427-3). David & Charles.
--West Coast Route to Scotland. LC 75-35925. 1976. 11.95 (ISBN 0-7153-7157-6). David & Charles.
Kicherer, F. Alkoholkonsum und Alkoholismus als didaktisches Problem. (Psychologische Praxis Ser.: Band 54). (Illus.). vi, 146p. 1980. pap. 17.50 (ISBN 3-8055-0957-X). S Karger.
Kickham, Charles J. Knocknagow; or, the Cabins of Tipperary. (Nineteenth Century Fiction Ser.: Ireland: No. 68). 1979. lib. bdg. 46.00 (ISBN 0-8240-3517-8). Garland Pub.
--Knocknagow or the Homes of Tipperary. abr. ed. 1978. pap. 3.50 (ISBN 0-85342-554-X). Irish Bk Ctr.
Kicklighter, Clois E. & Baird, Ronald J. Crafts, Illustrated Designs & Techniques. LC 79-23955. (Illus.). 384p. 1980. text ed. 14.64 (ISBN 0-87006-298-0). Goodheart.
Kidd, B. S. & Keith, John D. The Natural History & Progress in Treatment of Congenital Heart Defects. (Illus.). 360p. 1971. 26.50 (ISBN 0-398-02174-0). C C Thomas.
Kidd, Charles V. Manpower Policies for the Use of Science & Technology in Development. (Policy Studies). 1980. 22.00 (ISBN 0-08-025124-2). Pergamon.
Kidd, D. M. & Leighbody, G. B. Methods of Teaching Shop & Technical Subjects. LC 66-26821. 1968. pap. text ed. 6.60 (ISBN 0-8273-0360-2). Delmar.
Kidd, Eleanor. Threshold to Music, Level 1. 2nd ed. (gr. 2-4). 1974. pap. 8.80 teacher's resources book (ISBN 0-8224-9062-5); experience charts 48.00 (ISBN 0-8224-9063-3). Pitman Learning.
--Threshold to Music, Level 2. 2nd ed. (gr. 4-7). 1975. pap. 8.80 teacher's resource book (ISBN 0-8224-9064-1); experience charts 48.00 (ISBN 0-8224-9065-X). Pitman Learning.
--Threshold to Music: Early Childhood. 2nd ed. (gr. k-2). 1974. pap. 5.60 teacher's resource book (ISBN 0-8224-9060-9); experience charts 40.00 (ISBN 0-8224-9061-7). Pitman Learning.
--Threshold to Music: Higher Grades. 2nd ed. (gr. 3-5). 1978. pap. 8.80 tchr's. resource book (ISBN 0-8224-9068-4); experience charts 48.00 (ISBN 0-8224-9069-2). Pitman Learning.
Kidd, Flora. The Silken Bond. (Harlequin Presents Ser.). 192p. 1980. pap. 1.50 (ISBN 0-373-10379-4, Pub. by Harlequin). PB.
--Wife by Contract. (Harlequin Presents Ser.). 192p. 1980. pap. 1.50 (ISBN 0-373-10400-6, Pub. by Harlequin). PB.
Kidd, I. G., jt. ed. see Edelstein, L.
Kidd, James H. Historical Sketch of General Custer. (Custer Monograph: No. 3). 1978. pap. 8.00x (ISBN 0-686-27938-7). Monroe County.
Kidd, Jane. Drag Hunting. 1978. 5.25 (ISBN 0-85131-285-3, Dist. by Sporting Book Center). J A Allen.
--Horsemanship in Europe. (Illus.). 17.35 (ISBN 0-85131-243-8, Dist. by Sporting Book Center). J A Allen.
Kidd, Kenneth P., et al. The Laboratory Approach to Mathematics. 1970. pap. text ed. 11.14 (ISBN 0-574-34790-9, 3-4790). SRA.
Kidd, Roby, jt. ed. see Hall, Bud L.
Kidd, Virginia, ed. Millennial Women: Tales for Tomorrow. LC 77-86299. 1978. 8.95 o.s.i. (ISBN 0-440-05599-7). Delacorte.
Kidd, Virginia, jt. ed. see Le Guin, Ursula K.
Kidde, Janet. The Prophetess. 1978. pap. 1.95 o.s.i. (ISBN 0-515-04456-3). Jove Pubns.
Kiddell, John. Choogoowarra: Australian Sheep Station. LC 79-165575. (gr. 3-6). 1972. 4.95g o.s.i. (ISBN 0-02-750300-3). Macmillan.
Kidder, Frank E. & Parker, Harry. Architects' & Builders' Handbook. 18th ed. 1931. 75.00 (ISBN 0-471-47421-5, Pub. by Wiley-Interscience). Wiley.
Kidder, J. Edward. Jomon Pottery: Prehistoric Japanese Arts. LC 68-17458. (Illus.). 308p. 1968. 85.00 (ISBN 0-87011-095-0). Kodansha.
Kidder, Rushworth M. E. E. Cummings: An Introduction to the Poetry. LC 79-772. (Columbia Introductions to Twentieth-Century American Poetry Ser.). 1979. 15.95 (ISBN 0-231-04044-X). Columbia U Pr.
Kiddle, L. B., jt. ed. see Walsh, Donald.
Kiddle, Lawrence B., jt. ed. see Anderson-Imbert, Enrique.
Kidgell, John. The Card, 2 vols. in 1. (The Flowering of the Novel, 1740-1775 Ser: Vol. 43). 1974. Repr. of 1755 ed. lib. bdg. 50.00 (ISBN 0-8240-1142-2). Garland Pub.
Kidner, A. W. Asparagus. (Illus.). 1959. 6.95 (ISBN 0-571-06771-9, Pub. by Faber & Faber). Merrimack Bk Serv.
Kidney, Dorothy B. Wilderness Journey. (Illus.). 200p. (Orig.). 1980. pap. 7.95 (ISBN 0-930096-10-X). G Gannett.
Kid's Stuff People. The Elementary School Kid's Book of Lists. 240p. (gr. 1-8). 1981. pap. text ed. 7.95 (ISBN 0-86530-047-X, IP 47X). Incentive Pubns.
Kidson, C. & Tooley, M. J. The Quaternary History of the Irish Sea: Geological Journal Special Issue, No. 7. (Liverpool Geological Society & the Manchester Geological Association). 356p. 1980. 64.95 (ISBN 0-471-27754-1, Pub. by Wiley-Interscience). Wiley.
Kidwell, Clara S. & Roberts, Charles. Choctaws: A Critical Bibliography. LC 80-8037. (The Newberry Library Center for the History of the American Indian Bibliographical Ser.). 96p. 1980. pap. 3.95 (ISBN 0-253-34412-3). Ind U Pr.
Kidwell, Connie. House of Bisque & Sawdust. (Orig.). 1980. pap. 1.95 (ISBN 0-532-23205-4). Manor Bks.
Kidwell, David S. & Peterson, Richard L. Financial Institutions & Markets. LC 80-65804. 640p. 1981. text ed. 18.95 (ISBN 0-03-046066-2). Dryden Pr.
Kidwell, R. J. & DeWelt, Don. Ecclesiastes - Song of Solomon. LC 78-301088. (The Bible Study Textbook Ser.). 1977. 13.50 (ISBN 0-89900-019-3). College Pr Pub.
Kieburtz, Richard B. Structured Programming & Problem Solving with Algol W. (Illus.). 384p. 1975. 14.95 (ISBN 0-13-854737-8). P-H.
--Structured Programming & Problem Solving with Pascal. (Illus.). 1978. Cloth. 20.95 (ISBN 0-13-854877-3); pap. 14.95 (ISBN 0-13-854869-2). P-H.
Kieckhefer, Richard. European Witch Trials: Their Foundations in Popular Learned Culture, 1300-1500. 1976. 21.50x (ISBN 0-520-02967-4). U of Cal Pr.
--Repression of Heresy in Medieval Germany. LC 78-65112. (The Middle Ages Ser.). 1979. 14.00x (ISBN 0-8122-7758-9). U of Pa Pr.
Kiefer, Ferenc, jt. auth. see Abraham, Samuel.
Kiefer, Ferenc, ed. The Hungarian Language & General Linguistics. (Linguistic & Literary Studies in Eastern Europe Ser.: No. 4). 580p. 1980. text ed. 68.50x (ISBN 90-272-1508-1). Humanities.
Kiefer, H. & Maushart, R. Radiation Protection Measurement. Friese, Ralf, tr. LC 70-133884. 576p. 1972. text ed. 75.00 (ISBN 0-08-015838-2). Pergamon.
Kiefer, Irene. A Global Jigsaw Puzzle: The Story of Continental Drift. LC 77-16188. (Illus.). (gr. 5-8). 1978. 8.95 (ISBN 0-689-30621-0). Atheneum.
--Poisoned Land: The Problem of Hazardous Waste. LC 80-22120. (Illus.). 96p. (gr. 5-9). 1981. PLB 8.95 (ISBN 0-689-30837-X). Atheneum.
--Underground Furnaces, the Story of Geothermal Energy. LC 76-3606. (Illus.). (gr. 3-7). 1976. PLB 6.00 (ISBN 0-688-32075-9). Morrow.
Kiefer, Nicholas M. The Economic Benefits from Four Employment & Training Programs. LC 78-75061. (Outstanding Dissertations in Economics Ser.). 1979. lib. bdg. 15.00 (ISBN 0-8240-4138-0). Garland Pub.
Kiefer, Ralph W., jt. auth. see Lillesand, Thomas M.
Kiefer, Warren. The Pontius Pilate Papers. 1977. pap. 1.95 o.s.i. (ISBN 0-515-04441-5). Jove Pubns.
Kieffer. Mental Health & Industry. LC 80-18057. 1980. 18.95 (ISBN 0-87705-085-6). Human Sci Pr.
Kieffer, F., ed. Radiation Physics & Chemistry: Magat Memorial Issue, Vols. 2 & 3. 300p. 1980. pap. 42.00 (ISBN 0-08-025069-6). Pergamon.
--Trapped Charges. 236p. 1976. pap. text ed. 42.00 (ISBN 0-08-019961-5). Pergamon.
Kieffer, Joyce L. To Have, To Hold. 2nd ed. (Illus.). 80p. 1981. pap. 4.95 (ISBN 0-933794-02-9). Train Res Assoc.
Kieffer, W. F. & Rakestraw, eds. Cumulative Index to Journal of Chemical Education, 3 vols. index 7.50 ea. Vol. 1 (ISBN 0-910362-10-6, 1924-1949). Vol. 2 (ISBN 0-910362-11-4, 1949-1958). Vol. 3 (ISBN 0-910362-12-2, 1958-1968). Chem Educ.
Kieft, David O. Belgium's Return to Neutrality: An Essay in the Frustrations of Small Power Diplomacy. 200p. 1972. 16.50x (ISBN 0-19-821497-9). Oxford U Pr.
Kieft, Ruth M. Vande see Vande Kieft, Ruth M.
Kiehl, Charles, jt. auth. see Gallo, Michael.
Kiek, Edward S. The Modern Religious Situation. 227p. Repr. of 1926 ed. 2.95 (ISBN 0-567-02158-0). Attic Pr.
Kielar, Wieslaw. Anus Mundi: 1,500 Days in Auschwitz-Birkenau. Flatauer, Susanne, tr. 352p. 1980. 13.95 (ISBN 0-8129-0921-6). Times Bks.
Kielhorn, William. Welding Guidelines with Aircraft Supplement. (Aviation Maintenance Training Course Ser.). (Illus.). 187p. 1978. text ed. 10.95 (ISBN 0-89100-136-0, E*A-W*B-2). Aviation Maintenance.
Kiell, Norman, ed. Psychiatry & Psychology in the Visual Arts & Aesthetics: A Bibliography. 1965. 22.50x (ISBN 0-299-03500-X). U of Wis Pr.
--The Psychology of Obesity: Dynamics & Treatment. (Illus.). 480p. 1973. 19.75 (ISBN 0-398-02685-8). C C Thomas.
Kiell, Paul J. & Frelinghuysen, Joseph. Keep Your Heart Running. 1976. 11.95 (ISBN 0-87691-182-3). Winchester Pr.
Kiely, Dennis K. Essentials of Music for New Musicians. (Illus.). 192p. 1975. pap. text ed. 10.95 (ISBN 0-13-286492-4). P-H.
Kiely, Edmond R. Surveying Instruments: Their History. 1979. Repr. of 1947 ed. 19.50 (ISBN 0-686-25583-6). CARBEN Survey.
Kiemel, Ann. Hi, I'm Ann. (Direction Bks). pap. 1.75 (ISBN 0-8010-5346-3). Baker Bk.
--I'm Running to Win. 1980. 6.95 (ISBN 0-8423-1736-8). Tyndale.
Kienast, Walther. Unteraneid & Treuvorbehalt in Frankreich & England. LC 80-2022. 1981. Repr. of 1952 ed. 31.00 (ISBN 0-404-18572-X). AMS Pr.
Kieninger, Richard. Observations-Four. (Orig., Forty percent discount on ten or more books). 1979. pap. 3.00 ea. Stelle.
Kientzler, Kharma, jt. auth. see Jones, Jeanne.
Kienzle, O., et al. The Promotion of the Relationship Between Research & Industry in Mechanical Production. 1970. pap. 7.50 (ISBN 0-08-006607-0). Pergamon.
Kienzle, William. Death Wears a Red Hat. 288p. 1981. pap. 2.75 (ISBN 0-553-14429-4). Bantam.
--The Rosary Murders. 1979. 9.95 o.p. (ISBN 0-8362-6101-1). Andrews & McMeel.
Kienzle, William X. Mind Over Murder. (Father Koesler Mystery Ser.). 320p. 1981. 9.95 (ISBN 0-686-69587-9). Andrews & McMeel.
Kier, Lemont B. Molecular Orbital Theory in Drug Research. LC 73-137616. (Medicinal Chemistry Ser). 1971. 40.50 (ISBN 0-12-406550-3). Acad Pr.
Kieran, J. A., jt. ed. see Ogot, B. A.
Kieran, John & Daley, Arthur. The Story of the Olympic Games: 776 B. C. to 1976. LC 76-56106. (Illus.). 1977. 12.95 o.s.i. (ISBN 0-397-01168-7). Lippincott.
Kierkegaard, Soren. Christian Discourses. Lowrie, W., tr. 1971. pap. 5.95 (ISBN 0-691-01973-8). Princeton U Pr.
--Concluding Unscientific Postscript. Swenson, D. F. & Lowrie, W., trs. (American-Scandinavian Foundation). 1941. 25.00x (ISBN 0-691-07106-3); pap. 5.95 (ISBN 0-691-01960-6). Princeton U Pr.
--The Corsair Affair & Articles Related to the Writings. Hong, Howard V. & Hong, Edna H., trs. from Danish. LC 80-7538. (Kierkegaards Writings: No. XIII). (Illus.). 380p. 1981. 25.00x (ISBN 0-691-07246-9). Princeton U Pr.
--The Difficulty of Being Christian. Collette, Jacques, ed. McInery, M. & Turcotte, L., trs. from Danish. 1968. 24.50x (ISBN 0-89197-730-9). Irvington.
--Either-Or, 2 Vols. Lowrie, W., tr. 1971. Vol. 1. 19.50x (ISBN 0-691-07177-2); Vol. 2. pap. 4.95 (ISBN 0-691-07178-0); Vol 1. pap. 4.95 (ISBN 0-691-01976-2); Vol. 2. pap. 4.95 (ISBN 0-691-01977-0). Princeton U Pr.
--Present Age. Dru, Alexander, ed. & tr. pap. 3.95x (ISBN 0-06-130094-2, TB94, Torch). Har-Row.
--The Sickness Unto Death: A Christian Psychological Exposition for Upbuilding & Awakening. Hong, Howard V. & Hong, Edna H., trs. LC 79-3218. (Kierkegaard's Writings Ser.: Vol. XIX). 1980. 16.50x (ISBN 0-691-07247-7). Princeton U Pr.
--Soren Kierkegaard's Journals & Papers, 7 vols. Hong, Howard V. & Hong, Edna H., eds. Incl. Vol. 1. A-E. 572p. 1967. 25.00x (ISBN 0-253-18240-9); Vol. 2. F-K. 640p. 1970. 35.00x (ISBN 0-253-18241-7); Vol. 3. L-R. 944p. 1976. 40.00x (ISBN 0-253-18242-5); Vol. 4. S-Z. 800p. 1976. 40.00x (ISBN 0-253-18243-3); Vol. 5. Autobiographical, Part One, 1829-1848. 576p. 1978. 27.50x (ISBN 0-253-18244-1); Vol. 6. Autobiographical, Part Two, 1848-1855. 648p. 1978. 35.00x (ISBN 0-253-18245-X); Vol. 7. Index & Composite Collation. 160p. 1978. 20.00x (ISBN 0-253-18246-8). LC 67-13025. Set. 175.00x (ISBN 0-253-18239-5). Ind U Pr.
Kierkegaard, Soren A. The Internal Development of Man in Dynamio Representational Expressions. Karlweiss, Joseph R., ed. (Illus.). 107p. 1981. 49.75 (ISBN 0-89266-273-5). Am Classical Coll Pr.
Kiermaier, Constance. To Be on an Island. (Illus., Orig.). 1980. pap. 7.95 (ISBN 0-89272-098-0). Down East.
Kiernan, Frank A., tr. see Maspero, Henri.
Kiernan, Bernard P. United States, Communism & the Emergent World. LC 72-75636. 256p. 1972. 10.00x (ISBN 0-253-19009-6). Ind U Pr.
Kiernan, Chris & Jones, Malcolm. Behaviour Assessment Battery. (General Ser.). 1977. pap. text ed. 19.25x (ISBN 0-685-05810-7, NFER). Humanities.
Kiernan, K. A. Histological & Histochemical Methods: Theory & Practice. (Illus.). 400p. Date not set. 63.01 (ISBN 0-08-024936-1); pap. 27.01 (ISBN 0-08-024935-3). Pergamon.
Kiernan, R. H. The Unveiling of Arabia: The Story of Arabian Travel & Discovery. (Illus.). 360p. 1981. Repr. of 1937 ed. 27.50x (ISBN 0-7146-1990-6, F Cass Co). Biblio Dist.
Kiernan, Thomas. Roman Polanski: A Biography. LC 80-997. (Illus.). 1980. 12.95 (ISBN 0-394-51396-7, GP835). Grove.
Kiernan, Thomas, jt. auth. see Root, Leon.
Kiernan, Vernon. America: The New Imperialism. 306p. 1978. 19.00 (ISBN 0-905762-18-5, Pub. by Zed Pr). Lawrence Hill.
Kierulff, Herbert E. The Economics of Decision: A Practical Decision System for Business & Management. 1976. 13.50 (ISBN 0-8046-7107-9). Kennikat.
Kiesel & Gore. Problems for Chemistry. 3.95x o.p. (ISBN 0-205-04244-9, 6842445); instr's manual free o.p. (ISBN 0-685-47255-8, 6842453). Allyn.
Kiesel, Stanley. The War Between the Pitiful Teachers & the Splendid Kids. LC 80-13450. 256p. (gr. 6 up). 1980. 9.95 (ISBN 0-525-42201-3). Dutton.

Kiesewetter, Raphael G. History of the Modern Music of Western Europe: From the First Century of the Christian Era to the Present Day. LC 74-140375. (Music Ser). 354p. 1973. Repr. of 1848 ed. lib. bdg. 25.00 (ISBN 0-306-70089-1). Da Capo.
Kiesler, Charles A. & Kiesler, Sara B., eds. Conformity. (Topics in Social Psychology Ser). (Orig.). 1969. pap. text ed. 6.95 (ISBN 0-201-03664-9). A-W.
Kiesler, Charles A., ed. see Davis, James H.
Kiesler, Charles A., ed. see Gergen, Kenneth J.
Kiesler, Charles A., et al. Attitude Change: A Critical Analysis of Theoretical Approaches. LC 68-56162. (Psychology Ser). 1969. 24.95 (ISBN 0-471-47465-7). Wiley.
Kiesler, Donald J., jt. ed. see Anchin, Jack C.
Kiesler, Sara B. Interpersonal Processes in Groups & Organizations. Mackenzie, Kenneth D., ed. LC 77-86018. (Organizational Behavior Ser.). 1978. pap. text ed. 9.95x (ISBN 0-88295-451-2). AHM Pub.
Kiesler, Sara B., jt. ed. see Kiesler, Charles A.
Kieso, Donald E. & Weygandt, Jerry J. Intermediate Accounting. 1290p. 1980. text ed. 25.95 (ISBN 0-471-04819-4); write for info. (ISBN 0-471-05580-8); write for info. (ISBN 0-471-06439-4); 9.95 (ISBN 0-471-04821-6); practice set 7.65 (ISBN 0-471-06441-6). Wiley.
Kiess, Helmut. Camera Sensitive Electrophotography. (Illus.). 100p. 1980. 25.00 (ISBN 0-240-51067-4). Focal Pr.
Kiesselbach, T. A. The Structure & Reproduction of Corn. LC 79-19648. viii, 96p. 1980. 9.50x (ISBN 0-8032-2703-5); pap. 2.95x (ISBN 0-8032-7751-2, BB 724, Bison). U of Nebr Pr.
Kiev, Ari. Riding Through the Downers, Hassles, Snags & Funks. 96p. 1980. 7.95 (ISBN 0-525-93138-4). Dutton.
--A Strategy for Handling Executive Stress. LC 74-7319. 1974. 12.95 (ISBN 0-88229-153-X). Nelson-Hall.
--A Strategy for Success. 1977. 6.95 o.s.i. (ISBN 0-02-563100-4, 56310). Macmillan.
--Suicidal Patient: Recognition & Management. LC 76-47330. 1977. 15.95 (ISBN 0-88229-302-8). Nelson-Hall.
--Transcultural Psychiatry. LC 73-163235. 1973. 12.95 (ISBN 0-02-917180-6); pap. 3.50 (ISBN 0-02-917170-9). Free Pr.
Kiev, Ari, jt. auth. see Argandona, Mario.
Kifer, R. S. & Stewart, H. L. Farming Hazards in the Drought Area. LC 78-165600. (FDR & the Era of the New Deal Ser). 1971. Repr. of 1938 ed. lib. bdg. 25.00 (ISBN 0-306-70348-3). Da Capo.
Kiger, John, jt. auth. see Ayala, Francisco.
Kihara, T. Intermolecular Forces. LC 77-12353. 1978. 30.25 (ISBN 0-471-99583-5, Pub. by Wiley-Interscience). Wiley.
Kihlstrom, April L. Paris Summer. (YA) 1977. 5.95 (ISBN 0-685-74270-9, Avalon). Bouregy.
Kihlstrom, B., jt. auth. see Langefors, U.
Kihlstrom, J., jt. ed. see Cantor, N.
Kijek, Jean C., jt. auth. see Murray, Rosemary.
Kikkawa, H. see Shen, H. W.
Kikkawa, J., tr. see Ito, Y.
Kikuchi, Chihiro, jt. auth. see Duderstadt, James.
Kilander, Virginia C., jt. auth. see Crawford, Annie L.
Kilbourne, James W. Escape & Evasion: Seventeen Stories of Downed Pilots Who Made It Back. Glines, Carrol V., ed. (Air Force Academy Ser.). (Illus.). 192p. 1973. 9.95 (ISBN 0-02-563000-8). Macmillan.
Kilbride, Thomas. Spinning & Weaving at Home. (Illus.). 128p. 1981. pap. 5.95 (ISBN 0-8069-9272-7). Sterling.
Kilbride-Jones, H. E. Celtic Craftsmanship in Bronze. LC 80-10520. (Illus.). 320p. 1980. 35.00 (ISBN 0-312-12698-0). St Martin.
Kilburn, Robert E. & Howell, Peter S. Exploring Earth Science. (Junior High Science Program Ser.). (gr. 7-9). 1981. text ed. 15.52 (ISBN 0-205-06733-6, 6967337); tchrs'. guide & tests 9.96 (ISBN 0-205-06734-4); 7.20 (ISBN 0-205-06735-2, 6967353). Allyn.
--Exploring Life Science. (Junior High Science Program Ser.). (gr. 7-9). 1981. text ed. 15.52 (ISBN 0-205-06728-X, 6967280); tchrs'. ed. with tests 9.96 (ISBN 0-205-06729-8, 696739-0); record bk. 7.20 (6967302). Allyn.
--Exploring Physical Science. (Junior High Science Program Ser.). (gr. 7-9). 1981. text ed. 15.52 (ISBN 0-205-06738-7, 6967388); tchrs'. guide & tests 3.60 (ISBN 0-205-06739-5, 696739-6); record bk. 7.20 (ISBN 0-205-06740-9, 696740-X). Allyn.
Kilburn, Robert E., jt. auth. see Turber, Walter A.
Kilburn, Robert E., jt. auth. see Thurber, Walter A.
Kilby, B. A., jt. ed. see Candy, D. J.
Kilby, Clyde & Mead, Marj, eds. Brothers & Friends: An Intimate Portrait of C. S. Lewis; the Diaries of Major Warren Hamilton Lewis. LC 80-7756. (Illus.). 1981. 14.95 (ISBN 0-06-065244-6, HarpR). Har-Row.
Kilby, P. Entrepreneurship & Economic Development. LC 79-122279. 1971. 19.95 (ISBN 0-02-917270-5). Free Pr.
Kildeberg, Poul. Quantitative Acid-Base Physiology. (Illus.). 142p. 1981. 15.00. Igaku-Shoin.
Kilduff, Peter, tr. see Von Richthofen, Manfred.
Kiley, Dan. Keeping Parents Out of Trouble. (Orig.). 1981. 11.95 (ISBN 0-446-51221-4). Warner Bks.
--Nobody Said It Would Be Easy: Raising Responsible Kids -- and Keeping Them Out of Trouble. LC 77-11821. 1978. 10.95 o.s.i. (ISBN 0-06-012369-9, HarpT). Har-Row.
Kiley, Frederick T. & Shuttleworth, Jack M., eds. Satire: From Aesop to Buchwald. LC 70-134892. 1971. pap. 7.50 (ISBN 0-672-63110-5). Odyssey Pr.
Kiley, John C. Equilibrium. LC 79-54813. 1980. pap. 6.95 (ISBN 0-89615-047-X). Guild of Tutors.
Kiley, M. A. Personal & Interpersonal Appraisal Techniques: For Counselors, Teachers, Students. (Illus.). 264p. 1975. 17.50 (ISBN 0-398-03219-X); pap. 12.50 (ISBN 0-398-03240-8). C C Thomas.
Kiley-Worthington, M. Behavioral Problems of Farm Animals. (Illus.). 1977. pap. 15.00 (ISBN 0-85362-163-2, Oriel). Routledge & Kegan.
Kilgannon, Pete. Business Data Processing & Systems Analysis. (Illus.). 326p. 1980. pap. 21.00 (ISBN 0-7131-2755-4). Intl Ideas.
Kilgarriff, Michael, intro. by. The Golden Age of Melodrama. 499p. 1975. 14.95 o.p. (ISBN 0-8238-0190-X). Plays.
Kilgore, Axel. The Killer Genesis. (Orig.). 1980. pap. 2.25 (ISBN 0-89083-678-7, Kable News Co). Zebra.
Kilgore, Thomas, Jr. I Kept on Praying. (Prayer in My Life Ser.: Ser. II). 1974. pap. 1.00x (ISBN 0-8358-0315-5). Upper Room.
Kilgour, Gordon. Fundamentals of Biochemistry. Date not set. text ed. 21.95 (ISBN 0-442-25756-2); instr's. manual 2.00 (ISBN 0-442-25757-0). D Van Nostrand.
Kilgour, O. Multiple-Choice Questions in Biology & Human Biology. (Orig.). 1974. pap. text ed. 4.95x o.p. (ISBN 0-435-59502-4). Heinemann Ed.
Kilgour, O. F. At Home with Science. 1976. pap. text ed. 5.95x o.p. (ISBN 0-435-42231-6). Heinemann Ed.
--Introduction to Science for Catering & Homecraft Students. 3rd ed. (Illus.). 1976. pap. text ed. 15.95x (ISBN 0-434-91057-0). Intl Ideas.
--Introduction to the Chemical Aspects of Nursing Science. (Illus.). 1972. 19.95x (ISBN 0-433-18471-X). Intl Ideas.
--Multiple Choice Questions in the House & Its Services. 1978. pap. text ed. 4.95 o.p. (ISBN 0-435-42229-4). Heinemann Ed.
Kilham, Walter H., Jr. Raymond Hood, Architect of Ideas. Date not set. 12.50 (ISBN 0-8038-0218-8). Hastings.
Kiliper, R. Smith, jt. auth. see Schulz, Charles M.
Killam, G. D., ed. African Writers on African Writing. 1973. pap. text ed. 4.25x o.s.i. (ISBN 0-8101-0420-2). Northwestern U Pr.
Killanin, Lord. The Olympic Games. 272p. 1976. 22.95 (ISBN 0-02-563050-4). Macmillan.
Killeen. The Whole World Cookbook. 1979. text ed. 15.95 (ISBN 0-87002-913-4). Bennett IL.
Killeen, Jacqueline. Best Restaurants of San Francisco & Northern California. rev. ed. LC 80-18764. (Illus.). 220p. 1980. pap. 3.95 (ISBN 0-89286-160-6). One Hund One Prods.
Killeen, P. G. & Heier, K. S. Radioelement Distribution & Heat Production in Precambrian Granitic Rocks, Southern Norway. 1975. pap. 11.00x (ISBN 8-200-01463-0, Dist. by Columbia U Pr). Universitet.
Killeen, Veronica A., jt. auth. see Hayes, Walter M.
Killens, John O. Great Gittin up Morning: The Story of Denmark Vesey. Rivera, Louis R., ed. (Illus.). 128p. 1980. pap. 5.50 (ISBN 0-917886-06-2). Shamal Bks.
Killer, W. K. Illustrated Technical German for Builders-Bautechnisches Englisch Im Bild. LC 76-467695. 1977. pap. 12.50x (ISBN 3-7625-0898-4). Intl Pubns Serv.
Killgallon, Don. Sentence Composing Eleven. 152p. (gr. 10-12). 1979. pap. text ed. 5.20x (ISBN 0-8104-6123-4); teacher's guide 1.75 (ISBN 0-8104-6121-8). Hayden.
--Sentence Composing Ten. 160p. (gr. 10-12). 1980. pap. 5.20x (ISBN 0-8104-6122-6); tchr's. guide 1.75 (ISBN 0-8104-6121-8). Hayden.
--Sentence Composing Twelve. 160p. (gr. 10-12). 1979. pap. 5.20x (ISBN 0-8104-6124-2); 1.75 (ISBN 0-8104-6121-8). Hayden.
Killham, John, ed. Critical Essays on the Poetry of Tennyson. 1960. pap. 10.00 (ISBN 0-7100-4669-3). Routledge & Kegan.
Killian, H. Cold & Frost Injuries: Rewarming Damages. (Disaster Medicine: Vol. 3). (Illus.). 260p. 1981. pap. 49.60 (ISBN 0-387-08991-8). Springer-Verlag.
Killian, Lewis, jt. auth. see Turner, Ralph.
Killian, Ray A. Human Resource Management: An ROI Approach. LC 76-7058. (Illus.). 208p. 1976. 14.95 (ISBN 0-8144-5415-1). Am Mgmt.
Killigrew, Anne. Poems. LC 67-10177. 1967. Repr. of 1686 ed. 20.00x (ISBN 0-8201-1030-2). Schol Facsimiles.
Killigrew, John W. The Impact of the Great Depression on the Army. Freidel, Frank, ed. LC 78-62385. (Modern American History Ser.: Vol. 11). 1979. lib. bdg. 25.00 (ISBN 0-8240-3634-4). Garland Pub.
Killikelly, Sarah H. Curious Questions in History, Literature, Art, & Social Life, 3 Vols. LC 68-26581. 1968. Repr. of 1900 ed. Set. 58.00 (ISBN 0-8103-3091-1). Gale.
Killilea, Marie. Karen. pap. 1.75 o.s.i. (ISBN 0-440-14376-4). Dell.
--With Love from Karen. 1964. pap. 1.75 o.s.i. (ISBN 0-440-19615-9). Dell.
--With Love from Karen. (gr. 7-12). 1980. pap. 1.95 (ISBN 0-440-99615-5, LE). Dell.
Killingbeck, J. & Cole, G. H. Mathematical Techniques & Physical Applications. (Pure & Applied Physics Ser). 1971. text ed. 22.95 (ISBN 0-12-406850-2); solutions manual 3.00 (ISBN 0-12-406856-1). Acad Pr.
Killinger, John. A Devotional Guide to John. 144p. 1981. 7.95 (ISBN 0-8499-0256-8). Word Bks.
--Hemingway & the Dead Gods: A Study in Existentialism. LC 60-15379. 128p. 1960. 9.00x (ISBN 0-8131-1055-6). U Pr of Ky.
--His Power in You. LC 77-90811. 1978. 5.95 o.p. (ISBN 0-385-12717-0, Galilee). Doubleday.
--The Loneliness of Children. LC 79-56378. 320p. 1980. 12.95 (ISBN 0-8149-0830-6). Vanguard.
Killinger, Margaret, ed. see Painter, Desmond & Shepard, John.
Killingray, David. The Atom Bomb. Yapp, Malcolm, et al, eds. (World History Ser.). (Illus.). 32p. (gr. 10). 1980. Repr. of 1977 ed. lib. bdg. 5.95 (ISBN 0-89908-235-1); pap. text ed. 1.95 (ISBN 0-89908-210-6). Greenhaven.
--Nyerere & Nkrumah. Yapp, Malcolm & Killingray, Margaret, eds. (World History Ser.). (Illus.). 32p. (gr. 10). 1980. Repr. of 1977 ed. lib. bdg. 5.95 (ISBN 0-89908-129-0); pap. text ed. 1.95 (ISBN 0-89908-104-5). Greenhaven.
--A Plague of Europeans. (Education Ser.). 1974. pap. 3.65 o.p. (ISBN 0-14-080671-7). Penguin.
--Population. O'Connor, Edmund, ed. (World History Ser.). (Illus.). 32p. (gr. 10). 1980. Repr. of 1977 ed. lib. bdg. 5.95 (ISBN 0-89908-141-X); pap. text ed. 1.95 (ISBN 0-89908-116-9). Greenhaven.
--The Russian Revolution. Yapp, Malcolm, et al, eds. (World History Ser.). (Illus.). (gr. 10). 1980. Repr. of 1977 ed. lib. bdg. 5.95 (ISBN 0-89908-138-X); pap. text ed. 1.95 (ISBN 0-89908-113-4). Greenhaven.
--The Slave Trade. Yapp, Malcolm & Killingray, Margaret, eds. (World History Ser.). (Illus.). (gr. 10). 1980. Repr. of 1977 ed. lib. bdg. 5.95 (ISBN 0-89908-149-5); pap. text ed. 1.95 (ISBN 0-89908-124-X). Greenhaven.
--The Two World Wars. Yapp, Malcolm & Killlingray, Margaret, eds. (World History Ser.). (Illus.). 32p. (gr. 10). 1980. Repr. of 1977 ed. lib. bdg. 5.95 (ISBN 0-89908-234-3); pap. text ed. 1.95 (ISBN 0-89908-209-2). Greenhaven.
--A World Economy. Yapp, Malcolm, et al, eds. (World History Ser.). (Illus.). 32p. (gr. 10). 1980. Repr. of 1977 ed. lib. bdg. 5.95 (ISBN 0-89908-143-6); pap. text ed. 1.95 (ISBN 0-89908-118-5). Greenhaven.
Killingray, David, et al. Stalin. Yapp, Malcolm, et al, eds. (World History Ser.). (Illus.). 32p. (gr. 10). 1980. Repr. of 1977 ed. lib. bdg. 5.95 (ISBN 0-89908-126-6); pap. text ed. 1.95 (ISBN 0-89908-101-0). Greenhaven.
Killingray, Margaret. The Agricultural Revolution. Yapp, Malcolm & O'Connor, Edmund, eds. (World History Ser.). (Illus.). 32p. (gr. 10). 1980. Repr. of 1977 ed. lib. bdg. 5.95 (ISBN 0-89908-131-2); pap. text ed. 1.95 (ISBN 0-89908-106-1). Greenhaven.
--Ancient Greece. Yapp, Malcolm & O'Connor, Edmund, eds. (World History Ser.). Orig. Title: The Mediterranean. (Illus.). 32p. (gr. 10). 1980. Repr. of 1977 ed. lib. bdg. 5.95 (ISBN 0-89908-026-X); pap. text ed. 1.95 (ISBN 0-89908-001-4). Greenhaven.
--Constantine. Yapp, Malcolm, et al, eds. (Greenhaven World History Ser.). (Illus.). 32p. (gr. 10). 1980. lib. bdg. 5.95 (ISBN 0-89908-040-5); pap. text ed. 1.95 (ISBN 0-89908-015-4). Greenhaven.
Killingray, Margaret, ed. see Addison, John, et al.
Killingray, Margaret, ed. see Booth, Martin, et al.
Killingray, Margaret, ed. see Doncaster, Islay.
Killingray, Margaret, ed. see Duckworth, John, et al.
Killingray, Margaret, ed. see Harrison, John, et al.
Killingray, Margaret, ed. see Heater, Derek & Owen, Gwyneth.
Killingray, Margaret, ed. see Killingray, David.
Killingray, Margaret, ed. see O'Connor, Edmund.
Killingray, Margaret, ed. see Painter, Desmond.
Killingray, Margaret, ed. see Pearson, Eileen.
Killingray, Margaret, ed. see Read, James & Yapp, Malcolm.
Killingray, Margaret, ed. see Tames, Richard.
Killingray, Margaret, ed. see Yapp, Malcolm.
Killingray, Margaret, et al, eds. see Guyatt, John.
Killingray, Margaret, et al, eds. see Tames, Richard.
Killingray, Margaret, et al, eds. see Townson, Duncan.
Killingray, Margaret, et al, eds. see Vapp, Malcolm.
Killingray, Margaret, et al, eds. see Yapp, Malcolm.
Killingray, Marget, ed. see O'Connor, Edmund.
Killingsworth, Amy. Basic Physical Disabilities Procedures: A Manual in Occupational Therapy. (Illus.). 1976. pap. 15.00 (ISBN 0-930638-00-X). Cal-Syl Pr.
Killlingray, Margaret, ed. see Killingray, David.
Killogh, Lee. Deadly Silents. 256p. (Orig.). 1981. pap. 2.25 (ISBN 0-345-28780-0, Del Rey). Ballantine.
Killough, Larry N. & Leininger, Wayne F. Cost Accounting for Managerial Decision Making. LC 76-52741. 1977. 15.95 (ISBN 0-8221-0191-2). CBI Pub.
Killough, Lee. The Monitor, the Miners & the Shree. (Orig.). 1980. pap. 1.95 (ISBN 0-345-28456-9). Ballantine.
Killpatrick, James. An Impartial Account of the Late Expedition Against St. Augustine Under General Oglethorpe. LC 78-21956. (Bicentennial Floridiana Facsimile & Reprint Ser). 1978. Repr. of 1742 ed. 6.00 (ISBN 0-8130-0420-9). U Presses Fla.
Killy, Jean-Claude. One-Hundred & Thirty-Three Ski Lessons by Jean-Claude Killy. 80p. 1975. pap. 3.95 o.p. (ISBN 0-695-80628-9). Follett.
Killy, Jean-Claude & Halstead, Mike. Situation Skiing. LC 77-16927. 1978. 12.50 o.p. (ISBN 0-385-12189-X). Doubleday.
Kilmartin, Angela. Cystitis: The Complete Self-Help Guide. LC 79-26425. (Illus.). 256p. 1980. 9.95 (ISBN 0-446-51203-6); pap. 5.95 (ISBN 0-446-97720-9). Warner Bks.
--Understanding Cystitis. 1973. pap. 10.00x (ISBN 0-685-83939-7). Intl Ideas.
Kilmartin, Edward. Toward Reunion: The Orthodox & Roman Catholic Churches. LC 79-88570. 1979. pap. 4.95 (ISBN 0-8091-2236-7). Paulist Pr.
Kilmartin, Joanna, tr. see Sagan, Francoise.
Kilmartin, Terence, tr. see Aron, Raymond.
Kilmartin, Terence, tr. see Malraux, Andre.
Kilmarx, Robert A., jt. auth. see Jordan, Amos A.
Kilmarx, Robert A., jt. ed. see Alexander, Yonah.
Kilmeister, Clive W. The Nature of the Universe. Clarke, Robin, ed. (The World of Science Lib.). 1973. pap. 3.95 o.p. (ISBN 0-525-04005-6). Dutton.
Kilmister, C. W. Special Theory of Relativity. 1970. 35.00 (ISBN 0-08-006996-7); pap. 11.25 (ISBN 0-08-006995-9). Pergamon.
Kilner, Mary J. Memoirs of a Peg-Top. Lurie, Alison & Schiller, Justin G., eds. LC 75-32145. (Classics of Children's Literature Ser.: 1621-1932). PLB 38.00 (ISBN 0-8240-2268-8). Garland Pub.
Kiloh, L. G., jt. ed. see Smith, J. Sydney.
Kiloh, L. G., et al. Clinical Electroencephalography. 4th ed. 1981. text ed. price not set (ISBN 0-407-00160-3). Butterworth.
Kilpatrick, Anna G., jt. auth. see Kilpatrick, Jack F.
Kilpatrick, Franklin P., et al. Source Book of a Study of Occupational Values & the Image of the Federal Service. 1964. 13.95 (ISBN 0-8157-4928-7). Brookings.
Kilpatrick, Jack F. & Kilpatrick, Anna G. Shadow of Sequoyah: Social Documents of the Cherokees, 1862-1964. LC 65-24205. 1965. 7.95 (ISBN 0-8061-0677-8); pap. 3.50 (ISBN 0-8061-1274-3, CAI81). U of Okla Pr.
Kilpatrick, James J., jt. auth. see Bake, William A.
Kilpatrick, Jeremy, jt. auth. see Polya, George.
Kilpatrick, Sarah. Fanny Burney. LC 80-5891. (Illus.). 256p. 1981. 14.95 (ISBN 0-8128-2761-9). Stein & Day.
Kilpatrick, T. B. Bishop Butler's Three Sermons Upon Human Nature. (Handbooks for Bible Classes Ser.). 123p. 1949. text ed. 3.50 (ISBN 0-567-08142-7). Attic Pr.
--The Redemption of Man. (Short Course Ser.). 163p. 1920. text ed. 2.95 (ISBN 0-567-08320-9). Attic Pr.

Kilpatrick, Thomas L. & Hoshiko, Patsy Rose. Illinois! Illinois! An Annotated Bibliography of Fiction. LC 79-13011. 627p. 1979. 30.00 (ISBN 0-8108-1222-3). Scarecrow.

Kilpatrick, William H. Education for a Changing Civilization: Three Lectures Delivered on the Luther Laflin Kellogg Foundation at Rutgers University 1926. 143p. 1980. Repr. of 1926 ed. lib. bdg. 15.00 (ISBN 0-89760-426-1). Telegraph Bks.

Kilpatrick, William K. Identity & Intimacy. 272p. 1975. 8.95 o.p. (ISBN 0-440-04373-5). Delacorte.

Kilpatrik, Hilary, tr. see Kanafani, Ghassan.

Kilroy, James. The Playboy Riots. (Irish Theatre Ser.: No. 4). (Orig.). 1971. pap. text ed. 4.00x (ISBN 0-85105-199-5, Dolmen Pr). Humanities.

Kilroy, James, jt. auth. see Hogan, Robert.

Kilroy, James, ed. see Mangan, James C.

Kilshaw. Steroids & Non-Steroid Hormones. 1981. text ed. price not set. Butterworth.

Kilson, Marion D. African Urban Kinsman: The Ga of Central Accra. LC 74-79128. 1975. 21.95 (ISBN 0-312-01050-8). St Martin.

Kilthau, Gus. How to Write Dumb Poems. LC 79-88250. (Orig.). 1981. price not set (ISBN 0-89896-013-4). Larksdale.

Kilts, D. F., jt. auth. see Brill, E. L.

Kilvert, Ian S. see Scott-Kilvert, Ian.

Kilworth, Garry. The Night of Kadar. 208p. 1979. pap. 1.95 (ISBN 0-380-50070-1, 50070-1). Avon.

Kim & Roush. Introduction to Mathematical Concensus Theory. 192p. 1980. 25.00 (ISBN 0-8247-1001-0). Dekker.

Kim, B. S., jt. auth. see Wade, L. L.

Kim, C. I. & Kim, Han-Kyo. Korea & the Politics of Imperialism, 1876-1910. (Center for Japanese & Korean Studies, UC Berkeley). (Maps). 1968. 15.75x o.p. (ISBN 0-520-00646-1). U of Cal Pr.

Kim, C. I., jt. auth. see Zifing, Lawrence.

Kim, Chan-Hie. Form & Structure of the Familiar Greek Letter of Recommendation. LC 72-87887. (Society of Biblical Literature. Dissertation Ser.: No. 4). 1972. pap. 9.00 (ISBN 0-89130-160-7, 060104). Scholars Pr Ca.

Kim, Charles W., ed. Microbiology Review. 7th ed. LC 80-20088. 1980. pap. 8.50 spiral bdg. (ISBN 0-87488-203-6). Med Exam.

Kim, Chewon & Lee, L. Kim. Arts of Korea. LC 73-79768. (Illus.). 364p. 1974. 85.00 (ISBN 0-87011-206-6). Kodansha.

Kim, Choong H. Books by Mail: A Handbook for Libraries. LC 76-15335. (Illus.). 1977. lib. bdg. 22.50 (ISBN 0-8371-9029-0, KBM/). Greenwood.

Kim, Han-Kyo, jt. auth. see Kim, C. I.

Kim, Han Kyo, ed. Essays on Modern Politics & History. LC 75-91958. xiv, 255p. 1969. 13.95x (ISBN 0-8214-0079-7). Ohio U Pr.

Kim, Han-Kyo, ed. Studies on Korea: A Scholar's Guide. LC 79-26491. 576p. 1980. text ed. 25.00x (ISBN 0-8248-0673-5). U Pr of Hawaii.

Kim, Hei C., jt. auth. see Hurh, Won M.

Kim, Hong N. Scholars' Guide to Washington, D.C. for East Asian Studies. LC 79-17344. (Scholars' Guide to Washington, D.C. Ser.: No. 3). 413p. 1979. text ed. 19.95x (ISBN 0-87474-582-9); pap. text ed. 8.95x (ISBN 0-87474-581-0). Smithsonian.

Kim, Hyung I. Fundamental Legal Concepts of China & the West: A Comparative Study. (National University Publications, Multidisciplinary Studies in the Law). 1981. 17.50 (ISBN 0-8046-9275-0). Kennikat.

Kim, Ilpyong. The Politics of Chinese Communism: Kiangi Under Soviet Rule. 1974. 20.00x (ISBN 0-520-02438-9). U of Cal Pr.

Kim, Ilpyong J. Communist Politics in North Korea. LC 72-92887. (Special Studies). 130p. 1975. text ed. 24.95 (ISBN 0-275-09190-2). Praeger.

Kim, Jae-On & Mueller, Charles. Introduction to Factor Analysis: What It Is & How to Do It. LC 79-103006. (The University Papers Ser.: Quantitive Applications in the Social Sciences No. 13). 1978. pap. 3.50x (ISBN 0-8039-1165-3). Sage.

Kim, Jae T. New Readings in Public Administration. 320p. 1980. pap. text ed. 9.95 (ISBN 0-8403-2245-3). Kendall-Hunt.

Kim, Jai-Hyup. The Garrison State in Prewar Japan & Post-War Korea: A Comparative Analysis of Military Politics. LC 77-26344. 1978. 11.25 (ISBN 0-8191-0416-7). U Pr of Amer.

Kim, Jenny. Chinese Cooking Jenny Kim's Way. LC 78-71036. (Illus.). 1979. pap. 5.95 o.p. (ISBN 0-916076-29-6). Writing.

Kim, Key-Hiuk. The Last Phase of the East Asian World Order: Korea, Japan, & the Chinese Empire, 1860-1882. 1980. 22.75x (ISBN 0-520-03556-9). U of Cal Pr.

Kim, Kie-Taek & Kaulins, Andis, eds. The Foreign Policies & Foreign Trade of the German Democratic Republic & the Korean Democratic People's Republic. (German Korea Studies Group Ser.). 144p. 1980. pap. 15.00 (ISBN 0-8188-0117-4, Pub. by German Korea Stud Germany). Paragon.

Kim, Richard. The Weaponless Warriors. Scurra, John, ed. LC 74-21218. (Ser. 313). (Illus.). 1974. pap. text ed. 5.95 (ISBN 0-89750-041-5). Ohara Pubns.

Kim, Samuel S., jt. ed. see Falk, Richard A.

Kim, Samuel S., jt. ed. see Hsiung, James C.

Kim, Sang Ki. The Problem of the Contingency of the World in Husserl's Phenomenology. (Philosophical Currents: No. 17). 1976. pap. text ed. 17.25x (ISBN 90-6032-054-9). Humanities.

Kim, Scott. Inversions. 200p. 1980. pap. 8.95 (ISBN 0-07-034546-5). McGraw.

Kim, Suk H. An Introduction to International Financial Management. LC 80-5203. 302p. 1980. pap. text ed. 10.75 (ISBN 0-8191-1054-X). U Pr of Amer.

--An Introduction to International Financial Management. LC 80-5203. 272p. 1980. 13.50 o.p. U Pr of Amer.

Kim, Suk H. & Guithues, Henry J. Capital Expenditure Analysis. LC 80-6070. 338p. 1981. 20.00 (ISBN 0-8191-1462-6); pap. 11.25. U Pr of Amer.

Kim, Thomas K. Introductory Mathematics for Economic Analysis. 1971. 14.95x o.p. (ISBN 0-673-05144-7). Scott F.

Kim, Ung Chon. Policies of Publishers: A Handbook for Order Librarians, 1978 Edition. LC 77-25063. 1978. pap. 10.00 (ISBN 0-8108-1098-0). Scarecrow.

Kim, Yong C. Oriental Thought: An Introduction to the Philosophical & Religious Thought of Asia. (Littlefield, Adams Quality Paperback Ser.: No. 365). 130p. 1981. pap. 3.95 (ISBN 0-8226-0365-9). Littlefield.

Kim, Yong Choon. Oriental Thought: An Introduction to the Philosophical & Religious Thought of Asia. 130p. 1981. Repr. of 1973 ed. 8.95x (ISBN 0-8476-6972-6). Rowman.

Kim, Young C. Japanese Journalists & Their World. LC 80-25720. 1981. price not set (ISBN 0-8139-0877-9). U Pr of Va.

--Japanese-Soviet Relations. LC 74-27559. (The Washington Papers: No. 21). 1975. 3.50x (ISBN 0-8039-0377-4). Sage.

Kim, Young C. & Halpern, Abraham M., eds. The Future of the Korean Peninsula. LC 77-24407. (Praeger Special Studies). 1977. text ed. 25.95 (ISBN 0-03-021846-2). Praeger.

Kim, Young H., ed. East Asia's Turbulent Century: With American Diplomatic Documents. LC 66-10328. (Orig.). 1966. pap. text ed. 7.95x (ISBN 0-89197-513-6). Irvington.

Kim, Young-Pyoung. A Strategy for for Rural Development: Saemaeul Undong in Korea. 1980. pap. 5.00 (ISBN 0-89249-032-2). Intl Development.

Kimambo, Isaria, jt. ed. see Ranger, T. O.

Kimball. Culture & the Educative Process. LC 73-21760. 285p. 1974. text ed. 10.25x (ISBN 0-8077-2422-X); pap. text ed. 6.50x (ISBN 0-8077-2434-3). Tchrs Coll.

Kimball, Art & Kimball, Scott. Collecting Old Fishing Tackle. LC 80-122941. (Illus.). 1980. 30.00 (ISBN 0-9604906-0-4); pap. 19.00 (ISBN 0-9604906-1-2). Aardvark Pubs.

Kimball, Betsy, ed. see Wigmore, Ann.

Kimball, Chase P. The Biopsychosocial Approach to the Patient. (Illus.). 382p. 1981. softcover 24.00 (ISBN 0-686-69562-3, 9400-9). Williams & Wilkins.

Kimball, Don. Driftwood Prayers Passions & Permissions. LC 77-82766. 1978. Softbound 4.95 o.p. (ISBN 0-385-13369-3). Doubleday.

Kimball, Edward A. Lectures & Articles on Christian Science. (Illus.). 1976. 10.00 (ISBN 0-911588-01-9). N S Wait.

--Teaching & Addresses. 1944. 5.50 (ISBN 0-910964-01-7); deluxe ed. 8.75 o.p. (ISBN 0-686-66491-4). Metaphysical.

Kimball, Edward L., jt. auth. see Miner, Caroline E.

Kimball, George E., jt. auth. see Morse, Philip M.

Kimball, Gertrude S. Providence in Colonial Times. LC 76-87452. (The American Scene Ser.). (Illus.). 391p. 1972. Repr. of 1912 ed. lib. bdg. 49.50 (ISBN 0-306-71524-4). Da Capo.

Kimball, John. Biology. 4th ed. LC 77-74322. (Life Sciences Ser.). 1978. text ed. 21.95 (ISBN 0-201-03761-0); lab manual 8.50 (ISBN 0-201-03692-4); study guide 6.95 (ISBN 0-201-03764-5). A-W.

Kimball, John P. & Tedesch, Philip, eds. Syntax & Semantics, Vol. 14: Tense & Aspect. 1981. price not set (ISBN 0-12-613514-2). Acad Pr.

Kimball, John P., et al. Syntax & Semantics, 13 vols. Incl. Vol. 1. Studies in Language. 260p. 1973. 30.50 (ISBN 0-12-785421-5); Vol. 2. 1973. 30.50 (ISBN 0-12-785422-3); Vol. 3. 1975. 31.00 (ISBN 0-12-785423-1); Vol. 4. 1975. 35.00 (ISBN 0-12-785424-X); Vol. 5. Japanese Generative Grammar. 1975. 45.50 (ISBN 0-12-785425-8); Vol. 6. 1976. 42.50 (ISBN 0-12-785426-6); Vol. 7. 1976. 30.00 (ISBN 0-12-613507-X); Vol. 8. 1976. 30.00 (ISBN 0-12-613508-8); Vol. 9. Pragmatics. 1978. 27.00 (ISBN 0-12-613509-6); Vol. 10. 1979. 38.00 (ISBN 0-12-613510-X); Vol. 11. Presupposition. 1979. 35.00 (ISBN 0-12-613511-8); Vol. 12. Discourse & Syntax. 1979. 43.00 (ISBN 0-12-613512-6); Vol. 13. Current Approaches to Syntax. 1980. write for info. (ISBN 0-12-613513-4). Acad Pr.

Kimball, John W. Cell Biology. 2nd ed. LC 77-77742. (Life Sciences Ser.). (Illus.). 1978. pap. text ed. 16.95 (ISBN 0-201-03628-2). A-W.

--Man & Nature: Principles of Human & Environmental Biology. LC 74-19694. 480p. 1975. text ed. 18.95 (ISBN 0-201-03688-6). A-W.

Kimball, Kathleen M. Big Foot, Little Foot. LC 78-68822. (Illus.). (ps-3). 1979. 5.00 (ISBN 0-933308-00-0). West Village.

Kimball, P. The Disconnected. LC 72-6349. 1972. 17.50x (ISBN 0-231-03696-5). Columbia U Pr.

Kimball, Richard L. China Beginner's Traveler's Dictionary. 1980. pap. 6.95 (ISBN 0-8351-0732-9). China Bks.

Kimball, Robert C., ed. see Tillich, Paul.

Kimball, Scott, jt. auth. see Kimball, Art.

Kimball, Virginia. Earthquake Ready. LC 80-8997. (Illus.). 128p. (Orig.). (gr. 6 up). 1981. pap. 5.95 (ISBN 0-915238-46-2). Peace Pr.

Kimball, Warren F. Swords or Ploughshares? the Morgenthau Plan for Defeated Nazi Germany: 1943-1946. LC 75-33057. (America's Alternatives Ser.). 172p. 1976. pap. text ed. 3.25x o.p. (ISBN 0-397-47350-8). Lippincott.

Kimbell, R. B. Verdi in the Age of Italian Romanticism. (Illus.). 800p. Date not set. price not set (ISBN 0-521-23052-7). Cambridge U Pr.

Kimber, Edward. The History of the Life & Adventures of Mr. Anderson. Washburn, Wilcomb E., ed. LC 75-7026. (Narratives of North American Indian Captivities: Vol. 7). 1975. lib. bdg. 44.00 (ISBN 0-8240-1631-9). Garland Pub.

--The Juvenile Adventures of David Ranger, Esq. 1757, 2 vols. in 1. LC 74-17443. (Novel in England, 1700-1775 Ser.). 1974. lib. bdg. 50.00 (ISBN 0-8240-1148-1). Garland Pub.

--The Life & Adventures of Joe Thompson, 1750, 2 vols. in 1. LC 74-17302. (Novel in England, 1700-1775 Ser). 1974. lib. bdg. 50.00 (ISBN 0-8240-1130-9). Garland Pub.

--Maria: The Genuine Memoirs of a Young Lady of Rank & Fortune, 1765, 2 vols. in 1. LC 74-16057. (Novel in England, 1700-1775 Ser). 1974. lib. bdg. 50.00 (ISBN 0-8240-1171-6). Garland Pub.

Kimber, Richard T. & Boyd, A. Automation in Libraries. 2nd ed. 1974. text ed. 28.00 (ISBN 0-08-017969-X). Pergamon.

Kimber, Rita, tr. see Adams, Willi P.

Kimber, Rita, tr. see Chotjewitz, Peter O.

Kimber, Robert, tr. see Adams, Willi P.

Kimber, Robert, tr. see Chotjewitz, Peter O.

Kimberly, John R., et al. The Organizational Life Cycle: Issues in the Creation, Transformation, & Decline of Organizations. LC 79-92446. (Social & Behavioral Science Ser.). 1980. text ed. 19.95x (ISBN 0-87589-459-3). Jossey-Bass.

Kimberly, Robert C. Problems of Recurrent Hernia. (Illus.). 76p. 1975. pap. 9.50 (ISBN 0-398-03374-9). C C Thomas.

Kimble, Daniel P. Physiological Psychology. LC 63-13008. (Psychology Ser). (Orig., Prog. Bk.). 1963. 9.95 (ISBN 0-201-03683-5); manual with tests 1.00 (ISBN 0-201-03686-X). A-W.

Kimble, David. Political History of Ghana: The Rise of Gold Coast Nationalism, 1850-1928. 1963. 37.50x (ISBN 0-19-821623-8). Oxford U Pr.

Kimble, Gregory A., ed. Foundations of Conditioning & Learning. LC 67-10442. (Century Psychology Ser.). (Illus.). 1967. 38.50x (ISBN 0-89197-172-6); pap. text ed. 18.50x o. p. (ISBN 0-89197-762-7). Irvington.

--Hilgard & Marquis' Conditioning & Learning. 2nd ed. 1961. 21.95 (ISBN 0-13-388876-2). P-H.

Kimble, Gregory A., et al. Principles of General Psychology. 5th ed. LC 79-23269. 1980. 18.95x (ISBN 0-471-04469-5, Pub by Ronald Pr). Wiley.

Kimbrall, Grady. Introduction to Business & Office Careers. (gr. 7-10). 1975. pap. text ed. 5.00 activity ed. (ISBN 0-87345-181-3). McKnight.

Kimbrall, Mary E. Introduction to Health Careers. (gr. 7-10). 1975. pap. text ed. 5.00 activity ed (ISBN 0-87345-179-1). McKnight.

Kimbrell, Grady & Vineyard, Ben S. Activities for Succeeding in the World of Work. 1975. pap. 4.64 (ISBN 0-87345-526-6). McKnight.

--Individualized Related Instruction for Succeeding in the World of Work. pap. 4.64 (ISBN 0-87345-547-9). McKnight.

--Strategies for Implementing Work Experience Programs. 400p. 1975. text ed. 34.67 (ISBN 0-87345-528-2). McKnight.

--Succeeding in the World of Work. rev. ed. (gr. 10-12). 1975. text ed. 14.64 (ISBN 0-87345-525-8); filmstrip set 330.00 (ISBN 0-685-04243-X). McKnight.

Kimbro, Ralph H. The Art of Pipewelding. 1981. 10.00 (ISBN 0-8062-1633-6). Carlton.

Kimbrough, Emily. Time Enough. LC 74-1823. (Illus.). 256p. 1974. 10.00 o.s.i. (ISBN 0-06-012364-8, HarpT). Har-Row.

Kimbrough, Emily, jt. auth. see Skinner, Cornelia O.

Kimbrough, J. Defender of Angels. 1969. 6.95 o.s.i. (ISBN 0-02-563030-X). Macmillan.

Kimbrough, Katheryn. Ilene, the Superstitious. (The Saga of the Phenwick Women: No. 14). 1977. pap. 1.50 o.p. (ISBN 0-445-03181-6). Popular Lib.

--Joanne, the Unpredictable. (Saga of the Phenwick Women Ser.: Bk. 8). 256p. 1976. pap. 1.25 o.p. (ISBN 0-445-00347-2). Popular Lib.

Kimbrough, Kathryn. Alexandria, the Ambivalent. (Saga of the Phenwick Women Ser.: No. 36). 256p. 1981. pap. 2.25 (ISBN 0-445-04655-4). Popular Lib.

--Saga of the Phenwick Women: Letitia, the Dreamer, Vol. 35. 1981. pap. 2.25 (ISBN 0-445-04638-4). Popular Lib.

Kimbrough, Ralph B. & Nunnery, Michael Y. Politics, Power, Polls, & School Elections. LC 70-146308. 1971. 15.25x (ISBN 0-8211-1012-8); text ed. 13.75x (ISBN 0-685-04201-4). McCutchan.

Kimbrough, Robert. Sir Philip Sidney. (English Authors Ser.: No. 114). lib. bdg. 10.95 (ISBN 0-8057-1492-8). Twayne.

Kimbrough, Robert, ed. see Conrad, Joseph.

Kimche, David, jt. auth. see Kimche, Jon.

Kimche, Jon. Seven Fallen Pillars. LC 76-6848. (The Middle East in the 20th Century). 1976. Repr. of 1950 ed. lib. bdg. 39.50 (ISBN 0-306-70820-5). Da Capo.

Kimche, Jon & Kimche, David. Both Sides of the Hill: Britain & the Palestine War. (Return to Zion Ser.). (Illus.). 287p. 1981. Repr. of 1960 ed. lib. bdg. 20.00x (ISBN 0-87991-145-X). Porcupine Pr.

Kime, R., et al. Health Instruction: An Action Approach. 1977. text ed. 16.50 (ISBN 0-13-385252-0). P-H.

Kime, R. D., jt. auth. see Nelder, J. A.

Kime, Robert E. Health: A Consumer's Dilemma. 1970. pap. 4.95x (ISBN 0-534-00661-2). Wadsworth Pub.

Kime, Wayne. Washington Irving Miscellaneous Writings, 1803-1859. (Critical Editions Program). 1981. lib. bdg. 75.00 (ISBN 0-8057-8520-5). Twayne.

Kimeldorf, Donald J. & Hunt, Edward L. Ionizing Radiation: Neural Function & Behavior. (Atomic Energy Commission Monographs). 1965. 19.00 o.p. (ISBN 0-12-406950-9). Acad Pr.

Kimenyi, Alexandre. Linguistics: A Relational Grammar of Kinyarwanda. (UC Publications in Linguistics: Vol. 91). 1980. 13.00x (ISBN 0-520-09598-7). U of Cal Pr.

Kimes, Beverly R. The Cars That Henry Ford Built. LC 78-51029. 1978. 19.95 (ISBN 0-915038-08-0). Princeton Pub.

Kimes, Beverly R., ed. Packard: A History of the Motor Car & the Company. LC 78-71063. 1979. 75.00 (ISBN 0-915038-12-9); leather bdg. 95.00 (ISBN 0-915038-26-9). Princeton Pub.

Kimishima, Hisako. Lum Fu & the Golden Mountain. Tresselt, Alvin, tr. from Japanese. LC 77-136991. Orig. Title: Yama Ippai No Kinka. (Illus.). (gr. k-3). 1971. 5.95 o.s.i. (ISBN 0-8193-0469-7, Four Winds); PLB 5.41 o.s.i. (ISBN 0-8193-0470-0). Schol Bk Serv.

--Ma Lien & the Magic Brush. LC 68-21077. Orig. Title: Ma Lien to Haho No Fude. (Illus.). (gr. k-3). 1968. 5.95 o.s.i. (ISBN 0-8193-0343-7, Four Winds); PLB 5.41 o.s.i. (ISBN 0-8193-0344-5). Schol Bk Serv.

Kimmel, Carole A. & Buelke-Sam, Judith, eds. Developmental Toxicity. (Target Organ Toxicity Ser.). 1981. price not set. Raven.

Kimmel, Douglas C. Adulthood & Aging: An Interdisciplinary Developmental View. 2nd ed. LC 79-24037. 1980. text ed. 18.95x (ISBN 0-471-05229-9); tchrs. manual avail. (ISBN 0-471-05237-X). Wiley.

Kimmel, Eric A. Nicanor's Gate. 32p. (gr. k-4). 1979. 5.95 (ISBN 0-8276-0168-9). Jewish Pubn.

Kimmel, Jay M. Real Estate Investment. 1980. 9.95 (ISBN 0-346-12439-5). Cornerstone.

Kimmel, Jo. Steps to Prayer Power. 1976. pap. 1.25 (ISBN 0-685-84388-2). Jove Pubns.

Kimmel, K. & Walker, R. O. Practising Dentistry. (Illus.). 258p. 1972. 46.00. Quint Pub Co.

Kimmey, John & Brown, Ashley, eds. The World of Tragedy. 1981. pap. 3.95 (ISBN 0-451-61991-9, ME1991, Ment). NAL.

Kimmey, John L., jt. ed. see Brown, Ashley.

Kimmich, H. P. Implantable Telemetry Systems Based on Integrated Circuits. (Biotelemetry & Patient Monitoring: Vol. 6, No. 3). (Illus.). 1979. pap. 16.25 (ISBN 3-8055-0358-X). S Karger.

--Monitoring of Vital Parameters During Extracorporeal Circulation. (Illus.). 1981. soft cover 72.00 (ISBN 3-8055-2059-X). S Karger.

Kimmich, H. P., ed. Fifth International Symposium on Biotelemetry, Sapporo, June 1980 & Kyoto, June 1980. (Biotelemetry & Patient Monitoring Journal: Vol. 7, No. 1). 52p. 1980. 19.75 (ISBN 3-8055-1073-X). S Karger.

--Wildlife Biotelemetry. (Journal: Biotelemetry & Patient Monitoring: Vol. 7, No. 3-4). (Illus.). 116p. 1980. pap. write for info. (ISBN 3-8055-2093-X). S Karger.

Kimpel, Ben F. Philosophies of Life of Ancient Greeks & Israelites. LC 80-81697. 1981. 17.50 (ISBN 0-8022-2371-0). Philos Lib.

Kimpton, Robert S., jt. auth. see Stephenson, Hugh E.

Kimsey, Larry R. & Roberts, Jean L. Referring the Psychiatric Patient: A Guide for the Physician. (American Lectures in Clinical Psychiatry Ser.). 100p. 1973. text ed. 9.50 (ISBN 0-398-02725-0). C C Thomas.

Kimura, Gibun. Why Pursue the Buddha? Yokogawa, Ken'Ichi, tr. from Japanese. LC 75-14981. Orig. Title: Kagerinaki Daihi. (Illus.). 160p. 1976. 5.95 o.p. (ISBN 0-912624-00-0). Nembutsu Pr.

Kimura, Ken-Ichi. Scientific Basis of Air Conditioning. (Illus.). 1977. 46.70x (ISBN 0-85334-732-8, Pub. by Applied Science). Burgess-Intl Ideas.

Kimura, Motoo & Ohta, Tomoko. Theoretical Aspects of Population Genetics. LC 75-155963. (Monographs in Population Biology: No. 4). 1971. 16.50 o.p. (ISBN 0-691-08096-8); pap. 9.00 (ISBN 0-691-08098-4). Princeton U Pr.

Kimura, Ryozo. Color Atlas of Gonioscopy. (Illus.). 1973. 35.00 (ISBN 0-89640-037-9). Igaku-Shoin.

Kimzey, Bruce W. The Property Tax in New Mexico. 1977. pap. text ed. 7.50x (ISBN 0-8191-0131-1). U Pr of Amer.

Kinard, J. Spencer. The Worth of a Smile. LC 75-42298. 1976. 8.95 (ISBN 0-13-969139-1). P-H.

Kinard, Jerry, jt. auth. see Iverstine, Joe C.

Kincaid, A. N., ed. see Buck, George.

Kincaid, Charles A. Deccan Nursery Tales; or, Fairy Tales from the South. LC 76-78183. xiv, 135p. 1972. Repr. of 1914 ed. 18.00 (ISBN 0-8103-3815-7). Gale.

Kincaid, D. Lawrence, jt. auth. see Rogers, Everett M.

Kincaid, David, jt. auth. see Cheney, Ward.

Kincaid, Dennis. British Social Life in India 1608-1937. 2nd ed. (Illus.). 1973. 20.00 (ISBN 0-7100-7284-8). Routledge & Kegan.

Kincaid, Joseph J. Cristobal de Villalon. (World Authors Ser.: Spain: No. 264). 1971. lib. bdg. 10.95 (ISBN 0-8057-2963-1). Twayne.

Kincaid, William M. Promotion: Products, Servies & Ideas. (Illus.). 360p. 1981. text ed. 19.95 (ISBN 0-675-08082-7); tchr's. manual avail. Merrill.

Kincaid-Smith, P., et al. Progress in Glomerulonephritis. (Perspectives in Nephrology & Hypertension Ser.). 1979. 55.00 (ISBN 0-471-04424-5, Pub. by Wiley Med). Wiley.

Kincaid-Smith, Priscilla, jt. ed. see Hodson, John C.

Kincaid-Smith, Priscilla, et al. Glomerulonephritis: Morphology, Natural History, & Treatment, Pts. 1-2. LC 73-6562. (Perspectives in Nephrology & Hypertension Ser). 1238p. 1973. Set. 77.50 (ISBN 0-471-47762-1, Pub. by Wiley-Medical). Wiley.

Kincannon, James C. Fundamentals of Alcohol Problems. (Illus.). 300p. Date not set. pap. text ed. 10.50 (ISBN 0-8016-2695-1). Mosby. Postponed.

Kinchen, Oscar A. General Bennet H. Young. 1981. 8.95 (ISBN 0-8158-0404-0). Chris Mass.

Kinchin, F. & Melluish, J. W., eds. Catullus: Selections from the Poems. (Roman World Ser.). 1956. pap. text ed. 3.95x (ISBN 0-04-874001-2). Allen Unwin.

Kind, Stuart & Overman, Michael. Science Against Crime. LC 76-178896. 160p. 1972. PLB 7.95 o.p. (ISBN 0-385-09293-8). Doubleday.

Kindelehrer, Jane. The Art of Cooking with Love & Wheatgerm. Gerras, Charlie, ed. LC 76-49579. 1977. 9.95 (ISBN 0-87857-148-5); pap. 7.95 (ISBN 0-87857-280-5). Rodale Pr Inc.

Kinder, E. F., jt. auth. see Riesen, Austin H.

Kinder, Herman & Hilgemann, Werner. The Anchor Atlas of World History, Vol. 2. 1978. pap. 5.95 (ISBN 0-385-13355-3, Anch). Doubleday.

Kinder, Marsha & Houston, Beverle. The Self & Cinema. 1980. pap. 7.90 (ISBN 0-913178-62-4). Redgrave Pub Co.

Kinderlehrer, J. Kosher Cooking: The Natural Way. 1980. 12.50 o.p. (ISBN 0-8246-0240-4). Jonathan David.

Kinderlehrer, Jane. Cooking Kosher! The Natural Way. 1980. 12.50 (ISBN 0-8246-0240-4). Jonathan David.

--How to Feel Younger, Longer. LC 74-13909. (Illus.). 228p. 1974. 8.95 (ISBN 0-87857-083-7); pap. 6.95 (ISBN 0-87857-278-3). Rodale Pr Inc.

Kinderman, Katherine S., jt. auth. see La, Ruth E.

Kindermann, Ross & Snell, J. Laurie. Markov Random Fields & Their Applications. (Contemporary Mathematics Ser.: Vol. 1). 1980. 8.80 (ISBN 0-8218-5001-6). Am Math.

Kindersley, Anna. The Mountains of Serbia: Travels Through Inland Yugoslavia. (Illus.). 1977. 26.00 (ISBN 0-7195-3300-7). Transatlantic.

Kindersley, David. Optical Letterspacing. (Illus.). pap. 12.50 (ISBN 0-913720-05-4). Sandstone.

Kindersley, David & Cardozo, Lida L. Letters Slate Cut. (Illus.). 96p. 1981. pap. 9.95 (ISBN 0-8008-4741-5, Pentalic). Taplinger.

Kindilien, Carlin T. American Poetry in the Eighteen Nineties: A Study of American Verse, 1890-1899. LC 56-12410. (Brown University Studies: No. 20). 223p. 1956. 8.50x (ISBN 0-87057-039-0, Pub. by Brown U Pr). Univ Pr of New England.

Kindleberger, Charles P. America in the World Economy. (Headline Ser.: 237). (Illus.). 1977. pap. 3.00 (ISBN 0-87124-043-2, 77-86278). Foreign Policy.

--American Business Abroad: Six Lectures on Direct Investment. LC 69-12325. (Illus.). 1969. 16.00x o.p. (ISBN 0-300-01096-6); pap. 3.95 o.p. (ISBN 0-300-01085-0, Y213). Yale U Pr.

--The World in Depression, 1929-1939. (Library Reprint Ser: No. 64). 1975. 15.75 o.p. (ISBN 0-520-02912-7); pap. 4.95x (ISBN 0-520-02514-8). U of Cal Pr.

Kindleberger, Charles P. & Lindert, Peter. International Economics. 6th ed. 1978. text ed. 19.25 (ISBN 0-256-02028-0). Irwin.

Kindler, J., jt. ed. see Haimes, Y.

Kindred, Alton R. Data Systems & Management. 2nd ed. (Illus.). 1980. text ed. 18.95 (ISBN 0-13-196402-X). P-H.

--Data Systems & Management: An Introduction to Systems Analysis & Design. (Illus.). 368p. 1973. text ed. 15.95 o.p. (ISBN 0-13-196766-5); 5.95 o.p. study guide & wkbk. (ISBN 0-13-196865-3). P-H.

--Introduction to Computers. 1976. 19.95 (ISBN 0-13-480087-7). P-H.

Kindred, L. W., et al. The School & Community Relations. 2nd ed. LC 75-9699. (Illus.). 368p. 1976. 18.95 (ISBN 0-13-792259-0). P-H.

Kindred, Michael, et al. The Mentally Retarded Citizen & the Law: The President's Committee on Mental Retardation. LC 74-21489. 1976. 25.00 (ISBN 0-02-916860-0). Free Pr.

Kindrick, Robert L. Robert Henryson. (English Authors Ser.: No. 274). 1979. 14.50 (ISBN 0-8057-6758-4). Twayne.

Kine, Jack. Miniature Scenic Modelling. (Illus., Orig.). 1979. pap. 7.50x (ISBN 0-85242-650-X). Intl Pubns Serv.

Kine, R. Carole, et al. Basic Science Nursing Review. LC 80-22950. 208p. (Orig.). 1981. pap. text ed. 8.00 (ISBN 0-668-05133-7, 5133). Arco.

Kinert, Reed. Racing Planes & Air Races, Vol. 11. LC 67-16455. (Illus.). 96p. 1975. pap. 4.95 (ISBN 0-8168-7865-X). Aero.

King. Chemistry. 1979. 19.95 (ISBN 0-525-07926-2). Dutton.

--Land Reform: The Italian Experience. 34.95 (ISBN 0-408-70472-1). Butterworths.

--The Shining. 1980. pap. 2.75 o.p. (ISBN 0-451-09216-3, Sig). NAL.

King & Treat. Florida One Hundred Years Ago. (Sun Historical Ser.). (Illus.). pap. 3.50 (ISBN 0-89540-055-3). Sun Pub.

King, A. & Nicol, C. Venereal Diseases. 4th ed. 1980. text ed. 45.00 (ISBN 0-02-858270-5). Macmillan.

King, A. D. Colonial Urban Development: Culture, Social Power & Environment. 1977. 27.50x (ISBN 0-7100-8404-8). Routledge & Kegan.

King, A. L., jt. ed. see Bonnington, S. T.

King, A. L., jt. ed. see Pursall, B. R.

King, A. R., Jr. & Brownell, J. A. Curriculum & the Disciplines of Knowledge. LC 74-13124. 240p. 1976. Repr. of 1966 ed. 12.50 o.p. (ISBN 0-88275-211-1). Krieger.

King, A. S. & McLelland, J. Outlines of Avian Anatomy. 2nd ed. (Illus.). 154p. 1981. text ed. write for info. (ISBN 0-8121-0779-9). Lea & Febiger.

King, Alec H. Mozart Wind & String Concertos. LC 75-27957. (BBC Music Guides: No. 35). (Illus.). 64p. (Orig.). 1978. pap. 2.95 (ISBN 0-295-95478-7). U of Wash Pr.

--Printed Music in the British Museum: A Guide to the Catalogues & Their Construction. 208p. 1979. 33.00 (ISBN 0-89664-409-X, Pub. by K G Saur). Shoe String.

King, Alexander, ed. see International Symposium on Science & Technology for Development, Singapore, 1979.

King, Alexander, et al, eds. Bioresources for Development: The Renewable Way of Life. LC 79-28229. (Pergamon Policy Studies). (Illus.). 368p. 1980. 39.50 (ISBN 0-08-025581-7). Pergamon.

King, Alison. The Dreamer, Lost in Terror. 256p. 1976. pap. 1.25 o.p. (ISBN 0-445-00356-1). Popular Lib.

King, Allen L., ed. see International Working Seminar on the Role of the History of Physics in Physics Education.

King, Anita, compiled by. Quotations in Black. LC 80-1794. (Illus.). 320p. 1981. lib. bdg. 25.00 (ISBN 0-313-22128-6, KQB/). Greenwood.

King, Anthony. British Members of Parliament: A Self Portrait. 128p. 1975. 12.50 (ISBN 0-333-17170-5). Transatlantic.

King, B. J. & Beer, J. E. Home Heating. (Teach Yourself Ser.). 1974. pap. 2.95 o.p. (ISBN 0-679-10470-4). McKay.

King, Bart. How to Raise & Train a Gordon Setter. (Orig.). 1965. pap. 2.00 (ISBN 0-87666-307-2, DS1082). TFH Pubns.

King, Bert. Cocker Spaniels. (Illus.). 1979. 2.95 (ISBN 0-87666-692-6, KW-043). TFH Pubns.

King, Bert, et al, eds. Managerial Control & Organizational Democracy. LC 77-13200. (Scripta Ser. in Personality & Social Psychology). 1978. 22.95 (ISBN 0-470-99323-5). Halsted Pr.

King, Bill & King, Pat. Money Talks, It Says Good-by. 112p. 1977. 3.45 (ISBN 0-930756-31-2, 4230-K14). Women's Aglow.

King, C., jt. auth. see Hickey, M.

King, C. A., jt. auth. see Embleston, C.

King, C. Judson. Separation Processes. 2nd ed. (Chemical Engineering Ser.). (Illus.). 1979. text ed. 28.95 (ISBN 0-07-034612-7); solutions manual 8.50 (ISBN 0-07-034613-5). McGraw.

King, C. Richard. A Birthday in Texas. LC 80-11751. (Illus.). 64p. (gr. 3-6). 1980. 6.95 (ISBN 0-88319-051-6). Shoal Creek Pub.

--The Lady Cannoneer: A Biography of Angelina Belle Peyton Eberly, Heroine of Texas, Archives War. (Illus.). 192p. 1981. 12.95 (ISBN 0-89015-280-2). Eakins.

King, C. W. The Gnostics & Their Remains. LC 73-76092. (Illus.). 500p. 1981. Repr. of 1887 ed. 19.50 (ISBN 0-913510-34-3). Wizards.

King, Carlyle, jt. ed. see Chambers, Robert.

King, Carole. Professional Dining Room Management. (Ahrens Ser.). 160p. 1980. pap. 7.95 (ISBN 0-8104-9471-X). Hayden.

King, Cecil. With Malice Toward None: A War Diary by Cecil King. Armstrong, William, ed. LC 70-175619. 343p. 1971. 28.50 (ISBN 0-8386-1067-6). Fairleigh Dickinson.

King, Charles L. Ramon J. Sender. (World Authors Ser.: Spain: No. 307). 1974. lib. bdg. 12.50 (ISBN 0-8057-2815-5). Twayne.

--Ramon J. Sender: An Annotated Bibliography, 1928-1974. LC 76-9020. 301p. 1976. 14.50 (ISBN 0-8108-0933-8). Scarecrow.

King, Charles R., ed. see King, Rufus.

King, Cheryl N. see Wah-Be-Gwo-Nese, pseud.

King, Clarence. Mountaineering in the Sierra Nevada. LC 79-116056. 1970. pap. 3.95 (ISBN 0-8032-5716-3, BB 518, Bison). U of Nebr Pr.

King County Arts Commision, jt. ed. see Morris, Robert.

King County Historical Survey Committee. History of King County, Texas. (Illus.). 350p. 1975. 25.00 (ISBN 0-89015-106-7). Nortex Pr.

King County Physicians' Task Force. Your Guide to Physicians of King County, (Washington), 1978. 1978. pap. 5.95 (ISBN 0-685-91737-1). Madrona Pubs.

King, Cuchlaine. Introduction to Marine Geology & Geomorphology. LC 74-81340. 336p. 1975. pap. 19.50x (ISBN 0-8448-0401-0). Crane-Russak Co.

--Introduction to Physical & Biological Oceanography. LC 74-81339. 1974. pap. 19.50x (ISBN 0-8448-0400-2). Crane-Russak Co.

King, Cuchlaine A. Physical Geography. (Illus.). 332p. 1980. 34.50x (ISBN 0-389-20089-1). B&N.

King, David & Levine, Karen. Best Way in the World for a Woman to Make Money. 1980. pap. 4.95 (ISBN 0-446-97515-X). Warner Bks.

King, Derek & Bird, Peter. Small Boat Against the Sea. 1976. 12.95 (ISBN 0-236-40013-4, Pub. by Paul Elek). Merrimack Bk Serv.

King, Don R. Sex Self Taught: A Home - Study Course for Underachievers. LC 77-5909. 1977. 14.95 (ISBN 0-88229-386-9); pap. 7.95 (ISBN 0-88229-490-3). Nelson-Hall.

King, Donald B. Consumer Protection Experiments in Sweden. LC 73-89036. iv, 116p. (Orig.). 1974. pap. text ed. 10.00x (ISBN 0-8377-0728-5). Rothman.

--New Conceptualism of the Uniform Commercial Code. 126p. (Orig.). 1968. pap. text ed. 8.50x (ISBN 0-8377-0726-9). Rothman.

King, Donald W. & Bryant, Edward C. The Evaluation of Information Services & Products. LC 76-141595. (Illus.). 306p. 1971. text ed. 21.95 (ISBN 0-87815-003-X). Info Resources.

King, Donald W., et al, eds. Key Papers in the Economics of Information. 350p. 1980. text ed. 25.00 (ISBN 0-914236-62-8, ASIS). Knowledge Indus.

King, E. J. Education & Social Change. 1966. text ed. 15.00 (ISBN 0-08-012059-8); pap. text ed. 7.75 (ISBN 0-08-012058-X). Pergamon.

--The Teacher & the Needs of Society in Evolution. 1970. text ed. 19.50 (ISBN 0-08-016102-2); pap. text ed. 10.50 (ISBN 0-08-016103-0). Pergamon.

King, Edmanuel J., ed. see Hearnden, Arthur.

King, Edmund. Peterborough Abbey Ten Eighty-Six to Thirteen Ten. LC 72-91959. (Cambridge Studies in Economic History). (Illus.). 232p. 1972. 32.95 (ISBN 0-521-20133-0). Cambridge U Pr.

King, Edmund F., ed. Ten Thousand Wonderful Things. LC 75-124587. 1970. Repr. of 1860 ed. 25.00 (ISBN 0-8103-3009-1). Gale.

King, Edmund J. Comparative Studies & Educational Decision. LC 67-29489. 1968. 9.50 (ISBN 0-672-60627-5). Bobbs.

King, Edmund J., jt. auth. see Boyd, William.

King, Edmund J., ed. Education for Uncertainty. LC 78-63118. (Sage Annual Review of Social & Educational Change: Vol. 2). 1978. 18.50x (ISBN 0-8039-9896-1); pap. 9.95x (ISBN 0-8039-9897-X). Sage.

King, Edmund J., et al. Post Compulsory Education II. LC 74-31574. (Sage Studies in Social & Educational Change: Vol. 2). 1975. 17.50x (ISBN 0-8039-9953-4); pap. 8.95x (ISBN 0-8039-9950-X). Sage.

King, Edmund J., et al, eds. Post-Compulsory Education: A New Analysis in Western Europe. LC 74-76709. (Sage Studies in Social & Educational Change: Vol. 1). 1974. 22.50x (ISBN 0-8039-9900-3). Sage.

King, Edward L. Chemistry. 1100p. 1981. text ed. 23.95 (ISBN 0-394-32761-6). Random.

--How Chemical Reactions Occur. (Orig.). (YA) (gr. 9-12). 1963. pap. 8.95 (ISBN 0-8053-5401-8, 5401). Benjamin-Cummings.

King, Elbert A. Space Geology: An Introduction. LC 75-45357. 400p. 1976. text ed. 31.95 (ISBN 0-471-47810-5). Wiley.

King, Eleanor A. Bible Plants for American Gardens. LC 75-3646. (Illus.). 224p. 1975. pap. 3.50 (ISBN 0-486-23188-7). Dover.

King, Elizabeth C. Classroom Evaluation Strategies. LC 79-13907. (Illus.). 1979. pap. text ed. 11.50 (ISBN 0-8016-2674-9). Mosby.

King, Ernest & Whitehill, Walter. Fleet Admiral King. LC 78-11889. (Politics and Strategy of World War II Ser.). 1976. Repr. of 1952 ed. lib. bdg. 49.50 (ISBN 0-306-70772-1). Da Capo.

King, Everard H. James Beattie. (English Authors Ser.: No. 206). 1977. lib. bdg. 10.95 (ISBN 0-8057-6653-7). Twayne.

King, F. W. & Cree, D. Ann. English Business Letters. (Illus.). 1980. pap. text ed. 4.00x (ISBN 0-582-55353-9). Longman.

King Features. The Amazing Adventures of Flash Gordon, 6 vols. Incl. Vol. 1 (ISBN 0-448-17240-2); Vol. 2 (ISBN 0-448-17241-0); Vol. 3. 192p (ISBN 0-448-17242-9); Vol. 4 (ISBN 0-448-17155-4); Vol. 5 (ISBN 0-448-17208-9); Vol. 6 (ISBN 0-448-17245-3). (Flash Gordon Cartoon Ser.). 192p. 1980. pap. 1.75 ea. (Tempo). G&D.

King, Florence. Wasp, Where Is Thy Sting? pap. 4.95 (ISBN 0-8128-6025-X). Stein & Day.

King, Francis & Skinner, Stephen. Techniques of High Magic. (Warner Destiny Bk). (Orig.). 1976. pap. 1.95 o.s.i. (ISBN 0-446-89378-1). Warner Bks.

King, Francis H. Classical & Foreign Quotations. 3rd ed. LC 68-30647. 1968. Repr. of 1904 ed. 18.00 (ISBN 0-8103-3185-3). Gale.

King, Francis P., jt. auth. see Greenough, William C.

King, Frank A. The Missabe Road: The Duluth, Missabe & Iron Range Railway. LC 74-190177. (Illus.). 200p. 1972. 19.95 (ISBN 0-87095-040-1). Golden West.

King, Frank H. & King, Viola W. Aviation Safety Bibliography & Source Book. LC 80-21946. (Aviation Management Ser.). 80p. (Orig.). 1980. pap. write for info. (ISBN 0-89100-138-7). Aviation Maintenance.

King, Fred D. Palmer Method Cursive, Consumable. new ed. (Palmer Method Easy to Teach Ser.). (Illus.). (gr. 6). 1979. wkbk. 2.60 (ISBN 0-914268-68-6, 79-6C); tchr's ed. 5.32 (ISBN 0-914268-69-4, 79-6CTE). A N Palmer.

King, Fred M. Palmer Method Cursive, Consumable. new ed. (Palmer Method Easy to Teach Ser.). (Illus.). (gr. 4). 1979. wkbk 2.60 (ISBN 0-914268-64-3, 79-4C); tchr's ed. 5.32 (ISBN 0-914268-65-1, 79-4CTE). A N Palmer.

--Palmer Method Cursive, Consumable. (Palmer Method Easy to Teach Ser.). (Illus.). (gr. 4). 1976. wkbk. 2.60 (ISBN 0-914268-31-7, 76-4C); tchr's ed 5.32 (ISBN 0-914268-32-5, 76-4C-TE). A N Palmer.

--Palmer Method Cursive, Consumable. (Palmer Method Easy to Teach Ser.). (Illus.). (gr. 5). 1976. wkbk 2.60 (ISBN 0-914268-33-3, 76-5C); tchr's ed. 5.32 (ISBN 0-914268-34-1, 76-5C-TE). A N Palmer.

--Palmer Method Cursive, Consumable. (Palmer Method Easy to Teach Ser.). (Illus.). (gr. 6). 1976. wkbk. 2.60 (ISBN 0-914268-35-X, 76-6C); tchr's ed. 5.32 (ISBN 0-914268-36-8, 76-6C-TE). A N Palmer.

--Palmer Method Cursive, Grade 5, Consumable. new ed. (Palmer Method Easy to Teach Ser.). (Illus.). (gr. 5). 1979. wkbk. 2.60 (ISBN 0-914268-66-X, 79-5C); tchr's ed. 5.32 (ISBN 0-914268-67-8, 79-5CTE). A N Palmer.

--Palmer Method Cursive, Non-Consumable. (Palmer Method Easy to Teach Ser.). (gr. 8). 1979. wkbk 3.20 (ISBN 0-914268-86-4, N79-SL2); tchr's ed. 5.32 (ISBN 0-914268-87-2, N79-SL2TE). A N Palmer.

--Palmer Method Cursive, Non-Consumable. (Palmer Method Easy to Teach Ser.). (Illus.). 1979. wkbk 3.20 (ISBN 0-914268-84-8, N79-SL1); tchr's ed. 5.32 (ISBN 0-914268-85-6, N79-SL1TE). A N Palmer.

--Palmer Method Cursive, Non-Consumable. new ed. (Palmer Method Easy to Teach Ser.). (Illus.). (gr. 6). 1979. wkbk 3.20 (ISBN 0-914268-82-1, N79-6C); tchr's ed. 5.32 (ISBN 0-914268-83-X, N79-6CTE). A N Palmer.

--Palmer Method Cursive, Non-Consumable. new ed. (Palmer Method Easy to Teach Ser.). 1979. wkbk. 3.20 (ISBN 0-914268-80-5, N79-5C); tchr's ed. 5.32 (ISBN 0-914268-81-3, N79-5CTE). A N Palmer.

--Palmer Method Cursive, Non-Consumable. (Palmer Method Easy to Teach Ser.). (Illus.). (gr. 4). 1975. wkbk. 3.20 (ISBN 0-914268-45-7, N75-4C); tchr's ed. 5.32 (ISBN 0-914268-46-5, N75-4C-TE). A N Palmer.

--Palmer Method Cursive, Non-Consumable. (Palmer Method Easy to Teach Ser.). (Illus.). (gr. 5). 1975. wkbk. 3.20 (ISBN 0-914268-47-3, N75-5C); tchr's ed. 5.32 (ISBN 0-914268-48-1, N75-5C-TE). A N Palmer.

--Palmer Method Cursive, Non-Consumable. (Palmer Method Easy to Teach Ser.). (Illus.). (gr. 6). 1975. wkbk. 3.20 (ISBN 0-914268-49-X, N75-6C); tchr's ed. 5.32 (ISBN 0-914268-50-3, N75-6C-TE). A N Palmer.

--Palmer Method Cursive, Non-Consumable. (Palmer Method Easy to Teach Ser.). (Illus.). (gr. 7). 1976. wkbk 3.20 (ISBN 0-914268-51-1, N75-SL1); tchr's ed. 5.32 (ISBN 0-914268-52-X, N75-SL1-TE). A N Palmer.

--Palmer Method Cursive, Non-Consumable. (Palmer Method Easy to Teach Ser.). (Illus.). (gr. 8). 1976. wkbk. 3.20 (ISBN 0-914268-53-8, N75-SL2); tchr's ed. 5.32 (ISBN 0-914268-54-6, N75-SL2-TE). A N Palmer.

--Palmer Method Manuscript, Consumable. new ed. (Palmer Method Easy to Teach Ser.). (Illus.). (gr. 1). 1979. 2.60 (ISBN 0-914268-56-2, 79-1M); tchr's ed. 5.32 (ISBN 0-914268-57-0, 79-1MTE). A N Palmer.

--Palmer Method Manuscript, Consumable. new ed. (Palmer Method Easy to Teach Ser.). (Illus.). (gr. 2). 1979. wkbk. 2.60 (ISBN 0-914268-58-9, 79-2M); tchr's ed. 5.32 (ISBN 0-914268-59-7, 79-2MTE). A N Palmer.

--Palmer Method Manuscript, Consumable. (Palmer Method Easy to Teach Ser.). (Illus.). (gr. 1). 1976. tchr's ed. 5.32 (ISBN 0-914268-24-4, 76-IM-TE); wkbk. 2.60 (ISBN 0-914268-23-6, 76-1M). A N Palmer.

--Palmer Method Manuscript, Consumable. (Palmer Method Easy to Teach Ser.). (Illus.). (gr. 2). 1976. wkbk. 2.60 (ISBN 0-914268-25-2, 76-2M); tchr's man. 5.32 (ISBN 0-914268-26-0, 76-2M TE). A N Palmer.

--Palmer Method Manuscript, Non-Consumable. new ed. (Palmer Method Easy to Teach Ser.). (Illus.). (gr. 2). 1979. wkbk. 3.20 (ISBN 0-914268-72-4, N79-2M); tchr's ed. 5.32 (ISBN 0-914268-73-2, N79-2MTE). A N Palmer.

--Palmer Method Manuscript, Non-Consumable. new ed. (Palmer Method Easy to Teach Ser.). (Illus.). (gr. 1). 1979. wkbk. 3.20 (ISBN 0-914268-70-8, N79-1M); tchr's ed. 5.32 (ISBN 0-914268-71-6, N79-1MTE). A N Palmer.

--Palmer Method Manuscript, Non-Consumable. (Palmer Method Easy to Teach Ser.). (Illus.). (gr. 1). 1976. wkbk. 3.20 (ISBN 0-914268-37-6, N75-1M); tchr's ed. 5.32 (ISBN 0-914268-38-4, N75-1M-TE). A N Palmer.

--Palmer Method Manuscript, Non-Consumable. (Palmer Method Easy to Teach Ser.). (Illus.). (gr. 2). 1976. wkbk. 3.20 (ISBN 0-914268-39-2, N75-2M); tchr's ed. 5.32 (ISBN 0-914268-40-6, N75-2M-TE). A N Palmer.

--Palmer Method Transition on Cursive, Consumable. (Palmer Method Easy to Teach Ser.). (Illus.). (gr. 3). 1976. wkbk. 2.60 (ISBN 0-914268-29-5, 76-3TC); tchr's ed. 5.32 (ISBN 0-914268-30-9, 76-3TC-TE). A N Palmer.

--Palmer Method Transition on Cursive, Non-Consumable. (Palmer Method Easy to Teach Ser.). (gr. 3). 1979. wkbk 3.20 (ISBN 0-914268-76-7, N79-3TC); tchr's ed. 5.32 (ISBN 0-914268-77-5, N79-3TC TE). A N Palmer.

--Palmer Method Transition to Cursive, Consumable. new ed. (Palmer Method Easy to Teach Ser.). (Illus.). (gr. 2). 1979. wkbk. 2.60 (ISBN 0-914268-60-0, 79-2TC); tchr's ed. 5.32 (ISBN 0-914268-61-9, 79-2TCTE). A N Palmer.

--Palmer Method Transition to Cursive Consumable. (Palmer Method Easy to Teach Ser.). (Illus.). (gr. 2). 1976. tchr's ed. 5.32 (ISBN 0-914268-28-7, 76-2TC-TE); wkbk. 2.60 (ISBN 0-914268-27-9, 76-2TC). A N Palmer.

--Palmer Method Transition to Cursive, Non-Consumable. new ed. (Palmer Method Easy to Teach Ser.). (Illus.). (gr. 2). 1979. wkbk. 3.20 (ISBN 0-914268-74-0, N79-2TC); tchr's ed. 5.32 (ISBN 0-914268-75-9, N79-2TCTE). A N Palmer.

--Palmer Method Transition to Cursive, Non-Consumable. (Palmer Method Easy to Teach Ser.). (Illus.). (gr. 2). 1976. wkbk. 3.20 (ISBN 0-914268-41-4, N75-2TC); tchr's ed. 5.32 (ISBN 0-914268-42-2, N75-2TC-TE). A N Palmer.

--Palmer Method Transition to Cursive, Non-Consumable. (Palmer Method Easy to Teach Ser.). (Illus.). (gr. 3). 1975. 3.20 (ISBN 0-914268-43-0, N75-3TC); tchr's ed. 5.32 (ISBN 0-914268-44-9, N75-3TC-TE). A N Palmer.

--Palmer Method Writing Readiness, Consumable. new ed. (Illus.). (gr. k-1). 1979. wkbk. 2.60 (ISBN 0-914268-55-4, 79-WR). A N Palmer.

--Palmer Method Writing Readiness, Consumable. (Palmer Method Easy to Teach Ser.). (Illus.). (gr. k-1). 1976. wkbk 2.60 (ISBN 0-914268-22-8, 76-WR). A N Palmer.

King, Glen D. First-Line Supervisor's Manual. (Police Science Ser.). 160p. 1976. 10.75 (ISBN 0-398-01017-X). C C Thomas.

King, Gordon J. Audio Equipment Tests. (Illus.). 1979. text ed. 18.00 (ISBN 0-408-00336-7). Butterworths.

King, Guy. All Through the Day. 128p. 1980. pap. 3.95 (ISBN 0-310-41831-3). Zondervan.

--Joy Way. 1973. pap. 2.50 (ISBN 0-87508-280-7). Chr Lit.

King, H. F. Aeromarine Origins. (Illus.). 1966. 5.50 o.p. (ISBN 0-370-00058-7). Aero.

--Armament of British Aircraft Nineteen Hundred & Nine to Nineteen Thirty-Nine. (Putnam Aeronautical Ser.). (Illus.). 1980. 17.95 (ISBN 0-370-00057-9, Pub. by Chatto Bodley Jonathan). Merrimack Bk Serv.

--Sopwith Aircraft Nineteen Twelve to Nineteen Twenty. (Illus.). 320p. 1981. 36.00 (ISBN 0-370-30050-5, Pub. by Chatto-Bodley-Jonathan). Merrimack Bk Serv.

King, H. Gill, jt. auth. see Aceves, Joseph B.

King, Harold. Closing Ceremonies. 1980. pap. write for info. (ISBN 0-671-83396-0). PB.

King, Harold & Everett, Alan. Components & Finishes. (Mitchell's Building Construction Ser.). 1978. pap. 13.95 (ISBN 0-470-26351-2). Halsted Pr.

King, Harold V. & Campbell, Russell N. English Reading Test. 1956. pap. 15.00 set of 20 tests (ISBN 0-87789-029-3); pap. 0.50 eRT answer key (ISBN 0-87789-030-7). Eng Language.

King, Hazel. Elizabeth Macarthur & Her World. 240p. 1980. 27.50x (ISBN 0-424-00080-6, Pub. by Sydney U Pr Australia). Intl Schol Bk Serv.

King, Henry C. The History of the Telescope. LC 79-87811. (Illus.). 480p. 1980. Repr. of 1979 ed. 16.50x (ISBN 0-938164-05-8). Vintage Bk Co.

King, Horace M. A Clear Introduction to Business Mathematics. 2nd ed. 580p. pap. text ed. 15.95x (ISBN 0-89863-035-5). Star Pub CA.

--Songs in the Night: A Study of the Book of Job. (Illus.). 1969. pap. 2.95 (ISBN 0-685-20632-7). Transatlantic.

King, Howard S. You Were Meant to Be Wealthy & Can Be. (Orig.). 1969. pap. 1.00 o.p. (ISBN 0-8283-1041-6). Branden.

King, Imogene M. Toward a Theory for Nursing: General Concepts of Human Behavior. LC 70-136716. (Nursing Ser). 1971. pap. 9.50 (ISBN 0-471-47800-8, Pub. by Wiley-Medical). Wiley.

King, Ivan. The Universe Unfolding. LC 75-33369. (Illus.). 1976. 21.95x (ISBN 0-7167-0521-4); resource bk. & instructor's manual 6.95x (ISBN 0-7167-0288-6). W H Freeman.

King, J. E., ed. Readings in Labour Economics. (Illus.). 454p. 1980. text ed. 39.50x (ISBN 0-19-877132-0); pap. text ed. 13.95x (ISBN 0-19-877133-9). Oxford U Pr.

King, J. O. An Introduction to Animal Husbandry. LC 78-4883. 1978. pap. 28.95 (ISBN 0-470-26338-5). Halsted Pr.

King, J. R. Production Planning & Control: An Introduction to Quantitative Methods. 1974. text ed. 42.00 (ISBN 0-08-017721-2); pap. text ed. 24.00 (ISBN 0-08-018983-0). Pergamon.

King, Jack. A Closeter Look at Hamburger. 1981. 4.95 (ISBN 0-917530-12-8); pap. write for info. (ISBN 0-685-97205-4). Pig Iron Pr.

King, Jack, pseud. Play Winning Poker. (Gambler's Book Shelf). 64p. 1979. pap. 2.95 (ISBN 0-89650-542-1). Gamblers.

King, James & Ryskamp, Charles, eds. The Letters & Prose Writings of William Cowper, Volume II: Letters 1782-1786. (Illus.). 586p. 1981. 98.00 (ISBN 0-19-812607-7). Oxford U Pr.

King, James R. Studies in Six Seventeenth Century Writers. LC 65-24645. xv, 236p. 1966. 12.95x (ISBN 0-8214-0013-4). Ohio U Pr.

King, James R., jt. auth. see Farner, Donald S.

King, Jean C. & Esposito, Tony, eds. The Designer's Guide to Text Type. 320p. 1980. pap. 24.95 (ISBN 0-442-25425-3). Van Nos Reinhold.

King, Jeannette M. Tragedy of the Victorian Novel. LC 77-77762. 1978. 36.00 (ISBN 0-521-21670-2). Cambridge U Pr.

King, Jere C., ed. The First World War. LC 72-80545. (Documentary History of Western Civilization Ser). 350p. 1973. 15.00x o.s.i. (ISBN 0-8027-2047-1). Walker & Co.

King, John & King, Martha. Answers & Explanations to Commercial Pilot Written Test Guide. (Pilot Training Ser.). (Illus.). 68p. 1979. pap. 6.95 (ISBN 0-89100-153-0, E*A-61-71-B*G). Aviation Maintenance.

--Answers & Explanations to Instrument Rating Written Test Guide. (Pilot Training Ser.). (Illus.). 90p. 1978. pap. 7.95 (ISBN 0-89100-091-7, E*A-61-8A*D*G). Aviation Maintenance.

--Answers & Explanations to Private Pilot - Airplane Written Test Guide. (Pilot Training Ser.). 58p. 1979. pap. 6.95 (ISBN 0-89100-104-2, E*A-61-32C*G). Aviation Maintenance.

--Combined Commercial Pilot Written Test Questions, Answers & Explanations Book. (Pilot Training Ser.). (Illus.). 210p. 1979. pap. 10.95 (ISBN 0-89100-167-0, EA-A C61-71 B-1). Aviation Maintenance.

--Flight Instructor's Written Test Questions, Answers & Explanations. combined ed. (Pilot Training Ser.). 1980. pap. 13.95 (ISBN 0-89100-200-6, E*A-A*C61-72B-1). Aviation Maintenance.

--Fundamentals of Instruction. (Pilot Training Ser.). 1979. pap. 2.95 (ISBN 0-89100-134-4, E*A-A*C61-90). Aviation Maintenance.

--Instrument Pilot Airplane Written Test Guide, Including Answers & Explanations. (Pilot Training Ser.). (Illus.). 290p. 1978. pap. 10.95 (ISBN 0-89100-196-4, E*A-A*C61-8D*G-1). Aviation Maintenance.

--Private Pilot - Airplane Written Test Questions Including Answers & Explanations. combined ed. (Pilot Training Ser.). (Illus.). 206p. 1979. pap. 8.95 (ISBN 0-89100-197-2, E*A-A*C61-32C-1). Aviation Maintenance.

King, John, jt. auth. see Howard, Michael.

King, John, jt. auth. see King, Martha.

King, John L. Human Behavior & Wall Street. LC 71-189196. 226p. 1972. 11.95 (ISBN 0-8040-0562-1). Swallow.

King, John L. see Kraemer, Kenneth L.

King, John L., jt. ed. see Kraemer, Kenneth L.

King, John R. Stabilization Policy in an African Setting Nineteen Sixty-Three to Seventy-Three. LC 79-670197. (Studies in the Economics of Africa). 1979. text ed. 25.95x (ISBN 0-435-97375-4); pap. text ed. 10.95x (ISBN 0-686-65420-X). Heinemann Ed.

King, Judith. The Greatest Gift Guide Ever. LC 79-65184. (Illus., Orig.). 1980. pap. 4.00 (ISBN 0-9602776-0-9). Variety Pr.

King, Judith E., jt. auth. see Harrison, Richard J.

King, K. Introductory Algebra & Related Topics for Technicians. 1979. pap. 11.95 (ISBN 0-13-501585-5). P-H.

King, K. C., ed. see Bostock, J. Knight.

King, Kenneth. The African Artisan: Education & the Informal Sector in Kenya. LC 76-58316. 1977. pap. text ed. 8.75x (ISBN 0-8077-8023-5). Tchrs Coll.

King, L. Thomas. Problem Solving in a Project Environment: A Consulting Process. 168p. 1981. 19.95 (ISBN 0-471-08115-9, Pub. by Wiley-Interscience). Wiley.

King, Larry L. Of Outlaws, Whores, Politicians, Con Men & Other Artists. 288p. 1981. pap. 3.95 (ISBN 0-14-005755-2). Penguin.

King, Lawrence, et al. Municipal Bankruptcy Law & Its Implications. (COMP Papers: No. P-6). 81p. (Orig.). 1980. pap. 12.00 (ISBN 0-916450-39-2). Coun on Municipal.

King, Leslie J. & Golledge, Reginald G. Cities, Space & Behavior: The Elements of Urban Geography. (Illus.). 1978. ref. 20.95 (ISBN 0-13-134601-6). P-H.

King, Lis. Furniture: How to Make -Do, Make Over, Make Your Own. LC 76-16409. (Illus.). 1976. pap. 4.95 (ISBN 0-8069-8356-6). Sterling.

King, Louise T. & Wexler, Jean S. The Martha's Vineyard Cook Book. LC 70-144180. (Illus.). 1971. 12.50 o.p. (ISBN 0-06-012398-2, HarpT). Har-Row.

King, Mark. For We Are: Toward Understanding Your Personal Potential. LC 74-10354. 1975. text ed. 6.00 (ISBN 0-201-03747-5). A-W.

King, Martha & King, John. Flight Instructor Written Test Answers & Explanations. (Pilot Training Ser.). 1980. pap. 8.95 (ISBN 0-89100-191-3, E*A-61-72B*G). Aviation Mainenance.

King, Martha, jt. auth. see King, John.

King, Martha L., jt. ed. see Garnica, Olga K.

King, Martin L; see Lynd, Staughton.

King, Martin L., Jr. Strength to Love. LC 80-2374. 160p. 1981. pap. 4.25 (ISBN 0-8006-1441-0, 1-1441). Fortress.

--Trumpet of Conscience. LC 68-31061. 1968. 11.95 o.p. (ISBN 0-06-012396-6, HarpT). Har-Row.

--Why We Can't Wait. (Illus.). (RL 7). pap. 1.50 (ISBN 0-451-61887-4, MW1887, Ment). NAL.

King, Martin L., Sr. & Riley, Clayton. Daddy King. 1981. lib. bdg. 13.95 (ISBN 0-8161-3157-0, Large Print Bks). G K Hall.

King, Mary E. & Traylor, Idris R., Jr., eds. Art & Environment in Native America. (Special Publications: No. 7). (Illus., Orig.). 1974. pap. 8.00 (ISBN 0-89672-032-2). Tex Tech Pr.

King, Maurice. A Medical Laboratory for Developing Countries. (Illus.). 1973. pap. text ed. 22.50x (ISBN 0-19-264910-8). Oxford U Pr.

King, Maurice, ed. X-Ray Technology Examination Review Book, Vol. 1. 3rd ed. 186p. 1972. spiral bdg. 8.50 o.p. (ISBN 0-87488-441-1). Med Exam.

King, Michael. Childhood, Welfare & Justice. 160p. 1981. pap. 16.95 (ISBN 0-7134-3713-8, Pub. by Batsford England). David & Charles.

--New Zealand: Its Land & Its People. (Illus.). 152p. 1979. Repr. of 1977 ed. 19.95 (ISBN 0-589-01295-9, Pub. by Reed Bks Australia). C E Tuttle.

King, Michael, ed. see H. D.

King, Michael J. William Orlando Darby: A Military Biography. Date not set. 19.50 (ISBN 0-208-01867-0, Archon). Shoe String. Postponed.

King, Nancy R. Movement Approach to Acting. (P-H Ser. in Theatre & Drama). (Illus.). 288p. 1981. text ed. 13.95 (ISBN 0-13-604637-1). P-H.

King, Noel, ed. Islam & the Confluence of Religions in Uganda, 1840-1966. LC 73-85593. (American Academy of Religion. Studies in Religion). 1973. pap. 6.00 (ISBN 0-89130-157-7, 010006). Scholars Pr Ca.

King, Noel, tr. see Battuta, Ibn.

King, P. B. The Geology of the Glass Mountains, Texas: Part I, Descriptive Geology. (Illus.). 167p. 1930. 2.50 (BULL 3038). Bur Econ Geology.

King, P. B. & Flawn, P. T. Geology & Mineral Deposits of Pre-Cambrian Rocks of the Van Horn Area, Texas. (Illus.). 218p. 1953. 5.75 (PUB 5301). Bur Econ Geology.

King, P. D. Law & Society in the Visigothic Kingdom. LC 77-179163. (Cambridge Studies in Medieval Life & Thought: Third Ser., No. 5). 320p. 1972. 44.50 (ISBN 0-521-08421-0). Cambridge U Pr.

King, Pat, jt. auth. see King, Bill.

King, Pat, jt. auth. see Lance, Fran.

King, Paul. In the Chinese Customs Service: A Personal Record of Forty-Seven Years. LC 78-74327. (The Modern Chinese Economy Ser.). 299p. 1980. lib. bdg. 33.00 (ISBN 0-8240-4254-9). Garland Pub.

King, Peter, jt. ed. see Johnsen, Arne O.

King, Preston. Fear of Power: An Analysis of Anti-Statism in Three French Writers. 1967. text ed. 6.25x (ISBN 0-391-01977-5). Humanities.

King, R. School & College: Studies of Post-Sixteen Education. 1976. 16.95x (ISBN 0-7100-8359-9); pap. 9.50 (ISBN 0-7100-8360-2). Routledge & Kegan.

King, R., jt. ed. see Nugent, N.

King, R. A. Electronic Circuits & Systems. LC 74-31175. 1975. 19.95 (ISBN 0-470-47779-2); solutions to problems manual 3.50 (ISBN 0-470-01399-0). Halsted Pr.

King, R. D., ed. Developments in Food Analysis Techniques-2. (Illus.). ix, 268p. 1981. 46.00x (ISBN 0-85334-921-5). Burgess-Intl Ideas.

--Developments in Food Analysis Techniques, Vol. 1. (Illus.). 1978. text ed. 71.00x (ISBN 0-85334-755-7, Pub. by Applied Science). Burgess-Intl Ideas.

King, R. E. The Geology of the Glass Mountains, Texas: Part Ii, Faunal Summary & Correlation of the Permian Formations with Description of Brachiopoda. (Illus.). 146p. 1930. 2.50 (BULL 3042). Bur Econ Geology.

King, R. F., jt. auth. see Griffiths, D. H.

King, R. W., et al. Arrays of Cylindrical Dipoles. LC 67-26069. (Illus.). 1968. 68.50 (ISBN 0-521-05887-2, 2). Cambridge U Pr.

King, Ralph W. & Magid, John. Industrial Hazard & Safety Handbook. (Illus.). 1979. 74.95 (ISBN 0-408-00304-9). Butterworths.

King, Richard L. Airport Noise Pollution: A Bibliography of Its Effects on People & Property. LC 73-3370. 1973. 13.50 (ISBN 0-8108-0610-X). Scarecrow.

King, Robert C. Genetics. 2nd ed. (Illus.). 1965. 12.95x (ISBN 0-19-500932-0). Oxford U Pr.

King, Robert G. Forms of Public Address. LC 68-15020. (Speech Communication Ser). 1968. pap. 3.95 (ISBN 0-672-61077-9, SC6). Bobbs.

King, Robert R. A History of the Romanian Communist Party. (Publication Ser.: No. 206). 225p. (Orig.). 1980. pap. 8.95 (ISBN 0-8179-7332-X). Hoover Inst Pr.

King, Robert R. & Brown, James F., eds. Eastern Europe's Uncertain Future: A Selection of Radio Free Europe Research Reports. LC 77-10666. (Praeger Special Studies). 1977. 37.50 (ISBN 0-03-040861-X). Praeger.

King, Roger T. Perspectives in Bank Management: A Book of Readings. LC 79-63851. 1979. pap. text ed. 10.50 (ISBN 0-8191-0745-X). U Pr of Amer.

King, Roma A., Jr. The Focusing Artifice: The Poetry of Robert Browning. LC 68-20934. 1968. 10.00 o.p. (ISBN 0-8214-0042-8). Ohio U Pr.

King, Roma A., Jr., et al, eds. see Browning, Robert.

King, Ronald. All Things Bright & Beautiful? A Sociological Study of Infants' Classrooms. LC 78-4518. 1978. 25.25 (ISBN 0-471-99653-X, Pub. by Wiley-Interscience). Wiley.

--Education. 2nd ed. LC 77-1388. (Aspects of Modern Sociology: Social Structure of Modern Britain). 1977. pap. text ed. 10.50x (ISBN 0-582-48550-9). Longman.

--School Organisation & Pupil Involvement: A Study of Secondary Schools. (International Library of Sociology). (Illus.). 266p. 1973. 22.50 (ISBN 0-7100-7610-X). Routledge & Kegan.

King, Ronald W., et al. Antennas in Matter: Fundamentals, Theory & Applications. 784p. 1981. text ed. 75.00x (ISBN 0-262-11074-1). MIT Pr.

King, Roy D. & Elliott, Kenneth W. Albany: Birth of a Prison--End of an Era. (International Library of Social Policy Ser.). 1978. 25.00 (ISBN 0-7100-8727-6). Routledge & Kegan.

King, Roy D., et al. Patterns of Residential Care: Sociological Studies in Institutions for Handicapped Children. (International Library of Sociology). 1978. Repr. of 1971 ed. 23.50 (ISBN 0-7100-7038-1). Routledge & Kegan.

King, Rufus. The Drug Hang-up: America's Fifty Year Folly. 398p. 1974. pap. 12.75 (ISBN 0-398-03071-5). C C Thomas.

--The Life & Correspondence of Rufus King, 6 vols. King, Charles R., ed. LC 69-16653. (American Public Figures Ser.). 1971. Repr. of 1894 ed. Set. lib. bdg. 245.00 (ISBN 0-306-71125-7). Da Capo.

King, Russell. Land Reform: A World Survey. LC 77-24633. (Advanced Economic Geography Ser.). (Illus.). 1978. lib. bdg. 37.50x (ISBN 0-89158-819-1). Westview.

King, S. F. Making Large Toys & Play Equipment. (Illus.). 128p. 1980. 10.95 (ISBN 0-263-06399-2, Pub. by Mills & Boon England). Hippocrene Bks.

King, Serge. Imagineering for Health. LC 80-53949. 154p. (Orig.). 1980. pap. 4.95 (ISBN 0-8356-0546-9, Quest). Theos Pub Hse.

King, Sophia. Waldorf; or, the Dangers of Philosophy: A Philosophical Tale, 2 vols. Luria, Gina, ed. (The Feminist Controversy in England, 1788-1810 Ser.). 1974. Set. lib. bdg. 76.00 (ISBN 0-8240-0871-5); lib. bdg. 50.00 ea. Garland Pub.

King, Spencer B., Jr. Darien: The Death & Rebirth of a Southern Town. LC 80-83662. (Illus.). 100p. 1981. 13.95x (ISBN 0-86554-003-9). Mercer Univ Pr.

King, Stephen. Carrie. LC 73-9037. 216p. 1974. 7.95 (ISBN 0-385-08695-4). Doubleday.

--The Dead Zone. 1980. pap. 3.50 (ISBN 0-451-09338-0, E9338, Sig). NAL.

--Salem's Lot. LC 73-22804. 1975. 11.95 (ISBN 0-385-00751-5). Doubleday.

--Salem's Lot: TV Edition. (Illus.). (RL 10). 1979. pap. 2.75 (ISBN 0-451-09231-7, E9231, Sig). NAL.

--The Shining. (RL 6). 1978. pap. 2.95 o.p. (ISBN 0-451-07872-1, E7872, Sig). NAL.

King, Stephen W. Communication & Social Influence. 1975. text ed. 6.50 (ISBN 0-201-03720-3). A-W.

King, Syneta E. Real-Life Contemporary Poems. 1981. 4.95 (ISBN 0-8062-1584-4). Carlton.

King, Tabitha. Small World. 192p. 1981. 10.95 (ISBN 0-02-563190-X). Macmillan.

King, Thea, ed. see Thurston, Frederick.

King, Tom. In the Shadow of Giants: Mountain Ascents Past & Present. LC 77-84572. (Illus.). 1981. 14.95 (ISBN 0-498-02186-6). A S Barnes.

King, Ursula. Towards a New Mysticism: Teilhard de Chardin & Eastern Religions. 320p. 1980. 14.95 (ISBN 0-8164-0475-5). Seabury.

King, Victor T., ed. Essays on Borneo Societies. (Hull Monographs on South-East Asia: No. 7). (Illus.). 1979. pap. 24.95x (ISBN 0-19-713434-3). Oxford U Pr.

King, Viola W., jt. auth. see King, Frank H.

King, Virginia & Gerwig, Norma. Humanizing Nursing Education. LC 80-83678. (Nursing Dimensions Education Ser.). 200p. 1981. text ed. 15.95 (ISBN 0-913654-69-8). Nursing Res.

King, Warren B. Endangered Birds of the World: The ICPB Bird Red Data Book. 624p. 1981. text ed. 19.95x (ISBN 0-87474-584-5); pap. text ed. 8.95 (ISBN 0-87474-583-7). Smithsonian.

King, Willard F., tr. see Castro, Americo.

King, William. William King (Sixteen Fifty to Seventeen Twenty-Nine) LC 75-11228. (British Philosophers & Theologians of the 17th & 18th Centuries Ser.). 1978. lib. bdg. 42.00 (ISBN 0-8240-1782-X). Garland Pub.

King, William R. & Zaltman, Gerald, eds. Marketing Scientific & Technical Information. (Special Studies in Science & Technology). 1979. lib. bdg. 24.50x (ISBN 0-89158-397-1). Westview.

King, William S. & Jones, Delmos J. Papago Indians, Vol. Two: Papago Population Studies. (American Indian Ethnohistory Ser: Indians of the Southwest). (Illus.). lib. bdg. 42.00 (ISBN 0-8240-0701-8). Garland Pub.

King, Winston L. Theravada Meditation: The Buddhist Transformation of Yoga. LC 79-25856. 192p. 1980. 15.00x (ISBN 0-271-00254-9). Pa St U Pr.

King, Woodie, ed. Black Short Story Anthology. LC 72-6773. 600p. 1972. text ed. 20.00x (ISBN 0-231-03711-2). Columbia U Pr.

--Blackspirits. 1972. pap. 1.95 o.p. (ISBN 0-394-71701-5, V701, Vin). Random.

King, Woodie & Anthony, Earl, eds. Black Poets & Prophets. pap. 1.50 o.p. (ISBN 0-451-61126-8, MW1126, Ment). NAL.

King, Woodie & Milner, Ron, eds. Black Drama Anthology. LC 77-181833. 675p. 1972. 25.00x (ISBN 0-231-03644-2). Columbia U Pr.

King, Wuncz, ed. see Wellington, V. K.

King Abdallah Of Jordan. My Memoirs Completed: Al-Takmilah. (Illus.). 1978. text ed. 14.95x (ISBN 0-582-78082-9). Longman.

Kingbay, Keith, jt. auth. see Fichter, George S.

Kingdon, John W. Candidates for Office: Beliefs & Strategies. 6.00 (ISBN 0-8446-2377-6). Peter Smith.

--Congressmen's Voting Decisions. 2nd ed. 313p. 1980. pap. text ed. 13.50 scp (ISBN 0-06-043657-3, HarpC). Har-Row.

Kingdon, R., ed. see Palmer, H. E.

Kingery, Jul. Step into Skiing Discoveries. LC 77-91906. (Skiing Your Way Ser.). (Illus.). 1978. pap. 7.97 (ISBN 0-9604574-0-2). Alpine-Tahoe.

King-Farlow, John & Shea, William R., eds. Values & the Quality of Life. LC 75-55511. 1976. pap. text ed. 4.95 o.p. (ISBN 0-88202-045-5). N Watson.

Kingh, Henry C. Pictorial Guide to the Stars. (Illus.). 1967. 10.95 o.s.i. (ISBN 0-690-62513-8, TYC-T). T Y Crowell.

King-Hall, Stephen. The Communist Conspiracy. LC 79-2907. 239p. 1981. Repr. of 1953 ed. 19.75 (ISBN 0-8305-0077-4). Hyperion Conn.

Kinghorn, A. Douglas, ed. Toxic Plants. LC 79-16180. 1979. 21.50x (ISBN 0-231-04686-3). Columbia U Pr.

Kinghorn, A. M., ed. Middle Scots Poets. (York Medieval Texts). 1970. pap. 8.95 (ISBN 0-8101-0329-X). Northwestern U Pr.

Kinghorn, Kenneth C. Dynamic Discipleship. 160p. 1975. pap. 3.95 (ISBN 0-8010-5357-9). Baker Bk.

--Fresh Wind of the Spirit. LC 74-7415. 128p. 1975. pap. 4.95 (ISBN 0-687-13495-1). Abingdon.

Kinglake, A. W. Eothen. LC 71-93107. 1970. pap. 4.50x (ISBN 0-8032-5711-2, BB 509, Bison). U of Nebr Pr.

Kingman, Daniel. American Music: A Panorama. LC 78-22782. 1979. pap. text ed. 10.95 (ISBN 0-02-871260-9). Schirmer Bks.

Kingman, John F. & Taylor, S. J. Introduction to Measure & Probability. 1966. 44.50 (ISBN 0-521-05888-0). Cambridge U Pr.

Kingman, Lee. Break a Leg Betsy Maybe. (YA) 1979. pap. 1.50 (ISBN 0-440-90794-2, LFL). Dell.

--Goergina & the Dragon. (Illus.). (gr. 3-5). 1974. pap. 1.25 (ISBN 0-671-29892-5). PB.

--Head Over Wheels. (gr. 7 up). 1981. pap. 1.75 (ISBN 0-440-93129-0, LE). Dell.

--The Meeting Post: A Story of Lapland. LC 73-139105. (Stories from Many Lands Ser). (Illus.). (gr. 2-5). 1972. 3.95 o.p. (ISBN 0-690-52975-9, TYC-J); PLB 7.89 (ISBN 0-690-52976-7). T Y Crowell.

Kingman, Lee, ed. The Illustrator's Notebook. LC 77-20028. (Illus.). 1978. 28.00 (ISBN 0-87675-013-7). Horn Bk.

--Newbery & Caldecott Medal Books: 1956-1965. LC 65-26759. (Illus.). 1965. 17.00 (ISBN 0-87675-002-1). Horn Bk.

--Newbery & Caldecott Medal Books: 1966-1975. LC 75-20167. (Illus.). 325p. 1975. 17.00 (ISBN 0-87675-003-X). Horn Bk.

Kingman, Lee, et al, eds. Illustrators of Children's Books: 1957-1966, Vol. 3. LC 47-31264. (Illus.). 1968. 28.00 (ISBN 0-87675-017-X). Horn Bk.

--Illustrators of Children's Books: 1967-1976, Vol. 4. LC 78-13759. (Illus.). 1978. 35.00 (ISBN 0-87675-018-8). Horn Bk.

Kingsbury, A. A. Introduction to Security & Crime Prevention Surveys. (Illus.). 384p. 1973. 16.75 (ISBN 0-398-02836-2); pap. 11.95 (ISBN 0-398-02893-1). C C Thomas.

Kingsbury, Jack D. Jesus Christ in Matthew, Mark, & Luke. Krodel, Gerhard, ed. LC 80-69755. (Proclamation Commentaries Ser.: The New Testament Witnesses for Preaching). 144p. (Orig.). 1981. pap. 4.25 (ISBN 0-8006-0596-9, 1-596). Fortress.

--The Parables of Jesus in Matthew 13. LC 76-40850. 1976. pap. text ed. 10.50 (ISBN 0-915644-08-8). Clayton Pub Hse.

Kingsbury, Jack D. & Pennington, Chester. Lent. Achtemeier, Elizabeth, et al, eds. LC 79-7377. (Proclamation 2: Aids for Interpreting the Lessons of the Church Year, Ser. A). 64p. (Orig.). 1980. pap. 2.50 (ISBN 0-8006-4093-4, 1-4093). Fortress.

Kingsbury, Jack D., jt. auth. see Randolph, David.

Kingsbury, John M. Poisonous Plants of the United States & Canada. 3rd ed. 1964. 25.95 (ISBN 0-13-685016-2). P-H.

--Rocky Shore. LC 71-122758. (Illus.). 1970. 5.95 (ISBN 0-85699-015-9). Chatham Pr.

Kingsbury, Roy & O'Shea, Patrick. Sunday Afternoons. 1974. tchrs notes 2.50x (ISBN 0-582-55226-5); record 11.75x (ISBN 0-582-56732-7); cassette 12.50x (ISBN 0-582-56755-6). Longman.

Kingsford, Thomas R., jt. auth. see Shirts, Morris A.

Kingslake, R., ed. Applied Optics & Optical Engineering: A Comprehensive Treatise, 5 vols. Incl. Vol. 1. Light: Its Generation & Modification. 1965 (ISBN 0-12-408601-2); Vol. 2. The Detection of Light & Infrared Radiation. 1965 (ISBN 0-12-408602-0); Vol. 3. Optical Components. 1965 (ISBN 0-12-408603-9); Vol. 4. Optical Instruments, Part I. 1967 (ISBN 0-12-408604-7); Vol. 5. Optical Instruments, Part 2. 1969 (ISBN 0-12-408605-5). 48.50 ea.; Set. 197.50. Acad Pr.

Kingsland, L. W., tr. see Brodtkorb, Reidar.

Kingsley, Charles. Heroes. (New Children's Classics). (Illus.). (gr. 6 up). 1954. 4.95g o.s.i. (ISBN 0-02-750710-6). Macmillan.

--Hypatia; or, New Foes with an Old Face: 1853. Wolff, Robert L., ed. (Victorian Fiction Ser.). 1975. lib. bdg. 66.00 (ISBN 0-8240-1571-1). Garland Pub.

--The Water Babies. (Childrens Illustrated Classics Ser). (Illus.). 1975. Repr. of 1957 ed. 11.00x o.p. (ISBN 0-460-05037-0, Pub. by J. M. Dent England). Biblio Dist.

--The Water Babies. LC 75-32190. (Classics of Children's Literature, 1621-1932: Vol. 52). (Illus.). 1976. Repr. of 1885 ed. PLB 38.00 (ISBN 0-8240-2301-3). Garland Pub.

Kingsley, D. & Taylor, F. Albion in China: The First British Football Tour to China in Pictures. (Illus.). 1979. pap. 9.00 (ISBN 0-08-024496-3). Pergamon.

Kingsley, Emily P. Big Bird & Little Bird's Big & Little Book. (Sesame Street Shape Bks.). (Illus.). (ps-3). 1977. PLB 5.38 (ISBN 0-307-68875-5, Golden Pr). Western Pub.

--Farley Goes to the Doctor. (Sesame Street Early Bird Bks). (Illus.). 32p. (ps). 1981. 3.50 (ISBN 0-307-11605-0, Golden Pr). Western Pub.

--The Great Cookie Thief. (Sesame Street Shape Bks.). (Illus.). (ps-3). 1977. PLB 5.38 (ISBN 0-307-68877-1, Golden Pr). Western Pub.

--I Can Do It Myself. (Sesame Street Starter Bks). (Illus.). 32p. (ps). 1981. 3.50 (ISBN 0-307-11604-2, Golden Pr). Western Pub.

Kingsley, Henry. Ravenshoe. Scheuerle, William H., ed. LC 67-12117. 1967. pap. 4.95x (ISBN 0-8032-5109-2, BB 365, Bison). U of Nebr Pr.

Kingsley, Norman. Icecraft. (Illus.). 120p. 1975. wrappers 4.95 (ISBN 0-910856-59-1). La Siesta.

Kingsnorth, G. W., jt. auth. see Marsh, Zoe.

Kingsther, W. & Parish, W. Today's Business World. 1978. 16.95 (ISBN 0-8359-7761-7); study guide 6.95 (ISBN 0-8359-7762-5). instrs'. manual avail. Reston.

Kingston, Albert J., ed. Toward a Psychology of Language & Reading: Selected Papers of Wendell W. Weaver. LC 75-3816. 280p. 1976. 17.50x (ISBN 0-8203-0386-0). U of Ga Pr.

Kingston, Beryl. Lifting the Curse. 1980. 17.50x (ISBN 0-85223-176-8, Pub. by Telford England). State Mutual Bk.

Kingston, Ceylon S. The Inland Empire in the Pacific Northwest: The Historical Essays & Sketches of Ceylon S. Kingston. 1981. price not set (ISBN 0-87770-186-5). Ye Galleon.

Kingston, Irene & Benjamin, William A., eds. Directory of European Information. 590p. 1979. 85.00 (ISBN 2-85993-001-9). Ballinger Pub.

Kingston, Jeremy. Arts & Artists. (Horizons of Knowledge Ser.). (Illus.). 1980. lib. bdg. 19.95 (ISBN 0-87196-404-X). Facts on File.

--The Bird Who Saved the Jungle. (Illus.). 1977. 7.95 (ISBN 0-571-10303-0, Pub. by Faber & Faber); pap. 2.45 (ISBN 0-571-11130-0). Merrimack Bk Serv.

--The Dustbin Who Wanted to Be a General. (Illus.). (ps-5). 1970. 6.95 (ISBN 0-571-09517-8, Pub. by Faber & Faber). Merrimack Bk Serv.

Kingston, Maxine H. China Men. 288p. 1981. pap. 3.50 (ISBN 0-345-29482-3). Ballantine.

--The Woman Warrior: Memoirs of a Girlhood Among Ghosts. LC 77-3246. 1977. pap. 2.45 (ISBN 0-394-72392-9, Vin). Random.

Kingston, Meredith. Winter Love Song. (Second Chance at Love, Contemporary Ser.: No. 2). 192p. (Orig.). 1981. pap. 1.75 (ISBN 0-515-05637-5). Jove Pubns.

Kingston, William. Innovation. 1979. 11.95 (ISBN 0-7145-3540-0); pap. 4.95 (ISBN 0-7145-3611-3). Riverrun NY.

Kingstone, Brett M. The Student Entrepreneur's Guide. 192p. (Orig.). 1981. pap. 4.95 (ISBN 0-89815-045-0). Ten Speed Pr.

King-Stoops, Joyce B. Migrant Education: Teaching the Wandering Ones. LC 80-82678. (Fastback Ser.: No. 145). (Orig.). 1980. pap. 0.75 (ISBN 0-87367-145-7). Phi Delta Kappa.

King-Yi, Hsu. Political Mobilization & Economic Extraction: Chinese Communist Agrarian Policies During the Kiangi Period. LC 78-74335. (The Modern Chinese Economy Ser.). 400p. 1980. lib. bdg. 44.00 (ISBN 0-8240-4275-1). Garland Pub.

Kinietz, W. Vernon. Indians of the Great Lakes Region. 1965. pap. 4.95 (ISBN 0-472-06107-0, 107, AA). U of Mich Pr.

--Indians of the Western Great Lakes, 1615-1760. 1965. 8.95 (ISBN 0-472-09107-7). U of Mich Pr.

Kininmonth, Christopher. The Travellers' Guide to Morocco. rev. ed. (Illus.). 356p. 1981. pap. 10.95 (ISBN 0-224-01897-3, Pub. by Chatto-Bodley-Jonathan). Merrimack Bk Serv.

--The Travellers' Guide to Sicily. rev. ed. LC 74-158691. (Travellers' Guide Ser.). (Illus.). 1979. 9.95 (ISBN 0-224-00612-6, R75, Pub. by Chatto Bodley Jonathan). Merrimack Bk Serv.

--The Travellers' Guide to Sicily. rev. ed. (Illus.). 306p. 1981. pap. 7.95 (ISBN 0-224-01854-X, Pub. by Chatto-Bodley-Jonathan). Merrimack Bk Serv.

Kinkead, Duncan T. Juan De Valdes Leal (Sixteen Twenty-Two to Sixteen Ninety) His Life & Work. LC 77-94700. (Outstanding Dissertations in the Fine Arts Ser.). 1978. lib. bdg. 72.50 (ISBN 0-8240-3232-2). Garland Pub.

Kinkead, Eugene. A Concrete Look at Nature. (Illus.). 242p. 1974. 8.00x (ISBN 0-8129-0471-0). E Kinkead.

--Squirrel Book. (Illus.). 160p. 1980. 13.95 (ISBN 0-525-93137-6). Dutton.

--Wildness Is All Around Us. (Illus.). 178p. 1978. pap. 10.00x (ISBN 0-87690-277-8). E Kinkead.

Kinklighter, Clois E. Modern Masonry. (Illus.). 1980. text ed. 12.00 (ISBN 0-87006-296-4). Goodheart.

Kinlaw, Dennis C. Becoming an Effective Counselor: Skills for Interpersonal Problem Solving. LC 79-92072. (Illus.). 144p. (Orig.). 1981. pap. 6.50 (ISBN 0-8042-1108-6). John Knox.

--Helping Skills for Human Resource Development: A Facilitator's Package. 100p. (Orig.). 1980. pap. write for info. (ISBN 0-88390-163-3). Univ Assocs.

Kinley, David H., et al. Aid As Obstacle: Twenty Questions About Our Foreign Aid & the Hungry. (Illus., Orig.). 1980. pap. 4.95 (ISBN 0-935028-07-2). Inst Food & Develop.

Kinloch, G. C. Sociological Study of South Africa. 1972. text ed. 17.00x (ISBN 0-333-13101-0). Humanities.

Kinloch, Graham C. Racial Conflict in Rhodesia: A Socio-Historical Study. LC 78-64823. 1978. pap. text ed. 11.25 (ISBN 0-8191-0642-9). U Pr of Amer.

Kinmond, Jean. The Coats Book of Lacecrafts: Crochet, Tatting, Knitting. (Illus.). 1980. 19.95 (ISBN 0-7134-0783-2, Pub. by Batsford England). David & Charles.

--Fashion Crochet. (Illus.). 1972. 7.25 o.p. (ISBN 0-8231-5035-6). Branford.

Kinmond, William. The First Book of Communist China. rev. ed. (First Bks). (Illus.). 96p. (gr. 7 up). 1972. PLB 4.90 o.p. (ISBN 0-531-00506-2). Watts.

Kinmonth, Earl H. The Self-Made Man in Meija Japanese Thought: From Samurai to Salary Man. (Illus.). 400p. 1981. 22.50x (ISBN 0-520-04159-3). U of Cal Pr.

Kinn, Donald N. The Life Cycle & Behavior of Cercoleipus Coelontous (Acarina: Mesostigmata). Including a Survey of Phoretic Mite Associates of California Scolytidae. (U. C. Publ. in Entomology: Vol. 65). 1971. pap. 6.50x (ISBN 0-520-09379-8). U of Cal Pr.

Kinn, Mary E. Review of Medical Terminology. 1980. 7.50. Thieme Stratton.

Kinnaird, John. William Hazlitt, Critic of Power. (Illus.). 1978. 25.00x (ISBN 0-231-04600-6). Columbia U Pr.

Kinnaird, William. Joy Comes with the Morning. 1979. pap. 4.95 (ISBN 0-8499-2874-5). Word Bks.

Kinnamon, Kenneth, ed. James Baldwin: A Collection of Critical Essays. LC 74-6175. (Twentieth Century Views Ser). 192p. 1973. 10.95 (ISBN 0-13-055566-5, Spec). P-H.

Kinnane, Adrian. Policing. LC 78-2314. 1979. 15.95 (ISBN 0-88229-327-3). Nelson-Hall.

Kinnard, Douglas. President Eisenhower & Strategy Management: A Study in Defense Politics. LC 76-46031. 184p. 1977. 14.50x (ISBN 0-8131-1356-3). U Pr of Ky.

--The Secretary of Defense. LC 80-5178. 256p. 1981. 19.50 (ISBN 0-8131-1434-9). U Pr of Ky.

Kinnard, William N. & Messnen, Stephen D. Effective Business Relocation. LC 78-113590. 1970. 16.95 (ISBN 0-669-58420-7). Lexington Bks.

Kinne, O. Diseases of Marine Animals: Bivalvia to Arthopoda, Vol. 2. 1980. write for info. (ISBN 0-471-99585-1, Pub. by Wiley-Interscience). Wiley.

--Marine Ecology: A Comprehensive Integrated Treatise on Life in Oceans & Coastal Waters, Vols. 1-4. Incl. Vol. 1, 3 pts. 1970. Pt. 1. 69.95 (ISBN 0-471-48001-0); Pt. 2. 64.50 (ISBN 0-471-48002-9); Pt. 3. 69.95 (ISBN 0-471-48003-7); Vol. 2, 2 pts. 1975. Pt. 1. 68.25 (ISBN 0-471-48004-5); Pt. 2. 83.95 (ISBN 0-471-48006-1); Vol. 3, 3 pts. 1976. Pt. 1. 87.25 (ISBN 0-471-48005-3); Pt. 2. 113.50 (ISBN 0-471-01577-6); Pt. 3. 52.50 (ISBN 0-471-48007-X); Vol. 4. 1978. Pt. 1. 111.00 (ISBN 0-471-48008-8). LC 79-221779 (Pub. by Wiley-Interscience). Wiley.

Kinne, O. & Bulnheim, H. P. Cultivation of Marine Organisms & Its Importance for Marine Biology. (International Symposium Helgoland 1969 Ser.). (Illus.). 722p. 1973. pap. text ed. 93.60x (ISBN 3-87429-059-X). Lubrecht & Cramer.

Kinnear, Angus. Against the Tide: Watchman Nee. 1974. pap. 2.95 (ISBN 0-87508-408-7). Chr Lit.

Kinnear, Thomas C., jt. auth. see Bernhardt, Kenneth L.

Kinnear, Willis. Spiritual Healing. 110p. (Orig.). 1973. pap. 3.95 (ISBN 0-911336-50-8). Sci of Mind.

--Thirty Day Mental Diet. 1965. pap. 4.95 (ISBN 0-911336-20-6). Sci of Mind.

Kinnear, Willis, jt. auth. see Holmes, Ernest.

Kinnear, Willis, ed. The Creative Power of Mind. 1966. pap. 7.95 (ISBN 0-911336-01-X). Sci of Mind.

Kinnear, Willis, ed. see Holmes, Ernest.

Kinnear, Willis, ed. see Holmes, Ernest, et al.

Kinnear, Willis, ed. see Holmes, Ernest.

Kinnear, Willis, ed. see Seabury, David.

Kinnear, Willis H., jt. auth. see Holmes, Ernest.

Kinnear, Willis H., ed. Thought As Energy: Exploring the Spiritual Nature of Man. (Illus.). 96p. 1975. pap. 3.50 (ISBN 0-911336-62-1). Sci of Mind.

Kinnear, Willis H., ed. see Holmes, Ernest.

Kinneavy, James L. Theory of Discourse. 496p. 1980. pap. 7.95x (ISBN 0-393-00919-X). Norton.

Kinneir, Jock. Words & Buildings. 192p. 1981. 32.50 (ISBN 0-8230-7487-0, Whitney Lib). Watson-Guptill.

Kinnell, Galway. Black Light. rev. ed. 128p. 1980. pap. 5.00 (ISBN 0-86547-016-2). N Point Pr.

--Walking Down the Stairs. Hall, Donald, ed. LC 77-23752. (Poets on Poetry Ser.). pap. 5.95 (ISBN 0-472-52530-1). U of Mich Pr.

Kinnell, Galway, tr. see Bonnefoy, Yves.

Kinney, A. J. The Air Force Officer's Guide. 25th, rev. ed. (Illus.). 416p. 1981. pap. 10.95 (ISBN 0-8117-2055-1). Stackpole.

Kinney, Analee, jt. auth. see Schaller, Agnes P.

Kinney, Arthur F. Dorothy Parker. (United States Authors Ser.: No. 315). 1978. 9.95 (ISBN 0-8057-7241-3). Twayne.

Kinney, F. Markets of Bawdrie: The Dramatic Criticism of Stephen Gossor. (Salzburg Studies in English Literature, Elizabethan & Renaissance Studies: No. 4). 291p. 1974. pap. text ed. 25.00x (ISBN 0-391-01445-5). Humanities.

Kinney, Francis S. You Are First: The Story of Olin & Rod Stephens of Sparkman & Stephens, Inc. LC 78-8148. (Illus.). 1978. 17.95 (ISBN 0-396-07567-3). Dodd.

Kinney, Henry, ed. Replacement Parts Guide: 1980. 1980. pap. write for info. (ISBN 0-934890-02-1). Hoffman Pubns.

Kinney, J. S. Indeterminate Structural Analysis. 1957. 22.95 (ISBN 0-201-03695-9). A-W.

Kinney, Jean & Leaton, Gwen. Loosening the Grip: A Handbook of Alcohol Information. LC 78-2219. (Illus.). 1978. pap. text ed. 11.95 (ISBN 0-8016-2673-0). Mosby.

Kinney, John M., ed. see Committee on Pre & Postoperative Care American College of Surgeons.

Kinney, Noreen. Cooking Irish Style Today. 1977. pap. 4.50 (ISBN 0-85342-482-9). Irish Bk Ctr.

Kinney, Peter. The Early Sculpture of Bartolomeo Ammanati. LC 75-23798. (Outstanding Dissertations in the Fine Arts - 16th Century). (Illus.). 1976. lib. bdg. 41.00 (ISBN 0-8240-1993-8). Garland Pub.

Kinney, R. Transcending Dimensions to Another World. 6.95 o.p. (ISBN 0-8062-1069-9). Carlton.

Kinney, Ralph. Complete Book of Furniture Repair & Refinishing. rev. ed. LC 73-162743. (Illus.). 1981. 20.00x (ISBN 0-684-16839-1, ScribT). Scribner.

--Complete Book of Furniture Repair & Refinishing. LC 73-162743. (Illus.). 1971. 12.95 o.p. (ISBN 0-684-12437-8, ScribT). Scribner.

Kinney, William P. The Monetary Maze: Gold, the International Monetary System, & the Emerging World Economy. LC 76-52187. 1977. pap. text ed. 4.95 (ISBN 0-8403-1700-X). Kendall-Hunt.

Kinnibugh, William, jt. auth. see Short, Andrew.

Kinoshita Junji. Between God & Man: A Judgment on War Crimes; a Play in Two Parts. Gangloff, Eric J., tr. & intro. by. LC 79-84890. (Illus.). 180p. (Japanese., Pt. 1, The Judgement; Pt. 2, Summer, a Romance of the South Seas). 1979. 15.00 (ISBN 0-295-95670-4). U of Wash Pr.

Kinrade, Derek, jt. auth. see Darnbrough, Ann.

Kinsbourne, M., ed. Asymmetrical Function of the Brain. LC 77-8633. (Illus.). 1978. 39.50 (ISBN 0-521-21481-5). Cambridge U Pr.

Kinsbourne, Marcel & Smith, W. Lynn, eds. Hemispheric Disconnection & Cerebral Function. (Illus.). 316p. 1975. text ed. 29.75 (ISBN 0-398-02967-9). C C Thomas.

Kinsella, T., jt. auth. see Yeats, William B.

Kinsella, Thomas. Tain. (Illus.). 1970. pap. 8.95x (ISBN 0-19-281090-1, OPB). Oxford U Pr.

Kinsella, Thomas, jt. auth. see O'Tuama, Sean.

Kinser, Samuel, ed. see De Commynes, Philippe.

Kinsey, Anthony. The Art of Screen Printing. 1979. 24.00 (ISBN 0-7134-1544-4, Pub. by Batsford England). David & Charles.

Kinsey, W. Fred, ed. Archaeology in the Upper Delaware Valley: A Study of the Cultural Chronology of the Tocks Island Reservoir. LC 72-169104. (Pennsylvania Historical & Museum Commission Anthropological Ser.: No. 2). (Illus.). 499p. 1972. 13.00 (ISBN 0-911124-68-3). Pa Hist & Mus.

Kinsley, David R. The Sword & the Flute - Kali & Krsna: Dark Visions of the Terrible & the Sublime in Hindu Mythology. 175p. 1975. 18.50x (ISBN 0-520-02675-6); pap. 2.95 (ISBN 0-520-03510-0). U of Cal Pr.

Kinsley, Helen, jt. ed. see Kinsley, James.

Kinsley, James & Kinsley, Helen, eds. Dryden: The Critical Heritage. 1971. 38.00x (ISBN 0-7100-6977-4). Routledge & Kegan.

Kinsley, James, ed. see Austen, Jane.

Kinsley, James, ed. see Burns, Robert.

Kinsley, James, ed. see Dryden, John.

Kinsley, James, ed. see Dunbar, William.

Kinsman, Donald M. International Meat Science Dictionary. (Illus.). 282p. (Orig.). 1979. pap. 9.95x (ISBN 0-89641-029-3). American Pr.

Kinsman, Robert. Your New Swiss Bank Book. rev. ed. LC 78-74760. 1979. 17.50 (ISBN 0-87094-177-1). Dow Jones-Irwin.

Kinsman, Robert S. Darker Vision of the Renaissance: Beyond the Fields of Reason. 1975. 20.00x (ISBN 0-520-02259-9). U of Cal Pr.

Kinstler, Everett R. Painting Faces, Figures & Landscapes. 144p. 1981. 22.50 (ISBN 0-8230-3625-1). Watson-Guptill.

Kinton, J. American Ethnic Groups Sourcebook or Supplementary Text. 5th ed. 1980. lib. bdg. 10.95 (ISBN 0-915574-16-0). Soc Sci & Soc Res.

--Criminology & Criminal Justice in America: A Guide to the Literature. rev. ed. (Specialized Bibliography Ser.: No. 2). 1981. 3.95 (ISBN 0-685-53690-4). Soc Sci & Soc Res.

Kinton, J., ed. Criminology, Law Enforcement & Offender Treatment: A Sourcebook. rev. ed. 1981. write for info. (ISBN 0-685-96247-4). Soc Sci & Soc Res.

Kinton, Jack. American Family Styles. 1981. pap. 2.95 (ISBN 0-915574-22-5). Soc Sci & So.

Kinton, Jack F. Leaders in Anthropology: The Men & Women of the Science of Man. 1974. 8.95 (ISBN 0-685-79791-0); pap. 4.95 supplementary text (ISBN 0-685-79792-9). Soc Sci & Soc Res.

Kinton, Jack F., ed. Police Roles in the Seventies, Vol. 1. LC 75-271. (Society in Transition Ser.). 1975. 10.95 o.p. (ISBN 0-685-56482-7); pap. 6.95 o.p. (ISBN 0-685-56483-5). Soc Sci & Soc Res.

--Sociology in America: A Bicentennial Review. 1980. pap. 0.95 o.p. (ISBN 0-685-80070-9). Soc Sci & Soc Res.

Kinton, Ronald & Ceserani, Victor. The Theory of Catering. (Illus.). 412p. 1978. pap. 15.95x (ISBN 0-7131-0193-8). Intl Ideas.

Kinton, Ronald, jt. auth. see Ceserani, Victor.

Kintsch, W. Memory & Cognition. LC 76-49031. 1977. 22.95x (ISBN 0-471-48072-X). Wiley.

Kintsch, Walter. The Representation of Meaning in Memory. LC 74-17331. (Experimental Psychology Ser). 275p. 1974. 14.95 o.p. (ISBN 0-470-48074-2). Halsted Pr.

Kintzer, Frederick C. Middleman in Higher Education: Improving Articulation Among High School, Community College, & Senior Institutions. LC 72-11969. (Higher Education Ser.). 1973. 12.95x o.p. (ISBN 0-87589-160-8). Jossey-Bass.

Kintzinger, J. P. & Marsmann, H. Oxygen-Seventeen & Silicon-Twenty-Nine. (NMR-Basic Principles & Progress Ser.: Vol. 17). (Illus.). 250p. 1981. 48.00 (ISBN 0-387-10414-3). Springer-Verlag.

Kinyatti, Maina W., ed. Thunder from the Mountain: Mau Mau Patriotic Songs. 128p. (Orig.). 1980. 10.95 (ISBN 0-905762-83-5, Pub. by Zed Pr); pap. 5.95 (ISBN 0-905762-84-3). Lawrence Hill.

Kinzel, Marianne. Second Book of Modern Lace Knitting. rev. ed. LC 72-86064. (Illus.). 128p. 1973. pap. 4.00 (ISBN 0-486-22905-X). Dover.

Kinzer, David M. Health Controls Out of Control. 194p. 9.75 (ISBN 0-686-68584-9, 14918). Hospital Finan.

Kinzer, Nora S. Put Down & Ripped off: The American Woman & the Beauty Cult. LC 77-3619. 1977. 7.95 o.s.i. (ISBN 0-690-01243-8, TYC-T). T Y Crowell.

Kinzey, Bertram Y., Jr. & Sharp, H. M. Environmental Technologies in Architecture. (Illus.). 1963. ref. ed. 28.95 (ISBN 0-13-283226-7). P-H.

Kinzie, Juliette. Wau-Bun, the "Early" Days in the Northwest. LC 75-7095. (Indian Captivities Ser.: Vol. 70). 1976. Repr. of 1856 ed. lib. bdg. 44.00 (ISBN 0-8240-1694-7). Garland Pub.

Kinzie, Juliette A. see Hutchinson, K. M.

Kipler, James, ed. American Novelists Since World War II: Second Series. (Dictionary of Literary Biography Ser.: Vol. 6). (Illus.). 300p. 1980. 54.00 (ISBN 0-8103-0908-4). Gale.

Kipling. Walt Disney's the Jungle Book. (Illus.). 128p. 1980. 9.95 (ISBN 0-517-54324-9, Harmony); pap. 5.95 (ISBN 0-517-54328-1, Harmony); 24-copy prepak 142.80 (ISBN 0-686-68778-7). Crown.

Kipling, R. How the Leopard Got His Spots & Other Stories. (Peter Possum Paperbacks Ser). 1967. pap. 0.95 o.p. (ISBN 0-531-05124-2). Watts.

Kipling, Rudyard. Captains Courageous. (Classics Ser). (gr. 6 up). 1964. pap. 1.25 (ISBN 0-8049-0027-2, CL-27). Airmont.

--Captains Courageous. (Literature Ser.). (gr. 10-12). 1970. pap. text ed. 3.33 (ISBN 0-87720-722-4). AMSCO Sch.

--Elephant's Child. LC 73-104661. (gr. k-3). 1970. 7.95 (ISBN 0-8027-6020-1); PLB 7.85 o.s.i. (ISBN 0-8027-6021-X). Walker & Co.

--How the Leopard Got His Spots. LC 72-81373. (Just So Ser.). (Illus.). 32p. (gr. 2 up). 1972. 7.95 (ISBN 0-8027-6111-9); PLB 7.85 o.s.i. (ISBN 0-8027-6112-7). Walker & Co.

--How the Rhinoceros Got His Skin. LC 73-76356. (Just So Ser.). (Illus.). 32p. (gr. 1 up). 1974. 7.95 (ISBN 0-8027-6149-6); PLB 7.85 o.s.i. (ISBN 0-8027-6150-X). Walker & Co.

--If. pap. 2.50 (ISBN 0-385-04217-5, Dolp). Doubleday.

--Jungle Books. (gr. 5 up). 1964. 4.95g o.s.i. (ISBN 0-02-750800-5). Macmillan.

--Just So Stories. (Doubleday Classic). (Illus.). (gr. 1-6). 1946. 8.95a (ISBN 0-385-07352-6); PLB (ISBN 0-385-07110-8). Doubleday.

--Just So Stories: Anniversary Edition. LC 79-170932. 112p. (gr. 2-5). 1972. 12.95a (ISBN 0-385-07225-2); PLB (ISBN 0-385-07443-3). Doubleday.

--Rudyard Kipling's Verse. LC 40-29931. 1940. 12.95 (ISBN 0-385-04407-0). Doubleday.

Kipnis, Claude. The Mime Book. Kleinman, Neil, ed. LC 73-14266. (Illus.). 256p. (YA) 1974. 15.95 o.s.i. (ISBN 0-06-012404-0, HarpT). Har-Row.

Kipnis, Kenneth. Philosophical Issues in Law: Cases & Materials. 1977. pap. text ed. 12.95 (ISBN 0-13-662296-8). P-H.

Kipp, Jacob, jt. ed. see Higham, R.

Kipp, Jerry. Firefacts: The Consumer's Guide to Wood Heat. 256p. 1980. 14.95 (ISBN 0-914378-61-9); pap. 9.95 (ISBN 0-914378-58-9). Countryman.

Kipp, Maxine. Living Life to the Fullest. LC 79-52997. (Radiant Life Ser). 1980. pap. 2.95 (ISBN 0-88243-896-4, 02-0896); teacher's ed 2.95 (ISBN 0-88243-187-0, 32-0187). Gospel Pub.

Kipper, Lenore, jt. auth. see Kipper, Morris.

Kipper, Morris & Kipper, Lenore. God's Wonderful World. 1968 ed. LC 68-56182. (Illus.). (gr. k-3). text ed. 3.50 o.p. (ISBN 0-88400-026-5); teachers' ed. 6.50 o.p. (ISBN 0-88400-028-1). Shengold.

Kippley, Sheila. Breast-Feeding & Natural Child Spacing: The Ecology of Natural Mothering. 1975. pap. 3.50 (ISBN 0-14-003992-9). Penguin.

Kiraldi, Louis & Burk, Janet L., eds. Pollution: A Selected Bibliography of U.S. Government Publications on Air, Water, & Land Pollution 1965-1970. 1971. 3.00 (ISBN 0-932826-09-1). New Issues MI.

Kiraly, Bela. Ferenc Deak. Brown, Arthur W., et al, eds. (World Leaders Ser.: No. 39). 1975. lib. bdg. 10.95 (ISBN 0-8057-3030-3). Twayne.

Kiraly, Bela K. Hungary in the Late Eighteenth Century. LC 69-19459. (East Central European Studies). (Illus.). 1969. 20.00x (ISBN 0-231-03223-4). Columbia U Pr.

Kiraly, Bela K. & Rothenberg, Gunther E., eds. War & Society in East Central Europe During the Eighteenth & Nineteenth Centuries: Special Topics & Generalizations, Vol. 1. (Studies on Society in Change: No. 10). 1979. 22.50 (ISBN 0-930888-04-9). Brooklyn Coll Pr.

Kirban, Salem. Questions on Prophecy. 1979. pap. 2.95 (ISBN 0-8024-7055-6). Moody.

Kirby & Smith. Mechanical Ventilation of the Lungs. 1981. text ed. write for info. (ISBN 0-443-08063-1). Churchill.

Kirby, Alice M., ed. Curriculum: Content & Change. 128p. (Orig.). 1980. pap. 4.95 (ISBN 0-88200-141-8, C2883). Alexander Graham.

Kirby, Colleen & Roberts, Laura. Putting You in Creative Aerobic Dance: The Fun & Fitness of a Lifetime Sport Through Movement to Music. Fritze, David, ed. LC 80-84937. (Illus.). 150p. (Orig.). 1981. pap. write for info. Korakas-Roberts-Kirby.

Kirby, D. G., ed. see Paasivirt, Juhani.

Kirby, D. P., ed. St. Wilfrid at Hexham. 1974. 22.00 (ISBN 0-85362-155-1, Oriel). Routledge & Kegan.

Kirby, David. America's Hive of Honey: Foreign Influences on American Fiction Through Henry James. LC 80-20672. 231p. 1980. 12.50 (ISBN 0-8108-1349-1). Scarecrow.

Kirby, David & Dawson, John. Small Scale Retailing in the United Kingdom. 1979. text ed. 28.25 (ISBN 0-566-00164-0, Pub. by Gower Pub Co England). Renouf.

Kirby, David K., ed. American Fiction to Nineteen Hundred: A Guide to Information Sources. LC 73-16982. (American Literature, English Literature, & World Literatures in English Information Guide Ser.: Vol. 4). 260p. 1975. 30.00 (ISBN 0-8103-1210-7). Gale.

Kirby, E. T. Ur-Drama: The Origins of Theatre. LC 74-32656. 164p. 1975. 15.00x (ISBN 0-8147-4559-8); pap. 7.00x (ISBN 0-8147-4573-3). NYU Pr.

Kirby, F. E. Introduction to Western Music. LC 69-15248. 1970. text ed. 12.95 (ISBN 0-02-917360-4). Free Pr.

Kirby, G. W., jt. auth. see Bentley, K. W.

Kirby, G. W. see Weissberger, A.

Kirby, George. Looking at Germany. LC 77-37629. (Looking at Other Countries Ser.). (Illus.). (gr. 4-6). 1972. 8.95 (ISBN 0-397-31337-3). Lippincott.

Kirby, Jack T. Darkness at the Dawning: Race & Reform in the Progressive South. LC 77-161416. (Critical Periods of History Ser). 220p. 1972. 6.95 o.p. (ISBN 0-397-47225-0); pap. text ed. 2.95 o.p. (ISBN 0-397-47209-9). Lippincott.

--Media-Made Dixie: The South in the American Imagination. LC 77-14551. 1978. 11.95 (ISBN 0-8071-0375-6). La State U Pr.

--Westmoreland Davis: Virginia Planter - Politician 1859-1942. LC 68-22730. (Illus.). 232p. 1968. 9.95 (ISBN 0-8139-0158-8). U Pr of Va.

Kirby, John B. Black Americans in the Roosevelt Era: Liberalism & Race. LC 79-10315. (Twentieth Century America Ser.). 1980. 14.50x (ISBN 0-87049-279-9). U of Tenn Pr.

Kirby, John R. & Biggs, J. B., eds. Cognition, Development & Instruction. LC 80-523. (Educational Psychology Ser.). 1980. 19.00 (ISBN 0-12-409550-X). Acad Pr.

Kirby, Jonell H., et al. Manual for Users of Standardized Tests. 8.75 (ISBN 0-936224-01-0). Schol Test.

Kirby, L. & Scarry, S. From Writers to Writing: A College Reading & Writing Workbook. 364p. 1978. 10.95 (ISBN 0-471-01766-3). Wiley.

Kirby, M. J., jt. auth. see Wilson, A. G.

Kirby, M. W. The Decline of British Economic Power Since Eighteen Seventy. 216p. 1981. text ed. 24.95x (ISBN 0-04-942169-7, 2614). Allen Unwin.

Kirby, Michael. Futurist Performance. (Illus.). 1971. pap. 3.95 o.p. (ISBN 0-525-47280-0). Dutton.

Kirby, Money Alian. Dr. Jesus Christ & the Sick World. 1980. 4.50 o.p. (ISBN 0-682-49101-2). Exposition.

Kirby, P. A. & Nethercot, D. A. Design for Structural Stability. LC 79-754. 1979. 43.95 (ISBN 0-470-26691-0). Halsted Pr.

Kirby, R. S. Early Years of Modern Civil Engineering. 1932. 47.50x (ISBN 0-685-69833-5). Elliots Bks.

Kirby, Ronald F. Road User Charges-Some Practical Considerations. 17p. 1974. pap. 1.50 o.p. (ISBN 0-87766-115-4, 66000). Urban Inst.

Kirby, Ronald F. & Bhatt, Kiran U. Guidelines on the Operation of Subscription Bus Services. 76p. 1975. pap. 3.00 o.p. (ISBN 0-87766-141-3, 11100). Urban Inst.

Kirby, Ronald F., et al. Residential Zoning & Equal Housing Opportunities: A Case Study in Black Jack, Missouri. 34p. 1972. pap. 2.00 o.p. (ISBN 0-87766-075-1, 19000). Urban Inst.

Kirby, S. Woodburn. Singapore: The Chain of Disaster. (Illus.). 1971. 8.95 o.s.i. (ISBN 0-02-563200-0). Macmillan.

Kirby, Sheelah. The Yeats Country. 1977. pap. text ed. 4.00x (ISBN 0-391-00737-8, Dolmen Pr). Humanities.

Kirby, William C., tr. see Hillgruber, Andreas.

Kirbya, N. Personal Values in Primary Education. 1981. text ed. 18.35 (ISBN 0-06-318130-4, Pub. by Har-Row Ltd England); pap. 9.25 (ISBN 0-06-318131-2). Har-Row.

Kircheimer, Otto. Politics, Law, & Social Change: Selected Essays. LC 69-16955. 1969. 22.50x (ISBN 0-231-03191-2). Columbia U Pr.

Kirchem, Ronald, ed. see Jones, Ronald E.

Kirchenmann, Jorg C. & Muschalek, Christian. Residential Districts. (Illus.). 192p. 1980. 32.50 (ISBN 0-8230-7491-9). Watson-Guptill.

Kircher, Harry B., jt. auth. see McNall, Preston E.

Kircher, Harry B., jt. ed. see McNall, Preston E.

Kirchgassner, K., tr. see Collatz, Lothar & Albrecht, Julius.

Kirchheimer, Otto. Political Justice: The Use of Legal Procedure for Political Ends. LC 80-14279. xiv, 452p. 1980. Repr. of 1961 ed. lib. bdg. 34.50x (ISBN 0-313-22509-5, KIPJ). Greenwood.

Kirchhoff, Bodo. Body-Building: Erzaehlung, Schauspiel, Essay. (Edition Suhrkamp. Neue Folge: Es. NF 5). 130p. (Orig., Ger.). 1980. pap. text ed. 4.55 (ISBN 3-518-11005-5, Pub. by Insel Verlag Germany). Suhrkamp.

Kirchhoff, Frederick. William Morris. (English Authors Ser.: No. 262). 1979. lib. bdg. 14.50 (ISBN 0-8057-6723-1). Twayne.

Kirchman, Milton. Mannerism & Imagination: A Reexamination of Sixteenth Century Italian Aesthetic. (Elizabethan Studies: No. 88). 1980. pap. text ed. 25.00x (ISBN 0-391-02162-1). Humanities.

Kirchmayer, L. K., jt. ed. see Hafele, W.

Kirchner, Emil & Schwaiger, Konrad. Role of Interest Groups in the European Community. 1979. text ed. 22.25x (ISBN 0-566-00257-4, Pub. by Gower Pub Co England). Renouf.

Kirchner, Glenn, et al. Physical Education for Elementary School Children. 5th ed. 1981. text ed. 15.95x (ISBN 0-697-07175-8); instrs.' manual 1.00 (ISBN 0-697-07179-0); unit lesson plans avail. (ISBN 0-697-07180-4). Wm C Brown.

Kirchner, J. G. Techniques of Chemistry: Vol. 14 Thin Layer Chromatography. 2nd ed. 1137p. 1978. 77.00 (ISBN 0-471-93264-7). Wiley.

Kirchner, Jane. The Function of the Persona in the Poetry of Byron. (Salzburg Studies in English Literature, Romantic Reassessment: No.15). 1973. pap. text ed. 25.00x (ISBN 0-391-01446-3). Humanities.

Kirchner, Justus G. Techniques of Chemistry: Thin Layer Chromatography. 2nd ed. LC 78-9163. (Techniques of Chemistry Ser.: Vol. 14). 1978. 77.00 (ISBN 0-471-93264-7, Pub. by Wiley-Interscience). Wiley.

Kirchner, Peter T., ed. Nuclear Medicine Review Syllabus. LC 79-92990. (Illus.). 619p. 1980. pap. text ed. 32.50 (ISBN 0-932004-04-0). Soc Nuclear Med.

Kirchner, Walther. History of Russia. rev. 6th ed. LC 72-5830. (Illus.). 403p. 1976. pap. 5.50 (ISBN 0-06-460169-2, 169, COS). Har-Row.

--Western Civilization Since Fifteen Hundred. 2 nd ed. (gr. 9-12). 1975. pap. 4.95 (ISBN 0-06-460111-0, CO 111, COS). Har-Row.

--Western Civilization to Fifteen Hundred. (gr. 9-12). 1960. pap. text ed. 3.95 (ISBN 0-06-460110-2, CO 110, COS). Har-Row.

Kirchner, Wayne K., jt. auth. see Dunnette, Marvin D.

Kirchnoff, William E. Job Hunting Handbook for the Municipal Executive. (Illus.). 63p. 1980. pap. 8.50 (ISBN 0-9603848-0-4). Appellate Pub.

Kirchoff, William, jt. auth. see Collis, Martin.

Kiricuta, Ion. Use of the Omentum in Plastic Surgery. (Illus.). 320p. Date not set. 48.01 (ISBN 0-08-026352-6). Pergamon.

Kirillova, F. M., jt. ed. see Gabasov, R.

Kirk & Othmer. Encyclopedia of Chemical Technology, 12 vols. 3rd ed. Incl. Vol. 1. A-Alkanolamines. 967p (ISBN 0-471-02037-0); Vol. 2. Alkoxides, Metals & Antibiotics (Peptides) 1036p (ISBN 0-471-02038-9); Vol. 3. Antibiotics (Phenazines) 958p (ISBN 0-471-02039-7); Vol. 4. Blood, Coagulants & Anticoagulants to Cardiovascular Agents. 930p (ISBN 0-471-02040-0); Vol. 5. Castor Oil to Chlorosulfuric Acid. 880p (ISBN 0-471-02041-9); Vol. 6. Chocolate & Cocoa to Copper. 869p (ISBN 0-471-02042-7); Vol. 7. Copper Alloys to Distillations (ISBN 0-471-02043-5); Vol. 8. Diuretics to Emulsions (ISBN 0-471-02044-3); Vol. 9. Enamels: Porcelain or Vitreous to Ferrites. 902p (ISBN 0-471-02062-1); Vol. 10. Ferroelectrics to Fluorine Compounds. 962p (ISBN 0-471-02063-X); Vol. 11. Fluorine Compounds to Gold & Gold Compounds (ISBN 0-471-02064-8); Vol. 12. Gravity Concentration to Hidroxy Carboxylic Acids (ISBN 0-471-02065-6). 1978-80. 145.00 ea. (Pub. by Wiley-Interscience). Wiley.

Kirk, Albert & Obach, Robert E. Commentary on the Gospel of Matthew. LC 78-65715. 1978. pap. 4.95 (ISBN 0-8091-2173-5). Paulist Pr.

Kirk, Albert, jt. auth. see Obach, Robert E.

Kirk, Barbara. Grandpa, Me & Our House in the Tree. LC 78-9564. (Illus.). (gr. 3-6). 1978. 8.95 (ISBN 0-02-750750-5, 75075). Macmillan.

Kirk, C. J. Basic Medical Laboratory Technology. (Illus.). 1975. 21.00x o.s.i. (ISBN 0-8464-0179-7). Beekman Pubs.

Kirk, C. J., et al. Basic Medical Laboratory Technology. LC 76-3314. 1975. 26.50 o.p. (ISBN 0-471-01799-X, Pub. by Wiley Medical). Wiley.

Kirk, Clara M., jt. ed. see Kirk, Rudolf.

Kirk, D. Optimal Control Theory: An Introduction. 1970. ref. ed. 26.95 (ISBN 0-13-638098-0). P-H.

Kirk, D., jt. auth. see Milson, A.

Kirk, David, et al. Biology: The Unity & the Diversity of Life. 1978. text ed. 18.95x (ISBN 0-534-00540-3); wkbk. 6.95x (ISBN 0-534-00584-5). Wadsworth Pub.

Kirk, Donald. Tell It to the Dead: Memories of a War. LC 75-29137. 229p. 1975. 12.95 (ISBN 0-88229-287-0); pap. 6.95 (ISBN 0-88229-354-0). Nelson-Hall.

Kirk, Eugene P. Menippean Satire: An Annotated Catalogue of Texts & Criticism. LC 79-7921. (Garland Reference Library of the Humanities). 1980. lib. bdg. 40.00 (ISBN 0-8240-9533-2). Garland Pub.

Kirk, Francis G. Total System Development for Information Systems. LC 73-4359. (Business Data Processing: A Wiley Ser.). 284p. 1973. 32.95 (ISBN 0-471-48260-9, Pub. by Wiley-Interscience). Wiley.

Kirk, G. S. The Bacchae of Euripides. LC 78-31827. 1979. 21.95 (ISBN 0-521-22675-9); pap. 5.50x (ISBN 0-521-29613-7). Cambridge U Pr.

--Homer & the Oral Tradition. LC 76-7806. 1977. 28.50 (ISBN 0-521-21309-6). Cambridge U Pr.

--Myth: Its Meaning & Functions in Ancient & Other Cultures. (Sather Classical Lectures: No. 40). 1970. 17.50x (ISBN 0-520-01651-3); pap. 6.95x (ISBN 0-520-02389-7). U of Cal Pr.

Kirk, G. S., ed. see Heraclitus.

Kirk, Geoffrey S. Homer & the Epic. abr. ed. Orig. Title: Songs of Homer, II. pap. 8.50 (ISBN 0-521-09356-2, 356). Cambridge U Pr.

--Songs of Homer. 1962. 55.00 (ISBN 0-521-05890-2). Cambridge U Pr.

Kirk, Geoffrey S. & Raven, John E. Presocratic Philosophers. 1957. 47.50 (ISBN 0-521-05891-0); pap. 9.95x (ISBN 0-521-09169-1). Cambridge U Pr.

Kirk, Grayson & Wessell, Nils, eds. The Soviet Threat: Myths & Realities. LC 78-56914. 1978. 22.95 (ISBN 0-03-046591-5). Praeger.

Kirk, Grayson L. Philippine Independence: Motives, Problems & Prospects. LC 72-2377. (FDR & the Era of the New Deal Ser.). 278p. 1974. Repr. of 1936 ed. lib. bdg. 29.50 (ISBN 0-306-70486-2). Da Capo.

Kirk, H. David. Shared Fate. LC 64-13232. 1964. 12.95 (ISBN 0-02-917340-X). Free Pr.

Kirk, J. Andrew. Theology Encounters Revolution. LC 80-7471. 192p. (Orig.). 1980. pap. 4.95 (ISBN 0-87784-468-2). Inter-Varsity.

Kirk, James A. Stories of the Hindus: An Introduction Through Texts & Interpretations. LC 72-77651. 224p. 1972. 7.95 o.s.i. (ISBN 0-02-563230-2); pap. 2.95 o.s.i. (ISBN 0-02-086400-0). Macmillan.

Kirk, John. How to Manage Your Money. (Orig.). pap. 1.50 o.p. (ISBN 0-87502-007-0). Benjamin Co.

Kirk, John, jt. auth. see Professional Report Editors.

Kirk, John F. Supplement to Allibone's Critical Dictionary of English Literature & British & American Authors, 2 Vols. LC 67-296. 1965. Repr. of 1891 ed. 76.00 (ISBN 0-8103-3018-0). Gale.

Kirk, John M., jt. tr. see Prentice, Roger.

Kirk, K. E., ed. Epistle to the Romans. (Clarendon Bible Ser.). (Illus.). 1937. pap. 5.95x (ISBN 0-19-826116-0). Oxford U Pr.

Kirk, Kenneth E. The Vision of God: The Christian Doctrine of the Summum Bonum. abr. ed. Dunstan, G. R., ed. 1978. Repr. of 1934 ed. 13.95 (ISBN 0-227-67830-3). Attic Pr.

Kirk, Margaret. God Was a Stranger. 1980. pap. 2.75 (ISBN 0-85363-130-1). OMF Bks.

Kirk, Michael. Cargo Risk. LC 80-1123. (Crime Club Ser.). 1980. 8.95 (ISBN 0-385-17272-9). Doubleday.

Kirk, Nancy, jt. auth. see Conway, Madeleine.

Kirk, Nancye J., ed. Managing the Office Building. (Illus.). 400p. 1980. text ed. 21.95 (ISBN 0-912104-45-7). Inst Real Estate.

Kirk, Nancye J., ed. see Inst. Real Estate & U. S. Department of Energy.

Kirk, Nancye J., ed. see Institute of Real Estate Management Staff.

Kirk, Nancye J., ed. see Kelley, Edward N.

Kirk, Nancye J., ed. see Walters, William, Jr.

Kirk, Paul L. & Bradford, Lowell W. Crime Laboratory: Organization & Operation. (August Vollmer Criminalistics Ser). (Illus.). 132p. 1972. 9.50 (ISBN 0-398-01022-6). C C Thomas.

Kirk, Paul L., et al. Crime Investigation. 2nd ed. LC 73-19854. 1974. text ed. 23.95 (ISBN 0-471-48247-1). Wiley.

Kirk, Philip. Hydra Conspiracy. (Butler Ser.: No. 1). 1979. pap. 1.75 (ISBN 0-8439-0655-3, Leisure Bks). Nordon Pubns.

Kirk, R., jt. auth. see Scoles, C. A.

Kirk, R. E. & Othmer, D. F., eds. Encyclopedia of Chemical Technology, Vol. 1. 3rd ed. LC 64-22188. 1978. 145.00 o.p. (ISBN 0-471-02037-0, Pub. by Wiley-Interscience). Wiley.

--Encyclopedia of Chemical Technology, Vol. 2. 3rd ed. LC 77-15820. 1978. 145.00 o.p. (ISBN 0-471-02038-9, Pub. by Wiley-Interscience). Wiley.

Kirk, R. Wade, jt. auth. see Roueche, John E.

Kirk, Robert W. First Aid for Pets: The Pet Owner's Complete Guide to Emergency Care of Dogs, Cats & Other Small Animals. 1978. 10.95 o.p.; pap. 7.95 (ISBN 0-87690-275-1). Dutton.

Kirk, Robert W. & Bistner, Stephen I. Handbook of Veterinary Procedures & Emergency Treatment. 3rd ed. (Illus.). 928p. 1981. text ed. write for info. (ISBN 0-7216-5475-4). Saunders.

Kirk, Rudolf & Kirk, Clara M., eds. Types of English Poetry. LC 79-51972. (Granger Poetry Library). 1981. Repr. of 1940 ed. 42.50x (ISBN 0-89609-184-8). Granger Bk.

Kirk, Russell & Chamberlain, John. Great Issues 73: A Forum on Important Questions Facing the American Public, Vol. 5. 1974. 5.95. TSU Pr.

Kirk, Ruth. Exploring Crater Lake Country. LC 75-9506. (Illus.). 96p. 1975. pap. 4.95 o.p. (ISBN 0-295-95397-7). U of Wash Pr.

--Snow. 1978. 12.50 (ISBN 0-688-03268-0); pap. 5.95 (ISBN 0-688-08268-8). Morrow.

Kirk, Ruth & Daugherty, Richard D. Hunters of the Whale, an Adventure in Northwest Coast Archaeology. LC 73-17317. (Illus.). 160p. (gr. 5-9). 1974. 7.92 (ISBN 0-688-30109-6); 8.25 (ISBN 0-688-20109-1). Morrow.

Kirk, Samuel A. & Gallagher, James J. Educating Exceptional Children. 3rd ed. LC 78-69609. (Illus.). 1979. text ed. 17.95 (ISBN 0-395-26526-6); inst. manual 0.80 (ISBN 0-395-26529-0); test item supplement 0.75 (ISBN 0-395-28699-9). HM.

Kirk, Samuel A. & Lord, Francis E. Exceptional Children: Educational Resources & Perspectives. 464p. 1974. pap. text ed. 11.95 (ISBN 0-395-18027-9). HM.

Kirk, Samuel A. & McCarthy, Jeanne M. Learning Disabiliies: Selected ACLD Papers. LC 74-20857. 1975. 15.75 (ISBN 0-395-20200-0). HM.

Kirk, Samuel A., et al. Teaching Reading to Slow & Disabled Learners. LC 77-77655. (Illus.). 1978. text ed. 17.75 (ISBN 0-395-25821-9). HM.

Kirk, T. Kent, et al. Lignin Biodegradation: Microbiology, Chemistry & Potential Applications, 2 vols. 1980. 64.95 ea.; Vol. 2, 272p. (ISBN 0-8493-5459-5); Vol. 2. (ISBN 0-8493-5460-9). CRC Pr.

Kirk, Tim, illus. Fozzie's Big Book of Sidesplitting Jokes (Please Laugh) LC 80-23776. (Muppet Show Bks.). (Illus.). 32p. (gr. 1-5). 1981. pap. 1.95 (ISBN 0-394-84675-3). Random.

Kirk, W. Richard. Aim for a Job in Hospital Work. LC 74-114137. (Career Guidance Ser.). 124p. 1971. pap. 3.50 (ISBN 0-668-02230-2). Arco.

Kirkaldy, J. F. Study of Fossils. 1964. pap. text ed. 3.50x (ISBN 0-09-108391-5, Hutchinson U Lib). Humanities.

Kirkbridge, T., jt. ed. see Gage, Michael.

Kirkby, D. One Hundred Questions in Auditing with Suggested Answers for Accountancy Examinees. 1968. 15.00 (ISBN 0-08-012901-3); pap. 7.75 (ISBN 0-08-012900-5). Pergamon.

Kirkby, John. The Capacity & Extent of Human Understanding, Exemplified in the Extraordinary Case of Automathes. (The Flowering of the Novel, 1740-1775 Ser: Vol. 15). 1974. Repr. of 1745 ed. lib. bdg. 50.00 (ISBN 0-8240-1114-7). Garland Pub.

Kirkby, M. J., jt. auth. see Carson, M. A.

Kirkby, M. J., jt. auth. see Wilson, A. G.

Kirkby, M. J., ed. Hillslope Hydrology. LC 77-2669. (Landscape Systems-A Ser. in Geomorphology). 1978. 63.90 (ISBN 0-471-99510-X, Pub. by Wiley-Interscience). Wiley.

Kirkconnell, Watson, jt. tr. see Andrusyshen, C. H.

Kirke, et al. Michigan One Hundred Years Ago. (Sun Historical Ser.-). (Illus.). pap. 3.50 (ISBN 0-89540-053-7). Sun Pub.

--Ohio One Hundred Years Ago. (Sun Historical Ser.). (Illus.). pap. 3.50 (ISBN 0-89540-050-2). Sun Pub.

Kirkeby, Ed. Ain't Misbehavin: The Story of Fats Waller. LC 75-14123. (Roots of Jazz). 248p. 1975. lib. bdg. 22.50 (ISBN 0-306-70683-0); pap. 4.95 (ISBN 0-306-80015-2). Da Capo.

Kirkemo, Ronald B. An Introduction to International Law. LC 73-81677. 1974. 15.95 (ISBN 0-88229-118-1). Nelson-Hall.

Kirkendall, Carolyn A., ed. Directions for the Decade: Library Instruction in the 1980's. (Library Orientation Ser.: No. 12). 1980. 10.00. Pierian.

Kirkendall, Lester A. & Osborne, Ruth F. Sex Education: Syllabus. 1971. pap. text ed. 4.65 (ISBN 0-89420-087-9, 216786); cassette recordings 82.60 (ISBN 0-89420-184-0, 180800). Natl Book.

Kirkendall, Richard S. The Truman Period As a Research Field: A Reappraisal, 1972. LC 73-80585. 1973. 12.50x (ISBN 0-8262-0152-0). U of Mo Pr.

Kirkendall, Richard S., jt. auth. see Schutz, John A.

Kirkendall, Richard S., ed. The Truman Period As a Research Field. 1967. 12.00 o.p. (ISBN 0-8262-0598-4). U of Mo Pr.

Kirker, Harold. The Architecture of Charles Bulfinch. (Illus.). 1977. 18.50x (ISBN 0-674-04390-1). Harvard U Pr.

--California's Architectural Frontier. LC 73-77786. (In Search of California Ser). (Illus.). 1973. pap. 4.95 o.s.i. (ISBN 0-87905-011-X). Peregrine Smith.

Kirk-Greene, A. H., ed. West Africa Portraits: A Biographical Dictionary of West African Personalities, 1947-1977. 1981. 25.00x (ISBN 0-7146-3112-4, F Cass Co). Biblio Dist.

Kirk-Greene, A. H. M. African Administrators in Action. rev. ed. 1981. 29.50x (ISBN 0-7146-3134-5, F Cass Co). Biblio Dist.

Kirk-Greene, Anthony. A Biographical Dictionary of the British Colonial Governor: Volume I, Africa. LC 80-81949. 256p. 1980. 31.95 (ISBN 0-8179-2611-9). Hoover Inst Pr.
Kirk-Greene, Anthony H., tr. Hausa Ba Dabo Ba Ne: A Collection of Five Hundred Proverbs. 1966. 2.50x o.p. (ISBN 0-19-639390-6). Oxford U Pr.
Kirk-Greene, C. W. E. French False Friends. 272p. 1981. 18.95 (ISBN 0-7100-0741-8). Routledge & Kegan.
Kirkham, Don & Powers, W. L. Advanced Soil Physics. LC 74-153083. 1972. 53.50 (ISBN 0-471-48875-5, Pub. by Wiley-Interscience). Wiley.
Kirkham, Michael. Poetry of Robert Graves. 1969. text ed. 15.00x (ISBN 0-485-11103-9, Athlone Pr). Humanities.
Kirkham, Pat, jt. auth. see Hayward, Helena.
Kirkland, Frazar. Cyclopaedia of Commerical and Business Anecdotes: Comprising Interesting Reminiscences & Facts, Remarkable Traits & Humors, & Notable Sayings, Dealings, Experiences & Witticisms of Merchants, Etc, 2 vols. LC 73-95777. (Illus.). 1969. Repr. of 1864 ed. 38.00 (ISBN 0-8103-3131-4). Gale.
Kirkland, J. J., jt. auth. see Snyder, L. R.
Kirkland, Will, tr. see Lorca, Federico G.
Kirkley, George & Goodbody, John, eds. Manual of Weighttraining. 3rd ed. (Illus.). 1979. pap. text ed. 12.50x o.p. (ISBN 0-392-07003-0, SpS). Soccer.
Kirkman, Francis. The Counterfeit Lady Unveiled: Being a Full Account of the Birth, Life, Most Remarkable Actions, & Untimely Death of Mary Carleton, Known by the Name of the German Princess. Bd. with The Memoirs of Mary Carleton, Commonly Stiled, the German Princess: Being a Narrative of Her Life & Death. LC 80-2486. 1981. 74.50 (ISBN 0-404-19120-7). AMS Pr.
Kirkman, Francis, jt. auth. see Head, Richard.
Kirkman, Kay & Stinnett, Roger. Joplin: A Pictorial History. Friedman, Donna R., ed. (Illus.). 192p. 1980. pap. 13.95 (ISBN 0-89865-070-4). Donning Co.
Kirkpatrick. Alpha-Getoprotein: Laboratory Procedures & Clinical Applications. 1981. write for info. Masson Pub.
Kirkpatrick, C. A., jt. auth. see Levin, Richard I.
Kirkpatrick, C. A., jt. auth. see Tillman, Rollie.
Kirkpatrick, Charles A. & Russ, Frederick A. Business. 2nd ed. LC 77-13460. 544p. 1978. pap. text ed. 13.95 (ISBN 0-574-19365-0, 13-2365); instr's guide avail. (ISBN 0-574-19366-9, 13-2366); study guide 5.95 (ISBN 0-574-19367-7, 13-2367); trans. mstrs. 30.00 (ISBN 0-686-60861-5, 13-2369); test booklet 6.50 (ISBN 0-574-19368-5, 13-2368); instructor's presentation notebook 49.95 (ISBN 0-686-52458-6, 13-2309). SRA.
Kirkpatrick, Charles A., jt. auth. see Levin, Richard I.
Kirkpatrick, Daniel, jt. ed. see Vinson, James.
Kirkpatrick, Daniel, jt. ed. see Vinson, Jim.
Kirkpatrick, Donald L., et al. Selecting & Training First-Line Supervisors. 396p. 1980. 69.50 (ISBN 0-85013-114-6). Dartnell Corp.
Kirkpatrick, E. M. & Schwartz, C. M. Chambers Spell Well. 256p. 1980. 10.00x (ISBN 0-550-11821-7, Pub. by W & R Chambers Scotland). State Mutual Bk.
Kirkpatrick, E. M., ed. Chambers Universal Learners' Dictionary. 928p. 1980. 25.00x (ISBN 0-550-10632-4, Pub by W & R Chambers Scotland). State Mutual Bk.
Kirkpatrick, Frank. How to Buy a Country Business. 1981. 11.95 (ISBN 0-8092-5944-3). Contemp Bks.
Kirkpatrick, George. War - What for? LC 78-147519. (Library of War & Peace; Labor, Socialism & War). lib. bdg. 38.00 (ISBN 0-8240-0307-1). Garland Pub.
Kirkpatrick, Inez E. Stagecoach Trails in Iowa. LC 75-56295. (Illus.). 231p. 1976. 25.00 o.p. (ISBN 0-916170-03-9). J-B Pubs.
--Tavern Days in the Hawkeye State. (Illus.). 370p. (Orig.). (gr. 7 up). Date not set. pap. price not set (ISBN 0-916170-15-2). J B Pubs. Postponed.
Kirkpatrick, James J., et al. Testing & Fair Employment: Fairness & Validity Of Personnel Tests For Different Ethnic Groups. LC 68-28006. (Illus.). 1969. 10.00x (ISBN 0-8147-0234-1). NYU Pr.
Kirkpatrick, James M. & Weaver, Michael K. Automotive Air Conditioning & Climate Control. LC 78-994. 1978. pap. 14.85 (ISBN 0-672-97098-8); wkbk. 4.95 (ISBN 0-672-97099-6); tchr's manual 3.33 (ISBN 0-672-97100-3). Bobbs.
Kirkpatrick, Martha, ed. Women's Sexual Development: Outer Form & Inner Space. (Women in Context Ser.). (Illus.). 290p. 1980. 25.00 (ISBN 0-306-40375-7, Plenum Pr). Plenum Pub.
Kirkpatrick, P. B., jt. auth. see Room, Thomas G.
Kirkpatrick, R. Dante's Paradiso & the Limitations of Modern Criticism. LC 77-80839. 1978. 36.00 (ISBN 0-521-21785-7). Cambridge U Pr.
Kirkpatrick, Rena K. Look at Flowers. LC 77-27433. (Look at Science Ser.). (Illus.). (gr. k-3). 1978. PLB 9.95 (ISBN 0-8393-0061-1). Raintree Child.
--Look at Insects. LC 77-27130. (Look at Science Ser.). (Illus.). (gr. k-3). 1978. PLB 9.95 (ISBN 0-8393-0062-X). Raintree Child.
--Look at Leaves. LC 77-26662. (Look at Science Ser.). (Illus.). (gr. k-3). 1978. PLB 9.95 (ISBN 0-8393-0060-3). Raintree Child.
--Look at Magnets. LC 77-26665. (Look at Science Ser.). (Illus.). (gr. k-3). 1978. PLB 9.95 (ISBN 0-8393-0063-8). Raintree Child.
--Look at Pond Life. LC 77-27243. (Look at Science Ser.). (Illus.). (gr. k-3). 1978. PLB 9.95 (ISBN 0-8393-0059-X). Raintree Child.
--Look at Rainbow Colors. LC 77-27593. (Look at Science Ser.). (Illus.). (gr. k-3). 1978. PLB 9.95 (ISBN 0-8393-0064-6). Raintree Child.
--Look at Seeds & Weeds. LC 77-27459. (Look at Science Ser.). (Illus.). (gr. k-3). 1978. PLB 9.95 (ISBN 0-8393-0065-4). Raintree Child.
--Look at Shore Life. LC 77-27589. (Look at Science Ser.). (Illus.). (gr. k-3). 1978. PLB 9.95 (ISBN 0-8393-0067-0). Raintree Child.
--Look at Trees. LC 77-27242. (Look at Science Ser.). (Illus.). (gr. k-3). 1978. PLB 9.95 (ISBN 0-8393-0066-2). Raintree Child.
--Look at Weather. LC 78-6815. (Look at Science Ser.). (Illus.). (gr. k-3). 1978. PLB 9.95 (ISBN 0-8393-0069-7). Raintree Child.
Kirkpatrick, Samuel A., jt. auth. see Morgan, David R.
Kirkpatrick, Samuel A., ed. American Electoral Behavior: Change & Stability. LC 75-32374. (Sage Contemporary Social Science Issues Ser.: Vol. 24). 1976. 4.95x (ISBN 0-8039-0582-3). Sage.
Kirkup, James, tr. see Durrenmatt, Friedrich.
Kirkup, James see Ibsen, Henrik.
Kirkus, Virginia. Gardening. rev. ed. (First Bks.). (Illus.). 72p. (gr. 4 up). 1976. PLB 4.90 o.p. (ISBN 0-531-00540-2). Watts.
Kirkwood, James. Good Times, Bad Times. 1978. pap. 2.25 (ISBN 0-449-23975-6, Crest). Fawcett.
--Hit Me with a Rainbow. 1981. pap. 3.25 (ISBN 0-440-13622-9). Dell.
--P. S. Your Cat Is Dead. 224p. 1973. pap. 2.75 (ISBN 0-446-95948-0). Warner Bks.
Kirkwood, Patrica F., tr. see Lear, John.
Kirkwood, Robert T. Laboratory Exercises in Biology. 1981. pap. text ed. 5.95 (ISBN 0-8403-1754-9). Kendall-Hunt.
Kirman, B. H. Mental Retardation. 1968. 675.00 (ISBN 0-08-013371-1). Pergamon.
Kirmse, Wolfgang. Carbene Chemistry. 2nd ed. (Organic Chemistry Ser.: Vol. 1). 1971. 55.50 o.p. (ISBN 0-12-409956-4). Acad Pr.
Kirmser, Camille. Camille, a Boy in Love with Nature. 4.95 o.p. (ISBN 0-685-58638-3). Vantage.
Kirn, John. Cell. (Orig.). 1960. pap. 0.90 (ISBN 0-8054-9706-4). Broadman.
Kirp, David L. Doing Good by Doing Little: Race & Schooling in Britain. 1979. 12.95x (ISBN 0-520-03740-5). U of Cal Pr.
Kirp, David L. & Yudof, Mark G. Educational Policy & the Law. LC 73-17609. 1974. 32.00 (ISBN 0-8211-1015-2); text ed. 29.00x (ISBN 0-685-42636-X). McCutchan.
Kirsch, A., jt. auth. see Peacock, J.
Kirsch, Arthur C. Jacobean Dramatic Perspectives. LC 70-180964. 1972. 7.50x o.p. (ISBN 0-8139-0390-4). U Pr of Va.
Kirsch, Arthur C., ed. see Dryden, John.
Kirsch, Charlotte. A Survivor's Manual to Wills, Trusts, Maintaining Emotional Stability. LC 80-977. 240p. 1981. 11.95 (ISBN 0-385-15879-3, Anchor Pr). Doubleday.
Kirsch, Dietrich & Kirsch-Korn, Jutta. Make Your Own Rugs. 1970. 11.95 (ISBN 0-7134-2461-3, Pub. by Batsford England). David & Charles.
Kirsch, Donald. Documentary Supplement to Financial & Economic Journalism: Analysis, Interpretation & Reporting. LC 78-55415. 1978. pap. 8.00x (ISBN 0-8147-4572-5). NYU Pr.
Kirsch, Francine. Collecting Chromos. LC 80-26616. (Illus.). 288p. 1981. 25.00 (ISBN 0-498-02517-9). A S Barnes.
Kirsch, Jonathan. Lovers in a Winter Circle. (Orig.). 1978. pap. 1.75 o.p. (ISBN 0-451-08119-6, E8119, Sig). NAL.
Kirsch, Robert. Casino. Date not set. pap. 2.75 (ISBN 0-671-82931-9). PB.
Kirsch, Susan. What to Do Between Here & There: Activities for Families on the Go. (Illus.). 128p. 1980. 10.95 (ISBN 0-13-955112-3, Spec); pap. 3.95 (ISBN 0-13-955104-2). P-H.
Kirsch, Uri. Optimum Structural Design. (Illus.). 448p. 1981. text ed. write for info (ISBN 0-07-034844-8, C); write for info. solutions manual (ISBN 0-07-034845-6). McGraw.
Kirsch Company Publication, A. The Complete Window Book. 1978. 5.95 o.p. (ISBN 0-385-14524-1). Doubleday.
Kirschen, Etienne S., et al. Financial Integration in Western Europe. LC 68-58869. 1969. 20.00x (ISBN 0-231-03200-5). Columbia U Pr.
Kirschenbaum, Howard. Advanced Value Clarification. LC 76-50695. 188p. (Orig.). 1977. pap. 12.95 (ISBN 0-88390-132-3). Univ Assocs.
Kirschenbaum, Howard & Glaser, Barbara. Developing Support Groups: A Manual for Facilitators & Participants. LC 78-60280. 82p. 1978. pap. 8.50 (ISBN 0-88390-145-5). Univ Assocs.
Kirschenbaum, Howard & Simon, Sidney B. Readings in Values Clarification. 1973. pap. 8.95 (ISBN 0-03-011936-7, 861). Winston Pr.
Kirschenbaum, Howard & Stensrud, Rockwell. The Wedding Book: Alternative Ways to Celebrate Marriage. LC 73-17901. 1974. pap. 4.50 (ISBN 0-8164-2090-4). Crossroad NY.
Kirschenbaum, Michael A. Practical Diagnosis: Renal Disease. (Illus.). 1978. kroydenflex 14.00x (ISBN 0-89289-200-5). HM Prof Med Div.
Kirschke, James J. Henry James & Impressionism. LC 80-52732. 357p. 1981. 22.50x (ISBN 0-87875-206-4). Whitston Pub.
Kirsch-Korn, Jutta, jt. auth. see Kirsch, Dietrich.
Kirschman, John C., jt. ed. see Ayres, John C.
Kirschner, Allen. Film: Readings in the Mass Media. LC 70-158977. 1971. pap. 7.50 (ISBN 0-672-73221-1). Odyssey Pr.
Kirschner, Allen & Kirschner, Linda. Radio & Television: Readings in the Mass Media. LC 72-158975. 1971. pap. 8.50 (ISBN 0-672-73230-0). Odyssey Pr.
Kirschner, Allen & Kirschner, Linda, eds. Journalism: Readings in the Mass Media. LC 76-158976. 1971. pap. 7.95 (ISBN 0-672-73224-6). Odyssey Pr.
Kirschner, Heidi. Fireless Cookery. 144p. 1981. pap. 5.95 (ISBN 0-914842-58-7). Madrona Pubs.
Kirschner, L. H., jt. auth. see Folsom, M. M.
Kirschner, Linda, jt. auth. see Kirschner, Allen.
Kirschner, Linda, jt. ed. see Kirschner, Allen.
Kirschner, Stanley, ed. Coordination Chemistry. LC 77-81522. 331p. 1969. 32.50 (ISBN 0-306-30402-3, Plenum Pr). Plenum Pub.
Kirschner, Stephen M., jt. auth. see Pavelec, Barry J.
Kirsh, D. Y., jt. auth. see Chen, Reuven.
Kirshina, K. The Yard of Tame Birds. (Illus.). 20p. 1978. pap. 1.25 (ISBN 0-8285-0003-7). Progress Pubs.
Kirsner, Douglas. The Schizoid World of Jean-Paul Sartre & R. D. Laing. LC 76-44197. 1977. text ed. 23.50x (ISBN 0-391-00677-0). Humanities.
Kirsner, Joseph B. Inflammatory Bowel Disease. 2nd ed. Shorter, Roy G., ed. LC 79-8884. (Illus.). 693p. 1980. 74.00 (ISBN 0-8121-0698-9). Lea & Febiger.
Kirsner, Joseph B., jt. auth. see Schachter, Howard.
Kirsner, Robert. The Novels & Travels of Camilo Jose Cela. (Studies in the Romance Languages & Literatures: No. 43). 1964. pap. 8.50x (ISBN 0-8078-9043-X). U of NC Pr.
Kirst, Hans H. The Affairs of the Generals. 1980. pap. 2.50 o.p. (ISBN 0-449-24258-7, Crest). Fawcett.
--Hero in the Tower. 352p. 1973. pap. 1.50 o.p. (ISBN 0-523-00145-2). Pinnacle Bks.
Kirst, Michael, jt. auth. see Wirt, Frederick.
Kirst, Michael W. Politics of Education at the Local, State & Federal Levels. LC 75-100956. 1971. 19.50 (ISBN 0-8211-1009-8); text ed. 17.50x (ISBN 0-685-14294-9). McCutchan.
Kirstein, Lincoln. Flesh Is Heir. (Lost American Fiction Ser.). 1977. pap. 1.75 o.p. (ISBN 0-445-08548-7). Popular Lib.
Kirtisinghe, Parakrama. Sea Shells of Sri Lanka: Including Forms Scattered Throughout the Indian & Pacific Oceans. LC 77-72607. (Illus.). 1978. 12.50 (ISBN 0-8048-1189-X). C E Tuttle.
Kirtland, G. B. One Day in Aztec Mexico. LC 63-7897. (Illus.). (gr. 4-6). 1963. 4.50 o.p. (ISBN 0-15-258381-5, HJ). HarBraceJ.
Kirtland, Katheleen, jt. auth. see Kadish, Ferne.
Kirtland, Kathleen, jt. auth. see Kadish, Ferne.
Kirtley, Donald D. The Psychology of Blindness. LC 74-17155. 376p. 1974. 19.95 (ISBN 0-88229-178-5). Nelson-Hall.
Kirts, Donald K., jt. auth. see Powell, C Randall.
Kirvan, John, jt. auth. see Radlowski, Roger J.
Kirwan, Albert D., jt. auth. see Clark, Thomas D.
Kirwan, Albert D., ed. see Eaton, Clement.
Kirwan, Christopher, tr. see Aristotle.
Kirwin, Gerald J. & Grodzinsky, Stephen. Basic Circuit Analysis. LC 79-88449. (Illus.). 1980. text ed. 26.50 (ISBN 0-395-28488-0); solutions manual 0.75 (ISBN 0-395-28489-9). HM.
Kirzhnits, D. A. Field Theoretical Methods in Many-Body Systems. Meadows, A. J., tr. 1967. 60.00 (ISBN 0-08-011779-1). Pergamon.
Kirzner, Israel M. The Economic Point of View: An Essay in the History of Economic Thought. 2nd ed. LC 75-42449. (Studies in Economic Theory). 228p. 1976. 12.00; pap. 4.95. NYU Pr.
Kisdi, D., jt. auth. see Gombas, P.
Kiselev, A. V. & Lygin, V. I. Infrared Spectra of Surface Compounds. Slutzkin, D., ed. Kaner, N., tr. from Rus. LC 75-15866. 384p. 1975. 59.95 (ISBN 0-470-48905-7). Halsted Pr.
Kiseli, Karl. Incompatible Destinies. 1980. 10.95 (ISBN 0-533-04518-5). Vantage.
Kish, George. Bibliography of International Geographical Congresses, Eighteen Seventy-One to Nineteen Seventy-Six. (Reference Bks.). 1979. lib. bdg. 32.50 (ISBN 0-8161-8226-4). G K Hall.
Kish, Joseph L., Jr. Business Forms: Design & Control. 226p. 1971. 25.95 (ISBN 0-8260-5045-X, 57521). Ronald Pr.
Kish, Joseph L., Jr. & Morris, J. Microfilm in Business. (Illus.). 1966. 16.50 (ISBN 0-8260-5060-3). Ronald Pr.
Kish, Leslie. Survey Sampling. LC 65-19479. 1965. 29.95 (ISBN 0-471-48900-X). Wiley.
Kishi, Nami. Ogre & His Bride. Tresselt, Alvin, tr. from Jap. LC 73-136990. Orig. Title: Oni No Yomesan. (Illus.). (gr. k-3). 1971. 5.95 o.s.i. (ISBN 0-8193-0471-9, Four Winds); PLB 5.41 o.s.i. (ISBN 0-8193-0472-7). Schol Bk Serv.
Kishikawa, Shigemi. Stepping Stones to Go. LC 65-13411. (Illus.). 1965. pap. 5.95 (ISBN 0-8048-0547-4). C E Tuttle.
Kishlansky, Mark A. The Rise of the New Model Army. LC 79-4285. 1979. 21.50 (ISBN 0-521-22751-8). Cambridge U Pr.
Kisiel, Marie. Design for Change: A Guide to New Careers. (New Viewpoints Vision Bks.). 352p. 1980. 12.95 (ISBN 0-531-02374-5, EE40); pap. 8.95 (ISBN 0-531-06754-8). Watts.
Kismaric, Susan. American Children. 1981. 14.95 (ISBN 0-87070-229-7, 037338); pap. 7.95 (ISBN 0-87070-232-7, 037346). NYGS.
--American Children: Photographs in the Collection of the Museum of Modern Art. (Springs Mills Series on the Art of Photography). (Illus.). 80p. 1981. 14.95 (ISBN 0-87070-232-7); pap. 7.95 (ISBN 0-87070-229-7). Museum Mod Art.
Kismark, Carole. Andre Kertesz, No. 6. LC 77-70070. (Aperture History of Photography Ser.). 1977. pap. 8.95 (ISBN 0-912334-96-7). Aperture.
Kisner, James. Nero's Vice. LC 80-27484. 256p. 1981. 10.95 (ISBN 0-8253-0042-8). Beaufort Bks NY.
Kispert, Lowell D., jt. auth. see Kevan, Larry.
Kiss, Judit, ed. Agricultural Development Strategy in the Developing Countries. (Studies on Developing Countries: No. 103). (Illus.). 156p. (Orig.). 1979. pap. 12.50x (ISBN 963-301-060-8). Intl Pubns Serv.
Kissam, P., jt. auth. see Ives, Howard C.
Kissane, James. Alfred Tennyson. (English Authors Ser.: No. 110). lib. bdg. 9.95 (ISBN 0-8057-1544-4). Twayne.
Kissane, John M., jt. auth. see Anderson, W. A. D.
Kissel, P., et al. The Neurocristopathies. LC 79-89479. (Illus.). 1980. 57.50 (ISBN 0-89352-039-X). Masson Pub.
Kisselbach, Theo. Leica CL. (Illus.). 1978. 15.00 (ISBN 3-77632-550-X, 4550). Hove Camera.
Kissell, Mary L. Basketry of the Papago & Pima Indians: Anthropological Papers of the Am. Museum of Natural History, Vol. 17, Pt. 4. LC 72-8827. (Beautiful Rio Grande Classics Ser). lib. bdg. 10.00 o.s.i. (ISBN 0-87380-095-8); pap. 8.00 o.p. (ISBN 0-87380-133-4). Rio Grande.
Kissinger, Ellen M. A Sequential Curriculum for the Severely & Profoundly Mentally Retarded-Multi-Handicapped. 216p. 1981. pap. 22.75 spiral (ISBN 0-398-04145-8). C C Thomas.
Kissinger, Henry. For the Record: Selected Statements, 1977 to 1980. 288p. 1981. 12.95 (ISBN 0-316-49663-4). Little.
Kissinger, Henry A. The Necessity for Choice. LC 61-6187. 1961. 12.50 o.p. (ISBN 0-06-012410-5, HarpT). Har-Row.
--World Restored: Europe After Napoleon. 8.00 (ISBN 0-8446-2384-9). Peter Smith.
Kissinger, Warren S. The Parables of Jesus: A History of Interpretation & Bibliography. (American Theological Library Association (ATLA) Bibliography Ser.: No. 4). 463p. 1979. lib. bdg. 22.00 (ISBN 0-8108-1186-3). Scarecrow.
--Sermon on the Mount: A History of Interpretation & Bibliography. LC 75-29031. (ATLA Bibliography Ser.: No. 3). 1975. 15.00 (ISBN 0-8108-0843-9). Scarecrow.
Kissling, H. J., et al. Muslim World: A Historical Survey Part Three: The Last Great Muslim Empires. 1969. text ed. 44.50x (ISBN 90-040-2104-3). Humanities.

Kisslo, Joseph. Two-Dimensional Echocardiography. (Clinics in Diagnostic Ultrasound: Vol. 4). 1980. text ed. 20.50 (ISBN 0-443-08076-3). Churchill.

Kissock, Craig. Curriculum Planning for Social Studies & Teaching Cultural Approach. 125p. 1981. 28.00 (ISBN 0-471-27868-8, Pub. by Wiley Interscience). Wiley.

Kiste, R. C. The Bikinians: A Study in Forced Migration. LC 79-224. 1974. pap. 5.95 (ISBN 0-8465-3752-4). Benjamin-Cummings.

Kister, Kenneth F. Encyclopedia Buying Guide. 3rd ed. LC 76-645701. 388p. 1981. 22.50 (ISBN 0-8352-1353-6). Bowker.

Kister, M. J. Studies in Jahiliyya & Early Islam. 360p. 1980. 75.00x (ISBN 0-86078-068-6, Pub. by Variorum England). State Mutual Bk.

Kistler, Stan, jt. auth. see Duke, Donald.

Kitagawa, D. Issei & Nisei: The Internment Years. 1967. pap. 3.95 (ISBN 0-8164-9244-1). Continuum.

Kitagawa, Joseph M. Religion in Japanese History. LC 65-23669. 1966. 25.00x (ISBN 0-231-02834-2). Columbia U Pr.

Kitagawa, Joseph M., jt. auth. see Wach, Joachim.

Kitano, Harry H. Race Relations. 2nd ed. (Ser. in Sociology). (Illus.). 1980. text ed. 17.95 (ISBN 0-13-750091-2). P-H.

Kitano, Harry H., jt. auth. see Daniels, Roger.

Kitch, Edmund W. Regulation, Federalism, and Interstate Commerce. Tarlock, A. Dan, ed. LC 80-23166. 176p. 1981. lib. bdg. 20.00 (ISBN 0-89946-065-8). Oelgeschlager.

Kitchel, Denison. The Truth About the Panama Canal. (Illus.). 1978. 8.95 o.p. (ISBN 0-87000-409-3). Arlington Hse.

Kitchell, Marilyn. Weeds, Wood, Stone & Mettle. (Orig.). 1980. limited signed ed. 20.00x (ISBN 0-915316-77-3); pap. 7.50x (ISBN 0-915316-76-5). Pentagram.

Kitchen, Helen, jt. auth. see Commission on Critical Choices.

Kitchen, Jonathan S. The Employment of Merchant Seamen. 658p. 1980. 150.00x (ISBN 0-85664-527-3, Pub. by Croom Helm Ltd England). Biblio Dist.

Kitchen, Joseph W., jt. auth. see Bolker, Ethan D.

Kitchen, K. A. The Bible in Its World: The Bible & Archaeology Today. (Illus.). 1978. pap. 4.95 (ISBN 0-87784-797-5). Inter-Varsity.

Kitchen, Kenneth A. Ancient Orient & Old Testament. LC 66-30697. 1966. 5.95 (ISBN 0-87784-907-2). Inter-Varsity.

Kitchen, Martin. A Military History of Germany: From the Eighteenth Century to the Present Day. 1976. pap. 4.95 (ISBN 0-8065-0524-9). Citadel Pr.

--Military History of Germany from the 18th Century to the Present Day. LC 74-17022. 392p. 1975. 12.50x (ISBN 0-253-33838-7). Ind U Pr.

Kitchen, Martin, jt. auth. see Berghahn, Volker.

Kitchen, Ruben P., Jr. Pacific Carrier. (Zebra World at War Ser.: No. 23). (Orig.). 1980. pap. 2.50 (ISBN 0-89083-683-3, Kable News Co). Zebra.

Kitchens, James A. & Muessig, Raymond H. The Study & Teaching of Sociology. 2nd ed. (Social Science Seminar, Secondary Education Ser.: No. C28). 104p. 1980. pap. text ed. 5.95 (ISBN 0-675-08194-7). Merrill.

Kitchenside, G. M. Isle of Wight Album. 15.95x (ISBN 0-392-07972-0, SpS). Soccer.

Kitchin, Frances. Cook Out. (Illus.). 1978. 6.95 (ISBN 0-7153-7610-1). David & Charles.

--Granny's Cookery Book. LC 78-66798. (Illus.). 1978. 8.95 (ISBN 0-7153-7721-3). David & Charles.

Kitchin, G. W., ed. see Bacon, Francis.

Kitchin, Laurence. Mid-Century Drama. 1969. pap. 4.95 (ISBN 0-571-09077-X, Pub. by Faber & Faber). Merrimack Bk Serv.

Kitchin, M., jt. ed. see Yudelson, J.

Kitching, Frances, jt. auth. see Dowell, Susan S.

Kitching, Gavin. Class & Economic Change in Kenya: The Making of an African Petite Bourgeoisie, 1905-1970. LC 79-21804. 448p. 1980. text ed. 35.00x (ISBN 0-300-02385-5). Yale U Pr.

Kitching, J. A; see Dangeard, P.

Kitching, Jessie. Birdwatcher's Guide to Wildlife Sanctuaries. LC 76-5388. 1976. 8.95 (ISBN 0-668-03949-3). Arco.

Kitching, Jessie & Braun, Susan, eds. Dance & Mime Film & Videotape Catalog. rev. ed. (Orig.). 1980. pap. 10.95 (ISBN 0-914438-00-X). Dance Films.

Kitman, Marvin. The Coward's Almanac. 128p. 1976. pap. 1.50 o.p. (ISBN 0-345-25051-6). Ballantine.

--George Washington's Expense Account. 1976. pap. 1.95 o.p. (ISBN 0-345-25519-4). Ballantine.

Kitney, R. I. & Rompelman, O. The Study of Heart-Rate Variability. (Illus.). 220p. 1980. text ed. 65.00x (ISBN 0-19-857533-5). Oxford U Pr.

Kitov, A. E. The Jew & His Home. 10th ed. Bulman, Nathan, tr. LC 63-17660. 233p. 1976. 8.50 (ISBN 0-88400-004-4). Shengold.

Kitson, Charles H. The Art of Counterpoint. LC 75-4973. (Music Reprint Ser.). 344p. 1975. Repr. of 1924 ed. lib. bdg. 32.50 (ISBN 0-306-70668-7). Da Capo.

Kitson, Harry D. & Stover, Edgar M. Vocations for Boys. rev. ed. LC 55-8677. (gr. 9 up). 1955. 5.95 o.p. (ISBN 0-15-293917-2, HJ). HarBraceJ.

Kitson, Harry D., jt. auth. see Lingenfelter, Mary R.

Kitson, Michael. Claude Lorrain: Liber Veritatis. (Illus.). 1978. 40.00 o.p. (ISBN 0-684-15784-5, ScribT). Scribner.

Kitsuse, John, jt. auth. see Spector, Malcom.

Kitsuse, John I., jt. auth. see Broom, Leonard.

Kittel, Charles. Introduction to Solid State Physics. 5th ed. LC 75-25936. 560p. 1976. text ed. 28.95 (ISBN 0-471-49024-5). Wiley.

--Quantum Theory of Solids. LC 63-20633. 1963. 29.95 (ISBN 0-471-49025-3). Wiley.

Kittel, Charles & Kroemer, Herbert. Thermal Physics. 2nd ed. LC 79-16677. (Illus.). 1980. text ed. 22.95x (ISBN 0-7167-1088-9); instrs' guide avail. W H Freeman.

Kittlaus, Paul, jt. auth. see Leas, Speed.

Kittle, Linda, jt. ed. see Bereny, Justin.

Kittler, Glenn D. Laetrile Control for Cancer. 1963. 8.95 (ISBN 0-8392-1059-0). Astor-Honor.

Kittler, Glenn D., jt. auth. see Panzarella, Joseph J., M.D.

Kitto, H. D. Poiesis: Structure & Thought. (Sather Classical Lectures: No. 36). 1966. 21.50x (ISBN 0-520-00651-8). U of Cal Pr.

Kitto, John. Kitto's Comments & Applications, 2 vols. LC 80-8069. 1934p. 1981. Repr. of 1901 ed. Set. 49.95 (ISBN 0-8254-3025-9). Kregel.

Kittredge, George L. Chaucer & His Poetry. LC 78-135544. 1970. 10.00x (ISBN 0-674-11201-6); pap. 2.95 (ISBN 0-674-11210-5). Harvard U Pr.

Kittredge, George L., ed. see Shakespeare, William.

Kittredge, Richard & Lehrberger, John, eds. Sublanguage: Studies on Language in Restricted Semantic Domains. (Foundations of Communications Ser.). 240p. 1980. text ed. 52.50x (ISBN 3-11-008244-6). De Gruyter.

Kittrell, Beverly. Poems of Faith. 1981. 5.95 (ISBN 0-533-04798-6). Vantage.

Kittrie, Nicholas. The Right to Be Different. 1973. pap. 4.50 o.p. (ISBN 0-14-021538-7, Pelican). Penguin.

Kittrie, Nicholas N. & Susman, Jackwell, eds. Legality, Morality, & Ethics in Criminal Justice. (Praeger Special Studies). 1978. 25.95 (ISBN 0-03-047521-X). Praeger.

Kitts, Kent D., jt. auth. see Eliason, Alan.

Kittsley, Scott L. Physical Chemistry. 3rd ed. LC 68-26399. (Orig.). 1969. pap. 3.95 (ISBN 0-06-460097-1, CO 97, COS). Har-Row.

Kitzberger, Ingrid R. A Thousand Images of Loveliness in Percy Bysshe Shelley's Love Poetry. (Salzburg Studies in English Literature, Romantic Reassessment: No. 69). 1977. pap. text ed. 25.00x (ISBN 0-391-01447-1). Humanities.

Kitzing, Donald. Credit & Collections for Small Business. Newton, William R., ed. (Illus.). 192p. 1981. 15.95 (ISBN 0-07-034915-0, P&RB). McGraw.

Kitzinger, Ernst. Art of Byzantium & the Medieval West: Selected Studies. Kleinbauer, W. Eugene, ed. LC 75-34728. (Illus.). 448p. 1976. 22.50x (ISBN 0-253-31055-5). Ind U Pr.

Kitzinger, Sheila. Complete Book of Pregnancy & Childbirth. LC 80-7650. (Illus.). 336p. 1980. 14.95 (ISBN 0-394-51349-5). Knopf.

--The Experience of Breastfeeding. 255p. (Orig.). 1980. pap. 3.50 (ISBN 0-14-005591-6). Penguin.

Kitzinger, Sheila & Davis, John A., eds. The Place of Birth. (Illus.). 1978. text ed. 29.50x (ISBN 0-19-261125-9); pap. text ed. 15.95x (ISBN 0-19-261238-7). Oxford U Pr.

Kitzinger, U. The Second Try: Labour & the EEC. 1969. 25.00 (ISBN 0-08-012961-7); pap. 13.25 (ISBN 0-08-012960-9). Pergamon.

Kivelowitz, Terri. Diabetes: A Guide to Self-Management for Patients & Their Families. (Illus.). 224p. 1981. 12.95 (ISBN 0-13-208637-9, Spec); pap. 5.95 (ISBN 0-13-208629-8). P-H.

Kivenko. Managing Work in Process. Date not set. price not set (ISBN 0-8247-1268-4). Dekker.

Kiver & Kaufman. Television Simplified. 7th ed. LC 72-11273. 630p. 1973. pap. 16.40 (ISBN 0-8273-0492-7); instructor's guide 1.60 (ISBN 0-8273-0493-5). Delmar.

Kivley, Melvin. Hadlock Hill. LC 79-56885. 178p. 1981. 7.95 (ISBN 0-533-04545-2). Vantage.

--The Still & I. 1981. 8.95 (ISBN 0-533-04820-6). Vantage.

Kivlin. Innovation in Rural India. 1975. 10.00 (ISBN 0-87972-169-3). Bowling Green Univ.

Kivy, Peter. The Corded Shell: Reflections on Musical Expression. LC 80-7539. (Princeton Essays on the Arts: No. 9). 176p. 1980. 15.00 (ISBN 0-691-07258-2); pap. 5.95 (ISBN 0-691-02014-0). Princeton U Pr.

Kivy-Rosenberg, E., jt. auth. see Kaplan, S. J.

Kiyohara, Michiko. A Checklist of Monographs & Periodicals on the Japanese Colonial Empire. LC 80-84459. (Special Project Ser.: No. 28). 352p. 1981. pap. 11.95 (ISBN 0-8179-4284-X). Hoover Inst Pr.

Kiyohara, Michiko, compiled by. A Checklist of Monographs & Periodicals on the Japanese Colonial Empire. (Special Project: No.28). 352p. 1981. pap. 11.95 (ISBN 0-8179-4284-X). Hoover Inst Pr.

Kiyooka, E., tr. see Fukuzawa, Yukichi.

Kiyooka, Eiichi, tr. The Autobiography of Yukichi Fukuzawa. 407p. (Japanese.). 1980. pap. text ed. 10.00x (ISBN 0-231-08373-4). Columbia U Pr.

Kiyosaki, Wayne S. North Korea's Foreign Relations: The Politics of Accomodation, 1945-75. LC 76-19548. (Special Studies). 1976. 24.95 (ISBN 0-275-23490-8). Praeger.

Kizziar, Janet & Hagedorn, Judy. Search for Acceptance: The Adolescent & Self-Esteem. LC 78-11491. 1979. 13.95 (ISBN 0-88229-369-9); pap. 6.95 (ISBN 0-88229-648-5). Nelson-Hall.

Kjekshus, Helge. Ecology Control & Economic Developement in East African History: The Case of Tanganyika 1850-1950. 1977. 20.00x (ISBN 0-520-03384-1). U of Cal Pr.

Kjeldsen, Kitty. Women's Gymnastics. 2nd ed. 100p. 1975. pap. text ed. 3.95x o.p. (ISBN 0-205-04841-2, 6248411). Allyn.

Kjelgaard, Jim. Boomerang Hunter. 1978. pap. 1.25 (ISBN 0-686-68376-5, 37408, Camelot). Avon.

--Irish Red. 192p. (gr. 4-6). 1981. pap. 1.95 (ISBN 0-553-15008-1, Skylark). Bantam.

--Lion Hound. (gr. 4-8). 1980. pap. 1.75 (ISBN 0-686-57992-5). Bantam.

Kjelgaard, Jim A. Explorations of Pere Marquette. (Landmark Ser.: No. 17). (Illus.). (gr. 4-6). 1951. PLB 5.99 (ISBN 0-394-90317-X). Random.

Kjellerup, Hope R. Molly the Mule. 1981. 5.95 (ISBN 0-533-04776-5). Vantage.

Kjellstrom, Bjorn. Be Expert with Map & Compass: The Orienteering Handbook. rev. ed. LC 76-12550. (Illus.). 176p. 1976. pap. 7.95 (ISBN 0-684-14270-8, SL595, ScribT). Scribner.

Klaassen, Leo H., jt. auth. see Vanhove, Norbert.

Klaassen, Leo K., et al. Spatial Systems: A General Introduction. 1979. 24.95 (ISBN 0-566-00263-9, 02930-0, Pub. by Saxon Hse England). Lexington Bks.

Klabunde, Kenneth J. Chemistry of Free Atoms & Particles. 1980. 29.50 (ISBN 0-12-410750-8). Acad Pr.

Klachko, David M., et al, eds. Hormone Receptors. LC 77-25856. (Advances in Experimental Medicine & Biology Ser.: Vol. 96). 224p. 1978. 27.50 (ISBN 0-306-32696-5, Plenum Pr). Plenum Pub.

Klachko, Wolodymyr, jt. auth. see Dickey, Ronald W.

Klaeser, Barbara M. Reading Improvement: A Complete Course for Increasing Speed and Comprehension. LC 76-49042. 384p. 1977. 16.95 (ISBN 0-88229-232-3); pap. 8.95 (ISBN 0-88229-406-7). Nelson-Hall.

Klaessig, Janet, jt. ed. see Katz, William A.

Klaf, A. Albert. Calculus Refresher for Technical Men. 1957. pap. text ed. 5.00 (ISBN 0-486-20370-0). Dover.

Klafs, Carl E. & Arnheim, Daniel D. Modern Principles of Athletic Training. 5th ed. (Illus.). 580p. 1981. text ed. 21.95 (ISBN 0-8016-2682-X). Mosby.

Klafs, Carl E. & Lyon, M. Joan. The Female Athlete: A Coach's Guide to Conditioning & Training. 2nd ed. LC 77-27418. (Illus.). 1978. pap. text ed. 11.95 (ISBN 0-8016-2681-1). Mosby.

Klafs, Carl E., jt. auth. see Arnheim, Daniel D.

Klaften, E. B. & Allison, F. C. German-English, English-German Patent Terminological Dictionary. 1971. 50.00 (ISBN 0-685-12020-1). Heinman.

Klagsbrun, Francine. Psychiatry: What It Is, What It Does, a Book for Young People. LC 75-79669. (Illus.). (gr. 7 up). 1969. PLB 3.90 o.p. (ISBN 0-531-01911-X). Watts.

--Read About the Sanitation Man. LC 71-171903. (Read About Bks). (Illus.). 72p. (gr. 4 up). 1972. PLB 4.47 o.p. (ISBN 0-531-01268-9). Watts.

--Story of Moses. LC 68-27403. (Immortals Biography Ser). (gr. 7 up). 1968. PLB 6.90 (ISBN 0-531-00905-X). Watts.

Klagsbrun, Francine & Klagsbrun, Samuel. Your Health: Nutrition. LC 75-87930. (gr. 4-6). PLB 3.90 o.p. (ISBN 0-531-01906-3). Watts.

Klagsbrun, Samuel, jt. auth. see Klagsbrun, Francine.

Klahr, Saulo. Essentials of Renal Pathophysiology. 1981. 10.95 (ISBN 0-8036-5377-8). Davis Co.

Klain, Peter. Food Service Lodging English. (Illus., Prog. Bk.). 1971. pap. 7.95 (ISBN 0-8436-0531-6). CBI Pub.

Klainer, Albert & Klainer, Jo-Ann. The Judas Gene. 258p. 1981. pap. 2.95 (ISBN 0-441-39298-9). Charter Bks.

Klainer, Jo-Ann, jt. auth. see Klainer, Albert.

Klais, Hans G. Reflections on the Organ Stoplist: Theory & Practice from the Organ Workshop. Blanchard, Homer D., tr. from Ger. (Illus.). 1975. 17.50 o.s.i. (ISBN 0-930112-00-8). Praestant.

Klaits, Barrie. When You Find a Rock: A Field Guide. LC 75-38519. (Illus.). 64p. (gr. 3-7). 1976. 8.95 (ISBN 0-02-750790-4, 75079). Macmillan.

Klamkin, Charles. Photographica: A Guide to the Value of Historic Cameras & Images. LC 77-2849. (Funk & W Bk.). (Illus.). 1978. 17.95 (ISBN 0-308-10298-3, TYC-T). T Y Crowell.

--Railroadiana: The Collectors Guide to Railroad Memorabilia. LC 75-26977. (Funk & W Bk.). (Illus.). 1977. 10.95 o.s.i. (ISBN 0-308-10221-5, TYC-T); pap. 5.95 o.s.i. (ISBN 0-308-10319-X, TYC-T). T Y Crowell.

Klamkin, Charles, jt. auth. see Fetterman, Elsie.

Klamkin, Charles, jt. auth. see Klamkin, Marian.

Klamkin, Marian. The Carnival Glass Collector's Price Guide. LC 77-92365. (Illus., Orig.). 1978. pap. 5.95 (ISBN 0-8015-1094-5, Hawthorn). Dutton.

--The Collector's Guide to Carnival Glass. 224p. 1976. 21.50 (ISBN 0-8015-1396-0, Hawthorn); pap. 9.95 (ISBN 0-8015-1397-9, Hawthorn). Dutton.

--The Collector's Guide to Depression Glass. (Illus.). 288p. 1973. pap. 12.95 (ISBN 0-8015-1399-5, Hawthorn). Dutton.

--The Depression Glass Collector's Price Guide. (Illus.). 96p. 1974. pap. 4.50 (ISBN 0-8015-2018-5, Hawthorn). Dutton.

Klamkin, Marian & Klamkin, Charles. Collectibles: A Compendium. LC 77-37677. (Illus.). 288p. 1981. pap. 10.95 (ISBN 0-385-12176-8, Dolp). Doubleday.

Klane, Robert. Fire Sale. 1977. pap. 1.75 o.p. (ISBN 0-449-23350-2, Crest). Fawcett.

Klann, Margaret L. Target Archery. (Health & Physical Education Ser). 1970. pap. 7.95 (ISBN 0-201-03765-3). A-W.

Klapp, O. E. Opening & Closing. LC 77-87382. (A.S.A. Rose Monograph Ser.). (Illus.). 1978. 19.95 (ISBN 0-521-21923-X); pap. 6.95x (ISBN 0-521-29311-1). Cambridge U Pr.

Klapp, Orrin E. Currents of Unrest: An Introduction to Collective Behavior. LC 76-189252. 1972. 24.00x (ISBN 0-03-085305-2); pap. text ed. 12.95x (ISBN 0-89197-717-1). Irvington.

--Symbolic Leaders: Public Dramas & Public Men. LC 64-23369. 1964. 24.00x (ISBN 0-202-30024-2); pap. text ed. 2.95. Irvington.

Klapper, Charles. The Golden Age of Tramways. new ed. 1974. 13.50 o.p. (ISBN 0-7153-6458-8). David & Charles.

Klapper, Gilbert & Murphy, M. A. Silurian-Lower Devonian Conodont Sequence in the Roberts Mountains Formation of Central Nevada. (Publications in Geological Sciences: Vol. 3). 1975. pap. 10.00x (ISBN 0-520-09517-0). U of Cal Pr.

Klapper, Joseph T. Effects of Mass Communication. LC 60-14402. 1960. text ed. 14.95 (ISBN 0-02-917380-9). Free Pr.

Klapper, M. Roxana. The German Literary Influence on Byron. (Salzburg Studies in English Literature, Romantic Reassessment Ser.: No. 43). 1975. pap. text ed. 25.00x (ISBN 0-391-01448-X). Humanities.

Klapper, Roxana M. The German Literary Influence on Shelley. (Salzburg Studies in English Literature, Romantic Reassessment: No. 42). 1974. pap. text ed. 25.00x (ISBN 0-391-01449-8). Humanities.

Klar, Kathryn, et al, eds. American Indian & Indo-European Studies: Papers in Honor of Madison S. Beeler. 1980. text ed. 79.50x (ISBN 90-279-7876-X). Mouton.

Klare, George R. Measurement of Readability. facsimile ed. 1963. pap. 6.90x o.p. (ISBN 0-8138-2385-4). Iowa St U Pr.

Klare, H. J. & Haxby, D., eds. Frontiers of Criminology. 1967. 21.00 (ISBN 0-08-011579-9). Pergamon.

Klare, Michael T. Beyond the "Vietnam Syndrome". U. S. Interventionism in the 1980's. 80p. (Orig.). 1981. pap. 4.95 (ISBN 0-89758-027-3). Inst Policy Stud.

Klare, Michael T., jt. auth. see Arnson, Cynthia.

Klaren, Peter F. Modernization, Dislocation & Aprismo: Origins of the Peruvian Aprista Party, 1870-1932. LC 73-4915. (Latin American Monographs, No. 32). (Illus.). 282p. 1973. 10.00 (ISBN 0-292-76001-9). U of Tex Pr.

Klarman, Herbert E. Economics of Health. LC 65-14323. 1965. 17.50x (ISBN 0-231-02797-4). Columbia U Pr.

Klarner, David A., ed. The Mathematical Gardiner. 382p. 1980. 19.95x (ISBN 0-534-98015-5). Wadsworth Pub.

Klarner, Walter E., et al. Writing by Design. LC 76-14652. (Illus.). 1977. pap. text ed. 9.50 (ISBN 0-395-24428-5); inst. manual 0.25 (ISBN 0-395-24429-3). HM.

Klarsfeld, Beate. Wherever They May Be: One Woman's Battle Against Nazism. LC 74-81809. 352p. 1975. 10.00 (ISBN 0-8149-0748-2). Vanguard.

Klass, jt. auth. see Weiss.

Klass, Donald L., ed. Biomass As a Nonfossil Fuel Source. LC 80-26044. (ACS Symposium Ser.: No. 144). 1981. 42.00 (ISBN 0-8412-0599-X). Am Chemical.

Klass, Donald W. & Daly, David D., eds. Current Practice of Clinical Electroencephalography. LC 75-32088. 1979. text ed. 52.00 (ISBN 0-89004-088-5). Raven.

Klass, Michael W., ed. see Landis, Robin C.

Klass, Michael W., et al. International Mineral Cartels & Embargoes: Policy Implications for the United States. LC 80-11123. 350p. 1980. 22.95 (ISBN 0-03-044366-0). Praeger.

Klass, Morton & Hellman, Hal. The Kinds of Mankind: An Introduction to Race & Racism. 1971. text ed. write for info. scp (ISBN 0-397-31129-X, HarpC); pap. text ed. 4.50 o.p (ISBN 0-397-47267-6). Har-Row.

Klass, Richard A. The Physician's Business Manual. 400p. 1980. 23.50x (ISBN 0-8385-7850-0). ACC.

Klass, Sheila S. Nobody Knows Me in Miami. 156p. (gr. 4-6). 1981. 8.95 (ISBN 0-684-16851-0). Scribner.

Klassen, A. J. A Bonhoeffer Legacy: Essays in Understanding. 186p. (Orig.). 1981. pap. 13.95 (ISBN 0-8028-1744-0). Eerdmans.

Klassen, A. J., ed. Essays on Bonhoeffer. 1981. pap. 5.95 (ISBN 0-8028-1744-0). Eerdmans.

Klassen, Peter. The Reformation. LC 79-54030. (Problems in Civilization Ser.). (Orig.). 1980. pap. text ed. 3.95x (ISBN 0-88273-408-3). Forum Pr MO.

Klassen, Peter J. Europe in the Reformation. (Illus.). 1979. pap. text ed. 13.95 (ISBN 0-13-292136-7). P-H.

Klastersky, J., ed. Infections in Cancer Chemotherapy. 1976. text ed. 27.50 (ISBN 0-08-019964-X). Pergamon.

Klastersky, Jean & Staquet, Maurice J., eds. Medical Complications in Cancer Patients. (European Organization for Research on Treatment of Cancer (EORTC), Monograph: Vol. 7). Orig. Title: Medical Disorders in Cancer Patients. 323p. 1980. text ed. 31.50 (ISBN 0-89004-519-4). Raven.

Klatt, Edmund, et al. Langenscheidt's Standard German Dictionary: German-English, English-German. Orig. Title: Standard German Dictionary. 1264p. 1974. 11.95 (ISBN 0-685-39723-8). Hippocrene Bks.

Klatt, Edmund, et al, eds. Langenscheidt's Taschenworterbuch. 6th ed. 1264p. 1970. 10.95 (ISBN 3-468-11121-5). Hippocrene Bks.

Klatt, Lawrence A. & Urban, Thomas F. KUBSIM: A Simulation in Collective Bargaining. (Management Ser.). 1975. pap. text ed. 5.95 o.p. (ISBN 0-88244-101-9). Grid Pub.

Klatt, Lawrence A., et al. Human Resources Management: A Behavioral Systems Approach. 1978. text ed. 18.95x (ISBN 0-256-02045-0). Irwin.

Klauber, John. Difficulties in the Analytic Encounter. LC 80-69670. 200p. 1981. 25.00 (ISBN 0-87668-430-4). Aronson.

Klauber, Laurence M. Rattlesnakes: Their Habits, Life Histories, & Influence on Mankind. abr. ed. (Illus.). 400p. 1981. 14.95 (ISBN 0-520-04038-4). U of Cal Pr.

--Rattlesnakes: Their Habits, Life Histories & Influence on Mankind, 2 vols. 2nd ed. LC 56-5002. (Illus.). 1973. Boxed Set. 75.00 (ISBN 0-685-26757-1). Vol. 1 (ISBN 0-520-01775-7). Vol. 2 (ISBN 0-520-02286-6). U of Cal Pr.

Klauder, Francis J. The Wonder of Intelligence. LC 73-79083. (Illus.). 144p. 1973. 6.95 (ISBN 0-8158-0307-9). Chris Mass.

Klauder, John R., ed. Magic Without Magic: John Archibald Wheeler, a Collection of Essays in Honor of His 60th Birthday. LC 75-183745. (Illus.). 1972. text ed. 28.95x (ISBN 0-7167-0337-8). W H Freeman.

Klaus & Kennell. Maternal-Infant Bonding: The Impact of Early Separation or Loss on Family Development. LC 76-5397. Orig. Title: Care of the Family of the Normal or Sick Newborn. (Illus.). 224p. 1976. text ed. 14.95 (ISBN 0-8016-2631-5); pap. 11.95 (ISBN 0-8016-2630-7). Mosby.

Klaus, Bille & Stefan, Raymond J. Physical Assessment & Diagnosis in Primary Care. (Illus.). 704p. 1981. text ed. 24.95 (ISBN 0-86542-003-3). Blackwell Sci.

Klaus, Billie J. Protocols Handbook for Nurse Practitioners. LC 79-14389. 1979. 13.95 (ISBN 0-471-05219-1, Pub. by Wiley-Medical). Wiley.

Klaus, Rudi, jt. ed. see Honadle, George.

Klaus, Samuel, ed. Milligan Case. LC 78-118031. (Civil Liberties in American History Ser). 1970. Repr. of 1929 ed. lib. bdg. 42.50 (ISBN 0-306-71945-2). Da Capo.

Klauser, Theodor. A Short History of the Western Liturgy. Halliburton, John, tr. from Ger. 1979. text ed. 14.95x (ISBN 0-19-213224-5); pap. text ed. 6.95x (ISBN 0-19-213223-7). Oxford U Pr.

Klausmeier, Herbert J. Learning & Teaching Concepts: A Strategy for Testing Applications Theory. Sipple, Thomas S., ed. LC 80-758. (Educational Psychology Ser.). 1980. 22.50 (ISBN 0-12-411450-4). Acad Pr.

Klausmeier, Herbert J. & Goodwin, William. Learning & Human Abilities: Educational Psychology. 4th ed. 576p. 1975. text ed. 20.95 scp (ISBN 0-06-043695-6, HarpC); avail instrs' manual (ISBN 0-06-363694-8). Har-Row.

Klausner, Carla L. & Schultz, Joseph P. From Destruction to Rebirth: The Holocaust & the State of Israel. LC 78-62262. 1978. pap. text ed. 11.25 (ISBN 0-8191-0574-0). U Pr of Amer.

Klausner, Larry. Son of Sam: Based on the Authorized Transcription of the Tapes, Official Documents & Diaries of David Berkowitz. (Illus.). 400p. 1980. 12.95 (ISBN 0-07-035027-2). McGraw.

Klavan, Laurence. I Watch Lois. 192p. (Orig.). 1981. pap. 1.95 (ISBN 0-523-41318-1). Pinnacle Bks.

Klawans, Harold L. Clinical Neuropharmacology, Vol. 4. 1979. 24.50 (ISBN 0-89004-350-7). Raven.

Klawans, Harold L., ed. Clinical Neuropharmacology, Vol. 1. LC 75-14581. 1976. 26.00 (ISBN 0-89004-035-4). Raven.

--Clinical Neuropharmacology, Vol. 2. LC 75-14581. 1977. 24.00 (ISBN 0-89004-171-7). Raven.

--Clinical Neuropharmacology, Vol. 3. LC 75-14581. 1978. 24.50 (ISBN 0-89004-266-7). Raven.

--Clinical Neuropharmacology, Vol. 5. 1981. text ed. price not set (ISBN 0-89004-648-4). Raven.

Klawans, Harold L., et al. Textbook of Clinical Neuropharmacology. 1981. text ed. write for info. (ISBN 0-89004-430-9). Raven.

Klay, Frank. The Samuel E. Dyke Collection of Kentucky Pistols. 30p. 1980. 2.00 (ISBN 0-88227-004-4). Gun Room.

Klayman, Daniel L. & Gunther, Wolfgang H. Organic Selenium Compounds: Their Chemistry & Biology. LC 72-5448. (Organometallic Compounds Ser.). 1024p. 1972. 105.00 (ISBN 0-471-49032-6, Pub. by Wiley-Interscience). Wiley.

Klebba, A. Joan. Mortality from Diseases Associated with Smoking: United States, 1960-77. Shipp, Audrey, ed. (Ser. 20, No. 17). 50p. Date not set. pap. text ed. price not set (ISBN 0-8406-0208-1). Natl Ctr Health Stats.

Kleber, George F. Pictorial Mementoes of the Romantic Age. (Illus.). 1979. deluxe ed. 29.75 (ISBN 0-930582-34-9). Gloucester Art.

Klechkovskii, V. M., et al. Radioecology. LC 73-4697. 371p. 1973. 51.95 (ISBN 0-470-49035-7). Halsted Pr.

Klecka, William R. Discriminant Analysis. LC 80-50927. (Quantitative Applications in the Social Sciences Ser.: No. 19). (Illus.). 71p. 1980. pap. 3.50 (ISBN 0-8039-1491-1). Sage.

Kleckner, Simone-Marie, tr. from Romanian. The Penal Code of the Romanian Socialist Republic. LC 76-17385. (American Series of Foreign Penal Codes: Vol. 20). 1976. text ed. 17.50x (ISBN 0-8377-0040-X). Rothman.

Klee, Albert J. Quantitative Decision-Making, Vol. 3. Vesilind, P. Aarne, ed. (Design & Management for Resource Recovery Ser.). 1980. 39.00 (ISBN 0-250-40313-7). Ann Arbor Science.

Klee, Gary A. World Systems of Traditional Resources Management. LC 80-17711. (Scripta Ser. in Geography). 290p. 1980. 29.95 (ISBN 0-470-27008-X). Halsted Pr.

Klee, Paul. Paul Klee. Grohmann, Will, ed. (Library of Great Painters Ser). 1967. 35.00 (ISBN 0-8109-0228-1). Abrams.

--Paul Klee on Modern Art. 1966. pap. 5.95 (ISBN 0-571-06682-8, Pub. by Faber & Faber). Merrimack Bk Serv.

Klee, V., ed. see Symposia in Pure Mathematics-Seattle-1961.

Kleeberg, Irene. Bicycle Repair. LC 73-4798. (Career Concise Guide Ser.). (gr. 5 up). 1973. PLB 4.90 o.p. (ISBN 0-531-02636-1). Watts.

Kleeberg, Irene C. Bicycle Touring. LC 75-8999. (Career Concise Guide Ser.). (Illus.). 72p. (gr. 5 up). 1975. PLB 4.90 o.p. (ISBN 0-531-02838-0). Watts.

--Going to Camp. (First Bks.). (Illus.). (gr. 4-6). 1978. PLB 6.45 s&l (ISBN 0-531-01488-6). Watts.

Kleefeld, Carolyn M. Climates of the Mind. Karahan, Patricia, ed. LC 78-73648. 240p. 1980. signed ed. 27.00 (ISBN 0-9602214-1-7); pap. 8.95 (ISBN 0-9602214-2-5). Horse & Bird.

Kleek, Peter E. Van see Van Kleek, Peter E.

Kleeman, Charles R., jt. auth. see Maxwell, Morton H.

Kleeman, Walter. The Challenge of Interior Design. 304p. 1981. 19.95 (ISBN 0-8436-0133-7). CBI Pub.

Klees, Fredric. Pennsylvania Dutch. 1950. 9.95 o.s.i. (ISBN 0-02-563820-3). Macmillan.

Kleffner, Frank R. Language Disorders in Children. LC 73-3116. (Studies in Communicative Disorders Ser). 60p. 1973. pap. text ed. 2.95 (ISBN 0-672-61292-5). Bobbs.

Klehr, Harvey E. Communist Cadre: The Social Background of the American Communist Party Elite. LC 78-58488. (Publications 198). 168p. 9.95 (ISBN 0-8179-6981-0). Hoover Inst Pr.

Klei, Herbert E., jt. auth. see Sundstrom, Donald W.

Kleid, Jack J. & Schiller, Nelson B. Echocardiography Case Studies. 1974. spiral bdg. 12.00 o.p. (ISBN 0-87488-040-8). Med Exam.

Kleid, Jack J., jt. ed. see Feinsmith, Leslie S.

Kleid, Jack J., et al. Textbook Study Guide of Internal Medicine. 3rd ed. (Medical Examination Review Book: Vol. 2A). 1976. pap. 8.50 spiral bdg. (ISBN 0-87488-123-4). Med Exam.

Kleiman, Devra G., ed. The Biology & Conservation of the Callitrichidae. LC 78-2428. (Illus.). 1978. text ed. 25.00x (ISBN 0-87474-586-1); pap. text ed. 12.50x (ISBN 0-87474-587-X). Smithsonian.

Kleiman, Robert. Atlantic Crisis. (Orig.). 1964. pap. 2.95x (ISBN 0-393-09753-6). Norton.

Kleimola, Ann M. Justice in Medieval Russia: Muscovite Judgment Characters (Pravye Gramoty) of the 15th & 16th Centuries. LC 75-7171. (Transactions Ser: Vol. 65, Pt. 6). 1975. pap. 5.00 o.p. (ISBN 0-87169-656-8). Am Philos.

Klein, jt. auth. see Kazanas.

Klein, Aaron E. Beyond Time & Matter. LC 73-79684. 120p. (gr. 7-9). 1973. 4.95 o.p. (ISBN 0-385-06106-4). Doubleday.

--The Complete Beginner's Guide to Microscopes & Telescopes. LC 78-22334. (Illus.). 224p. 1980. 9.95a (ISBN 0-385-14854-2); PLB (ISBN 0-385-14855-0). Doubleday.

--The Parasites We Humans Harbor. (Illus.). 1981. 12.95 (ISBN 0-525-66693-1). Elsevier-Nelson.

--Science & the Supernatural: A Scientific Overview of the Occult. LC 76-42339. (gr. 7-9). 1979. 7.95a (ISBN 0-385-12036-2); PLB (ISBN 0-385-12037-0). Doubleday.

--You & Your Body. (gr. 3-5). 1980. pap. 1.50 (ISBN 0-671-29899-2). Archway.

Klein, Aaron E. & Klein, Cynthia L. The Better Mousetrap: A Miscellany of Gadgets, Labor-Saving Devices, & Inventions That Intrigue. (Illus.). 192p. (gr. 6 up). 1981. 10.95 (ISBN 0-8253-0030-4). Beaufort Bks NY.

Klein, Barry L., jt. auth. see Frost, Joe L.

Klein, Bertram. How to Make Money Listing Business Opportunities. 1981. 9.95 (ISBN 0-533-04710-2). Vantage.

Klein, Bob. Wounded Men, Broken Promises. 300p. 1981. 10.95 (ISBN 0-02-563930-7). Macmillan.

Klein, Carole. Aline. (Illus.). 1980. pap. 2.95 (ISBN 0-446-93526-3). Warner Bks.

Klein, Cecilia F. The Face of the Earth: Frontality in Two-Dimensional Mesoamerican Art. LC 75-23799. (Outstanding Dissertations in the Fine Arts - Native American Art). (Illus.). 1976. lib. bdg. 41.00 (ISBN 0-8240-1994-6). Garland Pub.

Klein, Charles M., jt. auth. see Title, Stanley H.

Klein, Chuck. So You Want to Get into the Race. 1980. 2.95 (ISBN 0-8423-6082-4). Tyndale.

Klein, Cornelis, jt. auth. see Hurlbut, Cornelius S., Jr.

Klein, Cynthia L., jt. auth. see Klein, Aaron E.

Klein, D. C. Community Dynamics & Mental Health. LC 68-8105. 1968. 19.95 (ISBN 0-471-49050-4, Pub. by Wiley-Interscience). Wiley.

Klein, Dennis A. Peter Shaffer. (English Authors Ser.: No. 261). 1979. lib. bdg. 12.50 (ISBN 0-8057-6738-X). Twayne.

Klein, Donald, jt. auth. see Israel, John.

Klein, Donald F. & Rabkin, Judith G., eds. Anxiety: New Research & Changing Concepts. 325p. 1981. 29.50 (ISBN 0-686-69136-9). Raven.

Klein, Donald F., jt. ed. see Spitzer, Robert L.

Klein, Ed. Parachutists. LC 77-82953. 406p. 1981. 10.95 (ISBN 0-385-12573-9). Doubleday.

Klein, Elinor, jt. auth. see Landey, Dora.

Klein, Elizabeth. Approaches. Bensen, Robert, ed. (Chapbook: No. 5). 1980. pap. 3.75. Red Herring.

Klein, Elizabeth P. The Break-Even Point: A Guide to the Process of Management for the Medical Office. LC 79-90728. (Illus.). 237p. 1979. wkbk. 30.00 (ISBN 0-9604250-0-4). E P Klein.

Klein, Eugene. United States Waterway Packet-Marks. 1981. 35.00x (ISBN 0-88000-076-7). Quarterman.

Klein, F., jt. auth. see Grove, A. T.

Klein, Fannie J., ed. Federal & State Court Systems: A Guide. LC 76-47480. 1977. 18.50 (ISBN 0-88410-219-X); pap. 9.95 (ISBN 0-88410-795-7). Ballinger Pub.

Klein, Felix. Nicht-Euklidische Geometrie. LC 59-10281. (Ger). 12.00 (ISBN 0-8284-0129-2). Chelsea Pub.

Klein, Felix see Sierpinski, Waclaw, et al.

Klein, G. deVries, ed. Holocene Tidal Sedimentation. (Benchmark Papers in Geology Ser.: Vol. 30). 432p. 1976. 46.50 (ISBN 0-12-786859-3). Acad Pr.

Klein, George, ed. Viral Oncology. 1980. text ed. 92.00 (ISBN 0-89004-390-6). Raven.

Klein, George & Weinhouse, Sidney, eds. Advances in Cancer Research, Vol. 31. LC 52-13360. 1980. 35.00 (ISBN 0-12-006631-9). Acad Pr.

--Advances in Cancer Research, Vol. 32. 1980. 36.00 (ISBN 0-12-006632-7). Acad Pr.

--Advances in Cancer Research, Vol. 33. 1980. 37.50 (ISBN 0-12-006633-5). Acad Pr.

Klein, George see Greenstein, Jesse P. & Haddow, Alexander.

Klein, George, jt. ed. see Weinhouse, Sidney.

Klein, George D. Sandstone Depositional Models for Exploration for Fossil Fuels. (Illus.). 1975. pap. 12.00 (ISBN 0-89469-083-3, CEPCO). Burgess.

Klein, George DeVries see Klein, George D.

Klein, Gerard. Star Masters' Gambit. (Daw Science Fiction Ser.). 1979. pap. 1.75 o.p. (ISBN 0-87997-464-8, UE1464). DAW Bks.

Klein, H. Arthur. Holography. Hale, Helen, ed. LC 77-117232. (Introducing Modern Science Ser). (Illus.). (gr. 7 up). 1970. 8.95 o.p. (ISBN 0-397-31122-2). Lippincott.

--Oceans & Continents in Motion. LC 72-3731. (Introducing Modern Science Ser). (Illus.). 192p. (gr. 8 up). 1972. 7.95 o.p. (ISBN 0-397-31271-7). Lippincott.

Klein, H. Arthur, jt. auth. see Klein, Mina C.

Klein, H. Arthur, jt. ed. see Klein, Nina C.

Klein, Henriette, ed. see Rado, Sandor.

Klein, Herbert S., jt. auth. see Kelley, Jonathan.

Klein, Herman. The Golden Age of Opera. (Music Reprint Ser.). 1979. 29.50 (ISBN 0-306-70840-X). Da Capo.

--The Reign of Patti. LC 77-17874. (Music Reprint Ser.: 1978). (Illus.). 1978. Repr. of 1920 ed. lib. bdg. 35.00 (ISBN 0-306-77530-1). Da Capo.

--Unmusical New York: A Brief Criticism of Triumphs, Failures, & Abuses. (Music Reprint Ser.). 1979. Repr. of 1910 ed. lib. bdg. 19.50 (ISBN 0-306-79517-5). Da Capo.

Klein, Herman, ed. Polycythemia: Theory & Management. (American Lectures in Hematology). (Illus.). 280p. 1973. text ed. 19.75 (ISBN 0-398-02684-X). C C Thomas.

Klein, Hermann. Musicians & Mummers. LC 80-2284. (Illus.). 1981. Repr. of 1925 ed. 38.50 (ISBN 0-404-18850-8). AMS Pr.

--Thirty Years of Musical Life in London. LC 78-2565. (Music Reprint Ser., 1978). (Illus.). 1978. Repr. of 1903 ed. lib. bdg. 32.50 (ISBN 0-306-77586-7). Da Capo.

Klein, Irving. I Remember My Brother Morris. 1978. 4.50 o.p. (ISBN 0-682-48992-1). Exposition.

Klein, Irving J. Law of Evidence for Police. 2nd ed. (Criminal Justice Ser.). 1978. text ed. 16.95 o.p. (ISBN 0-8299-0149-3); instrs.' manual avail. o.p. (ISBN 0-8299-0149-3). West Pub.

Klein, James H., et al. The Skin Book: Looking & Feeling Your Best Through Proper Skin Care. 1980. 10.95 (ISBN 0-02-563920-X). Macmillan.

Klein, Jerry. Father's Day. 176p. 1981. pap. 4.95 (ISBN 0-933180-24-1). Kickapoo.

Klein, John F. & Montague, Arthur. Check-Forgers. LC 77-14869. 1978. 16.95 (ISBN 0-669-01993-3). Lexington Bks.

Klein, Karl K. The Knees. 6.95 (ISBN 0-8363-0060-2). Jenkins.

Klein, Karl K. & Allman, Fred L., Jr. Knee in Sports. (Illus.). 6.95 o.p. (ISBN 0-8363-0061-0). Jenkins.

Klein, Kenneth. You Might Save Someone's Life Someday. 324p. 1981. 11.95 (ISBN 0-316-49838-6). Little.

Klein, Lawrence R. & Burmeister, Edwin, eds. Econometric Model Performance: Comparative Simulation Studies of the U. S. Economy. LC 76-20145. (Orig.). 1976. 15.00x (ISBN 0-8122-7714-7). U of Pa Pr.

Klein, Lawrence R. & Young, Richard M., eds. An Introduction to Econometric Forecasting & Forecasting Models. LC 79-1542. (Wharton Econometric Forecasting Studies: No. 3). 176p. 1980. 18.95 (ISBN 0-669-02896-7). Lexington Bks.

Klein, Leonard S., ed. Encyclopedia of World Literature in the Twentieth Century. 2nd rev. ed. (Illus.). Date not set. 75.00 (ISBN 0-8044-3135-3). Ungar.

Klein, Leonore. Only One Ant. 32p. (gr. k-3). 1971. 5.95g (ISBN 0-8038-5362-9). Hastings.

Klein, Lisl. New Forms of Work Organization. LC 75-22556. 1976. 18.95 (ISBN 0-521-21055-0). Cambridge U Pr.

--Social Scientist in Industry. LC 75-41612. 257p. 1976. 19.95 (ISBN 0-470-15004-1). Halsted Pr.

Klein, Malcolm, jt. auth. see Carter, Robert M.

Klein, Malcolm W., ed. The Juvenile Justice System. LC 75-14632. (Sage Criminal Justice System Annuals: Vol. 5). 1976. 20.00x (ISBN 0-8039-0450-9); pap. 9.95x (ISBN 0-8039-0451-7). Sage.

Klein, Malcolm W & Teilmann, Katherine S., eds. Handbook of Criminal Justice Evaluation. LC 80-16909. (Illus.). 693p. 1980. 39.95 (ISBN 0-8039-1052-5). Sage.

Klein, Martin A., ed. Peasants in Africa: Historical & Contemporary Perspectives. LC 79-23415. (Sage Series on African Modernization & Development: Vol. 4). (Illus.). 1980. 20.00x (ISBN 0-8039-1406-7); pap. 9.95x (ISBN 0-8039-1407-5). Sage.

Klein, Maury. History of the Louisville & Nashville Railroad. (Railroads of America Ser.). (Illus.). 384p. 1972. 10.95 o.s.i. (ISBN 0-02-563890-4). Macmillan.

Klein, Maury & Kantor, Harvey A. Prisoners of Progress: American Industrial Cities, 1850-1920. (Illus.). 1976. 13.95 o.s.i. (ISBN 0-02-563880-7). Macmillan.

Klein, Mavis. How to Choose a Mate. 160p. 1981. 12.00 (ISBN 0-7145-2727-0, Pub. by M. Boyars). Merrimack Bk Serv.

Klein, Maxine. Time, Space & Designs for Actors. 1975. pap. text ed. 12.95 (ISBN 0-395-18612-9). HM.

Klein, Melanie. Envy & Gratitude. 1975. 17.50 o.p. (ISBN 0-440-05014-6, Sey Lawr). Delacorte.

--Love, Guilt & Reparation. 1975. 20.00 o.p. (ISBN 0-440-05021-9, Sey Lawr). Delacorte.

--Psychoanalysis of Children. 396p. 1975. 17.50 o.s.i. (ISBN 0-440-06085-0, Sey Lawr). Delacorte.

Klein, Miles V. Optics. LC 73-107584. 1970. 31.95 (ISBN 0-471-49080-6). Wiley.

Klein, Milton M. Politics of Diversity: Essays in the History of Colonial New York. new ed. LC 74-77647. (National University Publications Ser.). 212p. 1974. 17.50 (ISBN 0-8046-9081-2). Kennikat.

Klein, Milton M., ed. New York: The Centennial Years, 1676-1976. (Interdisciplinary Urban Ser.). (Illus.). 250p. 1976. 13.95 (ISBN 0-8046-9143-6, Natl U). Kennikat.

Klein, Milton M., jt. ed. see Hershkowitz, Leo.

Klein, Mina C. & Klein, H. Arthur. The Kremlin: Citadel of History. (Illus.). 176p. (gr. 7 up). 1973. 8.95g (ISBN 0-02-750830-7). Macmillan.

Klein, Nina C. & Klein, H. Arthur, eds. The Kidnapped Saint & Other Stories by B. Traven. LC 74-9349. 1977. 8.95 (ISBN 0-88208-049-0); pap. 5.95 (ISBN 0-88208-074-1). Lawrence Hill.

Klein, Norma. Domestic Arrangements. Katz, Herbert M., ed. 224p. 1981. 11.95 (ISBN 0-87131-343-X). M Evans.

--Give Me One Good Reason. (YA) 1977. pap. 2.25 (ISBN 0-380-00166-7, 51292). Avon.

--A Honey of a Chimp. LC 79-20951. (gr. 3-7). 1980. 6.95 (ISBN 0-394-84412-2); PLB 6.99 (ISBN 0-394-94412-7). Pantheon.

--It's Ok If You Don't Love Me. 1978. pap. 1.95 (ISBN 0-449-23526-2, Crest). Fawcett.

--Mom, the Wolfman & Me. (gr. 5-9). 1974. pap. 1.95 (ISBN 0-380-00791-6, 53595). Avon.

--Mom the Wolfman & Me. (gr. 5-9). 1977. pap. 1.95 (ISBN 0-380-01725-3, 49502, Camelot). Avon.

--Naomi in the Middle. (Illus.). (gr. 3-5). 1978. pap. 1.50 (ISBN 0-671-56070-0). PB.

--Tomboy. LC 78-4337. 128p. (gr. 3-7). 1978. 6.95 (ISBN 0-590-07521-7, Four Winds). Schol Bk Serv.

--Tomboy. (gr. 3-5). 1980. pap. 1.75 (ISBN 0-671-56033-6). PB.

--What It's All About. (YA) (gr. 7-10). 1978. pap. 1.75 (ISBN 0-671-29997-2). PB.

Klein, Norman, ed. Culture, Curers, & Contagion. LC 79-10888. (Anthropology Ser.). 256p. 1979. pap. text ed. 6.95x (ISBN 0-88316-531-7). Chandler & Sharp.

Klein, Philip. From Philanthropy to Social Welfare: An American Cultural Perspective. LC 68-18617. (Social & Behavioral Science Ser.). 1968. 14.95x o.p. (ISBN 0-87589-012-1). Jossey-Bass.

Klein, Philip S. & Hoogenboom, Ari. A History of Pennsylvania. 2nd enlarged ed. LC 79-1731. (Illus.). 620p. 1980. 17.50 (ISBN 0-271-00216-6). Pa St U Pr.

Klein, Raymond M., jt. ed. see Jusczyk, Peter W.

Klein, Richard B., ed. see Calvo-Sotelo, Joaquin.

Klein, Robert. Form & Meaning: Writings on the Renaissance & Modern Art. Jay, Madeline & Wieseltier, Leon, trs. LC 80-8772. 276p. 1981. pap. 7.95 (ISBN 0-691-00328-9). Princeton U Pr.

Klein, Robert E., et al, eds. Evaluating the Impact of Nutrition & Health Programs. LC 79-11321. 476p. 1979. 29.50 (ISBN 0-306-40164-9, Plenum Pr). Plenum Pub.

Klein, Roger D., et al, eds. Behavior Modification in Educational Settings. (Illus.). 568p. 1973. 21.75 (ISBN 0-398-02538-X). C C Thomas.

Klein, Sonia, jt. ed. see Adams, F. Gerard.

Klein, Stanley, jt. ed. see Aylesworth, Thomas C.

Klein, Stuart M. Workers Under Stress: The Impact of Work Pressure on Group Cohesion. LC 75-160046. (Illus.). 136p. 1971. 9.50x (ISBN 0-8131-1253-2). U Pr of Ky.

Klein, Stuart M. & Ritti, Richard R. Understanding Organizational Behavior. 592p. 1980. text ed. 19.95x (ISBN 0-534-00755-4, Kent Pub.). Kent Pub Co.

Klein, Ted, tr. see Husserl, Edmund.

Klein, Theodore M., jt. ed. see Aycock, Wendell M.

Klein, Thomas A. Social Costs & Benefits of Business. 1977. 12.95 (ISBN 0-13-815837-1); pap. 9.95 (ISBN 0-13-815829-0). P-H.

Klein, Viola, jt. auth. see Myrdal, Alva.

Klein, William. William Klein: Photographs. Heilpern, John, ed. (Monograph). (Illus.). 1980. 40.00 (ISBN 0-89381-049-5); ltd. ed. 300.00 (ISBN 0-89381-053-3). Aperture.

Klein, Woody. Lindsay's Promise. (Illus.). 1970. 6.95 o.s.i. (ISBN 0-02-563910-2). Macmillan.

Klein, Zanvel E., jt. ed. see Newman, Sidney H.

Klein, Zev. Integrating Jerusalem Schools. (Quantitative Studies in Social Relations Ser.). 1980. 19.50 (ISBN 0-12-413250-2). Acad Pr.

Kleinau, Marion & McHughes, Janet. Theatres for Literature. LC 79-24492. 1980. pap. 11.50 (ISBN 0-88284-096-7). Alfred Pub.

Kleinbauer, W. Eugene, ed. see Kitzinger, Ernst.

Kleinberg, Harry. How You Can Learn to Live with Computers. 1977. 8.95 o.p. (ISBN 0-397-01226-8). Lippincott.

Kleinberg, Seymour. Alienated Affections. 320p. 1981. 13.95 (ISBN 0-312-01857-6). St Martin.

Kleinberger, A. F. Society, Schools & Progress in Israel. LC 73-92460. 1969. 25.00 (ISBN 0-08-006494-9); pap. 14.50 (ISBN 0-08-006493-0). Pergamon.

Kleiner, Art. Robots. LC 80-11681. (Look Inside Ser.). (Illus.). 48p. (gr. 4-12). 1981. PLB 10.25 (ISBN 0-8172-1401-1). Raintree Child.

Kleiner, Diana E. Roman Group Portraiture: The Funerary Reliefs of the Late Republic & Early Empire. LC 76-23634. (Outstanding Dissertations in the Fine Arts - 2nd Series - Ancient). (Illus.). 1977. Repr. lib. bdg. 63.00 (ISBN 0-8240-2703-5). Garland Pub.

Kleiner, Dick, jt. auth. see Cooper, Jackie.

Kleiner, Richard, jt. auth. see Isaac, Godfrey.

Kleinfeld, ed. see Newmyer, Joseph, Jr. & Klentos, Gus.

Kleinfeld, Gerald R. & Tambs, Lewis A. Hilter's Spanish Legion: The Blue Division in Russia. LC 78-15677. (Illus.). 446p. 1979. 25.95 (ISBN 0-8093-0865-7). S Ill U Pr.

Kleinfeld, Judith S. Eskimo School on the Andreafsky: A Study of Effective Bicultural Education. LC 79-4520. 22.95 (ISBN 0-03-048366-2). Praeger.

Kleinfield, Sonny. The Biggest Company on Earth: A Profile of AT&T. LC 80-13095. 352p. 1981. 14.95 (ISBN 0-03-045326-7). HR&W.

Kleinke, Chris L. Self-Perception: The Psychology of Personal Awareness. LC 78-1370. (Psychology Ser.). (Illus.). 1978. pap. text ed. 8.95x (ISBN 0-7167-0062-X). W H Freeman.

Kleinman, Arthur. Patients & Healers in the Context of Culture: An Exploration of the Borderland Between Anthropology, Medicine, & Psychiatry. (Comparative Studies of Health Systems & Medical Care). 1979. 27.50x (ISBN 0-520-03706-5). U of Cal Pr.

Kleinman, Carol. Women's Networks. 1981. pap. 2.95 (ISBN 0-345-29355-X). Ballantine.

Kleinman, David S. Human Adaptation & Population Growth: A Non-Malthusian Perspective. LC 78-59176. 296p. 1980. text ed. 23.50 (ISBN 0-916672-18-2). Allanheld.

Kleinman, Neil, ed. see Kipnis, Claude.

Kleinman, Ronald L., ed. see International Planned Parenthood Federation.

Kleinpeter, Joseph. Executive Air Fleet. (Illus.). 1979. pap. 4.95 (ISBN 0-911721-52-5, Pub. by J Kleinpeter). Aviation.

Kleinrock, Leonard. Queueing Systems, 2 vols. Incl. Vol. 1. Theory. 432p. 30.00 (ISBN 0-471-49110-1); Vol. 2. Computer Applications. 512p. 32.00 (ISBN 0-471-49111-X). LC 74-9846. 1975-76 (Pub. by Wiley-Interscience). Wiley.

Kleinschrod, Walter. Management's Guide to Word Processing. 1980. 59.50 (ISBN 0-85013-070-0). Dartnell Corp.

Kleinschrod, Walter, et al. Word Processing: Operations, Applications, & Administration. LC 79-13613. 1980. 19.95 (ISBN 0-672-97270-0); tchrs. manual 3.33 (ISBN 0-672-97271-9). Bobbs.

Kleinsinger, Irene J. Wine Log. (Illus.). 96p. 1980. 9.95 (ISBN 0-9605146-1-9); pap. 4.95 (ISBN 0-9605146-0-0). Kleinsinger.

Kleist, Heinrich von. An Abyss Deep Enough: The Letters of Heinrich Von Kleist with a Selection of Essays & Anecdotes. Miller, Philip B., ed. & tr. from Ger. 288p. 1981. 16.95 (ISBN 0-525-05479-0); pap. 8.95 o.p. (ISBN 0-525-03008-5). Dutton.

Klekamp, Robert C., jt. auth. see Thierauf, Robert J.

Klem, Joan R. & Rodemacher, P. G. How to Raise & Train a Rottweiler. (Orig.). pap. 2.00 (ISBN 0-87666-373-0, DS1110). TFH Pubns.

Klem, Kaye W. Defiant Desire. 1977. pap. 1.75 o.p. (ISBN 0-449-13741-4, GM). Fawcett.

Klement, Frank L. The Limits of Dissent: Clement L. Vallandigham & the Civil War. LC 71-111512. (Illus.). 367p. 1970. 16.00x (ISBN 0-8131-1218-4). U Pr of Ky.

Klemer, D. J., ed. Modern Love Poems. LC 61-12542. 1961. 4.95 o.p. (ISBN 0-385-03266-8). Doubleday.

Klemke, E. D., ed. The Meaning of Life. 288p. 1981. pap. text ed. 6.95x (ISBN 0-19-502871-6). Oxford U Pr.

Klemke, E. D., et al, eds. Introductory Readings in the Philosophy of Science. LC 80-65940. 373p. 1980. pap. text ed. 11.95 (ISBN 0-87975-134-7). Prometheus Bks.

Klemm, Friedrich. History of Western Technology. (Illus.). 1964. pap. 9.95x (ISBN 0-262-61001-9). MIT Pr.

Klemm, W. R. Applied Electronics for Veterinary Medicine & Animal Physiology. (Illus.). 484p. 1976. 41.50 (ISBN 0-398-03477-X). C C Thomas.

Klemperer, D., tr. see Welder, G.

Klemperer, Lily von see Garraty, John A. & Von Klemperer, Lily.

Klemperer, O. Electron Physics: The Physics of the Free Electron. 2nd ed. 280p. 1972. 14.50x (ISBN 0-408-70223-0); pap. 10.95x (ISBN 0-408-70229-X). Butterworths.

Klemperer, O. E. & Barnett, M. E. Electron Optics. 3rd ed. LC 74-118065. (Cambridge Physics Monographs). (Illus.). 1970. 68.50 (ISBN 0-521-07928-4). Cambridge U Pr.

Klempner, D. & Frisch, K. C., eds. Polymer Alloys II: Blends, Blocks, Grafts, & Interpenetrating Networks. (Polymer Science & Technology Ser.: Vol. 11). 290p. 1980. 35.00 (ISBN 0-306-40346-3, Plenum Pr). Plenum Pub.

Klenck, Robert H. Words Fitly Spoken: Reflections & Prayers. LC 79-13449. 1979. 7.95 (ISBN 0-396-07764-1, 07764-1, Dist. by W.W. Norton). Dembner Bks.

Klenk, Robert W. & Ryan, Robert M. Practice of Social Work. 2nd ed. 1974. pap. 11.95x (ISBN 0-534-00341-9). Wadsworth Pub.

Klenke, William W. Art of Wood Turning. (gr. 7-12). 1954. 11.60 (ISBN 0-87002-104-4). Bennett IL.

Klenke-Hamel, Karen, jt. auth. see Janda, Louis.

Klentos, Gus & Newmyer, Joseph, Jr. Elementary Functions: Algebra & Analytic Geometry. 448p. 1975. pap. text ed. 15.95 (ISBN 0-675-08827-5); media: audiocassettes 160.00, 2-6 sets, 100.00 ea., 7 or more sets, 75.00 ea. (ISBN 0-675-08774-0); instructor's manual 3.95 (ISBN 0-686-67047-7). Merrill.

--Elementary Functions: Trigonometry. LC 73-87838. 1974. text ed. 15.95 (ISBN 0-675-08864-X); media: audiocassettes 140.00, 2-6 sets, 95.00 ea., 7 or more sets, 70.00 ea. (ISBN 0-675-08865-8). Merrill.

Klentos, Gus, jt. auth. see Newmyer, Joseph.

Klentos, Gus, jt. auth. see Newmyer, Joseph, Jr.

Klenze, Camillo Von. From Goethe to Hauptmann: Studies in a Changing Culture. LC 66-23519. 1926. 10.50x (ISBN 0-8196-0178-0). Biblo.

Klepczynski, W. J., jt. ed. see Cristescu, Cornelia.

Kleppner, D. Advertising Procedure. 6th ed. 1973. 16.95 o.p. (ISBN 0-13-018069-6). P-H.

Kleppner, Otto & Govoni, Norman. Advertising Procedure. 7th ed. LC 78-5728. 1979. 21.00 (ISBN 0-13-018119-6). P-H.

Kleppner, Otto & Settel, Irving, eds. Exploring Advertising. (Illus.). 1969. pap. text ed. 10.95 (ISBN 0-13-296020-6). P-H.

Klerman, Lorraine V. & Jekel, James F. School-Age Mothers: Problems, Programs & Policy. 256p. (Orig.). 1973. 6.00 o.p. (ISBN 0-208-01412-8, Linnet); pap. 2.95 (ISBN 0-208-01413-6, Linnet). Shoe String.

Klesney, S. P., jt. ed. see Rigaudy, J.

Klett, C. James, jt. auth. see Overall, John E.

Kleverbring, Bjorn, jt. auth. see Alexandersson, Gunnar.

Klevin. That's My Girl. (gr. 7-12). 1980. pap. 1.50 (ISBN 0-590-31274-X, Schol Pap). Schol Bk Serv.

Klevins, Gil. Your Career in Office Occupations. LC 77-17377. (Arco Career Guidance Ser.). (Illus.). 1978. lib. bdg. 6.95 (ISBN 0-668-04449-7); pap. 3.50 (ISBN 0-668-04434-9). Arco.

Kliban, B. Cat. LC 75-7285. (Illus.). 160p. (Orig.). 1975. pap. 3.50 (ISBN 0-911104-54-2). Workman Pub.

--The Cat Calender Book. LC 80-54618. 144p. 1981. 17.50 (ISBN 0-89480-155-4). Workman Pub.

--Whack Your Porcupine & Other Drawings. LC 76-52861. (Illus.). 1977. pap. 3.50 (ISBN 0-911104-92-5). Workman Pub.

Klibanksy, Raymond, ed. see Mussolini, Benito.

Klibbe, Lawrence. Monarch Notes on Hemingway's for Whom the Bell Tolls. (Orig.). pap. 1.75 (ISBN 0-671-00672-X). Monarch Pr.

Klibbe, Lawrence H. Fernan Caballero. (World Authors Ser.: Spain: No. 259). 1971. lib. bdg. 10.95 (ISBN 0-8057-2187-8). Twayne.

Kliebard, Herbert E., jt. ed. see Bellack, Arno A.

Kliever, Lonnie D. The Shattered Spectrum: A Survey of Contemporary Theology. LC 80-82184. 276p. (Orig.). 1981. pap. 9.95 (ISBN 0-8042-0707-0). John Knox.

Kliewer, Vernon L. Music Reading: A Comprehensive Approach, Vol. 1. LC 72-3870. (Illus.). 352p. 1973. pap. text ed. 12.95 (ISBN 0-13-607903-2). P-H.

--Music Reading, a Comprehensive Approach, Vol. 2. LC 72-3870. (Illus.). 272p. 1973. pap. text ed. 12.95 (ISBN 0-13-607911-3). P-H.

Kligerman, Jack. A Fancy for Pigeons. LC 77-92316. (Illus.). 1978. 12.00 o.p. (ISBN 0-8015-4043-7). Dutton.

Kligman, Albert M., jt. auth. see Magnusson, Bertil.

Kligman, Gail. Calus: Symbolic Transformation in Romanian Ritual. LC 80-21372. (Chicago Originals Ser.). (Illus.). 240p. 1981. lib. bdg. 12.00x (ISBN 0-226-44221-7). U of Chicago Pr.

Kliman, Ann S. Crisis: Psychological First Aid for Recovery & Growth. LC 77-133353. 1978. 8.95 o.p. (ISBN 0-03-019461-X). HR&W.

Klimas, John E. Wildflowers of Western America. 1974. write for info. o.p. Knopf.

Klimas, Paul C., jt. auth. see Sladky, Joseph F.

Kliment, C. K., jt. auth. see Doyle, H. C.

Klimke, Reiner. Cavalletti. Goodall, Daphne M., tr. (Illus.). pap. 7.85 (ISBN 0-85131-192-X, Dist. by Sporting Book Center). J A Allen.

Klimo, Kate, ed. My Cash Register Book. (Playboards Ser.). (Illus.). 12p. (ps-k). Date not set. boards 2.95 (ISBN 0-671-42527-7, Little Simon). S&S.

--My Clock Book. (Playboards Ser.). (Illus.). 12p. (ps-k). Date not set. boards 2.95 (ISBN 0-671-42528-5, Little Simon). S&S.

--My Color Book. (Playboards Ser.). (Illus.). 12p. (ps-k). Date not set. boards 2.95 (ISBN 0-671-42529-3, Little Simon). S&S.

--My Telephone Book. (Playboards Ser.). (Illus.). 12p. (ps-k). Date not set. boards 2.95 (ISBN 0-671-42526-9, Little Simon). S&S.

Klimo, Vernon & Oursler, Will. Hemingway & Jake. 224p. 1973. pap. 1.25 o.p. (ISBN 0-445-00176-3). Popular Lib.

Klimontovich, Yu L. The Statistical Theory of Non-Equilibrium Processes in a Plasma. 1967. text ed. 40.00 (ISBN 0-08-011966-2). Pergamon.

Klimova, Nina T. Folk Embroidery of the USSR. 152p. 1981. 19.95 (ISBN 0-442-24464-9). Van Nos Reinhold.

Klimovitch, Don, et al. The Chicago Book. (Illus., Orig.). 1981. pap. 5.95 (ISBN 0-8092-5893-5). Contemp Bks.

Klimsch, Karl. Florid Victorian Ornament. LC 76-58573. (Pictorial Archive Ser.). (Illus.). 1977. pap. 4.00 (ISBN 0-486-23490-8). Dover.

Klin, George & Marsland, Amy L. Les Miserables Notes. (Orig.). 1968. pap. 2.25 (ISBN 0-8220-0735-5). Cliffs.

Klinck, Carl F. Robert Service: A Biography. LC 76-22706. (Illus.). 1977. 8.95 (ISBN 0-396-07391-3). Dodd.

Klinck, Carl F., ed. see Richardson, John.

Klindt, Steven, ed. New American Photography. (Illus.). 48p. 1981. pap. 10.00 (ISBN 0-932026-06-0). Chicago Contemp Photo.

Klindt, Steven, ed. see Jachna, Joseph.

Klindt, Steven, ed. see Uelsmann, Jerry N.

Kline, Daniel L. & Reddy, K. N. Fibrinolysis. 256p. 1980. 64.95 (ISBN 0-8493-5425-0). CRC Pr.

Kline, Donald L. Susanna Wesley: God's Catalyst for Revival. (Orig.). 1980. pap. text ed. 4.35 (ISBN 0-89536-450-6). CSS Pub.

Kline, Draza & Jaffee, Benson. New Payment Patterns & the Foster Parent Role. LC 76-129456. (Orig.). 1970. pap. 2.00 o.p. (ISBN 0-87868-044-5). Child Welfare.

Kline, Draza & Overstreet, Helen-Mary F. Foster Care of Children: Nurture & Treatment. LC 78-186386. (Studies of the Child Welfare League of America). 385p. 1972. 17.50x (ISBN 0-231-03601-9). pap. 8.00x (ISBN 0-231-08337-8). Columbia U Pr.

Kline, F. Gerald & Clarke, Peter, eds. Mass Communications & Youth: Some Current Perspectives. LC 73-89939. (Sage Contemporary Social Science Issues: No. 5). 1974. 4.95x (ISBN 0-8039-0335-9). Sage.

Kline, Gary, jt. auth. see Agee, Anne.

Kline, George L. Spinoza in Soviet Philosophy: A Series of Essays. LC 79-2908. 190p. 1981. Repr. of 1952 ed. 18.00 (ISBN 0-8305-0078-2). Hyperion Conn.

Kline, Jacob. Biological Foundations of Biomedical Engineering. LC 74-20221. 1976. text ed. 42.50 (ISBN 0-316-49857-2). Little.

Kline, Leslie L. The Sayings of Jesus in the Pseudo-Clementine Homilies. LC 75-1645. (Society of Biblical Literature. Dissertation Ser.). ix, 198p. 1975. pap. 7.50 (ISBN 0-89130-060-0, 060114). Scholars Pr Ca.

Kline, Mary-Jo, ed. see Hamilton, Alexander.

Kline, Milton V., et al. Obesity: Etiology, Treatment, & Management. (Illus.). 480p. 1976. 29.50 (ISBN 0-398-03369-2). C C Thomas.

Kline, Morris. Calculus: An Intuitive & Physical Approach. 2nd ed. LC 76-22760. 1977. text ed. 27.95x (ISBN 0-471-49116-0); solutions manual avail. (ISBN 0-471-02396-5). Wiley.

--Mathematical Thought from Ancient to Modern Times. 1300p. 1972. 60.00 (ISBN 0-19-501496-0). Oxford U Pr.

--Mathematics: A Cultural Approach. 1962. text ed. 19.95 (ISBN 0-201-03770-X). A-W.

--Mathematics & the Physical World. (Illus.). 496p. 1981. pap. price not set (ISBN 0-486-24104-1). Dover.

--Mathematics for Liberal Arts. 1967. text ed. 18.95 (ISBN 0-201-03771-8); instr's manual 2.50 (ISBN 0-201-03772-6). A-W.

--Mathematics in Western Culture. 1953. 19.95 (ISBN 0-19-500603-8). Oxford U Pr.

--Mathematics in Western Culture. (Illus.). 1964. pap. 8.95 (ISBN 0-19-500714-X, GB). Oxford U Pr.

--Mathematics: The Loss of Certainty. (Illus.). 400p. 1980. 19.95 (ISBN 0-19-502754-X). Oxford U Pr.

--Why Johnny Can't Add: The Failure of the New Math. LC 72-80894. 256p. 1973. 7.95 o.p. (ISBN 0-312-87780-3, W3500). St Martin.

Kline, Morris, intro. by. Mathematics: An Introduction to Its Spirit & Use: Readings from Scientific American. LC 78-7878. (Illus.). 1979. text ed. 19.95x (ISBN 0-7167-0370-X); pap. text ed. 9.95x (ISBN 0-7167-0369-6). W H Freeman.

Kline, Nathan. From Sad to Glad: Kline on Depression. 224p. 1975. pap. 1.95 (ISBN 0-345-28502-6). Ballantine.

Kline, Nathan S. From Sad to Glad. 1981. pap. 2.95 (ISBN 0-345-29545-5). Ballantine.

Kline, Nathan S., ed. Factors in Depression. LC 74-77571. 1974. 24.50 (ISBN 0-911216-79-0). Raven.

Kline, Nathan S., jt. ed. see Evans, Wayne O.

Kline, Otis A. Jan in India. LC 80-23787. 128p. 1980. Repr. of 1973 ed. lib. bdg. 10.95x (ISBN 0-89370-090-8). Borgo Pr.

Kline, Otis Adelbert. Jan in India. LC 73-94035. (Illus.). 1974. pap. 5.00 (ISBN 0-87707-131-4). Fictioneer Bks.

Kline, Paula. Urban Needs: A Bibliography & Directory for Community Resource Centers. LC 78-9265. 1978. 13.50 (ISBN 0-8108-1148-0). Scarecrow.

Kline, Peter. Theatre Student-Diary of Producing a Play. (Theatre Student Ser.). (Illus.). 140p. 1981. lib. bdg. 12.50 (ISBN 0-8239-0523-3). Rosen Pr.

Kline, Raymond M. Digital Computer Design. (Illus.). 1977. 27.95 (ISBN 0-13-214205-8). P-H.

Kline, Robert D., jt. ed. see Murphy, Thomas P.

Kline, Thomas J. Andre Malraux & the Metamorphosis of Death. 250p. 1973. 15.00x (ISBN 0-231-03608-6). Columbia U Pr.

Kline, Tilde S. Handbook of Fine Needle Aspiration Biopsy Cytology. (Illus.). 210p. 1981. text ed. 27.50 (ISBN 0-8016-2701-X). Mosby.

Klineberg, Otto & Hull, W. Frank, IV. At a Foreign University: An International Study of Adaptation & Coping. 22.95 (ISBN 0-03-052486-5). Praeger.

Klineberg, Otto, et al. Students, Values, & Politics: A Cross-Cultural Comparison. LC 77-94082. 1979. 19.95 (ISBN 0-02-916770-1). Free Pr.

Klineberg, Stephen L., jt. auth. see Cottle, Thomas J.

Kline-Graber, Georgia & Graber, Benjamin. Woman's Orgasm. 1976. pap. 2.25 (ISBN 0-445-08537-1). Popular Lib.

Kling, Bernard & Plehn, Heinz. Elvis Presley. 1980. pap. 12.95 (ISBN 0-8256-3945-X). Music Sales.

Kling, Blair. Blue Mutiny. LC 64-24507. 1966. 9.00x o.p. (ISBN 0-8122-7475-X). U of Pa Pr.

Kling, Blair B. Partner in Empire: Dwarkanath Tagore & the Age of Enterprise in Eastern India. LC 74-27293. 1977. 20.00x (ISBN 0-520-02927-5). U of Cal Pr.

Kling, Samuel G. The Complete Guide to Everyday Law. 1975. pap. 3.95 (ISBN 0-515-05824-6, Y3703). Jove Pubns.

Klingaman, David & Vedder, Richard, eds. Essays in Nineteenth Century Economic History: The Old Northwest. LC 74-80811. xiv, 356p. 1975. 16.00x (ISBN 0-8214-0170-X). Ohio U Pr.

Klingbeil, Jerome R., jt. auth. see Grazer, Frederick M.

Klingbeil, Louis J. & Klingbeil, Reinhold L. Battle to Breathe. LC 76-170374. (Better Living Ser). (Illus.). 64p. 1971. pap. 0.95 (ISBN 0-8127-0059-7). Southern Pub.

Klingbeil, Reinhold L. Hazards to Health. LC 78-17381. (Better Living Ser.). 1978. pap. 0.95 (ISBN 0-8127-0185-2). Southern Pub.

Klingbeil, Reinhold L., jt. auth. see Klingbeil, Louis J.

Klingberg, F. J. & Klingberg, F. W. The Correspondence Between Henry Stephens Randall & Hugh Blair Grigsby 1856-1861. LC 73-37530. (The American Scene Ser). 196p. 1972. Repr. of 1952 ed. lib. bdg. 22.50 (ISBN 0-306-70429-3). Da Capo.

Klingberg, F. W., jt. auth. see Klingberg, F. J.

Klinge, Peter L., ed. American Education in the Electric Age: New Perspectives on Media & Learning. LC 74-1220. 224p. pap. 10.95 (ISBN 0-87778-069-2). Educ Tech Pubns.

Klingel, Gilbert & Colvin, Thomas. Boatbuilding with Steel (Including Boatbuilding with Aluminum) LC 72-97402. 260p. 1973. 17.50 (ISBN 0-87742-029-7). Intl Marine.

Klingele, William E. Teaching in Middle Schools. 1979. text ed. 16.95 (ISBN 0-205-06526-0, 236526X). Allyn.

Klingender, Francis D. Animals in Art & Thought to the End of the Middle Ages. Antal, Evelyn & Harthan, John, eds. 1971. 50.00x (ISBN 0-262-11040-7). MIT Pr.

Klinger, A., jt. ed. see Tanimoto, S.

Klinger, Judith L. The Food Inflation Fighters Handbook. (Illus.). 1980. pap. 5.95 (ISBN 0-449-90030-4, Columbine). Fawcett.

Klinger, M. I. Problems of Linear Electron Transport Theory in Semiconductors. LC 78-40821. 1979. text ed. 190.00 (ISBN 0-08-018224-0). Pergamon.

Klinger, W., jt. ed. see Chambers, P. L.

Klinghammer, Erich. The Behavior & Ecology of Wolves. new ed. LC 77-89306. (Illus.). 1980. lib. bdg. 37.50 (ISBN 0-8240-7019-4, Garland STPM Pr). Garland Pub.

Klinghoffer, Arthur J. The Soviet Union & International Oil Politics. LC 76-52411. 1977. 22.50x (ISBN 0-231-04104-7). Columbia U Pr.

Klingman, Ed. Microprocessor Systems Design. LC 76-45190. (Illus.). 1977. 26.95 (ISBN 0-13-581413-8). P-H.

Klingman, Glenn C. & Ashton, Floyd M. Weed Science: Principles & Practices. LC 75-8908. 431p. 1975. 22.50 (ISBN 0-471-49171-3, Pub. by Wiley-Interscience). Wiley.

Klingner, Donald E., ed. Public Personnel Management: Readings in Contexts & Strategies. (Illus.). 500p. (Orig.). 1981. write for info (ISBN 0-87484-517-3). Mayfield Pub.

Klink, Jerry. The Mighty Cortez Fish Trap. LC 72-6388. (Illus.). 256p. 1973. 8.95 o.p. (ISBN 0-498-01172-0). A S Barnes.

Klink, Johanna L. Your Child & Religion. Wilson, R. A., tr. LC 72-1764. 256p. 1972. 6.95 (ISBN 0-8042-2239-8). John Knox.

Klink, William. Sentence Writing. LC 80-5805. (Illus.). 141p. (Orig.). 1981. pap. text ed. 7.50 (ISBN 0-8191-1430-8). U Pr of Amer.

Klink, William R. S.N. Behrman: The Major Plays. (Costerus: New Ser.: No. 11). 1978. pap. text ed. 25.75x (ISBN 90-6203-512-4). Humanities.

Klinkel, Sheryl, ed. see Pelton, Charles L.

Klinkerman, Oscar J. Welcome to a New Life. LC 75-31786. 32p. 1976. pap. 1.50 (ISBN 0-570-03720-4, 12-2622). Concordia.

Klinkowitz, Jerome. The American Nineteen Sixties: Imaginative Acts in a Decade of Change. 116p. (gr. 9-12). 1980. 10.95 (ISBN 0-8138-1380-8). Iowa St U Pr.

--Literary Disruptions: The Making of a Post-Contemporary American Fiction. 2nd ed. LC 80-1592. 280p. 1980. 15.95 (ISBN 0-252-00809-X); pap. 6.50 (ISBN 0-252-00810-3). U of Ill Pr.

--Practice of Fiction in America: Writers from Hawthorne to the Present. 140p. (gr. 9-12). 1980. text ed. 10.95 (ISBN 0-8138-1420-0). Iowa St U Pr.

Klinowski, Jacek, jt. auth. see Garbicz, Adam.

Klintworth, Gordon K. The Eye: Structure & Function in Disease. 200p. 1976. 19.50 o.p. (ISBN 0-683-04628-4). Williams & Wilkins.

Klintworth, Gordon K. & Landers, Maurice B. The Eye. LC 75-19061. 236p. 1976. 18.50 (ISBN 0-683-04628-4). Krieger.

Klinzing, Dene, jt. auth. see Klinzing, Dennis.

Klinzing, Dennis & Klinzing, Dene. The Hospitalized Child: Communication Techniques for Health Personnel. (Illus.). 1977. pap. text ed. 9.95 (ISBN 0-13-394817-X). P-H.

Klinzing, George E. Gas-Solid Transport. (Chemical Engineering Ser.). (Illus.). 358p. 1981. text ed. 28.50 (ISBN 0-07-035047-7, C). McGraw.

Kliot, Jules & Kliot, Kaethe. Honiton Bobbin Lace: Designs for Prickling from Traditional Pieces. 1979. pap. 8.95 (ISBN 0-916896-16-1). Lacis Pubns.

--The Stitches of Bobbin Lace: Structure & Classification. 60p. 1973. spiral bdg. 4.95 o.p. (ISBN 0-916896-02-1). Lacis Pubns.

Kliot, Jules & Kliot, Kaethe, eds. Battenberg & Point Lace: Techniques, Stitches & Designs from Victorian Needlework. (Illus.). 1978. pap. text ed. 3.50 o.p. (ISBN 0-916896-12-9). Lacis Pubns.

--Needle Lace: Battenberg, Point & Reticella. (Illus.). 1981. pap. 5.95 (ISBN 0-916896-18-8). Lacis Pubns.

--Tatting: Designs from Victorian Lace Craft. (Illus.). 1978. pap. text ed. 5.95 (ISBN 0-916896-13-7). Lacis Pubns.

Kliot, Kaethe, jt. auth. see Kliot, Jules.

Kliot, Kaethe, jt. ed. see Kliot, Jules.

Klippart, John H. The Wheat Plant: Its Origin, Culture, Growth, Development, Composition, Varieties Together with Information on Corn & Its Culture, 2 vols. 1980. Set. lib. bdg. 200.00 (ISBN 0-8490-3119-2). Gordon Pr.

Klippel, C. H., jt. auth. see El'Shafie, M.

Klipper, Ilse. My Magic Garden. (Illus., Orig.). (gr. 2-6). 1980. pap. 4.95 (ISBN 0-9605022-0-3). Pathway Pr.

Klitz, J. Kenneth. North Sea Oil: Resource Requirements for UK Development. (Illus.). 1981. 36.00 (ISBN 0-08-024442-4). Pergamon.

Klobukowski, Christopher J., jt. auth. see Frey, G. Donald.

Klock, David R., jt. auth. see Pfeffer, Irving.

Klock, Mary E., ed. Bibliography of Creative Dramatics. 40p. 1975. pap. 2.00 ATA members 1.00 (ISBN 0-686-13201-7). Am Theatre Assoc.

Klockars, Carl B. The Professional Fence. LC 74-483. 1976. pap. text ed. 6.95 (ISBN 0-02-917820-7). Free Pr.

Klockars, Carl B. & O'Connor, Finbarr W., eds. Deviance & Decency: The Ethics of Research with Human Subjects. LC 79-18034. (Sage Annual Reviews of Studies in Deviance: Vol. 3). (Illus.). 1979. 20.00x (ISBN 0-8039-1359-1); pap. 9.95x (ISBN 0-8039-1360-5). Sage.

Klocker, Harry R., ed. Thomism & Modern Thought. LC 62-9414. 1962. 28.00x (ISBN 0-89197-451-2). Irvington.

Kloefkorn, William. Alvin Turner As Farmer. 1977. pap. 4.00 (ISBN 0-931534-02-X). Windflower Pr.

--Ludi Jr. LC 76-2268. (Orig.). 1976. limited signed 10.00x (ISBN 0-915316-24-2); pap. 5.95 (ISBN 0-915316-23-4). Pentagram.

Kloefkorn, William & Kooser, Ted. Cottonwood County. 1980. pap. 3.00 (ISBN 0-931534-08-9). Windflower Pr.

Kloepfer, Marquerite. The Heart & the Scarab. 288p. 1981. pap. 2.50 (ISBN 0-380-77610-3). Avon.

Kloesel, Christion J. & Smitten, Jeffrey R. English Novel Explication: Supplement II, Through 1979. (Novel Explication Ser.). 312p. 1981. 27.50 (ISBN 0-208-01709-7). Shoe String.

Kloman, Erasmus H., ed. Cases in Accountability: The Work of the Gao. 1979. lib. bdg. 24.50x (ISBN 0-89158-395-5); pap. text ed. 9.50x (ISBN 0-89158-494-3). Westview.

Klong-Chen Rab-'Byams-Pa. Kindly Bent to Ease Us. Guenther, Herbert V., tr. LC 75-29959. (Tibetan Translation Ser.: Vol. 5). 1975. 14.95 (ISBN 0-913546-39-9); pap. 7.95 (ISBN 0-913546-40-2). Dharma Pub.

--Kindly Bent to Ease Us: Meditation, Pt. 2. LC 75-29959. (Tibetan Translation Ser.: Vol. 6). (Illus., Orig.). 1976. 12.95 (ISBN 0-913546-42-9); pap. 6.50 (ISBN 0-913546-43-7). Dharma Pub.

--Kindly Bent to Ease Us: Wonderment, Part 3. Guenther, Herbert V., tr. from Tibetan. LC 75-29959. (Tibetan Translation Ser.: Vol. 7). (Illus.). 1976. 12.95 (ISBN 0-913546-44-5); pap. 6.50 (ISBN 0-913546-45-3). Dharma Pub.

Kloos, Peter. Maroni River Caribs of Surinam. (Studies of Developing Countries). 1971. pap. text ed. 26.50x (ISBN 90-232-0903-6). Humanities.

Klopf, A. Harry. The Hedonistic Neuron: A Theory of Memory, Learning, & Intelligence. LC 80-16410. (Illus.). 112p. Date not set. pap. 14.95 (ISBN 0-89116-202-X). Hemisphere Pub. Postponed.

Klopf, Donald & McCroskey, James. Elements of Debate. LC 69-17545. (Orig.). 1969. lib. bdg. 6.50 o. p. (ISBN 0-668-01899-2); pap. 5.00 (ISBN 0-668-01901-8). Arco.

Klopf, Donald W. & Cambra, Ronald E. Personal & Public Speaking. 208p. 1981. pap. text ed. 8.95 (ISBN 0-89582-042-0). Morton Pub.

Klopf, Gordon J. & Laster, Israel, eds. Integrating the Urban School. LC 60-13467. (Orig.). 1963. pap. text ed. 4.25x (ISBN 0-8077-1632-4). Tchrs Coll.

Klopfer, Peter H. & Hailman, Jack P. An Introduction to Animal Behavior: Ethology's First Century. 2nd ed. (Biological Sciences Ser). (Illus.). 304p. 1974. 18.95x (ISBN 0-13-477935-5). P-H.

Klopfer, Peter H., jt. ed. see Bateson, P. P.

Klopfer, Peter H., jt. ed. see Gubernick, David J.

Klopman, Gilles, ed. Chemical Reactivity & Reaction Paths. LC 73-17325. 369p. 1974. 32.50 (ISBN 0-471-49355-4, Pub. by Wiley-Interscience). Wiley.

Kloppenborg, Anne, et al. Vancouver's First Century: A City Album, 1860-1960. (Illus.). 172p. 1978. 25.00 (ISBN 0-295-95600-3). U of Wash Pr.

Kloppenburg-Versteegh, J. The Traditional Use of Malay Plants & Herbs. Kaufman, Aileen, tr. from Dutch. LC 79-89939. Orig. Title: Het Gebruik Van Indische Planten. (Illus.). Date not set. price not set (ISBN 0-89793-014-2). Hunter Hse.

Klose, Al P. Democracy, Technology, Collision. (ITT Key Issues Lecture Ser.). 1980. pap. 4.95 (ISBN 0-672-97676-5). Bobbs.

Klose, Kevin, jt. auth. see Shaffer, Ron.

Klose, Nelson. Concise Study Guide to the American Frontier. LC 64-15180. (Illus.). 1964. 13.95x (ISBN 0-8032-0093-5); pap. 2.75x (ISBN 0-8032-5110-6, BB 190, Bison). U of Nebr Pr.

--U. S. History, 2 vols. rev. ed. 480p. (gr. 7-12). Date not set. Vol. 1. pap. text ed. 5.50 (ISBN 0-8120-2250-5); Vol. 2. pap. text ed. 5.50 (ISBN 0-8120-2251-3). Barron. Postponed.

Kloskowska, Antonia & Martinotti, Guido, eds. Education in a Changing Society. LC 76-22903. (Sage Studies in International Sociology: Vol. 11). 1977. 18.00x (ISBN 0-8039-9983-6); pap. 9.95x (ISBN 0-8039-9984-4). Sage.

Kloss, et al. Sociology-with a Human Face: Sociology As If People Mattered. (Illus.). 352p. 1976. text ed. 13.95 o.p. (ISBN 0-8016-2718-4); pap. 9.50 o.p. (ISBN 0-8016-2712-5). Mosby.

Kloss, Doris. Sarah Winnemucca. LC 81-390. (Story of an American Indian Ser.). (Illus.). (gr. 5 up). 1981. PLB 6.95 (ISBN 0-87518-178-3). Dillon.

Kloss, Gunther. West Germany: An Introduction. LC 75-25564. 180p. 1976. text ed. 28.95 (ISBN 0-470-49357-7). Halsted Pr.

Kloss, Robert, jt. auth. see Kaplan, Morton.

Kloss, Robert M., jt. auth. see Roberts, Ron E.

Klosty, James. Merce Cunningham. 1975. 15.95 o.p. (ISBN 0-8415-0359-1); pap. 8.95 (ISBN 0-8415-0372-9). Dutton.

Klotman, Phyllis R. Another Man Gone: The Black Runner in Contemporary Afro-American Literature. (Literary Criticism Ser). 1976. 12.00 (ISBN 0-8046-9149-5, Natl U). Kennikat.

Klotman, Robert H. The School Music Administrator & Supervisor: Catalysts for Change in Music Education. LC 72-6635. (Illus.). 256p. 1973. ref. ed. 13.95 (ISBN 0-13-793711-3). P-H.

Klotman, Robert H. & Harris, Ernest E. Learning to Teach Through Playing: String Techniques & Pedagogy. LC 77-116861. (Music Ser). 1971. pap. 17.95 (ISBN 0-201-03775-0). A-W.

Klots, Alexander B., Dr. & Klots, Elsie B. Living Insects of the World. LC 59-9100. 1975. 19.95 o.p. (ISBN 0-385-06873-5). Doubleday.

Klots, Elsie B., jt. auth. see Klots, Alexander B., Dr.

Klotter, James C., jt. ed. see Tapp, Hambleton.

Klotter, John C. Criminal Evidence. 3rd rev. ed. LC 79-55201. (Criminal Justice Studies). 500p. 1980. text ed. 18.95 (ISBN 0-87084-500-4). Anderson Pub Co.

--Techniques for Police Instructors. 180p. 1978. 12.75 (ISBN 0-398-01029-3). C C Thomas.

Klotter, John C. & Kanovitz, Jacqueline R. Constitutional Law. 4th ed. (Justice Administration Legal Ser.). 900p. Date not set. price not set (ISBN 0-87084-492-X). Anderson Pub Co.

Klotter, John C & Meier, Carl L. Criminal Evidence for Police. 2nd ed. 1975. text ed. 16.95 o.p. (ISBN 0-87084-499-7). Anderson Pub Co.

Klotter, John C. & Rosenfeld, Joseph. Criminal Justice Instructional Techniques. (Illus.). 216p. 1979. text ed. 16.75 (ISBN 0-398-03887-2); pap. text ed. 7.50 student workbook, 80p. (ISBN 0-398-03892-9). C C Thomas.

Klotter, John C., et al. Legal Aspects of Private Security. LC 79-55202. 368p. 1981. text ed. price not set (ISBN 0-87084-488-1). Anderson Pub Co.

Klotz, E. A., jt. auth. see Brinkmann, H. W.

Klotz, Hans. Organ Handbook. LC 69-11068. 1969. 9.75 (ISBN 0-570-01306-2, 99-1187). Concordia.

Klotz, Irving M. Energy Changes in Biochemical Reactions. (Orig.). 1967. pap. text ed. 7.95 (ISBN 0-12-416260-6). Acad Pr.

Klotz, Irving M. & Rosenberg, R. M. Chemical Thermodynamics. 3rd ed. 1972. 21.95 (ISBN 0-8053-5506-5). Benjamin-Cummings.

Klouwen, H. M., et al, eds. Cell Nucleus: Metabolism & Radiosensitivity. 1966. pap. text ed. 17.95x (ISBN 0-685-83716-5). Intl Ideas.

Klubertanz, George P. Habits & Virtues: A Philosophical Analysis. LC 65-23606. 1965. 27.50x (ISBN 0-89197-196-3). Irvington.

--Philosophy of Human Nature. LC 53-6357. 1953. 34.50x (ISBN 0-89197-343-5). Irvington.

Klubertanz, George P. & Holloway, Maurice R. Being & God: Introduction to the Philosophy of Being & to Natural Theology. LC 63-15359. 1963. 29.00x (ISBN 0-89197-045-2); pap. text ed. 16.50x (ISBN 0-89197-674-4). Irvington.

Kluckhohn, Clyde. Anthropology & the Classics. LC 61-11106. 76p. 1961. 5.00 (ISBN 0-87057-065-X, Pub. by Brown U Pr). Univ Pr of New England.

Kludas, Arnold. Great Passenger Ships: 1936-1950, Vol. 4. (Illus.). 1977. 47.90 (ISBN 0-85059-253-4). Aztex.

--Great Passenger Ships: 1951-1976, Vol. 5. (Illus.). 1977. 47.95 (ISBN 0-85059-265-8). Aztex.

Klug, Anthony, jt. ed. see Tsichritzis, Dennis.

Klug, Harold P. & Alexander, Leroy E. X-Ray Diffraction Procedures: For Polycrystalline & Amorphous Materials. 2nd ed. LC 73-21936. (Illus.). 864p. 1974. 60.00 (ISBN 0-471-49369-4, Pub. by Wiley-Interscience). Wiley.

Klug, Jay, jt. ed. see Brown, Barbara B.

Klug, John R. Basic Book of Business. 350p. 1980. Repr. of 1977 ed. 50.00 (ISBN 0-932648-16-9). Boardroom.

--The Book of Business Answers. 1981. 50.00 (ISBN 0-932648-16-9). Boardroom.

Klug, Ron. Psalms: A Guide to Prayer & Praise. (Fisherman Bible Study Guides). 1979. saddlestitched 1.95 (ISBN 0-87788-699-7). Shaw Pubs.

Klug, Ronald. Following Christ. 1981. pap. 3.50 (ISBN 0-570-03826-X, 12-2791). Concordia.

Kluge, Eike-Henner W. The Ethics of Deliberate Death. (National University Publications, Multidisciplinary Studies in the Law). 1981. 17.50 (ISBN 0-8046-9264-5). Kennikat.

Kluger, Phyllis. Victorian Designs for Needlepoint. LC 78-2396. (Illus.). 1978. 12.95 o.p. (ISBN 0-03-020436-4); pap. 7.95 o.p. (ISBN 0-686-66723-9). HR&W.

Kluger, Rivkah S. Psyche & Bible: Three Old Testament Themes. Hillman, James, ed. 130p. (Orig.). 1973. pap. 7.50 (ISBN 0-88214-107-4). Spring Pubns.

Klugh, Henry E. Statistics: The Essentials for Research. 2nd ed. LC 73-16182. 416p. 1974. text ed. 22.95 (ISBN 0-471-49372-4). Wiley.

Klugman, Edgar. Teaching in the Elementary School: A Guide to Placement. LC 77-116889. (Illus., Orig.). 1970. pap. 3.50 o.p. (ISBN 0-8224-6825-5). Pitman Learning.

Kluser, Bernd, jt. ed. see Schellmann, Jorg.

Klust, Gerhard. Netting Materials for Fishing Gear. (Illus.). 184p. 8.75 (ISBN 0-85238-060-7, FN). Unipub.

Kluwer, R., jt. ed. see Eckstaedt, A.

Klyne & Buckingham, J. Atlas of Stereochemistry: Absolute Configurations of Organic Molecules, 2 vols. 2nd ed. (Illus.). 1978. 49.95 ea. Vol. I (ISBN 0-19-520058-6). Vol. II (ISBN 0-19-520059-4). Oxford U Pr.

Klyvert, Marlene, jt. auth. see Moss-Salentijn, Letty.

Kmenta, Jan & Ramsey, James B., eds. Evaluation of Econometric Models. 1980. 39.50 (ISBN 0-12-416550-8). Acad Pr.

Kmoch, Hans. Pawn Power in Chess. (Illus.). 1959. pap. 5.95 (ISBN 0-679-14028-X, Tartan). McKay.

Knaap G. A. Van, Der see Van Der Knaap, G. A.

Knack, John W., Sr., jt. auth. see Grimes, Harriette H.

Knack, Martha C. Life Is with People: Household Organization of the Contemporary Paiute Indians. (Anthropological Papers Ser.: No. 19). 106p. (Orig.). 1981. pap. 6.95 (ISBN 0-87919-091-4). Ballena Pr.

Knackstedt, Mary V. Interior Design for Profit. Haney, Laura J., ed. 1980. 17.00 (ISBN 0-9604676-0-2). Kobro Pubns.

Knafl, Kathleen A., jt. auth. see Kviz, Frederick J.

Knafla, L. A. Law & Politics in Jacobean England. LC 76-4757. (Cambridge Studies in English Legal History). (Illus.). 1977. 59.00 (ISBN 0-521-21191-3). Cambridge U Pr.

Knap, Jerome, ed. All About Wildfowling in America. 1976. 11.95 (ISBN 0-87691-177-7). Winchester Pr.

Knape, Beth J., jt. ed. see Garigliano, Leonard J.

Knapke, William F. & Hubbard, Freeman. Railroad Caboose. LC 67-28316. (Illus.). (gr. 10 up). 1968. 13.95 (ISBN 0-87095-011-8). Golden West.

Knaplund, Paul. British Empire, Eighteen Fifteen to Nineteen Thirty. LC 68-9617. (Illus.). 1970. Repr. 27.50 (ISBN 0-86527-017-1). Fertig.

Knapp, Alozis, tr. see Frankhauser, Eduard.

Knapp, B. J. Elements of Geographical Hydrology. (Illus.). 1978. pap. text ed. 6.95x (ISBN 0-04-551030-X). Allen Unwin.

--Soil Processes. (Process in Physical Geography Ser.: No. 2). (Illus.). 1979. pap. text ed. 5.95x (ISBN 0-04-631011-8). Allen Unwin.

Knapp, B. J., ed. Practical Foundations of Physical Geography. (Illus.). 152p. 1981. pap. text ed. 11.50x (ISBN 0-04-551035-0, 2590); tchr's ed. 13.50x (ISBN 0-04-551034-2, 2589). Allen Unwin.

Knapp, Bert van der see Odell, P. R. & Van Der Knapp, Bert.

Knapp, Bert Vander see Odell, P. R. & Van Der Knapp, Bert.

Knapp, Bettina L. Anais Nin. LC 78-57692. (Modern Literature Ser.). 1978. 10.95 (ISBN 0-8044-2481-0); pap. 3.45 (ISBN 0-8044-6371-9). Ungar.

--Antonin Artaud: Man of Vision. LC 79-9637. 233p. 1980. pap. 5.95 (ISBN 0-8040-0809-4). Swallow.

--Emile Zola. LC 79-48079. (Modern Literature Ser.). 160p. 1980. 10.95 (ISBN 0-8044-2482-9). Ungar.

--Fernand Crommelynck. (World Authors Ser.: No. 444). 1978. lib. bdg. 12.50 (ISBN 0-8057-6286-8). Twayne.

--Georges Duhamel. (World Authors Ser.: France: No. 199). lib. bdg. 10.95 (ISBN 0-8057-2272-6). Twayne.

--Maurice Maeterlinck. (World Authors Ser.: France: No. 342). 1975. lib. bdg. 10.95 (ISBN 0-8057-2562-8). Twayne.

--Theatre & Alchemy. 320p. 1981. 19.95 (ISBN 0-8143-1656-5). Wayne St U Pr.

Knapp, Daniel. California Woman. (Orig.). 1980. pap. 2.50 o.s.i. (ISBN 0-440-11035-1). Dell.

Knapp, Daniel & Dennis, John. Writing for Real. (Illus.). 192p. 1972. pap. text ed. 6.95 (ISBN 0-13-970525-2). P-H.

Knapp, Daniel R. Handbook of Analytical Derivatization Reactions. LC 78-12944. 1979. 45.00 (ISBN 0-471-03469-X, Pub. by Wiley-Interscience). Wiley.

Knapp, David A., jt. auth. see Smith, Mickey C.

Knapp, Elsie M. Horary Art & It's Synthesis. 1974. 5.00x (ISBN 0-686-17210-8). Sandollar Pr.

Knapp, Elsie M. & Faithful, Denise. Numbers Mean More Than You Think. 51p. (gr. 6 up). 1974. pap. 1.50 (ISBN 0-686-05514-4). Sandollar Pr.

Knapp, Herbert, jt. auth. see Knapp, Mary.

Knapp, James F. Ezra Pound. (United States Author Ser.: No. 348). 1979. 9.95 (ISBN 0-8057-7286-3). Twayne.

Knapp, Sr. Justina. Christian Symbols & How to Use Them. LC 74-8172. (Illus.). 164p. 1975. Repr. of 1935 ed. 20.00 (ISBN 0-8103-4050-X). Gale.

Knapp, Martin, jt. auth. see Davies, Bleddyn.

Knapp, Mary & Knapp, Herbert. One Potato, Two Potato: The Folklore of American Children. 1978. pap. text ed. 4.95x (ISBN 0-393-09039-6). Norton.

Knapp, Peggy A. & Stugrin, Michael A., eds. Assays: Critical Approaches to Medieval & Renaissance Texts, Vol. 1. LC 80-54059. 200p. 1981. 15.95x (ISBN 0-8229-3439-6). U of Pittsburgh Pr.

Knapp, Rebecca G. Basic Statistics for Nurses. LC 77-26950. 1978. pap. 10.95 (ISBN 0-471-03545-9, Wiley Medical). Wiley.

Knapp, Rebecca G., jt. auth. see Miller, M. Clinton.

Knapp, Robert R. Handbook for the Personal Orientation Inventory. LC 75-17256. 1976. text ed. 12.95 (ISBN 0-912736-17-8). EDITS Pubs.

Knapp, Robert W., jt. ed. see Couger, J. Daniel.

Knapp, Ron. Tutankhamun & the Mysteries of Ancient Egypt. LC 79-15504. (Illus.). 96p. (gr. 4-6). 1979. PLB 7.79 (ISBN 0-671-33036-5). Messner.

Knapp, Ronald G., ed. China's Island Frontier: Studies in the Historical Geography of Taiwan. LC 80-18578. 368p. 1980. text ed. 20.00x (ISBN 0-8248-0705-7). U Pr of Hawaii.

Knapp, Ruediger. Gegenseitige Beeinflussung und Temperatur-Wirkung bei tropischen und subtropischen Pflanzen: Bericht ueber neue experimentelle Untersuchungen an Nutzpflanzen und Arten der spontanen Vegetation. (Illus.). 1967. pap. 6.00 (ISBN 3-7682-0576-2). Lubrecht & Cramer.

Knapp, Susan, jt. auth. see Wolman, Benjamin B.

Knapp, Vincent J. Austrian Social Democracy, Eighteen Eighty-Nine to Nineteen Fourteen. LC 79-5509. 1980. text ed. 19.50 (ISBN 0-8191-0906-1); pap. text ed. 11.25 (ISBN 0-8191-0907-X). U Pr of Amer.

Knapp, William I. Life, Writings & Correspondence of George Borrow, 2 Vols. LC 67-23870. 1967. Repr. of 1899 ed. Set. 28.00 (ISBN 0-8103-3051-2). Gale.

Knapper, Arno & Newcomb, Loda. Style Manual for Written Communications. (Business English Ser.). 1974. pap. text ed. 8.95 (ISBN 0-88244-053-5). Grid Pub.

Knapper, Arno F. Cases in Personnel Management. LC 76-11577. (Management Ser.). 1977. pap. text ed. 6.95 o.p. (ISBN 0-88244-121-3). Grid Pub.

Knapper, Christopher K. Evaluating Instructional Technology. (New Pattern in Learning Ser.). 163p. 1980. 26.95x (ISBN 0-470-26994-4). Halsted Pr.

Knappert, Jan. Bantu Myths & Other Tales. (Nisaba Ser.: No. VII). 1977. text ed. 20.50x (ISBN 90-04-05423-5). Humanities.

Knapton, Ernest J. Revolutionary & Imperial France: 1750-1815. LC 76-181037. 150p. 1972. 6.95 o.p. (ISBN 0-684-12718-0, ScribT). Scribner.

Knarr, Patricia. Curse of the Pennsylvania Dutch. 1980. 4.50 o.p. (ISBN 0-8062-1226-8). Carlton.

Knatz, Hilary F., jt. auth. see Sprague, Norman.

Knauerhase, Ramon. The Saudi Arabian Economy. LC 75-8407. (Special Studies). (Illus.). 390p. 1975. text ed. 37.50 (ISBN 0-275-09000-0). Praeger.

Knauff, Ellen R. The Ellen Knauff Story. LC 73-21679. (Civil Liberties in American History Ser.). 242p. 1974. Repr. of 1952 ed. lib. bdg. 29.50 (ISBN 0-306-70238-X). Da Capo.

Knauff, Thomas. Glider Basics from Frist Flight to Solo. Northcut, Allan & Northcut, Debbie, eds. LC 80-81375. (Illus.). 155p. 1980. text ed. 12.95. Knauff.

Knaupp, Jonathan, et al. Patterns & Systems of Elementary Mathematics. LC 76-13087. (Illus.). 1977. pap. text ed. 17.75 (ISBN 0-395-20638-3); instructors' manual 3.25 (ISBN 0-395-20639-1). HM.

Knaus, Jakob. Hofmannsthals Weg Zur Oper, Die Frau Ohne Schatten: Ruecksichten und Einfluesse auf die Musik. (Quellen und Forschungen zur Sprach-und Kulturgeschichte der germanischen Volker, N. F. 38). (Ger). 1971. 29.40 (ISBN 3-11-001865-9). De Gruyter.

Knaus, William A. Inside Russian Medicine. 1981. 14.95. Everest Hse.

Knaus, William J., jt. auth. see Ellis, Albert.

Knauth, Percy. The Metalsmiths. (The Emergence of Man Ser.). (Illus.). 1974. 9.95 (ISBN 0-8094-1308-6); lib. bdg. avail. (ISBN 0-685-48124-7). Time-Life.

--The Metalsmiths. LC 73-89680. (Emergence of Man Ser.). (gr. 6 up). 1973. PLB 9.63 o.p. (ISBN 0-8094-1309-4, Pub. by Time-Life). Silver.

--The North Woods. (The American Wilderness Ser.). (Illus.). 1972. 12.95 (ISBN 0-8094-1164-4). Time-Life.

--The North Woods. LC 72-88525. (American Wilderness Ser). (Illus.). (gr. 6 up). 1972. lib. bdg. 11.97 (ISBN 0-8094-1165-2, Pub. by Time-Life). Silver.

--A Season in Hell. LC 74-1826. 124p. 1975. 7.95 o.p. (ISBN 0-06-012421-0, HarpT). Har-Row.

Knauth, Percy, jt. auth. see Bubley, Esther.

Kneafsey, James T. Transporation Economic Analysis. LC 74-2203. (Illus.). 1975. 21.95x (ISBN 0-669-93211-6). Lexington Bks.

Knebel, Fletcher. Dave Sulkin Cares! LC 77-25600. 1978. 8.95 o.p. (ISBN 0-385-13693-5). Doubleday.

Kneberg, Madeline, jt. auth. see Lewis, Thomas M.

Knecht, Charles D., et al. Fundamental Techniques Veterinary Surgery. (Illus.). 250p. 1981. text ed. price not set (ISBN 0-7216-5463-0). Saunders.

Knecht, Ken. Microsoft Basic. LC 79-53476. 225p. 1979. pap. 10.95 (ISBN 0-918398-23-1). Dilithium Pr.

Knee, Allan. Second Avenue Rag. (Phoenix Theatre Ser.). pap. 2.95 (ISBN 0-912262-71-0). Proscenium.

Kneedler, Rebecca D. & Tarver, Sara G. Changing Perspectives in Special Education. 1977. pap. text ed. 12.50 (ISBN 0-675-08529-2). Merrill.

Kneese, Allen V. & Bower, Blair T. Environmental Quality & Residuals Management. LC 79-2181. (Resources for the Future Ser.). 1979. 25.00x (ISBN 0-8018-2245-9); pap. 7.95x (ISBN 0-8018-2286-6). Johns Hopkins.

Kneese, Allen V. & Schultze, Charles L. Pollution, Prices & Public Policy. 125p. 1975. 11.95 (ISBN 0-8157-4994-5); pap. 4.95 (ISBN 0-8157-4993-7). Brookings.

Kneeter, Robert. America's Gauntlet: Manuscript 1 of the Humanist Papers. pap. 5.00 (ISBN 0-938722-01-8). Word Ent.

--The Humanist Papers, 4 vols, Vols. 1 & 2. pap. write for info. (ISBN 0-938722-00-X). Word Ent.

Knef, Hildegard. The Verdict. 1977. pap. 1.95 o.p. (ISBN 0-345-25401-5). Ballantine.

Kneider, A. P. Mathematics of Merchandising. 2nd ed. (Illus.). 320p. 1981. pap. text ed. 15.95 (ISBN 0-686-63445-4). P-H.

Kneip, Theo J. & Lioy, Paul J., eds. Aerosols: Anthropogenic & Natural, Sources & Transport. LC 80-12891. (N.Y. Academy of Sciences Annals: Vol. 338). 618p. Date not set. 108.00x (ISBN 0-89766-064-1); pap. price not set (ISBN 0-89766-065-X). NY Acad Sci.

Knei-Paz, Baruch. The Social & Political Thought of Leon Trotsky. 1978. 29.50x o.p. (ISBN 0-19-827233-2). Oxford U Pr.

Kneisl, Carol R. Current Perspectives in Psychiatric Nursing: Issues & Trends, Vol. 1. 228p. 1976. case bound 11.95 o.p. (ISBN 0-8016-2714-1); pap. 8.95 o.p. (ISBN 0-8016-2713-3). Mosby.

Kneisl, Carol R. & Ames, Sue Ann. Mental Health Concepts in Medical-Surgical Nursing: A Workbook. 2nd ed. LC 78-16371. (Illus.). 1979. pap. 9.50 (ISBN 0-8016-0161-4). Mosby.

Kneisl, Carol R., jt. auth. see Wilson, Holly S.

Kneitel, Tom. CBers' SSB Handbook. (gr. 10 up). 1977. pap. 7.15 (ISBN 0-8104-0857-0). Hayden.

Kneller, E., jt. ed. see Berkowitz, A. E.

Kneller, G. E. Educational Philosophy of National Socialism. 1941. 42.50x (ISBN 0-685-69834-3). Elliots Bks.

Kneller, George F. Educational Anthropology: An Introduction. LC 65-14252. 171p. 1965. pap. text ed. 9.50x o.p. (ISBN 0-471-49513-1). Wiley.

--Introduction to the Philosophy of Education. 2nd ed. LC 78-168637. 1971. pap. text ed. 7.25 (ISBN 0-471-49515-8). Wiley.

--Science As a Human Endeavor. LC 77-19167. 1978. 17.50x (ISBN 0-231-04206-X). Columbia U Pr.

Kneller, George F., ed. Foundations of Education. 3rd ed. LC 78-138913. 1971. text ed. 22.95 (ISBN 0-471-49505-0). Wiley.

Kneller, J. W., jt. auth. see Grubbs, H. A.

Kneller, Richard, jt. auth. see Dobkins, David H.

Knerr, Michael E. Heavy Weather. 1979. pap. 1.75 (ISBN 0-505-51426-5). Tower Bks.

Kneubuhl, Fritz, ed. see International Conference on Infrared Physics, 2nd, (CIRP 2), Zurich, 1979.

Knewstubb, P. F. Mass Spectrometry & Ion-Molecule Reactions. LC 69-16282. (Cambridge Chemistry Textbooks Ser). (Illus.). 1969. 27.50 (ISBN 0-521-07489-4); pap. 11.50x (ISBN 0-521-09563-8). Cambridge U Pr.

Knezevich, Stephen J. Program Budgeting. LC 72-5703. 1973. 17.90x (ISBN 0-8211-1014-4); text ed. 16.20x (ISBN 0-685-36206-X). McCutchan.

Knibb, M. A., ed. The Ethiopic Book of Enoch, 2 vols. 1979. 89.00x set (ISBN 0-19-826163-2). Oxford U Pr.

Knickerbocker, K. L., jt. ed. see Litzinger, Boyd.

Knickmeyer, Steve. Straight. 1976. 6.95 o.p. (ISBN 0-394-40190-5). Random.

Knies, Earl A. The Art of Charlotte Bronte. LC 69-15917. x, 234p. 1969. 11.95x (ISBN 0-8214-0059-2). Ohio U Pr.

Knies, Elizabeth. Streets After Rain. LC 80-66181. 64p. 1980. pap. 4.95 (ISBN 0-914086-31-6). Alicejamesbooks.

Kniesner, Thomas J., jt. auth. see Fleisher, Belton M.

Knigge, R. Silver Spurs. LC 75-10111. 1973. 4.25 (ISBN 0-915614-01-4); incl. record 5.95 (ISBN 0-685-57207-2). Knollwood Pub.

Knight, Alanna. Castle of Foxes. LC 80-952. 312p. 1981. 11.95 (ISBN 0-385-15327-9). Doubleday.

Knight, Allan. Asthma, Hay Fever & Other Allergies. LC 80-22839. (Positive Health Guides Ser.). (Illus.). 112p. 1981. 9.95 (ISBN 0-668-04675-9); pap. 5.95 (ISBN 0-668-04681-3). Arco.

Knight, Allen W. & Simmons, Mary Ann, eds. Water Pollution: A Guide to Information Sources. LC 73-17537. (Man & the Environment Information Guide Ser.: Vol. 9). 1980. 30.00 (ISBN 0-8103-1346-4). Gale.

Knight, Alma T. Behold the Man, Jesus. 3.95 o.p. (ISBN 0-685-48827-6). Nortex Pr.

Knight, Anthony, tr. see Ecke, Wolfgang.
Knight, Arthur. The Liveliest Art: A Panoramic History of the Movies. rev. ed. (Illus.). 1978. 19.95 (ISBN 0-02-564210-3). Macmillan.
Knight, Arthur R. Introductory Physical Chemistry. 1969. text ed. 20.95 (ISBN 0-13-502203-7). P-H.
Knight, B. C., jt. ed. see Charles, H. P.
Knight, Bernard. Discovering the Human Body: How Pioneers of Modern Medicine Solved the Mysteries of the Body's Structure & Surface & Function. LC 80-7886. (Illus.). 192p. 1980. 17.95 (ISBN 0-690-01928-9). Lippincott & Crowell.
Knight, Brenda. Runaway's Chance. 1973. 6.50 (ISBN 0-571-10208-5, Pub. by Faber & Faber). Merrimack Bk Serv.
Knight, Brian. Rugweaving: Technique & Design. (Illus.). 1981. 22.50 (ISBN 0-7134-2582-2, Pub. by Batsford England). David & Charles.
Knight, Bryan M. Enjoying Single Parenthood. 176p. 1981. pap. 6.95 (ISBN 0-442-29623-1). Van Nos Reinhold.
Knight, C. & Newman, J. Contemporary Africa: Geography & Change. 1976. 22.95 (ISBN 0-13-170035-9). P-H.
Knight, C. A. Chemistry of Viruses. (Protoplasmatologia: Vol. 4, Pt. 2). (Illus.). 1963. pap. 29.50 o.p. (ISBN 0-387-80652-0). Springer-Verlag.
Knight, C. Gregory & Wilcox, R. Paul. Triumph or Triage? The World Food Problem in Geographical Persective. Natoli, Salvatore J., ed. LC 76-29265. (Resource Papers for College Geography Ser.). 1977. pap. text ed. 4.00 (ISBN 0-89291-115-8). Assn Am Geographers.
Knight, C. Morley. Hints on Driving. (Illus.). 12.25 (ISBN 0-85131-040-0, Dist. by Sporting Book Center). J A Allen.
Knight, Cecil B. Pentecostal Worship. 1974. pap. 2.25 (ISBN 0-87148-684-9). Pathway Pr.
Knight, Charles. Passages of a Working Life: During Half a Century with a Prelude of Early Reminiscences, 3 vols. (The Development of Industrial Society Ser.). 1026p. 1980. Repr. 50.00x (ISBN 0-7165-1568-7, Pub. by Irish Academic Pr). Biblio Dist.
Knight, Charles R. Animal Drawing-Anatomy & Action for Artists. (Orig.). 1959. pap. text ed. 4.50 (ISBN 0-486-20426-X). Dover.
--Animal Drawing: Animal Anatomy & Psychology for Artists & Laymen. (Illus.). 8.50 (ISBN 0-8446-0742-8). Peter Smith.
Knight, Charles W. Secrets of Green Thumb Gardening. LC 64-17301. (gr. 9 up). 1964. 6.95 (ISBN 0-8119-0154-8). Fell.
Knight, Connie, jt. ed. see Levin, L. Stefan.
Knight, D. The Other Foot. pap. text ed. 7.00 (ISBN 0-08-007043-4). Pergamon.
Knight, Damon. A for Anything. 1980. pap. 1.95 (ISBN 0-380-48553-2, 48553). Avon.
--Science Fiction in the Thirties. 1977. pap. 4.95 (ISBN 0-380-00904-8, 31708). Avon.
Knight, Damon, ed. Best from Orbit One to Ten. pap. 1.95 o.p. (ISBN 0-425-03161-6). Berkley Pub.
--Orbit Fifteen. LC 74-1890. 224p. (YA) 1974. 9.95 o.p. (ISBN 0-06-012439-3, HarpT). Har-Row.
--Orbit Sixteen. LC 74-15875. (Illus.). 280p. (YA) 1975. 9.95 o.p. (ISBN 0-06-012437-7, HarpT). Har-Row.
--Orbit Thirteen. LC 66-15585. (YA) 1974. 5.95 o.p. (ISBN 0-399-11222-7, Dist. by Putnam). Berkley Pub.
--Orbit Twenty. LC 77-11784. 1978. 9.95 o.p. (ISBN 0-06-012429-6, HarpT). Har-Row.
--Orbit Twenty One. LC 78-20207. 224p. 1980. 12.95 (ISBN 0-06-012426-1, HarpT). Har-Row.
--Turning Points: Essays on the Art of Science Fiction. LC 76-5135. (YA) 1977. 12.50 o.s.i. (ISBN 0-06-012432-6, HarpT). Har-Row.
Knight, David. Colonies in Orbit: The Coming Age of Human Settlements in Space. (gr. 5-9). 1977. 6.25 o.p. (ISBN 0-688-22096-7); PLB 6.96 (ISBN 0-688-32096-1). Morrow.
--Eavesdropping on Space: The Quest of Radio Astronomy. LC 74-19285. (Illus.). 96p. (gr. 5-9). 1975. PLB 6.96 (ISBN 0-688-32019-8). Morrow.
--Harnessing the Sun: The Story of Solar Energy. (Illus.). 128p. (gr. 5-9). 1976. PLB 6.96 (ISBN 0-688-32070-8). Morrow.
--Helps for Family Prayer. (Illus.). 1977. 0.50 (ISBN 0-89570-109-X). Claretian Pubns.
--Let's Find Out About Sound. LC 74-2997. (Let's Find Out Bks). (gr. k-2). 1975. PLB 6.45 (ISBN 0-531-00103-2). Watts.
--Tiny Planets: Asteroids of Our Solar System. (Illus.). 96p. (gr. 3-7). 1973. PLB 6.96 (ISBN 0-688-30072-3). Morrow.
Knight, David C. Bees Can't Fly, but They Do: Things That Are Still a Mystery to Science. LC 76-8491. 48p. (gr. 3 up). 1976. 7.95 (ISBN 0-02-750860-9, 75086). Macmillan.
--Comets. LC 68-16015. (First Bks). (Illus.). (gr. 4-6). 1968. PLB 4.90 o.p. (ISBN 0-531-00505-4). Watts.
--First Book of Air. (First Bks). (Illus.). (gr. 4-6). 1961. PLB 4.90 o.p. (ISBN 0-531-00453-8). Watts.
--First Book of Deserts. (First Bks). (Illus.). (gr. 4-6). 1964. PLB 4.90 o.p. (ISBN 0-531-00515-1). Watts.
--The First Book of Mars. rev ed. LC 72-8123. (First Bks). (Illus.). 96p. (gr. 4-6). 1973. 6.45 (ISBN 0-531-00797-9). Watts.
--First Book of Meteors & Meteorites. LC 69-11190. (First Bks). (Illus.). (gr. 4-6). 1969. PLB 4.90 o.p. (ISBN 0-531-00582-8). Watts.
--Galaxies, Islands in Space. (Illus.). (gr. 4-6). 1979. 6.50 (ISBN 0-688-22180-7); PLB 6.24 (ISBN 0-688-32180-1). Morrow.
--The Haunted Souvenir Warehouse. LC 77-76251. (gr. 3-7). 1978. PLB 5.95 (ISBN 0-385-12729-4). Doubleday.
--Isaac Newton: Mastermind of Science. (Biography Ser). (Illus.). (gr. 7 up). 1961. PLB 5.90 o.p. (ISBN 0-531-00910-6). Watts.
--Let's Find Out About Earth. LC 74-3501. (Let's Find Out Bks). (Illus.). 48p. (gr. k-3). 1975. PLB 4.90 o.p. (ISBN 0-531-00111-3). Watts.
--Let's Find Out About Mars. LC 66-10159. (Let's Find Out Bks). (Illus.). (gr. k-3). 1966. PLB 4.47 o.p. (ISBN 0-531-00032-X). Watts.
--Let's Find Out About Telephones. LC 67-10006. (Let's Find Out Bks). (Illus.). (gr. k-3). 1967. PLB 4.47 o.p. (ISBN 0-531-00048-6). Watts.
--Let's Find Out About the Ocean. LC 77-100095. (Let's Find Out Bks). (Illus.). (gr. k-3). 1970. PLB 4.47 o.p. (ISBN 0-531-00056-7). Watts.
--Let's Find Out About Weather. LC 67-10010. (Let's Find Out Bks). (Illus.). (gr. k-3). 1967. PLB 4.47 o.p. (ISBN 0-531-00053-2). Watts.
--Naval War with France, 1798-1800: "Millions for Defense, but Not One Cent for Tribute". LC 70-119577. (Focus Books). (Illus.). (gr. 7 up). 1970. PLB 6.45 (ISBN 0-531-01017-1). Watts.
--Poltergeists: Hauntings & the Haunted. LC 72-2449. (Illus.). 160p. (gr. 5-9). 1972. 7.95 o.p. (ISBN 0-397-31488-4); pap. 1.95 o.p. (ISBN 0-397-31416-7, LSC-19). Lippincott.
--Robert Koch: Father of Bacteriology. (Biography Ser). (Illus.). (gr. 7 up). 1961. PLB 5.90 o.p. (ISBN 0-531-00891-6). Watts.
--Silent Sound: The World of Ultrasonics. LC 80-19118. (Illus.). 96p. (gr. 4-6). 1980. 6.95 (ISBN 0-688-22244-7); PLB 6.67 (ISBN 0-688-32244-1). Morrow.
--The Spy Who Never Was & Other True Spy Stories. LC 77-15162. (A Signal Book). (gr. 9 up). 1978. 6.95 (ISBN 0-385-13108-9). Doubleday.
--Those Mysteriuos UFO's: The Story of Unidentitied Flying Objects. LC 74-31465. (Finding-Out Book). (Illus.). 64p. (gr. 2-4). 1979. Repr. of 1975 ed. PLB 6.95 (ISBN 0-89490-032-3). Enslow Pubs.
Knight, David M. Confession Can Change Your Life. (Illus.). 40p. 1977. pap. 1.50 (ISBN 0-89570-102-2). Claretian Pubns.
--Natural Science Books in English, Sixteen Hundred to Nineteen Hundred. 1972. 60.00 (ISBN 0-7134-0728-X, Pub. by Batsford England). David & Charles.
Knight, Debby. Death by Narration. 48p. 1981. 5.95 (ISBN 0-89962-051-5). Todd & Honeywell.
Knight, Douglas A. Rediscovering the Traditions of Israel: The Development of the Tradition-Historical Research of the Old Testament, with Special Consideration of Scandinavian Contributions. LC 75-6868. (Society of Biblical Literature. Dissertation Ser.). 1975. pap. 9.00 (ISBN 0-89130-235-2, 060109). Scholars Pr Ca.
Knight, E. Leslie, jt. auth. see Davis, J. Boyce.
Knight, Frank. Ships: From Noah's Ark to Nuclear Submarine. LC 70-124418. (Illus.). (gr. 5-8). 1971. 4.95 o.s.i. (ISBN 0-02-750890-0, CCPr). Macmillan.
Knight, Frank B., ed. Essentials of Brownian Motion & Diffusion. (Mathematical Surveys: Vol. 18). Date not set. cancelled (ISBN 0-8218-1518-0). Am Math.
Knight, Frank H. The Ethics of Competition. (Midway Reprint Ser.). 1935. pap. 15.00x (ISBN 0-226-44687-5). U of Chicago Pr.
Knight, Franklin W. The African Dimension in Latin American Societies, Vol. 3. LC 73-11732. (Latin American Ser.). (Illus.). 180p. 1974. 9.95 o.s.i. (ISBN 0-02-564200-6). Macmillan.
--The Caribbean: The Genesis of a Fragmented Nationalism. (Latin American History Ser.). 1978. 14.95 (ISBN 0-19-502242-4); pap. 4.95x (ISBN 0-19-502243-2). Oxford U Pr.
--Slave Society in Cuba During the Nineteenth Century. LC 76-121770. (Illus.). 1970. 25.00 (ISBN 0-299-05790-9); pap. 7.50x (ISBN 0-299-05793-3). U of Wis Pr.
Knight, Frida. Cambridge Music: From the Middle Ages to Modern Times. (Cambridge Town, Gown & Country Ser.: Vol. 29). (Illus.). 1980. 16.50 (ISBN 0-900891-51-3). Oleander Pr.
Knight, Gareth. Experience of the Inner Worlds. 1975. 12.50 (ISBN 0-685-67326-X). Weiser.
Knight, George W. Church Bulletin Bits. 160p. 1976. pap. 3.45 (ISBN 0-8010-5368-4). Baker Bk.
Knight, Gilda, jt. ed. see Barrett, Stephen.
Knight, H. Gary. Managing the Sea's Living Resources. LC 76-20042. (Lexington Books Studies in Marine Affairs). 1977. 17.95 (ISBN 0-669-00874-5). Lexington Bks.
Knight, H. Gary, et al, eds. Ocean Thermal Energy Conversion: Legal, Political & Institutional Aspects. LC 77-2049. 1977. 22.95 (ISBN 0-669-01441-9). Lexington Bks.
Knight, Harold, ed. see Barth, Karl.
Knight, Hilary. The Circus Is Coming. (Illus.). (ps-2). 1979. 3.95 (ISBN 0-307-13737-6, Golden Pr); PLB 9.15 (ISBN 0-307-63377-2). Western Pub.
Knight, Hilary, jt. auth. see Maiden, Cecil.
Knight, J. W. The Starch Industry. 1969. 15.00 o.p. (ISBN 0-08-013044-5). Pergamon.
Knight, Jackson W. Selections from Eclogues Georgies & Aeneid: Selections from Eclogues,Georgics & Aeneid. (Roman World Ser.). 1970. pap. text ed. 3.95x (ISBN 0-04-873001-7). Allen Unwin.
Knight, Jacqueline E. The Hunter's Game Cookbook. (Illus.). 1978. 12.95 (ISBN 0-87691-252-8). Winchester Pr.
Knight, James T. Commutative Algebra. LC 76-152625. (London Mathematical Society Lecture Notes Ser.: No. 5). (Illus.). 1971. pap. 14.50 (ISBN 0-521-08193-9). Cambridge U Pr.
Knight, James W., jt. ed. see Otto, Herbert A.
Knight, Jesse F. The World of O. Henry - Five One Act Plays. LC 77-15687. (Lion Theatrical Ser.: No. 1). 1980. pap. 3.50 (ISBN 0-930962-03-6). Lion Ent.
Knight, John F. What a Married Couple Should Know About Sex. LC 78-71469. 1979. pap. 5.95 (ISBN 0-8163-0388-6, 23104-3). Pacific Pr Pub Assn.
--What a Young Man Should Know About Sex. LC 76-48572. 1977. pap. 5.95 (ISBN 0-8163-0312-6, 23111-8). Pacific Pr Pub Assn.
--What a Young Woman Should Know About Sex. LC 76-48571. 1977. pap. 5.95 (ISBN 0-8163-0311-8, 23112-6). Pacific Pr Pub Assn.
Knight, Karl F., jt. auth. see Moore, L. Hugh.
Knight, Kenneth. Matrix Management. LC 78-1516. 1978. text ed. 20.00 (ISBN 0-89433-082-9). Petrocelli.
Knight, Kenneth, jt. auth. see Guest, David.
Knight, Kenneth L. & Stone, Alan. A Catalog of the Mosquitos of the World, Vol. 6. 2nd ed. LC 77-82735. 1977. 20.50 (ISBN 0-686-04889-X); supplement 1978 3.35 (ISBN 0-686-28524-7). Entomol Soc.
Knight, Kenneth L., jt. auth. see Harbach, R. E.
Knight, Lucian L., ed. Biographical Dictionary of Southern Authors. LC 75-26631. (Library of Southern Literature). (Illus.). 1978. Repr. of 1929 ed. 38.00 (ISBN 0-8103-4269-3). Gale.
Knight, Margaret. Teaching Nutrition & Food Science. 1976. pap. 13.50 (ISBN 0-7134-3099-0, Pub. by Batsford England). David & Charles.
Knight, Max, ed. see Maenchen-Helfen, Otto J.
Knight, Max, tr. see Kelsen, Hans.
Knight, Max, tr. & intro. by see Morgenstern, Christian.
Knight, Max, tr. see Strauss, Richard & Zweig, Stefan.
Knight, Maxwell E. The German Executive, 1890-1933. LC 78-80560. (Illus.). 52p. 1973. Repr. of 1952 ed. 9.00 (ISBN 0-86527-079-1). Fertig.
Knight, Norman, jt. auth. see Pick, Fred L.
Knight, Richard V., jt. auth. see Stanback, Thomas M.
Knight, Richard V., jt. auth. see Stanback, Thomas M., Jr.
Knight, Robert. Manual for News Writing. (Lucas Text Ser). 1970. text ed. 2.00x spiral bdg. (ISBN 0-87543-070-8). Lucas.
Knight, Robert E. Industrial Relations in the San Francisco Bay Area, 1900-1918. (Institute of Industrial Relations, UC Berkeley). 1960. 28.50x (ISBN 0-520-00658-5). U of Cal Pr.
Knight, S. A. Electronics for Technicians Three. (Newnes-Butterworth Technical Ser.). (Illus.). 192p. 1980. pap. text ed. 15.95 (ISBN 0-408-00458-4). Butterworths.
Knight, Spencer. Frank Bear. (Orig.). 1979. pap. 1.95 (ISBN 0-532-23112-0). Manor Bks.
Knight, Stanley, jt. auth. see Hawes, Gordon.
Knight, Stephen A. Electronics for Technicians Two. (TEC Technicians Ser.). (Illus.). 1978. pap. 9.95 (ISBN 0-408-00324-3). Butterworths.
Knight, Thomas J. Latin America Comes of Age. LC 79-18702. 335p. 1979. 19.00 (ISBN 0-8108-1243-6). Scarecrow.
--Technology's Future: The Hague Congress Technology Assessment. 566p. 1981. Repr. of 1976 ed. text ed. price not set (ISBN 0-89874-283-8). Krieger.
Knight, U. G. Power Systems Engineering & Mathematics. 304p. 1972. 40.00 (ISBN 0-08-016603-2); pap. 23.00 (ISBN 0-08-018294-1). Pergamon.
Knight, Vick. The Night the Crayons Talked. 1974. 4.95 (ISBN 0-686-64102-7). Borden.
Knight, Walker & Touchton, Ken. Seven Beginnings. LC 75-44496. (Human Torch Ser.: 2nd). (Illus.). 1976. 5.95 (ISBN 0-937170-17-8). Home Mission.
Knight, Walker & Wall, Steve. Chaplaincy: Love on the Line. Furlow, Elaine S., ed. (Human Touch Photo-Text Ser.). (Illus.). 1978. 6.95 (ISBN 0-937170-12-7). Home Mission.
Knight, William A. Through the Wordsworth Country. 268p. 1980. Repr. of 1887 ed. lib. bdg. 35.00 (ISBN 0-8482-4196-7). Norwood Edns.
Knight, William F. Accentual Symmetry in Virgil. Commager, H. Steele, ed. LC 77-70820. (Latin Poetry Ser.). 1979. Repr. of 1939 ed. lib. bdg. 13.00 (ISBN 0-8240-2971-2). Garland Pub.
Knight, William F., tr. see Virgil.
Knights, B. The Idea of the Clerisy, in the Nineteenth Century. LC 77-80840. 1978. 42.00 (ISBN 0-521-21798-9). Cambridge U Pr.
Knights, B., jt. auth. see Phillips, J.
Knights, Jack. Sail Racer. (Illus.). 235p. 1974. 15.00 (ISBN 0-229-98674-9). Transatlantic.
Knights, L. C. Some Shakespearean Themes & an Approach to Hamlet. 1961. 16.50x (ISBN 0-8047-0300-0); pap. 3.95 o.p. (ISBN 0-8047-0301-9). Stanford U Pr.
Knights, Peter R. The Plain People of Boston, 1830-1860: A Study in City Growth. (Urban Life in America Ser.). 1973. 14.95 (ISBN 0-19-501488-X). Oxford U Pr.
Knights, R. Treatment of Hyperactivity & Learning Disorders. 1979. 24.50 (ISBN 0-8391-1515-6). Univ Park.
Knights, Ward A., Jr., ed. Sermons from Hell: Help for the Distressed. LC 75-4830. 192p. (Orig.). 1975. pap. 1.25 (ISBN 0-8272-3414-7). Bethany Pr.
Knightsfield, P. F., tr. see Lange, Oskar.
Kniker, Charles. You & Values Education. (Educational Foundations Ser.). 1977. pap. text ed. 8.50 (ISBN 0-675-08516-0). Merrill.
Kniker, Charles R. & Naylor, Natalie A. Teaching Today & Tomorrow. (Special Education Ser.). (Orig.). 1981. pap. text ed. 15.95 (ISBN 0-675-08034-7); instrs'. manual 3.95. Merrill.
Kniker, Charles R., jt. auth. see Smith, Glenn.
Kniker, H. T., jt. auth. see Beede, J. W.
Knill, J. L., ed. Industrial Geology. (Illus.). 1979. 29.95x (ISBN 0-19-854520-7). Oxford U Pr.
Kniskern, David P., jt. auth. see Gurman, Alan S.
Knister, Raymond. The First Day of Spring & Other Prose: Stories & Other Prose. Stevens, Peter, ed. LC 76-10475. (Literature of Canada Ser: No. 17). 376p. 1975. pap. 7.95 (ISBN 0-8020-6198-2). U of Toronto Pr.
Kniveton, Bromley & Towers, Brian. Training for Negotiating. 213p. 1978. text ed. 21.00x (ISBN 0-220-66347-5, Pub. by Busn Bks England). Renouf.
Knoben, James E., et al. Handbook of Clinical Drug Data. rev. 4th ed. LC 77-89811. 1979. 16.00 (ISBN 0-914768-27-1). Drug Intl Pubns.
Knobloch, Hilda, et al. Manual of Developmental Diagnosis: The Administration & Interpretation of the Revised Gesell & Amtruda Developmental & Neurologic Examination. (Illus.). 286p. 1980. text ed. write for info. (ISBN 0-06-141437-9, Harper Medical). Har-Row.
Knobloch, Irving W. Selected Botanical Papers. (Illus.). 1963. pap. text ed. 11.95 (ISBN 0-13-800300-9). P-H.
Knoch, A E., ed. Concordant Greek Text. rev. ed. 1975. lea. bdg. 20.00 (ISBN 0-910424-32-2). Concordant.
Knoche, Grace F., ed. see De Purucker, G.
Knoche, Grace F., ed. see Ryan, Charles J.
Knoche, H. Flora Balearica Etude Phytogeographique Sur les Iles Baleares, 4vols. (Illus.). 240.00 (ISBN 3-87429-061-1). Lubrecht & Cramer.
Knoche, Keith. The Incredible Voyage. (Uplook Ser.). 1975. pap. 0.75 (ISBN 0-8163-0184-0, 09446-6). Pacific Pr Pub Assn.
--Knoche's Law. LC 73-85432. (Agape Ser.). 128p. (YA) 1973. pap. 2.50 o.p. (ISBN 0-8163-0011-9, 11380-3). Pacific Pr Pub Assn.
--Lord, Give Me Patience. LC 77-93362. (Agape Ser.). 1978. pap. 3.50 (ISBN 0-8163-0205-7, 12611-0). Pacific Pr Pub Assn.
Knoche, Philip B. Has God Given You up. (Uplook Ser). 1970. pap. 0.75 (ISBN 0-8163-0257-X, 08165-3). Pacific Pr Pub Assn.
--Married to the Enemy. (Uplook Ser.). 1976. pap. 0.75 (ISBN 0-8163-0262-6, 13263-9). Pacific Pr Pub Assn.

--Your Ups & Downs. (Uplook Ser.). 32p. 1970. pap. 0.75 (ISBN 0-8163-0085-2, 24535-7). Pacific Pr Pub Assn.

Knocher, Editha, tr. see Mozart, Leopold.

Knock. Perspectives on the Preparation of Student Affairs Professionals. (ACPA Monograph). 1977. pap. 7.25 (ISBN 0-686-23072-8). Am Personnel.

Knodel, Arthur J., ed. see Perse, John.

Knodt, Kenneth S., ed. Pursuing the American Dream. 336p. 1976. pap. text ed. 9.50 (ISBN 0-13-742742-5). P-H.

Knoedel, W. & Schneider, H. J., eds. Parallel Processes & Related Automata. (Computing Supplementum Ser.: No. 3). 203p. 1981. pap. 59.00 (ISBN 0-387-81606-2). Springer-Verlag.

Knoefel, P. R. Radio Contrast Agents, 2 Vols. 1971. Set. 165.00 (ISBN 0-08-016144-8). Pergamon.

Knoefel, Peter K., et al. Absorption, Distribution, Transformation & Excretion of Drugs. (Illus.). 220p. 1972. 18.75 (ISBN 0-398-02518-5). C C Thomas.

Knoepfle, John. Thinking of Offerings: Poems Nineteen Seventy - Nineteen Seventy-Three. 1979. 9.00 (ISBN 0-686-65851-5); signed ed. 16.00 (ISBN 0-686-61893-9); pap. 4.00 (ISBN 0-686-61894-7). Juniper Pr WI.

Knoepflmacher, U. C. Laughter & Despair: Readings in Ten Novels of the Victorian Era. 1973. 17.50x (ISBN 0-520-01907-5); pap. 2.95x (ISBN 0-520-02352-8). U of Cal Pr.

--Religious Humanism & the Victorian Novel: George Eliot, Walter Pater, & Samuel Butler. 1970. 18.00 o.p. (ISBN 0-691-06112-2); pap. 3.95 o.p. (ISBN 0-691-01295-4, 187). Princeton U Pr.

Knoepflmacher, U. C. & Tennyson, G. B., eds. Nature & the Victorian Imagination. 1978. 27.50 (ISBN 0-520-03229-2). U of Cal Pr.

Knoerle, Jeanne. Dream of the Red Chamber: A Critical Study. LC 72-183609. (East Asian Ser). 170p. 1973. 8.95x (ISBN 0-253-39102-4). Ind U Pr.

Knoke, David & Burke, Peter J. Log-Linear Models. LC 80-17031. (Quantitative Applications in the Social Sciences Ser.: No. 20). (Illus.). 80p. 1980. pap. 3.50 (ISBN 0-8039-1492-X). Sage.

Knolie, G., jt. auth. see Strassburg, M.

Knoll. Symposium on Analgesics: 1974. 1979. 14.00 (ISBN 0-9960007-4-7, Pub. by Kaido Hungary). Heyden.

Knoll, Charles M. The Water Level Route. (Illus.). 64p. (Orig.). 1977. pap. 5.95 (ISBN 0-686-61272-8). Natl Rail Rochester.

--The Water Level Route. 2nd ed. 1981. pap. 5.95 (ISBN 0-686-64650-9). Natl Rail Rochester.

Knoll, J., jt. ed. see Darvas, F.

Knoll, J., jt. ed. see Furst, Susanna.

Knoll, J., ed. see Hungarian Pharmacological Society, 3rd Congress, Budapest, 1979.

Knoll, J., jt. ed. see Kecskemeti, Valeria.

Knoll, Michael. The Woman at the End of the Mattress. Lee, Joan H., ed. 64p. 1981. pap. 4.95 (ISBN 0-932220-12-6). Broken Whisker.

Knoll, Robert E. Christopher Marlowe. LC 68-17237. (English Authors Ser.: No. 74). 1969. lib. bdg. 10.95 (ISBN 0-8057-1376-X). Twayne.

Knoll, Robert E., ed. Conversations with Wright Morris: Critical Views & Responses. LC 76-25497. (Illus.). 1977. 10.95x (ISBN 0-8032-0904-5); pap. 3.95 (ISBN 0-8032-5854-2, BB 630, Bison). U of Nebr Pr.

Knoll, Sheila. Power Places. (Illus.). 40p. (Orig.). 1980. pap. 4.95 (ISBN 0-937962-00-7). Indian Feather.

Knoop, Hans. The Menten Affair. 1979. 12.95 (ISBN 0-02-564500-5). Macmillan.

Knopf, Irwin J. Childhood Psychopathology: A Developmental Approach. (Illus.). 1979. text ed. 19.95 (ISBN 0-13-130336-8). P-H.

Knopf, Mel. The Batting Machine. 192p. 1981. 9.95 (ISBN 0-89962-205-4). Todd & Honeywell.

Knopp, Anthony, compiled by. Brazil Books. 20p. 1970. pap. 1.00 (ISBN 0-913456-76-4, Pub by Ctr Inter-Am Rel). Interbk Inc.

Knopp, Konrad. Elements of the Theory of Functions. Bagemihl, Frederick, tr. 1952. pap. text ed. 2.75 (ISBN 0-486-60154-4). Dover.

--Infinite Sequences & Series. Bagemihl, Frederick, tr. 1956. pap. text ed. 3.00 (ISBN 0-486-60153-6). Dover.

--Problem Book in the Theory of Functions, 2 vols. Incl. Vol. 1. Problems in the Elementary Theory of Functions. Bers, Lipman, tr (ISBN 0-486-60158-7); Vol. 2. Problems in the Advanced Theory of Functions (ISBN 0-486-60159-5). 1968. pap. text ed. 3.00 ea. Dover.

--Theory of Functions, 2 vols. (Illus.). Vol. 1. pap. 2.75 (ISBN 0-486-60156-0); Vol. 2. pap. text ed. 2.75 (ISBN 0-486-60157-9). Dover.

Knorr, Karin D. The Manufacture of Knowledge: An Essay on the Constructivist & Contextual Nature of Science. 200p. Date not set. 39.01 (ISBN 0-08-025777-1); pap. 19.21 (ISBN 0-08-025778-X). Pergamon.

Knorr, Karin D., et al, eds. The Social Process of Scientific Investigation. (Sociology of the Sciences Ser.: No. IV). 356p. 1980. lib. bdg. 34.50 (ISBN 90-277-1174-7, Pub. by D. Reidel); pap. 15.95 (ISBN 90-277-1175-5). Kluwer Boston.

Knorr, Susan. C. Jane. Lawrence, Joseph, ed. (Orig.). 1979. pap. 3.25 (ISBN 0-89144-103-4). Crescent Pubns.

Knorre, D. G., jt. auth. see Emanuel', N. M.

Knorre, Marty, et al. Puntas de Partida: An Invitation to Spanish. Incl. Arana, Alice & Arana, Oswaldo. 224p. wkbk. 6.95; Yates, Maria S. 196p. lab manual 6.95 (ISBN 0-394-32630-X). 608p. 1981. text ed. 17.95 (ISBN 0-394-32618-0). Random.

Knorring, L. von see Perris, C. & Von Knorring, L.

Knott, A. E., et al. Australian Schools & the Law. 2nd ed. (Educational Organization & Administration Ser.). 180p. (Orig.). 1981. pap. text ed. 10.25 (ISBN 0-7022-1549-X). U of Queensland Pr.

Knott, Bill. Selected & Collected Poems. LC 77-3473. 1977. 10.00 (ISBN 0-915342-17-0); pap. 4.00 (ISBN 0-915342-16-2). SUN.

Knott, J. Eugene, jt. auth. see Drum, David J.

Knott, J. F. Fundamentals of Fracture Mechanics. LC 73-15844. 1974. 35.95 o.p. (ISBN 0-470-49565-0). Halsted Pr.

Knott, Thomas A., jt. auth. see Kenyon, John S.

Knott, Will C. Kiowa Blood. 1980. pap. 1.75 o.p. (ISBN 0-425-04679-6). Berkley Pub.

Knotts, G. R. & McGovern, J. P. School Health Problems. (Illus.). 352p. 1976. 26.75 (ISBN 0-398-03220-3). C C Thomas.

Knotts, Howard. The Summer Cat. LC 79-9610. (Illus.). 48p. (gr. k-4). 1981. 7.95 (ISBN 0-06-023178-5, HarpJ); PLB 7.89g (ISBN 0-06-023179-3). Har-Row.

Knotts, Ulysses S. & Swift, Ernest W. Management Science for Management Decisions. 1978. text ed. 19.95 (ISBN 0-205-06039-0, 1060392); instr's man. avail. (ISBN 0-205-06040-4, 1060406); sol. man. avail. (ISBN 0-205-06041-2, 1060414). Allyn.

Knower, Barry, jt. auth. see Roberts, Jane.

Knowland, W. E., jt. ed. see Smil, V.

Knowledge Industry Publication Editors. The Professional Librarian's Reader in Library Automation & Technology. LC 80-11636. (Professional Librarian Ser.). (Illus.). 256p. 1980. text ed. 24.50 (ISBN 0-914236-59-8); pap. text ed. 17.50 (ISBN 0-914236-57-1). Knowledge Indus.

Knowles. More by Alison Knowles. pap. write for info. (ISBN 0-914162-41-1). Knowles.

--Natural Assemblages & the True Crow. pap. write for info. (ISBN 0-914162-47-0). Knowles.

Knowles, A. V., ed. Tolstoy: The Critical Heritage. 1978. 32.00x (ISBN 0-7100-8947-3). Routledge & Kegan.

Knowles, Anne. The Halcyon Island. LC 80-7909. 128p. (gr. 5 up). 1981. 8.95 (ISBN 0-06-023203-X, HarpJ); PLB 8.79g (ISBN 0-06-023204-8). Har-Row.

Knowles, Christopher J. Diversity of Bacterial Respiratory Systems, 2 vols. (Vol. 1-256pp., vol. 2-240pp.). 1980. 59.95 ea. Vol. 1 (ISBN 0-8493-5399-8). Vol. 2 (ISBN 0-8493-5400-5). CRC Pr.

Knowles, D., et al, eds. Heads of Religious Houses, England & Wales, 940-1216. LC 79-171676. 336p. 1972. 47.95 (ISBN 0-521-08367-2). Cambridge U Pr.

Knowles, David. Episcopal Colleagues of Archbishop Thomas Becket. 1971. Repr. 14.95 (ISBN 0-521-05493-1). Cambridge U Pr.

--Monastic Order in England. 2nd ed. 1963. 67.50 (ISBN 0-521-05479-6). Cambridge U Pr.

--Religious Orders in England. Incl. Vol. 1. The Old Orders. 1948. 47.50 (ISBN 0-521-05480-X); pap. 14.50 (ISBN 0-521-29566-1); Vol. 2. End of the Middle Ages. 1955. 53.50 (ISBN 0-521-05481-8); pap. 15.50 (ISBN 0-521-29567-X). Cambridge U Pr.

--The Religious Orders in England: The Tudor Age, Vol. 3. LC 78-73953. 1979. 59.50 (ISBN 0-521-05482-6); pap. 19.50 (ISBN 0-521-29568-8). Cambridge U Pr.

Knowles, David H. Consumer Math Series, 7 bks. 1972. pap. 9.00 ea. (ISBN 0-8449-0200-4). Learning Line.

Knowles, F., jt. ed. see Eckstein, P.

Knowles, Henry P. & Saxberg, Borje O. Personality & Leadership Behavior. LC 73-125609. (Business Ser). (Illus.). 1971. pap. text ed. 8.95 (ISBN 0-201-03781-5). A-W.

Knowles, John. Peace Breaks Out. LC 80-19678. 192p. 1981. 9.95 (ISBN 0-03-056908-7). HR&W.

--Separate Peace. (gr. 9 up). 1960. 11.95 (ISBN 0-02-564840-3); large print ed. 6.95 (ISBN 0-02-489390-0). Macmillan.

Knowles, John, jt. auth. see Atkins, Chet.

Knowles, John H., ed. Doing Better & Feeling Worse. 1977. 9.95 (ISBN 0-393-06419-0); pap. text ed. 5.95 (ISBN 0-393-06423-9). Norton.

Knowles, Louis & Prewitt, Kenneth, eds. Institutional Racism in America. 1969. pap. 3.95 o.p. (ISBN 0-13-467738-2). P-H.

Knowles, Malcolm S. The Modern Practice of Adult Education: Andragogy Versus Pedragogy. rev. ed. 400p. 1980. 17.95 (ISBN 0-695-81472-9, Assn Pr). Follett.

Knowles, Nathaniel. The Torture of Captives by the Indians of Eastern North America: In: Proceedings of the American Philosophical Society, Vol. 8I, No. 2, March 22, 1940, Repr. Of 1940 Ed. Bd. with Captivity of Jonathan Alder. Repr. of 1944 ed; Horrors of Captivity: Authentic & Thrilling Sketches of Tragedies That Occurred on the Texas Frontier During Indian Times. Hunter, John M. Repr. of 1954 ed; Indian John: Life of John W. Johnson. Repr. of 1861 ed. LC 75-7139. (Indian Captivities Ser.: Vol. 111). 1977. lib. bdg. 44.00 (ISBN 0-8240-1735-8). Garland Pub.

Knowles, Peter. Design of Structural Steelwork. (Illus.). 1977. 24.95x (ISBN 0-903384-16-7). Intl Ideas.

Knowles, R. North America in Maps: Topographical Map Studies of Canada and the USA. (Illus.). 1976. pap. text ed. 12.95x (ISBN 0-582-31017-2). Longman.

Knowles, Ruth S. America's Energy Famine: Its Cause & Cure. LC 80-8040. 337p. 1980. 14.95 (ISBN 0-8061-1669-2). U of Okla Pr.

--The Greatest Gamblers. Orig. Title: The Epic of American Oil Exploration. 376p. 1980. pap. 7.95 (ISBN 0-8061-1654-4). U of Okla Pr.

Knowles, Wendell. Sweet Skunks & Sneaky Butter. LC 79-92619. 3.95. Heritage Kansas.

Knowlson, James. Journal of Beckett, Nos. 3 & 4. 1978. pap. text ed. 8.00x (ISBN 0-685-59433-5). Vol. 3. Vol. 4. pap. text ed. 8.25x (ISBN 0-7145-3709-8). Humanities.

--Journal of Beckett Studies. 1975. pap. 5.00 (ISBN 0-7145-3669-5). Riverrun NY.

Knowlson, James & Pilling, John. Frescoes of the Skull: The Later Prose & Drama of Samuel Beckett. LC 79-6153. 320p. (Orig.). 1980. pap. 4.95 postponed (ISBN 0-394-17610-3, E735, Ever). Grove.

Knowlson, T. Sharper. The Origins of Popular Superstitutions & Customs. LC 80-329. 242p. 1980. Repr. of 1972 ed. lib. bdg. 9.95x (ISBN 0-89370-613-2). Borgo Pr.

Knowlson, Thomas S. Origins of Popular Superstitions & Customs. LC 68-30946. 1968. Repr. of 1910 ed. 18.00 (ISBN 0-8103-3357-0). Gale.

Knowlton, Derrick. The Naturalist in Central Southern England: Hampshire, Berkshire, Wiltshire, Dorset & Somerset. (Regional Naturalist Ser.). (Illus.). 13.95 o.p. (ISBN 0-7153-5876-6). David & Charles.

--The Naturalist in Scotland. LC 74-78250. 1975. 7.50 o.p. (ISBN 0-7153-6627-0). David & Charles.

--Naturalist in the Hebrides. 1977. 17.95 (ISBN 0-7153-7446-X). David & Charles.

Knowlton, Winthrop & Furth, John L. Shaking the Money Tree: New Growth Opportunities in Common Stocks. LC 76-156529. 192p. 1972. 7.50 o.s.i. (ISBN 0-06-012441-5, HarpT). Har-Row.

Knox. Power Cable Handbook. 1981. text ed. price not set. Butterworths.

Knox, tr. see Hegel, Friedrich.

Knox, Alan B., et al. Developing, Administering, & Evaluating Adult Education. LC 80-7998. (Higher Education Ser.). 1980. text ed. 15.95x (ISBN 0-87589-467-4). Jossey-Bass.

Knox, Albert. Cloth. (Easy-Read Fact Book Ser.). (Illus.). 48p. (gr. 2-4). 1976. PLB 4.47 o.p. (ISBN 0-531-00353-1). Watts.

Knox, Alexander. Glossary of Geographical & Topographical Terms. LC 68-30592. 1968. Repr. of 1904 ed. 15.00 (ISBN 0-8103-3236-1). Gale.

Knox, Bill. A Killing in Antiques. LC 80-2967. 192p. 1981. 9.95 (ISBN 0-385-17625-2). Doubleday.

Knox, Carol & Rowsey, Katheryn. Problems in Biology. (Illus.). 90p. (Orig.). (gr. 10-11). 1980. lab manual 2.95 (ISBN 0-88334-132-8). Ind Sch Pr.

Knox, D. Marriage: Who, When & Why? 1974. pap. 9.95 (ISBN 0-13-559336-0). P-H.

Knox, D. E. The Making of a New Eastern Question: British Palestine Policy & the Origins of Israel, 1917-1925. 1981. 17.95 (ISBN 0-8132-0555-7). Cath U Pr.

Knox, D. M. The Neolithic Revolution. Yapp, Malcolm, et al, eds. (World History Ser.). (Illus.). 32p. (gr. 10). 1980. lib. bdg. 5.95 (ISBN 0-89908-130-4); pap. text ed. 1.95 (ISBN 0-89908-105-3). Greenhaven.

Knox, David. Exploring Marriage & the Family. 1979. text ed. 16.95x (ISBN 0-673-15046-1). Scott F.

Knox, Diana. The Industrial Revolution. Yapp, Malcolm, et al, eds. (World History Ser.). (Illus.). (gr. 10). pap. text ed. 1.95 (ISBN 0-89908-133-9); pap. text ed. 2.75 (ISBN 0-89908-108-8). Greenhaven.

Knox, Edward. Jean de la Bruyere. (World Authors Ser.: France: No. 298). 1973. lib. bdg. 10.95 (ISBN 0-8057-2507-5). Twayne.

Knox, Edward C. & Rifelj, Carol D. C'Est-a-Dire. 352p. 1980. pap. text ed. write for info. (HC). HarBraceJ.

Knox, F. Governments & Growth. 1976. 18.95 (ISBN 0-347-01153-5, 00787-0, Pub. by Saxon Hse). Lexington Bks.

Knox, Francis. Labour Supply in Economic Development. 1979. text ed. 20.50x (ISBN 0-566-00238-8, Pub. by Gower Pub Co England). Renouf.

Knox, Frank M. Managing Paperwork: The Key to Productivity. LC 80-19685. 1980. 16.95 (ISBN 0-444-00452-1, Thomond Pr). Elsevier.

Knox, George. Giambattista & Domenico Tiepolo: A Study & Catalogue Raisonne of the Chalk Drawings. (Illus.). 632p. 1980. 180.00 (ISBN 0-19-817313-X). Oxford U Pr.

Knox, George L. Slave & Freeman: The Autobiography of George L. Knox. Gatewood, Willard B., Jr., ed. LC 78-21058. 256p. 1979. 17.00x (ISBN 0-8131-1384-9). U Pr of Ky.

Knox, Israel. Aesthetic Theories of Kant, Hegel & Schopenhauer. 1978. Repr. of 1936 ed. text ed. 12.50x (ISBN 0-391-00929-X). Humanities.

Knox, John. Humanity & Divinity of Christ. (Orig.). 18.95 (ISBN 0-521-05486-9); pap. 5.50x (ISBN 0-521-09414-3). Cambridge U Pr.

Knox, John H. High Performance Liquid Chromatography. 205p. 1981. pap. 17.00x (ISBN 0-85224-383-9, Pub. by Edinburgh U Pr Scotland). Columbia U Pr.

Knox, Katherine M. The Sharples. LC 70-87456. (Library of American Art Ser.). 133p. 1972. Repr. of 1930 ed. lib. bdg. 35.00 (ISBN 0-306-71529-5). Da Capo.

Knox, Margaret. Betsey's Bbee Ree. (Illus.). 32p. (gr. k-4). 1980. 7.95 (ISBN 0-88319-055-9). Shoal Creek Pub.

Knox, Marlys, jt. auth. see Lande, Rivian.

Knox, Norman D. The Word Irony & Its Context: 1500-1755. LC 60-13606. 1961. 14.75 o.p. (ISBN 0-8223-0100-8). Duke.

Knox, Peter, ed. The Cell Surface, Vol. IV. (Biochemistry of Cellular Regulation). 304p. 1981. 69.95 (ISBN 0-8493-5457-9). CRC Pr.

Knox, R. Foundations of Astronomy: From Big Bang to Black Holes. LC 79-13. 1979. 12.95 (ISBN 0-470-26638-4). Halsted Pr.

Knox, Robert S. Theory of Excitons. (Solid State Physics: Advances in Research & Applications Suppl. 5). 1964. 31.50 (ISBN 0-12-607765-7). Acad Pr.

Knox, T. M., ed. see Collingwood, Robin G.

Knox, T. M., tr. see Hegel, G. W.

Knox, Thomas W. Camp-Fire & Cotton-Field. LC 75-84186. (American Scene Ser.). 1969. Repr. of 1865 ed. lib. bdg. 49.50 (ISBN 0-306-71782-4). Da Capo.

Knox, Vera H., ed. Public Finance Information Sources. LC 64-16503. (Management Information Guide Ser.: No. 3). 1964. 30.00 (ISBN 0-8103-0803-7). Gale.

Knox-Johnston, Robin. Sailing. (International Library). (Illus.). 128p. (gr. 7 up). 1976. PLB 6.90 o.p. (ISBN 0-531-02125-4). Watts.

Knox-Mawer, June. Gift of Islands: Living in Figi. 8.75 (ISBN 0-7195-0780-4). Transatlantic.

Knox-Wagner, Elaine. The Oldest Kid. Tucker, Kathleen, ed. (Concept Bks.). (Illus.). 32p. (gr. k-3). 1981. 6.50 (ISBN 0-8075-5986-5). A Whitman.

Knox-Wagner, Elaine, jt. auth. see Delton, Judy.

Knuchell. How to Win at Pocket Billiards. pap. 4.00 (ISBN 0-87980-069-0). Wilshire.

Knudsen, Carol J., tr. see Stang, N. C.

Knudsen, Charles W. Evaluation & Improvement of Teaching (in Secondary Schools) 538p. 1980. Repr. of 1932 ed. lib. bdg. 30.00 (ISBN 0-89984-302-6). Century Bookbindery.

Knudsen Corporation. Cooking for Compliments. LC 77-88223. (Illus.). 1977. pap. 5.95 (ISBN 0-912656-91-3). H P Bks.

Knudsen, Estelle H. & Christensen. Children's Art Education. (YA) (gr. 9 up). 1971. 11.52 (ISBN 0-87002-060-9). Bennett IL.

Knudsen, Franklin. I Was Quisling's Secretary. 192p. 1967. 6.00 (351, Pub. by Britons England). Inst Hist Rev.

--I Was Quisling's Secretary. 192p. 1967. 6.00 (ISBN 0-911038-96-5, 351, Inst Hist Rev). Noontide.

Knudsen, Harald. Expropriation of Foreign Investments in Latin America. 356p. 1975. pap. 19.50x (ISBN 8-200-01385-5, Dist. by Columbia U Pr). Universitet.

Knudsen, James G., jt. ed. see Somerscales, Euan F.

Knudsen, Johannes, ed. N. F. S. Grundtvig: Selected Writings. LC 76-7873. 192p. 1976. pap. 5.95 (ISBN 0-8006-1238-8, 1-1238). Fortress.

Knudson, Mary, jt. auth. see Solomon, Neil.

Knudson, R. R. Jesus Song. LC 73-1067. (Illus.). 160p. (gr. 5-9). 1973. 5.95 o.s.i. (ISBN 0-440-04215-1). Delacorte.

--Rinehart Lifts. LC 80-66825. 192p. (gr. 4 up). 1980. 8.95 (ISBN 0-374-36294-7). FS&G.
--You Are the Rain. LC 73-15397. 160p. (gr. 7 up). 1974. 5.95 o.p. (ISBN 0-440-08759-7). Delacorte.
--Zanboomer. (gr. 7-12). 1980. pap. 1.50 (ISBN 0-440-99908-1, LFL). Dell.
Knudson, Richard L. Fabulous Cars of the 1920s & 1930s. LC 80-343. (Superwheels & Thrill Sports Bks.). (Illus.). (gr. 4 up). 1981. PLB 6.95 (ISBN 0-8225-0504-5). Lerner Pubns.
--Land Speed Recordbreakers. LC 80-12385. (Superwheels & Thrill Sports Bks.). (Illus.). (YA) (gr. 4 up). 1981. PLB 6.95g (ISBN 0-8225-0438-3). Lerner Pubns.
--Model Cars. LC 80-17153. (Superwheels & Thrill Sports Bks.). (Illus.). (YA) (gr. 4 up). 1981. PLB 6.95g (ISBN 0-685-96939-8). Lerner Pubns.
--Rallying. LC 80-17863. (Superwheels & Thrill Sports Bks.). (Illus.). 48p. (gr. 4 up). 1981. PLB 6.95g (ISBN 0-686-63304-0). Lerner Pubns.
Knudten, Richard D., jt. ed. see Schafer, Stephen.
Knust, H. Texte und Ubungen: Intermediate Readings & Exercises. 1977. pap. 9.50 (ISBN 0-13-903526-5). P-H.
Knuth, A. M. The Wink of the Word: A Study of James Joyce's Phatic Communication. 1976. pap. text ed. 17.25x (ISBN 0-391-02068-4). Humanities.
Knuth, Donald E. Art of Computer Programming: Semi-Numerical Algorithms, Vol. 2. 2nd ed. 1981. text ed. 25.95 (ISBN 0-201-03822-6). A-W. Postponed.
--Art of Computer Programming, Vol. 1: Fundamental Algorithms. 2nd ed. LC 73-1830. 640p. 1974. 25.95 (ISBN 0-201-03809-9). A-W.
--The Art of Computer Programming, Vol. 3: Sorting & Searching. 1973. 25.995 (ISBN 0-201-03803-X). A-W.
--Surreal Numbers. LC 74-5998. 1974. pap. text ed. 5.95 (ISBN 0-201-03812-9). A-W.
Knuth, Larry, jt. auth. see Bullard, Ernie.
Knutson, jt. auth. see Kowitz.
Knutson, Andie L. The Individual, Society, & Health Behavior. 533p. (Orig.). 1982. pap. 6.95 (ISBN 0-87855-685-0). Transaction Bks. Postponed.
Knutzleman, Charles T. & Cryderman, Lynx. They Accepted the Challenge. (Illus.). 304p. 1981. 11.95 (ISBN 0-312-79971-3). St Martin.
Ko, Won. The Turn of Zero. (Poetry Ser.). (Illus.). 1974. o. p. 10.00x (ISBN 0-89304-021-5, CCC103); signed ltd. ed. 15.00x (ISBN 0-89304-048-7); pap. 4.50x (ISBN 0-89304-003-7); pap. 4.00x signed ltd. ed. o.p. (ISBN 0-89304-049-5). Cross Cult.
Kobal, John. Film-Star Portraits of the Fifties: 163 Glamor Photos. (Illus.). 164p. (Orig.). 1980. pap. 6.95 (ISBN 0-486-24008-8). Dover.
Kobayashi, Akira. Machining of Plastics. LC 79-20877. 270p. 1980. Repr. of 1967 ed. lib. bdg. 24.50 (ISBN 0-89874-007-X). Krieger.
Kobayashi, Hisashi. Modeling & Analysis: An Introduction to System Performance Evaluation Methodology. LC 77-73946. (IBM Ser.). (Illus.). 1978. text ed. 20.95 (ISBN 0-201-14457-3). A-W.
Kobayashi, Keizo. Shojin Cooking: The Buddhist Vegeterian Cook Book. Ooka, D., tr. from Japanese. (Illus.). 1977. 7.95 o.p. (ISBN 0-89346-013-3). Heian Intl.
Kobayashi, M. Azasulfones: Versatile Precursors for Aryl Free Radicals & Aryl Cations. (Sulfur Reports Ser.). 28p. flexicover 7.50 (ISBN 3-7186-0040-4). Harwood Academic.
Kobayashi, N., jt. auth. see Adams, T. F. M.
Kobayashi, T., et al. Geology & Palaeontology of Southeast Asia, Vol. XXI. 381p. 1980. 52.00x (ISBN 0-86008-263-6, Pub. by U of Tokyo Pr Japan). Intl Schol Bk Serv.
Kobayashi, Tetzuya. Society, Schools & Progress in Japan. 222p. 1976. text ed. 23.00 (ISBN 0-08-019936-4); pap. text ed. 12.25 (ISBN 0-08-019935-6). Pergamon.
Kobernick, Sidney D., tr. see Masson, Pierre.
Kobert, Norman. Managing Time. LC 80-13891. 140p. 1980. flexible cover 50.00 (ISBN 0-932648-11-8). Boardroom.
Koblas, John J. F. Scott Fitzgerald in Minnesota: His Homes & Haunts. LC 78-21979. (No. 18). 1978. pap. 3.75 (ISBN 0-87351-134-4). Minn Hist.
Kobler, Jay, jt. auth. see Isaacs, Benno.
Kobler, John. Capone. 416p. 1977. pap. 1.95 o.p. (ISBN 0-449-22824-X, C2824, Crest). Fawcett.
Koblitz, N. P-Adic Analysis. (London Mathematical Society Lecture Note Ser.: No. 46). 150p. 1980. pap. 14.95 (ISBN 0-521-28060-5). Cambridge U Pr.
Kobrak, Peter. Private Assumption of Public Responsibilities: The Role of American Business in Urban Manpower Programs. LC 72-83571. (Special Studies in U.S. Economic, Social & Political Issues). 1973. 29.50x (ISBN 0-275-07030-1). Irvington.
Kobre, Ken. Photojournalism: The Professionals' Approach. (Illus.). 368p. (Orig.). 1980. 24.95 (ISBN 0-930764-16-1); pap. text ed. 15.95 (ISBN 0-930764-15-3). Curtin & London.
Kobre, Sidney. Backgrounding the News: The Newspaper & the Social Sciences. LC 70-137063. (Illus.). 271p. 1974. Repr. of 1939 ed. lib. bdg. 23.00x (ISBN 0-8371-5526-6, KOBN). Greenwood.
Kobrin, Janet, jt. auth. see Bernstein, Margery.
Kobrin, Leon. A Lithuanian Village. Goldberg, Isaac, tr. from Yiddish. LC 79-53454. (Short Story Index in Reprint Ser.). Date not set. Repr. of 1920 ed. 18.75x (ISBN 0-8486-5007-7). Core Collection. Postponed.
Kobryn, A. P. Poseidon's Shadow. 1980. pap. 2.75 (ISBN 0-440-16899-6). Dell.
Kobs, Betty & Kobs, Douglas. Magic: An Introduction. LC 75-42496. (Games & Activities Ser.). (Illus.). (gr. k-3). 1976. PLB 9.30 (ISBN 0-8172-0058-4). Raintree Pubs.
--Magic, Magic. LC 76-53540. (Games & Activities Ser.). (Illus.). (gr. k-5). 1977. PLB 9.30 (ISBN 0-8172-0070-3). Raintree Pubs.
Kobs, Douglas, jt. auth. see Kobs, Betty.
Kocaoglu, Dundar F., jt. auth. see Cleland, David I.
Koch, A., jt. ed. see Bettex, M.
Koch, Adrienne. Jefferson & Madison: The Great Collaboration. 1964. pap. 8.95 (ISBN 0-19-500420-5, GB). Oxford U Pr.
--The Philosophy of Thomas Jefferson. 8.00 (ISBN 0-8446-1270-7). Peter Smith.
Koch, Adrienne, ed. The American Enlightment: The Shaping of the American Experiment & a Free Society. LC 64-21765. (American Epochs Ser.). 1965. 10.00 o.s.i. (ISBN 0-8076-0278-7); pap. 4.95 o.s.i. (ISBN 0-8076-0393-7). Braziller.
Koch, Anna P. Let's Read Hebrew. rev. ed. 1974. pap. 2.95x (ISBN 0-8197-0029-0). Bloch.
Koch, Charlotte. Susan B. Anthony. LC 78-73539. (Illus.). (gr. 2-5). Date not set. price not set (ISBN 0-89799-162-1); pap. price not set (ISBN 0-89799-080-3). Dandelion Pr. Postponed.
Koch, Don. The Colorado Pass Book: A Guide to Colorado's Back Road Mountain Passes. (Illus.). 120p. (Orig.). 1980. 14.95 (ISBN 0-87108-566-6). Pruett.
Koch, Donald. Chilton's Complete Guide to Motorcycles & Motorcycling. LC 74-17365. (Illus.). 240p. 1974. pap. 5.95 o.p. (ISBN 0-8019-6089-4). Chilton.
Koch, E. E., et al, eds. Vacuum Ultraviolet Radiation Physics: Proceedings of the 4th International Conference. 848p. 1976. text ed. 125.00 (ISBN 0-08-018942-3). Pergamon.
Koch, Gebhard & Richter, Dietmar. Biosynthesis, Modification & Processing of Cellular & Viral Polyproteins. 1980. 29.00 (ISBN 0-12-417560-0). Acad Pr.
Koch, George S., Jr. & Link, Richard F. Statistical Analysis of Geological Data. 850p. 1981. pap. 12.50 (ISBN 0-486-64040-X). Dover.
Koch, H. Gilbert, jt. auth. see Strong, F. M.
Koch, H. W. A History of Prussia. (Illus.). 1978. text ed. 25.00x (ISBN 0-582-48189-9); pap. text ed. 12.50x (ISBN 0-582-48190-2). Longman.
Koch, Hal. Pronoia und Paideusis: Studien Uber Origenes und Sein Verhaltnis Zum Platonismus. LC 78-66597. (Ancient Philosophy Ser.). 347p. 1980. lib. bdg. 34.00 (ISBN 0-8240-9592-8). Garland Pub.
Koch, Harvey. Fastest Way to Get Rich: Trading in Financial Futures. LC 80-6155. 224p. 1981. 12.95 (ISBN 0-8128-2782-1). Stein & Day.
Koch, Howard. Koch: As Time Goes by, Memoirs of a Writer. LC 78-22260. 1979. 10.95 (ISBN 0-15-109769-0). HarBraceJ.
Koch, Hugo, jt. auth. see Sirrocco, Al.
Koch, James H. Profits from Country Property: How to Select, Buy, Improve & Maintain Your Country Property. (Illus.). 320p. 1980. 12.95 (ISBN 0-07-035248-8, P&RB). McGraw.
Koch, James V. Industrial Organization & Prices. 2nd ed. (Illus.). 1980. text ed. 17.95 (ISBN 0-13-462481-5). P-H.
Koch, James V., jt. auth. see Ostrosky, Anthony L., Jr.
Koch, Karen. A Special Look. 1973. pap. 1.00x (ISBN 0-88323-115-8, 220). Richards Pub.
Koch, Kenneth. The Burning Mystery of Ana in Nineteen Fifty-One. LC 78-21608. 1979. 8.95 (ISBN 0-394-50473-9). Random.
--The Duplications. 1977. 6.95 o.p. (ISBN 0-394-40614-1); pap. 3.95 (ISBN 0-394-73368-1). Random.
Koch, Kenneth, tr. see Roussel, Raymond.
Koch, Klaus. Growth of the Biblical Tradition. 1968. lib. rep. ed. 17.50x (ISBN 0-684-14524-3, ScribT). Scribner.
Koch, Kurt E. Charismatic Gifts. 1975. pap. 2.95 (ISBN 0-8254-3023-2). Kregel.
--Christian Counseling & Occultism. LC 65-23118. 1972. pap. 5.95 (ISBN 0-8254-3010-0). Kregel.
--The Coming One. LC 72-85597. 1972. pap. 2.50 (ISBN 0-8254-3011-9). Kregel.
--Day X. LC 70-160688. 1969. pap. 2.50 (ISBN 0-8254-3005-4). Kregel.
--Demonology, Past & Present. LC 72-93353. 1973. pap. 2.95 (ISBN 0-8254-3013-5). Kregel.
--Devil's Alphabet. LC 76-160692. 1972. pap. 2.95 (ISBN 0-8254-3004-6). Kregel.
--Occult ABC. 1980. 7.95 (ISBN 0-8254-3031-3). Kregel.
--Satan's Devices. LC 78-5066. 1978. pap. 7.95 o.p. (ISBN 0-8254-3024-0). Kregel.
--Wine of God. LC 74-81561. 1974. pap. 2.95 (ISBN 0-8254-3017-8). Kregel.
Koch, Polly, ed. see Alsup, Fisher.
Koch, Rudolf. The Book of Signs. (Illus.). 8.50 (ISBN 0-8446-0744-4). Peter Smith.
--Little ABC Book of Rudolf Koch. LC 76-14224. (Illus.). 1980. pap. 6.95 (ISBN 0-87923-295-1). Godine.
Koch, S., jt. auth. see Wentink, S.
Koch, Stephen. Night Watch. 1979. 10.95 (ISBN 0-7145-0411-4, Pub. by M Boyars). Merrimack Bk Serv.
--Night Watch. 212p. 1981. pap. 6.95 (ISBN 0-7145-2736-X, Pub. by M. Boyars). Merrimack Bk Serv.
Koch, Stuart G. Water Resources Planning in New England. LC 79-66453. (Illus.). 200p. 1980. 12.00x (ISBN 0-87451-176-3). U Pr of New Eng.
Koch, Tom & Clarke, Bob. The Mad Worry Book. (Mad Ser.). (Illus.). 1980. pap. 1.75 (ISBN 0-446-94448-3). Warner Bks.
Koch, Walter A. & Schaeck, Elisabeth. Birthplace Tables of Houses. LC 75-22416. 1975. 12.00 (ISBN 0-88231-020-8); pap. text ed. 8.95 (ISBN 0-88231-021-6). ASI Pubs Inc.
Kochan, Lionel, jt. ed. see Kochan, Miriam.
Kochan, Miriam. Prisoners of England. 288p. 1980. text ed. 37.50x (ISBN 0-391-01738-1). Humanities.
Kochan, Miriam & Kochan, Lionel, eds. Russian Themes. LC 67-106641. (Selections from History Today Ser.: No. 3). (Illus.). 1967. 5.00 (ISBN 0-685-09196-1); pap. 3.95 (ISBN 0-685-09197-X). Dufour.
Kochan, Miriam L. The Last Days of Imperial Russia: 1910-1917. 1976. 5.98 o.s.i. (ISBN 0-02-564900-0). Macmillan.
Kochan, Stephen, jt. auth. see Mullish, Henry.
Kochan, Thomas A. Collective Bargaining & Industrial Relations. 1980. 19.95x (ISBN 0-256-02353-0). Irwin.
Kochan, Thomas A., et al. The Effectiveness of Union-Management Safety & Health Committees. LC 77-22038. 1977. pap. 2.75 (ISBN 0-911558-02-0). Upjohn Inst.
Kochanek, Stanley A. Business & Politics in India. 1974. 23.75x o.p. (ISBN 0-520-02377-3). U of Cal Pr.
Kochar, Mahendra S. & Daniels, Linda M. Hypertension Control: A Manual for Nurses & Other Allied Health Professionals. LC 78-3750. 1978. pap. text ed. 11.95 (ISBN 0-8016-2717-6). Mosby.
Kochen, Manfred. Principles of Information Retrieval. LC 74-1204. (Information Sciences Ser). 256p. 1974. 23.95 (ISBN 0-471-49697-9, Pub. by Wiley-Interscience). Wiley.
Kochen, Manfred, ed. Information for Action: From Knowledge to Wisdom. (Library & Information Science Ser.). 256p. 1975. 20.00 o.s.i. (ISBN 0-12-417950-9). Acad Pr.
Kochenberger, Gary A., jt. auth. see Plane, Donald R.
Kocherga, O. D., tr. see Sitenko, A. G.
Kochetkov, N. K., et al, eds. Radiation Chemistry of Carbohydrates. (Illus.). 1979. 50.00 (ISBN 0-08-022962-X). Pergamon.
Kochetkova, Natalya. Nikolay Karamazin. (World Authors Ser.: Russia: No. 250). 1974. lib. bdg. 12.50 (ISBN 0-8057-2488-5). Twayne.
Kochhar, A. K. Development of Computer-Based Production Systems. LC 79-902. 274p. 1979. 38.95 (ISBN 0-470-26693-7). Halsted Pr.
Kochi, Jay K., ed. Free Radicals, 2 vols. LC 72-6105. (Reactive Intermediates in Organic Chemistry Ser). 713p. 1973. Vol. 1. 68.95 (ISBN 0-471-49701-0); Vol. 2. 75.00 (ISBN 0-471-49702-9, Pub by Wiley-Interscience). Wiley.
Kochis, Jon. Chrystal Beauty & Other Poems. 1981. 5.75 (ISBN 0-8062-1688-3). Carlton.
Kochiss, John M. Oystering from New York to Boston. LC 74-5965. (The American Maritime Library: Vol. 7). (Illus.). 264p. 1974. 14.95 (ISBN 0-8195-4074-9); ltd. edition 30.00 (ISBN 0-8195-4075-7). Mystic Seaport.
Kochman, Stanley O. The Symplectic Cobordism Ring. LC 79-27872. 1980. 9.60 (ISBN 0-8218-2228-4). Am Math.
Kochmann, K., ed. Index on Trademarks of German-Austrian-Swiss-French Industrialized Clockmakers. 240p. 1980. softcover 10.50 (ISBN 0-686-12238-0). Antique Clocks.
Koci, Marta. Blackie & Marie. Crawford, Elizabeth D., tr. from Ger. (Junior Bks.). Orig. Title: Schwarzack. (Illus.). 32p. (gr. k-3). 1980. 8.95 (ISBN 0-688-00217-X); PLB 8.59 (ISBN 0-688-00236-6). Morrow.
--Ivan, Divan, & Zariman. LC 76-25196. (Illus.). (gr. k-3). 1977. 5.95 o.s.i. (ISBN 0-8193-0893-5, Four Winds); PLB 5.41 o.s.i. (ISBN 0-8193-0894-3). Schol Bk Serv.
Kock, Eric, jt. auth. see Fischer, Hans C.
Kock, M. A. de see De Kock, M. A.
Kock, Winston E. Lasers & Holography: An Introduction to Coherent Optics. 2nd, rev. ed. (Illus.). 128p. 1981. pap. price not set (ISBN 0-486-24041-X). Dover.
Kock, Winston E., ed. The Creative Engineer: The Art of Inventing. new ed. (Illus.). 399p. 1978. 25.00 (ISBN 0-306-30987-4, Plenum Pr). Plenum Pub.
Kocka, Jurgen. White Collar Workers in America Eighteen Ninety to Nineteen Forty: A Social-Political History in International Perspective. LC 80-40572. (Sage Studies in 20th Century History: Vol. 10). (Illus.). 1980. 25.00x (ISBN 0-8039-9844-9); pap. 12.50x (ISBN 0-8039-9845-7). Sage.
Kockarts, G., jt. auth. see Banks, P. M.
Kockelmans, Joseph J., ed. Philosophy of Science: The Historical Background. LC 68-14108. 1968. pap. text ed. 6.95 o.s.i. (ISBN 0-02-917530-5). Free Pr.
Kocsis, James J., et al, eds. The Effects of Taurine on Excitable Tissue. 1980. write for info. (ISBN 0-89335-125-3). Spectrum Pub.
Kocsis, Miklos. High Speed Silicon Planar-Epitaxial Switching Diodes. LC 75-19391. 1976. 34.95 (ISBN 0-470-49707-6). Halsted Pr.
Kodama, Goji, jt. auth. see Parry, Robert W.
Kodet, Ambrose S., jt. auth. see Stelter, Gayle A.
Kodjak, Andrej. Alexander Solzhenitsyn. (Twayne's World Author Ser.: No. 479). 1978. lib. bdg. 9.95 (ISBN 0-8057-6320-1). Twayne.
Kodjak, Andrej, et al, eds. The Structural Analysis of Narrative Texts, Conference Papers. (New York University Slavic Papers: Vol. II). (Illus.). 203p. (Orig.). 1980. pap. 10.95 (ISBN 0-89357-071-0). Slavica.
--Alexander Pushkin Symposium II. (New York University Slavic Papers Ser.: Vol. III). (Illus.). 131p. (Orig.). 1980. pap. 8.95 (ISBN 0-89357-067-2). Slavica.
Kodyen, Charlott M. Here, There & Everywhere. 1981. 4.95 (ISBN 0-8062-1571-2). Carlton.
Koebner, Hans K. Lasers in Medicine, Vol. 1. LC 79-40525. 1980. 64.75 (ISBN 0-471-27602-2, Pub. by Wiley-Interscience). Wiley.
Koechlin-Schwartz, Dorothee, jt. auth. see LeComte, Jacques.
Koefoed, H., jt. auth. see Norlev, E.
Koegler, Horst, jt. auth. see Spatt, Leslie.
Koehler, Edward W. A. Summary of Christian Doctrine. 1971. 11.95 (ISBN 0-570-03216-4, 15-2117). Concordia.
Koehler, J. The Epistle of Paul to the Galatians. Sauer, E. E., tr. 1957. 2.95 (ISBN 0-8100-0038-5). Northwest Pub.
Koehler, Jerry. The Corporation Game. LC 75-14061. 224p. 1975. 8.95 o.s.i. (ISBN 0-02-564950-7). Macmillan.
Koehler, Jerry W. & Sisco, John I. Public Communication in Business & the Professions. 300p. 1981. text ed. 11.36 (ISBN 0-8299-0417-4). West Pub.
Koehler, Lyle. A Search for Power: The Weaker Sex in Seventeenth Century New England. LC 80-16666. 570p. 1980. 25.00 (ISBN 0-252-00808-1). U of Ill Pr.
Koehler, Robert E., jt. ed. see Class, Robert A.
Koehler, S. R. American Etchings. Bd. with American Art. LC 75-28876. (Art Experience in Late 19th Century America Ser.: Vol. 12). (Illus.). 1976. Repr. of 1886 ed. lib. bdg. 72.50 (ISBN 0-8240-2236-X). Garland Pub.
--The United States Art Directory & Year-Book. Weinberg, H. Barbara, ed. Incl. Vol. 1. A Guide for Artists, Art Students, Travellers, Etc; Vol. 2. A Chronicle of Events in the Art World, & a Guide for All Interested in the Progress of Art in America. LC 75-28874. (Art Experience in Late 19th Century America Ser.: Vol. 10). (Illus.). 1976. Repr. of 1884 ed. lib. bdg. 72.50 (ISBN 0-8240-2234-3). Garland Pub.
Koehler, Vera J., jt. auth. see Weaver, Mabel E.
Koehmstedt, Carol L. Plot Summary Index. LC 72-13726. 1973. 11.50 (ISBN 0-8108-0584-7). Scarecrow.
Koehn, Ilse. Mischling, Second Degree: My Childhood in Nazi Germany. LC 77-6189. (gr. 7 up). 1977. 8.95 (ISBN 0-688-80110-2); PLB 8.59 (ISBN 0-688-84110-4). Greenwillow.
Koehn, Michael F. Bankruptcy Risk in Financial Depository Intermediaries: Assessing Regulatory Effects. LC 79-2411. (Arthur D. Little Bk.). (Illus.). 176p. 1979. 20.95- (ISBN 0-669-03169-0). Lexington Bks.

Koehn, Peter & Waldron, Sidney R. Afocha: A Link Between Community & Administration in Harar Ethiopia. LC 78-27903. (Foreign & Comparative Studies-African Ser.: No. XXXI). (Illus.). 120p. 1979. pap. 7.00x (ISBN 0-915984-53-9). Syracuse U Foreign Comp.

Koelbel, Fritz, jt. auth. see Philbin, Tom.

Koella, W. P., ed. see Fifth European Congress on Sleep Research, Amsterdam, September 1980.

Koelle, Sigismund W. Polyglotta Africana. LC 65-82544. 1963. Repr. of 1854 ed. 42.50x (ISBN 3-201-00766-8). Intl Pubns Serv.

Koelsch, William A., jt. ed. see Rosenkrantz, Barbara G.

Koen, Ross Y. China Lobby in American Politics. 1974. pap. 4.95x o.p. (ISBN 0-06-138885-8, HR1833, Torch). Har-Row.

Koenig. Illnesses of Our Time. 1980. pap. 3.25x (ISBN 0-906492-36-X, Pub. by Kolisko Archives). St George Bk Serv.

Koenig, Alfred E., et al, eds. Philosophy of the Humanistic Society. LC 80-1425. 290p. (Orig.). 1981. lib. bdg. 22.50 (ISBN 0-8191-1414-6); pap. text ed. 11.75 (ISBN 0-8191-1415-4). U Pr of Amer.

Koenig, Allen E., ed. Broadcasting & Bargaining: Labor Relations in Radio & Television. 1970. 25.00 (ISBN 0-299-05521-3). U of Wis Pr.

Koenig, Denes. Endlichen und Unendlichen Graphen. LC 51-3002. (Ger). 12.95 (ISBN 0-8284-0072-5). Chelsea Pub.

Koenig, E. G. Magnetic Properties of Coordination & Organometallic Transition Metal Compounds: Supplement Three, (1971, 1972) (Landolt-Boernstein-Numerical Data & Functional Relationships in Science & Technology: Group II, Vol. 11 (Supplement to Vol. 2)). (Illus.). 800p. 1980. 702.10 (ISBN 0-387-09908-5). Springer-Verlag.

Koenig, Gloria K. Patent Invalidity: A Statistical & Substantive Analysis. LC 73-89532. 1974. looseleaf with 1980 rev. pages 60.00 (ISBN 0-87632-127-9). Boardman.

Koenig, Jack L. Chemical Microstructure of Polymer Chains. LC 80-15165. 450p. 1980. 42.50 (ISBN 0-471-07725-9, Pub. by Wiley Interscience). Wiley.

Koenig, John. The Boy Who Was Afraid of the Dark. (Illus.). (ps-3). 0.35 o.s.i. (ISBN 0-8198-0208-5). Dghtrs St Paul.

Koenig, Karl. Brothers & Sisters. 1980. pap. 6.95 (ISBN 0-903540-38-X, Pub. by Floris Books). St George Bk Serv.

Koenig, Karl R. Virginia & Truckee Locomotives. LC 80-67819. (Illus.). 88p. 1980. pap. 14.00 (ISBN 0-89685-102-8). Chatham Pub CA.

Koenig, Marion & Speirs, Gill. Making Rugs for Pleasure & Profit. LC 80-17110. (Illus.). 80p. 1980. 10.95 (ISBN 0-668-05079-9, 5079-9). Arco.

Koenig, Michael, ed. Budgeting Techniques for Libraries & Information Centers. (Professional Development Ser.: No. 1). 1980. pap. write for info. (ISBN 0-87111-278-7). SLA.

Koenig, Norma E. The Runaway Heart. (Orig.). (gr. 4-6). 1981. pap. 4.95 (ISBN 0-377-00112-0). Friend Pr.

Koenig, Rush, tr. see Karkoschka, Erhard.

Koenig, Samuel. Sociology: An Introduction to the Science of Society. (Orig.). 1957. pap. 3.95 (ISBN 0-06-463268-7, EH 268, EH). Har-Row.

Koenigsbergen, T., jt. auth. see Tobias, S. A.

Koenigsberger, Dorothy. Renaissance Man & Creative Thinking: A History of Concepts of Harmony 1400-1700. LC 78-956. 1979. text ed. 27.50x (ISBN 0-391-00851-X). Humanities.

Koenigsberger, F. & Tlusty, J. Machine Tool Structures, Vol. 1. LC 79-84073. 1970. 94.00 (ISBN 0-08-013405-X). Pergamon.

Koenigsberger, F., ed. see Machine Tool Design & Research International Conference, 12th.

Koenigsberger, F., ed. see Machine Tool Design & Research International Conference 15th.

Koenigsberger, F., jt. ed. see Tobias, S. A.

Koenigsberger, H. G. Estates & Revolutions: Essays in Early Modern European History. LC 71-132141. (Illus.). 1971. 18.50x o.p. (ISBN 0-8014-0605-6). Cornell U Pr.

Koenigsberger, H. G. & Mosse, George L. Europe in the Sixteenth Century. (General History of Europe Ser.). (Illus.). 1971. pap. text ed. 9.95x (ISBN 0-582-48345-X). Longman.

Koenigsberger, O. H., jt. ed. see Groak, S.

Koenigsberger, O. H., et al. Manual of Tropical Housing & Building Design: Climatic Design, Pt. 1. (Illus.). 344p. 1974. pap. text ed. 14.95x (ISBN 0-582-44546-9). Longman.

Koenigsberger, O. H., et al, eds. Work of Charles Abrams: Housing & Urban Renewal in the U. S. A. & the Third World. (Illus.). 264p. 1980. 55.00 (ISBN 0-08-026111-6). Pergamon.

Koenigsberger, Otto, et al, eds. Land Policy. 200p. 1980. 50.00 (ISBN 0-08-026078-0). Pergamon.

Koenigsberger, T. & Tobias, S. A., eds. Proceedings of the Sixteenth Machine Tool Design & Research Conference. LC 76-5219. (International Machine Tool Design & Research Conference Ser.). 599p. 1976. text ed. 99.95 (ISBN 0-470-15100-5). Halsted Pr.

Koeninger, Jimmy & Hephner, Thomas. Jeffrey's Department Store: A Retailing Simulation-Employee's Guide. (Illus.). (gr. 11-12). 1978. pap. text ed. 6.96x (ISBN 0-07-035231-3, G); replacement forms 75.00x (ISBN 0-07-086511-6); general mgr's manual 6.95x (ISBN 0-07-035230-5); store box 150.00x (ISBN 0-07-086510-8). McGraw.

Koenker, Diane. Moscow Workers & the Nineteen Seventeen Revolution. LC 80-8557. (Studies of the Russian Institute, Columbia University). (Illus.). 456p. 1981. 30.00x (ISBN 0-691-05323-5). Princeton U Pr.

Koenner, Alfred. The Peacock's Wedding. (Illus.). 1978. 7.95 (ISBN 0-7011-5019-X, Pub. by Chatto Bodley Jonathan). Merrimack Bk Serv.

Koentjaraningrat, R. M. Introduction to the Peoples & Cultures of Indonesia & Malaysia. LC 75-4078. 1975. pap. 6.95 (ISBN 0-8465-1670-5). Benjamin-Cummings.

Koeper, Frederick, jt. auth. see Whiffen, Marcus.

Koepke, John A. Guide to Clinical Laboratory Diagnosis. 2nd. ed. (Illus.). 320p. 1979. pap. 15.50x (ISBN 0-8385-3518-6). ACC.

Koepp, D. W. Public Library Government: Seven Case Studies. (U. C. Publ. in Librarianship: Vol. 6). 1968. pap. 10.00x (ISBN 0-520-09209-0). U of Cal Pr.

Koeppen, Wolfgang. Tauben Im Gras. (Suhrkamp Taschenbuecher: No. 37101). (Illus.). 224p. 1980. pap. text ed. 4.55 (ISBN 3-518-37101-0, Pub. by Insel Verlag Germany). Suhrkamp.

Koerber, Hildegard Von see Lorber, Jakob.

Koerber, Nordewin Von see Lorber, Jakob.

Koerner, E. F. The Importance of Techmer's Internationale Zeitschrift Fur Allgemeine Sprachwissenschaft in the Development of General Linguistics. (Studies in the History of Linguistics: No. 1). 1973. pap. 17.25x (ISBN 0-391-01661-X). Humanities.

Koerner, E. F., ed. Progress in Linguistic Historiography: Papers from the International Conference on the History of the Language Sciences. (Studies in the History of Linguistics: No. 20). 400p. 1980. text ed. 51.50x (ISBN 90-272-4501-0). Humanities.

Koerner, Thomas F., ed. see Kelley, Edgar A.

Koerner, Thomas F., ed. see National Association of Secondary School Principals.

Koerner, Wolfgang. The Green Frontier. Crampton, Patricia, tr. from Ger. (gr. 7 up). 1977. 8.25 (ISBN 0-688-22124-6); lib. bdg. 7.92 (ISBN 0-688-32124-0). Morrow.

Koertge, Noretta. Who Was That Masked Woman? 266p. 1981. 11.95 (ISBN 0-312-87032-9). St Martin.

Koertge, Ronald. Cheap Thrills. 28p. 1976. pap. 2.00 (ISBN 0-935390-01-4). Wormwood Rev.

--The Hired Nose. 1980. 2.50 (ISBN 0-917554-15-9). Maelstrom.

--The Jockey Poems. 1980. 2.50 (ISBN 0-917554-12-4). Maelstrom.

Koestenbaum, Peter. The New Image of the Person: The Theory & Practice of Clinical Philosophy. LC 77-84764. (Contributions in Philosophy: No. 9). 1978. lib. bdg. 22.50 (ISBN 0-8371-9888-7, KNI/). Greenwood.

Koester, Arthur R. The Cymbidium List: Species, Hybirds & Awards 1799-1976, Vol. 1. LC 79-84474. (Orig.). 1979. pap. 11.00x (ISBN 0-9602558-0-X). A R Koester Bks.

Koester, Edwin H., jt. auth. see Mercer, James L.

Koester, Helmut, jt. auth. see Robinson, James M.

Koester, Helmut, jt. auth. see Smith, Charles W.

Koester, Helmut, ed. see Dibelius, Martin.

Koester, Helmut, ed. see Dibelius, Martin & Conzelmann, Hans.

Koester, Helmut, ed. see Lohse, Eduard.

Koester, John, jt. ed. see Byrne, John H.

Koester, Mary C. Into This Land: Centennial History of the Cleveland Poor Clare Monestary of the Blessed Sacrament. (Illus.). 274p. 1980. write for info. (ISBN 0-934906-03-3); pap. write for info. (ISBN 0-934906-04-1). R J Liederbach.

Koestler, A. Darkness at Noon. 1941. 12.95 (ISBN 0-02-565200-1). Macmillan.

--Yogi & the Commissar. 1967. 5.95 o.s.i. (ISBN 0-02-565850-6). Macmillan.

Koestler, Arthur. Arrow in the Blue. LC 77-85781. (Danube Edition Ser). 1970. 12.95 (ISBN 0-02-565020-3). Macmillan.

--The Case of the Midwife Toad. 1972. 8.95 o.p. (ISBN 0-394-48037-6). Random.

--Invisible Writing. LC 70-85782. (Danube Edition Ser). 1970. 10.95 o.s.i. (ISBN 0-02-565190-0). Macmillan.

--Die Nachtwandler. (Suhrkamp Taschenbuecher: 579). 576p. (Ger.). 1980. pap. text ed. 7.80 (ISBN 3-518-37079-0, Pub. by Insel Verlag Germany). Suhrkamp.

--Thieves in the Night. 1967. 12.95 (ISBN 0-02-565670-8). Macmillan.

Koestline, K. Henry. What Jesus Said About It. pap. 1.50 (ISBN 0-451-07763-6, W7763, Sig). NAL.

Koethe, John. Domes: "The Frank O'Hara Award Series". (A Full Court Rebound Bk.). 1978. 14.95 (ISBN 0-231-03743-0); pap. 66.00 (ISBN 0-231-03744-9). Full Court NY.

Koetschau, K., jt. ed. see Boeheim, W.

Koetting, Michael. Nursing-Home Organization & Efficiency: Profit Versus Non Profit. LC 79-2796. 160p. 1980. 19.95 (ISBN 0-669-03290-5). Lexington Bks.

Kofele-Kale, Ndiva. Tribesmen & Patriots: Political Culture in a Poly-Ethnic African State. LC 80-5734. 375p. 1981. lib. bdg. 22.00 (ISBN 0-8191-1395-6); pap. text ed. 12.75 (ISBN 0-8191-1396-4). U Pr of Amer.

Kofele-Kale, Ndiva, ed. An African Experiment in Nation Building: The Bilingual Cameroon Republic. (Westview Special Studies on Africa). 1980. lib. bdg. 26.50x (ISBN 0-89158-685-7). Westview.

Koff. Hospice: A Caring Community. (Illus.). 192p. 1980. text ed. 13.95 (ISBN 0-87626-332-5); pap. text ed. 7.95 (ISBN 0-87626-331-7). Winthrop.

Koff, Raymond S. Liver Disease in Primary Care Medicine. 256p. 1980. 19.95x (ISBN 0-8385-5678-7). ACC.

--Viral Hepatitis. LC 78-17013. (Clinical Gastroenterology Monographs). 1978. 24.95 (ISBN 0-471-03695-1, Pub. by Wiley Medical). Wiley.

Koff, Richard. Home Computers: A Manual of Possibilities. 1979. 7.95 o.p. (ISBN 0-15-142163-3). HarBraceJ.

Koffarnus, Richard. Why Believe? LC 80-53673. 96p. (Orig.). 1981. pap. 2.25 (ISBN 0-87239-425-5, 40090). Standard Pub.

Koffler, Richard, jt. ed. see Cheuse, Alan.

Koffman, Elliot, jt. auth. see Friedman, Frank.

Koffman, Elliot B. & Friedman, Frank L. Problem Solving & Structured Programming in BASIC. LC 78-65355. 1979. pap. text ed. 13.95 (ISBN 0-201-03888-9). A-W.

Kofoid, C. A. & Swezy, Olive. Free-Living Unarmoured Dinoflagellata. (Univ. of California Memoirs Ser.). (Illus.). 540p. 1974. Repr. of 1921 ed. lib. bdg. 105.00 (ISBN 3-87429-066-2). Lubrecht & Cramer.

Koga, T. Introduction to Kinetic Theory. LC 76-93474. 1970. 82.00 (ISBN 0-08-006538-4); pap. 27.00 (ISBN 0-08-018993-8). Pergamon.

Kogan, Gerald, ed. Your Body Works: A Guide to Health, Energy & Balance. LC 77-79272. (Illus.). 177p. (Orig.). 1980. pap. 10.95 (ISBN 0-930162-02-1). Transform Berkeley.

Kogan, Herman, jt. auth. see Wendt, Lloyd.

Kogan, Jerry. Gestalt Therapy Resources. 3rd ed. 44p. 1980. pap. 5.00 (ISBN 0-930162-03-X). Transform Berkeley.

Kogan, Josef. Crane Design: Theory & Calculations of Reliability. LC 75-38664. 365p. 1976. 63.95 (ISBN 0-470-15224-9). Halsted Pr.

Kogan, Leonard S. & Jenkins, Shirley. Indicators of Child Health & Welfare: Development of the DIPOV Index. LC 74-16402. 176p. 1974. 17.50x (ISBN 0-231-03951-4). Columbia U Pr.

Kogan, M. & Pope, M., eds. The Challenge of Change: A Multi-Disciplinary Symposium. Lord Cohen of Birkenhead. (General Ser.). 110p. 1972. pap. text ed. 9.50x (ISBN 0-85633-013-2, NFER). Humanities.

Kogan, Maurice. Educational Policy-Making: A Study of Interest Groups & Parliament. 1975. pap. text ed. 9.95x o.p. (ISBN 0-04-370064-0). Allen Unwin.

--The Politics of Educational Change. LC 78-66344. 1978. 19.95 (ISBN 0-03-046246-0). Praeger.

Kogiku, K. C. Microeconomic Models. LC 78-11695. 320p. 1981. Repr. of 1971 ed. lib. bdg. write for info. (ISBN 0-88275-781-4). Krieger.

Koh, Gertrude. Revised Chapter Six of the Anglo-American Cataloging Rules. pap. 1.00 (ISBN 0-686-24157-6). CHCUS Inc.

Kohak, E. V., tr. see Ricoeur, Paul.

Kohak, Erazim. Idea & Experience: Edmund Husserl's Project of Phenomenology in Ideas, I. LC 78-661. xvi, 250p. 1980. pap. 5.95 (ISBN 0-226-45020-1, P901, Phoen). U of Chicago Pr.

Kohan, Rhea. Hand-Me-Downs. 1980. 11.95 (ISBN 0-394-51161-1). Random.

Kohanski, Alexander. Analytical Interpretation of Martin Buber's 'I & Thou' LC 74-4349. 1975. pap. 2.75 (ISBN 0-8120-0505-8). Barron.

Kohe, J. Martin. Your Greatest Power. 1977. 5.95 (ISBN 0-685-74305-5). Success Unltd.

Kohl, Benjamin G. & Witt, Ronald G. The Earthly Republic: Italian Humanists on Government & Society. LC 78-53335. 1978. 22.00x (ISBN 0-8122-7752-X); pap. 9.50x (ISBN 0-8122-1097-2). U of Pa Pr.

Kohl, Herbert. Growing with Your Children. 256p. 1981. pap. 2.95 (ISBN 0-553-13923-1). Bantam.

Kohl, Herbert & Kohl, Judith. The View from the Oak. (Sierra Club-Scribner's Juvenile Ser.). 1977. 8.95 (ISBN 0-684-15016-6); pap. 4.95 (ISBN 0-684-15017-4). Sierra.

Kohl, James A. How to Save Money on Your Auto Insurance. LC 79-84203. (Illus.). 88p. 1980. pap. 10.00 (ISBN 0-935674-00-4). Jaks Pub Co.

Kohl, Judith, jt. auth. see Kohl, Herbert.

Kohl, Margaret, tr. see Moltmann, Jurgen.

Kohl, Marvin, ed. Infanticide & the Value of Life. LC 77-26376. 252p. 1978. 15.95 (ISBN 0-87975-100-2). Prometheus Bks.

Kohl, Philip L., ed. A New Bronze Age Civilization in the USSR: Archeological Findings. Mandell, William, tr. from Rus. LC 80-5454. (Illus.). 300p. 1981. 30.00x (ISBN 0-87332-169-3). M E Sharpe.

Kohl, Sam & Goldstein, Catherine. All Breed Dog Grooming Guide. LC 72-86425. (Illus.). 288p. 1973. spiral bdg. 11.95 (ISBN 0-668-02729-0). Arco.

Kohl, Wilfred L., ed. Economic Foreign Policies of Industrial States. LC 76-43584. 1977. 21.50 (ISBN 0-669-00958-X). Lexington Bks.

Kohlberg, Lawrence. The Philosophy of Moral Development: Essays in Moral Development, Vol. 1. LC 80-8902. 256p. 1981. 17.95 (ISBN 0-06-064760-4). Har-Row.

Kohlenberger, John P., jt. auth. see Goodrick, Edward W.

Kohlenberger, John R., ed. The NIV Triglot Old Testament. 1334p. 1981. 49.95 (ISBN 0-310-43820-9). Zondervan.

Kohlenberger, John R., III. The Niv Interlinear Hebrew-English Old Testament. 544p. 1980. Vol. 1. 19.95 (ISBN 0-310-38890-2, 6281); Vol. 2. 19.95 (ISBN 0-310-38890-2). Zondervan.

Kohler, Carl. History of Costume. (Illus.). 10.00 (ISBN 0-8446-2393-8). Peter Smith.

Kohler, Carolyn & Westfall, Gloria. Documentation of Intergovernmental Organizations: Proceedings of the Workshop, Indiana U., 24-26 May 1978. 70p. 1980. 29.90 (ISBN 0-08-024670-2). Pergamon.

Kohler, Heinz, jt. ed. see Cohen, Edward P.

Kohler, Wolfgang. The Mentality of Apes. rev. 2nd ed. Winter, Ella, tr. from Ger. (International Library of Psychology). (Illus.). 344p. 1973. 32.00 (ISBN 0-7100-7525-1). Routledge & Kegan.

Kohli, Devindra. Kamala Das. Narasimhaiah, C. D., ed. (Indian Writers Ser.). 128p. 1976. 8.50 (ISBN 0-89253-046-4). Ind-US Inc.

--Virgin Whiteness: The Poetry of Kamala Das. (Greybird Ser.). 1975. 8.00 (ISBN 0-88253-668-0); pap. text ed. 4.00 (ISBN 0-88253-667-2). Ind-US Inc.

Kohli, Suresh. Death's Epicure. 5.00 (ISBN 0-89253-695-0). Ind-US Inc.

Kohli, Suresh, ed. Modern Indian Short Stories. (Indian Short Stories Ser.). 164p. 1975. 5.00 (ISBN 0-88253-737-7). Ind-US Inc.

Kohli, Suresh, tr. see Sehgal, Lalit.

Kohlman, David L. Introduction to V-STOL Airplanes. (Illus.). 1981. write for info. (ISBN 0-8138-0660-7). Iowa St U Pr.

Kohlmann, G., jt. ed. see De Boor, W.

Kohlmeier, Louis, et al, eds. Reporting on Business & the Economy. 336p. 1981. text ed. 14.95 (ISBN 0-13-773879-X). P-H.

Kohlschmidt, Werner. A History of German Literature, 1760-1805. Hilton, Ian, tr. from Ger. LC 74-32062. 420p. 1975. text ed. 35.00x (ISBN 0-8419-0195-3). Holmes & Meier.

Kohmescher, Matthew F. Catholicism Today. LC 80-82085. 160p. (Orig.). 1980. pap. 3.50 (ISBN 0-8091-2335-5). Paulist Pr.

Kohn, A. see Hertmann, A. I., et al.

Kohn, B. Chipmunks. 1979. pap. 1.50 (ISBN 0-13-133090-X). P-H.

Kohn, Bernice. Communications Satellites: Message Centers in Space. LC 74-26872. (Illus.). 64p. (gr. 2-5). 1975. 5.95 (ISBN 0-590-07356-7, Four Winds). Schol Bk Serv.

--Out of the Cauldron. LC 74-150030. (Illus.). (gr. 5-9). 1971. reinforced bdg. 5.95 o.p. (ISBN 0-03-088367-9). HR&W.

Kohn, Clyde F., jt. ed. see Mayer, Harold M.

Kohn, Eugene. Photography: A Manual for Shutterbugs. (Illus.). (gr. 3-7). 1965. pBL o.p. 4.95 (ISBN 0-13-665000-7); pap. 1.25 (ISBN 0-13-665018-X). P-H.

Kohn, Hans. Nationalism & Imperialism in the Hither East. 1932. 17.00 (ISBN 0-86527-139-9). Fertig.

Kohn, Ira, jt. auth. see Clarke, Kenneth.

Kohn, Kate H., et al. Physical Medicine & Rehabilitation. 3rd ed. (Medical Examination Review Bk.: Vol. 20). 1979. spiral bdg. 19.50 (ISBN 0-87488-128-5). Med Exam.

Kohn, Mervin. Dynamic Managing: Principles, Process, Practice. LC 76-14002. 1977. pap. text ed. 18.95 (ISBN 0-8465-3676-5); instr's guide 3.50 (ISBN 0-8465-3677-3). Benjamin-Cummings.

Kohn, Michael. There Was an Old Woman Who Swallowed a Fly. LC 78-74130. (Illus.). 32p. (gr. k-5). Date not set. price not set (ISBN 0-89799-166-4); pap. price not set (ISBN 0-89799-165-6). Dandelion Pr. Postponed.

Kohn, Rita & Tepper, Krysta. You Can Do It: A PR Skills Manual for Librarians. LC 80-24217. xii, 232p. 1981. pap. 12.50 (ISBN 0-8108-1401-3). Scarecrow.

Kohn, Robert R. Principles of Mammalian Aging. 2nd ed. (Illus.). 1978. 21.95 (ISBN 0-13-709352-7). P-H.

Kohn, S. & Meyendorff, Alexander F. The Cost of the War to Russia. 15.00 (ISBN 0-86527-034-1). Fertig.

Kohner, Frederick. The Delights of Olding. LC 77-74004. (Illus.). 1979. 7.00 o.p. (ISBN 0-89430-012-1). Morgan-Pacific.

--The Magician of Sunset Boulevard. Anderson, C. N., ed. LC 78-175270. 10.00 (ISBN 0-89430-004-0). Morgan-Pacific.

Kohno, Sadako. Home Style Japanese Cooking in Pictures. (Illus., Orig.). 1978. pap. 8.95 (ISBN 0-87040-423-7). Japan Pubns.

Kohonen, T. Associative Memory: A System-Theoretical Approach. (Communication & Cybernetics Ser.: Vol. 17). 1977. 27.70 (ISBN 0-387-08017-1). Springer-Verlag.

Kohrs, Karl, jt. auth. see Cross, Milton.

Kohs, Ellis B. Musical Form: Studies in Analysis & Synthesis. 1976. text ed. 19.95 (ISBN 0-395-18613-7). HM.

Kohut, Daniel L. Instrumental Music Pedagogy. (Illus.). 256p. 1973. ref. ed. 14.50 (ISBN 0-13-467944-X). P-H.

Koichi, Marquis K. Diary of Marquis Kido, Nineteen Thirty-One to Nineteen Forty-Five: Selected Translation Selected Translations into English. 500p. 1980. 34.00 (ISBN 0-89093-273-5). U Pubns Amer.

Koike, Yujiro. Electron Tubes. (Eng.). 1972. 37.50x (ISBN 0-8002-1389-0). Intl Pubns Serv.

Koistinen, Paul A. C. The Military-Industrial Complex: A Historical Perspective. LC 79-20569. 186p. 1980. 19.95 (ISBN 0-03-055766-6). Praeger.

Kojeve, Alexandre. Introduction to the Reading of Hegel: Lectures on the "Phenomenology of Spirit". Bloom, Allan, ed. LC 70-78467. (Cornell Paperbacks Ser.). 304p. 1980. pap. 7.95 (ISBN 0-8014-9203-3). Cornell U Pr.

Kojima, Kiyoshi. Direct Foreign Investment: A Japanese Model of Multinational Business Operations. LC 78-61337. (Praeger Special Studies). 1979. 27.95 (ISBN 0-03-047471-X). Praeger.

--Japan & a New World Economic Order. LC 76-5808. 1977. 22.50 o.p. (ISBN 0-89158-607-5). Westview.

Kojima, Naomi. Mr. & Mrs. Thief. LC 79-7902. (Illus.). 32p. (gr. k-4). 1980. 6.95 (ISBN 0-690-04021-0, TYC-J); PLB 6.89 (ISBN 0-690-04022-9). T Y Crowell.

Kojima, Takashi. Advanced Abacus: Japanese Theory & Practice. LC 62-15064. (Illus.). 160p. 1963. pap. 5.25 (ISBN 0-8048-0003-0). C E Tuttle.

--Japanese Abacus: Its Use & Theory. LC 55-3550. (Illus.). (YA) (gr. 7 up). 1955. pap. 3.75 (ISBN 0-8048-0278-5). C E Tuttle.

Kok, J. F. Structopathic Children. Incl. Pt. 1. Description of Disturbance Type & Strategies. (Modern Approaches to the Diagnosis & Instruction of Milti-Handicapped Children: Vol. 9). 126p (ISBN 90-237-4109-9); Pt. 2. Results of Experimental Research of Structuring Group Therapy. (Modern Approaches to the Diagnosis & Instruction of Multi-Handicapped: Vol. 10). 122p (ISBN 90-237-4110-2). 1972. text ed. 26.00 ea. (Pub. by Swets Pub Serv Holland). Swets North Am.

Kok, J. F. W. Structopathic Children, 2 pts. Incl. Pt. 1. Description of Disturbance Type & Strategies. 1126p (ISBN 90-237-4109-9); Pt. 2. Results of Experimental Research of Structuring Group Therapy. 122p (ISBN 90-237-4110-2). (Modern Approaches to the Diagnosis & Instruction of Multi-Handicapped Children Ser.: Vols. 9 & 10). 1972. text ed. 26.00 ea. (Pub. by Swets Pub Serv Holland). Swets North Am.

Kokaska, Charles J., jt. auth. see Brolin, Donn E.

Koke, Richard J. A Checklist of the American Engravings of John Hill, 1770-1850. LC 61-66305. (Illus.). 1961. pap. 4.50x o.p. (ISBN 0-685-73878-7, New York Historical Society). U Pr of Va.

Kokette, Stephen. Money Saving Conservation Products & Projects for the Homeowner. LC 78-55883. 1978. pap. 5.95 (ISBN 0-932314-07-4). Aylmer Pr.

Kokorin, A. I. & Kopytov, V. M. Fully Ordered Groups. Louvish, D., tr. from Rus. LC 73-22108. 147p. 1974. 32.95 (ISBN 0-470-49887-0). Halsted Pr.

Kolafova, V. & Slaba, D. Czech-English-Czech Dictionary. (For Travel Ser.). 394p. 1979. text ed. write for info. (ISBN 0-89918-302-6). Vanous.

Kolakowski, Leszek. Main Currents of Marxism, 3 vols. 1980. Vol. 1. 26.50x (ISBN 0-19-824547-5); Vol. 2. 26.50x (ISBN 0-19-824569-6); Vol. 3. 26.50x (ISBN 0-19-824570-X). Oxford U Pr.

Kolankiewicz, George, jt. auth. see Lane, David.

Kolar, Carol K., compiled by. Plot Summary Index. 2nd rev. & enl. ed. LC 80-27112. 544p. 1981. 25.00 (ISBN 0-8108-1392-0). Scarecrow.

Kolar, Vladimir. Islands of the Adriatic. (Illus.). 1978. 19.95 (ISBN 0-8467-0465-X, Pub. by Two Continents). Hippocrene Bks.

Kolar, Walter W., ed. The Folk Arts of Hungary. LC 80-54019. (Illus.). 190p. (Orig.). 1980. pap. 10.00 (ISBN 0-936922-01-X). Tamburitza.

Kolasa, Blair, jt. auth. see Meyer, Bernadine.

Kolasa, Blair J. Responsibility in Business: Issues & Problems. LC 72-170645. 1972. pap. text ed. 9.95 (ISBN 0-13-773739-4). P-H.

Kolatch. The Jonathan David Dictionary of First Names. 1980. 19.95 (ISBN 0-8246-0234-X). Jonathan David.

Kolatch, Alfred J. Jewish Info. Quiz Book. LC 66-30508. 250p. 1980. 9.95 (ISBN 0-8246-0248-X). Jonathan David.

Kolath, Anna B. The Lost Star & Other Tales. 4.50 (ISBN 0-8062-1655-7). Carlton.

Kolb, Avery. The Great Founding Clans of America. 1980. 20.00 o.p. (ISBN 0-8424-0158-X). Caroline Hse.

Kolb, Bryan & Whishaw, Ian Q. Fundamentals of Human Neuropsychology. LC 80-17987. (Psychology Ser.). (Illus.). 1980. text ed. 17.95x (ISBN 0-7167-1219-9). W H Freeman.

Kolb, Carolyn. New Orleans. LC 71-160873. 1972. pap. 3.95 (ISBN 0-385-02460-6, Dolp). Doubleday.

Kolb, D., et al. Organizational Psychology: An Experimental Approach. 3rd ed. 1979. pap. 14.95 (ISBN 0-13-641258-0). P-H.

Kolb, David A. & McIntyre, James M. Organizational Psychology: A Book of Readings. (Ser. in Behavior Sciences in Business). 1979. text ed. 12.95 (ISBN 0-13-641274-2). P-H.

Kolb, Harold H., Jr. A Field Guide to the Study of American Literature. LC 75-22033. 1976. 10.00x (ISBN 0-8139-0626-1); pap. 4.95x (ISBN 0-8139-0664-4). U Pr of Va.

--Illusion of Life: American Realism As a Literary Form. LC 76-93186. 1969. 9.95x (ISBN 0-8139-0286-X). U Pr of Va.

Kolb, Patricia A. H.I.T. A Manual for the Classification, Filing, & Retrieval of Palmprints. (Illus.). 112p. 1979. text ed. 16.50 spiral bdg. (ISBN 0-398-03855-4). C C Thomas.

Kolb, Peter. The Present State of the Cape of Good-Hope: Or, a Particular Account of the Several Nations of the Hottentots, 2 vols. (Anthropology Ser.). 1969. Repr. of 1731 ed. Vol. 1. 27.00 (ISBN 0-384-30100-2); Vol. 2. 34.50 (ISBN 0-685-13553-5). Johnson Repr.

Kolb, Robert. Andreae & the Formula of Concord. 1977. pap. 7.50 (ISBN 0-570-03741-7, 12-2645). Concordia.

Kolb, W. J., jt. auth. see Gould, Julius.

Kolbas, Grace H. Ecology: Cycle & Recycle. LC 72-81035. (Basic Biology in Color Ser.). (Illus.). 192p. (gr. 9 up). 1972. 12.95 (ISBN 0-8069-3558-8); PLB 11.69 (ISBN 0-8069-3559-6). Sterling.

Kolbe, Hartmut. Ornamental Waterfowl. Lindsay, Ilse, tr. from Ger. (Illus.). 260p. 1979. 22.50x (ISBN 0-8002-2277-6). Intl Pubns Serv.

Kolbe, Helen K. Intrauterine Devices Abstracts: A Guide to the Literature, 1976-1979. (Population Information Library Ser.: Vol. 1). 575p. 1980. 75.00 (ISBN 0-306-65191-2, IFI). Plenum Pub.

--Oral Contraceptives Abstracts--a Guide to the Literature: 1977-1979. (Population Information Library Ser.: Vol. 2). 565p. 1980. 75.00 (ISBN 0-306-65192-0). IFI Plenum.

Kolchin, Valentin F., et al. Random Allocations. Balakrishnan, A. V., tr. (Scripta Ser. in Mathematics). 1978. 25.95 (ISBN 0-470-99394-4). Halsted Pr.

Kolde, E. International Business Enterprise. 2nd ed. LC 78-37518. (Illus.). 672p. 1973. ref. ed. 21.95 (ISBN 0-13-472381-3). P-H.

Kolde, Endel. The Pacific Quest: The Concept & Scope of an Oceanic Community. LC 76-41117. (Pacific Rim Research Series: No. 1). 1976. 17.95 (ISBN 0-669-00978-4). Lexington Bks.

Kolenda, Konstantin. Philosophy's Journey: An Historical Introduction. LC 73-9126. 1974. text ed. 14.95 (ISBN 0-201-03811-0). A-W.

Kolenda, Konstantin, ed. see Kegley, Jacquelyn A., et al.

Kolenda, Konstantin, tr. see Schopenhauer, Arthur.

Kolenda, Pauline. Caste in Contemporary India. LC 77-74109. 1978. pap. text ed. 6.95 (ISBN 0-8053-5602-9). Benjamin-Cummings.

Kolers, Paul A. Aspects of Motion Perception. LC 73-188746. 232p. 1972. text ed. 32.00 (ISBN 0-08-016843-4). Pergamon.

Kolers, Paul A., et al, eds. Processing of Visible Language, Vol. 2. 620p. 1980. 49.50 (ISBN 0-306-40576-8, Plenum Pr). Plenum Pub.

Koleshnik, Eugene, et al, eds. The Encyclopedia of Ships & Seafaring. (Illus.). 256p. 1980. 14.95 (ISBN 0-517-53738-9, Michelman Bks). Crown.

Kolesnik, Walter B. Educational Psychology. 2nd ed. 1970. text ed. 15.95 o.p. (ISBN 0-07-035303-4, C); instructor's manual 3.95 o.p. (ISBN 0-07-035305-0). McGraw.

--Learning: Educational Applications. 240p. 1976. pap. text ed. 11.50 (ISBN 0-205-05443-9). Allyn.

--Motivation: Understanding & Influencing Human Behavior. 1978. pap. text ed. 11.50 (ISBN 0-205-05973-2, 2459736). Allyn.

Kolevzon, Edward R. The Afro-Asian World: A Cultural Understanding. rev. ed. (gr. 7-12). 1972. text ed. 16.80 (ISBN 0-205-03298-2, 7832982); tchrs'. guide 4.40 (ISBN 0-205-03299-0, 7832990); wkbk. & tchrs'. ed. 5.12 ea. (7822960, 7822979); tests & tchrs'. ed. 4.80 ea. (ISBN 0-205-02294-4, 7822944, 7822952). Allyn.

--The Afro-Asian World: A Cultural Understanding. (gr. 7-12). 1978. text ed. 16.80 (ISBN 0-205-05608-3, 7856083); 14.12 (ISBN 0-205-02294-4). Allyn.

Kolevzon, Edward R. & Heine, John A. Our World & Its Peoples. rev. ed. (gr. 9-12). 1977. text ed. 17.24 (ISBN 0-205-04853-6, 7748531); tchrs'. guide 7.32 (ISBN 0-205-04854-4, 774854X); wkbk 44.00 (ISBN 0-205-05606-7, 7756062); tests 36.00 (ISBN 0-205-05607-5, 7756070). Allyn.

Kolig, Erich. Silent Revolution: The Effects of Westernization on Aboriginal Religion. (Illus.). 240p. 1981. text ed. 18.50x (ISBN 0-89727-020-7). Inst Study Hum.

Kolin, jt. auth. see Kolin, Philip C.

Kolin, Michael J. & De La Rosa, Denise M. The Custom Bicycle: Buying, Setting Up & Riding the Quality Bicycle. 12.95 (ISBN 0-87857-254-6); pap. 8.95 (ISBN 0-87857-255-4). Rodale Pr Inc.

--The Ten Speed Bicycle. (Illus.). 1979. 12.95 (ISBN 0-87857-268-6); pap. 9.95 (ISBN 0-87857-281-3). Rodale Pr Inc.

Kolin, Philip C. The Elizabethan Stage Doctor As a Dramatic Convention. (Salzburg Studies in English Literature, Elizabethan & Renaissance Studies Ser.: No. 41). 212p. (Orig.). 1975. pap. text ed. 25.00x (ISBN 0-391-01450-1). Humanities.

Kolin, Philip C. & Kolin. Professional Writing for Nurses in Education, Practice & Research. LC 79-29258. 1980. pap. text ed. 10.95 (ISBN 0-8016-2724-9). Mosby.

Kolinski, Charles J. Historical Dictionary of Paraguay. LC 72-13238. (Latin American Historical Dictionaries Ser.: No. 8). 1973. 10.00 (ISBN 0-8108-0582-0). Scarecrow.

Kolinsky, Martin & Bell, D. S., eds. Divided Loyalties: British Regional Assertion & European Integration. 1978. text ed. 33.50x (ISBN 0-7190-0694-5). Humanities.

Koliopoulos, John S. Greece & the British Connection, 1935-1941. 1978. 37.50x (ISBN 0-19-822523-7). Oxford U Pr.

Kolis, Annette, ed. see Mandelker, et al.

Kolisko, E. Lead & the Human Organism. 1980. pap. 3.95x (ISBN 0-906492-31-9, Pub. by Kolisko Archives). St George Bk Serv.

Kolisko, Eugen. Geology. 1979. pap. 3.95x (ISBN 0-906492-01-7, Pub. by Kolisko Archives). St George Bk Serv.

--Human Organism in the Light of Anthropasaphy. 1980. pap. 1.95x (ISBN 0-906492-11-4, Pub. by Kolisko Archives). St George Bk Serv.

--Medical Work in Education. 1980. pap. 1.95x (ISBN 0-906492-38-6, Pub. by Kolisko Archives). St. George Bk Serv.

--Natural History. 1980. pap. 3.25x (ISBN 0-906492-21-1, Pub. by Kolisko Archives). St George Bk Serv.

--Zoology for Everybody, Vol. 1: A General Survey. 2nd ed. 1977. pap. 3.95x (ISBN 0-906492-05-X, Pub. by Kolisko Archives). St George Bk Serv.

--Zoology for Everybody, Vol. 3: Mammals. (Illus.). 1979. pap. 4.50x (ISBN 0-906492-15-7, Pub. by Kolisko Archives). St George Bk Serv.

--Zoology for Everybody, Vol. 4: Protozoa. 1980. pap. 4.25x (ISBN 0-906492-24-6, Pub. by Kolisko Archives). St George Bk Serv.

Kolisko, Eugen, ed. Zoology for Everybody, Vol. 2: Birds. 2nd ed. 1978. pap. 3.95x (ISBN 0-906492-08-4, Pub. by Kolisko Archives). St George Bk Serv.

Kolko, Gabriel. Main Currents in Modern American History. LC 76-5138. 416p. 1976. 17.50 o.s.i. (ISBN 0-06-012451-2, HarpT). Har-Row.

--The Triumph of Conservatism: A Reinterpretation of American History, 1900-1916. LC 63-16588. 1977. pap. text ed. 7.95 (ISBN 0-02-916650-0). Free Pr.

--Wealth & Power in America: An Analysis of Social Class & Income Distribution. LC 62-11584. 178p. 1962. pap. text ed. 4.95x (ISBN 0-03-037491-X). Praeger.

Kollaritsch, Felix P. Cost Systems for Planning, Decisions & Controls: Concepts & Techniques. LC 78-6799. (Accounting Ser.). 1979. text ed. 20.95 (ISBN 0-88244-172-8). Grid Pub.

Kolle, Gert, ed. see Zweigert, Konrad & Kropholler, Jan.

Koller, Earl L., jt. auth. see Benczer-Koller, Noemie.

Koller, Lawrence R. Shots at Whitetails. rev. ed. LC 78-98642. (Illus.). 1970. 12.50 o.p. (ISBN 0-394-44526-0). Knopf.

Koller, Marvin R. & Ritchie, Oscar W. Sociology of Childhood. 2nd ed. LC 77-13314. (P-H Ser. in Sociology). (Illus.). 1978. text ed. 17.95 (ISBN 0-13-821074-8). P-H.

Koller, William. Your Career in Computer-Related Occupations. LC 78-13700. 1979. lib. bdg. 6.95 (ISBN 0-668-04610-4); pap. 3.50 (ISBN 0-668-04622-8). Arco.

--Your Career in Construction. LC 77-17396. (Arco Career Guidance Ser.). (Illus.). 1978. lib. bdg. 6.95 (ISBN 0-668-04453-5); pap. 3.50 (ISBN 0-668-04435-7). Arco.

Koller, William D. The Dare. (Pal Paperbacks, - Pal Skills II Ser.). (Illus.). (gr. 5-12). 1980. pap. 1.25 (ISBN 0-8374-6805-1). Xerox Ed Pubns.

--I Am the Greatest. (Pal Paperbacks, - Pal Skills II Ser.). (Illus.). (gr. 5-12). 1980. pap. text ed. 1.25 (ISBN 0-8374-6813-2). Xerox Ed Pubns.

Kollet, et al. Strategic Marketing. 1972. 20.95 (ISBN 0-03-078770-X). Dryden Pr.

Kollmar, Kerry & Mason, Melody. Roller Disco Dancing: The Basic Steps on Wheels. LC 79-63091. (Illus.). 1979. pap. 3.95 o.p. (ISBN 0-8069-8858-4). Sterling.

Kollock, John. The Long Afternoon. 8.95 (ISBN 0-932298-01-X). Green Hill.

--Meg's World. 4.95 (ISBN 0-932298-15-X). Green Hill.

--These Gentle Hills. 14.95 (ISBN 0-932298-14-1). Green Hill.

Kollwitz, Kathe. Prints & Drawings of Kathe Kollwitz. (Illus.). 12.50 (ISBN 0-8446-0745-2). Peter Smith.

Kolm, Ronald A. Welcome to the Barbecue. 65p. (Orig.). 1981. pap. 2.95 (ISBN 0-9605626-0-5). Low-Tech.

Kolman, Bernard & Beck, Robert. Elementary Linear Programming with Applications. (Computer Science & Applied Mathematics Ser.). 1980. text ed. 19.95 (ISBN 0-12-417860-X). Acad Pr.

Kolman, Bernard & Shapiro, Arnold. Algebra for College Students. 1980. text ed. 17.95 (ISBN 0-12-417880-4); instr's manual 3.00 (ISBN 0-12-417885-5). Acad Pr.

Kolman, Bernard, jt. auth. see Anton, Howard.

Kolman, Bernard, jt. auth. see Trench, William F.

Kolmar, Gertrud. Dark Soliloquy: The Selected Poems of Gertrud Kolmar. Smith, Henry A., tr. from Ger. LC 75-2239. 192p. 1975. 9.95 o.p. (ISBN 0-8164-9199-2). Continuum.

Kolmogorov, Andrei N. Foundations of the Theory of Probability. 2nd ed. LC 56-11512. 7.50 (ISBN 0-8284-0023-7). Chelsea Pub.

Kolnai, Aurel. Ethics, Value, & Reality: Selected Papers of Aurel Kolnai. LC 77-83145. 1978. 25.00 (ISBN 0-915144-39-5); pap. text ed. 12.50 (ISBN 0-915144-40-9). Hackett Pub.

Kolneder, Walter. Anton Webern: An Introduction to His Works. Searle, Humphrey, tr. 1968. 18.50x o.p. (ISBN 0-520-00662-3). U of Cal Pr.

Kolodin, Irving. In Quest of Music. LC 78-22336. (Illus.). 360p. 1980. 14.95 (ISBN 0-385-13061-9). Doubleday.

--Metropolitan Opera. rev. ed. (Illus.). 1966. 17.50 o.p. (ISBN 0-394-40837-3). Knopf.

Kolodny, Gerald M. Eukaryotic Gene Regulation, 2 vols. 1980. Vol. 1, 224p. 55.95 (ISBN 0-8493-5225-8); Vol. 2, 256p. 59.95 (ISBN 0-8493-5226-6). CRC Pr.

Kolowrat, Ernest, et al. What You Should Know About Medical Lab Tests. LC 79-7092. (Illus.). 1979. 10.95 (ISBN 0-690-01831-2, TYC-T). T Y Crowell.

Kolsky, H. Stress Waves in Solids. 2nd ed. (Illus.). 1963. pap. text ed. 4.00 (ISBN 0-486-61098-5). Dover.

Kolson, Clifford, jt. auth. see Kaluger, George.

Kolson, Clifford J. & Kaluger, George. Clinical Aspects of Remedial Reading. (Illus.). 160p. 1972. pap. 14.95 photocopy ed., spiral (ISBN 0-398-01038-2). C C Thomas.

Kolstee, Hans M. Motion & Power. (Illus.). 256p. 1981. text ed. 19.95 (ISBN 0-13-602953-1). P-H.

Kolstoe, Oliver P. College Professoring: Or, Through Academia with Gun & Camera. LC 75-1237. (Illus.). 159p. 1975. pap. 4.95 (ISBN 0-8093-0712-X). S Ill U Pr.

Kolthoff, I. M. & Elving, P. J. Treatise on Analytical Chemistry, 3 pts. Incl. Pt. 1, Vols. 10-12. Theory & Practice of Analytical Chemistry. Vol. 10, 1972, 595p. 46.50 (ISBN 0-470-49966-4); Vol. 11, 1975. 60.00 (ISBN 0-471-49967-6); Vol. 12, 1976. 32.50 (ISBN 0-471-49968-4); Pt. 2, Vols. 4, 10, 12 & 14-15. Analytical Chemistry of the Elements & of Inorganic & Organic Compounds. Vol. 4, 1966, 452p. 39.50 (ISBN 0-470-49986-9); Vol. 10, 1978. 50.00 (ISBN 0-471-49998-6); Vol. 12, 1976. 27.25 (ISBN 0-470-50002-6); Vol. 14, 1971. 44.95 (ISBN 0-471-50005-4); Vol. 15, 1976. 50.00 (ISBN 0-471-50009-7); Pt. 3, Vols. 3-4. Analytical Chemistry in Industry. 60.00 (ISBN 0-471-50012-7); 60.00 (ISBN 0-471-02765-0). LC 59-12439 (Pub. by Wiley-Interscience). Wiley.

--Treatise on Analytical Chemistry, 3 pts. Incl. Pt. 1, Vols. 1-9. Theory & Practice of Analytical Chemistry. Vol. 1, 1959, 835p (ISBN 0-470-49950-8). Vol. 2, 1961, 520p (ISBN 0-470-49952-4). Vol. 3, 1961, 458p (ISBN 0-470-49954-0). Vol. 4, 1963, 955p (ISBN 0-470-49956-7). Vol. 5, 1964, 640p (ISBN 0-470-49958-3). Vol. 6, 1965, 899p (ISBN 0-470-49960-5). Vol. 7, 1967. 622p (ISBN 0-470-49962-1). Vol. 8, 1968, 515p (ISBN 0-470-49964-8). Vol. 9, 1971, 552p (ISBN 0-471-49965-X); Pt. 2, Vols. 1-3, 5-9, 11 & 13. Analytical Chemistry of the Elements & of Inorganic & Organic Compounds. 1966. Vol. 1, 1961, 471p (ISBN 0-470-49980-X). Vol. 2, 1962, 471p (ISBN 0-470-49982-6). Vol. 3, 1961, 398p (ISBN 0-470-49984-2). Vol. 5, 1961, 409p (ISBN 0-470-49988-5). Vol. 6, 1964, 627p (ISBN 0-470-49990-7); Vol. 7, 1962, 568p (ISBN 0-470-49992-3). Vol. 8, 1963, 556p (ISBN 0-470-49994-X). Vol. 9, 1962, 491p (ISBN 0-470-49996-6). Vol. 11 (ISBN 0-470-50000-X). Vol. 13, 1966, 528p (ISBN 0-470-50004-2); Pt. 3, Vols. 1-2. Analytical Chemistry in Industry. Vol. 1, 1967, 457p (ISBN 0-470-50010-7). Vol. 2, 1971, 597p (ISBN 0-471-50011-9). LC 59-12439. (Pub. by Wiley-Interscience). Wiley.

Koltun, Jan F. Eat & Run: Your 1980 Diet, Exercise & Engagement Calendar. (Illus., Orig.). 1979. pap. 6.95 o.p. (ISBN 0-03-044571-X). HR&W.

Koltz, Charles J. Private Practice in Nursing. LC 79-9311. 1979. text ed. 25.50 (ISBN 0-89443-158-7). Aspen Systems.

Kolupaev, Victor. Hermit's Swing. Jacobson, Helen S., tr. (Best of Soviet Science Fiction Ser.). 174p. 1980. 9.95 (ISBN 0-02-566350-X). Macmillan.

Kolvin, I. Bladder Control & Enuresis. MacKeith, R. C., ed. (Clinics in Developmental Medicine Ser.: Vols. 48 & 49). 328p. 1973. 32.00 (ISBN 0-685-59043-7). Lippincott.

Kolzow, L. V. I.D.E.A. Power for Reading Comprehension. 336p. 1976. pap. text ed. 9.95 (ISBN 0-13-450551-4). P-H.

Kolzow, Lee & Lehman, Jane. College Reading: Strategies for Success. (Illus.). 352p. 1981. pap. text ed. 8.95 (ISBN 0-13-150052-X). P-H.

Komar, John J. The Resume Builder. 120p. 1980. pap. 4.95 (ISBN 0-695-81437-0). Follett.

Komarik, Stephan, et al. Food Products Formulary: Meats, Poultry, Fish & Shellfish. (Illus.). 1974. text ed. 49.50 (ISBN 0-87055-152-3). AVI.

Komarov, Boris. The Destruction of Nature in the Soviet Union. Vale, Michel, tr. from Rus. Orig. Title: Unichtozhenie Prioroda Obostrenie Ekologicheskogo Krizi Sa V SSSR. 192p. 1980. 15.00 (ISBN 0-87332-157-X). M E Sharpe.

Komarov, F., jt. auth. see Kumakhov, M.

Komarovsky, Mirra. Women in the Modern World. (Reprints in Sociology Ser). 1971. lib. bdg. 28.50x (ISBN 0-697-00213-6); pap. text ed. 8.95x (ISBN 0-89197-979-4). Irvington.

Komey, Ellis A., ed. see Mphalele, Ezekiel.

Komi, P. V., ed. Biomechanics V. (International Series on Biomechanics: Vol. Va & Vb). (Illus.). 700p. 1976. 39.50 ea. Vol. VA (ISBN 0-8391-0947-4). Vol. VB (ISBN 0-8391-0946-6). Univ Park.

Kominsky, Nancy. Paint Along with Nancy Kominsky: Landscapes. (Illus., Orig.). 1979. pap. 7.95 (ISBN 0-446-97880-9). Warner Bks.

--Paint Along with Nancy Kominsky: Still Lifes. (Orig.). 1981. pap. 7.95 (ISBN 0-446-87792-1). Warner Bks.

Komisar, Lucy. Down & Out in the USA: A History of Social Welfare. updated ed. 256p. (gr. 6 up). 1977. PLB 7.45 (ISBN 0-531-02647-7). Watts.

--New Feminism. LC 70-149011. (Illus.). (gr. 7 up). 1971. PLB 6.88 o.p. (ISBN 0-531-01981-0). Watts.

Komjathy, Anthony T. The Crisis of France's East Central European Diplomacy, 1933-1938. (East European Monographs: No. 21). 1977. 14.50x o.p. (ISBN 0-914710-14-1, Dist. by Columbia U Pr). East Eur Quarterly.

Komnenich, Pauline, et al, eds. The Menstrual Cycle, Vol. 2: Research & Implications for Women's Health. 256p. 1981. text ed. 25.50 (ISBN 0-8261-2980-3). Springer Pub.

Komoda, Beverly. The Lake Mess Monster. LC 80-17569. (Illus.). 48p. (ps-3). 1981. 4.95 (ISBN 0-8193-1033-6); PLB 5.95 (ISBN 0-8193-1034-4). Parents.

Komoda, Shusul & Pointer, Horst. Ikebana: Spirit & Technique. (Illus.). 224p. 1980. 15.95 (ISBN 0-7137-1040-3, Pub. by Blandford Pr England). Sterling.

Kompaneyets, Alexander. Theoretical Physics. MIR Publishers, tr. from Rus. (Illus.). 592p. 1975. text ed. 17.50x o.p. (ISBN 0-8464-0918-6). Beekman Pubs.

Komroff, Manuel. Battle of Waterloo: The End of an Empire. (gr. 5-9). 1964. 8.95g (ISBN 0-02-750920-6). Macmillan.

Kon, S. K. & Cowie, Alfred T., eds. Milk: The Mammary Gland & Its Secretion, 2 Vols. (Illus.). 1961. Vol. 1. 49.00 (ISBN 0-12-418701-3); Vol. 2. 49.00 (ISBN 0-12-418702-1); Set. 80.00 (ISBN 0-685-05135-8). Acad Pr.

Konarski, M. M. Russian-English Dictionary of Modern Terms in Aeronautics & Rocketry. 1962. 82.00 (ISBN 0-08-009658-1). Pergamon.

Konczacki, J. M., jt. ed. see Konczacki, Z. A.

Konczacki, Z. A. & Konczacki, J. M., eds. An Economic & Social History of Southern Africa, Vol. 3. 1981. 27.50x (ISBN 0-7146-3099-3, F Cass Co). Biblio Dist.

Kondo, Herbert. First Book of the Moon. rev. ed. LC 72-139484. (First Bks). (Illus.). (gr. 7 up). 1971. PLB 4.90 o.p. (ISBN 0-531-00740-5). Watts.

Kondo, Herbert, ed. New Book of Popular Science, 6 vols. LC 79-55175. (Illus.). 1980. write for info o.p. (ISBN 0-7172-1210-6). Grolier Ed Corp.

Kondo, Herbert, ed. see Grolier Incorporated.

Kondo, Yoichiro, jt. auth. see Okabayashi, Atsushi.

Kondor, R., tr. see Emanuel', N. M. & Knorre, D. G.

Kondor, R., tr. see Entelis, S. G. & Tiger, R. P.

Kondor, R., tr. see Gur'Yanova, E. N., et al.

Kondor, R., tr. see Kozhevnikov, A. V.

Kondor, R., tr. see Lipatov, Yu. S & Sergeeva, L. M.

Kondor, R., tr. see Paushkin, Ya. M., et al.

Kondratiev, V. N. Chemical Kinetics of Gas Reactions. 1964. text ed. 37.00 o.p. (ISBN 0-08-010108-9). Pergamon.

Kondratiev, V. N. & Nikitin, E. E. Gas-Phase Reactions: Kinetics & Mechanisms. (Illus.). 250p. 1980. 63.80 (ISBN 0-387-09956-5). Springer-Verlag.

Kondratyav, K. Ya. Radiation in the Atmosphere. (International Geophysics Ser.: Vol. 12). 1969. 75.50 (ISBN 0-12-419050-2). Acad Pr.

Konecsni, Johnemery. A Post-Kantian Anthropology. 1978. pap. text ed. 9.00x (ISBN 0-8191-0374-8). U Pr of Amer.

Konefsky, Samuel J. The Legacy of Holmes & Brandeis. LC 78-157828. (American Constitutional & Legal History, Ser.). 316p. 1974. Repr. of 1956 ed. lib. bdg. 29.50 (ISBN 0-306-70215-0). Da Capo.

Konek, Carol, et al. The Source Book. 192p. (Orig.). 1981. pap. text ed. 7.95 (ISBN 0-582-28201-2); tchrs'. manual free (ISBN 0-582-28252-7). Longman.

Kones, Richard J. Basic Science & Diagnosis, Vol. I. LC 79-89752. (New Horizons in Cardiovascular Disease Ser.). (Illus.). 288p. 1980. 32.50 (ISBN 0-87993-101-9). Futura Pub.

--Basic Science & Diagnosis, Vol. 2. LC 79-89752. (New Horizons in Cardiovascular Disease Ser.). 272p. 1980. 29.50 (ISBN 0-87993-144-2). Futura Pub.

Kong, Bucksam & Ho, Eugene H. Hung Gar Kung-Fu Chinese Art of Self-Defense. Scurra, John, ed. LC 73-75551. (Ser. 310). 1973. pap. text ed. 6.95 (ISBN 0-89750-038-5). Ohara Pubns.

Kong, F. K. & Evans, R. H. Reinforced & Prestressed Concrete. 1975. text ed. 29.95x (ISBN 0-17-761040-9). Intl Ideas.

Kong, Les, jt. auth. see Heaser, Eileen.

Konheim, Alan G. Crytography: A Primer. 450p. 1981. 25.00 (ISBN 0-471-08132-9, Pub. by Wiley-Interscience). Wiley.

Koniecko, Edward S. Handbook for Meat Chemists. 1979. pap. text ed. 20.00 (ISBN 0-89529-097-9). Avery Pub.

--Nutritional Encyclopedia for the Elderly. 1981. 12.95 (ISBN 0-8062-1676-X). Carlton.

Konig, Hans. Amsterdam. (The Great Cities Ser.). (Illus.). 1977. lib. bdg. 14.94 (ISBN 0-686-51000-3). Silver.

Konig, Hans-Jost. Geheime Mission. LC 75-2362. 1975. pap. 4.25 (ISBN 0-88436-181-0). EMC.

Konig, Imre. Chess from Morphy to Botwinnik. 2nd ed. LC 77-72873. 1977. pap. 3.75 (ISBN 0-486-23503-3). Dover.

Konigsburg, E. L. From the Mixed-up Files of Mrs. Basil E. Frankweiler. 1977. pap. 1.50 (ISBN 0-440-43180-8, YB). Dell.

--Jennifer, Hecate, Macbeth, William McKinley, & Me, Elizabeh. (gr. 3-6). 1967. pap. 2.95 (ISBN 0-689-70296-5, Aladdin). Atheneum.

--Throwing Shadows. (gr. 5-9). pap. 2.95 (ISBN 0-689-70491-7, A-118, Aladdin). Atheneum.

Konigsson, Lars-Konig & Sundstrom, Stephan, eds. Current Argument on Early Man: Nobel Symposium "Current Argument on Early Man" Royal Swedish Academy of Sciences & the Nobel Foundation, Karlskoga, Sweden, May 21-27, 1978. (Illus.). 1980. 69.00 (ISBN 0-08-024956-6). Pergamon.

Koning, Hans. Amsterdam. Time-Life Books, ed. (The Great Cities Ser.). (Illus.). 1977. 14.95 (ISBN 0-8094-2290-5). Time-Life.

--World of Vermeer. (Library of Art). (Illus.). 1967. 15.95 (ISBN 0-8094-0237-8). Time-Life.

--World of Vermeer. LC 67-15299. (Library of Art Ser.). (Illus.). (gr. 6 up). 1967. 12.96 (ISBN 0-8094-0266-1, Pub. by Time-Life). Silver.

Koningsberger, Hans. The Revolutionary. 212p. 1967. 4.95 (ISBN 0-374-24984-9). FS&G.

Konior, Mary, jt. auth. see Calder, Louisa.

Konizeski, Dick. The Montanans' Fishing Guide: West of the Continental Divide, Vol. I. rev. ed. Fbursk, Dale A., ed. (Illus.). 325p. 1980. pap. 7.95 (ISBN 0-87842-139-4). Mountain Pr.

Konkel, Gilbert, jt. auth. see Peck, Phyllis.

Konkel, Wilbur. Living Hymn Stories. 1971. pap. 2.50 (ISBN 0-87123-334-7, 210334). Bethany Fell.

Konner. Roller Fever. (gr. 7-12). 1980. pap. 1.50 (ISBN 0-590-30029-6, Schol Pap). Schol Bk Serv.

Konnully, George L. Network Analysis & Transmission Lines. 1967. pap. 10.00x (ISBN 0-210-26907-3). Asia.

Konopacki, Steven A. The Descent into Words: Jakob Bohme's Transcendental Linguistics. (Linguistica Extranea: Studia: No. 7). 201p. 1979. pap. 7.50 (ISBN 0-89720-019-5). Karoma.

Konopinski, Emil. Electromagnetic Fields & Relativistic Particles. (International Series in Pure & Applied Physics). (Illus.). 640p. 1981. text ed. 25.95x (ISBN 0-07-035264-X, C). McGraw.

Konopka, Ursula & Guggenmos, Josef. Dragon Franz. LC 76-40986. (Illus.). (gr. k-3). 1977. 8.25 (ISBN 0-688-80077-7); PLB 7.92 (ISBN 0-688-84077-9). Greenwillow.

Konoplyova, N. P. & Popov, V. N. Gauge Fields. 300p. 1981. 60.00 (ISBN 3-7186-0045-5). Harwood Academic.

Konovalov, S. M. Differentiation of Local Populations of Sockeye Salmon Oncorhynchus Nerka. Sagen, Leda V., tr. from Rus. LC 75-14733. (Publications in Fisheries, Ser.: No. 6). (Illus.). 256p. (Orig.). 1975. pap. text ed. 12.50 (ISBN 0-295-95406-X). U of Wash Pr.

Konrad, Evelyn. Indiscretions. 1980. pap. 2.50 o.s.i. (ISBN 0-440-14079-X). Dell.

Konrad, George & Szelenyi, Ivan. The Intellectuals on the Road to Class Power. LC 77-92547. 1979. 10.00 (ISBN 0-15-177860-4). HarBraceJ.

--The Road of the Intellectuals to Class Power: A Sociological Study of the Role of the Intelligentsi in Socialism. Arato, Andrew & Allen, Richard E., trs. LC 77-92547. 1979. 10.00 o.p. (ISBN 0-685-94990-7). HarBraceJ.

Konrad, Herman W. A Jesuit Hacienda in Colonial Mexico: Santa Lucia, 1576-1767. LC 79-65518. (Illus.). 472p. 1980. 28.50x (ISBN 0-8047-1050-3). Stanford U Pr.

Konrad, Patricia & Ertl, John. Pediatric Oncology. (Medical Outline Ser.). 1978. spiral 14.50 (ISBN 0-87488-673-2). Med Exam.

Konrad, Roselinde. Reviewing German Grammar & Building Vocabulary. 1977. pap. text ed. 10.95 scp o.p. (ISBN 0-06-043752-9, HarpC); instructor's manual avail. o.p. (ISBN 0-06-363700-6). Har-Row.

Konrad, Z., ed. see International Experts Discussion on Lead Occurrence, Fate & Pollution in the Marine Environment, Rovinj, Yugoslavia, 18-22 October 1977.

Konsalik, Heinz G. Strike Force Ten. 320p. 1981. 12.95 (ISBN 0-399-12615-5). Putnam.

Konsler, Runelle & Mirabella, Lauren, eds. Cruising into Measurements. 1980. pap. text ed. 8.95 (ISBN 0-8302-2140-9). Goodyear.

Konstantinovic, Radomir. Exitus. 1980. 10.95 (ISBN 0-7145-0223-5). Riverrun NY.

Kontopoulos, Kyriakos M. Knowledge & Determination: The Transition from Hegel to Marx. 1980. text ed. 23.00x (ISBN 90-6032-125-1). Humanities.

Kontos, Joan F. Red Cross, Black Eagle: A Biography of Albania's American School. (East European Monographs: No. 75). 240p. 1981. text ed. 17.00x (ISBN 0-914710-69-9). East Eur Quarterly.

Kontrul, Jamgon. The Torch of Certainty. Hanson, Judith, tr. from Tibetan. LC 76-53359. (Illus.). 179p. (Orig.). 1981. pap. 7.95 (ISBN 0-87773-101-2). Great Eastern.

Konuk, Mutlu, tr. see Hikmet, Nazim.

Konvitz, Milton, ed. see Pekelis, Alexander H.

Konvitz, Milton R. A Century of Civil Rights. LC 61-8988. 1967. pap. 6.00x (ISBN 0-231-08577-X). Columbia U Pr.

Konvitz, Milton R. & Kennedy, Gail, eds. American Pragmatists. (Orig.). 1960. pap. 4.95 o.p. (ISBN 0-452-00105-6, F105, Mer). NAL.

Konvitz, Milton R., ed. see Liberia, Republic of.

Konwicki. The Polish Complex. 1981. 10.00 (ISBN 0-374-23548-1). FS&G.

Konwicki, Tadeusz. Anthropos-Specter-Beast. Korwin-Rodziszewski, George & Korwin-Rodziszewski, Audrey, trs. from Pol. LC 77-13500. 320p. (gr. 9 up). 1977. 9.95 (ISBN 0-87599-218-8). S G Phillips.

--Dreambook for Our Time. Welsh, David, tr. 1970. 17.50x o.p. (ISBN 0-262-11035-0). MIT Pr.

Konz, Stephan. Work Design. LC 78-50042. (Industrial Engineering Ser.). 1979. text ed. 22.50 (ISBN 0-88244-162-0). Grid Pub.

Koo, Joo Ok, jt. auth. see Dudewicz, Edward J.

Koob, Derry D. & Boggs, William E. The Nature of Life. LC 73-140837. (Life Science Ser). 1972. text ed. 18.95 (ISBN 0-201-03815-3). A-W.

Koocher, Gerald P. & O'Malley, John E. The Damocles Syndrome: Psychosocial Consequences of Surviving Childhood Cancer. 1981. 15.95 (ISBN 0-07-035340-9). McGraw.

Koocher, Gerald P., ed. Children's Rights & the Mental Health Professions. LC 76-16062. (Personality Processes Ser.). 1976. 26.95 (ISBN 0-471-01736-1, Pub. by Wiley-Interscience). Wiley.

Kooi, E. Surface Properties of Oxidized Silicon. (Illus.). 1967. 5.60 o.p. (ISBN 0-387-91009-3). Springer-Verlag.

Kooi, Kenneth A. & Marshall, Robert E. Visual Evoked Potentials in Central Disorders of the Visual System. (Illus.). 1979. text ed. 25.00 (ISBN 0-06-141477-8, Harper Medical). Har-Row.

Kooiker, Leonie. The Magic Stone. Winston, Richard & Winston, Clara, trs. from Dutch. (Illus.). (gr. 3-7). 1978. 7.95 (ISBN 0-688-22143-2); PLB 7.63 (ISBN 0-688-32143-7). Morrow.

Kooiman, Gladys, jt. auth. see Decker, Beatrice.

Koolhaas, Rem. Delirious New York: A Retroactive Manifesto for Manhattan. LC 77-17418. (Illus.). 1978. 39.95 (ISBN 0-19-520035-7). Oxford U Pr.

Koon, Helene, jt. ed. see Mahl, Mary R.

Koons, Walter E. The Mystery of Music. 1977. 7.50 o.p. (ISBN 0-533-02422-6). Vantage.

Koontz, Charles W. Koontz Child Developmental Program: Training Activities for the First 48 Months. LC 73-91239. 1974. pap. 17.50x (ISBN 0-87424-136-7). Western Psych.

Koontz, Dean R. Whispers. 1981. pap. 2.95 (ISBN 0-425-04707-5). Berkley Pub.

Koontz, Harold. Board of Directors & Effective Management. 2nd ed. 286p. 1981. Repr. lib. bdg. write for info. (ISBN 0-89874-188-2). Krieger.

Koontz, Harold & Fulmer, Robert M. A Practical Introduction to Business. rev. ed. 1978. text ed. 17.95 (ISBN 0-256-02012-4). Irwin.

Koontz, Harold, et al. Management. 7th, rev. ed. (Illus.). 1980. text ed. 18.95 (ISBN 0-07-035377-8); instructor's manual 9.95 (ISBN 0-07-035378-6); study guide 6.95 (ISBN 0-07-035379-4). McGraw.

Koonz, Claudia, jt. auth. see Bridenthal, Renate.

Koop, Albert J. & Inada, Hogitaro. Japanese Names & How to Read Them: A Manual for Art-Collectors & Students. 1972. 75.00 (ISBN 0-7100-1707-3). Routledge & Kegan.

Koop, Gordon, et al. The Deni of Western Brazil. (Museum of Anthropology Ser.: No. 7). 200p. 1980. write for info. (ISBN 0-88312-156-5); price not set microfiche (ISBN 0-88312-243-X). Summer Inst Ling.

Koopman, Bernard O. Search & Screening: General Principles with Historical Applications. LC 79-16909. (Illus.). 400p. 1980. 50.00 (ISBN 0-08-023136-5); pap. 21.00 (ISBN 0-08-023135-7). Pergamon.

Koopman, LeRoy. Beauty Care for the Eyes. 96p. 1975. pap. 2.50 (ISBN 0-310-26832-X). Zondervan.

--Beauty Care for the Tongue. (Illus.). 96p. (Orig.). 1974. pap. 2.25 (ISBN 0-310-26842-7). Zondervan.

--Devotions for Christian Workers. (Good Morning Lord Ser.). 96p. 1980. 3.95 (ISBN 0-8010-5418-4). Baker Bk.

Koopmans. An Introduction to Contemporary Statistics. (Illus.). 500p. 1981. text ed. 20.95. Duxbury Pr.

Koops, Willem R., ed. see IFLA Council Meeting, 44th, Strbske, Pleso, et al.

Koops, Willem R., et al, eds. IFLA Annual 1977: Proceedings. (IFLA Annual 1977). 275p. 1978. text ed. 31.25 (ISBN 3-7940-4303-0, Pub. by K G Saur). Shoe String.

Koops, Willeur R. & Stellingwerf, Johannes. Developments in Collection Building in University Libraries in Western Europe. 109p. 1977. text ed. 17.00 (ISBN 3-7940-7020-8, Pub. by K G Saur). Shoe String.

Kooser, Ted. The Blizzard Voices. 1981. price not set (ISBN 0-931460-17-4). Bieler.

--Not Coming to Be Barked at. LC 76-21422. (Illus.). 1976. 15.00x (ISBN 0-915316-45-5); pap. 4.50x (ISBN 0-915316-25-0); ltd. signed ed. 5.00 (ISBN 0-915316-26-9). Pentagram.

Kooser, Ted, jt. auth. see Kloefkorn, William.

Koosis, Donald J. & Coladarci, Arthur P. Statistics. 2nd ed. LC 77-10201. (Self-Teaching Guides Ser.). 1977. pap. text ed. 6.95 (ISBN 0-471-03391-X). Wiley.

Koosis, P. J. Introduction to Hp Spaces. LC 80-65175. (London Mathematical Society Lecture Note Ser.: No. 40). (Illus.). 380p. (Orig.). 1980. pap. 23.95 (ISBN 0-521-23159-0). Cambridge U Pr.

Kooy, Alide see Wilson, Francis.

Kooyman, Gerald L. Weddell Seal, Consummate Diver. LC 80-18794. (Illus.). 176p. Date not set. price not set (ISBN 0-521-23657-6). Cambridge U Pr.

Kopaczynski, Germain. Linguistic Ramifications of the Essence-Existence Debate. LC 79-5373. 1979. pap. text ed. 9.50 (ISBN 0-8191-0865-0). U Pr of Amer.

Kopal, Zdenek. The Realm of the Terrestrial Planets. LC 79-40449. 223p. 1979. 22.95 (ISBN 0-470-26688-0). Halsted Pr.

Kopan, Alice, jt. auth. see Kowtaluk, Helen.

Kopan, Andrew & Walberg, Herbert. Rethinking Educational Equality. LC 73-20856. 1974. 15.25x (ISBN 0-8211-0012-2); text ed. 13.75x (ISBN 0-685-42637-8). McCutchan.

Kopan, Andrew T. see Walberg, Herbert J.

Kopay, David & Young, Perry D. The David Kopay Story. 1980. pap. 5.95 (ISBN 0-87795-290-6). Arbor Hse.

Kopel, Zdenek & Mikhailov, Z. K., eds. The Moon. 1963. 49.00 (ISBN 0-12-419362-5). Acad Pr.

Kopelev, Lev. The Education of a True Believer. Kern, Gary, tr. from Rus. LC 79-3397. 15.95 (ISBN 0-06-012476-8, HarpT). Har-Row.

--Utoli Moi Pechali. (Rus.). 1981. 16.50 (ISBN 0-88233-483-2); pap. 9.00 (ISBN 0-88233-484-0). Ardis Pubs.

Kopelev, Lev Z. Vera V. Slovo. (Illus., Rus.). 1977. 10.00 o.p. (ISBN 0-88233-301-1). Ardis Pubs.

Kopelman, Arie, jt. auth. see Crawford, Tad.

Kopf, Alfred W., et al. Atlas of Tumors of the Skin. new ed. 1978. text ed. 80.00 (ISBN 0-7216-5487-8). Saunders.

--Malignant Melanoma. LC 78-71687. (Illus.). 256p. 1979. 57.25 (ISBN 0-89352-040-3). Masson Pub.

Kopf, David. British Orientalism & the Bengal Renaissance: The Dynamics of Indian Modernization, 1773-1835. 1969. 20.00x (ISBN 0-520-00665-8). U of Cal Pr.

Kopin, Irwin J., ed. Neurotransmitters. LC 72-75942. (ARNMD Research Publications Ser: Vol. 50). 1972. 34.50 (ISBN 0-683-00244-9). Raven.

Kopin, Irwin J., jt. ed. see Ehrenpreis, Seymour.

Kopit, Arthur. The Day the Whores Came Out to Play Tennis & Other Plays. Incl. Chamber Music; The Questioning of Nick; Sing to Me Through Open Windows; The Hero; The Conquest of Everest. 140p. (Orig.). 1965. pap. 3.95 (ISBN 0-8090-0736-3, Mermaid). Hill & Wang.

Kopit, Arthur L. Wings. 78p. 1978. 8.95 (ISBN 0-8090-9756-7, Mermaid); pap. 3.95 (ISBN 0-8090-1239-1). Hill & Wang.

Kopland, Roger. An Empty Place to Stay & Other Selected Poems. Leigh-Loohuizen, Ria, tr. from Dutch. 74p. 1980. pap. text ed. 4.00 (ISBN 0-918786-22-3). Lost Roads.

Kopp, Claire B., ed. Readings in Early Development: For Occupational Physical Therapy Students. (Illus.). 576p. 1971. 21.50 (ISBN 0-398-02333-6). C C Thomas.

Kopp, Ernestine, et al. Designing Apparel Through the Flat Pattern. 4th ed. LC 73-132040. 1971. 13.50 o.p. (ISBN 0-87005-094-X). Fairchild.

--New Fashion Areas - For Designing Apparel Through the Flat Pattern. LC 72-82160. (Illus.). 350p. 1972. 14.50 (ISBN 0-87005-111-3). Fairchild.

--Designing Apparel Through the Flat Pattern. 5th, new ed. (Illus.). 250p. 1980. pap. text ed. 18.95 (ISBN 0-87005-258-6). Fairchild.

Kopp, Richard D. & Fraser, Theodore P. Readings in French Literature. 1975. pap. text ed. 8.80 (ISBN 0-395-13638-5). HM.

Kopp, Ruth & Sorenson, Stephen. Encounter with Terminal Illness. 256p. 1980. 9.95 (ISBN 0-310-41600-0). Zondervan.

Kopp, Sheldon. An End to Innocence: Facing Life Without Illusions. 208p. 1981. pap. 2.95 (ISBN 0-553-13327-6). Bantam.

--The Naked Therapist. LC 76-17939. 1976. 11.95 (ISBN 0-912736-18-6). EDITS Pubs.

Kopp, Sheldon B. An End to Innocence. 1978. 9.95 (ISBN 0-02-566470-0). Macmillan.

Kopp, T., jt. auth. see Linde, T. F.

Koppelman, Lee E., et al. The Urban Sea: Long Island Sound. LC 74-3161. (Illus.). 1976. text ed. 29.95 (ISBN 0-275-09010-8). Praeger.

Koppenhaver, April M., ed. see Frompovich, Catherine J.

Kopper, Edward J., Jr. Lady Isabella Persse Gregory. (English Authors Ser: No. 194). 1976. lib. bdg. 12.50 (ISBN 0-8057-6658-8). Twayne.

Kopper, Philip. The Wild Edge: Life & Lore of the Great Atlantic Beaches. 288p. 1981. pap. 6.95 (ISBN 0-14-046497-2). Penguin.

Koppisch, Michael S. The Dissolution of Character: Changing Perspectives in La Bruyere's Caracteres. (French Forum Monographs: No.24). 120p. (Orig.). 1981. pap. 10.50 (ISBN 0-917058-23-2). French Forum.

Kopplin, Dorothea S. Something to Live By. 4.95 o.p. (ISBN 0-385-00155-X). Doubleday.

Koppman, Lionel, jt. auth. see Postal, Bernard.

Kops, W. J., jt. auth. see Owen, Brian E.

Kopta, Joseph A., et al, eds. Orthopedic Surgery Continuing Education Review. LC 80-80366. 1980. pap. 14.50 (ISBN 0-87488-398-9). Med Exam.

Kopycinski, Joseph V., ed. Textile Industry Information Sources. LC 64-25644. (Management Information Guide Ser.: No. 4). 1964. 30.00 (ISBN 0-8103-0804-5). Gale.

Kopytoff, Igor, jt. ed. see Miers, Suzanne.

Kopytov, V. M., jt. auth. see Kokorin, A. I.

Korach. Manual of Radiographic Techniques of the Skull. 1981. write for info (ISBN 0-89352-098-5). Masson Pub.

Koral, Bella. Abraham Lincoln. (Illus.). (gr. k-3). 1952. 1.95 o.p. (ISBN 0-394-80625-5, BYR). Random.

Koral, Richard L., jt. ed. see Stamper, Eugene.

Koralek, Jenny, tr. see Zuber, Rene.

Koran, Al. How to Bring Out the Magic in Your Mind. 272p. 1976. pap. 4.95 o.s.i. (ISBN 0-88391-046-2). Fell.

Koranyi, Erwin K. Transsexuality in the Male: The Spectrum of Gender Dysphoria. (Behavioral Science & Law Ser.). (Illus.). 192p. 1980. text ed. 18.75 (ISBN 0-398-03924-0). C C Thomas.

Koranyi, Erwin K., jt. auth. see Smith, Selwyn M.

Korb, Lawrence J. Joint Chiefs of Staff: The First 25 Years. LC 75-16839. (Illus.). 224p. 1976. 10.95x (ISBN 0-253-33169-2). Ind U Pr.

Korb, Lawrence J., jt. auth. see Laird, Melvin R.

Korbel, Josef. Communist Subversion of Czechoslovakia, 1938-1948: The Failure of Coexistence. 1959. 16.50x o.p. (ISBN 0-691-08705-9); pap. 4.95 o.p. (ISBN 0-691-02502-9). Princeton U Pr.

--Twentieth Century Czechoslovakia: The Meanings of Its History. LC 76-54250. 1977. 20.00x (ISBN 0-231-03724-4). Columbia U Pr.

Korbonski, Stefan. Polish Underground State. 288p. 1981. pap. 7.95 (ISBN 0-88254-517-5). Hippocrene Bks.

Korchnoi, Victor. Victor Korchnoi's Best Games. 1978. text ed. 13.00 (ISBN 0-08-023028-8). Pergamon.

Korchnoi, Viktor & Zak, Vladimir. King's Gambit. 1975. 14.95 (ISBN 0-7134-2914-3). David & Charles.

Korcok, Milan, jt. ed. see D'Amanda, Christopher.

Korda, Michael. Charmed Lives. 560p. 1981. pap. 3.50 (ISBN 0-380-53017-1, 53017). Avon.

Kordel, Lelord. Secrets for Staying Slim. 208p. 1972. pap. 2.25 (ISBN 0-451-09220-1, E9220, Sig). NAL.

Kordo, Herbert, ed. New Book of Popular Science, 6 vols. LC 80-83090. (Illus.). 1981. write for info. (ISBN 0-7172-1211-4). Grolier Ed Corp.

Korean Traders Association. Korean Trade Directory, 1979 to 1980. 21st ed. LC 60-45910. 579p. 1979. 35.00x (ISBN 0-8002-2520-1). Intl Pubns Serv.

Korelitz, Burton I., ed. Inflammatory Bowel Diseases. 332p. 1981. text ed. 27.50 (ISBN 0-88416-310-5). PSG Pub.

Korem, Danny & Meier, Paul. The Fakers. 1980. cancelled o.p. (ISBN 0-8007-1130-0). Revell.

--The Fakers: Exploding the Myths of the Supernatural. (Illus.). 1981. 8.95 (ISBN 0-8010-5431-1). Baker Bk.

Koren, Henry J. Marx & the Authentic Man: A First Introduction to the Philosophy of Karl Marx. 1973. Repr. of 1967 ed. text ed. 5.00x o.p. (ISBN 0-391-00315-1, J26202). Humanities.

Koren, Herman. Environmental Health & Safety. LC 72-11634. 338p. 1974. text ed. 26.00 o.p. (ISBN 0-08-017077-3); pap. text ed. 14.50 (ISBN 0-08-017623-2). Pergamon.

--Handbook of Environmental Health & Safety: Principles & Practices. 1980. 99.50 (ISBN 0-08-023900-5). Pergamon.

Korenman, Stanley G., et al. Practical Diagnosis: Endocrine Diseases. (Illus.). 1978. pap. 14.00x (ISBN 0-89289-201-3). HM Prof Med Div.

Korfhage, Robert R., ed. Computer Networks & Communication. (The Information Technology Ser.: Vol. IV). 150p. 1977. pap. 20.00 (ISBN 0-88283-017-1). AFIPS Pr.

Korfhage, Robert R., ed. see National Computer Conference, 1977.

Korg, Jacob. Dylan Thomas. (English Authors Ser.: No. 20). 1964. lib. bdg. 10.95 (ISBN 0-8057-1548-7). Twayne.

Korg, Jacob, ed. see Browning, Robert.

Korg, Jacob, ed. see Gissing, George.

Koriwn. Vark' Mastotsi: Life of Mastots. Maksoudian, Krikor, ed. 1981. write for info. (ISBN 0-88206-030-9). Caravan Bks.

Korkisch, J. Modern Methods for the Separation of Rarer Metal Ions. 1969. text ed. 60.00 (ISBN 0-08-012921-8). Pergamon.

Korman, Abraham. Organizational Behavior. (Illus.). 1977. 19.95 (ISBN 0-13-640938-5). P-H.

Korman, Abraham & Korman, Rhoda. Career Success - Personal Failure. 150p. 1980. text ed. 12.95 (ISBN 0-13-114777-3). P-H.

Korman, Abraham K. The Psychology of Motivation. (Experimental Psychology Ser). (Illus.). 288p. 1974. ref. ed. 18.95 (ISBN 0-13-733279-3). P-H.

Korman, Keith. Swan Dive. 1981. pap. 2.95 (ISBN 0-440-18423-1). Dell.

Korman, Rhoda, jt. auth. see Korman, Abraham.

Kormendi, Roger G., jt. auth. see Mussa, Michael L.

Korn, Alfons L., tr. see De Varigny, Charles.

Korn, Arthur. Glass in Modern Architecture of the Bauhaus Period. LC 68-11357. (Illus.). 1968. 15.00 o.s.i. (ISBN 0-8076-0440-2). Braziller.

Korn, Bernhard C. The Story of Bay View. LC 80-83069. (Illus.). 136p. (gr. 6-12). 1980. 5.00 (ISBN 0-938076-05-1). Milwaukee County.

Korn, Donald H., jt. auth. see Bradley, James W.

Korn, Errol R. & Johnson, Karen. Visualization: The Uses of Imagery in the Health Professions. 1981. write for info. (ISBN 0-88416-300-8). PSG Pub.

Korn, Francis. Elementary Structures Reconsidered: Levi-Strauss on Kinship. 1973. 17.50x (ISBN 0-520-02476-1). U of Cal Pr.

Korn, Granino A. & Wait, John V. Digital Continuous System Simulation. (Illus.). 1978. ref. ed. 21.95 (ISBN 0-13-212274-X). P-H.

Korn, Harold A., jt. auth. see Sampson, Edward E.

Korn, Henri, jt. ed. see Faber, Donald.

Korn, Henry J. A Difficult Act to Follow. LC 79-57461. 80p. 1981. 15.00 (ISBN 0-686-69412-0); pap. 5.95 (ISBN 0-686-69413-9). Assembling Pr.

Korn, Henry J., jt. ed. see Kostelanetz, Richard.

Korn, J. Hydrostatic Transmission Systems. 1970. pap. 10.00 (ISBN 0-7002-0189-0). Transatlantic.

Korn, Richard. Union & Its Retired Workers: A Case Study of the UMW. (Key Issues Ser.: No. 21). 1976. pap. 3.00 (ISBN 0-87546-230-8). NY Sch Indus Rel.

Korn, Walter. Modern Chess Openings. 11th ed. 1978. 12.50 (ISBN 0-679-13056-X, 13056X). McKay.

Korn, Wolfgang. The Traditional Architecture of the Kathmandu Valley. (Ratna Pustak Bhandar Bibliotheca Himalayica Ser.). (Illus.). 1977. 17.50x (ISBN 0-685-89504-1). Himalaya Hse.

Kornberg, Arthur. DNA Replication. LC 79-19543. (Illus.). 1980. text ed. 34.95x (ISBN 0-7167-1102-8). W H Freeman.

--DNA Synthesis. LC 74-3005. (Illus.). 1974. text ed. 30.95x (ISBN 0-7167-0586-9). W H Freeman.

Kornblatt, Joyce R. Nothing to Do with Love. LC 80-52006. 204p. 1981. 11.95 (ISBN 0-670-48020-7, Studio). Viking Pr.

Kornbluh, jt. auth. see Neinstein.

Kornbluh, Elaine, jt. auth. see Neinstein, Murray.

Kornbluh, Elaine, ed. Business English. 1981. pap. text ed. 2.25 (ISBN 0-8120-0669-0). Barron. Postponed.

Kornbluh, Joyce, jt. auth. see Craig, Bette.

Kornblum, Allan. Awkward Song. LC 80-18370. 54p. 1980. 20.00 (ISBN 0-915124-33-5, Bookslinger); pap. 5.00 (ISBN 0-915124-32-7). Toothpaste.

Kornblum, Allan N. The Moral Hazards: Police Strategies for Honesty & Ethical Behavior. LC 75-34614. 224p. 1976. 22.95 (ISBN 0-669-00378-6). Lexington Bks.

Kornblum, William. Blue Collar Community. LC 74-5733. (Studies of Urban Society Ser). 1976. pap. 6.50 (ISBN 0-226-45038-4, P699, Phoen). U of Chicago Pr.

Kornbluth, C. M. The Syndic. 1978. pap. 1.50 (ISBN 0-380-00093-8, 39404). Avon.

Kornbluth, C. M., jt. auth. see Pohl, Frederik.

Korneff, Theodore. Introduction to Electronics. 1966. text ed. 19.95 (ISBN 0-12-421150-X). Acad Pr.

Korner, J. G., et al, eds. Current Induced Reactions. (Lecture Notes in Physics: Vol. 56). 1976. soft cover 22.00 (ISBN 3-540-07866-5). Springer-Verlag.

Korner, S. Experience & Conduct. LC 75-44578. 1976. 38.50 (ISBN 0-521-21075-5). Cambridge U Pr.

--Experience & Conduct: A Philosophical Enquiry into Practical Thinking. LC 75-44578. 270p. 1980. pap. 13.50 (ISBN 0-521-29943-8). Cambridge U Pr.

Korner, S., ed. see McPherson, Thomas.

Korner, Sten. The Battle of Hastings, England & Europe, 1035-1066. LC 80-2221. 1981. Repr. of 1964 ed. 38.00 (ISBN 0-404-18765-X). AMS Pr.

Korner, Stephan. Experience & Theory. 1966. text ed. 19.25x (ISBN 0-7100-3628-0). Humanities.

Korner, Stephan, ed. Philosophy of Logic. 1976. 25.00x (ISBN 0-520-03235-7). U of Cal Pr.

Korner, Stephen. The Philosophy of Mathematics: An Introductory Essay. 1979. pap. text ed. 5.75x (ISBN 0-09-056642-4, Hutchinson U Lib). Humanities.

Kornetsky, Conan. Pharmacology: Drugs Affecting Behavior. LC 76-6062. 1976. 25.95 (ISBN 0-471-50410-6, Pub. by Wiley-Interscience). Wiley.

Kornfeld, Anita. Vintage. 1980. 13.95 (ISBN 0-671-25308-5). S&S.

Kornhaber, Arthur & Woodward, Kenneth L. Grandparents - Grandchildren: The Vital Connection. LC 79-6083. (Illus.). 312p. 1981. 11.95 (ISBN 0-385-15577-8, Anchor Pr). Doubleday.

Kornhauser, Alain L., jt. ed. see Kerr, Arnold D.

Kornhauser, William. Politics of Mass Society. LC 59-6820. 1959. text ed. 15.95 (ISBN 0-02-917620-4). Free Pr.

Kornilovich, Yu. E. & Belokhovstikova, V. I. Ultrasound in the Production & Inspection of Concrete: Pt. 1, Production Applications. 1965. 29.50 (ISBN 0-306-17035-3, Consultants). Plenum Pub.

Korniss, Peter. Passing Times. (Illus.). 1979. 17.50x (ISBN 963-13-0733-6). Intl Pubns Serv.

Kornweibel, Theodore, Jr., ed. In Search of the Promised Land: Essays in Black Urban History. (National University Publications, Interdisciplinary Urban Ser.). 237p. 1981. 17.50 (ISBN 0-8046-9267-X). Kennikat.

Korochkin, L. I. Gene Interactions in Development. (Monographs on Theoretical & Applied Genetics: Vol. 4). (Illus.). 340p. 1980. 59.80 (ISBN 0-387-10112-8). Springer-Verlag.

Korones, Sheldon B. High Risk Newborn Infants. 3rd ed. (Illus.). 350p. 1981. text ed. 16.95 (ISBN 0-8016-2738-9). Mosby.

Koropeckyj, I. S., ed. The Ukraine Within the USSR: An Economic Balance Sheet. LC 77-7817. (Praeger Special Studies). 1977. text ed. 32.50 (ISBN 0-03-022356-3). Praeger.

Korotky, V., tr. see Anpilogova, B. B., et al.

Korpi, Walter. The Working Class in Welfare Capitalism. (International Library of Sociology). 1978. 28.00x (ISBN 0-7100-8848-5). Routledge & Kegan.

Korr, Charles P. Cromwell & the New Model Foreign Policy. 1975. 19.50x (ISBN 0-520-02281-5). U of Cal Pr.

Korr, David. Cookie Monster & the Cookie Tree. LC 79-10796. (Big Picture Bks.). (Illus.). (ps-k). 1979. 1.95 (ISBN 0-307-10821-X, Golden Pr); PLB 7.62 (ISBN 0-307-60821-2); PLB 5.00 Little Golden Reader (ISBN 0-307-60159-5). Western Pub.

Korr, H. Proliferation of Different Cell Types in the Brain. (Advances in Anatomy, Embryology & Cell Biology Ser.: Vol. 61). (Illus.). 80p. 1980. pap. 28.30 (ISBN 0-387-09899-2). Springer-Verlag.

Kors, Alan C. & Peters, Edward, eds. Witchcraft in Europe, 1100-1700: A Documentary History. LC 71-170267. (Illus.). 1973. 17.50x (ISBN 0-8122-7645-0); pap. 9.95x (ISBN 0-8122-1063-8, Pa Paperbks). U of Pa pr.

Korsch, Karl. Marxism & Philosophy. Halliday, Fred, tr. from Ger. LC 71-158921. 1971. 7.50 o.p. (ISBN 0-85345-153-2, CL-1532); pap. 3.45 (ISBN 0-85345-189-3, PB-1893). Monthly Rev.

Korsching, Peter F., jt. auth. see Stofferahn, Curtis W.

Korshak, V. V. Heat Resistant Polymers. 1969. 43.95 o.p. (ISBN 0-470-50426-9). Halsted Pr.

--Heat-Resistant Polymers. 43.95 o.p. (ISBN 0-87245-446-0). Textile Bk.

Korshin, Paul J., et al, eds. The Widening Circle: Essays on the Circulation of Literature in Eighteenth-Century Europe. 1976. 17.50x (ISBN 0-8122-7717-1). U of Pa Pr.

Kort, Carol, jt. ed. see Friedland, Ronnie.

Kort, Wolfgang. Alfred Doblin. LC 73-16222. (World Author Ser.: Germany: No. 290). 1974. lib. bdg. 10.95 (ISBN 0-8057-2266-1). Twayne.

Korte, F., jt. ed. see Coulston, F.

Kortepeter, Carl Max. Ottoman Imperialism During the Reformation: Europe & The Caucasus. LC 72-75005. (Illus.). 278p. 1972. 17.50x (ISBN 0-8147-4552-0). NYU Pr.

Korth, Leslie O. Tensions: A Practical Method for Their Release. 1980. 4.00x (ISBN 0-8464-1053-2). Beekman Pubs.

Kortian, Garbis. Metacritique. Habermas, J., tr. from Fr. LC 79-7652. 140p. 1980. 24.95 (ISBN 0-521-22374-1); pap. 8.95 (ISBN 0-521-29618-8). Cambridge U Pr.

Korting. Practical Dermatology of the Genital Region. 1981. text ed. price not set (ISBN 0-7216-5498-3). Saunders.

Kortner, Peter. Breakfast with a Stranger. LC 76-28043. 1977. 7.95 o.p. (ISBN 0-312-09520-1). St Martin.

Kortright, E. H. Ducks, Geese & Swans of North America. rev. ed. Bellrose, Frank C., rev. by. LC 75-33962. (Illus.). 568p. 1981. 24.95 (ISBN 0-8117-0535-8). Stackpole.

Kortvelyessy, Eniko, tr. see Flandorffer, Tamas & Hajas, Jozsef.

Koruza, Colleen M. Macromolecular Science. (IRS Physical Chemistry Ser. Two: Vol. 8). 1975. 29.95 (ISBN 0-408-70607-4). Butterworths.

Korwin, Yala H. Index to Two-Dimensional Art Works, 2 vols. LC 80-25002. 1519p. 1981. 69.50 (ISBN 0-8108-1381-5). Scarecrow.

Korwin-Rodziszewski, Audrey, tr. see Konwicki, Tadeusz.

Korwin-Rodziszewski, George, tr. see Konwicki, Tadeusz.

Koryta, J. Ion Selective Electrodes. LC 75-9090. (Physical Chemistry Monographs). (Illus.). 250p. 1975. 42.50 (ISBN 0-521-20569-7). Cambridge U Pr.

Korzybski, Alfred. General Semantics Bulletin: Official Annual Journal of the Institute of General Semantics. Pula, Robert, ed. 20.00 (ISBN 0-910780-00-5). Inst Gen Semantics.
--General Semantics Seminar Nineteen Thirty Seven. 2nd ed. 1964. pap. 5.00x (ISBN 0-910780-02-1). Inst Gen Semantics.
--Manhood of Humanity. 2nd ed. 326p. 1950. 9.00x (ISBN 0-937298-00-X). Inst Gen Semantics.
--Science & Sanity: An Introduction to Non-Aristotelian Systems & General Semantics. 4th ed. LC 58-6260. 806p. 1958. 19.50x (ISBN 0-937298-01-8). Inst Gen Semantics.
--Time-Binding: The General Theory. pap. 4.00x (ISBN 0-910780-01-3). Inst Gen Semantics.

Korzybski, T., et al, eds. Antibiotics: Origin, Nature & Properties, 3 vols. 1979. 48.00 (ISBN 0-914826-14-X). Am Soc Microbio.

Kos, Leon, jt. auth. see Sani, Guelfo.

Kosaka, Masataka. One Hundred Million Japanese. LC 72-76298. (Illus.). 282p. 1972. 10.00x (ISBN 0-87011-182-5). Kodansha.

Kosberg, Jordan I. Abuse & Maltreatment of the Aged. 400p. Date not set. text ed. 30.00 (ISBN 0-88416-353-9). PSG Pub.

Koschitz. Koschitz's Manual of Useful Information. (Gambler's Book Shelf). 1976. pap. 2.95 (ISBN 0-89650-569-3). Gamblers.

Kosecoff, Jacqueline, jt. auth. see Fink, Arlene.

Kosel, Janice. Bankruptcy: Do It Yourself. (Illus.). 192p. 1980. write for info (ISBN 0-201-08305-1). A-W.
--Bankruptcy: Do It Yourself in California. 1980. 12.00 (ISBN 0-917316-29-0). Nolo Pr.

Koshel, Jeffrey, jt. auth. see Gutowski, Michael.

Koshel, Patrica P., jt. auth. see Gramlich, Edward M.

Koshland, Daniel E., Jr. Bacterial Chemotaxis As a Model Behavioral System. (Distinguished Lecture Ser. of the General Physiologists: Vol. 2). 210p. 1980. text ed. 19.50 (ISBN 0-89004-468-6). Raven.

Kosimaki, George E. D-Day with the Screaming Eagles. (Illus.). 1977. 10.00 (ISBN 0-686-22784-0). One Hund First Air.

Kosinski, Jerzy. Devil Tree. 256p. 1981. 11.95 (ISBN 0-312-19794-2). St Martin.
--Passion Play. 1980. pap. 2.95 (ISBN 0-553-13656-9). Bantam.

Kosinski, Leszek A., ed. Demographic Developments in Eastern Europe. LC 76-12858. (Special Studies). 1977. text ed. 32.50 (ISBN 0-275-56180-1). Praeger.

Koskoff, David E. The Mellons: The Chronicle of America's Richest Family. LC 77-25947. (Illus.). 1978. 14.50 o.s.i. (ISBN 0-690-01190-3, TYC-T). T Y Crowell.

Kosloff, Albert. Textile-Garment Screen Printing. (Illus.). 1980. 12.00 (ISBN 0-911380-39-6). Signs of Times.

Koslow, Jules. The Despised & the Damned: The Russian Peasant Through the Ages. (Russia Old & New Ser.). (Illus.). 192p. 1972. 5.95 o.s.i. (ISBN 0-02-566500-6). Macmillan.

Koslow, Jules, ed. see Parry, Albert.

Koslow, Stephen, jt. ed. see Hanin, Israel.

Kosman, William Y. Sadat's Realistic Peace Initiative. Date not set. 8.95 (ISBN 0-533-04614-9). Vantage.

Kosnioswski, C. A First Course in Algebraic Topology. LC 79-41682. 280p. 1980. 44.50 (ISBN 0-521-23195-7); pap. 15.95 (ISBN 0-521-29864-4). Cambridge U Pr.

Kosniowski, C., ed. Transformation Groups. LC 76-40837. (London Mathematical Society Lecture Notes Ser.: No. 26). 1977. limp bdg. 17.95x (ISBN 0-521-21509-9). Cambridge U Pr.

Kosolapoff, G. M. & Maier, L., eds. Organic Phosphorus Compounds, Vols. 1-3, 5-6. LC 72-1359. 2304p. 1972. Vol. 2. 50.95 (ISBN 0-471-50441-6); Vol. 5. 50.95 (ISBN 0-471-50444-0); Vol. 6. o.p. (ISBN 0-471-50445-9, Pub. by Wiley-Interscience). Wiley.

Kosow, I. L. Study Guide in Direct Current Circuits: A Personalized System of Instruction. LC 77-1739. (Ser. in Electronic Technology). 1977. 9.95 (ISBN 0-471-01664-0); solutions manual avail. (ISBN 0-471-03081-3). Wiley.

Kosow, Irving. Study Guide in Alternating Current Circuits: A Personalized System of Instruction. LC 77-22152. (Electronic Technology Ser.). 1977. pap. text ed. 10.95 (ISBN 0-471-02665-4); solutions manual avail. (ISBN 0-471-03218-2). Wiley.

Kosow, Irving L. Control of Electric Machines. LC 72-5631. (Electronic Technology Ser). (Illus.). 368p. 1973. ref. ed. 21.95 (ISBN 0-13-171785-5). P-H.

Kosoy, Ted. A Budget Guide to New York & New England: Special Bicentennial Edition. LC 75-40795. (Illus.). 288p. 1976. pap. 3.95 o.p. (ISBN 0-685-63268-7). St Martin.
--A Budget Guide Washington, D. C. & the Central Atlantic States: Special Bicentennial Edition. (Illus.). 288p. 1976. 7.95 o.p. (ISBN 0-685-63269-5); pap. 3.95 o.p. (ISBN 0-685-63270-9). St Martin.

Koss, Leopold G. & Coleman, Dulcie V. Advances in Clinical Cytology. LC 80-49874. 380p. 1980. text ed. 66.95 (ISBN 0-407-00174-3). Butterworths.

Koss, Stephen. Sir John Brunner, Radical Plutocrat. (Conference on British Studies Biographical Ser). (Illus.). 1970. 47.50 (ISBN 0-521-07906-3). Cambridge U Pr.

Koss, Stephen E. Lord Haldane: Scapegoat for Liberalism. LC 69-19460. (Illus.). 1969. 17.50x (ISBN 0-231-03201-3). Columbia U Pr.

Kossma, E. H., jt. ed. see Bromley, J. S.

Kossman, E. H. The Low Countries 1780-1940. (History of Modern Europe Ser.). 1978. 49.50x (ISBN 0-19-822108-8). Oxford U Pr.

Kossoff, G., ed. Diagnostic Ultrasound. 1980. with 400 slides 609.75 (ISBN 0-444-90056-X, Excerpta Medica). Elsevier.

Kost, Mary Lu. Success or Failure Begins in the Early School Years. (Amer. Lec. Special Education Ser.). (Illus.). 500p. 1972. 22.75 (ISBN 0-398-02334-4); pap. 19.50 (ISBN 0-398-02486-3). C C Thomas.

Kostelanetz, Richard. Autobiographies. LC 79-87601. (Rockbottom Prosework Ser.). 288p. (Orig.). 1980. pap. 8.00 (ISBN 0-930012-42-9); 15.00 o.p. (ISBN 0-930012-41-0). Mudborn.
--Come Here. 1975. 2.50, signed & lettered A-Z 25.00 ea. (ISBN 0-685-56017-1). Assembling Pr.
--End Essentials. Bd. with End Appendix. LC 79-313. LC 79-51582. 1979. 5.95 (ISBN 0-686-59587-4). Assembling Pr.
--The End-Essentials. Bd. with End - Appendix "Intelligent Writing" Reconsidered. LC 79-51580 (ISBN 0-8108-1246-0). LC 79-57582. 1979. 12.50 (ISBN 0-8108-1247-9). Scarecrow.
--Exhaustive Parallel Intervals. LC 79-51581. 1980. 15.00; signed & lettered, A-Z 50.00; pap. 5.95 (ISBN 0-918406-09-9). Future Pr.
--Extrapolate. 50p. 1975. pap. 2.00 (ISBN 0-685-61221-X); signed 50.00 (ISBN 0-685-61222-8). Assembling Pr.
--Master Minds: Portraits of Contemporary American Artists & Intellectuals. 1969. 7.95 o.s.i. (ISBN 0-02-566510-3). Macmillan.
--Metamorphosis in the Arts. LC 80-68968. 328p. 1981. 18.00 (ISBN 0-686-69406-6); pap. 8.00 (ISBN 0-686-69407-4). Assembling Pr.
--More Short Fictions. LC 80-58969. (Illus.). 224p. (Orig.). 1981. 15.00 (ISBN 0-686-69408-2); pap. 6.96 (ISBN 0-686-69409-0). Assembling Pr.
--Portraits from Memory. 1975. 7.95 (ISBN 0-932360-21-1); signed & numbered, 1-10 75.00 (ISBN 0-685-58447-X); pap. 3.00 (ISBN 0-932360-20-3). RK Edns.
--Prunings-Accruings. 24p. 1978. pap. 25.00 signed & lettered. a-z (ISBN 0-932360-22-X). RK Edns.
--The Theatre of Mixed Means. 1978. pap. 15.00 (ISBN 0-932360-06-8). RK Edns.

Kostelanetz, Richard, ed. A Critical Ninth Assembling. LC 78-72282. (Illus.). 1979. pap. text ed. 10.00 (ISBN 0-915066-33-5). Assembling Pr.
--John Cage. LC 70-12174. (Illus.). 1978. 12.50 (ISBN 0-932360-09-2); pap. 4.95 (ISBN 0-932360-10-6). RK Edns.
--Scenarios. LC 80-68155. (Illus.). 1981. pap. 16.00 (ISBN 0-686-69411-2). Assembling Pr.

Kostelanetz, Richard & Korn, Henry J., eds. Eighth A-J Assembling. (Illus.). 1978. pap. 4.95 (ISBN 0-685-49935-9). Assembling Pr.
--Fifth Assembling. new ed. (Illus.). 300p. (Orig.). 1974. pap. 4.95 (ISBN 0-685-49921-9). Assembling Pr.

Kostelanetz, Richard, et al, eds. Complete Assembling. (Orig.). 1979. pap. 60.00 (ISBN 0-915066-34-3). Assembling Pr.
--Tenth Assembling. LC 80-68188. (Assembling Ser.). (Illus.). 200p. 1981. pap. 4.95 (ISBN 0-686-69410-4). Assembling Pr.

Kosten, L. Stochastic Theory of Service Systems. LC 72-10124. 180p. 1973. text ed. 30.00 (ISBN 0-08-016948-1). Pergamon.

Kosten, Richard, ed. Teacher Absenteeism. 1977. pap. 9.00 o.p. (ISBN 0-686-00913-4, D-111). Essence Pubns.

Kostenbaum, Peter. Is There an Answer to Death. LC 76-1939. (Illus.). 224p. 1976. pap. 3.95 (ISBN 0-13-506097-4). P-H.

Koster, Donald N. Transcendentalism in America. (World Leaders Ser.). 1975. lib. bdg. 10.95 (ISBN 0-8057-3727-8). Twayne.

Koster, Jan, et al. Locality Principles in Syntax. (Studies in Generative Grammar: No. 5). (Orig.). 1979. pap. text ed. 20.00x (ISBN 90-70176-06-8). Humanities.

Koster, M. D. The Peshitta of Exodus, the Development of Its Text in the Course of Fifteen Centuries. (Studia Semitica Neerlandica: No. 19). 1977. text ed. 116.85x (ISBN 90-232-1503-6). Humanities.

Koster, R. M. The Dissertation. LC 80-20066. 438p. 1981. pap. 7.95 (ISBN 0-688-00043-6, Quill). Morrow.
--Mandragon. 346p. 1981. pap. 5.95 (ISBN 0-688-00348-6, Quill). Morrow.
--The Prince. LC 78-155996. 1979. pap. 5.95 (ISBN 0-688-05108-1, Quill). Morrow.

Kosterlitz, H. W. & Terenius, L. Y., eds. Pain & Society. (Dahlem Workshop Reports, Life Sciences Research Report Ser.: No. 17). (Illus.). 523p. (Orig.). 1980. pap. text ed. 39.40 (ISBN 0-89573-099-5). Verlag Chemie.

Kostich, Dragos. The Land & People of the Balkans. rev. ed. LC 73-7709. (Portraits of the Nations Series). (Illus.). 1973. 8.95 (ISBN 0-397-31397-7). Lippincott.

Kostich, Dragos D., rev. by see Kelly, Eric P.

Kostick, Marilyn, jt. auth. see Aukema, Susan.

Kostick, Marilyn, ed. see Murphy, Margaret D.

Kostka, Matthew. Climb to the Top. LC 62-14787. (gr. 6-9). 1962. 5.95 o.p. (ISBN 0-385-02581-5). Doubleday.

Kostof, Spiro, ed. The Architect: Chapters in the History of the Profession. LC 75-46368. (Illus.). 1976. 25.00x (ISBN 0-19-502067-7). Oxford U Pr.

Kostruba, T., tr. from Ukrainian. Halyts'ko-Volyns'kyi Litopys, 2 vols. 258p. 1967. 17.50. Slavia Lib.

Kostrubala, Thaddeus. The Joy of Running. LC 76-9835. 1976. 8.95 o.p. (ISBN 0-397-01110-5); pap. 4.95 o.p. (ISBN 0-397-01169-5). Lippincott.

Kostuik, J. P. & Gillespie, Robert, eds. Amputation Surgery & Rehabilitation: The Toronto Experience. (Illus.). 1981. text ed. price not set (ISBN 0-443-08024-0). Churchill. Postponed.

Kostyu, Frank A. The Time of Your Life Is Now. 1977. 6.95 (ISBN 0-8164-0375-9). Crossroad NY.

Kosygin, A. N. Selected Speeches & Writings. LC 80-41077. 352p. 1981. 100.00 (ISBN 0-08-023610-3). Pergamon.

Koszarowski, Tadeusz. Cancer Surgery. LC 78-27389. (Illus.). 1981. text ed. 25.00 (ISBN 0-8067-1021-7). Urban & S.

Koszarski, Richard, ed. Hollywood Directors, 1941-1976. LC 76-51716. (Illus.). 1977. 19.95 (ISBN 0-19-502217-3). Oxford U Pr.
--Hollywood Directors, 1941-1976. LC 76-51716. (Illus.). 1977. pap. 6.95 (ISBN 0-19-502218-1, GB 509, GB). Oxford U Pr.

Koszarski, Richard, et al. The Rivals of D.W. Griffith: Alternate Auteurs, 1913 to 1918. (Illus.). 58p. (Orig.). 1980. pap. 4.95 (ISBN 0-918432-32-4). Ny Zoetrope.

Kosztolnyik, Z. J. Five Eleventh Century Hungarian Kings: Their Policies & Their Relations with Rome. (East European Monographs: No. 79). 288p. 1981. text ed. 20.00x (ISBN 0-914710-73-7). East Eur Quarterly.

Kotani, M., ed. Advances in Biophysics, 12 vols, Vols. 7-12. (Illus.). Vols. 7-10. 19.50 ea. Vol. 7, 1975 (ISBN 0-8391-0104-X). Vol. 8, 1975 (ISBN 0-8391-0105-8). Vol. 9, 1977 (ISBN 0-8391-0106-6). Vol. 10, 1978 (ISBN 0-8391-0107-4). Vols. 11 & 12. 29.50 ea. Vol. 11, 1979 (ISBN 0-8391-0108-2). Vol. 12, 1979 (ISBN 0-8391-0109-0). Vol. 13. 39.50 (ISBN 0-8391-0110-4). Univ Park.

Kotas, Richard & Kreul, L. Management Accounting for Hotels & Restaurants. (gr. 10 up). 1979. text ed. 15.50x (ISBN 0-8104-9472-8). Hayden.

Kotelnikov, Vladimir A. Theory of Optimum Noise Immunity. Silverman, R. A., tr. LC 68-20594. (Illus.). 1960. pap. text ed. 3.50 (ISBN 0-486-61952-4). Dover.

Kothari, C. R. Quantitative Techniques. 1979. text ed. 18.95 (ISBN 0-7069-0642-X, Pub. by Vikas India). Advent Bk.

Kothari, L. S., jt. auth. see Ghatak, A. K.

Kothari, M. L. & Mehta, L. A. Cancer: Myths & Realities of Cause & Cure. (Ideas in Progress Ser.). 1979. 12.00 (ISBN 0-7145-2665-7, Pub. by M Boyars); pap. 5.95 (ISBN 0-7145-2666-5). Merrimack Bk Serv.

Kothari, Rajni. Footsteps into the Future. LC 74-31357. (Preferred Worlds for the 1990's Ser.). 1975. 8.95 (ISBN 0-02-917570-4); pap. text ed. 7.95 (ISBN 0-02-917580-1). Free Pr.

Kothari, Ranji. Democratic Polity & Social Change in India: Crisis & Opportunities. LC 76-904213. 1976. text ed. 7.50x o.p. (ISBN 0-88386-881-4); pap. text ed. 4.00x o.p. (ISBN 0-685-74909-6). South Asia Bks.

Kothari, Sunil, ed. Bharata Natyam: Indian Classical Dance Art. LC 80-901925. (Illus.). 212p. 1979. 37.50x (ISBN 0-8002-2441-8). Intl Pubns Serv.

Kothe, Gottfried, ed. see Toeplitz, Otto.

Kotheimer, William J. Applied Chiropractic in Distortion Analysis. (Illus.). 200p. 1976. 8.95 (ISBN 0-8059-2329-2). Dorrance.

Kotik, Charlotta, ed. With Paper, About Paper. LC 80-69318. (Illus.). 1980. pap. 7.50 (ISBN 0-914782-35-5). Buffalo Acad.

Kotker, Norman. The Israelites. (Emergence of Man Ser.). (Illus.). 1975. 9.95 (ISBN 0-8094-1294-2); lib. bdg. avail. (ISBN 0-685-72431-X). Time-Life.

Kotker, Zane. White Rising. LC 80-20011. 288p. 1981. 11.95 (ISBN 0-394-40776-8). Knopf.

Kotkin, G. I. & Serbo, V. G. Collection of Problems in Classical Mechanics. 1971. 18.00 (ISBN 0-08-015843-9). Pergamon.

Kotlar, Barbara, jt. auth. see Silva, Tony.

Kotler, Milton. Neighborhood Government: The Local Foundations of Political Life. LC 69-13097. 1969. pap. 4.50 (ISBN 0-672-60720-4). Bobbs.

Kotler, Philip. Marketing Management: Analysis, Planning & Control. 4th ed. 1980. text ed. 21.00 (ISBN 0-13-557975-9). P-H.

Kotler, Philip & Cox, Keith. Marketing Management & Strategy: A Reader. rev. ed. (Illus.). 1980. pap. text ed. 12.95 (ISBN 0-13-558122-2). P-H.
--Readings in Marketing Management. 1972. pap. text ed. 9.95 o.p. (ISBN 0-13-759241-8). P-H.

Kotler, Phillip. Marketing for Non-Profit Organizations. (Illus.). 448p. 1975. ref. ed. 19.95 (ISBN 0-13-556084-5). P-H.
--Marketing Management: Analysis, Planning & Control. 3rd ed. 1976. 17.95 o.p. (ISBN 0-13-557959-7). P-H.

Kotliar, B. C. X. Neutral Mechanism of Conditioning. LC 80-25451. 205p. 1981. 11.00 (ISBN 0-08-026334-8). Pergamon.

Kotosixin, Grigorij. Russia in the Reign of Aleksej Mixajlovic: Text & Commentary. Pennington, A. E., ed. (Illus.). 740p. 1980. 165.00x (ISBN 0-19-815639-1). Oxford U Pr.

Kotov, Alexander. Alexander Alekhine. 1975. 18.95 (ISBN 0-7134-2963-1, Pub. by Batsford England). David & Charles.
--Play Like a Grandmaster. 1978. pap. 12.50 (ISBN 0-7134-1807-9). David & Charles.
--Think Like a Grandmaster. 1976. pap. 12.50 (ISBN 0-7134-3160-1, Pub. by Batsford England). David & Charles.
--Train Like a Grandmaster. (Clubplayer's Library Ser.). (Illus.). 112p. 1981. pap. 11.95 (ISBN 0-7134-3609-3, Pub. by Batsford England). David & Charles.

Kotrba, Danella G. God's Helper. (Come Unto Me Ser.: Year 2, Bk. 1). 32p. (ps). 1980. pap. 1.50 (ISBN 0-8127-0211-5). Southern Pub.

Kotre, John N. The Best of Times, the Worst of Times: Andrew Greeley & American Catholicism, 1950-1975. LC 78-14224. 1978. 14.95 (ISBN 0-88229-380-X); pap. 7.95 (ISBN 0-88229-597-7). Nelson-Hall.

Kotschevar, Lendal H. Foodservice for the Extended Care Facility. LC 72-75295. 1973. text ed. 21.95 (ISBN 0-8436-0548-0). CBI Pub.
--Quantity Food Production. 3rd ed. (Illus.). 1975. 33.60x (ISBN 0-85334-632-1). Intl Ideas.

Kotschevar, Lendal H., jt. auth. see Lunberg, Donald.

Kotsiubynsky, Mykhailo. Shadows of Forgotten Ancestors. Carynnk, Marco, tr. from Ukrainian. (Ukrainian Classics in Translation Ser.: No. 4). 215p. 1981. lib. bdg. 9.50 (ISBN 0-87287-205-X, Ukrainian Acad Pr). Libs Unl.

Kottak, Conrad P. Anthropology: The Exploration of Human Diversity. 2nd ed. 1978. text ed. 16.95 (ISBN 0-394-31276-7); study guide 4.25 (ISBN 0-394-31836-6). Random.

--Cultural Anthropology. 2nd ed. LC 78-15704. (Illus.). 1978. pap. text ed. 10.95x (ISBN 0-394-32221-5). Random.
--The Past in the Present: History, Ecology, and Cultural Variation in Highland Madagascar. (Illus.). 406p. 1980. 18.95x (ISBN 0-472-09323-1); pap. 9.95x (ISBN 0-472-06323-5). U of Mich Pr.
Kottegoda, N. T. Stochastic Water Resources Technology. LC 79-23032. 1980. 53.95x (ISBN 0-470-98975-0). Halsted Pr.
Kotter, John P. Organizational Dynamics: Diagnosis & Intervention. 1978. pap. text ed. 6.50 (ISBN 0-201-03890-0). A-W.
Kotter, John P., et al. Organization. 1979. 18.95 (ISBN 0-256-02226-7). Irwin.
Kottke, Frank. The Promotion of Price Competition Where Sellers Are Few. LC 77-18328. (Illus.). 1978. 19.95 (ISBN 0-669-02094-X). Lexington Bks.
Kotz, David M. Bank Control of Large Corporations in the United States. 1978. 14.50x (ISBN 0-520-03321-3); pap. 3.95 (ISBN 0-520-03937-8). U of Cal Pr.
Kotz, Mary L., jt. auth. see Kotz, Nick.
Kotz, Mary L., jt. auth. see West, J. B.
Kotz, Nick & Kotz, Mary L. A Passion for Equality. 1977. pap. text ed. 3.95x (ISBN 0-393-09006-X). Norton.
Kotz, S. I., jt. auth. see Johnson, N. L.
Kotz, Samuel, jt. auth. see Johnson, Norman.
Kotz, Samuel, jt. auth. see Johnson, Norman L.
Kotz, Samuel I., jt. auth. see Johnson, Norman L.
Kotz, Sanuel. Russian-English - English-Russian Glossary of Statistical Terms. new ed. 1973. 13.75 o.s.i. (ISBN 0-02-848030-9, 84803). Hafner.
Kotze, D. A. African Politics in South Africa: Parties & Issues. LC 75-6050. 350p. 1975. 29.95 (ISBN 0-312-01015-X). St Martin.
Kotzwinkle, William. The Elephant Boy. (ps-3). 1970. 3.95 o.p. (ISBN 0-374-32013-6). FS&G.
--Fata Morgana. 208p. 1980. pap. 2.95 (ISBN 0-553-11736-X). Bantam.
--The Leopard's Tooth. LC 75-25504. (Illus.). 96p. (gr. 3-6). 1976. 6.95 (ISBN 0-395-28862-2, Clarion). HM.
--The Leopard's Tooth. 1978. pap. 1.25 (ISBN 0-686-68379-X, 37382, Camelot). Avon.
--The Nap Master. LC 78-12178. (Illus.). 32p. 1979. 7.95 (ISBN 0-15-256704-6, HJ). HarBraceJ.
--Night Book. 1980. pap. 2.50 (ISBN 0-380-49106-0, 49106, Bard). Avon.
--Up the Alley with Jack & Joe. LC 74-2127. (Ready-to-Read Ser.). (Illus.). 64p. (gr. 1-3). 1974. 7.95g (ISBN 0-02-750940-0). Macmillan.
Koulischer, Lucien, jt. auth. see Cervenka, Jaroslav.
Koulomzin, Sophie. Many Worlds: A Russian Life. LC 80-19332. 368p. 1980. pap. 8.95. St Vladimirs.
--Many Worlds: A Russian Life. LC 80-19332. 368p. 1980. pap. 8.95 (ISBN 0-913836-72-9, BS597 K64A35). St Martin.
--Our Church & Our Children. LC 75-20215. 158p. 1975. pap. 4.95 (ISBN 0-913836-25-7). St Vladimirs.
Koumoulides, John T. Cyprus & the War of Greek Independence 1821-1829. (Bibliothea Historica Cyprica). (Illus.). 1977. text ed. 13.00x (ISBN 0-900834-81-1); pap. text ed. 8.00x (ISBN 0-900834-82-X). Humanities.
Koumoulides, John T., ed. Hellenic Perspectives: Essays in the History of Greece. LC 80-5475. 398p. 1980. lib. bdg. 20.75 (ISBN 0-8191-1107-4); pap. text ed. 12.75 (ISBN 0-8191-1108-2). U Pr of Amer.
Kounovsky, Nicholas. Kounovsky's Instant Fitness: How to Stay Fit & Healthy in 6 Minutes a Day. 1978. 8.95 (ISBN 0-394-41316-4). Random.
Kounovsky, Nicholas, jt. auth. see Crenshaw, Mary A.
Kour, Z. H. The History of Aden 1839-1872. 1980. 29.50x (ISBN 0-7146-3101-9, F Cass Co). Biblio Dist.
Kourouma, Ahmadu. The Suns of Independence. Adams, Adrian, tr. from Fr. LC 80-8891. 160p. 1981. text ed. 24.50x (ISBN 0-8419-0626-2, Africana); pap. text ed. 9.75x (ISBN 0-8419-0688-2). Holmes & Meier.
Koury, Enver M. The Balance of Economic Power: North-South Confrontation on Raw Materials. LC 76-23819. 125p. 1977. pap. 6.00 (ISBN 0-934484-09-0). Inst Mid East & North Africa.
--The Balance of Military Power: The Arab-Israeli Conflict. LC 76-57912. 111p. 1977. pap. 5.00 (ISBN 0-934484-10-4). Inst Mid East & North Africa.
--The Middle East & North Africa: Definition & Analysis of Regional Balances of Power. LC 74-84755. 132p. 1974. pap. 6.00 (ISBN 0-934484-06-6). Inst Mid East & North Africa.
--Oil & Geopolitics in the Persian Gulf Area: A Center of Power. LC 73-85565. 96p. 1973. pap. 5.00 (ISBN 0-934484-03-1). Inst Mid East & North Africa.
--The Saudi Decision-Making Body: The House of Al-Saud. LC 77-90773. 96p. 1978. pap. 5.00 (ISBN 0-934484-12-0). Inst Mid East & North Africa.
--The Superpowers & the Balance of Power in the Arab World. LC 79-131974. 208p. 1970. pap. 7.00 (ISBN 0-934484-01-5). Inst Mid East & North Africa.
--The United Arab Emirates: Its Political System & Politics. LC 79-90997. 147p. (Orig.). 1980. pap. 8.00 (ISBN 0-934484-15-5). Inst Mid East & North Africa.
Koury, Enver M. & Nakhleh, Emile A., eds. The Arabian Peninsula, Red Sea, & Gulf: Strategic Considerations. LC 79-88430. 100p. 1979. pap. 6.00 (ISBN 0-934484-14-7). Inst Mid East & North Africa.
Koushakdjian, Mardiros & Khantrouni, Dicran. Armenian-English - English-Armenian Dictionary. 2nd, rev. ed. 1372p. 1976. 35.00 (ISBN 0-686-68934-8). Heinman.
Koushanpour, Esmail. Renal Physiology: Principles & Functions. LC 75-12489. (Illus.). 1976. pap. 13.50 o.p. (ISBN 0-7216-5493-2). Saunders.
Kouts, H. H., jt. ed. see Henley, E. J.
Koutsoyiannis, A. Theory of Econometrics: An Introductory Exposition of Econometric Methods. 2d ed. LC 76-53202. 1978. pap. 20.50x (ISBN 0-06-493949-9). B&N.
Kouymjian, Dickran, ed. see Lazar Of Pharbi.
Kovacevic, Ivanka. Fact into Fiction: English Literature & the Industrial Scene 1750-1850. 416p. 1975. text ed. 16.00x (ISBN 0-7185-1130-1, Leicester). Humanities.
Kovach, A. G. B., et al, eds. Cardiovascular Physiology, Microcirculation & Capillary Exchange: Proceedings of the 28th International Congress of Physiological Sciences, Budapest, 1980. LC 80-41873. (Advances in Physiological Sciences: Vol. 7). (Illus.). 400p. 1981. 50.00 (ISBN 0-08-026819-6). Pergamon.
--Cardiovascular Physiology, Heart, Peripheral Circulation & Methodology: Proceedings of the 28th International Congress of Physiological Sciences, Budapest, Hungary, 1980. LC 80-41875. (Advances in Physiological Sciences). (Illus.). 400p. 1981. 50.00 (ISBN 0-08-026820-X). Pergamon.
--Cardiovascular Physiology-Neural Control Mechanisms: Proceedings of the 28th International Congress of Physiological Sciences, Budapest, 1980. LC 80-41927. (Advances in Physiological Sciences: Vol. 9). (Illus.). 400p. 1981. 50.00 (ISBN 0-08-026821-8). Pergamon.
Kovach, E. G., ed. Technology of Efficient Energy Utilization: Report, Nato Science Committee Conference, les Arcs, France, Oct. 1973. LC 74-19839. 82p. 1976. pap. text ed. 10.00 (ISBN 0-08-018314-X). Pergamon.
--Thermal Energy Storage. LC 77-71233. 1977. pap. text ed. 9.50 (ISBN 0-08-021724-9). Pergamon.
Kovach, Francis J. & Shahan, Robert W., eds. Albert the Great: Commemorative Essays. LC 79-6713. 250p. 1980. 12.95x (ISBN 0-8061-1666-8). U of Okla Pr.
Kovach, Kenneth A. Readings & Cases in Contemporary Labor Relations 1980. LC 80-1429. 359p. 1981. pap. text ed. 12.00 (ISBN 0-8191-1362-X). U Pr of Amer.
Kovacic, Michael L. Business & Consumer Mathematics. 1978. text ed. 17.80 (ISBN 0-205-05963-5); instr's man. avail. (ISBN 0-205-05964-3). Allyn.
Kovaco, W. & Holtz, R. Introduction to Geotechniical Engineering. 1981. 28.95 (ISBN 0-13-484394-0). P-H.
Kovacs, David. The Andromache Oof Euripides: An Interpretation. LC 80-11220. write for info. (ISBN 0-89130-389-8); lib. bdg. 10.00x (ISBN 0-89130-390-1). Scholars Pr CA.
Kovacs, E. Biochemistry of the Poliomyelitis Viruses. 1964. 18.75 (ISBN 0-08-010111-9). Pergamon.
Kovacs, Ferenc. Linguistic Structures & Linguistic Laws. Simon, Sandor, tr. from Hungarian. 1971. text ed. 42.75x (ISBN 90-6032-492-7). Humanities.
Kovacs, G., et al. Subterranean Hydrology. 1981. 45.00 (ISBN 0-918334-35-7). WRP.
Kovacs, Kalman, et al. Pituitary Diseases. 256p. 1980. lib. bdg. 69.95 (ISBN 0-8493-5435-8). CRC Pr.
Kovacs, Klara L. Collected Poems of Klara L. Kovacs: Eszmeles. (Rainbow Bks.: No. 1). (Illus.). 1980. write for info. (ISBN 0-936398-01-9). Framo Pub.
Kovacs, L. G., ed. see International Conference on the Theory of Groups, 1969.
Kovacs, T. & Zsoldos, L. Dislocations & Plastic Deformations. LC 73-6995. 364p. 1974. 23.00 (ISBN 0-08-017062-5). Pergamon.
Kovacs, William D. & Holtz, Robert D. An Introduction to Geotechnical Engineering. (Illus.). 720p. 1981. text ed. 28.95 (ISBN 0-13-484394-0). P-H.
Kovaleff, Theodore P. Business & Government During the Eisenhower Administration: A Study of the Anti-Trust Policy of the Anti-Trust Division of the Justice Department. LC 79-25590. x, 313p. 1980. 17.95x (ISBN 0-8214-0416-4). Ohio U Pr.
Kovalenko, Y. G. English-Russian Dictionary of Reliability & Quality Control. LC 77-70279. 1977. text ed. 67.00 (ISBN 0-08-021933-0). Pergamon.
Kovalevsky, J., ed. see COSPAR-IAU-IUTAM Symposium, Paris, 1965.
Kovash, Sr. Emily. How to Have Fun Making Cards. LC 74-10532. (Creative Craft Bks.). (Illus.). 32p. (gr. 2-6). 1974. PLB 5.95 (ISBN 0-87191-360-7). Creative Ed.
Kovda, Viktor. Land Aridization & Drought Control. (Westview Special Studies in Natural Resources & Energy Management). 1980. lib. bdg. 27.50x (ISBN 0-89158-259-2). Westview.
Kovesi, Julius. Moral Notions. 1967. text ed. 7.00x (ISBN 0-7100-2984-5); pap. text ed. 5.25x (ISBN 0-7100-7167-1). Humanities.
Kovetz, Albert. Silent Partners. 400p. (Orig.). 1980. pap. 2.50 (ISBN 0-89083-688-4). Zebra.
Kovi, Paul, jt. auth. see Margittai, Tom G.
Kovner, Anthony R. & Neuhauser, Duncan, eds. Health Services Management: An Anthology. LC 78-4567. 1978. text ed. 27.50 (ISBN 0-914904-17-5). Health Admin Pr.
Kovoor, A., tr. see Gabe, M.
Kovrig, Bennett. Communism in Hungary from Kun to Kadar. Staar, Richard F., ed. LC 78-59863. (Publications Ser.: No. 211). (Illus.). 1979. pap. 10.95 (ISBN 0-8179-7112-2). Hoover Inst Pr.
Kowakami, Kiyoshi K; see Lay, Arthur H.
Kowal, J. M. & Kassam, A. H. Agricultural Ecology of Savanna: A Study of West Africa. LC 77-30412. (Illus.). 1979. 59.00x (ISBN 0-19-859462-3). Oxford U Pr.
Kowalczyk, J. Orthodox View on Abortion. 1979. pap. 1.50 (ISBN 0-686-27070-3). Light&Life Pub Co MN.
Kowalewski, Gerhard. Determinantentheorie. 3rd ed. LC 49-22682. (Ger). 14.95 (ISBN 0-8284-0039-3). Chelsea Pub.
--Kontinuierliche Gruppen. LC 51-3003. (Ger). 14.95 (ISBN 0-8284-0070-9). Chelsea Pub.
Kowalik, Janusz S., jt. auth. see Jacoby, Samuel L.
Kowalski, Casimir, jt. auth. see Cangemi, Joseph.
Kowalski, Casimir J. & Cangemi, Joseph P. Higher Education in the United States & Latin America. 128p. (Orig.). 1981. 8.50 (ISBN 0-8022-2385-0). Philos Lib.
Kowalski, Gene. How to Eat Cheap but Good. 1977. pap. 1.75 o.p. (ISBN 0-445-08601-7). Popular Lib.
Kowalski, Ludwik & Hellman, Hal. Understanding Physics. 1978. text ed. 17.95x (ISBN 0-534-00596-9). Wadsworth Pub.
Kowalski, R., jt. ed. see Bibel, W.
Kowalski, Rosemary R. Women & Film: A Bibliography. LC 76-25051. 1976. 13.50 (ISBN 0-8108-0974-5). Scarecrow.
Kowalski, T., ed. Floating Breakwater Conference Papers, 1974. (Marine Technical Report Ser.: No. 24). 1974. pap. 5.00 (ISBN 0-938412-10-8). URI MAS.
Ko Wang Mei, jt. auth. see Singh, Baljit.
Kowet, Don. The Soccer Book. LC 76-8131. (gr. 5-9). 1976. pap. 4.95 (ISBN 0-394-93250-1, BYR); pap. 5.95 (ISBN 0-394-83250-7). Random.
Kowet, Donald K. Land, Labour Migration & Politics in Southern Africa: Botswana, Lesotho & Swaziland. 1978. pap. text ed. 18.00x (ISBN 0-8419-9734-9). Holmes & Meier.
Kowit, Steve, tr. see Neruda, Pablo.
Kowit, Steven. Cutting Our Losses. 60p. (Orig.). 1981. pap. 3.00 (ISBN 0-686-69322-1). Contact Two.
Kowitz & Knutson. Decision Making in Small Groups: The Search for Alternatives. 1980. text ed. 16.95 (ISBN 0-205-06650-X, 486650-9). Allyn.
Kowta, Makoto. The Sayles Complex: A Late Milling Stone Horizon Assemblage from Cajon Pass, California, & the Ecological Implications of Its Scraper Planes. (U. C. Publ. in Anthropology: Vol. 6). 1969. pap. 6.50x (ISBN 0-520-09005-5). U of Cal Pr.
Kowtaluk. Discovering Foods. (gr. 9-12). 1978. pap. 5.80 o.p. (ISBN 0-87002-272-5). Bennett IL.
Kowtaluk, Helen. Discovering Food. (gr. 9-12). 1978. 8.64 (ISBN 0-87002-270-9); pap. 5.96 (ISBN 0-87002-272-5); student guide 3.96 (ISBN 0-87002-278-4); tchrs. guide 7.36 (ISBN 0-87002-280-6). Bennett IL.
--Discovering Nutrition. 1980. text ed. 9.28 (ISBN 0-87002-310-1); tchr's guide 6.00 (ISBN 0-87002-318-7); student guide 2.64 (ISBN 0-87002-317-9). Bennett IL.
--Discovering Nutrition. (gr. 7-12). 1980. text ed. 9.28 o.p. (ISBN 0-87002-310-1); tchr's guide avail. o.p.; student guide avail. o.p. Bennett IL.
Kowtaluk, Helen & Kopan, Alice. Food for Today. 1977. 15.00 (ISBN 0-87002-181-8); pap. 16.80 tchr. resource guide (ISBN 0-87002-187-7); student activity guide 2.60 (ISBN 0-87002-197-4). Bennett IL.
Kozak, Lola J. The Status of Hospital Discharge Data, in Denmark, Scotland, West Germany, & the United States. Cox, Klaudia, ed. (Ser. Two: No. 88). 55p. 1981. pap. 1.75 (ISBN 0-8406-0211-1). Natl Ctr Health Stats.
Kozar, L. A., jt. ed. see Chibisova, O. I.
Kozhevnikov, A. V. Electron-Ion Exchangers: A New Group of Redoxites. Pick, A., ed. Kondor, R., tr. from Rus. LC 74-32247. 129p. 1975. 27.95 (ISBN 0-470-50626-1). Halsted Pr.
Koziakin, Vladimir. Science Fiction Mazes. 128p. (gr. 4 up). pap. 1.50 (ISBN 0-448-17259-3, Tempo). G&D.
Kozicki, Henry, jt. ed. see Canary, Robert H.
Kozier, Barbara B. & Erb, Glenora L. Fundamentals of Nursing: Concepts & Procedures. LC 78-7776. 1979. 23.95 (ISBN 0-201-03904-4, 03904, M&N Div); instr's guide 3.95 (ISBN 0-686-52327-X, 03905). A-W.
Kozloff & Solis. Microaggragates: Experimental & Clinical Aspects. 1981. write for info. (ISBN 0-87527-177-4). Green.
Kozloff, M. Educating Children with Learning & Behavior Problems. LC 74-11304. 1974. 29.95 (ISBN 0-471-50630-3, Pub. by Wiley-Interscience). Wiley.
Kozloff, Martin A. A Program for Families of Children with Learning & Behavior Problems. LC 78-26578. 1979. 28.95 (ISBN 0-471-04434-2, Pub. by Wiley-Interscience). Wiley.
Kozlov, Valery A., jt. auth. see Malinovsky, Nikolai N.
Kozlovsky, Daniel G., ed. An Ecological & Evolutionary Ethic. (Illus.). 128p. 1974. pap. 10.95 (ISBN 0-13-222935-8). P-H.
Kozlowski, Andrezj, jt. ed. see Roedder, Edwin.
Kozlowski, T. K., jt. ed. see Tibbitts, T.
Kozlowski, T. T. Growth & Development of Trees, 2 Vols. LC 70-127688. (Physiological Ecology Ser). 1971. Vol. 1. 48.00 (ISBN 0-12-424201-4); Vol. 2. 58.00 (ISBN 0-12-424202-2); Set. 86.50 (ISBN 0-685-03085-7). Acad Pr.
--Water Deficits & Plant Growth: Woody Plant Communities, Vol. 6. 1981. write for info. (ISBN 0-12-424156-5). Acad Pr.
Kozlowski, Theodore T., ed. Tree Growth. (Illus.). 1962. 21.50 (ISBN 0-8260-5090-5, Pub. by Wiley-Interscience). Wiley.
--Water Deficits & Plant Growth, 5 vols. LC 68-14658. Vol. 1 1968. 48.00 (ISBN 0-12-424150-6); Vol. 2 1968. 40.50 (ISBN 0-12-424152-2); Vol. 3 1972. 40.50 (ISBN 0-12-424153-0); Vol. 4 1976. 48.50 (ISBN 0-12-424154-9); Vol. 5, 1978. 39.50 (ISBN 0-12-424155-7); Set. 176.50. Acad Pr.
Kozmetsky, George, jt. auth. see Kozmetsky, Ronya.
Kozmetsky, Ronya & Kozmetsky, George. Making It Together: A Survival Manual for the Executive Family. LC 80-69284. 1981. 12.95 (ISBN 0-02-917910-6). Free Pr.
Kozol, Jonathan. On Being a Teacher. 208p. 1981. 12.95 (ISBN 0-8264-0035-3). Continuum.
Kozoll, Charles E. Staff Development in Organizations: A Cost Evaluation for Managers & Trainers. 124p. 1974. text ed. 8.95 (ISBN 0-201-03864-1). A-W.
Kozuki, Russel. Junior Karate. (Illus.). (gr. 4-6). 1977. pap. 1.50 (ISBN 0-686-68483-4). PB.
Kozuki, Russell. Junior Karate. LC 71-167665. (Illus.). (gr. 3 up). 1971. 6.95 (ISBN 0-8069-4446-3); PLB 6.69 (ISBN 0-8069-4447-1). Sterling.
--Junior Karate. (gr. 4-6). 1977. pap. 1.75 (ISBN 0-671-42065-8). Archway.
--Karate for Young People. LC 73-93590. (Athletic Institute Ser.). (Illus.). 128p. (gr. 3 up). 1974. 6.95 (ISBN 0-8069-4074-3); PLB 6.69 (ISBN 0-8069-4075-1). Sterling.
Kozuki, Russell & Lee, Douglas. Kung Fu for Young People: The Ving Tsun System. LC 75-14504. (Illus.). 128p. 1975. 5.95 o.p. (ISBN 0-8069-4094-8); PLB 5.89 o.p. (ISBN 0-8069-4095-6). Sterling.
Kozuszek, Jane E. Hygiene. (First Bks.). (Illus.). (gr. 4 up). 1978. PLB 6.45 s&l (ISBN 0-531-01410-X). Watts.
Kozyrev, B. M., jt. auth. see Al'tshuler, S. A.
Kra, I. & Maskit, B., eds. Riemann Surfaces & Related Topics: Proceedings of the 1978 Stony Brook Conference. 1980 (ISBN 0-691-08264-2). pap. 9.50 (ISBN 0-691-08267-7). Princeton U Pr.

--Riemann Surfaces & Related Topics: Proceedings of the 1978 Stony Brook Conference. LC 79-27923. (Annals of Mathematics Studies: No.97). 400p. 1981. 25.00x (ISBN 0-691-08264-2); pap. 9.50x (ISBN 0-691-08267-7). Princeton U Pr.

Kra, S. Basic Correlative Echocardiography Technique & Interpretation. 1977. spiral bdg. 16.00 o.p. (ISBN 0-87488-978-2). Med Exam.

Kra, Siegfried J. & Boltax, Robert S. Is Surgery Necessary. 256p. 1981. 10.95 (ISBN 0-02-566560-X). Macmillan.

Kraak, A. Linguistics in the Netherlands. 280p. 1974. text ed. 13.75x (ISBN 90-232-1251-7). Humanities.

Kraas, Helen L. How to Start in Photography. (Illus.). 88p. (Orig.). 1981. pap. 4.95 (ISBN 0-934616-08-6). Valkyrie Pr.

Kraay, C. M., jt. auth. see Carson, R. A.

Kraay, C. M., jt. auth. see Sutherland, C. H.

Krabbe, M., jt. auth. see Vogel, R. A.

Krabill, Willard, jt. auth. see Lind, Loren.

Kracauer, Siegfried. History: The Last Things Before the Last. 1969. text ed. 16.95x (ISBN 0-19-500604-6). Oxford U Pr.

--Theory of Film: The Redemption of Physical Reality. (Illus.). 1965. pap. 6.95 (ISBN 0-19-500721-2, GB). Oxford U Pr.

Kracum, Vincent D. Respiratory Therapy Examination Review Book, Vol. 1. 3rd ed. 1975. spiral bdg. 9.50 (ISBN 0-87488-471-3). Med Exam.

Krader, Lawrence. The Asiatic Mode of Production: Sources Development & Critique in the Writings of Karl Marx. 454p. 1975. text ed. 58.25x (ISBN 90-232-1289-4). Humanities.

Krader, Lawrence, ed. see Marx, Karl.

Krader, Ruth, tr. see Pavlovsky, Michel N.

Kraditor, Aileen S. The Idea's of the Woman's Suffrage Movement 1880-1920. 1980. pap. 6.95 (ISBN 0-393-00039-7). Norton.

Kraegel, Janet, ed. Organization-Environment Relationships. LC 79-90380. (The Management Anthology Ser.). 1980. pap. text ed. 12.95 (ISBN 0-913654-58-2). Nursing Res.

Kraeling, Emil G., ed. see Bewer, Julius A.

Kraemer, Hans Joachim. Platonismus und hellenistische Philosophie. 368p. 1971. 60.60x (ISBN 3-11-003643-6). De Gruyter.

Kraemer, Hendrik. Christian Message in a Non-Christian World. LC 56-10732. 1961. 12.95 (ISBN 0-8254-3002-X). Kregel.

Kraemer, Joel L., ed. Jerusalem: Problems & Prospects. 256p. 1980. 25.95 (ISBN 0-03-057733-0); pap. 9.95 (ISBN 0-03-057734-9). Praeger.

Kraemer, Kenneth L. Policy Analysis in Local Government. LC 73-83294. (Municipal Management Ser.). 1973. pap. 12.50 o.p. (ISBN 0-87326-003-1). Intl City Mgt.

Kraemer, Kenneth L., ed. Computers & Local Government: A Review of the Research, Vol. 2. King, John L. LC 77-23886. (Praeger Special Studies). 1978. 32.95 (ISBN 0-03-040761-3). Praeger.

Kraemer, Kenneth L. & King, John L., eds. Computers & Local Government: A Manager's Guide, Vol. 1. LC 77-23886. (Praeger Special Studies). 1977. 22.95 (ISBN 0-03-040846-6). Praeger.

Kraemer, Kenneth L., jt. ed. see Perry, James L.

Kraemer, Kenneth L., et al. The Management of Information Systems. 416p. 1980. 25.00 (ISBN 0-231-04886-6). Columbia U Pr.

--The Municipal Information Systems Directory. LC 75-22891. (Illus.). 1976. 41.95 (ISBN 0-669-00469-3). Lexington Bks.

Kraemer, Richard & Newell, Charldean. Texas Politics. (Illus.). 1979. pap. text ed. 11.50 (ISBN 0-8299-0286-4); instrs.' manual avail. (ISBN 0-8299-0499-9). West Pub.

Kraemer, Richard, et al. American Democracy: The Third Century. (Illus.). 1978. pap. text ed. 13.50 (ISBN 0-8299-0160-4); instrs.' manual avail. (ISBN 0-8299-0498-0). West Pub.

Kraenzlin, R. Monographie von Masdevallia Ruiz et Pavon Lothiana Kraenz: Scaphosepalum Pfitzer, Cryptophorantus Bearb, Rodr., Pseudostomeria Kraenzl. (Feddes Repertorium: Beiheft 34). 240p. (Ger.). 1980. Repr. of 1925 ed. lib. bdg. 47.85x (Pub. by Koeltz Germany). Lubrecht & Cramer.

Kraepelin, Emil. Clinical Psychiatry. LC 80-25289. (History of Psychology Ser.). 1981. write for info. (ISBN 0-8201-1352-2). Schol Facsimilies.

Kraft, Barbara S. The Peace Ship: Henry Ford's Pacifist Adventure in the First World War. 1978. 17.95 o.s.i. (ISBN 0-02-566570-7). Macmillan.

Kraft, Betsy H. Careers in the Energy Industry. (Career Concise Guides Ser.). (Illus.). (gr. 7 up). 1977. PLB 6.45 s&l (ISBN 0-531-01305-7). Watts.

--Coal. (First Books Ser.). (Illus.). 72p. (gr. 4-6). 1977. PLB 6.45 (ISBN 0-531-00336-1). Watts.

--Oil & Natural Gas. (First Bks). (Illus.). (gr. 4 up). 1978. PLB 6.45 (ISBN 0-531-01411-8). Watts.

Kraft, Carlotte, jt. auth. see Allen, Robert F.

Kraft, Charles H. Communicating the Gospel God's Way. LC 80-53945. 60p. 1980. pap. 2.95x (ISBN 0-87808-742-7). William Carey Lib.

--Hausa Reader: Cultural Materials with Helps for Use in Teaching Intermediate & Advanced Hausa. 1974. pap. 22.75x (ISBN 0-520-02067-7). U of Cal Pr.

Kraft, Charles H. & Kraft, Marguerite G. Introductory Hausa. LC 79-92676. 1974. 22.75x (ISBN 0-520-01988-1). U of Cal Pr.

Kraft, Charlotte, jt. auth. see Allen, Robert F.

Kraft, David. The Compleat Oak Leaves. LC 80-23937. 192p. 1980. Repr. of 1979 ed. lib. bdg. 16.95x (ISBN 0-89370-092-4). Borgo Pr.

Kraft, Dean. Portrait of a Psychic Healer. 192p. 1981. 10.95 (ISBN 0-686-69592-5). Putnam.

Kraft, Eva, ed. Japanese Institutions. 611p. (Japanese, Eng.). 1972. text ed. 42.00 (ISBN 3-7940-5041-X, Pub. by K G Saur). Gale.

Kraft, George D. & Toy, Wing N. Microprogrammed Control & Reliable Design of Small Computers. (Illus.). 248p. 1981. text ed. 21.95 (ISBN 0-13-581140-6). P-H.

--Mini-Microcomputer Hardware Design. (Illus.). 1978. ref. ed. 24.95 (ISBN 0-13-583807-X). P-H.

Kraft, Herbert C., ed. A Delaware Indian Symposium. (Pennsylvania Historical & Museum Comm. Anthropological Ser., No. 4). (Illus.). 160p. 1974. 7.00 (ISBN 0-911124-77-2); pap. 4.00 (ISBN 0-911124-76-4). Pa Hist & Mus.

Kraft, James, ed. see Bynner, Wittter.

Kraft, James, ed. see Bynner, Wytter.

Kraft, Julius, ed. see Nelson, Leonard.

Kraft, Ken & Kraft, Pat. Exotic Vegetables: How to Grow & Cook Them. (Illus.). 1977. 8.95 o.s.i. (ISBN 0-8027-0560-X); pap. 3.95 o.s.i. (ISBN 0-8027-7109-2). Walker & Co.

Kraft Kitchens. The Parkay Margarine Cookbook. (Orig.). pap. 5.95 (ISBN 0-87502-074-7). Benjamin Co.

--Salads from Beginning to Endive. (Orig.). pap. 5.95 (ISBN 0-87502-073-9). Benjamin Co.

--Travel Your Taste with Kraft Foodservice: International Recipes from the World of Foodservice. LC 78-5909. (Illus.). 1978. 25.95 (ISBN 0-8436-2171-0). CBI Pub.

Kraft, Leo. New Approach to Ear Training. (Orig., Prog. Bk.). 1967. 5.95x (ISBN 0-393-09764-1, NortonC); tapes 185.00 (ISBN 0-393-09916-4); tchrs. manual free (ISBN 0-393-09788-9). Norton.

Kraft, Lisbeth M., tr. see Ramon Y Cajal, Santiago.

Kraft, Marguerite G., jt. auth. see Kraft, Charles H.

Kraft, Michael E. & Schneider, Mark, eds. Population Policy Analysis. LC 77-221. (Policy Studies Organization Ser.). 1978. 18.95 (ISBN 0-669-01456-7). Lexington Bks.

Kraft, Pat, jt. auth. see Kraft, Ken.

Kraft, Robert A. Septuagintal Lexicography. LC 75-15894. (Society of Biblical Literature. Septuagint & Cognate Studies). 1975. pap. 7.50 (ISBN 0-89130-008-2, 060401). Scholars Pr Ca.

--The Testament of Job. LC 74-15201. (Society of Biblical Literature. Text & Translation-Psuedepigrapha Ser.). 1974. pap. 6.00 (ISBN 0-88414-044-X, 060205). Scholars Pr Ca.

Kraft, Robert A. & Purintun, Ann-Elizabeth. Paraleipomena Jeremiou. LC 72-88436. (Society of Biblical Literature. Texts & Translation-Psuedepigrapha Ser.). 1972. pap. 4.50 (ISBN 0-89130-169-0, 060201). Scholars Pr Ca.

Kraft, Thomas L., jt. auth. see Harvill, Lawrence R.

Kraft, William. Sexual Dimensions of the Celibate Life. 1979. 12.95 o.p. (ISBN 0-8362-3908-3). Andrews & McMeel.

Kraft, Wolfgang S. Deutsch: Aktuell 1. LC 78-11445. 1979. 8.95 (ISBN 0-88436-539-5); pap. 5.95 (ISBN 0-88436-537-9). EMC.

--Deutsch: Aktuell 2. LC 79-12315. (Illus.). 1980. 9.50 (ISBN 0-88436-542-5); pap. 6.50 (ISBN 0-88436-540-9, GEA 132021). EMC.

Krag, Erik. Dostoevsky: The Literary Artist. 1976. pap. text ed. 26.00x (ISBN 8-200-01450-9, Dist. by Columbia U Pr). Universitet.

Kragelsky, I. V., et al. Friction & Wear: Calculation Methods. LC 80-41669. (Illus.). 450p. 1981. 75.00 (ISBN 0-08-025461-6); pap. 60.00 (ISBN 0-08-027320-3). Pergamon.

Kragen, Adrian A. & McNulty, John K. Cases & Materials on Federal Income Taxation: Taxation of Corporations, Shareholders, Partnerships & Partners, Vol. II. (American Casebook Ser.). 976p. 1981. text ed. 24.95 (ISBN 0-8299-2133-8). West Pub.

--Cases & Materials on Federal Income Taxation: Taxation of Individuals, Vol. 1. 3rd ed. LC 79-16910. (American Casebook Ser.). 1236p. 1979. text ed. 24.95 (ISBN 0-8299-2058-7). West Pub.

Kragten, J. Atlas of Metal-Ligand Equilibria in Aqueous Solution. LC 77-12168. 1978. 149.95 (ISBN 0-470-99309-X). Halsted Pr.

Krahn, Cornelius. Dutch Anabaptism. 320p. 1981. pap. 18.00 (ISBN 0-8361-1243-1). Herald Pr.

Krahn, Fernando. Arthur's Adventure in the Abandoned House. LC 80-22249. (Illus.). (ps-1). 1981. PLB 7.95 (ISBN 0-525-25945-7). Dutton.

--The Family Minus. LC 76-18093. (Illus.). 40p. (ps-3). 1977. 5.95 o.s.i. (ISBN 0-8193-0860-9, Four Winds); PLB 5.41 o.s.i. (ISBN 0-8193-0861-7). Schol Bk Serv.

--The Great Ape. (Puffin Picture Bks.). (Illus.). 1980. 1.95 (ISBN 0-14-005744-7). Penguin.

--Here Comes Alex Pumpernickel. (Illus.). 32p. (ps up). 1981. 7.95 (ISBN 0-316-50311-8, Atlantic). Little.

--How Santa Claus Had a Long & Difficult Journey Delivering His Presents. LC 72-122769. (Illus.). (ps-3). 1970. PLB 7.45 (ISBN 0-440-03887-1, Sey Lawr); 7.95 (ISBN 0-440-03886-3). Delacorte.

--The Self-Made Snowman. LC 74-551. (gr. 1-3). 1974. PLB 7.89 (ISBN 0-397-31472-8). Lippincott.

Kraig, Bruce, jt. auth. see Stover, Leon E.

Krailsheimer, Alban. Pascal. 84p. 1980. 9.95 (ISBN 0-8090-7550-4); pap. 2.95 (ISBN 0-8090-1412-2). Hill & Wang.

Krailsheimer, A. J. Armand-Jean De Rance, Abbot of la Trappe: His Influence in the Cloister & the World. (Illus.). 384p. 1974. text ed. 34.50x (ISBN 0-19-815744-4). Oxford U Pr.

Krailsheimer, A. J., ed. Continental Renaissance, Fifteen Hundred to Sixteen Hundred. (Pelican Guides to European Literature). 1978. Repr. of 1971 ed. text ed. 28.50x (ISBN 0-391-00816-1). Humanities.

Krailsheimer, A. J., tr. see Pascal, Blaise.

Kraines, Samuel H. & Thetford, Eloise S. Help for the Depressed. (Illus.). 272p. 1979. pap. 11.75 (ISBN 0-398-02335-2). C C Thomas.

Krajenke, Robert W. Psychic Side of American Dream. 1976. pap. 2.00 o.p. (ISBN 0-87604-093-8). ARE Pr.

Krajewski, Lee J. & Thompson, Howard E., eds. Management Science: Quantitative Methods in Context. LC 80-17103. (Management Ser.). 560p. 1981. text ed. write for info. (ISBN 0-471-06109-3). Wiley.

Krakauer, Henry, jt. ed. see Lalezari, Parviz.

Krakel, Dean, II. Season of the Elk. LC 75-42982. (Illus.). 128p. 1980. 20.00 (ISBN 0-913504-28-9); pap. 12.95 (ISBN 0-913504-29-7). Lowell Pr.

Krakowka, Steven, jt. auth. see Olsen, Richard G.

Kral, Brian. Ransom of Red Chief. (Orig.). 1980. playscript 2.00 (ISBN 0-87602-227-1). Anchorage.

--Special Class. (Orig.). 1981. playscript 2.50 (ISBN 0-87602-235-2). Anchorage.

Kral, J. Integral Operators in Potential Theory. (Lecture Notes in Mathematics Ser.: Vol. 823). 171p. 1981. pap. 11.80 (ISBN 0-387-10227-2). Springer-Verlag.

Kral, Stephen. Power Game. LC 78-78052. 1979. pap. 1.95 o.p. (ISBN 0-87216-548-5). Playboy Pbks.

Kram, Mark, jt. auth. see Selmier, Dean.

Kramarae, Cheris, ed. The Voices & Words of Women & Men. 195p. 1981. 28.80 (ISBN 0-08-026106-X). Pergamon.

Kramer. Phonics Crossword Puzzles Series. Incl. Early Phonics Crossword Puzzle Book. (gr. k). 1974. pap. text ed. 1.60 (ISBN 0-8009-0438-9); tchr's. ed. 3.00 (ISBN 0-8009-0450-8); spirit masters (ISBN 0-8009-0440-0); Bk. A. (gr. 1-2). 1971. pap. text ed. (ISBN 0-8009-0441-9); tchr's. ed. (ISBN 0-8009-0443-5); spirit masters (ISBN 0-8009-0442-7); Bk. B. (gr. 3-4). 1970. pap. text ed. (ISBN 0-8009-0445-1); tchr's. ed. (ISBN 0-8009-0447-8); spirit masters (ISBN 0-8009-0444-3); Bk. C. (gr. 5-6). 1971. pap. text ed. (ISBN 0-8009-0449-4); tchr's. ed. (ISBN 0-8009-0451-6); spirit masters (ISBN 0-8009-0448-6). (gr. k-6). Bks. A-C. pap. text ed. 1.76 ea.; tchr's. eds. Bks. A-C 3.32 ea.; spirit masters Early Phonics-Bk. C 6.88 ea. McCormick-Mathers.

--Your Trellis Garden. Date not set. 1.49 (ISBN 0-517-31432-0). Bonanza.

Kramer & Krause. Lehigh & New England. (Carstens Hobby Bks.: No. C41). 1980. pap. 9.95 (ISBN 0-911868-41-0). Carstens Pubns.

Kramer, et al. Sculpture of Gaston Lachaise. LC 67-17017. (Illus., Orig.). 1967. 15.00x (ISBN 0-87130-016-8); pap. 9.00x (ISBN 0-87130-017-6). Eakins.

Kramer, A. L., Sr. Van Goor's Concise Indonesian Dictionary: English-Indonesian Indonesian-English. LC 66-23535. 1966. Repr. 8.95 (ISBN 0-8048-0611-X). C E Tuttle.

Kramer, Aaron, ed. On Freedom's Side: An Anthology of American Poems of Protest. (gr. 7up). 1972. 5.95 o.s.i. (ISBN 0-02-750950-8). Macmillan.

Kramer, Amihud. Food & the Consumer. (Illus.). 1973. pap. text ed. 8.50 o.p. (ISBN 0-87055-148-5). AVI.

--Food & the Consumer. rev. ed. (Illus.). 1980. pap. text ed. 12.50 (ISBN 0-87055-339-9). AVI.

Kramer, Amihud & Twigg, Bernard. Quality Control for the Food Industry: Vol. 2, Applications. 3rd ed. (Illus.). 1973. text ed. 29.50 (ISBN 0-87055-127-2). AVI.

Kramer, Amihud & Twigg, Bernard A. Quality Control for the Food Industry Vol. 1: Fundamentals. 3rd ed. (Illus.). 1970. text ed. 29.50 (ISBN 0-87055-072-1). AVI.

Kramer, Amihud, jt. auth. see Green, John H.

Kramer, Carol, ed. Ethnoarchaeology. 1979. 25.00x (ISBN 0-231-04182-9). Columbia U Pr.

--Ethnoarchaeology. 1980. pap. 10.00x (ISBN 0-231-04182-9). Columbia U Pr.

Kramer, Charles H. Becoming a Family Therapist: Developing an Integrated Approach to Working with Families. LC 80-11322. 256p. 1980. text ed. 19.95 (ISBN 0-87705-470-3). Human Sci Pr.

Kramer, Charles H. & Kramer, Jeannette R. Basic Principles of Long-Term Patient Care: Developing a Therapeutic Community. (Illus.). 380p. 1976. 26.75 (ISBN 0-398-03453-2). C C Thomas.

Kramer, Dale. Charles Robert Maturin. (English Authors Ser.: No. 156). 1973. lib. bdg. 10.95 (ISBN 0-8057-1382-4). Twayne.

Kramer, Fred A. Perspectives on Public Bureaucracy. 3rd ed. (Illus.). 236p. 1981. pap. text ed. 7.95 (ISBN 0-87626-659-6). Winthrop.

Kramer, Geneal. Welcome to God's Family. (Illus.). 40p. (gr. k-5). 1980. pap. 1.25 (ISBN 0-912228-66-0). St Anthony Mess Pr.

Kramer, Hilton. Richard Lindner. LC 74-78458. (Illus.). 256p. 1975. 42.50 (ISBN 0-8212-0513-7, 743224). NYGS.

Kramer, I. R., jt. auth. see Pindborg, J. J.

Kramer, Jack. Cacti As Decorative Plants. LC 73-172694. (Illus.). 128p. 1974. encore ed. 2.95 o.p. (ISBN 0-684-15711-X, ScribT); pap. 3.95 o.p. (ISBN 0-684-13718-6, SL510, ScribT). Scribner.

--The Complete Book of Terrarium Gardening. LC 73-17253. (Illus.). 160p. 1974. encore ed. 3.95 o.p. (ISBN 0-684-15707-1, ScribT). Scribner.

--Easy Plants for Difficult Places. 1977. pap. 1.50 o.p. (ISBN 0-345-24865-1). Ballantine.

--Fences, Hedges & Walls. LC 74-11055. (Illus.). 128p. 1975. 8.95 o.p. (ISBN 0-684-13891-3, ScribT). Scribner.

--Ferns & Palms for Interior Decoration: Garden Library. LC 73-326. (Illus.). 128p. 1972. pap. 4.95 o.p. (ISBN 0-684-12931-0, SL365, ScribT); encore edition 2.95 o.p. (ISBN 0-684-15255-X, ScribT). Scribner.

--Flowering House Plants Month by Month. 126p. 1973. pap. 1.95 o.s.i. (ISBN 0-346-12085-3). Cornerstone.

--Gardens Without Soil. LC 75-22408. (Encore Edition). (Illus.). 1976. 3.95 o.p. (ISBN 0-684-15698-9, ScribT). Scribner.

--Growing Beautiful Flowers Indoors. (Illus.). 1980. 24.95 (ISBN 0-312-35120-8). St Martin.

--Growing Orchids at Your Window. 1979. pap. 4.50 (ISBN 0-8015-3175-6, Hawthorn). Dutton.

--Indoor Trees. 1980. 25.00x (ISBN 0-232-51399-6, Pub. by Darton-Longman-Todd England). State Mutual Bk.

--Once-a-Week Indoor Gardening Guide. (Orig.). pap. 1.75 (ISBN 0-515-04475-X). Jove Pubns.

--One Thousand Beautiful Garden Plants & How to Grow Them. 256p. 1976. 12.95 o.p. (ISBN 0-688-03025-4). Morrow.

--Orchids: Flowers of Romance & Mystery. (Illus.). 156p. 1980. 20.00 (ISBN 0-686-62708-3, 1401-8); pap. 9.95 (ISBN 0-686-62709-1, 2171-5). Abrams.

--Orchids: Flowers of Romance & Mystery. concise ed. (Illus.). 1979. 20.00 o.p. (ISBN 0-8109-1401-8); pap. 9.95 (ISBN 0-8109-2171-5). Abrams.

--Outdoor Garden Build-It Book. LC 76-52761. (Illus.). 1977. 14.95 o.p. (ISBN 0-684-14762-9, ScribT); pap. 7.95 o.p. (ISBN 0-684-15039-5, SL716, ScribT). Scribner.

--Picture Encyclopedia of Small Plants. LC 78-1089. 192p. 1981. pap. 8.95 (ISBN 0-8128-6083-7). Stein & Day.

--Plant Sculptures: Making Miniature Indoor Topiaries. (Illus.). (gr. 3-12). 1978. 6.95 (ISBN 0-688-22144-0); PLB 6.67 (ISBN 0-688-32144-5). Morrow.

--Planters: Make Your Own Containers for Indoor & Outdoor Plants. 1977. pap. 3.95 o.p. (ISBN 0-345-25534-8). Ballantine.

--Starting from Seed. 1977. pap. 1.50 o.p. (ISBN 0-685-75040-X, 345-25502-X-150). Ballantine.

--The Trellis Garden Book: How to Build It, How to Grow It, How to Show It. LC 75-43989. (Illus.). 96p. 1976. 7.95 o.s.i. (ISBN 0-8027-0532-4). Walker & Co.

--Underwater Gardens. LC 73-8031. (Illus.). 128p. 1974. 6.95 o.p. (ISBN 0-684-13601-5, ScribT). Scribner.

--Victorian Gardens: How to Plan, Plant, & Enjoy Nineteenth Century Beauty Today. LC 80-8342. (Illus.). 160p. 1981. 14.95 (ISBN 0-06-250480-0, HarpR); pap. 9.95 (ISBN 0-06-250481-9). Har-Row.
--Your First Garden. LC 73-1102. (Encore Editions). (Illus.). 128p. 1973. pap. 3.50 o.p. (ISBN 0-684-15413-7, ScribT). Scribner.
--Your Homemade Greenhouse. 1980. pap. 5.95 (ISBN 0-346-12442-5). Cornerstone.
Kramer, Jack & Sheehan, Larry. How to Play Your Best Tennis All the Time. LC 76-53402. (Illus.). 1978. pap. 6.95 (ISBN 0-689-70576-X). Atheneum.
Kramer, James R., jt. ed. see Allen, Herbert E.
Kramer, Jane. Honor to the Bride Like the Pigeon That Guards Its Grain Under the Clove Tree. 1970. 5.95 o.p. (ISBN 0-374-17257-9). FS&G.
--The Last Cowboy. LC 77-6150. 1978. 9.95 o.s.i. (ISBN 0-06-012454-7, HarpT). Har-Row.
Kramer, Janice. El Buen Samaritano. Rodriguez, Eliseo, tr. from Eng. (Libros Arco Ser.). (Illus.). 32p. (Orig., Span.). (gr. 1-3). 1979. pap. 0.95 (ISBN 0-89922-147-5). Edit Caribe.
--La Princesa y el Ninito. Villalobos, Fernando, tr. from Eng. (Libros Arco Ser.). (Illus.). 32p. (Orig., Span.). (gr. 1-3). 1978. pap. 0.95 (ISBN 0-89922-127-0). Edit Caribe.
Kramer, Jeannette R., jt. auth. see Kramer, Charles H.
Kramer, Jerry. Lombardi: Winning Is the Only Thing. LC 76-3503. (Illus.). 1976. 14.95 o.p. (ISBN 0-690-01131-8, TYC-T). T Y Crowell.
Kramer, John, jt. auth. see Clare, Paul.
Kramer, John L. & Englebrecht, Ted D. A Practical Guide to Farm & Ranch Taxation. 1978. pap. text ed. 10.50 o.p. (ISBN 0-88450-550-2, 1716-B). Lawyers & Judges.
Kramer, K. Erdoel-Lexikon (Crude Oil Dictionary) 5th rev. ed. LC 72-313250. 1972. 20.00x (ISBN 3-7785-0233-6). Intl Pubns Serv.
Kramer, Kenneth L., jt. ed. see Colton, Kent W.
Kramer, Klaas. Teaching Elementary School Mathematics. 4th ed. 1978. text ed. 18.95 (ISBN 0-205-06054-4, 2360543); instr's man. o.p. avail. (ISBN 0-205-06055-2); performance based study guide 6.95 (ISBN 0-205-06056-0, 2360543). Allyn.
Kramer, Leo & Clague, Ewan, eds. The Health-Impaired Miner Under Black Lung Legislation. LC 73-9385. (Special Studies in U.S. Economic, Social & Political Issues). 1973. 28.50x (ISBN 0-275-28759-9); pap. text ed. 12.50x (ISBN 0-89197-783-X). Irvington.
Kramer, Mark. Three Farms: Making Milk, Meat & Money from the American Soil. 1980. 12.95 (ISBN 0-316-50315-0). Little.
Kramer, Marlene. Reality Shock: Why Nurses Leave Nursing. LC 73-22243. (Illus.). 1974. pap. text ed. 16.95 (ISBN 0-8016-2741-9). Mosby.
Kramer, Marlene & Schmalenberg, Claudia. Path to Biculturalism. LC 77-7202. 1977. pap. text ed. 12.95 (ISBN 0-913654-30-2). Nursing Res.
Kramer, Mary. Illustrated Guide to Foreign & Fancy Foods. LC 75-20972. (Illus.). 1975. pap. 11.95x spiral bdg. (ISBN 0-916434-14-1). Plycon Pr.
Kramer, Matt. Smoke Cooking. pap. 3.95 (ISBN 0-8015-6896-X, Hawthorn). Dutton.
Kramer, Melinda G., jt. auth. see Rigg, Donald C.
Kramer, Paul J., jt. auth. see Raper, C. David.
Kramer, Ralph M. Voluntary Agencies in the Welfare State. 400p. 1981. 24.95x (ISBN 0-520-04290-5). U of Cal Pr.
Kramer, Ralph M. & Specht, Harry, eds. Readings in Community Organization Practice. 2nd ed. (Illus.). 432p. 1975. pap. text ed. 14.95 (ISBN 0-13-755769-8). P-H.
Kramer, Rita. Giving Birth: Childbearing in America Today. 1979. 10.95 o.p. (ISBN 0-8092-7859-6). Contemp Bks.
Kramer, Ruth, jt. auth. see Hale, Lloyd S.
Kramer, Samuel N. Cradle of Civilization. LC 67-29528. (Great Ages of Man). (Illus.). (gr. 6 up). 1967. PLB 11.97 (ISBN 0-8094-0378-1, Pub. by Time-Life). Silver.
--Cradle of Civilization. (Great Ages of Man Ser). (Illus.). 1967. 12.95 (ISBN 0-8094-0356-0); lib. bdg. avail. (ISBN 0-685-20547-9). Time-Life.
--From the Poetry of Sumer: Creation, Glorification, Adoration. LC 78-57321. 1979. 11.95x (ISBN 0-520-03703-0). U of Cal Pr.
--Sumerian Mythology. (Illus.). 1972. pap. 5.95x (ISBN 0-8122-1047-6, Pa Paperbks). U of Pa Pr.
Kramer, Samuel N., jt. ed. see Gurney, Oliver R.
Kramer, Samuel Noah, ed. Mythologies of the Ancient World. LC 60-13538. 1961. pap. 2.95 (ISBN 0-385-09567-8, A229, Anch). Doubleday.
Kramer, Steven P. & Welsh, James M. Abel Gance. (Theatrical Arts Ser.). 1978. lib. bdg. 12.50 (ISBN 0-8057-9254-6). Twayne.
Kramer, Theodore T. Comparative Pathogenic Bacteriology. 32p. 1972. pap. 37.50, incl. film strips o.p. (ISBN 0-7216-9829-8). Saunders.
Kramer, Victor A. James Agee. LC 74-23882. (U. S. Authors Ser.: No. 252). 1975. lib. bdg. 9.95 (ISBN 0-8057-0006-4). Twayne.
Kramer, William. Here & Hereafter. 1978. pap. 4.95 (ISBN 0-8100-0053-9, 15-0365). Northwest Pub.
Kramer, William A. God's People. LC 75-16790. 1975. lib. bdg. 7.25 (ISBN 0-8100-0010-5, 06N552). Northwest Pub.
--Teenagers Pray. LC 55-12193. (gr. 8-12). 1956. 3.95 (ISBN 0-570-03018-8, 6-1054). Concordia.
Kramer, William A., ed. Building for Eternity. rev. ed. (Units in Religion: Bk. 5, 2-V). (gr. 5-6). 1958. pap. text ed. 3.50 (ISBN 0-686-57525-3, 22-1125); teachers' manual 4.65 (ISBN 0-570-06755-3, 22-1126). Concordia.
Kramer, Wolfgang. Tortula Hedw. Sect. Rurales De Not. Pottiaceae, Musci in der Oestlichen Holarktis. (Bryophytorum Bibliotheca: 21). 250p. (Ger.). 1980. lib. bdg. 30.00x (ISBN 3-7682-1266-1). Lubrecht & Cramer.
Kramerae, Cheris. Women & Men Speaking. (Orig.). 1981. pap. text ed. 11.95 (ISBN 0-88377-179-9). Newbury Hse.
Kramer-Greene, Judith, compiled by. A Bibliography of Noise for Nineteen Seventy-Five. LC 72-87107. 171p. 1977. 10.00x (ISBN 0-87875-099-1). Whitston Pub.
Kramers, J. H., jt. ed. see Gibb, H. A.
Kramlich, W. E., et al. Processed Meats. (Illus.). 1973. 29.50 (ISBN 0-87055-141-8). AVI.
Kramnick, Isaac & Watkins, Frederick. Age of Ideology: Political Thought 1750 to the Present. 2nd ed. (Foundations of Modern Political Science Ser.). 1979. pap. 6.95 ref. ed. (ISBN 0-13-018499-3). P-H.
Krampitz, Sydney D. & Pavlovich, Natalie. Readings for Nursing Research. LC 80-18125. (Illus.). 285p. 1980. pap. text ed. 9.95 (ISBN 0-8016-2747-8). Mosby.
Kramrisch, Stella. Indian Sculpture in the Philadelphia Museum of Art. LC 60-14837. 1961. 12.00x o.p. (ISBN 0-8122-7276-5). U of Pa Pr.
--The Presence of Siva. LC 80-8558. (Illus.). 550p. 1981. 37.50x (ISBN 0-691-03964-X); pap. 16.50x (ISBN 0-691-10115-9). Princeton U Pr.
Kramsky, Jiri. The Phoneme: Introduction to the History & Theories of a Concept. 1974. 25.00 (ISBN 3-7705-0945-5); pap. 16.25 (ISBN 0-686-67210-0). Adler.
Krane, Ronald E. International Labor Migration in Europe. LC 78-19746. (Praeger Special Studies). 1979. 24.95 (ISBN 0-03-022361-X). Praeger.
Kranes, David. Criminals. 256p. (Orig.). pap. 2.50 (ISBN 0-441-12174-8). Charter Bks.
Kranich, Roger E. & Messec, Jerry L. Visual Data. 1979. pap. 2.50 (ISBN 0-88323-153-0, 243); free answer key 1.00 (ISBN 0-88323-157-3). Richards Pub.
Kranich, Rogert E. & Messec, Jerry L. Learning to Use Maps. (Illus.). 1978. text ed. write for info. (ISBN 0-88323-150-6, 236); 2.25x (ISBN 0-686-67722-6); teacher's answer key free (239). Richards Pub.
Krannich, Caryl R. & Krannich, Ronald L. Politics of Family Planning Policy: Thailand--A Case of Successful Implementation. 1980. 12.50. UC Ctr for S&SE Asian.
Krannich, Caryl R., jt. auth. see Krannich, Ronald L.
Krannich, Ronald L. & Krannich, Caryl R. The Politics of Family Planning Policy: Thailand--a Case of Successful Implementation. (Monograph: No. 19). 115p. 1980. pap. 9.00x (Pub. by Northern Ill Univ Ctr S E Asian Stud); pap. text ed. 9.00. Cellar.
Krannich, Ronald L., jt. auth. see Krannich, Caryl R.
Krant, Melvin J. Dying & Dignity: The Meaning & Control of a Personal Death. 164p. 1974. 11.75 (ISBN 0-398-02995-4); pap. 8.50 (ISBN 0-398-02996-2). C C Thomas.
Krantz, Grover S. Climatic Races & Descent Groups. 288p. 1980. 14.95 (ISBN 0-8158-0390-7). Chris Mass.
Krantz, Hazel. Freestyle for Michael. LC 64-16255. (Illus.). (gr. 5-8). 3.95 (ISBN 0-8149-0345-2). Vanguard.
--One Hundred Pounds of Popcorn. LC 61-15479. (Illus.). (gr. 3-6). 1961. 4.95 (ISBN 0-8149-0344-4). Vanguard.
--Secret Raft. LC 65-17372. (Illus.). (gr. 5-8). 1965. 6.95 (ISBN 0-8149-0343-6). Vanguard.
--Tippy. LC 68-14335. (gr. 7-10). 6.95 (ISBN 0-8149-0342-8). Vanguard.
Krantz, Judith. Princess Daisy. 512p. 1981. pap. 3.95 (ISBN 0-553-14200-3). Bantam.
--Scruples. 1979. pap. 3.50 (ISBN 0-446-96743-2). Warner Bks.
Krantz, Les. Portrait of Chicago. Pfeiffer, Douglas, ed. (Portrait of America Ser.). (Illus.). 80p. (Orig.). 1981. pap. text ed. 5.95 (ISBN 0-912856-70-X). Graphic Arts Ctr.
Krantz, Leslie J. The Wahington, D. C. Review of Art. LC 79-56026. (Illus.). 124p. 1980. pap. 8.95 (ISBN 0-8149-0832-2). Vanguard.
Krantz, Lucretia, jt. auth. see Zim, Herbert S.
Krantz, Sheldon. Cases & Materials on the Law of Corrections & Prisoners' Rights. 2nd ed. (American Casebook Ser.). 786p. 1981. text ed. 22.95 (ISBN 0-8299-2127-3). West Pub.
--Law of Corrections & Prisoners' Rights, 1977 Supplement: Cases & Materials. (American Casebook Ser.). 1973. pap. 5.95 o.p. (ISBN 0-685-80683-9). West Pub.
Krantz, Sheldon, jt. auth. see Bittner, Egon.
Krantzler, Harold I. Your Congregation's Adult Jewish Education Committee: A Manual. 1978. pap. 2.50 (ISBN 0-8074-0013-0, 181730). UAHC.
Krantzler, Mel. Creative Divorce: A New Opportunity for Personal Growth. LC 73-82863. 268p. 1974. 8.95 (ISBN 0-87131-131-3). M Evans.
--Learning to Love Again. LC 77-6347. 1977. 7.95 o.s.i. (ISBN 0-690-01456-2, TYC-T). T Y Crowell.
Kranz, Harry. The Participatory Bureaucracy: Women & Minorities in a More Representative Public Service. LC 75-44600. (Illus.). 1976. 21.95 (ISBN 0-669-00556-8). Lexington Bks.
Kranz, J., et al, eds. Diseases, Pests & Weeds in Tropical Crops. LC 78-6212. 1978. 79.25 (ISBN 0-471-99667-X, Pub. by Wiley-Interscience). Wiley.
Kranzberg, Melvin, ed. Ethics in an Age of Pervasive Technology. 220p. 1980. lib. bdg. 25.00x (ISBN 0-89158-686-5). Westview.
Kranzberg, Melvin, et al, eds. Energy & the Way We Live. LC 79-25054. (Illus.). 520p. 1980. lib. bdg. 16.00x (ISBN 0-87835-092-6); pap. text ed. 7.95x (ISBN 0-87835-084-5); study guide 2.95x (ISBN 0-87835-089-6); pap. text bd. with study guide 9.95 (ISBN 0-87835-090-X). Boyd & Fraser.
Kranzdorf, Hermie. Cooking for the Eighties. (Illus.). 256p. 1980. 10.95 (ISBN 0-916838-31-5). Schiffer.
Krapp, George P., ed. Junius Manuscript. LC 31-8589. 1931. 17.50x (ISBN 0-231-08765-9). Columbia U Pr.
--Paris Psalter & Meters of Boethius. LC 33-2302. 1932. 17.50x (ISBN 0-231-08769-1). Columbia U Pr.
--Vercelli Book. LC 32-10861. 1932. 17.50x (ISBN 0-231-08766-7). Columbia U Pr.
Krapp, George P. & Dobie, Elliott V., eds. Exeter Book. LC 36-30684. 1936. 20.00x (ISBN 0-231-08767-5). Columbia U Pr.
Krappe, Alexander H., tr. see Grimm Brothers.
Krar, S. F. & Oswald, J. W. Drilling Technology. LC 73-13486. 1977. pap. text ed. 7.40 (ISBN 0-8273-0210-X). Delmar.
--Grinding Technology. LC 72-7935. 1974. pap. text ed. 11.60 (ISBN 0-8273-0208-8); instructor's guide 1.60 (ISBN 0-8273-0209-6). Delmar.
--Turning Technology: Engine & Turret Lathes. LC 78-153723. 1971. pap. text ed. 11.60 (ISBN 0-8273-0206-1); instructor's guide 1.60 (ISBN 0-8273-0207-X). Delmar.
Krashen, Stephen. Second Language Acquisition & Second Language Learning. (Language Teaching Methodology Ser.). 176p. 1981. pap. 9.95 (ISBN 0-08-025338-5). Pergamon.
Krashen, Stephen D., jt. ed. see Scarcella, Robin C.
Krasheninnikov, Stepan P. Explorations of Kamchatka: North Pacific Scimitar. Crownhart-Vaughan, E. A., tr. LC 72-79116. (North Pacific Studies Ser.: No. 1). (Illus.). 1972. 14.95 (ISBN 0-87595-033-7). Oreg Hist Soc.
Krasilovsky, Phyllis. Cow Who Fell in the Canal. (gr. k-3). 1950. pap. 1.49 (ISBN 0-385-08096-4, Zephyr). Doubleday.
--Man Who Didn't Wash His Dishes. (Illus.). (gr. k-3). 1950. pap. 1.95 (ISBN 0-385-13343-X, Zephyr). Doubleday.
--Scaredy Cat. (gr. k-2). 1959. 6.95g (ISBN 0-685-15889-6). Macmillan.
--Susan Sometimes. (Illus.). (gr. k-1). 1962. 1.95 o.s.i. (ISBN 0-02-751160-X). Macmillan.
--Very Little Boy. LC 62-7276. (gr. k-1). pap. 1.95 (ISBN 0-385-00947-X, Zephyr). Doubleday.
--Very Little Boy. LC 62-7276. (gr. k-1). pap. 5.95a (ISBN 0-385-02756-7). Doubleday.
--Very Little Girl. (gr. k-1). 1953. 5.95a (ISBN 0-385-07552-9); PLB (ISBN 0-385-07666-5). Doubleday.
Kraske, Robert. Clara Barton. new ed. (Stories About Christian Heroes Ser.). (Illus.). (gr. 1-3). 1980. pap. 1.95 (ISBN 0-03-049436-2). Winston Pr.
--Treason of Benedict Arnold, 1780: An American General Becomes His Country's First Traitor. LC 72-115774. (Focus Bks). (Illus.). (gr. 7 up). 1970. PLB 4.47 o.p. (ISBN 0-531-01016-3). Watts.
Krasner, L., ed. see Hersen, Michel & Barlow, David H.
Krasner, Leonard, jt. auth. see Ullmann, Leonard.
Krasner, Leonard, ed. Environmental Design & Human Behavior: A Psychology of the Individual in Society. (Pergamon General Psychology Ser.). 1980. 29.50 (ISBN 0-08-023858-0). Pergamon.
Krasnoff, Barbara. Mirrors. 464p. (Orig.). 1980. pap. 2.75 (ISBN 0-89083-690-6). Zebra.
Krasnoff, Julienne, ed. see Lewis, Alfred A.
Krasnoshchekov, V. V., jt. auth. see Myshlyaeva, L. V.
Krasnov, Mikhail M. Microsurgery of Glaucoma. LC 78-26221. (Illus.). 1979. text ed. 35.00 (ISBN 0-8016-2743-5). Mosby.
Krasnow, Donna C., jt. auth. see Levy, Tedd.
Krassner, Paul. Tales of Tongue Fu. LC 80-16192. (Illus.). 130p. 1981. pap. 4.95 (ISBN 0-915904-55-1). And-or Pr.
Kratcoski. Correctional Counseling & Treatment. (Illus.). 432p. 1980. pap. text ed. 10.95 (ISBN 0-686-65821-3). Duxbury Pr.
Kratcoski, Peter C. & Walker, Donald B. Criminal Justice in America: Process & Issues. 1978. 16.95x (ISBN 0-673-15051-8). Scott F.
Krathwohl, David R., jt. auth. see Bloom, Benjamin S.
Krathwohl, David R., et al. Taxonomy of Educational Objectives: Handbook 2: Affective Domain. 1969. pap. 7.95x (ISBN 0-582-28239-X). Longman.
Kratochvil, P., ed. see Hsun Lu.
Kratochvil, Paul. Chinese Language Today: Features of an Emerging Standard. (Illus.). 1968. pap. text ed. 6.00x (ISBN 0-09-084651-6, Hutchinson U Lib). Humanities.
Kratochwil, Friedrich V. International Order & Foreign Policy: A Theoretical Sketch of Post-War Internaional Politics. LC 77-94107. (Westview Replica Edition Ser.). 1978. lib. bdg. 28.00 (ISBN 0-89158-065-4). Westview.
Kratochwill, Thomas R. Advances in School Psychology, Vol. 1. (Advances in School Psychology Ser.). 368p. 1981. profess. & reference 24.95 (ISBN 0-89859-076-0). L Erlbaum Assocs.
--Selective Mutism: Implications for Research & Treatment. LC 80-18631. 224p. 1981. profess. & reference 19.95 (ISBN 0-89859-064-7). L Erlbaum Assocs.
Kratovil, Robert & Werner, Raymond J. Real Estate Law. 7th ed. (P-H Ser. in Real Estate). (Illus.). 1979. 25.95 (ISBN 0-13-763268-1); text ed. 19.95 student ed. (ISBN 0-686-67336-0). P-H.
Kratt, Mary. Charlotte: Spirit of the New South. Blakey, Ellen S. & Silvey, Larry P., eds. LC 80-66341. (The American Portrait Ser.). (Illus.). 224p. 1980. 24.95 (ISBN 0-932986-14-5). Continent Herit.
Kratz, Charlotte R., jt. ed. see Barber, J. H.
Kratzmann, G. Anglo-Scottish Literary Relations: Fourteen Thirty to Fifteen Fifty. LC 78-74537. 1980. 36.00 (ISBN 0-521-22665-1). Cambridge U Pr.
Kraus & Rollain. Exploring Electricity-Electronics with the Electrical Team. LC 76-3947. (Illus.). 1979. pap. 10.80 (ISBN 0-8273-1166-4); research manual 3.40 (ISBN 0-8273-1167-2); instructor's guide 2.00 (ISBN 0-8273-1168-0). Delmar.
Kraus, Alan. Basic College Issues. (Orig.). 1968. pap. text ed. 3.95 o.p. (ISBN 0-394-30339-3, RanC). Random.
Kraus, Albert L. The New York Times Guide to Business & Finance: The American Economy & How It Works. LC 70-138745. (Illus.). 352p. 1972. 10.95 o.p. (ISBN 0-06-012462-8, HarpT). Har-Row.
Kraus, Barbara. Barbara Kraus Calories & Carbohydrates. 1979. pap. 4.95 o.p. (ISBN 0-452-25207-5, Z5207, Plume). NAL.
--Barbara Kraus Guide to Calories: 1981 Edition. (Orig.). 1981. pap. 1.75 (ISBN 0-451-09580-4, E9580, Sig). NAL.
--Barbara Kraus Guide to Carbohydrates: 1981 Edition. (Orig.). 1981. pap. 1.75 (ISBN 0-451-09581-2, E9581, Sig). NAL.
--Barbara Kraus Guide to Fibers in Foods. 1980. 7.95 (ISBN 0-453-00368-0, H368). NAL.
--Barbara Kraus 1980 Calorie Guide to Brand Names & Basic Foods. (Orig.). 1980. pap. 1.50 (ISBN 0-451-09032-2, W9032, Sig). NAL.
--Barbara Kraus 1980 Carbohydrate Guide to Brand Names & Basic Foods. (Orig.). 1980. pap. 1.50 (ISBN 0-451-09033-0, W9033, Sig). NAL.
--Calories & Carbohydrates. rev. ed. 1980. pap. 4.95 (ISBN 0-452-25207-5, 25207, Plume). NAL.
--Calories & Carbohydrates. 4th, rev. ed. 1981. pap. 5.95 (Z5267, Plume). NAL.
--Calories & Carbohydrates. 4th, rev. ed. (Orig.). 1981. pap. 3.50 (ISBN 0-451-09774-2, E9774, Sig). NAL.
Kraus, Bruce. According to Mork: The World As Mork Sees It. (Illus.). 1980. pap. cancelled (ISBN 0-671-41486-0). Wanderer Bks.
Kraus, David, tr. see Zubov, V. P.

Kraus, E. Philip. Yesterday's Children: A Longitudinal Study of Children from Kindergarten into the Adult Years. 208p. 1981. Repr. of 1973 ed. lib. bdg. price not set (ISBN 0-89874-311-7). Krieger.
Kraus, Edward H. & Hunt, W. F. Mineralogy. 5th ed. (Illus.). 1959. text ed. 23.00 o.p. (ISBN 0-07-035388-3, C). McGraw.
Kraus, Ernest A. Pathways Back to the Community. LC 71-100099. 1970. Set. pap. 18.50 (ISBN 0-8261-1093-2); 3.95 (ISBN 0-686-66539-2). Springer Pub.
Kraus, George. By Word & Prayer. 1981. 8.95 (ISBN 0-570-03045-5, 6-1169). Concordia.
Kraus, Gerhard. Homo Sapiens in Decline: A Reappraisal of Natural Selection. 189p. 1973. text ed. 8.00x (ISBN 0-7121-5601-1). Humanities.
Kraus, Hans. Clinical Treatment of Back & Neck Pain. LC 70-79496. (Illus.). 1970. 23.50 o.p. (ISBN 0-07-035415-4, HP). McGraw.
Kraus, Harry. Creep Analysis. LC 80-15242. 250p. 1980. 28.75 (ISBN 0-471-06255-3, Pub. by Wiley-Interscience). Wiley.
Kraus, Henry. Gold Was the Mortar: The Economics of Cathedral Building. (Illus.). 1979. 35.00 (ISBN 0-7100-8728-4). Routledge & Kegan.
--The Living Theater of Medieval Art. LC 67-24004. (Illus.). 272p. 1972. pap. 7.50x (ISBN 0-8122-1056-5, Pa Paperbks). U of Pa Pr.
Kraus, John L. John Locke: Empiricist, Atomist, Conceptualist & Agnostic. LC 68-22348. 1969. 4.95 o.p. (ISBN 0-8022-2257-9). Philos Lib.
Kraus, Milton N., ed. see Chemical Engineering Magazine.
Kraus, Oskar, ed. see Brentano, Franz.
Kraus, Pam, jt. auth. see Kraus, Robert.
Kraus, Pam, ed. see Kraus, Robert.
Kraus, Philip E. Yesterday's Children: A Longitudinal Study of Children from Kindergarten into the Adult Years. LC 72-14108. 224p. 1973. 17.95 o.p. (ISBN 0-471-50722-9, Pub. by Wiley-Interscience). Wiley.
Kraus, R. Square Dances of Today & How to Teach & Call Them. 124p. 1950. 14.95 (ISBN 0-471-07097-1). Wiley.
Kraus, Richard. A Cotton & Cotton Goods in China. LC 78-22779. (The Modern Chinese Economy Ser.). 500p. 1980. lib. bdg. 50.00 (ISBN 0-8240-4276-X). Garland Pub.
--History of the Dance: In Art & Education. LC 69-13716. 1969. ref. ed. 15.95 (ISBN 0-13-390054-1). P-H.
--Square Dances of Today & How to Teach & Call Them. (Illus.). (gr. 5-9). 1950. 14.95 (ISBN 0-8260-5120-0). Ronald Pr.
--Urban Parks & Recreation: Challenges of the 1970's. 1972. pap. 1.50 (ISBN 0-86671-006-X). Comm Coun Great NY.
Kraus, Richard & Charman, Sarah. A History of the Dance in Art & Education. 2nd ed. (Illus.). 432p. 1981. text ed. 15.95 (ISBN 0-13-390021-5). P-H.
Kraus, Richard G. Social Recreation: A Group Dynamics Approach. LC 79-16634. (Illus.). 1979. pap. text ed. 11.00 (ISBN 0-8016-2742-7). Mosby.
Kraus, Richard G. & Curtis, Joseph E. Creative Administration in Recreation & Parks. 2nd ed. LC 76-29696. (Illus.). 1977. text ed. 16.95 (ISBN 0-8016-2739-7). Mosby.
Kraus, Robert. Animal Families. LC 80-51360. (Windmill Board Bks.). (Illus.). 16p. (ps). 1980. board book 3.50 (ISBN 0-671-41532-8, Pub. by Windmill). S&S.
--Bunya the Witch. LC 80-13252. (Illus.). 32p. (ps-2). 1980. pap. 3.95 (ISBN 0-671-96038-5, Pub. by Windmill). S&S.
--The Christmas Cookie Sprinkle Snitcher. LC 80-13641. (Illus.). 32p. (gr. k-3). 1980. pap. 3.95 (ISBN 0-671-41199-3, Pub. by Windmill). S&S.
--Daddy Long Ears. (Illus.). 32p. (ps-2). Date not set. pap. 1.95 (ISBN 0-671-42582-X, Pub. by Windmill). S&S.
--Goodnight Little One. (Illus.). 32p. (ps-2). 1981. paper over board 1.95 (ISBN 0-671-41091-1, Pub. by Windmill). S&S.
--Goodnight Richard Rabbit. (Illus.). 32p. (ps-2). 1981. paper over board 1.95 (ISBN 0-671-41090-3, Pub. by Windmill). S&S.
--Herman the Helper Cleans up. (Tubby Bks). (Illus.). 10p. (ps). 1981. vinyl 2.95 (ISBN 0-671-42555-2). Windmill Bks.
--How Spider Saved Christmas. LC 80-13662. (Illus.). 40p. (ps-2). 1980. pap. 2.50 (ISBN 0-671-41201-9, Pub. by Windmill). S&S.
--How Spider Saved Halloween. LC 80-16778. (Illus.). 40p. (ps-3). 1980. Repr. of 1973 ed. 7.95 (ISBN 0-590-07769-4, Four Winds). Schol Bk Serv.
--How Spider Saved Halloween. LC 80-13661. (Illus.). 32p. (ps-2). 1980. pap. 2.50 (ISBN 0-671-96086-5, Pub. by Windmill). S&S.
--The King's Trousers. LC 79-14569. (Illus.). 40p. (gr. 1-4). 1981. 8.95 (ISBN 0-671-42259-6). Windmill Bks.
--Leo the Late Bloomer. abr. ed. LC 80-51357. (Windmill Board Bks.). (Illus.). 16p. (ps). 1980. board book 3.50 (ISBN 0-671-41202-7, Pub. by Windmill). S&S.
--Leo the Late Bloomer Takes a Bath. (Tubby Bks.). (Illus.). 10p. (ps). 1981. vinyl 2.95 (ISBN 0-671-42554-4). Windmill Bks.
--Milton the Early Riser. 2nd, abr. ed. LC 80-51358. (Windmill Board Bks.). (Illus.). 16p. (ps). 1980. 3.50 (ISBN 0-671-41203-5, Pub. by Windmill). S&S.
--Mouse Work. LC 80-51359. (Windmill Board Bks.). (Illus.). 16p. (ps). 1980. 3.50 (ISBN 0-671-41531-X, Pub. by Windmill). S&S.
--The Old-Fashioned Raggedy Ann ABC Book. Kraus, Pam, ed. (Illus.). 32p. (ps-2). 1980. 4.95 (ISBN 0-671-42552-8). Windmill Bks.
--See the Moon: A Glow-in-the-Dark Book. LC 80-51361. (Windmill Board Bks.). (Illus.). 8p. (ps). 1980. 3.95 (ISBN 0-671-41206-X, Pub. by Windmill). S&S.
Kraus, Robert & Aruego, Jose. Mert the Blurt. LC 80-14508. (Illus.). 32p. (ps-2). 1980. 8.95 (ISBN 0-671-96265-5, Pub. by Windmill). S&S.
Kraus, Robert & Kraus, Pam. Box of Brownies, 4 bks. Incl. The Brownie's ABC. 32p; The Brownie's Joke Book. 32p; The Brownie's Song & Dance Book. 32p; You Can Count on Brownies. 32p. LC 80-50808. (Illus.). Date not set. Set. 7.95 (ISBN 0-671-41193-4, Pub. by Windmill). S&S.
Kraus, Ronnie. Goofy Goes to the Hospital. LC 79-91868. (Illus.). 48p. (gr. 1-3). 1981. 4.95 (ISBN 0-448-16583-X); PLB 9.30 (ISBN 0-448-13642-2). G&D.
Kraus, Sidney, ed. Great Debates, Carter Vs. Ford, 1976. LC 78-62422. (Midland Bks.: No. 229). (Illus.). 568p. 1979. 29.95x (ISBN 0-253-30363-X); pap. 19.50x (ISBN 0-253-20229-9). Ind U Pr.
--Great Debates: Kennedy vs. Nixon, 1960. LC 62-7487. 1977. 17.50x (ISBN 0-253-32630-3); pap. text ed. 5.95x (ISBN 0-253-32631-1). Ind U Pr.
Kraus, William A. Collaboration in Organizations: Alternatives to Hierarchy. LC 80-11291. 274p. 1980. text ed. 19.95 (ISBN 0-87705-491-6). Human Sci Pr.
Krause & Crist. Susquehanna: NYS&W. (Carstens Hobby Bks.: No. C38). (Illus.). 1980. pap. 12.00 (ISBN 0-9604188-38-0). Carstens Pubns.
Krause & Grenard. East Broad Top. (Carstens Hobby Bks: No. C40). 1980. pap. 9.95 (ISBN 0-911868-40-2). Carstens Pubns.
--Steam in the Alleghenies: Western Maryland. (Carstens Hobby Bks.: No. C37). (Illus.). 1980. pap. 10.00 (ISBN 0-911868-37-2). Carstens Pubns.
Krause, jt. auth. see Kramer.
Krause, Aurel. The Tlingit Indians: Results of a Trip to the Northwest Coast of America & the Bering Straits. Gunther, Erna, tr. LC 56-3408. (American Ethnological Society Monographs: No. 26). (Illus.). 320p. 1970. 9.95 o.p. (ISBN 0-295-73971-1); pap. 6.95 (ISBN 0-295-95075-7, WP58). U of Wash Pr.
Krause, Charles, jt. auth. see Speiser, Stuart.
Krause, Chester L. & Mishler, Clifford. Standard Catalog of World Coins. rev. 6th ed. Bruce, Colin R., ed. LC 79-65719. (Illus.). 1979. pap. 24.50 o.s.i. (ISBN 0-87341-050-5). Krause Pubns.
Krause, Corinne. How to up Your Potassium. 5.95 (ISBN 0-9604104-0-6). Green Hill.
Krause, David. Sean O'Casey & His World. LC 76-7182. (Encore Edition). (Illus.). 128p. 1976. 3.95 (ISBN 0-684-16547-3, ScribT). Scribner.
--Sean O'Casey: The Man & His World. rev. ed. LC 74-11129. 416p. 1975. 8.95 o.s.i. (ISBN 0-02-566640-1, 50664). Macmillan.
--A Self Portrait of the Artist As a Man: Sean O'Casey's Letters. 40p. 1968. pap. text ed. 2.50x (ISBN 0-85105-127-8, Dolmen Pr). Humanities.
Krause, David, ed. The Letters of Sean O'Casey: 1910-1941, Vol. 1. (Illus.). 800p. 1975. 60.00 (ISBN 0-02-566660-6). Macmillan.
Krause, David & Lowery, Robert G., eds. Sean O'Casey: Centenary Essays. (Irish Literary Studies 7). 257p. 1981. 24.75x (ISBN 0-389-20096-4). B&N.
Krause, E. Taxicab Geometry. (gr. 9-12). 1976. pap. text ed. 4.40 o.p. (ISBN 0-201-03934-6, Sch Div). A-W.
Krause, Emil. Book of Cons. LC 80-68663. (Illus.). 96p. (Orig.). 1980. pap. 4.95 (ISBN 0-89708-029-7). And Bks.
Krause, Eugene, jt. auth. see Brumfiel, Charles.
Krause, Eugene F. Mathematics for Elementary Teachers. (Illus.). 1978. text ed. 17.95 (ISBN 0-13-562702-8). P-H.
Krause, F. & Radler, K-H. Mean-Field Magnetohydrodynamics & Dynamo Theory. (Illus.). 270p. Date not set. 36.00 (ISBN 0-08-025041-6). Pergamon.
Krause, Frank, jt. auth. see Dimick, Kenneth.
Krause, Herbert. The Oxcart Trail. LC 54-6495. 1976. Repr. of 1954 ed. 9.95 (ISBN 0-88498-047-2). leatherette 12.95 (ISBN 0-88498-047-2). Brevet Pr.
--The Thresher. LC 76-29325. 1976. Repr. of 1946 ed. 9.95 (ISBN 0-88498-046-4); text ed. 9.95 o.p. (ISBN 0-685-71795-X); leatherette 12.95 (ISBN 0-685-71796-8). Brevet Pr.
--Wind Without Rain. LC 76-28868. 1976. Repr. of 1939 ed. 9.95 (ISBN 0-88498-045-6); text ed. 9.95 o.p. (ISBN 0-685-71797-6); leatherette 12.95 (ISBN 0-685-71798-4). Brevet Pr.
Krause, Herbert & Olson, Gary D. Prelude to Glory. LC 74-80769. (Illus.). 279p. (Orig.). 1974. 19.95 (ISBN 0-88498-018-9); ltd. lea. ed. 75.00 (ISBN 0-685-50460-3); pap. 10.95 (ISBN 0-88498-019-7); pap. text ed. 7.45 o.p. (ISBN 0-685-50461-1). Brevet Pr.
Krause, J. V. & Barham, Jerry N. The Mechanical Foundations of Human Motion: A Programmed Text. (Illus.). 1975. pap. text ed. 13.95 (ISBN 0-8016-0474-5). Mosby.
Krause, Kathalyn. The Blue Key. (Orig.). 1980. pap. 2.25 (ISBN 0-505-51536-9). Tower Bks.
--Mellona. 1979. pap. 2.25 (ISBN 0-505-51360-9). Tower Bks.
Krause, Lawrence B. European Economic Integration & the United States. 1968. 11.95 (ISBN 0-8157-5034-X). Brookings.
--Sequel to Bretton Woods: A Proposal to Reform the World Monetary System. 50p. 1971. pap. 2.95 (ISBN 0-8157-5035-8). Brookings.
Krause, Lawrence B. & Salant, Walter S., eds. European Monetary Unification & Its Meaning for the United States. LC 73-1084. 1973. 12.95 (ISBN 0-8157-5032-3). Brookings.
--Worldwide Inflation: Theory & Recent Experience. LC 76-51580. 1976. 21.95 (ISBN 0-8157-5030-7); pap. 11.95 (ISBN 0-8157-5029-3). Brookings.
Krause, Lawrence B., jt. ed. see Bergsten, A. C. Fred.
Krause, Lawrence B., jt. ed. see Caves, Richard E.
Krause, Patricia A., jt. auth. see Carper, Jean.
Krause, Paul M. Planning a Christian Wedding. 1963. pap. 0.95 (ISBN 0-570-03504-X, 14-2010). Concordia.
Krause, Peter, jt. auth. see Shull, Henry A.
Krause, Richard M., jt. ed. see Haber, Edgar.
Krause, Sydney J., ed. see Brown, Charles B.
Krause, William J. & Cutts, J. Jarry. Concise Text of Histology. (Illus.). 175p. 1981. write for info. soft cover (4784-1). Williams & Wilkins.
Krauss, Beatrice, jt. auth. see Krauss, Herbert.
Krauss, Bob. Kauai. LC 77-82233. (Illus.). 1978. pap. 4.95 (ISBN 0-89610-067-7). Island Her.
Krauss, Ellis S. Japanese Radicals Revisited: Student Protest in Postwar Japan. 1974. 20.00x (ISBN 0-520-02467-2). U of Cal Pr.
Krauss, Herbert & Krauss, Beatrice. Living with Anxiety & Depression. encore ed. 1980. Encore Ed. pap. 4.95 (ISBN 0-88347-035-7). Thomas More.
Krauss, Irving. Stratification, Class & Conflict. LC 75-12060. (Illus.). 1976. text ed. 15.95 (ISBN 0-02-917690-5). Free Pr.
Krauss, Judith B. & Slavinsky, Ann T. Chronic Psychiatric Illness. (Illus.). 288p. 1981. text ed. 14.95 (ISBN 0-86542-006-8). Blackwell Sci.
Krauss, Leonard I. SAFE: Security Audit & Field Evaluation for Computer Facilities & Information Systems. 308p. 1981. 29.95 (ISBN 0-8144-5526-3). Am Mgmt.
Krauss, Melvyn B. A Geometric Approach to International Trade. LC 77-20676. 1979. text ed. 34.95 (ISBN 0-470-99353-7). Halsted Pr.
--The New Protectionism: The Welfare State & International Trade. LC 78-19545. 1978. cOBE 10.00x (ISBN 0-8147-4570-9); pap. 5.00x cobe (ISBN 0-8147-4571-7). NYU Pr.
Krauss, Melvyn B., ed. The Economics of Integration: A Book of Readings. 1973. pap. text ed. 14.95x (ISBN 0-04-330222-X). Allen Unwin.
Krauss, Paul G. German Review & Reference Grammar. (Orig.). 1962. pap. text ed. 7.95 o.p. (ISBN 0-13-354100-2). P-H.
Krauss, Ruth. Somebody Spilled the Sky. LC 78-14306. (Illus.). (gr. k-3). 1979. 7.50 (ISBN 0-688-80186-2); PLB 7.20 (ISBN 0-688-84186-4). Greenwillow.
--What a Fine Day For. LC 67-18464. (gr. k-2). 1967. 5.95 o.s.i. (ISBN 0-8193-0197-3, Four Winds). Schol Bk Serv.
Krauss, S., et al. Encyclopedic Handbook of Medical Psychology. LC 75-33106. 1976. 19.95 (ISBN 0-407-00044-5). Butterworths.
Krausz, A. S. & Eyring, H. Deformation Kinetics. LC 75-12554. 398p. 1975. 39.95 (ISBN 0-471-24983-1, Pub. by Wiley-Interscience). Wiley.
Krausz, John. The Bicycling Book. (Illus.). 1980. 10.00 (ISBN 0-686-65922-8). Times Bks.
Kraut, Florence R. From My Israel Journal. LC 80-80528. 56p. (Orig.). 1980. pap. 2.95 (ISBN 0-686-28879-3). Preston St Pr.
Krautkramer, H., jt. auth. see Krautkramer, J.
Krautkramer, J. & Krautkramer, H. Ultrasonic Testing of Materials. LC 76-12561. 1977. 71.70 (ISBN 0-387-07716-2). Springer-Verlag.
Kravette, Steve. Complete Meditation. Dodge, Plunkett, tr. (Illus.). 356p. (Orig.). 1981. pap. 9.95 (ISBN 0-914918-28-1). Para Res.
Kravis, Judy. The Prose of Mallarme. LC 75-22977. 272p. 1976. 42.00 (ISBN 0-521-20921-8). Cambridge U Pr.
Kravitol, R. Buying, Owning & Selling a Home in the Nineteen Eighties. 1981. pap. 9.95 (ISBN 0-13-109504-8). P-H.
Kravitz, Wallace W. Developing Bookkeeping Skills. (gr. 10-11). 1978. wkbk 9.42 (ISBN 0-87720-404-7). AMSCO Sch.
--Modern Business Mathematics. (Orig.). (gr. 7-12). 1973. pap. text ed. 5.33 (ISBN 0-87720-400-4). AMSCO Sch.
Krawczyk, Chess J. Mountaineering: A Bibliography of Books in English to 1974. LC 76-45415. 1977. 8.50 o.p. (ISBN 0-8108-0979-6). Scarecrow.
Krawiec, T. S., ed. The Psychologists, Vol. 2. (Illus.). 350p. 1974. text ed. 12.95x (ISBN 0-19-501726-9); pap. text ed. 7.95x (ISBN 0-19-501725-0). Oxford U Pr.
--The Psychologists: What They Do & How They Came to Do It, Vol. 1. (Illus.). 350p. 1972. text ed. 12.95x (ISBN 0-19-501568-1); pap. text ed. 7.95x (ISBN 0-19-501567-3). Oxford U Pr.
--A Road Not Taken: The Editorial Opinions of Frederick C. Thorne. 1981. pap. 11.95 (ISBN 0-88422-013-3). Clinical Psych.
Krawitt, Laura P. & Weinberger, Emily K. Practical Low Protein Cookery. (Illus.). 128p. 1971. pap. 10.50 (ISBN 0-398-01049-8). C C Thomas.
Krawitz, Henry. A Post-Symbolist Bibliography. LC 73-1181. 1973. 10.00 (ISBN 0-8108-0594-4). Scarecrow.
Krayenbuehl, H., et al, eds. Advances & Technical Standards in Neurosurgery, Vol. 5. LC 74-10499. (Illus.). 1978. 46.00 (ISBN 0-387-81441-8). Springer-Verlag.
--Advances & Technical Standards in Neurosurgery, Vol. 7. (Illus.). 270p. 1980. 57.90 (ISBN 0-387-81592-9). Springer-Verlag.
--The Management of Head Injuries. (Progress in Neurological Surgery: Vol. 10). (Illus.). 1981. 75.00 (ISBN 3-8055-0134-X). S Karger.
Krcma, Vaclav. Identification & Registration of Firearms. (Illus.). 200p. 1971. 19.75 (ISBN 0-398-02336-0). C C Thomas.
Kreal, Louis. Clark's Positioning in Radiography, Vol. 1. 10th ed. (Illus.). 500p. 1980. 45.95 (ISBN 0-8151-5190-X). Year Bk Med.
Krebs, A., jt. auth. see Zuercher, K.
Krebs, Carl. Dittersdorfiana. LC 72-166092. (Music Ser.). 1972. Repr. of 1900 ed. lib. bdg. 19.50 (ISBN 0-306-70259-2). Da Capo.
Krebs, John G. Your People Problems. LC 68-25949. (Harvest Ser.). 1978. pap. 3.95 (ISBN 0-686-63846-8, 24510-0). Pacific Pr Pub Assn.
Krebs, John R. & Davies, Nicholas B., eds. Behavioural Ecology. LC 78-8414. (Illus.). 1978. text ed. 34.00x (ISBN 0-87893-433-2); pap. text ed. 19.50x (ISBN 0-87893-434-0). Sinauer Assoc.
Krebs, Margie M., jt. auth. see Edwards, Lisa A.
Krech, Inez M., jt. auth. see Celli, Elisa.
Krech, Shepard, III. Praise the Bridge That Carries You Over: The Life of Joseph L. Sutton. (University Books Ser.). 1981. lib. bdg. 18.50 (ISBN 0-8161-9038-0). G K Hall.
Krech, Shepard, 3rd. Praise the Bridge That Carries You Over: The Life of Joseph Sutton. 1981. pap. text ed. 11.25x (ISBN 0-87073-650-7). Schenkman.
Kreck, Lothar A. Menus: Analysis & Planning. LC 74-28068. (Illus.). 200p. 1975. 16.95 (ISBN 0-8436-2050-1). CBI Pub.
--Operational Problem Solving for the Hotel & Restaurant Industry. LC 78-15134. 1978. pap. 10.95 (ISBN 0-8436-2132-X). CBI Pub.
Kreck, Lothar A. & McConnell, Jon P. Hospitality Management: Avoiding Legal Pitfalls. 1976. 16.95 (ISBN 0-8436-2064-1). CBI Pub.
Kredenser, Gail. One Dancing Drum. LC 79-146845. (Illus.). (gr. k-3). 1971. 8.95 (ISBN 0-87599-178-5). S G Phillips.
--Write It Right. 1972. pap. 2.95 (ISBN 0-06-463329-2, EH 329, EH). Har-Row.
Kreeft, Peter J. Heaven: The Heart's Deepest Longing. LC 80-7747. 160p. 1980. 8.95 (ISBN 0-06-064776-0, HarpR). Har-Row.
Kregel-Javaux, M. P., tr. see Abraham-Frois, Gilbert & Berrebi, E.
Kreh, Lefty & Kessler, Hermann. Fly Casting with Lefty Kreh. LC 73-16374. (Illus.). 1974. 8.95 o.s.i. (ISBN 0-397-00999-2). Lippincott.
Kreh, Richard T. Advanced Masonry Skills. LC 77-78176. 1978. pap. text ed. 11.44 (ISBN 0-8273-1636-4); instructor's guide 1.60 (ISBN 0-8273-1637-2). Delmar.
--Masonry Skills. LC 75-27994. 1976. pap. 10.80 (ISBN 0-8273-1090-0); instructor's guide 1.60 (ISBN 0-8273-1091-9). Delmar.

--Safety for Masons. LC 78-53663. 1979. pap. text ed. 3.60 (ISBN 0-8273-1668-2); instructor's guide 0.75 (ISBN 0-8273-1669-0). Delmar.

Krehbiel, Henry. Chapters of Opera. (Music Reprint Ser.). (Illus.). xvii, 435p. 1980. Repr. of 1909 ed. lib. bdg. 45.00 (ISBN 0-306-76036-3). Da Capo.

Krehbiel, Henry E. A Book of Operas, Their Histories, Their Plots & Their Music. LC 80-2279. 1981. Repr. of 1919 ed. 42.50 (ISBN 0-404-18851-6). AMS Pr.

--More Chapters of Opera: Being Historical & Critical Observations & Records Concerning the Lyric Drama in New York from 1908-1918. LC 78-66910. (Encore Music Editions Ser.). 1981. Repr. of 1919 ed. 45.00 (ISBN 0-686-66139-7). Hyperion Conn.

--A Second Book of Operas, Their Histories, Their Plots & Their Music. LC 80-2280. 1981. Repr. of 1917 ed. 36.50 (ISBN 0-404-18852-4). AMS Pr.

Krehel, Peter. Spiritual Fingerprint. 1981. 10.95 (ISBN 0-8062-1675-1). Carlton.

Krehl, Willard A. The Role of Citrus in Health & Disease. LC 76-4502. 1976. 6.50 (ISBN 0-8130-0532-9); pap. 2.95 o.p. (ISBN 0-8130-0571-X). U Presses Fla.

Kreidberg, Marjorie. Food on the Frontier: Minnesota Cooking from 1850 to 1900, with Selected Recipes. LC 75-34214. (Illus.). 313p. 1975. 10.50 (ISBN 0-87351-096-8); pap. 6.50 (ISBN 0-87351-097-6). Minn Hist.

Kreider, Barbara A. Index to Children's Plays in Collections. 2nd ed. LC 76-49666. 1977. 11.50 (ISBN 0-8108-0992-3). Scarecrow.

Kreider, Donald L., et al. Introduction to Linear Analysis. 1966. 22.95 (ISBN 0-201-03949-4). A-W.

Kreider, Jan F. The Solar Heating Design Process: Active & Passive. (Illus.). 432p. 1981. 21.50 (ISBN 0-07-035478-2, P&RB). McGraw.

Kreider, Jan F., jt. auth. see Kreith, Frank.

Kreider, Jan F. & Kreith, Frank, eds. Solar Energy Handbook. (Illus.). 1099p. 1981. 49.50 (ISBN 0-07-035474-X). McGraw.

Kreidl, John F. Nicholas Ray. (Theatrical Arts Ser.). 1977. lib. bdg. 12.50 (ISBN 0-8057-9250-3). Twayne.

Kreidolf, Ernst. Servants of the Spring. (Illus.). 1979. 9.95 (ISBN 0-914676-11-3); pap. write for info (ISBN 0-914676-19-9). Green Tiger.

Kreier, Julius P., ed. Malaria: Epidemiology, Chemotherapy, Morphology & Metabolism, Vol. 1. LC 80-530. 1980. 49.00 (ISBN 0-12-426101-9). Acad Pr.

--Malaria: Pathology, Vecter Studies & Culture, Vol. 2. LC 80-530. 1980. 38.50 (ISBN 0-12-426102-7). Acad Pr.

Kreighbaum, Ellen. Qualitative Biomechanics. (Orig.). 1980. write for info. (ISBN 0-8087-1155-5). Burgess.

Kreiler, Kurt & Sloterdijk, Peter, eds. In Irrer Gesellschaft: Verstaendigungstexte Zur Psychtherapie und Selbsterfahrung. (Edition Suhrkamp: No. 435). 528p. (Orig.). 1980. pap. text ed. 10.40 (ISBN 0-686-64715-7, Pub. by Insel Verlag Germany). Suhrkamp.

Krein, M. G., et al. Functional Analysis & Measure Theory. rev. ed. (Translations Ser.: No. 1, Vol. 10). 1980. 37.20 (ISBN 0-8218-1610-1, TRANS 1-10). Am Math.

Krein, S. G., et al. Interpolation of Linear Operators. (Mathematical Monographs). 1981. cancelled (ISBN 0-8218-4504-7). Am Math.

Kreinin, Mordechai E. International Economics: A Policy Approach. 3rd ed. 464p. 1979. text ed. 18.95 (ISBN 0-15-541540-9, HC). HarBraceJ.

Kreis, Bernadine & Pattie, Alice. Up from Grief: Patterns of Recovery. LC 69-13542. 1969. 6.95 (ISBN 0-8164-0198-5). Crossroad NY.

Kreissman, Bernard, ed. see Scott, Sir Walter.

Kreith, Frank & Kreider, Jan F. Principles of Solar Engineering. LC 77-27861. (McGraw-Hill - Hemisphere Thermal & Fluids Engineering Ser). (Illus.). 1978. pap. 24.95 (ISBN 0-07-035476-6, C). McGraw.

Kreith, Frank & West, R. E. Economics of Solar Energy & Conservation Systems, 3 vols. 1980. 69.95 ea. Vol. 1, 320p (ISBN 0-8493-5229-0). Vol. 2, 32 O.p (ISBN 0-8493-5230-4). Vol. 3, 288p (ISBN 0-8493-5231-2). CRC Pr.

Kreith, Frank & Wrenn, Catherine B. The Nuclear Impact: A Case Study of the Plowshare Program to Produce Natural Gas by Underground Nuclear Stimulation in the Rocky Mountains. LC 75-31708. (Special Studies on Technology, Natural Resources & the Environment). 250p. 1976. 26.75 o.p. (ISBN 0-89158-005-0). Westview.

Kreith, Frank, jt. ed. see Kreider, Jan F.

Kreitler, Hans & Kreitler, Shulamith. Psychology of the Arts. LC 70-185566. (Illus.). 1972. 18.75 (ISBN 0-8223-0269-1); pap. 9.75 (ISBN 0-8223-0437-6). Duke.

Kreitler, Peter, et al. Affair Prevention. 256p. 1981. 10.95 (ISBN 0-02-566710-6). Macmillan.

Kreitler, Shulamith, jt. auth. see Kreitler, Hans.

Kreitlow, Burton W. Examining Controversies in Adult Education. LC 80-27058. (Higher Education Ser.). 1981. text ed. price not set (ISBN 0-87589-488-7). Jossey-Bass.

Kreitlow, Burton W., et al. Leadership for Action in Rural Communities. LC 65-20644. (Illus.). 1965. 11.35 (ISBN 0-8134-0532-7); text ed. 8.50x (ISBN 0-685-12632-3, 532). Interstate.

Kreitner, Robert. Management: A Problem-Solving Process. LC 79-88719. (Illus.). 1980. text ed. 18.75 (ISBN 0-395-28490-2); inst. manual 1.75 (ISBN 0-395-28491-0). HM.

Kreitner, Robert & Sova, Margaret. Understanding Management: Study Guide to Management: A Problem-Solving Process. LC 79-88719. (Illus.). pap. 6.95 (ISBN 0-395-28492-9). HM.

Kreitzman, Stephen & Kreitzman, Susan. The Nutrition Cookbook: 123 Gourmet Recipes Computer Analyzed for Your Specific Daily Requirements. LC 76-54565. 1977. 12.95 o.p. (ISBN 0-15-167750-6). HarBraceJ.

Kreitzman, Susan, jt. auth. see Kreitzman, Stephen.

Kreivsky, Joseph & Linfield, Jordon L. The Bad Spellers Dictionary. 1967. 2.50 (ISBN 0-394-49199-8). Random.

Krejcarek, Philip. Photography: Simple Truths. (Illus.). 1978. pap. 4.00 (ISBN 0-686-15968-3). P Krejcarek.

Krejci, Jaroslav. Social Change & Stratification in Postwar Czechoslovakia. (Social & Political Processes in Eastern Europe Ser.). 1972. 20.00x (ISBN 0-231-03685-X). Columbia U Pr.

Krejci, Jaroslav & Velimsky, V. Ethnic & Political Nations in Europe. 1980. write for info. St Martin.

Krejewski, Robert J. & Shuman, R. Baird. The Beginning Teacher: A Practical Guide to Problem Solving. 128p. 1979. pap. 5.75 (ISBN 0-686-63677-5, 1489-8-06). NEA.

Krekic, Barisa. Dubrovnik in the Fourteenth & Fifteenth Centuries: A City Between East & West. LC 76-177340. (Center of Civilization Ser.: Vol. 30). 188p. 1972. 5.95 o.p. (ISBN 0-8061-0999-8). U of Okla Pr.

--Dubrovnik, Italy & the Balkans in the Late Middle Ages. 332p. 1980. 75.00x (ISBN 0-86078-070-8, Pub. by Variorum England). State Mutual Bk.

Krell, Edwin D. & Vasel, Major J. Killer Cops. (Orig.). 1979. pap. 1.95 (ISBN 0-532-23265-8). Manor Bks.

Krementz, Jill. How It Feels When a Parent Dies. LC 80-8808. (Illus.). 128p. 1981. 9.95 (ISBN 0-394-51911-6). Knopf.

--Writer's Image: The Literary Portraits of Jill Krementz. LC 80-66461. (Illus.). 112p. 1980. 25.00 (ISBN 0-87923-349-4). Godine.

Kremer, et al. Missouri's Black Heritage. LC 79-54887. (Orig.). 1980. pap. text ed. 6.95x (ISBN 0-88273-115-7). Forum Pr MO.

Kremer, Karl, jt. auth. see Grewe, Horst-Eberhard.

Kremmer, T. & Boross, L. Gel Chromatography. LC 77-24994. 1980. 57.00 (ISBN 0-471-99548-7, Pub. by Wiley-Interscience). Wiley.

Krenek, Ernst. Exploring Music. 1980. pap. 4.95 (ISBN 0-7145-0226-X). Riverrun NY.

--Horizons Circled: Reflections on My Music. (Illus.). 1975. 15.75x (ISBN 0-520-02338-2). U of Cal Pr.

--Modal Counterpoint in the Style of the Sixteenth Century. LC 59-45012. 21p. 1959. pap. 3.50 (ISBN 0-913932-11-6). Boosey & Hawkes.

Krenkel, John H., ed. Richard Yates: Civil War Governor. LC 65-16499. 1966. text ed. 8.95x (ISBN 0-8134-0821-0, 821). Interstate.

Krenkel, Peter A. & Novotny, Vladimir. Water Quality Management. LC 80-516. 1980. 65.00 (ISBN 0-12-426150-7). Acad Pr.

Krenov, James. James Krenov Worker in Wood. (Illus.). 128p. 1981. 24.95 (ISBN 0-442-26336-8). Van Nos Reinhold.

Krensky. The Dragon Circle. (gr. 3-5). 1980. pap. 1.25 (ISBN 0-590-30069-5, Schol Pap). Schol Bk Serv.

Krentz, Edgar & Vogel, Arthur A. Easter. Achtemeier, Elizabeth, et al, eds. LC 79-7377. (Proclamation 2: Aids for Interpreting the Lessons of the Church Year, Ser. C). 64p. 1980. pap. 2.50 (ISBN 0-8006-4080-2, 1-4080). Fortress.

Krentzman, Harvey C. Successful Management Strategies for Small Business. (Illus.). 208p. 1981. text ed. 13.95 o.p. (ISBN 0-13-863126-3, Spec); pap. text ed. 6.95 (ISBN 0-13-863118-2, Spec). P-H.

Krenz, Jerrold H. Energy: Conversion & Utilization. 448p. 1976. text ed. 23.95x (ISBN 0-205-05421-8). Allyn.

--Energy: From Opulence to Sufficiency. LC 79-15059. 24.95 (ISBN 0-03-057001-8). Praeger.

Krepel, Wayne J. & Duvall, Charles R. Education & Education-Related Serials: A Directory. LC 76-47040. 1977. lib. bdg. 15.00x o.p. (ISBN 0-87287-131-2). Libs Unl.

Kreps, Georgian, tr. see Imbo, M.

Kreps, Georgian, tr. see Mann, Philip.

Kreps, Juanita, et al. Contemporary Labor Economics: Issues Analysis & Policies. 3rd ed. 1974. 16.95x o.p. (ISBN 0-534-00303-6). Wadsworth Pub.

Kreps, Juanita M. Women and the American Economy: A Look to the 1980's. LC 76-4105. (American Assembly Ser.). (Illus.). 192p. 1976. pap. 4.00 (ISBN 0-13-962316-7, Spec). P-H.

Kreps, Juanita M., et al. Contemporary Labor Economics & Labor Relations. 2nd ed. 496p. 1980. text ed. 21.95x (ISBN 0-534-00810-0). Wadsworth Pub.

Kresin, V. Z., jt. auth. see Geilikman, B. T.

Kress, George J. Marketing Research. (Illus.). 1979. text ed. 18.95 (ISBN 0-8359-4271-6); instrs'. manual avail. (ISBN 0-8359-4272-4). Reston.

Kress, Gunther. Language As Ideology. 1981. pap. price not set (ISBN 0-7100-0795-7). Routledge & Kegan.

Kress, Gunther & Hodge, Robert. Language As Ideology. 1979. 18.00x (ISBN 0-7100-0215-7). Routledge & Kegan.

Kress, Jack M. Prescripton for Justice: The Theory & Practice of Sentencing Guidelines. 368p. 1980. reference 25.00 (ISBN 0-88410-792-2). Ballinger Pub.

Kress, Jack M., jt. ed. see Brantingham, Paul J.

Kress, John R. & Singer, James. HMO Handbook. LC 75-18637. 206p. 1975. text ed. 22.00 (ISBN 0-912862-14-9). Aspen Systems.

Kress, Stephen W. Audubon Society Handbook for Birders. (Illus.). 320p. 1981. 14.95 (ISBN 0-684-16336-5, ScribT). Scribner.

Kretchmer & Brasel. Biomedical & Social Bases of Pediatrics. 1981. write for info. (ISBN 0-89352-093-4). Masson Pub.

Kretchmer, Norman see Walcher, Dwain N., et al.

Kretchmer, Norman, intro. by. Human Nutrition: Readings from Scientific American. LC 78-17367. (Illus.). 1978. pap. text ed. 10.95x (ISBN 0-7167-0182-0). W H Freeman.

Kretchmer, Norman, jt. ed. see Quilligan, E. J.

Kreter, L. Sight & Sound: A Manual of Aural Musicianship, 2 vols. 1976. Vol. 1. pap. 12.95 (ISBN 0-13-809905-7); Vol. 2. pap. 13.50 (ISBN 0-13-809913-8); Recording Vols. 1 & 2. 150.00 (ISBN 0-13-809921-9). P-H.

Kretlow, William, jt. auth. see Moyer, Charles R.

Kretschmer, Joan. The Bestseller. 1980. pap. write for info. (ISBN 0-671-83277-8). PB.

Kretschmer, V. Leukozytenseparation und Transfusion. (Beitraege Zu Infusionstherapie und Klinische Ernaehrung Ser.: Vol. 6). (Illus.). viii, 200p. 1981. 18.00 (ISBN 3-8055-1946-X). S Karger.

Kretzschmar, Hermann. Geschicte der Oper. LC 80-2285. 1981. Repr. of 1919 ed. 33.50 (ISBN 0-404-18853-2). AMS Pr.

Kreul, L., jt. auth. see Kotas, Richard.

Kreuter, Gretchen. Running the Twin Cities. (Illus.). 95p. 1980. pap. 3.95 (ISBN 0-931714-08-7). Nodin Pr.

Kreuter, Gretchen, jt. auth. see Kreuter, Kent.

Kreuter, Gretchen, jt. ed. see Stuhler, Barbara.

Kreuter, Kent & Kreuter, Gretchen. An American Dissenter: The Life of Algie Martin Simons, 1870-1950. LC 68-55042. (Illus.). 248p. 1969. 12.00x (ISBN 0-8131-1177-3). U Pr of Ky.

Kreutler, Patricia. Nutrition in Perspective. (Illus.). 1980. text ed. 17.95 (ISBN 0-13-627752-7); wkbk. 6.95 (ISBN 0-13-627778-0). P-H.

Kreutzberg, G. W., ed. Physiology & Pathology of Dendrites. LC 74-14474. (Advances in Neurology Ser: Vol. 12). 523p. 1975. 43.50 (ISBN 0-911216-99-5). Raven.

Kreuzer, H. J. Non-Equilibrium Thermodynamics & Its Statistical Foundations. (Monographs on the Physics & Chemistry of Materials). (Illus.). 500p. 1981. 105.00 (ISBN 0-19-851361-5). Oxford U Pr.

Kreuzer, Rudolf, ed. Freezing & Irradiation of Fish. (Illus.). 548p. 41.25 (ISBN 0-85238-008-9, FN). Unipub.

Kreveld, D. Van see Van Kreveld, D.

Krevelen, Alice Van see Van Krevelen, Alice.

Krewer, Semyon E. The Arthritis Exercise Book. 256p. (Orig.). 1981. pap. 7.95 (ISBN 0-346-12497-2). Cornerstone.

Krey, A. C., jt. auth. see Kelley, Truman L.

Kreye, Eric & Youngberg, Norma R. Under the Blood Banner. LC 68-21461. 1968. pap. 4.95 (ISBN 0-8163-0148-4, 21190-4). Pacific Pr Pub Assn.

Kreyemborg, Alfred. Troubadour: An American Autobiography. 1957. pap. 1.75 o.p. (ISBN 0-8090-0022-9, AmCen). Hill & Wang.

Kreyszig, Erwin. Introductory Mathematical Statistics: Principles & Methods. LC 70-107583. 1970. 26.95 (ISBN 0-471-50730-X). Wiley.

Krichbaum, Jorg & Zondergeld, Rein. Dictionary of Fantastic Art. (Pocket Art Ser.). (Illus.). 1981. pap. 5.95 (ISBN 0-8120-2110-X). Barron.

Krichmar, Albert, et al. The Women's Movement in the Seventies: An International English-Language Bibliography. LC 77-21416. 1977. 35.00 (ISBN 0-8108-1063-8). Scarecrow.

--The Women's Rights Movement in the United States 1848-1970: A Bibliography & Sourcebook. LC 72-4702. 1972. 15.00 o.p. (ISBN 0-8108-0528-6). Scarecrow.

Krick. The Confederate Death Roster at Gettysburg. 10.00. Pr of Morningside.

Krick, Edward V. Introduction to Engineering: Methods, Concepts & Issues. LC 75-41432. 351p. 1976. text ed. 17.95x (ISBN 0-471-50750-4); instructor's manual avail. (ISBN 0-471-01912-7). Wiley.

--Methods Engineering. LC 62-8775. (Illus.). 1962. text ed. 28.95x (ISBN 0-471-50754-7). Wiley.

Krick, L., tr. see Makrakis, Apostolos.

Kricka, L. J. & Clark, P. M. Biochemistry of Alcohol & Alcoholism. LC 79-40252. 1979. 59.95 (ISBN 0-470-26712-7). Halsted Pr.

Kricka, L. J., jt. auth. see Clark, P. M.

Kriedl, John F. Alain Resnais. (Theatrical Art Ser.). 1978. 12.50 (ISBN 0-8057-9256-2). Twayne.

Kriegel, Annie. Eurocommunism: A New Kind of Communism? Stern, Peter S., tr. LC 77-92081. (Publications 194). 145p. 1978. 12.00 (ISBN 0-8179-6941-1). Hoover Inst Pr.

Krieger, Dorothy T., ed. Endocrine Rhythms: Comprehensive Endocrinology. LC 77-75655. 1979. 34.50 (ISBN 0-89004-234-9). Raven.

Krieger, Dorothy T. & Hughes, Joan, eds. Neuroendocrinology. LC 79-28123. (Illus.). 1980. 25.00x (ISBN 0-87893-425-1). Sinauer Assoc.

Krieger, Henry A. Measure-Theoretic Probability. LC 80-1431. 394p. 1980. lib. bdg. 20.50 (ISBN 0-8191-1228-3); pap. text ed. 12.50 (ISBN 0-8191-1229-1). U Pr of Amer.

Krieger, M., jt. auth. see Corbman, B. P.

Krieger, Murray. Arts on the Level: The Fall of the Elite Object. LC 80-25401. (The Hodges Lectures). (Illus.). 112p. 1981. text ed. 7.50x (ISBN 0-87049-308-6). U of Tenn Pr.

--The Complete Dictionary of Buying & Merchandising. 125p. 1980. pap. text ed. 3.95 (ISBN 0-686-60189-0, M47780). Natl Ret Merch.

--Practical Merchandising Math for Everyday Use. 700p. 1980. pap. text ed. 21.75 (ISBN 0-686-60196-3, M47680). Natl Ret Merch.

--Student's Workbook for the Buyer's Manual. 300p. 1980. pap. text ed. 13.50 (ISBN 0-686-60198-X, M47579). Natl Ret Merch.

Krieger, Murray, jt. auth. see Corbman, Bernard P.

Krieger, Murray & Dembo, L. S., eds. Directions for Criticism: Structuralism & Its Alternatives. 1977. 17.50 (ISBN 0-299-07390-4, 739); pap. text ed. 5.95 (ISBN 0-299-07394-7). U of Wis Pr.

Kriegman, George, et al, eds. American Psychiatry: Past, Present, & Future. LC 75-8962. 200p. 1975. 9.95x (ISBN 0-8139-0571-0). U Pr of Va.

Kriehn, George. The English Rising in Fourteen Fifty. (Perspectives in European History Ser.: No. 37). vii, 131p. 1980. Repr. of 1882 ed. lib. bdg. 15.00x (ISBN 0-87991-081-X). Porcupine Pr.

Kriek, E., ed. see International Conference on Environmental Carcinogenesis, Amsterdam, May 1979.

Krier, James E., jt. auth. see Stewart, Richard B.

Kriesberg, Louis. Social Inequality. (P-H Ser. in Sociology). (Illus.). 1979. ref. ed. 17.95 (ISBN 0-13-815860-6). P-H.

--Sociology of Social Conflicts. (General Sociology Ser.). (Illus.). 304p. 1973. text ed. 15.95 (ISBN 0-13-821546-4). P-H.

Krige, D. G. Lognormal: De Wijsian Geostatistics for Ore Evaluation. 50p. 1980. 18.50x (ISBN 0-620-03006-2, Pub. by Mining Journal England). State Mutual Bk.

Krige, John. Science, Revolution & Discontinuity. (Harvester Studies in Philosophy: No. 10). 220p. Date not set. text ed. 30.00x (ISBN 0-391-02094-3). Humanities.

Krikler, Dennis M. & Goodwin, John F., eds. Cardiac Arrhythmias. LC 75-11582. (Illus.). 255p. 1975. text ed. 26.00 (ISBN 0-7216-5516-5). Saunders.

Krikorian, A. D., jt. auth. see Steward, F. C.

Krikorian, Mesrob K. Armenians in the Service of the Ottoman Empire, 1860-1908. (Direct Editions Ser.). (Orig.). 1978. pap. 10.50 (ISBN 0-7100-8564-8). Routledge & Kegan.

Krikorian, Yervant H., ed. Naturalism & the Human Spirit. LC 44-2760. 1944. 20.00x (ISBN 0-231-01424-4). Columbia U Pr.

Krim, Seymour. Views of a Nearsighted Cannoneer. 1968. pap. 1.95 o.p. (ISBN 0-525-47214-2). Dutton.

Krimm, Bernard G. W. B. Yeats & the Emergence of the Irish Free State, 1918-1939: Living in the Explosion. 324p. 1981. 20.00x (ISBN 0-87875-200-5). Whitston Pub.

Krimmer, Sally, ed. see Baynton, Barbara.

Krimsky, Emanuel. The Corneal Light Reflex: A Guide to Binocular Disorders. (Illus.). 212p. 1972. 21.50 (ISBN 0-398-02596-7). C C Thomas.

Krimsky, Joseph. The Wonder of Man. 1968. pap. 3.95 (ISBN 0-911336-21-4). Sci of Mind.

Krimsley, Victor S., et al. Introductory General Chemistry: Laboratory Manual. 2nd ed. (Illus.). 114p. 1976. pap. text ed. 5.50 o.p. (ISBN 0-8016-2744-3). Mosby.

Kring, Hilda A. The Harmonists: A Folk-Cultural Approach. (ATLA Monograph: No. 3). 1973. 10.00 (ISBN 0-8108-0603-7). Scarecrow.

Krinsky, Carol. Rockefeller Center. (Illus.). 1978. 19.95 (ISBN 0-19-502317-X). Oxford U Pr.

Krinsky, Fred & Boskin, Joseph. Welfare State: Who Is My Brother's Keeper. (Insight Ser). 144p. (Orig.). 1968. pap. text ed. 4.95x (ISBN 0-02-476040-4, 47604). Macmillan.

Krinsky, Fred, jt. auth. see Boskin, Joseph.

Krinsky, Fred, jt. auth. see Tapp, June L.

Krinsky, Fred, ed. Democracy & Complexity: Who Governs the Governors. (Insight Series: Studies in Contemporary Issues). 128p. 1968. pap. text ed. 4.95x (ISBN 0-02-476030-7, 47603). Macmillan.

--Politics of Religion in America. 128p. 1968. pap. text ed. 4.95x (ISBN 0-02-476020-X, 47602). Macmillan.

Krinsky, Fred, ed. see Boskin, Joseph.

Krinsky, Fred, ed. see Brown, Michael.

Krinsky, Fred, ed. see Hickman, Martin.

Krinsky, Fred, ed. see McGrath, Edward.

Krinsky, Fred, ed. see Rosenstone, Robert A.

Krinsky, Fred, ed. see Wolf, Jerome.

Krinsky, R., et al. Concepts & Issues in American Government. 1976. pap. 6.95x (ISBN 0-02-475160-X). Macmillan.

Krinsley, Jeanette. The Cow Went Over the Mountain. (Illus.). (ps-2). 1963. PLB 5.00 (ISBN 0-307-60576-0, Golden Pr). Western Pub.

Kripke, Dorothy K. Debbie in Dreamland. (gr. 2-5). 1960. 3.95x (ISBN 0-685-06929-X). Bloch.

--Let's Talk About the Jewish Holidays. LC 75-104328. (Illus.). (gr. k-4). 1970. 5.95 (ISBN 0-8246-0106-8). Jonathan David.

Krippendorff, Ekkehart & Rittberger, Volker, eds. The Foreign Policy of West Germany: Formation & Contents. LC 80-40149. (German Political Studies: Vol. 4). (Illus.). 372p. 1980. 20.00 (ISBN 0-8039-9818-X); pap. 9.95 (ISBN 0-8039-9819-8). Sage.

Krippendorff, Klaus. Content Analysis: An Introduction to Its Methodology. LC 80-19166. (CommText Ser.: Vol. 5). (Illus.). 191p. 1980. 15.00 (ISBN 0-8039-1497-0); pap. 7.95 (ISBN 0-8039-1498-9). Sage.

Krippner, Stanley. Human Possibilities: Mind Exploration in the USSR & Eastern Europe. LC 80-953. 360p. 1980. 14.95 (ISBN 0-385-12805-3, Anchor Pr). Doubleday.

Krippner, Stanley, jt. auth. see Ullman, Montague.

Krippner, Stanley & Rubin, Daniel, eds. The Kirlian Aura: The Galaxies of Life. LC 73-10733. 224p. 1974. pap. 3.95 (ISBN 0-385-06574-4, Anch). Doubleday.

Krippner, Stanley, jt. ed. see White, John.

Kris, Ernst & Kurz, Otto. Legend, Myth & Magic in the Image of the Artists: A Historical Experiment. 1979. 17.50x (ISBN 0-300-02205-0). Yale U Pr.

--Legend, Myth, & Magic in the Image of the Artist: A Historical Experiment. LC 78-24024. (Illus.). 175p. 1981. pap. 5.95 (ISBN 0-300-02669-2). Yale U Pr.

Krisberg, Barry & Austin, James, eds. The Children of Ishmael: Critical Perspectives on Juvenile Delinquency. LC 77-89919. 1978. pap. text ed. 11.95 (ISBN 0-87484-387-1). Mayfield Pub.

Krisberg, Jane, jt. auth. see Geismar, Ludwig.

Krisch, Henry. The German Democratic Republic: A Profile. (Nations of Contemporary Eastern Europe Ser.). 128p. 1981. lib. bdg. 16.50x (ISBN 0-89158-850-7). Westview.

--German Politics Under Soviet Occupation. LC 74-3288. 1974. 20.00x (ISBN 0-231-03835-6). Columbia U Pr.

Krishef, Curtis H., jt. auth. see Ehlers, Walter H.

Krishef, Robert K. Dolly Parton. LC 79-28247. (Country Music Bks.). (Illus.). (YA) (gr. 4 up). 1980. PLB 5.95g (ISBN 0-8225-1411-7). Lerner Pubns.

Krishna, G. & Rajhan, S. K. Advanced Laboratory Manual: Nutrition Research. 176p. 1980. text ed. 15.00 (ISBN 0-7069-1125-3, Pub. by Vikas India). Advent Bk.

Krishna, G. & Ranjhan, S. K. Advanced Laboratory Manual for Nutrition Research. 150p. 1980. text ed. 13.95 (ISBN 0-7069-1125-3, Pub by Vikas India). Advent Bk.

Krishna, Gopal, ed. Contributions to South Asian Studies I. (Illus.). 206p. 1979. text ed. 13.95x (ISBN 0-19-520252-X). Oxford U Pr.

Krishna, Gopi. Riddles of Consciousness. 160p. 1977. pap. 3.95 o.s.i. (ISBN 0-8334-1779-7). Multimedia.

Krishna, Kumar & Weesner, Frances M., eds. Biology of Termites, 2 Vols. 1969-70. Vol. 1. 69.00 (ISBN 0-12-426301-1); Vol. 2. 72.75 (ISBN 0-12-426302-X); Set. 115.00 (ISBN 0-685-05123-4). Acad Pr.

Krishna, P. Journey from the East. pap. 0.50 o.p. (ISBN 0-87784-140-3). Inter-Varsity.

Krishnaiah, P., ed. Multivariate Analysis. 1966. 55.25 (ISBN 0-12-426650-9). Acad Pr.

Krishnaiah, P. R., ed. Developments in Statistics, Vol. 3. 1980. 35.00 (ISBN 0-12-426603-7). Acad Pr.

Krishnamachar, P., jt. auth. see Manohar, M.

Krishna Menon, K. Outlines of Jurisprudence. 4.25x o.p. (ISBN 0-210-33910-1). Asia.

Krishnamoorthy, H. N. Gibberellins & Plant Growth. LC 74-10469. 1976. 25.95 (ISBN 0-470-50797-7). Halsted Pr.

Krishnamoorthy, P. N. & Ahmed, J. U. Radiation Protection Procedures. (Safety Ser.: No. 38). (Illus.). 198p. (Orig.). 1973. pap. 15.75 (ISBN 92-0-123373-6, IAEA). Unipub.

Krishnamurthi, M. G., jt. auth. see McCormack, William.

Krishnamurthi, M. G., jt. ed. see Ramanujan, A. K.

Krishnamurthy, R. The Saints of the Cauvery Delta. 1979. text ed. 10.00x (ISBN 0-391-01844-2). Humanities.

Krishnamurti, Bhadriraju. Telugu Verbal Bases. 1972. 12.50 (ISBN 0-89684-328-9). Orient Bk Dist.

Krishnamurti, J. Talks & Dialogues of J. Krishnamurti. (Orig.). 1976. pap. 2.25 (ISBN 0-380-01573-0, 38133). Avon.

--Truth & Actuality: Conversations on Science & Consciousness. LC 77-20450. 176p. 1980. pap. 5.95 (ISBN 0-06-064875-9, RD 334, HarpR). Har-Row.

--You Are the World. LC 73-172504. 1972. pap. 1.95 (ISBN 0-06-064871-6, RD 303, HarpR). Har-Row.

Krishnamurti, Jiddu. Beyond Violence. LC 72-9875. 176p. 1973. pap. 3.95 (ISBN 0-06-064839-2, RD 61, HarpR). Har-Row.

--The First & Last Freedom. LC 74-25687. 228p. 1975. pap. 4.95 (ISBN 0-06-064831-7, RD 91, HarpR). Har-Row.

--Freedom from the Known. LC 69-17013. 128p. 1975. pap. 3.95 (ISBN 0-06-064808-2, RD 90, HarpR). Har-Row.

--Only Revolution. Lutyens, Mary, ed. LC 77-109066. 1970. 5.95 o.p. (ISBN 0-06-064869-4, HarpR). Har-Row.

--The Only Revolution. Lutyens, Mary, ed. 1977. pap. 1.95 o.p. (ISBN 0-06-080410-6, P410, PL). Har-Row.

Krishnan, P., ed. Mathematical Models of Sociology. (Sociological Review Monograph: No. 24). 229p. 1979. pap. 22.50x (ISBN 0-8476-2297-5). Rowman.

Krishnan, R. S., et al. Thermal Expansion of Crystals. LC 77-30620. (International Ser. in the Science of the Solid State: Vol. 12). 1980. 41.00 (ISBN 0-08-021405-3). Pergamon.

Krishnan, S. S. An Introduction to Modern Criminal Investigation: With Basic Laboratory Techniques. (Illus.). 440p. 1978. 29.75 (ISBN 0-398-03722-1); pap. 22.00 (ISBN 0-398-03723-X). C C Thomas.

Krishnan-Kutty, G. Money & Banking. 1979. text ed. 9.25x (ISBN 0-391-01815-9). Humanities.

Krishnaswami, S. Musical Instruments of India. (Illus.). 1967. 2.50x (ISBN 0-88253-378-9); pap. 1.00x (ISBN 0-88253-915-9). Ind-US Inc.

Krishnaswamy, S., jt. auth. see Barnouw, Erik.

Krishtalka, Leonard. Late Paleocene Mammals from the Cypress Hills, Alberta. (Special Publications: No. 2). (Illus., Orig.). 1973. pap. 4.00 (ISBN 0-89672-027-6). Tex Tech Pr.

Krislov, Samuel. Representative Bureaucracy. LC 73-21814. (Foundations of Public Administration Ser.). (Illus.). 160p. 1974. pap. text ed. 7.95 (ISBN 0-13-773747-5). P-H.

Kriss, Eric, jt. ed. see Guitar Player Magazine.

Kristek, Vladimir. Theory of Box Girders. LC 78-8637. 1980. 40.50 (ISBN 0-471-99678-5, Pub. by Wiley-Interscience). Wiley.

Kristeller, Paul O. Renaissance Thought & Its Sources. Mooney, Michael, ed. 352p. 1981. Repr. 9.50 (ISBN 0-231-04513-1). Columbia U Pr.

--Renaissance Thought & Its Sources. Mooney, Michael, ed. LC 79-15521. 1979. 27.50x (ISBN 0-231-04512-3). Columbia U Pr.

Kristeva, Julia. Desire in Language: A Semoitic Approach to Literature & Art. Roudiez, Leon S., ed. Jardine, Alice & Gora, Thomas, trs. from Fr. LC 80-10689. (European Perspectives Ser.). (Illus.). 336p. 1980. 16.95 (ISBN 0-231-04806-8). Columbia U Pr.

Kristiansen, M., jt. auth. see Hagler, M. O.

Kristol, Irving, jt. ed. see Bell, Daniel.

Kristol, Irving, ed. see Commission on Critical Choices.

Kristos, Kyle. Voodoo. LC 76-18989. (gr. 4-8). 1976. 7.95 (ISBN 0-397-31706-9); pap. 2.95 (ISBN 0-397-31707-7). Lippincott.

Kristy, Norton F. Staying in Love: Reinventing Marriage & Other Realationships. (Orig.). pap. 2.75 (ISBN 0-515-05089-X). Jove Pubns.

Kritchevsky, D., jt. auth. see Pollak, O. J.

Kritchevsky, D., jt. ed. see Paoletti, R.

Kritchevsky, David & Paoletti, Rodolfo, eds. Advances in Lipid Research, Vol. 17. LC 63-22330. (Serial Publication). 1980. 31.00 (ISBN 0-12-024917-0); lib ed. 40.50 (ISBN 0-12-024980-4); microfiche 20.50 (ISBN 0-12-024981-2). Acad Pr.

Kritchevsky, David, jt. ed. see Alfin-Slater, Roslyn.

Kritsch, Erna. Modernes Deutsch: Eine Wiederholung der Grammatik Mit Modernes Autoren. 2nd ed. (Illus., Ger.). (gr. 10-12). 1966. pap. text ed. 8.95 o.p. (ISBN 0-13-595033-3); tapes 75.00 o.p. (ISBN 0-13-595017-1). P-H.

Kritzeck, James, ed. Anthology of Islamic Literature: From the Rise of Islam to Modern Times. 1975. pap. 5.95 (ISBN 0-452-00498-5, F498, Mer). NAL.

Kritzer, Hildreth, jt. auth. see Fenson, Harry.

Kritzman, Lawrence D. Destruction-Decouverte: Le Fontionnement de la Rhetorique dans les Essais de Montaigne. LC 80-66329. (French Forum Monographs: No. 21). 187p. (Orig.). 1980. pap. 11.50 (ISBN 0-917058-20-8). French Forum.

Krivchenkov, V. D., jt. auth. see Goldman, I.

Krivonos, Paul, jt. auth. see Sussman, Lyle.

Kriyananda, Swami. The Story of Search for Meaning: An Autobiography. abr. ed. 240p. 1980. pap. 3.95 (ISBN 0-916124-19-3). Ananda.

Kriz, Caroline. Convection Cookery. LC 80-19915. (Illus.). 152p. (Orig.). 1980. pap. 5.95 (ISBN 0-89286-181-9). One Hund One Prods.

Kriz, Wilhelm, jt. auth. see Jamison, Rex L.

Krizek, Thomas J., jt. ed. see Touloukian, Robert J.

Krleza, Miroslav. The Cricket Beneath the Waterfall & Other Stories. Lenski, Branko, ed. LC 72-83354. 256p. 1972. 8.95 (ISBN 0-8149-0699-0). Vanguard.

--On the Edge of Reason. LC 74-81810. 1977. 8.95 (ISBN 0-8149-0747-4). Vanguard.

--Return of Philip Latinovicz. LC 67-29443. 1968. 8.95 (ISBN 0-8149-0136-0). Vanguard.

Kroch, Anthony S. The Semantics of Scope in English. Hankamer, Jorge, ed. LC 78-66559. (Outstanding Dissertations in Linguistics Ser.). 1979. lib. bdg. 30.00 (ISBN 0-8240-9681-9). Garland Pub.

Krochmal, Arnold & Krochmal, Connie. The Complete Illustrated Book of Dyes from Natural Sources. LC 73-9167. 288p. 1974. pap. 4.95 o.p. (ISBN 0-385-05656-7). Doubleday.

Krochmal, Connie, jt. auth. see Krochmal, Arnold.

Krockover, Gerald & Devito, Alfred. Activities Handbook for Energy Education. (Illus.). 192p. (Orig.). 1981. pap. 10.95 (ISBN 0-8302-2717-2). Goodyear.

Krockover, Gerald H. & Krockover, Sharon D. Uncle Bill's Ice Cream Shop. 1978. 4.50 o.p. (ISBN 0-533-03191-5). Vantage.

Krockover, Sharon D., jt. auth. see Krockover, Gerald H.

Krodel, ed. & tr. from Ger. Luther's Works, Vol. 49: Letters II. LC 55-9893. 480p. 1972. 9.50 (ISBN 0-8006-0349-4, 1-349). Fortress.

Krodel, Gerhard. Acts. LC 80-2395. (Proclamation Commentaries: the New Testament Witnesses for Preaching). 128p. (Orig.). 1981. pap. 3.95 (ISBN 0-8006-0585-3, 1-585). Fortress.

Krodel, Gerhard, jt. auth. see Watermulder, David B.

Krodel, Gerhard, ed. see Danker, Frederick W.

Krodel, Gerhard, ed. see Kingsbury, Jack D.

Krodel, Gottfried G. & Lehman, Helmut T., eds. Luther's Works: Letters I, Vol. 48. LC 55-9893. 1963. 15.95 (ISBN 0-8006-0348-6, 1-348). Fortress.

Krodel, Gottfried G. & Lehmann, Helmut T., eds. Luther's Works: Letters III, Vol. 50. LC 74-76934. 416p. 1975. 16.95 (ISBN 0-8006-0350-8, 1-350). Fortress.

Kroeber, A. L. & Gifford, E. W. Karok Myths. Buzaljko, Grace, ed. 450p. 1980. 25.00 (ISBN 0-520-03870-3). U of Cal Pr.

Kroeber, A. L., et al. The Diegueno Indians. 1975. pap. 2.00 (ISBN 0-916552-02-0). Acoma Bks.

Kroeber, Alfred L. Configurations of Culture Growth. 1944. 22.75x (ISBN 0-520-00669-0). U of Cal Pr.

--Mohave Indians. Horr, David A., ed. (American Indian Ethnohistory Ser.). 1978. lib. bdg. 42.00 (ISBN 0-8240-0738-7). Garland Pub.

--More Mojave Myths. (U. C. Publ. in Anthropological Records: Vol. 27). 1972. pap. 11.00x (ISBN 0-520-09373-9). U of Cal Pr.

--Nature of Culture. (Illus.). 1952. 20.00x (ISBN 0-226-45422-3). U of Chicago Pr.

Kroeber, Karl. Romantic Landscape Vision: Constable & Wordsworth. LC 74-5905. 176p. 1975. 17.50x (ISBN 0-299-06710-6). U of Wis Pr.

--Romantic Narrative Art. (Illus.). 1960. pap. 7.50x (ISBN 0-299-02244-7). U of Wis Pr.

Kroeber, Karl, ed. Traditional Literatures of the American Indian: Texts & Interpretations. LC 80-18338. x, 162p. 1981. 16.50x (ISBN 0-8032-2704-3, Bison); pap. 5.95 (ISBN 0-8032-7753-9, BB 765). U of Nebr Pr.

Kroeber, Theodora. Alfred Kroeber: A Personal Configuration. LC 71-94983. (Illus.). 1970. 14.50 (ISBN 0-520-01598-3); pap. 4.95 (ISBN 0-520-03720-0). U of Cal Pr.

Kroeger, Arthur, jt. auth. see Dirksen, Charles J.

Kroell, Maurice. L Immunite Franque. LC 80-2021. 1981. Repr. of 1910 ed. 39.50 (ISBN 0-404-18573-8). AMS Pr.

Kroemer, Herbert, jt. auth. see Kittel, Charles.

Kroenke, David M. Business Computer Systems: An Introduction. (Illus.). 576p. 1980. 15.95x (ISBN 0-938188-00-3). Mitchell Pub.

--Database Processing: Fundamentals, Modeling, Applications. LC 76-41803. 416p. 1977. text ed. 20.95 (ISBN 0-574-21100-4, 13-4100); instr's guide avail. (ISBN 0-574-21101-2, 13-4101). SRA.

Kroepelin, H., et al. Thermodynamic Diagrams for High Temperature Plasmas of Air-Carbon, Carbon-Hydrogen Mixtures & Argon. 1971. 51.00 (ISBN 0-08-017581-3). Pergamon.

Kroes, William H. Society's Victim -- the Policeman: An Analysis of Job Stress in Policing. (Illus.). 144p. 1980. 13.75 (ISBN 0-398-03479-6). C C Thomas.

Kroes, William H., jt. auth. see Margolis, Bruce L.

Krog, Hildur, jt. auth. see Dahl, Eilif.

Krogdahl, Wasley S. Tensor Analysis: Fundamentals & Applications. LC 78-62755. 1978. pap. text ed. 18.50 (ISBN 0-8191-0594-5). U Pr of Amer.

Krogh, August. Anatomy & Physiology of Capillaries. 1929. 65.00x (ISBN 0-685-89734-6). Elliots Bks.

Krogman, David W. The Biochemistry of Green Plants. LC 73-7637. (Foundatons of Modern Biochemistry Ser). (Illus.). 224p. 1973. pap. 12.95 ref. ed. (ISBN 0-13-076455-8). P-H.

Krogman, W. M. Child Growth. (Ann Arbor Science Library). 1972. pap. 5.50 (ISBN 0-472-05019-2, AA). U of Mich Pr.

Krogman, W. M., jt. auth. see Moyers, R. E.

Krogman, William, et al. Medicine Among the American Indians: CIBA Symposia, 1939, Vol. 1, No. 1. 1981. pap. 4.95 (ISBN 0-686-69101-6). Acoma Bks.

Krogman, Wilton M. Human Skeleton in Forensic Medicine. (Illus.). 364p. 1978. 19.75 (ISBN 0-398-01054-4). C C Thomas.

Krohn, Ernst C. The History of Music. LC 65-23398. (Music Reprint Ser.). 1973. Repr. of 1958 ed. lib. bdg. 27.50 (ISBN 0-306-70595-8). Da Capo.

--Missouri Music. LC 65-23398. (Music Ser.). xlvi, 380p. 1971. Repr. of 1924 ed. lib. bdg. 37.50 (ISBN 0-306-70932-5). Da Capo.

Krohn, Lawrence H. High-Resolution Electrocardiography: A Superior Diagnostic Modality. (Illus.). 304p. 1976. 37.50 (ISBN 0-398-03515-6). C C Thomas.

Krohne, Heinz W. & Laux, Lothar, eds. Achievement, Stress & Anxiety. LC 79-28840. (Clinical & Community Psychology Ser.). (Illus.). 448p. Date not set. text ed. 24.95 (ISBN 0-89116-187-2). Hemisphere Pub. Postponed.

Krois, John M., tr. see Apel, Karl-Otto.

Kroitor, Harry. The Five Hundred Word Theme Workbook. (Illus.). 224p. 1981. pap. 6.95 (ISBN 0-13-321612-8). P-H.

Kroitor, Harry P., jt. auth. see Martin, Lee J.

Krolick, Robert S. Administrator's Manual for Plastics Education. LC 78-8937. 1978. pap. 5.95 (ISBN 0-672-97186-0). Bobbs.

Kroll. Fat Magic. (ps-3). 1980. pap. 1.50 (ISBN 0-590-38332-9, Schol Pap). Schol Bk Serv.

Kroll, Arthur M., et al. Career Development: Growth & Crisis. LC 79-96048. 1970. 20.00 (ISBN 0-471-50850-0, Pub. by Wiley-Interscience). Wiley.

Kroll, Carol. The Whole Craft of Spinning from the Raw Material to the Finished Yarn. 1980. pap. 1.75 (ISBN 0-486-23968-3). Dover.

Kroll, Edite, tr. see Richter, Hans P.

Kroll, Larry J. & Silverman, Manuel S. Opiate Addiction: Theory & Process. LC 80-8283. 199p. 1980. lib. bdg. 17.50 (ISBN 0-8191-1324-7); pap. text ed. 9.00 (ISBN 0-8191-1325-5). U Pr of Amer.

Kroll, Morton, ed. Libraries & Librarians of the Pacific Northwest. LC 60-9873. (PNLA Library Development Project Reports, Ser.: Vol. 4). 281p. 1960. 10.50 (ISBN 0-295-73827-8). U of Wash Pr.

--Public Libraries of the Pacific Northwest. LC 60-9873. (PNLA Library Development Project Reports, Ser.: Vol. 1). 461p. 1960. 9.50 (ISBN 0-295-73897-9). U of Wash Pr.

Kroll, Steven. The Candy Witch. LC 79-10141. (Illus.). 32p. (gr. k-3). 1979. PLB 8.95 (ISBN 0-8234-0359-9). Holiday.
--Dirty Feet. LC 80-17570. (Illus.). 48p. (ps-3). 1981. 4.95 (ISBN 0-8193-1035-2); PLB 5.95 (ISBN 0-8193-1036-0). Parents.
--Giant Journey. LC 80-20512. (Illus.). 32p. (ps-3). 1981. PLB 7.95 (ISBN 0-8234-0381-5). Holiday.
--Santa's Crash-Bang Christmas. LC 77-3025. (Illus.). (gr. k-3). 1977. reinforced bdg. 8.95 (ISBN 0-8234-0302-5). Holiday.
--Space Cats. (Illus.). (gr. 1-4). 1981. pap. 1.95 (ISBN 0-380-53371-5, 53371, Camelot). Avon.
--T. J. Folger, Thief. (gr. k-6). Date not set. pap. price not set (ISBN 0-440-48668-8, YB). Dell.
Kroll, Wilhelm. Studien zum Verstaendnis der Romischen Literatur. Commager, Steele, ed. LC 77-70839. (Latin Poetry Ser.: Vol. 23). 1978. lib. bdg. 41.00 (ISBN 0-8240-2972-0). Garland Pub.
Kroll, William A., jt. auth. see Stone, William J.
Krolow, Karl. Poems Against Death. Salinger, Herman, tr. LC 71-82716. 1980. 7.50 (ISBN 0-685-39468-9). Charioteer.
Kroman, Vera. How to Raise & Train a Samoyed. (Orig.). pap. 2.00 (ISBN 0-87666-378-1, DS1113). TFH Pubns.
Kromer, Helen. Amistad Revolt, Eighteen Thirty-Nine: The Slave Uprising Aboard the Spanish Schooner. LC 72-5731. (Focus Bks.). (Illus.). 96p. 1973. PLB 4.90 o.p. (ISBN 0-531-02456-3). Watts.
Krommer-Benz, Magdalena. World Guide to Terminological Activities. (Infoterm Ser.: Vol. 4). 311p. 1977. pap. text ed. 45.00 (ISBN 3-7940-5504-7, Pub. by K G Saur). Gale.
Krompart, Janet, ed. Biographical Dictionary of Republican China: A Personal Name Index, Vol. 5. 1979. 27.50 (ISBN 0-231-04558-1). Columbia U Pr.
Kromschlies, C., jt. auth. see Mrachek, L.
Kron, Thora. The Management of Patient Care: Putting Leadership Skill to Work. 4th ed. LC 75-38153. (Illus.). 1976. pap. text ed. 9.95 (ISBN 0-7216-5528-9). Saunders.
--The Management of Patient Care: Putting Leadership Skills to Work. (Illus.). 247p. 1981. pap. text ed. 9.95 (ISBN 0-7216-5529-7). Saunders.
Kronberger, Helge F., tr. see ARE Study Group No. 1.
Kronberger, Helge F., tr. see Sechrist, Elsie.
Kroncke, Charles, et al. Managerial Finance: Essentials. 2nd ed. (Illus.). 1978. text ed. 19.50 (ISBN 0-8299-0159-0); study guide 6.95 (ISBN 0-8299-0161-2); instrs.' manual avail. (ISBN 0-8299-0550-2). West Pub.
Krone, Chester. Blood Wrath. LC 80-82852. 272p. (Orig.). 1981. pap. 2.50 (ISBN 0-87216-778-X). Playboy Pbks.
Kronecker, Leopold. Werke, 5 vols. LC 66-20394. 1969. Repr. Set. 99.50 (ISBN 0-8284-0224-8). Chelsea Pub.
Kronenberg, M. Machining Science & Applications. 1966. text ed. 60.00 (ISBN 0-08-011627-2). Pergamon.
Kronenberger, Louis. The Last Word: Portraits of Fourteen Master Aphorists. LC 75-186440. 252p. 1972. 7.95 o.s.i. (ISBN 0-02-567100-6). Macmillan.
Kronenberger, Louis, ed. see Ferguson, Francis.
Kronenberger, Louis, ed. see Fowlie, Wallace.
Kronenberger, Louis, ed. & intro. by see Sheridan, Richard B.
Kronenfeld, Jennie J., jt. ed. see Charles, Edgar D.
Kroner, R., tr. see Hegel, G. W.
Kronick, David A. History of Scientific & Technical Periodicals: The Origins & Development of the Scientific & Technical Press, 1665-1790. 2nd ed. LC 75-41487. 1976. 15.00 o.p. (ISBN 0-8108-0844-7). Scarecrow.
Kronman, Anthony T. & Posner, Richard A. The Economics of Contract Law. 1979. pap. text ed. 6.95 (ISBN 0-316-50471-8). Little.
Kronmiller, Theodore G., ed. The Lawfullness of Deep Seabed Mining, Vols. 1 & 2. LC 79-23232. 1980. Set. lib. bdg. 80.00 (ISBN 0-686-61308-2). Vol. 1, 521p (ISBN 0-379-20461-4). Vol. 2, 460p (ISBN 0-379-20462-2). Oceana.
Kronovet, Esther & Shirk, Evelyn, eds. In Pursuit of Awareness: The College Student in the Modern World. LC 67-14573. (Orig.). 1967. pap. text ed. 10.95x (ISBN 0-89197-229-3). Irvington.
Kronzek, Allan Z. The Secrets of Alkazar: A Book of Magic. LC 80-11436. (Illus.). 128p. (gr. 7 up). 1980. 9.95 (ISBN 0-590-07425-3, Four Winds). Schol Bk Serv.
Krook, Dorothea. Ordeal of Consciousness in Henry James. (Orig.). 1968. pap. 13.95x (ISBN 0-521-09449-6). Cambridge U Pr.
Krooss, Herman E. & Gilbert, Charles. American Business History. 352p. 1972. pap. 11.95x ref ed. (ISBN 0-13-024083-4). P-H.
Krooss, Herman E., ed. Documentary History of Banking & Currency in the U. S, 4 vols. LC 69-16011. 3300p. 1981. Set. pap. 67.50 (ISBN 0-87754-209-0). Chelsea Hse.
Kropf, William, jt. auth. see Houben, Milton.
Kropholler, Jan, jt. auth. see Zweigert, Konrad.
Kropotkin, Peter. The Conquest of Bread. LC 75-188871. 235p. 1972. 12.00x (ISBN 0-8147-4554-7). NYU Pr.
--Fields, Factories & Workshops Tomorrow. Ward, Colin, ed. 1975. pap. 3.45x o.p. (ISBN 0-06-131858-2, TB1858, Torch). Har-Row.
--Modern Science & Anarchism. 1980. lib. bdg. 49.95 (ISBN 0-8490-3125-7). Gordon Pr.
--Mutual Aid: A Factor of Evolution. LC 79-188872. 277p. 1972. 12.00x (ISBN 0-8147-4555-5). NYU Pr.
Krosby, H. Peter. Finland, Germany & the Soviet Union, 1940-1941: The Petsamo Dispute. (Illus.). 1968. 22.50x (ISBN 0-299-05140-4). U of Wis Pr.
Krotee, Richard, jt. auth. see Krotee, Walter.
Krotee, Walter & Krotee, Richard. Shipwrecks off the New Jersey Coast. (Illus.). cancelled o.s.i. (ISBN 0-913352-07-1). Mariners Boston.
Kroth, Earl, et al. Soils Manual. (Lucas Text Ser). 1980. text ed. 3.95x unbound (ISBN 0-87543-073-2). Lucas.
Kroth, Jerome A. Child Sexual Abuse: Analysis of a Family Therapy Approach. (Illus.). 216p. 1979. text ed. 19.25 (ISBN 0-398-03906-2). C C Thomas.
--Counseling Psychology & Guidance: An Overview in Outline. 272p. 1973. 12.75 (ISBN 0-398-02726-9). C C Thomas.
--Programmed Primer in Learning Disabilities. (Illus.). 296p. 1974. 14.75 (ISBN 0-398-01055-2). C C Thomas.
Krout, J. A. American Themes. LC 63-17362. 1963. 20.00x (ISBN 0-231-02633-1). Columbia U Pr.
Krout, John A. United States to Eighteen Seventy-Seven. 7th rev. ed. (Orig.). 1971. pap. 3.95 (ISBN 0-06-460029-7, CO 29, COS). Har-Row.
Krout, John A see Gabriel, Ralph H.
Krow, Harvey A. Stock Market Behavior: The Technical Approach to Understanding Wall Street. LC 69-18405. Orig. Title: Technical Analysis in the Stock Market. 1969. 15.00 o.p. (ISBN 0-394-44809-X). Random.
Krown, Sylvia. Threes & Fours Go to School. (Early Childhood Ser.). (Illus.). 288p. 1974. ref. ed. 15.95 (ISBN 0-13-920322-2). P-H.
Kroy, Moshe. The Conscience: A Structural Theory. LC 74-10912. 1974. 32.50 (ISBN 0-470-50856-6). Halsted Pr.
Krueckeberg, Donald A. & Silvers, Arthur L. Urban Planning Analysis: Methods & Models. LC 74-7087. 1974. text ed. 24.95 (ISBN 0-471-50858-6). Wiley.
Kruegar, Janelle C. & Nelson, Allen H. Nursing Research: Development, Collaboration & Utilization. LC 78-26215. (Illus.). 1978. text ed. 25.00 (ISBN 0-89443-082-3). Aspen Systems.
Krueger, Anne O., et al. Trade & Employment in Developing Countries, Vol. 1: Individual Studies. LC 80-15826. (National Bureau of Economic Research Ser.). (Illus.). 1981. lib. bdg. 39.00x (ISBN 0-226-45492-4). U of Chicago Pr.
Krueger, Caryl W. Six Weeks to Better Parenting: The Complete Guide for Creative Raising of Children 2-12. 348p. 1981. pap. 8.95 (ISBN 0-938632-05-1). Belleridge.
Krueger, Catherine M. How Oft Shall Phoenix Rise. Date not set. 5.95 (ISBN 0-533-04837-0). Vantage.
Krueger, Elizabeth A. Hypodermic Injection: A Programed Unit. LC 66-17379. (Orig.). 1965. pap. 7.50x (ISBN 0-8077-1650-2). Tchrs Coll.
Krueger, John, tr. see Gronbech, Vilhelm.
Krueger, John R., tr. see Gronbech, Kaare.
Krueger, John R., tr. see Gronbech, Vilhelm.
Krueger, Lorenz. Begriff des Empirismus: Erkenntnistheoretische Studien am Beispiel John Lockes. (Quellen und Studien zur Philosophie, Vol. 6). xii, 283p. 1973. 41.75x (ISBN 3-11-004133-2). De Gruyter.
Krug, Edward A., ed. Charles W. Eliot & Popular Education. LC 61-17886. (Orig.). 1961. text ed. 8.75 (ISBN 0-8077-1656-1); pap. text ed. 4.00x (ISBN 0-8077-1653-7). Tchrs Coll.
Krug, Joseph P. Credit & Free Enterprise: A Chance to Survive. 1977. pap. 5.50 (ISBN 0-934914-04-4). NACM.
Krug, Samuel E. A Sixteen PF Codebook. 1981. pap. price not set (ISBN 0-918296-16-1). Inst Personality & Ability.
Kruger, Arthur N. Argumentation & Debate: A Classified Bibliography. 2nd ed. LC 74-17198. 1975. 21.00 (ISBN 0-8108-0749-1). Scarecrow.
Kruger, Dreyer. An Introduction to Phenomenological Psychology. LC 80-29203. 212p. 1981. pap. text ed. 8.95 (ISBN 0-8207-0150-5). Duquesne.
Kruger, Gustav O. Textbook of Oral & Maxillofacial Surgery. 5th ed. (Illus.). 1979. 29.95 o.p. (ISBN 0-8016-2792-3). Mosby.
Kruger, Hayes & Kruger, Jane M. Movement & Education in Physical Education: A Guide to Teaching & Planning. 2nd ed. 1981. pap. text ed. 12.95x (ISBN 0-697-07181-2). Wm C Brown.
Kruger, Jane M., jt. auth. see Kruger, Hayes.
Kruger, Maximilian. The Maximal Problems of Philosophy. (Illus.). 137p. 1981. 39.45 (ISBN 0-89266-274-3). Am Classical Coll Pr.
Kruger, Mollee. Yankee Shoes: A Light Verse Saunter Through Our Second Hundred Years. LC 75-21446. 100p. 1975. pap. 2.50 (ISBN 0-913184-03-9). Maryben Bks.
Kruglak, Gregory T. The Politics of United States Decision-Making in United Nations Specialized Agencies: The Case of the International Labor Organization. LC 80-5318. 300p. 1980. lib. bdg. 18.50 (ISBN 0-8191-1075-2); pap. text ed. 10.75 (ISBN 0-8191-1076-0). U Pr of Amer.
Krugman, Richard D. Review of Pediatrics. 400p. Date not set. text ed. 10.95 (ISBN 0-7216-5549-1). Saunders. Postponed.
Krugman, Richard D. & Welch, Thomas R. Pediatrics Continuing Education Review. 1976. spiral bdg. 12.00 o.p. (ISBN 0-87488-342-3). Med Exam.
Krugman, Saul. Infectious Diseases of Children. 7th ed. LC 80-24696. (Illus.). 607p. 1980. text ed. 39.95 (ISBN 0-8016-2796-6). Mosby.
Krugman, Saul, ed. see Symposium by the New York University Medical Center & the National Foundation-March of Dimes, New York City, Mar. 1975.
Kruijsen, Joep, ed. Liber Amicorum Weijnen: A Collection on Essays Presented to Professor Dr. A. Weijnen on the Occasion of His Seventieth Birthday. 396p. 1980. pap. text ed. 42.75 (ISBN 90-232-1749-7). Humanities.
Kruk, Z. L. & Pycock, C. J. Neurotransmitters & Drug. 160p. 1980. 35.00x (ISBN 0-85664-865-5, Pub. by Croom Helm England). State Mutual Bk.
Kruk, Z. L., jt. auth. see Williams, R. A. D.
Krull, Kathleen, jt. auth. see Allington, Richard L.
Krumbein, William C. & Graybill, F. A. Introduction to Statistical Models in Geology. (International Ser.in the Earth & Planetary Sciences). 1965. text ed. 21.95 o.p. (ISBN 0-07-035555-X, C). McGraw.
Krumbein, William C. & Sloss, L. L. Stratigraphy & Sedimentation. 2nd ed. LC 61-11422. 1963. 27.95x (ISBN 0-7167-0219-3). W H Freeman.
Krumbein, William C., jt. auth. see Croneis, Carey G.
Krumbhaar, E. B. Pathology. (Illus.). 1962. Repr. of 1937 ed. pap. 8.75 o.s.i. (ISBN 0-02-848090-2). Hafner.
Krumboltz, Helen, jt. auth. see Krumboltz, John D.
Krumboltz, John D. & Krumboltz, Helen. Changing Children's Behavior. (Counseling & Guidance Ser). 1972. 14.95 (ISBN 0-13-127951-3); pap. text ed. 10.50 (ISBN 0-13-127944-0). P-H.
Krumgold, Joseph. And Now Miguel. LC 53-8415. (Illus.). (gr. 6 up). 1953. 9.95 (ISBN 0-690-09118-4, TYC-J). T Y Crowell.
--Onion John. LC 59-11395. (Illus.). (gr. 5 up). 1959. 9.95 (ISBN 0-690-59957-9, TYC-J). T Y Crowell.
Krumm, John M., jt. auth. see Kelleran, Marion.
Krumm, John W. Why Choose the Episcopal Church? 1974. 1.35 (ISBN 0-686-28800-9). Forward Movement.
Krummel, D. W., et al, eds. Resources of American Music History: A Directory of Source Materials from Colonial Times to World War II. LC 80-14873. (Music in American Life Ser.). 500p. 1981. lib. bdg. 44.95 (ISBN 0-252-00828-6). U of Ill Pr.
Krummel, Donald W. Bibliotheca Bolduaniana: A Renaissance Music Bibliography. LC 71-175176. (Detroit Studies in Music Bibliography Ser.: No. 22). 1972. 8.00 (ISBN 0-685-24023-1); pap. 6.50 (ISBN 0-685-24023-1). Info Coord.
Krummel, Donald W., ed. Organizing the Library's Support: Donors, Volunteers, Friends. (Allerton Park Institute Proceedings Ser.: No. 25). 1980. 10.00 (ISBN 0-87845-054-8). U of Ill Lib Sci.
Krump, John. Hope for the Future? Youth & the Church. (Orig.). 1979. pap. 4.95 (ISBN 0-88347-092-6). Thomas More.
--What a Modern Catholic Believes About Eucharist. 96p. (Orig.). 1974. pap. 4.95 (ISBN 0-88347-040-3). Thomas More.
Krupar, Karen D. Communication Games. LC 73-76074. (Orig.). 1973. pap. text ed. 6.95 (ISBN 0-02-917710-3). Free Pr.
Krupin, Theodore, jt. auth. see Waltman, Stephen R.
Krupinski, Jerzy & Stoiler, Alan. The Family in Australia: Social, Demographic & Psychological Aspects. 273p. 1974. text ed. 18.70 o.p. (ISBN 0-08-017374-8). Pergamon.
--The Family in Australia: Social, Demographic & Psychological Aspects. 2nd ed. 1978. text ed. 31.00 (ISBN 0-08-022260-9); pap. text ed. 13.25 (ISBN 0-08-022259-5). Pergamon.
Krupp, Marcus A. & Chatton, Milton J., eds. Current Medical Diagnosis & Treatment. rev. ed. LC 74-641062. (Illus.). 1100p. 1981. lexotone cover 21.00 (ISBN 0-87041-251-5). Lange.
--Current Medical Diagnosis & Treatment. rev. ed. LC 74-641062. 1116p. 1980. lexotone cover 19.00 (ISBN 0-87041-250-7). Lange.
Krupskaya, N. K. Reminiscences of Lenin. LC 67-27253. (Illus.). 1970. 7.50 (ISBN 0-7178-0253-1); pap. 4.95 (ISBN 0-7178-0254-X). Intl Pub Co.
Krusch, Werner E., jt. auth. see Wohlrabe, Raymond A.
Kruse, et al. Cancer: Pathophysiology Etiology, Management: Selected Readings. LC 78-27228. (Illus.). 1979. pap. text ed. 16.95 (ISBN 0-8016-2794-X). Mosby.
Kruse, Alexander Z. How to Draw & Paint. (Orig.). 1962. pap. 2.95 o.p. (ISBN 0-06-463244-X, 244, EH). Har-Row.
Kruse, Christine G. Patient Centered Audit. (Illus.). 180p. (Orig.). 1981. 14.50 (ISBN 0-87527-247-9). Green.
Kruse Classic Auction Co. The Kruse Professional Price Guide to Collector Cars. LC 78-55416. (Collector Ser.). (Illus.). 1979. pap. 7.95 o.p. (ISBN 0-87637-337-6). Hse of Collectibles.
--Official Price Guide to Collector Cars. 2nd ed. (Collector Ser.). (Illus.). 400p. 1980. pap. 9.95 (ISBN 0-87637-119-5, 119-05). Hse of Collectibles.
Kruse, Douglas C. Monetary Integration in Western Europe. LC 80-40980. (European Studies Ser.). (Illus.). 256p. 1980. text ed. 42.95 (ISBN 0-408-10666-2). Butterworths.
Kruse, Olan E. General Physics Demonstration Manual. 1973. Repr. pap. 4.50x wkbk. (ISBN 0-934786-06-2). G Davis.
Kruse, Olan E., et al. Technical Physics Laboratory Manual. 1971. Repr. workbook 5.50x (ISBN 0-934786-07-0). G Davis.
Krushkal, Samuel L. Quasiconformal Mappings & Riemann Surfaces. LC 79-995. (Scripta Series in Mathematics). 1979. 27.95 (ISBN 0-470-26695-3). Halsted Pr.
Kruss, James. Three by Three. (Illus.). (ps-k). 1965. 4.75 o.s.i. (ISBN 0-02-751210-X). Macmillan.
Kruszewski, Mikolaj, ed. Writings in General Linguistics: Vocal Alternation & "Prinzipien der Sprachentwicklung". Austerlitz, Robert & Techmer, Fredrich, trs. from Ger. (Amsterdam Classics in Linguistics Ser.: No. 11). 190p. 1980. text ed. 31.50x (ISBN 90-272-0972-3). Humanities.
Krutch, Joseph W. Comedy & Conscience After the Restoration. rev. ed. LC 24-28256. 1924. pap. 7.50x (ISBN 0-231-08516-8). Columbia U Pr.
--Henry David Thoreau. LC 73-16724. 1974. pap. 4.75 (ISBN 0-688-06774-3). Morrow.
--Henry David Thoreau. LC 80-2511. 1981. Repr. of 1948 ed. 34.00 (ISBN 0-404-19059-6). AMS Pr.
--A Krutch Omnibus: Forty Years of Social & Literary Criticism. LC 80-14794. 342p. 1980. 6.95 (ISBN 0-688-00389-3, Quill). Morrow.
Krutza, William J. Graduate's Guide to Success. 96p. 1976. 3.95 (ISBN 0-8010-5374-9). Baker Bk.
--So Now You're a Graduate. 88p. 1981. 4.95 (ISBN 0-8010-5433-8). Baker Bk.
Krutza, William J. & DiCicco, Philip P. Living That Counts. (Contemporary Discussion Ser.). 1972. pap. 2.50 (ISBN 0-8010-5318-8). Baker Bk.
--Youth Face Today's Issues One. (Contemporary Discussion Ser.). (Orig.). 1970. pap. 2.45 (ISBN 0-8010-5304-8). Baker Bk.
--Youth Face Today's Issues Two. (Contemporary Discussion Ser.). pap. 2.45 (ISBN 0-8010-5311-0). Baker Bk.
Kruzas, Anthony T., jt. auth. see Sullivan, Linda E.
Kruzas, Anthony T., ed. Encyclopedia of Information Systems & Services. 3rd ed. LC 78-14575. 1030p. 1978. 135.00 o.p. (ISBN 0-8103-0940-8). Gale.
--Medical & Health Information Directory: A Guide to Professional & Nonprofit Organizations, Government Agencies, Educational Institutons, Grant Award Sources, Health Care Insurers, Journals, Newsletters, Review Serials, Etc. 2nd ed. LC 77-82802. 1980. 92.00 (ISBN 0-8103-0267-5). Gale.
Kruzas, Anthony T. & Thomas, Robert C., eds. Business Organizations & Agencies Directory. LC 80-32. 1980. 85.00 (ISBN 0-8103-1135-6). Gale.
Kruzas, Anthony T., jt. ed. see Schmittroth, John, Jr.
Kryer, M. Pathophysiology of Respiration. (Wiley Pathophysiology Ser.). 384p. 1981. 17.50 (ISBN 0-471-05923-4, Pub. by Wiley Med). Wiley.

Krygier, Martin, jt. ed. see Kamenka, Eugene.

Krylov. The Soviet Economy: How It Really Works. LC 78-22286. (Illus.). 1979. 18.95 (ISBN 0-669-02743-X). Lexington Bks.

Krynski, Magnus J., tr. see Szymborska, Wislawa.

Krysl, Marilyn. Honey You've Been Dealt a Winning Hand. 140p. (Orig.). 1980. pap. 6.50 (ISBN 0-88496-154-0). Capra Pr.

Krystal, Henry & Raskin, Herbert A. Drug Dependence: Aspects of Ego Functions. LC 76-121920. 1970. text ed. 8.95x (ISBN 0-8143-1419-8). Wayne St U Pr.

Krystufek, Zdenek. The Soviet Regime in Czechoslovakia. (East European Monographs: No. 81). 320p. 1981. text ed. 21.00x (ISBN 0-914710-75-3). East Eur Quarterly.

Kryszak, Wayne D. The Small Business Index. LC 78-17540. 1978. 12.00 (ISBN 0-8108-1150-2). Scarecrow.

Kryt, Dobromila & Semniuk, Bazyli, eds. English-Polish-Polish-English Chemical Dictionary. LC 79-393179. 912p. 1979. 32.50x (ISBN 83-204-0004-X). Intl Pubns Serv.

Krythe, Maymie R. All About American Holidays. LC 61-6450. (Illus.). 1962. 9.95 o.p. (ISBN 0-06-003090-9, HarpT). Har-Row.

--All About Christmas. LC 54-8965. 1954. lib. bdg. 8.97 o.s.i. (ISBN 0-06-003151-4, HarpT). Har-Row.

--What So Proudly We Hail: All About Our American Flag, Monuments & Symbols. LC 68-15993. (YA) 1968. 9.95 o.s.i. (ISBN 0-06-003157-3, HarpT); lib. bdg. 8.97 (ISBN 0-06-012464-4). Har-Row.

Krzyzanowski, Jerzy. Wladyslaw Stanislaw Reymont. (World Authors Ser.: Poland: No. 248). lib. bdg. 10.95 (ISBN 0-8057-2758-2). Twayne.

Krzyzanowski, Julian. A History of Polish Literature. Ronowicz, Doris, tr. from Polish. (Illus.). 807p. 1979. 39.95x (ISBN 0-686-60390-7, Pub. by Polish Scientific Pubs Poland). Hippocrene Bks.

Krzyzanowski, Ludwik, jt. ed. see Gillon, Adam.

Kuan, L. K., jt. auth. see Raven, A. J.

Kubach, H. Erich. Romanesque Architecture. LC 73-21549. (History of World Architecture Ser.). 1975. 45.00 (ISBN 0-8109-1024-1). Abrams.

Kubala, T. S. Circuit Concepts: Direct & Alternating Current. LC 75-19521. 1976. pap. 8.80 (ISBN 0-8273-1169-9); instructor's guide 1.60 (ISBN 0-8273-1170-2). Delmar.

Kubala, Thomas S. Electricity One: Devices, Circuits, Materials. LC 79-93322. (Electrical Trades Ser.). 98p. 1981. pap. text ed. 4.80 (ISBN 0-8273-1357-8); instr's manual 1.00 (ISBN 0-8273-1358-6). Delmar.

--Electricity Two: Devices, Circuits, Materials. LC 79-93323. (Electrical Trades Ser.). 104p. 1981. pap. text ed. 4.40 (ISBN 0-8273-1151-6); instr's guide 1.45 (ISBN 0-8273-1152-4). Delmar.

Kubalak, Janet. Directory of Online Information Resources: Semi-Annual. 6th ed. Orig. Title: Directory of on-Line Bibliographic Services. 55p. pap. 12.00 (ISBN 0-686-28098-9); four issue subscription 38.00 (ISBN 0-686-28099-7). CSG Pr.

Kuballa. Seeing the Real Moscow. Date not set. pap. 7.95 (ISBN 0-8120-2180-0). Barron. Postponed.

Kubat, Daniel, ed. The Politics of Migration Policies: The First World in the 1970's. LC 77-93185. 1979. pap. 9.95x (ISBN 0-913256-34-X, Dist. by Ozer). Ctr Migration.

Kubat, Daniel, jt. ed. see Richmond, Anthony.

Kubie, Nora B. First Book of Archaeology. (First Bks). (Illus.). (gr. 4-6). 1957. PLB 6.90 (ISBN 0-531-00470-8). Watts.

--First Book of Israel. rev. ed. LC 74-31166. (First Bks). (Illus.). (gr. 4-6). 1968. PLB 6.45 (ISBN 0-531-00563-1). Watts.

--Israel. 2nd rev. ed. (First Bks). (Illus.). (gr. 4-6). 1978. PLB 6.45 s&l (ISBN 0-531-02239-0). Watts.

Kubik, Richard S. Baseball Transition Nineteen Fifty to Nineteen Seventy-Nine. (Illus.). 124p. 1981. 10.00 (ISBN 0-682-49676-6). Exposition.

Kubisz, John B. How to Serve Your Dog. LC 79-56249. (Illus.). 1980. 7.95 o.s.i. (ISBN 0-931866-05-7). Alpine Pubns.

Kubler, Hans. Wood As Building & Hobby Material: How to Use Lumber & Wood-Base Panels & Wood Wisely in Construction, for Furniture, & As Fuel. LC 80-13380. 256p. 1980. 19.95 (ISBN 0-471-05390-2, Pub. by Wiley-Interscience). Wiley.

Kubler, Rolf. Light in the Aquarium. Ahrens, Christa, tr. from Ger. 1973. pap. 2.95 (ISBN 0-87666-096-0, PS-301). TFH Pubns.

Kubler-Ross, Elisabeth. Coping with Death & Dying. (Illus.). 192p. 1980. 9.95 (ISBN 0-686-69030-3). Macmillan.

Kubler-Ross, Elisabeth, ed. Death: The Final Stage of Growth. (Human Development Ser.). (Illus.). 192p. 1975. 13.95 (ISBN 0-13-197012-7, Spec); pap. 2.95 (ISBN 0-13-196998-6, Spec). P-H.

Kublin, Hyman. Africa: Regional Study. rev. ed. 1974. pap. 6.60 (ISBN 0-395-17716-2). HM.

--Africa: Selected Readings. rev. ed. 1974. pap. 6.60 (ISBN 0-395-17743-X). HM.

--China: Regional Study. 2nd ed. Anderson, Howard R., ed. (World Regional Studies). (gr. 7-12). 1976. pap. text ed. 6.60 (ISBN 0-395-21686-9, 2-31023). HM.

--China: Selected Readings. 2nd ed. Anderson, Howard R., ed. (World Regional Studies). (gr. 7-12). 1976. pap. text ed. 6.60 (ISBN 0-395-21686-9, 2-31029). HM.

--India. rev. ed. LC 72-3351. (Illus.). 228p. (gr. 9-12). 1973. pap. text ed. 6.60 (ISBN 0-395-13928-7, 2-31034). HM.

--India: Selected Readings. rev. ed. LC 72-7637. 230p. (gr. 9-12). 1973. pap. text ed. 6.60 (ISBN 0-395-13929-5, 2-31040). HM.

--Japan: Regional Study. (World Regional Studies). (gr. 7-12). 1973. pap. 6.60 (ISBN 0-395-13830-2, 2-31046). HM.

--Japan: Selected Readings. rev. ed. LC 72-84106. (Illus.). 228p. (gr. 6-9). 1973. pap. text ed. 6.60 (ISBN 0-395-13930-9, 2-31046). HM.

--The Middle East: Selected Readings. rev ed. LC 72-12182. (World Regional Studies). (Illus.). 246p. (gr. 9-12). 1973. pap. text ed. 6.60 (ISBN 0-395-13932-5, 2-31076). HM.

--Russia: Regional Study. (World Regional Studies). (Orig.). (gr. 7 up). 1970. pap. 6.60 (ISBN 0-395-17718-9, 2-31056). HM.

--Russia: Selected Readings. (World Regional Studies). (Orig.). (gr. 7 up). 1969. pap. 6.60 (ISBN 0-395-17715-4, 2-31062). HM.

Kublin, Hyman, et al. Middle East: Regional Study. rev. ed. (World Regional Studies). (gr. 9-12). 1973. pap. text ed. 6.60 (ISBN 0-395-13931-7). HM.

Kubly, Herbert. Native's Return. LC 80-5894. 408p. 1981. 14.95 (ISBN 0-8128-2768-6). Stein & Day.

Kubo, Sakae. Acquitted! Message from the Cross. LC 74-28685. (Stories That Win Ser.). 1975. pap. 0.95 o.p. (ISBN 0-8163-0190-5, 01070-2). Pacific Pr Pub Assn.

--A Beginner's New Testament Greek Grammar. LC 79-64247. 1979. pap. text ed. 9.50 (ISBN 0-8191-0761-1). U Pr of Amer.

--God Meets Man: A Theology of the Sabbath & the Second Advent. LC 78-6616. (Anvil Ser.). 1978. pap. 7.95 (ISBN 0-8127-0171-2). Southern Pub.

--A Reader's Greek-English Lexicon of the New Testament. 1975. text ed. 11.95 (ISBN 0-310-26920-2). Zondervan.

Kubota, Takayuki. Gosoku Ryu Karate: Kumite I. LC 80-53036. (Illus.). 160p. (Orig.). 1980. pap. 6.95 (ISBN 0-86568-010-8). Unique Pubns.

Kubota, Takayuki & McCaul, Paul F. Baton Techniques & Training. (Illus.). 320p. 1974. 14.75 (ISBN 0-398-02338-7). C C Thomas.

Kubovy, Michael & Pomerantz, James, eds. Perceptual Organization. 608p. 1981. text ed. 39.95 (ISBN 0-89859-056-6). L Erlbaum Assocs.

Kucera, Vladimir. Discrete Linear Control: The Polynomial Equation Approach. LC 78-12956. 1980. 40.95 (ISBN 0-471-99726-9, Pub. by Wiley-Interscience). Wiley.

Kuchhal, M. C. Mercantile Law. (Illus.). 1979. text ed. 20.00x (ISBN 0-7069-0641-1, Pub. by Vikas India). Advent Bk.

Kuchler, A. W. Vegetation Mapping. (Illus.). 1967. 27.00 (ISBN 0-8260-5150-2, Pub. by Wiley-Interscience). Wiley.

Kuchler, F. Law of Support. 3rd ed. 1980. 5.95 (ISBN 0-379-11135-7). Oceana.

Kuchowicz, B. Nuclear & Relativistic Astrophysics & Nuclidic Cosmochemistry: 1963-1967, 4 vols. 1976. Vol. 1. 62.50 (ISBN 0-677-02760-5); Vol. 2. microform 35.00; Vol. 3. microform 32.00 (ISBN 0-677-02780-X); Vol. 4. 62.50 (ISBN 0-677-02790-7). Gordon.

Kuck, David J. The Structure of Computers & Computations, Vol. 1. LC 78-5412. 1978. text ed. 29.95 (ISBN 0-471-02716-2); tchr's manual avail. (ISBN 0-471-05294-9). Wiley.

Kuck, Loraine. The World of the Japanese Garden: From Chinese Origins to Modern Landscape Art. LC 68-26951. (Illus.). 413p. 1980. 37.50 (ISBN 0-8348-0029-2, Pub. by John Weatherhill Inc Japan). C E Tuttle.

Kuczkir, Mary. My Dish Towel Flies at Half-Mast. 288p. 1980. pap. 2.25 (ISBN 0-345-27855-0). Ballantine.

Kuczkowski, jt. auth. see Gersting, Judith L.

Kuczynski, ed. Sintering Processes. (Materials Sciences Research Ser.: Vol. 13). 585p. 1980. 55.00 (ISBN 0-306-40336-6, Plenum Pr). Plenum Pub.

Kuczynski, Robert R. Balance of Births & Deaths, 2 vols. Incl. Vol. I. Western & Northern Europe. Repr. of 1928 ed (ISBN 0-697-00159-8); Vol. 2. Eastern & Southern Europe. Repr. of 1931 ed (ISBN 0-697-00160-1). (Brookings Institution Reprint Ser). lib. bdg. 22.50x ea. Irvington.

Kuder, John, tr. see Keysser, Christian.

Kudo, Kazuyoshi. Japanese Bamboo Baskets. LC 78-71255. (Form & Function Ser.: Vol. 4). (Illus.). 80p. 1981. pap. 8.95 (ISBN 0-87011-394-1). Kodansha.

Kudo, Kazuzo. Judo in Action: Throwing Techniques. LC 67-20768. (Illus.). pap. 5.95 (ISBN 0-87040-073-8). Japan Pubns.

Kudo, Masanobu, jt. auth. see Seike, Kiyoshi.

Kudo, Richard R. Protozoology. 5th ed. (Illus.). 1188p. 1977. 33.75 (ISBN 0-398-01058-7). C C Thomas.

Kudrna, C. Imbior. Two-Way Words. LC 80-10468. (Illus.). 32p. (gr. 1-3). 1980. 5.95g (ISBN 0-687-42785-1). Abingdon.

Kudrna, Dennis A. Purchasing Manager's Decision Handbook. LC 74-23120. 224p. 1975. 17.95 (ISBN 0-8436-1307-6). CBI Pub.

Kudrow, Lee. Cluster Headache: Mechanisms & Management. (Illus.). 200p. 1981. 29.50 (ISBN 0-19-261169-0). Oxford U Pr.

--Cluster Headache: Mechanisms & Management. (Illus.). 200p. 1980. text ed. 29.50x (ISBN 0-19-261169-0). Oxford U Pr.

Kuebler, Roy R., Jr. & Smith, Harry, Jr. Statistics: A Beginning. LC 75-35719. 1976. text ed. 19.50 (ISBN 0-471-50928-0); instructor's manual avail. (ISBN 0-471-01541-5); wkbk. avail. (ISBN 0-471-02638-7); answers avail. (ISBN 0-471-02757-X). Wiley.

Kuecken, John A. Handbook of Microprocessor Applications. (Illus.). 308p. (Orig.). 1980. 14.95 (ISBN 0-8306-9935-X); pap. 8.95 (ISBN 0-8306-1203-3). Tab Bks.

--Solid-State Motor Controls. (Illus.). 1978. pap. 8.95 (ISBN 0-8306-7929-4, 929). TAB Bks.

Kuehl, John. John Hawkes & the Craft of Conflict. 1975. 14.00 (ISBN 0-8135-0802-9). Rutgers U Pr.

Kuehn, Dieter. Josephine. (Suhrkamp Taschenbuch: No. 587). 176p. 1980. pap. text ed. 3.90 (ISBN 3-518-37087-1, Pub. by Insel Verlag Germany). Suhrkamp.

Kuehn, Douglas. Takeovers & the Theory of the Firm: An Empirical Analysis for the United Kingdom 1957-69. 189p. 1975. 29.75x (ISBN 0-8419-5000-8). Holmes & Meier.

Kuehn, Robert E., ed. Aldous Huxley: A Collection of Critical Essays. (Twentieth Century Views Ser.). 192p. 1974. 10.95 (ISBN 0-13-448514-9, Spec); pap. 2.45 o.p. (ISBN 0-13-448506-8, Spec). P-H.

Kuehneli, Erik M. Von see Faulk, Odie B. & Von Kuehneli, Erik M.

Kuehnemund, Terry M., ed. Treasure House: Museums of the Empire State. LC 79-53226. (Illus.). 1979. pap. 10.00 (ISBN 0-89062-042-3). Pub Ctr Cult Res.

Kuehni, Rolf G. Computer Colorant Formulation. 128p. 1975. 17.95 (ISBN 0-669-03335-9). Lexington Bks.

Kuenzlen, Martin. Playing Urban Games: The Systems Approach to Planning. LC 75-189032. 8.95x (ISBN 0-262-11069-5); pap. 4.95x (ISBN 0-262-61028-0, Pub. by I Pr). MIT Pr.

Kueren, Dolores Van see Siegel, Murray J. & Van Kueren, Dolores.

Kuerti, G. see Von Mises, Richard & Von Karman, Theodore.

Kueter, Roger A. & Miller, Janeen. Slides. Duane, James E., ed. LC 80-21335. (The Instructional Media Library: Vol. 13). (Illus.). 104p. 1981. 13.95 (ISBN 0-87778-173-7). Educ Tech Pubns.

Kuethe, Arnold M. & Chow, Chuen-Yen. Foundations of Aerodynamics: Bases of Aerodynamic Design. 3rd ed. LC 76-20761. 1976. text ed. 29.95 (ISBN 0-471-50953-1). Wiley.

Kufeld, William M., ed. see Bicks, Alexander.

Kuffel & Abdullah, M. High Voltage Engineering. 1970. text ed. 28.00 (ISBN 0-08-006383-7); pap. text ed. 11.25 (ISBN 0-08-006382-9). Pergamon.

Kuffler, Stephen W. & Nicholls, John G. From Neuron to Brain: A Cellular Approach to the Function of the Nervous System. LC 75-32228. 1976. text ed. 19.50x (ISBN 0-87893-442-1). Sinauer Assoc.

Kugel, James L. The Idea of Biblical Poetry: Parallelism & Its History. LC 80-25227. 320p. 1981. 27.50x (ISBN 0-300-02474-6). Yale U Pr.

Kugel, Yerachmiel & Gruenberg, Gladys W. Ethical Perspectives on Business & Society. LC 77-3106. 1977. 16.95 (ISBN 0-669-01482-6). Lexington Bks.

Kugel, Yerachmiel & Gruenberg, Gladys. International Payoffs: A Dilemma for Business. LC 76-48404. 1977. 18.95 (ISBN 0-669-01150-9). Lexington Bks.

--Selected Readings on International Payoffs. LC 76-48404. 1977. 19.95 (ISBN 0-669-01458-3). Lexington Bks.

Kugelmass, I. Newton. Adolescent Immaturity: Prevention & Treatment. (American Lectures in Living Chemistry Ser.). (Illus.). 320p. 1973. text ed. 17.50 (ISBN 0-398-02707-2). C C Thomas.

--Adolescent Medicine: Principles & Practice. (American Lectures in Living Chemistry Ser.). (Illus.). 584p. 1975. 31.75 (ISBN 0-398-03288-2). C C Thomas.

--Autistic Child. (Illus.). 382p. 1974. 22.75 (ISBN 0-398-01059-5). C C Thomas.

--Mastering Adolescence in a Dangerous World. LC 77-81795. 264p. 1981. 22.50 (ISBN 0-87527-167-7). Green.

Kugler, Hans J. Slowing Down the Aging Process. (Orig.). 1973. pap. 1.95 (ISBN 0-515-05333-3, A3099). Jove Pubns.

Kuh, Katharine. Art Has Many Faces. LC 51-13484. (Illus.). 1951. 10.95 o.s.i. (ISBN 0-06-003180-8, HarpT). Har-Row.

--Artist's Voice. LC 62-9893. (Illus.). 1962. 10.95 o.p. (ISBN 0-06-012465-2, HarpT). Har-Row.

Kuhaulua, Jesse & Wheeler, John. Takamiyama: The World of Sumo. LC 72-96129. (Illus.). 176p. 1973. 12.95 (ISBN 0-87011-195-7). Kodansha.

Kuhl, Ingrid K. The Executive Role in Health Service Delivery Organizations. 1977. 5.00. Assn Univ Progs Hlth.

Kuhle, Leo & Monroe, Debbie. The Shortcut Gourmet Cookbook. (Illus., Orig.). 1981. pap. 6.95 (ISBN 0-933474-20-2, Gabriel Bks). Minn Scholarly.

Kuhlenbeck, H. The World of Natural Sciences & Its Phenomenology: The Human Brain & Its Universe. 2nd ed. Gerlach, J., ed. (Vol. 1). viii, 320p. 1981. 118.75 (ISBN 3-8055-1817-X). S Karger.

Kuhlenbeck, H. & Gerlach, J. The Brain & Its Mind. 2nd ed. (The Human Brain & Its Universe: Vol. 2). (Illus.). x, 398p. 1981. 118.75 (ISBN 3-8055-2403-X). S Karger.

Kuhlig, Clemens & Kuhlig, Ruth. Building the Skiff Cabin Boy: A Step by Step Pictoral Guide. LC 76-8775. (Illus.). 1977. 15.00 (ISBN 0-87742-064-5). Intl Marine.

Kuhlig, Ruth, jt. auth. see Kuhlig, Clemens.

Kuhlman, James A., jt. auth. see Hopple, Gerald W.

Kuhlman, James A., jt. ed. see Gyorgy, Andrew.

Kuhlman, Kath. I Believe in Miracles. 1975. pap. 1.50 (ISBN 0-89129-003-6). Jove Pubns.

Kuhlman, Kathryn. Captain LeVrier Believes in Miracles. 90p. 1973. pap. 0.95 (ISBN 0-87123-077-1, 200077). Bethany Fell.

--From Medicine to Miracles. LC 78-67100. 1978. pap. 1.50 (ISBN 0-87123-383-5, 200383). Bethany Fell.

--How Big Is God? LC 74-12775. 96p. (Orig.). 1974. pap. 1.75 (ISBN 0-87123-222-7, 200222). Bethany Fell.

--I Believe in Miracles. 1969. pap. 1.95 o.s.i. (ISBN 0-515-04684-1). Jove Pubns.

--Never Too Late. LC 75-32235. 80p. 1975. pap. 1.50 (ISBN 0-87123-397-5, 200387). Bethany Fell.

--Nothing Is Impossible with God. (Orig.). pap. 1.75 (ISBN 0-89129-084-2). Jove Pubns.

--Standing Tall. LC 74-28755. (Kathryn Kuhlman Ser.). 96p. 1975. pap. 0.95 (ISBN 0-87123-534-X, 200534). Bethany Fell.

--Ten Thousand Miles for a Miracle. LC 74-4851. (Kathryn Kuhlman Ser). 96p. 1974. pap. 0.95 (ISBN 0-87123-536-6, 200536). Bethany Fell.

Kuhlman, Kathryn, tr. Dios Quiere Sanarte y Revolucionar Tu Vida. (Spanish Bks.). (Span.). 1977. 2.25 (ISBN 0-8297-0751-4). Life Pubs Intl.

Kuhn, Alfred. Unified Social Science: A System-Based Introduction. 1975. text ed. 17.95x (ISBN 0-256-01444-2). Dorsey.

Kuhn, Annette & Wolpe, Annmarie, eds. Feminism & Materialism. 1978. 22.50x (ISBN 0-7100-0072-3); pap. 9.00 (ISBN 0-7100-0074-X). Routledge & Kegan.

Kuhn, Arthur K. Pathways in International Law, a Personal Narrative. Repr. of 1953 ed. lib. bdg. 15.00x (ISBN 0-8371-2211-2, KUPI). Greenwood.

Kuhn, Barbara. The Whole Lay Ministry Catalog. (Orig.). 1979. pap. 8.95 (ISBN 0-8164-2187-0). Crossroad NY.

Kuhn, Charles L. The Police Officer's Memorandum Book. (Illus.). 80p. 1964. pap. 5.00 spiral (ISBN 0-398-01062-5). C C Thomas.

Kuhn, Delia, jt. ed. see Kuhn, Ferdinand.

Kuhn, Ferdinand & Kuhn, Delia, eds. Adventures in Public Service. LC 63-21855. 3.95 (ISBN 0-8149-0137-9). Vanguard.

Kuhn, Fritz. Decorative Work in Wrought Iron & Other Metals. Date not set. 24.95 (ISBN 0-8038-0060-6). Hastings.

Kuhn, G. & Weiss, D. Guide to Illinois Real Estate License Preparation. 1979. pap. 16.95 (ISBN 0-13-370254-5). P-H.
Kuhn, H. W., ed. see International Summer School on Mathematical Systems Theory & Economics, Varenna, Italy, 1967.
Kuhn, Isobel. In the Arena. 1960. pap. 3.50 (ISBN 0-85363-023-2). OMF Bks.
--Nests Above the Abyss. pap. 3.95 (ISBN 0-85363-031-3). OMF Bks.
--Stones of Fire. 1951. pap. 2.95 (ISBN 0-85363-049-6). OMF Bks.
Kuhn, Jerold R. Marriage Counseling: Fact or Fallacy? LC 80-22269. 146p. 1980. Repr. of 1973 ed. lib. bdg. 9.95x (ISBN 0-89370-622-1). Borgo Pr.
Kuhn, Phyllis. Dazzled by Diamonds. (Orig.). 1981. pap. 1.50 o.s.i. (ISBN 0-440-11710-0). Dell.
Kuhn, Ryan A., jt. ed. see Paulsen, Kathryn.
Kuhn, Terry L., jt. auth. see Madsen, Clifford K.
Kuhn, U., tr. see Gashutz, W.
Kuhn, Ursula. English Literary Terms in Poetological Texts of the Sixteenth Century, 3 vols. (Salzburg Studies in English Literature, Elizabethan & Renaissance Studies: Nos. 32-34). 1071p. 1974. Set. pap. text ed. 75.25x (ISBN 0-391-01452-8). Humanities.
Kuhn, W., jt. auth. see Graeff, H.
Kuhne, Cecil. Advanced River Rafting. LC 80-14073. (Illus.). 224p. (Orig.). 1980. pap. 4.95 (ISBN 0-89037-183-0). Anderson World.
Kuhne, Robert J. Co-Determination in Business: Workers Representatives in the Boardroom. LC 79-21415. (Praeger Special Study Ser.). (Illus.). 1980. 19.95 (ISBN 0-03-052386-9). Praeger.
Kuhne, Walter G. The Liassic Therapsid Oligokyphus. (Illus.). iii, 150p. 1956. 16.50x (ISBN 0-565-00115-9, Pub. by British Mus Nat Hist England). Sabbot-Natural Hist Bks.
Kuhner, Herbert, tr. see Herzele, Margarethe.
Kuhner, Herbert, tr. see Wiplinger, Peter P.
Kuhnert-Brandstatter, M. Thermomicroscopy in the Analysis of Pharmaceuticals. 424p. 1972. 72.00 (ISBN 0-08-006990-8). Pergamon.
Kuhns, Richard. The House, the City & the Judge: The Growth of Moral Awareness in the Oresteia. LC 61-18061. 1962. 20.00x (ISBN 0-672-51317-X). Irvington.
Kuhr, R. J., jt. ed. see Staples, R. C.
Kuhrt, Emilie. Ancient Civilizations. (Visual World Ser.). 1978. s&l 7.90 (ISBN 0-531-09073-6); lib. bdg. 5.95 (ISBN 0-531-09091-4). Watts.
Kuiper, Gerard P. & Middlehurst, Barbara M., eds. Planets & Satellites. LC 54-7183. (Solar System Ser: Vol. 3). 1961. 23.00x (ISBN 0-226-45927-6). U of Chicago Pr.
Kuiper, R. B. The Bible Tells Us So: Twelve Short Chapters on Major Themes of the Bible. 1978. pap. 2.95 (ISBN 0-85151-001-9). Banner of Truth.
--God Centred Evangelism. 1978. pap. 3.95 (ISBN 0-85151-110-4). Banner of Truth.
Kuipers, A. H., jt. ed. see Rainich, Gabrielle.
Kuipers, J. F. J. World's Truck Catalogue: International Listings. (Illus.). Date not set. pap. 16.95 (ISBN 0-89404-013-8). Aztex. Postponed.
Kuipers, Katharina, jt. auth. see Dalton, J. Michael.
Kuipers, L. & Niederreiter, H. Uniform Distribution of Sequences. LC 73-20497. (Pure & Applied Mathematics Ser.). 416p. 1974. 37.50 (ISBN 0-471-51045-9, Pub. by Wiley-Interscience). Wiley.
Kuipers, L. & Timman, R. Handbook of Mathematics. 1969. 60.00 (ISBN 0-08-011857-7); pap. 21.00 (ISBN 0-08-018996-2). Pergamon.
Kuisel, Richard F. Capitalism & the State in Modern France: Renovation & Economic Management in the Twentieth Century. 352p. Date not set. price not set (ISBN 0-521-23474-3). Cambridge U Pr.
Kuist, ed. The Nichols File of "The Gentleman's Magazine". 300p. 1981. 50.00 (ISBN 0-299-08480-9). U of Wis Pr.
Kujath, Mentor, ed. see Becker, Siegbert.
Kujath, Mentor, ed. see Gedde, Palmer.
Kujath, Mentor, ed. see Lauterbach, William.
Kujawa, D. Employment Effects of Multinational Enterprises: The Case of the United States. International Labour Office, ed. (Research on Employment Effects of Multinational Enterprises. Working Papers Ser.: No. 12). 53p. (Orig.). 1980. pap. 8.55. Intl Labour Office.
Kujawa, Duane, ed. American Labor & the Multinational Corporation. LC 72-85977. (Special Studies in International Economics & Development). 1973. 28.50x (ISBN 0-275-28717-3); pap. text ed. 12.95x (ISBN 0-89197-657-4). Irvington.
Kujoth, Jean S. Best-Selling Children's Books. LC 72-11692. 1973. 10.00 (ISBN 0-8108-0571-5). Scarecrow.
--Subject Guide to Humor: Anecdotes, Facetiae & Satire from 365 Periodicals, 1968-74. LC 76-4865. 206p. 1976. 10.00 (ISBN 0-8108-0924-9). Scarecrow.
Kujoth, Jean S., ed. Book Publishing: Inside Views. LC 76-155284. 1971. 15.50 (ISBN 0-8108-0420-4). Scarecrow.
--Teacher & School Discipline. LC 75-9770. 1970. 10.00 (ISBN 0-8108-0300-3). Scarecrow.
Kujoth, Richard K., jt. auth. see Blum, Lawrence P.
Kukarkin, B. V., ed. Pulsating Stars. Hardin, R. R., tr. from Rus. LC 75-17851. 320p. 1975. 54.95 (ISBN 0-470-51035-8). Halsted Pr.
Kukiel, Marian. Czartoryski & European Unity: 1770-1861. LC 80-22899. (Poland's Millenium Ser. of the Kosciuszko Foundation). (Illus.). xvii, 354p. 1981. Repr. of 1955 ed. lib. bdg. 35.00x (ISBN 0-313-22511-7, KUCZ). Greenwood.
Kukla, Robert J. Gun Control: A Written Record of Efforts to Eliminate the Private Possession of Firearms in America. LC 73-9505. 448p. 1973. pap. 4.95 (ISBN 0-8117-2057-8). Stackpole.
Kuklick, Bruce, ed. see James, William.
Kuklick, Henrika. The Imperial Bureaucrat: The Colonial Administrative Service in the Gold Coast,1920-1939. LC 79-2463. (Publications Ser.: No. 217). 256p. 1979. 10.95 (ISBN 0-8179-7171-8). Hoover Inst Pr.
Kukuk, Jack W. Musical Sketchbook Two. (Illus., Orig.). (gr. 2-4). 1968. pap. 1.40 (ISBN 0-8224-9012-9); tchrs' manual free (ISBN 0-8224-9016-1). Pitman Learning.
Kulaev, I. S. The Biochemistry of Inorganic Polyphosphates. LC 78-31627. 1980. 61.50 (ISBN 0-471-27574-3, Pub. by Wiley-Interscience). Wiley.
Kulas, Jim. Let's Count All the Animals. (A Tell-a-Tale Reader Ser.). (Illus.). (gr. k-3). 1979. PLB 4.77 (ISBN 0-307-68407-5, Golden Pr). Western Pub.
--Puppy's One-Two-Three Book. (Illus.). (gr. k-1). 1978. PLB 5.38 (ISBN 0-307-68990-5, Golden Pr). Western Pub.
Kulas, Jim E. My Little Book of Big Animals. (Tell-a-Tale Readers). (Illus.). (gr. k-3). 1979. PLB 4.77 (ISBN 0-307-68645-0, Whitman). Western Pub.
Kulash, Damian J. Congestion Pricing: A Research Summary. 33p. 1974. pap. 2.50 o.p. (ISBN 0-87766-125-1, 83000). Urban Inst.
--Income-Distributional Consequences of Roadway Pricing. 32p. 1974. pap. 2.50 o.p. (ISBN 0-87766-126-X, 84000). Urban Inst.
--Parking Taxes As Roadway Prices: A Case Study of the San Francisco Experience. 46p. 1974. pap. 2.50 o.p. (ISBN 0-87766-116-2, 68000). Urban Inst.
--Parking Taxes for Congestion Relief: A Survey of Related Experience. 1974. pap. 2.50 o.p. (ISBN 0-87766-114-6). Urban Inst.
Kulash, Damian J. & Silverman, William. Discrimination in Mass Transit. 1974. pap. 2.25 o.p. (ISBN 0-87766-112-X, 64000). Urban Inst.
Kulawiec, E. P. The Warsaw Ghetto Memoirs of Janusz Korczak. LC 78-63065. 1978. pap. text ed. 8.00 (ISBN 0-8191-0611-9). U Pr of Amer.
Kulczycki, John J. School Strikes in Prussian Poland, 1901 to 1907: The Struggle Over Bilingual Education. (East Eropean Monographs: No. 82). 320p. 1981. 21.00x (ISBN 0-914710-76-1). East Eur Quarterly.
Kulicke, Barbara & Wood, Peter. All About Frames. (Illus.). 1980. cancelled (ISBN 0-394-41461-6). Pantheon.
Kulig, B. M., ed. see Workshop Held in the Leeuwenhorst Congress Centre Noordwijkerhout, Nov. 23-25, 1979.
Kulik, I. O. & Yanson, I. K. Josephson Effect in Superconducting Tunneling Structures. Gluck, P., tr. from Rus. LC 75-184438. 182p. 1972. 32.50 (ISBN 0-470-51050-1). Halsted Pr.
Kulikowski, M. Karl. Oedipus Rex. (Orig.). 1979. pap. 4.75 (ISBN 0-933906-06-4). Gusto Pr.
Kulikowski, M. Karl, ed. see McDowell, Leonora.
Kulikowski, M. Karl, ed. see Marie, Jean.
Kulikowski, M. Karl, ed. see Shaffer, Joe.
Kulikowski, M. Karl, ed. see Speer, Laurel.
Kulisch, Ulrich W. & Miranker, Willard L. Computer Arithmetic in Theory & Practice. LC 80-765. (Computer Science & Applied Mathematics Ser.). 1980. 25.00 (ISBN 0-12-428650-X). Acad Pr.
Kulish, Mykola. Sonata Pathetique. Luckyj, George S., tr. from Ukrainian. LC 73-91177. (Ukrainian Classics in Translation Ser: No. 3). 120p. 1975. lib. bdg. 11.50x (ISBN 0-87287-092-8). Ukrainian Acad.
Kulish, Panteleimon. The Black Council. Luckyj, George S. & Luckyj, Moira, trs. from Ukrainian. LC 72-97984. (Ukrainian Classics in Translation Ser.: No. 2). 1973. lib. bdg. 11.50x (ISBN 0-87287-063-4). Ukrainian Acad.
Kulk, W. Van Der see Schouten, Jan A. & Van Der Kulk, W.
Kulkarni, jt. auth. see Barlingay.
Kullak, Adolf. The Aesthetics of Pianoforte-Playing. LC 69-16652. (Music Reprint Ser.). 340p. 1972. Repr. of 1893 ed. lib. bdg. 27.50 (ISBN 0-306-71095-1). Da Capo.
Kullak, Franz. Beethoven's Piano-Playing: With an Essay on the Execution of the Trill. LC 72-14059. 110p. 1973. Repr. of 1901 ed. lib. bdg. 14.95 (ISBN 0-306-70564-8). Da Capo.
Kullen, Patrick & Roche, Thomas P., Jr., eds. Spenser Studies: A Renaissance Poetry Annual, Vol. II. (Illus.). 320p. 1981. 20.95x (ISBN 0-8229-3433-7). U of Pittsburgh Pr.
Kuller. Guide to Private Schools: Eastern Ed. 1981. pap. 4.95 (ISBN 0-8120-0837-5). Barron.
Kullman, Harry. The Battle Horse. Blecher, George & Blecher, Lone T., trs. from Swedish. Orig. Title: Stridshasten. 192p. (gr. 6 up). 1981. 8.95 (ISBN 0-87888-175-1). Bradbury Pr.
Kullmann, Wolfgang. Wissenschaft und Methode: Interpreationen Zur aristotelischen Theorie der Naturwissenschaft. (Ger.). 1974. 85.30x (ISBN 3-11-004481-1). De Gruyter.
Kulonen, E. & Kulonen, E., eds. Biology of Fibroblast. 1974. 97.00 (ISBN 0-12-428950-9). Acad Pr.
Kulp, C. A. & Hall, J. W. Casualty Insurance. 4th ed. 1072p. 1968. 28.95 (ISBN 0-471-06568-4). Wiley.
Kulp, C. A. & Hall, John W. Casualty Insurance. 4th ed. LC 68-30893. 1968. 28.95 (ISBN 0-8260-5165-0, 58871). Ronald Pr.
Kulshrestha, V. V. Experimental Physiology. 1977. 8.95 (ISBN 0-7069-0551-2, Pub. by Vikas India). Advent Bk.
Kultermanh, Udo. Architecture in the Seventies. (ABPC Ser.). (Illus.). 160p. 1980. 29.95 (ISBN 0-8038-0019-3). Hastings.
Kultermann, Udo. Trova. LC 77-1915. (Contemporary Artist Ser.). (Illus.). 1978. 65.00 o.p. (ISBN 0-8109-0502-7); ltd. ed. signed 600.00 o.p. (ISBN 0-686-68042-1). Abrams.
Kulvinskas, Viktoras. Sprout for the Love of Everybody: Nutritional Evaluation of Sprouts & Grasses. pap. 2.45 (ISBN 0-933278-03-9). OMango.
--Survival into the Twenty-First Century. Hurlbut, Hermine & Newman, Joan, eds. (Illus.). 1975. pap. 12.95 (ISBN 0-933278-04-7). OMango.
Kumakhov, M. Energy Losses & Ion Ranges in Solids. 1981. cancelled (ISBN 3-7186-0059-5). Harwood Academic.
Kumakhov, M. & Komarov, F. Energy Losses & Ion Ranges in Solids. 400p. 1981. price not set (ISBN 0-677-21220-8). Gordon.
Kuman, Alexandra, jt. ed. see DuBane, Janet.
Kumar, Dharma. India & the European Economic Community. 1967. 8.50x (ISBN 0-210-27182-5). Asia.
Kumar, Girja & Aurora, V. K. Documents on Indian Affairs: 1960. 1965. 20.00x o.p. (ISBN 0-210-22619-6). Asia.
Kumar, Girja & Kumar, Krishan. Theory of Cataloguing. 1975. 12.50 (ISBN 0-7069-0361-7, Pub. by Vikas India). Advent Bk.
Kumar, H. D. Modern Concepts of Ecology. 1977. 14.00 (ISBN 0-7069-0501-6, Pub. by Vikas India). Advent Bk.
Kumar, Krishan. Reference Service. 2nd rev. ed. 390p. 1980. text ed. 18.95 (ISBN 0-7069-0637-3, Pub. by Vikas India). Advent Bk.
Kumar, Krishan, jt. auth. see Ali, Asghar.
Kumar, Krishan, jt. auth. see Kumar, Girja.
Kumar, Krishna & McLeod, Maxwell G., eds. Multinationals from Developing Countries. LC 80-8531. 1981. write for info. (ISBN 0-669-04113-0). Lexington Bks.
Kumar, Krishnan. Theory of Classification. 1980. text ed. 18.95x (ISBN 0-7069-0797-3, Pub. by Vikas India). Advent Bk.
Kumar, Martha J., jt. auth. see Grossman, Michael B.
Kumar, Rajendra. Physical Metallurgy of Iron & Steel. 1968. 20.00x (ISBN 0-210-22658-7). Asia.
Kumar, Ram. Stories. 1976. lib. bdg. 9.00 (ISBN 0-89253-085-5); flexible bdg. 6.00 (ISBN 0-89253-267-X). Ind-US Inc.
Kumar, Ram, jt. auth. see Chopra, M. G.
Kumar, S. & Rathi, M., eds. Perinatal Medicine: Clinical & Biochemical Aspects of the Evaluation, Diagnosis & Management of the Fetus & Newborn. LC 78-40219. 1978. text ed. 45.00 (ISBN 0-08-021517-3). Pergamon.
Kumar, S., et al, eds. Clinical Cancer - Principal Sites One: International Cancer Congress, 12th, Buenos Aires, 1978. LC 79-40710. (Advances in Medical Oncology, Research & Education: Vol. X). (Illus.). 1979. 68.00 (ISBN 0-08-024393-2). Pergamon.
Kumar, Satish. Cryptodiplomacy: CIA & the Third World. 210p. 1981. text ed. 22.50x (ISBN 0-7069-1292-6, Pub by Vikas India). Advent Bk.
Kumar, Satish, ed. The Schumacher Lectures. LC 80-8408. 288p. (Orig.). 1981. pap. 4.95 (ISBN 0-06-090843-2, CN 843, CN). Har-Row.
Kumar, Sharat. The Storm & Other Stories. 1976. 9.00 (ISBN 0-89253-815-5); flexible cloth 6.75 (ISBN 0-89253-816-3). Ind-US Inc.
Kumar, Shiv K. Articulate Silences. (Writers Workshop Redbird Ser). 34p. 1975. 6.75 (ISBN 0-88253-500-5); pap. text ed. 4.00 (ISBN 0-88253-499-8). Ind-US Inc.
Kumar, Shiv K., ed. Indian Verse in English 1970. (Writers Workshop Redbird Ser.). 1977. flxible bdg. 6.75 (ISBN 0-89253-752-3); text ed. 15.00 (ISBN 0-89253-751-5). Ind-US Inc.
Kumar, Shrawan & Machwe, Prabhar, eds. Hindi Short Stories. Kumar, Shrawan & Machwe, Prabhar, trs. 175p. 1970. pap. 1.80 (ISBN 0-88253-053-4). Ind-US Inc.
Kumar, Shrawan, tr. see Kumar, Shrawan & Machwe, Prabhar.
Kumar, Sudhir, jt. ed. see Rathi, Manohar.
Kumar, Vinay. Experimental Techniques in Quantitative Chemical Analysis. LC 80-69043. 183p. (Orig.). 1981. pap. text ed. 10.00 (ISBN 0-8191-1509-6). U Pr of Amer.
Kumar, Virendra. Committees & Commissions in India 1947-73: Vols. 1-10, 1947-73. 1979. text ed. 25.00x ea. (ISBN 0-391-01934-1). Humanities.
Kumarappa, B. The Hindu Conception of the Deity. 1979. text ed. 17.50x (ISBN 0-391-01848-5). Humanities.
Kumarappa, Bharatan, ed. see Gandhi, Mohandas K.
Kumin, Maxine. House, Bridge, Fountain, Gate. LC 75-1353. 1975. pap. 3.50 o.p. (ISBN 0-670-00592-4). Penguin.
--The Nightmare Factory. LC 77-108941. 1970. 8.95 o.p. (ISBN 0-06-012481-4, HarpT). Har-Row.
--To Make a Prairie: Essays on Poets, Poetry, & Country Living. LC 79-13289. (Poets on Poetry Ser.). 1979. pap. 5.95 (ISBN 0-472-06306-5). U of Mich Pr.
Kumli, Karl F. Introductory Chemistry: A Survey of General, Organic, & Biological Chemistry. (Illus.). 608p. 1974. text ed. 20.95 (ISBN 0-13-501668-1); study guide pap. 4.95 (ISBN 0-13-501684-3). P-H.
Kumm, Alan, jt. auth. see Evans, Hazel.
Kumm, Patsy. The Busy Mother's Cook Book. 1972. 4.95 o.p. (ISBN 0-571-09899-1, Pub. by Faber & Faber). Merrimack Bk Serv.
Kummer, B. Spiele Auf Graphen. (Internationale Schriftenreihe zur numerischen Mathematik: No. 44). 88p. (Ger.). 1979. pap. 18.50 (ISBN 3-7643-1077-4). Birkhauser.
Kummer, Hans. Primate Societies: Group Techniques of Ecological Adaptations. LC 78-140010. (Worlds of Man Ser.). 1971. text ed. 11.00x (ISBN 0-88295-612-4); pap. text ed. 5.75x (ISBN 0-88295-613-2). AHM Pub.
Kummings, Gail, ed. see Burch, Monte.
Kump, Peter. Breakthrough Rapid Reading. 256p. 1980. 5.95 (ISBN 0-13-081554-3, Reward). P-H.
Kunar, Raj. The New Concept of the Novel. 49p. 1980. Repr. of 1959 ed. lib. bdg. 6.00 (ISBN 0-8482-1446-3). Norwood Edns.
Kundell, James E., ed. Georgia Water Resources: Issues & Options. 114p. 1980. pap. 10.00x. U of GA Inst Govt.
Kundera, Milan. The Book of Laughter & Forgetting. LC 80-7657. 224p. 1980. 10.95 (ISBN 0-394-50896-3). Knopf.
--Laughable Loves. Rappaport, Suzanne, tr. from Czech. 266p. 1975. pap. 4.50 (ISBN 0-14-004044-7). Penguin.
Kundis, Lawrence E. Point, Line, Plane & Solid: A Basic Text Workbook for Engineering Graphics. 2nd ed. 368p. 1980. pap. text ed. 16.95 (ISBN 0-8403-2310-7). Kendall-Hunt.
Kundu, M. R., ed. see IUA Symposium, College Park, Md., Aug. 7-10, 1979.
Kunen, James S. Strawberry Statement: Notes of a College Revolutionist. LC 69-16455. 1969. 6.95 o.p. (ISBN 0-394-44753-0). Random.
Kunene, D. P. Heroic Poetry of the Basotho. (Oxford Library of African Literature Ser). 1971. 14.95x (ISBN 0-19-815132-2). Oxford U Pr.
Kung, Andres. Bruce Olson: Missionary of American Colonizer? LC 80-69309. 1981. pap. 5.95 (ISBN 0-915684-83-7). Christian Herald.
Kung, Hans. Art & the Question of Meaning. 96p. (Ger.). 1981. 7.95 (ISBN 0-8245-0016-4). Crossroad NY.
--The Church. 600p. 1976. pap. 3.95 (ISBN 0-385-11367-6, Im). Doubleday.
--The Church-Maintained in Truth: A Theological Meditation. 87p. 1980. 6.95 (ISBN 0-8164-0454-2). Crossroad NY.
--Does God Exist? An Answer for Today. Quinn, Edward, tr. LC 79-6576. 864p. 1980. 17.50 (ISBN 0-385-13592-0). Doubleday.
--Justification: The Doctrine of Karl Barth & a Catholic Reflection. LC 80-26001. 1981. pap. price not set (ISBN 0-664-24364-9). Westminster.
--Papal Ministry in the Church. (Concilium Ser.: Religion in the Seventies: Vol. 64). 1971. pap. 4.95 (ISBN 0-8164-2520-5). Crossroad NY.

--Signposts for the Future. LC 77-75387. 1978. 7.95 o.p. (ISBN 0-385-13151-8). Doubleday.
Kung, Hans, ed. The Plurality of Ministries. (Concilium Ser.: Religion in the Seventies: Vol. 74). 1972. pap. 4.95 (ISBN 0-8164-2530-2). Crossroad NY.
--Post-Ecumenical Christianity. (Concilium Ser.: Religion in the Seventies: Vol. 54). 1970. pap. 4.95 (ISBN 0-8164-2510-8). Crossroad NY.
Kung, Hans & Kasper, Walker, eds. Christians & Jews: Concilium Ser.: Religion in the Seventies. (Vol. 98). 1976. pap. 4.95 (ISBN 0-8164-2095-5). Crossroad NY.
Kung, Hans & Kasper, Walter, eds. Polarization in the Church. LC 73-6435. (Concilium Ser.: Religion in the Seventies: Vol. 88). 156p. 1973. pap. 4.95 (ISBN 0-8164-2572-8). Crossroad NY.
Kung, Hans & Moltmann, Jurgen, eds. Conflicting Ways of Interpreting the Bible, Concilium 138. (New Concilium 1980). 128p. 1981. pap. 5.95 (ISBN 0-8245-4771-3). Crossroad NY.
--Conflicts About the Holy Spirit. (The New Concilium: Vol. 128). 120p. (Orig.). 1980. pap. 4.95 (ISBN 0-8164-2035-1). Crossroad NY.
--An Ecumenical Creed? (Concilium Ser.: Vol. 118). (Orig.). 1978. pap. 4.95 (ISBN 0-8164-2198-6). Crossroad NY.
--Why Did God Make Me? Concilium, Vol. 108. 1978. pap. 4.95 (ISBN 0-8164-2167-6). Crossroad NY.
Kunhardt, Dororthy. Tiny Golden Library: A Dozen Animal Nonsense Tales. (Illus.). 24p. (gr. 4-8). 1980. 6.95 (ISBN 0-307-13618-3, Golden Pr). Western Pub.
Kuniczak, W. S. My Name Is Million: An Illustrated History of the Poles in America. LC 77-82954. 1978. 12.95 o.p. (ISBN 0-385-12228-4). Doubleday.
--Thousand Hour Day. 628p. 1980. cancelled (ISBN 0-88254-506-X). Hippocrene Bks.
Kunin, Madeleine & Stout, Marilyn. The Big Green Book: A Four-Season Guide to Vermont. (Illus.). 352p. 1976. pap. 6.95 (ISBN 0-517-52517-8). Crown.
Kunin, Richard A. Mega-Nutrition: The New Prescription for Maximum Health,Energy & Longevity. 1981. pap. 6.95 (ISBN 0-452-25271-7, Z5271, Plume Bks). NAL.
Kunishi, Marilyn M., jt. auth. see Ahana, Doris N.
Kunitz, Stanley, ed. see Keats, John.
Kunitz, Stanley J. & Haycraft, Howard, eds. British Authors Before Eighteen Hundred. (Illus.). 1952. 15.00 (ISBN 0-8242-0006-3). Wilson.
--British Authors of the Nineteenth Century. (Illus.). 1936. 18.00 (ISBN 0-8242-0007-1). Wilson.
--Junior Book of Authors. 2nd rev. ed. (Illus.). 1951. 12.00 (ISBN 0-8242-0028-4). Wilson.
--Twentieth Century Authors. (Illus.). 1942. 35.00 (ISBN 0-8242-0049-7); 1st suppl. 1955. 27.00 (ISBN 0-8242-0050-0). Wilson.
Kunitz, Stephen J., jt. auth. see Levy, Jerrold E.
Kunkel, Barbara K., jt. auth. see Gibson, Robert W., Jr.
Kunkel, H. G. & Dixon, F. J., eds. Advances in Immunology, Vol. 30. 1980. 35.00 (ISBN 0-12-022430-5). Acad Pr.
Kunkel, Henry G. & Dixon, Frank J., eds. Advances in Immunology, Vol. 29. (Serial Pub.). 1980. 35.00 (ISBN 0-12-022429-1). Acad Pr.
Kunkel, Henry G. see Taliaferro, W. H. & Humphrey, J. H.
Kunkel, Wolfgang. An Introduction to Roman Legal & Constitutional History. 2nd ed. Kelly, J. M., tr. 1973. 22.50x (ISBN 0-19-825317-6). Oxford U Pr.
Kunos, George. Adrenoceptors & Catecholamine Action. (Neurotransmitter Receptors Ser.: Vol. 1). 300p. 1981. 29.50 (ISBN 0-471-05725-8, Pub. by Wiley-Interscience). Wiley.
Kunreuther, Howard. Disaster Insurance Protection: Public Policy Lessons. LC 77-179. 1978. 34.95 (ISBN 0-471-03259-X, Pub. by Wiley-Interscience). Wiley.
Kunstadt, Leonard, jt. auth. see Charters, Samuel.
Kunstadt, Robert M. The Protection of Personal & Commercial Reputation. (IIC Studies in Industrial Property & Copyright Law: Vol. 3). 1980. pap. 36.30 (ISBN 0-89573-028-6). Verlag Chemie.
Kunstler, James H. A Clown in the Moonlight. 256p. 1981. 10.95 (ISBN 0-312-14495-4). St Martin.
Kuntscher, Gerhard. Practice of Intramedullary Nailing. (Illus.). 388p. 1967. photocopy ed. 35.75 (ISBN 0-398-01067-6). C C Thomas.
Kuntsevich, I. M. & Sheleg, A. V. Tables of Trigonometric Functions for the Numerical Computation of Electron Density in Crystals. 1967. 22.95 (ISBN 0-470-51090-0). Halsted Pr.
Kuntz, Arnold G. Serving God Always. 1966. pap. text ed. 2.15 (ISBN 0-570-06645-X, 22-2014); pap. 4.85 manual (ISBN 0-570-06646-8, 22-2015). Concordia.
Kuntzleman, Charles T. The Complete Book of Walking. 1980. lib. bdg. 14.95 (ISBN 0-8161-6768-0). G K Hall.
Kunz, Marilyn & Schell, Catherine. Efesios y Filemon. Orozco, Julio, tr. from Eng. LC 77-83811. (Encuentros Biblicos Ser.). 55p. (Orig., Span.). 1977. pap. 1.25 (ISBN 0-89922-095-9). Edit Caribe.
--El Evangelio Segun San Lucas. Roberts, Grace S., tr. from Eng. LC 75-42950. (Encuentros Biblicos). 64p. (Orig., Span.). pap. 1.25 (ISBN 0-89922-063-0). Edit Caribe.
--Mark, Neighborhood Bible Study. pap. 1.75 (ISBN 0-8423-4101-3). Tyndale.
--Se Encontraron Con Jesus. Velez, Jose R., tr. from Eng. LC 76-1299. (Encuentros Biblicos). 55p. (Orig., Span.). 1976. pap. 1.25 (ISBN 0-89922-065-7). Edit Caribe.
--Uno Corintios: Llamado a la Madurez. Velez, Jose R., tr. from Eng. LC 76-1298. (Encuentros Biblicos). 77p. (Orig., Span.). 1976. pap. 1.25 (ISBN 0-89922-064-9). Edit Caribe.
Kunz, Werner & Rittel, Horst. Systems Analysis of the Logic of Research & Information Processes. 74p. 1977. text ed. 13.00 (ISBN 3-7940-3455-4, Pub. by K G Saur). Shoe String.
Kunz, Werner, et al. Methods of Analysis & Evaluation of Information Needs. 84p. 1976. text ed. 18.00 (ISBN 3-7940-3450-3, Pub. by K G Saur). Shoe String.
Kunz-Bircher, Ruth. The Bircher-Benner Health Guide. Shed, Rosemarie, tr. from Fr. LC 80-93644. Orig. Title: Le Guide De Sante Bircher. 160p. 1980. pap. 3.95 (ISBN 0-912800-87-9). Woodbridge Pr.
Kunze, Ray, jt. auth. see Hoffman, Kenneth.
Kunzer, Ruth G., jt. auth. see Bahr, Ehrhard.
Kunzle, David. Fashion & Fetishism: A Social History of the Corset, Tight-Lacing & Other Forms of Body-Sculpture in the West. (Illus.). 300p. 1981. 27.50x (ISBN 0-8476-6276-4). Rowman.
Kunzle, David, tr. see Dorfman, Ariel & Mattelart, Armand.
Kuo, Benjamin C. Automatic Control Systems. 3rd ed. (Illus.). 640p. 1975. ref. ed. 27.95 (ISBN 0-13-054973-8). P-H.
Kuo, Benjamin C., jt. auth. see Tabak, Daniel.
Kuo, Chia-Ling. Social & Political Change in New York's Chinatown: The Role of Voluntary Associations. LC 77-5328. (Special Studies). 1977. text ed. 24.95 (ISBN 0-03-021951-5). Praeger.
Kuo, Leslie T. The Technical Transformation of Agriculture in Communist China. LC 73-181867. (Special Studies in International Economics & Development). 1971. 29.50x (ISBN 0-275-28276-7). Irvington.
Kuo, Ping-Chia. China: New Age & New Outlook. LC 74-30084. (China in the 20th Century Ser). xix, 231p. 1975. Repr. of 1956 ed. lib. bdg. 22.50 (ISBN 0-306-70679-2). Da Capo.
Kuo, Shan S. Assembler Language for Fortran, Cobol & PL-1 Programmers. new ed. LC 73-2138. 1974. text ed. 20.95 (ISBN 0-201-03954-0). A-W.
--Computer Applications of Numerical Methods. LC 78-164654. 1972. text ed. 18.95 (ISBN 0-201-03956-7). A-W.
Kuo-Ching Tu. Li Ho. (World Authors Ser.: No. 537). 1979. lib. bdg. 14.95 (ISBN 0-8057-6379-1). Twayne.
Kuo-Nan Liou, ed. An Introduction to Atmospheric Radiation. LC 80-769. (International Geophysics Ser.). 1980. 32.50 (ISBN 0-12-451450-2). Acad Pr.
Kuong, Javier F., jt. auth. see Perry, William E.
Kupchella, Charles E. Sights & Sounds: The Very Special Senses. LC 75-1446. 1976. pap. text ed. 6.95 (ISBN 0-672-63695-6). Bobbs.
Kupelnick, Bruce S., ed. see Gibbon, Monk.
Kupelnick, Bruce S., ed. see Hill, W. Aber.
Kuper. The Social Anthropology of Radcliffe-Brown. 1977. 22.00x (ISBN 0-7100-8556-7); pap. 10.00 (ISBN 0-7100-8557-5). Routledge & Kegan.
Kuper, Adam. Changing Jamaica. 160p. 1975. 18.50x (ISBN 0-7100-8241-X). Routledge & Kegan.
Kuper, Jessica, ed. The Anthropologists' Cookbook. LC 77-80179. (Illus.). 1978. text ed. 12.50x (ISBN 0-87663-301-7); pap. 6.95 (ISBN 0-87663-971-6). Universe.
Kupferle, Mary L. God Never Fails. 1958. 2.95 o.p. (ISBN 0-87159-045-X). Unity Bks.
Kupferman, Martin. Slowth: The Changing Economy & How You Can Successfully Cope. Levi, Maurice D., ed. LC 80-18863. 225p. 1980. 13.95 (ISBN 0-471-08090-X). Wiley.
Kupinsky, Stanley, ed. The Fertility of Working Women: A Synthesis of International Research. LC 76-12861. (Praeger Special Studies). 1977. text ed. 37.50 (ISBN 0-275-23100-3). Praeger.
Kupka, I. & Wilsing, N. Conversational Languages. LC 80-40120. (Computing Ser.). 128p. 1980. text ed. 27.75 (ISBN 0-471-27778-9, Pub. by Wiley-Interscience). Wiley.
Kupper, Mike. Driven to Win: A. J. Foyt. LC 75-19276. (Sports Profiles Ser.). (Illus.). 48p. (gr. 4-11). 1975. PLB 8.50 (ISBN 0-8172-0120-3). Raintree Pubs.
Kupper, Mike & Sanders, Peter. Racing to Indy. LC 74-34462. (The Venture Ser, a Reading Incentive Program). (Illus.). 80p. (gr. 7-12,RL 4.5-6.5). 1975. In Packs Of 5. text ed. 23.25 ea. pack (ISBN 0-8172-0212-9). Follett.
Kupperman, Robert & Trent, Darrel. Terrorism: Threat, Reality, Response. LC 78-70394. (Publications Ser.: No. 204). 1979. 14.95 (ISBN 0-8179-7041-X). Hoover Inst Pr.
Kuppers, Harald. Basic Law of Color Theory. (Illus.). 224p. 1981. pap. text ed. 2.95 (ISBN 0-8120-2173-8). Barron.
--Kupper's Color Atlas. (Pocket Art Ser.). (Illus.). 170p. (gr. 9-12). 1981. pap. 4.95 (ISBN 0-8120-2172-X). Barron.
Kuppinger, Roger. Everything You Always Wanted to Know About Mergers, Acquisitions & Divestitures but Didn't Know Whom to Ask. LC 78-71201. 1978. 12.95 (ISBN 0-686-24646-2). R Kuppinger.
Kuppuswamy, Gowry, ed. Indian Music: A Perspective. 1980. 32.50x (ISBN 0-8364-0629-X, Pub. by Sundeep). South Asia Bks.
Kupsh, Joyce, et al. Machine Transcription & Dictation. LC 77-15790. (Wiley Word Processing Ser.). 1978. 13.95 (ISBN 0-471-02734-0); tchrs. manual 2.00 (ISBN 0-471-04211-0). Wiley.
Kupst, Mary J., jt. auth. see Schulman, Jerome L.
Kurata, M. Thermodynamics of Polymer Solutions. Fujita, H., tr. from Jap. (Mmi Press Polymer Monographs). 310p. 1981. 62.00 (ISBN 3-7186-0023-4). Harwood Academic.
Kurata, Satoru. Bibliography of Forest Botany in Japan: 1940 to 1963. 160p. 1966. 12.50x o.p. (ISBN 0-8002-0695-9). Intl Pubns Serv.
Kurath, Hans. Phonology & Prosody of Modern English. LC 64-13467. 1949. 10.00x (ISBN 0-472-08530-1). U of Mich Pr.
--Word Geography of the Eastern United States. 1949. pap. 7.95x (ISBN 0-472-08532-8). U of Mich Pr.
Kurath, Hans & McDavid, Raven I., Jr. Pronunciation of English in the Atlantic States: Based Upon the Collections of the Linguistic Atlas of the Eastern United States. LC 60-5671. (Illus.). 1961. 15.00 o.p. (ISBN 0-472-04541-5). U of Mich Pr.
Kuratowski, K. A Half Century of Polish Mathematics: Remembrances & Reflections. (International Series in Pure & Applied Mathematics: Vol. 108). (Illus.). 212p. 1980. 26.00 (ISBN 0-08-023046-6). Pergamon.
--Introduction to Set Theory & Topology. 2nd, rev. ed. 356p. 1972. text ed. 19.50 (ISBN 0-08-016160-X). Pergamon.
Kurban, Roy. Kicking Techniques. LC 79-65639. (Ser. 211). (Illus.). 1979. pap. 5.95 (ISBN 0-89750-065-2). Ohara Pubns.
Kurdi, Kevin J., ed. see Kurdi, William J.
Kurdi, William J. The Kurdi I. V. Antibiotic Therapy Handbook. Kurdi, Kevin J., ed. pap. 5.95. Med Educ.
Kurdys, Douglas B. Form in Modern Verse Drama, 2 vols. (Salzburg Studies in English Literature Poetic Drama & Poetic Theory Ser.: No. 17). 1972. Set. pap. 50.25x (ISBN 0-391-01454-4). Humanities.
Kureshy, K. U. A Geography of Pakistan. 4th ed. (Illus.). 1978. pap. text ed. 5.95x (ISBN 0-19-577222-9). Oxford U Pr.
Kurian, George T. Historical & Cultural Dictionary of India. LC 76-16186. (Historical & Cultural Dictionaries of Asia Ser.: No. 8). 1976. 14.50 (ISBN 0-8108-0951-6). Scarecrow.
Kurien, C. T. Theoretical Approach to the Indian Economy. (Asia Monographs,: No. 18). 1970. 4.00x o.p. (ISBN 0-210-22261-1). Asia.
Kuriyama, Kurt Y. Humanists & Technocrats: Political Conflict in Contemporary China. LC 79-66648. 1979. pap. text ed. 9.50 (ISBN 0-8191-0846-4). U Pr of Amer.
Kurl, Shreeprakash, tr. The Devotional Poems of Mirabai. (Writers Workshop Saffronbird Ser.). 87p. 1975. 15.00 (ISBN 0-88253-722-9); pap. 6.75 (ISBN 0-89253-539-3). Ind-US Inc.
Kurland, David J., jt. auth. see Weiss, Kenneth L.
Kurland, Gerald. Nikita Sergeievich Khrushchev: Modern Dictator of the USSR. Rahmas, D. Steve, ed. LC 74-185668. (Outstanding Personalities Ser.: No. 12). 32p. 1972. lib. bdg. 2.75 incl. catalog cards (ISBN 0-87157-512-4); pap. 1.50 vinyl laminated covers (ISBN 0-87157-012-2). SamHar Pr.
--Seth Low: The Patrician As Social Reformer; the Patrician As Social Architect--a Biography. LC 76-125816. 415p. 1971. text ed. 24.50x (ISBN 0-8290-0205-7). Irvington.
Kurland, Howard. Back Pains. (Illus.). 1981. 12.95 (ISBN 0-671-41379-1). S&S.
Kurland, Michael. Ten Years to Doomsday. 1977. pap. 1.50 o.s.i. (ISBN 0-515-04458-X). Jove Pubns.
--Transmission Error. 1978. pap. 1.50 o.s.i. (ISBN 0-515-04514-4). Jove Pubns.
Kurland, Philip B., jt. auth. see Supreme Court of the United States.
Kurmit, A. A. Information-Lossless Automata of Finite Order. Louvish, D., tr. LC 74-8183. 186p. 1974. 37.95 (ISBN 0-470-51099-4). Halsted Pr.
Kuroda, Alice K. & Kuroda, Yasumasa. Palestinians Without Palestine: A Study of Political Socialization Among Palestinian Youths. LC 78-51851. 1978. pap. text ed. 10.25x (ISBN 0-8191-0479-5). U Pr of Amer.
Kuroda, K., jt. auth. see Burton, L.
Kuroda, S. Y. Generative Grammatical Studies in the Japanese Language. Hankamer, Jorge, ed. LC 78-66564. (Outstanding Dissertations in Linguistics Ser.). 1979. lib. bdg. 27.50 (ISBN 0-8240-9680-0). Garland Pub.
--The (W) Hole of the Doughnut. (Studies in Generative Linguistic Analysis: No. 1). 258p. 1980. text ed. 62.25x (ISBN 90-6439-161-0). Humanities.
Kuroda, Yasumasa, jt. auth. see Kuroda, Alice K.
Kurokawa, Kisho. Metabolism in Architecture. (Illus.). 1977. 35.00 o.p. (ISBN 0-89158-734-9). Westview.
Kurokawa, S. A Monograph of the Genus Anaptychia. 1962. pap. 20.00 (ISBN 3-7682-5406-2). Lubrecht & Cramer.
Kurosawa, Akira. Rashomon. (Illus.). 1969. pap. 17.25 (ISBN 0-686-66133-8, ST00051). Grove.
Kurpel, N. S. Projection-Iterative Methods for Solution of Operator Equations. Douglas, R. G., ed. Israel Program for Scientific Translations, tr. LC 76-17114. (Translations of Mathematical Monographs). 1976. 24.80 (ISBN 0-8218-1596-2, MMONO-46). Am Math.
Kurrel, N. S. Iterative Methods for Solution of Operator Equations. LC 76-1711. (Translations of Mathematical Monographs: Vol. 46). 1976. 24.80 o.p. (ISBN 0-8218-1596-2, MMONO-46). Am Math.
Kurrik, Maire J. Literature & Negation. LC 79-15949. (Illus.). 1979. 25.00x (ISBN 0-231-04342-2). Columbia U Pr.
Kursunogl, Behram, ed. see Center for Theoretical Studies.
Kursunoglu, Behram & Perlmutter, Arnold, eds. Directions in Energy Policy: A Comprehensive Approach to Energy Resource Decision-Making. LC 79-21524. 736p. reference 38.00 (ISBN 0-88410-089-8). Ballinger Pub.
Kursunoglu, Behram, et al, eds. Recent Developments in High-Energy Physics. (Studies in the Natural Sciences Ser.: Vol. 17). 320p. 1980. 39.50 (ISBN 0-306-40565-2, Plenum Pr). Plenum Pub.
Kurt, Franklin T. Water Flying. LC 73-13362. (Illus.). 288p. 1974. 12.95 (ISBN 0-02-567130-8). Macmillan.
Kurten, Bjorn. The Age of Mammals. LC 79-177479. (Illus.). 1972. 17.50x (ISBN 0-231-03624-8). Columbia U Pr.
--The Age of Mammals. (Illus.). 1972. pap. 7.50 (ISBN 0-231-03647-7). Columbia U Pr.
--Dance of the Tiger: A Novel of the Ice Age. 1980. 10.95 (ISBN 0-394-51267-7). Pantheon.
Kurten, Bjory. The Cave Bear Story. Life & Death of a Vanished Animal. LC 76-3723. (Illus.). 144p. 1976. 15.00x (ISBN 0-231-04017-2). Columbia U Pr.
Kurten, Nancy N. Needlepoint: In Stitches. pap. 3.95 o.p. (ISBN 0-684-13843-3, SL530, ScribT). Scribner.
Kurth, Ann. Prescription: Murder. (Illus.). 1981. pap. 2.50 (ISBN 0-451-09997-4, E9997, Sig). NAL.
Kurth, Edwin W. Catechetical Helps. (gr. 4-12). 1981. pap. text ed. 4.50 (ISBN 0-570-03507-4, 14-1261). Concordia.
Kurth, Rudolf. Dimensional Analysis & Group Theory in Astrophysics. 249p. 1972. text ed. 55.00 (ISBN 0-08-016616-4). Pergamon.
--Elements of Analytical Dynamics. 200p. 1976. text ed. 28.00 (ISBN 0-08-019848-1). Pergamon.
Kurtis, Arlene H. Jews Helped Build America. LC 74-19114. (Illus.). (gr. 4-6). 1970. PLB 4.64 o.p. (ISBN 0-671-32707-0). Messner.
Kurtsin, I. T. Theoretical Principles of Psychosomatic Medicine. Kaner, N., tr. from Rus. LC 75-5587. 257p. 1976. 53.95 (ISBN 0-470-51100-1). Halsted Pr.
Kurtz, jt. auth. see Boone.
Kurtz, David L. & Boone, Louis E. Marketing. LC 80-65788. 736p. 1981. text ed. 18.95 (ISBN 0-03-057431-5). Dryden Pr.
--Principles of Management. Incl. Student Mastery Guide. Baird, James, et al. 265p. wkbk. 5.95 (ISBN 0-394-32697-0). 624p. 1981. pap. text ed. 18.95 (ISBN 0-394-32246-0). Random.
Kurtz, David L., jt. auth. see Boone, Louis E.

Kurtz, David L., et al. Professional Selling. rev. ed. 1979. text ed. 16.95x (ISBN 0-256-02211-9). Business Pubns.

Kurtz, Edwin B. & Shoemaker, Thomas M. The Lineman's & Cableman's Handbook. 6th ed. 768p. Date not set. 32.50 (ISBN 0-07-035678-5, P&RB). McGraw. Postponed.

Kurtz, H. P. Public Relations & Fund Raising for Hospitals. (Illus.). 208p. 1980. 23.50 (ISBN 0-398-04082-6). C C Thomas.

Kurtz, Harold & Burrows, Margaret. Effective Use of Volunteers in Hospitals, Homes & Agencies. 132p. 1971. pap. 12.50 photocopy ed., spiral (ISBN 0-398-01069-2). C C Thomas.

Kurtz, Henry I. Captain John Smith. LC 75-20148. (Visual Biographies Ser). (Illus.). 64p. (gr. 4-6). 1976. PLB 4.90 o.p. (ISBN 0-531-01105-4). Watts.

Kurtz, John W. John Frederick Oberlin. rev. ed. LC 76-25211. 1977. lib. bdg. 24.50 o.p. (ISBN 0-89158-118-9). Westview.

Kurtz, Katherine. Camber of Culdi. 336p. 1976. pap. 1.95 o.p. (ISBN 0-345-24590-3). Ballantine.

--Deryni Checkmate. 1976. pap. 2.25 (ISBN 0-345-29224-3). Ballantine.

--Deryni Rising. 1976. pap. 2.25 (ISBN 0-345-29105-0). Ballantine.

--High Deryni. 1976. pap. 2.25 (ISBN 0-345-28614-6). Ballantine.

Kurtz, Laura S. Historical Dictionary of Tanzania. LC 77-25962. (African Historical Dictionaries Ser.: No. 15). 1978. 18.00 (ISBN 0-8108-1101-4). Scarecrow.

Kurtz, M. A. & Phillips, H. L. Technical Typewriting. (gr. 9 up). 1968. text ed. 14.95 (ISBN 0-201-03970-2). A-W.

Kurtz, Margaret, jt. auth. see Adams, Dorothy.

Kurtz, Max. Structural Engineering for Professional Engineer's Examination. 3rd ed. (Illus.). 1978. 19.50 (ISBN 0-07-035657-2, P&RB). McGraw.

Kurtz, O. Art Forgeries & How to Examine Paintings Scientifically. (Illus.). 1979. deluxe ed. 57.45 (ISBN 0-930582-32-2). Gloucester Art.

Kurtz, Paul, ed. A Secular Humanist Declaration. 40p. 81. pap. 1.95 (ISBN 0-87975-149-5). Prometheus Bks.

Kurtz, Paul W., ed. Classics in the History of Thought, 2 vols. Incl. Vol. 1. American Thought Before 1900. text ed. 5.95 (ISBN 0-685-22913-0, 56654); Vol. 2. American Philosophy in the Twentieth Century. text ed. 6.95 (ISBN 0-02-566550-2, 56655). 1966. Macmillan.

Kurtz, Regina & Van Gieson, Susan. Interior Planting Line Art. (Illus.). 1980. pap. text ed. 25.00 (ISBN 0-918436-13-3). Environ Design.

Kurtz, Richard A. Social Aspects of Mental Retardation. LC 76-42693. 1977. 18.95 (ISBN 0-669-01054-5). Lexington Bks.

Kurtz, Rosemary B. & Miller, Nancy F. Clinical Workbook in Medical-Surgical Nursing. (Illus.). 1978. pap. text ed. 9.95 (ISBN 0-7216-5580-7). Saunders.

Kurtz, Stephen G. Presidency of John Adams. LC 57-7764. 1957. 10.00x o.p. (ISBN 0-8122-7101-7). U of Pa Pr.

Kurtz, Stephen G. & Hutson, James H., eds. Essays on the American Revolution. 350p. 1973. pap. text ed. 5.95x (ISBN 0-393-09419-7). Norton.

Kurtz, V. Ray. Metrics for Elementary & Middle Schools. 120p. 1978. pap. 4.50 (ISBN 0-686-63709-7, 1714-5-06). NEA.

Kurtz, Venjamin P. The Pursuit of Death. 339p. 1980. Repr. of 1933 ed. lib. bdg. 30.00 (ISBN 0-8495-3051-2). Arden Lib.

Kurtzman, Joel, jt. ed. see Laszlo, Ervin.

Kurtzman, Neil A. & Martinez-Maldonado, Manuel. Pathophysiology of the Kidney. (Illus.). 1104p. 1977. 99.50 (ISBN 0-398-03600-4). C C Thomas.

Kurtzman, Neil A. & Rogers, Philip W. A Handbook of Urinalysis & Urinary Sediment. (Illus.). 112p. 1974. 12.75 (ISBN 0-398-02918-0). C C Thomas.

Kury, Gloria. The Early Work of Signorelli: 1465-1490. LC 77-94701. (Outstanding Dissertations in the Fine Arts Ser.). (Illus.). 1978. lib. bdg. 45.00 (ISBN 0-8240-3233-0). Garland Pub.

Kurylowicz, W., et al, eds. Numerical Taxonomy of Streptomycetes. (Illus.). 1975. 6.00 (ISBN 0-685-88610-7). Am Soc Microbio.

Kurz, Edmund P. & Ruhleder, Karl H., eds. Probleme Unserer Zeit. LC 72-130785. (Orig., Ger.). 1971. pap. text ed. 4.95x (ISBN 0-89197-359-1). Irvington.

Kurz, Otto, jt. auth. see Kris, Ernst.

Kurzban, Stan, et al. The Compleat Cruciverbalist: How to Solve & Compose Crossword Puzzles for Fun & Profit. 156p. 1980. 9.95 (ISBN 0-442-25738-4). Van Nos Reinhold.

Kurzhals, Ina W., jt. auth. see Halliday, Carol.

Kurzig, Carol, et al, eds. Foundation Grants to Individuals. 2nd ed. LC 79-90273. 236p. 1979. pap. 15.00 (ISBN 0-87954-025-7). Foundation Ctr.

Kurzig, Carol M. Foundation Fundamentals: A Guide for Grantseekers. LC 80-67501. (Illus.). 148p. (Orig.). 1980. pap. 4.95 (ISBN 0-87954-026-5). Foundation Ctr.

Kusche, Larry. The Disappearance of Flight Nineteen. (Illus.). 224p. 1981. 3.95 (ISBN 0-06-464044-2, BN4044, BN). Har-Row.

--Popcorn Cookery. LC 77-83276. 1977. pap. 7.95 (ISBN 0-912656-62-X). H P Bks.

Kusche, Lawrence D. The Bermuda Triangle Mystery Solved. 1975. pap. 2.50 (ISBN 0-446-91489-4). Warner Bks.

Kuschevsky, Ivan. Nikolai Negorev. Costello, Bella, tr. 1980. pap. 4.95 (ISBN 0-7145-0414-9). Riverrun NY.

Kuse, James & Luedke, Ralph D., eds. The Ideals Farmhouse Cookbook. 1978. pap. 2.95 o.p. (ISBN 0-89542-609-9). Ideals.

Kusel, George. The Marching Drummer's Companion. 2nd ed. 52p. 1981. pap. 4.95 (ISBN 0-9604476-0-1). Kusel.

--The Martial Musician's Mentor: A Complete Course of Instruction for the Fife, Pt. 1. rev., 2nd ed. (Illus.). 52p. (gr. 6 up). 1979. pap. 4.95 (ISBN 0-9604476-1-X). Kusel.

Kushel, Lillian. Fashion Textiles & Laboratory Workbook. 2nd ed. 1971. pap. 15.15 (ISBN 0-672-96046-X); wkbk & kit 28.75 (ISBN 0-672-96049-4); textile kit 15.50 (ISBN 0-686-68511-3). Bobbs.

Kushi, Aveline T. How to Cook with Miso. (Orig.). 1979. pap. 7.95 (ISBN 0-87040-450-4). Japan Pubns.

Kushi, Michio. The Book of Do-In: Exercise for Physical & Spiritual Development. (Illus.). 176p. (Orig.). 1979. pap. 10.95 (ISBN 0-87040-382-6). Japan Pubns.

--The Book of Macrobiotics: The Universal Way of Health & Happiness. LC 76-29341. (Illus.). 176p. (Orig.). 1977. pap. 10.95 (ISBN 0-87040-381-8). Japan Pubns.

--How to See Your Health: The Book of Oriental Diagnosis. LC 79-89346. (Illus.). 208p. (Orig.). 1980. pap. 9.95 (ISBN 0-87040-467-9). Japan Pubns.

Kushner, Bill, jt. auth. see Tatum, Jack.

Kushner, Harvey W. & De Maio, Gerald. Understanding Basic Statistics. LC 78-54195. 1980. text ed. 17.95 (ISBN 0-8162-4874-5); sol. manual 5.00 (0-8162-8475). Holden-Day.

Kushner, Howard I. & Sherrill, Anne H. John Milton Hay. (World Leaders Ser.: No. 69). 1977. lib. bdg. 12.50 (ISBN 0-8057-7719-9). Twayne.

Kushner, James A. Apartheid in America: An Historical & Legal Analysis of Contemporary Racial Residential Segregation in the United States. LC 80-67048. (Scholarly Monographs). 135p. 1980. pap. 12.00 (ISBN 0-8408-0509-8). Carrollton Pr.

Kushner, M. & Zucker, C. RPG: Language & Techniques. LC 73-8644. 1974. pap. 20.95 (ISBN 0-471-51117-X). Wiley.

Kushyar Ibn Labban. Principles of Hindu Reckoning. Levey, Martin, ed. Petruck, Marvin, tr. (Medieval Science Pubns., No. 8). 1965. 17.50x (ISBN 0-299-03610-3). U of Wis Pr.

Kusin, Vladimir V. Intellectual Origins of the Prague Spring: The Development of Reformist Ideas in Czechoslovakia, 1958-1967. (Soviet & East European Studies Monographs). 1971. 21.50 (ISBN 0-521-08124-6). Cambridge U Pr.

Kuskin, Karla. Dogs & Dragons, Trees & Dreams: A Collection of Poems. LC 79-2814. (Illus.). 96p. (gr. 1-6). 1980. 8.95 (ISBN 0-06-023543-8, HarpJ); PLB 8.79 (ISBN 0-06-023544-6). Har-Row.

--Night Again. (Illus.). 32p. (ps-1). 1981. 6.95 (ISBN 0-316-50721-0, Atlantic). Little.

Kusko, A. C., jt. auth. see Timbie, William H.

Kusko, Alexander, ed. see Veinott, Cyril G.

Kusler, Jon A. Regulating Sensitive Lands. 256p. 1980. 25.00 (ISBN 0-88410-095-2). Ballinger Pub.

Kusmer, Kenneth L. A Ghetto Takes Shape: Black Cleveland, 1870-1930. (Blacks in the New World Ser.). (Illus.). 320p. 1976. 15.00 (ISBN 0-252-00289-X); pap. 4.50 (ISBN 0-252-00690-9). U of Ill Pr.

Kusnetz, Len. Your Child Can Be a Super Reader. LC 79-84790. 128p. 1980. pap. 3.95. Liberty Pub.

--Your Child Can Be a Super-Reader: A Fun & Easy Approach to Reading Improvement. LC 79-84790. (Illus.). 132p. (Orig.). 1980. pap. 3.95 (ISBN 0-9602730-0-X, Dist. by Liberty Pub. Co). Learning Hse.

Kuspit, Donald B., ed. see Falkenheim, Jacqueline V.

Kuspit, Donald B., ed. see Foster, Stephen C.

Kuspit, Donald B., ed. see Gamwell, Lynn.

Kuspit, Donald B., ed. see Gelber, Lynne L.

Kuspit, Donald B., ed. see Halperin, Joan U.

Kuspit, Donald B., ed. see Janzen, Reinhild.

Kuspit, Donald B., ed. see Johnson, Lee M.

Kuspit, Donald B., ed. see Olson, Arlene R.

Kuspit, Donald B., ed. see Zemel, Carol M.

Kuster, Gustavo G. Hepatic Support in Acute Liver Failure. (Illus.). 320p. 1976. 31.75 (ISBN 0-398-03539-3). C C Thomas.

Kusterer, Ken. Know-How on the Job. 1978. lib. bdg. 20.00 o.p. (ISBN 0-89158-260-6). Westview.

Kusterer, Ken C. Know-How on the Job: The Important Working Knowledge of "Unskilled" Workers. (Westview Replica Edition Ser.). 202p. 1980. pap. text ed. 9.50x (ISBN 0-89158-916-3). Westview.

Kustom, R. L. Thyristor Networks for the Transfer of Energy Between Superconducting Coils. LC 79-5410. 1980. 23.00 (ISBN 0-299-08050-1). U of Wis Pr.

Kustra, Mary E., jt. ed. see Elliott, Norman F.

Kut, D. Heating & Hot Water Services in Buildings. 1968. 32.00 (ISBN 0-08-012218-3). Pergamon.

--Warm Air Heating. LC 71-122009. 1971. 42.00 (ISBN 0-08-015853-6); pap. 21.00 (ISBN 0-08-019006-5). Pergamon.

Kutak, Rosemary. I Am the Cat. 1964. pap. 0.95 o.s.i. (ISBN 0-02-022030-8, Collier). Macmillan.

Kutash, Irwin L., et al. Handbook on Stress & Anxiety: Contemporary Knowledge, Theory, & Treatment. LC 80-8014. (Social & Behavioral Science Ser.). 1980. text ed. 27.95x (ISBN 0-87589-478-X). Jossey-Bass.

Kuten, Jay. Coming Together, Coming Apart. LC 73-1961. 212p. 1974. 5.95 o.s.i. (ISBN 0-02-567000-X). Macmillan.

Kutie, Rita & Huffman, Virginia. The WP Book. LC 79-18274. 1980. pap. text ed. 10.95 (ISBN 0-471-03881-4); study guide avail. (ISBN 0-471-07863-8). Wiley.

Kutler, Stanley E., ed. see Wolters, Raymond.

Kutner, Marc L., jt. auth. see Pasachoff, Jay M.

Kutsche, Paul & Van Ness, John R. Canones: Values, Crisis, & Survival in a Northern New Mexico Village. (Illus.). 280p. 1981. 17.50x (ISBN 0-8263-0570-9). U of NM Pr.

Kutscher, A. H., jt. auth. see Seeland, Irene.

Kutscher, Austin H. Death & Bereavement. 392p. 1974. 16.75 (ISBN 0-398-01070-6); pap. 12.50 (ISBN 0-398-03293-9). C C Thomas.

Kutscher, Austin H. & Goldberg, Ivan K. Oral Care of the Aging & Dying Patient. (American Lectures in Dentistry Ser.). (Illus.). 236p. 1973. text ed. 17.50 (ISBN 0-398-02714-5). C C Thomas.

Kutscher, Austin H., jt. auth. see Bane, Donald.

Kutscher, Austin H. see Reiffel, James, et al.

Kutscher, Lillian G., ed. see McGill, Frances.

Kuttner, Monroe S. Managing the Paperwork Pipeline: Achieving Cost-Effective Paperwork & Information Processing. LC 77-15041. 1978. 27.95 (ISBN 0-471-03154-2, Pub. by Wiley-Interscience). Wiley.

Kuttner, Paul. The Man Who Lost Everything. LC 76-17142. 352p. 1976. 8.95 (ISBN 0-8069-0152-7); lib. bdg. 7.49 (ISBN 0-8069-0153-5). Sterling.

Kuttner, Paul, tr. see Bauzen, Peter & Bauzen, Susanne.

Kuttner, Paul, tr. see Strose, Susanne.

Kuttner, Paul, tr. see Zechlin, Katharina.

Kuttner, Stephan. Medieval Councils, Decretals & Collections of Canon Law: Selected Essays. 338p. 1980. 75.00x (ISBN 0-86078-071-6, Pub. by Variorum England). State Mutual Bk.

Kuttruff, H. Room Acoustics. LC 73-16149. (Illus.). 298p. 1973. 43.95 (ISBN 0-470-51105-2). Halsted Pr.

Kuttruff, K. H. Room Acoustics. 2nd ed. (Illus.). 1979. 49.20x (ISBN 0-85334-813-8, Pub. by Applied Science). Burgess-Intl Ideas.

Kutty, K. Madhaven, jt. auth. see Subrahmanyam, Sarada.

Kutty, K. Madhaven, jt. ed. see Subrahmanyam, Sarada.

Kuttykrishnan, P. C. The Beloved. Menon, R. R., tr. from Malayalam. 194p. 1975. pap. 2.80 (ISBN 0-88253-696-6). Ind-US Inc.

Kutz, Myer. Midtown North. 1976. pap. 1.25 o.p. (ISBN 0-685-69154-3, LB351ZK, Leisure Bks). Nordon Pubns.

Kutza, Elizabeth A. The Benefits of Old Age: Social Welfare Policies for the Elderly. LC 80-24241. 192p. 1981. lib. bdg. 18.00 (ISBN 0-226-46565-9); pap. 5.95 (ISBN 0-226-46566-7). U of Chicago Pr.

Kutzbach, J. E., jt. ed. see Bryson, R. E.

Kuusi, Juha. Host State & the Transnational Corporation. 1980. text ed. 25.25x (ISBN 0-566-00249-3, Pub. by Gower Pub Co England). Renouf.

Kuvas, J., ed. Boss Nineteen Seventy-Six: Proceedings of an International Conference on the Behavior of off-Shore Structures, Norwegian Institute of Technology, Trondheim, 2-5 August 1976. LC 77-75338. 1977. text ed. 110.00 o.p. (ISBN 0-08-021739-7). Pergamon.

Kuvshinoff, B. W., et al, eds. Fire Sciences Dictionary. LC 77-3489. 1977. 20.50 (ISBN 0-471-51113-7, Pub. by Wiley-Interscience). Wiley.

Kuwata, Mashiro. Theory & Practice of Ceramo Metal Restorations. (Illus.). 150p. 1980. 58.00 (ISBN 0-931386-15-2). Quint Pub Co.

Kuwayama, George. Chinese Jade from Southern California Collections. LC 76-43233. (Illus.). 1976. pap. 4.95 o.p. (ISBN 0-87587-074-0). LA Co Art Mus.

Kuwayama, George, jt. auth. see Keyes, Roger.

Kuyk, W., ed. see International Summer School, University of Antwerp, 1972.

Kuykendall, Crystal. Developing Leadership for Parent-Citizen Groups. 1976. pap. 3.50 (ISBN 0-934460-02-7). NCCE.

Kuykendall, Jack L., jt. auth. see Unsinger, Peter C.

Kuykendall, John W., jt. auth. see Lingle, Walter L.

Kuyper, Lester. The Scripture Unbroken. 1978. pap. 6.95 o.p. (ISBN 0-8028-1734-3). Eerdmans.

Kuzma, Jan & Kuzma, Jay. Building Character. LC 79-83592. (Harvest Ser.). 1979. pap. 4.50 (ISBN 0-8163-0233-2, 02625-2). Pacific Pr Pub Assn.

Kuzma, Jay, jt. auth. see Kuzma, Jan.

Kuzma, Kay. Understanding Children. LC 78-50449. (Harvest Ser.). 1978. pap. 3.95 (ISBN 0-8163-0212-X, 21198-7). Pacific Pr Pub Assn.

Kuzmanovic, B. O. & Williams, N. Steel Design for Structural Engineers. (Illus.). 1977. 25.95 (ISBN 0-13-846352-2). P-H.

Kuzmin, A. D. & Salomonovich, A. E. Radioastronomical Methods of Antenna Measurements. (Electrical Science Monographs). 1967. 27.50 (ISBN 0-12-431150-4). Acad Pr.

Kuz'Minskii, A. S., ed. Ageing & Stabilisation of Polymers. Leyland, B. N., tr. from Rus. (Illus.). 1971. text ed. 48.50x (ISBN 0-444-20076-2, Pub. by Applied Science). Burgess-Intl Ideas.

Kuznets, Simon. Population, Capital & Growth. 1974. 14.95x (ISBN 0-393-05497-7). Norton.

--Six Lectures on Economic Growth. LC 59-13596. 1959. 19.95 (ISBN 0-02-917700-6). Free Pr.

Kuznetsov, B., ed. Russian-English Polytechnical Dictionary. LC 80-41193. 900p. 1981. 100.00 (ISBN 0-08-023609-X). Pergamon.

Kuznetsov, Boris, tr. see Bessonov, L.

Kvale, O., jt. ed. see Hoyem, T.

Kvam, Wayne. Hemingway in Germany. LC 79-181689. x, 214p. 1973. 12.95x (ISBN 0-8214-0126-2). Ohio U Pr.

Kvan, Erik, tr. see From, Franz.

Kvasnicka, Robert M. & Viola, Herman J., eds. The Commissioners of Indian Affairs, 1824-1977. LC 79-12336. 1979. 19.75x (ISBN 0-8032-2700-0). U of Nebr Pr.

Kvavik, Robert B. Interest Groups in Norwegian Politics. 1976. pap. 17.00x (ISBN 8-200-01477-0, Dist. by Columbia U Pr). Universitet.

Kviz, Frederick J. & Knafl, Kathleen A. Statistics for Nurses: An Introductory Text. 330p. 1980. pap. text ed. 9.95 (ISBN 0-316-50750-4). Little.

Kvols-Riedler, Bill & Kvols-Riedler, Kathy. Understanding Yourself & Others. (Illus.). 222p. (Orig.). 1981. pap. 6.95 (ISBN 0-933450-01-X). RDIC Pubns.

Kvols-Riedler, Kathy, jt. auth. see Kvols-Riedler, Bill.

Kwak, N. K. Mathematical Programming with Business Applications. (Illus.). 384p. 1972. text ed. 21.50 (ISBN 0-07-035717-X, C); instructor's manual 4.95 (ISBN 0-07-035718-8). McGraw.

Kwak, No Kyoon & DeLurgio, Stephen A. Quantitative Models for Business Decisions. LC 78-27175. (Illus.). 1979. text ed. 19.95 (ISBN 0-87872-215-7). Duxbury Pr.

Kwakernaak, Huibert & Sivan, Raphael. Linear Optimal Control Systems. LC 72-3576. 544p. 1972. 44.00 (ISBN 0-471-51110-2, Pub. by Wiley-Interscience). Wiley.

Kwang, Eu-Yang. Political Reconstruction of China. (Studies in Chinese Government & Law). 190p. 1977. Repr. of 1922 ed. 18.50 (ISBN 0-89093-058-9). U Pubns Amer.

Kwanten, Luc & Hesse, Susan. Tangut (Hsi Hsia) Studies: A Bibliography. Sinor, Denis, ed. (Indiana University Uralic & Altaic Ser.: Vol. 137). 125p. 1980. pap. text ed. 9.00 (ISBN 0-933070-05-5). Ind U Res Inst.

Kwapinski, J. B., ed. Molecular Microbiology. LC 80-11813. 494p. 1981. Repr. of 1974 ed. lib. bdg. write for info. (ISBN 0-89874-148-3). Krieger.

Kwapiszewski, Michael, tr. see Modjeska, Helena.

Kwawer, Jay S. & Lerner, Howard D., eds. Borderline Phenomena & the Rorschach Test. 515p. 1980. text ed. 30.00 (ISBN 0-8236-0577-9, 00-0577). Intl Univs Pr.

Kwiatkowska, Hanna Y. Family Therapy & Evaluation Through Art. (Illus.). 304p. 1978. 26.75 (ISBN 0-398-03729-9). C C Thomas.
Kwiatkowski, Diana. Panorama. (Gusto Press Poetry Discovery Ser.). 61p. 1979. 9.00 (ISBN 0-933906-07-2). Gusto Pr.
Kwiatkowski, Diana, ed. The Poet Pope. 67p. 1981. 9.50 (ISBN 0-933906-16-1); pap. 4.50 (ISBN 0-933906-15-3). Gusto Pr.
Kwiatkowski, Joan, jt. auth. see Shribert, Lawrence D.
Kwitko, Marvin L. & Praeger, Donald L. Pseudophakia: Current Trends & Concepts. (Illus.). 456p. 1980. lib. bdg. 50.00 (ISBN 0-683-04800-7). Williams & Wilkins.
Kwitny, Jonathan. Vicious Circles: The Mafia in the Marketplace. 432p. 1981. pap. 6.95 (ISBN 0-393-00029-X). Norton.
Kwitz, Mary. Little Chick's Big Day. LC 80-7905. (Early I Can Read Bks.). (Illus.). 32p. (ps-3). 1981. 6.95 (ISBN 0-06-023667-1, HarpJ); PLB 7.89g (ISBN 0-06-023668-X). Har-Row.
Kwo, David, ed. Chinese Brushwork. 200p. 1981. text ed. 46.50 (ISBN 0-8390-0267-X). Allanheld.
Kwock, C. H. & McHugh, Vincent, trs. Old Friend from Far Away: One Hundred Fifty Chinese Poems from the Great Dynasties. 192p. 1980. 15.00 (ISBN 0-86547-017-0); pap. 6.50 (ISBN 0-86547-018-9). N Point Pr.
Kwok, D. W. Scientism in Chinese Thought, 1900-1950. LC 73-162297. 231p. 1972. Repr. of 1965 ed. 12.00x (ISBN 0-8196-0275-2). Biblo.
Kwong, Laura. Dark Eyes of the Soul. (Illus.). 1979. pap. cancelled (ISBN 0-9601428-6-X). Entwhistle Bks.
Kwong Ki Chaou. Dictionary of English Phrases with Illustrative Sentences. LC 74-136559. (Illus.). 1971. Repr. of 1881 ed. 38.00 (ISBN 0-8103-3386-4). Gale.
Kwun Sup Chung, et al. Modernization & Its Impact Upon Korean Law. (Korea Research Monographs: No. 3). 150p. 1981. pap. 12.50 (ISBN 0-686-69422-8). IEAS Ctr Chinese Stud.
Kybett, Harry. The Complete Handbook of Videocassette Recorders. LC 77-79347. (Illus.). 1977. 9.95 o.p. (ISBN 0-8306-7811-5); pap. 5.95 o.p. (ISBN 0-8306-6811-X, 811). TAB Bks.
Kyd, Stewart. A Treatise on the Law of Corporations, 2 vols. Berkowitz, David & Thorne, Samuel, eds. LC 77-86637. (Classics of English Legal History in the Modern Era Ser.: Vol. 89). 1979. Repr. of 1794 ed. Set. lib. bdg. 55.00 ea. (ISBN 0-8240-3076-1). Garland Pub.
Kyd, T., tr. see Tasso, Torquato.
Kyd, Thomas. The First Part of Hieronimo. Cairncross, Andrew S., ed. Bd. with The Spanish Tragedy. LC 66-20826. (Regent Renaissance Drama Ser). 1967. 10.95x (ISBN 0-8032-0267-9); pap. 2.65x (ISBN 0-8032-5267-6, BB 221, Bison). U of Nebr Pr.
Kydonieus, Agis F. Controlled Release Theologies, 2 vols. 1980. Vol. 1, 272p. 69.95 (ISBN 0-8493-5641-5); Vol. 2, 288p. 69.95 (ISBN 0-8493-5642-3). CRC Pr.
Kyes, Joan J. & Hofling, Charles K. Basic Psychiatric Concepts in Nursing. 4th ed. LC 79-23254. 736p. 1980. text ed. 17.75 (ISBN 0-397-54246-1). Lippincott.
Kyle. Sylvia Plath: A Dramatic Portrait. 1976. pap. 4.95 (ISBN 0-571-10698-6, Pub. by Faber & Faber). Merrimack Bk Serv.
Kyle, James. Crohn's Disease. (Illus.). 1972. 17.50x (ISBN 0-433-18900-2). Intl Ideas.
--Electronics Unraveled: A New Commonsense Approach. LC 74-79583. (Illus.). 228p. 1974. pap. 5.95 o.p. (ISBN 0-8306-3691-9, 691). TAB Bks.
Kyle, Louisa V. Country Woman's Scrapbook. Dunn, Joseph, ed. LC 80-84557. (Illus.). 120p. 1980. 10.95 (ISBN 0-938694-02-2). JCP Corp VA.
Kyle, R. A. & Shampo, M. A. Medicine & Stamps, 2 vols. LC 79-26733. 528p. 1980. Vol. 1. lib. bdg. 11.50 (ISBN 0-89874-085-1); Vol. 2. lib. bdg. 13.50 (ISBN 0-89874-072-X); Set. lib. bdg. 20.00 (ISBN 0-89874-234-X). Krieger.
Kyle, Robert A. & Bayrd, Edwin A. The Monoclonal Gammopathies: Multiple Myeloma & Related Plasma-Cell Disorders. (Amer. Lec. Living Chemistry Ser.). (Illus.). 432p. 1976. 48.75 (ISBN 0-398-03545-8). C C Thomas.
Kyles, I. & Sumner, R. Tests of Attainment Mathematics in Schools: Vol. 2, Continuation of Monitoring Feasibility Study, Vol. 1. (Occasional Reports Ser.: No. 2). (Illus.). 1977. pap. text ed. 9.00x (ISBN 0-85633-135-X, NFER). Humanities.
Kylie, Edward, tr. see Boniface, St., et al.
Kyne, Peter. The Long Chance. 1976. lib. bdg. 14.85x (ISBN 0-89968-054-2). Lightyear.
--Valley of the Giants. 1976. lib. bdg. 17.25x (ISBN 0-89968-056-9). Lightyear.
Kyner, James H. & Daniel, Hawthorne. End of Track. LC 60-12942. (Illus.). 1960. pap. 2.75 (ISBN 0-8032-5115-7, BB 101, Bison). U of Nebr Pr.
Kyner, Walter T., jt. auth. see Moser, Jurgen.
Kyrala, A. Applied Functions of a Complex Variable. LC 74-176285. 1972. 35.00 (ISBN 0-471-51129-3, Pub. by Wiley-Interscience). Wiley.
Kyriacou, Demetrios. Basics of Electroorganic Synthesis. 230p. 1980. 24.50 (ISBN 0-471-07975-8, Pub. by Wiley-Interscience). Wiley.
Kyriakopoulos, Irene, jt. auth. see Binkin, Martin.
Kyriss, S. E. & Dodge, D. O. Seamanship: Fundamentals for the Deck Officer. 2nd ed. LC 80-81089. (Fundamentals of Naval Science: Vol. 2). 272p. 1981. text ed. 16.95 (ISBN 0-87021-613-9). Naval Inst Pr.
Kyrk, Hazel. The Family in the American Economy. LC 53-12266. (Midway Reprint). (Illus.). 1976. pap. text ed. 18.00x (ISBN 0-226-46621-3). U of Chicago Pr.
Kysar, Robert. John, the Maverick Gospel. LC 76-12393. (Biblical Foundations Ser.). 1976. pap. 4.95 (ISBN 0-8042-0302-4). John Knox.
Kysar, Robert & Kaysar, Myrna. The Asundered: Biblical Teachings on Divorce & Remarriage. LC 77-79591. 1978. 6.95 (ISBN 0-8042-1096-9). John Knox.
Kyte, Barbara & Greenberg, Kathy. Low Calorie Way. LC 80-84335. (Illus.). 1981. pap. 2.50 (ISBN 0-915942-17-8). Owlswood Prods.
--Versatile Vegetables. LC 80-83403. (Illus.). 1980. pap. 2.50 (ISBN 0-915942-16-X). Owlswood Prods.
Kytle, Ray, Jr. Concepts in Context: Aspects of the Writer's Craft. LC 73-16245. 208p. 1974. 10.50 (ISBN 0-471-51127-7). Wiley.

L

L. H. Selman Ltd., ed. see Ingold, Gerard.
L. Sachse & Co. Full-Color Uniforms of the Prussian Army: Seventy-Two Plates from the Year 1830. (Illus.). 80p. 1981. pap. price not set (ISBN 0-486-24085-1). Dover.
La, Ruth E. & Kinderman, Katherine S. In the Eye of the Typhoon. LC 80-7937. (Illus.). 288p. 1980. 12.95 (ISBN 0-15-144374-2). HarBraceJ.
la, Walter Mare de see De La Mare, Walter.
Laak, Rein. Wastewater Engineering Design for Unsewered Areas. LC 80-65509. (Illus.). 172p. 1980. 28.00 (ISBN 0-250-40373-0). Ann Arbor Science.
Laakso, Elia, ed. see Central Statistical Office of Finland.
Laane, Henk-Maarten. The Arterial Pole of the Embryonic Heart. 160p. 1978. pap. text ed. 26.50 (ISBN 90-265-0297-4, Pub. by Swets Pub Serv Holland). Swets North Am.
Labalme, Patricial H., ed. Beyond Their Sex: Learned Women of the European Past. LC 79-56638. 208p. 1980. 17.50x (ISBN 0-8147-4998-4). NYU Pr.
Laban. Modern Educational Dance. (Orig.). 1980. pap. 5.95 (ISBN 0-8238-0165-9). Plays.
Laban, Rudolf. Life for Dance. LC 74-32538. (Illus.). 1975. 10.45 (ISBN 0-87830-073-2). Theatre Arts.
La Barba, Richard. Foundations of Developmental Psychology. LC 80-615. 1980. lib ed 18.95 (ISBN 0-12-432350-2); write for info. (ISBN 0-12-432355-3). Acad Pr.
LaBarca, Angela, jt. auth. see Hendrickson, James M.
La Barca Pedro Calderon, De see Calderon De La Barca, Pedro.
Labaree, Benjamin W. The Boston Tea Party. 2nd ed. (Illus.). 347p. 1981. Repr. of 1966 ed. price not set (ISBN 0-930350-16-2). NE U Pr.
La Barge, Lura. Basketmaking from the Beginning. LC 75-38908. (Funk & W Bk.). (Illus.). 112p. 1976. 7.95 o.s.i. (ISBN 0-308-10243-6, TYC-T); pap. 4.95 o.s.i. (ISBN 0-308-10244-4, TYC-T). T Y Crowell.
LaBarge, Lura, jt. auth. see Hartzell, Warren.
Labarge, Margaret W. A Baronial Household of the Thirteenth Century. (Illus.). 235p. 1980. 22.50x (ISBN 0-389-20068-9); pap. 9.95x (ISBN 0-389-20034-4). B&N.
--Court, Church & Castle. (Illus.). 112p. 1972. pap. 2.95 (ISBN 0-88884-431-X, 56310-3, Pub. by Natl Mus Canada). U of Chicago Pr.
--Gascony: England's First Colony 1204-1453. (Illus.). 276p. 1980. 24.50x (ISBN 0-389-20142-1). B&N.
LaBarr, Dorothy F. & Singer, J. David. The Study of International Politics: A Guide to the Sources for the Student, Teacher, & Researcher. LC 76-12545. 211p. 1976. text ed. 10.00 (ISBN 0-87436-233-4). ABC-Clio.
Labarre, Anthony E. Elementary Mathematical Analysis. 1961. 15.95 (ISBN 0-201-04110-3). A-W.
Labarre, E. J. Dictionary & Encyclopaedia of Paper & Paper-Making. 2nd, rev. ed. 500p. 1952. text ed. 71.50 (ISBN 90-265-0037-8, Pub. by Swets Pub Serv Holland). Swets North Am.
Labarre, Harriet. Live Alone & Be Happier Than Anybody. 1977. pap. 1.75 o.p. (ISBN 0-445-08613-0). Popular Lib.
La Barre, Weston. Culture in Context: Selected Writings of Weston La Barre. LC 78-74728. (Illus.). viii, 338p. 1980. 19.75 (ISBN 0-8223-0424-4). Duke.
Labastida, Aurora, jt. auth. see Ets, Marie H.
LaBastille, Anne. Assignment Wildlife. (Illus.). 1980. 11.95 (ISBN 0-525-05910-5). Dutton.
--The Opossums. Bourne, Russell & Rifkin, Natalie, eds. LC 73-89876. (Ranger Rick's Best Friends Ser.: No. 2). (Illus.). 32p. (gr. 1-6). 1974. 2.50 o.p. (ISBN 0-912186-08-9). Natl Wildlife.
--The Seal Family. Bourne, Russell & Rifkin, Natalie, eds. LC 73-91356. (Ranger Rick's Best Friends Ser.: No. 2). (Illus.). 32p. (gr. 1-6). 1974. 2.50 o.p. (ISBN 0-912186-09-7). Natl Wildlife.
--White-Tailed Deer. Bourne, Russell & Lawrence, Bonnie S., eds. (Ranger Rick's Best Friends Ser.: No. 1). (Illus.). (gr. 1-6). 1973. 2.50 o.p. (ISBN 0-912186-00-3). Natl Wildlife.
--Wild Bobcats. Bourne, Russell & Lawrence, Bonnie S., eds. LC 73-89875. (Ranger Rick's Best Friends Ser.: No. 2). (Illus.). 32p. (gr. 1-6). 1973. 2.50 (ISBN 0-912186-07-0). Natl Wildlife.
--Women & Wilderness: Women in Wilderness Professions & Lifestyles. LC 80-14369. (Illus.). 320p. 1980. 12.95 (ISBN 0-87156-234-0). Sierra.
--Woodswoman. LC 75-34071. 1976. 10.95 (ISBN 0-525-23715-1); pap. 4.50 (ISBN 0-525-47504-4). Dutton.
Labat, Elisabeth-Paule. The Presence of God. Smith, N. D., tr. from Fr. LC 80-82089. Orig. Title: Presences De Dieu. 224p. 1980. pap. 7.95 (ISBN 0-8091-2336-3). Paulist Pr.
Labat, Rene. L' Akkadien de Boghaz-Koi. LC 78-72748. (Ancient Mesopotamian Texts & Studies). 1979. Repr. of 1932 ed. 37.50 (ISBN 0-685-91790-8). Ams Pr.
L'Abate, Bess, jt. auth. see L'Abate, Luciano.
Labate, Christina, jt. auth. see Platt, Jerome.
L'Abate, Luciano & L'Abate, Bess. How to Avoid Divorce. LC 76-12389. 1976. pap. 4.95 (ISBN 0-8042-1118-3). John Knox.
LaBau, Tom, jt. auth. see Quick, John.
Labay, jt. auth. see Boyarsky.
Labbe, Dominique. Le Discours Communiste. 1977. lib. bdg. 27.50x o.p. (ISBN 2-7246-0380-X); pap. 20.00x o.p. (ISBN 0-685-86514-2). Clearwater Pub.
Labbett, Peter. Military Small Arms Ammunition of the World, 1945-1980. (Illus.). 160p. 1980. 18.95 (ISBN 0-89141-116-X). Presidio Pr.
La Beau, Dennis, ed. Author Biographies Master Index, 2 vols. LC 76-27212. (Gale Biographical Index: No. 3). 1978. Set. 98.00 (ISBN 0-8103-1085-6). Gale.
--Theatre, Film, & TV Biographies Master Index. 1st ed. LC 77-2470. (Gale Biographical Index Ser.: No. 5). 1979. 52.00 (ISBN 0-8103-1081-3). Gale.
LaBeau, Dennis & Tarbert, Gary, eds. Biographical Dictionaries Master Index - 1975-76: A Guide to More Than 800,000 Listings in Over 50 Current Who's Whos & Other Works of Collective Biography, 3 vols. LC 75-19059. (Gale Biographical Index: No. 1). 1975. 140.00 (ISBN 0-8103-1077-5). Gale.
LaBelle, Maurice M. Alfred Jarry: Nihilism & the Theatre of the Absurd. LC 79-3009. (The Gotham Library). 1980. 15.00x (ISBN 0-8147-4995-X); pap. 7.00x (ISBN 0-8147-4996-8). NYU Pr.
Laber, Jeri. Woman's Day Plain & Fancy Ground Beef Cookbook. 1978. 8.95 (ISBN 0-394-41372-5). Random.
LaBerge, Armand J., jt. auth. see Fryklund, Verne C.
Labiche, Eugene M. Italian Straw Hat. Davies, Frederick, tr. Bd. with Spelling Mistakes. LC 67-28051. (Orig.). (gr. 8up). 1967. pap. 2.65x (ISBN 0-87830-543-2). Theatre Arts.
Labor, Earle. Jack London. (U. S. Authors Ser.: No. 230). 184p. 1974. lib. bdg. 10.95 (ISBN 0-8057-0455-8). Twayne.
Laborde, E. D., tr. see Gourou, Pierre.
LaBossiere, Eileen. Histological Processing for the Neural Sciences. (Illus.). 100p. 1976. pap. 10.75 (ISBN 0-398-03516-4). C C Thomas.
Labov, William. Language in the Inner City: Studies in the Black English Vernacular. LC 72-80376. (Conduct & Communication Ser). 438p. 1973. text ed. 18.00x (ISBN 0-8122-7658-2); pap. 7.95x (ISBN 0-685-29061-1, Pa Paperbks). U of Pa Pr.
--Sociolinguistic Patterns. LC 72-80375. (Conduct & Communication Ser). 360p. 1973. 15.00x (ISBN 0-8122-7657-4); pap. 6.95x (ISBN 0-8122-1052-2, Pa Paperbks). U of Pa Pr.
Labov, William, ed. Locating Language in Time & Space, Vol. I. LC 80-757. (Quantitative Analysis of Linguistic Structure Ser.). 1980. 24.50 (ISBN 0-12-432101-1). Acad Pr.
Labov, William, ed. see Weinreich, Uriel.
Labowitz, L. C. & Arents, J. S. Physical Chemistry Problems & Solutions. 1969. text ed. 12.95 (ISBN 0-12-432150-X). Acad Pr.
Labrie, Fernand, et al, eds. Hypothalamus & Endocrine Functions. LC 76-13912. (Current Topics in Molecular Endocrinology Ser.: Vol. 3). 508p. 1976. 42.50 (ISBN 0-306-34003-8, Plenum Pr). Plenum Pub.
Labrie, Roger, ed. SALT Handbook: Key Documents & Issues, 1972-1979. 1979. pap. 12.25 (ISBN 0-8447-3316-4). Am Enterprise.
Labriola, Antonio. Socialism & Philosophy. LC 79-90007. 223p. 1980. 12.00 (ISBN 0-914386-21-2); pap. 4.50 (ISBN 0-914386-22-0). Telos Pr.
Labrousse, E., ed. see Bayle, Pierre.
Labrow, S., jt. auth. see Manning, W. R.
Labuza, T. P. & Sloan, A. Elizabeth. Food for Thought. 2nd ed. (Illus.). 1977. pap. text ed. 8.50 (ISBN 0-87055-244-9). AVI.
Labuza, Theodore P. Food & Your Well-Being. (Illus.). 1977. pap. text ed. 11.95 (ISBN 0-8299-0129-9); instrs.' manual & study guide 4.95 (ISBN 0-8299-0162-0). West Pub.
Laby, T. H., jt. auth. see Kaye, G. W.
Labys, Walter & Granger, Clive W. Speculation, Hedging, & Commodity Price Forecasts. 1971. 19.95 (ISBN 0-669-61051-8). Lexington Bks.
Labys, Walter C. Market Structure, Bargaining Power, & Resource Price Formation. LC 78-19541. 256p. 1980. 23.95 (ISBN 0-669-02511-9). Lexington Bks.
Labys, Walter C., ed. Quantitative Models of Commodity Markets. LC 74-13784. 400p. 1975. text ed. 25.00 o.p. (ISBN 0-88410-254-8). Ballinger Pub.
Labys, Walter C., et al, eds. Commodity Markets & Latin American Development: A Modeling Approach. LC 79-16533. 1980. 25.00 (ISBN 0-88410-481-8). Ballinger Pub.
La Capria, Raffaele. The Mortal Wound. Waldman, M., tr. from It. Orig. Title: Ferito a Morte. 1964. 4.75 o.p. (ISBN 0-374-21317-8). FS&G.
La Casce, Steward, jt. auth. see Balanger, Terry.
Lacasse, Walter J., jt. auth. see Carpenter, Stanley J.
Lacaze, Andre. Tunnel at Loibl Pass. Dower, W. Barrett, tr. LC 79-7112. 1981. 14.95 (ISBN 0-385-15015-6). Doubleday.
Lacaze, Charlotte. The Vie De St. Denis Manuscript. LC 78-74369. (Fine Arts Dissertations, Fourth Ser.). (Illus.). 1980. lib. bdg. 50.00 (ISBN 0-8240-3957-2). Garland Pub.
Laccetti, Silvio R., ed. The Outlook on New Jersey. new ed. LC 79-64897. 488p. 1979. 14.95x (ISBN 0-8349-7540-8). W H Wise.
Lace, Vivian, ed. Ohio Industrial Directory: 1981. rev. ed. LC 75-42929. (Illus., Annual). 1981. 65.00 (ISBN 0-916512-55-X). Harris Pub.
LaCerra, Charles, Jr. Looking at the American Government: Past & Present. LC 78-61390. 1978. pap. text ed. 9.00 (ISBN 0-8191-0602-X). U Pr of Amer.
Lacey, A. R. A Dictionary of Philosophy. 1976. 16.00x (ISBN 0-7100-8361-0). Routledge & Kegan.
Lacey, Douglas R. Dissent & Parliamentary Politics in England 1661-1689: A Study in the Perpetuation & Tempering of Parliamentarianism. 1969. 35.00 (ISBN 0-8135-0594-1). Rutgers U Pr.
Lacey, E. A., tr. see Zapata, Luis.
Lacey, Henry C. To Raise, Destroy, & Create. LC 80-50078. 1981. 15.00 (ISBN 0-87875-185-8). Whitston Pub.
Lacey, Jim & Keough, Allen. Radiation Curing: A Discussion of Advantages, Features & Applications. LC 80-52815. (Illus.). 89p. (Orig.). 1980. pap. text ed. 8.50 (ISBN 0-87263-060-9). SME.
Lacey, John M., jt. auth. see Flamholtz, Eric G.
Lacey, P. R. Life with the Mentally Sick Child. LC 71-97950. 1970. 11.25 (ISBN 0-08-006978-9); pap. 5.75 (ISBN 0-08-006977-0). Pergamon.
Lacey, Robert E., ed. see Membrane Processes for Industry, Symposium, May 19-20, 1966.
Lacey, Roy. Cowpasture: The Every Day Life of an English Allotment. LC 79-56041. (Illus.). 1980. 17.95 (ISBN 0-7153-7916-X). David & Charles.
Lach, Donald F. & Wehrle, Edmund S. International Politics in East Asia Since World War Two. LC 75-58. (Illus.). 400p. 1975. text ed. 27.95 o.p. (ISBN 0-275-05420-9); pap. text ed. 8.95 o.p. (ISBN 0-275-89380-4). Praeger.
LaChapelle, Dolores. D. H. Lawrence: Future Primitive. LC 80-67900. 1981. 12.95 (ISBN 0-89615-027-5); pap. 7.95 (ISBN 0-89615-028-3). Guild of Tutors.

LaChapelle, Edward R. Field Guide to Snow Crystals. LC 70-85215. (Illus.). 108p. 1969. pap. 7.95 (ISBN 0-295-95040-4). U of Wash Pr.

Lachar, David & Gdowski, Charles. Actuarial Assesment of Child & Adolescent Personality: An Interpretive Guide for the Personality Inventory for Children Profile. LC 79-66985. 186p. 1979. text ed. 19.75x (ISBN 0-87424-305-X). Western Psych.

La Charite, Raymond, jt. tr. see La Charite, Raymond C.

La Charite, Raymond C. & La Charite, Raymond, trs. Bonaventure Des Periers's Novel Pastimes & Merry Tales. LC 70-190532. (Studies in Romance Languages: No. 6). 264p. 1972. 13.00x (ISBN 0-8131-1279-6). U Pr of Ky.

La Charite, Virginia A. Henri Michaux. (World Authors Ser.: No. 465). 1977. lib. bdg. 11.95 (ISBN 0-8057-6302-3). Twayne.

La Chavignerie, Emile B. De see De La Chavignerie, Emile B. & Auvray, Louis.

Lachenmeyer, Charles. Productive Performance. (Analysis). 51p. (Orig.). 1980. pap. text ed. 14.95 (ISBN 0-938526-01-4). Inst Analysis.

Lachenmeyer, Charles W. The Essence of Social Research: A Copernican Revolution. LC 72-87692. 1973. 14.95 (ISBN 0-02-917720-0). Free Pr.

--Language of Sociology. LC 72-164501. 125p. 1971. 15.00x (ISBN 0-231-03556-X); pap. 6.00x (ISBN 0-231-08338-6). Columbia U Pr.

Lachenmeyer, Juliana R., jt. auth. see Gibbs, Margaret S.

Lacher, Mortimer J., ed. Hodgkin's Disease. LC 75-25644. 464p. 1976. 50.50 (ISBN 0-471-51149-8, Pub. by Wiley Medical). Wiley.

Lachman, Ernest & Faulkner, Kenneth K. Case Studies in Anatomy. 3rd ed. (Illus.). 432p. 1981. pap. text ed. 9.95x (ISBN 0-19-502813-9). Oxford U Pr.

Lachman, L., jt. ed. see Lieberman, H.

Lachman, Ruth. Boats. (ps-1). 1951. PLB 4.57 o.p. (ISBN 0-307-61501-4, Golden Pr). Western Pub.

Lachman, Sheldon J. Psychosomatic Disorders: A Behavioristic Interpretation. LC 78-37936. (Approaches to Behavior Pathology Ser.). 1972. pap. text ed. 10.95 (ISBN 0-471-51146-3). Wiley.

Lachmann, Karl. Kleinere Schriften 2. Band: Zur Classischen Philologie. Vahlen, J., ed. viii, 274p. 1974. Repr. of 1876 ed. 38.25x (ISBN 3-11-002399-7). De Gruyter.

Lachmann, Ludwig M. Capital & Its Structure. LC 77-82807. (Studies in Economic Theory). 130p. 1977. 15.00; pap. 4.95. NYU Pr.

--Capital, Expectations, & the Market Process: Essays on the Theory of the Market Economy. Grinder, Walter E., ed. & intro. by. 1977. write for info. NYU Pr.

--Capital, Expectations, & the Market Process: Essays on the Theory of the Market Econony. LC 77-1357. (Studies in Economic Theory). 352p. 1977. 15.00; pap. 4.95. NYU Pr.

Lachs, John, ed. Animal Faith & Spiritual Life: Previously Unpublished & Uncollected Writings by George Santayana with Critical Essays on His Thought. LC 67-20665. (Century Philosophy Ser.). 1967. 28.50x (ISBN 0-89197-607-8). Irvington.

Lachs, John & Scott, Charles E., eds. The Human Search: An Introduction to Philosophy. 528p. 1981. pap. text ed. 10.95x (ISBN 0-19-502675-6). Oxford U Pr.

Lachs, Samuel T. & Wachs, Saul P. Judaism. (Illus.). 1978. pap. 3.95 (ISBN 0-89505-023-4). Argus Comm.

Lack, David. Darwin's Finches: An Essay on the General Biological Theory of Evolution. (Illus.). 7.75 (ISBN 0-8446-1275-8). Peter Smith.

Lack, Sylvia, ed. A Hospice Program. 1981. cancelled (ISBN 0-88416-298-2). PSG Pub.

Lacker, Marty, et al. Elvis: Portrait of a Friend. 384p. 1980. pap. 2.95 (ISBN 0-553-13824-3). Bantam.

Lackey, Robert T. Fisheries Management. LC 80-20028. 422p. 1980. 34.95 (ISBN 0-470-27056-X). Halsted Pr.

Lackner, Bede K. & Philp, Kenneth R., eds. Essays on Medieval Civilization. LC 77-17068. (Walter Prescott Webb Memorial Lecture Ser: No. 12). 1978. 10.95 (ISBN 0-292-72023-8). U of Tex Pr.

Laclos, Choderlos de. Les Liaisons Dangereuses. Stone, P. W., tr. (Classics Ser). 1977. pap. 2.95 (ISBN 0-14-044116-6). Penguin.

LaClotte, Michel. The Louvre. LC 79-57409. (Abbeville Library of Art: No. 3). (Illus.). 112p. 1980. pap. 4.95 (ISBN 0-89659-097-6). Abbeville Pr.

Laclotte, Michel & Cuzin, Jean-Pierre. One Hundred Favorite Old Master Paintings from the Louvre Museum, Paris. LC 79-64988. (Illus.). 160p. 1979. 17.95 (ISBN 0-89659-065-8). Abbeville Pr.

Lacocque, Andre & Lacocque, Pierre. Jonah Complex. LC 80-84649. 1981. 14.00 (ISBN 0-8042-0091-2); pap. 7.95 (ISBN 0-8042-0092-0). John Knox.

Lacocque, Andre, jt. auth. see Niedenthal, Morris.

Lacocque, Pierre, jt. auth. see Lacocque, Andre.

Laconte, M. Pierre & Lambert, Richard D., eds. Changing Cities: A Challenge to Planning. (The Annals of the American Academy of Political & Social Science Ser.: No. 451). 250p. 1980. 7.50 (ISBN 0-87761-254-4); pap. text ed. 6.00 (ISBN 0-87761-255-2). Am Acad Pol Soc Sci.

Laconte, Pierre, et al, eds. see World Environment & Resources Council (WERC) Brussels, Apr. 1976.

Lacosa, Jaime, jt. auth. see Noble, Judith.

Lacosta, Francisco C., ed. see Poncela, Enrique J.

LaCoste, Edward. Black Nations in Action. 3.75 o.p. (ISBN 0-685-26056-9). Vantage.

La Cour, F. L., jt. auth. see Darlington, C. D.

LaCour, L. F., jt. auth. see Darlington, C. D.

LaCour, Pierre. Manufacture of Liquers, Wines, & Cordials Without the Aid of Distillation. (Illus.). 1980. Repr. of 1853 ed. lib. bdg. 25.00 (ISBN 0-915262-52-5). S J Durst.

LaCoursiere, Roy. The Life Cycle of Groups: Group Developmental Stage Theory. LC 79-27112. 320p. 1980. text ed. 24.95 (ISBN 0-87705-469-X). Human Sci Pr.

La Croix, Grethe. Beads Plus Macrame: Applying Knotting Techniques to Beadcraft. LC 78-151710. (Little Craft Book Ser). (Illus.). (gr. 8 up). 1971. 5.95 (ISBN 0-8069-5168-0); PLB 6.69 (ISBN 0-8069-5169-9). Sterling.

Lacroix, Leona. Just for Me Poems. (gr. k-4). 1977. pap. text ed. 2.25x (ISBN 0-933892-02-0). Child Focus Co.

Lacroix, Paul. Bibliotheque Dramatique de Monsieur de Soleinne, 9 vols. in 8. Incl. Bibliotheque Dramatique de Pont de Vesle, vii, 279p; Essai d'une Bibliographie General du Theatre, Ou Catalogue Raisonne de la Bibliotheque d'un Amateur. De Filippi, Joseph. xiii, 224p; Table des Pieces de Theatre Descrites dans le Catalogue de la Bibliotheque de M. de Soleinne, par Charles Brunet. iv, 491p. Repr. 32.50 (ISBN 0-8337-1817-7). B Franklin.

Lacue, Juan J., tr. see Francisco, C. T.

Lacy, Dan. The Colony of North Carolina. LC 74-22217. (First Bks). (Illus.). (gr. 5-8). 1975. PLB 4.90 o.p. (ISBN 0-531-00830-4). Watts.

--The Colony of Virginia. LC 72-10780. (First Bks). (Illus.). 72p. (gr. 6-8). 1973. PLB 4.90 o.p. (ISBN 0-531-00784-7). Watts.

--The Lewis & Clark Expedition: 1804-1806. LC 73-12088. (Focus Bks). (Illus.). 72p. (gr. 7 up). 1974. PLB 4.47 o.p. (ISBN 0-531-01048-1). Watts.

--The Lost Colony. LC 70-182898. (First Bks). (Illus.). 72p. (gr. 4 up). 1972. PLB 4.90 o.p. (ISBN 0-531-00761-8). Watts.

Lacy, Edward A. How to Cut Your Electric Bill & Install Your Own Emergency Power System. (Illus.). 1978. pap. 2.95 (ISBN 0-8306-1036-7, 1036). TAB Bks.

Lacy, Gerald M., ed. see Lawrence, D. H.

Lacy, Joseph R. & Penry, J. Kiffin. Infantile Spasms. LC 76-25378. 1976. pap. 15.50 (ISBN 0-89004-018-4). Raven.

Lacy, Leslie. First Book of Black Africa on the Move. LC 77-75874. (First Bks). (Illus.). (gr. 7 up). 1969. PLB 4.90 o.p. (ISBN 0-531-00702-2). Watts.

--Native Daughter. LC 73-10785. 256p. 1974. 9.95 o.s.i. (ISBN 0-02-567220-7). Macmillan.

Lacy, Madison S. & Morgan, Don. Leg Art: Sixty Years of Hollywood Cheesecake. (Illus.). 256p. 1981. 24.95 (ISBN 0-8065-0734-9). Citadel Pr.

Lacy, Mary L. And God Wants People. LC 62-11717. 1976. pap. 1.25 o.p. (ISBN 0-8042-3594-5). John Knox.

--Springboard to Discovery. 1976. 1.25 o.p. (ISBN 0-8042-3595-3). John Knox.

--Woman Wants God. 1959. pap. 1.25 o.p. (ISBN 0-8042-3596-1). John Knox.

Lacy, Susana B., tr. see Winley, Jesse.

Laczay, Eteka de see Hajdu, Tibor.

Laczniak, Gene R., jt. auth. see Udell, Jon G.

La Dage, John H. Modern Ships: Elements of Their Design, Construction, & Operation. LC 65-21747. (Illus.). 1965. 8.50x (ISBN 0-87033-065-9). Cornell Maritime.

La Dage, John H. & Van Gemert, Lee. Stability & Trim for the Ship's Officer. 2nd ed. LC 56-6885. 1956. 8.50x (ISBN 0-87033-167-1). Cornell Maritime.

Ladame, Cathryn. Winters Heart. 192p. 1981. pap. 1.50 (ISBN 0-671-57055-2). S&S.

Ladas, Gerasimbs E., jt. auth. see Grove, Edward A.

Ladas, Gerasimos, jt. auth. see Finizio, Norman.

Ladbury, Ann. Batsford Book of Sewing. 1978. pap. 13.50 (ISBN 0-7134-0199-0, Pub. by Batsford England). David & Charles.

--Dressmaking with Basic Patterns. 1976. pap. 8.95 (ISBN 0-7134-3226-8). David & Charles.

--Improve Your Dressmaking. 1978. 17.95 (ISBN 0-7134-0031-5, Pub. by Batsford England). David & Charles.

--Practical Sewing. LC 78-50819. 1978. pap. 7.95 (ISBN 0-528-88198-1); pap. 7.95 (ISBN 0-528-88198-1). Rand.

--Short Cuts for Busy Dressmakers. (Illus.). 144p. 1980. 24.00 (ISBN 0-7134-1811-7, Pub. by Batsford England); pap. 11.95 (ISBN 0-7134-1812-5). David & Charles.

Ladd. Meg of Heron's Neck. 1977. pap. 3.50 (ISBN 0-89272-035-2). Down East.

--Meg's Mysterious Island. 1977. pap. 3.50 (ISBN 0-89272-034-4). Down East.

--Mystery for Meg. 1977. pap. 3.50 (ISBN 0-89272-033-6). Down East.

Ladd, D. Robert, Jr. Structure of Intonational Meaning: Evidence from English. LC 79-3093. 256p. 1980. 18.50x (ISBN 0-253-15864-8). Ind U Pr.

Ladd, Doris M. The Mexican Nobility at Independence, 1780-1826. LC 75-720106. (Latin American Monographs: No. 40). 1976. 15.95x (ISBN 0-292-75026-9); pap. 7.95 (ISBN 0-292-75027-7). U of Tex Pr.

Ladd, Everett C., jt. auth. see Carnegie Commission on Higher Education.

Ladd, Everett C., Jr. & Hadley, Charles D. Transformations of the American Party System: Political Coalitions from the New Deal to the 1970's. 2nd ed. 1978. 16.95 (ISBN 0-393-05660-0); pap. 6.95x (ISBN 0-393-09065-5). Norton.

Ladd, George E. El Apocalipsis de Juan: Un Comentario. Canclini, Arnoldo, tr. from Eng. LC 78-50625. 269p. (Orig., Span.). 1978. pap. 5.50 (ISBN 0-89922-111-4). Edit Caribe.

--Creo en la Resurreccion de Jesus. Blanch, Miguel, tr. from Eng. LC 77-79934. (Serie Creo). 204p. (Orig., Span.). 1977. pap. 3.95 (ISBN 0-89922-091-6). Edit Caribe.

--New Testament & Criticism. 1966. pap. 3.95 (ISBN 0-8028-1680-0). Eerdmans.

--The Presence of the Future: The Eschatology of Biblical Realism. 1973. pap. 7.95 (ISBN 0-8028-1531-6). Eerdmans.

Ladd, George T., tr. see Lotze, Hermann.

Ladd, John, tr. see Kant, Immanuel.

Ladd, M. F. Structure & Bonding in Solid State Chemistry. LC 78-41289. 1979. 52.95 (ISBN 0-470-26597-3). Halsted Pr.

Ladd, M. F. & Palmer, R. A., eds. Structure Determination by X-Ray Crystallography. (Illus.). 393p. 1977. 29.50 (ISBN 0-306-30844-4, Plenum Pr); pap. 14.75 (ISBN 0-306-40032-4). Plenum Pub.

Ladde, G. S. & Laksmikantham, V. Random Differential Inequalities. LC 80-521. (Mathematics in Science & Engineering Ser.). 1980. 30.00 (ISBN 0-12-432750-8). Acad Pr.

Ladebat De, Monique P. see De Ladebat, Monique P.

Ladefoged, Peter. Preliminaries to Linguistic Phonetics. LC 75-179318. 1972. 6.95x o.s.i. (ISBN 0-226-46786-4). U of Chicago Pr.

--Preliminaries to Linguistic Phonetics. pap. 5.00 (ISBN 0-226-46787-2). U of Chicago Pr.

La Dell, Edwin. Your Book of Landscape Drawing. (Your Book Ser.). (Illus.). 1964. 7.95 (ISBN 0-571-05888-4, Pub. by Faber & Faber). Merrimack Bk Serv.

Laden, Alice & Minney, R. J. The George Bernard Shaw Vegetarian Cookbook. 1974. pap. 1.50 o.s.i. (ISBN 0-515-03465-7, A3465). Jove Pubns.

Laden, Caroline S., ed. see Institute for Paralegal Training.

Ladenheim, J., jt. auth. see Olivecrona, H.

Lader, Malcolm. Priorities in Psychiatric Research. LC 80-40583. 256p. 1980. 37.00 (ISBN 0-471-27833-5, Pub. by Wiley-Interscience). Wiley.

--Psychophysiology of Mental Illness. (Social & Psychological Aspects of Medical Practice Ser.). 1975. 24.00x (ISBN 0-7100-8091-3). Routledge & Kegan.

Lader, Martin, jt. auth. see Kelley, Red.

Ladewig, D., ed. Drogen & Alkohol. (Illus.). xii, 220p. 1980. pap. 23.50 (ISBN 3-8055-1624-X). S Karger.

Ladies Aid of the Northern Maine Universalist-Unitarian Churches. The Great State of Maine Cookbook. 180p. 1981. 8.95 (ISBN 0-89975-002-8). World Authors.

Ladley, Barbara. Money & Finance: Sources of Print & Nonprint Materials. (Neal-Schuman Sourcebook Ser.). 1980. 19.95x (ISBN 0-918212-23-5). Neal-Schuman.

Ladley, Betty A. & Patt, Jerry. Office Procedures for the Dental Team. new ed. LC 77-23557. 1977. pap. text ed. 16.95 (ISBN 0-8016-2815-6). Mosby.

Ladley, Betty A. & Wilson, Shirley A. Review of Dental Assisting. LC 79-18921. 1979. pap. text ed. 10.95 (ISBN 0-8016-2806-7). Mosby.

Ladman, Jerry R., et al, eds. United States-Mexico Energy Relationships: Realities & Prospects. 350p. 1980. lib. bdg. cancelled (ISBN 0-86531-066-1). Westview.

--U.S.-Mexican Energy Relationships: Realities & Prospects. LC 80-8878. 1981. price not set (ISBN 0-669-04398-2). Lexington Bks.

Ladner, Joyce, ed. The Death of White Sociology. 1973. 12.50 o.p. (ISBN 0-394-48208-5). Random.

Ladner, Joyce A., Ph.D. Tomorrow's Tomorrow. LC 78-139038. 320p. 1972. pap. 2.95 (ISBN 0-385-00941-0, Anch). Doubleday.

Lado, Robert. Lado English Series, Bk. 1. (Illus.). (gr. 7-12). 1977. pap. text ed. 3.45 (ISBN 0-88345-328-2); wkbk 2.25 (ISBN 0-88345-334-7); cassettes 80.00 (ISBN 0-685-89607-2); teacher's manual 4.95 (ISBN 0-88345-340-1). Regents Pub.

--Lado English Series, Bk. 2. 1978. pap. text ed. 3.45 (ISBN 0-88345-329-0); tchr's manual 4.95 (ISBN 0-88345-341-X); wkbk. 2.25 (ISBN 0-88345-335-5); cassettes 80.00 (ISBN 0-686-59595-5); testbook 20.00 (ISBN 0-88345-382-7). Regents Pub.

--Lado English Series, Bk. 3. 1978. pap. text ed. 3.45 (ISBN 0-88345-330-4); tchr's manual 4.95 (ISBN 0-88345-342-8, 18759); wkbk. 2.25 (ISBN 0-88345-336-3); cassettes 80.00 (ISBN 0-685-92972-8). Regents Pub.

--Lado English Series, Bk. 4. 1978. pap. text ed. 3.45 (ISBN 0-88345-331-2); tchr's manual 4.95 (ISBN 0-88345-343-6, 18760); wkbk. 2.25 (ISBN 0-88345-337-1). Regents Pub.

--Lado English Series, Bk. 5. (Illus.). 198p. (gr. 7-12). 1980. pap. text ed. 3.75 (ISBN 0-88345-307-X, 18749); tchr's manual 4.95 (ISBN 0-88345-344-4); wkbk., 132 pp. 2.25 (ISBN 0-88345-338-X, 18755). Regents Pub.

--Lado English Series, Bk. 6. (Illus.). 1980. pap. text ed. 3.75 (ISBN 0-88345-333-9); tchr's manual 4.95 (ISBN 0-88345-345-2); wkbk. 2.25 (ISBN 0-88345-339-8). Regents Pub.

--Lado English Series, Bk. 6. (Illus.). 202p. (gr. 7-12). 1980. pap. text ed. 3.75 (ISBN 0-88345-333-9); wkbk 2.25 (ISBN 0-88345-339-8). Regents Pub.

--Linguistics Across Cultures: Applied Linguistics for Language Teachers. 1957. pap. 4.95x (ISBN 0-472-08542-5). U of Mich Pr.

Ladoo, Harold S. Yesterdays. LC 74-75919. (Anansi Fiction Ser.: No. 29). 110p. 1974. 10.95 (ISBN 0-88784-431-6, Pub. by Hse Anansi Pr Canada); pap. 4.95 (ISBN 0-88784-329-8). U of Toronto Pr.

Ladouceur, Paul A. Chiefs & Politicians: Regional & Political Development in North Ghana. (LEGON History Ser.). (Illus.). 1979. text ed. 40.00 (ISBN 0-582-64646-4). Longman.

Ladurie, Emmanuel L. The Mind & Method of the Historian. Reynolds, Sian & Reynolds, Ben, trs. 224p. 1981. price not set (ISBN 0-226-47326-0). U of Chicago Pr.

Ladusaw, William A. & Hankamer, Jorge. Polarity Sensitivity As Inherent Scope Relations. LC 79-6614. (Outstanding Dissertations in Linguistics Ser.). 236p. 1980. lib. bdg. 27.50 (ISBN 0-8240-4555-6). Garland Pub.

Ladyzenskaja, O. A., ed. Boundary Value Problems of Mathematical Physics. (Trudy Steklov: No. 147). Date not set. cancelled (ISBN 0-8218-3068-6). Am Math.

Ladyzenskaja, O. A., ed. see Steklov Institute of Mathematics, Academy of Sciences, U S S R, No. 102.

Laertacher, David V. A Nonbook Cataloguing Sampler. 100p. 1975. pap. 5.00 (ISBN 0-912556-04-8). Hi Willow.

Laerum, O. D., ed. Flow Cytometry, Four. 550p. 1981. 64.00x (ISBN 8-20005-399-7). Universitet.

Laevastu, Taivo, jt. auth. see Hela, Ilmo.

Lafarge, Henry, ed. see Benson, Elizabeth & Conklin, William.

LaFarge, Henry A., ed. see El Mallakh, Kamal & Bianchi, Robert S.

LaFarge, Henry A., et al, eds. The Splendors of Dresden: Critical Texts by Licia Collobi Ragghianti. LC 79-3547. (Illus.). 1980. 19.95 (ISBN 0-88225-286-0). Newsweek.

La Farge, John. Artist's Letters from Japan. LC 74-130311. (Library of American Art Ser.). (Illus.). 1970. Repr. of 1897 ed. lib. bdg. 35.00 (ISBN 0-306-70064-6). Da Capo.

--Considerations on Painting. LC 70-9611. (Library of American Art Ser). 1969. Repr. of 1895 ed. lib. bdg. 35.00 (ISBN 0-306-71824-3). Da Capo.

La Farge, John, et al, eds. Noteworthy Paintings in American Private Collections, 2 vols. LC 75-28888. (Art Experience in Late 19th Century America Ser.: Vol. 21). (Illus.). 1976. Repr. of 1907 ed. Set. lib. bdg. 218.00 (ISBN 0-8240-2245-9). Garland Pub.

La Farge, Oliver & Morgan, Arthur N. Santa Fe: The Autobiography of a Southwestern Town. (Illus.). 1959. 14.95 o.p. (ISBN 0-8061-0434-1). U of Okla Pr.

La Farge, Phyllis. Granny's Fish Story. LC 74-545. (Illus.). 36p. (ps-3). 1975. 5.95 o.s.i. (ISBN 0-8193-0760-2, Four Winds); PLB 5.41 o.s.i. (ISBN 0-8193-0761-0). Schol Bk Serv.

La Farge, Phyllis, tr. see Giraudoux, Jean.

La Farge, Sheila, tr. see Bodker, Cecil.

Lafarge, Sheila, tr. see Carpelan, Bo.

La Farge, Sheila, tr. see Gripe, Maria.

La Farge, W. E. The Changing & Unchanging Harvest. (Orig.). 1980. pap. 4.95 (ISBN 0-935598-00-6). Heartwork Pr.

LaFargue, Thomas E. China & the World War. 16.50 (ISBN 0-86527-023-6). Fertig.

La Faso, John, jt. auth. see Flynn, Elizabeth.

La Fauci, H. M. & Richter, P. Team Teaching at the College Level. LC 73-88573. 1970. 16.50 (ISBN 0-08-006946-0). Pergamon.

LaFave, Wayne R. Principles of Criminal Law. abr. ed. (Criminal Justice Ser.). 1978. text ed. 17.95 (ISBN 0-8299-0215-5); instrs.' manual avail. (ISBN 0-8299-0595-2). West Pub.

LaFave, Wayne R., jt. auth. see Israel, Jerold H.

LaFave, Wayne R., ed. Law in the Soviet Society. LC 65-19109. 297p. 1965. pap. 1.95 (ISBN 0-252-72524-7). U of Ill Pr.

La Fayette, Marie-Madeleine De see De La Fayette, Marie-Madeleine.

La Feber, Walter. America in the Cold War: Twenty Years of Revolution & Response, 1947-1967. LC 70-38955. (Problems in American History Ser.). 232p. 1969. 9.95x (ISBN 0-471-51133-1). Wiley.

LaFeber, Walter. The Panama Canal: The Crisis in Historical Perspective. 1978. 13.95 (ISBN 0-19-502360-9). Oxford U Pr.

Lafehr, Thomas R. Integrated Geophysics for Exploration Geologists. text ed. write for info. o.p. (ISBN 0-8087-3802-X, CEPCO); pap. text ed. write for info. o.p. (ISBN 0-8087-3803-8). Burgess.

Laferriere, Daniel. Sign & Subject: Semiotic & Psychoanalytic Investigations into Poetry. (Studies in Semiotics Ser.: No. 14). (Orig.). 1978. pap. text ed. 11.50x (ISBN 9-0316-0138-1). Humanities.

Lafever, Minard. Beauties of Modern Architecture. 2nd ed. LC 68-29602. (Architecture & Decorative Art Ser.: Vol. 18). (Illus.). 1968. Repr. of 1835 ed. lib. bdg. 25.00 (ISBN 0-306-71040-4). Da Capo.

LaFevor, C. S., jt. auth. see Hendrix, T. G.

Laffal, Florence. Primitive & Early Breads. LC 77-9240. (Illus.). Date not set. pap. cancelled (ISBN 0-913622-06-0). Gallery Pr. Postponed.

Laffal, Julius. A Concept Dictionary of English. LC 72-97927. 305p. 1973. 19.95 (ISBN 0-470-51160-5). Halsted Pr.

--Concept Dictionary of English. LC 72-97927. 1973. text ed. 13.50 (ISBN 0-470-51160-5). Gallery Pr.

Laffer & Miles. International Economics: In an Integrated World. 416p. 1981. pap. write for info. (ISBN 0-8302-4028-4). Goodyear.

Lafferty, J. M., ed. Vacuum Arcs: Theory & Application. LC 79-15654. 1980. 29.95 (ISBN 0-471-06506-4). Wiley.

Lafferty, Maude W. Lure of Kentucky: A Historical Guide Book. LC 71-153018. (Illus.). 1971. Repr. of 1939 ed. 18.00 (ISBN 0-8103-3344-9). Gale.

Lafferty, Michael B., ed. Ohio's Natural Heritage. LC 78-60505. 1979. 23.95 (ISBN 0-933128-01-0). Ohio Acad Sci.

Lafferty, Perry. How to Lose Your Fear of Flying. (Illus., Orig.). 1980. pap. 2.95 (ISBN 0-8431-0654-9). Price Stern.

Lafferty, R. A. Past Master. 1977. pap. 1.95 (ISBN 0-441-65302-2). Ace Bks.

--Strange Doings. LC 72-162759. 1972. 5.95 o.p. (ISBN 0-684-12530-7, ScribT). Scribner.

Laffin, John. The Dagger of Islam. 224p. 1981. pap. 2.95 (ISBN 0-553-14287-9). Bantam.

Laffin, Richard F. Jewelers' Inventory Manual. 1981. 24.95 (ISBN 0-931744-04-0). Jewelers Circular.

Lafleur, Mark H. Anti-Hegelianism & the Theory of the Infinite. (Illus.). 131p. 1981. 31.45 (ISBN 0-89266-281-6). Am Classical Coll Pr.

Lafitte, Lucette. Eau Trouble. 1963. text ed. 2.95x (ISBN 0-521-05506-7). Cambridge U Pr.

--Ferme Du Pere Mathieu. 1958. text ed. 2.95x (ISBN 0-521-05508-3). Cambridge U Pr.

Lafkas, C. & Paterson, J. G. A Survey of Resources & a Production Cycle for the Non-Ferrous Metals. 60p. (Orig.). 1978. pap. text ed. 3.00x (ISBN 0-686-63136-6, Pub. by Ctr Resource Stud Canada). Renouf.

La Flesche, Francis, jt. auth. see Fletcher, Alice C.

La Fleur, Ida, jt. auth. see Gardner, Joyce.

Lafleur, Laurence J., tr. see Descartes.

Lafleur, Laurence J., tr. see Descartes, Rene.

LaFleur, Lydia, jt. auth. see Robotham, John S.

LaFleur, N. Kenneth, jt. auth. see Cook, David R.

LaFleur, Tom, jt. auth. see Brennan, Gale.

LaFollette, B. C. & LaFollette, F. Robert M. LaFollette, 2 vols. 1971. Repr. of 1953 ed. 38.50 o.s.i. (ISBN 0-02-848290-5). Hafner.

LaFollette, F., jt. auth. see LaFollette, B. C.

LaFollette, Hugh, jt. ed. see Aiken, William.

La Follette, P., jt. auth. see Hunter, W. F.

Lafont, Pierre-Bernard, ed. Bibliographie Du Laos. 2nd ed. Incl. Vol. 1. 1666-1961. 269p; Vol. 2. 1962-1975. 413p. LC 65-53527. (Orig., Fr.). 1978. pap. 55.00x. Intl Pubns Serv.

LaFontaine, Herman see Dodge, James W.

Laforce, J. Clayburn, jt. auth. see Scoville, Warren C.

Laforet, Carmen. Nada. Mulvihill, Edward R. & Sanchez, Roberto G., eds. (Orig., Sp). 1958. pap. 5.95x (ISBN 0-19-500942-8). Oxford U Pr.

--Un Noviazgo. Galerstein, Carolyn L., ed. LC 72-85231. 100p. 1973. pap. 3.95 (ISBN 0-672-63131-8). Odyssey Pr.

Laforet, Claude. La Vie Musicale Au Temps Romantique. LC 77-4153. (Music Reprint Ser., 1977). 1977. Repr. of 1929 ed. lib. bdg. 19.50 (ISBN 0-306-70890-6). Da Capo.

Laforgue, Jules. Les Complaintes. Collie, Michael, ed. (Athlone French Poets Ser). 192p. 1977. text ed. 30.00x (ISBN 0-485-14713-0, Athlone Pr); pap. text ed. 13.00x (ISBN 0-485-12713-X). Humanities.

La Fountaine, George. Flashpoint. 1978. pap. 1.75 o.p. (ISBN 0-449-23644-7, Crest). Fawcett.

--Two Minute Warning. 240p. 1977. pap. 1.75 o.p. (ISBN 0-449-23080-5, Crest). Fawcett.

Lafranche, Gaston M. The Intimate Memoirs of Barbara, the Duchess of Cleveland. (The Great Women of History Library). (Illus.). 93p. 1981. 19.85 (ISBN 0-89266-276-X). Am Classical Coll Pr.

--The Intimate Memoirs of Louise Renee De Kerouaille, Duchess of Portsmouth & Aubigny. (The Great Women of History Library). (Illus.). 94p. 1981. 19.85 (ISBN 0-89266-275-1). Am Classical Coll Pr.

Lafreniere, Gyslaine F., jt. auth. see Persinger, Michael A.

LaFreniere, Joan G. The Low Back Patient. (Illus.). 208p. 1979. 20.50 (ISBN 0-89352-033-0). Masson Pub.

Lag, Jul, ed. Survey of Geomedical Problems. 272p. 1980. 24.00x (ISBN 82-00-12654-4). Universitet.

Lagan, Jake. Slocums Code. LC 80-85107. (Jake Logan Ser.). 224p. (Orig.). 1981. pap. 1.95 (ISBN 0-87216-823-9). Playboy Pbks.

Lagane, Rene, jt. auth. see Dubois, Jean.

Lagarde, A. & Michard, L. Collection Litteraire, 6 vols. Incl. Vol. 1. Moyen Age. 9.60 (ISBN 0-685-58371-6); Vol. 2. Seizieme Siecle. 9.60 (ISBN 0-685-58372-4); Vol. 3. Dix-Septieme Siecle. 10.90 (ISBN 0-685-58373-2); Vol. 4. Dix-Huitieme Siecle. 12.25 (ISBN 0-685-58374-0); Vol. 5. Dix-Neuvieme Siecle. 13.65 (ISBN 0-685-58375-9); Vol. 6. Vingtieme Siecle. 17.25 (ISBN 0-685-58376-7). (Fr.). Schoenhof.

Lagarde, Alexis, ed. see I.U.T.A.M Symposium on Optical Methods in Mechanics of Solids.

Lager, James L. Leica Illustrated Guide, No. 2. LC 78-54092. 1978. pap. 19.95 (ISBN 0-87100-138-1). Morgan.

--Leica Illustrated Guide III. LC 79-90513. (Orig.). 1979. pap. 14.95 (ISBN 0-87100-161-6). Morgan.

--Leica Literature. 512p. 1980. pap. 22.95 (ISBN 0-87100-174-8). Morgan.

Lagercrantz, H., jt. ed. see Von Euler, C.

Lagerkvist, Par. The Dwarf. Dick, Alexandra, tr. 228p. (Orig.). 1958. pap. 4.25 (ISBN 0-8090-1303-7). Hill & Wang.

--The Marriage Feast. Blair, Alan & Lindin, Carl E., trs. 1973. 6.95 o.p. (ISBN 0-8090-6786-2); pap. 2.95 o.p. (ISBN 0-8090-1372-X). Hill & Wang.

Lagerkvist, Par & Buckman, Thomas R. Modern Theatre: Seven Plays & an Essay. LC 64-11582. 1966. 14.95x (ISBN 0-8032-0098-6). U of Nebr Pr.

Lagerlof, Selma. Christ Legends. 1977. 8.95 (ISBN 0-903540-06-1, Pub. by Floris Books). St George Bk Serv.

--Marbacka. Howard, Velma S., tr. LC 70-167024. (Illus.). viii, 288p. 1974. Repr. of 1926 ed. 18.00 (ISBN 0-8103-4031-3). Gale.

Lagnado, J. R. see Bull, Alan T., et al.

Lagnado, J. R., tr. see Youdim, M. B. & Lovenberg, W.

Lago, G. & Benningfield, L. M. Circuit & System Theory. LC 79-10878. 1979. text ed. 29.95 (ISBN 0-471-04927-1). Wiley.

Lago, Mary M. Rabindranath Tagore. (World Authors Ser.: No. 402). 1976. lib. bdg. 12.50 (ISBN 0-8057-6242-6). Twayne.

Lagos Conference, 1964. Final Report. 1964. pap. 2.50 (ISBN 92-3-100565-0, U243, UNESCO). Unipub.

Lagoulle, Henri. Essai Sur la Conception Juridique De la Propriete Fonciere Dans le Tres Anciendroit Normand: Premiere Partie, la Conception Feodale. LC 80-2020. 1981. Repr. of 1902 ed. 47.50 (ISBN 0-404-18574-6). AMS Pr.

Lagowski, J. M., jt. ed. see Katritzky, Alan R.

Lagowski, Joseph J., jt. auth. see Sorum, Henry.

La Grande, Hypolite. Economics for the Smart Businessman Who knows Nothing of Economics. (Illus.). 50p. 1974. 37.50 (ISBN 0-913314-25-0). Am Classical Coll Pr.

La Grande, Hyppolite. The Deceit of the New Economics. (Illus.). 150p. 1975. 37.50 (ISBN 0-913314-50-1). Am Classical Coll Pr.

La Guardia, Robert. From Ma Perkins to Mary Hartman: The Illustrated History of Soap Operas. 1977. pap. 1.95 o.p. (ISBN 0-345-25562-3). Ballantine.

Laguerre, E. Oeuvres, 2 Vols. LC 70-125075. (Fr). 1971. Repr. of 1905 ed. text ed. 39.50 (ISBN 0-8284-0263-9). Chelsea Pub.

Laguerre, Michel S. Voodoo Heritage. LC 79-25318. (Sage Library of Social Research: No. 98). (Illus.). 231p. 1980. 18.00x (ISBN 0-8039-1402-4); pap. 8.95x (ISBN 0-8039-1403-2). Sage.

La Guma, A. In the Fog of the Season's End. LC 72-93381. 1973. 8.95 (ISBN 0-89388-058-2). Okpaku Communications.

LaGumina, Salvatore J. An Album of the Italian American. LC 72-6275. (Picture Albums Ser.). (Illus.). 96p. (gr. 4 up). 1972. PLB 5.90 o.p. (ISBN 0-531-01514-9). Watts.

LaGumina, Salvatore J., ed. The Immigrants Speak: The Italian Americans Tell Their Story. (Illus.). 200p. 1979. lib. bdg. 14.95x (ISBN 0-913256-37-4). Ctr Migration.

Laguna, Asela Rodriguez-Seda De see Rodriguez-Seda de Laguna, Asela.

Laham, Sandra L., jt. auth. see Popovich, Dorothy.

LaHaye, Beverly. Le Femme Dirigee Par l'Esprit. Cosson, Annie, ed. Schneider, Michele, tr. from Eng. 175p. (Fr. & English.). 1979. pap. 1.85 (ISBN 0-8297-0972-X). Vida Pubs.

LaHaye, Beverly, jt. auth. see LaHaye, Tim.

La Haye, Tim. Understanding the Male Temperament: What Every Man Would Like to Tell His Wife About Himself...but Won't. 1977. 6.95 o.p. (ISBN 0-8007-0863-6); pap. 3.95 (ISBN 0-8007-0864-4); power ed. o.p. 3.95 (ISBN 0-8007-5009-8). Revell.

LaHaye, Tim & LaHaye, Beverly. The Act of Marriage. 316p. 1981. pap. 2.95. Zondervan.

--The Act of Marriage. 1976. o. p. 7.95 (ISBN 0-310-27060-X); pap. 5.95 (ISBN 0-310-27061-8); pap. 2.95 (ISBN 0-310-27062-6). Zondervan.

--Spirit Controlled Family Living. 1978. 7.95 (ISBN 0-8007-0950-0); pap. 4.95 (ISBN 0-8007-0951-9). Revell.

LaHaye, Tim, tr. Como Vencer a Depressao. (Portuguese Bks.). 1979. 1.50 (ISBN 0-8297-0648-8). Life Pubs Intl.

--Como Vencer la Depresion. (Spanish Bks.). (Span.). 1978. 1.95 (ISBN 0-8297-0515-5). Life Pubs Intl.

La Haye, Yves De see Marx, Karl & Frederick, Engels.

Lahey, Benjamin B. & Johnson, Martha S. Psychology & Instruction: A Practical Approach to Educational Psychology. 1978. pap. 12.95x (ISBN 0-673-15040-2). Scott F.

Lahey, Benjamin B., ed. Behavior Therapy with Hyperactive & Learning Disabled Children. (Illus.). 1979. text ed. 16.95x (ISBN 0-19-502478-8); pap. text ed. 8.95x (ISBN 0-19-502479-6). Oxford U Pr.

Lahey, Francis J., jt. auth. see Moroni, J. Alfred.

Lahey, Gerald, ed. see Hazlitt, William.

Lahey, Gerald B., ed. see Farquhar, George.

Lahey, Gerald B., ed. see Goldsmith, Oliver.

Lahey, Gerald B., jt. ed. see Hopper, Vincent F.

Lahey, Gerald B., ed. see Webster, John.

Lahey, James F., jt. auth. see Wahl, Eberhard W.

Lahey, James F., et al. Atlas of Five-Day Normal Sea-Level Pressure Charts for the Northern Hemisphere. 1958. wired bdg. 50.00x (ISBN 0-299-01663-3). U of Wis Pr.

--Atlas of Five Hundred Mb Wind Characteristics for the Northern Hemisphere. 1958. wired bdg. 50.00x (ISBN 0-299-01703-6). U of Wis Pr.

--Atlas of Three Hundred Mb Wind Characteristics for the Northern Hemisphere. 1960. wired bdg. 50.00x (ISBN 0-299-01963-2). U of Wis Pr.

Lahey, Margaret, jt. auth. see Bloom, Lois.

Lahey, Margaret, ed. Readings in Childhood Language Disorders. LC 77-21408. (Communications Disorders Ser.). 1978. text ed. 20.50 (ISBN 0-471-51167-6). Wiley.

Lahiri, R. K. Family Farming in a Developing Economy. 1979. pap. text ed. 8.00x (ISBN 0-391-01851-5). Humanities.

Lahlou, B., ed. Epithelial Transport in the Lower Vertebrates. LC 79-50884. (Illus.). 1980. 55.00 (ISBN 0-521-22748-8). Cambridge U Pr.

LaHoye, Tim. The Battle for the Mind. 1980. 8.95 (ISBN 0-8007-5043-8); pap. 4.95 (ISBN 0-8007-1121-1). Revell.

Lahr, Georgiana L. The Heart Sings. 3.50 o.p. (ISBN 0-685-26028-3). Vantage.

Lahr, John. Prick up Your Ears. 1979. pap. 3.50 (ISBN 0-380-48629-6, 48629, Discus). Avon.

Lahr, Theis. Congress: Power & Purpose on Capitol Hill. (gr. 9-12). 1974. pap. text ed. 5.40 (ISBN 0-205-03972-3, 7639724). Allyn.

Lahue, Kalton C. The Darkroom Guide. (Petersen's Photographic Library). (Illus.). 160p. 1980. pap. 8.95 o.p. (ISBN 0-8227-4039-7). Petersen Pub.

--Telephoto Photography. LC 77-74103. (PhotoGraphic How to Library). (Illus.). (gr. 9-12). 1977. pap. 3.95 o.p. (ISBN 0-8227-4021-4). Petersen Pub.

Lahue, Kalton C., ed. Big Book of Auto Repair, 1981. LC 76-18639. 896p. 1980. pap. 14.95 (ISBN 0-8227-5054-6). Petersen Pub.

Lahue, Kalton C., et al. Photographing Children. LC 74-78333. (Illus.). 1974. pap. 3.95 o.p. (ISBN 0-8227-0063-8). Petersen Pub.

Lahue, Robert, ed. Methods in Neurobiology. 1981. 50.00 ea.; Set. 89.50 (ISBN 0-686-69459-7); Vol. 1, 640 Pp. for two vol. set 89.50 (ISBN 0-306-40517-2). Vol. Ii, 700 Pp (ISBN 0-306-40518-0). Plenum Pub.

Lai, T. C. Chinese Seals. LC 76-7789. (Illus.). 224p. 1976. 10.00 (ISBN 0-295-95517-1). U of Wash Pr.

Lai, W. M., et al. Introduction to Continuum Mechanics: In SI-Metric Units. rev. ed. 1978. text ed. 45.00 (ISBN 0-08-022698-1); pap. text ed. 19.75 (ISBN 0-08-022699-X). Pergamon.

--Introduction to Continuum Mechanics. LC 72-10904. 1974. text ed. 24.20 o.p. (ISBN 0-08-017622-4). Pergamon.

Lai, Whalen, jt. ed. see Lancaster, Lewis.

Laidlaw, J. C., ed. Poetical Works of Alain Chartier. LC 73-77177. 576p. 1974. 110.00 (ISBN 0-521-07940-3). Cambridge U Pr.

Laidlaw, Karen A., jt. auth. see Stockwell, Edward G.

Laidlaw, Mary V. Epilepsy Explained. (Patient Handbook Ser.). 1980. pap. text ed. 3.50 (ISBN 0-443-01962-2). Churchill.

Laidlaw, Robert A. The Reason Why. 48p. 1975. pap. 0.95 (ISBN 0-310-27112-6). Zondervan.

Laidlaw-Dickson, D. J. The Book of the Unimat. LC 79-300391. (Illus.). 128p. (Orig.). 1977. pap. 9.50x (ISBN 0-85242-591-0). Intl Pubns Serv.

--Radio Control Model Cars Manual. (Illus.). 128p. (Orig.). 1979. pap. 10.00x (ISBN 0-906958-00-8). Intl Pubns Serv.

Laidler, Harry W. & Thomas, Norman. The Socialism of Our Times: A Symposium, Prelude to Depression. LC 76-27725. 1976. Repr. of 1929 ed. lib. bdg. 35.00 (ISBN 0-306-70850-7). Da Capo.

Laidler, K. J. Reaction Kinetics, 2 vols. 1963. Vol. 1. text ed. 16.00 (ISBN 0-08-009834-7); Vol. 2. text ed. 13.75 (ISBN 0-08-009836-3); Vol. 1. pap. text ed. 7.75 (ISBN 0-08-009833-9); Vol. 2. pap. text ed. 6.25 (ISBN 0-08-009835-5). Pergamon.

Laidler, K. J., jt. ed. see Back, M.

Laidler, Keith. Squirrels in Britain. LC 80-66421. (Illus.). 176p. 1980. 19.95 (ISBN 0-7153-7825-2). David & Charles.

Laidler, Kieth. The Talking Ape. LC 80-5388. (Illus.). 160p. 1980. 11.95 (ISBN 0-8128-2731-7). Stein & Day.

Laidman, Hugh. The Complete Book of Drawing & Painting. (Handbooks Ser.). (Illus.). 1978. pap. 14.95 (ISBN 0-14-046349-6). Penguin.

Laiken, D. S., jt. auth. see Rowan, Lilian.

Laiken, Nora, et al. Interpretation of Electrocardiograms: A Self-Instructional Approach. (Illus.). 1978. 13.95 (ISBN 0-8385-4047-3). ACC.

Laikin, Judith L. Krishna Smiled: Assignment in Southeast Asia. LC 72-737. 268p. 1972. 9.95x (ISBN 0-8143-1473-2). Wayne St U Pr.

Laine, Denny. Denny Laine: How to Play the Guitar. (Illus.). 110p. 1980. 10.95 (ISBN 0-517-54207-2, Harmony); pap. 6.95 (ISBN 0-517-54208-0, Harmony). Crown.

Laine, Michael. Checklist of Works on John Stuart Mill. 176p. 1981. 25.00x (ISBN 0-686-69479-1). U of Toronto Pr.

Laing, A. F., jt. auth. see Hussell, C. G.

Laing, Alexander. The American Heritage History of Seafaring America. Thorndike, Joseph J., ed. LC 74-5301. (Illus.). 352p. 1974. deluxe ed. 30.00 (ISBN 0-8281-0266-X, BO35D); 25.00 (ISBN 0-8281-0265-1, BO35R). Am Heritage.

Laing, Donald A. An Annotated Bibliography of the Published Writings of Roger Fry. LC 78-68305. (Garland Reference Library of the Humanities Ser.). 200p. 1979. lib. bdg. 25.00 (ISBN 0-8240-9838-2). Garland Pub.

Laing, Frederick. Tales from Scandinavia. LC 78-56060. (The World Folktale Library). (Illus.). 1979. lib. bdg. 7.65 (ISBN 0-686-51165-4). Silver.

Laing, Gordon. Survivals of Roman Religion. LC 63-10280. (Our Debt to Greece & Rome Ser). 1963. Repr. of 1930 ed. 22.50x (ISBN 0-8154-0130-2). Cooper Sq.

Laing, Jean, ed. see Mackenzie, David.

Laing, Jenniger. Finding Roman Britain. 1977. 11.50 o.p. (ISBN 0-7153-7406-0). David & Charles.

Laing, Lloyd. Orkney & Shetland: An Archaeological Guide. LC 74-76182. 1974. 16.95 (ISBN 0-7153-6305-0). David & Charles.
Laing, Peter, jt. auth. see Hill, Michael.
Lainiotis, D. G. & Tzannes, N. S., eds. A Selection of Papers from Info II, 3 vols. 1980. lib. bdg. 47.50 ea. Vol. 1, 530p (ISBN 90-277-1140-2). Vol. 2, 600p (ISBN 90-277-1129-1). Vol. 3, 530p (ISBN 90-277-1143-7). Kluwer Boston.
Lair, Jacqueline, jt. auth. see Lair, Jess.
Lair, Jess. Sex-If I Didn't I'd Cry. LC 77-27678. 1979. pap. 5.95 (ISBN 0-385-13391-X). Doubleday.
--Sex: If I Didn't Laugh, I'd Cry. 1980. pap. 2.50 (ISBN 0-449-24336-2, Crest). Fawcett.
Lair, Jess & Lair, Jacqueline. Hey, God, What Should I Do Now? 240p. 1978. pap. 2.50 (ISBN 0-449-23586-6, Crest). Fawcett.
Laird, A. D., jt. ed. see Spiegler, K. S.
Laird, Antonia B. A Melody of Words. 1978. 5.00 o.p. (ISBN 0-8233-0286-5). Golden Quill.
Laird, Betty A., jt. auth. see Francisco, Ronald A.
Laird, Carobeth. Encounter with an Angry God. 1977. pap. 2.25 (ISBN 0-345-28464-X). Ballantine.
--Limbo. LC 79-10937. 190p. 1979. pap. 5.95 (ISBN 0-88316-536-8). Chandler & Sharp.
Laird, Charles, et al. Modern English Reader. 2nd ed. (Illus.). 416p. 1977. pap. text ed. 9.95 (ISBN 0-13-594176-8). P-H.
Laird, Charlton, jt. auth. see Gorrell, Robert.
Laird, Charlton, jt. auth. see Gorrell, Robert M.
Laird, Charlton, ed. Webster's New World Thesaurus. pap. 5.95 (ISBN 0-452-00535-3, F535, Mer). NAL.
Laird, Dugan. Approaches to Training & Development. LC 77-81193. (Illus.). 1978. text ed. 14.95 (ISBN 0-201-04112-X). A-W.
--Writing for Results: Principles & Practice. LC 77-88052. 1978. pap. text ed. 8.95 (ISBN 0-201-04114-6). A-W.
Laird, Elizabeth. Adult Medicine. (Modern Practical Nursing Ser.: No. 9). 1972. pap. 9.95x (ISBN 0-433-19050-7). Intl Ideas.
Laird, J. T. The Shaping of Tess of the D'Urbervilles. (Illus.). 202p. 1975. 29.95x o.p. (ISBN 0-19-812060-5). Oxford U Pr.
Laird, Jean. Homemaker's Book of Time & Money Savers. 1980. pap. 2.50 (ISBN 0-446-91562-9). Warner Bks.
Laird, Melvin R. & Korb, Lawrence J. Problem of Military Readiness. 1980. pap. 3.75 (ISBN 0-8447-1087-3). Am Enterprise.
Laird, R. D. The Soviet Paradigm. LC 75-122278. 1970. text ed. 9.95 o.s.i. (ISBN 0-02-917750-2). Free Pr.
Laird, Roy, et al, eds. Future of Agriculture in the Soviet Union & Eastern Europe: The 1976-1980 Five-Year Plans. LC 77-582. (Westview Special Studies on the Soviet Union & Eastern Europe). 1977. lib. bdg. 27.50x (ISBN 0-89158-302-5). Westview.
Laird, Walter. Technique of Latin Dancing. rev. ed. (Illus.). 180p. 1980. pap. text ed. 19.50 (ISBN 0-392-07535-0, LTB). Soccer.
Laite, Jordon, illus. Cinderella & Snow White & Rose Red. (Illus.). 24p. (gr. k-3). 1976. PLB 7.15 o.p. (ISBN 0-307-69052-0, Golden Pr). Western Pub.
Laithwaite. Exciting Electric Machine Inventions. pap. 3.95 (ISBN 0-08-017249-0). Pergamon.
Laithwaite, E. R., ed. Transport Without Wheels. LC 76-53107. (Illus.). 1977. lib. bdg. 50.00x (ISBN 0-89158-724-1). Westview.
Laitos, Jan G. A Legal-Economic History of Air Pollution Controls. LC 80-67046. (Scholarly Monograph Ser.). 350p. 1980. pap. 27.50 (ISBN 0-8408-0507-1). Carrollton Pr.
Laity, Edward. Priesthood, Old & New. 1980. 1.95 (ISBN 0-86544-012-3). Salvation Army.
--Tabernacle Types & Teaching. 1980. pap. 1.25 (ISBN 0-86544-011-5). Salvation Army.
La Jonchere, E. L. De see De La Jonchere, E. L.
Lajtha, Abel, ed. Handbook of Neurochemistry, Vols. 1-7. Incl. Vol. 1. Chemical Architecture of the Nervous System. 484p. 1969 (ISBN 0-306-37701-2); Vol. 2. Structural Neurochemistry. 562p. 1969 (ISBN 0-306-37702-0); Vol. 3. Metabolic Reactions in the Nervous System. 590p. 1970 (ISBN 0-306-37703-9); Vol. 4. Control Mechanisms in the Nervous System. 516p. 1970 (ISBN 0-306-37704-7); Vol. 5A. Metabolic Turnover in the Nervous Systems. 438p. 1971 (ISBN 0-306-37705-5); Vol. 5B. Metabolic Turnover in the Nervous System. 399p. 1971 (ISBN 0-306-37715-2); Vol. 6. Alterations of Chemical Equilibrium in the Nervous System. 584p. 1971 (ISBN 0-306-37706-3); Vol. 7. Pathological Chemistry of the Nervous System. 675p. 1972 (ISBN 0-306-37707-1). LC 68-28097. 45.00 ea. (Plenum Pr). Plenum Pub.
Lak, Richard K., jt. auth. see Leh, Francis K.
Lakatos, E. Proofs & Refutations. Worrall, J., ed. LC 75-32478. 160p. 1976. 32.50 (ISBN 0-521-21078-X); pap. 8.95 (ISBN 0-521-29038-4). Cambridge U Pr.
Lakatos, I. Mathematics, Science & Epistomology: Philosophical Papers, Vol. 2. Worrall, J. & Currie, G., eds. LC 77-71415. 1978. 32.50 (ISBN 0-521-21769-5). Cambridge U Pr.
--The Methodology of Scientific Research Programmes: Philosophical Papers, Vol. 1. Worrall, J. & Currie, G., eds. LC 77-71415. 1978. 32.50 (ISBN 0-521-21644-3). Cambridge U Pr.
Lakatos, Imre. Philosophical Papers: Mathematics, Science & Epistemology, Vol. 2. Worrall, J. & Currie, G., eds. LC 77-14374. 295p. 1980. pap. 13.50 (ISBN 0-521-28030-3). Cambridge U Pr.
--Philosophical Papers: The Methodology of Scientific Research Programmes, Vol. 1. Worrall, J. & Currie, G., eds. LC 77-71415. 258p. 1980. pap. 12.50 (ISBN 0-521-28031-1). Cambridge U Pr.
Lake, Anthony, ed. The Legacy of Vietnam: The War, American Society, & the Future of American Foreign Policy. LC 75-13571. 440p. 1976. 22.50x (ISBN 0-8147-4964-X); pap. 7.00x (ISBN 0-8147-4997-6). NYU Pr.
Lake, Antony. The "Tar Baby" Option: American Policy Toward Southern Rhodesia. 288p. 1976. 20.00x (ISBN 0-231-04066-0); pap. 6.50x (ISBN 0-231-04067-9). Columbia U Pr.
Lake, D. J. The Canon of Thomas Middleton's Plays. LC 74-25651. (Illus.). 354p. 1975. 49.50 (ISBN 0-521-20741-X). Cambridge U Pr.
Lake, Dale. Perceiving & Behaving. LC 72-77891. (Illus.). 1970. text ed. 10.50x (ISBN 0-8077-1658-8). Tchrs Coll.
Lake, Dale G., et al, eds. Measuring Human Behavior: Tools for the Assessment of Social Functioning. LC 72-82083. 1973. pap. text ed. 11.75x (ISBN 0-8077-1648-0). Tchrs Coll.
Lake, Elizabeth, et al. Who Pays for Clean Water? (A Westview Replica Edition Ser.). (An Urban systems research report). 1979. lib. bdg. 24.00x (ISBN 0-89158-586-9). Westview.
Lake, Frances & Neiomark, Joseph. Mathematics As a Second Language. 2nd ed. LC 76-14659. (Illus.). 1977. text ed. 17.95 (ISBN 0-201-04099-9). A-W.
Lake, H. S., tr. see Van Eeden, Frederik.
Lake, J., ed. see ICN-UCLA Symposium, Keystone, Colo., February 1979.
Lake, Joe. What a Way to Go. 1980. 6.95 (ISBN 0-533-04440-5). Vantage.
Lake, Laura M., ed. Environmental Mediation: The Search for Consensus. (Social Impact Assessment Ser.). 1979. lib. bdg. 24.00x (ISBN 0-89158-587-7). Westview.
Lake, Sara, ed. Children & Television. (Special Interest Resource Guides in Education Ser.). (Orig.). 1981. pap. 8.50x (ISBN 0-912700-87-4). Oryx Pr.
--Declining Enrollments, Declining Resources. (Special Interest Resource Guides in Education Ser.). (Orig.). 1981. pap. text ed. 9.50x (ISBN 0-912700-86-6). Oryx Pr.
Lake, Sara, compiled by. Discipline & Classroom Control. (Special Interest Resource Guides in Education). 1980. pap. text ed. 7.50x (ISBN 0-912700-71-8). Oryx Pr.
Lake, Sara, ed. Drug Abuse. (Special Interest Resource Guides in Education). 1980. pap. text ed. 8.50 (ISBN 0-912700-72-6). Oryx Pr.
--Mainstreaming. (Special Interest Resource Guides in Education). 1980. pap. text ed. 7.50x (ISBN 0-912700-73-4). Oryx Pr.
Lake, Tony. Affairs: How to Cope with Extra-Marital Relationships. 224p. 1981. 10.95 (ISBN 0-13-018671-6, Spec); pap. 5.95 (ISBN 0-13-018663-5). P-H.
Lakela, Olga & Wonderlin, Richard P. Trees of Central Florida. (Illus.). 1980. 14.95 (ISBN 0-916224-51-1). Banyan Bks.
Lakeman, Enid. How Democracies Vote. 1974. 10.95 (ISBN 0-571-09690-5, Pub. by Faber & Faber). Merrimack Bk Serv.
Laker, K., jt. auth. see Ghausi, M.
Laker, Mark. Nursing Home Activities for the Handicapped. 98p. 1980. 9.75 (ISBN 0-398-04074-5). C C Thomas.
Laker, Rosalind. Banners of Silk. LC 80-1453. 480p. 1981. 13.95 (ISBN 0-385-15902-1). Doubleday.
--Ride the Blue Riband. 1978. pap. 1.95 o.p. (ISBN 0-451-08252-4, J8252, Sig). NAL.
--Ride the Blue Riband. LC 76-29791. 1977. 7.95 o.p. (ISBN 0-385-12416-3). Doubleday.
--Warwick's Choice. 1981. pap. 2.50 (ISBN 0-451-09664-9, E9664, Sig). NAL.
Lakey, George. Manifesto for a Nonviolent Revolution. 1980. staple back bdg. 1.75 (ISBN 0-86571-004-X). Movement New Soc.
Lakey, H. L. I David: Double Murder on Capitol Hill. Platt, Deborah, ed. 186p. 1981. 12.50 (ISBN 0-934506-03-5). Westminster Comm Pubns.
Lakey, Harold. I, David. Platt, Deborah & Wiesley, Keith, eds. 250p. 1980. 10.95 (ISBN 0-934506-03-5). Westminster Comm & Pubns.
Lakey, Steven D. Bamboo Horses: Wooden Dragons - .22 Hornet. LC 80-69817. 60p. (Orig.). 1980. text ed. 4.95 (ISBN 0-936748-03-6, 0003); pap. text ed. 3.25 (ISBN 0-936748-04-4). Fade In.
--The Nickel Chimera. LC 80-65824. (Illus.). 60p. 1980. 4.95 (ISBN 0-936748-00-1); pap. 2.95 (ISBN 0-936748-01-X). Fade In.
Laki, Kolomon, ed. Contractile Proteins & Muscle. 1971. 89.75 o.p. (ISBN 0-8247-1394-X). Dekker.
Laking, Guy F. A Record of European Armour & Arms Through Seven Centuries, 5 vols. LC 79-8365. (Illus.). Repr. 295.00 set (ISBN 0-404-18344-1). AMS Pr.
Laklan, Carli. Nurse in Training. LC 65-15667. 5.95 o.p. (ISBN 0-385-05816-0). Doubleday.
--Second Year Nurse: Nancy Kimball at City Hospital. LC 67-10052. (gr. 5-9). 1967. 5.95 o.p. (ISBN 0-385-06288-5). Doubleday.
Laklan, Carli, ed. see Collins, Wilkie.
Lakoff, Robin. Language & Woman's Place. 160p. (Orig.). 1975. pap. 4.95 (ISBN 0-06-090389-9, CN389, CN). Har-Row.
Lakoff, Sanford A., ed. Knowledge & Power. LC 66-23079. 1966. 14.95 o.s.i. (ISBN 0-02-917760-X). Free Pr.
--Science & Ethical Responsibility. 1980. pap. text ed. 17.50 (ISBN 0-201-03993-1). A-W.
Lakond, Wladimir, tr. see Tchaikovsky, Petr I.
Lakritz, Esther. Randy Visits the Doctor. LC 61-5063. (Illus.). (ps). 1962. pap. 0.60 (ISBN 0-8054-4119-0); board 1.35 (ISBN 0-686-66386-1). Broadman.
Lakshin, Vladimir. Solzhenitsyn, Tvardovsky & Novy Mir. 176p. 1980. 10.00 (ISBN 0-262-12086-0). MIT Pr.
Lakshmanan, T. R. & Chatterjee, Lata. Urbanization & Environmental Quality. Natoli, Salvatore, ed. LC 76-57032. (Resource Papers for College Geography Ser.). 1977. pap. text ed. 4.00 (ISBN 0-89291-122-0). Assn Am Geographers.
Lakshmanan, T. R., ed. Economic-Environmental-Energy Interactions. Nijkamp, P. (Studies in Applied Regional Science: Vol. 16). 224p. 1980. lib. bdg. 18.95 (ISBN 0-89838-023-5, Martinus Nijhoff Pubs). Kluwer Boston.
Lakshmikantham, V., jt. auth. see Bernfeld, Stephen R.
Laksmikantham, V., jt. auth. see Ladde, G. S.
Lal, jt. auth. see Sachchidananda.
Lal, Basant K. Contemporary Indian Philosophy. 1979. 14.00x (ISBN 0-89684-012-3). South Asia Bks.
Lal, Chaman. The Crown & the Loincloth: A Novel. 432p. 1981. 22.50x (ISBN 0-7069-1285-3, Pub. by Vikas India). Advent Bk.
Lal, Kundan, jt. auth. see Agrawal, A. N.
Lal, P. An Annotated Mahabharata Bibliography. 31p. 1973. 10.00 (ISBN 0-88253-306-1); pap. text ed. 5.00 (ISBN 0-89253-786-8). Ind-US Inc.
--The Concept of an Indian Literature: Six Essays by P. Lal. 49p. 1973. 10.00 (ISBN 0-88253-303-7). Ind-US Inc.
--David McCutchion: Shraddanjali. 15.00 (ISBN 0-89253-671-3); flexible cloth 6.75 (ISBN 0-89253-672-1). Ind-US Inc.
--Draupadi & Jayadratha & Other Poems. 18p. 1973. 5.00 (ISBN 0-88253-271-5); bdg. 4.00flexible (ISBN 0-89253-540-7). Ind-US Inc.
--The Farce of the Drunk Monk. Lal, P., tr. from Sanskrit. 30p. 1973. pap. text ed. 4.00 (ISBN 0-88253-301-0). Ind-US Inc.
--The First Writers Workshop Story Anthology. 9.00 (ISBN 0-89253-762-0); flexible cloth 5.00 (ISBN 0-89253-763-9). Ind-US Inc.
--The Lemon Tree of Modern Sex. (Writers Workshop Greybird Ser.). 106p. 1975. 12.00 (ISBN 0-88253-572-2); pap. text ed. 6.75 (ISBN 0-88253-571-4). Ind-US Inc.
--Love's the First. 32p. 1973. 5.00 (ISBN 0-88253-263-4); flexible bdg. 4.00 (ISBN 0-89253-602-0). Ind-US Inc.
--The Man of Dharma & the Rasa of Silence. (Redbird Book). 61p. 1975. 8.00 (ISBN 0-88253-831-4); pap. 4.80 (ISBN 0-88253-832-2). Ind-US Inc.
--The Parrot's Death & Other Poems. 13p. 1973. 5.00 (ISBN 0-88253-268-5); pap. 4.00 (ISBN 0-88253-806-3). Ind-US Inc.
--T. S. Eliot: Homage from India. 12.00 (ISBN 0-88253-300-2). Ind-US Inc.
--Transcreation: Two Essays. 29p. 1973. 8.00 (ISBN 0-88253-269-3). Ind-US Inc.
--Yakshi from Didarganj. 42p. 1973. 8.00 (ISBN 0-88253-267-7); flexible bdg. 4.00 (ISBN 0-89253-518-0). Ind-US Inc.
Lal, P., jt. auth. see Shastri, P. N.
Lal, P., ed. The First Writers Workshop Literary Reader: An Anthology. (Writers Workshop Greybird Book Ser.). 107p. 1975. 15.00 (ISBN 0-88253-542-0); pap. text ed. 6.75 (ISBN 0-88253-541-2). Ind-US Inc.
--Modern Indian Poetry in English. 733p. 1973. 15.00 (ISBN 0-88253-273-1); pap. text ed. 10.00 (ISBN 0-88253-986-8). Ind-US Inc.
--New English Poetry by Indian Women. (Writers Workshop Redbird Ser.). 1977. flexible bdg. 8.00 (ISBN 0-89253-804-X); text ed. 14.00 (ISBN 0-89253-803-1). Ind-US Inc.
--The Second Writers Workshop Literary Reader: An Anthology. 72p. 1975. 15.00 (ISBN 0-88253-624-9); pap. text ed. 6.75 (ISBN 0-88253-623-0). Ind-US Inc.
Lal, P., ed. see Derozio, Henry.
Lal, P., jt. ed. see Nopany, Nandini.
Lal, P., tr. from Sanskrit. The Avyakta Upanisad. 25p. 1973. 8.00 (ISBN 0-88253-272-3). Ind-US Inc.
--The Bhagavad Gita. 71p. 1973. 8.00 (ISBN 0-88253-304-5); flexible bdg. 4.80 (ISBN 0-89253-542-3). Ind-US Inc.
Lal, P., tr. The Bhagavadgita. 107p. 1971. pap. 2.00 (ISBN 0-88253-054-2). Ind-US Inc.
Lal, P., tr. from Sanskirt. The Brhadaranyaka Upanisad. (Saffronbird Book). 117p. (Eng.). 1975. text ed. 15.00 (ISBN 0-88253-827-6); pap. text ed. 6.75 (ISBN 0-88253-828-4). Ind-US Inc.
Lal, P., tr. from Sanskrit. The Golden Womb of the Sun (Rig Veda) 40p. 1973. 6.75 (ISBN 0-89253-787-6); pap. text ed. 4.80 (ISBN 0-88253-305-3). Ind-US Inc.
Lal, P., tr. from Punjabi. The Japji (Adi Granth) 38p. 1973. 4.80 (ISBN 0-88253-262-6); pap. text ed. 4.00 (ISBN 0-89253-788-4). Ind-US Inc.
Lal, P., tr. Mahabharata, 114 vols. 1973. 6.00 ea. Ind-US Inc.
Lal, P., tr. from Punjabi. More Songs from the Jap-Ji: Selections from the Adi-Granth. 20p. 1975. 4.80 (ISBN 0-88253-708-3); pap. text ed. 4.00 (ISBN 0-89253-789-2). Ind-US Inc.
Lal, P., tr. from Sanskrit. Sanskrit Love Lyrics. 31p. 1973. 6.75 (ISBN 0-88253-265-0); flexible bdg. 4.80 (ISBN 0-89253-525-3). Ind-US Inc.
--Some Sanskrit Poems. 16p. 1973. 8.00 (ISBN 0-88253-266-9); flexible bdg. 4.00 (ISBN 0-89253-520-2). Ind-US Inc.
Lal, P., tr. see Das, Jibanananda.
Lal, P., tr. see Premchand.
Lal, P., tr. see Roy, Tarapada.
Lal, P, tr. see Tagore, Rabindranath.
Lal, P., tr. see Upanisads.
Lal, R., jt. ed. see Greenland, D. J.
Lal, R. B. Art of Working. 5.00 o.p. (ISBN 0-210-34038-X). Asia.
Lala Kalyan Kumar Dey. The Intermediary World & Patterns of Perfection in Philo & Hebrews. LC 75-22457. (Society of Biblical Literature. Dissertation Ser.). 1975. pap. 7.50 (ISBN 0-89130-022-8, 060125). Scholars Pr Ca.
La Laurencie, Lionel de. Les Createurs De l'Opera Francais. LC 80-2287. 1981. Repr. of 1921 ed. 26.00 (ISBN 0-404-18854-0). AMS Pr.
Lalezari, Parviz & Krakauer, Henry, eds. Organ Specific Alloantigens. (Transplantations Proceedings Reprint Ser.). 1980. 24.50 (ISBN 0-8089-1324-7). Grune.
Laliberte, Elizabeth & Daisy, Carol A., eds. Nursing Care of Children: PreTest Self-Assessment & Review. LC 78-50595. (PreTest Self-Assessment & Review Ser.). (Illus.). 1978. pap. 6.95 (ISBN 0-07-051568-9). McGraw-Pretest.
Laliberte, Norman, jt. auth. see Morman, Jean M.
Laliberty, Rene, jt. auth. see Bean, Joseph J., Jr.
Laliberty, Rene, jt. auth. see Bean, Joseph, Jr.
Lalique, Rene. Latique Glass: The Complete Illustrated Catalogue for 1932. (Illus.). 160p. 1981. pap. price not set (ISBN 0-486-24122-X). Dover.
Lall, Arthur. The Emergence of Modern India. LC 80-25028. 288p. 1981. 17.95 (ISBN 0-231-03430-X). Columbia U Pr.
--How Communist China Negotiates. LC 67-29051. 1968. 17.95x (ISBN 0-231-02958-6); pap. 7.50x (ISBN 0-231-08592-3). Columbia U Pr.
--Modern International Negotiation. LC 66-17587. 1966. 22.50x (ISBN 0-231-02935-7). Columbia U Pr.
--U N & the Middle East Crisis. LC 68-8879. (Paperback Ser.: No. 103). 1970. 20.00x (ISBN 0-231-03173-4); pap. 5.00x (ISBN 0-231-08635-0). Columbia U Pr.
Lall, Bernard & Lall, Geeta. Dynamic Leadership. 1979. pap. 6.95 o.p. (ISBN 0-8163-0323-1, 04900-7). Pacific Pr Pub Assn.
--Marijuana--Friend or Foe? LC 78-23656. (Better Living Ser.). 1979. pap. 0.95 (ISBN 0-8127-0222-0). Southern Pub.
Lall, Geeta, jt. auth. see Lall, Bernard.
Lall, K. B. & Chopra, H. S., eds. EEC & The Third World. 500p. 1980. text ed. 31.00x (ISBN 0-391-02004-8). Humanities.
Lall, Samuel B. Cactus Love. flexible cloth 4.80 (ISBN 0-89253-578-4). Ind-US Inc.
Lall, Sanjaya. The Multinational Corporation. 224p. 1980. 32.50 (ISBN 0-8419-5083-0). Holmes & Meier.

Lallez, Raymond. The TEVEC Case: An Experiment in Adult Education Using the Multi-Media System. LC 72-93793. (Experiments & Innovations in Education Ser., No. 1). 659p. (Orig.). 1973. pap. 2.50 (ISBN 92-3-101007-7, U676, UNESCO). Unipub.

Lalli, Judi. At Least I'm Getting Better: Poems for Kids & Other People. (Orig.). 1981. pap. 4.95t (ISBN 0-915166-49-6). Impact Pubs CA.

Lally, Richard. A Bartender's Guide to Baseball. 304p. (Orig.). 1981. pap. 2.50 (ISBN 0-446-91736-2). Warner Bks.

Lal Mani Joshi. God's Alternative: Swami Vivekenanda's Attitude to Buddhism. (God Ser.: No. 841). Date not set. cancelled (ISBN 0-89007-841-6). C Stark. Postponed.

La Lone, Mary. Gabrielino Indians of Southern California: An Annotated Ethnohistoric Bibliography. (Occasional Papers: No. 6). 72p. 1980. pap. 4.50 (ISBN 0-917956-15-X). UCLA Arch.

La Luz, Antonio De see De La Luz, Antonio.

Lam, Basil. Beethoven String Quartets, 2 vols. Incl. Vol. 1. (BBC Music Guides Ser.: No. 32). 64p. pap. (ISBN 0-295-95423-X); Vol. 2. (BBC Music Guides Ser.: No. 33). 64p. pap. (ISBN 0-295-95424-8). LC 75-5008. (Illus.). 1975. pap. 1.95 ea. U of Wash Pr.

Lam, Sau-Hai, jt. auth. see Li, Wen-Hsiung.

Lama Chimpa, Alaka Chattopadhyaya, tr. see Chattopadhyaya, Debiprasad.

Lamadrid, Enrique E., et al. Communicating in Spanish, Level I. 800p. (Sp.). 1974. text ed. 18.25 (ISBN 0-686-57707-8); instructors' manual 12.10 (ISBN 0-395-17530-5); wkbk. 6.95 (ISBN 0-395-17531-3); tapes 158.76 (ISBN 0-395-17534-8). HM.

Lamanna, Carl, et al. Basic Bacteriology. 4th ed. (Illus.). 1973. 26.50 o.p. (ISBN 0-683-04854-6). Williams & Wilkins.

Lamantia, Philip. Becoming Visible. (Pocket Poet Ser.: No. 39). 72p. 1981. pap. 3.00 (ISBN 0-686-69340-X). City Lights.

LaMar, Virginia, ed. see Shakespeare, William.

LaMar, Virginia A., ed. see Shakespeare, William.

LaMarche, Robert J., ed. see Smith, Stan, et al.

Lamare, James W. Texas Politics: Economics, Power, & Policy. 225p. 1981. pap. text ed. 7.16 (ISBN 0-8299-0390-9). West Pub.

La Mare, Walter De see De La Mare, Walter.

Lamarsh, J. R. Introduction to Nuclear Reactor Theory. 1966. 26.95 (ISBN 0-201-04120-0). A-W.

Lamarsh, John R. Introduction to Nuclear Engineering. LC 74-4718. (Nuclear Science & Engineering Ser.). (Illus.). 600p. 1975. text ed. 26.95 (ISBN 0-201-04160-X). A-W.

Lamartine, Alphonse de. A Pilgrimage to the Holy Land. LC 78-14368. 1978. Repr. of 1838 ed. 40.00x (ISBN 0-8201-1323-9). Schol Facsimiles.

Lamb, Beatrice P. India. (Illus.). (gr. 7 up). 1965. 4.95 o.s.i. (ISBN 0-02-751340-8). Macmillan.

--Nehrus of India: Three Generations of Leadership. (gr. 7 up). 1967. 5.95 o.s.i. (ISBN 0-02-751320-3). Macmillan.

Lamb, Brian, jt. auth. see Lamb, Edgar.

Lamb, Charles. Essays of Elia. Incl. Last Essays of Elia. 1954. 11.50x (ISBN 0-460-00014-4, Evman); pap. 4.50 (ISBN 0-460-01014-X, Evman). Dutton.

--Lamb As Critic. Park, Roy, ed. LC 78-73572. xii, 367p. 1980. 21.50x (ISBN 0-8032-8700-3). U of Nebr Pr.

--Lamb: Selected Essays. Nabholtz, John R., ed. LC 67-13464. (Crofts Classics Ser.). 1967. pap. text ed. 1.25x (ISBN 0-88295-052-5). AHM Pub.

Lamb, Charles & Lamb, Mary. Tales from Shakespeare. (New Children's Classics). (Illus.). (gr. 5-8). 1963. 4.95g o.s.i. (ISBN 0-02-751260-6). Macmillan.

--Tales from Shakespeare. Shakespeare Library, ed. LC 79-89991. (Illus.). 1979. 35.00 (ISBN 0-918016-04-5); pap. 19.95 (ISBN 0-918016-17-7). Folger Bks.

Lamb, Charles see Fenwick, Eliza.

Lamb, Charles, jt. ed. see Vernon, Ivan, Jr.

Lamb, Charles W., Jr., ed. see Theory Conference, Phoenix, Arizona, February, 1980.

Lamb, Charlotte. Compulsion. (Harlequin Presents Ser.). 192p. 1981. pap. 1.50 (ISBN 0-373-10422-7, Pub. by Harlequin). PB.

--The Cruel Flame. (Harlequin Presents Ser.). 192p. 1980. pap. 1.50 (ISBN 0-373-10387-5, Pub. by Harlequin). PB.

--A Frozen Fire. (Harlequin Presents Ser.). 192p. 1980. pap. 1.50 (ISBN 0-373-10380-8, Pub. by Harlequin). PB.

--Man's World. (Harlequin Presents Ser.). 192p. (Orig.). 1981. pap. 1.50 (ISBN 0-373-10412-X, Pub. by Harlequin). PB.

--Night Music. (Harlequin Presents Ser.). 192p. (Orig.). 1981. pap. 1.50 (ISBN 0-373-10404-9, Pub. by Harlequin). PB.

--Savage Surrender. (Harlequin Presents Ser.). 192p. 1980. pap. 1.50 (ISBN 0-373-10401-4, Pub. by Harlequin). PB.

--Seduction. (Harlequin Presents Ser.). 192p. 1981. pap. 1.50 (ISBN 0-373-10428-6, Pub. by Harlequin). PB.

--The Silken Trap. (Harlequin Presents Ser.). 192p. 1980. pap. 1.50 (ISBN 0-373-10374-3, Pub. by Harlequin). PB.

--Star-Crossed. (Alpha Books). 1978p. (Orig.). 1979. pap. text ed. 2.25x (ISBN 0-19-424160-2). Oxford U Pr.

--Stranger in the Night. (Harlequin Presents Ser.). 192p. 1981. pap. 1.50 (ISBN 0-373-10417-0, Pub. by Harlequin). PB.

Lamb, David. Hegel: From Foundation to System. (Martinus Nijhoff Philosophy Library: No. 1). 252p. 1980. lib. bdg. 34.50 (ISBN 90-247-2359-0, Martinus Nijhoff Pubs). Kluwer Boston.

Lamb, Edgar & Lamb, Brian. Colorful Cacti of the American Deserts. LC 74-8615. (Pocket Encyclopedias in Color Ser). (Illus.). 208p. 1974. 9.95 (ISBN 0-02-567670-9). Macmillan.

--The Illustrated Reference on Cacti & Other Succulents in 5 Volumes. Incl. Vol. 1. 1955 (ISBN 0-7137-0681-3); Vol. 2. 1959 (ISBN 0-7137-0623-6); Vol. 3. 1963 (ISBN 0-7137-0009-2); Vol. 4. 1966 (ISBN 0-7137-0691-0). (Illus.). 20.95 ea. (Pub. by Blandford Pr England). Sterling.

--Illustrated Reference on Cacti & Succulents, Vol. 5. (Illus.). 1978. 20.95 (ISBN 0-7137-0852-2, Pub. by Blandford Pr England). Sterling.

Lamb, Edgar & Lamp, Brian. Pocket Encyclopedia of Cacti in Color. (Illus.). 217p. 1980. 9.95 (ISBN 0-7137-0506-X, Pub. by Blandford Pr England). Sterling.

Lamb, G. Victorian Magic. (Illus.). 1976. 15.00 (ISBN 0-7100-8453-6). Routledge & Kegan.

Lamb, G. B., jt. auth. see Wraith, R. E.

Lamb, Geoffrey. Card Tricks. LC 72-13357. (Illus.). 80p. (gr. 6 up). 1973. 6.95 o.p. (ISBN 0-525-66300-2). Elsevier-Nelson.

--Illustrated Magic Dictionary. (Illus.). 160p. 1980. 7.95 (ISBN 0-525-66689-3). Elsevier-Nelson.

--Pencil & Paper Tricks. LC 77-12102. (Illus.). (gr. 5 up). 1977. Repr. 6.95 o.p. (ISBN 0-525-66565-X). Elsevier-Nelson.

Lamb, Geoffrey F. Magicians. LC 79-366524. (Pegasus Books: No. 15). (Illus.). 1968. 7.50x (ISBN 0-234-77022-8). Intl Pubns Serv.

Lamb, George L. Elements of Solition Theory. LC 80-13373. (Pure & Applied Mathematics: Texts & Monographs). 1980. 29.95 (ISBN 0-471-04559-4, Pub. by Wiley-Interscience). Wiley.

Lamb, H. Richard, et al, eds. Handbook of Community Mental Health Practices: The San Mateo Experience. LC 72-92886. (Behavioral Sciences Ser). 1969. 18.95x o.p. (ISBN 0-87589-040-7). Jossey-Bass.

Lamb, Harold. Babur the Tiger. 1979. pap. 1.95 o.p. (ISBN 0-523-40473-5). Pinnacle Bks.

Lamb, Horace. Hydrodynamics. 6th ed. (Illus.). 1932. pap. text ed. 8.95 (ISBN 0-486-60256-7). Dover.

Lamb, Hugh, ed. Tide of Terror: An Anthology of Rare Horror Stories. LC 73-6181. 1973. 7.95 o.p. (ISBN 0-8008-7695-4). Taplinger.

Lamb, Jackie & Lamb, Wesley. Parent Education & Elementary Counseling. Walz, Garry R. & Benjamin, Libby, eds. LC 77-12942. (New Vistas in Counseling Ser.: Vol. 5). 1978. 14.95 (ISBN 0-87705-318-9). Human Sci Pr.

Lamb, Jefferson D. The Development of the Agrarian Movement & Agrarian Legislation in China. LC 78-74319. (Modern Chinese Economy Ser.: Vol. 12). 254p. 1980. lib. bdg. 33.00 (ISBN 0-8240-4261-1). Garland Pub.

Lamb, John. Running & Maintenance of the Marine Diesel Engine. 722p. 1977. 57.95x (ISBN 0-85264-105-2, Pub. by Griffin England). State Mutual Bk.

Lamb, Karl A. As Orange Goes: Twelve California Families & the Future of American Politics. 1974. 8.95x (ISBN 0-393-05520-5); pap. 6.95x (ISBN 0-393-09235-6). Norton.

Lamb, Lowry, jt. auth. see Wells, Ted.

Lamb, M. J. Biology of Aging. LC 77-9528. (Tertiary Level Biology Ser.). 1977. 24.95 (ISBN 0-470-99221-2). Halsted Pr.

Lamb, M. W. & Harden, M. L. Meaning of Human Nutrition. 1973. text ed. 18.50 (ISBN 0-08-017078-1); pap. text ed. 9.50 (ISBN 0-08-017079-X). Pergamon.

Lamb, Margaret. Colorado High Country. LC 64-7814. (Illus., Orig.). 1965. pap. 2.95 (ISBN 0-8040-0053-0, CB6, SB). Swallow.

Lamb, Mary, jt. auth. see Lamb, Charles.

Lamb, Max & Sanford, Harry. The Last Nazi. (Orig.). 1980. pap. 2.25 (ISBN 0-505-51486-9). Tower Bks.

Lamb, Michael E. The Role of the Father in Child Development. LC 76-21778. (Personality Processes Ser.). 1976. 23.50 (ISBN 0-471-51172-2, Pub. by Wiley-Interscience). Wiley.

Lamb, Michael E. & Brown, Ann L., eds. Advances in Developmental Psychology, Vol. 1. (Advances in Developmental Psychology Ser.). 400p. 1981. prof. ref. 24.95 (ISBN 0-89859-094-9). L Erlbaum Assocs.

Lamb, Michael E. & Sherrod, Lonnie R., eds. Infant Social Cognition: Empirical & Theoretical Considerations. LC 80-21137. 438p. 1981. text ed. 29.95 (ISBN 0-89859-058-2). L Erlbaum Assocs.

Lamb, Michael E., et al, eds. Social Interaction Analysis: Methodological Issues. LC 78-53287. 1979. 21.50 (ISBN 0-299-07590-7). U of Wis Pr.

Lamb, Norman. Guide to Teaching Strings. 3rd ed. (Instrumental Technique Ser.). 225p. 1980. pap. text ed. 7.95 (ISBN 0-697-03603-0). Wm C Brown.

Lamb, Peter, jt. auth. see Hastenrath, Stefan L.

Lamb, Peter J., jt. auth. see Hastenrath, Stefan.

Lamb, Pose & Arnold, Richard. Teaching Reading: Foundations & Strategies. 2nd ed. 432p. 1980. text ed. 16.95x (ISBN 0-534-00847-X). Wadsworth Pub.

Lamb, Pose M. & Arnold, Richard D. Reading: Foundations & Instructional Strategies. 1976. text ed. 15.95x o.p. (ISBN 0-534-00423-7). Wadsworth Pub.

Lamb, Robert, et al, eds. Business, Media & the Law: The Troubled Confluence. LC 78-55569. 1980. 15.00x (ISBN 0-8147-0565-0). NYU Pr.

Lamb, Robert P., jt. auth. see Swaggart, Jimmy.

Lamb, V. B. The Betrayal of Richard III. 128p. 1980. 9.75x (ISBN 0-7050-0066-4, Pub. by Skilton & Shaw England). State Mutual Bk.

Lamb, Warren & Watson, Elizabeth. Body Code: The Meaning in Movement. (Illus.). 1979. 16.00 (ISBN 0-7100-0017-0). Routledge & Kegan.

Lamb, Wesley, jt. auth. see Lamb, Jackie.

Lamballe, Nathaniel. Art Secrets Artists Follow in Their Search for Greatness. (Illus.). 90p. 1975. 37.50 (ISBN 0-913314-48-X). Am Classical College Pr.

--The Bold Approach & Tested Advice of Benefit to Artists Valiantly Struggling for Artistic Success. (The Institute for Human Development Ser.). (Illus.). 1978. deluxe bdg. 37.50 (ISBN 0-930582-03-9). Gloucester Art.

Lambard, Wliiam. The Duties of Constables, Borsholders, Tithing-Men, & Such Other Low Ministers of the Peace. LC 70-25853. (English Experience Ser.: No. 176). 1969. Repr. of 1583 ed. 8.00 (ISBN 90-221-0176-2). Walter J Johnson.

Lambdin, Thomas O. An Introduction to Biblical Hebrew. 1971. text ed. 17.95x (ISBN 0-684-41322-1, ScribC). Scribner.

--Introduction to Classical Ethiopic (Ge'ez) LC 78-12895. (Harvard Semitic Museum. Harvard Semitic Studies: No. 24). 1978. 15.00 (ISBN 0-89130-263-8, 040424). Scholars Pr Ca.

Lambe, Dwight W., et al, eds. Anaerobic Bacteria: Selected Topics. 324p. 1980. 29.50 (ISBN 0-686-63458-6, Plenum Pr). Plenum Pub.

Lambe, T. William. Soil Testing for Engineers. (Soil Engineering Ser.). 1951. pap. text ed. 24.95x (ISBN 0-471-51183-8). Wiley.

Lambe, T. William & Whitman, Robert V. Soil Mechanics. LC 68-30915. (Soil Engineering Ser). 1969. 29.95 (ISBN 0-471-51192-7). Wiley.

Lambeck, K. The Earth's Variable Rotation. LC 79-7653. (Cambridge Monographs on Mechanics & Applied Mathematics). (Illus.). 400p. 1980. 92.50 (ISBN 0-521-22769-0). Cambridge U Pr.

Lambek, Joachim. Lectures in Rings & Modules. 2nd ed. LC 75-41494. viii, 184p. 1976. 9.95 (ISBN 0-8284-1283-9). Chelsea Pub.

Lamberg, Stanley L. & Rothstein, Robert. Histology & Cytology: Functional Medical Laboratory Manual. (Illus.). 1978. lab. manual 10.50 (ISBN 0-87055-272-4). AVI.

Lamberg-Karlovsky, C. C. Excavations at Tepe Yahya, Iran, 1967-1969: Progress Report No. 1. LC 74-143902. (ASPR Bulletin: No. 27). 1970. pap. text ed. 12.00 (ISBN 0-87365-528-1). Peabody Harvard.

Lamberg-Karlovsky, C. C., intro. by. Hunters, Farmers, & Civilizations: Old World Archaeology: Readings from Scientific American. LC 78-27049. (Illus.). 1979. text ed. 19.95x (ISBN 0-7167-1073-0); pap. text ed. 9.95x (ISBN 0-7167-1074-9). W H Freeman.

Lamberson, L. K., jt. auth. see Kapur, K. C.

Lambert. De Ferri Metallographia: Recent Examination Methods in Metallography & the Metallography of Welds, Vol. 4. 1980. write for info. (ISBN 0-85501-165-3). Heyden.

Lambert, Anthony J. Victorian & Edwardian Country House Life. (Illus.). 120p. 1981. 21.20x (ISBN 0-8419-0684-X). Holmes & Meier.

Lambert, Betty. Bring Down the Sun. 300p. 1980. 10.95 (ISBN 0-670-24857-6). Viking Pr.

Lambert, Byron C., ed. The Essential Paul Elmer More: A Selection of His Writings. 1972. 12.95 o.s.i. (ISBN 0-87000-162-0). Arlington Hse.

Lambert, Carla. Melinda. (Orig.). 1979. pap. 1.95 (ISBN 0-532-23285-2). Manor Bks.

Lambert, Charles E. & Stone, Donald. Orthopaedic Physician's Assistant Techniques. LC 74-77819. (Allied Health Ser). 1975. pap. 7.05 (ISBN 0-672-61388-3). Bobbs.

Lambert, Clark. Field Sales Performance Appraisal. LC 79-18567. (Marketing Management Ser.). 1979. 24.95 (ISBN 0-471-04781-3, Pub by Ronald Pr). Wiley.

Lambert, Clinton E., Jr., jt. auth. see Lambert, Vickie A.

Lambert, David. Exploring the Age of Dinosaurs. (Explorer Bks). (Illus.). (gr. 3-5). 1978. 2.95 o.p. (ISBN 0-531-09095-7); PLB 4.90 s&l o.p. (ISBN 0-531-09101-5). Watts.

--Seashore. (Modern Knowledge Library). (Illus.). (gr. 5 up). 1978. 3.95 o.p. (ISBN 0-685-86307-7); PLB 5.90 s&l o.p. (ISBN 0-531-09061-2). Watts.

Lambert, Dennis & Zalkind, Ronald. Producing Hit Records. LC 79-91505. (Illus.). 1980. 17.50 (ISBN 0-02-871950-6); pap. 9.95 (ISBN 0-02-871960-3). Schirmer Bks.

Lambert, E. N. & Mohammed, M. J. Comprehensive Qualitative Analysis for Advanced Level Chemistry. 1978. pap. text ed. 5.95x (ISBN 0-435-65537-X). Heinemann Ed.

Lambert, Frederick. Letter Forms: 110 Complete Alphabets. 128p. 1972. pap. 3.50 (ISBN 0-486-22872-X). Dover.

Lambert, Gussie. Christ at Corinth. rev. ed. pap. 3.95 (ISBN 0-89315-008-8). Lambert Bk.

--Gleaning from Galatians. (Ser. Outlines). 4.95 (ISBN 0-89315-075-4). Lambert Bk.

Lambert, H. M. Gujarati Language Course. LC 68-23180. 1970. 44.00 (ISBN 0-521-07157-7). Cambridge U Pr.

Lambert, H. P., jt. ed. see Caldwell, A. D.

Lambert, Herbert G., ed. see Plywood Clinic, 3rd, Portland, Mar.1975.

Lambert, Herbert H. Getting Inside the Bible. 144p. 1976. pap. 1.50 (ISBN 0-8272-1218-6). Bethany Pr.

Lambert, Hugh, jt. auth. see Parker, Watson.

Lambert, J., jt. auth. see Holderness, A.

Lambert, J. D. Vibrational & Rotational Relaxation in Gases. (International Series of Monographs on Chemistry). (Illus.). 1978. 34.95x (ISBN 0-19-855605-5). Oxford U Pr.

Lambert, Jean-Clarence, ed. Karel Appel: Works on Paper. White, Kenneth, tr. LC 79-92227. (Illus.). 256p. 1980. 65.00 (ISBN 0-89659-069-0); limited ed. 2500.00 (ISBN 0-89659-140-9). Abbeville Pr.

Lambert, Karel & Brittan, Gordon G., Jr. An Introduction to the Philosophy of Science. rev. 2nd ed. 1979. lib. bdg. 22.00 (ISBN 0-917930-37-1); pap. text ed. 7.50x (ISBN 0-917930-17-7). Ridgeview.

Lambert, Karel, ed. Logical Way of Doing Things. LC 69-15450. 1969. 20.00x o.p. (ISBN 0-300-01133-4). Yale U Pr.

Lambert, M. B. Volcanoes. LC 78-64573. (Illus.). 70p. 1979. pap. 7.95 (ISBN 0-295-95783-2). U of Wash Pr.

Lambert, Mark. Dickins & the Suspended Quotation. LC 80-22072. 208p. 1981. 16.50 (ISBN 0-300-02555-6). Yale U Pr.

--Malory: Style & Vision in "le Morte d'Arthur". LC 74-29727. (Studies in English Ser.: No. 186). 224p. 1975. 15.00x o.p. (ISBN 0-300-01835-5). Yale U Pr.

Lambert, O. C. Catholicism Against Itself, Vol. 1. 7.50 (ISBN 0-89315-005-3). Lambert Bk.

--Catholicism Against Itself, Vol. 2. 7.50 (ISBN 0-89315-006-1). Lambert Bk.

Lambert, R. M., jt. auth. see Thomas, J. M.

Lambert, R. W. The Wolfman Cometh. 4.00 o.p. (ISBN 0-8062-1057-5). Carlton.

Lambert, Richard D., ed. Resources for South Asian Area Studies in the United States. LC 62-11263. 1962. 9.00x o.p. (ISBN 0-8122-7362-1). U of Pa Pr.

Lambert, Richard D., jt. ed. see Cook, Philip J.

Lambert, Richard D., jt. ed. see Gordon, Milton M.

Lambert, Richard D., jt. ed. see Laconte, M. Pierre.

Lambert, Richard D., jt. ed. see Sherman, Lawrence W.

Lambert, Richard D., ed. see Shur, Irene G. & Littell, Franklin H.

Lambert, Richard D., jt. ed. see Taeuber, Conrad.

Lambert, Richard D., jt. ed. see Wolfgang, Marvin E.

Lambert, Rosemary. The Twentieth Century. LC 80-40456. (Cambridge Introduction to the History of Art: No. 7). (Illus.). 90p. Date not set. 19.95 (ISBN 0-521-22715-1); pap. 6.95 (ISBN 0-521-29622-6). Cambridge U Pr.

Lambert, Royston. New Wine in Old Bottles? 171p. 1968. pap. text ed. 5.00x (Pub. by Bedford England). Renouf.

Lambert, Sheila. Bills & Acts: Legislative Procedure in Eighteenth Century England. 1971. 39.00 (ISBN 0-521-08119-X). Cambridge U Pr.

Lambert, Terence. Lambert's Birds of Shore & Estuary. (Encore Edition). (Illus.). 1979. 5.95 (ISBN 0-684-16906-1, ScribT). Scribner.

Lambert, Terence & Mitchell, Alan. Lambert's Birds of Garden & Woodland. LC 76-21893. (Encore Edition). (Illus.). 1976. 4.95 o.p. (ISBN 0-684-15416-1, ScribT). Scribner.

Lambert, Theresa N., jt. auth. see Hirschfield, Ira S.

Lambert, Vickie A. & Lambert, Clinton E., Jr. The Impact of Physical Illness & Related Mental Health Concepts. (Illus.). 1979. pap. 11.95 ref. ed. (ISBN 0-13-451732-6). P-H.

Lambert, Wallace E., jt. auth. see Lambert, William W.

Lambert, Wallace E., et al. Child Rearing Values: A Cross National Study. LC 78-19747. 1979. 29.95 (ISBN 0-03-049086-3). Praeger.

Lambert, Wilfred G. Babylonian Wisdom Literature. (Illus.). 1960. 37.50x (ISBN 0-19-815424-0). Oxford U Pr.

Lambert, William W. & Lambert, Wallace E. Social Psychology. 2nd ed. (Foundations of Modern Psychology Ser.). (Illus.). 192p. (Reference eds.). 1973. ref. ed 12.95 (ISBN 0-13-818021-0); pap. 7.95 (ISBN 0-13-818013-X). P-H.

Lambert, William W., jt. auth. see Triandis, Harry C.

Lamberth, John, et al. Personality: An Introduction. 1978. 14.95x (ISBN 0-394-31190-6). Random.

Lamberton, Charles. Selected Papers on the Subfossil Lemurs of Madagascar: 1934-1956. LC 78-72726. 1980. 67.50 (ISBN 0-404-18297-6). AMS Pr.

Lamberts, J. J. A Short Introduction to English Usage. 400p. 1981. Repr. lib. bdg. write for info. (ISBN 0-89874-328-1). Krieger.

Lamberts, Steven W. & MacLeod, Robert M. Physiological & Pathological Aspects of Prolactin Secretion, Vol. 1, 1977. Horrobin, David F., ed. (Annual Research Reviews Ser.). 1978. 19.20 (ISBN 0-88831-034-X). Eden Med Res.

Lambeth, M. Strawcraft. 72p. 1974. 9.95 (ISBN 0-212-97010-0). Transatlantic.

Lambeth, R. J. Templeman on Marine Insurance: Its Principles & Practice. 5th ed. 500p. 1981. 48.00x (ISBN 0-7121-1395-9). Sheridan.

Lambley, Peter. The Psychology of Apartheid. LC 80-53595. 312p. 1981. lib. bdg. 16.50x (ISBN 0-8203-0548-0). U of Ga Pr.

Lamblin, Simone. Le Larousse des enfants. (Illus., Fr.). (gr. 3 up). 1979. 33.75 (ISBN 2-03-051421-7). Larousse.

Lambo, J. O. Catalogue of African Herbs. (Traditional Healing Ser.: Vol. 5). 1981. 39.50 (ISBN 0-932426-04-2). Trado-Medic.

Lamborn, George D., ed. Entirely Entertaining. 212p. (Orig.). 1979. pap. 5.95. Jr League Montclair-Newark.

Lambourne, Lionel. British Watercolours in the Victoria & Albert Museum: An Illustrated Summary Catalogue of the National Collection. (Illus.). 455p. 1980. 125.00x (ISBN 0-85667-067-7, Pub. by Sotheby Parke Bernet England). Biblio Dist.

Lambrecht, Ann. Step-by-Step Plumbing. (Step-by-Step Home Repair Ser.). (Illus.). 96p. 1981. 4.95 (ISBN 0-696-00575-1). Meredith Corp.

Lambrick, George & Robinson, Mark. Iron Age & Roman Riverside Settlements at Farmoor, Oxfordshire. 160p. 1980. pap. 54.00x (ISBN 0-900312-57-2, Pub. by Coun Brit Arch England). Intl Schol Bk Serv.

Lambright, W. Henry, et al. Technology Transfer to Cities: Process of Choice at the Local Level. (Special Studies in Public Policy & Public Systems Management). 1979. lib. bdg. 21.50x (ISBN 0-89158-366-1). Westview.

Lambro, Donald. The Federal Rathole. 1975. 7.95 o.p. (ISBN 0-87000-294-5). Arlington Hse.

Lambros, Paul. Unpublished Coins of the Medieval Kingdom of Cyprus. Toumazou, Michael, tr. from Gr. (Illus.). 170p. (Eng., Fr., Gr.). 20.00 (ISBN 0-916710-76-9). Obol Intl.

Lambton, A. K. Theory & Practice in Medieval Persian Government. 332p. 1980. 75.00x (ISBN 0-86078-067-8, Pub. by Variorum England). State Mutual Bk.

Lambton, Ann, jt. ed. see Holt, P. M.

Lambton, Ann K. Persian Grammar. 1953-1960. pap. 16.95x (ISBN 0-521-09124-1). Cambridge U Pr.

--Persian Vocabulary. 1954-1962. pap. 18.95x (ISBN 0-521-09154-3, 154). Cambridge U Pr.

Lambton, Anne. Lady. 352p. (Orig.). 1981. pap. 2.75 (ISBN 0-515-05532-8). Jove Pubns.

Lambuth, Letcher. The Angler's Workshop. 212p. 1979. 49.50x (ISBN 0-918400-01-5, Pub. by Champoeg Pr). Intl Schol Bk Serv.

Lamd, Hugh, ed. Wave of Fear: A Classic Horror Anthology. LC 74-1963. 1974. 7.95 o.p. (ISBN 0-8008-8063-3). Taplinger.

Lamdrum, Phil, jt. tr. see Brant, Henry.

Lameijer, J. N., jt. auth. see Cockcroft, A. N.

Lamennais, Hughes F. Words of a Believer & the Past & Future of the People. vi, 208p. 1972. Repr. of 1891 ed. 15.00 (ISBN 0-86527-212-3). Fertig.

Lamere, Bernard. Guide to Home Air Conditioners & Refrigeration Equipment. (Illus., Orig.). 1963. pap. 6.50 (ISBN 0-8104-0294-7). Hayden.

Lamers, William M., Jr., jt. auth. see Semmens, James P.

La Meslee, Edmond M. The New Australia, 1883. Ward, Russel, tr. 1973. text ed. 13.95x o.p. (ISBN 0-435-32895-6). Heinemann Ed.

Laming, Roy. Fun with Building Models. (Learning with Fun Ser.). (Illus.). 64p. 1980. text ed. 11.50x (ISBN 0-7182-1322-X, SpS). Soccer.

Lamit, Gary. Industrial Model Building. (Illus.). 528p. 1981. text ed. 38.00 (ISBN 0-13-461566-2). P-H.

Lamkin, Jill S. Getting Started: Career Education Activities for Exceptional Students. 144p. 1980. pap. 5.50 (ISBN 0-86586-113-7). Coun Exc Child.

Lamm, Michael. The Great Camaro. (Illus.). 144p. 1978. 16.95 (ISBN 0-932128-00-9). Lamm-Morada.

Lamm, Nathaniel, jt. auth. see Geier, Alvin E.

Lamm, Ursula, tr. see Bauer, Arnold.

Lamm, Zvi. Conflicting Theories of Instruction: Conceptual Dimensions. LC 76-9238. 1976. 17.50x (ISBN 0-8211-1112-4); text ed. 15.75x (ISBN 0-685-73826-4). McCutchan.

Lammer, Jutta. Fun with Felt. 1970. 14.95 (ISBN 0-7134-2459-1, Pub. by Batsford England). David & Charles.

Lammers, Lawrence P., jt. auth. see Hardy, Owen B.

Lammich, G. & Kadow, H. Warm up for Soccer. LC 74-31697. (Illus.). 128p. (gr. 5 up). 1975. 8.95 (ISBN 0-8069-4090-5); PLB 8.29 (ISBN 0-8069-4091-3). Sterling.

Lamming, George. Of Age & Innocence. 414p. 1981. 13.95 (ISBN 0-8052-8095-2, Pub. by Allison & Busby England); pap. 5.95 (ISBN 0-8052-8094-4). Schocken.

LaMond, Annette M. Competition in the General-Freight Motor-Carrier Industry. LC 79-3048. 1980. 16.95x (ISBN 0-669-03308-1). Lexington Bks.

LaMond, Annette M., jt. ed. see Wallace, Phyllis A.

Lamond, Ross, jt. auth. see Jochle, Wolfgang.

La Monica, Elaine L. The Nursing Process: A Humanistic Approach. 1979. text ed. 13.95 (ISBN 0-201-04138-3, 04138, M&N Div). A-W.

Lamont, Barbara. City People. 224p. 1975. 7.95 o.s.i. (ISBN 0-02-567690-3). Macmillan.

Lamont, Bette. Island Time. LC 75-26998. (Illus.). (gr. k-3). 1976. 7.95 (ISBN 0-397-31568-6). Lippincott.

Lamont, Claire, ed. see Scott, Sir Walter.

Lamont, Corliss. Freedom Is As Freedom Does. LC 74-171384. (Civil Liberties in American History Ser.). 1972. Repr. of 1956 ed. lib. bdg. 35.00 (ISBN 0-306-70498-6). Da Capo.

--Freedom Is As Freedom Does: Civil Liberties in America. 330p. (Orig.). 1981. pap. 5.95 (ISBN 0-8180-0350-2). Horizon.

--Humanist Funeral Service. LC 77-76001. 48p. 1977. 6.95 (ISBN 0-87975-093-6); pap. 2.95 (ISBN 0-87975-090-1). Prometheus Bks.

--A Humanist Wedding Service. 32p. pap. 2.95 saddle bdg. (ISBN 0-87975-000-6). Prometheus Bks.

--Illusion of Immortality. 4th ed. LC 65-25140. 1965. pap. 4.45 (ISBN 0-8044-6377-8). Ungar.

--Voice in the Wilderness: Collected Essays of Corliss Lamont. new ed. LC 74-75351. 327p. 1974. 10.00 (ISBN 0-87975-044-8); pap. 5.95 (ISBN 0-87975-060-X). Prometheus Bks.

Lamont, Corliss, ed. Dialogue on George Santayana. 115p. (Orig.). 1981. pap. 4.95 (ISBN 0-8180-1327-3). Horizon.

--Dialogue on John Dewey. 155p. (Orig.). 1981. pap. 4.95 (ISBN 0-8180-1328-1). Horizon.

--Freedom of Choice Affirmed. 214p. (Orig.). 1981. pap. 4.95 (ISBN 0-8180-1329-X). Horizon.

Lamont, Daniel. Christ & the World of Thought. 2nd ed. 309p. 1935. text ed. 6.50 (ISBN 0-567-02160-2). Attic Pr.

Lamont, Rosette C., ed. Ionesco: A Collection of Critical Essays. (Twentieth Century Views Ser). (Illus.). 192p. 1973. 10.95 o.p. (ISBN 0-13-504977-6); pap. 1.95 o.p. (ISBN 0-13-504969-5). P-H.

LaMonte, John L. World of the Middle Ages: A Reorientation of Medieval History. (Illus.). 1949. 34.50x (ISBN 0-89197-473-3); pap. text ed. 19.50x (ISBN 0-89197-980-8). Irvington.

Lamore, Lee. Stop Trying to Stop Smoking, & Do It This Time: Secrets of a Mad Smoker. LC 80-69207. 112p. pap. 3.95 (ISBN 0-938318-00-4). Britton Pub.

La Mothe, Francois De Salignac De see Fenelon & De Salignac De La Mothe, Francois.

Lamott, Kenneth. Escape from Stress. 1975. pap. 1.95 o.p. (ISBN 0-425-03212-4). Berkley Pub.

LaMotta, Jake & Carter, Joseph. Raging Bull. 160p. 1980. pap. 2.25 (ISBN 0-553-13981-9). Bantam.

L'Amour. Fallon. 160p. (Orig.). 1981. pap. 2.25 (ISBN 0-553-14534-7). Bantam.

L'Amour, Louis. Bendigo Shafter. 1980. lib. bdg. 15.95 (ISBN 0-8161-3144-9, Large Print Bks). G K Hall.

--Brionne. 160p. (Orig.). 1981. pap. 2.25 (ISBN 0-553-14754-4). Bantam.

--Complete L'amour, 9 bks. Incl. To Tame a Land; Heller with a Gun; The Tall Stranger; Last Stand at Papago Wells; Hondo; Kilkenny; Showdown at Yellow Butte; Utah Blaine; Crossfire Trail. (Western Fiction Ser.). 1981. Repr. of 1978 ed. Set. lib. bdg. 74.50 (ISBN 0-8398-2662-1). Gregg.

--The Comstock Lode. 384p. 1981. 14.95 (ISBN 0-553-05001-X); pap. 7.95 (ISBN 0-553-01307-6). Bantam.

--Crossfire Trail. 1978. pap. 1.95 (ISBN 0-449-14276-0, GM). Fawcett.

--Fair Blows the Wind. 1978. 7.95 o.p. (ISBN 0-525-10260-4). Dutton.

--The First Fast Draw. 160p. (Orig.). 1980. pap. 2.25 (ISBN 0-553-14538-X). Bantam.

--Heller with a Gun. (Western Fiction Ser.). 1981. lib. bdg. 11.95 (ISBN 0-8398-2696-6). Gregg.

--The Iron Marshal. 1980. pap. 8.95 (ISBN 0-8161-3101-5, Large Print Bks). G K Hall.

--Kiowa Trail. 160p. (Orig.). 1980. pap. 1.95 (ISBN 0-553-13882-0). Bantam.

--L'amour Westerns: Part Two, 4 bks. Incl. To Tame a Land; Heller with a Gun; The Tall Stranger; Last Stand at Papago Wells. (Western Fiction Ser.). 1981. Set. lib. bdg. 40.00 (ISBN 0-8398-2661-3). Gregg.

--Last Stand at Papago Wells. (Western Fiction Ser.). 1981. lib. bdg. 10.95 (ISBN 0-8398-2694-X). Gregg.

--Matagorda. 176p. (Orig.). 1981. pap. 2.25 (ISBN 0-553-14743-9). Bantam.

--Over the Dry Side. 192p. 1981. pap. 2.25 (ISBN 0-553-14536-3). Bantam.

--Shalako. 176p. (Orig.). 1980. pap. 1.95 (ISBN 0-553-14013-2). Bantam.

--The Tall Stranger. (Western Fiction Ser.). 1981. lib. bdg. 10.95 (ISBN 0-8398-2695-8). Gregg.

--To Tame a Land. (Western Fiction Ser.). 1981. lib. bdg. 11.95 (ISBN 0-8398-2697-4). Gregg.

--To the Far Blue Mountains. 1977. pap. 2.25 (ISBN 0-685-78253-0, T12721-7). Bantam.

--The Warrior's Path. 240p. (Orig.). 1980. pap. 1.95 (ISBN 0-553-14207-0). Bantam.

--The Warrior's Path. 1981. lib. bdg. 13.95 (ISBN 0-8161-3145-7, Large Print Bks). G K Hall.

Lamoureux, Denis, jt. auth. see Blandy, Thomas.

Lamoureux, Richard E. Alberti's Church of San Sebastiano in Mantua. Freedberg, Sydney J., ed. LC 78-74370. (Oustanding Dissertations in the Fine Arts Ser.). (Illus.). 1979. lib. bdg. 38.00 (ISBN 0-8240-3958-0). Garland Pub.

Lamp, Brian, jt. auth. see Lamb, Edgar.

Lampe, G. W., ed. Patristic Greek Lexicon, Fascicle 5. 1968. 22.00x (ISBN 0-19-864212-1). Oxford U Pr.

--Patristic Greek Lexicon Nineteen Sixty-One to Sixty-Eight. 165.00x (ISBN 0-19-864213-X). Oxford U Pr.

Lampe, Gerald N., jt. auth. see Mannheimer, Jeffrey S.

Lampen, Nevada. Fat-Free Recipes. 1977. pap. 4.95 (ISBN 0-571-11026-6, Pub. by Faber & Faber). Merrimack Bk Serv.

Lampert, L. M. Modern Dairy Products. 3rd ed. (Illus.). 1975. 39.50 (ISBN 0-8206-0230-2). Chem Pub.

Lamperti, Claudia M., ed. Woman Space: Future & Fantasy Stories by Women. 60p. (Orig.). 1981. pap. 3.95. New Victoria Pubs.

Lamperti, Noelle, et al. Noelle's Brown Book. LC 79-89574. (Illus., Orig.). (ps). 1979. pap. 1.50 (ISBN 0-934678-03-0). New Victoria Pubs.

Lamphear, F. Charles, jt. auth. see Emerson, M. Jarvin.

Lamphear, John. The Traditional History of the Jie of Uganda. (Oxford Studies in African Affairs). (Illus.). 1976. 37.50x (ISBN 0-19-821692-0). Oxford U Pr.

Lampkin, G. V. God's Word As It Was in the Beginning. 1981. 6.95 (ISBN 0-533-04646-7). Vantage.

Lampl, Paul. Cities & Planning in the Ancient Near East. LC 68-14699. (Planning & Cities Ser). (Illus., Orig.). (YA) (gr. 9-12). 1968. 7.95 (ISBN 0-8076-0465-8); pap. 4.95 (ISBN 0-8076-0469-0). Braziller.

Lamplugh, Lois. Winter Donkey. (gr. 3-7). 1980. 8.95 (ISBN 0-233-97198-X). Andre Deutsch.

Lampman, Ben H. How Could I Be Forgetting. (Illus.). 1980. pap. 4.95 (ISBN 0-8323-0379-8). Binford.

Lampman, Evelyn S. Bargain Bride. (gr. 7 up). pap. 2.95 (ISBN 0-689-70493-3, A-120, Aladdin). Atheneum.

--Shy Stegosaurus of Cricket Creek. LC 55-9233. (gr. 3-7). 1955. 6.95 o.p. (ISBN 0-385-07490-5). Doubleday.

--Squaw Man's Son. LC 77-17503. (gr. 5-9). 1978. 7.95 (ISBN 0-689-50102-1, McElderry Bk). Atheneum.

--Year of Small Shadow. LC 73-152694. 190p. (gr. 5-7). 1971. 5.95 o.p. (ISBN 0-15-299815-2, HJ). HarBraceJ.

Lampman, Henry P. The Wire Womb: Life in a Girls' Penal Institution. LC 72-90555. 1973. 12.95 (ISBN 0-911012-23-0). Nelson-Hall.

Lampman, Linda & Sterling, Julie. The Portland Guidebook. LC 78-17274. (Illus.). 1978. pap. 3.95 o.p. (ISBN 0-916076-25-3). Writing.

Lamport, Felicia. Light Metres: Poems. (Illus.). 120p. 1981. 9.95 (ISBN 0-89696-090-0). Everest Hse.

Lamprecht, Sterling P. Metaphysics of Naturalism. LC 67-18049. (Century Philosophy Ser.). 1967. 24.00x (ISBN 0-89197-302-8). Irvington.

--Our Philosophical Traditions: A Brief History of Philosophy in Western Civilization. LC 55-9432. (Century Philosophy Ser.). 1980. 29.50x (ISBN 0-89197-325-7); pap. text ed. 16.95x (ISBN 0-89197-873-9). Irvington.

Lamprey, Louise. All the Ways of Building. (Illus.). (gr. 7 up). 1933. 5.95 o.s.i. (ISBN 0-02-751380-7). Macmillan.

--Children of Ancient Gaul. LC 60-16708. (Illus.). (gr. 7-11). 8.50x (ISBN 0-8196-0109-8). Biblo.

--Children of Ancient Rome. LC 61-12876. (Illus.). (gr. 7-11). 8.50x (ISBN 0-8196-0114-4). Biblo.

Lampton. Black Holes & Other Secrets of the Universe. (gr. 7 up). 1980. PLB 6.90 (ISBN 0-531-02284-6). Watts.

Lana, Robert, ed. see Goldstein, Jeffrey H.

Lanarkshire Physics Group. H Grade Questions in Physics. 1972. pap. text ed. 4.95x o.p. (ISBN 0-435-68200-8). Heinemann Ed.

Lancashire, Anne, ed. The Editing of Renaissance Dramatic Texts: English, Italian, & Spanish. LC 76-7324. (Conference on Editorial Problems Ser.: No. 11). 1976. lib. bdg. 16.50 (ISBN 0-8240-2410-9). Garland Pub.

Lancashire, Anne B., ed. see Lyly, John.

Lancaster, Arnold. Nursery & Midwifery Sourcebook. 304p. 1980. 25.00x (Pub. by Beaconsfield England). State Mutual Bk.

Lancaster, Brown P. Planet Earth in Color. (Macmillan Color Ser.). (Illus.). 1976. 9.95 (ISBN 0-02-567710-1). Macmillan.

Lancaster, Bruce. The American Heritage Book of the Revolution. Ketchum, Richard M., ed. LC 58-10707. (Illus.). 384p. 1958. deluxe ed. 22.00 slipcased (ISBN 0-8281-0351-8, BO19D). Am Heritage.

--No Bugles Tonight. 1977. pap. 1.95 o.p. (ISBN 0-685-78260-3, 40-074-2). Pinnacle Bks.

Lancaster, Chet S. The Goba of the Zambezi: Sex Roles, Economics & Change. LC 80-24220. (Illus.). 350p. 1980. 19.95x (ISBN 0-8061-1613-7). U of Okla Pr.

Lancaster, David. Caroline R. 1980. 11.95 (ISBN 0-87795-285-X). Arbor Hse.

Lancaster, F. W. Information Retrieval Systems: Characteristics, Testing & Evaluation. 2nd ed. LC 78-11078. (Information Sciences Ser.). 1979. 23.95 (ISBN 0-471-04673-6, Pub. by Wiley-Interscience). Wiley.

Lancaster, F. W. & Fayen, E. G. Information Retrieval on-Line. LC 73-9697. (Information Sciences Ser.). 512p. 1973. 29.95 (ISBN 0-471-51235-4, Pub. by Wiley-Interscience). Wiley.

Lancaster, F. W., ed. see Library Applications of Data Processing Clinic, 1979.

Lancaster, F. Wilfrid. Vocabulary Control for Information Retrieval. LC 78-186528. (Illus.). xiv, 233p. 1972. text ed. 25.00 (ISBN 0-87815-006-4). Info Resources.

Lancaster, Fidelity. The Bedouin. LC 78-2679. (Civilization Library). (Illus.). (gr. 5 up). 1978. PLB 6.90 s&l (ISBN 0-531-01447-9). Watts.

Lancaster, G. T. Programming in COBOL. 152p. 1972. pap. 11.25 (ISBN 0-08-016384-X). Pergamon.

Lancaster, H. O. Bibliography of Statistical Bibliographies. 1968. 11.75 (ISBN 0-934454-12-4). Lubrecht & Cramer.

--An Introduction to Medical Statistics. LC 73-11323. (Ser. in Probability & Mathematical Statistics). 1974. 34.50 (ISBN 0-471-51250-8, Pub. by Wiley-Interscience). Wiley.

Lancaster, Helen. Aging. 1980. pap. 2.50 (ISBN 0-8309-0290-2). Herald Hse.

Lancaster, Janet & Gaunt, Joan. Developments in Early Childhood Education. (Changing Classroom). 1976. text ed. 11.75x (ISBN 0-7291-0027-8); pap. text ed. 4.75x (ISBN 0-7291-0022-7). Humanities.

Lancaster, Jeanette, ed. Community Mental Health Nursing: An Ecological Perspective. LC 79-26185. (Illus.). 1980. pap. text ed. 10.95 (ISBN 0-8016-2816-4). Mosby.

Lancaster, John. Introducing Op Art. LC 72-10428. (Illus.). 112p. 1973. 9.95 o.p. (ISBN 0-8230-6267-8). Watson-Guptill.
--Introducing Op Art. 1973. 16.95 (ISBN 0-7134-2438-9, Pub. by Batsford England). David & Charles.
--Lettering Techniques. LC 79-56448. (Illus.). 120p. 1980. 24.00 (ISBN 0-7134-0220-2, Pub. by Batsford England). David & Charles.
Lancaster, Kelvin. Consumer Demand: A New Approach. LC 76-164502. (Study in Economics: No. 5). 1971. 17.50x (ISBN 0-231-03357-5). Columbia U Pr.
--Variety, Equity, & Efficiency. LC 78-24616. 1979. 25.00x (ISBN 0-231-04616-2). Columbia U Pr.
Lancaster, Larry E. The Patient with End Stage Renal Disease. LC 78-23659. 1979. 18.50 (ISBN 0-471-03564-5, Pub. by Wiley Medical). Wiley.
Lancaster, Lewis. The Mad Monk. (Lancaster - Miller Art Ser.). (Illus.). 1980. 7.95 (ISBN 0-89581-017-4). Lancaster-Miller.
Lancaster, Lewis & Gomez, Luis O., eds. Prajnaparamita & Related Systems. 1980. 20.00 (ISBN 0-89581-150-2). Lancaster-Miller.
Lancaster, Lewis & Lai, Whalen, eds. Early Ch'an in China & Tibet. 1981. 22.50 (ISBN 0-89581-152-9). Lancaster-Miller.
Lancaster, Lydia. Passion & Proud Hearts. (Orig.). 1978. pap. 2.25 o.s.i. (ISBN 0-446-82548-4). Warner Bks.
--The Temptation. 1979. pap. 2.50 o.s.i. (ISBN 0-446-81771-6). Warner Bks.
Lancaster, Osbert, jt. auth: see Scott-James, Anne.
Lancaster, Sheila. Dark Sweet Wanton. (Historical Romance). 256p. (Orig.). 1981. pap. 2.50 (ISBN 0-515-05759-2). Jove Pubns.
Lancaster, William. The Rwala Bedouin Today. (Changing Cultures Ser.). (Illus.). 192p. Date not set. price not set (ISBN 0-521-23877-3); pap. price not set (ISBN 0-521-28275-6). Cambridge U Pr.
Lancaster-Gaye, Derek, ed. Personal Relationships, the Handicapped & the Community: Some European Thoughts & Solutions. (Illus.). 156p. 1972. 12.00 (ISBN 0-7100-7478-6). Routledge & Kegan.
Lance, Fran & King, Pat. Fran. 132p. 1980. pap. 4.95 (ISBN 0-930756-51-7, 4230-LK1). Women's Aglow.
Lance, H. Darrell. The Old Testament & the Archaeologist. Tucker, Gene M., ed. LC 80-2387. (Guides to Biblical Scholarship: Old Testament Ser.). 112p. (Orig.). 1981. pap. 4.50 (ISBN 0-8006-0467-9, 1-467). Fortress.
Lance, J. G. & McLeod, J. G. A Physiological Approach to Clinical Neurology. 2nd ed. LC 80-49872. 1975. 32.95 (ISBN 0-407-00022-4). Butterworths.
Lance, James W. Headache: Understanding, Alleviation. LC 75-11809. (Illus.). 1975. pap. 0.95 o.p. (ISBN 0-684-14372-0, ScribT); pap. 0.95 (ISBN 0-684-16373-X, SL657, ScribT). Scribner.
Lance, James W. & McLeod, James G. A Physiological Approach to Clinical Neurology. 3rd ed. (Illus.). 368p. 1981. text ed. 49.95 (ISBN 0-407-00196-4). Butterworth.
Lance, Leslie. The House in the Woods. 1980. pap. 1.95 (ISBN 0-441-34382-1). Ace Bks.
Lancelot, Claude, jt. auth. see Arnauld, Antoine.
Lancer, Cynthia A., jt. auth. see Fisk, Donald M.
Lanciano, Claude O., Jr. Captain John Sinclair of Virginia. LC 72-93109. (Illus.). 1973. 7.50 (ISBN 0-9603558-2-0). Lands End Bks.
--Legends of Lands End. LC 72-18023. (Illus.). 1971. 4.30 (ISBN 0-9603558-1-2). Lands End Bks.
--Our Most Skillful Architect Richard Taliaferro & Associated Colonial Virginia Constructions. Date not set. text ed. price not set (ISBN 0-9603558-0-4). Lands End Bks.
--Rosewell Garland of Virginia. (Illus.). 1978. 12.50 (ISBN 0-9603558-3-9). Lands End Bks.
Lancour, Gene. Sword for the Empire. LC 77-11750. 1978. 7.95 o.p. (ISBN 0-385-13067-8). Doubleday.
Lancourt, Joan E. Confront or Concede: The Alinsky Citizen-Action Organizations. (Illus.). 1979. 19.50 (ISBN 0-669-02715-4). Lexington Bks.
Lanczos, C. Discourse on Fourier Series. 1966. 16.25 o.s.i. (ISBN 0-02-848310-3). Hafner.
Lanczos, Cornelius. Variational Principles of Mechanics. 4th ed. LC 70-151376. 1970. 17.50x o.p. (ISBN 0-8020-1743-6). U of Toronto Pr.
Land, Barbara. The New Explorers: Women in Antarctica. LC 80-2778. (Illus.). 224p. (gr. 7 up). 1981. PLB 8.95 (ISBN 0-396-07924-5). Dodd.
Land, Brian, ed. Directory of Associations in Canada. 3rd ed. 696p. cancelled o.s.i. (ISBN 0-8020-4531-6, Pub.by U. of Toronto Pr). Bowker.
Land, Charles. Land's Industrial Machinery & Epuipment Pricing Guide. 1980. pap. text ed. 29.95 (ISBN 0-442-28820-4). Van Nos Reinhold.
Land, D. G. & Nursten, H. E., eds. Progress in Flavour Research. (Illus.). 1979. 57.00x (ISBN 0-85334-818-9). Intl Ideas.
Land, Hilarly. Large Families in London. 154p. 1969. pap. text ed. 6.25x (ISBN 0-7135-1577-5, Pub. by Bedford England). Renouf.
Land, Jane, ed. To Walk the Night. 192p. (Orig.). Date not set. pap. 2.25 (ISBN 0-345-28603-0). Ballantine.
Land, L. K., ed. see Nicholson, H. B. & Cordy-Collins, Alana.
Land, Stephen K. From Signs to Propositions: The Concept of Form in 18th-Century Semantic Theory. LC 74-189426. (Linguistics Library). (Illus.). 224p. 1974. text ed. 14.95x (ISBN 0-582-55046-7). Longman.
Land Tenure Center. Land Tenure & Agrarian Reform in Asia: An Annotated Bibliography. 1980. lib. bdg. 45.00 (ISBN 0-8161-8221-3). G K Hall.
Land Use Subcommittee. Urban Growth & Land Development. 1972. pap. 2.95 (ISBN 0-309-02044-1). Natl Acad Pr.
Landa, Henry C. Gambling Probabilities. (Illus.). 1979. pap. 4.00 (ISBN 0-931974-05-4). FICOA.
Landa, Louis A. Essays in Eighteenth-Century English Literature. LC 80-7541. (Princeton Ser. of Collected Essays). 270p. 1980. 20.00 (ISBN 0-691-06449-0); pap. 7.95 (ISBN 0-691-01375-6). Princeton U Pr.
Landa, S., jt. auth. see Weisser, Otto.
Landau see Weyl, Hermann, et al.
Landau, Alice. My Thoughts in Verse. Date not set. 5.95 (ISBN 0-533-04817-6). Vantage.
Landau, Anneliese. The Lied: The Unfolding of Its Style. LC 79-6725. 1980. text ed. 15.00 (ISBN 0-8191-0935-5); pap. text ed. 7.50 (ISBN 0-8191-0936-3). U Pr of Amer.
Landau, Barbara R. Essential Human Anatomy & Physiology. 2nd ed. 1980. text ed. 20.95x (ISBN 0-673-15249-9). Scott F.
Landau, E. D., et al. The Teaching Experience: An Introduction to Education Through Literature. (Illus.). 496p. 1976. pap. text ed. 11.95 (ISBN 0-13-892539-9). P-H.
Landau, Edmund. Algebraische Zahlen. 2nd ed. (Ger). 8.95 (ISBN 0-8284-0062-8). Chelsea Pub.
--Elementare Zahlentheorie. LC 49-235. (Ger). 9.95 (ISBN 0-8284-0026-1). Chelsea Pub.
--Elementary Number Theory. 2nd ed. LC 57-8494. 12.00 (ISBN 0-8284-0125-X). Chelsea Pub.
--Foundations of Analysis. 2nd ed. LC 60-15580. (gr. 9 up). 1960. text ed. 8.95 (ISBN 0-8284-0079-2). Chelsea Pub.
--Handbuch der Lehre von der Verteilung der Primzahlen, 2 vols. in 1. 3rd ed. LC 73-21539. 1974. text ed. 39.50 (ISBN 0-8284-0096-2). Chelsea Pub.
--Vorlesungen Ueber Zahlentheorie, 3 Vols. in One. LC 49-235. (Ger). 29.95 (ISBN 0-8284-0032-6). Chelsea Pub.
Landau, Elliot, et al. The Exceptional Child Through Literature. (Illus.). 1978. ref. ed. 10.95 (ISBN 0-13-293860-X). P-H.
Landau, Elliott D. Today's Family. LC 74-28592. 246p. 1974. 5.95 o.p. (ISBN 0-87747-543-1); pap. 3.95 o.p. (ISBN 0-87747-552-0). Deseret Bk.
Landau, Elliott D. & Egan, M. Winston. Guiding Your Child: A 60-Point Checklist for Parents. LC 78-70361. 1978. pap. 2.95 (ISBN 0-88290-103-6). Horizon Utah.
Landau, Genevieve M., jt. auth. see Piers, Maria W.
Landau, Jacob M. Parliaments & Parties in Egypt. LC 79-1632. 1981. Repr. of 1954 ed. 19.50 (ISBN 0-88355-936-6). Hyperion Conn.
Landau, Jacob M., et al, eds. Electoral Politics in the Middle East: Issues, Voters & Elites. (Publication Ser.: No. 241). 400p. 1980. 29.95 (ISBN 0-8179-7411-3). Hoover Inst Pr.
Landau, L. D. & Lifshitz, E. M. Course on Theoretical Physics: Statistical Physics, Vol. 5, Pt. 1. new ed. (Illus.). 1980. text ed. 69.00 (ISBN 0-08-023039-3); pap. text ed. 22.00 (ISBN 0-08-023038-5). Pergamon.
Landau, L. D., et al. General Physics: Mechanics & Molecular Physics. 1967. 21.00 (ISBN 0-08-009106-7). Pergamon.
Landau, Robert, jt. auth. see Henderson, Sally.
Landau, Rom. Morocco. 1967. 21.95 (ISBN 0-236-30866-1, Pub. by Paul Elek). Merrimack Bk Serv.
Landau, Sarah B. Edward T. & William A. Potter, American Victorian Architects. Freedberg, Sydney J., ed. LC 78-74371. (Outstanding Dissertations in the Fine Arts Ser.). (Illus.). 1979. lib. bdg. 60.50 (ISBN 0-8240-3955-6). Garland Pub.
Landau, Saul, jt. auth. see Dinges, John.
Landau, Sidney & Bogus, Ronald, eds. Doubleday Dictionary: For Home, School & Office. LC 74-3543. 936p. 1975. 5.95 (ISBN 0-385-04099-7); thumb-indexed 7.95 (ISBN 0-385-03368-0). Doubleday.
--Doubleday Roget's Thesaurus in Dictionary Form. LC 76-7696. 564p. 1977. 6.95 (ISBN 0-385-01236-5); thumb-indexed 7.95 (ISBN 0-385-12379-5). Doubleday.
Landau, Simha F. & Sebba, Leslie. Criminology in Perspective: Essays in Honor of Israel Drapkin. LC 76-50437. 1978. 19.95 (ISBN 0-669-01281-5). Lexington Bks.
Landau, Susanne & Bailey, Geoffrey. The Landau Strategy: How Working Women Win Top Jobs. LC 80-83564. 224p. 1981. pap. 2.50 (ISBN 0-87216-806-9). Playboy Pbks.
Landau, Suzanne & Bailey, Geoffrey. The Landau Strategy: How Working Women Win Top Jobs. 1981. pap. 4.95 (ISBN 0-686-68906-2). Bantam.
Landau, Yehuda H., et al, eds. Rural Communities: Inter-Cooperation & Development. LC 75-19779. (Special Studies). (Illus.). 175p. 1976. text ed. 22.95 (ISBN 0-275-55700-6). Praeger.
Landauer, Gustav. For Socialism. Parent, David J., tr. from Ger. LC 78-51081. 1978. 12.00 (ISBN 0-914386-10-7); pap. 3.95 (ISBN 0-914386-11-5). Telos Pr.
Landauer, Thomas K. Psychology: A Brief Overview. (Illus.). 416p. 1972. text ed. 16.95 o.p. (ISBN 0-07-036113-4, C); instructor's manual 2.95 o.p. (ISBN 0-07-036117-7); wkbk. & study guide 6.50 o.p. (ISBN 0-07-043625-8). McGraw.
Landaw, Jonathan, ed. see Gyatso, Geshe.
Lande, Nathaniel. Cricket. 1981. 12.95 (ISBN 0-453-00392-3, H392). NAL.
Lande, Rivian & Knox, Marlys. Concepts of Genetics. (Orig.). 1980. 5.95 (ISBN 0-8087-3826-7). Burgess.
Landeck, Terry, jt. auth. see Busch, H. Ted.
Landecker, Mildred N. Creative Music Theory. (gr. 8-12). 1972. pap. text ed. 13.20 o.p. (ISBN 0-205-02775-X, 5827752); tchr's guide 2.00 o.p. (ISBN 0-205-02776-8, 5827760). Allyn.
Landecker, Werner S. Class Crystallization. 272p. 1981. 19.00 (ISBN 0-8135-0918-1). Rutgers U Pr.
Landeira, Ricardo. Ramiro De Maeztu. (World Authors Ser.: No. 484). 1978. lib. bdg. 12.50 (ISBN 0-8057-6325-2). Twayne.
Lander, J. R. Conflict & Stability in Fifteenth Century England. 3rd ed. 1977. pap. 5.75x (ISBN 0-09-095741-5, Hutchinson U Lib). Humanities.
Lander, Jeannette. Ezra Pound. LC 71-134828. (Modern Literature Ser.). 1971. 10.95 (ISBN 0-8044-2486-1); pap. 3.45 (ISBN 0-8044-6380-8). Ungar.
Lander, L., tr. see Brocker, T. H.
Lander, Patricia S. In the Shadow of the Factory: Social Change in a Finnish Community. LC 75-37634. 198p. 1976. text ed. 12.50 o.p. (ISBN 0-470-01379-6); pap. text ed. 5.95 (ISBN 0-470-01380-X). Halsted Pr.
Landers, jt. auth. see Kelly.
Landers, Ann. The Ann Landers Encyclopedia A to Z. Date not set. 7.95 (ISBN 0-345-28892-0). Ballantine.
--Ann Landers Talks to Teenagers about Sex. 1978. pap. 1.95 (ISBN 0-449-24208-0, Crest). Fawcett.
Landers, Daniel & Roberts, Glyn, eds. Psychology of Motor Behavior & Sport 1980. 1981. text ed. 12.00x (ISBN 0-931250-19-6). Human Kinetics.
Landers, Gunnard. The Hunting Shack. 1980. pap. 2.50 (ISBN 0-440-13300-9). Dell.
Landers, Jack M. Construction. LC 75-4032. (Illus.). 1976. text ed. 10.64 (ISBN 0-87006-291-3); lab manual 3.20 (ISBN 0-87006-214-X). Goodheart.
Landers, Jonathan M. & Martin, James A. Basic Civil Procedure: Cases & Materials. 1196p. 1981. price not set. Little.
Landers, Maurice B., jt. auth. see Klintworth, Gordon K.
Landes, David S. Unbound Prometheus: Technological Change & Industrial Development in Western Europe from 1750 to the Present. 41.50 (ISBN 0-521-07200-X); pap. 9.95x (ISBN 0-521-09418-6). Cambridge U Pr.
Landes, Kenneth K. Petroleum Geology. LC 74-26700. 458p. 1975. Repr. of 1959 ed. 22.50 (ISBN 0-88275-226-X). Krieger.
Landesman, Alter F. A History of New Lots, Brooklyn to Eighteen Eighty-Seven. LC 76-30367. 1977. 12.50 (ISBN 0-8046-9172-X). Kennikat.
Landesman, Bill, jt. auth. see Berman, Kathleen.
Landesman, Fran. More Truth Than Poetry. 64p. (Orig.). 1981. pap. 5.95 (ISBN 0-932966-13-6). Permanent Pr.
Landess, Thomas H. Julia Peterkin. (U.S. Authors Ser.: No. 273). 1976. lib. bdg. 10.95 (ISBN 0-8057-7173-5). Twayne.
Landey, Dora & Klein, Elinor. Dazzle. 416p. 1981. pap. 2.95 (ISBN 0-446-93476-3). Warner Bks.
Landfield, A. W., ed. Personal Construct Psychology: Psychotherapy & Personality. Leitner, L. M. LC 80-16938. (Personality Processes Ser.). 400p. 1980. 28.00 (ISBN 0-471-05859-9, Pub. by Wiley-Interscience). Wiley.
Landgarten, Helen B. Clinical Art Therapy. 416p. 1981. 27.50 (ISBN 0-87630-237-1). Brunner-Mazel.
Landgrebe, Gary. Tofu at Center Stage. LC 80-69560. (Illus.). 112p. (Orig.). 1981. pap. 5.95 (ISBN 0-9601398-3-4). Fresh Pr.
Landgrebe, John A. Theory & Practice in the Organic Laboratory. 2nd ed. 1976. pap. text ed. 15.95x (ISBN 0-669-99937-7). Heath.
Landis. Building a Successful Marriage. 7th ed. 1977. 17.95 (ISBN 0-13-087007-2). P-H.
Landis, Arthur H. The Magick of Camelot. 1981. pap. 2.25 (ISBN 0-87997-623-3, UE1623, Daw Bks). NAL.
Landis, Benson Y. Outline of the Bible: Book by Book. (Orig.). 1963. pap. 3.50 (ISBN 0-06-463263-6, EH 263, EH). Har-Row.
Landis, Carolyn R., jt. ed. see Hamblen, John W.
Landis, Fred S., jt. auth. see Freed, Donald.
Landis, James M. The Administrative Process. LC 73-17952. 160p. 1974. Repr. lib. bdg. 17.50x (ISBN 0-8371-7284-5, LAAP). Greenwood.
Landis, Joseph C., ed. & tr. The Great Jewish Plays. LC 66-14720. 360p. 1972. 8.95 o.s.i. (ISBN 0-8180-0504-1). Horizon.
Landis, Joseph C., ed. The Great Jewish Plays. 1980. pap. 3.50 (ISBN 0-380-51573-3, 51573, Bard). Avon.
Landis, Judson R. Sociology: Concepts & Characteristics. 4th ed. 416p. 1979. pap. text ed. 13.95x (ISBN 0-534-00784-8). Wadsworth Pub.
Landis, Judson R., Jr. Sociology: Concepts & Characteristics. 3rd ed. 1977. pap. 10.95x o.p. (ISBN 0-534-00492-X). Wadsworth Pub.
Landis, Paul H. Making the Most of Marriage. 5th ed. 624p. 1975. text ed. 17.95 (ISBN 0-13-547968-1). P-H.
Landis, Robin C. OPEC: Policy Implications for the United States. Klass, Michael W., ed. LC 78-19457. (Praeger Special Studies). (Illus.). 304p. 1980. 29.95 (ISBN 0-03-044361-X). Praeger.
Landman, Uzi, ed. Aspects of the Kinetics & Dynamics of Surface Reactions. LC 80-68004. (AIP Conference Proceedings: No. 61). 343p. 1980. lib. bdg. 22.25 (ISBN 0-88318-160-6). Am Inst Physics.
Landon, H. C. Chronicle & Works, 5 vols. Incl. Haydn: The Early Years, 1732-1765. Vol. 1 Haydn: the Early Years, 1732-1765. 640p. 1980. 75.00x (ISBN 0-253-37001-9); Vol. 2. Haydn at Eszterhaza; 1766-1790. 820p. 1978. 60.00x (ISBN 0-253-37002-7); Vol. 3. Haydn in England, 1791-1795. 640p. 1976. 55.00x (ISBN 0-253-37003-5); Vol. 4. Haydnn: the Years of "The Creation" 1796-1800. 640p. 1976. 55.00x (ISBN 0-253-37004-3); Vol. 5. Haydn: the Late Years, 1801-1809. 496p. 1977. 55.00x (ISBN 0-253-37005-1). Set. 300.00x. Ind U Pr.
--Essays on the Viennese Classical Style: Gluck, Haydn, Mozart, Beethoven. LC 74-119133. 1970. 6.95 o.s.i. (ISBN 0-02-567890-6). Macmillan.
Landon, H. Robbins, jt. auth. see Raynor, Henry.
Landon, Mary T. & Swan, Susan B. American Crewel Work. LC 79-104869. (Illus.). 1970. 9.95 o.s.i. (ISBN 0-02-567870-1). Macmillan.
--American Crewel Work. (Illus.). 1976. pap. 5.95 o.s.i. (ISBN 0-02-011730-2, Collier). Macmillan.
Landon, Michael L. Erin & Britannia: The Historical Backround to a Modern Tragedy. LC 79-27005. (Illus.). 288p. 1981. text ed. 18.95 (ISBN 0-88229-643-4); pap. text ed. 8.95 (ISBN 0-88229-766-X). Nelson-Hall.
Landon, Perceval. Nepal, 2 vols. (Illus.). 27.95 o.s.i. (ISBN 0-685-89507-6). Himalaya Hse.
Landon, Robbins H. & Chapman, Roger. Studies in Eighteenth Century Music: A Tribute to Karl Geiringer on His 70th Birthday. (Music Reprint Ser.). 1979. Repr. of 1970 ed. lib. bdg. 35.00 (ISBN 0-306-79519-1). Da Capo.
Landorf, Joyce. Fragrance of Beauty. LC 74-76813. 1973. pap. 2.95 (ISBN 0-88207-231-5). Victor Bks.
--I Came to Love You Late. 1981. pap. 2.50 (ISBN 0-451-09897-8, E9897, Sig). NAL.
--Joyce, I Feel Like I Know You. 1976. pap. 2.95 (ISBN 0-88207-742-2). Victor Bks.
--Let's Have a Banquet. 1968. pap. 3.95 (ISBN 0-310-27131-2). Zondervan.
--Mix Butter with Love. LC 74-18857. 1974. gift ed. 8.95 (ISBN 0-89081-035-4, 0354). Harvest Hse.
--The Richest Lady in Town. 1979. pap. 2.25 (ISBN 0-310-27142-8). Zondervan.

Landorf, Joyce, tr. La Belleza Radiante. (Spanish Bks.). (Span.). 1978. 1.90 (ISBN 0-8297-0807-3). Life Pubs Intl.

--Fortaleza y Ternura. (Spanish Bks.). (Span.). 1978. 1.90 (ISBN 0-8297-0806-5). Life Pubs Intl.

--La Mujer Mas Rica De la Ciudad. (Spanish Bks.). (Span.). 1979. 1.65 (ISBN 0-8297-0587-2). Life Pubs Intl.

--Se Eu Posso, Tu Podes. (Portuguese Bks.). 1979. 1.30 (ISBN 0-8297-0769-7). Life Pubs Intl.

--Seu Obstinado Amor. (Portuguese Bks.). 1979. 1.35 (ISBN 0-8297-0691-7). Life Pubs Intl.

--Su Obstinado Amor. (Spanish Bks.). (Span.). 1978. 1.80 (ISBN 0-8297-0600-3). Life Pubs Intl.

--Tarde Te Ame. (Spanish Bks.). (Span.). 1979. 1.95 (ISBN 0-8297-0906-1). Life Pubs Intl.

Landovitz, Leon F., jt. auth. see Schwartz, Edmund I.

Landow, George. William Holman Hunt & Typological Symbolism. LC 77-91017. 1979. 30.00x (ISBN 0-300-02196-8). Yale U Pr.

Landow, George P. Victorian Types, Victorian Shadows: Biblical Typology in Victorian Literature, Art & Thought. 256p. 1980. 24.95 (ISBN 0-7100-0598-9). Routledge & Kegan.

Landreth, Garry L. & Berg, Robert C. Counseling the Elderly: For Professional Helpers Who Work with the Aged. (Illus.). 532p. 1980. 26.75 (ISBN 0-398-04058-3); pap. 19.75 (ISBN 0-398-04059-1). C C Thomas.

Landreth, Harry H. History of Economic Theory: Scope, Method & Content. LC 75-31003. (Illus.). 512p. 1976. text ed. 20.95 (ISBN 0-395-19234-X). HM.

Landru, H. C. The Blue Parka Man: Alaskan Gold Rush Bandit. LC 79-25575. (Illus.). 208p. 1980. 8.95 (ISBN 0-396-07821-4). Dodd.

Landrum, Phil, jt. auth. see Armerding, George D.

Landrum, Phil, jt. auth. see Brandt, Henry.

Landrum, Phil, jt. tr. see Brant, Henry.

Landry, Hilton. Interpretations in Shakespeare's Sonnets. LC 76-1901. (Perspectives in Criticism Ser.: No. 14). (Illus.). 185p. 1976. Repr. of 1963 ed. lib. bdg. 16.75x (ISBN 0-8371-8749-4, LAIS). Greenwood.

Landry, Hilton, et al. A Concordance to the Poems of Hart Crane. LC 72-10663. (Concordances Ser.: No. 4). 1973. 16.50 (ISBN 0-8108-0564-2). Scarecrow.

Landry, Judith, tr. see Benevolo, Leonard.

Landry, Lenore L. & Jorde, Emma M. Creating a Tailored Garment. rev ed. (Illus.). 1977. pap. text ed. 3.95 o.s.i. (ISBN 0-89534-005-4). Am Pub Co WI.

Landsberg, G., jt. auth. see Hensel, Kurt.

Landsberg, H. E., ed. Advances in Geophysics, 19 vols. Incl. Vol. 1. 1952 (ISBN 0-12-018801-5); Vol. 2. 1955 (ISBN 0-12-018802-3); Vol. 3. 1956 (ISBN 0-12-018803-1); Vol. 4. Landsberg, H. E. & Van Mieghen, J., eds. 1958 (ISBN 0-12-018804-X); Vol. 5. 1958 (ISBN 0-12-018805-8); Vol. 6. Atmospheric Diffusion & Air Pollution: Proceedings. Frenkiel, F. N. & Sheppard, P. A., eds. 1959 (ISBN 0-12-018806-6); Vol. 7. 1961 (ISBN 0-12-018807-4); Vol. 8. 1961 (ISBN 0-12-018808-2); Vol. 9. 1962 (ISBN 0-12-018809-0); Vol. 10. 1964 (ISBN 0-12-018810-4); Vol. 11. 1965 (ISBN 0-12-018811-2); Vol. 12. 1967 (ISBN 0-12-018812-0); Vol. 13. 1969 (ISBN 0-12-018813-9); Vol. 14. 1970 (ISBN 0-12-018814-7); Vol. 15. 1971 (ISBN 0-12-018815-5); Suppl. 1. Biometeorological Methods. Munn, R. E. 1966. 30.50 (ISBN 0-12-018861-9); Vol. 16. 1973 (ISBN 0-12-018816-3); Vol. 17. 1974 (ISBN 0-12-018817-1); Vol. 18A. 1974. 33.00 (ISBN 0-12-018818-X); Vol. 19. 1976. 48.00 (ISBN 0-12-018819-8). Vols. 1-17. 52.50 ea. Acad Pr.

Landsberg, H. E., ed. see International Biometeorological Congress, 7th, College Park, MD 1975.

Landsberg, Hans, ed. Energy: The Next Twenty Years. LC 79-5226. 656p. 1979. reference 27.00 (ISBN 0-88410-092-8); pap. 11.95 (ISBN 0-88410-094-4). Ballinger Pub.

--Selected Studies on Energy: Background Papers for Energy: the Next Twenty Years. LC 79-24800. 1980. 35.00 (ISBN 0-88410-093-6). Ballinger Pub.

Landsberg, Helmut. The Urban Climate. (International Geophysics Ser.). 1981. write for info. (ISBN 0-12-435960-4). Acad Pr.

Landsberg, P. R. & Evans, D. A. Mathematical Cosmology. 1980. pap. 14.95x (ISBN 0-19-851147-7). Oxford U Pr.

Landsberg, Peter T. & Evans, David. Mathematical Cosmology: An Introduction. (Illus.). 1978. pap. 18.95x o.p. (ISBN 0-19-851136-1). Oxford U Pr.

Landsberger, Frank R., jt. ed. see Scanu, Angelo M.

Landsburg, Alan. Secrets of the Bermuda Triangle. (Orig.). 1978. pap. 1.95 (ISBN 0-446-89626-8). Warner Bks.

Landsburg, Harry F., et al. Retailer's Basic Accounting Handbook: A Manual Retail Accounting System. 80p. 1980. 15.00 (C15080). Natl Ret Merch.

Landsburg, Sally, jt. auth. see Derenski, Arlene.

Landsburgh, Alan. The Insects Are Coming. (Illus., Orig.). 1978. pap. 2.25 o.s.i. (ISBN 0-446-82595-6). Warner Bks.

Landscape Architecture Magazine. Home Landscape Nineteen Eighty-One. Clay, Grady & Johnson, Norman, eds. (Landscape Architecture Magazine Ser.). 168p. 1981. 7.95 (ISBN 0-07-036193-2). McGraw.

--Home Landscape, 1980. (Illus.). 1980. pap. 5.95 o.p. (ISBN 0-07-036192-4). McGraw.

--Landscapes for Living. (Illus.). 1980. 19.95 (ISBN 0-07-036191-6). McGraw.

Landshoff, P. V. & Metherell, A. J. Simple Quantum Physics. LC 78-73244. (Illus.). 1980. 29.95 (ISBN 0-521-22498-5); pap. 9.95 (ISBN 0-521-29538-6). Cambridge U Pr.

Landsittell, David L., jt. auth. see Hall, William D.

Landsman, Stephen, et al. What to Do Until the Lawyer Comes. LC 76-2802. 1977. pap. 2.95 (ISBN 0-385-11163-0, Anch). Doubleday.

Landstreet, Barent F. The Drinking Driver. 128p. 1977. 14.75 (ISBN 0-398-03560-1). C C Thomas.

Landstrom, Bjorn. Sailing Ships. 2nd ed. LC 78-1011. 1978. 8.95 o.p. (ISBN 0-385-14408-3). Doubleday.

Landsverk, O. G. Runic Records of the Norsemen in America. (Library of Scandinavian Literature). 1974. lib. bdg. 20.00x (ISBN 0-8057-5457-1). Irvington.

Landweber, Lawrence H., jt. auth. see Brainerd, Walter S.

Landwehr, John. Fable-Books Printed in the Low Countries: A Concise Bibliography Until 1800. 1963. text ed. 16.00x (ISBN 90-6004-096-1). Humanities.

Landwehr, William C., ed. see Albin, Edgar A., et al.

Landy, Frank J. & Trumbo, Don A. Psychology of Work Behavior. rev. ed. 1980. text ed. 18.95x (ISBN 0-256-02324-7). Dorsey.

Landy, Jacob. Architecture of Minard Lafever. LC 69-19461. (Illus.). 1970. 22.50x (ISBN 0-231-03132-7). Columbia U Pr.

Lane. Princess. (gr. 4-6). 1980. pap. 0.95 (ISBN 0-590-30383-X, Schol Pap). Schol Bk Serv.

Lane, jt. auth. see Miles.

Lane, Alaine, ed. Developmental Psychology: The Problems of Disordered Mental Development. (Special Education Ser.). (Illus., Orig.). 1979. pap. text ed. 9.95 o.p. (ISBN 0-89568-108-0). Spec Learn Corp.

Lane, Alexander. Functional Human Anatomy: The Regional Approach. 3rd ed. 1981. pap. text ed. 15.95 (ISBN 0-8403-2340-9). Kendall-Hunt.

Lane, Ann J. The Brownsville Affair: National Crisis & Black Reaction. LC 73-139357. 1973. 13.50 (ISBN 0-8046-9008-1); pap. 6.50 (ISBN 0-8046-9045-6). Kennikat.

Lane, Arthur. English Porcelain Figures of the Eighteenth Century. 1961. 23.00 (ISBN 0-571-04027-6, Pub. by Faber & Faber). Merrimack Bk Serv.

--Greek Pottery. 3rd ed. 1971. 38.00 (ISBN 0-571-04701-7, Pub. by Faber & Faber). Merrimack Bk Serv.

--Italian Porcelain. 1954. 19.95 o.p. (ISBN 0-571-05331-9, Pub. by Faber & Faber). Merrimack Bk Serv.

--Later Islamic Pottery. 2nd ed. 1971. 24.95 o.p. (ISBN 0-571-04736-X, Pub. by Faber & Faber). Merrimack Bk Serv.

Lane, Arthur, jt. auth. see Poynter, Margaret.

Lane, Billy & Graham, Colin. Billy Lanes Encyclopaedia of Float Fishing. (Illus.). 1971. 9.50 (ISBN 0-7207-0514-2). Transatlantic.

Lane, Byron. How to Free Yourself in a Business of Your Own. (Illus.). 176p. 1980. 11.95 (Spec); pap. 5.95. P-H.

Lane, Byron, jt. auth. see Fisher, Ida.

Lane, Calvin W. Evelyn Waugh. (English Authors Ser.: No. 301). 1981. lib. bdg. 9.95 (ISBN 0-8057-6793-2). Twayne.

Lane, Carl D. Boatowner's Sheet Anchor. 1973. pap. 3.50 o.p. (ISBN 0-8015-0774-X). Dutton.

Lane, Carolyn. Echoes in an Empty Room. LC 80-20278. 160p. (gr. 4-7). 1981. 8.95 (ISBN 0-03-057477-3). HR&W.

Lane, D. R. Jones' Animal Nursing. 3rd. ed. (Illus.). Date not set. 67.50 (ISBN 0-08-024945-0); pap. 36.00 (ISBN 0-08-024944-2). Pergamon. Postponed.

Lane, David. Leninism: A Sociological Interpretation. (Themes in the Social Sciences Ser.). (Illus.). 176p. Date not set. price not set (ISBN 0-521-23855-2); pap. price not set (ISBN 0-521-28259-4). Cambridge U Pr.

--Politics & Society in the U.S.S.R. 2nd ed. LC 78-53993. 1978. uSA 25.00x (ISBN 0-8147-4988-7); pap. 13.00x usa (ISBN 0-8147-4989-5). NYU Pr.

--The Socialist Industrial State: Toward a Political Sociology of State Socialism. LC 75-33036. 220p. 1976. 24.50x (ISBN 0-89158-523-0). Westview.

Lane, David & Kolankiewicz, George. Social Groups in Polish Society. (Political Social Processes in Eastern Europe Ser.). 250p. 1973. 22.50x (ISBN 0-231-03729-5). Columbia U Pr.

Lane, Elizabeth. Drums of Darkness. 304p. (Orig.). 1981. pap. 2.75 (ISBN 0-515-05664-2). Jove Pubns.

--Mistress of the Morning Star. 1980. 2.75 (ISBN 0-515-05467-4). Jove Pubns.

Lane, G. W. Bring the Book. 158p. 1968. 2.95 (ISBN 0-87148-104-9); pap. 2.25 (ISBN 0-87148-105-7). Pathway Pr.

--But This Man. 105p. 1960. pap. 1.50 (ISBN 0-87148-107-3). Pathway Pr.

--Doctrine of the New Testament in Ten Great Subjects. 127p. 1964. pap. 1.50 (ISBN 0-87148-250-9). Pathway Pr.

Lane, Gary. A Concordance to the Poems of Dylan Thomas. LC 76-18078. (Concordances Ser.: No. 5). 1976. 27.50 (ISBN 0-8108-0971-0). Scarecrow.

--A Concordance to the Poems of Theodore Roethke. (Concordances Ser.: No. 3). 1972. 20.50 (ISBN 0-8108-0514-6). Scarecrow.

--I Am: A Study of E. E. Cummings' Poems. LC 75-38757. (Illus.). 144p. 1976. pap. 4.00x (ISBN 0-7006-0142-2). Regents Pr Ks.

Lane, Gary & Stevens, Maria. Sylvia Plath: A Bibliography. LC 78-834. (Author Bibliographies Ser.: No. 36). 1978. 10.00 (ISBN 0-8108-1117-0). Scarecrow.

Lane, Hana U., ed. The World Almanac & Book of Facts Nineteen Eighty-One. 976p. 1980. 8.95 (ISBN 0-911818-17-0); pap. 4.50 (ISBN 0-911818-09-X). World Almanac.

Lane, Helen R., tr. see Burch, Noel.

Lane, Irving M., jt. auth. see Siegel, Laurence.

Lane, Jack C., ed. America's Military Past: A Guide to Information Sources. LC 74-11517. (The American Government & History Information Guide Ser.: Vol. 7). 1980. 30.00 (ISBN 0-8103-1205-0). Gale.

Lane, James B., ed. Jacob A. Riis: The American City. LC 74-77650. 267p. 1974. 17.50 (ISBN 0-8046-9058-8, Natl U). Kennikat.

Lane, James B., jt. ed. see Goldfield, David R.

Lane, Jim & Schaaf, Dick. Wheelchair Bowling: A Complete Guide to Bowling for the Handicapped. LC 78-24103. (Illus.). 96p. (Orig.). 1980. pap. 7.95 (ISBN 0-9605306-0-6). Wheelchair Bowlers.

Lane, John, jt. auth. see Hammel, Eric.

Lane, John R. Stuart Davis: Art & Art Theory. LC 77-17452. (Illus.). 1978. pap. 11.95 o.p. (ISBN 0-87273-067-0). Bklyn Mus.

Lane, Joseph E., Jr., jt. auth. see Miles, Catherine E.

Lane, Ken. Sport Stars. Mooney, Thomas, ed. (Pal Paperbacks Kit A Ser.). (Illus., Orig.). (gr. 7-12). 1974. pap. text ed. 1.25 (ISBN 0-8374-3469-6). Xerox Ed Pubns.

Lane, Ken, ed. Champions All. (Pal Paperbacks Ser., Kit B). (Illus., Orig.). (gr. 7-12). 1972. pap. text ed. 1.25 (ISBN 0-8374-3510-2). Xerox Ed Pubns.

Lane, Leonard C. Simplified Radiotelephone License Course, 3 Vols. (Illus.). 1971. combined ed. 18.50 (ISBN 0-8104-0755-8); Set. pap. 24.05 (ISBN 0-8104-0751-5); Vol. 1. pap. 7.75 (ISBN 0-8104-0752-3); Vol. 2. pap. 8.60 (ISBN 0-8104-0753-1); Vol. 3. pap. 7.70 (ISBN 0-8104-0754-X). Hayden.

Lane, Maggie. Maggie Lane's Needlepoint Pillows. LC 76-24824. (Illus.). 96p. 1976. encore ed. 4.95 o.p. (ISBN 0-684-16199-0, ScribT); pap. 6.95 o.p. (ISBN 0-684-14724-6, SL672, ScribT). Scribner.

--Maggie Lane's Oriental Patchwork: Elegant Designs for Easy Living. LC 78-7957. (Encore Edition). (Illus.). 1978. 6.95 (ISBN 0-684-16907-X, ScribT). Scribner.

--More Needlepoint by Design. LC 72-1205. (Illus.). 192p. 1972. 17.50 (ISBN 0-684-12906-X, ScribT). Scribner.

--Needlepoint by Design. LC 71-123842. 1970. 17.50 (ISBN 0-684-10338-9, ScribT). Scribner.

--Rugs & Wall Hangings. LC 76-10177. (Illus.). 160p. 1976. 14.95 o.p. (ISBN 0-684-14670-3, ScribT). Scribner.

Lane, Marc J. The Doctor's Lawyer: A Legal Handbook for Doctors. (Illus.). 112p. 1974. text ed. 17.50 (ISBN 0-398-02988-1). C C Thomas.

--Taxation for the Computer Industry. 165p. 1980. 24.95 (ISBN 0-471-05710-X). Wiley.

Lane, Margaret. Edgar Wallace. 423p. 1980. Repr. lib. bdg. 30.00 (ISBN 0-8495-3259-0). Arden Lib.

--Frances Wright & the "Great Experiment". (Illus.). 50p. 1972. bds. 5.00x (ISBN 0-87471-090-1). Rowman.

Lane, N. Gary. Life of the Past. 1978. pap. text ed. 13.95 (ISBN 0-675-08411-3). Merrill.

Lane, Paula, ed. The New Hamshire Atlas & Gazatteer. 2nd ed. 67p. 1979. pap. 6.95 (ISBN 0-89933-004-5). DeLorme Pub.

Lane, Peter. China in the Twentieth Century. 16.95 (ISBN 0-7134-0973-8, Pub. by Batsford England). David & Charles.

--China in the Twentieth Century. 1978. 14.00 (ISBN 0-7134-0973-8, Pub. by Batsford England). David & Charles.

--Europe in the Twentieth Century. (Twentieth Century World History Ser.). 1978. 16.95 (ISBN 0-7134-0984-3). David & Charles.

--Georgian England. (Visual Sources Ser.). (Illus.). 96p. (gr. 7-9). 1981. 16.95 (ISBN 0-7134-3358-2, Pub. by Batsford England). David & Charles.

--The Middle Ages. 96p. 1980. 14.95 (ISBN 0-7134-0033-1, Pub. by Batsford England). David & Charles.

--Norman England. (Visual Sources Ser.). (Illus.). 96p. (gr. 7 up). 1980. text ed. 14.95 (ISBN 0-7134-3356-6, Pub. by Batsford England). David & Charles.

--Roman Britain. (Visual Sources Ser.). (Illus.). 96p. (gr. 7 up). 1980. text ed. 14.95 (ISBN 0-7134-3354-X, Pub. by Batsford England). David & Charles.

--The Stuart Age. 96p. 1980. 16.95 (ISBN 0-7134-0037-4, Pub. by Batsford England). David & Charles.

--Studio Porcelain. LC 80-50884. 244p. Date not set. 30.00 (ISBN 0-8019-7001-6). Chilton.

--Success in British History Seventeen Sixty to Nineteen Fourteen. (Success Ser). (Illus.). 1978. pap. 9.95 (ISBN 0-7195-3483-6). Transatlantic.

--Tudor England. (Visual Source Ser.). 96p. 1980. 14.95 (ISBN 0-7134-0035-8, Pub. by Batsford England). David & Charles.

--The Twentieth Century. (Visual Sources Ser.). 1972. 16.95 (ISBN 0-7134-1722-6, Pub. by Batsford England). David & Charles.

--The U.S.A. in the Twentieth Century. 1978. 16.95 (ISBN 0-7134-0975-4, Pub. by Batsford England). David & Charles.

--The U.S.S.R. in the Twentieth Century. 1978. 16.95 (ISBN 0-7134-0977-0, Pub. by Batsford England). David & Charles.

--The Victorian Age. (Visual Sources Ser.). 1972. 16.95 (ISBN 0-7134-1721-8, Pub. by Batsford England). David & Charles.

Lane, Robert. The Regulation of Businessmen: Social Conditions of Government Economic Control. LC 66-14606. 1966. Repr. of 1954 ed. 13.50 (ISBN 0-208-00515-3, Archon). Shoe String.

Lane, Robert, et al. Analytical Transport Planning. LC 72-11852. 283p. 1973. 26.95 (ISBN 0-470-51440-X). Halsted Pr.

Lane, Robert E. Political Life. LC 58-6485. 1965. pap. text ed. 3.00 (ISBN 0-02-917870-3). Free Pr.

Lane, Robert E. & Sears, David O. Public Opinion. (Orig.). 1964. pap. 6.95 ref. ed. (ISBN 0-13-737809-2). P-H.

Lane, Robert S., jt. auth. see Middlekauff, Woodrow W.

Lane, Rose W. & MacBride, Roger L. Rose Wilder Lane: Her Story. LC 77-12072. 238p. 1980. pap. 6.95 (ISBN 0-8128-6077-2). Stein & Day.

Lane, Saunders M., jt. ed. see Fitzgerald, Anne.

Lane, Theodore. Life, the Individual, the Species. LC 75-43551. (Illus.). 720p. 1976. text ed. 15.95 o.p. (ISBN 0-8016-2814-8). Mosby.

Lane, Walter P. Adventures & Recollections of Walter P. Lane, a San Jacinto Veteran Containing Sketches of the Texan, Mexican, & Civil Wars with Several Indian Fights Thrown In. (Illus.). 15.00 (ISBN 0-8363-0001-7). Jenkins.

Lane, William. Moonlight Standing in As Cordelia. 1980. pap. 2.50 (ISBN 0-914610-20-1). Hanging Loose.

Lane, William G. Richard Harris Barham. 1967. 11.00 (ISBN 0-8262-0070-2). U of Mo Pr.

Lane, William L. Highlights of the Bible: New Testament. LC 80-50543. 160p. 1980. pap. 2.50 (ISBN 0-8307-0676-3, S343118). Regal.

Lane, Wilson H., et al. Wordworld. (Illus.). (gr. k-3). 1976. pap. 6.99 pupil's materials (ISBN 0-87892-880-4); tchr's handbook 3.99 (ISBN 0-87892-881-2); tapes 144.30 (ISBN 0-87892-878-2); duplicating masters 4.59 (ISBN 0-87892-882-0). Economy Co.

Lane, Wm. An Arabic English Lexicon in 8 Volumes. 230.00x (ISBN 0-685-77121-0). Intl Bk Ctr.

Lane-Petter, W. & Pearson, A. E., eds. The Laboratory Animal: Principles & Practices. 1972. 40.50 (ISBN 0-12-435760-1). Acad Pr.

Lane-Petter, William, jt. ed. see Porter, George.

Lanes, Selma G. The Art of Maurice Sendak. (Illus.). 264p. 1980. 45.00 (ISBN 0-8109-1600-2, 1600-2). Abrams.

Laney, jt. auth. see Delaney.

Lanford, H. W. System Management: Planning & Control. (National University Publications Ser.). 200p. 1981. 15.00 (ISBN 0-8046-9223-8). Kennikat.

Lanfranc. The Letters of Lanfranc, Archbishop of Canterbury. Clover, Helen & Gibson, Margaret, eds. (Oxford Medieval Texts Ser.). (Illus.). 218p. 1979. text ed. 47.00x (ISBN 0-19-822235-1). Oxford U Pr.

Lang. Absorption Spectra, Vols. 18 & 19. 1974. Vol. 18. 55.25 (ISBN 0-12-436318-0); Vol. 19. 55.25 (ISBN 0-12-436319-9). Acad Pr.

--Real Analysis. 1976. 22.95 (ISBN 0-201-04179-0). A-W.

Lang, A. G., jt. auth. see Amos, H. D.

Lang, Andrew. The Book of Dreams & Ghosts. LC 80-19690. 301p. 1980. Repr. of 1972 ed. lib. bdg. 9.95x (ISBN 0-89370-610-8). Borgo Pr.

--Favorite Andrew Dang Fairy Tale Books in Many Colors: Red, Green & Blue Fairy Tale Books. (Illus.). 1979. pap. 14.95 boxed set (ISBN 0-486-23407-X). Dover.

--The Lilac Fairy Book. (Illus.). 7.50 (ISBN 0-8446-2425-X). Peter Smith.

--Modern English Writers, Alfred Tennyson. 233p. 1980. Repr. lib. bdg. 25.00 (ISBN 0-89984-321-2). Century Bookbindery.

--The Orange Fairy Book. 7.00 (ISBN 0-8446-4770-5). Peter Smith.

--Prince Prigio, Repr. Of 1889 Ed. Bd. with Prince Ricardo of Pantouflia. Repr. of 1893 ed. LC 75-32195. (Classics of Children's Literature, 1621-1932: Vol. 57). (Illus.). 1976. PLB 38.00 (ISBN 0-8240-2306-4). Garland Pub.

--Prince Prigio & Prince Ricardo of Pantouflia. (Illus.). 156p. (gr. 1-6). 1980. 10.00 (ISBN 0-87923-390-7). Godine.

--The Red Fairy Book. (gr. 6-8). 7.00 (ISBN 0-8446-0756-8). Peter Smith.

--Selection from Andrew Lang's Fairy Tales. Dickinson, Alice, ed. (Keith Jennison Large Type Bks). (Illus.). (gr. 4-7). 1971. 8.95 o.p. (ISBN 0-531-00316-7). Watts.

--The Violet Fairy Book. (Illus.). (gr. 6-8). 7.00 (ISBN 0-8446-0757-6). Peter Smith.

Lang, Andrew, ed. Blue Fairy Book. (Illus.). (gr. 1-6). 1965. pap. 3.95 (ISBN 0-486-21437-0). Dover.

--Green Fairy Book. (gr. 4-6). 1965. pap. 4.00 (ISBN 0-486-21439-7). Dover.

--Yellow Fairy Book. (Illus.). (gr. 4-6). pap. 4.00 (ISBN 0-486-21674-8). Dover.

Lang, Berel. Philosophical Style: An Anthology About the Writng & Reading of Philosophy. LC 79-20424. 1980. 27.95 (ISBN 0-88229-230-7). Nelson-Hall.

Lang, Brad. Crockett: Brand of Fear. 1976. pap. 1.25 o.p. (ISBN 0-685-69159-4, LB367ZK, Leisure Bks). Nordon Pubns.

--Crockett on the Loose. (Crockett Ser). (Orig.). 1975. pap. 1.25 o.p. (ISBN 0-685-53900-8, LB283ZK, Leisure Bks). Nordon Pubns.

--The Perdition Express. (Orig.). 1976. pap. 1.25 o.p. (ISBN 0-685-62587-7, LB328, Leisure Bks). Nordon Pubns.

Lang, Cynthia, tr. see Friedman, Yona.

Lang, D. M. Armenia: Cradle of Civilisation. 3rd ed. (Illus.). 330p. 1980. 35.00 (ISBN 0-04-956009-3, 2619). Allen Unwin.

Lang, Daniel. A Backward Look: Germans Remember. (Illus.). 144p. (Orig.). 1981. pap. 4.95 (ISBN 0-07-036241-6). McGraw.

Lang, David. Oedipus Burning. LC 80-5408. 204p. 1981. 11.95 (ISBN 0-8128-2722-8). Stein & Day.

Lang, David C. Orchids of Britain: A Field Guide. (Illus.). 256p. 1980. 26.50x (ISBN 0-19-217692-7). Oxford U Pr.

Lang, David M. & Walker, Christopher. Armenians. (MRG Reports Ser.: No. 32). 1976. pap. 2.50 (ISBN 0-89192-170-2). Interbk Inc.

Lang, Eleanor M., ed. Art of the Real World. (Masterworks of Literature Ser.). 1979. pap. 5.50x (ISBN 0-686-68076-6, M50). Coll & U Pr.

Lang, Elizabeth. Anna's Country. 320p. (Orig.). 1981. pap. 6.95 (ISBN 0-930044-19-3). Naiad Pr.

Lang, Ewald & Taylor, William L. The Semantics of Coordination. (Studies in Language Companion Ser.: 9). 350p. Date not set. text ed. 54.25x (ISBN 90-272-3008-0). Humanities.

Lang, George. Lang's Compendium of Culinary Nonsense & Trivia. (Illus.). 1980. 10.00 (ISBN 0-517-54148-3). Potter.

Lang, Gerald S. & Dickie, Kenneth J. The Practice-Oriented Medical Record. LC 78-1931. (Illus.). 1978. text ed. 27.95 (ISBN 0-89443-032-7). Aspen Systems.

Lang, Grace. Love a Hostage. (YA) 1970. 5.95 (ISBN 0-685-07445-5, Avalon). Bouregy.

Lang, Iain. Jazz in Perspective. LC 76-6985. (Roots of Jazz Ser.). 1976. lib. bdg. 18.50 (ISBN 0-306-70814-0). Da Capo.

Lang, J. David. Devotion for Everyday: 1980-1981. 1980. pap. 2.95 (ISBN 0-87239-399-2, 4081); pap. 4.95 large print ed. (ISBN 0-87239-400-X). Standard Pub.

Lang, J. David, ed. Devotion for Every Day, 1981-1982: Third Annual. 384p. (Orig.). 1981. pap. 5.50 large type ed. (ISBN 0-87239-434-4, 4082). Standard Pub.

Lang, James. Portuguese Brazil: The King's Plantation. (Studies in Social Discontinuity). 1979. 24.00 (ISBN 0-12-436480-2). Acad Pr.

Lang, Jovian P. Your Search Key to L. C. (Library Learning Laboratory: No. 4). 1980. pap. 23.95 o.p.; tchr's ed. 9.95 (ISBN 0-913308-06-4); wkbk. 9.95 (ISBN 0-913308-07-2); set of nine transparencies 10.90 ea.; 94.50 set (ISBN 0-686-66113-3); library congress oversized catalog card 27.95; dewey classification-Library of congress poster 14.50. Fordham Pub.

Lang, K. Monographie der Harpacticiden. (Illus.). 1682p. (Ger.). 1975. Repr. of 1948 ed. lib. bdg. 240.00x (ISBN 3-87429-089-1). Lubrecht & Cramer.

Lang, K. R. Astrophysical Formulae: A Compendium for the Physicist & Astrophysicist. (Illus.). 735p. 1980. pap. 49.50 (ISBN 0-387-09933-6). Springer-Verlag.

--Astrophysical Formulae: A Compendium for the Physicist & Astrophysicist. LC 73-20809. 800p. 1974. 95.20 o.p. (ISBN 0-387-06605-5). Springer-Verlag.

--Astrophysical Formulae: A Compendium for the Physicist & Astrophysicist. (Springer Study Edition). (Illus.). 1979. pap. 31.00 o.p. (ISBN 0-387-09064-9). Springer-Verlag.

Lang, L., ed. Absorption Spectra in the Ultraviolet & Visible Region. Incl. Vols. 3-4. 1962-63. 52.25 ea. Vol. 3 (ISBN 0-12-436303-2). Vol. 4 (ISBN 0-12-436304-0); Vol. 5. 1965. 52.25 (ISBN 0-12-436305-9); Vols. 6-12. 1966-73. 55.25 ea. Vol. 6 (ISBN 0-12-436306-7). Vol. 7 (ISBN 0-12-436307-5). Vol. 8 (ISBN 0-12-436308-3). Vol. 9 (ISBN 0-12-436309-1). Vol. 10 (ISBN 0-12-436310-5). Vol. 11. (ISBN 0-12-436311-3); Vol. 12. (ISBN 0-12-436312-1); Index to Volumes. 1969. 21.00 (ISBN 0-12-436356-3); Vols. 13-15. 1970. 52.25 ea. Vol. 13 (ISBN 0-12-426313-5). Vol. 14 (ISBN 0-12-436314-8). Vol. 15 (ISBN 0-12-436315-6); Index to Volumes 11-15. 1971. 27.00 (ISBN 0-686-57637-3); Vols. 16-17. 1972-73. 55.25 ea. Vol. 16 (ISBN 0-12-436316-4). Vol. 17 (ISBN 0-12-436317-2). Acad Pr.

Lang, Larry. Strategy for Personal Finance. 2nd ed. 1981. text ed. 17.95 (ISBN 0-07-036281-5, C); instructor's manual 4.95 (ISBN 0-07-036283-1); wkbk. 5.95 (ISBN 0-07-036282-3). McGraw.

Lang, M. see Blegen, C. W. & Rawson, M.

Lang, Michael. Gentrification & the Resegregation of American Cities. 1981. price not set professional reference (ISBN 0-88410-697-7). Ballinger Pub.

Lang, Nancy M. Getting Started in Plastics. 104p. 1972. pap. 2.95 o.s.i. (ISBN 0-02-011720-5, Collier). Macmillan.

Lang, Paul H. George Frederic Handel. (Illus.). 1966 22.95 (ISBN 0-393-02131-9); pap. 7.95, 1977 (ISBN 0-393-00815-0). Norton.

--What an Altar Guild Should Know. 1964. ring bdg. 5.95 (ISBN 0-570-03501-5, 14-1528). Concordia.

Lang, Robert E., jt. auth. see Ma, T. S.

Lang, Serge. Calculus of Several Variables. 2nd ed. LC 78-55822. (Mathematics Ser.). (Illus.). 1979. text ed. 20.95 (ISBN 0-201-04299-1). A-W.

--First Course in Calculus. 4th ed. LC 77-76193. (Mathematics Ser.). (Illus.). 1978. text ed. 20.95 (ISBN 0-201-04149-9). A-W.

--Introduction to Algebraic & Abelian Functions. LC 72-1765. 1972. text ed. 16.50 (ISBN 0-201-04163-4, Adv Bk Prog). A-W.

Lang, Serge A. Algebra. 1965. 23.95 (ISBN 0-201-04177-4). A-W.

--Algebraic Structures. 1967. 12.95 (ISBN 0-201-04173-1). A-W.

--Analysis One. 1968. 20.95 (ISBN 0-201-04172-3). A-W.

--Analysis Two. 1969. text ed. 22.95 (ISBN 0-201-04179-0). A-W.

--Differential Manifolds. LC 71-161227. (Mathematics Ser). 1972. text ed. 17.95 (ISBN 0-201-04166-9). A-W.

--Introduction to Algebraic Geometry. 3rd ed. 1958. 16.50 (ISBN 0-201-04164-2, Adv Bk Prog). A-W.

--Introduction to Linear Algebra. LC 77-100872. (Mathematics Ser). 1970. pap. 10.95 (ISBN 0-201-04206-1). A-W.

--Linear Algebra. 2nd ed. LC 70-129520. (Mathematics Ser). 1971. text ed. 16.95 (ISBN 0-201-04211-8). A-W.

Lang, Serge R. Complex Analysis. LC 76-15463. (Illus.). 1977. text ed. 19.95 (ISBN 0-201-04137-5). A-W.

Lang, Steven & Spectre, Peter. On the Hawser: A Tugboat Album. LC 79-67416. (Illus.). 506p. 1980. 30.00 (ISBN 0-89272-071-9). Down East.

Lang, V. Paul. Heating & Cooling Safety. LC 76-24983. (gr. 9-12). 1977. pap. 3.80 (ISBN 0-8273-1011-0); instructor's guide 1.00 (ISBN 0-8273-1012-9). Delmar.

--Principles of Air Conditioning. LC 77-78900. (Air Conditioning, Refrigeration Ser.). 1979. text ed. 14.52 (ISBN 0-8273-1001-3); pap. text ed. 12.20 (ISBN 0-8273-1009-9); instructor's guide 1.50 (ISBN 0-8273-1002-1). Delmar.

Lang, Virgil, ed. see Bulgakov, Sergei.

Lang, William. Montana: Our Land & People. (Illus.). 1981. pap. 11.95 (ISBN 0-87108-586-0). Pruett.

Langaard, Johan H. & Revold, Reidar. Edvard Munch: Masterpieces from the Artist's Collection in the Munch Museum in Oslo. LC 64-20212. (Illus.). 72p. 1972. 25.00x o.p. (ISBN 0-87663-175-8). Universe.

Langan, John. English Skills. 2nd ed. (Illus.). 416p. 1980. text ed. 7.95x (ISBN 0-07-036265-3, C); instructor's manual 3.95x (ISBN 0-07-036266-1). McGraw.

Langan, John & Clapp, Jeremy, eds. Ligand Assay: Analysis of International Developments on Isotopic & Nonisotopic Immunoassay. (Illus.). 304p. 1980. 37.50 (ISBN 0-89352-094-2). Masson Pub.

Langbaine, Gerard. An Account of the English Dramatick Poets. LC 71-170468. (The English Stage Ser.: Vol. 20). lib. bdg. 50.00 (ISBN 0-8240-0603-8). Garland Pub.

--Momus Truimphans: The Plagiaries of the English Stage-Expos'd in a Catalogue. Bd. with The Lives & Characters of the English Dramatic Poets. (The English Stage Ser.: Vol. 19). lib. bdg. 50.00 (ISBN 0-8240-0602-X). Garland Pub.

Langballe, Hans, jt. auth. see Hellstrom, Pontus.

Langbaum, Robert. The Mysteries of Identity: A Theme in Modern Literature. LC 76-42657. 1977. 17.95 (ISBN 0-19-502189-4). Oxford U Pr.

Langbein, John H. Prosecuting Crime in the Renaissance: England, Germany, France. LC 73-81670. (Studies in Legal History). 336p. 1974. text ed. 16.50x (ISBN 0-674-71675-2). Harvard U Pr.

Langbridge, R. H. Edwardian Shopping. LC 75-24631. 1976. 25.00 (ISBN 0-7153-7068-5). David & Charles.

Langdell, C. C. A Summary of the Law of Contracts. xiv, 278p. 1980. Repr. of 1880 ed. lib. bdg. 26.00x (ISBN 0-8377-0809-5). Rothman.

Langdon, Bill. Movable Insulation. (Illus.). 1980. 14.95 (ISBN 0-87857-298-8); pap. 9.95 (ISBN 0-87857-310-0). Rodale Pr Inc.

Langdon, Margaret, jt. auth. see Couro, Ted.

Langdon, Rohen. Lighthouse of Langdon: Presenting Twentieth Century Jeharah to Doomsday Man. 64p. 1980. 9.00 (ISBN 0-682-49637-5). Exposition.

Langdon-Davies, John. Columbus & Discovery of America. (Jackdaw Ser: No. 4). (gr. 7 up). 1972. 5.95 o.p. (ISBN 0-670-23092-8). Viking Pr.

--Crimean War. (Jackdaw Ser: No. 11). (Illus.). 1968. 5.95 o.p. (ISBN 0-670-24748-0, Grossman). Viking Pr.

--Plague & Fire of London. (Jackdaw Ser: No. 2). (Illus.). 1968. 5.95 o.p. (ISBN 0-670-55770-6, Grossman). Viking Pr.

--Slave Trade & Its Abolition. (Jackdaw Ser: No. 12). (Illus.). 1970. 5.95 o.s.i. (ISBN 0-670-65082-X, Grossman). Viking Pr.

--The South Sea Bubble. (Jackdaw Ser: No. 19). (Illus.). 1968. 5.95 o.p. (ISBN 0-670-65912-6, Grossman). Viking Pr.

--Ten Sixty-Six. (Jackdaw Ser: No. 38). (Illus.). 1969. 5.95 o.p. (ISBN 0-670-69600-5, Grossman). Viking Pr.

Lange, jt. auth. see Mason.

Lange, Charles H. Cochiti: New Mexico Pueblo, Past & Present. LC 58-10852. (Illus.). 642p. 1968. lib. bdg. 14.95x (ISBN 0-8093-0295-0). S Ill U Pr.

--Cochiti: New Mexico Pueblo, Past & Present. LC 58-10852. (Arcturus Books Paperbacks). (Illus.). 642p. pap. 11.95 (ISBN 0-8093-0296-9). S Ill U Pr.

Lange, Charles H., ed. see Hill, W. W.

Lange, Charles H., et al, eds. The Southwestern Journals of Adolph F. Bandelier, 3 vols. Incl. Vol. 1. 1880-1882. 462p. 1966. 15.00x (ISBN 0-8263-0061-8); Vol. 2. 1883-1884. 546p. 1970. 20.00x (ISBN 0-8263-0153-3); Vol. 3. 1885-1888. 702p. 1975. 20.00x o.p. (ISBN 0-8263-0352-8). LC 65-17862. (Illus.). o.p. 30.00x set (ISBN 0-8263-0419-2). U of NM Pr.

Lange, Dale L. & Clifford, Ray T. Testing in Foreign Languages, ESL, & Bilingual Education, 1966-1979: A Select, Annotated ERIC Bibliography. (Language in Education Ser.: No. 24). 337p. 1980. pap. text ed. 7.95 (ISBN 0-87281-112-3, V-24). Ctr Appl Ling.

Lange, E., et al. Shameless Nude. (Illus.). 12.50 (ISBN 0-910550-14-X). Elysium.

Lange, Ed. Nudist Nudes. 4.95 (ISBN 0-910550-12-3). Elysium.

Lange, Francois-Joseph. Plaintes et Representations. (Fr.). 1977. lib. bdg. 13.75x o.p. (ISBN 0-8287-0506-2); pap. text ed. 3.75x o.p. (ISBN 0-685-77006-0). Clearwater Pub.

--Remede a Tout, Ou Constitution Invulnerable De la Felicite Publique. (Fr.). 1977. lib. bdg. 23.75x o.p. (ISBN 0-8287-0507-0); pap. text ed. 13.75x o.p. (ISBN 0-685-77004-4). Clearwater Pub.

Lange, John P. Lange's Commentary on the Holy Scriptures, 12 vols. 1980. Repr. Set. 219.00 (ISBN 0-310-27198-3). Zondervan.

Lange, Julian E. & Mills, Daniel Q. The Construction Industry: Balance-Wheel of the Economy. LC 79-1562. 256p. 1979. 18.95 (ISBN 0-669-02913-0). Lexington Bks.

Lange, June. Wonderful Webbers. (Illus.). 1967. 12.95 (ISBN 0-910550-19-0). Elysium.

Lange, Luise, tr. see Toeplitz, Otto.

Lange, Monique. Plane Trees. Calder, J. M., tr. 1980. pap. 2.95 (ISBN 0-7145-0446-7). Riverrun NY.

--The Plane Trees. Calder, J. M., tr. pap. 2.95 (ISBN 0-7145-0446-7). Riverrun NY.

Lange, Muriel W. Geometry in Modules A-D, Bks. 1-4. (gr. 10-12). 1975. pap. text ed. 4.24 ea. (Sch Div); No. 1. pap. text ed. (ISBN 0-201-04125-1); No. 2. pap. text ed. 4.24 (ISBN 0-201-04126-X); No. 3. pap. text ed. 4.24 (ISBN 0-201-04127-8); No. 4. pap. text ed. 4.24 (ISBN 0-201-04128-6); tchr's commentary 12.44 (ISBN 0-201-04129-4). A-W.

Lange, N. R. De see De Lange, N. R.

Lange, Nicholas De see Oz, Amos.

Lange, O. H. see Ordway, Frederick I., 3rd.

Lange, Oskar. Introduction to Econometrics. 2nd ed. 1963. text ed. 9.65 (ISBN 0-08-009759-6); pap. text ed. 8.00 (ISBN 0-08-013560-9). Pergamon.

--Introduction to Economic Cybernetics. Banasinski, Antoni, ed. Stadler, Jozef, tr. LC 73-106449. 1970. 19.50 (ISBN 0-08-006652-6). Pergamon.

--On Political Economy & Econometrics. 1965. 56.00 (ISBN 0-08-011588-8). Pergamon.

--Optimal Decisions. 304p. 1972. text ed. 32.00 (ISBN 0-08-016053-0). Pergamon.

--Papers in Economics & Sociology, 1930-1960. Knightsfield, P. F., tr. LC 68-22080. 1970. 50.00 (ISBN 0-08-012352-X). Pergamon.

--Political Economy, 2 vols. LC 65-367. Vol. 1, 1963. text ed. 13.75 (ISBN 0-08-013561-7); Vol. 2, 1972. text ed. 26.00 (ISBN 0-08-016572-9). Pergamon.

Lange, Oskar & Banasinski, A. Theory of Reproduction & Accumulation. 1969. 27.00 (ISBN 0-08-012256-6). Pergamon.

Lange, Peter & Tarrow, Sidney, eds. Italy in Transition: Conflict & Consensus. 186p. 1980. 25.00x (ISBN 0-7146-3147-7, F Cass Co). Biblio Dist.

Lange, Peter & Vannicelli, Maurizio, eds. The Communist Parties of Italy France & Spain: Postwar Change & Continuity, a Casebook. (Casebook Series on European Politics & Society: No. 1). 392p. 1981. text ed. 42.00x (ISBN 0-04-329033-7, 2644-5); pap. text ed. 18.50 (ISBN 0-686-69601-8). Allen Unwin.

Lange, Suzanne. The Year. LC 78-120787. (gr. 8 up). 1970. 9.95 (ISBN 0-87599-173-4). S G Phillips.

Langefors, U. & Kihlstrom, B. The Modern Technique of Rock Blasting. 3rd ed. LC 77-23895. 1978. 34.95 (ISBN 0-470-99282-4). Halsted Pr.

Langellier, Alice & Langellier, Paul. Billet Circulaire. LC 66-12110. 1966. pap. text ed. 3.95x (ISBN 0-89197-516-0). Irvington.

Langellier, Paul, jt. auth. see Langellier, Alice.

Langeluttig, Albert. Department of Justice of the United States. (Brookings Institution Reprint Ser). Repr. of 1927 ed. lib. bdg. 28.50x (ISBN 0-697-00161-X). Irvington.

Langen, Dietrich. Speaking of: Sleeping Problems. Humphreys, Martha, tr. from Ger. LC 78-72874. (Medical Adviser Ser.). (Illus.). 1979. pap. 3.95 (ISBN 0-8326-2234-6, 7452). Delair.

Langen, P., jt. ed. see Skoda, J.

Langenbach, Michael & Neskora, Teanna W. Day Care: Curriculum Considerations. (Elementary Education Ser.). 1977. text ed. 16.95 (ISBN 0-675-08544-6). Merrill.

Langenderfer, Harold Q. & Yager, E. Ben. CPA Examination: A Comprehensive Review, Problems & Solutions. 3rd ed. (Business Ser.). 1979. text ed. 24.95 (ISBN 0-675-08298-6). Merrill.

Langenkamp, R. D. Handbook of Oil Industry Terms & Phrases. 2nd ed. LC 74-80034. 176p. 1977. 14.00 (ISBN 0-87814-034-4). Pennwell Pub.

Langer, Alvin, jt. auth. see Iffy, Leslie.

Langer, Ellen J. & Dweck, Carol S. Personal Politics: The Psychology of Making It. (Illus.). 192p. 1973. pap. text ed. 9.95x (ISBN 0-13-657247-2). P-H.

Langer, Herbert. Thirty Years War. Orig. Title: Horticus Bellicus. (Illus.). 260p. 1980. 35.00 (ISBN 0-88254-497-7). Hippocrene Bks.

Langer, Howard J., ed. Directory of Speakers. 1981. lib. bdg. 32.00x (ISBN 0-912700-26-2). Oryx Pr.
Langer, James S., et al, eds. see International Conference on Collective Phenomena, 3rd, et al.
Langer, Paul F. & Zasloff, Joseph J. North Vietnam & the Pathet Lao: Partners in the Struggle for Laos. LC 73-134326. (Rand Corporation Research Studies). 1970. 12.50x (ISBN 0-674-62675-3). Harvard U Pr.
Langer, Richard W. The After-Dinner Gardening Book: The Avocado-Gift Edition. (Illus.). 198p. 1974. 9.95 o.s.i. (ISBN 0-02-567940-6). Macmillan.
--Grow It Indoors. (Illus.). 1976. pap. 2.50 (ISBN 0-446-91022-8). Warner Bks.
Langer, Robert. Seizure of Territory, the Stimson Doctrine & Related Principles in Legal Theory & Diplomatic Practice. Repr. of 1947 ed. lib. bdg. 18.75x (ISBN 0-8371-0907-8, LASD). Greenwood.
Langer, S. Z., et al. Presynadtic Receptors: Proceedings of the Satellite Symposium, Paris, July 22-23 1978, 7th International Congress of Pharmacology. (Illus.). 414p. 1979. 65.00 (ISBN 0-08-023190-X). Pergamon.
Langer, Sidney. Scared Straight: Fear in the Deterrence of Delinquency. LC 80-5859. 141p. 1981. lib. bdg. 15.50 (ISBN 0-8191-1494-4); pap. text ed. 6.75 (ISBN 0-8191-1495-2). U Pr of Amer.
Langer, Steven. Compensation of Industrial Engineers. 5th ed. 1980. pap. 50.00 (ISBN 0-916506-50-9). Abbott Langer Assocs.
--Income in Sales-Marketing Management. 1981. pap. 85.00 (ISBN 0-916506-58-4). Abbott Langer Assocs.
--Inter-City Wage & Salary Differentials 1980. 3rd ed. 1980. pap. 50.00 (ISBN 0-916506-36-3). Abbott Langer Assocs.
--The Personnel-Industrial Relations Report, Pt. III: Departmental Budgets & Staffing Ratios. 1980. pap. 85.00 (ISBN 0-916506-35-5). Abbott Langer Assocs.
--The Personnel-Industrial Relations Report, Pt. II: Income by Type & Size of Employer. 1980. pap. 85.00 (ISBN 0-916506-53-3). Abbott Langer Assocs.
--Salaries & Related Matters in the Service Department 1980. 1980. pap. 60.00 (ISBN 0-916506-38-X). Abbott Langer Assocs.
Langer, Steven, ed. The Accounting-Financial Report, 2 pts. Incl. Pt. 1. Public Accounting Firms (ISBN 0-916506-48-7); Pt. 2. Industry, Government, Education, Non-Profit (ISBN 0-916506-49-5). 1980. pap. 60.00 ea. Abbot Langer Assocs.
--The Accounting-Financial Report: Industry-Government-Education-Non-Profit, Pt. II. 2nd ed. 1981. pap. 75.00 (ISBN 0-916506-61-4). Abbott Langer Assocs.
--The Accounting-Financial Report: Public Accounting Firms, Pt. I. 2nd ed. 1981. pap. 75.00 (ISBN 0-916506-60-6). Abbott Langer Assocs.
--Available Pay Survey Reports: An Annotated Bibliography. 2nd ed. 1980. Pt. I. pap. 89.50 (ISBN 0-916506-21-5). Abbott Langer Assocs.
--Available Pay Survey Reports: An Annotated Bibliography, Pts. 2 & 3. 2nd ed. 1980. Pt. 1. pap. 39.50 (ISBN 0-916506-45-2); Pt. 2. pap. 19.50 (ISBN 0-916506-46-0). Abbott Langer Assocs.
--College Recruiting Report. 1979. pap. 50.00 o.p. (ISBN 0-916506-43-6). Abbott Langer Assocs.
--College Recruiting Report: 1980. pap. 75.00 (ISBN 0-916506-57-6). Abbott Langer Assocs.
--Compensation in Human Resource Development. 1981. pap. 75.00 (ISBN 0-916506-59-2). Abbott Langer Assocs.
--Compensation in Manufacturing: Engineers & Managers. 3rd ed. 1980. pap. 75.00 (ISBN 0-916506-56-8). Abbott Langer Assocs.
--Compensation of Attorneys, Pt. I: Non-Law Firms. 2nd ed. 1980. pap. 50.00 (ISBN 0-916506-51-7). Abbott Langer Assocs.
--Compensation of Industrial Engineering. 6th ed. 1981. 60.00 (ISBN 0-916506-63-0). Abbott Langer Assocs.
--Inter-City Wage & Salary Differentials, 1981. 1981. pap. 75.00 (ISBN 0-916506-62-2). Abbott Langer Assocs.
--Personnel-Industrial Relations Report, Pt. I: Income by Individual Variables. 1980. pap. 85.00 (ISBN 0-916506-54-1). Abbott Langer Assocs.
--Salaries & Related Matters in the Service Department, 1981. 1981. pap. 85.00 (ISBN 0-686-69467-8). Abbott Langer Assocs.
Langer, Susanne K. Introduction to Symbolic Logic. 3rd ed. 1953. pap. text ed. 5.00 (ISBN 0-486-60164-1). Dover.
Langer, Suzanne K. Problems of Art. 1957. pap. text ed. 5.95x (ISBN 0-684-15346-7, ScribC). Scribner.
Langer, William L., ed. see O'Connell, Marvin R.
Langer, William L., et al. Western Civilization, 2 vols. 2nd ed. Incl. Vol. 1. Prehistory to the Peace of Utrecht. 526p (ISBN 0-06-043844-4); Vol. 2. The Expansion of Empire to Europe in the Modern World. 485p (ISBN 0-06-043846-0). 1975. pap. text ed. 15.50 scp ea. (ISBN 0-686-67088-4, HarpC); test item to accompany vol. 1 avail. (ISBN 0-06-363843-6); test item to accompany vol. 2 avail. (ISBN 0-06-363844-4). Har-Row.
Langeren, Jacob Van. Direction for the English Traveller. LC 72-211. (English Experience Ser.: No. 197). 1969. Repr. of 1635 ed. 8.00 (ISBN 90-221-0197-5). Walter J Johnson.
Langeron, jt. auth. see Loquin.
Langerton, Edward P. The Busing Coverup. LC 75-34839. 182p. 1975. pap. 2.95. Quam Pr.
Langfeldt, Steffen. The Energy to Prosper. 138p. (Orig.). 1980. pap. 6.95x (ISBN 0-935190-04-X). AM Books CA.
Langford, Alec J. Meditations & Devotions for Adults. LC 76-223. 1976. 4.95 o.p. (ISBN 0-687-24090-5). Abingdon.
Langford, Cooper H. & Beebe, Ralph A. The Development of Chemical Principles. 1969. text ed. 16.95 (ISBN 0-201-04207-X). A-W.
Langford, Gerald, ed. see Clark, Emily.
Langford, Glenn & O'Connor, D. J., eds. New Essays in the Philosophy of Education. (International Library of the Philosophy of Education). 1973. 22.50x (ISBN 0-7100-7690-8). Routledge & Kegan.
Langford, Herbert G. & Watson, Robert. Preventing Hypertension. 280p. 1981. 22.50 (ISBN 0-87527-185-5). Green. Postponed.
Langford, Jerome J. Galileo, Science & the Church. rev. ed. 1971. pap. 4.95 (ISBN 0-472-06173-9, 173, AA). U of Mich Pr.
Langford, Michael. The Darkroom Handbook. LC 80-2703. (Illus.). 352p. 1981. 25.00 (ISBN 0-394-51370-3). Knopf.
--Starting Photography. (Illus.). (gr. 4 up). 1976. 8.95 o.p. (ISBN 0-8038-6736-0); pap. 6.95 o.p. (ISBN 0-8038-6757-3). Hastings.
--Story of Photography. (Illus.). 1980. 14.95 (ISBN 0-240-51044-5). Focal Pr.
Langford, Michael J., ed. The Camera Book. (Illus.). 256p. 1980. 25.00 (ISBN 0-87165-073-8). Ziff-Davis Pub.
Langford, Nathaniel P. Discovery of Yellowstone Park: Journal of the Washburn Expedition to the Yellowstone & Firehole Rivers in the Year 1870. LC 78-93106. (Illus.). 1972. 9.75x (ISBN 0-8032-0710-7); pap. 3.95 (ISBN 0-8032-5705-8, BB 508, Bison). U of Nebr Pr.
Langford, Paul. The Excise Crisis: Society & Politics in the Age of Walpole. 194p. 1975. 23.00x (ISBN 0-19-822437-0). Oxford U Pr.
Langford, Teddy. Managing & Being Managed: Preparation for Professional Nursing Practice. (Illus.). 304p. 1981. text ed. 15.95 (ISBN 0-13-550525-9); pap. text ed. 10.95 (ISBN 0-13-550517-8). P-H.
Langford, Thomas A. Christian Wholeness. LC 78-58011. 1979. pap. 3.50x (ISBN 0-8358-0383-X). Upper Room.
Langford, Thomas A., jt. auth. see Abernathy, George L.
Langford, W. J., ed. see Neville, Eric H.
Langfors, Arthur, ed. see Amauri, Maurice & Decraon, Pierre.
Langhaar, Henry L. Energy Methods in Applied Mechanics. LC 62-10925. 1962. 28.95 (ISBN 0-471-51711-9, Pub. by Wiley-Interscience). Wiley.
Langham, James M. Planetary Effects on Stock Market & Commodity Prices: The Influence of Certain Planetary Positions & Commodity Futures Prices, 2 vols. in 1. (Illus.). 1979. Repr. deluxe ed. 135.85 (ISBN 0-918968-42-9). Inst Econ Finan.
Langham, M. J., jt. auth. see Hussey, David.
Langham, Wright H., ed. see Space Science Board.
Langhans, Edward A. Restoration Promptbooks. LC 80-15626. 704p. 1981. price not set (ISBN 0-8093-0855-X). S Ill U Pr.
Langhans, Edward A., ed. Restoration Adaptations. LC 78-66611. (Eighteenth Century English Drama Ser.). 1980. lib. bdg. 50.00 (ISBN 0-8240-3575-5). Garland Pub.
Langhans, Robert W. Greenhouse Management: A Guide to Structures, Environmental Control, Materials Handling, Crop Programming & Business Analysis. (Illus.). 239p. 1980. 14.50 (ISBN 0-9604006-0-5). Halcyon Ithaca.
Langhans, Robert W., ed. A Growth Chamber Manual: Environmental Control for Plants. LC 77-90906. (Illus.). 240p. 1978. 19.50x (ISBN 0-8014-1169-6). Comstock.
Langhenkel, de Boer. Two Hundred Carp Tips. (Illus.). 96p. (Orig.). 1979. pap. 5.00x (ISBN 0-85242-614-3). Intl Pubns Serv.
Langholm, Odd. Price & Value in the Aristotelian Tradition: A Study in Scholastic Economics. 1979. 28.00x (ISBN 82-00-01840-7, Dist. by Columbia U Pr.). Universitet.
Langill, Ellen. Carroll College, the First Century, 1846-1946. LC 79-54879. (Illus.). 1980. text ed. 20.95 (ISBN 0-916120-06-6). Carroll Coll.
Langiulli, Nino, ed. Existentialist Tradition. LC 78-150930. 1971. pap. 2.95 o.p. (ISBN 0-385-04567-0, Anch). Doubleday.
Langiulli, Nino, ed. see Abbagnano, Nicola.
Langlais, Robert, jt. auth. see Kasle, Myron J.
Langland. Vision of Piers Plowman. 1979. 14.00x (ISBN 0-460-10571-X, Everyman); pap. 8.95 (ISBN 0-460-11571-5, Everyman). Dutton.
Langland, Olaf E. & Sippy, Francis H. Textbook of Dental Radiography. rev. ed. (Illus.). 400p. 1978. text ed. 24.75 (ISBN 0-398-02746-3). C C Thomas.
Langland, William. Piers the Ploughman. Goodridge, J. F., tr. (Classics Ser.). (Orig.). 1959. pap. 3.50 (ISBN 0-14-044087-9). Penguin.
--Visions from Piers Plowman. Coghill, Nevill, tr. 1953. 3.50x o.p. (ISBN 0-19-519578-7). Oxford U Pr.
Langlands, R. Base Change for GL (2) LC 79-28820. (Annals of Mathematics Studies: No. 96). 225p. 1980. 17.50x (ISBN 0-691-08263-4); pap. 7.00x (ISBN 0-691-08272-3). Princeton U Pr.
Langle, James I. Representation & Presidential Primaries: The Democratic Party in the Post-Reform Era. LC 80-1791. (Contributions in Political Science Ser.: No. 57). (Illus.). 192p. 1981. lib. bdg. 25.00 (ISBN 0-313-22482-X, LEP/). Greenwood.
Langley. Workbook in Accounting. 3rd ed. 1981. text ed. price not set (ISBN 0-408-10680-8). Butterworth.
Langley, Billy C. Comfort Heating. 2nd ed. (Illus.). 1978. ref. 17.50 (ISBN 0-87909-091-X); instrs'. manual avail. Reston.
--Electric Controls for Refrigeration & Air Conditioning. 1974. 18.95 (ISBN 0-13-247072-1); pap. 13.95 ref. ed. (ISBN 0-13-247064-0). P-H.
Langley, Bob. Death Stalk. (Penguin Crime Monthly). 1980. pap. 2.75 (ISBN 0-14-005328-X). Penguin.
--War of the Running Fox. LC 78-15445. 1979. 6.95 o.p. (ISBN 0-684-15918-X, ScribT). Scribner.
--Warlords. LC 80-20572. 223p. 1981. 9.95 (ISBN 0-688-00069-X). Morrow.
Langley, F. A., jt. auth. see Fox, H.
Langley, J. Ayodele. Pan-Africanism & Nationalism in West Africa 1900-1945. (Oxford Studies in African Affairs). 340p. 1973. 33.00x (ISBN 0-19-821689-0). Oxford U Pr.
Langley, Jean. Australian Bushflowers. (Illus.). 19.50x (ISBN 0-7018-0330-4, ABC). Soccer.
Langley, Lee. From the Broken Tree. 1978. 10.95 o.p. (ISBN 0-525-10988-9). Dutton.
Langley, Lee & Christensen, John B. Structure & Function of the Human Body: An Introduction to Anatomy & Physiology. LC 77-75791. 1978. text ed. 16.95 o.p. (ISBN 0-8087-1241-1). Burgess.
Langley, Lester D. Struggle for the American Mediterranean: United States-European Rivalry in the Gulf-Caribbean, 1776-1904. LC 74-84527. 240p. 1975. 15.00x (ISBN 0-8203-0364-X). U of Ga Pr.
--U. S., Cuba & the Cold War: American Failure or Communist Conspiracy. (Problems in American Civilization Ser). 1970. pap. text ed. 4.95x o.p. (ISBN 0-669-51839-5). Heath.
Langley, Lester D., jt. ed. see Glauert, Earl T.
Langley, Michael. Inchon: Macarthur's Last Triumph. 1979. 24.00 (ISBN 0-7134-3346-9, Pub. by Batsford England). David & Charles.
Langley, Noel. Dream of Dragon Flies. Bartholomew, Alick, ed. 1971. 4.95 o.s.i. (ISBN 0-02-567900-7). Macmillan.
Langley, Ray A. Basic Patterns of Historical Action in the Chematized Analysis of the Philosophy of History. (The Major Currents in Contemporary World History Library). (Illus.). 129p. 1981. 49.25 (ISBN 0-930008-84-7). Inst Econ Pol.
Langley, Roger & Levy, Richard C. Wife Beating: The Silent Crisis. 1977. 9.95 (ISBN 0-87690-231-X). Dutton.
Langley, Stephen. Producers on Producing. LC 75-26817. (Illus.). 1976. 12.50x (ISBN 0-910482-68-3). Drama Bk.
Langlois, Arthur C. Palms of the World: Supplement. LC 77-161006. (Illus.). 252p. 1977. 25.00 o.p. (ISBN 0-8130-0329-6). U Presses Fla.
Langlois, John D., Jr., ed. China Under Mongol Rule. LC 80-8559. (Illus.). 532p. 1981. 30.00x (ISBN 0-691-03127-4); pap. 12.50x (ISBN 0-691-10110-8). Princeton U Pr.
Langlois, Marc H. The Art & Life of Jean-Francois Millet. (Illus.). 121p. 1980. 33.45 (ISBN 0-930582-76-4). Gloucester Art.
Langlois, Wilfred V. Keynes & the Economic Bankruptcy of the United States. (Illus.). 139p. 1980. deluxe ed. 49.85 (ISBN 0-918968-71-2). Inst Econ Finan.
Langman, Harry. Play Mathematics: Mathematical Puzzler with Graded Exerciser. 1962. 7.50 o.p. (ISBN 0-02-848360-X). Hafner.
Langman, Jan. Medical Embryology. 4th ed. 328p. 1981. write for info. (4858-9). Williams & Wilkins.
Langmead, W. A., ed. Manual of Good Practice for Radiation Protection of the Patient: Diagnostic Radiology. 1980. Part 1. 15.00x (Pub. by Brit Inst Radiology). State Mutual Bk.
Langmuir, Janet. The Death of Bragg. LC 80-27109. (Prime Time Adventures Ser.). (Illus.). 64p. (gr. 4 up). 1981. PLB 7.95 (ISBN 0-516-02103-6). Childrens.
Langner, Lawrence. Play's the Thing. 1960. text ed. 7.95 o.p. (ISBN 0-87116-036-6). Writer.
Langner, Nola. Miss Lucy. LC 74-78082. (Illus.). (gr. k-3). 1969. 4.95g o.s.i. (ISBN 0-02-751450-1). Macmillan.
Langner, T. S. & Michael, S. T. Life Stress & Mental Health. LC 63-16587. 1963. 14.95 o.s.i. (ISBN 0-02-917900-9). Free Pr.
Langness, L. L. & Frank, Gelya F. Lives: An Anthropological Approach to Biography. Edgerton, R. N., ed. (Chandler & Sharp Publications in Anthropology Ser.). 224p. (Orig.). 1981. pap. 5.95 (ISBN 0-88316-542-2). Chandler & Sharp.
Langone, John. Like, Love, Lust: A View of Sex & Sexuality. 144p. 1981. pap. 2.25 (ISBN 0-380-54189-0, 54189). Avon.
--Like, Love, Lust: A View of Sex & Sexuality. 204p. (gr. 7 up). 1980. 7.95 (ISBN 0-316-51429-2). Little.
Langre, de Jacques see De Langre, Jacques.
Langre, Jacques De see De Langre, Jacques.
Langre, Jacques De see De Langre, Yvette.
Langre, Jacques de see Kervan, L. C.
Langre, Yvette De see De Langre, Yvette.
Langrish, J., et al. Wealth from Knowledge. 1972. 24.95 (ISBN 0-470-51721-2). Halsted Pr.
Langrognet, Michel, et al, eds. Larousse des jeunes, 8 vols. new ed. (Illus.). 192p. (Fr.). (gr. 6-12). 1975. 23.25 ea. Vol. 1 (ISBN 2-03-051601-5, 3080). Vol. 2 (ISBN 2-03-051602-3, 3081). Vol. 3 (ISBN 2-03-051603-1, 3082). Vol. 4 (ISBN 2-03-051604-X, 3086). Vol. 5 (ISBN 2-03-051605-8, 3087). Vol. 6 (ISBN 2-03-051606-6, 3088). Vol. 7 (ISBN 2-03-051607-4, 3089). Vol. 8 (ISBN 2-03-051608-2, 3090). Larousse.
Langs, Robert. Interactions: The Realm of Transference & Countertransference. LC 80-68042. 575p. 1980. 30.00 (ISBN 0-87668-425-8). Aronson.
--Resistances & Interventions. LC 80-69667. 460p. 1981. 30.00 (ISBN 0-87668-433-9). Aronson.
--The Supervisory Experience. LC 79-51514. 1979. 30.00 (ISBN 0-87668-342-1). Aronson.
--The Therapeutic Environment. 1979. 30.00x (ISBN 0-87668-385-5). Aronson.
Langs, Robert & Stone, Leo. Psychoanalytic Dialogues Two: The Clinical Experience & Its Setting. LC 79-64457. 1979. 30.00x (ISBN 0-87668-383-9). Aronson.
Langs, Robert, ed. Classics in Psychoanalytic Technique. LC 80-66919. 750p. 1981. 50.00 (ISBN 0-87668-417-7). Aronson.
--International Journal of Psychoanalytic Psychotherapy, Vol. 8. LC 75-648853. 705p. 1980. 35.00 (ISBN 0-87668-428-2). Aronson.
Langsdale, Richard. Getting Ready for Living Together. LC 74-76918. (Illus.). 96p. (Orig.). 1974. pap. 1.95 o.p. (ISBN 0-8006-1302-3, 1-1302). Fortress.
Langsley, Donald G., et al, eds. Mental Health Education in the New Medical Schools. LC 73-48. (Social & Behavioral Science Ser.). 1973. 13.95x o.p. (ISBN 0-87589-167-5). Jossey-Bass.
Langstaff, Anne L. & Volkmor, Cora B. Contingency Management. (Educational Psychology Ser.). (Illus.). 96p. 1975. pap. text ed. 6.95x (ISBN 0-675-08708-2); instructor's manual 3.95 (ISBN 0-686-67123-6). Merrill.
Langstaff, Eleanor. Andrew Lang. (English Authors Ser.: No. 241). 1978. 12.50 (ISBN 0-8057-6719-3). Twayne.
--Panama. (World Bibliographical Ser.: No. 14). 1981. write for info. (ISBN 0-903450-26-7). ABC-Clio.
Langstaff, Nancy. Teaching in an Open Classroom. (Illus.). 1975. pap. 4.75 o.p. (ISBN 0-934338-24-8). NAIS.
Langton, Algernon, tr. see Espinel, Vincente.
Langton, Christopher. An Introduction into Physicke. LC 75-25797. (English Experience Ser.: No. 281). 1970. Repr. of 1550 ed. 16.00 (ISBN 90-221-0281-5). Walter J Johnson.
Langton, J. Geographical Change & Industrial Revolution. LC 78-67428. (Cambridge Geographical Studies: No. 11). (Illus.). 1980. 53.50 (ISBN 0-521-22490-X). Cambridge U Pr.

Langton, Jane. Dark Nantucket Noon. LC 74-5799. (Harper Novel of Suspense). (Illus.). 302p. (YA) 1975. 8.95 o.p. (ISBN 0-06-012502-0, HarpT). Har-Row.
--The Fledgling. LC 79-2008. 192p. (gr. 3-7). 1981. pap. 2.95 (ISBN 0-06-440121-9, Trophy). Har-Row.
--The Memorial Hall Murder. 1981. pap. 2.95 (ISBN 0-14-005704-8). Penguin.
Langton, Jane, ed. see Dickinson, Emily.
Langton, Kenneth P. Political Socialization. (Studies in Behavioral Political Science Ser). 1969. pap. 5.95x (ISBN 0-19-500945-2). Oxford U Pr.
Langton, Stuart, ed. Citizen Participation in America. LC 78-19913. 1978. 14.95 (ISBN 0-669-02651-4); pap. 9.95 (ISBN 0-669-02465-1). Lexington Bks.
Languirand, Yolande, jt. auth. see Durand, Pauline.
Languis, Marlin, et al. Brain & Learning: Directions in Early Childhood Education. LC 80-81273. (Illus.). 72p. (Orig.). 1980. pap. text ed. 2.75 (ISBN 0-912674-72-5, NAEYC 111). Natl Assn Child Ed.
Langville, Alan R., compiled By. Modern World Rulers: A Chronology. LC 79-19294. 372p. 1979. 20.00 (ISBN 0-8108-1251-7). Scarecrow.
Langworth, Richard M. The Thunderbird Story: Personal Luxury. LC 80-20358. 1980. 28.95 (ISBN 0-87938-093-4). Motorbooks Intl.
Langworthy, Franklin. Scenery of the Plains, Mountains & Mines. LC 76-87645. (American Scene Ser). (Illus.). 292p. 1972. Repr. of 1932 ed. lib. bdg. 32.50 (ISBN 0-306-71785-9). Da Capo.
Lanham, Richard A. Revising Prose. 1979. pap. text ed. 3.95x (ISBN 0-684-15987-2, ScribC). Scribner.
Lanham, Url. The Sapphire Planet. LC 77-13160. 1978. 20.00x (ISBN 0-231-03956-5). Columbia U Pr.
Lanham, Url N. The Bone Hunters. LC 73-5596. (Illus.). 336p. 1973. 20.00x (ISBN 0-231-03152-1). Columbia U Pr.
--The Fishes. LC 62-9366. (Illus.). 1967. pap. 5.00 (ISBN 0-231-08581-8, 81). Columbia U Pr.
--The Insects. LC 64-14235. (Illus.). 1967. 17.50x (ISBN 0-231-02603-X); pap. 5.00 (ISBN 0-231-08582-6, 82). Columbia U Pr.
--Origins of Modern Biology. LC 68-24478. (gr. 11-12). 1968. 17.50x (ISBN 0-231-02872-5); pap. 4.50x (ISBN 0-231-08660-1, 123). Columbia U Pr.
Lanier, Alison. Update -- Taiwan. (Country Orientation Ser.). 1980. pap. text ed. 25.00 (ISBN 0-933662-30-0). Intercult Network.
Lanier, Alison R. Living in the U. S. A. rev. ed. LC 72-2212. 1978. pap. text ed. 6.75x (ISBN 0-933662-10-6, Pub. by Overseas Brief). Intercult Pr.
--Update -- Arab Emirates. (Country Orientation Ser.). 1980. pap. text ed. 25.00 (ISBN 0-933662-42-4). Intercult Network.
--Update -- Bahrain-Qatar. (Country Orientation Ser.). 1980. pap. text ed. 25.00 (ISBN 0-933662-44-0). Intercult Network.
--Update -- Belgium. (Country Orientation Ser.). 1980. pap. text ed. 25.00 (ISBN 0-933662-28-9). Intercult Network.
--Update -- Brazil. (Country Orientation Ser.). 1980. pap. text ed. 25.00 (ISBN 0-933662-36-X). Intercult Network.
--Update -- Britain. (Country Orientation Ser.). 1980. pap. text ed. 25.00 (ISBN 0-933662-35-1). Intercult Network.
--Update -- Egypt. (Country Orientation Ser.). 1980. pap. text ed. 25.00 (ISBN 0-933662-32-7). Intercult Network.
--Update -- France. (Country Orientation Ser.). 1980. pap. text ed. 25.00 (ISBN 0-933662-41-6). Intercult Pr.
--Update -- Germany. (Country Orientation Ser.). 1980. pap. text ed. 25.00 (ISBN 0-933662-40-8). Intercult Network.
--Update -- Hong Kong. (Country Orientation Ser.). 1980. pap. 25.00 (ISBN 0-933662-38-6). Intercult Pr.
--Update -- Indonesia. (Counry Orientation Ser.). 1980. pap. text ed. 25.00 (ISBN 0-933662-37-8). Intercult Network.
--Update -- Japan. (Country Orientation Ser.). 1980. pap. text ed. 25.00 (ISBN 0-933662-39-4). Intercult Network.
--Update -- Kuwait. (Country Orientation Ser.). 1980. pap. text ed. 25.00 (ISBN 0-933662-29-7). Intercult Network.
--Update -- Mexico. (Country Orientation Ser.). 150p. (Orig.). 1980. pap. text ed. 25.00 (ISBN 0-933662-25-4). Intercult Pr.
--Update -- Nigeria. (Country Orientation Ser.). 1980. pap. text ed. 25.00 (ISBN 0-933662-27-0). Intercult Network.
--Update -- Saudi Arabia. (Country Orientation Ser.). 150p. 1980. pap. text ed. 25.00 (ISBN 0-933662-26-2). Intercult Network.
--Update -- Singapore. (Country Orientation Ser.). 1980. pap. text ed. 25.00 (ISBN 0-686-28735-5). Intercult Network.
--Update -- South Korea. (Country Orientation Ser.). 1980. pap. text ed. 25.00 (ISBN 0-933662-33-5). Intercult Network.
--Update -- Venezuela. (Country Orientation Ser.). 1980. pap. text ed. 25.00 (ISBN 0-686-28736-3). Intercult Network.
--Update: Peoples Republic of China. Pusch, Margaret D., ed. (Country Orientation Ser.). 150p. (Orig.). 1980. pap. 25.00 (ISBN 0-933662-44-0). Intercult Pr.
Lanier, Mary, ed. Poems of Sidney Lanier. LC 80-29576. 262p. 1981. Repr. of 1884 ed. 12.50 (ISBN 0-8203-0560-X). U of Ga Pr.
Lanier, Roy H., jt. auth. see Whitten, D. J.
Lanigan, Anne. Cookie & Cracker Cookbook. 1980. pap. 6.95 (ISBN 0-8256-3166-1). Music Sales.
--The Cookie & Cracker Cookbook. (Illus.). 1980. cancelled (ISBN 0-8256-3188-2, Quick Fox). Music Sales.
Lankford, T. Randall. Integrated Science for Health Students. 2nd ed. (Illus.). 1979. text ed. 18.95 (ISBN 0-8359-3103-X); pap. 7.95 lab manual (ISBN 0-8359-3105-6); instrs' manual avail. (ISBN 0-687-01281-3). Reston.
Lanman, Charles. Biographical Annals of the Civil Government of the United States. LC 68-30626. 1976. Repr. of 1876 ed. 42.00 (ISBN 0-8103-4300-2). Gale.
Lanmon, Dwight P., jt. auth. see Hollister, Paul.
Lanner, Ronald M. The Pinon Pine: A Natural & Cultural History. (Illus.). 160p. 1981. price not set (ISBN 0-87417-065-6). U of Nev Pr.
Lanners, E. Illusions. 1977. 12.95 o.p. (ISBN 0-03-020891-2); pap. 6.95 o.p. (ISBN 0-03-020886-6). HR&W.
Lannie, Vincent P. Henry Barnard: American Educator. LC 74-4827. 1974. text ed. 8.75 (ISBN 0-8077-2441-6); pap. text ed. 4.00 (ISBN 0-8077-2443-2). Tchrs Coll.
Lanning, Sereta. Escape from Tomorrow. LC 78-16559. (Pacesetters Ser.). (Illus.). (gr. 4 up). 1978. PLB 7.95 (ISBN 0-516-02169-9). Childrens.
Lannois, Georges. Modern French Writing. 1969. pap. text ed. 2.95x o.p. (ISBN 0-435-37550-4). Heinemann Ed.
Lannois, Georges, ed. Pages francaises. 1969. 14.50 (ISBN 0-08-006379-9). Pergamon.
Lannoy, Richard. India: People & Places. (Illus.). 1955. 17.50 o.s.i. (ISBN 0-8149-0139-5). Vanguard.
Lano, David. Wandering Showman I. viii, 290p. 1957. 5.75 o.p. (ISBN 0-87013-027-7). Mich St U Pr.
LaNoue, George R. Educational Vouchers: Concepts & Controversies. LC 78-187726. (Illus.). 1972. text ed. 8.95x (ISBN 0-8077-1660-X); pap. text ed. 5.75x (ISBN 0-8077-1661-8). Tchrs Coll.
Lanoux, Armand, ed. Dreams of the Chateaux of the Loire. (Illus.). 92p. 1967. 13.50x (ISBN 0-8002-0758-0). Intl Pubns Serv.
Lanphere, Marvin A., jt. auth. see Dalrymple, G. Brent.
Lanros. Assessment Intervention in Emergency Nursing. LC 78-9832. 19.95 (ISBN 0-87618-990-7). R J Brady.
Lansburg, A. Early American Song Book. LC 74-76864. 1974. 12.95 o.p. (ISBN 0-13-222778-9). P-H.
Lansbury, Coral. The Reasonable Man: Trollope's Legal Fictions. LC 80-8560. 260p. 1981. 16.50x (ISBN 0-691-06457-1). Princeton U Pr.
Lansbury, George. Why Pacifists Should Be Socialists. LC 72-147520. (Library of War & Peace; Labor, Socialism & War). lib. bdg. 38.00 (ISBN 0-8240-0454-X). Garland Pub.
Lansdale, Merton. Twenty-Four Ways of Becoming a Millionaire in Less Than One Year. (The Essential Knowledge Library). (Illus.). 1979. spiral bdg. 6.00 (ISBN 0-89266-174-7). Am Classical Coll Pr.
Lansdowne, J. F. Birds of the West Coast, Vol. 2. 1980. 40.00 (ISBN 0-395-29546-7). HM.
Lansford, Henry, jt. auth. see Roberts, Walter O.
Lansing, Alfred, jt. auth. see Modell, Walter.
Lansing, John B. & Morgan, James N. Economic Survey Methods. LC 71-633672. 448p. 1971. cloth 14.00 (ISBN 0-87944-009-0); pap. 8.00 (ISBN 0-87944-008-2). U of Mich Soc Res.
Lansing, John R. Delegate from New York. Strayer, J. R., ed. LC 67-27618. 1967. Repr. of 1939 ed. 12.00 (ISBN 0-8046-0262-X). Kennikat.
Lansing, John S. Evil in the Morning of the World: Phenomenological Approaches to a Balinese Community. LC 74-620023. (Michigan Papers on South & South East Asia No. 6). (Illus.). 104p. 1974. pap. 4.50x (ISBN 0-89148-006-4). Ctr S&SE Asian.
Lansky, Lester L. Pediatric Neurology: A Practitioner's Guide. 1975. spiral bdg. 12.00 o.p. (ISBN 0-87488-712-7). Med Exam.
Lansky, Vicki. Feed Me, I'm Yours. 176p. 1981. pap. 2.25 (ISBN 0-553-12640-7). Bantam.
Lanslots. The Primitive Church. LC 79-67862. 291p. 1980. write for info. o.p. (ISBN 0-89555-134-9). Tan Bks Pubs.
Lanson, Lucienne. From Woman to Woman: A Gynecologist Answers Questions About You & Your Body. rev. ed. LC 80-11226. (Illus.). 352p. 1981. 15.00 (ISBN 0-394-51293-6); pap. 8.95 (ISBN 0-394-73996-5). Knopf.
Lant, A. F., ed. Advanced Medicine - XI: Proceedings of the 11th Annual Symposium on Advanced Medicine 1975. (Illus.). 450p. (Orig.). 1975. pap. text ed. 30.00x (ISBN 0-8464-0112-6). Beekman Pubs.
Lantern, John De see Fidell, Linda S. & De Lamater, John.
Lanting, Fred L. Canine Hip Dysplasia & Orthopedic Problems. LC 79-54235. (Illus.). 100p. 1981. 12.95 (ISBN 0-931866-06-5). Alpine Pubns.
Lantz, Alma E., et al. Re-Entry Programs for Female Scientists. 1980. 21.95 (ISBN 0-03-055771-2). Praeger.
Lantz, Herman R. People of Coal Town. LC 58-7169. (Arcturus Books Paperbacks). 332p. 1971. pap. 2.85 (ISBN 0-8093-0531-3). S Ill U Pr.
Lantz, Kenneth. Nikoly Leskov. (World Authors Ser.: No. 523). 1979. lib. bdg. 12.95 (ISBN 0-8057-6364-3). Twayne.
Lantz, Sherlee. Trianglepoint. LC 76-3550. 1976. 12.95 o.p. (ISBN 0-670-73030-0, Studio). Viking Pr.
Lanyon, Andrew. A St. Ives Album. 72p. 1980. 10.00x (ISBN 0-906720-00-1, Pub. by Hodge England). State Mutual Bk.
Lanyon, R. I. & Goodstein, L. D. Personality Assessment. LC 75-140552. 1971. 23.95 (ISBN 0-471-51740-2). Wiley.
Lanyon, Richard I., jt. auth. see Goodstein, Leonard D.
Lanzano, Susan & Abreu, Rosendo. Preparacion Para el Examen de Equivalencia de la Escuela Superior. 3rd ed. Ringel, Martin & Banks, William K., eds. LC 80-17685. 368p. (Span.). 1981. pap. 6.95 (ISBN 0-668-05095-0, 50950). Arco.
Lanzillotti, Robert F., jt. ed. see Blair, Roger D.
Lanzmann, Claude, ed. The Bird Has No Wings: The Letters of Peter Schwiefert. Lucas, Barbara, tr. (Illus.). 224p. 1976. 8.95 o.p. (ISBN 0-312-08085-9). St Martin.
Lao Tzu. Way of Lao Tzu: Tao-Te Chins. Chan, Wing-Tsit, tr. LC 62-21266. (Orig.). 1963. 5.95 (ISBN 0-672-60350-0, LLA139). Bobbs.
Lapage, Geoffrey. Animals Parasitic in Man. rev. ed. (Illus.). 8.75 (ISBN 0-8446-2427-6). Peter Smith.
LaPalma, ed. see Wong, Nellie, et al.
LaPalombara, Joseph & Blank, Stephen. Multinational Corporations & National Elites: A Study in Tensions. LC 76-48768. (Report Ser: No. 702). (Illus.). 1976. pap. 15.00 o.p. (ISBN 0-8237-0136-0). Conference Bd.
LaPalombra, Joseph. Politics Within Nations. (Contemporary Comparative Politics Ser.). 608p. 1974. text ed. 17.95 (ISBN 0-13-687814-8). P-H.
Lapan, Stephen D., jt. auth. see House, Ernest R.
Lapanje, Savo. Physicochemical Aspects of Protein Denaturation. LC 78-1919. 1978. 34.50 (ISBN 0-471-03409-6, Pub. by Wiley-Interscience). Wiley.
Lapati, Americo D. John Henry Newman. (English Authors Ser.: No. 140). lib. bdg. 10.95 (ISBN 0-8057-1416-2). Twayne.
LaPatra, J. W. Public Welfare Systems. (Illus.). 232p. 1975. 17.75 (ISBN 0-398-03469-9). C C Thomas.
LaPatra, Jack. Analyzing the Criminal Justice System. LC 77-2678. (Illus.). 1978. 17.95 (ISBN 0-669-01625-X). Lexington Bks.
Lapchick, Richard E. The Politics of Race & International Sport: The Case of South Africa. LC 74-11705. (Studies in Human Rights: No. 1). 268p. 1975. lib. bdg. 16.95 (ISBN 0-8371-7691-3, LPR/). Greenwood.
Lape, Fred. A Farm & Village Boyhood. LC 80-17303. (Illus.). 200p. 9.95 (ISBN 0-8156-0162-X, York State Bks). Syracuse U Pr.
Lapenna, Ivo. Soviet Penal Policy. (Background Ser.). 1968. 6.25 (ISBN 0-8023-1196-2). Dufour.
La Pice, Margaret. Been There: Post Office Poems & Other Poems. pap. 3.95 (ISBN 0-9604508-0-7). M La Pice.
Lapide, Pinchas & Moltmann, Jurgen. Jewish Monotheism & Christian Trinitarian Doctrine. Swidler, Leonard, tr. from Ger. LC 80-8058. 96p. 1981. pap. 4.50 (ISBN 0-8006-1405-4, 1-1405). Fortress.
LaPidus, Anne, jt. auth. see Rucker, Marion E.
Lapidus, Jacqueline. Starting Over. (Illus.). 1977. pap. 3.50 (ISBN 0-918314-03-8). Out & Out.
Lapidus, Saul, ed. Ceramics, Mosaics, Stained Glass. 1977. 9.95 o.p. (ISBN 0-679-50761-2); pap. 6.95 o.p. (ISBN 0-679-50762-0). McKay.
--Wood, Metal & Plastic: A Creative Introduction to Methods & Materials. (Illus.). 1978. 12.50 o.p. (ISBN 0-679-50757-4); pap. 6.95 o.p. (ISBN 0-679-50808-2). McKay.
Lapierre, Dominique, jt. auth. see Collins, Larry.
Lapin, Howard S. Structuring the Journey to Work. LC 63-15012. 1964. 9.00x o.p. (ISBN 0-8122-7424-5). U of Pa Pr.
Lapin, Jackie, jt. auth. see Parkhouse, Bonnie L.
Lapin, Lynne. Craftworker's Market 1980. 2nd ed. (Illus.). 1979. 11.95 o.p. (ISBN 0-89879-004-2). Writers Digest.
Lapin, Lynne, ed. Artist's Market Nineteen Eighty. (Illus.). 480p. 1980. 11.95 (ISBN 0-89879-029-8). Writers Digest.
Lapis, K., ed. Developments of Cancer Chemotherapy. (Journal: Oncology: Suppl. 1, Vol. 37). (Illus.). iv, 120p. 1980. pap. 19.75 (ISBN 3-8055-1588-X). S Karger.
Lapis, Karoly & Johannessen, Jan V., eds. Liver Carcinogenesis. LC 79-134. (Illus.). 1979. text ed. 40.00 (ISBN 0-89116-149-X, Co-Pub. by McGraw Intl). Hemisphere Pub.
Laplace, John. Health. 2nd ed. 1976. pap. text ed. 12.95 o.p. (ISBN 0-13-385369-1). P-H.
--Health. 3rd ed. (Illus.). 1980. text ed. 13.95 (ISBN 0-13-385393-4); cloth 16.95 (ISBN 0-13-385427-2). P-H.
Laplace, Pierre S. Celestial Mechanics, Vols. 1-4. LC 69-11316. Set. text ed. 175.00 (ISBN 0-8284-0194-2). Chelsea Pub.
--Celestial Mechanics, Vol. 5. LC 63-11316. (Mecanique Celeste, Tome V, Fr). 1969. Repr. of 1832 ed. text ed. 20.00 (ISBN 0-8284-0214-0). Chelsea Pub.
LaPoint, Diana. The Gold of Karinthy. 1978. pap. 1.95 (ISBN 0-505-51261-0). Tower Bks.
Lapointe, Francois. Edmund Husserl & His Critics: An International Bibliography (1894-1979) (Bibliographies of Famous Philosophers: Vol. 4). 352p. 1980. 27.50 (ISBN 0-912632-42-9). Philos Document.
Lapointe, Francois H., compiled by. Soren Kierkegaard & His Critics: An International Bibliography of Criticism. LC 80-783. viii, 430p. 1980. lib. bdg. 37.50 (ISBN 0-313-22333-5, LKI/). Greenwood.
LaPointe, Frank. The Sioux Today. LC 73-189727. 144p. (gr. 7 up). 1972. 5.95g o.s.i. (ISBN 0-02-751600-8, CCPr). Macmillan.
Lapointe, Juliet G., tr. see Bosquet, Alain.
Laponce, J. A. Left & Right: The Topography. 284p. 1981. 27.50x (ISBN 0-8020-5533-8). U of Toronto Pr.
Laporte, Genevieve. Sunshine at Midnight. 136p. 1975. 6.95 o.s.i. (ISBN 0-02-568300-4). Macmillan.
Laporte, Leo F., intro. by. Evolution & the Fossil Record: Readings from Scientific American. LC 77-26073. (Illus.). 1978. text ed. 19.95x (ISBN 0-7167-0291-6); pap. text ed. 9.95x (ISBN 0-7167-0290-8). W H Freeman.
LaPorte, Valerie & Rubin, Jeffrey, eds. Reform & Regulation of Long Term Care. LC 79-9761. 230p. 1979. 22.95 (ISBN 0-03-049341-2). Praeger.
Lapp, Eleanor. The Mice Came in Early This Year. Rubin, Caroline, ed. LC 76-45629. (Self-Starter Bks). (Illus.). (ps-2). 1976. 6.50g (ISBN 0-8075-5111-2). A Whitman.
Lapp, Eleanor J. In the Morning Mist. Pacini, Kathy, ed. LC 77-28442. (Self-Starter Bks.). (Illus.). (gr. k-3). 1978. 6.50g (ISBN 0-8075-3634-2). A Whitman.
Lapp, John. Dream for America. Orig. Title: Bicentennial. 1976. pap. 1.50 (ISBN 0-89129-159-8). Jove Pubns.
Lapp, John C. Esthetics of Negligence: La Fontaine's Contes. LC 72-142130. 1971. 42.00 (ISBN 0-521-08067-3). Cambridge U Pr.
Lapp, John C., ed. & tr. see Corneille, Pierre.
Lapp, Nancy L., ed. The Tale of the Tell: Archaeological Studies by Paul W. Lapp. LC 75-5861. (Pittsburgh Theological Monographs: No. 5). 1975. pap. text ed. 6.50 (ISBN 0-915138-05-0). Pickwick.
Lapp, Ralph & Andrews, Howard. Nuclear Radiation Physics. 4th ed. (Illus.). 1972. 21.95 (ISBN 0-13-625988-X). P-H.
Lapp, Ralph E. Matter. LC 63-21668. (Life Science Library). (Illus.). (gr. 5 up). 1969. PLB 8.97 o.p. (ISBN 0-8094-0459-1, Pub. by Time-Life). Silver.
Lappe, Frances M. Diet for a Small Planet. rev ed. 432p. 1975. spiral bdg. 7.95 (ISBN 0-345-28919-6); pap. 2.75 (ISBN 0-345-29515-3). Ballantine.
Lappe, Frances M. & Beccar-Varela, Adele. Mozambique & Tanzania: Asking the Big Questions. (Illus.). 128p. 1980. pap. 4.75 (ISBN 0-935028-05-6). Inst Food & Develop.
Lappe, Frances M. & Collins, Joseph. Food First. 1979. pap. 2.95 (ISBN 0-345-29045-3). Ballantine.
Lappe, Frances M. & Ewald, Ellen B. Great Meatless Meals. (Orig.). 1976. pap. 2.25 (ISBN 0-345-29501-3). Ballantine.
Lappe, Francis M. & Ewald, Ellen B. Great Meatless Meals. 160p. (Orig.). 1981. pap. 2.50. Ballantine.

Lappe, Marc & McCurdy, John C. Of All Things Most Yielding. Brower, David R., ed. Moulton, Betty L., tr. LC 73-8379. (Celebrating the Earth Ser). (Illus.). 128p. 1973. 14.95 o.p. (ISBN 0-913890-25-1); pap. 6.95 o.p. (ISBN 0-685-56641-2, Co-Pub. by Ballantine). Friends Earth.

Lappenberg, Johann M. A History of England Under the Anglo-Saxon Kings, 2 vols. Thorpe, Benjamin, rev. by. & tr. LC 80-2209. 1981. Repr. of 1845 ed. 97.50 (ISBN 0-404-18740-4). AMS Pr.

Lappin, Kendall E. Baudelaire Revisited: Forty-One Poems. Pheiffer, Susan G., ed. (Illus.). 196p. 1981. 11.95 (ISBN 0-9605710-1-9); pap. 7.95 (ISBN 0-9605710-0-0). KEL Pubns.

Lappin, Peter. Dominic Savio: Teenage Saint. LC 54-11044. (gr. 5-10). 1954. 2.75 (ISBN 0-89944-034-7); pap. 1.25 (ISBN 0-89944-033-9). D Bosco Pubns.

--Halfway to Heaven. 240p. (Orig.). 1980. pap. write for info. (ISBN 0-89944-052-5). D Bosco Pubns.

Lappo-Danilevskii, J. A. Systemes Des Equations Differentielles, 3 Vols. in 1. LC 53-7110. (Fr). 22.50 (ISBN 0-8284-0094-6). Chelsea Pub.

Lapuerta, Leopoldo. Blood Gases in Clinical Practice. (Illus.). 132p. 1976. 16.75 (ISBN 0-398-03527-X). C C Thomas.

Lapwood, E. R. Ordinary Differential Equations. LC 68-21278. 1968. 25.00 (ISBN 0-08-012551-4). Pergamon.

Lapwood, E. R. & Usami, T. Free Oscillations of the Earth. (Cambridge Monographs on Mechanics & Applied Mathematics). (Illus.). 168p. Date not set. price not set (ISBN 0-521-23536-7). Cambridge U Pr.

LaQue, Francis L. Marine Corrosion: Causes & Prevention. LC 75-16307. (Corrosion Monograph Ser). 332p. 1975. 32.50 (ISBN 0-471-51745-3, Pub. by Wiley-Interscience). Wiley.

Laquer, Walter. Fate of the Revolution. 1967. 5.95 o.s.i. (ISBN 0-02-568330-6). Macmillan.

--Road to Jerusalem. 1968. 6.95 o.s.i. (ISBN 0-02-568360-8). Macmillan.

La Queriere, Yves de. Celine et les mots: Etude stylistique des effets de mots dans le Voyage au bout de la nuit. LC 70-160050. (Studies in Romance Languages: No. 7.). 172p. 1973. 10.00x (ISBN 0-8131-1268-0). U Pr of Ky.

Laqueur, Thomas W. Religion & Respectability: Sunday Schools & English Working Class Culture, 1780-1850. LC 74-29728. 1976. 27.50x (ISBN 0-300-01859-2). Yale U Pr.

Laqueur, Walter. Dictionary of Politics. rev. ed. LC 74-9232. 1974. 17.95 (ISBN 0-02-917950-5). Free Pr.

--Farewell to Europe. 336p. 1981. 12.95 (ISBN 0-316-51475-6). Little.

--Struggle for the Middle East: The Soviet Union & the Middle East 1958-1968. 1969. 12.95 o.s.i. (ISBN 0-02-568320-9). Macmillan.

--The Terrible Secret. 276p. 1980. 12.95 (ISBN 0-316-51474-8). Little.

Laragh, John H., ed. Topics in Hypertension. LC 80-52799. (Illus.). 644p. 1980. 49.00 (ISBN 0-914316-20-6). Yorke Med.

La Ramee, Pierre De. The Latine Grammar of P. Ramus. LC 78-26236. (English Experience Ser.: No. 289). 1971. Repr. of 1585 ed. 16.00 (ISBN 90-221-0289-0). Walter J Johnson.

--The Logike of the Most Excellent Philosopher P. Ramus, Martyr. Makilmenaeus, Rolandus, tr. LC 77-26225. (English Experience Ser.: No. 107). 101p. 1969. Repr. of 1555 ed. 11.50 (ISBN 90-221-0107-X). Walter J Johnson.

Larbalestrier, D. Paralegal Practice & Procedure: A Practical Guide for the Legal Assistant. 1979. pap. 9.95 (ISBN 0-13-648691-6). P-H.

Larcher, Fabian R., tr. see Aquinas, Thomas.

Larcher, W. Physiological Plant Ecology. rev. ed. Biederman-Thorson, M. A., tr. from Ger. LC 79-26396. (Illus.). 340p. 24.00 (ISBN 3-540-09795-3). Springer-Verlag.

Larcom, Lucy. Childhood Songs. LC 77-20397. (Granger Poetry Library Ser.). (Illus.). 1978. Repr. of 1874 ed. 19.00x (ISBN 0-89609-069-8). Granger Bk.

Larden, Ida C., jt. auth. see Hull, Raymond.

Lardner, R. W., jt. auth. see Arya, J. C.

Lardner, Rex. Downhill Lies & Other Falsehoods; or, How to Play Dirty Golf. (Illus.). 192p. 1973. pap. 3.50 (ISBN 0-8015-2198-X, Hawthorn). Dutton.

--Finding & Exploiting Your Opponents Weaknesses. LC 74-12730. 1978. 4.95 o.p. (ISBN 0-385-09103-6). Doubleday.

--The Fine Art of Tennis Hustling. 128p. (Orig.). 1975. pap. 3.50 (ISBN 0-8015-2638-8, Hawthorn). Dutton.

--Tactics in Women's Singles, Doubles & Mixed Doubles. LC 74-12731. 125p. 1975. 4.95a o.p. (ISBN 0-385-09044-7); pap. 2.50 o.p. (ISBN 0-385-06733-X). Doubleday.

--Underhanded Serve, or How to Play Dirty Tennis. (Illus.). 1968. pap. 2.95 (ISBN 0-8015-8142-7, Hawthorn). Dutton.

Lardner, Ring. The Best Short Stories of Ring Lardner. LC 57-13394. 346p. 1957. lib. rep. ed. 17.50x (ISBN 0-684-14743-2, ScribT); pap. 4.95 (ISBN 0-684-13648-1, SL494, ScribT). Scribner.

--Letters from Ring. Caruthers, Clifford M., ed. 1979. 10.95 (ISBN 0-911938-08-7); pap. 6.95 (ISBN 0-911938-09-5). Walden Pr.

--Ring Lardner Reader. Geismar, Maxwell, ed. 1963. 25.00x (ISBN 0-684-15365-3, ScribT). Scribner.

--Some Champions: Previously Uncollected Autobiographical Sketches & Fiction. Bruccoli, Matthew J. & Layman, Richard, eds. 208p. 1976. encore ed. o.p. 3.50 (ISBN 0-684-15681-4, ScribT); pap. 3.95 (ISBN 0-684-15065-4, SL729, ScribT). Scribner.

Lardner, Robin W., jt. auth. see Arya, Jagdish C.

Lardy, N. Economic Growth & Distribution in China. (Illus.). 1978. 29.95 (ISBN 0-521-21904-3). Cambridge U Pr.

Lare, Gary, jt. auth. see Schroeder, Don.

Larew, James C. A Party Reborn: The Democrats of Iowa, 1950-1974. LC 80-51855. (Illus.). 216p. 1980. 12.00x (ISBN 0-89033-002-6); pap. 6.00. State Hist Iowa.

Larew, Walter B. Automatic Transmissions. LC 66-27600. (Illus.). 1966. 11.50 o.p. (ISBN 0-8019-5184-4). Chilton.

--Carburetors & Carburetion. LC 66-27600. (Illus.). 1967. 9.50 o.p. (ISBN 0-8019-5224-7). Chilton.

--Fluid Clutches & Torque Converters. LC 68-8908. (Illus.). 1968. 9.95 o.p. (ISBN 0-8019-5383-9). Chilton.

Larfillon, L. One Hundred Hours to Visit the Chateaux of the Loire. new ed. (Illus.). 95p. 1973. pap. 5.95 o.p. (ISBN 0-88332-016-9, 4103). Larousse.

Larg, David G. Andre Maurois. 239p. 1980. Repr. of 1931 ed. lib. bdg. 25.00 (ISBN 0-8492-1633-8). R West.

Largay, James A. & Livingstone, J. L. Accounting for Changing Prices: Replacement Cost & General Price Level Adjustments. LC 76-7491. (Accounting, Management & Information Systems Ser.). 1976. text ed. 24.95 (ISBN 0-471-54210-5). Wiley.

Large, Brian, ed. see Wagner, Richard.

Large, George E. & Chen, T. Y. Reinforced Concrete Design. 3rd ed. LC 69-14677. (Illus.). 1969. 27.95 (ISBN 0-8260-5225-8). Wiley.

Large, John, ed. Contributions of Voice Research to Singing. LC 79-57539. (Illus.). 432p. 1980. pap. text ed. 30.00 (ISBN 0-933014-53-8). College-Hill.

Largen, Velda L. Guide to Nutrition. LC 80-25186. (Illus.). 144p. 1981. text ed. 8.96 (ISBN 0-87006-312-X). Goodheart.

Largent, David. How to Identify Mushrooms (to Genus I) Macroscopic Features. 2nd ed. (Illus.). 1977. pap. 4.85x (ISBN 0-916422-00-3). Mad River.

Largent, David, et al. How to Identify Mushrooms (to Genus III) Microscopic Features. (Illus.). 1977. pap. 8.25x (ISBN 0-916422-09-7). Mad River.

Largent, David L. & Thiers, H. How to Identify Mushrooms (to Genus II): Field Identification of Genera. (Illus.). 1977. pap. 3.50x (ISBN 0-916422-08-9). Mad River.

Largo, Gerald A. Community & Liturgy: An Historical Overview. LC 80-1434. 151p. 1980. lib. bdg. 16.25 (ISBN 0-8191-1302-6); pap. text ed. 7.75 (ISBN 0-8191-1303-4). U Pr of Amer.

Larimer, Sarah L. The Capture & Escape: Or, Life Among the Sioux. LC 75-7110. (Indian Captivities Ser.: Vol. 84). 1976. Repr. of 1870 ed. lib. bdg. 44.00 (ISBN 0-8240-1708-0). Garland Pub.

Larit, Barry. Pro Basketball, 1976-1977. 1976. pap. 1.75 o.p. (ISBN 0-345-25442-2). Ballantine.

--Pro Hockey, 1976-1977. 1976. pap. 1.75 o.p. (ISBN 0-345-25443-0). Ballantine.

Larit, Barry, ed. Major League Baseball, 1976. 1976. pap. 1.75 o.p. (ISBN 0-345-25441-4). Ballantine.

Lark, Karl G. The Mystery of DNA Replication. (The Universsity of Utah Frederick William Reynolds Lecture Ser.: No. 43). 1980. 4.00 (ISBN 0-87480-179-6). U of Utah Pr.

Lark, P. D., et al. The Handling of Chemical Data. LC 66-17264. 1968. 32.00 (ISBN 0-08-011849-6). Pergamon.

Larkcom, Joy. Vegetables from Small Gardens. 1977. 9.95 (ISBN 0-571-10644-7, Pub. by Faber & Faber). Merrimack Bk Serv.

Lark-Horovitz, Betty, et al. Understanding Children's Art for Better Teaching. 2nd ed. LC 73-81970. 1973. text ed. 17.95 (ISBN 0-675-08927-1). Merrill.

Lark-Horovitz, K. see Marton, L.

Larkin. Zachary Goes Groundfishing. 1980. 6.95 (ISBN 0-89272-084-0). Down East.

Larkin, David, ed. Christmas Book. (Encore Ed.). (Illus.). 1975. 3.95 o.p. (ISBN 0-685-99258-6, ScribT). Scribner.

--Dulac. (Encore Ed.). (Illus.). 1975. 3.95 o.p. (ISBN 0-684-16161-3, ScribT). Scribner.

--Fantastic Art. (Illus., Orig.). 1975. pap. 5.95 o.p. (ISBN 0-345-25038-9). Ballantine.

--Innocent Art. (Gift Bks). (Illus.). 96p. (Orig.). 1974. pap. 4.95 o.p. (ISBN 0-345-24244-0). Ballantine.

--Magritte. 1976. pap. 6.95 (ISBN 0-345-25593-3). Ballantine.

Larkin, Elinor. Love's Tempest. (Orig.). 1981. pap. 1.50 (ISBN 0-440-14948-7). Dell.

Larkin, Emmett. James Larkin, Irish Labor Leader, 1876-1947. (Illus.). 1977. Repr. of 1965 ed. 28.00x (ISBN 0-7100-8606-7). Routledge & Kegan.

Larkin, Francis. Understanding the Heart. rev. ed. LC 80-81066. 127p. 1980. pap. write for info. (ISBN 0-89870-007-8). Ignatius Pr.

Larkin, James F. & Hughes, Paul L., eds. Stuart Royal Proclamations: Royal Proclamations of King James I 1603-1625, Vol. 1. 716p. 1974. 79.00x (ISBN 0-19-822372-2). Oxford U Pr.

Larkin, Joan. Housework. (Illus.). 1976. pap. 3.50 (ISBN 0-918314-02-X). Out & Out.

Larkin, Joan & Bulkin, Elly, eds. Amazon Poetry: An Anthology. 1975. pap. 3.50 (ISBN 0-918314-07-0). Out & Out.

Larkin, Joan, jt. ed. see Bulkin, Elly.

Larkin, Philip. The North Ship. 1974. pap. 4.95 (ISBN 0-571-10503-3, Pub. by Faber & Faber). Merrimack Bk Serv.

--The Whitsun Weddings. 46p. 1964. 8.95 (ISBN 0-571-05750-0, Pub. by Faber & Faber). Merrimack Bk Serv.

--The Whitsun Weddings. 46p. 1971. pap. 3.95 (ISBN 0-571-09710-3, Pub. by Faber & Faber). Merrimack Bk Serv.

Larkin, Phyllis, ed. see Doty, Jean & Doty, Roy.

Larkin, R. T. The Sexual Superstars. 1976. pap. 1.75 o.p. (ISBN 0-685-69155-1, LB363KK, Leisure Bks). Nordon Pubns.

Larkin, Robert P., et al. Geology Field Guide: The Southern Rocky Mountains. 176p. (Orig.). 1980. pap. text ed. 9.95 (ISBN 0-8403-2207-0). Kendall-Hunt.

--People, Environment & Place: An Introduction to Human Geography. (Illus.). 368p. 1981. text ed. 20.95 (ISBN 0-675-08085-1); instr's. manual 3.95 (ISBN 0-686-69496-1). Merrill.

Larkin, Rochelle. Glitterball. (Orig.). 1980. pap. 2.50 (ISBN 0-451-09525-1, E9525, Sig). NAL.

Larkins, A. Guy, jt. auth. see Shaver, James P.

Larma, Dominique-Rene De see De Larma, Dominique-Rene.

Larn, Richard. Devon Shipwrecks. LC 74-76178. 1974. 14.95 (ISBN 0-7153-6337-9). David & Charles.

--Goodwin Sands Shipwrecks. (Shipwrecks Ser.). 1977. 14.95 (ISBN 0-7153-7202-5). David & Charles.

--Shipwrecks of Great Britain & Ireland. LC 80-68898. (Illus.). 1981. 24.00 (ISBN 0-7153-7491-5). David & Charles.

Larner, Jeremy. Nobody Knows. 1968. 4.95 o.s.i. (ISBN 0-02-568390-X). Macmillan.

Larner, John. Culture & Society in Italy: Twelve Ninety to Fourteen Twenty. 1971. 38.00 (ISBN 0-7134-1521-5, Pub. by Batsford England). David & Charles.

--Italy in the Age of Dante & Petrarch: 1216-1380. (Longman History of Italy Ser.). (Illus.). 288p. 1980. text ed. 43.00 (ISBN 0-686-27681-7). Longman.

LaRocca, Joseph & Turen, Jerry. The Application of Technological Developments to Physically Disabled People. (An Institute Paper). 113p. 1978. pap. 3.50 (ISBN 0-87766-225-8, 23200). Urban Inst.

La Roche, Mazo De see De La Roche, Mazo.

LaRoche, Nancy & Urdang, Laurence, eds. Picturesque Expressions: A Thematic Dictionary. LC 80-22705. 300p. 1980. 35.00 (ISBN 0-8103-1122-4). Gale.

La Rochefoucauld, Francois. Maximes. (Documentation thematique). (Illus., Fr.). pap. 2.95 (ISBN 0-685-13985-9, 123). Larousse.

La Rochelle, Pierre Drieu see Drieu La Rochelle, Pierre.

La Roe, Marlene S. & Herrick, Lee. How Not to Ruin a Perfectly Good Marriage. 208p. 1980. pap. 2.50 (ISBN 0-553-13818-9). Bantam.

Laron, Elaine. Giggles Goggles. (Electric Company Ser.). (Illus.). (gr. 1-5). 1973. PLB 5.38 (ISBN 0-307-64825-7, Golden Pr). Western Pub.

La Rosa, Frank E., ed. see Heywood, John.

LaRosa, Linda J. & Tanenbaum, Barry. The Random Factor. (Orig.). 1979. pap. 2.95 (ISBN 0-515-05166-7). Jove Pubns.

--The Random Factor. LC 77-82764. 1978. 8.95 o.p. (ISBN 0-385-13282-4). Doubleday.

La Rosa, Michael M. de see Kolin, Michael J. & De La Rosa, Denise M.

LaRouche, Lyndon H., Jr. Basic Economics for Conservative Democrats. LC 80-5684. (Illus.). 172p. (Orig.). 1980. pap. 3.95 (ISBN 0-933488-04-1). New Benjamin.

--The Case of Walter Lippmann: A Presidential Strategy, Vol. 3. Stevens, Kathy, ed. (American History Ser.). 1978. pap. 5.95 (ISBN 0-918388-06-6, Univ Edns). New Benjamin.

--What Every Conservative Should Know About Communism. LC 80-20325. (Illus.). 149p. (Orig.). 1980. pap. 3.95 (ISBN 0-933488-06-8). New Benjamin.

--Why Revival of "SALT" Won't Stop War. 116p. (Orig.). 1980. pap. 3.95 (ISBN 0-933488-08-4). New Benjamin.

LaRouche, Lyndon H., Jr. & Goldman, David. The Ugly Truth About Milton Friedman. LC 80-20623. (Illus.). 350p. (Orig.). 1980. pap. 3.95 (ISBN 0-933488-09-2). New Benjamin.

Larousse And Co. Dictionnaire complet des mots croises. (Fr). 27.50 (ISBN 2-03-020294-0, 3617). Larousse.

--Dictionnaire du francais contemporain. (Fr). 27.50 (ISBN 0-685-13872-0, 3745). Larousse.

--Dictionnaire du vocabulaire essentiel. (Illus., Fr.). pap. 12.25 (ISBN 0-685-13873-9, 3753). Larousse.

Larousse & Co. Grammaire Larousse du francais contemporain. (Fr). 18.00 (ISBN 2-03-070031-2, 3746). Larousse.

Larousse And Co. Interprete Larousse, francais-allemand et allemand-francais. pap. 3.95 (ISBN 0-685-13946-8, 3782). Larousse.

--Interprete Larousse, francais-italien et italien-francais. (Fr. & It.). pap. 3.95 (ISBN 0-685-13947-6, 3787). Larousse.

--Interprete Larousse, French-Spanish & Spanish-French. (Fr. & Span.). pap. 3.95 (ISBN 0-685-13948-4, 3777). Larousse.

--Larousse classique. (Illus., Fr.). 28.25 (ISBN 0-685-13957-3, 3747). Larousse.

--Larousse de poche. (Fr.). pap. 6.95 (ISBN 2-03-020166-9, 1008). Larousse.

--Larousse de poche, francais-allemand et allemand-francais. pap. 5.95 (ISBN 0-685-13959-X). Larousse.

--Larousse de poche francais-espagnol, et espanol-frances. (Fr. & Span.). pap. 5.95 (ISBN 0-685-13961-1, 1010). Larousse.

--Larousse de poche, francais-italien et italien-francais. (Fr. & It.). pap. 5.98 (ISBN 0-685-13960-3, 1012). Larousse.

--Larousse de poche French-English & English-French. (Fr. & Eng.). pap. 5.95 (ISBN 2-03-029203-6, 1009). Larousse.

--Larousse des debutants. (Illus., Fr.). 12.25 (ISBN 2-03-020151-0, 3752). Larousse.

--Larousse medical illustre. (Illus., Fr.). 72.50x (ISBN 2-03-008500-6, 3912). Larousse.

--Larousse pour tous. (Fr). 11.50 (ISBN 0-685-13965-4, 3751). Larousse.

--Ma Premiere Encyclopedie. (Illus., Fr.). 12.95x (ISBN 0-685-13974-3, 3797). Larousse.

--Mon Premier Larousse francais-anglais, anglais-francais en couleurs. (Fr. & Eng.). (gr. 6-9). 23.75 (ISBN 2-03-051431-4, 3794). Larousse.

--Nouveau Larousse elementaire. (Illus., Fr.). 23.95 (ISBN 0-685-14003-2). Larousse.

--Nouveau Larousse universel, 2 Vols. (Illus., Fr.). 91.00x ea. Larousse.

--Nouveau Petit Larousse en couleurs. (Illus., Fr.). 1974. 83.00 (ISBN 2-03-020111-1, 3676). Larousse.

--Nuevo Larousse manual illustrado. (Span). 17.95 o.p. (ISBN 2-03-020546-X, 21121). Larousse.

--Petit Dictionnaire bilingue Larousse, francais-espagnol, espanol-frances. (Adonis). (Fr & Span). plastic bdg. 5.95 (ISBN 0-685-14033-4, 3775). Larousse.

--Petit Dictionnaire francais Larousse. (Illus., Fr.). 10.50 (ISBN 0-685-14034-2, 3754). Larousse.

--Plus Petit Larousse. (Fr). plastic bdg. 6.25 (ISBN 0-685-14044-X, 3756). Larousse.

Larousse, Pierre, jt. auth. see Clement, Felix.

Larrabeiti, Michael De see De Larrabeiti, Michael.

Larrain, Jorge. The Concept of Ideology. LC 79-53386. 250p. 1980. 18.00x (ISBN 0-8203-0490-5). U of Ga Pr.

Larralde, Carlos, et al, eds. Molecules, Cells & Parasites in Immunology. 1980. 19.50 (ISBN 0-12-436840-9). Acad Pr.

Larrauri, A. Dictionary of Oto-Rhino-Laryngology in Five Languages: English-French-Spanish-German-Italian. LC 71-501781. 1008p. 1971. 48.00x (ISBN 0-8002-0197-3). Intl Pubns Serv.

Larrea, Victoria de see Hiller, Catherine.

Larreche, Jean-Claude & Strong, Edward C. Readings in Marketing Strategy. 1981. pap. text ed. 13.50x (ISBN 0-89426-030-8). Scientific Pr.

Larrew, Christopher E. The Thinking Processes of the Human Mind. (Illus.). 1980. 37.50 (ISBN 0-89266-218-2). Am Classical Coll Pr.

Larrick, Gail, ed. see Hobbs, Fredric & Hobbs, Deborah.

Larrick, Gail, ed. see Orlando, Joseph.

Larrick, Gail, ed. see Van Der Zee, John & Jacobson, Boyd.

Larrick, Nancy, ed. Bring Me All of Your Dreams. LC 79-26892. (Illus.). 128p. (gr. 5 up). 1980. 7.95 (ISBN 0-87131-313-8). M Evans.
--Crazy to Be Alive in Such a Strange World. LC 76-49667. (Illus.). 192p. (gr. 5 up). 1977. 7.95 (ISBN 0-87131-225-5). M Evans.
--I Heard a Scream in the Street: Poetry by Young People in the City. LC 79-122820. (Illus.). 144p. (gr. 5 up). 1970. 7.95 (ISBN 0-87131-064-3). M Evans.
--On City Streets: An Anthology of Poetry. LC 68-30505. (Illus.). 160p. (gr. 5-8). 1968. 7.95 (ISBN 0-87131-080-5). M Evans.
--Room for Me & a Mountain Lion: Poetry of Open Space. LC 73-87710. (Illus.). 192p. (gr. 5 up). 1974. 7.95 (ISBN 0-87131-124-0). M Evans.
Larrick, Nancy & Merriam, Eve, eds. Male & Female Under 18. (YA) 1973. pap. 1.50 (ISBN 0-380-00711-8, 76448, Discus). Avon.
Larrie, Reginald R. Makin' Free: African - Americans in the Northwest Territory. (Illus.). 1981. 6.95 (ISBN 0-87917-072-7). Blaine Ethridge.
Larrison, Earl J. & Johnson, Donald R. Mammals of Idaho. LC 80-51876. (GEM Bks-Natural History Ser.). (Illus.). 200p. 1981. pap. 6.95 (ISBN 0-89301-070-7). U Pr of Idaho.
Larsen, Bent A. Anna & Bent. (Destiny Ser.). 1979. pap. 4.95 (ISBN 0-8163-0330-4, 01617-0). Pacific Pr Pub Assn.
--Jungle Journey. LC 76-7856. (Destiny Ser.). 1977. pap. 4.50 o.p. (ISBN 0-8163-0283-9). Pacific Pr Pub Assn.
Larsen, Carl. Even the Dog Won't Eat My Meat Loaf. LC 79-19887. 1980. pap. 5.95 (ISBN 0-89645-011-2). Media Ventures.
Larsen, Carl, jt. auth. see Milts, Michael H.
Larsen, Earnest. Something Wonderful Is Happening. LC 76-24443. (Emmaus Book Ser.). 1977. pap. 1.95 (ISBN 0-8091-1987-0). Paulist Pr.
--Spiritual Renewal of the American Parish. 64p. (Orig.). 1975. pap. 1.50 o.p. (ISBN 0-89243-021-4, 29560). Liguori Pubns.
Larsen, Egon, jt. ed. see Salis, Richard.
Larsen, Egon, tr. see Salis, Richard & Larsen, Egon.
Larsen, Gerald. Classical Samkhya. LC 79-26238. 332p. 1980. pap. 8.95 (ISBN 0-915520-27-3). Ross-Erikson.
Larsen, Hanne. Don't Forget Tom. LC 77-20953. (John Day Bk.). (Illus.). (gr. k-4). 1978. PLB 7.89 (ISBN 0-381-99554-2, TYC-J). T Y Crowell.
Larsen, Jack L., jt. auth. see Constantine, Mildred.
Larsen, Jackie. Arrows to the Heart. LC 77-91631. 1977. softcover 4.95 (ISBN 0-9602474-1-6). J Larsen.
--Beyond This Colored Glass. LC 79-83904. (Illus.). 1970. softcover 4.95 (ISBN 0-9602474-2-4). J Larsen.
--Steps Across Life. LC 80-80720. (Illus.). 1980. soft cover 4.95 (ISBN 0-9602474-3-2). J Larsen.
--Weaving Life's Story. (Illus.). 1978. soft cover 4.95x (ISBN 0-686-14922-X). J Larsen.
Larsen, Jens P., et al, eds. Haydn Studies. 1981. 29.95 (ISBN 0-393-01454-1). Norton.
Larsen, Judith L., jt. auth. see Waugh, Carol A.
Larsen, Knud S. Aggression: Myths & Models. LC 76-5882. 416p. 1976. 19.95x (ISBN 0-911012-71-0); pap. 9.95x (ISBN 0-88229-452-0). Nelson-Hall.
Larsen, L. Competencies for Effective Teaching of the Severely & Profoundly Handicapped in Classroom Settings. Date not set. 16.50 (ISBN 0-8391-1260-2). Univ Park. Postponed.
Larsen, M. D. & Shumway, R. J. Essentials of Precalculus Mathematics. (Mathematics Ser.). 1971. 12.95 (ISBN 0-201-04123-5); instructor's manual 4.00 (ISBN 0-201-04124-3). A-W.
Larsen, Madelyn, ed. see Wasserman, Pauline & Wasserman, Sheldon.
Larsen, Max D. & Fejfar, James L. Essentials of Elementary School Mathematics. 1974. text ed. 18.95 (ISBN 0-12-438640-7); solution manual 3.00 (ISBN 0-12-438642-3). Acad Pr.
Larsen, Max D., jt. auth. see Boisen, Monte B., Jr.
Larsen, Otto N., jt. ed. see Coser, Lewis A.
Larsen, Paul E. Wise up & Live. 2nd ed. LC 73-86222. pap. 2.75 (ISBN 0-8307-0453-1, S274-1-24). Regal.
Larsen, R. & Marx, M. Introduction to Mathematical Statistics & Its Applications. 1981. 22.95 (ISBN 0-13-487744-6). P-H.
Larsen, R. R., jt. auth. see Chance, M. R.
Larsen, Richard J. Statistics for the Allied Health Sciences. 320p. 1975. text ed. 19.95 (ISBN 0-675-08782-1). Merrill.
Larsen, Richard W. Bundy: The Deliberate Stranger. LC 80-15795. 1980. 10.95 (ISBN 0-13-089185-1). P-H.
Larsen, Robert P., jt. auth. see Wrenn, C. Gilbert.
Larsen, Sherman J. Close Encounters: A Factual Report on UFOs. LC 78-2322. (Illus.). (gr. 4-12). 1978. PLB 16.50 (ISBN 0-8172-1200-0). Raintree Pubs.
Larsen, Stein U., ed. Who Were the Fascists? Social Roots of European Fascism. 800p. 1981. 44.00x (ISBN 8-20005-331-8). Universitet.
Larsen, Stephen. The Shaman's Doorway. 1977. pap. 4.95 (ISBN 0-06-090547-6, CN 547, CN). Har-Row.
Larsen, Stephen C., jt. auth. see Ehly, Stewart W.
Larsen, Stephen C., jt. auth. see Wallace, Gerald.
Larsen-Freeman, Diane, ed. Discourse Analysis in Second Language Research. 283p. (Orig.). 1980. pap. text ed. 11.95 (ISBN 0-88377-163-2). Newbury Hse.
Larsgaard, Mary. Map Librarianship: An Introduction. LC 77-28821. (Library Science Text Ser.). 1978. 22.50x (ISBN 0-87287-182-7). Libs Unl.
Larson, jt. auth. see Pyle.
Larson, Allan L. Comparative Political Analysis. 1980. 14.95x (ISBN 0-88229-257-9); pap. 8.95 (ISBN 0-88229-729-5). Nelson-Hall.
Larson, Arlene & Logan, Carolyn. How Does Language Work? 208p. (Orig.). 1980. pap. text ed. 11.95 (ISBN 0-8403-2199-6). Kendall-Hunt.
Larson, Arthur D., ed. National Security Affairs: A Guide to Information Sources. LC 70-184013. (Management Information Guide Ser.: No. 27). 350p. 1973. 30.00 (ISBN 0-8103-0827-4). Gale.
Larson, Betsy. Kidstories: Seasonal & Topical Sermons for Children. (Paperback Program Ser.). 128p. 1980. pap. 2.95 (ISBN 0-8010-5598-9). Baker Bk.
Larson, Bob. Rock. 1980. pap. write for info. (ISBN 0-8423-5685-1). Tyndale.
Larson, Boyd. Transistor Fundamentals & Servicing. (Illus.). 480p. 1974. 20.95 (ISBN 0-13-929992-0). P-H.
Larson, Bruce. Dare to Live Now. 1967. pap. 1.75 (ISBN 0-310-27202-5). Zondervan.
--The One & Only You. (Orig.). 1976. pap. 1.50 (ISBN 0-89129-135-0). Jove Pubns.
--Thirty Days to a New You. 1977. pap. 2.50 (ISBN 0-310-27242-4). Zondervan.
Larson, Bruce, jt. auth. see Deegan, Paul.
Larson, Bruce, jt. auth. see Miller, Keith.
Larson, Bruce L. & Smith, Vearl R., eds. Lactation: A Comprehensive Treatise. Incl. Vol. 1, 1974. Development, Lactogenesis. 55.50 (ISBN 0-12-436701-1); subscription 47.50 (ISBN 0-686-67530-4); Vol. 2. 1974. 48.75, by subscription 41.75 (ISBN 0-12-436702-X); Vol. 3. Milk, Nutrution & Maintenance. 1974. 48.75, by subscription 41.75 (ISBN 0-12-436703-8); Vol. 4. 1978. 58.00, by subscription 50.00 (ISBN 0-12-436704-6). Acad Pr.
Larson, C. Basic Retailing. 2nd ed. 1981. 20.95 (ISBN 0-13-068072-9). P-H.
Larson, C. F., jt. ed. see Smith, W. Novis.
Larson, Calvin J. Major Themes in Sociological Theory. 2nd ed. LC 77-77775. 1977. pap. 9.95x (ISBN 0-679-30348-0, Pub. by MacKay). Longman.
Larson, Calvin J. & Nikkel, Stan R. Urban Problems: Perspectives on Corporations, Governments, & Cities. 1978. pap. text ed. 12.95 (ISBN 0-205-06530-9, 8165300); instr's man. o.p. avail. (ISBN 0-205-06547-3). Allyn.
Larson, Carl, jt. auth. see Goldberg, Alvin.
Larson, Carl F., compiled by. American Regional Theatre History to 1900: A Bibliography. LC 79-11282. 1979. 11.00 (ISBN 0-8108-1216-9). Scarecrow.
Larson, Carroll B. & Gould, Marjorie. Orthopedic Nursing. 9th ed. LC 77-3429. (Illus.). 1978. text ed. 18.95 (ISBN 0-8016-2866-0). Mosby.
Larson, Charles, jt. auth. see Wickstrom, Ralph.
Larson, Charles H., ed. see Greene, Robert.
Larson, Charles R. The Insect Colony. LC 78-4701. 1978. 7.95 o.p. (ISBN 0-03-041896-8). HR&W.
Larson, Charles U. Communication: Everyday Encounters. 240p. pap. text ed. 10.95 (ISBN 0-917974-60-3). Waveland Pr.
--Persuasion: Reflection & Responsibility. 2nd ed. 1979. pap. text ed. 11.95x (ISBN 0-534-00689-2). Wadsworth Pub.
Larson, Clinton F. Counterpoint: A Book of Poems. LC 73-15889. 111p. 1973. 6.95 o.p. (ISBN 0-8425-0449-4). Brigham.
Larson, David, et al. Eighty-Eighty, Eighty-Eighty-Five, Software Design, Bk. 1. LC 78-57207. 1978. pap. 10.95 (ISBN 0-672-21541-1). Sams.
Larson, David L. United States Foreign Policy Toward Yugoslavia, 1943-1963. LC 78-71369. 1979. pap. 12.25 (ISBN 0-8191-0669-0). U Pr of Amer.
Larson, Diane, jt. auth. see Carrenno, Josephine.
Larson, Donald N. & Smalley, William A. Becoming Bilingual: A Guide to Language Learning. LC 74-8839. (Applied Cultural Anthropology Ser.). 425p. (Orig.). 1974. pap. 6.95x (ISBN 0-87808-718-4). William Carey Lib.
Larson, Donna R. Guide to U. S. Government Directories. 1981. lib. bdg. 27.50x (ISBN 0-912700-63-7). Oryx Pr.
Larson, Doris, jt. auth. see Larson, Roland.
Larson, E. Great Ideas in Engineering. 6.00 o.p. (ISBN 0-08-007078-7). Pergamon.
Larson, E. Richard. Sue Your Boss. 1981. 14.95 (ISBN 0-374-27161-5); pap. 6.95 (ISBN 0-374-51608-1). FS&G.
Larson, E. Richard & McDonald, Laughlin. The Rights of Racial Minorities. 1979. pap. 1.95 (ISBN 0-380-75077-5, 75077, Discus). Avon.
Larson, Emil. Arizona School Law. LC 64-17272. 1964. 2.00 (ISBN 0-8165-0277-3). U of Ariz Pr.
Larson, Gene F. The Unforgettable. rev. ed. 1978. 10.00 (ISBN 0-686-68574-1, 1491). Hospital Finan.
Larson, George C. Fly on Instruments. LC 79-7602. (Illus.). 240p. 1980. 12.95 (ISBN 0-385-14619-1). Doubleday.
Larson, Glen A. & Thurston, Robert. Battlestar Galactica: Flight to Kobal, No. 3. 1979. pap. 2.25 (ISBN 0-425-04992-2). Berkley Pub.
--Battlestar Galactica Four: the Young Warriors. 288p. 1980. pap. 2.25 (ISBN 0-425-04997-3). Berkley Pub.
Larson, Harold J. Statistics: An Introduction. LC 74-13460. 1975. 20.95 (ISBN 0-471-51770-4); tchrs. manual avail. (ISBN 0-471-51771-2). Wiley.
Larson, J. L., jt. auth. see Thorpe, Azalea S.
Larson, James S. Why Government Programs Fail: Improving Policy Implementation. LC 79-26917. 140p. 1980. 18.95 (ISBN 0-03-053956-0). Praeger.
Larson, Jim, ed. Make Learning a Joy. (Illus.). 80p. (Orig.). 1975. pap. 1.65 o.p. (ISBN 0-8307-0362-4, 54-023-01). Regal.
Larson, Kathryn, jt. auth. see Editors of Farm Journal.
Larson, Kathryn, jt. auth. see Halpern, Bomie.
Larson, Kay. Artists' Vehicles & Metaphorical Machinery. (Illus.). 1980. pap. 8.00 (ISBN 0-904540-26-X). U of Pa Contemp Art.
Larson, Kermit D., jt. auth. see Pyle, William W.
Larson, Lane, jt. auth. see Larson, Peggy.
Larson, Lars L., jt. ed. see Hunt, James G.
Larson, Lewis H. Aboriginal Subsistence Technology on the Southeastern Coastal Plain During the Late Prehistoric Period. LC 80-16279. (Ripley P. Bullen Monographs in Anthropology & History: No. 2). (Illus.). 1980. 20.00 (ISBN 0-8130-0675-9). U Presses Fla.
Larson, Linda, jt. auth. see Baeckler, Virginia.
Larson, Loren C. Algebra & Trigonometry Refresher for Calculus Students. LC 79-20633. (Mathematical Sciences Ser.). (Illus.). 1979. pap. 6.95x (ISBN 0-7167-1110-9). W H Freeman.
Larson, Magali S. The Rise of Professionalism: A Sociological Analysis. 1977. 20.00x (ISBN 0-520-02938-0); pap. 7.50x (ISBN 0-520-03950-5). U of Cal Pr.
Larson, Martin. A Manual on How to Establish a Trust & Reduce Taxation. 195.00 (ISBN 0-935036-01-6). Liberty Lobby.
Larson, Martin A. Church Wealth & Business Income. LC 65-20799. 1965. 3.95 o.p. (ISBN 0-8022-0930-0). Philos Lib.
Larson, Milton E. Teaching Related Subjects in Trade & Industrial & Technical Education. LC 72-80235. 1972. text ed. 19.95 (ISBN 0-675-09073-3). Merrill.
Larson, Muriel K. Are You Real, God? pap. 2.95 (ISBN 0-89728-020-2, 654470). Omega Pubns OR.
Larson, Norita. Walt Disney. LC 74-14925. 40p. (gr. 4-8). 1975. PLB 5.75 o.p. (ISBN 0-87191-407-7). Creative Ed.
Larson, Norita & Taylor, Paula. Walter Cronkite. LC 75-2103. (Creative Education Closeup Bks.). (Illus.). 32p. (gr. 3-6). 1975. PLB 5.75 o.p. (ISBN 0-87191-424-7). Creative Ed.
Larson, Norita D. Langston Hughes, Poet of Harlem. Redpath, Ann, ed. (People to Remember Ser.). (Illus.). 32p. (gr. 5-9). 1981. PLB 5.95 (ISBN 0-87191-798-X). Creative Ed.
Larson, Orvin. When It's Your Turn to Speak. new & enl. ed. LC 70-108942. 1971. 9.95 o.s.i. (ISBN 0-06-012526-8, HarpT). Har-Row.
Larson, Peggy & Larson, Lane. Sierra Club Naturalist's Guide to the Deserts of the Southwest. LC 76-24835. (Naturalist's Guide Ser). (Illus.). 1977. pap. 5.95 (ISBN 0-87156-186-7). Sierra.
Larson, R. & Odoni, A. Urban Operations Research. 1981. 32.00 (ISBN 0-13-939447-8). P-H.
Larson, Richard C. Urban Public Safety Systems: New Tools for Planners. LC 77-9135. (IRP Ser.: Vol. 1). (Illus.). 1978. 23.95 (ISBN 0-669-01783-3). Lexington Bks.
--Urban Public Safety Systems: Police Accountability Systems & Unionism. LC 77-9136. (IRP Ser.: Vol. 2). 1978. 22.95 (ISBN 0-669-01785-X). Lexington Bks.
Larson, Richard C., jt. ed. see Willemain, Thomas R.
Larson, Richard L. Studies in John Dryden's Dramatic Technique. (Salzburg Studies in English Literature, Poetic Drama & Poetic Theory Ser.: No. 9). 320p. (Orig.). 1975. pap. text ed. 25.00x (ISBN 0-391-01455-2). Humanities.
Larson, Roland & Larson, Doris. I Need to Have You Know Me. (Orig.). 1980. pap. 7.95 (ISBN 0-03-053431-3). Winston Pr.
Larson, Roland E. & Hostetler, Robert P. Calculus with Analytic Geometry. 1979. text ed. 27.95 (ISBN 0-669-01301-3); solution manuals 5.95 ea. Vol. 1 (ISBN 0-669-03187-9). Vol. 2 (ISBN 0-669-03188-7). Vol. 3 (ISBN 0-669-03189-5). Differential Equations suppl. free (ISBN 0-669-03204-2); student manual 6.95 (ISBN 0-669-01705-1); Appendix D free (ISBN 0-669-03190-9); instructor's manual free (ISBN 0-669-01302-1). Heath.
Larson, Ronald C. see Garrett, Jessie A.
Larson, Ross. Fantasy & Imagination in the Mexican Narrative. LC 77-3019. 1977. pap. 8.50x (ISBN 0-87918-032-3). ASU Lat Am St.
Larson, Roy A. Introduction to Floriculture. 1980. text ed. 29.50 (ISBN 0-12-437650-9). Acad Pr.
Larson, T. A., ed. see Nye, Bill.
Larson, Taft A. Wyoming: A History. LC 77-3592. (The States & the Nation Ser.). (Illus.). 1977. 12.95 (ISBN 0-393-05626-0, Co-Pub by AASLH). Norton.
Larson, Thomas B. Soviet-American Rivalry. 320p. 1981. pap. 6.95 (ISBN 0-393-95145-6). Norton.
Larson, Vernon D., et al, eds. Auditory & Hearing Prosthetic Research. 1979. 21.50 (ISBN 0-685-67602-1). Grune.
Larson, William H., ed. Seven Great Detective Stories. (gr. 3 up). 1979. pap. 1.25 (ISBN 0-307-21627-6, Golden Pr). Western Pub.
Larsori, Muriel. You Are What You Think. pap. 1.95 (ISBN 0-89728-063-6, 658463). Omega Pubns OR.
Larssen, A. K. & Jaeger, Sig. The ABC's of Fo'c'sle Living. LC 76-17265. (Illus.). 1976. pap. 3.95 (ISBN 0-914842-11-0). Madrona Pubs.
Larsson, Bo, ed. The Scandinavian Psychoanalytic Review. 1978. pap. 18.00x (ISBN 82-00-05174-9, Dist. by Columbia U Pr). Universitet.
Larsson, Kaye. Your Book of the Weather. (Your Book Ser.). (Illus.). 1966. 4.95 o.p. (ISBN 0-571-06610-0, Pub. by Faber & Faber). Merrimack Bk Serv.
LaRue, Charlotte, tr. see Petersen, Carol.
Larue, Gerald A. Ancient Myth & Modern Man. LC 74-9527. 320p. (Orig.). 1975. 11.95 (ISBN 0-13-035493-7); pap. 10.50 (ISBN 0-13-035485-6). P-H.
Larwood, Laurie & Wood, Marion M. Women in Management. LC 76-27033. 1977. 19.95 (ISBN 0-669-00973-3). Lexington Bks.
Lary, N. M. Dostoevsky & Dickens: A Study of Literary Influence. 188p. 1973. 17.00 (ISBN 0-7100-7554-5). Routledge & Kegan.
Lasagna, Louis, ed. Clinical Pharmacology, 2 Vols. 1966. Set. 34.00 (ISBN 0-08-012067-9). Pergamon.
LaSalle, Herbert J., jt. auth. see Riese, Alan W.
La Salle, Innocent De see De La Salle, Innocent.
Lasansky, Jeannette. Made of Mud: Stoneware Potteries in Central Pennsylvania, 1831-1929. LC 79-2708. (Illus.). 1979. pap. 7.95 (ISBN 0-271-00228-X, Keystone Bks). Pa St U Pr.
--To Draw, Upset, & Weld: The Work of the Pennsylvania Rural Blacksmith, 1742-1935. LC 80-15912. (Illus.). 84p. 1980. pap. 7.95 (ISBN 0-271-00265-4, Keystone Bks). Pa St U Pr.
Lasarte, Francisco, tr. see Crane, Barbara J.
La Sasso, Wilma R. Regional Italian Cooking: From the Alps to the Mediterranean. (Illus.). 268p. 1975. 5.95 o.s.i. (ISBN 0-02-568400-0). Macmillan.
Lascari, Andre D. Leukemia in Childhood. (Illus.). 504p. 1973. 22.75 (ISBN 0-398-02810-9). C C Thomas.
Lascelles, Mary. The Story-Teller Retrieves the Past: Historical Fiction & Fictitious History in the Art of Scott, Stevenson, Kipling, & Some Others. 116p. 1980. 29.50x (ISBN 0-19-812802-9). Oxford U Pr.
Lasch, Christopher. The Culture of Narcissism. 1979. pap. 3.50 (ISBN 0-446-93264-7); pap. 6.95 (ISBN 0-446-97495-1). Warner Bks.
Lash, James & Burger, Max M., eds. Cell & Tissue Interactions. LC 77-83689. (Society of General Physiologists Ser: Vol. 32). 1977. 29.50 (ISBN 0-89004-180-6). Raven.
Lash, Joseph P. Helen & Teacher: The Story of Helen Keller & Anne Sullivan Macy. 1980. 17.95 (ISBN 0-440-03654-2). Delacorte.

Lash, Nicholas. Theology on Dover Beach. LC 79-88760. (Orig.). 1979. pap. 9.95 (ISBN 0-8091-2241-3). Paulist Pr.

Lasher, H. L. Cop Out. 1978. pap. 1.75 (ISBN 0-505-51284-X). Tower Bks.

Lasher, Miriam G., jt. auth. see Braun, Samuel J.

Lashings, Edwina G. Chocolate & Chortles. 64p. (Orig.). 1975. pap. 1.95 (ISBN 0-686-10979-1). MTM Pub Co.

Lasjaunias, Pierre. Craniofacial & Upper Cervical Arteries: Functional, Clinical & Angiographic Aspects. (Illus.). 220p. 1980. lib. bdg. write for info. (ISBN 0-683-04900-3). Williams & Wilkins.

Laska, John A., jt. auth. see Gillett, Margaret.

Laska, Shirley & Spain, Daphne. Back to the City: The Making of a Movement? (Pergamon Policy Studies). 1980. 42.00 (ISBN 0-08-024641-9); pap. 9.95 (ISBN 0-08-024640-0). Pergamon.

Lasker, Anabel, jt. auth. see Fischer, Pauline.

Lasker, Bruno, jt. auth. see Rountree, B. Seebohm.

Lasker, Edward. Chess for Fun & Chess for Blood. 2nd ed. (Illus.). 1942. pap. 3.50 (ISBN 0-486-20146-5). Dover.

--Go & Go Moku. (Illus.). 1960. pap. 3.50 (ISBN 0-486-20613-0). Dover.

Lasker, Emanuel. Lasker's Manual of Chess. (YA) (gr. 7-12). pap. 5.00 (ISBN 0-486-20640-8). Dover.

Lasker, Gabriel, ed. Process of Ongoing Human Evolution. (Publications on Human Evolution Ser). 1960. 5.95x o.p. (ISBN 0-8143-1144-X). Wayne St U Pr.

Lasker, Joe. He's My Brother. LC 73-7318. (Concept Bks.). (Illus.). 40p. (gr. 1-3). 1974. 6.95g (ISBN 0-8075-3218-5). A Whitman.

--Lentil Soup. LC 77-7145. (Illus.). (gr. k-3). 1977. 6.50g o.p. (ISBN 0-8075-4438-8). A Whitman.

--Mothers Can Do Anything. LC 72-83684. (Concept Bks.). (Illus.). 32p. (gr. k-3). 1972. 6.95g (ISBN 0-8075-5287-9). A Whitman.

--Nick Joins in. Tucker, Kathleen, ed. LC 79-29637. (Concept Bk.: Level 1). (Illus.). (gr. 1-3). 1980. PLB 6.95g (ISBN 0-8075-5612-2). A Whitman.

Lasker, Judith, jt. auth. see Borg, Susan O.

Lasker, Michael & Simmons, Richard A. The Gangster Chronicles: TV Lie-In. 224p. (Orig.). 1981. pap. 2.50 (ISBN 0-515-05808-4). Jove Pubns.

Lasker-Schuler, Else. Hebrew Ballads & Other Poems. 128p. 1980. 10.95 (ISBN 0-8276-0179-4, 460); pap. 6.95 (ISBN 0-8276-0180-8, 459). Jewish Pubn.

Laski, Harold J. A Grammar of Politics. 1925. 47.50x o.p. (ISBN 0-686-51396-7). Elliots Bks.

--Studies in the Problem of Sovereignty. 1968. Repr. 17.50 (ISBN 0-86527-191-7). Fertig.

Laskiewicz, H. J. & Zaremba, M., eds. Pneumatic & Hydraulic Components & Instruments in Automatic Control: Proceedings of the IFAC Symposium, Warsaw, Poland, 20-23 May 1980. (IFAC Proceedings Ser.). (Illus.). 308p. 1981. 75.00 (ISBN 0-08-027317-3). Pergamon.

Laskin, A. I., jt. ed. see Perlman, D.

Laskin, A. I., jt. ed. see Sebek, O. K.

Laskin, Allen I. & Lechevalier, Hubert, eds. Handbook of Microbiology, CRC, Vol. 3: Amino Acids & Proteins. 2nd ed. LC 77-12460. 576p. 1981. 64.95 (ISBN 0-8493-7203-8). CRC Pr.

--Handbook of Microbiology, CRC, Vol. 4: Carbohydrates, Lipids & Minerals. 2nd ed. 480p. 1981. 59.95 (ISBN 0-8493-7204-6). CRC Pr.

Laskin, Daniel M. Oral & Maxillofacial Surgery, Vol. 1. 6th. ed. LC 79-18723. 1979. text ed. 75.00 (ISBN 0-8016-2822-9). Mosby.

Lasky, Jesse, Jr. & Silver, Pat. Love Scene: The Story of Laurence Olivier & Vivien Leigh. LC 78-4765. (Illus.). 1978. 10.95 o.p. (ISBN 0-690-01413-9, TYC-T). T Y Crowell.

Lasky, Jesse L. & Silver, Pat. The Offer. LC 80-1813. (Illus.). 800p. 1981. 15.95 (ISBN 0-385-15767-3). Doubleday.

Lasky, Jesse L., Jr. & Silver, Pat. Love Scene. 1981. pap. 2.75 (ISBN 0-425-05022-X). Berkley Pub.

Lasky, Kathryn. The Weaver's Gift. LC 80-12042. (Illus.). 64p. (gr. 3-7). 1981. 8.95g (ISBN 0-7232-6191-1). Warne.

Lasky, Lila & Mukerji, Rose. Art: Basic for Young Children. (Illus.). 148p. (Orig.). 1980. pap. text ed. write for info. (ISBN 0-912674-73-3). Natl Assn Child Ed.

Lasky, Michael S. & Harris, Robert A. The Films of Alfred Hitchcock. (Illus.). pap. 7.95 (ISBN 0-8065-0619-9). Citadel Pr.

Lasky, Victor. Never Complain, Never Explain. 338p. 1981. 15.00 (ISBN 0-399-90104-3). Marek.

Laslett, P. & Wall, R., eds. Household & Family in Past Time. LC 77-190420. 608p. 1972. 49.95 (ISBN 0-521-08473-3); pap. 15.95x (ISBN 0-521-09901-3). Cambridge U Pr.

Laslett, Peter. Family Life & Illicit Love in Earlier Generations. 1977. 47.50 (ISBN 0-521-21408-4); pap. 12.95x (ISBN 0-521-29221-2). Cambridge U Pr.

Laslett, Peter, ed. Philosophy, Politics & Society. Incl. First Series. 1975. Repr. of 1956 ed (ISBN 0-631-16810-9); Second Series. 1979 (ISBN 0-631-04880-4); Third Series. 1978. Repr. of 1956 ed (ISBN 0-631-17730-2); Fourth Series (ISBN 0-631-17740-X). pap. 12.50 ea. (Pub. by Basil Blackwell England). Biblio Dist.

--Philosophy, Politics & Society: Second Series. 1980. 27.50x (ISBN 0-686-28141-1, Pub. by Basil Blackwell England); pap. 12.50x (ISBN 0-631-04880-4, Pub. by Basil Blackwell England). Biblio Dist.

Laslett, Peter, ed. see Locke, John.

Lasley, John F. Genetics of Livestock Improvement. 3rd ed. LC 77-22807. (Illus.). 1978. ref. ed. 22.95 (ISBN 0-13-351106-5). P-H.

Lasnik, Robert S. A Parent's Guide to Adoption. LC 78-56845. 192p. 1980. pap. 5.95 (ISBN 0-8069-8956-4). Sterling.

--A Parent's Guide to Adoption. LC 78-56895. 1979. 12.95 (ISBN 0-8069-8830-4); PLB 10.79 (ISBN 0-8069-8831-2). Sterling.

Lasocki, David, ed. see Le Romain, Jacques H.

Lasok, D., et al, eds. Fundamental Duties. 275p. 1980. 30.00 (ISBN 0-08-024048-8); pap. 12.00 (ISBN 0-08-024049-6). Pergamon.

Lasor, B. & Elliot, M. Issues in Canadian Nursing. 1977. 9.95 o.p. (ISBN 0-13-506220-9); pap. 9.25 (ISBN 0-13-506238-1). P-H.

Lasor, William, jt. auth. see Gasque, Ward.

LaSor, William S. Handbook of Biblical Hebrew, 3 vols. Set. 12.95x (ISBN 0-8028-2379-3). Eerdmans.

--Handbook of New Testament Greek: An Inductive Approach Based on the Greek Text of Acts, 2 vols. 1973. pap. text ed. 10.95x (ISBN 0-8028-2341-6). Eerdmans.

--Men Who Knew Christ. LC 70-135026. (Orig.). 1971. pap. 1.95 o.p. (ISBN 0-8307-0086-2, S252-1-04). Regal.

--Men Who Knew God. LC 72-109369. pap. 1.65 o.p. (ISBN 0-8307-0064-1, S251108). Regal.

Lasry, George. Valuing Common Stock: The Power of Prudence. 1979. 16.95 (ISBN 0-8144-5491-7). Am Mgmt.

Lass, A. H. Business Spelling & Word Power. 7th ed. 1961. text ed. 8.95 (ISBN 0-672-96012-5); tchr's key (2nd ed.) 6.67 (ISBN 0-672-96014-1); tchr's manual (2nd ed.) 5.00 (ISBN 0-672-96013-3); 3.30 (ISBN 0-672-96015-X). Bobbs.

Lass, A. H., jt. auth. see Flesch, Rudolf.

Lass, Abraham & Tasman, Norma, eds. Twenty-One Great Stories. (Orig.). 1969. pap. 1.95 (ISBN 0-451-61843-2, MJ1843, Ment). NAL.

Lass, Abraham H. & Tasman, Norma L., eds. Going to School: An Anthology of Prose About Teachers & Students. 1981. pap. 2.95 (ISBN 0-451-61905-6, ME1905, Ment). NAL.

Lass, Harry. Vector & Tensor Analysis. (International Ser. in Pure & Applied Mathematics). 1950. text ed. 19.95 o.p. (ISBN 0-07-036520-2, C). McGraw.

Lass, Norman J., ed. Speech & Language: Advances in Basic Research & Practice, Vol. 3. (Serial Publication). 1980. 29.50 (ISBN 0-12-608603-6). Acad Pr.

--Speech & Language: Advances in Basic Research & Practice, Vol. 4. 1980. 35.00 (ISBN 0-12-608604-4). Acad Pr.

Lass, R. English Phonology & Phonological Theory. LC 76-650. (Studies in Linguistics: No. 17). 240p. 1976. 39.50 (ISBN 0-521-21039-9). Cambridge U Pr.

Lass, R. & Anderson, J. M. Studies in Old English Phonology. LC 74-80360. (Studies in Linguistics: No. 14). 352p. 1975. 49.50 (ISBN 0-521-20531-X). Cambridge U Pr.

Lass, R., tr. see Wunderlich, D.

Lass, Roger. On Explaining Language Change. LC 79-51825. (Studies in Linguistics Ser.: No. 27). (Illus.). 1980. 29.95 (ISBN 0-521-22836-0). Cambridge U Pr.

Lass, Roger, ed. Approaches to English Historical Linguistics: An Anthology. LC 69-14526. 1969. pap. text ed. 12.95x (ISBN 0-03-074505-5). Irvington.

Lass, William E. Minnesota: A History. (States & the Nation Ser.). (Illus.). 1977. 12.95 (ISBN 0-393-05651-1, Co-Pub. by AASLH); pap. 3.95 (ISBN 0-393-00937-8). Norton.

--Minnesota's Boundary with Canada: Its Evolution Since 1783. LC 80-21644. (Minnesota Public Affairs Center Publication Ser.). 141p. 1980. 16.50 (ISBN 0-87351-147-6); pap. 8.75 (ISBN 0-87351-153-0). Minn Hist.

Lassaigne, Jack. El Greco. (Illus.). 264p. 1974. 28.00 (ISBN 0-500-18142-X); pap. 11.50 (ISBN 0-500-20136-6). Transatlantic.

Lassaigne, Jacques. Toulouse-Lautrec & the Paris of the Cabarets. (Illus.). 1975. Repr. 5.95 o.p. (ISBN 0-88308-005-2). Lamplight Pub.

Lassam, Robert. Fox Talbot, Photographer. (Illus.). 94p. 1981. 22.50 (ISBN 0-900193-77-8, Pub. by Compton Pr England); pap. 9.95 (ISBN 0-686-69417-1). Kent St U Pr.

Lassau. Anatomical Atlas of the Neonate. 1981. write for info. Masson Pub.

Lassea, Paul. Graphic Problem Solving for Architects & Builders. LC 75-8607. 1975. 18.95 (ISBN 0-8436-0154-X); pap. 12.75 (ISBN 0-685-93090-4). CBI Pub.

Lassen, Niels A. & Perl, William. Tracer Kinetic Methods in Medical Physiology. LC 75-43198. 1979. text ed. 26.00 (ISBN 0-89004-114-8). Raven.

Lassen, Richard. Currency Management. 168p. 1980. 40.00x (ISBN 0-85941-154-0, Pub. by Woodhead-Faulkner England). State Mutual Bk.

Lasser, Elliot C., jt. auth. see Berk, Robert N.

Lasser, S. Jay. Everyone's Income Tax Guide. rev. ed. 192p. 1980. write for info. (ISBN 0-937782-00-9). Hilltop Pubns.

Lassey, jt. auth. see Carlson.

Lassia, Margaret R. Games for Information Skills. 80p. 1980. pap. text ed. 8.58x (ISBN 0-931510-06-6). Hi Willow.

Lassila, Jean D., et al. Programmed Reviews of Chemical Principles. 3rd ed. 1979. 9.95 (ISBN 0-8053-6027-1). Benjamin-Cummings.

Lassimonne, Denise & Ferguson, Howard, eds. Myra Hess by Her Friends. LC 67-29444. (Illus.). 6.95 (ISBN 0-8149-0140-9). Vanguard.

Lassiter, J. W. & Edwards, Hardy M. Animal Nutrition. 1982. text ed. 17.95 (ISBN 0-8359-0222-6); instr's. manual free (ISBN 0-8359-0223-4). Reston.

Lassiter, Perry. Once Saved...Always Saved. new ed. LC 74-15289. 98p. 1975. pap. 2.95 (ISBN 0-8054-1931-4). Broadman.

Lasson, Frans, ed. see Dinesen, Isak.

Lasson, Georg, ed. see Hegel, Georg W.

Lasson, Nelson B. History & Development of the Fourth Amendment to the United States Constitution. LC 75-87389. (American Constitutional & Legal History Ser.). 1970. Repr. of 1937 ed. lib. bdg. 22.50 (ISBN 0-306-71532-5). Da Capo.

Lasson, Robert & Shupak, Sidney. Glue It Yourself: Woodworking Without Nails. (Illus.). (YA) 1978. PLB 8.95 o.p. (ISBN 0-525-30722-2). Dutton.

Lasswell, Harold D. Harold D. Lasswell on Political Sociology. Marvick, Dwaine, ed. LC 76-22961. (Heritage of Sociology Ser.). vi, 456p. 1980. pap. text ed. 7.00x (ISBN 0-226-46921-2). U of Chicago Pr.

--National Security & Individual Freedom. LC 71-139193. (Civil Liberty in American History Ser). 1970. Repr. of 1950 ed. lib. bdg. 25.00 (ISBN 0-306-70085-9). Da Capo.

--Politics: Who Gets What, When & How. 7.25 (ISBN 0-8446-1277-4). Peter Smith.

--Propaganda Technique in World War One. 1971. pap. 4.95 (ISBN 0-262-62018-9). MIT Pr.

Lasswell, Harold D., jt. auth. see Arens, Richard.

Lasswell, Harold D. & Lerner, Daniel, eds. World Revolutionary Elites: Studies in Coercive Ideological Movements. LC 80-21600. xi, 478p. 1980. Repr. of 1965 ed. lib. bdg. 39.75x (ISBN 0-313-22572-9, LAWE). Greenwood.

Lasswell, Marcia & Lobsenz, Norman. Styles of Loving: Why You Love the Way You Do. 192p. 1981. pap. 2.50 (ISBN 0-345-29228-6). Ballantine.

Last, Jack, et al. Everyday Law Made Simple. LC 77-15164. 1978. softbound 3.50 (ISBN 0-385-12921-1, Made). Doubleday.

Last, Joan. The Young Pianist: An Approach for Teachers & Students. 2nd ed. (Illus.). 168p. 1972. pap. 9.95x (ISBN 0-19-318420-6). Oxford U Pr.

Last, John M., ed. Maxcy-Rosenau Public Health & Preventive Medicine. 11th ed. 1492p. 1980. text ed. 64.50x (ISBN 0-8385-6186-1). ACC.

Last, Murray. Sokoto Caliphate. LC 67-16974. (Ibadan History Ser.). (Illus.). 1967. pap. text ed. 8.00x (ISBN 0-582-64504-2). Humanities.

Last, R. W. Hans Arp: The Poet of Dadaism. LC 79-84905. (Modern German Authors Texts & Contexts: Vol. 1). 8.95 (ISBN 0-8023-1227-6). Dufour.

Last, R. W., tr. see Keith-Smith, B.

Last, R. W., tr. see Schneede, Uwe M.

Last, Rex W. German Dadaist Literature. (World Authors Ser.: Germany: No. 272). 1973. lib. bdg. 10.95 (ISBN 0-8057-2361-7). Twayne.

Laster, Ann A., jt. auth. see Pickett, Nell A.

Laster, Israel, jt. ed. see Klopf, Gordon J.

Lasure, Charles F. Dollars from Washington: An Individual's. 64p. 1980. 5.00 (ISBN 0-682-49647-2). Exposition.

Laszlo, Ervin. The Inner Limits of Mankind: Heretical Reflections on Today's Values, Culture & Politics. LC 77-30732. 1978. text ed. 21.00 (ISBN 0-08-023013-X); pap. text ed. 9.75 (ISBN 0-08-023012-1). Pergamon.

--The Systems View of the World. LC 71-188357. 1972. 7.95 (ISBN 0-8076-0637-5); pap. 3.95 (ISBN 0-8076-0636-7). Braziller.

Laszlo, Ervin, ed. Goals in a Global Community: Studies on the Conceptual Foundations, Vol. I. LC 77-79971. 1977. text ed. 32.00 (ISBN 0-08-022221-8). Pergamon.

--Regionalism & the New World Order: A Strategy for Progress. 375p. Date not set. 45.01 (ISBN 0-08-026318-6). Pergamon.

Laszlo, Ervin & Bierman, Judah, eds. Goals in a Global Community, Vol. II. 1978. text ed. 49.00 (ISBN 0-08-022973-5). Pergamon.

Laszlo, Ervin & Keys, Donald, eds. Disarmament: The Human Factor: Pproceedings of a Colloquium on the Societal Context for Disarmament. 200p. 1981. 25.00 (ISBN 0-08-024703-2). Pergamon.

Laszlo, Ervin & Kurtzman, Joel, eds. Eastern Europe & the New International Economic Order: A Review of Four Representative Samples of Socialist Perspectives. LC 79-20028. (Pergamon Policy Studies). 110p. 1980. 16.50 (ISBN 0-08-025115-3). Pergamon.

--The Structure of the World Economy & Economic Order: Prospects for a New International. LC 79-23350. 1980. 16.50 (ISBN 0-686-64334-8). Pergamon.

--The Structure of the World Economy & Prospects for a New International Economic Order. LC 79-23350. (Pergamon Policy Studies on the New International Economic Order Ser.). 120p. 1980. 16.50 (ISBN 0-08-025119-6). Pergamon.

--The United States, Canada & the New International Economic Order. (Policy Studies). 1979. 20.00 (ISBN 0-08-025113-7). Pergamon.

--Western Europe & the New International Economic Order: Representative Samples of European Perspectives. LC 80-16620. (Pergamon Policy Studies). 120p. 1980. 16.50 (ISBN 0-08-025114-5). Pergamon.

Laszlo, Ervin, ed. see Sutherland, John W.

Laszlo, Ervin, et al. The Objectives of the New International Economic Order. LC 78-14766. (Pergamon Policy Studies). 288p. 1978. 20.00 (ISBN 0-08-023697-9). Pergamon.

--The Obstacles to the New International Economic Order. LC 79-28723. (Pergamon Policy Studies on the New International Economic Order). 170p. 1980. 20.00 (ISBN 0-08-025110-2); pap. 7.95 (ISBN 0-08-025970-7). Pergamon.

Laszlo, F. A. Renal Cortical Necrosis. (Contributions to Nephrology Ser.: Vol. 28). (Illus.). vi, 210p. 1981. pap. 45.00 (ISBN 3-8055-2109-X). S Karger.

Laszlo, F. A., ed. Recent Results in Peptide Hormone & Androgenic Steroid Research. (Illus.). 325p. 1979. 30.00x (ISBN 963-05-2292-6). Intl Pubns Serv.

Laszt, L. & Schaad, R. Luftverunreinigung und Herz-Kreislauf-System. (Illus.). viii, 140p. 1980. pap. 28.75 (ISBN 3-8055-3067-6). S Karger.

Latane, Bibb & Darley, John M. Unresponsive Bystander: Why Doesn't He Help? LC 79-123548. (Psychology Ser). (Orig.). 1970. 10.95 (ISBN 0-13-938613-0). P-H.

Latane, Henry A., et al. Security Analysis & Portfolio Management. 2nd ed. 1975. 24.95 (ISBN 0-8260-5256-8). Wiley.

Latanision, R. M. & Courtel, R. Advances in Mechanics & Physics of Surfaces. 262p. 1981. 35.50 (ISBN 3-7186-0026-9). Harwood Academic.

Latchaw, Marjorie. Pocket Guide of Movement Activities for the Elementary School. 2nd ed. 1970. pap. 10.95 (ISBN 0-13-684852-4). P-H.

Latempa, Susan see La Tempa, Susan.

La Tempa, Susan, ed. New Plays by Women. Sullivan, L. M. & Latempa, Susan. 1979. pap. 3.95 (ISBN 0-915288-41-9). Shameless Hussy.

La Terreur, Marc see Halpenny, Francess.

Latham, A. J. Old Calabor, Sixteen Hundred to Eighteen Ninety One: The Impact of the International Economy Upon a Traditional Society. 1973. 33.00x (ISBN 0-19-821687-4). Oxford U Pr.

Latham, Agnes M., ed. see Raleigh, Walter.

Latham, Bryan. Victorian Staffordshire Portrait Figures. (Illus.). 5.95 (ISBN 0-85670-073-8). Transatlantic.

Latham, Calvin, ed. see Clar, Lawrence M, et al.

Latham, Edward. Dictionary of Names, Nicknames, & Surnames. LC 66-22674. 1966. Repr. of 1904 ed. 22.00 (ISBN 0-8103-0157-1). Gale.

--Famous Sayings & Their Authors: A Collection of Historical Sayings in English, French, German, Greek, Italian, & Latin. LC 68-26582. 1970. Repr. of 1904 ed. 18.00 (ISBN 0-8103-3141-1). Gale.

Latham, Elizabeth D. Happiness Is a Warm Fuzzy. (Illus.). 64p. 1981. 5.00 (ISBN 0-682-49682-0). Exposition.

Latham, Frank B. Dred Scott Decision, March 6, 1857: Slavery & the Supreme Court's Self-Inflicted Wound. LC 68-25729. (Focus Bks). (Illus.). (gr. 7 up). 1968. PLB 4.90 o.p. (ISBN 0-531-01000-7); pap. 1.25 o.p. (ISBN 0-531-02329-X). Watts.
--F. D. R. & the Supreme Court Fight, Nineteen Thirty-Seven: A President Tries to Reorganize the Federal Judiciary. LC 71-180166. (Focus Books). (Illus.). 72p. (gr. 7 up). 1971. PLB 4.90 o.p. (ISBN 0-531-02451-2). Watts.
--Lincoln & the Emancipation Proclamation, January 1, 1863: The Document That Turned the Civil War into a Fight for Freedom. LC 69-13759. (Focus Bks). (Illus.). (gr. 7 up). 1969. PLB 4.90 o.p. (ISBN 0-531-01002-3); pap. 1.25 o.p. (ISBN 0-531-02331-1). Watts.
--Panic of 1893: A Time of Strikes, Riots, Hobo Camps, Coxey's Army, Starvation, Withering Droughts & Fears of Revolution. LC 70-132067. (Focus Bks). (Illus.). (gr. 7 up). 1971. PLB 4.90 o.p. (ISBN 0-531-01022-8). Watts.
--Rise & Fall of Jim Crow: The Long Struggle Against the Supreme Court's Separate-But-Equal Ruling. LC 70-80897. (Focus Bks). (gr. 7 up). 1969. PLB 4.47 o.p. (ISBN 0-531-01011-2); pap. 0.95 o.p. (ISBN 0-531-02335-4). Watts.
--The Transcontinental Railroad, 1862-69: A Great Engineering Feat Links America Coast to Coast. LC 73-1222. (Focus Bks). (Illus.). (gr. 7-12). 1973. text ed. 4.47 o.p. (ISBN 0-531-01025-2). Watts.
--Trial of John Peter Zenger, August 1735: An Early Fight for America's Freedom of the Press. LC 71-101751. (Focus Books). (Illus.). (gr. 7 up). 1970. PLB 1.25 o.p. (ISBN 0-531-02333-8). Watts.
Latham, Gary P. & Wexley, Kenneth N. Increasing Productivity Through Performance Appraisal. (Managing Human Resources Ser.). 175p. 1980. pap. 6.95 (ISBN 0-201-04217-7). A-W.
Latham, Hugh, tr. Mother Goose in French. LC 64-10863. (Illus., Fr). (gr. 4 up). 1964. 8.79 o.p. (ISBN 0-690-56265-9, TYC-J); PLB 6.79 o.p. (ISBN 0-690-56266-7). T Y Crowell.
Latham, R. E., compiled by. Dictionary of Medieval Latin from British Sources: Fascicule I, A-B. 280p. 1975. pap. 49.00x (ISBN 0-19-725948-0). Oxford U Pr.
Latham, Richard T. Law & the Commonwealth. Repr. of 1949 ed. lib. bdg. 16.75x (ISBN 0-8371-3974-0, LALC). Greenwood.
Latham, Robert. Catalogue of the Pepys Library at Magdalene College, Cambridge, Vol. 3: Pt. 1 - Prints & Drawings (General) Aspitall, A., ed. 160p. 1981. 135.00x (ISBN 0-8476-3637-2). Rowman.
Latham, Robert, ed. Catalogue of the Pepys Library, Vol. 1. (Printed Bks.). 201p. 1978. 89.50x (ISBN 0-87471-819-8). Rowman.
Latham, Robert, ed. see Pepys, Samuel.
Latham, Robert O. Trail Maker (David Livingstone) 1973. pap. 1.95 (ISBN 0-87508-626-8). Chr Lit.
Latham, Ronald E., ed. Revised Medieval Latin Word-List from British & Irish Sources. (British Academy Ser.). 1965. 49.00x (ISBN 0-19-725891-3). Oxford U Pr.
Latham, Shyree A. Melange. (Contemporary American Poets Ser.). 51p. (Orig.). 1981. 10.95 (ISBN 0-86663-702-8); pap. 8.95 (ISBN 0-86663-703-6); delux ed. 20.95 (ISBN 0-86663-704-4). Ide Hse.
--Peppertree III. (Illus.). 100p. (Orig.). 1981. pap. 12.95 (ISBN 0-86663-600-5). Ide Hse.
Latham, Sid. Great Sporting Posters of the Golden Age. LC 77-76772. (Illus.). 48p. 1978. pap. 11.95 (ISBN 0-8117-2115-9). Stackpole.
--Knifecraft. LC 78-16825. (Illus.). 240p. 1978. 18.95 (ISBN 0-8117-0927-2). Stackpole.
--Knives & Knifemakers. 1973. 17.50 (ISBN 0-87691-109-2). Winchester Pr.
--Knives & Knifemakers. (Illus.). 160p. 1974. pap. 7.95 (ISBN 0-02-011750-7, Collier). Macmillan.
--Leathercraft. (Illus.). 1977. 13.95 (ISBN 0-87691-227-7). Winchester Pr.
--Leathercraft. (Illus.). 1978. pap. 6.95 o.p. (ISBN 0-695-80936-9). Follett.
Latham, Willoughby. The Future of Academic Community Medicine in Development Countries. LC 78-24484. 1979. 22.95 (ISBN 0-03-051116-X). Praeger.
Lathem, Edward C., ed. see Coolidge, Calvin.
Lathem, Edward C., ed. see Dickey, John S.
Lathem, Edward C., ed. see Frost, Robert.
Lathen, Emma. Death Shall Overcome. 1981. pap. 2.50 (ISBN 0-671-83675-7). PB.
--Going for the Gold. 1981. 10.95 (ISBN 0-671-41407-0). S&S.
--Pick up Sticks. 1981. pap. 2.50 (ISBN 0-671-83674-9). PB.
Lathrap, Donald W., et al. Ancient Ecuador: Culture, Clay & Creativity, 3000-300 B.C. LC 74-25248. (Illus.). 110p. (Orig., Eng. & Span.). 1980. pap. 5.95 (ISBN 0-914868-07-1). Field Mus.
Lathrop, D. P. Bouncing Betsy. 1964. 3.95 o.s.i. (ISBN 0-02-753150-3). Macmillan.
Lathrop, Dorothy P. Animals of the Bible. (Illus.). (ps-6). 1969. 9.79 (ISBN 0-397-31536-8). Lippincott.
--Let Them Live. (Illus.). (gr. 4-6). 1966. 6.95g (ISBN 0-02-753800-1). Macmillan.
--Who Goes There. (Illus.). (gr. 1-3). 1963. 4.95g o.s.i. (ISBN 0-02-754350-1). Macmillan.
Lathrop, Gilbert. Rio Grande Glory Days. LC 76-45760. (Illus.). 356p. 1976. 14.95 (ISBN 0-87095-056-8). Golden West.
Lathrop, Irving T., jt. auth. see Lindbeck, John R.
Lathrop, Mary L. & Lathrop, Norman M., eds. Index to Model Making & Miniatures. 1980. pap. 15.00 (ISBN 0-910868-20-4). Lathrop.
Lathrop, Norma J. Herbs. (Orig.). 1981. pap. 7.95 (ISBN 0-89586-077-5). H P Bks.
Lathrop, Norman M., jt. ed. see Lathrop, Mary L.
Lathrop, Richard. Don't Use a Resume. 1980. pap. 1.95 (ISBN 0-89815-027-2). Ten Speed Pr.
Latil, M. Enhanced Recovery. 275p. 1980. 24.95 (ISBN 0-87201-775-3). Gulf Pub.
Latilla, Gaetano. La Finta Cameriera. Brown, Howard M., ed. LC 76-21007. (Italian Opera 1640-1770 Ser.: Vol. 37). 1978. lib. bdg. 75.00 (ISBN 0-8240-2636-5). Garland Pub.
Latimer, Charles, et al. Legal Environment of Business Study Guide. 2nd ed. 105p. 1980. pap. text ed. 7.50 (ISBN 0-88244-215-5). Grid Pub.
Latimer, George W. & Ragsdale, Ronald O. Modern Experimental Chemistry. 279p. 1971. text ed. 8.95 (ISBN 0-12-437250-3). Acad Pr.
Latner, jt. ed. see Bodansky, Oscar.
Latner, A. L. & Schwartz, Morton K., eds. Advances in Clinical Chemistry, Vol. 21. LC 58-12341. (Serial Publication). 1980. 29.00 (ISBN 0-12-010321-4); library ed. 37.50 (ISBN 0-12-010382-6); microfiche 20.50 (ISBN 0-12-010383-4). Acad Pr.
Latner, Albert L. Cantarow & Trumper Clinical Biochemistry. 7th ed. LC 73-89933. 770p. 1975. text ed. 34.00 (ISBN 0-7216-5637-4). Saunders.
Latner, Helen. The Book of Modern Jewish Etiquette: A Guide to All Occasions. LC 80-22537. (Illus.). 416p. 19.95 (ISBN 0-8052-3757-7). Schocken.
Latorre, G., jt. auth. see Ewer, J. R.
LaTorre, Ronald A. Sexual Identity: Implications for Mental Health. LC 78-26442. 1979. 16.95 (ISBN 0-88229-360-5). Nelson-Hall.
Latourette, Jane. El Arca de Noe. Villalobos, Fernando, tr. from Eng. (Libros Arco). Orig. Title: Story of Noah's Ark. (Illus.). 32p. (Orig., Span.). (gr. 1-3). 1975. pap. 0.95 o.s.i. (ISBN 0-89922-036-3). Edit Caribe.
--Jonatan y el Corderito Travieso. Ross, Ronald, tr. from Eng. (Libros Arco). (Illus.). 32p. (Orig., Span.). (gr. 1-3). 1972. pap. 0.95 o.s.i. (ISBN 0-89922-040-1). Edit Caribe.
Latourette, Kenneth S. Chinese: Their History & Culture, 2 Vols in 1. 4th, rev. ed. 1964. 15.95 o.s.i. (ISBN 0-02-568920-7). Macmillan.
--Desde el Siglo XVI hasta el Siglo XX. Quarles, Jaime C. & Quarles, Lemuel C., trs. (Historia del Cristianismo: Tomo II). Orig. Title: A History of the Expansion of Christianity. 968p. 1980. pap. 10.80 (ISBN 0-311-15012-8). Casa Bautista.
--Historia del Cristianismo, Tomo I. Quarles, Jaime C. & Quarles, Lemuel C., trs. from Eng. (Illus.). 1980. pap. 10.80 (ISBN 0-311-15010-1). Casa Bautista.
--A History of Christianity. rev. ed. Incl. Vol. 1. Beginnings to 1500. 758p (ISBN 0-06-064952-6, RD-93); Vol. 2. Reformation to the Present. 922p (ISBN 0-06-064953-4, RD-94). LC 74-25692. 1975. pap. 9.95 ea. (HarpR). Har-Row.
La Tourrette, Jacqueline. The Pompeii Scroll. 256p. 1975. 7.95 o.p. (ISBN 0-440-06091-5). Delacorte.
Latsis, S. J., ed. Method & Appraisal in Economics. LC 75-44581. 220p. 1976. 38.50 (ISBN 0-521-21076-3). Cambridge U Pr.
Latta, Gordon, jt. auth. see Polya, George.
Latta, Gordon, tr. see Jacquemard, Yves & Senecal, Jean-Michel.
Latta, L., jt. auth. see Sarmiento, A.
Latta, Richard. Games for Travel, No. 3. 1981. 1.50 (ISBN 0-8431-0242-X). Price Stern.
--Games for Travel, No. 3. 48p. (Orig.). 1981. pap. 1.75 (ISBN 0-8431-0312-4). Price Stern.
--Rain. 1972. 12.00 o.p. (ISBN 0-685-67926-8). Windless Orchard.
Lattes, Raffaele, jt. auth. see Enzinger, Franz M.
Lattimer, John K. Lincoln & Kennedy: Medical & Ballistic Comparisons of Their Assassinations. 1980. 19.95 (ISBN 0-15-152281-2). HarBraceJ.
Lattimore. Which Way, Black Cat? (gr. 3-5). 1980. pap. 1.25 (ISBN 0-590-30040-7, Schol Pap). Schol Bk Serv.
Lattimore, David, tr. The Harmony of the World: Chinese Poems. rev. & enl. ed. (Illus.). 1980. pap. 4.50 (ISBN 0-914278-31-2). Cooper Beech.
Lattimore, Eleanor F. Adam's Key. LC 76-13013. (Illus.). (gr. 2-5). 1976. PLB 6.96 (ISBN 0-688-32089-9). Morrow.
--The Bus Trip. (Illus.). (gr. 2-5). 1965. 7.25 (ISBN 0-688-21133-X). Morrow.
--Little Pear & His Friends. LC 34-27286. (Illus.). (gr. k-3). 5.95 o.p. (ISBN 0-15-246861-7, HJ). HarBraceJ.
--Little Pear & the Rabbits. (Illus.). (gr. 2-5). 1956. 6.25 o.p. (ISBN 0-688-21715-X). Morrow.
--More About Little Pear. LC 71-151939. (Illus.). (gr. 2-5). 1971. 7.25 (ISBN 0-688-21892-X). Morrow.
--Proudfoot's Way. LC 77-20057. (Illus.). (gr. 2-5). 1978. 7.95 (ISBN 0-688-22145-9); PLB 7.63 (ISBN 0-688-32145-3). Morrow.
Lattimore, Owen. The Mongols of Manchuria. LC 68-9626. 1969. Repr. of 1934 ed. 18.00 (ISBN 0-86527-132-1). Fertig.
Lattimore, Richard, ed. see Euripides.
Lattimore, Richard, tr. The Iliad of Homer. 63p. pap. 3.95 (ISBN 0-226-46940-9). U of Chicago Pr.
Lattimore, Richmond, jt. ed. see Grene, David.
Lattimore, Richmond, tr. from Greek. The Four Gospels & Revelation. 320p. 1979. 10.95 (ISBN 0-374-15801-0). FS&G.
Lattimore, Richmond, tr. Greek Lyrics. rev ed. LC 60-51619. 1960. 5.00x o.s.i. (ISBN 0-226-46943-3). U of Chicago Pr.
Lattimore, Richmond, tr. see Euripides.
Lattimore, Richmond, tr. see Willcock, Malcolm M.
Lattin, Gerald W. Modern Hotel & Motel Management. 3rd ed. LC 77-10007. (Illus.). 1977. text ed. 16.95x (ISBN 0-7167-0483-8). W H Freeman.
Latzko, D. G., ed. Post-Yield Fracture Mechanics. (Illus.). 1979. 72.50x (ISBN 0-85334-775-1). Intl Ideas.
Lau, James B. Behavior in Organizations. rev. ed. 1979. pap. text ed. 13.50x (ISBN 0-256-02122-8). Irwin.
Lau, Joseph, et al, eds. Modern Chinese Stories & Novellas, Nineteen Nineteen to Nienteen Forty-Nine. LC 80-27572. (Modern Asian Literature Ser.). 608p. (Eng.). 1981. 35.00x (ISBN 0-231-04202-7); pap. 15.00x (ISBN 0-231-04203-5). Columbia U Pr.
Lau, Joseph S. & Ross, Timothy A., eds. Chinese Stories from Taiwan, Nineteen Sixty to Nineteen Seventy. 336p. 1976. 22.50x (ISBN 0-231-04007-5); pap. 10.00x (ISBN 0-231-04008-3). Columbia U Pr.
Lau, Joseph S., jt. ed. see Hsia, Chih-Tsing.
Lau, Joseph S., jt. ed. see Ma, Y. W.
Lau, Joseph S., tr. see Ts'ao Yu.
Lau, Lillian see Penney, William M.
Laub, Bryna, ed. The Official Soap Opera Annual. 1977. pap. 1.95 (ISBN 0-345-25695-6, 345-25695-6). Ballantine.
Laub, Donald R., ed. see Vistnes, Lars M., et al.
Laub, Richard J. & Pecsok, Robert L. Physiochemical Applications of Gas Chromatography. LC 78-5493. 1978. 31.95 (ISBN 0-471-51838-7, Pub. by Wiley-Interscience). Wiley.
Laubach, David C. Introduction to Folklore. 192p. (gr. 10-12). 1980. pap. 6.25 (ISBN 0-8104-6039-4). Hayden.
Laubenthal, Sanders A. Excalibur. 1977. pap. 1.95 o.p. (ISBN 0-345-25635-2). Ballantine.
Lauber, John. Sir Walter Scott. (English Authors Ser.: No. 39). 1966. lib. bdg. 10.95 (ISBN 0-8057-1476-6). Twayne.
Lauber, Patricia. Bats: Wings in the Night. LC 68-23672. (Gateway Ser.: No. 47). (Illus.). (gr. 3-6). 1968. PLB 5.39 (ISBN 0-394-90147-9, BYR). Random.
--Friendly Dolphins. (Gateway Ser.: No. 28). (Illus.). (gr. 3-6). 1963. 3.95 (ISBN 0-394-80128-8, BYR); PLB 5.99 (ISBN 0-394-90128-2). Random.
--Look-It-Up Book of Stars and Planets. (Look-It-up Books Ser.). (Illus.). (gr. 1-6). 1967. 4.95 o.p. (ISBN 0-394-81683-8, BYR); PLB 5.99 (ISBN 0-394-91683-2). Random.
--Science Book of Volcanoes. (Illus.). (gr. 4-6). 1972. pap. 1.25 (ISBN 0-590-02560-0, Schol Pap). Schol Bk Serv.
--Your Body & How It Works. (Gateway Ser.: No. 25). (Illus.). (gr. 3-5). 1962. 2.95 o.p. (ISBN 0-685-19707-7, BYR); PLB 5.99 (ISBN 0-394-90125-8). Random.
Lauber, R., ed. Safety of Computer Control Systems: Proceedings of the IFAC Workshop, Stuttgart, Federal Republic of Germany, 16-18 May 1979. (Illus.). 230p. 1980. 52.00 (ISBN 0-08-024453-X). Pergamon.
Laubin, Gladys, jt. auth. see Laubin, Reginald.
Laubin, Reginald & Laubin, Gladys. The Indian Tipi: Its History... (Illus.). 288p. 1976. pap. 1.95 o.p. (ISBN 0-345-25034-6). Ballantine.
Lauckner, Edie. Signs of Celebration. 1978. 2.25 (ISBN 0-570-03770-0, 12-2706). Concordia.
Laucks, Eulah C. The Meaning of Children: Attitudes & Opinions of a Selected Group of U.S. University Graduates. (Special Studies in Contemporary Social Issues). 225p. 1981. lib. bdg. 20.00x (ISBN 0-89158-881-7). Westview.
Laudan, Larry. Progress & Its Problems: Towards a Theory of Scientific Growth. 1977. 15.75x (ISBN 0-520-03330-2); pap. 4.95 (ISBN 0-520-03721-9). U of Cal Pr.
Lauder, Phyllis. Batsford Book of the Siamese Cat. 1974. 14.95 (ISBN 0-7134-2828-7, Pub. by Batsford England). David & Charles.
--The Siamese Cat. 1978. 19.95 (ISBN 0-7134-1733-1, Pub. by Batsford England). David & Charles.
--The Siamese Cat. (Illus.). 1979. 9.95 o.p. (ISBN 0-684-16078-1, ScribT). Scribner.
Lauderdale, Beverly & Shelgren, Margaret. Ten Women & God. LC 78-75316. (Illus.). Date not set. cancelled (ISBN 0-498-02329-X). A S Barnes.
Laudicina, Paul A. World Poverty & Development: A Survey of American Opinion. LC 73-89873. (Monographs: No. 8). 126p. 1973. 2.50 (ISBN 0-686-28687-1). Overseas Dev Council.
Laudicina, R. & Tramutola, J. A Legal Perspective for Student Personnel Administrators. (Illus.). 152p. 1974. 14.75 (ISBN 0-398-03080-4). C C Thomas.
Laudicina, Robert A. & Tramutola, Joseph L., eds. A Legal Overview of the New Student: As Educational Consumer, Citizen & Bargainer. (Illus.). 316p. 1976. 24.50 (ISBN 0-398-03575-X). C C Thomas.
Laudon, Kenneth C. Communications Technology & Democratic Participation. LC 77-7471. (Special Studies). 1977. text ed. 21.95 (ISBN 0-03-021836-5). Praeger.
Laue, Theodore H. Von see Von Laue, Theodore H.
Lauer, A. R. The Psychology of Driving: Factors of Traffic Enforcement. (Illus.). 352p. 1972. 15.75 (ISBN 0-398-02337-9). C C Thomas.
Lauer, Judith A. Computers for Pharmacy. LC 78-68406. (Illus.). 1978. 15.00 (ISBN 0-917330-21-8). Am Pharm Assn.
Lauer, Kenneth R. Structural Engineering for Architects. (Illus.). 672p. 1981. text ed. 25.95 (ISBN 0-07-036622-5, C). McGraw.
Lauer, Quentin. Hegel's Idea of Philosophy. LC 74-152244. xii, 159p. 1971. 9.00 o.p. (ISBN 0-8232-0925-3). Fordham.
Lauer, Quentin, tr. see Husserl, Edmund.
Lauer, R. M. & Shekelle, R. B., eds. Childhood Prevention of Atherosclerosis. 1979. 48.50 (ISBN 0-89004-381-7). Raven.
Lauer, Robert H. Perspectives on Social Change. 2nd ed. 1977. text ed. 16.95 (ISBN 0-205-05846-9, 8158460). Allyn.
Lauer, Robert H. & Handel, Warren H. Social Psychology: The Theory & Application of Symbolic Interactionism. LC 76-10895. 512p. 1977. text ed. 16.95 (ISBN 0-395-24333-5); inst. manual 1.25 (ISBN 0-395-24334-3). HM.
Lauer, Robert H., jt. auth. see Hampton, Bill R.
Lauerhass, Ludwig & A Raujo-Haugse, Vera L. De. Education in Latin America: A Bibliography. (Reference Books Ser.). lib. bdg. 55.00 (ISBN 0-8161-8516-6). G K Hall.
Lauersen, Neils H. & Hochberg, Howard. Clinical Perinatal Biochemical Monitoring. 271p. 1981. write for info. (1901-1). Williams & Wilkins.
Lauf, Detlef-Ingo. Secret Revelations of Tibetan Thangkas. (Illus.). 1979. 40.00 (ISBN 3-591-08025-X, Pub. by Aurum Verlag Germany). Hunter Hse.
Laufeld, Sven. Silurian Chitinozoa from Gotland. (Fossils & Strata Ser: No. 5). 1974. pap. 25.00x (ISBN 8-200-09358-1, Dist. by Columbia U Pr). Universitet.
Laufer, R. Introduction a la textologie: Verification...etablissement, edition des textes. (Collection L). 160p. (Orig., Fr.). 1972. pap. 13.95 (ISBN 2-03-036006-6). Larousse.
Lauffer, Armand. Grantsmanship. LC 77-10013. (Sage Human Services Guides: Vol. 1). 1977. pap. 6.00x (ISBN 0-8039-0880-6). Sage.
--Resources: For Child Placement & Other Human Services. LC 78-26352. (Sage Human Service Guides: Vol. 6). 1979. pap. 8.00x (ISBN 0-8039-1218-8). Sage.
--Social Planning at the Community Level. (P-H Ser. in Social Work Practice). (Illus.). 1978. 15.95 (ISBN 0-13-817189-0). P-H.
Lauffer, Armand & Gorodezky, Sarah. Volunteers. LC 77-9003. (Sage Human Services Guides: Vol. 5). 1977. pap. 6.00x (ISBN 0-8039-0884-9). Sage.
Lauffer, Armand, jt. auth. see Manela, Roger.
Lauffer, Armand, et al. Understanding Your Social Agency. LC 77-10012. (Sage Human Services Guides: Vol. 3). 1977. pap. 6.00x (ISBN 0-8039-0882-2). Sage.
Lauffer, Max A., et al, eds. Advances in Virus Research, Vol. 26. (Serial Publication). 1981. write for info. (ISBN 0-12-039826-5). Acad Pr.

Laufman, Harold. Hospital Special Care Facilities: Planning for User Needs. (Clinical Engineering Ser.). 1981. price not set (ISBN 0-12-437740-8). Acad Pr.
Laufman, Harold, jt. auth. see Banks, Sam W.
Laughin, James. Confidential Report: Selected Poems. 1959. 3.95 (ISBN 0-8112-0781-1). New Directions.
Laughlin. Roe's Laboratory Guide in Chemistry. 7th ed. (Illus.). 1976. pap. text ed. 8.50 (ISBN 0-8016-1473-2). Mosby.
--Simple Method of Solving Equations of the Fourth Degree. 2.00 o.p. (ISBN 0-686-00168-0). Columbia Graphs.
Laughlin, Blanche. Guidebook to Mathematics. (Remedial). (gr. 7 up). 1967. pap. text ed. 2.19 (ISBN 0-87892-611-9); tchrs' handbook 2.19 (ISBN 0-87892-612-7). Economy Co.
Laughlin, Charles D. & D'Aquili, Eugene G. Biogenetic Stucturalism. (Illus.). 1974. text ed. 12.00x (ISBN 0-231-03817-8). Columbia U Pr.
Laughlin, Charles D., Jr. & Brady, Ivan A., eds. Extinction & Survival in Human Populations. LC 76-17596. 1978. 22.50x (ISBN 0-231-04418-6); pap. 10.00x (ISBN 0-231-04419-4). Columbia U Pr.
Laughlin, Eugene J. The Basis of Accounting. LC 76-15721. (Accounting Ser.). 1977. text ed. 17.50 o.p. (ISBN 0-88244-137-X). Grid Pub.
Laughlin, Florence. Little Leftover Witch. (Illus.). (gr. 4-5). 1960. 7.95 (ISBN 0-02-754560-1). Macmillan.
--The Mystery of the McGilley Mansion. (Illus.). (gr. 4-6). 1963. 6.95 (ISBN 0-688-41398-6). Lothrop.
--Seventh Cousin. (Illus.). (gr. 4-6). 1966. 3.95g o.s.i. (ISBN 0-02-754540-7). Macmillan.
Laughlin, J., et al, eds. New Directions Forty-One: Anthology. LC 37-1751. 192p. 1980. 15.95 (ISBN 0-8112-0770-6); pap. 5.95 (ISBN 0-8112-0771-4, NDP505). New Directions.
--New Directions Forty-Two: Anthology. LC 37-1751. 192p. 1981. 15.95 (ISBN 0-8112-0783-8); pap. 5.95 (ISBN 0-8112-0784-6, NDP510). New Directions.
Laughlin, Jerry & Osterhout, Connie, eds. Salvage & Overhaul Practices: FSTA, 104. 6th ed. LC 79-84252. 1979. pap. text ed. 7.00 (ISBN 0-87939-030-1). Intl Fire Serv.
Laughlin, Jerry, ed. see IFSTA Committee.
Laughlin, Jerry, jt. ed. see Peige, John D.
Laughlin, Ruth. Natural Sweets & Treats. new ed. LC 75-17275. (Illus.). 176p. (Orig.). 1975. pap. 5.95 (ISBN 0-912800-17-8). Woodbridge Pr.
Laughlin, William. Survivors of the Bering Land Bridge. (Case Studies in Cultural Anthropology). 128p. 1980. pap. text ed. 4.95 (ISBN 0-03-081269-0, HoltC). HR&W.
Laugwitz, D. Differential & Riemannian Geometry. Steinhardt, F., tr. 1965. 33.50 (ISBN 0-12-437750-5). Acad Pr.
Laumann, Edward O. Prestige & Association in an Urban Community: An Analysis of an Urban Stratification System. LC 66-29709. (Orig.). 1966. pap. 4.95 (ISBN 0-672-60620-8). Bobbs.
Laumann, Edward O., ed. Social Stratification: Research & Theory for the 1970's. LC 77-135769. (Illus., Orig.). 1970. 8.50 (ISBN 0-672-51402-8); pap. 6.95 (ISBN 0-672-61195-3). Bobbs.
Laumark, Eleanor & Christianson, Victoria. Keeping Track: A Personal Medical Record System. LC 80-22042. (Illus., Orig.). 1980. pap. 7.95 (ISBN 0-912800-79-8). Woodbridge Pr.
Laumer, Keith. Bolo. 1978. pap. 1.50 o.p. (ISBN 0-425-03450-X). Berkley Pub.
--Bolo: The Annals of the Dinochrome Brigade. LC 76-9769. (YA) 1976. 6.95 o.p. (ISBN 0-399-11794-6, Dist. by Putnam). Berkley Pub.
--Retief & the Rebels. 1980. pap. write for info. (ISBN 0-671-81866-X). PB.
Launay, Andre & Pendered, Maureen. Madrid & Southern Spain. 19.95 (ISBN 0-7134-3081-8). David & Charles.
Launey, Andre. Morrocco. 1976. 19.95 (ISBN 0-7134-3182-2). David & Charles.
Laure, Ettagale, jt. auth. see Laure, Jason.
Laure, Jason & Laure, Ettagale. Jovem Portugal: After the Revolution. LC 77-8127. (Illus.). 160p. (gr. 7 up). 1977. 8.95 (ISBN 0-374-33934-1). FS&G.
Laurello, Bartholomeo J. Ministering to the Aging. LC 79-90992. (Paths of Life Ser.). 90p. (Orig.). 1979. pap. 2.45 (ISBN 0-8091-2268-5). Paulist Pr.
Lauren, Paul, jt. auth. see Geffner, Saul.
Laurence, D. R. & Bacharach, A. L., eds. Evaluation of Drug Activities: Pharmacometrics, 2 Vols. 1965. Vol. 1. 59.00 (ISBN 0-12-438301-7); Vol. 2. 59.00 (ISBN 0-12-438302-5). Acad Pr.
Laurence, Dan, ed. Bernard Shaw: Platform & Pulpit. 1979. 9.95x (ISBN 0-8464-0088-X). Beekman Pubs.
--Bernard Shaw: The Matter with Ireland. 1979. 9.95x (ISBN 0-8464-0087-1). Beekman Pubs.
Laurence, Dan H., ed. Shaw's Music: The Complete Musical Criticism, 3 vols. LC 80-1113. 1981. Boxed Set. 150.00 (ISBN 0-686-69572-0). Vol. 1 (ISBN 0-396-07960-1). Vol. 2 (ISBN 0-396-07961-X). Vol. 3 (ISBN 0-396-07962-8). Dodd.
Laurence, Frank M. Hemingway & the Movies. LC 79-1437. 336p. 1980. 20.00 (ISBN 0-87805-115-5). U Pr of Miss.
Laurence, Jeanne. My Life with Sydney Laurence. LC 74-75661. (Illus.). 180p. 1974. 35.00 o.p. (ISBN 0-87564-010-9). Superior Pub.
Laurence, John C. Race, Propaganda & South Africa: The Manipulation of Western Opinion & Policies by the Forces of White Supremacy. 1981. text ed. 19.25 (ISBN 0-575-02691-X, Pub. by Gollancz England). Humanities.
Laurence, Margaret. Jason's Quest. 144p. 1981. pap. 2.50 (ISBN 0-686-68905-4). Bantam.
Laurence, Theodor. The Sexual Key to the Tarot. 1973. pap. 1.50 (ISBN 0-451-07581-1, W7581, Sig). NAL.
Laurence Urdang Associates. Longman Dictionary of English Idioms. (Illus.). 1979. 15.95x (ISBN 0-582-55524-8). Longman.
Laurencie, Lionel de la see La Laurencie, Lionel de.
Laurene, Ruth. Bellringer. LC 74-75851. (Illus.). 1974. 20.00x (ISBN 0-933652-08-9). Domjan Studio.
Laurenson, Diana, ed. The Sociology of Literature: Applied Studies. (Sociological Review Monograph: No. 26). 284p. 1978. pap. 28.00x (ISBN 0-8476-2299-1). Rowman.
Laurent, J. P., ed. Coordination Chemistry-Twenty One: Twenty First International Conference on Coodination Chemistry, Toulouse, France 7-11 July 1980. (IUPAC Symposium Ser.). 200p. 1981. 54.00 (ISBN 0-08-025300-8). Pergamon.
Laurent, Laurence L., jt. auth. see Gotshall, Daniel W.
Laurenti, Joseph L. & Poqueras-Mayo, A. The Spanish Golden Age. (Reference Books). 1979. lib. bdg. 45.00 (ISBN 0-8161-8286-8). G K Hall.
Laurenti, Joseph L. & Siracusa, Joseph. Federico Garcia Lorca y Su Mundo: Ensayo De una Bibliografia General. LC 74-2252. (Author Bibliographies Ser.: No. 15). 1974. 11.00 (ISBN 0-8108-0713-0). Scarecrow.
Laurentian Hormone Conferences. Recent Progress in Hormone Research: Proceedings. Pincus, Gregory, ed. Incl. Vols. 1-5. 1947-50. Set (ISBN 0-685-30520-1). Vol. 1. 47.50 (ISBN 0-12-571101-8); Vol. 2. 47.50 (ISBN 0-12-571102-6); Vol. 3. 48.50 (ISBN 0-12-571103-4); Vol. 4. 48.50 (ISBN 0-12-571104-2); Vol. 5. 48.50 (ISBN 0-12-571105-0); Vols. 6-11. 1951-55. 48.50 ea.; Vol. 6. o.s.i (ISBN 0-12-571106-9). Vol. 7 (ISBN 0-12-571107-7). Vol. 8 (ISBN 0-12-571108-5). Vol. 9 (ISBN 0-12-571109-3). Vol. 10 (ISBN 0-12-571110-7). Vol. 11 (ISBN 0-12-571111-5); Vol. 12. 1956. 48.50 (ISBN 0-12-571112-3); Vol. 13. 1957. 48.50 (ISBN 0-12-571113-1); Vols. 14-15. 1958-59. 48.50 ea. Vol. 14 (ISBN 0-12-571114-X). Vol. 15 (ISBN 0-12-571115-8); Vol. 16. 1960. 48.50 (ISBN 0-12-571116-6); Vols. 17-18. 1961-62. 48.50 ea. Vol. 17 (ISBN 0-12-571117-4). Vol. 18 (ISBN 0-12-571118-2); Vol. 19. 1963. 54.00 (ISBN 0-12-571119-0); Vol. 20. 1964. 54.00 (ISBN 0-12-571120-4); Vol. 21. 1965. 54.00 (ISBN 0-12-571121-2); Vol. 22. 1966. 54.00 (ISBN 0-12-571122-0); **Vol. 23. 1967. 61.00 (ISBN 0-12-571123-9); Vol. 24. Astwood, E. B., ed. 1968. 61.00 (ISBN 0-12-571124-7); Vol. 25. 1969. 61.00 (ISBN 0-12-571125-5); Vols. 26-27. 1970-71. 61.00 ea. Vol. 26 (ISBN 0-12-571126-3). Vol. 27 (ISBN 0-12-571127-1); Vol. 28. 1972. 58.00 (ISBN 0-12-571128-X); Vol. 29. 1973. 61.00 (ISBN 0-12-571129-8); Vol. 32. Greep, Roy O., ed. 1976. 61.00 (ISBN 0-12-571132-8); Vol. 33. Greep, Roy O., ed. 1977. 52.50 (ISBN 0-12-571133-6); Vol. 34. Greep, Roy O., ed. 1978. 51.50 (ISBN 0-12-571134-4). Acad Pr.**
Lauria, Frank. Lady Sativa. 1979. pap. 1.95 o.p. (ISBN 0-345-27328-1). Ballantine.
Laurie, Bruce, jt. ed. see Cantor, Milton.
Laurie, Edward J. Computers, Automation, & Society. 1979. pap. 13.95x (ISBN 0-256-02140-6). Irwin.
Laurie, Peter. Electronics Explained: A Handbook for the Layman. (Illus.). 144p. 1980. 31.95 (ISBN 0-571-11514-4, Pub. by Faber & Faber); pap. 16.95 (ISBN 0-571-11593-4, Pub. by Faber & Faber). Merrimack Bk Serv.
Laurie, Rona & Vann, Barbara, eds. One Hundred Speeches from the Theater. LC 72-81070. 208p. (gr. 9-12). 1973. 5.95g o.s.i. (ISBN 0-02-754610-1, CCPr). Macmillan.
Laurie, Sanders, et al. Centering: Your Guide to Inner Growth. 1978. 2.25 (ISBN 0-446-82750-9). Inner Tradit.
Laurie, Simon S. Studies in the History of Educational Opinion from the Renaissance. LC 72-93272. Repr. of 1903 ed. 22.50x (ISBN 0-678-05086-4). Kelley.
Laurila, Simo H. Electronic Surveying & Navigation. LC 75-41461. 512p. 1976. 37.50 (ISBN 0-471-51865-4, Pub. by Wiley-Interscience). Wiley.
Laurin, Anne. Perfect Crane. LC 80-7912. (Illus.). 32p. (gr. 1-4). 1981. 8.95 (ISBN 0-06-023743-0, HarpJ); PLB 8.79g (ISBN 0-06-023744-9). Har-Row.
Lauritzen, Peter. Palaces of Venice. (Illus.). 1978. 35.00 o.p. (ISBN 0-670-53724-1, Studio). Viking Pr.
--Venice: A Thousand Years of Culture & Civilization. LC 78-2690. 1978. 12.95 (ISBN 0-689-10897-4); pap. 6.95 (ISBN 0-689-70603-0). Atheneum.
Laursen, Gary A. Bradley CPA Review Q & A Law. LC 79-83862. 1979. pap. 12.00 (ISBN 0-932788-09-2). Bradley CPA.
--Q & A Law. LC 79-83862. 12.00 (ISBN 0-932788-09-2). Bradley CPA.
Laury, Jean R. & Aiken, Joyce. The Pantyhose Craft Book: Making Things from Run Pantyhose & Nylons. LC 76-53871. (Illus.). 1977. 12.95 (ISBN 0-8008-6235-X); pap. 5.95 (ISBN 0-8008-6234-1). Taplinger.
Laus, Michael D. Travel Instruction for the Handicapped. 164p. 1977. 14.75 (ISBN 0-398-03637-3). C C Thomas.
Lauter, Paul, jt. ed. see Kampf, Louis.
Lauterbach, William. The Crucial Hours. 1977. pap. 4.95 (ISBN 0-8100-0050-4, 15-0358). Northwest Pub.
--Es Will Abend Werden. Kujath, Mentor, ed. 1978. pap. 1.95 (ISBN 0-8100-0101-2, 26-0511). Northwest Pub.
Lauterbach, William A. Through Cloud & Sunshine. (Illus.). 1979. 4.95 (ISBN 0-570-03056-0, 6-1181). Concordia.
--When Shadows Fall. 1945. pap. 0.85 (ISBN 0-570-03537-6, 14-1573). Concordia.
Lauterbach, Wolf. Soviet Psychotherapy. Date not set. 24.01 (ISBN 0-08-024291-X). Pergamon.
Lauterpacht, Elihu & Collier, John G. Individual Rights & the State in Foreign Affairs: An International Compendium. LC 77-8010. (Praeger Special Studies). 1977. text ed. 52.95 (ISBN 0-275-24350-8). Praeger.
Lauton, Barry & Freese, Arthur. You & Your Adolescent. 2244p. 1981. 9.95 (ISBN 0-684-16819-7, ScribT). Scribner.
Lauton, Barry & Freese, Arthur S. The Healthy Adolescent: A Parent's Manual. 224p. 1981. 10.95 (ISBN 0-684-16819-7). Scribner.
Laux, Lothar, jt. ed. see Krohne, Heinz W.
La Vada, Weir. Skateboards & Skateboarding. (gr. 4-6). 1977. pap. 1.75 (ISBN 0-671-41136-5). PB.
Lavalla, Patrick, jt. auth. see Stoffel, R.
Lavalla, Rick, jt. auth. see Stoffer, R.
LaValle, Teresa, tr. see Ralph, Margaret.
Lavallee, Hugues, jt. auth. see Shephard, Roy J.
LaValley, Albert J., ed. Mildred Pierce. LC 80-5107. (Wisconsin - Warner Bros. Screenplay Ser.). (Illus.). 228p. 1980. 15.00 (ISBN 0-299-08370-5); pap. 5.95 (ISBN 0-299-08374-8). U of Wis Pr.
Lavan, S., jt. auth. see Fletcher, B.
Lavan, Spencer. The Ahmadiyah Movement: A History & Perspective. LC 74-901627. ix, 220p. 1974. 10.00x o.p. (ISBN 0-88386-455-X). South Asia Bks.
Lavanda, Violet, jt. auth. see Finocchiaro, Mary.
Lavater. Melodie De Tur-Di-Di. Date not set. 12.95 (ISBN 0-8120-5312-5). Barron. Postponed.
LaVeck, G. D., jt. ed. see De La Cruz, F.
Lavedan, Pierre. French Architecture. (Illus.). 304p. 1980. 15.95 (ISBN 0-85967-366-9, Pub. by Scolar Pr England); pap. 7.95 (ISBN 0-85967-365-0). Biblio Dist.
La Vega, Garcilasco De see De La Vega, Garcilasco.
Lavelle, C. L., et al. Evolutionary Changes to the Primate Skull & Dentition. (Illus.). 308p. 1977. 43.75 (ISBN 0-398-03618-7). C C Thomas.
Lavelle, Doris. Latin & American Dances. (gr. 7 up). 1979. text ed. 17.95x (ISBN 0-273-41640-5, LTB). Soccer.
Lavelle, Mike, ed. The Many Faces of Jane Fonda: An A-Z Miscellany. (Illus.). 260p. (Orig.). 1980. pap. 7.95 (ISBN 0-89803-037-4). Caroline Hse.
Lavenberg, Robert J., jt. auth. see Fitch, John E.
Lavenda, B. H. Thermodynamics of Irreversible Processes. LC 76-22604. 1978. 39.95x (ISBN 0-470-98898-3). Halsted Pr.
Lavenda, Violet H., jt. auth. see Finocchiaro, Mary.
Lavendar, William. Children of the River. 448p. (Orig.). 1980. pap. 2.50 (ISBN 0-515-05388-0). Jove Pubns.
--Fields Above the Sea. (Orig.). pap. 2.75 (ISBN 0-515-05390-2). Jove Pubns.
Lavender, David. The American Heritage History of the Great West. Josephy, Alvin M., Jr., ed. LC 65-23041. (Illus.). 416p. 1973. Repr. of 1965 ed. 19.95 (ISBN 0-8281-0303-8, B037R). Am Heritage.
--Bent's Fort. LC 54-7322. (Illus.). 1972. pap. 4.95 (ISBN 0-8032-5753-8, BB 545, Bison). U of Nebr Pr.
--California: Land of New Beginnings. LC 70-181630. (Regions of America Ser.). (Illus.). 512p. (YA) 1972. 14.95 o.p. (ISBN 0-06-012524-1, HarpT). Har-Row.
--Los Angeles: Two Hundred. Blakey, Ellen S. & Silvey, Larry P., eds. LC 80-66342. (The American Portrait Ser.). (Illus.). 240p. 1980. 24.95 (ISBN 0-932986-08-0). Continent Herit.
--One Man's West. LC 76-45450. 1977. 14.95x (ISBN 0-8032-0908-8); pap. 3.95 (ISBN 0-8032-5855-0, BB 633, Bison). U of Nebr Pr.
--The Rockies. rev. ed. LC 75-6345. (Regions of America Ser.). (Illus.). 448p. (YA) 1975. 13.95 o.p. (ISBN 0-06-012522-5, HarpT). Har-Row.
Lavender, J. P., ed. Clinical & Experimental Applications of Krypton 81m. 1980. 75.00x (Pub. by Brit Inst Radiology England). State Mutual Bk.
Lavender, John A. Your Marriage Needs Three Love Affairs. LC 77-91492. 1978. pap. 2.95 o.p. (ISBN 0-916406-91-1). Accent Bks.
Lavender, William. Chinaberry. (Orig.). 1976. pap. 2.95 (ISBN 0-515-05838-6). Jove Pubns.
--Journey to Quiet Waters. 496p. 1980. pap. 2.75 (ISBN 0-515-05389-9). Jove Pubns.
Laver, tr. see Barthes, Roland.
Laver, J. The Phonetic Description of Voice Quality. LC 77-82501. (Cambridge Studies in Linguistics: No. 31). (Illus.). 225p. 1980. 34.50 (ISBN 0-521-23176-0). Cambridge U Pr.
Laver, J., jt. ed. see Jones, W. E.
Laver, James. Concise History of Costume & Fashion. LC 73-18802. (Illus.). 1974. pap. write for info. (ISBN 0-684-13522-1, SL477, ScribT). Scribner.
Laver, John. Voice Quality: A Classified Bibliography of Research. (Library & Information Sources in Linguistics: No. 5). 1978. text ed. 30.25x (ISBN 90-272-0996-0). Humanities.
Laver, M. An Introduction to the Uses of Computers. LC 75-23535. (Cambridge Computer Science Texts Ser.). (Illus.). 187p. 1976. 11.95x (ISBN 0-521-29035-X). Cambridge U Pr.
Laver, Michael. The Politics of Private Desires. 272p. 1981. pap. 3.95 (ISBN 0-14-022316-9, Pelican). Penguin.
Laver, Murray. Computers & Social Change. (Cambridge Computer Science Texts Ser.: No. 10). 128p. 1980. 10.95 (ISBN 0-521-23027-6); pap. 7.95x (ISBN 0-521-29771-0). Cambridge U Pr.
--Computers, Communications, & Society. (Science & Engineering Policy Ser.). (Illus.). 104p. 1975. 18.50x (ISBN 0-19-858323-0). Oxford U Pr.
Laverack, Elizabeth. With This Ring... One Hundred Years of Marriage. (Illus.). 138p. 1980. pap. 17.95 (ISBN 0-241-89895-1, Pub. by Hamish Hamilton England). David & Charles.
Laverack, M. S. & Dando, J., eds. Essential Invertebrate Zoology. 2nd ed. LC 78-25963. 1979. pap. text ed. 14.95 (ISBN 0-470-26605-8). Halsted Pr.
LaVerdiere, Eugene. Luke. (New Testament Message Ser.). 10.95 (ISBN 0-89453-128-X); pap. 5.95 (ISBN 0-89453-193-X). M Glazier.
--The New Testament in the Life of the Church. LC 80-67403. 192p. (Orig.). 1980. pap. 4.95 (ISBN 0-87793-213-1). Ave Maria.
LaVerdiere, Eugene A. The Year of Matthew. LC 80-82553. (Illus.). 200p. (Orig.). 1981. pap. 6.95 (ISBN 0-934134-06-5, Celebration Bks). Natl Cath Reporter.
Lavers, Annette, tr. see Barthes, Roland.
Lavers, Norman. Mark Harris. (United States Authors Ser.: No. 304). 1978. lib. bdg. 12.50 (ISBN 0-8057-7209-X). Twayne.
Lavery, Brian. Deane's Doctrine of Naval Architecture 1670. 192p. 1980. 69.50x (ISBN 0-85177-180-7, Pub. by Conway Maritime England). State Mutual Bk.
La Vey, Anton S. Satanic Bible. 1969. pap. 2.75 (ISBN 0-380-01539-0, 53207). Avon.
LaVey, Anton S. The Satanic Rituals. (Orig.). 1972. pap. 2.75 (ISBN 0-380-01392-4, 76877). Avon.
Lavier, J. Chinese Micro-Massage. 1978. pap. 3.95 o.s.i. (ISBN 0-7225-0362-8). Newcastle Pub.
--Points of Chinese Acupuncture. Chancellor, Philip, tr. from Fr. 115p. 1974. text ed. 10.95x (ISBN 0-8464-1038-9). Beekman Pubs.
Laviera, Tato. La Carreta Made a U-Turn. LC 79-90764. (Orig.). 1980. pap. 5.00x (ISBN 0-934770-01-8). Arte Publico.
Lavigne, D. M., et al. Remote Sensing & Ecosystem Management. (Norsk Polarinstitutt Skrifter: Vol. 166). (Illus.). 51p. 1980. pap. text ed. 5.00x. Universitet.

Lavigne, Marie. The Socialist Economies of the Soviet Union & Europe. Waywell, T. G., tr. from Fr. LC 74-83551. 396p. 1974. 25.00 o.p. (ISBN 0-87332-063-8). M E Sharpe.
Laville, Henri, et al. Rock Shelters of the Perigord: Geological Stratigraphy & Archaeological Succession. LC 80-511. (Studies in Archaeology). 1980. 29.50 (ISBN 0-12-438750-0). Acad Pr.
Lavin, David E., et al. Right Versus Privilege: The Open Admissions Experiment at the City University of New York. LC 80-69571. (Illus.). 1981. 24.95 (ISBN 0-02-918080-5). Free Pr.
Lavin, Irving. Bernini & the Unity of the Visual Arts, 2 vols. (Illus.). 498p. 1980. text ed. 89.00x (ISBN 0-19-520184-1). Oxford U Pr.
Lavin, Mary A., jt. auth. see Hamilton, William P.
Lavin, Mary A., jt. ed. see Gebbie, Kristine M.
Lavine, Emanuel H. The Third Degree: A Detailed Account of Police Brutality. LC 74-676. (Civil Liberties in American History Ser.). 248p. 1974. Repr. of 1930 ed. lib. bdg. 27.50 (ISBN 0-306-70601-6). Da Capo.
Lavine, Harold & Wechsler, James. War Propaganda & the United States. 1940. 18.50x (ISBN 0-686-50035-0). Elliots Bks.
Lavine, Harold, jt. auth. see Wechsler, James.
Lavine, Irvin, jt. auth. see Zimmerman, O. T.
Lavine, Robert L., jt. ed. see Rose, Leslie I.
Lavine, Sigmund A. A Beginner's Book of Vegetable Gardening. LC 76-53439. (gr. 7 up). 1977. 5.95 (ISBN 0-396-07410-3). Dodd.
--Wonders of Camels. LC 78-22436. (Wonder Ser.). (Illus.). (gr. 4 up). 1979. 5.95 (ISBN 0-396-07670-X). Dodd.
--Wonders of Herbs. LC 75-38356. (Wonders Ser.). (gr. 5 up). 1976. 5.95 (ISBN 0-396-07294-1). Dodd.
--Wonders of Mice. LC 80-1018. (Wonders Ser.). (Illus.). 80p. (gr. 4 up). 1980. PLB 5.95 (ISBN 0-396-07891-5). Dodd.
--Wonders of Terrariums. LC 77-6493. (Wonders Se). (Illus.). (gr. 5 up). 1977. PLB 5.95g. (ISBN 0-396-07488-X). Dodd.
--Wonders of the Owl World. LC 77-143288. (gr. 3-7). 1971. PLB 5.95 (ISBN 0-396-06321-7). Dodd.
Lavine, Sigmund A. & Scuro, Vincent. Wonders of Donkeys. LC 78-7737. (Wonders Ser.). (Illus.). (gr. 4 up). 1979. 5.95 (ISBN 0-396-07592-4). Dodd.
--Wonders of Pigs. (Wonders Ser.). (Illus.). 80p. (gr. 4 up). 1981. PLB 6.95 (ISBN 0-396-07943-1). Dodd.
Lavington, S. H. Logical Design of Computers. 50p. 1972. 18.00x (ISBN 0-7190-0480-2, Pub. by Manchester U Pr England). State Mutual Bk.
Lavington, Simon. Early British Computers. (History of Computing). (Illus.). 140p. 1980. pap. 8.00 (ISBN 0-932376-08-8). Digital Pr.
LaViolette, Paul, ed. see Von Bertalanffy, Ludwig.
Lavitt, jt. auth. see McDowell.
La Vopa, Anthony J. Prussian Schoolteachers: Profession & Office, 1763-1848. LC 79-24873. 230p. 1980. 19.50x (ISBN 0-8078-1426-1). U of NC Pr.
Lavrin, Janko. Lermontov. 1959. pap. text ed. 3.25x (ISBN 0-391-02003-X). Humanities.
Lavrov, Peter. Historical Letters. Scanlan, James P., tr. 1967. 25.00x (ISBN 0-520-01136-8). U of Cal Pr.
Law, Averill M. & Kelton, David. Simulation Modeling & Analysis. (Illus.). 416p. 1981. text ed. 25.95 (ISBN 0-07-036696-9). McGraw.
Law, Beverly, ed. Cryogenics Handbook. 1980. text ed. 39.00 (ISBN 0-86103-021-4). Butterworths.
Law, Christopher M. British Regional Development Since World War I. LC 80-66425. 176p. 1980. 38.00 (ISBN 0-7153-7974-7). David & Charles.
Law, Donald. The Concise Herbal Encyclopedia. LC 73-87589. (Illus.). 266p. 1974. 7.95 o.p. (ISBN 0-312-16135-2). St Martin.
--The Concise Herbal Encyclopedia. LC 73-87589. (Illus.). 1976. pap. 4.95 o.p. (ISBN 0-312-16170-0). St Martin.
--Herbs for Health & Flavor. LC 76-28046. 1977. 5.95 o.p. (ISBN 0-312-36960-3). St Martin.
--How to Keep Your Hair On. 70p. 1968. pap. 4.00x (ISBN 0-8464-1025-7). Beekman Pubs.
--Starting Mountaineering & Rockclimbing. 1977. 10.50 (ISBN 0-7153-7322-6). David & Charles.
Law, Edmund. An Enquiry into the Ideas of Space & Time. Wellek, Rene, ed. LC 75-11230. (British Philosophers & Theologians of the 17th & 18th Century: Vol. 31). 1976. Repr. of 1734 ed. lib. bdg. 42.00 (ISBN 0-8240-1783-8). Garland Pub.
Law Enforcement. National Crime Surveys: National Sample, 1973-1978. LC 78-71979. 1979. 10.00 (ISBN 0-89138-991-1). ICPSR.
Law Enforcement Assistance Administration. National Crime Surveys: Cities Attitude Sub-Sample, 1972-1975. 1979. codebook 12.00 (ISBN 0-89138-970-9). ICPSR.
--National Crime Surveys: Cities, 1972-1975. LC 78-71978. 1978. codebook 12.00 (ISBN 0-89138-992-X). ICPSR.
--Public Image of Courts, Nineteen Seventy-Seven: General Public Data. LC 79-91248. 1980. 16.00 (ISBN 0-89138-962-8). ICPSR.
Law, Henry. The Gospel in Exodus. 1967. pap. 1.95 (ISBN 0-686-12516-9). Banner of Truth.
Law, Joy. Learning to Cook the Girl Way. pap. 4.50x o.p. (ISBN 0-392-06191-0, LTB). Soccer.
Law, Richard D. & Luther, Craig W. Rommel: A Narrative & Pictorial History. (Illus.). 368p. 1980. 17.95 (ISBN 0-912138-20-3). Bender Pub CA.
Law, Robin. The Oyo Empire: A West African Imperialism in the Era of the Atlantic Slave Trade. (Oxford Studies in African Matters). (Illus.). 1977. 48.00x (ISBN 0-19-822709-4). Oxford U Pr.
Law, T. S. & Berwick, Thurso, eds. The Socialist Poems of Hugh MacDiarmid. (Orig.). 1978. pap. 8.95 (ISBN 0-7100-8914-7). Routledge & Kegan.
Law, William. The Absolute Unlawfulness of the Stage Entertainment Fully Demonstrated. Bd. with The Stage Defended. Dennis, John; Law Outlaw'd: A Short Reply to Mr. Law's Long Declamation Against the Stage. LC 75-170493. (The English Stage Ser.: Vol. 49). lib. bdg. 50.00 (ISBN 0-8240-0632-1). Garland Pub.
--Freedom from a Self-Centered Life. Murray, Andrew, ed. LC 77-71426. 1977. pap. 2.25 (ISBN 0-87123-104-2, 200104). Bethany Fell.
--The Power of the Spirit. Murray, Andrew, ed. LC 76-57110. (Classics of Devotions Ser). 1977. pap. 2.50 (ISBN 0-87123-463-7, 200463). Bethany Fell.
--Spirit of Prayer & Spirit of Love. 1969. 13.95 (ISBN 0-227-67720-X). Attic Pr.
--Wholly for God. Murray, Andrew, ed. LC 76-6622. 336p. 1976. pap. 3.50 (ISBN 0-87123-602-8, 200602). Bethany Fell.
--William Law on Christian Perfection. 144p. 1981. pap. 2.95 (ISBN 0-87123-117-4, 210117). Bethany Fell.
Lawall, David B. Asher Brown Durand: His Art & Art Theory in Relations to His Times. LC 76-23635. (Outstanding Dissertations in the Fine Arts Ser.). 1978. lib. bdg. 97.00x (ISBN 0-8240-2704-3). Garland Pub.
Lawall, Sarah N. Critics of Consciousness: The Existential Structures of Literature. LC 68-25614. 1968. 15.00x (ISBN 0-674-17750-9). Harvard U Pr.
Lawden, D. F. Electromagnetism. (Problem Solvers Ser.). (Illus.). 1973. pap. text ed. 6.50x o.p. (ISBN 0-04-538002-3). Allen Unwin.
Lawder, Standish D. The Cubist Cinema. LC 72-96466. 1975. 20.00x (ISBN 0-8147-4956-9); pap. 12.00 (ISBN 0-8147-4957-7). NYU Pr.
Lawford, James P. Clive: Proconsul of India. 1976. text ed. 25.00x o.p. (ISBN 0-04-923067-0). Allen Unwin.
Lawhead, Terry. The Ferry Story. LC 78-16743. (Illus.). (gr. k-6). 1978. pap. 4.95 o.p. (ISBN 0-914718-33-9). Pacific Search.
Lawhead, Wendell H., jt. auth. see Farnsworth, Kirk E.
Lawhorne, Clifton O. The Supreme Court & Libel. (New Horizons in Journalism Ser.). 1981. 19.95 (ISBN 0-8093-0998-X). S Ill U Pr.
Lawler, Ann. The Substitute. LC 77-23303. (Illus.). 40p. (gr. k-4). 1977. 5.95 o.s.i. (ISBN 0-8193-0902-8, Four Winds); PLB 5.41 o.s.i. (ISBN 0-8193-0903-6). Schol Bk Serv.
Lawler, Donald L. Approaches to Science Fiction. LC 77-77995. (Illus.). 1978. pap. text ed. 10.50 (ISBN 0-395-25496-5); inst. manual 0.50 (ISBN 0-395-25497-3). HM.
Lawler, James. IQ, Heritability & Racism. 1978. 12.00 o.p. (ISBN 0-7178-0499-2); pap. 3.95 (ISBN 0-7178-0554-9). Intl Pub Co.
Lawler, James H. Patterns of Civilizations. LC 77-18670. 1978. pap. text ed. 6.75x (ISBN 0-8191-0431-0). U Pr of Amer.
Lawler, James J., jt. auth. see Spurrier, Robert L.
Lawler, James R. The Poet As Analyst: Essays on Paul Valery. 1974. 22.75x (ISBN 0-520-02450-8). U of Cal Pr.
Lawler, John. Book Auctions in England in the Seventeenth Century. LC 68-30614. 1968. Repr. of 1898 ed. 15.00 (ISBN 0-8103-3310-4). Gale.
Lawler, Louise. Untitled, Red, Blue, 2 vols. LC 78-59796. (Illus.). 1978. Set. pap. text ed. 7.95 (ISBN 0-931706-00-9). Vol. 1 (ISBN 0-931706-01-7). Vol. 2 (ISBN 0-931706-02-5). L Lawler.
Lawler, Marcella R., ed. Strategies for Planned Curricular Innovation. LC 78-106048. 1970. text ed. 9.25x (ISBN 0-8077-1667-7); pap. text ed. 6.00x (ISBN 0-8077-1666-9). Tchrs Coll.
Lawler, Thomas, tr. see Augustine, St.
Lawler, Traugott. The One & the Many in the Canterbury Tales. 209p. 1980. 17.50 (ISBN 0-208-01842-5, Archon). Shoe String.
Lawless, Agnes & Goodboy, Eadie. The Word. (Aglow Bible Study Bk.: No. E-4). (Illus.). 64p. (Orig.). 1980. pap. 1.95 (ISBN 0-930756-59-2, 4220-E4). Women's Aglow.
Lawless, David J. Organizational Behavior: The Psychology of Effective Management. 2nd ed. (Illus.). 1979. text ed. 19.95 (ISBN 0-13-640706-4). P-H.
Lawless, Emily. Grania: The Story of an Island. Wolff, Robert L., ed. (Ireland Nineteenth Century Fiction - Ser. Two: Vol. 73). 592p. 1979. lib. bdg. 32.00 (ISBN 0-8240-3522-4). Garland Pub.
--Hurrish: A Study. Wolff, Robert L., ed. (Ireland Nineteenth Century Fiction - Ser. Two: Vol. 71). 584p. 1979. lib. bdg. 32.00 (ISBN 0-8240-3520-8). Garland Pub.
--Maelcho: A Sixteenth-Century Narrative. Wolff, Robert L., ed. (Ireland Nineteenth Century Fiction - Ser. Two: Vol. 74). 672p. 1979. lib. bdg. 32.00 (ISBN 0-8240-3523-2). Garland Pub.
--Poems. Fallon, Padraic, ed. (Arts Council Ser). 1964. 4.25 (ISBN 0-85105-090-5). Dufour.
--Traits & Confidences. Wolff, Robert L., ed. (Ireland Nineteenth Century Fiction - Ser. Two: Vol. 75). 280p. 1979. lib. bdg. 32.00 (ISBN 0-8240-3524-0). Garland Pub.
--With Essex in Ireland. Wolff, Robert L., ed. (Ireland Nineteenth Century Fiction - Ser. Two: Vol. 72). 348p. 1979. lib. bdg. 32.00 (ISBN 0-8240-3521-6). Garland Pub.
Lawless, Joann. The Complete Book of Women's Sports. LC 78-22816. (Illus.). 512p. 1981. 17.95 (ISBN 0-385-14175-0, Anchor Pr); pap. 10.95 (ISBN 0-385-17199-4). Doubleday.
Lawless, Joann, jt. auth. see Brady, Frank.
Lawless, Joann A. Mysteries of the Mind. LC 77-10726. (Great Unsolved Mysteries Ser.). (Illus.). (gr. 4-5). 1977. PLB 9.65 (ISBN 0-8172-1066-0). Raintree Pubs.
--Strange Stories of Life. LC 77-10866. (Great Unsolved Mysteries Ser.). (Illus.). (gr. 4-5). 1977. PLB 9.65 (ISBN 0-8172-1062-8). Raintree Pubs.
Lawless, P. Britain's Inner Cities. 1981. text ed. 25.85 (ISBN 0-06-318184-3, Pub. by Har-Row Ltd England); pap. text ed. 13.10 (ISBN 0-06-318185-1). Har-Row.
Lawless, R. I., jt. ed. see Blake, G. H.
Lawless, Richard. Algeria. (World Bibliographical Ser.: No. 19). 1981. write for info. (ISBN 0-903450-32-1). Abc-Clio.
--The Middle East in the Twentieth Century. (Illus.). 96p. 1980. 16.95 (ISBN 0-7134-2494-X, Pub. by Batsford England). David & Charles.
Lawley, Francis E. The Growth of Collective Economy, 2 vols. (Studies in International Economics: No. 1). Repr. of 1938 ed. Set. lib. bdg. 57.50x (ISBN 0-87991-850-0). Porcupine Pr.
Lawley, K., ed. Potential Energy Surfaces. (Advances in Chemical Physics: Vol. 42). 1980. 90.25 (ISBN 0-471-27633-2, Pub. by Wiley-Interscience). Wiley.
Lawlis, Frank, jt. auth. see Achterberg, Jeanne.
Lawlon, Timothy E. Handbook to the Families & Orders of Living Mammals. 2nd ed. (Illus.). 1979. 9.40x (ISBN 0-916422-16-X). Mad River.
Lawlor, Edward E., III. Pay & Organization Development. 230p. 1981. pap. text ed. 6.95 (ISBN 0-201-03990-7). A-W.
Lawlor, Elizabeth P. Research in Science Education: 1953 Through 1957. LC 70-112927. 1970. text ed. 12.75x (ISBN 0-8077-1669-3). Tchrs Coll.
Lawlor, John, ed. New University. LC 68-8250. 1968. 15.00x (ISBN 0-231-03217-X). Columbia U Pr.
Lawlor, Peter, ed. see Aigner, Hal, et al.
Lawlor, Steven. BASIC. 1979. pap. text ed. 11.95x (ISBN 0-534-00694-9). Wadsworth Pub.
Lawman, Anthony. A Private Truce. 1981. 11.95 (ISBN 0-671-25408-1). S&S.
Lawn, B. R. & Wilshaw, T. R. Fracture of Brittle Solids. LC 74-12970. (Solid State Science Ser). (Illus.). 160p. 1975. 47.00 (ISBN 0-521-20654-5); pap. 17.50x (ISBN 0-521-09952-8). Cambridge U Pr.
Lawn, Brian, ed. The Prose Salernitan Questions: An Anonymous Collection Dealing with Science & Medicine Written by an Englishman Circa 1200, with an Appendix of Ten Related Collections. (British Academy: Auctores Britannici Medii Aevi: Vol. V). 1979. 89.00x (ISBN 0-19-725978-2). Oxford U Pr.
Lawn, Martin. Rethinking Curriculum Studies. 224p. 27.95 (ISBN 0-470-27097-7). Halsted Pr.
--Rethinking Curriculum Studies: A Radical Approach. 224p. 1981. 27.95 (ISBN 0-470-27097-7). Halsted Pr.
Lawrence. Growth in Animals. LC 79-41574. (SAFS). 1980. 52.95 (ISBN 0-408-10638-7). Butterworths.
Lawrence, Alfred. Columbo No. 1. 1975. pap. 1.25 o.p. (ISBN 0-445-08382-4). Popular Lib.
Lawrence, Berta. Somerset Legends. 11.95 (ISBN 0-7153-6185-6). David & Charles.
Lawrence, Bonnie S., ed. see Hay, Keith, et al.
Lawrence, Bonnie S., ed. see Johnson, Fred.
Lawrence, Bonnie S., ed. see LaBastille, Anne.
Lawrence, Brother Of The Resurrection see Delaney, John J.
Lawrence, Bruce. Notes from a Distant Flute. LC 78-62007. 1979. 8.00 (ISBN 0-87773-735-5). Great Eastern.
Lawrence, Carl. Majken. 192p. 1981. pap. 4.95 (ISBN 0-8407-5762-X). Nelson.
Lawrence, Carol & Zimmer, Norma. Top Entertainers Are Born Again. LC 77-78464. (Lifeline Ser.). pap. 0.95 o.p. (ISBN 0-88419-142-7). Creation Hse.
Lawrence, Cherrie M. & Anzaldua, Gloria, eds. This Bridge Called My Back: Writings by Radical Women of Color. (Orig.). 1981. pap. price not set (ISBN 0-930436-10-5). Persephone.
Lawrence, Clifford H., ed. English Church & the Papacy in the Middle Ages. 1965. 20.00 o.p. (ISBN 0-8232-0645-9). Fordham.
Lawrence, D. H. Aaron's Rod. 1976. pap. 2.95 (ISBN 0-14-000755-5). Penguin.
--The Boy in the Bush. 1981. pap. 3.95 (ISBN 0-14-001935-9). Penguin.
--The Escaped Cock. Lacy, Gerald M., ed. 175p. 1976. pap. 4.00 (ISBN 0-87685-170-7). Black Sparrow.
--Lady Chatterly's Lover. 384p. (Orig.). 1981. pap. 2.50 (ISBN 0-553-13530-9). Bantam.
--Letters to Thomas & Adele Seltzer. Lacy, Gerald M., ed. (Illus.). 290p. (Orig.). 1976. 14.00 (ISBN 0-87685-225-8); pap. 6.00 (ISBN 0-87685-224-X). Black Sparrow.
--Sons & Lovers. Salgado, Gamini, ed. LC 75-127570. (Casebook Ser). 1970. pap. text ed. 2.50 o.s.i. (ISBN 0-87695-041-1). Aurora Pubs.
--Sons & Lovers. 1976. pap. 2.95 (ISBN 0-14-004217-2). Penguin.
Lawrence, D. H., jt. ed. see Schorer, Mark.
Lawrence, Edgar D. Focus on Deafness: Selected Readings on Deafness for Paraprofessionals. 1978. pap. text ed. 10.50x (ISBN 0-8191-0389-6). U Pr of Amer.
Lawrence, G. Allen, jt. auth. see Harley, Randall K.
Lawrence, G. H., ed. Adanson: The Bicentennial of Michel Adanson's "Familles des plantes", 2 vols. (Illus.). 1965. Vol. 1. 19.00 (ISBN 0-913196-23-1); Vol. 2. 15.00 (ISBN 0-686-65641-5); Vol. 1. soft cover 17.00 (ISBN 0-913196-25-8); Vol. 2. soft cover 13.00 (ISBN 0-913196-26-6). Hunt Inst Botanical.
Lawrence, G. H., et al. Catalogue of the Strandell Collection at the Hunt Institute for Botanical Documentation. 1000p. 1980. 180.00 (ISBN 0-913196-21-5). Hunt Inst Botanical.
Lawrence, George see Tocqueville, Alexis de.
Lawrence, George, tr. see De Tocqueville, Alexis C.
Lawrence, Henry W. The Not-Quite Puritans: Some Genial Follies & Peculiar Frailities of Our Revered New England Ancestors. (Illus.). 1975. Repr. of 1928 ed. 18.00 (ISBN 0-8103-3993-5). Gale.
Lawrence, Herbert. The Contemplative Man; or, the History of Christopher Crab, Esq., of North Wales, 1771, 2 vols. in 1. (The Flowering of the Novel, 1740-1775 Ser: Vol. 96). 1974. lib. bdg. 50.00 (ISBN 0-8240-1195-3). Garland Pub.
--The Life & Adventures of Common Sense, 1769, 2 vols. in 1. LC 74-23918. (Novel in England, 1700-1775 Ser). 1974. lib. bdg. 50.00 (ISBN 0-8240-1187-2). Garland Pub.
Lawrence, Ian, jt. ed. see Burnett, Michael.
Lawrence, Irene. Linguistics & Theology: The Significance of Noam Chomsky for Theological Construction. LC 80-24210. (ATLA Monograph: No. 16). 214p. 1980. 12.50 (ISBN 0-8108-1347-5). Scarecrow.
Lawrence, J. Dennis. Catalog of Special Plane Curves. LC 72-80280. (Illus.). 218p. 1972. pap. text ed. 4.50 (ISBN 0-486-60288-5). Dover.
Lawrence, J. F., jt. auth. see Smith, R. F.
Lawrence, J. S. Rheumatism in Populations. (Illus.). 1977. 70.00x (ISBN 0-433-19070-1). Intl Ideas.
Lawrence, Jerome & Lee, Robert E. The Incomparable Max. 1972. pap. 2.45 o.p. (ISBN 0-8090-1227-8, Mermaid). Hill & Wang.
Lawrence, John F. The Ciid Beetles of California: Coleoptera, Ciid. (California Insect Survey Bulletin, Vol. 17). 1974. pap. 6.25x (ISBN 0-520-09489-1). U of Cal Pr.
Lawrence, John H., et al. Radioisotopes & Radiation. LC 69-20423. (Illus.). 1969. pap. text ed. 3.00 (ISBN 0-486-62296-7). Dover.
Lawrence, John R., ed. see Society of the Plastics Industry.
Lawrence, Joseph, ed. see Knorr, Susan.

Lawrence, Joseph, ed. see Mundy, Mary-Ruth C.
Lawrence, Joseph, ed. see Runyon, Mary B.
Lawrence, Joy & Ferguson, John. A Musician's Guide to Church Music. 280p. 1981. 16.95 (ISBN 0-8298-0424-2). Pilgrim NY.
Lawrence, Louise. The Earth Witch. LC 80-8431. 224p. (YA) (gr. 7 up). 1981. 9.95 (ISBN 0-06-023751-1, HarpJ); PLB 9.89g (ISBN 0-06-023752-X). Har-Row.
Lawrence, M. J. & Mason, K. L. Key to Advanced Spanish Course. LC 78-122008. 1970. 4.80 (ISBN 0-08-016084-0); pap. 3.85 (ISBN 0-08-016083-2). Pergamon.
Lawrence, Marjorie K. Misty Meadows. 96p. 1981. 6.00 (ISBN 0-682-49742-8). Exposition.
Lawrence, Mary C. Captain's Best Mate: The Journal of Mary Chipman Lawrence on the Whaler Addison, 1856-1860. Garner, Stanton, ed. LC 66-19585. (Illus.). 311p. 1966. 15.00 (ISBN 0-87057-099-4, Pub. by Brown U Pr). Univ Pr of New England.
Lawrence, Michael. How to Read Your Opponent's Cards: The Bridge Experts' Way to Locate Missing High Cards. LC 73-7820. 176p. 1973. 7.95 o.p. (ISBN 0-13-431122-1); pap. 3.95 (ISBN 0-13-431114-0). P-H.
--Surrealism in Perspective. LC 79-51630. (Themes in Art Ser.). (Illus., Orig.). Date not set. pap. 7.95 o.p. (ISBN 0-910386-54-4, Pub. by Cleveland Mus Art). Ind U Pr. Postponed.
--Working with Wood. LC 78-65631. (Illus.). 1979. 11.95 (ISBN 0-690-01810-X, TYC-T); pap. 5.95 (ISBN 0-690-01820-7, TYC-T). T Y Crowell.
Lawrence, Mildred. No Slipper for Cinderella. LC 65-17990. (gr. 7 up). 1965. 5.25 o.p. (ISBN 0-15-257575-8, HJ). HarBraceJ.
--One Hundred White Horses. LC 53-7866. (Illus.). (gr. 4-6). 1953. 5.25 o.p. (ISBN 0-15-258675-X, HJ). HarBraceJ.
--Sand in Her Shoes. LC 49-10407. (Illus.). (gr. 4-7). 1949. 4.95 o.p. (ISBN 0-15-270129-X, HJ). HarBraceJ.
--Treasure & the Song. LC 66-10203. (gr. 7 up). 1966. 4.95 o.p. (ISBN 0-15-289950-2, HJ). HarBraceJ.
Lawrence, Nelda R. Writing Communications in Business & Industry. 2nd ed. 176p. 1974. pap. text ed. 10.95 (ISBN 0-13-970491-4). P-H.
Lawrence, Nelda R. & Tebeaux, Elizabeth. Writing Communications in Business & Industry. 3rd ed. (Illus.). 272p. 1981. 12.95 (ISBN 0-13-970467-1). P-H.
Lawrence, P. & Meggitt, M. J., eds. Gods, Ghosts & Men in Melanesia. 1965. pap. 12.95x (ISBN 0-19-550147-0). Oxford U Pr.
Lawrence, P. A. Insect Development. LC 76-8196. (Royal Entomological Society of London Symposium Ser.). 1976. 30.95 (ISBN 0-470-15098-X). Halsted Pr.
Lawrence, Patricia A., jt. auth. see Steiner, George.
Lawrence, Paul, jt. auth. see Brown, Robert M.
Lawrence, Paul A. In Praise of Chocolate. (Illus.). 60p. (Orig.). 1981. pap. 6.95 (ISBN 0-938034-03-0). PAL Pr.
--Lomi-Lomi Hawaiian Massage. LC 80-83756. (Positive Health Ser.). (Illus.). 80p. 1981. 12.95 (ISBN 0-938034-01-4); pap. 5.95 (ISBN 0-938034-02-2). PAL Pr.
Lawrence, Paul R. & Lorsch, Jay W. Developing Organizations: Diagnosis & Action. LC 78-93985. (Organization Development Ser). (Orig.). 1969. pap. text ed. 6.50 (ISBN 0-201-04204-5). A-W.
--Organization & Environment: Managing Differentiation & Integration. 1969. pap. text ed. 8.50x (ISBN 0-256-00314-9). Irwin.
Lawrence, Paul R., jt. auth. see Lorsch, Jay W.
Lawrence, Paul R., jt. ed. see Dalton, Gene W.
Lawrence, Paul R., et al, eds. Organizational Behavior & Administration: Cases & Readings. 3rd ed. 1976. text ed. 19.50x (ISBN 0-256-01760-3). Irwin.
Lawrence, R. D. Paddy: A Naturalist's Story of an Orphaned Beaver. 1978. pap. 1.95 (ISBN 0-380-42580-7, 42580). Avon.
--The Study of Life: A Naturalist's View. (Illus.). 43p. 1980. pap. 1.50 (ISBN 0-913098-37-X). Myrin Institute.
--The Zoo That Never Was. LC 80-18956. (Illus.). 304p. 1981. 12.95 (ISBN 0-03-056811-0). HR&W.
Lawrence, Richard, tr. The Book of Enoch. LC 80-65736. 96p. 1980. pap. 3.00 (ISBN 0-934666-06-7). Artisan Sales.
Lawrence, Richard D. & Record, K. Jeffrey. U. S. Force Structure in NATO: An Alternative. (Studies in Defense Policy). 136p. 1974. pap. 3.95 (ISBN 0-8157-5171-0). Brookings.
Lawrence, Richard H. The Paduans, Medals by Giovanni Cavino. (Illus.). pap. 5.00 (ISBN 0-916710-74-2). Obol Intl.
Lawrence, Robert. Arms Control & Disarmament. LC 72-88750. (Burgess Critical Issues in Political Science Ser.). 1973. pap. text ed. 2.95 o.p. (ISBN 0-8087-1222-5). Burgess.
--New Dimensions to Energy Policy. LC 78-389. (Policy Studies Organization Ser.). 1979. 22.95 (ISBN 0-669-02172-5). Lexington Bks.
Lawrence, Robert M. & Heisler, Martin O., eds. International Energy Policy. LC 79-4748. (A Policy Studies Organization Book). 240p. 1980. 23.95 (ISBN 0-669-02929-7). Lexington Bks.
Lawrence, Roger, jt. auth. see Dell, Sidney.
Lawrence, Roger, jt. ed. see Kenen, Peter B.
Lawrence, Roy. Christian Healing Rediscovered. LC 80-7470. 128p. (Orig.). 1980. pap. 3.95 (ISBN 0-87784-621-9). Inter-Varsity.
Lawrence, Roy T. The Two Basic Psychological Forces Prompting Men to Action & How to Utilize Them Effectively. (Essential Knowledge Library Bk.). (Illus.). 1979. 6.00 (ISBN 0-89266-158-5). Am Classical Coll Pr.
Lawrence, Ruth A. Breast Feeding: A Practical Guide for the Medical Profession. LC 79-17277. (Illus.). 1979. pap. text ed. 17.50 (ISBN 0-8016-2897-0). Mosby.
Lawrence, Steven C. The Naked Range. Orig. Title: Thruway West. 1976. pap. 0.95 o.p. (ISBN 0-685-69152-7, LB354NK, Leisure Bks). Nordon Pubns.
--Slattery Stands Alone. (Slattery Ser.). (Orig.). 1976. pap. 0.95 o.p. (ISBN 0-685-64017-5, LB337NK, Leisure Bks). Nordon Pubns.
--Slattery's Gun Says No. 1975. pap. 0.95 o.p. (ISBN 0-685-52942-8, LB258NK, Leisure Bks). Nordon Pubns.
Lawrence, Vera B. Music for Patriots, Politicans & Presidents. (Illus.). 480p. 1975. 35.00 o.s.i. (ISBN 0-02-569390-5). Macmillan.
Lawrenson, Helen. Stranger at the Party: A Memoir. 1975. 8.95 o.p. (ISBN 0-394-48900-4). Random.
Lawrie, Norman & Veitch, Helen. Timetabling & Organization in Secondary Schools. (General Ser.). 160p. 1975. pap. text ed. 13.75x (ISBN 0-85633-057-4, NFER). Humanities.
Lawrie, R. A. Meat Science. 2nd ed. 1974. text ed. 38.00 o.p. (ISBN 0-08-017133-8); pap. text ed. 17.05 o.p. (ISBN 0-08-017811-1). Pergamon.
Lawrie, W. H. All Fur Flies & How to Dress Them. LC 68-14407. (Illus.). 1968. 7.95 o.p. (ISBN 0-498-06796-3). A S Barnes.
Lawry, Antje, tr. see Balthasar, Hans Urs Von.
Lawrynowicz, J., ed. Analytic Functions Kozubnik 1979: Proceedings. (Lecture Notes in Mathematics: Vol. 798). 476p. 1980. pap. 27.00 (ISBN 0-387-09985-9). Springer-Verlag.
Laws, Edward A. Aquatic Pollution. LC 80-23311. (Environmental Science & Technology Ser.). 600p. 1981. 35.00 (ISBN 0-471-05797-5, Pub. by Wiley-Interscience). Wiley.
Laws, Peter. A Guide to the National Trust in Devon & Cornwall. LC 77-91765. (Illus.). 1978. 14.95 (ISBN 0-7153-7581-4). David & Charles.
Laws, Peter, jt. auth. see Todd, A. C.
Laws, Phe. International Gourmet Cooking with Microwave. LC 76-12163. 1976. pap. 5.95 (ISBN 0-8256-3811-9, Hidden Hse). Music Sales.
--Vegetable Cookery. 256p. 1980. pap. 6.95 (ISBN 0-8256-3828-3, Quick Fox). Music Sales.
Laws, Sophie. The Epistle of James. LC 80-8349. (Harper's New Testament Commentaries Ser.). 288p. 1981. 14.95 (ISBN 0-06-064918-6, HarpR). Har-Row.
Lawson. Terrific Gifts to Make & Give. (gr. 7-12). 1980. pap. 1.25 (ISBN 0-590-30885-8, Schol Pap). Schol Bk Serv.
Lawson, Alan, jt. auth. see Lock, Fred.
Lawson, Alan, ed. see Baynton, Barbara.
Lawson, Andrew. Discover Unexpected London. LC 77-82736. (Illus.). 1978. 8.95 (ISBN 0-8467-0369-6, Pub. by Two Continents). Hippocrene Bks.
Lawson, Archie. Freight Trains West. (Illus.). 150p. (Orig.). 1980. 9.95 (ISBN 0-9604806-0-9); pap. 5.95 (ISBN 0-9604806-1-7). Lucas Pubs CA.
Lawson, Audrey & Lawson, Herbert. Man Who Freed the Slaves: The Story of William Wilberforce. (gr. 7 up). 4.95 (ISBN 0-571-05061-1). Transatlantic.
Lawson, Cecil C. P. A History of the Uniforms of the British Army, Vols. 1-2, 4-5. Vol. 1. 18.00 o.p. (ISBN 0-498-09865-6); Vol. 2. 18.00 o.p. (ISBN 0-498-06080-2); Vol. 3. 18.00 o.p. (ISBN 0-498-01529-7); Vol. 4. 18.00 o.p. (ISBN 0-498-07562-1); Vol. 5. 18.00 o.p. (ISBN 0-498-06692-4). A S Barnes.
Lawson, Charles L. & Hanson, Richard J. Solving Least Squares Problems. (Illus.). 384p. 1974. 22.95 (ISBN 0-13-822585-0). P-H.
Lawson, D. Photomicrography. 1973. 69.50 (ISBN 0-12-439750-6). Acad Pr.
Lawson, Don. The Changing Face of the Constitution. LC 78-11570. (gr. 7 up). 1979. PLB 7.45 s&l (ISBN 0-531-02923-9). Watts.
--Democracy. LC 78-1860. (First Bks). (Illus.). (gr. 4-6). 1978. PLB 6.45 s&l (ISBN 0-531-01487-8). Watts.
--Education Careers. (Career Concise Guides Ser.). (Illus.). (gr. 7-12). 1977. lib. bdg. 6.45 s&l (ISBN 0-531-01281-6). Watts.
--F D R's New Deal. LC 78-4775. (Illus.). (gr. 7 up). 1979. 8.95 (ISBN 0-690-03953-0, TYC-J). T Y Crowell.
--The Kennedy Brothers. 160p. (gr. 8-12). 1981. 8.95 (ISBN 0-416-30731-0). Methuen Inc. Postponed.
--Morocco, Algeria, Tunisia & Libya. (First Bks). (Illus.). (gr. 4-6). 1978. PLB 6.45 s&l (ISBN 0-531-02233-1). Watts.
Lawson, Douglas. Fund Raising by Parent-Citizen Groups. 1976. pap. 3.50 (ISBN 0-934460-04-3). NCCE.
Lawson, Douglas E. Wisdom & Education. LC 61-11660. 168p. 1961. 4.95x (ISBN 0-8093-0048-6). S Ill U Pr.
Lawson, Douglas E. & Lean, Arthur E., eds. John Dewey & the World View. LC 64-11170. 1964. lib. bdg. 6.00x o.p. (ISBN 0-8093-0130-X). S Ill U Pr.
--John Dewey & the World View. LC 64-11170. (Arcturus Books Paperbacks). 168p. 1966. pap. 2.25 (ISBN 0-8093-0224-1). S Ill U Pr.
Lawson, Fred. Hotels, Motels & Condominiums: Design, Planning & Maintenance. (Illus.). 1976. 49.95 (ISBN 0-8436-2109-5). CBI Pub.
Lawson, Frederick H., jt. auth. see Keir, David L.
Lawson, George. Esther. LC 80-8072. (Kregal Timeless Classics Ser.). 1981. 9.95 (ISBN 0-8254-3124-7). Kregel.
--Exposition of Proverbs, 2 vols. in 1. LC 80-8070. (Kregal Timeless Classics Ser.). 796p. 1981. Repr. of 1810 ed. 14.95 (ISBN 0-8254-3123-9). Kregel.
--The History of Joseph. 7.95 o.p. (ISBN 0-686-12473-1). Banner of Truth.
--Joseph & His Brethren in Genesis. LC 80-8071. 1981. 12.95 (ISBN 0-8254-3122-0). Kregel.
Lawson, Harry O., et al. Personnel Administration in the Courts. (A Westview Special Study). 1979. lib. bdg. 32.50x (ISBN 0-89158-588-5). Westview.
Lawson, Helen. How to Make Good Curries. (Illus.). 80p. 1980. 11.95 (ISBN 0-600-34408-8). Transatlantic.
Lawson, Herbert, jt. auth. see Lawson, Audrey.
Lawson, J. D. The Physics of Charged-Particle Beams. (International Series of Monographs on Physics). (Illus.). 1977. 67.00x (ISBN 0-19-851278-3). Oxford U Pr.
Lawson, J. W. & Smith, Ballard. Managements Complete Guide to Employee Benefits. 259p. 1980. 69.50 (ISBN 0-85013-119-7). Dartnell Corp.
Lawson, James. The Girl Watcher. 1977. pap. 1.95 o.s.i. (ISBN 0-446-89330-7). Warner Bks.
Lawson, James G., ed. World's Best Loved Poems. 1927. 9.95 (ISBN 0-06-065210-1, HarpR). Har-Row.
Lawson, Jennifer A. A Right to Love. 64p. 1980. 5.00 (ISBN 0-682-49651-0). Exposition.
Lawson, Jill, tr. Gueri Du Cancer. (French Bks.). (Fr.). 1979. 1.85 (ISBN 0-686-28820-3). Life Pubs Intl.
--Sanado De Cancer. (Spanish Bks.). 1979. 1.40 (ISBN 0-8297-0532-5). Life Pubs Intl.
Lawson, Joan. Teaching Young Dancers: Muscular Coordination in Classical Ballet. LC 75-15369. (Illus.). 1975. 16.95 (ISBN 0-87830-144-5). Theatre Arts.
Lawson, John. The High Hills. (Illus.). 220p. (Orig.). 1981. pap. 4.95 (ISBN 0-938658-01-8). West SW Pub Co.
--Medieval Education & the Reformation. LC 67-18836. (Students Library of Education). 1967. pap. text ed. 3.00x (ISBN 0-7100-4209-4). Humanities.
Lawson, John D., ed. American State Trials: 1659-1920, 17 vols. LC 74-182150. 1972. Repr. of 1914 ed. Set. lib. bdg. 295.00 (ISBN 0-8420-0510-2). Scholarly Res Inc.
Lawson, K., ed. see Jones, Peter.
Lawson, K., ed. see Sommer, Elyse & Sommer, Mike.
Lawson, Ken, intro. by. Radiation Curing V: A Look to the 80's. LC 80-52816. (Illus.). 544p. 1980. pap. text ed. 55.00 (ISBN 0-87263-059-5). SME.
Lawson, Kenneth, jt. auth. see Murdock, Carol V.
Lawson, LeRoy. The Family of God: The Meaning of Church Membership. LC 80-53497. 64p. (Orig.). 1981. pap. 1.50 (ISBN 0-87239-432-8, 39970). Standard Pub.
--The New Testament Church Then & Now. (Orig.). 1981. pap. 3.95 (ISBN 0-87239-443-3, 88585). Standard Pub.
Lawson, Lewis A., ed. Kierkegaard's Presence in Contemporary American Life: Essays from Various Disciplines. LC 76-142237. 1971. 10.00 (ISBN 0-8108-0358-5). Scarecrow.
Lawson, Maron. Maggie Flying Bird. LC 74-6551. (Illus.). 160p. (gr. 7 up). 1974. 6.75 o.p. (ISBN 0-688-21825-3); PLB 6.96 (ISBN 0-688-31825-8). Morrow.
Lawson, Richard H. Edith Wharton. LC 77-40. (Modern Literature Ser.). 1977. 10.95 (ISBN 0-8044-2496-9). Ungar.
Lawson, Robert. Ben & Me. (gr. 3-6). 1973. pap. 1.50 (ISBN 0-440-42038-5, YB). Dell.
--Mr. Revere & I. (gr. 3-6). 1973. pap. 1.25 (ISBN 0-440-45897-8, YB). Dell.
--Principles & Methods of Social Psychology. 3rd ed. (Illus.). 750p. 1976. text ed. 13.95x (ISBN 0-19-501850-8). Oxford U Pr.
--Rabbit Hill. (Illus.). (gr. 4-6). 1944. PLB 8.95 (ISBN 0-670-58675-7). Viking Pr.
--Rabbit Hill. (Illus.). (gr. 1-3). 1977. pap. 1.75 (ISBN 0-14-031010-X, Puffin). Penguin.
Lawson, Robert B., jt. auth. see Gulick, W. Lawrence.
Lawson, Roger, jt. ed. see George, Vic.
Lawson, Steven F. Black Ballots: Voting Rights in the South 1944-1969. LC 76-18886. (Contemporary American History Ser.). 1976. 25.00x (ISBN 0-231-03978-6); pap. 10.00x (ISBN 0-231-08352-1). Columbia U Pr.
Lawson, T. V. Wind Effects on Buildings: Vol. 1, Design Applicatons. (Illus.). xii, 344p. 1980. 55.00x (ISBN 0-85334-887-1). Burgess-Intl Ideas.
--Wind Effects on Buildings: Volume 2--Statistics & Meteorology. (Illus.). xii, 160p. 1980. 30.00x (ISBN 0-85334-893-6). Burgess-Intl Ideas.
Lawson, Ted. Thirty Seconds Over Tokyo. LC 53-6522. (Landmark Bks.). (Illus.). 208p. (gr. 5-9). 1981. pap. 2.95 (ISBN 0-394-84698-2). Random.
Lawson, Ted, jt. auth. see Considine, Bob.
Lawson, Tom E., jt. auth. see Wentling, Tim L.
Lawson-Wood, D. & Lawson-Wood, J. Acupuncture Handbook. 6.00 o.p. (ISBN 0-685-36226-4). Weiser.
--Acupuncture Vitality & Revival Points. 56p. 1975. 6.00x (ISBN 0-8464-0990-9). Beekman Pubs.
--First Aid at Your Fingertips. 56p. 1976. pap. 4.00x (ISBN 0-8464-1009-5). Beekman Pubs.
--Five Elements of Acupuncture & Chinese Massage. 96p. 1976. 8.95x (ISBN 0-8464-1010-9). Beekman Pubs.
--Glowing Health Through Diet & Posture. 62p. 1973. pap. 2.50x (ISBN 0-686-68110-X). Beekman Pubs.
--Progressive Vitality & Dynamic Posture. 88p. 1977. 12.00x (ISBN 0-8464-1043-5). Beekman Pubs.
Lawson-Wood, D., jt. auth. see Lawson-Wood, J.
Lawson-Wood, J. & Lawson-Wood, D. Acupuncture Handbook. 141p. 1973. 6.75x (ISBN 0-8464-0989-5). Beekman Pubs.
Lawson-Wood, J., jt. auth. see Lawson-Wood, D.
Lawther, John D. The Learning & Performance of Physical Skills. 2nd ed. (Illus.). 1977. text ed. 12.95 (ISBN 0-13-527325-0). P-H.
Lawton, A. T. A Window in the Sky. 1979. 19.25 (ISBN 0-08-024663-X). Pergamon.
Lawton, Anna. Vadim Shershenevich. 1981. 15.00 (ISBN 0-88233-681-9). Ardis Pubs.
Lawton, Ben, ed. see Buscombe, et al.
Lawton, Ben, ed. see Glasser, et al.
Lawton, Denis. Class, Culture & the Curriculum. (Students Library of Education). 1975. 12.75x o.s.i. (ISBN 0-7100-8053-0); pap. 7.00 (ISBN 0-7100-8054-9). Routledge & Kegan.
--Education & Social Justice. LC 74-31568. (Sage Studies in Social & Educational Change: Vol 7). 1977. 18.00x (ISBN 0-8039-9946-1); pap. 9.95x (ISBN 0-8039-9867-8). Sage.
Lawton, Denis, jt. auth. see Gordon, Peter.
Lawton, Denis, et al. Theory & Practice of Curriculum Studies. (Education Bks). 1978. 22.00x (ISBN 0-7100-0028-6); pap. 8.95 (ISBN 0-7100-0029-4). Routledge & Kegan.
Lawton, M. Murray, et al. Lawton's & Foy's Textbook for Medical Assistants. 4th ed. LC 80-15524. (Illus.). 456p. 1980. text ed. 17.95 (ISBN 0-8016-2893-8). Mosby.
Lawton, M. Powell. Environment & Aging. LC 79-26816. (Social Gerontology Ser.). (Orig.). 1980. pap. text ed. 7.95 (ISBN 0-8185-0378-5). Brooks-Cole.
--Planning & Managing Housing for the Elderly. LC 74-28099. 304p. 1975. 32.50 (ISBN 0-471-51894-8, Pub. by Wiley-Interscience). Wiley.
Lawton, Richard. A World of Movies: Seventy Years of Film History. (Illus.). 384p. 1974. 25.00 o.s.i. (ISBN 0-440-08586-1). Delacorte.
Lawyer, Kenneth, jt. auth. see Baumback, Clifford M.
Lawyers & Judges Publishing Staff. About Divorce: Eighty-Two Questions & Answers. rev. ed. 1978. pap. 0.95 (ISBN 0-88450-052-7, 6110-B). Lawyers & Judges.
--About Your Deposition: Ninety-Five Questions & Answers. rev. ed. 1979. pap. 0.95 (ISBN 0-88450-051-9, 6109-B). Lawyers & Judges.
Lawyers Co-Op Editorial Staff. Medical Malpractice: ALR 20 Cases & Annotations, 3 vols. LC 70-1405. 1966. 105.00 (ISBN 0-686-14517-8). Lawyers Co-Op.
Lawyers Co-Operative Publishing Company Staff. Decisions of the United States Supreme Court: 1963-64, 1964-65, 1965-66, 1966-67, 1967-68, 1968-69, 1969-70, 1970-71, 1971-72, 1972-73, 1973-74, 1974-75, 1975-76, 1976-77, 1977-78, 1978-79, 1979-80, 1980-81, 18 vols. 25.00 ea.; 376.00 set (ISBN 0-686-28514-X). Lawyers Co-Op.

Lax, Melvin. Symmetry Principles in Solid State & Molecular Physics. LC 74-1215. 592p. 1974. 26.95 o.p. (ISBN 0-471-51903-0, Pub. by Wiley-Interscience); pap. 23.95x (ISBN 0-471-51904-9). Wiley.

Lax, Peter D., ed. Mathematical Aspects of Production & Distribution of Energy. LC 77-7174. (Proceedings of Symposia in Applied Mathematics: No. 21). 1979. Repr. of 1977 ed. with corrections 12.80 (ISBN 0-8218-0121-X, PSAPM-21). Am Math.

Lay, Arthur H. Brief Sketch of the History of Political Parties in Japan. Bd. with Political Ideas of Modern Japan: An Interpretation Studies in Japanese Law & Government. Kowakami, Kiyoshi K. 461p. 1979. Repr. of 1902 ed. 22.00 (ISBN 0-89093-222-0). U Pubns Amer.

Lay, Beirne, Jr. & Bartlett, Sy. Twelve O'Clock High. LC 80-16525. (Great Classic Stories of World War II Ser.). 1980. pap. 5.95 (ISBN 0-396-07867-2). Dodd.

Lay, Colin, jt. auth. see Broyles, Robert.

Lay, Margaret Z. & Dopyera, John E. Becoming a Teacher of Young Children. 1977. text ed. 15.95x (ISBN 0-669-99796-X). Heath.

Lay, N., jt. auth. see Fassler, D.

Layamon. Brut, Vol. 1. Brook, George L. & Leslie, R. F., eds. (Early English Text Society Ser.). 1963. 36.00x (ISBN 0-19-722250-1). Oxford U Pr.

Layard, John. A Celtic Quest: Soul & Sexuality in Individuation. (Seminar Ser.). 220p. 1975. 12.00 o.p. (ISBN 0-88214-110-4). Spring Pubns.

--The Virgin Archetype. (Dunquin Ser.). (Orig.). 1973. pap. 6.50 o.p. (ISBN 0-88214-205-4). Spring Pubns.

Laycock, Frank. Gifted Children. 1979. pap. text ed. 8.95x (ISBN 0-673-15142-5). Scott F.

Laycock, George. Autumn of the Eagle. LC 73-1368. (Illus.). 256p. 1973. 6.95 o.p. (ISBN 0-684-13413-6, ScribT). Scribner.

--Bats in the Night. LC 80-25834. (Illus.). 64p. (gr. 1-5). 1981. 9.95 (ISBN 0-590-07653-1, Four Winds). Schol Bk Serv.

--Beyond the Arctic Circle. LC 77-15844. (Illus.). 128p. (gr. 5-9). 1978. 7.95 (ISBN 0-590-07481-4, Four Winds). Schol Bk Serv.

--Caves. LC 76-15194. (Illus.). 112p. (gr. 5-9). 1976. 6.95 (ISBN 0-590-07392-3, Four Winds). Schol Bk Serv.

--Deer Hunter's Bible. rev. ed. LC 76-50875. 1971. softbound 3.50 (ISBN 0-385-12896-7). Doubleday.

--How to Buy & Enjoy a Small Farm: Your Comprehensive Guide to the Country Life. (Illus.). 1978. 12.95 o.p. (ISBN 0-679-50858-9); pap. 5.95 (ISBN 0-679-50865-1). McKay.

--People & Other Mammals. LC 74-4874. 160p. (gr. 4-5). 1975. 5.95 o.p. (ISBN 0-385-00227-0). Doubleday.

--Strange Monsters & Great Searches. LC 72-76185. 120p. (gr. 4-7). 1973. 6.95 (ISBN 0-385-03463-6). Doubleday.

Laycock, George & Bauer, Erwin. Hunting with Bow & Arrow. LC 65-28519. 1965. lib. bdg. 3.95 o.p. (ISBN 0-668-01417-2). Arco.

Laycock, Mary & McLean, Peggy. Skateboard Practice: Multiplication & Division. (Illus.). (gr. 3-6). 1979. pap. text ed. 4.95 (ISBN 0-918932-65-3). Activity Resources.

Laycock, T., tr. see Prochaska, Georg.

Layde, Durwood C. & Busch, Daryle H. Introduction to Qualitative Analysis. 2nd ed. (Illus.). 1968. pap. text ed. 12.95x (ISBN 0-205-02334-7, 6823343). Allyn.

Laye, Camara. Enfant Noir. Hutchinson, Joyce A., ed. 1966. pap. text ed. 5.95x (ISBN 0-521-05357-9). Cambridge U Pr.

Layman, Earl D. The Sights of Seattle: Downtown. (Illus.). 96p. (Orig.). 1981. pap. 6.95 (ISBN 0-914842-59-5). Madrona Pubs.

Layman, Emma M. Buddhism in America. LC 76-4566. (Illus.). 344p. 1976. 19.95x (ISBN 0-88229-166-1); pap. 10.95 (ISBN 0-88229-436-9). Nelson-Hall.

Layman, J. C. At the Last Moment. LC 78-63646. 1979. 6.95 (ISBN 0-533-03994-0). Vantage.

Layman, N. Kathryn & Renner, Adrienne G. Word Processors: A Programmed Training Guide with Practical Applications. (Illus.). 352p. 1981. text ed. 19.95 (ISBN 0-13-963520-3). P-H.

Layman, Richard. The Shadow Man: A Documentary Life of Dashiell Hammett. 300p. 1981. 14.95 (ISBN 0-15-181459-7). HarBraceJ.

Layman, Richard, jt. ed. see Bruccoli, Matthew J.

Layman, Richard, ed. see Lardner, Ring.

Laymon, Richard. The Cellar. (Orig.). 1980. pap. 2.25 (ISBN 0-446-92246-3). Warner Bks.

Layne, James N. Old Testament Study Simplified. new ed. LC 77-23715. 1978. pap. 3.25 (ISBN 0-87148-656-3). Pathway Pr.

Layne, Marion M. The Balloon Affair. 202p. 1981. 8.95 (ISBN 0-396-07951-2). Dodd.

Layton, R. B. A Parents Introduction to the New Mathematics. LC 65-24340. (Illus.). 43p. 1964. pap. 1.50x o.p. (ISBN 0-685-36217-5). Nature Bks Pubs.

Layton, R. B., illus. Thirty Birds That Will Build in Bird Houses. LC 77-81805. 1977. pap. 5.95 (ISBN 0-912542-03-9). Nature Bks Pubs.

Layton, R. C., jt. auth. see Marr, G. W.

Layton, Robert. Dvorak Symphonies & Concertos. LC 77-82650. (BBC Music Guides: No. 38). (Illus.). 64p. (Orig.). 1978. pap. 2.95 (ISBN 0-295-95505-8). U of Wash Pr.

Layton, Thomas N., jt. auth. see Yee, Min S.

Lazar, Arpad Von. Conference on Community Development in Latin America & the U. S., October 15-17, 1970. LC 74-150597. 1970. pap. 1.25 o.p. (ISBN 0-913456-79-9). Interbk Inc.

Lazard, Naomi. What Amanda Saw. LC 80-14516. (Illus.). 32p. (gr. k-3). 1981. 7.95 (ISBN 0-688-80272-9); PLB 7.63 (ISBN 0-688-84272-0). Greenwillow.

Lazare, jt. auth. see Burgess, A. W.

Lazare, Aaron, jt. auth. see Burgess, Ann W.

Lazareth, William H., ed. see Bonino, Jose M.

Lazareth, William H., jt. ed. see Forell, George W.

Lazarillo de Tormes. The Pleasant History of Lazarillo de Tormes, His Fortunes & Adversities, Containing the Strange Adventures That Befell Him in the Service of Sundry Masters, As Written Supposedly by Diego Hurtado de Mendoza: Together with the Pursuit or Second Part of His Life, As Related by Juan de Luna. LC 80-2487. 1981. Repr. of 1926 ed. 35.00 (ISBN 0-404-19121-5). AMS Pr.

Lazaro, Eric J., ed. Colon & Rectal Surgery: Continuing Education Review. 1973. spiral bdg. 12.00 o.p. (ISBN 0-87488-338-5). Med Exam.

Lazar Of Pharbi. Patmowtiwn Hayots. Date not set. Repr. of 1904 ed. cancelled. Caravan Bks.

--Patmowtiwn Hayots: History of the Armenians. Kouymjian, Dickran, ed. 1981. write for info. (ISBN 0-88206-031-7). Caravan Bks.

Lazarsfeld, P. F. & Katz, E. Language of Social Research: A Reader in the Methodology of Social Research. LC 55-7342. 1965. pap. text ed. 7.95 (ISBN 0-02-918270-0). Free Pr.

Lazarsfeld, Paul, jt. auth. see Boudon, Raymond.

Lazarsfeld, Paul, jt. auth. see Katz, Elihu.

Lazarsfeld, Paul, jt. ed. see Boudon, Raymond.

Lazarsfeld, Paul, et al, eds. Continuities in the Language of Social Research. 2nd ed. LC 77-143525. 1972. 19.95 (ISBN 0-02-918250-6). Free Pr.

Lazarsfeld, Paul F. Qualitative Analysis: Historical & Critical Essays. 1971. pap. text ed. 14.95x o.p. (ISBN 0-205-03221-4, 8132216). Allyn.

Lazarsfeld, Paul F., et al. The People's Choice: How the Voter Makes up His Mind in a Presidential Campaign. LC 68-20443. (Illus.). 15.00x (ISBN 0-231-03158-0); pap. 5.00 (ISBN 0-231-08583-4, 83). Columbia U Pr.

Lazarus, A. L. & Jones, Victor H. Beyond Graustark: George Barr McCutcheon - Playwright Discovered. (National University Publications, Literary Criticism Ser.). 1981. 15.00 (ISBN 0-8046-9280-7). Kennikat.

Lazarus, Alan, jt. auth. see Funes, Marilyn.

Lazarus, Arnold A. The Practice of Multimodal Therapy. (Illus.). 256p. 1981. 18.95 (ISBN 0-07-036813-9, P&R&B). McGraw.

Lazarus, Arnold L., ed. Indiana Experience: An Anthology. LC 76-50528. 448p. 1977. 15.00x (ISBN 0-253-14156-7); pap. text ed. 4.95x (ISBN 0-253-32986-8). Ind U Pr.

Lazarus, D., jt. auth. see Hulsizer, R. I.

Lazarus, Mell. Miss Peach. 128p. (Orig.). 1981. pap. 1.75 (ISBN 0-553-14789-7). Bantam.

--Momma. 128p. (Orig.). 1981. pap. 1.75 (ISBN 0-553-14788-9). Bantam.

--The Momma Treasury. (Illus.). 1978. 12.95 o.p. (ISBN 0-8362-1102-2); pap. 7.95 o.p. (ISBN 0-8362-1101-4). Andrews & McMeel.

Lazarus, Mitchel. Goodbye to Excellence: A Critical Look at Minimum Competency Testing. (NAESP Studies in Education & Public Policy). 192p. (Orig.). 1981. lib. bdg. 16.00x (ISBN 0-89158-771-3); pap. text ed. 6.50x (ISBN 0-89158-897-3). Westview.

Lazarus, Mitchell. Educating the Handicapped: Where We've Been, Where We're Going. 1980. pap. 11.95 (ISBN 0-87545-019-9). Natl Sch PR.

Lazarus, Richard S., jt. ed. see Monat, Alan.

Lazarus, Stephen M. Self-Assessment of Current Knowledge in Urology. 2nd ed. 1974. spiral bdg. 12.00 o.s.i. (ISBN 0-87488-251-6). Med Exam.

Lazarus, Stephen M., ed. Urology. 4th ed. (Medical Examination Review Bk.: Vol. 14). 1977. pap. 16.50 (ISBN 0-87488-114-5). Med Exam.

Lazarus, Sy. Loud & Clear: A Guide to Effective Communication. LC 75-4925. 152p. 1975. 10.95 (ISBN 0-8144-5375-9). Am Mgmt.

Lazdina, Tereza B. Teach Yourself Latvian. (Teach Yourself Ser). 1966. pap. 3.95 o.p. (ISBN 0-679-10219-1). McKay.

Lazear, Robert. Maestro de Dolores. (Illus.). 342p. (Orig., Span.). 1979. pap. 4.50 (ISBN 0-89922-138-6). Edit Caribe.

Lazell, David. Gipsy Smith: From the Forest I Came. 224p. 1973. pap. 2.50 (ISBN 0-8024-2959-9). Moody.

Lazenby, David & Phillips, Paul. Cutting for Construction: A Handbook of Methods & Applications of Hard Cutting & Breaking on Site. LC 78-40610. 1978. 24.95 (ISBN 0-470-26437-3). Halsted Pr.

Lazenby, Walter. Arthur Wing Pinero. (English Authors Ser.: No. 150). lib. bdg. 10.95 (ISBN 0-8057-1444-8). Twayne.

Lazer, William & Kelley, Eugene J. Social Marketing: Perspectives & Viewpoints. 1973. pap. text ed. 12.50x (ISBN 0-256-00284-3). Irwin.

Lazere, M. R. Commercial Financing. 310p. 1968. 23.95 (ISBN 0-471-06570-6). Wiley.

Lazere, Monroe R., ed. Commercial Financing. 1968. 23.95 (ISBN 0-8260-5300-9). Ronald Pr.

Lazerowitz, Morris. Structure of Metaphysics. 1963. text ed. 17.75x (ISBN 0-7100-3148-3). Humanities.

Lazerowitz, Morris, jt. ed. see Ambrose, Alice.

Lazerson, Marvin & Grubb, W. Norton, eds. American Education & Vocationalism: A Documentary History 1870-1970. LC 73-87511. 1974. text ed. 8.75 (ISBN 0-8077-2413-0); pap. text ed. 4.00x (ISBN 0-8077-2414-9). Tchrs Coll.

Lazes, Peter, ed. The Handbook of Health Education. LC 79-50. 1979. 29.95 (ISBN 0-89443-085-8). Aspen Systems.

Lazlo, Kate. Forever After. 288p. 1981. 10.95 (ISBN 0-686-69084-2). Dial.

Lazreg, Marnia. The Emergence of Classes in Algeria: Colonialism & Socio-Political Change. LC 76-7955. (Westview Special Studies on Social Political, & Economic Development Ser). 250p. 1976. 30.00x (ISBN 0-89158-107-3). Westview.

Lazzarini, John & Lazzarini, Roberta. Pavlova: Repertoire of a Legend. LC 80-5560. (Illus.). 1980. 35.00 (ISBN 0-02-871970-0). Schirmer Bks.

Lazzarini, Roberta, jt. auth. see Lazzarini, John.

Lazzaro, Victor. Systems & Procedures: A Handbook for Business & Industry. 2nd ed. 1968. text ed. 25.95 (ISBN 0-13-881425-2). P-H.

Lazzerini, Edward J., jt. auth. see Yang, Richard.

LBJ School of Public Affairs. Feasibility of Health Maintenance Organizations in Texas. LC 75-620099. (Policy Research Project Report Ser.: No. 11). 1975. 3.00 (ISBN 0-89940-607-6). LBJ Sch Public Affairs.

--Health of Mexican - Americans in South Texas. LC 79-88345. (Policy Research Project Report Ser.: No. 32). 1979. 6.00 (ISBN 0-89940-628-9). LBJ Sch Public Affairs.

Lea, Alice & Tasman, Nast. Wedding Album: Custom & Lore Through the Ages. (Illus.). 96p. cancelled o.s.i. (ISBN 0-8027-0653-3); pap. cancelled o.s.i. (ISBN 0-8027-7159-9). Walker & Co. Postponed.

Lea, Henry C. The Duel & the Oath. (Middle Ages Ser). Orig. Title: Superstition & Force. 1974. 12.00x (ISBN 0-8122-7681-7); pap. 4.95x (ISBN 0-8122-1080-8). U of Pa Pr.

--The Ordeal. (Middle Ages Ser). 224p. 1973. pap. 5.95x (ISBN 0-8122-1061-1, Pa Paperbks). U of Pa Pr.

--Torture. (Middle Ages Ser). 192p. 1973. pap. 6.95x (ISBN 0-8122-1062-X, Pa Paperbks). U of Pa Pr.

Lea, K. J., et al. Geography of Scotland. LC 77-76096. 1977. 21.95 o.p. (ISBN 0-7153-7422-2). David & Charles.

Lea, May V. Health & Social Education. 1975. pap. text ed. 8.95x (ISBN 0-435-60601-8). Heinemann Ed.

Lea, Sydney L. Gothic to Fantastic: Readings in Supernatural Fiction. Varma, Devendra P., ed. LC 79-8463. (Gothic Studies & Dissertations Ser.). 1980. lib. bdg. 22.00x (ISBN 0-405-12653-0). Arno.

Lea, Tom. Ranger Escort West of the Pelos. 3.00 o.p. (ISBN 0-292-77003-0). U of Tex Pr.

Lea, W. Trends in Speech Recognition. 1980. text ed. 30.00 (ISBN 0-13-930768-0). P-H.

Lea, William S. Faith & Science: Mutual Responsibility for a Human Future. 1979. 1.50 (ISBN 0-686-28776-2). Forward Movement.

Leab, Daniel, jt. ed. see Leab, Katherine.

Leab, Daniel J. Union of Individuals: The Formation of the American Newspaper Guild, 1933-36. LC 75-110603. 1970. 20.00x (ISBN 0-231-03367-2). Columbia U Pr.

Leab, Daniel J. & Leab, Katherine K. The Auction Companion. LC 80-8208. 224p. 1981. 12.95 (ISBN 0-06-012556-X, HarpT); pap. 5.95 (ISBN 0-06-090850-5, CN 850). Har-Row.

Leab, Daniel J., jt. ed. see Leab, Katharine K.

Leab, Katharine K. & Leab, Daniel J., eds. American Book Prices Current Index: Nineteen Seventy Five to Nineteen Seventy-Nine, 2 vols. 1980. Set. 250.00x (ISBN 0-914022-10-5, 314557). Vol. 1, 1020p. Vol. 2, 1030p. Bancroft Parkman.

--American Book Prices Current: 1980, Vol. 86. 1200p. 1981. 79.75 (ISBN 0-914022-10-5); prepub. 62.30 (ISBN 0-686-68816-3). Bancroft Parkman.

Leab, Katherine & Leab, Daniel, eds. American Book Prices Current, Vol. 86. 1981. 79.75 (ISBN 0-914022-11-3). Am Book Prices.

Leab, Katherine K., jt. auth. see Leab, Daniel J.

Leabo, Dick A. Basic Statistics. 5th ed. (Illus.). 1976. text ed. 18.95x (ISBN 0-256-01835-9). Irwin.

Leach, Barry. German Strategy Against Russia, 1939-1941. (Illus.). 1973. 29.00x o.p. (ISBN 0-19-821495-2). Oxford U Pr.

Leach, Bernard. Hamada, Potter. LC 75-11394. (Illus.). 305p. 1975. 60.00 (ISBN 0-87011-252-X). Kodansha.

--Potter's Book. (gr. 9-12). 20.00 (ISBN 0-693-01117-3); pap. 10.00 (ISBN 0-693-01157-2). Transatlantic.

Leach, Berton J. The Structure & Development of Vertebrates. (Lucas Text Ser). 1973. text ed. 3.95x (ISBN 0-87543-086-4). Lucas.

Leach, C. E. The Goat Owners' Scrapbook. Date not set. 7.50 (ISBN 0-686-26682-X). Dairy Goat.

Leach, Catherine S., ed. see Pasek, Jan C.

Leach, Corl A. Aids to Goatkeeping. Date not set. 10.00 (ISBN 0-686-26686-2). Dairy Goat.

Leach, D. J. & Raybould, E. C. Learning & Behaviour Difficulties in School. (Psychology & Education Ser.). 1977. text ed. 11.75x (ISBN 0-7291-0076-6); pap. text ed. 5.25x (ISBN 0-7291-0071-5). Humanities.

Leach, Donald P. Experiments in Digital Principles. 2nd ed. (Illus.). 176p. 1980. 14.95x (ISBN 0-07-036916-X, G). McGraw.

Leach, Douglas E. The Northern Colonial Frontier, 1607-1763. LC 66-10083. (Histories of the American Frontier Ser.). (Illus.). 282p. 1966. pap. 6.50x (ISBN 0-8263-0337-4). U of NM Pr.

Leach, Douglas E. & Buchanan, Patrick J. Great Issues 78: A Forum on Important Questions Facing the American Public, Vol.10. LC 75-648855. 1979. 13.95 (ISBN 0-916624-28-5). TSU Pr.

Leach, Duane, jt. ed. see Billington, Monroe.

Leach, E. Culture & Communication. LC 75-30439. (Themes in the Social Sciences Ser.). (Illus.). 120p. 1976. 16.95 (ISBN 0-521-21131-X); pap. 5.95x (ISBN 0-521-29052-X). Cambridge U Pr.

Leach, E. R. Political Systems of Highland Burma: A Study of Kachin Social Structure. (Monographs on Social Anthropology Ser: No. 44). 1977. text ed. 15.00x (ISBN 0-391-00147-7, Athlone Pr); pap. text ed. 13.00x (ISBN 0-391-00975-3). Humanities.

--Rethinking Anthropology. (Monographs on Social Anthropology Ser: No. 22). 1971. text ed. 15.75x (ISBN 0-391-02078-1, Athlone Pr); pap. text ed. 9.50x (ISBN 0-391-00146-9). Humanities.

Leach, Edmund. Claude Levi-Strauss. rev. ed. (Modern Masters Ser.). 1976. pap. 3.50 (ISBN 0-14-004300-4). Penguin.

Leach, F., jt. auth. see De Noriega, L. A.

Leach, Geraldine M. Victims of an Unknown Wrath. 440p. (Orig.). 1981. pap. write for info. (ISBN 0-9605274-0-0). Albion Am Bks.

Leach, Joan & St. Louis, Patricia. Caring for Babies. LC 78-52432. (Illus.). 1978. pap. 3.50 (ISBN 0-87239-220-1, 7963). Standard Pub.

Leach, K. G. The Physica Aspects of Radioisotopic Organ Imaging. 1980. 10.00x (Pub. by Brit Inst Radiology). State Mutual Bk.

Leach, MacEdward & Glassie, Henry. A Guide for Collectors of Oral Traditions & Folk Cultural Materials in Pennsylvania. (Illus., Orig.). 1973. pap. 2.00 (ISBN 0-911124-60-8). Pa Hist & Mus.

Leach, MacEdward, ed. Studies in Medieval Literature: In Honor of Albert Croll Baugh. LC 61-15274. 1961. 9.00x o.p. (ISBN 0-8122-7294-3). U of Pa Pr.

Leach, Maria. Whistle in the Graveyard: Folktales to Chill Your Bones. 128p. (gr. 4-6). 1974. 7.95 (ISBN 0-670-76245-8). Viking Pr.

Leach, Mark, ed. Netherlandish Artists. LC 79-50679. (The Illustrated Bartsch: Vol. II). 1979. 120.00 (ISBN 0-89835-002-6). Abaris Bks.

Leach, Penelope. Your Baby & Child: From Birth to Age Five. pap. 9.95 (ISBN 0-394-73509-9). Knopf.

Leach, R. & Palmer, R., eds. Folk Music in School. LC 77-71416. (Resources of Music Ser.). 1978. 17.50 (ISBN 0-521-21595-1); pap. 6.95 (ISBN 0-521-29206-9). Cambridge U Pr.

Leach, R. J. International Schools & Their Role in the Field of International Education. 1969. 22.00 (ISBN 0-08-013037-2); pap. 10.75 (ISBN 0-08-013036-4). Pergamon.

Leach, R. M., jt. auth. see Milton, J. H.
Leach, Richard H. Interstate Relations in Australia. LC 65-11828. 200p. 1965. 9.50x (ISBN 0-8131-1101-3). U Pr of Ky.
Leach, Richard H., jt. auth. see Mason, Alpheus T.
Leach, Robert A. The Chiropractic Theories: A Synopsis of Scientific Research. LC 79-92761. (Illus.). 300p. 1980. pap. text ed. 16.95 (ISBN 0-935974-00-8). Mid South Sci Pubs.
Leach, Ronald & Stamp, Edward. British Accounting Standards: The First Ten Years. 160p. 1980. 40.00x (ISBN 0-85941-149-4, Pub. by Woodhead-Faulkner England). State Mutual Bk.
Leach, Sidney J., ed. Physical Principles & Techniques of Protein Chemistry. (Molecular Biology Ser.). 1969-1973. Pt. A. 59.00 (ISBN 0-12-440101-5); Pt. B. 55.25 (ISBN 0-12-440102-3); Pt. C. 68.50 (ISBN 0-12-440103-1); 148.25 set (ISBN 0-686-57487-7). Acad Pr.
Leach, Virgil. Attitudes I. Date not set. pap. 2.95 (ISBN 0-89137-803-0). Quality Pubns.
--Attitudes II. 1981. pap. 2.95 (ISBN 0-89137-804-9). Quality Pubns.
--Get Behind Me Satan. 1977. 6.95 (ISBN 0-89137-521-X); pap. 4.95 (ISBN 0-89137-520-1). Quality Pubns.
Leach, William. True Love & Perfect Union: The Feminist Reform of Sex & Society. LC 80-50557. 320p. 1980. 17.50 (ISBN 0-465-08752-3). Basic.
Leachman, Robert B. & Althoff, Philip, eds. Preventing Nuclear Theft: Guidelines for Industry & Government. LC 72-76452. (Special Studies in U.S. Economic, Social & Political Issues). 1972. 28.50x (ISBN 0-275-28618-5). Irvington.
Leacock, Eleanor see Etienne, Mona.
Leacock, Eleanor, jt. ed. see Etienne, Mona.
Leacock, Stephen. Humor & Humanity. 232p. 1980. Repr. of 1938 ed. lib. bdg. 35.00 (ISBN 0-89984-322-0). Century Bookbindery.
--The Social Criticism of Stephen Leacock: The Unsolved Riddle of Social Justice & Other Essays. LC 73-78960. (Social History of Canada Ser.). 1973. pap. 3.95 (ISBN 0-8020-6201-6). U of Toronto Pr.
Leacroft, Helen. Buildings of Byzantium. LC 76-54979. (gr. 8-12). 1977. PLB 7.95 (ISBN 0-201-09266-2, A-W Childrens). A-W.
Leadbeater, C. W. The Art & Science of Clairvoyance. (Illus.). 1979. 47.50 (ISBN 0-89266-182-8). Am Classical Coll Pr.
Leadbeater, Charles W. Astral Plane. 1973. 3.75 (ISBN 0-8356-7093-7). Theos Pub Hse.
--Chakras. 10th ed. 1973. 7.25 (ISBN 0-8356-7016-3). Theos Pub Hse.
--Clairvoyance. 10th ed. 1968. 4.50 (ISBN 0-8356-7095-3). Theos Pub Hse.
--Man Visible & Invisible. rev. ed. (Illus.). 1969. pap. 6.50 (ISBN 0-8356-0311-3, Quest). Theos Pub Hse.
Leadbeater, Charles W., jt. auth. see Besant, Annie.
Leader, Alan H. Problems & Opportunities in Economic Development. (Illus.). 1977. pap. text ed. 2.95x (ISBN 0-932826-11-3). New Issues MI.
Leader, John P., jt. ed. see Macknight, Anthony D.
Leader, Ninon A. Hungarian Classical Ballads & Their Folklore. 1967. 72.00 (ISBN 0-521-05526-1). Cambridge U Pr.
Leader, Zachery. Reading Blake's Poems. (Illus.). 256p. 1981. 27.50 (ISBN 0-7100-0635-7). Routledge & Kegan.
Leaf, Alexander & Cotran, Ramzi. Renal Pathophysiology. 2nd ed. (Illus.). 448p. 1980. text ed. 18.95x (ISBN 0-19-502688-8); pap. text ed. 11.95x (ISBN 0-19-502689-6). Oxford U Pr.
Leaf, Alexander, et al, eds. Renal Pathophysiology - Recent Advances. 1980. text ed. 35.50 (ISBN 0-89004-399-X). Raven.
Leaf, Carol A., jt. auth. see Fordham, Sheldon L.
Leaf, Hayim, jt. ed. see Ben-Asher, Naomi.
Leaf, Munro. Manners Can Be Fun. rev. ed. LC 58-5611. (Illus.). (gr. k-3). 1958. 7.95 (ISBN 0-397-31603-8). Lippincott.
--Metric Can Be Fun. LC 75-29223. (gr. 1-3). 1976. 6.79 (ISBN 0-397-31679-8); pap. 1.95 (ISBN 0-397-31680-1). Lippincott.
--Safety Can Be Fun. rev. ed. LC 61-14579. (Illus.). (gr. k-3). 1961. 7.89 (ISBN 0-397-31593-7). Lippincott.
--Science Can Be Fun. LC 58-10135. (Illus.). (gr. k-3). 1958. 4.50 o.p. (ISBN 0-397-30431-5); PLB 4.82 o.p. (ISBN 0-397-30430-7). Lippincott.
--Who Cares? I Do. LC 74-15172. 48p. (ps-3). 1971. 7.89 (ISBN 0-397-31521-X); pap. 2.25 (ISBN 0-397-31276-8). Lippincott.
Leaf, Murray J. Information & Behavior in a Sikh Village: Social Organization Reconsidered. LC 78-172390. (Illus.). 300p. 1972. 20.00x (ISBN 0-520-02115-0). U of Cal Pr.
Leaf, VaDonna. Robbie & the Stolen Minibike. LC 77-78849. (Robbie Ser.). (gr. 4-9). 1978. pap. 2.95 (ISBN 0-88419-127-3). Creation Hse.
League for Social Reconstruction. Social Planning for Canada. LC 72-94917. (Social History of Canada Ser.). 1975. pap. 7.50 (ISBN 0-8020-6178-8). U of Toronto Pr.
League, Nehume see DeCrow, Roger.
League of Women Voters Education Fund. Choosing the President. 108p. 1980. pap. 1.95 (ISBN 0-8407-5726-3). Nelson.
--Choosing the President: 1980 Edition. (Illus.). 1980. pap. 1.95 (ISBN 0-89959-100-0, 420). LWV US.
League of Women Voters of New York State. New York State: A Citizen's Handbook. Richman, Jeanne, ed. LC 79-24095. (Illus.). 119p. (Orig.). 1979. pap. 2.95 (ISBN 0-938588-03-6). LWV NYS.
--Toward an Evaluation of the Property Tax System in New York State. Amlung, Susan, ed. (Illus.). 125p. (Orig.). 1979. pap. 4.00 (ISBN 0-938588-02-8). LWV NYS.
Leahey, Joseph, tr. see Idung Of Prufening.
Leahey, Thomas H. A History of Psychology. (Illus.). 1980. text ed. 18.95 (ISBN 0-13-391755-X). P-H.
Leahy, Frederick. Satan Cast Out. 1975. pap. 4.45 (ISBN 0-85151-234-8). Banner of Truth.
Leahy, Irene M., et al. The Nurse & Radiotherapy: A Manual for Daily Care. LC 78-12296. 1978. pap. text ed. 11.95 (ISBN 0-8016-2896-2). Mosby.
Leahy, James. The Cinema of Joseph Losey. (Film Guide Ser.). 1967. pap. 4.95 o.p. (ISBN 0-498-06749-1). A S Barnes.
Leahy, Syrell R. A Book of Ruth. 384p. 1978. pap. 1.95 o.p. (ISBN 0-449-22689-1, Crest). Fawcett.
Leahy, W. H., et al. Urban Economics. LC 75-88859. 1970. pap. text ed. 10.95 (ISBN 0-02-918280-8). Free Pr.
Leake, B. E., jt. auth. see Bowes, D. R.
Leake, Charles, jt. auth. see Lieblich, Gerald S.
Leake, Chauncey D. An Historical Account of Pharmacology to the Twentieth Century. (Illus.). 224p. 1975. 16.00 (ISBN 0-398-03277-7); pap. 11.75 (ISBN 0-398-03278-5). C C Thomas.
Leake, Chauncey D., tr. see Harvey, William.
Leake, I. Q. Memoir of the Life & Times of General John Lamb. LC 72-152230. (Era of the American Revolution Ser). 1971. Repr. of 1850 ed. lib. bdg. 49.50 (ISBN 0-306-70122-7). Da Capo.
Leake, Laura, jt. auth. see Riley, Bill.
Leake, Lucy D. Comparative Histology: An Introduction to the Microscopic Structure of Animals. 1976. 97.50 (ISBN 0-12-441050-2). Acad Pr.
Leake, Lucy D. & Walker, Robert J. Invertebrate Neuropharmacology. LC 79-21390. 358p. 1980. 64.95x (ISBN 0-470-26857-3). Halsted Pr.
Leakey, C. L. & Wills, J. B., eds. Food Crops of the Lowland Tropics. 1977. 45.00x (ISBN 0-19-854517-7). Oxford U Pr.
Leakey, John & Yost, Nellie S. West That Was: From Texas to Montana. LC 58-14110. (Illus.). 1965. pap. 2.95 (ISBN 0-8032-5117-3, BB 304, Bison). U of Nebr Pr.
Leakey, L. S. White African. (Walden Editions). 1973. pap. 1.50 o.p. (ISBN 0-685-32481-8, 345-23566-5-150). Ballantine.
Leakey, L. S. & Bestor, William S., eds. Adam or Ape: A Sourcebook of Discoveries About Early Man. 540p. 1981. text ed. 15.95x (ISBN 0-87073-700-7); pap. text ed. 8.95x (ISBN 0-87073-701-5). Schenkman.
Leakey, L. S. & Tobias, P. V., eds. Olduvai Gorge, Vol. 1 & 2: Nineteen Fifty-One - Nineteen Sixty-One. 1965. Vol. 1. 65.00 (ISBN 0-521-05527-X); Vol. 2. 72.50 (ISBN 0-521-06901-7). Cambridge U Pr.
Leakey, L. S., et al, eds. Fossil Vertebrates of Africa, 3 vols. Vol. 1, 1969. 28.60 (ISBN 0-12-440401-4); Vol. 2, 1971. 46.00 (ISBN 0-12-440402-2); Vol. 3, 1973. 29.00 (ISBN 0-12-440403-0). Acad Pr.
Leakey, M. D., ed. Olduvai Gorge, Vol. 3: Nineteen Sixty - Nineteen Sixty-Three. 1972. 110.00 (ISBN 0-521-07723-0). Cambridge U Pr.
Leakey, Meave G. & Leakey, Richard E., eds. Koobi Fora: Research Projects, Vol. 1. (Illus.). 1978. text ed. 49.00x (ISBN 0-19-857392-8). Oxford U Pr.
Leakey, Richard E. The Making of Mankind. (Illus.). 256p. 1981. 25.00 (ISBN 0-525-15055-2). Dutton.
Leakey, Richard E., jt. ed. see Leakey, Meave G.
Leal, Emily B. & Hamilton, Susan. Beginning Spanish by Easy Steps. (Orig.). (gr. 7-10). 1975. wkbk. 7.58 (ISBN 0-87720-507-8). AMSCO Sch.
Leal, Luis. Mexico: Civilizaciones y Culturas. rev. ed. (Illus.). 1971. pap. text ed. 7.50 (ISBN 0-395-12744-0, 3-32161). HM.
Leal, V. N. Coronelismo. Henfrey, J., tr. LC 76-46044. (Cambridge Latin American Studies: No. 28). 1977. 29.95 (ISBN 0-521-21488-2). Cambridge U Pr.
Leamer, Laurence. Assignment. 256p. 1981. 10.95 (ISBN 0-8037-0266-3). Dial.
Leaming, Majorie P. & Motley, Robert J. Administrative Office Management: A Practical Approach. 1979. text ed. 14.95x (ISBN 0-697-08030-7); instr. manual 4.00 (ISBN 0-685-91852-1). Wm C Brown.
Lean, Arthur E. And Merely Teach: Irreverent Essays on the Mythology of Education. 2nd ed. LC 75-42233. 164p. 1976. 8.95x (ISBN 0-8093-0744-8); pap. 4.95 (ISBN 0-8093-0745-6). S Ill U Pr.
Lean, Arthur E., jt. ed. see Lawson, Douglas E.
Lean, Garth. Strangely Warmed. 1979. pap. 3.95 (ISBN 0-8423-6662-8). Tyndale.
Lean, Geoffrey. Rich World, Poor World. 1979. text ed. 17.95x (ISBN 0-04-309010-9); pap. 13.50 (ISBN 0-04-309012-5). Allen Unwin.
Lean, Vincent S. Lean's Collectanea, 5 vols. LC 68-26583. 1969. Repr. of 1902 ed. Set. 130.00 (ISBN 0-8103-3203-5). Gale.
Leana, Frank C. Getting into College. 1980. 11.95 (ISBN 0-8090-4921-X); pap. 5.95 (ISBN 0-8090-1393-2). Hill & Wang.
Lear, Denise Van see Van Lear, Denise.
Lear, E. The Owl & the Pussycat & Other Verses. (Peter Possum Paperbacks Ser). 1967. pap. 0.95 o.p. (ISBN 0-531-05119-6). Watts.
Lear, Edward. A Book of Nonsense. LC 80-5355. (Illus.). 56p. (gr. 4 up). 1980. 8.95 (ISBN 0-87099-241-4). Metro Mus Art.
--The Book of Nonsense, Repr. Of 1846 Ed. Bd. with The English Struwwelpeter. Hoffman, Heinrich. Repr. of 1848 ed; The Fairy Library Series. Cruikshank, George. Repr. of 1864 ed. LC 75-32161. (Classics of Children's Literature, 1621-1932: Vol. 26). 1976. PLB 38.00 (ISBN 0-8240-2275-0). Garland Pub.
--The Complete Nonsense of Edward Lear. Jackson, Holdrook, ed. (Illus.). 7.50 (ISBN 0-8446-0722-3). Peter Smith.
--Edward Lear's Nonsense. (Illus.). 1977. pap. 1.75 (ISBN 0-486-22744-8). Dover.
--Nonsense Alphabets. (Peter Possum Paperbacks). (gr. k-3). 1975. pap. 0.95 o.p. (ISBN 0-531-05129-3). Watts.
--The Pelican Chorus & Quangle Wangle's Hat. LC 80-53511. (Illus.). 32p. 1981. 7.95 (ISBN 0-670-54613-5). Viking Pr.
Lear, John. Kepler's Dream: With the Full Text & Notes of Somnium Sive Astronomia Lunaris, Joannis Kepleri. Kirkwood, Patrica F., tr. 1965. 15.75x (ISBN 0-520-00716-6). U of Cal Pr.
Lear, Martha W. Heartsounds. 1981. pap. price not set (ISBN 0-671-41986-2). PB.
Lear, Roma. Play Helps: Toys & Activities for Handicapped Children. 1977. pap. 12.95x (ISBN 0-433-19085-X). Intl Ideas.
Learmonth, Larry, tr. see Nation, Terry.
Learmonth, Nancy. The Australians: How They Live & Work. LC 72-89452. 166p. 1973. text ed. 8.95 (ISBN 0-03-029571-8, HoltC). HR&W.
Learmouth, John & Whitaker, Keith. Movement in Practice. LC 76-41142. (Illus.). 1977. pap. 7.95 (ISBN 0-8238-0209-4). Plays.
Learn, C. R. & Lewis, Jack, eds. Backpacker's Digest. 2nd. rev. ed. (DBI Bks). 288p. (Orig.). 1976. pap. 7.95 o.p. (ISBN 0-695-80645-9). Follett.
Learned, Edmund P. & Sproat, Audrey T. Organization Theory & Policy: Notes for Analysis. 1966. pap. text ed. 6.25x o.p. (ISBN 0-256-00310-6). Irwin.
Learner, Howard. White Paper on Science Museums. (Orig.). 1979. pap. 4.00 (ISBN 0-89329-095-5). Ctr Sci Public.
Learning Achievement Corp. Decimals, Percent & Money: Measurement & Transportation. Zak, Therese A., ed. (MATCH Ser.). (Illus.). 144p. 1981. text ed. 5.28 (ISBN 0-07-037114-8, G). McGraw.
Learning Achievement Corporation. Fractions & Food: Fractions, Decimals & Electronic Communications. Zak, Therese A., ed. (MATCH Ser.). (Illus.). 144p. Date not set. text ed. 5.28 (ISBN 0-07-037113-X, G). McGraw.
--Geometry & Design & Maintenance: Ratio, Proportion, Reading Graphs & Data. Zak, Therese A., ed. (MATCH Ser.). (Illus.). 128p. 1981. text ed. 5.28 (ISBN 0-07-037115-6, G). McGraw.
--Multiplication & Energy & Construction: Division & Medicine. Zak, Therese A., ed. (MATCH Ser.). (Illus.). 144p. 1980. text ed. 5.28 (ISBN 0-07-037112-1, G). McGraw.
Learning Systems Ltd. Break-Even Charts: Their Interpretation & Construction. 1968. pap. text ed. 6.00 o.p. (ISBN 0-08-014050-5). Pergamon.
--Effective Communication. 1968. pap. text ed. 4.20 (ISBN 0-08-014048-3). Pergamon.
Learning Systems Ltd, ed. Elements of Injection Moulding of Thermoplastics. (Illus., Orig.,). (gr. 10 up). 1969. pap. text ed. 5.95 (ISBN 0-85334-043-9). Transatlantic.
Learning Technology Incorporated. Basic Spelling Skills. 2nd ed. Raygor, Alton L., ed. (Basic Skills Ser.). 1979. pap. text ed. 7.95x (ISBN 0-07-044415-3); cassette tapes & transcripts 25.00 (ISBN 0-07-044416-1). McGraw.
Learsi, Rufus. Prince of Judah & Other Stories of a Great Journey. 1962 ed. LC 62-21985. (Illus.). (gr. 5-9). 5.95 (ISBN 0-88400-031-1). Shengold.
Leary, Daniel J., ed. see Shaw, George B.
Leary, Helen F. & Stirewalt, Maurice R., eds. North Carolina Research: Genealogy & Local History. LC 80-50414. (Illus.). 672p. 1980. 21.50 (ISBN 0-936370-00-9). Natl Genealogical.
Leary, Lewis. John Greenleaf Whittier. (U. S. Authors Ser.: No. 6). lib. bdg. 10.95 (ISBN 0-8057-0796-4). Twayne.
--Norman Douglas. LC 68-19753. (Columbia Ser.: No. 32). (Orig.). 1968. pap. 2.00 (ISBN 0-231-02874-1, MW32). Columbia U Pr.
Leary, Lewis, intro. by. American Literature to Nineteen Hundred. 1981. pap. 8.95 (ISBN 0-312-02876-8). St Martin.
Leary, Lewis, ed. see Clemens, Samuel L.
Leary, Lewis, ed. see Thoreau, Henry D.
Leary, Lewis, ed. see Twain, Mark.
Leary, Lewis G., ed. Bible When You Want It. 1951. 1.95 o.p. (ISBN 0-8096-1023-X). Follett.
--Motive & Method in the Cantos of Ezra Pound. LC 54-11609. 1961. 12.50x (ISBN 0-231-02060-0); pap. 4.00x (ISBN 0-231-08520-6). Columbia U Pr.
Leary, Norma E., jt. auth. see Hohman, Edward J.
Leary, Paul M. The Northern Marianas Covenant & American Territorial Relations. LC 80-10945. (IGS Research Report: No. 80-1). 55p. (Orig.). 1980. pap. 3.50x (ISBN 0-87772-269-2). Inst Gov Stud Berk.
Leary, T. Interpersonal Diagnosis of Personality: A Functional Theory & Methodology for Personality Evaluation. 518p. 1957. 24.95 (ISBN 0-471-06915-9). Wiley.
Leary, Timothy. Interpersonal Diagnosis of Personality: A Functional Theory & Methodology for Personality Evaluation. (Illus.). 1957. 24.95 (ISBN 0-8260-5315-7). Ronald Pr.
Leary, William. Hidden Bible. 1955. 8.50 (ISBN 0-910140-07-3). Anthony.
Leary, William M., Jr. & Link, Arthur S., eds. The Progressive Era & the Great War: 1896-1920. 2nd ed. LC 78-70030. (Goldentree Bibliographies in American History). 1978. pap. text ed. 12.95x (ISBN 0-88295-575-6). AHM Pub.
Leas, Speed & Kittlaus, Paul. The Pastoral Counselor in Social Action. Clinebell, Howard J. & Stone, Howard W., eds. LC 80-8059. (Creative Pastoral Care & Counseling Ser.). 96p. (Orig.). 1981. pap. 3.25 (ISBN 0-8006-0565-9, 1-565). Fortress.
Lea-Scarlett, Errol. Roots & Branches: Ancestry for Australians. 256p. 1980. pap. 6.95x (ISBN 0-00-216415-9, Pub. by W Collins Australia). Intl Schol Bk Serv.
Leason, Barney. Rodeo Drive. 416p. (Orig.). 1981. pap. 2.95 (ISBN 0-523-41031-X). Pinnacle Bks.
Leasor, James. The Unknown Warrior. 272p. 1981. 10.95 (ISBN 0-395-30228-5). HM.
Leasure, Jan. Jan's Consumer Savings. (Illus.). 175p. 1981. pap. write for info. (ISBN 0-930256-08-5). Almar.
Leathard, Audrey. The Fight for Family Planning. 1980. text ed. 37.50x (ISBN 0-8419-5068-7). Holmes & Meier.
Leathart, Scott. Trees of the World. LC 76-52282. (Illus.). 1977. 19.95 o.p. (ISBN 0-89479-000-5). A & W Pubs.
Leathem, James. Protein Nutrition & Free Amino Acid Patterns. 1968. 15.00x (ISBN 0-8135-0572-0). Rutgers U Pr.
Leather, E. Hartley. Combat Without Weapons. (Illus.). 1975. pap. 3.00 (ISBN 0-87364-060-8). Paladin Ent.
Leather, John. Colin Archer & the Seaworthy Double-Ender. LC 78-55782. (Illus.). 1979. 20.00 (ISBN 0-87742-086-6). Intl Marine.
Leather, John, jt. auth. see Cannell, David.
Leather, Kate. Fashion with Leather. 1978. 17.95 (ISBN 0-7134-1015-9, Pub. by Batsford England). David & Charles.
Leatherbarrow, Canon. Worchestershire. (Batsford Britain Ser.). (Illus.). 1974. 8.95 o.p. (ISBN 0-8038-8068-5). Hastings.
Leatherbarrow, Margaret. Gold in the Grass. Bargyla & Rateaver, Gylver, eds. LC 75-23179. (Conservation Gardening & Farming Ser: Ser. C). 1975. pap. 10.00 (ISBN 0-9600698-8-7). Rateavers.

Leatherdale, C. So You Want to Teach English to Foreigners. 112p. 1980. 16.95x (ISBN 0-85626-191-2, Pub. by Abacus Pr England); pap. 8.95x (ISBN 0-85626-192-0). Intl Schol Bk Serv.
Leathers. Orientations to Researching Communication. Applbaum, Ronald & Hart, Roderick, eds. LC 77-20988. (MODCOM - Modules in Speech Communication). 1978. pap. text ed. 2.25 (ISBN 0-574-22535-8, 13-5535). SRA.
Leathers, Dale. Nonverbal Communications Systems. 288p. 1976. pap. text ed. 10.95 (ISBN 0-205-04894-3, 4848942). Allyn.
Leatherwood, Stephen & Mate, Bruce R. Marine Mammals of the World, 2 vols. 1980. 90.00 set (ISBN 0-525-10474-7). Dutton.
Leaton, Gwen, jt. auth. see Kinney, Jean.
Leavell, L. P., jt. auth. see Bunyan, Juan.
Leavell, Robert N., et al. Cases & Materials on Equitable Remedies & Restitution. 3rd ed. LC 79-27903. (American Casebook Ser.). 736p. 1980. text ed. 19.95 (ISBN 0-8299-2084-6). West Pub.
Leavell, Stuart & Bungay, Stanley. Standard Aircraft Handbook. 3rd ed. LC 80-67736. (Illus.). 1980. pap. 5.95 (ISBN 0-8168-8502-8). Aero.
Leavens, John, ed. The Catboat Book. LC 73-88648. 168p. 1973. 15.00 (ISBN 0-87742-034-3). Intl Marine.
Leavenworth, C., jt. auth. see Hendricks, C.
Leavenworth, Carol. Love & Commitment: You Don't Have to Settle for Less. (Illus.). 192p. 1981. 10.95t (ISBN 0-13-540971-3, Spec); pap. 5.95b (ISBN 0-13-540963-2). P-H.
Leavenworth, Richard, jt. auth. see Grant, Eugene L.
Leaver, C. J., ed. Genome Organization & Expression in Plants. (NATO Advanced Study Institutes Ser., Series A, Life Sciences: Vol. 29). 600p. 1980. 59.50 (ISBN 0-306-40340-4). Plenum Pub.
Leaver, K. D. & Chapman, B. N. Thin Films. LC 75-153871. (Wykeham Science Ser.: No. 17). 1971. 9.95x (ISBN 0-8448-1119-X). Crane Russak Co.
Leaver, R. H. & And Thomas, T. R. Analysis & Presentation of Experimental Results. LC 74-30111. 1974. text ed. 10.95 (ISBN 0-470-52027-2). Halsted Pr.
Leavey, John P., Jr., tr. see Derrida, Jacques.
Leavis, F. R. Education & the University. 1979. 23.95 (ISBN 0-521-22610-4); pap. 6.50 (ISBN 0-521-29573-4). Cambridge U Pr.
--English Literature in Our Time & the University. LC 78-73128. 1979. 26.50 (ISBN 0-521-22609-0); pap. 7.50 (ISBN 0-521-29574-2). Cambridge U Pr.
--The Great Tradition: George Eliot, Henry James, Joseph Conrad. (Gotham Library). 1963. pap. 5.00x, usa (ISBN 0-8147-0254-6). NYU Pr.
--Thought, Words & Creativity: Art & Thought in Lawrence. 1976. 12.95 (ISBN 0-19-519884-0). Oxford U Pr.
--Towards Standards of Criticism. 200p. 1981. pap. 7.25x (ISBN 0-85315-388-4, Pub. by Lawrence & Wishart Ltd England). Humanities.
Leavis, Q. D., ed. see Bronte, Charlotte.
Leavitt, Charles. Monarch Notes on Twain's the Prince & the Pauper. (Orig.). pap. 1.95 (ISBN 0-671-00878-1). Monarch Pr.
Leavitt, Dinah L. Feminist Theatre Groups. LC 80-10602. 159p. 1980. lib. bdg. 10.95x (ISBN 0-89950-005-6). McFarland & Co.
Leavitt, Emily S., et al. Animals & Their Legal Rights. rev. ed. Stevens, Christine, ed. LC 77-70142. (Illus.). 215p. 1978. pap. text ed. 2.00 (ISBN 0-938414-00-3). Animal Welfare.
Leavitt, G. S. Oral-Aural Communications (OAC) A Teacher's Manual. (Illus.). 136p. 1974. 11.75 (ISBN 0-398-03061-8); pap. 8.25 (ISBN 0-398-03063-4). C C Thomas.
Leavitt, Harold, et al, eds. Organizations of the Future: Interaction with the External Environment. LC 74-1733. (Special Studies). (Illus.). 220p. 1974. text ed. 25.95 (ISBN 0-275-28864-1). Praeger.
Leavitt, Harold J. & Pondy, Louis R., eds. Readings in Managerial Psychology. 2nd ed. LC 64-15811. 1974. 17.50x o.s.i. (ISBN 0-226-46984-0); pap. 8.50x o.s.i. (ISBN 0-226-46985-9). U of Chicago Pr.
Leavitt, John F. The Charles W. Morgan. LC 73-83835. (Illus.). 131p. 1973. 14.00 (ISBN 0-913372-09-9); pap. 8.00 (ISBN 0-913372-10-2). Mystic Seaport.
Leavitt, Judith W. & Numbers, Ronald L., eds. Sickness & Health in America: Readings in the History of Medicine & Public Health. LC 78-53288. 1978. 27.50 (ISBN 0-299-07620-2); pap. 10.95 (ISBN 0-299-07624-5). U of Wis Pr.
Leavitt, Sophie. All New Sophie Lavitt's Penny Pincher's Cookbook. 512p. 1980. pap. 2.95 (ISBN 0-553-13329-2). Bantam.
Leavy, Herbert T. Successful Small Farms: Building Plans & Methods. LC 78-7987. 1978. 14.00 (ISBN 0-912336-67-6); pap. 7.95 (ISBN 0-912336-68-4). Structures Pub.
Lebar, Lois & Berg, Miguel. Llamados a Ensenar. Blanch, Jose M., tr. from Eng. LC 77-5183. Orig. Title: Called to Teach. (Illus.). 160p. (Orig., Span.). 1970. pap. 2.50 o.s.i. (ISBN 0-89922-006-1). Edit Caribe.
Le Bar, Lois E. Education That Is Christian. 9.95 (ISBN 0-8007-0078-3). Revell.
LeBaron, Charles. Gentle Vengeance. 1981. 12.95 (ISBN 0-399-90112-4). Marek.
LeBaron, Dean. The Ins and Outs of Institutional Investing. LC 76-40961. 176p. 1976. 14.95 (ISBN 0-88229-343-5). Nelson-Hall.
Lebaron, John. Making Television: A Video Guide for Teachers. (Orig.). 1981. pap. 12.50 (ISBN 0-8077-2636-2). Tchrs Coll.
Lebas, Elizabeth, tr. see Castells, Manuel.
Lebeck, M., tr. see Nossack, Hans E.
Lebeck, Robert. The Kiss. (Illus.). 176p. 1981. pap. 6.95 (ISBN 0-312-45687-5). St Martin.
--Playgirls of Yesteryear. (Illus.). 176p. 1981. pap. 6.95 (ISBN 0-312-61553-1). St Martin.
Lebedev, N. I. A New Stage in International Relations. LC 77-30488. 1978. text ed. 30.00 (ISBN 0-08-022246-3). Pergamon.
Lebel, J. J. & Marowitz, Charles. New Writers Four. 1980. pap. 6.00 (ISBN 0-7145-0403-3). Riverrun NY.
Lebell, Frank. Independent Marketing-Selling. 288p. 1980. 19.95 (ISBN 0-9600762-3-9). Herman Pub.
--The Manufacturer's Representative. 192p. 1981. 19.95 (ISBN 0-89047-037-5). Herman Pub.
--Professional Sales Representation. 208p. 1981. 19.95 (ISBN 0-89047-038-3). Herman Pub.
Le Bendig, Michael & Diamond, Elliot. Podiatric Resource Guide for Preventive & Rehabilitative Foot & Leg Care. LC 75-45780. 1976. m0n0graph 18.25 (ISBN 0-87993-080-2). Futura Pub.
Lebens, Ralph M. Passive Solar Heating Design. 234p. 1980. 49.95x (ISBN 0-470-26977-4). Halsted Pr.
Lebenthal, Emanuel, ed. Gastroenterology & Nutrition in Infancy, 2 vols. 1980. Set. text ed. 115.00 (ISBN 0-89004-526-7) (ISBN 0-89004-533-X). Raven.
Le Berrurier, Diane O. The Pictorial Sources of Mythological & Scientific Illustrations in Hrabanus Maurus' De rerum naturis. LC 77-94732. (Outstanding Dissertations in the Fine Arts Ser.). (Illus.). 263p. 1980. lib. bdg. 31.00 (ISBN 0-8240-3234-9). Garland Pub.
Le Blanc, Charles, ed. see Bodde, Derk.
Leblanc, Hugues & Wisdom, William. Deductive Logic. 2nd ed. 354p. 1976. text ed. 19.95 (ISBN 0-205-05496-X). Allyn.
LeBlanc, Jacques. Man in the Cold. (American Lectures in Environmental Studies Ser.). (Illus.). 208p. 1975. 21.75 (ISBN 0-398-03429-X). C C Thomas.
LeBlanc, John F., et al. Mathematics-Methods Program: Addition & Subtraction. (Mathematics Ser). 176p. 1976. pap. text ed. 4.25 (ISBN 0-201-14608-8); instr's man. 1.50 (ISBN 0-201-14609-6). A-W.
--Mathematics-Methods Program: Analysis of Shapes. (Mathematics Ser.). (Illus.). 112p. 1976. pap. text ed. 3.25 (ISBN 0-201-14618-5); instr's man. 1.50 (ISBN 0-201-14619-3). A-W.
--Mathematics Methods Program: Awareness Geometry. 40p. 1976. pap. text ed. 2.95 (ISBN 0-201-14614-2); instructor's manual 1.50 (ISBN 0-201-14615-0). A-W.
--Mathematics-Methods Program: Experiences in Problem Solving. (Mathematics Ser). 64p. 1976. pap. text ed. 2.95 (ISBN 0-201-14628-2); instr's man. 1.50 (ISBN 0-201-14629-0). A-W.
--Mathematics-Methods Program: Graphs, the Picturing of Information. (Mathematics Ser.). (Illus.). 160p. 1976. pap. text ed. 3.95 (ISBN 0-201-14622-3); instr's man. 1.50 (ISBN 0-201-14623-1). A-W.
--Mathematics-Methods Program: Measurement. (Mathematics Ser.). (Illus.). 144p. 1976. pap. text ed. 3.50 (ISBN 0-201-14620-7); instr's man. 1.50 (ISBN 0-201-14621-5). A-W.
--Mathematics-Methods Program: Number Theory. (Mathematics Ser.). (Illus.). 128p. 1976. pap. text ed. 3.50 (ISBN 0-201-14624-X); instr's manual 1.50 (ISBN 0-201-14625-8). A-W.
--Mathematics-Methods Program: Numeration. (Mathematics Ser.). 128p. 1976. pap. 3.95 (ISBN 0-201-14606-1); instr's man. 1.50 (ISBN 0-201-14607-X). A-W.
--Mathematics-Methods Program: Probability & Statistics. (Mathematics Ser). 128p. 1976. pap. text ed. 3.25 (ISBN 0-201-14626-6); instr's man. 1.50 (ISBN 0-201-14627-4). A-W.
--Mathematics Methods Program: Rational Numbers with Integers & Reals. (Mathematics Ser). (Illus.). 240p. 1976. pap. text ed. 4.50 (ISBN 0-201-14612-6); instructor's manual 1.50 (ISBN 0-201-14613-4). A-W.
--Mathematics-Methods Program: Transformational Geometry. (Mathematics Ser.). (Illus.). 132p. 1976. pap. text ed. 3.50 (ISBN 0-201-14616-9); instr's manual 1.50 (ISBN 0-201-14617-7). A-W.
--Mathematics-Methods Program: Multiplication & Division. (Mathematics Ser.). (Illus.). 1976. 3.95 (ISBN 0-201-14610-X); instr's man. 1.50 (ISBN 0-201-14611-8). A-W.
LeBlanc, Maurice. The Confessions of Arsene Lupin. 327p. 1980. Repr. of 1912 ed. lib. bdg. 15.50x (ISBN 0-89968-202-2). Lightyear.
--The Crystal Stopper. 287p. 1980. Repr. of 1913 ed. lib. bdg. 14.25x (ISBN 0-89968-201-4). Lightyear.
--The Hollow Needle. 325p. 1980. Repr. of 1910 ed. lib. bdg. 15.50x (ISBN 0-89968-203-0). Lightyear.
--Teeth of the Tiger. 490p. 1980. Repr. of 1914 ed. lib. bdg. 17.95x (ISBN 0-89968-204-9). Lightyear.
Le Blon, J. C. Coloritto. 98p. 1980. 12.50 (ISBN 0-442-24723-0). Van Nos Reinhold.
Leblond, C. P., ed. see International Society For Cell Biology.
LeBoeuf. Imagineering: How to Think & Act Creatively. 88p. Date not set. 9.95 (ISBN 0-07-036952-6). McGraw.
LeBoeuf, Michael. Imagineering: How to Profit from Your Creative Powers. LC 80-13232. 240p. 1980. 9.95 (ISBN 0-07-036952-6). McGraw.
--Working Smart: How to Accomplish More in Half the Time. 1980. pap. 2.50 (ISBN 0-446-91273-5). Warner Bks.
LeBoit, Joseph & Capponi, Attilio. Advances in Psychotherapy of the Borderline Patient. LC 79-50292. Date not set. 35.00x (ISBN 0-87668-365-0). Aronson.
LeBon, Gustave. The French Revolution & the Psychology of Revolution. (Social Science Classics Ser.). 337p. 1980. 19.95 (ISBN 0-87855-310-X); pap. 6.95 (ISBN 0-87855-697-4). Transaction Bks.
Le Bon, Gustave. The Psychology of Socialism. Repr. of 1965 ed. flexible cover 12.00 (ISBN 0-87034-025-5). Fraser Pub Co.
Lebon, J. H. Introduction to Human Geography. 1966. text ed. 5.50x (ISBN 0-09-031612-6, Hutchinson U Lib). Humanities.
Lebour, M. V. The Planktonic Diatoms of Northern Seas. (Ray Society Publication: No. 116). (Illus.). 244p. 1978. Repr. of 1930 ed. lib. bdg. 30.00x (ISBN 3-87429-147-2). Lubrecht & Cramer.
LeBow, Michael D., ed. Weight Control: The Behavioural Strategies. LC 79-41728. 352p. 1981. 35.75 (ISBN 0-471-27745-2, Pub. by Wiley-Interscience). Wiley.
Lebow, Richard N. Between War & Peace: The Nature of International Crisis. LC 80-21982. 410p. 1981. text ed. 24.50 (ISBN 0-8018-2311-0). Johns Hopkins.
Lebow, Ruth & Garrison, Tom. Oceanus: The Marine Environment. 204p. 1979. 7.95x (ISBN 0-534-00841-0). Wadsworth Pub.
Lebowitz, Carl R., jt. auth. see Edwards, Charles M., Jr.
Lebowitz, Naomi. Italo Svevo. 1978. 16.50 (ISBN 0-8135-0848-7). Rutgers U Pr.
Lebowitz, Philip W., ed. see Massachusetts General Hospital.
Lebra, Joyce, et al, eds. Women in Changing Japan. LC 75-33663. (Special Studies on China & East Asia Ser). 250p. 1976. 26.50x (ISBN 0-89158-019-0). Westview.
Lebra, Joyce C. Japanese-Trained Armies in Southeast Asia: Independence & Volunteer Forces in World War 2. LC 75-16116. 264p. 1977. 17.50x (ISBN 0-231-03995-6). Columbia U Pr.
Lebra, Joyce C., ed. Japan's Greatest East Asia Co-Prosperity Sphere in World War Two: Selected Readings & Documents. 234p. 1975. 27.50x (ISBN 0-19-638265-3). Oxford U Pr.
Lebra, Takie S. Japanese Patterns of Behavior. LC 76-110392. 1976. pap. text ed. 5.95x (ISBN 0-8248-0460-0, Eastwest Ctr). U Pr of Hawaii.
Lebredo, Raquel, jt. auth. see Jarvis, Ana C.
Le Breton, Preston P., ed. The Evaluation of Continuing Education for Professionals: A Systems View. LC 79-4923. 340p. (Orig.). 1979. pap. 11.50 (ISBN 0-295-95693-3, Pub. by Div Acad Prof Progs). U of Wash Pr.
Lebrun, Rico. Rico Lebrun Drawings. 1961. 21.50x (ISBN 0-520-00717-4). U of Cal Pr.
Lebrun, Yvan & Hoops, Richard. Intelligence & Aphasia. (Neurolinguistics Ser.: Vol. 2). 140p. 1974. pap. text ed. 15.75 (ISBN 90-265-0182-X, Pub. by Swets Pub Serv Holland). Swets North Am.
Lebrun, Yvan & Hoops, Richard, eds. The Management of Aphasia. (Neurolinguistics Ser.: Vol. 8). 124p. 1978. text ed. 26.00 (ISBN 90-265-0280-X, Pub. by Swets Pub Serv Holland). Swets North Am.
--Problems of Aphasia. (Neurolinguistics Ser.: Vol. 9). 198p. 1979. text ed. 36.00 (ISBN 90-265-0309-1, Pub. by Swets Pub Serv Holland). Swets North Am.
--Recovery in Aphasics. (Neurolinguistics Ser.: Vol. 4). 270p. 1976. text ed. 34.50 (ISBN 90-265-0228-1, Pub. by Swets Pub Serv Holland). Swets North Am.
Lebrun, Yvan, ed. see International Symposium Held at St. Ode, Belgium, Oct. 1-3, 1979.
Lebrun, Yvan, jt. ed. see Von Raffler-Engel, Walburga.
Lebrun, Yvan, et al. The Artificial Larynx. (Neurolinguistics Ser.: Vol. 1). 90p. 1973. pap. text ed. 15.75 (ISBN 90-265-0173-0, Pub. by Swets Pub Serv Holland). Swets North Am.
Leca, Ange-Pierre. The Egyptian Way of Death: Mummies & the Cult of the Immortal. LC 78-68326. (Illus.). 312p. 1981. 12.95 (ISBN 0-385-14609-4). Doubleday.
LeCain, Errol. The Cabbage Princess. (Illus.). (ps-5). 1969. 6.95 (ISBN 0-571-09155-5, Pub. by Faber & Faber). Merrimack Bk Serv.
--King Arthur's Sword. (Illus.). (ps-5). 1968. 5.95 o.p. (ISBN 0-571-08637-3, Pub. by Faber & Faber). Merrimack Bk Serv.
Le Camus, A. Abdeker; or, the Art of Preserving Beauty, 1754. Shugrue, Michael F., ed. (The Flowering of the Novel, 1740-1775 Ser: Vol. 41). 1974. lib. bdg. 50.00 (ISBN 0-8240-1140-6). Garland Pub.
Le Camus, E. The Children of Nazareth. 131p. 1901. text ed. 2.95 (ISBN 0-567-02162-9). Attic Pr.
Le Carre, John. Smiley's People. 1980. pap. 3.50. Bantam.
Lecca, Pedro J. & Tharp, C. Patrick. Pharmacy in Health Care & Institutional Systems. LC 77-27655. (Illus.). 1978. text ed. 17.95 (ISBN 0-8016-2904-7). Mosby.
Lecerf, Auguste. An Introduction to Reformed Dogmatics. Leigh-Hunt, S., tr. (Twin Brooks Ser.). 408p. (Orig.). 1981. pap. 9.95 (ISBN 0-8010-5603-9). Baker Bk.
Lechat, P. Local Anesthetics. 1971. 55.00 (ISBN 0-08-015836-6). Pergamon.
Lecherbonnier, Bernard, jt. auth. see Du, Gerard.
Lecherbonnier, Bernard, jt. auth. see Durozoi, Gerard.
Lechevalier, Hubert, jt. ed. see Laskin, Allen I.
Lechner, H. & Aranibar, A., eds. EEG & Clinical Neurophysiology. (International Congress Ser.: No. 506). 128p. 1979. 24.50 (ISBN 0-444-90111-6, Excerpta Medica). Elsevier.
Lecht, Jane, ed. see Population Reference Bureau.
Lecht, Leonard A. Occupational Choices & Training Needs. LC 76-24356. (Special Studies). 1977. text ed. 23.95 (ISBN 0-275-23960-8). Praeger.
Lecht, Leonard A., et al. Changes in Occupational Characteristics: Planning Ahead for the 1980's. LC 76-20179. (Report Ser.: No. 691). (Illus.). 1976. pap. 30.00 o.p. (ISBN 0-8237-0125-5). Conference Bd.
Lechtman, Max D., jt. auth. see Wistreich, George A.
Lechtman, Max D., et al. The Games Cells Play. LC 78-57373. 1979. text ed. 7.50 (ISBN 0-8053-6094-8). Benjamin-Cummings.
Leck, J. H. Theory of Semiconductor Junction Devices. 1967. 7.00 o.p. (ISBN 0-08-012173-X). Pergamon.
Leckel, John, jt. auth. see Feeney, Agnes.
Lecker, Sidney. How to Get Lucky: Stacking the Odds in Your Favor in Life, Love, & Work. LC 80-681. 256p. 1980. 10.95 (ISBN 0-672-52660-3). Bobbs.
Leckie, James O., jt. ed. see Kavanaugh, Michael.
Leckie, Jim, et al. More Other Homes & Garbage: Designs for Self-Sufficient Living. (Illus.). 416p. 1981. pap. 14.95 (ISBN 0-87156-274-X). Sierra.
--Other Homes & Garbage: Designs for Self-Sufficient Living. LC 75-8913. (Illus.). 320p. (Orig.). 1975. pap. 9.95 (ISBN 0-87156-141-7). Sierra.
Leckie, R. William, Jr. The Passage of Dominion: Geoffrey of Monmouth & the Periodization of Insular History in the Twelfth Century. 184p. 1981. 20.00x (ISBN 0-8020-5495-1). U of Toronto Pr.
Leckie, Robert. Battle for Iwo Jima. (gr. 5-9). 1967. 2.95 o.p. (ISBN 0-394-80418-X, BYR). Random.
--The Bloodborn. (Americans at War Ser.: No. 1). (Orig.). 1981. pap. 2.95 (ISBN 0-451-09801-3, E9801, Signet Bks). NAL.
--The Wars of America. rev. ed. LC 78-4735. (Illus.). 1981. 20.00 (ISBN 0-06-012571-3, HarpT). Har-Row.

Leckie, William H. Buffalo Soldiers: A Narrative of the Negro Cavalry in the West. (Illus.). 1967. 12.95 (ISBN 0-8061-0734-0); pap. 5.95 (ISBN 0-8061-1244-1). U of Okla Pr.
Lecky, W. E. A History of Ireland in the Eighteenth Century. abr. ed. Curtis, L. P., Jr., ed. LC 78-184286. (Classics of British Historical Literature Ser.). 576p. 1972. 15.00x o.s.i. (ISBN 0-226-46994-8). U of Chicago Pr.
Lecky, William E. Democracy & Liberty. LC 80-82371. 1981. Set. 18.00 (ISBN 0-913966-80-0); Vol. I, 520p. (ISBN 0-913966-82-7); Vol. II 528p. (ISBN 0-913966-83-5); Set. pap. 6.00 (ISBN 0-913966-81-9). Vol. I (ISBN 0-913966-84-3). Vol. II. (ISBN 0-913966-85-1). Liberty Fund.
Lecky, Wm. Edward. Leaders of Public Opinion in Ireland, 2 vols. LC 76-159800. (Europe 1815-1945 Ser.). 720p. 1973. Repr. of 1903 ed. Set. lib. bdg. 59.50 (ISBN 0-306-70574-5). Da Capo.
Leclerc, Ivor. Whitehead's Metaphysics. 1978. Repr. of 1958 ed. text ed. 15.00x (ISBN 0-391-00570-7). Humanities.
Leclercq, H. Manuel D'archeologie Chretienne: Depuis les origines jusqu'au VIII siecle, 2 vols. (Illus., Fr.). 1981. Repr. of 1907 ed. lib. bdg. 160.00x (ISBN 0-89241-148-1). Vol. 1, 592p. Vol. 2, 682p. Caratzas Bros.
Leclercq, Jacques. This Day Is Ours. Livingstone, Dinah, tr. LC 80-50314. Orig. Title: Le Jour de L'Homme. 160p. 1980. pap. 6.95 (ISBN 0-88344-504-2). Orbis Bks.
Le Clercq, Jacques, tr. see Goncourt, Edmond L.
Leclercq, Jean. Monks & Love in Twelfth-Century France: Psycho-Historical Essays. 156p. 1979. text ed. 28.50x (ISBN 0-19-822546-6). Oxford U Pr.
Leclerque, James R. Nature & the Fibonacci's Conception of the Universe. (Illus.). 123p. 1980. deluxe ed. 59.85 (ISBN 0-89266-263-8). Am Classical Coll Pr.
Lecomber, Brian. Talk Down. 1979. pap. 2.25 o.p. (ISBN 0-425-04196-4). Berkley Pub.
LeComber, P. G. & LeComber, P. G., eds. Electronic & Structural Properties of Amorphous Semiconductors. 1973. 87.50 (ISBN 0-12-440550-9). Acad Pr.
Lecomber, Richard. Economic Growth Versus the Environment. LC 75-5605. 1975. pap. 6.50x (ISBN 0-470-52100-7). Halsted Pr.
--Economics of Natural Resources. LC 78-23595. 247p. 1979. 24.95 (ISBN 0-470-26546-9). Halsted Pr.
LeCompte, Herman, jt. auth. see Parkinson, C. Northcote.
Lecompte, Janet. Pueblo, Hardscrabble, Greenhorn: The Upper Arkansas, 1832-1856. LC 77-18616. (Illus.). 354p. 1981. pap. 7.95 (ISBN 0-8061-1723-0). U of Okla Pr.
Le Comte, Edward. Dictionary of Puns in Milton's English Poetry. 240p. 1981. text ed. 25.00x (ISBN 0-231-05102-6). Columbia U Pr.
LeComte, Edward. Milton & Sex. LC 77-1081. 1978. 15.00x (ISBN 0-231-04340-6). Columbia U Pr.
--Milton's Unchanging Mind: Three Essays. LC 73-83266. 132p. 1974. 11.00 (ISBN 0-8046-9060-X). Kennikat.
--Poet's Riddles: Essays in Seventeenth Century Explication. LC 74-77656. 1975. 12.50 (ISBN 0-8046-9065-0, Natl U). Kennikat.
LeComte, Jacques & Koechlin-Schwartz, Dorothee. How to Talk to the Birds & the Beasts. LC 79-54013. (Illus.). 1980. 9.95 (ISBN 0-87795-252-3). Arbor Hse.
Le Corbeiller, Clara. China Trade Porcelain: Patterns of Exchange. LC 74-2097. (Illus.). 1974. 15.00 o.p. (ISBN 0-87099-089-6, 139092). Metro Mus Art.
Le Corbusier, see Jeanneret, Charles E., pseud.
Lecourt, Nancy. Rainbow. (Books I Can Read). 32p. (gr. 2). 1980. pap. 1.25 (ISBN 0-8127-0290-5). Southern Pub.
Le Cren, E. D. & Lowe-McConnell, R. H., eds. The Functioning of Freshwater Ecosystems. LC 79-50504. (International Biological Programme Ser.: No. 22). (Illus.). 1980. 95.00 (ISBN 0-521-22507-8). Cambridge U Pr.
Lectures, International Winter College, Trieste, 1973. Atoms, Molecules & Lasers. (Illus.). 710p. 1975. pap. 50.50 (ISBN 92-0-130374-2, IAEA). Unipub.
Le Cuff, Madeleine see Cuff, Madeleine Le.
Lecyn, Nancy, jt. ed. see Germano, William P.
Ledbetter, Elaine & Young, Jay. Keys to Chemistry: Metric. 2nd ed. (gr. 11-12). 1977. text ed. 15.40 (ISBN 0-201-04361-0, Sch Div); tchr's ed. 5.28 (ISBN 0-201-04362-9); lab man. 5.72 (ISBN 0-201-04363-7). A-W.
Ledbetter, Marie, jt. auth. see Thiel, Linda.
Ledbetter, Steven, ed. see Marenzio, Luca.
Ledd, Paul. Chain Gang Kill. (Shelter Ser.: No. 3). 256p. (Orig.). 1980. pap. 1.95 (ISBN 0-89083-658-2). Zebra.
--China Doll. (Shelter Ser.: No. 5). 1980. pap. 1.95 (ISBN 0-89083-682-5, Kable News Co). Zebra.
--The Lazarus Guns. (Shelter Ser.: No. 5). 256p. (Orig.). 1980. pap. 1.95 (ISBN 0-89083-694-9). Zebra.
Ledda, Gavino. Padre Padrone...My Father, My Master. Salamanazar, George, tr. 1979. 12.95 (ISBN 0-89396-003-9); pap. 6.95 (ISBN 0-89396-006-3). Urizen Bks.
Ledebur, L. C., jt. auth. see Henderson, W. L.
Ledeen, Michael & Lewis, William. Debacle: The American Failure in Iran. LC 80-27149. 320p. 12.95 (ISBN 0-686-69414-7). Knopf.
Leder, Dora, illus. Mother Goose in the City. (ps-2). 1974. PLB 5.00 (ISBN 0-307-60336-9, Golden Pr). Western Pub.
Leder, Lawrence H. Dimensions of Change: Problems & Issues of American Colonial History. LC 72-75882. 1972. pap. text ed. 6.95 o.p. (ISBN 0-8087-1220-9). Burgess.
Lederach, John & Lederach, Naomi. Marriage in Today's World: Student Activity Book. 56p. 1980. pap. 2.50 (ISBN 0-8361-1946-0). Herald Pr.
Lederach, Naomi, jt. auth. see Lederach, John.
Lederach, Paul M. A Third Way. LC 80-26280. 152p. 1980. pap. 6.95 (ISBN 0-8361-1934-7). Herald Pr.
Lederer, Emil. State of the Masses. 1967. Repr. 14.00 (ISBN 0-86527-190-9). Fertig.
Lederer, Emil & Lederer-Seidler, Emy. Japan in Transition. 1938. 32.50x o.p. (ISBN 0-685-69837-8). Elliots Bks.
Lederer, Katherine. Lillian Hellman. (United States Authors Ser.: No. 338). 1979. 9.95 (ISBN 0-8057-7275-8). Twayne.
Lederer, Laura, ed. Take Back the Night: Women on Pornography. LC 80-23701. 352p. (Orig.). 1980. pap. 7.95 (ISBN 0-688-08728-0, Quill). Morrow.
--Take Back the Night: Women on Pornography. LC 80-17084. 352p. 1980. 14.95 (ISBN 0-688-03728-3). Morrow.
Lederer, Muriel. Blue-Collar Jobs for Women. 1979. 12.95 o.p.; pap. 7.95 (ISBN 0-87690-319-7). Dutton.
Lederer, Rhoda, jt. auth. see Cohen, Ben.
Lederer, Richard, jt. auth. see Burnham, Philip.
Lederer, Richard, jt. auth. see Burnham, Phillip.
Lederer, W., jt. auth. see Burdick, E.
Lederer, William J. Marital Choices: Forecasting, Assesing & Improving a Relationship. 1981. 12.95 (ISBN 0-393-01412-6). Norton.
Lederer, William J. & Jackson, Don D. Mirages of Marriage. LC 67-16608. 1968. 14.95 (ISBN 0-393-08400-0). Norton.
Lederer-Seidler, Emy, jt. auth. see Lederer, Emil.
Lederman, D., tr. see Dukhin, S. S. & Shilov, V. N.
Lederman, D., tr. see Sedunov, Yu. S.
Lederman, E. K. Existential Neurosis. (Illus.). 150p. 1972. 10.60 (ISBN 0-407-17040-5). Butterworths.
Lederman, Minna, ed. Stravinsky in the Theatre. LC 74-34377. (Music Reprint Ser.). (Illus.). 228p. 1975. Repr. of 1949 ed. lib. bdg. 22.50 (ISBN 0-306-70665-2); pap. 4.95 (ISBN 0-306-80022-5). Da Capo.
Lederman, N., ed. see Shostakovskii, M. F.
Ledermann, W. Introduction to Group Characters. LC 76-46858. (Illus.). 1977. 47.00 (ISBN 0-521-21486-6); pap. 12.95 (ISBN 0-521-29170-4). Cambridge U Pr.
Ledermann, Walter. Complex Numbers. (Library of Mathematics). 1971. pap. 5.00 (ISBN 0-7100-4345-7). Routledge & Kegan.
--Handbook of Applicable Mathematics, Vol. 1: Algebra. LC 79-42724. (Handbook of Applicable Mathematics Ser.). 1980. text ed. 85.00 (ISBN 0-471-27704-5, Pub. by Wiley-Interscience). Wiley.
--Integral Calculus. (Library of Mathematics). 1967. pap. 5.00 (ISBN 0-7100-4355-4). Routledge & Kegan.
--Multiple Integrals. (Library of Mathematics Ser.). (Illus.). 1966. pap. 5.00 (ISBN 0-7100-4358-9). Routledge & Kegan.
Ledford, A. A. Pathways to Prophetic Fulfillment. LC 78-53118. 1978. pap. 3.25 (ISBN 0-87148-695-4). Pathway Pr.
Ledgard, Henry F. Programming Proverbs. (Computer Programming Ser.). (Illus.). 144p. 1975. pap. text ed. 8.50x (ISBN 0-8104-5522-6). Hayden.
--Programming Proverbs for FORTRAN Programmers. LC 74-22074. (Computer Programming Ser.). (Illus.). 144p. (Orig.). 1975. pap. text ed. 8.35x (ISBN 0-8104-5820-9). Hayden.
Ledgard, Henry F. & Chmura, Louis J. FORTRAN with Style. (Computer Programming Ser.). (gr. 12 up). 1978. pap. text ed. 8.35x (ISBN 0-8104-5682-6). Hayden.
Ledgard, Henry F. & Chmura, Louis J., Jr. COBOL with Style: Programming Proverbs. (Computer Programming Ser.). 1976. pap. text ed. 8.35x (ISBN 0-8104-5781-4). Hayden.
Ledgard, Henry F., jt. auth. see Nagin, Paul.
Ledgard, Henry F., et al. Pascal with Style: Programming Proverbs. 1979. pap. text ed. 7.70 (ISBN 0-8104-5124-7). Hayden.
Ledger, John, ed. see Skaife, Sydney H.
Ledin, George. A Structured Approach to General BASIC. 1978. pap. 10.95x (ISBN 0-87835-070-5). Boyd & Fraser.
Ledin, George, Jr. A Structured Approach to Essential Basic. 176p. 1979. pap. text ed. 7.95x (ISBN 0-87835-077-2). Boyd & Fraser.
Ledin, George, Jr. & Ledin, Victor. The Programmer's Book of Rules. LC 79-13746. 1979. pap. 9.95 (ISBN 0-534-97993-9). Lifetime Learn.
Ledin, Victor, jt. auth. see Ledin, George, Jr.
Lednicer, Daniel & Mitscher, Lester A. Organic Chemistry of Drug Synthesis, 2 vols. LC 76-28387. Vol. 1, 1977. 28.50 (ISBN 0-471-52141-8, Pub. by Wiley-Interscience); Vol. 2, 1980. 28.00 (ISBN 0-471-04392-3). Wiley.
Le Douarin, N., ed. Cell Lineage, Stem Cells & Cell Determination. (INSERM: No. 10). 378p. 1979. 56.00 (ISBN 0-7204-0673-0, North Holland). Elsevier.
Le Duc, Barbara. Safe Food Guide. 1979. pap. 1.95 (ISBN 0-345-28424-0). Ballantine.
Leduc, Lucien P. Behavior Modification Comes to Camelot. (Scholarly Monograph Ser.). 140p. 1980. pap. 9.00 (ISBN 0-686-64783-1). Carrollton Pr.
Leduc, Violette. La Batarde. Coltman, Derek, tr. 488p. 1965. 12.95 o.p. (ISBN 0-374-18232-9); pap. 7.95 (ISBN 0-374-51371-6). FS&G.
--Mad in Pursuit. Coltman, Derek, tr. from Fr. 351p. 1971. 8.95 o.p. (ISBN 0-374-19508-0). FS&G.
--The Taxi. Weaver, Helen, tr. from Fr. 96p. 1972. 4.95 o.p. (ISBN 0-374-27253-0). FS&G.
Le Duc, William G. Recollections of a Civil War Quartermaster. LC 63-64537. 167p. 1963. 3.75 (ISBN 0-685-47098-9). Minn Hist.
Lee. The Hidden Events: Incredible Life & Behavior of Insects. 1981. 12.95 (ISBN 0-8120-5340-0). Barron.
Lee, A. G. Chemistry of Thallium. (Illus.). 1971. text ed. 59.60x (ISBN 0-444-20112-2, Pub. by Applied Science). Burgess-Intl Ideas.
Lee, A. G., ed. see Ovid.
Lee, A. R. Blast Furnaces & Steel Slag: Production, Properties & Uses. LC 74-521. 119p. 1974. 16.95 (ISBN 0-470-52151-1). Halsted Pr.
Lee, Albert. Henry Ford & the Jews. LC 79-3694. 252p. 1980. 12.95 (ISBN 0-8128-2701-5). Stein & Day.
--How to Profit from Your Arts & Crafts. 1978. 9.95 o.p. (ISBN 0-679-50831-7); pap. 4.95 o.p. (ISBN 0-679-50868-6). McKay.
--Slumlord: The True Story of the Man Who Is Beating America's Biggest Problem. LC 76-4784. 1976. 7.95 o.s.i. (ISBN 0-87000-360-7). Arlington Hse.
Lee, Alfred M., et al, eds. Principles of Sociology. 3rd ed. LC 75-89671. 1969. pap. 5.50 (ISBN 0-06-460026-2, CO 26, COS). Har-Row.
Lee, Amy F. & Lowman, Alintro. by. Watercolor, Wax & Wool: The Art of Janet Shook Lacoste. LC 80-82780. (Illus.). 88p. (Orig.). 1980. pap. 10.00 (ISBN 0-933164-81-5). U of Tex Inst Tex Culture.
Lee, Anthony A. The Black Rose: A Story About 'Abdu'l-Baha in America. (Stories About 'abdu'l-Baha in America Ser.). (Illus.). 24p. (gr. k-5). 1979. pap. 2.50 (ISBN 0-933770-00-6). Kalimat.
--The Scottish Visitors: A Story About 'Abdu'l-Baha in Britain. (Stories About 'abdu'l-Baha Ser.). (Illus.). 24p. (Orig.). (gr. k-5). 1981. pap. 2.50 (ISBN 0-933770-05-7). Kalimat.
--The Unfriendly Governor. (Stories About Abdul'l-Baha Ser.). (Illus.). 24p. (gr. k-5). 1980. pap. 2.50 (ISBN 0-933770-02-2). Kalimat.
Lee, Bennett & Barme, Geremie. China Traveler's Phrasebook. 1980. pap. 5.95 (ISBN 0-8351-0729-9). China Bks.
Lee, Betsy. Mother Teresa: Caring for All God's Children. LC 80-20286. (Taking Part Ser.). (Illus.). 48p. (gr. 3 up). 1981. PLB 6.95 (ISBN 0-87518-205-4). Dillon.
Lee, Bob, jt. auth. see Arnold, Henri.
Lee, Bok Y. Handbook of Noninvasive Diagnostic Techniques. 352p. 1981. pap. 15.00 (ISBN 0-8385-3620-4). ACC.
Lee, Brian. The Novels of Henry James: A Study of Culture & Consciousness. LC 78-16902. 1979. 16.95 (ISBN 0-312-57969-1). St Martin.
--Theory & Personality: The Significance of T. S. Eliot's Criticism. 1979. text ed. 26.00x (ISBN 0-485-11185-3, Athlone Pr). Humanities.
Lee, Brian N. British Bookplates: A Pictorial History. LC 79-53732. (Illus.). 1979. 45.00 (ISBN 0-7153-7785-X). David & Charles.
Lee, Byung S. & Huang, Lien-Fu. Fundamental Statistics in Business & Economics. LC 78-68690. 1979. pap. text ed. 17.25 (ISBN 0-8191-0701-8). U Pr of Amer.
Lee, C., ed. see Carnegie Commission on Higher Education.
Lee, C. H. British Regional Employment Statistics: 1841-1971. LC 78-25698. 1980. 52.50 (ISBN 0-521-22666-X). Cambridge U Pr.
Lee, C. K., ed. Developments in Food Carbohydrate, Vol. 2. (Illus.). 402p. 1980. 75.00x (ISBN 0-85334-857-X, Pub. by Applied Science). Burgess-Intl Ideas.
Lee, C. M. & Inglis, J. K. Science for Hairdressing Students. 2nd ed. 1972. text ed. 16.50 (ISBN 0-08-016665-2); pap. text ed. 7.75 (ISBN 0-08-016666-0). Pergamon.
Lee, C. Y. Land of the Golden Mountain. 1977. pap. 1.50 o.p. (ISBN 0-445-03213-8). Popular Lib.
--Lover's Point. 1958. 3.75 o.p. (ISBN 0-374-19380-0). FS&G.
Lee, Catherine. The Growth & Development of Children. 2nd ed. LC 76-56438. 1977. pap. text ed. 7.95x (ISBN 0-582-48828-1). Longman.
Lee, Changsoo & DeVos, George. Koreans in Japan: Ethnic Conflict & Accommodation. (Illus.). 448p. 1981. 30.00x (ISBN 0-520-04258-1). U of Cal Pr.
Lee, Charlotte. Oral Interpretations. 5th ed. LC 76-13095. (Illus.). 1976. text ed. 16.50 (ISBN 0-395-24547-8). HM.
Lee, Charlotte E. Oral Reading of the Scriptures. 1974. text ed. 14.75 (ISBN 0-395-18940-3). HM.
Lee, Chin-Chuan. Media Imperialism Reconsidered: The Homogenizing of Television Culture. LC 80-16763. (People & Communication Ser.: Vol. 10). (Illus.). 276p. 1980. 20.00 (ISBN 0-8039-1495-4). Sage.
--Media Imperialism Reconsidered: The Homogenizing of Television Culture. LC 80-16763. (People & Communication Ser.: Vol. 10). (Illus.). 276p. 1980. pap. 9.95 (ISBN 0-8039-1496-2). Sage.
Lee, Chip. Progressions in Climbing. (Illus.). 250p. 1981. pap. price not set (ISBN 0-910146-35-7). Appalach Mtn.
Lee, Chong. Dynamic Kicks: Essentials for Free Fighting. Johnson, Gilbert, ed. LC 75-36052. (Ser. 122). (Illus.). 1975. pap. text ed. 5.95 (ISBN 0-89750-017-2). Ohara Pubns.
--Super Dynamic Kicks, Vol. 3. LC 80-84496. 1980. pap. 5.50 (ISBN 0-89750-072-5). Ohara Pubns.
Lee, Chong-Sik, jt. auth. see Scalapino, Robert A.
Lee, Clarence L., ed. see Carpenter, H. J.
Lee, Clarence L., ed. see Jones, A. H.
Lee, Colin. Models in Planning. LC 72-8442. 152p. 1973. text ed. 21.00 (ISBN 0-08-017020-X); pap. text ed. 9.75 (ISBN 0-08-017021-8). Pergamon.
Lee County Historical Survey Committee. History of Lee County, Texas. (Illus.). 480p. 1974. 25.00 (ISBN 0-685-53907-5). Nortex Pr.
Lee, D., jt. auth. see Leggett, G.
Lee, Danise L. Surgery Without Fear. (Illus.). 48p. 1980. pap. 4.95 (ISBN 0-937210-00-5). Time-Lee Pubns.
Lee, David. Cocaine Handbook. 192p. 1981. price not set. And-or Pr.
Lee, David E. The Motivating Administrator. 128p. 1981. 6.95 (ISBN 0-88289-255-X). Pelican.
Lee, David W., et al, eds. The Soviet Merchant Marine: Economic Aid & Strategic Challenge to the West. 1979. pap. text ed. 6.50x (ISBN 0-686-59447-9). Westview.
Lee, Deemer. Esther's Town. 190p. 1980. 12.95 (ISBN 0-8138-0460-4). Iowa St U Pr.
Lee, Derek. Regional Planning & Location of Industry. 3rd ed. (Studies in the British Economy). 1980. pap. text ed. 6.50 (ISBN 0-435-84577-2). Heinemann Ed.
Lee, Donald Lewis & Atkinson, H. J. Physiology of Nematodes. 2d ed. LC 77-1232. (Illus.). 1977. 20.00x (ISBN 0-231-04358-9). Columbia U Pr.
Lee, Dorothy E. & Clifton, A. Kay. Minority Status: The Position of Women. LC 79-65259. 155p. 1981. perfect bdg. 13.50 (ISBN 0-86548-044-3). Century Twenty One.
Lee, Dorris M. & Allen, Richard V. Learning to Read Through Experience. 2nd ed. (Illus.). (YA) (gr. 9-12). 1966. pap. text ed. 8.95 (ISBN 0-13-527523-7). P-H.
Lee, Douglas, jt. auth. see Kozuki, Russell.
Lee, Douglas H., ed. Environmental Factors in Respiratory Disease. (Environmental Science Ser.). 1972. 22.00 (ISBN 0-12-440655-6). Acad Pr.
Lee, Dwight E. Europe's Crucial Years: The Diplomatic Background of World War I, 1902-1914. LC 73-91315. (Illus.). 500p. 1974. text ed. 27.50x (ISBN 0-87451-094-5). U Pr of New Eng.
Lee, Dwight R. & McNown, Robert F. Economics in Our Time: Concepts & Issues. LC 74-18924. 224p. 1975. pap. text ed. 5.95 (ISBN 0-574-18222-5, 13-2220); instr's guide avail. (ISBN 0-574-18221-7, 13-2221). SRA.
Lee, Dwight R., jt. auth. see McNown, Robert F.
Lee, E. B. & Markus, L. Foundations of Optimal Control Theory. LC 67-22414. (SIAM Series in Applied Mathematics). 1967. 44.50 (ISBN 0-471-52263-5, Pub. by Wiley-Interscience). Wiley.

Lee, E. H. & Symonds, P. S., eds. Plasticity: Proceedings, Symposium on Naval Structural Mechanics - 2nd - Brown Univ. - 1960. 1960. 17.00 o.p. (ISBN 0-08-009459-7). Pergamon.

Lee, E. Lawrence. Indian Wars in North Carolina, 1663-1763. (Illus.). 1968. pap. 1.00 (ISBN 0-86526-084-2). NC Archives.

Lee, E. Stanley, jt. ed. see Wen, C. Y.

Lee, Earl G. Recycled for Living. LC 72-94753. 128p. (Orig.). 1973. pap. 1.65 o.p. (ISBN 0-8307-0217-2, 50-091-03). Regal.

Lee, Ed, jt. ed. see Vulliamy, Graham.

Lee, Elbert. How to Make Money 24 Hours a Day. 140p. 1980. pap. 9.95 (ISBN 0-686-28038-5). Positive Pub.

Lee, Elisa T. Statistical Methods for Survival Data Analysis. LC 80-24720. 557p. 1980. text ed. 26.95 solutions manual (ISBN 0-534-97987-4). Lifetime Learn.

Lee, Elizabeth, ed. A Quorum of Cats. 1976. 9.95 (ISBN 0-236-40019-3, Pub. by Paul Elek). Merrimack Bk Serv.

Lee, Elsie. Nabob's Widow. 1976. 7.95 o.p. (ISBN 0-440-06305-1). Delacorte.

--The Nabob's Widow. 1977. pap. 1.75 o.s.i. (ISBN 0-440-16398-6). Dell.

--The Wicked Guardian. 1979. pap. 1.95 o.s.i. (ISBN 0-440-19801-1). Dell.

Lee, Ernest M. Story of Opera. LC 69-16803. (Music Story Ser). 1968. Repr. of 1909 ed. 15.00 (ISBN 0-8103-3359-7). Gale.

--Story of Symphony. LC 69-16804. (Illus.). 1968. Repr. of 1916 ed. 21.00 (ISBN 0-8103-3568-9). Gale.

Lee, Eugene C. The Politics of Nonpartisanship: A Study of California City Elections. 1960. 18.50x (ISBN 0-520-00719-0). U of Cal Pr.

Lee, Eugene C. & Keith, Bruce E. California Votes, Nineteen Sixty to Nineteen Seventy-Two: A Review & Analysis of Registration & Voting. new ed. LC 74-12271. (Illus.). 172p. 1974. 7.50x (ISBN 0-87772-201-3); 1974 supplement 1.50x (ISBN 0-685-51351-3). Inst Gov Stud Berk.

Lee, Eugene H., jt. ed. see Ballon, Robert J.

Lee, Eve. An American in Saudi Arabia. 2nd ed. LC 80-83093. (Country Orientation Ser.). (Illus.). 100p. 1980. pap. text ed. 7.50 (ISBN 0-933662-11-4). Intercult Pr.

Lee, Frank A. Basic Food Chemistry. (Illus.). 1975. pap. text ed. 19.50 (ISBN 0-87055-289-9). AVI.

Lee, Frederick G. A Glossary of Liturgical & Ecclesiastical Terms. LC 76-174069. (Tower Bks). (Illus.). xl, 452p. 1972. Repr. of 1877 ed. 21.00 (ISBN 0-8103-3949-8). Gale.

Lee, Georgia. The Portable Cosmos: Effigies, Ornaments & Incised Stone from the Chumash Area. (Ballena Press Anthropological Papers: No. 21). (Illus.). 114p. (Orig.). 1981. pap. 6.95 (ISBN 0-87919-093-0). Ballena Pr.

Lee, Georgia, et al. An Uncommon Guide to San Luis Obispo County, California. LC 75-2794. (Padre Productions Uncommon Guide Ser.). (Illus.). 1977. pap. 4.95 o.p. (ISBN 0-914598-18-X). Padre Prods.

Lee, Gerard. Pieces for Glass Piano. (Paperback Prose Ser.). 1978. pap. 7.25x (ISBN 0-7022-1169-9). U of Queensland Pr.

Lee, Gordon C., ed. Crusade Against Ignorance: Thomas Jefferson on Education. LC 61-10961. (Orig.). 1961. text ed. 8.75 (ISBN 0-8077-1671-5); pap. text ed. 4.00x (ISBN 0-8077-1668-5). Tchrs Coll.

Lee, Hanka, jt. auth. see Lee, Michael.

Lee, Harper. To Kill a Mockingbird. LC 60-7847. 1960. 10.95 (ISBN 0-397-00151-7). Lippincott.

Lee, Harry O. & LeForestier, Wilford A. Review & Reduction of Real Property Assessments in New York. 2nd ed. LC 77-14270. 1978. 45.00 (ISBN 0-87632-214-3); 1979 supplement incl. (ISBN 0-685-99204-7). Boardman.

Lee, Helen B. Joy Supplement Two: Descendants of Thomas Joy, Pt. 1. LC 76-45277. (Illus.). 1976. pap. 2.50 (ISBN 0-87106-074-4). Globe Pequot.

--Joy Supplement, Two: Descendants of Thomas Joy, Pt.2. LC 76-45277. (Illus.). 1980. pap. write for info. (ISBN 0-87106-075-2). Globe Pequot.

Lee, Henry. Report of a Committee of Citizens of Boston & Vicinity, Opposed to a Further Increase of Duties on Importations. Bd. with An Examination of the Report, & Review of the Report. (The Neglected American Economists Ser.). 1974. lib. bdg. 50.00 (ISBN 0-8240-1004-3). Garland Pub.

Lee, Henry, jt. auth. see Forbes, Crosby.

Lee, Hollis. Cattle, Sheep & Hogs. (Country Home & Small Farm Guides Ser.). (Illus.). 1978. pap. 2.95 (ISBN 0-88453-005-1). Barrington.

--Crops on a Few Acres. (Country Home & Small Farm Guides Ser.). (Illus.). 1978. pap. 2.95 (ISBN 0-88453-010-8). Barrington.

--Goats, Rabbits & Chickens. (Country Home & Small Farm Guides Ser.). (Illus.). 1978. pap. 2.95 (ISBN 0-88453-006-X). Barrington.

--Nuts, Berries & Grapes. (Country Home & Small Farm Guides Ser.). (Illus.). 1978. pap. 2.95 (ISBN 0-88453-009-4). Barrington.

--Orchard Handbook. (Country Home & Small Farm Guides Ser.). 1978. pap. 2.95 (ISBN 0-88453-007-8). Barrington.

--Planning a Country Place. (Country Home & Small Farm Guides Ser.). (Illus.). 1978. pap. 2.95 (ISBN 0-88453-003-5). Barrington.

--The Pleasure Horse. (Country Home & Small Farm Guides Ser.). (Illus.). 1978. pap. 2.95 (ISBN 0-88453-004-3). Barrington.

--Vegetable Farming. (Country Home & Small Farm Guides Ser.). (Illus.). 1978. pap. 2.95 (ISBN 0-88453-008-6). Barrington.

Lee, Hong Y. The Politics of the Chinese Cultural Revolution: A Case Study. 1978. 22.75x (ISBN 0-520-03297-7); pap. 7.95x (ISBN 0-520-04065-1). U of Cal Pr.

Lee, Howard. Kung Fu No. 3: Superstition. (Kung Fu Ser). 176p. (Orig.). 1973. pap. 1.25 o.s.i. (ISBN 0-446-76466-3). Warner Bks.

Lee, Ian. The Third Word War. (Illus.). 1978. pap. 4.95 (ISBN 0-89104-115-X). A & W Pubs.

Lee, J. Fletcher, ed. Pain Management. 1977. 21.00 (ISBN 0-683-04918-6). Williams & Wilkins.

Lee, J. M. The Churchill Coalition, Nineteen Forty to Nineteen Forty-Five. 192p. 1980. 20.00 (ISBN 0-208-01880-8, Archon). Shoe String.

Lee, J. M., et al. The Scope of Local Initiative: A Study of Cheshire County Council 1961-1974. 208p. 1974. 30.50x (ISBN 0-85520-059-6, Pub by Martin Robertson England). Biblio Dist.

Lee, J. Yimm. Wing Chun Kung-Fu. LC 72-87863. (Ser. 309). (Illus.). 1972. pap. 7.95 (ISBN 0-89750-037-7). Ohara Pubns.

Lee, James, jt. auth. see Falk, Nicholas.

Lee, James A. The Gold & the Garbage in Management Theories & Prescriptions. LC 80-12758. (Illus.). x, 480p. 1980. 22.95x (ISBN 0-8214-0436-9, 0436E); pap. 10.95x (ISBN 0-8214-0578-0). Ohio U Pr.

Lee, James B., ed. Renal Prostaglandins, Vol. 1. (Annual Research Reviews Ser.). 1979. 28.80 (ISBN 0-88831-037-4). Eden Med Res.

Lee, James L. & Pulvino, Charles J. Educating the Forgotten Half: Structured Activities for Learning. 1978. pap. text ed. 7.95 (ISBN 0-8403-1873-1). Kendall-Hunt.

Lee, James M. The Flow of Religious Instruction. 4.95 o.p. (ISBN 0-686-13703-5). Pflaum Pr.

Lee, James M. & Rooney, Patrick, eds. Toward a Future for Religious Education. 1969. 2.95 o.p. (ISBN 0-8278-9043-5); pap. 2.95 o.p. (ISBN 0-685-19394-2, 90043). Pflaum Pr.

Lee, Jasper S. Commercial Catfish Farming. 2nd ed. (Illus.). 1981. 10.00 (ISBN 0-8134-2156-X, 2156). Interstate.

--Commercial Catfish Farming. LC 73-75382. (Illus.). 1973. 10.00 o.p. (ISBN 0-8134-1570-5, 1570). Interstate.

Lee, Jasper S., ed. see Long, Don L., et al.

Lee, Jasper S., ed. see Miller, Larry.

Lee, Joan H., ed. see Knoll, Michael.

Lee, John. Lago. 1981. pap. 2.95 (ISBN 0-440-14788-3). Dell.

--The Thirteenth Hour. 1979. pap. 2.50 o.s.i. (ISBN 0-440-18751-6). Dell.

Lee, John E. & Sears, Francis W. Thermodynamics: An Introductory Text for Engineering Students. 2nd ed. 1963. 22.95 (ISBN 0-201-04190-1). A-W.

Lee, John F., et al. Statistical Thermodynamics. 2nd ed. LC 78-183672. 1973. 20.95 (ISBN 0-201-04214-2). A-W.

Lee, John R. Teaching Social Studies in the Elementary School. LC 73-14017. (Illus.). 1974. 12.95 (ISBN 0-02-918360-X); pap. text ed. 7.95 (ISBN 0-02-918370-7). Free Pr.

Lee, John R., et al. Teaching Social Studies in the Secondary School. LC 72-91998. (Orig.). 1973. pap. text ed. 7.95 (ISBN 0-02-918380-4). Free Pr.

Lee, John W. & Pierce, Milton. Hour Power: How to Have More Time for Work & Play. LC 80-70146. 260p. 1981. 11.95 (ISBN 0-87094-186-0). Dow Jones-Irwin.

Lee, Joo B. HWA Rang Do. LC 78-52313. (Ser. 131). 1979. pap. 6.95 (ISBN 0-89750-070-9). Ohara Pubns.

Lee, Joseph R. Advanced Calculus with Linear Analysis. 1972. text ed. 20.95 (ISBN 0-12-440750-1). Acad Pr.

Lee, Josephine. The Fabulous Manticora. LC 75-25784. 1976. 6.95 o.p. (ISBN 0-381-99619-0, JD-J). John Day.

Lee, Joshua A. With Their Ears Pricked Forward: Tales of Mules I've Known. 1980. 8.95 (ISBN 0-89587-018-5). Blair.

Lee, Jung Y. Korean Shamanistic Rituals. (Religion & Society Ser.). 1979. text ed. 44.50x (ISBN 90-279-3378-2). Mouton.

Lee, K. Francis & Shu-Ren Lin. Neuroradiology of Sellar & Juxtasellar Lesions. (Illus.). 512p. 1979. 84.75 (ISBN 0-398-03717-5). C C Thomas.

Lee, K. S., ed. see Heinisch, K. F.

Lee, Kaiman & Donnelly, Linda. Solar Failure. LC 80-130467. (Illus.). 1980. 30.00 (ISBN 0-915250-36-5). Environ Design.

Lee, Kaiman & Yang, Rita. Encyclopedia of Financial & Personal Survival: Six Hundred Fifty Coping Strategies. LC 80-130472. 1980. 210.00 (ISBN 0-915250-34-9). Environ Design.

Lee, Kay & Lee, Marshall. America's Favorites. (Illus.). 160p. 1980. 17.95 (ISBN 0-399-12514-0). Putnam.

Lee, Kay, jt. auth. see Clark, Linda.

Lee, Keat-Jin, ed. Essential Otolaryngology: A Board Preparation & Concise Reference. 2nd ed. 1977. spiral bdg. 19.50 (ISBN 0-87488-313-X). Med Exam.

Lee, Kyung-Shik, tr. see Han, Woo-Keun.

Lee, L. H., ed. Characterization of Metal & Polymer Surfaces, 2 vols. 1977. Vol. 1. 37.00 (ISBN 0-12-442101-6); Vol. 2. 36.00 (ISBN 0-12-442102-4). Acad Pr.

Lee, L. Kim, jt. auth. see Kim, Chewon.

Lee, L. L. Vladimir Nabokov. (U. S. Authors Ser.: No. 266). 1976. lib. bdg. 12.50 (ISBN 0-8057-7166-2). Twayne.

Lee, Larry. American Eagle: The Story of a Navajo Vietnam Veteran. 1977. pap. text ed. 3.50 (ISBN 0-686-12227-5). Packrat Pr.

Lee, Laurel. Barnaby Frost Plants a Seed. (ps-3). 1980. 5.95 (ISBN 0-8423-0118-6). Tyndale.

--Signs of Spring. 128p. 1981. pap. 2.25 (ISBN 0-553-14342-5). Bantam.

--Walking Through the Fire: A Hospital Journal. 1977. 6.95 o.p. (ISBN 0-525-22955-8). Dutton.

Lee, Lauri F. Foundations. (Gateway to English Program). (Illus.). 128p. (Orig.). 1981. tchrs' bk. 4.95 (ISBN 0-88377-176-4); student wkbk 1.95 (ISBN 0-88377-177-2). Newbury Hse.

Lee, Lawrence. The Grants Game: How to Win the First Time You Play. 224p. (Orig.). 1981. 11.95 (ISBN 0-936602-18-X); pap. 7.95 (ISBN 0-686-69117-2). Harbor Pub CA.

--The Grants Game: How to Win the First Time You Play. 224p. 1981. 11.95 (ISBN 0-936602-18-X); pap. 7.95 (ISBN 0-936602-03-1). Harbor Pub CA.

--New Hanover County: a Brief History. rev. ed. (Illus.). 1977. pap. 2.00 (ISBN 0-86526-128-8). NC Archives.

Lee, Leo Ou-fan, ed. see Prusek, Jaroslav.

Lee, Leonard S., jt. auth. see Kalthoff, Robert J.

Lee, Leslie & Comte, Robert. Management Procedures. LC 74-18677. (Allied Health Ser). 1975. pap. 6.35 (ISBN 0-672-61397-2). Bobbs.

Lee, Linda. Bruce Lee: The Man Only I Knew. 1975. pap. 1.95 o.s.i. (ISBN 0-446-89407-9). Warner Bks.

--Today I Am a Woman. 2.95 (ISBN 0-912216-17-4). Green Hill.

Lee, Linsey. Edible Wild Plants of Martha's Vineyard: And Other Coastal Parts of New England. LC 75-24889. (Illus., Orig.). 1979. pap. 4.95 (ISBN 0-932384-03-X). Tashmoo.

Lee, Lorenzo P. History of the Spirit Lake Massacre! 8th March, 1857 & of Miss Abigail Gardiner's 3 Month's Captivity Among the Indians. According to Her Own Account, As Given to L. P. Lee, Repr. Of 1857 Ed. Bd. with History of the Spirit Lake Massacre & Captivity of Miss Abbie Gardner. Sharp, Abigail. Repr. of 1885 ed. LC 75-7097. (Indian Captivities Ser.: Vol. 72). 1976. lib. bdg. 44.00 (ISBN 0-8240-1696-3). Garland Pub.

Lee, Lynn. Don Marquis. (United States Authors Ser: No. 393). 1981. lib. bdg. 11.95 (ISBN 0-8057-7282-0). Twayne.

Lee, M. J. The United Nations & World Realities. 1966. 22.00 (ISBN 0-08-011350-8); pap. 10.75 (ISBN 0-08-011349-4). Pergamon.

Lee, Mark W. How to Have a Good Marriage. LC 78-56794. 1981. pap. 5.95 (ISBN 0-915684-89-6). Christian Herald.

--How to Have a Good Marriage. LC 78-56974. 1978. 7.95 (ISBN 0-915684-39-X); pap. 5.95 (ISBN 0-915684-89-6). Christian Herald.

Lee, Marshall, jt. auth. see Lee, Kay.

Lee, Marshall, ed. Bookmaking: The Illustrated Guide to Design, Production, Editing. rev & enlarged ed. LC 79-65014. 1980. 29.50 (ISBN 0-8352-1097-9). Bowker.

Lee, Mary P. The Team That Runs Your Hospital. LC 80-36762. 1980. write for info. (ISBN 0-664-32669-2). Westminster.

Lee, Maurice. Government by Pen: The Scotland of James VI & I. LC 79-16830. 224p. 1980. 16.00 (ISBN 0-252-00765-4). U of Ill Pr.

Lee, Maurice, Jr., ed. Dudley Carleton to John Chamberlain 1603-1624: Jacobean Letters. LC 76-185391. 1972. 22.50 (ISBN 0-8135-0723-5). Rutgers U Pr.

Lee, Maurice W. Macroeconomics. 5th ed. 1971. text ed. 18.95x (ISBN 0-256-00296-7). Irwin.

Lee, Melicent H. Indians of the Oaks. rev. ed. (Illus.). 1978. pap. 6.95 (ISBN 0-916552-17-9). Acoma Bks.

Lee, Melissa. Shadow of Reddoch's Landing. 1976. pap. 1.25 o.p. (ISBN 0-685-74576-7, LB424ZK, Leisure Bks). Nordon Pubns.

Lee, Michael & Lee, Hanka. Cyprus. (Islands Ser.). 1974. 14.95 (ISBN 0-7153-5980-0). David & Charles.

Lee, Mildred. Fog. LC 72-81259. 250p. (gr. 7 up). 1972. 9.95 (ISBN 0-395-28911-4, Clarion). HM.

--The People Therein. 320p. (gr. 7 up). 1980. 10.95 (ISBN 0-395-29434-7, Clarion). HM.

--Skating Rink. LC 69-13443. (gr. 5 up). 1969. 6.95 (ISBN 0-395-28912-2, Clarion). HM.

--Sycamore Year. 160p. (RL 6). Date not set. pap. 1.25 (ISBN 0-451-07073-9, Y7073, Sig). NAL.

Lee, Milton L., et al. Analytical Chemistry of Polycyclic Aromatic Compounds. 1981. write for info. (ISBN 0-12-440840-0). Acad Pr.

Lee, Molly K., ed. East Asian Economies: A Guide to Information Sources. LC 78-13114. (Economics Information Guide Ser.: Vol. 1). 1979. 30.00 (ISBN 0-8103-1427-4). Gale.

Lee, Nancy. Targeting the Top: Everything a Woman Needs to Know to Develop a Successful Career in Business Year After Year. LC 78-22736. 408p. 1980. 11.95 (ISBN 0-385-13244-1). Doubleday.

Lee, Nathaniel. Lucius Junius Brutus. Loftis, John, ed. LC 67-12644. (Regents Restoration Drama Ser). 1967. 7.25x (ISBN 0-8032-0363-2); pap. 1.65x (ISBN 0-8032-5362-1, BB 266, Bison). U of Nebr Pr.

--Rival Queens. Vernon, P. F., ed. LC 72-91330. (Regents Restoration Drama Ser). 1970. 7.95x (ISBN 0-8032-0375-6); pap. 1.65x (ISBN 0-8032-5374-5, BB 273, Bison). U of Nebr Pr.

Lee, Owen. Skin Diver's Bible. LC 67-11191. pap. 3.50 (ISBN 0-385-03737-6). Doubleday.

Lee, P. J. see Dickinson, A. K.

Lee, Peter & Bearman, Graham. Russia in Revolution. 1974. pap. text ed. 6.95x (ISBN 0-435-31176-X). Heinemann Ed.

Lee, Peter H., ed. & tr. from Korean. Poems from Korea: A Historical Anthology. rev. ed. LC 73-80209. 196p. 1974. 8.50x (ISBN 0-8248-0263-2, Eastwest Ctr). U Pr of Hawaii.

Lee, Peter H., ed. The Silence of Love: Twentieth-Century Korean Poetry. LC 80-21999. 368p. 1980. text ed. 17.95x (ISBN 0-8248-0711-1); pap. 8.95 (ISBN 0-8248-0732-4). U Pr of Hawaii.

Lee, Philip R., jt. auth. see Silverman, Milton.

Lee, Philip R., et al, eds. The Nation's Health. 560p. 1980. lib. bdg. 16.00x (ISBN 0-87835-107-8); pap. 8.95x (ISBN 0-87835-108-6). Boyd & Fraser.

Lee, R. Alton. A History of Regulatory Taxation. LC 73-80460. 240p. 1973. 16.00x (ISBN 0-8131-1303-2). U Pr of Ky.

Lee, R. E. Phycology. LC 79-25402. (Illus.). 450p. 1980. 49.50 (ISBN 0-521-22530-2); pap. 16.95 (ISBN 0-521-29541-6). Cambridge U Pr.

Lee, R. G. How to Lead a Soul to Christ. 448p. 1974. pap. 1.25 (ISBN 0-310-27461-3). Zondervan.

Lee, R. J. English County Maps: Their Indentification, Cataloguing & Physical Care of a Collection. 1955. pap. 4.30x (ISBN 0-85365-002-0, Pub. by Lib Assn England). Oryx Pr.

Lee, R. M., jt. auth. see Lipson, H.

Lee, Rebecca S., ed. see Duval, John C.

Lee, Reginald. Building Maintenance Management. 194p. 1976. pap. text ed. 17.50x (ISBN 0-258-96947-4, Pub. by Granada England). Renouf.

Lee, Rex E. A Lawyer Looks at the Constitution. (Illus.). 256p. 1981. 19.95 (ISBN 0-8425-1904-1). Brigham.

--A Lawyer Looks at the Equal Rights Amendment. LC 80-22202. (Illus.). 150p. 1980. pap. 7.95 (ISBN 0-8425-1883-5). Brigham.

Lee, Richard. Forest Microclimatology. LC 77-21961. (Illus.). 1978. 20.00x (ISBN 0-231-04156-X). Columbia U Pr.

Lee, Richard B. The Kung San: Men, Women, & Work in a Foraging Society. LC 78-29504. (Illus.). 1979. 42.50 (ISBN 0-521-22578-7); pap. 11.95x (ISBN 0-521-29561-0). Cambridge U Pr.

Lee, Richard B. & De Vore, Irven, eds. Man the Hunter. LC 67-17603. 1968. pap. 11.50x (ISBN 0-202-33032-X). Aldine Pub.

Lee, Richard C., jt. auth. see Karnes, Merle B.

Lee, Richard M. Civil War Washington: A Guide to Mr. Lincoln's City. 272p. 1981. pap. price not set (ISBN 0-914440-48-9). EPM Pubns.

Lee, Richard V., jt. auth. see Smith, Tony.

Lee, Robert. China Journal: Glimpses of a Nation in Transition. (Illus., Orig.). 1980. 9.25 (ISBN 0-934788-00-6); pap. 5.25 (ISBN 0-686-28891-2). E-W Pub Co.

--Faith & the Prospects of Economic Collapse. LC 80-82187. 144p. 1981. pap. 6.95 (ISBN 0-8042-0814-X). John Knox.

Lee, Robert C. Summer of the Green Star. LC 80-27427. (Junior Literary Guild Ser.). (gr. 5-9). 1981. price not set (ISBN 0-664-32681-1). Westminster.

Lee, Robert E. North Carolina Family Law, 3 vols. 3rd ed. 1963. 1979-1980 100.00 (ISBN 0-87215-098-4). Michie.

Lee, Robert E., jt. auth. see Lawrence, Jerome.
Lee, Ronald R. Clergy & Clients: The Practice of Pastoral Psychotherapy. 1980. 9.95 (ISBN 0-8164-0115-2). Crossroad NY.
Lee, Russell V., jt. auth. see Eimerl, Sarel.
Lee, Ruth M. Orientation to Health Services. LC 77-15094. pap. 8.85 (ISBN 0-672-61434-0); tchr's manual 3.33 (ISBN 0-672-61435-9). Bobbs.
Lee, S., ed. Syriac Bible, Peshitta Version. 9.40 (ISBN 0-564-03212-3, 82566). United Bible.
Lee, Samuel C. Modern Switching Theory & Digital Design. 1978. ref. 25.95x (ISBN 0-13-598680-X). P-H.
Lee, Samuel C., jt. auth. see Kandel, Abraham.
Lee, Sang M. Goal Programming Methods for Multiple Objective Integer Programs. 1979. pap. text ed. 12.00 (ISBN 0-89806-001-X, 125). Am Inst Indus Eng.
--Management by Multiple Objective. (Illus.). 240p. 1981. 20.00 (ISBN 0-89433-083-7). Petrocelli.
Lee, Sang M., jt. auth. see Green, Thaddeus B.
Lee, Sang M., ed. Personnel Management: A Computer Based System. Thorp, Cary. 1979. text ed. 17.50 (ISBN 0-89433-052-7); pap. 14.00 (ISBN 0-89433-053-5). Petrocelli.
Lee, Sang M., et al. Management Science. 1050p. 1981. write for info. (ISBN 0-697-08046-3); instr's manual avail. Wm C Brown.
Lee, Sherman E. Asian Art: Selections from the Collection of Mr. and Mrs. John D. Rockefeller, 3rd. (Illus.). 1970. pap. text ed. 35.00 (ISBN 0-89192-278-4). Interbk Inc.
--Chinese Landscape Painting. LC 62-11141. (Illus.). 168p. 1962. 15.00x (ISBN 0-910386-02-1, Pub. by Cleveland Mus Art). Ind U Pr.
--The Genius of Japanese Design. LC 79-66246. (Illus.). 1981. 39.50 (ISBN 0-87011-395-X). Kodansha.
--A History of Far Eastern Art. rev. ed. 528p. 1974. text ed. 21.95 (ISBN 0-13-390088-6). P-H.
Lee, Si D. & Grant, Lester, eds. Toxicology & Toxicological Health Assessment for Polycyclic Agents. 1980. pap. text ed. 13.50 (ISBN 0-930376-20-X). Pathotox Pubs.
Lee, Sidney, ed. see Smith, George.
Lee, Simon, ed. see Anouilh, Jean.
Lee, Stan. The Best of the Worst. LC 79-1671. (Illus.). 1979. pap. 4.95 (ISBN 0-06-090728-2, CN 728, CN). Har-Row.
Lee, Stewart, jt. auth. see Gordon, Leland.
Lee, T. A. Company Financial Reporting: The Measurement & Communication of Accounting Information. 1976. text ed. 24.00x (ISBN 0-17-761041-7). Intl Ideas.
Lee, T. D. Field Theory & Particle Analysis. (Contemporary Concepts in Physics Ser.). 1981. 35.00 (ISBN 0-686-69595-X); pap. 14.00 (ISBN 0-686-69596-8). Harwood Academic.
--Statistical Mechanics. (Concepts in Contemporary Physics Ser.). 550p. 1981. lib. bdg. 35.00 (ISBN 0-686-65737-3); pap. 14.50 (ISBN 3-7186-0053-6). Harwood Academic. Postponed.
Lee, T. D., ed. Field Theory & Particle Physics. (Concepts in Contemporary Physics Ser.: Vol. 1). 575p. 1981. 35.00 (ISBN 0-686-65734-9); pap. 14.00 (ISBN 0-686-65735-7). Harwood Academic.
Lee, T. H., et al. Computer Process Control: Modeling & Optimization. LC 67-30914. 1968. 29.95 o.p. (ISBN 0-471-52207-4, Pub. by Wiley-Interscience). Wiley.
Lee, Tanith. Animal Castle. 40p. (gr. 2 up). 1972. 4.95 (ISBN 0-374-30337-1). FS&G.
--Day by Night. (Science Fiction Ser.). 1980. pap. 2.25 (ISBN 0-87997-576-8, UE1576). DAW Bks.
--East of Midnight. LC 77-15867. 1978. 7.95 o.p. (ISBN 0-312-22494-X). St Martin.
--Kill the Dead. (Science Fiction Ser.). 1980. pap. 1.75 (ISBN 0-87997-562-8, UE1562). Daw Bks.
--Lycanthia. 1981. pap. 2.25 (ISBN 0-87997-610-1, UE1610). DAW Bks.
--Volkhavaar. (Science Fiction Ser). 1977. pap. 1.75 (ISBN 0-87997-312-9, UE1539). DAW Bks.
Lee, Tina. Manners to Grow On. LC 54-9846. (gr. 4-7). 1955. 4.95 o.p. (ISBN 0-385-07398-4); PLB (ISBN 0-385-07664-9). Doubleday.
Lee, Tong H., et al. Regional & Interregional Intersectoral Flow Analysis: The Method & an Application to the Tennessee Economy. LC 72-187360. 168p. 1973. 10.50x (ISBN 0-87049-139-3). U of Tenn Pr.
Lee, Trevor R. Race & Residence: The Concentration & Dispersal of Immigrants in London. (Oxford Research Studies in Geography Ser). (Illus.). 1977. 29.95x (ISBN 0-19-823215-2). Oxford U Pr.
Lee, Trevor R. & Wood, L. J. Adjustment in the Urban System: The Tasman Bridge Collapse & Its Effects on Metropolitan Hobart. 85p. 1980. pap. 13.50 (ISBN 0-08-026810-2). Pergamon.
Lee, Vera G., ed. see Ionesco, Eugene.
Lee, Vernon. Handling of Words & Other Studies in Literary Psychology. LC 68-13649. 1968. pap. 4.95x o.p. (ISBN 0-8032-5118-1, 376, Bison). U of Nebr Pr.
--Miss Brown. Fletcher, Ian & Stokes, John, eds. LC 76-20088. (Decadent Consciousness Ser.). 1978. lib. bdg. 38.00 (ISBN 0-8240-2766-3). Garland Pub.
--Renaissance Fancies & Studies: Being a Sequel to Euphorion. LC 76-20099. (The Decadent Consciousness Ser.: Vol. 19). 1977. Repr. of 1895 ed. lib. bdg. 38.00 (ISBN 0-8240-2767-1). Garland Pub.
Lee, Vernon & Paget, Violet. Studies of the Eighteenth Century in Italy. LC 77-17466. (Music Reprint Ser.: 1978). 1978. Repr. of 1887 ed. lib. bdg. 27.50 (ISBN 0-306-77517-4). Da Capo.
Lee, Victor. Language Development. LC 78-9081. 1979. 21.95x (ISBN 0-470-26432-2). Halsted Pr.
Lee, Virginia. The Magic Moth. LC 73-171862. (Illus.). 64p. (gr. 3 up). 1972. 6.95 (ISBN 0-395-28863-0, Clarion). HM.
--The Magic Moth. (Illus.). 64p. (gr. 3-6). 1981. pap. 2.95 (ISBN 0-395-30008-8, Clarion). HM.
Lee, Virginia, jt. auth. see Claiborne, Craig.
Lee, W. A. Administration of Solvent Deceased Estates in Queensland. 1973. pap. 2.50x (ISBN 0-7022-0856-6). U of Queensland Pr.
Lee, W. R., jt. auth. see Haycraft, Brita.
Lee, W. R., ed. Current Research in Ophthalmic Electron Microscopy, 3. (Illus.). 160p. 1980. 28.40 (ISBN 0-686-62616-8). Springer-Verlag.
Lee, W. R., jt. ed. see Evans, Richard.
Lee, Walter D. The Alpha Curse. 1981. 8.95 (ISBN 0-8062-1578-X). Carlton.
Lee, Warren F., et al. Agricultural Finance. 7th ed. Nelson, Aaron G. & Murray, William G., eds. 1980. text ed. 17.50 (ISBN 0-8138-0050-1). Iowa St U Pr.
Lee, Wayne. Experimental Design & Analysis. LC 74-12241. (Psychology Ser.). (Illus.). 1975. text ed. 23.95x (ISBN 0-7167-0772-1); wkbk. 5.95x (ISBN 0-7167-0763-2). W H Freeman.
Lee, Wayne C. Skirmish at Fort Phil Kearny. (YA) 1977. 5.95 (ISBN 0-685-74268-7, Avalon). Bouregy.
--Trails of the Smoky Hill. LC 79-67199. (Illus., Orig.). 1980. cancelled (ISBN 0-87004-288-2); pap. 12.95 (ISBN 0-87004-276-9). Caxton.
Lee, Welton L., ed. Carotenoproteins in Animal Colorations. (Benchmark Papers in Biological Concepts Ser.: Vol. 3). 1977. 42.50 (ISBN 0-12-786935-2). Acad Pr.
Lee, William R. Language Teaching Games & Contests. 2nd ed. 1979. pap. text ed. 5.95x (ISBN 0-19-432716-7). Oxford U Pr.
Lee, William T. The Estimation of Soviet Defense Expenditures, 1955-75: An Unconventional Approach. LC 76-24357. (Special Studies). 1977. text ed. 36.50 (ISBN 0-275-56900-4). Praeger.
Lee, Won R. Essentials of Clinical Cardiology. (Illus.). 443p. (Orig.). 1980. pap. text ed. 24.95 (ISBN 0-89303-008-2). Charles.
Lee, Y., jt. auth. see Termini, B.
Lee, Young-Sook C., jt. auth. see Martin, Samuel E.
Leebaert, ed. European Security: Prospects for the 1980's. (Illus.). 1979. 15.95 (ISBN 0-669-02518-6). Lexington Bks.
Leech, Clifford. Shakespeare - the Tragedies: A Collection of Critical Essays. LC 65-17295. (Midway Reprint Ser.). xxxii, 256p. 1975. pap. 11.00x (ISBN 0-226-47018-0). U of Chicago Pr.
Leech, Clifford see Henderson, Philip.
Leech, Clifford, ed. see World Shakespeare Congress, Vancouver, August 1971.
Leech, Frederick B. & Sellers, Kenneth C. Statistical Epidemiology in Veterinary Science. LC 78-75106. 1979. 26.95 (ISBN 0-02-848430-4). Macmillan.
Leech, G. N. & Short, M. H. Style in Fiction. (English Language Ser.). 384p. 1981. text ed. 32.00 (ISBN 0-582-29102-X); pap. text ed. 16.95 (ISBN 0-582-29103-8). Longman.
Leech, Geoffrey & Svartvik, Jan. A Communicative Grammar of English. (Illus.). 368p. 1975. pap. text ed. 12.50x (ISBN 0-582-55238-9). Longman.
Leech, Geoffrey N. Meaning & the English Verb. 1971. pap. text ed. 4.25x (ISBN 0-582-52214-5). Longman.
Leech, J. Computational Problems in Abstract Algebra. 1970. 60.00 (ISBN 0-08-012975-7). Pergamon.
Leech, Jay & Spencer, Zane. Moon of the Big-Dog. LC 79-7893. (Illus.). 64p. (gr. 2-6). 1980. 6.95 (ISBN 0-690-04001-6, TYC-J); PLB 6.89 (ISBN 0-690-04002-4). T Y Crowell.
Leech, Kenneth. True Prayer: An Invitation to Christian Spirituality. 208p. 1981. 9.95 (ISBN 0-06-065227-6, HarpR). Har-Row.
Leech, Kenneth & Jordan, Brenda. Drugs for Young People: Their Use & Misuse. 2nd ed. 1974. 3.85 (ISBN 0-08-017938-X). Pergamon.
Leech, Kenneth, ed. see Lull, Ramon.
Leech, Michael. Italy. LC 75-44863. (Macdonald Countries). (Illus.). (gr. 6 up). 1976. PLB 7.95 (ISBN 0-382-06107-1, Pub. by Macdonald Ed). Silver.
Leech, Rachel M., jt. auth. see Reid, Robert A.
Lee-Chon, Seunghi. Daily Pursuits & Timeless Values: A Woman's View. LC 78-729955. 1978. 6.30 (ISBN 0-930878-11-6). Hollym Intl.
Leecing, W. & Armstrong, J. L. Curious Eye. 1970. text ed. 10.50 o.p. (ISBN 0-07-037006-0, C); instructor's guide 3.95 o.p. (ISBN 0-07-037007-9). McGraw.
Leed, E. J. No Man's Land. LC 78-73601. 1979. 21.50 (ISBN 0-521-22471-3). Cambridge U Pr.
Leed, Roger, ed. Shorelines Management: The Washington Experience. (Washington Sea Grant Ser.). 184p. 1973. pap. 6.50 (ISBN 0-295-95309-8). U of Wash Pr.
Leed, Theodore W. & German, Gene A. Food Merchandising: Principles & Practices. LC 73-88739. (Illus.). 1973. 14.95 (ISBN 0-686-01267-4). Lebhar Friedman.
Leedam, Elizabeth J. Community Nursing Manual: A Guide for Auxiliary Public Health Nurses. (McGraw-Hill International Health Ser.). (Illus.). 1977. pap. text ed. 6.95 o.p. (ISBN 0-07-099412-9, C). McGraw.
Leeder, Ellen L. Justo Sierra Y el Mar. LC 78-58669. (Coleccion Polymita Ser.). 83p. (Orig., Span.). 1979. pap. 6.95 (ISBN 0-89729-202-2). Ediciones.
Leedham, Charles G., jt. auth. see Pearsall, Milo.
Leedham, L., ed. see Gresh, Sean.
Leedham, L., ed. see Wurzer, Karl.
Leedham, Linnea, ed. see Haponski, William C. & McCabe, Charles.
Leedom, William S. The Vintage Wine Book. rev. ed. 1975. pap. 2.45 o.p. (ISBN 0-394-70230-1, Vin). Random.
Leeds, Arthur, jt. auth. see Esenwein, J. Berg.
Leeds, C. A. European History Seventeen Eighty-Nine to Nineteen Fourteen. 448p. 1979. pap. 13.95x (ISBN 0-7121-0575-1, Pub. by Macdonald & Evans England). Intl Ideas.
--Twentieth-Century History Nineteen Hundred to Nineteen Forty-Five. (Illus.). 224p. 1979. pap. text ed. 9.95x (ISBN 0-7121-2025-4, Pub. by Macdonald & Evans England). Intl Ideas.
Leeds, C. S., et al. Management & Business Studies. 2nd ed. 448p. 1978. pap. text ed. 16.95x (ISBN 0-7121-1298-7, Pub. by Macdonald & Evans England). Intl Ideas.
Leeds, E. Thurlow. Archaeology of the Anglo-Saxon Settlements. (Oxford Reprints Ser). (Illus.). 1913. 19.50x (ISBN 0-19-813161-5). Oxford U Pr.
Leeds, M. A. Handbook of Electronic Materials, Vol. 9: Electronic Properties of Composite Materials. LC 76-147312. 103p. 1972. 37.00 (ISBN 0-306-67109-3). IFI Plenum.
Leeds, Margaret, jt. auth. see Farkas, Emil.
Leeds, Norman E., jt. auth. see Burrows, E. H.
Leeds, Roger S. Co-Financing for Development: Why Not More? LC 80-80117. (Development Papers Ser.: No. 92). 64p. 1980. pap. 3.00 (ISBN 0-686-28119-5). Overseas Dev Council.
Leeds University Institute of Education. Objectives of Teacher Education. (General Ser.). 45p. 1973. pap. text ed. 5.75x (ISBN 0-85633-028-0, NFER). Humanities.
--Teacher Education: The Teacher's Point of View. (General Ser.). 85p. (Orig.). 1974. pap. text ed. 5.75x (ISBN 0-85633-050-7, NFER). Humanities.
Leeds, Wendy. The Child Sellers. 1981. pap. 2.25 (ISBN 0-8439-0889-0, Leisure Bks). Nordon Pubns.
Leedy, Jack J., ed. Compensation in Psychiatric Disability & Rehabilitation. (Illus.). 384p. 1971. 36.75 (ISBN 0-398-02186-4). C C Thomas.
Leefe, Christopher, ed. Rolls-Royce Alpine Compendium: 1913-1973. (Illus.). 164p. 1973. 12.95 o.p. (ISBN 0-85184-005-1, Pub. by Transport Bkman England). Motorbooks Intl.
Leefeldt, Christine & Callenbach, Ernest. The Art of Friendship. 1980. pap. 2.75 (ISBN 0-425-04674-5). Berkley Pub.
Leek, Sybil. How to Be Your Own Astrologer. 1974. pap. 1.75 (ISBN 0-451-09426-3, E9426, Sig). NAL.
--Moon Signs. 1977. 2.25 (ISBN 0-425-04364-9, Pub. by Putnam). Berkley Pub.
--The Night Voyagers: You & Your Dreams. 192p. 1976. pap. 1.50 o.p. (ISBN 0-345-24850-3). Ballantine.
--Phrenology. 1970. pap. 2.95 o.s.i. (ISBN 0-02-077250-5, Collier). Macmillan.
--The Story of Faith Healing. 160p. 1973. 6.95 o.s.i. (ISBN 0-02-570150-9). Macmillan.
--Sybil Leek's Book of Herbs. 1980. pap. 3.95 (ISBN 0-346-12435-2). Cornerstone.
--Sybil Leek's Book of the Curious & the Occult. 1976. pap. 1.75 o.p. (ISBN 0-345-25385-X). Ballantine.
Leeker, Robert, ed. The Annotated Bibliography of Canada's Major Authors: Margaret Atwood, Leonard Cohen, Archibald Lampman, E. J. Pratt, & Al Purdy, Vol. I. (Reference Book Ser.). 1981. 26.00 (ISBN 0-8161-8552-2). G K Hall.
Leekley, Thomas B. King Herla's Quest & Other Medieval Stories from Walter Map. LC 56-12037. (Illus.). (gr. 6-9). 6.95 (ISBN 0-8149-0348-7). Vanguard.
--Rescue for Brownie. LC 59-15202. (gr. 4-8). 3.95 (ISBN 0-8149-0350-9). Vanguard.
--Riddle of the Black Knight & Other Stories from the Middle Ages Based on the Gesta Romanorum. LC 57-12262. (Illus.). (gr. 3-7). 1957. 6.95 (ISBN 0-8149-0347-9). Vanguard.
Leeman, Fred. Hidden Images-Games of Perception: Anamorphic Art Illusion. LC 76-3736. (Illus.). 1976. pap. 9.85 o.p. (ISBN 0-8109-9019-9); Anamorphic Jigsaw Puzzle 9.00 o.p. (ISBN 0-685-73055-7). Abrams.
Leemhuis, Roger P. James L. Orr & the Sectional Conflict. LC 78-65850. 1979. pap. text ed. 9.75 (ISBN 0-8191-0679-8). U Pr of Amer.
Leeming, David A. Mythology: The Voyage of the Hero. 2nd ed. (Illus.). 370p. 1980. pap. text ed. 10.50 scp (ISBN 0-06-043942-4, HarpC); avail. Har-Row.
Leeming, Donald, jt. auth. see Tidg, Michael.
Leeming, Joseph. Costume Book for Parties & Plays. LC 38-27654. (Illus.). (gr. 7-9). 1938. PLB 8.95 o.p. (ISBN 0-397-30052-2). Lippincott.
--The First Book of Chess. rev. ed. Fenton, Robert S., ed. (First Bks.). (Illus.). (gr. 4-6). 1977. lib. bdg. 4.90 s&l o.p. (ISBN 0-531-01290-5). Watts.
--Fun with Clay. (Illus.). (gr. 7-9). 1944. 8.95 o.p. (ISBN 0-397-30095-6). Lippincott.
--Fun with Paper. (Illus.). (gr. 4-6). 1939. 6.50 o.p. (ISBN 0-397-30061-1). Lippincott.
--Fun with Shells. (Illus.). (gr. 7-9). 1958. 4.82 o.p. (ISBN 0-397-31384-5). Lippincott.
--Holiday Craft & Fun. (Illus.). (gr. 7-9). 1950. 7.50 (ISBN 0-397-30168-5). Lippincott.
--Riddles, Riddles, Riddles. 1979. pap. 1.75 (ISBN 0-449-14014-8, GM). Fawcett.
Leeming, Joseph, ed. Riddles, Riddles, Riddles. (Terrific Triple Titles Ser). (gr. 4-6). 1953. PLB 7.90 (ISBN 0-531-01777-X). Watts.
Leemon, Thomas A. The Rites of Passage in a Student Culture. LC 72-81190. 1972. pap. text ed. 7.50x (ISBN 0-8077-1673-1). Tchrs Coll.
Leen, Edie. Complete Women's Weight Training Guide. LC 78-64384. (Illus.). 176p. 1980. pap. 6.95 (ISBN 0-89037-161-X). Anderson World.
Leen, Nina. Rare & Unusual Animals. (Illus.). 80p. (gr. 3-7). 1981. 8.95 (ISBN 0-03-057478-1). HR&W.
--Taking Pictures. (gr. 6-10). 1980. pap. 1.75 (ISBN 0-380-49205-9, 49205, Camelot). Avon.
Leenders, Michael R., et al. Purchasing & Materials Management. 7th ed. 1980. 21.50x (ISBN 0-256-02374-3). Irwin.
Leenhardt, Franz J., jt. auth. see Cullmann, Oscar.
Leenhouts, H. P., jt. auth. see Chadwick, K. H.
Leenhouts, Keith. A Father...a Son...& a Three-Mile Run. 1977. pap. 2.25 (ISBN 0-310-27512-1). Zondervan.
--Un Pai, un Filho, e Uma Corrida de Amor. Caruso, Luiz A., ed. Balthazar, Vera, tr. 156p. (Portuguese.). 1980. pap. 1.50 (ISBN 0-8297-0676-3). Vida Pubs.
Leenhouts, Keith, tr. Una Carrera De Amor. (Spanish Bks.). (Span.). 1978. 1.75 (ISBN 0-8297-0849-9). Vida Pub.
Leepa, Allen, ed. see Rattner, Abraham.
Leeper, Nancy C., jt. auth. see Canning, Richard G.
Leer, E. Fleseman-Van see Flesseman-Van Leer, E.
Leer, J. Arthur, jt. auth. see Horngren, Charles T.
Lees, David H. & Singer, Albert. Surgery of Conditions Complicating Pregnancy, Vol. 6. (Illus.). 1981. write for info. (ISBN 0-8151-5356-2). Year Bk Med.
Lees, F. A. International Banking & Finance. LC 73-11884. 419p. 1974. text ed. 32.95 (ISBN 0-470-52273-9). Halsted Pr.
Lees, Francis & Brooks, Hugh C. The Economic & Political Development of the Sudan. LC 77-5252. (Illus.). 1978. lib. bdg. 28.50x (ISBN 0-89158-816-7). Westview.
Lees, Francis A. Foreign Banking & Investment in the United States: Issues & Alternatives. LC 76-4782. 1976. 22.95 (ISBN 0-470-15212-5). Halsted Pr.
Lees, Francis A. & Eng, Maximo. International Financial Markets: Development of the Present System & Future Prospects. LC 73-13345. (Special Studies). (Illus.). 576p. 1975. text ed. 32.95 o.p. (ISBN 0-275-28789-0); pap. text ed. 12.95 (ISBN 0-275-89180-1). Praeger.
Lees, Frank P. Loss Prevention in the Process Industry, 2 vols. new ed. 1980. 195.00 set (ISBN 0-408-10604-2); Vol. 1. 99.00 (ISBN 0-408-10697-2); Vol. 2. 99.00 (ISBN 0-408-10698-0). Butterworths.

Lees, Herbert, jt. auth. see Lovell, Mary.

Lees, James. The Masting & Rigging of English Ships of War 1625-1860. LC 76-45985. (Illus.). 1979. 36.95 (ISBN 0-87021-847-6). Naval Inst Pr.

Lees, John D. The Political Systems of the United States. (Orig.). 1975. pap. 9.95 (ISBN 0-571-04878-1, Pub. by Faber & Faber). Merrimack Bk Serv.

Lees, Susan H., jt. auth. see Bates, Daniel G.

Leeser, I., jt. auth. see Fox, D. J.

Leeser, Ilse R., et al. Community Health Nursing. (Nursing Outline Ser.). 1975. spiral bdg. 6.00 o.p. (ISBN 0-87488-382-2). Med Exam.

Lees-Haley, Paul R. The Questionnaire Design Handbook. LC 80-82969. 150p. (Orig.). 1980. pap. 9.95 (ISBN 0-938124-00-5). Innova Assoc.

Leesley, Michael E. Freshman Chemical Engineering. 1979. 15.95 (ISBN 0-87201-106-2). Gulf Pub.

Lees-Milne, J. Worchestershire: A Shell Guide. (Illus.). 1964. 12.95 (ISBN 0-571-05936-8, Pub. by Faber & Faber). Merrimack Bk Serv.

Lees-Milne, James. Ancestral Voices. 1978. 10.95 o.p. (ISBN 0-684-15647-4, ScribT). Scribner.

--Heretics in Love. 1976. pap. 1.50 o.p. (ISBN 0-445-03167-0). Popular Lib.

--Prophesying Peace: A Sequel to "Ancestral Voices". 1978. 10.95 o.p. (ISBN 0-684-15646-6, ScribT). Scribner.

--Round the Clock. 1978. 7.95 o.p. (ISBN 0-684-15882-5, ScribT). Scribner.

Leeson, C. Roland, jt. auth. see Leeson, Thomas S.

Leeson, Kenneth W., jt. auth. see Machlup, Fritz.

Leeson, Lewis J. & Carstenpen, J. Thuro. Dissolution Technology. 1974. 21.00 (ISBN 0-917330-15-3). Am Pharm Assn.

Leeson, Marjorie. Computer Operations: Procedures & Management. LC 77-14204. 480p. 1978. pap. text ed. 15.95 (ISBN 0-574-21155-1, 13-4155); instr's guide avail. (ISBN 0-574-21156-X, 13-4156). SRA.

--Delta Products Case Study. 112p. 1980. pap. text ed. 6.95t (ISBN 0-574-21288-4, 13-4288); solutions manual avail. (ISBN 0-574-21289-2, 13-4289). SRA.

--Systems Analysis & Design. 464p. 1980. text ed. 14.95 (ISBN 0-574-21279-5, 13-4285); instr's. guide avail. (ISBN 0-574-21286-8, 13-4286); write for info. transparency masters (ISBN 0-574-21287-6, 13-4287). SRA.

Leeson, Richard. Fluency & Language Teaching. (Applied Linguistics & Language Study). 1976. pap. text ed. 9.00x (ISBN 0-582-55078-5). Longman.

Leeson, Thomas S. & Leeson, C. Roland. Histology. 1981. text ed. price not set (ISBN 0-7216-5704-4). Saunders.

Lees-Smith, Hastings B., ed. The Encyclopaedia of the Labour Movement, 3 vols. 7th ed. LC 73-167033. xxv, 1132p. 1972. Repr. of 1928 ed. Set. 115.00 (ISBN 0-8103-3028-8). Gale.

Leet, Don R. & Shaw, John A. Economics: Concepts, Themes & Applications. 464p. 1980. pap. text ed. 14.95x (ISBN 0-534-00793-7); 6.95xwkbk. (ISBN 0-534-00826-7). Wadsworth Pub.

Leet, L. Don, et al. Physical Geology. 5th ed. 1978. ref. ed. 20.95 (ISBN 0-13-669739-9); study guide 5.95 (ISBN 0-13-669747-X). P-H.

Leet, Lewis D. Vibrations from Blasting Rock. LC 60-10037. 1960. 7.95x (ISBN 0-674-93526-8). Harvard U Pr.

Lee Tan, Paul. The Interpretation of Prophecy. 1975. 8.95 (ISBN 0-88469-000-8). BMH Bks.

Leeuw, Adele De see De Leeuw, Adele.

Leeuw, Frank De see De Leeuw, Frank & Tarutis, Eleanor L.

Leeuw, Frank de, et al. The Web of Urban Housing. 240p. 1975. 10.00 (ISBN 0-87766-151-0, 12900); pap. 4.95 (ISBN 0-87766-151-0, 12700). Urban Inst.

Leeuwen, J. Van, jt. ed. see Bakker, J. W.

Leeuwen, Jean Van see Van Leeuwen, Jean.

Leeuwenhoek, Antoni van see Van Leeuwenhoek, Antoni.

Leevy, Carroll M. Liver Regeneration in Man. (Amer. Lec. in Living Chemistry Ser.). (Illus.). 128p. 1973. 13.75 (ISBN 0-398-02776-5). C C Thomas.

Lee-Warner, William. The Life of the Marquis of Dalhousie, 2 vols. (Illus.). 896p. 1972. Repr. of 1904 ed. Set. 70.00x (ISBN 0-686-28321-X, Pub. by Irish Academic Pr). Biblio Dist.

Le Fanu, J. Sheridan. Uncle Silas. 1966. pap. 6.00 (ISBN 0-486-21715-9). Dover.

Le Fanu, Joseph S. The Cock & the Anchor: Being a Chronicle of Old Dublin City. (Nineteenth Century Fiction Ser.: Ireland: Vol. 59). 1036p. 1979. lib. bdg. 46.00 (ISBN 0-8240-3508-9). Garland Pub.

--The House by the Church-Yard. (Nineteenth Century Fiction Ser.: Ireland: Vol. 60). 952p. 1979. lib. bdg. 46.00 (ISBN 0-8240-3509-7). Garland Pub.

--The Purcell Papers with a Memoir by Alfred Perceval Graces. (Nineteenth Century Fiction Ser.: Ireland: Vol. 58). 840p. 1979. lib. bdg. 46.00 (ISBN 0-8240-3507-0). Garland Pub.

Lefco, Helene. Dance Therapy: Narrative Case Histories of Therapy Sessions with Six Patients. LC 73-88511. 1974. 13.95 (ISBN 0-911012-93-1). Nelson-Hall.

Lefcoe, George. An Introduction to American Land Law: Cases & Materials. LC 74-2945. (Contemporary Legal Education Ser). 1974. text ed. 18.00 (ISBN 0-672-81893-0, Bobbs-Merrill Law). Michie.

Lefcoe, George, ed. Respective Roles of State & Local Governments in Land Policy & Taxation. (Lincoln Institute Monograph: No. 80-7). 271p. 1980. write for info. Lincoln Inst Land.

Lefcowitz. Writer's Handbook. 1976. text ed. 10.50 (ISBN 0-13-969923-6); pap. text ed. 6.95 wkbk. (ISBN 0-13-969907-4); pap. text ed. 12.00 net, diagnostic test (ISBN 0-13-970012-9). P-H.

Lefebvre, Adrian. The New Frontiers of Interior Decoration. (Illus.). 1980. deluxe ed. 41.75 (ISBN 0-930582-60-8). Gloucester Art.

Lefebvre, Arthur H., ed. Gas Turbine Combustor Design Problems. LC 79-22350. 431p. 1979. text ed. 51.75 (ISBN 0-89116-177-5). Hemisphere Pub.

Lefebvre, Georges. The French Revolution, 2 vols. Incl. From Its Origins to 1793. Evans, Elizabeth M., tr. Vol. 1. 20.00x (ISBN 0-231-02342-1); Vol. 1. pap. 6.00 (ISBN 0-231-08598-2); From 1793 to 1799. Stewart, John H. & Friguglietti, James, trs. Vol. 2. 20.00x (ISBN 0-231-02519-X); pap. 6.00 (ISBN 0-231-08599-0). LC 64-11939. 1962-64. Columbia U Pr.

--Napoleon: From Eighteen Brumaire to Tilsit, 1799-1807. Stockhold, Henry F., tr. LC 68-29160. 1969. 20.00x (ISBN 0-231-02558-0). Columbia U Pr.

--Napoleon: From Tilsit to Waterloo, 1807-1815. Anderson, J. E., tr. LC 74-79193. 1969. 20.00x (ISBN 0-231-03313-3). Columbia U Pr.

Lefebvre, Henri. The Survival of Capitalism. (Allison & Busby Motive Ser.). 140p. 1981. pap. 7.95 (ISBN 0-8052-8076-6, Pub. by Allison & Busby England). Schocken.

Lefebvre, Jacques. Clinical Practice in Pediatric Radiology: The Heart & Great Vessels, Vol. I. Kaufmann, Herbert J., ed. LC 79-83739. (Great Pediatric Radiology Ser.). Orig. Title: Radiopediatrie. 1979. 54.50 (ISBN 0-89352-015-2). Masson Pub.

--Clinical Practice in Pediatric Radiology: The Respiratory System, Vol. II. Kaufman, Herbert J., ed. LC 79-83739. 448p. 1979. 65.50 (ISBN 0-89352-066-7). Masson Pub.

Lefer, Allan M., ed. see Papers from the First Annual Conference on Shock, Airlie, Va., June 1978.

Lefer, Allan M., ed. see Papers from the Second Annual Conference on Shock, Williamsburg, Va. June 1979.

Lefer, Allan M., ed. see Third Annual Conference on Shock, Lake of the Ozarks, Missouri, June 1980.

Lefever, Ernest. Amsterdam to Nairobi: The World Council of Churches & the Third World. 126p. 1979. 10.00 (ISBN 0-89633-025-7); pap. 5.00 (ISBN 0-89633-024-9). Ethics & Public Policy.

Lefever, Ernest, ed. Will Capitalism Survive? A Challenge by Paul Johnson with Twelve Responses. 79p. 1979. pap. 3.00 (ISBN 0-89633-026-5). Ethics & Public Policy.

Lefever, Ernest W. Crisis in the Congo: A U.N. Force in Action. 1965. 11.95 (ISBN 0-8157-5198-2); pap. 4.95 (ISBN 0-8157-5197-4). Brookings.

--Nuclear Arms in the Third World: U. S. Policy Dilemma. 1979. 11.95 (ISBN 0-8157-5202-4); pap. 4.95 (ISBN 0-8157-5201-6). Brookings.

--Spear & Scepter: Army, Police, & Politics in Tropical Africa. 1970. 11.95 (ISBN 0-8157-5200-8). Brookings.

Lefever, Ernest W. & Godson, Roy. The C. I. A. & the American Ethic: An Unfininished Debate. 176p. 1980. 9.50 (ISBN 0-89633-032-X); pap. 5.00 (ISBN 0-89633-031-1). Ethics & Public Policy.

Lefever, Ernest W., ed. Morality & Foreign Policy: A Symposium on President Carter's Stance. 82p. 1977. pap. 3.00 (ISBN 0-89633-005-2). Ethics & Public Policy.

Lefever, Ernest W., ed. see Novak, Michael, et al.

Lefever, R. & Goldbeter, A., eds. Molecular Movements & Chemical Reactivity As Conditioned by Membranes, Enzymes & Other Macromolecules. LC 58-9935. (Advances in Chemical Physics Ser.: Vol. 39). 1978. 46.50 (ISBN 0-471-03541-6, Pub. by Wiley-Interscience). Wiley.

Lefever, R., jt. ed. see Nicolis, G.

LeFevre, Adam. Everything All at Once. LC 77-14847. (Wesleyan Poetry Program: Vol. 89). 1978. pap. 10.00x (ISBN 0-8195-2089-6, Pub. by Wesleyan U Pr); pap. 4.95 (ISBN 0-8195-1089-0). Columbia U Pr.

Lefevre, Carl A. Linguistics, English & the Language Arts. LC 73-15655. 371p. 1974. Repr. of 1970 ed. text ed. 8.00x (ISBN 0-8077-2428-9). Tchrs Coll.

Lefevre, Edwin. Reminiscences of a Stock Operator. 1980. Repr. of 1923 ed. flexible cover 12.00 (ISBN 0-87034-058-1). Fraser Pub Co.

LeFevre, Gregg. Creating with Sheet Plastic. LC 74-82326. (Little Craft Bk.). (Illus.). 48p. (gr. 10 up). 1974. 4.95 o.p. (ISBN 0-8069-5314-4); PLB 5.89 o.p. (ISBN 0-8069-5315-2). Sterling.

--Junk Sculpture. LC 72-95204. (Little Craft Book Ser.). (Illus.). 50p. 1972. 4.95 o.p. (ISBN 0-8069-5258-X); lib. bdg. 5.89 o.p. (ISBN 0-8069-5259-8). Sterling.

Le Fevre, P. G. Active Transport Through Animal Cell Membranes. (Protoplasmatologia: Vol. 8, Pt. 7a). (Illus.). 1955. pap. 33.70 o.p. (ISBN 0-387-80387-4). Springer-Verlag.

LeFevre, Perry D., ed. Conflict in a Voluntary Association: A Case Study of a Classic Suburban Church Fight. LC 75-12388. (Studies in Ministry & Parish Life). 1975. 12.95x (ISBN 0-913552-03-8); pap. 5.00x (ISBN 0-913552-09-7). Exploration Pr.

Leff, Gordon. Dissolution of the Medieval Outlook. (Orig.). 1976. pap. 4.95x o.p. (ISBN 0-06-131897-3, TB1897, Torch). Har-Row.

--The Dissolution of the Medieval Outlook: An Essay on Intellectual & Spiritual Change in the Fourteenth Century. LC 76-48865. 154p. 1976. 10.00x (ISBN 0-8147-4974-7). NYU Pr.

Leffert, H. L., ed. Growth Regulation by Ion Fluxes. LC 80-13986. (N.Y. Academy of Sciences Annals: Vol. 339). 340p. 60.00x (ISBN 0-89766-049-8). NY Acad Sci.

Leffert, Robert. Lesions of the Brachial Plexus. (Illus.). Date not set. text ed. price not set (ISBN 0-443-08026-7). Churchill. Postponed.

Lefferts, Robert. Elements of Graphics: How to Prepare Charts & Graphs for Effective Reports. LC 80-8209. (Illus.). 192p. 1981. 12.95 (ISBN 0-06-012578-0, HarpT). Har-Row.

Leffland, Ella. Rumors of Peace. 1980. pap. 2.50 (ISBN 0-445-04587-6). Popular Lib.

Leffler, G. L. & Farwell, L. C. The Stock Market. 3rd ed. (Illus.). 1963. 18.95 (ISBN 0-8260-5360-2). Ronald Pr.

--The Stock Market. 3rd ed. 654p. 1963. 18.95 (ISBN 0-471-06571-4). Wiley.

Lefkovits, I., jt. ed. see Steinberg, C. M.

Lefkovits, Ivan, ed. Immunological Methods, Vol. 2. 1981. write for info. (ISBN 0-12-442702-2). Acad Pr.

Lefkovitz, Ivan & Waldmann, Hermann. Limiting Dilution Analysis of Cells in the Immune System. LC 77-82502. (Illus.). 1980. 43.50 (ISBN 0-521-22771-2). Cambridge U Pr.

Lefkowitz, Irene, et al, trs. see Prichard, Elizabeth, et al.

Lefkowitz, M. M., et al. Growing up to Be Violent: A Longitudinal Study of the Development of Agression. 1976. text ed. 18.15 (ISBN 0-08-019515-6); pap. 10.25 (ISBN 0-08-019514-8). Pergamon.

Lefkowitz, Robert J., jt. auth. see Williams, Lewis T.

Lefkowitz, William. Fight for Freedom. Mooney, Thomas J., ed. (Pal Paperbacks Ser., Kit A). (Illus., Orig.). (gr. 7-12). 1976. pap. text ed. 1.25 (ISBN 0-8374-3503-X). Xerox Ed Pubns.

Leflar, Robert A. American Conflicts Law. 3rd ed. 1977. 35.00 (ISBN 0-672-83415-4, Bobbs-Merrill Law). Michie.

LeFlore, Ron & Hawkins, Jim. One in a Million: The Ron LeFlore Story. 1978. pap. 1.95 o.s.i. (ISBN 0-446-89976-3). Warner Bks.

LeForestier, Wilford A., jt. auth. see Lee, Harry O.

Leforge, Thomas H. Memoirs of a White Crow Indian. Marquis, Thomas B., narrated by. LC 74-6222. xxiv, 356p. 1974. 14.95x (ISBN 0-8032-0885-5); pap. 6.50 (ISBN 0-8032-5800-3, BB 584, Bison). U of Nebr Pr.

Lefrak, Edward & Starr, Albert. Cardiac Valve Prostheses. LC 79-46. (Illus.). 1979. 25.50 (ISBN 0-8385-1049-3). ACC.

Lefrancais, Gustave. Etude Sur le Mouvement Communaliste a Paris En 1871. (Commune De Paris en 1871). (Fr.). 1977. lib. bdg. 28.75x o.p. (ISBN 0-8287-0520-8); pap. text ed. 18.75x o.p. (ISBN 0-685-77002-8). Clearwater Pub.

Le Francois, Guy. Adolescents. 1976. text ed. 18.95x (ISBN 0-534-00433-4). Wadsworth Pub.

Lefrancois, Guy R. Of Children: An Introduction to Child Development. 3rd ed. 560p. 1979. text ed. 19.95x (ISBN 0-534-00806-2); study guide 6.95x (ISBN 0-534-00840-2). Wadsworth Pub.

--Of Humans: Introductory Psychology by Kongor. LC 73-91422. 1974. text ed. 13.95 o.p. (ISBN 0-8185-0120-0); instructor's manual avail. o.p. (ISBN 0-685-42222-4). Brooks-Cole.

--Psychological Theories & Human Learning: Kongor's Report. LC 76-164998. (Core Bks. in Psychology Ser.). 384p. 1971. text ed. 14.95 (ISBN 0-8185-0014-X); test items avail. (ISBN 0-685-23472-X). Brooks-Cole.

--Psychology. 672p. 1979. 19.95x (ISBN 0-534-00712-0); study guide 7.95x (ISBN 0-534-00844-5). Wadsworth Pub.

--Psychology for Teaching: A Bear Sometimes Faces the Front. 3rd ed. 1979. pap. text ed. 14.95x (ISBN 0-534-00602-7). Wadsworth Pub.

Lefrox, A. H., tr. see Girard, Paul F.

Lefschetz, Solomon. Algebraic Topology. LC 41-6147. (Colloquium Pbns. Ser.: Vol. 27). 1980. 31.60 (ISBN 0-8218-1027-8, COLL-27). Am Math.

--Selected Papers. LC 73-113137. 1971. text ed. 27.50 (ISBN 0-8284-0234-5). Chelsea Pub.

--Topology. 2nd ed. LC 56-11513. 13.95 (ISBN 0-8284-0116-0). Chelsea Pub.

Lefton, Lester A. Psychology. 1979. text ed. 18.95 (ISBN 0-205-06421-3, 7964218); instr's man. o.p. avail. (ISBN 0-205-06422-1); study guide 7.95 (ISBN 0-205-06423-X, 7964234). Allyn.

Lefton, Robert, et al. Improving Productivity Through People Skills. 1980. 22.50 (ISBN 0-88410-498-2). Ballinger Pub.

Leftwich. Price Systems Res. Alloc. 1979. 20.95 (ISBN 0-03-045421-2). Dryden Pr.

Leftwich, A. W. A Dictionary of Entomology. LC 75-27143. 1976. 27.50x (ISBN 0-8448-0820-2). Crane-Russak Co.

--A Dictionary of Zoology. 3rd ed. 487p. 1973. 27.50x (ISBN 0-8448-0845-8). Crane-Russak Co.

Leftwich, Richard H. A Basic Framework for Economics. 1980. pap. 9.95x (ISBN 0-256-02309-3); student wkbk. avail. (ISBN 0-256-02358-1). Business Pubns.

Leftwich, Richard H. & Sharp, Ansel M. Economics of Social Issues. 4th ed. 1980. pap. text ed. 9.95x (ISBN 0-256-02310-7); write for info. wkbk. & student guide (ISBN 0-256-02355-7). Business Pubns.

Le Gall, A., et al. Present Problems in the Democratization of Secondary & Higher Education. LC 72-97137. (The Development of Higher Education Ser.). (Illus.). 238p. (Orig.). 1973. pap. 9.25 (ISBN 92-3-101068-9, U477, UNESCO). Unipub.

Le Gallienne, Eva. The Mystic in the Theatre: Eleonora Duse. LC 72-11975. (Arcturus Books Paperbacks). 189p. 1973. pap. 5.45 (ISBN 0-8093-0631-X). S Ill U Pr.

LeGallienne, Eva, tr. see Ibsen, Henrik.

Legare, H. S. Writings of Hugh Swinton Legare. Bullen, Mary S. L., ed. LC 70-107413. (American Public Figures Ser). 1970. Repr. of 1846 ed. lib. bdg. 27.50 (ISBN 0-306-71885-5). Da Capo.

Le Gassick, Trevor, tr. see Mahfouz, Naguib.

LeGassick, Trevor J. Major Themes in Modern Arabic Thought: An Anthology. 1979. text ed. 12.50 (ISBN 0-472-08561-1). U of Mich Pr.

LeGates, Richard T., jt. auth. see Phillips, E. Barbara.

Legato, Marianne J. The Myocardial Cell for the Clinical Cardiologist. LC 73-80701. (Illus.). 196p. 1973. 20.00 o.p. (ISBN 0-87993-024-1). Futura Pub.

Leger, Robert G. & Stratton, John R. The Sociology of Corrections: A Book of Readings. LC 76-51462. 1977. text ed. 15.95x (ISBN 0-471-01680-2). Wiley.

Legere, J. Roy. Commissioned by the Lord Himself. 168p. 1980. 7.95 (ISBN 0-935488-00-6); pap. 3.95 (ISBN 0-935488-01-4). Apostolic Formation.

Legesse, Asmarom. Gada: Three Approaches to the Study of African Society. LC 72-87783. 1973. 25.00 (ISBN 0-02-918400-2). Free Pr.

Legeza, Irenus. Descriptive & Illustrated Catalogue of the Malcolm Macdonald Collection of Chinese Ceramics. Orig. Title: Laszlo. (Illus.). 1972. pap. 65.00 (ISBN 0-19-713135-2). Oxford U Pr.

Legg, Phyllida, jt. auth. see Harrold, Robert.

Legg, Stuart. The Heartland. 1970. 8.95 o.p. (ISBN 0-374-16866-0). FS&G.

Leggat, Robert. Photography in School. 1975. 16.95 o.p. (ISBN 0-85242-404-3, Pub. by Fountain). Morgan.

Leggatt, Alex. Carpentry for the Home. (Illus.). 144p. 1981. 22.50 (ISBN 0-7134-1886-9, Pub. by Batsford England). David & Charles.

Legge, tr. see Mueller, F. Max.

Legge, James, tr. Book of Poetry. (Eng. & Chinese.). 1967. Repr. of 1923 ed. 11.00 o.p. (ISBN 0-8188-0061-5). Paragon.

Legge, James, tr. see I Ching.

Legge, K. & Mugford, E. Designing Organisations for Satisfaction & Efficiency. 160p. 1978. text ed. 24.00x (ISBN 0-566-02102-1, Pub. by Gower Pub Co England). Renouf.

--Designing Organisations for Satisfaction & Efficiency. 1978. text ed. 24.00x (ISBN 0-566-02102-1, Pub. by Gower Pub Co England). Renouf.
Legge, Karen, jt. ed. see Gowler, Dan.
Legge, Sylvia. Affectionate Cousins: T. Sturge Moore & Maria Appia. (Illus.). 288p. 1980. text ed. 24.50x (ISBN 0-19-211761-0). Oxford U Pr.
Legge, Thomas. Richardus Tertius. Lordi, Robert J. & Orgel, Stephen, eds. LC 78-66843. (Renaissance Drama Ser.). 1979. lib. bdg. 50.00 (ISBN 0-8240-9741-6). Garland Pub.
Leggert, Glenn H., et al. Prentice-Hall Handbook for Writers. 7th ed. 1978. text ed. 10.50 (ISBN 0-13-695767-6). P-H.
Legget, Robert F. Rideau Waterway. rev. ed. LC 56-1252. (Illus.). 1972. pap. 6.95 (ISBN 0-8020-6156-7). U of Toronto Pr.
Leggett, B. J. Housman's Land of Lost Content: A Critical Study of "A Shropshire Lad". LC 71-100407. 172p. 1970. 10.00x (ISBN 0-87049-106-7). U of Tenn Pr.
Leggett, G. & Lee, D. Writers Workbook A: Form D. 1967. pap. text ed. 5.95 o.p. (ISBN 0-13-970087-0). P-H.
Leggett, Gary. Letters to Timothy. LC 80-82830. (Radiant Life Ser.). 128p. 1981. 1.95 (ISBN 0-88243-877-8, 02-0877). Gospel Pub.
Leggett, Gerene C. How to Raise & Train a Bouvier Des Flandres. (Orig.). 1965. pap. 2.00 (ISBN 0-87666-252-1, DS1061). TFH Pubns.
Leggett, Linda & Andrews, Linda. The Rose Colored Glasses: Melanie Adjusts to Poor Vision. LC 79-12501. 1979. 8.95 (ISBN 0-87705-408-8). Human Sci Pr.
Leggett, Trevor. Zen & the Ways. (Illus.). 1978. 18.00 (ISBN 0-7100-8598-2). Routledge & Kegan.
Leggett, Trevor P. First Zen Reader. LC 60-12739. (Illus.). 1960. pap. 5.50 (ISBN 0-8048-0180-0). C E Tuttle.
Leggewie, Robert, jt. ed. see Clouard, Henri.
Leggitt, Hunter, jt. auth. see Myers, Lonny.
Legner, E. F., jt. auth. see Moore, Ian.
Le Goff, Jacques. Time, Work, & Culture in the Middle Ages. Goldhammer, Arthur, tr. LC 79-25400. 1980. lib. bdg. 22.50x (ISBN 0-226-47080-6). U of Chicago Pr.
Le Goff, T. J. Vannes & Its Region: A Study of Town & Country in Eighteenth-Century France. (Illus.). 496p. 1981. 69.00x (ISBN 0-19-822515-6). Oxford U Pr.
Legon, Ronald P. Megara: The Political History of a Greek City-State to 336 B. C. LC 80-69828. (Illus.). 344p. 1981. 25.00x (ISBN 0-8014-1370-2). Cornell U Pr.
Legouix, Susan. Botticelli. LC 77-10355. (The Oresko Art Book). (Illus.). 1977. 15.95 (ISBN 0-8467-0376-9, Pub. by Two Continents); pap. 9.95 (ISBN 0-8467-0379-3). Hippocrene Bks.
Legrand, Louis, ed. Educational Research on New Developments in Primary Education. (Council of Europe Trends Ser.). 206p. 1980. pap. text ed. 29.75x (ISBN 0-85633-190-2, NFER). Humanities.
LeGrand, R. J. Advanced French Unseens. 1970. pap. text ed. 4.95x o.p. (ISBN 0-435-37536-9). Heinemann Ed.
Le Grand Richards. A Marvelous Work & a Wonder. 424p. 14.00 (ISBN 0-87747-686-1); pap. 1.50 (ISBN 0-87747-614-4). Deseret Bk.
Legras, R., jt. auth. see Mercier, J. P.
Le Grice, E. B. Rose Growing for Everyone. (Illus.). 1969. 7.95 o.p. (ISBN 0-571-08682-9, Pub. by Faber & Faber). Merrimack Bk Serv.
Legros, G. V. Fabre: Poet of Science. LC 73-152059. 1971. 7.50 o.p. (ISBN 0-8180-0218-2). Horizon.
Legros, Lucien & Grant, John C. Typographical Printing-Surfaces: The Technology & Mechanism of Their Production. Bidwell, John, ed. LC 78-74403. (Nineteenth-Century Book Arts & Printing History Ser.: Vol. 16). (Illus.). 1980. lib. bdg. 87.00 (ISBN 0-8240-3890-8). Garland Pub.
Legters, Lyman H., ed. The German Democratic Republic. LC 77-578. 1977. lib. bdg. 24.50 o.p. (ISBN 0-89158-142-1). Westview.
Le Guern, M. & Le Guern, M. R. Les Pensees de Pascal: De l'anthropologie a la theologie. (Collection themes et textes). 244p. (Fr.). 1972. pap. 6.75 (ISBN 2-03-035005-2, 2697). Larousse.
Le Guern, M. R., jt. auth. see Le Guern, M.
LeGuin, Ursula. The Beginning Place. 192p. 1981. pap. 2.25 (ISBN 0-553-14259-3). Bantam.
Le Guin, Ursula. The Dispossessed. 1975. pap. 2.50 (ISBN 0-380-00382-1, 51284). Avon.
LeGuin, Ursula. Hard Words & Other Poems. LC 80-8210. 96p. 1981. 10.00 (ISBN 0-06-012579-9, HarpT); pap. 4.95 (ISBN 0-06-090848-3, CN 848). Har-Row.
--The Lathe of Heaven. 1973. pap. 1.95 (ISBN 0-380-01320-7, 43547). Avon.
Leguin, Ursula K. City of Illusion. 160p. (Orig.). 1976. pap. 2.25 (ISBN 0-441-10705-2). Ace Bks.
--The Left Hand of Darkness. 320p. (Orig.). 1976. pap. 2.25 (ISBN 0-441-47805-0). Ace Bks.
--Rocannon's World. Del Rey, Lester, ed. LC 75-419. (Library of Science Fiction). 1975. lib. bdg. 17.50 (ISBN 0-8240-1424-3). Garland Pub.
Le Guin, Ursula K. The Word for World Is Forest. LC 75-37085. (YA) 1976. 6.95 o.p. (ISBN 0-399-11716-4, Dist. by Putnam). Berkley Pub.
LeGuin, Ursula K., ed. Nebula Award Stories Eleven. LC 66-20974. (YA) 1977. 8.95 o.p. (ISBN 0-06-012564-0, HarpT). Har-Row.
Le Guin, Ursula K. & Kidd, Virginia, eds. Edges. 1980. pap. write for info. (ISBN 0-671-83532-7). PB.
Legum, Colin. Africa Contemporary Record, Vol. 12. LC 70-7957. 1400p. 1981. text ed. 125.00x (ISBN 0-8419-0550-9, Africana). Holmes & Meier.
--Pan-Africanism: A Short Political Guide. LC 75-25492. (Illus.). 1976. Repr. of 1962 ed. lib. bdg. 22.75x (ISBN 0-8371-8420-7, LEPA). Greenwood.
Legum, Colin, ed. Africa Contemporary Record, Vol. 9. LC 70-7957. (Illus.). 1977. 125.00x (ISBN 0-8419-0158-9, Africana). Holmes & Meier.
--Africa Contemporary Record, Vol. 10. LC 70-7957. 1979. 125.00x (ISBN 0-8419-0159-7, Africana). Holmes & Meier.
--Africa Contemporary Record, Vol. 11. LC 70-7957. 1980. 125.00x (ISBN 0-8419-0160-0, Africana). Holmes & Meier.
--Africa Contemporary Record: Annual Survey & Documents. Incl. Vol. 1. 1968-69. 904p (ISBN 0-8419-0150-3); Vol. 2. 1969-70. 1213p (ISBN 0-8419-0151-1); Vol. 3. 1970-71. 1065p (ISBN 0-8419-0152-X); Vol. 4. 1971-1972. 1100p (ISBN 0-8419-0153-8); Vol. 5. 1972-73. Legum, Colin, ed (ISBN 0-8419-0154-6). LC 70-7957. 125.00 ea. (Africana). Holmes & Meier.
--Africa Contemporary Record: 1973-74, Vol. 6. LC 70-7957. (Illus.). 1200p. 1974. 125.00x (ISBN 0-8419-0155-4, Africana). Holmes & Meier.
--Africa Contemporary Record: 1974-75, Vol. 7. LC 70-7957. (Illus.). 1100p. 1975. 125.00x (ISBN 0-8419-0156-2, Africana). Holmes & Meier.
Legum, Colin & Shaked, Haim, eds. Middle East Contemporary Survey, Vol. 2. LC 78-648245. (Illus.). 1979. text ed. 77.50x (ISBN 0-8419-0398-0). Holmes & Meier.
--Middle East Contemporary Survey: 1978-1979, Vol. 3. LC 78-648245. (Illus.). 1980. text ed. 97.50x (ISBN 0-8419-0609-2). Holmes & Meier.
Legunn, Joel. Famous Americans, 2 bks. (Janus Stamp & Story Ser.). (Illus.). 64p. (gr. 6-12). 1980. 2.85 ea. Bk. 1 Before 1860 (ISBN 0-915510-44-8). Bk. 2 After 1860 (ISBN 0-915510-45-6). Janus Bks.
--Highlights of American History, 2 bks. (Janus Stamp & Story Ser.). (Illus.). 64p. (gr. 7-12). 1979. Bk. 1 Before 1850. pap. text ed. 2.85 (ISBN 0-915510-31-6); Bk. 2 After 1850. pap. text ed. 2.85 (ISBN 0-915510-32-4). Janus Bks.
--Motion. Liberty, Gene, ed. LC 73-128852. (Understanding Bks.). Orig. Title: Investigating Motion. (gr. 6-9). 1971. PLB 7.95 (ISBN 0-87191-041-1). Creative Ed.
Leh, Francis K. & Lak, Richard K. Environment & Pollutions: Sources, Health Effects, Monitoring & Control. (Illus.). 308p. 1974. 19.75 (ISBN 0-398-03030-8). C C Thomas.
Lehan, Richard D. F. Scott Fitzgerald & the Craft of Fiction. LC 66-5059. (Crosscurrents-Modern Critiques Ser.). 221p. 1966. 13.95 (ISBN 0-8093-0216-0). S Ill U Pr.
Lehane, B. Dublin. Time-Life Books, ed. (Great Cities Ser.). (Illus.). 1979. 14.95 (ISBN 0-8094-2343-X). Time-Life.
--Dublin. (The Great Cities Ser.). (Illus.). 1978. lib. bdg. 14.94 (ISBN 0-686-51002-X). Silver.
Lehman, Carolyn. One Hundred & Ten Helps for Teachers. 64p. (Orig.). 1980. pap. text ed. 3.50 (ISBN 0-87239-413-1, 3070). Standard Pub.
Lehman, Charles. Italic Handwriting & Calligraphy for the Beginner: A Craft Manual. (Illus.). 160p. (Orig.). 1981. pap. 3.95 (ISBN 0-8008-4290-1, 80-53415, Pentalic). Taplinger.
Lehman, Charles A. Emergency Survival. Fessler, Diane M., ed. (Illus.). 160p. 1979. pap. 6.95 (ISBN 0-935810-03-X). Primer Pubs.
Lehman, Chester K. Gospels & the Acts. rev. ed. (Bible Survey Course No. 4). 1956. pap. 1.00 o.p. (ISBN 0-8361-1319-5). Herald Pr.
Lehman, Edna. Talking to Children About Sex. pap. 0.95 o.p. (ISBN 0-06-087001-X, HW). Har-Row.
Lehman, Edward W. Coordinating Health Care. LC 75-691. (Sage Library of Social Research: Vol. 17). 1975. 18.00x (ISBN 0-8039-0442-8); pap. 7.95x o.p. (ISBN 0-8039-0512-2). Sage.
--Political Society: A Macrosociology of Politics. LC 77-23887. 1977. 17.50x (ISBN 0-231-04003-2). Columbia U Pr.
Lehman, Ernest. The French Atlantic Affair. 1978. pap. 2.75 (ISBN 0-446-95258-3). Warner Bks.
Lehman, Helmut H., jt. ed. see Bergendoff, Conrad.
Lehman, Helmut T., jt. ed. see Krodel, Gottfried G.
Lehman, Helmut T., jt. ed. see Lehman, Martin E.
Lehman, Helmut T., jt. ed. see Sherman, Franklin.
Lehman, Helmut T., jt. ed. see Wiencke, Gustav K.
Lehman, James. The Old Brethren. (Orig.). 1976. pap. 2.45 (ISBN 0-89129-155-5). Jove Pubns.
Lehman, Jane, jt. auth. see Kolzow, Lee.
Lehman, John. The Executive, Congress, & Foreign Policy: Studies of the Nixon Administration. LC 76-13835. (Special Studies). 1976. text ed. 23.95 (ISBN 0-275-56490-8). Praeger.
Lehman, John W. Operational Organic Chemistry: A Laboratory Course. new ed. 640p. 1981. text ed. 19.95 (ISBN 0-205-07146-5, 687146-1); tchr's. ed. free (ISBN 0-205-07147-3). Allyn.
Lehman, Martin E. & Lehman, Helmut T., eds. Luther's Works: Word & Sacrament IV, Vol. 38. LC 55-9893. 1971. 16.95 (ISBN 0-8006-0338-9, 1-338). Fortress.
Lehman, Maxwell, ed. Communication Technologies & Information Flow. (PPS on Science & Technology Ser.). (Illus.). 175p. 1981. 20.00 (ISBN 0-08-027169-3); pap. 12.50 (ISBN 0-08-027528-1). Pergamon.
Lehman, P. Thirteen Ivenrow. 4.00 o.p. (ISBN 0-8062-1101-6). Carlton.
Lehman, Paul E. Bandit in Black. 1979. pap. 1.25 (ISBN 0-505-51368-4). Tower Bks.
--Blood of the West. 1979. pap. 1.50 (ISBN 0-505-51410-9). Tower Bks.
--Calamity Range: Valley of Hunted Men. 1979. pap. 2.25 (ISBN 0-8439-0679-0). Nordon Pubns.
--Gun-Whipped. 1979. pap. 1.25 (ISBN 0-505-51369-2). Tower Bks.
--Idaho & Only the Brave. 1979. pap. 2.25 (ISBN 0-505-51429-X). Tower Bks.
Lehman, Wallace B. The Clubfoot. (Illus.). 114p. 1980. 27.50 (ISBN 0-397-50457-8). Lippincott.
Lehmann, jt. ed. see Wentz, Abdel R.
Lehmann, A. Church Musicians Enchiridon. 1979. 3.25 (ISBN 0-8100-0111-X). Northwest Pub.
Lehmann, A. G. The Symbolist Aesthetic in France, 1885-1895. 2nd ed. 1968. 30.25x (ISBN 0-631-10380-5, Pub. by Basil Blackwell). Biblio Dist.
Lehmann, Armin D. Travel & Tourism: An Introduction to Travel Agency Operations. LC 77-12589. 1978. pap. 18.95 (ISBN 0-672-97090-2). Bobbs.
Lehmann, E. L. Nonparametrics: Statistical Methods Based on Ranks. LC 72-93538. 1975. text ed. 29.95x (ISBN 0-8162-4994-6). Holden-Day.
Lehmann, H. L., tr. see Heckner, Fritz.
Lehmann, H. Peter, ed. see Heckner, Fritz.
Lehmann, Helmut T. & Atkinson, James, eds. Luther's Works: The Christian in Society I, Vol. 44. LC 55-9893. 1966. 16.95 (ISBN 0-8006-0344-3, 1-344). Fortress.
Lehmann, Helmut T. & Doberstein, John W., eds. Luther's Works: Sermons I, Vol. 51. Doberstein, John W., tr. LC 55-9893. 1959. 16.95 (ISBN 0-8006-0351-6, 1-353). Fortress.
Lehmann, Helmut T. & Gritsch, Eric W., eds. Luther's Works: Church & Ministry III, Vol. 41. LC 55-9893. 1966. 16.95x (ISBN 0-8006-0341-9, 1-341). Fortress.
Lehmann, Helmut T., jt. ed. see Bachmann, Theodore.
Lehmann, Helmut T., jt. ed. see Brandt, Walter I.
Lehmann, Helmut T., jt. ed. see Dietrich, Martin O.
Lehmann, Helmut T., jt. ed. see Fischer, Robert H.
Lehmann, Helmut T., jt. ed. see Forell, George W.
Lehmann, Helmut T., jt. ed. see Grimm, Harold J.
Lehmann, Helmut T., jt. ed. see Gritsch, Eric W.
Lehmann, Helmut T., jt. ed. see Hillerbrand, Hans J.
Lehmann, Helmut T., jt. ed. see Krodel, Gottfried G.
Lehmann, Helmut T., jt. ed. see Leupold, Ulrich S.
Lehmann, Helmut T., jt. ed. see Schultz, Robert C.
Lehmann, Helmut T., jt. ed. see Spitz, Lewis W.
Lehmann, Helmut T., jt. ed. see Tappert, Theodore G.
Lehmann, Helmut T., jt. ed. see Watson, Philip S.
Lehmann, Jerry. We Walked to Moscow. (Illus.). 1966. pap. 3.00 (ISBN 0-934676-07-0). Greenlf Bks.
Lehmann, John. Edward Lear & His World. LC 77-73133. (Enore Edition). (Illus.). 1977. 3.95 (ISBN 0-684-16548-1, ScribT). Scribner.
--The Strange Destiny of Rupert Brooke. LC 80-13822. (Illus.). 228p. 1981. 12.95 (ISBN 0-03-057479-X). HR&W.
Lehmann, Karl & Lehmann, P. W., eds. Samothrace Excavations: Conducted by the Institute of Fine Arts of New York University, 4 vols. Incl. Vol. 1. Ancient Literary Sources. Lewis, Naphtali, ed. & tr. 1958. 20.00x (ISBN 0-691-09820-4); Vol. 2, Pt. 1. Inscriptions on Stone. Fraser, P. M. 1960. 25.00x (ISBN 0-691-09821-2); Vol. 2, Pt. 2. Inscriptions on Ceramics & Minor Objects. Lehmann, Karl. 1960. 25.00x (ISBN 0-691-09822-0); Vol. 3. The Hieron. Lehmann, P. 1969. 3 vols. boxed set 70.00 (ISBN 0-691-09823-9); Vol. 4, Pt. 1. Hall of Votive Gifts. Lehmann, Karl. 1962. 25.00x (ISBN 0-691-09824-7); Vol. 4, Pt. 2. Altar Court. Lehmann, Karl & Spittle, Denys. 1964. 30.00x (ISBN 0-691-09825-5). (Bollingen Ser.: Vol. 60). Princeton U Pr.
Lehmann, Lilli. My Path Through Life. Seligman, Alice B., tr. LC 80-2286. (Illus.). 1981. Repr. of 1914 ed. 54.50 (ISBN 0-404-18855-9). AMS Pr.
Lehmann, Linwood, tr. see Jefferson, Thomas.
Lehmann, Liza. The Life of Liza Lehmann. (Music Reprint Ser.: 1980). (Illus.). 1980. Repr. of 1918 ed. lib. bdg. 22.50 (ISBN 0-306-76010-X). Da Capo.
Lehmann, P. see Lehmann, Karl & Lehmann, P. W.
Lehmann, P. W., jt. ed. see Lehmann, Karl.
Lehmann, R. C. The Adventures of Picklock Holes. (Illus.). 64p. 1975. 10.00 o.p. (ISBN 0-915230-07-0); pap. 5.00 o.p. (ISBN 0-915230-08-9). Rue Morgue.
Lehmann, Walter J. Atomic & Molecular Structure: The Development of Our Concepts. LC 70-37434. 1972. text ed. 21.50x o.p. (ISBN 0-471-52440-9). Wiley.
Lehmann, Winfred P. Proto-Indo-European Syntax. LC 52-2570. 382p. 1974. 20.00x (ISBN 0-292-76419-7). U of Tex Pr.
Lehmann, Winfred P., ed. see Bennett, William H.
Lehmann, Winfred P., et al. Introduction to Scholarship in Modern Languages & Literatures. Gibaldi, Joseph, ed. 160p. 1981. 10.50x (ISBN 0-87352-092-0); pap. 6.00x (ISBN 0-87352-093-9). Modern Lang.
Lehmberg, Paul. In the Strong Woods. 160p. 1981. pap. 4.95 (ISBN 0-312-41173-1). St Martin.
Lehmberg, S. E. The Later Parliaments of Henry VIII, 1536-1547. LC 76-7804. 1977. 49.95 (ISBN 0-521-21256-1). Cambridge U Pr.
--Reformation Parliament Fifteen Twenty-Nine - Fifteen Thirty-Six. LC 70-85723. (Illus., Orig.). 1970. 35.50 (ISBN 0-521-07655-2). Cambridge U Pr.
Lehmbruch, Gerhard, jt. ed. see Schmitter, Philippe C.
Lehnen, Robert G. & Forthofer, Ronald N. Program Analysis: The GSK Categorical Data Approach. (Illus.). 225p. 1981. text ed. 25.00 (ISBN 0-534-97974-2). Lifetime Learn.
Lehner, Ernst. Alphabets & Ornaments. (Pictorial Archive Series). (Illus.). 1968. pap. 6.50 (ISBN 0-486-21905-4). Dover.
Lehnert, Bruce E. & Schachter, E. Neil. The Pharmacology of Respiratory Care. LC 79-28446. (Illus.). 1980. pap. text ed. 13.95 (ISBN 0-8016-2921-7). Mosby.
Lehning, James R. The Peasants of Mahrles: Economic Development & Family Organization in Nineteenth-Century France. LC 79-18707. 280p. 1980. 19.50x (ISBN 0-8078-1411-3). U of NC Pr.
Lehninger, Albert L. Biochemistry: The Molecular Bases of All Structure & Function. 2nd ed. LC 75-11082. 1975. text ed. 33.95x (ISBN 0-87901-047-9). Worth.
--A Short Course in Biochemistry. LC 72-93199. (Illus.). 400p. 1973. text ed. 21.95x (ISBN 0-87901-024-X). Worth.
Lehnus, Donald J. Book Numbers: Their History, Principles, and Application. LC 80-23100. 158p. 1980. pap. 7.50 (ISBN 0-8389-0316-9). ALA.
--Enquiridion De Mecanografiar Fichas Catalograficas Segun las Normas De la Descripcion Bibliografica Internacionel Para Monografias Publicadadas for Separado, Manual 1. (Serie Bibliotecologica). pap. 1.85 o.s.i. (ISBN 0-8477-0901-9). U of PR Pr.
--Milestones in Cataloging: Famous Catalogers & Their Writings, 1835-1969. LC 73-94030. (Research Studies in Library Science Ser.: No. 13). 1974. lib. bdg. 10.00 o.p. (ISBN 0-87287-090-1). Libs Unl.
--Who's on Time? LC 79-17330. 177p. 1980. lib. bdg. 17.50 (ISBN 0-379-20684-6). Oceana.

Lehr, J. Harry. A Catalogue of the Flora of Arizona. 1978. 4.75 (ISBN 0-9605656-0-4). Desert Botanical.

Lehr, R. E. & Manchard, Alan. Orbital Symmetry Relationships. 1972. text ed. 12.50 (ISBN 0-12-441150-9); pap. text ed. 6.95 (ISBN 0-12-441156-8). Acad Pr.

Lehr, Sally T., jt. auth. see Shipes, Ellen A.

Lehrberger, John, jt. ed. see Kittredge, Richard.

Lehrburger, Egon. Inventors. LC 68-2276. (Pegasus Books: No. 5). (Illus.). 1965. 7.50x (ISBN 0-234-77841-5). Intl Pubns Serv.

Lehrer, Keith, ed. Freedom & Determinism. 204p. 1976. pap. text ed. 5.95x (ISBN 0-391-00537-5). Humanities.

Lehrer, Keith, ed. see Feigl, Herbert.

Lehrer, Keith, ed. see Reid, Thomas.

Lehrer, Robert N. Work Simplification: Creative Thinking About Work Problems. 1957. ref. ed. 16.95x o.p. (ISBN 0-13-965319-8). P-H.

Lehrer, Stanley, jt. ed. see Brickman, William.

Lehrer, Stanley, jt. ed. see Brickman, William W.

Lehrer, Steven. Alternative Treatments for Cancer. LC 78-31430. (Illus.). 1979. 13.95 (ISBN 0-88229-473-3); pap. 7.95 (ISBN 0-88229-666-3). Nelson-Hall.

Lehrling, George. Machinist: Basic Skill Development. (Illus.). 1978. pap. text ed. 10.65 o.p. (ISBN 0-8269-1950-2). Am Technical.

Lehrman, Alexander, tr. see Apresjan, Yuri D.

Lehrman, Irving. In the Name of God. LC 79-51518. 1979. 12.00x (ISBN 0-8197-0467-9). Bloch.

Lehrman, Jonathan W., et al. A Practical Guide for Handling Drug Crises. 134p. 1980. text ed. 12.75 (ISBN 0-398-04095-8); pap. text ed. 7.50 (ISBN 0-398-04100-8). C C Thomas.

Lehrman, Lewis. Dining Room Service. LC 70-142510. 1971. text ed. 14.50 (ISBN 0-672-96065-6); tchr's manual 5.90 (ISBN 0-672-96067-2); wkbk. 6.50 (ISBN 0-672-96066-4). Bobbs.

Lehrman, Nat. Masters & Johnson Explained. rev. ed. LC 76-19839. 272p. 1981. pap. 2.75 (ISBN 0-87216-808-5). Playboy Pbks.

Lehrman, Robert & Clark, Phyllis E. Doing Time: A Look at Crime & Prisons. new ed. (Illus.). 160p. 1980. 10.95 (ISBN 0-8038-1566-2). Hastings.

Lehrman, Steve, jt. auth. see Allis, John.

Lehrs, Ernst, jt. auth. see Roeschl, Maria.

Le Huray, P. Music & the Reformation in England: Fifteen Forty-Nine to Sixteen Sixty. LC 77-87383. (Studies in Music). (Illus.). 1978. 64.50 (ISBN 0-521-21958-2); pap. 14.95x (ISBN 0-521-29418-5). Cambridge U Pr.

Le Huray, Peter & Day, James. Music & Aesthetics in the Eighteenth & Early Nineteenth Centuries. (Cambridge Studies in Music: Readings in the Literature of Music). (Illus.). 700p. Date not set. price not set (ISBN 0-521-23426-3). Cambridge U Pr.

Le Huray, Peter, et al. Anthems for Men's Voices, 2 vols. Incl. Vol. 1. Altos, Tenors & Basses. 6.75x o.p. (ISBN 0-19-353234-4); Vol. 2. Tenors & Basses. 6.75x o.p. (ISBN 0-19-353235-2). 1965. Oxford U Pr.

Leib, Hans-Heinrich. International Linguistics: Volume 5, Morphology & Morphosemant-Tics. (Current Issues in Linguistic Theory Ser.: No. 17). 250p. 1981. text ed. 27.50x (ISBN 90-272-3508-2). Humanities.

Leibenstein, Harvey. Beyond Economic Man: A New Approach to Micro-Economic Theory. (Illus.). 288p. 1976. 16.50x (ISBN 0-674-06891-2); pap. 6.95 (ISBN 0-674-06892-0). Harvard U Pr.

Leiber, Fritz. Swords Against Wizardry. Baen, James P., ed. (Fafhrd & the Grey Mouser Ser.). 1976. pap. 1.95 (ISBN 0-441-79164-6). Ace Bks.

--Swords & Ice Magic. 1977. pap. 1.95 (ISBN 0-441-79168-9). Ace Bks.

--Swords in the Mist. Baen, James P., ed. (Fafhrd & the Grey Mouser Ser.). 1976. pap. 1.95 (ISBN 0-441-79184-0). Ace Bks.

--The Swords of Lankhmar. Baen, James P., ed. (Fafhrd & the Grey Mouser Ser.). 1974. pap. 1.95 (ISBN 0-441-79223-5). Ace Bks.

Leiber, Fritz & Spinrad, Norman. Destiny Times Three & Riding the Torch. (Binary Star: No. 1). 1978. pap. 1.75 o.s.i. (ISBN 0-440-10564-1). Dell.

Leiber, Jerry. Selected Lyrics: Nineteen Fifty to Nineteen Eighty. 1981. 12.95 (ISBN 0-89396-015-2); pap. 5.95 (ISBN 0-89396-016-0). Urizen Bks.

Leiber, Justin. Structuralism. 1978. lib. bdg. 12.50 (ISBN 0-8057-7721-0). Twayne.

Leibholz, S. W. & Wilson, L. D. User's Guide to Computer Crime: Its Commission, Detection & Prevention. LC 74-10662. 1974. 9.95x o.p. (ISBN 0-8019-6095-9). Chilton.

Leibling, Louis, jt. auth. see Riemer, Edwin.

Leibniz. The Leibniz-Clarke Correspondence. Alexander, H. G., ed. 200p. 1977. 15.00x (ISBN 0-7190-0669-4, Pub. by Manchester U Pr England). State Mutual Bk.

Leibniz, G. W. New Essays on Human Understanding. Remnant, Peter & Bennett, Jonathan, eds. 610p. Date not set. price not set (ISBN 0-521-23147-7); pap. price not set (ISBN 0-521-29836-9). Cambridge U Pr.

Leibniz, Gottfried. Logical Papers: A Selection. Parkinson, G. H., tr. 1966. 24.00x (ISBN 0-19-824306-5). Oxford U Pr.

--Monadology & Other Philosophical Essays. Schrecker, Paul & Schrecker, Anne, trs. LC 65-26531. (Orig.). 1965. pap. 4.95 (ISBN 0-672-60426-4, LLA188). Bobbs.

Leibovic, K. N. Nervous System Theory: An Introductory Study. 1973. 33.00 (ISBN 0-12-441250-5). Acad Pr.

Leibovitch, D. A., tr. see Neuhaus, Heinrich.

Leibowitz, Arleen A., ed. Wealth Redistribution & the Income Tax. LC 77-18652. 1978. 15.95 (ISBN 0-669-01506-7). Lexington Bks.

Leibowitz, Arnold H. Bilingual Education Act: A Legislative Analysis. LC 80-80121. 70p. (Orig.). 1980. pap. 4.20 (ISBN 0-89763-022-X). Natl Clearinghse Bilingual Ed.

--Colonial Emancipation in the Pacific and the Caribbean: A Legal and Political Analysis. LC 75-19801. (Prae Ger Special Studies Ser.). 240p. 1976. text ed. 23.95 (ISBN 0-275-56000-7). Praeger.

Leibowitz, Herbert A. Hart Crane: An Introduction to the Poetry. LC 68-13559. 1968. 17.50x (ISBN 0-231-03014-2); pap. 5.00 (ISBN 0-231-08670-9). Columbia U Pr.

Leibowitz, J. O. & Marcus, Shlomo, eds. Moses Maimonides on the Causes of Symptoms. 1974. 19.50x (ISBN 0-520-02224-6). U of Cal Pr.

Leibowitz, Paul J. see Bourne, G. H. & Danielli, J. F.

Leibowitz, Rene. Schoenberg & His School: The Contemporary Stage of the Language of Music. Newlin, Dika, tr. from Fr. LC 75-115338. (Music Ser). 1970. Repr. of 1949 ed. lib. bdg. 27.50 (ISBN 0-306-71930-4). Da Capo.

Leibowitz, Uri, ed. Progress in Multiple Sclerosis: Research & Treatment. 1973. 33.00 (ISBN 0-12-441350-1). Acad Pr.

Leiby, James. Charity & Correction in New Jersey: A History of State Welfare Institutions. 1967. 27.50 (ISBN 0-8135-0560-7). Rutgers U Pr.

Leicester, Henry M. Historical Background of Chemistry. LC 79-166426. (Illus.). 1971. pap. text ed. 3.50 (ISBN 0-486-61053-5). Dover.

Leicester, Henry M., ed. Chymia, Vols. 7, 9-12, 1961-1967. LC 48-7051. (Vol. 8 o.p.). 10.00x ea. o.p. U of Pa Pr.

Leicester, J. H. & Farndale, W. A., eds. Trends in the Services for Youth. 1967. 46.00 (ISBN 0-08-011604-3). Pergamon.

Leicht, Kathleen F. Understanding Yourself. LC 73-3156. (Concise Guides Ser.). (gr. 7-12). 1973. PLB 4.47 o.p. (ISBN 0-531-02629-9). Watts.

Leichter, H. M. The Comparative Study of Public Policy. LC 79-50625. (Illus.). 1979. 27.50 (ISBN 0-521-22648-1); pap. 8.95x (ISBN 0-521-29601-3). Cambridge U Pr.

Leichter, Hope. Families & Communities As Educators. LC 79-63. 1979. text ed. 11.95 o.p. (ISBN 0-8077-2560-9); pap. text ed. 10.95 (ISBN 0-8077-2559-5). Tchrs Coll.

Leichter, Hope J. & Mitchell, William E. Kinship & Casework. rev. ed. LC 78-15482. 1978. pap. text ed. 11.75x (ISBN 0-8077-2530-7). Tchrs Coll.

Leichter, Hope J., ed. The Family As Educator. LC 75-16252. 1975. 8.75x (ISBN 0-8077-2497-1); pap. 6.00x (ISBN 0-8077-2496-3). Tchrs Coll.

Leichter, Larry R. Epidemic! 368p. (Orig.). 1980. pap. 2.50 (ISBN 0-89083-644-2). Zebra.

Leichtman, Robert R. & Japikse, Carl. The Art of Living, Vol. 1. 242p. Date not set. pap. 5.00 (ISBN 0-89804-032-9). Ariel Pr.

--The Art of Living, Vol. 2. (Illus.). 249p. (Orig.). 1980. pap. 5.00 (ISBN 0-89804-033-7). Ariel Pr.

--The Way to Health. (The Art of Living). 90p. Date not set. pap. 3.00 (ISBN 0-89804-037-X). Ariel Pr.

Leiden, Carl & Schmitt, Karl M. The Politics of Violence: Revolution in the Modern World. LC 80-23161. x, 244p. 1980. Repr. of 1968 ed. lib. bdg. 27.50x (ISBN 0-313-22463-3, LEPV). Greenwood.

Leider, Emily W., ed. see Zunser, Miriam S.

Leider, Frida. Playing My Part. Osborne, Charles, tr. LC 77-26171. (Music Reprint Ser., 1978). (Illus.). 1978. Repr. of 1959 ed. lib. bdg. 22.50 (ISBN 0-306-77535-2). Da Capo.

Leider, Robert. Am I Eligible? The Easy Way to Calculate the Beog Index, 1980-1981. 16p. 1980. pap. 1.00 (ISBN 0-917760-20-4). Octameron Assocs.

--The A's & B's of Academic Scholarships: A Guide to Current Programs, 1980-1982. 3rd ed. LC 78-52571. 52p. 1980. pap. 2.00 (ISBN 0-917760-18-2). Octameron Assocs.

--Help from the Governor & Locating Lenders: Two Contact Directories for Scholarships & Student Loans, 1980-1982. 16p. (Orig.). 1980. pap. 1.00 (ISBN 0-917760-21-2). Octameron Assocs.

--Your Own Financial Aid Factory: The Guide to Locating College Money. rev. ed. LC 80-11185. 184p. 1981. pap. 5.95 (ISBN 0-917760-22-0). Octameron Assocs.

Leiderman, David & Liederman, Susan V. David's Cookies Cookie Cookbook. (Illus.). 128p. 1981. 8.95 (ISBN 0-89480-151-1); pap. 4.95 (ISBN 0-89480-149-X). Workman Pub.

Leidy, W. Philip. A Popular Guide to Government Publications. 4th ed. LC 76-17803. 384p. 1976. 27.50x (ISBN 0-231-04019-9). Columbia U Pr.

Leif, Irving P. Community Power & Decision Making: An International Handbook. LC 74-4171. 1974. 10.00 (ISBN 0-8108-0717-3). Scarecrow.

Leifchild, J. R. Cornwall: Its Mines & Miners. 2nd ed. LC 68-58855. Repr. of 1857 ed. 17.50x (ISBN 0-678-05064-3). Kelley.

--Our Coal & Our Coal-Pits. 2nd ed. LC 68-58856. Repr. of 1856 ed. 22.00x (ISBN 0-678-05065-1). Kelley.

Leifer, M. Malacca, Singapore & Indonesia. (International Straits of the World: No. 2). 288p. 1978. 35.00x (ISBN 90-286-0778-1). Sijthoff & Noordhoff.

Leifer, Michael. The Foreign Relations of the New States. (Studies in Contemporary Southeast Asia). 128p. 1974. text ed. 8.50x (ISBN 0-582-71042-1); pap. text ed. 5.50x (ISBN 0-582-71043-X). Longman.

Leifer, Myra. Psychological Effects of Motherhood: A Study of First Pregnancy. 22.95 (ISBN 0-03-055781-X); pap. 8.95 (ISBN 0-03-055776-3). Praeger.

Leifermann, Henry P. Crystal Lee: A Woman of Inheritance. LC 75-14118. 192p. 1975. 8.95 o.s.i. (ISBN 0-02-570220-3). Macmillan.

Leigh, Ana. Love's Long Journey. 1981. pap. 2.250 (ISBN 0-8439-0884-X, Leisure Bks). Nordon Pubns.

Leigh, Hoyle & Reiser, Morton F. The Patient: Biological, Psychological, & Social Dimensions of Medical Practice. (Illus.). 370p. 1980. 19.50 (ISBN 0-306-40207-6, Plenum Pr). Plenum Pub.

Leigh, James. The Ludi Victor. 320p. Date not set. 11.95 (ISBN 0-698-11038-2). Coward.

Leigh, James H. & Martin, Claude R., Jr., eds. Current Issues & Research in Advertising, 1980. (Illus.). 250p. 1980. pap. 7.00 (ISBN 0-87712-209-1). U Mich Busn Div Res.

Leigh, John. Young People & Leisure. (International Library of Sociology & Social Reconstruction). 1971. text ed. 9.00x (ISBN 0-7100-7059-4). Humanities.

Leigh, L. H. Economic Crime in Europe. Date not set. write for info. (ISBN 0-312-22788-4). St Martin.

Leigh, Petra. Coral. 1979. pap. 2.50 (ISBN 0-446-91088-0). Warner Bks.

Leigh, R. John & Zee, David S. The Neurology of Ocular Movement. (Contemporary Neurology Ser.: No. 22). 350p. 1981. 35.00 (ISBN 0-8036-5524-X). Davis Co.

Leigh, Richard. The Copie of a Letter Sent Out of England to don B. Mendoza. LC 72-6010. (English Experience Ser.: No. 536). 1973. Repr. of 1588 ed. 6.00 (ISBN 90-221-0536-9). Walter J Johnson.

Leigh, Robert. Index to Song Books. LC 72-8344. (Music Ser). 242p. 1973. Repr. of 1964 ed. lib. bdg. 18.50 (ISBN 0-306-70553-2). Da Capo.

Leigh, Roberta. Cupboard Love. (Alpha Books). 78p. 1979. pap. text ed. 2.25x (ISBN 0-19-424165-3). Oxford U Pr.

Leigh, Tom, illus. Sesame Street What's Inside? (Touch & Feel Bk.). (Illus.). 18p. (ps). Date not set. 3.95 (ISBN 0-307-12153-4, Golden Pr). Western Pub.

Leighbody, G. B., jt. auth. see Kidd, D. M.

Leigh-Hunt, S., tr. see Lecerf, Auguste.

Leigh-Loohuizen, Ria, tr. see Kopland, Roger.

Leighly, John, ed. see Sauer, Carl O.

Leight, Edward, jt. auth. see Moore, Nancy.

Leighton, Alexander. Commonwealth Tracts 1625-1650: A Shorte Treatise Against Stage-Playes. Bd. with The Stage Players Complaint; Declaration...Also an Ordinance of Both Houses, for the Supression of Stage Playes; The Actors Remonstrance; Two Ordinances; An Ordinance for the Utter Suppression & Abolishing of All Stage-Playes & Interludes; The Dagonizing of Bartholomew Fayre; The Humble Petition of Diverse Poor & Distressed Men, Heretofore the Actors of Blackfriers & the Cock-Pit. LC 71-170417. (The English Stage Ser.: Vol. 14). lib. bdg. 50.00 (ISBN 0-8240-0597-X). Garland Pub.

Leighton, Alexander H. Governing of Men. 1945. 20.00x o.p. (ISBN 0-691-08607-9). Princeton U Pr.

Leighton, David & Simmonds, Kenneth. Case Problems in Marketing. 1973. pap. text ed. 12.95 (ISBN 0-17-771026-8). Intl Ideas.

Leighton, F., jt. auth. see Carter, Hugh.

Leighton, Ford. The Christian Persuader. LC 66-22043. 1977. pap. 4.95 (ISBN 0-06-062679-8, RD 157, HarpR). Har-Row.

Leighton, Frances S., jt. auth. see Bryant, Traphes L.

Leighton, Frances S., jt. auth. see Caprio, Frank S.

Leighton, Frances S., jt. auth. see Parks, Lillian R.

Leighton, Frances S., jt. auth. see Szostak, John M.

Leighton, Gerald. Huxley: His Life & Work. 94p. 1980. Repr. lib. bdg. 15.00 (ISBN 0-8492-1649-4). R West.

Leighton, Hal. The Harmonica for Fun & Profit. 1978. pap. 4.00 (ISBN 0-87980-354-1). Wilshire.

Leighton, Jack R. Progressive Weight Training. (Illus.). 1961. 14.95 (ISBN 0-8260-5375-0). Wiley.

Leighton, Lee. Law Man. 1977. pap. 1.75 (ISBN 0-441-47492-6). Ace Bks.

Leighton, Philip. Coins & Tokens. (Junior Reference Ser.). (Illus.). 64p. (gr. 7 up). 1972. 7.95 (ISBN 0-7136-1238-X). Dufour.

Leighton, Robert B. & Vogt, Rochus E. Exercises in Introductory Physics. (Physics Ser). (Orig.). 1969. pap. text ed. 4.95 (ISBN 0-201-04215-0). A-W.

Leighton, Terrance & Loomis, William F., eds. The Molecular Genetics of Development. LC 80-532. (Molecular Biology Ser.). 1980. 49.50 (ISBN 0-12-441960-7). Acad Pr.

Leighton, Thomas. The Phoenix Formula. (Orig.). 1980. pap. 2.50 (ISBN 0-440-14649-6). Dell.

Leighton, Walter. First Course in Ordinary Differential Equations. 4th ed. 1976. text ed. 21.95x (ISBN 0-534-00435-0). Wadsworth Pub.

--First Course in Ordinary Differential Equations. 5th ed. 304p. 1980. text ed. 21.95x (ISBN 0-534-00837-2). Wadsworth Pub.

Leijonhufvud, Axel. Information & Coordination: Essays in Macroeconomic Theory. (Illus.). 320p. 1981. text ed. 15.95x (ISBN 0-19-502814-7); pap. text ed. 9.95x (ISBN 0-19-502815-5). Oxford U Pr.

--On Keynesian Economics & the Economics of Keynes: A Study in Monetary Theory. 1968. text ed. 12.95x (ISBN 0-19-500948-7). Oxford U Pr.

Leik, Robert K. Methods, Logic, & Research of Sociology. LC 72-85667. (Studies in Sociology Ser). 1972. 2.95- (ISBN 0-672-61242-9). Bobbs.

Leik, Robert K. & Meeker, Barbara F. Mathematical Sociology. LC 74-22271. (Methods of Social Science Ser.). (Illus.). 272p. 1975. 19.95 (ISBN 0-13-562108-9). P-H.

Leikur & Torshavn. Islands & People. 150p. 1980. 27.50 (ISBN 0-906191-22-X, Pub. by Thule Pr England). Intl Schol Bk Serv.

Leiman, M. Jacob N. Cardozo. LC 66-27478. 1966. 20.00x (ISBN 0-231-09608-9). Columbia U Pr.

Leiman, Melvin, jt. auth. see Romano, Richard.

Leimas, Brooke. The Intruder. (Orig.). 1980. pap. 2.50 (ISBN 0-451-09524-3, E9524, Sig). NAL.

Leimberg, Stepan R., et al. The Tools & Techniques of Estate Planning. 3rd ed. 376p. 1980. pap. 20.00 (ISBN 0-87218-406-4). Natl Underwriter.

Lein, Allen. The Cycling Female: Her Menstrual Rhythm. LC 78-23675. (Illus.). 1979. pap. text ed. 7.95x (ISBN 0-7167-1038-2). W H Freeman.

Lein, Charles F., Jr. The Farmer's Tax Guide. LC 77-99077. (Illus.). 1978. pap. 3.95 o.p. (ISBN 0-8015-2558-6). Dutton.

Leiner, Katherine & Arthur, Michael. The Greatest Show on Earth. LC 80-17776. (Old Friends Ser.: Old Friends Ser.). (Illus.). 80p. 1980. 6.95 (ISBN 0-916392-62-7). Oak Tree Pubns.

--The Real Flash Gordon. LC 80-17779. (Old Friends Ser.). (Illus.). 80p. 1980. 6.95 (ISBN 0-916392-54-6). Oak Tree Pubns.

Leinhardt, Samuel, ed. Sociological Methodology Nineteen Eighty-One. LC 68-54940. (Social & Behavioral Science Series). 1981. text ed. price not set (ISBN 0-87589-490-9). Jossey-Bass.

Leininger, Joseph E. & Gilchrist, Bruce, eds. Computers, Society & Law: The Role of Legal Education. LC 73-93427. (Illus.). 264p. 1973. pap. 6.00 (ISBN 0-88283-001-5). AFIPS Pr.

Leininger, Madeleine. Transcultural Nursing: Concepts, Theories & Practices. LC 77-28250. 1977. text ed. 22.50 (ISBN 0-471-52608-8, Pub by Wiley Medical). Wiley.

Leininger, Madeline, ed. Transcultural Nursing, 1979. (Illus.). 742p. 1979. text ed. 32.50 (ISBN 0-89352-079-9). Masson Pub.

Leininger, Sheryl, ed. Internal Theft: Investigation & Control. LC 75-17137. 256p. (Anthology). 1975. 15.95 (ISBN 0-913708-21-6). Butterworths.
Leininger, Steve. The Official Russian Joke Book. 192p. (Orig.). 1981. pap. 1.95 (ISBN 0-523-41427-7). Pinnacle Bks.
Leininger, Wayne E., jt. auth. see Hicks, James O., Jr.
Leininger, Wayne F., jt. auth. see Killough, Larry N.
Leinsdorf, Erich. The Composer's Advocate: A Radical Orthodoxy for Musicians. LC 80-17614. (Illus.). 232p. 1981. 14.95 (ISBN 0-300-02427-4). Yale U Pr.
Leinster, Murray. Doctor to the Stars. 1977. pap. 1.50 o.s.i. (ISBN 0-515-04482-2). Jove Pubns.
Leinwand, Gerald. The Pageant of American History. (gr. 7-9). 1975. text ed. 17.24 (ISBN 0-205-03849-2, 7838492); tchrs'. guide 3.60 (ISBN 0-205-03850-6, 7838506); dup. masters 44.00 (ISBN 0-205-05391-2, 7853912). Allyn.
--The Pageant of World History. new rev. ed. (gr. 9-12). 1977. text ed. 16.80 (ISBN 0-205-05392-0, 7853920); tchrs'. guide 5.40 (ISBN 0-205-05393-9, 7853939); wkbk 60.00 (ISBN 0-205-05657-1, 786571); tests-duplicator masters 48.00 (ISBN 0-205-05658-X, 785658X). Allyn.
Leinwoll, Stanley. The Book of Pets. LC 80-17598. (Illus.). 128p. (gr. 7 up). 1980. PLB 8.79 (ISBN 0-671-33071-3). Messner.
--Candles & Candlecrafting. LC 72-6556. (Illus.). 128p. 1973. 8.95 o.p. (ISBN 0-684-13187-0, ScribT). Scribner.
--So You Think You're Covered? A Consumer's Guide to Home Fire Insurance. LC 76-44842. 1978. pap. 2.95 o.p. (ISBN 0-684-15580-X, ScribT). Scribner.
Leipsic, Reggie. Save Money Buying Meat, Poultry, & Fish. (Illus.). 200p. (Orig.). 1981. pap. 6.95 (ISBN 0-89141-113-5). Presidio Pr.
Leipunskii, O. I., et al. The Propagation of Gamma Quanta in Matter. 1965. 37.00 (ISBN 0-08-010553-X); pap. 22.00 (ISBN 0-08-013564-1). Pergamon.
Leipziger, Danny M., ed. The Basic Human Needs Approach to Development: Some Policy Issues. LC 80-19938. 256p. 1981. lib. bdg. 20.00 (ISBN 0-89946-021-6). Oelgeschlager.
Leirfall, Jon. West Over Sea. 160p. 1980. 14.95 (ISBN 0-906191-15-7, Pub. by Thule Pr England). Intl Schol Bk Serv.
Leiris, Michael & Mourlot, Fernand. Joan Miro, Lithographs, Vol. 1. (Illus.). 231p. 1972. 150.00x (ISBN 0-8148-0494-2, Pub. by Tudor). Hennessey.
Leiris, Michel. Race & Culture. 1965. pap. 2.50 (ISBN 92-3-100435-2, U506, UNESCO). Unipub.
Leiser, Erwin. Nazi Cinema. (Illus.). 1975. pap. 4.95 o.s.i. (ISBN 0-02-012400-7, Collier). Macmillan.
Leish, Kenneth W., ed. see American Heritage Editors.
Leishman, J. B., tr. see Rilke, Rainer M.
Leisman, Gerald. Basic Visual Processes & Learning Disability. (Illus.). 456p. 1976. 35.75 (ISBN 0-398-03454-0). C C Thomas.
Leissler, Frederick. Roads & Trails of Olympic National Park. 2nd ed. (Illus.). 114p. 1976. pap. 6.95 (ISBN 0-295-95533-3). U of Wash Pr.
--Roads & Trails of Olympic National Park. 4th rev. ed. LC 57-3575. (Illus.). 114p. 1981. pap. 6.95 (ISBN 0-295-95819-7). U of Wash Pr.
Leissner, Aryeh. Family Advice Services. 1967. pap. text ed. 3.00x (ISBN 0-582-32408-4). Humanities.
--Street Club Work in Tel Aviv & New York. (Studies in Child Development). (Illus., Orig.). 1969. pap. text ed. 5.75x (ISBN 0-582-32444-0). Humanities.
Leister, Mary. Flying Fur, Fin & Scale: Strange Animals That Swoop and Soar. LC 77-7620. (Illus.). (gr. 4 up). 1977. 9.95 (ISBN 0-916144-07-0). Stemmer Hse.
--Wee Green Witch. LC 78-12380. (Illus.). (ps up). 1978. 9.95 (ISBN 0-916144-30-5); pap. 3.95 (ISBN 0-916144-31-3). Stemmer Hse.
--Wildlings. LC 76-2063. (Illus.). 192p. 1976. 8.95 (ISBN 0-916144-06-2). Stemmer Hse.
Leistner, Georg. Abbreviations Guide to French Forms in Justice & Administration. 191p. 1975. 17.25 (ISBN 3-7940-3016-8, Pub. by K G Saur). Shoe String.
Leistritz, F. Larry & Murdock, Steven H. The Socioeconomic Impact of Resource Development: Methods for Assessment. (Social Impact Assessment Ser.: No. 6). 250p. 1981. lib. bdg. 22.50x (ISBN 0-89158-978-3). Westview.
Leistritz, F. Larry, jt. auth. see Murdock, Steven H.
Leisy, James. Calories in - Calories Out Calorie Counter: The Calorie Counter That Counts Both Ways. 96p. (Orig.). 1980. pap. 3.95 (ISBN 0-8289-0401-4). Greene.
--The Calories in - Calories Out Diary: A Daily Program for Fitness & Weight Control. 256p. (Orig.). 1980. pap. 9.95 (ISBN 0-8289-0412-X). Greene.
--Calories in - Calories Out: The Energy Budget Way to Fitness & Weight Control. 128p. 1980. 10.95 (ISBN 0-8289-0413-8); pap. 6.95 (ISBN 0-8289-0414-6). Greene.
Leitch, Cynthia J., jt. auth. see Chinn, Peggy L.
Leitch, David B. Railways of New Zealand. 11.95 (ISBN 0-7153-5496-5). David & Charles.
Leitch, Susan M. A Child Learns to Speak: A Guide for Parents & Teachers of Preschool Children. (Illus.). 104p. 1977. 11.75 (ISBN 0-398-03599-7); pap. 8.25 (ISBN 0-398-03602-0). C C Thomas.
Leite, Elizabeth. Simply Beautiful: Living with the Earth in Mind. (Illus., Orig.). 1980. lib. bdg. 7.95 (ISBN 0-87961-106-5); pap. 3.95 (ISBN 0-87961-107-3). Naturegraph.
Leitenberg, Milton, jt. auth. see Burns, Richard D.
Leitenberg, Milton & Sheffer, Gabriel, eds. Great Power Intervention in the Middle East. LC 79-341. (Pergamon Policy Studies). 400p. 1979. 28.00 (ISBN 0-08-023867-X). Pergamon.
Leiter, Robert D. Costs & Benefits of Education. (Illus.). 215p. 1975. text ed. 15.00x (ISBN 0-8290-0398-3). Irvington.
--Modern Economics. 2nd rev. ed. (Orig.). 1976. pap. 3.95 (ISBN 0-06-460138-2, CO 138, COS). Har-Row.
Leiter, Robert D. & Friedlander, Stanley L., eds. Economics of Resources. (Illus.). 250p. 1976. text ed. 18.00x (ISBN 0-8290-0396-7). Irvington.
Leiter, Robert D. & Sirkin, Gerald, eds. Economics of Public Choice. (Illus.). 202p. 1976. text ed. 18.00x (ISBN 0-8290-0397-5). Irvington.
Leiter, Samuel. From Belasco to Brook: Great Stage Directors of the Twentieth Century. 1981. 16.95 (ISBN 0-89676-057-X); pap. 12.95 (ISBN 0-89676-063-4). Drama Bk.
Leith, John. The Church: A Believing Fellowship. rev. ed. LC 80-82192. 1980. 6.95 (ISBN 0-8042-1813-7). John Knox.
Leith, John H. The Church, a Believing Fellowship. LC 80-82192. 192p. 1981. pap. 6.95 (ISBN 0-8042-0518-3). John Knox.
Leith, John H., ed. Creeds of the Churches: A Reader in Christian Doctrine from the Bible to the Present. rev. ed. LC 73-5346. 608p. 1973. pap. 5.95 (ISBN 0-8042-0515-9). John Knox.
Leithauser, Gladys & Breitmeyer, Lois. The Rabbit Is Next. (Young Reader Ser.). (Illus.). (gr. k-3). PLB 5.00 (ISBN 0-307-60173-0, Golden Pr). Western Pub.
Leithold, Louis. Calculo. (Span.). 1973. pap. 12.00 (ISBN 0-06-315010-7, IntlDept). Har-Row.
--El Calculo, Vols. I & II. (Sp.). 1979. Vol. I. pap. text ed. 7.00 (ISBN 0-06-315008-5, Pub. by HarLA Mexico); Vol. II. pap. text ed. 6.00 (ISBN 0-06-359009-3). Har-Row.
Leitmann, George, ed. Optimization Techniques with Applications to Aerospace Systems. (Mathematics in Science & Engineering,: Vol. 5). 1962. text ed. 44.50 (ISBN 0-12-442950-5). Acad Pr.
Leitner, Bernhard. Architecture of Ludwig Wittgenstein: A Documentation with Excerpts from the Family Recollections by Hermine Wittgenstein. LC 72-97706. (The Nova Scotia Ser). (Illus.). 127p. 1976. 22.50x (ISBN 0-8147-4968-2); pap. 12.95 (ISBN 0-8147-4969-0). NYU Pr.
Leitner, L. M. see Landfield, A. W.
Leitritz, Earl & Lewis, Robert C. Trout & Salmon Culture (Hatchery Methods) (Illus.). 1980. pap. 5.00x (ISBN 0-931876-36-2, 4100). Ag Sci Pubns.
Leitz, Pierr M., jt. auth. see Edge, Nellie.
Leitz, Robert C., et al, eds. The Selected Letters of W. D. Howells, Vol. III. (Critical Editions Program Ser.). 1980. lib. bdg. 27.50 (ISBN 0-8057-8529-9). Twayne.
Leiva, Erasmo, tr. see Muggeridge, Malcolm, et al.
Leiva, Erasmo, tr. see Von Balthasar, Hans Urs.
Lejeune, H., jt. auth. see Richelle, M.
Lejeune-Dirichlet, P. G. & Dedekind, R. Zahlentheorie. 4th ed. LC 68-54716. (Ger). 1969. text ed. 29.95 (ISBN 0-8284-0213-2). Chelsea Pub.
Le Journeau, Roger. L' Islam Contemporain. LC 80-1922. 1981. Repr. of 1950 ed. write for info. (ISBN 0-404-18975-X). AMS Pr.
Lekachman, Robert. Capitalism for Beginners. Van Loon, Bron, tr. (Pantheon Documentary Comic Books). 1981. 8.95 (ISBN 0-394-51027-5); pap. 2.95 (ISBN 0-394-73863-2). Pantheon.
Lekatsos, Anthony, tr. see Makrakis, Apostolos.
Lekovic, Zdravko & Bjelica, Mihalo. Communication Policies in Yugoslavia. 66p. 1977. pap. 4.75 (ISBN 92-3-101409-9, U88, UNESCO). Unipub.
Leland, Charles G. Algonquin Legends of New England. LC 68-31217. 1968. Repr. of 1884 ed. 22.00 (ISBN 0-8103-3468-2). Gale.
--English Gypsies & Their Language. LC 68-22035. 1969. Repr. of 1874 ed. 22.00 (ISBN 0-8103-3883-1). Gale.
--Legends of Florence, 2 Vols. LC 68-27173. 1969. Repr. of 1895 ed. 15.00 ea. Vol. 1, First Ser (ISBN 0-8103-3843-2). Vol. 2, Second Ser. (ISBN 0-8103-3844-0); Set. write for info. (ISBN 0-8103-3899-8). Gale.
--Memoirs. LC 68-22036. 1968. Repr. of 1893 ed. 20.00 (ISBN 0-8103-3533-6). Gale.
Leland, Charles G., ed. see Barrere, Albert.
Leland, Henry & Deutsch, Marilyn W., eds. Abnormal Behavior: A Guide to Information Sources. LC 80-65. (The Psychology Informationguide Ser.: Vol. 5). 261p. 1980. 30.00 (ISBN 0-8103-1416-9). Gale.
Leland, Howe W. Taking Charge of Your Life. LC 77-86340. 1977. pap. 3.95 (ISBN 0-913592-93-5). Argus Comm.
Leland, John. The Labouryouse Journey & Serche of Johan Leylande for Englandes Antiquitees. LC 74-28871. (English Experience Ser.: No. 750). 1975. Repr. of 1549 ed. 7.00 (ISBN 90-221-0750-7). Walter J Johnson.
Leland, Thomas. Longsword, Earl of Salisbury. Shugrue, Michael F., ed. (Flowering of the Novel Ser.: 1740-1775). lib. bdg. 50.00 (ISBN 0-8240-1159-7). Garland Pub.
Leleux, Robin. A Regional History of the Railways of Great Britain: The East Midlands, Vol. 9. LC 76-8786. (Regional Railway History Ser). (Illus.). 1976. 19.95 (ISBN 0-7153-7165-7). David & Charles.
Le Lievre, Audrey. Miss Willmott of Warley Place. (Illus.). 240p. 1981. 28.00 (ISBN 0-571-11622-1, Pub. by Faber & Faber). Merrimack Bk Serv.
Lellis, Geore, jt. auth. see Wead, George.
Lellis, George, jt. auth. see Wead, George.
LeLorenzo, Ronald. Problem Solving in General Chemistry. 496p. 1980. pap. text ed. 10.95 (ISBN 0-669-02924-6). Heath.
LeLoup, Lance T. The Fiscal Congress: Legislative Control of the Budget. LC 79-6823. (Contributions in Political Science: No. 47). (Illus.). xii, 227p. 1980. lib. bdg. 25.00 (ISBN 0-313-22009-3, LFC/). Greenwood.
Lely, James A. Aquarius. (Sun Signs Ser.). (Illus.). (gr. 4-12). 1978. PLB 5.95 (ISBN 0-87191-651-7); pap. 2.95 (ISBN 0-89812-080-2). Creative Ed.
--Battlestar Galactica. (T. V. & Movie Tie-Ins Ser.). 32p. (gr. 4-12). 1979. PLB 5.95 (ISBN 0-87191-701-7); pap. 2.95 (ISBN 0-89812-033-0). Creative Ed.
--Libra. (Sun Signs Ser.). (Illus.). (gr. 4-12). 1978. PLB 5.95 (ISBN 0-87191-647-9); pap. 2.95 (ISBN 0-685-86522-3). Creative Ed.
--Star Wars. (T.V. & Movie Tie-Ins Ser.). (Illus.). (gr. 4-12). 1979. PLB 5.95 (ISBN 0-87191-700-9); pap. 2.95 (ISBN 0-89812-036-5). Creative Ed.
--Virgo. (Sun Signs Ser.). (Illus.). (gr. 4-12). 1978. PLB 5.95 (ISBN 0-87191-646-0); pap. 2.95 (ISBN 0-89812-076-4). Creative Ed.
Lem, Dean P. Graphics Master, No. 2. LC 76-41508. (Illus.). 113p. 1977. 47.50 (ISBN 0-914218-02-6). D Lem Assocs.
Lem, Stanislaw. The Chain of Chance. 1979. pap. 1.75 (ISBN 0-515-05138-1). Jove Pubns.
--The Cosmic Carnival of Stanislaw Lem: An Anthology of Entertaining Stories by the Modern Master of Science Fiction. Kandel, Michael, ed. 256p. (Orig.). 1981. pap. 7.95 (ISBN 0-8264-0043-4). Continuum.
--More Tales of Pirx the Pilot. Iribarne, Louis, tr. (Helen & Kurt Wolff Bk.). 1981. 9.95 (ISBN 0-15-162138-1). HarBraceJ.
--Mortal Engines. Kandel, Michael, tr. from Polish. LC 76-54758. 1977. 9.95 (ISBN 0-8164-9296-4). Continuum.
--Return from the Stars. Marszal, Barbara & Simpson, Frank, trs. LC 79-3358. (Helen & Kurt Wolff Bk.). 312p. 1980. 9.95 (ISBN 0-15-177082-4). HarBraceJ.
--Solaris. 1976. pap. 1.75 o.p. (ISBN 0-425-03380-5). Berkley Pub.
Lemagny, J. C. & De Menil, Dominiqueintro. by. Visionary Architects: Boullee, Ledoux, Lequeu. (Illus.). 1968. pap. 8.00 (ISBN 0-914412-21-3). Inst for the Arts.
Le Mair, Henrietta W., illus. The Mullberry Bush. (Illus.). 1978. Repr. of 1911 ed. 7.50 o.p. (ISBN 0-85249-338-X, Star & Elephant). Green Tiger.
Le Mair, Henriette W., illus. Christmas Carols for Young Children. (Illus.). 32p. pap. 4.95 o.s.i. (ISBN 0-914676-42-3). Green Tiger.
Lemaire, Anika. Jacques Lacan. Macey, David, tr. from Fr. 21.00 (ISBN 0-7100-8621-0). Routledge & Kegan.
Le Maitre, Alexandre. La Metropolitee. (Principal French Demographic Works of the 18th Century Ser.). (Fr.). 1976. lib. bdg. 35.00x o.p. (ISBN 0-8287-0530-5); pap. text ed. 25.00x o.p. (ISBN 0-685-71515-9). Clearwater Pub.
Leman, A., et al, eds. Diseases of Swine. 5th ed. (Illus.). 1981. 60.00 (ISBN 0-8138-0440-X). Iowa St U Pr.
Leman, Kevin. Sex Begins in the Kitchen. LC 80-54004. 144p. 1981. text ed. 7.95 (ISBN 0-8307-0787-5). Regal.
Lemann, Nicholas. The Fast Track: Texans & Other Strivers. 1981. 12.95 (ISBN 0-393-01436-3). Norton.
Lemarchand, Elizabeth. Change for the Worse. 192p. 1981. 9.95 (ISBN 0-8027-5429-5). Walker & Co.
--Suddenly While Gardening. 1978. 7.95 o.s.i. (ISBN 0-8027-5395-7). Walker & Co.
--Unhappy Returns. LC 77-80205. 1978. 7.95 o.s.i. (ISBN 0-8027-5375-2). Walker & Co.
Lemarchand, Rene & Martin, David. Selective Genocide in Burundi. (Minority Rights Group: No. 20). 1974. pap. 2.50 (ISBN 0-89192-106-0). Interbk Inc.
Lemarchand, Rene, ed. African Kingships in Perspective: Political Change & Modernization in Monarchical Settings. 325p. 1977. 32.50x (ISBN 0-7146-3027-6, F Cass Co). Biblio Dist.
--American Policy in Southern Africa: The Stakes & the Stance. 2nd ed. LC 80-6222. 513p. 1981. lib. bdg. 22.75 (ISBN 0-8191-1436-7); pap. text ed. 12.50 (ISBN 0-8191-1437-5). U Pr of Amer.
Lemarechale, C & Mifflin, R., eds. Nonsmooth Optimization: Proceedings of an IIASA Workshop, 28 March-8 April 1977. 1979. text ed. 37.00 (ISBN 0-08-023428-3). Pergamon.
LeMassena, Robert. Rio Grande... to the Pacific! (Illus.). 416p. 35.00 (ISBN 0-913582-10-7). Sundance.
LeMassena, Robert A. Articulated Steam Locomotives of North America: A Catalogue of "Giant Steam". (Illus.). 416p. 45.00 (ISBN 0-913582-26-3). Sundance.
Le Massena, Robert A. Rio Grande...to the Pacific. Collman, Russ, ed. (Illus.). 1974. 35.00 (ISBN 0-913582-10-7). Sundance.
LeMaster, jt. auth. see Jordan.
LeMaster, J. R. Jesse Stuart: Kentucky's Chronicler-Poet. LC 79-28224. 1980. 14.95x (ISBN 0-87870-049-8). Memphis St Univ.
Lemaster, J. R. & Clarke, Mary W., eds. Jesse Stuart: Essays on His Work. LC 76-46032. 176p. 1977. 15.00x (ISBN 0-8131-1352-0). U Pr of Ky.
Le Master, Richard. Wildlife in Wood. 1978. 19.95 (ISBN 0-9601840-1-5, Pub. by Model Tech). Contemp Bks.
LeMasters, E. E. Blue Collar Aristocrats: Life Styles at a Working Class Tavern. LC 74-27309. 233p. 1975. 17.50 (ISBN 0-299-06550-2); pap. 5.95 (ISBN 0-299-06554-5). U of Wis Pr.
--Parents in Modern America. 3rd ed. 1977. pap. text ed. 9.50x (ISBN 0-256-01972-X). Dorsey.
LeMasurier, John & Watts, Denis. Athletics: Track Events. (Pelham Pictorial Sports Instruction Ser.). (Illus.). 1979. 9.95 (ISBN 0-7207-0970-9). Transatlantic.
LeMay, Alan. The Searchers. (Western Fiction Ser.). 1978. lib. bdg. 9.95 (ISBN 0-8398-2464-5). Gregg.
LeMay, H. E., jt. auth. see Brown, Theodore L.
LeMay, H. Eugene, jt. auth. see Brown, Theodore L.
LeMay, H. Eugene, Jr., jt. auth. see Brown, T. L.
Lemay, Harding. Eight Years in Another World. LC 80-69363. 1981. 10.95 (ISBN 0-689-11149-5). Atheneum.
Le May, I., ed. Advances in Materials Technology in the Americas, 2 vols. Incl. Vol. 1. Materials Recovery & Utilization: Bk. No. H00161, MD1; Vol. 2. Materials Processing & Performance: Bk. No. H00162, MD2. 1980. Set. 30.00. ASME.
Lemay, J. A., ed. The Oldest Revolutionary: Essays on Benjamin Franklin. LC 75-41618. 176p. 1976. 15.00x (ISBN 0-685-63233-4). U of Pa Pr.
Lemay, J. A., ed. see Franklin, Benjamin.
Lemay, J. Leo. Ebenezer Kinnersley: Franklin's Friend. LC 64-10894. 1964. 9.00x o.p. (ISBN 0-8122-7425-3). U of Pa Pr.
--Men of Letters in Colonial Maryland. LC 79-177357. (Illus.). 428p. 1972. 18.50x (ISBN 0-87049-137-7). U of Tenn Pr.
Lemay, Leo J. The Frontiersman from Lout to Hero: Notes on the Significance of the Comparative Method & the Stage Theory in Early American Literature & Culture. 1979. pap. 3.50 (ISBN 0-912296-39-9, Dist. by U Pr of Va). Am Antiquarian.
Lemay, Nita K., jt. auth. see Newman, Matt.
Lemberg. Vectorcardiography: A Programmed Introduction. 2nd ed. (Illus.). 1975. pap. 17.00 o.p. (ISBN 0-8385-9396-8). ACC.
Lembke, Janet. Bronze & Iron: Old Latin Poetry from Its Beginning to 100 B. C. 1973. 16.75x (ISBN 0-520-02164-9). U of Cal Pr.
Lembke, Janet, tr. see Aeschylus.
Leme, J. Garcia, jt. auth. see Rocha E Silva, M.

Lemelin, Robert. Pathway to the National Character, 1830-1861. LC 74-80589. 1974. 12.50 (ISBN 0-8046-9087-1, Natl U). Kennikat.

Lemerise, Bruce. Sheldon's Lunch. LC 80-10449. (Illus.). 48p. (ps-3). 1980. 4.95 (ISBN 0-8193-1025-5); PLB 5.95 (ISBN 0-8193-1026-3). Parents.

Lemert, Charles, ed. French Sociology: Rupture & Renewal Since 1968. 528p. 1981. 22.50x (ISBN 0-231-04698-7); pap. 10.00x (ISBN 0-231-04699-5). Columbia U Pr.

Lemert, Charles C. Sociology & the Twilight of Man: Homocentrism & Discourse in Sociological Theory. LC 78-17146. 274p. 1980. pap. 8.95 (ISBN 0-8093-0975-0). S Ill U Pr.

Lemert, Edwin M. & Dill, Forrest. Offenders in the Community. LC 77-87184. 1978. 19.95 (ISBN 0-669-01981-X). Lexington Bks.

Lemert, James B. Does Mass Communication Change Public Opinion, After All? A New Approach to Effects Analysis. LC 80-23826. 260p. 1981. text ed. 17.95 (ISBN 0-88229-474-1); pap. text ed. 8.95 (ISBN 0-88229-764-3). Nelson-Hall.

Lemeshow, Stanley, jt. auth. see Levy, Paul S.

Lemesurier, Peter. Gospel of the Stars: A Celebration of the Mystery of the Zodiac. LC 78-61013. 1979. 7.95 o.p. (ISBN 0-312-34067-2). St Martin.

LeMieux, Joan, jt. auth. see Nelson, Sharlene.

Lemire, Ronald J., et al. Normal & Abnormal Development of the Human Nervous System. (Illus.). 1975. 34.00x o.p. (ISBN 0-06-141530-8, Harper Medical). Har-Row.

--Anencephaly. LC 77-83688. 1977. 28.00 (ISBN 0-89004-179-2). Raven.

Lemisch, Jesse, ed. & intro. by see Franklin, Benjamin.

Lemke, Bernhard C. & Edwards, J. Don. Administrative Control & Executive Action. 2nd ed. LC 71-161870. 564p. 1971. text ed. 21.95 (ISBN 0-675-09792-4). Merrill.

Lemke, C. E., ed. see Society for Industrial & Applied Mathematics-American Mathematical Society Symposia-New York, March 1975.

Lemke, Donald A., jt. auth. see Cummings, Richard L.

Lemlich, Robert. Adsorptive Bubble Separation Techniques. 1972. 48.50 (ISBN 0-12-443350-2). Acad Pr.

Lemmel, Maurice. Gambling Nevada Style. LC 64-16205. pap. 2.95 (ISBN 0-385-07257-0, C476, Dolp). Doubleday.

Lemmerz, A. H. & Schmidt, R. R. Auswertung und Deutung Des EKG. 12th ed. (Illus.). xii, 260p. 1981. pap. 29.50 (ISBN 3-8055-1932-X). S Karger.

Lemmon, Ed. Boss Cowman: The Recollections of Ed Lemmon, 1857-1946. Yost, Nellie S., ed. LC 69-10313. (Pioneer Heritage Ser: Vol. 6). (Illus.). xiv, 321p. 1969. 14.50x (ISBN 0-8032-0102-8); pap. 4.25 (ISBN 0-8032-5810-0, BB 5595, Bison). U of Nebr Pr.

Lemmon, John, ed. Family Law & Child Welfare: Selected Current Trends in Legal Social Work Practice. (Law & Social Work Quarterly Ser.: Vol. 1, No. 1). 112p. 1981. text ed. 12.95 (ISBN 0-917724-64-X). Haworth Pr.

Lemmon, Kenneth. The Gardens of Britain, Five: Yorkshire & Humberside. 1979. 24.00 (ISBN 0-7134-1743-9, Pub. by Batsford England). David & Charles.

Lemmon, Robert S. All About Moths & Butterflies. (gr. 4-6). 1956. 2.95 o.p. (ISBN 0-394-80215-2, BYR). Random.

--Parks & Gardens. LC 60-6114. (Illus.). (gr. 4-8). 1967. PLB 7.45 (ISBN 0-87191-018-7). Creative Ed.

Lemmon, Sarah M. North Carolina & the War of 1812. (Illus.). 1971. pap. 1.00 (ISBN 0-86526-087-7). NC Archives.

--North Carolina's Role in the First World War. (Illus.). 1975. pap. 1.00 (ISBN 0-86526-094-X). NC Archives.

--North Carolina's Role in World War Two. (Illus.). 1969. pap. 1.00 (ISBN 0-86526-095-8). NC Archives.

Lemmons, Reuel G., et al, eds. see Smith, William.

Lemoine, Serge, jt. auth. see Coolican, Don.

Lemon, Anthony. Apartheid: A Geographical Perspective. 1977. 19.95 (ISBN 0-347-01106-3, 00313-1, Pub. by Saxon Hse). Lexington Bks.

Lemon, H. How to Find Out About the Wool Textile Industry. 1969. 29.00 (ISBN 0-08-012984-6); pap. 14.00 (ISBN 0-08-012983-8). Pergamon.

Lemon, Jane. Embroidered Boxes. (Illus.). 208p. 1980. 30.00 (ISBN 0-571-11606-X, Pub. by Faber & Faber). Merrimack Bk Serv.

Lemon, Lee T. & Reis, Marion J., trs. Russian Formalist Criticism: Four Essays. LC 65-21899. (Regents Critics Ser). 1965. 9.50x (ISBN 0-8032-0460-4); pap. 3.50x (ISBN 0-8032-5460-1, BB 405, Bison). U of Nebr Pr.

Lemon, Mark. The Enchanted Doll, Repr. Of 1849 Ed. Bd. with Tinykin's Transformations. Repr. of 1869 ed. LC 75-32163. (Classics of Children's Literature, 1621-1932: Vol. 27). (Illus.). 1977. PLB 38.00 (ISBN 0-8240-2276-9). Garland Pub.

Lemon, Nigel. Attitudes & Their Measurement. 1973. 38.00 (ISBN 0-7134-0983-5, Pub. by Batsford England). David & Charles.

LeMond, Alan, jt. auth. see Spitz, Mark.

Lemons, Frank W. In Remembrance of Me. 1975. 3.95 (ISBN 0-87148-430-7); pap. 2.95 (ISBN 0-87148-431-5). Pathway Pr.

--Looking Beyond. 78p. 1969. 2.95 (ISBN 0-87148-506-0); pap. 2.25 (ISBN 0-87148-507-9). Pathway Pr.

--Perennial Pentecost. 1971. pap. 2.25 (ISBN 0-87148-679-2). Pathway Pr.

--Profiles of Faith. 1971. pap. 2.25 (ISBN 0-87148-683-0). Pathway Pr.

Lemons, J. Stanley. The Woman Citizen: Social Feminism in the 1920's. LC 72-75488. 280p. 1975. pap. 3.45 (ISBN 0-252-00563-5). U of Ill Pr.

Lemons, Wayne & Price, Bill. How to Repair Home & Auto Air Conditioners. LC 74-120384. 1970. pap. 5.95 (ISBN 0-8306-9520-6, 520). TAB Bks.

Lemons, Wayne & Price, Billy. Major Appliance Repair Guide. LC 70-162406. (Illus.). 1971. 8.95 o.p. (ISBN 0-8306-1555-5); pap. 5.95 o.p. (ISBN 0-8306-0555-X, 555). TAB Bks.

Lemordant, Jean-Julien. Jean-Juliem Lemordant: Ensemble of the Decorative Works of the Painter. (Illus.). 1919. pap. 32.50x (ISBN 0-686-51409-2). Elliots Bks.

Lemos, M. De. Aboriginal Students in Victoria. (ACER Research Monograph: No. 3). 1979. pap. 18.00 (ISBN 0-85563-193-7). Verry.

Lemos, Ramon M. Hobbes & Locke: Power & Consent. LC 77-7482. 190p. 1978. 13.50x (ISBN 0-8203-0428-X). U of Ga Pr.

--Rousseau's Political Philosophy: An Exposition & Interpretation. LC 74-18584. 344p. 1977. 18.00x (ISBN 0-8203-0388-7). U of Ga Pr.

Lempriere, Raoul. Portrait of the Channel Islands. LC 70-515033. (Portrait Bks.). (Illus.). 1970. 10.50x (ISBN 0-7091-5152-7). Intl Pubns Serv.

Lemu, B. Aisha & Heeren, Gatima. Woman in Islam. 51p. 1980. pap. 2.95x (ISBN 0-86037-004-6, Pub. by Islamic Council of Europe England). Intl Schol Bk Serv.

Lemus, jt. auth. see Dominguez.

Lenard, A., ed. Statistical Mechanics & Mathematical Problems. (Lecture Notes in Physics: Vol. 20). (Illus.). viii, 246p. 1973. pap. 14.70 o.p. (ISBN 0-387-06194-0). Springer-Verlag.

Lenard, Alexander, tr. see Milne, A. A.

Lenard, Yvone. Fenetres Sur la France. new ed. (Verbal-Active French Ser.). (Illus.). (gr. 11-12). 1976. text ed. 15.68 (ISBN 0-06-582101-7, SchDept); tchr's ed. 22.36 (ISBN 0-06-582205-6); wkbk. 4.00 (ISBN 0-06-582303-6); tests 3.56 (ISBN 0-06-582603-5); tchrs. test ed. 4.00 (ISBN 0-06-582701-5); tapes 216.04 (ISBN 0-06-582802-X). Har-Row.

--Jeunes Voix, Jeunes Visages. (Verbal-Active French Ser.). text ed. 12.76 (ISBN 0-06-582100-9, SchDept); tchr's ed. 22.32 (ISBN 0-06-582204-8); wkbk 4.00 (ISBN 0-06-582300-1); tests 3.56 (ISBN 0-06-582602-7); tchrs.' tests 3.56 (ISBN 0-06-582700-7); tapes 252.84 (ISBN 0-06-582801-1); study prints 48.08 (ISBN 0-06-582800-3). Har-Row.

--Tresors Du Temps. (Verbal-Active French Ser.). text ed. 15.68 (ISBN 0-06-582102-5, SchDept); tchr's. ed. 12.36 (ISBN 0-06-582206-4). Har-Row.

Lenardon, Robert J., jt. auth. see Morford, Mark P.

Lenburg, Carrie. The Clinical Performance Examination. 384p. 1979. 14.75 (ISBN 0-8385-1168-6). ACC.

Lenburg, Carrie B. Open Learning & Career Mobility in Nursing. LC 74-20887. 1975. pap. 12.95 o.p. (ISBN 0-8016-2938-1). Mosby.

Lenburg, Jeff. The Complete Encyclopedia of Animated Cartoon Series. (Illus.). 192p. 1981. 24.95 (ISBN 0-87000-495-6). Arlington Hse.

--The Encyclopedia of Animated Cartoon Series: Nineteen Hundred & Nine to Nineteen Seventy-Nine. (Illus.). 1981. 24.95 (ISBN 0-87000-441-7). Arlington Hse.

Lenci, Francesco & Colombetti, Giuliano, eds. Photoreception & Sensory Transduction in Aneural Organisms. (Nato Advanced Study Institutes Ser., Ser. A: Life Sciences: Vol. 33). 430p. 1980. 45.00 (Plenum Pr). Plenum Pub.

Lenczner, D. Elements of Loadbearing Brickwork. 125p. 1972. text ed. 19.50 (ISBN 0-08-016814-0). Pergamon.

--Movement in Buildings. LC 73-4253. 108p. 1974. text ed. 13.25 (ISBN 0-08-017136-2). Pergamon.

--Movements in Buildings. 2nd ed. LC 80-49947. (Illus.). 105p. 1981. 18.00 (ISBN 0-08-024755-5); pap. 12.00 (ISBN 0-08-024756-3). Pergamon.

Lenczowski, George. The Middle East in World Affairs. 4th ed. LC 79-17059. (Illus.). 1980. 29.50 (ISBN 0-8014-0255-7); pap. 14.95 (ISBN 0-8014-9872-4). Cornell U Pr.

Lenczowski, George, ed. Political Elites in the Middle East. LC 75-10898. 1975. 13.25 (ISBN 0-8447-3164-1); pap. 7.25 (ISBN 0-8447-3163-3). Am Enterprise.

Lender, Mark, jt. auth. see Martin, James K.

Lenderink, R. S. & Siebrand, J. C. A Disequalibrium of the Labour Market. 1979. text ed. 17.00x (ISBN 90-237-2277-9, Pub. by Gower Pub Co England). Renouf.

Lendvai, Emo. Bela Bartok: An Analysis of His Music. (Illus.). 115p. 1971. text ed. 10.50x (ISBN 0-900707-04-6). Humanities.

Lendvai, Paul. The Bureaucracy of Truth. 350p. 1981. lib. bdg. 20.00x (ISBN 0-86531-142-0). Westview.

Lenel, Fritz V. Powder Metallurgy: Principles & Applications. LC 80-81830. (Illus.). 608p. 1980. 55.00 (ISBN 0-918404-48-7). Metal Powder.

Le Neve, John. Fasti Ecclesiae Anglicanae: Series 1541-1857. Incl. Vol. 1. St. Paul's, London. 1969. text ed. o.p. (ISBN 0-685-37486-6); Vol. 2. Chichester Diocese. 1971. text ed. o.p. (ISBN 0-685-37487-4); Vol. 3. Canterbury, Rochester & Winchester Dioceses. 1974. text ed. 12.00x (ISBN 0-685-37488-2). Athlone Pr). Humanities.

Leng, Shao-Chuan, ed. Post-Mao China & U.S. China Trade. LC 77-20811. 1978. 10.95x (ISBN 0-8139-0733-0). U Pr of Va.

Lengenfelder, Helga, ed. International Bibliography of Directories. 6th rev. ed. 1978. 72.00 (ISBN 0-89664-002-7, Pub. by K G Saur). Gale.

--International Bibliography of the Book Trade & Librarianship 1976-79. (Handbook of International Documentation & Information Ser.: Vol. 2). 800p. 1981. 95.00 (ISBN 3-598-20504-X, Dist. by Gale Research). K G Saur.

Lengerova, Alena. Membrane Antigens. (Illus.). 1977. 38.80 (ISBN 0-685-85899-5). Adler.

L'Engle, Madeleine. The Anti-Muffins. (The Education of the Public & the Public School Ser.). (Illus.). 48p. (gr. 3-6). 1981. 7.95 (ISBN 0-8298-0415-3). Pilgrim NY.

--A Circle of Quiet. 246p. 1972. 10.95 (ISBN 0-374-12374-8). FS&G.

--Dance in the Desert. LC 68-29465. (Illus.). (gr. 4 up). 1969. 8.95 (ISBN 0-374-31684-8). FS&G.

--The Irrational Season. 1977. 8.95 (ISBN 0-8164-0324-4). Crossroad NY.

--Love Letters. 365p. 1966. 7.95 (ISBN 0-374-19325-8). FS&G.

--Meet the Austins. (YA) (gr. 7-12). 1981. pap. 1.95 (ISBN 0-440-95777-X, LE). Dell.

--The Moon by Night. (YA) (gr. 7-12). 1981. pap. 1.95 (ISBN 0-440-95776-1, LE). Dell.

--Prelude. LC 68-56600. (gr. 7 up). 6.95 (ISBN 0-8149-0351-7). Vanguard.

--A Ring of Endless Light. LC 79-27679. 356p. (gr. 4 up). 1980. 9.95 (ISBN 0-374-36299-8). FS&G.

--The Summer of the Great Grandmother. 1980. 5.95 (ISBN 0-8164-2259-1). Seabury.

--A Swiftly Tilting Planet. (YA) 1980. pap. 1.75 (ISBN 0-440-90158-6, LFL). Dell.

--The Time Trilogy: A Wrinkle in Time; A Wind in the Door; A Swiftly Moving Planet, 3 vols. (gr. 4 up). 1979. Boxed Set. 23.85 (ISBN 0-374-37592-5). FS&G.

--Walking on Water. LC 80-21066. (Wheaton Literary Ser.). 200p. 1980. text ed. 7.95 (ISBN 0-87788-918-X). Shaw Pubs.

L'Engle, Madeleine, jt. ed. see Green, William B.

L'Engle, Madelene. Meet the Austins. LC 60-9726. (gr. 3-8). 1960. 6.95 (ISBN 0-8149-0352-5). Vanguard.

L'Engle, Madeline. The Arm of the Starfish. (YA) (gr. 7-12). 1979. pap. 1.75 (ISBN 0-440-90183-9, LFL). Dell.

--The Summer of the Great Grandmother. LC 74-13157. 1974. 10.95 (ISBN 0-374-27174-7). FS&G.

--The Young Unicorns. (YA) (gr. 7-12). 1980. pap. 1.75 (ISBN 0-440-99919-7, LFL). Dell.

Lengyel, Bela A. Lasers. 2nd ed. LC 77-139279. (Ser. in Pure & Applied Optics). 1971. 36.50 (ISBN 0-471-52620-7, Pub. by Wiley-Interscience). Wiley.

Lengyel, Cornel. Presidents of the United States. (Illus.). PLB 12.23 (ISBN 0-307-67863-6, Golden Pr). Western Pub.

Lengyel, Emil. Asoka the Great: India's Royal Missionary. LC 71-83650. (Biography Ser). (gr. 7 up). 1969. PLB 6.90 (ISBN 0-531-00947-5). Watts.

--Cattle Car Express: A Prisoner of War in Siberia. LC 79-53452. (Short Story Index in Reprint Ser.). Date not set. Repr. of 1931 ed. 21.50x (ISBN 0-8486-5008-5). Core Collection. Postponed.

--The Colony of New Hampshire. LC 74-12036. (First Bks). (Illus.). 72p. (gr. 5-8). 1975. PLB 4.90 o.p. (ISBN 0-531-02776-7). Watts.

--The Colony of Pennsylvania. LC 74-846. (First Bks). (Illus.). 72p. (gr. 4-7). 1974. PLB 6.45 (ISBN 0-531-02721-X). Watts.

--The Congress of Vienna, Eighteen-Fourteen to Eighteen-Fifteen: The Diplomacy Surrounding the End of the Napoleonic Era. LC 73-12440. (World Focus Bks). (Illus.). 72p. (gr. 7 up). 1974. PLB 6.45 (ISBN 0-531-02169-6). Watts.

--First Book of Turkey. LC 77-94770. (First Bks). (Illus.). (gr. 4-6). 1970. PLB 4.90 o.p. (ISBN 0-531-00695-6). Watts.

--Iran. LC 72-180169. (First Bks). (Illus.). 72p. (gr. 6-9). 1972. PLB 6.45 (ISBN 0-531-00760-X). Watts.

--Iran. rev. ed. (First Bks). (Illus.). (gr. 4-6). 1978. PLB 6.45 s&l (ISBN 0-531-02242-0). Watts.

--Jawaharlal Nehru. the Brahman from Kashmir. LC 68-17704. (Biography Ser). (Illus.). (gr. 7 up). 1968. PLB 5.90 o.p. (ISBN 0-531-00908-4). Watts.

--Lajos Kossuth: Hungary's Great Patriot. LC 69-12097. (Biography Ser). (Illus.). (gr. 7 up). 1969. PLB 6.90 (ISBN 0-531-00892-4). Watts.

--The Land & People of Hungary. rev. ed. LC 72-37763. (Portraits of the Nations Ser.). (Illus.). (gr. 6 up). 1972. 8.79 (ISBN 0-397-31545-7). Lippincott.

--Modern Egypt. rev. ed. (First Bks). (Illus.). (gr. 5-7). 1978. PLB 6.45 s&l (ISBN 0-531-02240-4). Watts.

--The Oil Countries of the Middle East. LC 73-5891. (First Bks). (gr. 6-9). 1973. PLB 4.90 o.p. (ISBN 0-531-00809-6). Watts.

--Pakistan & Bangladesh. LC 75-8996. (First Bks.). (Illus.). 72p. (gr. 6-9). 1975. PLB 4.90 o.p. (ISBN 0-531-00762-6). Watts.

--Siberia. LC 73-14873. (First Bks). (Illus.). 72p. (gr. 5-8). 1974. PLB 4.90 o.p. (ISBN 0-531-00821-5). Watts.

Lenham, B. J., jt. auth. see Titow, W. V.

Lenihan, J. M. & Thompson, S. J., eds. Activation Analysis: Principles & Applications. (Illus.). 1966. 32.00 (ISBN 0-12-443650-1). Acad Pr.

Lenihan, J. M., ed. see Weber, Robert L.

Lenin. What the "Friends of the People" Are & How They Fight the Social-Democrats. 1978. 3.95 (ISBN 0-8351-0524-5); pap. 1.95 (ISBN 0-8351-0491-5). China Bks.

Lenin, V. I. Marx, Engels, Marxism. 1978. 7.95 (ISBN 0-8351-0553-9); pap. 4.95 (ISBN 0-8351-0545-8). China Bks.

--One Step Forward, Two Steps Back. 1976. 3.95 (ISBN 0-8351-0232-7); pap. 2.25 (ISBN 0-8351-0233-5). China Bks.

--Selected Works, 1-vol. ed. LC 75-175177. 800p. 1971. pap. 5.75 (ISBN 0-7178-0300-7). Intl Pub Co.

--The Tasks of the Youth Leagues. 1975. pap. 0.75 (ISBN 0-8351-0396-X). China Bks.

Lenin, Vladimir I. Imperialism. 1965. pap. 1.95 (ISBN 0-8351-0113-4). China Bks.

--Left-Wing Communism. 1965. pap. 1.95 (ISBN 0-8351-0128-2). China Bks.

--Lenin on War & Peace. 1966. pap. 1.25 (ISBN 0-8351-0130-4). China Bks.

--Materialism & Empirio-Criticism. pap. 3.25 (ISBN 0-8351-0151-7). China Bks.

--Proletarian Revolution & the Renegade Kautsky. 1965. pap. 1.95 (ISBN 0-8351-0279-3). China Bks.

--State. 1965. pap. 0.75 (ISBN 0-8351-0371-4). China Bks.

--State & Revolution. 1965. pap. 1.95 (ISBN 0-8351-0372-2). China Bks.

--Two Tactics of Social Democracy in the Democratic Revolution. 1965. pap. 1.95 (ISBN 0-8351-0413-3). China Bks.

Lenk. How to Troubleshoot & Repair Microcomputers. 304p. 1980. pap. 7.95 (ISBN 0-8359-2981-7). Reston.

Lenk, J. Manual for Integrated Circuit Users. LC 72-96757. 1973. 19.95 (ISBN 0-87909-482-6). Reston.

--Manual for M. O. S. Users. 1975. 18.95 (ISBN 0-87909-478-8). Reston.

Lenk, John D. Handbook for Transistors. (Illus.). 320p. 1976. 18.95 (ISBN 0-13-382259-1); pap. 7.95 (ISBN 0-13-382267-2). P-H.

--Handbook of Controls & Instrumentation. (Illus.). 1980. text ed. 19.95 (ISBN 0-13-377069-9). P-H.

--Handbook of Digital Electronics. (Illus.). 384p. 1981. text ed. 21.95 (ISBN 0-13-377184-9). P-H.

--Handbook of Electronic Charts, Graphs & Tables. 1970. ref. ed. 18.95 (ISBN 0-13-377275-6). P-H.

--Handbook of Electronic Circuit Design. (Illus.). 320p. 1976. 19.95 (ISBN 0-13-377309-4). P-H.

--Handbook of Electronic Components & Circuits. LC 73-11038. (Illus.). 224p. 1973. ref. ed. 18.95x (ISBN 0-13-377283-7). P-H.

--Handbook of Electronic Meters: Theory & Application. 1969. ref. ed. 18.95 (ISBN 0-13-377358-2). P-H.

--Handbook of Electronic Test Equipment. LC 78-135753. 1971. ref. ed. 21.95 (ISBN 0-13-377366-3). P-H.

--Handbook of Integrated Circuits: For Engineers & Technicians. (Illus.). 1978. ref. 19.95 (ISBN 0-8359-2744-X). Reston.
--Handbook of Modern Solid State Amplifiers. (Illus.). 400p. 1974. ref. ed 19.95 (ISBN 0-13-380394-5); pap. 7.95 (ISBN 0-13-380386-4). P-H.
--Handbook of Practical Electronic Tests & Measurements. 1969. ref. ed. 19.95 (ISBN 0-13-380626-X). P-H.
--Handbook of Practical Microcomputer Troubleshooting. (Illus.). 1979. text ed. 19.95 (ISBN 0-8359-2757-1). Reston.
Lenk, John D., jt. auth. see Marcus, Abraham.
Lenk, Torsten. Flintlock: Its Origin & Development. 45.00 (ISBN 0-87556-149-7). Saifer.
Lenkerd, Barbara, jt. ed. see Reining, Priscilla.
Lenman, Bruce. The Jacobite Rising in Britain Sixteen Eighty-Nine to Seventeen Forty-Six. 1980. text ed. 34.00x (ISBN 0-8419-7004-1). Holmes & Meier.
Lenna, Harry R., jt. auth. see Woodman, Natalie J.
Lennard, Henry L. The Valium Papers. LC 80-84546. 150p. (Orig.). 1981. pap. 9.95 (ISBN 0-935824-02-2). Gondolier.
Lennard, Reginald V. Rural England, Ten Eighty-Six to Eleven Thirty-Five: A Study of Social & Agrarian Conditions. LC 80-2222. 1981. Repr. of 1959 ed. 49.50 (ISBN 0-404-18767-6). AMS Pr.
Lennarz, William J., ed. The Biochemistry of Glycoproteins & Proteoglycans. (Illus.). 395p. 1980. 35.00 (ISBN 0-306-40243-2, Plenum Pr). Plenum Pub.
Lenneberg, E. H. Foundations of Language Development a Multidisciplinary Approach, 2 vols. Lenneberg, Elizabeth, ed. 1975. Vol. 1. 35.50 (ISBN 0-12-443701-X); Vol. 2. 35.50 (ISBN 0-12-443702-8); Set. 57.00. Acad Pr.
Lenneberg, Elizabeth, ed. see Lenneberg, E. H.
Lenneberg, Eric H. Biological Foundations of Language. LC 66-28746. 1967. 32.95 (ISBN 0-471-52626-6). Wiley.
Lennerstrand, G. & Bach-Y-Rita, P., eds. Basic Mechanisms of Ocular Motility & Their Clinical Implications. 1975. text ed. 115.00 (ISBN 0-08-018885-0). Pergamon.
Lennert, K. Histopathology of Non-Hodgkin Lymphomas: Kiel Classification. (Illus.). 130p. 1981. 46.00 (ISBN 0-387-10445-3). Springer-Verlag.
Lennette, E. H., et al, eds. Manual of Clinical Microbiology. 3rd ed. (Illus.). 1980. 25.00 (ISBN 0-914826-24-7). Am Soc Microbio.
Lennette, Edwin H., et al, eds. Manual of Clinical Microbiology. LC 74-81968. (Illus.). 1974. text ed. 20.00 o.p. (ISBN 0-914826-00-X); pap. text ed. 16.00 o.p. (ISBN 0-914826-01-8). Am Soc Microbio.
Lenning, Larry G. Blessing in Mosque & Mission. LC 80-25110. 176p. (Orig.). 1980. pap. write for info. (ISBN 0-87808-433-9). William Carey Lib.
Lennon, Colm. Richard Stanihurst the Dubliner Fifteen Forty-Seven-Sixteen Eighteen. 200p. 1981. 27.50x (Pub. by Irish Academic Pr Ireland). Biblio Dist.
Lennon, Cynthia. A Twist of Lennon. 1979. pap. 2.50 (ISBN 0-380-45450-5, 45450). Avon.
Lennon, John. The Writings of John Lennon: In His Own Write, a Spaniard in the Works. 1981. 9.95 (ISBN 0-671-43257-5). S&S.
Lennon, Lynn, photos by. Categorically Speaking. (Illus.). 128p. (Orig.). 1981. pap. 6.95 (ISBN 0-670-20685-7, Studio). Viking Pr.
Lennon, Thomas H., jt. auth. see Tucker, Spencer A.
Lennox, Augustus. The Stock Market Metaphysical Significance of Elliott's Principles & Theories. (Illus.). 1978. deluxe bdg. 79.75 (ISBN 0-918968-07-0). Inst Econ Finan.
Lennox, Charlotte. The Female Quixote: or the Adventures of Arabella, 1752, 2 vols. in 1. Shugrue, Michael F., ed. (The Flowering of the Novel, 1740-1775 Ser: Vol. 36). 1974. lib. bdg. 50.00 (ISBN 0-8240-1135-X). Garland Pub.
--Henrietta, 2 vols. in 1. (The Flowering of the Novel Ser, 1740-1775: Vol. 50). 1974. Repr. of 1758 ed. lib. bdg. 50.00 (ISBN 0-8240-1149-X). Garland Pub.
--Sophia, 2 vols. in 1. Shugrue, Michael F., ed. (The Flowering of the Novel, 1740-1775 Ser: Vol. 61). 1974. Repr. of 1762 ed. lib. bdg. 50.00 (ISBN 0-8240-1160-0). Garland Pub.
Lennox, Margaret, jt. auth. see Branson, Joan C.
Lennox, Stanley C. & Chadwick, Mary. Mathematics for Engineers & Applied Scientists. LC 79-670196. 1977. pap. text ed. 15.50x o.p. (ISBN 0-435-71282-9). Heinemann Ed.
Lenoe, Edward M., et al, eds. Fibrous Composites in Structural Design. 900p. 1980. 85.00 (ISBN 0-306-40354-4). Plenum Pub.
Lenormand, Rene & Carner, Mosco. A Study of Twentieth-Century Harmony: Harmony in France to 1914 & Contemporary Harmony, 2 vols. in 1. LC 76-40058. (Music Reprint Ser). 1975. Repr. of 1940 ed. lib. bdg. 22.50 (ISBN 0-306-70717-9). Da Capo.
LeNotre, Gaston. LeNotre's Book of Desserts & Pastries. Hyman, Philip & Hyman, Mary, trs. from Fr. LC 77-13231. 1977. 17.95 (ISBN 0-8120-5137-8). Barron.
Lenowitz, Harris, jt. ed. see Doria, Charles.
Lenrow, Gerald, et al. Federal Income Taxation of Insurance Companies. 3rd ed. LC 78-26091. 1979. 46.50 (ISBN 0-471-05193-4, Pub. by Ronald). Wiley.
Lens, Sidney. Poverty: America's Enduring Paradox. LC 69-11085. 1969. 8.95 o.s.i. (ISBN 0-690-64927-4, TYC-T). T y Crowell.
Lens, Willy, jt. ed. see D'Ydewalle, Gery.
Lenski, B. A. Jean Anouilh: Stages in Rebellion. LC 73-12687. 109p. 1974. text ed. 7.50x (ISBN 0-391-00323-2). Humanities.
Lenski, Branko, ed. Death of a Simple Giant & Other Modern Yugoslav Stories. LC 64-23319. 1964. 7.95 (ISBN 0-8149-0143-3). Vanguard.
Lenski, Branko, ed. see Krleza, Miroslav.
Lenski, Lois. Blue Ridge Billy. (Regional Stories Ser). (Illus.). (gr. 4-6). 1946. PLB 9.79 (ISBN 0-397-30120-0). Lippincott.
--Houseboat Girl. (Regional Stories Ser.). (Illus.). (gr. 4-6). 1957. 7.95 o.p. (ISBN 0-397-30366-1). Lippincott.
--Indian Captive: The Story of Mary Jemison. LC 41-51956. (Illus.). (gr. 7-9). 1941. 9.79 (ISBN 0-397-30072-7). Lippincott.
--Judy's Journey. LC 47-4504. (Regional Stories Ser). (Illus.). (gr. 4-6). 1947. 9.79 (ISBN 0-397-30131-6). Lippincott.
--Mama Hattie's Girl. (Regional Stories Ser). (Illus.). (gr. 4-6). 1953. 5.95 o.p. (ISBN 0-397-30243-6). Lippincott.
--We Live in the City: Short Stories. (Roundabout America Stories Ser). (Illus.). (gr. k-3). 1954. PLB 4.82 o.p. (ISBN 0-397-30291-6). Lippincott.
Lenskii, V. S., jt. auth. see Ilyushin, A. A.
Lent, Henry B. Jet Pilot. (Illus.). (gr. 7-9). 1958. 4.50g o.s.i. (ISBN 0-02-756350-2). Macmillan.
Lent, John A. Caribbean Mass Communications: A Comprehensive Bibliography. (Archival & Bibliographic Ser.). 152p. 1981. pap. 20.00 (ISBN 0-918456-39-8). African Studies Assn.
Lent, William T. Speed Sketching. LC 77-82957. 1978. 8.95 o.p. (ISBN 0-385-13089-9). Doubleday.
Lenthall, Ben, jt. auth. see Friedhoff, Herman.
Lenthall, Patricia R. Carlotta & the Scientist. 2nd ed. LC 76-20841. 47p. (gr. k-4). 1976. 6.50 (ISBN 0-914996-14-2); pap. 2.75 (ISBN 0-914996-12-6). Lollipop Power.
Lenton, Roberto L., jt. auth. see Major, David C.
Lenton, Trevor. British Escort Ships. (Fact Files on World War 2 Ser). (Illus.). 64p. 1975. 5.95 o.p. (ISBN 0-668-03507-2); pap. 3.95 o.p. (ISBN 0-668-03609-5). Arco.
Lentricchia, Frank & Lentricchia, Melissa C. Robert Frost: A Bibliography, 1913-1974. LC 75-44093. (Author Bibliographies Ser.: No. 25). 1976. 11.00 (ISBN 0-8108-0896-X). Scarecrow.
Lentricchia, Melissa C., jt. auth. see Lentricchia, Frank.
Lenz. Lotte soll nicht sterben. (Easy Reader, A). pap. 3.75 (ISBN 0-88436-039-3, GEA110052). EMC.
Lenz, Elinor. Once My Child Now My Friend. (Orig.). 1981. 12.95 (ISBN 0-446-51224-9). Warner Bks.
Lenz, Hermann. Der Innere Bezirk: Roman in Drei Buechern. 680p. (Ger.). 1980. write for info. (Pub. by Insel Verlag Germany). Suhrkamp.
Lenz, John W., ed. see Hume, David.
Lenz, Matthew, Jr. Risk Management Manual. 225p. 1971. 122.00, incl. supplemental service o.p. (ISBN 0-88245-011-5). Merritt Co.
--Risk Management Manual. 1981. 188.00 (ISBN 0-930868-02-1). Merritt Co.
Lenz, Millicent & Mahood, Ramona, eds. Young Adult Literature: Background & Criticisms. LC 80-23489. 524p. 1980. 30.00 (ISBN 0-8389-0302-9). ALA.
Lenz, Robert R. Explosives & Bomb Disposal Guide. (Illus.). 320p. 1976. 15.75 (ISBN 0-398-01097-8). C C Thomas.
Lenz, Wilhelm Von see Von Lenz, Wilhelm.
Leo, Alan. The Art of Synthesis. (Astrologer's Library). 1979. pap. 6.95 (ISBN 0-89281-178-1). Inner Tradit.
--Astrology for All. (Astrologer's Library). 1979. pap. 6.95 (ISBN 0-89281-175-7). Inner Tradit.
--Casting the Horoscope. (Astrologer's Library). 1979. pap. 6.95 (ISBN 0-89281-176-5). Inner Tradit.
--The Complete Dictionary of Astrology. (Astrologer's Library). 1978. pap. 6.95 (ISBN 0-89281-182-X). Inner Tradit.
--The Complete Dictionary of Astrology. 1978. pap. 6.95 (ISBN 0-685-62084-0). Weiser.
--Esoteric Astrology. (Astrologer's Library). 1978. pap. 6.95 (ISBN 0-89281-181-1). Inner Tradit.
--Esoteric Astrology. 1978. pap. 6.95 (ISBN 0-685-62085-9). Weiser.
--How to Judge a Nativity. (Astrologer's Library). 1979. pap. 6.95 (ISBN 0-89281-177-3). Inner Tradit.
--The Key to Your Own Nativity. 1978. pap. 6.95 (ISBN 0-685-62086-7). Weiser.
--The Progressed Horoscope. 1978. pap. 6.95 (ISBN 0-685-62087-5). Weiser.
Leo, Francisco D. & Amador, Antonio A. Corporate Taxation of the Netherlands Antilles. 1978. pap. 18.00x o.p. (ISBN 0-8464-0292-0). Beekman Pubs.
Leoff, Eve. Monarch Notes on Shakespeare's a Midsummer Night's Dream. (Orig.). pap. 1.95 (ISBN 0-671-00638-X). Monarch Pr.
--A Study of Keats's Isabella. (Salzburg Studies in English Literature, Romantic Reassessment: No. 17). 217p. 1972. pap. text ed. 25.00x (ISBN 0-391-01457-9). Humanities.
LeoGrande, William M. Cuba's Policy in Africa, Nineteen Fifty-Nine to Nineteen Eighty. (Policy Papers in International Affairs: No. 13). vi, 80p. 1980. pap. 3.25x (ISBN 0-87725-513-X). U of Cal Intl St.
Leokum, Arkady. The Curious Book: Fascinating Facts About People, Places & Things. LC 76-19772. (Illus.). (gr. 10 up). 1976. 7.95 o.p. (ISBN 0-8069-0100-4); PLB 7.49 o.p. (ISBN 0-8069-0101-2). Sterling.
Leokum, Leonard & Posnick, Paul. Weather War. 1978. pap. 2.25 o.p. (ISBN 0-523-40229-5). Pinnacle Bks.
Leon, Aimee. Of Life & Love & Such. 1981. 5.95 (ISBN 0-533-04860-5). Vantage.
Leon, D. Kibbutz: New a of Life. 1969. 16.50 (ISBN 0-08-013357-6); pap. 7.75 (ISBN 0-08-013356-8). Pergamon.
Leon, Dorothy. One Eye, Two Eyes, Three Eyes, Four... The Many Ways Animals See. LC 80-15468. (Illus.). (gr. 4-6). 1980. PLB 7.29 (ISBN 0-671-34001-8). Messner.
Leon, George & Sands, Leo G. Dial Nine One One: Modern Emergency Communications Networks. (Illus.). 128p. 1975. pap. 3.95 o.p. (ISBN 0-8104-0343-9). Hayden.
Leon, George D. The ABC Book of Hi-Fi-Audio Projects. (Illus.). 1977. pap. 5.95 (ISBN 0-8306-6921-3, 921). TAB Bks.
Leon, Gloria R. Case Studies in Deviant Behavior: An Interactional Perspective. 2nd ed. 1977. pap. 11.95 (ISBN 0-205-05847-7, 795847-1). Allyn.
Leon, H. & Alain, Hermano. Flora de Cuba, 2 vols. (Illus.). 2317p. (Span., Lat.). 1979. Repr. of 1946 ed. lib. bdg. 280.80 five parts bound in 2 vols. (ISBN 3-87429-077-8). Lubrecht & Cramer.
Leon, Jorge A. Cada Muchacho Necesita un Modelo Vivo. 96p. (Span.). 1981. pap. write for info. (ISBN 0-311-46087-9). Casa Bautista.
--Psicologia Pastoral de la Iglesia. LC 77-43121. 192p. (Orig., Span.). 1978. pap. 4.95 (ISBN 0-89922-113-0). Edit Caribe.
--Psicologia Pastoral para Todos los Cristianos. LC 76-43121. 181p. (Orig., Span.). 1976. pap. 4.95 (ISBN 0-89922-020-7). Edit Caribe.
--Lo Que Todos Debemos Saber Sobre la Homosexualidad. LC 76-19206. 136p. (Orig., Span.). 1976. pap. 2.95 (ISBN 0-89922-071-1). Edit Caribe.
Leon, Joseph M. World Civilization, 2 vols. Incl. Vol. 1. To 1715. 1970. pap. text ed. 4.95 (ISBN 0-8220-1509-9); Vol. 2. Since 1650. 1969. pap. text ed. 4.95 (ISBN 0-8220-1510-2). (Cliffs Course Outlines Ser.). Cliffs.
Leon, Ruth. What Am I? A Picture Quiz Book. (Illus.). (ps-2). 1949. PLB 4.57 o.p. (ISBN 0-307-60509-4, Golden Pr). Western Pub.
Leonard, Anne & Terrell, John. Patterns of Paradise. Bushman, Tanisse, ed. (Illus.). 76p. 1980. pap. 9.95 (ISBN 0-914868-05-5). Field Mus.
Leonard, Charles A. Search for a Judicial Philosophy: Mr. Justice Roberts & the Constitutional Revolution of 1937. LC 77-139358. (National University Publications). 1971. 15.00 (ISBN 0-8046-9009-X). Kennikat.
Leonard, Charles B., Jr. Concentrations of Solutions. 120p. 1971. spiral bdg. 6.00 (ISBN 0-87488-602-3). Med Exam.
Leonard, Constance. The Marina Mystery. LC 80-2781. 160p. (gr. 8 up). 1981. PLB 7.95 (ISBN 0-396-07930-X). Dodd.
Leonard, Dick & Valentine, Herman, eds. The Backbencher & Parliament. LC 78-185906. 1972. 18.95 (ISBN 0-312-06475-6). St Martin.
Leonard, Donna. Lord, I'm Listening. 1979. pap. 2.95 (ISBN 0-88207-745-7). Victor Bks.
Leonard, Donna, jt. auth. see Leonard, Stan.
Leonard, Ellen M., ed. Wood Burning for Power. 135p. 1980. pap. 14.95 (ISBN 0-89934-048-2, B048-PP). Solar Energy Info.
Leonard, Elmore. Hombre. 1974. pap. 1.75 (ISBN 0-345-28850-5). Ballantine.
--Last Stand at Saber River. 176p. 1980. pap. 1.75 (ISBN 0-553-13696-8). Bantam.
--Swag. 240p. 1976. 7.95 o.p. (ISBN 0-440-08449-0). Delacorte.
Leonard, Eugenie A. Dear-Bought Heritage. LC 64-24496. (Illus.). 1965. 15.00x o.p. (ISBN 0-8122-7436-9). U of Pa Pr.
Leonard, Frances M. Laughhter in the Court of Love: Comedy in Allegory, from Chaucer to Spencer. 192p. 1981. 18.95 (ISBN 0-937664-54-5). Pilgrim Bks OK.
Leonard, George. Alien. LC 76-49397. 256p. 1980. pap. 2.25 (ISBN 0-87216-746-1). Playboy Pbks.
--Beyond Control. LC 75-17505. 200p. 1975. 7.95 o.s.i. (ISBN 0-02-570350-1, 57035). Macmillan.
--The Silent Pulse. 208p. 1981. pap. 2.95 (ISBN 0-553-14368-9). Bantam.
Leonard, George B. The Transformation. 288p. 1981. pap. 5.95 (ISBN 0-87477-169-2). J P Tarcher.
--The Transformation. 288p. 1972. 7.95 o.s.i. (ISBN 0-440-09031-8). Delacorte.
Leonard, Irving A. Baroque Times in Old Mexico: Seventeenth-Century Persons, Places, & Practices. LC 80-29256. (Illus.). xi, 260p. 1981. Repr. of 1978 ed. lib. bdg. 25.50x (ISBN 0-313-22826-4, LEBT). Greenwood.
--Baroque Times in Old Mexico: Seventeenth-Century Persons, Places, & Practices. (Illus.). 1959. pap. 4.95 (ISBN 0-472-06110-0, 110, AA). U of Mich Pr.
Leonard, Irving A., tr. see Picon-Salas, Mariano.
Leonard, Jan, ed. see Adams, Gerald.
Leonard, Jan, ed. see Butler, Phyllis.
Leonard, Jan, ed. see Kamin, Ira.
Leonard, Jan, ed. see Olmstead, Marty & Weimer, Jan.
Leonard, Jerry. Kart Racing. LC 79-26985. (Illus.). 160p. (gr. 7 up). 1980. PLB 7.79 (ISBN 0-671-34033-6). Messner.
Leonard, Jon N. & Taylor, Elaine A. The Live Longer Now Cookbook. 384p. 1981. pap. 2.50 (ISBN 0-441-48521-9). Charter Bks.
Leonard, Jon N., et al. Live Longer Now. 236p. 1981. pap. 2.50 (ISBN 0-441-48516-2). Charter Bks.
Leonard, Jonathan. Ancient America. LC 67-15619. (Great Ages of Man). (Illus.). (gr. 6 up). 1967. PLB 11.97 (ISBN 0-8094-0374-9, Pub. by Time-Life). Silver.
--Atlantic Beaches. LC 72-79775. (American Wilderness Ser). (Illus.). (gr. 6 up). 1972. lib. bdg. 11.97 (ISBN 0-8094-1157-1, Pub. by Time-Life). Silver.
Leonard, Jonathan N. American Cooking: New England. (Foods of the World Ser). (Illus.). 1970. 14.95 (ISBN 0-8094-0049-9). Time-Life.
--American Cooking: New England. LC 70-133841. (Foods of the World Ser.). (Illus.). (gr. 6 up). 1970. lib. bdg. 14.94 (ISBN 0-8094-0076-6, Pub. by Time-Life). Silver.
--American Cooking: The Great West. (Foods of the World Ser). (Illus.). 1971. 14.95 (ISBN 0-8094-0053-7). Time-Life.
--American Cooking: The Great West. LC 76-156273. (Foods of the World Ser.). (Illus.). (gr. 6 up). 1971. 14.94 (ISBN 0-8094-0080-4, Pub. by Time-Life). Silver.
--Ancient America. (Great Ages of Man Ser). (Illus.). 1967. 12.95 (ISBN 0-8094-0352-8). Time-Life.
--Atlantic Beaches. LC 72-79775. (The American Wilderness Ser.). (Illus.). 1972. 12.95 (ISBN 0-8094-1156-3). Time-Life.
--Early Japan. (Great Ages of Man Ser). (Illus.). 1968. 12.95 (ISBN 0-8094-0360-9). Time-Life.
--Early Japan. LC 68-27297. (Great Ages of Man). (Illus.). (gr. 6 up). 1968. PLB 11.97 (ISBN 0-8094-0382-X, Pub. by Time-Life). Silver.
--The First Farmers. LC 73-85264. (Emergence of Man Ser). (Illus.). (gr. 6 up). 1973. lib. bdg. 9.63 o.p. (ISBN 0-8094-1305-1, Pub. by Time-Life). Silver.
--The First Farmers. (Emergence of Man Ser.). (Illus.). 1973. 9.95 (ISBN 0-8094-1304-3); lib. bdg. avail. (ISBN 0-685-41616-X). Time-Life.
--Latin American Cooking. LC 68-58451. (Foods of the World Ser). (Illus.). (gr. 6 up). 1968. PLB 14.94 (ISBN 0-8094-0063-4, Pub. by Time-Life). Silver.
--Latin American Cooking. (Foods of the World Ser). (Illus.). 1968. 14.95 (ISBN 0-8094-0036-7). Time-Life.
--World of Gainsborough. (Library of Art). (Illus.). 1969. 15.95 (ISBN 0-8094-0253-X). Time-Life.
--World of Gainsborough. LC 73-84574. (Library of Art Ser.). (Illus.). (gr. 6 up). 1969. 12.96 (ISBN 0-8094-0282-3, Pub. by Time-Life). Silver.
Leonard, Joseph W., ed. Coal Preperation. 4th ed. LC 79-52245. (Illus.). 1204p. 1979. text ed. 42.00x (ISBN 0-89520-258-1). Soc Mining Eng.
Leonard, Karen I. Social History of an Indian Caste: The Kayasths of Hyderabad. LC 76-52031. (Center for South & Southeast Asian Studies). 1978. 19.50x (ISBN 0-520-03431-7). U of Cal Pr.

Leonard, Lawrence E., et al. Centralized Book Processing: A Feasibility Study Based on Colorado Academic Libraries. LC 77-4903. 1969. 13.50 (ISBN 0-8108-0263-5). Scarecrow.
Leonard, Marcia & Cricket Magazine Editors. Cricket's Jokes, Riddles & Other Stuff. LC 77-3164. (Illus.). (gr. 1-6). 1977. 2.95 (ISBN 0-394-83545-X); PLB 3.99 (ISBN 0-394-93545-4). Random.
Leonard, Margery B., jt. auth. see Harrison, Henry S.
Leonard, Phyllis. Warrior's Woman. 1978. pap. 2.25 (ISBN 0-515-04620-5). Jove Pubns.
Leonard, R. C., jt. auth. see Wooldridge, P. J.
Leonard, R. M., jt. auth. see Jerrold, Walter C.
Leonard, Ray. AMC Guide to Backcountry Facilities. (Illus.). 250p. (Orig.). 1980. pap. 6.95 (ISBN 0-910146-31-4). Appalach Mtn.
Leonard, Richard. South Africa at War: The Crisis in South Africa & U. S. Policy. (Orig.). 1981. 12.95 (ISBN 0-88208-108-X); pap. 5.95 (ISBN 0-88208-109-8). Lawrence Hill.
Leonard, Stan & Leonard, Donna. Games to Grow on. 1976. pap. 1.50 o.p. (ISBN 0-88207-254-4). Victor Bks.
Leonard, Thomas C. Above the Battle: War-Making in America from Appomattox to Versailles. (Illus.). 1978. 15.95 (ISBN 0-19-502239-4). Oxford U Pr.
Leonard, V. A. Criminal Investigation & Identification. (Illus.). 160p. 1971. 10.75 (ISBN 0-398-01098-6). C C Thomas.
--The New Police Technology. (Illus.). 360p. 1980. 29.75 (ISBN 0-398-03967-4). C C Thomas.
--Police Communications System. 96p. 1970. 8.75 (ISBN 0-398-01106-0). C C Thomas.
--Police Crime Prevention. (Illus.). 210p. 1972. text ed. 14.75 (ISBN 0-398-02339-5). C C Thomas.
--Police Detective Function. 124p. 1970. 9.75 (ISBN 0-398-01099-4). C C Thomas.
--Police Enterprise: Its Organization & Management. (Illus.). 104p. 1969. 8.75 (ISBN 0-398-01100-1). C C Thomas.
--Police Patrol Organization. (Illus.). 116p. 1970. 11.50 (ISBN 0-398-01102-8). C C Thomas.
--Police Personnel Administration. 144p. 1970. 12.75 (ISBN 0-398-01103-6). C C Thomas.
--Police Pre-Disaster Preparation. (Illus.). 344p. 1973. 15.75 (ISBN 0-398-02693-9). C C Thomas.
--The Police Records System. (Illus.). 104p. 1977. 10.75 (ISBN 0-398-01104-4). C C Thomas.
--Police Science for the Young American. (Illus.). 80p. 1968. 6.75 (ISBN 0-398-01105-2). C C Thomas.
--The Police, the Judiciary, & the Criminal. 2nd ed. (Illus.). 320p. 1975. 18.75 (ISBN 0-398-03332-3). C C Thomas.
--Police Traffic Control. 176p. 1971. 11.75 (ISBN 0-398-01107-9). C C Thomas.
Leonard, William E., tr. from Gr. & see Empedocles.
Leonard, William L., ed. Radiologic Technology Examination Review Book, Vol. 1. 4th ed. 1979. pap. 9.50 (ISBN 0-87488-441-1). Med Exam.
Leonardson, jt. auth. see Briscoe.
Leondes, C. T., ed. Advances in Control & Dynamic Systems: Theory & Application, Vol. 17. (Serial Publication). 1981. price not set (ISBN 0-12-012717-2). Acad Pr.
--Control of Dynamic Systems: Advances in Theory & Application, Vols. 9, 10, 13 & 15. Incl. Vol. 9. 44.00 (ISBN 0-12-012709-1); Vol. 10. 44.00 (ISBN 0-12-012710-5); Vol. 13. 1977. 39.00 (ISBN 0-12-012713-X); Vol. 15. 1979. 22.50 (ISBN 0-12-012715-6). 1973. Acad Pr.
Leon-Dufour, Xavier. Dictionary of the New Testament. Prendergast, Terrence, tr. LC 79-3004. (Illus.). 448p. (Fr.). 1980. 19.95 (ISBN 0-06-062100-1, HarpR). Har-Row.
Leon-Dufour, Xavier, ed. Dictionary of Biblical Theology. new ed. Cahill, P. Joseph, tr. from Fr. LC 73-6437. 710p. 1973. Repr. 22.50 (ISBN 0-8164-1146-8). Crossroad NY.
Leone, Bruno. Maria Montessori: Knight of the Child. Bender, David L. & McCuen, Gary E., eds. (Focus on Famous Women Ser.). (Illus.). (gr. 3 up). 1978. 6.95 (ISBN 0-912616-47-4); read along cassette 9.95 (ISBN 0-89908-246-7). Greenhaven.
Leone, Bruno, ed. Capitalism: Opposing Viewpoints. (ISMS Ser.). (Illus.). (gr. 9-12). 1978. 8.95 (ISBN 0-912616-51-2); pap. 3.95 (ISBN 0-912616-50-4). Greenhaven.
--Communism: Opposing Viewpoints. (ISMS Ser.). (Illus.). (gr. 9-12). 8.95 (ISBN 0-912616-53-9); pap. 3.95 (ISBN 0-912616-52-0). Greenhaven.
--Internationalism: Opposing Viewpoints. (ISMS Ser.). (Illus.). (gr. 9-12). 8.95 (ISBN 0-912616-59-8); pap. 3.95 (ISBN 0-912616-58-X). Greenhaven.
--Nationalism: Opposing Viewpoints. (ISMS Ser.). (Illus.). (gr. 9-12). 1978. 8.95 (ISBN 0-912616-57-1); pap. 3.95 (ISBN 0-912616-56-3). Greenhaven.
--Racism: Opposing Viewpoints. (ISMS Ser.). (Illus.). (gr. 9-12). 1978. 8.95 (ISBN 0-912616-61-X); pap. 3.95 (ISBN 0-912616-60-1). Greenhaven.
--Socialism: Opposing Viewpoints. (ISMS Ser.). (Illus.). (gr. 9-12). 1978. 8.95 (ISBN 0-912616-55-5); pap. 3.95 (ISBN 0-912616-54-7). Greenhaven.
Leone, Mark P., ed. Contemporary Archaeology: A Guide to Theory & Contributions. LC 79-156779. 476p. 1972. pap. 12.95x (ISBN 0-8093-0534-8). S Ill U Pr.
Leone, Nicholas C. & Phillips, Elisabeth C. The Farmer's & Rancher's Medical Guide. 1980. 12.95 (ISBN 0-679-51025-7). McKay.
Leone, Robert, jt. auth. see Martin, Curtis H.
Leone, Robert A. Environmental Controls: The Impact on Industries. LC 75-32222. 304p. 1976. 16.95 (ISBN 0-669-00345-X). Lexington Bks.
Leong, Charles L., jt. auth. see Kan, Johnny.
Leong, Y. S. Silver: An Analysis of Factors Affecting Its Price. 2nd ed. (Brookings Institution Reprint Ser). Repr. of 1934 ed. lib. bdg. 28.00x (ISBN 0-697-00162-8). Irvington.
Leonhardy, Adele. Introductory College Mathematics. 2nd ed. LC 63-12284. 1963. text ed. 22.95 (ISBN 0-471-52736-X). Wiley.
Leoni, Bruno. Freedom & the Law. LC 71-167535. 204p. 1961. 7.50x o.p. (ISBN 0-8402-1215-1); pap. text ed. 4.95x o.p. (ISBN 0-686-65432-3). Nash Pub.
--Freedom & the Law. LC 71-167535. 1976. 7.50x o.p. (ISBN 0-916054-18-7); pap. 4.95x o.p. (ISBN 0-8402-1215-1). Green Hill.
Leonidas. Secrets of Stage Hypnotism. LC 80-19741. 149p. 1980. Repr. of 1975 ed. lib. bdg. 9.95x (ISBN 0-89370-629-9). Borgo Pr.
Leonor, M., jt. auth. see Richards, P.
Leonov, Alexei. Sun's Wind. (Let There Always Be Sunshine Ser.). (Illus.). (gr. k-3). 1977. 2.75 (ISBN 0-8285-8829-5). Progress Pubs.
Leonov, Leonid M. Soviet River. Montagu, Ivor & Nalbandov, Sergei, trs. from Rus. LC 72-90298. (Soviet Literature in English Translation Ser.). 383p. 1981. Repr. 21.50 (ISBN 0-88355-009-1). Hyperion Conn.
Leon-Portilla, Miguel. Pre-Columbian Literatures of Mexico. Lobanov, Grace, tr. (Civilization of the American Indian Ser: No. 92). (Illus.). 1969. 9.95 (ISBN 0-8061-0818-5). U of Okla Pr.
Leontiades, Milton. Management Policy: Strategies & Plans. 680p. 1981. text ed. 18.95 (ISBN 0-316-52104-3); tchrs'. manual free (ISBN 0-316-52105-1). Little.
Leontief, W., ed. Structure, System & Economic Policy. LC 77-8581. 1977. 35.50 (ISBN 0-521-21724-5). Cambridge U Pr.
Leontief, Wassily W. Input-Output Economics. 1966. 19.95x (ISBN 0-19-500616-X). Oxford U Pr.
Leontiev, A. Activity Conscientiousness & Personality. 1978. 23.95 (ISBN 0-13-003533-5). P-H.
Leontiev, Aleksei A. Psychology & the Language Learning Process. LC 80-41819. 160p. 1981. 11.95 (ISBN 0-08-024601-X); pap. 5.95 (ISBN 0-08-024600-1). Pergamon.
Leontiev, Konstantin. Analiz, Stil' I Veyanie: O Romanakh Gr. L. N. Tolstogo. LC 65-24667. (Slavic Reprint Ser.: No. 3). 158p. (Rus.). 1968. pap. 3.00 (ISBN 0-87057-090-0, Pub. by Brown U Pr). Univ Pr of New England.
Leontovich, M. A., ed. Reviews of Plasma Physics, Vol. 8. 425p. 1980. 42.50 (ISBN 0-306-17068-X, Consultants Bureau). Plenum Pub.
Leopold, A. Starker. Desert. LC 61-18379. (Life Nature Library). (Illus.). (gr. 5 up). 1961. PLB 8.97 o.p. (ISBN 0-8094-0615-2, Pub. by Time-Life). Silver.
--The Desert. (Young Readers Library). (Illus.). 1977. lib. bdg. 7.95 (ISBN 0-686-51086-0). Silver.
--Wildlife of Mexico: The Game Birds & Mammals. LC 59-6865. (Illus.). 568p. 1959. 35.00 (ISBN 0-520-00724-7). U of Cal Pr.
Leopold, Aldo. A Sand County Almanac, & Sketches Here & There. (Illus.). 1949. pap. 4.95 (ISBN 0-19-500777-8, GB). Oxford U Pr.
--Sand County Almanac: With Other Essays on Conservation from Round River. (Illus.). 1966. 15.95 (ISBN 0-19-500619-4). Oxford U Pr.
Leopold, Carolyn C. School Libraries Worth Their Keep: A Philosophy Plus Tricks. LC 72-7497. (Illus.). 1972. 13.50 (ISBN 0-8108-0503-0). Scarecrow.
Leopold, I. H. Cases in Diagnostic Ultrasound. 224p. 1980. 22.00 (ISBN 0-471-08731-9, Pub. by Wiley Med). Wiley.
Leopold, Irving H. Proceedings, Vol. 8. Burns, R. P., ed. LC 66-22972. (Wiley Ser. in Clinical Opthalmology). 144p. 1976. 28.00 o.p. (ISBN 0-471-05151-9, Pub. by Wiley Medical). Wiley.
Leopold, Irving H. & Burns, Robert P. Symposium on Ocular Therapy. LC 76-645664. (Clinical Opthalmology Ser.: Vol. 11). 1979. 20.95 o.p. (ISBN 0-471-05151-9, Pub. by Wiley Medical). Wiley.
Leopold, Irving H., ed. see Symposium on Ocular Therapy.
Leopold, Jules, jt. auth. see Wiswell, Tom.
Leopold, Luna, jt. auth. see Davis, Kenneth S.
Leopold, Luna B. Water: A Primer. LC 73-19844. (Geology Ser.). (Illus.). 1974. text ed. 16.95x (ISBN 0-7167-0264-9); pap. text ed. 8.95x (ISBN 0-7167-0263-0). W H Freeman.
Leopold, Luna B., jt. auth. see Dunne, Thomas.
Leopold, Luna B., ed. Round River: From the Journals of Aldo Leopold. (Illus.). 188p. 1972. pap. 3.95 (ISBN 0-19-501563-0, 372, GB). Oxford U Pr.
Leopold, Luna B., et al. Fluvial Processes in Geomorphology. LC 64-10919. (Geology Ser.). (Illus.). 1964. 27.95x (ISBN 0-7167-0221-5). W H Freeman.
Leopoldo & De Meis. The Sarcoplasmic Reticulum: With Special Reference to Transport & Energy Transduction. (Transport in the Life Sciences Ser.). 150p. 1981. 25.00 (ISBN 0-471-05025-3, Pub. by Wiley-Interscience). Wiley.
Leopoldt, Heinrich W., ed. see Hasse, Helmut.
Lep, Antoinette. Traditional Quilt Block Patterns for Crocheting. 48p. (Orig.). 1981. pap. write for info. (ISBN 0-486-23967-5). Dover.
Lepa, E., tr. see Scharf, C.
Le Page, R. B., jt. ed. see Cassidy, F. G.
LePage, Wilbur, jt. auth. see Balabanian, Norman.
LePage, Wilbur R. Applied APL Programming. LC 78-6619. (Illus.). 1978. pap. 15.95 ref. (ISBN 0-13-040063-7). P-H.
--Complex Variables & the Laplace Transform for Engineers. (Illus.). 1980. pap. text ed. 6.00 (ISBN 0-486-63926-6). Dover.
Le Paillot, Jean. Caroline & the King's Hunt. Saunders, Rubie, tr. LC 72-673. (Illus.). 36p. (ps-3). 1972. Repr. 5.95 o.s.i. (ISBN 0-8193-0604-5, Four Winds); PLB 5.41 o.s.i. (ISBN 0-8193-0605-3). Schol Bk Serv.
--Caroline at the King's Ball. Saunders, Rubie, tr. from Fr. LC 75-183378. Orig. Title: Caroline Au Bal Du Roi. (Illus.). (gr. k-3). 1972. Repr. of 1968 ed. 5.95 o.s.i. (ISBN 0-8193-0551-0, Four Winds); PLB 5.41 o.s.i. (ISBN 0-8193-0552-9). Schol Bk Serv.
LePak, Roy C. A Theology of Christian Mystical Experience. 1977. pap. text ed. 12.00x (ISBN 0-8191-0148-6). U Pr of Amer.
Le Patourel, John. The Norman Empire. (Illus.). 426p. 1977. 49.50x (ISBN 0-19-822525-3). Oxford U Pr.
Lepawsky, Albert, et al, eds. Search for World Order: Studies by Students & Colleagues of Quincy Wright. LC 75-147119. (Orig.). 1971. 38.50x (ISBN 0-89197-479-2). Irvington.
LePeau, Andrew T. & LePeau, Phyllis J. Faith That Works: Eleven Studies in James. 72p. (Orig.). 1980. pap. 2.25 (ISBN 0-87784-365-1). Inter Varsity.
Le Peau, Andrew T., jt. auth. see Le Peau, Phyllis J.
Le Peau, Phyllis J. & Le Peau, Andrew T. One Plus One Equals One. 96p. (Orig.). 1981. pap. 2.95 (ISBN 0-87784-803-3). Inter-Varsity.
LePeau, Phyllis J., jt. auth. see LePeau, Andrew T.
Le Petit, Jean Francois. The Low Country Commonwealth. Grimeston, E., tr. LC 72-25634. (English Experience Ser.: No. 208). 1969. Repr. of 1609 ed. 30.00 (ISBN 90-221-0208-4). Walter J Johnson.
Leplin, Jarrett. Propositional Logic. LC 79-63560. 1979. pap. text ed. 7.50 (ISBN 0-8191-0728-X). U Pr of Amer.
Lepori, N. G. Sex Differentiation, Hermaphroditism & Intersexuality in Vertebrates Including Man. (Illus.). 372p. 1980. text ed. 49.50x (ISBN 88-212-0747-1, Pub. by Piccin Italy). J K Burgess.
Lepp, Henry. Identifying & Collecting Rocks & Minerals. LC 78-69632. (Illus.). 1979. 14.50 o.p. (ISBN 0-498-02208-0). A S Barnes.
Lepp, Ignace. Ways of Friendship. 1968. 8.95 (ISBN 0-02-570410-9); pap. 1.25 (ISBN 0-02-086650-X). Macmillan.
Lepper, John H. Famous Secret Societies. LC 73-143638. 1971. Repr. of 1932 ed. 20.00 (ISBN 0-8103-3648-0). Gale.
Leppert, Mary, ed. see Ekern, Doris.
Leppert, Mary, ed. see Oblander, Ruth.
Leppert, Richard D. Arcadia at Versailles: Noble Amateur Musicians & Their Musettes & Hurdy-Gurdies at the French Court (C. 1660-1789), a Visual Study. 138p. 1978. pap. text ed. 32.50 (ISBN 90-265-0246-X, Pub. by Swets Pub Serv Holland). Swets North Am.
Leppzer, Robert. Voices from Three-Mile Island: The People Speak Out. LC 80-20933. (Illus.). 1980. 8.95 (ISBN 0-89594-041-8); pap. 3.95 (ISBN 0-89594-042-6). Crossing Pr.
Leprohon, Rosanna E. The Poetical Works of Mrs. Leprohon. (Toronto Reprint Library of Canadian Prose & Poetry). 1973. Repr. of 1881 ed. 16.75x (ISBN 0-8020-7523-1). U of Toronto Pr.
Lepsius, Richard. Standard Alphabet for Reducing Unwritten Languages & Foreign Graphic Systems to a Uniform Orthography in European Letters. (Amsterdam Classics in Linguistics Ser.: No. 5). 375p. 1980. text ed. 45.75x (ISBN 90-272-0876-X). Humanities.
Lepson, Ruth. Dreaming in Color. LC 79-54882. 72p. 1980. pap. 4.95 (ISBN 0-914086-27-8). Alicejamesbooks.
Leptich, Anne & Evans, Jacque. Calligrapher's Reference Book. pap. 6.00 (ISBN 0-87980-386-X). Wilshire.
--Calligraphy for Fun & Profit. pap. 6.00 (ISBN 0-87980-385-1). Wilshire.
Lerch, Constance & Bliss, Jane. Maternity Nursing: A Self Study Guide. 4th ed. (Illus.). 1978. pap. text ed. 9.50 (ISBN 0-8016-2959-4). Mosby.
Lerch, Constance & Bliss, Virginia. Maternity Nursing. 3rd ed. LC 77-13983. (Illus.). 1978. text ed. 18.95 (ISBN 0-8016-2961-6). Mosby.
Lerch, Harold A., jt. auth. see Welch, Paula D.
Lerch, Harold H. Active Learning Experiences for Teaching Elementary School Mathematics. (Illus.). 592p. 1981. pap. text ed. price not set (ISBN 0-395-29764-8). HM.
--Teaching Elementary School Mathematics: An Active Learning Approach. (Illus.). 416p. 1981. text ed. price not set (ISBN 0-395-29762-1); price not set instr's. manual (ISBN 0-395-29763-X). HM.
Lerche, Charles Q., jt. auth. see Said, Abdul A.
LeRette, Jon M. Airline Job Kit. (Illus.). 82p. 1980. pap. text ed. 3.50 (ISBN 0-686-28722-3). Airline Job.
Lerin, A., jt. auth. see Sloan, W. H.
Lerin, Alfredo, compiled by. Quinientas Ilustraciones. 324p. (Span.). 1980. pap. 4.95 (ISBN 0-311-42037-0). Casa Bautista.
Lerin, Olivia de see Crane, J. D.
Lerin, Olivia S. D. de see Sutton, Joan L. & Watson de Barros, Leda.
Lerin, Olivia S. de see De Lerin, Olivia S.
Lerin, Olivia Y Alfredo, tr. see Brown, Raymond B.
Lerin, S. D. De, tr. see Stowell, Gordon.
Lerin, S. D. de, tr. see Stowell, Gordon.
Lerma, Dominique-Rene De see De Lerma, Dominique-Rene.
Lerman, Arthur J. Taiwan's Politics: The Provincial Assemblyman's World. LC 78-64524. 1978. pap. text ed. 11.25 (ISBN 0-8191-0632-1). U Pr of Amer.
Lerman, Eleanor. Armed Love. (Wesleyan Poetry Program: Vol. 68). 1973. pap. 4.95 (ISBN 0-8195-1068-8, Pub. by Wesleyan U Pr). Columbia U Pr.
Lerman, J. W., jt. auth. see Damste, P. H.
Lerman, Paul. Community Treatment & Social Control: A Critical Analysis of Juvenile Correctional Policy. LC 74-11629. (Studies in Crime & Justice). xvi, 254p. 1975. 12.50x o.s.i. (ISBN 0-226-47307-4). U of Chicago Pr.
Lerman, Rhoda. Eleanor: A Novel. LC 78-15140. 304p. 1980. 10.95 (ISBN 0-03-021066-6); pap. 4.95 (ISBN 0-03-057643-1). HR&W.
Lermontov, Mihail. Hero of Our Time. pap. 4.95 (ISBN 0-385-09344-6, A133, Anch). Doubleday.
Lerner, Abba & Colander, David. MAP: A Market Anti-Inflation Plan. 128p. 1980. pap. text ed. write for info. (HC). HarBraceJ.
Lerner, Alan J. & Loewe, Frederick. Camelot. 1961. 6.95 (ISBN 0-394-40521-8). Random.
Lerner, Allan W. The Politics of Decision-Making: Strategy, Cooperation, & Conflict. LC 76-22632. (Sage Library of Social Research: Vol. 34). 1976. 18.00x (ISBN 0-8039-0694-3); pap. 8.95x (ISBN 0-8039-0695-1). Sage.
Lerner, Carol. On the Forest Edge. (Illus.). (gr. k-3). 1978. 6.95 (ISBN 0-688-22162-9); PLB 6.67 (ISBN 0-688-32162-3). Morrow.
Lerner, Craig Alan, ed. Grants Register: Nineteen Eighty-One-Eighty-Three. 7th ed. 800p. 1980. 32.50x (ISBN 0-312-34407-4). St Martin.
Lerner, Daniel, jt. ed. see Lasswell, Harold D.
Lerner, Gerda. The Majority Finds Its Past: Placing Women in History. (A Galaxy Book: No. 624). 250p. 1981. pap. 5.95 (ISBN 0-19-502899-6). Oxford U Pr.
--The Majority Finds Its Past: Placing Women in History. 250p. 1981. pap. 5.95 (ISBN 0-19-502899-6, GB 624, OPB). Oxford U Pr.
--The Majority Finds Its Past: Placing Women in History. 1979. 14.95 (ISBN 0-19-502597-0). Oxford U Pr.
Lerner, Gerda, ed. The Female Experience: An American Documentary AHS-90. 1977. 13.95 (ISBN 0-672-51555-5); pap. text ed. 9.95 (ISBN 0-672-61248-8). Bobbs.
Lerner, Howard D., jt. ed. see Kwawer, Jay S.
Lerner, I. Michael & Libby, William J. Heredity, Evolution, & Society. 2nd ed. LC 75-33968. (Illus.). 1976. text ed. 22.95x (ISBN 0-7167-0576-1); tchr's manual avail. W H Freeman.

Lerner, Janet, et al. Cases in Learning & Behavior Problems: A Guide to Individualized Education Programs. LC 79-88101. 1979. pap. text ed. 9.50 (ISBN 0-395-28493-7); instructor's manual 0.25 (ISBN 0-395-28494-5). HM.
Lerner, Janet W. Children with Learning Disabilities. 2nd ed. LC 75-26085. (Illus.). 448p. 1976. text ed. 17.95 (ISBN 0-395-20474-7); inst. manual 1.25 (ISBN 0-395-20473-9). HM.
--Learning Disabilities: Theories, Diagnosis, & Teaching Strategies. (Illus.). 560p. 1981. text ed. 17.95 (ISBN 0-395-29710-9); write for info. set study guide (ISBN 0-395-30371-0); write for info. instr's manual (ISBN 0-395-29711-7). HM.
Lerner, Janet W., et al. Special Education for the Early Childhood Years. 416p. 1981. text ed. 17.95 (ISBN 0-13-826461-9). P-H.
Lerner, Joel J., jt. auth. see Cashin, James A.
Lerner, Joel L., jt. auth. see Cashin, James A.
Lerner, Laurence. Thomas Hardy's "The Mayor of Casterbridge: Tragedy or Social History? (Text & Context Ser.). 1975. text ed. 6.25x (ISBN 0-85621-042-0); pap. text ed. 2.75x (ISBN 0-85621-043-9). Humanities.
Lerner, Laurence, ed. The Victorians. LC 78-15642. (Context of English Literature). 1978. text ed. 25.50x (ISBN 0-8419-0419-7); pap. text ed. 12.50x (ISBN 0-8419-0420-0). Holmes & Meier.
Lerner, Lawrence S., jt. auth. see Eisberg, Robert M.
Lerner, Lily & Stuart, S. L. The Silence. 1980. 10.95 (ISBN 0-8184-0306-3). Lyle Stuart.
Lerner, Marguerite. Medical School: The Interview & the Applicant. rev ed. 175p. 1980. pap. 3.95 (ISBN 0-8120-0752-2). Barron.
Lerner, Mark. Careers at a Zoo. LC 80-19614. (Early Career Bks.). (Illus.). (gr. 2-5). 1980. PLB 4.95g (ISBN 0-8225-0342-5). Lerner Pubns.
--Careers in Auto Racing. LC 80-12047. (Illus.). (gr. 2-5). 1980. PLB 4.95 (ISBN 0-8225-0343-3). Lerner Pubns.
--Careers in Toy Making. LC 80-11293. (Early Career Bks.). (Illus.). (gr. 2-5). 1980. PLB 4.95g (ISBN 0-8225-0340-9). Lerner Pubns.
--Quarter-Midget Racing Is for Me. LC 81-41. (Sports for Me Bks.). (Illus.). (gr. 2-5). 1981. PLB 5.95 (ISBN 0-8225-1125-8). Lerner Pubns.
Lerner, Melvin J. The Belief in a Just World: A Fundamental Delusion. (Perspectives in Social Psychology Ser.). (Illus.). 200p. 1980. 22.50 (ISBN 0-306-40495-8, Plenum Pr). Plenum Pub.
Lerner, Michael. The New Socialist Revolution. 488p. 1973. 8.95 o.p. (ISBN 0-440-06372-8). Delacorte.
Lerner, Michael G. Pierre Loti. (World Authors Ser.: France: No. 277). 1974. lib. bdg. 12.50 (ISBN 0-8057-2546-6). Twayne.
Lerner, Natan. U. N. Convention on the Elimination of Al Forms of Racial Discrimination. LC 80-51738. 278p. 1980. 37.50x (ISBN 90-286-0160-0). Sijthoff & Noordhoff.
Lerner, Norbert, jt. auth. see Sobel, Max A.
Lerner, Norbert, jt. auth. see Sobol, Max A.
Lerner, Richard M. Concepts & Theories of Human Development. LC 75-12098. 1976. text ed. 14.95 (ISBN 0-201-04342-4). A-W.
Lerner, Rita G. & Trigg, George L., eds. Encyclopedia of Physics. 1980. text ed. 99.50 (ISBN 0-201-04313-0). A-W.
Lerner, Robert E. The Heresy of the Free Spirit in the Later Middle Ages. LC 78-145790. 1972. 20.00x (ISBN 0-520-01908-3). U of Cal Pr.
Lerner, Sharon. Nitty-Gritty Rhyming Riddle Book. (Electric Company Ser.). (Illus.). (gr. 1-5). 1973. PLB 5.38 (ISBN 0-307-64823-0, Golden Pr). Western Pub.
LeRoi, David. The Aquarium. 5.50x (ISBN 0-392-06613-0, LTB). Soccer.
Le Romain, Jacques H. Principles of the Flute, Recorder & Oboe. Lasocki, David, ed. 1978. 7.50 o.p. (ISBN 0-214-65942-9, 8026, Dist. by Arco). Barrie & Jenkins.
Le Rossignol, J. N. & Holliday, C. B. A Pharmacopoeia for Chiropodists. 8th ed. 1971. 5.95 o.p. (ISBN 0-571-04728-9, Pub. by Faber & Faber). Merrimack Bk Serv.
Leroux, Gaston. The Mystery of the Yellow Room. lib. bdg. 13.95x (ISBN 0-89966-141-6). Buccaneer Bks.
LeRoy, Dave, jt. auth. see Brosius, Jack.
LeRoy, David. The Outdoorsman's Guide to Government Surplus. 1978. 9.95 (ISBN 0-8092-7612-7); pap. 5.95 o.p. (ISBN 0-8092-7611-9). Contemp Bks.
Leroy, Douglas. I Didn't Know That. 1973. pap. 1.75 (ISBN 0-87148-425-0). Pathway Pr.
Leroy, F., ed. Blastocyst-Endometrium Relationships. (Progress in Reproductive Biology Ser.: Vol. 7). (Illus.). 338p. 1980. 118.75 (ISBN 3-8055-0988-X). S Karger.
LeRoy, Gen. Cold Feet. (gr. 7 up). 1981. pap. 1.75 (ISBN 0-440-91336-5, LE). Dell.
Lerrigo, Marion O. & Cassidy, Michael. Doctor Talks to Nine to Twelve Year Olds. (Illus.). 1980. pap. 2.50 (ISBN 0-910304-03-3). Budlong.
Lertz, Richard. Dracula's Children. 208p. 1981. 12.95 (ISBN 0-932966-15-2). Permanent Pr.
Lerumo, A. Fifty Fighting Years: The Communist Party of South Africa, 1921-1971. (Illus.). 1971. 4.00 o.p. (ISBN 0-8285-9101-6). Inkululeko.
Le Sage, Alain R. The Bachelor of Salamanca, 2 vols. in 1. Lockman, John, tr. LC 80-2488. 1981. Repr. of 1767 ed. 98.50 (ISBN 0-404-19122-3). AMS Pr.
--Le Diable Boiteux, or the Devil Upon Two Sticks. LC 73-170518. (Foundations of the Novel Ser.: Vol. 13). lib. bdg. 50.00 (ISBN 0-8240-0525-2). Garland Pub.
--The History & Adventures of Gil Blas of Santillane. LC 74-170537. (Foundations of the Novel Ser.: Vol. 27). Part 1. lib. bdg. 50.00 (ISBN 0-8240-0539-2). Garland Pub.
--The History & Adventures of Gil Blas of Santillane. LC 71-170539. (Foundations of the Novel Ser.: Vol. 28). Part 2. lib. bdg. 50.00 (ISBN 0-8240-0540-6). Garland Pub.
--The History of Vanillo Gonzales, Surnamed the Merry Bachelor. LC 80-2489. 1981. Repr. of 1881 ed. 48.00 (ISBN 0-404-19123-1). AMS Pr.
Lesavoy, Malcolm A. Reconstruction of the Head & Neck. (Illus.). 350p. 1981. write for info. (ISBN 0-683-04949-6). Williams & Wilkins.
Lesavoy, Malcolm A., jt. auth. see Meals, Roy.
Lesberg, Sandy. Violence in Our Time. (Illus.). 256p. 19.95x (ISBN 0-8464-0988-7). Beekman Pubs.
Lesburg, Sandy. Sandy Lesburg's One Hundred Great Restaurants of America. Michaelman, Herbert, ed. 1981. 12.95 (ISBN 0-517-53988-8, Michaelman Books). Crown.
Leschot, N., jt. auth. see Harris, M.
Lescroart, John. Sunburn. 224p. (Orig.). 1981. pap. 2.25 (ISBN 0-523-41187-1). Pinnacle Bks.
Lescroat, John, ed. see Fahey, John.
LeSeuer, Joe, jt. ed. see Berkson, Bill.
Le Seur, Jean F. Ossian Ou les Bardes. Geosset, Philip & Rosen, Charles, eds. LC 76-49219. (Early Romantic Opera Ser.). 1979. lib. bdg. 82.00 (ISBN 0-8240-2936-4). Garland Pub.
Lesgold, Alan M. & Perfetti, Charles A., eds. Interactive Processes in Reading. LC 80-21048. 448p. 1981. professional reference text 24.95 (ISBN 0-89859-079-5). L Erlbaum Assocs.
Lesh, Donald. Treatise on Thoroughbred Selection. new ed. 12.25 (ISBN 0-85131-296-9, Dist. by Sporting Book Center). J A Allen.
LeShan, Eda. Learning to Say Good-by: When a Parent Dies. LC 76-15155. (Illus.). (gr. 3 up). 7.95 (ISBN 0-02-756360-X, 75636). Macmillan.
--The Roots of Crime: What You Need to Know About Crime & What You Can Do About It. LC 80-69999. 192p. (gr. 7 up). 1981. 8.95 (ISBN 0-590-07532-2, Four Winds). Schol Bk Serv.
--What's Going to Happen to Me? When Parents Separate or Divorce. LC 78-4340. (Illus.). 144p. (gr. 3 up). 1978. 7.95 (ISBN 0-590-07535-7, Four Winds). Schol Bk Serv.
--What's the Matter with Me? (gr. 7-12). 1976. pap. 1.25 o.p. (ISBN 0-590-10162-5, Schol Pap). Schol Bk Serv.
--Winning the Losing Battle. 176p. (Orig.). 1981. pap. 2.50 (ISBN 0-553-14147-3). Bantam.
--The Wonderful Crisis of Middle Age. 320p. 1974. pap. 2.95 (ISBN 0-446-93746-0). Warner Bks.
--You & Your Feelings. 128p. (gr. 7 up). 1975. 7.95 (ISBN 0-02-757330-3). Macmillan.
LeShan, Eda, jt. auth. see Polk, Lee.
LeShan, Eda J. Conspiracy Against Childhood. LC 67-28453. 1967. pap. 5.95 (ISBN 0-689-70276-0, 182). Atheneum.
LeShan, Lawrence. Alternate Realities. 252p. 1976. 8.95 (ISBN 0-87131-217-4). M Evans.
--The Medium, the Mystic & the Physicist. 304p. 1975. pap. 1.95 o.p. (ISBN 0-685-50990-7, 24408-7-195). Ballantine.
--Toward a General Theory of the Paranormal. 3rd ed. LC 73-80027. (Parapsychological Monograph No. 9). 1969. pap. 4.00 (ISBN 0-912328-13-4). Parapsych Foun.
--You Can Fight for Your Life. 1978. pap. 1.95 (ISBN 0-515-04502-0). Jove Pubns.
Leshem, Y. The Molecular & Hormonal Basis of Plant Growth Regulation. LC 73-6802. 168p. 1974. 14.50 (ISBN 0-08-017649-6). Pergamon.
Leshin, Geraldine. Nineteen Eighty Report on Equal Employment Opportunity & Affirmative Action: The Roots Grow Deeper. 526p. 1980. pap. text ed. 14.00 (ISBN 0-89215-110-2). U Cal LA Indus Rel.
Lesick, Lawrence T. The Lane Rebels: Evangelicalism & Antislavery in Antebellum America. LC 80-24123. (Studies in Evangelicalism: No. 2). 287p. 1980. 15.00 (ISBN 0-8108-1372-6). Scarecrow.
Le Sieg, Theodore. I Can Write - by Me, Myself. (Illus.). (ps-1). 1971. 3.95 (ISBN 0-394-82323-0, BYR). Random.
Lesikar, Raymond V. Basic Business Communication. 1979. 16.95x (ISBN 0-256-02141-4). Irwin.
--Business Communication: Theory & Application. 4th ed. 1980. 18.50x (ISBN 0-256-02332-8). Irwin.
--Business Communication: Theory & Application. 3rd ed. 1976. text ed. 16.50x o.p. (ISBN 0-256-01818-9). Irwin.
--Report Writing for Business. 5th ed. 1977. text ed. 17.25x (ISBN 0-256-01900-2). Irwin.
Lesikar, Raymond V., jt. auth. see Perlick, Walter W.
Lesko, Leonard H. The Ancient Egyptian Book of Two Ways. (California Library Reprint Ser.). 1978. 15.00x (ISBN 0-520-03514-3). U of Cal Pr.
--Index of the Spells on Egyptian Middle Kingdom Coffins & Related Documents. LC 79-66500. (Orig.). 1979. pap. text ed. 6.00x (ISBN 0-930548-02-7). B C Scribe.
Lesko, Leonard H., ed. Dictionary of Late Egyptian, 2 vols. 1980. lib. bdg. write for info. (ISBN 0-930548-03-5); pap. text ed. write for info. (ISBN 0-930548-04-3). B C Scribe.
Leslau, Wolf. Concise Amharic Dictionary. LC 73-90668. 1976. 65.00x (ISBN 0-520-02660-8). U of Cal Pr.
--Ethiopians Speak: Studies in Cultural Background. Incl. No. I. Harari. (U. C. Publ. in Near Eastern Studies: Vol. 7). 1965. pap. 11.50x (ISBN 0-520-09300-3); No. II. Chaha. (U. C. Publ. in Near Eastern Studies: Vol. 9). 1966. pap. 10.50x (ISBN 0-520-09303-8). U of Cal Pr.
--Etymological Dictionary of Harari. (U. C. Publ. in Near Eastern Studies: Vol. 1). 1963. pap. 9.00x (ISBN 0-520-09293-7). U of Cal Pr.
Leslie, Charles, ed. Asian Medical Systems: A Comparative Study. LC 73-91674. 1976. 23.75x (ISBN 0-520-02680-2); pap. 7.95x (ISBN 0-520-03511-9). U of Cal Pr.
Leslie, D. C. Developments in the Theory of Turbulence. (Illus.). 368p. 1973. 38.50x o.p. (ISBN 0-19-856318-3). Oxford U Pr.
Leslie, Douglas. Cases & Materials on Labor Law. 1979. 21.00 (ISBN 0-316-52157-4); pap. 3.95 statutory supplement (ISBN 0-316-52158-2). Little.
Leslie, Douglas L. Labor Law in a Nutshell. LC 79-158396. (Nutshell Ser.). 403p. 1979. pap. text ed. 6.95 (ISBN 0-8299-2053-6). West Pub.
Leslie, Elizabeth M., jt. auth. see Leslie, Gerald R.
Leslie, Gerald R. The Family in Social Context. 4th ed. (Illus.). 1979. text ed. 15.95x (ISBN 0-19-502423-0). Oxford U Pr.
Leslie, Gerald R. & Leslie, Elizabeth M. Marriage in a Changing World. 2nd ed. LC 79-16195. 1980. text ed. 16.95x (ISBN 0-471-05593-X); tchrs'. manual avail. (ISBN 0-471-06271-5); study guide avail. (ISBN 0-471-06104-2). Wiley.
Leslie, Gerald R., jt. auth. see Horton, Paul B.
Leslie, Glenn F. & Gold, Marvin. Meet the Meters. 1976. pap. 2.95 o.p. (ISBN 0-345-25246-2). Ballantine.
Leslie, J. D., ed. see Solar Energy Conversion Course, 5th, University of Waterloo, Ontario, August 6-19, 1978.
Leslie, John K. Spanish for Conversation. 4th ed. LC 75-3774. 1976. text ed. 17.95 (ISBN 0-471-52810-2); instructor's manual avail. (ISBN 0-471-01417-6); wkbk avail (ISBN 0-471-52811-0); tapes avail. (ISBN 0-471-01841-4). Wiley.
Leslie, John W. Seeking the Competitive Dollar: College Management in the Seventies. 1971. pap. 3.00 (ISBN 0-89964-033-8). CASE.
Leslie, L. Et Al & Zoubek, C. Gregg Shorthand for Colleges, Transcription. 2nd ed. LC 79-11916. (Series 90). (Illus.). 448p. 1980. text ed. 16.50 (ISBN 0-07-037760-X, G); instructor's manual 4.90 (ISBN 0-07-037764-2); wkbk. 5.95 (ISBN 0-07-037762-6); key to wkbk. 3.40 (ISBN 0-07-037763-4); student's trans. 4.45 (ISBN 0-07-037761-8); teach. dict. 12.80 (ISBN 0-686-62427-0). McGraw.
Leslie, Larry L., jt. auth. see Richardson, Richard C., Jr.
Leslie, Louis A. & Zoubek, Charles E. Gregg Shorthand, Functional Method. (Diamond Jubilee Ser.). 1963. text ed. 10.68 (ISBN 0-07-037310-8, G); wkbk. 4.40 (ISBN 0-07-037308-6). McGraw.
--Gregg Shorthand Functional Method. 2nd ed. (Diamond Jubilee Ser). 1971. text ed. 9.96 (ISBN 0-07-037255-1, G); inst. handbk. 3.90 (ISBN 0-07-037256-X); wkbk. 4.40 (ISBN 0-07-037250-0); key to wkbk. 2.70 (ISBN 0-07-037251-9). McGraw.
Leslie, Louis A., et al. Gregg Dictation: Diamond Jubilee Series. 2nd ed. 1970. text ed. 9.96 (ISBN 0-07-037257-8, G); instructor's handbk 3.90 (ISBN 0-07-037258-6); student transcript 3.76 (ISBN 0-07-037259-4); wkbk 4.40 (ISBN 0-07-037260-8); key to wkbk 2.90 (ISBN 0-07-037261-6); tapes avail. (ISBN 0-07-086052-1) (ISBN 0-07-087482-4). McGraw.
--Gregg Notehand. 2nd ed. 1968. text ed. 11.04 (ISBN 0-07-037331-0, G); instructor's guide 4.30 (ISBN 0-07-037338-8); exercises 5.18 (ISBN 0-07-037343-4); inst. key to exercises 4.30 (ISBN 0-07-037344-2). McGraw.
--Gregg Shorthand for Colleges, Vol. 2. 2nd ed. (Diamond Jubilee Ser.). (Illus.). 448p. 1973. text ed. 14.95 (ISBN 0-07-037406-6, G); instructor's handbk. 4.35 (ISBN 0-07-037409-0); wkbk. 5.45 (ISBN 0-07-037408-2); key to wkbk. 3.10 (ISBN 0-07-037410-4); tapes avail. (ISBN 0-07-086345-8); student transcript 4.45 (ISBN 0-07-037407-4); cassettes avail. (ISBN 0-07-087615-0). McGraw.
Leslie, Mary, jt. auth. see Seltz, David D.
Leslie, R. F. History of Poland Since Eighteen Sixty-Three. LC 78-73246. (Soviet & East European Studies). 528p. 1980. 45.00 (ISBN 0-521-22645-7). Cambridge U Pr.
Leslie, R. F., ed. see Layamon.
Leslie, Robert C. Jesus & Logotherapy. LC 65-11077. (Series AD). 1968. pap. 2.25 (ISBN 0-687-19927-1, Apex). Abingdon.
Leslie, Rochelle. Tears of Passion, Tears of Shame. 384p. (Orig.). 1980. pap. 2.25 (ISBN 0-515-05445-3). Jove Pubns.
Leslie, William. Message from Angola. Date not set. 4.95 (ISBN 0-8062-1654-9). Carlton.
Leslie, William C. The Physical Metallurgy of Steels. (M-H Materials Science & Engineering Ser.). 368p. 1981. text ed. 29.50 (ISBN 0-07-037780-4). McGraw.
Leslie-Melville, Betty & Leslie-Melville, Jock. Elephant Have Right of Way. LC 72-84927. 264p. 1973. 6.95 o.p. (ISBN 0-385-07943-5). Doubleday.
--Raising Daisy Rothschild. (Illus.). 1979. pap. 1.95 o.s.i. (ISBN 0-446-89948-8). Warner Bks.
Leslie-Melville, Jock, jt. auth. see Leslie-Melville, Betty.
Lesnin, I. M. & Petrova, Luba. Spoken Russian. Incl. Bk. 1, Units 1-12. vii, 382p. 10.00x (ISBN 0-87950-190-1); Bk. 2, Units 13-30. 397p. 10.00x (ISBN 0-87950-191-X); Records Six 12-Inch lp (33.3 rpm) o.s.i (ISBN 0-87950-194-4); Record Course-Bk. 1 & Records. text ed. o.s.i (ISBN 0-87950-195-2); Cassettes I, Six Dual Track. 60.00x (ISBN 0-87950-196-0); Cassette Course-Bk. 1 & Cassettes I. text ed. 65.00x (ISBN 0-87950-197-9); Cassettes IE for Bk. 1, 28 Dual Track. 135.00 (ISBN 0-87950-200-2); Cassettes IE & Bk. 1. text ed. 140.00 (ISBN 0-87950-202-9); Cassettes II E for Bk. 2, 11 Dual Track. 95.00 (ISBN 0-87950-201-0); Book 2 & Cassettes II. text ed. 100.00 (ISBN 0-87950-203-7); Combined Reel Tape Course, Books 1 & 2 Plus Reel Tapes 1 & 2. text ed. 220.00 (ISBN 0-87950-109-X). LC 74-176010. (Spoken Lang Ser). (Prog. Bk.). 1971. Spoken Lang Serv.
Lesnoff-Caravaglia, Gari. Education As Existential Possibility. LC 76-171469. 112p. 1972. 7.50 o.p. (ISBN 0-8022-2068-1). Philos Lib.
--Health Care of the Elderly: Strategies for Prevention & Intervention. LC 79-19192. 1980. text ed. 22.95x (ISBN 0-87705-417-7); pap. text ed. 9.95x (ISBN 0-87705-486-X). Human Sci Pr.
Lesowitz, Robert I. Rules for Raising Kids. (Illus.). 200p. 1974. pap. 9.50 (ISBN 0-398-03146-0). C C Thomas.
L'Esperance, Frances, jt. ed. see Friedman, Eli A.
L'Esperance, Francis A., Jr. Stereoscopic Atlas of Ocular Photocoagulation. LC 75-33111. (Illus.). 338p. 1975. text ed. 77.50 (ISBN 0-8016-2824-5). Mosby.
L'Esperance, Francis A., Jr., ed. Current Diagnosis & Management of Chorioretinal Diseases. (Illus.). 1977. text ed. 67.50 o.p. (ISBN 0-8016-2949-7). Mosby.
Lessa, William A. More Tales from Ulithi Atoll. (U. C. Publications in Folklore & Mythology Studies: Vol. 32). 1980. pap. 15.00 (ISBN 0-520-09615-0). U of Cal Pr.
Lessard, Victoria C., jt. auth. see Hall, Jack.
Lesse, Nicholas, tr. see Melanchthon, Philipp.
Lesse, Stanley. The Future of the Health Sciences. 216p. 1981. text ed. 18.50x (ISBN 0-8290-0250-2). Irvington.
Lessem, Don. Life Is No Yuk for the Yak. 1977. 5.95 o.p. (ISBN 0-686-58576-3). Scribner.
Lesser, Alexander. The Pawnee Ghost Dance Hand Game: A Study of Cultural Change. LC 79-82340. (Illus.). 1978. 20.00 (ISBN 0-299-07480-3); pap. 7.95 (ISBN 0-299-07484-6). U of Wis Pr.
Lesser, Melvin P. The United States in the 20th Century: A Programed Approach. 2nd ed. 1975. spiral bdg. 8.50x (ISBN 0-87543-158-5). Lucas.

Lesser, Michael. Nutrition & Vitamin Therapy. 224p. 1981. pap. 2.50 (ISBN 0-553-14437-5). Bantam.

Lesser, Milton, et al. Contemporary Science Book 2. (gr. 6-10). 1977. pap. text ed. 7.33 (ISBN 0-87720-006-8). AMSCO Sch.

--Contemporary Science Book 3. (gr. 6-10). 1978. pap. text ed. 8.33 (ISBN 0-87720-008-4). AMSCO Sch.

--Contemporary Science Book,1. (gr. 6-10). 1977. pap. text ed. 7.33 (ISBN 0-87720-002-5). AMSCO Sch.

Lesser, Milton S. Life Science: Intermediate Level. (gr. 7-10). 1967. pap. text ed. 5.42 (ISBN 0-87720-005-X); tchr's ed. 4.00 (ISBN 0-87720-004-1); wkbk ed. plus free unit tests 6.42 (ISBN 0-87720-003-3). AMSCO Sch.

Lesser, Milton S., jt. auth. see Hall, Mark A.

Lesser, R. H. Indian Mosaic. (Writers Workshop Greybird Book Ser.). 41p. 1975. 12.00 (ISBN 0-88253-564-1); pap. text ed. 4.80 (ISBN 0-88253-563-3). Ind-US Inc.

Lesser, Rika, tr. see Ekelof, Gunnar.

Lessin, Roy. Dads Are God's Idea. (God's Idea Books Ser.). (Illus.). 32p. (ps-4). 1981. pap. 1.25 (ISBN 0-87123-176-X, 210176). Bethany Fell.

--Families Are God's Idea. (God's Idea Books Ser.). (Illus.). 32p. (ps-4). 1981. pap. 1.25 (ISBN 0-87123-177-8, 210177). Bethany Fell.

--How to Be Parents of Happy Obedient Children. 1978. 6.95 (ISBN 0-89728-003-2, 702120); pap. 3.95 (ISBN 0-686-67298-4). Omega Pubns OR.

--Kids Are God's Idea. (God's Idea Books Ser.). (Illus.). 32p. (ps-4). 1981. pap. 1.25 (ISBN 0-87123-178-6, 210178). Bethany Fell.

--Moms Are God's Idea. (God's Idea Books Ser.). (Illus.). 32p. (ps-4). 1981. pap. 1.25 (ISBN 0-87123-175-1, 210175). Bethany Fell.

Lessing, Doris. The Grass Is Singing. 288p. 1976. pap. 1.75 o.p. (ISBN 0-445-08391-3). Popular Lib.

--In Pursuit of the English. 1979. 16.95x (ISBN 0-8464-0089-8). Beekman Pubs.

--The Sirian Experiments. LC 79-27710. 304p. 1981. 11.95 (ISBN 0-394-51231-6). Knopf.

Lessing, Erich, jt. auth. see Westerman, Claus.

Lessing, Gotthold. Emilia Galotti. Stahl, E. L., ed. (Blackwell's German Text Ser.). 1973. pap. 9.95x (ISBN 0-631-01390-3, Pub. by Basil Blackwell). Biblio Dist.

Lessing, Gotthold E. Laocoon & Other Writings. 1959. 12.95x (ISBN 0-460-00843-9, Evman). Dutton.

Lester & Levy. Jacob Epstein. LC 78-50724. Date not set. price not set casebound (ISBN 0-916526-05-4). Maran Pub.

Lester, Andrew D. & Lester, Judith L. Understanding Aging Parents. LC 80-17832. (A Christian Care Bk.). 1980. pap. 5.95 (ISBN 0-664-24329-0). Westminster.

Lester, C. Edwards. The Glory & Shame of England, 2 vols. (The Development of Industrial Society Ser.). 905p. 1980. Repr. 36.00x (ISBN 0-7165-1789-2, Pub. by Irish Academic Pr). Biblio Dist.

Lester, Charles E. Artists of America: S. T. A Series of Biographical Sketches of American Artists. LC 68-8689. (American Art Ser). (Illus.). 1970. Repr. of 1846 ed. lib. bdg. 29.50 (ISBN 0-306-71169-9). Da Capo.

Lester, David. Gambling Today. 160p. 1979. text ed. 13.75 (ISBN 0-398-03952-6). C C Thomas.

--A Physiological Basis for Personality Traits: A New Theory of Personality. (Illus.). 138p. 1974. 13.75 (ISBN 0-398-03078-2). C C Thomas.

--The Psychological Basis of Handwriting Analysis: The Relationship of Handwriting to Personality & Psychopathology. LC 79-23957. 192p. 1981. text ed. 18.95 (ISBN 0-88229-533-0). Nelson-Hall.

--Unusual Sexual Behavior: The Standard Deviations. 256p. 1976. 22.75 (ISBN 0-398-03343-9). C C Thomas.

--The Use of Alternative Modes for Communication in Psychotherapy: The Computer,The Book,The Telephone,The Television,The Tape Recorder. 120p. 1977. 14.75 (ISBN 0-398-03655-1). C C Thomas.

Lester, David & Brockopp, Gene W. Crisis Intervention & Counseling by Telephone. (Illus.). 336p. 1976. pap. 29.50 photocopy ed., spiral (ISBN 0-398-02641-6). C C Thomas.

Lester, David & Lester, Gene. Crime of Passion: Murder & the Murderer. LC 74-20788. 1975. 15.95 (ISBN 0-88229-139-4). Nelson-Hall.

Lester, David, et al, eds. Suicide: A Guide to Information Sources. LC 80-71. (Social Issues & Social Problems Information Guide Ser.: Vol. 3). 30.00 (ISBN 0-8103-1415-0). Gale.

Lester, G. A. The Anglo Saxons: How They Lived & Worked. LC 76-20156. 1976. 11.95 (ISBN 0-8023-1266-7). Dufour.

Lester, Gene, jt. auth. see Lester, David.

Lester, Henry M., jt. auth. see Morgan, Willard D.

Lester, J. C. & Wilson, D. L. Ku Klux Klan. LC 71-114758. (Civil Liberties in Amer. History Ser.). (Illus.). 208p. 1973. Repr. of 1905 ed. lib. bdg. 22.50 (ISBN 0-306-71927-4). Da Capo.

Lester, Judith L., jt. auth. see Lester, Andrew D.

Lester, Julius. All Is Well. 1976. 9.95 o.p. (ISBN 0-688-03045-9). Morrow.

Lester, Julius, jt. ed. see Alexander, Rae P.

Lester, Katherine, et al. Historic Costume. rev. ed. (gr. 10-12). 1977. text ed. 12.00 (ISBN 0-87002-174-5). Bennett IL.

Lester, Malcom. Anthony Merry Redivivus: A Reappraisal of the British Minister to the United States, 1803-6. LC 77-20910. 1978. 13.95x (ISBN 0-8139-0750-0). U Pr of Va.

Lester, Mary. A Woman's Guide to Starting a Small Business. LC 80-24298. pap. 2.50 (ISBN 0-87576-093-7). Pilot Bks.

Lester, Richard I. Confederate Finance & Purchasing in Great Britain. LC 74-13916. (Illus.). 1975. 17.50x (ISBN 0-8139-0513-3). U Pr of Va.

Lester, Richard K., jt. auth. see Willrich, Mason.

Lester, Ronald H. & Enrick, Norbert Lloyd. Quality Control for Profit. LC 76-58534. (Illus.). 1977. 23.00 (ISBN 0-8311-1117-8). Indus Pr.

Lester-Smith, L. H., ed. The Universal Flame. 263p. 1975. 6.50 (ISBN 0-8356-7506-8). Theos Pub Hse.

Le Strange, Nicholas. Merry Passages & Jeasts: A Manuscript Jestbook of Sir Nicholas le Strange, 1603-1655. Lippincott, H. F., ed. (Salzburg Studies in English Literature, Elizabethan & Renaissance Studies: No. 29). (Illus.). 266p. 1974. pap. text ed. 25.00x (ISBN 0-391-01460-9). Humanities.

L'Estrange, Roger, ed. see Castillo Solorzano, Alonso De.

Le Sueur, Meridel. Conquistadores. LC 72-6051. (First Bks). (Illus.). 96p. (gr. 5-7). 1973. PLB 4.90 o.p. (ISBN 0-531-00744-8). Watts.

--The Mound Builders. LC 73-22497. (First Bks). (Illus.). 72p. (gr. 5-7). 1974. PLB 4.90 o.p. (ISBN 0-531-02717-1). Watts.

Lesy, Michael. Time Frames: The Meaning of Family Pictures. (Illus.). 1980. 20.00 (ISBN 0-394-42456-5); pap. 8.95 (ISBN 0-394-73958-2). Pantheon.

Lesznai, Anna. The Wanderings of the Little Blue Butterfly in Fairyland. Bodoczky, Caroline, tr. from Hungarian. (Illus.). 23p. 1978. 7.50x (ISBN 963-13-0618-6). Intl Pubns Serv.

Letarouilly, Paul. Buildings of Renaissance Rome: An American Student Edition. abr. ed. Bayley, John B., ed. (Classical America Series in Art & Architecture). (Illus.). 96p. text ed. cancelled (ISBN 0-8038-0076-2); pap. text ed. cancelled (ISBN 0-8038-0075-4). Architectural.

Letcher, John. Self-Contained Celestial Navigation with H.O. 208. LC 76-8782. (Illus.). 1977. 17.50 (ISBN 0-87742-082-3). Intl Marine.

Letchworth, L. Tom. Sun of Superlove. LC 80-53694. (Illus.). 120p. (Orig.). (gr. 7 up). 1980. pap. 3.95 (ISBN 0-9602334-1-5). Superlove.

Leth, Pamela C. & Leth, Steven A. Public Communications. Brooks, W. D. & Vogel, R. A., eds. LC 76-44139. (Ser. in Speech Communication). 1977. pap. text ed. 5.95 (ISBN 0-8465-7604-X); instr's guide 3.95 (ISBN 0-8465-7607-4). Benjamin-Cummings.

Leth, Steven A., jt. auth. see Leth, Pamela C.

Lethaby, et al. Life & Work. Stansky, Peter & Shewan, Rodney, eds. LC 76-17779. (Aesthetic Movement & the Arts & Crafts Movement Ser.). (Illus.). 1978. Repr. of 1926 ed. lib. bdg. 44.00x (ISBN 0-8240-2485-0). Garland Pub.

Letham, D. S., jt. ed. see Stewart, P. R.

Lethbridge, David G., ed. Government & Industry Relationships: The Lubbock Memorial Lectures, 1975. 200p. 1976. text ed. 25.00 (ISBN 0-08-019733-7); pap. text ed. 17.50 (ISBN 0-08-019732-9). Pergamon.

Lethbridge, T. C. ESP: Beyond Time & Distance. 1965. 10.00 (ISBN 0-7100-1740-5). Routledge & Kegan.

--The Legend of the Sons of God: A Fantasy? (Illus.). 1972. 12.00 (ISBN 0-7100-7159-0). Routledge & Kegan.

--The Monkey's Tail: A Study in Evolution & Parapsychology. (Illus.). 1969. 12.00 (ISBN 0-7100-6598-1). Routledge & Kegan.

--The Power of the Pendulum. 1976. 12.00 (ISBN 0-7100-8337-8). Routledge & Kegan.

--A Step in the Dark. 1967. 12.00 (ISBN 0-7100-1741-3). Routledge & Kegan.

Lethbridge, Thomas C. Herdsmen & Hermits. 1950. text ed. 4.25x (ISBN 0-391-01986-4). Humanities.

Letherman, K. M. Automatic Controls for Heating & Airconditioning: Principles & Applications. (International Series on Heating, Ventilation & Refrigeration: Vol. 15). (Illus.). 220p. 1981. 30.00 (ISBN 0-08-023222-1). Pergamon.

Letkemann, Peter. Crime As Work. LC 73-12071. (Illus.). 192p. 1973. pap. 2.95 o.p. (ISBN 0-13-192922-4, S308, Spec). P-H.

Letokhov, V. S., jt. ed. see Feld, M. S.

Le Tord, Bijou. The Generous Cow. LC 76-14464. (Illus.). 40p. (ps-2). 1977. 5.95 o.s.i. (ISBN 0-8193-0852-8, Four Winds); PLB 5.41 o.s.i. (ISBN 0-8193-0853-6). Schol Bk Serv.

--Nice & cozy. LC 80-11376. (Illus.). 32p. (ps-3). 1980. 8.95 (ISBN 0-590-07668-X, Four Winds). Schol Bk Serv.

--A Perfect Place to Be. LC 75-33098. (Illus.). 40p. (ps-3). 1976. 5.95 o.s.i. (ISBN 0-8193-0842-0, Four Winds); PLB 5.41 o.s.i. (ISBN 0-8193-0843-9). Schol Bk Serv.

--Picking & Weaving. LC 79-23457. (Illus.). 32p. (gr. k-3). 1980. 8.95 (ISBN 0-590-07642-6, Four Winds). Schol Bk Serv.

Letourneau, Gene. Sportsmen Say. 1977. 8.95 (ISBN 0-930096-01-0). G Gannett.

LeTourneau, Richard H. Success Without Compromise. 1977. pap. 3.50 (ISBN 0-88207-757-0). Victor Bks.

Le Tourneau, Roger. Fez in the Age of the Marinides. Clement, Besse A., tr. LC 61-6496. (Centers of Civilization Ser: No. 4). 1961. 5.95 (ISBN 0-8061-0482-1); pap. 3.95 (ISBN 0-8061-1198-4). U of Okla Pr.

Letournel, E. & Judet, R. Fracture to the Acetabulum. (Illus.). 420p. 1981. 162.00 (ISBN 0-387-09875-5). Springer-Verlag.

Lett, J. T. & Adler, H. I., eds. Advances in Radiation Biology, Vol. 9. (Serial Publication Ser.). 1981. write for info. (ISBN 0-12-035409-8). Acad Pr.

Lett, J. T. & Edler, Howard, eds. Advances in Radiation Biology, Vol. 7. 1978. 52.50 (ISBN 0-12-035407-1); lib. ed. 67.50 (ISBN 0-12-035478-0); microfiche 34.50 (ISBN 0-12-035479-9). Acad Pr.

Lettau, Reinhard. Breakfast in Miami. Pradi, Julie & Lettau, Reinhard, trs. 1981. lib. bdg. 14.95 (ISBN 0-7145-3831-0); pap. 5.95 (ISBN 0-7145-3834-5). Riverrun NY. Postponed.

Lettau, Reinhard & Ferlinghetti, Lawrence, eds. Love Poems of Karl Marx. LC 76-8200. 1977. pap. 2.00 o.p. (ISBN 0-87286-087-6). City Lights.

Lettau, Reinhard, tr. see Lettau, Reinhard.

Lettis, Richard. Catcher in the Rye by J. D. Salinger. LC 63-17168. (Orig.). 1964. pap. text ed. 1.95 (ISBN 0-8120-0001-3). Barron.

Letton, Jeannette. The Haunting of Cliffside. LC 74-7668. 250p. 1975. 7.95 o.s.i. (ISBN 0-8027-5326-4). Walker & Co.

Letts, Rosa M. The Renaissance. (Cambridge Introduction to the History of Art Ser.: No. 3). (Illus.). 100p. Date not set. 19.95 (ISBN 0-521-23394-1); pap. 6.95 (ISBN 0-521-29957-8). Cambridge U Pr.

Lettvin, Maggie. The Beautiful Machine. 448p. 1975. pap. 2.95 o.p. (ISBN 0-345-27350-8). Ballantine.

Letwin, William. Law & Economic Policy in America: The Evolution of the Sherman Antitrust Act. LC 80-21868. xi, 304p. 1980. Repr. of 1965 ed. lib. bdg. 27.50x (ISBN 0-313-22651-2, LELE). Greenwood.

--Sir Josiah Child, Merchant Economist. (Kress Library of Business & Economics: No. 14). (Illus.). 1959. pap. 5.00x (ISBN 0-678-09909-X, Baker Lib). Kelley.

Leuba, jt. auth. see McCullough.

Leuba, James H. The Psychological Origin & the Nature of Religion. 94p. 1980. Repr. of 1909 ed. lib. bdg. 12.50 (ISBN 0-8482-1622-9). Norwood Edns.

--The Psychology of Religious Mysticism. 1972. 22.50 (ISBN 0-7100-7317-8). Routledge & Kegan.

Leuchtenburg, William E. Age of Change, from Nineteen Forty-Five. LC 63-8572. (Life History of the United States). (Illus.). (gr. 5 up). 1974. PLB 9.96 (ISBN 0-8094-0561-X, Pub. by Time-Life). Silver.

--Flood Control Politics: The Connecticut River Valley Problem, 1927-1950. LC 73-38834. (FDR & the Era of the New Deal Ser.). (Illus.). 1972. Repr. of 1953 ed. lib. bdg. 32.50 (ISBN 0-306-70446-3). Da Capo.

--New Deal & War, 1933-1945. LC 63-8572. (Life History of the United States). (Illus.). (gr. 5 up). 1974. PLB 9.96 (ISBN 0-8094-0560-1, Pub. by Time-Life). Silver.

--Perils of Prosperity: Nineteen Fourteen - Thirty Two. LC 58-5680. (Chicago History of America Civilization Ser). pap. 5.50 (ISBN 0-226-47369-4, CHAC12). U of Chicago Pr.

Leukart, R. H., jt. auth. see Otis, Jay L.

Leukel, Francis. Introduction to Physiological Psychology. 3rd ed. LC 75-33031. (Illus.). 1976. text ed. 17.95 (ISBN 0-8016-2974-8). Mosby.

--Physiological Psychology: A Study Guide. 2nd ed. 208p. 1976. pap. text ed. 8.00 (ISBN 0-8016-2968-3). Mosby.

Leukocyte Culture Conference, 9th. Immune Recognition: Proceedings. Rosenthal, Alan S., ed. 1975. 43.50 (ISBN 0-12-597850-2). Acad Pr.

Leuner, H. D. When Compassion Was a Crime: Germany's Silent Heroes, 1933-1945. 1978. pap. 12.95 (ISBN 0-85496-138-0). Dufour.

Leung, Chi-Keung. China: Railway Patterns & National Goals. LC 80-17030. (Research Papers). (Illus.). 233p. 1980. pap. 8.00 (ISBN 0-89065-102-7). U Chicago Dept Geog.

Leupold, Herbert C. Exposition of Genesis, 2 Vols. Vol. 1. 12.95 (ISBN 0-8010-5549-0); Vol. 2. 12.95 (ISBN 0-8010-5522-9). Baker Bk.

Leupold, Nancy S., tr. see Sandberg, Inger.

Leupold, Ulrich S. & Lehmann, Helmut T., eds. Luther's Works: Liturgy & Hymns, Vol. 53. LC 55-9893. 1965. 12.95 (ISBN 0-8006-0353-2, 1-353). Fortress.

Leusen, Isadore, jt. ed. see Vanhoutte, Paul M.

Leutenegger, Ralph R. Patient Care & Rehabilitation of Communication-Impaired Adults. (Illus.). 196p. 1975. 17.50 (ISBN 0-398-03473-7). C C Thomas.

--Sounds of American English: An Introduction to Phonetics. 1963. pap. 7.95x o.p. (ISBN 0-673-05702-X). Scott F.

Leuthold, D. A. Electioneering in a Democracy: Campaigns for Congress. LC 68-22891. 1968. pap. text ed. 6.95x o.p. (ISBN 0-471-52991-5). Wiley.

Leuthold, Steven. The Myths of Inflation & Investing. LC 80-67811. 1980. 27.50 (ISBN 0-87251-048-4). Crain Bks.

Leutwiler, Heinz, jt. auth. see Arsove, Maynard.

Leuv, John H. Van de see American College of Emergency Physicians.

Lev, Baruch. Financial Statement Analysis: A New Approach. (Contemporary Topics in Accounting Ser: Foundations of Finance). (Illus.). 288p. 1974. pap. text ed. 8.95 (ISBN 0-13-316364-4). P-H.

Lev, Daniel S. Islamic Courts in Indonesia: A Study in the Political Bases of Legal Institutions. LC 78-182281. 304p. 1972. 21.50x (ISBN 0-520-02173-8). U of Cal Pr.

Lev, Donald. Footnotes. Barkan, Stanley H., ed. (Cross-Cultural Review Chapbook 11). 16p. 1980. pap. 2.00 (ISBN 0-89304-810-0). Cross Cult.

Leva, Laudia. Hard to Kill. 1981. 6.95 (ISBN 0-533-04672-6). Vantage.

Levack, Daniel J., compiled by. Dune Master: A Pictorial Frank Herbert Bibliography. (Illus.). 96p. 1980. 17.50 (ISBN 0-934438-38-2); pap. 6.95 (ISBN 0-934438-37-4). Underwood-Miller.

--PKD: A Pictorial Philip K. Dick Bibliography. (Illus.). 144p. 1980. 17.50 (ISBN 0-934438-34-X); pap. 6.95 (ISBN 0-934438-33-1). Underwood-Miller.

Levack, Daniel J. & Owings, Mark, eds. Amber Dreams: A Pictorial Roger Zelazny Bibliography. (Illus.). 128p. 1980. 17.50 (ISBN 0-934438-40-4); pap. 6.95 (ISBN 0-934438-39-0). Underwood-Miller.

Levan, Susan. The Vegetable Parade. LC 77-8078. (Orig.). 1979. pap. 10.00 (ISBN 0-914908-90-1). Street Fiction.

Levandowsky, M. & Hunter, S. H., eds. Biochemistry & Physiology of Protozoa, Vol. 4. 2nd ed. 1980. write for info. (ISBN 0-12-444604-3). Acad Pr.

Levandowsky, Michael, ed. Biochemistry & Physiology of Protozoa, Vol. I. 2nd ed. LC 78-20045. 1979. 48.00, by subscription 41.50 (ISBN 0-12-444601-9). Acad Pr.

Levandowsky, Michael & Hutner, S. H., eds. Biochemistry & Physiology of Protozoa, Vol. 2. 2nd ed. 1979. 51.00 (ISBN 0-12-444602-7); subscription 44.00 (ISBN 0-12-444602-7). Acad Pr.

--Biochemistry & Physiology of Protozoa, Vol. 3. 2nd ed. LC 79-2045. 1980. 42.00 (ISBN 0-12-444603-5); subscription 35.50 (ISBN 0-12-444603-5). Acad Pr.

Levant, Lorna, jt. ed. see Clements, Robert J.

Levanthal, Lance. Z-Eighty Assembly Language Programming. (Assembly Language Programming Ser.: No. 3). (Orig.). 1979. pap. text ed. 16.99 (ISBN 0-931988-21-7). Osborne-McGraw.

Levanthal, Lance A. & Walsh, Colin. Microcomputer Experimentation with Intel SDK-85. 1980. text ed. 15.95 (ISBN 0-13-580860-X). P-H.

Levanway, Russell W. Advanced General Psychology. LC 70-145878. 1972. 17.75x (ISBN 0-88295-206-4). AHM Pub.

Levarie, Siegmund. Guillaume De Machaut. LC 70-98309. (Music Ser). 1969. Repr. of 1954 ed. lib. bdg. 15.00 (ISBN 0-306-71831-6). Da Capo.

--Mozart's Le Nozze Di Figaro. LC 77-5150. (Music Reprint Ser.). 1977. Repr. of 1952 ed. lib. bdg. 27.50 (ISBN 0-306-70897-3). Da Capo.

Levarie, Siegmund & Levy, Ernst. Tone: A Study in Musical Acoustics. 2nd ed. LC 80-29383. (Illus.). xvii, 256p. 1981. Repr. of 1980 ed. lib. bdg. 27.50x (ISBN 0-313-22499-4, LETO). Greenwood.

--Tone: A Study in Musical Acoustics. rev. ed. LC 80-16794. (Illus.). 280p. 1980. pap. 6.75x (ISBN 0-87338-250-1). Kent St U Pr.

Levasseur, Alain A. Precis in Conventional Obligations. 300p. 1980. text ed. 18.00 (ISBN 0-87215-334-7). Michie.

Levasseur, Georges, jt. auth. see Butler, William J.

Levater. Cendrillon (Cinderella) Date not set. 12.95 (ISBN 0-8120-5311-7). Barron. Postponed.

Levchev, Lyumbomir. The Mysterious Man. Phillipov, Vladimir, tr. LC 80-83426. (International Poetry: Vol. 4). 40p. 1981. 10.95 (ISBN 0-8214-0594-2); pap. 6.95 (ISBN 0-8214-0595-0). Ohio U Pr.

Leveen, Jacob. The Hebrew Bible in Art. LC 74-78239. (Illus.). 208p. 1974. Repr. 14.50 (ISBN 0-87203-045-8). Hermon.

Level, Dale A., Jr. & Galle, William P., Jr. Business Communication: Theory & Practice. 1980. 17.95x (ISBN 0-256-02203-8). Business Pubns.

Leven, Charles L., ed. The Mature Metropolis. LC 77-10363. 1978. 24.95 (ISBN 0-669-01844-9). Lexington Bks.

Leven, Charles L., et al. Analytical Framework for Regional Development Policy. 1970. 17.50x (ISBN 0-262-12036-4). MIT Pr.

Leven, Merwin. Accounting for Nonfinancial Managers. LC 80-19502. 175p. 1980. 50.00 (ISBN 0-932648-16-9). Boardroom.

Levenbach, Hans & Cleary, James P. The Forecasting Process for the Beginning Forecaster. (Illus.). 350p. 1981. text ed. 29.95 (ISBN 0-534-97975-0). Lifetime Learn.

Levendosky, Charles. Distances. 24p. 1980. pap. 4.50 (ISBN 0-937160-01-6). Dooryard.

--Perimeters. LC 78-105508. (Wesleyan Poetry Program: Vol. 49). 1970. 10.00x (ISBN 0-8195-2049-7, Pub. by Wesleyan U Pr); pap. 4.95 (ISBN 0-8195-1049-1). Columbia U Pr.

Levenfish & Smuslov. Rook Endings. pap. 10.95 (ISBN 0-7134-0449-3, Pub. by Batsford England). David & Charles.

Levenkron, Steven. The Best Little Girl in the World. 1979. pap. 2.50 (ISBN 0-446-91836-9). Warner Bks.

Levens, Alexander & Chalk, William. Graphics in Engineering Design. 3rd ed. LC 79-17291. 1980. text ed. 25.95 (ISBN 0-471-01478-8); tchrs' manual (ISBN 0-471-04998-0); wkbk. 1 a (ISBN 0-471-03133-X); wkbk. 2 a (ISBN 0-471-03214-X); wkbk. 3 a (ISBN 0-471-07749-6); solution manual 1 a; solution manual 2 a (ISBN 0-471-08104-3). Wiley.

Levens, R. G. Cicero: Verrine Orations V. 1946. 6.95 (ISBN 0-312-13825-3). St Martin.

Levenson, Alvin, ed. The Neuropsychiatric Side Effects of Drugs in the Elderly. LC 78-55806. (Aging Ser.: Vol. 9). 1979. 24.00 (ISBN 0-89004-285-3). Raven.

Levenson, Alvin J. & Hall, Richard C., eds. Neuropsychiatric Manifestations of Physical Disease in the Elderly. (Aging Ser.: Vol. 14). 175p. 1980. text ed. 17.00 (ISBN 0-89004-493-7). Raven.

Levenson, Alvin J. & Tollett, Susan M., eds. Multidisciplinary Assessment of the Geriatric Patient. 1981. text ed. price not set (ISBN 0-89004-492-9). Raven.

Levenson, Dorothy. First Book of Reconstruction. LC 78-117941. (First Bks). (Illus.). (gr. 4-6). 1970. PLB 4.90 o.p. (ISBN 0-531-00715-4). Watts.

--The First Book of the Civil War. rev. ed. (First Bks.). (Illus.). (gr. 4-7). lib. bdg. 6.45 s&l (ISBN 0-531-01291-3). Watts.

--Homesteaders & Indians. LC 79-136832. (First Bks). (Illus.). (gr. 4-6). 1971. PLB 4.90 o.p. (ISBN 0-531-00734-0); pap. 1.25 o.p. (ISBN 0-531-02314-1). Watts.

--Women of the West. LC 72-10441. (First Bks). (Illus.). 96p. (gr. 4-7). 1973. PLB 4.90 o.p. (ISBN 0-531-00793-6). Watts.

Levenson, Eleanore, jt. auth. see Goldberg, Louis P.

Levenson, Jon D. Theology of the Program of Restoration of Ezekiel Forty to Forty-Eight. LC 76-3769. (Harvard Semitic Museum, Monographs). 1976. 7.50 (ISBN 0-89130-105-4, 040010). Scholars Pr Ca.

Levenson, Jon D., jt. ed. see Halpern, Baruch.

Levenson, Jordan. Poor Man's Route to Rich Man's Stock Market Wealth. 120p. 1980. pap. 18.00x (ISBN 0-914442-08-2). Levenson Pr.

--Retail Fruit Species: Your Shopper's Guide to Their Best Varieties. 2nd ed. LC 79-369. (Illus.). 1980. pap. 9.87x (ISBN 0-914442-06-6). Levenson Pr.

Levenson, Joseph R. Confucian China & Its Modern Fate: A Trilogy. 1968. 21.50x (ISBN 0-520-00736-0); pap. 9.95x (ISBN 0-520-00737-9, CAMPUS12). U of Cal Pr.

--Revolution & Cosmopolitanism: The Western Stage & the Chinese Stages. LC 73-121188. (Illus.). 1971. 13.75x (ISBN 0-520-01737-4). U of Cal Pr.

Levenson, Joseph R. & Schurmann, Franz. China-An Interpretive History: From the Beginnings to the Fall of Han. 1969. 14.50x (ISBN 0-520-01440-5); pap. 4.75x (ISBN 0-520-01892-3, CAMPUS46). U of Cal Pr.

Levenson, Sam. You Don't Have to Be in Who's Who to Know What's What. (gr. 7-12). 1980. lib. bdg. 11.95 (ISBN 0-8161-3056-6, Large Print Bks). G K Hall.

Levenstein, Aaron. Use Your Head. (Illus.). 1965. 4.95 o.s.i. (ISBN 0-685-16181-1). Macmillan.

Levenstein, Harvey. Communism, Anticommunism, & the CIO. LC 80-787. (Contributions in American History Ser.: No. 91). 360p. 1981. lib. bdg. 29.95 (ISBN 0-313-22072-7, LEC/). Greenwood.

Levenstein, Sidney. Private Practice in Social Casework. LC 64-18471. 1964. 20.00x (ISBN 0-231-02712-5). Columbia U Pr.

Leventhal, Herbert. In the Shadow of the Enlightenment: Occultism & Renaissance Science in Eighteenth-Century America. LC 75-13762. 336p. 1976. 17.50x (ISBN 0-8147-4965-8). NYU Pr.

Leventhal, Lance. Assembly Language Programming: 6502. (Assembly Language Programming: No. 4). (Orig.). 1979. pap. text ed. 16.99 (ISBN 0-931988-27-6). Osborne-McGraw.

--Assembly Language Programming: 6809. (Assembly Language Programming: No. 5). (Orig.). 1980. pap. text ed. 16.99 (ISBN 0-931988-35-7). Osborne-McGraw.

--Six Eight Zero Nine Assembly Language Programming. (Assembly Language Programming Ser.: No. 6). 530p. 1980. pap. text ed. 16.99 (ISBN 0-931988-35-7). Osborne-McGraw.

Leventhal, Lance, et al. Z Eight Thousand Assembly Language Programming. (Assembly Language Programming Ser.: No.5). 930p. (Orig.). 1980. pap. text ed. 19.99 (ISBN 0-931988-36-5). Osborne-McGraw.

--Assembly Language Programming: Z8000. (Assembly Language Programming: No. 6). (Orig.). 1980. pap. 19.99 (ISBN 0-931988-36-5). Osborne-McGraw.

Leventhal, Lance A. Eighty-Eighty A - Eighty Eighty-Five Assembly Language Programming. (Assembly Language Programming Ser.: No. 1). (Orig.). 1978. pap. text ed. 15.99 (ISBN 0-931988-10-1). Osborne-McGraw.

--Introduction to Microprocessors: Software, Hardware, Programming. LC 78-7800. (Illus.). 1978. ref. ed. 27.95 (ISBN 0-13-487868-X). P-H.

--The Six-Eight Hundred Microprocessor: A Self-Study Course with Applications. (gr. 10 up). 1978. pap. text ed. 9.55 (ISBN 0-8104-5120-4). Hayden.

--Sixty-Eight Hundred Assembly Language Programming. (Assembly Language Programming Ser.: No. 2). (Orig.). 1978. pap. text ed. 15.99 (ISBN 0-931988-12-8). Osborne-McGraw.

Leventhal, Lance A. & Stafford, Irving. Why Do You Need a Personal Computer. LC 80-2391. (Self-Teaching Guide Ser.). 320p. 1980. pap. text ed. 8.95 (ISBN 0-471-04784-8). Wiley.

Leventman, Paula G. Professionals Out of Work. LC 80-1645. (Illus.). 1981. 19.95 (ISBN 0-02-918800-8). Free Pr.

Leventman, Seymour, jt. auth. see Figley, Charles R.

Leveque, Jean-Jacques. Jean Francois Milet. 1977. pap. text ed. 5.95 (ISBN 0-8120-0712-3). Barron.

LeVeque, William J. Fundamentals of Number Theory. LC 76-55645. 1978. text ed. 19.95 (ISBN 0-201-04287-8). A-W.

Lever, Charles J. Confessions of Con Cregan, the Irish Gil Blas, 2 vols. in 1. LC 80-2490. 1981. Repr. of 1877 ed. 98.50 (ISBN 0-404-19124-X). AMS Pr.

Lever, Christopher. Goldsmiths and Silversmiths of England. LC 75-314072. (Illus.). 1975. pap. text ed. 15.75x (ISBN 0-09-121220-0). Humanities.

Lever, J. W. Sonnets of the English Renaissance. (Athlone Renaissance Library). 192p. 1974. text ed. 18.75x (ISBN 0-485-13604-X, Athlone Pr); pap. text ed. 10.00x (ISBN 0-485-12604-4, Athlone Pr). Humanities.

Lever, Jill, jt. auth. see Harris, John.

Lever, Judy. T V Studio. LC 78-61232. (Careers Ser.). (Illus.). 1979. lib. bdg. 7.95 (ISBN 0-686-50004-0). Silver.

Lever, Wayne. Profile of Selected Senior Citizen Programs. 72p. (Orig.). 1980. pap. text ed. 3.95 (ISBN 0-89536-458-1). CSS Pub.

Leverant, Robert. Photographic Notations. LC 80-8094. (Illus.). 1980. 54.50 (ISBN 0-9600374-6-2). Images Pr.

Levere, Trevor H. Affinity & Matter: Elements of Chemical Philosophy, 1800-1865. 248p. 1971. 28.00x (ISBN 0-19-858134-3). Oxford U Pr.

Leverich, Kathleen & Cricket Magazine Editors. Cricket's Expeditions: Outdoor & Indoor Activities. LC 77-3231. (Illus.). (gr. 1-6). 1977. 2.95 (ISBN 0-394-83543-3, BYR); PLB 3.99 (ISBN 0-394-93543-8). Random.

Levering, Robert. Beating the Used Car Hustle. LC 79-18647. 1980. pap. 5.95 (ISBN 0-87701-150-8). Chronicle Bks.

Levering, Robert, jt. auth. see Shepard, Susan.

Levernier, James A., ed. Souldiery Spiritualized: Seven Sermons Preached Before the Artillery Companies of New England, 1674-1774. LC 79-9727. 1979. 50.00x (ISBN 0-8201-1325-5). Schol Facsimiles.

Levertov, Denise. Life in the Forest. LC 78-9356. 1978. 8.00 (ISBN 0-8112-0692-0); pap. 3.95 (ISBN 0-8112-0693-9). New Directions.

--Relearning the Alphabet. LC 72-103373. 1970. 6.00 (ISBN 0-8112-0303-4); pap. 3.95 (ISBN 0-8112-0085-X, NDP290). New Directions.

Leverty, Maureen J., compiled by. Guide to Records of Northern Pacific Branch Lines, Subsidiaries, & Related Companies in the Minnesota Historical Society. LC 77-227041. 1977. pap. 2.00 (ISBN 0-87351-117-4). Minn Hist.

Leveson, David J. Geology & the Human Environment. (Illus.). 1980. text ed. 17.95x (ISBN 0-19-502578-4). Oxford U Pr.

Leveson, Irving. Economic Future of the United States. (Hudson Institute Studies on the Prospects for Mankind). 300p. 1981. lib. bdg. 27.50x (ISBN 0-86531-097-1). Westview.

Levesque, Jacques. The USSR & the Cuban Revolution: Soviet Ideological & Strategical Perspectives, 1959-77. LC 78-16188. (Praeger Special Studies). 1978. 24.95 (ISBN 0-03-042261-2). Praeger.

Levesque, Jacques, jt. ed. see Desfosses, Helen.

Levett, M. J., tr. see Plato.

Levey, A. B., jt. auth. see Martin, I.

Levey, Martin, ed. see Kushyar Ibn Labban.

Levey, Martin, tr. see Al-Kindi.

Levey, Martin, tr. see Shuja Ibn Aslam, Abukamil.

Levey, Michael. A Concise History of Painting: From Giotto to Cezanne. (World of Art Ser.). (Illus.). 1962. pap. 9.95 (ISBN 0-19-519942-1). Oxford U Pr.

--A History of Western Art. (World or Art Ser.). (Illus.). 1968. pap. 9.95 (ISBN 0-19-519943-X). Oxford U Pr.

--Painting at Court. LC 75-124528. (Wrightsman Lectures: Vol. 5). (Illus.). 1971. 20.00 (ISBN 0-8147-4950-X). NYU Pr.

--Painting in Eighteenth-Century Venice. rev. ed. LC 80-549. (Cornell-Phaidon Bks.). (Illus.). 264p. 1980. 38.50 (ISBN 0-8014-1331-1). Cornell U Pr.

--Rococo to Revolution: Major Trends in Eighteenth-Century Painting. (World of Art Ser.). (Illus.). 1966. pap. 9.95 (ISBN 0-19-519960-X). Oxford U Pr.

--The World of Ottoman Art. LC 76-40383. (Encore Edition). 1977. 4.95 o.p. (ISBN 0-684-16200-8, ScribT). Scribner.

Levey, Samuel & Loomba, Narendra P., eds. Health Care Administration: A Selected Bibliography. LC 72-11486. 149p. 1973. pap. 4.00 o.p. (ISBN 0-397-52060-3). Lippincott.

Levi, Donald R. Real Estate Law. (Illus.). 1980. text ed. 16.95 (ISBN 0-8359-6536-8). Reston.

Levi, Donald R., jt. auth. see Matthews, Stephen F.

Levi, Eliphas. History of Magic. 1980. pap. 7.95 (ISBN 0-87728-077-0). Weiser.

--The Key of the Mysteries. 1980. pap. 6.95 (ISBN 0-87728-078-9). Weiser.

Levi, Giulio, ed. Transport Phenomena in the Nervous System: Physiological & Pathological Aspects. LC 76-4839. (Advances in Experimental Medicine & Biology Ser.: Vol. 69). 541p. 1976. 45.00 (ISBN 0-306-39069-8, Plenum Pr). Plenum Pub.

Levi, L. Applied Optics: A Guide to Optical Systems Design, 2 vols. LC 67-29942. (Pure & Applied Optics Ser.). Vol. 1, 1968. 41.95 (ISBN 0-471-53110-3, Pub. by Wiley-Interscience); Vol. 2, 1980. 75.00 (ISBN 0-471-05054-7). Wiley.

Levi, Lennart. Occupational Stress: Sources, Management & Prevention. (Occupational Stress Ser.). 143p. 1981. pap. text ed. 6.50 (ISBN 0-201-04317-3). A-W.

--Society, Stress, & Disease: The Productive & Reproductive Age-Male-Female Roles & Relationships, Vol. 3. (Illus.). 1978. 67.50x (ISBN 0-19-261306-5). Oxford U Pr.

Levi, Lennart, ed. Emotions: Their Parameters & Measurement. LC 74-80539. 1975. 46.50 (ISBN 0-89004-019-2). Raven.

--Society, Stress & Disease, Vol. 1. 1971. 67.50x (ISBN 0-19-264416-5). Oxford U Pr.

--Society, Stress, & Disease: Working Life, Vol. 4. 1981. text ed. 75.00x (ISBN 0-19-264421-1). Oxford U Pr.

Levi, Leone. Wages & Earnings of the Working Class. 151p. 1971. Repr. of 1885 ed. 23.00x (ISBN 0-686-28331-7, Pub. by Irish Academic Pr). Biblio Dist.

Levi, M., tr. see Vinnichenko, N. K. & Gorelik, A. G.

Levi, Maurice. Economics Deciphered: A Layman's Guide. LC 80-68173. 192p. 1981. 11.95 (ISBN 0-465-01794-0). Basic.

Levi, Maurice D., ed. see Kupferman, Martin.

Levi, Peter. Atlas of Greek World. 239p. 1981. 29.95 (ISBN 0-87196-448-1). Facts on File.

--John Clare & Thomas Hardy. (John Coffin Memorial Lecture Ser., 1975). 1976. pap. text ed. 2.50x (ISBN 0-485-16210-5, Athlone Pr). Humanities.

Levi, Peter, ed. see Porter, Eliot.

Levi, Peter S. Water, Rock & Sand: Poems. 1962. 5.95 (ISBN 0-8023-1071-0). Dufour.

Levi, Renato S. Dhows to Deltas. 255p. 1980. 15.00x (ISBN 0-245-59956-8, Pub. by Nautical England). State Mutual Bk.

Levi, Wendell M. The Pigeon. 1981. Repr. 42.50 (ISBN 0-910876-01-0). Levi Pub.

Levi, Werner. Contemporary International Law: A Concise Introduction. 1978. lib. bdg. 28.50x (ISBN 0-89158-184-7); pap. text ed. 11.00x (ISBN 0-89158-187-1). Westview.

Leviant, Curt. Passion in the Desert. 160p. 1980. pap. 2.50 (ISBN 0-380-76125-4, 76125). Avon.

Leviatan, Uri, ed. Work & Organization in Kibbutz Industry. Rosner, Menachem, tr. 204p. 1980. lib. bdg. 20.00 (ISBN 0-8482-1640-7). Norwood Edns.

Levich, Richard M. & Wihlborg, Clas G., eds. Exchange Risk & Exposure: Current Developments in International Financial Management. LC 79-5181. (Illus.). 224p. 1980. 22.95 (ISBN 0-669-03246-8). Lexington Bks.

Levich, V. Physiochemical Hydrodynamics. 1962. ref. ed. 35.95 (ISBN 0-13-674440-0). P-H.

Levi-Civita, Tullio. The Absolute Differential Calculus: Calculus of Tensors. Persico, Enrico, ed. Long, Marjorie, tr. from Italian. LC 76-27497. (Illus.). 480p. 1977. pap. text ed. 6.50 (ISBN 0-486-63401-9). Dover.

Levidow, Les & Young, Bob. Science, Technology & the Labor Process. (Marxist Studies: Vol. 1). 1980. pap. text ed. write for info. (ISBN 0-906336-20-1); pap. text ed. write for info. (ISBN 0-906336-21-X). Humanities.

Levie, Albert. The Meat Handbook. 4th ed. (Illus.). 1979. text ed. 21.00 (ISBN 0-87055-315-1). AVI.

Levie, Robert C. & Ballard, Lou E. Writing Effective Reports on Police Investigations: Concepts, Procedures, Samples. 1978. text ed. 17.95 (ISBN 0-205-06098-6, 826098-2). Allyn.

Levien, Roger, ed. see Carnegie Commission on Higher Education.

Levieux, Eleanor, tr. see Duby, Georges.

Levin, Alexandra L. Dare to Be Different: A Biography of Louis H. Levin of Baltimore. 1972. 7.50x (ISBN 0-8197-0280-3). Bloch.

Levin, Arnie. I'll Skip the Appetizer--I Ate the Flowers. 1980. pap. 4.95 (ISBN 0-452-25242-3, 25242, Plume). NAL.

Levin, Arthur, ed. Health Services: The Local Perspective. LC 77-73219. (Praeger Special Studies). 1977. text ed. 26.95 (ISBN 0-03-039731-6). Praeger.

Levin, Beatrice. Hidden Treasures. LC 79-87530. 232p. 1981. 3.95 (ISBN 0-89896-049-5, Pub. by the Lindahl Press). Larksdale.

Levin, Beatrice S. Women & Medicine. LC 80-12705. 272p. 1980. 13.50 (ISBN 0-8108-1296-7). Scarecrow.

Levin, Betsy, et al. The High Cost of Education in Cities: An Analysis of the Purchasing Power of the Educational Dollar. 1973. pap. 2.50 o.p. (ISBN 0-87766-056-5, 31000). Urban Inst.

Levin, Betty. The Beast on the Brink. (Illus.). (gr. 5-7). 1980. pap. 1.95 (ISBN 0-380-76141-6, 76141, Camelot). Avon.

--A Griffon's Nest. 352p. (gr. 5-9). 1975. 10.95 (ISBN 0-02-757350-8, 75735). Macmillan.

--The Keeping Room. LC 80-23931. 256p. (gr. 5 up). 1981. 8.95 (ISBN 0-688-80300-8). Greenwillow.

--The Sword of Culann. LC 73-583. 288p. (gr. 5-8). 1973. PLB 8.95 (ISBN 0-02-757340-0). Macmillan.

Levin, Boris J. Distribution of Zeros of Entire Functions. rev. ed. LC 63-15661. (Translations of Mathematical Monographs: Vol. 5). 1980. 27.60 (ISBN 0-8218-4505-5, MMONO-5). Am Math.

Levin, Charles, tr. see Baudrillard, Jean.

Levin, Daniel L., et al. A Practical Guide to Pediatric Intensive Care. LC 79-13793. (Illus.). 1979. pap. text ed. 24.50 (ISBN 0-8016-3011-8). Mosby.

Levin, David, ed. English Institute-Emerson: Prophecy, Metamorphosis, & Influence. (Selected Papers from the English Institute Ser). 192p. 1975. 12.50x (ISBN 0-231-04000-8). Columbia U Pr.

Levin, Flora R. The Harmonics of Nicomachus & the Pythagorean Tradition. (American Philological Association, American Classical Studies). 1975. pap. 4.50 (ISBN 0-89130-241-7, 400401). Scholars Pr Ca.

Levin, Gail. Edward Hopper: The Art & the Artist. (Illus.). 1980. 29.95 (ISBN 0-393-01374-X). Norton.

Levin, Gerald. Richardson the Novelist: The Psychological Patters. (Costerus New Ser.: No. 9). 1978. pap. text ed. 17.25x (ISBN 90-6203-410-1). Humanities.

--A Self-Directing Guide to the Study of Child Psychology. LC 72-92046. (Statistics Ser.). (Illus., Orig.). 1973. pap. text ed. 10.95 o.p. (ISBN 0-8185-0076-X); instructor's manual avail. o.p. (ISBN 0-685-28534-0). Brooks-Cole.

--Sigmund Freud. LC 74-31135. (World Authors Ser.: Austria: No. 357). 1975. lib. bdg. 12.50 (ISBN 0-8057-2330-7). Twayne.

Levin, Gilbert, et al. The Persistent Poppy: A Computer-Aided Search for Heroin Policy. LC 75-4656. 184p. 1975. text ed. 17.50 o.p. (ISBN 0-88410-031-6). Ballinger Pub.

Levin, Harold L. & Wallace, Robert J. Life Through Time. 2nd ed. Date not set. pap. text ed. cancelled (ISBN 0-697-05036-X). Wm C Brown.

Levin, Harry. Christopher Marlowe: The Over-Reacher. (Orig.). 1965. pap. 2.95 o.p. (ISBN 0-571-07028-0, Pub. by Faber & Faber). Merrimack Bk Serv.

--Grounds for Comparison. LC 72-75402. (Studies in Comparative Literature: No. 32). (Illus.). 448p. 1972. 18.50x (ISBN 0-674-36335-3). Harvard U Pr.

--Memories of the Moderns. LC 80-36827. 256p. 1980. 15.95 (ISBN 0-8112-0733-1). New Directions.

--Myth of the Golden Age in the Renaissance. 167p. 1972. pap. 4.95 (ISBN 0-19-501602-5, GB). Oxford U Pr.

--The Power of Blackness: Hawthorne, Poe, Melville. LC 80-83221. xxii, 263p. 1980. pap. 6.95x (ISBN 0-8214-0581-0). Ohio U Pr.

--Refractions: Essays in Comparative Literature. 1968. pap. 5.95 (ISBN 0-19-500771-9, GB). Oxford U Pr.

--Shakespeare & the Revolution of the Times: Perspectives & Commentaries. 1978. pap. 5.95 (ISBN 0-19-502362-5, GB528, GB). Oxford U Pr.

Levin, Harry, ed. see Shakespeare, William.

Levin, Henry M., et al, eds. Community Control of Schools. (Studies in Social Economics). 318p. 1970. 12.95 (ISBN 0-8157-5224-5). Brookings.

Levin, Ilya, tr. see Schmidt, Paul.

Levin, Ira. A Kiss Before Dying. 1975. pap. 1.95 (ISBN 0-515-05127-6). Jove Pubns.

--This Perfect Day. 1970. 6.95 o.p. (ISBN 0-394-44858-8). Random.

Levin, Jack. Estadistica en Investigacion. (Span.). 1979. pap. text ed. 7.80 (ISBN 0-06-315012-3, Pub. by HarLA Mexico). Har-Row.

Levin, Jack & Levin, William. Ageism: Prejudice & Discrimination Against the Elderly. 168p. 1980. pap. text ed. 7.95x (ISBN 0-534-00881-X). Wadsworth Pub.

Levin, Jack, jt. auth. see Zieve, Philip D.

Levin, Jennifer. Charter Controversy in the City of London, 1660-1688, & Its Consequence. 1969. text ed. 17.50x (ISBN 0-485-13409-8, Athlone Pr). Humanities.

Levin, Jules F. The Slavic Element in the Old Prussian Elbing Vocabulary. (U. C. Publ. in Linguistics: Vol. 77). pap. 10.50x (ISBN 0-520-09473-5). U of Cal Pr.

Levin, L. Stefan & Knight, Connie, eds. Genetic & Environmental Hearing Loss: Syndromic & Nonsyndromic. (Birth Defects: Oringinal Article Ser.: Vol. XVI, No. 7). 100p. 1980. write for info. (ISBN 0-8451-1040-3). A R Liss.

Levin, Lowell & Idler, Ellen. The Hidden Health Care System: Mediating Structures & Health. 1980. 19.00 (ISBN 0-88410-822-8). Ballinger Pub.

Levin, Marcia, jt. auth. see Bendick, Jeanne.

Levin, Martin, ed. How to Get from January Through December in Powerboating. LC 77-11815. (Illus.). 1979. 14.95 o.s.i. (ISBN 0-06-012558-6, HarpT). Har-Row.

Levin, Melvin R. Community & Regional Planning: Issues in Public Policy. 3rd ed. LC 76-12862. (Special Studies). 1977. text ed. 29.95 (ISBN 0-275-23690-0); pap. 11.95 (ISBN 0-275-85740-9). Praeger.

Levin, Melvin R. & Shank, Alan, eds. Educational Investment in an Urban Society: Costs, Benefits, & Public Policy. LC 70-110397. (Illus.). 1970. pap. text ed. 12.75x (ISBN 0-8077-1684-7). Tchrs Coll.

Levin, Milton. Noel Coward. LC 68-24285. (English Authors Ser.: No. 73). 1969. lib. bdg. 10.95 (ISBN 0-8057-1120-1). Twayne.

Levin, Moshe Chaim, ed. see Schneersohn, Y. Y.

Levin, Murray B. & Blackwood, George. The Compleat Politician: Political Strategy in Massachusetts. LC 62-18204. 1962. 24.50x (ISBN 0-672-51133-9); pap. text ed. 12.95x (ISBN 0-8290-0138-7). Irvington.

Levin, Noel A. Guidelines for Fiduciaries of Taft-Hartley Trusts: An ERISA Manual. 137p. 1980. 25.00 (ISBN 0-89154-135-7). Intl Found Employ.

Levin, P. H. Government & the Planning Process. 1976. text ed. 25.00x o.p. (ISBN 0-04-352059-6). Allen Unwin.

Levin, Rich. Magic Johnson: Court Magician. LC 80-25814. (Sports Stars Ser.). (Illus.). 48p. (gr. 2-8). 1981. PLB 7.35 (ISBN 0-516-04313-7). Childrens.

Levin, Richard. The Executive's Illustrated Primer of Long-Range Planning. (Illus.). 240p. 1981. text ed. 11.95 (ISBN 0-13-294140-6). P-H.

Levin, Richard, ed. see Middleton, Thomas.

Levin, Richard I. & Kirkpatrick, C. A. Planning & Control with PERT-CPM. 1966. 20.95 (ISBN 0-07-037364-7, C); pap. 12.95 (ISBN 0-07-037365-5). McGraw.

Levin, Richard I. & Kirkpatrick, Charles A. Quantitative Approaches to Management. 4th ed. (Illus.). 1978. text ed. 20.95 (ISBN 0-07-037423-6, C); instructor's manual 4.95 (ISBN 0-07-037424-4); student wkbk. 6.95 (ISBN 0-07-037434-1). McGraw.

Levin, Richard M. Pediatric Respiratory Intensive Care Handbook. 1976. spiral bdg. 13.75 (ISBN 0-87488-649-X). Med Exam.

Levin, Richard M., ed. Pediatric Anesthesia Handbook. 2nd. ed. (Illus.). 1980. pap. 14.75 (ISBN 0-87488-637-6). Med Exam.

Levin, Shirley, jt. auth. see Feingold, S. Norman.

Levin, Susan K., jt. ed. see Slater, Lloyd E.

Levin, William, jt. auth. see Levin, Jack.

Levine. Cancer in the Young. 1981. write for info. Masson Pub.

--Realtors' Liability. LC 79-4133. (Real Estate for Professional Practitioners Ser.). 1979. 23.95 (ISBN 0-471-05208-6, Pub. by Ronald). Wiley.

Levine, Arthur. When Dreams & Heroes Died: A Portrait of Today's College Student. LC 80-8005. (Carnegie Council Ser.). 1980. text ed. 13.95x (ISBN 0-87589-481-X). Jossey-Bass.

Levine, Arthur E. & Weingart, John R. Reform of Undergraduate Education. LC 73-7154. (Higher Education Ser). 176p. 1973. 11.95x o.p. (ISBN 0-87589-186-1). Jossey-Bass.

Levine, Barbara see Dewey, John.

Levine, Baroch. Group Psychotherapy: Practice & Development. 1979. 17.95 (ISBN 0-13-365296-3). P-H.

Levine, Betty K. Great Burgerland Disaster. LC 80-36713. 120p. (gr. 5-9). 1981. PLB 8.95 (ISBN 0-689-30815-9). Atheneum.

Levine, Carol, jt. auth. see Hitchner, Dell G.

Levine, Charles H., ed. Managing Fiscal Stress: The Crisis in the Public Sector. LC 79-27266. (Chatham House Series on Change in American Politics). 1980. pap. text ed. 11.95x (ISBN 0-934540-02-0). Chatham Hse Pubs.

--Managing Human Resources: A Challenge to Urban Governments. LC 77-79869. (Urban Affairs Annual Reviews Ser.: Vol. 13). (Illus.). 1977. 20.00x (ISBN 0-8039-0741-9); pap. 9.95x (ISBN 0-8039-0938-1). Sage.

Levine, D., jt. auth. see Berenson, M.

Levine, D., ed. Family Formation in an Age of Nascent Capitalism. 1977. 20.00 (ISBN 0-12-445050-4). Acad Pr.

Levine, Daniel, jt. auth. see Yett, Donald E.

Levine, Daniel H., ed. Churches & Politics in Latin America. LC 79-23827. (Sage Focus Editions: Vol. 14). 288p. 1980. 18.95 (ISBN 0-8039-1298-6); pap. 9.95x (ISBN 0-8039-1299-4). Sage.

Levine, Daniel U., jt. auth. see Havighurst, Robert J.

Levine, Daniel V. & Havighurst, Robert J., eds. The Future of Big-City Schools: Desegregation Policies & Magnet Alternatives. LC 76-62900. 1977. 17.50x (ISBN 0-8211-1113-2); text ed. 15.75x 10 or more copies (ISBN 0-685-75000-0). McCutchan.

Levine, David, jt. auth. see Wrightson, Keith.

Levine, David P. Economic Studies: Contributions to the Critique of Economic Theory. 1977. 28.00x (ISBN 0-7100-8573-7). Routledge & Kegan.

--Economic Theory: The Elementary Relations of Economic Life. 1978. 28.00 (ISBN 0-7100-8837-X). Routledge & Kegan.

Levine, Edna, jt. auth. see Garrett, James.

Levine, Edna S. Psychology of Deafness. LC 60-7250. 1960. 20.00x (ISBN 0-231-02394-4). Columbia U Pr.

Levine, Elieba. Friends. 288p. (Orig.). 1980. pap. 2.25 (ISBN 0-89083-645-0). Zebra.

Levine, Erwin L. Theodore Francis Green: The Rhode Island Years, 1906-1936. LC 63-18096. (Illus.). 222p. 1963. 8.50 (ISBN 0-87057-077-3, Pub. by Brown U Pr). Univ Pr of New England.

--Theodore Francis Green: The Washington Years, 1937-1960. LC 73-127366. (Illus.). 179p. 1971. 8.50 (ISBN 0-87057-126-5, Pub. by Brown U Pr). Univ Pr of New England.

Levine, George. The Realistic Imagination: English Fiction from Frankenstein to Lady Chatterley. LC 80-17444. 1981. lib. bdg. 25.00x (ISBN 0-226-47550-6). U of Chicago Pr.

Levine, George & Madden, William. Art of Victorian Prose. 1968. pap. 6.95x (ISBN 0-19-500953-3). Oxford U Pr.

Levine, George L., ed. Emergence of Victorian Consciousness. LC 66-24458. 1967. pap. text ed. 6.95 (ISBN 0-02-918890-3). Free Pr.

Levine, Gustav. Introductory Statistics for Psychology: The Logic & the Methods. LC 80-81254. 1981. write for info. (ISBN 0-12-445480-1). Acad Pr.

Levine, Gustav & Burke, C. Mathematical Model Techniques for Learning Theories. 1972. text ed. 17.95 (ISBN 0-12-445250-7). Acad Pr.

Levine, H. B. & Levine, Marlene. Urbanization in Papua New Guinea. LC 78-58795. (Urbanization in Developing Countries Ser.). 1979. 24.95 (ISBN 0-521-22230-3); pap. 9.95x (ISBN 0-521-29410-X). Cambridge U Pr.

Levine, Harold. Comprehensive English Review Text. 4th ed. (Orig.). 1980. pap. text ed. 5.83 (ISBN 0-87720-390-3). AMSCO Sch.

--English: A Comprehensive Course. (Orig.). (gr. 11-12). 1970. pap. text ed. 4.83 (ISBN 0-87720-303-2). AMSCO Sch.

--Vocabulary & Composition Through Pleasurable Reading, Bk. 3. (Orig.). (gr. 10-12). 1976. wkbk. 6.75 (ISBN 0-87720-306-7); pap. text ed. 5.92 (ISBN 0-87720-377-6). AMSCO Sch.

--Vocabulary & Composition: Through Pleasurable Reading, Book 4. (gr. 11-12). 1978. wkbk 6.75 (ISBN 0-87720-376-8); pap. text ed. 5.92 (ISBN 0-87720-378-4). AMSCO Sch.

--Vocabulary & Composition Through Pleasurable Reading, Bk. 5. (gr. 10-12). 1979. pap. text ed. 5.92 (ISBN 0-87720-385-7); wkbk 6.75 (ISBN 0-87720-379-2). AMSCO Sch.

--Vocabulary & Composition Through Pleasurable Reading, Bk. 6. (gr. 11-12). 1979. pap. text ed. 5.92 (ISBN 0-87720-388-1); wkbk. 6.75 (ISBN 0-87720-387-3). AMSCO Sch.

--Vocabulary for the College-Bound Student. (Orig.). (gr. 9-12). 1964. text ed. 8.83 (ISBN 0-87720-367-9); pap. text ed. 4.92 (ISBN 0-87720-366-0); wkbk. 5.58 (ISBN 0-87720-312-1); with answers 3.25 (ISBN 0-87720-313-X). AMSCO Sch.

--Vocabulary for the High School Student. (Orig.). (gr. 9-12). 1967. text ed. 8.83 (ISBN 0-87720-365-2); pap. text ed. 4.92 (ISBN 0-87720-364-4); wkbk. 5.58 (ISBN 0-87720-310-5); with answer 3.25 (ISBN 0-87720-311-3). AMSCO Sch.

--Vocabulary Through Pleasurable Reading, Bk. 1. (Orig.). (gr. 7-10). 1974. pap. text ed. 5.92 (ISBN 0-87720-373-3); wkbk. 6.75 (ISBN 0-87720-368-7). AMSCO Sch.

--Vocabulary Through Pleasurable Reading Book, Bk. 2. (gr. 7-12). 1974. wkbk 6.75 (ISBN 0-87720-369-5); pap. text ed. 5.92 (ISBN 0-87720-374-1). AMSCO Sch.

Levine, Harold & Levine, Robert T. Vocabulary Foundations for the College Student. (Orig.). 1980. pap. text ed. 7.50 (ISBN 0-87720-962-6). AMSCO Sch.

Levine, Harriet, jt. auth. see Feinstein, Maurice B.

Levine, Harriet & Minno, Frances P., eds. History & Law of Nursing. (Nursing Examination Review Books: Vol. 10). 1971. spiral bdg. 6.00 (ISBN 0-87488-510-8). Med Exam.

Levine, Harriet, jt. ed. see Holmes, Marguerite C.

Levine, Harvey A. National Transportation Policy: A Study of Studies. new ed. LC 78-7156. 1978. 18.95 (ISBN 0-669-02393-0). Lexington Bks.

Levine, Harvey R. Legal Dimensions of Drug Abuse in the United States. (Criminal Law Education & Research Center Ser.). 208p. 1974. 13.75 (ISBN 0-398-02876-1). C C Thomas.

Levine, Herbert M. Point-Counterpoint: Readings in American Government. 1979. pap. text ed. 8.95x (ISBN 0-673-15297-9). Scott F.

Levine, Herbert M. & Owen, Dolores B. An American Guide to British Social Science Resources. LC 76-22690. 1976. 13.50 (ISBN 0-8108-0950-8). Scarecrow.

Levine, I. E. The Many Faces of Slavery. LC 74-28162. 192p. (gr. 9 up). 1975. PLB 5.29 o.p. (ISBN 0-671-32713-5). Messner.

Levine, Ira N. Molecular Spectroscopy. LC 74-30477. 480p. 1975. 32.50 (ISBN 0-471-53128-6, Pub. by Wiley-Interscience). Wiley.

--Quantum Chemistry. 2nd ed. 592p. 1974. text ed. 26.95 (ISBN 0-205-04305-4, 6843050). Allyn.

Levine, Israel E. Conqueror of Smallpox: Dr. Edward Jenner. LC 60-7817. (Biography Ser.). (gr. 7 up). 1960. 3.34 o.p. (ISBN 0-671-06900-4). Messner.

Levine, James. Who Will Raise the Children? New Options for Fathers (Mothers) LC 76-18743. 1976. 8.95 o.p. (ISBN 0-397-01120-2). Lippincott.

Levine, Joseph, jt. auth. see Pine, Tillie S.

Levine, Joseph M. Dr. Woodward's Shield: History, Science, & Satire in Augustan England. 1977. 28.50x (ISBN 0-520-03132-6). U of Cal Pr.

Levine, Karen, jt. auth. see King, David.

Levine, Larry. Snowbird. 1977. pap. 1.75 o.p. (ISBN 0-449-13866-6, GM). Fawcett.

Levine, Lawrence W. Black Culture & Black Consciousness: Afro-American Folk Thought from Slavery to Freedom. LC 76-9223. 1978. pap. 7.95 (ISBN 0-19-502374-9, GB530, GB). Oxford U Pr.

Levine, Lenore, jt. ed. see New, Maria.

Levine, Linda, jt. auth. see Barbach, Lonnie.

Levine, Lois. Delicious Diet Cookbook: The Sensible Way to Slim. (Illus.). 192p. 1974. 6.95 o.s.i. (ISBN 0-02-570400-1). Macmillan.

Levine, Lois, jt. auth. see Burros, Marian.

Levine, Louis. Biology for a Modern Society. LC 76-46318. (Illus.). 1977. pap. 11.95 (ISBN 0-8016-2990-X). Mosby.

--Biology of the Gene. 2nd ed. LC 72-89495. (Illus.). 400p. 1973. text ed. 13.95 o.p. (ISBN 0-8016-2987-X). Mosby.

--Biology of the Gene. 3rd ed. LC 80-10730. (Illus.). 1980. pap. text ed. 17.95 (ISBN 0-8016-2988-8). Mosby.

Levine, Louis S. Heart Attack! LC 75-30337. 128p. 1976. 6.95 o.p. (ISBN 0-06-012595-0, HarpT). Har-Row.

Levine, M. Digital Theory & Experimentation Using Integrated Circuits. LC 73-12863. 1974. pap. 14.95 ref. ed. (ISBN 0-13-212258-8). P-H.

Levine, Madeline, tr. see Bialoszewski, Miron.

Levine, Mark L. Real Estate Fundamentals. LC 76-3508. 375p. 1976. text ed. 17.95 (ISBN 0-8299-0095-0); review manual 5.95 (ISBN 0-8299-0553-7); instrs.' manual avail. (ISBN 0-8299-0552-9). West Pub.

Levine, Marlene, jt. auth. see Levine, H. B.

Levine, Marvin J., ed. Public Personnel Management: Readings, Cases & Contingency Plans. 1979. pap. text ed. 11.95 (ISBN 0-89832-006-2). Brighton Pub Co.

Levine, Melvin D., et al. Pediatric Approach to Learning Disorders. LC 79-21839. 1980. 20.00 (ISBN 0-471-04736-8, Pub. by Wiley-Medical). Wiley.

LeVine, Michael. Johnny Horton-Your Singing Fisherman. Date not set. 10.95 (ISBN 0-533-04802-8). Vantage.

Levine, Michael L. Moviemaking: A Guide for Beginners. LC 80-19314. (Illus.). 48p. (gr. 5 up). 1980. 9.95 (ISBN 0-684-16707-7). Scribner.

Levine, Michael W. & Shefner, Jeremy M. Fundamentals of Sensation & Perception. (Psychology Ser.). (Illus.). 480p. 1981. text ed. 19.95 (ISBN 0-201-04339-4). A-W.

Levine, Milton, jt. auth. see Seligmann, Jean.

Levine, Morris E. Digital Theory & Practice Using Integrated Circuits. 1978. ref. 19.95 (ISBN 0-13-212613-3). P-H.

Levine, Mortimer. Tudor Dynastic Problems, 1462-1571. (Historical Problems: Studies & Documents). 1973. pap. text ed. 8.95x o.p. (ISBN 0-04-942111-5). Allen Unwin.

Levine, Mortimer, ed. Bibliographical Handbook on Tudor England, Fourteen Eighty-Five to Sixteen Hundred Three. (Bibliographical Handbooks of the Conference on British Studies). 1968. 17.50 (ISBN 0-521-05543-1). Cambridge U Pr.

Levine, Murray. From State Hospital to Psychiatric Center. 1980. 15.95 (ISBN 0-669-03810-5). Lexington Bks.

Levine, Nancy. Hard Core Crafts. (Illus.). 120p. 1976. pap. 7.95 o.p. (ISBN 0-345-24997-6). Ballantine.

Levine, Nathan. Typing Made Simple. 1958. pap. 3.50 (ISBN 0-385-01224-1, Made). Doubleday.

Levine, Norman. The Tragic Deception: Marx Ontra Engels. new ed. LC 74-14193. (Twentieth Century Ser.: No. 8). 259p. 1975. text ed. 5.75 (ISBN 0-87436-192-3); pap. text ed. 2.50 (ISBN 0-87436-193-1). ABC-Clio.

Levine, Norman D. Nematode Parasites of Animals & of Man. 2nd ed. 477p. 1980. 68.95 (ISBN 0-8087-1299-3). Burgess.

Levine, Philip. Not This Pig. LC 68-16006. (Wesleyan Poetry Program: Vol. 38). (Orig.). 1968. 10.00x (ISBN 0-8195-2038-1, Pub. by Wesleyan U Pr); pap. 2.45 o.p. (ISBN 0-8195-1038-6). Columbia U Pr.

Levine, Philip, tr. see Sabines, Jaime.

Levine, R. & Luft, R., eds. Advances in Metabolic Disorders, Vols. 1-6. Incl. Vol. 1. 1964 (ISBN 0-12-027301-2); Vol. 2. 1965. o.s.i. (ISBN 0-12-027302-0); Vol. 3. 1968 (ISBN 0-12-027303-9); Vol. 4. 1970 (ISBN 0-12-027304-7); Vol. 5. 1971 (ISBN 0-12-027305-5); Vol.6. 1972 (ISBN 0-12-027306-3). 48.00 ea. Acad Pr.
Levine, R. D. & Jortner, J. Molecular Energy Transfer. LC 75-37726. 1976. 44.95 (ISBN 0-470-15205-2). Halsted Pr.
Levine, Raphael, jt. auth. see Treacy, William.
Levine, Raphael D. Quantum Mechanics of Molecular Rate Processes. 1969. 45.00x (ISBN 0-19-855343-9). Oxford U Pr.
Levine, Richard A., ed. The Victorian Experience: The Novelists. LC 75-15338. 273p. 1976. 15.95x (ISBN 0-8214-0190-4). Ohio U Pr.
Levine, Robert. A Comparison of Sidney's Old & New Arcadia. (Salzburg Studies in English Literature, Elizabethan & Renaissance Studies: No.13). 122p. 1976. pap. text ed. 25.00x (ISBN 0-391-01458-7). Humanities.
--The Uniform Commercial Code: An Operational Translation. LC 80-68569. 1980. 16.50 (ISBN 0-933718-00-4). Browning Pubns.
LeVine, Robert A., ed. Culture & Personality: Contemporary Readings. LC 79-16915. 1974. lib. bdg. 22.95x (ISBN 0-202-01121-6); pap. text ed. 13.95x (ISBN 0-202-01122-4). Aldine Pub.
--Culture, Behavior & Personality. 2nd ed. LC 75-169514. 320p. 1979. text ed. 17.95x (ISBN 0-202-01085-6). Aldine Pub.
Levine, Robert M. Historical Dictionary of Brazil. LC 78-10178. (Latin American Historical Dictionaries: No. 19). 1979. lib. bdg. 13.50 (ISBN 0-8108-1178-2). Scarecrow.
--Vargas Regime. LC 78-115222. 1970. 17.50x (ISBN 0-231-03370-2). Columbia U Pr.
Levine, Robert T., jt. auth. see Levine, Harold.
Levine, Robert T., ed. see Middleton, Thomas.
Levine, Ruth R. Pharmacology: Drug Actions & Reactions. 2nd ed. (Illus.). 1978. 18.95 (ISBN 0-316-52226-0); pap. 12.95 (ISBN 0-316-52227-9). Little.
Levine, Samuel. Vocational & Technical Mathematics in Action. (Illus., Orig.). 1969. pap. 11.95x (ISBN 0-8104-5717-2); inst. guide & ans. bk. 1.95x (ISBN 0-8104-5719-9); transparencies 102.15 (ISBN 0-8104-8851-5). Hayden.
--You Take Jesus, I'll Take God. LC 80-82731. 134p. (Orig.). 1980. 9.95 (ISBN 0-9604754-2-7); pap. 6.95 (ISBN 0-9604754-1-9). Hamoroh Pr.
Levine, Sol. Your Future in NASA: National Aeronautic & Space Administration. LC 78-114111. (Career Guidance Ser). 1971. pap. 3.50 (ISBN 0-668-02255-8). Arco.
Levine, Stephen. A Gradual Awakening. LC 77-27712. 1979. pap. 4.95 (ISBN 0-385-14164-5, Anch). Doubleday.
Levine, Steven I., tr. see Rubin, Vitaly A.
Levine, Steven Z. Monet & His Critics. LC 75-23800. (Outstanding Dissertations in the Fine Arts - 19th Century). (Illus.). 1976. lib. bdg. 45.00 (ISBN 0-8240-1995-4). Garland Pub.
Levine, Stuart & Lurie, Nancy. American Indian Today. 2nd ed. LC 67-24839. (Illus.). 1971. lib. bdg. 6.00 o.p. (ISBN 0-912112-13-1). Everett-Edwards.
Levine, Stuart, ed. see Poe, Edgar A.
Levine, Summer N., ed. Financial Analyst's Handbook. Incl. Vol. 1. Portfolio Management. 1540p. 37.50 (ISBN 0-87094-082-1); Vol. 2. Analysis by Industry. 1032p. o.p. (ISBN 0-87094-083-X). LC 74-81386. 1975. Dow Jones-Irwin.
Levine, Sumner N., ed. The Dow Jones-Irwin Business Almanac, Nineteen Eighty-One. LC 76-53629. 800p. 1981. 16.95 (ISBN 0-87094-225-5). Dow Jones-Irwin.
--Selected Papers on New Techniques for Energy Conversion. pap. text ed. 6.00 (ISBN 0-486-60037-8). Dover.
Levine, Susan, ed. see Poe, Edgar A.
Levine, Suzanne, et al. The Decade of Women: A Ms. History of the Seventies in Words & Pictures. 17.95 (ISBN 0-399-12490-X). Putnam.
Levine, Suzanne J., tr. see Fuentes, Carlos.
Levine, Talya. Chronic Cholecystitis: Its Pathology & the Role of Vascular Factors in Its Pathogenesis. LC 75-6842. 1975. 33.95 (ISBN 0-470-53122-3). Halsted Pr.
Levine, Victor T. & Luke, Timothy W. The Arab-African Connection: Political & Economic Realities. (Special Studies on Africa & the Middle East). 1979. lib. bdg. 18.00x (ISBN 0-89158-398-X). Westview.
Le Vine, Victor T. & Nye, Roger. Historical Dictionary of Cameroon. LC 74-901. (African Historical Dictionaries Ser.: No. 1). 1974. 10.00 (ISBN 0-8108-0707-6). Scarecrow.
Levine, W. G., ed. The Chelation of Heavy Metals. 1979. text ed. 9.00 (ISBN 0-08-017719-0). Pergamon.
Levings, Pat. Profit from Foodservice: A Q & A Approach. LC 74-706. 160p. 1974. 11.95 (ISBN 0-8436-0584-7). CBI Pub.
Levins, Richard. Evolution in Changing Environments: Some Theoretical Explorations. LC 68-20871. (Monographs in Population Biology: No. 2). (Illus.). 1968. 12.50x (ISBN 0-691-07959-5); pap. 5.50x (ISBN 0-691-08062-3). Princeton U Pr.
Levinson, A. A. & Taylor, Ross. Moon Rocks & Minerals. 240p. 1976. text ed. 31.00 (ISBN 0-08-016669-5). Pergamon.
Levinson, Alfred see Corrigan, Robert W.
Levinson, Alfred L. Energy & Materials in Three Sectors of the Economy: A Dynamic Model with Technological Change As an Endogenous Variable. LC 78-75010. (Outstanding Dissertations on Energy Ser.). 1979. lib. bdg. 15.50 (ISBN 0-8240-3983-1). Garland Pub.
Levinson, Boris M. Pet-Oriented Child Psychotherapy. 228p. 1969. 13.75 (ISBN 0-398-01118-4). C C Thomas.
--Pets & Human Development. 256p. 1972. 14.75 (ISBN 0-398-02358-1). C C Thomas.
Levinson, Charles. Capital, Inflation & the Multinationals. 1971. text ed. 12.50x o.p. (ISBN 0-04-330196-7). Allen Unwin.
--Industry's Democratic Revolution. (Ruskin House Ser in Trade Union Studies). 1974. text ed. 13.50x o.p. (ISBN 0-04-331062-1). Allen Unwin.
--International Trade Unionism. (Ruskin House Series in Trade Union Studies). 1972. text ed. 15.95x (ISBN 0-04-331049-4). Allen Unwin.
Levinson, David & Malone, Martin. Toward Explaining Human Culture. LC 80-83324. (Comparative Studies Ser.). 400p. 1980. 25.00 (ISBN 0-87536-339-3); pap. 15.00 (ISBN 0-87536-340-7). HRAFP.
Levinson, H. N. A Solution to the Riddle Dyslexia. (Illus.). 398p. 1981. 24.80 (ISBN 0-387-90515-4). Springer-Verlag.
Levinson, Hanna, jt. auth. see Reif, Joseph A.
Levinson, Harry. Emotional Health: In the World of Work. LC 63-20323. 1964. 12.95x o.p. (ISBN 0-06-033540-8, HarpT). Har-Row.
Levinson, Irving J. Introduction to Mechanics. 2nd ed. 1968. text ed. 18.95 (ISBN 0-13-487660-1). P-H.
--Mechanics of Materials. 2nd ed. 1970. text ed. 19.95 (ISBN 0-13-571380-3). P-H.
Levinson, Leonard L. The Eating Rich Cookbook. LC 73-12700. 1977. pap. 7.95 o.p. (ISBN 0-8128-2257-9). Stein & Day.
Levinson, Louis, jt. ed. see Singer, Richard B.
Levinson, Michael see Wruble, Lawrence D., et al.
Levinson, Nancy. World of Her Own. LC 80-81791. (Illus.). 128p. (gr. 5 up). 1981. PLB 6.59 (ISBN 0-8178-0014-X). Harvey.
Levinson, Nancy S. Contributions of Women: Business. LC 80-36667. (Contributions of Women Ser.). (Illus.). (gr. 6 up). 1981. PLB 8.95 (ISBN 0-87518-200-3). Dillon.
Levinson, Norman & Redheffer, Raymond. Complex Variables. LC 76-113833. (Illus.). 1970. text ed. 24.95x (ISBN 0-8162-5104-5); sol. man. 2.95 (ISBN 0-8162-5114-2). Holden-Day.
Levinson, Richard & Link, William. Stay Tuned. 256p. 1981. 10.95 (ISBN 0-312-76136-8). St Martin.
Levinthal, Charles F. The Physiological Approach in Psychology. (Illus.). 1979. 19.95 (ISBN 0-13-674796-5). P-H.
Levis, John H. Foundations of Chinese Musical Art. 2nd ed. (Illus.). 1963. Repr. of 1933 ed. 13.50 o.p. (ISBN 0-8188-0064-X). Paragon.
Levis, Larry. The Dollmaker's Ghost. 1981. 9.95 (ISBN 0-525-09450-4); pap. 5.95 (ISBN 0-525-47662-8). Dutton.
Levison, Arnold B. Knowledge & Society: An Introduction to the Philosophy of the Social Sciences. LC 72-88122. 1974. pap. 7.50 (ISBN 0-672-63661-1). Pegasus.
--Knowledge & Society: An Introduction to the Philosophy of the Social Sciences. LC 72-88122. 1974. 20.00x (ISBN 0-672-53661-7). Irvington.
Levison, Peter K., ed. see Committee on Substance Abuse & Habitual Behavior.
Levison, Wilhelm. England & the Continent in the Eighth Century. (Ford Lectures Ser). 1946. 24.95x (ISBN 0-19-821232-1). Oxford U Pr.
Levi-Strauss, Claude. The Naked Man. Weightman, John & Weightman, Doreen, trs. from Fr. LC 79-3399. (Introduction to a Science of Mythology Ser.). (Illus.). 440p. 1981. 30.00 (ISBN 0-06-012584-5, HarpT). Har-Row.
--The Origin of Table Manners. Weightman, John & Weightman, Doreen, trs. from Fr. LC 77-11810. (Science of Mythology Ser.: Vol. 3). (Illus.). 1979. 30.00 o.s.i. (ISBN 0-06-012587-X, HarpT). Har-Row.
Levitan, Lois. Improve Your Gardening with Backyard Research. (Illus.). 1980. 12.95 (ISBN 0-87857-306-2); pap. 6.95 (ISBN 0-87857-267-8). Rodale Pr Inc.
Levitan, Max & Montagu, Ashley. Textbook of Human Genetics. 2nd ed. (Illus.). 1977. text ed. 22.95x (ISBN 0-19-502101-0). Oxford U Pr.
Levitan, Sar A. Programs in Aid of the Poor for the 1980's. LC 80-8093. (Policy Studies in Employment & Welfare: No. 1). (Illus.). 166p. 1980. text ed. 11.00 (ISBN 0-8018-2483-4); pap. text ed. 3.95 (ISBN 0-8018-2484-2). Johns Hopkins.
Levitan, Sar A. & Alderman, Karen C. Warriors at Work: The Volunteer Armed Force. LC 77-21234. (Sage Library of Social Research: Vol. 58). 1977. 18.00x (ISBN 0-8039-0932-2); pap. 8.95x (ISBN 0-8039-0933-0). Sage.
Levitan, Sar A. & Zickler, Joyce K. Too Little but Not Too Late: Federal Aid to Lagging Areas. LC 76-12363. (Illus.). 1976. 16.95 (ISBN 0-669-00721-8). Lexington Bks.
Levitas, G. B., ed. Culture & Consciousness: Perspectives in the Social Sciences. LC 67-24209. (Science Ser). 1967. 7.50 (ISBN 0-8076-0431-3). Braziller.
Levitas, Maurice. Marxist Perspectives in the Sociology of Education. 216p. 1974. 21.00x (ISBN 0-7100-7896-X); pap. 8.95 (ISBN 0-7100-7897-8). Routledge & Kegan.
Levith, Murray J., ed. Fiddlers in Fiction. (Illus.). 220p. 1979. 9.95 (ISBN 0-87666-616-0, Z-27). Paganiniana Pubns.
Levitin, Isabella, tr. see Yanovsky, V. S.
Levitin, Sonia. The No-Return Trail. LC 77-88964. (gr. 7 up). 1978. 6.95 (ISBN 0-15-257545-6, HJ). HarBraceJ.
Levitine, George. Girodet-Trioson: An Iconographical Study. LC 77-94702. (Outstanding Dissertations in the Fine Arts Ser.). 1978. lib. bdg. 52.00x (ISBN 0-8240-3235-7). Garland Pub.
Leviton, Alan E., jt. ed. see Taylor, Ronald J.
Leviton, Sharon, jt. auth. see Greenstone, James L.
Levitt. Sensory Aids of the Hearing Impaired. LC 76-28875. 640p. 1980. 46.95 (ISBN 0-471-08436-0, Pub. by Wiley-Interscience); pap. 30.50 (ISBN 0-471-08437-9). Wiley.
Levitt, Arthur, Jr. How to Make Your Money Make Money. LC 80-70617. 220p. 1981. 11.95 (ISBN 0-87094-236-0). Dow Jones-Irwin.
Levitt, Barbara, jt. auth. see Levitt, Leonard S.
Levitt, Dulcie. Plants & People: Aboriginal Uses of Plants on Groote Eylandt. (Australian Institute of Aboriginl Studies). 1981. text ed. price not set (ISBN 0-391-02195-8); pap. text ed. write for info. Humanities.
Levitt, Eleanor. Natural Food Cookery. Orig. Title: The Wonderful World of Natural-Food Cookery. (Illus.). 320p. 1979. pap. 3.95 (ISBN 0-486-23851-2). Dover.
Levitt, Eugene E. Primer on the Rorshach Technique: A Method of Administration, Scoring & Interpretation. (Illus.). 116p. 1980. 14.50 (ISBN 0-398-04048-6); pap. 8.95 (ISBN 0-398-04081-8). C C Thomas.
Levitt, H., et al, eds. Sensory Aids for the Hearing Impaired. LC 76-28875. 1980. 46.95 (ISBN 0-87942-133-9). Inst Electrical.
Levitt, J. Frost, Drought & Heat Resistance. (Protoplasmatologia: Vol. 8, Pt. 6). (Illus.). 1958. pap. 30.70 o.p. (ISBN 0-387-80490-0). Springer-Verlag.
Levitt, Kent. Kidnapped for My Faith. 1978. pap. cancelled o.s.i. (ISBN 0-89728-006-7). Omega Pubns OR.
Levitt, Leonard S. & Levitt, Barbara. Comprehensive Solved Problems in Organic Chemistry. LC 78-54189. Date not set. text ed. 12.95x (ISBN 0-8162-5151-7). Holden-Day.
Levitt, Morris J. & Feldbaum, Eleanor G. Of, by & for the People: State & Local Governments & Politics. 300p. 1980. lib. bdg. 27.00x (ISBN 0-89158-591-5); pap. text ed. 12.00x (ISBN 0-89158-896-5). Westview.
Levitt, Mortimer. The Executive Look. LC 80-66011. (Illus.). 1981. 14.95 (ISBN 0-689-11078-2). Atheneum.
Levitt, Morton. Freud & Dewey on the Nature of Man. 1960. 3.75 (ISBN 0-8022-0966-1). Philos Lib.
Levitt, Morton & Rubenstein, Ben, eds. Youth & Social Change. LC 73-157414. 1972. 14.95x (ISBN 0-8143-1450-3). Wayne St U Pr.
Levitt, Morton, ed. see Meeting of the American Orthopsychiatric Assoc., 47th.
Levitt, P. John Millington Synge: A Bibliography of Published Criticism. 224p. 1974. 10.00x (ISBN 0-7165-2155-5, Pub. by Irish Academic Pr). Biblio Dist.
Levitt, Paul, et al. Cancer Reference Book. (Orig.). 1980. pap. 4.95 (ISBN 0-440-51353-7, Delta). Dell.
Levitt, Paul M., et al. The Cancer Reference Book: Direct & Clear Answers to Everyone's Questions. 271p. 1978. 12.95 (ISBN 0-87196-317-5). Facts on File.
Levitt, Paul R., jt. auth. see Boorman, Scott A.
Levitt, Ruth. Implementing Public Policy. 256p. 1981. 30.00x (ISBN 0-7099-0068-6, Pub. by Croom Helm Ltd England). Biblio Dist.
Levitt, Ruth, jt. auth. see Simpson, Peter.
Levitt, Saul. Jim Thorpe, All American. (Orig.). 1980. playscript 2.50 (ISBN 0-87602-237-9). Anchorage.
Levitt, Zola. Creation: A Scientist's Choice. 132p. 1976. pap. 2.95 o.p. (ISBN 0-88207-629-9). Victor Bks.
--Some of My Best Friends Are Christians. LC 77-90581. 1978. pap. 3.25 o.p. (ISBN 0-8307-0591-0, 54-085-04). Regal.
Levitt, Zola & McCall, Tom. Once Through the New Testament. LC 80-69306. 160p. 1981. pap. 5.95 (ISBN 0-915684-78-0). Christian Herald.
Levitt, Zola, jt. auth. see McCall, Thomas S.
Levmore, Saul. Super Strategies: Games & Puzzles for Strategy Training. (Illus.). 168p. 1981. 10.95 (ISBN 0-385-17165-X). Doubleday.
Le Vois, Camille, jt. auth. see Dondo, Muthurin.
Levorsen, A. I. Geology of Petroleum. 2nd ed. LC 65-25242. (Geology Ser.). (Illus.). 1967. 30.95x (ISBN 0-7167-0230-4). W H Freeman.
Levoy, Myron. A Shadow Like a Leopard. LC 79-2812. 192p. (YA) (gr. 7 up). 1981. 8.95 (ISBN 0-06-023816-X, HarpJ); PLB 8.79g (ISBN 0-06-023817-8). Har-Row.
Levstik, Frank R., compiled by. A Directory of State Archives in the United States. 66p. (Orig.). 1980. pap. 8.00 (ISBN 0-931828-26-0). Soc Am Archivists.
Levtzion, N. & Hopkins, J. F. Corpus of Early Arabic Sources for West African History. LC 78-67628. (Illus.). 448p. Date not set. 85.00 (ISBN 0-521-22422-5). Cambridge U Pr.
Levtzion, Nehemia. Ancient Ghana & Mali. LC 79-27281. 1980. text ed. 18.75x (ISBN 0-8419-0431-6, Africana); pap. text ed. 9.75x (ISBN 0-8419-0432-4). Holmes & Meier.
Levy. The New Language of Psychiatry: Learning & Using DSM-III. 384p. 1981. text ed. 16.95 (ISBN 0-87626-610-3). Winthrop.
Levy, jt. auth. see Lester.
Levy, A., et al, eds. Endogenous Peptides & Centrally Acting Drugs. (Progress in Biochemical Pharmacology Ser.: Vol. 16). (Illus.). 200p. 1980. 49.25 (ISBN 3-8055-0831-X). S Karger.
Levy, Alan. The Bluebird of Happiness: The Memoirs of Jan Peerce. LC 75-25055. (Illus.). 1976. 12.50 o.p. (ISBN 0-06-013311-2, HarpT). Har-Row.
--Many Heroes. 2nd ed. LC 80-65002. 384p. 1980. Repr. of 1972 ed. 12.50 (ISBN 0-933256-12-4, Pub. by Second Chance Pr). Watts.
--So Many Heroes. 2nd, rev. ed. LC 80-65002. Orig. Title: Rowboat to Prague. 384p. 1980. 15.95 (ISBN 0-933256-12-4); pap. 7.95 (ISBN 0-933256-16-7). Second Chance.
Levy, Babette M. Cotton Mather. (United States Authors Ser.: No. 328). 1979. lib. bdg. 9.95 (ISBN 0-8057-7261-8). Twayne.
Levy, Bernard & Szarmach, Paul, eds. The Alliterative Tradition in the Fourteenth Century. LC 80-84665. 230p. 1980. write for info. (ISBN 0-87338-255-2). Kent St U Pr.
Levy, Bert Y. Guerrilla Warfare. Brown, Robert K., ed. LC 64-6189. (Illus.). 119p. 1965. pap. 5.00 (ISBN 0-87364-020-9). Paladin Ent.
Levy, Charles. Social Work Ethics. 266p. 1980. pap. text ed. 9.95 (ISBN 0-87705-493-2). Human Sci Pr.
--Social Work Ethics. LC 75-11007. 240p. 1976. text ed. 22.95 (ISBN 0-87705-254-9). Human Sci Pr.
Levy, D. A. The Madison Poems & Collages. 1980. 12.00. Quixote.
Levy, D. N. Sacrifices in the Sicilian. (Batsford Chess Ser.). 196p. 1981. 19.95 (ISBN 0-7134-2596-2, Pub. by Batsford England); pap. 10.95 (ISBN 0-7134-2597-0). David & Charles.
--Sicilian Dragon: Classical & Levenfish Variations. 96p. 1981. pap. 11.95 (ISBN 0-7134-2744-2, Pub. by Batsford England). David & Charles.
Levy, Daniel C. University & Government in Mexico: Autonomy in a Authoritarian System. LC 79-21134. 190p. 1980. 20.95 (ISBN 0-03-055276-1). Praeger.
Levy, Darline G., et al, eds. Women in Revolutionary Paris, Seventeen Eighty-Nine to Seventeen Ninety-Five. LC 79-4102. 1979. text ed. 22.50 (ISBN 0-252-00409-4); pap. 10.00 (ISBN 0-252-00855-3). U of Ill Pr.
Levy, David. Play Chess: Combinations & Sacrifices. 256p. 1980. pap. cancelled o.p. (ISBN 0-19-217589-0). Oxford U Pr.
--Sicilian Accelerated Dragons. 1975. 17.50 (ISBN 0-7134-3031-1, Pub. by Batsford England). David & Charles.
--Sicilian Dragon. 1976. 19.95 (ISBN 0-7134-2931-3, Pub. by Batsford England). David & Charles.
Levy, David, jt. auth. see Keene, R. D.
Levy, David, jt. auth. see Keene, Raymond.
Levy, David, jt. auth. see O'Connell, K. J.

Levy, David N. L., ed. Learn Chess from the World Champions. 1978. text ed. 22.00 (ISBN 0-08-021387-1); pap. text ed. 9.50 (ISBN 0-08-021388-X). Pergamon.

Levy, Diana. Memories Are Like Dying Embers. 40p. 1980. 4.95 (ISBN 0-533-04286-0). Vantage.

Levy, Donald L., tr. see Haggai, J. E.

Levy, E. E., ed. Dental Hygienist "Mock" National Board. (Illus.). 128p. 1976. 13.75 (ISBN 0-398-03176-2); pap. 9.25 (ISBN 0-398-03177-0). C C Thomas.

Levy, Edward. The Beast Within. LC 78-73871. 1981. 10.95 (ISBN 0-87795-225-6). Arbor Hse.

Levy, Elizabeth. The Case of the Counterfeit Racehorse. (A Jody & Jake Mystery Bk.: No. 2). (Orig.). (gr. 5-7). 1980. pap. 1.95 (ISBN 0-671-29965-4). Archway.

--The Case of the Dark Horse: A Judy & Jake Mystery, No. 2. (Orig.). (gr. 4-7). 1980. pap. write for info. PB.

--The Case of the Fired-up Gang. (Jody & Jake Mystery: No. 3). (gr. 3-6). 1981. pap. 1.95 (ISBN 0-671-41140-3). Archway.

--The Case of the Frightened Rock Star: A Jody & Jake Mystery Bk. (No. 1). (Orig.). 1980. pap. 1.95 (ISBN 0-671-29964-6). Archway.

--Come Out Smiling. LC 80-68734. 192p. (YA) (gr. 8-12). 1981. 8.95 (ISBN 0-440-01378-X). Delacorte.

--Frankenstein Moved in on the Fourth Floor. LC 78-19830. (Illus.). 64p. (gr. 2-5). 1981. pap. 1.95 (ISBN 0-06-440122-7, Trophy). Harrow.

--Mr. Big Time. (Orig.). (gr. k-6). 1981. pap. 1.95 (ISBN 0-440-46184-7, YB). Dell.

--Mom or Pop. (Orig.). (gr. k-6). pap. 1.95 (ISBN 0-440-45779-3, YB). Dell.

--Nice Little Girls. LC 73-15394. (Illus.). 48p. (gr. k-3). 1974. 6.95 o.s.i. (ISBN 0-440-06207-1); PLB 6.46 o.s.i. (ISBN 0-440-06193-8). Delacorte.

--The People Lobby: The SST Story. LC 72-1385. 160p. (gr. 7 up). 1973. 4.95 o.s.i. (ISBN 0-440-07234-4). Delacorte.

--Running Out of Time. LC 79-28064. (Capers Ser.). (Illus.). 128p. (gr. 3-6). 1980. PLB 4.99 (ISBN 0-394-94422-4); pap. 1.95 (ISBN 0-394-84422-X). Knopf.

--The Runt. (Orig.). (gr. k-6). 1981. pap. 1.95 (ISBN 0-440-47538-4, YB). Dell.

--The Shuttered Window. (Orig.). (gr. k-6). 1981. pap. 1.95 (ISBN 0-440-47980-0, YB). Dell.

--Something Queer at the Ballpark. LC 74-16332. 48p. (gr. 1-3). 1975. 6.95 o.s.i. (ISBN 0-440-05992-5); PLB 6.46 o.s.i. (ISBN 0-440-05993-3). Delacorte.

--Something Queer on Vacation. LC 78-72858. (gr. 1-3). 1980. 6.95 (ISBN 0-440-08346-X); PLB 6.46 (ISBN 0-440-08347-8). Delacorte.

--Take Two, They're Small. (Orig.). (gr. k-6). 1981. pap. 1.95 (ISBN 0-440-48517-7, YB). Dell.

--The Tryouts. LC 78-22125. (Illus.). 112p. (gr. 3-7). 1979. 7.95 (ISBN 0-590-07487-3, Four Winds). Schol Bk Serv.

Levy, Elizabeth & Richards, Tad. Struggle & Lose, Struggle & Win: The United Mine Workers Union. LC 76-56703. 144p. (gr. 7-11). 1977. 6.95 (ISBN 0-590-07355-9, Four Winds). Schol Bk Serv.

Levy, Emanuel. The Habima--Israel's National Theater 1917-1977. LC 79-12486. 1979. 25.00x (ISBN 0-231-04582-4). Columbia U Pr.

Levy, Ernst, jt. auth. see Levarie, Siegmund.

Levy, Frank. The Harried Staffer's Guide to Current Welfare Reform Proposals. (Welfare Reform Policy Analysis Ser.: No. 4). 83p. 1978. pap. 3.50 (ISBN 0-87766-231-2, 23400). Urban Inst.

--The Logic of Welfare Reform. (Welfare Reform Policy Analysis Ser.: No. 6). 81p. 1981. pap. 6.00 (ISBN 0-87766-282-7, 29700). Urban Inst.

Levy, Frank S., et al. Urban Outcomes: Schools, Streets, & Libraries. (The Oakland Project). 1974. 20.00x (ISBN 0-520-02546-6); pap. 6.95x (ISBN 0-520-03045-1). U of Cal Pr.

Levy, Fritz J., ed. see Bacon, Francis.

Levy, G. & Amitai, P. Scorpiones: Arachnida I, Vol. 3. (Fauna Palestina Ser.). (Illus.). 132p. 1981. text ed. 25.00x (ISBN 0-87474-606-X). Smithsonian.

Levy, George C., et al. Carbon-Thirteen Nuclear Magnetic Resonance. 2nd ed. LC 80-17289. 300p. 1980. 22.50 (ISBN 0-471-53157-X, Pub. by Wiley-Interscience). Wiley.

Levy, Gerald. Ghetto School: Class Warfare in an Elementary School. LC 70-116067. 1970. pap. 4.95 (ISBN 0-672-63543-7). Pegasus.

Levy, H. & Sarnat, M. Capital Investment & Financial Decisions. 1978. 21.95 (ISBN 0-13-113423-X). P-H.

Levy, Haim & Sarnat, Marshall. Investment & Portfolio Analysis. LC 74-175793. (Ser. in Finance). 568p. 1972. 26.50 (ISBN 0-471-53152-9). Wiley.

Levy, Haim, jt. auth. see Ben-Horim, Moshe.

Levy, Harold L., ed. The Language Teacher. Incl. Foreign Language Program: Grades 3-12. Eaton, Margaret E; The Ghosts in the Language Classroom. Walsh, Donald D; Means of Meeting the Shortage of Teachers. Bock, Carolyn E; Patterns As Grammar. Brodin, Dorothy; Single vs. Multiple Languages in Secondary Schools; The Teaching of Writing. Atkins, Jeannette. 84p. 1958. pap. 7.95x (ISBN 0-915432-58-7). NE Conf Teach Foreign.

Levy, Henry M., jt. auth. see Eckhouse, Richard H.

Levy, Hermann. Economic Liberalism. LC 79-51864. 1981. Repr. of 1913 ed. 14.50 (ISBN 0-88355-956-0). Hyperion Conn.

--Large & Small Holdings. LC 67-42. Repr. of 1911 ed. 25.00x (ISBN 0-678-05067-8). Kelley.

Levy, Howard & Ross-Molloy, Lynn. Beginning a Community Museum. LC 75-27098. 84p. 1975. pap. 3.00 (ISBN 0-89062-009-1, Pub. by NYSCA.). Pub Ctr Cult Res.

Levy, Howard S., jt. auth. see Ishihara, Akira.

Levy, Ian H., tr. from Japanese. The Ten Thousand Leaves: A Translation of Man'yoshu, Japan's Premier Anthology of Classical Poetry, Vol. 1. LC 80-8561. (Princeton Library of Asian Translations). (Illus.). 280p. 1981. 20.00x (ISBN 0-691-06452-0). Princeton U Pr.

Levy, J. Literary Translation As an Art Form. Flatauer, S., tr. (Approaches to Translation Studies: No. 6). 1980. pap. text ed. write for info. (ISBN 0-391-01196-0). Humanities.

Levy, Janine. You & Your Toddler: Sharing the Developing Years. (Illus.). 1981. 10.95 (ISBN 0-394-51532-3); pap. 6.95 (ISBN 0-394-74806-9). Pantheon.

Levy, Jerrold E. & Kunitz, Stephen J. Indian Drinking: Navajo Practices & Anglo-American Theories. LC 73-17173. 320p. 1974. 20.95 o.p. (ISBN 0-471-53163-4, Pub. by Wiley-Interscience). Wiley.

Levy, Joseph. Play Behavior. LC 77-12504. 1978. pap. text ed. 19.95 (ISBN 0-471-01712-4). Wiley.

Levy, Joyce I., jt. auth. see Cormier, Patricia P.

Levy, Juliette D. Herbal Handbook for Farm & Stable. LC 76-2734. 1976. pap. 5.95 (ISBN 0-87857-115-9); 5.95 o.p. (ISBN 0-87857-120-5). Rodale Pr Inc.

Levy, Leon, et al. Essentials of Merchandise Information: Nontextiles. LC 66-10398. 1968. pap. text ed. 9.20 o.p. (ISBN 0-8224-0273-4); wkbk 3.16 o.p. (ISBN 0-8224-0250-5); tchrs'. manual & key 2.80 o.p. (ISBN 0-8224-0613-6). Pitman Learning.

Levy, Leon S. Discrete Structures of Computer Science. LC 79-11218. 1980. text ed. 20.95 (ISBN 0-471-03208-5). Wiley.

Levy, Leonard. Blasphemy in Massachusetts. LC 70-16634. 592p. 1974. lib. bdg. 55.00 (ISBN 0-306-70221-5). Da Capo.

Levy, Leonard W. Law of the Commonwealth & Chief Justice Shaw. 1957. 7.50x o.p. (ISBN 0-8377-2401-5). Rothman.

--Origins of the Fifth Amendment: The Right Against Self-Incrimination. 1971. pap. 7.95 (ISBN 0-19-501356-5, GB34, GB). Oxford U Pr.

Levy, Leonard W., ed. Essays on the Making of the Constitution. (Orig.). 1969. pap. 5.95x (ISBN 0-19-500954-1). Oxford U Pr.

Levy, Leonard W. & Jones, Douglas L., eds. Jim Crow in Boston: The Origin of the "Separate but Equal Doctrine". LC 73-39622. (Civil Liberties in American History Ser). 1974. lib. bdg. 25.00 (ISBN 0-306-70157-X). Da Capo.

Levy, Madeleine R., jt. auth. see Tigar, Michael E.

Levy, Matthew N., jt. auth. see Berne, Robert M.

Levy, Maurice, et al, eds. Quarks & Leptons: Cargese Nineteen Seventy-Nine. (NATO Advanced Study Institutes Ser. (Series B--Physics): Vol. 61). 760p. 1981. 75.00 (ISBN 0-306-40560-1, Plenum Pr). Plenum Pub.

Levy, Milton L. Media Awards Handbook. LC 68-24272. 190p. 1980. pap. 20.00 (ISBN 0-910744-03-3). Media Awards.

Levy, Miriam, jt. auth. see Fraser, Kathleen.

Levy, Morton. Accounting Goes Public. LC 77-81445. 1977. 13.95 (ISBN 0-8122-7733-3). U of Pa Pr.

Levy, Norman. Living or Dying: Adaptation to Hemodialysis. 164p. 1974. pap. 16.75 photocopy ed., spiral (ISBN 0-398-02987-3). C C Thomas.

Levy, Norman B., ed. Psychonephrology One: Psychological Factors in Hemodialysis & Transplantation. 280p. 1981. 25.00 (ISBN 0-306-40586-5, Plenum Pr). Plenum Pub.

Levy, Paul S. & Lemeshow, Stanley. Sampling for Health Professionals. LC 80-14733. 320p. 1980. pap. text ed. 22.95 solutions manual (ISBN 0-534-97986-6). Lifetime Learn.

Levy, R. I Can Only Touch You Now. 1973. ref. ed. 13.95 (ISBN 0-13-448746-X); pap. text ed. 10.95 (ISBN 0-13-448738-9). P-H.

Levy, Reuben. An Introduction to Persian Literature. LC 68-8876. 194p. 1969. 17.50x (ISBN 0-231-03177-7). Columbia U Pr.

Levy, Reynold. Nearing the Crossroads: Contending Approaches to Contemporary American Foreign Policy. LC 74-21490. 1975. 10.95 o.s.i. (ISBN 0-02-918810-5). Free Pr.

Levy, Richard C., jt. auth. see Langley, Roger.

Levy, Robert I., et al, eds. Nutrition, Lipids & Coronary Heart Disease. LC 78-67020. (Nutrition in Health & Disease Ser.: Vol. 1). 1979. 52.00 (ISBN 0-89004-181-4). Raven.

Levy, Robert J., jt. auth. see Feld, Barry.

Levy, Ronald. Self-Revelation Through Relationships. LC 73-167896. 1972. 7.95 (ISBN 0-13-803569-5). P-H.

Levy, Salomon see Heat Transfer & Fluid Mechanics Institute.

Levy, Sara G. Mother Goose Rhymes for Jewish Children. (Illus.). (ps-2). 1979. Repr. of 1945 ed. 6.95 (ISBN 0-8197-0254-4). Bloch.

Levy, Sidney J. & Zaltman, Gerald. Marketing, Society, & Conflict. (Economic Institutions & Social Systems Ser). (Illus.). 176p. 1975. text ed. 12.95 ref. ed. (ISBN 0-13-557819-1); pap. text ed. 9.95 (ISBN 0-13-557801-9). P-H.

Levy, Tedd & Krasnow, Donna C. A Guidebook for Teaching United States History: Earliest Times to the Civil War. 1979. pap. text ed. 18.95 (ISBN 0-205-06503-1). Allyn.

--A Guidebook for Teaching United States History: Mid-Nineteenth Century to Present. 1979. pap. text ed. 18.95 (ISBN 0-205-06496-5). Allyn.

Levy, Wilbert J. Man Studies Himself. (gr. 10-12). 1973. pap. text ed. 3.83 (ISBN 0-87720-370-9). AMSCO Sch.

--Man Studies His Past. (gr. 10-12). 1973. pap. text ed. 3.83 (ISBN 0-87720-371-7). AMSCO Sch.

--Man Studies the World Around Him. (gr. 10-12). 1973. pap. text ed. 3.83 (ISBN 0-87720-372-5). AMSCO Sch.

--More Powerful Reading. (Orig.). (gr. 10-12). 1969. pap. text ed. 6.17 (ISBN 0-87720-325-3). AMSCO Sch.

--Paragraph Composition. (gr. 10-12). 1977. wkbk 5.67 (ISBN 0-87720-957-X). AMSCO Sch.

--Paragraph Power. (gr. 10-12). 1977. pap. 5.67 wkbk. (ISBN 0-87720-334-2). AMSCO Sch.

--Reading & Growing. (gr. 7-10). 1975. pap. text ed. 5.42 (ISBN 0-87720-328-8). AMSCO Sch.

--Sense of Sentences. (Orig.). (gr. 9-12). 1976. wkbk 5.67 (ISBN 0-87720-336-9). AMSCO Sch.

--Sentence Composition. (Orig.). 1976. wkbk 5.67 (ISBN 0-87720-950-2). AMSCO Sch.

Levy, Wilbert J. & Farber, Carol R. Patterns of Meaning. 1977. pap. text ed. 6.92 (ISBN 0-87720-956-1). AMSCO Sch.

Levy, Wilbert J., jt. auth. see Zimbal, Samuel F.

Levy, William S. Skin Problems of the Amputee. LC 78-50196. (Illus.). 320p. 1981. 55.00 (ISBN 0-87527-181-2). Green.

Lew, Irving, ed. see De Vinne, Theodore L.

Lew, Irving, ed. see Watkins, George T.

Lew, Irving, ed. see Willett, Ralph.

Lew, Marvin I. Hospital Pharmacy Journal Articles. 3rd ed. 1977. spiral bdg. 15.50 (ISBN 0-87488-799-2). Med Exam.

Lewald, H. Ernest. Eduardo Mallea. (World Authors Ser.: No. 433). 1977. lib. bdg. 12.50 (ISBN 0-8057-6273-6). Twayne.

Lewald, H. Ernest, ed. The Cry of Home: Cultural Nationalism & the Modern Writer. LC 76-173656. 412p. 1972. 15.50x (ISBN 0-87049-135-0). U of Tenn Pr.

Lewalski, Barbara K. Milton's Brief Epic: The Genre, Meaning, & Art of Paradise Regained. LC 66-10282. 436p. 1967. Repr. of 1966 ed. 16.00x (ISBN 0-87057-095-1, Pub. by Brown U Pr). Univ Pr of New England.

Lewalski, Barbara K. & Sabol, Andrew J., eds. Major Poets of the Earlier Seventeenth Century. LC 70-789379. 1973. 28.90 o.p. (ISBN 0-672-53184-4); pap. 17.50 o.p. (ISBN 0-672-63184-9). Odyssey Pr.

Lewellen, Ted. The Ruthless Gun. 160p. 1981. pap. 1.75 (ISBN 0-449-12796-6, GM). Fawcett.

Lewellen, Theodore C. Peasants in Transition: The Changing Economy of the Peruvian Aymara: a General Systems Approach. LC 78-343. (A Westview Replica Edition Ser.). 1978. lib. bdg. 24.00x (ISBN 0-89158-076-X). Westview.

Lewen, Si. A Journey. LC 80-67120. 88p. 1980. 15.00 (ISBN 0-87982-032-2). Art Alliance.

Lewenhak, Shiela. History of Wool in Britain. (Jackdaw Ser: No. 96). (Illus.). 1972. 5.95 o.p. (ISBN 0-670-78213-0, Grossman). Viking Pr.

Lewerth, Margaret. Hester-Roundtree Women, Bk. III. 1979. pap. 2.50 o.s.i. (ISBN 0-440-14884-7). Dell.

--Lilith: The Roundtree Women. (Orig.). 1981. pap. 3.25 (ISBN 0-440-14630-5). Dell.

Lewery, A. J. Narrow Boat Painting: A History & Description of the English Narrow Boats' Traditional Paintwork. LC 74-81074. 1975. 16.95 (ISBN 0-7153-6771-4). David & Charles.

Lewes, George H. The Life of Goethe. LC 65-21308. (Illus.). 604p. 1980. 15.00 (ISBN 0-8044-2521-3). Ungar.

--Literary Criticism of George Henry Lewes. Kaminsky, Alice R., ed. LC 64-17230. (Regents Critics Ser). 1965. 9.95x (ISBN 0-8032-0456-6); pap. 2.75x (ISBN 0-8032-5455-5, BB 402, Bison). U of Nebr Pr.

--Study of Psychology. (Contributions to the History of Psychology Ser.: No. 6, Pt. A Orientations). 1978. Repr. of 1879 ed. 30.00 (ISBN 0-89093-155-0). U Pubns Amer.

Lewicki, Tadeusz. Arabic External Sources for the History of Africa to the South of Sahara. (Illus.). 102p. (Orig.). 1974. pap. text ed. 6.50x (ISBN 0-7007-0020-X). Humanities.

Lewick-Wallace, Mary. Vocabulary Building & Word Study. Raygor, Alton, ed. (Communication Skills Ser.). 240p. (Orig.). 1981. pap. text ed. 8.95 (ISBN 0-07-067902-9, C). McGraw.

Lewin, A. C. Housing Cooperatives in Developing Countries: A Manual for Self-Help in Low Cost Housing Schemes. 192p. 1981. 35.75 (ISBN 0-471-27820-3, Pub. by Wiley-Intrscience); pap. write for info. (ISBN 0-471-27819-X). Wiley.

Lewin, Arie Y. & Shakum, Melvin F., eds. Policy Science: Methodologies & Cases. 450p. 1975. 50.00 (ISBN 0-08-019601-2); pap. text ed. 24.00 (ISBN 0-08-019600-4). Pergamon.

Lewin, Benjamin. Gene Expression, Vol. 3: Plasmids & Phages. LC 73-14382. 1977. 41.95 (ISBN 0-471-53170-7, Pub. by Wiley-Interscience); pap. 18.95 (ISBN 0-471-02715-4). Wiley.

Lewin, Betsy. Cat Count: LC 80-25849. (Illus.). 32p. (ps-2). 1981. PLB 5.95 (ISBN 0-396-07928-8). Dodd.

Lewin, Douglas. Computer Aided Design of Digital Systems. LC 76-250. (Computer Systems Engineering Ser.). 1977. 27.50x (ISBN 0-8448-0918-7). Crane-Russak Co.

--Theory & Design of Digital Computer Systems. 2nd ed. 472p. 1980. pap. text ed. 24.95x (ISBN 0-470-26959-6). Halsted Pr.

Lewin, Jane E., tr. see Genette, Gerard.

Lewin, Leonard. Theory of Waveguides. LC 72-389. 320p. 1975. 37.95 (ISBN 0-471-53165-0). Halsted Pr.

Lewin, Michael Z. Ask the Right Question. 1979. pap. 1.95 o.p. (ISBN 0-425-04027-5). Berkley Pub.

--The Enemies Within. 1979. pap. 1.75 o.p. (ISBN 0-425-04029-1). Berkley Pub.

--Night Cover. 1980. pap. 1.95 o.p. (ISBN 0-425-04030-5). Berkley Pub.

--Outside in. Date not set. pap. 2.25 (ISBN 0-425-05006-8). Berkley Pub.

--The Way We Die Now. 1979. pap. 1.95 o.p. (ISBN 0-425-04028-3). Berkley Pub.

Lewin, Miriam. Understanding Psychological Research: The Student Researcher's Handbook. LC 78-27842. 1979. text ed. 21.95 (ISBN 0-471-65837-5); tchrs. manual avail. (ISBN 0-471-05037-7). Wiley.

Lewin, Ralph A. The Genetics of Algae. LC 75-27297. (Botanical Monographs: Vol 12). 1976. 40.00x (ISBN 0-520-03149-0). U of Cal Pr.

Lewin, Roger, jt. ed. see Cherfas, Jeremy.

Lewin, Ronald. The Chief: Field Marshal Lord Wavell, Commander-in-Chief & Viceroy 1939-47. 1980. 10.95 (ISBN 0-374-12112-5). FS&G.

--Churchill As Warlord. LC 72-96544. (Illus.). 308p. 1981. pap. 6.95 (ISBN 0-8128-6099-3). Stein & Day.

Lewin, Stephen, ed. Crime & Its Prevention. LC 68-17131. (Reference Shelf Ser: Vol. 40, No. 4). 1968. 6.25 (ISBN 0-8242-0103-5). Wilson.

--Nation's Health. (Reference Shelf Ser: Vol. 43, No. 3). 1971. 6.25 (ISBN 0-8242-0448-4). Wilson.

Lewin, Ted. World Within a World: Baja. LC 78-7740. (Illus.). (gr. 5 up). 1979. 5.95 (ISBN 0-396-07615-7). Dodd.

Lewine, Richard R. J., jt. auth. see Bernheim, Kayla F.

Lewington, Mike, jt. ed. see Cook, Jim.

Le Winn, Edward B. Human Neurological Organization. (Illus.). 244p. 1977. 14.75 (ISBN 0-398-01122-2). C C Thomas.

Lewins, J. Nuclear Reactor Kinetics & Control. LC 77-8107. 1978. text ed. 45.00 (ISBN 0-08-021682-X); pap. text ed. 18.00 (ISBN 0-08-021681-1). Pergamon.

Lewinski, Jorge & Clark, Bob. Colour in Focus. 1978. 16.95 o.p. (ISBN 0-85242-439-6, Pub. by Fountain). Morgan.

Lewis. Criminal Procedure: The Supreme Court's View - Cases. (Criminal Justice Ser.). 131p. 1980. pap. text ed. write for info. (ISBN 0-8299-0321-6); 1980 supplement avail. West Pub.

--How to Find a Job. 1981. pap. 2.95 (ISBN 0-8120-2298-X). Barron.

Lewis & Lyman. Essential English. 1981. pap. text ed. write for info. Goodyear.

Lewis, jt. auth. see Ray.

Lewis, A. H., jt. auth. see McEwen, W. A.

Lewis, A. S., ed. see Romen, A. S.

Lewis, Alan E. Graves' Disease. LC 80-15624. (Discussions in Patient Management Ser.). 1980. pap. 12.00 (ISBN 0-87488-870-0). Med Exam.

Lewis, Albert C., intro. by. Albert Einstein: Four Commemorative Lectures. 1980. 3.50 (ISBN 0-87959-093-9). U of Tex Hum Res.

Lewis, Alec. The Quotable Quotations Book. 352p. 1981. pap. 5.95 (ISBN 0-346-12523-5). Cornerstone.

--The Quotable Quote Book. LC 78-22461. 1980. 12.95 (ISBN 0-690-01489-9, TYC-T). T y Crowell.

Lewis, Alfred A. Everybody's Weaving Book. Krasnoff, Julienne, ed. LC 75-31512. (Illus.). 192p. 1976. 14.95 o.s.i. (ISBN 0-02-571270-5, 57127). Macmillan.

--The Mountain Artisans Quilting Book. LC 72-91259. (Illus.). 120p. 1973. 15.00 o.s.i. (ISBN 0-02-571260-8). Macmillan.

Lewis, Alfred A. & Berns, Barrie. Three Out of Four Wives. 288p. 1975. 7.95 o.s.i. (ISBN 0-02-570500-8). Macmillan.

Lewis, Allan. Ionesco. (World Authors Ser.: France: No. 239). lib. bdg. 10.95 (ISBN 0-8057-2452-4). Twayne.

Lewis, Alun. Alun Lewis: Selected Poetry & Prose. 1966. text ed. 8.95x o.p. (ISBN 0-04-821011-0). Allen Unwin.

--The Last Inspection & Other Stories. 1942. text ed. 3.95x (ISBN 0-04-823032-4). Allen Unwin.

Lewis, Anne. A Guide to Basic Riding Instruction. (Illus.). pap. 4.35 (ISBN 0-85131-218-7, Dist. by Sporting Book Center). J A Allen.

Lewis, Anthony, jt. ed. see Fortune, Nigel.

Lewis, Anthony J. Mechanisms of Neurological Disease. 1976. 27.95 (ISBN 0-316-52336-4). Little.

Lewis, Archibald R. The Development of Southern French & Catalan Society Seven Eighteen to Ten Fifty. LC 80-2019. 1981. Repr. of 1965 ed. 47.50 (ISBN 0-404-18575-4). AMS Pr.

Lewis, Arnold & Morgan, Keith. American Victorian Architecture: American Victorian Architecture: a Survey of the 70's & 80's in Contemporary Photographs. 12.50 (ISBN 0-8446-5217-2). Peter Smith.

Lewis, Arnold & Morgan, Keith, eds. American Victorian Architecture. LC 73-92261. Orig. Title: L' Architecture American. (Illus.). 160p. 1975. pap. 6.95 (ISBN 0-486-23177-1). Dover.

Lewis, Arthur H. Dark Side of the Millennium: The Problem of Evil in Revelation 20: 1-10. 96p. (Orig.). 1980. pap. 4.95 (ISBN 0-8010-5596-2). Baker Bk.

--Murder by Contract: The People Vs. "Tough Tony" Boyle. LC 75-6721. 400p. 1975. 10.95 o.s.i. (ISBN 0-02-570520-2, 57052). Macmillan.

Lewis, Arthur J., jt. ed. see Gonzales, Gertrude D.

Lewis, Arthur O., Jr., ed. Of Men & Machines. 1963. pap. 3.95 o.p. (ISBN 0-525-47130-8). Dutton.

Lewis, B., et al, eds. Encyclopedia of Islam, 5 vols. Incl. Vol. 1. A-B: Fasc. 1-22. Gibb, H. A., et al, eds. 1960. text ed. 182.25x (ISBN 90-040-0530-7); Vol. 2. C-G: Fasc. 23-40. Lewis, B., et al, eds. 1965. 178.75x (ISBN 90-040-0531-5); Vol. 3. H-Iram: Fasc. 41-60. 1969. text ed. 217.75x (ISBN 90-040-3275-4); Vols. 4 & 5. I-Ram &K-Ha: Fasc. 61-78. 1978. text ed. 275.00 (ISBN 0-685-23323-5). Humanities.

Lewis, B. A. The Murle: Red Chiefs & Black Commoners. (Oxford Monographs in Social Anthropology). 1972. 11.00x o.p. (ISBN 0-19-823172-5). Oxford U Pr.

Lewis, Benjamin & Wilkin, Leon O., Jr. Veterinary Drug Index. LC 78-64717. 600p. 1981. text ed. write for info. (ISBN 0-7216-5764-8). Saunders.

Lewis, Bernard. Islam, 2 vols. 1976. 15.00 ea. o.s.i.; Vol. 1. (ISBN 0-8027-2023-4); Vol. 2. (ISBN 0-8027-2055-2). Walker & Co.

--Istanbul & the Civilization of the Ottoman Empire. (Centers of Civilization Ser.: No. 9). (Illus.). 1972. 6.95x (ISBN 0-8061-0567-4); pap. 4.95x (ISBN 0-8061-1060-0). U of Okla Pr.

--Studies in Classical & Ottoman Islam (7th-16th Centuries) 414p. 1980. 68.00x (ISBN 0-902089-97-8, Pub. by Variorum England). State Mutual Bk.

Lewis, Bernard, ed. Islam, from the Prophet Muhammad to the Capture of Constantinople Vol. 1: Politics & War. (Documentary History of Western Civilization Ser.). 1973. pap. 6.95x (ISBN 0-06-131749-7, TB1749, Torch). Harper Row.

Lewis, Bernard, jt. ed. see Braude, Benjamin.

Lewis, Bernard, ed. see Goldziher, Ignaz.

Lewis, Bessie. Walks of Jesus. 1976. 1.25 o.p. (ISBN 0-8042-3598-8). John Knox.

Lewis, Beth I. George Grosz: Art & Politics in the Weimar Republic. LC 79-143764. (Illus.). 1971. 25.00 (ISBN 0-299-05901-4). U of Wis Pr.

Lewis, Betty. Monterey Bay Yesterday: A Nostalgic Era in Post Cards. LC 77-93856. (Illus.). 1977. 3.98 (ISBN 0-913548-48-0, Valley Calif). Western Tanager.

--Watsonville: Memories That Linger. LC 76-41500. (Illus.). 1976. 10.00 o.p. (ISBN 0-913548-37-5, Valley Calif). Western Tanager.

--Watsonville: More Memories That Linger, Vol. 2. LC 76-41500. (Illus.). 168p. 1980. 11.95 (ISBN 0-934136-08-4, Valley Calif). Western Tanager.

Lewis, Brenda R. Growing up in Ancient Rome. LC 79-56455. (Growing up Ser.). (Illus.). 72p. (gr. 7 up). 1980. text ed. 14.95 (ISBN 0-7134-3374-4, Pub. by Batsford England). David & Charles.

--Growing up in Aztec Times. (Growing up Ser.). (Illus.). 72p. (gr. 7-9). 1981. 15.95 (ISBN 0-7134-2734-5, Pub. by Batsford England). David & Charles.

--Growing up in Inca Times. (Growing up Ser.). (Illus.). 72p. (gr. 7-9). 1981. 15.95 (ISBN 0-7134-2736-1, Pub. by Batsford England). David & Charles.

--Growing up in the Dark Ages. LC 79-56478. (Growing up Ser.). (Illus.). 72p. (gr. 7 up). 1980. text ed. 16.95 (ISBN 0-7134-3362-0, Pub. by Batsford England). David & Charles.

Lewis, Bruce. Meet the Computer. LC 77-2856. (gr. 4-5). 1977. 5.95 (ISBN 0-396-07456-1). Dodd.

--What Is a Laser? LC 78-11100. (Skylight Bks.). (Illus.). (gr. 3-5). 1979. 5.95 (ISBN 0-396-07646-7). Dodd.

Lewis, C. A. see Bowen, D. Q.

Lewis, C. D. Operations Management in Practice. 304p. 1980. 36.00x (ISBN 0-86003-511-5, Pub. by Allan Pubs England); pap. 18.00x (ISBN 0-86003-611-1). State Mutual Bk.

Lewis, C. S. Case for Christianity. 1943. 7.95 (ISBN 0-02-570490-7). Macmillan.

--Christianismo...y Nada Mas. Orozco, Julio, tr. from Eng. LC 77-85609. 216p. (Orig., Span.). 1977. pap. 3.50 (ISBN 0-89922-096-7). Edit Caribe.

--Great Divorce. 1946. 4.95 o.p. (ISBN 0-02-570550-4); pap. 1.95 (ISBN 0-02-086780-8). Macmillan.

--Grief Observed. 1963. 4.95 (ISBN 0-8164-0137-3). Crossroad NY.

--A Grief Observed. (Orig.). 1966. pap. 3.95 (ISBN 0-571-06624-0, Pub. by Faber & Faber). Merrimack Bk Serv.

--Horse & His Boy. (Illus.). (gr. 4-6). 1954. 8.95 (ISBN 0-02-757670-1). Macmillan.

--The Joyful Christian: 100 Readings from the Works of C. S. Lewis. LC 77-21685. 1977. 8.95 (ISBN 0-02-570900-3). Macmillan.

--Last Battle. (Illus.). (gr. 4-6). 1956. 8.95 (ISBN 0-02-757890-9). Macmillan.

--El Leon, la Brula y el Guardarropa. Orozco, Julio, tr. from Eng. LC 76-55492. (Cronicas de Narnia). 171p. (Orig., Span.). (gr. 4 up). 1977. pap. 2.95 (ISBN 0-89922-081-9). Edit Caribe.

--Letters to Malcolm: Chiefly on Prayer. LC 64-11536. 124p. 1973. pap. 2.50 (ISBN 0-15-650880-X, HB250, Harv). HarBraceJ.

--Lion, the Witch & the Wardrobe. (Illus.). (gr. 4-6). 1951. 8.95 (ISBN 0-02-758110-1). Macmillan.

Lewis, C S. Literary Impact of the Authorized Version. Reumann, John, ed. LC 63-17883. (Facet Bks). 48p. (Orig.). 1963. pap. 1.00 (ISBN 0-8006-3003-3, 1-3003). Fortress.

Lewis, C. S. Mere Christianity. 1964. 8.95 (ISBN 0-02-570610-1); pap. 2.95 (ISBN 0-02-086810-3). Macmillan.

--A Mind Awake. LC 80-14133. 1980. pap. 3.95 (ISBN 0-15-659772-1, Harv). HarBraceJ.

--Out of the Silent Planet. 1943. 10.95 (ISBN 0-02-570790-6); large print ed. 9.95 (ISBN 0-02-489400-1). Macmillan.

--Perelandra. 1968. 10.95 (ISBN 0-02-570840-6); pap. 1.95 (ISBN 0-02-086900-2). Macmillan.

--Prince Caspian. (Illus.). (gr. 4-6). 1951. 8.95 (ISBN 0-02-758550-6). Macmillan.

--El Principe Caspian. Orozco, Julio, tr. from Eng. LC 77-14649. (Cronicas De Narnia Ser.). 223p. (Orig., Span.). (gr. 4 up). 1978. pap. 2.95 (ISBN 0-89922-105-X). Edit Caribe.

--Problem of Pain. 1943. 7.95 (ISBN 0-02-570910-0); pap. 1.65 (ISBN 0-02-086840-5). Macmillan.

--El Problema del Dolor. Vilela, Ernesto S., tr. from Eng. LC 77-16715. 156p. (Orig., Span.). 1977. pap. 2.95 (ISBN 0-89922-097-5). Edit Caribe.

--The Screwtape Letters. LC 80-18591. (Illus.). 136p. 1980. Repr. of 1979 ed. 9.95 (ISBN 0-8006-0650-7, 1-650). Fortress.

--La Silla de Plata. Orozco, Julio, tr. from Eng. (Cronicas de Narnia Ser.). 251p. (Orig., Span.). (gr. 4 up). 1979. pap. 2.95 (ISBN 0-89922-137-8). Edit Caribe.

--Silver Chair. (Illus.). (gr. 4-6). 1953. 8.95 (ISBN 0-02-758770-3). Macmillan.

--Six by Lewis. 1978. pap. 12.95 (ISBN 0-02-086770-0). Macmillan.

--Spenser's Images of Life. Fowler, A., ed. LC 77-82504. (Illus.). 1978. pap. 6.50 (ISBN 0-521-29284-0). Cambridge U Pr.

--Studies in Medieval & Renaissance Literature. 1980. 23.95 (ISBN 0-521-05545-8); pap. 7.95 (ISBN 0-521-29701-X). Cambridge U Pr.

--That Hideous Strength. LC 68-7663. 1968. 11.95 (ISBN 0-02-571250-0). Macmillan.

--El Viaje del "Aurora". Ingledew, Roberto, tr. from Eng. LC 78-54297. (Cronicas de Narnia Ser.). 239p. (Orig., Span.). (gr. 4 up). 1978. pap. 2.95 (ISBN 0-89922-119-X). Edit Caribe.

--Voyage of the Dawn Treader. (Illus.). (gr. 4-6). 1952. 8.95 (ISBN 0-02-758800-9). Macmillan.

Lewis, C. S., ed. George MacDonald: An Anthology. 1978. 7.95 (ISBN 0-02-570530-X). Macmillan.

Lewis, C. V., jt. auth. see Armstrong, H. C.

Lewis, Canella. The Music of Aquarius. 1977. pap. 1.50 o.p. (ISBN 0-425-03292-2). Berkley Pub.

Lewis, Carol & Sternheimer, Stephen. Soviet Urban Management: With Comparisons to the United States. LC 78-19748. (Praeger Special Studies). 1979. 28.95 (ISBN 0-03-046136-7). Praeger.

Lewis, Carolyn K. The Villa Giustinian at Roncade. LC 76-23636. (Outstanding Dissertations in the Fine Arts). (Illus.). 643p. 1980. Repr. of 1973 ed. lib. bdg. 91.00 (ISBN 0-8240-2705-1). Garland Pub.

Lewis, Carroll. Treasures of Galveston Bay. (Illus.). 1967. 8.95 (ISBN 0-87244-052-4). Texian.

Lewis, Cecil D., ed. A Book of English Lyrics. 1979. 5.95 (ISBN 0-7011-0909-2, Pub. by Chatto Bodley Jonathan). Merrimack Bk Serv.

Lewis, Charles, et al. A Right to Health: The Problem of Access to Primary Medical Care. LC 76-18129. (Health, Medicine, & Society Ser.). 416p. 1976. 27.95 (ISBN 0-471-01494-X, Pub. by Wiley-Interscience). Wiley.

Lewis, Charles E. Health & Medical Care Services: Current Critical Issues. LC 80-17126. (Collected Essay Ser.). 64p. 1981. pap. text ed. 6.95 (ISBN 0-917724-17-8). Haworth Pr.

Lewis, Charles L. Matthew Fontaine Maury. LC 79-6116. (Navies & Men Ser.). (Illus.). 1980. Repr. of 1927 ed. lib. bdg. 25.00x (ISBN 0-405-13045-7). Arno.

--Philander Priestley Claxton: Crusader for Public Education. 1948. 10.00x o.p. (ISBN 0-87049-002-8). U of Tenn Pr.

Lewis, Chris, jt. auth. see Slesser, Malcolm.

Lewis, Christa. Boobies on My Bowsprit. 1981. 8.75 (ISBN 0-8062-1598-4). Carlton.

Lewis, Clara M. Nutrition & Therapy. 1981. write for info. (ISBN 0-8036-5615-7). Davis Co.

Lewis, Clara M., jt. auth. see Bailey, Carolyn S.

Lewis, Clarence I. Mind & the World Order. 1924. pap. 6.50 (ISBN 0-486-20359-X). Dover.

Lewis, Claudia. Writing for Young Children. LC 79-6588. 168p. 1981. 10.95 (ISBN 0-385-15392-9, Anchor Pr). Doubleday.

Lewis, Cleona. International Accounts. (Brookings Institution Reprint Ser.). Repr. of 1927 ed. lib. bdg. 28.00x (ISBN 0-697-00163-6). Irvington.

Lewis, Clive S. Allegory of Love: A Study of Medieval Tradition. 1936. 22.00x (ISBN 0-19-811562-8); pap. 4.95x (ISBN 0-19-500343-8). Oxford U Pr.

--Discarded Image. LC 64-21555. (Orig.). 1968. 29.95 (ISBN 0-521-05551-2); pap. 7.50 (ISBN 0-521-09450-X). Cambridge U Pr.

--English Literature in the Sixteenth Century Excluding Drama. (Oxford History of English Literature Ser.). 1954. 37.50x (ISBN 0-19-812204-7). Oxford U Pr.

--Experiment in Criticism. 1961. 23.95 (ISBN 0-521-05553-9); pap. 6.50 (ISBN 0-521-09350-3). Cambridge U Pr.

--Selected Literary Essays. Hooper, Walter, ed. LC 74-85724. 1969. 42.00 (ISBN 0-521-07441-X); pap. 8.95 (ISBN 0-521-29680-3). Cambridge U Pr.

--Spenser's Image of Life. Fowler, A., ed. 1967. 29.95 (ISBN 0-521-05546-6). Cambridge U Pr.

--Studies in Words. 2nd ed. 1960. 32.50 (ISBN 0-521-05547-4); pap. 9.95 (ISBN 0-521-09371-6). Cambridge U Pr.

--Surprised by Joy: The Shape of My Early Life. LC 56-5329. 1956. 12.95 (ISBN 0-15-187011-X). HarBraceJ.

Lewis, Colin D. Demand Analysis & Inventory Control. 1974. 23.50 (ISBN 0-347-01038-5, 93518-2, Pub. by Saxon Hse England). Lexington Bks.

Lewis, Collin A. Hunting in Ireland. (Illus.). 26.25 (ISBN 0-85131-213-6, Dist. by Sporting Book Center). J A Allen.

Lewis, D. & Bartenieff, I. Body Movement: Coping with the Environment. 1980. 42.50 (ISBN 0-677-05500-5). Gordon.

Lewis, D. B. & Gower, D. M. Biology of Communication. LC 79-20920. (Tertiary Level Biology Ser.). 1980. 29.95x (ISBN 0-470-26859-X). Halsted Pr.

Lewis, D. G. Assessment in Education. 198p. 1975. 17.95 (ISBN 0-470-53197-5). Halsted Pr.

Lewis, D. G., jt. auth. see Oliver, R. A.

Lewis, Dan, jt. auth. see Reginald, R.

Lewis, Daniel, jt. auth. see Helberg, Kristen.

Lewis, Daniel E. At the Crossroads. 64p. 1980. 6.50 (ISBN 0-682-49631-6). Exposition.

Lewis, Darrell R. & Becker, William E., eds. Academic Rewards in Higher Education. LC 79-11692. 1979. 19.50 (ISBN 0-88410-189-4). Ballinger Pub.

Lewis, David. La Casa Apinada. (Calle Lucas). 1978. pap. 0.40 o.p. (ISBN 0-311-38520-6, Edit Mundo). Casa Bautista.

--La Casa Del Cobrador. (Calle Lucas). 1978. pap. 0.40 o.p. (ISBN 0-311-38524-9, Edit Mundo). Casa Bautista.

--La Casa Del Lider. (Calle Lucas). 1978. pap. 0.40 o.p. (ISBN 0-311-38522-2, Edit Mundo). Casa Bautista.

--La Casa Del Rico. (Calle Lucas). 1978. pap. 0.40 o.p. (ISBN 0-311-38521-4, Edit Mundo). Casa Bautista.

--La Casa En las Afueras. 1978. pap. 0.40 o.p. (ISBN 0-311-38526-5, Edit Mundo). Casa Bautista.

--La Casa Hospedadora. (Calle Lucas). pap. 0.40 o.p. (ISBN 0-311-38523-0, Edit Mundo). Casa Bautista.

--La Casa Secreta. (Calle Lucas). 1978. pap. 0.40 o.p. (ISBN 0-311-38525-7, Edit Mundo). Casa Bautista.

--La Casa Triste. (Calle Lucas). 1978. pap. 0.40 o.p. (ISBN 0-311-38519-2, Edit Mundo). Casa Bautista.

--Growth of Cities. LC 70-171916. 1971. 32.95 (ISBN 0-471-53198-7). Halsted Pr.

--How to Be a Gifted Parent: Realize Your Child's Full Potential. 1981. 14.95 (ISBN 0-393-01394-4). Norton.

--The Secret Language of Your Child. pap. 2.75 (ISBN 0-425-04547-1). Berkley Pub.

--Sexpionage. 1977. pap. 1.75 o.p. (ISBN 0-345-25714-6). Ballantine.

Lewis, David, jt. auth. see Sharpe, Robert.

Lewis, David, jt. ed. see Meiggs, Russell.

Lewis, David A. & Hicks, Darryl E. The Presidential Zero-Year Mystery. (Orig.). 1980. pap. 2.95 (ISBN 0-88270-490-7). Logos.

Lewis, David L. The Book of Ford Books. (Illus.). 200p. 1981. price not set (ISBN 0-934780-04-8); pap. price not set (ISBN 0-934780-05-6). Bookman Dan.

--District of Columbia: A Bicentennial History. (States & the Nation Ser.). (Illus.). 1976. 12.95 (ISBN 0-393-05601-5, Co-Pub by AASLH). Norton.

--When Harlem Was in Vogue. LC 80-2704. (Illus.). 400p. 1981. 17.95 (ISBN 0-394-49572-1). Knopf.

Lewis, David Maybury see Maybury-Lewis, David.

Lewis, Diehl & Loh, May. Patternless Fashions: How to Design & Make Your Own Fashions. (Illus.). 1980. 14.95 (ISBN 0-87491-416-7); pap. 8.95 (ISBN 0-87491-413-2). Acropolis.

Lewis, Dorothy O., ed. Psychobiological Vulnerabilities to Delinquency. 1981. text ed. write for info. (ISBN 0-89335-136-9). Spectrum Pub.

Lewis, Douglas. The Late Baroque Churches of Venice. LC 78-94704. (Outstanding Dissertations in the Fine Arts Ser.). 1979. lib. bdg. 52.00 (ISBN 0-8240-3236-5). Garland Pub.

Lewis, Douglass. Resolving Church Conflicts: A Case Study Approach for Local Congregations. LC 80-8347. 192p. (Orig.). 1981. pap. 6.95 (ISBN 0-06-065244-6, HarpR). Har-Row.

Lewis, E. R. Life & Teaching of Jesus Christ. (London Divinity Ser.). pap. 3.95 (ISBN 0-227-67519-3). Attic Pr.

Lewis, E. S. see Weissberger, A.

Lewis, Edith. Willa Cather Living: A Personal Record. LC 76-17551. 1976. pap. 2.95 (ISBN 0-8032-5849-6, BB 623, Bison). U of Nebr Pr.

Lewis, Edith P. & Browning, Mary H. Nurse in Community Health. (Contemporary Nursing Ser). 1972. 6.50 o.p. (ISBN 0-686-02586-5, C04). Am Journal Nurse.

Lewis, Edward. Be a Winner. (Gamblers Book Shelf). 160p. 1979. pap. 2.95 (ISBN 0-89650-530-8). Gamblers.

Lewis, Edward V. & O'Brien, Robert. Ships. LC 65-28353. (Life Science Library). (Illus.). (gr. 5 up). 1970. PLB 8.97 o.p. (ISBN 0-8094-0472-9, Pub. by Time-Life). Silver.

Lewis, Edwin. A Manual of Christian Beliefs. 162p. 1927. text ed. 2.95 (ISBN 0-567-02170-X). Attic Pr.

Lewis, Eils M. The Snug Little House. LC 80-24282. (Illus.). 32p. (ps-3). 1981. 8.95 (ISBN 0-689-50177-3, McElderry Bk). Atheneum.

Lewis, Eleanor. Darkroom. (Illus., Orig.). 1979. pap. 17.50 (ISBN 0-912810-19-X). Lustrum Pr.

Lewis, Elliott. Bennett, Number Three: People in Glass Houses. 192p. (Orig.). Date not set. pap. 1.95 (ISBN 0-523-41437-4). Pinnacle Bks.

Lewis, Ernest L., jt. auth. see Beggs, Donald L.

Lewis, Evelyn, jt. auth. see Ray, Mary.

Lewis, Evelyn L. Housing Decisions. LC 80-19068. 1980. text ed. 13.20 (ISBN 0-87006-302-2). Goodheart.

Lewis, Felice F. Literature, Obscenity, & Law. LC 75-42094. 310p. 1978. pap. 8.95 (ISBN 0-8093-0870-3). S Ill U Pr.

Lewis, Ferris E. Michigan Yesterday & Today. rev., 8th ed. (Illus.). (gr. 10-12). 1975. text ed. 12.20x o.p. (ISBN 0-910726-50-7); tchrs'. guide 3.00x o.p. (ISBN 0-910726-51-5). Hillsdale Educ.

--My State & Its Story: Michigan History. rev., 16th ed. (Illus.). (gr. 8 up). 1972. text ed. 10.45x o.p. (ISBN 0-910726-10-8); wkbk. 2.40x o.p. (ISBN 0-910726-15-9). Hillsdale Educ.

--Our Own State, Michigan. rev., 14th ed. LC 78-66800. (Illus.). (gr. 7-10). 1978. pap. text ed. 5.25x (ISBN 0-910726-21-3); questions & ans. for tchr's. 8.00x (ISBN 0-910726-23-X). Hillsdale Educ.

Lewis, Ferris E. & McConnell, David B. Learning About Michigan's Government. rev., 2nd ed. (Illus.). (gr. 7-10). 1973. text ed. 9.20x o.p. (ISBN 0-910726-30-2). Hillsdale Educ.

--State & Local Government of Michigan. rev., 8th ed. LC 78-66807. (Illus.). (gr. 10-12). 1979. pap. text ed. 7.75x (ISBN 0-910726-41-8); questions & answers for tchrs. 3.00x (ISBN 0-910726-42-6). Hillsdale Educ.

Lewis, Florence. Help Wanted: A Guide to Career Counseling in the Bay Area. 4.95 (ISBN 0-931018-03-X). Green Hill.

Lewis, Frank. Average Length of Stay on Short-Stay Hospitals United States, 1977. Shipp, Audrey, ed. (Ser. 13-50). 50p. 1980. pap. text ed. 1.75 (ISBN 0-8406-0198-0). Natl Ctr Health Stats.

Lewis, Frederick P. The Dilemma in the Congressional Power to Enforce the Fourteenth Amendment. 110p. 1980. text ed. 15.50 (ISBN 0-8191-1045-0); pap. text ed. 7.50 (ISBN 0-8191-1046-9). U Pr of Amer.

Lewis, G. J. Rural Communities: A Social Geography. LC 78-74090. (Modern Geography Ser.). 1979. 28.00 (ISBN 0-7153-7768-X). David & Charles.

Lewis, G. M. & Wheatley, G. A. Neutrinos. LC 73-135382. (Wykeham Science Ser.: No. 12). 1970. 9.95x (ISBN 0-8448-1114-9). Crane-Russak Co.

Lewis, Gaspar. Cabinetmaking, Patternmaking & Millwork. LC 79-50917. (Carpentry-Cabinetmaking Ser.). 448p. 1981. text ed. 14.60 (ISBN 0-8273-1814-6); instructor's guide 2.55 (ISBN 0-8273-1815-4). Delmar.

--Safety for Carpenters & Woodworkers. LC 80-66859. (Carpentry-Cabinetmaking Ser.). 1981. pap. text ed. 4.40 (ISBN 0-8273-1869-3); instructor's guide 0.85 (ISBN 0-8273-1870-7). Delmar.

Lewis, Gaspar J. Cabinetmaking, Pattermaking, & Millwork. 448p. 1981. 18.95 (ISBN 0-442-24785-0). Van Nos Reinhold.

Lewis, Geoffrey, jt. ed. see Spink, Martin S.

Lewis, Geoffrey L. Turkish Grammar. 1967. 24.95x (ISBN 0-19-815375-9). Oxford U Pr.

Lewis, Gerald E. My Big Buck: Outdoor Stories of Maine. LC 78-26185. (Illus.). 1978. lib. bdg. 9.50 o.p. (ISBN 0-89621-021-9); pap. 4.95x (ISBN 0-89621-020-0). Thorndike Pr.

Lewis, Gilbert. Day of Shining Red. LC 78-68354. (Studies in Social Anthropology: No. 27). 1980. 24.95 (ISBN 0-521-22278-8). Cambridge U Pr.

--Knowledge of Illness in a Sepik Society: A Study of the Gnau, New Guinea. (Monographs on Social Anthropology). (Illus.). 372p. 1975. text ed. 42.00x (ISBN 0-391-00389-5, Athlone Pr). Humanities.

Lewis, Gogo, jt. ed. see Manley, Seon.

Lewis, Gordon K. Notes on the Puerto Rican Revolution: An Essay on American Dominance & Caribbean Resistance. LC 74-7791. 192p. 1975. 9.50 o.p. (ISBN 0-85345-341-1, CL-3411). Monthly Rev.

--Puerto Rico: Freedom & Power in the Caribbean. LC 63-20065. 640p. 1975. Repr. of 1963 ed. 17.50 o.p. (ISBN 0-85345-316-0, CL-3160). Monthly Rev.

Lewis, Greg. Wedding Photography for Today. (Illus.). 136p. 1980. 19.95 (ISBN 0-8174-6410-7); pap. 9.95 (ISBN 0-8174-6411-5). Amphoto.

Lewis, Gregg, jt. auth. see Lewis, Margie M.

Lewis, Gwynne. The Second Vendee: The Continuity of Counter-Revolution in the Department of the Gard 1789-1815. (Illus.). 1978. 37.50x (ISBN 0-19-822544-X). Oxford U Pr.

Lewis, H. D. Contemporary British Philosophy, Vol. 4. (Muirhead Library of Philosophy). 1976. text ed. 24.75x (ISBN 0-391-00716-5). Humanities.

--Elusive Mind. (Muirhead Library of Philosophy). 1969. text ed. 26.00x (ISBN 0-00-430013-0). Humanities.

Lewis, H. D., ed. Logic, Ontology & Action, Vol. 1. (Jadavpur Studies in Philosophy). 1980. text ed. write for info. (ISBN 0-391-01764-0). Humanities.

Lewis, H. G. How to Handle Your Own Public Relations. LC 76-20710. 1976. 12.95 (ISBN 0-88229-319-2); pap. 8.95 (ISBN 0-88229-408-3). Nelson-Hall.

Lewis, H. R., tr. see Pauli, Wolfgang.

Lewis, H. T. & Culliton, J. W. Role of Airfreight in Physical Distribution: Including Two Cases by J. D. Steele. 1970. Repr. of 1956 ed. 18.50 (ISBN 0-08-018744-7). Pergamon.

Lewis, Harrison. Ancient Malta & Its Antiquities. 1977. pap. text ed. 10.50x (ISBN 0-901072-25-7). Humanities.

Lewis, Harry. Elementary Algebra Skills for College. (Orig.). 1980. pap. text ed. 14.95 (ISBN 0-442-20396-9). D Van Nostrand.

--Intermediate Algebra Skills for College. (Orig.). Date not set. pap. text ed. price not set (ISBN 0-442-23163-6); price not set instr's. manual (ISBN 0-442-28663-5). D Van Nostrand.

--An Introduction to Computer Programming & Data Structures Using MACRO-11. 188p. 1981. text ed. 18.95 (ISBN 0-8359-3143-9); soln. manual avail. (ISBN 0-8359-3144-7). Reston.

Lewis, Harry D. College Business Mathematics. LC 76-19528. 1976. pap. 13.20 (ISBN 0-8273-0289-4); instructor's guide 2.75 (ISBN 0-8273-0290-8); test bklet 2.80 (ISBN 0-8273-0299-1). Delmar.

Lewis, Harry R. & Papadimitriou, Christos H. Elements of the Theory of Computation. (Software Ser.). (Illus.). 496p. 1981. text ed. 22.50 (ISBN 0-13-273417-6). P-H.

Lewis, Harvey S. & Waller, E. Nolan. Commercial Banking in Mississippi, 1940-1975. 1977. pap. 3.00 (ISBN 0-938004-07-7). U MS Bus Econ.

Lewis, Helen B. Freud & Modern Psychology: The/Emotional Basis of Mental Illness, Vol. 1. (Emotions Personality & Psychotherapy Ser.). 240p. 1981. 19.50 (ISBN 0-306-40525-3, Plenum Pr). Plenum Pub.

Lewis, Helen Block. Psychic War in Men & Women. LC 74-21634. 321p. 1976. 12.00 (ISBN 0-8147-4960-7); pap. 6.00 (ISBN 0-8147-4982-8). NYU Pr.

Lewis, Herbert S. Galla Monarchy: Jimma Abba Jifar, Ethiopia, 1830-1932. (Illus.). 1965. 17.50x (ISBN 0-299-03690-1). U of Wis Pr.

Lewis, Hilda. Ship That Flew. LC 58-5903. (Illus.). (gr. 3-7). 1958. 9.95 (ISBN 0-87599-067-3). S G Phillips.

Lewis, Howard L., jt. auth. see Brown, Montague.

Lewis, I. M. A Modern History of Somalia: Nation & State in the Horn of Africa. (Illus.). 248p. 1980. pap. text ed. 10.95 (ISBN 0-582-64657-X). Longman.

Lewis, I. M., ed. Islam in Tropical Africa. 2nd ed. LC 79-3292. 352p. 1980. 25.00x (ISBN 0-253-14956-8); pap. 10.95x (ISBN 0-253-28514-3). Ind U Pr.

Lewis, Isabelle, jt. auth. see Sparling, Joseph.

Lewis, J. History of Philosophy. (Teach Yourself Ser.). 1974. pap. 2.95 o.p. (ISBN 0-679-10440-2). McKay.

Lewis, J. David & Smith, Richard L. American Sociology & Pragmatism: Mead, Chicago Sociology, & Symbolic Interaction. LC 80-15489. (Illus.). 1981. lib. bdg. 25.00 (ISBN 0-226-47697-9). U of Chicago Pr.

Lewis, J. G. The Biology of Centipedes. (Illus.). 350p. Date not set. price not set (ISBN 0-521-23413-1). Cambridge U Pr.

--Introduction to Medicine: 100 Topics. (Illus.). 1975. 17.95x (ISBN 0-433-19253-4). Intl Ideas.

Lewis, J. R. Cases for Discussion. 1966. 13.75 (ISBN 0-08-011352-4); pap. 6.25 (ISBN 0-08-011351-6). Pergamon.

Lewis, J. W., ed. Party Leadership & Revolutionary Power in China. (Publications of the Contemporary China Institute Ser). 1970. 39.95 o.p. (ISBN 0-521-07792-3); pap. 11.50x (ISBN 0-521-09614-6). Cambridge U Pr.

Lewis, Jack. The Digest Book of Horse Care. (The Sports & Leisure Library). (Illus.). 96p. 1979. pap. 2.95 (ISBN 0-695-81325-0). Follett.

--The Gospel According to Matthew, Pt. 1. Ferguson, Everett, ed. LC 75-21256. (The Living Word Commentary Ser.: Vol. 2). 1976. 7.95 (ISBN 0-8344-0094-4). Sweet.

--Law Enforcement Handgun Digest. 3rd ed. 288p. 1980. pap. 8.95 (ISBN 0-695-81413-3). Follett.

--Modern Gun Values. 3rd ed. (Illus.). 384p. (Orig.). 1981. pap. 9.95 (ISBN 0-910676-19-4, 5836). DBI.

Lewis, Jack & Mitchell, Jack. Shotgun Digest. 2nd ed. 288p. 1980. pap. 8.95 (ISBN 0-910676-13-5). DBI.

Lewis, Jack, jt. ed. see Learn, C. R.

Lewis, Jack P. The English Bible: From KJV to NIV. 400p. 1981. 15.95 (ISBN 0-8010-5599-7). Baker Bk.

--The Gospel According to Matthew. Ferguson, Everett, ed. LC 75-21256. (Living Word Commentary Ser.: Vol. 2). 1976. 7.95 (ISBN 0-8344-0065-0). Sweet.

Lewis, James. West Virginia Pilgrim. 228p. 1976. 8.95 (ISBN 0-8164-0297-3). Crossroad NY.

Lewis, James C. The World of the Wild Turkey. LC 72-2923. (Living World Bks.). (Illus.). (YA) 1973. 8.95 (ISBN 0-397-00788-4). Lippincott.

Lewis, James K. The Pony Club Book. LC 79-87794. (Illus.). 128p. 1981. 8.95 (ISBN 0-498-02257-9). A S Barnes.

Lewis, Jane. The Politics of Motherhood: Child & Maternal Welfare in England, 1900-1939. 240p. 1980. 27.95 (ISBN 0-7735-0521-0). McGill-Queens U Pr.

Lewis, Janet. The Ancient Ones. (Illus.). 1979. pap. 7.50 o.p. (ISBN 0-931832-12-8). No Dead Lines.

--Birthday of the Infanta. 1980. s & l, wrappers 25.00 (ISBN 0-936576-03-0). Symposium Pr.

--Ghost of Monsieur Scarron. LC 65-16520. 378p. 1959. 10.95 (ISBN 0-8040-0076-X); pap. 6.95 (ISBN 0-8040-0133-2, 70). Swallow.

--Poems Old & New, Nineteen Eighteen to Nineteen Seventy-Eight. LC 80-26209. xvi, 112p. 1981. 11.00 (ISBN 0-8040-0371-8); pap. 5.95 (ISBN 0-8040-0372-6). Swallow.

--Poems Old & New: 1918-1978. LC 80-26209. xvi, 112p. 1981. 11.00 (ISBN 0-8040-0371-8); pap. 5.95 (ISBN 0-8040-0372-6). Swallow.

--Wife of Martin Guerre. LC 70-135357. 109p. 1941. 5.00 o.s.i. (ISBN 0-8040-0079-4); pap. 3.95 (ISBN 0-8040-0321-1). Swallow.

Lewis, Jean. Benji the Detective. (Tell-a-Tale Readers). (Illus.). (gr. k-3). PLB 4.77 (ISBN 0-307-68640-X, Whitman). Western Pub.

--Bugs Bunny: Too Many Carrots. (Illus.). 24p. (ps-4). 1977. PLB 5.00 (ISBN 0-307-60145-5, Golden Pr). Western Pub.

Lewis, Jill, jt. auth. see Joseph, Gloria.

Lewis, Joe O. Layman's Bible Book Commentary: 1 & 2 Samuel & 1 Chronicles. LC 79-54796. 1981. 4.25 (ISBN 0-8054-1175-5). Broadman.

Lewis, John. The Anatomy of Printing. 1970. 45.00 o.p. (ISBN 0-571-08768-X, Pub. by Faber & Faber). Merrimack Bk Serv.

--The Chinese Man...& the Chinese Woman. (The Chinese Word for...Ser). (Illus.). 1977. pap. 3.95 (ISBN 0-8467-0384-X, Pub. by Two Continents). Hippocrene Bks.

--The Chinese Word for Horse. (The Chinese Word for...Ser.). (Illus.). 1977. pap. 3.95 (ISBN 0-8467-0383-1, Pub. by Two Continents). Hippocrene Bks.

--The Chinese Word for Thief. (The Chinese Word for...Ser.). (Illus., Orig.). 1978. pap. 3.95 (ISBN 0-8467-0431-5, Pub. by Two Continents). Hippocrene Bks.

--The Marxism of Marx. 266p. 1972. pap. text ed. 8.95x o.p. (ISBN 0-8464-0614-4). Beekman Pubs.

--Religions of the World Made Simple. rev. ed. 1958. pap. 3.50 (ISBN 0-385-02276-X, Made). Doubleday.

--Repair of Wooden Boats. 1977. 14.95 (ISBN 0-7153-7378-1). David & Charles.

--Restoring Vintage Boats. LC 75-4329. (Illus.). 192p. 1975. 22.50 (ISBN 0-87742-054-8). Intl Marine.

--Rowland Hilder: Artist & Illustrator. (Illus.). 1979. 29.95 o.p. (ISBN 0-214-20425-1, 8059, Dist. by Arco). Barrie & Jenkins.

Lewis, John & Smith, Edwin. The Graphic Reproduction & Photography of Works of Art. 1969. 12.95 o.p. (ISBN 0-571-09034-6, Pub. by Faber & Faber). Merrimack Bk Serv.

Lewis, John & Towers, Bernard. Naked Ape or Homo Sapiens: A Reply to Desmond Morris. 2nd ed. (Teilhard Study Library). 1972. text ed. 6.25x (ISBN 0-900391-21-9). Humanities.

Lewis, John L., ed. Teaching School Physics: A UNESCO Source Bk. (Illus., Orig.). pap. 11.50 (ISBN 92-3-100937-0, U662, UNESCO). Unipub.

Lewis, John R. First Year College Chemistry. 9th ed. (Illus., Orig.). 1971. pap. 3.95 (ISBN 0-06-460005-X, CO 5, COS). Har-Row.

Lewis, Jona. Creative Imagination: Your Key to High Accomplishment. (Illus.). 1980. pap. 12.95 o.p. (ISBN 0-930490-27-4). Future Shop.

Lewis, Joseph. Lincoln the Atheist. 1979. pap. 3.00. Am Atheist.

Lewis, Judith A. & Lewis, Michael D. Community Counseling: A Human Services Approach. LC 76-15274. (Wiley Series in Counseling & Human Development). 1977. text ed. 19.95 (ISBN 0-471-53203-7). Wiley.

Lewis, K. R., jt. auth. see John, B.

Lewis, K. R., jt. ed. see Pearson, P. L.

Lewis, K. R., jt. ed. see Wahrman, J.

Lewis, L. A. & Opplt, J. J., eds. Handbook of Electrophoresis, CRC, 2 vols. 1980. Vol. 1, 336p. 56.95 (ISBN 0-8493-0571-3); Vol. 2, 400p. 59.95 (ISBN 0-8493-0572-1). CRC Pr.

Lewis, L. J. Society, Schools & Progress in Nigeria. 1965. 22.00 (ISBN 0-08-011340-0); pap. 11.25 (ISBN 0-08-011339-7). Pergamon.

Lewis, Laverne W. Fundamental Skills in Patient Care. 2nd ed. LC 79-27050. 1980. pap. text ed. 14.95 (ISBN 0-397-54283-6, 408 PGS.); 8.75 (ISBN 0-397-54335-2, 257 PGS. FOR WKBK.). Lippincott.

--Fundamental Skills in Patient Care. LC 75-26993. 495p. 1976. pap. 13.75 o.p. (ISBN 0-397-54174-0). Lippincott.

Lewis, Lawrence. Guido Cantelli: Portrait of a Maestro. LC 80-29385. (Illus.). 176p. 1981. 11.95 (ISBN 0-498-02493-8). A S Barnes.

Lewis, Linda. The Ultimate Dessert Book. (Illus.). 1979. cancelled o.p. (ISBN 0-394-41276-1). Random.

Lewis, Lucia. The First Book of Microbes. LC 72-254. (First Bks). (Illus.). 96p. (gr. 4 up). 1972. PLB 4.90 o.p. (ISBN 0-531-00677-8). Watts.

Lewis, Luverne W. Lippincott's State Board Examination Review for Nurses. LC 77-27368. 1978. pap. text ed. 13.95 (ISBN 0-397-54214-3). Lippincott.

Lewis, M. D. Philosophy of Religion. (Teach Yourself Ser.). 1975. pap. 4.95 o.p. (ISBN 0-679-10441-0). McKay.

Lewis, M. J. Libraries for the Handicapped. 1969. pap. 3.30x (ISBN 0-85365-281-3, Pub. by Lib Assn England). Oryx Pr.

Lewis, M. M. Language & the Child. 1969. pap. text ed. 3.00x (ISBN 0-901225-07-X, NFER). Humanities.

Lewis, Mack O. How to Franchise Your Business. rev. ed. LC 74-8015. 1980. 3.50 (ISBN 0-87576-007-4). Pilot Bks.

Lewis, Margie M. & Lewis, Gregg. The Hurting Parent. 160p. (Orig.). 1980. pap. 3.95 (ISBN 0-310-41731-7). Zondervan.

Lewis, Marlo & Lewis, Mina B. Prime Time. LC 79-89529. 1979. 10.00 o.p. (ISBN 0-312-90785-0). St Martin.

--Prime Time... LC 79-89529. (Illus.). 1979. 10.00 (ISBN 0-87477-107-2). J P Tarcher.

Lewis, Martha B. Sentence Analysis in Modern Malay. LC 69-10062. 1969. 54.00 (ISBN 0-521-05554-7). Cambridge U Pr.

Lewis, Mary. Midsummer Bride. 192p. (Orig.). 1980. pap. 1.50 (ISBN 0-671-57007-2). S&S.

Lewis, Mel. Collecting for Fun... & Profit. (Illus.). 228p. (Orig.). 1981. pap. 9.95 (ISBN 0-906071-23-2). Proteus Pub NY.

--How to Make Money from Antiques. (Illus.). 160p. 1981. 12.50 (ISBN 0-7137-1084-5, Pub. by Blandford Pr England). Sterling.

Lewis, Meriwether & Clark, William. The History of the Lewis & Clark Expedition, 3 vols. Coues, Elliot, ed. (Illus.). 1508p. 1979. pap. 5.00 ea. Vol. 1 (ISBN 0-486-21268-8). Vol. 2 (ISBN 0-486-21269-6). Vol. 3 (ISBN 0-486-21270-X). Dover.

Lewis, Michael & Rosenblum, Leonard, eds. The Uncommon Child. (Genesis of Behavior Ser.: Vol. 3). 335p. 1981. 25.00 (ISBN 0-306-40499-0, Plenum Pr). Plenum Pub.

Lewis, Michael D., jt. auth. see Lewis, Judith A.

Lewis, Mina B., jt. auth. see Lewis, Marlo.

Lewis, Myron see Wruble, Lawrence D., et al.

Lewis, Nancy & Lewis, Richard. Keeping in Shape. LC 75-29267. (Career Concise Guides Ser.). (Illus.). 72p. (gr. 5-9). 1976. PLB 4.90 o.p. (ISBN 0-531-02848-8). Watts.

Lewis, Nancy, ed. My Roots Be Coming Back. (Illus.). 24p. 1973. pap. 3.50x (ISBN 0-89062-034-2, Pub. by Touchstone). Pub Ctr Cult Res.

--Out of My Body. (Illus.). 20p. 1974. pap. 3.00x (ISBN 0-89062-035-0, Pub. by Touchtone). Pub Ctr Cult Res.

Lewis, Naomi. The Butterfly Collector. (ps-2). 1979. 7.95 (ISBN 0-13-108852-1). P-H.

Lewis, Naomi, ed. see Bronte, Emily.

Lewis, Naphtali see Lehmann, Karl & Lehmann, P. W.

Lewis, Norman. Instant Spelling Power. (Orig.). 1976. wkbk 8.42 (ISBN 0-87720-952-9). AMSCO Sch.

--Instant Word Power. (Orig.). 1981. pap. text ed. price not set (ISBN 0-87720-963-4). AMSCO Sch.

--Power with Words. rev. ed. (Apollo Eds.). pap. 4.50 o.s.i. (ISBN 0-8152-0079-X, A79, TYC-T). T Y Crowell.

--Reading, Spelling, Vocabulary, Pronunciation, 3 vols. Incl. Book 1. text ed. 8.75 (ISBN 0-87720-357-1); pap. text ed. 4.42 (ISBN 0-87720-356-3); tchr's ed 3.10 (ISBN 0-87720-315-6); wkbk 5.25 (ISBN 0-87720-314-8); Book 2. text ed. 8.75 (ISBN 0-87720-359-8); pap. text ed. 4.42 (ISBN 0-87720-358-X); tchr's ed. 3.10 (ISBN 0-87720-317-2); wkbk 5.25 (ISBN 0-87720-316-4); Book 3. text ed. 8.75 (ISBN 0-87720-361-X); pap. text ed. 4.42 (ISBN 0-87720-360-1); tchr's ed 3.10 (ISBN 0-87720-319-9); wkbk 5.25 (ISBN 0-87720-318-0). (RSVP Ser). (gr. 7-9). 1967. Amsco Sch.

--RSVP for College English Power, Bk. 1. 1977. wkbk 6.92 (ISBN 0-87720-953-7). Amsco Sch.

--RSVP for College English Power, Bk. 2. 1978. wkbk. 6.33 (ISBN 0-87720-959-6). AMSCO Sch.

--RSVP for College English Power, Bk. 3. 1979. 6.33 (ISBN 0-87720-960-X). AMSCO Sch.

--RSVP with Etymology, Bk. I. (Orig.). (gr. 7-9). 1981. pap. text ed. price not set (ISBN 0-87720-395-4). AMSCO Sch.

--See, Say & Write, Bk. 1. (Orig.). (gr. 6-8). 1973. 6.17 (ISBN 0-87720-346-6). AMSCO Sch.

--See, Say & Write, Bk. 2. (Orig.). (gr. 7-9). 1973. 6.17 (ISBN 0-87720-348-2). AMSCO Sch.

--Word Power Made Easy. pap. 2.95 (ISBN 0-671-42416-5). PB.

--Word Power Made Easy: The Complete Handbook for Building a Bigger & Better Vocabulary. LC 77-14894. 1978. 10.95 o.p. (ISBN 0-385-14085-1). Doubleday.

Lewis, Norman, jt. auth. see Funk, Wilfred.

Lewis, Oscar. Life in a Mexican Village: Tepoztlan Restudied. 8.50 (ISBN 0-8446-2469-1). Peter Smith.

--La Vida: A Puerto Rican Family in the Culture of Poverty--San Juan & New York. 1980. Repr. of 1966 ed. text ed. 24.50x (ISBN 0-8290-0074-7). Irvington.

Lewis, P., et al. Visual Blight in America. LC 73-88850. (CCG Resource Papers Ser.: No. 23). (Illus.). 1973. pap. text ed. 4.00 (ISBN 0-89291-070-4). Assn Am Geographers.

Lewis, P. M., II, jt. ed. see Freeman, Herbert.

Lewis, Paul G. & Potter, David C., eds. The Practice of Comparative Politics: A Reader. 2nd ed. (Open University Set Bk.). 1979. pap. text ed. 10.95 (ISBN 0-582-49033-2). Longman.

Lewis, Paul H. Paraguay Under Stroessner. LC 79-28554. xi, 256p. 1980. 22.00x (ISBN 0-8078-1437-7). U of NC Pr.

Lewis, Paul M. Beautiful Alaska. Shangle, Robert D., ed. LC 78-102338. (Illus.). 72p. 1976. 14.95 (ISBN 0-915796-14-7); pap. 7.95 (ISBN 0-915796-13-9). Beautiful Am.

--Beautiful America. Shangle, Robert D., ed. LC 79-22245. (Illus.). 1979. 27.50 (ISBN 0-89802-000-X). Beautiful Am.

--Beautiful Arizona. Shangle, Robert D., ed. LC 78-8732. (Illus.). 72p. 1978. 14.95 (ISBN 0-915796-40-6); pap. 7.95 (ISBN 0-915796-39-2). Beautiful Am.

--Beautiful Atlanta. Shangle, Robert D., ed. LC 80-25850. (Illus.). 72p. 1980. 14.95 (ISBN 0-89802-121-9); pap. 7.95 (ISBN 0-89802-120-0). Beautiful Am.

--Beautiful Boston. Shangle, Robert D., ed. LC 80-15184. (Illus.). 72p. 1980. 14.95 (ISBN 0-89802-172-3); pap. 7.95 (ISBN 0-89802-171-5). Beautiful Am.

--Beautiful California Coast. Shangle, Robert D., ed. LC 79-13134. 72p. 1979. 14.95 (ISBN 0-915796-97-X); pap. 7.95 (ISBN 0-915796-96-1). Beautiful Am.

--Beautiful California Desert. Shangle, Robert D., ed. LC 78-14890. (Illus.). 72p. 1979. 14.95 (ISBN 0-89802-067-0); pap. 7.95 (ISBN 0-89802-066-2). Beautiful Am.

--Beautiful California Mountains. Shangle, Robert D., ed. LC 80-11107. (Illus.). 72p. 1980. 14.95 (ISBN 0-89802-127-8); pap. 7.95 (ISBN 0-89802-126-X). Beautiful Am.

--Beautiful Colorado. Shangle, Robert D., ed. LC 75-27463. 72p. 1979. 14.95 (ISBN 0-915796-08-2); pap. 6.95 (ISBN 0-915796-07-4). Beautiful Am.

--Beautiful Colorado Country. Shangle, Robert D., ed. LC 80-18366. (Illus.). 72p. 1980. 14.95 (ISBN 0-89802-058-1); pap. 6.95 (ISBN 0-89802-057-3). Beautiful Am.

--Beautiful Denver. Shangle, Robert D., ed. (Illus.). 72p. 1981. 14.95 (ISBN 0-89802-119-7); pap. 7.95 (ISBN 0-89802-118-9). Beautiful Am.

--Beautiful Florida. Shangle, Robert D., ed. LC 79-1428. (Illus.). 72p. 1979. 14.95 (ISBN 0-915796-71-6); pap. 7.95 (ISBN 0-915796-70-8). Beautiful Am.

--Beautiful Georgia. Shangle, Robert D., ed. LC 78-7895. 72p. 1978. 14.95 (ISBN 0-915796-42-2); pap. 7.95 (ISBN 0-915796-41-4). Beautiful Am.

--Beautiful Hawaii. rev. ed. (Illus.). 72p. 1980. 14.95 (ISBN 0-89802-109-X); pap. 7.95 (ISBN 0-89802-108-1). Beautiful Am.

--Beautiful Idaho. Shangle, Robert D., ed. LC 79-779. 72p. 1979. 14.95 (ISBN 0-915796-93-7); pap. 7.95 (ISBN 0-915796-92-9). Beautiful Am.

--Beautiful Massachusetts. 72p. 1980. 14.95 (ISBN 0-915796-57-0); pap. 7.95 (ISBN 0-915796-56-2). Beautiful Am.

--Beautiful Missouri. LC 80-14717. (Illus.). 72p. 1980. 14.95 (ISBN 0-89802-123-5); pap. 7.95 (ISBN 0-89802-122-7). Beautiful Am.

--Beautiful New Jersey. Shangle, Robert D., ed. LC 80-23325. (Illus.). 72p. 1980. 14.95 (ISBN 0-89802-113-8); pap. 7.95 (ISBN 0-89802-112-X). Beautiful Am.

--Beautiful North Idaho. LC 79-4546. 72p. 1979. 14.95 (ISBN 0-915796-95-3); pap. 7.95 (ISBN 0-915796-94-5). Beautiful Am.

--Beautiful Orange County. Shangle, Robert D., ed. LC 80-25846. (Illus.). 72p. 1980. 14.95 (ISBN 0-89802-174-X); pap. 7.95 (ISBN 0-89802-173-1). Beautiful Am.

--Beautiful Oregon. Shangle, Robert D., ed. LC 75-314222. (Illus.). 72p. 1974. 14.95 (ISBN 0-915796-04-X); pap. 7.95 (ISBN 0-915796-00-7). Beautiful Am.

--Beautiful Oregon, Vol. II. Shangle, Robert D., ed. LC 78-13762. (Illus.). 72p. 1978. 14.95 (ISBN 0-915796-79-1); pap. 7.95 (ISBN 0-915796-78-3). Beautiful Am.

--Beautiful Oregon Coast. Shangle, Robert D., ed. LC 78-102344. (Illus.). 72p. 1977. 14.95 (ISBN 0-915796-21-X); pap. 7.95 (ISBN 0-915796-20-1). Beautiful Am.

--Beautiful Oregon Mountains. (Illus.). Date not set. 14.95 (ISBN 0-915796-99-6); pap. 7.95 (ISBN 0-915796-98-8). Beautiful Am. Postponed.

--Beautiful Pacific Coast. Shangle, Robert D., ed. (Illus.). 72p. 1980. 14.95 (ISBN 0-89802-125-1); pap. 7.95 (ISBN 0-89802-124-3). Beautiful Am.

--Beautiful Pennsylvania. LC 79-26331. (Illus.). 72p. 1980. 14.95 (ISBN 0-915796-59-7); pap. 7.95 (ISBN 0-915796-58-9). Beautiful Am.

--Beautiful Philadelphia. Shangle, Robert D., ed. (Illus.). 72p. 1980. 14.95 (ISBN 0-89802-115-4); pap. 7.95 (ISBN 0-89802-114-6). Beautiful Am.

--Beautiful Utah. Shangle, Robert D., ed. LC 78-102331. (Illus.). 72p. 1976. 14.95 (ISBN 0-915796-30-9); pap. 7.95 (ISBN 0-915796-29-5). Beautiful Am.

--Beautiful Utah Country. Shangle, Robert D., ed. LC 80-11826. (Illus.). 72p. 1980. 14.95 (ISBN 0-89802-162-6); pap. 7.95 (ISBN 0-89802-161-8). Beautiful Am.

--Beautiful Washington. LC 75-314223. (Illus.). 72p. 1974. 14.95 (ISBN 0-915796-05-8); pap. 7.95 (ISBN 0-915796-02-3). Beautiful Am.

--Beautiful Washington, Vol. II. LC 75-31422. (Illus.). 72p. 1978. 14.95 (ISBN 0-915796-81-3); pap. 7.95 (ISBN 0-915796-80-5). Beautiful Am.

--Beauty of California. Shangle, Robert D., ed. LC 79-9212. (Illus.). 1979. 27.50 (ISBN 0-89802-002-6). Beautiful Am.

--Beauty of Washington. Shangle, Robert D., ed. (Illus.). 160p. 1980. 27.50 (ISBN 0-89802-129-4). Beautiful Am.

--Colorful California, Vol. II. Shangle, Robert D., ed. LC 78-12042. (Illus.). 72p. 1978. 14.95 (ISBN 0-915796-85-6); pap. 7.95 (ISBN 0-915796-84-8). Beautiful Am.

Lewis, Peter. The British Bomber Since 1914. LC 67-15743. 1967. 9.95 (ISBN 0-370-00121-4). Aero.

--British Fighter Since 1912. LC 65-19381. (Illus.). 1965. 12.95 (ISBN 0-370-00063-3). Aero.

Lewis, Peter J. & O'Grady, John M., eds. Clinical Pharmacology of Prostacyclin. 1981. price not set (ISBN 0-89004-591-7). Raven.

Lewis, Peter W. Criminal Procedure: The Supreme Court's View Cases. (Criminal Justice Ser.). (Illus.). 1979. pap. text ed. 14.95 (ISBN 0-8299-0236-8); resource manual avail. (ISBN 0-8299-0597-9). West Pub.

Lewis, Philip M., 2nd, et al. Compiler Design Theory. LC 75-9012. (Illus.). 672p. 1976. text ed. 21.95 (ISBN 0-201-14455-7). A-W.

Lewis, Phillip & Williams, John W. Readings for Organizational Communications. LC 79-19091. (Grid Ser. in Management). 1980. pap. text ed. 10.50 (ISBN 0-88244-200-7). Grid Pub.

Lewis, Phillip V. Organizational Communication: The Essence of Effective Management. 2nd ed. LC 79-19572. (Management Ser.). 1980. text ed. 18.95 (ISBN 0-88244-203-1). Grid Pub.

Lewis, Phillip V. & Baker, William H. Business Report Writing. LC 78-50045. (Business English Ser.). 1978. text ed. 17.95 (ISBN 0-88244-084-5). Grid Pub.

Lewis, R., ed. Computers in Life Sciences. 128p. 1980. 25.00x (Pub. by Croom Helm England). State Mutual Bk.

Lewis, R. W. & Morgan, K. Numerical Methods in Heat Transfer. Zienkiewicz, O. C., ed. (Numerical Methods in Engineering Ser.). 1981. price not set (ISBN 0-471-27803-3, Pub. by Wiley-Interscience). Wiley.

Lewis, R. W. B., ed. see Wharton, Edith.

Lewis, Ralph. Making & Managing an Art & Craft Shop. LC 80-68685. (Making & Managing Ser.). (Illus.). 128p. 1981. 16.95 (ISBN 0-7153-8065-6). David & Charles.

Lewis, Rena, jt. auth. see McLoughlin, James.

Lewis, Rhys. Electrical Engineering Principles & Testing Methods. (Illus.). 1973. 22.30x (ISBN 0-85334-564-3, Pub. by Applied Science). Burgess-Intl Ideas.

--Engineering Quantities & Systems of Units. LC 72-3115. (Illus.). 176p. 1972. 13.95 o.p. (ISBN 0-470-53377-3). Halsted Pr.

Lewis, Richard. Reading for Adults. (Illus.). 1977. Bk. 1. pap. text ed. 4.50x (ISBN 0-582-52790-2); Bk. 2. pap. text ed. 4.50x (ISBN 0-582-52791-0); Bk. 3. pap. text ed. 4.50x (ISBN 0-582-52792-9). Longman.

Lewis, Richard, jt. auth. see Lewis, Nancy.

Lewis, Richard B., jt. ed. see Brown, James W.

Lewis, Robert A. & Rowland, Richard H. Population Redistribution in the USSR: Its Impact on Society 1897-1977. LC 79-18076. (Praeger Special Studies Ser.). 510p. 1979. 41.50 (ISBN 0-03-050641-7). Praeger.

Lewis, Robert A., ed. Men in Difficult Times: Masculinity Today & Tomorrow. (Illus.). 352p. 1981. 14.95 (ISBN 0-13-574418-0, Spectrum); pap. 7.95 (ISBN 0-13-574400-8). P-H.

Lewis, Robert A., et al. Nationality & Population Change in Russia & the USSR: An Evaluation of Census Data, 1897-1970. LC 76-6942. (Special Studies). (Illus.). 465p. 1976. text ed. 31.95 o.p. (ISBN 0-275-56480-0). Praeger.

Lewis, Robert C., jt. auth. see Leitritz, Earl.

Lewis, Robert E., ed. De Miseria Condicionis Humane. LC 75-26119. 310p. 1978. 25.00 (ISBN 0-8203-0395-X). U of Ga Pr.

Lewis, Robert J. & Hart, David G. Business FORTRAN: A Structured Approach. 480p. 1980. pap. text ed. 14.95x (ISBN 0-534-00778-3). Wadsworth Pub.

Lewis, Robert S. & Clark, G. B. Elements of Mining. 3rd ed. LC 64-14990. 1964. 49.95 (ISBN 0-471-53331-9). Wiley.

Lewis, Robin J. E. M. Forster's Passages to India. LC 79-843. 1979. 17.50x (ISBN 0-231-04508-5). Columbia U Pr.

Lewis, Roger. Color & the Edgar Cayce Readings. 48p. 1973. pap. 1.95 (ISBN 0-87604-068-7). Are Pr.

Lewis, Roger, ed. The New Roget's Thesaurus in Dictionary Form. 1977. pap. 1.95 (ISBN 0-425-04727-X). Berkley Pub.

Lewis, Ronald L. see Foner, Philip S.

Lewis, Ronald L., jt. auth. see Foner, Philip S.

Lewis, Rose. Mademoiselle. 192p. (Orig.). 1981. pap. 1.95 (ISBN 0-523-40962-1). Pinnacle Bks.

Lewis, Roy. A Certain Blindness. 180p. 1981. 9.95 (ISBN 0-312-12782-0). St Martin.

Lewis, Roy H. The Book Browser's Guide: Britain's Secondhand & Antiquarian Bookshops. LC 75-10562. 224p. 1975. 14.95 (ISBN 0-7153-7038-3). David & Charles.

Lewis, Ruth P., jt. ed. see Browning, Mary H.

Lewis, S. Architectural Draftsman's Reference Handbook. 1981. 25.00 (ISBN 0-13-044164-3). P-H.

Lewis, Sasha G. Slave Trade Today: American Exploitation of Illegal Aliens. LC 79-51151. 256p. 1980. pap. 5.95 (ISBN 0-8070-0490-1, BP 610). Beacon Pr.

Lewis, Shari. The Do-It-Better Book. LC 79-3839. (Kids-Only Club Bks.). (Illus.). 96p. (Orig.). (gr. 3-6). 1981. 6.95 (ISBN 0-03-049721-3); pap. 3.95 (ISBN 0-03-049726-4). HR&W.

--Magic Show in a Book. LC 79-23941. (Kids-Only Club Bks.). (Illus.). 96p. (Orig.). (gr. 3-6). 1980. pap. 3.95 (ISBN 0-03-049746-9). HR&W.

--Secrets, Signs, Signals & Codes. LC 79-3837. (Kids-Only Club Bks.). (Illus.). 96p. (gr. 3-6). 1980. 6.95 (ISBN 0-03-049711-6); pap. 3.95 (ISBN 0-03-049716-7). HR&W.

--Things Kids Collect. LC 79-3838. (Kids-Only Club Bks.). (Illus.). 96p. (Orig.). (gr. 3-6). 1981. 6.95 (ISBN 0-03-049731-0); pap. 3.95 (ISBN 0-03-049736-1). HR&W.

Lewis, Sinclair. Arrowsmith. pap. 1.95 (ISBN 0-451-51371-1, CJ1371, Sig Classics). NAL.

--Elmer Gantry. LC 79-15937. 1979. Repr. of 1927 ed. lib. bdg. 12.50x (ISBN 0-8376-0441-9). Bentley.

--Free Air. 370p. 1980. Repr. of 1919 ed. lib. bdg. 35.00 (ISBN 0-8495-3330-9). Arden Lib.

Lewis, Sinclair & Schary, Dore. Storm in the West. rev. ed. LC 63-13228. (Illus.). 200p. 1981. pap. 5.95 (ISBN 0-8128-6079-9). Stein & Day.

Lewis, Stanley, jt. auth. see Lidstone, John.

Lewis, Stephen. How's It Made? A Photo Tour of Seven Small Factories. LC 77-5485. (gr. 1-5). 1977. 8.25 (ISBN 0-688-80111-0); PLB 7.92 (ISBN 0-688-84111-2). Greenwillow.

--Massage: The Loving Touch. 1974. pap. 1.95 o.p. (ISBN 0-523-25135-1). Pinnacle Bks.

--Natural Victims. 1978. pap. 1.95 o.p. (ISBN 0-449-14042-3, GM). Fawcett.

--The Regulars. (Orig.). 1980. pap. 2.50 (ISBN 0-8439-0735-5, Leisure Bks). Nordon Pubns.

--Zoo City. LC 75-35659. 32p. (gr. k-3). 1976. 8.25 (ISBN 0-688-86000-1). Greenwillow.

Lewis, Steven. Exits off a Toll Road. LC 75-6211. 53p. 1975. pap. 5.00 (ISBN 0-915316-11-0); pap. 2.50 limited signed ed. (ISBN 0-685-56251-4). Pentagram.

Lewis, Sulwyn. Principles of Cultural Cooperation. (Orig.). 1971. pap. 2.50 (ISBN 92-3-100810-2, U482, UNESCO). Unipub.

Lewis, Sylvan. Doctor's Diet & Fitness Guide. 1979. pap. cancelled (ISBN 0-686-26708-7). Haldon Pubns.

Lewis, Sylvan R. Doctor's Carbohydrate Diet List. 128p. 1981. pap. 1.95 (ISBN 0-936320-12-5). Compact Pubns.

Lewis, T. G. How to Profit from Your Personal Computer: Professional, Business, & Home Applications. 1978. pap. 10.75 (ISBN 0-8104-5761-X). Hayden.

--The Mind Appliance: Home Computer Applications. 1978. pap. 9.55 (ISBN 0-8104-5112-3). Hayden.

--Software Engineering for Micros: The Electrifying Streamlined Blueprint Speedcode Method. 168p. 1979. pap. 7.70 (ISBN 0-8104-5166-2). Hayden.

Lewis, Taylor B., Jr. & Young, Joanne B. Christmas in Williamsburg. rev. ed. LC 76-11598. 1976. 5.95 o.p. (ISBN 0-03-089945-1). HR&W.

Lewis, Ted. Boldt. 1976. 9.95 o.p. (ISBN 0-7181-1460-4, Pub. by Michael Joseph). Merrimack Bk Serv.

--Boldt. (Orig.). pap. 2.25 (ISBN 0-515-05640-5). Jove Pubns.

--Grievous Bodily Harm. (Orig.). pap. 2.25. Jove Pubns.

Lewis, Theodore & Doerr, Jerry. Minicomputers: Structure & Programming. (Illus.). 1976. text ed. 16.60x (ISBN 0-8104-5642-7). Hayden.

Lewis, Theodore & Smith, Brian J. Computer Principles of Modeling & Simulation. LC 78-69604. (Illus.). 1979. text ed. 21.95 (ISBN 0-395-27143-6); instrs'. manual 0.65 (ISBN 0-395-27144-4). HM.

Lewis, Theodore G. Distribution Sampling for Computer Simulation. LC 74-25058. 128p. 1975. 19.95 (ISBN 0-669-97139-1). Lexington Bks.

--Pascal Programming for the Apple. 224p. 1981. 14.95 (ISBN 0-8359-5455-2); pap. 9.95 (ISBN 0-8359-5454-4). Reston.

Lewis, Theodore G. & Smith, Marilyn Z. Applying Data Structures. LC 75-25004. (Illus.). 1976. text ed. 21.95 (ISBN 0-395-24060-3). HM.

Lewis, Theodore H., jt. ed. see Hodge, Frederick W.

Lewis, Thomas E. & Griffith, H. Winter. Instructions for Dental Patients. LC 75-5052. (Illus.). 114p. 1975. pap. text ed. 24.00 o.p. (ISBN 0-7216-5760-5). Saunders.

Lewis, Thomas M. & Kneberg, Madeline. Tribes That Slumber: Indians of the Tennessee Region. LC 58-12085. (Illus.). 1958. pap. 7.95 (ISBN 0-87049-021-4). U of Tenn Pr.

Lewis, Thomas P. Call for Mr. Sniff. LC 79-2679. (I Can Read Bks.). (Illus.). 64p. (gr. k-3). 1981. 6.95 (ISBN 0-06-023814-3, HarpJ); PLB 7.89g (ISBN 0-06-023815-1). Har-Row.

Lewis, Thomas R. Near the Tidal River: Readings in the Historical Geography of Central Connecticut. LC 80-6181. 156p. 1981. lib. bdg. 17.50 (ISBN 0-8191-1464-2); pap. text ed. 8.00 (ISBN 0-8191-1465-0). U Pr of Amer.

Lewis, Thomas S. Letters of Hart Crane & His Family. LC 73-21675. 704p. 1974. 30.00 (ISBN 0-231-03740-6). Columbia U Pr.

Lewis, Tom. Rooftops. 300p. 1981. 11.95 (ISBN 0-87131-345-6). M Evans.

--Rooftops: A Novel. Graver, Fred, ed. 300p. 1981. 10.95 (ISBN 0-87131-345-6). M Evans.

Lewis, Trevor & Taylor, L. R. Introduction to Experimental Ecology. 1967. 30.50 o.p. (ISBN 0-12-447150-1). Acad Pr.

Lewis, W. Engine Service. 256p. 1980. pap. 11.95 (ISBN 0-13-277236-1). P-H.

Lewis, W., tr. see Gall, Franz J.

Lewis, W. Arhtur. The Theory of Economic Growth. 1955. pap. text ed. 13.50x (ISBN 0-04-330054-5). Allen Unwin.

Lewis, W. Arthur. Development Planning. 1966. pap. text ed. 11.50 (ISBN 0-04-330049-9). Allen Unwin.

--Development Planning: The Essentials of Economic Policy. LC 66-10655. 1966. 10.95x o.p. (ISBN 0-06-033615-3, HarpT). Har-Row.

--Economic Survey 1919-1939. 1949. pap. text ed. 9.95x (ISBN 0-04-330051-0). Allen Unwin.

Lewis, W. M., ed. Developments in Water Treatment - One. (Illus.). xii, 195p. 1980. 42.50x (ISBN 0-85334-902-9). Burgess-Intl Ideas.

--Developments in Water Treatment-2. (Illus.). xii, 225p. 1981. 39.00x (ISBN 0-85334-903-7). Burgess-Intl Ideas.

Lewis, Walter H., ed. Polyploidy: Biological Relevance. (Basic Life Sciences Ser.: Vol. 13). 590p. 1980. 55.00 (ISBN 0-306-40358-7, Plenum Pr). Plenum Pub.

Lewis, Warren, ed. Towards a Global Congress of the World's Religions. LC 80-53764. (Conference Ser.: No. 7). (Illus.). xiv, 78p. (Orig.). 1980. pap. text ed. 3.25x (ISBN 0-932894-07-0). Unif Theol Seminary.

Lewis, Wilfred, Jr. Federal Fiscal Policy in the Postwar Recessions. (Studies of Government Finance). 311p. 1962. 9.95 (ISBN 0-8157-5242-3). Brookings.

Lewis, Wilfred, Jr., ed. Budget Concepts for Economic Analysis. LC 68-26185. (Studies of Government Finance). 198p. 1968. pap. 3.95 (ISBN 0-8157-5237-7). Brookings.

Lewis, William. Son of Sato. 1978. 15.00 (ISBN 0-918824-10-9); pap. 3.00 (ISBN 0-918824-09-5). Turkey Pr.

Lewis, William, jt. auth. see Ledeen, Michael.

Lewis, William D. Mathematics Makes Sense. LC 66-21185. 1969. pap. 1.45 o.p. (ISBN 0-668-01854-2). Arc Bks.

Lewis, William D., ed. Great American Lawyers, 8 Vols. LC 75-157105. (Illus.). 1971. Repr. of 1909 ed. Set. text ed. 245.00x (ISBN 0-8377-2402-3). Rothman.

Lewis, William M. Maintaining Fishes for Experimental & Instructional Purposes. LC 62-15001. (Arcturus Books Paperbacks Ser.). 109p. 1963. pap. 3.95 (ISBN 0-8093-0078-8). S Ill U Pr.

Lewis, Wyndham. The Apes of God. (Illus.). 625p. (Orig.). 1981. 20.00 (ISBN 0-87685-513-3); deluxe ed. 30.00 (ISBN 0-87685-514-1); pap. price not set (ISBN 0-87685-512-5). Black Sparrow.

--Blasting & Bombardiering. 2nd rev. ed. 1967. 21.50c (ISBN 0-520-00742-5). U of Cal Pr.

--Collected Poems & Plays. Munton, Alan, ed. (Poetry Ser.). 229p. 1979. 14.95 o.s.i. (ISBN 0-85635-171-7, Pub. by Carcanet New Pr England). Persea Bks.

--Wyndham Lewis on Art: Collected Writings 1913-1956. 480p. 12.95x (ISBN 0-912158-33-6). Hennessey.

Lewis, Wyndham, ed. The Tyro: A Review of the Arts of Painting, Sculpture & Design, Nos. 1 & 2, 1921-22. new ed. (Illus.). 120p. 1970. 55.00x (ISBN 0-7146-2116-1, F Cass Co). Biblio Dist.

Lewis-Beck, Michael S. Applied Regression: An Introduction. LC 80-5821. (Quantitative Applications in the Social Sciences Ser.: No. 22). (Illus.). 79p. 1980. pap. 3.50 (ISBN 0-8039-1494-6). Sage.

Lewisohn, Leonard, tr. see Nurbaksh, Javad.

Lewison, Edward F. & Montague, Albert C. Diagnosis & Treatment of Breast Cancer: International Clinical Congress. (Illus.). 268p. 1981. write for info. (4954-2). Williams & Wilkins.

Lewison, Lawrence. You & Your Eyes. 2nd rev. ed. 1978. 10.00 o.p. (ISBN 0-682-48926-3). Exposition.

Lewiton, Mina. Rachel. (Illus.). (gr. 4-6). 1954. PLB 3.90 o.p. (ISBN 0-531-01908-X). Watts.

LeWitt, Sol. On the Walls of the Lower East Side. (Illus.). 72p. (Orig.). 1981. pap. 20.00 (ISBN 0-9601068-8-X). Agrinde Pubns.

Lewman, Harry. Managing an Appraisal Office. 1971. 3.00 o.s.i. (ISBN 0-911780-27-0). Am Inst Real Estate Appraisers.

Lewontin, R. C. The Genetic Basis of Evolutionary Change. (Biological Ser.: Vol. 25). 336p. 1974. 20.00 (ISBN 0-231-03392-3); pap. 8.00x (ISBN 0-231-08318-1). Columbia U Pr.

Lewontin, R. C., et al, eds. see Dobzhansky, Theodosius.

Lewty, Marjorie. A Certain Smile. (Harlequin Romances Ser.). (Orig.). 1980. pap. 1.25 o.p. (ISBN 0-373-02331-6, Pub. by Harlequin). PB.

--Prisoner in Paradise. (Harlequin Romances Ser.). 192p. (Orig.). 1981. pap. 1.25 (ISBN 0-373-02382-0, Pub. by Harlequin). PB.

Lewy, Arieh & Nevo, David. Evaluation Roles. 500p. 1981. price not set (ISBN 0-677-16290-1). Gordon.

Lewy, C. Meaning & Modality. LC 76-11084. 1977. 23.50 (ISBN 0-521-21314-2). Cambridge U Pr.

Lewy, C., jt. auth. see Broad, C. D.

Lewy, C., ed. see Broad, O. D.

Lewy, Robert. Preventive Primary Medicine: Reducing the Major Causes of Mortality. 1980. pap. text ed. 9.95 (ISBN 0-316-52401-8). Little.

Lewytzki, Borys. The Soviet Union: Figures - Facts - Data. 614p. 1979. 85.00 (ISBN 0-89664-010-8, Pub. by K G Saur). Gale.

Lewytzkyi, Borys & Stroynowski, Julius. Who's Who in the Socialist Countries. new ed. 736p. 1978. 140.00 (ISBN 0-89664-011-6, Pub. by K G Saur). Gale.

Lexau, Joan. Archimedes Takes a Bath. LC 69-11084. (Illus.). (gr. 2-5). 1969. PLB 6.89 o.p. (ISBN 0-690-09900-2, TYC-J). T Y Crowell.

Lexau, Joan M. Becky & the Bookworm. LC 78-73526. (Illus.). (gr. 2-5). Date not set. 3.50 (ISBN 0-89799-150-8); pap. price not set (ISBN 0-89799-068-4). Dandelion Pr. Postponed.

--Striped Ice Cream. LC 68-10774. (gr. 1-6). 1968. 7.95 (ISBN 0-397-31046-3). Lippincott.

Ley, Alice C. The Clandestine Betrothal. 192p. (Orig.). 1976. pap. 1.50 (ISBN 0-345-28576-X). Ballantine.

--A Season at Brighton. 192p. (Orig.). 1976. pap. 1.50 (ISBN 0-345-28577-8). Ballantine.

Ley, Ralph. Brecht As Thinker: Studies in Literary Marxism & Existentialism. Parent, David J., ed. LC 79-14407. (Illinois Language & Culture Ser.: No. 6). 604p. 1979. 37.75 (ISBN 0-8357-0413-0, IS-00077, Pub. by Applied Lit Pr). Univ Microfilms.

Ley, Rosamond, tr. see Busoni, Ferruccio.

Ley, Sandra J. Foodservice Refrigeration. (Illus.). 1980. 21.50 (ISBN 0-8436-2146-X). CBI Pub.

Ley, Willy. Our Work in Space. (gr. 7 up). 4.50 o.s.i. (ISBN 0-02-758980-3). Macmillan.

--Poles. LC 62-13534. (Life Nature Library). (Illus.). (gr. 5 up). 1962. PLB 8.97 o.p. (ISBN 0-8094-0617-9, Pub. by Time-Life). Silver.

Leyda, Jay. Kino: A History of the Russian & Soviet Film. (Illus.). 528p. 1973. pap. 4.95 o.s.i. (ISBN 0-02-012430-9, Collier). Macmillan.

--Voices of Film Experience, 1894 to the Present. 1977. 24.95 (ISBN 0-02-571600-X, 57160). Macmillan.

Leyda, Jay, jt. auth. see Bertensson, Sergei.

Leyda, Jay, ed. Eisenstein: Three Films: Battleship Potemkin, October, Alexander Nevsky. LC 74-6548. (Icon Editions: Masterworks Film Ser). (Illus.). 1974. pap. 4.95 o.s.i. (ISBN 0-06-430055-2, IN-55, HarpT). Har-Row.

Leyda, Jay & Bertensson, Sergei, eds. Mussorgsky Reader: A Life of Modeste Petrovich Mussorgsky in Letters & Documents. LC 70-87393. (Music Ser). (Illus.). 1970. Repr. of 1947 ed. lib. bdg. 32.50 (ISBN 0-306-71534-1). Da Capo.

Leyda, Seraphia De Ville. The Serpent Is Shut Out from Paradise: A Revaluation of Romantic Love in Shelley. (Salzburg Studies in English Literature, Romantic Reassessment: No. 4). 1972. pap. text ed. 25.00x (ISBN 0-391-01459-5). Humanities.

Leyden, D. & Collins, W. Silyated Surfaces, Vol. 7. (Midland Macromolecular Monographs). 1980. 63.50 (ISBN 0-677-13370-7). Gordon.

Leyden, D. E. & Cox, R. H. Analytical Applications of NMR. LC 77-1229. (Chemical Analysis Ser: Vol. 48). 1977. 40.00 (ISBN 0-471-53403-X, Pub. by Wiley-Interscience). Wiley.

Leydenfrost, Robert. Ten Little Elephants. LC 74-19313. 48p. 1975. 5.95 o.p. (ISBN 0-385-08360-2). Doubleday.

Leydet, Francois. Time & the Flowing River. 1978. pap. 3.95 (ISBN 0-345-21143-X). Ballantine.

Leyel, Mrs. C. F., ed. see Grieve, M.

Leyer, Albert. Machine Design. 1974. 19.95x (ISBN 0-216-87457-2). Intl Ideas.

Leyerle, Anne & Leyerle, William D. Song Anthology One. rev. 2nd ed. LC 79-90829. 144p. (gr. 9 up). 1980. pap. 8.95 plastic comb. (ISBN 0-9602296-1-2). W D Leyerle.

Leyerle, John & Quick, Anne, eds. Chaucer: A Selected Bibliography. (Toronto Medieval Bibliographies). 224p. 1981. 20.00x (ISBN 0-8020-2375-4); pap. 8.95x (ISBN 0-8020-6408-6). U of Toronto Pr.

Leyerle, John, jt. ed. see Benson, Larry D.

Leyerle, William D., jt. auth. see Leyerle, Anne.

Leyland, B. N., tr. see Kuz'Minskii, A. S.

Leyland, Eric. Budgerigars for Pleasure & Profit. 6.50x (SpS). Soccer.

Leyland, Winston. Orgasms of Light: The Gay Sunshine Anthology. (Poetry, Short Fiction, Graphics). (Illus.). 1977. lib. bdg. 20.00 (ISBN 0-917342-53-4, Pub. by Gay Sunshine); pap. 5.95 o.p. (ISBN 0-917342-54-2). Bookpeople.

Leyland, Winston, ed. Orgasms of Light. (Illus.). 264p. 1980. 20.00 (ISBN 0-917342-53-4); pap. 7.95 o.p. (ISBN 0-917342-54-2). Gay Sunshine.

Leyland, Winston, ed. see Ginsberg, Allen & Orlovsky, Peter.

Leys, Colin. Underdevelopment in Kenya: The Political Economy of Neo-Colonialism, 1964-71. LC 74-76387. 1975. 17.50x (ISBN 0-520-02731-0); pap. 6.95x (ISBN 0-520-02770-1). U of Cal Pr.

Leys, Simon. Broken Images. (Allison & Busby's Motive Ser.). 160p. 1981. pap. 8.95 (ISBN 0-8052-8069-3, Pub. by Allison & Busby England). Schocken.

--The Chairman's New Clothes: Mao & the Cultural Revolution. LC 77-12772. 1978. 18.95 (ISBN 0-312-12791-X). St Martin.

--The Chairwoman's New Clothes: Mao & the Cultural Revolution. (Allison & Busby Motive Ser.). 270p. 1981. pap. 8.95 (ISBN 0-8052-8080-4, Pub. by Allison & Busby England). Schocken.

Leyshon, Glynn. Programmed Functional Anatomy. LC 73-22279. 1974. pap. text ed. 10.00 (ISBN 0-8016-2999-3). Mosby.

Leyton, Leonard. Fluid Behaviour in Biological Sciences. (Illus.). 250p. 1975. 39.95x (ISBN 0-19-854126-0). Oxford U Pr.

L'Heureux, Conrad E. Rank Among the Canaanite Gods: El, Baal, & the Raphaim. LC 79-15582. (Harvard Semitic Monographs: No. 21). 1979. 10.50 (ISBN 0-89130-326-X, 040021). Scholars Pr Ca.

L'Heureux, John. Desires. LC 80-20228. 1981. 11.95 (ISBN 0-03-058902-9). HR&W.

L'Hommedieu, Dorothy K. Little Black Chaing. (Illus.). (ps-4). 1958. 2.75 o.p. (ISBN 0-374-34587-2). FS&G.

Lhuede, E. P. & Davern, W. A. Noise Levels in Australian Sawmills. 1980. 10.00x (ISBN 0-643-00348-7, Pub. by CSJRO Australia). State Mutual Bk.

Li. Accounting for Management Analysis. 1964. 18.95 (ISBN 0-675-09814-9). Merrill.

--Cost Accounting for Management Application. 1966. text ed. 18.95x (ISBN 0-675-09883-1); instructor's manual 3.95 (ISBN 0-686-66973-8). Merrill.

Li, Charles N. & Thompson, Sandra A. Mandarin Chinese: A Functional Reference Grammar. 1981. price not set (ISBN 0-520-04286-7). U of Cal Pr.

Li, Charles N., ed. Mechanisms of Syntactic Change. 1977. 20.00x (ISBN 0-292-75035-8). U of Tex Pr.

Li, Choh H., ed. Hormonal Proteins & Peptides, 7 vols. Incl. Vol. 1. 1973. 31.00 (ISBN 0-12-447201-X); Vol. 2. 1973. 37.50 (ISBN 0-12-447202-8); Vol. 3. 1975. 43.00 (ISBN 0-12-447203-6); Vol. 4. 1977. 33.00 (ISBN 0-12-447204-4); Vol. 5. Lipotropin & Related Peptides. 1978. 29.00 (ISBN 0-12-447205-2); Vol. 6. Thyroid Hormones. 1978. 48.50 (ISBN 0-12-447206-0); Vol. 7. Hypothalmic Hormones. 1979. 32.50 (ISBN 0-12-447207-9). LC 78-5444. Acad Pr.

Li, Choh-ming. The Statistical System of Communist China. 1962. 18.50x (ISBN 0-520-00746-8). U of Cal Pr.

Li, Christine, jt. auth. see Stanwick, Kathy.

Li Ho. Poems of Li Ho, 791-817. Frodsham, J. D., tr. (Oxford Library of East Asian Literature Ser). 1970. 24.95x (ISBN 0-19-815436-4). Oxford U Pr.

Li, Jeanette. Autobiography of Jeanette Li. Huston, Rose A., tr. 1971. pap. 3.95 (ISBN 0-686-12522-3). Banner of Truth.

Li, Ju-chen. Flowers in the Mirror. Tai-yi Lin, ed. & tr. 1965. 20.00x (ISBN 0-520-00747-6). U of Cal Pr.

Li, Lillian Ming-tse see Ming-tse Li, Lillian.

Li, Norman N., ed. Recent Developments in Separation Science, 5 vols. LC 72-88417. (Uniscience Ser.). Vol. 1. 54.95 (ISBN 0-8493-5029-8); Vol. 2, 1972, 292p. 59.95 (ISBN 0-8493-5030-1); Vol. 3A, 1977, 224p. 55.95 (ISBN 0-8493-5481-1); Vol. 3B, 1977, 200p. 49.95 (ISBN 0-8493-5482-X); Vol. 4, 1978, 248p. 58.95 (ISBN 0-8493-5483-8). CRC Pr.

Li, Sui-Fong. Studies on the Tolerance to Elevated Temperatures in Pleurotus Ostreatus (Jacq. Ex Fr.) Kummer: A Contribution to Taxonomy & the Genetics of the Fruiting Process. (Bibliotheca Mycologica: No. 76). (Illus.). 88p. 1981. pap. text ed. 15.00x (ISBN 3-7682-1276-9). Lubrecht & Cramer.

Li, Tien-Min. Mao's First Heir-Apparent. LC 72-152427. (Special Project). 223p. 1975. 10.00 (ISBN 0-8179-4141-X). Hoover Inst Pr.

Li, Tze-Chung. A List of Doctoral Dissertations by Chinese Students in the United States: 1961-1964. LC 67-30284. 1967. pap. 3.50 (ISBN 0-686-24155-X). CHCUS Inc.

--Mah Jong: The Rules to Play the Chinese Game. 1981. write for info. (ISBN 0-937256-02-1). Chinese Culture.

Li, Tze-Chung & Chang, Roy. Directory of Chinese American Librarians. LC 77-373584. 1977. pap. 5.00 (ISBN 0-686-24156-8). CHCUS Inc.

Li, Victor H. Law Without Lawyers: A Comparative View of Law in the United States & China. LC 78-568. 1978. lib. bdg. 16.50x (ISBN 0-89158-160-X); pap. text ed. 7.50 (ISBN 0-89158-161-8). Westview.

Li, Victor H., ed. Law & Politics in China's Foreign Trade. LC 76-7790. (Asian Law Ser: No.4). 488p. 1977. 22.50 (ISBN 0-295-95512-0). U of Wash Pr.

Li, Wen-Hsiung & Lam, Sau-Hai. Principles of Fluid Mechanics. 1964. 20.95 (ISBN 0-201-04240-1). A-W.

Lial, Margaret A. & Miller, Charles D. Study Guide to Accompany Intermediate Algebra. 3rd ed. 1981. pap. text ed. 5.95x (ISBN 0-673-15480-7). Scott F.

Lial, Margaret L. & Miller, Charles D. Algebra & Trigonometry. 2nd ed. 1980. text ed. 18.95x (ISBN 0-673-15272-3). Scott F.

--Beginning Algebra. 3rd ed. 1980. text ed. 16.95x (ISBN 0-673-15330-4). Scott F.

--College Algebra. 3rd ed. 1981. text ed. 16.95x (ISBN 0-673-15407-6); pap. text ed. 5.95x study guide (ISBN 0-673-15477-7). Scott F.

--Essential Calculus: With Applications in Business, Biology, & Behavioral Sciences. 346p. 1975. 16.95x o.p. (ISBN 0-673-07959-7). Scott F.

--Finite Mathematics: With Applications in Business, Biology, & Behavioral Sciences. 1977. 17.95x (ISBN 0-673-15044-5). Scott F.

--Intermediate Algebra. 3rd ed. 1981. text ed. 15.95x (ISBN 0-673-15406-8). Scott F.

--Mathematics: With Applications in the Management, Natural, & Social Sciences. 2nd ed. 1979. text ed. 18.95x (ISBN 0-673-15185-9); study guide 5.95x (ISBN 0-673-15187-5). Scott F.

--Trigonometry. 2nd ed. 1981. text ed. 16.95x (ISBN 0-673-15432-7). Scott F.

Lial, Margaret L., jt. auth. see Miller, Charles D.

Liang, Daniel S. Facts About Aging. 120p. 1973. pap. 6.75 (ISBN 0-398-02727-7). C C Thomas.

Liang, Hsi-huey. The Berlin Police Force in the Weimar Republic, 1918-1933. LC 74-85452. (Illus.). 1970. 20.00x (ISBN 0-520-01603-3). U of Cal Pr.

--The Sino-German Connection: Alexander von Falckenhausen Between China & Germany. (Van Gorcum Historical Library: No. 94). (Illus.). 1978. pap. text ed. 23.75x (ISBN 90-232-1554-0). Humanities.

Liang, Lucille. Chinese Regional Cooking: Authentic Recipies of the Liang School. LC 79-65067. (Illus.). 1979. 12.95 (ISBN 0-8069-0148-9); lib. bdg. 11.69 (ISBN 0-8069-0149-7). Sterling.

Liao, David C., ed. World Christianity: Eastern Asia. 198p. 1979. pap. 9.00 (ISBN 0-912552-31-X). MARC.

Liao, S. Microwave Devices & Circuits. 1980. 29.95 (ISBN 0-13-581207-0). P-H.

Liban, Felicia & Mitchell, Louise K. Cloisonne Enameling & Jewelry. 256p. 1980. 18.95 (ISBN 0-8019-6900-X). Chilton.

Libbey, James K. Alexander Gumberg & Soviet-American Relations, 1917-1933. LC 77-73704. 248p. 1978. 17.00x (ISBN 0-8131-1361-X). U Pr of Ky.

Libby, Bill. Baseball's Greatest Sluggers. (Major League Baseball Library: No. 19). (Illus.). (gr. 5 up). 1973. 2.50 o.p. (ISBN 0-394-82538-1, BYR); PLB 3.69 (ISBN 0-394-92538-6). Random.

--Champions of the Indianapolis 500. LC 76-87. (Illus.). 1976. 7.95 (ISBN 0-396-07306-9). Dodd.

--Goliath: The Wilt Chamberlain Story. LC 76-50104. 1977. 8.95 (ISBN 0-396-07392-1). Dodd.

--Great Stanley Cup Playoffs. (Pro Hockey Library: No. 4). (Illus.). (gr. 5 up). 1972. 2.50 o.p. (ISBN 0-394-82404-0, BYR); PLB 3.69 (ISBN 0-394-92404-5). Random.

--Star Running Backs of the NFL. (NFL Punt, Pass & Kick Library: No. 15). (Illus.). (gr. 5-9). 1971. 2.50 o.p. (ISBN 0-394-82285-4, BYR); PLB 3.69 (ISBN 0-394-92285-9). Random.

--They Didn't Win the Oscars. (Illus.). 256p. 1980. 18.95 (ISBN 0-87000-455-7). Arlington Hse.

Libby, Bill, jt. auth. see O'Neil, Kitty.

Libby, Bill, jt. auth. see O'Neill, Frank.

Libby, Dorothy see Horr, David A.

Libby, Larry, jt. auth. see McMinn, Gordon.

Libby, P. A. & Williams, F., eds. Turbulent Reacting Flows. (Topics in Applied Physics Ser.: Vol. 44). (Illus.). 260p. 1981. 49.50 (ISBN 0-387-10192-6). Springer Verlag.

Libby, Paul A., et al see Heat Transfer & Fluid Mechanics Institute.

Libby, Roger W. & Whitehurst, Robert N. Marriage & Alternatives: Exploring Intimate Relationships. 1977. pap. 9.95x (ISBN 0-673-15050-X). Scott F.

Libby, William J., jt. auth. see Lerner, I. Michael.

Libecap, Gary. Locking up the Range: Federal Land Controls & Grazing. (Pacific Institute for Public Policy Research Ser.). 1981. price not set professional reference (ISBN 0-88410-382-X). Ballinger Pub.

Liben, Lynn S., et al, eds. Spatial Representation & Behavior: Application & Theory Across the Life Span. (Developmental Psychology Ser.). 1980. 27.50 (ISBN 0-12-447980-4). Acad Pr.

Liber, Maurice. Rashi: His Life & Works. Szold, Adele, tr. from Fr. LC 70-136767. (Illus.). 1971. Repr. of 1906 ed. 12.50 (ISBN 0-87203-021-0). Hermon.

Liberatore, E. K. Liberation Manifesto. 1981. softbound 9.95 (ISBN 0-87100-177-2). Morgan.

Liberia, Republic of. Opinions of the Attorney General of the Republic of Liberia, September, 1964-August 1968. Konvitz, Milton R., ed. LC 28-17298. (Liberian Law Reports Ser). 1969. 25.00x (ISBN 0-8014-0529-7). Cornell U Pr.

Liberman, R. P. A Guide to Behavioral Analysis & Therapy. 368p. 1972. text ed. 17.25 (ISBN 0-08-016645-8); pap. text ed. 9.25 (ISBN 0-08-016786-1). Pergamon.

Liberman, R. P., et al. The Handbook of Marital Therapy: A Positive Approach to Helping Troubled Relationships. (Applied Clinical Psychology Ser.). (Illus.). 250p. 1980. 19.50 (ISBN 0-306-40235-1, Plenum Pr). Plenum Pub.

Liberman, Robert P., et al. Personal Effectiveness: Guiding People to Assert Themselves & Improve Their Social Skills. (Illus., Orig.). 1975. basic manual 7.95 (ISBN 0-87822-163-8); program guide 3.95 (ISBN 0-87822-164-6); client's introduction set 5.95 (ISBN 0-87822-165-4). Res Press.

Liberson, W. T., tr. see Maigne, Robert.

Libert, Jack. Brothers & Sisters of the January Moon. (Illus., Orig.). 1971. pap. 2.00 (ISBN 0-911732-58-6). Irego.

--Children of the Twenty Third Century Beautiful As You Will Be I Know Your Hair. (Illus.). 69p. 1980. pap. 4.00 (ISBN 0-911732-08-X). Irego.

--The Doorman. (Orig.). 1966. 6.00 (ISBN 0-911732-50-0); pap. 4.00 (ISBN 0-911732-51-9). Irego.

--Myself Exactly. (Illus., Orig.). 1971. pap. 2.00 (ISBN 0-911732-56-X). Irego.

--Sun a Honeydew, Moon a Cantaloupe. (Illus., Orig.). 1970. pap. 2.00 (ISBN 0-911732-53-5). Irego.

--Waiting for Me Waiting for the Train Hilda Dearwater. (Illus.). 1972. pap. 2.00 (ISBN 0-911732-59-4). Irego.

--You. (Orig.). 1971. pap. 2.00 (ISBN 0-911732-57-8). Irego.

Liberty, Gene. The Continuation of Life. (Orig.). (gr. 7-10). 1975. pap. text ed. 6.42 (ISBN 0-87720-012-2). AMSCO Sch.

--First Book of the Human Senses. (First Bks). (Illus.). (gr. 4-6). 1961. PLB 4.90 o.p. (ISBN 0-531-00555-0). Watts.

--The Meaning of Life. (Orig.). (gr. 7-10). 1975. pap. text ed. 5.50 (ISBN 0-87720-010-6). AMSCO Sch.

--The Support of Life. (Orig.). (gr. 7-10). 1975. pap. text ed. 6.00 (ISBN 0-87720-011-4). AMSCO Sch.

Liberty, Gene, ed. see Alvarez, Joseph.

Liberty, Gene, ed. see Cohen, Daniel.

Liberty, Gene, ed. see Legunn, Joel.

Liberty, Gene, ed. see Lowenherz, Robert J.

Liberty, Margot, jt. auth. see Stands In Timber, John.

Liberty, Margot, jt. ed. see Wood, W. Raymond.

Libes, Sol. Fundamentals & Applications of Digital Logic Circuits. 2nd ed. 1978. pap. 9.75 (ISBN 0-8104-5661-3); exam 1.30 (ISBN 0-8104-0916-X); final exam 0.30 (ISBN 0-685-93591-4). Hayden.

--Small Computer Systems Handbook. (gr. 12 up). 1978. pap. 9.95 (ISBN 0-8104-5678-8). Hayden.

Libes, Sol, jt. auth. see Towers, T. D.

Libes, Soloman. Interfacing to S-100 IEEE 696 Microcomputers. (Orig.). 1981. pap. text ed. 15.99 (ISBN 0-931988-37-3). Osborne-McGraw.

Libien, Lois & Strong, Margaret. Paint It Yourself: The Complete Indoor House-Painting Book. LC 78-6692. 1978. 9.95 o.p. (ISBN 0-688-03289-3); pap. 5.95 o.p. (ISBN 0-688-08289-0). Morrow.

Libig, Mark C. Surgical Technology: The 70's. 432p. 1981. text ed. 26.50 (ISBN 0-8403-2336-0). Kendall-Hunt.

Liblich, Garnet Mills, ed. Qualified Products List & Sources. 60th ed. 300p. 1981. lib. bdg. 65.00 perfect bdg (ISBN 0-912702-03-6). Global Eng.

Libman, Gary. Bjorn Borg. (Sports Superstars Ser.). (Illus.). (gr. 3-9). 1979. PLB 5.95 (ISBN 0-87191-721-1); pap. 2.95 (ISBN 0-89812-161-2). Creative Ed.

--An Interview with Lynne Cox. (Interviews Ser.). (Illus.). (gr. 3-8). 1977. PLB 6.75 (ISBN 0-87191-571-5). Creative Ed.

--Reggie Jackson. (Sports Superstars Ser.). (Illus.). (gr. 3-9). 1979. PLB 5.95 (ISBN 0-87191-724-6); pap. 2.95 (ISBN 0-89812-162-0). Creative Ed.

Libo, Kenneth, jt. auth. see Howe, Irving.

Libow, Leslie S. & Sherman. The Core of Geriatric Medicine: A Guide for Students & Practitioners. (Illus.). 354p. 1980. text ed. 22.95 (ISBN 0-8016-3096-7). Mosby.

Libra, C. Aq. Astrology: Its Techniques & Ethics. LC 80-23764. 259p. 1980. Repr. of 1976 ed. lib. bdg. 10.95x (ISBN 0-89370-635-3). Borgo Pr.

Library & Information Technology Association, jt. ed. see Gapen, D. Kaye.

Library & Information Technology Association. The Closing the Catalog: Proceedings of the LITA Institute. Gapen, D. Kaye & Juergens, Bonnie, eds. 1980. lib. bdg. 18.50x (ISBN 0-912700-56-4). Oryx Pr.

Library Applications of Data Processing Clinic, 1979. The Role of the Library in an Electronic Society: Proceedings. Lancaster, F. W., ed. LC 79-19449. 200p. 1980. 9.00 (ISBN 0-87845-053-X). U of Ill Lib Sci.

Library Association & National Association for Partially Handicapped Conference. Print for the Visually Handicapped Reader: Proceedings. 1971. 5.50x (ISBN 0-85365-394-1, Pub. by Lib Assn England). Oryx Pr.

Library Association (London), ed. British Humanities Index 1978. LC 63-24940. 802p. 1979. 175.00x (ISBN 0-85365-901-X). Intl Pubns Serv.

Library Association, London, ed. British Technology Index: Annual Volume 1978. LC 63-23735. 828p. 1979. 285.00x (ISBN 0-85365-911-7). Intl Pubns Serv.

Library Association-the Working Party on Community Information, ed. Community Information: What Libraries Can Do. 1980. pap. 9.25x (ISBN 0-85365-872-2, Pub. by Lib Assn England). Oryx Pr.

Library Assoociation (London) British Humanities Index 1979. LC 63-24940. 744p. 1980. 190.00x (ISBN 0-85365-583-9). Intl Pubns Serv.

Library of Congress. Bibliographic Guide to Law. 1979. lib. bdg. 99.50 (ISBN 0-8161-6873-3). G K Hall.

--Bibliographic Guide to Law: Nineteen Seventy-Eight. (Library Catalogs-Bib. Guides). 1979. lib. bdg. 95.00 (ISBN 0-8161-6856-3). G K Hall.

--Charles Fenderich: Lithographer of American Statesmen. Miller, Lillian B., ed. (Illus.). 1978. text ed. 25.00 incl. microfiche (ISBN 0-226-69243-4). U of Chicago Pr.

Library of Congress, jt. auth. see New York Public Library, Research Libraries.

Library of Congress, ed. see New York Public Library Research Library.

Library of Congress & the Research Libraries of the New York Public Library. Bibliographic Guide to Psychology: Nineteen Seventy-Eight. (Library Catalogs-Bib. Guides). 1979. lib. bdg. 60.00 (ISBN 0-8161-6859-8). G K Hall.

Library of Congress & University of Texas Library (Austin) Bibliographic Guide to Latin American Studies: 1979. (Library Catalogs-Bib. Guides). 1980. lib. bdg. 245.00 (ISBN 0-8161-6872-5). G K Hall.

Library of Congress, Geography & Map Division (Washington, D. C.) The Bibliography of Cartography, First Supplement. 1979. lib. bdg. 250.00 (ISBN 0-8161-0259-7). G K Hall.

Library of Congress Research Library, jt. auth. see New York Public Library Research Library.

Libris, Edouard, jt. ed. see Porter, Edwin.

Licart, Jean. Basic Equitation. (Illus.). pap. 6.10 (ISBN 0-85131-202-0, Dist. by Sporting Book Center). J A Allen.

Licata, Salvatore J. & Petersen, Robert, eds. Historical Perspectives on Homosexuality. LC 80-6262. 240p. 1981. 14.95 (ISBN 0-8128-2810-0). Stein & Day.

Lichello, Robert. How to Make a Million Dollars in the Stock Market - Automatically. rev. ed. 1980. pap. 2.25 (ISBN 0-451-09461-1, E9461, Sig). NAL.

--How to Make a Million Dollars in the Stock Market---Automatically. (Orig.). 1977. pap. 1.95 o.p. (ISBN 0-451-07619-2, J7619, Sig). NAL.

Lichfield, N., et al. Evaluation in the Planning Process. 336p. 1976. text ed. 36.00 (ISBN 0-08-017843-X); pap. text ed. 19.50 (ISBN 0-08-018243-7). Pergamon.

Lichfield, Nathaniel & Darin-Drabkin, Haim. Land Policy in Planning. (Urban & Regional Studies: No. 8). (Illus.). 334p. 1981. text ed. 39.95 (ISBN 0-04-333017-7, 2540). Allen Unwin.

Lichine, Alexis. Alexis Lichine's New Encyclopedia of Wines & Spirits. 3rd ed. LC 80-22385. (Illus.). 736p. 1981. 29.95 (ISBN 0-394-51781-4). Knopf.

Licht, Paul & Gorman, George. Reproductive & Fat Cycles in Caribbean Anolis Lizards. (U. C. Publ. in Zoology: Vol. 95). 1971. pap. 7.00x (ISBN 0-520-09374-7). U of Cal Pr.

Lichtblau, Myron I. Manuel Galvez. (World Authors Ser.: Argentina: No. 203). lib. bdg. 10.95 (ISBN 0-8057-2340-4). Twayne.

Lichten, William. Physics. new ed. (Orig.). (gr. 7-12). 1973. 6.44 (ISBN 0-201-04242-8, Sch Div); tchr's manual 2.84 (ISBN 0-201-04243-6). A-W.

Lichtenberg, Jacqueline. The House of Zeor. LC 80-83565. 224p. 1981. pap. 2.25 (ISBN 0-87216-801-8). Playboy Pbks.

--Mahogany Trinrose. LC 79-8563. (Double D Science Fiction Ser.). 256p. 1981. 10.95 (ISBN 0-385-15476-3). Doubleday.

Lichtenberg, Marc L., jt. auth. see Tarlow, David M.

Lichtenberger, James P. Development of Social Theory. 482p. 1980. Repr. of 1925 ed. lib. bdg. 45.00 (ISBN 0-89987-508-4). Darby Bks.

Lichtendorf, Susan & Gillis, Phyllis. The New Pregnancy: The Active Woman's Guide to Work, Legal Rights, Health Care, Travel, Sports, Dress, Sex, & Emotonal Well-Being. 1979. 9.95 (ISBN 0-394-50210-8). Random.

Lichtenstadter, Ilse. Islam & the Modern Age. 228p. 1980. text ed. 21.00x (ISBN 0-8290-0179-4). Irvington.

Lichtenstein, Edward. Psychotherapy: Approaches & Applications. LC 79-25036. 1980. text ed. 14.95 (ISBN 0-8185-0381-5). Brooks-Cole.

Lichtenstein, Edward, jt. auth. see Danaher, Brian G.

Lichtenstein, Grace. A Long Way, Baby: Behind-the-Scenes in Women's Pro Tennis. LC 74-1166. 1974. 6.95 o.p. (ISBN 0-688-00263-3). Morrow.

--Machisma: Women & Daring. LC 79-7114. 360p. 1981. 14.95 (ISBN 0-385-15109-8). Doubleday.

Lichtenstein, L. M. & Austen, K. F., eds. Asthma-Physiology, Immunopharmacology & Treatment. 1974. 37.00 (ISBN 0-12-068450-0). Acad Pr.

Lichtenstein, L. M., et al, eds. Asthma: Physiology, Immunopharmacology & Treatment, Vol. 2. 1977. 37.00 (ISBN 0-12-448502-2). Acad Pr.

Lichtenstein, Louis. Bone Tumors. 5th ed. LC 77-22264. (Illus.). 1977. 47.50 (ISBN 0-8016-3005-3). Mosby.

Lichtenstein, Roy, illus. Roy Lichtenstein Drawings & Prints. LC 73-90344. (Illus.). 276p. 1981. pap. 19.95 (ISBN 0-87754-203-1). Chelsea Hse.

Lichtenstein, Sara. Delacroix & Raphael. Freedberg, Sydney J., ed. LC 78-74970. (Outstanding Dissertations in the Fine Arts Ser.). (Illus.). 1979. lib. bdg. 44.00 (ISBN 0-8240-3972-6). Garland Pub.

Lichter, Henry, jt. auth. see Piscano, John.

Lichter, Paul. The Boy Who Dared to Rock: The Definitive Elvis. LC 76-52006. 1978. pap. 8.95 (ISBN 0-385-12636-0, Dolp). Doubleday.

Lichter, Solomon O., et al. Drop-Outs: A Treatment Study of Intellectually Capable Students Who Drop Out of High School. LC 62-11853. 1962. 12.95 (ISBN 0-02-918900-4). Free Pr.

Lichtheim, George. From Marx to Hegel. LC 70-167871. 1971. pap. 3.95 (ISBN 0-8164-9188-7); 7.95 o.p. (ISBN 0-8164-9120-8, Continuum). Continuum.

--Marxism in Modern France. LC 66-14788. 1966. 20.00x (ISBN 0-231-02908-X); pap. 6.00x (ISBN 0-231-08584-2). Columbia U Pr.

Lichtheim, Miriam. Ancient Egyptian Literature, Vol. 3: A Book of Readings. 1980. 15.75x (ISBN 0-520-03882-7); pap. 3.95 (ISBN 0-520-04020-1). U of Cal Pr.

--Demotic Ostraca from Medinet Habu. LC 57-9105. (Oriental Institute Pubns. Ser: No. 80). (Illus.). 1957. 25.00x o.s.i. (ISBN 0-226-62181-2). U of Chicago Pr.

Lichtman, Allan J. & Challinor, Joan R. Kin & Communities: Families in America. LC 78-24246. (Illus.). 335p. 1979. text ed. 19.95x (ISBN 0-87474-608-6); pap. text ed. 8.95x (ISBN 0-87474-609-4). Smithsonian.

Lichtman, Allan J. & French, Valerie. Historians & the Living Past: The Theory & Practice of Historical Study. LC 77-86035. 1978. pap. text ed. 8.95x (ISBN 0-88295-773-2). AHM Pub.

Licklider, Heath. Architectural Scale. LC 66-14230. (Illus.). 1966. 5.00 o.p. (ISBN 0-8076-0351-1). Braziller.

Licklider, Patricia. Building a College Vocabulary. 256p. (Orig.). 1981. pap. text ed. 7.95 (ISBN 0-316-52424-7); tchrs'. manual free (ISBN 0-316-52425-5). Little.

Lickteig, Mary J. An Introduction to Children's Literature. 448p. 1975. text ed. 17.95x (ISBN 0-675-08716-3). Merrill.

Lickwar, Vasily, tr. see Chetverikov, Sergii.

Lid, R. W. Ford Madox Ford: The Essence of His Art. 1964. 15.75x (ISBN 0-520-00748-4). U of Cal Pr.

--Grooving the Symbol. LC 78-98886. 1970. pap. text ed. 6.95 (ISBN 0-02-918960-8). Free Pr.

Liddell, H. G. & Scott, Robert, eds. Intermediate Greek-English Lexicon. 1959. text ed. 29.50x (ISBN 0-19-910206-6). Oxford U Pr.

Liddell, Hart A., jt. auth. see Liddell, Hart B.

Liddell, Hart B. & Liddell, Hart A. The Sword & the Pen: A Collection of the World's Greatest Military Writings. 304p. 1976. 10.95 o.p. (ISBN 0-690-00052-9, TYC-T). T Y Crowell.

Liddell, Heather. Computer-Aided Techniques for the Design of Multilayer Filters. 1981. 49.00 (ISBN 0-9960020-2-2, Pub. by a Hilger England). Heyden.

Liddell, Henry G. & Scott, Robert. Greek-English Lexicon: A Supplement. Barber, E. A., et al, eds. 1968. 22.00x (ISBN 0-19-864210-5). Oxford U Pr.

Liddell, Henry G. & Scott, Robert, eds. Greek-English Lexicon. 9th ed. 1940. 74.00x (ISBN 0-19-864214-8). Oxford U Pr.

Liddell, Louise A. Clothes & Your Appearance. rev. ed. LC 80-25167. (Illus.). 352p. 1981. text ed. 13.20 (ISBN 0-87006-311-1). Goodheart.

--Clothes & Your Appearance. rev. ed. LC 80-25167. (Illus.). 352p. 1980. 13.20 (ISBN 0-87006-311-1). Good Heart.

--Clothes & Your Appearance. LC 80-25167. (Illus.). 1981. text ed. 12.80 (ISBN 0-87006-311-1). Goodheart.

Liddell, Robert. Some Principles of Fiction. LC 73-433. 162p. 1974. Repr. of 1954 ed. lib. bdg. 9.50x o.p. (ISBN 0-8371-6764-7, LIPF). Greenwood.

Liddell Hart, Basil H. The Revolution in Warfare. LC 79-22632. 1980. Repr. of 1947 ed. lib. bdg. 16.75x (ISBN 0-313-22173-1, LHRW). Greenwood.

Lidden, H. P. & Orr, J. The Birth of Christ. Date not set. 13.95 (ISBN 0-86524-058-2). Klock & Klock.

Liddie, Alexander S., ed. see Armin, Robert.

Liddle, William. EARS. (Illus., Orig.). (gr. k-3). 1974. student's bk. 3.60 (ISBN 0-87892-854-5); tchr's handbook 3.60 (ISBN 0-87892-856-1); tapes 84.90 (ISBN 0-87892-857-X). Economy Co.

Liddon, Henry P. The Divinity of Our Lord. 1978. 20.25 (ISBN 0-686-12948-2). Klock & Klock.

--The First Epistle to Timothy. 1978. 6.00 (ISBN 0-686-12944-X). Klock & Klock.

Liddy, G. Gordon. Will. 1981. pap. 3.50 (ISBN 0-440-09666-9). Dell.

Liddy, James. Corca Bascinn. 1977. pap. text ed. 6.50x (ISBN 0-85105-314-9, Dolmen Pr). Humanities.

Lider, Julian. The Political & Military Laws of War. 1979. text ed. 29.00x (ISBN 0-566-00231-0, Pub. by Gower Pub Co England). Renouf.

Lidicker, W. Z., Jr. & Ziegler, A. C. Report on a Collection of Mammals from Eastern New Guinea, Including Species Keys for Fourteen Genera. (U. C. Publ. in Zoology: Vol. 87). 1968. pap. 6.50x (ISBN 0-520-09344-5). U of Cal Pr.

Lidstone, Herrick K., ed. A Tax Guide for Artists & Arts Organizations. LC 76-53905. (Illus.). 1979. 24.95 (ISBN 0-669-01294-7); pap. 14.95 (ISBN 0-669-01295-5). Lexington Bks.

Lidstone, John. Motivating Your Sales Force. 1978. text ed. 25.25 (ISBN 0-566-02082-3, Pub. by Gower Pub Co England). Renouf.

--Recruiting & Selecting Salesmen. 1979. text ed. 28.50x (ISBN 0-566-02153-6, Pub. by Gower Pub Co England). Renouf.

Lidstone, John & Lewis, Stanley. Reinhold Visuals Study Guide. 160p. 1980. pap. 8.95 (ISBN 0-442-25399-0). Van Nos Reinhold.

Lidvall, jt. auth. see Minish.

Lie, Sophus. Transformationsgruppen, 3 Vols. 2nd ed. LC 76-113135. (Ger). 1970. 79.50 set (ISBN 0-8284-0232-9). Chelsea Pub.

Lie, T. S., ed. see International Microsurgical Society, 5th, Germany, Oct. 1978.

Lieb, Hans-Heinrich. International Linguistiics: Volume 4, Syntax & Semantics. (Current Issues in Linguistic Theory Ser.: No. 17). 250p. 1981. text ed. 27.50x (ISBN 90-272-3508-2). Humanities.

Lieb, Robert. Transportation: The Domestic System. 2nd ed. 1980. text ed. 18.95 (ISBN 0-8359-7826-5). Reston.

Lieb, Robert C. Transportation: The Domestic System. LC 77-5432. 1978. 16.95 (ISBN 0-87909-843-0); instrs'. manual avail. Reston.

Lieb, Thom. Everybody's Book of Bicycle Riding. McCullagh, Chuck, ed. (Illus.). 336p. 1981. 12.95 (ISBN 0-87857-322-4); pap. 9.95 (ISBN 0-87857-323-2). Rodale Pr Inc.

Lieban, Richard W. Cebuano Sorcery: Malign Magic in the Philippines. 1967. 14.75x (ISBN 0-520-00749-2); pap. 3.95x (ISBN 0-520-03420-1). U of Cal Pr.

Liebb, Julius, jt. auth. see Bromberg, Murray.

Liebeck, Pamela. Vectors & Matrices. 192p. 1971. 25.00 (ISBN 0-08-015823-4); pap. 12.75 (ISBN 0-08-015822-6). Pergamon.

Liebenow, J, Gus. Colonial Rule & Political Development in Tanzania: The Case of the Makonde. LC 72-126898. 1971. 14.75x o.s.i. (ISBN 0-8101-0332-X). Northwestern U Pr.

Lieber, Francis. Notes on Fallacies of American Protectionists. Bd. with Lectures on the History of Protection in the United States. Sumner, William. (The Neglected American Economists Ser.). 1974. lib. bdg. 50.00 (ISBN 0-8240-1018-3). Garland Pub.

--On Civil Liberty & Self Government. LC 76-169655. (Civil Liberties in American History Ser). 1972. Repr. of 1877 ed. lib. bdg. 59.50 (ISBN 0-306-70284-3). Da Capo.

Lieber, Fritz. The Book of Fritz Leiber, Vols. I & II. (Science Fiction Ser.). 1980. lib. bdg. 19.95 (ISBN 0-8398-2638-9). Gregg.

--Gather, Darkness! (Science Fiction Ser.). 1980. lib. bdg. 14.95 (ISBN 0-8398-2639-7). Gregg.

--The Green Millenium. (Science Fiction Ser.). 1980. lib. bdg. 14.95 (ISBN 0-8398-2641-9). Gregg.

--The Sinful Ones. (Science Fiction Ser.). 1980. lib. bdg. 13.95 (ISBN 0-8398-2643-5). Gregg.

--The Wanderer. (Science Fiction Ser.). 1980. lib. bdg. 15.95 (ISBN 0-8398-2642-7). Gregg.

Lieber, Harvey. Federalism & Clean Waters: The 1972 Water Pollution Control Act. LC 74-33980. (Illus.). 288p. 1975. 22.50 (ISBN 0-669-99150-3). Lexington Bks.
Lieber, Justin. Noam Chomsky: A Philosophic Overview. (World Leaders Ser: No. 36). 1975. lib. bdg. 9.95 (ISBN 0-8057-3661-1). Twayne.
Lieber, Michael. Street Life: Afro-American Culture in Urban Trinidad. (University Book Ser.). 1981. lib. bdg. 15.95 (ISBN 0-8161-9033-X). G K Hall.
Lieber, Robert J. British Politics & European Unity: Parties, Elites & Pressure Groups. LC 70-104104. 1970. 20.00x (ISBN 0-520-01675-0). U of Cal Pr.
Lieberman & Schimmel. Personal Typing in Thirty Days. 1981. pap. 3.75 (ISBN 0-8120-2284-X). Barron.
Lieberman, Ann & Miller, Lynn. Staff Development: New Demands, New Realities, New Perspectives. LC 78-27453. 1979. 10.95 (ISBN 0-8077-2512-9). Tchrs Coll.
Lieberman, Bernhardt, ed. Human Sexual Behavior: A Book of Readings. LC 70-162422. 1971. pap. text ed. 13.95x o.p. (ISBN 0-471-53423-4). Halsted Pr.
Lieberman, Bonnie, ed. see Reynolds, Lloyd G.
Lieberman, Chaim. The Grave Concern. LC 68-58650. 202p. 1968. 4.95 (ISBN 0-88400-016-8). Shengold.
Lieberman, David E., ed. Computer Methods: The Fundamentals of Digital Nuclear Medicine. LC 77-10999. (Illus.). 1977. pap. 20.00 (ISBN 0-8016-3009-6). Mosby.
Lieberman, E. J. & Peck, Ellen. Sex & Birth Control: A Guide for the Young. rev. ed. LC 79-7094. (Illus.). 304p. 1981. 10.95 (ISBN 0-690-01837-1, HarpT). Har-Row.
Lieberman, Florence. Social Work with Children. LC 78-23287. 1979. text ed. 24.95 (ISBN 0-87705-255-7); pap. text ed. 9.95 (ISBN 0-87705-257-3). Human Sci Pr.
Lieberman, Fred. A Chinese Zither Tutor: The Mei-an Ch'in-p'u. 1981. write for info. U of Wash Pr.
Lieberman, Fredric. Chinese Music: An Annotated Bibliography. LC 72-101135. (A (Bibliographies), No. 1). xii, 158p. (Orig.). 1970. pap. text ed. 7.50x (ISBN 0-913360-02-3). Asian Music Pub.
Lieberman, Gerald J., jt. auth. see Hillier, Frederick S.
Lieberman, H. & Lachman, L., eds. Pharmaceutical Dosage Forms: Tablets, Vol. 1. 536p. 1980. 59.75 (ISBN 0-8247-6918-X). Dekker.
Lieberman, Herbert. Brilliant Kids. 384p. 1975. 8.95 o.s.i. (ISBN 0-02-571810-X). Macmillan.
--Crawlspace. 1981. pap. 2.50 (ISBN 0-671-43068-8). PB.
Lieberman, J. Ben. Arts & Crafts As Root Technologies. (The Root Technologies Ser.: Bk. I). Date not set. write for info (ISBN 0-918142-14-8); pap. write for info (ISBN 0-918142-15-6). Myriade. Postponed.
--Printing As a Hobby. 3rd ed. 1980. pap. 5.95 o.p. (ISBN 0-918142-07-5). Caroline Hse.
--Printing As a Hobby. 2nd ed. (Illus.). 1981. write for info. (ISBN 0-918142-08-3); pap. write for info. (ISBN 0-918142-07-5). Myriade.
--Simple Printing. 1980. pap. 6.95 o.p. (ISBN 0-918142-11-3). Caroline Hse.
--Simple Printing. (Root Technologies Ser.: Bk. II). (Illus.). Date not set. write for info. (ISBN 0-918142-09-1); pap. write for info. (ISBN 0-918142-11-3). Myriade. Postponed.
Lieberman, Jerry. Three Thousand Five Hundred Good Jokes for Speakers. LC 74-29354. 480p. 1975. pap. 4.50 (ISBN 0-385-00545-8, Dolp). Doubleday.
Lieberman, Jethro. The Litigious Society. LC 80-68181. 256p. 1980. 13.95 (ISBN 0-465-04134-5). Basic.
Lieberman, Jethro K. & Rhodes, Neil S. The Complete Nineteen Eighty CB Handbook. 1980. pap. 2.95 (ISBN 0-380-48587-7, 48587). Avon.
Lieberman, Laurence. The Osprey Suicides: Poems. LC 72-87164. 96p. 1973. pap. 1.95 o.s.i. (ISBN 0-02-069790-2, Collier). Macmillan.
--Unblinding. 1968. 9.95 (ISBN 0-02-571830-4). Macmillan.
Lieberman, Lawrence. Osprey Suicides. 1973. 6.95 o.s.i. (ISBN 0-02-571820-7). Macmillan.
Lieberman, Leo, ed. Dictionary of Correct English Usage. LC 63-15604. 1963. 4.75 o.p. (ISBN 0-8022-0973-4). Philos Lib.
Lieberman, M. & Sano, T., eds. Developmental & Physiological Correlates of Cardiac Muscle: Perspectives in Cardiovascular Research, Vol. 1. LC 74-21979. 336p. 1976. 34.50 (ISBN 0-89004-027-3). Raven.
Lieberman, Mark. Zion South. LC 80-66494. 1981. 12.95 (ISBN 0-87795-269-8). Arbor Hse.
Lieberman, Myron. Public-Sector Bargaining: A Policy of Reappraisal. LC 80-8426. 1980. 19.95 (ISBN 0-669-04110-6). Lexington Bks.
Lieberman, Philip. Intonation, Perception, & Language. LC 67-13392. (Press Research Monographs: No. 38). 1967. 16.00x (ISBN 0-262-12024-0); pap. 4.95x o.p. (ISBN 0-262-62031-6). MIT Pr.
--Speech Acoustics & Perception. LC 70-183114. (Studies in Communicative Disorders Ser). 1972. 2.50 (ISBN 0-672-61293-3). Bobbs.
Lieberman, Philip H. & Good, Robert A., eds. Diseases of Hematopoietic System. (Anatomic Pathology Slide Seminar Ser.). (Illus.). 137p. 1981. pap. text ed. 18.00 (ISBN 0-89189-085-8); slides 85.00 (ISBN 0-686-69528-3). Am Soc Clinical.
Lieberman, Robert. Goobersville Breakdown. (Illus.). 221p. 1979. 10.95 (ISBN 0-686-60866-6); pap. 4.95 (ISBN 0-933124-00-7). Gamma Bks.
Lieberman, S. The Growth of European Mixed Economics 1945-1970: A Concise Study of the Economic Evolution of Six Countries. 347p. 1979. 22.95 (ISBN 0-470-99168-2). Halsted Pr.
Lieberman, Samuel S. An Economic Approach to Differential Demographic Behavior in Turkey. LC 78-75054. (Outstanding Dissertations in Economics Ser.). 1979. lib. bdg. 25.00 (ISBN 0-8240-4132-1). Garland Pub.
Lieberman, Saul. The Tosefta, 13 vols. 125.00 ea. (ISBN 0-685-31430-8, Pub. by Jewish Theol Seminary). KTAV.
Lieberman, Saul & Hyman, Arthur, eds. Salo Wittmayer Baron Jubilee Volume: On the Occasion of His Eightieth Birthday, 3 vols. new ed. LC 74-82633. 1533p. 1975. 90.00x set (ISBN 0-685-51945-7); Vol. 1. (ISBN 0-231-03911-5); Vol. 2. (ISBN 0-231-03912-3); Vol. 3. (ISBN 0-231-03913-1). Columbia U Pr.
Lieberman, Stephen J. The Sumerian Loanwords in Old-Babylonian Akkadian: Prolegomena & Evidence. LC 76-54167. (Illus.). 1977. 15.00 (ISBN 0-89130-122-4, 040422). Scholars Pr Ca.
Lieberman, Stuart. Transgenerational Family Therapy. 240p. 1980. 39.00x (ISBN 0-85664-776-4, Pub. by Croom Helm England). State Mutual Bk.
--Transgenerational Family Therapy. (Illus.). 234p. 1979. 35.00x (ISBN 0-85664-776-4, Pub. by Croom Helm Ltd England). Biblio Dist.
Lieberman, William S. Art of the Twenties. LC 79-62957. (Illus.). 144p. 1979. pap. 8.95 (ISBN 0-87070-216-5). Museum Mod Art.
--Matisse: Fifty Years of His Graphic Art. 12.50 o.s.i. (ISBN 0-8076-0037-7). Braziller.
Liebers, Arthur. Housebreak & Train Your Dog. (Orig.). 1958. pap. 2.00 (ISBN 0-87666-318-8, DS1020). TFH Pubns.
--How to Raise & Train a German Short-Haired Pointer. pap. 2.00 (ISBN 0-87666-301-3, DS1016). TFH Pubns.
--How to Raise & Train a Maltese. pap. 2.00 (ISBN 0-87666-335-8, DS1025). TFH Pubns.
--How to Raise & Train a Mixed or Pedigreed Puppy. pap. 2.00 (ISBN 0-87666-370-6, DS1027). TFH Pubns.
--How to Raise & Train an English Springer Spaniel. pap. 2.00 (ISBN 0-87666-398-6, DS1034). TFH Pubns.
--Jobs in Construction. LC 73-4944. (Exploring Careers Ser.). (Illus.). 96p. (gr. 5 up). 1973. 7.25 o.p. (ISBN 0-688-75004-4). Lothrop.
Liebers, Arthur & Hardy, Dorothy. How to Raise & Train a Basset Hound. pap. 2.00 (ISBN 0-87666-240-8, DS1003). TFH Pubns.
Liebers, Arthur & Jeffries, Paul. How to Raise & Train a Weimaraner. pap. 2.00 (ISBN 0-87666-405-2, DS1035). TFH Pubns.
Liebers, Arthur & Miller, Dana. How to Raise & Train a Yorkshire Terrier. (Illus.). pap. 2.00 (ISBN 0-87666-410-9, DS1037). TFH Pubns.
Liebers, Arthur & Sheppard, Georgie M. How to Raise & Train a Pomeranian. (Illus.). pap. 2.00 (ISBN 0-87666-352-8, DS1029). TFH Pubns.
Lieberson, Stanley. Ethnic Patterns in American Cities. LC 63-7551. 1962. 15.95 (ISBN 0-02-918980-2). Free Pr.
--Language Diversity & Language Contact: Essays by Stanley Lieberson. Dil, Anwar S., ed. (Language Science & National Development Ser.). 416p. 1981. 18.75x (ISBN 0-8047-1098-8). Stanford U Pr.
--A Piece of the Pie: Blacks & White Immigrants Since 1880. 420p. 1981. 19.95 (ISBN 0-520-04123-2). U of Cal Pr.
Liebert, jt. auth. see Johnson, M.
Liebert, Burt & Liebert, Marjorie. A Schoolwide Secondary Reading Program: Here's How. LC 78-10904. 1979. text ed. 18.95x (ISBN 0-471-03549-1). Wiley.
Liebert, Marjorie, jt. auth. see Liebert, Burt.
Liebert, R. M., et al. The Early Window: the Effect of Television on Children & Youth. 1976. 21.00 (ISBN 0-08-017091-9); pap. 8.75 (ISBN 0-08-017780-8). Pergamon.
Liebert, Robert M. & Pelson, Wickes. Developmental Psychology. 3rd ed. (Illus.). 640p. 1981. text ed. 18.95 (ISBN 0-13-208256-X). P-H.
Liebert, Robert M., jt. auth. see Neale, John M.
Liebert, Robert M. & Spiegler, Michael D., eds. Personality: Strategies for the Study of Man. 3rd ed. 1978. text ed. 18.95x (ISBN 0-256-02059-0). Dorsey.
Liebert, Robert M., et al. Developmental Psychology. 2nd ed. (Illus.). 1977. text ed. 18.95 (ISBN 0-13-208231-4). P-H.
Liebert, Roland J. & Imershein, Allen W., eds. Power, Paradigms, & Community Research. LC 76-54539. (Sage Studies in International Sociology: Vol. 9). 1977. 18.00x (ISBN 0-8039-9850-3); pap. 9.95x (ISBN 0-8039-9875-9). Sage.
Lieberthal, E. A., jt. auth. see Gurau, Peter K.
Lieberthal, Edwin M., jt. auth. see Gurau, Peter K.
Lieberthal, Kenneth G. Revolution & Tradition in Tientsin, 1949-1952. LC 79-64215. 1980. 18.50x (ISBN 0-8047-1044-9). Stanford U Pr.
Liebeschuetz, J. H. Antioch: City & Imperial Administration in the Later Roman Empire. 312p. 1972. 29.95x (ISBN 0-19-814295-1). Oxford U Pr.
Liebesny, Herbert J., jt. ed. see Khadduri, Majid.
Liebetrau, Preben. Oriental Rugs in Color. 1963. 8.95 (ISBN 0-02-571840-1). Macmillan.
Liebing, Ralph W. & Paul, Mimi F. Architectural Working Drawings. LC 76-48154. 1977. 22.50 (ISBN 0-471-53432-3, Pub. by Wiley-Interscience). Wiley.
Liebknecht, Karl. Militarism & Anti-Militarism. 1969. 11.00 (ISBN 0-86527-130-5). Fertig.
--Militarism & Antimilitarism: With Special Regard to the International Young Socialist Movement. Lock, Grahame, tr. from Ger. 162p. 1974. text ed. 10.00x (ISBN 0-9502495-7-2); pap. text ed. 4.00x (ISBN 0-9502495-8-0). Humanities.
Liebler, Joan G. Managing Health Records: Administrative Principles. 306p. 1979. text ed. 26.50 (ISBN 0-89443-168-4, 79-22455). Aspen Systems.
Lieblich, Garnet M. Qualified Products List & Sources. 59th ed. Orig. Title: Military Specifications & Sources. 1980. 65.00x o.p. (ISBN 0-912702-01-X). Global Eng.
Lieblich, Gerald S. & Leake, Charles. Pre-Algebra Mathematics. new ed. LC 72-92569. (Illus.). 318p. (gr. 8-10). 1973. text ed. 13.95 (ISBN 0-675-09007-5). Merrill.
Lieblich, Jerome H., ed. Dimension & Tolerances (an Interpretation of ANSI y14.5) 1973. pap. 3.75x (ISBN 0-912702-05-2). Global Eng.
--Drawing Requirement Manual. 4th ed. 624p. 1981. lib. bdg. 21.95x perfect bdg (ISBN 0-912702-02-8). Global Eng.
--Drawing Requirements Manual. 3rd ed. (Illus.). 1979. pap. text ed. 19.95 o.p. (ISBN 0-685-96581-3). Global Eng.
Liebling, A. J. The Press. 1981. pap. 6.95 (ISBN 0-394-74849-2). Pantheon.
Liebling, Herman I. U. S. Corporate Profitability & Capital Formation: Are Rates of Return Sufficient? (Pergamon Policy Studies). 1980. 22.00 (ISBN 0-08-024622-2). Pergamon.
Liebman, Arthur. Jews & the Left. LC 78-20871. (Contemporary Religious Movements Ser.). 1979. 19.50 (ISBN 0-471-53433-1, Pub. by Wiley-Interscience). Wiley.
--Science Fiction: Masters of Today. 140p. 1981. lib. bdg. 7.97 (ISBN 0-8239-0537-3). Rosen Pr.
--Tales of Espionage & Intrigue. (Masterworks of Mystery Ser). 274p. (gr. 7-12). 1976. PLB 7.97 (ISBN 0-8239-0411-3); tchr's manual 1.50 (ISBN 0-685-66609-3). Rosen Pr.
Liebman, Seymour B. Exploring the Latin American Mind. LC 76-6847. 225p. 1976. 14.95 (ISBN 0-88229-134-3). Nelson-Hall.
Liebman, William. Pediatric Gastroenterology Case Studies. 1980. pap. 18.50 (ISBN 0-87488-084-X). Med Exam.
Liebner, Janos. Mozart on the Stage. 1980. pap. 4.95 (ISBN 0-7145-1070-X). Riverrun NY.
Liebow, Averill A., jt. auth. see Bloor, Colin M.
Liebow, Gina, jt. auth. see Ress, Etta S.
Liebowitz, H., ed. Combined Nonlinear & Linear (Micro & Macro) Fracture Mechanics: Applications to Modern Engineering Structures - Selected Papers, U.S.-Japan Seminar. 1976. pap. text ed. 46.00 (ISBN 0-08-019982-8). Pergamon.
Liebowitz, Harold A. A Treatise on Fracture, 7 vols. Incl. Vol. 1. Microscopic & Macroscopic Fundamentals of Fracture. 1969. 62.50 (ISBN 0-12-449701-2); Vol. 2. Mathematical Fundamentals of Fracture. 1969. 75.50 (ISBN 0-12-449702-0); Vol. 3. Engineering Fundamentals & Environmental Effects. 1971. 75.50 (ISBN 0-12-449703-9); Vol. 4. 1969. 51.25 (ISBN 0-12-449704-7); Vol. 5. 1969. 58.50 (ISBN 0-12-449705-5); Vol. 6. 1969. 58.50 (ISBN 0-12-449706-3); Vol. 7. 1972. 97.50 (ISBN 0-12-449707-1). Set. 387.75 (ISBN 0-685-23225-5). Acad Pr.
Liebowitz, M., jt. auth. see Johnston, P. M.
Liebson, Philip R., jt. ed. see Shakibi, Jami G.
Liechty, Richard D. & Soper, Robert T. Synopsis of Surgery. 4th ed. LC 80-12884. (Illus.). 1980. pap. text ed. 24.50 (ISBN 0-8016-3012-6). Mosby.
Liederman, Judith. The Moneyman. 1980. pap. 2.75 (ISBN 0-451-09164-7, E9164, Sig). NAL.
Liederman, Susan V., jt. auth. see Leiderman, David.
Liedloff, Helmut, jt. auth. see Moeller, Jack.
Lief, Alfred, compiled by see Holmes, Oliver W., Jr.
Liefrink, Frans. Semantico-Syntax. (Linguistics Library Ser). 192p. 1974. text ed. 15.95x (ISBN 0-582-55035-1). Longman.
Lieh, David A. Controlling the World with Your TRS-80. Gunzel, David, ed. (Compusoft Learning Ser.). (Illus.). 300p. (gr. 7 up). 1981. pap. 19.95 (ISBN 0-932760-03-1). CompuSoft.
Liehm, Antonin, jt. auth. see Liehm, Mira.
Liehm, Mira & Liehm, Antonin. The Most Important Art: East European Film After 1945. 1977. 24.95 (ISBN 0-520-03157-1); pap. 10.95 (ISBN 0-520-04128-3, CAL 474). U of Cal Pr.
Liem Thanh Nguyen, jt. auth. see Henkin, Alan B.
Lien, Arnold J. & Lien, Harriet S. Measurement & Evaluation of Learning. 4th ed. 1980. text ed. 13.95x (ISBN 0-697-06128-0) (ISBN 0-697-06124-8). instructor's manual available. Wm C Brown.
Lien, David A. The BASIC Handbook: An Encyclopedia of the BASIC Computer Language. 2nd ed. Gunzel, Dave, ed. LC 78-64886. (CompuSoft Learning Ser.). 1981. pap. 19.95 (ISBN 0-932760-00-7). CompuSoft.
--Learning Disc Basis & DOS. Gunzel, David, ed. (CompuSoft Learning Ser.). (Illus.). 300p. 1980. pap. 19.95 (ISBN 0-932760-02-3). CompuSoft.
--Learning Disk Basic & Dos. Gunzel, David, ed. (CompuSoft Learning Ser.). (Illus.). 400p. (gr. 7 up). 1981. pap. 19.95 (ISBN 0-932760-02-3). CompuSoft.
--Learning Level II. 2nd ed. Gunzel, David, ed. LC 79-91309. (CompuSoft Learning Ser.). (Illus.). 360p. 1980. pap. 15.95 (ISBN 0-932760-01-5). CompuSoft.
Lien, Harriet S., jt. auth. see Lien, Arnold J.
Liener, Irvin E. Toxic Constitutuents of Plant Foodstuffs. 2nd ed. LC 79-51681. (Food Science & Technology Ser.). 1980. 39.50 (ISBN 0-12-449960-0). Acad Pr.
Lienhard, John. A Heat Transfer Textbook. (Illus.). 480p. 1981. text ed. 24.95 (ISBN 0-13-385112-5). P-H.
Lienhard, John H., jt. auth. see Tien, Chang-Lim.
Lienhardt, Godfrey. Divinity & Experience: The Religion of the Dinka. 1961. 37.50x (ISBN 0-19-823119-9). Oxford U Pr.
Lienhardt, R. G., jt. ed. see Beattie, J. H.
Lientz, Bennet P. & Swanson, E. Burton. Software Maintenance Management. LC 80-12154. 160p. 1980. pap. text ed. 8.95 (ISBN 0-201-04205-3). A-W.
Lier, Bruno, et al. Bruno Lier: Ad Topica Carminum Amatorium Symbolae, Repr. Of 1914 Ed. Commager, Steele, ed. Bd. with Keith Preston: Studies in the Diction of the Sermo Amatorius in Roman Comedy. Repr. of 1916 ed; Alfons Spies: Militat Omnis Amons. Repr. of 1930 ed. LC 77-70837. (Latin Poetry Ser.). 1979. lib. bdg. 25.00 (ISBN 0-8240-2973-9). Garland Pub.
Lier, Hal & Peterson, Howard, eds. I Hope I Get a Purple Ribbon. LC 80-50645. (Illus.). 110p. 1980. pap. text ed. 7.95 (ISBN 0-9604162-0-X). US Ski.
Liers, Emil E. A Groundhog's Story. LC 76-25629. (Crown Ser.). (primer). 1976. pap. 4.50 (ISBN 0-8127-0130-5). Southern Pub.
Lierse, W. & Beck, F., eds. Normal & Impaired Differentiation Processes in the Nervous System. (Bibliotheca Anatomica Ser.: No. 19). (Illus.). 1980. soft cover 112.00 (ISBN 3-8055-1039-X). S Karger.
--Studies of Normal & Abnormal Devlopment, of the Nervous System. (Bibliotheca Anatomica Ser.: No. 19). (Illus.). viii, 328p. 1980. softcover 112.00 (ISBN 3-8055-1039-X). S Karger.
Lieser, Marie Y. & Hargreaves, Marjorie K. Lent...Easter...Pentecost. (gr. k-4). 1978. with duplicating masters 9.95 (ISBN 0-686-13701-9). Pflaum Pr.
Lieshout, Cornelis F. & Ingram, David J., eds. Stimulation of Social Development in School. 234p. 1977. pap. text ed. 25.25 (ISBN 90-265-0258-3, Pub. by Swets Pub Serv Holland). Swets North Am.
Lieu, Bing H. Digital Computer Programming: Principles, Techniques, & Applications. (Illus., Orig.). 1974. pap. text ed. 4.00 (ISBN 0-486-22948-3). Dover.
Lieuwen, Edwin. Mexican Militarism: The Political Rise & Fall of the Revolutionary Army, 1910-1940. LC 80-28937. (Illus.). xiii, 194p. 1981. Repr. of 1968 ed. lib. bdg. 23.50x (ISBN 0-313-22911-2, LIMM). Greenwood.
Lievano, Francisco, tr. see Johnson, James L.

Lievsay, John L. The Seventeenth Century Resolve: A Historical Anthology of a Literary Form. LC 79-4004. 224p. 1980. 15.50x (ISBN 0-8131-1393-8). U Pr of Ky.

Liew, Kit S. Struggle for Democracy: Sung Chiao-Jen & the 1911 Revolution. LC 74-123623. 1971. 20.00x (ISBN 0-520-01760-9). U of Cal Pr.

Lifchez, Aaron S., jt. auth. see Fenton, Judith A.

Life Editors, ed. Guide to Science & Index to Life Science Library. LC 67-29962. (Life Science Library). (Illus.). (gr. 5 up). 1967. PLB 8.97 o.p. (ISBN 0-8094-0936-4, Pub. by Time-Life). Silver.

Life, Nancy. Move Over, Mountain. LC 74-31682. 144p. (Orig.). 1975. pap. 2.45 (ISBN 0-87123-375-4, 210375). Bethany Fell.

Life Office Management Association, ed. Readings for the Group Insurance Specialty. (FLMI Insurance Education Program Ser.). (Orig.). 1980. pap. 3.75 (ISBN 0-915322-40-4). Loma.

--Readings for the Information Systems Specialty. (FLMI Insurance Education Program Ser.). (Illus.). 186p. (Orig.). 1980. pap. text ed. 10.00x (ISBN 0-915322-39-0). Loma.

--Readings for the Personnel Administration Specialty. (FLMI Insurance Education Program Ser.). 95p. (Orig.). 1980. pap. 6.00x (ISBN 0-915322-41-2). Loma.

--Readings in Management Principles. (FLMI Insurance Education Program Ser.). 68p. (Orig.). 1980. pap. text ed. 5.00x (ISBN 0-915322-37-4). Loma.

--Student Guide to Accounting for Life Insurance Companies. (FLMI Insurance Education Program Ser.). 97p. (Orig.). 1980. wkbk. 4.00x (ISBN 0-915322-42-0). Loma.

Life, Page W. Sir Thomas Malory & the Morte Darthur: A Survey of Scholarship & Annotated Bibliography. LC 80-16180. 1980. 13.50x (ISBN 0-8139-0868-X). U Pr of Va.

Liffick, Blaise W. Bits & Pieces. (Orig.). 1980. pap. 8.95 (ISBN 0-07-037828-2, BYTE Bks). McGraw.

Liffick, Blaise W., ed. The Byte Book of Pascal. 1980. 25.00 (ISBN 0-07-037823-1, BYTE Bks). McGraw.

Lifland, William T., jt. auth. see Van Cise, Jerrold G.

Lifschitz, Danielle. France. LC 75-44867. (Macdonald Countries). (Illus.). (gr. 7 up). 1976. PLB 7.95 (ISBN 0-382-06099-7, Pub. by Macdonald Ed). Silver.

Lifshin, Lyn. Paper Apples. 32p. 1975. pap. 2.00 (ISBN 0-935390-00-6). Wormwood Rev.

Lifshin, Lyn, ed. Tangled Vines: A Collection of Mother & Daughter Poems. LC 77-88340. 1978. 9.95 (ISBN 0-8070-6366-5); pap. 4.95 (ISBN 0-8070-6367-3, BP574). Beacon Pr.

Lifshitz. Clinical Disorders in Pediatric Gastroenterology & Nutrition. 488p. 1980. 44.50 (ISBN 0-8247-6954-6). Dekker.

Lifshitz, A. Test Your Chess IQ, 2 bks. Neat, K. P., ed. Incl. Bk. 1. 128p. 15.70 (ISBN 0-08-023120-9); pap. 8.90 (ISBN 0-08-024118-2); Bk. 2. 224p. 20.00 (ISBN 0-08-026881-1); pap. 13.40 (ISBN 0-08-026880-3). LC 80-41072. (Pergamon Russian Chess Ser.). (Illus.). 1981. Pergamon.

Lifshitz, E. M., jt. auth. see Landau, L. D.

Lifshitz, Samuel & Buchsbaum, Herbert. Gynecologic Oncology Case Studies. 1978. spiral bdg. 14.75 (ISBN 0-87488-005-X). Med Exam.

Lifton, Betty J. I'm Still Me. LC 80-24372. 224p. (YA) 1981. 8.95 (ISBN 0-394-84783-0); PLB 8.99 (ISBN 0-394-94783-5). Knopf.

Lifton, David S. Best Evidence: Deception & Disguise in the Assassination of John F. Kennedy. 1981. 16.95 (ISBN 0-02-571870-3). Macmillan.

Lifton, Robert. The Broken Connection. 1980. pap. 7.95 (ISBN 0-671-41386-4, Touchstone). S&S.

Ligare, Kathleen M. Illinois Women's Directory: A Comprehensive Guide to Women's Organizations & Programs Throughout Illinois and Northwestern Indiana. LC 78-66125. (Illus.). 168p. 1978. pap. 5.95 (ISBN 0-8040-0802-7). Swallow.

Ligeti, Louis, ed. Mongolian Studies: Dedicated to the Second International Congress of Mongolists, to Its Organizers, the Mongolian Scholars, Budapest, 1970. (Bibliotheca Orientalis Hungrica). 1970. text ed. 48.50x (ISBN 90-6032-352-1). Humanities.

Liggett, John V. Fundamentals of Position Tolerance. (Manufacturing Data Ser.). (Illus.). 1970. pap. 11.75 (ISBN 0-87263-020-X). SME.

Light, Donald, Jr. & Spiegel, John D., eds. Dynamics of University Protest. LC 77-2364. 1977. 14.95 (ISBN 0-88229-164-5). Nelson-Hall.

Light, Ivan H. Ethnic Enterprise in America: Business & Welfare Among Chinese, Japanese, & Blacks. 1972. 15.75x (ISBN 0-520-01738-2); pap. 5.75x (ISBN 0-520-02485-0). U of Cal Pr.

Light, J. O. & White, William L. The Financial System. 1979. 19.95x (ISBN 0-256-02120-1). Irwin.

Light, Mary. God's Guidance at Dawn. pap. 1.00 o.p. (ISBN 0-910924-68-6). Macalester.

Light, P. The Development of Social Sensitivity. LC 78-12415. (Illus.). 1979. 17.95 (ISBN 0-521-22372-5). Cambridge U Pr.

Light, Patricia K. Let the Children Speak. LC 74-313. 1975. 14.95 (ISBN 0-669-92676-0). Lexington Bks.

Lightbody, Nancy K. & Malley, Sarah H. Observa-Story: Portland to Cut & Color. LC 76-54460. (Illus.). (gr. 1-4). 1976. pap. 1.25 (ISBN 0-9600612-5-8). Greater Portland.

Lightbown, R. W., jt. auth. see Corbett, Margery.

Lightbown, Ronald, tr. see Piccolpasso, Cipriano.

Lightfoot, D. W. Principles of Diachronic Syntax. LC 78-54717. (Cambridge Studies in Linguistics Monograph: No. 23). (Illus.). 1979. 69.50 (ISBN 0-521-22082-3); pap. 17.50x (ISBN 0-521-29350-2). Cambridge U Pr.

Lightfoot, E. N. Transport Phenomena & Living Systems: Biomedical Applications of Momentum & Mass Transfer. LC 73-9541. 495p. 1974. 36.50 (ISBN 0-471-53515-X, Pub. by Wiley-Interscience). Wiley.

Lightfoot, Frederick, jt. auth. see Johnson, Harry.

Lightfoot, J. B. Apostolic Fathers. (Twin Brooks Ser). pap. 5.95 (ISBN 0-8010-5514-8). Baker Bk.

--Notes on the Epistles of St. Paul. Date not set. 12.95 (ISBN 0-88469-137-3). BMH Bks.

Lightfoot, J. B., ed. Commentary on St. Paul's Epistle to the Colossians & Philemon. 1957. 11.95 (ISBN 0-310-27630-6). Zondervan.

--Commentary on St. Paul's Epistle to the Philippians. 1957. 14.95 (ISBN 0-310-27650-0). Zondervan.

Lightfoot, Keith. Philippines. (Nations of the Modern World). 1977. lib. bdg. 19.75x (ISBN 0-89158-735-7). Westview.

Lightfoot, Neil R. Lessons from the Parables. (Minister's Paperback Library). 184p. 1976. pap. 3.95 (ISBN 0-8010-5564-4). Baker Bk.

Lightfoot, Sara L. Worlds Apart: Relationships Between Families & Schools. LC 78-54506. 257p. 1981. pap. 5.95 (ISBN 0-465-09243-8). Basic.

Lighthill, J. Waves in Fluids. LC 77-8174. (Illus.). 1978. 56.50 (ISBN 0-521-21689-3); pap. 22.95x (ISBN 0-521-29233-6). Cambridge U Pr.

Lighthill, J. & Pearce, R. P., eds. Monsoon Dynamics. LC 78-72091. (Illus.). 700p. Date not set. 130.00 (ISBN 0-521-22497-7). Cambridge U Pr.

Lightner, Kevin M., jt. auth. see Buckley, John W.

Lightner, Robert. Triumph Through Tragedy. 70p. (Orig.). (gr. 7 up). 1980. pap. 2.00 (ISBN 0-89323-008-1). BMA Pr.

Lighton, Merle. Addict to Yearning: Inspirational Philosophy & Religion. 1952. 5.00 (ISBN 0-910892-00-8, 910892). Lighton Pubns.

Lightwood, Martha B., ed. Public & Business Planning in the United States: A Bibliography. LC 79-165488. (Management Information Guide Ser.: No. 26). 1972. 30.00 (ISBN 0-8103-0826-6). Gale.

Ligon, Linda, ed. see Strickler, Carol & Taggart, Barbara.

Ligon, Mary G. & McDaniel, Sarah W. Teachers Role in Counseling. (Foundations of Secondary Education Ser). 1970. pap. 9.95x ref. ed. (ISBN 0-13-891119-3). P-H.

Ligtelijn, V., jt. auth. see Saariste, R.

Liguori, St. Alphonsus. How to Face Death Without Fear. 1976. pap. 1.50 (ISBN 0-89243-029-X, 28376). Liguori Pubns.

--Love Is Prayer - Prayer Is Love. LC 72-97592. 1973. pap. 2.50 (ISBN 0-89243-047-8, 41500). Liguori Pubns.

Liguori, F., ed. Automatic Test Equipment: Hardware, Software, & Management. LC 74-18892. (IEEE Press Selected Reprint Ser). 253p. 1974. 17.95 (ISBN 0-471-53536-2, Pub. by Wiley-Interscience); pap. 8.95x o.p. (ISBN 0-471-53537-0). Wiley.

Lihani, John. Bartolome De Torres Naharro. (World Authors Ser.: No. 522). 1979. lib. bdg. 14.50 (ISBN 0-8057-6363-5). Twayne.

--Lucas Fernandez. (World Authors Ser.: Spain: No. 251). 1971. lib. bdg. 10.95 (ISBN 0-8057-2290-4). Twayne.

Liholiho, Alexander. Journal of Prince Alexander Liholiho: Voyages Made to the United States, England, & France in 1849-50. Adler, Jacob, ed. LC 67-27052. (Personal Diary, Photos, Index, Notes, 188p). 1967. 10.00 (ISBN 0-87022-009-8). U Pr of Hawaii.

Li Hui-Lin. The Origin & Cultivation of Shade & Ornamental Trees. LC 62-11271. (Illus.). 288p. 1974. pap. 5.95 (ISBN 0-8122-1070-0, Pa Paperbks). U of Pa Pr.

Trees of Pennsylvania, the Atlantic States, & the Lake States. LC 72-80377. (Illus.). 1972. 17.50 (ISBN 0-8122-7665-5); pap. 9.95 (ISBN 0-8122-1064-6, Pa Paperbks). U of Pa Pr.

Li Hui-Lin, tr. see Chi Han.

Lijnen, H. R., et al, eds. Synthetic Substrates in Clinical Blood Coagulation Assays. (Developments in Hematology Ser.: No. 1). 142p. 1981. PLB 23.50 (ISBN 90-247-2409-0, Pub. Bymartinus Nijhoff). Kluwer Boston.

Lijphart, Arend. The Politics of Accommodation: Pluralism & Democracy in the Netherlands. new ed. 1976. 20.00x (ISBN 0-520-02918-6); pap. 6.95x (ISBN 0-520-02900-3). U of Cal Pr.

Likes, Robert C. & Day, Glenn R. From This Mountain-Cerro Gordo. LC 75-44236. (Illus.). 86p. 1975. 7.95 (ISBN 0-912494-16-6); pap. 3.95 (ISBN 0-912494-15-8). Chalfant Pr.

Likins, Peter. Elements of Engineering Mechanics. (Illus.). 550p. 1973. text ed. 24.50 o.p. (ISBN 0-07-037852-5, C); solutions manual 4.50 o.p. (ISBN 0-07-037853-3). McGraw.

Likoff, William, et al. Your Heart: Complete Information for the Family. (Illus.). 1972. 6.95 o.s.i. (ISBN 0-397-00789-2). Lippincott.

--Management of the Cardiac Patient with Renal Failure. 1981. 25.00 (ISBN 0-8036-5643-2). Davis Co.

Likoudis, James & Whitehead, K. D. The Pope, the Council, & the Mass. 1981. 14.95 (ISBN 0-8158-0400-8). Chris Mass.

Liles, B. Basic Grammar of Modern English. 1979. 14.95 (ISBN 0-13-061853-5). P-H.

Liles, Bruce L. An Introduction to Linguistics. 368p. 1975. ref. ed. 14.50 (ISBN 0-13-486134-5); pap. text ed. 9.95 (ISBN 0-13-486126-4). P-H.

--Introductory Transformational Grammar. LC 70-122388. (Illus.). 1971. pap. text ed. 8.95x (ISBN 0-13-502286-X). P-H.

Liles, Patrick R. New Business Ventures & the Entrepreneur. 1974. text ed. 18.50x (ISBN 0-256-01560-0). Irwin.

Liley, H. M., jt. auth. see Day, Beth.

Lilge, Frederic, tr. see Bernfeld, Siegfried.

Lilienfeld, Abraham M. Foundations of Epidemiology. 275p. 1976. text ed. 12.95x o.p. (ISBN 0-19-502072-3); pap. text ed. 9.95x o.p. (ISBN 0-19-502071-5). Oxford U Pr.

Lilienfeld, Robert. Learning to Read Music. (Funk & W Bk.). 128p. 1976. pap. 4.95 o.s.i. (ISBN 0-308-10249-5, TYC-T). T Y Crowell.

--The Rise of Systems Theory: An Ideological Analysis. LC 77-12609. 1978. 26.95 (ISBN 0-471-53533-8, Pub. by Wiley-Inerscience). Wiley.

Lilienthal, Alfred M. The Zionist Connection: What Price Peace? LC 78-10556. 1978. 19.95 (ISBN 0-396-07564-9). Dodd.

Lilienthal, David E. The Journals of David E. Lilienthal, 6 vols. Incl. Vol. 1. The TVA Years, 1939-45. 1964 (ISBN 0-06-012610-8); Vol. 2. The Atomic Energy Years, 1945-50. 1964. o.p. (ISBN 0-06-012611-6); Vol. 3. Venturesome Years, 1950-55. 1966 (ISBN 0-06-012612-4); Vol. 4. The Road to Change, 1955-59. 1969 (ISBN 0-06-012613-2); Vol. 5. The Harvest Years, 1959-63. 1971 (ISBN 0-06-012614-0); Vol. 6. Creativity & Conflict, 1964-1967. 1976. o.p. (ISBN 0-06-012619-1). LC 64-18056. (Illus.). 20.00 ea. o.s.i. (HarpT). Har-Row.

--Management: A Humanist Art. LC 67-20667. (B. F. Fairless Memorial Lectures). 1967. 9.00x (ISBN 0-231-03064-9). Columbia U Pr.

Lilius, Irmelin S. Gold Crown Lane. Helweg, Marianne, tr. from Swedish. LC 79-2103. (gr. 5 up). 1980. 7.95 (ISBN 0-440-04231-3, Sey Lawr); PLB 7.45 (ISBN 0-440-04232-1). Delacorte.

--The Goldmaker's House. Helweg, Marianne, tr. from Swedish. LC 79-2104. (gr. 5 up). 1980. 7.95 (ISBN 0-440-04200-3, Sey Lawr); PLB 7.45 (ISBN 0-440-04201-1). Delacorte.

--Horses of the Night. Tate, Joan, tr. from Swedish. LC 79-2105. (gr. 5 up). 1980. 7.95 (ISBN 0-440-04450-2, Sey Lawr); PLB 7.45 (ISBN 0-440-04451-0). Delacorte.

Lilja, Saara. The Roman Elegists' Attitude Towards Women. Commager, Steele, ed. LC 77-70836. (Latin Poetry Ser.: Vol. 25). 1979. Repr. of 1965 ed. lib. bdg. 31.00 (ISBN 0-8240-2974-7). Garland Pub.

Liljedahl, J. B., et al. Tractors & Their Power Units. 3rd ed. LC 79-10180. 1979. text ed. 25.95 (ISBN 0-471-01905-4). Wiley.

Lill, A. Lek Behavior in the Golden-Headed Manakin, Pipra erythrocephala in Trinidad (West Indies) (Advances in Ethology Ser.: Vol. 18). (Illus.). 84p. (Orig.). 1976. pap. text ed. 34.00 (ISBN 3-489-72536-0). Parey Sci Pubs.

Lillard, Richard G. The Great Forest. LC 72-8129. (Illus.). 452p. 1973. Repr. of 1947 ed. lib. bdg. 39.50 (ISBN 0-306-70534-6). Da Capo.

Lillard, Richard G., jt. auth. see Coan, Otis W.

Lillegraven, Jason A., et al, eds. Mesozoic Mammals: The First Two-Thirds of Mammalian History. 1980. 37.50x (ISBN 0-520-03582-8); pap. 10.75x (ISBN 0-520-03951-3, CAMPUS NO. 234). U of Cal Pr.

Lillesand, Thomas M. & Kiefer, Ralph W. Remote Sensing & Image Interpretation. LC 78-27846. 1979. text ed. 27.95 (ISBN 0-471-02609-3). Wiley.

Lillesand, Thomas M., intro. by. Thermosense I: Proceedings. 244p. 1978. pap. 15.00 (ISBN 0-686-27662-0). ASP.

Lilley. Information Sources in Agriculture & Food Science. (Butterworths Guides to Information Sources Ser.). 1981. text ed. price not set (ISBN 0-408-10612-3). Butterworth.

Lilley, A. E. & Midgley, W. A Book of Studies in Plant Form: With Some Suggestions for Their Application to Design. LC 70-89276. (Tower Bks). (Illus.). xvi, 131p. 1972. Repr. of 1896 ed. 15.00 (ISBN 0-8103-3947-1). Gale.

Lilley, David G., jt. auth. see Croft, David R.

Lilley, Irene M., ed. see Froebel, Fred.

Lilley, S. Discovering Relativity for Yourself. LC 80-40263. (Illus.). 425p. Date not set. 49.50; pap. 19.95 (ISBN 0-521-29780-X). Cambridge U Pr.

Lilley, T. Problems of Accelerating Aircraft Production During World War II. (Harvard Graduate School of Business Administration: Studies in Aviation Research). 1970. Repr. of 1957 ed. 16.00 (ISBN 0-08-018743-9). Pergamon.

Lillibridge, G. D. Images of American Society: A History of the United States, 2 vols. LC 75-31017. (Illus.). 736p. 1976. pap. text ed. 10.75 ea.; Vol. 1. pap. text ed. (ISBN 0-395-21873-X); Vol. 2. pap. text ed. (ISBN 0-395-21874-8); inst. manual 2.25 (ISBN 0-395-20371-6). HM.

Lillich, Meredith, et al, eds. Studies in Cistercian Art & Architecture I. (Cistercian Studies: No. 66). (Illus., Orig.). 1981. pap. price not set (ISBN 0-87907-866-9). Cistercian Pubns.

Lillich, Richard B., ed. U. S. Ratification of the Human Rights Treaties: With or Without Reservations? (Procedural Aspects of International Law Ser.). 1980. write for info. (ISBN 0-8139-0881-7). U Pr of Va.

Lillico, Michael. Managerial Communication. LC 77-188641. 168p. 1972. text ed. 18.00 (ISBN 0-08-016633-4). Pergamon.

Lillicrap, D. H. Food & Beverage Service. (Illus.). 218p. 1971. pap. 13.95x (ISBN 0-7131-1664-1). Intl Ideas.

Lillie, John. Lectures on the First & Second Epistles of Peter. 1978. 18.25 (ISBN 0-686-12954-7). Klock & Klock.

Lillie, Sally L. Judging the Dreamer. 52p. 1980. pap. 4.50x (ISBN 0-938564-00-5). P a Abbott.

Lillis, B. Lauren. Instant Speaking Course. 1981. pap. 1.50 (ISBN 0-8134-2176-4). Interstate.

Lilliston, Lynn. Megavitamins: A New Key to Health. 224p. 1976. pap. 1.50 o.p. (ISBN 0-449-13736-8, GM). Fawcett.

Lillo, George. Fatal Curiosity. McBurney, William H., ed. LC 66-15130. (Regents Restoration Drama Ser). 1967. 5.95x (ISBN 0-8032-0364-0); pap. 1.65x (ISBN 0-8032-5364-8, BB 258, Bison). U of Nebr Pr.

--London Merchant. McBurney, William, ed. LC 65-11521. (Regents Restoration Drama Ser). 1965. 7.50x (ISBN 0-8032-0365-9); pap. 2.50x (ISBN 0-8032-5365-6, BB 252, Bison). U of Nebr Pr.

Lilly, Gene. God Is Calling His People to Forgiveness. 1977. pap. 2.25 (ISBN 0-917726-15-4). Hunter Bks.

Lilly, John C. The Scientist: A Novel Autobiography. LC 78-3545. (Illus.). 1978. 10.00 o.p. (ISBN 0-397-01274-8). Lippincott.

Lilly, John C., M.D. Lilly on Dolphins-Humans of the Sea. LC 75-2854. 520p. 1975. pap. 4.50 (ISBN 0-385-11037-5, Anch). Doubleday.

Lilly, John R., et al. Pediatric Surgery Case Studies. 1978. spiral bdg. 19.50 (ISBN 0-87488-069-6). Med Exam.

Lilly, William. An Introduction to Astrology. LC 80-19691. 346p. 1980. Repr. of 1972 ed. lib. bdg. 11.95x (ISBN 0-89370-614-0). Borgo Pr.

Lillyquist, Michael J. Understanding & Changing Criminal Behavior. (Ser. in Criminal Justice). 1980. text ed. 17.95 (ISBN 0-13-935528-6). P-H.

Lillywhite, Bryant. London Signs: A Reference Book of London Signs from Earliest Times to About Mid-Nineteenth Century. 1972. 25.00 o.p. (ISBN 0-04-942101-8). Allen Unwin.

Lillywhite, Gordon, jt. auth. see Weiss, Curtis E.

Lillywhite, Harold S., jt. auth. see Weiss, Curtis E.

Lim, jt. auth. see Grady.

Lim, Arthur & Constable, Ian J. Colour Atlas of Ophthalmology. (Illus.). 1979. 14.00x (ISBN 0-89289-409-1). HM Prof Med Div.

Lim, Arthur S., ed. Ocular Microsurgery. (Developments in Opthamology Ser.: Vol. 1). (Illus.). 130p. 1981. 36.00 (ISBN 3-8055-1106-X). S Karger.

Lim, Edward C., ed. Excited States, Vols. 1 & 2. Vol. 1, 1974. 46.00 (ISBN 0-12-227201-3); Vol. 2, 1975. 52.50 (ISBN 0-12-227202-1); Vol. 3, 1978. 40.00 (ISBN 0-12-227203-X). Acad Pr.

Lim, Paulino, Jr. The Style of Lord Byron's Plays. (Salzburg Studies in English Literature, Poetic Drama & Poetic Theory: No. 3). 177p. 1973. pap. text ed. 25.00x (ISBN 0-391-01461-7). Humanities.

Lim, R. K., ed. Pharmacology of Pain: Proceedings - Vol. 9. 1968. 27.25 o.p. (ISBN 0-08-012374-0). Pergamon.

Lim, Thomas P. Respiratory System Basic Sciences. 1972. spiral bdg. 7.00 o.p. (ISBN 0-87488-213-3). Med Exam.

Lima, Robert F., ed. Arco Motor Vehicle Dictionary: English & Spanish. LC 76-77605. 368p. 1980. pap. 7.95 (ISBN 0-668-04982-0, 4982-0). Arco.

Liman, Ellen. Money Saver's Guide to Decorating. LC 74-109451. 1971. 7.95 o.s.i. (ISBN 0-02-572300-6). Macmillan.

--The Money Saver's Guide to Decorating. (Illus.). 296p. 1972. pap. 1.95 o.s.i. (ISBN 0-02-080530-6, Collier). Macmillan.

Liman, Ellen & Panter, Carol. Decorating Your Room: A Do-It-Yourself Guide. LC 73-9999. (Illus.). 128p. (gr. 5 up). 1974. 9.90 o.p. (ISBN 0-531-02651-5). Watts.

Limardo, Miguel. Luces Encendidas Para Cada Dia. 1978. 2.95 (ISBN 0-311-40038-8). Casa Bautista.

Limaye, B. V. Functional Analysis. LC 80-84533. 400p. 1981. 17.95 (ISBN 0-470-26933-2). Halsted Pr.

Limbacher, James L. Film Music: From Violins to Video. LC 73-16153. 1974. 25.00 (ISBN 0-8108-0651-7). Scarecrow.

--Keeping Score: Film Music 1972-1979. LC 80-26474. 519p. 1981. 22.50 (ISBN 0-8108-1390-4). Scarecrow.

Limbacher, Walter J. Here I Am. 2nd ed. (Dimensions of Personality Ser). (gr. 4). text ed. 4.75x o.p. (ISBN 0-686-66516-3); pap. text ed. 3.95x (ISBN 0-88320-637-4); tchrs' ed. pap. 5.95x (ISBN 0-88320-639-0); spirit masters 12.95x (ISBN 0-88320-640-4, 10198). Pflaum-Standard.

Limbrey, Susan & Evans, J. G., eds. The Effect of Man on the Landscape: The Lowland Zone. 160p. 1980. pap. 29.95x (ISBN 0-900312-60-2, Pub. by Council Brit Arch England). Intl Schol Bk Serv.

Limburg, James. The Prophets & the Powerless. LC 76-12397. 1976. pap. 3.95 (ISBN 0-8042-0156-0). John Knox.

Limburg, Peter R. Chickens, Chickens, Chickens. LC 75-16378. (Illus.). 160p. (gr. 5 up). 1975. 7.95 (ISBN 0-525-66463-7). Elsevier-Nelson.

--Deceived: The Story of the Donner Party. (Illus.). 256p. (gr. 7 up). Date not set. PLB 7.95 (ISBN 0-396-07942-3). Dodd. Postponed.

--Engines. LC 74-77243. (First Bks). (gr. 4-6). 1969. PLB 4.90 o.p. (ISBN 0-531-00705-7). Watts.

--Farming the Waters. LC 80-23362. (Illus.). 256p. 1981. 10.95 (ISBN 0-8253-0009-6). Beaufort Bks NY.

Limentani, Uberto. Mind of Dante. 1966. 37.50 (ISBN 0-521-05560-1). Cambridge U Pr.

Liming, Roy A. Mathematics for Computer Graphics. LC 79-65814. 1979. 35.00 (ISBN 0-8168-6751-8). Aero.

Limmer, Ruth. Journey Around My Room: The Autobiography of Louise Bogan. LC 79-56279. (Illus.). 224p. 1980. 13.95 (ISBN 0-670-40942-1). Viking Pr.

Limos, Antonio A. Briquet De see Briquet de Limos, Antonio A.

Lin, Adet, tr. see Hsieh Pingying.

Lin, Anor, tr. see Hsieh Pingying.

Lin, Florence. Florence Lin's Chinese One-Dish Meals: The Fastest Way of Cooking Delicious, Economical, Well Balanced Meals. 192p. 1981. pap. 5.95 (ISBN 0-8015-2672-8, Hawthorn). Dutton.

--Florence Lin's Chinese Regional Cookbook. 288p. 1975. 15.95 (ISBN 0-8015-2674-4, Hawthorn); text ed. 8.95 (ISBN 0-8015-2673-6, Hawthorn). Dutton.

--Florence Lin's Chinese Vegetarian Cookbook. LC 75-28686. 1977. pap. 4.95 (ISBN 0-8015-2677-9, Hawthorn). Dutton.

Lin, Hazel. Weeping May Tarry: My Long Night with Cancer. LC 79-55554. 1980. 9.95 (ISBN 0-8283-1738-0). Branden.

Lin, James C. Microwave Auditory Effects & Applications. (Illus.). 232p. 1978. 29.75 (ISBN 0-398-03704-3). C C Thomas.

Lin, Jan. Living Out God's Love. 128p. 1981. pap. 4.95 (ISBN 0-8170-0897-7). Judson.

Lin, Julia C. Modern Chinese Poetry: An Introduction. LC 70-152330. (Washington Paperback Ser: No. 66). 278p. 1972. 11.50 (ISBN 0-295-95145-1); pap. 2.95 (ISBN 0-295-95281-4). U of Wash Pr.

Lin, Nan. The Study of Human Communication. LC 72-77128. 1973. 7.65 o.p. (ISBN 0-672-61340-9); pap. 6.50 (ISBN 0-672-61206-2). Bobbs.

Lin, P., jt. auth. see Chua, L.

Lin, Shu. Introduction to Error-Correcting Codes. LC 76-124417. 1970. ref. ed. 24.95 (ISBN 0-13-482810-0). P-H.

Lin, T. Y. & Burns, Ned H. Design of Prestressed Concrete Structures. 3rd ed. 752p. 1981. text ed. 28.95 (ISBN 0-471-01898-8); tchrs.' ed. avail. (ISBN 0-471-08788-2). Wiley.

Lin Yu-Sheng. The Crisis of Chinese Consciousness: Radical Antitraditionalism in the May Fourth Era. LC 77-91057. 1978. 20.00 (ISBN 0-299-07410-2). U of Wis Pr.

Lin, Yu-T'Ang. The Little Critic: Essays, Satires & Sketches on China. (First Series: 1930-1932) LC 79-2831. 299p. 1981. Repr. of 1936 ed. 22.50 (ISBN 0-8305-0009-X). Hyperion Conn.

--The Little Critic: Essays, Satires & Sketches on China (Second Series: 1933-1935. LC 79-2832. 258p. 1981. Repr. of 1939 ed. 19.50 (ISBN 0-8305-0010-3). Hyperion Conn.

Lin, Yu-T'Ang, jt. auth. see Hu, Shih.

Lin Adet. Dawn Over Chungking. LC 74-31239. (China in the 20th Century Ser). 240p. 1975. Repr. of 1941 ed. lib. bdg. 22.50 (ISBN 0-306-70692-X). Da Capo.

Linaker, Michael R. Scorpion. 1981. pap. 1.95 (ISBN 0-451-09606-1, J9606, Sig). NAL.

Linakis, Steven. Diva: The Life & Death of Maria Callas. LC 80-18919. 1980. 10.95 (ISBN 0-13-216572-4). P-H.

Linam, Gail. God's Winter Gifts. 1980. pap. 2.95 (ISBN 0-8054-4158-1). Broadman.

Linares, Olga F. & Ranere, Anthony J. Adaptive Radiation in Prehistoric Panama. Condon, Lorna, ed. (Peabody Museum Monograph: No. 5). (Orig.). 1980. pap. text ed. 20.00 (ISBN 0-87365-905-8). Peabody Harvard.

Linch, Adrian L. Evaluation of Ambient Air Quality by Personnel Monitoring, Vols. 1 & 2. 2nd ed. (Vol. 1-336pp., vol. 2-304pp.). 1981. Vol. 1. 69.95 (ISBN 0-8493-5293-2); Vol. 2. 69.95 (ISBN 0-8493-5294-0). CRC Pr.

Lincicome, David R., ed. International Review of Tropical Medicine. Incl. Vol. 1. 1960 (ISBN 0-12-367501-4); Vol. 2. 1963 (ISBN 0-12-367502-2); Vol. 3. 1969 (ISBN 0-12-367503-0); Vol. 4. Lincicome, David R. & Woodruff, A. W., eds. 1971 (ISBN 0-12-367504-9). 43.50 ea. Acad Pr.

Lincks, John, jt. auth. see Taaffe, James G.

Lincoln, Abraham. The Collected Works of Abraham Lincoln, 9 vols. Basler, Roy P., ed. 1953. Set. 275.00 (ISBN 0-8135-0172-5). Rutgers U Pr.

Lincoln, Andrew T. Paradise Now & Not Yet. LC 80-41024. (Society for the New Testament Studies Monographs: No. 43). 240p. Date not set. price not set (ISBN 0-521-22944-8). Cambridge U Pr.

Lincoln, Bruce. Emerging from the Chrysalis: Studies in Rituals of Women's Initiation. LC 80-24189. (Illus.). 208p. 1981. text ed. 18.50 (ISBN 0-674-24840-6). Harvard U Pr.

--Priests, Warriors & Cattle: A Study in the Ecology of Religions. LC 78-68826. (Hermeneutics: Studies in the History of Religions). 240p. 1981. 20.00x (ISBN 0-520-03880-0). U of Cal Pr.

Lincoln, C. Eric, ed. The Black Experience in Religion: A Collection of Readings. LC 73-16508. 384p. 1974. pap. 4.50 (ISBN 0-385-01884-3, Anch). Doubleday.

Lincoln, Edmond E., tr. Du Pont De Nemours on the Dangers of Inflation. (Kress Library of Business & Economics: No. 7). 1949. pap. 5.00x (ISBN 0-678-09902-2, Baker Lib). Kelley.

Lincoln, John E., jt. auth. see Heffernan, James A.

Lincoln, Nina, jt. auth. see Schalkwijk, Bob.

Lincoln, R. J. & Sheals, J. G. Collecting Invertebrate Animals. LC 79-14530. (Illus.). 1980. 22.50 (ISBN 0-521-22851-4); pap. 6.95 (ISBN 0-521-29677-3). Cambridge U Pr.

Lincoln, Victoria. Everyhow Remarkable. (gr. 2-4). 1967. 3.50 o.s.i. (ISBN 0-02-759130-1, CCPr). Macmillan.

Lincoln, W. Bruce. Nicholas I: Emperor & Autocrat of All the Russias. LC 77-15764. 424p. 1980. pap. 7.95x (ISBN 0-253-20254-X). Ind U Pr.

Lincoln, William C. Personal Bible Study. LC 75-2345. 160p. 1975. pap. 4.95 (ISBN 0-87123-458-0, 210458). Bethany Fell.

Lincoln, Yvonna S., jt. auth. see Guba, Egon G.

Lind, Aulis O. Coastal Landforms of Cat Island, Bahamas: A Study of Holocene Accretionary Topography & Sea Level Change. LC 76-77892. (Research Papers Ser.: No. 122). 156p. 1969. pap. 8.00 (ISBN 0-89065-029-2). U Chicago Dept Geog.

Lind, Carolyn P., pseud. One Hundred Four Ideas for Improving Your Young Child's Language Skills. (Illus.). 80p. (Orig.). 1980. pap. 10.00 (ISBN 0-9604940-0-6). Lindell Pubs.

Lind, E. M. & Tallantire, A. C. Some Common Flowering Plants of Uganda. 1971. pap. 4.50x o.p. (ISBN 0-19-644104-8). Oxford U Pr.

Lind, Ernie. Complete Book of Trick & Fancy Shooting. (Illus.). 1972. 6.95 o.p. (ISBN 0-87691-045-2). Winchester Pr.

Lind, J., et al, eds. Children & Parents in Hospitals. (Journal: Pediatrician: Vol. 9, No. 3-4). (Illus.). 120p. 1980. pap. 12.00 (ISBN 3-8055-1476-X). S Karger.

Lind, L. F. & Nelson, J. C. Analysis & Design of Sequential Digital Systems. LC 76-49959. 1977. 25.95 (ISBN 0-470-99021-X). Halsted Pr.

Lind, L. R., ed. Twentieth Century Italian Poetry: A Bilingual Anthology. LC 73-11343. (LLA Ser). 432p. 1974. 10.50 (ISBN 0-672-51409-5); pap. 9.70 (ISBN 0-672-61220-8). Bobbs.

Lind, L. R., tr. from Fr. Andre Chenier: Elegies & Camille. Bilingual ed. LC 77-18578. 1978. pap. text ed. 7.75 (ISBN 0-8191-0412-4). U Pr of Amer.

Lind, L. R., tr. see Ovid.

Lind, Loren & Krabill, Willard. Tobacco & Your Life. LC 64-8550. (Family Life Ser.). (Orig.). 1964. pap. 0.35 o.p. (ISBN 0-8361-1498-1). Herald Pr.

Lind, Margot, jt. auth. see Rapoport, Roger.

Lind, Millard C. Yahweh Is a Warrior. LC 80-16038. (Christian Peace Shelf Selection Ser.). 240p. 1980. pap. 9.95x (ISBN 0-8361-1233-4). Herald Pr.

Lind, Owen T. Handbook of Common Methods in Limnology. 2nd ed. LC 78-21173. (Illus.). 1979. pap. text ed. 11.95 (ISBN 0-8016-3019-3). Mosby.

Lind, Roger M., jt. auth. see Tropman, John E.

Lindahl, Judy. Decorating with Fabric: An Idea Book. rev. ed. 128p. 1980. pap. 4.95 (ISBN 0-9603032-1-9). Lindahl.

--Energy Saving Decorating. new ed. (Illus.). 128p. (Orig.). 1981. pap. 4.95 (ISBN 0-9603032-3-5). Lindahl.

--The Shade Book. rev. ed. (Illus.). 128p. pap. 4.95 (ISBN 0-9603032-2-7). Lindahl.

Lindars, B. & Smalley, S. S. Christ & Spirit in the New Testament. LC 72-91367. 300p. 1974. 63.00 (ISBN 0-521-20148-9). Cambridge U Pr.

Lindars, Barnabas, jt. ed. see Ackroyd, Peter R.

Lindau, Joan. Hrs. Cooper's Boardinghouse. 1980. lib. bdg. write for info. (Large Print Bks). G K Hall.

Lindauer. Communicating in Business. 2nd ed. 1979. 17.95 (ISBN 0-7216-5794-X). Dryden Pr.

Lindauer, John. Macroeconomic Readings. LC 68-9816. (Orig.). 1968. pap. text ed. 9.95 (ISBN 0-02-919110-6). Free Pr.

Lindauer, M. S. Perceptual Psychology. 1978. text ed. 23.50 o.p. (ISBN 0-08-019517-2); pap. text ed. 17.00 o.p. (ISBN 0-08-019516-4). Pergamon.

Lindauer, Martin S. The Psychological Study of Literature: Limitations, Possibilities & Accomplishments. LC 73-80499. 250p. 1974. 15.95 (ISBN 0-911012-74-5). Nelson-Hall.

Lindbeck. Metric Practices in Drafting. 1979. pap. 2.64 (ISBN 0-87002-298-9). Bennett IL.

Lindbeck, jt. auth. see Feirer.

Lindbeck, jt. auth. see Feirer, John L.

Lindbeck, et al. Basic Crafts. (gr. 7-12). 1979. text ed. 11.00 (ISBN 0-87002-275-X); student guide 2.60 (ISBN 0-87002-296-2). Bennett IL.

Lindbeck, Assar. The Political Economy of the New Left: An Outsider's View. 2nd ed. LC 77-83267. 1977. 15.00x (ISBN 0-8147-4979-8). NYU Pr.

--Swedish Economic Policy. 1973. 19.50x (ISBN 0-520-02422-2). U of Cal Pr.

Lindbeck, John R. Designing Today's Manufactured Products. LC 72-79110. 225p. (gr. 10-12). 1972. text ed. 17.16 (ISBN 0-87345-440-5). McKnight.

--Metrics in Career Education. 120p. (gr. 7-12). 1975. pap. text ed. 3.60 (ISBN 0-87002-082-X). Bennett IL.

Lindbeck, John R. & Lathrop, Irving T. General Industry. (Illus.). (gr. 7-9). 1977. 15.28 (ISBN 0-87002-185-0). student guide 4.64 (ISBN 0-87002-196-6). answer sheet free. Bennett IL.

Lindbeck, John R., jt. auth. see Feirer, John L.

Lindberg, Conrad, ed. The Middle English Bible: Prefatory Epistles of Saint Jerome. 1979. pap. 19.50x (ISBN 82-00-01773-7, Dist. by Columbia U Pr.). Universitet.

Lindberg, David C., ed. Science in the Middle Ages. LC 78-5367. (The Chicago History of Science & Medicine). 1980. pap. 9.95 (ISBN 0-226-48233-2, P870, Phoen). U of Chicago Pr.

Lindberg, Donald A. The Computer & Medical Care. (Illus.). 224p. 1971. 17.50 (ISBN 0-398-01131-1). C C Thomas.

--The Growth of Medical Information Systems in the United States. LC 79-1555. 208p. 1979. 21.95 (ISBN 0-669-02911-4). Lexington Bks.

Lindberg, G. U. Fishes of the World: A Key to Families & a Checklist. LC 73-16382. (Illus.). 545p. 1974. 59.95 (ISBN 0-470-53565-2). Halsted Pr.

Lindberg, Leon N. The Energy Syndrome: Comparing National Responses to the Energy Crisis. LC 76-6772. (Illus.). 1977. 17.95 (ISBN 0-669-00662-9). Lexington Bks.

Lindberg, Lucile & Swedlow, Rita. Early Childhood Education: A Guide for Observation & Participation. 320p. 1976. pap. text ed. 7.95x o.s.i. (ISBN 0-205-05442-0). Allyn.

--Early Childhood Education: A Guide for Observation & Participation. 2nd ed. LC 23-67203. 1980. pap. text ed. 10.50 (ISBN 0-205-06720-4, 2367203). Allyn.

Lindberg, O. & Ernster, L. Chemistry & Physiology of Mitochondria & Microsomes. (Protoplasmatologia: Vol. 3, Pt. 4). (Illus.). 1954. 30.70 o.p. (ISBN 0-387-80346-7). Springer-Verlag.

Lindberg, Olov, ed. see I U B - I U B S Joint Symposium - 1st - Stockholm - 1960.

Lindberg Press. Scandanavian Charted Designs. (Illus.). 1979. pap. 1.75 (ISBN 0-486-23787-7). Dover.

Lindberg, Rick. Stuck on the Sox. 192p. (Orig.). 1978. pap. 1.95 (ISBN 0-930528-02-6). Sassafras Pr.

Lindberg, Roy, jt. auth. see Austin, L.

Lindberg, Roy A. Materials & Manufacturing Technology. (Illus.). 1968. text ed. 23.95x (ISBN 0-205-01947-1, 321947X). Allyn.

--Processes & Materials of Manufacture. 2nd ed. 1977. text ed. 25.95x (ISBN 0-205-05414-5, 32544143); a. b. avail. (ISBN 0-205-05492-7, 3254143). Allyn.

Lindberg, Roy A. & Braton, Norman R. Welding & Other Joining Processes. 544p. 1976. text ed. 26.95x (ISBN 0-205-05000-X, 3250008). Allyn.

Lindberg, Wayne see Foster, Rick.

Lindbergh, Anne M. Bring Me a Unicorn: Diaries & Letters of Anne Morrow Lindbergh, 1922-1928. LC 71-182329. (Helen & Kurt Wolff Bk). 288p. 1972. 7.95 o.p. (ISBN 0-15-114180-0). HarBraceJ.

--War Within & Without: Diaries & Letters, Nineteen Thirty-Nine to Nineteen Forty-Four. 1980. 14.95 (ISBN 0-15-194661-2). HarBraceJ.

Lindbergh, Charles A. Spirit of St. Louis. hudson river ed. (Illus.). 1953. lib. rep. ed. 20.00x (ISBN 0-684-14421-2, ScribT); slip case ed. 17.50 (ISBN 0-684-10362-1, ScribT). Scribner.

Lindblom, C. Policy Making Process. 2nd ed. 1980. pap. 6.95 (ISBN 0-13-686543-7). P-H.

Lindblom, Charles E., jt. auth. see Braybrooke, David.

Lindblom, J. Prophecy in Ancient Israel. LC 63-907. 480p. 1962. 16.50 (ISBN 0-8006-0916-6, 1-916). Fortress.

Lindblom, P., jt. auth. see Dodge, R.

Lindblom, Steven. The Fantastic Homemade Book. (gr. 1-12). 1979. 8.95 (ISBN 0-395-28481-3); pap. 3.95 (ISBN 0-395-28482-1). HM.

Linde, Richard W. Te see Te Linde, Richard W. & Mattingly, Richard F.

Linde, Shirley, jt. auth. see Allen, Robert.

Linde, Shirley M. & Savary, Louis M. The Joy of Sleep: Facts, Fantasy, & Folklore Relating to the Mystery of Sleep with 22 Remedies for Insomniacs. LC 73-7066. 192p. 1980. pap. 4.95 (ISBN 0-06-250515-7, BN 3002, HarpR). Har-Row.

Linde, T. F. & Kopp, T. Training Retarded Babies & Preschoolers. (Illus.). 200p. 1974. 17.50 (ISBN 0-398-02825-7). C C Thomas.

Lindeboom, G. A. Descartes & Medicine. (Nieuwe Nederlandse Bijdragen Tot De Geschiedenis der Geneekundem: No. 1). (Illus.). 1978. pap. text ed. 17.25x (ISBN 90-6203-882-4). Humanities.

--The Letters of Jan Swammerdam to Melchisedec Thevenot, with English Translation & a Biographical Sketch. 202p. 1975. text ed. 47.50 (ISBN 90-265-0222-2, Pub. by Swets Pub Serv Holland). Swets North Am.

Lindeburg, Michael R. Civil Engineering Review Manual. 2nd ed. LC 80-81798. (Engineering Review Manual Ser.). (Illus.). 688p. (Orig.). 1980. pap. 29.50 (ISBN 0-932276-15-6); wkbk. 4.00 (ISBN 0-932276-17-2). Prof Engine.

--Engineer-in-Training Review Manual. 5th ed. LC 80-81799. (Engineering Review Manual Ser.). (Illus.). 760p. 1980. pap. 26.50 (ISBN 0-932276-14-8); wkbk. 7.00 (ISBN 0-932276-16-4). Prof Engine.
--Engineering Economic Analysis & Expanded Interest Tables. 2nd ed. (Engineering Review Manual Ser.). 134p. 1980. pap. 8.50 (ISBN 0-932276-25-3). Prof Engine.
--Mechanical Engineering Review Manual. 5th ed. LC 80-83176. (Engineering Review Manual Ser.). (Illus.). 704p. 1980. pap. 26.50 (ISBN 0-932276-21-0); wkbk. 7.00 (ISBN 0-932276-23-7). Prof Engine.
--Seismic Design for the Professional Engineering Examination. LC 80-81796. (Engineering Review Manual Ser.). (Illus.). 104p. 1980. pap. 9.50 (ISBN 0-932276-20-2). Prof Engine.
--Surveying Law for the California Civil Professional Engineering Exam. (Engineering Review Manual Ser.). (Illus.). 154p. 1981. pap. 9.50 (ISBN 0-932276-26-1). Prof Engine.
Lindegren, Carl C. The Theory & Practice of Natural Healing. LC 80-50132. 1981. 7.95 (ISBN 0-533-04595-9). Vantage.
Lindeke, W. Four-Language Technical Dictionary of Heating, Ventilation & Sanitary Engineering: English, German, French, Russian. LC 79-81248. 1971. 50.00 (ISBN 0-08-006426-4). Pergamon.
Lindell, Anne. Intensive English for Communication: Book Two. (Illus.). 294p. 1980. pap. text ed. 6.95x (ISBN 0-472-08572-7). U of Mich Pr.
Lindell, Anne & Hagiwara, M. Peter. Intensive English for Communication, Bk. 1. LC 78-58152. (Illus.). 1979. pap. text ed. 6.95x (ISBN 0-472-08570-0, 08570); pap. text ed. 4.95x wkbk. (ISBN 0-472-08571-9). U of Mich Pr.
Lindell, Kristina, et al. Folktales from Kammu Two: A Story-Teller's Tales. (Scandanavian Institute of Asian Studies Monograph: No. 40). (Orig.). 1980. pap. text ed. 10.50x (ISBN 0-7007-0131-1). Humanities.
Lindeman, Bruce. Real Estate Brokerage. 450p. 1981. text ed. 16.95 (ISBN 0-8359-6517-1); instr's. manual free (ISBN 0-8359-6518-X). Reston.
Lindeman, J. Bruce & Friedman, Jack P. How to Prepare for the Real Estate Licensing Examination -- Salesman & Broker. LC 78-17332. 1979. pap. text ed. 7.95 (ISBN 0-8120-0771-9). Barron.
Lindeman, Joyce & Jones, F. L. The Components of Synchronized Swimming. (Illus.). 336p. 1975. 15.95 (ISBN 0-13-164814-4). P-H.
Lindeman, Richard, et al. Introduction to Bivariate & Multivariate Statistics. 1980. text ed. 19.95x (ISBN 0-673-15099-2). Scott F.
Lindeman, Richard H. & Merenda, Peter F. Educational Measurement. 2nd ed. 1979. pap. text ed. 9.95x (ISBN 0-673-15096-8). Scott F.
Lindemann. Arnoldwesker Als Gesellschaftskritiker. (Poetic Drama & Poetic Theory Ser.). 1980. pap. text ed. 25.00x. Humanities.
Lindemann, Albert S. The Red Years: European Socialism Versus Bolshevism, 1919-1921. LC 73-80834. 1975. 23.75x (ISBN 0-520-02511-3). U of Cal Pr.
Lindemann, Valeska. Arnold Wesker Als Gesellschaftskritiker. (Poetic Drama Ser.: No.60). (Ger.). 1980. pap. text ed. 25.00 (ISBN 0-391-02204-0). Humanities.
Linden, Catherine. Close Associates. 1980. pap. 1.95 (ISBN 0-380-75473-8, 75473). Avon.
--Wakefield's Passion. 208p. 1981. pap. 2.25 (ISBN 0-380-77626-X). Avon.
Linden, Eugene. The Alms Race: The Impact of American Voluntary Aid Abroad. 1976. 10.00 o.p. (ISBN 0-394-49607-8). Random.
Linden, Frank van der see Van Der Linden, Frank.
Linden, Ian & Linden, Jane. Catholics, Peasants & Chewa Resistance in Nyasaland, 1889-1939. 1974. 23.75x (ISBN 0-520-02500-8). U of Cal Pr.
Linden, James D., jt. auth. see Shertzer, Bruce.
Linden, Jane, jt. auth. see Linden, Ian.
Linden, Ronald, ed. The Foreign Policy of Eastern Europe: New Approaches. (Praeger Special Studies). 290p. 1980. 27.95 (ISBN 0-03-056136-1). Praeger.
Linden, Ronald H., jt. ed. see Eckhard, Frederic.
Lindenberg, Marc & Crosby, Benjamin. Managing Development: The Political Dimension. LC 80-83345. (Library of Management for Development). 228p. (Orig.). 1981. 19.50x (ISBN 0-931816-49-1); pap. 9.95x (ISBN 0-931816-49-1). Kumarian Pr.
Lindenberger, Herbert. Georg Buchner. LC 64-16355. (Crosscurrents-Modern Critiques Ser.). 169p. 1964. 6.95 (ISBN 0-8093-0138-5). S Ill U Pr.
--Georg Trakl. (World Authors Ser.: Germany: No. 171). lib. bdg. 10.95 (ISBN 0-8057-2886-4). Twayne.
Lindenfeld, Jacqueline. Yaqui Syntax. (U. C. Publ. in Linguistics: Vol. 76). 1974. pap. 12.50x (ISBN 0-520-09470-0). U of Cal Pr.
Lindenfeld, David. The Transformation of Positivism: Alexius Meinong & European Thought, 1880-1920. 304p. 1981. 25.00x (ISBN 0-520-03994-7). U of Cal Pr.
Lindenmann, Walter K. Attitude & Opinion Research: Why You Need It, How to Do It. 1977. 9.50 (ISBN 0-89964-028-1). CASE.
Linder, Bill R. How to Trace Your Family History. 1979. pap. 2.25 o.p. (ISBN 0-445-04508-6). Popular Lib.
Linder, Darwyn E., ed. Psychological Dimensions of Social Interaction: Readings & Perspectives. LC 72-4707. 1973. pap. text ed. 9.95 (ISBN 0-201-04246-0). A-W.
Linder, Enid, ed. see Potter, Beatrix.
Linder, Erik H. Hjalmar Bergman. LC 74-23060. (World Authors Ser.: Sweden: No. 356). 1975. lib. bdg. 12.50 (ISBN 0-8057-2147-9). Twayne.
Linder, Marc. The Anti-Samuelson. Incl. Vol. I. Macroeconomics: Basic Problems of Capitalist Economy (ISBN 0-916354-14-8) (ISBN 0-916354-15-6); Vol. II. Microeconomics: Money & Banking (ISBN 0-916354-16-4) (ISBN 0-916354-17-2). 1977. 20.00 ea.; pap. text ed. 6.95 ea. Urizen Bks.
Linder, P. Air Filters for Use at Nuclear Facilities. (Technical Reports Ser.: No. 122). (Illus.). 76p. (Orig.). 1970. pap. 6.50 (ISBN 92-0-125670-1, IDC122, IAEA). Unipub.
Linder, Robert D. & Pierard, Richard V. Politics: A Case for Christian Action. LC 73-77850. 160p. 1973. pap. 1.95 o.p. (ISBN 0-87784-356-2). Inter-Varsity.
Linder, Robert D., ed. God & Caesar: Case Studies in the Relationship Between Christianity & the State. LC 78-187900. 140p. 1971. pap. 1.95 o.p. (ISBN 0-913446-00-9). Conf Faith & Hist.
Linder, Staffan B. Harried Leisure Class. LC 73-92909. 1970. 17.50x (ISBN 0-231-03302-8); pap. 6.00x (ISBN 0-231-08649-0). Columbia U Pr.
Linderman, Charles W., ed. International Technical Conference on Slurry Transportation: Proceedings. 5th ed. LC 79-92621. (Illus.). 296p. (Orig.). 1980. pap. 65.00 (ISBN 0-932066-05-4). Slurry Transport.
Linderman, Charles W., ed. see International Technical Conference on Slurry Transportation, 2nd.
Linderman, Frank B. Plenty-coups, Chief of the Crows. LC 30-11369. (Illus.). 1962. pap. 3.95 (ISBN 0-8032-5121-1, BB 128, Bison). U of Nebr Pr.
--Pretty-shield, Medicine Woman of the Crows. LC 72-3273. (Illus.). 256p. 1974. pap. 4.95 (ISBN 0-8032-5791-0, BB 580, Bison). U of Nebr Pr.
--Recollections of Charley Russell. Merriam, H. G., ed. LC 63-18074. 148p. 1963. 9.95 (ISBN 0-8061-0582-8). U of Okla Pr.
Lindert, Peter, jt. auth. see Kindleberger, Charles P.
Lindert, Peter H., jt. auth. see Williamson, Jeffrey G.
Lindey, A., jt. auth. see Ernst, M. L.
Lindey, Alexander. Entertainment, Publishing & the Arts: Agreement & the Law, 3 vols. LC 80-10991. 1963. 60.00 ea. (ISBN 0-87632-005-1). Boardman.
Lindfors, Bernth. Mazungumzo: Interviews with East African Writers, Publishers, Editors & Scholars. LC 80-25684. (Africa Ser., Ohio University Papers in International Studies). 179p. 1981. pap. 13.00 (ISBN 0-89680-108-X). Ohio U Ctr Intl.
Lindfors, Bernth, ed. Black African Literature in English: A Guide to Information Sources. LC 73-16983. (American Literature, English Literature, & World Literatures in English Information Guide Ser.: Vol. 23). 1979. 30.00 (ISBN 0-8103-1206-9). Gale.
--Critical Perspectives on Amos Tutuola. LC 75-13706. 318p. (Orig.). 1975. 20.00 (ISBN 0-914478-05-2); pap. 9.00 (ISBN 0-914478-06-0). Three Continents.
--Critical Perspectives on Nigerian Literatures. 1976. cased 20.00 (ISBN 0-914478-27-3); pap. 9.00 (ISBN 0-914478-28-1). Three Continents.
Lindfors, Judith W. Children's Language & Learning. (Illus.). 1980. text ed. 17.95 (ISBN 0-13-131953-1). P-H.
Lindfors, Viveca & Austin, Paul. I Am a Woman. LC 76-740002. (Orig.). pap. 4.95 (ISBN 0-916840-01-8). Slohm Assoc.
Lindgren, Alvin J. & Shawchuck, Norman L. Management for Your Church: How to Realize Your Church Potential Through Systems Approach. LC 77-425. 1977. 8.95 (ISBN 0-687-23062-4). Abingdon.
Lindgren, Astrid. Children on Troublemaker Street. Bothner, Gerry, tr. (Illus.). (gr. 2-5). 1964. 7.95g (ISBN 0-02-759100-X). Macmillan.
--Emil & the Piggy Beast. Heron, Michael, tr. LC 72-91228. 128p. (gr. 2-6). 1973. 5.95 o.p. (ISBN 0-695-80356-5, T0356). Follett.
--Emil in the Soup Tureen. LC 79-93795. (Illus.). (gr. 2-6). 1970. 5.95 o.p. (ISBN 0-695-82210-1). Follett.
--Emil's Pranks. (gr. 1-3). PLB 5.97 o.p. (ISBN 0-695-40158-0). Follett.
--I Want a Brother or Sister. Lucas, Barbara, tr. from Swedish. (Illus.). 32p. (ps-3). 1981. 7.95 (ISBN 0-15-239387-0, HJ). HarBraceJ.
--Lotta on Troublemaker Street. (gr. k-2). 1963. 4.25 o.s.i. (ISBN 0-02-759030-5). Macmillan.
--Of Course Polly Can Do Almost Everything. (Illus.). 1978. 6.95 o.p. (ISBN 0-695-80967-9); lib. bdg. 6.99 o.p. (ISBN 0-695-40967-0). Follett.
--Of Course Polly Can Ride a Bike. (Picture Bk). (Illus.). 32p. (gr. k-3). 1972. 6.95 o.p. (ISBN 0-695-40349-4). Follett.
--Pippi Goes on Board. (Illus.). (gr. 4-6). 1957. PLB 6.95 (ISBN 0-670-55677-7). Viking Pr.
Lindgren, Claire. Classical Art Forms & Celtic Mutations: Figural Art in Roman Britain. LC 80-18987. (Illus.). 244p. (Orig.). 1981. 24.00 (ISBN 0-8155-5057-X, NP). Noyes.
Lindgren, Eric. Wildlife in Papua New Guinea. (Illus.). 1976. 12.50 o.p. (ISBN 0-584-97052-8). R Curtis Bks.
Lindgren, Ernest. Art of the Film. 2nd ed. (Illus.). 1970. pap. 2.95 o.s.i. (ISBN 0-02-061190-0, Collier). Macmillan.
Lindgren, Henry C. The Psychology of College Success: A Dynamic Approach. LC 79-25614. 158p. 1980. Repr. lib. bdg. 6.50 (ISBN 0-89874-035-5). Krieger.
Lindgren, Henry C. & Byrne, Donn. Psychology: An Introduction to a Behavioral Science. 4th ed. LC 74-23293. 448p. 1975. text ed. 19.95 (ISBN 0-471-53603-2). Wiley.
Lindgren, Henry C. & Fisk, Leonard W., Jr. Psychology of Personal Development. 3rd ed. LC 75-34926. 1976. 19.95x (ISBN 0-471-53769-1). Wiley.
Lindgren, Henry C. & Harvey, John H. An Introduction to Social Psychology. 3rd ed. (Illus.). 500p. 1981. text ed. 17.95 (ISBN 0-8016-3038-X). Mosby.
Lindgren, Kenneth E., jt. auth. see Wright, D. Franklin.
Lindguist, A. W., ed. Insect Population Control by the Sterile-Male Technique. (Technical Reports Ser.: No. 21). (Illus., Orig.). 1963. pap. 2.75 (ISBN 92-0-115063-6, IAEA). Unipub.
Lindh, Gunnar, jt. auth. see Falkenmark, Malin.
Lindhe, Richard & Grossman, Steven D. Accounting Information Systems. 500p. 1980. text ed. 18.95x (ISBN 0-931920-23-X). Dame Pubns.
Lindholm, Dan. How the Stars Were Born. Twyman, Leo, tr. 1975. 7.95 o.p. (ISBN 0-904822-01-X, Pub by Henry Goulden, Ltd). St George Bk Serv.
Lindholm, Richard W. The Economics of VAT: Preserving Efficiency, Capitalism & Social Progress. LC 80-8428. 1980. 19.95 (ISBN 0-669-04111-4). Lexington Bks.
--Property Taxation & the Finance of Education. LC 73-2046. (TRED Ser.). 1974. 25.00x (ISBN 0-299-06440-9, 644). U of Wis Pr.
--Value-Added Tax & Other Tax Reforms. LC 76-24827. (Illus.). 332p. 1976. 21.95 (ISBN 0-911012-87-7). Nelson-Hall.
Lindholm, Richard W. & Wignjowijoto, Hortojo. Financing & Managing State & Local Government. LC 78-19227. (Illus.). 1979. 29.95 (ISBN 0-669-02434-1). Lexington Bks.
Lindholm, Richard W., ed. Property Taxation, USA: Proceedings. (Committee on Taxation, Resources and Economic Development Ser. No. 2). (Illus.). 1967. pap. 7.95 (ISBN 0-299-04544-7). U of Wis Pr.
Lindin, Carl E., tr. see Lagerkvist, Par.
Lindisfarne Association, ed. Earth's Answer: Exploring Planetary Culture at the Lindisfarne Conferences. LC 76-26240. (Illus.). 1977. pap. 6.95 o.s.i. (ISBN 0-06-012632-9, TD276, HarpT). Har-Row.
Lindlahr, Victor H. Eat - & - Reduce. LC 80-19206. 194p. 1980. Repr. of 1972 ed. lib. bdg. 9.95x (ISBN 0-89370-615-9). Borgo Pr.
--The Lindlahr Vitamin Cookbook. LC 80-19202. 319p. 1980. Repr. of 1972 ed. lib. bdg. 9.95x (ISBN 0-89370-611-6). Borgo Pr.
--The Natural Way to Health. LC 80-19863. 255p. 1980. Repr. of 1973 ed. lib. bdg. 9.95x (ISBN 0-89370-617-5). Borgo Pr.
--Victor Lindlahr's Seven-Day Reducing Diet. LC 80-20589. 128p. 1980. Repr. of 1977 ed. lib. bdg. 9.95x (ISBN 0-89370-640-X). Borgo Pr.
--You Are What You Eat. LC 80-19722. 128p. 1980. Repr. of 1971 ed. lib. bdg. 9.95x (ISBN 0-89370-604-3). Borgo Pr.
Lindley, Betty & Lindley, E. K. A New Deal for Youth. LC 72-172687. (FDR & The Era of the New Deal Ser). (Illus.). 316p. 1972. Repr. of 1938 ed. lib. bdg. 32.50 (ISBN 0-306-70382-3). Da Capo.
Lindley, D. V. Introduction to Probability & Statistics from a Bayesian Viewpoint: Pt. 1 Probability. (Illus.). 270p. 1980. pap. 15.50x (ISBN 0-521-29867-9). Cambridge U Pr.
--Introduction to Probability & Statistics from a Bayesian Viewpoint: Pt. 2: Inference. (Illus.). 300p. 1980. pap. 15.50x (ISBN 0-521-29866-0). Cambridge U Pr.
Lindley, Dennis V. Introduction to Probability & Statistics from a Bayesian Viewpoint, 2 Pts. Pt. 1. Probability. text ed. 34.95x (ISBN 0-521-05562-8); Pt. 2. Inference. text ed. 34.95 (ISBN 0-521-05563-6). Cambridge U Pr.
Lindley, Dennis V. & Miller, Jeffrey C. Cambridge Elementary Statistical Tables. 1953. text ed. 4.50x (ISBN 0-521-05564-4). Cambridge U Pr.
Lindley, Denver, tr. see Pilhes, Rene-Victor.
Lindley, E. K. Franklin Delano Roosevelt: A Career in Progressive Democracy. rev. ed. LC 73-21771. (FDR & the Era of the New Deal Ser.). 366p. 1974. Repr. of 1933 ed. lib. bdg. 32.50 (ISBN 0-306-70634-2). Da Capo.
Lindley, E. K., jt. auth. see Lindley, Betty.
Lindley, Erica. Devil in Crystal. 1977. pap. 1.95 (ISBN 0-451-07643-5, E7643, Sig). NAL.
Lindley, Ernest K. Half Way with Roosevelt. LC 75-8789. (FDR & the Era of the New Deal Ser.). x, 449p. 1975. Repr. of 1937 ed. lib. bdg. 32.50 (ISBN 0-306-70706-3). Da Capo.
--The Roosevelt Revolution, First Phase. LC 74-637. (FDR & the Era of the New Deal Ser.). 328p. 1974. Repr. of 1933 ed. lib. bdg. 32.50 (ISBN 0-306-70651-2). Da Capo.
Lindley, Helen, tr. see Pilhes, Rene-Victor.
Lindley, K. Appreciation of Architecture: Landscape & Buildings. (Illus.). 58p. 1972. text ed. 4.65 o.p. (ISBN 0-08-015677-0). Pergamon.
Lindley, Letty A. Leaping into Language with Sound-a-Roo. 1981. pap. 9.95 (ISBN 0-8134-2165-9). Interstate.
Lindman, Harold R. Analysis of Variance in Complex Experimental Designs. LC 74-11211. (Illus.). 1974. text ed. 24.95x (ISBN 0-7167-0774-8); answers to exercises avail. W H Freeman.
Lindman, Maj. Flicka, Ricka, Dicka & a Little Dog. LC 48-3307. (Illus.). (gr. k-2). 1946. 5.75g (ISBN 0-8075-2486-7). A Whitman.
--Flicka, Ricka, Dicka & the Big Red Hen. LC 60-13634. (Illus.). (gr. k-2). 1960. 5.75g (ISBN 0-8075-2481-6). A Whitman.
--Flicka, Ricka, Dicka & the Girl Next Door. (Illus.). (gr. k-2). 5.75g (ISBN 0-8075-2483-2). A Whitman.
--Flicka, Ricka, Dicka & the New Dotted Dresses. (Illus.). (gr. k-2). 5.75g (ISBN 0-8075-2482-4). A Whitman.
--Flicka, Ricka, Dicka & the Strawberries. (Illus.). (gr. k-2). 1944. 5.75g (ISBN 0-8075-2489-1). A Whitman.
--Flicka, Ricka, Dicka & the Three Kittens. LC 41-17581. (Illus.). (gr. k-2). 1941. 5.75g (ISBN 0-8075-2490-5). A Whitman.
--Flicka, Ricka, Dicka & Their New Friend. (Illus.). (gr. k-2). 1942. 5.75g (ISBN 0-8075-2487-5). A Whitman.
--Flicka, Ricka, Dicka & Their New Skates. (Illus.). (gr. k-2). 1950. 5.75g (ISBN 0-8075-2488-3). A Whitman.
--Flicka, Ricka, Dicka Bake a Cake. LC 55-7571. (Illus.). (gr. k-2). 1955. 5.75g (ISBN 0-8075-2480-8). A Whitman.
--Flicka, Ricka, Dicka Go to Market. LC 58-9950. (Illus.). (gr. k-2). 1958. 5.75g (ISBN 0-8075-2485-9). A Whitman.
--Snipp, Snapp, Snurr & the Big Surprise. LC 37-35180. (Illus.). (gr. k-2). 1937. 5.75g (ISBN 0-8075-7503-8). A Whitman.
--Snipp, Snapp, Snurr & the Buttered Bread. LC 34-37832. (Illus.). (gr. k-2). 1934. 5.75g (ISBN 0-8075-7504-6). A Whitman.
--Snipp, Snapp, Snurr & the Gingerbread. LC 36-32643. (Illus.). (gr. k-2). 1936. 5.75g (ISBN 0-8075-7505-4). A Whitman.
--Snipp, Snapp, Snurr & the Seven Dogs. LC 59-14391. (Illus.). (gr. k-2). 1959. 5.75g (ISBN 0-8075-7512-7). A Whitman.
--Snipp, Snapp, Snurr Learn to Swim. LC 54-9945. (Illus.). (gr. k-2). 1954. 5.75g (ISBN 0-8075-7506-2). A Whitman.
Lindmayer, Joseph, et al. Fundamentals of Semiconductor Devices. LC 76-16765. 506p. 1977. Repr. of 1965 ed. 26.50 (ISBN 0-88275-424-6). Krieger.
Lindner, Burkhardt & Luedke, Martin, eds. Materialien Zur Asthetischen Theorie Adornos. (Suhrkamp Taschenbuecher Wissenschaft). 560p. (Orig.). pap. text ed. 11.70 (ISBN 3-518-07722-8). Suhrkamp.
Lindner, Rhoda, jt. auth. see Lindner, William A.
Lindner, Vicki, jt. auth. see Jody, Ruth.
Lindner, Vicki, jt. auth. see Walden, Barbara.
Lindner, William A. & Lindner, Rhoda. Statistics for Students in the Behavioral Sciences. 1979. pap. text ed. 17.95 (ISBN 0-8053-6576-1); instr's guide 3.95 (ISBN 0-8053-6577-X); wkbk 5.95 (ISBN 0-8053-6578-8). Benjamin-Cummings.

Lindon, Edmund. Cuba. (gr. 4 up). 1980. PLB 6.90 (ISBN 0-531-04101-8). Watts.

Lindon, J. C., jt. auth. see Emsley, J. W.

Lindop, Edmund. An Album of the Fifties. (Illus.). (gr. 6 up). 1978. PLB 7.90 s&l (ISBN 0-531-01505-X). Watts.

--Dazzling Twenties. LC 75-94767. (Modern America Ser). (Illus.). (gr. 7 up). 1970. PLB 4.33 o.p. (ISBN 0-531-01840-7). Watts.

--The First Book of Elections. rev. ed. LC 68-10435. (First Bks). (Illus.). 72p. (gr. 4-6). 1972. PLB 4.90 o.p. (ISBN 0-531-00521-6). Watts.

--Turbulent Thirties. LC 78-114923. (Illus.). (gr. 7 up). 1970. PLB 3.90 o.p. (ISBN 0-531-01945-4). Watts.

Lindop, Patricia J. & Sacher, G. A., eds. Radiation & Aging. 1966. pap. text ed. 18.95x (ISBN 0-685-83895-1). Intl Ideas.

Lindow, Ch. W. Historic Organs in France, No.1. Blanchard, Homer D., tr. (The Little Organ Books Ser.). (Illus.). 1980. pap. 21.00 (ISBN 0-930112-03-2). Praestant.

Lindow, Ch. W. & Blanchard, Homer D. A Little Organ Lexicon. (The Little Organ Book Ser.: No. 2). 44p. 1981. pap. write for info. Praestant.

Lindquist, Donald. The Red Gods. 1981. 11.95 (ISBN 0-440-07349-9). Delacorte.

Lindquist, Mary M., ed. Selected Issues in Mathematics Education. LC 80-82903. 250p. 1981. write for info (ISBN 0-8211-1114-0); text ed. write for info. McCutchan.

Lindquist-Cock, Elizabeth. The Influence of Photography on American Landscape Painting, 1839-1880. LC 76-23608. (Outstanding Dissertations in the Fine Arts - 2nd Series - American). (Illus.). 1977. Repr. of 1967 ed. lib. bdg. 48.00 (ISBN 0-8240-2680-2). Garland Pub.

Lindsay, A. D., tr. see Plato.

Lindsay, B. R., ed. Applications of Energy: Nineteenth Century. (Benchmark Papers in Energy Ser.: Vol. 2). 1976. 47.00 (ISBN 0-12-786961-1). Acad Pr.

Lindsay, Beverly, ed. Comparative Perspectives of Third World Women: The Impact of Race, Sex, & Class. LC 78-19793. (Praeger Special Studies). 334p. 1980. 24.95 (ISBN 0-03-046651-2). Praeger.

Lindsay, C. School & Community. 1970. pap. 7.00 (ISBN 0-08-016043-3). Pergamon.

Lindsay, Cotton M., ed. Pharmaceutical Industry: Economics, Performance & Government Regulation. LC 77-27062. 1978. 17.50 (ISBN 0-471-04077-0, Pub. by Wiley Medical). Wiley.

Lindsay, Cynthia. Dear Boris: The Life of William Henry Pratt, a.k.a. Boris Karloff. 1975. 12.50 o.p. (ISBN 0-394-47579-8). Knopf.

Lindsay, D. B., jt. auth. see Buttery, P. J.

Lindsay, David. The Haunted Woman. new ed. LC 74-30384. (Forgotten Fantasy Library: Vol. 4). 176p. 1975. pap. 2.85 (ISBN 0-87877-103-4, F-104). Newcastle Pub.

--The Haunted Woman. Reginald, R. & Menveille, Douglas, eds. LC 80-19459. (Newcastle Forgotten Fantasy Library: Vol. 4). 176p. 1980. Repr. of 1975 ed. lib. bdg. 9.95x (ISBN 0-89370-503-9). Borgo Pr.

Lindsay, Devon. Crimson Intrigue. (Orig.). 1981. pap. write for info. (ISBN 0-671-41781-9). PB.

Lindsay, Diana E. Our Historic Desert. Puurade, Richard F., ed. LC 73-11878. (Illus.). 160p. 1973. 14.50 (ISBN 0-913938-15-7). Copley Bks.

Lindsay, Donald & Price, Mary R. Authority & Challenge: A Portrait of Europe 1300-1600. (A Portrait of Europe Ser). (Illus.). 360p. 1975. 16.00x (ISBN 0-19-913118-X); pap. 9.95x (ISBN 0-19-913220-8). Oxford U Pr.

Lindsay, Donald & Washington, E. S. Portrait of Britain Between the Exhibitions: 1851-1951. (Oxford Introduction to British History Ser.). (Illus.). 1952. 6.95x o.p. (ISBN 0-19-831513-9). Oxford U Pr.

Lindsay, Frank W., ed. see Simenon, Georges.

Lindsay, Frannie. The Horse We Lie Down in: Eight Poems. (Pikestaff Poetry Chapbooks: No. 1). 10p. 1980. pap. 1.00 (ISBN 0-936044-02-0). Pikestaff Pr.

Lindsay, Gordon. Abraham, Friend of God. (Old Testament Ser.). 1.25 (ISBN 0-89985-126-6). Christ Nations.

--The Art of Successful Praying. (School of Prayer Ser.). 1.25 (ISBN 0-89985-079-0). Christ Nations.

--The Creation. (Old Testament Ser.). 1.25 (ISBN 0-89985-123-1). Christ Nations.

--David Comes into the Kingdom. (Old Testament Ser.). 1.25 (ISBN 0-89985-142-8). Christ Nations.

--David Reaping the Whirlwind. (Old Testament Ser.). 1.25 (ISBN 0-89985-143-6). Christ Nations.

--The Decline & Fall of Israel & Judah. (Old Testament Ser.). 1.25 (ISBN 0-89985-153-3). Christ Nations.

--The Early Kings of Israel. (Old Testament Ser.). 1.25 (ISBN 0-89985-147-9). Christ Nations.

--The Early Kings of Judah. (Old Testament Ser.). 1.25 (ISBN 0-89985-146-0). Christ Nations.

--The Early Life of David. (Old Testament Ser.). 1.25 (ISBN 0-89985-141-X). Christ Nations.

--The Eighteen Silent Years. (Life of Christ & Parable Ser.). 0.95 o.p. (ISBN 0-89985-162-2). Christ Nations.

--Elijah, the Man Who Did Not Die. (Old Testament Ser.). 1.25 (ISBN 0-89985-149-5). Christ Nations.

--Elijah, The Whirlwind Prophet. (Old Testament Ser.). 1.25 (ISBN 0-89985-148-7). Christ Nations.

--Enoch & Noah, Patriarchs of the Deluge. (Old Testament Ser.). 1.25 (ISBN 0-89985-125-8). Christ Nations.

--Ezra & Nehemiah & the Return from Babylon. (Old Testament Ser.). 1.25 (ISBN 0-89985-154-1). Christ Nations.

--Flying Saucers. pap. 0.95 (ISBN 0-89985-199-1). Christ Nations.

--Forty-Eight Signs in the Land of Israel. 1.25 (ISBN 0-89985-186-X). Christ Nations.

--The Four Hundred Silent Years. (Old Testament Ser.). 1.25 (ISBN 0-89985-158-4). Christ Nations.

--Gideon & the Early Judges. (Old Testament Ser.). 1.25 (ISBN 0-89985-135-5). Christ Nations.

--God's Master Key to Prosperity. 1.95 (ISBN 0-89985-001-4). Christ Nations.

--Isaac & Rebekah. (Old Testament Ser.). 1.25 (ISBN 0-89985-127-4). Christ Nations.

--Isaiah & Jeremiah. (Old Testament Ser.). 1.25 (ISBN 0-89985-155-X). Christ Nations.

--Jacob & His Son, Joseph. (Old Testament Ser.). 1.25 (ISBN 0-89985-129-0). Christ Nations.

--Jacob, The Supplanter Who Became a Prince with God. (Old Testament Ser.). 1.25 (ISBN 0-89985-128-2). Christ Nations.

--Jephthah & Samson. (Old Testament Ser.). 1.25 (ISBN 0-89985-136-3). Christ Nations.

--John Alexander Dowie: A Life of Tragedies & Triumphs. 1980. 4.95 (ISBN 0-89985-985-2). Christ Nations.

--John G. Lake: Apostle to Africa. 1.50 (ISBN 0-89985-011-1). Christ Nations.

--Joseph & His Brethren. (Old Testament Ser.). 1.25 (ISBN 0-89985-130-4). Christ Nations.

--Joshua, Conqueror of Canaan. (Old Testament Ser.). 1.25 (ISBN 0-89985-134-7). Christ Nations.

--The Last Days of David & His Contemporaries. (Old Testament Ser.). 1.25 (ISBN 0-89985-144-4). Christ Nations.

--Life & Teachings of Christ, Vol. 1. (Life of Christ & Parable Ser.). pap. 4.00 (ISBN 0-89985-967-4). Christ Nations.

--Life & Teachings of Christ, Vol. 2. (Life of Christ & Parable Ser.). pap. 4.00 (ISBN 0-89985-968-2). Christ Nations.

--Life & Teachings of Christ, Vol. 3. (Life of Christ & Parable Ser.). pap. 4.00 (ISBN 0-89985-969-0). Christ Nations.

--Lot & Lots Wife. (Old Testament Ser.: Vol. 4). pap. 1.25 (ISBN 0-89985-958-5). Christ Nations.

--The Minor Prophets: Hosea, Joel, Amos, Obadiah, Jonah, Micah. (Old Testament Ser.). 1.25 (ISBN 0-89985-156-8). Christ Nations.

--The Minor Prophets: Nahum, Habakkuk, Zephaniah, Haggai. Zechariah, Malachi. (Old Testament Ser.). 1.25 (ISBN 0-89985-157-6). Christ Nations.

--Moses & His Contemporaries. (Old Testament Ser.). 1.25 (ISBN 0-89985-133-9). Christ Nations.

--Moses & the Church in the Wilderness. (Old Testament Ser.). 1.25 (ISBN 0-89985-132-0). Christ Nations.

--Moses, The Deliverer. (Old Testament Ser.). 1.25 (ISBN 0-89985-131-2). Christ Nations.

--Moses the Lawgiver. (Old Testament Ser.: Vol. 10). pap. 1.25 (ISBN 0-89985-959-3). Christ Nations.

--Red China in Prophecy. (Prophecy Ser.). 1.25 (ISBN 0-89985-059-6). Christ Nations.

--The Revolution & After. (Old Testament Ser.). 1.25 (ISBN 0-89985-152-5). Christ Nations.

--Ruth, The Gleaner, & the Boy Samuel. (Old Testament Ser.). 1.25 (ISBN 0-89985-137-1). Christ Nations.

--Samuel, The Prophet. (Old Testament Ser.). 1.25 (ISBN 0-89985-138-X). Christ Nations.

--Saul & Jonathan. (Old Testament Ser.). 1.25 (ISBN 0-89985-140-1). Christ Nations.

--Saul, Israel's First King. (Old Testament Ser.). 1.25 (ISBN 0-89985-139-8). Christ Nations.

--Seven Keys to Triumphant Christian Living. 1.25 (ISBN 0-89985-006-5). Christ Nations.

--Should Christians Smoke? 1.00 o.p. (ISBN 0-89985-009-X). Christ Nations.

--Solomon & Rehoboam. (Old Testament Ser.). 1.25 (ISBN 0-89985-145-2). Christ Nations.

--Spiritual Hunger. 2.25 (ISBN 0-89985-020-0). Christ Nations.

--The Story of Adam & Eve. (Old Testament Ser.). 1.25 (ISBN 0-89985-124-X). Christ Nations.

--Will Our President Die in Office? (Prophecy Ser.). 1980. 2.25 (ISBN 0-89985-984-4). Christ Nations.

Lindsay, Ilse, tr. see Kolbe, Hartmut.

Lindsay, J. V., et al. Urban Crisis: A Symposium. LC 71-146555. (Symposia on Law & Society Ser). 1971. Repr. of 1969 ed. lib. bdg. 15.00 (ISBN 0-306-70115-4). Da Capo.

Lindsay, Jack. Crisis in Marxism. 1981. 22.50x (ISBN 0-389-20185-5). B&N.

--Thomas Gainsborough: His Life & Art. LC 80-54397. (Illus.). 248p. 1981. 25.00 (ISBN 0-87663-352-1, Pica Pr). Universe.

Lindsay, Jean. A History of the North Wales Slate Industry. 1974. 25.00 (ISBN 0-7153-6265-8). David & Charles.

--The Trent & Mersey Canal. LC 78-51089. (Illus.). 1979. 17.95 (ISBN 0-7153-7781-7). David & Charles.

Lindsay, Jeanne W. Pregnant Too Soon: Adoption Is an Option. LC 79-93356. (Illus.). 208p. (gr. 8-12). 1980. write for info. Morning Glory.

--Pregnant Too Soon: Adoption Is an Option. LC 79-93356. (Illus.). (gr. 7-12). 1980. pap. text ed. 5.95 (ISBN 0-88436-778-9); tchr's ed. avail. (ISBN 0-88436-780-0); wkbk. avail. (ISBN 0-88436-779-7). EMC.

--Teens Parenting: The Challenge of Babies & Toddlers. (Illus.). 320p. 1981. 14.95 (ISBN 0-930934-07-5); pap. 9.95 (ISBN 0-930934-06-7); price not set tchr's guide (ISBN 0-930934-09-1); wkbk. 2.50 (ISBN 0-930934-08-3). Morning Glory.

Lindsay, L. Brooks, jt. auth. see Simmons, W. T.

Lindsay, Maurice. History of Scottish Literature. 1977. 22.50 (ISBN 0-7091-5642-1). Dufour.

Lindsay, Merrill. The New England Gun: The First 200 Years. (Illus.). 190p. 1976. 20.00 o.p. (ISBN 0-679-50586-5); pap. 12.50 o.p. (ISBN 0-679-50621-7). McKay.

Lindsay, Michael. China & the Cold War: A Study in International Politics. LC 79-2834. 286p. 1981. Repr. of 1955 ed. 22.50 (ISBN 0-8305-0011-1). Hyperion Conn.

--The Unknown War: North China, 1937-1945. LC 76-54567. (Illus.). 1977. 10.00 (ISBN 0-8467-0260-6). Hippocrene Bks.

Lindsay, Noel, tr see Marczewski, Jan.

Lindsay, Norman, ed. see Bott, Ross, et al.

Lindsay, Oliver. At the Going Down of the Sun: Hong Kong & South East Asia, 1914-45. (Illus.). 250p. 1981. 25.00 (ISBN 0-241-10542-0, Pub. by Hamish Hamilton England). David & Charles.

--The Lasting Honour: The Fall of Hong Kong Nineteen Forty-One. (Illus.). Date not set. cancelled (ISBN 0-241-89946-X). Hippocrene Bks.

Lindsay, P. A. Introduction to Quantum Electronics. LC 75-15696. 202p. 1975. 27.95 (ISBN 0-470-53891-0). Halsted Pr.

Lindsay, Peter H. & Norman, Donald A. Human Information Processing: An Introduction to Psychology. 2nd ed. 1977. 18.95 (ISBN 0-12-450960-6); test bklet. avail. Acad Pr.

Lindsay, R. B. Julius Robert Mayer, Prophet of Energy. LC 72-8045. (Men of Physics Ser.). 1973. 22.00 (ISBN 0-08-016985-6). Pergamon.

--Lord Rayleigh, the Man & His Work. LC 79-94934. (Men of Physics Ser.). 1970. 23.00 (ISBN 0-08-006821-9); pap. 11.25 (ISBN 0-08-006820-0). Pergamon.

Lindsay, R. Bruce, ed. Physical Acoustics. (Benchmark Papers in Acoustics Ser). 480p. 1974. 44.50 (ISBN 0-12-786964-6). Acad Pr.

Lindsay, R. K., et al. Applications of Artificial Intelligence for Organic Chemistry: The Dendral Project. (Artificial Intelligence Ser.). (Illus.). 208p. 1980. text ed. 35.00 (ISBN 0-07-037895-9, C). McGraw.

Lindsay, Rachel. Love & No Marriage. (Harlequin Presents Ser.). 192p. 1980. pap. 1.50 (ISBN 0-373-10381-6, Pub. by Harlequin). PB.

--Rent a Wife. (Harlequin Presents Ser.). 192p. 1980. pap. 1.50 (ISBN 0-373-10375-1, Pub. by Harlequin). PB.

--Wife for a Year. (Harlequin Presents Ser.). 192p. (Orig.). 1981. pap. 1.50 (ISBN 0-373-10413-8, Pub. by Harlequin). PB.

Lindsay, Rae. How to Look As Young As You Feel. (Illus.). 320p. 1980. pap. 2.50 o.p. (ISBN 0-523-40843-9). Pinnacle Bks.

--The Left-Handed Book. (gr. 4 up). 1980. PLB 6.45 (ISBN 0-531-02258-7). Watts.

--Sleep & Dreams. LC 78-5519. (First Bks.). (Illus.). (gr. 4-6). 1978. PLB 6.45 s&l (ISBN 0-531-01493-2). Watts.

Lindsay, Ray, jt. auth. see Michael, George.

Lindsay, Robert B. Nature of Physics: A Physicist's Views on the History & Philosophy of His Science. LC 68-10642. 212p. 1971. Repr. of 1968 ed. 10.00 (ISBN 0-87057-107-9, Pub. by Brown U Pr). Univ Pr of New England.

Lindsay, Robert O. & Neu, John. Mazarinades: A Checklist of Copies in Major Collections in the United States. LC 74-150720. 1972. 20.50 (ISBN 0-8108-0369-0). Scarecrow.

Lindsay, Robert O. & Neu, John, eds. French Political Pamphlets, Fifteen Forty-Seven to Sixteen Forty-Eight: A Catalog of Major Collections in American Libraries. LC 78-84953. 1969. 35.00 (ISBN 0-299-04990-6). U of Wis Pr.

Lindsay, T. M. Acts, Vol. 2, Chapts. 13-28. (Handbooks for Bible Classes). 165p. 1950. text ed. 3.50 (ISBN 0-567-08117-6). Attic Pr.

--History of the Reformation: In Germany, Vol. 1. 2nd ed. (International Theological Library). 544p. 1907. text ed. 13.95x. Attic Pr.

--History of the Reformation: In Lands Beyond Germany, Vol. 2. 2nd ed. (International Theological Library). 648p. 1908. text ed. 13.95x (ISBN 0-567-07212-6). Attic Pr.

--The Reformation. (Handbooks for Bible Classes). 224p. 1977. text ed. 8.95. Attic Pr.

Lindsay, Thomas. History of the Reformation, 2 vols. Repr. 48.00 o.p. (ISBN 0-686-12348-4). Church History.

--Plant Names. LC 75-16423. viii, 93p. 1976. Repr. of 1923 ed. 18.00 (ISBN 0-8103-4160-3). Gale.

Lindsay, Vachel. Collected Poems. rev. ed. (Illus.). 1925. 17.50 (ISBN 0-02-572530-0). Macmillan.

Lindsay, W. M., ed. see Plautus.

Lindsay, W. M., ed. see Terence.

Lindsay, Willard L. Chemical Equilibria in Soils. LC 79-12151. 1979. 28.95 (ISBN 0-471-02704-9, Pub. by Wiley-Interscience). Wiley.

Lindsay, William L. Mind in the Lower Animal in Health & Disease. (Contributions to the History of Psychology Ser.: Pts. 6 & 7, Comparative Psychology). 1980. Repr. of 1879 ed. 30.00 ea. U Pubns Amer.

Lindsell, Harold. God's Incomparable Word. 1978. pap. 2.95 (ISBN 0-88207-774-0). Victor Bks.

Lindsey, Bonnie J. The Administrative Medical Assistant. 184p. 1979. pap. text ed. 9.95 (ISBN 0-87619-435-8). R J Brady.

--Clinical Medical Assistant. (Illus.). 169p. (Orig.). 1980. pap. text ed. 9.95 (ISBN 0-87619-714-4). R J Brady.

Lindsey, David. Americans in Conflict: The Civil War & Reconstruction. 208p. 1974. pap. text ed. 7.75 (ISBN 0-395-14068-4, 3-33320). HM.

Lindsey, Dawn. Victory Summer. 304p. 1981. pap. 2.25 (ISBN 0-553-13647-X). Bantam.

Lindsey, Forrest R. Pipefitters Handbook. 3rd ed. (Illus.). 1967. text ed. 15.00 (ISBN 0-8311-3019-9). Indus Pr.

Lindsey, Hal. The Events That Changed My Life. 1977. pap. 0.98 o.s.i. (ISBN 0-88449-026-2). Vision Hse.

--Late Great Planet Earth. 1976. pap. 2.50 mass market (ISBN 0-310-27772-8); pap. 4.95 (ISBN 0-310-27771-X); study guide 0.75 (ISBN 0-310-27773-6). Zondervan.

--The Liberation of Planet Earth. 244p. 1974. pap. 5.95 (ISBN 0-310-27721-3, 18193P); pap. 3.95 mass market (ISBN 0-310-27722-1); study guide 0.75 (ISBN 0-310-27723-X). Zondervan.

--The Nineteen Eighties Countdown to Armageddon. 192p. 1981. pap. 6.92 (ISBN 0-553-01303-3). Bantam.

--The World's Final Hour: Evacuation or Extinction? Orig. Title: Homo Sapiens. 1976. pap. 1.25 (ISBN 0-310-27732-9). Zondervan.

Lindsey, Hal & Carlson, C. C. The Late Great Planet Earth. 176p. 1980. pap. 2.50. Zondervan.

--The Late Great Planet Earth. 192p. 1980. pap. 2.50 (ISBN 0-553-14096-5). Bantam.

--Satan Is Alive & Well on Planet Earth. large print ed. 1974. kivar 4.95 o.p. (ISBN 0-310-27797-3). Zondervan.

--The Terminal Generation. 1976. pap. 1.95 o.p. (ISBN 0-8007-8305-0, Spire Bks). Revell.

Lindsey, J. P. & Gilbertson, R. L. Basidiomycetes That Decay Aspen in North America. (Bibliotheca Mycologica Ser.: No. 63). 1978. lib. bdg. 60.00 (ISBN 3-7682-1193-2). Lubrecht & Cramer.

Lindsey, Jon. Accounts for the Year. 1981. 8.95 (ISBN 0-533-04793-5). Vantage.

Lindsey, Karen. Falling off the Roof. LC 75-21788. 72p. 1975. pap. 4.95 (ISBN 0-914086-08-1). Alicejamesbooks.

Lindsey, M., jt. auth. see Stratemeyer, Florence B.

Lindsey, Robert. The Falcon & the Snowman: A True Story of Friendship & Espionage. 1980. pap. 2.95 (ISBN 0-671-41160-8). PB.

Lindsey, William C. & Simon, Marvin K. Telecommunication Systems Engineering. (Illus.). 672p. 1972. ref. ed. 32.95 (ISBN 0-13-902429-8). P-H.

Lindskold, Svern, jt. auth. see Tedeschi, James T.

Lindskoog, Kathryn. A Partir del Eden. Orozco, Julio, tr. from Eng. LC 77-73843. 144p. (Orig., Span.). 1977. pap. 2.50 (ISBN 0-89922-092-4). Edit Caribe.

Lindskoog, Kay. C. S. Lewis: Mere Christian. rev. ed. 192p. 1981. pap. 5.95 (ISBN 0-87784-466-6). Inter-Varsity.
Lindsley, E. F. Welding, Brazing & Soldering. LC 77-26479. (Illus.). 1980. pap. 4.95 (ISBN 0-06-090723-1, CN 723, CN). Har-Row.
Lindstrom, Aletha J. Sojourner Truth: Slave, Abolitionist, Fighter for Women's Rights. LC 79-25576. (Illus.). 128p. (gr. 4-6). 1980. PLB 7.79 (ISBN 0-671-32988-X). Messner.
Lindstrom, Diane. Economic Change in the Philadelphia Region, 1810-1850. LC 77-23582. 1978. 17.50x (ISBN 0-231-04272-8). Columbia U Pr.
Lindstrom, Miriam. Children's Art: A Study of Normal Development in Children's Modes of Visualization. LC 57-10499. (Illus.). 1957. 10.00 o.p. (ISBN 0-520-01441-3); pap. 3.95 (ISBN 0-520-00752-2, CAL8). U of Cal Pr.
Lindstrom, Stephen E. Death on a Birthday Morning. 1977. 8.95 o.p. (ISBN 0-533-02709-8). Vantage.
Lindstrom, Talbot S. & Tighe, Kevin P. Antitrust Consent Decrees, 2 vols. LC 74-76323. 1974. Set. 94.00 (ISBN 0-686-14482-1). Lawyers Co-Op.
Lindstrom, Thais. A Concise History of Russian Literature, Vol. 1: From the Beginnings to Chekhov. LC 66-22218. (Gotham Library). (Orig.). 1966. 12.50x (ISBN 0-8147-0260-0); pap. 6.00x (ISBN 0-8147-0261-9). NYU Pr.
Lindstrom, Thais S. A Concise History of Russian Literature, Vol. 2: 1900 to the Present. LC 77-14671. 1979. 17.50x (ISBN 0-8147-4980-1); pap. 8.00x (ISBN 0-8147-4981-X). NYU Pr.
--Nikolay Gogol. (World Authors Ser.: Russia: No. 299). 1974. lib. bdg. 12.50 (ISBN 0-8057-2377-3). Twayne.
Linduff, Katheryn M. Tradition, Phase & Style of Shang & Chow Bronze Vessels. LC 77-94705. (Outstanding Dissertations in the Fine Arts Ser.). (Illus.). 254p. 1980. lib. bdg. 27.50 (ISBN 0-8240-3237-3). Garland Pub.
Lindwall, Ted. Poder Espiritual. 1978. Repr. of 1977 ed. 0.60 (ISBN 0-311-46068-2). Casa Bautista.
Lindzey, Gardner. A History of Psychology in Autobiography, Vol. 6. 480p. 1974. Repr. text ed. 21.95 (ISBN 0-13-392274-X). P-H.
--Projective Techniques & Cross-Cultural Research. LC 61-15951. (Century Psychology Ser.). 1976. 24.00x (ISBN 0-89197-361-3); pap. text ed. 10.95x (ISBN 0-89197-908-5). Irvington.
Lindzey, Gardner, jt. auth. see Hall, Calvin S.
Lindzey, Gardner, ed. A History of Psychology in Autobiography, Vol. VII. LC 30-20129. (A Series of Books in Psychology). (Illus.). 1980. text ed. 24.95x (ISBN 0-7167-1119-2); pap. text ed. 15.95x (ISBN 0-7167-1120-6). W H Freeman.
Lindzey, Gardner & Thiessen, Delbert D., eds. Contributions to Behavior - Genetic Analysis. LC 73-92661. (Century Psychology Ser). 1970. 28.00x (ISBN 0-89197-109-2); pap. text ed. 8.95x (ISBN 0-89197-110-6). Irvington.
Lindzey, Gardner, et al. Psychology. 2nd ed. LC 77-86622. (Illus.). 1978. 18.95x (ISBN 0-87901-089-4); study guide 6.95x (ISBN 0-87901-090-8). Worth.
Lindzey, Gardner, et al, eds. Theories of Personality: Primary Sources & Research. 2nd ed. LC 72-6983. 512p. 1973. pap. text ed. 17.95x (ISBN 0-471-53901-5). Wiley.
Line, Francis & Line, Helen. Our Road to Prayer. (Prayer in My Life Ser.: Ser. I). 1974. pap. 1.00x (ISBN 0-8358-0305-8). Upper Room.
Line, Helen, jt. auth. see Line, Francis.
Line, Les, ed. The Pleasure of Birds: An Audubon Treasury. LC 75-17948. (Illus.). 240p. 1975. 14.95 o.p. (ISBN 0-397-01065-6). Lippincott.
Line, Walter C. News Writing for Non-Professionals. LC 78-20771. 1979. 12.95 (ISBN 0-88229-348-6). Nelson-Hall.
Lineaweaver, Thomas H., 3rd & Backus, Richard H. Natural History of Sharks. LC 75-109174. (Illus.). 1970. 9.95 (ISBN 0-397-00660-8). Lippincott.
Lineback, Neal G. Laboratory Manual in Physical Geography. 2nd ed. 1976. pap. text ed. 7.95 (ISBN 0-8403-1089-7). Kendall-Hunt.
Lineback, Richard H. Ethics: A Bibliography. LC 76-24747. (Reference Library of the Humanities Ser.: Vol. 65). 1976. lib. bdg. 25.00 o.p. (ISBN 0-8240-9933-8). Garland Pub.
Linebarger, J. M. John Berryman. (U. S. Authors Ser.: No. 244). 1974. lib. bdg. 10.95 (ISBN 0-8057-0054-4). Twayne.
Lineberry, William P. Priorities for Survival. (Reference Shelf Ser: Vol. 44, No. 6). 223p. 1972. 6.25 (ISBN 0-8242-0469-7). Wilson.
Lineberry, William P., ed. American Colleges: The Uncertain Future. (Reference Shelf Ser: Vol. 47, No. 3). 1975. 6.25 (ISBN 0-8242-0571-5). Wilson.
--Business of Sports. (Reference Shelf Ser.). 1973. 6.25 (ISBN 0-8242-0506-5). Wilson.
--Colleges at the Crossroads. (Reference Shelf Ser: Vol. 37, No. 6). 1966. 6.25 (ISBN 0-8242-0088-8). Wilson.
--East Africa. (Reference Shelf Ser: Vol. 40, No. 2). 1968. 6.25 (ISBN 0-8242-0101-9). Wilson.
--Justice in America. (Reference Shelf Ser: Vol. 44, No. 1). 200p. 1972. 6.25 (ISBN 0-8242-0464-6). Wilson.
--Mass Communications. (Reference Shelf Ser: Vol. 41, No. 3). 1969. 6.25 (ISBN 0-8242-0108-6). Wilson.
--The Struggle Against Terrorism. (Reference Shelf Ser.). 1977. 6.25 (ISBN 0-8242-0605-3). Wilson.
Linecar, Howard. An Advanced Guide to Coin Collecting. (Illus.). 1970. 9.95 o.p. (ISBN 0-7207-0224-0, Pub. by Michael Joseph). Merrimack Bk Serv.
--Beginner's Guide to Coin Collecting. 9.95 (ISBN 0-7207-0015-9). Transatlantic.
--Observer's Book of Coins. (Observer Bks.). (Illus.). 1977. 4.95 (ISBN 0-684-15207-X, ScribT). Scribner.
Linecar, Howard A. The Commemorative Medal: Its Appreciation & Collection. LC 72-12989. (Illus.). 250p. 1974. 16.00 (ISBN 0-8103-2012-6). Gale.
Linedecker, Cliff, jt. auth. see Yance, Becky.
Linedecker, Cliff, jt. auth. see Yancy, Becky.
Linedecker, Clifford L. The Man Who Killed Boys. 1980. 10.00 (ISBN 0-312-51157-4). St Martin.
Linehan, Peter. Spanish Church & the Papacy in the Thirteenth Century. LC 75-154505. (Studies in Medieval Life & Thought, Third Ser: No. 4). (Illus.). 1971. 46.95 (ISBN 0-521-08039-8). Cambridge U Pr.
Linehan, Peter, jt. ed. see Tierney, Brian.
Lines, James. Beyond the Balance Sheet: Evaluating Profit Potential. LC 74-5512. 1974. 18.95 (ISBN 0-470-53906-2). Halsted Pr.
--The Role of the Chief Executive. 172p. 1978. text ed. 24.50x (ISBN 0-220-66355-6, Pub. by Busn Bks England). Renouf.
Lines, Kathleen. The Faber Storybook. (Illus.). (ps-5). 1972. pap. 3.95 o.p. (ISBN 0-571-10176-3, Pub. by Faber & Faber). Merrimack Bk Serv.
Lines, Kathleen, ed. Faber Book of Greek Legends. 1973. 9.95 (ISBN 0-571-09830-4, Pub. by Faber & Faber). Merrimack Bk Serv.
Lines, Kathleen, ed. see Uttley, Alison.
Linesberry, Robert L. & Masotti, Louis H., eds. Urban Problems & Public Policy. (Policy Studies Organization Ser.). 192p. 1975. 19.95 (ISBN 0-669-00017-5). Lexington Bks.
Linet, Beverly. Susan Hayward: Portrait of a Survivor. LC 80-66003. 1980. 12.95 (ISBN 0-686-68614-4). Atheneum.
Linfante, Michele see Foster, Rick.
Linfert, Carl. Bosch. LC 71-149853. (Library Great Painters Ser). (Illus.). 136p. 1971. 35.00 (ISBN 0-8109-0043-2). Abrams.
Linfield, Esther, tr. see Hobson, Sam B. & Hobson, George.
Linfield, Jordon L., jt. auth. see Kreivsky, Joseph.
Linfoot, John A., ed. Recent Advances in the Diagnosis & Treatment of Pituitary Tumors. LC 78-64817. 1979. text ed. 44.50 (ISBN 0-89004-365-5). Raven.
Ling, Agnes H., jt. auth. see Ling, Daniel.
Ling, Daniel & Ling, Agnes H. Aural Habilitation: The Foundations of Verbal Learning in Hearing-Impaired Children. 1978. 12.50 (ISBN 0-88200-121-3). Bell Assn Deaf.
Ling, Dwight L. Morocco & Tunisia: A Comparative History. LC 79-5364. 1979. pap. text ed. 9.50 (ISBN 0-8191-0873-1). U Pr of Amer.
Ling, Robert F. & Roberts, Harry V. Users Manual for IDA. (Data Analysis Ser.). 300p. 1980. pap. text ed. 12.50 (ISBN 0-07-037905-X, C). McGraw.
Ling, Trevor. Buddha, Marx & God: Some Aspects of Religion in the Modern World. 2nd ed. 1979. 25.00 (ISBN 0-685-62341-6). St Martin.
--Buddhism. (Living Religions Series). (Illus.). 1976. pap. 3.50x (ISBN 0-7062-3594-0). Intl Pubns Serv.
--Buddhist Revival in India: Aspects of the Sociology of Buddhism. LC 79-20167. 1980. 22.50x (ISBN 0-312-10681-5). St Martin.
Lingard, Joan. Across the Barricades. LC 72-8915. 160p. (gr. 7 up). 1973. 7.95 o.p. (ISBN 0-525-66280-4). Elsevier-Nelson.
--The Clearance. LC 74-1289. 160p. (gr. 7 up). 1974. 6.95 o.p. (ISBN 0-525-66400-9). Elsevier-Nelson.
--Greenyards. 396p. 1981. 12.95 (ISBN 0-399-12513-2). Putnam.
--A Proper Place. LC 75-6591. (gr. 6 up). 1975. 7.95 o.p. (ISBN 0-525-66425-4). Elsevier-Nelson.
Lingat, Robert. The Classical Law of India. Derrett, J. Duncan, tr. from Fr. LC 76-81798. Orig. Title: Sources Du Droit Dans le Systeme Traditionnel De L'inde. 1973. 25.00x (ISBN 0-520-01898-2). U of Cal Pr.
Linge, G. J., jt. auth. see Hamilton, F. E.
Lingeman, Richard R. Drugs from A to Z: A Dictionary. 2nd ed. (McGraw-Hill Paperbacks). 320p. (Orig.). 1974. text ed. 4.95 (ISBN 0-07-037913-0, SP); pap. 3.95 (ISBN 0-07-037912-2). McGraw.
Lingenberg, Rolf. Metric Planes & Metric Vector Spaces. LC 78-21906. (Pure & Applied Mathematics: Texts, Monographs & Tracts). 1979. 25.50 (ISBN 0-471-04901-8, Pub. by Wiley-Interscience). Wiley.
Lingenfelter, Mary R. & Kitson, Harry D. Vocations for Girls. rev. ed. LC 39-22231. (gr. 7 up). 1951. 5.95 o.p. (ISBN 0-15-294096-0, HJ). HarBraceJ.
Lingens, Barbara, jt. auth. see Lingens, Hans G.
Lingens, Hans G. & Lingens, Barbara. Education in West Germany: A Quest for Excellence. LC 79-93116. (Fastback Ser.: No. 140). (Orig.). 1980. pap. 0.75 (ISBN 0-87367-140-6). Phi Delta Kappa.
Linger, R. C., et al. Structured Programming: Theory & Practice. LC 78-18641. 1979. text ed. 19.95 (ISBN 0-201-14461-1). A-W.
Lingertwood, Kenneth. Huntsman of Our Time. 15.00x (ISBN 0-392-07938-0, SpS). Soccer.
Lingle, Walter L. & Kuykendall, John W. Presbyterians: Their History & Beliefs. LC 77-15750. 1978. pap. 4.50 (ISBN 0-8042-0985-5). John Knox.
Lingren, Wesley E. Inorganic Nomenclature: A Programmed Approach. (Illus.). 1980. pap. text ed. 8.95 (ISBN 0-13-466607-0). P-H.
Lings, Martin. A Sufi Saint of the Twentieth Century: Shaikh Ahmad al-'Alawi, His Spiritual Heritage & Legacy. (Illus.). 242p. 1972. 17.50x (ISBN 0-520-02174-6); pap. 4.95 (ISBN 0-520-02486-9). U of Cal Pr.
Lingua Press. Lingua Press Collection Three Catalogue, Vol. 3. Gaburo, Kenneth, ed. (Illus.). 150p. 1981. softcover 8.50. Lingua Pr.
--Lingua Press Collection Two Catalogue, Vol. 2. Gaburo, Kenneth, ed. 132p. 1978. soft cover 3.95. Lingua Pr.
Linguet, S. N. H. Du Plus Heureux Gouvernement...Servant D'introduction a la Theorie Des Loix Civiles. (Fr.). 1977. Repr. of 1774 ed. lib. bdg. 41.25x o.p. (ISBN 0-8287-0548-8). Clearwater Pub.
Linguistic Association of Canada & the U.S. The First LACUS Forum: Proceedings. Makkai, Adam & Makki, Valerie, eds. pap. text ed. 10.95 (ISBN 0-685-69725-8). Hornbeam Pr.
--The Second LACUS Forum: Proceedings. Reich, Peter A., ed. pap. text ed. 10.95 (ISBN 0-685-69722-3). Hornbeam Pr.
--Third LACUS Forum: Proceedings. Di Pietro, Robert J. & Blansitt, Edward L., Jr., eds. pap. text ed. 10.95 (ISBN 0-685-82432-2). Hornbeam Pr.
Lingwood, Rex. Leather in Three Dimensions. 144p. 1980. pap. 12.95 (ISBN 0-442-29733-5). Van Nos Reinhold.
Ling Yu. Cooking the Chinese Way. (Easy Menu Ethnic Cookooks). (Illus.). (YA) (gr. 5 up). 1981. PLB 4.95g (ISBN 0-8225-0902-4). Lerner Pubns.
Linh, Tran C., jt. auth. see Dam, Nguyen C.
Linhart, Robert. The Asssembly Line. Rosland, Margaret, tr. from Fr. Orig. Title: L'Etabli. 144p. (Orig.). 1981. pap. text ed. 6.95x (ISBN 0-87023-322-X). U of Mass Pr.
Liniger-Goumaz, Max. Historical Dictionary of Equatorial Guinea. LC 79-15914. (African Historical Dictionaries Ser.: No. 21). 246p. 1979. 13.00 (ISBN 0-8108-1230-4). Scarecrow.
Linington, Elizabeth. Perchance of Death. LC 76-52221. 1977. 6.95 o.p. (ISBN 0-385-13081-3). Doubleday.
Link, A. Anything Book. 1981. 28.50 o.p. (ISBN 0-686-68301-3). Porter.
Link, Albert N. Research & Development in U.S. Manufacturing. 124p. 1981. 18.95 (ISBN 0-03-057677-6). Praeger.
Link, Arthur S., jt. ed. see Leary, William M., Jr.
Link, Arthur S., ed. see Wilson, Woodrow.
Link, Arthur S., et al. The American People: A History. (Illus.). 1008p. 1981. text ed. 16.95 (ISBN 0-88295-804-6); Vol. I. pap. text ed. 8.95 (ISBN 0-88295-805-4); Vol. II. pap. text ed. 8.95 (ISBN 0-88295-806-2). AHM Pub.
Link, Arthur S., et al, eds. The Papers of Woodrow Wilson: Vol. 34, July-September, 1915. LC 66-10880. (Illus.). 1980. 30.00x (ISBN 0-691-04673-5). Princeton U Pr.
--The Papers of Woodrow Wilson, Vol. 36: January-May, 1916. LC 66-10880. (Illus.). 648p. 1981. 30.00x (ISBN 0-691-04682-4). Princeton U Pr.
--The Papers of Woodrow Wilson: Volume 35, October 1915 to January 1916. LC 66-10880. (Illus.). 568p. 1981. 30.00 (ISBN 0-691-04676-X). Princeton U Pr.
Link, David E., ed. Residential Designs: How to Get the Most for Your Housing Dollar. LC 73-76442. 1972. 15.95 o.p. (ISBN 0-8436-0116-7). CBI Pub.
Link, Frederick M., ed. English Drama, Sixteen Sixty-Eighteen Hundred: A Guide to Information Sources. LC 73-16984. (American Literature English Literature & World Literatures in English Information Guide Ser.: Vol.9). 360p. 1976. 30.00 (ISBN 0-8103-1224-7). Gale.
Link, Frederick M. & Backscheider, Paula R., eds. The Plays of Hannah Cowley, 2 vols. LC 78-66646. (Eighteenth-Century English Drama Ser.: Vol. 12). 1980. Set. lib. bdg. 100.00 (ISBN 0-8240-3586-0); lib. bdg. 50.00 ea. Garland Pub.
Link, Frederick M., ed. see Behn, Aphra.
Link, Frederick M., ed. see Dryden, John.
Link, Frederick M., ed. see Scott, Sir Walter.
Link, Howard A., et al. Primitve Ukiyo-E: From the James A. Michener Collection in the Honolulu Academy of Arts. LC 79-6397. (Illus.). 384p. 1980. 55.00 (ISBN 0-8248-0483-X). U Pr of Hawaii.
Link, Irene, jt. auth. see Farnham, Rebecca.
Link, Mark. The Seventh Trumpet. 1978. 6.95 (ISBN 0-89505-014-5). Argus Comm.
Link, Martin, jt. auth. see Blood, Charles L.
Link, Perry. Mandarin Ducks & Butterflies: Popular Fiction in the Early Twentieth-Century Chinese Cities. (Illus.). 352p. 1981. 20.00x (ISBN 0-520-04111-9). U of Cal Pr.
Link, Richard F., jt. auth. see Koch, George S., Jr.
Link, Werner & Feld, Werner J., eds. The New Nationalism: Implications for Transatlantic Relations. new ed. LC 78-17144. (Pergamon Policy Studies). 1979. text ed. 19.25 (ISBN 0-08-023370-8); pap. text ed. 7.95 (ISBN 0-08-023369-4). Pergamon.
Link, William, jt. auth. see Levinson, Richard.
Linke, Frances. Space Patrol III. (Space Patrol Ser.: No. 3). 205p. 20.00 (ISBN 0-933276-06-0). Nin-Ra Ent.
--Space Patrol III. Linke, Ray, ed. (Illus.). 205p. 1980. 25.00 (ISBN 0-933276-07-9). Nin-Ra Ent.
Linke, Ray, ed. see Linke, Frances.
Linke, Russell. Environmental Education in Australia. 300p. 1980. text ed. 17.50x (ISBN 0-86861-361-4, 2339). Allen Unwin.
Linkhart, Luther. The Sawtooth National Recreation Area. Winnett, Thomas, ed. LC 79-57594. (Illus., Orig.). 1981. pap. 9.95 (ISBN 0-911824-96-0). Wilderness.
Linklater, Andro, jt. auth. see Linklater, Eric.
Linklater, Eric. God Likes Them Plain. LC 79-53455. (Short Story Index in Reprint Ser.). Date not set. Repr. of 1935 ed. 24.50x (ISBN 0-8486-5009-3). Core Collection. Postponed.
--Orkney & Shetland: An Historical, Geographical, Social & Scenic Survey. 3rd ed. Nicolson, James R., rev. by. (Illus.). 285p. 1980. 20.00x (ISBN 0-7091-8142-6). Intl Pubns Serv.
--Stories of Eric Linklater. LC 76-85336. 1969. 6.50 o.p. (ISBN 0-8180-0602-1). Horizon.
Linklater, Eric & Linklater, Andro. The Black Watch: The History of the Royal Highland Regiment. (Illus.). 1979. 19.95 o.p. (ISBN 0-214-20083-3, 8087-6, Dist. by Arco). Barrie & Jenkins.
Linklater, Kristin & Florian, Douglas. Freeing the Natural Voice. LC 75-28172. (Illus.). 1976. text ed. 12.50x (ISBN 0-910482-67-5). Drama Bk.
Linkletter, Art & Gallup, George, Jr. My Child on Drugs? Youth & the Drug Culture. (Orig.). 1981. pap. 3.50 (ISBN 0-87239-456-5, 5015). Standard Pub.
Linko, P., et al, eds. Food Process Engineering: Vol. 1 Food Processing Systems. (Illus.). xii, 981p. 1980. 210.00x (ISBN 0-85334-896-0). Burgess-Intl Ideas.
--Food Process Engineering: Volume 2--Enzyme Engineering in Food Processing. (Illus.). vii, 328p. 1980. 75.00x (ISBN 0-85334-897-9). Burgess-Intl Ideas.
Links, J. G. Canaletto & His Patrons. LC 76-39696. (Illus.). 1977. 25.00x, cusa (ISBN 0-8147-4975-5). NYU Pr.
--The Ruskins in Normandy: A Tour in 1848 with Murrays Handbook. LC 78-134669. (Illus.). Date not set. 6.95 (ISBN 0-8149-0689-3). Vanguard. Postponed.
--Venice for Pleasure. (Illus.). 1968. 7.50 o.p. (ISBN 0-8023-1136-9). Dufour.
Links, J. G., ed. see Constable, W. G.
Links, Jay, jt. auth. see Wheatley, Dennis.
Linn, Bill. Missing in Action. 224p. (Orig.). 1981. pap. 2.25 (ISBN 0-380-77370-8, 77370). Avon.
Linn, Charles F. Estimation. LC 75-106574. (Young Math Ser.). (Illus.). (gr. 1-4). 1970. PLB 6.89 o.p. (ISBN 0-690-27028-3, TYC-J); filmstrip with record 12.85 o.p. (ISBN 0-690-27029-1); filmstrip with cassette 15.85 o.p. (ISBN 0-690-27031-3). T Y Crowell.
--Estimation. LC 75-106574. (Crocodile Paperbacks Ser.). (Illus.). 40p. (gr. 1-4). 1972. pap. 1.45 o.p. (ISBN 0-690-27033-X, TYC-J). T Y Crowell.

--Probability. LC 79-171006. (Young Math Ser.). (Illus.). 40p. (gr. 1-4). 1972. PLB 7.89 (ISBN 0-690-65602-5, TYC-J). T Y Crowell.

Linn, Dennis & Linn, Matthew. Healing Life's Hurts. LC 77-14794. 1978. 7.95 (ISBN 0-8091-0231-5); pap. 4.95 (ISBN 0-8091-2059-3). Paulist Pr.

Linn, Edward, jt. auth. see Sutton, Willie.

Linn, Jo W. People Named Hanes. LC 80-52426. (Illus.). 300p. 1980. 25.00 (ISBN 0-918470-12-9). J W Linn.

Linn, Jo W. & Gray, Gordon. The Gray Family & Allied Lines. LC 76-42358. (Illus.). 1976. 27.50 (ISBN 0-918470-01-3). J W Linn.

Linn, Louis C. Eastern North America's Wildflowers: A Full-Color Guide of 373 Life-Size Paintings for Easy Flower Identification. 1978. pap. 9.95 o.p. (ISBN 0-87690-262-X). Dutton.

Linn, Matthew, jt. auth. see Linn, Dennis.

Linn, Patricia. I Can Wait. (Orig.). 1980. pap. 2.25 (ISBN 0-505-51526-1). Tower Bks.

Linn, Robert. Basic Training for the Second Half of Life. 1980. pap. write for info. PB.

Linn, Rolf N. Schillers Junge Idealisten. (U. C. Publ. in Modern Philology: Vol. 106). 1973. 8.00 (ISBN 0-520-09429-8). U of Cal Pr.

Linn, W. A. Horace Greeley. LC 80-26831. (American Men & Women of Letters Ser.). 275p. 1981. pap. 4.95 (ISBN 0-87754-165-5). Chelsea Hse.

Linn, William A. Horace Greeley. (American Newspapermen 1790-1933 Ser.). (Illus.). xiii, 267p. 1974. Repr. of 1903 ed. 16.00x o.s.i. (ISBN 0-8464-0015-4). Beekman Pubs.

Linnaeus, Carl von. Carl von Linnaeus's Plants. Black, David, ed. (Encore Edition). (Illus.). 1979. pap. 4.95 (ISBN 0-684-16821-9, ScribT). Scribner.

Linneaweaver, Charles. First Book of Canada. rev. ed. LC 67-17788. (First Bks). (Illus.). (gr. 4-6). 1967. PLB 4.90 o.p. (ISBN 0-531-00495-3). Watts.

Linneman, R. Shirt Sleeve Approach to Long Range Planning for the Smaller Growing Corporation. 1980. 15.95 (ISBN 0-13-808972-8). P-H.

Linneman, William R. Richard Hovey. (U. S. Authors Ser.: No. 263). 1976. lib. bdg. 10.95 (ISBN 0-8057-7162-X). Twayne.

Linney, et al. Southern Directions: Gallimaufry 15. MacArthur, Mary & Crone, Moira, eds. Date not set. pap. cancelled (ISBN 0-916300-19-6). Gallimaufry.

Linney, Romulus. Jesus Tales, a Novel. 208p. 1980. 10.00 (ISBN 0-86547-020-0). N Point Pr.

Linnik, Ju. V. Dispersion Method in Binary Additive Problems. LC 63-15660. (Translations of Mathematical Monographs: Vol. 4). 1979. Repr. of 1963 ed. 17.60 (ISBN 0-8218-1554-7, MMONO-4). Am Math.

Linowes, R. Robert & Allensworth, Don T. The States & Land-Use Control. LC 75-3624. (Special Studies). (Illus.). 262p. 1975. text ed. 27.95 (ISBN 0-275-05210-9). Praeger.

Lins, David A., jt. auth. see Penson, John B., Jr.

Linscott, William D. Linscotts Catalog of Immunological & Biological Reagents. 112p. (Orig.). 1979. 20.00 (ISBN 0-9604920-0-3). W D Linscott.

Linsdale, Jean M. & Tevis, Lloyd P., Jr. The Dusky-Footed Wood Rat: A Record of Observations Made on the Hastings Natural History Reservation. (Illus.). 1951. 25.00x (ISBN 0-520-00754-9). U of Cal Pr.

Linskill, Joseph, ed. The Poems of the Troubadour Raimbaut De Vaqueiras. LC 80-2190. 1981. Repr. of 1964 ed. 45.00 (ISBN 0-404-19014-6). AMS Pr.

Linsley, E. G. & MacSwain, J. W. Nesting Biology & Associates of Melitoma (Hymenoptera, Anthrophoridae) (U. C. Publications in Entomolgy: Vol. 90). 1980. pap. 6.00 (ISBN 0-520-09618-5). U of Cal Pr.

Linsley, E. G., et al. Comparative Behavior of Bees & Onagraceae. V. Camissonia & Oenothera Bees of Cismontane California. (U. C. Publ. in Entomology: Vol. 71). 1973. pap. 8.50x (ISBN 0-520-09474-3). U of Cal Pr.

Linsley, E. Gorton, jt. auth. see Hurd, Paul D., Jr.

Linsley, Leslie. Decoupage: A New Look at an Old Craft. LC 73-168290. (Illus.). 160p. 1972. pap. 3.95 o.p. (ISBN 0-385-08863-9). Doubleday.

--Decoupage for Young Crafters. (Illus.). (gr. 1-5). 1977. PLB 7.95 (ISBN 0-525-28614-4). Dutton.

--Scrimshaw: A Traditional Folk Art, a Contemporary Craft. (Illus.). 1979. pap. 6.95 (ISBN 0-8015-6609-6, Hawthorn). Dutton.

Linstone, Harold A. & Simmonds, W. H., eds. Futures Research: New Directions. 1977. text ed. 25.50 (ISBN 0-201-04096-4, Adv Bk Prog). A-W.

Linstone, Harold A. & Turoff, Murray, eds. Delphi Method: Techniques & Applications. LC 75-25650. 672p. 1975. text ed. 35.50 (ISBN 0-201-04294-0, Adv Bk Prog); pap. text ed. 21.50 (ISBN 0-201-04293-2, Adv Bk Prog). A-W.

Linstromberg, Walter W. & Baumgarten, Henry E. Organic Chemistry: A Brief Course. 4th ed. 1978. text ed. 17.95x (ISBN 0-669-00637-8); study guide with problems & solutions manual 7.95x (ISBN 0-669-00640-8). Heath.

Linstromberg, Walter W. & Baumgarten, Henry F. Organic Experiments. 4th rev. ed. 1980. pap. text ed. 7.95 (ISBN 0-669-02902-5). Heath.

Lint, Alice M., jt. auth. see Lint, Kenton C.

Lint, J. H. Van see Cameron, P. J. & Van Lint, J. H.

Lint, J. Van see Van Lint, J. H.

Lint, Kenton C. & Lint, Alice M. Diets for Birds in Captivity. (Illus.). 192p. 1981. 50.00 (ISBN 0-7137-1087-X, Pub. by Blandford Pr England). Sterling.

Linton, Adelin & Wagley, Charles. Ralph Linton. LC 76-174708. (Leaders of Modern Anthropology Ser). 1971. 15.00x (ISBN 0-231-03355-9); pap. 6.00x (ISBN 0-231-03398-2). Columbia U Pr.

Linton, Anthony. Newes of the Complement of the Art of Navigation & of the Mightie Empire of Cataia. LC 72-215. (English Experience Ser.: No. 204). 1969. Repr. of 1609 ed. 8.00 (ISBN 90-221-0204-1). Walter J Johnson.

Linton, Eliza L. The Autobiography of Christopher Kirkland, 1885. Wolff, Robert L., ed. LC 75-1532. (Victorian Fiction Ser.). 1975. lib. bdg. 66.00 (ISBN 0-8240-1604-1). Garland Pub.

--The True History of Joshua Davidson, 1872. Wolff, Robert L., ed. LC 75-1524. (Victorian Fiction Ser). 1975. lib. bdg. 66.00 (ISBN 0-8240-1596-7). Garland Pub.

--Under Which Lord? A Novel, 1879. LC 75-482. (Victorian Fiction Ser). 1975. lib. bdg. 66.00 (ISBN 0-8240-1559-2). Garland Pub.

Linton, James M., jt. auth. see Jowett, Garth.

Linton, Marigold. A Simplified Style Manual: For the Preparation of Journal Articles in Psychology, Social Sciences, Education & Literature. 200p. 1972. 9.95 (ISBN 0-13-810135-3). P-H.

Linton, Ralph. The Cultural Background of Personality. LC 80-29240. xix, 157p. 1981. Repr. of 1945 ed. lib. bdg. 17.50x (ISBN 0-313-22783-7, LICU). Greenwood.

Linton, Robert R. Atlas of Vascular Surgery. LC 72-80791. (Illus.). 504p. 1973. text ed. 80.00 (ISBN 0-7216-5783-4). Saunders.

Linton, Sydney, tr. see Sjogren, Per-Olof.

Linton, Virginia. Heading Out. LC 80-23182. 1981. 8.95 (ISBN 0-87233-054-0). Bauhan.

Lintz, Joseph, Jr. & Simonett, David S., eds. Remote Sensing of Environment. LC 76-47661. (Illus.). 1976. text ed. 35.50 (ISBN 0-201-04245-2, Adv Bk Prog). A-W.

Linville, Barbara. God Made the One & Only Me. LC 76-8737. (Illus.). (ps). 1976. pap. text ed. 2.25 (ISBN 0-916406-28-8). Accent Bks.

Lin Yu Shen see Kann, Eduard A.

Linz, Peter. Theoretical Numerical Analysis: An Introduction to Advanced Techniques. LC 78-15178. (Pure & Applied Mathematics: Texts, Monographs & Tracts). 1979. 23.50 (ISBN 0-471-04561-6, Pub. by Wiley-Interscience). Wiley.

Linzee, David. Belgravia. 1981. pap. 2.25 o.s.i. (ISBN 0-440-10472-6). Dell.

Linzell, J. L., jt. auth. see Peaker, M.

Linzey, Alicia V. & Linzey, Donald W. Mammals of Great Smoky Mountains National Park. LC 74-111048. (Illus.). 1971. pap. 4.95 (ISBN 0-87049-114-8). U of Tenn Pr.

Linzey, Donald W., jt. auth. see Linzey, Alicia V.

Lion, John R. Evaluation & Management of the Violent Patient: Guidelines in the Hospital & Institution. 88p. 1972. 8.75 (ISBN 0-398-02542-8). C C Thomas.

Lionetti, Harold E., jt. auth. see Castells, Matilde.

Lionni, Leo. A Flea Story: I Want to Stay Here! I Want to Go There! LC 77-4322. (Illus.). (ps-2). 1977. 5.95 (ISBN 0-394-83498-4); PLB 6.99 (ISBN 0-394-93498-9). Pantheon.

--Theodore & the Talking Mushroom. (Illus.). (gr. k-3). 1971. PLB 6.99 o.s.i. (ISBN 0-394-92312-X). Pantheon.

Lions, J. L. & Glowinski, R. Computing Methods in Applied Sciences & Engineering, 2 pts. Incl. Pt. 1. (Lecture Notes in Computer Science: Vol. 10). 497p. pap. 17.60 o.p. (ISBN 0-387-06768-X); Pt. 2. (Lecture Notes in Computer Science: Vol. 11). 434p. (12 contributions in Fr., 8 in Eng.). pap. 17.60 o.p. (ISBN 0-387-06769-8). (Illus.). 1974. Springer-Verlag.

Lions, J. L., jt. ed. see Bensoussan, A.

Lioy, Paul J., jt. ed. see Kneip, Theo J.

Lipatov, Yu. S & Sergeeva, L. M. Absorption of Polymers. Slutzkin, D., ed. Kondor, R., tr. from Rus. LC 74-12194. 177p. 1974. 28.95 (ISBN 0-470-54040-0). Halsted Pr.

Lipe, Dewey & Wolff, Jurgen. Help for the Over-Weight Child: A Parent's Guide to Helping Children Lose Weight. 1978. 8.95 (ISBN 0-8128-2507-1). Stein & Day.

--Slimmanship. LC 74-17808. (Illus.). 224p. 1974. pap. 13.95 (ISBN 0-88229-161-0). Nelson-Hall.

Lipetz, Marcia. Studying Life Designs. 1978. pap. 4.95x (ISBN 0-673-15121-2). Scott F.

Lipinsky, Deward S., jt. ed. see McClure, Thomas A.

Lipke, Jean C. Birth. LC 71-104891. (Being Together Books). (Illus.). (gr. 5-11). 1971. PLB 4.95 o.p. (ISBN 0-8225-0596-7). Lerner Pubns.

--Dating. LC 79-104893. (Being Together Books). (Illus.). (gr. 5-11). 1971. PLB 4.95 o.p. (ISBN 0-8225-0592-4). Lerner Pubns.

Lipke, Paul. Plank on Frame: The Who, What & Where of 150 Boatbuilders. LC 80-80779. (Illus.). 320p. 1980. pap. 19.95 (ISBN 0-87742-121-8). Intl Marine.

Lipke, William C., ed. Shelburne Farms: The History of an Agricultural Estate. (Illus.). 79p. (Orig.). 1979. pap. 7.50 (ISBN 0-87451-990-X). U Pr of New Eng.

Lipke, William C., jt. ed. see Kebabian, Paul B.

Lipkin, Mack. Straight Talk About Your Health Care. LC 75-25046. 1977. 8.95 o.s.i. (ISBN 0-06-012638-8, HarpT). Har-Row.

Lipkin, Semen. Volia: Izbrannoe. (Rus.). 1981. 14.00 (ISBN 0-88233-674-6). Ardis Pubs.

Lipman, J., ed. see Zariski, Oscar.

Lipman, Jean. American Primitive Painting. (Illus.). 11.00 (ISBN 0-8446-4574-5). Peter Smith.

--Rufus Porter Rediscovered. (Illus.). 224p. 1980. 16.95 (ISBN 0-517-54115-7). Potter.

Lipman, Jean & Aspinwall, Margaret. Sandy Calder & His Magical Mobiles. (Illus.). (ps up). 1981. 15.00 (ISBN 0-933920-17-2); pap. 7.00 (ISBN 0-933920-18-0). Hudson Hills.

Lipman, Jean & Winchester, Alice. The Flowering of American Folk Art, 1776-1876. LC 73-3081. (Illus.). 288p. 1974. 25.00 o.s.i. (ISBN 0-670-32120-6, Studio). Viking Pr.

Lipman, Matthew. El Descubrimiento De Harry Stottlemeier. Marti, Oscar R., tr. from Eng. (Philosophy for Children). 190p. (Orig., Eng. & Span.). (gr. 5-6). pap. 10.00 (ISBN 0-916834-16-6). Inst Adv Philo.

--Discovering Philosophy. 1981. Repr. of 1969 ed. text ed. 14.95x (ISBN 0-8290-0049-6). Irvington.

--Harry Stottlemeier's Discovery. rev. ed. 96p. (gr. 5-6). 1980. pap. 6.00 (ISBN 0-916834-06-9). Inst Adv Philo.

--Pixie. (Philosophy for Children). 90p. (Orig.). (gr. 3-4). pap. 6.00 (ISBN 0-916834-17-4). Inst Adv Philo.

--What Happens in Art. LC 66-27473. (Century Philosophy Ser.). (Orig.). 1967. pap. text ed. 8.95x (ISBN 0-89197-470-9). Irvington.

Lipman, Matthew & Sharp, Ann M. Social Inquiry: Instructional Manual to Accompany Mark. 396p. 1980. tchr's. ed. 30.00 (ISBN 0-916834-15-8). Inst Adv Philo.

Lipman, Matthew, ed. Contemporary Aesthetics. LC 73-76197. 1973. 28.50x (ISBN 0-89197-711-2); pap. text ed. 8.95x (ISBN 0-89197-712-0). Irvington.

Lipman, Matthew & Sharp, Ann M., eds. Writing How & Why: Instructional Manual to Accompany Suki. 384p. 1980. tchrs ed. 30.00 (ISBN 0-916834-14-X). Inst Adv Philo.

Lipman, Miriam H., jt. auth. see Jacobsen, Gertrude A.

Lipman, Richard, ed. Pediatrics: PreTest Self-Assessment & Review. LC 77-78444. (Clinical Sciences: PreTest Self-Assessment & Review Ser.). (Illus.). 1978. pap. 9.95 (ISBN 0-07-051603-0). McGraw-Pretest.

Lipman-Blumen, Jean & Bernard, Jessie, eds. Sex Roles & Social Policy: A Complex Social Science Equation. LC 77-90858. (Sage Studies in International Sociology: Vol. 14). 1979. 18.00x (ISBN 0-8039-9870-8); pap. 9.95x (ISBN 0-8039-9871-6). Sage.

Lipmann, Joel. Sweet Home Chicago. 1980. pap. 2.00. Quixote.

Lipner, Barbara E. & Fredericks, Robert F. How to Prepare for the Regents Competency Exam in Reading. 340p. (gr. 9-12). 1981. pap. text ed. 6.95 (ISBN 0-8120-2287-4). Barron.

Lipnick, Bernard. An Experiment That Works. 1976. 12.50x (ISBN 0-914536-02-8). Bloch.

Lipow, Myron, jt. auth. see Lloyd, David K.

Lipowski, Z. J. Delirium. 1980. 39.75 o.p. (ISBN 0-398-03909-7). C C Thomas.

--Delirium: Acute Brain Failure in Man. (American Lecture in Living Chemistry Ser.). 576p. 1980. text ed. 39.75 (ISBN 0-398-03909-7). C C Thomas.

Lipp, Frederick J. Some Lose Their Way. LC 80-13510. 132p. (gr. 5-9). 1980. 7.95 (ISBN 0-689-50178-1, McElderry Bk). Atheneum.

Lipp, Martin R. The Bitter Pill: Doctors, Patients & Failed Expectations. LC 79-1673. 288p. 1980. 10.95 (ISBN 0-06-012649-3, HarpT). Har-Row.

Lippard, Lucy, jt. auth. see Delehanty, Suzanne.

Lippard, Lucy R. Eva Hesse. LC 76-17380. (Illus.). 1976. 25.00x (ISBN 0-8147-4971-2); pap. 10.95 (ISBN 0-8147-4972-0). NYU Pr.

--Pop Art. (World of Art Ser.). (Illus.). 1966. pap. text ed. 9.95 (ISBN 0-19-519937-5). Oxford U Pr.

Lippard, Stephen J. Progress in Inorganic Chemistry. LC 59-13035. (Progress in Inorganic Chemistry Ser.). Vol. 26, 1979. 38.50 (ISBN 0-471-04944-1, Pub. by Wiley-Interscience); Vol. 28, 1980. 54.00 (ISBN 0-471-08310-0). Wiley.

Lippard, Stephen J., ed. Progress in Inorganic Chemistry. (Progress in Inorganic Chemistry Ser.). Vol. 12, 1970. 38.50 o.p. (ISBN 0-471-54082-X); Vol. 15, 1972. 32.50 o.p. (ISBN 0-471-54085-4); Vol. 18, 1973. 45.50 o.p. (ISBN 0-471-54088-9); Vol. 20, 1976. 41.95 (ISBN 0-471-54090-0); Vol. 21, 1976. 33.50 (ISBN 0-471-54091-9); Vol. 22, 1976. 38.50 (ISBN 0-471-54092-7); Vol. 23, 1977. 40.50 (ISBN 0-471-02186-5); Vol. 24, 1978. 41.50 (ISBN 0-471-03874-1); Vol. 25, 1979. 33.95 (ISBN 0-471-04943-3). Wiley.

Lippett, Peter E. Estate Planning: What Anyone Who Owns Anything Must Know. (Illus.). 1979. 16.95 (ISBN 0-8359-1778-9). Reston.

Lippi, Otty. The Second Time Around: An Honest Widow Reveals Her Intimate & Humorous Experiences in the Dating & Mating Game. LC 80-27189. 1981. 12.95 (ISBN 0-934878-03-X). Dembner Bks.

Lippin, Gerard. Circuit Problems & Solutions, Vol. 2: Network Theorems. 128p. 1971. pap. 6.45 o.p. (ISBN 0-8104-5755-5). Hayden.

--Circuit Problems & Solutions, Vol. 3: Transistor & Tube Circuits. 96p. 1971. pap. 5.95 o.p. (ISBN 0-8104-5756-3). Hayden.

Lippincott, David. Tremor Violet. 1976. pap. 1.75 (ISBN 0-451-06947-1, E6947, Sig). NAL.

--The Voice of Armageddon. 1975. pap. 1.75 o.p. (ISBN 0-451-06949-8, E6949, Sig). NAL.

Lippincott, H. F., ed. see Le Strange, Nicholas.

Lippincott, Joseph W. Black Wings: The Unbeatable Crow. (Illus.). (gr. 7-9). 1947. 5.95 o.p. (ISBN 0-397-30123-5). Lippincott.

--Chisel-Tooth the Beaver. (Illus.). (gr. 4-6). 1936. 3.95 o.p. (ISBN 0-397-30028-X). Lippincott.

--Wilderness Champion: The Story of a Great Hound. (Illus.). (gr. 7-9). 1944. 9.95 (ISBN 0-397-30099-9). Lippincott.

Lippincott, W. T. Chemistry, a Study of Matter. 3rd ed. 1977. 21.95x (ISBN 0-471-29246-X); study guide 7.95 (ISBN 0-471-02221-7); tchrs' manual avail. (ISBN 0-471-02689-1). Wiley.

Lippit, Noriko M. Reality & Fiction in Modern Japanese Literature. LC 79-67859. 1980. 20.00 (ISBN 0-87332-137-5). M E Sharpe.

Lippitt, Gordon & Lippitt, Ronald. The Consulting Process in Action. LC 77-15681. 130p. 1978. pap. 13.50 (ISBN 0-88390-141-2). Univ Assocs.

Lippitt, Gordon L. Visualizing Change: Model Building & the Change Process. LC 73-81361. (Illus.). 370p. 1973. pap. 14.50 (ISBN 0-88390-125-0). Univ Assocs.

Lippitt, Gordon L., jt. auth. see Ford, George A.

Lippitt, Ronald, jt. auth. see Lippitt, Gordon.

Lippitt, Ronald, jt. auth. see Schindler-Rainman, Eva.

Lippman, Edward A. Musical Thought in Ancient Greece. LC 74-23415. (Music Reprint Ser.). 1975. Repr. of 1964 ed. lib. bdg. 22.50 (ISBN 0-306-70669-5). Da Capo.

Lippman, Leopold. Attitudes Toward the Handicapped: A Comparison Between Europe & the United States. (American Lecture in Special Education Ser.). 136p. 1972. text ed. 10.50 (ISBN 0-398-02341-7). C C Thomas.

Lippman, Marc E., jt. auth. see Thompson, E. Brad.

Lippman, Peter. The Amazing Travels of Ingrid Our Turtle. (ps-3). 1973. PLB 7.15 o.p. (ISBN 0-307-62050-6, Golden Pr). Western Pub.

--Animals! Animals! (Illus.). (gr. k-4). 1976. 5.95 (ISBN 0-307-16808-5, Golden Pr); PLB 10.69 o.p. (ISBN 0-307-66808-8). Western Pub.

--Busy Boats. LC 79-29636. (Picturebacks Ser.). (Illus.). 32p. (gr. 2-3). 1980. PLB 3.99 (ISBN 0-394-93731-7); pap. 1.25 (ISBN 0-394-83731-2). Random.

--Busy Wheels. (ps-1). 1973. pap. 1.25 (ISBN 0-394-82706-6, BYR). Random.

--The Mix or Match Storybook: 2,097,152 Silly Stories. LC 73-18934. (Illus.). 9p. 1974. 2.50 (ISBN 0-394-82808-9, BYR). Random.

Lippman, Richard W. Urine & the Urinary Sediment: A Practical Manual & Atlas. 2nd ed. (Illus.). 152p. 1977. text ed. 18.95 (ISBN 0-398-01133-8). C C Thomas.

Lippman, William J., jt. ed. see Jackson, F. Scott.

Lippmann, H., ed. see CISM (International Center for Mechanical Sciences), Dept. for General Mechanics, Technical Univ. of Brunswick, 1970.

Lippmann, Walter. Public Philosophy. pap. 1.50 (ISBN 0-451-61866-1, MW1866, Ment). NAL.

Lips, Claude. Art & Stained Glass. LC 72-92255. 96p. 1973. pap. 5.95 (ISBN 0-385-08286-X). Doubleday.

Lips, Hilary M. & Colwill, Nina L. The Psychology of Sex Differences. (Illus.). 1978. 13.95 (ISBN 0-13-736561-6, Spec); pap. 5.95 (ISBN 0-13-736553-5). P-H.

Lipscomb, jt. auth. see Graham.

Lipscomb, A. B. Around the Lord's Table. 1.75 (ISBN 0-89225-020-8). Gospel Advocate.

Lipscomb, David M. An Introduction to the Laboratory Study of the Ear. (Illus.). 296p. 1974. 26.75 (ISBN 0-398-02938-5). C C Thomas.

Lipscomb, Delores H., et al. The Mature Student's Guide to Reading & Composition, Bk. 1. 280p. pap. text ed. 9.27 (ISBN 0-574-26000-5, 3-46000); tchr's manual avail. (ISBN 0-574-26002-1, 3-46002); Set Of 150. flash cards 10.30 (ISBN 0-574-26004-8, 3-46004); phono record avail. (3-46003). SRA.

--The Mature Student's Guide to Reading & Composition: A Guide to Composition & Reading, Bk. 2. pap. text ed. 9.27 (ISBN 0-574-26005-6, 3-46005); intr's. guide 3.47 (ISBN 0-574-26008-0). SRA.

Lipscomb, F. W. The British Submarine. 298p. 1980. 29.95x (ISBN 0-85177-086-X, Pub. by Cornell England.). State Mutual Bk.

--The Wise Men of the Wires: The History of Farady House. (Illus.). 1973. text ed. 9.25x (ISBN 0-09-117060-5). Humanities.

Lipscomb, Shirley F., jt. auth. see Ireson, Amy G.

Lipscombe, Joan & Williams, Bill. Are Science & Technology Neutral? (Science in a Social Context Ser.). 1979. pap. 3.95 (ISBN 0-408-71312-7). Butterworths.

Lipset, S. M., jt. ed. see Bendix, Reinhard.

Lipset, S. M., ed. see Carnegie Commission on Higher Education.

Lipset, Seymour M. Agrarian Socialism: The Cooperative Commonwealth Federation in Saskatchewan: A Study in Political Sociology. rev. ed. 1971. 10.00 o.p.; pap. 6.95x (ISBN 0-520-02056-1, CAMPUS64). U of Cal Pr.

--Political Man: The Social Bases of Politics. LC 80-8867. 584p. 1981. pap. text ed. 7.50x (ISBN 0-8018-2522-9). Johns Hopkins.

Lipset, Seymour M & Rokkan, S. Party Systems & Voter Alignments. LC 67-25332. 1967. 12.95 o.s.i. (ISBN 0-02-919150-5). Free Pr.

Lipset, Seymour M., jt. auth. see Horowitz, Irving L.

Lipset, Seymour M., ed. Politics & the Social Sciences. LC 70-75604. 1969. 17.95 (ISBN 0-19-500628-3). Oxford U Pr.

--The Third Century: America As a Post-Industrial Society. LC 78-70400. (Publications Ser.: No. 203). 468p. 1979. 14.95 (ISBN 0-8179-7031-2). Hoover Inst Pr.

Lipset, Seymour M., ed. see Martineau, Harriet.

Lipset, Seymour M., et al. Union Democracy: The Internal Politics of the International Typographical Union. LC 56-6202. (Illus.). 1977. pap. text ed. 8.95 (ISBN 0-02-919210-2). Free Pr.

Lipsey, Sally I. Mathematics for Nursing Science: A Programmed Text. 2nd ed. LC 76-44843. 1977. text ed. 10.95 (ISBN 0-471-01798-1, Pub. by Wiley-Medical). Wiley.

Lipshitz, Susan, ed. Tearing the Veil: Essays on Femininity. (Orig.). 1978. pap. 7.95 (ISBN 0-7100-8721-7). Routledge & Kegan.

Lipshitz, Susan, tr. see Frederic, Helene & Malinsky, Martine.

Lipsitt, L. P., jt. ed. see Reese, H. W.

Lipsitt, Lewis P., ed. Advances in Infancy Research. 300p. 1981. price not set (ISBN 0-89391-045-7). Ablex Pub.

Lipsitt, Lewis P. see Reese, Hayne.

Lipsitt, Lewis P see Reese, Hayne.

Lipsitz, Joan. Growing up Forgotten: A Review of Research & Programs Concerning Early Adolescence. LC 76-28621. 1976. 18.95 (ISBN 0-669-00975-X). Lexington Bks.

Lipsitz, Lou. Cold Water. LC 67-15228. (Wesleyan Poetry Program: Vol. 34). (Orig.). 1967. 10.00x (ISBN 0-8195-2034-9, Pub. by Wesleyan U Pr); pap. 4.95 (ISBN 0-8195-1034-3). Columbia U Pr.

Lipsius, Justus. Sixe Bookes of Politickes or Civil Doctrine. Jones, W., tr. LC 79-25633. (English Experience Ser.: No. 287). 1970. Repr. of 1594 ed. 22.00 (ISBN 90-221-0287-4). Walter J Johnson.

Lipsky, M., jt. auth. see Hawley, W. D.

Lipson, Alexander. A Russian Course. Date not set. price not set (ISBN 0-89357-040-0). Slavica.

Lipson, Goldie. Beyond Yoga. 1977. pap. 1.50 o.s.i. (ISBN 0-515-04419-9). Jove Pubns.

--Rejuvenation Through Yoga. 1978. pap. 1.50 o.s.i. (ISBN 0-515-04480-6). Jove Pubns.

Lipson, Greta. Fact, Fantasy, Folklore. (gr. 3-12). 1977. 9.95 (ISBN 0-916456-11-0, GA71). Good Apple.

--It's a Special Day. (gr. k-4). tchrs. ed. 9.95 (ISBN 0-916456-25-0, GA87). Good Apple.

Lipson, H. & Lee, R. M. Crystals & X-Rays. (Wykeham Science Ser.: No. 13). 1970. 9.95x (ISBN 0-8448-1115-7). Crane Russak Co.

Lipson, H., jt. auth. see Lipson, S. G.

Lipson, Harry A. & Darling, John R. Marketing Fundamentals: Texts & Cases. LC 80-12441. 590p. 1980. Repr. of 1974 ed. lib. bdg. 22.00 (ISBN 0-89874-166-1). Krieger.

Lipson, John D. Elements of Algebra & Algebraic Computing. 420p. 1980. text ed. 34.50 (ISBN 0-201-04115-4). A-W.

Lipson, Leon, tr. see Stern, August.

Lipson, Leslie. Great Issues of Politics. 5th ed. (Illus.). 528p. 1976. text ed. 16.95 (ISBN 0-13-363895-2). P-H.

Lipson, S. G. & Lipson, H. Optical Physics. LC 67-15308. (Illus.). 1969. 39.95 (ISBN 0-521-06926-2). Cambridge U Pr.

--Optical Physics. 2nd ed. LC 79-8963. (Illus.). 496p. Date not set. 55.00 (ISBN 0-521-22630-9); pap. 22.50 (ISBN 0-521-29584-X). Cambridge U Pr.

Lipson, Stephen H. & Hensel, Mary D. Hospital Manpower Budget Preparation Manual. LC 75-20992. 200p. 1975. pap. text ed. 15.00 (ISBN 0-914904-11-6). Health Admin Pr.

--Hospital Manpower Budget Preparation Manual. 200p. 1975. 12.00 (ISBN 0-686-68583-0, 14917). Hospital Finan.

Lipsyte, Robert. Summer Rules. LC 79-2816. (An Ursula Nordstrom Bk.). (YA) (gr. 7 up). 1981. 8.95 (ISBN 0-06-023897-6, HarpJ); PLB 8.79g (ISBN 0-06-023898-4). Har-Row.

Lipsyte, Robert, ed. see Gregory, Dick.

Liptak, David Q. Biblical-Caatechetical Homilies for Sundays & Holy Days (A, B & C) Based on the Lectionary & Reflecting the Syllabus of the Pastoral Homiletic Plan. LC 79-27895. 370p. (Orig.). 1980. pap. 10.95 (ISBN 0-8189-0400-3). Alba.

--Sacramental & Occasional Homilies. LC 80-29287. 96p. (Orig.). 1981. pap. 4.95 (ISBN 0-8189-0406-2). Alba.

Lipton, Dean. Bluegrass Frontier. 368p. (Orig.). 1980. pap. 2.50 (ISBN 0-89083-667-1). Zebra.

Lipton, Douglas, et al. The Effectiveness of Correctional Treatment: A Survey of Treatment Evaluation Studies. LC 74-14730. (Illus.). 768p. 1975. text ed. 46.50 (ISBN 0-275-05580-9). Praeger.

Lipton, Eunice. Picasso Criticism, Nineteen One to Nineteen Thirty-Nine: The Making of an Artist-Hero. LC 75-23801. (Outstanding Dissertations in the Fine Arts - 20th Century). (Illus.). 1976. lib. bdg. 45.00 (ISBN 0-8240-1996-2). Garland Pub.

Lipton, Gladys & Munoz, Olivia. Diccionario Del Ingles Americano. (Illus.). 368p. (gr. 10-12). 1981. pap. 2.95 (ISBN 0-8120-2319-6). Barron.

Lipton, James. Mirrors. 352p. 1981. 12.95 (ISBN 0-312-53438-8). St Martin.

Lipton, James M., ed. Fever. 1980. text ed. 34.50 (ISBN 0-89004-451-1). Raven.

Lipton, L. Super Eight Book. 1975. 6.95 (ISBN 0-671-22082-9). S&S.

Lipton, Morris A., et al, eds. Psychopharmacology: A Generation of Progress. LC 77-83697. 1978. 69.50 (ISBN 0-89004-191-1). Raven.

Lipton, Werner J., jt. auth. see Ryall, A. Lloyd.

Liquori, Marty & Parker, John L. Playboy's Book of Real Running. 1980. 10.95 (ISBN 0-87223-625-0). Playboy.

--Playboy's Elite Runner's Manual. LC 80-7728. (Playboy's Lifestyles Library). 224p. 1980. 10.95 (ISBN 0-87223-625-0, Dist. by Har-Row). Playboy.

Liroff, Richard A. Air Pollution Offsets: Trading Selling & Banking. LC 80-66464. 54p. (Orig.). 1980. pap. 5.00 (ISBN 0-89164-061-4). Conservation Foun.

--National Policy for the Environment: NEPA & Its Aftermath. LC 75-28910. 288p. 1976. 10.00x (ISBN 0-253-33973-1). Ind U Pr.

Liroff, Richard A. & Davis, G. Gordon. Conflict in the North Country: A Study of the Implementation of Regional Land Use Controls by the Adirondack Park Agency. 1981. price not set (ISBN 0-88410-643-8). Ballinger Pub.

Lisann, Maury. Broadcasting to the Soviet Union: International Politics & Radio. LC 74-14046. (Illus.). 224p. 1975. text ed. 23.95 (ISBN 0-275-05590-6). Praeger.

Lisboa, Henriqueta. Selected Poems. 119p. 1980. Repr. of 1978 ed. lib. bdg. 20.00 (ISBN 0-8414-5761-1). Folcroft.

Lisca, Peter. John Steinbeck: Nature & Myth. LC 77-11556. (Twentieth Century American Writers Ser.). (gr. 7 up). 1978. 7.95 (ISBN 0-690-01315-9, TYC-J); PLB 7.89 o.p. (ISBN 0-690-03835-6). T Y Crowell.

--The Wide World of John Steinbeck. 332p. 1981. Repr. of 1958 ed. 15.00 (ISBN 0-87752-217-0). Gordian.

Lischer, Richard. A Theology of Preaching: The Dynamics of the Gospel. (Preacher's Library). (Orig.). 1981. pap. 4.95 (ISBN 0-687-41570-5). Abingdon.

Liscomb, Robie. Limits. 1980. pap. 3.00. Pentagram.

--Traces. 1981. pap. 3.00 (ISBN 0-915316-88-9). Pentagram.

Liscombe, R. W. William Wilkins, Seventeen Seventy-Eight to Eighteen Thirty-Nine. LC 78-73247. 320p. 1980. 49.50 (ISBN 0-521-22528-0). Cambridge U Pr.

Lisenko, Alexander I., tr. see Chetverikov, Sergii.

Lish, Gordon. English Grammar, 2 vols. (gr. 9-12). 1972. pap. text ed. 9.00 each incl. tchrs' manual & test (ISBN 0-8449-2700-7). Learning Line.

Lish, Kenneth C. Nuclear Power Plant Systems & Equipment. new ed. 160p. 1972. 24.50 (ISBN 0-8311-1078-3). Indus Pr.

Lishfin, Lyn. Shaker House Peoms. 1976. 3.95 (ISBN 0-915298-02-3). Sagarin Pr.

Lishida, Ichiro, jt. ed. see Brown, Delmer M.

Lishka, Gerald R. Handbook for the Ballet Accompanist. LC 78-2051. (Illus.). 256p. 1979. 15.00x (ISBN 0-253-32704-0). Ind U Pr.

Lisiero, Dario. People Ideology-People Theology: New Perspectives on Religious Dogma. 64p. 1980. 10.95 (ISBN 0-682-49664-2, Banner). Exposition.

Lisitsyn, G. M. & Cafferty, B. First Book of Chess Strategy. 1978. pap. 9.95 (ISBN 0-7134-1423-5, Pub. by Batsford England). David & Charles.

Lisitsyn, G. M. & Cafferty, Bernard. The Second Book of Chess Strategy. 1978. pap. 8.95 (ISBN 0-7134-1425-1, Pub. by Batsford England). David & Charles.

Lisitsyn, G. M. & Caffery, B. Second Book of Chess Strategy. (The Chess Player Ser.). (Illus.). 1978. pap. 3.95 o.p. (ISBN 0-900928-83-2). Hippocrene Bks.

Lisitzky, Gene. Four Ways of Being Human. 1976. pap. 3.50 (ISBN 0-14-004391-8). Penguin.

Liske, C. T., jt. ed. see Raichur, S.

Lisker, Leigh. Spoken Telugu. Incl. Book, Units 1-30. pap. 10.00x (ISBN 0-87950-376-9); Cassettes, Six Dual Track. 60.00x (ISBN 0-87950-377-7); Cassette Course-Bk. & Cassettes. pap. 65.00x (ISBN 0-87950-378-5). LC 63-12992. (Spoken Language Ser). (Prog. Bk.). 1976. cassettes 2 for units 13-30 5 dual trac 50.00x (ISBN 0-87950-379-3). Spoken Lang Serv.

Lisker, Tim. Nellie Bly: First Woman of the News. LC 78-14382. (Famous Firsts Ser.). (Illus.). 1978. lib. bdg. 7.35 (ISBN 0-686-51113-1). Silver.

Lisker, Tom. First to the Top of the World: Admiral Peary at the North Pole. LC 78-14924. (Famous Firsts Ser.). (Illus.). 1978. lib. bdg. 7.35 (ISBN 0-686-51107-7). Silver.

--Tall Tales: American Myths. LC 77-11104. (Myth, Magic & Superstition Ser.). (Illus.). (gr. 4-5). 1977. PLB 9.65 (ISBN 0-8172-1039-3). Raintree Pubs.

--Terror in the Tropics: The Army Ants. LC 77-10765. (Great Unsolved Mysteries Ser.). (Illus.). (gr. 4-5). 1977. PLB 9.65 (ISBN 0-8172-1060-1). Raintree Pubs.

Lismore, Thomas. Welcome to English, 5 bks. rev. ed. Incl. Bk. 1. pap. text ed. 2.75 (ISBN 0-88345-190-5, 18073); cassettes 25.00 (ISBN 0-685-48094-1); Bk. 2. pap. text ed. 2.75 (ISBN 0-88345-191-3, 18074); cassettes 40.00 (ISBN 0-685-48095-X); Bk. 3. pap. text ed. 3.25 (ISBN 0-88345-192-1, 18075); cassettes 40.00 (ISBN 0-685-48096-8); Bk. 4. pap. text ed. 3.25 (ISBN 0-88345-193-X, 18076); cassettes 40.00 (ISBN 0-685-48097-6); Bk. 5. pap. text ed. 3.25 (ISBN 0-88345-194-8, 18077); cassettes 40.00 (ISBN 0-685-48098-4). (gr. 1-6). 1973-74. tchr's manual, bks. 4 & 5 4.95. Regents Pub.

Lisney, M. I., tr. see Makrakis, Apostolos.

Lisowsky, G., ed. Konkordanz Zum Hebraeischen Alten Testaments. 2nd ed. 1958. 31.75 (ISBN 0-686-20117-5, 60910). United Bible.

Liss, Howard. Baseball's Zaniest Stars. LC 71-146650. (Major League Baseball Library: No. 15). (Illus.). (gr. 5-9). 1971. 2.50 o.p. (ISBN 0-394-82142-4, BYR); PLB 3.69 (ISBN 0-394-92142-9). Random.

--Bowling Talk. (gr. 4-6). 1974. pap. 0.75 o.s.i. (ISBN 0-671-29619-1). Archway.

--Bowling Talk. (gr. 4-6). 1974. pap. 0.75 (ISBN 0-671-29619-1). PB.

--Football Talk. 1980. pap. 1.50 (ISBN 0-671-56037-9). Archway.

--The Giant Book of Strange but True Sports Stories. LC 76-8132. (Illus.). (gr. 5-9). 1976. 3.95 (ISBN 0-394-83287-6, BYR); PLB 6.99 (ISBN 0-394-93287-0). Random.

--Hockey Talk. (gr. 4-6). pap. 0.95 (ISBN 0-686-68482-6). PB.

--More Strange but True Baseball Stories. (Major League Baseball Library: No. 16). (Illus.). (gr. 5-9). 1972. 2.95 o.p. (ISBN 0-394-82390-7, BYR); PLB 4.39 (ISBN 0-394-92390-1). Random.

--The Pocket Book of Baseball. 1981. pap. 2.75 (ISBN 0-671-41862-9). PB.

--Soccer. (Illus.). pap. 3.50 o.p. (ISBN 0-8015-6910-9). Dutton.

Liss, Leopold, ed. Aluminum Toxicology Symposium. (Neurotoxicology Ser.: Vol. 1, No. 4). (Illus.). 1980. text ed. 29.00 (ISBN 0-930376-18-8). Pathotox Pubs.

Liss, P., et al. Environmental Chemistry. LC 80-12132. (Resource & Environmental Science). 184p. 1980. pap. text ed. 14.95x (ISBN 0-470-26968-5). Halsted Pr.

Lissagaray, H. Les Huits Journees De Mai Derriere les Barricades. (Commune De Paris En 1871 Ser). 332p. (Fr.). 1977. lib. bdg. 20.00x o.p. (ISBN 0-8287-0549-6); pap. text ed. 10.00x o.p. (ISBN 0-685-75631-9). Clearwater Pub.

Lissak. Results in Neurochemistry, Neuroendocrinology, Neurophysiology & Behavior, Neuropharmacology, Neuropathology, Cybernetics. 1976. 19.50 (ISBN 0-9960007-2-0, Pub. by Kaido Hungary). Heyden.

Lissak, K., ed. Results in Neuroendocrinology, Neurochemistry & Sleep Research. LC 76-379912. (Recent Developments of Neurobiology in Hungary: Vol. VII). (Illus.). 190p. 1978. 20.00x (ISBN 963-05-1587-3). Intl Pubns Serv.

Lissak, Moshe. Military Roles in Moderization: Civil-Military Relations in Thailand & Burma. LC 75-5015. (Armed Forces & Society Ser.: Vol. 8). 1976. 20.00x o.p. (ISBN 0-8039-0436-3). Sage.

Lissitzyn, Oliver J. The International Court of Justice: Its Role in the Maintenance of International Peace & Security. LC 78-2885. (Carnegie Endowment for International Peace, United Nations Studies: No. 6). 1978. Repr. of 1951 ed. lib. bdg. 15.25x (ISBN 0-313-20333-4, LICJ). Greenwood.

Lisska. Philosophy Matters. 1977. 12.95 (ISBN 0-675-08592-6). Merrill.

List, Ely, ed. see Girl Scouts of the U. S. A.

List, Friedrich. National System of Political Economy. Colwell, Stephen, ed. Matile, G. A., tr. (The Neglected American Economists Ser.). 1974. lib. bdg. 50.00 (ISBN 0-8240-1013-2). Garland Pub.

List, W., et al, eds. Systolic Time Intervals. (International Boehringer Mannheim Symposia). (Illus.). 300p. 1980. pap. 31.90 (ISBN 0-387-09871-2). Springer-Verlag.

Lister, D., et al, eds. Meat Animals: Growth & Productivity. LC 76-985. (NATO Advanced Study Institutes Ser., Series A: Life Sciences: Vol. 8). 541p. 1976. 42.50 (ISBN 0-306-35608-2, Plenum Pr). Plenum Pub.

Lister, Florence C., jt. auth. see Lister, Robert H.

Lister, Hal. The Suburban Press: A Separate Journalism. 1975. pap. text ed. 5.25x (ISBN 0-87543-124-0). Lucas.

Lister, John W., et al. Arrhythmia Analysis by Intracardiac Electrocardiography. (Illus.). 360p. 1976. 44.75 (ISBN 0-398-03423-0). C C Thomas.

Lister, Louis & Lister, Rebecca. The Religious School Board: A Manual. 1978. pap. 5.00 (ISBN 0-8074-0014-9, 243870). UAHC.

Lister, R. P. Marco Polo's Travels in Xanadu with Kublai Khan. (Illus.). 1976. 13.95 o.p. (ISBN 0-86033-008-7). Gordon-Cremonesi.

Lister, Raymond. Little Treasury of Familiar Prose. (Little Treasury Ser.). 1964. 2.50 (ISBN 0-212-35942-8). Dufour.

--Little Treasury of Familiar Verse. (Little Treasury Ser). 2.50 (ISBN 0-212-35912-6). Dufour.

--Little Treasury of Love Lyrics. (Little Treasury Ser.). 1963. 2.50 (ISBN 0-685-09180-5). Dufour.

--Little Treasury of Religious Verse. (Little Treasury Ser.). 1964. 2.50 (ISBN 0-212-35941-X). Dufour.

--Samuel Palmer: A Biography. 1974. 17.95 (ISBN 0-571-09732-4, Pub. by Faber & Faber). Merrimack Bk Serv.

Lister, Rebecca, jt. auth. see Lister, Louis.

Lister, Robert H. & Lister, Florence C. Chaco Canyon: Archaeology & Archaeologists. (Illus.). 312p. 1981. 29.95 (ISBN 0-8263-0574-1). U of NM Pr.

Lister, Rota H., ed. see Fletcher, John.

Lister, Thomas M. The Superior Sex. 237p. 1980. 7.95 (ISBN 0-8059-2732-8). Dorrance.

Lister, Timothy R. & Yourdon, Edward. Learning to Program in Structured COBOL, Part 2. LC 77-99232. 1977. pap. 12.00 (ISBN 0-917072-03-0). Yourdon.

Liston, Hattye H., et al. Basic Mathematical Statistics for Behavioral Sciences & Techniques for Data Compilation in Ecological Studies. 1976. text ed. 13.50x (ISBN 0-8191-0093-5). U Pr of Amer.

Liston, L. L., ed. see Myhra, David.

Liston, Mary D., jt. ed. see Stapp, William B.

Liston, Robert A. The Edge of Madness: Prisons & Prison Reform in America. LC 79-186756. 128p. (gr. 7 up). 1972. PLB 5.88 o.p. (ISBN 0-531-02025-8). Watts.

--Getting in Touch with Your Government. LC 75-22333. 160p. (gr. 7 up). 1975. PLB 6.64 o.p. (ISBN 0-671-32763-1). Messner.

--On the Job Training & Where to Get It. rev. ed. LC 72-11898. (Career Bks.). (Illus.). 192p. (gr. 7 up). 1973. PLB 7.29 o.p. (ISBN 0-671-32590-6). Messner.

--The Right to Know: Censorship in America. LC 73-1266. 192p. (gr. 7 up). 1973. PLB 5.90 o.p. (ISBN 0-531-02612-4). Watts.

--The Ugly Palaces: Housing in America. LC 74-1044. 160p. (gr. 7 up). 1974. PLB 6.88 o.p. (ISBN 0-531-02673-6). Watts.

--Why We Think As We Do. (gr. 7 up). 1977. PLB 6.90 s&l o.p. (ISBN 0-531-00390-6). Watts.

Listowel. Modern Aesthetics: An Historical Introduction. LC 67-14767. (Orig.). 1967. text ed. 10.25 (ISBN 0-8077-1696-0); pap. text ed. 7.00x (ISBN 0-8077-1695-2). Tchrs Coll.

Liszt, Rudolph. The Last Word in Make-up: A Practical Illustrated Handbook. rev. ed. (Illus.). 1980. 6.00 (ISBN 0-686-68849-X). Dramatists Play.

Litchfield, Ada B. A Button in Her Ear. Rubin, Caroline, ed. LC 75-28390. (Concept Bks.). (Illus.). 32p. (gr. 2-4). 1976. 6.95g (ISBN 0-8075-0987-6). A Whitman.

--A Cane in Her Hand. Rubin, Caroline, ed. LC 77-14255. (Concept Books Ser.). (Illus.). (gr. 1-3). 1977. 6.95g (ISBN 0-8075-1056-4). A Whitman.

--It's Going to Rain. LC 80-12732. (Illus.). 32p. (ps-2). 1980. 8.95 (ISBN 0-689-30779-9). Atheneum.

--Words in Our Hands. Tucker, Kathleen, ed. LC 79-28402. (Concept Bk.: Level 2). (Illus.). (gr. 2-6). 1980. 6.95g (ISBN 0-8075-9212-9). A Whitman.

Liteanu, C. & Gocan, S. Gradient Liquid Chromatography. LC 74-1008. (Ser. in Analytical Chemistry). 1974. text ed. 44.95 (ISBN 0-470-54124-5). Halsted Pr.

Liteanu, C. & Rica, I. Statistical Theory & Methodlogy of Trace Analysis. (Ellis Horwood Ser. in Analytical Chemistry). 1980. 94.95x (ISBN 0-470-26797-6). Halsted Pr.

Litfin, Duane. Public Speaking: A Handbook for Christians. 400p. (Orig.). 1981. pap. 9.95 (ISBN 0-8010-5605-5). Baker Bk.

Lithgow, Marilyn. Quiltmaking & Quiltmakers. (Funk & W Bk.). 128p. 1974. pap. 4.50 o.s.i. (ISBN 0-308-10089-1, TYC-T). T Y Crowell.

Litka, Michael P. Business Law. 2nd ed. LC 76-2999. (Law Ser.). 1977. text ed. 20.50 (ISBN 0-88244-108-6). Grid Pub.

Litka, Michael P. & Shillif, Karl A. Contemporary Real Estate Incidents. LC 79-27028. (Real Estate Ser.). 189p. 1980. pap. text ed. 8.50 (ISBN 0-88244-222-8). Grid Pub.

Litka, Michael P., jt. auth. see Pearson, Karl G.

Litlienfeld, Abraham M. Times, Places & Persons: Aspects of the History of Epidemiology. LC 80-8090. (The Henry F. Sigerist Supplements to the Bulletin of the History of Medicine, New Ser.: No. 4). 160p. 1980. pap. text ed. 9.00x (ISBN 0-8018-2425-7). Johns Hopkins.

--Times, Places & Persons: Aspects of the History of Epidemiology. LC 80-8090. (The Henry E. Sigerist Supplements to the Bulletin of the History of Medicine, New Ser.: No. 4). 160p. pap. text ed. 9.00x (ISBN 0-8018-2425-7). Johns Hopkins.

Litoff, Judy B. American Midwives: 1860 to the Present. LC 77-83893. (Contributions in Medical History: No. 1). 1978. lib. bdg. 17.50 (ISBN 0-8371-9824-0, LAM/). Greenwood.

Litsky, Frank. The Summer Olympics. 4th rev. ed. (First Bks.). (Illus.). (gr. 4-6). 1979. PLB 6.45 s&l (ISBN 0-531-02935-2). Watts.

--Winners in Gymnastics. (Picture Life Books Ser.). (Illus.). (gr. 2 up). 1978. PLB 6.45 s&l (ISBN 0-531-02887-9). Watts.

--Winners on Ice. (Picture Life Bks.). (Illus.). (gr. k-3). 1979. PLB 6.45 s&l (ISBN 0-531-02291-9). Watts.

--The Winter Olympics. (First Bks.). (Illus.). (gr. 4 up). 1979. PLB 6.45 s&l (ISBN 0-531-02946-8). Watts.

Litt, Edgar & Parkinson, Michael. U. S. & U. K. Education Policy: A Decade of Reform. LC 78-19759. (Praeger Special Studies). 1979. 22.95 (ISBN 0-03-046706-3). Praeger.

Litt, Iris F., jt. auth. see Gersh, Marvin J.

Litt, Jerome Z. Your Skin & How to Live in It. LC 80-65323. 223p. 1980. pap. 4.95 (ISBN 0-86551-011-3). Corinthian.

Litt, M., jt. auth. see Ponting, Kenneth G.

Litt, Mitchell, jt. auth. see Gabelnick, Henry L.

Littauer, Florence. Blow Away the Black Clouds. LC 80-85334. 1981. pap. 3.95 (ISBN 0-89081-285-3). Harvest Hse.

--The Pursuit of Happiiness. LC 80-85333. 1981. pap. 4.95 (ISBN 0-89081-284-5). Harvest Hse.

Littauer, U. Z., jt. auth. see Weizman Institute of Science, Rehovot, Israel, Feb. 1980.

Littell, Franklin H. Macmillan Atlas History of Christianity. LC 75-22113. (Illus.). 163p. 1976. 21.95 (ISBN 0-02-573140-8, 57314). Macmillan.

Littell, Franklin H., jt. auth. see Shur, Irene G.

Littell, Robert. The Amateur. 1981. 12.95 (ISBN 0-671-41873-4). S&S.

--The Debriefing. 1981. pap. 2.75 (ISBN 0-440-11873-5). Dell.

Litterer, J. Organizations: Structure & Behavior. 3rd ed. LC 80-15645. (Wiley Series in Management). 600p. 1980. pap. 14.95 (ISBN 0-471-07786-0). Wiley.

Litterer, Joseph A. The Analysis of Organizations. 2nd ed. LC 72-8586. (Management & Administration Ser). (Illus.). 640p. 1973. text ed. 23.50x (ISBN 0-471-54106-0). Wiley.

--An Introduction to Management. LC 77-23820. (Ser. in Management & Administration). 1978. text ed. 20.95 (ISBN 0-471-54100-1); tchrs. manual avail. Wiley.

--Management: Concepts & Controversies. LC 77-20031. 1978. pap. text ed. 11.50 (ISBN 0-471-03611-0). Wiley.

Littke, Lael. Cave In! (Prime Time Adventures Ser.). (Illus.). 64p. (gr. 4 up). 1981. PLB 7.95 (ISBN 0-516-02102-8). Childrens.

Little, Brown Editiors, ed. Birds: West Coast Edition. (Explorer's Notebooks). (Illus.). 32p. (Orig.). (gr. 5 up). 1981. pap. 1.95 (ISBN 0-316-52776-9). Little.

Little, Brown Editorial Staff, ed. Trees: West Coast Ed. (Explorer's Notebooks Ser.). (Illus.). 32p. (Orig.). (gr. 5 up). 1981. pap. 1.95 (ISBN 0-316-52769-6). Little.

Little, Brown Editors, ed. Birds: East Coast Edition. (Explorer's Notebooks). (Illus.). 32p. (Orig.). (gr. 5 up). 1981. pap. 1.95 (ISBN 0-316-52775-0). Little.

--Flowers: East Coast Edition. (Explorer's Notebooks). (Illus.). 32p. (Orig.). (gr. 5 up). 1981. pap. 1.95 (ISBN 0-316-52773-4). Little.

--Flowers: West Coast Edition. (Explorer's Notebooks). (Illus.). 32p. (Orig.). (gr. 5 up). 1981. pap. 1.95 (ISBN 0-316-52774-2). Little.

--Insects: East Coast Edition. (Explorer's Notebooks). (Illus.). 32p. (Orig.). (gr. 5 up). 1981. pap. 1.95 (ISBN 0-316-52771-8). Little.

--Insects: West Coast Edition. (Explorer's Notebooks). (Illus.). 32p. (Orig.). (gr. 5 up). 1980. pap. 1.95 (ISBN 0-316-52772-6). Little.

--Trees: East Coast Edition. (Explorer's Notebooks). (Illus.). 32p. (Orig.). (gr. 5 up). 1981. pap. 1.95 (ISBN 0-316-52769-6). Little.

Little, Bryan. Portrait of Somerset. LC 77-444966. (Portrait Bks.). (Illus.). 224p. 1976. 10.50x (ISBN 0-7091-5791-6). Intl Pubns Serv.

Little, C. Challenge of the Land. 1969. 12.25 (ISBN 0-08-006913-4). Pergamon.

Little, Charles E. Cyclopedia of Classified Dates, with Exhaustive Index. LC 66-27839. 1967. Repr. of 1900 ed. 56.00 (ISBN 0-8103-3334-1). Gale.

--Historical Lights, 2 vols. 3rd ed. LC 68-27175. 1968. Repr. of 1886 ed. Set. 25.00 (ISBN 0-8103-3186-1). Gale.

Little, Craig B., jt. ed. see Traub, Stuart H.

Little, Dennis L., et al, eds. Renewable Natural Resources: A Management Handbook for the Eighties. (Special Studies in Natural Resources & Energy Management). 375p. (Orig.). 1981. lib. bdg. 19.50x (ISBN 0-89158-665-2). Westview.

Little, Edward A. Automechanics: An Introduction & Guide. LC 73-14689. (Illus.). 128p. (gr. 7 up). 1974. PLB 5.88 o.p. (ISBN 0-531-02670-1). Watts.

Little, Elbert L. Forest Trees of the United States & Canada, & How to Identify Them. LC 79-52527. (Illus.). 1980. pap. text ed. 2.00 (ISBN 0-486-23902-0). Dover.

Little, Elbert L., Jr. Audubon Field Guide to North American Trees. western ed. 1980. 9.95 o.p. (ISBN 0-394-50761-4). Knopf.

Little, Elsie, ed. see Monroe City County Fine Arts Council.

Little, Gilbert. Nervous Christians. 1956. pap. 1.50 (ISBN 0-8024-5878-5). Moody.

Little, H. Ganse, Jr. Decision & Responsibility: A Wrinkle in Time. LC 74-24729. (American Academy of Religion. Studies in Religion). 1974. pap. 7.50 (ISBN 0-88420-122-8, 010008). Scholars Pr Ca.

Little, I. M. Aid to Africa. 1964. 3.30 o.p. (ISBN 0-08-010938-1). Pergamon.

Little, J. Miles. Major Amputations for Vascular Disease. LC 74-84692. (Illus.). 128p. 1975. text ed. 21.00 (ISBN 0-443-01250-4). Churchill.

Little, James H., jt. auth. see Emery, Jared M.

Little, James W. & Falace. Dental Management of the Medically Compromised Patient. LC 80-15164. (Illus.). 300p. 1980. pap. text ed. 14.95 (ISBN 0-8016-3045-2). Mosby.

Little, Jane. Danger at Sneaker Hill. (Illus.). (gr. 3-5). 1975. pap. 1.25 (ISBN 0-671-29734-1). PB.

Little, Janet. Hecate the Bandicoot. LC 80-69437. 32p. 1980. 5.95 (ISBN 0-396-07893-1). Dodd.

Little, Jean. Mine for Keeps. (Illus.). (gr. 4-6). 1962. 8.95 (ISBN 0-316-52793-9). Little.

--Mine for Keeps. (gr. 4-6). 1973. pap. 1.75 (ISBN 0-671-42455-6). Archway.

--Nine for Keeps. (Illus.). (gr. 4-6). 1974. pap. 1.75 (ISBN 0-671-29993-X). PB.

Little, Jeffrey B. & Rhodes, Lucien. Understanding Wall Street. LC 78-54787. (Illus.). 220p. 1980. pap. 7.95 (ISBN 0-89709-010-1). Liberty Pub.

Little, Julia, jt. auth. see Macdonald, Eleanor.

Little, Kenneth. The Sociology of Urban Women's Image in African Literature. 174p. 1980. 27.50x (ISBN 0-8476-6290-X). Rowman.

--Urbanization As a Social Process: An Essay on Movement & Change in Contemporary Africa. (Library of Man Ser.). 1974. 14.00x (ISBN 0-7100-7931-1). Routledge & Kegan.

Little, Lessie J. & Greenfield, Eloise. I Can Do It by Myself. LC 77-11554. (Illus.). (gr. k-2). 1978. 8.95 (ISBN 0-690-01369-8, TYC-J); PLB 7.89 (ISBN 0-690-03851-8). T Y Crowell.

Little, Margaret. Transference Neurosis & Transference Psychosis. LC 80-66925. 350p. 1980. 25.00 (ISBN 0-87668-421-5). Aronson.

Little, Meredith, jt. auth. see Foster, Steven.

Little, Michael A., jt. ed. see Baker, P. T.

Little, Mildred J. Camper's Guide to Texas Parks, Lakes & Forests. LC 77-73561. (Illus.). 1978. pap. 5.95 (ISBN 0-88415-097-6). Pacesetter Pr.

Little, Nina F. American Decorative Wall Painting: 1700-1850. 1972. pap. 7.50 o.p. (ISBN 0-525-47335-1). Dutton.

Little, Paul. Faith Is for People. (Orig.). 1977. pap. 3.95 (ISBN 0-88449-057-2). Vision Hse.

Little, Paul E. Know What You Believe. LC 76-105667. 192p. 1970. pap. 2.95 (ISBN 0-88207-024-X). Victor Bks.

--Know Why You Believe. LC 67-12231. 1967. pap. 2.95 (ISBN 0-88207-022-3). Victor Bks.

--Paul Little's Why & What Book. 240p. 1980. text ed. 8.95 (ISBN 0-88207-814-3). Victor Bks.

Little, Paul E., et al. His Guide to Evangelism. LC 77-72523. 1977. pap. 2.50 o.p. (ISBN 0-87784-488-7). Inter-Varsity.

Little, R. E. & Jebe, E. H. Statistical Design of Fatigue Experiments. LC 74-14802. 280p. 1975. 44.95 (ISBN 0-470-54115-6). Halsted Pr.

Little, Roger. Guillaume Apollinaire. (Athlone French Poets Ser). 160p. 1976. text ed. 20.00x (ISBN 0-485-14608-8, Athlone Pr); pap. text ed. 10.00x (ISBN 0-485-12208-1). Humanities.

--Saint-John Perse. (Athlone French Poets Ser.). 1973. text ed. 16.25x (ISBN 0-485-14602-9, Athlone Pr); pap. text ed. 8.75x (ISBN 0-485-12202-2, Athlone Pr). Humanities.

Little, Roger, ed. see Perse, Saint-John.

Little, Roger W., ed. Handbook of Military Institutions. LC 78-127989. (Sage Ser. on Armed Forces & Society: Vol. 1). 1971. 27.50x (ISBN 0-8039-0078-3). Sage.

Little, Sara. Language of the Christian Community. (Illus., Orig.). (gr. 11-12). 1965. pap. 3.45 (ISBN 0-8042-9240-X); tchrs' guide pap. 2.60. John Knox.

--Learning Together in the Christian Fellowship. LC 56-9220. (Orig.). 1956. pap. 3.95 (ISBN 0-8042-1320-8). John Knox.

Little, Stuart & Cantor, Arthur. Playmakers. 1971. pap. 2.95 o.p. (ISBN 0-525-47278-9). Dutton.

Little, T. R. The Arab World in the Twentieth Century. LC 77-179782. (Young Historian Ser.). (Illus.). 112p. (gr. 8-10). 1972. 4.50 o.p. (ISBN 0-381-99763-4, A05300, JD-J). John Day.

Little, William A. Gottfried August Burger. (World Authors Ser.: Germany: No. 270). 1974. lib. bdg. 12.50 (ISBN 0-8057-2185-1). Twayne.

Littlechild, S. C. Operational Research for Managers. 256p. 1977. 33.00x (ISBN 0-86003-504-2, Pub. by Allan Pubs England); pap. 16.50 (ISBN 0-86003-604-9). State Mutual Bk.

Littledale. Pinocchio. (ps-3). 1978. pap. 1.95 (ISBN 0-590-12070-0, Schol Pap). Schol Bk Serv.

Littledale, Freya. The Elves & the Shoemaker. LC 75-12500. (Illus.). 32p. (gr. k-3). 1975. 4.95 (ISBN 0-590-07426-1, Four Winds). Schol Bk Serv.

--The Elves & the Shoemaker. (Illus.). (gr. k-3). 1977. pap. 1.95 (ISBN 0-590-01441-2, Schol Pap); pap. 3.50 bk. & record (ISBN 0-590-20615-X). Schol Bk Serv.

--Seven at One Blow. (gr. k-3). 1977. pap. 1.50 (ISBN 0-590-10319-9, Schol Pap); pap. 3.50 bk. & record (ISBN 0-590-20600-1). Schol Bk Serv.

Littledale, Harold. Alexander. LC 64-10365. (Illus.). (gr. k-3). 1964. 5.95 o.s.i. (ISBN 0-8193-0086-1, Four Winds). Schol Bk Serv.

Littlefield, C. L., et al. Management of Office Operations. (Illus.). 1978. ref. 18.95 (ISBN 0-13-548834-6). P-H.

Littlefield, Charles W. Man, Minerals, & Masters. (Illus.). 140p. 1980. pap. 5.50 (ISBN 0-89540-059-6). Sun Pub.

Littlefield, Daniel F., Jr. Africans & Seminoles: From Removal to Emancipation. LC 77-86. (Contributions in Afro-American & African Studies: No. 32). 1977. lib. bdg. 17.95x (ISBN 0-8371-9529-2, LAS/). Greenwood.

--The Chickasaw Freedmen: A People Without a Country. LC 79-6192. (Contributions in Afro-American and African Studies: No. 54). xii, 248p. 1980. lib. bdg. 25.00 (ISBN 0-313-22313-0, LCF/). Greenwood.

Littlefield, Henry W. History of Europe Since Eighteen Fifteen. 21st ed. 1963. pap. 3.95 (ISBN 0-06-460012-2, CO 12, COS). Har-Row.

Littlefield, James E., jt. auth. see Kerr, John R.

Littlefield, James E. & Shawver, Donald L., eds. Doctoral Programs in Marketing: Proceedings of the Educational Workshop on Doctoral Education in Marketing, Univ. of N. C., Spring, 1976. LC 77-6724. 1977. pap. text ed. 7.00 o.p. (ISBN 0-87757-096-5). Am Mktg.

Littlefield, Larry J. Biology of the Plant Rusts: An Introduction. (Illus.). 112p. 1981. text ed. 9.00. Iowa St U Pr.

Littlefield, Mark G. A Bibliographic Index to Romance Philology, Vols. 1-25. 1974. 34.50x (ISBN 0-520-02455-9). U of Cal Pr.

Littlefield, Roy E., III. William Randolph Hearst: His Role in American Progressivism. LC 80-5729. 405p. 1980. lib. bdg. 22.75 (ISBN 0-8191-1320-4); pap. text ed. 13.75 (ISBN 0-8191-1321-2). U Pr of Amer.

Littlejohn, Bruce. Laugh with the Judge. LC 74-22868. 1974. 6.95 o.p. (ISBN 0-87844-025-9). Sandlapper Store.

Littlejohn, G. N., jt. auth. see Freebairen-Smith, S. J.

Littlejohn, G. N., jt. auth. see Freebairn-Smith, S. J.

Littlejohn, Stephen, jt. auth. see Jabusch, David M.

Littlejohn, Stephen W. Theories of Human Communication. 1978. text ed. 15.95 (ISBN 0-675-08431-8). Merrill.

Littlepage, Loyd. Why David Can. (Illus.). (ps-3). 1977. 2.50 (ISBN 0-911336-67-2). Sci of Mind.

Littleton, August V. The Art & Science of Psychomancy with Concrete & Practical Applications. (Library of Scientific Psychology Bk.). (Illus.). 107p. 1981. 29.45 (ISBN 0-89920-022-2). Am Inst Psych.

Littleton, C. Scott. The New Comparative Mytholgy: An Anthropological Assessment of the Theories of Georges Dumezil. 3rd ed. 1980. pap. 5.95 (ISBN 0-520-04103-8, CAMPUS 216). U of Cal Pr.

--The New Comparative Mythology: An Anthropological Assessment of the Theories of George Dumezil. 2nd ed. 1974. pap. 5.95x o.p. (ISBN 0-520-02403-6). U of Cal Pr.

Littleton, Harvey. Glassblowing: A Search for Form. 136p. 1980. pap. 9.95 (ISBN 0-442-24341-3). Van Nos Reinhold.

Littlewood, Barbara, tr. see Press, Hans J.

Littlewood, Barbara S., jt. auth. see Davies, Julian.

Littlewood, Cyril. The World's Vanishing Birds. LC 72-92101. (Illus.). 64p. 1973. lib. bdg. 5.95 o.p. (ISBN 0-668-02889-0). Arco.

Littlewood, Thomas B. Horner of Illinois. LC 70-78329. 1969. 12.95x o.s.i. (ISBN 0-8101-0250-1). Northwestern U Pr.

Littlton, Thomas. Lyttleton: His Treatise of Tenures. Berkowitz, David S. & Thorne, Samuel E., eds. LC 77-89237. (Classics of English Legal History in the Modern Era Ser.: Vol. 73). 727p. 1979. lib. bdg. 40.00 (ISBN 0-8240-3172-5). Garland Pub.

Littman, Connie. Basic Pattern Making: An Individualized Approach. LC 76-14097. (gr. 9-12). 1977. pap. text ed. 7.20 (ISBN 0-8273-0581-8); instructor's guide 1.50 (ISBN 0-8273-0582-6). Delmar.

--Pattern Making Design: Skirts & Pants. LC 76-14096. (gr. 9-12). 1977. pap. text ed. 4.80 (ISBN 0-8273-0583-4). Delmar.

--Pattern Making Design: Sleeved & Tailored Garments. LC 76-14096. (gr. 9-12). 1977. pap. text ed. 4.80 (ISBN 0-8273-0585-0). Delmar.

--Pattern Making Design: Sleeveless Dresses. LC 76-14096. (gr. 9-12). 1977. pap. text ed. 4.80 (ISBN 0-8273-0584-2). Delmar.

Littmark, U. & Ziegler, J. F. Handbook of Range Distributions for Energetic Ions in All Elements. LC 79-27825. (The Stopping & Ranges of Ions in Matter Ser.: Vol. 6). 490p. 72.00 (ISBN 0-08-023879-3). Pergamon.

Littner, Ner. Five More. LC 80-80866. 56p. (Orig.). 1980. pap. text ed. 3.95 (ISBN 0-87868-189-2). Child Welfare.

Litton. Microwave Cooking: Everyday Dinners in Half an Hour. 1980. 10.95 (ISBN 0-442-24851-2). Van Nos Reinhold.

--Microwave Cooking on a Diet. 160p. 1981. 10.95 (ISBN 0-442-24526-2). Van Nos Reinhold.

Litton, E. A. Introduction to Dogmatic Theology. 1960. 16.00 (ISBN 0-227-67501-0). Attic Pr.

Litton, Freddie W. Education of the Trainable Mentally Retarded: Curriculum, Methods, Materials. LC 77-10772. (Illus.). 1978. text ed. 16.95 (ISBN 0-8016-3023-1). Mosby.

Litton, Freddie W., jt. auth. see Gearheart, Bill R.

Litton, Gaston, jt. auth. see Dale, E. E.

Litton, Glenn, jt. auth. see Smith, Cecil.

Littrell, W. Boyd. Bureaucratic Justice: Police, Prosecutors, & Plea Bargaining. LC 79-18158. (Sage Library of Social Research: Vol. 93). (Illus.). 1979. 18.00x (ISBN 0-8039-1264-1); pap. 8.95x (ISBN 0-8039-1265-X). Sage.

Litvag, I. Singer in the Shadows. 1972. 7.95 o.s.i. (ISBN 0-02-573350-8). Macmillan.

Litvak, Stuart. Unstress Yourself. LC 79-89639. 172p. (Orig.). 1980. pap. 4.95 (ISBN 0-686-64397-6). Ross-Erikson.

Litvak, Stuart B. Unstress Yourself! (gr. 9 up). 1979. pap. 4.95x (ISBN 0-686-24982-8, Pub. by Mainstream). Ross-Erikson.

Litwack, G., ed. Biochemical Actions of Hormones, Vol. 8. 1981. write for info. (ISBN 0-12-452808-2). Acad Pr.

Litwack, Gerald, ed. Biochemical Actions of Hormones, 7 vols. Incl. Vol. 1. 1970. 52.75 (ISBN 0-12-452801-5); Vol. 2. 1972. 52.75 (ISBN 0-12-452802-3); Vol. 3. 1975. 51.50 (ISBN 0-12-452803-1); Vol. 4. 1977. 47.00 (ISBN 0-12-452804-X); Vol. 5. 1978. 42.50 (ISBN 0-12-452805-8); Vol. 6. 1979. 42.50 (ISBN 0-12-452806-6); Vol. 7. 1980. 45.00 (ISBN 0-12-452807-4). LC 70-107567. Acad Pr.

Litwack, Lawrence, et al. Health Counseling. 290p. 1980. 13.50 (ISBN 0-8385-3665-4). ACC.

Litwack, Leon, jt. auth. see Graham, Otis L., Jr.

Litwak, Eugene & Meyer, Henry. School, Family, & Neighborhood. 400p. 1974. 17.50x (ISBN 0-231-03354-0). Columbia U Pr.

Litwiller, Bonnie & Duncan, David. Activities for the Maintenance of Computational Skills. 1980. pap. 3.20 (ISBN 0-87353-169-8). NCTM.

Litwinski, Wiktor, tr. see Duleba, Wladyslaw & Sokolowska, Zofia.

Litz, A. Walton. Art of James Joyce: Method & Design in Ulysses & Finnegans Wake. 1964. pap. 3.95 (ISBN 0-19-500258-X, GB). Oxford U Pr.

--James Joyce. (English Authors Ser.: No. 31). 1966. lib. bdg. 9.95 (ISBN 0-8057-1300-X). Twayne.

Litzenburg, Thomas V., Jr., jt. auth. see Diamond, Malcolm L.

Litzinger, Boyd & Knickerbocker, K. L., eds. The Browning Critics. LC 65-27008. 448p. 1965. pap. 7.50x (ISBN 0-8131-0113-1). U Pr of Ky.

Litzinger, F. D., et al. Elementary Accounting: A Logical Approach. LC 77-86162. (Accounting Ser.). 1978. pap. text ed. 18.95 o.p. (ISBN 0-88244-160-4). Grid Pub.

Litzmann, Berthold. Clara Schumann: An Artist's Life, 2 vols. (Music Reprint Ser.). 1979. Repr. of 1913 ed. Set. lib. bdg. 69.50 (ISBN 0-306-79582-5). Da Capo.

Liu, Alan P. Communications & National Integration in Communist China. (Center for Chinese Studies, Univ. of Michigan). 1971. 20.00 (ISBN 0-520-01882-6); pap. 6.95x (ISBN 0-520-02901-1). U of Cal Pr.

--Political Culture & Group Conflict in Communist China. LC 74-14195. (Studies in International & Comparative Politics: No. 4). 205p. 1976. text ed. 19.40 (ISBN 0-87436-196-6); pap. text ed. 6.00 (ISBN 0-87436-197-4). ABC-Clio.

Liu, Allan J., ed. The American Sporting Collector's Handbook. 1976. 13.95 (ISBN 0-87691-217-X). Winchester Pr.

Liu, Bede, jt. auth. see Peled, Abraham.

Liu, Jin-An. Sino-American Juvenile Justice System. LC 80-67051. (Scholarly Monographs). 340p. 1980. pap. 27.50 (ISBN 0-8408-0512-8). Carrollton Pr.

Liu, Kwang-Ching, jt. auth. see Fairbank, John K.

Liu, Leonard Y., ed. see National Computer Conference, 1978.

Liu, P. T. & Sutinen, J. G. Control Theory & Mathematical Economics: Proceedings of the Third Kingston Conference, Pt. B. 26.50 (ISBN 0-8247-6852-3). Dekker.

Liu, Pon-Tai, ed. Dynamic Optimization & Mathematical Economics. (Mathematical Concepts & Methods in Science & Engineering Ser.: Vol. 19). (Illus.). 280p. 1980. 29.50 (ISBN 0-306-40245-9, Plenum Pr). Plenum Pub.

Liu, Sarah & Vittitow, Mary L. Games Without Losers. LC 75-25279. (Illus.). 112p. 1975. pap. 5.95 (ISBN 0-913916-17-X). Incentive Pubns.

Liu, Shih S., tr. from Chinese. Chinese Classical Prose: The Eight Masters of the T'ang-Sung Period. LC 79-129782. (A Renditions Bk.). (Illus.). 3384p. 1980. 20.00 (ISBN 0-295-95662-3). U of Wash Pr.

Liu Ts'un-Yan. Buddhist & Taoist Influences on Chinese Novels: The Authorship of the Feng Shen Yen I, Vol. 1. LC 70-222767. 334p. 1962. 32.50x (ISBN 3-447-00564-5). Intl Pubns Serv.

Liu, William T., ed. Methodological Problems in Minority Research. (Orig.). 1981. pap. write for info. (ISBN 0-934584-09-5). Pacific-Asian.

Liu, Wu-chi & Lo, Irving Y., eds. K'uei Yeh Chi. LC 76-12366. 288p. (Chinese.). 1976. 19.50x (ISBN 0-253-33177-3); pap. text ed. 6.95x (ISBN 0-253-33178-1). Ind U Pr.

Liu, Yu-Cheng, jt. auth. see Gibson, Glenn A.

Liu Da. Ta'i Chi Chu'uan & I Ching: A Choreography of Body & Mind. LC 79-183640. (Illus.). 1972. pap. 1.95 o.p. (ISBN 0-06-061667-9, RD-46, HarpR). Har-Row.

Liu Kwang-Ching, ed. Americans & Chinese: A Historical Essay & a Bibliography. LC 63-19141. 1963. 10.00x (ISBN 0-674-03000-1). Harvard U Pr.

--Anglo-American Steamship Rivalry in China, 1862-1874. LC 62-9426. (East Asian Ser: No. 8). (Illus.). 1962. 10.00x (ISBN 0-674-03601-8). Harvard U Pr.

Liungman, Karl. What Is I.Q.? 1975. pap. 5.95 (ISBN 0-86033-040-0). Gordon-Cremonesi.

Liu Shao-Chi. How to Be a Good Communist. LC 75-26943. 1967. Repr. of 1964 ed. 4.00 o.p. (ISBN 0-87364-079-9). Paladin Ent.

Liuzzi, Fernando. La Lauda e i Primordi Della Melodia Italiana, 2 vols. LC 80-2238. 1981. Repr. of 1935 ed. 185.00 (ISBN 0-404-19037-5). AMS Pr.

Livadeas, Themistocles & Charitos, Minas. The Real Truth Concerning Apostolos Makrakis. Orthodox Christian Educational Society, ed. Cummings, Denver, tr. from Hellenic. 230p. (Orig.). 1952. pap. 4.00x (ISBN 0-938366-30-0). Orthodox Chr.

Livanova. L. D. Landau. Sykes, J., tr. 1980. 26.00 (ISBN 0-08-023076-8). Pergamon.

Lively, C. E. & Taeuber, Conrad. Rural Migration in the United States. LC 71-165601. (FDR & the Era of the New Deal Ser.). 1971. Repr. of 1939 ed. pap. 19.50 (ISBN 0-306-70351-3). Da Capo.

Lively, Chauncy K. Chauncy Lively's Flybox: A Portfolio of Modern Trout Flies. (Illus.). 96p. 1980. pap. 9.95 (ISBN 0-8117-2078-0). Stackpole.

Lively, Jeanne. Howdy: Stories About the Uncommon West Texans. Roy, Linda, ed. (Illus.). 70p. 1974. 5.50 o.p. (ISBN 0-89015-070-2). Nortex Pr.

Lively, Penelope. The Ghost of Thomas Kempe. 192p. (gr. 3-6). 1973. PLB 8.95 (ISBN 0-525-30495-9). Dutton.

--Judgment Day. LC 80-2749. 192p. 1981. 11.95 (ISBN 0-385-15814-9). Doubleday.

Liverani, Giuseppe. Italian Ceramics. Charleston, Robert J., ed. LC 78-55079. (Masterpieces of Western & Near Eastern Ceramics Ser.: Vol. V). (Illus.). 308p. 1981. 200.00 (ISBN 0-87011-346-1); pre-April 1981 165.00 (ISBN 0-686-63472-1). Kodansha.

Liveright, James. Simple Methods for Detecting Buying & Selling Points in Securities. Repr. of 1968 ed. flexible cover 3.50 (ISBN 0-87034-028-X). Fraser Pub Co.

Livermore, Ann. A Short History of Spanish Music. 262p. 1972. 40.50x (ISBN 0-7156-0634-4, Pub. by Duckworth England); pap. 13.50x (ISBN 0-7156-0886-X). Biblio Dist.

Livermore, Harold. The Origins of Spain & Portugal. 1971. text ed. 13.50x o.p. (ISBN 0-04-946005-6). Allen Unwin.

Livermore, Harold U. New History of Portugal. 2nd ed. (Illus.). 1977. 51.95 (ISBN 0-521-21320-7); pap. 12.95x (ISBN 0-521-29103-8). Cambridge U Pr.

Livermore, Mary A., jt. auth. see Willard, Frances E.

Livermore, Sarah, et al, eds. The American Bar - The Canadian Bar - The International Bar: 1981. 63rd ed. LC 18-21110. 3062p. 1981. 130.00 (ISBN 0-931398-06-1). R B Forster.

Livermore, Seward W. Woodrow Wilson & the War Congress, 1916-18. LC 66-14666. Orig. Title: Politics Is Adjourned. 335p. 1968. pap. 2.95 (ISBN 0-295-78564-0, WP42). U of Wash Pr.

Livernash, E. Robert, jt. auth. see Peach, David A.

Livernash, E. Robert, ed. Comparable Worth: Issues & Alternatives. LC 80-67644. 260p. 1980. 21.00 (ISBN 0-937856-01-0). Equal Employ.

Liversidge, Douglas. First Book of Arctic Exploration. LC 75-114925. (First Bks). (Illus.). (gr. 4-6). 1970. PLB 4.90 o.p. (ISBN 0-531-00711-1). Watts.

--First Book of the Arctic. LC 67-10058. (First Bks). (Illus.). (gr. 4-6). 1967. PLB 4.90 o.p. (ISBN 0-531-00472-4). Watts.

--The Luddites: Machine-Breakers of the Early Nineteenth Century. (World Focus Bks.). (Illus.). 96p. (gr. 7-12). 1972. PLB 5.90 (ISBN 0-531-02162-9). Watts.

--Peter the Great: The Reformer-Tsar. LC 68-18579. (Biography Ser). (Illus.). (gr. 7 up). 1968. PLB 5.90 o.p. (ISBN 0-531-00914-9). Watts.

--Saint Francis of Assisi. LC 68-10187. (Biography Ser). (Map). (gr. 7 up). 1968. PLB 5.90 o.p. (ISBN 0-531-00922-X). Watts.

Livesay, Harold C. American Made: Men Who Shaped the American Economy. LC 79-15971. (Illus.). 1980. Repr. of 1979 ed. 11.95 (ISBN 0-316-52871-4); pap. text ed. 6.95 (ISBN 0-316-52874-9). Little.

Livesay, John. Bible Beasts. LC 74-84764. 1976. 3.00 (ISBN 0-8309-0130-2). Herald Hse.

Livesey, Herbert B. Second Chance: Blueprints for Life Change. LC 77-8571. 1977. 8.95 o.p. (ISBN 0-397-01223-3). Lippincott.

Livesley, R. K. Matrix Methods of Structural Analysis. 2nd ed. 208p. 1975. text ed. 28.00 (ISBN 0-08-018888-5); pap. text ed. 15.00 (ISBN 0-08-018887-7). Pergamon.

Livezey, William E. Mahan on Sea Power. rev. ed. LC 79-6720. (Illus.). 389p. 1981. 15.95 (ISBN 0-8061-1569-6). U of Okla Pr.

Living Art Company. Aspen: The One Hundred Year High. LC 79-55797. (Illus.). 1980. 34.95 (ISBN 0-916728-30-7). Bks in Focus.

Livingood, James W. Hamilton County. Dunn, Joy B. & Crawford, Charles W., eds. (Tennessee County History Ser.: No. 33). 144p. 1981. 12.50 (ISBN 0-87870-120-6). Memphis St Univ.

--Philadelphia-Baltimore Trade Rivalry: 1780-1860. LC 47-29. 195p. 1947. 5.00 (ISBN 0-911124-35-7). Pa Hist & Mus.

Livingston, A. D. Advanced Bass Tackle & Boats. LC 75-15557. (Illus.). 240p. 1975. 9.95 o.p. (ISBN 0-397-01100-8). Lippincott.

--Fishing for Bass: Modern Tactics & Tackle. LC 74-8026. 1974. 8.95 o.s.i. (ISBN 0-397-01017-6). Lippincott.

--Fly-Rodding for Bass. LC 75-38710. 1976. 8.95 o.p. (ISBN 0-397-01112-1). Lippincott.

Livingston, Arthur, ed. see Mosca, Gaetano.

Livingston, Carole. I'll Never Be Fat Again. 224p. 1981. pap. 2.50 (ISBN 0-345-28659-6). Ballantine.

Livingston, Dennis, jt. auth. see Diwan, Romesh K.

Livingston, E. A., ed. see International Congress on Biblical Studies.

Livingston, G. E. & Chang, Charlotte M., eds. Food Service Systems: Analysis, Design & Implementation. 1980. 30.50 (ISBN 0-12-453150-4). Acad Pr.

Livingston, G. Herbert. The Pentateuch in Its Cultural Environment. 1974. 11.95 (ISBN 0-8010-5540-7). Baker Bk.

Livingston, James. The Ethics of Belief. LC 74-18616. (American Academy of Religion. Studies in Religion). 1974. pap. 7.50 (ISBN 0-88420-121-X, 010009). Scholars Pr Ca.

Livingston, John C. Fair Game? Inequality & Affirmative Action. LC 79-13422. 1979. text ed. 14.95x (ISBN 0-7167-1131-1); pap. text ed. 7.95x (ISBN 0-7167-1132-X). W H Freeman.

Livingston, Jon, et al. The Japan Reader, 2 vols. LC 73-7015. 1974. Vol. 1. pap. 7.95 (ISBN 0-394-70668-4); Vol. 2. pap. 7.95 (ISBN 0-394-70669-2). Pantheon.

Livingston, Kimball. Sailing the Bay. (Illus.). 128p. (Orig.). 1981. pap. 5.95 (ISBN 0-87701-180-X). Chronicle Bks.

Livingston, Lida & Schrader, Constance. Wrinkles. Date not set. pap. 2.50 (ISBN 0-345-29418-1). Ballantine.

Livingston, Lida, jt. auth. see Fillian, Barbie.

Livingston, Margie. The Yachtsman's Mate's Guide. (Yachtman's Guide Ser.). (Illus.). 128p. 1980. 8.95 (ISBN 0-87165-087-8, ZD Bks). Ziff-Davis Pub.

Livingston, Myra C. No Way of Knowing: Dallas Poems. LC 80-14584. 64p. (gr. 5 up). 1980. 7.95 (ISBN 0-689-50179-X, McElderry Bk). Atheneum.

--O Sliver of Liver. LC 78-23681. (Illus.). (gr. 4-7). 1979. 7.95 (ISBN 0-689-50133-1, McElderry Bk). Atheneum.

--Poems of Christmas. LC 80-13627. 132p. (gr. 5 up). 1980. 9.95 (ISBN 0-689-50180-3, McElderry Bk). Atheneum.

Livingston, Myra C. & Blegvad, Erik. I'm Hiding. LC 61-6119. (Illus.). (gr. k-2). 1961. 4.50 o.p. (ISBN 0-15-238090-6, HJ). HarBraceJ.

Livingston, Myra C., ed. Speak Roughly to Your Little Boy: A Collection of Parodies & Burlesques. LC 71-140779. (Illus.). (gr. 3 up). 1971. 8.50 o.p. (ISBN 0-15-277859-4, HJ). HarBraceJ.

Livingston, Myra C., compiled by see Carroll, Lewis.

Livingston, Peter, et al. The Complete Book of Country Swing & Western Dance. LC 80-70555. 1981. pap. 9.95 (ISBN 0-385-17601-5, Dolp). Doubleday.

Livingston, Robert B. Sensory Processing, Perception, & Behavior. LC 76-19854. 1978. soft cover 10.50 (ISBN 0-89004-134-2). Raven.

Livingston, Robert B., ed. Lung Cancer. (Cancer Treatment & Research Ser.: No. 1). (Illus.). 320p. 1981. PLB 47.50 (ISBN 90-247-2394-9, Pub. by Martinus Nijhoff). Kluwer Boston.

Livingston, Samuel. Comprehensive Management of Epilepsy in Infancy, Childhood & Adolescence. (Illus.). 672p. 1972. 39.75 (ISBN 0-398-02342-5). C C Thomas.

--Living with Epileptic Seizures. (Illus.). 368p. 1963. 9.75 (ISBN 0-398-01135-4). C C Thomas.

Livingston, Samuel A. & Stoll, Clarice S. Simulation Games: An Introduction for the Social Studies Teacher. LC 77-171567. (Orig.). 1973. pap. text ed. 8.95 (ISBN 0-02-919240-4). Free Pr.

Livingston, William S. Federalism & Constitutional Change. LC 74-9226. 380p. 1974. Repr. of 1956 ed. lib. bdg. 29.00x (ISBN 0-8371-7623-9, LIFC). Greenwood.

Livingstone, Arthur. Social Policy in Developing Countries. (Library of Social Policy & Administration). 1969. pap. text ed. 2.50x (ISBN 0-7100-6443-8). Humanities.

Livingstone, David. Livingstone's Missionary Correspondence, 1841-1856. Schapera, I., ed. & intro. by. (Illus.). 1961. 20.00x (ISBN 0-520-00761-1). U of Cal Pr.

Livingstone, Dinah, tr. see Leclercq, Jacques.

Livingstone, E. A., ed. The Concise Oxford Dictionary of the Christian Church. 1978. 18.95 (ISBN 0-19-211549-9). Oxford U Pr.

Livingstone, E. A., ed. see Sixth International Congress on Biblical Studies, Oxford, 3-7 April 1978.

Livingstone, Elizabeth, jt. auth. see Norman, Claude E.

Livingstone, Elizabeth A., jt. auth. see Cross, F. L.

Livingstone, Hugh. University: An Organizational Analysis. 1974. 14.95x (ISBN 0-216-89705-X). Intl Ideas.

Livingstone, Ian, ed. Development Economics & Policy Readings. (Illus.). 368p. (Orig.). 1981. text ed. 38.95x (ISBN 0-04-382025-5, 2581); pap. text ed. 15.00x (ISBN 0-04-382026-3, 2582). Allen Unwin.

Livingstone, J. L. Managerial Accounting: The Behavioral Foundations. LC 74-23018. (Accounting Ser.). 1975. pap. text ed. 8.95 o.p. (ISBN 0-88244-079-9). Grid Pub.

Livingstone, J. L. & Kerrigan, Harry D. Financial Accounting: An Introductory Study. LC 76-5615. (Accounting Ser.). 1977. text ed. 19.95 o.p. (ISBN 0-88244-100-0). Grid Pub.

Livingstone, J. L., jt. auth. see Largay, James A.

Livingstone, James V. The British Economy in Theory & Practice. LC 74-13513. 240p. 1975. 18.95 (ISBN 0-312-10080-9). St Martin.

Livingstone, Richard. Electricity from the Sun: Photovoltaic Energy. (Energy Systems Bks.). (Illus.). 160p. 1981. pap. 7.95 (ISBN 0-07-038150-X). McGraw.

Livingstone, Richard W. Greek Ideals & Modern Life. LC 72-82814. 1969. Repr. of 1935 ed. 10.50x (ISBN 0-8196-0245-0). Biblo.

Livingstone, S. E. The Chemistry of Ruthenium, Rhodium, Palladium, Osmium, Iridium & Platinum. (Pergamon Texts in Inorganic Chemistry: Vol. 25). 208p. 1975. text ed. 32.00 (ISBN 0-08-018876-1); pap. text ed. 17.50 (ISBN 0-08-018875-3). Pergamon.

Livinston, Pat. The Pittsburgh Steelers: A Pictorial History. LC 79-91292. 198p. 1980. 14.95 (ISBN 0-918908-11-6). Jordan & Co.

Livolsi, Virginia A. & Logerfo, Paul. Thyroiditis. 192p. 1981. 54.95 (ISBN 0-8493-5705-5). CRC Pr.

Liv Tieh-Yua, jt. auth. see Shadick, Harold.

Livy. Ab Urbe Condita, 5 vols. Incl. Vol. 1. Books 1-5. 2nd ed. Ogilvie, R. M., et al, eds. 1974. 18.50x (ISBN 0-19-814661-2); Vol. 2. Books 6-10. Conway, R. S., et al, eds. 1920. 18.50x (ISBN 0-19-814621-3); Vol. 3. Books 21-25. Conway, R. S. & Johnson, S. K., eds. 1929. 24.00x (ISBN 0-19-814622-1); Vol. 4. Books 26-30. Conway, R. S. & Johnson, S. K., eds. 1934. 22.50x (ISBN 0-19-814623-X); Vol. 5. Books 31-35. McDonald, Alexander H., ed. 1965. 18.50x (ISBN 0-19-814646-9). (Oxford Classical Texts Ser.). Oxford U Pr.

--The Early History of Rome. DeSelincourt, Aubrey, tr. lib. bdg. 10.50x (ISBN 0-88307-393-5). Gannon.

--War with Hannibal. De Selincourt, Aubrey, tr. (Classics Ser.). (Orig.). 1965. pap. 5.95 (ISBN 0-14-044145-X). Penguin.

Li Yu. Twelve Towers. Mao, Nathan K., tr. from Chinese. LC 73-92416. 154p. 1979. pap. 5.95 (ISBN 0-295-95640-2). U of Wash Pr.

Lizardi, Jose J. Fernandez De see Fernandez De Lizardi, Jose J.

Lizarralde, German, jt. auth. see Colwell, John A.

Lize, Diana & Lize, Emile. Dear Teacher. (Illus.). 75p. 1980. pap. 3.95 o.p. (ISBN 0-919676-22-7, 1657). Caroline Hse.

Lize, Emile, jt. auth. see Lize, Diana.

Lizot, Jacques. Circle of Fires: Life Among the Yanomami. Simon, Ernest, tr. from Fr. 224p. 1981. 22.50x (ISBN 0-8476-6968-8). Rowman.

Ljung, Magnus. Reflections on the English Progressive. (Gothenberg Studies in English: 46). 166p. 1981. pap. text ed. 19.75x (ISBN 91-7346-080-X, Pub. by Acta Univertatis, Sweden). Humanities.

Ljungmark, Lars. Swedish Exodus. Westerberg, Kermit B., tr. from Swedish. LC 79-10498. 192p. 1979. 12.95 (ISBN 0-8093-0905-X). S Ill U Pr.

Llamzon, Benjamin S. Reason, Experience & the Moral Life. LC 78-58444. 1978. pap. text ed. 10.25 (ISBN 0-8191-0534-1). U Pr of Amer.

Llaurado, J. G., et al, eds. Biologic & Clinical Effects of Low-Frequency Magnetic & Electric Fields. (Illus.). 384p. 1974. 44.75 (ISBN 0-398-03024-3). C C Thomas.

Llewellyn, David T. International Financial Integration: The Limits of Sovereignty. 200p. 1980. 29.95x (ISBN 0-470-26960-X). Halsted Pr.

Llewellyn, Meyer. The Stray Cow. pap. 2.15 o.p. (ISBN 0-08-015697-5). Pergamon.

Llewellyn, Richard. How Green Was My Valley. (gr. 9 up). 1941. 15.95 (ISBN 0-02-573430-X); pap. 2.75 (ISBN 0-02-022550-4, 02255). Macmillan.

--How Green Was My Valley. Date not set. Repr. lib. bdg. 18.65x (ISBN 0-88411-936-X). Amereon Ltd.

--Tell Me Now, & Again. LC 77-80895. 1978. 8.95 o.p. (ISBN 0-385-12123-7). Doubleday.

Llewellyn, Sam. Hell Bay. 1981. pap. 2.50 (ISBN 0-345-29642-7). Ballantine.

Llewellyn-Jones, Derek. Everywoman: A Gynaecological Guide for Life. (Illus.). 1978. 11.95 (ISBN 0-571-04961-3, Pub. by Faber & Faber); pap. 4.95 (ISBN 0-571-04960-5). Merrimack Bk Serv.

--Fundamentals of Obstetrics & Gynaecology, Vol. 2: Gynaecology. (Illus.). 1978. 29.00 (ISBN 0-571-04929-X, Pub. by Faber & Faber); pap. 18.00 (ISBN 0-571-04958-3). Merrimack Bk Serv.

--Sex & V. D. 1975. 8.95 (ISBN 0-571-10482-7, Pub. by Faber & Faber); pap. 3.50 (ISBN 0-571-10483-5). Merrimack Bk Serv.

Llobera, Josep, jt. ed. see Kahn, Joel.

Llosa, M. V., jt. ed. see Brotherston, G.

Lloyd, A. C., et al. Gregg Typing for Colleges: Intensive Course. (Gregg College Typing Ser.: Series 4). 1978. pap. text ed. 9.95 (ISBN 0-07-038252-2, G); instructor's manual 12.95 (ISBN 0-07-038259-X); proofguide for lessons 2.80 (ISBN 0-07-038261-1); wk. guide for lessons 5.95 (ISBN 0-686-60821-6). McGraw.

Lloyd, A. L. Folk Song in England. 1968. pap. 3.65 o.p. (ISBN 0-7178-0278-7). Intl Pub Co.

Lloyd, Alan C., et al. Typing One: General Course. (Illus.). (gr. 9-12). 1976. text ed. 11.28x (ISBN 0-07-038241-7, G); wkbks. 3.96x ea.; course management manual 12.75x (ISBN 0-07-038247-6). McGraw.

--Typing Two, Advanced Course. (Illus.). (gr. 9-12). 1977. text ed. 10.72 (ISBN 0-07-038257-3, G); wkbks. 3.76 ea.; tchrs manual & key 11.65 (ISBN 0-07-038247-6). McGraw.

Lloyd, Albert. Deutsch und Deutschland Heute. 2nd ed. 1981. text ed. price not set (ISBN 0-442-24461-4). D Van Nostrand.

Lloyd, Anne, jt. auth. see Weber, Michael.

Lloyd, Barbara & Gay, J., eds. Universals of Human Thought. LC 79-41471. (Illus.). 300p. Date not set. 47.50 (ISBN 0-521-22953-7); pap. 14.95 (ISBN 0-521-29818-0). Cambridge U Pr.

Lloyd, Charles. Desultory Thoughts in London; Titus & Gisippus; with Other Poems. 1821. Reiman, Donald H., ed. LC 75-31227. (Romantic Context Ser.: Poetry 1789-1830). 1978. lib. bdg. 47.00 (ISBN 0-8240-2177-0). Garland Pub.

--Nugae Canorae: Poems. 1819. Reiman, Donald H., ed. LC 75-31226. (Romantic Context Ser.: Poetry 1789-1830). 1978. lib. bdg. 47.00 (ISBN 0-8240-2176-2). Garland Pub.

--Poems. Reiman, Donald H., ed. Incl. Blank Verse by Charles Lloyd & Charles Lamb. Repr. of 1798 ed; Poetical Essays on the Character of Pope. Repr. of 1821 ed; Poems. Repr. of 1823 ed. LC 75-31225. (Romantic Context Ser.: Poetry 1789-1830). 1978. lib. bdg. 47.00 (ISBN 0-8240-2175-4). Garland Pub.

Lloyd, Christopher. A Catalogue of the Earlier Italian Paintings in the Ashmolean Museum. (Illus.). 1977. 49.50x (ISBN 0-19-817342-3). Oxford U Pr.

--Masacio. (Oresko-Jupiter Art Bks). (Illus.). 96p. 1981. 17.95 (ISBN 0-933516-86-X, Pub. by Oresko-Jupiter England). Hippocrene Bks.

Lloyd, Christopher, jt. ed. see Brettell, Richard.

Lloyd, Cynthia, et al, eds. Women in the Labor Market. LC 79-15547. 1977. 27.50x (ISBN 0-231-04638-3). Columbia U Pr.

Lloyd, Cynthia B., ed. Sex, Discrimination, & the Division of Labor. LC 74-32175. 432p. 1975. 25.00x (ISBN 0-231-03750-3); pap. 10.00x (ISBN 0-231-03751-1). Columbia U Pr.

Lloyd, D. G. Modern Syllabus Algebra. 1971. 19.50 (ISBN 0-08-015965-6); pap. 9.75 (ISBN 0-08-015964-8). Pergamon.

Lloyd, D. I., ed. Philosophy & the Teacher. (Students' Library of Education). 180p. 1975. 16.00 (ISBN 0-7100-8282-7); pap. 7.95 (ISBN 0-7100-8288-6). Routledge & Kegan.

Lloyd, David K. & Lipow, Myron. Reliability: Management, Methods & Mathematics. 2nd rev. ed. LC 77-80554. 1977. Repr. of 1962 ed. 17.50 (ISBN 0-9601504-1-2). Lloyd & Lipow.

Lloyd, E. Handbook of Applicable Mathematics: Probability, Vol. 2. (Handbook of Applicable Mathematics Ser.). 444p. 1980. 32.50 (ISBN 0-471-27821-1, Pub. by Wiley-Interscience). Wiley.

Lloyd, E. Keith, ed. see Tomescu, Ioan.

Lloyd, Ernest. The Book That Lives. (Uplook Ser.). 31p. 1954. pap. 0.75 (ISBN 0-8163-0065-8, 02435-6). Pacific Pr Pub Assn.

--This Was Abe Lincoln. 30p. 1954. pap. 0.75 (ISBN 0-8163-0077-1, 20365-3). Pacific Pr Pub Assn.

Lloyd, Eva B. Annie: Herald of Home Missions. (Orig.). 1981. pap. 1.25 (ISBN 0-8054-9502-9). Broadman.

Lloyd, G. A. Egypt Since Cromer, 2 Vols. LC 68-9625. 1970. Repr. Set. 28.50 (ISBN 0-86527-056-2). Fertig.

--Radiology of the Orbit. (Monographs in Clinical Radiology: Vol. 7). (Illus.). 250p. 1975. text ed. 28.00 (ISBN 0-7216-5792-3). Saunders.

Lloyd, G. E. Greek Science After Aristotle. LC 72-11959. (Ancient Culture & Society Ser.). (Illus.). 208p. 1973. 6.95x (ISBN 0-393-04371-1); pap. 4.95 (ISBN 0-393-00780-4). Norton.

Lloyd, G. E. & Owen, G. E., eds. Aristotle on Mind & the Senses. LC 77-9389. (Classical Studies). 1978. 38.50 (ISBN 0-521-21669-9). Cambridge U Pr.

Lloyd, G. R. Magic, Reason & Experience: Studies in the Origin & Development of Greek Science. LC 78-25710. (Illus.). 1979. 59.50 (ISBN 0-521-22373-3); pap. 19.95 (ISBN 0-521-29641-2). Cambridge U Pr.

Lloyd, Geoffrey E. Aristotle: Growth & Structure of His Thought. LC 68-21195. (Orig.). 1968. 38.50 (ISBN 0-521-07049-X); pap. 9.95x (ISBN 0-521-09456-9). Cambridge U Pr.

--Polarity & Analogy. 1966. 59.50 (ISBN 0-521-05578-4). Cambridge U Pr.

Lloyd, H. The Legal Limits of Journalism. 1968. pap. 4.20 (ISBN 0-08-012914-5). Pergamon.

Lloyd, H. G. The Red Fox. (Illus.). 320p. 1980. 45.00 (ISBN 0-7134-1190-2, Pub. by Batsford England). David & Charles.

Lloyd, Howell A., jt. auth. see Connell-Smith, Gordon.

Lloyd, J., tr. see Detienne, Marcel & Vernant, Jean-Pierre.

Lloyd, J. Guth de see Guth de Lloyd, J.

Lloyd, J. W. Case-Studies in Groundwater Resources Evaluation. (Illus.). 250p. 1981. 82.50 (ISBN 0-19-854530-4). Oxford U Pr.

Lloyd, Janet, tr. see Agulhon, Maurice.

Lloyd, Janet, tr. see Vernant, Jean-Pierre & Vidal-Naquet, Pierre.

Lloyd, Joan B. African Animal in Rennaissance Literature & Art. (Oxford Studies in the History of Art & Architecture Ser). (Illus.). 1971. 27.00x (ISBN 0-19-817180-3). Oxford U Pr.

Lloyd, John U. Etidorhpa. 386p. 1981. pap. 15.00 (ISBN 0-89540-004-9). Sun Pub.

Lloyd, June C., jt. auth. see Bryce, Marvin.

Lloyd, L. E., et al. Fundamentals of Nutrition. 2nd ed. LC 77-16029. (Animal Science Ser.). (Illus.). 1978. text ed. 23.95x (ISBN 0-7167-0566-4). W H Freeman.

Lloyd, Lorna & Sims, Nicholas. British Writing on Disarmament Nineteen Fourteen - Nineteen Seventy Eight: A Bibliography. 1979. 37.25x (ISBN 0-89397-052-2). Nichols Pub.

Lloyd, Lyle L. & Kaplan, Harriet. Audiometric Interpretation: A Manual of Basic Audiometry. 1978. pap. 19.95 (ISBN 0-8391-0759-5). Univ Park.

Lloyd, N. G. Degree Theory. LC 77-3205. (Tracts in Mathematics Ser.: No. 73). (Illus.). 1978. 35.50 (ISBN 0-521-21614-1). Cambridge U Pr.

Lloyd, Nathaniel. The History of the English House. Date not set. 36.95 (ISBN 0-8038-0107-6). Hastings.

Lloyd, Norris. Desperate Dragons. (Illus.). (gr. 2-4). 1966. PLB 3.99 o.s.i. (ISBN 0-8038-1522-0). Hastings.

Lloyd, P. The Young Towns of Lima. LC 79-51826. (Urbanization in Developing Countries Ser.). (Orig.). 1980. 34.50 (ISBN 0-521-22871-9); pap. 9.95 (ISBN 0-521-29688-9). Cambridge U Pr.

Lloyd, P. C. Power & Independence: Urban Africans' Perception of Social Inequality. (International Library of Anthropology Ser). (Illus.). 1974. 24.00x (ISBN 0-7100-7973-7). Routledge & Kegan.

Lloyd, P. J., jt. auth. see Grubel, H. G.

Lloyd, Paul M. Desarrollando Destrezas En Preparacion Para el Examen de Equivalencia De Escuela Superior En Espanol: El Escribir. (Span.). (gr. 9-12). Date not set. pap. text ed. 3.75 (ISBN 0-8120-0559-7). Barron.

Lloyd, Peter & Dicken, Peter. Location in Space. 2nd ed. 1977. text ed. 19.80 (ISBN 0-06-318058-8, IntlDept); pap. text ed. 16.75 (ISBN 0-06-318059-6). Har-Row.

Lloyd, Peter, jt. auth. see Dicken, Peter.

Lloyd, Peter C. Slums of Hope? Shanty Towns of the Third World. LC 78-24770. 1979. 17.95x (ISBN 0-312-72963-4). St Martin.

Lloyd, Richard & Alabaster, J. S., eds. Water Quality Criteria for Fresh Water Fish. LC 79-41350. 1980. text ed. 52.50 (ISBN 0-408-10673-5). Butterworths.

Lloyd, Robert M. Systematics of the Onocleoid Ferns. (U. C. Publ. in Botany: Vol. 61). 1972. pap. 7.50x (ISBN 0-520-09411-5). U of Cal Pr.

Lloyd, Robin. For Money or Love: Boy Prostitution in America. LC 75-40691. 1976. 8.95 (ISBN 0-8149-0773-3). Vanguard.

--For Money or Love: Boy Prostitution in America. 1977. pap. 1.95 (ISBN 0-345-27577-2). Ballantine.

Lloyd, Ronald. France. (Illus.). (gr. 5-9). 1975. PLB 3.90 o.p. (ISBN 0-531-02777-5). Watts.

Lloyd, Rosemary H. Baudelaire et Hoffmann. LC 78-58796. (Fr.). 1979. 38.00 (ISBN 0-521-22459-4). Cambridge U Pr.

Lloyd, Seton. The Archaeology of Mesopotamia: From the Old Stone Age to the Persian Conquest. 1980. pap. 8.95 (ISBN 0-500-79007-8). Thames Hudson.

--The Art of the Ancient Near East. (World of Art Ser.). (Illus.). 1961. pap. 9.95 (ISBN 0-19-519919-7). Oxford U Pr.

--Foundations in the Dust: The Story of Mesopotamian Exploration. rev. enl. ed. (Illus.). 216p. 1981. 19.95 (ISBN 0-500-05038-4). Thames Hudson.

Lloyd, Seton, et al. Ancient Architecture: Egypt, Mesopotamia, Crete, Greece. LC 73-2843. (History of World Architecture Ser.). (Illus.). 418p. 1975. 45.00 (ISBN 0-8109-1020-9). Abrams.

Lloyd, T. H. The English Wool Trade in the Middle Ages. LC 76-11086. (Illus.). 1977. 53.50 (ISBN 0-521-21239-1). Cambridge U Pr.

Lloyd, T. O. Empire to Welfare State: English History Nineteen Six to Nineteen Seventy-Six. 2nd ed. (Short Oxford History of the Modern World Ser.). (Illus.). 1979. 37.50x (ISBN 0-19-913132-5); pap. 12.95x (ISBN 0-19-913243-7). Oxford U Pr.

Lloyd, William, jt. auth. see Salter, Christopher.

Lloyd, William B., Jr. Waging Peace: The Swiss Experience. LC 80-15577. (Illus.). xii, 101p. 1980. Repr. of 1958 ed. lib. bdg. 16.75x (ISBN 0-313-22506-0, LLWP). Greenwood.

Lloyd Evans, Barbara, jt. auth. see Lloyd Evans, Gareth.

Lloyd Evans, Gareth & Lloyd Evans, Barbara. The Shakespeare Companion. (Encore Edition). (Illus.). 1978. 5.95 (ISBN 0-684-16908-8, ScribT). Scribner.

Lloyd George, David. Memoirs of the Peace Conference, 2 vols. 1939. Set. 75.00x (ISBN 0-686-51415-7). Elliots Bks.

--The Truth About Reparations & War Debts. LC 68-9609. 1970. Repr. 12.50 (ISBN 0-86527-197-6). Fertig.

Lloyd-Jones, D. M. El Sermon Del Monte, Vol. 1. 1978. 3.95 (ISBN 0-686-12554-1). Banner of Truth.

Lloyd-Jones, D. Martyn. Christian Unity: An Exposition of Ephesians 4: 1-16. 280p. 1981. 9.95 (ISBN 0-8010-5607-1). Baker Bk.

--Preaching & Preachers. 325p. 1972. 10.95 (ISBN 0-310-27870-8). Zondervan.

--Romans: Assurance, Vol. 2. 272p. 1972. 10.95 (ISBN 0-310-27890-2). Zondervan.

--Romans: The Law-Chapter 7: 1 to 8: 4, 6 vols. 368p. 1974. 11.95 (ISBN 0-310-27910-0); Six-volume Set. text ed. 65.70 (ISBN 0-310-27948-8, 10575). Zondervan.

--Romans: The New Man, Vol. 3. 1973. text ed. 11.95 (ISBN 0-310-27900-3). Zondervan.

--Studies in the Sermon on the Mount. 11.95 (ISBN 0-8028-3175-3). Eerdmans.

Lloyd-Jones, Esther, jt. auth. see Estrin, Herman A.

Lloyd-Jones, Hugh. The Justice of Zeus. (Sather Classical Lectures: No. 41). 1971. 17.50x (ISBN 0-520-01739-0); pap. 3.45x (ISBN 0-520-02359-5). U of Cal Pr.

Lloyd-Jones, Hugh, ed. Maurice Bowra: A Celebration. (Illus.). 156p. 1974. 10.50x (ISBN 0-7156-0789-8, Pub. by Duckworth England). Biblio Dist.

Lloyd-Jones, Hugh, tr. see Aeschylus & Aeschylus.

Lloyd-Jones, Martyn D. God's Way of Reconciliation: Studies in Ephesians II. 1972. 10.95 (ISBN 0-8010-5519-9). Baker Bk.

Lloyd-Roberts, G. C. Clinical Surgery: Orthopaedics. (Illus.). 1968. 22.50 o.p. (ISBN 0-397-58016-9). Lippincott.

Lloyd-Roberts, G. C. & Ratliff, A. H. Hip Disorders in Children. (Postgraduate Orthopedics Ser.). 1978. 57.95 (ISBN 0-407-00132-8). Butterworths.

Lloyd-Watts, Valery, jt. auth. see Bigler, Carole L.

Lluch, Constantino, et al. Patterns in Household Demand & Saving. (World Bank Research Publications Ser.). (Illus.). 1977. 14.95x (ISBN 0-19-920097-1); pap. 7.95x (ISBN 0-19-920100-5). Oxford U Pr.

Llywelyn, Morgan. Lion of Ireland. LC 80-84371. 560p. 1981. pap. 3.50 (ISBN 0-87216-825-5). Playboy Pbks.

--The Wind from Hastings. 1979. pap. 2.50 (ISBN 0-446-82969-2). Warner Bks.

Lo, Hui-Min, ed. Correspondence of G. E. Morrison, 2 vols. Set. 249.00 (ISBN 0-521-08779-1); Vol. 1 1895-1912. 119.00 (ISBN 0-521-20486-0); Vol. 2 1912-1920. 150.00 (ISBN 0-521-21561-7). Cambridge U Pr.

Lo, Irving Y., jt. ed. see Liu, Wu-chi.

Lo, Kenneth. Chinese Regional Cooking. 1981. pap. 4.95 (ISBN 0-394-73870-5). Pantheon.

Lo, Sara De Mundo see De Mundo Lo, Sara.

Loach, Jennifer, jt. ed. see Tittler, Robert.

Loader, Anne, compiled by. Pregnancy & Parenthood. (Illus.). 226p. 1980. 16.95 (ISBN 0-19-217684-6); pap. 8.95 (ISBN 0-19-286006-2). Oxford U Pr.

Loader, Jamer A. Polar Structures in the Book of Qohelet. (Beihefte aur Zeitschrift fuer die alttestamentliche Wissenschaft). 150p. 1979. text ed. 34.50x (ISBN 3-11-007636-5). De Gruyter.

Loades, D. M. Politics & the Nation, Fourteen Fifty-Sixteen Sixty: Obedience, Resistance & Public Order. Elton, Y. R., ed. (Fontana Library of English History). 484p. 1974. text ed. 22.25 (ISBN 0-901759-34-1). Humanities.

--Politics & the Nation 1450-1660: Obedience, Resistance & Public Order. 1974. pap. 4.95 o.p. (ISBN 0-531-06053-5, Fontana Pap). Watts.

--Two Tudor Conspiracies. 1965. 41.95 (ISBN 0-521-05580-6). Cambridge U Pr.

Loague, Nehume, jt. ed. see Grabowski, Stanley M.

Loane, M. From Their Point of View: London Nineteen Eight. LC 79-56961. (The English Working Class Ser.). 1980. lib. bdg. 27.00 (ISBN 0-8240-0113-3). Garland Pub.

Loane, Marcus L. Makers of Puritan History. (Canterbury Bks). Orig. Title: Pioneers of Religious Freedom. 240p. 1980. pap. 6.95 (ISBN 0-8010-5593-8). Baker Bk.

Loasby, B. J. Choice, Complexity & Ignorance. LC 75-22558. 1976. 38.50 (ISBN 0-521-21065-8). Cambridge U Pr.

Loavenbruck, Angela M. & Madell, Jane, eds. Hearing Aid Dispensing for Audiologists: A Guide for Clinical Service. 1980. 16.50 (ISBN 0-8089-1323-9). Grune.

Loban, Walter & Watkins, Lillian, eds. Best in Children's Literature. Incl. Sense & Nonsense. record ed. o.p. (ISBN 0-8372-1936-1); cassette o.p. (ISBN 0-8372-1942-6); Ocean Capers. record ed. (ISBN 0-8372-1933-7); cassette (ISBN 0-8372-1939-6); Never Never Land. record ed. (ISBN 0-8372-1934-5); cassette; Myths & Legends Around the World. record ed. (ISBN 0-8372-1932-9); cassette (ISBN 0-8372-1938-8). (Ser. 4). (gr. k-4). set 54.75 ea. Bowmar-Noble.

--Best in Children's Literature. Incl. Funny Bones. record ed. (ISBN 0-8372-0932-3); cassette; Friendly Dragons. record ed. (ISBN 0-8372-0937-4); cassette; Ecology. record ed. (ISBN 0-8372-0941-2); cassette (ISBN 0-8372-1056-9); Folktales from Other Lands. record ed (ISBN 0-8372-1011-9); cassette. (Ser. 3). (gr. k-4). set 54.75 ea. Bowmar-Noble.

Lobanov, Grace, tr. see Leon-Portilla, Miguel.

Lobb, Charlotte. Exploring Careers in Animal Care. (Careers in Depth Ser.). (Illus.). 140p. (gr. 7-12). 1980. lib. bdg. 5.97 (ISBN 0-8239-0536-5). Rosen Pr.

Lobb, Edward. T. S. Eliot & the Romantic Critical Tradition. 208p. 1981. 20.00 (ISBN 0-7100-0636-5). Routledge & Kegan.

Lobb, Frances, tr. see Mussolini, Benito.

Lobban, J. H., intro. by. English Essays. 257p. 1980. Repr. lib. bdg. 30.00 (ISBN 0-89987-507-6). Century Bookbindery.

Lobban, R. D. Edinburgh & the Medical Revolution. LC 78-51669. (Cambridge Introduction to the History of Mankind Ser.). (Illus.). (YA) 1980. pap. 3.95 (ISBN 0-521-22028-9). Cambridge U Pr.
Lobban, Richard. Historical Dictionary of the Republics of Guinea-Bissau & Cape Verde. LC 79-18227. (African Historical Dictionaries Ser.: No. 22). 209p. 1979. 11.00 (ISBN 0-8108-1240-1). Scarecrow.
Lobeck, Armin K. Things Maps Don't Tell Us: Adventure into Map Interpretation. (Illus.). 1956. 10.95 (ISBN 0-02-573790-2). Macmillan.
Lobel. A Holiday for Mr. Muster. (gr. 2-3). 1980. pap. 3.50 incl. record (ISBN 0-590-24003-X, Schol Pap). Schol Bk Serv.
Lobel, Arnold. Fables. LC 79-2004. (Illus.). 48p. (gr. 1-4). 1980. 8.95 (ISBN 0-06-023973-5, HarpJ); PLB 8.79 (ISBN 0-06-023974-3). Har-Row.
--The Frog & Toad Coloring Book. (Illus.). 32p. (ps-3). 1981. pap. 1.95 (ISBN 0-06-023978-6, HarpJ). Har-Row.
--Gregory Griggs & Other Nursery Rhyme People. LC 77-22209. (Illus.). (gr. k-3). 1978. 9.25 (ISBN 0-688-80128-5); PLB 8.88 (ISBN 0-688-84128-7). Greenwillow.
--How the Rooster Saved the Day. LC 76-17602. (Illus.). (gr. k-3). 1977. 7.95 (ISBN 0-688-80063-7); PLB 7.92 (ISBN 0-688-84063-9). Greenwillow.
--The Ice-Cream Cone Coot & Other Rare Birds. LC 80-15290. (Illus.). 48p. (ps-3). 1980. Repr. of 1971 ed. 9.95 (ISBN 0-686-65811-6, Four Winds). Schol Bk Serv.
--On Market Street. LC 80-21418. (Illus.). 40p. (gr. k-3). 1981. 8.95 (ISBN 0-688-80309-1); PLB 8.59 (ISBN 0-688-84309-3); prepack. Greenwillow.
--Treeful of Pigs. LC 78-1810. (Illus.). (gr. k-3). 1979. 8.50 (ISBN 0-688-80177-3); PLB 8.16 (ISBN 0-688-84177-5). Greenwillow.
Lobell, John. Between Silence & Light: Spirit in the Architecture of Louis I. Kahn. LC 78-65437. (Illus.). 1979. pap. 7.95 (ISBN 0-394-73687-7). Shambhala Pubns.
--The Little Green Book: A Guide to Self-Reliant Living in the '80s. LC 80-53445. (Illus.). 224p. (Orig.). 1981. pap. 5.95 (ISBN 0-394-74924-3). Shambhala Pubn.
Lo Bello, Nino. European Detours: A Trave Guide to Unsual Sights. (Illus.). 176p. 1981. 8.95 (ISBN 0-8437-3375-6). Hammond Inc.
Lobley, Priscilla. Making Children's Costumes. LC 77-185256. 7.95 (ISBN 0-8008-5077-7, K872). Taplinger.
--Your Book of Flower Making. 1970. 6.95 (ISBN 0-571-09294-2, Pub. by Faber & Faber). Merrimack Bk Serv.
Lobley, Priscilla & Lobley, Robert. Your Book of English Country Dancing. (Your Book Ser.). (Illus.). (gr. 4 up). 1980. 8.95 (ISBN 0-571-11522-5, Pub. by Faber & Faber). Merrimack Bk Serv.
Lobley, Robert. Your Book of Painting. (Your Book Ser). (Illus.). 1978. 7.95 (ISBN 0-571-10776-1, Pub. by Faber & Faber). Merrimack Bk Serv.
Lobley, Robert, jt. auth. see Lobley, Priscilla.
Lobo, Gerald & Maher, Michael, eds. Information Economics & Accounting Research: A Workshop Conducted by Joel S. Demski. (Michigan Business Papers: No. 65). (Illus.). 240p. 1980. 9.00 (ISBN 0-87712-204-0). U Mich Busn Div Res.
Lobsenz, Norman, jt. auth. see Lasswell, Marcia.
Lobstein, A., jt. auth. see Weigelin, E.
LoBue, Joseph & Gordon, Albert S., eds. Humoral Control of Growth & Differentiation, 2 vols. Incl. Vol. 1. Vertebrate Regulatory Factors. 1973. 52.50 (ISBN 0-12-453801-0); Vol. 2. Nonvertebrate Neuroendocrinology & Ageing. 1974. 45.00 (ISBN 0-12-453802-9). Set. 79.00 (ISBN 0-686-66930-4). Acad Pr.
Locander, William B., ed. Marketing Looks Outward: 1976 International Marketing Conference Proccedings. LC 76-30865. 1977. 10.00 o.p. (ISBN 0-87757-087-6). Am Mktg.
Lochak, Michele & Mangin, Marie-France. Suzette & Nicholas & the Sunijudi Circus. (Illus.). 32p. (gr. 4-8). 1981. 7.95 (ISBN 0-399-20750-3); lib. bdg. 7.99 (ISBN 0-399-61160-6). Philomel.
Locher, Frances C., ed. Contemporary Authors: A Bio-Bibliographical Guide to Current Writers in Fiction, General Non-Fiction, Poetry, Journalism, Drama, Motion Pictures, Television & Other Fields. LC 62-52046. (Contemporary Author Ser.: Vols. 97-100). 900p. 1980. 58.00 (ISBN 0-8103-1900-4). Gale.
--Contemporary Authors: A Bio-Bibliographical Guide to Current Writers in Fiction, General Non-Fiction, Poetry, Journalism, Drama, Motion Pictures, Television & Other Fields, Vol. 101. LC 62-52046. 900p. 1981. 58.00 (ISBN 0-8103-1901-2). Gale.
Locher, Frances C. & Evory, Ann, eds. Contemporary Authors: A Bibliographical Guide to Current Writers in Fiction, General Nonfiction, Poetry, Journalism, Drama, Motion Pictures, Television, & Other Fields. Incl. Vols. 1-4. rev. ed. 1967. (ISBN 0-8103-0000-1); Vols. 5-8. rev. ed. 1969. (ISBN 0-8103-0001-X); Vols. 9-12. rev. ed. 1974. (ISBN 0-8103-0002-8); Vols. 13-16. rev. ed. 1975. (ISBN 0-8103-0027-3); Vol. 17-20. rev. ed. 1976. (ISBN 0-8103-0032-X); Vols. 21-24. rev. ed. 1976. (ISBN 0-8103-0033-8); Vols. 25-28. rev. ed. 1977. (ISBN 0-8103-0034-6); Vols. 29-32. rev. ed. 1978. (ISBN 0-685-59670-2); Vols. 33-36. rev. ed. 1978. (ISBN 0-8103-0014-1); Vols. 37-40. rev. ed. 1979. (ISBN 0-8103-0016-8); Vols. 41-44. rev. ed. 1979. (ISBN 0-8103-0041-9); Vols. 45-48. 1974. (ISBN 0-8103-0020-6); Vols. 49-52. 1974. (ISBN 0-8103-0024-9); Vols. 53-56. 1975. (ISBN 0-8103-0022-2); Vols. 57-60. 1976. (ISBN 0-8103-0026-5); Vols. 61-64. 1976. (ISBN 0-8103-0028-1); Vols. 69-72. 1978. (ISBN 0-8103-0030-3); Vols. 73-76. (ISBN 0-**8103-0031-1); Vol. 77-80. 1978 (ISBN 0-8103-0039-7); Vols. 81-84. 1979 (ISBN 0-8103-0046-X); Vols. 85-88. 1979 (ISBN 0-8103-0047-8); Vols. 89-92. 1980 (ISBN 0-8103-0048-6); Vols. 93-96. 1980 (ISBN 0-8103-0049-4). LC 62-52046. sold in 4 vol. units 58.00 ea. Gale.**
Lochhead, Jack, jt. auth. see Whimbey, Arthur.
Lochhead, Marion. Portrait of the Scott Country. LC 68-119619. (Portrait Bks.). (Illus.). 1968. 10.50x (ISBN 0-7091-3957-8). Intl Pubns Serv.
Lochman, Jan M. Reconciliation & Liberation: Challenging a One-Dimensional View of Salvation. LC 80-24060. 160p. (Orig.). 1980. pap. 6.95 (ISBN 0-8006-1340-6, 1-1340). Fortress.
Lochner, Barbara, jt. auth. see Daley, Maxime.
Łochovsky, F. H., jt. auth. see Tsichritzis, Dennis C.
Lock, B. E., et al. The Geology of Edgeoya & Barentsoya: Svalbard. (Norsk Polarinstitutt Skrifter: Vol. 168). (Illus.). 64p. 1980. pap. text ed. 7.50x. Universitet.
Lock, D. S. Engineers' Metric Manual & Buyers' Guide. 1975. text ed. 230.00 (ISBN 0-08-018220-8). Pergamon.
Lock, F. P. The Politics of Gulliver's Travels. 166p. 1980. text ed. 22.00x (ISBN 0-19-812656-5). Oxford U Pr.
--Susanna Centlivre. (English Authors Ser.: No. 254). 1979. lib. bdg. 13.95 (ISBN 0-8057-6744-4). Twayne.
Lock, Fred & Lawson, Alan. Austalian Literature: A Reference Guide. 2nd ed. (Australian Bibliographies Ser.). 134p. 1980. pap. text ed. 10.95x (ISBN 0-19-554214-2). Oxford U Pr.
Lock, Grahame, tr. see Liebknecht, Karl.
Lock, Margaret M. East Asian Medicine in Urban Japan: Varieties of Medical Experience. 1980. 20.00x (ISBN 0-520-03820-7). U of Cal Pr.
Lock, S. Thorne's Better Medical Writing. 2nd ed. 1977. 11.95 (ISBN 0-471-03062-7, Pub. by Wiley-Medical). Wiley.
Lock, W. Pastoral Epistles. (International Critical Commentary Ser.). 212p. 1924. text ed. 17.50x (ISBN 0-567-05033-5). Attic Pr.
Lockaby, George W. Sermon Outlines on the Person & Work of Christ. 1981. pap. 2.25 (ISBN 0-8054-2238-2). Broadman.
Lockard, Joan S. & Ward, Arthur A., Jr., eds. Epilepsy: A Window to Brain Mechanisms. 296p. 1980. text ed. 29.50 (ISBN 0-89004-499-6). Raven.
Lockard, William K. Design Drawing. LC 74-16003. (Illus.). 1974. pap. text ed. 12.50x (ISBN 0-914468-01-4). Pepper Pub.
--Design Drawing. 2nd rev. ed. LC 79-65405. (Illus.). 1981. pap. 15.00x (ISBN 0-914468-06-5). Pepper Pub.
--Design Drawing Experiences. 4th. rev. ed. LC 79-65404. (Illus.). 1979. pap. text ed. 12.50x (ISBN 0-914468-07-3). Pepper Pub.
Lockavitch, Joseph, jt. auth. see Mauser, August.
Locke, Alain, ed. Negro in Art: A Pictorial Record of the Negro Artist & of the Negro Theme in Art. LC 68-9006. (Illus.). 1971. Repr. of 1940 ed. lib. bdg. 30.00 buckram (ISBN 0-87817-013-8). Hacker.
Locke, Alain L. Plays of Negro Life: A Sourcebook of Native American Drama. LC 77-132077. Repr. of 1927 ed. 25.00x (ISBN 0-8371-5037-X). Negro U Pr.
Locke, Don. A Fantasy of Reason: The Life & Thought of William Godwin. (Illus.). 1980. 28.00 (ISBN 0-7100-0387-0). Routledge & Kegan.
Locke, Duane, ed. The Immanentists Anthology: Art of the Superconscious. LC 72-96447. (Illus.). 120p. 1973. pap. 2.50 (ISBN 0-912292-30-X). The Smith.
Locke, Edith R. Red Door. LC 65-20821. (Illus.). (gr. k-3). 1965. 4.50 (ISBN 0-8149-0353-3). Vanguard.
Locke, F. W., ed. see Capellanus, Andreas.
Locke, Flora M. College Mathematics for Business. 2nd ed. LC 73-10090. 384p. 1974. text ed. 17.95x (ISBN 0-471-54321-7); wkbk. 7.95x (ISBN 0-471-54319-5). Wiley.
--Electronic Calculators for Business Use. LC 78-1852. 1978. pap. text ed. 15.95 (ISBN 0-471-03579-3); tchrs. manual avail. (ISBN 0-471-03766-4). Wiley.
Locke, J. Courtney, tr. see Grillot De Givry.
Locke, John. The Correspondence of John Locke: Vol. 5, Letters 1702-2198 Covering the Years 1694-1697. DeBeer, E. S., ed. 808p. 1979. text ed. 89.00x (ISBN 0-19-824562-9). Oxford U Pr.
--Educational Writings. Axtell, James L., ed. LC 68-18341. (Illus.). 1968. 42.50 (ISBN 0-521-04073-6). Cambridge U Pr.
--An Essay Concerning Human Understanding. 1979. pap. 11.50x (ISBN 0-460-00984-2, Evman). Dutton.
--Isometric Perspective Designs & How to Create Them. (Illus.). 64p. (Orig.). 1981. pap. price not set (ISBN 0-486-24123-8). Dover.
--Letter Concerning Toleration. 2nd ed. 1955. pap. 2.50 (ISBN 0-672-60183-4, LLA22). Bobbs.
--Second Treatise of Government. Peardon, Thomas P., ed. LC 52-14648. (gr. 11 up). 1952. pap. 3.95 (ISBN 0-672-60193-1, LLA31). Bobbs.
--Second Treatise of Government. Macpherson, C. B., ed. (Philosophical Classsics Ser.). 138p. 1980. lib. bdg. 12.50 (ISBN 0-915144-93-X); pap. text ed. 2.75 (ISBN 0-915144-86-7). Hackett Pub.
--Some Thoughts Concerning Education. Garforth, F. W., ed. LC 65-16960. (Orig.). 1964. text ed. 6.00 o.p. (ISBN 0-8120-5057-6); pap. 2.50 o.p. (ISBN 0-8120-0129-X). Barron.
--Treatise of Civil Government & a Letter Concerning Toleration. Sherman, Charles L., ed. 1965. pap. text ed. 5.95x (ISBN 0-89197-519-5). Irvington.
--Two Tracts on Government. Abrams, Philip, ed. 1967. 32.50 (ISBN 0-521-05583-0). Cambridge U Pr.
--Two Treatises of Government. Laslett, Peter, ed. 1960. 39.95 (ISBN 0-521-06903-3). Cambridge U Pr.
Locke, Lawrence F. & Wyrick-Spirduso, Waneen. Proposals That Work: A Guide for Planning Research. LC 76-4965. 1976. pap. 8.25x (ISBN 0-8077-2495-5). Tchrs Coll.
Locke, M., ed. see Society For The Study Of Developmental Biology - 24th Symposium.
Locke, Michael. Power & Politics in the School System: A Guidebook. 192p. 1974. 16.00x (ISBN 0-7100-7732-7); pap. 7.95 (ISBN 0-7100-7733-5). Routledge & Kegan.
Locke, Michael & Smith, D. S. Insect Biology in the Future: "VBW 80". 1980. 50.00 (ISBN 0-12-454340-5). Acad Pr.
Locke, Michael & Locke, Michael, eds. Control Mechanisms in Developmental Processes. 1968. 37.50 (ISBN 0-12-612950-9); pap. 28.50 o.p. (ISBN 0-12-612956-8). Acad Pr.
Locke, Michael, ed. see Society For The Study Of Developmental Biology - 25th Symposium.
Locke, S. R., jt. ed. see Otte, H. M.
Locke, Sam, jt. auth. see Clark, L. Roy.
Locke, Sam, jt. auth. see Karpman, Harold L.
Locke, Simeon, et al. A Study in Neurolinguistics. (Illus.). 160p. 1973. text ed. 13.75 (ISBN 0-398-02738-2). C C Thomas.
Locke, William & Schally, Andrew V., eds. The Hypothalamus & Pituitary in Health & Disease. (Illus.). 624p. 1972. 41.75 (ISBN 0-398-02526-6). C C Thomas.
Lockerbie, D. Bruce. The Apostles' Creed: Do You Really Believe It? 1977. pap. 2.50 (ISBN 0-88207-748-1). Victor Bks.
--Asking Questions: A Classroom Model for Teaching the Bible. Zimmerman, Diane, ed. LC 80-18198. (Orig.). 1980. pap. text ed. 4.95 (ISBN 0-915134-75-6). Mott Media.
--Fatherlove: Learning to Give the Best You've Got. LC 80-711. 240p. 1981. 10.95 (ISBN 0-385-15865-3, Galilee). Doubleday.
--Timeless Moment. LC 80-65332. 126p. 1980. pap. 3.95 (ISBN 0-89107-181-4, Cornerstone Bks). Good News.
--The Timeless Moment: Creativity & the Christian Faith. 1980. pap. 3.95 (ISBN 0-89107-181-4). Good News.
--Who Educates Your Child? 216p. (Orig.). 1981. pap. 5.95 (ISBN 0-310-44001-7). Zondervan.
Lockerbie, Jeanette. Forgive, Forget & Be Free. LC 80-69304. 148p. 1981. 7.95 (ISBN 0-915684-76-4). Christian Herald.
--More Salt in My Kitchen. (Moody Quiet Time Ser.). 1980. pap. 1.95 (ISBN 0-8024-5668-5). Moody.
Lockett, David. Getting New Business Leads: A Guide for Advertising Agencies. LC 80-70204. 1980. 6.95 (ISBN 0-87251-062-X). Crain Bks.
Lockett, F. J. Nonlinear Viscoelastic Solids. 1973. 28.00 (ISBN 0-12-454350-2). Acad Pr.
Lockey, Richard F., ed. Allergy & Clinical Immunology. LC 78-62073. 1979. 42.50 (ISBN 0-87488-665-1). Med Exam.
Lockhart, Aileene S. & Pease, Esther E. Modern Dance: Building & Teaching Lessons. 5th ed. 1977. 9.95x (ISBN 0-697-07430-7). Wm C Brown.
Lockhart, Charles. Bargaining in International Conflicts. 1979. 15.00x (ISBN 0-231-04560-3). Columbia U Pr.
Lockhart, J. & Otte, E. Letters & People of the Spanish Indies. LC 75-6007. (Cambridge Latin American Studies: No. 22). 322p. 1976. 29.95 (ISBN 0-521-20883-1); pap. 8.95x (ISBN 0-521-20990-0). Cambridge U Pr.
Lockhart, J. A. & Wiseman, A. J. Introduction to Crop Husbandry. rev. 3rd ed. LC 74-10000. 1975. text ed. 23.10 o.p. (ISBN 0-08-018115-5); pap. text ed. 9.90 o.p. (ISBN 0-08-018105-8). Pergamon.
--Introduction to Crop Husbandry. 4th ed. 1978. text ed. 45.00 (ISBN 0-08-022653-1); pap. text ed. 14.00 (ISBN 0-08-022652-3). Pergamon.
Lockhart, J. Stewart. The Lockhart Collection of Chinese Copper Coins. LC 74-27610. (Illus.). 240p. 1975. Repr. 35.00x (ISBN 0-88000-056-2). Quarterman.
Lockhart, James. The Men of Cajamarca: A Social & Biographical Study of the First Conquerors of Peru. LC 72-185236. (Latin American Monographs: No. 27). 490p. 1972. 17.95 (ISBN 0-292-75001-3). U of Tex Pr.
--Spanish Peru, Fifteen Thirty-Two to Fifteen Sixty: A Colonial Society. LC 68-14032. (Illus.). 1968. 25.00 (ISBN 0-299-04660-5); pap. 7.95x (ISBN 0-299-04664-8). U of Wis Pr.
Lockhart, James, jt. auth. see Karttunen, Frances.
Lockhart, John G. Curses, Lucks & Talismans. LC 70-132016. (Illus.). 1971. Repr. of 1938 ed. 20.00 (ISBN 0-8103-3376-7). Gale.
Lockhart, Noble L. & Rice, Ona E. AC Circuit Analysis. LC 75-27997. 1976. pap. 8.00 (ISBN 0-8273-1136-2); instructors guide 1.60 (ISBN 0-8273-1137-0). Delmar.
Lockhart, R. D. Living Anatomy. 1970. pap. 6.95 (ISBN 0-571-09177-6, Pub. by Faber & Faber). Merrimack Bk Serv.
Lockhart, R. D., et al. Anatomy of the Human Body. (Illus.). 698p. 1981. pap. 35.00 (ISBN 0-571-07037-X, Pub. by Faber & Faber). Merrimack Bk Serv.
Lockhart, Robert D., et al. Anatomy of the Human Body. (Illus.). 1969. text ed. 23.50 o.p. (ISBN 0-397-58090-8). Lippincott.
Lockhart, William B., et al. The American Constitution, Cases-Comments-Questions. 5th ed. LC 80-54210. 1181p. 1980. text ed. 20.95 (ISBN 0-8299-2132-X). West Pub.
--Cases & Materials on Constitutional Rights & Liberties. 5th ed. LC 80-54541. (American Casebook Ser.). 1298p. 1980. text ed. 21.95 (ISBN 0-8299-2135-4). West Pub.
--Constitutional Law: Cases-Comments-Questions. 5th ed. LC 80-21518. (American Casebook Ser.). 1829p. 1980. text ed. 23.95 (ISBN 0-8299-2110-9). West Pub.
Lockhart, William E. English & Pre-Test: Placement Tests. (Michigan Prescriptive Program Ser.). (gr. 10). 1975. wkbk. 1.50 (ISBN 0-89039-125-4). Ann Arbor Pubs.
--English Study Material: High School Equivalency-GED. (Michigan Prescriptive Program Ser.). 1975. pap. text ed. 4.50 (ISBN 0-89039-121-1). Ann Arbor Pubs.
--Mathematics Study Material: High School Equivalency-GED. (Michigan Prescriptive Program Ser.). (gr. 10). 1975. pap. text ed. 8.00 (ISBN 0-89039-120-3). Ann Arbor Pubs.
Lockhead, Marian. John Gibson Lockhart. 324p. 1980. lib. bdg. 30.00 (ISBN 0-8482-1621-0). Norwood Edns.
Lockheed Aircraft Corporation. Of Men & Stars: A History of Lockheed Aircraft Corporation. Gilbert, James, ed. LC 79-7280. (Flight: Its First Seventy-Five Years Ser.). (Illus.). 1979. Repr. of 1957 ed. lib. bdg. 21.00x (ISBN 0-405-12189-X). Arno.
Locklear, Edmond, Jr. Your Future in Accounting. LC 73-114134. (Career Guidance Ser). 1971. pap. 3.50 (ISBN 0-668-02232-9). Arco.
Lockley, Arthur S. How to Raise & Train a Giant Schnauzer. (Orig.). pap. 1.79 o.p. (ISBN 0-87666-305-6, DS1081). TFH Pubns.
Lockley, Fred. The Lockley Files. Helm, Mike, ed. (Illus.). 300p. (Orig.). 1981. pap. 9.95 (ISBN 0-931742-08-9). Rainy Day Oreg.
Lockley, R. M. Britain in Colour. 1976. 11.95 (ISBN 0-7134-0016-1, Pub. by Batsford England). David & Charles.
--The Naturalist in Wales. 232p. 1970. 14.95 (ISBN 0-7153-4900-7). David & Charles.
--The Private Life of the Rabbit. (Illus.). 1975. pap. 4.95 (ISBN 0-380-00447-X, 38224). Avon.

--The Private Life of the Rabbit: An Account of the Life History & Social Behavior of the Wild Rabbit. LC 74-8855. (Illus.). 1974. 8.95 o.s.i. (ISBN 0-02-573900-X). Macmillan.
Lockley, Ronald. Orielton-the Human & Natural History of a Welsh Manor. (Illus.). 1978. 15.00 (ISBN 0-233-96928-4). Transatlantic.
Lockley, Ronald M. Whales, Dolphins, & Porpoises. LC 79-88317. (Illus.). 1979. 15.95 (ISBN 0-393-01283-2). Norton.
Locklin, D. Philip. Economics of Transportation. 7th ed. 1972. text ed. 19.25x (ISBN 0-256-00301-7). Irwin.
Locklin, Gerald. The Four Day Week & Other Stories. 1980. 3.00 (ISBN 0-917554-06-X). Maelstrom.
--Frisco Epic. 1980. 1.50 (ISBN 0-917554-07-8). Maelstrom.
--Locked in. 1980. 3.00 (ISBN 0-917554-18-3). Maelstrom.
--Poop & Other Poems. 1980. 3.00 (ISBN 0-917554-13-2). Maelstrom.
--Pronouncing Borges. 32p. 1977. pap. 2.00 (ISBN 0-935390-02-2). Wormwood Rev.
--Son of Poop. 1980. 2.00 (ISBN 0-917554-14-0). Maelstrom.
--Two for the Seesaw, One for the Road. LC 80-80783. 1980. 10.95 (ISBN 0-89002-155-4); pap. 3.50 (ISBN 0-89002-154-6). Northwoods Pr.
--Two Summer Sequences. 1980. 2.50 (ISBN 0-917554-10-8). Maelstrom.
Locklin, Gerald, et al. Tarzan & Shane Meet the Toad. limited ed. 1980. 2.00 (ISBN 0-917554-01-9). Maelstrom.
Lockman, John, tr. see Le Sage, Alain R.
Lockmiller, D. A. Scholars on Parade. 1969. 6.95 o.s.i. (ISBN 0-02-573960-3). Macmillan.
Lockridge, Ernest, ed. Twentieth Century Interpretations of The Great Gatsby. (Orig.). (YA) (gr. 9-12). 1968. 8.95 (ISBN 0-13-363820-0, Spec); pap. 2.95 (ISBN 0-13-363812-X, Spec). P-H.
Lockridge, Kenneth A. Literacy in Colonial New England: An Inquiry into the Social Context of Literacy in the Early Modern West. (Illus.). 1974. 6.95x (ISBN 0-393-05522-1); pap. 3.95x (ISBN 0-393-09263-1). Norton.
--Settlement & Unsettlement in Early America: The Crisis of Political Legitimacy Before the Revolution. LC 80-25658. (Illus.). 96p. Date not set. price not set (ISBN 0-521-23707-6). Cambridge U Pr.
Lockridge, Richard. Inspector's Holiday: An Inspector Heimrich Mystery. new ed. LC 79-134933. 1971. 4.95 o.p. (ISBN 0-397-00702-7). Lippincott.
--The Tenth Life. LC 77-6673. 1977. 8.95 o.p. (ISBN 0-397-01237-3). Lippincott.
Locks, Mitchell O. Reliability, Maintainability, and Availability Assessment. (Illus.). 1973. 15.95x o.p. (ISBN 0-8104-9204-0, Spartan). Hayden.
Locks, Norman. Familiar Subjects: Polaroid SX-70 Impressions. LC 78-4754. (Illus.). 1978. 12.95 o.p. (ISBN 0-685-29945-7, HarpR); pap. 6.95 o.p. (ISBN 0-06-250530-0, RD 282, HarpR). Har-Row.
Locks, Renee & McHugh, Joseph. Abandon Yourself to Love. LC 80-67343. (Illus.). 112p. 1981. 4.95 (ISBN 0-89087-304-6). Celestial Arts.
Lockspeiser, E. Debussy: His Life & Mind. LC 78-51668. (Illus.). 1979. Vol. 1. 39.50 (ISBN 0-521-22053-X); pap. 10.50 (ISBN 0-521-29341-3); Vol. 2. 49.50 (ISBN 0-521-22054-8); pap. 12.50 (ISBN 0-521-29342-1). Cambridge U Pr.
Lockspeiser, Edward. Debussy, His Life & Mind, 2 Vols. 8.00 ea. o.s.i. Macmillan.
--Music & Painting: A Study in Comparative Ideas from Turner to Schoenberg. LC 73-7979. (Icon Editions). 208p. 1973. pap. 4.95x o.s.i. (ISBN 0-06-430040-4, IN-40, HarpT). Har-Row.
Lockward, George, tr. see Elwood, Roger.
Lockward, J. Alfonso, tr. see Scheck, Joann.
Lockward, J. Alfonso, tr. see Warren, Mary.
Lockwood & Sheldon. Poodle Guide. 6.98 o.p. (ISBN 0-385-01598-4). Doubleday.
Lockwood, A. P. Aspects of the Physiology of Crustacea. (Illus.). 1968. 21.95x (ISBN 0-7167-0667-9). W H Freeman.
Lockwood, A. P., ed. Effects of Pollutants on Aquatic Organisms. LC 75-32448. (Society for Experimental Biology Seminar Ser.: No. 2). 180p. 1976. 39.50 (ISBN 0-521-21103-4); pap. 14.95x (ISBN 0-521-29044-9). Cambridge U Pr.
Lockwood, Albert. Notes on the Literature of the Piano. LC 67-30400. (Music Ser). 1968. Repr. of 1940 ed. lib. bdg. 22.50 (ISBN 0-306-70983-X). Da Capo.
Lockwood, Allison. Passionate Pilgrims: The American Traveler in Great Britain, 1800-1914. LC 78-66808. 600p. 1981. 25.00 (ISBN 0-8386-2272-0). Fairleigh Dickinson.
Lockwood, Barbara, jt. auth. see Sheldon, Margaret.
Lockwood, E. H. & Macmillan, R. H. Geometric Symmetry. LC 77-77713. (Illus.). 1978. 28.50 (ISBN 0-521-21685-0). Cambridge U Pr.
Lockwood, Edward H. & Prag, A. Book of Curves. 1961. 32.95 (ISBN 0-521-05585-7). Cambridge U Pr.
Lockwood, Guy. Raising & Caring for Animals, a Handbook of Animal Husbandry & Veterinary Care. LC 79-14025. 1979. pap. 8.95 (ISBN 0-684-16299-7). Scribner.
Lockwood, John G. Causes of Climate. 1979. 32.95 o.p. (ISBN 0-470-26657-0); pap. 16.95 (ISBN 0-470-26658-9). Halsted Pr.
Lockwood, Lee, jt. auth. see Berrigan, Daniel.
Lockwood, M. S. The Art Book of Spanish, Italian, French & Egyptian Pottery. 1979. deluxe ed. 37.45 (ISBN 0-930582-41-1). Gloucester Art.
Lockwood, M. S. & Glaister, E. Art Embroidery. LC 76-17758. (Aesthetic Movement Ser.: Vol. 13). (Illus.). 1977. Repr. of 1878 ed. lib. bdg. 44.00x (ISBN 0-8240-2462-1). Garland Pub.
Lockwood, Margo, jt. auth. see Nyhart, Nina.
Lockwood, Myra. A Mouse Is Miracle Enough. 1965. 3.95 o.p. (ISBN 0-374-21429-8). FS&G.
Lockwood, Stan. Kaleidoscope of Char-a-Bancs & Coaches. (Illus.). 1980. 20.00x (ISBN 0-906116-02-3). Intl Pubns Serv.
Lockwood, Tim. Kawasaki Service - Repair Handbook: 250 & 350cc Twins, All Years. Robinson, Jeff, ed. (Illus.). 144p. 1972. pap. text ed. 9.95 (ISBN 0-89287-016-8, M352). Clymer Pubns.
--Motorcycle Repair Encyclopedia. 2nd ed. Robinson, Jeff, ed. (Illus.). 472p. 1976. pap. text ed. 10.00 o.p. (ISBN 0-89287-021-4, M430). Clymer Pubns.
--Recreational Vehicle Maintenance. Robinson, Jeff, ed. (Illus.). 232p. 1973. pap. text ed. 8.95 (ISBN 0-89287-081-8, X930). Clymer Pubns.
Lockwood, W. B. Indo-European Philology: Historical & Comparative. 1968. pap. text ed. 7.00x (ISBN 0-09-095581-1, Hutchinson U Lib). Humanities.
--Languages of the British Isles, Past & Present. (Andre Deutsch Language Library). 1977. lib. bdg. 29.50x (ISBN 0-233-96666-8). Westview.
Lockwood, W. D. A Panorama of Indo-European Languages. 1972. text ed. 14.50x (ISBN 0-09-111020-3, Hutchinson U Lib); pap. text ed. 7.50x (ISBN 0-09-111021-1, Hutchinson U Lib). Humanities.
Lockwood, William W. Economic Development of Japan: Growth & Structural Change, 1868-1938. rev. ed. 23.50 (ISBN 0-691-03014-6); pap. 7.50 o.p. (ISBN 0-691-00001-8). Princeton U Pr.
Lockyer. All the Apostles of the Bible. 1972. 10.95 (ISBN 0-310-28010-9, 10052). Zondervan.
--All the Prayers All the Pomises. Date not set. Set. 24.90 (ISBN 0-686-69347-7, 10089). Zondervan. Postponed.
--All the Promises of the Bible. 1962. 10.95 (ISBN 0-310-28130-X, 10074). Zondervan.
Lockyer, Herbert. All About Bible Study. 1977. 9.95 (ISBN 0-310-28160-1). Zondervan.
--The All Series, Bks. 1-4. Incl. Bk. 1. All the Apostles of the Bible. 11.95 (ISBN 0-310-28010-9); Bk. 2. All the Books & Chapters of the Bible. 10.95 (ISBN 0-310-28020-6); Bk. 3. All the Doctrines of the Bible. 11.95 (ISBN 0-310-28050-8); Bks. 2 & 3 Set. 21.90 (ISBN 0-310-28168-7); Bk. 4. All the Children of the Bible. 12.95 (ISBN 0-310-28030-3); Bk. 5. All the Holy Days & Holidays. 11.95 (ISBN 0-310-28060-5); Bk. 6. All the Kings & Queens of the Bible. 10.95 (ISBN 0-310-28070-2); Bks. 5 & 6 Set. 21.90 (ISBN 0-310-28178-4); Bk. 7. All the Men of the Bible. 11.95 (ISBN 0-310-28080-X); Bk. 8. All the Women of the Bible. 9.95 (ISBN 0-310-28150-4); Bks. 7 & 8 Set. 20.90 (ISBN 0-310-28188-1); Bk. 9. All the Miracles of the Bible. 10.95 (ISBN 0-310-28100-8); Bk. 10. All the Parables of the Bible. 12.95 (ISBN 0-310-28110-5); Bks. 9 & 10 Set. 21.90 (ISBN 0-310-28198-9); Bk. 11. All the Prayers of the Bible. 11.95 (ISBN 0-310-28120-2); Bk. 12. All the Promises of the Bible. 11.95 (ISBN 0-310-28130-X); Bks. 11 & 12 Set. 24.90 (ISBN 0-310-28208-X); Bk. 13. All the Trades & Occupations of the Bible. 11.95 (ISBN 0-310-28140-7); Bk. 14. All the Messianic Prophecies of the Bible. 14.95 (ISBN 0-310-28090-7). Zondervan.
--All the Divine Names & Titles in the Bible. 352p. 1975. 12.95 (ISBN 0-310-28040-0). Zondervan.
--The Holy Spirit of God. 1981. 9.95 (ISBN 0-8407-5234-2). Nelson.
--Last Words of Saints & Sinners. LC 78-85429. 1975. pap. 4.50 (ISBN 0-8254-3111-5). Kregel.
--Light to Live by (Wedding Edition) 384p. 1981. 7.95 (ISBN 0-310-28260-8). Zondervan.
--Revelation: Drama of the Ages. LC 80-80639. 475p. 1980. pap. 6.95 (ISBN 0-89081-247-0). Harvest Hse.
Lockyer, Herbert, Sr. The Person & Power of Satan. 1980. pap. 5.95 (ISBN 0-8499-2921-0). Word Bks.
Lockyer, K. G. Factory Management. 24.50x (ISBN 0-392-07793-0, SpS). Soccer.
Lockyer, K. G. & McEwan-Young, W. Short Cases in Industrial Management. 1972. text ed. 14.75x (ISBN 0-7002-0177-7). Intl Ideas.
Lockyer, Roger. Habsburg & Bourbon Europe, 1470-1720. LC 75-328564. (Illus.). 1974. pap. text ed. 10.95x (ISBN 0-582-35029-8). Longman.
Locurto, C. M., et al, eds. Autoshaping & Conditioning Theory. 1980. 30.00 (ISBN 0-12-454480-0). Acad Pr.
Loda, Charles J., jt. auth. see Winder, Alan A.
Loder, Dorothy. The Land & People of Belgium. rev. ed. LC 72-13301. (Portraits of the Nations Series). (Illus.). 1973. 8.79 (ISBN 0-397-31462-0). Lippincott.
--The Land & People of Spain. new rev. ed. LC 72-1368. (Portrait of the Nation Series). (Illus.). (gr. 6 up). 1972. 8.79 (ISBN 0-397-31303-9). Lippincott.
Loder, James E. The Transforming Moment: Understanding Convictional Experiences. LC 80-8354. 256p. 1981. 12.95 (ISBN 0-06-065276-4, HarpR). Har-Row.
Lodge, Arthur S. Body Tensor Fields in Continuum Mechanics. 1975. 48.00 (ISBN 0-12-454950-0). Acad Pr.
Lodge, Bernard, jt. auth. see Roffey, Maureen.
Lodge, David. Evelyn Waugh. LC 78-136497. (Columbia Essays on Modern Writers Ser.: No. 58). 48p. 1971. pap. 2.00 (ISBN 0-231-03258-7, MW58). Columbia U Pr.
--The Language of Fiction: Essays in Criticism & Verbal Analysis of the English Novel. LC 66-10731. 1967. 17.50x (ISBN 0-231-02854-7); pap. 6.00x (ISBN 0-231-08580-X, 80). Columbia U Pr.
--The Modes of Modern Writing: Metaphor, Metonymy, & the Modern Literature. LC 76-51544. 1977. 19.50x o.p. (ISBN 0-8014-1046-0). Cornell U Pr.
--Working with Structuralism: Essays & Reviews on Nineteenth & Twentieth-Century Literature. 240p. 1981. 30.00 (ISBN 0-7100-0658-6). Routledge & Kegan.
Lodge, David, ed. Twentieth Century Literary Criticism: A Reader. 1977. pap. text ed. 14.95x (ISBN 0-582-48422-7). Longman.
Lodge, George C. Engines of Change: United States Interests & Revolution in Latin America. (YA) 1970. 8.95 o.p. (ISBN 0-394-42344-5). Knopf.
Lodge, H. C. & Redmond, C. F., eds. Selections from the Correspondence of Theodore Roosevelt & Henry Cabot Lodge, 1884-1918, 2 Vols. LC 72-146156. (American Public Figures Ser). 1971. Repr. of 1925 ed. Set. lib. bdg. 95.00 (ISBN 0-306-70129-4). Da Capo.
Lodge, Henry C. Alexander Hamilton. LC 80-22082. (American Statesmen Ser.). 310p. 1981. pap. 4.95 (ISBN 0-87754-179-5). Chelsea Hse.
--Daniel Webster. LC 80-24628. (American Statesmen Ser.). 370p. 1981. pap. 5.95 (ISBN 0-87754-184-1). Chelsea Hse.
Lodge, Henry C., ed. see Cabot, George.
Lodge, Thomas. A Treatise of the Plague: Containing the Nature, Signes, & Accidents of the Same. LC 79-84119. (English Experience Ser.: No. 938). 92p. 1979. Repr. of 1603 ed. lib. bdg. 10.50 (ISBN 90-221-0938-0). Walter J Johnson.
--Wounds of Civil War. Houppert, J. W., ed. LC 68-63050. (Regents Renaissance Drama Ser). 1969. 7.95x (ISBN 0-8032-0269-5); pap. 1.65x (ISBN 0-8032-5268-4, BB 230, Bison). U of Nebr Pr.
Lodge, Thomas see Gosson, Stephen.
Lodhi, M. A., ed. see International Symposium on Superheavy Elements, March 9-11, 1978, Lubbock, Texas.
Lodowick, Lloyd. A Briefe Conference of Divers Laws: Divided into Certain Regiments. Berkowitz, David & Thorne, Samuel, eds. LC 77-86562. (Classics of English Legal History in the Modern Era Ser.: Vol. 64). 1979. Repr. of 1602 ed. lib. bdg. 55.00 (ISBN 0-8240-3051-6). Garland Pub.
Lodrick, Deryck O. Sacred Cows, Sacred Places: Origins & Survivals of Animal Homes in India. (Illus.). 350p. 1981. 20.00x (ISBN 0-520-04109-7). U of Cal Pr.
Loe, Kelley, jt. auth. see Neuberger, Richard L.
Loeb, Catherine, jt. auth. see Stineman, Esther.
Loeb, James R. & Kahn, Harold L. New York Supplement for Modern Real Estate Practice. 130p. (Orig.). 1980. pap. 7.95 (ISBN 0-88462-375-0). Real Estate Ed Co.
Loeb, Jo & Loeb, Paul. Cathletics: Ways to Amuse & Exercise Your Cat. LC 80-39813. (Illus.). 96p. 81. pap. 4.50 (ISBN 0-13-121004-1). P-H.
--Supertraining Your Dog. LC 80-10623. (Illus.). 1980. 9.95 (ISBN 0-13-876730-0). P-H.
--You Can Train Your Cat. 1979. pap. 3.95 (ISBN 0-671-25147-3, Fireside). S&S.
Loeb, Judy, ed. Feminist Collage: Educating Women in the Visual Arts. LC 79-15468. 1979. 14.95x (ISBN 0-8077-2561-7). Tchrs Coll.
Loeb, Leonard B. Electrical Coronas: Their Basic Physical Mechanisms. 1965. 35.00x o.p. (ISBN 0-520-00765-4). U of Cal Pr.
Loeb, O. W. & Prittie, Terence. Moselle. (Illus.). 1972. 9.95 o.p. (ISBN 0-571-08199-1, Pub. by Faber & Faber). Merrimack Bk Serv.
Loeb, Paul, jt. auth. see Loeb, Jo.
Loeb, Robert. Crime & Capital Punishment. (Impact Books Ser.). (Illus.). (gr. 7 up). 1978. PLB 6.90 s&l (ISBN 0-531-01453-3). Watts.
Loeb, Robert H. Your Guide to Voting. (gr. 7 up). 1977. PLB 7.90 s&l (ISBN 0-531-00391-4). Watts.
Loeb, Robert H., Jr. Marriage: For Better or for Worse? (gr. 9 up). 1980. PLB 8.90 (ISBN 0-686-65254-1, G25). Watts.
--Meet the Real Pilgrims: Everyday Life on Plimouth Plantation in 1627. LC 78-1208. 1979. 7.95a (ISBN 0-385-14152-1); PLB (ISBN 0-385-14153-X). Doubleday.
Loeb, Robert H., Jr. & Maloney, John P. Your Legal Rights As a Minor. LC 73-6955. (gr. 7 up). 1974. PLB 5.88 o.p. (ISBN 0-531-02650-7). Watts.
Loeb, Robert L. & Clay, Vidal S. Breaking the Sex Role Barrier. (gr. 6 up). 1977. lib. bdg. 7.45 (ISBN 0-531-00120-2). Watts.
Loebbecke, J., jt. auth. see Arens, A.
Loebbecke, J, jt. auth. see Arens, A.
Loebbecke, James K. & Arens, Alvin A. Applications of Statistical Sampling to Auditing. (Illus.). 400p. 1981. 23.95 (ISBN 0-13-039156-5). P-H.
Loebel, Arnold B. Chemical Problem Solving by Dimensional Analysis. 2nd ed. LC 77-78565. (Illus.). 1978. pap. text ed. 9.50 (ISBN 0-395-25516-3). HM.
Loebel, JoAnn, jt. auth. see Cramblit, Joella.
Loebell, E., ed. see International Association of Logopedics & Phoniatrics, 18th Congress, Washington, D.C. August, 1980.
Loeber, E. G., ed. Supplement to E. J. Labarre's Dictionary & Encyclopaedia of Paper & Paper-Making. 114p. text ed. 23.75 (ISBN 90-265-0038-6, Pub. by Swets Pub Serv). Swets North Am.
Loebl, Eugen, jt. auth. see Roman, Stephen B.
Loebl, Suzanne, et al. The Nurses Drug Book. 2nd ed. LC 80-15274. 889p. 1980. 19.95 (ISBN 0-471-06092-5, Pub. by Wiley Med); pap. 14.95 (ISBN 0-471-06017-8, Pub. by Wiley-Med). Wiley.
Loechel, William E. Medical Illustration: A Guide for the Doctor-Author & Exhibitor. (Illus.). 360p. 1964. pap. 34.75 photocopy ed., spiral (ISBN 0-398-01139-7). C C Thomas.
Loef, A. Rutgers Van Der see Van Der Loef, A. Rutgers.
Loeffler, Chris. Eydie Mae: How I Conquered Cancer Naturally. pap. 2.95 (ISBN 0-686-10146-4). Prod Hse.
Loeffler, Chris, jt. auth. see Mae, Eydie.
Loeffler, F. J. & Proctor, C. R., eds. Units & Bulk Materials Handling. 289p. 1980. 60.00 (H00163). ASME.
Loehlin, John C., et al. Race Differences in Intelligence. LC 75-1081. (Psychology Ser.). (Illus.). 1975. text ed. 22.95x (ISBN 0-7167-0754-3); pap. text ed. 12.95x (ISBN 0-7167-0753-5). W H Freeman.
Loehman, Edna, jt. ed. see Conner, J. Richard.
Loehr, Franklin. Diary After Death. 1976. pap. 1.50 (ISBN 0-89129-057-5). Jove Pubns.
Loehr, Max. The Great Painters of China. LC 79-6030. (Icon Editions). (Illus.). 336p. 1980. 29.95 (ISBN 0-06-435326-5, HarpT). Har-Row.
Loehr, Raymond C., ed. Phosphorus Management Strategies for Lakes. LC 79-55150. (Illus.). 1980. 39.95 (ISBN 0-250-40332-3). Ann Arbor Science.
Loehr, Wm. & Powelson, J. Economic Development, Poverty & Income Distribution. LC 77-23270. 1977. lib. bdg. 27.50x (ISBN 0-89158-248-7). Westview.
Loeliger, Ronald. Threaded Interpretive Languages. 272p. 1980. 18.95 (ISBN 0-07-038360-X, BYTE Bks). McGraw.
Loening, K. L., ed. Nomenclature of Regular Single-Strand Organic Polymers. 1977. pap. text ed. 10.00 (ISBN 0-08-021579-3). Pergamon.
Loeper, Eisenhart Von see Teutsch, Gotthard M. & Von Loeper, Eisenhart.
Loeper, John. By Hook & Ladder. LC 80-36738. (Illus.). 96p. (gr. 4-6). 1981. PLB 7.95 (ISBN 0-689-30816-7). Atheneum.
--Going to School in 1776. LC 72-86940. 112p. (gr. 4-6). 1973. 8.95 (ISBN 0-689-30089-1). Atheneum.

Loer, Barbara. Das Absolute & die Wirklichkeit in Schellings Philosophie: Mit der Erstedition einer Handschrift aus dem Berliner Schelling-Nachlass. LC 73-93164. (Quellen & Studien zur Philosophie, Vol. 7). (Illus.). viii, 288p. 1974. 60.59x (ISBN 3-11-004329-7). De Gruyter.

Loerg, Ernest A. Electrical Guide to DC-AC Circuit Analysis. 1979. pap. text ed. 9.95 (ISBN 0-89669-006-7). Collegium Bk Pubs.

Loero, Guido. Boundary Conditions & Global Management. 1975. 25.50 (ISBN 0-12-455050-9). Acad Pr.

Loeschen, John R. Wrestling with Luther. LC 75-33815. 232p. 1976. 10.50 (ISBN 0-570-03256-3, 15-2164). Concordia.

Loeschen, R., jt. auth. see Bauer, R.

Loescher, Ann D., jt. auth. see Loescher, Gil.

Loescher, Gil & Loescher, Ann D. China: Pushing Toward the Year 2000. LC 80-8802. (Illus.). 160p. (gr. 7 up). 1981. 10.95 (ISBN 0-15-217506-7, HJ). HarBraceJ.

Loesser, Arthur. Humor in American Song. LC 79-181804. (Illus.). 317p. 1975. Repr. of 1942 ed. 18.00 (ISBN 0-8103-4040-2). Gale.

Loether & McTavish. Descriptive & Inferential Statistics: An Introduction. 2nd ed. 624p. 1980. text ed. 20.95 (ISBN 0-205-06905-3, 8169055). Allyn.

--Statistical Analysis for Sociologists: A Student Manual. 1974. 4.95x o.p. (ISBN 0-205-04434-4, 8144346). Allyn.

Loether, Herman J. & McTavish, Donald G. Descriptive & Inferential Statistics: An Introduction. 640p. 1976. text ed. 14.95x o.p. (ISBN 0-205-05476-5). Allyn.

--Descriptive Statistics for Sociologists: An Introduction. 368p. 1974. pap. text ed. 13.60x (ISBN 0-205-04435-2). Allyn.

--Inferential Statistics for Sociologists: An Introduction. 304p. 1974. pap. text ed. 10.45x (ISBN 0-205-03737-2, 8137374). Allyn.

Loetscher, Lefferts A. Broadening Church. LC 54-7110. 1957. 9.00x o.p. (ISBN 0-8122-7018-5). U of Pa Pr.

Loew, H. Assessing Study Abroad Programs for Secondary School Students. (Language in Education Ser.: No. 29). 1980. pap. text ed. 2.95 (ISBN 0-87281-128-X). Ctr Appl Ling.

Loew, Reinhard. Philosophie Des Lebendigen Kants Begriff Des Organischen, Seine Wurzlen und Seine Aktualiat. 360p. 1980. text ed. 31.20 (ISBN 0-686-64717-3, 3-518-7499, Pub. by Insel Verlag Germany); pap. 22.40 quality paper (ISBN 3-518-07540-3). Suhrkamp.

Loewe, Frederick, jt. auth. see Lerner, Alan J.

Loewe, Michael. Records of Han Administration, 2 Vols. (University of Cambridge Oriental Pubns.). 1967. Vol. 1. 47.00 (ISBN 0-521-05586-5); Vol. 2. 79.00 (ISBN 0-521-05587-3). Cambridge U Pr.

Loewe, Ralph E. The Writing Clinic. 2nd ed. LC 77-17542. (Illus.). 1978. pap. text ed. 9.95 (ISBN 0-13-970434-5). P-H.

Loewen, Jacob A. Culture & Human Values: Christian Intervention in Anthropological Perspective. Smalley, William A., ed. LC 75-12653. (Applied Cultural Anthropology Ser.). 443p. (Orig.). 1975. pap. 6.95x (ISBN 0-87808-722-2). William Carey Lib.

Loewenberg, tr. see Moerikke, Eduard.

Loewenberg, Frank & Dolgoff, Ralph, eds. Practice of Social Intervention: Goals, Roles & Strategies: a Book of Readings in Social Work Practice. LC 74-174169. 1972. pap. text ed. 11.50 (ISBN 0-87581-121-3). Peacock Pubs.

Loewenberg, Frank M. Fundamentals of Social Intervention: Core Concepts & Skills for Social Work Practice. LC 76-23290. 1977. 13.50x (ISBN 0-231-03611-6). Columbia U Pr.

Loewenberg-Wertheim, tr. see Von Chamisso, Adelbert.

Loewenfeld, Claire. Herb Gardening. (Illus.). 1964. 9.95 (ISBN 0-571-06024-2, Pub. by Faber & Faber); pap. 5.50 (ISBN 0-571-09475-9). Merrimack Bk Serv.

Loewenfeld, Claire, et al. Britain's Wild Larder. LC 80-66426. (Illus.). 192p. 1980. 19.95 o.p. (ISBN 0-7153-7971-2). David & Charles.

Loewenstein, Louis K., ed. Urban Studies: An Introductory Reader. 2nd ed. LC 76-19644. 1977. 19.95 (ISBN 0-02-919470-9); pap. text ed. 10.95 (ISBN 0-02-919440-7). Free Pr.

Loewenthal, Leo & Dubiel, Helmut. Mitmachen Wollte Ich Nie: Gespraeche. (Edition Suhrkamp: Neue Folge). 240p. (Orig.). 1980. pap. text ed. 7.80 (ISBN 3-518-11014-4, Pub. by Insel Verlag Germany). Suhrkamp.

Loewenthal, R. E. & Marais, G. V. Carbonate Chemistry of Aquatic Systems, Vol. 2. LC 76-24963. 1981. price not set (ISBN 0-250-40150-9). Ann Arbor Science. Postponed.

Loewenthal, Rudolf, jt. auth. see Pokotilov, Dmitri.

Loewer, H. Peter. Evergreens. (Illus.). 144p. Date not set. 11.95 (ISBN 0-8027-0662-2). Walker & Co.

--The Indoor Water Gardener's How to Handbook. 5.95 o.s.i. (ISBN 0-8027-0404-2). Walker & Co.

Loewer, Peter. The Indoor Water Gardener's How-to Handbook. 1976. pap. 1.25 o.p. (ISBN 0-445-08270-4). Popular Lib.

Loewi, G., tr. see Fassbender, H. G.

Loewy, Arnold H. Criminal Law in a Nutshell. (Nutshell Ser.). 302p. 1980. pap. text ed. 6.95 (ISBN 0-8299-2067-6). West Pub.

Lofchie, Michael F., jt. auth. see Bates, Robert H.

Lofchie, Michael F., ed. The State of the Nations: Constraints on Development in Independent Africa. (African Studies Center, UCLA). 1971. 19.50x (ISBN 0-520-01740-4); pap. 3.25 o.p. (ISBN 0-520-02360-9). U of Cal Pr.

Loffler, Bertold. Die Sieben Zwerge Scheewittchens. (Insel Taschbuecher Fuer Kinder: It 489). 40p. (Ger.). pap. text ed. 4.55 (ISBN 3-458-32189-6, Pub. by Insel Verlag Germany). Suhrkamp.

Lofland, John. Analyzing Social Settings. 1971. pap. 7.95x (ISBN 0-534-00631-0). Wadsworth Pub.

--Deviance & Identity. 1969. pap. text ed. 12.95 (ISBN 0-13-208413-9). P-H.

--Doomsday Cult: A Study of Conversion, Proselytization, & Maintenance of Faith. enl. ed. LC 77-23028. 1981. pap. text ed. 9.50x (ISBN 0-8290-0095-X). Irvington.

Lofland, John, ed. Interaction in Everyday Life: Social Strategies. LC 78-51495. (Sage Contemporary Social Science Anthologies Ser.: No. 1). 1978. pap. 5.50x (ISBN 0-8039-1035-5). Sage.

Lofland, Lyn H., ed. Toward a Sociology of Death & Dying. LC 75-32378. (Sage Contemporary Social Science Issues Ser.: Vol. 28). 1976. 4.95x (ISBN 0-8039-0586-6). Sage.

Loflis, Anne, jt. auth. see Meister, Richard.

Lofthouse, Jessica. Portrait of Lancashire. LC 67-92282. (Portrait Bks.). (Illus.). 1967. 10.50x (ISBN 0-7091-6359-2). Intl Pubns Serv.

Loftie, M. J., et al. The Dining Room & the Drawing Room & the Bedroom & the Boudoir. Stansky, Peter & Shewan, Rodney, eds. LC 76-18321. (Aesthetic Movement & the Arts & Crafts Movement Ser.). 1978. lib. bdg. 44.00x (ISBN 0-8240-2461-3). Garland Pub.

Loftie, W. J., et al. A Plea for Art in the House & House Decoration & Dress & Music in the House. Stansky, Peter & Shewan, Rodney, eds. LC 76-18320. (Aesthetic Movement & the Arts & Crafts Movement Ser.). 1978. Repr. lib. bdg. 44.00x (ISBN 0-8240-2460-5). Garland Pub.

Loftin, Horace, jt. auth. see Edwards, Ernest P.

Loftin, Tee, ed. see Nault, Andy.

Lofting, Hugh. Doctor Dolittle: A Treasury. LC 67-19270. (Illus.). (gr. 4-6). 1967. 8.95 o.p. (ISBN 0-397-30937-6). Lippincott.

--Doctor Dolittle & the Green Canary. (Illus.). (gr. 4-6). 1950. 10.95 (ISBN 0-397-30166-9). Lippincott.

--Doctor Dolittle & the Secret Lake. (Illus.). (gr. 4-6). 1948. 10.95 (ISBN 0-397-30135-9). Lippincott.

--Doctor Dolittle's Birthday Book. LC 68-8923. (Illus.). (gr. 4-6). 1968. 7.95 (ISBN 0-397-30996-1). Lippincott.

--Doctor Dolittle's Caravan. (Illus.). (gr. 4-6). 1926. 10.95 (ISBN 0-397-30011-5). Lippincott.

--Doctor Dolittle's Circus. (Illus.). (gr. 4-6). 1924. 6.50 o.p. (ISBN 0-397-30008-5). Lippincott.

--Doctor Dolittle's Garden. (Illus.). (gr. 4-6). 1927. 5.50 o.p. (ISBN 0-397-30012-3). Lippincott.

--Doctor Dolittle's Zoo. (Illus.). (gr. 4-6). 1925. 10.95 (ISBN 0-397-30009-3). Lippincott.

Loftis, Anne. California: Where the Twain Did Meet. LC 72-11278. 324p. 1973. 7.95 o.s.i. (ISBN 0-02-574100-4). Macmillan.

Loftis, John see Dryden, John.

Loftis, John, ed. see Lee, Nathaniel.

Loftis, John, et al see Dryden, John.

Lofts, Norah. Bride of Moat House. 208p. 1976. pap. 1.50 o.p. (ISBN 0-449-22527-5, Crest). Fawcett.

--The Brittle Glass. 1977. pap. 1.75 o.p. (ISBN 0-449-23037-6, Crest). Fawcett.

--The Concubine. 336p. 1975. pap. 1.50 o.p. (ISBN 0-449-22405-8, Q2405, Crest). Fawcett.

--Crown of Aloes. 1977. pap. 1.75 o.p. (ISBN 0-449-23030-9, Crest). Fawcett.

--The Day of the Butterfly. 320p. 1981. pap. 2.95 (ISBN 0-449-24359-1, Crest). Fawcett.

--Hauntings. 1977. pap. 1.75 o.p. (ISBN 0-449-23393-6, Crest). Fawcett.

--The Homecoming. 1977. pap. 1.95 o.p. (ISBN 0-449-23166-6, Crest). Fawcett.

--The House at Sunset. 1978. pap. 1.95 o.p. (ISBN 0-449-23676-5, Crest). Fawcett.

--How Far to Bethlehem? 320p. 1977. pap. 1.95 o.p. (ISBN 0-449-23277-8, Crest). Fawcett.

--Knight's Acre. 320p. 1976. pap. 1.75 o.p. (ISBN 0-449-22685-9, X2685, Crest). Fawcett.

--Little Wax Doll. 1975. pap. 1.25 o.p. (ISBN 0-449-22270-5, P2270, Crest). Fawcett.

--The Lost Queen. 288p. 1975. pap. 1.50 o.p. (ISBN 0-449-22154-7, Q2154, Crest). Fawcett.

--Lovers All Untrue. 1977. pap. 1.50 o.p. (ISBN 0-449-22792-8, Q2792, Crest). Fawcett.

--Lute Player. 1976. pap. 1.95 o.p. (ISBN 0-449-22948-3, Crest). Fawcett.

--Nethergate. 256p. 1977. pap. 1.75 o.p. (ISBN 0-449-23095-3, Crest). Fawcett.

--Out of the Dark. 1978. pap. 1.75 o.p. (ISBN 0-449-23479-7, Crest). Fawcett.

--Scent of Cloves. 256p. 1981. pap. 2.50 o.p. (ISBN 0-449-22977-7, Crest). Fawcett.

--To See a Fine Lady. 272p. 1976. pap. 2.25 (ISBN 0-449-22890-8, Crest). Fawcett.

--The Town House. 384p. 1976. pap. 1.75 o.p. (ISBN 0-449-22793-6, X2793, Crest). Fawcett.

--Two by Norah Lofts. Bd. with Requiem for Idols; You're Best Alone. 240p. 1981. 12.95 (ISBN 0-385-01768-5). Doubleday.

--A Wayside Tavern. LC 80-954. 384p. 1980. 11.95 (ISBN 0-385-17201-X). Doubleday.

--Winter Harvest. 1976. pap. 1.75 o.p. (ISBN 0-449-22855-X, X2855, Crest). Fawcett.

Loftsgaarden, Don O., jt. auth. see Reinhardt, Howard E.

Loftus, Elizabeth & Wortman, Camille. Psychology. 672p. 1981. text ed. 18.95 (ISBN 0-394-32428-5); wkbk. 6.95 (ISBN 0-394-32730-6). Knopf.

Loftus, Elizabeth, et al. Cognitive Processes. LC 78-16953. (P-H Ser. in Experimental Psychology). 1979. ref. ed. 19.95 (ISBN 0-13-139634-X). P-H.

Loftus, Elizbeth. Memory: Surprising New Insights into How We Remember & Why We Forget. (Illus.). 224p. 1980. (ISBN 0-201-04473-0); pap. 5.95 (ISBN 0-201-04474-9). A-W.

Lo Fu-Chen & Salih, K., eds. Growth Pole Strategy & Regional Development Policy: Asian Experiences & Alternative Approaches. (Illus.). 1978. text ed. 55.00 (ISBN 0-08-021984-5). Pergamon.

Logan & Edwards. Manual of Laparoscopy & Culdoscopy. 1981. text ed. price not set. Butterworth.

Logan, Albert B. Justice in Jeopardy: Strategy to Revitalize the American Dream. (Illus.). 260p. 1973. text ed. 12.50 (ISBN 0-398-02694-7); pap. text ed. 8.25 (ISBN 0-398-02764-1). C C Thomas.

Logan, Ben, jt. auth. see Palomares, Uvaldo.

Logan, Bob. Denim & Dogwood. (Illus.). 96p. 1981. 5.95 (ISBN 0-89962-049-3). Todd & Honeywell.

Logan, Carolyn, jt. auth. see Larson, Arlene.

Logan, Elizabeth D. Shell Craft. LC 74-2018. (Illus.). 224p. 1974. 14.95 o.p. (ISBN 0-684-13863-8, ScribT). Scribner.

Logan, Frank A. Incentive: How the Conditions of Reinforcement Affect the Performance of Rats. 1960. 42.50x (ISBN 0-686-51403-3). Elliots Bks.

Logan, Frank A. & Ferraro, Douglas P. Systematic Analyses of Learning & Motivation. LC 78-6870. 1978. text ed. 21.95x (ISBN 0-471-04130-0). Wiley.

Logan, Frank A. & Gordon, William C. Fundamentals of Learning & Motivation. 3rd ed. 250p. 1981. pap. text ed. write for info. (ISBN 0-697-06634-7). Wm C Brown.

Logan, George H. Tax Reduction for Small Business & Self Employed. 1981. pap. 9.95 (ISBN 0-914598-08-2). Padre Prods.

Logan, Hugh L. Stress Corrosion of Metals. LC 66-2651. (Corrosion Monograph Ser.). 1966. 30.50 o.p. (ISBN 0-471-54340-3, Pub. by Wiley-Interscience). Wiley.

Logan, Jake. Across the Rio Grande. LC 75-23640. (John Slocum Ser.: No. 4). 224p. 1975. pap. 1.50 (ISBN 0-87216-702-X). Playboy Pbks.

--Bloody Trail to Texas. LC 76-1706. (John Slocum Ser.: No. 7). 192p. 1976. pap. 1.75 (ISBN 0-87216-736-4). Playboy Pbks.

--The Comanche's Woman. LC 75-36298. (John Slocum Ser.: No. 5). 192p. 1975. pap. 1.75 (ISBN 0-87216-722-4, B16301). Playboy Pbks.

--Hellfire. LC 80-83591. (Jake Logan Ser.). 256p. (Orig.). 1981. pap. 1.95 (ISBN 0-87216-795-X). Playboy Pbks.

--Iron Mustang. LC 78-54989. (Jake Logan Ser.: No. 15). 1978. pap. 1.75 (ISBN 0-87216-740-2). Playboy Pbks.

--North to Dakota. LC 76-9581. (John Slocum Ser.: No. 8). 1976. pap. 1.75 (ISBN 0-87216-742-9). Playboy Pbks.

--Ride, Slocum, Ride. LC 75-14619. (John Slocum Ser.: No. 2). 192p. 1975. pap. 1.50 (ISBN 0-87216-679-1, B16281). Playboy Pbks.

--Slocum & the Widow Kate. LC 75-21634. (John Slocum Ser.: No. 3). 224p. 1975. pap. 1.75 (ISBN 0-87216-744-5, B16287). Playboy Pbks.

--Slocum's Flag. LC 81-80091. (Slocum Ser.). 224p. (Orig.). 1981. pap. 1.95 (ISBN 0-87216-856-5). Playboy Pbks.

--Slocum's Gold. LC 75-40704. (John Slocum Ser.: No. 6). 1976. pap. 1.75 (ISBN 0-87216-738-0). Playboy Pbks.

--Slocum's Woman. LC 76-9585. (John Slocum Ser.: No. 9). 1977. pap. 1.75 (ISBN 0-87216-745-3). Playboy Pbks.

--White Hell. LC 76-49402. (Slocum Ser: No. 10). 1977. pap. 1.50 (ISBN 0-87216-648-1). Playboy Pbks.

--White Hell. LC 76-49402. (Jake Logan Ser.). 192p. (Orig.). 1981. pap. 1.95 (ISBN 0-87216-864-6). Playboy Pbks.

Logan, Janice L. Breaking the Language Barrier with Spanish. 1977. pap. text ed. 8.95 (ISBN 0-89420-035-6, 176040); cassette recordings 237.60 (ISBN 0-89420-127-1, 176000). Natl Book.

Logan, John. Ghosts of the Heart. LC 60-7239. 1960. 4.50x o.s.i. (ISBN 0-226-49110-2). U of Chicago Pr.

--Only the Dreamer Can Change the Dream: Selected Poems. LC 80-23184. (The American Poetry Ser.: Vol. 21). 256p. 1981. 14.95 (ISBN 0-912946-77-6). Ecco Pr.

Logan, John A. No Transfer: An American Security Principle. 1961. 42.50x (ISBN 0-685-69838-6). Elliots Bks.

Logan, Larry L. The Professional Photographer's Handbook. LC 80-80056. (Illus.). 128p. (Orig.). 1980. pap. 14.95 (ISBN 0-9603856-0-6). Logan Design.

Logan, Mark. Brumaire. LC 77-15864. 1978. 8.95 o.p. (ISBN 0-312-10677-7). St Martin.

Logan, R. W. Betrayal of the Negro: From Rutherford B. Hayes to Woodrow Wilson. Orig. Title: Negro in American Life & Thought. 1965. pap. 1.50 o.s.i. (ISBN 0-02-034490-2, Collier). Macmillan.

Logan, Rayford W. Haiti & the Dominican Republic. (Royal Institute of International Affairs Ser.). 1968. 13.95x (ISBN 0-19-214966-0). Oxford U Pr.

--The Senate & the Versailles Mandate System. LC 74-14357. 112p. 1975. Repr. of 1945 ed. lib. bdg. 11.75x (ISBN 0-8371-7798-7, LOVM). Greenwood.

Logan, Robert. The Bulls & Chicago: A Stormy Affair. (Illus.). 256p. 1975. 7.95 o.p. (ISBN 0-695-80619-X). Follett.

Logan, Roderick M., jt. auth. see Carroll, John E.

Logan, Wende W. Breast Carcinoma: The Radiologist's Expanded Role. LC 77-13047. 1977. 53.50 (ISBN 0-471-03023-6, Pub. by Wiley Medical). Wiley.

Logan, Wende W. & Muntz, E. Phillip. Reduced Dose Mammography. LC 79-63202. (Illus.). 576p. 1979. 41.25 (ISBN 0-89352-060-8). Masson Pub.

Logan, William & Petras, Herman. Handbook of the Martial Arts & Self-Defense. LC 74-26776. (Funk & W Bk.). (Illus.). 1975. 10.95 o.s.i. (ISBN 0-308-10104-9, TYC-T). T Y Crowell.

Logan, William H. Pedlar's Pack of Ballads & Songs. LC 67-23929. 1968. Repr. of 1869 ed. 21.00 (ISBN 0-8103-3534-4). Gale.

Logerberg, Ted & Logerberg, Vi. Collectible Glass, 4 bks. Incl. Bk. I. o.p. (ISBN 0-87069-232-1); Bk. II. o.p. (ISBN 0-87069-233-X); Bk. III. Durand Glass (ISBN 0-87069-234-8); Bk. IV. British Glass (ISBN 0-87069-235-6). (Illus.). 1978. ringbound 6.95 ea. Wallace-Homestead.

Logerberg, Vi., jt. auth. see Logerberg, Ted.

Logerfo, Paul, jt. auth. see Livolsi, Virginia A.

Loggins, Vernon. Andre Cnenier: His Life, Death & Glory. LC 65-13701. xii, 292p. 1965. 12.95x (ISBN 0-8214-0009-6). Ohio U Pr.

Logic Colloquim '79 Leeds, August 1979, et al. Recursion Theory: Its Generalisations & Applications; Proceedings. Drake, F. R. & Wainer, S. S, eds. (London Mathematical Society Lecture Notes Ser.: No. 45). 300p. 1980. pap. 24.50 (ISBN 0-521-23543-X). Cambridge U Pr.

Logier, Johann B. Logier's Comprehensive Course in Music: Harmony & Practical Composition. LC 76-15186. (Music Reprint Ser.). 1976. Repr. of 1888 ed. lib. bdg. 32.50 (ISBN 0-306-70794-2). Da Capo.

--A System of the Science of Music & Practical Composition: Incidentally Comprising What Is Usally Understood by the Term Through Bass. LC 76-20715. (Music Reprint Ser.). 1976. Repr. of 1897 ed. lib. bdg. 32.50 (ISBN 0-306-70793-4). Da Capo.

Logoreci, Anton. The Albanians: Europe's Forgotton Survivors. LC 77-14985. 1978. lib. bdg. 22.50x (ISBN 0-89158-827-2). Westview.

Logsdon, Joseph, ed. see Northup, Solomon.

Logsdon, Syd. A Fond Farewell to Dying. (Orig.). 1981. pap. text ed. 2.25 (ISBN 0-671-41099-7). PB.

Logsdon, Tom. Computers & Social Controversy. (Illus.). 123p. 1980. pap. text ed. write for info. wkbk (ISBN 0-914894-68-4). Computer Sci.

--Programming in BASIC. LC 77-75505. 1977. pap. 9.95x (ISBN 0-88236-179-1). Anaheim Pub Co.

--Programming in BASIC with Applications. LC 77-75504. 1977. pap. 10.95x (ISBN 0-88236-180-5). Anaheim Pub Co.

Logue, Christopher. Abecedary. (Illus.). 1979. 7.50 (ISBN 0-224-01562-1, Pub. by Chatto Bodley Jonathan). Merrimack Bk Serv.

Logue, Christopher, jt. auth. see Anderson, Wayne.

Logue, Christopher, compiled by. The Children's Book of Comic Verse. (Illus.). 160p. 1980. 17.95 (ISBN 0-7134-1528-2, Pub. by Batsford England). David & Charles.

Logue, Christopher, ed. The Children's Book of Comic Verse. (Illus.). 1979. 10.25 o.s.i. (ISBN 0-7134-1528-2, Pub. by Batsford). Hippocrene Bks.

Logue, Dennis E. Legislative Influences on Corporate Pension Plans. 1979. pap. 5.25 (ISBN 0-8447-3337-7). Am Enterprise.

Logue, H. E. & Simms, John D. Auburn: A Pictorial History. (Illus.). 192p. 1980. ltd. ed. 29.95 (ISBN 0-89865-048-8); pap. 12.95 (ISBN 0-89865-049-6). Donning Co.

Logue, Kenneth J. Popular Disturbances in Scotland, 1780-1815. (Illus.). 1979. text ed. 21.00x (ISBN 0-85976-037-5). Humanities.

Logue, Patrick E. Understanding & Living with Brain Damage. 116p. 1975. 11.75 (ISBN 0-398-03419-2); pap. 7.75 (ISBN 0-398-03420-6). C C Thomas.

Logue, Valentine. Neurosurgery. Rob, C. & Smith, R., eds. (Operative Surgery, Vol. 14). 1970. 20.00 o.p. (ISBN 0-685-14248-5). Lippincott.

Loh, Horace H. & Ross, David H., eds. Neurochemical Mechanisms of Opiates & Endorphins. LC 78-24623. (Advances in Biochemical Pharmacology Ser.: Vol. 20). 1979. text ed. 44.50 (ISBN 0-89004-166-0). Raven.

Loh, I. & Nida, E. A. Translators Handbook on Paul's Letter to the Philippians. (Helps for Translators Ser.). 1979. Repr. of 1977 ed. soft cover 1.70 (ISBN 0-8267-0144-2, 08528). United Bible.

Loh, Jules. Lords of the Earth: The History of the Navajo Indians. LC 76-150671. (Illus.). (gr. 7-12). 1971. 5.95 o.s.i. (ISBN 0-02-759290-1, CCPr). Macmillan.

Loh, May, jt. auth. see Lewis, Diehl.

Loh, Pai Ye. The Chinese Connection. 1978. 6.95 o.p. (ISBN 0-8007-0954-3). Revell.

Loham, Sandra L., jt. auth. see Popovich, Dorothy.

Lohan, Frank J. Pen & Ink Themes. (Illus.). 1981. 12.95 (ISBN 0-8092-7016-1); pap. 5.95 (ISBN 0-8092-7015-3). Contemp Bks.

Lohman, Joseph D. Cultural Patterns in Urban Schools: A Manual for Teachers, Counselors, & Administrators. (Orig.). 1967. pap. 5.95x (ISBN 0-520-01424-3, CAMPUS24). U of Cal Pr.

Lohmann, Jeanne. Where the Field Goes. 1976. pap. 3.00 (ISBN 0-686-17445-3). J A Lohmann.

Lohner, Edgar & Hannum, H. G. Modern German Drama. LC 66-3026. 1966. text ed. 21.30 (ISBN 0-395-04808-7, 3-35585). HM.

Lohner, Edgar, jt. ed. see Foulkes, A. Peter.

Lohnes, P. R., jt. auth. see Cooley, W. W.

Lohnes, Paul R., jt. auth. see Ackerman, Winona B.

Lohnes, Paul R., jt. auth. see Gribbons, Warren D.

Lohnes, Walter & Strothman, F. W. German: A Structural Approach. 2nd ed. (Illus.). 500p. 1973. text ed. 11.95x (ISBN 0-393-09345-X); tchr's ed. 3.95x (ISBN 0-393-09360-3); study guide 4.45x (ISBN 0-393-09352-2). Norton.

Lohnes, Walter F. & Strothmann, F. W. German: A Structural Approach. 3rd ed. 1980. text ed. 13.95x (ISBN 0-393-95059-X); tchrs'. manual avail. (ISBN 0-393-95068-9); study guide 4.95x (ISBN 0-393-95064-6). Norton.

Lohrentz, Kenneth P., jt. auth. see Easterbrook, David L.

Lohse, B., jt. auth. see Busch, H.

Lohse, Eduard. Colossians & Philemon. Koester, Helmut, ed. Poehlman, William R. & Karris, Robert J., trs. from Ger. LC 76-157550. (Hermeneia: A Critical & Historical Commentary on the Bible Ser). 256p. 1971. 14.95 (ISBN 0-8006-6001-3, 20-6001). Fortress.

--The Formation of the New Testament. Boring, M. Eugene, tr. LC 80-27032. 256p. (Orig.). 1981. pap. 8.95 (ISBN 0-687-13294-0). Abingdon.

Lohse, Eduard, jt. auth. see Hermission, Hans-Jurgen.

Lohse, Eduard, jt. auth. see Kaiser, Otto.

Lohwater, A. J. Russian-English Dictionary of the Mathematical Sciences. LC 61-15685. 267p. (Eng. & Rus.). 1979. Repr. of 1974 ed. 7.60 (ISBN 0-8218-0036-1, RED). Am Math.

Loinaz, George, ed. & tr. see Toboldt, William K.

Loiry, William S. Winning with Science: Source Book of Grants, Prizes & Awards for Science Competition. (Illus.). 224p. 1981. 11.95 (ISBN 0-87460-355-2). Lion.

Loiseaux, Pierre R. & Hawkland, William. Cases & Materials on Debtor-Creditor Relations. (Contemporary Legal Education Ser.). 1979. 22.50 (ISBN 0-672-82028-5, Bobbs-Merrill Law); statutory appendix 4.50 (ISBN 0-672-83731-5). Michie.

Lojko, Grace R. Typewriting Techniques for the Technical Secretary. LC 70-148198. 1972. pap. 10.95 ref. ed. (ISBN 0-13-935288-0). P-H.

Loke, Margarett. The World As It Was: A Photographic Portrait 1865 to 1921. LC 80-13031. (Illus.). 220p. 1980. 24.95 (ISBN 0-671-25376-X). Summit Bks.

Loken, Newton C. Tumbling & Trampolining. LC 78-90802. (Athletic Institute Ser). (Illus.). (gr. 5 up). 1969. 6.95 (ISBN 0-8069-4336-X); PLB 7.49 (ISBN 0-8069-4337-8). Sterling.

Loken, Newton C. & Willoughby, Robert J. The Complete Book of Gymnastics. 3rd ed. (Illus.). 256p. 1977. text ed. 16.95 (ISBN 0-13-157172-9). P-H.

Loken, Newton C., jt. auth. see Wachtel, Erna.

Lokich, Jacob J. Clinical Cancer Medicine: Treatment Tactics. (Medical Bks.). 1980. lib. bdg. 37.50 (ISBN 0-8161-2103-6, Hall Medical). G K Hall.

Lokke, Virgil L., jt. ed. see Thompson, G. R.

Lokken, Roy N. David Lloyd, Colonial Lawmaker. LC 59-13419. (Publications in History). (Illus.). 319p. 1959. 9.50 (ISBN 0-295-73762-X). U of Wash Pr.

Lokken, Roy N., ed. Meet Dr. Franklin. 2nd ed. 295p. 1981. 20.00 (ISBN 0-89168-035-7). Franklin Inst Pr.

Loll, Leo, Jr. & Buckley, Julian. Questions & Answers on the Securities Markets: A Quick Review Guide to Preparing for Securities Examinations. 1968. 15.95 (ISBN 0-13-749374-6). P-H.

Loll, Leo M., Jr. & Buckley, Julian G. The Over-the-Counter Securities Markets. 3rd ed. (Illus.). 560p. 1973. 19.95x (ISBN 0-13-647180-3). P-H.

Loller, Sherry G. The Super Food Cookbook for Kids. Van Dolson, Bobbie J., ed. (Illus.). (gr. k-5). 1976. pap. 2.95 (ISBN 0-8280-0060-3). Review & Herald.

Lollerstrom, Nick, jt. auth. see Best, Simon.

Lolley, R. N., jt. ed. see Bazan, N. G.

Lolli, F., jt. auth. see Bosco, F. J.

Lollis, Nicholas J. De see De Lollis, Nicholas J.

Lolme, Jean L. de see De Lolme, Jea L.

Lolme, Jean L. de see De Lolme, Jean L.

Lom, Herbert. Enter a Spy: The Double Life of Christopher Marlowe. (Illus.). 112p. 1978. 9.00x (ISBN 0-8476-6258-6). Rowman.

Lom, W. L. & Williams, A. F. Substitute Natural Gas: Manufacture & Properties. 1976. 44.95 (ISBN 0-470-15018-1). Halsted Pr.

Lom, W. L., jt. auth. see Williams, A. F.

Lomas, Geoffrey. Hostages. 1979. 8.95 o.p. (ISBN 0-684-16072-2, ScribT). Scribner.

Lomask, Martha. Low, Slow, Delicious: Recipes for Casseroles & Electric Slow-Cooking Pots. (Illus.). 160p. 1981. 19.95 (ISBN 0-571-11384-2, Pub. by Faber & Faber). Merrimack Bk Serv.

Lomask, Milton. Secret of Grandfather's Diary. (Illus.). (gr. 4-6). 1968. pap. 1.25 (ISBN 0-671-29797-X). PB.

--Seed Money: The Guggenheim Story. 1964. 6.50 o.p. (ISBN 0-374-25741-8). FS&G.

Lomax, Alan. Folk Songs of North America. LC 60-1043. (Illus.). 1960. 14.95 o.p. (ISBN 0-385-04844-0). Doubleday.

--The Folk Songs of North America. (Illus.). 656p. 1975. pap. 8.95 (ISBN 0-385-03772-4, Dolp). Doubleday.

Lomax, D. F. & Gutmann, P. T. The Euromarkets & International Financial Policies. 275p. 1980. 29.95x (ISBN 0-470-26923-5). Halsted Pr.

Lomax, Derek W. The Reconquest of Spain. LC 77-3030. (Illus.). 1978. text ed. 19.50x (ISBN 0-582-50209-8). Longman.

Lomax, Elizabeth M., et al. Science & Patterns of Child Care. LC 78-4972. (Psychology Ser.). 1978. text ed. 15.95x (ISBN 0-7167-0296-7); pap. text ed. 8.95x (ISBN 0-7167-0295-9). W H Freeman.

Lomax, Joseph F., ed. see Bright, Susan.

Lomax, Louis E. Negro Revolt. LC 62-7911. 1962. 8.95 o.p. (ISBN 0-06-012660-4, HarpT). Har-Row.

Lomazzo, Giovanni P. A Tracte Containing the Artes of Curious Paintinge. Haydocke, R., tr. LC 75-25632. (English Experience Ser.: No. 171). 1969. Repr. of 1598 ed. 42.00 (ISBN 90-221-0171-1). Walter J Johnson.

--Trattato dell'arte della pittura, scoltura, et architettura. (Documents of Art & Architectural History Series 2: Vol. 4). 754p. (Italian.). 1981. Repr. of 1585 ed. 65.00x (ISBN 0-89371-204-3). Broude Intl Edns.

Lombard. Biostatistics for the Health Professions. 1975. 12.95 o.p. (ISBN 0-8385-0664-X). ACC.

Lombard, Charles. Xavier De Maistre. (World Authors Ser.: No. 447). 1977. lib. bdg. 12.50 (ISBN 0-8057-6284-1). Twayne.

Lombard, Charles M. Joseph de Maistre. LC 76-13846. (World Authors Ser: No. 407). 1976. lib. bdg. 12.50 (ISBN 0-8057-6247-7). Twayne.

--Lamartine. (World Authors Ser.: France: No. 254). 1973. lib. bdg. 10.95 (ISBN 0-8057-2510-5). Twayne.

--Thomas Holley Chivers. (United States Authors Ser.: No. 325). 1979. lib. bdg. 12.50 (ISBN 0-8057-7258-8). Twayne.

Lombard, G. F., jt. auth. see Turner, A. N.

Lombardi, Donald. Search for Significance. LC 75-17676. (Illus.). 144p. 1975. 10.95 (ISBN 0-88229-109-2). Nelson-Hall.

Lombardi, Felipe R. A to Z No-Cook Cookbook. LC 72-79753. 1975. 5.95 (ISBN 0-910294-12-7). Brown Bk.

Lombardi, Frances G., jt. auth. see Lombardi, Gerald S.

Lombardi, George. The Jerry Ford Joke Book. 1976. pap. 0.95 o.p. (ISBN 0-685-69157-8, LB365, Leisure Bks). Nordon Pubns.

Lombardi, Gerald S. & Lombardi, Frances G. The Circle Without End: A Sourcebook of American Indian Ethics. (Illus.). 212p. 1981. lib. bdg. 9.95 (ISBN 0-87961-114-6); pap. 5.95 (ISBN 0-87961-117-0). Naturegraph.

Lombardi, Ronald P. & De Peters, Amalia B. Modern Spoken Spanish: An Interdisciplinary Perspective. LC 80-1442. 507p. (Orig.). 1981. pap. text ed. 16.75 (ISBN 0-8191-1513-4). U Pr of Amer.

Lombardi, Tarky, Jr. & Hoffman, Gerald N. Medical Malpractice Insurance: A Legislator's View. 1978. 11.95x (ISBN 0-8156-0128-X). Syracuse U Pr.

Lombardi, Thomas P. Career Adaptive Behavior Inventory Activity Book. Preston, J. B., ed. 88p. (Orig.). 1980. pap. text ed. 10.00x (ISBN 0-87562-066-3). Spec Child.

Lombardo, Guy & Altshul, Jack. Auld Acquaintance: An Autobiography. 1976. pap. 1.95 o.p. (ISBN 0-345-25244-6). Ballantine.

Lombardo, Victor S. Paraprofessionals in Special Education. (Illus.). 304p. 1980. text ed. 24.50 (ISBN 0-398-04105-9). C C Thomas.

Lombardy, Dana, ed. The Gamesmaster Catalog. (Illus., Orig.). 1980. pap. 6.95 (ISBN 0-933168-02-0). Boynton & Assoc.

Lombardy, William & Daniels, David. Guide to Tournament Chess. 1977. 8.95 o.p. (ISBN 0-679-13049-7); pap. 4.95 o.p. (ISBN 0-679-14041-7). McKay.

Lombroso, Cesare. Basic Characteristics Typical of Women Criminals. (The Library of Scientific Psychology). (Illus.). 1981. 74.95 (ISBN 0-89901-032-6). Found Class Reprints.

Lommasson, Robert C. Nebraska Wild Flowers. LC 70-188343. (Illus.). x, 185p. 1973. 16.50 (ISBN 0-8032-0816-2); pap. 10.50 (ISBN 0-8032-5768-6, BB 559, Bison). U of Nebr Pr.

Lomnicki, A. J. Summary of Landlord & Tenant Law. 1975. 25.00 (ISBN 0-7134-2923-2, Pub. by Batsford England); pap. 14.95 (ISBN 0-7134-2924-0). David & Charles.

--A Summary of Town & Country Planning Law. 1973. pap. 19.95 o.p. (ISBN 0-7134-0531-7, Pub. by Batsford England). David & Charles.

Londis, James. Abortion: Mercy or Murder? LC 79-25126. (Better Living Ser.). 1980. pap. 0.95 (ISBN 0-8127-0257-3). Southern Pub.

London, Barbara & Boyer, Richard. Photographing Indoors with Your Automatic Camera. (Your Automatic Camera Ser.). (Illus.). 144p. (Orig.). 1981. pap. 6.95 (ISBN 0-930764-18-8). Curtin & London.

--Photographing Outdoors with Your Automatic Camera. (Your Automatic Camera Ser.). (Illus.). 144p. (Orig.). 1981. pap. 6.95 (ISBN 0-930764-19-6). Curtin & London.

--Your Automatic Camera Indoors. 1981. pap. 6.95 (ISBN 0-442-21956-3). Van Nos Reinhold.

--Your Automatic Camera Outdoors. 1981. pap. 6.95 (ISBN 0-442-21955-5). Van Nos Reinhold.

London, Barbara, jt. auth. see Curtin, Dennis.

London, Barbara, jt. auth. see Witkin, Lee D.

London, Carolyn. Cat-Alog. (Children's Bks). (Illus.). 128p. (gr. 5 up). 1971. pap. 1.50 (ISBN 0-8024-1120-7). Moody.

--The Rat-Catcher's Son & Other Stories. (Children's Bks). (Illus.). 128p. (gr. 3-7). 1971. pap. 1.50 (ISBN 0-8024-1710-8). Moody.

London College of Physicians. Certain Necessary Directions Aswell for the Cure of the Plague As for Preventing the Infection: Also Certaine Select Statutes. LC 79-84120. (English Experience Ser.: No. 939). 148p. 1979. Repr. of 1636 ed. lib. bdg. 14.00 (ISBN 90-221-0939-9). Walter J Johnson.

London, Duke. Beautiful Las Vegas. Shangle, Robert D., ed. LC 79-18837. (Illus.). 72p. 1980. 14.95 (ISBN 0-89802-079-4); pap. 7.95 (ISBN 0-89802-078-6). Beautiful Am.

London, H. H. Principles & Techniques of Vocational Guidance. LC 73-78475. 1973. text ed. 18.95 (ISBN 0-675-08949-2). Merrill.

London, Harvey & Exner, John E., Jr. Dimensions of Personality. LC 77-25328. (Wiley Series on Personality Processes). 1978. 28.95 (ISBN 0-471-54392-6, Pub. by Wiley-Interscience). Wiley.

London, Harvey, ed. Personality: A New Look at Metatheories. LC 78-7022. (Series in Clinical Community Psychology). 1976. 12.95 (ISBN 0-470-26381-4). Halsted Pr.

London, Herbert I. The Overheated Decade. LC 76-5960. 200p. 1976. 12.00x (ISBN 0-8147-4966-6); pap. 6.95x (ISBN 0-8147-4967-4). NYU Pr.

--Social Science Theory, Structure & Application. LC 74-17461. 361p. 1975. 17.50x (ISBN 0-8147-4958-5). NYU Pr.

London, Herbert I. & Weeks, Albert. Myths That Rule America. LC 80-5866. 176p. 1981. lib. bdg. 13.50 (ISBN 0-8191-1446-4); pap. text ed. 6.95 (ISBN 0-8191-1447-2). U Pr of Amer.

London, Howard B. The Culture of a Community College. LC 78-8697. (Praeger Special Studies). 1978. 22.95 (ISBN 0-03-044701-1). Praeger.

London, Jack. Best Short Stories of Jack London. LC 45-3830. 1953. 8.95 (ISBN 0-385-00021-9). Doubleday.

--To Build a Fire. (Creative's Classics Ser.). (Illus.). 48p. (gr. 4-9). 1980. PLB 6.95 (ISBN 0-87191-769-6). Creative Ed.

--Call of the Wild. (gr. 6 up). 1963. 7.95 (ISBN 0-02-759510-2). Macmillan.

--Call of the Wild. (Literature Ser). (gr. 7-12). 1969. pap. text ed. 3.33 (ISBN 0-87720-704-6). AMSCO Sch.

--The Call of the Wild & Selected Stories. (RL 6). 1971. pap. 1.75 (ISBN 0-451-51383-5, CE1383, Sig Classics). NAL.

--The Call of the Wild, White Fang & Other Stories. Sinclair, Andrew, ed. (Penguin American Classics). (Orig.). 1980. pap. 2.95 (ISBN 0-14-039001-4). Penguin.

--Call of the Wild with Reader's Guide. (Literature Program). (gr. 10-12). 1970. pap. text ed. 3.92 (ISBN 0-87720-804-2); tchrs' ed. 2.60 (ISBN 0-87720-904-9). AMSCO Sch.

--Diable, a Dog. Pauk, Walter & Harris, Raymond, eds. (Classics Ser). (Illus.). (gr. 6-12). 1976. pap. text ed. 1.60x (ISBN 0-89061-046-0, 513); tchrs. ed. 3.00 (ISBN 0-89061-047-9, 515). Jamestown Pubs.

--The Iron Heel. rev. ed. 228p. 1980. pap. 4.95 (ISBN 0-88208-118-7). Lawrence Hill.

--The Iron Heel. (Arabic.). pap. 7.95x (ISBN 0-686-63557-4). Intl Bk Ctr.

--Jack London in the High School Aegis. Sisson, Jim, ed. (Illus.). 125p. (Orig.). (gr. 7-12). 1980. pap. 3.95 (ISBN 0-932458-01-7). Star Rover.

--The Law of Life. Pauk, Walter & Harris, Raymond, eds. (Classics Ser). (Illus.). (gr. 6-12). 1976. pap. text ed. 1.60x (ISBN 0-89061-040-1, 501); tchrs. ed. 3.00 (ISBN 0-89061-041-X, 503). Jamestown Pubs.

--The Marriage of Lit-Lit. Pauk, Walter & Harris, Raymond, eds. (Classics Ser). (Illus.). (gr. 6-12). 1976. pap. text ed. 1.60x (ISBN 0-89061-044-4, 509); tchrs. ed. 3.00 (ISBN 0-89061-045-2, 511). Jamestown Pubs.

--Martin Eden. (Literature Ser). (gr. 7-12). 1969. pap. text ed. 3.67 (ISBN 0-87720-709-7). AMSCO Sch.

--Martin Eden. 1957. 12.95 (ISBN 0-02-574510-7). Macmillan.

--Martin Eden with Reader's Guide. (AMSCO Literature Program Ser). (gr. 10-12). 1971. pap. text ed. 4.33 (ISBN 0-87720-812-3); tchr's ed. 2.80 (ISBN 0-87720-912-X). AMSCO Sch.

--Nam Bok. 250p. (Orig.). pap. 3.95 (ISBN 0-932458-03-3). Star Rover.

--Nam-Bok, the Liar. Pauk, Walter & Harris, Raymond, eds. (Classics Ser). (Illus.). (gr. 6-12). 1976. pap. text ed. 1.60x (ISBN 0-89061-042-8, 505); tchrs. ed. 3.00 (ISBN 0-89061-043-6, 507). Jamestown Pubs.

--The People of the Abyss. rev. ed. Simon, Myron, ed. (The Mind of Man Ser.). (Illus.). 224p. 1980. text ed. 25.00x (ISBN 0-686-64380-1). J Simon.

--The Sea Wolf. 351p. Repr. of 1904 ed. lib. bdg. 14.30x (ISBN 0-89190-657-6). Am Repr-Rivercity Pr.

--Selected Science Fiction & Fantasy Stories. LC 76-52712. (Illus.). 1979. 8.50 (ISBN 0-934882-03-7). Fictioneer Bks.

--Son of the Wolf. (Illus.). 250p. 1980. pap. 3.95 (ISBN 0-932458-02-5). Star Rover.

--South Sea Tales. 1961. 3.95 o.s.i. (ISBN 0-02-574690-1). Macmillan.

--Star Rover. (gr. 7 up). 1963. 4.95 o.s.i. (ISBN 0-02-759550-1). Macmillan.

--The Unabridged Jack London. Teacher, Lawrence, ed. 1250p. (Orig.). 1981. lib. bdg. 19.80 (ISBN 0-89471-123-7); pap. 9.95 (ISBN 0-89471-124-5). Running Pr.

--White Fang. (gr. 7 up). 1935. 10.95 (ISBN 0-02-574750-9). Macmillan.

--White Fang. (gr. 7-12). 1972. pap. 1.50 (ISBN 0-590-03130-9, Schol Pap). Schol Bk Serv.

London, Julius. Weather & Climate. LC 59-13618. (Illus.). (gr. 4-6). 1960. PLB 6.95 (ISBN 0-87396-012-2). Stravon.

London, Laura, ed. The Gypsy Heiress. (Orig.). 1981. pap. 1.50 (ISBN 0-440-12960-5). Dell.

London Magazine, ed. London Magazine Poems, Nineteen Sixty-One-Sixty-Six. 1966. pap. 3.50 (ISBN 0-85105-003-4). Dufour.

London Mathematical Society Committee, ed. see **Hardy, Godfrey H.**

London, Mel. Bread Winners. (Illus.). 1979. 14.95 (ISBN 0-87857-269-4). Rodale Pr Inc.

--Easy Going: A Guide to Good Health & Good Spirits on Your Journey Away from Home. (Illus.). 320p. (Orig.). 1981. 12.95 (ISBN 0-87857-331-3); pap. 9.95 (ISBN 0-87857-345-3). Rodale Pr Inc.

London, Mel & London, Sheryl. The Fish-Lovers Cookbook. (Illus.). 1980. 16.95 (ISBN 0-87857-299-6). Rodale Pr Inc.

London, P., jt. auth. see Heilbroner, R. L.

London, P. S. Modern Trends in Accident Surgery & Medicine-2. 1970. 17.95 (ISBN 0-407-28001-4). Butterworths.

London, Perry. Beginning Psychology. rev. ed. 1978. text ed. 18.95x (ISBN 0-256-02057-4). Dorsey.

London, Sheryl, jt. auth. see London, Mel.

London Stationers' Company. An Analytical Index to the Ballad-Entries (1557-1709) in the Registers of the Company of Stationers of London. LC 67-1586. xviii, 324p. Repr. of 1967 ed. 15.00 (ISBN 0-8103-5019-X). Gale.

London Sunday Times. Suffer the Children: The Story of Thalidomide. 1979. 12.95 o.p. (ISBN 0-670-68114-8). Viking Pr.

Londonderry, Robert S. A Journey to Damascus, Through Egypt, Nubia, Arabia Petroea, Palestine & Syria. LC 80-1925. 1981. Repr. of 1947 ed. 69.50 (ISBN 0-404-18976-8). AMS Pr.

Lone, Mary La see La Lone, Mary.

Lonergan, Bernard. Method in Theology. (Library of Contemporary Theology). 1979. pap. 9.95 (ISBN 0-8164-2204-4). Crossroad NY.

Lonergan, Bernard J. Insight: A Study of Human Understanding. LC 77-20441. 1977. pap. 11.95x (ISBN 0-06-065269-1, RD 251, HarpR). Har-Row.

Loney, Glenn, ed. The House of Mirth: The Play of the Novel. LC 78-75192. 220p. 1981. 13.50 (ISBN 0-8386-2416-2). Fairleigh Dickinsonn.

Loney, Glenn M., jt. ed. see Corrigan, Robert W.

Loney, Jan, jt. ed. see Gadow, Kenneth D.

Long. Transmission: Communication Skills for Technicians. (Illus.). 1980. pap. text ed. 12.95 (ISBN 0-8359-7816-8); instrs' manual avail. Reston.

Long & Prophit. Understanding-Responding. (Illus.). 225p. 1980. pap. text ed. 9.95 (ISBN 0-87872-284-X). Duxbury Pr.

Long, A. A. Hellenistic Philosophy: Stoics, Epicureans, Sceptics. (Classical Life & Letters Ser.). 262p. 1974. 40.50x (ISBN 0-7156-0667-0, 298, Pub. by Duckworth England). Biblio Dist.

Long, B., et al. Group Performance of Literature. (Illus.). 1977. pap. text ed. 15.95 (ISBN 0-13-365346-3). P-H.

Long, Barbara, jt. auth. see Long, E. B.

Long, Calvin T. Elementary Introduction to Number Theory. 2nd ed. 208p. 1972. text ed. 13.95x o.p. (ISBN 0-669-62703-8). Heath.

Long, Catherine. Sir Roland Ashton: A Tale of the Times, 1841. Wolff, Robert L., ed. Bd. with Mary Spencer: A Tale for the Times, 1844. Howard, Anne. (Victorian Fiction Ser.). 1975. lib. bdg. 66.00 (ISBN 0-8240-1565-7). Garland Pub.

Long, Cathryn & Tretten, Rudie. The Future of American Government: What Will It Be? (Crucial Issues in American Government). (gr. 9-12). 1978. pap. text ed. 4.96 (ISBN 0-205-05523-0, 7655231). Allyn.

--Social Policy: What Is It & How Is It Formed? (Crucial Issues in American Government). (gr. 9-12). 1978. pap. text ed. 4.96 (ISBN 0-205-05518-4, 7655185). Allyn.

Long, Charles. Prevention & Rehabilitation in Ischemic Heart Disease. (Rehabilitation Medicine Library Ser.). (Illus.). 424p. 1980. 39.95 (ISBN 0-683-05150-4). Williams & Wilkins.

Long, Charles H. Alpha the Myths of Creation. (Patterns of Myth Ser.). 6.00 o.s.i. (ISBN 0-8076-0238-8). Braziller.

Long, Charles H., ed. Partners in Prayer. 1980. 1.50 (ISBN 0-686-28786-X). Forward Movement.

Long, Dale D. Physics Around You. 608p. 1980. text ed. 17.95x (ISBN 0-534-00770-8). Wadsworth Pub.

Long, David. Early Returns: Poems. 55p. 1981. 15.00 (ISBN 0-918116-21-X); pap. 5.00 (ISBN 0-918116-20-1). Jawbone Pr.

Long, David E. The Persian Gulf: An Introduction to Its Peoples, Politics, & Economics. rev. ed. LC 76-6531. (Westview Special Studies on the Middle East Ser.). (Illus.). 1978. lib. bdg. 20.00 o.p. (ISBN 0-89158-826-4). Westview.

Long, David E. & Reich, Bernard, eds. The Government & Politics of the Middle East & North Africa. 465p. 1980. text ed. 30.00x (ISBN 0-89158-593-1); pap. text ed. 13.50x (ISBN 0-89158-871-X). Westview.

Long, David F. How to Organize & Raise Funds for Small Non-Profit Organizations. 283p. 1979. 19.95 (ISBN 0-916068-09-9); pap. 10.95 (ISBN 0-916068-12-9). Groupwork Today.

--Ready to Hazard: A Biography of Commodore William Bainbridge, Seventeen Seventy-Two to Eighteen Thirty-Three. (Illus.). 400p. 1980. text ed. 20.00 (ISBN 0-8357-0579-X). Univ Microfilms.

Long, Delbert & Long, Roberta. Education in the U.S.S.R. LC 80-82681. (Fastback Ser.: No. 148). (Orig.). 1980. pap. 0.75 (ISBN 0-87367-148-1). Phi Delta Kappa.

Long, Don L., et al. Introduction to Agribusiness Management. Lee, Jasper S., ed. (Careeer Preparation for Agriculture-Agribusiness). 1979. pap. text ed. 5.80x (ISBN 0-07-038665-X, G); activity guide 3.60x (ISBN 0-07-038666-8); tchrs manual & key 2.75x (ISBN 0-07-038667-6). McGraw.

Long, E. B. The Saints & the Union: Utah Territory During the Civil War. LC 80-16775. (Illus.). 292p. 1981. 17.95 (ISBN 0-252-00821-9). U of Ill Pr.

Long, E. B. & Long, Barbara. Civil War Day by Day: An Almanac 1861-1865. LC 73-163653. 1971. 11.95 (ISBN 0-385-01264-0). Doubleday.

Long, E. Hudson, compiled by. American Drama from Its Beginnings to the Present. LC 79-79170. (Goldentree Bibliographies in Language & Literature). (Orig.). 1970. pap. 6.95x (ISBN 0-88295-522-5). AHM Pub.

Long, Earlene. Johnny's Egg. LC 79-21248. (Illus.). 1980. 6.95 (ISBN 0-201-04153-7, 4153). A-W.

Long, Elton, et al. American Minorities: The Justice Issue. (Law Enforcement Ser.). (Illus.). 256p. 1975. pap. 9.95x (ISBN 0-13-028118-2). P-H.

Long, Eugene T., ed. Experience, Reason & God, Vol. 8. (Studies in Philosophy & the History of Philosophy: Vol. 8). 1980. write for info. (ISBN 0-8132-0553-0, Dist. by Isbs). Intl Schol Bk Serv.

Long, Frank, ed. Economic Planning Studies. (International Studies in Economics & Econometrics: No. 8). 198p. 1980. pap. 11.95 (ISBN 90-277-1194-1, Pub. by D. Reidel). Kluwer Boston.

--The Political Economy of EEC Relations with African, Caribbean & Pacific States: Contributions to the Understanding of the Lome Convention on North-South Relations. 192p. 1980. 26.00 (ISBN 0-08-024077-1). Pergamon.

Long, Frank B. The Hounds of Tinaldos: The Early Long. 1978. pap. 1.75 o.s.i. (ISBN 0-515-04655-8). Jove Pubns.

Long, Franklin A. & Rathjens, George W., eds. Arms, Defense Policy & Arms Control. 1976. 8.95x (ISBN 0-393-05573-6); pap. text ed. 6.95x (ISBN 0-393-09188-0). Norton.

Long, Franklin A. & Reppy, Judith, eds. The Genesis of New Weapons: Decision Making for Military R&D. LC 80-12243. 1980. 25.00 (ISBN 0-08-025973-1). Pergamon.

Long, George. Folklore Calendar. LC 76-78191. 1970. Repr. of 1930 ed. 19.00 (ISBN 0-8103-3367-8). Gale.

Long, Haniel. Walt Whitman & the Springs of Courage. LC 38-27504. (National University Publications Literary Criticism Ser.). 1977. 7.50 (ISBN 0-8046-9190-8). Kennikat.

Long, Harriet G. Public Library Service to Children: Foundation & Development. LC 70-8592. 1970. 10.00 (ISBN 0-8108-0291-0). Scarecrow.

Long, Howard De see DeLong, Howard.

Long, Howard R., ed. Main Street Militants: An Anthology from "Grassroots Editor". LC 78-16336. (Arcturus Books Paperbacks Ser.). 178p. 1979. pap. 5.95 (ISBN 0-8093-0894-0). S Ill U Pr.

Long, Huey P. My First Days in the White House. LC 70-171695. (FDR & the Era of the New Deal Ser). (Illus.). 146p. 1972. Repr. of 1935 ed. lib. bdg. 15.00 (ISBN 0-306-70383-1). Da Capo.

Long, Hugh W., jt. auth. see Bourdeaux, Kenneth J.

Long, J., et al, trs. see Raspe, G.

Long, James. The German-Russians: A Bibliography. LC 78-19071. 136p. 1978. text ed. 11.95 (ISBN 0-87436-282-2). ABC-Clio.

--Life: Jesus-Style. 1978. pap. 2.50 (ISBN 0-88207-575-6). Victor Bks.

--Living in Sonshine! 1980. pap. 2.50 (ISBN 0-88207-576-4). Victor Bks.

Long, Jean. How to Paint the Chinese Way. (Illus.). 1979. 14.95 (ISBN 0-7137-0999-5, Pub by Blandford Pr England). Sterling.

Long, Joan & Long, Ronald. Writer's & Photographer's Guide to Newspaper Markets. 2nd ed. 175p. 1981. pap. price not set (ISBN 0-936940-01-8). Helm Pub.

Long, John, et al, eds. Menus of the Valley's Finest Restaurants: Nineteen Eighhty-One Edition. 176p. 1980. pap. 5.95 (ISBN 0-930380-12-6, 0148-4133). Quail Run.

Long, John D. & Gregg, Davis W., eds. Property & Liability Insurance Handbook. 1965. text ed. 16.95x o.p. (ISBN 0-256-00302-5). Irwin.

Long, John H. Shakespeare's Use of Music: A Study of the Music & Its Performance in the Original Production of Seven Comedies. LC 77-5643. (Music Reprint Ser.). 1977. Repr. of 1955 ed. lib. bdg. 22.50 (ISBN 0-306-77423-2). Da Capo.

--Shakespeare's Use of Music: The Final Comedies. LC 77-5644. (Music Reprint Ser.). 1977. Repr. of 1961 ed. lib. bdg. 22.50 (ISBN 0-306-77424-0). Da Capo.

Long, John V., jt. auth. see Green, Samuel.

Long, Joseph K., ed. Extrasensory Ecology: Parapsychology & Anthropology. LC 77-6367. 1977. 19.50 (ISBN 0-8108-1036-0). Scarecrow.

Long, Judy. Volunteer Spring. LC 75-38365. (gr. 5). 1976. 5.95 (ISBN 0-396-07304-2). Dodd.

--Volunteer Spring. (YA) (gr. 7-9). 1977. pap. 1.50 (ISBN 0-671-56002-6). PB.

Long, Kenneth. Introduction to Economics. (Illus.). Date not set. text ed. price not set (ISBN 0-442-23894-0). D Van Nostrand.

Long, Lynette, et al. Questioning: Skills for the Helping Process. LC 80-24385. (Orig.). 1980. pap. text ed. 8.95 (ISBN 0-8185-0371-8). Brooks-Cole.

Long, Marguerite. At the Piano with Faure. LC 79-63623. (Illus.). 1981. 11.75 (ISBN 0-8008-0505-4, Crescendo). Taplinger.

Long, Marjorie, tr. see Levi-Civita, Tullio.

Long, Maurice W. Radar Reflectivity of Land & Sea. LC 75-13435. (Illus.). 400p. 1975. 26.95 (ISBN 0-669-00050-7). Lexington Bks.

Long, Max F. Introduction to Huna. 3.00 (ISBN 0-89861-004-4). Esoteric Pubns.

Long, Michael, et al. Reading English for Academic Study. Potvin, Douglas, ed. (Illus.). 160p. (Orig.). 1980. pap. text ed. 6.95 (ISBN 0-88377-108-X). Newbury Hse.

Long, Nicholas J., et al. Conflict in the Classroom: The Education of Children with Problems. 3rd ed. 1976. pap. 11.95x o.p. (ISBN 0-534-00400-8). Wadsworth Pub.

--Conflict in the Classroom. 4th ed. 464p. 1980. pap. text ed. 12.95x (ISBN 0-534-00791-0). Wadsworth Pub.

Long, Norman & Roberts, Bryan R., eds. Peasant Cooperation & Capitalist Expansion in Central Peru. (Latin American Monographs: No. 46). 1978. pap. text ed. 9.95x (ISBN 0-292-76451-0); pap. text ed. 9.95x (ISBN 0-292-76452-9). U of Tex Pr.

Long, Patrick D. De see De Long, Patrick D.

Long, Paul E. Introduction to General Topography. LC 71-138370. 1971. text ed. 17.95 (ISBN 0-675-09253-1). Merrill.

Long, Richard. Tawfiq Al Hakim: Playwright of Egypt. (Illus.). 235p. 1979. 25.00x (ISBN 0-903729-35-0). Three Continents.

Long, Richard A. & Collier, Eugenia W., eds. Afro-American Writing: An Anthology of Prose & Poetry, 2 vols. LC 72-83827. 1972. 22.50x set (ISBN 0-8147-4954-2); pap. 10.00x set (ISBN 0-8147-4955-0). NYU Pr.

Long, Robert. Getting Out of Town. 16p. pap. 2.00 o.p. (ISBN 0-935252-19-3). Street Pr.

Long, Roberta, jt. auth. see Long, Delbert.

Long, Ronald, jt. auth. see Long, Joan.

Long, Rose-Carol W. Kandinsky: The Development of an Abstract Style. (Studies in the History of Art & Architecture). (Illus.). 224p. 1980. 98.00 (ISBN 0-19-817311-3). Oxford U Pr.

Long, Rosemary. Systematic Nursing Care. (Illus.). 96p. 1981. 21.00 (ISBN 0-571-11615-9, Pub. by Faber & Faber); pap. 7.95 (ISBN 0-686-28936-6). Merrimack Bk Serv.

Long, Samual, ed. The Universal Reference System - Nineteen Seventy-Nine Annual Supplement, 3 vols. 2412p. 1980. Set. 350.00 (ISBN 0-306-69029-2, IFI). Plenum Pub.

Long, T. H., jt. ed. see Clark, Sandra.

Long, Terry L. Granville Hicks. (United States Authors Ser.: No. 387). 1981. lib. bdg. 11.95 (ISBN 0-8057-7319-3). Twayne.

Long, Tony. Mountain Animals. LC 70-185892. (Animal Life Ser.). (Illus.). 152p. (YA) 1972. 8.95 o.s.i. (ISBN 0-06-012666-3, HarpT). Har-Row.

Long, William A. & Seo, K. K. Management in Japan & India: With Reference to the United States. LC 77-7824. (Praeger Special Studies). 1977. text ed. 34.50 (ISBN 0-03-022651-1). Praeger.

Long, William E. Getting Started in Electronic Troubleshooting. (Illus.). 1979. ref. 17.95 (ISBN 0-8359-2487-4); instrs'. manual avail. (ISBN 0-8359-2488-2). Reston.

Long, William S. The Exiles. 1980. pap. 2.75 o.s.i. (ISBN 0-440-12369-0). Dell.

--The Settlers. (Orig.). 1980. pap. 2.95 o.s.i. (ISBN 0-440-15923-7). Dell.

--The Traitors. (Orig.). 1981. pap. 3.50 (ISBN 0-440-18131-3). Dell.

Longacre, Doris. Living More with Less. LC 80-15461. 296p. 1980. pap. 6.95 (ISBN 0-8361-1930-4). Herald Pr.

--More-with-Less Cookbook. LC 75-23563. 320p. 1976. pap. 8.95 (ISBN 0-8361-1786-7). Herald Pr.

Longacre, Doris J. More with with Cookbook. 336p. 1981. pap. 3.95 (ISBN 0-553-13930-4). Bantam.

Longacre, J. J. Cleft Palate Deformation: Causation & Prevention. 128p. 1970. pap. 16.25 photocopy ed. spiral (ISBN 0-398-01142-7). C C Thomas.

--Rehabilitation of the Facially Disfigured. (Illus.). 144p. 1973. 21.50 (ISBN 0-398-02597-5). C C Thomas.

--Scar Tissue-Its Use & Abuse: The Surgical Correction of Deformation Due to Hypertrophic Scar & the Prevention of Its Formation. (Illus.). 192p. 1972. 25.75 (ISBN 0-398-02343-3). C C Thomas.

--The Ultrastructure of Collagen: Its Relation to the Healing of Wounds & to the Management of Hypertrophic Scars. (American Lectures in Plastic & Reconstructive Surgery Ser.). (Illus.). 538p. 1976. 54.75 (ISBN 0-398-03254-8). C C Thomas.

Longacre, Paul. Fund-Raising Projects with a World Hunger Emphasis. LC 80-83771. 72p. 1980. pap. 1.95 (ISBN 0-8361-1940-1). Herald Pr.

Longacre, R. E. An Anatomy of Speech Notions. (Pdr Press Publications in Tagmemics,: No. 3). 1976. pap. text ed. 20.00x (ISBN 90-316-0090-3). Humanities.

Longaker, Jon D. Art, Style & History: A Selective History of Art. 1970. pap. 8.95x (ISBN 0-673-05998-7). Scott F.

Longaker, Mark. Ernest Dowson. 3rd ed. LC 68-1016. 1967. 9.00x o.p. (ISBN 0-8122-7560-8). U of Pa Pr.

Longaker, Mark, ed. see Dowson, Ernest.

Longanesi & Co., tr. see De Rachewiltz, Boris.

Longbottom, Roy. Computer System Reliability. LC 79-40649. (Wiley Ser. in Computing). 1980. 36.50 (ISBN 0-471-27634-0, Pub. by Wiley-Interscience). Wiley.

Longchamps, Joanne de see De Longchamps, Joanne.

Longden, E. Densening & Chilling in Foundary Work. 178p. 1954. 10.95x (ISBN 0-85264-040-4, Pub. by Griffin England). State Mutual Bk.

Longenecker, Justin G. Essentials of Management: A Behavioral Approach. 1977. text ed. 14.95 (ISBN 0-675-08552-7); instructor's manual 3.95 (ISBN 0-686-67520-7). Merrill.

--Principles of Management & Organizational Behavior. 4th ed. 1977. text ed. 19.95 (ISBN 0-675-08556-X); instructor's manual 3.95 (ISBN 0-686-67528-2). Merrill.

Longenecker, Justin G. & Pringle, Charles D. Management. 5th ed. (Illus.). 544p. 1981. text ed. 19.95 (ISBN 0-675-08061-4); tchr's. manual avail.; study guide 6.95 (ISBN 0-675-09995-1). Merrill.

Longenecker, Richard N. The Christology of Early Jewish Christianity. (Twin Brooks Ser.). 178p. 1981. pap. 5.95 (ISBN 0-8010-5610-1). Baker Bk.

Longest, Beafort B., Jr. Management Practices for the Health Professional. 2nd ed. (Illus.). 1980. text ed. 15.95 (ISBN 0-8359-4224-4). Reston.

Longest, Beaufort B., Jr. Principles of Hospital Business Office Management. 1975. 11.75 (ISBN 0-930228-02-2); instr's manual 23.50 (1448). Hospital Finan.

Longfellow, Henry W. Evangeline & Other Poems. (Classics Ser). (gr. 7 up). pap. 1.50 (ISBN 0-8049-0094-9, CL-94). Airmont.

Longford, Elizabeth. The Royal House of Windsor. 1974. 15.00 o.p. (ISBN 0-394-47906-8). Knopf.

Longhurst, Jean, jt. auth. see Singelmann, Jay.

Longhurst, R. S. Geometrical & Physical Optics. 2nd ed. LC 74-169158. (Illus.). 704p. 1974. pap. text ed. 19.95x (ISBN 0-582-44099-8). Longman.

Longinus. On Great Writing on the Sublime. Grube, G. M., tr. LC 57-14628. 1957. pap. 2.40 o.p. (ISBN 0-672-60261-X, LLA79). Bobbs.

Longinus, Cassius. Longinus on the Sublime: The Peri Hupsous in Translations by Nicolas Boileau-Despreaux (1674) & William Smith (1739) LC 75-8892. 390p. 1975. lib. bdg. 40.00x (ISBN 0-8201-1153-8). Schol Facsimiles.

Longland, Ed J., ed. see British Daily Mirror Children's Lit. Competitions.

Longland, Jean. Selections from Contemporary Portugese Poetry. 1966. 3.50 (ISBN 0-8178-3782-5). Hispanic Soc.

Longley, Arthur. Earth Will Be Invaded from Outer Space. (Orig.). 1981. pap. 4.95 (ISBN 0-88270-505-9). Logos.

Longley, Lawrence D., jt. auth. see Peirce, Neal R.

Longley, Michael. Selected Poems, Nineteen Sixty-Three to Nineteen Eighty. LC 80-52997. 54p. pap. 5.50 (ISBN 0-916390-14-4). Wake Forest.

Longley, Peter. Contemporary Logic. LC 80-1443. 178p. (Orig.). 1981. pap. text ed. 8.75 (ISBN 0-8191-1458-8). U Pr of Amer.

Longley, Richmond W. Elements of Meteorology. LC 71-110172. 1970. text ed. 19.50 o.p. (ISBN 0-471-54445-0). Wiley.

Longley-Cook, L. H. Fun with Brain Puzzlers. 1977. pap. 1.25 o.p. (ISBN 0-449-13755-4, GM). Fawcett.

--More Puzzle Fun. 128p. 1977. pap. 1.25 o.p. (ISBN 0-449-13744-9, GM). Fawcett.

--Work This One Out. 1978. pap. 1.25 o.p. (ISBN 0-449-13933-6, GM). Fawcett.

Longley-Cook, Laurence H. Statistical Problems. LC 76-126340. (Illus., Orig.). 1971. pap. 4.50 (ISBN 0-06-460009-2, CO 9, COS). Har-Row.

Longman, Harold S., ed. see Ryan, Bernard, Jr.

Longman, W. Tokens of the Eighteenth Century, Connected with Booksellers & Bookmakers (Authors, Printers, Publishers, Engravers, & Paper Makers) LC 70-78192. (Illus.). 90p. 1970. Repr. of 1916 ed. 15.00 (ISBN 0-8103-3368-6). Gale.

Longnecker, O. M., Jr., jt. auth. see Reed, L. C.

Longo, Gianni, jt. auth. see Brambilla, Roberto.

Longo, Peter. Simplified Golf: There's No Trick to It! De Mente, Boye, ed. (Illus.). 144p. (Orig.). 1980. pap. 9.95 (ISBN 0-914778-34-X). Phoenix Bks.

Longo, Teodosio. Fundamentals of Singing & Speaking. 112p. 1945. 7.00x (ISBN 0-913298-54-9). S F Vanni.

Longo, V. G. Neuropharmacology & Behavior. LC 72-75588. (Illus.). 1972. text ed. 11.95x (ISBN 0-7167-0828-0); pap. text ed. 6.95x (ISBN 0-7167-0827-2). W H Freeman.

Longree, Karla. Quantity Food Sanitation. 3rd ed. LC 80-11551. 1980. 27.50 (ISBN 0-471-06424-6, Pub. by Wiley Interscience). Wiley.

Longrigg, Cecily, tr. see Bidermann, Jacob.

Longrigg, Stephen. Four Centuries of Modern Iraq. (Arab Background Ser.). 15.00x (ISBN 0-685-72044-6). Intl Bk Ctr.

--Iraq Nineteen Hundred to Nineteen Fifty. (Arab Background Ser.). 1968. 15.00x (ISBN 0-685-77098-2). Intl Bk Ctr.

--Syria & Lebanon Under French Mandate, 1968. (Arab Background Ser.). 15.00x (ISBN 0-685-72062-4). Intl Bk Ctr.

Longrigg, Stephen H. Middle East. 2nd ed. LC 75-91722. 1970. lib. bdg. 17.95x (ISBN 0-202-10008-1). Aldine Pub.

Longsdorf, Bob & Trailer Life Editors. Trailer Life's RV Travel Guide & Atlas: Everything You Need to Know to RV America: Where to Go, What to See, How to Get There. LC 79-66971. (Illus.). 1980. 14.98 (ISBN 0-934798-01-X); pap. 12.98 (ISBN 0-686-25974-2). Trailer Life.

Longstaff, R. W., jt. ed. see Orchard, D. B.

Longstaff, Thomas R. Evidence of Conflation in Mark? A Study in the Synoptic Problem. LC 76-40001. (Society of Biblical Literature. Dissertation Ser.: No. 28). (Illus.). 1977. pap. 7.50 (ISBN 0-89130-086-4, 060128). Scholars Pr Ca.

Longstreet, Stephen. The Pembroke Colors. 320p. 1981. 12.95 (ISBN 0-399-12582-5). Putnam.

--Storm Watch. 1981. pap. 2.50 (ISBN 0-8439-0882-3, Leisure Bks). Nordon Pubns.

Longstreet, Stephen, jt. auth. see Carmichael, Hoagy.

Longstreet, Wilma. Aspects of Ethnicity: Understanding Differences in Pluralistic Classrooms. LC 78-16631. (Orig.). 1978. pap. text ed. 10.50x (ISBN 0-8077-2529-3). Tchrs Coll.

Longstreth, Langdon E. Psychological Development of the Child. 2nd ed. (Illus.). 1974. 20.50x (ISBN 0-8260-5526-5); instr's manual avail. (ISBN 0-471-07541-8). Wiley.

Longstreth, T. Morris. Catskills. LC 75-118782. (Empire State Historical Publications Ser: No. 85). 1970. Repr. of 1918 ed. 10.00 o.p. (ISBN 0-87198-085-1). Friedman.

Longsworth, Polly. Emily Dickinson: Her Letter to the World. LC 65-14902. (gr. 7 up). 1965. 8.95 (ISBN 0-690-25945-X, TYC-J). T Y Crowell.

--I, Charlotte Forten, Black & Free. LC 79-109901. (gr. 5-8). 1970. 8.95 (ISBN 0-690-42869-3, TYC-J). T Y Crowell.

Longton, Tim & Hart, Edward. The Sheep Dog: Its Work & Training. (Illus.). 128p. 1976. 12.95 (ISBN 0-7153-7149-5). David & Charles.

Longuet-Higgins, H. C., ed. see Royal Society Discussion, March 7 & 8, 1979.

Longueville, Peter. The Hermit. LC 75-170572. (Foundations of the Novel Ser.: Vol. 51). lib. bdg. 50.00 (ISBN 0-8240-0563-5). Garland Pub.

Longueville, Thomas de. The Life of a Prig. Wolff, Robert L., ed. (Victorian Fiction Ser.). 1975. Repr. of 1885 ed. lib. bdg. 66.00 (ISBN 0-8240-1538-X). Garland Pub.

Longwill, L. G. An Index of Musical Wind-Instrument Makers. 6th, rev. enl. ed. (Illus.). 1980. 50.00 (ISBN 0-686-64771-8). Heinman.

Longworth, Ian. Yorkshire. 1967. 3.95x o.p. (ISBN 0-435-32960-X). Heinemann Ed.

Longyear, Barry B. Science Fiction Writer's Workshop: An Introduction to Fiction Mechanics, Vol. 1. 168p. 1980. pap. 5.95 (ISBN 0-913896-18-7). Owlswick Pr.

Longyear, Rey M. Nineteenth Century Romanticism in Music. 2nd ed. LC 72-3962. (History of Music Ser). (Illus.). 304p. 1973. pap. text ed. 10.95 (ISBN 0-13-622647-7). P-H.

Longy-Miquelle, Renee. Principles of Musical Theory. 1925. 5.00 (ISBN 0-911318-06-2). E C Schirmer.

Lon Hefferlin, JB & Phillips, Ellis L., Jr. Information Services for Academic Administration. LC 76-148659. (Higher Education Ser.). 1971. 9.95x o.p. (ISBN 0-87589-096-2). Jossey-Bass.

Lonidier, Lynn. A Lesbian Estate: Poems, 1970-1974. 1977. pap. 4.00 o.p. (ISBN 0-686-19040-8). Man-Root.

Lonik, Larry J. The Healthy Taste of Honey: Bee People's Recipes, Anecdotes & Lore. Campbell, Jean, ed. (Orig.). 1981. deluxe ed. write for info. (ISBN 0-89865-020-8). Donning Co.

Lonner, W., ed. see International Conference of Selected Papers, 2nd, Kingston. Ont. August, 6-10, 1974.

Lonnrot, Elias. Kalevala or, The Land of Heroes, 2 vols. in 1. 1978. 15.50x (ISBN 0-460-00259-7, Evman). Dutton.

Lonnroth, Lars. Njals Saga: A Critical Approach. LC 73-94437. 400p. 1976. 24.50x (ISBN 0-520-02708-6). U of Cal Pr.

Lonnroth, Mans & Steen, Peter. Energy in Transition: A Report on Energy Policy & Future Options. 1980. 10.95 (ISBN 0-520-03881-9). U of Cal Pr.

Lono, Luz P., ed. see Ozaeta, Pablo.

Lonsdale, Gill, et al. Children, Grief & Social Work. (Practice of Social Work Ser.: Vol. 4). 130p. 1979. 21.95x (ISBN 0-631-12191-9, Pub. by Basil Blackwell); pap. 9.95x (ISBN 0-631-12181-1). Biblio Dist.

Lonsdale, J. T., jt. auth. see Dietrich, J. W.

Lonsdale, Richard E. & Holmes, John H., eds. Settlement Systems in Sparsely Populated Regions: The United States & Australia. (Pergamon Policy Studies, Comparative Rural Transofrmation). 200p. Date not set. 40.01 (ISBN 0-08-023111-X). Pergamon.

--Settlement Systems in Sparsely Populated Regions: The United States & Australia. LC 80-27278. (Pergamon Policy Studies on Urban Affairs; Comparative Rural Transformation Ser.). (Illus.). 360p. 1981. 40.00 (ISBN 0-08-023111-X). Pergamon.

Lonsdale, Richard E., jt. ed. see Volgyes, Ivan.

Lonsdale, Roger. The Poems of Gray, Collins & Goldsmith. LC 76-4543. (Longman Annotated English Poets Ser.). 1976. pap. text ed. 18.00x (ISBN 0-582-48495-2). Longman.

Lonstein, Albert I. & Marino, Vito. The Revised Compleat Sinatra. new, rev. ed. LC 79-88307. (Illus.). 702p. 1980. 49.95 (ISBN 0-87990-000-8). Lonstein Pubns.

Loo, Yew C. & Cusens, Anthony R. The Finite-Strip Method in Bridge Engineering. (Viewpoint Publication Ser.). (Illus.). 1979. pap. text ed. 22.50 (ISBN 0-7210-1041-5). Scholium Intl.

Loofbourow, Leon. He Shall Be Like a Tree: An Interpretation of the Seguoias. (Illus.). 1968. pap. 1.50 (ISBN 0-918634-27-X). D M Chase.

Loofbourrow, Tod. How to Build a Computer-Controlled Robot. (gr. 10 up). 1978. pap. 9.75 (ISBN 0-8104-5681-8); computer program tape no. 00100 (kin) 14.95 (ISBN 0-686-66680-1). Hayden.

Loofs-Wissowa, H. H. E., ed. The Diffusion of Material Culture. (Asian & Pacific Archaeology Ser.: No.9). (Illus.). 393p. (Orig.). 1980. pap. 10.00x (ISBN 0-8248-0744-8). U Pr of Hawaii.

Look, Al. Sidelights of Colorado. 1967. 4.95 (ISBN 0-87315-073-2). Golden Bell.

Look, Mrs. Travis, jt. auth. see McCarty, Diane.

Loomba, N. Paul, jt. ed. see Turban, Efraim.

Loomba, Narendra P., jt. ed. see Levey, Samuel.

Loomer, Alice. Famous Flaws. LC 76-8411. 320p. 1976. 9.95 o.s.i. (ISBN 0-02-575101-8, 57510). Macmillan.

Loomes, Brian. Complete British Clocks. LC 78-66804. (Illus.). 1978. 25.00 (ISBN 0-7153-7567-9). David & Charles.

--Country Clocks & Their London Origins. LC 75-26361. (Illus.). 208p. 1976. 19.95 (ISBN 0-7153-7079-0). David & Charles.

--The White Dial Clock. LC 74-13515. (Illus.). 172p. 1975. 10.95 (ISBN 0-8069-8772-3). Sterling.

--White Dial Clocks: The Complete Guide. (Illus.). 192p. 1981. price not set (ISBN 0-7153-8073-7). David & Charles.

Loomes, Brian, jt. auth. see Baillie, G. H.

Loomis, Charles P., tr. see Tonnies, Ferdinand.

Loomis, Edward. The Charcoal Horse. LC 59-8210. 124p. 1959. 4.50 (ISBN 0-8040-0035-2). Swallow.

--On Fiction: Critical Essays & Notes. LC 66-30425. 71p. 1966. 3.25 (ISBN 0-8040-0231-2). Swallow.

--Vedettes: A Collection of Stories. LC 64-16117. 112p. (Orig.). 1964. 5.95 (ISBN 0-8040-0309-2); pap. 2.75 (ISBN 0-8040-0310-6, 64). Swallow.

Loomis, Forrest D., jt. auth. see Parmalee, Paul W.

Loomis, Lynn H. Calculus. 2nd ed. LC 76-12799. (Mathematics Ser). 1977. text ed. 25.95 (ISBN 0-201-04326-2); student supplement 6.95 (ISBN 0-201-04328-9). A-W.

--Introduction to Calculus. LC 74-30700. 804p. 1975. text ed. 20.95 (ISBN 0-201-04306-8). A-W.

Loomis, Lynn H. & Sternberg, Shlomo. Advanced Calculus. 1968. 25.95 (ISBN 0-201-04305-X). A-W.

Loomis, Maxine E. Group Process for Nurses. LC 78-31261. (Illus.). 1979. pap. text ed. 10.50 (ISBN 0-8016-3037-1). Mosby.

Loomis, Robert D. All About Aviation. (Allabout Ser, No. 51). (Illus.). (gr. 5-8). 1964. 4.39 o.p. (ISBN 0-394-90251-3, BYR). Random.

Loomis, Roger S., ed. Arthurian Literature in the Middle Ages: A Collaborative History. 1959. 59.00x (ISBN 0-19-811588-1). Oxford U Pr.

Loomis, William F., jt. ed. see Leighton, Terrance.

Loon, Hendrik W. Van see Van Loon, Hendrik W.

Loon, Jon C. Van see Van Loon, Jon C.

Looney, Gerald, jt. auth. see Newton, Kathleen.

Looney, J. W. Business Management for Farmers. LC 80-67888. (Illus.). 500p. 1981. 24.95 (ISBN 0-932250-11-4). Doane Agricultural.

Looney, J. W., jt. auth. see Uchtmann, Donald L.

Looney, Robert E. The Economic Consequences of World Inflation on Semi-Dependent Countries. LC 78-65351. 1978. pap. text ed. 10.75 (ISBN 0-8191-0654-2). U Pr of Amer.

--The Economic Development of Panama: The Impact of World Inflation on an Open Economy. LC 74-33038. (Illus.). 1976. text ed. 31.95 (ISBN 0-275-05390-3). Praeger.

--Mexico's Economy: A Policy Analysis with Forecasts to 1990. LC 78-3132. (Westview Special Studies on Latin America Ser.). 1978. lib. bdg. 28.50x (ISBN 0-89158-093-X). Westview.

Looney, Robert F., ed. Thirty-Two Picture Postcards of Old Philadelphia. (Dover Postcard Ser). (Illus., Orig.). 1977. pap. 2.50 (ISBN 0-486-23421-5). Dover.

Looper, Travis. Byron & the Bible: A Compendium of Biblical Usage in the Poetry of Lord Byron. LC 78-1518. 1978. 15.50 (ISBN 0-8108-1123-5). Scarecrow.

Loos, Anita. San Francisco: A Screenplay. LC 78-9034. (Screenplay Library). (Illus.). 212p. 1979. 10.00 (ISBN 0-8093-0876-2); pap. 6.95 (ISBN 0-8093-0877-0). S Ill U Pr.

--The Talmadge Girls. (Illus.). 1978. 12.50 o.p. (ISBN 0-670-69302-2). Viking Pr.

Loose, Frances F. Fractions, Book 1: Reusable Edition. (gr. 4). 1973. wkbk. 6.00 (ISBN 0-89039-064-9). Ann Arbor Pubs.

--Fractions, Book 2: Reusable Edition. (gr. 4-6). 1973. wkbk. 6.50 (ISBN 0-89039-066-5). Ann Arbor Pubs.

--Matrics: Reusable Edition. (gr. 9-12). 1975. wkbk. 3.00 (ISBN 0-89039-128-9). Ann Arbor Pubs.

Loose, Gerhard. Ernst Junger. (World Authors Ser.: Germany: No. 323). 1974. lib. bdg. 10.95 (ISBN 0-8057-2479-6). Twayne.

Loose Leaf Reference Service. Clinical Ophthalmology, 5 vols. & index. Duane, Thomas, ed. (Illus.). Set. looseleaf bdg. 325.00 (ISBN 0-06-148007-X, Harper Medical); annual revision pages 50.00 (ISBN 0-685-71848-4). Har-Row.

Loose Leaf Reference Services. Baker's Clinical Neurology, 3 vols. Baker, Abe B., et al, eds. loose leaf bdg. 250.00 (ISBN 0-06-148006-1, Harper Medical); revision pages 30.00 (ISBN 0-685-57884-4). Har-Row.

--Practice of Medicine, 10 vols. loose leaf bdg. 325.00 o.p. (ISBN 0-06-148005-3, Harper Medical); revision pages 55.00 o.p. (ISBN 0-685-57890-9). Har-Row.

Loose Leaf References Services. Laboratory Medicine, 4 vols. Race, George J., ed. loose leaf bdg. 275.00 (ISBN 0-06-148009-6, Harper Medical); revision pages 50.00 (ISBN 0-685-57897-6). Har-Row.

Looseley, William R. An Account of a Meeting with Denizens of Another World. 1980. 7.95 (ISBN 0-312-00233-5). St Martin.

Lopata, Helena Z. Occupation: Housewife. 400p. 1972. pap. 5.95 (ISBN 0-19-501564-9, GB374, GB). Oxford U Pr.

--Occupation: Housewife. LC 80-23658. (Illus.). xvi, 387p. 1980. Repr. of 1971 ed. lib. bdg. 25.00x (ISBN 0-313-22697-0, LOOH). Greenwood.

Lopata, Helena Z. & Brehm, Henry P. Widowhood. LC 78-19789. 1979. 18.95 (ISBN 0-03-046301-7). Praeger.

Lopata, Helena Z., jt. auth. see Brehm, Henry P.

Lopate, Phillip. The Daily Round: New Poems. LC 76-7709. 1976. 10.00 (ISBN 0-915342-15-4); pap. 4.00 (ISBN 0-915342-14-6). SUN.

--The Eyes Don't Always Want to Stay Open: Poems. LC 74-34536. 1976. pap. 4.00 (ISBN 0-915342-12-X). SUN.

Lopatin, Arthur D., jt. auth. see Gupa, Brijen K.

Lopatin, Arthur D., jt. auth. see Gupta, Brijan K.

Lope De Vega, Carpio. Caballero de Olmedo. Macdonald, I. T., ed. text ed. 6.50x (ISBN 0-521-06676-X). Cambridge U Pr.

Loper. Direct Current Fundamentals. LC 70-153729. 352p. 1978. 13.60 (ISBN 0-8273-1143-5); pap. 10.40 (ISBN 0-8273-1147-8); instructor's guide 2.00 (ISBN 0-8273-1145-1). Delmar.

Loper, Orla, et al. Introduction to Electricity & Electronics. LC 77-78174. 1979. text ed. 15.80 (ISBN 0-8273-1160-5); instructor's guide 2.25 (ISBN 0-8273-1162-1). Delmar.

Lopes, Duarte. A Report of the Kingdome of Congo, Gathered by P. Pigafetta. Hartwell, A., tr. LC 75-25675. (English Experience Ser.: No. 260). 1970. Repr. of 1597 ed. 35.00 (ISBN 90-221-0260-2). Walter J Johnson.

Lopez, Albert C., tr. see Ray, C. A.

Lopez, Alberto, tr. see Edge, Findley B.

Lopez, Arcadia. Los Animales Del Parque. (Illus.). 1973. pap. 2.00 (ISBN 0-913632-06-6). Am Univ Artforms.

Lopez, Arcadia & Smith, John. El Parque Paquete. (Illus.). 1976. pap. 86.50 teaching system (ISBN 0-913632-09-0). Am Univ Artforms.

Lopez, Barry. Winter Count. (Illus.). 96p. 1981. 9.95 (ISBN 0-684-16817-0, ScribT). Scribner.

Lopez, Barry H. Desert Notes: Reflections in the Eye of the Raven. 96p. pap. 2.25 (ISBN 0-380-53819-9, 53819, Bard). Avon.

--Of Wolves & Men. LC 78-6070. (Encore Edition). (Illus.). 1979. 5.95 (ISBN 0-684-16909-6, ScribT); pap. 7.95 (ISBN 0-684-16322-5, SL882, ScribT). Scribner.

--River Notes: The Dance of the Herons. 96p. 1980. pap. 2.25 (ISBN 0-380-52514-3, 52514). Avon.

Lopez, Cruz, jt. auth. see Tejera, Gomez.

Lopez, Donald S., jt. ed. see Boyne, Walter J.

Lopez, E. H. Katherine Anne Porter. 352p. 1981. 14.95 (ISBN 0-316-53199-5). Little.

Lopez, J. A. La Tecnica. (Span.). 7.95 (ISBN 84-241-5628-5). E Torres & Sons.

Lopez, Juan E. & Cabat, Louis. How to Prepare for College Board Achievement Tests -- Spanish. rev. ed. (gr. 11-12). 1982. pap. 3.95 (ISBN 0-8120-0978-9). Barron. Postponed.

Lopez, Manuel D. New York: A Guide to Information & Reference Sources. LC 80-18634. x, 307p. 1980. 17.50 (ISBN 0-8108-1326-2). Scarecrow.

Lopez, Nancy. The Education of a Woman Golfer. 192p. 1980. pap. 6.95 (ISBN 0-346-12492-1). Cornerstone.

Lopez, R. S. The Commercial Revolution of the Middle Ages, 950-1350. LC 75-35453. (Illus.). 204p. 1976. 21.50 (ISBN 0-521-21111-5); pap. 7.95x (ISBN 0-521-29046-5). Cambridge U Pr.

Lopez, Robert S. Byzantium & the World Around It: Economic & Institutional Relations. 318p. 1980. 50.00x (ISBN 0-86078-030-9, Pub. by Variorum England). State Mutual Bk.

Lopez, Ulises M. & Warrin, George E. Electronic Drawing & Technology. LC 77-16452. (Electronic Technology Ser.). 1978. text ed. 19.95 (ISBN 0-471-02377-9); solutions manual avail. (ISBN 0-471-03715-X). Wiley.

Lopez-Antunez, Luis. Atlas of Human Anatomy. Monsen, Harry, tr. LC 69-17808. (Illus.). 1971. 29.00 (ISBN 0-7216-5790-7). Saunders.

Lopez de Thorogood, Lucy, tr. see Robson, Ernest.

Lopez Gonzalez, Julio. El Ensayo y Su Ensenanza: Dos Ejemplos Puertorriquenos. LC 80-17712. (Coleccion Mente y Palabra). 146p. 1980. 6.25 (ISBN 0-8477-0568-4); pap. 5.00 (ISBN 0-8477-0569-2). U of PR Pr.

Lopez-Morillas, Frances M., tr. see Arzans de Orsua y Vela, Bartolome.

Lopez-Morrillas, J. The Krausist Movement & Ideological Change in Spain: Eighteen Fifty-Four to Eighteen Seventy-Four. 180p. Date not set. price not set (ISBN 0-521-23256-2). Cambridge U Pr.

Lopez-Rey, Jose. Velazquez: A Catalogue Raissonne of His Oeuvre. 1963. 58.00 (ISBN 0-571-05465-X, Pub. by Faber & Faber). Merrimack Bk Serv.

LoPinto, Maria & Miloradovich, Milo. Art of Italian Cooking. 1948. 7.95 o.p. (ISBN 0-385-06603-1). Doubleday.

Lopo, Ana, jt. auth. see Murphy, Bruce.

Lopo, Ana G. & Murphy, Bruce. The Needlecraft Manual. LC 77-80197. (Illus.). 1977. pap. 7.95 (ISBN 0-8069-8532-1). Sterling.

LoPreato, Joseph, jt. auth. see Jackson, Eugene.

Lopreato, Sally C., jt. auth. see Cunningham, William H.

Lopshire, Robert. It's Magic. LC 78-78075. (Illus.). (gr. 1-4). 1969. 6.95 o.s.i. (ISBN 0-02-761430-1). Macmillan.

--It's Magic? LC 78-78075. (Illus.). 32p. (gr. k-3). 1973. pap. 1.25 o.s.i. (ISBN 0-02-044360-9, Collier). Macmillan.

Lopshits, A. M. Computation of Areas of Oriented Figures. (Topics in Mathematics Ser). 1963. pap. text ed. 2.95x o.p. (ISBN 0-669-19570-7). Heath.

Lopukhin, Y. M. & Molodenkov, M. N. Hemosorption. LC 79-1273. (Illus.). 1979. 35.00 (ISBN 0-8016-3029-0). Mosby.

Loquin & Langeron. Microscopy Handbook. 1981. text ed. price not set. Butterworth.

Lora, G. A History of the Bolivian Labour Movement 1848-1971. Whitehead, L., ed. Whitehead, Christine, tr. LC 76-22988. (Latin American Studies: No. 27). 1977. 44.50 (ISBN 0-521-21400-9). Cambridge U Pr.

Lorain, Pierre. Clandestine Armament, 1941-1944. (Illus.). 192p. 1981. 12.50 (ISBN 0-02-575200-6). Macmillan.

Loraine, John. Syndromes of the Seventies: Population, Sex & Social Change. (Contemporary Issues Ser.: No. 11). 1977. text ed. 15.75x (ISBN 0-7206-0404-4). Humanities.

Loran, Eric, et al. African & Ancient Mexican Art: The Loran Collection. LC 74-84681. (Illus.). 1974. pap. 4.95 (ISBN 0-88401-004-X, Pub. by Fine Arts Mus). C E Tuttle.

Lorand, Rhoda L. Love, Sex & the Teenager. 1965. 6.95 o.s.i. (ISBN 0-685-15488-2). Macmillan.

L'Orange, H. P. Apotheosis in Ancient Portraiture. (Illus.). 156p. 1981. Repr. of 1947 ed. lib. bdg. 40.00x (ISBN 0-89241-149-X). Caratzas Bros.

--Studies in the Iconography of Cosmic Kingship in the Ancient World. (Illus.). 206p. 1981. Repr. of 1953 ed. lib. bdg. 45.00x (ISBN 0-89241-150-3). Caratzas Bros.

Lorange, Peter. Corporate Planning: An Executive Viewpoint. (Illus.). 1980. text ed. 19.95 (ISBN 0-13-174755-X). P-H.

Lorange, Peter & Vancil, Richard F. Strategic Planning Systems. (Illus.). 1977. ref. ed. 18.95 (ISBN 0-13-851006-7). P-H.

Loranz, Bob. Fifty Best of Baltimore & Ohio Railroad, Bk. 5. (Illus.). 1979. 12.00 (ISBN 0-934118-04-3). Barnard Robert.

Lorayne, Harry. Good Memory-Good Student: A Guide to Remembering What You Learn. LC 72-6851. 160p. (gr. 5-9). 1972. Vol. 1. 7.95 o.p. (ISBN 0-525-66322-3). Elsevier-Nelson.

--How to Develop a Super-Power Memory. LC 57-7884. (gr. 9 up). 1956. 8.95 (ISBN 0-8119-0078-9). Fell.

--Remembering People: The Key to Success. 1976. pap. 2.25 o.s.i. (ISBN 0-446-82922-6). Warner Bks.

--Secrets of Mind Power. LC 61-9267. 242p. 1961. 9.95 (ISBN 0-8119-0156-4). Fell.

Lorayne, Harry, jt. auth. see Lucas, Jerry.

Lorber, Jakob. The Lord's Sermons. Ozols, Violet & Von Koerber, Hildegard, trs. from Ger. LC 80-50280. (Jakob Lorber Ser.). 278p. 1981. 12.95 (ISBN 0-934616-06-X). Valkyrie Pr.

--The Three Days Scene at the Temple in Jerusalem. 2nd ed. Von Koerber, Nordewin, tr. from Ger. Date not set. pap. 4.95 (ISBN 0-934616-10-8). Valkyrie Pr.

Lorber, Jokob. The Dream of Zorel. Ozols, Violet, tr. from Ger. 124p. Date not set. pap. 5.00 (ISBN 0-934616-17-5). Valkyrie Pr.

Lorber, Judith, jt. ed. see Freidson, Eliot.

Lorca see Bentley, Eric.

Lorca, Federico G. The Cricket Sings. Kirkland, Will, tr. LC 80-15560. (Illus.). 64p. (Orig.). 1980. pap. 4.95 (ISBN 0-8112-0734-X, NDP506). New Directions.

Lorca, Federico G. & Honig, Edward. Divan & Other Writings. (Illus.). 1977. pap. 4.50 (ISBN 0-914278-14-2). Copper Beech.

Lorca, Federico Garcia. Selected Poems. Allen, Donald M., ed. LC 54-9872. (Span. & Eng., Cloth 1955; pap 1968). pap. 3.95 (ISBN 0-8112-0091-4, NDP114). New Directions.

Lorca, Federico Gracia see Watson, E. Bradlee & Pressey, Benfield.

Lorca, Garcia. Libro De Poemas, Poema Del Cante Jondo, Romancero Gitano, Poeta En Nueva York, Odas, Llanto Por Sanchez Mejias, Bodas De Sangre, Yerma. Date not set. 4.50x o.s.i. (ISBN 0-686-09290-2). Colton Bk.

--Mariana Pineda, la Zapatera, la Casa De Romancero Gitano, Poeta En Nueva York, Odas, Llanto Por Sanchez Mejias, Bodas De Sangre, Yerma (in Spanish) 4.50x o.s.i. (ISBN 0-686-12053-1). Colton Bk.

Lorch. An Amateur's Guide to Foaling. (Illus.). 1978. 4.37 (ISBN 0-85131-302-7, Dist. by Sporting Book Center). J A Allen.

Lorch, Robert S. Democratic Process & Administrative Law. rev. ed. LC 69-10420. (Waynebooks Ser: No. 39). 1973. pap. 6.50x (ISBN 0-8143-1513-5). Wayne St U Pr.

Lorch, Sue. Basic Writing: A Practical Approach. 300p. 1981. pap. text ed. 8.95. Winthrop.

Lord, Alexandra. A Harmless Ruse. (Orig.). 1981. pap. 1.50 (ISBN 0-440-13582-6). Dell.

Lord, Athena V. Pilot for Spaceship Earth: R. Buckminster Fuller, Architect, Inventor & Poet. LC 77-12629. (Illus.). (gr. 5 up). 1978. 8.95 (ISBN 0-02-761420-4, 76142). Macmillan.

Lord, B. I. & Potten, C. S., eds. Stem Cells & Tissue Homeostasis. LC 77-80844. (British Society for Cell Biology Symposium Ser.). (Illus.). 1978. 68.00 (ISBN 0-521-21799-7). Cambridge U Pr.

Lord, Beman. The Perfect Pitch. (Children's Literature Ser.). 1981. PLB 7.95 (ISBN 0-8398-2724-5). Gregg.

Lord, Clifford L. Teaching History with Community Resources. LC 64-15864. (Orig.). 1967. pap. 4.50x (ISBN 0-8077-1710-X). Tchrs Coll.

Lord Cohen of Birkenhead see Kogan, M. & Pope, M.

Lord, Eliot. Comstock Miners & Mining. (Illus.). 578p. Repr. of 1959 ed. 20.00 (ISBN 0-8310-7008-0). A S Barnes.

--Comstock Miners & Mining. (Illus.). 578p. 1981. Repr. of 1959 ed. 20.00 (ISBN 0-8310-7008-0). Howell-North.

Lord, Francis E., jt. auth. see Kirk, Samuel A.

Lord, Frederic M. Applications of Item Response Theory to Practical Testing Problems. LC 79-24186. (Illus.). 288p. 1980. text ed. 29.95 (ISBN 0-89859-006-X). L Erlbaum Assocs.

Lord, Frederic M. & Novick, Melvin R. Statistical Theories of Mental Test Scores. 1968. text ed. 26.95 (ISBN 0-201-04310-6). A-W.

Lord, Gabrielle. Fortress. 154p. 1981. 8.95 (ISBN 0-312-29978-8). St Martin.

Lord, Guy. The French Budgetary Process. LC 70-186113. 1973. 28.50x (ISBN 0-520-02196-7). U of Cal Pr.

Lord, Harold W., et al. Noise Control for Engineers. (Illus.). 448p. 1979. text ed. 24.95x (ISBN 0-07-038738-9); solutions manual 4.95 (ISBN 0-07-038739-7). McGraw.

--Noise Control for Engineers. (Illus.). 1980. text ed. 24.95 (ISBN 0-07-038738-9); solutions manual 4.95 (ISBN 0-07-038739-7). McGraw.

Lord, J. Dennis. Spatial Perspectives on School Desegregation & Busing. Natoli, Salvatore J., ed. LC 76-57034. (Resource Papers for College Geography Ser.). (Illus.). 1977. pap. text ed. 4.00 (ISBN 0-89291-124-7). Assn Am Geographers.

Lord, Jeffrey. Treasure of the Stars. (Blade Ser.: No. 29). 1978. pap. 1.50 (ISBN 0-523-40207-4, Dist. by Independent News Co.). Pinnacle Bks.

Lord, John V. & Maschler, Fay. Miserable Aunt Bertha. (gr. k-3). 1980. 8.95 (ISBN 0-224-01613-X, Pub. by Chatto Bodley Jonathan). Merrimack Bk Serv.

Lord, Kenniston W., Jr. Design of the Industrial Classroom. LC 76-46605. (Illus.). 1977. text ed. 10.95 (ISBN 0-201-04357-2). A-W.

Lord, Lindsay. Nautical Etiquette & Customs. LC 76-44659. 1976. pap. 3.00 (ISBN 0-87033-225-2). Cornell Maritime.

Lord, Peter. Portrait of the River Trent. LC 68-117316. (Portrait Bks.). (Illus.). 1968. 10.50x (ISBN 0-7091-0210-0). Intl Pubns Serv.

Lord, Robert. Russian Literature: An Introduction. LC 79-63625. 1980. 9.95 (ISBN 0-8008-6940-0). Taplinger.

--Teach Yourself Comparative Linguistics. rev. ed. 1966. pap. 4.95 o.p. (ISBN 0-679-10210-8). McKay.

Lord, Robert, tr. see Dianin, Sergei A.

Lord, Robert W. Running Conventions, Conferences & Meetings. 400p. 1981. 21.95 (ISBN 0-8144-5643-X). Am Mgmt.

Lord, Russell. Behold Our Land. LC 74-2395. (FDR & the Era of the New Deal Ser.). 309p. 1974. Repr. of 1938 ed. lib. bdg. 27.50 (ISBN 0-306-70593-1). Da Capo.

--To Hold This Soil. LC 78-171385. (FDR & the Era of the New Deal Ser). (Illus.). 124p. 1972. Repr. of 1938 ed. lib. bdg. 17.50 (ISBN 0-306-70384-X). Da Capo.

--The Wallaces of Iowa. LC 76-167843. (FDR & the Era of the New Deal Ser.). (Illus.). 615p. 1972. Repr. of 1947 ed. lib. bdg. 49.50 (ISBN 0-306-70325-4). Da Capo.

Lord, Russell, ed. see Wallace, Henry A.

Lord, Shirley. The Easy Way to Good Looks. LC 75-20216. (Illus.). 224p. 1976. 10.00 o.s.i. (ISBN 0-690-00763-9, TYC-T). T y Crowell.

Lord, Vivian. The Voyagers. 1980. pap. 2.75 (ISBN 0-449-14358-9, GM). Fawcett.

Lord, William G. History of the 508th Parachute Infantry. (Airborne Ser.: No. 2). (Illus.). 1977. 20.00 o.p. (ISBN 0-89839-002-8); pap. 15.00 (ISBN 0-89839-001-X). Battery Pr.

Lord, William H. Stagecraft One: Your Introduction to Backstage Work. (Illus.). 126p. 1979. pap. 9.45 (ISBN 0-686-27395-8). W H Lord.

Lord Beveridge. Full Employment in a Free Society. 1960. text ed. 55.00x (ISBN 0-04-331004-4). Allen Unwin.

Lorde, Audre. The Cancer Journals. LC 80-53110. 80p. (Orig.). 1980. pap. 4.00 (ISBN 0-933216-03-3). Spinsters Ink.

--Uses of the Erotic: The Erotic As Power. (Out & Out Pamphlet Ser.). pap. 1.00 (ISBN 0-918314-09-7). Out & Out.

Lord Easu. Book of Revelations for the Aquarian Age. Rodehaver, Gladys K., compiled by. (Illus., Orig.). 1980. pap. 6.95 (ISBN 0-930208-19-6). Mangan Bks.

Lordi, Robert J. The Revenge of Bussy D'Ambois by George Chapman. (Salzburg Studies in English Literature, Jacobean Drama Studies: No. 75). (Illus.). 1977. pap. text ed. 25.00x (ISBN 0-391-01463-3). Humanities.

Lordi, Robert J., ed. see Chapman, George.

Lordi, Robert J., ed. see Legge, Thomas.

Lord Kinross. The Ottoman Centuries: The Rise & Fall of the Turkish Empire. LC 76-28498. (Illus.). 1979. pap. 7.95 (ISBN 0-688-08093-6, Quill). Morrow.

Lord Lugard, et al. The Diaries of Lord Lugard: East Africa 1889-92, 3 vols. Perham & Bull, eds. (Illus.). 1959. 39.00 set o.p. (ISBN 0-571-03632-5, Pub. by Faber & Faber). Vol. 1 (ISBN 0-571-03634-1). Vol. 2 (ISBN 0-571-03633-3). Vol. 3 (ISBN 0-571-03632-5). Merrimack Bk Serv.

Lord Montague. Jaguar. 2nd rev. ed. LC 80-27039. (Illus.). 240p. 1981. 19.95 (ISBN 0-498-02547-0). A S Barnes.

Lord Reay, jt. auth. see Archer, Peter.

Lord Walston. Dealing with Hunger. 1977. 10.00 (ISBN 0-370-10464-1). Transatlantic.

Lore, Ann. Effective Therapeutic Communications. (Illus.). 128p. 1981. pap. 10.95 (ISBN 0-87619-842-6). R J Brady.

Lore, Mary S., jt. auth. see Farmer, Geraldine M.

Lore, Segal, tr. see Grimm, Jacob & Grimm, Wilhelm.

Loredano, Giovanni. Life of Adam. LC 67-26617. 1967. Repr. of 1659 ed. 20.00x (ISBN 0-8201-1031-0). Schol Facsimiles.

Loree, M. Ray. Psychology of Education. 2nd ed. 666p. 1970. 18.50 o.p. (ISBN 0-8260-5555-9); instr's manual avail. o.p. (ISBN 0-471-07539-6). Wiley.

Loree, Sharron. The Sunshine Family & the Pony. LC 71-171859. (Illus.). 48p. (ps-2). 1972. 5.95 (ISBN 0-395-28816-9, Clarion). HM.

Loren, Amii. The Tawny Gold Man. 1980. pap. 1.50 (ISBN 0-440-18978-0). Dell.

Loren, Donald P. Shape up! LC 79-88437. 73p. 1980. 11.00x (ISBN 0-87021-626-0). Naval Inst Pr.

Lorena, Hickok, jt. auth. see Gould, Jean.

Lorence, Harry E. Hay, How's Your Lawn? (Illus.). spiral bdg. 6.50 o.p. (ISBN 0-686-19186-2). Thomson Pub CA.

Lorente De No, Raphael, ed. The Primary Acoustic Nuclei. Orig. Title: The Cochlear Nuclei. (Illus.). 189p. 1981. text ed. 25.00 (ISBN 0-89004-318-3). Raven.

Lorentz, H. A. A View of Chinese Rugs: From the Seventeenth to the Twentieth Century. (Illus.). 216p. 1973. 95.00 (ISBN 0-7100-6912-X). Routledge & Kegan.

Lorentzen, John F. The Manager's Personal Problem Solver: A Handbook of Creative Solutions to Human Relations Problems in Your Organization. 1980. 15.95 (ISBN 0-13-549915-1, Spec); pap. 6.95 (ISBN 0-13-549907-0, Spec). P-H.

Lorentzen, Karen M. A New Approach to the Secondary School Health Education Curriculum: Reading Proficiency. 1981. 11.95 (ISBN 0-533-04633-5). Vantage.

Lorenz, Alice D. Reach for Reading. rev. ed. 128p. (gr. 4 up). 1981. write for info. wkbk. (ISBN 0-87895-904-1); write for info. manual with ans. key (ISBN 0-87895-905-X). Modern Curr.

Lorenz, Bob. Fifty Best of Pennsylvania Railroad, Bk. 4. (Illus.). 1979. 12.00 (ISBN 0-934118-08-6). Barnard Robert.

Lorenz, Felix A. The Only Hope. LC 75-43059. 112p. 1976. pap. 4.50 (ISBN 0-8127-0108-9). Southern Pub.

Lorenz, Konrad. Civilized Man's Eight Deadly Sins. Kerr-Wilson, Marjorie, tr. LC 73-20189. (Helen & Kurt Wolff Bk). 1974. 4.95 o.p. (ISBN 0-15-118061-X). HarBraceJ.

--Studies in Animal & Human Behaviour, 2 vols. LC 75-11087. Vol. 1. 1970. 18.50x (ISBN 0-674-84630-3); Vol. 2. 1971. 18.50x (ISBN 0-674-84631-1). Harvard U Pr.

Lorenz, Konrad Z. King Solomon's Ring. LC 52-7373. (Apollo Eds.). (YA) (gr. 9-12). pap. 3.95 o.s.i. (ISBN 0-8152-0016-1, A16, TYC-T). T y Crowell.

--King Solomon's Ring. (Illus.). 1952. 6.95 o.s.i. (ISBN 0-690-47460-1, TYC-T). T Y Crowell.

Lorenz, L. Scornful Simkin. 1980. pap. 8.95 (ISBN 0-13-796664-4). P-H.

Lorenz, Rita, jt. auth. see Adolph, L.

Lorenz, Tom. Guys Like Us. 252p. 1980. 11.95 (ISBN 0-670-35815-0). Viking Pr.

Lorenzen, Betty. Dental Assistant Techniques. LC 74-18674. (Allied Health Ser). 1975. pap. 10.25 (ISBN 0-672-61395-6). Bobbs.

Lorenzen, Betty Jo. Examination Review for Dental Assistants. LC 79-53191. (Dental Assisting Ser.). 1981. 6.60 (ISBN 0-8273-1672-0). Delmar.

Lorenzen, David N. The Kapalikas & Kalamukhas: Two Lost Saivite Sects. LC 70-138509. (Center for South & Southeast Asia Studies, UC Berkeley). 1972. 20.00x (ISBN 0-520-01842-7). U of Cal Pr.

Lorenzen, Lilly. Of Swedish Ways. (Illus.). 1978. pap. 3.95 (ISBN 0-06-464021-3, BN 4025, BN). Har-Row.

Lorenzini, Jean. Medical Phrase Index. 1978. 28.50 (ISBN 0-87489-149-3); pap. 21.50 (ISBN 0-87489-198-1). Med Economics.

Lorie, James H. & Hamilton, Mary T. The Stock Market: Theories & Evidence. 1973. pap. text ed. 10.95 (ISBN 0-256-01450-7). Irwin.

Lorillard, Didi. New York City Slicker: A Counterchic Guide to Manhattan. (Richard Seaver Book). (Orig.). 1979. pap. 7.95 o.p. (ISBN 0-670-50911-6). Viking Pr.

Lorimer, Anne, jt. auth. see Seaman, Florence.

Lorimer, Claire. Chantal. 480p. (Orig.). 1981. pap. 2.95 (ISBN 0-553-13992-4). Bantam.

Lorimer, J. W. Alkaline-Earth Sulfates in All Solvents: Solubilities of Solids. (IUPAC Solubility Data Ser.: Vol. 6). 1981. 100.00 (ISBN 0-08-023916-1). Pergamon.

Lorimer, John G. Gazetteer of the Persian Gulf, 'Oman & Central Arabia, 2 vols. 1970. Repr. of 1914 ed. 650.00x o.p. (ISBN 0-7165-0993-8, Pub. by Irish Academic Pr Ireland). Biblio Dist.

Lorimer, Lawrence T. & Devaney, John. The Football Book. LC 77-74461. (Illus.). (gr. 5 up). 1977. PLB 5.99 (ISBN 0-394-93574-8, BYR); pap. 3.95 (ISBN 0-394-83574-3). Random.

Lorimer, Lawrence T., ed. Breaking in. LC 74-18743. (Illus.). 224p. (gr. 7 up). 1974. PLB 4.69 (ISBN 0-394-92653-6). Random.

Lorimer, Lawrence T., retold by. Noah's Ark. LC 77-92377. (Picturebacks Ser.). (Illus.). (ps-2). 1978. PLB 4.99 (ISBN 0-394-93861-5, BYR); pap. 1.25 (ISBN 0-394-83861-0). Random.

Lorimor, E. S., jt. auth. see Dunn, S. Watson.

Lorin, Amii. The Game Is Played. (Orig.). 1981. pap. 1.50 (ISBN 0-440-12835-8). Dell.

--Morgan Wade's Woman. (Orig.). 1981. pap. 1.50 (ISBN 0-440-15507-X). Dell.

Lorin, Harold. Aspects of Distributed Computer Systems. LC 80-16689. 450p. 1980. 27.50 (ISBN 0-471-08114-0, Pub. by Wiley-Interscience). Wiley.

--Sorting & Sort Systems. (Illus.). 480p. 1975. 18.95 (ISBN 0-201-14453-0). A-W.

Lorin, Harold & Deitel, Harvey. Operating Systems. LC 80-10625. (Computer Science: Systems Programming (IBM) Ser.). (Illus.). 480p. 1981. text ed. 18.95 (ISBN 0-201-14464-6). A-W.

Lorin, Martin I. The Parents' Book of Physical Fitness for Children. LC 78-3151. (Illus.). 290p. 1981. pap. 5.95 (ISBN 0-689-70608-1). Atheneum.

Loring, Andrew. Rhymers' Lexicon. 2nd. ed. LC 78-156926. 1971. Repr. of 1905 ed. 26.00 (ISBN 0-8103-3341-4). Gale.

Loring, Emile. The Shadow of Suspicion, No. 7. 208p. 1981. pap. 1.95 (ISBN 0-553-14296-8). Bantam.

Loring, Emilie. Behind the Cloud. 208p. 1981. pap. 1.95 (ISBN 0-553-14295-X). Bantam.

--A Certain Crossroad. 224p. 1981. pap. 1.95 (ISBN 0-553-14511-8). Bantam.

--Here Comes the Sun. 224p. 1980. pap. 1.95 (ISBN 0-553-14290-9). Bantam.

--It's a Great World. 224p. 1980. pap. 1.75. Bantam.

--A Key to Many Doors. 208p. 1980. pap. 1.95 (ISBN 0-553-14289-5). Bantam.

--Miranda No. Sixty. 208p. 1981. pap. cancelled (ISBN 0-553-14294-1). Bantam.

--Today Is Yours, No. 24. 224p. 1981. pap. 1.95 (ISBN 0-553-14656-4). Bantam.

--Trail of Conflict. 208p. 1981. pap. 1.95 (ISBN 0-553-14521-5). Bantam.

--Where Beauty Dwells. 1976. Repr. of 1941 ed. lib. bdg. 13.20 (ISBN 0-88411-364-7). Amereon Ltd.
Loring, James & Burn, Graham, eds. Integration of Handicapped Children in Society. 172p. 1975. 16.00x (ISBN 0-7100-8269-X). Routledge & Kegan.
Loring, Kate & Fries, James F. Arthritis Helpbook: What You Can Do for Your Arthritis. (Illus.). 160p. 1980. 11.95 (ISBN 0-201-03796-3); pap. 6.95 (ISBN 0-201-03797-1). A-W.
Loring, L. M. Two Kinds of Values. 1966. text ed. 11.50x (ISBN 0-7100-1760-X). Humanities.
Loring, Murray. Bees & the Law. LC 80-66362. 128p. 1981. 6.95 (ISBN 0-915698-07-2). Dadant & Sons.
Lorit, Sergius C. The Last Days of Maximilian Kolbe. Moran, Hugh, tr. from Ital. LC 80-82418. Orig. Title: Kolbe: Cronaca Degli Ultimi Giorni. 144p. 1980. pap. 2.95 (ISBN 0-911782-35-4). New City.
Loroch, Kim J. Vessel Voyage Data Analysis: A Comparative Study. LC 65-20766. (Illus.). 1966. 10.00x (ISBN 0-87033-131-0). Cornell Maritime.
Lorrah, Jean. Savage Empire. LC 80-83592. 224p. (Orig.). 1981. pap. 2.25 (ISBN 0-87216-794-1). Playboy Pbks.
Lorrah, Jean, et al. Pandora, No. 6. Wickstrom, Lois, ed. (Illus.). 60p. (Orig.). 1980. pap. 2.50 (ISBN 0-916176-11-8). Sproing.
Lorrain, Dorothee, tr. see Guinier, A.
Lorrain, Paul & Corson, Dale R. Electromagnetic Fields & Waves. 2nd ed. LC 72-94872. (Illus.). 1970. text ed. 25.95x (ISBN 0-7167-0331-9); solutions to problems avail. W H Freeman.
--Electromagnetism: Principles & Applications. LC 78-1911. (Illus.). 1979. pap. text ed. 14.95x (ISBN 0-7167-0064-6); sol. manual 3.95x (ISBN 0-7167-1105-2). W H Freeman.
Lorrain, Paul, tr. see Guinier, A.
Lorraine, Marian. The Enterprising Minx. (Orig.). 1981. pap. 1.50 (ISBN 0-440-12270-8). Dell.
Lorrance, Arleen. Born of Love. (Illus., Orig.). 1981. pap. write for info. L P Pubns.
--Hello, Goodbye, I Love You. (Illus., Orig.). 1981. pap. price not set (ISBN 0-916192-18-0). L P Pubns.
Lorrance, Arleen & Pike, Diane K. The Love Project Way. 216p. (Orig.). 1980. pap. 6.95 (ISBN 0-916192-15-6). L P Pubns.
Lorrimer, Claire. Relentless Storm. 224p. 1981. pap. 2.25 (ISBN 0-553-13658-5). Bantam.
Lorris, Guillaume De see De Lorris, Guillaume & De Meun, Jean.
Lorsch, Jay W. & Barnes, Louis B. Managers & Their Careers. 1972. pap. text ed. 8.95 (ISBN 0-256-01296-2). Irwin.
Lorsch, Jay W. & Lawrence, Paul R. Managing Group & Intergroup Relations. 1972. pap. text ed. 10.95 (ISBN 0-256-00264-9). Irwin.
--Organizational Planning: Cases & Concepts. LC 72-79316. 1972. pap. text ed. 10.95 (ISBN 0-256-00456-0). Irwin.
Lorsch, Jay W., jt. auth. see Lawrence, Paul R.
Lortie, Dan C. Schoolteacher: A Sociological Study. LC 74-11428. 1977. 6.95 (ISBN 0-226-49351-2); pap. 4.95 (ISBN 0-226-49354-7, P748, Phoen). U of Chicago Pr.
Lortie, Pierre. Economic Integration & the Law of Gatt. LC 75-3626. (Special Studies). (Illus.). 202p. 1975. text ed. 25.95 (ISBN 0-275-05230-3). Praeger.
Lorton, Mary B., jt. auth. see Baratta.
Lortz, Richard. The Valdepenas. LC 79-66114. 220p. 1980. 15.95 (ISBN 0-933256-06-X); pap. 7.95 (ISBN 0-933256-07-8). Second Chance.
Los Angeles County Museum of Art Curatorial Staff. Three Decades of Collecting: Gifts of Anna Bing Arnold. D'Andrea, Jeanne & West, Stephen, eds. (Los Angeles County Museum of Art Bulletin 1980: Vol. 26). (Illus.). 96p. (Orig.). 1981. pap. 6.00 (ISBN 0-87587-099-6). La Co Art Mus.
Los Angeles Press Photographers. Just One More. (Illus.). 1981. lib. bdg. 14.95 (ISBN 0-912076-41-0); pap. 9.95 (ISBN 0-912076-45-3). ESE Calif.
Los Angeles Public Library. Catalog of the Police Library of the Los Angeles Public Library, First Supplement. (Library Catalogs). 1980. lib. bdg. 220.00 (ISBN 0-8161-0328-3). G K Hall.
Los Angeles Unified School District. Drafting. Vorndran, Richard A., ed. LC 77-73291. 64p. (gr. 7-9). 1978. pap. text ed. 3.64 (ISBN 0-02-820410-7). Glencoe.
--Electricity. Vorndran, Richard A., ed. LC 77-73243. 96p. (gr. 7-9). 1978. pap. text ed. 4.40 (ISBN 0-02-820440-9). Glencoe.
--General Industrial Education. Vorndran, Richard A., ed. LC 77-73280. 552p. (gr. 7-9). 1978. text ed. 15.96 (ISBN 0-02-820350-X). Glencoe.
--Graphic Arts. Vorndran, Richard A., ed. LC 77-73302. 128p. (gr. 7-9). 1978. pap. text ed. 4.40 (ISBN 0-02-820430-1). Glencoe.
--Metalworking. Vorndran, Richard A., ed. LC 77-73297. 96p. (gr. 7-9). 1978. pap. text ed. 4.40 (ISBN 0-02-820420-4). Glencoe.
--Woodworking. Vorndran, Richard A., ed. LC 77-73286. 96p. (gr. 7-9). 1978. pap. text ed. 4.40 (ISBN 0-02-820400-X). Glencoe.
Los, F. J. The Franks. Wardle, John P., tr. from Dutch. 112p. 1940. pap. 3.50x (ISBN 0-911038-79-5, N League). Noontide.
Los, Pieter. An Entire New Healing Approach. 1981. 8.95 (ISBN 0-533-04361-1). Vantage.
Losang, Rato K. My Life & Lives: The Story of a Tibetan Incarnation. Campbell, Joseph, ed. 1977. pap. 4.95 o.p. (ISBN 0-525-47480-3). Dutton.
Loschburg, Winfried. A History of Travel. Michaelis-Jena, Ruth & Murray, Patrick, trs. from Ger. LC 80-461783. (Illus.). 190p. 1979. 37.50x (ISBN 0-8002-2423-X). Intl Pubns Serv.
Lose, M. Phyllis. Blessed Are the Brood Mares. (Illus.). 1978. 14.95 (ISBN 0-02-575250-2). Macmillan.
Losee, John. Historical Introduction to the Philosophy of Science. (Oxford Paperbacks University Ser.). (Illus.). 224p. (Orig.). 1972. pap. 5.95x o.p. (ISBN 0-19-888077-4). Oxford U Pr.
--An Historical Introduction to the Philosophy of Science. 2nd ed. (Illus.). 256p. 1980. 14.95x (ISBN 0-19-219156-X); pap. 6.95x (ISBN 0-19-289143-X). Oxford U Pr.
Losen, Stuart & Diament, Bert. Parent Conferences in the Schools: Procedures for Building Effective Partnership. new ed. 1978. text ed. 18.95 (ISBN 0-205-06094-3). Allyn.
Losey, Eugene see Chang, Raymond.
Loshak, Lionel, jt. auth. see Frishman, Bernard L.
Loshor, J. K., tr. see Ilyushin, A. A. & Lenskii, V. S.
Losoncy. Turning People on: How to Be an Encouraging Person. LC 77-4686. 1977. 11.95 (ISBN 0-13-933242-1, Spec); pap. 5.95 (ISBN 0-13-933234-0). P-H.
Losoncy, Lewis E. You Can Do It! How to Encourage Yourself. (Illus.). 1980. 10.95 (ISBN 0-13-976605-7, Spec); pap. 5.95 (ISBN 0-13-976597-2). P-H.
Loss, Joan. What Is It? LC 73-9038. 48p. (gr. 5-7). 1974. 4.95 o.p. (ISBN 0-385-06703-8). Doubleday.
Loss, Louis. Securities Regulation, 6 vols. 2nd ed. Incl. 1969 Supplement, 3 vols. 2053p. 1969. 260.00 (ISBN 0-316-53320-3). 2199p. 1961. Little.
--Securities Regulation: Student Edition. 2nd ed. 1234p. 1961. 20.00 (ISBN 0-316-53313-0). Little.
Loss, Richard, ed. see Gentz, Friedrich Von.
Lossing, Benson J. Harper's Encyclopaedia of United States History, from 458 A. D. to 1905: With Special Contributions Covering Every Phase of American History & Development by Eminent Authorities, 10 vols. new ed. LC 73-22093. (Illus.). 1974. Repr. of 1915 ed. 265.00 (ISBN 0-8103-3954-4). Gale.
--The Life & Times of Philip Schuyler, 2 vols. LC 78-167944. (Era of the American Revolution Ser). 1052p. 1973. Repr. of 1873 ed. Set. lib. bdg. 75.00 (ISBN 0-306-70533-8). Da Capo.
--Pictorial Field Book of the Revolution, 2 vols. LC 72-77516. (Illus.). (gr. 9 up). 1972. Repr. of 1859 ed. Set. 25.00 o.p. (ISBN 0-8048-1046-X). C E Tuttle.
--Seventeen Seventy-Six: Or, the War of Independence. LC 74-99070. (Illus.). 1970. Repr. of 1847 ed. 20.00 (ISBN 0-8103-3584-0). Gale.
Lossky, Andrew, ed. Seventeenth Century. LC 67-10426. (Orig.). 1967. pap. text ed. 7.95 (ISBN 0-02-919400-8). Free Pr.
Lossky, Vladimir. In the Image & Likeness of God. LC 76-383878. 232p. 1974. pap. 5.95 (ISBN 0-913836-13-3). St Vladimirs.
Lot, Ferdinand. L Art Militaire et les Armees Au Moyen Age En Europe et Dans le Proche Orient, 2 vols. LC 80-2017. 1981. Repr. of 1946 ed. 90.00 (ISBN 0-686-28932-3). AMS Pr.
--L' Impot Foncier et la Capitation Personnelle Sous le Bas-Empire et a l'epoque Franque. LC 80-2018. 1981. Repr. of 1928 ed. 21.50 (ISBN 0-404-18576-2). AMS Pr.
Lot, Ferdinand Vols., ed. Histoire Des Institutions Francaises Au Moyen Age, Publiee Sous la Direction De Ferdinand Lot et Robert Fawtier. LC 80-2204. 1981. Repr. of 1957 ed. 110.00 (ISBN 0-404-18606-8). AMS Pr.
Lotchin, Roger W. San Francisco, Eighteen Forty-Six to Eighteen Fifty-Six: From Hamlet to City. (Urban Life in America Ser.). (Illus.). 340p. 1974. 17.95 (ISBN 0-19-501749-8). Oxford U Pr.
Lotfi, Nasser. Iranian Christian. 160p. 1980. 8.95 (ISBN 0-8499-0275-4). Word Bks.
Loth, David G. Chief Justice: John Marshall & the Growth of the Republic. Repr. of 1949 ed. lib. bdg. 18.75x (ISBN 0-8371-2450-6, LOJM). Greenwood.
Lothers, John E. Design in Structural Steel. 3rd ed. LC 71-160254. (Civil Engineering & Engineering Mechanics Ser). (Illus.). 1972. 26.95 (ISBN 0-13-201921-3). P-H.
Lothian, Elizabeth. Country House Cookery from the West. LC 77-85035. (Illus.). 1978. 11.95 (ISBN 0-7153-7476-1). David & Charles.
Lothrop, Eaton S., Jr. Century of Cameras. rev. ed. 1981. pap. 12.95 (ISBN 0-87100-163-2). Morgan.
Lothrop, Harriet M. Five Little Peppers & How They Grew. LC 75-32184. (Classics of Children's Literature, 1621-1932: Vol. 47). (Illus.). 1976. Repr. of 1880 ed. PLB 38.00 (ISBN 0-8240-2296-3). Garland Pub.
Lotka, Alfred J. Elements of Mathematical Biology. Orig. Title: Elements of Physical Biology. 1957. pap. text ed. 6.00 (ISBN 0-486-60346-6). Dover.
Lotman, Iu. M. Lektsii Po Struktural'noi Poetike: Vvedenie, Teoriia Stikha. LC 68-10643. (Slavic Reprint Ser.: No. 5). 191p. (Rus). 1968. pap. 4.00 (ISBN 0-87057-106-0, Pub. by Brown U Pr). Univ Pr of New England.
--Struktura Khudozhestvennogo Teksta. LC 70-158681. (Slavic Reprint Ser.: No. 9). 381p. (Rus.). 1971. pap. 6.00 (ISBN 0-87057-129-X, Pub. by Brown U Pr). Univ Pr of New England.
Lotman, Lydia. Afanasy Fet. (World Author Ser.: Russia: No. 279). 1976. lib. bdg. 12.50 (ISBN 0-8057-2309-9). Twayne.
Lotman, Yury. Analysis of the Poetic Text. 296p. 1981. pap. 6.50 (ISBN 0-88233-107-8). Ardis Pubs.
Lott. Plaid for COBOL: A First Course. 1977. 5.50 (ISBN 0-256-01981-9, 14-1262-01). Learning Syst.
Lott, Arnold, jt. auth. see Engle, Eloise.
Lott, B. Becoming a Woman. 1980. pap. cancelled (ISBN 0-398-04053-2); pap. write for info. (ISBN 0-398-04067-2). C C Thomas.
Lott, Bernard, ed. Hamlet. (New Swan Shakespeare Advanced Ser.). (Illus.). pap. text ed. 4.50x (ISBN 0-582-52741-4). Longman.
Lott, Bernice. Becoming a Woman: The Socialization of Gender. (Illus.). 464p. 1980. 24.75 (ISBN 0-398-04053-2); pap. 18.50 (ISBN 0-398-04067-2). C C Thomas.
Lott, Clarinda H., jt. auth. see DeFord, Sara.
Lott, George & Bairstow, Jeffrey. How to Play Winning Doubles. LC 77-92904. (Illus.). 144p. 1979. pap. 6.95 (ISBN 0-914178-30-X). Golf Digest.
--How to Play Winning Doubles. LC 77-92904. (Illus.). 1979. 10.95 (ISBN 0-914178-20-2, 24923, Pub. by Tennis Mag). Golf Digest.
Lott, John N. A Scanning Electron Microscope Study of Green Plants. LC 75-33863. (Illus.). 192p. 1976. text ed. 14.95 o.p. (ISBN 0-8016-3033-9); pap. text ed. 8.25 o.p. (ISBN 0-8016-3034-7). Mosby.
Lott, R. E., ed. Juan Valera: Pepita Jimenez. 1974. 25.00 (ISBN 0-08-017918-5); pap. 10.75 (ISBN 0-08-017919-3). Pergamon.
Lott, Richard W. Auditing the Data Processing Function. (Illus.). 1980. 17.95 (ISBN 0-8144-5527-1). Am Mgmt.
Lotta, Raymond, et al. America in Decline: Imperialism's Greatest Crisis, Developments Toward War & Revolution, in the U.S. & Worldwide in the 1980's. (Illus.). 600p. (Orig.). 1981. 30.00 (ISBN 0-916650-12-X); pap. 9.95 (ISBN 0-916650-13-8). Banner Pr IL.
Lottinville, Savoie, ed. see Hyde, George E.
Lottinville, Savoie, ed. see Nuttall, Thomas.
Lottinville, Savoie, ed. see Wilhelm, Paul.
Lottman, Eileen. All Night Long. 192p. (Orig.). 1981. pap. 2.50 (ISBN 0-515-06000-3). Jove Pubns.
--Bionic Woman: Extracurricular Activities, No. 2. 1977. pap. 1.25 o.p. (ISBN 0-425-03326-0). Berkley Pub.
Lotz, Wolfgang. Studies in Italian Renaissance Architecture. (Illus.). 256p. 1980. 20.00x (ISBN 0-262-12073-9); pap. 7.95 (ISBN 0-262-62036-7). MIT Pr.
Lotze, Dieter P. Wilhelm Busch. (World Authors Ser.: No. 525). 1979. lib. bdg. 14.50 (ISBN 0-8057-6365-1). Twayne.
Lotze, Hermann. Logic, 2 vols. Natanson, Maurice, ed. LC 78-66738. (Phenomenology Background, Foreground & Influences Ser.: Vol. 8). 1980. Set. lib. bdg. 77.00 (ISBN 0-8240-9562-6). Garland Pub.
--Outlines of Psychology. Ladd, George T., tr. from Ger. (Contributions to the History of Psychology Ser.: Orientations). 1978. Repr. of 1886 ed. 30.00 (ISBN 0-89093-155-0). U Pubns Amer.
Loubere, Leo A. Louis Blanc: His Life & His Contribution to the Rise of French Jacobin-Socialism. LC 80-23424. (Northwestern University Studies in History: No.1). xii, 256p. 1980. Repr. of 1961 ed. lib. bdg. 27.50x (ISBN 0-313-22690-3, LOBL). Greenwood.
Louberge, Henri, jt. auth. see Giarini, Orio.
Loubser, Jan J., et al, eds. Explorations in General Theory in Social Science: Essays in Honor of Talcott Parsons, Vol. 1 & 2. LC 75-8427. (Illus.). 1976. Vol. 1. 40.00 (ISBN 0-02-919370-2); Vol. 2. 40.00 (ISBN 0-02-919380-X); 75.00 set (ISBN 0-02-919360-5). Free Pr.
Loucks, Celeste & Hullum, Everett. American Montage. Furlow, Elaine S., ed. (Human Touch: No. 3). (Illus.). 1976. 6.95 (ISBN 0-686-16312-5); lib. bdg. 6.95 (ISBN 0-937170-10-0). Home Mission.
Loucks, Celeste, et al. And a Cast of Thousands. Furlow, Elaine S., ed. (The Human Touch Photo-Text Ser.). (Illus.). 1978. 6.95 (ISBN 0-937170-11-9). Home Mission.
Louden, Louise. Forensic Paper Examination & Analysis. LC 79-55266. (Bibliographic Ser.: No. 286). 1979. pap. 10.00 (ISBN 0-87010-057-2). Inst Paper Chem.
--Toxicity of Chemicals & Pulping Wastes to Fish. LC 79-64742. (Bibliographic Ser.: No. 265, Suppl. I). 1979. pap. 60.00 (ISBN 0-87010-058-0). Inst Paper Chem.
Louderback, Joseph G., jt. auth. see Block, Stanley B.
Loudin, Jo. Act Yourself: How to Stop Playing Roles & Unmask Your True Feeings. (Illus.). 1979. 9.95 (ISBN 0-13-003715-X, Spec); pap. 3.95 (ISBN 0-13-003707-9). P-H.
--The Hoax of Romance. (Transformation Ser.). 320p. 1981. 12.95 (ISBN 0-13-392456-4, Spec); pap. 6.95 (ISBN 0-13-392449-1). P-H.
Loudon, Archibald. A Selection, of Some of the Most Interesting Narratives, of Outrages, Committed by the Indians, in Their Wars, with the White People, 2 vols. LC 75-7052. (Indian Captivities Ser.: Vols. 29 & 30). 1977. Repr. of 1811 ed. Vol. 1. lib. bdg. 44.00 (ISBN 0-8240-1653-X); Vol. 2. lib. bdg. 44.00 (ISBN 0-8240-1654-8). Garland Pub.
Loudon, F. H. James Scott & William Scott, Bookbinders. (Illus.). 1980. 65.00 (ISBN 0-89679-003-7). Moretus Pr.
Loudon, Rodney. The Quantum Theory of Light. (Illus.). 350p. 1973. 47.50 (ISBN 0-19-851130-2). Oxford U Pr.
Loudon, Rodney, jt. auth. see Hayes, William.
Louf, Andre. Teach Us to Pray: Learning a Little About God. 1977. pap. 2.95 (ISBN 0-8091-2001-1). Paulist Pr.
Lough, John. Encyclopedie of Diderot & D'Alembert. 42.00 (ISBN 0-521-07604-8). Cambridge U Pr.
--Seventeenth-Century French Drama: The Background. (Illus.). 1979. 14.95x (ISBN 0-19-815756-8). Oxford U Pr.
--Writer & Public in France: From the Middle Ages to the Present Day. 1978. text ed. 49.50x (ISBN 0-19-815749-5). Oxford U Pr.
Loughary, John W. & Ripley, Theresa M. This Isn't Quite What I Had in Mind: A Career Planning Program for College Students. 1978. pap. 3.95 o.p. (ISBN 0-695-80921-0). Follett.
Loughlin, R. L. Verses Vice Verses. LC 80-81692. 120p. 1981. 8.95 (ISBN 0-911906-18-5); pap. 5.95 (ISBN 0-911906-19-3). Harian Creative.
Loughman, Michael. Learning to Rock Climb. (Outdoor Activities Guides). (Illus.). 192p. (Orig.). 1981. 14.95 (ISBN 0-87156-281-2); pap. 9.95 (ISBN 0-87156-279-0). Sierra.
Louie, Kamm. Critiques of Confucius in Contemporary China. LC 80-214. 210p. 1980. 22.50 (ISBN 0-312-17645-7). St Martin.
Louis, Arthur. The Tycoons. 1981. 11.95 (ISBN 0-671-24974-6). S&S.
Louis, Cameron. Commonplace Book of Robert Reynes. LC 79-7933. (Medieval Texts Ser.: Vol. I). 630p. 1980. lib. bdg. 50.00 (ISBN 0-8240-9539-1). Garland Pub.
Louis, Frances. Swift's Anatomy of Misunderstanding: A Study of Swift's Epistemological Imagination in "a Tale of a Tub" & "Gulliver's Travels". 220p. 1980. 18.00x (ISBN 0-389-20074-3). B&N.
Louis Harris & Associates, Inc. Harris Nineteen Seventy-Two American Women's Opinion Poll. 1975. codebk. 12.00 (ISBN 0-89138-114-7). ICPSR.
Louis, Harry & Curry, Bob. The Story of Triumph Motorcycles. 3rd ed. (Illus.). 144p. 1981. 37.95 (ISBN 0-85059-480-4). Aztex.
Louis, Jennifer, jt. auth. see Louis, Victor.
Louis, Louise. Consulate of One. (Illus.). 16p. 1977. lib. bdg. 1.99. Pen-Art.
--The Dervish Dance. 40p. 1971. Repr. of 1958 ed. text ed. 4.95. Pen-Art.
--Honeybee Cousin. (Illus.). 88p. (gr. 4-11). 1979. PLB 5.99. Pen-Art.
--The Lillibooks, 3 bks. Incl. Marriage Idyll. 8p; Persistent Pilgrim. 16p; Sheltered Hours. 16p. (Illus.). 1979. Set. pap. 3.99. Pen-Art.
--The Lillibooks & Consulate of One, 4 bks. 1977. Set. pap. 3.99. Pen-Art.

--The Miraculous Affair. (Illus.). 75p. 1974. text ed. 12.00. Pen-Art.
--Path to the Peak. (Illus.). 176p. 1971. pap. 2.50. Pen-Art.
--Peopled Parables. (Illus.). 100p. text ed. 6.50. Pen-Art.
--Perennial Promise: First Lillibook Anthology. 48p. pap. 3.95. Pen-Art.
--The Scarlet Net. (Illus.). 68p. 1972. text ed. 7.50. Pen-Art.
--Trible Candle. 74p. 1977. pap. 4.95. Pen-Art.
--Twin Playlets for Children: Mr. Wishing Match & Community Sing, 2 bks. (gr. 4-11). 1979. pap. 3.99 (ISBN 0-345-54321-1). Pen-Art.

Louis, Louise, jt. auth. see Monaghan, William.

Louis, Victor & Louis, Jennifer. The Complete Guide to the Soviet Union. 1980. pap. 9.95 o.p. (ISBN 0-312-15753-3). St Martin.

Louisell, David W. & Kaplan, John. Cases & Materials on Evidence. 4th ed. (University Casebook Ser.). 899p. 1981. write for info. (ISBN 0-88277-018-7). Foundation Pr.

Louisell, David W. & Mueller, Christopher B. Federal Evidence, Vol. 5. LC 76-46689. 1978. 275.00 (ISBN 0-686-22901-0). Lawyers Co-Op.

Loukopoulos, Louisa D., ed. see Andronicos, Manolis, et al.

Lounds, Morris, Jr. Israel's Black Hebrews: Black Americans in Search of Identity. LC 80-5651. 231p. 1981. lib. bdg. 18.25 (ISBN 0-8191-1400-6); pap. text ed. 9.75 (ISBN 0-8191-1401-4). U Pr of Amer.

Lounsbury, John F. & Aldrich, Frank T. Introduction to Geographic Field Methods & Techniques. 1979. pap. text ed. 11.95 (ISBN 0-675-08304-4). Merrill.

Lounsbury, John F. & Ogden, Lawrence. Earth Science. 3rd ed. LC 78-21130. 1979. text ed. 19.50 scp (ISBN 0-06-044059-7, HarpC); inst. manual avail. Har-Row.

Lounsbury, T. R. James Fenimore Cooper. LC 80-29308. (American Men & Women of Letters Ser.). 310p. 1981. pap. 4.95 (ISBN 0-87754-156-6). Chelsea Hse.

Lounsbury, Thomas R. James Fenimore Cooper. LC 67-23882. 1968. Repr. of 1882 ed. 20.00 (ISBN 0-8103-3037-7). Gale.

Lourie, Margaret A., ed. William Morris's "the Defence of Guenevere", & Other Poems. LC 80-83223. 275p. 1981. lib. bdg. 33.00 (ISBN 0-8240-9452-2). Garland Pub.

Lourie, Richard. Sagittarius in Warsaw. LC 73-83036. 192p. 1973. 7.95 (ISBN 0-8149-0729-6). Vanguard.

Lous, Anne B. An Immigrant Speaks. 1981. 12.95 (ISBN 0-533-04294-1). Vantage.

Lousteau, Rod. Guide to the Ski Touring Centers of New England. LC 80-82792. (Illus.). 144p. (Orig.). 1980. pap. 5.95 (ISBN 0-87106-046-9). Globe Pequot.

Loutfi, Martha F. Rural Women: Unequal Partners in Development, a WEP Study. Intl Labour Office, ed. (Illus.). iii, 81p. 1980. pap. 7.15 (ISBN 92-2-102389-3). Intl Labour Office.

Louthan, Doniphan. The Poetry of John Donne: A Study in Explication. LC 75-40927. 193p. 1976. Repr. of 1951 ed. lib. bdg. 19.25x (ISBN 0-8371-8693-5, LOPJ). Greenwood.

Louthan, Robert. Shrunken Planets. LC 79-54883. 64p. 1980. pap. 4.95 (ISBN 0-914086-28-6). Alicejamesbooks.

Louthan, William C. Politics of Justice: A Study in Law, Social Science & Public Policy. (National University Pubns. Legal Series). 1979. 12.95 (ISBN 0-8046-9218-1). Kennikat.

Louvish, D., tr. see Demyanov, V. & Malozemov, V. N.

Louvish, D., tr. see Girsanov, I. V.

Louvish, D., tr. see Kokorin, A. I. & Kopytov, V. M.

Louvish, D., tr. see Kurmit, A. A.

Loux, Michael J., intro. by. The Possible & the Actual: Readings in the Metaphysics of Modality. LC 79-7618. 1979. 19.50x (ISBN 0-8014-1238-2); pap. 6.95x (ISBN 0-8014-9178-9). Cornell U Pr.

Lovaas, Ivar & Bucker, Bradley. Perspectives in Behavior Modification with Deviant Children. LC 7-18357. (Illus.). 512p. 1974. 20.95 (ISBN 0-13-657130-1). P-H.

Lovaas, Ole I. The Autistic Child. LC 76-5890. 256p. 1977. text ed. 16.95 (ISBN 0-8290-0253-7). Irvington.

Lovaglia, Florence. Algebra. (Span.). 1974. pap. 7.40 (ISBN 0-06-315513-3, IntlDept). Har-Row.

Lovan, Nora G., jt. auth. see Solomon, Martin B., Jr.

Lovato, Rebecca. All the Days of My Life. LC 77-74003. 1977. 6.00 (ISBN 0-89430-014-8). Morgan-Pacific.
--Carlos at the Fiesta (Carlos En la Fiesta) Cardona, Consuelo M., tr. LC 76-42856. (gr. 6-12). 1976. pap. 1.95 (ISBN 0-89430-000-8). Morgan-Pacific.

Lovberg, Ralph H. see Marton, L.

Love & Brealy. Modern Development in Invest. Mngt. 2nd ed. 1978. pap. 15.95 (ISBN 0-03-040716-8). Dryden Pr.

Love, A. & Love, D. Cytotaxonomical Atlas of the Arctic Flora. (Cytotaxonomical Atlases: Vol. 2). (Illus.). 598p. 1975. lib. bdg. 100.00x (ISBN 3-7682-0976-8). Lubrecht & Cramer.

Love, A. W., ed. Electromagnetic Horn Antennas. LC 75-44649. 1976. 28.95 (ISBN 0-87942-075-8). Inst Electrical.

Love, Alan C., jt. auth. see O'Neal, Robert.

Love, Augustus E. Some Problems of Geodynamics. 1967. pap. text ed. 2.50 (ISBN 0-486-61766-1). Dover.
--Treatise on the Mathematical Theory of Elasticity. 4th ed. (Illus.). 1927. pap. text ed. 8.00 (ISBN 0-486-60174-9). Dover.

Love, Barbara, ed. Handbook of Circulation Management. 1980. 49.95 (ISBN 0-918110-02-5). Folio.

Love, D., jt. auth. see Love, A.

Love, Diane. Flowers Are Fabulous: For Decorating. (Illus.). 144p. 1975. 17.50 (ISBN 0-02-575560-9). Macmillan.

Love, Frank. Arizona's Story: A Short History. (Illus.). 1979. pap. 7.95x (ISBN 0-87108-218-7); tchr's ed. 3.95 (ISBN 0-87108-234-9). Pruett.

Love, Frank & Feitz, Leland. Brothel to Boomtown: Yuma's Lively Past. (Illus., Orig.). 1981. pap. 2.95 (ISBN 0-936564-19-9). Little London.

Love, G. B., jt. ed. see Irwin, Walter.

Love, G. D., et al, eds. Clinical Aspects of Blood Viscosity & Ceell Deformability. (Illus.). 250p. 1981. 41.30 (ISBN 0-387-10299-X). Springer-Verlag.

Love, Glen A., jt. ed. see Bingham, Edwin R.

Love, Harold D. Educating Exceptional Children in a Changing Society. (Illus.). 264p. 1974. 13.75 (ISBN 0-398-02905-9). C C Thomas.
--The Mentally Retarded Child & His Family. (Illus.). 216p. 1973. text ed. 11.25 (ISBN 0-398-02728-5); pap. text ed. 7.95 (ISBN 0-398-02760-9). C C Thomas.
--Teaching Physically Handicapped Children: Methods & Materials. (Illus.). 176p. 1978. 15.75 (ISBN 0-398-03703-5). C C Thomas.
--Youth & the Drug Problem: A Guide for Parents & Teachers. 116p. 1971. photocopy ed. 12.00 (ISBN 0-398-01152-4). C C Thomas.

Love, Harold D. & Osborne, W. H. Early Childhood Education: A Methods & Materials Book. 160p. 1971. 9.75 (ISBN 0-398-02344-1). C C Thomas.

Love, Harold D. & Walthall, Joe E. A Handbook of Medical, Educational, & Psychological Information for Teachers of Physically Handicapped Children. (Illus.). 232p. 1977. 16.75 (ISBN 0-398-03629-2). C C Thomas.

Love, Harold D., jt. auth. see Mainord, James C.

Love, Harold D., jt. auth. see Walthall, Joe E.

Love, Harold D., et al. Your Child Goes to the Hospital: A Book for Parents. 112p. 1972. pap. 6.75 (ISBN 0-398-02346-8). C C Thomas.
--Language Development of Exceptional Children. (Illus.). 244p. 1977. 17.50 (ISBN 0-398-03573-3). C C Thomas.

Love, Jeff. The Quantum Gods. 1979. pap. 7.95 (ISBN 0-87728-476-8). Weiser.

Love, John & Hodgkins, John. Chess Battle Strategies. LC 79-65066. (Illus.). 1979. 9.95 (ISBN 0-8069-4952-X); lib. bdg. 9.29 (ISBN 0-8069-4953-8). Sterling.

Love, Kathleen, ed. Little Laughter. LC 57-10283. (Illus.). (gr. 1 up). 1957. 6.95 (ISBN 0-690-49804-7, TYC-J). T Y Crowell.

Love, Louise. Complete Book of Pizza. 2nd ed. (Illus.). 1981. pap. write for info. Sassafras Pr.

Love, Nigel H. Generative Phonology: A Case Study from French. (Linguisticae Investigationes Supplementa: No. 4). 300p. 1980. text ed. 34.25x (ISBN 90-272-3113-3). Humanities.

Love, Ralph N., jt. ed. see Goodman, Louis J.

Love, Robert W., ed. Changing Interpretations & New Sources in Naval History. LC 80-5. (Papers from the Third United States Naval Academy History Symposium). 500p. 1980. lib. bdg. 44.00 (ISBN 0-8240-9517-0). Garland Pub.

Love, Robert W., Jr. The Chiefs of Naval Operations. LC 80-12253. 1980. 28.95x (ISBN 0-87021-115-3). Naval Inst Pr.

Love Set, Inc. Staff, jt. ed. see Friedman, Sandra C.

Love, William D. The Colonial History of Hartford. LC 73-85465. (Illus.). 416p. 1974. casebound 15.00 (ISBN 0-87106-133-3). Globe Pequot.

Lovecraft, H. P. The Dunwich Horror & Others. 1978. pap. 1.75 o.s.i. (ISBN 0-685-86424-3). Jove Pubns.
--Lurking Fear & Other Stories. 1975. pap. 1.50 o.p. (ISBN 0-345-24690-X). Ballantine.
--Shuttered Room & Other Tales of Horror. 1974. pap. 1.50 o.p. (ISBN 0-345-24302-1). Ballantine.

Loveday, George C. Practical Algebra. LC 73-18336. (Self-Teaching Guides Ser). 384p. 1974. pap. text ed. 7.95x (ISBN 0-471-77557-6). Wiley.

Loveday, George C. & Seidman, Arthur H. Troubleshooting Solid State Circuits. LC 80-21954. 112p. 1981. pap. text ed. 7.95 (ISBN 0-471-08371-2). Wiley.

Loveday, R. First Course in Statistics. text ed. 6.95x (ISBN 0-521-05601-2). Cambridge U Pr.
--Practical Statistics & Probability. 256p. 1974. pap. text ed. 6.95x (ISBN 0-521-20291-4). Cambridge U Pr.

Loveday, Robert. Statistical Mathematics. 1973. text ed. 5.95x (ISBN 0-521-08643-4). Cambridge U Pr.
--Statistics. 2nd ed. LC 74-96095. Orig. Title: Second Course in Statistics. (Illus.). 1969. text ed. 10.95x (ISBN 0-521-07234-4). Cambridge U Pr.

Lovejoy, David S. The Glorious Revolution in America. 1974. pap. 3.95x o.p. (ISBN 0-06-131775-6, TB1775, Torch). Har-Row.
--Rhode Island Politics & the American Revolution, 1760-1776. LC 58-10478. (Brown University Studies: No. 23). (Illus.). 256p. 1969. Repr. of 1958 ed. 10.00 (ISBN 0-87057-053-6, Pub. by Brown U Pr). Univ Pr of New England.

Lovejoy, W., jt. auth. see Garfield, Paul.

Lovelace, Linda & McGrady, Mike. Ordeal. 1981. pap. 2.95 (ISBN 0-425-04749-0). Berkley Pub.

Lovelace, Maud H. Betsy & Joe. LC 48-8096. (Illus.). (gr. 5-11). 1948. 9.95 (ISBN 0-690-13378-2, TYC-J). T Y Crowell.
--Betsy & Tacy Go Downtown. LC 43-51264. (Illus.). (gr. 3-6). 1943. PLB 8.79 (ISBN 0-690-13450-9, TYC-J). T Y Crowell.
--Betsy & Tacy Go Over the Big Hill. LC 42-23557. (Illus.). (gr. 3-7). 1942. 9.95 (ISBN 0-690-13521-1, TYC-J); PLB 8.79 (ISBN 0-690-13521-1). T Y Crowell.
--Betsy & the Great World. LC 52-8657. (Illus.). (gr. 5-11). 1952. 9.95 (ISBN 0-690-13591-2, TYC-J). T Y Crowell.
--Betsy in Spite of Herself. LC 46-11995. (Illus.). (gr. 5-11). 1946. 9.95 (ISBN 0-690-13662-5, TYC-J). T Y Crowell.
--Betsy-Tacy. LC 40-30965. (Illus.). (gr. 1-5). 1940. PLB 8.79- (ISBN 0-690-13805-9, TYC-J). T Y Crowell.
--Betsy-Tacy & Tib. LC 41-18714. (Illus.). (gr. 3-7). 1941. PLB 8.79 (ISBN 0-690-13876-8, TYC-J). T Y Crowell.
--Betsy Was a Junior: A Betsy-Tacy High School Story. LC 46-11995. (Illus.). (gr. 5-11). 1947. 9.95 (ISBN 0-690-13946-2, TYC-J). T Y Crowell.
--Betsy's Wedding. LC 55-11108. (Illus.). (gr. 5-11). 1955. 9.95 (ISBN 0-690-13733-8, TYC-J). T Y Crowell.
--Heaven to Betsy. LC 45-9806. (Illus.). (gr. 5-11). 1945. 9.95 (ISBN 0-690-37449-6, TYC-J). T Y Crowell.

Lovelace, T. A. Engineering Principles for Electrical Tehcnicians, 2 vols. 1975. pap. text ed. 19.95x. Vol. 1 (ISBN 0-17-741108-2). Vol. 2 (ISBN 0-17-741109-0). Intl Ideas.

Loveland, Anne C. Southern Evangelicals & the Social Order Eighteen Hundred to Eighteen Sixty. LC 80-11200. 368p. 1980. 30.00x (ISBN 0-8071-0690-9); pap. 12.95 (ISBN 0-8071-0783-2). La State U Pr.

Loveland, Roger P. Photomicrography, 2 vols. LC 80-12428. 1981. Vol. 1. lib. bdg. write for info.; Vol. 2. lib. bdg. write for info. (ISBN 0-89874-209-9). Krieger.

Loveless, E. E., jt. auth. see Davis, Jack.

Loveless, Ganelle, jt. auth. see Bullock, Waneta B.

Lovell, Bernard. The Origins & International Economics of Space Exploration. LC 73-18325. 104p. 1973. 7.95 (ISBN 0-470-54851-7). Halsted Pr.

Lovell, Ernest J., Jr. Captain Medwin: Friend of Byron & Shelley. 1962. pap. 6.95 (ISBN 0-292-73180-9). U of Tex Pr.

Lovell, J. P. The British Isles Through Geological Time: A Northward Drift. (Illus.). 1977. pap. text ed. 6.95x (ISBN 0-04-554003-9). Allen Unwin.

Lovell, John. British Trade Unions, Eighteen Seventy-Five to Nineteen Thirty-Three. (Studies in Economic & Social History). 1977. pap. text ed. 5.00x (ISBN 0-333-17926-9). Humanities.

Lovell, John, ed. see Hammond, J. L. & Hammond, B.

Lovell, John, Jr. Black Song: The Forge & the Flame. (Illus.). 1972. 15.00 o.s.i. (ISBN 0-02-575700-8). Macmillan.

Lovell, M. Macroeconomics: Measurement, Theory & Policy. LC 75-2001. 541p. 1975. 23.50 (ISBN 0-471-54850-2). Wiley.

Lovell, Marc. The Spy Game. LC 80-499. (Crime Club Ser.). 192p. 1980. 8.95 (ISBN 0-385-17073-4). Doubleday.
--A Voice from the Living. LC 77-92221. 1978. 7.95 o.p. (ISBN 0-385-14104-1). Doubleday.

Lovell, Mary & Lees, Herbert. The New Iris Syrett Cookery Book. (Illus.). 1973. 10.95 o.p. (ISBN 0-571-09613-1, Pub. by Faber & Faber). Merrimack Bk Serv.

Lovell, Ned B., jt. auth. see Riegel, Rodney P.

Lovell, Ronald P. The Newspaper: An Introduction to Newswriting & Reporting. 1979. pap. text ed. 12.95x (ISBN 0-534-00729-5). Wadsworth Pub.

Lovell, S. An Introduction to Radiation Dosimetry, No. 4. LC 78-67261. (Techniques of Measurement in Medicine Ser.). (Illus.). 1979. 21.95 (ISBN 0-521-22436-5); pap. 6.50x (ISBN 0-521-29497-5). Cambridge U Pr.

Lovell, S. D. The Presidential Election of Nineteen Sixteen. LC 79-25689. 288p. 1980. 22.50x o.p. (ISBN 0-8093-0965-3). S Ill U Pr.

Lovelock, David & Rund, Hanno. Tensors, Differential Forms, & Variational Principles. LC 75-2261. (Pure & Applied Mathematics Ser). 364p. 1975. 35.00 (ISBN 0-471-54840-5, Pub. by Wiley-Interscience). Wiley.

Lovelock, James. Climbing. 1975. 7.50 o.p. (ISBN 0-7134-0326-8). Hippocrene Bks.

Lovelock, William. Common Sense in Music Teaching. (Illus.). 1968. Repr. of 1965 ed. 6.95 (ISBN 0-7135-0682-2). Dufour.

Loveman, Brian. Chile: The Legacy of Hispanic Capitalism. LC 78-13965. (Latin American Histories Ser.). (Illus.). 1979. 14.95x (ISBN 0-19-502518-0); pap. text ed. 6.95x (ISBN 0-19-502520-2). Oxford U Pr.

Loveman, Brian & Davies, Thomas M., Jr., eds. The Politics of Antipolitics: The Military in Latin America. LC 77-25256. 1978. 19.95x (ISBN 0-8032-0954-1); pap. 5.95x (ISBN 0-8032-7900-0, BB 672, Bison). U of Nebr Pr.

Lovenberg, W., jt. ed. see Youdim, M. B.

Lovenberg, Walter, ed. Iron-Sulfur Proteins, 3 vols. Incl. Biological Properties. Vol. 1, 1973. 53.00 (ISBN 0-12-456001-6); Molecular Properties. Vol. 2, 1974. 49.00 (ISBN 0-12-456002-4); Vol. 3. 1977. 55.00 (ISBN 0-12-456003-2). 1973. 127.50 set (ISBN 0-685-40605-9). Acad Pr.

Lover, Stanley. Association Football (Soccer) Laws Illustrated. 1977. 12.95 (ISBN 0-7207-0879-6). Transatlantic.

Loveridge, John W., jt. auth. see McArthur, Alfred G.

Loveridge, Mark. Laurence Sterne & the Argument About Design. 1981. 26.50x (ISBN 0-389-20106-5). B&N.

Lovering, David G., jt. ed. see Inman, Douglas.

Lovesey, Peter. Abracadaver. 1981. pap. 2.95 (ISBN 0-14-005803-6). Penguin.
--Five Fings of Distance. (Illus.). 197p. 1981. 10.95 (ISBN 0-312-29484-0). St Martin.
--Invitation to a Dynamite Party. (Crime Ser.). 176p. 1981. pap. 3.50 (ISBN 0-14-004029-3). Penguin.
--Mad Hatter's Holiday. 1981. pap. 2.95 (ISBN 0-14-005804-4). Penguin.
--Swing, Swing Together. LC 76-14865. 1976. 6.95 (ISBN 0-396-07327-1). Dodd.

Lovesey, S. W., jt. auth. see Marshall, W.

Lovestedt, L. K. Reclaiming Funational Communication. 1980. pap. 19.75 spiral (ISBN 0-398-03994-1). C C Thomas.

Lovet, Mrs. Heather M., jt. auth. see Gray, J. A.

Lovett, C. S. C. S. Lovett: Maranatha Man. (Illus.). 1978. pap. 4.95 (ISBN 0-938148-02-8). Personal Christianity.
--Latest Word on the Last Days. (Illus., Orig.). 1980. pap. 5.95 (ISBN 0-938148-00-1). Personal Christianity.
--Witnessing Made Easy. 1971. pap. 4.95 (ISBN 0-938148-01-X). Personal Christianity.

Lovett, Clara M., jt. ed. see Berkin, Carol R.

Lovett, Gabriel. The Duke of Rivas. (World Authors Ser.: No. 452). 1977. lib. bdg. 12.50 (ISBN 0-8057-6289-2). Twayne.

Lovett, Robert W., ed. American Economic & Business History Information Sources. LC 78-137573. (Management Information Guide Ser.: No. 23). 1971. 30.00 (ISBN 0-8103-0823-1). Gale.

Lovett, William & Collins, John. Chartism: A New Organization of the People. (Victorian Library). 1969. Repr. of 1840 ed. text ed. 5.50x (ISBN 0-7185-5006-4, Leicester). Humanities.

Lovewisdom, Johnny. Modern Juice Therapy. pap. 2.00 (ISBN 0-933278-08-X). OMango.
--Spiritualizing Dietetics. 5.00 (ISBN 0-933278-09-8). OMango.

Loving, Jerome. Walt Whitman's Champion: William Douglas O'Connor. LC 77-89511. 248p. 1978. 13.50 (ISBN 0-89096-039-9). Tex A&M Univ Pr.

Lovinger, Sophie L. Learning Disabilities & Games. LC 78-24619. (Illus.). 1979. text ed. 14.95x (ISBN 0-88229-353-2); pap. 7.95 (ISBN 0-88229-652-3). Nelson-Hall.

Lovinggood, Penman. Famous Modern Negro Musicians. LC 77-22215. (Music Reprint Ser.). (Illus.). 1977. Repr. lib. bdg. 15.00 (ISBN 0-306-77523-9). Da Capo.

Lovins, Amory & Evans, Philip H. Eryri: The Mountains of Longing. Brower, David R., ed. & pref. by. (The Earth's Wild Places Ser). (Illus.). 177p. 1971. 19.95 o.s.i. (ISBN 0-8415-0129-7). Friends Earth.

Lovins, Amory B. & Lovins, L. H. Energy- War: Breaking the Nuclear Links. LC 80-8713. 228p. 1981. pap. 4.95 (ISBN 0-06-090852-1, CN 852, CN). Har-Row.

Lovins, Amory B. & Lovins, L. Hunter. Energy & War: Breaking the Nuclear Link. 180p. 1980. 10.00 (ISBN 0-913890-44-8). Friends Earth.

Lovins, Amory B. & Price, John H. Non-Nuclear Futures: The Case for an Ethical Energy Strategy. LC 75-20260. 1980. pap. 3.95 (ISBN 0-06-090777-0, CN777, CN). Har-Row.

Lovins, L. H., jt. auth. see Lovins, Amory B.

Lovins, L. Hunter, jt. auth. see Lovins, Amory B.

Lovitt, Thomas C. In Spite of My Resistance, I've Learned from Children. (Special Education Ser.). 1977. pap. text ed. 8.95 (ISBN 0-675-08528-4). Merrill.

--Managing Inappropriate Behaviors in the Classroom. LC 78-54144. 1978. pap. text ed. 5.00 (ISBN 0-86586-055-6). Coun Exc Child.

Lovset, Ilona Skupinska. The Ustinov Collection: Terracottas. 1979. pap. 23.00x (ISBN 82-00-01786-9, Dist. by Columbia U Pr.). Universitet.

Lovset, Ilona-Skupinska. The Ustinov Collection: The Palestinian Pottery. 1976. pap. 23.00x (ISBN 82-00-01564-5, Dist. by Columbia U Pr). Universitet.

Lovy, Charles W. Silhouette De la France: A First Reader in French Civilization. LC 67-10548. (Fr). 1967. pap. 8.95x o.p. (ISBN 0-471-00346-8). Wiley.

Low, Abraham A. Lectures to Relatives of Former Patients. 1967. 6.95 (ISBN 0-8158-0139-4). Chris Mass.

Low, Albert. Zen & Creative Management. LC 74-33609. 288p. 1976. pap. 3.50 (ISBN 0-385-04669-3, Anch). Doubleday.

Low, Anthony. Blaze of Noon: A Reading of Samson Agonistes. 224p. 1974. 15.00x (ISBN 0-231-03842-9). Columbia U Pr.

--Love's Architecture: Devotional Modes in Seventeenth-Century English Poetry. LC 77-94391. 1978. 17.50x (ISBN 0-8147-4984-4); pap. 8.00x (ISBN 0-8147-4985-2). NYU Pr.

Low, D. A. Buganda in Modern History. LC 73-10019. (Illus.). 1971. 20.00x (ISBN 0-520-01640-8). U of Cal Pr.

Low, D. A., ed. History of East Africa, Vol. 3. 1976. 49.50x (ISBN 0-19-821680-7). Oxford U Pr.

--The Mind of Buganda: Documents of the Modern History of an African Kingdom. (Illus.). 1971. 20.00x (ISBN 0-520-01969-5). U of Cal Pr.

--Soundings in Modern South Asian History. LC 68-20442. (Illus.). 1968. 20.00x (ISBN 0-520-00770-0). U of Cal Pr.

Low, Donald A., ed. Robert Burns: The Critical Heritage. (Critical Heritage Ser.). 1974. 38.00 (ISBN 0-7100-7797-1). Routledge & Kegan.

Low, Jacqueline & Jacot, Yves. Adventures in Urban Reading Series. Incl. Choosing Sides (ISBN 0-8224-9401-9); The Daydreamer (ISBN 0-8224-9406-X); The Dope Pusher (ISBN 0-8224-9402-7); Good Joss Means Good Luck (ISBN 0-8224-9403-5). (gr. 4-8). 1974. pap. 2.00 ea. Pitman Learning.

Low, Jennie & Yee, Diane. The Chinese Restaurant Experience. Silva, Sharon, ed. LC 80-66946. 192p. 1981. pap. 5.95 (ISBN 0-89395-058-0). Cal Living Bks.

Low, Joseph. Boo to a Goose. LC 74-18188. 1975. 5.95 (ISBN 0-689-50009-2, Mcelderry Bk). Atheneum.

--The Christmas Grump. LC 77-3903. (Illus.). (ps-3). 1977. 7.95 (ISBN 0-689-50092-0, McElderry Bk). Atheneum.

--Five Men Under One Umbrella: And Other Ready-to-Read Riddles. (Ready-to-Read Ser.). (Illus.). 64p. (gr. 1-3). 1975. 7.95 (ISBN 0-02-761460-3). Macmillan.

--Mice Twice. LC 79-23274. (Illus.). 32p. (ps-3). 1980. 9.95 (ISBN 0-689-50157-9, McElderry Bk). Atheneum.

--My Dog, Your Dog. LC 77-12032. (Illus.). (ps-3). 1978. 7.95 (ISBN 0-02-761400-X, 76140). Macmillan.

Low, Peter W., jt. ed. see Greenawalt, R. Kent.

Low, Richard E. Modern Economic Organization. 1970. text ed. 17.50 (ISBN 0-256-00315-7). Irwin.

Low, Rosemary. Beginner's Guide to Birdkeeping. (Illus.). 217p. 1975. 14.95 (ISBN 0-7207-0673-4). Transatlantic.

--Lories & Lorikeets. (Illus.). 1979. pap. 6.95 (ISBN 0-87666-980-1, PS-773). TFH Pubns.

Low, Shirley P., jt. auth. see Alderson, William T.

Low, V. O., jt. auth. see Warner, Lloyd W.

Low, Victor N., ed. African History & Societies to 1914, a Critical Survey of Relevant Books with Special References to West Africa. Incl. Vol. 1. Africa at Large; Vol. 2. West Africa Region by Region. 1700p. 1981. 65.00x ea (ISBN 0-7146-3056-X, F Cass Co). Biblio Dist.

--From West Africa: A Social, Political & Economic Record 1917-1977, 4 vols. 1981. Set. 130.00x (ISBN 0-7146-3055-1, F Cass Co). Biblio Dist.

Low, Will H. A Painter's Progress. LC 75-28889. (Art Experience in Late 19th Century America Ser.: Vol. 22). (Illus.). 1976. Repr. of 1910 ed. lib. bdg. 37.00 (ISBN 0-8240-2246-7). Garland Pub.

Lowance, Mason I, Jr. The Language of Canaan: Metaphor & Symbol in New England from the Puritans to the Transcendentalists. LC 79-21179. 1980. 20.00x (ISBN 0-674-50949-8). Harvard U Pr.

Lowbury, E. J. & Ayliffe, G. A. Drug Resistance in Antimicrobial Therapy. (American Lectures in Living Chemistry Ser.). (Illus.). 168p. 1974. 22.50 (ISBN 0-398-02966-0). C C Thomas.

Lowden, J. Alexander, jt. ed. see Callahan, John W.

Lowder, Hughston E. & Scott, Jack. Batfish: The Champion "Submarine-Killer" Submarine of World War Ii. LC 80-12155. (Illus.). 300p. 1980. 10.95 (ISBN 0-13-066563-0). P-H.

Lowder, Richard E. Cribbage Is the Name of the Game. (Everday Handbook Ser.). (Illus.). 96p. 1975. pap. 2.50 (ISBN 0-06-463402-7, EH 402, Eh). Har-Row.

Lowdin, P. O. Complex Scaling in the Spectral Theory of the Hamiltonian: Proceedings of the 1978 Sanibel Workshop. (International Journal of Quantum Chemistry Ser.: Vol. XIII, No. 4). 1978. pap. 33.50 (ISBN 0-471-05774-6, Pub. by Wiley-Interscience). Wiley.

Lowdin, P. O. & Ohrn, Y. Proceedings. (International Journal of Quantum Chemistry-Quantum Chemistry Symposium: No. 12). 550p. 1978. 40.50 (ISBN 0-471-05633-2). Wiley.

Lowdin, Per-Olov, ed. Advances in Quantum Chemistry, Vols. 1-11. Incl. Vol. 1. 1964. 49.25 (ISBN 0-12-034801-2); Vol. 2. Vol. 2, 1966. 49.25 (ISBN 0-12-034802-0); Vol. 3. 1967. 49.25 (ISBN 0-12-034803-9); Vol. 4. 1968. 49.25 (ISBN 0-12-034804-7); Vol. 5. 1970. 49.25 (ISBN 0-12-034805-5); Vol. 6. 1972. 49.25 (ISBN 0-12-034806-3); Vol. 7. Vol. 7, 1973. 49.25 (ISBN 0-12-034807-1); Vol. 8. 1974. 49.25 (ISBN 0-12-034808-X); Vol. 9. 1975. 55.00 (ISBN 0-12-034809-8); Vol. 10. 1977. 50.00 (ISBN 0-686-66780-8); Vol. 11. 1979. 50.50 (ISBN 0-12-034811-X). Acad Pr.

--Advances in Quantum Chemistry, Vol. 12. LC 64-8029. 1980. 48.00 (ISBN 0-12-034812-8). Acad Pr.

Lowdin, Per-Olov, et al. Chemical Physics of Surfaces, Catalysis & Membranes. (International Journal of Quantum Chemistry Ser.: Supplement 2). 1978. pap. 21.95 (ISBN 0-471-05247-7, Pub. by Wiley-Interscience). Wiley.

--Quantum Chemistry: A Scientific Melting Pot. (International Journal of Quantum Chemistry Ser.: Vol. 12, Suppl.). 1978. 37.95 (ISBN 0-471-05248-5, Pub. by Wiley-Interscience). Wiley.

Lowe, jt. auth. see Seaborne.

Lowe, A. The Path of Economic Growth. LC 75-38186. (Illus.). 1976. 44.50 (ISBN 0-521-20888-2). Cambridge U Pr.

Lowe, Alfonso. The Culture & History of the Spanish. 1977. pap. 5.95 o.p. (ISBN 0-86033-050-8). Gordon-Cremonesi.

--The Spanish. 1976. 16.95 o.p. (ISBN 0-86033-006-0). Gordon-Cremonesi.

Lowe, Benjamin. The Beauty of Sport: A Cross-Disciplinary Inquiry. (Illus.). 1977. 14.95 (ISBN 0-13-066589-4). P-H.

Lowe, Brian. Hunting the Clean Boot: The Working Bloodhound. (Illus.). 240p. 1981. 22.50 (ISBN 0-7137-0950-2). Sterling.

Lowe, C. J. & Dockrill, M. L. The Mirage of Power, British Foreign Policy. Incl. Vol. 1. 1902-1914. 13.95x (ISBN 0-7100-7092-6); Vol. 2. 1914-1922. 18.00x (ISBN 0-7100-7093-4); Vol. 3. The Documents. 24.00x (ISBN 0-7100-7094-2). (Foreign Policies of the Great Powers Ser). 1972. Set. 50.00 (ISBN 0-685-25614-6). Routledge & Kegan.

Lowe, C. R., jt. auth. see McKeown, Thomas.

Lowe, C. W. Project Control by Critical Pathanalysis: A Basic Guide of CPA. 258p. 1978. text ed. 30.75x (ISBN 0-220-67012-9, Pub. by Busn Bks England). Renouf.

Lowe, Carl. New Alignments in American Politics. (Reference Shelf Ser.). 1980. 6.25 (ISBN 0-8242-0636-3). Wilson.

Lowe, Charles H., Jr. Arizona's Natural Environment: Landscapes & Habitats. 136p. 1972. pap. 3.95x (ISBN 0-8165-0349-4). U of Ariz Pr.

Lowe, Charles H., Jr., ed. The Vertebrates of Arizona: With Major Section on Arizona Habitats. LC 63-11981. 1964. pap. 5.95x (ISBN 0-8165-0348-6). U of Ariz Pr.

Lowe, Chuan-Hua. Facing Labor Issues in China. (Studies in Chinese History & Civilization). 1977. Repr. of 1938 ed. 17.50 (ISBN 0-89093-082-1). U Pubns Amer.

Lowe, D. Transport Manager's Handbook: United Kingdom 1980. 1979. 20.00 (ISBN 0-686-60661-2, Pub. by Kogan Pg). Nichols Pub.

Lowe, David, tr. see Annenkov, Yury.

Lowe, Elizabeth. Coping with Recurring Dreams & Nightmares. 1980. 1.50 (ISBN 0-686-28864-5). Dreams Unltd.

--Dreams & Spiritual Experiences. 1980. 1.50 (ISBN 0-686-28863-7). Dreams Unltd.

--How to Understand Dreams. 1979. 1.50 (ISBN 0-686-28862-9). Dreams Unltd.

Lowe, F. R. Milking Machines: A Comprehensive Guide for Farmers, Herdsmen & Students. (Illus.). 200p. 1981. 30.00 (ISBN 0-08-024381-9); pap. 15.00 (ISBN 0-08-024382-7). Pergamon.

Lowe, H., jt. auth. see McDonald, A. C.

Lowe, J. F., jt. auth. see Atkins, M. H.

Lowe, J. J., et al, eds. Studies in the Lateglacial of North-West Europe: Including Papers Presented at a Symposium of the Quaternary Research Association Held at University College London, January 1979. (Illus.). 215p. 1980. 44.00 (ISBN 0-08-024001-1). Pergamon.

Lowe, Jacqueline & Selber, Charles. The Language of Show Dancing. LC 80-10751. (Illus.). (gr. 5 up). 1980. 9.95 (ISBN 0-684-16431-0). Scribner.

Lowe, Jeff. The Ice Experience. 1979. 12.95 o.p. (ISBN 0-8092-7512-0); pap. 6.95 (ISBN 0-8092-7511-2). Contemp Bks.

Lowe, Jim & Taylor, Curtis B. Network. LC 75-44360. 304p. (Orig.). 1976. pap. 1.75 o.p. (ISBN 0-345-24970-4). Ballantine.

Lowe, John C. & Moryadas, S. Spatial Interaction: The Geography of Movement. 1975. text ed. 21.95 (ISBN 0-395-18584-X). HM.

Lowe, Joseph D. Dictionary of Military Terms: Chinese-English, English-Chinese. LC 76-7063. 1977. 50.00x (ISBN 0-89158-032-8). Westview.

Lowe, N. The Lancashire Textile Industry in the Sixteenth Century. 132p. 1972. 33.00x (ISBN 0-7190-1156-6, Pub. by Manchester U Pr England). State Mutual Bk.

Lowe, Pardee, Jr., tr. from Icelandic. King Harald & the Icelanders: Five Icelandic Stories. (Illus.). 1979. 12.00 (ISBN 0-915778-21-1); deluxe ed. 40.00x deluxe ed (ISBN 0-915778-22-X). Penmaen Pr.

Lowe, Patricia T., tr. see Pushkin, Alexander.

Lowe, Paul. Investment for Production: Managing the Plant Investment Process. LC 79-143. 1979. 29.95x (ISBN 0-470-26646-5). Halsted Pr.

Lowe, Percival G. Five Years a Dragoon ('49 to '54) And Other Adventures on the Great Plains. 1965. pap. 7.95 o.p. (ISBN 0-8061-1089-9). U of Okla Pr.

Lowe, Peter. Great Britain & the Origins of the Pacific War: A Study of British Policy in East Asia, 1937 to 1941. (Illus.). 330p. 1977. text ed. 39.00x (ISBN 0-19-822427-3). Oxford U Pr.

Lowe, Peter G. Classical Theory of Structures. (Illus.). 1971. 40.75 (ISBN 0-521-08089-4). Cambridge U Pr.

Lowe, Robert C. State Public Welfare Legislation. LC 75-165602. (FDR & the Era of the New Deal Ser.). 1971. Repr. of 1939 ed. lib. bdg. 37.50 (ISBN 0-306-70352-1). Da Capo.

Lowe, Robert W. Bibliographical Account of English Theatrical Literature. LC 66-27665. 1966. Repr. of 1888 ed. 22.00 (ISBN 0-8103-3216-7). Gale.

Lowe, Roger. The Diary of Roger Lowe of Ashton-in-Makerfield, Lancashire Sixteen Sixty-Three to Sixteen Seventy-Four. Sachse, W. L., ed. 1938. 27.50 (ISBN 0-686-51372-X). Elliots Bks.

Lowe, Stephen, jt. auth. see Robinson, J. F.

Lowe, Susan, jt. auth. see Campbell, Judy.

Lowe, Walter J. Mystery & the Unconscious: A Study in the Thought of Paul Ricoeur. LC 76-44865. (ATLA Monograph: No. 9). 1977. 10.00 (ISBN 0-8108-0989-3). Scarecrow.

Lowe, William C. Introduction to Acupuncture Anesthesia. 1973. 6.00 o.p. (ISBN 0-87488-753-4). Med Exam.

Lowell, Amy. Poetry & Poets. LC 77-162298. 1971. Repr. of 1930 ed. 10.50x (ISBN 0-8196-0274-4). Biblo.

Lowell, Cym H., jt. auth. see Weistart, John C.

Lowell, Elaine. This Time Forever. 256p. (YA) 1972. 5.95 (ISBN 0-685-27367-9, Avalon). Bouregy.

Lowell, Maria. The Poems of Maria Lowell, with Unpublished Letters & a Biography. Vernon, Hope J., ed. (Brown University Studies: No. 2). (Illus.). 187p. 1936. 7.50x (ISBN 0-87057-015-3, Pub. by Brown U Pr). Univ Pr of New England.

Lowell, Mark, jt. auth. see Potter, Jack.

Lowell, Mildred H. Library Management Cases. LC 75-23077. 1975. 10.00 (ISBN 0-8108-0845-5). Scarecrow.

--The Management of Libraries & Information Centers, 3 vols. Incl. Vol. 1. The Case Method in Teaching Library Management. 10.00 (ISBN 0-8108-0089-6); Vol. 2. The Process of Managing: Syllabus & Cases. 12.00 (ISBN 0-8108-0090-X); Vol. 4. Role Playing & Other Management Cases. 1971. 16.50 (ISBN 0-8108-0424-7). LC 68-12642. (Illus.). 1968. Scarecrow.

Lowell, Robert. Life Studies & For the Union Dead. 72p. 1967. pap. 3.95 (ISBN 0-374-50628-0, N329). FS&G.

Lowell, Robert see Raban, Jonathan.

Lowell, Robert, tr. Orestia of Aeschylus. 129p. 1978. 8.95 (ISBN 0-374-22723-3); pap. 6.95 (ISBN 0-374-51549-2). FS&G.

Lowell, Robert & Lowell, Robert, trs. from Fr. Racine's Phaedre. 213p. 1961. pap. 4.95 (ISBN 0-374-50911-5, N403). FS&G.

Lowell, Royal. Boatbuilding Down East: How to Build the Maine Lobsterboat. LC 76-52309. (Illus.). 1977. 20.00 (ISBN 0-87742-088-2). Intl Marine.

Lowell, S. Introduction to Powder Surface Area. LC 79-15878. 1979. 22.95 (ISBN 0-471-04771-6, Pub. by Wiley-Interscience). Wiley.

Lowe-McConnell, R. H., jt. ed. see Le Cren, E. D.

Lowe-McConnell, Rosemary. Fish Communities in Tropical Freshwaters. LC 74-75103. (Tropical Ecology Ser). Orig. Title: Ecology of Tropical Fish. (Illus.). 200p. (Orig.). 1975. 28.00x o.p. (ISBN 0-582-44348-2). Longman.

Lowen, Alexander. Betrayal of the Body. 1969. pap. 2.95 (ISBN 0-02-077300-5, Collier). Macmillan.

--Pleasure: A Creative Approach to Life. 1975. pap. 3.50 (ISBN 0-14-004033-1). Penguin.

Lowen, Walter. You & Your Job. rev. ed. 1962. pap. 0.95 o.s.i. (ISBN 0-02-080620-5, Collier). Macmillan.

Lowenberg, J. & Moskow, M. Collective Bargaining in Government: Readings & Cases. (Illus.). 1972. pap. text ed. 12.95 (ISBN 0-13-140483-0). P-H.

Lowenbraun, Sheila, et al. Teaching the Hearing Impaired. (Special Education Ser.). 224p. 1980. text ed. 14.95 (ISBN 0-675-08199-8). Merrill.

Lowenfeld, Berthold. The Changing Status of the Blind: From Separation to Integration. 352p. 1975. 31.75 (ISBN 0-398-03189-4). C C Thomas.

--Our Blind Children: Growing & Learning with Them. 3rd ed. (Illus.). 260p. 1977. 17.75 (ISBN 0-398-02200-3); pap. 11.75 (ISBN 0-398-03688-8). C C Thomas.

Lowenfeld, Berthold, ed. The Visually Handicapped Child in School. LC 72-12303. (John Day Bk.). 448p. 1973. 16.00 o.s.i. (ISBN 0-381-97097-3, TYC-T). T Y Crowell.

Lowenfeld, Berthold, et al. Blind Children Learn to Read. 196p. 1974. pap. 9.75 (ISBN 0-398-03205-X). C C Thomas.

Lowenfeld, V. Your Child & His Art. 1954. 8.95 o.s.i. (ISBN 0-02-575900-0). Macmillan.

Lowenheim, Frederick A. & Moran, Marguerite K. Faith, Keyes, & Clark's Industrial Chemicals. 4th ed. LC 75-17951. 904p. 1975. 74.95 (ISBN 0-471-54964-9, Pub. by Wiley-Interscience). Wiley.

Lowenherz, Lila, jt. auth. see Lowenherz, Robert J.

Lowenherz, Robert J. Population. Liberty, Gene, ed. LC 74-104928. (Creative Understanding Bks). (Illus.). (gr. 5-9). 1970. PLB 7.95 (ISBN 0-87191-042-X). Creative Ed.

Lowenherz, Robert J. & Lowenherz, Lila. Americans of Dream & Deed. (Orig.). (gr. 7-8). 1981. pap. text ed. 7.08 (ISBN 0-87720-397-0). AMSCO Sch.

Lowenkopf, Anne N., ed. see Schutz, Albert L.

Lowens, Irving. Bibliography of Songsters Printed in America Before Eighteen Twenty-One. LC 75-5021. 1976. 19.95x (ISBN 0-912296-05-4, Dist. by U Pr of Va). Am Antiquarian.

--Haydn in America. LC 79-92140. (Bibliographies in American Music Ser.: No. 5). 1980. 11.50 (ISBN 0-911772-99-5). Info Coord.

Lowenstein, Dino. Graphs. rev. ed. (First Bks.). (Illus.). 72p. (gr. 5 up). 1976. PLB 6.45 (ISBN 0-531-00679-4). Watts.

Lowenstein, Dyno. The First Book of Graphs. rev. ed. (First Bks.). (Illus.). 72p. (gr. 5 up). 1976. PLB 6.45 (ISBN 0-531-00679-4). Watts.

Lowenstein, Janet, jt. ed. see Julian, Alfred C.

Lowenstein, O., ed. Advances in Comparative Physiology & Biochemistry. Incl. Vol. 5. 1974. 40.50 (ISBN 0-12-011505-0); Vol. 6. 1975. 42.50 (ISBN 0-12-011506-9); lib. ed. 52.00 (ISBN 0-12-011574-3); microfiche 29.00 (ISBN 0-12-011575-1). Acad Pr.
--Advances in Comparative Physiology & Biochemistry, Vol. 7. 1978. 42.50 (ISBN 0-12-011507-7); lib. ed. 54.00 (ISBN 0-12-001576-5); microfiche 31.00 (ISBN 0-12-011577-8). Acad Pr.
Lowenstein, O. E., ed. Advances in Comparative Physiology & Biochemistry, Vols. 1-4. 52.50 ea. Vol. 1, 1962 (ISBN 0-12-011501-8). Vol. 2 (ISBN 0-12-011502-6). Vol. 3. o.s.i (ISBN 0-12-011503-4). Vol. 4, 1971 (ISBN 0-12-011504-2). Acad Pr.
Lowenstein, Ralph L., jt. auth. see Merrill, John C.
Lowenthal, Abraham F., et al. A New Treaty for Panama? (AEI Defense Review). 1.50 (ISBN 0-8447-1325-2). Am Enterprise.
Lowenthal, David & Bowden, Martyn J., eds. Geographies of the Mind: Essays in Historical Geosophy in Honor of John Kirtland Wright. (Illus.). 288p. 1976. text ed. 9.95x (ISBN 0-19-501970-9). Oxford U Pr.
Lowenthal, Joan. The All-Thumbs Color-Blind Book of Interior Decorating. (Illus.). 1977. 6.95 o.p. (ISBN 0-8092-7259-8). Contemp Bks.
Lowenthal, Mark M. Crispan Magicker. 1978. pap. 1.95 (ISBN 0-380-42333-2, 42333). Avon.
Lower, Mark A. English Surnames, 2 Vols. 4th ed. LC 68-22037. 1968. Repr. of 1875 ed. Set. 20.00 (ISBN 0-8103-3129-2). Gale.
Lowerre, George F. Critical Reading, Workbook B: Reusable Edition. (gr. 3-8). 1973. wkbk. 5.00 (ISBN 0-89039-072-X). Ann Arbor Pubs.
--Critical Reading: Workbook C Reusable Edition. (gr. 3-8). 1973. wkbk. 5.50 (ISBN 0-89039-074-6). Ann Arbor Pubs.
Lowerre, George F. & Scandure, Alice M. Critical Reading: Workbook A Reusable Edition. (gr. 3-8). 1973. 4.50 (ISBN 0-89039-070-3); tchrs' manual 2.00 (ISBN 0-686-67915-6). Ann Arbor Pubs.
--Critical Reading: Workbook D, Reusable Edition. (gr. 3-8). 1973. wkbk. 5.00 (ISBN 0-89039-076-2). Ann Arbor Pubs.
Lowers, James K. Shaw's Plays: Man & Superman Notes & Caesar & Cleopatra Notes. 1964. pap. 1.95 (ISBN 0-8220-0808-4). Cliffs.
Lowerson, John & Myerscough, John. Time to Spare in Victorian England. 1977. text ed. 13.00x (ISBN 0-391-00744-0). Humanities.
Lowery, Barbara. Mammals. (Easy-Read Fact Book Ser.). (Illus.). 48p. (gr. 2-4). 1976. PLB 4.47 o.p. (ISBN 0-531-01215-8). Watts.
--Oil. (Easy-Read Fact Bks.). (Illus.). 48p. (gr. 2-4). 1977. PLB 6.45 (ISBN 0-531-00357-4). Watts.
Lowery, Bruce. Scarred. LC 61-15476. 1961. 6.95 (ISBN 0-8149-0147-6). Vanguard.
--Werewolf. LC 72-139981. 1969. 7.95 (ISBN 0-8149-0669-9). Vanguard.
Lowery, H. Guide to Musical Acoustics. 1956. 6.95 (ISBN 0-234-77220-4). Dufour.
Lowery, Joan, jt. auth. see Nixon, Hershell H.
Lowery, Marilyn. The Reluctant Duke. (Orig.). 1981. pap. 1.50 (ISBN 0-440-17234-9). Dell.
Lowery, Mike. Masks of the Dreamer. LC 79-65336. (Wesleyan Poetry Program: Vol. 96). 1979. 10.00x (ISBN 0-8195-2096-9, Pub. by Wesleyan U Pr); pap. 4.95 (ISBN 0-8195-1096-3). Columbia U Pr.
Lowery, Robert. Robert Lowery: Radical & Chartist. Harrison, Brian & Hollis, Patrica, eds. LC 80-472644. (Illus.). 283p. 1979. 35.00x (ISBN 0-905118-31-6). Intl Pubns Serv.
Lowery, Robert G. Essays on Sean O'Casey's Autobiographies: Reflections Upon the Mirror. 1981. text ed. 22.50x (ISBN 0-06-494392-5). B&N.
Lowery, Robert G., ed. see Atkinson, Brooks.
Lowery, Robert G., jt. ed. see Krause, David.
Lowi, Theodore J. At the Pleasure of the Mayor. LC 64-11216. 1964. 12.95 (ISBN 0-02-919420-2). Free Pr.
Lowie, Robert H. Robert H. Lowie, Ethnologist: A Personal Record. (Illus.). 1959. 22.75x (ISBN 0-520-00775-1). U of Cal Pr.
Lowie, Robert H., tr. see Nimuendaju, Curt.
Lowinsky, Edward E., ed. Josquin Des Prez. (Illus.). 1977. incl. 3 seven inch discs 74.00x (ISBN 0-19-315229-0). Oxford U Pr.
Lowinson, Joyce & Ruiz, Pedro. Substance Abuse. (Illus.). 900p. 1981. write for info. (5210-1). Williams & Wilkins.
Lowitt, Richard. America in Depression & War. LC 73-810600. (Orig.). 1979. pap. text ed. 5.95x (ISBN 0-88273-022-3). Forum Pr MO.
Lowitt, Richard & Beasley, Maurine, eds. One Third of a Nation: Lorena Hickok Reports on the Great Depression. (Illus.). 450p. 1981. 18.95 (ISBN 0-252-00849-9). U of Ill Pr.
Lowman, Al see Lee, Amy F.
Lowman, Charles L., jt. auth. see Ellfeldt, Lois.
Lowman, J. Warren. Up from the Depths. 183p. 1926. pap. 3.00 (ISBN 0-917714-28-8). Beinfeld Pub.
Lowman, Joseph, et al. Predicting Achievement: A Ten-Year Followup of Black & White Adolescents. LC 80-17139. (IRSS Research Ser.). (Illus.). 102p. (Orig.). 1980. pap. text ed. 7.00 (ISBN 0-89143-100-4). U NC Inst Res Soc Sci.
Lowndes, D. Marketing: The Uses of Advertising. LC 72-97953. 1970. 19.50 (ISBN 0-08-006935-5); pap. 9.75 (ISBN 0-08-006934-7). Pergamon.
Lowndes, William T. Bibliographer's Manual of English Literature, 8 Vols. LC 66-28042. 1967. Repr. of 1864 ed. 135.00 (ISBN 0-8103-3217-5). Gale.
Lowney & Winslow. Deviant Reality: Alternative World Views. 2nd ed. 420p. 1980. pap. text ed. 10.95 (ISBN 0-205-07243-7, 8172439). Allyn.
Lowney, Paul B. The Big Book of Gleeb. (Illus.). 160p. 1975. 4.95 o.p. (ISBN 0-396-07223-2). Dodd.
Lowrey, Janette S. Poky Little Puppy. (Illus.). (gr. 1-3). 1942. 1.95 (ISBN 0-307-10418-4, Golden Pr); PLB 7.62 (ISBN 0-307-60418-7). Western Pub.
Lowrey, Lawson G. Psychiatry for Social Workers. 2nd ed. LC 50-8887. 1950. 20.00x (ISBN 0-231-01768-5). Columbia U Pr.
Lowrey, Paul B. The Best in OffBeat Humor. 1968. 2.95 (ISBN 0-442-82144-1). Peter Pauper.
Lowrie, Jean E. Elementary School Libraries. 2nd ed. LC 71-9962. 1970. 10.00 (ISBN 0-8108-0305-4). Scarecrow.
--School Libraries: International Developments. LC 72-3440. 1972. 10.00 (ISBN 0-8108-0505-7). Scarecrow.
Lowrie, W., tr. see Kierkegaard, Soren.
Lowrie, Walter. Art in the Early Church. rev. ed. 11.00 (ISBN 0-8446-2492-6). Peter Smith.
Lowry, Albert J. How to Become Financially Successful by Owning Your Own Business. 1981. 11.95 (ISBN 0-671-41261-2). S&S.
Lowry, B. Visual Experience. 1975. pap. 13.95 (ISBN 0-13-942490-3). P-H.
Lowry, Beverly. Come Back, Lolly Ray. 1978. pap. 1.95 o.p. (ISBN 0-445-04216-8). Popular Lib.
Lowry, Eugene. The Homiletical Plot: The Sermon As Narrative Art Form. LC 79-92074. 100p. (Orig.). 1980. pap. 3.95 (ISBN 0-8042-1652-5). John Knox.
Lowry, Gertrude S. The Wheel of Truth: An Ancestral Saga. (Illus.). 1977. 15.00 o.p. (ISBN 0-682-48886-0, University). Exposition.
Lowry, H. F., ed. see Arnold, Matthew.
Lowry, H. H. The Chemistry of Coal Utilization, Vols. 1 & 2. LC 45-5498. 1945. Set. 69.50 (ISBN 0-471-02494-5, Pub. by Wiley-Interscience); suppl. vol. (1963) 80.00 (ISBN 0-471-55158-9). Wiley.
Lowry, James. The Logical Principles of Proclus' As Systematic Ground of the Cosmos. (Elementa Ser.: No. 13). 118p. 1980. text ed. 17.25x (ISBN 90-6203-781-X). Humanities.
Lowry, Lois. Anastasia Krupnik. (Skylark Ser.). 128p. 1981. pap. cancelled (ISBN 0-686-69197-0). Bantam.
--Find a Stranger, Say Goodbye. (YA) (gr. 7-9). 1979. pap. 1.75 (ISBN 0-671-29999-9). PB.
--Find a Stranger, Say Goodbye. (gr. 7-9). 1979. pap. 1.95 (ISBN 0-671-42062-3). Archway.
Lowry, Lynn. Charmaine. 432p. (Orig.). 1981. pap. 2.75 (ISBN 0-553-14150-3). Bantam.
Lowry, M. J. The World of Aldus Manutius: Business & Scholarship in Renaissance Venice. LC 78-58631. (Illus.). 1979. 36.50x (ISBN 0-8014-1214-5). Cornell U Pr.
Lowry, Michael R. Preventing Mental Depression. 300p. 1981. 22.50 (ISBN 0-87527-186-3). Green.
Lowry, Richard. Evolution of Psychological Theory: 1650 to the Present. LC 70-116540. 1971. 14.95x (ISBN 0-202-25061-X). Aldine Pub.
Lowry, Ritchie P. & Rankin, Robert P. Sociology: Social Science & Social Concerns. 3rd ed. 1977. text ed. 16.95x (ISBN 0-669-99648-3); instructor's manual free (ISBN 0-669-03186-0); study guide 5.95x (ISBN 0-669-00339-5). Heath.
Lowry, S. M., et al. Time & Motion Study & Formulas for Wage Incentives. 3rd ed. LC 80-12407. 446p. 1981. Repr. of 1940 ed. write for info. (ISBN 0-89874-174-2, Pub. by McGraw). Krieger.
Lowry, T. Martin. Optical Rotatory Power. 1935. pap. 5.00 o.p. (ISBN 0-486-61197-3). Dover.
Lowry, Thomas P., ed. Camping Therapy, Its Use in Psychiatry & Rehabilitation. 160p. 1974. 11.75 (ISBN 0-398-02898-2). C C Thomas.
--The Classic Clitoris. LC 78-18298. (Illus.). 1978. text ed. 15.95 (ISBN 0-88229-387-7). Nelson-Hall.
Lowry, Timothy S. Rock Springs: Sodom & Gomorrah in America. LC 80-29293. (Illus.). 224p. 1981. 11.95 (ISBN 0-8253-0044-4). Beaufort Bks NY.
Lowry, William P. Weather & Life: An Introduction to Biometeorology. 1969. text ed. 17.95 (ISBN 0-12-457750-4); ans. bklet. 3.00 (ISBN 0-12-457756-3). Acad Pr.
Lowther, H. An Introduction to Organic Chemistry. 1964. text ed. 11.25 (ISBN 0-08-010819-9); pap. text ed. 5.75 (ISBN 0-08-010818-0). Pergamon.
Lowther, Kenneth, jt. ed. see Hammond, Reginald J.
Lowther, Kenneth E., ed. see Hammond, Reginald J.
Lowther, Kevin & Lucas, C. Payne. Keeping Kennedy's Promise: The Peace Corps: Unmet Hope of the New Frontier. LC 77-21187. 1978. 18.00x (ISBN 0-89158-422-6). Westview.
Lowy, George. A Searcher's Manual. 1965. 10.00 (ISBN 0-208-00789-X); pap. 6.50 (ISBN 0-686-68498-2). Shoe String.
Lowy, Louis. Social Policies & Programs on Aging. LC 78-55355. 1980. 21.95x (ISBN 0-669-02342-6). Lexington Bks.
Loxton, Howard. Guide to Cats of the World. (Illustrated Natural History Guides). (Illus.). 1977. pap. 4.95 (ISBN 0-8467-0366-1, Pub. by Two Continents). Hippocrene Bks.
Loxton, John. Practical Map Protection. LC 80-40118. 1980. 24.95 (ISBN 0-471-27782-7, Pub. by Wiley-Interscience); pap. 14.50 (ISBN 0-471-27783-5). Wiley.
Loy, John W., jt. auth. see Ball, Donald W.
Loy, John W., et al. Sport & Social Systems. (Social Significance of Sport Ser.). (Illus.). 1978. text ed. 17.95 (ISBN 0-201-04143-X). A-W.
Loy, Mira. The Last Lunar Baedeker: The Poems of Mira Loy. 1981. 25.00 (ISBN 0-912330-46-5, Dist by Gromon Press). Jargon Soc.
Loyen, Frances. The Thames & Hudson Manual of Silversmithing: The Constructional Processes. 1980. pap. 9.95 (ISBN 0-500-68021-3). Thames Hudson.
Lozaneo, Mary B., et al. Plants of Big Basin Redwooods State Park & the Northern Coastal Mountains of California. (Illus.). 160p. (Orig.). 1981. pap. 6.95 (ISBN 0-87842-135-1). Mountain Pr.
Lozano, Argentina D. And We Have to Live (y Tenemos Que Vivir) Sears, Lillian, tr. from Span. LC 78-59598. 1978. softcover 6.00 (ISBN 0-89430-032-6). Morgan-Pacific.
Lozano, Wendy. She Who Was King. 384p. 1980. pap. 2.50 (ISBN 0-345-28638-3). Ballantine.
Lozina-Lozinskii, L. K. Studies in Cryobiology. Harry, P., tr. from Rus. LC 74-8277. (Illus.). 259p. 1974. 44.95 (ISBN 0-470-54347-7). Halsted Pr.
Lozowick, Louis. William Gropper. (Illus.). 200p. 1981. 40.00 (ISBN 0-87982-033-0). Art Alliance.
Lozoya, Jorge & Estevez, Jaime, eds. Latin America & the New International Economic Order. LC 79-27384. (Pergamon Policy Studies in the New International Economic Order). 112p. 1980. 16.50 (ISBN 0-08-025118-8). Pergamon.
Lozoya, Jorge, et al. Alternative Views of the New International Economic Order: A Survey & Analysis of Major Academic Research Reports. (Pergamon Policy Studies). 1980. 20.00 (ISBN 0-08-024644-3). Pergamon.
Lozzio, Bismarck B. see Bourne, G. H. & Danielli, J. F.
Lozzio, Carmen see Bourne, G. H. & Danielli, J. F.
Lu, Gwei-Djen & Needham, J. Celestial Lancets: History & Rationale of Acupuncture & Moxa. LC 79-41734. (Illus.). 400p. 1980. 97.50 (ISBN 0-521-21513-7). Cambridge U Pr.
Lu, Y. C. Singularity Theory & Introduction to Catastrophe Theory. LC 76-48307. (Illus.). 1976. soft cover 16.80 (ISBN 0-387-90221-X). Springer-Verlag.
Lu, Yu. The Old Man Who Does As He Pleases. Watson, Burton, tr. from Chinese. (Translations from the Oriental Classics Ser). (Illus.). 128p. 1973. 12.50x (ISBN 0-231-03766-X). Columbia U Pr.
Luard, Evan. Types of International Society. LC 75-43173. 1976. 19.95 (ISBN 0-02-919450-4). Free Pr.
Luard, Nicholas. The Robespierre Serial. 1976. pap. 1.75 o.p. (ISBN 0-345-24902-X). Ballantine.
--The Shadow Spy. 1980. pap. 2.25 (ISBN 0-345-28789-4). Ballantine.
Lubachko, Ivan S. Belorussia Under Soviet Rule, Nineteen Seventeen to Nineteen Fifty-Seven. LC 79-160047. (Illus.). 240p. 1972. 13.00x (ISBN 0-8131-1263-X). U Pr of Ky.
Lubbock, Adelaide. People in Glass Houses: Growing up at Government House. 1978. 19.95 (ISBN 0-241-10059-3, Pub. by Hamish Hamilton England). David & Charles.
Lubbock, Sir John. A Contribution to Our Knowledge of Seedlings, 2 vols. (Landmark Reprints in Plant Science Ser.). 1978. Vol. 1. text ed. 29.50 (ISBN 0-86598-008-X); Vol. 2. text ed. 29.50 (ISBN 0-86598-025-X). Allanheld.
Lubec, G., ed. The Glomerular Basement Membrane. (Renal Physiology: Vol. 3, No. 1-6). (Illus.). viii, 434p. 1981. pap. write for info. (ISBN 3-8055-2398-X). S Karger.
Lubell, Cecil, jt. auth. see Lubell, Winifred.
Lubell, Samuel. The Future While It Happened. 162p. 1973. pap. 2.95x (ISBN 0-393-09321-2). Norton.
--Hidden Crisis in American Politics. LC 69-17630. 1971. 5.95 (ISBN 0-393-05370-9); pap. text ed. 4.95x (ISBN 0-393-09886-9, NortonC). Norton.
Lubell, Winifred & Lubell, Cecil. Street Markets Around the World. LC 74-805. (Finding-Out Book). (Illus.). 64p. (gr. 2-4). 1974. PLB 6.95 (ISBN 0-8193-0732-7). Enslow Pubs.
Lubic, Lowell G. & Palkovitz, Harry P. Stroke. (Discussions in Patient Management Ser.). 1979. pap. 9.50 (ISBN 0-87488-893-X). Med Exam.
Lubich, Chiara. A Little "Harmless" Manifesto: An Essay on the Spirituality of the Focolare Movement Based Upon Its Experiences. LC 72-97595. 1973. pap. 0.95 o.p. (ISBN 0-911782-17-6). New City.
--Meditations. LC 74-79452. 1974. pap. 1.95 (ISBN 0-911782-20-6). New City.
--Words to Live By. Moran, Hugh, ed. Dauphinais, Raymond, tr. from Fr. & Ital. LC 80-82419. Orig. Title: Paroles Pour Vivre. 160p. (Orig.). 1980. pap. 4.50 (ISBN 0-911782-08-7). New City.
Lubicz, Isha S. De see De Lubicz, Isha S.
Lubin, Bernard, et al, eds. Organizational Change Sourcebook I: Cases in Organization Development. LC 79-63006. 230p. 1979. pap. 12.95 (ISBN 0-88390-150-1). Univ Assocs.
Lubin, George. Handbook of Fiberglass & Advanced Plastics Composites. LC 75-1316. 912p. (Orig.). 1975. Repr. of 1969 ed. 44.00 (ISBN 0-88275-286-3). Krieger.
Lubin, Isador, jt. auth. see Hill, Arthur C.
Lubin, Leonard. The Elegant Beast. LC 80-52645. (Illus.). 48p. 1981. pap. 10.95 (ISBN 0-670-29097-1, Studio). Viking Pr.
Lubis, Mochtar. Twilight in Djakarta. Holt, Claire, tr. LC 64-16196. 1964. 7.95 (ISBN 0-8149-0148-4). Vanguard.
Lubkoll, Hans-Georg & Wiesnet, Eugen. Getting to Know Your Bible. Scheidt, David L., tr. from Ger. LC 75-34527. (Illus.). 64p. 1976. pap. 1.95 (ISBN 0-8006-1217-5, 1-1217). Fortress.
Lubliner, Jerry & Bednarski, Mary W. An Introduction to Medical Malpractice. (Learning Packages in Policy Issues: No. 1). 52p. 1976. pap. text ed. 3.00 (ISBN 0-936826-10-X). Pol Stud Assocs.
Lublinskaya, Alexandra D. French Absolutism: The Crucial Phase, 1620-1629. (Illus.). 1968. 44.50 (ISBN 0-521-07117-8). Cambridge U Pr.
Lubon, Miroslan, tr. see Jankowski, Stanislaw & Rafalski, Piotr.
Lubove, Roy. Professional Altruist: The Emergence of Social Work As a Career, 1880-1930. LC 65-12786. 1969. pap. text ed. 4.95x (ISBN 0-689-70130-6, 142). Atheneum.
Lubowe, Irwin I. & Huss, Barbara. A Teen-Age Guide to Healthy Skin & Hair. rev. ed. 1979. 12.50 o.p. (ISBN 0-87690-335-9); pap. 6.95 (ISBN 0-87690-334-0). Dutton.
Lubrano, Linda L. & Solomon, Susan G., eds. The Social Context of Soviet Science. (Special Studies on the Soviet Union & Eastern Europe). 1980. lib. bdg. 25.00x (ISBN 0-89158-450-1). Westview.
Lubs, Herbert & Cruz, Felix de la, eds. Genetic Counseling. LC 76-52601. 1977. 37.50 (ISBN 0-89004-150-4). Raven.
Luby, Barry J., jt. auth. see Brown, Robert B.
Luby, Sue. Hatha Yoga for Total Health: Handbook of Practical Programs. (Illus.). 1977. pap. 13.50 (ISBN 0-13-384123-5). P-H.
Luca, Stuart M. De see De Luca, Stuart M.
Lucafo, Rosemarie, jt. auth. see Hoemann, Harry W.
Lucano, James. Head Hunters. 320p. 1980. pap. 2.25 (ISBN 0-345-28529-8). Ballantine.
Lucas. First Science Dictionary: English with Arabic Glossary. 9.95x (ISBN 0-686-65474-9). Intl Bk Ctr.
Lucas, Alan. Illustrated Encyclopedia of Boating. LC 78-9809. (Illus.). 1978. 12.95 o.p. (ISBN 0-684-15900-7, ScribT). Scribner.
Lucas, Alec. Peter McArthur. (World Authors Ser.: Canada: No. 363). 1975. lib. bdg. 12.50 (ISBN 0-8057-6214-0). Twayne.
Lucas, Barbara, tr. see Lanzmann, Claude.
Lucas, Barbara, tr. see Lindgren, Astrid.
Lucas, Bryan K. & Richards, Peter G. A History of Local Government in the 20th Century. (New Local Government Ser.). 1978. text ed. 25.00x (ISBN 0-04-352070-7); pap. text ed. 9.95x (ISBN 0-04-352071-5). Allen Unwin.

Lucas, C. Payne, jt. auth. see Lowther, Kevin.

Lucas, Carol. Recreational Activity Development for the Aging in Homes, Hospitals, & Nursing Homes. (Illus.). 68p. 1978. pap. 5.75 (ISBN 0-398-03058-8). C C Thomas.

Lucas, Carol, jt. auth. see Rathbone, Josephine.

Lucas, Catherine, jt. auth. see Cunnington, Phillis.

Lucas, Christopher. Tiki & the Dolphin: The Adventures of a Boy in Tahiti. LC 74-76441. (gr. 4-6). 1974. 6.95 (ISBN 0-8149-0741-5). Vanguard.

Lucas, Christopher J. Challenge & Choice in Contemporary Education. (Illus.). 1976. text ed. 9.25 (ISBN 0-02-372180-4). Macmillan.

Lucas, Colin R. The Structure of the Terror. (Oxford Historical Monographs). 1973. 42.00x (ISBN 0-19-821843-5). Oxford U Pr.

Lucas, David G., jt. auth. see Hartlage, Lawrence C.

Lucas, Donna. Towards Reconstruction of an un-Paired Random Sample. 115p. 1979. pap. 3.60 (1252). U of NC Pr.

Lucas, Dorothy, jt. auth. see Hegarty, Seamus.

Lucas, E. V. The Gentlest Art. 422p. 1981. Repr. of 1913 ed. lib. bdg. 25.00 (ISBN 0-89987-509-2). Darby Bks.

Lucas, Ellyn. Semantic & Pragmatic Language Disorders: Assessment & Remediation. 250p. 1980. text ed. 21.95 (ISBN 0-89443-327-X). Aspen Systems.

Lucas, Ethel G., jt. auth. see Mansfield, Evelyn A.

Lucas, F. L. Tragedy: Serious Drama in Relation to Aristotle's "Poetics". rev. & enl. ed. 1981. pap. 5.95x (ISBN 0-389-20141-3). B&N.

Lucas, George. American Graffiti. 1979. pap. 1.75 (ISBN 0-394-17072-5, B373, BC). Grove.

Lucas, George L. Examination of the Hand. (Illus.). 248p. 1972. text ed. 19.75 (ISBN 0-398-02347-6). C C Thomas.

Lucas, George R. Two Views of Freedom in Process & Thought. LC 79-12287. (American Academy of Religion, Dissertation Ser.: No. 28). 1979. 12.00 (ISBN 0-89130-285-9, 010128); pap. 7.50 (ISBN 0-89130-304-9). Scholars Pr Ca.

Lucas, Glenn E. Effects of Anisotrophy & Irradiation on the Creep Behavior of Zircaloy-2. LC 78-75012. (Outstanding Dissertations on Energy Ser.). 1979. lib. bdg. 35.00 (ISBN 0-8240-3987-4). Garland Pub.

Lucas, Harold. Computers in Management & Business Studies. 2nd ed. (Illus., Orig.). 1979. pap. text ed. 19.95x (ISBN 0-7121-0390-2, Pub. by Macdonald & Evans England). Intl Ideas.

Lucas, Harry. Pensions & Industrial Relations: A Practical Guide for All Involved in Pensions. 1977. text ed. 26.00 (ISBN 0-08-021947-0); pap. text ed. 11.25 (ISBN 0-08-021946-2). Pergamon.

Lucas, Henry & Gibson, Cyrusf. Casebook for Management Information Systems. 2nd ed. (Management Information Systems Ser.). (Illus.). 480p. 1980. pap. text ed. 10.95 (ISBN 0-07-038939-X, C) (ISBN 0-686-68691-8). McGraw.

Lucas, Henry C. The Analysis, Design & Implementation of Information Systems. rev. ed. (Management Information Systems Ser.). (Illus.). 416p. 1981. text ed. 23.95 (ISBN 0-07-038927-6, C); instructor's manual 9.95 (ISBN 0-07-038928-4). McGraw.

--Computer-Based Information Systems in Organizations. LC 72-92561. (Illus.). 292p. 1973. text ed. 16.95 (ISBN 0-574-18590-9, 13-1590); instr's guide avail. (ISBN 0-574-18591-7, 13-1591). SRA.

--Toward Creative Systems Design. LC 74-4129. 1974. text ed. 15.00x (ISBN 0-231-03791-0). Columbia U Pr.

Lucas, Henry C., Jr. Implementation: The Key to Successful Information Systems. LC 80-27009. 224p. 1981. 30.00x (ISBN 0-231-04434-8). Columbia U Pr.

--Why Information Systems Fail. LC 74-18395. 144p. 1975. 12.50x (ISBN 0-231-03792-9). Columbia U Pr.

Lucas, J. A., jt. auth. see Dickinson, C. H.

Lucas, Jack. Our Polluted Food: A Survey of the Risks. LC 75-8700. 237p. 1975. 19.95 (ISBN 0-470-55285-9). Halsted Pr.

Lucas, Jay P. & Adams, Russell E., eds. Personal Computing: Proceedings. (Illus.). viii, 439p. 1979. pap. 12.00 (ISBN 0-88283-020-1). AFIPS Pr.

Lucas, Jerry & Lorayne, Harry. The Memory Book. 224p. 1975. pap. 1.95 (ISBN 0-345-27808-9). Ballantine.

Lucas, Jerry & Washburn, Del. Theomatics: God's Best Kept Secret Revealed. LC 76-49958. (Illus.). 1977. 8.95 (ISBN 0-8128-2181-5); pap. 6.95 (ISBN 0-8128-6017-9). Stein & Day.

Lucas, John. The Literature of Change: Studies in the Nineteenth Century Provincial Novel. 2nd ed. 217p. 1980. 20.00x (ISBN 0-389-20020-4); pap. 11.50x (ISBN 0-389-20021-2). B&N.

--The Melancholy Man: A Study of Dickens' Novels. 2nd ed. (Illus.). 375p. 1980. 20.00x (ISBN 0-389-20033-6). B&N.

Lucas, John, ed. see Austen, Jane.

Lucas, Katherine & Lucas, Louise. Hometown, U. S. A. (Illus., Orig.). 1980. pap. 4.95 (ISBN 0-914634-75-5, 8001). DOK Pubs.

Lucas, Katherine & Lucas, Louse. Who Owns the Unicorn. (Illus., Orig.). (gr. 4-12). 1980. pap. text ed. 3.95 (ISBN 0-914634-69-0, 7918). DOK Pubs.

Lucas, Louise, jt. auth. see Lucas, Katherine.

Lucas, Louse, jt. auth. see Lucas, Katherine.

Lucas, Lydia A., compiled by. Manuscripts Collections of the Minnesota Historical Society Guide, No. 3. LC 35-27911. 189p. 1977. pap. 7.00 (ISBN 0-87351-120-4). Minn Hist.

Lucas, N. J., ed. Local Energy Centres. (Illus.). 1978. text ed. 42.60x (ISBN 0-85334-782-4). Intl Ideas.

Lucas, Norm. Money Sermons. 94p. (Orig.). 1980. pap. text ed. 4.65 (ISBN 0-89536-457-3). CSS Pub.

Lucas, Paul R. Valley of Discord: Church & Society along the Connecticut River, 1636-1725. LC 75-22520. (Illus.). 288p. 1976. text ed. 15.00x (ISBN 0-87451-121-6). U Pr of New Eng.

Lucas, R. J. Fulness & Freedom. Motyer, J. A. & Stott, J. R., eds. LC 79-3635. (The Bible Speaks Today Ser.). 1980. pap. 4.95 (ISBN 0-87784-602-2). Inter-Varsity.

Lucas, Rex A. Minetown, Milltown, Railtown: Life in Canadian Communities of Single Industry. LC 70-166934. 1971. pap. 7.95 (ISBN 0-8020-6123-0). U of Toronto Pr.

Lucas, Robert E., Jr. & Sargent, Thomas J., eds. Rational Expectations & Econometric Practice. 672p. 1981. 35.00x (ISBN 0-8166-0916-0); pap. 14.95x (ISBN 0-8166-0917-9). U of Minn Pr.

Lucas, Ronald J. Pension Planning Within a Major Company. 1979. 35.00 (ISBN 0-08-024045-3). Pergamon.

Lucas, St. John & Dionisotti, C., eds. Oxford Book of Italian Verse, Thirteenth Century to Nineteenth Century. 1952. 24.95 (ISBN 0-19-812116-4). Oxford U Pr.

Lucas, St. John & Jones, P. M., eds. Oxford Book of French Verse, Thirteenth Century to Twentieth Century. 2nd ed. (Fr). 1957. 24.95 (ISBN 0-19-812109-1). Oxford U Pr.

Lucas, Spencer & Rigby, Keith, Jr., eds. Advances in San Juan Basin Paleontology. 440p. 1981. 27.50x (ISBN 0-8263-0554-7). U of NM Pr.

Lucas, Ted. How to Build a Solar Heater. rev. ed. 1980. pap. 6.95 (ISBN 0-517-54056-8, Michelman Books). Crown.

Lucas, Ted & Riess, Fred. How to Convert to an Electric Car. (Illus.). 192p. 1980. 10.00 (ISBN 0-517-54055-X); pap. 5.95 (ISBN 0-517-53990-X). Crown.

Lucas, Thomas E. Elder Olson. (U. S. Authors Ser.: No. 188). lib. bdg. 10.95 (ISBN 0-8057-0568-6). Twayne.

Lucas, Virginia H., et al. Kindergarten Program. (Illus.). 1980. pupil bk. 2.97 (ISBN 0-88309-101-1); tchr's guide 4.97 (ISBN 0-88309-102-X). Zaner-Bloser.

Lucchesi, Mario. Dizionario Medico Ragionato Inglese-Italiano: Termini, Abbreviazioni, Sigle, Eponimi e Sinonimi Medici, Medico-Biologici e Delle Specializzazionni Mediche. 1490p. 1978. 98.00x (ISBN 0-913298-52-2). S F Vanni.

Lucchi, Lorna De, tr. Anthology of Italian Poems, 13th-19th Century. LC 66-30496. (Eng. & Ital.). 1922. 14.00x (ISBN 0-8196-0198-5). Biblo.

Lucci, Jennie A. Occupational Therapy Case Studies. 2nd ed. 1980. pap. 14.00 (ISBN 0-87488-034-3). Med Exam.

Luccock, Halford E. American Mirror: Social, Ethical & Religious Aspects of American Literature, 1930-1940. LC 75-156806. 1971. Repr. of 1940 ed. lib. bdg. 27.50x (ISBN 0-8154-0385-2). Cooper Sq.

--Contemporary American Literature & Religion. 300p. 1980. Repr. of 1934 ed. lib. bdg. 30.00 (ISBN 0-89984-324-7). Century Bookbindery.

--In the Minister's Workshop. (Notable Books on Preaching). 1977. pap. 3.95 o.p. (ISBN 0-8010-5571-7). Baker Bk.

--A Sprig of Holly. new ed. Hartman, Charles S., ed. & intro. by. LC 78-17096. 64p. 1978. text ed. 3.50 (ISBN 0-8298-0354-8). Pilgrim NY.

Luccock, Robert E. Preaching Through Matthew. LC 80-12575. 240p. (Orig.). 1980. pap. 8.95 (ISBN 0-687-33908-1). Abingdon.

Luce, A., jt. tr. see Lund, A.

Luce, A. A. Berkeley & Malebranche: A Study in the Origins of Berkeley's Thought. 1934. 24.50x (ISBN 0-19-824319-7). Oxford U Pr.

--Logic. (Teach Yourself Ser.). 1975. pap. 2.95 o.p. (ISBN 0-679-10435-6). McKay.

Luce, Alice, tr. Mesajero y Su Mensaje. (Spanish Bks.). 1980. 1.25 (ISBN 0-8297-0582-1). Life Pubs Intl.

Luce, Alice A., tr. Evidencias Cristianas. (Spanish Bks.). (Span.). 1978. 1.25 (ISBN 0-8297-0554-6). Life Pubs Intl.

Luce, Gay G. Biological Rhythms in Human & Animal Physiology. Orig. Title: Biological Rhythms in Psychiatry & Medicine. 1971. Repr. of 1970 ed. pap. text ed. 4.00 (ISBN 0-486-22586-0). Dover.

Luce, Robert. Legislative Assemblies. LC 73-5617. (American Constitutional & Legal History Ser.). 692p. 1974. Repr. of 1924 ed. lib. bdg. 59.50 (ISBN 0-306-70583-4). Da Capo.

--Legislative Principles. LC 77-148083. (American Constitutional & Legal History Ser). 1971. Repr. of 1930 ed. lib. bdg. 59.50 (ISBN 0-306-70144-8). Da Capo.

--Legislative Problems. LC 76-152834. (American Constitutional & Legal History Ser). 1971. Repr. of 1935 ed. lib. bdg. 59.50 (ISBN 0-306-70153-7). Da Capo.

--Legislative Procedure. LC 72-6113. (American Constitutional & Legal History Ser). 640p. 1972. Repr. of 1922 ed. lib. bdg. 59.50 (ISBN 0-306-70522-2). Da Capo.

Luce, Robert D. & Raiffa, H. Games & Decisions: Introduction & Critical Survey. LC 57-12295. 1957. 27.95 (ISBN 0-471-55341-7). Wiley.

Lucey, jt. auth. see Clifton.

Luchene, Stephen R. Van see Van Luchene, Stephen R.

Luchins, Abraham S. & Luchins, Edith H. Revisting Wertheimer's Seminars, 2 vols. Incl. Vol. 1. Value, Social Influence, & Power (ISBN 0-8387-1227-4); Vol. 2. Problems in Social Psychology (ISBN 0-8387-1570-2). LC 72-3525. 1978. Set. 65.00 (ISBN 0-8387-1570-2); 32.50 ea. Bucknell U Pr.

Luchins, Edith H., jt. auth. see Luchins, Abraham S.

Luchka, Anton Y. Method of Averaging Functional Corrections: Theory & Applications. (Orig.). 1965. 22.00 o.p. (ISBN 0-12-458150-1). Acad Pr.

Luchs, Alison, tr. see Wackernagel, Martin.

Luchs, Allison. Cestello: A Cistercian Church of the Florentine Renaissance. LC 76-23642. (Outstanding Dissertations in the Fine Arts - 2nd Series - 15th Century). (Illus.). 1977. Repr. lib. bdg. 63.00 (ISBN 0-8240-2706-X). Garland Pub.

Luchs, Esther M. Yoga for Children. LC 77-7268. 1977. pap. 4.95 (ISBN 0-8091-2023-2). Paulist Pr.

Luchsinger, Richard & Arnold, Godfrey E. Voice-Speech-Language: Clinical Communicology - Its Physiology & Pathology. 1965. 34.95x (ISBN 0-534-00680-9). Wadsworth Pub.

Lucia, Ellis. Saga of Ben Holladay. 1959. 9.95 (ISBN 0-8038-6641-0). Hastings.

Lucia, Sr. Lucia Speaks: Memoirs & Letters of Sister Lucia. 272p. 1977. pap. 3.00 o.p. (ISBN 0-911988-04-1). AMI Pr.

Luciani, Vince. Amateur Radio: Super Hobby! LC 80-51260. (Illus.). 144p. 1981. 14.95x (ISBN 0-9602310-2-1); pap. 8.95x (ISBN 0-9602310-1-3). Cologne Pr.

Luciani, Vincent. Italian Idioms with Proverbs. 1964. 6.95 (ISBN 0-913298-15-8). S F Vanni.

Luciani, Vincent, ed. Betti: Corruzione Al Palazzo di Giustizia. 1980. pap. 4.95 (ISBN 0-913298-20-4). S F Vanni.

--Goldoni: La Locandiera. 1980. pap. 4.95 (ISBN 0-913298-18-2). S F Vanni.

Luciani, Vincent, tr. see De Beaumarchais, Pierre.

Luciano & Mayo, Gene. Stained Glass Home Studio Guide. (Illus.). 72p. 1981. pap. 4.95 (ISBN 0-8256-3844-5, Hidden Hse-Flash). Music Sales.

Luciano, Dorothy S., et al. Human Function & Structure. (Illus.). 1978. text ed. 19.95 (ISBN 0-07-038942-X, C); study guide 6.95 (ISBN 0-07-038944-6); inst's manual 5.95 (ISBN 0-07-038943-8). McGraw.

Lucier, Alvin & Simon, Douglas. Chambers. 173p. 1980. 15.00x (ISBN 0-8195-5042-6, Pub. by Wesleyan U Pr). Columbia U Pr.

Lucie-Smith, Edward. Art in the Seventies. (Illus.). 128p. 1980. 29.95 (ISBN 0-8014-1328-1); pap. 14.95 (ISBN 0-8014-9194-0). Cornell U Pr.

--A Concise History of French Painting. (World of Art Ser). (Illus.). 1978. pap. 9.95 (ISBN 0-19-520003-9). Oxford U Pr.

--Eroticism in Western Art. (World of Art Ser.). (Illus.). 1972. pap. 9.95 (ISBN 0-19-519946-4). Oxford U Pr.

--Furniture: A Concise History. (World of Art Ser.). (Illus.). 1979. 17.95 (ISBN 0-19-520145-0); pap. 9.95 (ISBN 0-19-520146-9). Oxford U Pr.

--Late Modern: The Visual Arts Since 1945. (World of Art Ser.). (Illus.). 1975. pap. 9.95 (ISBN 0-19-519938-3). Oxford U Pr.

--Symbolist Art. (World of Art Ser.). (Illus.). 1972. pap. 9.95 (ISBN 0-19-519947-2). Oxford U Pr.

--Thinking About Art. 1980. pap. 4.95 (ISBN 0-7145-0553-6). Riverrun NY.

Lucio-Meyer, J. De see De Lucio-Meyer, J.

Luciw, Wasyl. Ahapius Honcharenko & the Alaska Hearald: The Editor's Life & an Analysis of His Newspaper. LC 65-923. pap. text ed. 6.00 (ISBN 0-918884-10-1). Slavia Lib.

--Album Ex Medicorum: 115 American & European Book Plates. 1961. 15.00 o.p. (ISBN 0-685-89026-0). Slavia Lib.

--Het'man Ivan Mazepa. LC 59-19855. (Ukra.). 1954. text ed. 6.00 (ISBN 0-685-89027-9). Slavia Lib.

--Mandrivka U Viky. (Shkil'na Biblioteka). (Ukra.). 1970. pap. text ed. 6.00 (ISBN 0-685-89030-9). Slavia Lib.

--Pedahohichna Pratsia D-Ra Ivan Franke. (Ob'ednania Ukrains'kykh Pedahohiv U Kanadi). (Ukra.). 1956. pap. text ed. 1.50 (ISBN 0-918884-06-3). Slavia Lib.

--Pedahohichna Pratsia Tarasa Shevchenka. (Ob'ednannia Ukrains'kykj Pedahohiv U Kanadi). (Ukra.). 1959. pap. text ed. 1.50 (ISBN 0-918884-07-1). Slavia Lib.

--Slovo Pedahoha. LC 75-541045. (Seriia Shkil'na Biblioteka). (Ukra.). 1971. pap. text ed. 8.00 (ISBN 0-918884-01-2). Slavia Lib.

--Tvortsi Netlinnoi Krasy. (Ukra.). 1972. pap. text ed. 6.00 (ISBN 0-918884-05-5). Slavia Lib.

--Ukrainians & the Polish Revolt of 1863: A Contribution to the History of Ukrainian-Polish Relations. LC 62-67800. 1961. pap. text ed. 2.00 o.p. (ISBN 0-918884-08-X). Slavia Lib.

Luck, David J. & Ferrell, O. C. Marketing Strategy & Plans. (Illus.). 1979. ref. ed. 19.95 (ISBN 0-13-558254-7). P-H.

Luck, Edward C., jt. ed. see Albert, Stuart.

Luck, Gordon. A Guide to Practical Speech Training. 1979. 8.50 o.p. (ISBN 0-214-20036-1, 8033, Dist. by Arco). Barrie & Jenkins.

Luckau, Alma. The German Delegation at the Paris Peace Conference. LC 70-80569. 1971. Repr. 25.00 (ISBN 0-86527-078-3). Fertig.

Luckey, Carl. Old Fishing Lures & Tackle: A Collectors Identification & Value Guide. (Illus.). pap. 14.95 (ISBN 0-686-51464-5). Wallace-Homestead.

Luckey, T. D. Hormesis with Ionizing Radiation. 288p. 1980. 69.95 (ISBN 0-8493-5841-8). CRC Pr.

Luckey, T. D. & Venugopal, B. Metal Toxicity in Mammals. Incl. Vol. 1. Physiologic & Chemical Basis for Metal Toxicity. 238p. 29.50 (ISBN 0-306-37176-6); Vol. 2. Chemical Toxicity of Metals & Metalloids. 419p. 35.00 (ISBN 0-306-37177-4). (Illus.). 1977 (Plenum Pr). Plenum Pub.

Luckham, Robin. Nigerian Military: A Sociological Analysis of Authority & Revolt, 1960-67. (African Studies: No. 4). (Illus.). 1971. 39.95 (ISBN 0-521-08129-7); pap. 11.95x (ISBN 0-521-09882-3). Cambridge U Pr.

Luckhardt, C. G., tr. see Wittgenstein, Ludwig.

Luckiesh, M. Visual Illusions: Their Causes, Characteristics & Applications. (Illus.). 8.50 (ISBN 0-8446-0780-0). Peter Smith.

Lucking, Richard C. Mathematics for Management. LC 80-40127. 1980. 52.00 (ISBN 0-471-27779-7, Pub. by Wiley-Interscience); pap. write for info. (ISBN 0-471-27781-9). Wiley.

Luckner, M., ed. see FEBS Meeting, 12th, Dresden, 1978.

Luckock. Simon de Montfort: Reformer & Rebel. 3.38 (ISBN 0-08-008757-4). Pergamon.

Luckyj, G. S., ed. Shevchenko & the Critics, Eighteen Sixty-One to Nineteen Seventy-Eight. 1981. 30.00x (ISBN 0-8020-2346-0); pap. 8.50 (ISBN 0-8020-6377-2). U of Toronto Pr.

Luckyj, George S., tr. see Kulish, Mykola.

Luckyj, George S., tr. see Kulish, Panteleimon.

Luckyj, George S., tr. see Pidmohylny, Valerian.

Luckyj, George S., tr. see Sverstiuk, Ievhen.

Luckyj, Moira, tr. see Kulish, Panteleimon.

Lucovsky, et al. The Physics of MOS Insulators. 400p. 1980. 50.00 (ISBN 0-08-025969-3). Pergamon.

Lucretius. De Rerum Natura. Kenney, Ed, ed. (Cambridge Greek & Latin Classics Ser.: Bk. 3). 34.50 (ISBN 0-521-08142-4); pap. 11.95x (ISBN 0-521-29177-1). Cambridge U Pr.

--De Rerum Natura, Bk. 5. Duff, James D., ed. text ed. 4.50x (ISBN 0-521-05610-1). Cambridge U Pr.

--On Nature. Geer, Russel M., tr. LC 63-12204. (Orig.). 1965. pap. 5.95 (ISBN 0-672-60355-1, LLA142). Bobbs.

Lucy, Reda, pseud. The Lord's Prayer for Children. (Illus.). 24p. (Orig.). (ps-3). 1981. pap. 1.95 (ISBN 0-87516-437-4). De Vorss.

Lucy, Sean. Unfinished Sequence & Other Poems. 63p. 1980. pap. text ed. 5.25x (ISBN 0-905473-38-8). Humanities.

Ludel, Jacqueline. Introduction to Sensory Processes. LC 77-16785. (Psychology Ser.). (Illus.). 1978. text ed. 21.95x (ISBN 0-7167-0032-8); pap. text ed. 12.95 (ISBN 0-7167-0031-X). W H Freeman.

Ludeman, Annette. History of la Salle County, Texas. (Illus.). 300p. 1975. 17.95 (ISBN 0-89015-100-8). Nortex Pr.

Ludeman, Annette M. Pioneering in the Faith. 6.95 (ISBN 0-685-48819-5). Nortex Pr.

Luderer, Albert & Weetall, Howard, eds. Clinical Cellular Immunology. (Contemporary Immunology Ser.). (Illus.). 1981. 44.50 (ISBN 0-89603-011-3). Humana.

Ludins, George H. Seamanship for New Skippers. (Illus.). 1980. pap. 5.95 (ISBN 0-916224-54-6). Banyan Bks.

Ludlam, James E. Informed Consent. LC 78-24495. 96p. (Orig.). 1978. 8.75 (ISBN 0-87258-243-4, 1160). Am Hospital.

Ludlow, Edmund. A Voyce from the Watch Tower: Part Five, 1660-1662. Worden, A. B., ed. (Royal Historical Society: Camden Society Fourth Ser.: Vol. 21). 370p. 1980. 20.00x (ISBN 0-8476-3308-X). Rowman.

Ludlow, Norman H., Jr. Clip Book Number Eleven: Communicate the Action. (Illus.). 64p. (Orig.). 1980. pap. 13.95 (ISBN 0-916706-22-2). N H Ludlow.

Ludlum, Robert. The Bourne Identity. 544p. 1981. pap. 3.75 (ISBN 0-553-14300-X). Bantam.

Ludowyk, Evelyn F. Understanding Shakespeare. 1962. 32.50 (ISBN 0-521-05611-X); pap. 9.95x (ISBN 0-521-09242-6). Cambridge U Pr.

Luds, Peter, jt. auth. see Apel, Max.

Ludvigsen, Karl. Mercedes-Benz Racing Cars. (Illus.). 1971. 35.00 (ISBN 0-87880-009-3). Norton.

Ludvigsen, Karl, jt. auth. see Christy, John.

Ludvigsen, Karl, ed. The Best of Corvette News. LC 76-20955. 1976. 42.50 (ISBN 0-915038-07-2); leather bdg. 57.95 (ISBN 0-915038-20-X). Princeton Pub.

--Porsche: Excellence Was Expected. LC 77-83507. 1977. text ed. 64.95 (ISBN 0-915038-09-9). Princeton Pub.

Ludvik, J., ed. Progress in Protozoology. (Illus.). 1964. 62.50 (ISBN 0-12-459450-6). Acad Pr.

Ludwig & Bernal. California Story & Coloring Book. (Illus.). 32p. (Orig.). pap. 2.50 (ISBN 0-930504-01-1). Polaris Pr.

Ludwig & Santibanez. Mexican American Coloring Book. (Illus.). 32p. (gr. 4 up). pap. 2.50 (ISBN 0-930504-00-3). Polaris Pr.

Ludwig, Charles. At the Cross. 1975. pap. 1.25 (ISBN 0-515-03578-5). Jove Pubns.

--Sankey Still Sings. (Christian Biography Ser.). 176p. 1981. pap. 2.95 (ISBN 0-8010-5601-2). Baker Bk.

--Their Finest Hour. LC 74-82112. (Illus.). 128p. (Orig.). 1975. pap. 1.95 o.p. (ISBN 0-912692-45-6). Cook.

Ludwig, Edward W. The Chinese American Story. (Illus.). 32p. (Orig.). (gr. 4-12). 1981. pap. 2.95 (ISBN 0-930504-02-X). Polaris Pr. Postponed.

Ludwig, G. Wave Mechanics. 1968. 28.00 (ISBN 0-08-012302-3); pap. 10.75 (ISBN 0-08-012303-1). Pergamon.

Ludwig, Jan K., ed. Philosophy & Parapsychology. LC 77-91852. 454p. 1978. 16.95 (ISBN 0-87975-075-8); pap. 8.95 (ISBN 0-87975-076-6). Prometheus Bks.

Ludwig, Jerry. Little Boy Lost. 1977. 7.95 o.p. (ISBN 0-440-04796-X). Delacorte.

Ludwig, Myles, jt. auth. see Smyth, Frank.

Ludwig, Oswald A. & McCarthy, Willard J. Metalwork Technology & Practice. rev. & 5th ed. (Illus.). (gr. 11-12). 1975. text ed. 17.28 (ISBN 0-87345-117-1); study guide 5.00 (ISBN 0-87345-118-X); ans key avail. (ISBN 0-685-04228-6). McKnight.

Ludwig, Rita T., jt. auth. see Hoffman, Herbert H.

Ludwigson. Notes on Prophecy. pap. 2.95 o.p. (ISBN 0-686-12897-4). Schmul Pub Co.

Ludwigson, Kathryn R. Edward Dowden. (English Authors Ser.: No. 148). lib. bdg. 10.95 (ISBN 0-8057-1164-3). Twayne.

Ludwin, William G., jt. ed. see Worthley, John A.

Ludz, Peter C., et al. Dilemmas of the Atlantic Alliance: Two Germanys, Scandinavia, Canada, Nato & the EEC. LC 75-25737. (Atlantic Institute Studies: No. 1). 1975. text ed. 25.95 (ISBN 0-275-01490-8). Praeger.

Luebbers, D. W., ed. Progress in Enzyme & Ion-Selective Electrodes. (Illus.). 240p. 1981. pap. 34.30 (ISBN 0-387-10499-2). Springer-Verlag.

Luebering, Carol. To Comfort All Who Mourn: A Parish Handbook for Ministry to the Grieving. LC 80-82555. 112p. (Orig.). 1980. pap. 4.95 (ISBN 0-934134-07-3, Celebration Bks). Natl Cath Reporter.

Luebke, Frederick C., ed. Ethnic Voters & the Election of Lincoln. LC 72-139370. xxxii, 226p. 1971. 13.95x (ISBN 0-8032-0796-4); pap. 3.25x (ISBN 0-8032-5738-4, BB 567, Bison). U of Nebr Pr.

--Ethnicity on the Great Plains. LC 79-17743. (Illus.). xxxiv, 237p. 1980. 15.95x (ISBN 0-8032-2855-4). U of Nebr Pr.

Lueck, E. Antimicrobial Food Additives: Characteristics, Uses, Effects. (Illus.). 280p. 1980. 39.80 (ISBN 0-387-10056-3). Springer-Verlag.

Luecke, K., jt. ed. see Gottstein, G.

Luedke, Martin, jt. ed. see Lindner, Burkhardt.

Luedke, Ralph D., jt. ed. see Kuse, James.

Luedtke, Helmut, ed. Kommunikationstheoretische Grundlagen des Sprachwandels. (Grundlagen der Kommunikation). 280p. 1979. text ed. 58.00x (ISBN 3-11-007271-8). De Gruyter.

Luenberger, D. G. Optimization by Vector Space Methods. (Series in Decision & Control). 1969. 29.95 (ISBN 0-471-55359-X, Pub. by Wiley-Interscience). Wiley.

Luenberger, David G. Introduction to Dynamic Systems: Theory, Models & Applications. LC 78-12366. 1979. 24.95 (ISBN 0-471-02594-1); solutions manual avail. (ISBN 0-471-06081-X). Wiley.

--Introduction to Linear & Nonlinear Programming. LC 72-186209. 1973. text ed. 19.50 (ISBN 0-201-04347-5). A-W.

Lueneburg, H., ed. Translation Planes. 256p. 1980. 29.80 (ISBN 0-387-09614-0). Springer-Verlag.

Luening, Otto. The Odyssey of an American Composer. (Illus.). 1980. 22.50 (ISBN 0-684-16496-5, ScribT). Scribner.

Luer, Carlyle A. A Guide to Field Identification of Native Orchids of the U.S. & Canada. condensed ed. 1981. 15.95 (ISBN 0-8120-5191-2); pap. 10.95 (ISBN 0-8120-0933-9). Barron. Postponed.

Luetscher, G. D. Early Political Machinery in the United States. LC 70-155356. (Studies in American History & Government Ser.). 1971. Repr. of 1903 ed. lib. bdg. 20.00 (ISBN 0-306-70187-1). Da Capo.

Luetzelschwab, John. Household Energy Use & Conservation: How to Prepare an Energy Budget. 1980. 19.95x (ISBN 0-88229-476-8); pap. 11.95 (ISBN 0-88229-733-3). Nelson-Hall.

Lufburrow, Bill. The Most Honest People. LC 80-69253. (Illus., Orig.). 1980. pap. 4.95 (ISBN 0-918464-23-4). D Armstrong.

Luff, John N. The Postage Stamps of the United States. LC 80-54039. 320p. 1981. Repr. of 1940 ed. lib. bdg. 35.00 (ISBN 0-88000-121-6). Quarterman.

Luffman, George A., jt. auth. see Newbould, Gerald D.

Lufkin, Milton T. Henry, a Man of Aroostook: Pioneer in Northern Maine. LC 76-8088. (Illus.). 1976. 10.00 o.p. (ISBN 0-87027-173-3). Wheelwright.

Luft, Harold S. Health Maintenance Organization: Dimensions of Performance. LC 80-22420. (Health, Medicine & Society Ser.). 412p. 1981. 25.00 (ISBN 0-471-01695-0, Pub. by Wiley-Interscience). Wiley.

Luft, Joseph. Group Processes: An Introduction to Group Dynamics. 2nd ed. LC 76-107365. 1970. pap. 4.95 (ISBN 0-87484-146-1). Mayfield Pub.

Luft, R., jt. ed. see Levine, R.

Luftig, Milton. Computer Programmer: Analyst Trainee. 4th ed. LC 74-82865. (Illus., Orig.). 1975. o. p. 10.00 (ISBN 0-668-01344-3); pap. 8.00 (ISBN 0-668-01232-3). Arco.

Lugard, Frederick J. Political Memoranda: Revision of Instruction to Political Officers on Subjects Chiefly Political & Administrative, 1913-1918. 3rd rev. ed. 480p. 1970. 35.00x (ISBN 0-7146-1693-1, F Cass Co). Biblio Dist.

Lugenbeal, Edward. Who Killed Adam? A Look at the Major Types of Fossil Man. LC 78-8513. (Flame Ser.). 1978. pap. 0.95 (ISBN 0-8127-0186-0). Southern Pub.

Luger, Harriet. Chasing Trouble. (YA) (gr. 7-12). 1981. pap. price not set (ISBN 0-440-91568-6, LE). Dell.

Luger, Harriett. Lauren. (gr. 7-12). Date not set. pap. price not set (ISBN 0-440-94700-6, LE). Dell.

Lugg, George W. Religion? No! Good Living? Yes! LC 80-51444. 128p. (Orig.). 1980. pap. 3.95x (ISBN 0-935834-03-6). Rainbow-Betty.

Lugg, H. C., tr. see Fuze, M. M.

Lugones, Nestor, jt. ed. see Ramos-Garcia, Luis A.

Luh, B. S. & Woodroof, J. G. Commercial Vegetable Processing. (Illus.). 1975. text ed. 27.00 (ISBN 0-87055-186-8); pap. text ed. 19.00 o.p. (ISBN 0-87055-282-1). AVI.

Luh, B. S., jt. auth. see Woodroof, J. G.

Luh, Bor S. Rice: Production & Utilization. (Illus.). 1980. lib. bdg. 49.50 (ISBN 0-87055-332-1). AVI.

Luhan, Mabel L., et al. Three Fates in Taos. Moore, Harry T., ed. (Illus.). 228p. 1981. 20.00x (ISBN 0-933806-10-8). Black Swan CT.

Luhman, Reid & Gilman, Stuart. Race & Ethnic Relations: The Social & Political Experience of Minority Groups. 352p. 1980. pap. text ed. 12.95x (ISBN 0-534-00795-3). Wadsworth Pub.

Lu Hsun. Brief History of Chinese Fiction. 8.95 (ISBN 0-8351-0510-5). China Bks.

--Selected Stories. 3rd ed. 1972. 6.95 (ISBN 0-8351-0326-9); pap. 4.95 (ISBN 0-8351-0327-7). China Bks.

--Wild Grass. 1974. pap. 1.95 (ISBN 0-8351-0435-4). China Bks.

Lui, Adam Yuen-Chung. The Hanlin Academy: Training Ground for the Ambitious, 1644-1850. (Illus.). 1980. write for info. (ISBN 0-208-01833-6, Archon). Shoe String.

Luibheid, Colm. Eusebius of Caesarea & the Arian Crisis. 128p. 1981. 18.50x (ISBN 0-7165-2277-2, Pub. by Irish Academic Pr Ireland). Biblio Dist.

Luijpen, William A. What Can You Say About God? Except God. LC 76-171103. 1971. pap. 1.95 (ISBN 0-8091-1713-4). Paulist Pr.

Luikov, A. V. Analytical Heat Diffusion Theory. 1969. 43.50 (ISBN 0-12-459756-4). Acad Pr.

Luisada, Aldo A., et al. An Atlas of Non-Invasive Techniques: Sound & Pulse Tracings-Echograms. (Illus.). 568p. 1976. vinyl 45.75 (ISBN 0-398-03555-5). C C Thomas.

Luisi, Billie. Potworks: A First Book of Clay. (Illus.). 1973. 6.95 o.p. (ISBN 0-688-00157-2). Morrow.

Luk, Charles. The Vimalakirti Nirdesa Sutra. LC 71-189851. 1975. pap. 3.95 o.p. (ISBN 0-394-73065-8). Random.

Luk, Charles, tr. from Chinese. The Vimalakirti Nirdesa Sutra. LC 71-189851. 175p. 1981. pap. 5.95 (ISBN 0-87773-072-5). Great Eastern.

Luka, Ronald & Zlotowitz, Bernard. When a Christian & a Jew Marry. LC 73-77393. 96p. (Orig.). 1973. pap. 1.95 (ISBN 0-8091-1748-7). Paulist Pr.

Lukacs, Eugene. Probability & Mathematical Statistics: An Introduction. 1972. text ed. 19.95 (ISBN 0-12-459850-1). Acad Pr.

Lukacs, Georg. Essays on Realism. 1980. text ed. 26.00x (ISBN 0-391-02179-6). Humanities.

--Essays on Thomas Mann. Mitchell, Stanley, tr. from Ger. 1979. Repr. of 1965 ed. 16.50 (ISBN 0-86527-245-X). Fertig.

--Goethe & His Age. Anchor, Robert, tr. from Ger. 1978. Repr. of 1968 ed. 18.25 (ISBN 0-86527-256-5). Fertig.

Lukacs, John. Philadelphia: Patricians & Philistines 1900-1950. (Illus.). 1981. 15.00 (ISBN 0-374-23161-3). FS&G.

Lukan, Karl. Mountain Adventures. (International Library). (Illus.). 128p. (gr. 7 up). 1972. PLB 6.90 o.p. (ISBN 0-531-02110-6). Watts.

Lukas, Ellen, jt. auth. see Lukas, Mary.

Lukas, Mary & Lukas, Ellen. Teilhard. 360p. 1981. pap. 6.95 (ISBN 0-07-039047-9). McGraw.

Lukas, Richard C. From Metternich to the Beatles. 1973. pap. 1.95 o.p. (ISBN 0-451-61191-8, MJ1191, Ment). NAL.

--The Strange Allies: The United States & Poland, 1941-1945. LC 77-8585. 1978. 14.50x (ISBN 0-87049-229-2). U of Tenn Pr.

Lukas, Susan. Morgana's Fault. 228p. 1981. 10.95 (ISBN 0-399-12584-1). Putnam.

Lukash, William M. & Johnson, Raymond B., eds. The Systemic Manifestations of Inflammatory Bowel Disease. (Illus.). 368p. 1975. 21.75 (ISBN 0-398-03242-4). C C Thomas.

Lukasiewicz, J. Elements of Mathematical Logic. 2nd ed. (International Series in Pure & Applied Mathematics: Vol. 31). 1964. 12.10 o.p. (ISBN 0-08-010393-6); pap. 5.00 o.p. (ISBN 0-08-013695-8). Pergamon.

Luke, Barbara. Maternal Nutrition. 1980. text ed. 9.95 (ISBN 0-316-53610-5). Little.

Luke, Helen. Spirit Woman: The Spirirtuality of the Feminine in Symbol & Myth. 144p. 1981. 9.95 (ISBN 0-8245-0018-0). Crossroad NY.

Luke, Hugh J., ed. see Swinburne, Algernon C., Jr.

Luke, Hugh J., Jr., ed. see Shelley, Mary.

Luke, Peter. Under the Moorish Wall: Adventures in Andalusia. 176p. 1980. text ed. 18.75x (ISBN 0-85105-371-8, Dolmen Pr). Humanities.

Luke, Peter, ed. Enter Certain Players: Edwards, Mac Liammoir & the Gate 1928-1978. (Illus.). 1978. text ed. 26.00x (ISBN 0-85105-346-7, Dolmen Pr); pap. text ed. 9.25x (ISBN 0-85105-345-9). Humanities.

Luke, Timothy W., jt. auth. see Levine, Victor T.

Luke, Y. L., et al. Index to Mathematics of Computation, 1943-1969. 1972. 20.00 (ISBN 0-8218-4000-2, MCOMIN-1). Am Math.

Luke, Yudell L. Special Functions & Their Approximations, 2 Vols. LC 68-23498. (Mathematics in Science & Engineering Ser.,: Vol. 53). 1969. Vol. 1. 48.00 (ISBN 0-12-459901-X); Vol. 2. 55.00 (ISBN 0-12-459902-8). Acad Pr.

Lukeman, Tim. Koren. LC 79-7692. (Science Fiction Ser.). 192p. 1981. 9.95 (ISBN 0-385-15239-6). Doubleday.

Luken, Ralph A. Preservation Vs. Development: An Economic Analysis of San Francisco Bay Wetlands. LC 76-2907. (Special Studies). (Illus.). 150p. 1976. text ed. 24.95 (ISBN 0-275-56590-4). Praeger.

Lukens, Reaves C., Jr. The Appraiser & Real Estate Feasibility Studies. 1972. 5.00 (ISBN 0-911780-30-0). Am Inst Real Estate Appraisers.

Luker, Kristin. Taking Chances: Abortion & the Decision Not to Contracept. LC 74-22965. 200p. 1976. 10.95 o.p. (ISBN 0-520-02872-4); pap. 4.95 (ISBN 0-520-03594-1). U of Cal Pr.

Luker, Merville. They Came from the North. 1979. 5.95 o.p. (ISBN 0-8062-1157-1). Carlton.

Luker, Nicholas, ed. Russian Neo-Realism: An Anthology (the "Znanie" School of Writers) (Illus.). 1981. 20.00 (ISBN 0-88233-421-2); pap. 7.50 (ISBN 0-88233-422-0). Ardis Pubs.

Luker, Nicholas J. Alexander Kuprin. (World Authors Ser.: No. 481). 1978. lib. bdg. 12.50 (ISBN 0-8057-6322-8). Twayne.

Luker, William, et al. Hard Choices: The American Free Enterprise System at Work. (Illus.). (gr. 12). 1979. text ed. 9.95 (ISBN 0-88408-128-1); pap. text ed. 7.95 (ISBN 0-88408-123-0); tchrs.' manual avail. Sterling Swift.

Lukes, Edward A. De Witt Colony of Texas. LC 76-14583. (Illus.). 1976. 14.95 (ISBN 0-8363-0148-X). Jenkins.

Lukes, S. Development of the Sociology of Knowledge. (Studies in Sociology). 1980. pap. text ed. write for info. (ISBN 0-391-01130-8). Humanities.

Lukes, Steven. Essays in Social Theory. LC 77-8505. 1977. text ed. 17.50x (ISBN 0-231-04450-X). Columbia U Pr.

--Individualism. 1973. pap. text ed. 9.95x (ISBN 0-631-18750-2, Pub. by Basil Blackwell). Biblio Dist.

Lukman, Mphahlele K. The Critical Issues of Skin Colour: A Treatise on the Sociological, Economic & Political Reality of Blacks in a White Society. 125p. 1980. text ed. 10.50 (ISBN 0-9602660-0-3). M Lukman.

Lukoff, Herman. From Dits to Bits...a Personal History of the Electronic Computer. LC 79-90567. 200p. 1979. 14.95 (ISBN 0-89661-002-0). Robotics Pr.

Lukomsky, Genrikh I. Bronchology. LC 78-31431. (Illus.). 1979. 57.50 (ISBN 0-8016-3041-X). Mosby.

Lukovich, Istvan. Electric Foil Fencing. (Illus.). 1971. 16.50x (ISBN 0-392-05526-0, SpS). Soccer.

Lukowski, Susan & Grayson, Cary T., Jr., eds. State Information Book. 3rd, rev. ed. LC 73-80718. (Illus.). 310p. 1980. 18.50 (ISBN 0-87107-041-3). Potomac.

Luksa, Frank, jt. auth. see Staubach, Roger.

Lull, David J. The Spirit in Galatia: Paul's Interpretation of Pneuma As Divine Power. LC 79-26094. (Society of Biblical Literature Dissertation: No. 49). 13.50x (ISBN 0-89130-367-7, 06-01-49); pap. 9.00x (ISBN 0-89130-368-5). Scholars Pr CA.

Lull, Ramon. The Book of the Lover & the Beloved. Leech, Kenneth, ed. Peers, J. Allison, tr. LC 78-61666. (Spiritual Masters Ser.). 1978. pap. 2.95 (ISBN 0-8091-2135-2). Paulist Pr.

Lully, Jean B. Nine Seventeenth Century Organ Transcriptions from the Operas of Lully. Howell, Almonte C., Jr., ed. LC 62-19378. 1963. pap. 3.50x (ISBN 0-8131-1078-5). U Pr of Ky.

Lulow, JoAnn. Your Career in the Fashion Industry. LC 78-12724. (Arco Career Guidance Ser.). 1979. lib. bdg. 6.95 (ISBN 0-668-04613-9); pap. 3.50 (ISBN 0-668-04620-1). Arco.

Lum, Ada. How to Begin an Evangelistic Bible Study. pap. 1.95 (ISBN 0-87784-317-1). Inter-Varsity.

--Jesus the Life Changer. 40p. 1978. pap. 2.25 (ISBN 0-87784-316-3). Inter-Varsity.

Lum, Peter. Growth of Civilization in East Asia. LC 73-77311. (Illus.). (gr. 8 up). 1969. 10.95 (ISBN 0-87599-144-0). S G Phillips.

--Six Centuries in East Asia: China, Japan & Korea from the 14th Century to 1912. LC 72-12582. (Illus.). 288p. 1973. 10.95 (ISBN 0-87599-183-1). S G Phillips.

Lumb, Fred A. What Every Woman Should Know About Finances. LC 77-93504. 1978. 8.95 (ISBN 0-87863-148-8). Farnsworth Pub.

Lumbra, Elaine, ed. Hoosier Cookbook. LC 75-31420. (Illus.). 344p. 1976. 10.95x (ISBN 0-253-13865-5). Ind U Pr.

Lumbreras, Luis G. The Peoples & Cultures of Ancient Peru. LC 74-2104. (Illus.). 248p. 1974. 19.95 o.p. (ISBN 0-87474-151-3); pap. 9.95x (ISBN 0-87474-151-3). Smithsonian.

Lumby, Edmond W. The Transfer of Power in India: Nineteen Forty-Five to Nineteen Forty-Seven. LC 79-1634. 1981. Repr. of 1954 ed. 22.50 (ISBN 0-88355-938-2). Hyperion Conn.

Lumholtz, Carl. Among Cannibals. 1979. Repr. of 1888 ed. text ed. 26.00x (ISBN 0-904573-13-3). Humanities.

Lumiansky, R. M. Of Sondry Folk: The Dramatic Principles in the Canterbury Tales. (Illus.). 286p. 1980. pap. 6.95 (ISBN 0-292-76017-5). U of Tex Pr.

Lumley, Brian. The Clock of Dreams. 1978. pap. 1.75 o.s.i. (ISBN 0-685-86423-5). Jove Pubns.

--In the Moons of Borea. (Orig.). 1979. pap. 1.75 (ISBN 0-515-05125-X). Jove Pubns.

Lumley, Brian & McCauley, Kirby. Spawn of the Winds. 1978. pap. 1.75 o.s.i. (ISBN 0-515-04571-3). Jove Pubns.

Lumley, J. P., et al. Essential Anatomy. 3rd, rev. ed. (Illus.). 1981. pap. text ed. write for info. (ISBN 0-443-02003-5). Churchill.

Lumley, James E. Creative Sales Counseling: Using Psychology to Sell Real Estate. 1981. pap. 24.95 (ISBN 0-933928-04-1). Realvest Pub Co.

Lumley, Kay. District of Columbia. (Young People's Stories of Our States Ser.). (Illus.). 48p. (gr. 2-5). 1981. PLB 8.65g (ISBN 0-516-03951-2, Time Line). Childrens.

Lummis, Charles F. Land of Poco Tiempo. LC 66-22698. (Illus.). 1969. 8.95 o.p. (ISBN 0-8263-0070-7); pap. 5.95 (ISBN 0-8263-0071-5). U of NM Pr.

Lumpkin, Angela. Women's Tennis: A Historical Documentary. 200p. 1981. 15.00 (ISBN 0-87875-189-0). Whitston Pub.

Lumpkin, Katharine D. The Making of a Southerner. LC 80-24622. (Brown Thrasher Ser.). 264p. 1981. pap. 6.95 (ISBN 0-8203-0545-6). U of Ga Pr.

Lumpkin, Katharine Du Pre see Lumpkin, Katharine D.

Lumpkin, Thomas A. & Plucknett, Donald L. Azolla As an Aquatic Green Manure: Use & Management in Crop Production. (Tropical Agriculture Ser.: No. 15). 1981. lib. bdg. 22.50x (ISBN 0-89158-451-X). Westview.

Lumsden, jt. auth. see Attiyeh.

Lumsden, D. B., jt. ed. see Sherron, R. H.

Lumsden, E. S. Art of Etching. (Illus.). 8.50 (ISBN 0-8446-2497-7). Peter Smith.

Lumsden, Ian, ed. Close the Forty-Ninth Parallel Etc. The Americanization of Canada. LC 79-477171. 1970. pap. 6.50 (ISBN 0-8020-6111-7). U of Toronto Pr.

Lumsden, Robert J. Twenty-Three Steps to Success & Achievement. 1978. pap. 3.95 (ISBN 0-85454-024-5). Newcastle Pub.

Luna, David. The Lean Machine: David Luna's Guide to Total Fitness & the Sensible Diet. LC 79-89792. (Illus.). 131p. 1980. pap. 7.95 (ISBN 0-915238-34-9); 12.95 o.p. (ISBN 0-915238-36-5). Peace Pr.

Luna, Lee G., jt. auth. see Thompson, Samuel W., 2nd.

Luna, Roger M., tr. see Desramaut, Francis.

Lunar & Flanetary Science Conference, 9th, Houston, 1978. Proceedings, 3 vols. Lunar & Planetary Institute, Houston, Texas, compiled by. (Geochimica et Cosmochimicha Acta: Suppl. 10). 1979. Set. 245.00 (ISBN 0-08-022966-2). Pergamon.

Lunar & Planetary Institute, ed. The Ancient Sun: Proceedings of the Conference on the Ancient Sun: Fossil Record in the Earth, Moon & Meteorites, Boulder Colorado, October 16-19, 1979. LC 80-20084. (Geochimica & Cosmochimica Acta: Suppl. 13). 500p. 1980. 56.00 (ISBN 0-08-026324-0). Pergamon.

Lunar & Planetary Institute, compiled by. Proceedings: Eleventh Lunar & Planetary Science Conference, Houston, Texas, March 17-21, 1980, 3 vols. (Geochimica & Cosmochimica Acta: Suppl. 14). 3000p. 1981. Set. 200.00 (ISBN 0-08-026314-3). Pergamon.

Lunar & Planetary Institute, Houston, Texas, compiled by see Lunar & Flanetary Science Conference, 9th, Houston, 1978.

Lunar & Planetary Institute, Houston, Texas, ed. Mare Crisium: The View from Luna Twenty-Four. 733p. 1979. 49.00 (ISBN 0-08-022965-4). Pergamon.

Lunar & Planetary Science Conference, 10th, Houston, Texas, March 19-23, 1979. Proceedings. LC 79-22554. (Illus.). 3200p. 1980. 220.00 (ISBN 0-08-025128-5). Pergamon.

Lunar Science Conference, 8th, Houston, 1977. Proceedings. Lunar Science Institute, Houston, Texas, compiled by. (Lunar Science Ser.: No. 8). (Illus.). 1978. 255.00 (ISBN 0-08-022052-5). Pergamon.

Lunar Science Institute, Houston, Texas, compiled by see Lunar Science Conference, 8th, Houston, 1977.

Lunati, Rinaldo. Book Selection: Principles & Practice. Marulli, Luciana, tr. 1975. 10.00 (ISBN 0-8108-0846-3). Scarecrow.

Lunberg, Donald & Kotschevar, Lendal H. Understanding Cooking. 382p. 1970. pap. 10.95 (ISBN 0-685-04750-4). Radio City.

Lund, A. & Luce, A., trs. Hermeneutica. (Portuguese Bks.). 1979. 1.20 (ISBN 0-8297-0825-1). Life Pubs Intl.

--Hermeneutica E Introduccion Biblica. (Spanish Bks.). (Span.). 1978. 1.90 (ISBN 0-8297-0564-3). Life Pubs Intl.

Lund, Charles & Smart, Margaret. Focus on Calculator Math. (Illus.). (gr. 4-12). 1979. pap. text ed. 4.95 (ISBN 0-918932-66-1). Activity Resources.

Lund, Doris. Eric. LC 74-7061. 1974. 11.95 (ISBN 0-397-01046-X). Lippincott.

Lund, Doris H. Did You Ever. LC 64-19768. (Illus.). (gr. k-2). 1965. 5.95 o.s.i. (ISBN 0-8193-0088-8, Four Winds); PLB 5.41 o.s.i. (ISBN 0-8193-0089-6). Schol Bk Serv.

--You Ought to See Herbert's House. LC 77-185690. (gr. k-3). 1973. PLB 4.90 o.p. (ISBN 0-531-02595-0). Watts.

Lund, Gene J., tr. see Fagerberg, Holsten.

Lund, James. The Ultimate. 1979. 9.95 (ISBN 0-7145-3595-8). Riverrun NY.

Lund, Morten & Ski Magazine Editors. Ski Magazine's Complete Book of Ski Technique. LC 75-6362. (Illus.). 208p. 1975. 12.95 o.p. (ISBN 0-06-013904-8, HarpT). Har-Row.

Lund, P. C. Principles & Practice of Spinal Anesthesia. (Illus.). 892p. 1971. pap. 48.00 spiral (ISBN 0-398-01164-8). C C Thomas.

Lund, Peder C., ed. see Truby, J. David & Minnery, John.

Lund, Peter C., ed. see Thomas, Donald G.

Lund, Philip R. Compelling Selling. (AMACOM Executive Bks). 1978. pap. 5.95 (ISBN 0-8144-7506-X). Am Mgmt.

Lund, Shirley & Foster, Julia A. Variant Versions of Targumic Traditions Within Codex Neofiti 1. LC 77-5389. (Society of Biblical Literature. Aramaic Studies). 1977. pap. 7.50 (ISBN 0-89130-137-2, 061302). Scholars Pr Ca.

Lunday, Berneice. Unblessed. LC 78-15244. (Orion Ser). 1979. pap. 1.95 (ISBN 0-8127-0200-X). Southern Pub.

Lundberg, Donald E. The Hotel & Restaurant Business. 3rd ed. LC 79-207. 1979. text ed. 16.95 (ISBN 0-8436-2142-7); pap. text ed. 14.95 (ISBN 0-8436-2175-3). CBI Pub.

--The Tourist Business. 4th, rev. ed. LC 79-27512. 1980. 16.95 o.p. (ISBN 0-8436-2181-8); pap. 14.95x (ISBN 0-8436-2185-0). CBI Pub.

Lundberg, Donald E. & Amendola, Joseph. Understanding Baking. 1970. pap. 9.95 (ISBN 0-8436-0521-9). CBI Pub.

Lundberg, Eric. Inflation Theory & Anti-Inflation Policy. LC 76-30902. (International Economic Association Ser.). 1977. lib. bdg. 46.00 o.p. (ISBN 0-89158-729-2). Westview.

Lundberg, Margaret J. The Incomplete Adult. LC 74-67. (Illus.). 245p. 1974. lib. bdg. 16.95 (ISBN 0-8371-7362-0, LUA/). Greenwood.

Lundberg, N., ed. see International Symposium on Intracranial Pressure, 2nd.

Lundbom, Jack R. Jeremiah: A Study in Ancient Hebrew Rhetoric. LC 75-15732. (Society of Biblical Literature. Dissertation Ser.). xiv, 195p. 1975. pap. 9.00 (ISBN 0-89130-011-2, 060118). Scholars Pr Ca.

Lunde, Donald T. & Morgan, Jefferson. The Die Song. LC 80-83566. 288p. 1981. pap. 2.95 (ISBN 0-87216-803-4). Playboy Pbks.

Lundeen, Harry C. & Gibbs, Charles H., eds. Advances in Occlusion: Diagnoisis & Treatment. 1981. write for info. (ISBN 0-88416-168-4). PSG Pub.

Lundegren, Herberta M., jt. auth. see Farrell, Patricia.

Lundell, Torborg. Lars Ahlin. LC 76-40314. (World Authors Ser.: No. 430). 1977. lib. bdg. 12.50 (ISBN 0-8057-6270-1). Twayne.

Lundestad, Geir. America, Scandinavia, & the Cold War, Nineteen Forty-Five to Nineteen Forty Nine. LC 80-73048. 416p. 1980. 27.50x (ISBN 0-231-04974-9). Columbia U Pr.

Lundgren, Earl F. Organizational Management. LC 73-21940. (Illus.). 512p. 1974. text ed. 21.50 scp (ISBN 0-06-385355-8, HarpC). Har-Row.

Lundin, Robert W. An Objective Psychology of Music. 2nd ed. 1967. 15.95 (ISBN 0-8260-5600-8). Wiley.

--Theories & Systems of Psychology. 2nd ed. 1979. text ed. 15.95x (ISBN 0-669-01915-1). Heath.

Lundkvist, Artur. Agadir. Smith, William Jay & Sjoberg, Leif, trs. from Swedish. LC 80-15978. (International Poetry Ser.: Vol. 2). (Illus.). xiii, 57p. 1980. 10.95 (ISBN 0-8214-0444-X); pap. 5.95 (ISBN 0-8214-0561-6). Ohio U Pr.

Lundman, Bertil J. The Races & Peoples of Europe. Swan, Donald A., tr. from German. (Illus.). 78p. 1977. pap. 2.00x (ISBN 0-911038-72-8). Noontide.

Lundquist, James. Chester Himes. LC 75-42864. (Modern Literature Ser.). 170p. 1976. 10.95 (ISBN 0-8044-2561-2). Ungar.

--J. D. Salinger. LC 78-4301. (Modern Literature Ser.). 1978. 10.95 (ISBN 0-8044-2560-4); pap. 3.45 (ISBN 0-8044-6452-9). Ungar.

--Kurt Vonnegut. LC 76-15654. (Modern Literature Ser.). 1977. 10.95 (ISBN 0-8044-2564-7); pap. 3.45 (ISBN 0-8044-6458-8). Ungar.

--Sinclair Lewis. LC 72-76774. (Modern Literature Ser.). 10.95 (ISBN 0-8044-2562-0). Ungar.

--Theodore Dreiser. LC 73-84600. (Modern Literature Ser.). 150p. 1974. 10.95 (ISBN 0-8044-2563-9). Ungar.

Lundqvist, Bengt & Lundqvist, Stig, eds. Collective Properties of Physical Systems: Proceedings. 1974. 43.50 (ISBN 0-12-460350-5). Acad Pr.

Lundqvist, Jan. Local & Central Impulses for Change & Development. 1975. pap. text ed. 15.50x (ISBN 8-200-01457-6, Dist. by Columbia U Pr). Universitet.

Lundqvist, Lennart J. The Hare & the Tortoise: Clean Air Policy in the United States and Sweden. 248p. 1980. 15.00 (ISBN 0-472-09310-X). U of Mich Pr.

Lundqvist, Stig, jt. ed. see Lundqvist, Bengt.

Lundsted, Betty. Astrological Insights into Personality. 384p. (Orig.). 1980. pap. 9.95 (ISBN 0-917086-22-8, Pub. by Astro Computing Serv.). Para Res.

Lundsteen, S. Children Learn to Communicate: Language Arts Through Creative Problem Solving. (Illus.). 1976. ref. ed. 18.95 (ISBN 0-13-131888-8); ideas into practice companion guide 5.95 (ISBN 0-13-449231-5). P-H.

Lundsteen, Sara & Bernstein-Tarrow, Norma. Guiding Young Children's Learning. (Illus.). 528p. 1981. text ed. 16.95 (ISBN 0-07-039105-X, C); instrs'. manual avail. (ISBN 0-07-039106-8). McGraw.

Lundstrom, Lowell. How to Get up When You're Down. 1977. pap. 1.75 (ISBN 0-88207-502-0). Victor Bks.

Lundstrom, William J., jt. auth. see Zikmund, William.

Lundy, Kathryn R. Women View Librarianship: Nine Perspectives. LC 80-23611. (ACRL Publications in Librarianship: No. 41). 108p. 1980. pap. 7.00 (ISBN 0-8389-3251-7). ALA.

Lunetta, Vincent & Zalewski, Leon. Interactive Incidents from Classroom, School & Community. 1974. pap. 3.00 o.p. (ISBN 0-685-42403-0, 471-14668). Natl Sci Tchrs.

Lungmus, Dorothy, et al. Consumer Education Sourcebook. LC 80-11872. (Orig.). 1980. pap. 9.95 (ISBN 0-89994-246-6). Soc Sci Ed.

Lunin, Lois F., ed. Health Sciences & Services: A Guide to Information Sources. LC 77-80614. (Management Information Guide Ser.: No. 36). 1979. 30.00 (ISBN 0-8103-0836-3). Gale.

Lunn, David. The English Benedictines, Fifteen Forty to Sixteen Eighty-Eight: Reformation to Revolution. (Illus.). 282p. 1980. 24.95x. B&N.

Lunn, Eugene. Prophet of Community: The Romantic Socialism of Gustav Landauer. LC 70-186105. 1973. 25.00x (ISBN 0-520-02207-6). U of Cal Pr.

Lunn, Joan C. Social Class, Attitudes & Achievement: Two Subsidiary Studies from the Streaming Research Data. (Research Reports Ser.: No. 1). 35p. (Orig.). 1971. pap. text ed. 3.75x (ISBN 0-901225-92-4, NFER). Humanities.

Lunney, Rebecca J. When Trees Are Green & Daisies Dance. 1981. 4.75 (ISBN 0-8062-1622-0). Carlton.

Lunsted, Betty. Transits: The Time of Your Life. 1980. pap. 7.95 (ISBN 0-87728-503-9). Weiser.

Lunt, G., jt. auth. see Harrison, R.

Lunt, George G., jt. auth. see Harrison, Roger.

Lunt, James. Bokhara Burnes. (Great Travellers Ser.). (Illus.). 1969. 7.50 (ISBN 0-571-08935-6, Pub. by Faber & Faber). Merrimack Bk Serv.

Lunt, Peter. Udo Fahrt Nach Koln. LC 73-20464. (Ger). 1971. pap. text ed. 7.84 (ISBN 0-395-11058-0, 2-34500). HM.

Lunt, R. M. Handbook of Ultrasonic B-Scanning in Medicine. LC 77-22257. (Techniques of Measurement in Medicine Ser.: No. 1). (Illus.). 1978. 31.95 (ISBN 0-521-21753-9); pap. 8.50x (ISBN 0-521-29264-6). Cambridge U Pr.

Lunz, Mary E. Communication in Health Care Organizations. 420p. 1981. text ed. price not set (ISBN 0-914904-69-8). Health Admin Pr.

Lunzer, E. A. Recent Studies in Britain Based on the Work of Jean Piaget: 1970 Report of 1960 Edition. 1970. pap. text ed. 5.00x (ISBN 0-85633-024-8, NFER). Humanities.

Lunzer, E. A., tr. see Piaget, Jean, et al.

Luper, Harold L. & Mulder, Robert L. Stuttering: Therapy for Children. 1964. text ed. 13.95 (ISBN 0-13-858985-2). P-H.

Lupo, Alan, jt. auth. see Rivers, Caryl.

Lupoff, Richard, jt. auth. see Howard, Robert E.

Lupoff, Richard A. One Million Centuries. 1981. pap. 2.50 (ISBN 0-671-83226-3). PB.

--Space War Blues. 1978. pap. 1.95 o.s.i. (ISBN 0-440-16292-0). Dell.

--What If, Vol. 1. (Orig.). 1980. pap. write for info. (ISBN 0-671-83189-5). PB.

Lupton, D., tr. see Jacobus, Verheiden.

Lupton, Kenneth. Mungo Park: The African Traveler. (Illus.). 1979. 24.95x (ISBN 0-19-211749-1). Oxford U Pr.

Lupton, Martha. They Tell a Story. LC 74-167052. vi, 553p. 1972. Repr. of 1940 ed. 20.00 (ISBN 0-8103-3112-8). Gale.

Lupul, jt. auth. see Keiser.

Luray, Martin. Ski Racer. LC 75-38512. (Target Bks.). (Illus.). 48p. (gr. 3 up). 1976. PLB 6.45 (ISBN 0-531-01186-0). Watts.

Lurch, E. Norman. Fundamentals of Electronics. 2nd ed. LC 70-125273. 1971. text ed. 21.95x (ISBN 0-471-55520-7). Wiley.

Lurch, Norman E. Fundamentals of Electronics. 3rd ed. LC 79-18696. 624p. 1981. text ed. 19.95 (ISBN 0-471-03494-0); solution manual 7.00 (ISBN 0-471-03716-8). Wiley.

Luria, A. R. Neuropsychological Studies in Aphasia. (Neurolinguistics Ser.: Vol. 6). 184p. 1977. text ed. 26.00 (ISBN 90-265-0244-3, Pub. by Swets Pub Serv Holland). Swets North Am.

Luria, Aleksandr R. Higher Cortical Functions in Man. rev. & expanded ed. 655p. 1980. 27.50 (ISBN 0-306-10966-2, Consultants Bureau). Plenum Pub.

Luria, Gina, ed. The Female Aegis, or the Duties of Women from Childhood to Old Age. LC 74-8248. (The Feminist Controversy in England, 1788-1810 Ser.). 1974. lib. bdg. 50.00 (ISBN 0-8240-0858-8). Garland Pub.

Luria, Gina, ed. see Beckford, William.

Luria, Gina, ed. see Brunton, Mary.

Luria, Gina, ed. see Du Bois, Edward.

Luria, Gina, ed. see Edgeworth, Maria & Edgeworth, Richard L.

Luria, Gina, ed. see Fenwick, Eliza.

Luria, Gina, ed. see Gisborne, Thomas.

Luria, Gina, ed. see Gregory, John.

Luria, Gina, ed. see Hamilton, Elizabeth.

Luria, Gina, ed. see Hays, Mary.

Luria, Gina, ed. see King, Sophia.

Luria, Gina, ed. see More, Hannah.

Luria, Gina, ed. see Opie, Amelia.

Luria, Gina, ed. see Polwhele, Richard.

Luria, Gina, ed. see Porter, Anna Maria.

Luria, Gina, ed. see Robinson, Mary.

Luria, Gina, ed. see Smith, Charlotte.

Luria, Gina, ed. see Wakefield, Priscilla.

Luria, Gina, ed. see West, Jane.

Luria, Gina, ed. see Wollstonecraft, Mary.

Luria, Gina, ed. see Yearsley, Ann.

Luria, S. E. Life: The Unfinished Experiment. encore ed. LC 72-1179. (Encore Edition). 192p. 1973. pap. 0.95 (ISBN 0-684-16374-8, ScribT). Scribner.

--The Multiplication of Viruses. Bd. with Virus Inclusions in Plant Cells. Smith, K. M; Virus Inclusions in Insect Cells. Smith, K. M; Antibiotika Erzeugende Virus-Ahnliche Faktoren in Bakterien. Fredericq, P. (Protoplasmatologica: Vol. 4, Pts. 3, 4a, 4b, 5). (Illus.). iv, 118p. (Eng., Ger.). 1958. 32.50 o.p. (ISBN 0-387-80488-9). Springer-Verlag.

Luria, S. E., et al. General Virology. 3rd ed. LC 77-9498. 1978. text ed. 27.95 (ISBN 0-471-55640-8). Wiley.

Luria, Salvador E. Thirty Six Lectures in Biology. LC 74-19136. (Illus.). 439p. 1975. text ed. 19.95x o.p. (ISBN 0-262-12068-2); pap. text ed. 9.95x (ISBN 0-262-62029-4). MIT Pr.

Lurie, Alison. The Heavenly Zoo. LC 71-21263. (Illus.). 64p. (gr. k-4). 1980. 9.95 (ISBN 0-374-32910-9). FS&G.

--Nowhere City. 1976. pap. 1.65 (ISBN 0-380-00230-2, 23754). Avon.

--Real People. 1969. pap. 1.65 (ISBN 0-380-00227-2, 23747, Bard). Avon.

Lurie, Alison & Schiller, Justin G., eds. The History of Tom Thumb. Incl. Robin Hood's Garland; The Pleasant & Delightful History of Jack & the Giants, 2 pts; The Home Treasury. LC 75-32133. (Classics of Children's Literature 1621-1932 Ser.). PLB 38.00 (ISBN 0-8240-2250-5). Garland Pub.

Lurie, Alison, ed. see Ballantyne, Robert.

Lurie, Alison, ed. see Boreman, Thomas.

Lurie, Alison, ed. see Bunyan, John.

Lurie, Alison, ed. see Charlesworth, Maria L.

Lurie, Alison, ed. see D'Aulnoy, Marie C.

Lurie, Alison, ed. see Finley, Martha.

Lurie, Alison, ed. see Harris, Benjamin.

Lurie, Alison, ed. see Kilner, Mary J.

Lurie, Alison, ed. see Newbery, F.

Lurie, Alison, ed. see Perrault, Charles.

Lurie, Alison, ed. see Wilde, Oscar.

Lurie, Ann T., et al. Johann Liss: A German Painter of the European Baroque. LC 75-34907. (Illus.). 192p. 1975. pap. 10.00x (ISBN 0-910386-25-0, Pub. by Cleveland Mus Art). Ind U Pr.

Lurie, Charles N. Everyday Sayings: Their Meanings Explained, Their Origins Given. LC 68-28334. 1968. Repr. of 1928 ed. 24.00 (ISBN 0-8103-0158-X). Gale.

Lurie, Edward. Nature & the American Mind: Louis Agassiz & the Culture of Science. 128p. 1974. pap. text ed. 4.95x o.p. (ISBN 0-88202-011-0, Sci Hist). N Watson.
Lurie, Hannah R. Edge of an Era. 1974. 3.00 o.p. (ISBN 0-685-76701-9). Know Inc.
Lurie, Nancy, jt. auth. see Levine, Stuart.
Lurie, Nancy O. Wisconsin Indians. LC 80-10758. (Illus.). 66p. (Orig.). 1980. pap. 2.00 (ISBN 0-87020-195-6). State Hist Soc Wis.
Lurie, Nancy O., ed. Mountain Wolf Woman, Sister of Crashing Thunder: Autobiography of a Winnebago Indian. LC 61-5019. (Illus.). 1961. 5.00 o.p. (ISBN 0-472-09109-3). U of Mich Pr.
Lurie, Ranan R. Lurie's Worlds 1970-1980. LC 80-15526. (Illus.). 452p. 1980. 45.00 (ISBN 0-8248-0731-6); pap. 14.95 (ISBN 0-8248-0723-5). U Pr of Hawaii.
Lurker, Manfred. The Gods & Symbols of Ancient Egypt: An Illustrated Dictionary. Clayton, Peter A., rev. by. (Illus.). 144p. 1980. 16.95 (ISBN 0-500-11018-2, Quest). Thames Hudson.
Lury, D. A., jt. auth. see Casley, D. J.
Lury, D. A., jt. auth. see Fuller, M. F.
Lusch, Robert F. & Zinszer, Paul H., eds. Contemporary Issues in Marketing Channels. 187p. 1979. 10.00 (ISBN 0-931880-00-9). U OK Ctr Econ.
Luschen, Gunther & Sage, George, eds. Handbook of Social Science of Sport. 700p. 1981. text ed. 22.00 (ISBN 0-87563-191-6). Stipes.
Luscher, E. & Coufal, H., eds. Liquid & Amorphous Metals: Mechanics of Plastic Solids. (NATO-Advanced Study Institute Ser.). 672p. 1980. 75.00x (ISBN 9-0286-0680-7). Sijthoff & Noordhoff.
Luscher, Max. Luscher Color Test. 1980. pap. write for info. (ISBN 0-671-83170-4). PB.
--Personality Signs. (Orig.). pap. cancelled (ISBN 0-446-81317-6). Warner Bks.
Lusher. Acquired Bleeding Disorders in Children: Abnormalities of Hemostasis. (Monographs in Pediatric Hematology-Oncology: Vol. 3). 1981. price not set (ISBN 0-89352-127-2). Masson Pub.
Lushington, Nolan & Mills, Willis N., Jr. Libraries Designed for Users: A Planning Handbook. (Illus.). 1980. 24.50 (ISBN 0-208-01888-3, Lib Prof Pubns). Shoe String.
Lusk, Edward J. & Lusk, Janice G. Financial & Managerial Control: A Health Care Perspective. LC 78-10606. 1979. text ed. 38.50 (ISBN 0-89443-036-X). Aspen Systems.
Lusk, Harold F., jt. auth. see French, William B.
Lusk, Harold F., et al. Business Law: Principles & Cases, Fourth Uniform Commercial Code Edition. 1978. text ed. 20.95 (ISBN 0-256-02021-3). Irwin.
Lusk, Janice G., jt. auth. see Lusk, Edward J.
Luska, Sidney see Harland, Henry, pseud.
Lust, Benedict. About Herbs: Nature's Medicine. 1980. pap. 1.95 (ISBN 0-87904-045-9). Lust.
--About Prostate Trouble. 1980. pap. 1.95 (ISBN 0-87904-042-4). Lust.
--Superbath - The Blood - Washing Method. (Illus.). 1980. pap. 2.95 (ISBN 0-87904-027-0). Lust.
--Zone Therapy: Relieving Pain & Sickness by Nerve Pressure. (Illus.). 1980. pap. 3.95 (ISBN 0-87904-038-6). Lust.
Lust, John B. About Diabetes & the Diet. 1980. pap. 1.95 (ISBN 0-87904-046-7). Lust.
--About Raw Juices. 1980. pap. 1.95 (ISBN 0-87904-047-5). Lust.
--Drink Your Troubles Away. LC 66-28198. 1976. pap. 2.25 (ISBN 0-87904-006-8). Lust.
Lustbader, Eric V. Shallows of Night. 1979. pap. cancelled o.s.i. (ISBN 0-515-04715-5). Jove Pubns.
Lustbader, Eric Van see Van Lustbader, Eric.
Luster, Helen. Crystal, Bk. VII. 1980. pap. 5.00 (ISBN 0-686-28713-4). Man-Root.
--I (EE), Bk. 7, Crystal. (Illus.). 1979. 7.00 (ISBN 0-912662-22-0); pap. 5.00 (ISBN 0-912662-21-2). Fur Line Pr.
Lusterman, Don-David, jt. auth. see Smith, Jay M.
Lustgarten, Karen. The Complete Guide to Disco Dancing. (Illus., Orig.). 1978. pap. 5.95 (ISBN 0-446-97245-2). Warner Bks.
--The Complete Guide to Touch Dancing. (Illus., Orig.). 1979. pap. 5.95 (ISBN 0-446-97218-5). Warner Bks.
Lustick, Ian. Arabs in the Jewish State: Israel's Control of a National Minority. (Modern Middle East Ser.: No. 6). 400p. 1980. text ed. 19.95x (ISBN 0-292-70347-3); pap. 10.95 (ISBN 0-292-70348-1). U of Tex Pr.
Lustig, A. A Prayer for Katerina Horovitzova. 1975. pap. 1.50 o.s.i. (ISBN 0-380-00300-7, 23408). Avon.
Lustig, Arnost. A Prayer for Katerina Horovitzova. Nemcova, Jeanne, tr. from Czech. LC 73-4153. 172p. (YA) 1973. 9.95 o.s.i. (ISBN 0-06-012726-0, HarpT). Har-Row.
Lustig-Arecco, Vera. Technology: Strategies for Survival. Spindler, George & Spindler, Louise, eds. (Basic Anthropological Units Ser.). 96p. pap. text ed. 5.95x (ISBN 0-686-63841-7). Irvington.
Luter, James G., jt. auth. see Modisett, Noah F.
Lutgendorf, Philip. Addition & Subtraction. LC 79-730038. (Illus.). 1978. pap. text ed. 99.00 (ISBN 0-89290-092-X, A508-SATC). Soc for Visual.
Lutgendorf, Philip & Gray, Mary Jane. Punctuation. LC 77-731014. (Illus.). (gr. 7-9). 1977. pap. text ed. 99.00 (ISBN 0-89290-120-9, A149-SAR). Soc for Visual.
--Sentence Structure. LC 77-730353. (Illus.). (gr. 7-9). 1977. pap. text ed. 95.00 (ISBN 0-89290-119-5, A144). Soc for Visual.
Lutgendorf, Philip & James, Shirley M. The Parts of Speech. LC 77-730079. (Illus.). (gr. 7-9). 1976. pap. text ed. 95.00 (ISBN 0-89290-118-7, A134-SAR). Soc for Visual.
Lutgens, F. & Tarbuck, E. Atmosphere: An Introduction to Meteorology. 1979. 17.95 (ISBN 0-13-050104-2). P-H.
Lutgens, Fred, jt. auth. see Tarbuck, Edward.
Luthans, Fred. Introduction to Management: A Contingency Approach. 1975. text ed. 18.95x (ISBN 0-07-039125-4, C); instructors' manual 4.95 (ISBN 0-07-039126-2). McGraw.
Luthans, Fred & Thompson, Kenneth R. Contemporary Readings in Organizational Behavior. 3rd ed. (Illus.). 512p. Date not set. text ed. 11.95x (ISBN 0-07-039148-3, C). McGraw.
Luther, Craig W., jt. auth. see Law, Richard D.
Luther, Edward T. Our Restless Earth: The Geologic Regions of Tennessee. LC 77-21433. (Tennessee Three Star Bks. Ser.). (Illus.). 1977. lib. bdg. 8.50x (ISBN 0-87049-293-4); pap. 3.50x (ISBN 0-87049-293-4). U of Tenn Pr.
Luther, Frederic. MicroFilm: A History, 1839 to 1900. 1981. Repr. of 1959 ed. 25.00 (ISBN 0-913672-34-3). Microform Rev.
Luther, Mark, jt. auth. see McNell, Ken.
Luther, Martin. The Bondage of the Will. Packer, J. I. & Johnston, O. R., trs. from Ger. 323p. Repr. of 1957 ed. text ed. 14.95x (ISBN 0-227-67417-0). Attic Pr.
--The Large Catechism of Martin Luther. Fischer, Robert H., tr. from Ger. LC 61-3802. 112p. 1959. 4.95 (ISBN 0-8006-0885-2, 1-885). Fortress.
--Luther's Ninety-Five Theses. Jacobs, C. M., tr. 1957. pap. 0.95 (ISBN 0-8006-1265-5, 1-1265). Fortress.
--Three Treatises. rev. ed. LC 73-114753. 320p. 1970. pap. 3.50 (ISBN 0-8006-1639-1, 1-1639). Fortress.
Luther, Martin, tr. Bible in German: Old & New Testament. rev. ed. 15.00 o.p. (ISBN 3-4380-1221-9). Adler.
Luther, Susan M. Christable As Dream Reverie. (Salzburg Studies: Romantic Reassessment, Ser.: No. 61). 1976. pap. text ed. 25.00x (ISBN 0-391-01464-1). Humanities.
Luthi, Max. Once Upon a Time: On the Nature of Fairy Tales. Chadeayne, Lee & Gottwald, Paul, trs. from Ger. LC 76-6992. (Midland Bks.: No. 203). 192p. 1976. pap. 3.95x (ISBN 0-253-20203-5). Ind U Pr.
Luthman, Shirley G. Collection, Nineteen Seventy-Nine. LC 79-92404. (Orig.). 1980. pap. 7.95 (ISBN 0-936094-02-8). Mehetabel & Co.
Luttbeg. Plaid for American Government. 1976. pap. 5.50 (ISBN 0-256-01484-1, 09-1033-00). Learning Syst.
Luttbeg, Norman R. Public Opinion & Public Policy. 3rd ed. LC 80-52446. 475p. 1981. pap. text ed. 11.95 (ISBN 0-87581-259-7). Peacock Pubs.
Luttig, John C. Journal of a Fur Trading Expedition on the Upper Missouri, 1812-1813. (Illus.). 1964. Repr. of 1920 ed. 12.50 (ISBN 0-87266-019-2). Argosy.
Luttwak, Edward. Dictionary of Modern War. LC 77-159574. (Illus.). 1971. 12.50 o.p. (ISBN 0-06-012732-5, HarpT). Har-Row.
--The Strategic Balance, 1972. LC 72-6271. (The Washington Papers: No. 3). 1972. 3.50x (ISBN 0-8039-0277-8). Sage.
Luttwak, Edward & Horowitz, Dan. The Israeli Army. LC 73-14270. (Illus.). 480p. 1975. 15.00 o.p. (ISBN 0-06-012723-6, HarpT). Har-Row.
Lutyens, David B. The Creative Encounter. 200p. 1980. Repr. of 1960 ed. lib. bdg. 30.00 (ISBN 0-89987-506-8). Darby Bks.
Lutyens, Mary. Krishnamurti: The Years of Awakening. 1975. 8.95 o.p. (ISBN 0-374-18222-1). FS&G.
--Krishnamurti: The Years of Awakening. pap. 2.25 (ISBN 0-380-00734-7, 30072). Avon.
--Millais & the Ruskins. LC 68-8086. (Illus.). Date not set. 10.00 (ISBN 0-8149-0149-2). Vanguard. Postponed.
--The Ruskins & the Grays. LC 73-86125. (Illus.). 296p. Date not set. 10.00 (ISBN 0-8149-0737-7). Vanguard. Postponed.
--Young Mrs. Ruskin in Venice. LC 66-28881. (Illus.). 1966. 12.50 (ISBN 0-8149-0150-6). Vanguard.
Lutyens, Mary, ed. see Krishnamurti, Jiddu.
Lutz, Donald S. Popular Consent & Popular Control: Whig Political Theory in the Early State Constitutions. LC 78-17876. (Illus.). 1980. 21.50x (ISBN 0-8071-0596-1). La State U Pr.
Lutz, Frank W. & Iannacconne, Laurence. Understanding Educational Organizations: A Field Study Approach. 1969. text ed. 12.95 (ISBN 0-675-09540-9). Merrill.
Lutz, Frank W. & Iannaccone, Laurence, eds. Public Participation in Local School Districts. LC 77-260. (Politics of Education Ser.). 1978. 16.95- (ISBN 0-669-01466-4). Lexington Bks.
Lutz, Giles. The Echo. 160p. 1981. pap. 1.75 (ISBN 0-345-29100-X). Ballantine.
--Forked Tongue. 160p. 1981. pap. 1.75 (ISBN 0-345-29220-0). Ballantine.
--Man Hunt. 1981. pap. 1.75 (ISBN 0-345-29218-9). Ballantine.
Lutz, Giles A. The Great Railroad War. LC 80-1851. (Double D Western Ser.). 192p. 1981. 9.95 (ISBN 0-385-17348-2). Doubleday.
--Relentless Gun. 144p. 1981. pap. 1.75 (ISBN 0-449-13996-4, GM). Fawcett.
--Thieves' Brand. LC 80-2905. (Double D Western Ser.). 192p. 1981. 9.95 (ISBN 0-385-17487-X). Doubleday.
--The Turn Around. LC 78-3258. 1978. 7.95 o.p. (ISBN 0-385-14344-3). Doubleday.
Lutz, Henry F. Early Babylonian Letters from Larsa. (Yale Oriental Babylon Texts Ser.: No. II). 1917. 27.50x (ISBN 0-685-69839-4). Elliots Bks.
Lutz, James, jt. auth. see Green, Robert T.
Lutz, John. Jericho Man. LC 80-14988. 256p. 1980. 10.95 (ISBN 0-688-03719-4). Morrow.
Lutz, Lorry. Born to Loose, Bound to Win. LC 80-83877. 192p. (Orig.). 1981. pap. 5.95 (ISBN 0-89081-274-8). Harvest Hse.
Lutz, Ralph, jt. ed. see Bane, Suda L.
Lutz, Richard A., jt. ed. see Rhoads, Donald C.
Lutze. John Websters Tragodienstil Als Ausdruck der Leidenschaftlichkeit. (Jacobean Ser.). (Ger.). 1980. pap. text ed. 25.00x (ISBN 0-391-02196-6). Humanities.
Lutze, Lotha von see Von Lutze, Lotha.
Lutzeler, Paul M., ed. see Broch, Hermann.
Lutzer, Erwin. Managing Your Emotions. LC 80-69311. 128p. 1981. 7.95 (ISBN 0-915684-81-0). Christian Herald.
Lutzer, Erwin W. How in This World Can I Be Holy? Leader's Guide. (Leader's Guide Ser.). (Illus.). 1978. pap. 3.25 (ISBN 0-8024-3592-0). Moody.
--How to Say No to a Stubborn Habit. 1979. pap. 3.50 (ISBN 0-88207-787-2). Victor Bks.
--You're Richer Than You Think! 1978. pap. 2.50 (ISBN 0-88207-777-5). Victor Bks.
Lutzin, Sidney G., ed. Managing Municipal Leisure Services. LC 80-17378. (Municipal Management). 1980. pap. text ed. 12.95 (ISBN 0-87326-023-6). Intl City Mgt.
Lutzker, John & Martin, Jerry. Behavior Change. LC 80-20798. 400p. 1980. text ed. 18.95 (ISBN 0-8185-0420-X). Brooks-Cole.
Luukkanen, Eino. Fighter Over Finland: The Memorirs of a Fighter Pilot. Gilbert, James & Green, William, eds. Salo, Mauno A., tr. LC 79-7282. (Flight: Its First Seventy-Five Years Ser.). (Illus.). 1979. Repr. of 1963 ed. lib. bdg. 20.00x (ISBN 0-405-12191-1). Arno.
Lux, Don. Introduction to Construction Careers. (gr. 7-10). 1975. pap. text ed. 5.00 activity ed. (ISBN 0-87345-187-2). McKnight.
Lux, J. Richard & Pieters, Richard S. Basic Exercises in Algebra & Trigonometry. (Illus.). 365p. (Orig.). (gr. 10-12). 1979. pap. text ed. 5.50x (ISBN 0-88334-122-0). Ind Sch Pr.
--Exercises in Elementary Algebra. (gr. 8-9). 1977. pap. text ed. 4.75x (ISBN 0-88334-087-9) (ISBN 0-685-39242-2). Ind Sch Pr.
Lux, P. Fairy Tales from the Barbary Coast. (gr. 1-4). 1971. 7.95 (ISBN 0-584-62366-6). Transatlantic.
Luxem, Phyllis. Blue Harbor. (YA) 1966. 5.95 (ISBN 0-685-07425-0, Avalon). Bouregy.
Luxemburg, Rosa. The Industrial Development of Poland. DeCarlo, Tessa, tr. LC 77-2338. 1977. pap. 3.95 (ISBN 0-918388-00-7, Univ Edns). New Benjamin.
--The National Question: Selected Writings by Rosa Luxembourg. Davis, Horace B., ed. LC 74-2148. (Illus.). 320p. 1981. pap. 7.00 (ISBN 0-85345-577-5). Monthly Rev.
--The Russian Revolution, & Leninism or Marxism? LC 80-24374. (Ann Arbor Ser. for the Study of Communism & Marxism). 109p. 1981. Repr. of 1961 ed. lib. bdg. 18.75x (ISBN 0-313-22429-3, LURR). Greenwood.
--Selected Political Writings. Howard, Dick, ed. LC 75-142991. 1971. 11.50 o.p. (ISBN 0-85345-142-7, CL-1427); pap. 6.95 (ISBN 0-85345-197-4, PB-1974). Monthly Rev.
Luxenburg, Norman. Europe Since World War Two: The Big Chance. rev. enlarged ed. LC 78-26092. 330p. 1979. 18.95x (ISBN 0-8093-0911-4). S Ill U Pr.
Luxenburg, Norman, ed. see Skrjabina, Elena.
Luxenburg, Norman, ed. & illus. see Skrjabina, Elena.
Luxmoore, Edmund. Deer Stalking: The Whys & Wherefores. (Illus.). 160p. 1980. 22.50 (ISBN 0-7153-8063-X). David & Charles.
Luxton, Elsie. The Technique of Honiton Lace. 1979. 22.50 o.p. (ISBN 0-7134-1614-9, Pub. by Batsford England). David & Charles.
Luz, Antonio De La see De La Luz, Antonio.
Luzadder, Warren J. Fundamentals of Engineering Drawing. 1981. 21.95 (ISBN 0-13-338350-4). P-H.
--Fundamentals of Engineering Drawing for Design, Product Development & Numerical Control. 7th ed. (Illus.). 1977. text ed. 17.95 (ISBN 0-13-338368-7); problems book 9.95 (ISBN 0-13-716308-8). P-H.
--Innovative Design with an Introduction to Design Graphics. (Illus.). 496p. 1975. 21.95 (ISBN 0-13-465641-5). P-H.
Luzbetak, Louis J. The Church & Cultures: An Applied Anthropology for the Religious Worker. LC 75-108055. (Applied Cultural Anthropology Ser). 448p. 1976. pap. 6.95x (ISBN 0-87808-725-7). William Carey Lib.
Lwoff, Andre & Ullman, Agnes, eds. Origins of Molecular Biology: A Tribute to Jacques Monod. 1979. 23.50 (ISBN 0-12-460480-3). Acad Pr.
Lwoff, Andre, jt. ed. see Hutner, S. H.
Lwowski, Walter. Nitrenes. LC 76-97256. (Reactive Intermediates Ser). 1970. 44.95 (ISBN 0-471-55710-2, Pub. by Wiley-Interscience). Wiley.
Lyall, Alfred. The Rise & Expansion of the British Dominion in India. LC 67-24585. 1968. Repr. of 1894 ed. 15.50 (ISBN 0-86527-172-0). Fertig.
Lyall, Archibald. The Companion Guide to the South of France. (Illus.). 1977. pap. 6.95 o.p. (ISBN 0-684-14955-9, SL705, ScribT). Scribner.
Lyall, Charles J. Translations of Ancient Arabian Poetry. LC 79-2872. 142p. 1981. Repr. of 1885 ed. 18.00 (ISBN 0-8305-0042-1). Hyperion Conn.
Lyall, E. M. Flower Arrangement. 4.50x o.p. (ISBN 0-392-03016-0, LTB). Soccer.
Lyall, Leslie. Three of China's Mighty Men. pap. 3.95 (ISBN 0-85363-090-9). OMF Bks.
Lydall, Harold. Structure of Earnings. (Illus.). 1968. 29.95x (ISBN 0-19-828158-7). Oxford U Pr.
Lyday, David. Come Die for Me. 1977. pap. 1.50 o.p. (ISBN 0-445-04110-2). Popular Lib.
Lyday, Noreen. The Law of the Land: Debating National Land Use Legislation, 1970-75. 53p. 1976. pap. 3.00 (ISBN 0-87766-175-8, 15200). Urban Inst.
Lydecker, Beatrice. What the Animals Tell Me. LC 76-9997. (Illus.). 1977. 8.95 (ISBN 0-06-065316-7, HarpR). Har-Row.
Lydgate, J., tr. see Deguileville, Guillaume de.
Lydgate, John. Fall of Princes, 4 pts. Bergen, Henry, ed. Incl. Pt. 1. Books 1-2. o.p. (ISBN 0-19-722572-1); Pt. 2. Books 3-5. 19.95x o.p. (ISBN 0-19-722573-X); Pt. 3. Books 6-9. o.p. (ISBN 0-19-722574-8); Pt. 4. Biographical Introduction, Notes & Glossary. o.p. (ISBN 0-19-722575-6). (Early English Text Society Ser.). 1924. Oxford U Pr.
--Reason & Sensuality: Studies & Notes, Vol. 2. Sieper, Ernst, ed. (Early English Text Society Ser.). 1903. 9.95x (ISBN 0-19-722534-9). Oxford U Pr.
Lydon, F. D. Concrete Mix Design. (Illus.). 1972. text ed. 26.00x (ISBN 0-85334-552-X, Pub. by Applied Science). Burgess-Intl Ideas.
Lydon, F. D., ed. Developments in Concrete Technology, Vol. 1. (Illus.). 1979. 60.95x (ISBN 0-85334-855-3, Pub. by Applied Science). Burgess-Intl Ideas.
Lydon, James & Maccurtin, Margaret, eds. Gill History of Ireland, 11 vols. Set. pap. 60.10 (ISBN 0-686-16761-9). Irish Bk Ctr.
Lye, P. F. Creative Woodwork. (Illus.). 1974. cloth 15.95x (ISBN 0-245-53168-8); pap. 9.95x-. Intl Ideas.
Lye, William F. & Murray, Colin. Transformations on the Highveld: The Tswana & Southern Sotho. (The People of Southern Africa Ser.). (Illus.). 160p. 1980. bds. 21.50x (ISBN 0-389-20112-X). B&N.
Lyell, Charles. Principles in Geology, 3 vols. (Illus.). 1970. Repr. of 1833 ed. Set. text ed. 130.00 (ISBN 3-7682-0685-8). Lubrecht & Cramer.
Lyell, William A., Jr. Lu Hsun's Vision of Reality. LC 74-30527. 1976. 22.75x (ISBN 0-520-02940-2). U of Cal Pr.
Lyfick, Warren. Animal Tales. LC 79-56339. (Illus.). 48p. (gr. 2-6). PLB 5.39g (ISBN 0-933258-01-1). Riverhouse Pubns.
Lygin, V. I., jt. auth. see Kiselev, A. V.

Lygre, David G. Life Manipulation. 177p. 1980. pap. 7.95 (ISBN 0-8027-7162-9). Walker & Co.
Lykiard, Alexis, tr. see Ducasse, Isidore.
Lykken, David T. A Tremor in the Blood: Uses & Abuses of the Lie Detector. LC 80-10697. 320p. 1980. 14.95 (ISBN 0-07-039210-2). McGraw.
Lykos, Peter. Personal Computers in Chemistry. 250p. 1980. 25.00 (ISBN 0-471-08508-1, Pub. by Wiley-Interscience). Wiley.
Lyle. The Antique Dealers Pocketbook. LC 74-3739. 1974. 4.95 o.p. (ISBN 0-684-13828-X, ScribT). Scribner.
Lyle, Carl & Bianchi, Raymond. Common Clinical Perplexities. LC 78-71347. 1979. spiral 9.50 (ISBN 0-87488-958-8). Med Exam.
Lyle, Cynthia. Dancers on Dancing. LC 76-16375. 1976. pap. 4.95 o.p. (ISBN 0-8473-1313-1). Sterling.
Lyle, D. Clothing for Young Men. LC 78-135579. 1970. pap. 2.50 (ISBN 0-686-00148-6, 261-08302). Home Econ Educ.
Lyle, Dorothy S. Modern Textiles. LC 75-38558. 480p. 1976. text ed. 22.95 (ISBN 0-471-55726-9); instrs'. manual avail. (ISBN 0-471-01839-2). Wiley.
--Performance of Textiles. LC 76-54110. 1977. 26.95x (ISBN 0-471-01418-4). Wiley.
Lyle, Guy R., ed. Praise from Famous Men: An Anthology of Introductions. LC 76-55402. 1977. 10.00 (ISBN 0-8108-1002-6). Scarecrow.
Lyle, Katie L. Fair Day & Another Step Begun. LC 73-17014. 160p. (gr. 7 up). 1974. 8.95 (ISBN 0-397-31500-7). Lippincott.
Lyle, Rob. Mistral. 1953. 24.50x (ISBN 0-686-50050-4). Elliots Bks.
Lyle, Royster, Jr. & Simpson, Pamela H. The Architecture of Historic Lexington. LC 76-49890. 1980. Repr. of 1977 ed. 19.50x (ISBN 0-8139-0647-4). U Pr of Va.
Lyle, Sparky & Golenbeck, Peter. The Bronx Zoo. 1980. pap. 2.50 o.s.i. (ISBN 0-440-10764-4). Dell.
Lyle, William H., Jr. & Horner, Thetus W. Behavioral Science & Modern Penology: A Book of Readings. (Illus.). 376p. 1973. 16.50 (ISBN 0-398-02677-7). C C Thomas.
Lyly, John. Gallathea. Lancashire, Anne B., ed. Bd. with Midas. LC 69-11445. (Regents Renaissance Drama Ser). 1970. 10.95x (ISBN 0-8032-0268-7); pap. 2.65x (ISBN 0-8032-5269-2, BB 231, Bison). U of Nebr Pr.
--Mother Bombie. Andreadis, Harriette, ed. (Salzburg Studies in English Literature, Elizabethan & Renaissance Studies: No. 35). 248p. 1975. pap. text ed. 25.00x (ISBN 0-391-01465-X). Humanities.
Lyman, jt. auth. see Lewis.
Lyman, Daniel, jt. ed. see Clark, Stephen.
Lyman, E. R., ed. see Wong, Theodore R.
Lyman, Edna, pseud. Story Telling: What to Tell & How to Tell It. 3rd ed. LC 74-167166. 1971. Repr. of 1911 ed. 22.00 (ISBN 0-8103-3403-8). Gale.
Lyman, George R. The Art & Science of Effective Thinking. (Illus.). 1979. 37.45 (ISBN 0-89266-208-5). Am Classical Coll Pr.
Lyman, Henry. Successful Bluefishing. LC 73-93528. (Illus.). 120p. 1974. 15.00 (ISBN 0-87742-041-6). Intl Marine.
Lyman, Henry & Woolner, Frank. The Complete Book of Striped Bass Fishing. (Illus.). 1954. 6.95 o.p. (ISBN 0-498-08075-7). A S Barnes.
Lyman, Howard B. Test Scores & What They Mean. 3rd ed. (Illus.). 1978. ref. 10.95 (ISBN 0-13-903823-X); pap. 9.95 ref. ed. (ISBN 0-13-903815-9). P-H.
Lyman, Jerry, ed. see Electronics Magazine.
Lyman, Nanci A. The Colony of Delaware. LC 74-26676. (First Bks). (Illus.). (gr. 5-8). 1975. PLB 6.45 (ISBN 0-531-00829-0). Watts.
--The Colony of South Carolina. LC 74-22222. (First Bks). (Illus.). 96p. (gr. 5-8). 1975. PLB 4.90 o.p. (ISBN 0-531-00831-2). Watts.
--The School Newspaper: How It Works, How to Write for It. LC 73-6803. (First Bks.). (gr. 7 up). 1973. PLB 4.90 o.p. (ISBN 0-531-00810-X). Watts.
Lyman, Stanford. Chinese Americans. (Rose Ser: Ethnic Groups in Comparative Perspective). 1974. pap. text ed. 4.95 (ISBN 0-394-31157-4). Random.
--The Seven Deadly Sins. 1978. text ed. 15.95x (ISBN 0-312-71324-X); pap. text ed. 8.95x (ISBN 0-312-71325-8). St Martin.
Lyman, Stanford M. The Asian in North America. LC 77-9095. 299p. 1977. text ed. 15.00 (ISBN 0-87436-254-7). ABC-Clio.
Lyman, Theodore R., jt. auth. see Gardiner, John A.
Lyman, Thomas G. New, Tested Techniques for Independent Learning. (Human Development Library Bk). (Illus.). 131p. 1981. 27.85 (ISBN 0-89266-291-3). Am Classical Coll Pr.
Lyman, Tom & Riviere, Bill. The Field Book of Mountaineering & Rock Climbing. (Illus.). 256p. 1975. 9.95 (ISBN 0-87691-162-9). Winchester Pr.
--The Field Book of Mountaineering & Rock Climbing. LC 78-50762. (Illus.). 1978. pap. 5.95 o.p. (ISBN 0-684-15584-2, ScribT). Scribner.
Lynch, Bohun. A History of Caricature. LC 74-6414. (Illus.). 126p. 1975. Repr. of 1927 ed. 15.00 (ISBN 0-8103-4044-5). Gale.
--Max Beerbohm in Perspective. LC 74-13999. (Illus.). xx, 185p. 1975. Repr. of 1922 ed. 18.00 (ISBN 0-8103-4065-8). Gale.
Lynch, D. & Huntsberger, David V. Elements of Statistical Inference for Education & Psychology. 512p. 1976. text ed. 17.95x o.p. (ISBN 0-205-05014-X); man. of test items avail. o.p. (ISBN 0-205-05016-6); solutions manual avail. o.p. (ISBN 0-205-05017-4). Allyn.
Lynch, Daniel. Native & Naturalized Woody Plants of Austin & the Hill Country. Mosely, Jane, ed. LC 80-53737. (Illus.). 160p. (Orig.). 1980. pap. 6.95 (ISBN 0-938472-00-3). St Edwards Univ.
Lynch, David. Focalguide to Better Pictures. LC 80-41302. (Focalguide Ser.). 1981. pap. 7.95 (ISBN 0-240-51053-4). Focal Pr.
Lynch, Donald F., jt. auth. see Pearson, Roger W.
Lynch, Edith M. Decades: Lifestyle Changes in Career Expectations. 160p. 1980. 11.95 (ISBN 0-8144-5603-0). Am Mgmt.
Lynch, Frances. A Dangerous Magic. LC 77-17766. 1978. 8.95 o.p. (ISBN 0-312-18218-X). St Martin.
--The Fine & Handsome Captain. 1977. pap. 1.50 o.p. (ISBN 0-449-23269-7, Crest). Fawcett.
--Stranger at the Wedding. 1978. pap. 1.75 o.p. (ISBN 0-449-23555-6, Crest). Fawcett.
Lynch, Frederick H. Through Europe on the Eve of War: A Record of Personal Expeiences, Including an Account of the First World Conference of the Churches for International Peace. LC 78-147456. (Library of War & Peace; Peace Leaders: Biographies & Memoirs). lib. bdg. 38.00 (ISBN 0-8240-0252-0). Garland Pub.
Lynch, George. Canaries in Color. (Color Ser.). (Illus.). 1976. 9.95 (ISBN 0-7137-0540-X, Pub by Blandford Pr England). Sterling.
Lynch, H. T., ed. Cancer Genetics. (Illus.). 656p. 1976. 64.75 (ISBN 0-398-03222-X). C C Thomas.
Lynch, Hannah. George Meredith. 170p. 1980. Repr. of 1891 ed. lib. bdg. 10.00 (ISBN 0-8495-3335-X). Arden Lib.
Lynch, Henry T. Skin, Heredity, & Malignant Neoplasms. 1972. spiral bdg. 24.00 o.p. (ISBN 0-87488-744-5). Med Exam.
Lynch, Henry T., ed. Cancer & You. (Illus.). 338p. 1971. 22.75 (ISBN 0-398-01173-7). C C Thomas.
Lynch, Hollis R. Edward Wilmot Blyden: Pan-Negro Patriot, 1832-1912. (West African History Ser). (Illus.). 1970. pap. 4.95 (ISBN 0-19-501268-2, GB). Oxford U Pr.
Lynch, J. M. & Poole, N. J. Microbial Ecology: A Conceptual Approach. 1979. 49.50 o.p. (ISBN 0-470-26532-9); pap. 21.95 (ISBN 0-470-26533-7). Halsted Pr.
Lynch, Jacqueline M., ed. Students' Dictionary of Economics. (Students' Dictionary Ser.). 112p. (Orig.). (gr. 7 up). 1980. pap. text ed. 4.95 (ISBN 0-686-28479-8). Mara Pr MA.
Lynch, James & Plunkett, H. Dudley. Teacher Education & Cultural Change: England, France, West Germany. (Unwin Education Books). 1973. pap. text ed. 8.95x (ISBN 0-04-370046-2). Allen Unwin.
Lynch, James B., Jr., intro. by. Rufino Tamayo: Fifty Years of His Painting. LC 78-10760. (Illus.). 90p. 1981. 15.00 (ISBN 0-295-95816-2, Pub. by Phillips); pap. 7.50 (ISBN 0-295-95822-7). U of Wash Pr.
Lynch, Jane S., et al. Law & the Arts: Arts & the Law. Horwitz, Tem, ed. LC 79-54026. 240p. (Orig.). 1981. pap. 7.95x (ISBN 0-914090-71-2). Drama Bk.
Lynch, John. The Spanish American Revolutions, 1808-1862. (Revolutions in the Modern World Ser). (Illus.). 352p. 1973. text ed. 15.00x (ISBN 0-393-05388-1); pap. text ed. 6.95x (ISBN 0-393-09411-1). Norton.
Lynch, John G., tr. see Ganoczy, Alexander.
Lynch, John J., jt. auth. see Joseph, Lou.
Lynch, John W. A Woman Wrapped in Silence. 1976. pap. 3.45 (ISBN 0-8091-1905-6). Paulist Pr.
Lynch, Kathleen M. Jacob Tonson, Kit-Cat Publisher. LC 77-111046. (Illus.). 256p. 1971. 15.00x (ISBN 0-87049-122-9). U of Tenn Pr.
--Roger Boyle: First Earl of Orrery. LC 65-17438. (Illus.). 1965. 15.00x (ISBN 0-87049-060-5). U of Tenn Pr.
Lynch, Kathleen M., ed. see Congreve, William.
Lynch, Kevin. A Theory of Good City Form. (Illus.). 526p. 1981. text ed. 25.00x (ISBN 0-262-12085-2). MIT Pr.
Lynch, Louise. ABC's of Real Estate Exchanging. 1981. text ed. 12.95 (ISBN 0-8359-0015-0); instrs'. manual avail. (ISBN 0-8359-0016-9). Reston.
Lynch, Marilyn. Casino. 1979. pap. 2.50 (ISBN 0-441-09229-2). Ace Bks.
Lynch, Mervin D., et al, eds. Self Concept: Advances in Theory & Research. 1981. write for info. (ISBN 0-88410-376-5). Ballinger Pub.
Lynch, Michael see Foster, Rick.
Lynch, Miriam. Blacktower. (Orig.). 1974. pap. 0.95 o.p. (ISBN 0-345-26595-5). Ballantine.
--The Lonely Toys. 1978. pap. 1.50 o.p. (ISBN 0-523-40168-X). Pinnacle Bks.
Lynch, Owen M. Politics of Untouchability: Social Mobility & Social Change in a City of India. LC 76-87148. (Illus.). 1969. 17.50x (ISBN 0-231-03230-7). Columbia U Pr.
Lynch, P & Nicolaides, A. Worked Examples in Physical Electronics. (Illus.). 1972. pap. text ed. 15.95x (ISBN 0-245-50530-X). Intl Ideas.
Lynch, Patricia. Brogeen & the Bronze Lizard. LC 77-99123. (Illus.). (gr. 4-6). 1970. 4.95g o.s.i. (ISBN 0-02-761490-5). Macmillan.
--Brogeen Follows the Magic Tune. LC 68-24105. (Illus.). (gr. 4-6). 1968. 4.95g o.s.i. (ISBN 0-02-761480-8). Macmillan.
--Shane Comes to Dublin. LC 58-5902. (Illus.). (gr. 4-7). 1958. 8.95 (ISBN 0-87599-070-3). S G Phillips.
Lynch, Peter J. Dermatology for the House Officer: Problem Oriented Approach. 225p. 1981. write for info. softcover (5250-0). Williams & Wilkins.
Lynch, Philip F. Downhole Operations. (Basic Petroleum Production Operations Ser.: Vol. 3). (Illus.). 128p. (Orig.). 1981. pap. text ed. 14.95 (ISBN 0-87201-225-5). Gulf Pub.
Lynch, Robert E. & Swanzey, Thomas B. The Example of Science: An Anthology for College Composition. 320p. 1981. pap. text ed. 9.95 (ISBN 0-686-69275-6). P-H.
Lynch, Robert N., jt. ed. see Poggie, John J., Jr.
Lynch, Thomas, ed. Contemporary Public Budgeting. 250p. 1981. pap. text ed. 7.95 (ISBN 0-87855-722-9). Transaction Bks.
Lynch, Thomas F., ed. Guitarrero Cave: Early Man in the Andes. LC 79-8868. (Studies in Archaeology). 1980. 20.00 (ISBN 0-12-460580-X). Acad Pr.
Lynch, Valerie. Exploring the Past. LC 69-18749. (Finding Out About Science Ser). (Illus.). (gr. 3-6). 1970. PLB 5.79 o.p. (ISBN 0-381-99759-6, A24560, JD-J). John Day.
Lynch, William, tr. see Rahner, Karl.
Lynche, Richard see Batman, Stephen.
Lynch-Watson, Janet. The Shadow Puppet Book. LC 79-65069. (Illus.). (gr. 3 up). 1979. 9.95 (ISBN 0-8069-7030-8); PLB 9.29 (ISBN 0-8069-7031-6). Sterling.
Lynch-Watson, Janey. The Saffron Robe: The Dramatic & Intense Life of Renowned Christian Mystic, Sadhu Sundar Singh. 1977. pap. 1.75 o.p. (ISBN 0-310-28452-X). Zondervan.
Lynd, Staughton, ed. Nonviolence in America: A Documentary History. Incl. Civil Disobedience. Thoreau, Henry D; Moral Equivalent of War. James, William; Pilgrimage to Nonviolence. King, Martin L. LC 65-23010. 1966. pap. 8.20 o.p. (ISBN 0-672-60092-7, AHS60). Bobbs.
Lyndoe, Edward. Astrology for Everyone. rev. ed. (Illus.). 1970. 7.95 o.p. (ISBN 0-525-05919-9). Dutton.
Lyndon, Diana. The Country Rose. (Orig.). 1981. pap. 1.75 (ISBN 0-671-83448-7). PB.
Lyne, G. M., jt. auth. see Wormald, R. D.
Lyne, Michael. A Parson's Son. (Illus.). signed ed 87.50 (ISBN 0-85131-176-8, Dist. by Sporting Book Center). J A Allen.
Lyne, R. O. The Latin Love Poets from Catullus to Horace. 320p. 1981. 37.50 (ISBN 0-19-814453-9); pap. 15.95 (ISBN 0-19-814454-7). Oxford U Pr.
Lyne, R. O., ed. Ciris: A Poem Attributed to Vergil. LC 77-80845. (Classical Texts & Commentaries Ser.: No. 20). (Illus.). 1978. 65.00 (ISBN 0-521-21727-X). Cambridge U Pr.
--Selections from Catullus Handbook. (Cambridge Latin Texts Ser.). 96p. 1975. pap. text ed. 5.50x (ISBN 0-521-20490-9). Cambridge U Pr.
Lyneborg, Leif. Butterflies in Color. (European Ecology Ser.). (Illus.). 1974. 9.95 (ISBN 0-7137-0718-6, Pub by Blandford Pr England). Sterling.
--Mammals in Color. (European Ecology Ser.). (Illus.). 1971. 9.95 (ISBN 0-7137-0548-5, Pub by Blandford Pr England). Sterling.
Lyneis, James M. Corporate Planning & Policy Design. 520p. 1980. text ed. 29.95x (ISBN 0-262-12083-6). MIT Pr.
Lynes, A. How to Organize a Local Collection. (Grafton Books on Library Science). 1977. lib. bdg. 8.75x (ISBN 0-233-96452-5). Westview.
Lynes, C., ed. see Camus, A.
Lynes, David & Opdycke, Leonard E. Notes on Trusteeship. 1975. pap. 3.25 (ISBN 0-934338-29-9). NAIS.
Lynes, J. A. Principles of Natural Lighting. (Illus.). 1968. 22.30x (ISBN 0-444-20030-4). Intl Ideas.
Lynes, J. A., ed. Developments in Lighting, Vol. 1. (Illus.). 1978. text ed. 48.30x (ISBN 0-85334-774-3, Pub. by Applied Science). Burgess-Intl Ideas.
Lynes, Russell. The Tastemakers: The Development of American Popular Taste. (Illus.). 384p. 1980. pap. 6.50 (ISBN 0-486-23993-4). Dover.
Lynes, Tony. French Pensions. 163p. 1967. pap. text ed. 5.00x (Pub. by Bedford England). Renouf.
Lyngstad, Alexandra & Lyngstad, Sverre. Ivan Goncharov. (World Authors Ser.: Russia: No. 200). lib. bdg. 10.95 (ISBN 0-8057-2380-3). Twayne.
Lyngstad, Sverre. Jonas Lie. (World Authors Ser.: No. 434). 1977. lib. bdg. 12.50 (ISBN 0-8057-6274-4). Twayne.
Lyngstad, Sverre, jt. auth. see Lyngstad, Alexandra.
Lynn, Arthur D., Jr., ed. see Committee On Taxation - Resources - And Economic Development Symposium - 1967.
Lynn, Bill, jt. auth. see Drury, Kitty.
Lynn, Bruce G. Barbados: A Smiling Island. LC 78-113993. 1975. 6.50 (ISBN 0-910294-16-X). Brown Bk.
--The Virgin Islands: Pleasure Spots in the Caribbean. LC 74-113992. 1975. 6.50 (ISBN 0-910294-34-8). Brown Bk.
Lynn, Catherine. Wallpaper in America: From the Seventeenth Century to World War I. (Illus.). 1980. 45.00 (ISBN 0-393-01448-7, A Barra Foundation - Cooper-Hewitt Bk). Norton.
Lynn, Claire. Wjere Living Waters Flow. (Illus.). 99p. (Orig.). 1979. pap. 2.00 (ISBN 0-89323-002-2). BMA Pr.
Lynn, Claire, compiled by. Build on the Rock. (Illus.). 52p. (Orig.). (ps-7). 1979. pap. 2.50 (ISBN 0-89323-000-6). BMA Pr.
Lynn, David A. Air Pollution: Threat & Response. LC 74-12799. (Illus.). 400p. 1976. text ed. 9.95 (ISBN 0-201-04355-6). A-W.
Lynn, David B. The Father: His Role in Child Development. LC 74-77547. 1974. text ed. 12.95 (ISBN 0-8185-0302-5); pap. text ed. 10.95 (ISBN 0-686-66953-3). Brooks-Cole.
Lynn, Elizabeth A. The Dancers of Arun. 1979. 10.95 o.p. (ISBN 0-399-12329-6). Berkley Pub.
--A Different Light. 1980. pap. 2.25 (ISBN 0-425-04824-1). Berkley Pub.
--The Northern Girl. 1981. pap. 2.25 (ISBN 0-425-04725-3). Berkley Pub.
--The Northern Girls. 1979. 9.95 o.p. (ISBN 0-399-12409-8). Berkley Pub.
Lynn, Jack. The Turncoat. 1976. 8.95 o.p. (ISBN 0-440-09133-0). Delacorte.
Lynn, Jermyn Chi-Mung. Political Parties in China. (Studies in Chinese Government & Law). 255p. 1977. Repr. of 1930 ed. 19.50 (ISBN 0-89093-069-4). U Pubns Amer.
Lynn, Karen. Double Masquerade. LC 80-2944. 192p. 1981. 9.95 (ISBN 0-385-17467-5). Doubleday.
Lynn, Kenneth S. The Dream of Success: A Study of the Modern American Imagination. LC 73-176134. 269p. 1972. Repr. of 1955 ed. lib. bdg. 19.75x (ISBN 0-8371-6269-6, LYDS). Greenwood.
Lynn, Kenneth S., ed. Houghton Books in Literature. Incl. Designs for Reading, 4 bks. pap. 4.80 ea.; tchr's guide 4.80 (ISBN 0-395-11195-1); Plays (ISBN 0-395-02790-X); Poems (ISBN 0-395-02786-1); Short Stories (ISBN 0-395-02780-2); Nonfiction Prose (ISBN 0-395-02788-8); Range of Literature, 4 bks. tchr's guide 4.80 (ISBN 0-685-59075-5); Drama. pap. 6.48 (ISBN 0-395-02782-9); Poetry. pap. 4.80 (ISBN 0-395-02784-5); Fiction. pap. 5.60 (ISBN 0-395-02792-6); Nonfiction Prose. pap. 5.60 (ISBN 0-395-02794-2); Level 3, 4 bks. tchr's guide 4.80 (ISBN 0-395-13709-8); Five Comedies. pap. 6.96 (ISBN 0-395-12049-7); Tunnel & the Light: Readings in Modern Fiction. pap. 7.52 (ISBN 0-395-13452-8); Twentieth Century Poetry. pap. 6.48 (ISBN 0-395-12357-7); Scene Seventy: Recent Non Fiction. pap. 7.52 (ISBN 0-395-12505-7). HM.
Lynn, Laurence E., Jr. Managing the Public's Business: The Job of the Government Executive. LC 80-68176. 416p. 1981. 17.50 (ISBN 0-465-04378-X). Basic.
Lynn, Laurence E., Jr., ed. Studies in the Management of Social R & D: Selected Policy Areas. (Study Project on Social Research & Development). vii, 218p. (Orig.). 1979. pap. text ed. 12.50 (ISBN 0-309-02930-9). Natl Acad Pr.
Lynn, Loretta & Vecsey, George. Coal Miner's Daughter. Orig. Title: Loretta Lynn: Coal Miner's Daughter. (Illus.). 1977. pap. 2.50 (ISBN 0-446-91477-0). Warner Bks.
Lynn, Paul P., jt. auth. see Boresi, Arthur P.

Lynn, R. Attention, Arousal & the Orientation Reaction. 1966. text ed. 19.50 (ISBN 0-08-011524-1); pap. text ed. 9.50 (ISBN 0-08-013840-3). Pergamon.
--Personality & National Character. 1971. 27.00 (ISBN 0-08-016516-8). Pergamon.
Lynn, R., ed. Dimensions of Personality: Essays in Honour of H. J. Eysenck. (Illus.). 490p. 1981. 95.00 (ISBN 0-08-024294-4). Pergamon.
Lynn, Roa, et al. Learning Disabilities: An Overflow of Theories, Approaches & Politics. LC 79-7477. (Illus.). 1979. text ed. 15.95 (ISBN 0-02-919490-3). Free Pr.
Lynn, Robert H. All the King's Men Notes. (Orig.). pap. 1.95 (ISBN 0-8220-0146-2). Cliffs.
Lynn, Robert W. & Wright, Elliott. The Big Little School. 2nd rev. & enl. ed. LC 79-27864. 178p. 1980. pap. 6.95 (ISBN 0-89135-021-7). Religious Educ.
Lynn, Theodore S., et al. Real Estate Limited Partnerships. LC 77-11616. (Real Estate for Professional Practitioners Ser.). 1977. 31.50 (ISBN 0-471-55734-X, Pub. by Wiley-Interscience). Wiley.
Lynott, John. Loaded & Rollin' Trucks & Their Drivers. rev. ed. (Encore Edition). (Illus.). 1979. pap. 2.95 (ISBN 0-684-16911-8, SL856, ScribT). Scribner.
Lynton, Harriet R. & Rajan, Mohini. The Days of the Beloved. 1974. 15.75 (ISBN 0-520-02442-7); pap. 5.95 (ISBN 0-520-03939-4). U of Cal Pr.
Lyon, A. J. Dealing with Data. LC 76-92111. 1970. text ed. 28.00 (ISBN 0-08-006398-5); pap. text ed. 17.00 (ISBN 0-08-006397-7). Pergamon.
Lyon, Barbara. Dance Toward Wholeness: Moving Methods to Heal Individuals & Groups. Adams, Doug, ed. (Illus.). 112p. 1981. pap. text ed. 5.95 (ISBN 0-686-28737-1). Sharing Co.
Lyon, Bryce & Verhulst, A. E. Medieval Finance: A Comparison of Financial Institutions in Northwestern Europe. LC 67-19657. 100p. 1968. Repr. of 1967 ed. 5.00x (ISBN 0-87057-102-8, Pub. by Brown U Pr). Univ Pr of New England.
Lyon, Bryce, ed. High Middle Ages, 1000-1300. LC 64-21207. (Orig.). 1964. pap. text ed. 5.95 (ISBN 0-02-919480-6). Free Pr.
Lyon, Bryce, tr. see Ganshof, Francois L.
Lyon, Danny. Danny Lyon. 144p. 1981. 35.00 (ISBN 0-89381-073-8). Aperture.
Lyon, Danny & McCune, Billy. Conversations with the Dead: Photographs of Prison Life. (Illus.). 1970. pap. 0.25 (ISBN 0-914412-00-0). Inst for the Arts.
Lyon, H. H., jt. auth. see Johnson, Warren T.
Lyon, H. H., jt. auth. see Mai, W. F.
Lyon, Harold C., Jr. It's Me & I'm Here: From West Point to Esalen: How a Rigid Overachiever Revolutionized His Life. 224p. 1974. 6.95 o.p. (ISBN 0-440-04355-7). Delacorte.
--Learning to Feel: Feeling to Learn. LC 74-148507. 1971. pap. text ed. 7.95 (ISBN 0-675-09232-9). Merrill.
Lyon, Hugh. An Illustrated Guide to Modern Warships. LC 80-65166. (Illustrated Military Guides Ser.). (Illus.). 160p. 1980. 7.95 (ISBN 0-668-04966-9, 4966-9). Arco.
Lyon, James. Urania: A Choice Collection of Psalm-Tunes, Anthems & Hymns. LC 69-11667. (Music Reprint Ser.). 198p. 1974. Repr. of 1761 ed. lib. bdg. 27.50 (ISBN 0-306-71198-2). Da Capo.
Lyon, James K. Bertolt Brecht in America. LC 80-7543. (Illus.). 428p. 1980. 19.75 (ISBN 0-691-06443-1). Princeton U Pr.
Lyon, John K. The Database Administrator. LC 75-42442. (Business Data Processing Ser). 240p. 1976. 23.50 (ISBN 0-471-55741-2, Pub. by Wiley-Interscience). Wiley.
--Introduction to Data Base Design. LC 75-155904. (Communigraph Business Data Processing Ser). 1971. 24.50 (ISBN 0-471-55735-8, Pub. by Wiley-Interscience). Wiley.
Lyon, Laurie A. Guidelines for High School Students on Conducting Research in the Sciences. 1980. 1.25 (ISBN 0-87716-114-3). Moore Pub Co.
Lyon, Leverett, et al. The National Recovery Administration. LC 71-171386. (FDR & the Era of the New Deal Ser.). 1972. Repr. of 1935 ed. lib. bdg. 75.00 (ISBN 0-306-70385-8). Da Capo.
Lyon, Lorraine D. & Karplus, Elizabeth. Math in & Out of the Mainstream. 112p. (Orig.). 1980. pap. text ed. 7.00 (ISBN 0-87879-245-7). Acad Therapy.
Lyon, M. Joan, jt. auth. see Klafs, Carl E.
Lyon, Mary, ed. see Thorpe, Azalea S. & Larson, J. L.
Lyon, Mary, tr. see Ganshof, Francois L.
Lyon, Nancy. The Mystery of Stonehenge. LC 77-10044. (Great Unsolved Mysteries Ser.). (Illus.). (gr. 4-5). 1977. PLB 9.65 (ISBN 0-8172-1049-0). Raintree Pubs.
--Totem Poles & Tribes. LC 77-23748. (Myth, Magic & Superstition Ser.). (Illus.). (gr. 4-5). 1977. PLB 9.65 (ISBN 0-8172-1044-X). Raintree Pubs.
Lyon, Ninette. Meat at Any Price. (Illus., Orig.). 1969. pap. 4.95 (ISBN 0-571-09078-8, Pub. by Faber & Faber). Merrimack Bk Serv.
Lyon, Ninette & Benton, Peggie. Eggs, Milk & Cheese. 288p. 1971. 12.50x (ISBN 0-571-08302-1). Intl Pubns Serv.
Lyon, Ninette, jt. auth. see Benton, Peggie.
Lyon, Patricia J., tr. see Gasparini, Graziano & Margolies, Luise.
Lyon, Peter. Neutralism. 1963. text ed. 5.75x (ISBN 0-7185-1038-0, Leicester). Humanities.
Lyon, Richard K., jt. auth. see Offut, Andrew J.
Lyon, Roy B. Bosquefos Utiles Para Laicos. (Illus.). 96p. (Span.). Date not set. pap. price not set (ISBN 0-311-42401-5). Casa Bautista.
Lyon, Thoburn C. Practical Air Navigation. rev ed. Sanderson, Jeppesen, ed. 1978. pap. text ed. 8.95 (ISBN 0-88487-053-7, JE314531). Jeppesen Sanderson.
Lyon, Thomas E. Juan Godoy. (World Authors Ser.: Chile: No. 189). lib. bdg. 10.95 (ISBN 0-8057-2376-5). Twayne.
Lyon, Thomas J. Frank Waters. (U. S. Authors Ser.: No. 225). 1973. lib. bdg. 10.95 (ISBN 0-8057-0775-1). Twayne.
Lyon, William. A Pew for One, Please. LC 76-41976. 1977. 6.95 (ISBN 0-8164-0374-0). Crossroad NY.
Lyon, William & Duke, Bill. Introduction to Human Services. (Illus.). 320p. 1981. pap. text ed. 14.95 (ISBN 0-8359-3216-8). Reston.
Lyonne, Susana De. Six Days, 5 Nites. 1978. pap. 1.75 o.p. (ISBN 0-449-14028-8, GM). Fawcett.
Lyons. Handbook of Industrial Lighting. 1981. text ed. price not set. Butterworth.
Lyons, Anne K. & Lyons, Thomas R. A Concordance to the Complete Nonsense of King Lear. Preston, Michael J., ed. 341p. 1980. lib. bdg. 30.00 (ISBN 0-8482-1636-9). Norwood Edns.
Lyons, Arthur. Hard Trade. LC 80-19679. (Rinehart Suspense Novel Ser.). 264p. 1981. 10.95 (ISBN 0-686-69123-7). HR&W.
Lyons, Bridget G. Voices of Melancholy. (Ideas & Forms in English Literature). 1971. 15.00 (ISBN 0-7100-7001-2). Routledge & Kegan.
Lyons, C. G., et al. Concise Textbook of Organic Chemistry. 1965. 14.50 (ISBN 0-08-010657-9); pap. 6.25 (ISBN 0-08-010656-0). Pergamon.
Lyons, Charles H. To Wash an Aethiop White: British Ideas About Black Educability, 1530-1960. LC 74-23396. 1975. text ed. 9.25x (ISBN 0-8077-2464-5). Tchrs Coll.
Lyons, Charles H., et al. Education for What? British Policy Versus Local Initiative. (Foreign & Comparative Studies-Eastern African Ser.: No. 13). 100p. 1973. pap. 4.50x (ISBN 0-915984-10-5). Syracuse U Foreign Comp.
Lyons, Dorothy. Red Embers. LC 48-8369. (Illus.). (gr. 7-9). 4.50 o.p. (ISBN 0-15-266014-3, HJ). HarBraceJ.
Lyons, E. A. A Color Atlas of Sectional Anatomy: Chest, Abdomen, Pelvis. LC 78-15746. 1978. text ed. 139.50 (ISBN 0-8016-3052-5). Mosby.
Lyons, Eugene. Life & Death of Sacco & Vanzetti. LC 74-107414. (Civil Liberties in American History Ser). 1970. Repr. of 1927 ed. lib. bdg. 20.00 (ISBN 0-306-71888-X). Da Capo.
Lyons, F. S. Charles Stewart Parnell. 1977. 25.00 (ISBN 0-19-519949-9). Oxford U Pr.
--Culture & Anarchy in Ireland Eighteen Nineteen to Nineteen Thirty-Nine: The Ford Lectures 1978. 1979. 14.95x (ISBN 0-19-822493-1). Oxford U Pr.
Lyons, F. S. & Hawkins, R. A., eds. Ireland Under the Union: Varieties of Tension. (Illus.). 348p. 1980. 42.00x (ISBN 0-19-822469-9). Oxford U Pr.
Lyons, Forrest, Jr. Collectors Guide to Post Cards. (Illus.). pap. 8.95 o.p. (ISBN 0-686-51578-1). Wallace-Homestead.
Lyons, Geoffrey. Head's Tasks: A Handbook of Secondary School Administration. (General Ser.). (Orig.). 1976. pap. text ed. 31.25x (ISBN 0-85633-068-X, NFER). Humanities.
Lyons, Gracie. Constructive Criticism: A Handbook. rev. ed. (Illus.). 112p. (Orig.). 1980. pap. 3.50 (ISBN 0-686-28724-X). IC&P.
Lyons, Grant. Mustangs, Six-Shooters & Barbed Wire. (Illus.). 96p. (gr. 3-5). 1981. PLB 7.29 (ISBN 0-686-69299-3). Messner.
Lyons, Ivan, jt. auth. see Lyons, Nan.
Lyons, J. Semantics One. LC 76-40838. (Illus.). 1977. 42.50 (ISBN 0-521-21473-4); pap. 11.95x (ISBN 0-521-29165-8). Cambridge U Pr.
--Semantics Two. LC 76-40838. (Illus.). 1977. 49.50 (ISBN 0-521-21560-9); pap. 13.95x (ISBN 0-521-29186-0). Cambridge U Pr.
Lyons, Sr. Jeanne M., tr. see Jassy, Marie-France P.
Lyons, John. Introduction to Theoretical Linguistics. (Illus., Orig.). 1968. 49.50 (ISBN 0-521-05617-9); pap. text ed. 13.95x (ISBN 0-521-09510-7). Cambridge U Pr.
Lyons, John, ed. Linguistique generale. (Langue et langage). (Fr). 1970. pap. 20.25 (ISBN 0-685-13970-0, 3635). Larousse.
Lyons, John H. Stories of Our American Patriotic Songs. LC 42-24375. (Illus.). (gr. 5-12). 7.95 (ISBN 0-8149-0354-1). Vanguard.
Lyons, John L. James Joyce's Miltonic Affliction. 52p. 1980. Repr. of 1973 ed. lib. bdg. 7.50 (ISBN 0-8492-1632-X). R West.
Lyons, John O. The Invention of the Self: The Hinge of Consciousness in the Eighteenth Century. LC 77-27103. (Illus.). 277p. 1978. 15.95x (ISBN 0-8093-0815-0). S Ill U Pr.
Lyons, John S. & Dublin, Stanley W. Electrical Engineering & Economics & Ethics for Professional Engineering Examinations. Hollander, Lawrence J., ed. (Professional Engineering Examinations Ser.). (Illus.). 320p. 1970. 23.95 (ISBN 0-8104-5715-6). Hayden.
Lyons, Len. The One Hundred & One Best Jazz Albums: A History of Jazz on Records. 1980. 17.95 (ISBN 0-688-03720-8, Quill); pap. 9.95 (ISBN 0-688-08720-5). Morrow.
--The One Hundred One Best Jazz Albums: A History of Jazz on Records. LC 80-20392. (Illus.). 640p. 1980. 17.95 (ISBN 0-688-03720-8). Morrow.
Lyons, Louis M. Newspaper Story: One Hundred Years of the Boston Globe. LC 74-152697. (Illus.). 1971. 20.00x (ISBN 0-674-62225-1, Belknap Pr). Harvard U Pr.
Lyons, M. France Under the Directory. (Illus.). 256p. 1975. 35.50 (ISBN 0-521-20785-1); pap. 10.50x (ISBN 0-521-09950-1). Cambridge U Pr.
Lyons, M. & Jackson, D. Saladin: Politics of Holy War. LC 79-13078. (Cambridge University Oriental Publications Ser.). (Illus.). 400p. Date not set. price not set (ISBN 0-521-22358-X). Cambridge U Pr.
Lyons, Maggie. Bayou Passions. (Orig.). 1979. pap. 1.95 (ISBN 0-515-04740-6, 04740-6). Jove Pubns.
--Flame of Savannah. (Orig.). 1980. pap. 2.25 (ISBN 0-515-04745-7). Jove Pubns.
Lyons, Marvin. Russia in Original Photographs: 1860-1920. LC 77-73931. (Illus.). 1978. 20.00 o.p. (ISBN 0-684-15274-6, ScribT). Scribner.
Lyons, Nan & Lyons, Ivan. Champagne Blues. 1980. pap. 2.25 (ISBN 0-449-24317-6, Crest). Fawcett.
--Someone Is Killing the Great Chefs of Europe. 1978. pap. 1.95 o.s.i. (ISBN 0-515-04834-8). Jove Pubns.
Lyons, Nick, jt. auth. see Tanzer, Herbert.
Lyons, Paul. Investing in Residential Real Estate: A Guide to Increasing Your Income & Profit. (Illus.). 1981. text ed. 16.95 (ISBN 0-8359-3304-0). Reston. Postponed.
--Real Estate Investor's Tax & Profit Planner. 1981. pap. 12.95 (ISBN 0-8359-6529-5). Reston.
Lyons, Paul R., ed. see National Fire Protection Association.
Lyons, Richard. Scanning the Land, Poems in North Dakota. 157p. 1970. 11.75 (ISBN 0-911042-23-7). N Dak Inst.
Lyons, S. L. Exterior Lighting for Industry & Security. (Illus.). xiv, 320p. 1980. 50.00x (ISBN 0-85334-879-0, Pub. by Applied Science). Burgess-Intl Ideas.
Lyons, T. P. Personnel Function in a Changing Environment. (Times Management Library). 1971. 13.95x (ISBN 0-8464-0709-4); pap. 7.95 (ISBN 0-8464-0710-8). Beekman Pubs.
Lyons, Thomas R., jt. auth. see Lyons, Anne K.
Lyons, Thomas T., jt. auth. see Frederick, Wayne A.
Lyons, W. Emotion. LC 79-2521. (Cambridge Studies in Philosophy). 240p. 1980. 35.50 (ISBN 0-521-22904-9). Cambridge U Pr.
Lyons, W. E. The Politics of City-County Merger: The Lexington-Fayette County Experience. LC 77-73706. (Illus.). 192p. 1978. 14.00x (ISBN 0-8131-1363-6). U Pr of Ky.
Lyons, William. Gilbert Ryle: An Introduction to His Philosophy. (Harvester Studies in Philosophy: No. 21). 1980. text ed. 30.00 (ISBN 0-391-01800-0). Humanities.
Lyons, William, ed. see Elder, Crawford.
Lyons, William E., ed. see Tiles, J. E.
Lyovin, Anatole, jt. ed. see Wang, William S-Y.
Lysaght, A. M., ed. Joseph Banks in Newfoundland & Labrador, 1766: His Diary, Manuscripts & Collections. LC 70-81800. (Illus.). 1971. 60.00 (ISBN 0-520-01780-3). U of Cal Pr.
Lysaught, Jerome P. Action in Affirmation: Towards an Unambiguous Profession of Nursing. (Illus.). 224p. 1981. pap. text ed. 13.95 (ISBN 0-07-039271-4, HP). McGraw.
Lysebeth, Andre Van see Van Lysebeth, Andre.
Lysons, Kenneth. Managing Your Money in Retirement. LC 79-56045. (Illus.). 1980. 17.95 (ISBN 0-7153-7736-1). David & Charles.
--Your Hearing Loss & How to Cope with It. 1978. 10.50 (ISBN 0-7153-7472-9). David & Charles.
Lyte, Charles. Sir Joseph Banks. (Illus.). 232p. 1980. 32.00 (ISBN 0-7153-7884-8). David & Charles.
Lyth, Mike. The War on Pollution. LC 76-52304. 1977. 9.95x (ISBN 0-8448-1137-8). Crane-Russak Co.
Lythall, R. The J & P Switchgear Book. 7th ed. LC 72-5777. 800p. 1972. 49.95 (ISBN 0-470-55790-7). Halsted Pr.
Lytle, C., jt. auth. see Cortner, R.
Lytle, Charles F. see Wodsedalek, J. E.
Lytle, Dan. How to Be Young, Rich & Free All Your Life. LC 80-66441. (Illus.). 117p. 1980. pap. 4.95 (ISBN 0-936956-00-3). Am Quality.
Lytle, Marie-Jeanne, jt. auth. see Banov, Abel.
Lytle, Marie-Jeanne, jt. auth. see Lytle, R. J.
Lytle, R. J. & Lytle, Marie-Jeanne. Book of Successful Fireplaces: How to Build, Decorate, & Use Them. 20th ed. LC 77-9166. (A Successful Book). (Illus.). 1977. 13.95 (ISBN 0-912336-52-8); pap. 6.95 (ISBN 0-912336-53-6). Structures Pub.
Lytle, Richard H., ed. Management of Archives & Manuscript Collections for Librarians. LC 79-92650. 124p. 1980. Repr. of 1975 ed. 7.00 (ISBN 0-931828-27-9). Soc Am Archivists.
Lyttle, Bradford. You Come with Naked Hands: The Story of the San Francisco to Moscow March for Peace. LC 66-1279. (Illus.). 289p. 1966. 15.00 (ISBN 0-934676-08-9). Greenlf Bks.
Lyttle, Jean. Threads of Destiny. LC 61-9821. 3.00 o.p. (ISBN 0-685-57231-5). Garrett-Helix.
Lyttle, Richard B. The Complete Beginner's Guide to Backpacking. LC 74-18817. 160p. (gr. 4-9). 1975. PLB 4.95 (ISBN 0-385-06885-9). Doubleday.
--The Complete Beginner's Guide to Physical Fitness. LC 77-80896. (gr. 1 up). 1978. 7.95a (ISBN 0-385-12773-1); PLB (ISBN 0-385-12774-X). Doubleday.
--Complete Beginner's Guide to Stereo. LC 79-8564. (Illus.). 192p. 1981. 9.95a (ISBN 0-385-15532-8); lib. bdg. (ISBN 0-385-15533-6). Doubleday.
--Getting into Pro Basketball. (Getting into the Pros Ser.). (Illus.). (gr. 6 up). 1979. PLB 6.45 s&l (ISBN 0-531-01451-7). Watts.
--Jogging & Running. (Concise Guides Ser.). (gr. 5 up). 1979. PLB 6.45 s&l (ISBN 0-531-02949-2). Watts.
--Soccer Fever: A Year with the San Jose Earthquakes. LC 76-18361. (gr. 4-9). 1977. PLB 7.95 (ISBN 0-385-11297-1). Doubleday.
Lyttle, Richard B., jt. auth. see Dolan, Edward F., Jr.
Lyttleton, George. The Court Secret: A Melancholy Truth, 1741. Shugrue, Michael F., ed. Bd. with A New Journey to the World in the Moon, 1741; A Court Intrigue; or, the Statesman Detected, 1741. (The Flowering of the Novel, 1740-1775 Ser: Vol. 5). 1974. lib. bdg. 50.00 (ISBN 0-8240-1104-X). Garland Pub.
Lyttleton, Humphrey. Humphrey Lyttelton's Jazz & Big Band Quiz. 1979. 14.95 (ISBN 0-7134-2011-1, Pub. by Batsford England). David & Charles.
Lytton, Edward B. Last Days of Pompeii. Date not set. pap. 5.95 (ISBN 0-912800-74-7). Woodbridge Pr. Postponed.
Lytton, Hugh. Parent-Child Interaction: The Socialization Process Observed in Twin & Singleton Families. 335p. 1980. 35.00 (ISBN 0-306-40521-0, Plenum Pr). Plenum Pub.
Lytton, Hugh & Craft, Maurice, eds. Guidance & Counselling in British Schools. 2nd ed. 1974. pap. 11.95x (ISBN 0-7131-1860-1). Intl Ideas.

M

M, pseud. The Condensed Gospel of Sri Ramakrishna. 1979. 10.50 o.s.i. (ISBN 0-87481-488-X); pap. 4.95 o.s.i. (ISBN 0-87481-489-8). Vedanta Pr.
M. D. Anderson Hospital & Tumor Institute, ed. see Annual Clinical Conference on Cancer, 22nd.
M. D. Anderson Symposia on Fundamental Cancer Research, 33rd. Genes, Chromosomes, & Neoplasia. Arrighi, Frances E., et al, eds. 550p. 1981. 49.50 (ISBN 0-89004-532-1). Raven.
M., J. C., tr. see Charnace, Guy.
Ma, Laurence J. & Hanten, Edward W., eds. Urban Development in Modern China. (Special Studies on China & East Asia). 250p. 1981. lib. bdg. 20.00x (ISBN 0-86531-120-X). Westview.
Ma, Nancy C. Mrs. Ma's Chinese Cookbook. LC 60-12197. (Illus.). 1960. bds. 18.50 (ISBN 0-8048-0410-9). C E Tuttle.
--Mrs. Ma's Favorite Chinese Recipes. LC 68-13739. (Illus.). 145p. 1980. pap. 7.95 (ISBN 0-87011-427-1). Kodansha.

Ma, Nancy Chih, et al. Don't Lick the Chopsticks: The Creative, Harmonious Ma Family Chinese Cookbook. LC 73-79770. (Illus.). 156p. 1973. 9.95 o.p. (ISBN 0-87011-201-5). Kodansha.

Ma, T. S. & Horak, V. Microscale Manipulations in Chemistry. LC 75-20093. (Chemical Analysis Ser: Vol. 44). 480p. 1976. 42.50 (ISBN 0-471-55799-4, Pub. by Wiley-Interscience). Wiley.

Ma, T. S. & Lang, Robert E. Quantitative Analysis of Organic Mixtures: Part 1, General Principles. LC 78-23202. 1979. 28.95 (ISBN 0-471-55800-1, Pub. by Wiley-Interscience). Wiley.

Ma, Y. W. & Lau, Joseph S., eds. Traditional Chinese Stories. LC 77-21133. 1978. 32.50x (ISBN 0-231-04058-X); pap. 12.00 (ISBN 0-231-04059-8). Columbia U Pr.

Maar, Len, jt. auth. see Doty, Roy.

Ma'Arri, Abu Ala Al. Saqt Al Zand (the Spark from the Flint) Wormhoudt, Arthur, tr. (Arab Translation Ser.: No. 2). 125p. 1972. pap. 6.50 (ISBN 0-916358-52-6). Wormhoudt.

Ma'Arri, Abu 'Ala Al see Al Ma 'arri, Abu 'Ala, pseud.

Maarseveen, H. Written Constitutions, a Computerized Comparative Study. 1978. 37.50 (ISBN 0-379-20361-8). Oceana.

Maas, Henry. The Letters of A. E. Housman. 488p. 1980. text ed. 14.50x (ISBN 0-246-64007-3). Humanities.

--Letters of A. E. Housman. 1979. 15.95x (ISBN 0-8464-0090-1). Beekman Pubs.

Maas, Henry S., ed. Five Fields of Social Service. 208p. 1966. pap. 8.00 (ISBN 0-87101-611-7, CBO-611-C). Natl Assn Soc Wkrs.

Maas, Henry S., et al, eds. Research in the Social Services: A Five-Year Review. LC 75-139833. 232p. (Orig.). 1971. pap. 8.00x (ISBN 0-87101-616-8, CBO-616-C). Natl Assn Soc Wkrs.

Maas, J. P., jt. auth. see Corey, D. Q.

Maas, James. Fifteen Over Seventy: Counsel from My Elders. (Illus.). 1980. pap. 3.95 (ISBN 0-915288-42-7). Shameless Hussy.

Maas, Peter. Made in America. 304p. 1980. pap. 2.50 (ISBN 0-553-13743-3). Bantam.

Maas, Willard, jt. ed. see Van Ghent, Dorothy.

Maass, Arthur. Muddy Waters: The Army Engineers & the Nation's Rivers. LC 73-20238. (FDR & the Era of the New Deal Ser). 306p. 1974. Repr. of 1951 ed. lib. bdg. 29.50 (ISBN 0-306-70607-5). Da Capo.

Maass, Arthur & Anderson, Raymond L. And the Desert Shall Rejoice: Conflict, Growth, & Justice in Arid Environments. LC 77-17866. 1978. 22.50x (ISBN 0-262-13134-X). MIT Pr.

Maass, Joachim. Kleist. Manheim, Ralph, tr. from Ger. 1981. 17.95 (ISBN 0-374-18162-4). FS&G.

Mabbott, J. D. State & the Citizen: An Introduction to Political Philosophy. 2nd ed. 1967. pap. text ed. 6.50x (ISBN 0-391-02081-1, Hutchinson U Lib). Humanities.

Mabbott, Thomas D., ed. The Poems of Edgar Allan Poe. (Harvard Paperbacks: No. 166). 512p. 1980. pap. 8.95 (ISBN 0-674-67780-3). Harvard U Pr.

Mabee, Carleton. Black Freedom: The Nonviolent Abolitionists from 1830 to the Civil War. 1969. 12.95 (ISBN 0-02-577170-1). Macmillan.

Mabie, Hamilton H. & Ocvirk, Fred W. Mechanisms & Dynamics of Machinery, SI Version. 3rd ed. LC 78-1382. 1978. text ed. 28.95 (ISBN 0-471-02380-9); solutions manual avail. (ISBN 0-471-04134-3). Wiley.

Mabogunje, Akin L. Urbanization in Nigeria. LC 76-80853. 1969. 24.50x (ISBN 0-8419-0002-7, Africana); pap. 10.75 o.p. (ISBN 0-8419-0097-3, Africana). Holmes & Meier.

Mabro, Robert. The Egyptian Economy 1952-1972. (Economies of the World Ser). 368p. 1974. text ed. 24.00x (ISBN 0-19-877030-8). Oxford U Pr.

--The Industrialization of Egypt 1939-1973: Policy & Performance. 1976. 29.95x (ISBN 0-19-828405-5). Oxford U Pr.

Mabro, Robert, jt. auth. see Oxford Energy Seminar, First.

Mabry, Edward A. & Barnes, Richard E. The Dynamics of Small Group Communication. (Illus.). 1980. text ed. 15.95 (ISBN 0-13-222000-8). P-H.

Mabry, Helga, jt. ed. see Harborne, J.

Mabry, T. J., ed. see Phytochemical Society of North American Symposium.

Macaba. The Road Back. 2nd ed. 200p. (Orig.). 1979. pap. 9.75 (ISBN 0-911038-89-2). Noontide.

McAdam, Robert. Play the Game, 4 bks. Incl. Forty for Sixty. (RL 2.5) (ISBN 0-8372-2264-8); Viva Gonzales. (RL 3) (ISBN 0-8372-2265-6); Chief Cloud of Dust. (RL 3.5) (ISBN 0-8372-2267-2); Bull on Ice. (RL 4) (ISBN 0-8372-2266-4). (gr. 3-8). pap. text ed. 2.52 ea. o.p.; tchrs' guide 2.10 o.p. (ISBN 0-8372-0728-2). cassettes 8.49 ea. o.p.; 48 bks, 6 ea. of 8 titles with 8 cassettes & spiritmasters avail. o.p. (ISBN 0-8372-2262-1). Bowmar-Noble.

--Play the Game, 4 bks. Incl. Climb Any Mountain (ISBN 0-8372-2268-0); The Skillful Rider (ISBN 0-8372-2269-9); Holdup at the Crossover (ISBN 0-8372-2270-2); More Than Speedy Wheels (ISBN 0-8372-2271-0). (gr. 3-8). 1976. pap. text ed. 2.52 ea. o.p.; cassette for ea. title 8.49 ea. o.p.; 6 ea. of 8 titles, spiritmasters 102.12 o.p. (ISBN 0-8372-3741-6). Bowmar-Noble.

McAdams, Alan K. Power & Politics in Labor Legislation. LC 64-11813. 1964. 20.00x (ISBN 0-231-02644-7). Columbia U Pr.

McAdams, Cliff. The Grand Canyon: Guide & Reference Book. (Illus.). 100p. (Orig.). 1981. pap. 5.95 (ISBN 0-87108-577-1). Pruett.

--Yellowstone National Park: Complete Guide & Reference Book. (Illus.). 100p. 1981. pap. 5.95 (ISBN 0-87108-571-2). Pruett.

MacAdams, Cynthia. Emergence. 1979. pap. 9.95 o.p. (ISBN 0-525-47522-2). Dutton.

McAdow, Berl. From Crested Peaks: The Story of Adams State College of Colorado. 1961. 3.95 (ISBN 0-8040-0335-1). Swallow.

McAfee, Oralie, jt. auth. see Nedler, Shari.

McAfee, Ward. California's Railroad Era Eighteen-Fifty to-Nineteen Eleven. LC 73-18280. (Illus.). 296p. 10.95 (ISBN 0-87095-048-7). Golden West.

MacAgy, Jermayne & Sourian, Etienne. Out of This World. (Illus.). 1964. pap. 2.00 (ISBN 0-914412-23-X). Inst for the Arts.

McAleer, Edward C. The Brownings of Casa Guidi. (Illus.). 15.00x (ISBN 0-685-99384-1, Pub. by Browning Inst); pap. 6.95x (ISBN 0-930252-03-9). Pub Ctr Cult Res.

McAleer, John & Dickson, Billy. Unit Pride. LC 80-1066. 528p. 1981. 13.95 (ISBN 0-385-15925-0). Doubleday.

McAleese, Ray & Hamilton, David, eds. Understanding Classroom Life. (General Ser.). 1978. pap. text ed. 15.00x (ISBN 0-85633-158-9, NFER). Humanities.

McAlester, A. Lee & Hay, Edward A. Physical Geology: Principles & Perspectives. (Illus.). 448p. 1975. 18.95 (ISBN 0-13-669523-X); study guide 4.25 (ISBN 0-13-669531-0). P-H.

McAlester, Lee, jt. auth. see Eicher, Don.

McAliskey, Bernadette D. The Irish Struggle: Nineteen Seventy to Nineteen Eighty. 1981. lib. bdg. 25.00 (ISBN 0-913460-80-X); pap. 6.95 (ISBN 0-913460-79-6). Monad Pr. Postponed.

MacAlister, Ian. Driscoll's Diamonds. 208p. 1977. pap. 1.50 o.p. (ISBN 0-449-13600-0, Gm). Fawcett.

--Valley of the Assassins. 1978. pap. 1.50 o.p. (ISBN 0-449-13948-4, GM). Fawcett.

McAlister, Joan. Radionuclide Techniques in Medicine. LC 78-68348. (Techniques of Measurement in Medicine: No. 3). 1980. 41.50 (ISBN 0-521-22402-0); pap. 12.50x (ISBN 0-521-29474-6). Cambridge U Pr.

McAlister, John T., Jr., ed. Southeast Asia: The Politics of National Integration. 576p. 1972. text ed. 15.95 (ISBN 0-394-31409-3). Random.

McAlister, Linda. The Development of Franz Brentano's Ethics. 170p. 1980. pap. text ed. 14.25x (ISBN 0-391-01954-6). Humanities.

McAlister, Linda L., ed. see Brentano, Franz.

McAlister, Linda L., tr. see Brentano, Franz.

McAlister, Linda L., tr. see Wittgenstein, Ludwig.

McAlister, Lyle N., ed. see Solis De Meras, Gonzalo.

McAlister, Robert, tr. El Dilema. (Spanish Bks.). 1978. 1.50 (ISBN 0-8297-0888-X). Life Pubs Intl.

--O Dilema. (Portuguese Bks.). 1979. write for info. (ISBN 0-8297-0654-2). Life Pubs Intl.

--Le Dilemme. (French Bks.). (Fr.). 1979. wirte for info. (ISBN 0-8297-0934-7). Life Pubs Intl.

McAlister, Walter E, compiled By. Listen to the King: Meditations Just from the Scriptures. (Direction Bks.). 96p. (Orig.). 1980. pap. 2.95 (ISBN 0-8010-6104-0). Baker Bk.

Macallan, E. S. & Jackson, Ian T. Plastic Surgery & Burn Treatments. (Modern Practical Nursing Ser.: No. 6). (Illus.). 159p. 1971. pap. 9.95x (ISBN 0-686-65687-3). Intl Ideas.

MacAllister, Archibald T; see Bree, Germaine.

McAllister, Arthur G., jt. auth. see Panckhurst, John.

McAllister, Chris. Planes & Airports. (Illus.). 64p. 1981. pap. 5.95 (ISBN 0-7134-3911-4, Pub. by Batsford England). David & Charles.

McAllister, Constance. Creative Writing Activities, 2-6. (gr. 2-6). 1980. write for info. (ISBN 0-87534-176-4). Highlights.

McAllister, D. E. & Coad, Brian W. Fishes of Canada's National Capital Region. (Illus.). 1974. pap. text ed. 5.00x (ISBN 0-660-02014-9, 56345-6, Pub. by Natl Gallery Canada). U of Chicago Pr.

McAllister, D. E. & Crossman, E. J. A Guide to the Freshwater Sport Fishes of Canada. (Illus.). 1973. pap. 4.95 (ISBN 0-660-00048-2, 56365-0, Pub. by Natl Mus Canada). U of Chicago Pr.

McAllister, Dawson. Discussion Manual for Student Relationships, Vol. 3. 1979. pap. 7.95 (ISBN 0-8024-2240-3). Moody.

--A Walk with Christ Through the Resurrection. (Discussion Manual Ser.). 150p. 1981. pap. 7.95 (ISBN 0-8024-9192-8). Moody.

--A Walk with Christ to the Cross. (Discussion Manual Ser.). 150p. 1981. pap. 7.95 (ISBN 0-8024-9193-6). Moody.

McAllister, Harry E. Elements of Business & Economic Statistics: Learning by Objectives. LC 74-23909. 576p. 1975. text ed. 23.95 (ISBN 0-471-58120-8); tchrs. manual avail. (ISBN 0-471-02113-X). Wiley.

McAllister, Ian, jt. auth. see Rose, Richard.

McAllister, M. & Madama, G. English for Electrical Engineers. (Illus.). 1977. pap. text ed. 10.25 (ISBN 0-582-52437-7). Longman.

McAllister, Mary A. Metric Made Easy. (Illus.). 1975. pap. 1.98x o.p. (ISBN 0-685-56032-5). Nature Bks Pubs.

McAllister, Mary A., illus. Easy Metric Cookbook. (Illus.). 1977. pap. 3.98x o.p. (ISBN 0-685-81817-9). Nature Bks Pubs.

McAllister, Robert. The Civil War Letters of General Robert McAllister. Robertson, James I., Jr., ed. (Illus.). 1965. 30.00 (ISBN 0-8135-0496-1). Rutgers U Pr.

McAlmon, Robert. A Hasty Bunch. 1978. pap. 1.95 o.p. (ISBN 0-445-04314-8). Popular Lib.

MacAloon, John J. This Great Symbol: Pierre De Courbertin & the Origins of the Modern Olympic Games. LC 80-21898. 1981. lib. bdg. 25.00x (ISBN 0-226-50000-4). U of Chicago Pr.

McAlpin, Janet. Magazine Picture Library. (Practical Language Teaching Ser.). (Illus.). 96p. 1980. pap. text ed. 6.95x (ISBN 0-04-371061-1, 2366). Allen Unwin.

McAlpine, Campbell. Alone with God: A Manual of Biblical Meditation. 1981. pap. 3.95 (ISBN 0-87123-000-3, 210000). Bethany Fell.

Macan, T. T. Freshwater Ecology. 2nd ed. LC 73-14419. 1974. pap. 13.95 o.p. (ISBN 0-470-56149-1). Halsted Pr.

--Ponds & Lakes. LC 73-91602. (Illus.). 148p. 1974. pap. 8.95x o.p. (ISBN 0-8448-0773-7). Crane-Russak Co.

McAnally, David R. Irish Wonders: The Ghosts, Giants, Pookas, Demons, Leprechauns, Banshees, Fairies, Witches, Widows, Old Maids, & Other Marvels of the Emerald Isle. Popular Tales As Told by the People. LC 79-175738. (Illus.). xii, 218p. 1971. Repr. of 1888 ed. 22.00 (ISBN 0-8103-3818-1). Gale.

McAnally, Mary, ed. Warning: Anthology of Poetry from Prisoners of Oklahoma. 1980. pap. 5.00 (ISBN 0-931350-03-4). Moonlight Pubns.

McAnally, Stanley R. Educational Fund Raising Manual: Major Gift Societies. 1970. pap. 5.00 (ISBN 0-89964-021-4). CASE.

McAnany, Emile, et al, eds. Structure & Communication: Critical Studies in Mass Media Research. 260p. 1981. 20.95 (ISBN 0-03-057954-6). Praeger.

McAnany, Emile G., jt. auth. see Jamison, Dean T.

McAnany, Emile G., ed. Communications in the Rural Third World: The Role of Information in Development. LC 79-21406. (Praeger Special Studies). 1980. 23.95 (ISBN 0-03-052986-7). Praeger.

McAnarney, Elizabeth R., jt. auth. see Aten, Marilyn J.

MacAndrew, Andrew R., tr. see Dostoevsky, Fyodor.

MacAndrew, Andrew R., tr. see Olesha, Yuri.

MacAndrew, Craig & Edgerton, Robert B. Drunken Comportment: A Social Explanation. LC 68-8154. 1969. 16.50x (ISBN 0-202-30095-1). Aldine Pub.

MacAndrew, Elizabeth. The Gothic Tradition. LC 79-9447. 1980. 20.00x (ISBN 0-231-04674-X). Columbia U Pr.

McAndrew, Patricia, tr. see Bournonville, August.

McAninch, Sandra, compiled by. Sun Power: A Bibliography of United States Government Documents on Solar Energy. LC 80-29037. 980p. 1981. lib. bdg. 75.00 (ISBN 0-313-20992-8, MSU/). Greenwood.

Macan-Markar, Ajwad, et al, trs. see Bawa Muhaiyaddeen, M. R.

Macardle, Dorothy. The Uninvited. 342p. 1976. Repr. of 1942 ed. lib. bdg. 15.95x (ISBN 0-89244-068-6). Queens Hse.

McArdle, Frank. Altopascio: A Study in Tuscan Rural Society, 1587-1784. LC 76-53261. (Cambridge Studies in Early Modern History). (Illus.). 1978. 34.95 (ISBN 0-521-21619-2). Cambridge U Pr.

McArdle, H. & Suggitt, G. Per Saecula. 1974. write for info. (ISBN 0-686-19161-7); Pt. 1. pap. 3.50; Pt. 2. pap. 3.50; Pt. 3. pap. 3.50. Longman.

McArdle, J. Functional Morphology of the Hip & Thigh of the Lorisiformes. (Contributions to Primatology Ser.: Vol. 17). (Illus.). 148p. 1981. pap. 19.25 (ISBN 3-8055-1767-X). S Karger.

McArdle, William D., jt. auth. see Katch, Frank I.

McArdle, William D., et al. Exercise Physiology: Energy, Nutrition & Human Performance. LC 80-20156. (Illus.). 508p. 1981. text ed. 17.50 (ISBN 0-8121-0682-2). Lea & Febiger.

Macaree, David, jt. auth. see Macaree, Mary.

Macaree, Mary & Macaree, David. One Hundred Three Hikes in Southwestern British Columbia. 2nd ed. LC 80-17573. (Illus.). 224p. (Orig.). 1980. pap. 7.95 (ISBN 0-916890-96-1). Mountaineers.

Macarius, Staretz. Russian Letters of Direction. LC 75-1064. 115p. 1975. pap. 3.95 (ISBN 0-913836-23-0). St Vladimirs.

Maca-Roueche, Suanne & Patterson, Dorothy. Awareness: Exercises in Basic Composition Skills. 2nd ed. LC 77-20918. 1978. pap. text ed. 10.50 (ISBN 0-471-03460-6). Wiley.

McArthur, Alfred G. & Loveridge, John W. Economic Theory & Organization. (Illus.). 400p. 1980. pap. 16.95x. Intl Ideas.

MacArthur, Douglas, 2nd, jt. auth. see Reynolds, Robert L.

MacArthur, John F., Jr. The Charismatics: A Doctrinal Perspective. 224p. (Orig.). (YA) 1980. pap. 4.95 (ISBN 0-310-28491-0). Zondervan.

--Liberated for Life: Galatians - a Bible Commentary for Laymen. LC 75-23511. (Orig.). 1976. pap. 2.25 (ISBN 0-8307-0363-2, S301-1-05). Regal.

Macarthur, John, Jr. Found: God's Will. Orig. Title: God's Will Is Not Lost. 1977. pap. 1.75 (ISBN 0-88207-503-9). Victor Bks.

--Jesus' Pattern of Prayer. 200p. 1981. 7.95 (ISBN 0-8024-4961-1). Moody.

--Kingdom Living Here & Now. 1980. 8.95 (ISBN 0-8024-4564-0). Moody.

--The Legacy of Jesus. 1981. text ed. 7.95 (ISBN 0-8024-8524-3). Moody.

MacArthur, Mary, ed. see Linney, et al.

MacArthur, Robert H. & Connell, J. H. Biology of Populations. LC 66-21070. 1966. text ed. 16.95x o.p. (ISBN 0-471-55974-1). Wiley.

Macartney, C. A. Hapsburg Empire Seventeen Ninety to Nineteen Eighteen. LC 69-12834. 1969. 19.95 (ISBN 0-02-577200-7). Macmillan.

Macartney, C. A., tr. see Shestov, Lev.

Macartney, Clarence E. The Chosen Twelve Plus One. LC 80-17881. (Illus.). 124p. 1980. 39.95 (ISBN 0-930014-43-X); ltd. ed. 200.00 (ISBN 0-930014-52-9). Multnomah.

McAsh, Iain F. The Films of Vincent Price. Castell, David, ed. (The Films of...Ser.). (Illus.). (gr. 7-12). 1978. Repr. of 1973 ed. PLB 5.95 (ISBN 0-912616-79-2). Greenhaven.

Macaskill, Frederick. In Search of Liberty. LC 78-74587. 1979. 12.95 (ISBN 0-916728-24-2). Bks in Focus.

--In Search of Liberty. 1980. pap. cancelled (ISBN 0-916728-25-0). Bks in Focus.

McAteer, J. Davitt. Coal Mine Health & Safety: The Case of West Virginia. LC 72-92460. (Special Studies in U.S. Economic, Social & Political Issues). 1973. 28.50x (ISBN 0-275-28693-2). Irvington.

Macaulay, jt. auth. see Friedman.

McAulay, Alastair. Women's Work & Wages in the Soviet Union. 248p. 1981. text ed. 28.50x (ISBN 0-04-339020-X, 2605). Allen Unwin.

Macaulay, Catharine. Letters on Education, with Observations on Religious & Metaphysical Subjects. (The Feminist Controversy in England, 1788-1810 Ser.). 1974. lib. bdg. 50.00 (ISBN 0-8240-0872-3). Garland Pub.

Macaulay, Ronald. Generally Speaking: How Children Learn Language. (Orig.). 1980. pap. text ed. 6.95 (ISBN 0-88377-162-4). Newbury Hse.

Macaulay, Susan S. Something Beautiful from God. LC 80-67388. 1980. 11.95 (ISBN 0-89107-189-X, Cornerstone Bks); pap. 6.95 (ISBN 0-89107-186-5). Good News.

Macaulay, Thomas B. Napoleon & the Restoration of the Bourbons: The Complete Portion of Macaulay's Projected History of France from the Restoration of the Bourbons to the Accession of Louis Phillipe. LC 77-7107. 1977. 15.00x (ISBN 0-231-04376-7). Columbia U Pr.

Macauley, Hugh, Jr. & Yandle, Bruce, Jr. Environmental Use & the Market. LC 77-91. 1977. 17.95 (ISBN 0-669-01431-1). Lexington Bks.

McAuley, Sara. Catch Rides. 1975. 7.95 o.p. (ISBN 0-394-49553-5). Knopf.

McAuliffe, C. A., ed. Techniques & Topics in Bioinorganic Chemistry. LC 74-5074. (Aspects of Inorganic Chemistry Ser.). 351p. 1974. 44.95 (ISBN 0-470-58119-0). Halsted Pr.

McAuliffe, Conn. Re-Action. LC 74-141218. (Illus.). 1971. pap. 5.95 o.p. (ISBN 0-87835-014-4). Boyd & Fraser.

McAuliffe, Kevin. The Great American Newspaper: The Story of the Village Voice. (Encore Edition). (Illus.). 1978. 4.95 (ISBN 0-684-16588-0). Scribner.

Macavoy, Paul W. Regulated Industries. 1979. 11.95 (ISBN 0-393-01280-8); pap. 4.95x (ISBN 0-393-95094-8). Norton.

MacAvoy, Paul W., jt. auth. see Breyer, Stephen G.

McBain, Ed. Blood Relatives. 1977. pap. 1.50 o.p. (ISBN 0-394-25462-7). Ballantine.

--Eighty Million Eyes. 192p. (Orig.). 1975. pap. 1.25 (ISBN 0-345-29292-8). Ballantine.

--Ghosts. (Large Print Bks.). 1980. lib. bdg. 12.95 (ISBN 0-8161-3128-7). G K Hall.

--Ghosts. 176p. 1981. pap. 2.25 (ISBN 0-553-14518-5). Bantam.

--Killer's Choice. 192p. 1975. pap. 1.25 (ISBN 0-345-29288-X). Ballantine.

--Killer's Choice - an 87th Precinct Mystery. 1981. pap. 2.50 (ISBN 0-345-29288-X). Ballantine.

--The Mugger. 160p. 1981. pap. 2.25. Ballantine.

--The Mugger. 160p. (Orig.). 1975. pap. 2.25 o.p. (ISBN 0-345-29290-1). Ballantine.

--Rumpelstiltskin. (A Matthew Hope Mystery Ser.). 1981. 12.95 (ISBN 0-670-61059-3). Viking Pr.

--Where There's Smoke. 1975. 6.95 o.p. (ISBN 0-394-49670-1). Random.

McBaine, Susan. Miniature Needlepoint Rugs for Dollhouses Charted for Easy Use. (Dover Needlework Ser). (Illus., Orig.). 1976. pap. 1.75 (ISBN 0-486-23388-X). Dover.

McBarnet, Doreen. Conviction: The Law, the State & the Construction of Justice. (Oxford Sociolegal Studies). 1980. text ed. 50.00 (ISBN 0-333-25536-4). Humanities.

McBarret, Doreen see Fryer, Bob, et al.

McBeath, Gerald A. & Morehouse, Thomas A. The Dynamics of Alaska Native Self-Government. LC 80-8166. 141p. 1980. lib. bdg. 16.75 (ISBN 0-8191-1171-6); pap. text ed. 7.50 (ISBN 0-8191-1172-4). U Pr of Amer.

McBeath, Gordon. Manpower Planning & Control. 218p. 1978. text ed. 24.50x (ISBN 0-220-66348-3, Pub. by Busn Bks England). Renouf.

--Organisation & Manpower Planning. 3rd ed. 1974. 21.00x o.p. (ISBN 0-8464-0691-8). Beekman Pubs.

McBee, M. & Blake, K. The American Woman. 1974. 7.95 (ISBN 0-02-476280-6, 47628); pap. 4.95x (ISBN 0-02-476270-9, 47627). Macmillan.

McBee, Mary L., jt. auth. see Blake, Kathryn A.

M'Bengue, Mamadou S. Cultural Policy in Senegal. (Studies & Documents on Cultural Policies). (Illus.). 61p. (Orig.). 1974. pap. 2.50 (ISBN 92-3-101118-9, U137, UNESCO). Unipub.

MacBeth, George. Poems of Love & Death. LC 79-55591. 1980. 9.95 (ISBN 0-689-11049-9); pap. 5.95 (ISBN 0-689-11064-2). Atheneum.

Macbeth, George & Booth, Martin, eds. The Book of Cats. LC 76-43568. (Illus.). 1977. 25.00 o.p. (ISBN 0-688-03159-5). Morrow.

McBirnie, S. C. & Fox, W. J. Marine Steam Engines & Turbines. 4th ed. (Illus.). 672p. 1980. text ed. 39.95 (ISBN 0-408-00387-1). Butterworths.

McBirnie, William. The Search for the Twelve Apostles. 1973. pap. 1.25 o.s.i. (ISBN 0-515-02902-5). Jove Pubns.

McBirnie, William S. How to Motivate Your Child Toward Success. 1979. pap. 2.95 (ISBN 0-8423-1528-4). Tyndale.

McBoyle, Geoffrey. Climate in Review. LC 72-3536. 1973. pap. text ed. 10.95 (ISBN 0-395-16007-3, 3-35100). HM.

McBriar, A. M. Fabian Socialism & English Politics, Eighteen Eighty-Four - Nineteen Eighteen. 1962. pap. 14.95x (ISBN 0-521-09351-1). Cambridge U Pr.

McBride & Moses. Acute Myocardial Infarction. 1979. pap. 6.95 (ISBN 0-8385-0049-8). ACC.

McBride, Alfred. Death Shall Have No Dominion. 208p. 1979. pap. 4.25 (ISBN 0-697-01700-1); tchrs'. manual 3.00 (ISBN 0-697-01707-9); pap. text ed. 4.25. Wm C Brown.

--Saints Are People: Church History Through the Saints. 144p. (Orig.). 1981. pap. 4.00 (ISBN 0-697-01783-4). Wm C Brown.

McBride, Angela B. The Growth & Development of Mothers. LC 72-9138. 250p. 1973. 9.95 o.s.i. (ISBN 0-06-012899-2, HarpT). Har-Row.

--Living with Contradictions: A Married Feminist. 1977. pap. 4.95 (ISBN 0-06-090556-5, CN 556, CN). Har-Row.

--A Married Feminist. LC 74-15839. 224p. 1976. 8.95 o.s.i. (ISBN 0-06-012881-X, HarpT). Har-Row.

McBride, Carmen. Silent Victory. LC 73-84602. 11.95 (ISBN 0-911012-03-6). Nelson-Hall.

McBride, Charles, tr. see Boal, Augusto.

McBride, Dean, ed. see Wolff, Hans W., Jr.

MacBride, Dexter D. Power & Process, a Commentary on Eminent Domain & Condemnation. LC 70-77921. (ASA Monograph: No. 1). 1969. 5.00 (ISBN 0-937828-10-6). Am Soc Appraisers.

McBride, E. F. Sedimentary Petrology & History of the Haymond Formation (Pennsylvanian), Marathon Basin, Texas. 101p. 1966. 2.50 (RI 57). Bur Econ Geology.

McBride, Harper. Gentleman in Paradise. (Orig.). 1981. pap. 1.50 (ISBN 0-440-12186-8). Dell.

McBride, Henry. The Flow of Art. LC 75-13774. 1975. 12.50 (ISBN 0-689-10692-0). Atheneum.

McBride, Joseph. High & Inside: The Complete Guide to Baseball Slang. 288p. (Orig.). 1981. pap. 2.50 (ISBN 0-446-91939-X). Warner Bks.

McBride, Joseph & Wilmington, Michael. John Ford. LC 75-19281. (Theatre, Film & the Performing Arts Ser.). (Illus.). 234p. 1975. lib. bdg. 18.95 (ISBN 0-306-70750-0); pap. 4.95 (ISBN 0-306-80016-0). Da Capo.

McBride, Lois. Western Cooking. (Illus.). 288p. 1976. 10.95 o.p. (ISBN 0-679-50598-9); pap. 5.95 o.p. (ISBN 0-679-50635-7). McKay.

McBride, Mary M. Growing up of Mary Elizabeth. LC 66-10854. (Illus.). (gr. 5-9). 1966. 4.50 (ISBN 0-396-05436-6). Dodd.

McBride, Peter, jt. auth. see Fenwick, Keith.

McBride, R., jt. auth. see Brearley, K.

McBride, Richard. Lonely the Autumn Bird: Two Novels. LC 63-21868. 93p. (Orig.). 1963. pap. 3.25 (ISBN 0-8040-0189-8). Swallow.

--Memoirs of a Natural-Born Expatriate. LC 66-25960. 115p. 1966. 5.95 (ISBN 0-8040-0201-0); pap. 2.75 (ISBN 0-8040-0202-9). Swallow.

McBride, Robert. The Sceptical Vision of Moliere: A Study in Paradox. LC 76-7847. 1977. text ed. 23.50x (ISBN 0-06-494676-2). B&N.

MacBride, Roger L., jt. auth. see Lane, Rose W.

McBrien, Richard P. Catholicism, 2 vols. 1368p. 1980. Set. 37.50 (ISBN 0-03-056907-9). Winston Pr.

McBryde, Isabel. Coast & Estuary: Archaeological Coast of New South Wales at Wombah & Schnapper Point. (Australian Institute of Aboriginal Studies). 1981. pap. text ed. write for info. (ISBN 0-391-02194-X). Humanities.

McBryde, W. A., ed. A Critical Review of Equilibrium Data for Proton-and Metal Complexes of 1,10-Phenanthroline, 2,2'-Bipyridyl & Related Compounds: Critical Evaluation of Equilibrium Const. in Solution; Part A: Stability Const. of Metal Complexes, Vol. 17. 1978. pap. text ed. 18.75 (ISBN 0-08-022344-3). Pergamon.

McBurney, D. & Collings. Introduction to Sensation-Perception. (Experimental Psychology Ser.). 1977. 18.95 (ISBN 0-13-496000-9). P-H.

McBurney, William, ed. see Lillo, George.

McBurney, William H., ed. Four Before Richardson: Selected English Novels, 1720-1727. LC 63-9095. (Landmark Edition). 1978. 21.50x (ISBN 0-8032-0114-1). U of Nebr Pr.

McBurney, William H., ed. see Lillo, George.

McBurney, William J., Jr. Where the Jobs Are. 320p. Date not set. pap. 6.95 (ISBN 0-8019-7025-3). Chilton.

McCabe & Bender. Speaking Is a Practical Matter. 4th ed. 384p. 1981. pap. text ed. 12.95 (ISBN 0-205-07230-5, 4872304); free tchr's ed. (ISBN 0-205-07231-3). Allyn.

McCabe, C. Kevin. Qwiktran. LC 79-63962. 250p. 1979. pap. 12.95 (ISBN 0-918398-24-X). Dilithium Pr.

McCabe, Charles, jt. auth. see Haponski, William C.

MacCabe, Colin. The Talking Cure: Essays in Psychoanalysis. 1981. 25.00 (ISBN 0-312-78474-0). St Martin.

McCabe, Colin, ed. Evaluating in-Service Training for Teachers. 129p. 1981. pap. text ed. 22.00x (ISBN 0-85633-205-4, NFER). Humanities.

McCabe, Eugene. Cancer. (Adaptations Ser.). pap. 2.95 (ISBN 0-912262-68-0). Proscenium.

McCabe, Inger. Week in Amy's World: New England. (Face to Face Bks). (Illus.). (gr. k-3). 1970. 4.50 o.p. (ISBN 0-685-04412-2, CCPr); text ed. 1.36 (ISBN 0-685-04413-0, CCPr). Macmillan.

--Week in Henry's World: El Barrio. LC 78-146609. (Face to Face Bks). (Illus.). (gr. k-2). 1971. 4.95g (ISBN 0-685-00338-8, CCPr); pap. text ed. 1.36 o.p. (ISBN 0-02-765380-3, CCPr). Macmillan.

McCabe, Joseph. The Logic & Virtue of Atheism. 1980. pap. 3.29. Am Atheist.

--Rationalist Encyclopaedia: A Book of Reference on Religion, Philosophy, Ethics, & Science. LC 79-164054. 1971. Repr. of 1948 ed. 26.00 (ISBN 0-8103-3754-1). Gale.

McCabe, Joseph, tr. see Haeckel, Ernst.

McCabe, Maureen, jt. auth. see Dannett, Sylvia G.

McCabe, Sarah & Sutcliffe, Frank. Defining Crime. 1978. pap. 6.00x o.p. (ISBN 0-631-14300-9, Pub. by Basil Blackwell England). Biblio Dist.

Maccabee, John. Miami Millions. 416p. (Orig.). 1980. pap. 2.50 (ISBN 0-553-13313-6). Bantam.

McC. Adams, Robert. Evolution of Urban Society: Early Mesopotamia & Prehispanic Mexico. LC 66-15195. (Lewis Henry Morgan Lectures Ser.). 1966. 13.95x (ISBN 0-202-33016-8). Aldine Pub.

McCadden, Joseph F. The Flight from Women in the Fiction of Saul Bellow. LC 80-5641. 299p. 1980. lib. bdg. 18.75 (ISBN 0-8191-1308-5); pap. text ed. 10.50 (ISBN 0-8191-1309-3). U Pr of Amer.

McCaffer, Ronald, jt. auth. see Harris, Frank.

McCaffery, Jerry & Mikesell, John, eds. Urban Finance & Administration: A Guide to Information Sources. (Urban Studies Information Guide Ser.: Vol. 12). 200p. 1980. 30.00 (ISBN 0-8103-1464-9). Gale.

McCaffrey, Anne. Decision at Doona. 256p. 1975. pap. 2.25 (ISBN 0-345-28506-9). Ballantine.

--Dinosaur Planet. (Del Rey Bks). 1978. 2.25 (ISBN 0-345-29593-5); pap. 1.95 (ISBN 0-345-28509-3). Ballantine.

--Dragonflight. 1975. pap. 2.50 (ISBN 0-345-29568-4). Ballantine.

--Dragonquest. 1975. pap. 2.50 (ISBN 0-345-29666-4). Ballantine.

--Get off the Unicorn. LC 77-1709. 1977. pap. 2.25 (ISBN 0-345-28508-5). Ballantine.

--Restoree. (A Del Rey Bk.). 1977. pap. 2.25 o.p. (ISBN 0-345-29179-4, 345-25744-8-150). Ballantine.

--To Ride Pegasus. (A Del Rey Bk.). Date not set. pap. 2.25 (ISBN 0-345-28507-7). Ballantine.

--The White Dragon. Date not set. pap. 2.50 (ISBN 0-345-29525-0, Del Rey Bks). Ballantine.

MacCaffrey, I., ed. see Milton, John.

McCaffrey, John. Tales of Padre Pio: The Friar of San Giovanni. 1979. 9.95 o.p. (ISBN 0-8362-3500-2). Andrews & McMeel.

McCaffrey, Lawrence J. Daniel O'Connell & the Repeal Year. LC 65-27011. 272p. 1966. 10.00x (ISBN 0-8131-1115-3). U Pr of Ky.

--Ireland: From Colony to Nation State. 1979. 14.95 (ISBN 0-13-506196-2); pap. 11.95 (ISBN 0-13-506188-1). P-H.

--Irish Diaspora in America. LC 75-23894. (Midland Bks.: No. 215). 224p. 1978. 8.50x o.p. (ISBN 0-253-33166-8); pap. 3.95x (ISBN 0-253-20215-9). Ind U Pr.

--The Irish Question, Eighteen Hundred to Nineteen Twenty-Two. LC 68-12962. 202p. 1968. pap. 4.00x (ISBN 0-8131-0117-4). U Pr of Ky.

McCaffrey, M. Stanislaus. The Dolores: A River Running Guide. 96p. (Orig.). 1981. pap. 4.95 (ISBN 0-87108-578-X). Pruett.

MacCaffrey, Wallace T. Queen Elizabeth & the Making of Policy, 1572-1588. LC 80-8564. 536p. 1981. 40.00x (ISBN 0-691-05324-3); pap. 15.00x (ISBN 0-691-10112-4). Princeton U Pr.

McCagg, William O. & Silver, Brian D., eds. Soviet Asian Ethnic Frontiers. LC 77-11796. (Pergamon Policy Studies). (Illus.). 1979. 36.00 (ISBN 0-08-024637-0). Pergamon.

McCahill, Thomas W. & Meyer, Linda C. The Aftermath of Rape. LC 79-1952. (Illus.). 288p. 1979. 22.95 (ISBN 0-669-03018-X). Lexington Bks.

McCaig, M. Permanent Magnets in Theory & Practice. LC 77-23949. 1977. 39.95 (ISBN 0-470-99269-7). Halsted Pr.

McCain, William D., Jr. Properties of Petroleum Fluids. LC 73-78008. 325p. 1974. 27.00 (ISBN 0-87814-021-2). Pennwell Pub.

McCaleb, Charles S. Surf, Sand & Streetcars. Walker, Jim, ed. LC 77-14900. (Special Ser.: No.67). (Illus.). 1977. 12.50 o.p. (ISBN 0-916374-28-9). Interurban.

McCall, Clark B. Putting up with Your Put Downs. (Uplook Ser.). 1978. pap. 0.75 (ISBN 0-8163-0093-3, 16970-6). Pacific Pr Pub Assn.

--You're Not Just a Statistic. (Uplook Ser.). 1977. pap. 0.75 (ISBN 0-8163-0313-4, 24539-9). Pacific Pr Pub Assn.

McCall, Dorothy K. Theatre of Jean-Paul Sartre. LC 74-91659. 1969. 20.00x (ISBN 0-231-03180-7); pap. 6.00 (ISBN 0-231-08657-1). Columbia U Pr.

McCall, Elizabeth B. Old Philadelphia Houses on Society Hill. Date not set. 16.50 (ISBN 0-8038-0194-7). Hastings.

McCall, G. J. Meteorites & Their Origins. LC 72-7640. 352p. 1973. 19.95 (ISBN 0-470-58115-8). Halsted Pr.

McCall, George A. Letters from the Frontiers Written During a Period of Thirty Years Service in the Army of the United States. LC 74-22038. (Bicentennial Floridiana Facsimile & Reprint Ser.). 1974. Repr. of 1868 ed. 13.50 (ISBN 0-8130-0374-1). U Presses Fla.

McCall, George J. Observing the Law: Field Methods in the Study of Crime & the Criminal Justice System. LC 77-99094. (Illus.). 1978. 19.95 (ISBN 0-02-920400-3). Free Pr.

McCall, George J. & Simmons, J. L. Identities & Interactions. rev. ed. LC 77-99093. 1978. 16.95 (ISBN 0-02-920630-8); pap. text ed. 9.95 (ISBN 0-02-920620-0). Free Pr.

--Issues in Participant Observation: A Text & Reader. (Orig.). 1969. pap. text ed. 11.95 (ISBN 0-201-07027-8). A-W.

McCall, George J., jt. ed. see Weber, George H.

McCall, Grant. Rapanui: Tradition & Survival on Easter Island. LC 80-54833. 176p. 1981. text ed. 16.95x (ISBN 0-8248-0746-4). U Pr of Hawaii.

McCall, Grant, ed. see Young Nations Conference, Sydney, 1976.

McCall, J. L. & French, P. M., eds. Metallography As a Quality Control Tool. 345p. 1980. 39.50 (ISBN 0-306-40423-0, Plenum Pr). Plenum Pub.

McCall, J. R. & McCall, V. M. Outdoor Recreation: Forest, Park & Wilderness. (gr. 11-12). 1977. text ed. 12.95x (ISBN 0-685-71817-4, 82047). Macmillan.

McCall, John. William Shakespeare: Spacious in the Possession of Dirt. 1978. pap. text ed. 12.00x (ISBN 0-8191-0378-0). U Pr of Amer.

McCall, M., Jr., ed. Aeschylus: A Collection of Critical Essays. 1972. 8.95 o.p. (ISBN 0-13-018317-2, STC99, Spec); pap. 1.95 o.p. (ISBN 0-13-018309-1). P-H.

McCall, Margaret, ed. My Drama School. (Illus.). 202p. 1978. 14.50x (ISBN 0-8476-3123-0). Rowman.

McCall, Raymond J. Basic Logic: The Fundamental Principles of Formal Deductive Reasoning. 2nd ed. 1962. pap. 3.95 (ISBN 0-06-460052-1, CO 52, COS). Har-Row.

--The Varieties of Abnormality: A Phenomenological Analysis. (Illus.). 592p. 1975. 29.75 (ISBN 0-398-03280-7); pap. 21.75 (ISBN 0-398-03281-5). C C Thomas.

Maccall, Seamus. A Little History of Ireland. LC 80-21515. 59p. (Orig.). 1980. pap. 3.50 (ISBN 0-937702-00-5). Irish Bks Media.

McCall, Thomas S. & Levitt, Zola. Coming Russian Invasion of Israel. 96p. 1976. 3.95 (ISBN 0-8024-1606-3). Moody.

McCall, Tom, jt. auth. see Levitt, Zola.

McCall, V. M., jt. auth. see McCall, J. R.

McCall, Virginia N. Civil Service Careers. (Career Concise Guides Ser.). (Illus.). (gr. 7 up). 1977. PLB 6.45 s&l (ISBN 0-531-01302-2). Watts.

McCall, William A. & Schroeder, Lelah Crabbs. McCall-Crabbs Standard Test Lessons in Reading, Books A-f. 4th ed. 1979. Kit & Manual. pap. text ed. 12.00 (ISBN 0-8077-5554-0). Tchrs Coll.

McCalla, Alix F. & Josling, Timothy E., eds. Imperfect Markets in Agricultural Trade. LC 80-67393. 182p. 1981. text ed. 28.00 (ISBN 0-916672-68-9). Allanheld.

McCalla, Douglas B., ed. see Federico, Pat A., et al.

McCalley, John. Natucket Yesterday & Today. (Illus.). 176p. (Orig.). 1981. pap. price not set (ISBN 0-486-24059-2). Dover.

McCallister, Chris. Aircraft Alive: Aviation & Air Traffic for Enthusiasts. LC 79-56459. 144p. 1980. 19.95 (ISBN 0-7134-1914-8, Pub. by Batsford England). David & Charles.

McCall's Editors. The McCall's Book of Handcrafts. (Illus.). 1972. 10.00 (ISBN 0-394-48300-6). Random.

McCallum, Andrew. Fun with Stagecraft. (Illus.). 64p. 1981. 8.95 (ISBN 0-89490-008-0). Enslow Pubs.

MacCallum, Elizabeth P. The Nationalist Crusade in Syria. LC 79-2873. (Illus.). 299p. 1981. Repr. of 1928 ed. 23.50 (ISBN 0-686-60185-8). Hyperion Conn.

McCallum, Geo. P., adapted by. Six Stories for Acting. 1976. pap. 2.95 (ISBN 0-89318-031-9); cassettes 29.50 (ISBN 0-89318-034-3). ELS Intl.

McCallum, George P. One Hundred & One Word Games. 176p. 1980. pap. text ed. 5.95x (ISBN 0-19-502742-6). Oxford U Pr.

McCallum, George P., adapted by. Seven Plays from American Literature. rev. ed. 1971. pap. 2.95 (ISBN 0-87789-062-5); cassette tapes 39.50 (ISBN 0-87789-126-5). Eng Language.

McCallum, Jack, jt. auth. see Sciacchetano, Larry.

McCallum, John. Big Eight Football: The Story, the Stars, the Stats of America's Toughest Conference. (Encore Edition). (Illus.). 1979. 5.95 (ISBN 0-684-16750-6). Scribner.

McCallum, John D. Getting into Pro Football. (Getting into the Pros Ser.). (Illus.). (gr. 6 up). 1979. PLB 6.45 s&l (ISBN 0-531-02279-X). Watts.

Maccallum, Spencer H. The Art of Community. LC 78-112866. 1976. 8.95x o.p. (ISBN 0-916054-12-8); pap. text ed. 3.95x o.p. (ISBN 0-916054-13-6). Green Hill.

McCallum, Tara, ed. Taft Corporate Foundation Directory. 1979. pap. 125.00 (ISBN 0-914756-30-3). Taft Corp.

--Taft Foundation Reporter: National Edition. 1980. pap. 150.00 (ISBN 0-914756-44-3). Taft Corp.

McCalmon, George & Moe, Christian. Creating Historical Drama: A Guide for the Community & the Interested Individual. LC 65-12501. (Illus.). 1965. 15.00x o.p. (ISBN 0-8093-0189-X). S Ill U Pr.

McCamant, John F., jt. auth. see Duff, Ernest A.

McCambridge, Mercedes. The Quality of Mercy: An Autobiography. 1981. 10.95 (ISBN 0-8129-0945-3). Times Bks.

McCameron, Fritz A. Cobol Logic & Programming. 3rd ed. 1974. pap. text ed. 10.95 (ISBN 0-256-01581-3). Irwin.

--Fortran IV. 3rd ed. 1978. pap. text ed. 10.95 (ISBN 0-256-02036-1). Irwin.

--FORTRAN Logic & Programming. 1968. pap. text ed. 7.25x o.p. (ISBN 0-256-00322-X). Irwin.

McCammon, Robert. Baal. 1980. pap. 2.25 (ISBN 0-686-69249-7, 36319). Avon.

McCammon, Robert A. The Night Boat. 1980. 2.50 (ISBN 0-380-75598-X, 75598). Avon.

McCammon, Robert W. Human Growth & Development. (Illus.). 308p. 1970. text ed. 12.75 (ISBN 0-398-01245-8). C C Thomas.

McCamy, James L. The Quality of the Environment. LC 72-80576. 1972. 12.95 (ISBN 0-02-920480-1). Free Pr.

McCamy, John C. & Presley, James. Human Life Styling: Keeping Whole in the Twentieth Century. LC 73-14271. 206p. (YA) 1975. 12.95 o.s.i. (ISBN 0-06-012894-1, HarpT). Har-Row.

McCance. Preventing Aging. 1981. write for info. (ISBN 0-87527-223-1). Green.

McCandless, Stanley. Method of Lighting the Stage. 4th ed. LC 56-10331. 1958. 7.45 (ISBN 0-87830-082-1). Theatre Arts.

McCanles, Michael. Dialectical Criticism & Renaissance Literature. 1975. 23.75x (ISBN 0-520-02694-2). U of Cal Pr.

McCanliss, Irene. Weight on the Thoroughbred Racehorse. 1967. lib. bdg. 7.50 o.p. (ISBN 0-686-28404-6). Thoroughbred Own and Breed.

McCann, Dennis P. Christian Realism & Liberation Theology: Practical Theologies in Conflict. LC 80-23163. 256p. (Orig.). 1981. pap. 9.95 (ISBN 0-88344-086-5). Orbis Bks.

MacCann, Donnarae & Woodard, Gloria. The Black American in Books for Children: Readings in Racism. LC 72-4490. 1972. 10.00 (ISBN 0-8108-0526-X). Scarecrow.

MacCann, Donnarae & Woodard, Gloria, eds. Cultural Conformity in Books for Children: Further Readings in Racism. LC 77-22174. 1977. 10.00 (ISBN 0-8108-1064-6). Scarecrow.

MacCann, Richard D. The People's Films: A Political History of U. S. Government Motion Pictures. (Studies in Public Communication). 1973. 11.50 o.s.i. (ISBN 0-8038-5795-0); pap. text ed. 6.75x (ISBN 0-8038-5796-9). Hastings.

McCannon, Dingda. Wilhemina Jones, Future Star. LC 79-53602. (YA) (gr. 8-12). 1980. 8.95 (ISBN 0-440-04572-X). Delacorte.

McCarney, Joe. The Real World of Ideology. (Philosophy Now Ser.). 1980. text ed. 32.50x (ISBN 0-391-01704-7); pap. text ed. 11.75x (ISBN 0-391-01705-5). Humanities.

McCarr & Wisser. Curriculum Material Useful for the Hearing Impaired. 204p. 1980. 12.95 (ISBN 0-86575-131-5). Dormac.

McCarrell, Jo, jt. ed. see Hooker, Linda.

McCarren, Vincent P. Michigan Papyri XIV. (American Studies in Papyrology: No. 22). 15.00x (ISBN 0-89130-295-6). Scholars Pr CA.

McCarrick, Earlean M., ed. United States Constitution: A Guide to Information Sources. LC 74-15403. (American Government & History Information Guide Ser.: Vol. 4). 1980. 28.00 (ISBN 0-8103-1203-4). Gale.

McCarroll, H. Relton, Jr., jt. auth. see Jewett, Don L.

McCarron, Margaret M., ed. Principles of Clinical Pharmacy Illustrated by Clinical Case Studies. LC 74-18578. 200p. 1974. pap. 6.50 (ISBN 0-914768-12-3). Drug Intl Pubns.

McCarry, Charles. The Secret Lovers. 1978. pap. 1.95 o.p. (ISBN 0-449-23549-1, Crest). Fawcett.

--The Southwest, No. XV. new ed. LC 78-21450. (Illus.). 1980. 6.95 (ISBN 0-87044-283-X); lib. bdg. 8.50 (ISBN 0-87044-288-0). Natl Geog.

--The Tears of Autumn. 320p. 1976. pap. 1.95 o.p. (ISBN 0-449-22649-2, C2649, Crest). Fawcett.

McCarter, Albert D. & Reed, Glenn. I'm Dancing! (Illus.). 32p. (gr. k-3). 1981. 9.95 (ISBN 0-686-69284-5). Scribner.

McCarter, Neely D. Hear the Word of the Lord. (Illus., Orig.). (gr. 11-12). 1964. pap. 3.45 (ISBN 0-8042-9210-8); tchrs' guide pap. 2.60. John Knox.

McCarter, Pender M., jt. ed. see Nyborg, Philip S.

McCarthy, Albert, jt. auth. see Hentoff, Nat.

McCarthy, Barbara P; see Bree, Germaine.

McCarthy, Barry. What You Still Don't Know About Male Sexuality. LC 77-4239. 1977. 8.95 o.s.i. (ISBN 0-690-01443-0, TYC-T). T Y Crowell.

McCarthy, Belinda R. Easy Time: The Experiences of Female Inmates on Temporary Release. LC 78-13819. 1979. 22.50 (ISBN 0-669-02669-7). Lexington Bks.

McCarthy, C., et al. Federal Income Tax: Its Sources & Applications. 1980. 20.95 o.p. (ISBN 0-13-308965-7). P-H.

McCarthy, Cavan. Developing Libraries in Brazil: with a Chapter on Paraguay. LC 74-23681. 1975. 10.00 (ISBN 0-8108-0750-5). Scarecrow.

McCarthy, Charlotte. The Fair Moralist; or, Love & Virtue, 1745. Shugrue, Michael F., ed. Bd. with The Case of John Nelson, Written by Himself, 1745. Nelson, John. (The Flowering of the Novel, 1740-1775 Ser: Vol. 16). 1974. lib. bdg. 50.00 (ISBN 0-8240-1115-5). Garland Pub.

McCarthy, Christopher. Explorers from Britain. 1978. 16.95 (ISBN 0-7134-0988-6, Pub. by Batsford England). David & Charles.

Maccarthy, D., tr. see Romains, Jules.

McCarthy, D. M. Colonial Bureaucracy & Creating Underdevelopment, Tanganyika, 1919-1940. 1981. 10.95 (ISBN 0-8138-1590-8). Iowa St U Pr.

McCarthy, Daniel J., et al. Business Policy & Strategy: Concepts & Readings. rev ed. 1979. pap. text ed. 12.95 (ISBN 0-256-02168-6). Irwin.

MacCarthy, Daphne, jt. auth. see Bonar, Ann.

McCarthy, Dennis J. Old Testament Covenant: A Survey of Current Opinions. LC 71-37117. (Growing Points in Theology Ser). (Orig.). 1972. pap. 4.95 (ISBN 0-8042-0020-3). John Knox.

McCarthy, E. Jerome. Basic Marketing: A Managerial Approach. 6th ed. 1978. text ed. 19.95 (ISBN 0-256-02048-5). Irwin.

--Essentials of Marketing. 1979. 18.50 (ISBN 0-256-02142-2); pap. 5.95x student aid (ISBN 0-256-02242-9). Irwin.

McCarthy, E. Jerome & Shapiro, Stanley J. Basic Marketing: A Managerial Approach. 2nd ed. 1979. text ed. 19.95 (ISBN 0-256-02138-4). Irwin.

McCarthy, E. Jerome, et al, eds. Readings in Basic Marketing. rev. ed. 1978. pap. text ed. 9.95 (ISBN 0-256-02050-7). Irwin.

McCarthy, Eugene. Frankly McCarthy. Rinzler, Carol E., ed. 1.00 (ISBN 0-8183-0169-4). Pub Aff Pr.

McCarthy, Eugene J. America Revisited: One Hundred & Fifty Years After Tocqueville. LC 77-92222. 1978. 7.95 o.p. (ISBN 0-385-03106-8). Doubleday.

--Crescent Dictionary of American Politics. 1962. 5.95 o.s.i. (ISBN 0-02-582810-X). Macmillan.

McCarthy, G. D. Acquisitions & Mergers. 1963. 29.95 (ISBN 0-8260-5810-8, Pub. by Wiley-Interscience). Wiley.

McCarthy, G. J., et al, eds. The Rare Earths in Modern Science & Technology, Vol. 2. 670p. 1980. 59.50 (ISBN 0-306-40347-1, Plenum Pr). Plenum Pub.

McCarthy, Gary. Explosion at Donner Pass. (Orig.). 1981. pap. 1.95 (ISBN 0-553-14745-5). Bantam.

--The Legend of the Lone Ranger: A Novelization. 160p. (Orig.). 1981. pap. 2.25 (ISBN 0-345-29438-6). Ballantine.

--Mustang Fever. 1981. pap. 1.95 (ISBN 0-440-15308-5). Dell.

--The Pony Express War. 176p. 1980. pap. 1.75 (ISBN 0-553-14185-6). Bantam.

--Winds of Gold. 1980. pap. write for info. (ISBN 0-671-82730-8). PB.

McCarthy, George D. & Healy, Robert E. Valuing a Company: Practices & Procedures. LC 74-166300. 521p. 1971. 38.95 (ISBN 0-8260-5825-6, Pub. by Wiley-Interscience). Wiley.

McCarthy, I. E. Nuclear Reactions. 1970. text ed. 35.00 (ISBN 0-08-006630-5); pap. text ed. 10.75 (ISBN 0-08-006629-1). Pergamon.

McCarthy, J. K. New Guineas, Our Nearest Neighbor: Australia. 1968. 7.50 o.p. (ISBN 0-7015-1245-8). Verry.

--Patrol into Yesterday: My New Guinea Years (1927-1962) 1967. 9.00 o.p. (ISBN 0-8426-1359-5). Verry.

McCarthy, J. Thomas. Trademarks & Unfair Competition, 2 vols. LC 72-91430. 1973. 100.00 (ISBN 0-686-14481-3). Lawyers Co-Op.

McCarthy, James B. Death Anxiety: The Loss of the Self. 1980. 19.95 (ISBN 0-470-26508-6). Halsted Pr.

McCarthy, Jane. All That Glitters. 192p. (YA) 1976. 4.95 o.p. (ISBN 0-685-64242-9, Avalon). Bouregy.

--Listen to the Skylark. 192p. (YA) 1975. 5.95 (ISBN 0-685-52912-6, Avalon). Bouregy.

--Nurse of Thorne Grotto. (YA) 1977. 4.95 o.p. (ISBN 0-685-73809-4, Avalon). Bouregy.

McCarthy, Jeanne M., jt. auth. see Kirk, Samuel A.

McCarthy, Joe P. Days & Nights at Costello's. 288p. 1980. 12.95 (ISBN 0-316-55373-5). Little.

McCarthy, John. LISP 1.5 Programmer's Manual. 1962. 6.00x (ISBN 0-262-13011-4). MIT Pr.

McCarthy, John A. Christoph Martin Wieland. (World Authors Ser.: No. 528). 1979. lib. bdg. 13.95 (ISBN 0-8057-6369-4). Twayne.

McCarthy, Joseph R. America's Retreat from Victory. (Americanist Classics Ser). 1965. pap. 1.00 pocketsize o.p. (ISBN 0-88279-002-1). Western Islands.

McCarthy, Marianthy. Readings in English: Careers, Bk 3. 112p. (gr. 9-12). 1981. pap. text ed. price not set (ISBN 0-88345-425-4, 18884). Regents Pub.

McCarthy, Martha M. How Can I Best Manage My Classroom? (Teachers Education Ser.: No. 2). 1980. pap. 1.25 (ISBN 0-934402-05-1). Byls Pr.

McCarthy, Mary. A Charmed Life. 256p. 1981. pap. 2.95 (ISBN 0-380-53884-9, Bard). Avon.

--The Group. 1980. pap. 2.75 (ISBN 0-686-69265-9, 52134). Avon.

--The Groves of Academe. 240p. 1981. pap. 2.95 (ISBN 0-380-52522-4, 52522, Bard). Avon.

--Ideas & the Novel. 7.95 (ISBN 0-15-143682-7). HarBraceJ.

--Memories of a Catholic Girlhood. LC 57-8842. (Illus.). 1957. 4.75 o.p. (ISBN 0-15-158859-7). HarBraceJ.

--Memories of a Catholic Girlhood. LC 57-8842. 1972. pap. 3.95 (ISBN 0-15-658650-9, HB231, Harv). HarBraceJ.

--Venice Observed. LC 64-49016. 1963. pap. 2.95 (ISBN 0-15-693521-X, HB61, Harv). HarBraceJ.

McCarthy, Mary A. Sappho by the Sea: An Illustrated Guide to the Hamptons. LC 76-21830. (Illus.). 98p. 1980. Repr. of 1976 ed. 7.95 (ISBN 0-87754-252-X). Chelsea Hse.

McCarthy, Mike, jt. auth. see Davis, Pedr.

McCarthy, Muriel. All Graduates & Gentlemen: Marsh's Library. (Illus.). 239p. 1980. 22.50x (ISBN 0-8476-3141-9). Rowman.

McCarthy, P., jt. auth. see Shklar, G.

McCarthy, Pat. America's Bad Men. Mooney, Thomas, ed. (Pal Paperbacks Ser., Kit A). (Illus., Orig.). (gr. 7-12). 1974. pap. text ed. 1.25 (ISBN 0-8374-3476-9). Xerox Ed Pubns.

McCarthy, Pat, ed. Great Disasters. (Pal Paperbacks Ser., Kit A). (Illus., Orig.). (gr. 7-12). 1974. pap. text ed. 1.25 (ISBN 0-8374-3477-7). Xerox Ed Pubns.

--True Ghost Stories. (Pal Paperbacks Kit A Ser.). (Illus., Orig.). (gr. 7-12). 1974. pap. text ed. 1.25 (ISBN 0-8374-3478-5). Xerox Ed Pubns.

McCarthy, Pat, ed. see Cohen, Carl.

McCarthy, Pat, ed. see Herrmann, Charles F., III.

McCarthy, Pat, ed. see Jameson, F. A.

McCarthy, Patricia, ed. see Arnold, Joanne M.

McCarthy, Patricia, ed. see Bacon, Jo A.

McCarthy, Patricia, ed. see Drozd, Ann M.

McCarthy, Patricia, ed. see Munat, Florence & Munat, Charles.

McCarthy, Patricia, ed. see Piddock, Charles A.

McCarthy, Patricia, ed. see Schleifer, Jay.

McCarthy, Patricia, ed. see Schwach, Howard.

McCarthy, Patricia, ed. see Townsend, Marvin.

McCarthy, Patrick A. The Riddles of Finnegans Wake. LC 79-24075. 184p. 1980. 16.50 (ISBN 0-8386-3005-7). Fairleigh Dickinson.

McCarthy, Patrick J. Matthew Arnold & the Three Classes. LC 64-14237. 1964. 20.00x (ISBN 0-231-02693-5). Columbia U Pr.

McCarthy, Paul. John Steinbeck. LC 78-20929. (Modern Literature Ser.). 1980. 10.95 (ISBN 0-8044-2606-6). Ungar.

McCarthy, Paul & Duncan, John, eds. Close Radio Catalog. LC 81-65198. (Illus.). 100p. (Orig.). 1981. pap. 5.00 (ISBN 0-937122-01-7). Astro Artz.

McCarthy, Paul J. Algebraic Extensions of Fields. 2nd ed. LC 75-41499. ix, 166p. 1976. 9.50 (ISBN 0-8284-1284-7). Chelsea Pub.

McCarthy, Philip L. & Shklar, Gerald. Diseases of the Oral Mucosa. 2nd ed. LC 80-10335. (Illus.). 579p. 1980. text ed. 47.50 (ISBN 0-8121-0641-5). Lea & Febiger.

McCarthy, Robert. World War Two German Military Collectibles. (Illus.). 1980. pap. 6.95 (ISBN 0-89145-135-8). Collector Bks.

McCarthy, Stephen, jt. auth. see Colclough, Christopher.

McCarthy, T. First Aid Step by Step. (Illus.). 1977. pap. 11.00x (ISBN 0-433-20451-6). Intl Ideas.

McCarthy, Thomas. The First Convention. 1978. pap. text ed. 6.25x (ISBN 0-85105-340-8, Dolmen Pr). Humanities.

McCarthy, Timothy. Marx & the Proletariat: A Study in Social Theory. LC 78-4025. (Contributions in Political Science: No. 18). 1978. lib. bdg. 15.00 (ISBN 0-313-20412-8, MPL/). Greenwood.

McCarthy, Todd, jt. ed. see Flynn, Charles.

McCarthy, Willard J. & Repp, Victor. Machine Tool Technology. (Illus.). (gr. 11-12). 1979. text ed. 18.60 (ISBN 0-87345-143-0); Study Guide 1. 3.68 (ISBN 0-87345-144-9); Study Guide 2. 3.68 (ISBN 0-87345-145-7); ans. key avail. McKnight.

McCarthy, Willard J., jt. auth. see Ludwig, Oswald A.

McCarthy, William E. The Closed Shop in Britain. 1964. 20.00x (ISBN 0-520-00837-5). U of Cal Pr.

McCartney, Clarence, et al. The Federal Income Tax, 1981 Edition: Its Sources & Applications. (Illus.). 912p. 1980. text ed. 21.95 (ISBN 0-13-309005-1). P-H.

McCartney, Earl J. Optics of the Atmosphere: Scattering by Molecules & Particles. LC 76-10941. (Pure & Applied Optics Ser). 1976. 37.95 (ISBN 0-471-01526-1, Pub. by Wiley-Interscience). Wiley.

McCartney, J. J., ed. see Caplan, A. L., et al.

McCartney, James, jt. auth. see Galliher, John F.

McCartney, Wilma M. Ring the Doorbell with Your Elbow: A Cookbook of "Portables". rev. ed. LC 80-84349. (Illus.). 136p. 1981. pap. 6.95 (ISBN 0-933050-07-0). New Eng Pr VT.

McCarty, Burke. The Suppressed Truth About the Assassination of Abraham Lincoln. 255p. 1960. Repr. of 1870 ed. 10.00 (Pub. by Chedney). Alpine Ent.

McCarty, Clifford. Film Composers in America: A Checklist of Their Work. LC 72-4448. (Music Ser.). 196p. 1972. Repr. of 1953 ed. lib. bdg. 19.50 (ISBN 0-306-70495-1). Da Capo.

McCarty, Colin T. Flow-Schemes in Organic Chemistry. 1976. 3.95x o.p. (ISBN 0-435-65575-2). Heinemann Ed.

McCarty, Daniel E., jt. auth. see Osteryoung, Jerome S.

McCarty, Diane. Great Danes. (Illus.). 125p. 1980. 2.95 (ISBN 0-87666-693-4, KW-082). TFH Pubns.

--Lhasa Apsos. (Illus.). 125p. 1979. 2.95 (ISBN 0-87666-681-0, KW-076). TFH Pubns.

McCarty, Diane & Henneberry, Mrs. Janet. English Springer Spaniels. (Illus.). 1980. 2.95 (ISBN 0-87666-687-X, KW-081). TFH Pubns.

McCarty, Diane & Kattell, Ted. Collies. (Illus.). 128p. 1980. 2.95 (ISBN 0-87666-684-5, KW-078). TFH Pubns.

McCarty, Diane & Look, Mrs. Travis. Basset Hounds. (Illus.). 125p. 1979. 2.95 (ISBN 0-87666-679-9, KW-069). TFH Pubns.

McCarty, Donald J. & Ramsey, Charles E. The School Managers: Power & Conflict in American Public Education. LC 70-105975. (Illus.). 281p. 1971. lib. bdg. 16.95 (ISBN 0-8371-3299-1, MSM/). Greenwood.

McCarty, Donald J., jt. ed. see Griffiths, Daniel E.

McCarty, Dwight G. Psychology for the Lawyer. (Historical Foundations of Forensic Psychiatry & Psychology Ser.). Date not set. lib. bdg. 49.50 (ISBN 0-306-76068-1). Da Capo.

McCarty, Frank, intro. by. Autofact West Proceedings, Vol. 2. LC 80-53423. (Illus.). 842p. 1980. pap. 55.00 (ISBN 0-87263-066-8). SME.

McCarty, George. Calculator Calculus. LC 75-27363. 1976. pap. 10.95 o.p. (ISBN 0-8087-3929-8). Burgess.

--Calculator Calculus. rev. ed. LC 75-27363. (Illus.). xiv, 258p. 1980. pap. 14.95 (ISBN 0-936356-00-6); pap. text ed. 14.95 (ISBN 0-471-27596-4). Educalc Pubns.

McCarty, Janet & Paterson, Betty J. Craft Fun. (Golden Funtime Ser). (Illus.). (ps-6). 1975. PLB 7.62 o.p. (ISBN 0-307-66305-1, Golden Pr). Western Pub.

McCarty, Jeanne. The Struggle for Sobriety. (Southwestern Studies: No. 62). 1980. pap. 3.00 (ISBN 0-87404-121-X). Tex Western.

McCarty, John L. Maverick Town: The Story of Old Tascosa. rev. ed. (Illus.). 1946. 13.95 (ISBN 0-8061-0157-1). U of Okla Pr.

McCarty, Marilu, jt. auth. see Chisholm, Roger.

McCarty, Marilu H. Dollars & Sense: An Introduction to Economics. 2nd ed. 1979. pap. text ed. 11.95x (ISBN 0-673-15230-8); study guide 4.95x (ISBN 0-673-15238-3). Scott F.

McCarty, Michele. Believing. 160p. 1980. pap. text ed. 4.25 (ISBN 0-697-01753-2); tchr's manual 5.00. Wm C Brown.

--Believing. 160p. 1980. pap. 4.25 (ISBN 0-697-01753-2); tchrs'. manual 5.00 (ISBN 0-697-01754-0). Wm C Brown.

--Deciding. (Orig.). (gr. 11-12). 1981. pap. text ed. 4.25 (ISBN 0-697-01778-8); tchrs' manual 5.00 (ISBN 0-697-01779-6). Wm C Brown.

--Relating. 128p. (Orig.). (gr. 11-12). 1979. pap. text ed. 4.00 (ISBN 0-697-01710-9); tchr's manual 5.00 (ISBN 0-697-01711-7). Wm C Brown.

McCarty, Raymond. Trumpet in the Twilight of Time. LC 80-53734. (Illus.). 144p. (Orig.). 1981. 10.95 (ISBN 0-938310-00-3); pap. 6.95 (ISBN 0-938310-01-1). Volunteer Pubns.

McCarty, Toni. The Skull in the Snow & Other Folktales. LC 80-68730. (Illus.). 96p. (gr. 4-7). 1981. 7.95 (ISBN 0-440-08028-2); PLB 7.45 (ISBN 0-440-08030-4). Delacorte.

McCarus, Ernest, et al, eds. A Course in Levantine Arabic. rev. ed. Qafisheh, Hamdi & Rammuny, Raji. (Orig.). 1978. pap. text ed. 6.00x (ISBN 0-916798-07-0, Pub. by U Mich Dept Near East Stud). Eisenbrauns.

McCary, Ben C. Indians in Seventhteenth Century Virginia. 93p. 1980. pap. 1.95x (ISBN 0-8139-0142-1). U Pr of Va.

McCary, James L. Freedom & Growth in Marriage. 2nd ed. LC 79-17199. 1980. text ed. 15.95 (ISBN 0-471-05341-4); tchrs' manual (ISBN 0-471-07845-X). Wiley.

MacCaskey, Michael, jt. auth. see Ray, Richard.

McCasland, David C. Open to Change. 144p. 1981. pap. 3.95 (ISBN 0-88207-258-7). Victor Bks.

McCasland, S. Vernon, et al. Religions of the World. (Illus.). 1969. 13.95 (ISBN 0-394-30384-9). Random.

McCaslin, Buddy. New Heartthrobs, Vol. II. (Illus.). 160p. (Orig.). (gr. 5 up). pap. 1.95 (ISBN 0-448-14152-3, Tempo). G&D.

McCaslin, Nellie. Act Now: Plays & Ways to Make Them. LC 75-25557. (Illus.). 134p. (gr. 4-7). 1975. 9.95 (ISBN 0-87599-216-1). S G Phillips.

--Children & Drama. 2nd ed. 320p. 1981. text ed. 9.95 (ISBN 0-686-28848-3). Longman.

--Creative Drama in the Classroom. 3rd ed. 1980. text ed. 10.95 (ISBN 0-582-28139-3). Longman.

--Creative Dramatics in the Classroom. 2nd ed. LC 73-88681. 1977. pap. 6.95x o.p. (ISBN 0-582-28007-9). Longman.

McCaslin, Nellie, ed. Children & Drama. LC 74-84081. 1975. pap. 8.95x (ISBN 0-679-30269-7, Pub. by MacKay). Longman.

McCaughan, Nano. Group Work: Learning & Practice. (National Institute Social Service Library). 1978. text ed. 22.50x (ISBN 0-04-361029-3); pap. text ed. 8.95x (ISBN 0-04-361030-7). Allen Unwin.

McCaughey, Patrick, ed. Australian Paintings of the Heidelberg School: The Jack Manton Collection. (Illus.). 160p. 1979. text ed. 65.00x (ISBN 0-19-550592-1). Oxford U Pr.

McCaul, Paul F., jt. auth. see Kubota, Takayuki.

McCauley, Carole S. Pregnancy After Thirty-Five. 1976. 7.95 (ISBN 0-87690-219-0). Dutton.

McCauley, Jane R. Zoos Without Cages. LC 79-3243. (Ser. Two). (Illus.). 100p. (gr. 3-8). 1981. 6.95 (ISBN 0-87044-335-6); PLB 8.50 (ISBN 0-87044-340-2). Natl Geog.

McCauley, Kirby, jt. auth. see Lumley, Brian.

McCauley, Kirby E. Night Chills. (Orig.). 1975. pap. 1.50 (ISBN 0-380-00397-X, 26856). Avon.

McCauley, Lois B. A. Hoen on Stone: E. Weber & Co. and A. Hoen & Co. Exhibition Catalogue. LC 79-87284. (Illus.). 1969. 4.50 (ISBN 0-938420-02-X). Md Hist.

McCauley, Martin. The Stalin File. 1979. 14.95 (ISBN 0-7134-1918-0, Pub. by Batsford England). David & Charles.

McCauley, Rosemarie. Mini Sims Temporaries: Modern Office Simulations 1. 1979. pap. 9.95 (ISBN 0-672-97167-4); tchr's. resource 6.67 (ISBN 0-672-97168-2). Bobbs.

--Mini Sims Temporaries: Modern Office Simulations 2. 1979. pap. 9.95 (ISBN 0-672-97424-X); tchr's. resource 6.67 (ISBN 0-672-97168-2). Bobbs.

McCaulley, Mary H. Application of the Myers-Briggs Type Indicator to Medicine & Other Health Professions, 2 vols. Incl. Monograph I. 554p. 1978. pap. 20.00 (ISBN 0-935652-03-5); Monograph II. 288p. 1977. pap. 15.00 (ISBN 0-935652-04-3). (Illus.). 842p. (Orig.). Set. pap. 30.00 (ISBN 0-935652-05-1). Ctr Applications Psych.

McCausland, Elizabeth. Eyewitness: The Growth of Photography. Peters, Susan D., ed. (Illus.). 250p. 1981. 22.50 (ISBN 0-8180-1421-0). Horizon.

--Life & Work of Edward Lamson Henry N. A. LC 74-100614. (Library of American Art Ser.). (Illus.). 1970. Repr. of 1945 ed. lib. bdg. 39.50 (ISBN 0-306-71866-9). Da Capo.

McCavitt, William. Television Studio Operations Manual. rev. ed. 106p. 1980. pap. 4.50 (ISBN 0-935648-05-4). Halldin Pub.

McCavitt, William E. Radio & Television: A Selected, Annotated Bibliography. LC 77-28665. 1978. 12.00 (ISBN 0-8108-1113-8). Scarecrow.

McCawley, James D. Everything That Linguists Have Always Wanted to Know About Logic: but Were Ashamed to Ask. LC 80-345. (Illus.). 528p. 1981. lib. bdg. 35.00x (ISBN 0-226-55617-4); pap. text ed. 12.50x (ISBN 0-226-55618-2). U of Chicago Pr.

McCawley, Peter. Industrialization in Indonesia: Developments & Prospects. (Development Studies Centre - Occasional Paper: No. 13). (Orig.). 1980. pap. text ed. 3.95 (ISBN 0-7081-1593-4, 0412, Pub. by ANUP Australia). Bks Australia.

McCay, Clive M. & McCay, Jeannette B. The Cornell Bread Book: Fifty-Four Recipes for Nutritious Loaves, Rolls & Coffee Cakes. rev ed. (Illus.). 52p. 1980. pap. 2.00 (ISBN 0-486-23995-0). Dover.

McCay, Jeannette B., jt. auth. see McCay, Clive M.

McCay, Winsor. Little Nemo in the Palace of Ice, & Further Adventures. LC 75-19834. (Illus.). 32p. (Orig.). 1976. pap. 4.50 (ISBN 0-486-23234-4). Dover.

McCGwire, Michael, ed. Soviet Naval Developments: Capability & Context. LC 73-9058. (Special Studies). (Illus.). 576p. 1973. text ed. 35.00 (ISBN 0-275-07590-7). Praeger.

McCgwire, Michael & McDonnell, John, eds. Soviet Naval Influence: Domestic & Foreign Dimensions. LC 75-23982. (Special Studies). 1977. text ed. 52.50 (ISBN 0-275-56290-5). Praeger.

McCGwire, Michael, et al, eds. Soviet Naval Policy: Objectives & Constraints. LC 74-11923. (Illus.). 350p. 1975. 45.00 (ISBN 0-275-09720-X). Praeger.

McChesney, et al. Guide to Language & Study Skills, for College Students of English As a Second Language. 1977. pap. text ed. 9.50 (ISBN 0-13-370452-1). P-H.

McChesney, Harry V., ed. see Clift, G. Glenn, et al.

Macchesney, J. Packaging of Cosmetics & Toiletries. 1974. text ed. 16.95 (ISBN 0-408-00125-9). Butterworths.

M'Cheyne, R. M. Sermons of R. M. M'Cheyne. pap. 1.95 o.p. (ISBN 0-686-12540-1). Banner of Truth.

Macchiavelli, Niccolo. The Arte of Warre, (Certain Waies of the Orderyng of Souldiours) Whitehorne, P., tr. LC 79-26097. (English Experience Ser.: No. 135). 1969. Repr. of 1562 ed. 42.00 (ISBN 90-221-0135-5). Walter J Johnson.

Macchiaverna, Paul R. Auditing Corporate Data-Processing Activities, No. 776. (Illus.). 85p. (Orig.). 1980. pap. 5.00 (ISBN 0-8237-0212-X); pap. text ed. 15.00 (ISBN 0-686-64787-4). Conference Bd.

McClain, Alva J. Bible Truths. 1981. pap. 1.00 (ISBN 0-88469-013-X). BMH Bks.

--The Greatness of the Kingdom. 10.95 (ISBN 0-88469-011-3). BMH Bks.

--Law & Grace. pap. 1.75 (ISBN 0-88469-001-6). BMH Bks.

--Romans, the Gospel of God's Grace. 8.95 (ISBN 0-88469-080-6). BMH Bks.

McClain, Charles A. First Came the Wings. LC 79-63893. 1979. pap. 3.95x (ISBN 0-8358-0387-2). Upper Room.

McClain, Ernest G. Meditations Through the Quran. (Illus.). 1980. write for info. N Hays.

McClain, Mary, illus. First Things to Touch. (Floppies Ser.). (Illus.). 6p. (ps-k). Date not set. 3.95 (ISBN 0-671-42533-1, Little Simon). S&S.

McClain, William B. Travelling Light. (Orig.). 1981. pap. 3.75 (ISBN 0-377-00109-0). Friend Pr.

McClamroch, N. H. State Models of Dynamic Systems. (Illus.). 248p. 1980. 17.80 (ISBN 0-387-90490-5). Springer-Verlag.

McClary, Ben H., ed. Washington Irving & the House of Murray: Geoffrey Crayon Charms the British, 1817-1856. LC 73-77843. (Illus.). 1969. 14.50x (ISBN 0-87049-094-X). U of Tenn Pr.

McClary, Douglas. The Show Racer. (Illus.). 1976. 11.95 (ISBN 0-571-10761-3, Pub. by Faber & Faber). Merrimack Bk Serv.

McClaskey, Marilyn J. & Swanson, Edward, eds. A Manual of AACR 2 Level 1 Examples. 50p. 1980. pap. 6.00 (ISBN 0-936996-03-X). Soldier Creek.

McClaskey, Marilyn J., ed. see Blixrud, Julia C.

McClaskey, Marilyn J, ed. see Hanley, Mary D.

McClaskey, Marilyn J., ed. see Marion, Phyllis.

McClaskey, Marilyn J., ed. see Moore, Barbara N.

McClaskey, Marilyn J., ed. see Schilling, Irene A.

McClaskey, Marilyn J., jt. ed. see Swanson, Edward.

McClasky, Marilyn J., ed. see Aichele, Jean & Olson, Nancy B.

McClasky, Marilyn J., ed. see Simonton, Wesley & Mannie, Phillip.

McClean, A. E., ed. see Royal Society of London.

McClean, J. D., jt. auth. see Bottoms, A. E.

MacClean, Katherine. The Trouble with You Earth People. Freas, Polly & Freas, Kelly, eds. LC 79-15246. (Illus.). 1980. pap. 4.95 (ISBN 0-915442-95-7, Starblaze). Donning Co.

McClearn, G. E. & DeFries, J. C. Introduction to Behavioral Genetics. LC 73-8862. (Psychology Ser.). (Illus.). 347p. 1973. text ed. 21.95x (ISBN 0-7167-0835-3). W H Freeman.

McCleary, George F. On Detective Fiction & Other Things. 161p. 1980. Repr. of 1960 ed. lib. bdg. 20.00 (0-8492-6600-9). R West.

McCleary, Richard. Dangerous Men: The Sociology of Parole. LC 78-19859. (Sage Library of Social Research: Vol. 71). 1978. 18.00x (ISBN 0-8039-1094-0); pap. 8.95x (ISBN 0-8039-1095-9). Sage.

McCleary, Richard, et al. Applied Time Series Analysis for the Social Sciences. LC 79-27873. (Illus.). 331p. 1980. 19.95 (ISBN 0-8039-1205-6); pap. 12.50 (ISBN 0-8039-1206-4). Sage.

McClellan, A. L. Tables of Experimental Dipole Moments. LC 63-14844. 1963. text ed. 32.95x (ISBN 0-7167-0122-7). W H Freeman.

McClellan, Brenda. Successful Home Decorating. Case, Virginia A., ed. (Successful Ser.). (Illus.). 136p. 1981. 18.95 (ISBN 0-89999-021-5); pap. 7.95 (ISBN 0-89999-022-3). Structures Pub.

McClellan, Grant, ed. Canada in Transition. (Reference Shelf Ser.). (Sold on service basis). 1977. 6.25 (ISBN 0-8242-0603-7). Wilson.

McClellan, Grant S., ed. American Youth in a Changing Culture. (Reference Shelf Ser.). 266p. 1972. 6.25 (ISBN 0-8242-0466-2). Wilson.

--Censorship in the United States. (Reference Shelf Ser: Vol. 39, No. 3). 1967. 6.25 (ISBN 0-8242-0096-9). Wilson.

--Civil Rights. (Reference Shelf Ser: Vol. 36, No. 6). 1964. 6.25 (ISBN 0-8242-0083-7). Wilson.

--Consuming Public. (Reference Shelf Ser: Vol. 40, No. 3). 1968. 6.25 (ISBN 0-8242-0102-7). Wilson.

--Crisis in Urban Housing. (Reference Shelf Ser.). 1974. 6.25 (ISBN 0-8242-0509-X). Wilson.

--Land Use in the United States. (Reference Shelf Ser: Vol. 43, No. 2). 1971. 6.25 (ISBN 0-8242-0447-6). Wilson.

--Protecting Our Environment. LC 72-95636. (Reference Shelf Ser: Vol. 42, No. 1). 1970. 6.25 (ISBN 0-8242-0409-3). Wilson.

--The Right to Privacy. (Reference Shelf Ser.). 1976. 6.25 (ISBN 0-8242-0595-2). Wilson.

--Safety on the Road. (Reference Shelf Ser: Vol. 38, No. 1). 1966. 6.25 (ISBN 0-8242-0089-6). Wilson.

--Southern Africa. (Reference Shelf Ser.). 1979. 6.25 (ISBN 0-8242-0633-9). Wilson.

--Spain & Portugal: Democratic Beginnings. (Reference Shelf Ser.: Vol. 50, No. 5). 1978. 6.25 (ISBN 0-8242-0626-6). Wilson.

--U. S. Policy in Latin America. (Reference Shelf Ser: Vol. 35, No. 1). 1963. 6.25 (ISBN 0-8242-0074-8). Wilson.

McClellan, Robert W. Claiming a Frontier: Ministry & Older People. LC 77-85413. 1977. 4.50 (ISBN 0-88474-040-4). USC Andrus Geron.

McClellan, Thomas L. Science of Mind Hymnal. 7.50 o.p. (ISBN 0-87516-343-2). De Vorss.

McClellan, Val J. This Is Our Land, Vol. 1. LC 77-151749. (Illus.). 1977. 12.50x (ISBN 0-533-02248-7). Western Pubs OH.

--This Is Our Land, Vol. 2. LC 77-151749. (Illus.). 1979. 13.95x (ISBN 0-9602218-0-8). Western Pubs OH.

McClelland, Ben W., jt. auth. see Donovan, Timothy R.

McClelland, Charles. State, Society & University in Germany, Seventeen Hundred to Nineteen Hundred & Fourteen. LC 79-13575. 1980. 34.95 (ISBN 0-521-22742-9). Cambridge U Pr.

McClelland, Charles E. German Historians & England: A Study in Nineteenth Century Views. LC 79-154514. 1971. 41.00 (ISBN 0-521-08063-0). Cambridge U Pr.

McClelland, David C. Achieving Society. LC 69-11373. 1967. pap. text ed. 8.95 (ISBN 0-02-920510-7). Free Pr.

--Personality. rev. ed. 672p. 1980. text ed. 34.50x (ISBN 0-8290-0400-9); pap. text ed. 18.50x (ISBN 0-8290-0243-X). Irvington.

--Power: The Inner Experience. LC 75-35603. (Social Relations Ser.). 436p. 1975. 16.95 o.p. (ISBN 0-470-58169-7). Halsted Pr.

--Roots of Consciousness. enl. ed. (Illus.). 1981. text ed. 18.50x (ISBN 0-8290-0124-7). Irvington.

McClelland, David C., ed. Development of Social Maturity. 1981. text ed. 18.50x (ISBN 0-8290-0089-5): Irvington.

--Education for Values. 1981. text ed. 18.50x (ISBN 0-8290-0090-9). Irvington.

McClelland, David C., et al. The Drinking Man. LC 79-143504. 1972. 15.95 (ISBN 0-02-920460-7). Free Pr.

McClelland, I. L. Diego De Torres Villarroel. (World Authos Ser.: Spain: No. 395). 1976. lib. bdg. 12.50 (ISBN 0-8057-6237-X). Twayne.

McClelland, Ivy L. Ignacio de Luzan. (World Authors Ser.: Spain: No. 221). lib. bdg. 10.95 (ISBN 0-8057-2552-0). Twayne.

McClelland, James N., jt. auth. see Bradley, Jack I.

McClelland, L., et al. English Sounds & Spelling. 1979. pap. 6.95 (ISBN 0-13-282954-1). P-H.

McClelland, Lucille H. Textbook for Psychiatric Technicians. 2nd rev. ed. LC 74-147167. (Illus.). 1971. pap. text ed. 10.95 o.p. (ISBN 0-8016-3216-1). Mosby.

McClelland, Peter D. & Magdovitz, Alan L. Crisis in the Making: The Political Economy of New York State Since Nineteen Forty-Five. LC 80-24167. (Studies in Economic History & Policy: the United States in the Twentieth Century). (Illus.). 512p. Date not set. price not set (ISBN 0-521-23807-2). Cambridge U Pr.

McClelland, Peter D., ed. Introductory Macroeconomics, 1980-81: Readings on Contemporary Issues. LC 80-66907. (Illus.). 224p. (Orig.). 1980. pap. 8.95x (ISBN 0-8014-9873-2). Cornell U Pr.

--Macroeconomics 1979: Readings on Contemporary Issues. LC 77-6193. (Continuation Ser.). (Orig.). 1979. text ed. 7.95x soft cover o.p. (ISBN 0-8014-9870-8). Cornell U Pr.

McClellen, Joseph H. & Rader, Charles M. Number Theory in Digital Signal Processing. (Signal Processing Ser.). (Illus.). 1979. ref. 23.95 (ISBN 0-13-627349-1). P-H.

McClenaghan, William A. Magruder's American Government Nineteen Eighty. (gr. 9-12). 1980. text ed. 17.60 (ISBN 0-205-06891-X, 7668910); tchrs'. guide 6.12 (ISBN 0-205-06892-8, 7668929). Allyn.

--Magruder's American Government: 1976. rev. ed. (gr. 9-12). 1976. text ed. 17.60 (ISBN 0-205-05651-2, 7656513); tchrs'. guide 6.12 (ISBN 0-205-05652-0, 7656521); dup. mast 42.00 (ISBN 0-205-05653-9, 765653X); tests 42.00 (ISBN 0-205-05654-7, 7656548). Allyn.

--Magruder's American Government, 1978. rev. ed. (gr. 9-12). 1978. text ed. 17.60 (ISBN 0-205-05862-0, 7658621); tchr's guide 6.12 (ISBN 0-205-05863-9, 765863X). Allyn.

--Magruder's American Government, 1979. annual rev. ed. (gr. 7-12). 1979. text ed. 17.60 (ISBN 0-205-06430-2, 7664303). Allyn.

McClendon, James W., ed. Philosophy of Religion & Theology: 1975 Proceedings. LC 75-26618. (American Academy of Religion. Section Papers). 1975. pap. 7.50 (ISBN 0-89130-024-4, 010916). Scholars Pr Ca.

McClendon, James W., Jr. Biography As Theology: How Life Stories Can Remake Today's Theology. LC 74-9715. 224p. 1974. 13.95 (ISBN 0-687-03540-6); pap. 6.50 (ISBN 0-687-03539-2). Abingdon.

McClennen, Sandra E., et al. Social Skills for Severely Retarded Adults: An Inventory & Training Program. LC 80-51546. 265p. 1980. 3-ring binder 34.95 (ISBN 0-87822-220-0, 2200). Res Press.

McClenney, Byron N. Management for Productivity. 126p. (Orig.). 1980. pap. 5.00 (ISBN 0-87117-103-1). Am Assn Comm Jr Coll.

McClintic, J. Robert. Physiology of the Human Body. 2nd ed. LC 77-27066. 1978. text ed. 23.95x (ISBN 0-471-02664-6). Wiley.

McClintock, Cynthia. Peasant Cooperatives & Political Change in Peru. LC 80-8563. (Illus.). 480p. 1981. 30.00x (ISBN 0-691-07627-8); pap. 7.95x (ISBN 0-691-02202-X). Princeton U Pr.

McClintock, Dalene & Holmes, Carolyn. Communication Skillbook Three: New Worlds in English. (Communication Skillbooks). 64p. 1980. pap. text ed. 3.95 (ISBN 0-88499-223-3). Inst Mod Lang.

McClintock, David W. U.S. Food: Making the Most of a Global Resource. 1979. lib. bdg. 20.00x (ISBN 0-89158-183-9). Westview.

MacClintock, Dorcas. A Natural History of Raccoons. (Illus.). 160p. (gr. 7 up). 1981. 10.95 (ISBN 0-684-16619-4). Scribner.

McClintock, F. A. & Argon, A. S. Mechanical Behavior of Materials. 1966. 27.95 (ISBN 0-201-04545-1). A-W.

McClintock, H. F. Handbook on the Traditional Old Irish Dress. (Illus.). 8.95. Dufour.

McClintock, Inez, jt. auth. see Barenholtz, Bernard.

McClintock, Jean & McClintock, Robert, eds. Henry Barnard's School Architecture. LC 72-729262. (Illus.). 1970. text ed. 15.70 (ISBN 0-8077-1725-8); pap. text ed. 6.75x (ISBN 0-8077-1724-X). Tchrs Coll.

McClintock, John & Strong, James. Cyclopedia of Biblical, Theological, & Ecclesiastical Literature, 12 vols. 12400p. 1961. text ed. 395.00 (ISBN 0-8010-6123-7). Baker Bk.

McClintock, Michael C. NLRB General Counsel: Unreviewable Power to Refuse to Issue an Unfair Labor Practice Complaint. LC 80-67049. (Scholarly Monographs). 180p. 1980. pap. 15.00 (ISBN 0-8408-0510-1). Carrollton Pr.
McClintock, Robert, jt. ed. see McClintock, Jean.
McClintock, Walter. The Old North Trail; or, Life, Legends & Religion of the Blackfeet Indians. LC 68-13651. (Illus.). 1968. pap. 5.95 (ISBN 0-8032-5130-0, BB 379, Bison). U of Nebr Pr.
McClinton, Barbara S. & Meier, Blanche G. Beginnings: The Psychology of Early Childhood. LC 77-17619. (Illus.). 1978. text ed. 16.95 (ISBN 0-8016-3217-X). Mosby.
McClinton, Katherine M. An Introduction to Lalique Glass. (Illus.). 1978. 17.95 (ISBN 0-87069-238-0). Wallace-Homestead.
McClory, Robert. The Man Who Beat Clout City. LC 77-88692. (Illus.). 224p. 1977. 11.95 (ISBN 0-8040-0777-2). Swallow.
McCloskey, A. L., jt. ed. see Steinberg, H.
McCloskey, D., jt. ed. see Floud, R.
McCloskey, Donald N. Enterprise & Trade in Victorian Britain: Essays in Historical Economics. (Illus.). 240p. 1981. text ed. 35.00x (ISBN 0-04-942170-0, 2617-8); pap. text ed. 14.95x (ISBN 0-04-942171-9). Allen Unwin.
McCloskey, Joanne C., et al. Current Issues in Nursing. (Illus.). 480p. (Orig.). 1981. pap. text ed. 14.95 (ISBN 0-86542-005-X). Blackwell Sci.
McCloskey, Mark, tr. see Herbert, George.
McCloskey, Paul N. United States Constitution. (gr. 10-12). 1972. pap. text ed. 9.00 incl. tchrs' manual & test (ISBN 0-8449-0901-7). Learning Line.
McCloskey, Richard V. Self-Assessment of Current Knowledge in Infectious Diseases. 2nd ed. 1974. spiral bdg. 14.00 (ISBN 0-87488-263-X). Med Exam.
McCloskey, Robert G. American Supreme Court. LC 60-14235. (History of American Civilization Ser.). 1960. 12.00x (ISBN 0-226-55673-5); pap. 5.95 (ISBN 0-226-55675-1, CHAC13). U of Chicago Pr.
McCloskey, Robert G., jt. ed. see Friedrich, Carl J.
McCloskey, William B., Jr. Highliners. 408p. 1981. pap. 5.95 (ISBN 0-07-044858-2). McGraw.
MacCloud, Malcolm. The Tera Beyond. LC 80-36728. 192p. (gr. 5-9). 1981. PLB 9.95 (ISBN 0-689-30817-5, Argo). Atheneum.
McCloy, D. Control of Fluid Power: Analysis & Design. 2nd rev. ed. LC 80-40027. 500p. 1980. 85.00 (ISBN 0-470-27012-8). Halsted Pr.
McCloy, D. & Martin, H. R. The Control of Fluid Power. LC 72-5349. 1973. 37.95 (ISBN 0-470-58195-6). Halsted Pr.
McCloy, Helen. Burn This. LC 80-26053. 287p. 1980. Repr. of 1980 ed. large print ed. 10.95 (ISBN 0-89621-261-0). Thorndike Pr.
--Burn This. LC 80-150. (A Dr. Basil Willing Mystery Novel Ser.). 212p. 1980. 7.95 (ISBN 0-396-07806-0). Dodd.
McClung, John A. Sketches of Western Adventure: Containing an Account of the Most Interesting Incidents Connected with the Settlement of the West from 1755 to 1794. LC 75-7072. (Indian Captivities Ser.: Vol. 50). 1976. Repr. of 1832 ed. lib. bdg. 44.00 (ISBN 0-8240-1674-2). Garland Pub.
McClung, Nellie. In Times Like These. LC 70-163829. (Social History of Canada Ser.). 160p. 1972. pap. 4.95 (ISBN 0-8020-6125-7). U of Toronto Pr.
McClung, Robert. Hunted Mammals of the Sea. (Illus.). (gr. 7 up). 1978. 8.95 (ISBN 0-688-22146-7); PLB 8.59 (ISBN 0-688-32146-1). Morrow.
McClung, Robert M. Amazing Egg. LC 79-23461. (Illus.). 128p. (gr. 4-6). 1980. 9.95 (ISBN 0-525-25480-3). Dutton.
--Bees, Wasps, & Hornets. LC 73-151942. (Illus.). (gr. 3-7). 7.95 (ISBN 0-688-21075-9); PLB 7.63 (ISBN 0-688-31075-3). Morrow.
--Black Jack: Last of the Big Alligators. (Illus.). (gr. 3-7). 1967. PLB 6.96 (ISBN 0-688-31103-2). Morrow.
--Gypsy Moth: Its History in America. LC 74-6245. (Illus.). (gr. 5-9). 1974. PLB 6.96 (ISBN 0-688-20124-5); PLB 6.00 o.p. (ISBN 0-688-30124-X). Morrow.
--Honker: The Story of a Wild Goose. (Illus.). (gr. 3-7). 1965. PLB 6.96 (ISBN 0-688-31399-X). Morrow.
--Lost Wild Worlds, the Story of Extinct & Vanishing Wildlife of the Eastern Hemisphere. (Illus.). 256p. (gr. 7 up). 1976. 9.50 (ISBN 0-688-22090-8). Morrow.
--Mice, Moose & Men: How Their Populations Rise & Fall. LC 73-4926. (Illus.). 64p. (gr. 3-7). 1973. 7.25 (ISBN 0-688-20087-7); PLB 6.96 (ISBN 0-688-30087-1). Morrow.
--Peeper, First Voice of Spring. LC 77-2410. (Illus.). (gr. 1-5). 1977. PLB 6.96 (ISBN 0-688-32116-X). Morrow.
--Possum. (gr. 1-5). 1963. PLB 7.44 (ISBN 0-688-31508-9). Morrow.
--Samson, Last of the California Grizzlies. (Illus.). 96p. (gr. 3-7). 1973. PLB 6.25 o.p. (ISBN 0-688-21935-7); PLB 6.48 (ISBN 0-688-31935-1). Morrow.
--Sea Star. LC 75-2247. (Illus.). 48p. (gr. k-3). 1975. PLB 6.96 (ISBN 0-688-32034-1). Morrow.
--Vanishing Wildlife of Latin America. LC 80-25639. (Illus.). 160p. (gr. 7-9). 1981. 8.95 (ISBN 0-688-00378-8); PLB 8.59 (ISBN 0-688-00379-6). Morrow.
McClung, William A. The Country House in English Renaissance Poetry. 1977. 17.50x (ISBN 0-520-03137-7). U of Cal Pr.
McClure, Carma. Managing Software Development & Maintenance. 224p. 1981. text ed. 16.95 (ISBN 0-442-22569-5). Van Nos Reinhold.
McClure, Charlotte S. Gertrude Atherton. (United States Authors Ser.: No. 324). 1979. lib. bdg. 10.95 (ISBN 0-8057-7216-2). Twayne.
McClure, Cole R., jt. ed. see Hatheway, Allen W.
McClure, Donald S., ed. see Brome, Richard.
McClure, Gillian. Prickly Pig. (Illus.). (ps-1). 1980. 6.95 (ISBN 0-233-96780-X). Andre Deutsch.
McClure, James. The Blood of an Englishman. LC 80-7607. 288p. 1981. 9.95 (ISBN 0-06-013046-6, HarpT). Har-Row.
--Rogue Eagle. 1978. pap. 1.75 (ISBN 0-380-42267-0, 42267). Avon.
--Rogue Eagle. LC 76-9211. 256p. 1976. 8.95 o.p. (ISBN 0-06-012949-2, HarpT). Har-Row.
--Snake. 1977. pap. 1.50 (ISBN 0-380-01683-4, 33548). Avon.
--The Steam Pig. LC 72-410. (Harper Novel of Suspense). 256p. 1972. 7.95 o.p. (ISBN 0-06-012896-8, HarpT). Har-Row.
McClure, Jon. Meat Eaters Are Threatened. (Health Ser.). (Orig.). 1973. pap. 1.25 o.s.i. (ISBN 0-515-02984-X, V2984). Jove Pubns.
--Stretching Your Meat Dollar. (Orig.). 1978. pap. 2.50 o.s.i. (ISBN 0-515-04563-2). Jove Pubns.
McClure, Michael. Hymms to St. Geryon & Dark Brown. LC 79-18173. 104p. 1980. pap. 5.95 (ISBN 0-912516-33-X). Grey Fox.
McClure, Ruth K. Coram's Children: The London Foundling Hospital in the Eighteenth Century. LC 80-21375. (Illus.). 336p. 1981. text ed. 27.50 (ISBN 0-300-02465-7). Yale U Pr.
McClure, Thomas A. & Lipinsky, Deward S., eds. Resource Materials. (Handbook of Biosolar Resources Ser.: Vol. 2). 560p. 1981. 69.95 (ISBN 0-8493-3473-X). CRC Pr.
McCluskey, Neil G., ed. Catholic Education in America: A Documentary History. LC 64-23904. (Orig.). 1964. text ed. 8.75 (ISBN 0-8077-1731-2); pap. text ed. 4.00x (ISBN 0-8077-1728-2). Tchrs Coll.
McCluskey, Robert T. & Pirani, Conrad L. Medical Diseases of the Kidney. (Anatomic Pathology Slide Seminar Ser.). (Illus.). 1972. atlas 63.50 o.p. (ISBN 0-89189-055-6, 15-1-012-00); slides 22.50 o.p. (ISBN 0-685-78075-9, 01-1-072-00). Am Soc Clinical.
McClusky, Mary. Bel-Air. 256p. (Orig.). 1981. pap. 2.50 (ISBN 0-523-41158-8). Pinnacle Bks.
McClymer, John. Thinking About the American People. 98p. 4.50 (ISBN 0-686-68744-2). Revisionary.
McClymer, John F. War & Welfare: Social Engineering in America, 1890-1925. LC 79-54060. (Contributions in American History: No. 84). xvi, 248p. 1980. lib. bdg. 22.95 (ISBN 0-313-21129-9, MWW/). Greenwood.
McClymonds, Marita P. Niccolo Jommelli: The Last Years, Seventeen Sixty-Nine to Seventeen Seventy-Four. Buelow, George, ed. (Studies in Musicology). 700p. 1981. 59.95 (ISBN 0-8357-1113-7, Pub. by UMI Res Pr). Univ Microfilms.
Maccoby, Eleanor E. & Jacklin, Carol N. The Psychology of Sex Differences. LC 73-94488. 1974. 18.95x (ISBN 0-8047-0859-2); Vol. I: Text. pap. 7.50x (ISBN 0-8047-0974-2); Vol. II: Annotated Bibliography. pap. 4.95x (ISBN 0-8047-0975-0). Stanford U Pr.
Maccoby, Hyam. Revolution in Judaea: Jesus & the Jewish Resistance. LC 80-16752. 256p. 1980. 9.95 (ISBN 0-8008-6784-X). Taplinger.
Maccoby, Hyam, tr. from Heb. The Day God Laughed: Sayings, Fables & Entertainments of the Jewish Sages. LC 78-53502. 1978. 10.00 o.p. (ISBN 0-312-18403-4). St Martin.
MacColl, Ewan & Seeger, Peggy. Travellers' Songs from England & Scotland. LC 76-2854. 1977. 23.50x (ISBN 0-87049-191-1). U of Tenn Pr.
MacColl, LeRoy A. Fundamental Theory of Servomechanisms. pap. 3.50 o.p. (ISBN 0-486-61916-8). Dover.
MacCollam, Joel A. Carnival of Souls: Religious Cults & Young People. 1979. 10.95 (ISBN 0-8164-0436-4); pap. 4.95 (ISBN 0-8164-2211-7). Crossroad NY.
McCollister. The Christian Catalogue. LC 77-29136. 1981. 12.50 (ISBN 0-8246-0226-9). Jonathan David.
McCollough, Major C., jt. auth. see Faulkner, Charles H.
McCollum, Audrey T. Coping with Prolonged Health Impairment in Your Child. 242p. 1975. 12.95 (ISBN 0-316-54185-0). Little.
McCollum, J. P., jt. auth. see Ware, George W.
McCollum, John I., Jr., ed. see Jonson, Ben.
McComas, Alan. Neuromuscular Functions & Disorders. 1977. 59.95 (ISBN 0-407-00058-5). Butterworths.
McComas, Tom & Tuohy, James. Lionel: A Collectors Guide & History, Vol. IV:1970-1980. 138p. 1980. 24.95 (ISBN 0-937522-00-7). TM Prods.
McComb, David. Big Thompson: Profile of a Natural Disaster. (Illus.). 1980. 19.95 (ISBN 0-87108-558-5). Pruett.
McComb, H. G., jt. ed. see Noor, A. K.
McCombie, Ian. The Piano Paperback. (Illus.). 1980. 12.50 (ISBN 0-684-16444-2, ScribT). Scribner.
McCombie, Sharon L., ed. The Rape Crisis Intervention Handbook: A Guide to Victim Care. (Illus.). 250p. 1980. 19.50 (ISBN 0-306-40401-X, Plenum Pr). Plenum Pub.
McCombs, Maxwell & Grey, David. Handbook of Reporting Methods. LC 75-31009. (Illus.). 1976. text ed. 14.95 (ISBN 0-395-18958-6); inst. manual 1.00 (ISBN 0-395-18957-8). HM.
MacConaill, M. A., tr. see Oliver, George.
MacConaugha, Carol. Five Hundred Things to Do in Los Angeles for Free. 140p. 1981. pap. 3.95 (ISBN 0-695-81562-8). Follett.
McConaughy, Paul D., jt. ed. see Grisham, Roy A., Jr.
McCone, R. Clyde. Culture & Controversy: An Investigation of the Tongues of Pentecost. 136p. 1978. 6.95 (ISBN 0-8059-2532-5). Dorrance.
McConica, James K. English Humanists & Reformation Politics Under Henry Eighth & Edward Sixth. 1965. 29.95x (ISBN 0-19-821450-2). Oxford U Pr.
McConkey, A., jt. auth. see Eastop, T. D.
McConkey, Dale D. No-Nonsense Delegation. (Illus.). 1979. pap. 5.95 (ISBN 0-8144-7517-5). Am Mgmt.
McConkey, James. Night Stand: A Book of Stories. 207p. 1965. 12.50x (ISBN 0-8014-0280-8). Cornell U Pr.
McConkey, James H. El Triple Secreto Del Espiritu Santo. Agostini, Beatrice, tr. from Eng. Orig. Title: The Three Fold Secret of the Holy Spirit. 106p. (Span.). Date not set. pap. price not set (ISBN 0-311-09090-7). Casa Bautista.
McConkey, Lois. Sea & Cedar: How the Northwest Coast Indians Lived. (Illus.). 1973. paper-0ver-boards 6.95 (ISBN 0-88894-158-7, Pub. by Douglas & McIntyre). Madrona Pubs.
McConkey, Sue. Jade Bough, White Shadows. 1970. 5.00 o.p. (ISBN 0-87482-000-6). Wake-Brook.
--View from Douglas Hill. 1958. 5.00 o.p. (ISBN 0-87482-051-0). Wake-Brook.
McConkie, Bruce R. The Mortal Messiah, from Bethlehem to Calvary, Bk. 3. LC 79-19606. 486p. 1980. 11.95 (ISBN 0-87747-825-2). Deseret Bk.
McConnall, James M., jt. auth. see Dismukes, Newton B., Jr.
McConnaughey, Bayard H. Introduction to Marine Biology. 3rd ed. LC 77-25826. (Illus.). 1978. text ed. 23.50 (ISBN 0-8016-3258-7). Mosby.
McConnaughhay, Conda L. Birth of a Dilettante. 1980. 7.95 (ISBN 0-533-04546-0). Vantage.
McConnell, Allen. A Russian Philosophe, Alexander Radischev, Seventeen Forty-Nine to Eighteen Hundred Two. LC 79-2911. 228p. 1981. Repr. of 1964 ed. 21.00 (ISBN 0-8305-0080-4). Hyperion Conn.
--Tsar Alexander First: Paternalistic Reformer. LC 70-101949. (AHM Europe Since 1500 Ser.). 1970. pap. 5.95x (ISBN 0-88295-745-7). AHM Pub.
McConnell, Brian. The History of Assassination. LC 78-114781. 360p. 1974. 6.95 o.s.i. (ISBN 0-87695-027-6). Aurora Pubs.
McConnell, Campbell R. Economics: Principles, Problems & Policies. 8th, rev. ed. (Illus.). 992p. 1980. text ed. 19.95x (ISBN 0-07-044930-9, C); instructor's manual 15.00 (ISBN 0-07-044931-7); study guide 7.95x (ISBN 0-07-044932-5); economics concepts 9.95x (ISBN 0-07-044936-8); transparency masters avail. (ISBN 0-07-044934-1). McGraw.
McConnell, David, jt. auth. see Parker, Lois.
McConnell, David B., jt. auth. see Lewis, Ferris E.
McConnell, F. M. McConnell's Manual for Baptist Churches. 1975. 5.00 (ISBN 0-8170-0100-X). Judson.
McConnell, Frank. The Science Fiction of H. G. Wells. (Science Fiction Writers Ser.). (Illus.). 250p. 1981. 18.95 (ISBN 0-19-502811-2). Oxford U Pr.
--The Science Fiction of H. G. Wells. (Science Fiction Writers Ser.: No. 622). (Illus.). 250p. 1981. pap. 4.95 (ISBN 0-19-502812-0, GB). Oxford U Pr.
McConnell, Frank D., ed. see Wells, H. G.
McConnell, Freeman E., jt. auth. see Bess, Fred H.
McConnell, Gerald, ed. Illustrators Twenty Two: The 22nd Annual of American Illustration. (Illus.). 368p. 1981. 37.50 (ISBN 0-8038-3433-0, Visual Communication). Hastings.
McConnell, Jean. The Detectives. 160p. 1976. 5.95 (ISBN 0-7153-7140-1). David & Charles.
McConnell, Joan & McConnell, Teena. Ballet As Body Language: The Anatomy of Ballet for Student & Dance Lover. 1977. 13.95 (ISBN 0-06-012957-3, HarpT); pap. 7.95 o.p. (ISBN 0-06-012964-6, TD-289, HarpT). Har-Row.
McConnell, Joan, tr. see Mazzolani, Lidia S.
McConnell, John W. Ideas of the Great Economists. rev ed. (No. 511). 224p. 1980. pap. 4.95 (ISBN 0-06-463511-2, EH 511, EH). Har-Row.
McConnell, Jon P., jt. auth. see Kreck, Lothar A.
McConnell, Malcolm. Just Causes. LC 80-23692. (Illus.). 384p. 1981. 13.95 (ISBN 0-670-41092-6). Viking Pr.
McConnell, Robert R. Modeling Glass Furnace, Refiner & Forehearth Design & Operation for Energy Efficiency & Improved Control. LC 78-75008. (Outstanding Dissertations on Energy Ser.). 1979. lib. bdg. 28.00 (ISBN 0-8240-3976-9). Garland Pub.
McConnell, Rosemary. The Amazon. LC 78-62990. (Rivers of the World Ser.). (Illus.). 1978. lib. bdg. 7.95 (ISBN 0-686-51133-6). Silver.
McConnell, Stephen R. & Usher, Carolyn E. Intergenerational House-Sharing. LC 80-67436. (Andrus Papers). 52p. 1980. pap. 3.25 (ISBN 0-88474-098-6). USC Andrus Geron.
McConnell, Teena, jt. auth. see McConnell, Joan.
McConnell-Ginet, Sally, et al, eds. Women & Language in Literature & Society. (Praeger Special Studies). 470p. 1980. 25.95 (ISBN 0-03-057892-2); pap. 11.95 (ISBN 0-03-057893-0). Praeger.
McConner, Vincent. The Riviera Puzzle: An Inspector Damiot Mystery. 228p. 1981. 10.95 (ISBN 0-02-582930-0). Macmillan.
McConnico, Charles T. Medical Transcriptionist Handbook. 256p. 1972. text ed. 12.75 (ISBN 0-398-02367-0). C C Thomas.
McConochie, Jean, jt. auth. see Osman, Alice H.
MacConomy, Alma D., ed. see Robinson, David F.
McConville, Michael J., jt. auth. see Baldwin, John.
McConville, Sean. A History of English Prison Administration: 1750-1877. 520p. 1981. price not set (ISBN 0-7100-0694-2). Routledge & Kegan.
McCool, Barbara P., jt. auth. see Brown, Montague.
McCool, Gerald, ed. Rahner Reader. (Orig.). 1975. 13.50 (ISBN 0-8164-1173-5); pap. 6.95 (ISBN 0-8164-2107-2). Crossroad NY.
McCool, Gerald A. Catholic Theology in the Nineteenth Century: The Quest for a Unitary Method. 1977. 14.95 (ISBN 0-8164-4710-1). Crossroad NY.
McCord, Arline, jt. auth. see McCord, William.
McCord, Clinton D., Jr. Oculoplastic Surgery. 300p. 1981. 29.00 (ISBN 0-89004-633-6). Raven.
McCord, David. As Built with Second Thoughts, Reforming What Was Old. pap. 3.00. Boston Public Lib.
McCord, Howard. The Great Toad Hunt & Other Expeditions. LC 79-23842. 1980. 7.95 (ISBN 0-89594-015-9); pap. 3.95 (ISBN 0-89594-014-0). Crossing Pr.
McCord, Norman. North East England: The Region's Development 1760-1914. 1979. 50.00 (ISBN 0-7134-1261-5, Pub. by Batsford England). David & Charles.
McCord, William & McCord, Arline. American Social Problems: Challenges to Existence. LC 76-47622. 1977. pap. 9.95 (ISBN 0-8016-3221-8). Mosby.
McCorduck, Pamela. Machines Who Think. LC 79-13809. (Illus.). 1979. text ed. 15.95x (ISBN 0-7167-1072-2). W H Freeman.
McCormac, Jack C. Structural Steel Design. 3rd ed. (Illus.). 640p. 1981. text ed. 27.50 scp (ISBN 0-06-044344-8, HarpC); avail. Har-Row.
McCormack. Prevention of Mental Retardation & Other Developmental Disabilities. 680p. 1980. 49.75 (ISBN 0-8247-6950-3). Dekker.
MacCormack, Carol & Strathern, Marilyn, eds. Nature, Culture & Gender. (Illus.). 1980. 24.95 (ISBN 0-521-23491-3); pap. 8.95 (ISBN 0-521-28001-X). Cambridge U Pr.

McCormack, Erliss. How to Raise & Train a Cairn Terrier. pap. 2.00 (ISBN 0-87666-262-9, DS1068). TFH Pubns.
McCormack, Jack S. Surveying. (Illus.). 288p. 1976. 16.95x (ISBN 0-13-879064-7). P-H.
McCormack, James E. & Chalmers, Amanda J. Early Cognitive Instruction for the Moderately & Severely Handicapped: Teaching Sequences. LC 78-62903. (Illus.). 1978. loose-leaf 34.95 (ISBN 0-87822-188-3). Res Press.
McCormack, Mark. Dunhill Golf Yearbook, Nineteen Seventy-Nine. (Illus.). 1979. 17.95 o.p. (ISBN 0-385-14940-9); pap. 9.95 o.p. (ISBN 0-385-14941-7). Doubleday.
McCormack, Mark H. Dunhill Golf Yearbook 1980. 448p. 1980. 18.95 (ISBN 0-385-14942-5); pap. 10.95 (ISBN 0-385-14943-3). Doubleday.
--The World of Professional Golf: Mark H. McCormack's Golf Annual 1978. LC 78-58848. 1978. pap. 8.95 o.p. (ISBN 0-385-14166-1); pap. 8.95 Softbound o.p. (ISBN 0-385-14179-3). Doubleday.
McCormack, R. M. & Watson, J. Plastic Surgery: Operative Surgery Ser. 3rd ed. LC 79-40787. (Illus.). 1979. 160.00 (ISBN 0-407-00637-0). Butterworths.
MacCormack, Sabine. Art & Ceremony in Late Antiquity. (The Transformation of the Classical Heritage Ser.). (Illus.). 450p. 1981. 35.00x (ISBN 0-520-03779-0). U of Cal Pr.
McCormack, Thomas, ed. Afterwords: Novelists on Their Novels. LC 68-28208. 1969. 7.95 o.s.i. (ISBN 0-06-012903-4, HarpT). Har-Row.
McCormack, Thomas J., ed. see Berkeley, George.
McCormack, W. J. Sheridan le Fanu & Victorian Ireland. (Illus.). 334p. 1980. text ed. 36.00x (ISBN 0-19-812629-8). Oxford U Pr.
McCormack, William & Krishnamurthi, M. G. Kannada: A Cultural Introduction to the Spoken Styles of the Language. 1966. text ed. 17.50 (ISBN 0-299-03840-8). U of Wis Pr.
McCormack, William G. & Izzo, Herbert J., eds. Sixth LACUS Forum Proceedings, Linguistic Association of Canada & the U.S. pap. 10.95 (ISBN 0-686-64345-3). Hornbeam Pr.
McCormick, Barnes W. Aerodynamics, Aeronautics, & Flight Mechanics. LC 79-11073. 1979. text ed. 30.95 (ISBN 0-471-03032-5). Wiley.
McCormick, Bill. The Complete Beginner's Guide to Golf. LC 73-78770. 144p. (gr. 5-9). 1974. PLB 4.95 (ISBN 0-385-05529-3). Doubleday.
McCormick, C. W., jt. ed. see Peerless, S.
McCormick, Charles T., et al. Cases & Materials on Evidence. 5th ed. LC 80-22463. 1083p. 1980. text ed. write for info. (ISBN 0-8299-2112-5). West Pub.
McCormick, Dell. Paul Bunyan Swings His Axe. (gr. 4-6). 1972. pap. 1.25 (ISBN 0-590-01327-0, Schol Pap). Schol Bk Serv.
McCormick, Donald. The Master Book of Escapes. LC 74-10347. (Illus.). 192p. (gr. 5 up). 1975. PLB 4.95 o.p. (ISBN 0-531-02801-1). Watts.
McCormick, E. A., jt. auth. see Ryder, F. G.
McCormick, Ernest J. & Tiffin, Joseph. Industrial Psychology. 6th ed. (Psychology Ser.). 624p. 1974. ref. ed. 17.95 o.p. (ISBN 0-13-463125-0). P-H.
McCormick, G. P., jt. auth. see Fiacco, A. V.
McCormick, Gene H. & Soltis, Andy. Bird's Defense to the Ruy Lopez. LC 80-28210. (Illus.). 220p. 1981. lib. bdg. write for info. McFarland & Co.
McCormick, J. Middle Distance. LC 76-139233. 1971. 9.25 o.s.i. (ISBN 0-02-920520-4). Free Pr.
McCormick, Jack. Atoms, Energy & Machines. LC 66-30642. (Creative Science Ser). (Illus.). (gr. 4-9). 1967. PLB 7.95 (ISBN 0-87191-010-1). Creative Ed.
--The Living Forest. LC 57-11791. (Illus.). 1959. lib. bdg. 8.79 o.p. (ISBN 0-06-071021-7, HarpT). Har-Row.
McCormick, Joe, tr. see Ford, LeRoy.
McCormick, John O., ed. see Faculty of Comparative Literature, Livingston College.
McCormick, Michael E. Ocean Wave Energy Conversion. (Alternate Energy Ser.). 300p. 1981. 30.00 (ISBN 0-471-08543-X, Pub. by Wiley-Interscience). Wiley.
McCormick, Michael E., ed. Anchoring Systems. 1979. pap. text ed. 40.00 (ISBN 0-08-022694-9). Pergamon.
--Port & Ocean Engineering Under Arctic Conditions: Selected Papers from the 3rd International Conference. 1977. pap. text ed. 24.00 (ISBN 0-08-021421-5). Pergamon.
McCormick, Norman J. Reliability & Risk Analysis: Methods & Nuclear Power Applications. 1981. write for info. (ISBN 0-12-482360-2). Acad Pr.
McCormick, Peter & Elliston, Frederick A., eds. Husserl: Shorter Works. LC 80-53178. 440p. 1981. text ed. 26.00 (ISBN 0-268-01703-4); pap. text ed. 10.95 (ISBN 0-268-01077-3). U of Notre Dame Pr.
McCormick, Regina. Ethnic Heritage Studies Program Catalog: 1974-1979. (Illus.). 152p. (Orig.). 1980. pap. 9.95 (ISBN 0-89994-247-4). Soc Sci Ed.
McCormick, Richard A. Ambiguity in Moral Choice. (Pere Marquette Theology Lectures). 1977. pap. 6.95 (ISBN 0-87462-505-X). Marquette.
--How Brave a New World: Dilemmas in Bioethics. LC 80-921. 456p. 1981. 15.95 (ISBN 0-385-17179-X). Doubleday.
--Notes on Moral Theology. LC 80-5682. 902p. 1981. lib. bdg. 24.50 (ISBN 0-8191-1439-1); pap. text ed. 15.00 (ISBN 0-8191-1440-5). U Pr of Amer.
McCormick, Richard A., jt. ed. see Curran, Charles E.
McCormick, Richard P. New Jersey. LC 65-15071. 1965. pap. 2.95 (ISBN 0-8077-1734-7). Tchrs Coll.
McCormick, Robert. The Concept of Happiness in the Spanish Poetry of the Eighteenth Century. LC 80-68000. (Hispanic Studies Collection Ser.). 206p. (Orig.). 1980. pap. 19.95 (ISBN 0-89729-264-2). Ediciones.
McCormick, Rose M. & Parkavich, Tamar J. Patient & Family Education: Tools, Techniques & Theory. LC 79-10014. 1979. 18.50 (ISBN 0-471-04269-2, Pub by Wiley Medical). Wiley.
McCormick, Thomas C. Comparative Study of Rural Relief & Non-Relief Households. LC 70-165684. (FDR & the Era of the New Deal Ser.). 1971. Repr. of 1935 ed. lib. bdg. 17.50 (ISBN 0-306-70334-3). Da Capo.
McCormick, William. Tennis. LC 73-3407. (First Bks.). (gr. 3-7). 1973. PLB 4.90 o.p. (ISBN 0-531-00803-7). Watts.
McCormick, William, jt. auth. see Bell, William E.
McCormick, William F., jt. auth. see Schochet, Sydney S., Jr.
McCort, James J. Radiographic Examination in Blunt Abdominal Trauma. LC 66-18500. (Illus.). 1966. 10.50 o.p. (ISBN 0-7216-5905-5). Saunders.
McCorvey, Thomas C. Alabama Historical Sketches. Johnston, G. B., ed. LC 60-16695. 254p. 1971. 9.95x (ISBN 0-8139-0377-7). U Pr of Va.
McCosh, Andrew, et al. Developing Managerial Information Systems. 1980. 29.95x (ISBN 0-470-26913-8). Halsted Pr.
McCosh, Andrew M. & Scott-Morton, Michael S. Management Decision Support Systems. LC 77-13305. 1978. 21.95 (ISBN 0-470-99326-X). Halsted Pr.
McCosh, James. The Scottish Philosophy, Biographical, Expository, Critical, from Hutcheson to Hamilton. LC 75-3266. (A. P. (Philo. in Amer)). 496p. 1980. Repr. of 1875 ed. 33.50 (ISBN 0-404-59255-4). AMS Pr.
McCoubrey, John W. American Tradition in Painting. LC 63-11371. (Illus.). (YA) (gr. 9 up). 1963. 7.95 o.p. (ISBN 0-8076-0215-9). Braziller.
McCoubrey, John W., ed. American Art, Seventeen Hundred to Nineteen Sixty: Sources & Documents. (Orig.). 1965. pap. 10.95x ref. ed. (ISBN 0-13-024521-6). P-H.
McCowen, Alec. Double Bill. LC 80-66018. 1981. 10.95 (ISBN 0-689-11070-7). Atheneum.
McCown, Elizabeth, jt. auth. see Washburn, Sherwood L.
McCown, Joe. Availability: Gabriel Marcel & the Phenomenology of Human Openness. LC 77-22358. (American Academy of Religion. Studies in Religion: No. 14). 1978. pap. 5.00 (ISBN 0-89130-144-5, 010014). Scholars Pr Ca.
McCoy & Berger. Algebra: Groups, Rings, & Other Topics. 1977. text ed. 23.05 (ISBN 0-205-05699-7). Allyn.
McCoy, Andrew. Atrocity Week. 1979. pap. 2.25 o.s.i. (ISBN 0-446-82534-4). Warner Bks.
McCoy, Carl, ed. see IFSTA Committee.
McCoy, Clyde B., jt. ed. see Philliber, William W.
McCoy, Dell. The Crystal River Pictorial. (Illus.). 224p. 27.00 (ISBN 0-913582-04-2). Sundance.
McCoy, Dell & Collman, Russell. The Rio Grande Pictorial. (Illus.). 216p. 30.00 (ISBN 0-913582-02-6). Sundance.
McCoy, Donald R. Angry Voices: Left-Of-Center Politics in the New Deal Era. LC 78-137975. (American History & Culture in the Twentieth Century Ser). 1971. Repr. of 1958 ed. 13.50 (ISBN 0-8046-1431-8). Kennikat.
--Calvin Coolidge. 1967. 8.95 o.s.i. (ISBN 0-02-583020-1). Macmillan.
McCoy, Dorothy S. Tradition & Convention: A Study of Periphrasis in English Pastoral Poetry from 1557-1715. (Studies in English Literature: No. 5). 1979. pap. text ed. 23.00x (ISBN 0-391-01604-0). Humanities.
McCoy, Doyle. Roadside Trees & Shrubs of Oklahoma. LC 80-5944. (Illus.). 180p. (Orig.). 1981. pap. 9.95 (ISBN 0-8061-1556-4). U of Okla Pr.
--Roadside Wild Fruits of Oklahoma. LC 79-6705. (Illus.). 96p. (Orig.). 1980. pap. 8.95 (ISBN 0-8061-1626-9). U of Okla Pr.
McCoy, Drew R. The Elusive Republic: Political Economy in Jeffersonian America. LC 79-20952. (Institute for Early American History & Culture Ser.). x, 268p. 1980. 21.50x (ISBN 0-8078-1416-4). U of NC Pr.
McCoy, Duke. How to Organize & Manage Your Own Religious Cult. 1980. pap. 6.95. Loompanics.
McCoy, Esther. Richard Neutra. LC 60-13309. (Masters of World Architecture Ser.). (Illus.). 1960. 7.95 o.s.i. (ISBN 0-8076-0132-2); pap. 3.95 o.s.i. (ISBN 0-8076-0229-9). Braziller.
McCoy, F. N. Researching & Writing in History. 1974. 11.95x (ISBN 0-520-02447-8); pap. 3.95 (ISBN 0-520-02621-7). U of Cal Pr.
--Robert Baillie & the Second Scots Reformation. 1974. 20.00x (ISBN 0-520-02385-4). U of Cal Pr.
McCoy, J. J. In Defense of Animals. LC 76-58508. (Illus.). (gr. 3-6). 1978. 8.95 (ISBN 0-395-28864-9, Clarion). HM.
--Pet Safety. (Illus.). (gr. 3 up). 1979. PLB 6.90 (ISBN 0-531-02926-3). Watts.
--Saving Our Wildlife. (Surveyor Bks). (Illus.). (gr. 7-12). 1970. 5.95 o.s.i. (ISBN 0-02-765420-6, CCPr). Macmillan.
--Shadows Over the Land. LC 77-111212. (gr. 5 up). 1970. 6.50 o.p. (ISBN 0-8164-3061-6, Clarion). HM.
McCoy, James W. Chemical Treatment of Boiler Water. (Illus.). 1981. 40.00 (ISBN 0-8206-0284-1). Chem Pub.
McCoy, John H. Livestock & Meat Marketing. 2nd ed. (Illus.). 1979. text ed. 26.50 (ISBN 0-87055-321-6). AVI.
McCoy, John R., jt. auth. see Ribelin, William E.
McCoy, Neal. Introduction to Modern Algebra. 3rd ed. 296p. 1975. text ed. 22.00x (ISBN 0-205-04545-6, 564545X). Allyn.
McCoy, Richard C. Sir Philip Sidney: Rebellion in Arcadia. 1979. 16.50 (ISBN 0-8135-0869-X). Rutgers U Pr.
McCoy, Robert A. Practical Photography. rev ed. (Illus.). (gr. 10-12). 1972. text ed. 13.00 (ISBN 0-87345-431-6). McKnight.
McCoy, Winston. Fellow-Crafts Ritual. 1981. 4.95 (ISBN 0-8062-1608-5). Carlton.
MacCracken. City Kid. 288p. 1981. 12.95 (ISBN 0-316-54186-9). Little.
McCracken, Daniel D. A Guide to Fortran IV Programming. 2nd ed. LC 72-4745. (Illus.). 256p. 1972. pap. 15.50 (ISBN 0-471-58281-6). Wiley.
--Guide to PL-M Programming for Microcomputer Applications. 1978. pap. text ed. 11.95 (ISBN 0-201-04575-3). A-W.
McCracken, Daniel D., jt. auth. see Dorn, William S.
McCracken, David. Junius & Philip Francis. (English Authors Ser.: No. 259). 1979. lib. bdg. 14.50 (ISBN 0-8057-6753-3). Twayne.
MacCracken, Mary. A Circle of Children. LC 73-10054. 192p. 1973. 7.95 o.s.i. (ISBN 0-397-00994-1). Lippincott.
--Lovey - a Very Special Child. LC 76-15389. 1976. 10.95 (ISBN 0-397-01129-6). Lippincott.
McCracken, May Lou. The Deep South Natural Foods Cookbook. 1977. pap. 1.75 (ISBN 0-515-03661-7). Jove Pubns.
McCracken, Paul W. & Izard, Ralph. Great Issues 77: A Forum on Important Questions Facing the American Public, Vol. 9. LC 78-65990. 1978. 12.95 (ISBN 0-916624-26-9). TSU Pr.
McCrary, J. A., ed. Pediatric Oculo-Neural Diseases Case Studies. 1973. spiral bdg. 14.50 (ISBN 0-87488-023-8). Med Exam.
McCraw, Louise H. As the Snow on the High Hills. 198p. (Orig.). 1979. pap. 2.00 (ISBN 0-89323-001-4). BMA Pr.
McCraw, Thomas K. TVA & the Power Fight: 1933-1939. LC 75-129670. (Critical Periods of History Ser). 1971. 5.95 o.p. (ISBN 0-397-47257-9); pap. text ed. 2.95 o.p. (ISBN 0-397-47256-0). Lippincott.
McCray, A. W. Petroleum Evaluations & Economic Decision. (Illus.). 544p. 1975. 33.95 (ISBN 0-13-662213-5). P-H.
McCray, Arthur W. & Cole, Frank W. Oil Well Drilling Technology. (Illus.). 1979. Repr. of 1959 ed. 15.95x (ISBN 0-8061-0423-6). U of Okla Pr.
McCray, Walter A. Black Spirituality. 150p. (Orig.). 1981. pap. 6.95 (ISBN 0-933176-04-X). Black Light Fellow.
--Discipling the Children of Black America: A Discussion of Christian Black Education for Black Youth. 50p. (Orig.). 1981. pap. 4.00 (ISBN 0-933176-02-3). Black Light Fellow.
--How to Stick Together During Times of Tension: Directives for Christian Black Unity. 200p. (Orig.). 1981. pap. 4.95 (ISBN 0-933176-03-1). Black Light Fellow.
--Who Says? A Black Perspective on the Authority of New Testament Exegesis Highlighting the Foundation for Its Interpretations & Applications. Bentley, William H., ed. 75p. (Orig.). 1981. pap. 3.00 (ISBN 0-933176-35-X). Black Light Fellow.
McCrea, Brian. Henry Fielding & the Poliitics of Mid-Eighteenth-Century England. LC 80-14711. (South Atlantic Modern Language Association Award Study, 1979). 328p. 1981. 20.00x (ISBN 0-8203-0531-6). U of Ga Pr.
McCrea, W. H., tr. see Unsoeld, A.
McCreadie, Charles & McGonigal, John. English "O". 1974. pap. text ed. 3.95x o.p. (ISBN 0-435-10500-0). Heinemann Ed.
McCready, Gerald. Canadian Marketing Trends. 1972. pap. text ed. 3.80x o.p. (ISBN 0-256-01392-6). Irwin.
McCready, Gerald B. Profile Canada: Social & Economic Projections. 1977. pap. 9.75x (ISBN 0-256-01703-4). Irwin.
McCready, Karen, jt. auth. see Azel, Jan.
McCready, Richard R. Business Mathematics. 3rd ed. 1978. pap. text ed. 13.95x (ISBN 0-534-00570-5). Wadsworth Pub.
--Learning Business Mathematics with Electronic Calculators. 2nd ed. 384p. 1979. pap. text ed. 13.95x (ISBN 0-534-00741-4). Wadsworth Pub.
--Solving Business Problems with Calculators. 5th ed. 1977. 12.95x (ISBN 0-534-00495-4). Wadsworth Pub.
McCready, William C. & Greeley, Andrew M. The Ultimate Values of the American Population. LC 75-40337. (Sage Library of Social Research: Vol. 23). 1976. 18.00x (ISBN 0-8039-0502-5); pap. 8.95x (ISBN 0-8039-0503-3). Sage.
McCready, William C., jt. auth. see Greeley, Andrew.
McCreary, Paul. The Maze Book. (Educational Ser.). (Illus.). (gr. 2-4). 1979. pap. 4.50 (ISBN 0-89039-218-8). Ann Arbor FL.
--Michigan Map Skills & Information Workbook. (Illus.). 32p. (Orig.). (gr. 6-10). 1978. wkbk. 4.50 (ISBN 0-910726-92-2). Hillsdale Educ.
--Perceptual Activities: A Multitude of Perceptual Actitivies,Level 2-Advanced,Consumerable (Coloring) Edition. (gr. 2-8). 1972. wkbk. 4.00 (ISBN 0-89039-049-5). Ann Arbor Pubs.
--Perceptual Activities: A Multitude of Reusable Perceptual Activities, Level 1-Primary. (gr. 2-8). 1972. 5.00 (ISBN 0-89039-046-0). Ann Arbor Pubs.
McCredie, John A., ed. Basic Surgery. (Illus.). 1977. pap. text ed. 18.50 (ISBN 0-02-378740-6). Macmillan Info.
McCreedy, Kenneth R. Juvenile Justice: System & Procedures. LC 75-6061. 1975. pap. 9.60 (ISBN 0-8273-0437-4); instructor's guide 1.60 (ISBN 0-8273-0438-2). Delmar.
--Theory & Methods of Police Patrol. LC 73-11823. 240p. 1974. pap. 9.20 (ISBN 0-8273-1427-2); instructor's guide 1.60 (ISBN 0-8273-1428-0). Delmar.
McCreery, jt. auth. see Turner.
McCreight, L. R., et al. Ceramic & Graphic Fibers & Whiskers: A Survey of Technology. (Refractory Materials Ser., Vol. 1). 1965. 41.00 (ISBN 0-12-482950-3). Acad Pr.
McCrimmon, Barbara. GK One: The Publication of the General Catalogue of Printed Books in British Museum, 1881-1900. 1980. write for info. (ISBN 0-208-01874-3, Linnet). Shoe String.
McCrimmon, James M. Teaching with a Purpose. 1.25 (ISBN 0-395-28254-3). HM.
--Writing with a Purpose. 6th ed. LC 75-24527. (Illus.). 1975. text ed. 10.95 o.p. (ISBN 0-395-19235-8). HM.
--Writing with a Purpose. short, 6th ed. LC 76-47875. 1977. text ed. 9.95 o.p. (ISBN 0-395-25004-8); inst. guide & resource bk. 1.10 o.p. (ISBN 0-395-25012-9). HM.
McCrimmon, James M., et al. Writing with a Purpose. 7th ed. LC 79-88599. 1980. text ed. 12.50 (ISBN 0-395-28253-5); instrs' manual 1.25 (ISBN 0-395-28254-3). HM.
--Writing with a Purpose: Short Edition. LC 79-90088. 1979. pap. text ed. 11.50 (ISBN 0-395-28939-4). HM.
McCrirrick, Margaret. Better Dressmaking. 1979. 18.95 (ISBN 0-7134-1092-2). David & Charles.
McCrory, Margaret. The Nineteen-Seventy's Divorce Revolution. pap. 3.95. Green Hill.
McCroskey, James. Introduction to Rhetorical Communication. 3rd ed. 1977. pap. 14.95 (ISBN 0-13-495432-7). P-H.
McCroskey, James, jt. auth. see Klopf, Donald.
McCroskey, James C., et al. Introduction to Interpersonal Communication. LC 71-126966. 1971. text ed. 14.95x (ISBN 0-13-485425-X). P-H.
McCubbin, Hamilton J., et al, eds. Families in the Military System. LC 75-44398. (Sage Ser. on Armed Forces & Society: Vol. 9). 1976. 24.00x (ISBN 0-8039-0667-6). Sage.
McCubbin, William E., jt. auth. see Sebolt, Don R.

McCue, C. F., et al, eds. Performance Testing of Lubricants for Automotive Engines & Transmissions. (Illus.). 1974. 89.50x (ISBN 0-85334-468-X). Intl Ideas.

McCue, James F., jt. auth. see Forell, George W.

McCue, Noelle B. Ocean of Regrets. (Orig.). 1981. pap. 1.50 (ISBN 0-440-16592-X). Dell.

McCuen, Gary & Bender, David L., eds. Radical Left & the Far Right: Fringe Groups Speak on the Problem of Race. rev. ed. (Opposing Viewpoints Ser.: Vol. 1). (Illus.). (gr. 9 up). 1973. lib. bdg. 10.60 o.p. (ISBN 0-912616-25-3); pap. text ed. 4.60 o.p. (ISBN 0-912616-07-5). Greenhaven.

McCuen, Gary E., ed. American Justice: Is America a Just Society? (Opposing Viewpoints Ser.: Vol. 9). (Illus.). 1975. lib. bdg. 8.95 (ISBN 0-912616-34-2); pap. text ed. 3.95 (ISBN 0-912616-15-6). Greenhaven.

--America's Prisons: Correctional Institutions or Universities of Crime. rev. ed. (Opposing Viewpoints Ser.: Vol. 5). (gr. 9 up). 1973. lib. bdg. 10.60 o.p. (ISBN 0-912616-29-6); pap. text ed. 4.60 o.p. (ISBN 0-912616-11-3). Greenhaven.

--The Racist Reader: Analyzing Primary Source Readings by American Race Supremacists. (Illus.). 1974. lib. bdg. 10.95 (ISBN 0-912616-33-4); pap. text ed. 4.95 (ISBN 0-912616-14-8). Greenhaven.

McCuen, Gary E. & Bender, David L., eds. Ecology Controversy: Opposing Viewpoints. rev. ed. (Opposing Viewpoints Ser.: Vol. 3). (Illus.). (gr. 9 up). 1973. lib. bdg. 8.95 (ISBN 0-912616-27-X); pap. text ed. 3.95 (ISBN 0-912616-09-1). Greenhaven.

McCuen, Gary E., jt. ed. see Bender, David L.

Mc Cuen, Gary E., ed. see Church, Carol B.

McCuen, Gary E., ed. see Church, Carol B.

Mc Cuen, Gary E., ed. see Church, Carol B.

McCuen, Gary E., ed. see Leone, Bruno.

McCuen, Jo Ray, jt. auth. see Winkler, Anthony.

McCuen, JoRay & Winkler, Anthony C. From Idea to Essay. 2nd ed. 1980. pap. text ed. 8.95 (ISBN 0-574-22055-0, 13-5055); instr's guide avail. (ISBN 0-574-22056-9, 13-5056). SRA.

McCuen, R. Fortran Programming for Civil Engineers. 1975. pap. 16.95 (ISBN 0-13-329417-X). P-H.

McCulla, Dorothy & Gray, J. S. Victorian & Edwardian Birmingham. 1972. pap. 11.95 (ISBN 0-7134-0150-8, Pub. by Batsford England). David & Charles.

McCullagh, Chuck, ed. see Lieb, Thom.

McCullagh, Patrick. Modern Concepts in Geomorphology. (Science in Geography Ser.). (Illus.). 128p. (Orig.). 1978. pap. text ed. 4.95x (ISBN 0-19-913236-4). Oxford U Pr.

Mc Cullers, Carson. Heart Is a Lonely Hunter. (Literature Ser). (gr. 9-12). 1940. pap. text ed. 4.25 (ISBN 0-87720-753-4). AMSCO Sch.

McCullers, Carson. Member of the Wedding. (Literature Ser). (gr. 10-12). 1970. pap. text ed. 3.58 (ISBN 0-87720-756-9). AMSCO Sch.

McCullers, Levi D. & Schroeder, Richard G. Accounting Theory: Text & Readings. LC 78-570. (Wiley Ser. in Accounting & Information Systems). 1978. text ed. 23.95x (ISBN 0-471-58364-2). Wiley.

McCullers, Levis D. & Van Daniker, Relmond P. Introduction to Financial Accounting. LC 74-23261. (Management, Accounting & Information Systems Ser.). 1975. text ed. 23.95x (ISBN 0-471-58365-0). Wiley.

McCulloch, A., jt. auth. see Abrams, P.

MacCulloch, Donald B. Staffa. new ed. LC 75-26360. (Island Ser.). (Illus.). 224p. 16.95 (ISBN 0-7153-7101-0). David & Charles.

McCulloch, Hugh. Men & Measures of Half a Century. LC 77-87404. (American Scene Ser.). 1969. Repr. of 1888 ed. lib. bdg. 55.00 (ISBN 0-306-71548-1). Da Capo.

McCulloch, J. Houston. Money & Inflation: Monetarist Approach. 121p. 1975. 7.95 (ISBN 0-12-483050-1). Acad Pr.

McCulloch, J. P., tr. see Propertius, Sextus.

McCulloch, J. W. & Philip, A. E. Suicidal Behavior. LC 72-188140. 133p. 1972. pap. text ed. 21.00 (ISBN 0-08-016855-8). Pergamon.

McCulloch, J. W., et al. Social Work Research & the Analysis of Social Data. LC 74-32369. 252p. 1975. text ed. 25.00 (ISBN 0-08-018213-5); pap. text ed. 12.75 (ISBN 0-08-018212-7). Pergamon.

McCulloch, James A. Medical Greek & Latin Workbook. 174p. 1977. pap. 8.50 (ISBN 0-398-01249-0). C C Thomas.

MacCulloch, John A. Childhood of Fiction. LC 74-78208. 1971. Repr. of 1905 ed. 28.00 (ISBN 0-8103-3628-6). Gale.

McCulloch, Lou W. Paper Americana: A Collector's Guide. LC 78-75317. (Illus.). 1980. 17.50 (ISBN 0-498-02392-3). A S Barnes.

MacCulloch, M., jt. auth. see Feldman, P.

Macculloch, M. J., jt. auth. see Feldman, M. P.

McCulloch, R. K., jt. auth. see Rosser, W. G.

McCulloch, Winifred. A Short History of the American Teilhard Association. 1979. pap. 2.00 (ISBN 0-89012-013-7). Anima Pubns.

McCulloh, Walter. Conservation of Water. (Illus.). 1913. 47.50x (ISBN 0-686-51362-2). Elliots Bks.

McCullough & Leuba. Pennsylvania Main Line Canal. 1976. 4.75 o.p. (ISBN 0-933788-26-6). Am Canal & Transport.

McCullough, Colleen. Tim. 1977. pap. 2.50 (ISBN 0-445-08545-2). Popular Lib.

McCullough, Constance M., jt. auth. see Tinker, Miles A.

McCullough, D. R. The Tule Elk: Its History, Behavior & Ecology. (California Library Reprint Series: No. 16). 1971. 20.00x (ISBN 0-520-01921-0); pap. 10.50x (ISBN 0-520-09345-3). U of Cal Pr.

McCullough, Dale R. The George Reserve Deer Herd: Population Ecology of a K-Selected Species. (Illus.). 1979. lib. bdg. 16.00x (ISBN 0-472-08611-1, 08611). U of Mich Pr.

McCullough, David G., ed. see Sulzberger, C. L.

McCullough, Helen C., tr. Yoshitsune: A Fifteenth-Century Japanese Chronicle. 1966. 18.95x (ISBN 0-8047-0270-5). Stanford U Pr.

McCullough, Joseph B. Hamlin Garland. (United States Authors Ser.: No. 299). 1978. lib. bdg. 9.95 (ISBN 0-8057-7203-0). Twayne.

McCullough, Kathleen, et al. Approval Plans & Academic Libraries. LC 77-8514. (Neal-Schuman Professional Bk). 1977. lib. bdg. 13.95x (ISBN 0-912700-05-X). Oryx Pr.

McCullough, Prudence. The Do-It-Yourself Super Spa Home Weekend. (Illus., Orig.). 1981. pap. 6.95 (ISBN 0-8092-7083-8). Contemp Bks.

McCullough, Robert J. & Everard, Kenneth. Bank Reconciliation Projects. 1959. pap. text ed. 1.48 o.p. (ISBN 0-8224-0165-7); key 0.72 o.p. (ISBN 0-8224-0233-5). Pitman Learning.

--Bank Reconciliation Projects. 2nd ed. 1979. pap. 2.40 (ISBN 0-8224-0634-9); key 1.00 (ISBN 0-8224-0635-7). Pitman Learning.

McCullough, W., jt. auth. see Munro, A.

McCullough, William W. Sticky Fingers: A Close Look at Embezzlement---America's Fastest Growing Crime. 259p. 1981. 10.95 (ISBN 0-8144-5688-X). Am Mgmt.

McCully, Emily Arnold, jt. auth. see Hoban, Russell.

McCully, Helen, jt. ed. see American Heritage.

McCully, Marylyn. Els Quatre Gats: Art in Barcelona Around Nineteen Hundred. LC 77-72143. 1978. 27.50 o.p. (ISBN 0-691-03928-3). Princeton U Pr.

McCully, Ron. Testing Program: Up with Math. Jacobs, Helen J., ed. 120p. (Orig.). (gr. 5-12). 1979. pap. 1.95 (ISBN 0-918272-05-X); tchrs. manual 1.50 (ISBN 0-918272-06-8). Jacobs.

McCune, Billy, jt. auth. see Lyon, Danny.

McCune, James A. America, the True Church & the End of the Age: Where the United States Fits in Biblical Prophecy. (Illus.). 227p. (Orig.). 1980. pap. 5.95 (ISBN 0-9604732-0-3). Yorkshire Pub.

--Why Deflation Is Coming in the Nineteen Eighties. (Illus.). 1981. 8.95 (ISBN 0-686-69292-6). Yorkshire Pub.

McCune, Wesley. Nine Young Men. Repr. of 1947 ed. lib. bdg. 17.50x (ISBN 0-8371-2247-3, MCNY). Greenwood.

McCunn, Donald H. Write, Edit, & Print: Word Processing with Personal Computers. LC 80-67880. 1981. write for info. (ISBN 0-932538-06-1). Design Ent SF.

McCunn, Ruthanne L. An Illustrated History of the Chinese in America. LC 79-50114. (Illus.). 136p. 1979. 11.95 (ISBN 0-932538-01-0); pap. 6.95 (ISBN 0-932538-02-9). Design Ent SF.

Maccurdy, Edward, ed. Notebooks of Leonardo DaVinci. (Illus.). 1956. 10.00 (ISBN 0-8076-0003-2). Braziller.

McCurdy, John C., jt. auth. see Lappe, Marc.

McCurdy, John W., Jr. The Complete Guide to Cosmetic Facial Surgery. LC 80-70945. (Illus.). 256p. 1981. 12.95 (ISBN 0-8119-0331-1). Fell.

--The Complete Guide to Your Sinuses, Allergies, & Nasal Problems. LC 80-70960. (Illus.). 256p. 1981. text ed. 12.95 (ISBN 0-8119-0429-6). Fell.

McCurdy, Michael & Peich, Michael. The First Ten: A Penmaen Press Bibliography. LC 78-52650. (Illus.). 1978. 12.50 (ISBN 0-915778-20-3); deluxe ed. 50.00 o.p. (ISBN 0-915778-19-X). Penmaen Pr.

MacCurdy, Raymond R., ed. Spanish Drama of the Golden Age. 1979. text ed. 29.50x (ISBN 0-89197-985-9); pap. text ed. 18.95x (ISBN 0-89197-986-7). Irvington.

McCurley, Foster R. Genesis, Exodus, Leviticus, Numbers. LC 78-14670. (Proclamation Commentaries: the Old Testament Witness for Preaching). 128p. 1979. pap. 3.95 (ISBN 0-8006-0593-4, 1-593). Fortress.

McCurry, Don M., ed. The Gospel & Islam: A Nineteen Seventy-Eight Compendium. 1979. pap. 9.00 (ISBN 0-912552-26-3). MARC.

--World Christianity: Middle East. 1979. pap. text ed. 9.00 (ISBN 0-912552-27-1). MARC.

Maccurtin, Margaret, jt. ed. see Lydon, James.

McCurtin, Peter. Ambush at Derati Wells. (Soldier of Fortune Ser). 1977. pap. 1.25 (ISBN 0-505-51153-3). Tower Bks.

--Apache War. (Sundaance Ser.). 1980. pap. 1.75 (ISBN 0-8439-0780-0). Nordon Pubns.

--Battle Pay. (Soldier of Fortune Ser.). 1978. pap. 1.50 (ISBN 0-505-51233-5). Tower Bks.

--Body Count. (Soldier of Fortune Ser.). 1977. pap. 1.50 (ISBN 0-505-51172-X). Tower Bks.

--Day of the Halfbreeds. (Sundance Ser.: No. 29). 1979. pap. 1.75 (ISBN 0-8439-0693-6, Leisure Bks). Nordon Pubns.

--Death Dance. (Sundance Ser.: No. 27). 1979. pap. 1.75 (ISBN 0-8439-0669-3, Leisure Bks). Nordon Pubns.

--Gold Strike. (Sundance Ser.: No. 35). 1980. pap. 1.75 (ISBN 0-8439-0819-X, Leisure Bks). Nordon Pubns.

--Hangman's Knot. (Sundance Ser.: No. 33). 1980. pap. 1.75 (ISBN 0-8439-0764-9, Leisure Bks). Nordon Pubns.

--Loanshark. 1979. pap. 1.75 (ISBN 0-505-51437-0). Tower Bks.

--Marauders. (Sundance Ser.: No. 31). 1980. pap. 1.75 (ISBN 0-8439-0740-1, Leisure Bks). Nordon Pubns.

--Minnesota Strip. 1979. pap. 1.75 (ISBN 0-505-51333-1). Tower Bks.

--Nightriders. (Sundance Ser.: No. 26). 1976. pap. 1.75 (ISBN 0-8439-0653-7, LB346NK, Leisure Bks). Nordon Pubns.

--Los Olvidados. (Sundance Ser.: No. 30). 1980. 1.75. Nordon Pubns.

--Operation Hong Kong. (Soldier of Fortune Ser). (Orig.). 1977. pap. text ed. 1.50 (ISBN 0-505-51161-4). Tower Bks.

--The Savage. (Sundance Ser.: No. 28). 1979. pap. 1.75 (ISBN 0-8439-0678-2, Leisure Bks). Nordon Pubns.

--Scorpion. (Sundance Ser.: No. 32). 1980. pap. 1.75 (ISBN 0-8439-0756-8, Leisure Bks). Nordon Pubns.

--Sundance: The Marauders. (Orig.). 1980. pap. 1.75 (ISBN 0-8439-0740-1, Leisure Bks). Nordon Pubns.

--Trail Drive. (Sundance Ser.: No. 36). 1981. pap. 1.95 (ISBN 0-8439-0878-5, Leisure Bks). Nordon Pubns.

McCusker, Honor. Fifty Years of Music in Boston. 3.00. Boston Public Lib.

McCuskey, S. W., jt. auth. see Blanco, V. M.

McCutchan, Nell. Focus on Reading. (English As a Second Language Ser.). (Illus.). 1980. pap. text ed. 9.95 (ISBN 0-13-322776-6). P-H.

McCutchan, Philip. Halfhyde & the Flag Captain. 196p. 1981. 9.95 (ISBN 0-312-35684-6). St Martin.

--Halfhyde Ordered South. 1980. 9.95 (ISBN 0-686-58172-5). St Martin.

McCutchan, Philip D. Halfhyde to the Narrows. LC 77-72303. 1977. 7.95 o.p. (ISBN 0-312-35690-0). St Martin.

McCutcheon, George B. Beverly of Graustark. 1976. lib. bdg. 16.25x (ISBN 0-89968-057-7). Lightyear.

--Brewster's Millions. Jasen, David A., ed. (A Continuum Classic of Humor Ser.). 224p. 1980. 11.95 (ISBN 0-8264-0019-1). Continuum.

--Brewster's Millions. 1976. lib. bdg. 15.25x (ISBN 0-89968-058-5). Lightyear.

--Castle Craneycrow. 1976. lib. bdg. 17.25x (ISBN 0-89968-059-3). Lightyear.

--The Daughter of Anderson Crow. 1976. lib. bdg. 15.75x (ISBN 0-89968-060-7). Lightyear.

--Graustark. 1976. lib. bdg. 19.25x (ISBN 0-89968-061-5). Lightyear.

--Jane Cable. 1976. lib. bdg. 15.25x (ISBN 0-89968-062-3). Lightyear.

--Nedra. 1976. lib. bdg. 15.75x (ISBN 0-89968-063-1). Lightyear.

McCutcheon, J. R. Business One Twenty One. 224p. 1981. pap. 9.95 lab manual (ISBN 0-8403-2368-9). Kendall-Hunt.

McCutcheon, Robert. Limits of a Modern World. (Science in a Social Context Ser.). 1979. pap. text ed. 3.95 (ISBN 0-408-71310-0). Butterworths.

McCutchion, David. The Epistles of David-Kaka to Plalm'n. (Writers Workshop Greybird Book Ser.). 94p. 1975. 12.00 (ISBN 0-88253-536-6); pap. text ed. 4.80 (ISBN 0-88253-535-8). Ind-US Inc.

--Indian Writing in English. (Writers Workshop Greybird Ser.). 142p. 1975. 12.00 (ISBN 0-89253-596-2); pap. text ed. 8.00 (ISBN 0-88253-726-1). Ind-US Inc.

--The Temples of Bankura District. 12.00 (ISBN 0-89253-673-X); flexible cloth 6.75 (ISBN 0-89253-674-8). Ind-US Inc.

McDanel, Ralph C. The Virginia Constitutional Convention of 1901-1902. LC 75-146556. (American Constitutional & Legal History Ser.). 1972. Repr. of 1928 ed. lib. bdg. 19.50 (ISBN 0-306-70204-5). Da Capo.

McDaniel, Carl, Jr. Marketing: An Integrated Approach. 1979. text ed. 20.50 scp (ISBN 0-06-044355-3, HarpC); inst. manual avail. (ISBN 0-06-364106-2); scp study guide 6.50 (ISBN 0-06-044356-1); test bank avail. (ISBN 0-06-364236-0); tapes o.p. 30.00 (ISBN 0-686-67347-6). Har-Row.

McDaniel, D. H., jt. auth. see Douglas, Bodie E.

McDaniel, G. Floral Design & Arrangement. 250p. 1981. text ed. 16.95 (ISBN 0-8359-2072-0); instr's. manual free (ISBN 0-8359-2073-9). Reston.

McDaniel, Herman. Careers in Computers & Data Processing. LC 77-25076. 1978. 11.50 (ISBN 0-89433-029-2); pap. 8.95 (ISBN 0-89433-030-6). Petrocelli.

--Personal Records Directory. 1978. text ed. 8.95 (ISBN 0-89433-088-8); pap. 7.50 (ISBN 0-89433-089-6). Petrocelli.

McDaniel, James W. Physical Disability & Human Behavior. 2nd ed. 232p. 1976. text ed. 16.00 (ISBN 0-08-019722-1); pap. text ed. 9.25 (ISBN 0-08-019721-3). Pergamon.

McDaniel, John N., tr. see Cocchiara, Giuseppe.

McDaniel, Robert A. The Shuster Mission & the Persian Constitutional Revolution. LC 72-96696. (Studies in Middle Eastern History: No. 1). 1974. 25.00x (ISBN 0-88297-004-6). Bibliotheca.

McDaniel, Sarah W., jt. auth. see Ligon, Mary G.

McDaniel, Timothy R. The Creational Theory of Man & of the Universe. (Illus.). 141p. 1980. deluxe ed. 36.35 (ISBN 0-89266-242-5). Am Classical Coll Pr.

McDaniel, Wilma E. Tollbridge. 32p. 1980. 3.00 (ISBN 0-936556-01-3). Contact Two.

McDaniels, Allen. Water: What's in It for You? A Concise Discussion of the Vital Role of Water in Your Health. 1972. pap. 1.50 o.p. (ISBN 0-9600300-2-6). Heather Foun.

McDaniels, Kathleen A. My Mom, the Truck Driver. (Illus., Orig.). 1980. pap. 3.95 (ISBN 0-935424-01-6). Daisy.

McDarrah, Fred W. Greenwich Village. (Orig.). 1963. pap. 1.45 o.p. (ISBN 0-87091-032-9). Corinth Bks.

McDavid, Raven I., Jr., jt. auth. see Kurath, Hans.

McDearmon, Kay. Cougar. LC 77-6086. (gr. 2-5). 1977. 4.95 (ISBN 0-396-07468-5). Dodd.

--Gorillas. LC 78-11292. (Skylight Bks.). (Illus.). (gr. 3-5). 1979. 4.95 (ISBN 0-396-07645-9). Dodd.

Macdermat, Clinker. History of the Western Railway 1863-1921. 19.25x (ISBN 0-392-07907-0, SpS). Soccer.

Macdermot, C. G., jt. auth. see Anderson, Norman E.

MacDermot, Violet. The Cult of the Seer in the Ancient Middle East: A Contribution to Current Research on Hallucinations Drawn from Coptic & Other Texts. LC 79-152047. (Wellcome Institute of the History of Medicine). 1971. 55.00x (ISBN 0-520-02030-8). U of Cal Pr.

McDermott, Anthony, jt. auth. see Short, Martin.

McDermott, Beatrice S. & Coleman, Freada A., eds. Government Regulation of Business Including Antitrust Information Sources. LC 67-25294. (Management Information Guide Ser.: No. 11). 229p. 1967. 30.00 (ISBN 0-8103-0810-X). Gale.

McDermott, F. E. Self Determination in Social Work: A Collection of Essays on Self-Determination & Related Concepts. (International Library of Welfare & Philosophy). 1975. 17.50x (ISBN 0-7100-7980-X); pap. 8.95 (ISBN 0-7100-7981-8). Routledge & Kegan.

McDermott, Gerald. Anansi the Spider: A Tale from the Ashanti. (Illus.). (gr. k-3). 1977. pap. 1.95 o.p. (ISBN 0-14-050216-5, Puffin). Penguin.

--Arrow to the Sun: A Pueblo Indian Tale. (Illus.). 48p. (gr. 1 up). 1974. PLB 10.95 (ISBN 0-670-13369-8). Viking Pr.

--The Knight of the Lion. LC 78-54680. (Illus.). 96p. (gr. 3 up). 1979. 9.95 (ISBN 0-590-07504-7, Four Winds). Schol Bk Serv.

--The Stonecutter: A Japanese Folk Tale. (Illus.). 32p. (gr. k-3). 1975. PLB 9.95 (ISBN 0-670-67074-X). Viking Pr.

--Sun Flight. LC 79-5067. (Illus.). 40p. 1980. 10.95 (ISBN 0-590-07632-9, Four Winds). Schol Bk Serv.

Mc Dermott, Irene E. & Nicholas, Jeanne L. Homemaking for Teenagers, Bk. 1. new ed. (gr. 7-12). 1975. Bk 1. 17.24 (ISBN 0-87002-070-6). Bennett IL.

McDermott, Irene E. & Norris, Jeanne L. Opportunities in Clothing. rev. ed. (Illus.). (gr. 9-12). 1972. text ed. 14.60 (ISBN 0-87002-140-0). Bennett IL.

McDermott, Irene E., et al. Food for Modern Living. rev. ed. 1973. text ed. 12.60 o.p. (ISBN 0-397-40201-5); 14.52 o.p. (ISBN 0-397-40202-3). Lippincott.

McDermott, John E., ed. Indeterminacy in Education. LC 76-2987. 1976. 17.90x (ISBN 0-8211-1251-1); text ed. 16.20x (ISBN 0-685-71411-X). McCutchan.

McDermott, John F., jt. ed. see Harrison, Saul I.

McDermott, John Francis, ed. see Pittman, Philip.

McDermott, John J. The Culture of Experience: Philosophical Essays in the American Grain. LC 76-5962. 237p. 1976. 15.00x (ISBN 0-8147-5406-6); pap. 6.00x (ISBN 0-8147-5424-4). NYU Pr.

McDermott, Robert A., et al. Six Pillars: Introduction to the Major Works of Sri Aurobindo. McDermott, Robert A., ed. LC 74-77411. 300p. 1974. pap. 5.95 (ISBN 0-89012-001-3). Anima Pubns.

McDermott, Russell H. Columbia Bookkeeping Systems Double Entry. (Accounting-Bookkeeping Systems Ser.). (Illus.). 130p. 1980. text ed. 49.95 (ISBN 0-9604828-3-0). Columbia Bookkeeping.

McDermott, Thomas J. Manual of Sailboat Racing. 1964. 10.95 (ISBN 0-02-583070-8). Macmillan.

McDermott, William C. see Peters, Edward.

McDermottt, Irene, et al. Homemaking for Teen-Agers, Bk. 2. rev. ed. (gr. 9-12). 1976. text ed. 17.28 (ISBN 0-87002-171-0). Bennett IL.

McDevitt, Matthew. Joseph McKenna. LC 73-21874. (American Constitutional & Legal History Ser.). 250p. 1974. Repr. of 1946 ed. lib. bdg. 27.50 (ISBN 0-306-70632-6). Da Capo.

McDevitt, Robert, jt. auth. see Matthews, Kenneth.

McDevitt, William. Jack London As Poet & As Platform Man. 32p. 1972. Repr. of 1947 ed. pap. 2.00 o.p. (ISBN 0-915046-03-2). Wolf Hse.

MacDiarmid, H., ed. The Golden Treasury of Scottish Poetry. LC 77-88076. (Granger Poetry Library). 1976. Repr. of 1940 ed. 29.50x (ISBN 0-89609-027-2). Granger Bk.

MacDiarmid, Hugh. The Company I've Kept: Essays in Autobiography. 1967. 17.50x (ISBN 0-520-00783-2). U of Cal Pr.

--Lucky Poet: A Self-Study in Literature & Political Ideas Being the Autobiography of Hugh Macdiarmid. LC 76-138287: 1972. 20.00x (ISBN 0-520-01852-4). U of Cal Pr.

--More Collected Poems. LC 68-31076. 108p. 1970. 7.95 (ISBN 0-8040-0213-4). Swallow.

MacDiarmid, Roy A., jt. auth. see Park, Charles F., Jr.

McDicken, W. N. Diagnostic Ultrasonics: Principles & Use of Instruments. 2nd ed. LC 80-20750. 360p. 1981. 39.50 (ISBN 0-471-05740-1, Pub. by Wiley Med). Wiley.

McDill, Edward L., jt. ed. see McPartland, James M.

McDonagh, et al. Engineering Science for Technicians, Vol. 2. (Illus.). 1978. pap. 11.00x (ISBN 0-7131-3398-8). Intl Ideas.

McDonagh, Don. The Complete Guide to Modern Dance. 1977. pap. 2.50 o.p. (ISBN 0-445-08623-8). Popular Lib.

--Rise & Fall & Rise of Modern Dance. (RL 7). 1971. pap. 1.25 o.p. (ISBN 0-451-61117-9, MY1117, Ment). NAL.

--Rise & Fall & Rise of Modern Dance. 1970. 7.95 (ISBN 0-87690-013-9). Dutton.

Macdonagh, Donagh & Robinson, Lennox, eds. Oxford Book of Irish Verse Seventeenth to Twentieth Century. 1958. 24.95 (ISBN 0-19-812115-6). Oxford U Pr.

McDonagh, Edna. Church & Politics: From Theology to a Case History of Zimbabwe. LC 80-53070. 200p. 1980. text ed. 12.95 (ISBN 0-268-00734-9); pap. text ed. 5.95 (ISBN 0-268-00736-5). U of Notre Dame Pr.

McDonagh, I., et al. Engineering Science for Technicians, Vol. 1. (Illus.). 1977. pap. 11.00x (ISBN 0-686-67754-4). Intl Ideas.

McDonagh, Ian. Mechanical Science for Technicians. (Illus.). 121p. 1979. pap. 11.95x (ISBN 0-7131-3411-9). Intl Ideas.

MacDonagh, Oliver. Ireland: The Union & Its Aftermath. 1977. text ed. 25.00x (ISBN 0-04-941004-0); pap. text ed. 8.95x (ISBN 0-04-941005-9). Allen Unwin.

McDonald. Clinical Kidney Disease & Hypertension. 1980. 32.00. Thieme Stratton.

McDonald, A. C. & Lowe, H. Feedback & Control Systems. 1981. text ed. 19.95 (ISBN 0-8359-1898-X). Reston.

MacDonald, Alan D. Euphrates Exile. LC 80-1920. 1981. Repr. of 1936 ed. 34.00 (ISBN 0-404-18979-2). AMS Pr.

McDonald, Alan T., jt. auth. see Fox, Robert W.

McDonald, Alexander H. see Livy.

MacDonald, Alison. Children of Very Low Birthweight, Vol. 1. (Clinics in Developmental Medicine Research Monographs). 1967. 4.50 o.p. (ISBN 0-685-34618-8). Lippincott.

Macdonald, Allan J. Lanfranc, a Study of His Life, Work & Writing. LC 80-2223. 1981. Repr. of 1926 ed. 37.50 (ISBN 0-404-18768-4). AMS Pr.

Macdonald, Andrew. The Turner Diaries. 2nd ed. LC 80-82692. 216p. (Orig.). 1980. pap. 4.95 (ISBN 0-937944-02-5). Natl Alliance.

MacDonald, Angus J. Power: Mechanics of Energy Control. (gr. 9-12). 1970. text ed. 14.64 (ISBN 0-87345-486-3); mechanical control man. 4.48 (ISBN 0-87345-484-7); fluid control man. 4.48 (ISBN 0-87345-488-X); electric control man. 4.48 (ISBN 0-87345-487-1); optional experiments 4.48 (ISBN 0-87345-489-8); wkbk. & tests 4.48 (ISBN 0-87345-498-7); tchr's guide 40.00 (ISBN 0-87345-497-9); lab manual set 17.16 (ISBN 0-685-04238-3). McKnight.

--Wind Loading on Buildings. LC 75-11988. 219p. 1975. 29.95 (ISBN 0-470-55976-4). Halsted Pr.

McDonald, Angus W., Jr. The Urban Origins of Rural Revolution: Elites & the Masses in Hunan Province, China, 1911-1927. 1978. 21.50x (ISBN 0-520-03228-4). U of Cal Pr.

McDonald, Archie. Travis. LC 76-55914. (Illus.). 1976. 15.00 (ISBN 0-8363-0147-1). Jenkins.

McDonald, Archie & Procter, Ben. Texas Heritage. LC 79-54886. (Orig.). 1980. pap. text ed. 6.95x (ISBN 0-88273-001-0). Forum Pr MO.

McDonald, Archie P., ed. Eastern Texas History: Selections from East Texas Historical Journal. 12.50 (ISBN 0-8363-0159-5). Jenkins.

Macdonald, Bernice. How to Use Reference Materials. (gr. 7 up). 1980. PLB 6.45 (ISBN 0-531-04134-4). Watts.

MacDonald, Betty. Egg & I. LC 45-336. 1963. 10.95 (ISBN 0-397-00279-3). Lippincott.

Macdonald, C., ed. Cicero: Pro Murena. (Modern School Classics Ser). (Illus.). (gr. 10-12). 1969. text ed. 5.95 (ISBN 0-312-13755-9). St Martin.

MacDonald, Charles G. Iran, Saudi Arabia, & the Law of the Sea: Political Interaction and Legal Development in the Persian Gulf. LC 79-6186. (Contributions in Political Science: No. 48). xv, 226p. 1980. lib. bdg. 28.50 (ISBN 0-313-20768-2, MLS/). Greenwood.

McDonald, Cleveland. Creating a Successful Christian Marriage. LC 74-20202. 1975. 10.95 (ISBN 0-87227-038-6). Reg Baptist.

Macdonald, D., jt. ed. see Amlaner, C.

McDonald, D. A. Blood Flow in Arteries. 450p. 1974. 48.00 o.p. (ISBN 0-683-05760-X). Williams & Wilkins.

MacDonald, D. F. Age of Transition: Britain in the Nineteenth Twentieth Centuries. 1967. 16.95 (ISBN 0-312-01330-2). St Martin.

McDonald, D. L. Comparative Accounting Theory. 1972. pap. text ed. 6.50 (ISBN 0-201-04535-4). A-W.

McDonald, Dan. The Clyde Puffer. LC 77-76092. 1977. 10.50 (ISBN 0-7153-7443-5). David & Charles.

McDonald, Dan, jt. auth. see Rubright, Bob.

McDonald, Daniel. The Language of Argument. 3rd ed. (Illus.). 1980. pap. text ed. 10.50 scp (ISBN 0-06-044358-8, HarpC). Har-Row.

McDonald, Daniel, jt. auth. see Harwell, Charles W.

McDonald, Daniel, ed. see Addison, Joseph & Steele, Richard.

McDonald, David R. & Mail, Patricia D. Tulapai to Tokay: A Bibliography of Alcohol Use & Abuse Among Native Americans of North America. LC 80-81243. (Bibliography Ser.). 1981. 18.00 (ISBN 0-87536-253-2). HRAFP.

MacDonald, David W. Rabies & Wildlife: A Biologist's Perspective. (Illus.). 160p. 1980. text ed. 38.00x (ISBN 0-19-857567-X); pap. 11.95 (ISBN 0-19-857576-9). Oxford U Pr.

McDonald, Dick, jt. auth. see McDonald, Paula.

MacDonald, Donald J. Clan Donald. (Illus.). 437p. 1980. 59.95 (ISBN 0-904265-21-8). Pelican.

MacDonald, Donald L. Corporate Risk Control. 1966. 21.95 (ISBN 0-8260-5615-6). Wiley.

McDonald, Donna, ed. see American Association for State & Local History.

McDonald, Doug. Julia Bulette & the Red Light Ladies of Nevada. (Illus.). 1980. 2.95 (ISBN 0-913814-29-6). Nevada Pubns.

McDonald, Douglas. Nevada Lost Mines & Buried Treasure. (Illus.). 1981. 6.95. Nevada Pubns.

MacDonald, Douglass, jt. auth. see Edwards, James.

Macdonald, Dwight. Henry Wallace: The Man & the Myth. Freidel, Frank, ed. LC 78-66546. (The History of the United States Ser.: Vol. 11). 188p. 1979. lib. bdg. 15.00 (ISBN 0-8240-9701-7). Garland Pub.

Macdonald, Dwight, ed. see Poe, Edgar A.

Macdonald, Eleanor & Little, Julia. The Successful Secretary. (Illus.). 176p. 1980. pap. 9.95x (ISBN 0-7121-1976-0). Intl Ideas.

Macdonald, Eleanor J. & Heinze, Evelyn B. Epidemiology of Cancer in Texas: Incidence Analyzed by Type, Ethnic Group, & Geographic Location. LC 77-85516. 1978. 56.00 (ISBN 0-89004-203-9). Raven.

Macdonald, Elisabeth. Watch for the Morning. LC 77-13662. 1978. 9.95 o.p. (ISBN 0-684-15358-0, ScribT). Scribner.

McDonald, Ellen E., jt. auth. see Karve, D. D.

McDonald, Elvin. Decorative Gardening in Containers. LC 77-92224. 1978. 8.95 o.p. (ISBN 0-385-09590-2). Doubleday.

--Easy Gardens. 1981. 8.95 (ISBN 0-916752-20-8). Green Hill.

--Easy Gardens: A Weed Eater Book. (Berkley-Dorison House Bks.). (Illus.). (YA) 1978. 6.95 o.p. (ISBN 0-685-85770-0, Dist. by Putnam). Berkley Pub.

--Making Your Lawn & Garden Grow. 7.95 (ISBN 0-916752-07-0). Green Hill.

--Stop Talking to Your Plants & Listen. LC 77-9024. (Funk & W Bk.). (Illus.). 1977. 8.95 o.s.i. (ISBN 0-308-10288-6, TYC-T); pap. 4.95 o.s.i. (ISBN 0-308-10333-5, TYC-T). T Y Crowell.

--The World Book of House Plants. rev. ed. LC 74-23165. (Funk & W Bk.). (Illus.). 320p. 1975. 9.95 o.s.i. (ISBN 0-308-10087-5, TYC-T). T Y Crowell.

McDonald, Elvin, jt. auth. see Guest, C. Z.

McDonald, Elvin, et al, eds. The Color Handbook of House Plants. 1976. 9.95 o.p. (ISBN 0-8015-1441-X). Dutton.

MacDonald, Fred J. Don't Touch That Dial. LC 79-87700. 1979. 16.95 (ISBN 0-88229-528-4); pap. 8.95 (ISBN 0-88229-673-6). Nelson-Hall.

Macdonald, G. F., intro. by. Perception & Identity: Essays Presented to A. J. Ayer with His Responses. LC 79-52503. (Illus.). 1979. 32.50 (ISBN 0-8014-1265-X). Cornell U Pr.

McDonald, Gary R. & Nybakken, James W. Guide to the Nudibranchs of California. Abbott, R. T., ed. (Illus.). 72p. (Orig.). 1981. pap. 13.50 (ISBN 0-915826-08-9). Am Malacologists.

MacDonald, George. Alec Forbes of Howglen, 1865. Wolff, Robert L., ed. LC 75-1509. (Victorian Fiction Ser.). 1975. lib. bdg. 66.00 (ISBN 0-8240-1583-5). Garland Pub.

--At the Back of the North Wind. (Illus.). (gr. 4-6). 1964. 4.95g o.s.i. (ISBN 0-02-761540-5). Macmillan.

--At the Back of the North Wind. (Childrens Illustrated Classics Ser). (Illus.). 1973. Repr. of 1956 ed. 9.00x o.p. (ISBN 0-460-05036-2, Pub. by J. M. Dent England). Biblio Dist.

--At the Back of the North Wind. LC 75-32174. (Classics of Children's Literature, 1621-1932: Vol. 37). (Illus.). 1976. Repr. of 1871 ed. PLB 38.00 (ISBN 0-8240-2286-6). Garland Pub.

--David Elginbrod, 1863. Wolff, Robert L., ed. LC 75-1502. (Victorian Fiction Ser.). 1975. lib. bdg. 66.00 (ISBN 0-8240-1577-0). Garland Pub.

--The Evolution of Coinage. viii, 148p. 1980. 20.00 (ISBN 0-916710-73-4). Obol Intl.

--Gifts of the Child Christ, 2 vols. LC 72-94606. 1972. pap. 9.95 (ISBN 0-8028-1518-9). Eerdmans.

--Golden Key & Other Fantasy Stories. Sadler, Glenn G., ed. (The Fantasy Stories of George MacDonald Ser.). 176p. 1980. pap. 2.95 (ISBN 0-8028-1859-5). Eerdmans.

--The Gray Wolf & Other Fantasy Stories. Sadler, Glenn G., ed. (The Fantasy Stories of George MacDonald Ser.). 200p. 1980. pap. 2.95 (ISBN 0-8028-1862-5). Eerdmans.

--Light Princess. LC 62-12814. (Illus.). (gr. 1-5). 1962. PLB 7.89 o.p. (ISBN 0-690-49308-8, TYC-J). T Y Crowell.

--The Light Princess & Other Fantasy Stories. Sadler, George G., ed. (The Fantasy Stories of George MacDonald Ser.). 176p. 1980. pap. 2.95 (ISBN 0-8028-1861-7). Eerdmans.

--The Lost Princess: A Double Story. (Childrens Illustrated Classics Ser). (Illus.). 1976. Repr. of 1967 ed. 9.00x o.p. (ISBN 0-460-05069-9, Pub. by J. M. Dent England). Biblio Dist.

--Paul Faber, Surgeon. Wolff, Robert L., ed. LC 75-1513. (Victorian Fiction Ser.). 1975. Repr. of 1879 ed. lib. bdg. 66.00 (ISBN 0-8240-1586-X). Garland Pub.

--Princess & Curdie. (New Children's Classics). (Illus.). (gr. 4-6). 1954. 3.95 o.s.i. (ISBN 0-02-761750-5). Macmillan.

--The Princess & Curdie. Watson, Jean, ed. (Family Library Ser.). (Illus.). 128p. 1980. 6.95 (ISBN 0-310-42310-4, 9062). Zondervan.

--The Princess & the Goblin. Watson, Jean, ed. (The Family Library Ser.). 128p. 1980. 6.95 (ISBN 0-310-42300-7, 9061). Zondervan.

--Robert Falconer. Wolff, Robert L., ed. LC 75-1510. (Victorian Fiction Ser.). 1975. Repr. of 1868 ed. lib. bdg. 66.00 (ISBN 0-8240-1584-3). Garland Pub.

--Wise Woman & Other Fantasy Stories. Sadler, Glenn G., ed. (The Fantasy Stories of George MacDonald Ser.). 176p. 1980. pap. 2.95 (ISBN 0-8028-1860-9). Eerdmans.

--The Wise Woman, or the Lost Princess. LC 75-32187. (Classics of Children's Literature, 1621-1932: Vol. 50). (Illus.). 1976. Repr. of 1882 ed. PLB 38.00 (ISBN 0-8240-2299-8). Garland Pub.

MacDonald, George see Watson, Jean.

McDonald, Gerald D., ed. & compiled by see Crane, Stephen.

McDonald, Gregory. Fletch's Fortune. 1978. pap. 2.25 (ISBN 0-380-37978-3, 76323). Avon.

--Love Among the Mashed Potatoes. 1978. 8.95 o.p. (ISBN 0-525-14905-8). Dutton.

--Running Scared. 1977. pap. 1.95 o.p. (ISBN 0-380-00924-2, 42481). Avon.

MacDonald, Gus. Camera: Victorian Eyewitness; A History of Photography, 1826-1913. LC 79-5296. (Illus.). 1980. 17.95 (ISBN 0-670-20056-5, Studio). Viking Pr.

MacDonald, Gwendoline. Development of Standards & Accreditation in Collegiate Nursing Education. (Nursing Education Monograph Series No. 8). 1965. pap. 3.75 o.p. (ISBN 0-397-54039-6). Lippincott.

McDonald, H. D. The Doctrine of Man. (Foundations for Faith Ser.). 5.95 (ISBN 0-89107-217-9). Good News.

--Salvation. (Foundations for Faith). 4.95 (ISBN 0-89107-225-X). Good News.

McDonald, Hope. Descubramos Como Orar. Coleman, F. G., tr. from Eng. (Span.). 1980. pap. 2.50 (ISBN 0-311-40040-X). Casa Bautista.

Macdonald, I., tr. see Dieudonne, Jean.

Macdonald, I. G., jt. auth. see Atiyah, Michael F.

McDonald, I. R., jt. auth. see Hansen, J. P.

Macdonald, I. T., ed. see Lope De Vega, Carpio.

MacDonald, Ian D. Theory of Groups. 1968. pap. 16.95x (ISBN 0-19-853138-9). Oxford U Pr.

McDonald, Irene B. Language: All About It. 112p. (Orig.). (gr. 10-12). 1980. pap. text ed. 3.25x (ISBN 0-88334-140-9). Ind-Sch Pr.

McDonald, J. The Magic Story: Message of a Master. pap. 1.50 (ISBN 0-910140-23-5). R Collier.

Macdonald, J. M. Burglary & Theft. 292p. 1980. 19.75 (ISBN 0-398-03962-3). C C Thomas.

Macdonald, J. Ransay, ed. Women in the Printing Trades: A Sociological Study, London Nineteen Four. LC 79-56961. (The English Working Class Ser.). 1980. lib. bdg. 18.00 (ISBN 0-8240-0114-1). Garland Pub.

MacDonald, James. Food from the Far West. or, American Agriculture. 1980. lib. bdg. 69.95 (ISBN 0-8490-3187-7). Gordon Pr.

MacDonald, James R; see Hardie, James K.

MacDonald, Janet & Francis, Valerie. Riding Side Saddle. (Pelham Horsemaster Ser.). (Illus.). 1979. 14.00 (ISBN 0-7207-1100-2). Transatlantic.

McDonald, Joan. Rousseau & the French Revolution 1762-91. (Univ. of London Historical Studies: No. 17). 1965. text ed. 20.75x (ISBN 0-485-13117-X, Athlone Pr). Humanities.

MacDonald, John. All These Condemned. 1981. pap. 1.95 (ISBN 0-449-14239-6, GM). Fawcett.

McDonald, John. The Game of Business. LC 74-5530. 1977. pap. 4.50 (ISBN 0-385-11671-3, Anch). Doubleday.

McDonald, John & Burleson, Clyde. Flight from Dhahran: The True Experiences of an American Businessman Held Hostage in Saudi Arabia. 256p. 1981. 10.95 (ISBN 0-13-322453-8). P-H.

MacDonald, John A. Facing the Scalpel: What to Expect, What to Beware of When You Have an Operation. (Illus.). 144p. 1981. 10.95 (ISBN 0-13-299198-5); pap. 4.95 (ISBN 0-13-299180-2). P-H.

MacDonald, John B. The Green Ripper. (gr. 7-12). 1980. lib. bdg. 12.95 (ISBN 0-8161-3023-X). G K Hall.

MacDonald, John D. Area of Suspicion. 208p. 1978. pap. 1.75 o.p. (ISBN 0-449-14008-3, GM). Fawcett.

--Ballroom of the Skies. 1979. pap. 1.95 (ISBN 0-449-14143-8, GM). Fawcett.

--The Beach Girls. 1978. pap. 1.75 o.p. (ISBN 0-449-14081-4, GM). Fawcett.

--The Brass Cupcake. 1981. pap. 1.95 (ISBN 0-449-14141-1, GM). Fawcett.

--Bright Orange for the Shroud. LC 72-396. 1972. 7.95 o.s.i. (ISBN 0-397-00793-0). Lippincott.

--Bright Orange for the Shroud. (Travis McGee Ser.). 1978. pap. 2.25 (ISBN 0-449-14243-4, GM). Fawcett.

--A Bullet for Cinderella. 1979. pap. 1.75 o.p. (ISBN 0-449-14106-3, GM). Fawcett.

--Cancel All Our Vows. 1977. pap. 1.75 o.p. (ISBN 0-449-13764-3, GM). Fawcett.

--Clemmie. 1978. pap. 1.75 o.p. (ISBN 0-449-14015-6, GM). Fawcett.

--Condominium. LC 76-30593. 1977. 10.00 o.p. (ISBN 0-397-01203-9). Lippincott.

--Contrary Pleasure. 1979. pap. 1.75 o.p. (ISBN 0-449-14104-7, GM). Fawcett.

--Contrary Pleasure. 256p. 1981. pap. 2.50 (ISBN 0-449-14104-7, GM). Fawcett.

--The Crossroads. 1978. pap. 1.75 o.p. (ISBN 0-449-14033-4, GM). Fawcett.

--Cry Hard, Cry Fast. 1978. pap. 1.50 o.p. (ISBN 0-449-13969-7, GM). Fawcett.

--The Damned. 1978. pap. 1.95 (ISBN 0-449-13997-2, GM). Fawcett.
--Darker Than Amber. (Travis McGee Ser.). 1979. pap. 2.25 (ISBN 0-449-14162-4, GM). Fawcett.
--Darker Than Amber: A Travis McGee Story. (Orig.). 1970. Repr. 5.95 o.s.i. (ISBN 0-397-00642-X). Lippincott.
--A Deadly Shade of Gold. LC 73-20286. 1974. 7.50 o.s.i. (ISBN 0-397-01032-X). Lippincott.
--Death Trap. 1981. pap. 1.95 (ISBN 0-449-14323-6, GM). Fawcett.
--The Deceivers. 1978. pap. 1.75 o.p. (ISBN 0-449-14016-4, GM). Fawcett.
--The Deep Blue Good-by. LC 75-1092. 204p. 1975. Repr. of 1964 ed. 6.95 o.s.i. (ISBN 0-397-01090-7). Lippincott.
--The Dreadful Lemon Sky. LC 74-23085. (Travis McGee Ser). 1975. 6.95 o.p. (ISBN 0-397-01074-5). Lippincott.
--The Dreadful Lemon Sky. (Travis McGee Ser.). 272p. 1978. pap. 2.25 (ISBN 0-449-14148-9, GM). Fawcett.
--Dress Her in Indigo. 1971. 8.95 (ISBN 0-397-00697-7). Lippincott.
--The Drowner. 160p. 1977. pap. 1.75 o.p. (ISBN 0-449-13582-9, GM). Fawcett.
--Executioners. 1978. pap. 1.75 o.p. (ISBN 0-449-14059-8, GM). Fawcett.
--A Flash of Green. 1979. pap. 2.25 (ISBN 0-449-14186-1, GM). Fawcett.
--Free Fall in Crimson. LC 80-7871. 224p. 1981. 9.95 (ISBN 0-06-014833-0, HarpT). Har-Row.
--Girl in the Plain Brown Wrapper. LC 72-8388. 1973. 8.95 (ISBN 0-397-00953-4). Lippincott.
--Judge Me Not. 1978. pap. 1.75 o.p. (ISBN 0-449-14057-1, GM). Fawcett.
--A Key to the Suite. 1978. pap. 1.95 (ISBN 0-449-13995-6, GM). Fawcett.
--The Last One Left. 1978. pap. 2.50 (ISBN 0-449-13958-1, GM). Fawcett.
--The Long Lavender Look. LC 78-37010. 1972. 5.50 o.s.i. (ISBN 0-397-00739-6). Lippincott.
--A Man of Affairs. 176p. 1978. pap. 1.75 o.p. (ISBN 0-449-14051-2, GM). Fawcett.
--Nightmare in Pink. LC 75-31753. (Travis McGee Mystery Ser.). 1976. 9.95 (ISBN 0-397-01116-4). Lippincott.
--On the Run. 1978. pap. 1.95 (ISBN 0-449-13983-2, GM). Fawcett.
--One Fearful Yellow Eye. LC 77-24165. 1978. 8.95 o.p. (ISBN 0-397-01191-1). Lippincott.
--The Only Girl in the Game. 1978. pap. 1.75 o.p. (ISBN 0-449-14032-6, GM). Fawcett.
--Pale Gray for Guilt. 1971. 5.50 o.s.i. (ISBN 0-397-00792-2). Lippincott.
--The Quick Red Fox. LC 73-16074. 1974. 8.95 (ISBN 0-397-01015-X). Lippincott.
--S E V E N. 1979. pap. 1.75 o.p. (ISBN 0-449-14126-8, GM). Fawcett.
--The Scarlet Ruse. (Travis McGee Ser.). 1978. pap. 2.25 o.p. (ISBN 0-449-13952-2, GM). Fawcett.
--The Scarlet Ruse. 320p. 1981. pap. 2.50 (ISBN 0-449-13952-2, GM). Fawcett.
--Slam the Big Door. 208p. 1977. pap. 1.95 o.p. (ISBN 0-449-13707-4, GM). Fawcett.
--Soft Touch. 1978. pap. 1.95 (ISBN 0-449-13957-3, GM). Fawcett.
--A Tan & Sandy Silence. 1979. 8.95 o.s.i. (ISBN 0-397-01343-4). Lippincott.
--You Live Once. 1978. pap. 1.75 o.p. (ISBN 0-449-14050-4, GM). Fawcett.

Macdonald, John M. Armed Robbery: Offenders & Their Victims. 456p. 1975. 24.75 (ISBN 0-398-03350-1). C C Thomas.
--Bombers & Firesetters. 264p. 1977. 18.50 (ISBN 0-398-03687-X). C C Thomas.
--Homicidal Threats. (Illus.). 136p. 1968. 9.75 (ISBN 0-398-01178-8). C C Thomas.
--Indecent Exposure. 180p. 1973. 11.75 (ISBN 0-398-02598-3). C C Thomas.
--Psychiatry & the Criminal: A Guide to Psychiatric Examinations for the Criminal Courts. 3rd ed. 524p. 1976. 37.75 (ISBN 0-398-03480-X). C C Thomas.
--Rape: Offenders & Their Victims. 352p. 1979. 21.75 (ISBN 0-398-01181-8). C C Thomas.

MacDonald, Joseph A., ed. see Professional Publications.

MacDonald, K. L. Automotive Air Conditioning. LC 78-57176. 1978. pap. 7.95 (ISBN 0-672-23318-5). Audel.
--Small Gasoline Engines Student's Workbook. 2nd ed. 1973. pap. 2.95 (ISBN 0-672-97632-3). Bobbs.

McDonald, Karen M., jt. auth. see McMichael, Betty.

McDonald, Kay L. Vision of the Eagle: A Novel. LC 77-2579. 1977. 9.95 o.s.i. (ISBN 0-690-01491-0, TYC-T). T Y Crowell.

McDonald, Kendall. Food from the Seashore. (Illus.). 128p. 1980. 11.95 (ISBN 0-7207-1183-5, Pub. by Michael Joseph); pap. 6.50 (ISBN 0-7207-1235-1). Merrimack Bk Serv.

McDonald, L. E., ed. Veterinary Endocrinology & Reproduction. 3rd ed. LC 79-22338. (Illus.). 560p. 1980. text ed. 39.50 (ISBN 0-8121-0712-8). Lea & Febiger.

MacDonald, Lachlan, jt. ed. see Gilmore, Elaine.

Macdonald, Lachlan P. An Uncommon Guide to San Luis Obispo County California. rev. 2nd ed. LC 75-2794. (Illus.). 1981. pap. 5.95 (ISBN 0-686-69421-X). Padre Prods.

McDonald, Laughlin, jt. auth. see Larson, E. Richard.

McDonald, Lois H. Fur Trade Letters of Francis Ermatinger. LC 80-65050. (Northwest Historical Ser.: Vol. 15). (Illus.). 317p. 1980. 29.00 (ISBN 0-87062-130-0). A H Clark.

McDonald, Lucile. The Arab Marco Polo: Ibn Battuta. LC 75-4651. (Illus.). 160p. (gr. 6 up). 1975. 7.95 (ISBN 0-525-66441-6). Elsevier-Nelson.
--The Lake Washington Story. LC 79-20102. (Illus.). 1981. 19.95 (ISBN 0-87564-635-2). Superior Pub.
--Washington's Yesterdays. (Illus.). 192p. 1975. pap. 3.95 o.p. (ISBN 0-8323-0258-9). Binford.
--Windmills: An Old-New Energy Source. (Illus.). (gr. 4 up). 1981. 10.95 (ISBN 0-525-66708-3). Elsevier-Nelson.

Macdonald, Lyn. French Cooking Without Tears. (Illus.). 192p. 1980. 16.95 (ISBN 0-241-10173-5, Pub. by Hamish Hamilton England). David & Charles.

Macdonald, Lynn. Bordeaux & Aquitane. 1976. 24.00 (ISBN 0-7134-3183-0). David & Charles.

McDonald, Lynn. The Sociology of Law & Order. LC 76-9753. 330p. 1976. 32.50 o.p. (ISBN 0-89158-614-8); text ed. 15.00 o.p. (ISBN 0-686-67421-9). Westview.

MacDonald, Malcolm. Birds in the Sun. (Illus.). 1962. 22.50 (ISBN 0-85493-077-9). Dufour.
--Collected Poems of Malcolm MacDonald. 1978. 4.75 o.p. (ISBN 0-533-02200-2). Vantage.
--Goldeneye. LC 80-23235. (Illus.). 544p. 1981. 15.00 (ISBN 0-394-51118-2). Knopf.
--Inside China. (Illus.). 208p. 1981. 19.95 (ISBN 0-316-54188-5). Little.

McDonald, Margaret L. The Independent Woman in the Restoration Comedy of Manners. (Salzburg Studies in English Literature: Poetic Drama & Poetic Theory: No. 32). 255p. 1976. pap. text ed. 25.00x (ISBN 0-391-01478-1). Humanities.

McDonald, Margaret R. The Storyteller's Sourcebook: An Index to Folklore Collections for Children. 500p. 1981. 49.95 (ISBN 0-918212-40-5). Neal-Schuman.

McDonald, Marian, ed. see Childbearing Rights Information Project.

McDonald, Neil A. Politics: A Study of Control Behavior. 1965. 16.50 (ISBN 0-8135-0488-0). Rutgers U Pr.

McDonald, P. & Edwards, R. A. Animal Nutrition. 2nd ed. (Illus.). 475p. 1976. pap. text ed. 18.95x (ISBN 0-582-44157-9). Longman.

McDonald, P. W., jt. auth. see Tisdell, C. A.

McDonald, Paula & McDonald, Dick. Life Scripts from Loving Free. 1977. pap. 2.25 o.p. (ISBN 0-345-25766-9). Ballantine.

MacDonald, R. P. see Reiner, Miriam, et al.

McDonald, Ralph E. & Avery, David R. Dentistry for the Child & Adolescent. 3rd ed. LC 73-11347. (Illus.). 1978. text ed. 32.50 (ISBN 0-8016-3276-5). Mosby.

McDonald, Ralph J. A Down-Home Gallery of American Wildlife. (Illus.). 101p. 1980. 39.95 (ISBN 0-9605428-1-7); signed numbered ed. 95.00 (ISBN 0-9605428-0-9). Countryside Studio.

McDonald, Robert. Modern Upholstery Techniques. 144p. 22.50 o.p. (ISBN 0-7134-2197-5). David & Charles.

MacDonald, Robert D. Chinchilla. (Phoenix Theatre Ser.). pap. 2.95 (ISBN 0-912262-73-7). Proscenium.

McDonald, Robert L., jt. auth. see Hesse, Walter H.

MacDonald, Ross. On Crime Writing. new ed. (Capra Chapbook Ser.: No. 11). (Illus.). 1973. pap. 2.50 o.p. (ISBN 0-912264-66-7). Capra Pr.

Macdonald, S., jt. auth. see Braun, E.

MacDonald, Scott. Critical Essays on Erskine Caldwell. (Critical Essays on American Literature). 1981. lib. bdg. 25.00 (ISBN 0-8161-8299-X). Twayne.

Macdonald, Shelagh. Five from Me, Five from You. LC 80-2695. 192p. (gr. 6 up). 1981. 8.95 (ISBN 0-233-96554-8). Andre Deutsch.
--No End to Yesterday. LC 78-74755. (Illus.). (gr. 7 up). 1979. 7.95 (ISBN 0-233-96865-2). Andre Deutsch.

MacDonald, Susan. Your Career in the Beauty Industry. LC 78-17138. (Arco Career Guidance Ser.). 1979. lib. bdg. 6.95 (ISBN 0-668-04612-0); pap. 3.50 (ISBN 0-668-04623-6). Arco.

McDonald, T. Marll. Mathematical Methods for Social & Management Scientists. 544p. 1974. text ed. 19.95 (ISBN 0-395-17089-3); instructor's manual pap. 2.25 (ISBN 0-395-17858-4). HM.

McDonald, Vincent R. The Caribbean Issues of Emergence: Socio-Economic & Political Perspectives. LC 79-6604. 1980. text ed. 22.00 (ISBN 0-8191-0925-8); pap. text ed. 12.25 (ISBN 0-8191-0926-6). U Pr of Amer.

MacDonald, W. Scott, jt. auth. see Oden, Chet.

MacDonald, W. Scott, et al. Focus on Classroom Behavior: Readings & Research. (Illus.). 170p. 1973. 11.75 (ISBN 0-398-02460-X). C C Thomas.

MacDonald, Wendy. Constitutional Change & the Mining Industry in Canada. 73p. 1890. write for info. (Pub. by Ctr. Resource Stud Canada). Renouf.

MacDonald, William. Chasing the Wind. 1981. pap. 1.95 (ISBN 0-937396-07-9). Walterick Pubs.
--Enjoying the Psalms, 2 vols. 1981. pap. 4.95 ea. Vol. 1 (ISBN 0-937396-34-6). Vol. 2 (ISBN 0-937396-35-4). Walterick Pubs.
--Let Me Introduce You to the Bible. 1981. pap. 1.95 (ISBN 0-937396-22-2). Walterick Pubs.
--Letter to Titus. 54p pap. 1.50. Walterick Pubs.
--Old Testament Digest: Gen-Deut, Vol. 1. 1981. pap. 7.50 (ISBN 0-937396-59-1). Walterick Pubs.
--Old Testament Digest: Vol. 3, Job-Malachi. 1981. pap. 6.95 (ISBN 0-937396-29-X). Walterick Pubs.
--Romans: Justification by Faith. (Orig.). 1981. pap. 6.50 (ISBN 0-937396-36-2). Walterick Pubs.
--To What Should We Be Loyal. 55p. pap. 0.75 (ISBN 0-937396-47-8). Walterick Pubs.
--True Discipleship. enl. ed. 58p. pap. 1.95 (ISBN 0-937396-50-8). Walterick Pubs.

MacDonald, William C. Hellgate. 1978. pap. 1.25 (ISBN 0-505-51298-X). Tower Bks.
--Incident at Horado City. 1978. pap. 1.25 (ISBN 0-505-51288-2). Tower Bks.

McDonald, William C. & Goebel, Ulrich. German Medieval Literary Patronage from Charlemagne to Maximilian the First: A Critical Commentary with Special Emphasis on Imperial Promotion of Literature. LC 73-82154. (Amsterdamer Publikationen Zur Sprache und Literatur: No. 10). 220p. (Orig.). 1973. pap. text ed. 23.00x (ISBN 90-6203-201-X). Humanities.

McDonald, William F., ed. Criminal Justice & the Victim. LC 75-42754. (Sage Criminal Justice System Annuals Ser.: Vol. 6). 1976. 20.00x (ISBN 0-8039-0508-4); pap. 9.95x (ISBN 0-8039-0509-2). Sage.
--The Prosecutor. LC 79-14388. (Sage Criminal Justice System Annuals Ser.: Vol. 11). (Illus.). 279p. 1979. 20.00 (ISBN 0-8039-0815-6); pap. 9.95 (ISBN 0-8039-0816-4). Sage.

MacDonald-Ross, Michael. Nimzo-Indian Defence: Leningrad System. 1979. pap. 14.95 (ISBN 0-7134-0947-9). David & Charles.

MacDonald-Taylor, Margaret. Dictionary of Marks. (Illus.). 1962. 7.95 o.p. (ISBN 0-8015-2088-6, Hawthorn); pap. 4.95 (ISBN 0-8015-2089-4, Hawthorn). Dutton.

Macdonell, A., jt. auth. see Martin, W.

Macdonell, Margaret. Songs of Highland Emigrants in North America. 208p. 1981. 18.95x (ISBN 0-8020-5469-2). U of Toronto Pr.

McDonnell. The Use of Hand Woodworking Tools. LC 76-48504. 301p. 1978. pap. 7.20 (ISBN 0-8273-1098-6); instructor's guide 1.60 (ISBN 0-8273-1099-4). Delmar.
--The Use of Portable Power Tools. LC 77-85761. 1979. pap. 8.40 (ISBN 0-8273-1100-1); instructor's guide 1.00 (ISBN 0-685-93221-4). Delmar.

McDonnell & Ball. Blueprinting Reading & Sketching for Carpenters. LC 73-2165. 208p. 1975. 9.20 (ISBN 0-8273-1067-6); instructor's guide 1.60 (ISBN 0-8273-1068-4). Delmar.

MacDonnell, Arthur A. Sanskrit Grammar for Students. 3rd ed. 1927. 16.50x (ISBN 0-19-815415-1). Oxford U Pr.

McDonnell, James, ed. see DeGiacomo, F. P.

McDonnell, John, jt. ed. see McCgwire, Michael.

MacDonnell, Kenneth F., jt. auth. see Berman, Bernard A.

McDonnell, Kilian. Charismatic Renewal & the Churches. 1976. 8.95 (ISBN 0-8164-0293-0). Crossroad NY.
--Presence, Power, Praise: Documents on Charismatic Renewal: National Documents, Vol. 2. 1980. 35.00 (ISBN 0-8146-1189-3). Liturgical Pr.

McDonnell, Kilian, ed. Presence, Power, Praise; Documents on Charismatic Renewal: International Documents, Vol. 3. 1980. 35.00 (ISBN 0-8146-1065-X). Liturgical Pr.
--Presence, Power, Praise: Documents on Charismatic Renewal: National Documents, Vol. 1. 1980. 35.00 (ISBN 0-8146-1066-8). Liturgical Pr.

McDonnell, Leo & Ball, John. Blueprint Reading & Sketching for Carpenters: Residential. 3rd ed. LC 80-66027. (Blueprint Reading Ser.). (Illus.). 160p. 1981. pap. text ed. 9.80 (ISBN 0-8273-1354-3); price not set instr's guide (ISBN 0-8273-1355-1). Delmar.

McDonnell, Thomas P., ed. A Thomas Merton Reader. LC 74-29. 600p. 1974. pap. 2.95 (ISBN 0-385-03292-7, Im). Doubleday.

McDonough, Adrian M. & Garrett, Leonard J. Management Systems. 1965. text ed. 17.95 (ISBN 0-256-00321-1). Irwin.

McDonough, B. T. Nietzsche & Kazantzakis. LC 78-61302. 1978. pap. text ed. 7.25 (ISBN 0-8191-0607-0). U Pr of Amer.

McDonough, Irma. Canadian Books for Young People. 3rd ed. 1980. pap. 15.00x (ISBN 0-8020-4594-4). U of Toronto Pr.

McDonough, James L. Stones River: Bloody Winter in Tennessee. LC 80-11580. 256p. 1980. 14.50 (ISBN 0-87049-301-9). U of Tenn Pr.

McDonough, James L. & Gardner, Richard S. The Skyriders: History of the 327-401 Glider Infantry. LC 80-67956. (Airborne Ser.: No. 11). (Illus.). 176p. 1980. 20.00 (ISBN 0-89839-034-6). Battery Pr.

McDonough, Martin & Hansen, Alvin J. The College Board's Examination. LC 75-21998. 416p. 1976. lib. bdg. 10.00 (ISBN 0-668-02624-3); pap. 6.00. Arco.

McDonough, Peter & Desouza, Amaury. The Politics of Population in Brazil: Elite Ambivalence & Public Demand. (Texas Pan American Ser). 190p. 1981. 19.95x (ISBN 0-292-76466-9). U of Tex Pr.

McDonough, Sheila. The Authority of the Past. LC 76-141690. (American Academy of Religion. Studies in Religion). 46p. 1970. pap. 4.50 (ISBN 0-89130-153-4, 010001). Scholars Pr Ca.

McDonough, Steven H. Psychology in Foreign Language Teaching. (Illus.). 176p. 1981. text ed. 25.00x (ISBN 0-04-418002-0, 2628-9); pap. text ed. 8.95x (ISBN 0-04-418003-9). Allen Unwin.

McDonough, Tom. Virgin with Child. 1981. 11.95 (ISBN 0-670-74721-1). Viking Pr.

McDougal, Duncan & Quirk, James. Economics. 800p. 1981. text ed. 18.95 (ISBN 0-574-19405-3, 13-2405); instr's. guide avail. (ISBN 0-574-19406-1, 13-2406); study guide 6.50 (ISBN 0-574-19407-X, 13-2407). SRA.

McDougal, Stan. The World's Greatest Golf Jokes. 1980. 9.95 (ISBN 0-686-65057-3). Lyle Stuart.

McDougal, W. Scott. Traumatic Injuries of the Genitourinary System. (Illus.). 139p. 1980. 26.95. Williams & Wilkins.

McDougall, Bonnie S. Mao Zedong's "Talks at the Yan'an Conference on Literature & Art". A Translation of the 1943 Text with Commentary. LC 80-18443. (Michigan Papers in Chinese Studies: No. 39). 128p. 1980. pap. 5.00 (ISBN 0-89264-039-1). U of Mich Ctr Chinese.

McDougall, Donald. Boswell & Son. LC 77-17765. 1978. 10.00 o.p. (ISBN 0-312-09324-1). St Martin.
--Davie: A Love Story. 1978. pap. 1.95 o.p. (ISBN 0-445-04293-1). Popular Lib.

McDougall, Duncan & Quirk, James P. Macroeconomics. 1981. pap. text ed. 11.95 (ISBN 0-574-19415-0, 13-2415); instr's guide avail. (ISBN 0-574-19416-9, 13-2416). SRA.

McDougall, Duncan, jt. auth. see Quirk, James P.

McDougall, E. J., jt. auth. see Verzar, F.

MacDougall, Hamilton C. Early New England Psalmody: An Historical Appreciation, 1620-1820. LC 79-87398. (Music Reprint Ser). 1969. Repr. of 1940 ed. lib. bdg. 19.50 (ISBN 0-306-71542-2). Da Capo.

MacDougall, John. Rural Life in Canada. LC 72-75735. (Social History of Canada Ser.). 216p. 1973. pap. 5.50 (ISBN 0-8020-6145-1). U of Toronto Pr.

McDougall, Richard, tr. Herculine Barbin: Being the Recently Discovered Memoirs of a Nineteenth-Century Hermaphrodite. Foucault, Michel, intro. by. 1980. 8.95 (ISBN 0-394-50821-1); pap. 4.95 (ISBN 0-394-73862-4). Pantheon.

MacDougall, Ruth D. The Flowers of the Forest. LC 80-22415. 1981. 11.95 (ISBN 0-689-11124-X). Atheneum.

McDougall, T. W., jt. auth. see MacNaughton, E. G.

McDowall, David, et al. Interrupted Time Series Analysis. LC 80-52761. (Quantitative Applications in the Social Sciences Ser.: No. 21). (Illus.). 96p. 1980. pap. 3.50 (ISBN 0-8039-1493-8). Sage.

MacDowall, David W. The Western Coinages of Nero. LC 74-82869. (Numismatic Notes & Monographs: No. 161). (Illus.). xvii, 256p. (Orig.). 1979. pap. 40.00 (ISBN 0-89722-176-1). Am Numismatic.

McDowall, R. M. Freshwater Fish in New Zealand. (Mobil New Zealand Nature Ser.). (Illus.). 80p. (Orig.). 1980. pap. 6.95 (ISBN 0-589-01327-0, Pub. by Reed Bks Australia). C E Tuttle.

--New Zealand Freshwater Fishes: A Guide and Natural History. (Illus.). 230p. 1972. text ed. 27.50x (ISBN 0-87474-632-9, Pub. by Heinemann New Zealand). Smithsonian.

McDowell & Lavitt. Third World Voices for Children. 1981. 7.95. Okpaku Communications.

McDowell, Barbara & Umlauf, Hana, eds. The Good Housekeeping Woman's Almanac. 1977. pap. 3.95 o.p. (ISBN 0-685-59257-X). Newspaper Ent.

McDowell, Barbara, jt. ed. see Umlauf, Hana.

McDowell, Charles P. Community Relations & Criminal Justice. 500p. Date not set. text ed. price not set (ISBN 0-87084-558-6). Anderson Pub Co.

McDowell, D. M. & O'Connor, B. A. Hydraulic Behaviour of Estuaries. 1977. 34.95x (ISBN 0-470-98922-X). Halsted Pr.

MacDowell, Douglas M., ed. see Aristophanes.

MacDowell, Edward. Critical & Historical Essays. 2nd ed. LC 69-11289. 1969. Repr. of 1912 ed. lib. bdg. 19.50 (ISBN 0-306-71098-6). Da Capo.

--Piano Pieces, (Opus 51, 55, 61, 62) LC 70-170391. (Earlier American Music Ser.: No. 8). 144p. 1972. Repr. lib. bdg. 25.00 (ISBN 0-306-77308-2). Da Capo.

--Songs (Opus 40, 47, 56, 58, 60) LC 73-170392. (Earlier American Music Ser.: No. 7). 1972. Repr. lib. bdg. 16.50 (ISBN 0-685-29163-4). Da Capo.

McDowell, Edwin, ed. To Keep Our Honor Clean. LC 79-56025. 320p. 1980. 10.95 (ISBN 0-8149-0831-4). Vanguard.

McDowell, Ernest R. North American F-86A-H Sabre, Vol. 1. LC 79-113953. (Arco-Aircam Aviation Ser., No. 19). 1970. pap. 2.95 o.p. (ISBN 0-668-02301-5). Arco.

--Republic P-Forty-Seven Thunderbolt. Ward, Richard, ed. & illus. LC 75-86566. (Arco-Aircam Aviation Ser., No. 2). (Illus., Orig.). 1968. pap. 2.95 o.p. (ISBN 0-668-02095-4). Arco.

McDowell, F., ed. see Canadian-American Conference on Parkinson's Disease, 2nd.

McDowell, Fletcher H., ed. Current Concepts in Cerebravascular Disease. (Progress in Cardiovascular Disease Ser.). 1980. write for info. (ISBN 0-8089-1353-0). Grune.

McDowell, Frank & Enna, Carl D. Surgical Rehabilitation in Leprosy. 450p. 1974. 44.00 o.p. (ISBN 0-683-05853-3). Williams & Wilkins.

McDowell, Frank, jt. auth. see American Society of Plastic & Reconstructive Surgeons.

McDowell, Frederick P. E. M. Forster. (English Authors Ser.: No. 89). lib. bdg. 10.95 (ISBN 0-8057-1208-9). Twayne.

McDowell, Frederick P., ed. Poet As Critic. 1967. 7.95x o.s.i. (ISBN 0-8101-0151-3); pap. 4.95x o.s.i. (ISBN 0-8101-0150-5). Northwestern U Pr.

McDowell, Gary L., jt. ed. see Rossum, Ralph A.

McDowell, Jack, jt. auth. see Ketels, Hank.

McDowell, Josh. Evidence That Demands a Verdict. rev. ed. LC 78-75041. 1979. 10.95 (ISBN 0-918956-57-9); pap. 6.95 (ISBN 0-918956-46-3). Campus Crusade.

--Givers, Takers, & Other Kinds of Lovers. 1980. pap. 4.95 (ISBN 0-8423-1033-9). Tyndale.

--The Resurrection Factor. 180p. (Orig.). 1981. 8.95 (ISBN 0-918956-71-4, Dist. by Here's Life Publishers Inc.); pap. 4.95 (ISBN 0-918956-72-2). Campus Crusade.

McDowell, Josh & Stewart, Don. Answers to Tough Questions Skeptics Ask About the Christian Faith. 190p. 1980. pap. 4.95 (ISBN 0-918956-65-X). Campus Crusade.

--Josh McDowell & Don Stewart Answer Tough Questions That Skeptics Ask About the Christian Faith. 190p. (Orig.). 1980. pap. 4.95 o.p. (ISBN 0-918956-65-X). Campus Crusade.

McDowell, Leonora. Moccasin Meanderings. Kulikowski, M. Karl, ed. (Gusto Press Poetry Discovery Ser.). (Orig.). 1979. pap. 3.95 (ISBN 0-933906-02-1). Gusto Pr.

McDowell, Margaret B. Edith Wharton. LC 75-44094. (U. S. Authors Ser.: No. 265). 1976. lib. bdg. 10.95 (ISBN 0-8057-7164-6). Twayne.

--Edith Wharton. LC 75-44094. (Twayne's U. S. Authors Ser.). 158p. 1976. pap. text ed. 4.95 (ISBN 0-672-61509-6). Bobbs.

McDowell, Michael. The Amulet. 352p. 1980. pap. 2.50 (ISBN 0-380-40584-9, 40584). Avon.

--Gilded Needles. 352p. 1980. pap. 2.50 (ISBN 0-380-76398-2, 76398). Avon.

McDowell, Milton C., jt. auth. see Crawford, H. W.

McDowell, Milton C., jt. auth. see Crawford, Hollie.

McDowell, Robert J., jt. auth. see Reid, Margaret I.

Mac Duff, J. N. & Currey, John R. Vibration Control. 2nd ed. 1981. write for info. (ISBN 0-89874-030-4). Krieger.

MacDuff, John R. The Bow in the Cloud: And the First Bereavement. (Summit Bks.). 148p. 1980. pap. 2.45 (ISBN 0-8010-6108-3). Baker Bk.

MacDuffee, Cyrus C. Theory of Matrices. 2nd ed. LC 49-2197. 8.95 (ISBN 0-8284-0028-8). Chelsea Pub.

McDuffie, Jack. Walk Out with Me. 1979. 1.80 (ISBN 0-686-28798-3). Forward Movement.

Mace, David R. A los Que Dios Ha Juntado En Matrimonio. 1978. pap. 1.80 (ISBN 0-311-40036-1, Edit Mundo). Casa Bautista.

--Success in Marriage. (YA) (gr. 9 up). 1965. pap. 1.95 o.p. (ISBN 0-687-40554-8, 405548, Apex). Abingdon.

Mace, Elisabeth. Brother Enemy. LC 80-29258. 128p. (gr. 6 up). 1981. 7.95 (ISBN 0-8253-0031-2). Beaufort Bks NY.

Mace, Gertrude. Elusive Memory. (YA) 1978. 5.95 (ISBN 0-685-85777-8, Avalon). Bouregy.

Mace, M. E. & Bell, A. A., eds. Fungal Wilt Diseases of Plants. 1981. price not set (ISBN 0-12-464450-3). Acad Pr.

McEachern, D. A Class Against Itself. 245p. 1980. 29.50 (ISBN 0-521-22985-5); pap. cancelled (ISBN 0-521-28054-0). Cambridge U Pr.

McEachern, George. Growing Fruits, Berries & Nuts in the South. LC 77-99266. (Illus.). 1978. pap. 3.95 (ISBN 0-88415-299-5). Pacesetter Pr.

Macedo, Suzette, tr. see Cruz Costa, Joao.

Macedo, Suzette, tr. see Furtado, Celso.

McElderry, Andrea L. Shanghai's Old-Style Bangles. (Michigan Papers in Chinese Studies Ser: No. 25). 1976. pap. 4.00 (ISBN 0-89264-025-1). U of Mich Ctr Chinese.

McElderry, B. R., Jr., ed. see Shelley, Percy B.

McElderry, Bruce R., Jr. Henry James. (U. S. Authors Ser.: No. 79). 1965. lib. bdg. 10.95 (ISBN 0-8057-0404-3). Twayne.

--Thomas Wolfe. (U. S. Authors Ser.: No. 50). 1963. lib. bdg. 9.95 (ISBN 0-8057-0833-2). Twayne.

McElderry, Bruce R., Jr., ed. Realistic Movement in American Writing: 1865-1900. LC 65-19410. (Orig.). 1965. pap. 8.50 (ISBN 0-672-63104-0). Odyssey Pr.

McElduff, Colin. Trans-Asia Motoring. (Illus.). 1976. 26.00 (ISBN 0-905064-01-1). Intl Learn Syst.

McEleney, Neil J. The Growth of the Gospels. LC 79-90141. (Orig.). 1980. pap. 3.95 (ISBN 0-8091-2243-X). Paulist Pr.

McElfresh, Beth. Chuck Wagon Cookbook. LC 60-8068. 72p. 1960. pap. 3.50 (ISBN 0-8040-0042-5, 1, SB). Swallow.

McElheny, Kenneth R., jt. ed. see Moffett, James.

McElheny, Ruth, ed. see Mandel, Abby.

McElhinney, M. W. Palaeomagnetism & Plate Tectonics. LC 72-80590. (Earth Science Ser). (Illus.). 368p. 1973. 57.50 (ISBN 0-521-08707-4); pap. 18.50x (ISBN 0-521-29753-2). Cambridge U Pr.

McEliece, R. J. The Theory of Information & Coding: A Mathematical Framework for Communication. (Encyclopedia of Mathematics & Its Applications: Vol. 3). 1977. text ed. 25.50 (ISBN 0-201-13502-7, Adv Bk Prog). A-W.

McElrath, Hugh T., jt. auth. see Eskew, Harry.

McElrath, Joseph E., Jr., ed. The Complete Works of Anne Bradstreet. (Critical Editions Program Ser.). 1981. lib. bdg. 35.00 (ISBN 0-8057-8533-7). Twayne.

McElrath, William N. Great Passages of the Bible. Barry, James C., ed. LC 63-8409. (Illus., Orig.). (gr. 6-7). 1963. pap. 3.25 tchrs' ed. (ISBN 0-8054-4907-8); pap. 1.95 students' ed. (ISBN 0-8054-4908-6). Broadman.

McElroy, Colleen. Winters Without Snow. new ed. LC 79-92501. 81p. 1980. pap. 5.95 (ISBN 0-918408-17-2). Reed & Cannon.

McElroy, Colleen J. Music from Home: Selected Poems. LC 76-14852. 118p. 1976. 8.95 o.p. (ISBN 0-8093-0774-X). S Ill U Pr.

McElroy, Colleen W. Speech & Language Development of the Preschool Child: A Survey. (Illus.). 236p. 1978. 16.50 (ISBN 0-398-02368-9). C C Thomas.

McElroy, Elam E. Applied Business Statistics: An Elementary Approach. 2nd ed. 1979. text ed. 18.95x (ISBN 0-8162-5535-0); inst. manual 4.95x (ISBN 0-8162-5537-7); wkbk. 6.95x (ISBN 0-8162-5536-9). Holden-Day.

McElroy, John. Andersonville: A Story of Rebel Military Prisons. abr. ed. 5.00 (ISBN 0-686-66276-8). Peter Smith.

--Andersonville: A Story of Rebel Military Prisons. abr. ed. 1977. pap. 1.75 o.p. (ISBN 0-449-30764-6, X764, Prem). Fawcett.

McElroy, John F. Parody & Burlesque in the Tragicomedies of Thomas Middleton. (Salzburg Studies in English Literature, Jacobean Drama Studies: No. 19). 1972. pap. text ed. 25.00x (ISBN 0-391-01479-X). Humanities.

McElroy, Lee. Joe Pepper. 1976. pap. 1.25 o.p. (ISBN 0-505-50986-5, BT50986). Tower Bks.

--Long Way to Texas. LC 76-2786. 192p. 1976. 5.95 o.p. (ISBN 0-385-12128-8). Doubleday.

McElroy, Wayne, jt. auth. see Shank, Paul.

McElroy, William, jt. ed. see Deluca, Marlene.

McElvaney, William K. The People of God in Ministry. LC 80-26077. 176p. (Orig.). 1981. pap. 6.95 (ISBN 0-687-30660-4). Abingdon.

McElveen, Floyd. The Mormon Revelations of Convenience. LC 78-72945. 1978. pap. 1.75 (ISBN 0-87123-385-1, 210385). Bethany Fell.

McElwee, William. Art of War: Waterloo to Mons. LC 74-17459. (Midland Bks.: No. 214). 352p. 1975. pap. 4.95x (ISBN 0-253-20214-0). Ind U Pr.

--The Story of England. 3rd ed. (Story Ser.). (Illus.). 1972. 6.95 (ISBN 0-571-09951-3, Pub. by Faber & Faber). Merrimack Bk Serv.

McEntee, Howard C. Radio Control Handbook. 4th, rev. ed. (Illus.). 1979. pap. 11.95 (ISBN 0-8306-9772-1, 1093). TAB Bks.

McEntee, Howard G. The Model Aircraft Handbook. rev. ed. LC 68-27317. (Funk & W Bk.). (Illus.). 240p. 1975. pap. 2.95 o.s.i. (ISBN 0-308-10150-2, F109, TYC-T). T Y Crowell.

McEntee, Howard G. & Winter, William. Model Aircraft Handbook. rev. ed. LC 68-27317. (Illus.). 1968. 8.95 o.s.i. (ISBN 0-690-54632-7, TYC-T). T Y Crowell.

McEntyre. Practical Guide to the Care of the Surgical Patient. LC 79-16116. 1979. pap. 11.50 (ISBN 0-8016-3056-8). Mosby.

McEntyre, John G. Land Survey Systems. LC 78-8551. 1978. text ed. 25.95 (ISBN 0-471-02492-9). Wiley.

McEoin, Gary & Riley, Nevita. Puebla: A Church Being Born. LC 79-91894. 160p. (Orig.). 1980. pap. 4.95 (ISBN 0-8091-2279-0). Paulist Pr.

MacEoin, Gary, tr. see Eisner, Sigmund.

Macesich, George, jt. auth. see Dimitrijevic, Dimitrije.

McEvedy, Colin. Atlas of African History. (Orig.). 1980. pap. 8.95 (ISBN 0-14-051083-4). Penguin.

McEvedy, Colin & McEvedy, Sarah. The Classical World. LC 75-653786. (The Atlas of World History Ser.). (Illus.). 64p. (gr. 6-12). 1974. 9.95 (ISBN 0-02-765550-4, 76555, CCPr). Macmillan.

--The Dark Ages. LC 72-178600. (Atlas of World History Ser). (Illus.). 64p. (gr. 6-12). 1972. 9.95 (ISBN 0-02-765540-7, CCPr). Macmillan.

--From the Beginning to Alexander the Great. LC 70-135199. (Atlas of World History Ser). (Illus.). (gr. 6-10). 1971. 5.95 o.s.i. (ISBN 0-02-765530-X, CCPr). Macmillan.

McEvedy, Sarah, jt. auth. see McEvedy, Colin.

McEvers, Joan, jt. auth. see March, Marion.

McEvoy, Donald, jt. ed. see Steinberg, J. Leonard.

McEvoy, Donald W. The Police & Their Many Publics. LC 76-6851. 154p. 1976. 10.00 (ISBN 0-8108-0925-7). Scarecrow.

McEvoy, James, III & Dietz, Thomas, eds. Handbook for Environmental Planning: The Social Consequences of Environmental Change. LC 76-57239. 1977. 32.00 (ISBN 0-471-58389-8, Pub. by Wiley-Interscience). Wiley.

MacEwan, A. & Weisskopf, T. Perspectives on the Economics Problem. 2nd ed. 1973. pap. 6.95 o.p. (ISBN 0-13-660928-7). P-H.

McEwan, J. R., ed. see Ogyu Sorai.

McEwan, John, jt. auth. see Diggory, Peter.

McEwan, M. J. & Phillips, L. F. The Chemistry of the Atmosphere. LC 75-14487. 1975. 39.95x (ISBN 0-470-58393-2). Halsted Pr.

McEwan, P. J., ed. Africa from Early Times to Eighteen Hundred. (Readings in African History Ser). 1968. 22.00x (ISBN 0-19-215661-6). Oxford U Pr.

--Twentieth-Century Africa. (Readings in African History Ser). 1968. 28.50x (ISBN 0-19-215663-2). Oxford U Pr.

McEwan, Peter J., ed. Second Special Conference Issue: Sixth International Conference on Social Science & Medicine, Amsterdam 1979. 80p. 1980. pap. 14.40 (ISBN 0-08-026763-7). Pergamon.

McEwan-Young, W., jt. auth. see Lockyer, K. G.

McEwen, jt. auth. see Merritt.

McEwen, E. C., et al. Language Proficiency in the Multiracial Junior School. (Research Reports Ser). 113p. 1975. pap. text ed. 12.50x (ISBN 0-85633-067-1, NFER). Humanities.

McEwen, Gilbert D. The Oracle of the Coffee House: John Dunton's Athenian Mercury. LC 78-171109. 1972. 12.50 (ISBN 0-87328-056-3). Huntington Lib.

McEwen, W., jt. auth. see Brewster, R.

McEwen, W. A. Blue Book of Questions & Answers for Second Mate, Chief Mate & Master. LC 62-15957. (Illus.). 320p. 1969. pap. 8.50x (ISBN 0-87033-007-1). Cornell Maritime.

--Blue Book of Questions & Answers for Third Mates. 2nd ed. LC 65-25384. (Illus.). 1965. pap. 6.00x (ISBN 0-87033-008-X). Cornell Maritime.

McEwen, W. A. & Lewis, A. H. Encyclopedia of Nautical Knowledge. LC 53-9685. 1953. 15.00 (ISBN 0-87033-010-1). Cornell Maritime.

McEwen, William J., jt. auth. see Hanneman, Gerhard J.

Macey, David, tr. see Lemaire, Anika.

Macey, Robert I. Human Physiology. 2nd ed. (Illus.). 224p. 1975. pap. 11.95 ref. ed. (ISBN 0-13-445288-7). P-H.

Macey, Samuel C. The Plays of Henry Carey. LC 78-66613. (Eighteenth Century English Drama Ser.). 1980. lib. bdg. 50.00 (ISBN 0-8240-3580-1). Garland Pub.

MacFadden, A., jt. ed. see Anderson, J. M.

McFadden, A. Elisabeth & Spalding, R. W. Fire in My Bones. LC 78-71387. (Destiny Ser.). 1979. pap. 4.95 (ISBN 0-8163-0319-3, 06217-4). Pacific Pr Pub Assn.

McFadden, D., ed. Neural Mechanisms in Behavior: A Texas Symposium. (Illus.). 350p. 1980. 24.90 (ISBN 0-387-90468-9). Springer-Verlag.

McFadden, Daniel, jt. ed. see Manski, Charles F.

McFadden, F., jt. auth. see Couger, J. D.

McFadden, F. Lee, ed. Consumer Math Cassettes. (Illus.). (gr. 8-10). 1979. manual & cassettes 169.95 (ISBN 0-917792-01-7). Math Hse.

McFadden, Fred, jt. auth. see Couger, Dan.

McFadden, Fred R., jt. auth. see Couger, J. Daniel.

McFadden, John, tr. see Erdozain, Placido.

McFadden, Johnnie & Rotter, Joseph C. Values Orientation in School. LC 80-69238. 90p. 1981. perfect bdg. 4.50 (ISBN 0-86548-045-1). Century Twenty One.

McFadden, S. Michele, ed. see Gilliland, Ken & Millard, J.

McFadden, S. Michele, ed. see Grice, Charles R., Jr.

McFadden, Thomas, ed. Liberation, Revolution & Freedom. 224p. 1975. 8.95 (ISBN 0-8164-0271-X). Crossroad NY.

McFadden, Thomas M., ed. America in Theological Perspective. 1976. 9.95 (ISBN 0-8164-0294-9). Crossroad NY.

McFadden, Thomas R., ed. Does Jesus Make a Difference? LC 73-17902. 1974. 7.95 (ISBN 0-8164-1151-4). Crossroad NY.

McFadden, William C. & Fuller, Reginald H. Holy Week. LC 74-24932. (Proclamation 1: Aids for Interpreting the Lessons of the Church Year, Ser. B). 64p. 1975. pap. 1.95 (ISBN 0-8006-4074-8, 1-4074). Fortress.

MacFaddin, Jean F. Biochemical Tests for Identification of Medical Bacteria. 2nd ed. (Illus.). 416p. 1980. softcover 26.50 (ISBN 0-683-05315-9). Williams & Wilkins.

McFadyen, Barbara & Hoff, Marilyn G. Bring Out Your Own Book. LC 80-67280. (Illus.). 96p. 1980. pap. 6.00 (ISBN 0-938018-00-0). Godiva Pub.

McFadyen, J. F. The Missionary Idea in Life & Religion. 194p. Repr. of 1926 ed. text ed. 3.50 (ISBN 0-567-02180-7). Attic Pr.

McFadzean, Ronald. The Life & Work of Alexander Thomson. (Illus.). 1979. 48.00 (ISBN 0-7100-8858-2). Routledge & Kegan.

McFall, Christie. Wonders of Dust. LC 80-14285. (Wonders Ser.). (Illus.). 80p. (gr. 5 up). 1980. PLB 6.95 (ISBN 0-396-07850-8). Dodd.

MacFall, Russell P. Rock Hunter's Guide. LC 78-22457. (Illus.). 1980. 12.95 (ISBN 0-690-01812-6, TYC-T). T Y Crowell.

McFall, Waddy F. Taxidermy Step by Step. (Illus.). 256p. 1975. 9.95 (ISBN 0-87691-209-9). Winchester Pr.

MacFarlan, Allan A. Boy's Book of Biking. (Illus.). 1970. pap. 1.25 (ISBN 0-671-29739-2). PB.

McFarlan, Donald M. Who & What & Where in the Bible. LC 74-3709. (Illus.). 216p. (Orig.). 1974. pap. 4.50 o.p. (ISBN 0-8042-0001-7). John Knox.

McFarland, Carl, jt. auth. see Cummings, Homer.

MacFarland, Charles S. The Christian Ministry & the Social Order: Lectures Delivered in the Course in Pastoral Functions at the Yale Divinity School, 1908-1909. 1913. 27.50x o.p. (ISBN 0-686-51352-5). Elliots Bks.

McFarland, D. J. Motivational Control Systems Analysis. 1975. 60.00 (ISBN 0-12-483860-X). Acad Pr.

McFarland, Dalton E. Managerial Innovation & Change in the Metropolitan Hospital. LC 79-14557. (Praeger Special Studies Ser.). 336p. 1979. 28.95 (ISBN 0-03-051341-3). Praeger.

McFarland, Dalton E., jt. ed. see Wickert, Frederic R.

McFarland, Daniel M. Historical Dictionary of Haute Volta. LC 77-14987. (African Historical Dictionaries Ser.: No. 14). (Illus.). 1978. 11.50 (ISBN 0-8108-1088-3). Scarecrow.

McFarland, Dorothy T. Flannery O'Connor. LC 74-78443. (Modern Literature Ser.). 140p. 1976. 10.95 (ISBN 0-8044-2609-0). Ungar.

--Willa Cather. LC 74-190351. (Modern Literature Ser.). 1972. 10.95 (ISBN 0-8044-2610-4). Ungar.

Mc Farland, Edward M. The Midland Route: A Colorado Midland Guide & Data Book. (Illus.). 300p. 1980. 44.95 (ISBN 0-87108-569-0). Pruett.

McFarland, Grace. Official Price Guide to Antique & Other Collectibles. LC 78-67961. 1979. pap. 8.95 o.p. (ISBN 0-87637-340-6). Hse of Collectibles.
McFarland, H. Neill. Rush Hour of the Gods. 1967. 9.95 (ISBN 0-02-583200-X). Macmillan.
McFarland, H. S. Psychological Theory & Educational Practice: Human Development, Learning & Assessment. 1971. 20.00x (ISBN 0-7100-7009-8); pap. 8.95 (ISBN 0-7100-7010-1). Routledge & Kegan.
McFarland, James W. see Ibsen, Henrik.
McFarland, John, ed. Basic Clinical Surgery for Nurses & Medical Students. 2nd ed. LC 80-40150. (Illus.). 1980. 31.95 (ISBN 0-407-80101-4). Butterworths.
McFarland, Kay F. & Bransome, Edwin D., Jr. Self-Assessment of Current Knowledge in Clinical Endocrinology, Metabolism & Diabetes. 1975. spiral bdg. 12.00 o.s.i. (ISBN 0-87488-297-4). Med Exam.
McFarland, Kenton & Sparks, James C., Jr. Midget Motoring & Karting. (Illus.). (gr. 7 up). 1961. PLB 10.95 (ISBN 0-525-34880-8). Dutton.
McFarland, M. Carter. The Federal Government & Urban Problems: HUD: Successes, Failures, & the Fate of Our Cities. LC 77-26301. 1978. lib. bdg. 28.00x (ISBN 0-89158-085-9). Westview.
McFarland, Philip J., et al. Focus on America. LC 76-53136. (Focus on Literature Ser.). (Illus.). (gr. 11). 1977. text ed. 15.32 (ISBN 0-395-24962-7); tchr's guide 5.76 (ISBN 0-395-24961-9). HM.
--Focus on Forms. LC 76-53136. (Focus on Literature Ser.). (Illus., Gr. 10). 1977. text ed. 14.80 (ISBN 0-395-24970-8); teachers guide 5.24 (ISBN 0-395-24963-5). HM.
--Focus on Ideas. LC 76-53136. (Focus on Literature Ser.). (Illus., Gr. 12). 1977. text ed. 15.32 (ISBN 0-395-24960-0); teachers guide 5.76 (ISBN 0-395-24959-7). HM.
--Focus on Viewpoints. LC 76-53136. (Focus on Literature Ser.). (Illus., Gr. 9). 1977. text ed. 14.80 (ISBN 0-395-24968-6); tcr's guide 5.24 (ISBN 0-395-24969-4). HM.
McFarland, Richard A. Physiological Psychology: The Biology of Human Behavior. (Illus.). 600p. 1981. text ed. price not set (ISBN 0-87484-500-9). Mayfield Pub.
McFarland, Thomas. Romanticism & the Forms of Ruin: Wordsworth, Coleridge & Modalities of Fragmentation. LC 80-7546. 432p. 1981. 30.00 (ISBN 0-691-06437-7); pap. 9.50 (ISBN 0-691-10108-6). Princeton U Pr.
McFarland, Wayne J. & Smith, Philip. Sports Illustrated Handball. LC 75-28486. (Sports Illustrated Ser). (Illus.). 1976. 5.95 (ISBN 0-397-01095-8); pap. 2.95 (ISBN 0-397-01106-7). Lippincott.
Macfarlane, A. The Origins of English Individualism. LC 78-73956. 1979. 26.95 (ISBN 0-521-22587-6); pap. 7.50x (ISBN 0-521-29570-X). Cambridge U Pr.
MacFarlane, A. A. Architectural Supervision on Site. (Illus.). 1973. text ed. 29.90x (ISBN 0-85334-574-0, Pub. by Applied Science). Burgess-Intl Ideas.
MacFarlane, A. G., ed. Frequency: Response Methods in Control Systems. LC 79-90572. 1979. 39.95 (ISBN 0-87942-125-8). Inst Electrical.
Macfarlane, Alan. The Justice & the Mare's Ale: Law & Disorder in Seventeenth-Century England. (Illus.). 225p. Date not set. 19.95 (ISBN 0-521-23949-4). Cambridge U Pr.
--Witchcraft in Tudor & Stuart England: A Regional & Comparative Study. 1970. 25.00 (ISBN 0-7100-6403-9). Routledge & Kegan.
Macfarlane, Alistair G. Frequency Response Methods in Control Systems. 1979. 39.95 (ISBN 0-471-06486-6, Pub. by Wiley-Interscience); pap. 25.95 (ISBN 0-471-06426-2). Wiley.
Macfarlane, Claire. The Mystic Experience & Other Essays, 2 vols. 460p. 1981. Set. 12.95 (ISBN 0-936632-07-0); Vol. 1. 6.50 (ISBN 0-936632-08-9); Vol. 2. 6.50 (ISBN 0-936632-09-7). Mann Pubs.
McFarlane, I. D., ed. see D'Aubigne, Agrippa.
McFarlane, I. D., ed. see Sceve, Maurice.
Macfarlane, Iris. The Black Hole: Or the Makings of a Legend. 1975. text ed. 25.00x (ISBN 0-04-954019-X). Allen Unwin.
--The Mouth of the Night: Gaelic Stories Retold. LC 75-31576. (Illus.). 160p. (gr. 4 up). 1976. 6.95 o.s.i. (ISBN 0-02-765430-3, 76543). Macmillan.
McFarlane, James, jt. ed. see Bradbury, Malcolm.
McFarlane, James, tr. see Hamsun, Knut.
McFarlane, James W., ed. see Ibsen, Henrik.
McFarlane, James W. see Ibsen, Henrik.
McFarlane, K. B. Lancastrian Kings & Lollard Knights. Highfield, J. R. & Harriss, G. L., eds. 268p. 1972. 27.00x (ISBN 0-19-822344-7). Oxford U Pr.
--The Nobility of Later Medieval England: The Ford Lectures for 1953 & Related Studies. 1973. 29.95x (ISBN 0-19-822362-5). Oxford U Pr.
McFarlane, Paul T., jt. auth. see Scarpitti, Frank R.
McFarlin, Annjennette S. Black Congressional Reconstruction Orators & Their Orations 1869-1879. LC 75-45194. 343p. 1976. 15.00 (ISBN 0-8108-0902-8). Scarecrow.
Macfarquhar, Roderick. The Origins of the Cultural Revolution: Contradictions Among the People 1956-1957, Vol. 1. 428p. 1974. 22.50x (ISBN 0-231-03841-0). Columbia U Pr.
McFather, Nelle. Ecstasy's Captive. 1979. pap. 2.50 (ISBN 0-505-51380-3). Tower Bks.
McFaul, John M., jt. ed. see Gatell, Frank O.
McFeat, Tom. Small-Group Cultures. 1974. text ed. 19.00 (ISBN 0-08-017073-0); pap. text ed. 12.00 (ISBN 0-08-017770-0). Pergamon.
McFee, Graham. Much of Jackson Pollock Is Vivid Wallpaper: An Essay in the Epistomology of Aesthetic Judgements. 1978. pap. text ed. 9.50x (ISBN 0-8191-0380-2). U Pr of Amer.
McFee, June K. & Degge, Rogena M. Art, Culture, & Environment: A Catalyst for Teaching. 416p. 1980. pap. text ed. 13.95 (ISBN 0-8403-2330-1). Kendall-Hunt.
McFeely, William S. Grant: A Biography. (Illus.). 1981. 19.95 (ISBN 0-393-01372-3). Norton.
Macffarlane, Alan, ed. see Josselin, Ralph.
MacFie, J. M. Myths & Legends of India: An Introduction to the Study of Hinduism. 357p. Repr. of 1924 ed. pap. text ed. 4.95 (ISBN 0-567-22181-4). Attic Pr.
McGachie, R. O., ed. Precious Metals: Proceedings of the Fourth International Precious Metals Conference, Toronto Canada, June 3-5, 1980. 400p. 1981. 50.01 (ISBN 0-08-025369-5). Pergamon.
McGahey, Stan. Playboys Guide to Good Times: Europe. LC 80-84372. 256p. (Orig.). 1981. pap. 2.95 (ISBN 0-87216-819-0). Playboy Pbks.
McGann, jt. auth. see Court, Margaret.
McGann, Anthony F., et al. Introduction to Business. LC 78-12146. 1979. text ed. 20.95 (ISBN 0-471-57240-3); tchrs. manual avail. (ISBN 0-471-57241-1); study guide avail. (ISBN 0-471-04864-X). Wiley.
McGann, Jerome J., ed. Lord Byron: The Complete Poetical Works, Vol. I. 516p. 1980. 98.00x (ISBN 0-19-811890-2); pap. 59.00 (ISBN 0-19-812763-4). Oxford U Pr.
McGann, Thomas F. A History of Philosophy in the West: A Synopsis from Descartes to Nietzsche. LC 79-66477. 1979. pap. text ed. 9.00 (ISBN 0-8191-0833-2). U Pr of Amer.
McGannon, Robert E. Firefighter, F. D. 7th ed. LC 80-25047. 256p. (Orig.). 1981. pap. 8.00 (ISBN 0-668-05170-1, 5170). Arco.
McGarey, William A., jt. auth. see Carter, Mary E.
McGarry, Daniel, tr. see John Of Salisbury.
McGarry, Daniel D. & White, Sarah H. World Historical Fiction Guide: Annotated Chronological, Geographical & Topical List of Selected Historical Novels. 2nd ed. LC 73-4367. 1973. 20.50 (ISBN 0-8108-0616-9). Scarecrow.
McGarry, Jane, jt. ed. see Corderman, Susan.
McGarry, Kevin. Communication, Knowledge & the Librarian. 207p. (Orig.). 1975. 12.50 o.p. (ISBN 0-208-01369-5, Linnet). Shoe String.
McGarry, Mark J. Sun Dogs. (Orig.). 1981. pap. 1.95 (ISBN 0-451-09620-7, J9620, Sig). NAL.
McGarry, Michael B. Christology After Auschwitz. LC 77-73977. 1977. pap. 3.95 (ISBN 0-8091-2024-0). Paulist Pr.
McGary, Jane. Bibliography of Educational Publications for Alaska Native Languages. 168p. (Orig.). 1979. pap. 5.00 (ISBN 0-89763-018-1). Natl Clearinghse Bilingual Ed.
McGaugh, James L., jt. auth. see Cotman, Carl W.
McGaughy, Lane C. A Descriptive Analysis of Einai. LC 72-88437. (Society of Biblical Literature, Dissertation Ser.). 1972. pap. 9.00 (ISBN 0-89130-162-3, 060106). Scholars Pr Ca.
--Workbook for a Beginning-Intermediate Grammar of Hellenistic Greek. LC 76-44351. (Society of Biblical Literature. Sources for Biblical Study). 1976. pap. text ed. 6.00 (ISBN 0-89130-093-7, 060306). Scholars Pr Ca.
McGavin, Gary L. Earthquake Protection of Essential Building Equipment: Design, Engineering, Installation. 496p. 1981. 25.00 (ISBN 0-471-06270-7, Pub. by Wiley-Interscience). Wiley.
McGavran, Donald, frwd. by. Christian Churches at the Crossroads. 160p. (Orig.). 1980. pap. write for info. (ISBN 0-87808-178-X). William Carey Lib.
McGavran, Donald A. Bridges of God. (Orig.). 1980. pap. 5.95 o.p. (ISBN 0-377-45071-5). Friend Pr.
--Church Growth & Group Conversion. new ed. LC 73-80163. 128p. 1973. pap. 3.95 (ISBN 0-87808-712-5). William Carey Lib.
McGavran, Donald A. & Arn, Winfield C. Ten Steps for Church Growth. LC 76-62950. 1977. pap. 4.95 (ISBN 0-06-065352-3, RD 215, HarpR). Har-Row.
McGaw, Dickinson, jt. auth. see Watson, George.
McGaw, Dickinson L. & Watson, George. Political & Social Inquiry. LC 75-31913. 336p. 1976. text ed. 18.95 (ISBN 0-471-58403-7); instructor's manual avail. (ISBN 0-471-01579-2). Wiley.
McGaw, Francis A. Praying Hyde. 1970. pap. 1.95 (ISBN 0-87123-454-8, 200454). Bethany Fell.
McGaw, Jessie B. Chief Red Horse Tells About Custer. (Illus.). 64p. (gr. 4 up). 1981. 8.95 (ISBN 0-525-66713-X). Elsevier-Nelson.
McGaw, Lisa, ed. see Brasher, Rex.
McGaw, William C. Savage Scene: The Life & Times of James Kirker, Frontier King. (Illus.). 288p. 1972. 9.95 (ISBN 0-8038-6712-3). Hastings.
McGeary, M. Nelson. Gifford Pinchot: Forester-Politician. Freidel, Frank, ed. LC 78-66552. (The History of the United States Ser.: Vol. 12). 481p. 1979. lib. bdg. 36.00 (ISBN 0-8240-9700-9). Garland Pub.
--Pennsylvania Government in Action: Governor Leader's Administration, 1955-1959. LC 72-78442. (gr. 8-12). 1972. 7.00 (ISBN 0-931992-27-3); pap. 3.95 (ISBN 0-931992-28-1). Penns Valley.
McGee, Charles T. How to Survive Modern Technology. LC 80-82327. (Orig.). 1981. pap. 2.95 (ISBN 0-87983-230-4). Keats.
McGee, Dennis. The Rescue. 1981. 8.95 (ISBN 0-533-04792-7). Vantage.
McGee, J. D. see Marton, L.
McGee, J. D., et al see Marton, L.
McGee, L. Randolph. Income & Employment in the Southeast: A Study in Cyclical Behavior. LC 67-17849. (Illus.). 152p. 1967. 9.00x (ISBN 0-8131-1141-2). U Pr of Ky.
McGee, R. Accounting for Inflation: Stating a True Financial Position. 15.95 (ISBN 0-13-002337-X); pap. 7.95 (ISBN 0-13-002329-9). P-H.
McGee, Reece. Academic Janus: The Private College & Its Faculty. LC 70-149913. (Higher Education Ser.). 1971. 13.95x o.p. (ISBN 0-87589-097-0). Jossey-Bass.
McGee, Vern, tr. see Schmidt, Paul.
McGeeney, Patrick, jt. auth. see Young, Michael.
McGeer, Edith G., et al, eds. Kainic Acid As a Tool in Neurobiology. LC 78-55812. 1978. 29.00 (ISBN 0-89004-279-9). Raven.
McGehee, Lucius P. Due Process of Law Under the Federal Constitution. (Studies in Constitutional Law). x, 452p. 1981. Repr. of 1906 ed. lib. bdg. 37.50x (ISBN 0-8377-0837-0). Rothman.
McGeoch, Dorothy M., et al. Learning to Teach in Urban Schools. LC 65-22440. 1965. pap. text ed. 4.75x (ISBN 0-8077-1737-1). Tchrs Coll.
McGerr, Celia. Rene Clair. (Theater Arts Ser.). 1980. lib. bdg. 12.95 (ISBN 0-8057-9262-7). Twayne.
McGervey, John D. Introduction to Modern Physics. 1971. text ed. 22.95 (ISBN 0-12-483550-3). Acad Pr.
Mc Gettigan, James P. Complete Book of Drills for Winning Soccer. 254p. 1980. 10.95 (ISBN 0-13-156356-4, Parker). P-H.
McGettrick, A. D. ALGOL Sixty-Eight. LC 77-1104. (Computer Science Texts Ser.: No. 8). (Illus.). 1978. 47.95 (ISBN 0-521-21412-2); pap. 16.95x (ISBN 0-521-29143-7). Cambridge U Pr.
McGettrick, Andrew. The Definition of Programming Languages. LC 79-21635. (Cambridge Computer Science Texts). 1980. 29.95 (ISBN 0-521-22631-7); pap. 12.95 (ISBN 0-521-29585-8). Cambridge U Pr.
McGrady, Pat. The Persecuted Drug: The Story of DMSO. 312p. (Orig.). 1981. pap. 2.50 (ISBN 0-441-15101-9). Charter Bks.
McGhee, Paul E. Humor: Its Origin & Development. LC 79-15401. (Psychology Ser.). (Illus.). 1979. text ed. 15.95x o.p. (ISBN 0-7167-1095-1); pap. text ed. 8.95x (ISBN 0-7167-1096-X). W H Freeman.
McGhee, Paul E. & Chapman, Antony J. Children's Humour. LC 79-40648. 1980. 40.25 (ISBN 0-471-27638-3, Pub. by Wiley-Interscience). Wiley.
McGhee, Richard D. Marriage, Duty, & Desire in Victorian Poetry & Drama. LC 80-11962. 336p. 1980. 22.50x (ISBN 0-7006-0203-8). Regents Pr KS.
McGiffert, A. C. A History of Christianity in the Apostolic Age. (International Theologica Library). 692p. Repr. of 1897 ed. text ed. 13.95x (ISBN 0-567-07207-X). Attic Pr.
McGiffert, Michael. The Higher Learning in Colorado: A Historical Study, 1860-1940. LC 64-18746. 307p. 1964. 13.95 (ISBN 0-8040-0085-9). Swallow.
McGiffert, Michael, jt. auth. see Skotheim, Robert A.
McGiffert, Michael, ed. Character of Americans: A Book of Readings. rev. ed. (Orig.). 1970. pap. text ed. 9.50x (ISBN 0-256-01138-9). Dorsey.
McGiffert, Michael & Bernhard, Winfred E., eds. God's Plot: The Paradoxes of Puritan Piety, Being the Autobiography & Journal of Thomas Shepard. LC 71-181364. (Commonwealth Ser.: Vol. 1). (Illus.). 250p. 1972. 15.00x (ISBN 0-87023-100-6). U of Mass Pr.
McGill, Arthur C., jt. ed. see Hick, John H.
McGill, Dan M. Financing the Civil Service Retirement System. 1979. 11.00x (ISBN 0-256-02250-X). Irwin.
--Fundamentals of Private Pensions. 4th ed. 1979. text ed. 17.95 (ISBN 0-256-02252-6). Irwin.
McGill, Dan M., jt. ed. see Gregg, Davis W.
McGill, Frances. Go Not Gently: Letters from a Patient with Amyotrophic Lateral Sclerosis. Kutscher, Lillian G., ed. LC 79-48047. (Foundation of Thanatology Ser.). 1980. lib. bdg. 16.00x (ISBN 0-405-12643-3). Arno.
McGill, Frederick T., Jr. Channing of Concord: A Life of William Ellery Channing 2nd. 1967. 15.00 (ISBN 0-8135-0558-5). Rutgers U Pr.
McGill, Gordon. The Final Conflict: Omen III. (Orig.). 1980. pap. 2.50 (ISBN 0-451-09584-7, E9584, Sig). NAL.
--War Story. 1981. pap. 2.75 (ISBN 0-440-19416-4). Dell.
McGill, Marcia K. Research: Its Role in Development: 1978. pap. 2.50 (ISBN 0-934338-34-5). NAIS.
McGill-Franzen, Anne. The Gingerbread Boy. LC 79-62980. (Learn-a-Tale). (Illus.). (gr. k-2). 1979. PLB 8.25 (ISBN 0-8393-0184-7). Raintree Child.
--The Three Bears. LC 79-62977. (Learn-a-Tale). (Illus.). (gr. k-2). 1979. PLB 8.25 (ISBN 0-8393-0182-0). Raintree Child.
--The Three Little Pigs. LC 79-62978. (Learn-a-Tale). (Illus.). (gr. k-2). 1979. PLB 8.25 (ISBN 0-8393-0183-9). Raintree Child.
McGilligan, Patrick. Cagney: The Actor As Auteur. LC 73-14028. (Illus.). 192p. 1975. 12.00 o.p. (ISBN 0-498-01462-2). A S Barnes.
MacGillivray, Ian, et al. Human Multiple Reproduction. LC 75-21750. (Illus.). 238p. 1975. text ed. 25.00 (ISBN 0-7216-5974-8). Saunders.
MacGillivray, Lois. Decision-Related Research on the Organization of Service Delivery Systems in Metropolitan Areas: Fire Protection. LC 79-83819. 1979. codebook 34.00 (ISBN 0-89138-985-7). ICPSR.
McGillivray, Robert G. Automobile Gasoline Conservation. (An Institute Paper). 67p. 1976. pap. 3.00 (ISBN 0-87766-162-6, 14100). Urban Inst.
McGimsey, Charles R., 3rd. Mariana Mesa. (Peabody Museum Papers Ser.: Vol. 72). pap. 25.00 (ISBN 0-87365-198-7). Peabody Harvard.
MacGinitie, Harry D. An Early Middle Eocene Flora from the Yellowstone-Absaroka Volcanic Province North-Western Wind River Basin, Wyoming. (Publications in Geological Sciences, Vol. 108). 1974. pap. 10.75x (ISBN 0-520-09496-4). U of Cal Pr.
MacGinitie, Walter, jt. auth. see Rosenstein, Joseph.
McGinley, Patrick. Bogmail. LC 80-26135. 264p. 1981. 9.95 (ISBN 0-89919-031-6). Ticknor & Fields.
McGinley, Phyllis. B Book. LC 68-19821. (Illus.). (gr. 1-3). 1968. 2.95g o.s.i. (ISBN 0-02-765370-6, CCPr). Macmillan.
--Sixpence in Her Shoe. 1964. 9.95 (ISBN 0-02-583360-X). Macmillan.
--Wreath of Christmas Legends. (gr. 1-6). 1967. 9.95 (ISBN 0-02-765410-9). Macmillan.
McGinn, Bernard. Visions of the End. LC 79-4303. (Records of Civilization XCVI). 1979. 27.50x (ISBN 0-231-04594-8). Columbia U Pr.
McGinn, Charles. Bet on Yourself. (Illus.). 153p. (Orig.). 1980. pap. 3.95 (ISBN 0-89260-193-0). Hwong Pub.
McGinn, Daniel F. Joint Trust Pension Plans. 1979. 12.95x (ISBN 0-256-02105-8). Irwin.
McGinn, Donald J. John Penry & the Marprelate Controversy. 1966. 17.50 (ISBN 0-8135-0513-5). Rutgers U Pr.
McGinn, J. C. Lawyers: A Client's Manual. 1979. 11.95 o.p. (ISBN 0-13-526814-1); pap. 5.95 o.p. (ISBN 0-13-526806-0); 14 sets tape 100.00 o.p. (ISBN 0-13-530444-X). P-H.
McGinnies, W. B., jt. auth. see Bishay, A.
McGinnies, W. B., ed. see Cairo International Workshop on Applications of Science & Technology for Desert Development September 9-15, 1978.
McGinnies, William G. Discovering the Desert: The Legacy of the Carnegie Desert Botanical Laboratory. 1981. text ed. 21.95x (ISBN 0-8165-0719-8); pap. text ed. 9.50x (ISBN 0-8165-0728-7). U of Ariz Pr.

McGinnis, Bruce. The Fence. LC 79-64395. 1979. 10.00 (ISBN 0-8149-0821-7). Vanguard.

McGinnis, H. J. The Osteology of Phlegethontia, a Carboniferous & Permian Aistopod Amphibian. (U. C. Publ. in Geological Sciences: Vol. 71). 1967. pap. 5.75x (ISBN 0-520-09174-4). U of Cal Pr.

McGinnis, Harry & Ruley, M. J. Basic Woodworking Projects. (gr. 7-9). 1959. text ed. 13.28 (ISBN 0-87345-043-4). McKnight.

McGinnis, Lila. What Will Simon Say? LC 73-89291. 236p. 1974. 4.95 o.p. (ISBN 0-88270-074-X); pap. 2.95 o.p. (ISBN 0-88270-075-8). Logos.

McGinnis, Lila S. Secret of the Porcelain Cats. Pacini, Kathy, ed. LC 78-15225. (Pilot Bks). (Illus.). (gr. 3-8). 1978. 6.95g (ISBN 0-8075-7288-8). A Whitman.

McGinnis, Marilyn. Give Me a Child Until He's Two: Then You Take Him till He's Four! LC 80-54005. 176p. pap. 4.95 (ISBN 0-8307-0785-9). Regal.

--Single. 1976. pap. 1.50 (ISBN 0-89129-164-4). Jove Pubns.

McGinnis, Ralph Y. Quotations from Abraham Lincoln. LC 77-24595. (Illus.). 1978. 15.95 (ISBN 0-88229-316-8); pap. 8.95 (ISBN 0-88229-507-1). Nelson-Hall.

McGiven, A. R., ed. Immunological Investigation of Renal Disease. (Practical Methods in Clinical Immunology Ser.: Vol. 1). (Illus.). 160p. 1980. text ed. 39.50 (ISBN 0-443-01899-5). Churchill.

McGivern, William P. The Seeing. (Orig.). 1980. pap. 2.50 (ISBN 0-505-51493-1). Tower Bks.

McGivney, Raymond, et al. Essential Precalculus. 464p. 1980. text ed. 18.95x (ISBN 0-534-00766-X); solutions manual 3.95 (ISBN 0-534-00842-9). Wadsworth Pub.

McGlashan, Alan. The Savage & Beautiful Country. LC 66-66707. 1979. 7.95 o.p. (ISBN 0-7011-0922-X, Pub. by Chatto Bodley Jonathan). Merrimack Bk Serv.

McGlashan, Charles F. History of the Donner Party: A Tragedy of the Sierra. rev. ed. Hinkle, George H. & Hinkle, Bliss M., eds. (Illus.). 1947. 10.95 (ISBN 0-8047-0366-3); pap. 4.95 (ISBN 0-8047-0367-1, SP26). Stanford U Pr.

McGlashan, N. D., ed. Health Problems in Australia & New Zealand. 180p. 1980. 20.00 (ISBN 0-08-026103-5). Pergamon.

McGlinchee, Claire. James Russell Lowell. (U. S. Authors Ser.: No. 120). lib. bdg. 10.95 (ISBN 0-8057-0460-4). Twayne.

McGlone, James P. & Fiskin, A. M. Volpone Notes & Alchemist Notes. (Orig.). 1967. pap. 1.95 o.s.i. (ISBN 0-8220-1349-5). Cliffs.

McGlynn, Daniel R. Personal Computing: Home, Professional & Small Business Applications. LC 79-1005. 1979. pap. 10.95 (ISBN 0-471-05380-5, Pub. by Wiley-Interscience). Wiley.

McGlynn, George H., ed. Issues in Physical Education & Sports. LC 73-91388. 1974. pap. text ed. 7.95 (ISBN 0-87484-238-7). Mayfield Pub.

McGlynn, June A. Instant Parliamentary Procedure. (Illus.). 1976. pap. 3.25 (ISBN 0-9601350-1-4). McGlynn.

McGoldrick, J. E. Luther's English Connection. 1979. pap. 7.50 (ISBN 0-8100-0070-9, 15-0368). Northwest Pub.

McGonigal, John, jt. auth. see McCreadie, Charles.

McGonnagle, W., ed. International Advances in Nondestructive Testing, Vol. 7. 348p. 1981. write for info. (ISBN 0-677-15700-2). Gordon.

McGough, Elizabeth. Dollars & Sense. LC 75-19109. (Illus.). 160p. (gr. 7 up). 1975. PLB 6.96 (ISBN 0-688-32046-5). Morrow.

--On Your Own in Europe: A Teen-Agers Travel Guide. (gr. 7 up). 1978. PLB 7.20 (ISBN 0-688-32163-1); pap. 5.50 (ISBN 0-688-27163-4). Morrow.

--Who Are You? A Teen-Ager's Guide to Self-Understanding. (Illus.). (gr. 7-9). 1976. 8.25 (ISBN 0-688-22091-6); PLB 7.92 (ISBN 0-688-32091-0). Morrow.

--Your Silent Language. LC 73-4253. (Illus.). 128p. (gr. 7 up). 1974. PLB 6.96 (ISBN 0-688-31820-7). Morrow.

McGough, Lucy S., jt. auth. see Read, Frank T.

McGovern, Ann. If You Lived with the Sioux Indians. LC 74-7327. (Illus.). 96p. (gr. 2-4). 1974. 5.95 (ISBN 0-590-07340-0, Four Winds). Schol Bk Serv.

--Mr. Skinner's Skinny House. LC 79-18360. (Illus.). 48p. (gr. 2-6). 1980. 7.95 (ISBN 0-590-07620-5, Four Winds). Schol Bk Serv.

--Question & Answer Book About the Human Body. (Illus.). 1965. PLB 4.99 (ISBN 0-394-90780-9, BYR). Random.

--The Secret Soldier: The Story of Deborah Sampson. LC 75-15819. (Illus.). 64p. (gr. 1-5). 1975. 5.95 (ISBN 0-590-07432-6, Four Winds). Schol Bk Serv.

--Shark Lady: True Adventures of Eugenie Clark. LC 78-22126. (Illus.). 96p. (gr. 1-5). 1979. 7.95 (ISBN 0-590-07604-3, Four Winds). Schol Bk Serv.

--Sharks. LC 76-17122. (Illus.). 48p. (gr. k-3). 1976. 7.95 (ISBN 0-590-07468-7, Four Winds). Schol Bk Serv.

--The Underwater World of the Coral Reef. LC 75-44305. (Illus.). 40p. (gr. k-3). 1977. 6.95 (ISBN 0-590-07467-9, Four Winds). Schol Bk Serv.

--Woody Woodpecker Takes a Trip. (Illus.). (gr. k-3). 1976. PLB 5.00 (ISBN 0-307-60445-4, Golden Pr). Western Pub.

McGovern, Anne, ed. Robin Hood of Sherwood Forest. LC 68-11066. (Hero Tales Ser). (Illus.). (gr. 3-6). 1968. 8.95 (ISBN 0-690-70607-3, TYC-J). T Y Crowell.

Mc Govern, Bernard S. Playleader's Handbook. 1976. 14.95 o.p. (ISBN 0-571-10643-9, Pub. by Faber & Faber). Merrimack Bk Serv.

--Playleadership. 1973. 12.95 (ISBN 0-571-10184-4, Pub. by Faber & Faber). Merrimack Bk Serv.

McGovern, Charles P. Collection of Poems. 1981. 5.95 (ISBN 0-533-04804-4). Vantage.

McGovern, Edythe M. They're Never Too Young for Books: Literature for Pre-Schoolers. LC 80-80216. 294p. (Orig.). 1980. pap. 10.00 (ISBN 0-9604064-0-9). Mar Vista.

McGovern, J. P., jt. auth. see Knotts, G. R.

McGovern, Jill, jt. auth. see Fallen, Nancy.

McGovern, John P., et al. Chronobiology in Allergy & Immunology. (Illus.). 308p. 1977. 27.75 (ISBN 0-398-03583-0). C C Thomas.

McGovern, V. J., jt. auth. see Goulston, S. J.

McGovern, Vincent J. Malignant Melanoma: Clinical & Histological Diagnosis. LC 76-3793. 1976. 36.95 (ISBN 0-471-58417-7, Pub. by Wiley Medical). Wiley.

McGovern, Vincent J. & Brown, Malcolm M. The Nature of Melanoma. (Amer. Lec. Living Chemistry Ser.). (Illus.). 196p. 1969. pap. 17.50 spiral (ISBN 0-398-01257-1). C C Thomas.

McGovern, Vincent J. & Tiller, David J. Shock: A Clinicopathologic Correlation. LC 79-87539. (Illus.). 192p. 1980. 27.00 (ISBN 0-89352-073-X). Masson Pub.

McGowan, A. C., jt. auth. see Fabb, John.

McGowan, Carl. Organization of Judicial Power in the United States. (Julius Rosenthal Memorial Lectures Ser.: 1967). 1969. 7.95x o.s.i. (ISBN 0-8101-0007-X). Northwestern U Pr.

McGowan, J. A., jt. auth. see Okutani, T.

McGowan, J. William. The Excited State in Chemical Physics, Vol. Two. (Advances in Chemical Physics: Vol. 45). 616p. 1981. 45.95 (ISBN 0-471-05119-5, Pub. by Wiley-Interscience). Wiley.

McGowan, John E., jt. auth. see Stone, Scott C.

MacGowan, Kenneth & Melnitz, W. Living Stage: A History of the World Theatre. 1955. text ed. 19.95 (ISBN 0-13-538942-9). P-H.

MacGowan, Michael. The Hard Road to Klondike. Iremonger, Valentin, tr. from Irish. 1973. pap. 6.95 (ISBN 0-7100-7686-X). Routledge & Kegan.

McGowan, Patrick J., ed. Sage International Yearbook of Foreign Policy Studies, Vol. 1. LC 72-98039. 1973. 20.00x (ISBN 0-8039-0202-6). Sage.

--Sage International Yearbook of Foreign Policy Studies, Vol. 2. LC 72-98039. 1974. 20.00x (ISBN 0-8039-0471-1); pap. 9.95x (ISBN 0-8039-0496-7). Sage.

--Sage International Yearbook of Foreign Policy Studies, Vol. 3. LC 72-98039. 1975. 20.00x (ISBN 0-8039-0323-5); pap. 9.95x (ISBN 0-8039-0324-3). Sage.

McGowan, Prudence R. Twinkie Flickertail. (Illus.). 1977. 3.95 (ISBN 0-8059-2379-9). Dorrance.

McGowen, Charles H. In Six Days. pap. 2.95 (ISBN 0-89728-039-3, 658621). Omega Pubns OR.

McGowen, J. H. & Brewton, J. L. Historical Changes & Related Coastal Processes, Gulf & Mainland Shorelines, Matagorda Bay Area, Texas. (Illus.). 72p. 1975. 6.00. Bur Econ Geology.

McGowen, J. H., jt. auth. see Fisher, W. L.

McGowen, J. H., et al. Geochemistry of Bottom Sediments Matagorda Bay System, Texas. (Illus.). 64p. 1979. 1.50 (GC 79-2). Bur Econ Geology.

McGowen, Tom. Album of Reptiles. (gr. 3-7). 1978. 5.95 (ISBN 0-528-82001-X); PLB 5.97 o.p. (ISBN 0-528-80014-0). Rand.

--Album of Sharks. LC 77-5172. (Illus.). (gr. 5-7). 1977. 5.95 (ISBN 0-528-82023-0); PLB 5.97 o.p. (ISBN 0-528-80212-7). Rand.

McGown, Elizabeth R., jt. auth. see Hamburg, David A.

McGown, Linda B. & Bockris, John O'M. How to Obtain Abundant Clean Energy. 275p. 1980. 14.95 (ISBN 0-306-40399-4, Plenum Pr). Plenum Pub.

McGrade, A. S. The Political Thought of William of Ockham. LC 73-86044. (Studies in Medieval Life & Thought). 264p. 1974. 35.50 (ISBN 0-521-20284-1). Cambridge U Pr.

McGrady, Donald. Jorge Isaacs. (World Authors Ser.: Colombia: No. 166). lib. bdg. 10.95 (ISBN 0-8057-2460-5). Twayne.

McGrady, Mike. The Motel Tapes. 352p. (Orig.). 1977. pap. 1.95 o.s.i. (ISBN 0-446-89332-3). Warner Bks.

McGrady, Mike, jt. auth. see Aronson, Harvey.

McGrady, Mike, jt. auth. see Lovelace, Linda.

McGrady, Patrick, Jr., jt. auth. see Pritkin, Nathan.

McGrain, John W. Good Old Company Towns. (Baltimore County Heritage Publication Ser.). (Illus.). 1981. pap. price not set (ISBN 0-937076-01-5). Baltimore Co Pub Lib.

--Grist Mills in Baltimore County, Maryland. (Baltimore County Heritage Publication). (Illus.). 40p. 1980. pap. 4.95 (ISBN 0-937076-00-7). Baltimore Co Pub Lib.

McGrath, jt. auth. see Tegner.

McGrath, A. Tony's Tunnel. 1980. 7.95 (ISBN 0-13-925099-9). P-H.

McGrath, Charles M., et al, eds. Cell Biology of Breast Cancer. LC 80-13804. 1981. 33.00 (ISBN 0-12-483940-1). Acad Pr.

McGrath, Daniel F., ed. Bookman's Price Index: A Guide to the Values of Rare & Other Out-of-Print Books. LC 64-8723. (Bookman's Price Index Ser.: Vol. 21). 900p. 1981. 78.00 (ISBN 0-8103-0621-2). Gale.

McGrath, Earl J., ed. Prospect for Renewal: The Future of the Liberal Arts College. LC 75-189040. (Higher Education Ser.). 1972. 11.95x o.p. (ISBN 0-87589-132-2). Jossey-Bass.

McGrath, Ed. The Superinsulated House: A Working Guide for Owner/Builders & Architects. (Illus.). 128p. 1981. 13.95 (ISBN 0-918270-11-1); pap. 9.95 (ISBN 0-918270-12-X). That New Pub.

McGrath, Edward. Is American Democracy Exportable. Krinsky, Fred & Boskin, Joseph, eds. (Insight Series: Studies in Contemporary Issues). 128p. 1968. pap. text ed. 4.95x (ISBN 0-02-476350-0, 47635). Macmillan.

McGrath, J. B., jt. auth. see Weiss, Harold.

McGrath, James, ed. The Poetry Makers: A Graded Anthology for Secondary Schools, 4 bks. 1969. Bk. 1. text ed. 3.95x o.p. (ISBN 0-435-14570-3); Bk. 2. text ed. 3.95x o.p. (ISBN 0-435-14571-1); Bk. 3. text ed. 3.95x o.p. (ISBN 0-435-14572-X); Bk. 4. text ed. 3.95x o.p. (ISBN 0-435-14573-8). Heinemann Ed.

McGrath, James E., jt. auth. see Noshay, Allen.

McGrath, Mary. Trespassing Stoplights & Attitudes. (Illus.). 44p. (Orig.). 1980. pap. 5.00 (ISBN 0-930012-43-7). Mudborn.

McGrath, Michael J., jt. ed. see Barber, Benjamin.

McGrath, Patrick, ed. see Browne, John.

McGrath, Thomas. Letter to an Imaginary Friend, Pt. 1 & 2. LC 77-81967. 214p. 1969. 11.95 (ISBN 0-8040-0185-5); pap. 5.95 (ISBN 0-8040-0186-3). Swallow.

--The Movie at the End of the World: Collected Poems. LC 72-91918. 188p. 1972. 10.95 o.p. (ISBN 0-8040-0605-9); pap. 5.95 (ISBN 0-8040-0606-7). Swallow.

McGrath, Thomas & Jenkyns, Chris. Beautiful Things. LC 60-15076. (Illus.). (gr. k-3). 1960. 3.50 (ISBN 0-8149-0364-9). Vanguard.

McGrath, Thomas see Judson, John.

McGraw-Hill Book Co. McGraw-Hill Encyclopedia of Energy. 2nd ed. Parker, Sybil P., ed. LC 80-18078. (Illus.). 856p. 1980. 34.50 (ISBN 0-07-045268-7). McGraw.

McGraw-Hill Encyclopedia of Science & Technology Staff. McGraw-Hill Encyclopedia of Ocean & Atmospheric Sciences. Parker, Sybil P., ed. (Illus.). 1979. write for info. (ISBN 0-07-045267-9). McGraw.

McGraw, Lee. Hatchett. 1976. pap. 1.50 o.p. (ISBN 0-345-25103-2). Ballantine.

McGraw, Lora, jt. auth. see Getz, Donald J.

McGraw, Robert P., ed. see Breyfogle, Newell D.

McGraw, Tug & Witte, Mike. Scroogie. (Orig.). 1976. pap. 0.95 o.p. (ISBN 0-451-06961-7, Q6961, Sig). NAL.

Macgraw, Williams. Geography of the United States. (gr. 8-12). 1972. pap. text ed. 9.00 each incl. 3 texts, 3 maps, tchr's manual & test (ISBN 0-8449-1000-7). Learning Line.

McGreal, John, tr. see Frederic, Helene & Malinsky, Martine.

MacGregor, A. & Greenwood, C. T. Polymers in Nature. LC 79-41787. 328p. 1980. 53.75 (ISBN 0-471-27762-2, Pub. by Wiley-Interscience); pap. write for info. (ISBN 0-471-27794-0). Wiley.

McGregor, Alexander C. From Bunchgrass to Agribusiness on the Columbia Plateau: The McGregor Land & Livestock Company, Eighteen Eighty-Two to Nineteen Seventy-Two. 1980. write for info. o.p. U of Wash Pr.

MacGregor, Anne & MacGregor, Scott. Bridges. LC 80-23305. (Illus.). 56p. (gr. 4 up). 1981. PLB 9.55 (ISBN 0-688-51997-0); pap. 5.95 (ISBN 0-688-41997-6). Morrow.

MacGregor, Barrie. Volleyball. (EP Sport Ser.). (Illus.). 1979. 12.95 (ISBN 0-8069-9160-7, Pub. by EP Publishing England). Sterling.

MacGregor, Bruce. South Pacific Coast: A Centennial. rev. ed. (Illus.). 1981. 34.95 (ISBN 0-87108-545-3). Pruett.

MacGregor, Carol. Storybook Cookbook. LC 67-15382. (gr. 3-7). PLB 4.95 o.p. (ISBN 0-385-06329-6). Doubleday.

McGregor, Craig. The Great Barrier Reef. (The World's Wild Places Ser). (Illus.). 1973. 12.95 (ISBN 0-8094-2006-6). Time-Life.

--The Great Barrier Reef. (The World's Wild Places Ser.). (Illus.). 1977. lib. bdg. 11.97 (ISBN 0-686-51018-6). Silver.

McGregor, Craig, ed. Bob Dylan: A Retrospective. (Illus.). 1972. 10.95 (ISBN 0-688-01175-6); pap. 6.95 (ISBN 0-688-06025-0). Morrow.

Macgregor, David R. Fast Sailing Ships. 316p. 1980. 57.00x (ISBN 0-245-51964-5, Pub. by Nautical England). State Mutual Bk.

McGregor, Don. Dragonflame, & Other Bedtime Nightmares. LC 80-197751. 128p. 1980. Repr. of 1977 ed. lib. bdg. 12.95 (ISBN 0-89370-093-2). Borgo Pr.

--Dragonflame & Other Bedtime Nightmares. LC 77-17761. (Illus.). 1978. pap. 5.00 (ISBN 0-934882-02-9). Fictioneer Bks.

--The Variable Syndrome. 192p. 1981. Repr. lib. bdg. 16.95x (ISBN 0-89370-091-6). Borgo Pr.

--The Variable Syndrome: A Science Fiction Story. (Also including: "Detectives, Inc." -- a memoir). 1981. pap. 10.00 (ISBN 0-934882-05-3). Fictioneer Bks.

McGregor, Donald. Louisiana Lil. (Orig.). 1980. pap. 1.75 (ISBN 0-8439-0737-1, Leisure Bks). Nordon Pubns.

--Renegade Riders. (Orig.). 1980. pap. 1.75 (ISBN 0-505-51549-0). Tower Bks.

McGregor, Donald R. The Inertia of the Vacuum: A New Foundation for Theoretical Physics. 96p. 1981. 6.00 (ISBN 0-682-49722-3). Exposition.

MacGregor, Ellen. Miss Pickerell & the Geiger Counter. 128p. (gr. 3-6). pap. 1.75 (ISBN 0-671-56019-0). Archway.

--Miss Pickerell Goes to Mars, No. 9. (gr. 4-6). 1980. pap. 1.75 (ISBN 0-671-56018-2). Archway.

McGregor, Ellen. Miss Pickerell Goes to the Arctic, No. 14. (Illus.). 1981. pap. 1.75 (ISBN 0-671-56021-2). Archway.

MacGregor, Ellen. Miss Pickerell Goes Undersea. 1981. pap. 1.75 (ISBN 0-671-56020-4). PB.

--Miss Pickerell Harvests the Sea, No. 8. (Illus.). 1980. pap. 1.75 (ISBN 0-671-56024-7). Archway.

MacGregor, Ellen & Pankell, Dora. Miss Pickerell & the Supertanker, No. 6. (Illus.). (gr. 4-6). 1980. pap. 1.75 (ISBN 0-671-56026-3). Archway.

MacGregor, Ellen & Pantell, Dora. Miss Pickerell & the Weather Satellite. (Illus.). (gr. 4-6). 1980. pap. 1.75 (ISBN 0-671-56027-1). PB.

--Miss Pickerell Goes on a Dig, No. 7. (Illus.). (gr. 4-6). 1980. pap. 1.75 (ISBN 0-671-56022-0). Archway.

--Miss Pickerell Meets Mr. H. U. M. (Illus.). (gr. 4-6). 1980. pap. 1.75 (ISBN 0-671-56028-X). PB.

--Miss Pickerell on the Moon. (Illus.). (gr. 4-6). 1965. PLB 6.95 o.p. (ISBN 0-07-044551-6, GB). McGraw.

--Miss Pickerell Tackles the Energy Crisis. LC 79-24149. (Illus.). (gr. 4-6). 1980. 7.95 (ISBN 0-07-044589-3). McGraw.

--Miss Pickerell Takes the Bull by the Horns. LC 75-41454. (Illus.). (gr. 4-6). 1976. 6.95 o.p. (ISBN 0-07-044582-6, GB). McGraw.

--Miss Pickerell Takes the Bull by the Horns. (Illus.). (gr. 4-6). 1980. pap. 1.75 (ISBN 0-671-56029-8). PB.

--Miss Pickerell Takes the Bull by the Horns, No. 4. (Illus.). (gr. 4-6). 1980. pap. 1.75 (ISBN 0-671-56029-8). Archway.

--Miss Pickerell to the Earthquake Rescue, No. 5. (Illus.). (gr. 4-6). 1980. pap. 1.75 (ISBN 0-671-56025-5). Archway.

Macgregor, Frances C. After Plastic Surgery: Adaptation & Adjustment. LC 79-11808. (Praeger Special Studies Ser.). 160p. 1980. 19.95 (ISBN 0-03-052131-9). Praeger.

MacGregor, Geddes. He Who Lets Us Be: A Theology of Love. 210p. 1975. 8.95 (ISBN 0-8164-1202-2). Crossroad NY.

--The Nicene Creed Illumined by Modern Thought. 1981. pap. 7.95 (ISBN 0-8028-1855-2). Eerdmans.

--Philosophical Issues in Religious Thought. LC 78-65851. pap. text ed. 11.50 (ISBN 0-8191-0677-1). U Pr of Amer.

--Rhythm of God: A Philosophy of Worship. LC 74-13598. 1974. 5.95 (ISBN 0-8164-1174-3). Crossroad NY.

--Scotland Forever Home: An Introduction to the Homeland for American & Other Scots. LC 79-24066. 284p. 1980. 9.95 (ISBN 0-396-07804-4). Dodd.

MacGregor, Iona. The Burning Hill. (gr. 5 up). 1970. 6.95 (ISBN 0-571-09318-3, Pub. by Faber & Faber). Merrimack Bk Serv.

--An Edinburgh Reel. (gr. 5 up). 1968. 5.95 o.p. (ISBN 0-571-08362-5, Pub. by Faber & Faber). Merrimack Bk Serv.
--The Snake & the Olive. 1974. 8.95 (ISBN 0-571-10582-3, Pub. by Faber & Faber). Merrimack Bk Serv.
--The Tree of Liberty. 1972. 6.50 (ISBN 0-571-10121-6, Pub. by Faber & Faber). Merrimack Bk Serv.
MacGregor, James. Beer Making for All. (Orig.). 1973. pap. 3.95 (ISBN 0-571-10252-2, Pub. by Faber & Faber). Merrimack Bk Serv.
--Wine Making for All. 1966. 3.95 o.p. (ISBN 0-571-06646-1, Pub. by Faber & Faber). Merrimack Bk Serv.
McGregor, Jim & Rapoport, Ron. Called for Traveling. (Illus.). 1978. 12.95 (ISBN 0-02-583350-2). Macmillan.
McGregor, Jim & Watt, Alan. Simple Pascal. 1981. text ed. price not set (ISBN 0-914894-72-2). Computer Sci. Postponed.
McGregor, Lynn. Developments in Drama Teaching. (Changing Classroom). 1976. text ed. 11.25 o.p. (ISBN 0-7291-0007-3); pap. text ed. 4.00x (ISBN 0-7291-0002-2). Humanities.
MacGregor, Malcolm. Financial Planning Guide for Your Money Matters. LC 78-55443. (Illus.). 1978. spiral wkbk 5.95 (ISBN 0-87123-154-9, 210154). Bethany Fell.
MacGregor, Malcolm & Baldwin, Stanley C. Your Money Matters. LC 75-56123. 1977. pap. 3.95 (ISBN 0-87123-662-1, 210662). Bethany Fell.
McGregor, Malcolm, jt. auth. see Mollo, Andrew.
MacGregor, Morna. Early Celtic Art in North Britain: A Study of the Decorative Metalwork from the Third Century BC to the Third Century AD, 2 vols. Incl. Vol. 1. (Illus.). 240p; Vol. 2. (Illus.). 322p. 1975. text ed. 57.50x (ISBN 0-7185-1135-2, Leicester). Humanities.
MacGregor, Morris J. & Nalty, Bernard C., eds. Blacks in the U. S. Armed Forces: Basic Documents, 13 vols. LC 76-5603. 1977. Set. 750.00 (ISBN 0-8420-2098-5). Scholarly Res Inc.
McGregor, R. S. Exercises in Spoken Hindi. (Illus.). 1970. 32.50 (ISBN 0-521-07487-8); tape 49.50 (ISBN 0-521-07488-6). Cambridge U Pr.
--Language of Indrajit of Orcha. LC 68-10472. (University of Cambridge Oriental Pubns.). 1968. 49.50 (ISBN 0-521-05630-6). Cambridge U Pr.
--An Outline of Hindi Grammar. 304p. 1977. 5.95x (ISBN 0-19-560797-X). Oxford U Pr.
MacGregor, Roderick. Structure of the Meat Animals: A Guide to Their Anatomy & Physiology. 2nd ed. (Illus.). 1965. pap. 14.95 (ISBN 0-291-39536-8). Intl Ideas.
MacGregor, Scott, jt. auth. see MacGregor, Anne.
MacGregor, W. G., jt. ed. see Dawkins, Michael.
MacGregor-Hastie, Roy, ed. Anthology of Contemporary Romanian Poetry. 1969. 13.95 (ISBN 0-7206-0280-7). Dufour.
McGrew, D. R. Traffic Accident Investigation & Physical Evidence. (Illus.). 132p. 1976. pap. 16.75 (ISBN 0-398-03503-2). C C Thomas.
McGrew, Roderick E. Russia & the Cholera, Eighteen Twenty-Three to Eighteen Thirty-Two. (Illus.). 1965. 20.00 (ISBN 0-299-03710-X). U of Wis Pr.
McGriggs, Lee A. The Odyssey of Martin Luther King, Jr. LC 77-26343. 1978. pap. text ed. 9.00x o.p. (ISBN 0-8191-0415-9). U Pr of Amer.
McGuane, George. New England Patriots: A Pictorial History. LC 80-84555. (Illus.). 176p. 1981. 16.95 (ISBN 0-938694-00-6). JCP Corp VA.
McGuane, Thomas. The Bushwhacked Piano. 1973. pap. 1.95 o.p. (ISBN 0-446-89477-X). Warner Bks.
--The Missouri Breaks. (Orig.). 1976. pap. 1.75 o.p. (ISBN 0-345-25218-7). Ballantine.
--An Outside Chance: Essays on Sport. 256p. 1980. 10.95 (ISBN 0-374-10472-7). FS&G.
McGue, Noelle. Only the Present. 1981. pap. 1.50 (ISBN 0-440-16597-0). Dell.
McGuffey Editions. McGuffey's Illustrated Address Book. 160p. 1980. 6.95 (ISBN 0-442-21257-7). Van Nos Reinhold.
McGuffey, William H. Old Favorites from the McGuffey Readers. Minnich, Harvey C., ed. LC 79-76081. 1969. Repr. of 1936 ed. 20.00 (ISBN 0-8103-3854-8). Gale.
McGuffey, William H. see Weems, Mason L.
McGuffey, William Holmes. McGuffey's Pictorial Eclectic Primer. (Illus.). 60p. (gr. k-3). 1965. pap. 3.50 (ISBN 0-917420-02-0). Buck Hill.
McGuffie, T. H. The Seige of Gibraltar, 1779-1783. (Illus.). 1965. 6.95 (ISBN 0-8023-1074-5). Dufour.
McGuigan, F. Cognitive Psychophysiology: Principles of Covert Behavior. LC 78-18542. 1978. 31.95 (ISBN 0-13-139519-X). P-H.
McGuigan, F. J., et al, eds. Stress & Tension Control. 330p. 1980. 29.50 (ISBN 0-306-40450-8, Plenum Pr). Plenum Pub.
McGuigan, Frank J. Experimental Psychology: A Methodological Approach. 3rd ed. LC 77-25206. (Illus.). 1978. ref. ed. 19.95 (ISBN 0-13-295162-2). P-H.
McGuigan, James R. & Moyer, R. Charles. Managerial Economics. 2nd ed. 1979. text ed. 19.50 (ISBN 0-8299-0176-0); solutions manual avail. (ISBN 0-8299-0558-8); study guide 6.95 (ISBN 0-8299-0287-2); study guide 6.95 (ISBN 0-8299-0559-6). West Pub.
McGuiness, Rosamond. English Court Odes 1660-1820. (Oxford Monographs on Music). (Illus.). 250p. 1971. 22.50x o.p. (ISBN 0-19-816119-0). Oxford U Pr.
McGuinness, B. F., tr. see Wittgenstein, Ludwig.
McGuinness, Brian, ed. see Frege, Gottlob.
McGuinness, William J. & Stein, Benjamin. Building Technology: Mechanical & Electrical Systems. LC 76-14961. 1977. text ed. 27.95 (ISBN 0-471-58433-9); tchrs'. manual avail. (ISBN 0-471-01601-2). Wiley.
McGuire. Clinical Simulations: Selected Problems in Patient Management. 2nd ed. 1976. pap. 25.50 (ISBN 0-8385-1161-9). ACC.
McGuire, Chester C. International Housing Policies: A Comparative Analysis. LC 80-8815. 1981. price not set (ISBN 0-669-04385-0). Lexington Bks.
McGuire, Diane K., ed. Beatrix Farrand's Plant Book for Dumbarton Oaks. LC 80-12169. (Illus.). 1980. 20.00x (ISBN 0-88402-095-9, Ctr Landscape Arch); pap. 10.00x. Dumbarton Oaks.
McGuire, E. Patrick, ed. Consumer Protection: Implications for the International Trade, Report No. 789. (Illus.). vii, 63p. (Orig.). 1980. pap. 15.00 (ISBN 0-8237-0225-1). Conference Bd.
McGuire, Eddie. Phantom of the Card Table. (Gambler's Book Shelf Ser.). 1969. pap. 2.95 (ISBN 0-89650-512-X). Gamblers.
McGuire, Edna. Peace Corps: Kindlers of the Spark. (gr. 7 up). 1966. 4.95g o.s.i. (ISBN 0-02-765450-8). Macmillan.
McGuire, Frederick L. & Kersh, Ronald C. An Evaluation of Driver Education: A Study of History, Philosophy, Research Methodology, & Effectiveness in the Field of Driver Education. (California Library Reprint Series: No. 24). 1971. 15.75x (ISBN 0-520-01931-8). U of Cal Pr.
MacGuire, Jillian. Threshold to Nursing. 271p. 1969. pap. text ed. 5.00x (Pub. by Bedford England). Renouf.
McGuire, Kenny. Kenny's Stories. 1981. 4.95 (ISBN 0-8062-1559-3). Carlton.
McGuire, Patrick, ed. see American Craft Council.
McGuire, Paul, tr. see Inkiow, Dimiter.
McGuire, Thomas. Psychotherapy & National Health Insurance: Issues & Evidence. 1981. price not set (ISBN 0-88410-711-6). Ballinger Pub.
McGuire, W. L., et al, eds. Estrogen Receptors in Human Breast Cancer. LC 74-14484. 1975. 27.00 (ISBN 0-89004-015-X). Raven.
McGuire, William. Steel Structures. 1968. text ed. 38.00 (ISBN 0-13-846493-6). P-H.
McGuire, William & Gallagher, Richard H. Matrix Structural Analysis. LC 78-8471. 1979. text ed. 31.95 (ISBN 0-471-03059-7); solution manual avail. (ISBN 0-471-05535-2). Wiley.
McGuire, William L., ed. Hormones, Receptors, & Breast Cancer. LC 77-90595. (Progress in Cancer Research & Therapy Ser.: Vol. 10). 1978. 31.50 (ISBN 0-89004-261-6). Raven.
McGuire, William L., et al, eds. Progesterone Receptors in Normal & Neoplastic Tissues. LC 77-72065. (Progress in Cancer Research & Therapy Ser.: Vol. 4). 1977. 31.50 (ISBN 0-89004-163-6). Raven.
McGuirt, W. Frederick, ed. Pediatric Otolaryngology Case Studies. LC 80-80367. 1980. pap. 18.50 (ISBN 0-87488-094-7). Med Exam.
McGurk, Frank C. Race Differences--Twenty Years Later. 56p. (Orig.). 1978. pap. 2.00x (ISBN 0-911038-73-6, IAAEE). Noontide.
McGusty, Moyra, ed. see Smith, Elizabeth.
McGuyer, Nadine. To Ravish Rani. (Orig.). 1979. pap. 1.95 (ISBN 0-532-23273-9). Manor Bks.
Mach, Elyse. Great Pianists Speak for Themselves. LC 79-28736. 1980. 9.95 (ISBN 0-396-07824-9). Dodd.
Machado, Antonio. Canciones. Bly, Robert, tr. from Span. LC 80-27641. 20p. 1980. 30.00 (ISBN 0-915124-45-9, Bookslinger); pap. 4.00 (ISBN 0-915124-46-7). Toothpaste.
--Juan de Mairena: Epigrams, Maxims, Memoranda, & Memoirs of an Apocryphal Professor. Belitt, Ben, tr. (Illus.). 1963. 12.95x (ISBN 0-520-00792-1); pap. 1.50 (ISBN 0-520-00794-8, CAL89). U of Cal Pr.
--Selected Poems of Antonio Machado. Craig, Betty, tr. LC 78-57504. 1978. 11.95x (ISBN 0-8071-0456-6). La State U Pr.
Machado, Jeanne. Early Childhood Experiences in Language Arts. LC 78-55972. 1980. pap. 9.80 (ISBN 0-8273-1573-2); instructor's guide 1.50 (ISBN 0-8273-1574-0). Delmar.
Machado, Luis A. The Right to Be Intelligent. 85p. 1980. 12.75 (ISBN 0-08-025781-X). Pergamon.
Machado, Manuel A., Jr. An Industry in Crisis: Mexican-United States Cooperation in the Control of Foot-And-Mouth Disease. (U. C. Publ. in History: Vol. 80). 1968. pap. 6.50x (ISBN 0-520-09191-4). U of Cal Pr.
--The North Mexican Cattle Industry, 1910-1975: Ideology, Conflict & Change. LC 80-5515. (Illus.). 184p. 1980. 14.50x (ISBN 0-89096-104-2). Tex A&M Univ Pr.
Machado de Assis, Joaquim M. Counselor Ayres' Memorial. Caldwell, Helen, tr. from Port. LC 72-187876. 1973. 15.95x (ISBN 0-520-02227-0). U of Cal Pr.
--Esau & Jacob. Caldwell, Helen, tr. 1965. 12.95 (ISBN 0-520-00788-3). U of Cal Pr.
McHale, John. Changing Information Environment. (Westview Environmental Studies: Vol. 4). 1976. 18.00x (ISBN 0-89158-623-7). Westview.
McHale, John & McHale, Magda C. The Futures Directory. LC 76-51285. 1977. lib. bdg. 50.00x (ISBN 0-89158-224-X). Westview.
McHale, M. Jerome. On the Wing: The Story of the Pittsburgh Sisters of Mercy. 284p. 1980. 15.00 (ISBN 0-8164-0466-6). Crossroad NY.
McHale, Magda C., jt. auth. see McHale, John.
McHale, Mary C., jt. auth. see McHale, Thomas R.
McHale, T. J. & Witzke, P. T. Arithmetic Modules. 125p. 1975. module 1 4.95 (ISBN 0-201-04751-9); module 2 4.95 (ISBN 0-201-04752-7); module 3 4.95 (ISBN 0-201-04753-5); module 4 4.95 (ISBN 0-201-04754-3); module 5 4.95 (ISBN 0-201-04756-X); test bklt 4.95 (ISBN 0-201-04758-6); ans. keys avail. (ISBN 0-685-52163-X). A-W.
McHale, Thomas J. & Witzke, Paul T. Applied Algebra II. 1980. pap. text ed. 12.95 (ISBN 0-201-04775-6). A-W.
McHale, Thomas R. & McHale, Mary C. Early American-Philippine Trade: The Journal of Nathaniel Bowditch in Manila, 1796. (Monograph: No. 2). viii, 63p. 1962. 3.25 o.p. (ISBN 0-686-63729-1). Yale U Pr.
McHale, Tom. The Lady from Boston. LC 76-42370. 1978. 8.95 o.p. (ISBN 0-385-01865-7). Doubleday.
--School Spirit. 1977. pap. 1.75 o.p. (ISBN 0-345-25760-X). Ballantine.
McHale, William R. A Silence at Yorktown. 1976. pap. 1.25 o.p. (ISBN 0-685-69512-3, LB372ZK, Leisure Bks). Nordon Pubns.
Machan, Lorraine. The Practitioner-Teacher Role. LC 80-80814. (Nursing Dimensions Education Ser.). 1980. pap. text ed. 9.50 (ISBN 0-913654-65-5). Nursing Res.
Machan, Tibor R. Human Rights & Human Liberties. LC 74-26864. 318p. 1975. 15.95 (ISBN 0-88229-159-9). Nelson-Hall.
--The Pseudo Science of B. F. Skinner. 1974. 9.95 o.p. (ISBN 0-87000-236-8). Arlington Hse.
Machan, Tibor R., ed. The Libertarian Alternative: Essays in Social & Political Philosophy. LC 73-80501. 1974. 18.95 (ISBN 0-911012-72-9); pap. 11.95 (ISBN 0-88229-511-X). Nelson-Hall.
McHardy, George. The Higher Powers of the Soul. (Short Course Ser.). 142p. Repr. of 1912 ed. text ed. 2.95 (ISBN 0-567-08321-7). Attic Pr.
McHargue, Georgess. The Horseman's Word: A Novel. LC 80-68736. 256p. (YA) (gr. 8-12). 1981. 9.95 (ISBN 0-440-04167-8). Delacorte.
--Meet the Vampire. LC 78-20393. (Eerie Ser.). (Illus.). (gr. 2-4). 1979. 7.95 (ISBN 0-397-31833-2); pap. 7.89 (ISBN 0-397-31851-0). Lippincott.
--The Talking Table Mystery. LC 76-23794. (gr. 5 up). 1977. 5.95a o.p. (ISBN 0-385-11353-6); PLB (ISBN 0-385-11354-4). Doubleday.
McHargue, Georgess, compiled by. Little Victories, Big Defeats: War As the Ultimate Pollution. LC 74-5749. 192p. (gr. 7 up). 1974. 6.95 o.s.i. (ISBN 0-440-04899-0). Delacorte.
McHargue, Georgess (Compiler) Facts, Frauds, & Phantasms: A Survey of the Spiritualist Movement. LC 73-180090. 312p. (gr. 6-9). 1972. PLB 4.95 o.p. (ISBN 0-385-05305-3). Doubleday.
Machem, J. Gresham. The New Testament: An Introduction to Its History & Literature. 1976. 11.95 (ISBN 0-85151-240-2). Banner of Truth.
Machen, Arthur. Tales of Horror & the Supernatural, Vol. 1. 1976. pap. 1.50 o.p. (ISBN 0-523-23891-6). Pinnacle Bks.
Machen, Elizabeth M. Christian Education Public Schools: A Teacher's Interpretation. 1978. 5.00 o.p. (ISBN 0-682-48990-5). Exposition.
Machen, J. Gresham. The Christian View of Man. pap. 1.95 o.p. (ISBN 0-686-12511-8). Banner of Truth.
--Virgin Birth of Christ. (Twin Brooks Ser). 1967. pap. 7.95 (ISBN 0-8010-5885-6). Baker Bk.
--Virgin Birth of Christ. 1958. Repr. of 1930 ed. 12.95 (ISBN 0-227-67630-0). Attic Pr.
McHenry, Dean E., jt. auth. see Ferguson, John H.
McHenry, Donald F. Ethics & Foreign Policy. LC 80-68410. (Distinguished Cria Lecture on Morality & Foreign Policy Ser.). 1980. pap. 4.00 (ISBN 0-87641-220-7). Coun Rel & Intl.
McHenry, E. W., jt. ed. see Beaton, G. H.
McHenry, J. Patrick. Short History of Mexico. rev. ed. LC 75-107354. 1970. pap. 1.95 (ISBN 0-385-02391-X, C363, Dolp). Doubleday.
McHenry, Lawrence C., Jr., ed. Garrison's History of Neurology. (Illus.). 568p. 1969. 22.75 (ISBN 0-398-01261-X). C C Thomas.
McHenry, R., jt. auth. see Cook, Mark.
McHenry, Ruth W. Self-Teaching Tests in Arithmetic for Nurses. 10th. ed. LC 80-10859. (Illus.). 1980. pap. text ed. 8.95 (ISBN 0-8016-2505-X). Mosby.
Macherey, Pierre. A Theory of Literary Production. Wall, Geoffrey, tr. from Fr. 1978. 27.50x (ISBN 0-7100-8978-3); pap. 12.75 (ISBN 0-7100-0087-1). Routledge & Kegan.
Machiavelli. The Prince. pap. 1.50. Bantam.
Machiavelli, Niccolo. Art of War. rev. ed. Farneworth, Ellis, tr. LC 64-66078. (Orig.). 1965. pap. 6.95 (ISBN 0-672-60434-5, LLA196). Bobbs.
--The Discourses, 2 vols. Walker, Leslie J., tr. 1975. Set. 65.00x (ISBN 0-7100-8076-X); 24.50x ea. Routledge & Kegan.
--Il Principe (De Principatibus) Richardson, Brian, ed. & intro. by. 153p. (Orig., Ital.). 1979. pap. 5.95x (ISBN 0-7190-0742-9, Pub. by Manchester England). S F Vanni.
--Machiavelli's Thoughts on the Management of Men. (Illus.). 1978. deluxe bdg. 47.45 (ISBN 0-918968-08-9). Inst Econ Finan.
--Mandragola. Paolucci, Anne & Paolucci, Henry, trs. LC 57-14629. 1957. pap. 2.50 (ISBN 0-672-60231-8, LLA58). Bobbs.
--Mandragola. Flaumenhaft, Mera J., tr. from It. 64p. pap. text ed. 2.50x (ISBN 0-917974-57-3). Waveland Pr.
--Prince. 1952. pap. 1.95 (ISBN 0-451-61857-2, MJ1857, Ment). NAL.
--The Prince. Atkinson, James, ed. LC 75-15946. (LLA Ser: Vol. 172). 448p. 1975. pap. 9.50 (ISBN 0-672-61244-5). Bobbs.
--The Prince. Adams, Robert M., ed. & tr. 1977. 12.95 (ISBN 0-393-04448-3); pap. 3.95x (ISBN 0-393-09149-X). Norton.
--Il Principe. Burd, L. Arthur, ed. 1891. 14.95x (ISBN 0-19-815388-0). Oxford U Pr.
Machin, Barrie & Scopes, Nigel. Chrysanthemums: Year Round Growing. (Illus.). 1978. 24.95 (ISBN 0-7137-0885-9, Pub. by Blandford Pr England). Sterling.
Machine Tool & Design Research International Conference, 14th. Proceedings. Tobias, S. A. & Tobias, S. A., eds. 1974. 114.95 (ISBN 0-470-49746-7). Halsted Pr.
Machine Tool Design & Research International Conference, 12th. Proceedings. Koenigsberger, F. & Tobias, S. A., eds. LC 72-6276. 582p. 1972. 98.95 (ISBN 0-470-49745-9). Halsted Pr.
Machine Tool Design & Research International Conference 15th. Proceedings. Tobias, S. A. & Koenigsberger, F., eds. LC 63-19240. 738p. 1975. 164.95 (ISBN 0-470-87532-1). Halsted Pr.
Machlin, Evangeline. Dialects for the Stage. LC 75-7880. 1975. 39.95; tapes incl. (ISBN 0-87830-040-6). Theatre Arts.
--Speech for the Stage. new & rev. ed. LC 80-51639. 1980. 9.95 (ISBN 0-87830-120-8); tchr's manual 2.45 (ISBN 0-87830-573-4). Theatre Arts.
Machlin, Milt. Atlanta. 1978. pap. 2.50 (ISBN 0-380-43539-X, 43539). Avon.
--Libby. (Orig.). 1980. pap. 2.75 (ISBN 0-505-51533-4). Tower Bks.
--Pipeline. (Orig.). 1976. pap. 2.50 (ISBN 0-515-05408-9). Jove Pubns.
Machlin, Milt & Beckley, Tim. UFO. (Illus.). 192p. 1981. pap. 8.95 (ISBN 0-8256-3182-3, Quick Fox). Music Sales.
Machlis, Joseph. The Enjoyment of Music. 4th ed. LC 76-62482. (Illus.). 1977. 16.95x (ISBN 0-393-09118-X); shorter 14.95x (ISBN 0-393-09125-2); workbk 4.95x (ISBN 0-393-09122-8); instructor's guide gratis (ISBN 0-393-09129-5). Norton.
Machlup, Fritz. A History of Thought on Economic Integration. LC 76-54770. 1977. 22.50x (ISBN 0-231-04298-1). Columbia U Pr.
--International Payments, Debts & Gold: Collected Essays. 2nd ed. LC 76-20371. 1976. pap. 9.00x (ISBN 0-8147-5412-0). NYU Pr.
--Knowledge: Its Creation, Distribution, & Economic Significance, Vol. 1, Knowledge & Knowledge Production. LC 80-7544. 264p. 1980. 17.50 (ISBN 0-691-04226-8). Princeton U Pr.

Machlup, Fritz & Leeson, Kenneth W. Information Through the Printed Word. Incl. Vol. 1. Book Publishing. 28.95 (ISBN 0-03-047401-9); Vol. 2. Journals. 30.95 (ISBN 0-03-047406-X); Vol. 3. Libraries. 25.95 (ISBN 0-03-047411-6). LC 78-19460. 1978. Praeger.

Machlup, Fritz, ed. see Congress of the International Economic Association, 4th, Budapest, Hungary.

Machlup, Fritz, et al. The Production & Distribution of Knowledge in the United States. 415p. 1972. 20.00x o.p. (ISBN 0-691-08608-7); pap. 6.95 (ISBN 0-691-00356-4). Princeton U Pr.

Macholoitz, Marilyn. Workaholics: Living with Them, Working with Them. 1981. pap. 2.95 (ISBN 0-451-61971-4, ME1971, Mentor Bks). NAL.

McHose, Allen I. Contrapuntal Harmonic Technique of the Eighteenth Century. 1947. 19.95 (ISBN 0-13-171843-6). P-H.

McHose, Allen I. & Tibbs, Ruth N. Sight-Singing Manual. 3rd ed. 1957. 10.95 (ISBN 0-13-809707-0). P-H.

McHose, Allen I. & White, Donald F. Keyboard & Dictation Manual. (Eastman School of Music Ser.). 1949. 29.50x (ISBN 0-89197-255-2); pap. text ed. 18.50x (ISBN 0-89197-819-4). Irvington.

Machotka, Pavel & Spiegel, John P. Articulate Body. (Illus.). 250p. 1980. 18.50 (ISBN 0-8290-0229-4). Irvington.

Machover, Karen. Personality Projection in the Drawing of the Human Figure: A Method of Personality Investigation. (American Lecture Psychology Ser). (Illus.). 192p. 1978. 11.75 (ISBN 0-398-01184-2). C C Thomas.

Machover, Solomon, jt. auth. see Malamud, Daniel I.

Macht, Joel. Teacher-Teachim: The Toughest Game in Town. LC 75-2082. 160p. 1975. pap. text ed. 10.95 (ISBN 0-471-56243-2). Wiley.

Machtiger, B., ed. see Happel, Margaret.

McHugh, Geolo. Baby's House. (Illus.). 24p. (gr. k-1). 1976. PLB 7.15 o.p. (ISBN 0-307-69051-2, Golden Pr). Western Pub.

McHugh, Heather. A World of Difference. 1981. 8.95 (ISBN 0-395-30231-5); pap. 4.95 (ISBN 0-395-30232-3). HM.

McHugh, Joseph, jt. auth. see Locks, Renee.

McHugh, Mary. Careers in Engineering & Engineering Technology. (Career Concise Guides Ser.). (Illus.). (gr. 7 up). 1978. PLB 6.45 s&l (ISBN 0-531-01424-X). Watts.

--Law & the New Woman. LC 75-15584. (Choosing Life Styles Ser). 128p. (gr. 7 up). 1975. PLB 5.90 o.p. (ISBN 0-531-01097-X). Watts.

--Psychology & the New Woman. (Choosing Careers & Life-Styles Ser.). 128p. (gr. 7 up). 1976. PLB 5.90 o.p. (ISBN 0-531-00348-5). Watts.

--Veterinary Medicine & Animal Care Careers. (Illus.). 1977. lib. bdg. 6.45 (ISBN 0-531-01282-4). Watts.

McHugh, Paul. The Search for Goodbye-to-Rains. LC 79-28565. 192p. 1980. pap. 7.50 (ISBN 0-933280-07-6). Island CA.

McHugh, Peter. Defining the Situation: The Organization of Meaning in Social Interaction. LC 68-2800. 1968. 7.50 o.p. (ISBN 0-672-51135-5); pap. 5.50 (ISBN 0-672-60812-X). Bobbs.

McHugh, Peter, et al. On the Beginning of Social Inquiry. 1974. 15.00x (ISBN 0-7100-7765-3); pap. 7.95 (ISBN 0-7100-7766-1). Routledge & Kegan.

McHugh, Roger, ed. Jack B. Yeats: A Centenary Gathering. (Tower Series of Anglo Irish Studies). 1971. pap. text ed. 4.75x (ISBN 0-85105-205-3, Dolmen Pr). Humanities.

McHugh, Vernon D. From Hell to Heaven: Memoirs from Patton's Third Army. 35p. 1980. 3.95 (ISBN 0-8059-2742-5). Dorrance.

McHugh, Vincent. Caleb Catlum's America. LC 71-156927. 1971. Repr. of 1936 ed. 18.00 (ISBN 0-8103-3717-7). Gale.

McHugh, Vincent, jt. tr. see Kwock, C. H.

McHughes, Janet, jt. auth. see Kleinau, Marion.

Machwe, Prabhar, jt. ed. see Kumar, Shrawan.

Machwe, Prabhar, tr. see Kumar, Shrawan & Machwe, Prabhar.

Maciariello, Joseph A. Program-Management Control Systems. LC 77-20030. (Systems & Controls for Financial Management Ser.). 1978. 29.50 (ISBN 0-471-01566-0, Pub. by Wiley-Interscience). Wiley.

Maciel, Gary E., et al. Chemistry. 1978. text ed. 21.95x (ISBN 0-669-84830-1); inst. manual free (ISBN 0-669-99945-8); lab manual 7.95x (ISBN 0-669-00999-7); study guide 6.95x (ISBN 0-669-01000-6); solutions manual 3.99 (ISBN 0-669-01027-8). Heath.

Mc Ilhany, William H. Klandestine. (Illus.). 1975. 8.95 o.p. (ISBN 0-87000-295-3). Arlington Hse.

McIlhany, William H., 2nd. The Tax-Exempt Scandal: America's Leftist Foundations. 1980. 20.00 (ISBN 0-87000-380-1). Arlington Hse.

McIlhenny, Edward A., ed. Befo'de War Spirituals: Words & Melodies. LC 72-1724. Repr. of 1933 ed. 21.50 (ISBN 0-685-02341-9). AMS Pr.

McIllhany, William H. The ACLU on Trial. 1976. 8.95 o.p. (ISBN 0-87000-337-2). Arlington Hse.

McIlroy, Robert J. Introduction to Tropical Grassland Husbandry. 2nd ed. 1972. pap. 13.95x (ISBN 0-19-859427-5). Oxford U Pr.

McIlwain, Charles H. The American Revolution: A Constitutional Interpretation. LC 74-166335. (Era of the American Revolution Ser.). 198p. 1973. Repr. of 1923 ed. lib. bdg. 22.50 (ISBN 0-306-70249-5). Da Capo.

McIlwain, K., jt. auth. see Pender, H.

Macilwaine, P. S., jt. auth. see Plumpton, C.

MacIlwaine, P. S., jt. auth. see Plumpton, C.

Macilwaine, P. S., jt. auth. see Plumpton, C.

McInerny, Derek. Tropical Fish. LC 76-10815. (Illus.). 1976. bds. 2.25 o.p. (ISBN 0-668-03991-4). Arco.

McInerny, Ralph. Bishop As Pawn: A Father Dowling Mystery. LC 78-54978. (Father Dowling Ser.). 1978. 8.95 (ISBN 0-8149-0806-3). Vanguard.

--Her Death by Cold. LC 76-39728. 1977. 7.95 (ISBN 0-8149-0781-4). Vanguard.

--Lying Three. LC 79-68734. (The Father Dowling Mystery Ser.). 1979. 8.95 (ISBN 0-8149-0819-5). Vanguard.

--Quick As a Dodo. LC 77-93301. (Illus.). 1978. 6.95 (ISBN 0-8149-0806-3). Vanguard.

--Romanesque. LC 77-6891. 1978. 8.95 o.s.i. (ISBN 0-06-012966-2, HarpT). Har-Row.

--Second Vespers. LC 79-56379. (Father Dowling Mystery Ser.). 256p. 1980. 9.95 (ISBN 0-8149-0837-3). Vanguard.

--The Seventh Station: A Father Dowling Mystery. LC 77-77417. 1977. 7.95 (ISBN 0-8149-0787-3). Vanguard.

McInerry, Ralph. Second Vespers. large print ed. 1981. Repr. of 1980 ed. 10.95 (ISBN 0-89621-272-6). Thorndike Pr.

McInery, M., tr. see Kierkegaard, Soren.

McInery, Ralph M., ed. New Themes in Christian Philosophy. LC 68-20439. 1968. text ed. 29.50x (ISBN 0-268-00192-8). Irvington.

McInnes. Radiographic Anatomy. (Illus.). 1975. 13.95 o.p. (ISBN 0-685-78464-9). ACC.

McInnes, Betty. Controlling the Spread of Infection: A Programmed Presentation. 2nd ed. LC 76-48945. (Illus.). 1977. pap. text ed. 8.00 (ISBN 0-8016-3334-6). Mosby.

--The Vital Signs with Related Clinical Measurement. 3rd ed. (Illus.). 1979. pap. 9.50 (ISBN 0-8016-3333-8). Mosby.

MacInnes, Colin. Westward to Laughter. LC 76-95637. 1970. 5.95 o.p. (ISBN 0-374-28764-3). FS&G.

MacInnes, David & MacInnes, Kathleen. Walking Through Scotland. LC 80-68895. (Illus.). 192p. 1981. 19.95 (ISBN 0-7153-8090-7). David & Charles.

MacInnes, Hamish. High Drama. (Illus.). 224p. 1981. 11.95 (ISBN 0-89886-031-8). Mountaineers.

MacInnes, Helen. Above Suspicion. 1978. pap. 2.25 (ISBN 0-449-23833-4, Crest). Fawcett.

--Decision at Delphi. 1979. pap. 2.50 (ISBN 0-449-24015-0, Crest). Fawcett.

--Horizon. 1979. pap. 1.95 o.p. (ISBN 0-449-24012-6, Crest). Fawcett.

--Horizon. 192p. 1981. pap. 2.50 (ISBN 0-449-24012-6, Crest). Fawcett.

--I & My True Love. 1978. pap. 2.25 (ISBN 0-449-23798-2, Crest). Fawcett.

--Message from Malaga. 1979. pap. 2.25 (ISBN 0-449-23795-8, Crest). Fawcett.

--Rest & Be Thankful. 1978. pap. 2.25 (ISBN 0-449-23621-8, Crest). Fawcett.

--While Still We Live. 448p. 1981. pap. 2.75 (ISBN 0-449-24054-1, Crest). Fawcett.

MacInnes, Kathleen, jt. auth. see MacInnes, David.

McInnes, Mary E., ed. Essentials of Communicable Disease. LC 74-28353. 402p. 1975. 14.95 (ISBN 0-8016-2545-9). Mosby.

Macinnis, Joe. Underwater Man. LC 75-680. (Illus.). 144p. 1975. 6.95 (ISBN 0-396-07142-2). Dodd.

McInnis, Philip. Decoding Keys for Reading Success. (gr. k-9). 1981. 298.00 (ISBN 0-8027-9129-8); Primary Level. 98.00 (ISBN 0-8027-9130-1); Intermediate Level. 96.00 (ISBN 0-8027-9131-X); Advanced Level. 108.00 (ISBN 0-8027-9132-8); 4.50 (ISBN 0-8027-9133-6). Walker & Co.

McInnis, Philip J. McInnis-Hammondsport Plan: A Manual. LC 77-78982. 72p. 1977. tchrs. ed. 6.50 o.s.i. (ISBN 0-8027-9047-X). Walker Educ.

McInroy, Edward A. Driving Safely. (Quick & Easy Ser). (Orig.). 1967. pap. 1.95 o.s.i. (ISBN 0-02-080850-X, Collier). Macmillan.

McIntire, C. T., ed. God, History, & Historians: An Anthology of Modern Christian Views of History. LC 76-47428. 1977. 22.95 (ISBN 0-19-502203-3). Oxford U Pr.

--God, History & Historians: Modern Christian Views of History. 1977. pap. 6.95 (ISBN 0-19-502204-1, GB496, GB). Oxford U Pr.

McIntire, Matilda S. Handbook on Accident Prevention: Injury Control for Children & Youth. (Illus.). 128p. 1980. pap. text ed. 7.95 (ISBN 0-06-141611-8, Harper Medical). Har-Row.

McIntire, Matilda S. & Angle, Carol R., eds. Suicide Attempts in Children & Youth. 96p. 1980. pap. text ed. 7.95 (ISBN 0-686-65758-6, 0-0614160-X). Har-Row.

Macintosh, A. A. Isaiah XXI: A Palimpsest. LC 79-41375. 160p. 1980. 29.50 (ISBN 0-521-22943-X). Cambridge U Pr.

McIntosh, Bruce A., jt. ed. see Halliday, Ian.

McIntosh, Christopher. Astrology. 128p. 1973. pap. 1.25 o.p. (ISBN 0-06-087041-9, HW). Har-Row.

McIntosh, D. H., et al. Essentials of Meteorology. (Wykeham Science Ser.: No. 3). 1973. pap. 11.75x (ISBN 0-8448-1354-0). Crane-Russak Co.

McIntosh, D. M. Statistics for the Teacher. 2nd ed. 1967. text ed. 13.75 (ISBN 0-08-012254-X); pap. text ed. 6.25 (ISBN 0-08-012255-8). Pergamon.

McIntosh, David. Terror in the Starboard Seat. 208p. 1980. 10.95 (ISBN 0-8253-0025-8). Beaufort Bks NY.

Macintosh, H. G., ed. Techniques & Problems of Assessment for Teachers. 1974. pap. 13.95x (ISBN 0-7131-1816-4). Intl Ideas.

MacIntosh, H. R. The Highway of God. (Scholar As Preacher Ser.). 263p. Repr. of 1931 ed. text ed. 7.75 (ISBN 0-567-04424-6). Attic Pr.

MacIntosh, Harold C. The Chain Saw Craft Book. (Illus.). 1980. pap. 6.95 (ISBN 0-87108-516-X). Pruett.

Macintosh, J. J. & Coval, S. C., eds. Business of Reason. LC 68-27430. (International Library of Philosophy & Scientific Method). 1969. text ed. 15.00x (ISBN 0-7100-6528-0). Humanities.

McIntosh, James R. Perspectives on Marginality: Understanding Deviance. 320p. 1974. pap. text ed. 8.95x o.p. (ISBN 0-205-04419-0). Allyn.

McIntosh, Mary. The Organization of Crime. (Studies in Sociology Ser). 1977. pap. text ed. 4.00x o.p. (ISBN 0-333-15837-7). Verry.

McIntosh, Michael. Best Shotguns Ever Made. (Illus.). 192p. 1981. 12.95 (ISBN 0-684-16825-1, ScribT). Scribner.

McIntosh, Michael, ed. see Madson, John.

McIntosh, Naomi E., et al. A Degree of Difference: The Open Uninversity of the United Kingdom. LC 77-23034. (Praeger Special Studies). 1977. 29.95 (ISBN 0-03-040341-3). Praeger.

McIntosh, P. C. Fair Play: Ethics in Sport & Education. 1979. text ed. 27.50 o.p. (ISBN 0-435-80579-7); pap. text ed. 14.95x. Heinemann Ed.

McIntosh, P. C., ed. Landmarks in the History of Physical Education. 1957. 9.75 o.p. (ISBN 0-7100-1814-2). Routledge & Kegan.

McIntosh, R. M., et al. Kidney Disease: Hematologic & Vascular Problems. LC 77-7529. (Perspectives in Nephrology & Hypertension Ser.). 1977. 34.50 (ISBN 0-471-01921-6, Pub. by Wiley Medical). Wiley.

McIntosh, Robert W. & Gupta, Shashikant. Tourism: Principles, Practices, Philosophies. 3rd ed. LC 79-18050. 1980. text ed. 19.95 (ISBN 0-88244-198-1). Grid Pub.

MacIntyre, Alasdair. After Virtue. LC 80-53073. 320p. 1981. text ed. 15.95 (ISBN 0-268-00662-8). U of Notre Dame Pr.

MacIntyre, Alasdair & Ricoeur, Paul. Religious Significance of Atheism. LC 68-28398. (Bampton Lectures in America Ser.: No. 18). 1969. 12.50x (ISBN 0-231-03139-4). Columbia U Pr.

MacIntyre, Angus, jt. ed. see Garlick, Kenneth.

McIntyre, Bill. Grambling: Cradle of the Pros. Woolfolk, Doug, ed. (Illus.). 110p. 1980. 12.50 (ISBN 0-86518-015-6). Moran Pub Corp.

MacIntyre, C. F., tr. see Corbiere, Tristan.

MacIntyre, Christine M. & Wessel, Janet A. Body Contouring & Conditioning Through Movement. 2nd ed. (Series in Basic Concepts & Skills of Physical Activity). 1977. pap. 4.95x o.p. (ISBN 0-205-05584-2). Allyn.

McIntyre, D. A. Indoor Climate. (Illus.). xix, 442p. 1980. 65.00x (ISBN 0-85334-868-5). Intl Ideas.

M'Intyre, David M. Hidden Life of Prayer. 1962. pap. 2.50 (ISBN 0-87123-214-6, 200214). Bethany Fell.

--Hidden Life of Prayer. (Summit Books Ser). 1979. pap. 1.95 (ISBN 0-8010-6071-0). Baker Bk.

MacIntyre, Elisabeth. The Purple Mouse. LC 75-1318. 128p. (gr. 6 up). 1975. 6.95 o.p. (ISBN 0-525-66424-6). Elsevier-Nelson.

McIntyre, H. G. The Theatre of Jean Anoulh. 1981. 18.00x (ISBN 0-389-20182-0). B&N.

McIntyre, James M., jt. auth. see Kolb, David A.

McIntyre, Joan. Mind in the Waters. LC 74-13000. 1975. pap. 12.95 (ISBN 0-684-14443-3, SL614, ScribT). Scribner.

McIntyre, Michael P. Physical Geography. 3rd ed. LC 79-19207. 1980. text ed. 18.95 (ISBN 0-471-05629-4); study guide 7.95 (ISBN 0-471-05933-1); tchrs'. manual avail. (ISBN 0-471-06367-3). Wiley.

Macintyre, S. A Proletarian Science: Marxism in Britain, 1917 to 1933. 1980. 27.50 (ISBN 0-521-50539-9). Cambridge U Pr.

Macintyre, Stuart. Little Moscows: Communism & Working-Class Militancy in Inter-War Britain. 213p. 1980. 30.00x (ISBN 0-7099-0083-X, Pub. by Croom Helm Ltd England). Biblio Dist.

Macintyre, Sylvia, jt. ed. see Martin, G. H.

McIntyre, Thomas J. & Obert, John C. The Fear Brokers: Peddling the Hate Politics of the New Right. LC 80-70413. 384p. 1981. pap. 7.95 (ISBN 0-8070-3247-6, BP 620). Beacon Pr.

McIntyre, Vonda. Fire Flood & Other Stories. 1981. pap. 2.50 (ISBN 0-671-83631-5). PB.

McIntyre, Vonda N., et al. The Crystal Ship: Three Original Novellas of Science Fiction. Silverberg, Robert, ed. LC 76-26902. (Nelson's Science Fiction Ser.). (gr. 8 up). 1976. 7.95 o.p. (ISBN 0-525-66527-7). Elsevier-Nelson.

MacIsaac, David, ed. The United States Strategic Bombing Survey, 10 vols. Incl. Vol. 1 (ISBN 0-8240-2026-X); Vol. 2 (ISBN 0-8240-2027-8); Vol. 3 (ISBN 0-8240-2028-6); Vol. 4 (ISBN 0-8240-2029-4); Vol. 5 (ISBN 0-8240-2030-8); Vol. 6 (ISBN 0-8240-2031-6); Vol. 7 (ISBN 0-8240-2032-4); Vol. 8 (ISBN 0-8240-2033-2); Vol. 9 (ISBN 0-8240-2034-0); Vol. 10 (ISBN 0-8240-2035-9). LC 75-26396. 1976. 44.00 ea. Garland Pub.

MacIsaac, Fred. The Hothouse World. (YA) 1971. 5.95 (ISBN 0-685-23398-7, Avalon). Bouregy.

McIver, A., jt. auth. see Darmady, E. M.

McIver, Gwen. The Potato Cookbook. 1977. 11.95 (ISBN 0-7134-0477-9, Pub. by Batsford England). David & Charles.

MacIver, Joyce. Mercy. 1976. pap. 1.95 (ISBN 0-380-00843-2, 31096). Avon.

MacIver, R. M. The Ramparts We Guard. 1952. 17.50x (ISBN 0-686-51296-0). Elliots Bks.

--Society. 596p. 1980. Repr. of 1937 ed. lib. bdg. 40.00 (ISBN 0-89984-338-7). Century Bookbindery.

MacIver, R. M., ed. Great Moral Dilemmas. (Religion & Civilization Ser). 1964. Repr. of 1956 ed. 19.50x (ISBN 0-8154-0145-0). Cooper Sq.

Macivers, Donald. Cult of Killers. 1976. pap. 1.50 o.p. (ISBN 0-685-69156-X, LB364DK, Leisure Bks). Nordon Pubns.

McJimsey, George. Dividing & Reuniting of America. LC 80-68811. (Orig.). 1981. pap. text ed. 7.95x (ISBN 0-88273-108-4). Forum Pr MO.

Mack, Amanda. Makeshift Mistress. (Orig.). 1981. pap. 1.50 o.s.i. (ISBN 0-440-15874-5). Dell.

Mack, Bruce. Jesse's Dream Skirt. LC 79-89892. 36p. (ps-1). 1979. pap. 3.00 (ISBN 0-914996-20-7). Lollipop Power.

Mack, Dorothy. The Belle of Bath. (Candelight Romance Ser.). (Orig.). Date not set. pap. 1.50 (ISBN 0-440-10617-6). Dell.

--The Substitute Bride. 1977. pap. 1.25 o.s.i. (ISBN 0-440-18375-8). Dell.

Mack, Earle & Barnes, Patricia. The Children of Theatre Street. (Large Format Ser.). (Illus.). 1978. pap. 7.95 o.p. (ISBN 0-14-005019-1). Penguin.

Mack, Effie M., et al. Nevada Government. 384p. 1953. octavo 5.00. Holmes.

Mack, Elsie. Magic Is Fragile. 256p. (YA) 1973. 5.95 (ISBN 0-685-27366-0, Avalon). Bouregy.

Mack, Gerstle. Nineteen Hundred Six: Surviving the Great Earthquake & Fire. 96p. (Orig.). pap. 5.95 (ISBN 0-87701-176-1). Chronicle Bks.

Mack, Helen. Unpacking a Bundle. 1977. 6.50 o.p. (ISBN 0-682-48921-2, Banner). Exposition.

Mack, Jack A., jt. auth. see Ernstine, Bill I.

Mack, Jacque. Stanley Meets Do Good & Be Bad. (Apple Bks.). (Illus.). 32p. (gr. 5 up). 1978. pap. 3.50 (ISBN 0-570-07900-4, 56-1600). Concordia.

Mack, Jim. Haleakala: The Story Behind the Scenery. DenDooven, Gweneth R., ed. LC 78-51407. (Illus.). 1979. 7.95 (ISBN 0-916122-54-9); pap. 3.50 (ISBN 0-916122-53-0). K C Pubns.

Mack, Maynard. King Lear in Our Time. (California Library Reprint Series: No. 17). 1971. 12.00 o.p. (ISBN 0-520-01922-9); pap. 2.35 (ISBN 0-520-02157-6, CAL239). U of Cal Pr.

Mack, Maynard, jt. auth. see Boynton, Robert F.

Mack, Maynard, jt. auth. see Boynton, Robert W.

Mack, Maynard, jt. ed. see Boynton, Robert W.

Mack, Maynard, ed. see Shakespeare, William.

Mack, Maynard, et al, eds. The Norton Anthology of World Masterpieces, 2 vols. 4th ed. 1979. text ed. 17.95x (ISBN 0-393-95036-0); Vol II. text ed. 17.95x (ISBN 0-393-95040-9); Vol I. pap. text ed. 14.95x (ISBN 0-393-95079-4); Vol II. pap. text ed. 14.95x (ISBN 0-393-95045-X). Vol. II (ISBN 0-393-95050-6). Norton.

--The Norton Anthology of World Masterpieces, 2 vols. in pap. 4th continental ed. 1980. pap. text ed. 16.95x one vol. (ISBN 0-393-95079-4); pap. text ed. 14.95x ea. Vol. I (ISBN 0-393-95082-4). Vol. II (ISBN 0-393-95090-5). Norton.

Mack, Maynard, Jr. Killing the King: Three Studies in Shakespeare's Tragic Structure. LC 72-91301. (Studies in English: No. 180). 240p. 1973. 15.00x o.p. (ISBN 0-300-01450-3). Yale U Pr.

Mack, Nancy. I'm Not Going. LC 76-12457. (Moods & Emotions Ser.). (Illus.). 32p. (gr. k-3). 1976. PLB 8.95 (ISBN 0-8172-0011-8). Raintree Pubs.

--Tracy. LC 76-12557. (Moods & Emotions Ser.). (Illus.). 32p. (gr. k-4). 1976. PLB 8.95 (ISBN 0-8172-0013-4). Raintree Pubs.

--Why Me? LC 76-13175. (Moods & Emotions Ser.). (Illus.). 32p. (gr. k-3). 1976. PLB 8.95 (ISBN 0-8172-0012-6). Raintree Pubs.

Mack, Nancy & Sanders, Peter. Fall Line. LC 75-22010. (The Venture Ser, a Reading Incentive Program). (Illus.). 76p. (gr. 7-12,RL 4.5-6.5). 1975. text ed. 23.25 ea. pack of 5 (ISBN 0-8172-0245-5). Follett.

--Flying High. LC 74-34425. (The Venture Ser, a Reading Incentive Program). (Illus.). 80p. (gr. 7-12,RL 4.5-6.5). 1975. In Packs Of 5. text ed. 23.25 ea. pack (ISBN 0-8172-0216-1). Follett.

Mack, Newell B., et al. Energy Research Guide. 1981. write for info (ISBN 0-88410-097-9). Ballinger Pub.

Mack, William P. & Connell, Royal W. Naval Ceremonies, Customs, & Traditions. LC 79-92236. 352p. 1980. 14.95 (ISBN 0-87021-412-8). Naval Inst Pr.

Mack, William P., jt. auth. see Ageton, Arthur A.

Mack, Zella. California Paralegal's Handbook. LC 77-71561. 1977. incl. 1980 suppl. 38.00 (ISBN 0-911110-23-2). Parker & Son.

McKaig, Charlene, et al. Self-Assessment of Current Knowledge in Child Health Nursing. 1975. spiral bdg. 8.00 o.p. (ISBN 0-87488-292-3). Med Exam.

McKaig, Thomas H. Field Inspection of Building Construction. 1958. 24.95 o.p. (ISBN 0-07-045108-7, P&RB). McGraw.

Mackail, J. W. Lectures on Greek Poetry. LC 66-23520. 1910. 10.50x (ISBN 0-8196-0180-2). Biblo.

Mackaill, A. W. & Maclean, J. A. Revision Questions & Worked Examples in "H" Grade Chemistry. 1975. pap. text ed. 3.75x o.p. (ISBN 0-435-65561-2). Heinemann Ed.

Mackaill, Alan W. O Grade Questions & Worked Examples in Chemistry. 1971. pap. text ed. 3.95x o.p. (ISBN 0-435-64563-3). Heinemann Ed.

McKain, Robert J., Jr. Realize Your Potential. 1979. pap. 5.95 (ISBN 0-8144-7515-9). Am Mgmt.

Mackal, Roy P. The Monsters of Loch Ness: The First Complete Scientific Study & Its Startling Conclusions. LC 76-3139. (Illus.). 401p. 1980. pap. 8.95 (ISBN 0-8040-0704-7). Swallow.

McKale, Donald M. Hitler: The Survival Myth. LC 80-5405. (Illus.). 264p. 1980. 14.95 (ISBN 0-8128-2724-4). Stein & Day.

Mackaness, George, ed. A Book of the Bounty' William Bligh & Others. Kennedy, Gavin. (Everyman's Reference Library). 1981. 14.50x (ISBN 0-460-00950-8, Pub. by J. M. Dent England). Biblio Dist.

McKaughan, Howard P., ed. see Wolfenden, E. P.

McKay & Patera. McKay & Patera Tables of Dimensions. 336p. Date not set. 39.75 (ISBN 0-8247-1227-7). Dekker.

Mackay, Alan L. Scientific Quotations: The Harvest of a Quiet Eye. Ebison, Maurice, ed. LC 76-48396. 1977. 22.50x (ISBN 0-8448-1050-9). Crane-Russak Co.

McKay, Charles L. Five Simple Keys to Effective Evangelism: You Too Can Do It. 1978. pap. text ed. 11.00x (ISBN 0-8191-0397-7). U Pr of Amer.

Mackay, Charles O., jt. auth. see Ellenwood, F. O.

McKay, Charles W. Digital Circuits: A Preparation for Microprocessors. LC 77-13058. (Illus.). 1978. ref. 19.95 (ISBN 0-13-212175-1). P-H.

McKay, Claude. Banana Bottom. LC 73-14676. 317p. 1974. pap. 5.95 (ISBN 0-15-610650-7, HB273, Harv). HarBraceJ.

Mackay, D., jt. ed. see Afghan, B. K.

Mackay, D., ed. see Mackenzie, Brian.

MacKay, D. I., jt. auth. see Buxton, N. K.

Mackay, David, et al. Breakthrough to Literacy, 45 bks. Incl. Animals; Birds; Birthday Party; Cat, the Bird & the Tree; Christmastime; Crocodiles Are Dangerous; Cup of Tea; Day We Went to the Beach; Doctors & Nurses; Dressing up; Fish Book; Getting Married; I Fell Down; In Bed; Loose Tooth; My Mom; My Story; My Teacher; Old Houses; Our Baby; People; People in Stories; Playhouse; Rainy Day; Shopping; Soccer Book; Students' Sentence Maker; Students' Word Maker; Things I Can Do; Weather; At School. (gr. k-3). 1973. 1 copy ea. of 45 titles 39.30 (ISBN 0-8372-2159-5); complete breakthrough to literary prog. 270.00 (ISBN 0-8372-0858-0). Bowmar-Noble.

MacKay, Donald. Brains, Machines, & Persons. 112p. 1980. pap. 4.95 (ISBN 0-8028-1817-X). Eerdmans.

--The Clockwork Image. LC 74-8347. 112p. (Orig.). 1974. pap. 3.95 o.p. (ISBN 0-87784-557-3). Inter-Varsity.

Mackay, Donald, ed. Scotland Nineteen Eighty: The Economics of Self-Government. 1979. text ed. 18.25x (ISBN 0-905470-03-6). Humanities.

MacKay, Donald I. & Mackay, George A. The Political Economy of North Sea Oil. LC 75-25633. 208p. 1976. 26.50x (ISBN 0-89158-515-X). Westview.

McKay, Donald M. Science, Chance & Providence. (Riddell Memorial Lectures Ser.). (Illus.). 78p. 1978. text ed. 13.95x. Oxford U Pr.

McKay, Douglas R. Carlos Arniches. (World Authors Ser.: Spain: No. 188). lib. bdg. 10.95 (ISBN 0-8057-2068-5). Twayne.

--Enrique Jardiel Poncela. LC 74-6487. (World Authors Ser.: Spain: No. 333). 1974. lib. bdg. 10.95 (ISBN 0-8057-2462-1). Twayne.

--Miguel Mihura. (World Authors Ser.: No. 436). 1977. lib. bdg. 12.50 (ISBN 0-8057-6191-8). Twayne.

McKay, Ernest. Henry Wilson, Practical Radical: A Portrait of a Politician. LC 70-139359. 1971. 17.00 (ISBN 0-8046-9010-3, Natl U Pub). Kennikat.

McKay, Ernest A. A World to Conquer: The Story of the First Around the World Flight. LC 80-23064. (Illus.). 224p. 1981. 10.95 (ISBN 0-668-05096-9, 5096). Arco.

McKay, G. W., ed. see Rilke, Rainer M.

McKay, Gary D., jt. auth. see Dinkmeyer, Don.

Mackay, George A., jt. auth. see MacKay, Donald I.

McKay, George L., ed. American Book Auction Catalogues, 1713-1934. 1967. Repr. of 1937 ed. 20.00 (ISBN 0-8103-3311-2). Gale.

McKay, Harvey J. St. Paul, Oregon, Eighteen Thirty to Eighteen Ninety. LC 80-69228. (Illus.). 1980. 15.00 (ISBN 0-8323-0384-4). Binford.

McKay, Heather & Batten, Jack. Heather McKay's Complete Book of Squash. (Illus.). 1979. 5.95 (ISBN 0-345-28250-7); pap. 10.95 (ISBN 0-345-28271-X). Ballantine.

McKay, Hugh B., jt. auth. see Ross, Robert R.

Mackay, J. S. The Analysis of Marine Steam Indicator Diagrams. 130p. 1949. 27.50x (ISBN 0-85264-019-6, Pub. by Griffin England). State Mutual Bk.

Mackay, James. Collectibles. (Illus.). 1979. 19.95x (ISBN 0-8464-0254-8). Beekman Pubs.

--Railway Antiques. (Orig.). 1980. pap. 8.95x (ISBN 0-8464-1046-X). Beekman Pubs.

McKay, John H. Football Coaching. (Illus.). 1966. 14.95 (ISBN 0-8260-5885-X). Wiley.

McKay, John P., et al. A History of Western Society. LC 78-69592. (Illus.). 1979. pap. text ed. 17.95 1 vol. ed. (ISBN 0-395-27276-9); pap. text ed. 13.75 ea. 2 vol. ed.; pap. text ed. 11.95 ea. 3 vol. ed.; inst. manual 0.65 (ISBN 0-395-27421-4); wkbk. study guide 7.50 (ISBN 0-395-27420-6). HM.

McKay, Margaret M. The Rev. Dr. John Walker's Report on the Hebrides of 1764 to 1771. 263p. 1980. text ed. 39.00x (ISBN 0-85976-043-X). Humanities.

Mackay, Marianne. Prisms. LC 80-52415. 384p. 1981. 11.95 (ISBN 0-87223-655-2). Seaview Bks.

McKay, Mary E., jt. auth. see Herman, Harold.

MacKay, R. & Mountford, A. English for Specific Purposes. (Applied Linguistics & Language Study). 1978. pap. text ed. 9.00x (ISBN 0-582-55090-4). Longman.

MacKay, Ray. New Guinea. (World's Wild Places Ser.). (Illus.). 1976. 12.95 (ISBN 0-8094-2056-2). Time-Life.

--New Guinea. (The World's Wild Places Ser.). (Illus.). 1978. lib. bdg. 11.97 (ISBN 0-686-51022-4). Silver.

McKay, Rena. Bridal Trap. 192p. (Orig.). 1980. pap. 1.50 (ISBN 0-671-57036-6). S&S.

McKay, Robert. Canary Red. (gr. 7-9). 1972. pap. 1.25 o.p. (ISBN 0-590-04435-4, Schol Pap). Schol Bk Serv.

--Skean. LC 76-6904. 160p. (YA) 1976. 7.95 o.p. (ISBN 0-525-66486-6). Elsevier-Nelson.

McKay, Ron, et al, eds. Monoclonal Antibodies Against Neural Antigens. (Cold Spring Harbor Reports in the Neurosciences). 300p. 1981. price not set (ISBN 0-87969-138-7). Cold Spring Harbor.

Mackay, Ronald & Palmer, Joe, eds. Languages for Specific Purposes: Program Design & Evaluation. 144p. (Orig.). 1981. pap. text ed. 9.95 (ISBN 0-88377-184-5). Newbury Hse.

Mackay, Ruddock F. Fisher of Kilverstone. (Illus.). 559p. 1974. 19.95x (ISBN 0-19-822409-5). Oxford U Pr.

Mackay, Sally, jt. auth. see Balfour, Neil.

McKay, Sandra & Rosenthal, Linda. Writing for a Specific Purpose. (Illus.). 1980. pap. text ed. 7.50 (ISBN 0-13-970269-5). P-H.

Mackaye, Percy. Mystery of Hamlet, King of Denmark. 1976. ltd. ed. 125.00 (ISBN 0-87027-177-6); pap. 9.95 (ISBN 0-87027-176-8). Wheelwright.

MacKaye, Percy, jt. auth. see Tatlock, John S.

MacKaye, Steele & Tourgee, Albion W. Fool's Errand. Keller, Dean H., ed. LC 79-6587. 1969. 8.00 o.p. (ISBN 0-8108-0279-1). Scarecrow.

McKClough, T. H. & Cummins, W. A., eds. Stone Axe Studies: Archaeological, Petrological, Experimental, & Ethnographic. 109p. 1980. pap. 35.00x (ISBN 0-900312-63-7, Pub. by Coun Brit Arch England). Intl Schol Bk Serv.

McKeachie, Wilbert J. Teaching Tips: A Guidebook for the Beginning College Teacher. 7th ed. 1978. pap. text ed. 7.95x (ISBN 0-669-01151-7). Heath.

McKeag, R. M. & MacNaghten, A. M., eds. On the Construction of Programs. 432p. 1980. 24.50 (ISBN 0-521-23090-X). Cambridge U Pr.

McKeague, Charles P. Beginning Algebra. 1980. pap. 13.95 (ISBN 0-12-484765-X). Acad Pr.

Mackean, D. J. Introduction to Genetics. 3rd ed. 1978. pap. text ed. 8.95 (ISBN 0-7195-3346-5). Transatlantic.

McKean, H. P., jt. auth. see Dym, H.

McKean, H. P., ed. see Bucy, R. S., et al.

McKean, Keith F. Cross Currents in the South. LC 60-14586. 50p. 1960. pap. 1.00 (ISBN 0-8040-0058-1). Swallow.

McKean, Margaret A. Environmental Protest & Citizen Politics in Japan. 300p. 1981. 28.50x (ISBN 0-520-04115-1). U of Cal Pr.

McKean, Roland N. Efficiency in Government Through Systems Analysis. LC 58-7902. 1958. 31.95 (ISBN 0-471-58773-7, Pub. by Wiley-Interscience). Wiley.

McKeaugue, Charles P. Intermediate Algebra. 494p. 1979. 16.95 (ISBN 0-12-484760-9); instr's. manual avail. Acad Pr.

McKechnie, A., jt. auth. see Roblee, C.

Mackechnie, John. Gaelic Without Groans. 3rd ed. 1974. pap. text ed. 4.50x (ISBN 0-05-002862-6). Longman.

McKechnie, Sue. British Silhouette Artists & Their Work: 1760-1860. (Illus.). 798p. 1978. 180.00x (ISBN 0-85667-036-7, Pub. by Sotheby Parke Bernet England). Biblio Dist.

McKee, D. L., et al. Regional Economics. LC 70-94625. 1970. pap. text ed. 7.25 o.s.i. (ISBN 0-02-920530-1). Free Pr.

McKee, David. The Magician & the Sorcerer. LC 73-22280. (Illus.). 32p. (ps-3). 1974. 5.95 o.s.i. (ISBN 0-8193-0772-6, Four Winds); PLB 5.41 o.s.i. (ISBN 0-8193-0773-4). Schol Bk Serv.

McKee, Gwen, ed. see Fellowship Church, Baton Rouge, La, Members.

McKee, John G. Literary Irony & the Literary Audience: Studies in the Victimization of the Reader in Augustan Fiction. LC 74-7611. (Orig.). 1976. pap. text ed. 9.25x (ISBN 90-6203-051-3). Humanities.

McKee, William D., ed. Environmental Problems in Medicine. (Illus.). 880p. 1975. text ed. 48.75 (ISBN 0-398-02962-8). C C Thomas.

MacKeen, D. L., tr. see Roth, H. W. & Roth-Wittig, M.

McKeever, J. Ross. Apartment Development: Strategy for Successful Decision Making. LC 74-79436. (Special Publications Ser.). (Illus.). 80p. 1974. pap. 9.75 (ISBN 0-87420-560-3). Urban Land.

--Shopping Center Zoning. LC 73-88224. (Illus.). 73p. 1973. pap. 9.75 (ISBN 0-87420-069-5). Urban Land.

McKeever, J. Ross, ed. Dollars & Cents of Shopping Centers: A Study of Receipts & Expenditures, 1972. 5th ed. LC 70-81240. (Special Publications Ser.). (Illus.). 1972. pap. 24.25 (ISBN 0-87420-906-4); pap. 16.25 o.p. (ISBN 0-686-66562-7). Urban Land.

--Dollars & Cents of Shopping Centers-1975. 6th ed. LC 75-799. (Special Publication Ser). (Illus.). 1975. pap. 42.00 (ISBN 0-87420-563-8). Urban Land.

McKeever, Jim. The Almighty & the Dollar. 400p. 1980. 10.95 (ISBN 0-931608-09-0); pap. 5.95 (ISBN 0-931608-10-4). Omega Pubns OR.

--Christians Will Go Through the Tribulation. LC 78-55091. (Illus.). 1978. 10.95 (ISBN 0-931608-01-5); pap. 5.95 (ISBN 0-931608-02-3). Omega Pubns OR.

--Close Encounters of the Highest Kind. LC 78-70089. 1978. 7.95 (ISBN 0-931608-04-X); pap. 3.95 (ISBN 0-931608-03-1). Omega Pubns OR.

--How You Can Be Prepared. 246p. (Orig.). 1980. 14.95 (ISBN 0-931608-12-0); pap. 12.95 (ISBN 0-931608-13-9). Alpha Omega.

--Now You Can Understand the Book of Revelation. 320p. 1980. 10.95 (ISBN 0-931608-07-4); pap. 5.95 (ISBN 0-931608-08-2). Omega Pubns OR.

MacKeever, Maggie. A Banbury Tale. 1977. pap. 1.50 o.p. (ISBN 0-449-23174-7, Crest). Fawcett.

--A Notorious Lady. 1978. pap. 1.50 o.p. (ISBN 0-449-23491-6, Crest). Fawcett.

MacKeith, R. C., ed. see Kolvin, I.

McKellar, J. F., jt. ed. see Allen, N. S.

MacKellar, Walter, ed. Variorum Commentary on the Poems of John Milton, Vol. 4. 400p. 1975. 30.00 (ISBN 0-231-08883-3). Columbia U Pr.

MacKellar, William. The Cat That Never Died. LC 75-38358. (Illus.). (gr. 5 up). 1976. 5.95 (ISBN 0-396-07303-4). Dodd.

--The Ghost of Grannoch Moor. LC 73-6028. (Illus.). (gr. 4 up). 1973. 3.95g o.p. (ISBN 0-396-06834-0). Dodd.

--The Silent Bells. LC 78-7744. (Illus.). (gr. 4 up). 1978. 5.95 (ISBN 0-396-07618-1). Dodd.

--The Soccer Orphans. LC 78-22435. (gr. 5 up). 1979. 5.95 (ISBN 0-396-07667-X). Dodd.

--The Witch of Glen Gowrie. LC 77-16864. (gr. 5-8). 1978. 5.95 (ISBN 0-396-07531-2). Dodd.

McKelvey, Blake. The Emergence of Metropolitan America, 1915-1966. LC 68-18695. (Illus.). 1968. 21.00 (ISBN 0-8135-0571-2). Rutgers U Pr.

--Urbanization of America, 1860-1915. 1963. 24.00 (ISBN 0-8135-0421-X). Rutgers U Pr.

McKelvey, James L. George Third & Lord Bute: The Leicester House Years. LC 72-96682. 160p. 1973. 9.75 (ISBN 0-8223-0292-6). Duke.

McKelvey, James M. Polymer Processing. LC 62-8780. 1962. 22.50 o.p. (ISBN 0-471-58443-6). Wiley.

McKelvey, John J., Jr., et al, eds. Vectors of Disease Agents: Interactions with Plants, Animals, & Men. 350p. 1980. 34.95 (ISBN 0-03-056887-0). Praeger.

McKelvey, John P. & Grotch, Howard. Fisica Paraciencias E Ingenieria, Vol. II. (Span.). 1981. pap. text ed. 14.50 (ISBN 0-06-315476-5, Pub. by HarLA Mexico). Har-Row.

McKelvy, James. Music for Conducting Class. LC 77-76862. 1977. wire bound 11.95 (ISBN 0-916656-10-1). Mark Foster Mus.

McKelvy, John E., Jr. Translantic Summer. 1981. 10.00 (ISBN 0-533-04786-2). Vantage.

Macken, Bob, et al. The Rock Music Source Book. LC 78-1196. 648p. (Orig.). 1980. pap. 9.95 (ISBN 0-385-14139-4, Anch). Doubleday.

Macken, Walter. Flight of the Doves. LC 68-12083. (gr. 4-6). 1968. 5.95g o.s.i. (ISBN 0-02-762060-3). Macmillan.

--Silent People. 1962. Repr. 10.95 (ISBN 0-02-578000-X). Macmillan.

MacKendrick, Louise. The Glory Seeker. 1978. pap. 1.95 (ISBN 0-505-51230-0). Tower Bks.

--Natchez. (Orig.). 1977. pap. 1.75 (ISBN 0-505-51138-X). Tower Bks.

McKendrick, Melveena. Cervantes. Plumb, J. H., ed. (Library of World Biography). 288p. 1980. 11.95 (ISBN 0-316-56054-5). Little.

--Woman & Society in the Spanish Drama of the Golden Age. LC 73-82457. 384p. 1974. 56.00 (ISBN 0-521-20294-9). Cambridge U Pr.

McKendrick, Melveena & Elliott, J. H. Ferdinand & Isabella. LC 68-14974. (Horizon Caravel Bks). (Illus.). 153p. (gr. 6 up). 1968. 9.95 (ISBN 0-8281-0395-X, J03501-03); PLB 12.89 (ISBN 0-06-024165-9, Dist. by Har-Row). Am Heritage.

MacKendrick, Paul. The North African Stones Speak. LC 79-18534. xxii, 434p. 1980. 21.00x (ISBN 0-8078-1414-8). U of NC Pr.

--The Roman Mind at Work. LC 80-13022. (ANVIL Ser.). 192p. 1980. pap. text ed. 4.95 (ISBN 0-89874-200-5). Krieger.

MacKendrick, Paul L & Howe, Herbert M, eds. Classics in Translation, 2 vols. Incl. Vol. 1. Greek Literature. 440p (ISBN 0-299-80895-5); Vol. 2. Latin Literature. 448p (ISBN 0-299-80896-3). 1952. text ed. 7.95 ea. U of Wis Pr.

McKendry, Ruth. Traditional Quilts & Bed Coverings. 240p. 1980. 37.50 (ISBN 0-442-29790-4). Van Nos Reinhold.

McKenna, Brian, jt. auth. see Maltby, Arthur.

McKenna, Brian, ed. Irish Literature, Eighteen Hundred-Eighteen Seventy-Five: A Guide to Information Sources. LC 74-11540. (American Literature, English Literature & World Literatures in English Information Guide Ser.: Vol. 13). 1978. 30.00 (ISBN 0-8103-1250-6). Gale.

McKenna, Christopher K. Quantitative Methods for Business Decisions. (Quantitative Methods for Management). (Illus.). 1980. text ed. 18.95 (ISBN 0-07-045351-9); instrs.' manual 4.95 (ISBN 0-07-045352-7). McGraw.

McKenna, Eugene F. The Management Style of the Chief Accountant: A Situational Perspective. 1978. 24.95 (ISBN 0-566-00216-7, 02176-8, Pub. by Saxon Hse England). Lexington Bks.

McKenna, Evelyn. Castle Light. (YA) 1976. 4.95 o.p. (ISBN 0-685-69051-2, Avalon). Bouregy.

McKenna, Frank. The Railway Workers, Eighteen Forty to Nineteen Seventy. (Illus.). 288p. 1980. 30.00 (ISBN 0-571-11563-2, Pub. by Faber & Faber). Merrimack Bk Serv.

McKenna, Joseph P. Aggregate Economic Analysis. 5th ed. LC 76-19362. 1977. text ed. 17.95 (ISBN 0-03-089707-6). Dryden Pr.

McKenna, Julie & Polden, Margaret. You -- After Childbirth. (Churchill Livingstone Patient Handbook Ser.). 1980. pap. text ed. 2.25x (ISBN 0-443-02128-7). Churchill.

McKenna, Marian. Concise History of Catholicism. (Quality Paperback: No. 143). 1962. pap. 2.95 (ISBN 0-8226-0143-5). Littlefield.

--Myra Hess: A Portrait. (Illus.). 1978. 22.50 (ISBN 0-241-89522-7, Pub. by Hamish Hamilton England). David & Charles.

McKenna, Richard. Sand Pebbles. LC 62-15726. 1963. 11.95 o.p. (ISBN 0-06-012910-7, HarpT). Har-Row.

McKenna, Stephen, tr. Plotunus: The Enneads. 4th ed. 1970. 19.95 o.p. (ISBN 0-571-04688-6, Pub. by Faber & Faber). Merrimack Bk Serv.

McKenna, Virginia. Some of My Friends Have Tails. LC 76-17730. 1970. 5.50 o.p. (ISBN 0-15-183745-7, HJ). HarBraceJ.

McKenna, Wendy, jt. auth. see Kessler, Suzanne.

McKenney, James L. & Rosenbloom, Richard S. Cases in Operations Management. LC 69-13680. (Management & Administration Ser). 1969. pap. text ed. 14.50x o.p. (ISBN 0-471-58451-7). Wiley.

McKenney, Kenneth. Fire Cloud. 1980. pap. 2.50 (ISBN 0-380-50054-X, 50054). Avon.

McKenney, Mary. Divorce: A Selected Annotated Bibliography. LC 74-22423. 1974. 10.00 (ISBN 0-8108-0777-7). Scarecrow.

McKenney, Thomas L. Memoirs, Official & Personal. LC 72-94789. xxvii, 340p. 1973. pap. 3.95 (ISBN 0-8032-5776-7, BB 565, Bison). U of Nebr Pr.

McKenny, Margaret. The Savory Wild Mushroom. rev. ed. Stuntz, Daniel E., ed. LC 78-160288. (Illus.). 296p. 1971. 15.95 (ISBN 0-295-95155-9); pap. 8.95 (ISBN 0-295-95156-7). U of Wash Pr.

MacKenzie. District Heating Thermal Generation & Distribution. 1979. text ed. 37.00 (ISBN 0-08-022711-2). Pergamon.

MacKenzie, Alastair, jt. auth. see Benson, Jeffrey.

MacKenzie, Alec & Waldo, Kay C. About Time! A Woman's Guide to Time Management. (McGraw-Hill Paperback Ser.). 224p. (Orig.). 1981. pap. price not set (ISBN 0-07-044651-2, GB). McGraw.

MacKenzie, Alex, jt. auth. see Engstrom, Ted W.

Mackenzie, Alexander. Mackenzie's Rock. 31p. Repr. of 1905 ed. pap. 2.50 (ISBN 0-8466-0048-X, SJS48). Shorey.

MacKenzie, Andrew. Riddle of the Future. (RL 10). 1978. pap. 1.75 o.p. (ISBN 0-451-08096-3, E8096, Sig). NAL.

McKenzie, Arthur E. Physics. 4th ed. 1970. 17.95x (ISBN 0-521-07698-6). Cambridge U Pr.

McKenzie, Barbara. Flannery O'Connor's Georgia. LC 80-10936. (Illus.). 132p. 1980. 24.95 (ISBN 0-8203-0517-0); pap. 12.50 (ISBN 0-8203-0518-9). U of Ga Pr.

Mackenzie, Brian. Behaviorism & the Limits of Scientific Method. Mackay, D., ed. (International Library of Philosophy & Scientific Method Ser.). 1977. text ed. 13.00x (ISBN 0-391-00620-7). Humanities.

Mackenzie, Brian W. Canada's Competitive Positon in Copper & Zinc Markets. 60p. (Orig.). 1979. pap. text ed. 4.00x (ISBN 0-686-63143-9, Pub. by Ctr Resource Stud Canada). Renouf.

Mackenzie, Brian W. & Bolodeau, Michel L. Effects of Taxation on Base Metal Mining in Canada. 190p. (Orig.). 1979. pap. text ed. 9.50x (ISBN 0-88757-012-7, Pub. by Ctr Resource Stud Canada). Renouf.

Mackenzie, Brian W., jt. auth. see Downing, Donald O.

McKenzie, Bruce A. & Zachariah, Gerald. Understanding & Using Electricity. 2nd ed. 1981. text ed. 1.95x. Interstate.

McKenzie, Bruce A & Zachariah, Gerald. Understanding & Using Electricity. LC 75-18492. 1975. text ed. 1.95x o.p. (ISBN 0-8134-1754-6, 1754). Interstate.

MacKenzie, Charles A. Experimental Organic Chemistry. 4th ed. LC 70-138824. (Illus.). 1971. pap. text ed. 17.95 (ISBN 0-13-294785-4). P-H.

Mackenzie, Charles E. Coded-Character Sets: History & Development. LC 77-90165. (IBM Ser.). 1980. text ed. 21.95 (ISBN 0-201-14460-3). A-W.

Mackenzie, Colin. Maky a Slip. 9.50 (ISBN 0-392-07132-0, SpS). Soccer.

Mackenzie, Compton. Little Cat Lost. (Illus.). (gr. 2-5). 1966. 4.95g o.s.i. (ISBN 0-02-761990-7). Macmillan.

--My Life & Times. Incl. Octave 1, 1883-1891. 253p. 8.75x (ISBN 0-7011-0933-5); Octave 2, 1891-1900. 327p. 8.75x (ISBN 0-7011-0934-3); Octave 3, 1900-1907. 294p. o.p. (ISBN 0-7011-0935-1); Octave 4, 1907-1914. 268p. 8.75x (ISBN 0-7011-0936-X); Octave 5, 1915-1923. 269p. 8.75x (ISBN 0-7011-0937-8); Octave 6, 1923-1930. 269p. 8.75x (ISBN 0-7011-0938-6); Octave 7, 1931-1938. 320p. 10.50x (ISBN 0-7011-1302-2); Octave 8, 1939-1946. 319p. 11.25x (ISBN 0-7011-1425-8); Octave 9, 1946-1953. 325p. 11.25x (ISBN 0-7011-1577-7); Octave 10, 1953-1963. 208p. 11.50x (ISBN 0-7011-1703-6). LC 63-6236. (Illus.). 1963-71. Intl Pubns Serv.

McKenzie, D. F. Cambridge University Press, Sixteen Ninety-Six to Seventeen Twelve, 2 vols. Set. 150.00 (ISBN 0-521-05632-2). Cambridge U Pr.

Mackenzie, David. Goat Husbandry. 16.75 o.p. (ISBN 0-685-20587-8). Transatlantic.

--Goat Husbandry. 4th ed. Laing, Jean, ed. (Illus.). 375p. 1981. 23.00 (ISBN 0-571-18024-8, Pub. by Faber & Faber); pap. 9.95 (ISBN 0-571-11322-2). Merrimack Bk Serv.

McKenzie, David. Wolfhart Pannenberg & Religious Philosophy. LC 80-8171. 169p. 1980. lib. bdg. 17.50 (ISBN 0-8191-1314-X); pap. text ed. 9.00 (ISBN 0-8191-1315-8). U Pr of Amer.

MacKenzie, David & Curran, Michael. A History of Russia & the Soviet Union. 1977. 18.25x (ISBN 0-256-01934-7). Dorsey.

Mackenzie, David, ed. A Manual of Manuscript Transcription for the Dictionary of the Old Spanish Language. 2nd ed. (Illus.). 122p. 1981. pap. 15.00. Hispanic Seminary.

McKenzie, Dennis J. California Real Estate Principles. 416p. 1980. text ed. 13.95 (ISBN 0-471-06316-9). Wiley.

McKenzie, Dennis J. & Betts, Richard M. Essentials of Real Estate Economics. 2nd ed. (California Real Estate Ser.). 304p. 1980. text ed. 18.95 (ISBN 0-471-08334-8). Wiley.

McKenzie, Dennis J., et al. California Real Estate Principles. LC 80-23243. (California Real Estate Ser.). 352p. 1981. text ed. 17.95 (ISBN 0-471-01729-9). Wiley.

MacKenzie, Donald. Raven in Flight. 1981. pap. 1.95 (ISBN 0-425-04718-0). Berkley Pub.

--Raven Settles a Score. 1981. pap. 1.95 (ISBN 0-425-04717-2). Berkley Pub.

Mackenzie, Donald A. Migration of Symbols & Their Relations to Beliefs & Customs. LC 68-18029. 1968. Repr. of 1926 ed. 18.00 (ISBN 0-8103-3074-1). Gale.

MacKenzie, Douglas F. The Water Gators in Hell. 1977. 4.50 o.p. (ISBN 0-533-02936-8). Vantage.

McKenzie, Duncan. Training the Boy's Changing Voice. 1956. 10.00x (ISBN 0-8135-0249-7). Rutgers U Pr.

McKenzie, E. C. Mac's Giant Book of Quips & Quotes. 1980. 14.95 (ISBN 0-8010-6075-3). Baker Bk.

--Salted Peanuts: Eighteen Hundred Little Known Facts. (Direction Bks). 1976. pap. 3.95 large print ed. (ISBN 0-8010-5914-3); pap. 1.25 (ISBN 0-8010-5914-3). Baker Bk.

Mackenzie, Fraser, et al, eds. Studies in French Language Literature & History. 258p. 1980. Repr. of 1949 ed. lib. bdg. 50.00 (ISBN 0-89760-736-8). Telegraph Bks.

MacKenzie, Fred. The Men of Bastogne. 1978. pap. 1.95 (ISBN 0-441-52442-7). Charter Bks.

Mackenzie, Fred T., jt. auth. see Garrels, Robert M.

MacKenzie, G. The Aristocracy of Labor. LC 73-80484. (Studies in Sociology). (Illus.). 208p. 1973. pap. 9.95x (ISBN 0-521-09825-4). Cambridge U Pr.

Mackenzie, G. Calvin. The Politics of Presidential Appointments. LC 80-1029. (Illus.). 1980. 19.95 (ISBN 0-02-919670-1). Free Pr.

Mackenzie, Gavin. Class Theory & the Division of Labour. (Studies in Sociology). 1980. pap. write for info. (ISBN 0-391-01128-6). Humanities.

McKenzie, George A. & Gregory, Sadie. Company's Comin' (Cookbook) (Lucas Text Ser). text ed. 3.95x (ISBN 0-87543-088-0). Lucas.

Mackenzie, Gregor. Memoirs of a Ghillie. LC 78-52176. 1978. 16.95 (ISBN 0-7153-7584-9). David & Charles.

McKenzie, Heather, jt. auth. see Gray, Muir.

MacKenzie, Henry. Julia de Roubiggne, 2 vols. Paulson, Ronald, ed. LC 78-60840. (Novel 1720-1805 Ser.: Vol. 7). 1979. Set. lib. bdg. write for info. (ISBN 0-8240-3656-5); lib. bdg. 50.00 ea. Garland Pub.

--The Man of Feeling. LC 74-18367. (Novel in England, 1700-1775 Ser). 1974. Repr. of 1771 ed. lib. bdg. 50.00 (ISBN 0-8240-1196-1). Garland Pub.

--The Man of the World, 2 vols. in 1. LC 74-17142. (Novel in England, 1700-1775 Ser). 1974. Repr. of 1773 ed. lib. bdg. 50.00 (ISBN 0-8240-1202-X). Garland Pub.

McKenzie, Howard L. Mealybugs of California: With Taxonomy, Biology, & Control of North American Species. (Illus.). 1968. 57.50x (ISBN 0-520-00844-8). U of Cal Pr.

McKenzie, Hugh A., ed. Milk Proteins, Vols. 1-2. 1971. Vol. 1. 62.00 (ISBN 0-12-485201-7); Vol. 2. 63.00 (ISBN 0-12-485202-5); Set. 101.25 (ISBN 0-685-02414-8). Acad Pr.

Mackenzie, Ian. Collecting Old Toy Soldiers. 1975. 30.00 (ISBN 0-7134-3036-2). David & Charles.

Mackenzie, Ian C., et al, eds. Oral Premalignancy: Proceedings of the First Dows Symposium. LC 80-17988. (Illus.). 336p. 1980. text ed. 32.50x (ISBN 0-87745-103-6). U of Iowa Pr.

McKenzie, J., et al, eds. Interactive Computer Graphics in Science Teaching. LC 78-40598. (Computers & Their Applications Ser.). 1979. 29.95 (ISBN 0-470-26419-5). Halsted Pr.

McKenzie, J. Alexander. The Jordan Intercept. (Canaan Trilogy Ser.). 266p. (Orig.). 1980. pap. 2.95 (ISBN 0-87123-269-3, 200269). Bethany Fell.

--The Omega Document. LC 79-53442. (Canaan Trilogy Ser.). 1979. pap. 2.50 (ISBN 0-87123-416-5, 200416). Bethany Fell.

McKenzie, J. L., ed. New Testament for Spiritual Reading, 25 vols. Incl. Vol. 1. Gospel According to St. Matthew, Pt. 1 (ISBN 0-8164-1072-0); Vol. 2. Gospel According to St. Matthew, Pt. 2 (ISBN 0-8164-1073-9); Vol. 3. Gospel According to St. Mark, Pt. 1 (ISBN 0-8164-1074-7); Vol. 4. Gospel According to St. Mark, Pt. 2 (ISBN 0-8164-1075-5); Vol. 5. Gospel According to St. Luke, Pt. 1 (ISBN 0-8164-1076-3); Vol. 6. Gospel According to St. Luke, Pt. 2 (ISBN 0-8164-1077-1); Vol. 7. Gospel According to St. John, Pt. 1 (ISBN 0-8164-1078-X); Vol. 8. Gospel According to St. John, Pt. 2 (ISBN 0-8164-1079-8); Vol. 9. Gospel According to St. John, Pt. 3 (ISBN 0-8164-1080-1); Vol. 10. Acts of the Apostles, Pt. 1 (ISBN 0-8164-1081-X); Vol. 11. Acts of the Apostles, Pt. 2 (ISBN 0-8164-1082-8); Vol. 12. Epistle to the Romans (ISBN 0-8164-1083-6); Vol. 13. First Epistle to the Corinthians (ISBN 0-8164-1084-4); Vol. 14. Second Epistle to the Corinthians (ISBN 0-8164-1085-2); Vol. 15. Epistle to the Galatians **(ISBN 0-8164-1086-0); Vol. 16. Epistle to the Ephesians (ISBN 0-8164-1087-9); Vol. 17. Epistle to the Philippians. Epistle to the Colossians (ISBN 0-8164-1088-7); Vol. 18. First Epistle to the Thessalonians. Second Epistle to the Thessalonians (ISBN 0-8164-1089-5); Vol. 19. First Epistle to Timothy. Second Epistle to Timothy (ISBN 0-8164-1090-9); Vol. 20. Epistle to Titus. Epistle to Philemon (ISBN 0-8164-1091-7); Vol. 21. Epistle to the Hebrews. Epistle to James (ISBN 0-8164-1092-5); Vol. 22. First Epistle to Peter. Second Epistle to Peter (ISBN 0-8164-1093-3); Vol. 23. Epistle to Jude. Three Epistles of John (ISBN 0-8164-1094-1); Vol. 24. The Revelation of St. John, Pt. 1 (ISBN 0-8164-1095-X); Vol. 25. The Revelation of St. John, Pt. 2 (ISBN 0-8164-1096-8). 6.00 ea; Set. 119.00 (ISBN 0-686-57583-0). Crossroad NY.**

Mackenzie, James, jt. ed. see Mitchell, Rose G.

McKenzie, John G. Nervous Disorders & Religion: A Study of Souls in the Making. LC 79-8719. 183p. 1981. Repr. of 1951 ed. lib. bdg. 18.75x (ISBN 0-313-22192-8, MCND). Greenwood.

McKenzie, John L. Light on the Epistles: A Reader's Guide. 204p. 1975. 12.95 (ISBN 0-88347-057-8). Thomas More.

--Light on the Gospels. 216p. 1976. 12.95 (ISBN 0-88347-065-9). Thomas More.

--The New Testament Without Illusion. 1980. 11.95 (ISBN 0-88347-109-4). Thomas More.

--The Old Testament Without Illusion. 1979. 11.95 o.p. (ISBN 0-88347-098-5). Thomas More.

--The Power & the Wisdom: An Interpretation of the New Testament. 320p. 1972. pap. 2.45 (ISBN 0-385-08082-4, Im). Doubleday.

--Roman Catholic Church. 1971. pap. 3.95 (ISBN 0-385-02944-6, Im). Doubleday.

--Two-Edged Sword: An Interpretation of the Old Testament. pap. 2.45 (ISBN 0-385-06969-3, D215, Im). Doubleday.

McKenzie, John L., jt. auth. see Wylie, Samuel.

MacKenzie, Joy, jt. auth. see Forte, Imogene.

Mackenzie, Kenneth D. Organizational Structures. LC 77-86209. (Organizational Behavior Ser.). 1978. pap. text ed. 9.95x (ISBN 0-88295-452-0). AHM Pub.

MacKenzie, Kenneth D., ed. see Jabes, Jak.

Mackenzie, Kenneth D., ed. see Kiesler, Sara B.

Mackenzie, Kenneth D., ed. see Pfeffer, Jeffrey.

Mackenzie, Kenneth D., ed. see Simmons, Richard E.

Mackenzie, Kenneth D., ed. see Tuggle, Francis D.

Mackenzie, Lachlan. The Happy Man. 1979. 8.95 (ISBN 0-85151-282-8). Banner of Truth.

McKenzie, Leon. Adult Education & the Burden of the Future. LC 78-50845. 1978. pap. text ed. 7.50 (ISBN 0-8191-0470-1). U Pr of Amer.

MacKenzie, M., ed. The Letters of Sidney & Beatrice Webb. Incl. Vol. 1.; Vol. 2. (ISBN 0-685-85982-7); Vol. 3.. LC 77-1665. 1978. 69.95 ea.; Set. 185.00 (ISBN 0-521-22015-7). Cambridge U Pr.

MacKenzie, Manfred. Communities of Honor & Love in Henry James. 292p. 1976. 12.50x (ISBN 0-674-15160-7). Harvard U Pr.

Mackenzie, Mary M. Plato on Punishment. 272p. 1981. 22.50x (ISBN 0-520-04169-0). U of Cal Pr.

MacKenzie, Norman. Dreams & Dreaming. LC 65-26071. (Illus.). 1965. 15.00 (ISBN 0-8149-0151-4). Vanguard.

McKenzie, Peter. Focalguide to Travel Photography. LC 80-41482. (Focalguide Ser.). (Illus.). 136p. 1981. pap. 7.95 (ISBN 0-240-51072-0). Focal Pr.

McKenzie, R. A., jt. tr. see Engstrom, Ted W.

Mackenzie, R. Alec. The Time Trap. LC 72-82874. 208p. 1972. 11.95 (ISBN 0-8144-5308-2). Am Mgmt.

MacKenzie, R. C. Differential Thermal Analysis, Vol. 1: Fundamental Aspects. 1970. 99.00 (ISBN 0-12-464401-5). Acad Pr.

McKenzie, Richard B. & Tullock, Gordon. The New World of Economics: Explorations into the Human Experience. rev. ed. 1978. pap. text ed. 9.95 (ISBN 0-256-02029-9). Irwin.

McKenzie, Richared B. Restrictions on Business Mobility: Political Rhetoric & Economic Reality. 1979. pap. 4.25 (ISBN 0-8447-3338-5). Am Enterprise.

Mackenzie, Robert. John Brown of Haddington. 1964. pap. 2.25 (ISBN 0-686-12523-1). Banner of Truth.

MacKenzie, Robin, ed. Auditorium Acoustics. LC 75-16445. 231p. 1975. 42.95 (ISBN 0-470-56284-6). Halsted Pr.

MacKenzie, Susan T. Group Legal Services. (Key Issues Ser.: No. 18). 1975. pap. 3.00 (ISBN 0-87546-231-6). NY Sch Indus Rel.

--Noise & Office Work. (Key Issues Ser.: No. 19). 1975. pap. 3.00 (ISBN 0-87546-232-4). NY Sch Indus Rel.

Mackenzie, Toni. A Small Place in the Country. 240p. 1980. pap. 6.95 (ISBN 0-00-216408-6, Pub. by W Collins Australia). Intl Schol Bk Serv.

MacKenzie, Virginia. The Wind in the Leaves. 89p. 1980. 5.95 (ISBN 0-8059-2743-3). Dorrance.

Mackenzie, W. J. Biological Ideas in Politics: An Essay in Political Adaptivity. LC 78-20278. 1979. 10.95x (ISBN 0-312-07869-2). St Martin.

Mackenzie, W. J. M. Explorations in Government: Collected Papers 1951-1968. LC 74-6722. 1975. 24.95 (ISBN 0-470-56285-4). Halsted Pr.

Mackenzie, W. Mackay, ed. see Dunbar, William.

Mackenzie, W. S. & Guilford, C. Atlas of Rock-Forming Minerals in Thin Section. 98p. 1980. pap. 22.50x (ISBN 0-470-26921-9). Halsted Pr.

Mackenzie, W. S., ed. The Feldspars. LC 73-87831. 700p. 1974. 59.50x (ISBN 0-8448-0251-4). Crane-Russak Co.

Mackenzie-Grieve, Averil. Clara Novello. (Music Reprint Ser.). 1980. Repr. of 1955 ed. lib. bdg. 29.50 (ISBN 0-306-76009-6). Da Capo.

--Last Years of the English Slave Trade. LC 68-21439. (Illus.). Repr. of 1941 ed. 25.00 (ISBN 0-678-05070-8). Kelley.

McKenzie-Paige. Astrology for the Working Girl. 1980. pap. 1.75 (ISBN 0-505-51467-2). Tower Bks.

McKeon, R., ed. Selections from Medieval Philosophers, 2 vols. 1971. pap. 2.95 ea. (ScribT). Vol. 1, O.p (ISBN 0-684-12552-8, SL309, ScribT). Vol. 2 (ISBN 0-684-12553-6, SL310). Scribner.

McKeone, Dermot. Small Computers for Business & Industry. 1979. text ed. 32.50x (ISBN 0-566-02096-3, Pub. by Gower Pub Co Englad). Renouf.

McKeown, Beverly. Guitar Songbook with Instructions. 1975. pap. text ed. 9.95 (ISBN 0-395-18648-X). HM.

McKeown, James M. & McKeown, Joan C. Price Guide to Antique & Classic Still Cameras 1981-1982. LC 81-65028. (Illus.). 176p. 1981. pap. 12.95 (ISBN 0-931838-01-0). Centennial Photo Serv.

McKeown, Joan C., jt. auth. see McKeown, James M.

McKeown, Martha F. Them Was the Days: An American Saga of the '70's. LC 50-7450. (Illus.). 1961. pap. 2.95 (ISBN 0-8032-5131-9, BB 117, Bison). U of Nebr Pr.

McKeown, Milfred R. A Practicebook for Aphasics. (Illus.). 236p. 1976. pap. 19.75 (ISBN 0-398-03484-2). C C Thomas.

McKeown, Pamela. Reading: A Basic Guide for Parents & Teachers. 170p. 1974. 16.00x (ISBN 0-7100-7418-2); pap. 4.95 (ISBN 0-7100-7424-7). Routledge & Kegan.

McKeown, Thomas & Lowe, C. R. An Introduction to Social Medicine. 2nd ed. (Illus.). 356p. 1974. 20.00 (ISBN 0-397-60221-9, Dist. by Mosby). Lippincott.

Mackerle, J. Air-Cooled Automotive Engines. 518p. 1972. 59.00x (ISBN 0-85264-205-9, Pub. by Griffin England). State Mutual Bk.

McKern, Sharon. Redneck Mothers, Good Ol' Girls & Other Southern Belles. 1979. 10.95 o.p. (ISBN 0-670-59249-8). Viking Pr.

McKern, Sharon S. & McKern, Thomas W. Living Prehistory: An Introduction to Physical Anthropology & Archaeology. LC 73-90645. 1974. pap. 10.95 (ISBN 0-8465-3753-2). Benjamin-Cummings.

McKern, Thomas W., jt. auth. see McKern, Sharon S.

Mackerness, E. D., ed. see Sturt, George.

McKerns, Kenneth W., jt. ed. see Jutisz, Marian.

Mackerras, Colin P. Rise of the Peking Opera 1770-1870: Social Aspects of the Theatre in Manchu China. (Illus.). 290p. 1972. 34.95x (ISBN 0-19-815137-3). Oxford U Pr.

McKerrow, R. B. Prolegomena for the Oxford Shakespeare: A Study in Editorial Method. 1939. 5.00x o.p. (ISBN 0-19-811685-3). Oxford U Pr.

McKerrow, Ray, jt. auth. see Allen, Ronald R.

McKerrow, Ronald B. Introduction to Bibliography for Literary Students. (Illus.). 1927. 24.95x (ISBN 0-19-818103-5). Oxford U Pr.

McKetta, John J., Jr., intro. by. Chemical Technology: An Encyclopedic Treatment, 7 vols. Incl. Vol. 1. Air, Water, Inorganic Chemicals & Nucleonics. 1968. o.p. (ISBN 0-06-491102-0); Vol. 2. Non-Metallic Ores, Silicate Industries & Solid Minerals Fuels. 1971 (ISBN 0-06-491103-9); Vol. 3. Metals & Ores. 1970 (ISBN 0-06-491104-7); Vol. 4. Petroleum & Organic Chemicals. 1972 (ISBN 0-06-491105-5); Vol. 5. Natural Organic Materials & Related Synthetic Products. 1972 (ISBN 0-06-491106-3); Vol. 6. Wood, Paper, Textiles, Plastics & Photographic Materials. 1973 (ISBN 0-06-491107-1); Vol. 7. Vegetable Food Products & Luxuries. 1975 (ISBN 0-06-491108-X); Vol. 8. Edible Oils & Fats & Animal Food Products. 1975 (ISBN 0-06-491109-8). (Illus.). 40.00x ea. B&N.

Mackevich, Gene. The Woman's Money Book. 224p. 1981. pap. 2.95 (ISBN 0-553-14711-0). Bantam.

Mackey, Carol, jt. auth. see Moseley, Michael E.

Mackey, David. Multiple Family Housing. Date not set. 32.50 (ISBN 0-8038-0164-5). Hastings.

Mackey, Howard. Wit & Whiggery: The Rev. Sydney Smith (1771-1845) LC 79-64194. 1979. pap. text ed. 16.25 (ISBN 0-8191-0756-5). U Pr of Amer.

Mackey, James P. Jesus, the Man & the Myth. LC 78-61627. 1979. pap. 8.95 (ISBN 0-8091-2169-7). Paulist Pr.

Mackey, Louis. Kierkegaard: A Kind of Poet. LC 75-157050. (Orig.). 1971. 15.00x (ISBN 0-8122-7641-8); pap. 5.95x (ISBN 0-8122-1042-5). U of Pa Pr.

Mackey, Margaret G. & Sooy, Louise P. Early California Costumes: 1769-1850. (Illus.). 1932. 9.50x (ISBN 0-8047-0994-7). Stanford U Pr.

Mackey, Mary S. & Mackey, Maryette G., eds. The Pronunciation of Ten Thousand Proper Names. 1979. Repr. of 1922 ed. 34.00 (ISBN 0-8103-4137-9). Gale.

Mackey, Maryette G., jt. ed. see Mackey, Mary S.

Mackey, Richard T. Bowling. 2nd ed. LC 74-75228. (Illus.). 71p. 1974. pap. 4.95 o.p. (ISBN 0-87484-305-7). Mayfield Pub.

--Bowling. 3rd, rev. ed. LC 80-82563. 89p. 1980. pap. text ed. 4.95 (ISBN 0-87484-513-0). Mayfield Pub.

Mackey, Sandra. Better Than Gold & Silver. 1975. pap. 3.75 (ISBN 0-89137-407-8). Quality Pubns.

McKibben, Jorge F., tr. see Davis, Guillermo H.

McKibben-Stockwell. Nuevo Lexico Griego Espanol. 1978. pap. 7.95 (ISBN 0-311-42058-3, Edit Mundo). Casa Bautista.

Mackichan, Kenneth A., jt. auth. see Hammer, Mark J.

Mackie, Andrew. A Practical Manual in Urban Design. Date not set. 30.01 (ISBN 0-08-023362-7); pap. 15.01 (ISBN 0-08-023361-9). Pergamon.

Mackie, Carey T., et al. Crescent City Silver. (Illus.). vi, 130p. 1980. pap. 15.00x (ISBN 0-917860-05-5). Historic New Orleans.

McKie, Christine, jt. auth. see McKie, Duncan.

McKie, Duncan & McKie, Christine. Crystalline Solids. LC 73-34. 628p. 1974. text ed. 24.95 (ISBN 0-470-58455-6). Halsted Pr.

Mackie, Dustin & Decker, Douglas. A Guide to Group & IPA HMO's. 250p. 1981. text ed. price not set (ISBN 0-89443-341-5). Aspen Systems.

MacKie, Euan. Scotland: An Archaeological Guide. LC 74-32286. (Illus.). 1975. 15.00 o.p. (ISBN 0-8155-5034-0, NP). Noyes.

Mackie, Euan W. Scotland: An Archaeological Guide. (Illus., Orig.). 1975. pap. 7.95 o.p. (ISBN 0-571-10735-4, Pub. by Faber & Faber). Merrimack Bk Serv.

Mackie, J. A. Konfrontasi: The Indonesia-Malaysia Dispute 1963-1966. (Illus.). 384p. 1974. 34.50x (ISBN 0-19-638247-5). Oxford U Pr.

Mackie, J. A., ed. The Chinese in Indonesia. LC 76-139. 296p. 1976. text ed. 12.00x (ISBN 0-8248-0449-X). U Pr of Hawaii.

Mackie, J. L. Ethics: Inventing Right & Wrong. 1977. pap. 2.50 (ISBN 0-14-021957-9, Pelican). Penguin.

--Truth, Probability, & Paradox: Studies in Philosophical Logic. (Clarendon Library of Logic & Philosophy Ser). (Illus.). 320p. 1973. 32.00x (ISBN 0-19-824402-9). Oxford U Pr.

Mackie, James. Mountains & the Woman. 31p. (Orig.). 1980. pap. 3.00x (ISBN 0-88235-038-2). San Marcos.

McKie, James D., ed. Social Responsibility & the Business Predicament. (Studies in the Regulation of Economic Activity). 361p. 1975. 15.95 (ISBN 0-8157-5608-9); pap. 6.95 (ISBN 0-8157-5607-0). Brookings.

Mackie, John D. Earlier Tudors, 1485-1558. (Oxford History of England Ser.). (Illus.). 1952. 34.00x (ISBN 0-19-821706-4). Oxford U Pr.

Mackie, Mary. Light in the Valley: No. 1. (Starlight Romances Ser.). 144p. 1981. pap. 1.75 (ISBN 0-553-14366-2). Bantam.

--Pamela, No. 3. (Starlight Romance Ser.). 144p. 1981. pap. cancelled (ISBN 0-553-14365-4). Bantam.

Mackie, R. K., et al. Mathematical Methods for Chemists. LC 72-4758. (Illus.). 154p. 1972. text ed. 13.95 (ISBN 0-470-56295-1). Halsted Pr.

Mackie, Robert L., ed. Book of Scottish Verse. (World's Classics Ser.). 1934. 7.95 (ISBN 0-19-250897-0). Oxford U Pr.

Mackie, Romaine. Special Education in the United States: Statistics 1948-1966. LC 69-18776. 1969. pap. 4.25x (ISBN 0-8077-1721-5). Tchrs Coll.

McKie, Ronald. The Crushing. LC 78-21981. 1979. 8.95 o.p. (ISBN 0-684-15919-8, ScribT). Scribner.

McKie, Roy. The Riddle Book. LC 77-85237. (Picturebacks Ser.). (ps-2). 1978. PLB 4.99 (ISBN 0-394-93732-5, BYR); pap. 1.25 (ISBN 0-394-83732-0). Random.

McKie, Roy, jt. auth. see Beard, Henry.

Mackie, Thomas T. & Rose, Richard. International Almanac of Electoral History. LC 74-11577. 1974. 19.95 (ISBN 0-02-919640-X). Free Pr.

McKillip, Patricia. Harpist in the Wind. LC 78-11410. (Illus.). (gr. 6 up). 1979. 8.95 (ISBN 0-689-30687-3, Argo). Atheneum.

--Heir of Sea & Fire. 1978. pap. 2.25 (ISBN 0-345-28882-3, Del Rey Bks). Ballantine.

McKillip, Patricia A. The Throme of the Erril of Sherill. LC 73-76324. (Illus.). 80p. (gr. 5 up). 1973. 4.95 o.p. (ISBN 0-689-30115-4). Atheneum.

McKillop, Alan D. English Literature from Dryden to Burns. (Illus.). 1948. 34.00x (ISBN 0-89197-145-9). Irvington.

McKillop, Allan A., et al see Heat Transfer & Fluid Mechanics Institute.

McKillop, Susan R. Franciabigio. (California Studies in the History of Art). (Illus.). 1974. 60.00x (ISBN 0-520-01688-2). U of Cal Pr.

McKim, Audrey & McKim, Dodie. Read-a-Riddle, Pick-a-Joke. (Illus.). (gr. 2-3). 1975. pap. 1.25 (ISBN 0-590-09877-2, Schol Pap). Schol Bk Serv.

McKim, Dodie, jt. auth. see McKim, Audrey.

McKim, Robert H. Experiences in Visual Thinking. 2nd ed. LC 80-437. (Orig.). 1980. pap. text ed. 12.95 (ISBN 0-8185-0411-0). Brooks-Cole.

--Thinking Visually: A Strategy Manual for Problem-Solving. rev. ed. LC 80-16526. 1980. text ed. 24.95 (ISBN 0-534-97984-X); pap. text ed. 14.95 (ISBN 0-534-97978-5). Lifetime Learn.

Mackin, Ronald. A Short Course in Spoken English. 1975. pap. 4.95 (ISBN 0-87789-137-0); cassettes 50.00 (ISBN 0-87789-140-0). Eng Language.

Mackin, Ronald & Evans, Marcia. A Short Course in Spoken English. 150p. 1975. pap. text ed. 4.95x (ISBN 0-19-453062-0). Oxford U Pr.

Mackin, Ronald & Seidl, Jennifer. Exercises in English Patterns & Usage. 2nd ed. 1979. pap. text ed. 6.95x (ISBN 0-19-432717-5). Oxford U Pr.

Mackin, Ronald, jt. auth. see Hawkins, William F.

McKinlay, A. F. Thermoluminescence Dosimetry. (Medical Physics Handbook: No. 5). 180p. write for info. (ISBN 0-9960020-4-9, Pub. by a Hilger England). Heyden.

McKinlay, Ian, jt. ed. see Gordon, Neil.

McKinley, Albert E., ed. see Jameson, J. Franklin.

McKinley, Brett, jt. auth. see Denver, Shad.

McKinley, Charles & Frase, Robert W. Launching Social Security: A Capture & Record Account, 1935-1937. LC 70-121771. 1970. 35.00 (ISBN 0-299-05800-X). U of Wis Pr.

McKinley, Daniel, jt. ed. see Shepard, Paul.

McKinley, James L., jt. auth. see Bent, Ralph D.

McKinley, John. Group Development Through Participation Training. LC 78-71870. 128p. (Orig.). 1980. pap. text ed. 9.95 (ISBN 0-8091-2247-2); participant's bk. 2.50 (ISBN 0-8091-2299-5). Paulist Pr.

Mackinley, Malcolm S. Garcia the Centenarian & His Times. LC 75-40206. (Music Reprint Ser.). 1975. Repr. of 1908 ed. lib. bdg. 29.50 (ISBN 0-306-70671-7). Da Capo.

McKinley, Mary B. Words in a Corner: Studies in Montaigne's Latin Quotations. (French Forum Monograraphs: No. 26). 120p. (Orig.). 1981. pap. 9.50 (ISBN 0-917058-25-9). French Forum.

McKinley, Mary B., jt. ed. see Frame, Donald M.

McKinley, Norma A. The Rediscovery of Christ. (Illus.). 1980. deluxe ed. 49.75 (ISBN 0-89266-224-7). Am Classical Coll Pr.

McKinley, Robin. The Door in the Hedge. LC 80-21903. 224p. (gr. 7 up). 1981. 8.95 (ISBN 0-688-00312-5). Greenwillow.

McKinley, Ruth. Inquiry & Inspiration. LC 79-54824. (Orig.). Date not set. pap. cancelled (ISBN 0-89793-021-5). Hunter Hse.

McKinley, William L. Karluk: The Great Untold Story of Arctic Exploration. (RL 10). 1978. pap. 1.95 o.p. (ISBN 0-451-08074-2, J8074, Sig). NAL.

McKinnell, R. G., ed. Differentiation & Neoplasia. (Results & Problems in Cell Differentiation: Vol. 11). (Illus.). 350p. 1980. 76.20 (ISBN 0-387-10177-2). Springer-Verlag.

McKinnell, Robert C. Cloning: A Biologist Reports. LC 79-10569. (Illus.). 1979. 8.95 (ISBN 0-8166-0883-0). U of Minn Pr.

McKinney, Douglas. Sam Peckinpah. (Theatrical Arts Ser.). 1979. lib. bdg. 10.95 (ISBN 0-8057-9264-3). Twayne.

McKinney, James D. Environmental Health Chemistry: The Chemistry of Environmental Agents As Potential Human Hazards. LC 80-65510. (Illus.). 656p. 1981. 47.50 (ISBN 0-250-40352-8). Ann Arbor Science.

McKinney, John. A Day Hiker's Guide to Southern California. 160p. (Orig.). 1981. pap. 8.85 (ISBN 0-88496-163-X). Capra Pr.

McKinney, John C. Constructive Typology & Social Theory. LC 66-25454. (Century Sociology Ser.). 1966. 20.00x (ISBN 0-89197-105-X); pap. text ed. 6.95x (ISBN 0-89197-106-8). Irvington.

McKinney, John P., jt. ed. see Fitzgerald, Hiram E.

McKinney, John P., et al. Developmental Psychology: The Adolescent & Young Adult. 1977. pap. 8.95x (ISBN 0-256-01940-1). Dorsey.

McKinney, Millard G., jt. auth. see Metz, Leon C.

McKinney, Peter & Cunningham, Bruce L. Handbook of Plastic Surgery. (Illus.). 150p. 1981. price not set softcover (ISBN 0-683-05865-7). Williams & Wilkins.

McKinney, Roland J. Famous French Painters. LC 60-9152. (Illus.). (gr. 7-9). 1960. 5.95 (ISBN 0-396-04360-7). Dodd.

McKinney, W. A., ed. Creation, Christ & Culture: Studies in Honor of T. F. Torrance. 336p. Repr. of 1976 ed. text ed. 17.95x (ISBN 0-567-01019-8). Attic Pr.

McKinnon, Alastair. Falsification & Belief. 1979. lib. bdg. 21.00 (ISBN 0-917930-33-9); pap. text ed. 5.50x (ISBN 0-917930-13-4). Ridgeview.

MacKinnon, Charles. The Matriarch. 312p. 1975. 8.95 o.p. (ISBN 0-440-05459-1). Delacorte.

--Mereford Tapestry. 480p. 1974. 8.95 o.p. (ISBN 0-440-05589-X). Delacorte.

MacKinnon, D. M. The Problem of Metaphysics. LC 73-79309. 180p. 1974. 23.50 (ISBN 0-521-20275-2). Cambridge U Pr.

MacKinnon, Frank. The Government of Prince Edward Island. LC 53-2186. 1974. 28.50x o.p. (ISBN 0-8020-7038-8). U of Toronto Pr.

Mackinnon, G. E., jt. ed. see Waller, T. G.

MacKinnon, Jack. The Andes. (The World's Wild Places Ser.). (Illus.). 1976. 12.95 (ISBN 0-8094-2050-3). Time-Life.

Mackinnon, Joan. A Checklist of Toronto Cabinet & Chair Makers, 1800 to 1865. (Illus.). 202p. 1975. pap. text ed. 3.95x (ISBN 0-660-00111-X, 56305-7, Pub. by Natl Mus Canada). U of Chicago Pr.

MacKinnon, John. Borneo. (The World's Wild Places Ser.). (Illus.). 184p. 1975. 12.95 (ISBN 0-8094-2018-X). Time-Life.

--Borneo. (The World's Wild Places Ser.). (Illus.). 1978. lib. bdg. 11.97 (ISBN 0-686-51017-8). Silver.

--In Search of the Red Ape. new ed. LC 73-15457. (Illus.). 256p. 1974. 8.95 o.p. (ISBN 0-03-012496-4). HR&W.

--In Search of the Red Ape. 248p. 1975. pap. 1.95 o.p. (ISBN 0-345-24525-3). Ballantine.

McKinnon, Karen. Spiralings: A Journal into Poems. (Illus.). 48p. (Orig.). 1980. pap. 5.00 (ISBN 0-88235-041-2). San Marcos.

MacKinnon, L. Mechanics & Motion. (Oxford Physics Ser.). (Illus.). 1978. 23.50x (ISBN 0-19-851825-0); pap. 9.95x (ISBN 0-19-851843-9). Oxford U Pr.

Mackinnon, Lillias. Music by Heart. LC 80-26551. xi, 141p. 1981. Repr. of 1954 ed. lib. bdg. 17.50x (ISBN 0-313-22810-8, MAMB). Greenwood.

McKinnon, Ronald I. Money & Capital in Economic Development. 1973. 11.95 (ISBN 0-8157-5614-3); pap. 4.95 (ISBN 0-8157-5613-5). Brookings.

--Money in International Exchange: The Convertible Currency System. 1979. text ed. 13.95x (ISBN 0-19-502408-7); pap. text ed. 7.95x (ISBN 0-19-502409-5). Oxford U Pr.

MacKinnon, Stephen R. Power & Politics in Late Imperial China: Yuan Shi-kai in Beijing & Tianjin, 1901-1908. (Center for Chinese Studies Ser.). (Illus.). 400p. 1981. 18.50x (ISBN 0-520-04025-2). U of Cal Pr.

MacKinnon, William A. On the Rise, Progress & Present State of Public Opinion, in Great Britain & Other Parts of the World. 343p. 1971. Repr. of 1828 ed. 30.00x (ISBN 0-686-28332-5, Pub. by Irish Academic Pr). Biblio Dist.

Mackintosh, A. Symbolism & Art Nouveau. LC 77-76764. (Modern Movements in Art Ser.). 1978. pap. 1.95 (ISBN 0-8120-0882-0). Barron.

Mackintosh, C. H. Genesis to Deuteronomy: Notes on the Pentateuch, 6 vols. in 1. LC 72-75082. 928p. 1972. 15.95 (ISBN 0-87213-617-5). Loizeaux.

Mackintosh, Douglas R. The Economics of Airborne Emissions. LC 72-89646. (Special Studies in U. S. Economic, Social & Political Issues). 1973. 29.50x (ISBN 0-275-28668-1); pap. text ed. 12.95x (ISBN 0-8290-0139-5). Irvington.

--Systems of Health Care. LC 78-3134. (Illus.). 1978. lib. bdg. 27.50x (ISBN 0-89158-330-0); pap. text ed. 13.50x (ISBN 0-89158-818-3). Westview.

Mackintosh, Helen K., ed. Language Arts for Today's Children. LC 54-8794. 1954. 20.00x (ISBN 0-89197-264-1). Irvington.

Mackintosh, John, ed. People & Parliament. LC 78-60433. 1978. 22.95 (ISBN 0-03-046231-2). Praeger.

Mackintosh, John J., ed. British Prime Ministers in the Twentieth Century, Vol. 1. LC 77-76542. 1977. 19.95x (ISBN 0-312-10517-7). St Martin.

Mackintosh, John P. Government & Politics of Britain. 4th rev. ed. 1977. pap. text ed. 8.50x (ISBN 0-09-118481-9, Hutchinson U Lib). Humanities.

Mackintosh, John P., ed. British Prime Ministers in the Twentieth Century, Vol. 2. LC 77-76542. 1978. 19.95 (ISBN 0-312-10518-5). St Martin.

Mackintosh, May. Highland Fling. 1975. 7.95 o.p. (ISBN 0-440-04564-9). Delacorte.

Mackintosh, Prudence. Thundering Sneakers. LC 80-1124. 192p. 1981. 9.95 (ISBN 0-385-12879-7). Doubleday.

McKisack, M., ed. see Clarke, Maude V.

McKisack, May. Fourteenth Century, 1307-1399. (Oxford History of England Ser.). 1959. 34.00x (ISBN 0-19-821712-9). Oxford U Pr.

McKitrick, Eric L. Andrew Johnson & Reconstruction. LC 60-5467. 1964. pap. 12.00x (ISBN 0-226-56046-5). U of Chicago Pr.

McKitrick, M. O., jt. auth. see Idleman, H. K.

McKitterick, D., ed. Stanley Morison: Selected Essays, 2 vols. LC 78-54718. (Illus.). 250p. Date not set. Set. 275.00 (ISBN 0-521-22338-5). Vol. 1 (ISBN 0-521-22456-X). Vol. 2 (ISBN 0-521-22457-8). Cambridge U Pr.
McKitterick, Nathaniel & Middleton, Jenkins B. The Bankers of the Rich & the Bankers of the Poor: The Role of Export Credit in Development Finance. LC 72-76253. (Monographs: No. 6). 70p. 1972. 2.00 (ISBN 0-686-28689-8). Overseas Dev Council.
Mackle, M. Computers in Business. 2nd ed. 80p. 1970. text ed. 3.40 (ISBN 0-7715-0724-0). Forkner.
Mackler, Bernard. Philippe Pinel, Unchainer of the Insane. LC 68-11330. (Biography Ser). (gr. 7 up). 1969. PLB 6.90 (ISBN 0-531-00915-7). Watts.
Macklin, June, jt. auth. see West, Stanley A.
McKlveen, John W. Fast Neutron Activation Analysis: Elemental Data Base. 306p. 1981. text ed. 39.95 (ISBN 0-250-40406-0). Ann Arbor Science.
Mackmin, David, jt. auth. see Baum, Andrew.
Mackmurdo, A. H., ed. Letters (Selwyn Image Letters) LC 76-17780. (Aesthetic Movement & the Arts & Crafts Movement Ser.: Vol. 37). 1977. Repr. of 1932 ed. lib. bdg. 44.00 (ISBN 0-8240-2486-9). Garland Pub.
Macknight, Anthony D. & Leader, John P., eds. Epithelial Ion & Water Transport. 380p. 1981. 35.00 (ISBN 0-89004-537-2). Raven.
McKnight, Brian E. The Quality of Mercy: Amnesties & Traditional Chinese Justice. LC 80-26650. 224p. 1981. pap. 15.00x (ISBN 0-8248-0736-7). U Pr of Hawaii.
McKnight, George H. Middle English Humorous Tales in Verse. LC 78-128190. 1971. Repr. of 1913 ed. text ed. 7.50 (ISBN 0-87752-131-X). Gordian.
McKnight Staff. Exploring Careers in Child Care. LC 74-82448. (gr. 8-12). 1974. text ed. 14.64 (ISBN 0-87345-573-8); teacher's guide 30.00 (ISBN 0-87345-576-2); activity manual 5.00 (ISBN 0-87345-574-6). McKnight.
--Exploring Careers in Hospitality & Food Service. LC 75-18678. (gr. 8-12). 1975. text ed. 16.64 (ISBN 0-87345-605-X); teacher's guide 30.00 (ISBN 0-87345-606-8). McKnight.
--Exploring Fabrics. LC 76-53072. (gr. 7-12). 1977. text ed. 14.64 (ISBN 0-87345-613-0); tchr's ed. 34.67 (ISBN 0-87345-615-7). McKnight.
--Exploring Living Environments. LC 77-82245. (gr. 7-12). 1977. text ed. 14.64 (ISBN 0-87345-619-X); tchr's ed. 34.67 (ISBN 0-87345-620-3). McKnight.
McKnight Staff Members & Miller, Wilbur R. Electricity. LC 78-53389. (Basic Industrial Arts Ser.). (Illus.). 1978. 6.00 (ISBN 0-87345-794-3); softbound 4.48 (ISBN 0-87345-786-2). McKnight.
--Graphic Arts. LC 78-53390. (Basic Industrial Arts Ser.). (Illus.). 1978. 6.00 (ISBN 0-87345-795-1); softbound 4.48 (ISBN 0-87345-787-0). McKnight.
--Metalworking. LC 78-53387. (Basic Industrial Arts Ser.). (Illus.). 1978. 6.00 (ISBN 0-87345-792-7); softbound 4.48 (ISBN 0-87345-784-6). McKnight.
--Photography. LC 78-53393. (Basic Industrial Arts Ser.). (Illus.). 1978. 6.00 (ISBN 0-87345-797-8); softbound 4.48 (ISBN 0-87345-789-7). McKnight.
--Plastics. LC 78-53391. (Basic Industrial Arts Ser.). (Illus.). 1978. 6.00 (ISBN 0-87345-796-X); softbound 4.48 (ISBN 0-87345-788-9). McKnight.
--Power Mechanics. LC 78-53394. (Basic Industrial Arts Ser.). (Illus.). 1978. 6.00 (ISBN 0-87345-798-6); softbound 4.48 (ISBN 0-87345-790-0). McKnight.
--Woodworking. LC 78-53386. (Basic Industrial Arts Ser.). (Illus.). 1978. 6.00 (ISBN 0-87345-791-9); softbound 4.48 (ISBN 0-87345-783-8). McKnight.
McKnight, Tom. Feral Livestock in Anglo-America. (Publications in Geography Ser.: Vol. 16). 1964. pap. 6.50x (ISBN 0-520-09146-9). U of Cal Pr.
McKnight, Tom L. Friendly Vermin: A Survey of Feral Livestock in Australia. (Publ. in Geography Ser.: Vol. 21). 1977. pap. 9.00x (ISBN 0-520-09558-8). U of Cal Pr.
McKoski, Martin M. & Hahn, Lynne C. The Developing Writer: A Guide to Basic Skills. LC 80-21912. 250p. 1981. text ed. 8.95 (ISBN 0-471-05812-2). Wiley.
McKown, Robin. Colonial Conquest of Africa. LC 71-158424. (First Bks). (Illus.). (gr. 4-6). 1971. PLB 4.90 o.p. (ISBN 0-531-00743-X). Watts.
--The Execution of Maximilian: A Hapsburg Emperor Meets Disaster in the New World. LC 73-3427. (World Focus Bks). (Illus.). (gr. 7 up). 1973. PLB 6.45 (ISBN 0-531-02165-3). Watts.
--The Opium War in China, 1840-1842: The British Resort to War in Order to Maintain Their Opium Trade. LC 74-2436. (World Focus Bks.). (Illus.). 72p. (gr. 7 up). 1974. PLB 4.47 o.p. (ISBN 0-531-02728-7). Watts.
--The Republic of Zaire. LC 72-1873. (First Bks). (Illus.). 96p. (gr. 4-6). 1972. PLB 4.47 o.p. (ISBN 0-531-00770-7). Watts.
--Seven Famous Trials in History. LC 63-13800. (Illus.). (gr. 7 up). 1963. 7.95 (ISBN 0-8149-0367-3). Vanguard.
McKown, Robin, ed. The Resignation of Nixon: A Discredited President Gives up the Highest Office. LC 75-8538. (Focus Bks). (Illus.). 72p. (gr. 7 up). 1975. PLB 6.45 (ISBN 0-531-01092-9). Watts.
Mackowski, Richard M. Jerusalem: City of Jesus. (Illus.). 224p. 1980. 29.95 (ISBN 0-8028-3526-0). Eerdmans.
McKray, George, jt. ed. see Roemer, Ruth.
Macksey, Kenneth. Invasion: The German Invasion of Britain-July 1940. (Illus.). 224p. 1981. 12.95 (ISBN 0-02-578030-1). Macmillan.
--Kesselring: The Making of the Luftwaffe. 1978. 27.00 (ISBN 0-7134-0862-6, Pub. by Batsford England). David & Charles.
--The Partisans of Europe in the Second World War. LC 74-78526. (Illus.). 304p. 1975. 35.00x (ISBN 0-8128-1724-9). Stein & Day.
--Tank Facts & Feats. (Guinness Superlatives Ser.). (Illus.). 256p. 1980. 17.95 (ISBN 0-8069-9248-4, Pub. by Guinness Superlatives England). Sterling.
Macksey, Kenneth, jt. auth. see Frere-Cook, Gervis.
Mack Smith, Denis. Italy: A Modern History. rev. & enl. ed. LC 69-15851. (History of the Modern World Ser). (Illus.). 1969. 12.50x (ISBN 0-472-07051-7). U of Mich Pr.
McKuen, Rod. Listen to the Warm. (Pocket ed.). 1969. 5.95 (ISBN 0-394-40378-9); deluxe ed. 5.00 pocket ed. (ISBN 0-394-40380-0). Random.
--The Power Bright & Shining. 1980. 8.95 (ISBN 0-686-62883-7, 41392); deluxe ed. 19.95 (ISBN 0-686-62884-5, 41393). S&S.
--Too Many Midnights. 1981. pap. price not set (ISBN 0-671-43111-0). PB.
McKusick, Victor. Human Genetics. 2nd ed. (Foundations of Modern Genetics Ser). 1969. pap. 10.95x ref. ed. (ISBN 0-13-445106-6). P-H.
McLachlan, Alexander. The Poetical Works of Alexander McLachlan: 1818-1896. LC 73-82589. (Literature of Canada Ser.). (Illus.). 1974. pap. 5.95 (ISBN 0-8020-6235-0). U of Toronto Pr.
McLachlan, Christopher A. Inflation-Wise: How to Do Almost Everything for Less. 1981. pap. 4.95 (ISBN 0-380-76836-4). Avon.
MacLachlan, Colin M. Criminal Justice in Eighteenth Century Mexico: A Study of the Tribunal of the Acordada. LC 72-97737. 1975. 18.50x (ISBN 0-520-02416-8). U of Cal Pr.
MacLachlan, Colin M. & Rodriguez, Jaime E. The Forging of the Cosmic Race: A Reinterpretation of Colonial Mexico. (Illus.). 408p. 1980. 25.00 (ISBN 0-520-03890-8). U of Cal Pr.
McLachlan, E. M. Fundamentals of Electrocardiography. (Illus.). 192p. 1981. text ed. 37.50x (ISBN 0-19-261237-9); pap. text ed. 22.50x (ISBN 0-19-261199-2). Oxford U Pr.
McLachlan, Gordon. A Question of Quality? Roads to Assurance in Medical Care. (The Nuffield Provincial Hospitals Trust Ser.). 1976. 34.00x (ISBN 0-19-721393-6). Oxford U Pr.
McLachlan, Gordon, jt. ed. see Cawley, Robert.
McLachlan, Gordon, et al, eds. Patterns for Uncertainty? Planning for the Greater Medical Profession. 1979. pap. 14.95 (ISBN 0-19-721223-9). Oxford U Pr.
Maclachlan, Gretchen, jt. auth. see Freedman, Marcia.
McLachlan, Ian. Helen in Exile. 384p. 1980. 11.95 (ISBN 0-8037-3561-8). Dial.
MacLachlan, Patricia. Moon. Stars, Frogs & Friends. (Illus.). (ps-3). 1980. 6.95 (ISBN 0-394-84138-7); PLB 6.99 (ISBN 0-394-94138-1). Pantheon.
McLackhlan, K. S., ed. The Developing Agriculture of the Middle East: Opportunities & Prospects. 74p. 1976. 43.00x (ISBN 0-86010-046-4, Pub. by Graham & Trotman England). State Mutual Bk.
McLafferty, Fred W. Interpretation of Mass Spectra. Turro, Nicholas J., ed. LC 80-51179. (Organic Chemistry Ser.). 303p. 1980. text ed. 13.00x (ISBN 0-935702-04-0). Univ Sci Bks.
Maclagan, Eric R. Italian Sculpture of the Renaissance: The Charles Eliot Norton Lectures for the Years 1927-1928. LC 70-110272. (Illus.). 1971. Repr. of 1935 ed. lib. bdg. 25.75x (ISBN 0-8371-4498-1, MAIS). Greenwood.
Maclagan, Michael, ed. see De Bury, Richard.
McLain, John D. Year-Round Education. LC 72-14044. 1973. 17.50x (ISBN 0-8211-1222-8); text ed. 15.75x (ISBN 0-685-36207-8). McCutchan.
McLain, Joseph H. Pyrotechnics. (Illus.). 225p. 1980. 24.50 (ISBN 0-89168-032-2). Franklin Inst.
MacLaine, Allan, intro. by. The Beginnings to Fifteen Fifty-Eight. 96p. 1981. pap. 4.95 (ISBN 0-312-07190-6). St Martin.
MacLaine, Allan H. Student's Comprehensive Guide to The Canterbury Tales. LC 64-22359. (Orig.). (gr. 10up). 1965. text ed. 5.95 (ISBN 0-8120-5016-9); pap. text ed. 4.50 (ISBN 0-8120-0040-4). Barron.
McLane, Charles B. Islands of the Mid-Maine Coast: Penobscot & Blue Hill Bays. (Illus.). 576p. 1981. 35.00 (ISBN 0-933858-00-0, Pub by Kennebec River Pr); signed & numbered limited ed 100.00 (ISBN 0-933858-01-9). TBW Bks.
McLane, Helen J. Selecting, Developing & Retaining Women Executives: A Corporate Strategy for the Eighties. 256p. 1980. 14.95 (ISBN 0-442-20165-6). Van Nos Reinhold.
MacLane, S. Categories for the Working Mathematician. LC 78-166080. (Graduate Texts in Mathematics: Vol. 5). 272p. 1972. 19.80 o.p. (ISBN 0-387-90035-7); pap. 9.50 o.p. (ISBN 0-387-90036-5). Springer-Verlag.
Maclaren, A. Allan. Religion & Social Class: The Disruption. (The Scottish Ser.). 1974. 22.00 (ISBN 0-7100-7789-0). Routledge & Kegan.
McLaren, A. D. & Shugar, D. Photochemistry of Proteins & Nucleic Acids. 1964. 46.00 (ISBN 0-08-010139-9); pap. text ed. 22.00 (ISBN 0-08-013569-2). Pergamon.
McLaren, Anne. Germ Cells & Soma: A New Look at Old Problem. LC 80-54221. (Silliman Lectures: No. 5). (Illus.). 128p. 1981. 15.00 (ISBN 0-300-02694-3). Yale U Pr.
--Mammalian Chimaeras. LC 75-40988. (Developmental and Cell Biology Ser.: No. 4). (Illus.). 160p. 1976. 35.50 (ISBN 0-521-21183-2). Cambridge U Pr.
McLaren, D. & Burman, D. Textbook of Paediatric Nutrition. LC 75-46569. (Illus.). 1976. text ed. 47.00x (ISBN 0-443-01413-2). Churchill.
McLaren, Dell. The Seduction of Lady Mattson. 1977. pap. 1.50 (ISBN 0-505-51179-7). Tower Bks.
McLaren, Diane J. Schistosoma Mansoni: The Parasite Surface in Relation to Host Immunity. (Tropical Medicine Research Studies Ser.). 1981. write for info. (ISBN 0-471-27869-6, Pub. by Wiley-Interscience). Wiley.
McLaren, Donald S. Malnutrition & the Eye. 1963. 49.00 o.p. (ISBN 0-12-484250-X). Acad Pr.
McLaren, Duncan. In Ruins: The Once Great Houses of Ireland. LC 80-7662. (Illus.). 96p. 1980. 22.50 (ISBN 0-394-51095-X). Knopf.
McLaren, Ian A. Education in a Small Democracy, New Zealand. (World Education Ser.). 1974. 16.00 (ISBN 0-7100-7798-X). Routledge & Kegan.
Maclaren, W. A. Rubber, Tea & Cacao with Special Sections on Coffee, Spices & Tobacco. 1980. lib. bdg. 75.00 (ISBN 0-8490-3110-9). Gordon Pr.
McLaren, Walter W. Japanese Government Documents: (of the Meiji Era, 2 vols. (Studies in Japanese History & Civilization). 1979. Repr. of 1914 ed. Set. 52.50 (ISBN 0-89093-265-4). U Pubns Amer.
McLarn, Jack C. Writing Part Time for Fun & Money. LC 78-50474. 1980. pap. 4.95 (ISBN 0-913864-39-0). Enterprise Del.
Mc Larty, Barbara L., ed. Charles Heaney: Master of the Oregon Scene. McLarty, Jack, tr. (Illus.). 65p. (Orig.). 1980. pap. 9.50. Image Gallery.
McLarty, Jack, tr. see Mc Larty, Barbara L.
McLauchlan, K. A. Magnetic Resonance. (Oxford Chemical Ser). 108p. 1972. pap. text ed. 7.95x (ISBN 0-19-855403-6). Oxford U Pr.
McLauchlan, William P. American Legal Processes. LC 76-26579. (Viewpoints on American Politics Ser.). 1977. pap. text ed. 9.95x (ISBN 0-471-58561-0). Wiley.
McLaughlin. Commentary on Acts. kivar 5.95 (ISBN 0-686-12858-3). Schmul Pub Co.
--Commentary on Luke. kivar 5.95 (ISBN 0-686-12859-1). Schmul Pub Co.
--Commentary on Mark. kivar 5.95 (ISBN 0-686-12860-5). Schmul Pub Co.
--Commentary on Matthew. kivar 5.95 (ISBN 0-686-12861-3). Schmul Pub Co.
--Commentary on Romans. kivar 5.95 (ISBN 0-686-12862-1). Schmul Pub Co.
--Commentary on St. John. kivar 5.95 (ISBN 0-686-12863-X). Schmul Pub Co.
McLaughlin, Andrew C. Constitutional History of the United States. 1935. 29.50x (ISBN 0-89197-103-3); pap. text ed. 12.95x (ISBN 0-89197-104-1). Irvington.
--The Courts, the Constitution & Parties. LC 70-87405. (The American Scene Ser.). 312p. 1972. Repr. of 1912 ed. lib. bdg. 32.50 (ISBN 0-306-71549-X). Da Capo.
--Lewis Cass. LC 80-24025. (American Statesmen Ser.). 390p. 1981. pap. 5.95 (ISBN 0-87754-192-2). Chelsea Hse.
McLaughlin, Arthur J., Jr. Organization & Management for Respiratory Therapists. LC 78-1577. (Illus.). 1979. pap. text ed. 10.95 (ISBN 0-8016-3311-7). Mosby.
McLaughlin, Barry. Learning & Social Behavior. LC 74-143176. 1971. 12.95 (ISBN 0-02-920570-0). Free Pr.
McLaughlin, Barry, ed. Studies in Social Movements. LC 69-17783. 1969. 16.95 (ISBN 0-02-920560-3). Free Pr.
McLaughlin, Charles C., jt. ed. see Beveridge, Charles E.
McLaughlin, Doris B. Michigan Labor: A Brief History from 1818 to the Present. LC 73-633304. (Orig.). 1970. 9.50x (ISBN 0-87736-312-9); pap. 4.50x (ISBN 0-87736-333-1). U of Mich Inst Labor.
McLaughlin, Eve, jt. auth. see McLaughlin, Terence.
McLaughlin, Frank S. & Pickhardt, Robert C. Quantitative Techniques for Management Decisions. LC 78-69586. (Illus.). 1978. text ed. 19.50 (ISBN 0-395-26669-6); inst. manual 2.90 (ISBN 0-395-26668-8). HM.
McLaughlin, Iona H. Triumph Over Tragedy. (Festival Ser.). 128p. 1981. pap. 1.50 (ISBN 0-687-42640-5). Abingdon.
McLaughlin, James, jt. auth. see Bush, Loren S.
McLaughlin, John B. Gypsy Lifestyles. LC 80-7572. 1980. 14.95 (ISBN 0-669-03754-0). Lexington Bks.
McLaughlin, John C. Aspects of the History of English. LC 75-94889. (Illus.). 1970. 29.00x (ISBN 0-89197-666-3). Irvington.
McLaughlin, Martin M. & Overseas Development Council. The United States & World Development: Agenda 1979. 1979. 23.95 (ISBN 0-03-049146-0); pap. 4.95 student ed (ISBN 0-03-049151-7). Praeger.
McLaughlin, Martin M. & Overseas Development Council Staff. The United States & World Development: Agenda 1979. LC 78-71589. (Agenda Ser.). 280p. 1979. pap. 5.95 (ISBN 0-686-28666-9). Overseas Dev Council.
McLaughlin, Mary M., tr. see Weston, Jessie L.
McLaughlin, Patsy A. Comparative Morphology of Recent Crustacea. LC 79-26066. (Illus.). 1980. text ed. 23.95x (ISBN 0-7167-1121-4). W H Freeman.
McLaughlin, Robert E., jt. auth. see Carron, Harold.
McLaughlin, Roberta & Wood, Lucille. Sing a Song of People. (ps-3). 1973. songbook 9.00 (ISBN 0-8372-0765-7); 3 lp records 8.49 ea.; sets 1-3, incl. 2 filmstrips lp record & 20 minibks 45.00 ea.; 3 sets incl. 2 filmstrips, 2 cassettes & 20 minibks 45.00 ea.; minibks. sep. sets of 10 6.00 (ISBN 0-685-24085-1); complete kit cassette ed. 171.00 (ISBN 0-8372-0219-1); flannelbd. figures 3.93 (ISBN 0-8372-0220-5); complete kit, record edition 171.00 (ISBN 0-8372-0218-3). Bowmar-Noble.
McLaughlin, Terence. Make Your Own Electricity. LC 76-54075. 1977. 10.50 (ISBN 0-7153-7418-4). David & Charles.
McLaughlin, Terence & McLaughlin, Eve. Cost-Effective Self-Sufficiency: Middle Class Peasant. 1978. 17.95 (ISBN 0-7153-7474-5). David & Charles.
McLaurin, A. Virginia Woolf: The Echoes Enslaved. LC 72-83589. 300p. 1973. 32.95 (ISBN 0-521-08704-X). Cambridge U Pr.
McLaurin, Allen, jt. ed. see Majumader, Robin.
McLaurin, Melton A. The Knights of Labor in the South. LC 77-87916. (Contributions in Labor History: No. 4). (Illus.). 1978. lib. bdg. 18.95 (ISBN 0-313-20033-5, MCK/). Greenwood.
McLaurin, Melton A. & Thomason, Michael V. The Image of Progress: Alabama Photographs, 1872-1917. LC 80-11441. (Illus.). 240p. (Orig.). 1980. pap. 19.95 (ISBN 0-8173-0043-0). U of Ala Pr.
McLaurin, R. D., jt. auth. see Jureidini, Paul.
McLaurin, R. D., ed. The Political Role of Minorities in the Middle East. LC 79-20588. (Praeger Special Studies). 328p. 1979. 27.95 (ISBN 0-03-052596-9). Praeger.
McLaurin, R. D., et al. Foreign Policy Making in the Middle East: Domestic Influences on Policy in Egypt, Iraq, Israel, & Syria. LC 76-24360. (Special Studies). 1977. text ed. 29.95 (ISBN 0-275-23870-9); pap. 9.95 (ISBN 0-275-65010-3). Praeger.
MacLaverty. Lamb. Date not set. 8.95 (ISBN 0-8076-0990-0). Braziller.
Maclay, Sarah. Weeding the Duchess. 1979. 25.00; pap. 5.00. Black Stone.
McLean, jt. auth. see Weber.
McLean, A., ed. Occupational Stress. (Illus.). 128p. 1974. 13.50 (ISBN 0-398-03067-7). C C Thomas.

Maclean, A. D. Winter's Tales 26. 224p. 1981. 11.95 (ISBN 0-312-88414-1). St Martin.
McLean, Adam & Gribble, Colin. Geology for Civil Engineers. (Illus.). 1979. text ed. 30.00x (ISBN 0-04-624002-0); pap. text ed. 14.95x (ISBN 0-685-94492-1). Allen Unwin.
McLean, Albert F., Jr. William Cullen Bryant. (U. S. Authors Ser.: No. 59). 1964. lib. bdg. 10.95 (ISBN 0-8057-0108-7). Twayne.
Maclean, Alistair. Athabasca. LC 80-1067. 336p. 1980. 11.95 (ISBN 0-385-17204-4). Doubleday.
--Athabasca. 1981. lib. bdg. 13.95 (ISBN 0-8161-3147-3, Large Print Bks). G K Hall.
--Bear Island. LC 77-163654. 1971. 5.95 o.p. (ISBN 0-385-07192-2). Doubleday.
--Bear Island. 1979. pap. 2.25 (ISBN 0-449-23560-2, Crest). Fawcett.
--Breakheart Pass. 224p. 1978. pap. 2.25 (ISBN 0-449-24092-4, Crest). Fawcett.
--Caravan to Vaccares. 224p. 1977. pap. 2.25 (ISBN 0-449-24082-7, Crest). Fawcett.
--Force Ten from Navarone. 1979. pap. 2.50 (ISBN 0-449-23934-9, Crest). Fawcett.
--The Golden Gate. 1977. pap. 2.50 (ISBN 0-449-23177-1, Crest). Fawcett.
--The Golden Rendezvous. 1978. pap. 2.25 (ISBN 0-449-23624-2, Crest). Fawcett.
--Lawrence of Arabia. (World Landmark Ser: No. 52). (Illus.). (gr. 7-9). 1962. PLB 4.39 (ISBN 0-394-90552-0, BYR). Random.
--Night Without End. 1978. pap. 2.25 (ISBN 0-449-14129-2, GM). Fawcett.
--When Eight Bells Toll. 1978. pap. 2.50 (ISBN 0-449-23893-8, Crest). Fawcett.
--Where Eagles Dare. 1979. pap. 2.50 (ISBN 0-449-24121-1, Crest). Fawcett.
MacLean, Angus. Cuentos. 205p. 1979. pap. 9.95 (ISBN 0-914330-26-8); pap. write for info. (ISBN 0-914330-26-8). Western Tanager.
--Legends of the California Bandidos. 235p. 1977. 4.95 (ISBN 0-914330-09-8). Western Tanager.
McLean, Beth B. Meal Planning & Service. rev. ed. (Illus.). (gr. 9-12). 1964. text ed. 12.60 (ISBN 0-87002-218-0). Bennett IL.
McLean, Claire. The Bouvier Des Flandres. 19.95 (ISBN 0-87714-077-4). Green Hill.
--Bouvier Des Flandres. 2nd ed. 1980. 19.95 (ISBN 0-87714-077-4). Caroline Hse.
--The Complete Bouvier Des Flandres. LC 74-75115. (Other Dog Bks.). (Illus.). 1981. write for info. (ISBN 0-87714-077-4). Denlingers.
Maclean, D. Typographia Scoto-Gadelica. 384p. 1972. Repr. of 1915 ed. 31.00x (ISBN 0-7165-2058-3, Pub. by Irish Academic Pr Ireland). Biblio Dist.
McLean, Daniels. Minnesota Legal Forms-Family Law. Mason Publishing Company Staff, ed. (Minnesota Legal Forms 1981 Ser.). 150p. 1981. ring binder 15.00 (ISBN 0-917126-85-8). Mason Pub.
MacLean, David. Engine Maintenance & Repair. (Boatowners How-to Guides). (Illus.). 1977. pap. 5.95 (ISBN 0-8306-6943-4, 943). TAB Bks.
--Hauling Out & Winterizing. (Boatowners How-to Guides). (Illus.). 1977. pap. 5.95 (ISBN 0-8306-6944-2). TAB Bks.
Maclean, Dorothy. To Hear the Angels Sing. 192p. (Orig.). 1980. pap. text ed. 7.00 (ISBN 0-936878-01-0). Lorian Pr.
MacLean, Douglas, jt. ed. see Brown, Peter G.
McLean, Ephraim R. & Soden, John V. Strategic Planning for MIS. LC 77-58483. 1977. 31.50 (ISBN 0-471-58562-9, Pub. by Wiley-Interscience). Wiley.
Maclean, Fitzroy. Tito: A Pictorial Biography. LC 80-18683. (Illus.). 128p. 1980. 14.95 (ISBN 0-07-044671-7); pap. 9.95 (ISBN 0-07-044660-1). McGraw.
McLean, George, ed. Man & Nature. 1979. 9.95 (ISBN 0-19-561093-8). Oxford U Pr.
McLean, George F., ed. Ethical Wisdom East &-or West. LC 78-106891. (Proceedings of the American Catholic Philosophical Association: Vol. 51). 1977. pap. 8.00 (ISBN 0-918090-11-3). Am Cath Philo.
--The Human Person. LC 80-66375. (Proceedings: Vol. 53). 1980. pap. 8.00 (ISBN 0-918090-13-X). Am Cath Philo.
--Myth & Philosophy. LC 72-184483. (Proceedings of the American Catholic Philosophical Association: Vol. 45). 1971. pap. 8.00 (ISBN 0-918090-05-9). Am Cath Philo.
--Scholasticism in the Modern World. (Proceedings of the American Catholic Philosophical Association: Vol. 40). 1966. pap. 8.00 o.p. (ISBN 0-918090-00-8). Am Cath Philo.
MacLean, Gilmour, tr. see Schleiermacher, Friedrich.
McLean, Gordon. Terror in the Streets. LC 77-74159. (Illus.). 1977. pap. 1.95 (ISBN 0-87123-558-7, 200558). Bethany Fell.
McLean, Gordon & Pestana, Ken. Devil at the Wheel. LC 74-28547. 144p. (Orig.). (YA) 1975. pap. 1.95 (ISBN 0-87123-101-8, 200101). Bethany Fell.
MacLean, Hugh. Ben Jonson & the Cavalier Poets. new ed. (Critical Editions Ser.). 1975. 12.50 (ISBN 0-393-04387-8); pap. 6.95x (ISBN 0-393-09308-5). Norton.
MacLean, Ian. Woman Triumphant: Feminism in French Literature 1610-1652. (Illus.). 1977. 45.00x (ISBN 0-19-815741-X). Oxford U Pr.
MacLean, J., jt. auth. see Biggs, E.
Maclean, J. A., jt. auth. see Mackaill, A. W.
McLean, J. Michael. The Impact of the Microelectronics Industry on the Structure of the Canadian Economy. 50p. 1979. pap. text ed. 3.00x (ISBN 0-920380-22-0, Pub. by Inst Res Pub Canada). Renouf.
MacLean, Jan. White Fire. (Harlequin Romances Ser.). 192p. 1980. pap. 1.25 (ISBN 0-373-02348-0, Pub. by Harlequin). PB.
MacLean, Jane. Deadfall. 1979. 9.95 o.p. (ISBN 0-525-10585-9, Thomas Congdon Book). Dutton.
McLean, Janice, jt. ed. see Wasserman, Paul.
Maclean, Joan. English in Basic Medical Science. (English in Focus Ser.). (Illus.). 1975. pap. text ed. 6.95x (ISBN 0-19-437515-3); tchr's ed. 11.00x (ISBN 0-19-437503-X). Oxford U Pr.
McLean, John. The Science & Art Dental Ceramics, Vol. 1. (Illus.). 334p. 1979. 42.00 (ISBN 0-931386-04-7). Quint Pub Co.
--The Science & Art of Dental Ceramics, Vol. II. (Illus.). 496p. 1978. 120.00 (ISBN 0-931386-11-X). Quint Pub Co.
MacLean, Katharine. Missing Man. LC 74-16610. (YA) 1975. 6.95 o.p. (ISBN 0-399-11474-2, Dist. by Putnam). Berkley Pub.
Maclean, Katherine. The Diploids. (Science Fiction Ser.). 1981. PLB 13.95 (ISBN 0-8398-2510-2). Gregg.
MacLean, Katherine, jt. auth. see De Vet, Charles.
McLean, Malcolm D., compiled by. Papers Concerning Robertson's Colony in Texas: Vol. VI, March 6 Through December 5, 1831; the Campaigns Against the Tawakoni, Waco, Towash, & Comanche Indians. LC 73-78014. (Illus.). 1979. lib. bdg. 25.00 (ISBN 0-932408-06-0). UTA Pr.
MacLean, Michael J., jt. auth. see Stone, Leroy O.
McLean, Peggy, jt. auth. see Laycock, Mary.
McLean, R. C. & Cook, W. R. Textbook of Theoretical Botany, Vol. 4. LC 72-6057. 1973. text ed. 52.95 (ISBN 0-470-58558-7). Halsted Pr.
McLean, R. J. Education for Crime Prevention & Control. (Criminal Law Education & Research Center Ser.). (Illus.). 168p. 1975. 13.75 (ISBN 0-398-03226-2). C C Thomas.
McLean, Robert, ed. India in Transition. 1981. 15.00x (ISBN 0-8364-0011-9). South Asia Bks.
McLean, Ruari. The Thames & Hudson Manual of Typography. (Illus.). 192p. 1980. 17.95 (ISBN 0-500-67022-6). Thames Hudson.
--Victorian Book Design & Colour Printing. 2nd ed. (Illus.). 256p. 1972. 52.50x (ISBN 0-520-02078-2). U of Cal Pr.
--The Wood Engravings of Joan Hassall. LC 80-6193. (Illus.). 120p. 1981. pap. 7.95 (ISBN 0-8052-0675-2). Schocken.
McLean, Ruari, intro. by. Edward Bawden: A Book of Cuts. (Illus.). 84p. 1979. 15.00 (ISBN 0-85967-456-8, Pub. by Scolar Pr England); pap. 7.95 (ISBN 0-85967-457-6, Pub. by Scolor Pr England). Biblio Dist.
McLean, Susan H. Pennies for the Piper. 132p. (gr. 5 up). 1981. 9.95 (ISBN 0-374-35791-9). FS&G.
MacLean, Theresa. Medieval English Gardens. LC 79-56277. (Illus.). 288p. 1981. 25.00 (ISBN 0-670-46482-1). Viking Pr.
Maclean, Una. Magical Medicine: A Nigerian Case Study. 1974. pap. 1.95 o.p. (ISBN 0-14-021220-5, Pelican). Penguin.
McLeary, Roy, ed. Jane's Surface Skimmers 1977-78: Hovercraft & Hydrofoils. (Illus.). 1978. 60.00 (ISBN 0-531-03283-3). Watts.
McLeave, Hugh. A Borderline Case. 1979. 7.95 o.p. (ISBN 0-684-15803-5, ScribT). Scribner.
--No Face in the Mirror. 192p. 1980. 9.95 o.s.i. (ISBN 0-8027-5421-X). Walker & Co.
--Rogues in the Gallery: The Modern Plague of Art Thefts. 1981. 14.95 (ISBN 0-87923-378-8). Godine.
--Second Time Around. 1981. 9.95 (ISBN 0-8027-5439-2). Walker & Co.
McLeavy. Surface Skimmers Nineteen Eighty. 1980. 85.00 (ISBN 0-531-03933-1). Watts.
McLeavy, Roy. Naval Fast Strike Craft & Patrol Boats. (Illus.). 1979. 10.95 (ISBN 0-7137-0866-2, Pub by Blandford Pr England). Sterling.
McLeavy, Roy, ed. Jane's Surface Skimmers 1976-77. 1976. 60.00 o.p. (ISBN 0-531-03266-3). Watts.
McLeish, John, et al. The Psychology of the Learning Group. 1973. text ed. 9.00x (ISBN 0-09-114010-2, Hutchinson U Lib); pap. text ed. 4.75x (ISBN 0-09-114011-0). Humanities.
McLeish, K. Greek Art & Architecture. (Aspects of Greek Life). (Illus.). 1975. pap. text ed. 2.95x (ISBN 0-582-20673-1). Longman.
McLeish, K., jt. auth. see Nichols, R.
McLeish, K., jt. ed. see Nichols, R.
McLeish, K., tr. Aristophanes: Clouds, Women in Power, Knights. LC 78-51680. (Translations from Greek & Roman Authors). 1980. 28.50 (ISBN 0-521-22009-2); pap. 7.95 (ISBN 0-521-29707-9). Cambridge U Pr.
McLeish, K., jt. tr. see Raphael, F.
McLeish, Kenneth. Greek Exploration & Seafaring. (Aspects of Greek Life). 1972. pap. text ed. 2.95x (ISBN 0-582-34402-6). Longman.
--The Greek Theatre. (Aspects of Greek Life Ser.). (Illus.). 1972. pap. text ed. 2.95x (ISBN 0-582-34400-X). Longman.
--The Theatre of Aristophanes. LC 79-3142. (Illus.). 183p. 1980. 11.95 (ISBN 0-8008-7630-X). Taplinger.
MacLeish, Norman. The Nature of Religious Knowledge. 174p. Repr. of 1938 ed. text ed. 3.50 (ISBN 0-567-02193-9). Attic Pr.
Macleish, Roderick. The First Book of Eppe. 384p. 1981. pap. 2.95 (ISBN 0-449-24405-9, Crest). Fawcett.
--The Man Who Wasn't There. 1976. 7.95 o.p. (ISBN 0-394-49361-3). Random.
McLellan, A. G. The Classical Thermodynamics of Deformable Materials. LC 76-2277. (Cambridge Monographs on Physics). (Illus.). 1980. 74.50 (ISBN 0-521-21237-5). Cambridge U Pr.
McLellan, David S. Dean Acheson: The State Department Years. LC 76-8482. (Illus.). 1976. 17.50 (ISBN 0-396-07313-1). Dodd.
McLellan, David S. & Acheson, David C., eds. Among Friends: Personal Letters of Dean Acheson. LC 79-24127. 1980. 17.95 (ISBN 0-396-07721-8). Dodd.
McLellan, H. J. Elements of Physical Oceanography. 1966. 18.00 (ISBN 0-08-011320-6). Pergamon.
McLellan, Joyce. Days of the Year. (gr. 2-6). 1976. 3.15 (ISBN 0-08-006799-9). Pergamon.
McLellan, Robert. Isle of Arran. LC 74-20460. 256p. 1976. 13.50 (ISBN 0-7153-6946-6). David & Charles.
--Jamie the Saxt. 1981. pap. 3.95 (ISBN 0-7145-0307-X). Riverrun NY.
McLelland, J., jt. auth. see King, A. S.
McLelland, Joseph. Trabajo y Justicia. 1978. 1.95 (ISBN 0-311-46060-7). Casa Bautista.
McLemore. Racial & Ethnic Relations in America. (Illus.). 1980. text ed. 16.95 (ISBN 0-205-06827-8, 816827X). Allyn.
McLemore, Patricia R., jt. auth. see Coleman, William V.
McLemore, William P., ed. Foundations of Urban Education. 1977. pap. text ed. 9.75x (ISBN 0-8191-0172-9). U Pr of Amer.
McLendon, Charles, jt. auth. see Blackistone, Mick.
McLendon, Gordon. Get Really Rich in the Coming Super Metals Boom. 1981. pap. 4.95 (ISBN 0-671-43202-8). PB.
McLendon, James. Deathwork. LC 77-4774. 1977. 8.95 o.p. (ISBN 0-397-01193-8). Lippincott.
--Eddie Macon's Run. 1980. pap. 2.95 (ISBN 0-451-09518-9, E9518, Sig). NAL.
McLendon, Will, tr. see Mauron, Charles.
McLenigham, Valjean. Ernie's Work of Art. (A Young Reader Ser.). (Illus.). (gr. k-3). 1979. PLB 5.00 (ISBN 0-307-60109-9, Golden Pr). Western Pub.
McLenighan, Valjean. I Know You Cheated. LC 77-8623. (Moods & Emotions Ser.). (Illus.). (gr. k-3). 1977. PLB 8.95 (ISBN 0-8172-0962-X). Raintree Pubs.
--International Games. LC 77-28069. (Games & Activities Ser.). (Illus.). (gr. k-3). 1978. PLB 9.30 (ISBN 0-8172-1162-4). Raintree Pubs.
--New Wheels. LC 77-27052. (Moods & Emotions Ser.). (Illus.). (gr. k-3). 1978. PLB 8.95 (ISBN 0-8172-1152-7). Raintree Pubs.
--Three Strikes & You're Out. (Beginning-to-Read Ser.). 32p. 1980. PLB 4.39 (ISBN 0-695-41462-3); pap. 1.50 (ISBN 0-695-31462-9). Follett.
Maclennan, Beryce W. & Felsenfeld, Naomi. Group Counseling & Psychotherapy with Adolescents. LC 68-18998. 1968-70. 13.50x (ISBN 0-231-03093-2); pap. 5.00x (ISBN 0-231-08640-7). Columbia U Pr.
Maclennan, Duncan & Parr, John B. Regional Policy: Past Experience & New Directions. 334p. 1979. 41.95x (ISBN 0-85520-217-3, Pub by Martin Robertson England); pap. 17.25x (ISBN 0-85520-216-5, Pub. by Martin Robertson England). Biblio Dist.
MacLennan, Hugh. A Voiles in Time. 320p. 1980. 12.95 (ISBN 0-312-59590-5). St Martin.
MacLennan, Malcolm. Gaelic Dictionary--Gaelic-English; English-Gaelic. 632p. 1980. 45.00 (ISBN 0-08-025713-5); pap. 22.00 (ISBN 0-08-025712-7). Pergamon.
MacLeod, A. J. Instrumental Methods of Food Analysis. LC 72-7618. (Illus.). 802p. 1973. 54.95 (ISBN 0-470-56308-7). Halsted Pr.
MacLeod, Allstair. Paul Tillich: An Essay on the Role of Ontology in His Philosophical Theology. (Contemporary Religious Thinkers Ser.). 1973. text ed. 17.95x o.p. (ISBN 0-04-111005-6); pap. text ed. 7.50x o.p. (ISBN 0-04-111006-4). Allen Unwin.
MacLeod, Angus. The Songs of Duncan MacIntyre. 1978. 25.00x (ISBN 0-7073-0040-1, Pub. by Scottish Academic Pr Scotland). Columbia U Pr.
MacLeod, Charlotte. The Luck Runs Out. 192p. 1981. pap. 2.25 (ISBN 0-380-54171-8, 54171). Avon.
--Next Door to Danger. (YA) 5.95 (ISBN 0-685-07450-1, Avalon). Bouregy.
--The Palace Guard. LC 80-2750. 192p. 1981. 9.95 (ISBN 0-385-17533-7). Doubleday.
McLeod, D. G. & Mittemeyer, B. T. The Urinary System: Disease, Diagnosis, Treatment. (Clinical Monographs Ser.). (Illus.). 1973. pap. 7.95 (ISBN 0-87618-059-4). R J Brady.
MacLeod, D. J. Slavery, Race & the American Revolution. LC 74-77382. 269p. 1975. 37.95 (ISBN 0-521-20502-6); pap. 11.50x (ISBN 0-521-09877-7). Cambridge U Pr.
MacLeod, Donald. Presbyterian Worship: Its Meaning & Method. rev. ed. LC 80-82226. (Illus.). 176p. 1981. 12.50 (ISBN 0-8042-1813-7). John Knox.
Macleod, Donald & Forestell, J. T. Pentecost 2. LC 74-76929. (Proclamation 1: Aids for Interpreting the Lessons of the Church Year, Ser. C). 64p. 1975. pap. 1.95 (ISBN 0-8006-4067-5, 1-4067). Fortress.
McLeod, Emilie W. One Snail & Me. (Illus.). (gr. k up). 1961. 6.95 o.p. (ISBN 0-316-56197-5, Pub. by Atlantic Monthly Pr). Little.
McLeod, Enid, tr. see Colette.
Macleod, G., jt. auth. see Macleod, W.
McLeod, G. C. Georges Bank: Past, Present, & Future. (Special Studies on Natural Resources & Energy Management). 225p. 1981. lib. bdg. 22.00x (ISBN 0-86531-199-4). Westview.
Macleod, Gael S., jt. auth. see Macleod, William M.
MacLeod, Innes, jt. auth. see Donnachie, Ian.
McLeod, J. G., jt. auth. see Lance, J. G.
McLeod, James G., jt. auth. see Lance, James W.
MacLeod, John. Scottish Theology: In Relation to Church History. 1974. 8.95 (ISBN 0-85151-193-7). Banner of Truth.
McLeod, Joseph A., jt. auth. see Brewster, John W.
McLeod, Kirsty. Drums & Trumpets: The House of Stuart. LC 77-1496. (gr. 6 up). 1977. 8.95 (ISBN 0-395-28918-1, Clarion). HM.
MacLeod, Lily. Cooking for the Wayward Diabetic. 1971. 6.25 o.p. (ISBN 0-571-04744-0). Transatlantic.
McLeod, Maxwell G., jt. ed. see Kumar, Krishna.
MacLeod, Murdo J. Spanish Central America: A Socioeconomic History, 1520-1720. LC 70-174456. 1973. pap. 8.95x (ISBN 0-520-02632-2). U of Cal Pr.
McLeod, Raymond. Management Information Systems. LC 78-14983. 1979. text ed. 18.95 (ISBN 0-574-21245-0, 13-4245); instr's guide avail. (ISBN 0-574-21246-9, 13-4246); casebook 4.95 (ISBN 0-574-21247-7, 13-4247). SRA.
MacLeod, Robert. The Californio. 1979. pap. 1.75 o.p. (ISBN 0-449-14301-5, GM). Fawcett.
--The Muleskinner. 1978. pap. 1.50 o.p. (ISBN 0-449-14054-7, GM). Fawcett.
MacLeod, Robert & Scapagnini, Umberto, eds. Central & Peripheral Regulation of Prolactin Function. 424p. 1980. text ed. 39.00 (ISBN 0-89004-489-9). Raven.
MacLeod, Robert M., jt. auth. see Lamberts, Steven W.
McLeod, Robin J. & Wachspress, Eugene L., eds. Frontiers of Applied Geometru: Proceedings of Symposium. Les Cruces, New Mexico, January 1980. 128p. 1980. pap. 23.40 (ISBN 0-08-026487-5). Pergamon.
MacLeod, Roy M. Treasury Control & Social Administration. 62p. 1968. pap. text ed. 5.00x (Pub. by Bedford England). Renouf.
McLeod, Sterling & Science Book Associates Editors. Challenging Careers in Urban Affairs. LC 76-26977. (Messner Career Bks.). (Illus.). 192p. (gr. 7-12). 1976. PLB 7.79 (ISBN 0-671-32810-7). Messner.
McLeod, Stuart R. Dreams: A Portrait of the Psyche. LC 80-65607. 170p. 1981. perfect bdg. 14.95 (ISBN 0-86548-046-X). Century Twenty One.
--Modern Verse Drama. (Salzburg Studies in English Literature, Poetic Drama & Poetic Theory: No. 2). 345p. 1972. pap. text ed. 25.00x (ISBN 0-391-01480-3). Humanities.
McLeod, Susan H. Dramatic Imagery in the Plays of John Webster. (Salzburg Studies in English Literature: Jacobean Drama Studies: No. 68). 1977. pap. text ed. 25.00x (ISBN 0-391-01481-1). Humanities.
McLeod, Thomas E. The Work of the Church Treasurer. 80p. 1981. pap. 6.95 (ISBN 0-8170-0908-6). Judson.

Macleod, W. & Macleod, G. M.I.N.D. Over Weight: How to Stay Slim the Rest of Your Life. 1981. pap. 7.95 (ISBN 0-13-583385-X). P-H.

MacLeod, W. C. The American Indian Frontier. 1968. Repr. of 1928 ed. 18.50 o.p. (ISBN 0-7129-0336-4, Dist by Shoe String). Dawson Pub.

Macleod, William M. & Macleod, Gael S. M. I. N. D Over Weight: "How to Stay Slim the Rest of Your Life". LC 80-21001. 1981. 7.95 (ISBN 0-13-583385-X). P-H.

Macleon, Lucian. Opera Tomus III: Libelli 44-68. (Oxford Classical Texts Ser.). 406p. 1980. text ed. 24.00x (ISBN 0-19-814592-6). Oxford U Pr.

MacLiammoir, Michael. The Importance of Being Oscar. 2nd ed. 1978. pap. text ed. 6.25x (ISBN 0-85105-348-3, Dolmen Pr). Humanities.

MacLiammoir, Micheal & Boland, Eavan. W. B. Yeats & His World. LC 77-90492. (Illus.). 1978. 10.95 o.p. (ISBN 0-684-15573-7, ScribT). Scribner.

McLintock, D. R., ed. see Bostock, J. Knight.

McLoughlin, Emmett. Crime & Immorality in the Catholic Church. LC 62-7778. 1962. 4.95 (ISBN 0-910294-19-4). Brown Bk.

McLoughlin, J. B., jt. ed. see Diamond, D. R.

McLoughlin, J. Brian. Urban & Regional Planning. (Orig.). 1978. pap. 9.95 (ISBN 0-571-09534-8, Pub. by Faber & Faber). Merrimack Bk Serv.

McLoughlin, James & Lewis, Rena. Assessing Special Students. (Special Education Ser.). (Illus.). 640p. 1981. text ed. 17.95 (ISBN 0-675-08151-3). Merrill.

McLoughlin, John C. Synapsida: A New Look into the Origin of Mammals. LC 79-56270. (Illus.). 160p. 1980. 14.95 (ISBN 0-670-68922-X). Viking Pr.

--The Tree of Animal Life: A Tale of Changing Forms & Fortunes. (Illus.). 128p. (gr. 5 up). 1981. PLB 8.95 (ISBN 0-396-07939-3). Dodd.

McLoughlin, Leslie. Course in Colloquial Arabic. 1974. 11.00 (ISBN 0-685-72032-2); with two cassettes 40.00 (ISBN 0-685-72033-0). Intl Bk Ctr.

McLoughlin, Leslie, tr. see Awwad, Tawfiq Y.

McLoughlin, William G. American Evangelicals, 1800-1900: An Anthology. 8.00 (ISBN 0-8446-0793-2). Peter Smith.

--Revivals, Awakening, & Reform: An Essay on Religion & Social Change in America, 1607 to 1977. LC 77-27830. xvi, 240p. 1980. pap. 5.95 (ISBN 0-226-56092-9, P891, Phoen). U of Chicago Pr.

--Revivals, Awakenings, & Reform. LC 77-27830. 1978. 15.00x (ISBN 0-226-56091-0). U of Chicago Pr.

--Rhode Island: A History. (States and the Nation Ser.). (Illus.). 1978. 12.95 (ISBN 0-393-05675-9). Norton.

McLoughlin, William G., ed. see Backus, Isaac.

McLoulin Bros. Cut & Assemble the Pretty Village. 1980. pap. 4.00 (ISBN 0-486-23938-1). Dover.

Mac Low. Asymmetries 1-260. pap. write for info. (ISBN 0-914162-38-1). Knowles.

Mac Low, Jackson. Phone. 1979. pap. 4.00 (ISBN 0-914162-29-2). Printed Edns.

--Representative Works. Rothenberg, Jerome, ed. (New Wilderness Poetics Ser.). 1981. 16.00 (ISBN 0-915520-35-4); special limited ed. 25.00 (ISBN 0-915520-36-2); pap. 7.95 (ISBN 0-915520-34-6). Ross-Erikson.

McLuhan, Marshall. Understanding Media: The Extensions of Man. 1964. pap. 3.95 (ISBN 0-07-045436-1, GB). McGraw.

McLure, Charles E., Jr. Must Corporate Income Be Taxed Twice? LC 78-27905. (Studies of Government Finance). 1979. 14.95 (ISBN 0-8157-5620-8); pap. 5.95 (ISBN 0-8157-5619-4). Brookings.

MacLure, Millar, ed. Marlowe: The Critical Heritage, Fifteen Eighty-Eight to Eighteen Ninety-Six. 1979. 24.00x (ISBN 0-7100-0245-9). Routledge & Kegan.

Maclure, Stuart, jt. ed. see Becher, Tony.

McLusky, D. S., ed. see European Symposium on Marine Biology, 12th.

McLusky, Donald S. Estuarine Ecosystem. (Tertiary Level Biology Ser.). 176p. 1981. 34.95 (ISBN 0-470-27127-2). Halsted Pr.

McLynn, Francis. France & the Jacobite Rising of Seventeen Forty-Five. 256p. 1981. 26.50x (ISBN 0-85224-404-5, Pub. by Edinburgh U Pr Scotland). Columbia U Pr.

MacLysaght, Edward. Changing Times: Ireland Since Eighteen Ninety-Eight. 1978. text ed. 16.50x (ISBN 0-901072-88-5). Humanities.

--The Families of Ireland. 450p. 1980. 40.00x (ISBN 0-686-26446-0, Pub. by Irish Academic Pr). Biblio Dist.

--Irish Life in the Seventeenth Century. 324p. 1979. 15.00x (ISBN 0-7165-2343-4, Pub. by Irish Academic Pr); pap. 7.50x (ISBN 0-7165-2342-6, Pub. by Irish Academic Pr). Biblio Dist.

--The Surnames of Ireland. 3rd ed. 336p. 1978. 15.00x (ISBN 0-7165-2164-4, Pub. by Irish Academic Pr Ireland); pap. 6.00x (ISBN 0-7165-2291-8). Biblio Dist.

McMackin, et al. Mathematics of the Shop. 4th ed. LC 76-6726. 1978. 13.60 (ISBN 0-8273-1297-0); tchr's ed. 1.60 (ISBN 0-8273-1298-9). Delmar.

McMahan, Elizabeth. A Crash Course in Composition. 3rd ed. 272p. 1980. pap. text ed. 8.95 (ISBN 0-07-045458-2, C); instructor's manual 4.95 (ISBN 0-07-045459-0). McGraw.

McMahan, Elizabeth, ed. Critical Approaches to Mark Twain's Short Stories. (National University Publications, Literary Criticism Ser.). 160p. 1981. 15.00 (ISBN 0-8046-9274-2). Kennikat.

MacMahon, A. W., et al. The Administration of Federal Work Relief. LC 73-167845. (FDR & the Era of the New Deal Ser.). 408p. 1971. Repr. of 1941 ed. lib. bdg. 39.50 (ISBN 0-306-70326-2). Da Capo.

McMahon, Agnes & Curriculm Development Unit Dublin Vocation Ed. Comm., eds. The Celtic Way of Life. (Illus.). 1977. pap. text ed. 4.95 (ISBN 0-905140-16-8). Irish Bk Ctr.

Macmahon, Arthur W. Delegation & Autonomy. 1962. 4.50x o.p. (ISBN 0-210-33833-4). Asia.

McMahon, Bernard. McMahon's American Gardener. LC 75-29506. (Funk & W Bk.). (Illus.). 640p. 1976. 10.00 o.s.i. (ISBN 0-308-10223-1, TYC-T); pap. 5.95 o.s.i. (ISBN 0-308-10224-X, TYC-T). T Y Crowell.

Macmahon, Brian, jt. ed. see Clark, Duncan W.

MacMahon, Candace W. Elizabeth Bishop: A Bibliography, 1927-1979. LC 79-13063. 1980. 20.00x (ISBN 0-8139-0783-7). U Pr of Va.

McMahon, Eileen, jt. auth. see Dunn, Christine.

McMahon, Frank B. Abnormal Behavior: Psychology's View. 1976. 20.95 (ISBN 0-13-000711-0). P-H.

--Psychology: The Hybrid Science. 3rd ed. (Illus.). 1977. 18.95 (ISBN 0-13-732958-X); study guide & wkbk. 6.95 (ISBN 0-13-732966-0). P-H.

McMahon, Gordon. Curriculum Development in Trade, Industrial, & Technical Education. LC 74-187804. 160p. 1972. pap. text ed. 12.95 (ISBN 0-675-09117-9). Merrill.

McMahon, J. J. Between You & You: The Art of Listening to Yourself. LC 79-89628. 1980. 9.95 (ISBN 0-8091-0300-1). Paulist Pr.

McMahon, Joan, jt. auth. see Zinner, Ellen.

McMahon, Kathryn K., jt. auth. see Azevedo, Milton M.

MacMahon, Kenneth A., jt. ed. see Gillett, Edward.

McMahon, Michael, ed. Nineteen Eighty-One Radio Contacts. 1981. pap. text ed. 126.00 (ISBN 0-935224-05-X). Larimi Comm.

--Nineteen Eighty-One Television Contacts. 1981. pap. text ed. 117.00 (ISBN 0-935224-04-1). Larimi Comm.

--Nineteen Eighty to Nineteen Eighty-One TV News. 1980. 70.00 (ISBN 0-935224-03-3). Larimi Comm.

--Television Contacts. rev. ed. 1980. pap. text ed. 80.00 (ISBN 0-935224-00-9). Larimi Comm.

McMahon, Sarah Lynne, jt. ed. see Carney, Clarke G.

McMahon, Thomas. McKay's Bees. 176p. 1981. pap. 2.75 (ISBN 0-380-53579-3, 53579, Bard). Avon.

--Principles of American Nuclear Chemistry: A Novel. 224p. 1981. pap. 2.95 (ISBN 0-380-54122-X, 54122, Bard). Avon.

McMahon, William. Pine Barrens Legends, Lore & Lies. LC 80-23518. (Illus.). 1980. 10.95 (ISBN 0-912608-12-9). Mid Atlantic.

McManamon, P. J., ed. see Hodson, C. J., et al.

MacManiman, Gen. Dry It, You'll Like It. (Illus.). 1973. pap. 3.95 (ISBN 0-685-52952-5, Pub. by MacManiman). Madrona Pubs.

McMann, Evelyn, ed. The Royal Canadian Academy of Arts: Exhibitions & Members, 1880-1979. 356p. 1981. 60.00x (ISBN 0-8020-2366-5). U of Toronto Pr.

McMann, Jean M. Riddles of the Stone Age. LC 79-67658. (Illus.). 160p. 1980. 16.95 (ISBN 0-500-05033-3). Thames Hudson.

McManners, Kelsey. Underwater Attack: The First Submarines. LC 78-15101. (Famous Firsts Ser.). (Illus.). 1978. lib. bdg. 7.35 (ISBN 0-686-51117-4). Silver.

MacManus, D. A. Between Two Worlds: True Ghost Stories of the British Isles. 1977. text ed. 11.25x (ISBN 0-900675-83-7). Humanities.

--The Middle Kingdom: The Faerie World of Ireland. 1973. pap. text ed. 6.75x (ISBN 0-900675-82-9). Humanities.

McManus, Leslie. Operation Backlash. LC 79-88066. 1979. pap. 1.50 o.p. (ISBN 0-87216-536-1). Playboy Pbks.

McManus, Patrick. They Shoot Canoes, Don't They? 228p. 1981. 10.95 (ISBN 0-03-058646-1). HR&W.

MacManus, Seumas, ed. Donegal Fairy Stories. (Illus.). (gr. 4-6). 1968. pap. 3.50 (ISBN 0-486-21971-2). Dover.

MacManus, Susan A. Revenue Patterns in U. S. Cities & Suburbs: A Comparative Analysis. LC 77-27499. (Praeger Special Studies). 1978. 25.95 (ISBN 0-03-022846-8). Praeger.

MacManus, Yvonne. Deadly Legacy. 256p. 1981. pap. 2.25 (ISBN 0-523-41259-2). Pinnacle Bks.

McMartin, Barbara. Fifty Hikes in the Adirondacks. LC 79-92569. (Fifty Hikes Ser.). (Illus., Orig.). 1980. pap. 8.95 (ISBN 0-89725-015-X). NH Pub Co.

McMaster, James H. The ABC's of Sports Injuries. LC 80-20636. 1981. lib. bdg. write for info. (ISBN 0-88275-890-X). Krieger.

McMaster, John & Stone, Frederick B. Pennsylvania & the Federal Constitution 1787-1788, 2 vols, Vol. 1. LC 74-87406. (American Constitutional & Legal History Ser). 1970. Repr. of 1888 ed. lib. bdg. 65.00 (ISBN 0-306-71550-3). Da Capo.

McMaster, John B. Benjamin Franklin. LC 80-23681. (American Men & Women of Letters Ser.). 300p. 1980. pap. 4.95 (ISBN 0-87754-161-2). Chelsea Hse.

--Optimum Management. (Illus.). 1980. 17.50 (ISBN 0-89433-120-5). Petrocelli.

McMaster, Juliet. Thackeray: The Major Novels. LC 76-151380. 1971. pap. 5.95 (ISBN 0-8020-6309-8). U of Toronto Pr.

McMaster, Mary. To Him Who Waits. (Aston Hall Romances Ser.). 192p. 1981. pap. 1.75 (ISBN 0-523-41129-4). Pinnacle Bks.

McMaster, R. D., ed. see Dickens, Charles.

McMaster, R. E., Jr. Cycles of War: The Next Six Years. 11.00 (ISBN 0-9604348-0-1). L McMaster.

McMath, George A., jt. auth. see Vaughan, Thomas.

McMenemy, William G. Place of the Circle in Elementary Geometry. LC 66-22004. 1967. 3.00 o.p. (ISBN 0-8022-1023-6). Philos Lib.

McMichael, Betty & McDonald, Karen M. Cooking with Love & Cereal. LC 80-69312. 224p. 1981. spiral bdg. 9.95 (ISBN 0-915684-80-2). Christian Herald.

McMichael, James. Against the Falling Evil. LC 72-17187. (New Poetry Ser.: No. 43). 55p. 1971. o.p 5.00 (ISBN 0-8040-0552-4); pap. 3.25 (ISBN 0-8040-0620-2). Swallow.

McMichael, Joan, ed. Health Care for the People: Studies from Vietnam. 352p. (Orig.). 1980. pap. 6.95 (ISBN 0-932870-04-X). Alyson Pubns.

Macmillan. The Cook's Guide. LC 77-7138. (Illus.). 1977. 8.95 o.s.i. (ISBN 0-02-578780-2). Macmillan.

--Embroidery: Step-by-Step. LC 76-8262. (Step-by-Step Craft Ser.). (Illus.). 1976. pap. 5.95 o.s.i. (ISBN 0-02-011820-1, 01182, Collier). Macmillan.

--Everlasting Flowers. (Illus.). 72p. 1976. 9.95 (ISBN 0-02-578300-9). Macmillan.

--Pottery: Step-by-Step. LC 76-8826. (Step-by-Step Craft Ser.). (Illus.). 1976. pap. 5.95 o.s.i. (ISBN 0-02-011810-4, 01181, Collier). Macmillan.

--Things to Do in a Day. LC 76-1991. 1976. pap. 5.95 o.s.i. (ISBN 0-02-011870-8, 01187, Collier). Macmillan.

--Tie Dye, Batik & Candlemaking: Step-by-Step. LC 76-8487. (Step-by-Step Craft Ser.). (Illus.). 1976. pap. 5.95 o.s.i. (ISBN 0-02-011790-6, 01179, Collier). Macmillan.

--The Wonders of Nature. (Illus.). 240p. 1981. 24.95 (ISBN 0-02-619550-X). Macmillan.

MacMillan, Annabelle, tr. see Gillsater, Sven & Gillsater, Pia.

McMillan, Bruce. The Alphabet Symphony. LC 77-5491. (ps-3). 1977. 7.25 (ISBN 0-688-80112-9); PLB 6.96 (ISBN 0-688-84112-0). Greenwillow.

--Making Sneakers. (gr. k-3). 1980. pap. 6.95 (ISBN 0-395-29161-5). HM.

MacMillan, Bruce. Surgical & Medical Support for Burn Patients. 1981. write for info. (ISBN 0-88416-301-6). PSG Pub.

McMillan, Bruce A. Finest Kind O'day: Lobstering in Maine. LC 77-3049. (gr. 2 up). 1977. 8.95 (ISBN 0-397-31763-8). Lippincott.

McMillan, Charles B. Magnet Schools: An Approach to Voluntary Desegregation. LC 79-93118. (Fastback Ser.: No. 141). 50p. (Orig.). 1980. pap. 0.75 (ISBN 0-87367-141-4). Phi Delta Kappa.

McMillan, Charles H., jt. ed. see Fallenbuchl, Zbigniew M.

McMillan, Claude. Mathematical Programming. 2nd ed. LC 74-23273. (Management & Administration Ser.). 650p. 1975. text ed. 27.95 (ISBN 0-471-58572-6); solutions manual avail. (ISBN 0-471-58573-4). Wiley.

McMillan, Claude & Gonzalez, Richard F. Systems Analysis: A Computer Approach to Decision Models. 3rd ed. 1973. text ed. 19.00 (ISBN 0-256-01439-6). Irwin.

McMillan, Claude, Jr., jt. auth. see Gonzalez, Richard F.

MacMillan, Colin & Paulden, Sydney. Sales Manager's Guide to Selection & Control of Export Agents. LC 68-58695. 1969. 14.95 (ISBN 0-8436-0900-1). CBI Pub.

McMillan, Dorothy. Instant Readers, 18 vols. Incl. Vol. 1. Farm Animals; Vol. 2. Round the House; Vol. 3. Grown Ups; Vol. 4. My Family; Vol. 5. Father; Vol. 7. Big Brother; Vol. 8. People We Know; Vol. 8. Where Are They Kept; Vol. 9. Animals at the Zoo; Vol. 10. Traffic; Vol. 11. Busy; Vo. 12. Me; Vol. 13. Mother; Vol. 14. Big Sister; Vol. 15. Baby; Vol. 16. In the Park; Vol. 17. We Like You; Vol. 18. Pets. (Illus.). (gr. k-4). 1976. Set Of 54 - 1 Copy Of 18 Titles. pap. text ed. 25.50 set large format (ISBN 0-8372-2184-6); small format-3 copies of 18 titles, 54 bks 28.50 (ISBN 0-8372-2203-6). Bowmar-Noble.

Macmillan, Duncan D. The Problem of the Economic & Political Survival of the United States. (The Major Currents in Contemporary World History Library). (Illus.). 117p. 1981. 37.85 (ISBN 0-930008-80-4). Inst Econ Pol.

McMillan, Earle. The Gospel According to Mark. Ferguson, Everett, ed. LC 73-8572. (Living Word Commentary Ser., Vol. 3). 1973. 7.95 (ISBN 0-8344-0066-9). Sweet.

McMillan, F. R. & Tuthill, Lewis H. Concrete Primer. 3rd ed. 1973. 6.50 (ISBN 0-685-85094-3, SP-1) (ISBN 0-685-85095-1). ACI.

MacMillan, Gail. Inherited Deception. 192p. (YA) 1976. 5.95 (ISBN 0-685-62626-1, Avalon). Bouregy.

Macmillan, Harold. Blast of War 1939-1945. LC 67-28810. 1968. 20.00 o.p. (ISBN 0-06-012748-1, HarpT). Har-Row.

--Pointing the Way 1959-1961. LC 72-79682. (Illus.). 487p. 1972. 20.00 o.p. (ISBN 0-06-012741-4, HarpT). Har-Row.

--Riding the Storm 1956-1959. LC 79-156535. (Illus.). 1971. 20.00 o.p. (ISBN 0-06-012744-9, HarpT). Har-Row.

--Sides of Fortune, Nineteen Fourty-Five to Nineteen Fifty-Five. LC 78-83609. (Illus.). 1969. 20.00 o.p. (ISBN 0-06-012746-5, HarpT). Har-Row.

--Winds of Change, 1914-1939. LC 66-21710. (Illus.). 1966. 20.00 o.p. (ISBN 0-06-012753-8, HarpT). Har-Row.

Macmillan, Ian. Blakely's Ark. 1981. pap. 2.25 (ISBN 0-425-04928-0). Berkley Pub.

McMillan, Ian, jt. auth. see Ashton, Gordon C.

Macmillan Information Division. Abbreviations in the African Press, a Transdex Book. new ed. 1973. 15.00 o.s.i. (ISBN 0-02-468060-5). Macmillan Info.

--Abbreviations in the Latin American Press, a Transdex Book. new ed. 1973. 15.00 o.s.i. (ISBN 0-02-468050-8). Macmillan Info.

--ERIC Educational Documents Index, 1966-1971: Institutions. new ed. 1973. 20.00 o.s.i. (ISBN 0-02-468840-1). Macmillan Info.

Macmillan, J., ed. Hormonal Regulation of Development I: Molcular Aspects of Plant Hormones. (Encyclopedia of Plant Physiology Ser.: Vol. 9). (Illus.). 681p. 1981. 134.60 (ISBN 0-387-10161-6). Springer-Verlag.

Macmillan, J. A., et al. Human Resources in Canadian Mining: A Preliminary Analysis. 176p. (Orig.). 1977. pap. 8.50x (ISBN 0-88757-004-6, Pub. by Ctr Resource Stud Canada). Renouf.

McMillan, J. Michael, jt. ed. see Scott, George P.

McMillan, James H., ed. The Social Psychology of School Learning. LC 79-6797. (Educational Psychology Ser.). 1980. 21.00 (ISBN 0-12-485750-7). Acad Pr.

McMillan, Joe. Route of the Warbonnets. LC 77-81470. (Illus.). 1977. 22.95 (ISBN 0-934228-01-9). McMillan Pubns.

MacMillan, John A. Encounter with Darkness. 116p. pap. 1.95 (ISBN 0-87509-287-X). Chr Pubns.

MacMillan, Keith, jt. auth. see Oliver, Hugh.

McMillan, Nora F. Observer's Book of Seashells. (Observer Bks.). (Illus.). 1977. 4.95 (ISBN 0-684-15206-1, ScribT). Scribner.

Macmillan, R. A. The Crowning Phase of the Critical Philosophy: A Study in Kant's Critique of Judgment. Beck, Lewis W., ed. LC 75-32041. (The Philosophy of Immanuel Kant Ser.: Vol. 4). 1977. Repr. of 1912 ed. lib. bdg. 33.00 (ISBN 0-8240-2328-5). Garland Pub.

Macmillan, R. H., jt. auth. see Lockwood, E. H.

McMillan, Richard C., ed. Education, Religion, & the Supreme Court. LC 78-74196. (Special Studies Ser.: No. 6). 1979. 4.95 (ISBN 0-932180-05-1). Assn Baptist Profs.

McMillan, Robert M. Faith Without Fantasy. LC 80-66541. 1981. 2.95 (ISBN 0-8054-5285-0). Broadman.

Macmillan, W. M. Cape Colour Question. 1968. Repr. of 1927 ed. text ed. 17.00x (ISBN 0-391-01964-3). Humanities.

McMillen, Donald H. Chinese Communist Power & Policy in Xinjiang, 1949-1977. 1979. lib. bdg. 27.50 o.p. (ISBN 0-89158-452-8). Westview.

MacMillen, Richard E. Population Ecology, Water Relations & Social Behavior of a Southern California Semidesert Rodent Fauna. (U. C. Publ. in Zoology: Vol. 71). 1964. pap. 4.50x (ISBN 0-520-09326-7). U of Cal Pr.

McMillen, S. I. None of These Diseases. (Orig.). pap. 1.50 (ISBN 0-515-04604-3). Jove Pubns.
McMillin, J. M., jt. auth. see Scott, George P.
McMillin, S. I. None of These Diseases. 1975. pap. 1.50 (ISBN 0-89129-011-7). Jove Pubns.
McMinn, Gordon & Libby, Larry. Taking Charge: The Dynamics of Personal Decision-Making & Self-Management. LC 80-65061. 192p. (Orig.). 1980. pap. 4.95 (ISBN 0-89636-043-1). Accent Bks.
McMinn, Howard E. An Illustrated Manual of California Shrubs. 1939. 25.00x (ISBN 0-520-00847-2). U of Cal Pr.
McMinn, Howard E. & Maino, Evelyn. An Illustrated Manual of Pacific Coast Trees. 1981. pap. 6.95 (ISBN 0-520-04364-2). U of Cal Pr.
McMinn, Winston G. A Constitutional History of Australia. 228p. 1979. text ed. 29.95x (ISBN 0-19-550562-X). Oxford U Pr.
McMordie, W., jt. auth. see Seidl, Jennifer.
McMullan, J. R., et al. Energy Resources. (Resource & Environmental Science Ser.). 1978. pap. text ed. 9.95 (ISBN 0-470-99377-4). Halsted Pr.
McMullan, J. T. Physical Techniques in Medicine, 2 vols. Incl. Vol. 1. LC 76-30281. 1977. 59.75 (ISBN 0-471-99468-5); Vol. 2. LC 79-42909. 160p. 1980. 45.00 (ISBN 0-471-27695-2). Pub. by Wiley-Interscience). Wiley.
McMullan, Randall. Physical Science for Technicians I. 1978. pap. text ed. 9.95 (ISBN 0-408-00332-4). Butterworths.
McMullen, Charles. Real Estate Investments: A Step by Step Guide. LC 80-20704. (Real Estate for Professional Practitioners Ser.). 156p. 1981. 19.95 (ISBN 0-471-08365-8, Pub. by Wiley-Interscience). Wiley.
McMullen, David. Atlantis: The Missing Continent. LC 77-22138. (Great Unsolved Mysteries Ser.). (Illus.). (gr. 4-5). 1977. PLB 9.65 (ISBN 0-8172-1047-4). Raintree Pubs.
--Mystery in Peru: The Lines of Nazca. LC 77-10456. (Great Unsolved Mysteries Ser.). (Illus.). (gr. 4-5). 1977. PLB 9.65 (ISBN 0-8172-1058-X). Raintree Pubs.
McMullen, David & McMullen, Susan. First into the Air: The First Airplanes. LC 78-15141. (Famous Firsts Ser.). (Illus.). 1978. lib. bdg. 7.35 (ISBN 0-686-51101-8). Silver.
McMullen, Lorraine. Sinclair Ross. (World Authors Ser.: No. 504). 1979. lib. bdg. 14.95 (ISBN 0-8057-6385-6). Twayne.
McMullen, Mary. A Dangerous Funeral. large print ed. 1981. Repr. of 1977 ed. 9.95 (ISBN 0-89621-269-6). Thorndike Pr.
--The Other Shoe. LC 80-2751. (Crime Club Ser.). 192p. 1981. 9.95 (ISBN 0-385-17534-5). Doubleday.
MacMullen, Ramsay. Paganism in the Roman Empire. LC 80-54222. 221p. 1981. 23.00x (ISBN 0-300-02655-2). Yale U Pr.
--Roman Social Relations, 50 B. C to A. D. 284. LC 73-86909. 317p. 1981. pap. 4.95x (ISBN 0-300-02702-8). Yale U Pr.
McMullen, Richard E. Rural Route, No. 2. LC 79-15513. (Poems for People Ser.). (Orig.). 1979. pap. cancelled (ISBN 0-914908-32-4). Street Fiction.
McMullen, Stewart Y. Financial Statements. 7th ed. 1979. 20.95 (ISBN 0-256-02165-1). Irwin.
McMullen, Susan, jt. auth. see McMullen, David.
MacMunn, George F. Slavery Through the Ages. 298p. 1974. Repr. of 1938 ed. 15.00x o.p. (ISBN 0-87471-463-X). Rowman.
McMurray, David, ed. see Guillen, Nicolas.
McMurray, George R. Gabriel Garcia Marquez. LC 76-20409. (Modern Literature Ser.). 1977. 10.95 (ISBN 0-8044-2620-1). Ungar.
--Jose Donoso. (World Authors Ser.: No. 517). 1979. lib. bdg. 13.95 (ISBN 0-8057-6358-9). Twayne.
MacMurray, John. Interpreting the Universe. 164p. 1980. Repr. lib. bdg. 25.00 (ISBN 0-89987-576-9). Darby Bks.
--Persons in Relation. 1979. pap. text ed. 4.95x (ISBN 0-571-09404-X). Humanities.
MacMurray, John V., ed. Treaties & Agreements with & Concerning China, 1894-1919, 2 vols. LC 77-114588. 1729p. 1974. Repr. of 1921 ed. Set. 80.00 (ISBN 0-86527-195-X). Fertig.
McMurry, John & Miller, R. Bryan, eds. Annual Reports in Organic Synthesis, Vols. 1-3. Vol. 1. 1971. 26.00 (ISBN 0-12-040801-5); Vol. 2. 1972. 26.00 (ISBN 0-12-040802-3); Vol. 3, 1973. 26.00 (ISBN 0-12-040803-1). Acad Pr.
McMurtrie, Douglas C. Wings for Words: The Story of Johann Gutenberg & His Invention of Printing. LC 78-167061. (Tower Bks). (Illus.). 175p. 1972. Repr. of 1940 ed. 20.00 (ISBN 0-8103-3936-6). Gale.
McMurtrie, Francis E., ed. Jane's Fighting Ships, 1939. LC 69-14519. (Illus.). 1979. lib. bdg. 29.95 o.s.i. (ISBN 0-668-02431-3). Arco.
McMurtry, James G., 3rd. Neurological Surgery. 2nd ed. (Medical Examination Review Bk.: Vol. 19). 1975. spiral bdg. 16.50 (ISBN 0-87488-119-6). Med Exam.
McMurtry, Larry. Hud. Orig. Title: Horseman, Pass by. 144p. 1974. pap. 0.95 o.p. (ISBN 0-445-08318-2). Popular Lib.
McMurtry, R. Gerald, jt. auth. see Harkness, David J.
McMurty. The Bunjee Venture. (gr. 3-5). 1980. pap. 1.25 (ISBN 0-590-30162-4, Schol Pap). Schol Bk Serv.
Macnab, Ian. Neck & Shoulder Pain. (Illus.). 300p. Date not set. lib. bdg. price not set (ISBN 0-683-05354-X). Williams & Wilkins. Postponed.
Macnab, P. A. The Isle of Mull. (Islands Ser.). (Illus.). 246p. 1974. 16.95 (ISBN 0-7153-4354-8). David & Charles.
McNab, Robert. The Old Whaling Days. 1977. 8.50 o.p. (ISBN 0-85558-432-7). Transatlantic.
MacNaghten, A. M., jt. ed. see McKeag, R. M.
MacNaghten, Patrick, jt. auth. see Heywood, Harry.
McNair, Arnold D. & Watts, A. D. Legal Effects of War. 4th ed. 69.00 (ISBN 0-521-05652-7). Cambridge U Pr.
MacNair, Donald J. The Living Church: A Guide for Revitalization. (Illus.). 167p. (Orig.). 1980. pap. 4.50 (ISBN 0-934688-00-1). Great Comm Pubns.
McNair, James K. Adventures in Italian Cooking. Ortho Books Editorial Staff, ed. LC 80-66345. (Illus.). 96p. (Orig.). 1981. pap. 4.95 (ISBN 0-917102-89-4). Ortho.
--Adventures in Italian Cooking. Ortho Books Editorial Staff, ed. LC 80-66345. (Illus.). 96p. (Orig.). 1981. pap. 4.95 (ISBN 0-917102-89-4, Ortho Bks). Chevron Chem.
McNair, Jim. Experiencing the Holy Spirit. LC 77-9262. 1977. pap. 3.50 (ISBN 0-87123-135-2, 210135). Bethany Fell.
--Love & Gifts. LC 76-6555. 1976. 3.50 (ISBN 0-87123-328-2, 210328). Bethany Fell.
McNair, Paul C. The Sportsman's Crafts Book. 1978. 12.95 (ISBN 0-87691-263-3). Winchester Pr.
McNair, Philip. Peter Martyr in Italy: An Anatomy of Apostasy. 1967. 12.00x o.p. (ISBN 0-19-821459-6). Oxford U Pr.
McNair, Will. Electric Drilling Rig Handbook. 256p. 1980. 37.50 (ISBN 0-87814-120-0). Pennwell Pub.
McNairn, Alan. The Young Van Dyck. (Illus.). 1980. 29.95 (ISBN 0-88884-456-5, 56579-3, Pub. by Natl Mus Canada); pap. 19.95 (ISBN 0-88884-468-9, 56578-5). U of Chicago Pr.
McNairn, Colin H. Governmental & Intergovernmental Immunity in Australia & Canada. 1977. 15.00x (ISBN 0-8020-2241-3). U of Toronto Pr.
McNair-Wilson, Diana. Hungary. 1976. 24.00 (ISBN 0-7134-3199-7). David & Charles.
McNall, Lee. Current Practice in Obstetric & Gynecologic Nursing, Vol. 3. (Current Practice Ser.). 1980. pap. 12.95 (ISBN 0-8016-3325-7). Mosby.
McNall, Leota K. Current Practice in Obstetric & Gynecologic Nursing, Vol. 1. LC 75-2940. (Illus.). 224p. 1976. case bound 11.95 o.p. (ISBN 0-8016-3328-1); pap. text ed. 8.95 case bound o.p. (ISBN 0-8016-3329-X). Mosby.
McNall, Leota K., ed. Current Practice in Obstetric & Gynecologic Nursing, Vol. 2. Galeener, Janet. LC 75-29240. (Current Practice Ser.). (Illus.). 1978. 12.50 (ISBN 0-8016-3326-5); pap. 9.50 (ISBN 0-8016-3327-3). Mosby.
McNall, Preston E. & Kircher, Harry B. Our Natural Resources. 4th ed. LC 75-14994. (Illus.). (gr. 7-12). 1976. text ed. 10.95x o.p. (ISBN 0-8134-1739-2, 1739). Interstate.
McNall, Preston E. & Kircher, Harry B., eds. Our Natural Resources. 5th ed. LC 80-83584. (Illus.). (gr. 7-12). 1981. text ed. 10.95x (ISBN 0-8134-2166-7, 2166). Interstate.
McNall, Scott. Political Economy: A Critique of American Society. 1981. pap. text ed. 7.95x (ISBN 0-673-15424-6). Scott F.
McNall, Scott G. The Career of a Radical Rightist: A Study in Failure. 1975. 15.00 (ISBN 0-8046-9099-5, Natl U). Kennikat.
McNally, Claire. Ghost House Revenge. 240p. (Orig.). 1981. pap. 2.50 (ISBN 0-553-14624-6). Bantam.
McNally, D. Positional Astronomy. LC 74-4819. 1975. text ed. 19.95 o.p. (ISBN 0-470-58980-9). Halsted Pr.
McNally, Kenneth. Batsford Colour Book of Ireland. 1975. 10.50 (ISBN 0-7134-2904-6, Pub. by Batsford England). David & Charles.
McNally, Raymond T., jt. auth. see Florescu, Radu.
McNally, Terrence. The Ritz & Other Plays. LC 76-17603. (Illus.). 1976. 9.95 (ISBN 0-396-07315-8). Dodd.
McNally, Tom. Hunting. LC 77-125023. (All Star Sports Bk). (Illus.). 128p. (gr. 4 up). 1972. 3.95 o.p. (ISBN 0-695-80194-5); lib. ed. 5.97 o.p. (ISBN 0-695-40194-7). Follett.
--Pocket Fishing Guide. 1981. pap. 1.95 (ISBN 0-528-84548-9). Rand.
McNamara, Bernard, jt. auth. see McNamara, Joan.
Macnamara, Donal E. & Reidei, Marc, eds. Police: Perspectives, Problems, Prospects. (Special Studies). (Illus.). 150p. 1974. text ed. 17.95 o.p. (ISBN 0-275-09660-2). Praeger.
McNamara, Joan. The Adoption Adviser. 256p. 1975. 9.95 o.p. (ISBN 0-8015-0068-0, Hawthorn); pap. 5.95 (ISBN 0-8015-0069-9). Dutton.
McNamara, Joan & McNamara, Bernard. The Special Child Handbook. LC 76-41976. 1978. 12.50 o.p. (ISBN 0-8015-6994-X). Dutton.
McNamara, John. Magic in Frosting. LC 72-79676. 1972. 10.95 o.p. (ISBN 0-686-60806-2). Exposition.
McNamara, John E. Technical Aspects of Data Communication. LC 77-93590. (Illus.). 1977. 25.00 (ISBN 0-932376-01-0). Digital Pr.
McNamara, Robert S. Accelerating Population Stabilization Through Social & Economic Progress. (Development Papers: No. 24). 64p. 1977. pap. 1.50 (ISBN 0-686-28675-8). Overseas Dev Council.
McNamara, Terry S. Numeracy & Accounting. (Illus.). 370p. 1979. pap. text ed. 16.95x (ISBN 0-7121-1411-4, Pub. by Macdonald & Evans England). Intl Ideas.
McNamara, William, O.C.D. Art of Being Human. pap. 1.95 (ISBN 0-385-08323-8, E45, Echo). Doubleday.
McNamee, Lawrence, ed. Dissertations in English & American Literature: Theses Accepted in American, British & German Universities, 1865-1964. LC 68-27446. 1124p. 1968. 23.50 o.p. (ISBN 0-8352-0043-4). Bowker.
McNames, Lucille. Startling Revelations. 120p. (Orig.). 1979. pap. 3.50 o.p. (ISBN 0-89861-022-2). Esoteric Pubns.
McNaspy, C. J. What a Modern Catholic Believes About Worship. 91p. (Orig.). 1972. pap. 4.95 (ISBN 0-88347-031-4). Thomas More.
McNatty, Kenneth P., jt. auth. see Peters, Hannah.
McNaughton, Colin. Soccer Crazy. LC 80-67834. (Illus.). 32p. (ps-4). 1981. 8.95 (ISBN 0-689-50189-7, McElderry Bk). Atheneum.
MacNaughton, E. G. & McDougall, T. W. A New Approach to Latin: 1. (Illus.). 1973. pap. text ed. 5.00x (ISBN 0-05-002185-0). Longman.
--A New Approach to Latin: 2. (Illus.). 1974. pap. text ed. 5.00x (ISBN 0-05-002365-9). Longman.
MacNaughton, Edgar. Elementary Steam Power Engineering. 3rd ed. 1948. text ed. 32.95x (ISBN 0-471-56034-0). Wiley.
Macnaughton, Edwin, jt. auth. see Paterson, James.
McNaughton, John H. Stewardship Myth & Methods: A Program Guide for Ministers & Lay Readers. 128p. 1975. pap. 3.95 (ISBN 0-8164-2112-9). Crossroad NY.
McNaughton, Kenneth J., et al. Controlling Corrosion in Process Industry. (Chemical Engineering Book Ser.). 288p. 1980. 24.50 (ISBN 0-07-010691-6). McGraw.
McNaughton, S. J. & Wolf, Larry L. General Ecology. 2nd ed. LC 78-23200. 702p. 1979. text ed. 17.95 (ISBN 0-03-019801-1, HoltC). HR&W.
McNaughton, William, ed. Chinese Literature: An Anthology from the Earliest Times to the Present Day. LC 73-75284. 1974. pap. 11.75 (ISBN 0-8048-0882-1). C E Tuttle.
McNeal, James U. An Introduction to Consumer Behavior. LC 72-6717. (Marketing Ser.). (Illus.). 400p. 1973. text ed. 19.95x o.p. (ISBN 0-471-58700-1). Wiley.
MacNeal, Kenneth. Truth in Accounting. LC 74-75709. 1970. Repr. of 1939 ed. text ed. 15.00 (ISBN 0-914348-04-3). Scholars Bk.
McNeal, Robert H. The Bolshevik Tradition: Lenin, Stalin, Khrushchev, Brezhnev. rev. ed. 224p. 1975. 8.95 o.p. (ISBN 0-13-079772-3, Spec); pap. 3.95 (ISBN 0-13-079764-2, Spec). P-H.
--Bride of the Revolution: Krupskaya & Lenin. (Illus.). 320p. 1972. 10.00 o.p. (ISBN 0-472-61600-5). U of Mich Pr.
--The Russian Revolution: Why Did the Bolsheviks Win? 62p. 1959. pap. 1.50 o.p. (ISBN 0-03-009145-4). Krieger.
McNeal, Robert H., ed. Resolutions & Decisions of the Communist Party of the Soviet Union: 1898-1964, 4 vols. Incl. Vol. 1. The Russian Social Democratic Labour Party, 1898-October 1917. Elwood, Ralph C., ed; Vol. 2. The Early Soviet Period, 1917-1929. Gregor, Richard, ed; Vol. 3. The Stalin Years, 1929-1953. McNeil, Robert H., ed; Vol. 4. The Khrushchev Years, 1953-1964. Hodnett, Grey, ed. LC 74-81931. 1974. Set. 95.00x (ISBN 0-8020-2157-3); 25.00 ea. U of Toronto Pr.
McNeal, S. R., jt. ed. see Bluth, B. J.
McNee, Robert B. Primer on Economic Geography. 1970. pap. text ed. 3.95 o.p. (ISBN 0-394-31019-5). Random.
McNeely, Harold E. & Obele, Norma. Psychotherapy: The Private & Very Personal Viewpoints of Doctor & Patient. LC 72-88581. 1973. 13.95 (ISBN 0-911012-35-4). Nelson-Hall.
McNeese, Donald G. & Hoag, Albert L. Engineering & Technical Handbook. 1957. ref. ed. 21.95 (ISBN 0-13-277434-8). P-H.
MacNeice see Bentley, Eric.
MacNeice, Louis. The Revenant: A Song-Cycle for Hedli Anderson. 1975. text ed. 19.50x (ISBN 0-391-01597-4). Humanities.
--Selected Poems. Auden, ed. (Orig.). 1964. pap. 5.95 (ISBN 0-571-06089-7, Pub. by Faber & Faber). Merrimack Bk Serv.
--Varieties of Parable. 1966. 28.50 (ISBN 0-521-05654-3). Cambridge U Pr.
MacNeice, Louis & Dodds, E. R., eds. Collected Poems (ISBN 0-571-04985-0, Pub. by Faber & Faber). pap. 11.50 (ISBN 0-571-11353-2). Merrimack Bk Serv.
McNeil, Alex. Total Television: A Comprehensive Guide to Programming from 1948 Through 1979. (Illus.). 1980. pap. 9.95 (ISBN 0-14-004911-8). Penguin.
McNeil, Barbara & Herbert, Miranda. Author Biographies Master Index - Supplement. 1980. pap. 65.00 (ISBN 0-8103-1088-0). Gale.
McNeil, Barbara & Herbert, Miranda C., eds. Historical Biographical Dictionaries Master Index. LC 80-10719. (Biographical Index Ser.: No. 7). 1980. 140.00 (ISBN 0-8103-1089-9). Gale.
McNeil, Barbara, jt. ed. see Herbert, Miranda C.
McNeil, Brian. Christ in the Psalms. 90p. 1980. pap. 2.95 (ISBN 0-8091-2341-X). Paulist Pr.
McNeil, Don. Moving Through Here. 252p. 10.95 (ISBN 0-934558-08-6); pap. 5.95 (ISBN 0-934558-09-4). Entwhistle Bks.
McNeil, Donald R. Fluoridation-For Your Community & Your State. rev. ed. pap. cancelled o.s.i. (ISBN 0-685-05573-6). Am Dental.
--Interactive Data Analysis: A Practical Primer. LC 76-46571. 1977. text ed. 14.95 (ISBN 0-471-02631-X, Pub. by Wiley-Interscience). Wiley.
MacNeil, Duncan. By Command of the Viceroy. LC 75-9492. 224p. 1975. 8.95 o.p. (ISBN 0-312-11060-X). St Martin.
--The Restless Frontier. 1980. 8.95 (ISBN 0-312-67782-0). St Martin.
McNeil, E. Quiet Furies: Man & Disorder. 1967. pap. text ed. 8.95 (ISBN 0-13-749770-9). P-H.
McNeil, Elton B. Neurosis & Personality Disorders. (Lives in Disorder Ser). 1970. pap. 8.95 ref. ed. (ISBN 0-13-611491-1). P-H.
--Psychoses. (Lives in Disorder Ser). 1970. pap. 8.95 ref. ed. (ISBN 0-13-736413-X). P-H.
McNeil, Elton B., jt. auth. see Fader, Daniel N.
McNeil, Elton B., jt. auth. see Rubin, Zick.
McNeil, John. The Consultant. 1979. pap. 2.25 o.p. (ISBN 0-345-28108-X). Ballantine.
McNeil, John D. Curriculum: A Comprehensive Approach. 2nd ed. 1981. text ed. 14.95 (ISBN 0-316-56308-0). Little.
McNeil, John T. & Institutes of the Christian Religion, eds. Calvin, 2 vols. (Library of Christian Classics Ser.). 1960. Set. 25.00 (ISBN 0-686-67721-8). Vol. 20 (ISBN 0-664-22020-7). Vol.21 (ISBN 0-664-22021-5). Westminster.
McNeil, Keith, et al. Testing Research Hypotheses Using Multiple Linear Regression. LC 75-6639. 600p. 1975. lib. bdg. 12.50x o.p. (ISBN 0-8093-0732-4); pap. text ed. 7.95x (ISBN 0-8093-0755-3). S Ill U Pr.
McNeil, M. Revised Token Test. 1978. 17.95 (ISBN 0-8391-1289-0); manual/score sheets 11.95 (ISBN 0-8391-1262-9). Univ Park.
McNeil, Margaret C. Come Sing with Me. (ps). 1971. pap. 2.95 (ISBN 0-8170-0535-8); bk. & record o.p. 5.95 (ISBN 0-685-01111-9). Judson.
McNeil, Marion. Sand in My Shoes. 1980. 6.95 (ISBN 0-89962-004-3). Todd & Honeywell.
McNeil, Robert H. see McNeal, Robert H.
McNeil, William J. & Himsworth, Daniel C., eds. Salmonid Ecosystems of the North Pacific. LC 80-17800. (Illus.). 348p. pap. 15.00 (ISBN 0-87071-335-3); pap. text ed. 15.00 (ISBN 0-686-68208-4). Oreg St U Pr.
McNeile, A. H. Gospel According to St. Matthew. (Thornapple Commentaries). 484p. 1980. pap. 8.95 (ISBN 0-8010-6099-0). Baker Bk.
McNeill, Alexander R. The Chordates. (Illus.). 500p. Date not set. text ed. price not set (ISBN 0-521-23658-4); pap. text ed. price not set (ISBN 0-521-28141-5). Cambridge U Pr.
McNeill, Earldene, et al. Cultural Awareness for Young Children at the Learning Tree. rev. ed. LC 75-34504. (Illus.). 252p. (Orig.). (gr. 2). 1976. pap. 11.95 (ISBN 0-686-28415-1). CAYC Learning Tree.
McNeill, Elizabeth. Nine & a Half Weeks: A Mamoir of a Love Affair. 1978. 7.95 o.p. (ISBN 0-525-16715-3). Dutton.
McNeill, John T., ed. see Calvin, John.

McNeill, Malvina R. Guidelines to Problems of Education in Brazil: A Review & Selected Bibliography. LC 76-120599. 1970. text ed. 6.00x (ISBN 0-8077-1789-4). Tchrs Coll.

McNeill, Moyra. Pulled Thread Embroidery. LC 70-185624. (Illus.). 207p. 1976. 9.95 (ISBN 0-8008-6562-6); pap. 5.95 (ISBN 0-8008-6563-4). Taplinger.

--Quilting for Today. (Illus.). 64p. 1976. 9.50 (ISBN 0-263-05601-5). Transatlantic.

McNeill, T. E. Anglo-Norman Ulster: The History & Archaeology of an Irish Barony 1177-1400. (Illus.). 166p. 1980. text ed. 32.50x (ISBN 0-686-64580-4). Humanities.

McNeill, William H. America, Britain & Russia: Their Co-Operation & Conflict 1941-1946. Repr. of 1953 ed. 50.00 (ISBN 0-685-92793-8); text ed. 45.00 (ISBN 0-686-64463-9). Johnson Repr.

--The Contemporary World: Nineteen Fourteen to Present. rev. ed. 184p. 1975. pap. 7.95x (ISBN 0-673-07908-2). Scott F.

--Europe's Steppe Frontier, Fifteen Hundred to Eighteen Hundred: A Study of the Eastward Movement in Europe. LC 64-22248. (Midway Reprint Ser.). 252p. 1964. 10.50x o.s.i. (ISBN 0-226-56151-8); pap. 9.50x (ISBN 0-226-56152-6). U of Chicago Pr.

--History of Western Civilization: A Handbook. rev. ed. LC 69-18121. 1969. text ed. 16.50x (ISBN 0-226-56137-2); pap. 8.95x (ISBN 0-226-56138-0). U of Chicago Pr.

--The Human Condition: An Ecological & Historical View. LC 80-7547. 100p. 1980. 8.50 (ISBN 0-691-05317-0). Princeton U Pr.

--Plagues & People. LC 76-2798. 10.00 (ISBN 0-385-11256-4); pap. 4.50 (ISBN 0-385-12122-9). Doubleday.

--Rise of the West: A History of the Human Community. LC 63-13067. 1970. pap. 9.95 (ISBN 0-226-56144-5, P385, Phoen). U of Chicago Pr.

--A World History. 3rd ed. (Illus.). 1979. 24.95 (ISBN 0-19-502554-7); pap. text ed. 11.95x (ISBN 0-19-502555-5). Oxford U Pr.

McNeill, William H. & Adams, Ruth S. Human Migration: Patterns & Policies. LC 77-23685. 1978. 22.50x (ISBN 0-253-32875-6). Ind U Pr.

McNeill, William H., et al. The World...Its History in Maps. rev. ed. (Illus.). 96p. 1980. pap. text ed. 9.10x (ISBN 0-87453-011-3, 81011). Denoyer.

McNeillie, Andrew. Guide to Pigeons of the World. (Illustrated Natural History Guides). (Illus.). 1977. pap. 4.95 (ISBN 0-8467-0367-X, Pub. by Two Continents). Hippocrene Bks.

McNeillie, Andrew, ed. see Woolf, Virginia.

MacNeish, Richard S., intro. by. Early Man in America: Readings from Scientific American. LC 72-12251. (Illus.). 1973. text ed. 15.95x (ISBN 0-7167-0864-7); pap. text ed. 7.95x (ISBN 0-7167-0863-9). W H Freeman.

MacNeish, Richard S., et al. Prehistory of the Ayacucho Basin, Peru, Vol. II: Excavations & Chronology. LC 80-13960. (Illus.). 368p. 1981. text ed. 45.00 (ISBN 0-472-04907-0). U of Mich Pr.

--The Prehistory of the Ayacucho Basin, Peru: Vol. Three: Nonceramic Artifacts. (Illus.). 360p. 45.00x (ISBN 0-472-02707-7). U of Mich Pr.

McNeil, Ken & Luther, Mark. How to Be a Successful Songwriter. LC 78-54699. (Illus.). 1978. 012.95 o.p. (ISBN 0-312-39586-8); pap. 5.95 (ISBN 0-312-39587-6), St Martin.

McNelly, Theodore. Politics & Government in Japan. 2nd ed. LC 74-186377. (Contemporary Government Ser.). (Illus.). 256p. (Orig.). 1972. pap. text ed. 9.50 (ISBN 0-395-12649-5, 3-37419). HM.

McNelly, Theodore, ed. Sources in Modern East Asian History & Politics. LC 67-18502. (Illus., Orig.). 1967. pap. text ed. 7.95x (ISBN 0-89197-419-9). Irvington.

McNely, James K. Holy Wind in Navajo Philosophy. 1981. text ed. 14.95x (ISBN 0-8165-0710-4); pap. 6.95x (ISBN 0-8165-0724-4). U of Ariz Pr.

McNemar, Quinn. Psychological Statistics. 4th ed. 1969. 24.95 (ISBN 0-471-58708-7). Wiley.

McNerney, Walter J., ed. Working for a Healthier America. 304p. 1980. 25.00 (ISBN 0-88410-718-3). Ballinger Pub.

McNichol, David L. Commodity Agreements & Price Stabilization. LC 77-75626. (Illus.). 1978. 16.95 (ISBN 0-669-01539-3). Lexington Bks.

Macnichol, Kenneth. Twelve Lectures on the Technique of Fiction Writing. 385p. 1980. lib. bdg. 40.00 (ISBN 0-89760-545-4). Telegraph Bks.

McNichol, Ronald W. Treatment of Delirium Tremens & Related States. (Illus.). 160p. 1970. 11.75 (ISBN 0-398-01270-9). C C Thomas.

McNicholas, John. The Design of English Elementary & Primary Schools: A Select Annotated Bibliography. (Select Bibliographies Ser.). (Illus.). 36p. 1974. pap. text ed. 3.75x (ISBN 0-85633-044-2, NFER). Humanities.

MacNicholas, John, ed. Twentieth-Century American Dramatists, 2 vols. (Dictionary of Literary Biography Ser.: Vol. 7). (Illus.). 300p. 1980. 108.00 set (ISBN 0-8103-0928-9). Gale.

McNichols, Charles L. Crazy Weather. LC 38-32977. 1967. pap. 2.95 (ISBN 0-8032-5132-7, BB 354, Bison). U of Nebr Pr.

McNickle, D'Arcy. Native American Tribalism. new ed. (Illus.). 120p. 1973. 9.95x (ISBN 0-19-501723-4). Oxford U Pr.

Macnicol, Fred, tr. see Forrai, Katalin, et al.

Macnicol, Fred, tr. see Hegyi, Erzsebet.

McNicol, John. Thinking Through the Bible, 4 vols. in one. LC 76-25079. 1976. text ed. 12.95 (ISBN 0-8254-3214-6). Kregel.

McNicoll, Geoffrey, jt. auth. see Hicks, George L.

MacNiece, Louis, tr. see Goethe, Johann W. Von.

McNiff, Shaun. The Arts & Psychotherapy. (Illus.). 280p. 19.75. C C Thomas.

MacNiochaill, Gearoid. Ireland Before the Vikings. (Gill History of Ireland: Vol. 1). (Illus.). 184p. 1972. pap. 6.95 (ISBN 0-7171-0558-X). Irish Bk Ctr.

Macnish, Robert. Philosophy of Sleep. (Contributions to the History of Psycholgy Ser.: Orientations). 1978. Repr. of 1834 ed. 30.00 (ISBN 0-89093-159-3). U Pubns Amer.

McNitt, Frank. The Indian Traders. LC 62-16469. 393p. 1962. 16.95 (ISBN 0-8061-0531-3). U of Okla Pr.

MacNiven, Ian S. & Moore, Harry T., eds. Literary Lifelines: The Richard Aldington-Larence Durrell Correspondence. 288p. 1981. 17.50 (ISBN 0-670-42817-5). Viking Pr.

McNown, Robert F. & Lee, Dwight R. Economics in Our Time: Macro Issues. LC 76-374. 224p. 1976. pap. text ed. 5.95 (ISBN 0-574-19260-3, 13-2260); instr's guide avail. (ISBN 0-574-19261-1, 13-2261). SRA.

McNown, Robert F., jt. auth. see Lee, Dwight R.

McNulty, Charles. China. (Orig.). (gr. 9-12). 1975. pap. text ed. 4.92 (ISBN 0-87720-615-5). AMSCO Sch.

--Japan. (Orig.). (gr. 9-12). 1975. pap. text ed. 4.50 (ISBN 0-87720-616-3). AMSCO Sch.

McNulty, Edward N. Television: A Guide for Christians. LC 76-1990. 96p. (Orig.). 1976. pap. 3.50 o.p. (ISBN 0-687-41220-X). Abingdon.

McNulty, Faith. The Wildlife Stories of Faith McNulty: A Reporter at Large in the Natural World. LC 79-7400. (Illus.). 480p. 1980. 17.95 (ISBN 0-385-14300-1). Doubleday.

McNulty, J. Bard. Modes of Literature. LC 76-10896. (Illus.). 1976. text ed. 15.70 (ISBN 0-395-24249-5); inst. manual 0.50 (ISBN 0-395-24248-7). HM.

McNulty, James G. Radiology of the Liver. LC 77-75536. (Monographs in Clinical Radiology: 13). (Illus.). 1977. text ed. 32.00 (ISBN 0-7216-5969-1). Saunders.

McNulty, John K., jt. auth. see Kragen, Adrian A.

McNulty, P. A., tr. see Cabasilas, Nicholas.

McNulty, Thomas F. & Stevens, Mary O. World of Variations. pap. 2.95 o.p. (ISBN 0-8076-0573-5). Braziller.

MacNutt, Francis. Healing. LC 74-81446. (Illus.). 336p. 1974. pap. 3.50 (ISBN 0-87793-074-0). Ave Maria.

--The Prayer That Heals. LC 80-69770. 120p. (Orig.). 1981. pap. 2.95 (ISBN 0-87793-219-0). Ave Maria.

McNutt, Robert D. West's Book of Legal Forms. 200p. 1981. pap. text ed. 3.96 (ISBN 0-8299-0516-2). West Pub.

Macomber, James. The Dynamics of Spectroscopic Transitions Illustrated by Magnetic Resonance & Laser Effects. LC 75-25852. (Monographs in Chemical Physics Ser). 332p. 1976. 29.95 o.p. (ISBN 0-471-56300-5, Pub. by Wiley-Interscience). Wiley.

Macon, Jorge & Merino Manon, Jose. Financing Urban & Rural Development Through Betterment Levies: The Latin American Experience. LC 76-24359. (Special Studies). 1977. text ed. 24.50 (ISBN 0-275-23970-5). Praeger.

Macourek, Milos. Curious Tales. 96p. (gr. 4 up). 1980. 11.95 (ISBN 0-19-271427-9). Oxford U Pr.

McPartland, James M. & McDill, Edward L., eds. Violence in Schools: Perspectives, Programs & Positions. 1977. 17.95 (ISBN 0-669-01082-0). Lexington Bks.

McPartland, Joseph F. McGraw-Hill's National Electrical Code Handbook. 16th ed. (Illus.). 1979. 19.95 (ISBN 0-07-045690-9). McGraw.

McPartland, Pamela. Take It Easy: American Indians & Two Word Verbs for Students of English As a Foreign Language. (ESL Ser.). 176p. 1981. pap. text ed. 6.95 (ISBN 0-13-882902-0). P-H.

McPeek, Mary, tr. & intro. by. Bobbin Lace, First Series: Les Dentelles Aux Fuseaux, 3 pts. rev. ed. LC 73-18373. (Illus.). 255p. 1974. Repr. Set. 42.00 (ISBN 0-8103-3955-2); 25 corner patterns incl. (ISBN 0-685-49538-8). Gale.

McPeters, Colin F. How to Start a Sideline Business of Your Own & Make a Success Out of It. (Illus.). 1980. 32.75 (ISBN 0-918968-57-7). Inst Econ Finan.

McPhail, David. Alligators Are Awful: And They Have Terrible Manners, Too. LC 79-7607. (Illus.). (gr. 1-3). 1980. 7.95a (ISBN 0-385-13582-3); PLB (ISBN 0-385-13583-1). Doubleday.

--The Bear's Toothache. (gr. 2-8). 1978. pap. 2.50 (ISBN 0-14-050263-7, Puffin). Penguin.

--Bumper Tubbs. (gr. k-3). 1980. 8.95 (ISBN 0-395-28477-5). HM.

--Pig Grows up. LC 80-350. (Illus.). 24p. (ps-3). 1980. PLB 8.95 (ISBN 0-525-37027-7, Unicorn). Dutton.

--Pig Pig Grows up. LC 80-377. (Illus.). 32p. (ps-2). 1980. 8.95 (ISBN 0-525-37027-7). Dutton.

--A Wolf Story. (Illus.). 32p. (gr. 1-5). 1981. 8.95 (ISBN 0-684-16713-1). Scribner.

Macphail, I. M. Dumbarton Castle. 2nd ed. 215p. 1980. text ed. 26.00x (ISBN 0-85976-051-0). Humanities.

MacPhail, Ralph, Jr., ed. see Gilbert, W. S.

McPhatter, William. The Business Beat: Its Impact & Its Problems. LC 80-16599. (ITT Key Issue Lecture Ser.). 168p. pap. text ed. 4.95. Bobbs.

McPhee, Colin. Music in Bali. LC 76-4979. (Music Reprint Ser.). 1976. Repr. of 1966 ed. lib. bdg. 45.00 (ISBN 0-306-70778-0). Da Capo.

MacPhee, Halsey M., jt. auth. see Jastak, Joseph F.

McPhee, John. Basin & Range. 1981. 10.95 (ISBN 0-374-10914-1). FS&G.

--The Curve of Binding Energy. 224p. 1974. 10.95 (ISBN 0-374-13373-5); pap. 5.95 (ISBN 0-374-51598-0). FS&G.

--The Curve of Binding Energy: A Journey into the Awesome & Alarming World of Theodore B. Taylor. 160p. 1976. pap. 2.25 (ISBN 0-345-28000-8). Ballantine.

--The Deltoid Pumpkin Seed. 192p. 1973. 12.95 (ISBN 0-374-13781-1). FS&G.

--The Deltoid Pumpkin Seed. 160p. 1976. pap. 2.25 (ISBN 0-345-27999-9). Ballantine.

--The Deltoid Pumpkin Seed. 1981. pap. 5.95 (ISBN 0-374-51635-9). FS&G.

--Giving Good Weight. 261p. 1979. 9.95 (ISBN 0-374-16306-5); pap. 5.95 (ISBN 0-374-51600-6). FS&G.

--Oranges. 1967. 7.50 (ISBN 0-374-22688-1); pap. 3.95 (ISBN 0-374-51297-3). FS&G.

--Pieces of the Frame. 1975. 10.00 (ISBN 0-374-23281-4); pap. 4.95 (ISBN 0-374-51498-4). FS&G.

--Pine Barrens. 1976. pap. 1.95 o.p. (ISBN 0-345-25788-X). Ballantine.

--A Roomful of Hovings & Other Profiles. LC 68-23746. 250p. 1969. 9.95 (ISBN 0-374-25208-4); pap. 4.95 (ISBN 0-374-51501-8). FS&G.

--A Sense of Where You Are. 1978. 9.95 o.p. (ISBN 0-374-26093-1); pap. 4.95 (ISBN 0-374-51485-2). FS&G.

--Survival of the Bark Canoe. 1977. pap. 4.95 (ISBN 0-446-97326-2). Warner Bks.

McPhee, John, ed. see Norquist, Marilyn.

McPhee, Nancy. Book of Insults II. 144p. 1981. 7.95 (ISBN 0-312-08930-9). St Martin.

McPhee, Norma. More Programs & Skits for Young Teens. 1980. pap. 3.50 (ISBN 0-8024-5669-3). Moody.

McPhee, Norma H. Programs & Skits for Young Teens. 1978. pap. 2.50 (ISBN 0-8024-6892-6). Moody.

MacPhee, R. D. Auditory Regiona of Primates & Eutherian Insectivores. (Contributions to Primatology Ser.: Vol. 18). (Illus.). 280p. 1981. pap. 35.00 (ISBN 3-8055-1963-X). S Karger.

McPhee, Robert D., jt. ed. see Cushman, Donald P.

Macpherson, A. I., et al. The Spleen. (American Lectures in Living Chemistry). (Illus.). 290p. 1973. 22.50 (ISBN 0-398-02806-0). C C Thomas.

MacPherson, Alan & MacPherson, Sue. Edible & Useful Wildplants. (Illus.). 1979. pap. 7.95 (ISBN 0-87108-533-X). Pruett.

McPherson, Alan & McPherson, Sue. Wild Food Plants of Indiana & Adjacent States. LC 76-48528. (Illus.). 192p. 1977. 12.50x (ISBN 0-253-19039-8); pap. 4.95x (ISBN 0-253-28925-4). Ind U Pr.

McPherson, Alexander. James Fraser. 1968. 8.95 o.p. (ISBN 0-686-12484-7). Banner of Truth.

McPherson, Alice. New & Controversial Aspects of Vitreoretinal Surgery. LC 77-1827. (Illus.). 1977. 52.50 o.p. (ISBN 0-8016-3321-4). Mosby.

McPherson, Andrew & Neave, Guy. The Scottish Sixth. (General Ser.). 170p. 1976. pap. text ed. 13.25x (ISBN 0-85633-093-0, NFER). Humanities.

McPherson, Andrew, jt. auth. see Gow, Lesley.

Macpherson, C. B. Democracy in Alberta: Social Credit & the Party System. LC 54-4046. (Canadian University Paperbooks). 1953. pap. 6.95 (ISBN 0-8020-6009-9). U of Toronto Pr.

--The Life & Times of Liberal Democracy. 1977. text ed. 6.95x (ISBN 0-19-219120-9); pap. text ed. 4.50x (ISBN 0-19-289106-5). Oxford U Pr.

Macpherson, C. B., ed. see Locke, John.

McPherson, Donald. The Traditions of Independence: British Cinema in the 30's. (BFI Ser.). (Orig.). 1980. pap. 11.50 (ISBN 0-85170-093-4). NY Zoetrope.

McPherson, Edward. Handbook of Politics, 4 Vols. LC 72-146558. (Law, Politics & History Ser.). 1973. Repr. of 1894 ed. lib. bdg. 45.00 ea.; Set. pap. 175.00. Da Capo.

--The Political History of the U. S. A. During the Period of Reconstruction. Hyman, Harold & Trefousse, Hans, eds. LC 77-127288. (Studies in American History & Government Ser.). 648p. 1972. Repr. of 1871 ed. lib. bdg. 55.00 (ISBN 0-306-71206-7). Da Capo.

--Political History of the United States of America During the Great Rebellion. LC 73-127287. (American Constitutional & Legal History Ser). 1972. Repr. of 1865 ed. lib. bdg. 55.00 (ISBN 0-306-71207-5). Da Capo.

McPherson, George. An Introduction to Electrical Machines & Transformers. 544p. 1981. text ed. 22.95 (ISBN 0-471-05586-7); tchrs.' ed. avail. (ISBN 0-471-07954-5). Wiley.

McPherson, Gertrude. Small Town Teacher. LC 71-188349. (Illus.). 449p. 1972. 12.50 (ISBN 0-674-81100-3); pap. 5.95 (ISBN 0-674-81101-1). Harvard U Pr.

Macpherson, Ian. Art of Illustrating Sermons. (Minister's Paperback Library). 220p. 1976. pap. 3.95 o.p. (ISBN 0-8010-5987-9). Baker Bk.

McPherson, Ian & Sutton, Andrew. Reconstructing Psychological Practice. 192p. 1981. 26.00x (ISBN 0-7099-0419-3, Pub. by Croom Helm LTD England). Biblio Dist.

MacPherson, Ian, ed. see Manuel, Don J.

McPherson, J. The Westminster Confession of Faith. (Handbooks for Bible Classes). 175p. pap. text ed. 8.95 (ISBN 0-567-28143-4). Attic Pr.

MacPherson, J. C., jt. auth. see Neilson, W. A.

McPherson, James A., jt. auth. see Williams, Miller.

Macpherson, John. Caribbean Lands. 4th ed. (Illus.). 192p. 1980. pap. text ed. 6.95x (ISBN 0-582-76565-X). Longman.

--Caribbean Lands. rev. 3rd ed. (Illus.). 192p. 1973. pap. text ed. 6.95x o.p. (ISBN 0-582-76615-X). Longman.

MacPherson, Malcolm. The Lucifer Key. 1981. 12.95 (ISBN 0-525-14985-6). Dutton.

--Protege. 256p. 1981. pap. 2.75 (ISBN 0-553-14706-4). Bantam.

MacPherson, Margaret M. Ponies for Hire. LC 67-10208. (Illus.). (gr. 6-7). 1967. 4.50 o.p. (ISBN 0-15-263165-8, HJ). HarBraceJ.

--Rough Road. LC 65-21701. (Illus.). (gr. 7-9). 1966. 4.75 o.p. (ISBN 0-15-269147-2, HJ). HarBraceJ.

Macpherson, Michael C. Family Years: A Guide to Positive Parenting. 146p. (Orig.). 1981. pap. 5.95 (ISBN 0-03-059131-7). Winston Pr.

MacPherson, Myra. The Power Lovers. 1976. pap. 1.95 o.p. (ISBN 0-345-25245-4). Ballantine.

Macpherson, Ruth. Be a Guest at Your Own Party. (Illus., Orig.). 1981. pap. 6.95 (ISBN 0-8437-3377-2). Hammond Inc.

McPherson, Steven P. Respiratory Therapy Equipment. 2nd ed. (Illus.). 514p. 1980. text ed. 24.95 (ISBN 0-8016-3313-3). Mosby.

MacPherson, Sue, jt. auth. see MacPherson, Alan.

McPherson, Sue, jt. auth. see McPherson, Alan.

McPherson, Thomas. Philosophy & Religious Belief. Korner, S., ed. (Illus.). 132p. 1974. text ed. 11.00x (ISBN 0-09-118750-8, Hutchinson U Lib); pap. text ed. 7.00x (ISBN 0-09-118751-6). Humanities.

--Political Obligation. (Library of Political Studies). 1967. text ed. 5.00x (ISBN 0-7100-3158-0); pap. text ed. 2.25x (ISBN 0-7100-3159-9). Humanities.

McPheters, Lee R. & Stronge, William B. The Economics of Crime & Law Enforcement. (Illus.). 520p. 1976. 26.75 (ISBN 0-398-03415-X). C C Thomas.

MacPike, Loralee. Dostoevsky's Dickens: A Study of Literary Influence. 270p. 1980. 19.50x (ISBN 0-389-20062-X). B&N.

McPolin, James. John. Harrington, Wilfrid & Senior, Donald, eds. (New Testament Message Ser.: Vol. 6). 244p. 1979. 10.95 (ISBN 0-89453-129-8); pap. 5.95 (ISBN 0-89453-194-8). M Glazier.

McQuade, Walter & Aikman, Ann. The Longevity Factor. 1981. pap. 2.95 (ISBN 0-671-81611-X). PB.

McQuade, Walter, ed. Cities Fit to Live In. 1971. pap. 3.50 o.s.i. (ISBN 0-02-087700-5, Collier). Macmillan.

McQuaid, Kim, jt. auth. see Berkowitz, Edward.

McQuaig, Jack, et al. How to Interview & Hire Productive People. LC 80-70952. 204p. 1981. 9.95 (ISBN 0-8119-0332-X). Fell.

McQuail, Denis. Communication. LC 75-11683. (A.O.M.S. Social Processes Ser.). (Illus.). 240p. 1975. text ed. 13.95x (ISBN 0-582-48710-2); pap. text ed. 9.50x (ISBN 0-582-48711-0). Longman.

McQuail, Denis, jt. auth. see Blumler, Jay G.

MacQuarrie, Gordon. Stories of the Old Duck Hunters & Other Drivel. Taylor, Zack, ed. LC 67-12929. 1967. 6.95 o.p. (ISBN 0-8117-1682-1). Stackpole.

Macquarrie, John. Christian Hope. 1978. 7.95 (ISBN 0-8164-0388-0). Crossroad NY.

--Existentialism. 1973. pap. 2.95 (ISBN 0-14-021569-7, Pelican). Penguin.

--God-Talk. (Library of Contemporary Theology). 1979. pap. 7.95 (ISBN 0-8164-2205-2). Crossroad NY.

--Martin Heidegger. LC 68-11970. (Makers of Contemporary Theology Ser). 1968. pap. 3.45 (ISBN 0-8042-0659-7). John Knox.

McQuay, Mike. Escape from New York. 192p. (Orig.). 1981. pap. 2.50 (ISBN 0-553-14914-8). Bantam.

MacQueen, Donald R., ed. Understanding Sociology Through Research. LC 72-581. 1973. pap. text ed. 12.50 (ISBN 0-201-04381-5). A-W.

M'Queen, James. Geographical Survey of Africa. 303p. Repr. of 1969 ed. 29.50x (ISBN 0-7146-1834-9, F Cass Co). Biblio Dist.

MacQueen, John & MacQueen, Winifred, eds. A Choice of Scottish Verse. 1972. 8.95 (ISBN 0-571-09532-1, Pub. by Faber & Faber); pap. 4.95 (ISBN 0-571-09686-7). Merrimack Bk Serv.

MacQueen, Sheila. Your Book of Flower Arranging. 1972. 5.95 (ISBN 0-571-09625-5, Pub. by Faber & Faber). Merrimack Bk Serv.

MacQueen, Winifred, jt. ed. see MacQueen, John.

McQueen-Williams, Morvyth & Appisson, Barbara. A Diet for One Hundred Healthy, Happy Years. 1978. pap. 1.95 (ISBN 0-515-04523-3). Jove Pubns.

McQuilkin, Frank. Thinking Black: An Introduction to Black Political Power. 1970. pap. 2.95 (ISBN 0-685-03350-3, 80510). Macmillan.

McQuilkin, Robert. Comfort Below Freezing. LC 79-28741. (Illus.). 176p. (Orig.). 1981. pap. 5.95 (ISBN 0-89037-184-9). Anderson World.

McQuillan, Florence. Realities of Nursing Management: How to Cope. LC 78-8298. 384p. 1978. text ed. 19.95 (ISBN 0-87618-991-5). R J Brady.

McQuillan, J., jt. auth. see Gardner, P. S.

McQuillan, Mary T. Somatostatin, Vol. 1. Horrobin, D. F., ed. (Annual Research Reviews Ser.). 1979. 24.00 (ISBN 0-88831-040-4). Eden Med Res.

McQuillen, K., jt. ed. see Mandelstam, J.

McQuillin, F. J. Alicyclic Chemistry. (Chemistry Texts Ser). (Illus.). 1972. 34.95 (ISBN 0-521-08216-1); pap. 11.95x (ISBN 0-521-09659-6). Cambridge U Pr.

McQuiston, L., jt. ed. see Bicknell, J.

McQuitty, Robert A. & Walker, James P. Fresh English. 3rd ed. 384p. 1980. pap. text ed. 17.95 (ISBN 0-8403-2244-5). Kendall-Hunt.

Macquitty, William. Island of Isis. LC 76-5574. (Encore Edition). (Illus.). 192p. 1976. 6.95 o.p. (ISBN 0-684-15694-6, ScribT). Scribner.

McQuown, Judith H. Inc. Yourself. 1981. pap. 5.95 (ISBN 0-446-97817-5). Warner Bks.

MacRae, Anita. Year the Dreams Came Back. (YA) (gr. 7-9). pap. 1.25 (ISBN 0-671-29875-5). PB.

Macrae, C. Duncan, jt. auth. see Fredland, J. Eric.

Macrae, Donald, ed. The World of J. B. Priestley. 1967. text ed. 5.95x o.p. (ISBN 0-435-82725-1). Heinemann Ed.

Macrae, Donald G. Ages & Stages. (Anguste Camte Memorial Institute Lecture Ser.: No. 9). 1973. pap. text ed. 2.50x o.p. (ISBN 0-485-19109-1, Athlone Pr). Humanities.

--Max Weber. LC 72-181978. (Modern Masters Ser). 1974. pap. 2.25 o.p. (ISBN 0-670-01976-3). Penguin.

MacRae, Duncan, Jr. The Social Function of Social Science. LC 75-32282. (Illus.). 376p. 1976. 25.00x (ISBN 0-300-01921-1). Yale U Pr.

--The Social Function of Social Science. LC 75-32282. 376p. 1981. pap. 7.95 (ISBN 0-300-02670-6). Yale U Pr.

McRae, Gail C. How to Raise & Train a Borzoi. (Illus., Orig.). pap. 2.00 (ISBN 0-87666-250-5, DS1043). TFH Pubns.

Macrae, George W., S.J. Invitation to John: A Commentary on the Gospel of John with Complete Text from the Jerusalem Bible. LC 77-91559. 1978. pap. 2.95 (ISBN 0-385-12212-8, Im). Doubleday.

McRae, James T. Emergency Medicine Case Studies. LC 79-88721. 1979. pap. 15.50 (ISBN 0-87488-002-5). Med Exam.

McRae, Jane C. Photographer in Lebanon: The Story of Said Jureidini. LC 69-19024. (Illus.). (gr. 4-5). 1969. pap. 0.75 (ISBN 0-8054-4313-4). Broadman.

McRae, John. Elderly in the Environment: Northern Europe. (Illus.). 119p. (Orig.). 1975. pap. 7.50 (ISBN 0-8130-0687-2). U Presses Fla.

McRae, Kimberleigh Ann. Parallels from Life-Parallels from Life. LC 79-57180. (Illus.). 59p. 1980. pap. 4.95 (ISBN 0-935054-01-4). Webb-Newcomb.

Macrae, Norman, et al. Day After Tomorrow in the Pacific Region, Nineteen Seventy-Eight. (Worldview Symposium Ser.). 1978. pap. 2.00 o.p. (ISBN 0-685-99241-1). Asia Soc.

McRae, R. & Walker, D. Foreign Exchange Management. 1981. 36.00 (ISBN 0-13-325357-0). P-H.

McRae, Shirley. Chatter with the Angels. 1980. pap. 5.50 (ISBN 0-918812-09-7). Magnamusic.

McRae, William J. Preparing for Your Marriage. 160p. (Orig.). 1980. pap. 5.95 (ISBN 0-310-42761-4, 9366P). Zondervan.

McRaven, Charles. Building with Stone. (Illus.). 1980. 14.95 (ISBN 0-690-01879-7); pap. 8.95 (ISBN 0-690-01912-2). Lippincott.

--Country Blacksmithing. LC 80-7876. (Illus.). 208p. 1981. 14.95 (ISBN 0-06-014870-5, HarpT). Har-Row.

--Country Blacksmithing. LC 80-7876. (Illus.). 208p. 1981. pap. 9.95 (ISBN 0-06-090870-X, CN870, CN). Har-Row.

Macready, Robert. The Reincarnation of Robert Macready. 336p. (Orig.). 1981. pap. 2.75 (ISBN 0-89083-703-1). Zebra.

McReynolds, Cliff. Revelation Art: All Things New. (Illus., Orig.). 1980. pap. 10.95 (ISBN 0-917556-04-6). Pomegranate Calif.

McReynolds, Edwin C. Seminoles. (Civilization of the American Indian Ser.: No. 47). (Illus.). 1957. 15.95 o.p. (ISBN 0-8061-0382-5); pap. 7.95 (ISBN 0-8061-1255-7). U of Okla Pr.

McReynolds, Edwin C., et al. Oklahoma: The Story of Its Past & Present. rev. ed. (Illus.). 1980. Repr. of 1961 ed. 12.50x (ISBN 0-8061-0509-7). U of Okla Pr.

McReynolds, Jeannie. Footprints of Providence. LC 77-25504. (Crown Ser.). 1978. pap. 4.50 (ISBN 0-8127-0172-0). Southern Pub.

McReynolds, S. R., jt. auth. see Dyer, P.

Macri, Angelika, tr. see Hartmann, Sven & Hartner, Thoman.

Macridis, Roy C. Modern Political Systems: Europe. 4th ed. 1978. ref. 17.95 (ISBN 0-13-597187-X). P-H.

Macridis, Roy C. & Brown, Bernard E., eds. Comparative Politics: Notes & Readings. 5th ed. 1977. pap. text ed. 12.95x (ISBN 0-256-01956-8). Dorsey.

MacRobbie, Bill. Add Spice to Your Travels. (Illus.). 196p. 1980. pap. 4.95 (ISBN 0-9605244-0-1). B Sales.

McRobie, George. Small Is Possible. LC 79-2634. 256p. 1981. 11.95 (ISBN 0-06-013041-5, CN694, HarpT); pap. 4.95 (ISBN 0-06-090694-4). Har-Row.

Macrorie, Ken. Searching Writing. 352p. 1980. pap. 8.95x (ISBN 0-8104-6037-8). Hayden.

--Telling Writing. 3rd ed. (English Language Ser.). (gr. 10 up). 1980. pap. 8.95x (ISBN 0-8104-6116-1). Hayden.

--A Vulnerable Teacher. 192p. (Orig.). 1974. 6.95 (ISBN 0-8104-5936-1). Hayden.

--Writing to Be Read. rev. 2nd ed. (English Language Ser.). 288p. 1976. 11.50x (ISBN 0-8104-5980-9); pap. 9.50x (ISBN 0-8104-5979-5). Hayden.

McSeveney, S., jt. auth. see Silbey, J.

McShane, E. J. Riemann-Type Integral That Includes Lebesgue-Stieltjes, Bochner & Stochastic Integrals. LC 52-42839. (Memoirs: No. 88). 1979. pap. 6.00 (ISBN 0-8218-1288-2, MEMO-88). Am Math.

MacShane, Frank. The Life of John O'Hara. (Illus.). 300p. 1981. 14.95 (ISBN 0-525-13720-3). Dutton.

MacShane, Frank, ed. see Ford, Ford M.

McShane, Ivan, pref. by. An Anthology of Mentor Poetry for the Sixties. pap. 3.00 (ISBN 0-87423-015-2). Westburg.

McShane, Mark. The Halcyon Way. (Orig.). 1980. pap. 1.95 (ISBN 0-532-23148-1). Manor Bks.

McShane, Philip. Music That Is Soundless: An Introduction to God for the Graduate. 1977. pap. text ed. 7.00 (ISBN 0-8191-0236-9). U Pr of Amer.

--The Shaping of the Foundations: Being at Home in the Transcendental Method. 9.50 (ISBN 0-8191-0209-1). U Pr of Amer.

McShane, Rudolph M. Pre-Trig. LC 61-13070. (Illus.). (gr. 10-12). 1961. pap. 1.00 (ISBN 0-910172-02-1). Astro Comp Serv.

McShine, Kynaston, ed. Joseph Cornell. (Illus.). 296p. 1980. 29.95 (ISBN 0-87070-271-8); pap. 13.50 (ISBN 0-87070-272-6). Museum Mod Art.

MacStravic, Robin E. Marketing Health Care. LC 76-58967. 1977. 25.75 (ISBN 0-912862-41-6). Aspen Systems.

MacStravic, Robin S. Marketing by Objectives for Hospitals. LC 80-10903. 280p. 1980. text ed. 26.95 (ISBN 0-89443-174-9). Aspen Systems.

MacSwain, J. W., jt. auth. see Linsley, E. G.

McSwain, John S. The Very Private Affairs of Jason Smith. LC 77-83885. 1979. 8.00 o.p. (ISBN 0-89430-015-6). Morgan-Pacific.

McSwain, Larry L. & Treadwell, William C., Jr. Conflict Ministry in the Church. 1981. pap. 6.95 (ISBN 0-8054-2540-3). Broadman.

McSwain, Norman E., Jr. Traumatic Surgery. (Medical Outline Ser.). 1976. spiral bdg. 12.00 o.p. (ISBN 0-87488-619-8). Med Exam.

McSwain, Norman, Jr. & Skelton, Mary B. Surgical Procedures in Emergency Medicine. 300p. 1982. text ed. 29.95 (ISBN 0-8359-7394-8). Reston.

McSweeney, Edward. Managing the Managers. LC 77-3761. 1978. 9.95 o.s.i. (ISBN 0-06-012959-X, HarpT). Har-Row.

McSweeney, Kerry. Tennyson & Swinburne As Romantic Naturalists. 240p. 1981. 25.00x (ISBN 0-8020-2381-9). U of Toronto Pr.

McTaggart, Aubrey C. & McTaggart, Lorna M. The Health Care Dilemma. 2nd ed. 275p. 1976. pap. text ed. 11.95 (ISBN 0-205-05446-3, 7154461). Allyn.

McTaggart, Lorna M., jt. auth. see McTaggart, Aubrey C.

McTaggart, Lynn. The Baby Brokers: The Marketing of White Babies in America. 1980. 10.95 (ISBN 0-8037-0354-6). Dial.

McTavish, jt. auth. see Loether.

McTavish, Donald G., jt. auth. see Loether, Herman J.

McTrusty, Ron. Dandelion Year. LC 74-83424. (Bks Without Words). (Illus.). 32p. (ps-5). 1974. PLB 4.95 (ISBN 0-8178-5292-1). Harvey.

Macuch, Rudolf. Handbook of Classical & Modern Mandaic. 1965. 123.55x (ISBN 3-11-000261-2). De Gruyter.

Maculay, Lord. Literary Essays: Contributed by the Edinburgh Review. 706p. 1980. Repr. of 1923 ed. lib. bdg. 30.00 (ISBN 0-89760-544-6). Telegraph Bks.

MacUlsten, Liam. Post Mortem. (Irish Play Ser.). pap. 2.50 (ISBN 0-912262-43-5). Proscenium.

Macur, Mary. Curious What You Might Find When You Go Out to Look for Elephants. LC 48-29. pap. 5.00 (ISBN 0-686-28865-3). First Amend.

Macurdy, Grace H. Hellenistic Queens. LC 75-16848. (Johns Hopkins University Studies in Archaeology: No. 14). (Illus.). 250p. 1975. Repr. of 1932 ed. lib. bdg. 19.50x (ISBN 0-8371-8271-9, MAHQ). Greenwood.

MacVaugh, Gilbert S. Frigidity: Its Cure with Hypnosis. LC 78-26958. 1979. 44.00 (ISBN 0-08-021748-6). Pergamon.

McVaugh, Michael R., jt. auth. see Mauskopf, Seymour H.

McVay, Kipling L. & Stubbs, Robert S. Governmental Ethics & Conflicts of Interest in Georgia. 227p. 1980. 15.00 (ISBN 0-87215-304-5). Michie.

Macvey, John W. How We Will Reach the Stars. 1969. pap. 1.25 o.s.i. (ISBN 0-02-093450-5, Collier). Macmillan.

McVey, Ruth J. Rise of Indonesian Communism. 1965. 24.50x o.p. (ISBN 0-8014-0287-5). Cornell U Pr.

McVey, Sheila, jt. auth. see Altbach, Philip G.

McVicar, Marjorie & Craig, Julia F. Minding My Own Business: Entrepreneurial Women Share Their Secrets for Success. 425p. 1981. 12.95 (ISBN 0-399-90116-7). Marek.

McVickar, Malcolm H. Approved Practices in Pasture Management. 3rd ed. LC 72-97443. (Illus.). (gr. 9-12). 1974. 13.00 o.p. (ISBN 0-8134-1547-0, 1547); text ed. 9.75x o.p. (ISBN 0-685-42160-0). Interstate.

McWane, John W. Introduction to Electronics & Instrumentation. 1981. text ed. 19.95 (ISBN 0-534-00938-7, Breton Pubs). Wadsworth Pub.

McWatters, Ann R. Financing Capital Formation for Local Governments. LC 79-10333. (Research Report: No. 79-3). 1979. pap. 3.00x (ISBN 0-87772-266-8). Inst Gov Stud Berk.

McWebb, Elizabeth U. Little Brown Bear. 2nd ed. (Illus.). 55p. 1978. Repr. of 1962 ed. 8.00x (ISBN 0-686-28491-7). Monroe County Lib.

McWeeny, R. & Sutcliffe, B. T. Methods of Molecular Quantum Mechanics. (Theoretical Chemistry Ser). 1970. 39.00 (ISBN 0-12-486550-X). Acad Pr.

McWeeny, R., ed. see Farina, John E.

McWeeny, Roy, ed. see Coulson, Charles A.

McWhiney, Grady. Braxton Bragg & Confederate Defeat: Field Command, Vol. 1. LC 69-19856. (Illus.). 1969. 20.00x (ISBN 0-231-02881-4). Columbia U Pr.

McWhinney, Edward. Conflict & Compromise: International Law & World Order in a Revolutionary Age. LC 80-29045. 152p. 1981. text ed. 14.00x (ISBN 0-8419-0694-7); pap. text ed. 8.75x (ISBN 0-8419-0696-3). Holmes & Meier.

--Constitution-Making. 240p. 1981. 20.00x (ISBN 0-8020-5553-2). U of Toronto Pr.

--Quebec & the Constitution: Nineteen Sixty to Nineteen Seventy Eight. 1979. 15.00x o.p. (ISBN 0-8020-5456-0); pap. 5.95 (ISBN 0-8020-6364-0). U of Toronto Pr.

McWhinney, Ian R. An Introduction to Family Medicine. (Illus.). 224p. 1981. text ed. 16.95x (ISBN 0-19-502807-4); pap. text ed. 9.95 (ISBN 0-19-502808-2). Oxford U Pr.

McWhinnie, M. A., et al. Euphausiacea Bibliography: A World Literature Survey. 1981. 50.01 (ISBN 0-08-024649-4). Pergamon.

McWhinnie, Mary A., ed. Polar Research: To the Present & the Future. LC 78-52068. (AAAS Selected Symposium Ser.: No. 7). (Illus.). 1978. lib. bdg. 28.50x (ISBN 0-89158-435-8). Westview.

McWhirter, David. Millenial Harbinger - Index. LC 81-65031. (Millenial Harbinger Ser.). 864p. 1981. 19.95 (ISBN 0-89900-228-5). College Pr Pub.

McWhirter, J. Jeffries. The Learning Disabled Child: A School & Family Concern. LC 77-81300. (Illus.). 1977. text ed. 8.95 (ISBN 0-87822-147-6); pap. text ed. 8.95 (ISBN 0-87822-142-5). Res Press.

McWhirter, J. R., ed. Use of High Purity Oxygen in the Activated Sludge Process, 2 vols. (Uniscience Ser.). 1978. Vol. 1, 296p. 59.95 (ISBN 0-8493-5101-4); Vol. 2, 292p. 59.95 (ISBN 0-8493-5102-2). CRC Pr.

McWhirter, Norris. Guinness Book of Superstunts & Staggering Statistics. LC 79-91387. (Guinness Illustrated Collection of World Records for Young Readers Ser.). (Illus.). 96p. (gr. 3-12). 1980. 5.95 (ISBN 0-8069-0180-2); PLB 6.69 (ISBN 0-8069-0181-0). Sterling.

--Guinness Book of World Records 1981. rev. ed. LC 65-24391. (Illus.). 652p. 1980. 10.95 (ISBN 0-8069-0196-9); deluxe ed. 15.95 (ISBN 0-8069-0198-5); lib. bdg. 10.79 (ISBN 0-8069-0197-7). Sterling.

--Guinness Sports Record Book, 1979-1980. LC 78-66316. (Illus.). 1979. 5.95 o.p. (ISBN 0-8069-0164-0); lib. bdg. 5.89 o.p. (ISBN 0-8069-0165-9). Sterling.

McWhirter, Norris & McWhirter, Ross. Guinness Book of Amazing Achievements. LC 75-14502. (Guinness Illustrated Collection for Young People Ser.). (Illus.). 96p. (YA) 1975. 5.95 (ISBN 0-8069-0034-2); lib. bdg. 6.69 (ISBN 0-8069-0035-0). Sterling.

--Guinness Book of Astounding Feats & Events. LC 75-14503. (Guinness Illustrated Collection for Young People Ser.). 96p. (YA) 1975. 5.95 (ISBN 0-8069-0036-9); lib. bdg. 6.69 (ISBN 0-8069-0037-7). Sterling.

--Guinness Book of Daring Deeds & Fascinating Facts. LC 78-66312. (Illus.). (gr. 3 up). 1979. 5.95 (ISBN 0-8069-0158-6); PLB 6.69 (ISBN 0-8069-0159-4). Sterling.

--Guinness Book of Extraordinary Exploits. LC 77-79505. (Guinness Illustrated Collection of World Records for Young Readers). (Illus.). (gr. 3 up). 1977. 5.95 (ISBN 0-8069-0118-7); PLB 6.69 (ISBN 0-8069-0119-5). Sterling.

--Guinness Book of Startling Acts & Facts. LC 78-57791. (Guinness Illustrated Collection of World Records for Young Readers). (Illus.). (gr. 2 up). 1978. 5.95 (ISBN 0-8069-0128-4); PLB 6.69 (ISBN 0-8069-0129-2). Sterling.

--Guinness Book of Surprising Accomplishments. LC 76-51178. (Guinness Illustrated Collection of World Records for Young People Ser.). (gr. 3 up). 1977. 5.95 (ISBN 0-8069-0046-6); PLB 6.69 (ISBN 0-8069-0047-4). Sterling.

--Guinness Book of Young Recordbreakers. LC 76-1161. (Illus.). 96p. (gr. 2-5). 1976. 5.95 (ISBN 0-8069-0038-5); PLB 6.69 (ISBN 0-8069-0039-3). Sterling.

McWhirter, Norris & Pallas, Norvin. Guinness Game Book. LC 77-93311. (Illus.). (gr. 3 up). 1978. 5.95 (ISBN 0-8069-0122-5); PLB 5.89 (ISBN 0-8069-0123-3). Sterling.

McWhirter, Norris, jt. auth. see McWhirter, Ross.

McWhirter, Norris, ed. Guinness Book of World Records. 19th ed. 672p. 1981. pap. 3.50 (ISBN 0-553-14500-2). Bantam.

McWhirter, Norris & McWhirter, Ross, eds. Guinness Book of Exceptional Experiences. LC 76-19801. (Guinness Illustrated Collection of World Records for Young People). (Illus.). 96p. (gr. 3 up). 1976. 5.95 (ISBN 0-8069-0042-3); PLB 6.69 (ISBN 0-8069-0043-1). Sterling.

--Guinness Book of Phenomenal Happenings. LC 76-1162. (Illus.). 96p. (gr. 4 up). 1976. 5.95 (ISBN 0-8069-0040-7); PLB 6.69 (ISBN 0-8069-0041-5). Sterling.

McWhirter, Norris, et al. Guinness Book of Women's Sports Records. LC 78-66315. (Illus.). 1979. 7.95 (ISBN 0-8069-0162-4); lib. bdg. 7.49 (ISBN 0-8069-0163-2). Sterling.

--Guinness Book of Sports Records, Winners & Champions. LC 79-91388. (Illus.). 320p. 1980. 10.95 (ISBN 0-8069-0182-9); lib. bdg. 9.89 (ISBN 0-8069-0183-7). Sterling.

McWhirter, Ross & McWhirter, Norris. Guinness Book of Dazzling Endeavors. LC 80-52330. (Guinness Illustrated Collection of World Records for Young Readers). (Illus.). 96p. (gr. 3 up). 1980. 5.95 (ISBN 0-8069-0194-2); PLB 6.69 (ISBN 0-8069-0195-0). Sterling.

--Guinness Book of Young Recordbreakers. rev. ed. LC 76-1161. (Guinness Illustrated Collection of World Records for Young Readers). (Illus.). 96p. (gr. 3 up). 1981. 5.95 (ISBN 0-8069-0216-7); PLB 6.69 (ISBN 0-8069-0217-5). Sterling.

McWhirter, Ross, jt. auth. see McWhirter, Norris.

McWhirter, Ross, jt. ed. see McWhirter, Norris.

McWhorter, Jane. Caterpillars or Butterflies. 1977. pap. 3.75 (ISBN 0-89137-410-8). Quality Pubns.

--Let This Cup Pass. 1979. pap. 3.75 (ISBN 0-89137-414-0). Quality Pubns.

--She Hath Done What She Could. 1973. 3.75 (ISBN 0-89137-405-1). Quality Pubns.

McWhorter, Margaret L. Poems That Tell Me Who I Am. LC 80-51481. (Illus.). 57p. 1980. pap. 3.95 (ISBN 0-9604342-0-8). Ransom Hill.

McWhorter, William L. Inmante Society: Legs, Half-Pants & Gunmen, a Study of Inmate Guards. LC 80-69327. 140p. 1981. perfect bdg. 11.95 (ISBN 0-86548-047-8). Century Twenty One.

McWilliams, Bernard, tr. see Paoli, Arturo.

McWilliams, Dean, tr. see Weisgerber, Jean.

McWilliams, John P., jt. ed. see Dekker, George.

McWilliams, K. Richard, jt. auth. see El-Najjar, Mahmoud Y.

McWilliams, Margaret. Experimental Foods Laboratory Manual. (Illus.). 1977. spiral bdg. 11.95x (ISBN 0-916434-22-2). Plycon Pr.

--Food Fundamentals. 3rd ed. LC 78-65888. 1979. 20.95x (ISBN 0-471-02691-3). Wiley.

--Fundamentals of Meal Management. LC 78-54660. (Illus.). 1978. text ed. 16.95 (ISBN 0-916434-29-X). Plycon Pr.

--Illustrated Guide to Food Preparation. 4th rev. ed. 1981. pns (ISBN 0-8087-3409-1). Burgess.

--Illustrated Guide to Food Preparation. 3rd ed. LC 76-13996. (Illus.). 1976. spiral bdg. 11.95x (ISBN 0-916434-17-6). Plycon Pr.

MacWilliams, Margaret. Mistral. LC 80-2056. (Starlight Romance Ser.). 192p. 1981. 9.95 (ISBN 0-385-17390-3). Doubleday.

McWilliams, Margaret. Nutrition for the Growing Years. 2nd ed. LC 74-28180. 452p. 1975. text ed. 18.95 o.p. (ISBN 0-471-58738-9). Wiley.

--Nutrition for the Growing Years. 3rd ed. LC 80-453. 491p. 1980. text ed. 20.50x (ISBN 0-471-02692-1). Wiley.

McWilliams, Margaret & Paine, Harriett. Modern Food Preservation. LC 77-76339. (Illus.). 1977. text ed. 11.95x (ISBN 0-916434-25-7). Plycon Pr.

McWilliams, Margaret, jt. auth. see Stare, Fredrick J.

McWilliams, Margaret, jt. auth. see State, Frederick J.

McWilliams, Peter, jt. auth. see Denniston, Denise.

McWilliams, Tennant S. Hannis Taylor: The New Southerner As an American. LC 77-17124. 192p. 1978. 12.95 (ISBN 0-8173-5114-0). U of Ala Pr.

McWilliams, Wilson C. The Idea of Fraternity in America. LC 73-101339. 1973. 21.50x (ISBN 0-520-01650-5); pap. 4.95 (ISBN 0-520-02772-8). U of Cal Pr.

McWirter, Norris, ed. Guinness Sports Record Book. 7th ed. 192p. 1980. pap. 2.25 (ISBN 0-553-13238-5). Bantam.

Macy, Christopher, jt. auth. see Falkner, Frank.

Macy, John W., Jr. Public Service: The Human Side of Government. LC 70-123950. 1971. 12.50 o.s.i. (ISBN 0-06-012769-4, HarpT). Har-Row.

--To Irrigate a Wasteland: The Struggle to Shape a Public Television System in the United States. 1974. 11.95x (ISBN 0-520-02498-2). U of Cal Pr.

Macy, Ralph W. & Berntzen, Allen K. Laboratory Guide to Parasitology: With Introduction to Experimental Methods. (Illus.). 316p. 1971. pap. 17.75 (ISBN 0-398-02154-6). C C Thomas.

Maczewski, J., tr. see Blume, Helmut.

Mad Magazine Editors. Boiling Mad. (Mad Ser). (Illus.). 192p. 1973. pap. 1.50 (ISBN 0-446-88740-4). Warner Bks.

--Burning Mad. (Mad Ser.). (Illus.). 1975. pap. 1.75 (ISBN 0-446-94360-6). Warner Bks.

--Dirty Old Mad. (Mad Ser: No. 30). (Illus.). 1971. pap. 1.75 (ISBN 0-446-94362-2). Warner Bks.

--Dr. Jekyll & Mr. Mad. (Mad Ser.: No. 38). (Illus.). 1975. pap. 1.75 (ISBN 0-446-94363-0). Warner Bks.

--Fighting Mad. (Mad Ser.). (Illus.). 192p. 1974. pap. 1.75 (ISBN 0-446-88872-9). Warner Bks.

--Good 'n' Mad. (Mad Ser.: No. 26). (Illus.). 1976. pap. 1.75 (ISBN 0-446-94365-7). Warner Bks.

--Hooked on Mad. (Mad Ser.: No.42). (Illus.). 192p. 1976. pap. 1.75 (ISBN 0-446-94587-0). Warner Bks.

--Hopping Mad. (Mad Ser.). (Illus.). 192p. 1976. pap. 1.75 (ISBN 0-446-94588-9). Warner Bks.

--Howling Mad. (Mad Ser.). (Illus.). 192p. 1974. pap. 1.75 (ISBN 0-446-94367-3). Warner Bks.

--The Ides of Mad. (Mad Ser.). (Illus.). 192p. 1974. pap. 1.50 (ISBN 0-446-88747-1). Warner Bks.

--The Indigestible Mad. (Mad Ser.: No. 24). (Illus.). 1975. pap. 1.75 (ISBN 0-446-94368-1). Warner Bks.

--The Invisible Mad. (Mad Ser.: No. 37). (Illus.). 1974. pap. 1.75 (ISBN 0-446-94369-X). Warner Bks.

--It's a World, World, World, World Mad. (Mad Ser.). (Illus.). 1973. pap. 1.75 (ISBN 0-446-94370-3). Warner Bks.

--Like Mad. (Mad Ser.). (Illus.). 1973. pap. 1.75 (ISBN 0-446-94371-1). Warner Bks.

--Mad at You! (Mad Ser.: No. 40). (Illus.). 1975. pap. 1.75 (ISBN 0-446-94590-0). Warner Bks.

--Mad for Kicks. (Mad Ser.: No. 54). (Illus., Orig.). 1980. pap. 1.50 (ISBN 0-446-98461-2). Warner Bks.

--Mad Frontier. (Mad Ser.). (Illus.). 1975. pap. 1.75 (ISBN 0-446-94373-8). Warner Bks.

--Mad in Orbit. (Mad Ser.). (Illus.). 1975. pap. 1.50 (ISBN 0-446-88762-5). Warner Bks.

--Mad Power. (Mad Ser.: No. 29). (Illus.). 1977. pap. 1.75 (ISBN 0-446-94375-4). Warner Bks.

--A Mad Scramble. (Mad Ser.: No. 45). (Illus.). 192p. 1977. pap. 1.75 (ISBN 0-446-94437-8). Warner Bks.

--The Non-Violent Mad. (Mad Ser.: No. 33). (Illus.). 1972. pap. 1.75 (ISBN 0-446-94593-5). Warner Bks.

--The Organization Mad. (Mad Ser.). (Illus.). 1973. pap. 1.50 (ISBN 0-446-88897-4). Warner Bks.

--The Pocket Mad. (Mad Ser.). (Illus.). 1974. pap. 1.75 (ISBN 0-446-94594-3). Warner Bks.

--The Portable Mad. (Mad Ser.). (Illus.). 1977. pap. 1.50 (ISBN 0-446-88765-X). Warner Bks.

--Pumping Mad. (Mad Ser.: No. 56). (Illus.). 192p. (Orig.). 1981. pap. 1.75 (ISBN 0-446-94820-9). Warner Bks.

--Raving Mad. (Mad Ser.). (Illus.). 192p. 1973. pap. 1.75 (ISBN 0-446-94382-7). Warner Bks.

--Rip off Mad. (Mad Ser.). (Illus.). 1973. pap. 1.50 (ISBN 0-446-88739-0). Warner Bks.

--Steaming Mad. (Mad Ser.: No. 39). (Illus.). 1975. pap. 1.75 (ISBN 0-446-94387-8). Warner Bks.

--The Token Mad. (Mad Ser.: No. 35). (Illus.). 192p. (Orig.). 1973. pap. 1.75 (ISBN 0-446-94389-4). Warner Bks.

--The Uncensored Mad. (Mad Ser.: No. 55). 192p. (Orig.). 1980. pap. 1.75 (ISBN 0-446-94462-9). Warner Bks.

Mad Magazine Editors, ed. The Bedside Mad. (Mad Ser.). (Illus.). 192p. 1973. pap. 1.75 (ISBN 0-446-94358-4). Warner Bks.

Madama, G., jt. auth. see McAllister, M.

Madame Guyon. Madame Guyon. new ed. 382p. 1974. pap. 6.95 (ISBN 0-8024-5135-7). Moody.

Madan, T. N., jt. auth. see Majumdar, D. N.

Madanes, Cloe. Strategic Family Therapy. LC 80-26286. (Social & Behavioral Science Ser.). 1981. text ed. 14.95 (ISBN 0-87589-487-9). Jossey-Bass.

Madaus, George F., jt. auth. see Bloom, Benjamin S.

Madaus, H. Michael. The Warner Collector's Guide to American Long Arms. (Orig.). 1981. pap. 9.95 (ISBN 0-446-97628-8). Warner Bks.

Madayag, A. G. Metal Fatigue: Theory & Design. 1969. 36.50 (ISBN 0-471-56315-3, Pub. by Wiley-Interscience). Wiley.

Madda, Frank C., ed. Outdoor Emergency Medicine. (Illus.). 277p. (Orig.). 1981. pap. 3.95 (ISBN 0-938278-00-2). BioServ Corp.

Maddala, G. S., et al. Econometric Studies in Energy Demand & Supply. LC 78-2886. (Praeger Special Studies). 1978. 22.95 (ISBN 0-03-042266-3). Praeger.

Maddalena, Lucille A. A Communications Manual for Nonprofit Organizations. 286p. 1981. 17.95 (ISBN 0-8144-5606-5). Am Mgmt.

Madden, A. F. & Morris-Jones, W. H., eds. Australia & Britain: Studies in a Changing Relationship. 191p. 1980. 25.00x (ISBN 0-7146-3149-3, F Cass Co). Biblio Dist.

Madden, Anne, ed. Best of Sail Navigation. (Illus.). 1980. 13.95 (ISBN 0-914814-27-3). Sail Bks.

Madden, Carl H., ed. The Case for the Multinational Corporation. LC 76-12863. (Special Studies). 1976. text ed. 25.95 (ISBN 0-275-23980-2). Praeger.

Madden, Daniel M. A Religious Guide to Europe. 384p. 1975. pap. 4.95 o.s.i. (ISBN 0-02-097950-9, Collier). Macmillan.

Madden, David. Poetic Image in Six Genres. LC 76-76189. (Arcturus Books Paperbacks). 271p. 1969. pap. 7.45 (ISBN 0-8093-0394-9). S Ill U Pr.

Madden, David & Powers, Richard. Writers' Revisions: An Annotated Bibliography of Articles & Books About Writers' Revisions & Their Comments on the Creative Process. LC 80-22942. 254p. 1981. 13.50 (ISBN 0-8108-1375-0). Scarecrow.

Madden, David, ed. American Dreams, American Nightmares. LC 72-5512. (Arcturus Books Paperbacks). 271p. 1972. pap. 7.95 (ISBN 0-8093-0600-X). S Ill U Pr.

--Proletarian Writers of the Thirties. LC 78-16323. (Arcturus Books Paperbacks). 320p. 1979. pap. 8.95 (ISBN 0-8093-0895-9). S Ill U Pr.

--Tough Guy Writers of the Thirties. LC 68-10115. (Crosscurrents-Modern Critiques Ser.). 287p. 1968. 16.95 (ISBN 0-8093-0287-X). S Ill U Pr.

--Tough Guy Writers of the Thirties. LC 78-24304. (Arcturus Bks Paperbacks). 287p. 1979. pap. 7.95 (ISBN 0-8093-0912-2). S Ill U Pr.

Madden, Donald L. Management Accounting. LC 80-17277. (Teaching Guides Ser.). 326p. 1980. 8.95 (ISBN 0-471-03135-6, Pub. by Wiley-Interscience). Wiley.

Madden, Edward H. Civil Disobedience & Moral Law in Nineteenth-Century American Philosophy. LC 68-11043. 222p. 1970. pap. 2.95 (ISBN 0-295-95070-6). U of Wash Pr.

Madden, Edward H., ed. see Blake, Ralph M., et al.

Madden, F. A., jt. auth. see Herman, H. A.

Madden, L. How to Find Out About the Victorian Period. LC 74-116777. 1970. text ed. 22.00 (ISBN 0-08-015834-X); pap. text ed. 10.75 (ISBN 0-08-015833-1). Pergamon.

Madden, Lionel, ed. Robert Southey: The Critical Heritage. (The Critical Heritage Ser). 1972. 38.50x (ISBN 0-7100-7375-5). Routledge & Kegan.

Madden, Mary B., jt. auth. see Madden, Myron C.

Madden, Myron C. & Madden, Mary B. For Grandparents: Wonders & Worries. LC 80-12778. (A Christian Care Bk.). 1980. pap. 5.95 (ISBN 0-664-24325-8). Westminster.

Madden, Samuel. Memoirs of the Twentieth Century: Being Original Letters of State Under George the Sixth. LC 74-170588. (Foundations of the Novel Ser.: Vol. 58). lib. bdg. 50.00 (ISBN 0-8240-0570-8). Garland Pub.

Madden, Susan K., jt. auth. see Borich, Gary D.

Madden, Virginia M. Across America on the Yellow Brick Road. (Illus.). 1980. pap. 8.95 (ISBN 0-937760-00-5). Crow Canyon.

Madden, William, jt. auth. see Levine, George.

Maddex, James L., Jr. Constitutional Law: Cases & Comments. 2nd ed. (Criminal Justice Ser.). 1978. text ed. 18.95 (ISBN 0-8299-0185-X); instrs.' manual avail. (ISBN 0-8299-0598-7). West Pub.

Maddi, Salvatore R., ed. Personality Theories: A Comparative Analysis. 4th ed. 1980. text ed. 18.95x (ISBN 0-256-02299-2). Dorsey.

Maddin, Stuart, ed. Current Dermatologic Management. 2nd ed. LC 74-3001. 480p. 1975. 45.00 o.p. (ISBN 0-8016-3061-4). Mosby.

Maddison, Angus. Class Structure & Economic Growth: India & Pakistan Since the Moghuls. 1972. 7.95x (ISBN 0-393-05467-5, 05467); pap. 3.95x (ISBN 0-393-09399-9). Norton.

Maddison, Francis & Pelling, Margaret, eds. Linacre Studies: Essays on the Life & Work of Thomas Linacre. (Illus.). 1977. 49.00x (ISBN 0-19-858150-5). Oxford U Pr.

Maddison, Pamela, jt. auth. see Cave, Cyril.

Maddison, R., jt. auth. see Vetter, M.

Maddock, Alison. Animals at Peace. LC 71-185643. (Animal Life Ser.). (Illus.). 152p. (YA) 1972. 8.95 o.s.i. (ISBN 0-06-012728-7, HarpT). Har-Row.

Maddock, Brent. The Films of Jacques Tati. LC 77-11084. 1977. 10.00 (ISBN 0-8108-1065-4). Scarecrow.

Maddocks, Melvin. The Atlantic Crossing. Time-Life Books, ed. (The Seafarers Ser.). (Illus.). 176p. 1981. 14.95 (ISBN 0-8094-2726-5). Time Life.

--The Great Liners. (The Seafarers). 1978. 13.95 (ISBN 0-8094-2662-5). Time-Life.

--The Great Liners. LC 78-1366. (The Seafarers Ser.). (Illus.). 1978. lib. bdg. 11.97 (ISBN 0-686-50986-2). Silver.

Maddow, Ben. Edward Weston: His Life & Photographs. rev. ed. LC 79-7058. (Illus.). 1979. 375.00 (ISBN 0-89381-043-6); ltd. ed. 300.00 (ISBN 0-89381-045-2). Aperture.

Maddox & Fuquay. State & Local Government. 4th ed. Date not set. pap. text ed. price not set (ISBN 0-442-24454-1). D Van Nostrand.

Maddox, Brenda. Who's Afraid of Elizabeth Taylor. 1978. pap. 1.95 o.s.i. (ISBN 0-515-04583-7). Jove Pubns.

Maddox, C. Collective Bargaining in Law Enforcement. (Illus.). 160p. 1975. 16.75 (ISBN 0-398-03192-4). C C Thomas.

Maddox, Gaynor. Food & Arthritis. (Illus.). 224p. 1973. pap. 1.25 o.p. (ISBN 0-445-00151-8). Popular Lib.

Maddox, George L., jt. auth. see Fann, William E.

Maddox, Harry. How to Study. 1978. pap. 2.25 (ISBN 0-449-30831-6, Prem). Fawcett.

--Your Garden Soil. (Illus.). 223p. 1975. 14.95 (ISBN 0-7153-6661-0). David & Charles.

Maddox, I. J. Elements of Functional Analysis. LC 71-85726. 1970. text ed. 29.95 (ISBN 0-521-07617-X); pap. 12.50x (ISBN 0-521-29266-2). Cambridge U Pr.

Maddox, James H., Jr. Joyce's Ulysses & the Assault Upon Character. 1978. 17.50 (ISBN 0-8135-0851-7). Rutgers U Pr.

Maddox, Robert J. The Unknown War with Russia: Wilson's Siberian Intervention. LC 76-58761. (Illus.). 1977. 9.95 o.s.i. (ISBN 0-89141-013-9). Presidio Pr.

Maddrell, Simon H. & Nordmann, Jean J. Neurosecretion. LC 79-63655. (Tertiary Level Biology Ser.). 173p. 1979. 24.95x (ISBN 0-470-26711-9). Halsted Pr.

Maddux, Bob. Gem of the Wanderer. 1979. 2.95 (ISBN 0-89728-009-1). Omega Pubns OR.

Maddux, Hilary C. Menstruation. 1981. pap. 2.50 (ISBN 0-440-05582-2). Dell.

Madeira, Louis C., compiled by. Music in Philadelphia & History of the Musical Fund Society. LC 78-169650. (Music Reprint Ser.). (Illus.). 234p. 1973. Repr. of 1896 ed. lib. bdg. 25.00 (ISBN 0-306-70260-6). Da Capo.

Madeja, Stanley, jt. auth. see Hurwitz, Al.

Madeleine, Marie, illus. Baby's Journal. (Illus.). 1978. 11.95 (ISBN 0-684-15979-1, ScribT). Scribner.

Madell, Jane, jt. ed. see Loavenbruck, Angela M.

Madelung, O. & Queisser, H. J., eds. Advances in Solid State Physics: Festkoerper Probleme, Vols. 9-15. Vol. 9. 1969. 60.00 (ISBN 0-08-015543-X). Vol. 10. 1971. 40.00 (ISBN 0-08-017563-5); Vol. 11. 1971. 30.00 (ISBN 0-08-017593-7); Vol. 12. 1972. 66.00 (ISBN 0-08-017285-7); Vol. 13, 1973. 42.50 (ISBN 0-08-017293-8); Vol. 14, 1974. 42.50 (ISBN 0-08-018206-2); Vol. 15, 1975. 55.00 (ISBN 0-08-019894-5). Pergamon.

Mader, Charles L., ed. LASL Phermex Data, Vol. 2. (The Los Alamos Scientific Series on Dynamic Material Properties). 768p. 1980. 42.50x (ISBN 0-520-04010-4). U of Cal Pr.

Mader, Charles L. & Neal, Timothy R., eds. LASL Phermex Data, Vol. 1. (Los Alamos Scientific Laboratory Series on Dynamic Material Properties). 1980. 52.50 (ISBN 0-520-04009-0). U of Cal Pr.

Mader, Charles S. Numerical Modeling of Detonations. (Los Alamos Ser. in Basic & Applied Sciences). 1979. 45.00x (ISBN 0-520-03655-7). U of Cal Pr.

Mader, Chris. The Dow Jones-Irwin Guide to Real Estate Investing. LC 74-25812. 206p. 1975. 12.95 o.p. (ISBN 0-87094-095-3). Dow Jones-Irwin.

--Dow Jones-Irwin Guide to Real Estate Investing. rev. ed. 1981. 14.95 (ISBN 0-87094-214-X). Dow Jones-Irwin.

--Information Systems: Technology, Economics, Applications, Management. 2nd ed. LC 78-13048. 1979. text ed. 17.95 (ISBN 0-574-21150-0, 13-4150); instr's guide avail. (ISBN 0-574-21151-9, 13-4151). SRA.

Mader, Chris & Hagin, Robert W. Dow Jones-Irwin Guide to Common Stocks. LC 75-43167. 300p. 1976. 12.95 o.p. (ISBN 0-87094-108-9). Dow Jones-Irwin.

Madero, Thomas P., tr. see Thies, Dagmar.

Mades, Leonard, tr. see Donoso, Jose.

Madge, David S. The Mammalian Alimentary System: A Functional Approach. LC 75-34543. (Special Topics in Biology Ser). 200p. 1976. pap. 14.50x (ISBN 0-8448-0850-4). Crane-Russak Co.

Madge, John H. Origins of Scientific Sociology. LC 62-11855. 1962. 14.95 (ISBN 0-02-919700-7); pap. text ed. 9.95 (ISBN 0-02-919710-4). Free Pr.

Madge, Sidney J. Domesday of Crown Lands. LC 67-31560. (Illus.). Repr. of 1938 ed. 26.00x (ISBN 0-678-05071-6). Kelley.

Madge, Violet. Children in Search of Meaning. (Orig.). 1966. pap. 3.25 o.p. (ISBN 0-8192-1051-X). Morehouse.

Madgic, Robert F. Relevance & the Social Studies: A Conceptual Analysis. LC 73-77590. 1973. pap. 3.60 (ISBN 0-8224-5840-3). Pitman Learning.

Madgulkar, V. The Village Had No Walls. 1972. pap. 3.75x (ISBN 0-210-31153-3). Asia.

Madgulkar, Vyankatesh. The Winds of Fire. Kale, Pramod, tr. from Marathi. 113p. 1975. pap. 1.95 (ISBN 0-88253-693-1). Ind-US Inc.

Madhavan, A. More Poems. (Redbird Bk.). 1976. 8.00 (ISBN 0-89253-698-5); pap. text ed. 4.80 (ISBN 0-89253-083-9). Ind-US Inc.

--Poems. 8.00 (ISBN 0-89253-772-8); flexible cloth 4.00 (ISBN 0-89253-773-6). Ind-US Inc.

Madhavananda, Swami, tr. see Shankara.

Madhubuti, Haki. Plan to Planet. 1980. pap. 3.95 (ISBN 0-88378-066-6). Third World.

Madhubuti, Safisha. Story of Kwanza. 1980. pap. 2.95 (ISBN 0-88378-001-1). Third World.

Madigan, Mary Jean S., intro. by. Eastlake-Influenced American Furniture, 1870-1890. LC 73-90034. (Illus.). 68p. 1974. pap. 5.00 (ISBN 0-87100-043-1, Pub. by Hudson River Mus). Pub Ctr Cult Res.

Madigan, Thomas F. Word Shadows of the Great: The Lure of Autograph Collecting. LC 70-145705. (Illus.). 1971. Repr. of 1930 ed. 20.00 (ISBN 0-8103-3378-3). Gale.

Madison, Arnold. Arson! LC 78-6877. (Illus.). (gr. 5 up). 1978. PLB 6.90 s&l (ISBN 0-531-02243-9). Watts.

--Aviation Careers. (Career Concise Guides Ser.). (Illus.). 1977. lib. bdg. 6.45 (ISBN 0-531-01300-6). Watts.

--Carry Nation. LC 76-58839. (gr. 8 up). 1977. Repr. 7.95 o.p. (ISBN 0-525-66540-4). Elsevier-Nelson.

--Great Unsolved Cases. LC 78-6932. (Triumph Bks). (Illus.). (gr. 6 up). 1978. PLB 6.90 s&l (ISBN 0-531-01465-7). Watts.

--Great Unsolved Cases. (gr. 7-12). 1980. pap. 1.25 (ISBN 0-440-93099-5, LFL). Dell.

--How to Play Girls' Softball. (Illus.). 128p. (gr. 4-6). 1981. PLB 7.29 (ISBN 0-686-69303-5). Messner.

--Suicide & Young People. 144p. (gr. 6 up). 1981. pap. 3.95 (ISBN 0-686-69043-5, Clarion). HM.

--Suicide & Young People. LC 77-13240. (gr. 5 up). 1978. 6.95 (ISBN 0-395-28913-0, Clarion). HM.

--Transplanted & Artificial Body Organs. (Illus.). 192p. (gr. 7 up). 1981. 8.95 (ISBN 0-8253-0050-9). Beaufort Bks NY.

--Vandalism: The Not-So-Senseless Crime. LC 70-125833. 1970. 5.50 (ISBN 0-395-28914-9, Clarion). HM.

--Vandalism: The Not-So-Senseless Crime. 160p. (gr. 6 up). 1981. pap. 3.95 (ISBN 0-395-30009-6, Clarion). HM.

--Vigilantism in America. LC 72-97771. (gr. 5 up). 6.95 (ISBN 0-395-28915-7, Clarion). HM.

Madison, Arnold & Drotar, David L. Pocket Calculators: How to Use & Enjoy Them. LC 78-707. (Illus.). (gr. 6 up). 1978. 7.95 (ISBN 0-525-66580-3). Elsevier-Nelson.

Madison, George. Eden's Horizon. 1977. pap. 1.50 o.p. (ISBN 0-445-04004-1). Popular Lib.

Madison, Hank. Riding High. 1979. pap. 1.50 (ISBN 0-505-51430-3). Tower Bks.

Madison, James. Notes of Debates in the Federal Convention of 1787 Reported by James Madison. LC 65-18705. 1976. 20.00x (ISBN 0-8214-0011-8). Ohio U Pr.

Madison, John H. Principles of Turfgrass Culture. 412p. 1981. Repr. of 1971 ed. lib. bdg. price not set (ISBN 0-89874-197-1). Krieger.

Madison, Winifred. The Genessee Queen. LC 77-72634. (gr. 7up). 1977. 6.95 o.p. (ISBN 0-440-02809-4). Delacorte.

--Getting Out. LC 75-34629. (gr. 7 up). 1976. 6.95 o.p. (ISBN 0-695-80634-3); PLB 6.99 o.p. (ISBN 0-695-40634-5). Follett.

--Growing up in a Hurry. (YA) (gr. 7-9). 1975. pap. 1.50 (ISBN 0-671-29988-3). PB.

--Maria Luisa. LC 79-159825. 192p. (gr. 4-9). 1971. PLB 8.79 (ISBN 0-397-31280-6). Lippincott.

Madlee, Dorothy, jt. auth. see Norton, Andre.

Madlener, Judith Cooper De see Cooper Madlener, Judith.

Madler, Trudy. Why Did Grandma Die? LC 79-23892. (Life & Living from a Child's Point of View Ser.). (Illus.). (gr. k-5). 1980. PLB 9.65 (ISBN 0-8172-1354-6). Raintree Child.

Madnick, Myra E., jt. auth. see OCHE.

Madore, B. F., jt. ed. see Hanes, D. A.

Madow, Pauline, ed. Peace Corps. (Reference Shelf Ser: Vol. 36, No. 2). 1964. 6.25 (ISBN 0-8242-0080-2). Wilson.

--Recreation in America. (Reference Shelf Ser: Vol. 37, No. 2). 1965. 6.25 (ISBN 0-8242-0085-3). Wilson.

Madrid, jt. auth. see Cohn.

Madrigal & Meyer. Invitacion al Ingles. (gr. 9 up). 1965. pap. text ed. 3.50 (ISBN 0-88345-072-0, 17398); cassettes 40.00 (ISBN 0-685-48113-1); tapes o.p. 22.50 (ISBN 0-685-48114-X); records o.p. 9.95 (ISBN 0-685-48115-8); ans. key 1.00 (ISBN 0-686-67015-9). Regents Pub.

Madrigal, Margarita. First Steps in Spanish. 111p. (gr. 3-6). 1961. pap. text ed. 2.75 (ISBN 0-88345-177-8, 17448). Regents Pub.

--Open Door to Spanish, 2 bks. (gr. 7 up). 1972. Bk. 1. pap. text ed. 3.50 o.p. (ISBN 0-88345-186-7, 18098); Bk. 2. pap. text ed. 2.75 (ISBN 0-88345-187-5, 17704); records 20.00 ea.; tapes o.p. 30.00 ea.; cassettes 40.00 ea. Regents Pub.

--Open Door to Spanish, Bk. 1. new ed. (Illus.). 223p. (gr. 5-12). 1980. pap. text ed. 3.75 (ISBN 0-88345-420-3, 18469); cassettes 40.00. Regents Pub.

--Open Door to Spanish, Bk. 2. (Open Door to Spanish Ser.). 200p. (gr. 5-12). 1981. pap. text ed. 3.75 (ISBN 0-88345-427-0, 18470). Regents Pub.

Madrigal, Margarita & Dulac, Colette. Open Door to French. (gr. 7-10). 1963. pap. text ed. 2.95 (ISBN 0-88345-121-2, 17476). Regents Pub.

Madrigal, Margarita & Dulac, Collette. See It & Say It in French. (Orig.). pap. 1.75 (ISBN 0-451-08941-3, E8941, Sig). NAL.

Madrigal, Margarita & Salvadori, Giuseppina. See It & Say It in Italian. (Orig.). pap. 1.75 (ISBN 0-451-09399-2, E9399, Sig). NAL.

Madruga, Lenor. One Step at a Time. 1980. pap. 2.25 (ISBN 0-451-09407-7, E9407, Sig). NAL.

Madsen & Madsen. Teaching Discipline: A Positive Approach for Educational Development. 3rd. ed. 336p. 1980. text ed. 17.95 (ISBN 0-205-07143-0); pap. text ed. 9.95 (0247143-4). Allyn.

Madsen, A. A., jt. auth. see Curtis, E. L.

Madsen, Axel. Borderlines. 228p. 1975. 6.95 o.s.i. (ISBN 0-02-579180-X). Macmillan.

--John Huston. LC 78-55842. 1978. 10.00 o.p. (ISBN 0-385-11070-7). Doubleday.

--Malraux. LC 76-7558. 1976. 11.95 o.p. (ISBN 0-688-03075-0). Morrow.

--Private Power: Multinational Corporations for the Survival of Our Planet. LC 80-19372. 256p. 1980. 12.95 (ISBN 0-688-03735-6). Morrow.

Madsen, Betty M. & Madsen, Brigham D. North to Montana! Jehus, Bullwhackers & Mule Skinners on the Montana Trail. (University of Utah Publications in the American West). (Illus.). 1980. 20.00 (ISBN 0-87480-130-3). U of Utah Pr.

Madsen, Brigham D. The Northern Shoshoni. LC 78-53138. (Illus., Orig.). 1980. 17.95 (ISBN 0-87004-289-0); pap. 12.95 (ISBN 0-87004-266-1). Caxton.

Madsen, Brigham D., jt. auth. see Madsen, Betty M.

Madsen, Charles H., Jr. & Madsen, Clifford K. Teaching-Discipline: A Positive Approach for Educational Development. 2nd ed. 421p. 1975. text ed. 14.95 o.p. (ISBN 0-205-04413-1); pap. text ed. 5.95x o.p. (ISBN 0-205-04407-7). Allyn.

Madsen, Claudia, jt. auth. see Madsen, William.

Madsen, Clifford K. & Kuhn, Terry L. Contemporary Music Education. LC 77-90672. (Illus.). 1978. pap. text ed. 7.50x (ISBN 0-88295-350-8). AHM Pub.

Madsen, Clifford K., jt. auth. see Madsen, Charles H., Jr.

Madsen, Clifford K., et al, eds. Research in Music Behavior: Modifying Music Behavior in the Classroom. LC 74-13632. 1975. text ed. 16.50x (ISBN 0-8077-2436-X). Tchrs Coll.

Madsen, J. H., jt. ed. see Dupont, J. L.

Madsen, J. M. Aquarium Fishes in Color. LC 74-31451. (Illus.). 224p. 1975. 6.95 o.s.i. (ISBN 0-02-579170-2, 57917). Macmillan.

Madsen, Paul O. The Person Who Chairs the Meeting. (Illus.). 96p. (Orig.). 1973. tanalin 2.50 (ISBN 0-8170-0582-X). Judson.

Madsen, Richard W. & Moeschberger, Melvin L. Statistical Concepts: With Applications to Business & Economics. (Illus.). 1980. text ed. 21.00 (ISBN 0-13-844878-7). P-H.

Madsen, Richard W., jt. auth. see Isaacson, Dean L.

Madsen, S. A., et al. New Writers Eleven. (New Writing & Writers Ser.). 1974. text ed. 13.00x (ISBN 0-7145-0813-6). Humanities.

Madsen, Stephan T. Sources of Art Noveau. Christopherson, Ragnar, tr. LC 74-34464. (Architecture & Decorative Arts Ser). (Illus.). 488p. 1975. Repr. of 1956 ed. lib. bdg. 42.50 (ISBN 0-306-70733-0). Da Capo.

--Sources of Art Noveau. LC 75-26819. (Architecture & Decorative Arts Ser.). (Illus.). 1976. pap. 8.95 (ISBN 0-306-80024-1). Da Capo.

Madsen, Svend A., et al. New Writers Eleven. 1980. pap. 6.00 (ISBN 0-7145-0814-4). Riverrun NY.

Madsen, William. The American Alcoholic: The Nature-Nurture Controversy in Alcoholic Research & Therapy. (Illus.). 272p. 1980. 15.50 (ISBN 0-398-02926-1). C C Thomas.

Madsen, William & Madsen, Claudia. A Guide to Mexican Witchcraft. (Illus.). 1979. pap. 4.00 (ISBN 0-912434-10-4). Ocelot Pr.

Madson, John. John Madson: Out Home. McIntosh, Michael, ed. (Illus.). 1979. 11.95 (ISBN 0-87691-285-4). Winchester Pr.

Madu, Oliver V. Models of Class Domination in Plural Societies of Central Africa. LC 77-18595. 1978. pap. text ed. 15.45x o.p. (ISBN 0-8191-0407-8). U Pr of Amer.

Madubuike, Ihechukwu. A Handbook of African Names. LC 75-25943. (Illus.). 1976. 10.00 (ISBN 0-914478-13-3); pap. 5.00 (ISBN 0-89410-029-7). Three Continents.

Madura, Jeffrey. Basic Accounting, 2 vols. (Illus.). 1981. pap. text ed. 8.50 (ISBN 0-686-66062-5). Bk. 1 (ISBN 0-916780-16-3). Bk. 2 (ISBN 0-916780-17-1). Set. pap. text ed. 17.00 (ISBN 0-916780-19-8). CES.

Mae, Eydie & Loeffler, Chris. How I Conquered Cancer Naturally. LC 75-29754. 1976. 9.95 (0362); pap. 3.95 (ISBN 0-89081-036-2). Harvest Hse.

Maeda, Robert J. Two Sung Texts on Chinese Painting & the Landscape Styles of the 11th & 12th Centuries. LC 77-94706. (Outstanding Dissertations in the Fine Arts Ser.). 1978. lib. bdg. 27.50 (ISBN 0-8240-3238-1). Garland Pub.

Maegraith, Brian. One World. (Heath Clark Lectures 1970). 250p. 1973. text ed. 18.75x (ISBN 0-485-26323-8, Athlone Pr). Humanities.

Maeki, S. The Determination of Units in Real Cyclic Sextic Fields. (Lecture Notes in Mathematics: Vol. 797). 1980. pap. 14.00 (ISBN 0-387-09984-0). Springer-Verlag.

Maeland, A., jt. ed. see Andresen, A. F.

Maenchen-Helfen, Otto J. The World of the Huns: Studies in Their History & Culture. Knight, Max, ed. LC 79-94985. 1973. 30.00x (ISBN 0-520-01596-7). U of Cal Pr.

Maestas, jt. auth. see Griego, Jose.

Maestri, Vic. Little Eva, Baby Doll, & Blondy Ryan. (Orig.). pap. 4.50 (ISBN 0-682-49710-X). Exposition.

Maestri, Victor De see De Maestri, Victor.

Maestri, William. The God for Every Day. 204p. 1981. 8.95 (ISBN 0-88347-123-X). Thomas More.

Maestro, Betsy. Fat Polka-Dot Cat & Other Haiku. (Illus.). 32p. (ps-1). 1976. PLB 6.95 o.p. (ISBN 0-525-29625-5). Dutton.

Maevis, Alfred C., ed. see Rapid Excavation & Tunneling Conference, 1979.

Mafeje, Archie. Science Ideology & Development-Three Essays on Development Theory. 1978. pap. text ed. 9.50x (ISBN 0-8419-9731-4). Holmes & Meier.

Maffei, Anthony C. & Buckley, Patricia. Teaching Preschool Math: Foundations & Activities. LC 79-27448. 176p. 1980. text ed. 14.95 (ISBN 0-87705-492-4). Human Sci Pr.

Maffei, Paolo. Beyond the Moon. 1980. pap. 7.95 (ISBN 0-380-48744-6, 48744). Avon.

Magar, Kurt, jt. auth. see Schuter, Hans.

Magarian, Judith A. Measurement Comparisons. (Illus.). 24p. (gr. k-3). 1980. pap. 3.95 (ISBN 0-933358-64-4). Enrich.

Magarian, Judith A. & Horton, Patricia M. Sweepstakes. (Illus.). 13p. (gr. 4-6). 1980. pap. 4.95 (ISBN 0-933358-74-1). Enrich.

Magarick, Pat. Excessive Liability - Duties & Responsibilities of the Insurer. LC 75-44308. 1976. with 1978 suppl. 30.00 (ISBN 0-87632-157-0). Boardman.

--Successful Handling of Casualty Claims. LC 73-91720. 1974. 37.50 (ISBN 0-87632-168-6). Boardman.

Magaro, Peter A. Construction of Madness: Emerging Conceptions & Interventions into Psychotic Process. 240p. 1976. text ed. 26.00 (ISBN 0-08-019904-6); pap. text ed. 12.00 (ISBN 0-08-019903-8). Pergamon.

Magaro, Peter A., et al. The Mental Health Industry: A Cultural Phenomenon. LC 77-14434. (Series on Personality Processes). 1978. 23.95 (ISBN 0-471-02406-6, Pub. by Wiley-Interscience). Wiley.

Magarshack, David, tr. see Chekhov, Anton.

Magarshack, David, tr. see Dostoyevsky, Fedor.

Magarshack, David, tr. see Gogol, Nicolai V.

Magarshack, David, tr. see Gogol, Nikolai.

Magarshack, David, tr. see Pasternak, Boris.

Magarshack, David, tr. see Schneider, Ilya I.

Magarshack, David, tr. see Turgenev, Ivan.

Magary, Alan & Magary, Kerstin F. Across the Golden Gate: California's North Coast, Wine Country & Redwoods. LC 78-2149. (Illus.). 320p. (Orig.). 1980. pap. 6.95 (ISBN 0-06-090821-1, CN 821, CN). Har-Row.

--East Africa: A Travel Guide. LC 74-1836. (Illus.). 736p. 1975. 10.00 o.s.i. (ISBN 0-06-012792-9, HarpT); pap. 7.95 o.p. (ISBN 0-06-012808-9, TD-237, HarpT). Har-Row.

Magary, Kerstin F., jt. auth. see Magary, Alan.

Magazine, Alan H. Environmental Management in Local Government: A Study of Local Response to Federal Mandate. LC 77-12818. (Praeger Special Studies). 1977. 22.95 (ISBN 0-03-040786-9). Praeger.

Magazine, Sail, ed. The Best of Sail Navigation. (Illus.). 1981. 13.95 (ISBN 0-393-03261-2). Norton.

Magdoff, Harry & Sweezy, Paul M. The Deepening Crisis of U.S. Capitalism: Essays by Harry Magdoff & Paul M. Sweezy. LC 80-8935. 256p. 1981. 16.00 (ISBN 0-85345-573-2); pap. 6.50 (ISBN 0-85345-574-0). Monthly Rev.

Magdoff, L. Age of Imperialism. 1979. 24.50 o.p. (ISBN 0-685-67797-4). Porter.

Magdovitz, Alan L., jt. auth. see McClelland, Peter D.

Magee, C. C. Framework for Accountancy. 2nd ed. 336p. 1979. pap. text ed. 14.95x (ISBN 0-7121-0631-6, Pub. by Macdonald & Evans England). Intl Ideas.

Magee, David S. Everything Your Heirs Need to Know About You. Dugan, J. Magee, ed. 160p. 1980. write for info. Jama Bks.

Magee, Dennis W. Freshwater Wetlands: A Guide to Common Indicator Plants of the Northeast. LC 80-26876. (Illus.). 240p. 1981. lib. bdg. 17.50x (ISBN 0-87023-316-5); pap. text ed. 7.95x (ISBN 0-87023-317-3). U of Mass Pr.

Magee, Doug. Slow Coming Dark: Interviews on Death Row. LC 80-19747. (Illus.). 181p. 1980. 10.95 (ISBN 0-8298-0400-5). Pilgrim NY.

Magee, J. O. Basic Accounting. 2nd ed. 352p. 1979. pap. text ed. 11.95x (ISBN 0-7121-0284-1, Pub. by Macdonald & Evans England). Intl Ideas.

--Basic Bookeeping. 256p. (Orig.). 1979. pap. text ed. 10.00x (ISBN 0-7121-0274-4, Pub. by Macdonald & Evans England). Intl Ideas.

--Company Accounts. 2nd ed. 386p. 1978. pap. 12.95x (ISBN 0-7121-0384-8, Pub. by Macdonald & Evans England). Intl Ideas.

Magee, John. Northern Ireland: Crises & Conflict. (World Studies). (Illus.). 212p. 1974. 16.00x (ISBN 0-7100-7946-X); pap. 7.95 (ISBN 0-7100-7947-8). Routledge & Kegan.

Magee, R. J. Selected Readings in Chromatography. (Selected Readings in Analytical Chemistry). (Illus.). 1970. pap. 6.00 o.p. (ISBN 0-08-015851-X). Pergamon.

Magee, Robert. Classic World of Horses. LC 73-93951. (Orig.). 1974. 15.00 o.p. (ISBN 0-668-03466-1). Arco.

Magel, Charles R. A Bibliography on Animal Rights & Related Matters. LC 80-5636. 622p. 1981. lib. bdg. 28.50 (ISBN 0-8191-1488-X). U Pr of Amer.

Magendie, Francois. Elementary Treatise on Human Physiology. Revere, John, tr. from Fr. Bd. with Mind & the Brain. Binet, Alfred; An Essay. Huxley, T. H. (Contributions to the History of Psychology, Vol. IV, Pt. E: Physiological Psychology). 1978. Repr. of 1844 ed. 30.00 (ISBN 0-89093-177-1). U Pubns Amer.

Mager, George C., jt. auth. see Gray, Farnum.

Mager, Robert F. Developing Attitude Toward Learning. LC 68-54250. 1968. pap. 4.50 (ISBN 0-8224-2000-7). Pitman Learning.

--Goal Analysis. LC 77-189630. (Illus., Orig.). 1972. pap. 4.50 (ISBN 0-8224-3476-8). Pitman Learning.

--Measuring Instructional Intent, or Got a Match? LC 73-80970. 1973. pap. 4.95 (ISBN 0-8224-4462-3). Pitman Learning.

--Preparing Instructional Objectives. 2nd. ed. LC 75-16518. 1975. pap. 4.95 (ISBN 0-8224-5601-X). Pitman Learning.

Mager, Robert F. & Pipe, Peter. Analyzing Performance Problems; or, You Really Oughta Wanna. LC 73-140896. 1970. pap. text ed. 4.50 (ISBN 0-8224-0301-3); quick reference checklist, set of 25 3.95 (ISBN 0-8224-0302-1); performance analysis poster 3.50 (ISBN 0-8224-0303-X). Pitman Learning.

Maggio, Edward T. Enzyme Immunoassay. 304p. 1980. lib. bdg. 69.95 (ISBN 0-8493-5617-2). CRC Pr.

Maggio, Elio. The Psychiatry-Law Dilemma. 1980. 13.95 (ISBN 0-533-04795-1). Vantage.

Maggio, Frank. Las Vegas Calling. (Illus.). 1975. 6.50 (ISBN 0-913814-34-2). Nevada Pubns.

Maggiore, Josephine, jt. auth. see Zaccarelli, Bro. Herman E.

Maggs, Colin G. The Midland & South Western Junction Railway. LC 79-56254. (Illus.). 184p. 1980. 17.95 (ISBN 0-7153-7978-X). David & Charles.

Maggs, Tim, ed. Major Rock Paintings of Southern Africa. LC 80-7664. (Illus.). 96p. 1980. 50.00x (ISBN 0-253-19226-9). Ind U Pr.

Maghroori, Ray & Gorman, Stephen M. The Yom Kippur War: A Case Study in Crisis Decision Making in American Foreign Policy. LC 80-5811. 98p. 1981. lib. bdg. 14.75 (ISBN 0-8191-1373-5); pap. text ed. 6.75 (ISBN 0-8191-1374-3). U Pr of Amer.

Magi, Giovanna. All Paris. LC 77-365195. (Illus.). 128p. (Orig.). 1975. pap. 15.00x (ISBN 88-7009-055-8). Intl Pubns Serv.

Magid, Alvin. Men in the Middle: Leadership & Role Conflict in a Nigerian Society. LC 75-42145. 1976. text ed. 29.50x o.p. (ISBN 0-8419-0254-2, Africana). Holmes & Meier.

Magid, John, jt. auth. see King, Ralph W.

Magid, Ken & Schreibman, Walt. Divorce Is a Kid's Coloring Book. LC 80-80436. (Illus.). 62p. 1980. pap. 4.95 (ISBN 0-88289-276-2). Pelican.

Magid, Leonard M. Electromagnetic Fields, Energy, & Waves. 808p. 1981. Repr. of 1972 ed. text ed. write for info. (ISBN 0-89874-221-8). Krieger.

Magida, Phylis. Eating, Drinking, & Thinking: A Gourmet Perspective. LC 73-86024. 1973. 14.95 (ISBN 0-911012-91-5). Nelson-Hall.

Magida, Phylis & Staff of the Culinary Arts Institute. Cake Decorating Book. Finnegan, Edward G., ed. LC 78-54619. (Adventures in Cooking Ser). (Illus.). 1981. cancelled (ISBN 0-8326-0604-9, 1516); pap. 3.95 (ISBN 0-8326-0603-0, 2516). Delair.

Magidson, Jay, ed. see Goodman, Leo A.

Magie, Allan. Pets, People, Plagues. LC 79-19321. (Better Living Ser.). 1979. pap. 0.95 (ISBN 0-8127-0233-6). Southern Pub.

Magill, C. P., ed. see Schiller, Johann.

Magill, Frank N., ed. Cyclopedia of Literary Characters. 1964. 22.50 (ISBN 0-06-003990-6, HarpT); PLB 19.79 o.p (ISBN 0-06-003991-4, HarpT). Har-Row.

--Cyclopedia of World Authors. 1958. lib. bdg. 19.79 o.s.i. (ISBN 0-06-003960-4, HarpT). Har-Row.

--Magill Books Index. LC 80-53597. 800p. 1980. 35.00 (ISBN 0-89356-200-9). Salem Pr.

--Magills Quotations in Context, First Series. 1966. 20.00 o.s.i. (ISBN 0-06-003657-5, HarpT); lib. bdg. 16.29 o.s.i. (ISBN 0-06-003658-3). Har-Row.

--Masterpieces of World Literature in Digest Form, 4 vols. Incl. Series 1. 1952. o.p. (ISBN 0-06-003870-5); Series 2. 1956. o.p. (ISBN 0-06-003690-7); lib. bdg. 19.79 (ISBN 0-06-003900-0); Series 3. 1960. 22.50 (ISBN 0-06-003750-4); Series 4. 1969. 22.50 (ISBN 0-06-003751-2); lib. bdg. 19.79 (ISBN 0-06-003752-0). HarpT). Har-Row.

Magill, M. J. On a General Economic Theory of Motion. LC 74-135961. (Lecture Notes in Operations Research & Mathematical Systems: Vol. 36). 1970. pap. 10.70 o.p. (ISBN 0-387-04959-2). Springer-Verlag.

Magill, Robert S. Community Decision-Making for Social Welfare: Federalism, City Government, & the Poor. LC 79-301. 1979. text ed. 19.95 (ISBN 0-87705-378-2); pap. text ed. 8.95 (ISBN 0-87705-398-7). Human Sci Pr.

Maginley, C. J. Toys You Can Build. 1975. pap. 3.95 (ISBN 0-8015-7860-4, Hawthorn). Dutton.

--Toys You Can Build. 8.95 o.p. (ISBN 0-498-01179-8). A S Barnes.

Maginnis, James B. Fundamental ANSI Cobol Programming. 1975. Repr. text ed. 16.95x (ISBN 0-13-339218-X). P-H.

Maginnis, John J. Profile of a Citizen Soldier. (Illus.). 254p. 1981. 9.95 (ISBN 0-89962-046-9). Todd & Honeywell.

Magito, Suria, ed. see Andersen, Hans C.

Magliato, Joe. The Wall Street Gospel. LC 80-84629. (Orig.). 1981. pap. 4.95 (ISBN 0-89081-279-9). Harvest Hse.

Maglio, Rodolfo, jt. auth. see Jaffe, Philip M.

Maglione, Harry, jt. ed. see Emmens, Carol A.

Magnan, Mark W., Jr. Epilogue. 1979. 9.95 (ISBN 0-533-04507-X). Vantage.

Magnani, Bruno, ed. Beta-Adrenergic Blocking Agents in the Management of Hypertension & Angina Pectoris. LC 74-15629. 1974. 19.50 (ISBN 0-89004-013-3). Raven.

Magnani, Franco, ed. Country Houses. (Illus.). 1981. 22.50 (ISBN 0-8230-7132-4). Watson-Guptill.

Magnant, Robert S. Domestic Satellite Policy: An FCC Giant Step Toward Competitive Telecommunications Policy. LC 76-30840. (Illus.). 1977. PLB 27.50x (ISBN 0-89158-226-6). Westview.

Magner, J., jt. auth. see Magner, K.

Magner, James. Till No Light Leaps: The Selected Poems. 1981. 8.00 (ISBN 0-8233-0327-6). Golden Quill.

Magner, K. & Magner, J. Liberated Sex. (Orig.). 1977. pap. 1.50 o.p. (ISBN 0-425-03407-0). Berkley Pub.

Magnifico, G. European Monetary Unification. LC 73-303. 1973. 21.95 (ISBN 0-470-56525-X). Halsted Pr.

Magnus, I. A. Clinical Aspects of Dermatological Photobiology. (Blackwell Scientific Pubns.). (Illus.). 1976. 40.00 (ISBN 0-8016-3082-7, Blackwell). Mosby.

Magnus, Laurie. A Dictionary of European Literature, Designed As a Companion to English Studies. rev. ed. LC 74-6269. xii, 605p. 1975. Repr. of 1927 ed. 32.00 (ISBN 0-8103-4014-3). Gale.

Magnus, Leonard A. Russian Folk-Tales with Introduction & Notes. LC 74-6486. 1974. Repr. of 1916 ed. 20.00 (ISBN 0-8103-3654-5). Gale.

Magnus, Margaret. Fundamentals of Nursing. (Nursing Examination Review Books: Vol. 11). 1972. pap. 6.00 (ISBN 0-87488-511-6). Med Exam.

Magnus, Wilhelm & Winkler, Stanley. Hill's Equation. LC 78-74114. 1979. pap. text ed. 3.00 (ISBN 0-486-63738-7). Dover.

Magnuson, James. The Rundown. 1979. pap. 1.75 o.s.i. (ISBN 0-515-04725-2). Jove Pubns.

Magnuson, Norris. Salvation in the Slums: Evangelical Social Welfare Work, 1865-1920. LC 76-54890. (No. 10). 1977. 14.50 (ISBN 0-8108-1001-8). Scarecrow.

Magnussen, Daniel O. Thompson's Narrative of the Little Big Horn 1876. (Illus.). 1974. 22.50 o.p. (ISBN 0-87062-108-4). A H Clark.

Magnusson, Bertil & Kligman, Albert M. Allergic Contact Dermatitis in the Guinea Pig: Identification of Contact Allergens. (Illus.). 160p. 1970. 23.75 (ISBN 0-398-01200-8). C C Thomas.

Magnusson, D., et al. Adjustment: A Longitudinal Study. LC 75-11593. 1975. 17.95 (ISBN 0-470-56347-8). Halsted Pr.

Magnusson, David. Test Theory. 1966. 17.95 (ISBN 0-201-04395-5). A-W.

--Toward a Psychology of Situations. 488p. 1981. ref. ed. 24.95 (ISBN 0-89859-061-2). L Erlbaum Assocs.

Magnusson, Magnus. Landlord or Tenant? LC 79-305778. (Illus.). 1979. 10.50 (ISBN 0-370-30130-7, Pub. by Chatto Bodley Jonathan). Merrimack Bk Serv.

--Vikings! (Illus.). 320p. 1980. 20.00 o.p. (ISBN 0-525-22892-6). Dutton.

Magnusson, Magnus & Palsson, Hermann, trs. Njal's Saga. (Classics Ser.). (Orig.). 1960. pap. 3.50 (ISBN 0-14-044103-4). Penguin.

Magocsi, Paul R. Let's Speak Rusyn: Transcarpathian Edition. LC 79-18393. (Illus.). 106p. 1979. pap. 6.95 (ISBN 0-917242-01-7). Carpatho-Rusyn Res Ctr.

Magoffin, Susan S. Down the Santa Fe Trail & into Mexico: The Diary of Susan Shelby Magoffin, 1846-1847. Drumm, Stella M., ed. LC 75-31417. (Illus.). 344p. 1975. Repr. of 1962 ed. 25.00 o.p. (ISBN 0-88307-518-0). Gannon.

Magonet, Philip. Practical Hypnotism. pap. 3.00 (ISBN 0-87980-123-9). Wilshire.

Magoon, T. M., et al. Mental Health Counsellors at Work. 1971. 32.00 (ISBN 0-08-006422-1). Pergamon.

Magorian, James. Imaginary Radishes. LC 79-53857. 32p. 1980. 5.00 (ISBN 0-930674-03-0). Black Oak.

--Plucked Chickens. LC 80-68263. 32p. 1981. 5.00 (ISBN 0-930674-04-9). Black Oak.

Magoun, Francis P., Jr. The Anglo-Saxon Poems. 49p. 1980. Repr. of 1965 ed. write for info. (ISBN 0-89984-334-4). Century Bookbindery.

Magoun, Francis P., Jr. & Walker, James A. An Old English Anthology. 108p. 1980. Repr. of 1950 ed. lib. bdg. 15.00 (ISBN 0-89760-542-X). Telegraph Bks.

Magoun, Francis P., Jr., tr. see Grimm Brothers.

Magoun, Horace W. Waking Brain. 2nd ed. (A Salmon Lecture Ser). (Illus.). 196p. 1969. 111.75 (ISBN 0-398-01201-6). C C Thomas.

Magrab, Edward B. Environmental Noise Control. LC 75-20233. 299p. 1975. 27.50 (ISBN 0-471-56344-7, Pub. by Wiley-Interscience). Wiley.

Magrab, Phyllis R. & Elder, Jerry O., eds. Planning for Services to Handicapped Persons: Community, Education, Health. LC 79-21474. 1979. text ed. 14.50 (ISBN 0-933716-04-4). P H Brookes.

Magrab, Phyllis R., jt. ed. see Elder, Jerry O.

Magrath, C. Peter. Yazoo: Law & Politics in the New Republic. LC 66-19584. (Illus.). 243p. 1966. 10.00x (ISBN 0-87057-100-1, Pub. by Brown U Pr). Univ Pr of New England.

Magret, Guillem see Pistoleta.

Magretta, Joan, jt. ed. see Horton, Andrew S.

Magri, Iole F. A Ciascuno Il Suo. LC 75-29713. 1976. pap. text ed. 7.20 (ISBN 0-395-13398-X). HM.

Magrill, Rose M., jt. auth. see Bonk, Wallace J.

Magriso, Yitzchak. Avoth. Barocas, David N., tr. Kaplan, Aryeh, intro. by. & 400p. 14.95 (ISBN 0-686-27542-X). Maznaim.

Magruder, Jeb S. An American Life. LC 74-78466. (Illus.). 352p. 1974. 10.00 o.p. (ISBN 0-689-10603-3). Atheneum.

Magsam, Charles. Experience of God. LC 73-89314. 256p. 1975. 7.95x o.p. (ISBN 0-88344-123-3); pap. 4.95x o.p. (ISBN 0-88344-124-1). Orbis Bks.

Magubane, Bernard. The Political Economy of Race & Class in South Africa. LC 78-13917. 1979. 18.50 o.p. (ISBN 0-85345-463-9, CL-4639). Monthly Rev.

Maguire, Anne. Nurse at Towpath Lodge. (YA) 1976. 4.95 o.p. (ISBN 0-685-68910-7, Avalon). Bouregy.

Maguire, B. Carpentry in Commercial Construction. 1976. 17.00 (ISBN 0-87909-124-X); text ed. 13.50 (ISBN 0-87909-124-X). Reston.

Maguire, Byron. Carpentry: Framing & Finishing. (Illus.). 1979. 18.95 (ISBN 0-8359-0701-5); instrs'. manual avail. (ISBN 0-8359-0702-3). Reston.

--The Complete Book of Woodworking & Cabinetmaking. (Illus.). 1974. 16.95 (ISBN 0-87909-153-3); pap. text ed. 6.95 (ISBN 0-87909-182-7). Reston.

Maguire, Byron W. Carpentry in Residential Construction. (Illus.). 416p. 1975. 18.95 (ISBN 0-87909-118-5). Reston.

--Construction Materials. 375p. 1981. text ed. 19.95 (ISBN 0-8359-0935-2). Reston.

--Masonry & Concrete. (Illus.). 1978. ref. ed. 18.95 (ISBN 0-87909-521-0). Reston.

Maguire, Daniel C. The Moral Choice. 1979. pap. 9.95 (ISBN 0-03-053796-7). Winston Pr.

--A New American Justice: Ending the White Male Monopolies. LC 78-20084. (Illus.). 240p. 1980. 9.95 (ISBN 0-385-14325-7). Doubleday.

Maguire, Gregory. The Daughter of the Moon. LC 79-25683. 257p. (gr. 3 up). 1980. 9.95 (ISBN 0-374-31705-4). FS&G.

--Lights on the Lake. 262p. (gr. 5 up). 1981. 9.95 (ISBN 0-374-34463-9). FS&G.

Maguire, J. M. Marx's Theory of Politics. LC 77-90214. 1979. 29.95 (ISBN 0-521-21955-8). Cambridge U Pr.

Maguire, Jack R. Talk of Texas. LC 73-84554. (Illus.). 160p. 1980. 7.95 (ISBN 0-88319-014-1). Shoal Creek Pub.

Maguire, Kitty. Heart to Hand: A Calligraphy Manual. (Illus.). 68p. 1980. text ed. 25.00 limited ed of 50 (ISBN 0-9604818-0-X); pap. 12.00 (ISBN 0-9604818-1-8). Anemone Edns.

Maguire, R., tr. see Gippius, V. V.

Maguire, Robert A., tr. see Szymborska, Wislawa.

Maguire, W. A. The Downshire Estates in Ireland 1801-1845: The Management of Irish Landed Estates in the Early Nineteenth Century. (Illus.). 282p. 1972. text ed. 34.50x (ISBN 0-19-822357-9). Oxford U Pr.

Magyar, K., ed. Monoamine Oxidases & Their Selective Inhibition: Proceedings of the Third Congress of the Hungarian Pharmacological Society, Budapest, 1979. LC 80-41281. (Advances in Pharmacological Research Practice Ser.: Vol. IV). 165p. 1981. 30.00 (ISBN 0-08-026389-5). Pergamon.

Magyari, E., jt. auth. see Constantinescu, F.

Magyesy, Eugene F. Pressure Vessel Handbook. 5th ed. (Illus.). Date not set. 35.00 (ISBN 0-914458-07-8). Pressure.

Mahadev, K. Gaslights in Calcutta. 8.00 (ISBN 0-89253-677-2); flexible cloth 4.80 (ISBN 0-89253-678-0). Ind-US Inc.

--The Testament of Nizamulmulk. (Writers Workshop Redbird Ser.). 1975. 8.00 (ISBN 0-88253-654-0); pap. text ed. 4.00 (ISBN 0-88253-653-2). Ind-US Inc.

Mahadevan, Meera. Shulamith. (Indian Novel Ser.). 208p. 1976. 8.50 (ISBN 0-89253-047-2). Ind-US Inc.

Mahadevan, T. M. The Hymns of Sankaras. (Illus.). 188p. 1980. text ed. 16.50 (ISBN 0-8426-1652-7). Verry.

--Invitation to Indian Philosophy. (Orig.). 1979. pap. 5.95 (ISBN 0-89684-090-5, Pub. by Arnold Heinemann India). Orient Bk Dist.

--Sankaracharya. (Orig.). 1979. pap. 2.50 (ISBN 0-89744-204-0). Auromere.

Mahadevan, T. M., tr. see Anantendra-Yati.

Mahadevan, T. M., tr. see Sankaracharya.

Mahadevan, T. M., tr. see Shankara.

Mahadevan, T. M. P. Upanisads: The Selections from 108 Upanisads. Mahadevan, T. M. P., tr. from Sanskrit. 240p. (Orig.). 1975. pap. 3.20 (ISBN 0-88253-985-X). Ind-US Inc.

Mahadevan, T. M. P., ed. The Sage of Kanchi. 93p. 1975. lib. bdg. 6.25 (ISBN 0-89253-018-9). Ind-US Inc.

--Spiritual Perspectives: Essays in Mysticism & Metaphysics. 303p. 1975. lib. bdg. 15.00 (ISBN 0-89253-021-9). Ind-US Inc.

Mahaffey, Michael, jt. auth. see Hooten, Joseph.

Mahain, Jo, jt. auth. see Pal, George.

Mahajan, Ashok. The Garden of Fand. (Redbird Bk.). 1976. lib. bdg. 6.75 (ISBN 0-89253-122-3); flexible bdg. 4.80 (ISBN 0-89253-143-6). Ind-US Inc.

Mahajan, B. N. Consumer Behaviour in India: An Econometric Study. 1980. text ed. 20.50x (ISBN 0-391-01834-5). Humanities.

Mahajan, V. S. Development Planning: Lessons from the Japanese Model. LC 76-52207. 1977. 8.50x (ISBN 0-88386-805-9). South Asia Bks.

Mahajan, Vijay & Pegels, C. Carl, eds. Systems Analysis in Health Care. 1979. 34.50 (ISBN 0-03-046656-3). Praeger.

Mahalanobis, P. C. Approach of Operational Research to Planning in India. 1964. 6.50x o.p. (ISBN 0-210-27055-1). Asia.

Mahalmobis, Parasanta C. The University Teaching of Social Sciences: Statistics. 1957. pap. 3.00 (ISBN 92-3-100424-7, U710, UNESCO). Unipub.

Mahan. Christian Perfection. pap. 3.95 o.p. (ISBN 0-686-12855-9). Schmul Pub Co.

Mahan, A. & Preston, A. Influence of Seapower in History. 29.95 (ISBN 0-13-464537-5). P-H.

Mahan, Alfred T. From Sail to Steam: Recollections of Naval Life. LC 68-26817. (American Scene Ser). 1968. Repr. of 1907 ed. lib. bdg. 29.50 (ISBN 0-306-71148-6). Da Capo.

--Is the Panama Canal Still Essential to the Defense of the Uniited States & the Safety of the Free World? (Illus.). 1977. 39.50 (ISBN 0-930008-01-4). Inst Econ Pol.

--The Panama Canal & Sea Power in the Pacific. (Illus.). 1977. 45.15 (ISBN 0-89266-044-9). Am Classical Coll Pr.

Mahan, Bill. The Boy Who Looked Like Shirley Temple. 1981. lib. bdg. 14.95 (ISBN 0-8161-3155-4, Large Print Bks). G K Hall.

Mahan, Bruce H. College Chemistry. 1966. text ed. 19.95 (ISBN 0-201-04404-8). A-W.

--University Chemistry. 3rd ed. LC 74-19696. 1975. text ed. 21.95 (ISBN 0-201-04405-6). A-W.

Mahan, Gary P. The Demand for Residential Telephone Service. LC 79-620020. 1979. pap. 6.00 (ISBN 0-87744-158-8). Mich St U Busn.

Mahan, Gerald D. Many-Particle Physics. (Physics of Solids & Liquids Ser.). 980p. 1981. 85.00 (ISBN 0-306-40411-7, Plenum Pr). Plenum Pub.

Mahan, Harold D., jt. auth. see Wallace, George J.

Mahanand, Marilyn, jt. auth. see Cunningham, William.

Mahaney, W. C., ed. see Quarternary Stratigraphy Symposium, 1975.

Mahaney, William E. John Webster: A Classified Bibliography. (Salzburg Studies in English Literature, Jacobean Drama Studies: No. 10). 319p. 1973. pap. text ed. 25.00x (ISBN 0-391-01471-4). Humanities.

--Workbook of Current English. 2nd ed. 1981. pap. text ed. 6.95x (ISBN 0-673-15405-X). Scott F.

Mahaney, William E. & Sherwin, Walter K. Two University Latin Plays: Philip Parsons' "Atlanta" & Thomas Atkinson's "Homo". Sherwin, W. K., et al, trs. (Salzburg Studies in English Literature, Elizabethan & Renaissance Studies: No. 16). 191p. 1973. pap. text ed. 25.00x (ISBN 0-391-01470-6). Humanities.

Mahaney, William E. & Sherwin, Walter K., eds. Antoninus Bassianus Caracalla: An Edition & Translation. Sherwin, Walter K. & Freyman, Jay M., trs. from Lat. (Salzburg Studies in English Literature, Elizabethan & Renaissance Studies: No. 52). 189p. (Orig.). 1976. pap. text ed. 25.00x (ISBN 0-391-01467-6). Humanities.

Mahanta, K. C. Veterinary Microbiology. 1966. pap. 7.25x (ISBN 0-210-26947-2). Asia.

Mahanthappa, K. T. & Randa, James, eds. Quantum Flavordynamics, Quantum Chromodynamics & Unified Theories. (NATO Advanced Study Institute Ser., Ser. B: Physics: Vol. 54). 505p. 1980. 59.50 (ISBN 0-306-40436-2, Plenum Pr). Plenum Pub.

Mahanty, Aroop K. Intermediate Microeconomics with Applications. 1980. 17.95 (ISBN 0-12-465150-X). Acad Pr.

Mahapatra, Jayanta. Svayamvara & Other Poems. (Redbird Bk.). 1976. 6.75 (ISBN 0-89253-091-X); flexible bdg. 4.00 (ISBN 0-685-69683-9). Ind-US Inc.

Mahapatra, Sitakant. The Empty Distance Carries... Munda & Oraon Folk - Songs. 1976. lib. bdg. 14.00 (ISBN 0-89253-096-0); flexible bdg. 4.80 (ISBN 0-89253-146-0). Ind-US Inc.

--The Other Silence. (Redbird Ser.). 1975. 6.75 (ISBN 0-88253-600-1); pap. text ed. 4.80 (ISBN 0-88253-599-4). Ind-US Inc.

--Quiet Violence. (Translated from Oriya). 6.75 (ISBN 0-89253-604-7); flexible cloth 4.80 (ISBN 0-89253-605-5). Ind-US Inc.

--Staying Is Nowhere: An Anthology of Kondh & Paraja Poetry. (Saffronbird Bk.). 1976. lib. bdg. 12.00 (ISBN 0-89253-126-6); flexible bdg. 6.75 (ISBN 0-89253-142-8). Ind-US Inc.

Mahar, Dennis J. Frontier Development Policy in Brazil: A Study of Amazonia. LC 78-19750. (Praeger Special Studies). 1979. 21.95 (ISBN 0-03-047091-9). Praeger.

Maharaj, B., jt. auth. see Charran, R.

Maharshi, Ramana. The Spiritual Teaching of Ramana Maharshi. (Clear Light Ser). 112p. (Orig.). 1972. pap. 5.95 (ISBN 0-394-73015-1). Shambhala Pubns.

Mahbub ul Haq. The Third World & the International Economic Order. (Development Papers: No. 22). 54p. 1976. pap. 1.50 (ISBN 0-686-28676-6). Overseas Dev Council.

Mahdi, Ali-Akbar. A Selected Bibliography on Political Economy of Iran. (Public Administration Ser.: Bibliography P-598). 104p. 1980. pap. 15.25. Vance Biblios.

Mahelona, John, jt. auth. see Johnson, Rubellite K.

Mahendra Nath Gupta, see M, pseud.

Maher, B., ed. Progress in Experimental Personality Research. Incl. Vol. 1. 1964. 32.50 (ISBN 0-12-541401-3); Vol. 2. 1965. 32.50 (ISBN 0-12-541402-1); Vol. 3. 1966. 32.50 (ISBN 0-12-541403-X); Vol. 4. 1968. 32.50 (ISBN 0-12-541404-8); Vol. 5. 1970. 32.50 (ISBN 0-12-541405-6); Vol. 6. 1972. 32.50 (ISBN 0-12-541406-4); Vol. 7. 1974. 32.50 (ISBN 0-12-541407-2). Acad Pr.

Maher, Brendan A. Principles of Psychopathology. (Psychology Ser.). 1966. text ed. 19.95 o.p. (ISBN 0-07-039610-8, C); instructor's manual 2.95 o.p. (ISBN 0-07-039613-2). McGraw.

Maher, Brendan A., tr. see From, Franz.

Maher, Carolyn A., et al. Math, No. 1. Gafney, Leo, ed. (General Math Ser.). (Illus.). (gr. 7-9). 1981. text ed. write for info pupil's ed. (ISBN 0-07-039591-8, W); tchr's ed., 448 p. 13.20 (ISBN 0-07-039592-6); wkbk. to pupils ed. 4.80 (ISBN 0-07-039593-4); wkbk. to tchrs. ed. 5.20 (ISBN 0-07-039594-2). McGraw.

--General Math. Gafney, Leo, ed. 160p. 1980. pupil's ed. 4.80 (ISBN 0-07-039593-4, W); tchrs. ed. 5.20 (ISBN 0-07-039594-2). McGraw.

Maher, Charles A., jt. ed. see Hoover, J. Gary.

Maher, Donald J., jt. auth. see Mehta, Nitin H.

Maher, Frank J., jt. auth. see Cleary, Denis J.

Maher, George F. Hostage: A Police Approach to a Contemporary Crisis. (Illus.). 100p. 1977. 12.75 (ISBN 0-398-03698-5). C C Thomas.

Maher, J. Peter. Linguistics & Evolutionary Theory. (Amsterdam Classics in Linguistics Ser.: No. 6). 165p. 1980. text ed. 25.75x (ISBN 90-272-0877-8). Humanities.

Maher, John. Ideas About Taxes. LC 79-182292. (Ideas About Ser). (Illus.). 48p. (gr. 1-3). 1972. PLB 3.90 o.p. (ISBN 0-531-02021-5). Watts.

Maher, John E. Ideas About Measuring & Accounting. LC 73-8977. (Ideas About Ser). (Illus.). 48p. (gr. 1-4). 1974. PLB 5.90 (ISBN 0-531-02657-4). Watts.

--Ideas About Money. LC 77-115412. (Ideas About Ser). (gr. k-3). 1970. PLB 4.33 o.p. (ISBN 0-531-01947-0). Watts.

Maher, Marina. Marina Maher's Terrific Tips. (Orig.). Date not set. pap. 4.95 (ISBN 0-440-58369-1, Dell Trade Pbks). Dell.

Maher, Michael, jt. ed. see Lobo, Gerald.

Maher, Tom & Schwartz, Malcolm. Doctor Discusses Cancer. (Illus.). 1981. pap. 2.50 (ISBN 0-686-69338-8). Budlong.

Maher, Vanessa. Women & Property in Morocco. LC 74-80351. (Studies in Social Anthropology: No. 10). (Illus.). 164p. 1975. 27.50 (ISBN 0-521-20548-4). Cambridge U Pr.

Maheshawari, S. R. The Civil Service in Great Britain. 1977. 7.00x o.p. (ISBN 0-88386-948-9). South Asia Bks.

Maheshwari, B. L. Decision Styles & Organizational Effectiveness. 240p. 1980. text ed. 22.50 (ISBN 0-7069-1032-X, Pub. by Vikas India). Advent Bk.

Maheu, R., pref. by. Main Trends of Research in the Social & Human Sciences: Social Sciences, Part 1. LC 70-114641. 1970. 65.25 (ISBN 92-3-100828-5, U363, UNESCO); Part 2, (vols. 1 & 2) 137.50 (ISBN 92-3-101013-1). Unipub.

Mahfouz, Nagib. The Beggar. (Arabic.). pap. 5.50 (ISBN 0-685-82811-5). Intl Bk Ctr.

--Beginning & the End. (Arabic.). pap. 5.50x (ISBN 0-685-82812-3). Intl Bk Ctr.

--The Honeymoon. (Arabic). pap. 5.50 (ISBN 0-685-82831-X). Intl Bk Ctr.

--Khan el Khalili. pap. 5.50 arabic ed. (ISBN 0-685-82837-9). Intl Bk Ctr.

--Love in the Rain. pap. 5.50 arabic (ISBN 0-685-82841-7). Intl Bk Ctr.

--Madak Alley. pap. 5.50 arabic (ISBN 0-685-82842-5); pap. 3.95 English (ISBN 0-686-67892-3). Intl Bk Ctr.

--The Mirror. (Arabic.). pap. 5.50 (ISBN 0-685-82846-8). Intl Bk Ctr.

--The Road. pap. 5.50 arabic (ISBN 0-685-82870-0). Intl Bk Ctr.

--Tales of Old Cairo. pap. 5.50 arabic (ISBN 0-685-82882-4). Intl Bk Ctr.

--Tales of the Black Cat. pap. 5.50 arabic (ISBN 0-685-82881-6). Intl Bk Ctr.

--The Thief & the Dogs. (Arabic.). pap. 5.50 (ISBN 0-685-82888-3). Intl Bk Ctr.

Mahfouz, Nagrib. The Crime. pap. 5.50 arabic (ISBN 0-685-82818-2). Intl Bk Ctr.

Mahfouz, Naguib. Children of Gebelawi. Stewart, Philip, tr. from Arabic. (Arab Writers Series). 400p. (Orig.). 1980. 14.00x (ISBN 0-89410-212-5); pap. 7.00x (ISBN 0-686-64483-2). Three Continents.

--Midaq Alley. Le Gassick, Trevor, tr. 9.00 (ISBN 0-914478-53-2, Co-Pub. by Heinemann Educ.-Bks); pap. 5.00 (ISBN 0-914478-54-0). Three Continents.

--Miramar. Moussa-Mahmoud, Fatma, tr. from Arabic. LC 78-72968. (Orig.). 1978. pap. 5.00 (ISBN 0-89410-020-3). Three Continents.

Mahl, Huey. Average Purse Tables. (Gambler's Book Shelf). 64p. 1976. pap. 2.95 (ISBN 0-89650-564-2). Gamblers.

--Baccarat Decisions. (System Check Ser.). 1978. pap. 2.95 (ISBN 0-89650-614-2). Gamblers.

--Beating the Bookie. (Gambler's Book Shelf Ser.). 1975. pap. 2.95 (ISBN 0-89650-547-2). Gamblers.

--Craps Line Decisions. (System Check Ser.). 1978. pap. 2.95 (ISBN 0-89650-660-6). Gamblers.

--Crossbet Two. (Gambler's Book Shelf). 64p. 1975. pap. 2.95 (ISBN 0-89650-551-0). Gamblers.

--How They Ran - S. A. Seventy Five. (Gambler's Book Shelf). 64p. 1975. pap. 2.95 (ISBN 0-89650-553-7). Gamblers.

--The Race Is Pace. (Gambler's Book Shelf). 64p. 1975. pap. 2.95 (ISBN 0-89650-550-2). Gamblers.

--Roulette by the Numbers. (System Check Ser.). 1978. pap. 2.95 (ISBN 0-89650-888-9). Gamblers.

Mahl, Mary R. & Koon, Helene, eds. Female Spectator: English Women Writers Before 1800. LC 76-26430. (Midland Bks.: No. 224). 320p. 1977. 15.00x (ISBN 0-253-32166-2); pap. 5.95x (ISBN 0-253-20224-8). Ind U Pr.

Mahlendorf, tr. see Bienek, Horst.

Mahler, Alma. Gustav Mahler: Memories & Letters. 3rd ed. Mitchell, Donald & Martner, Knud, eds. LC 74-26502. (Illus.). 409p. 1968. pap. 7.95 (ISBN 0-295-95378-0). U of Wash Pr.

Mahler, Henry R. see Bourne, G. H. & Danielli, J. F.

Mahler, K. P-adic Numbers & Their Functions. LC 79-20103. (Cambridge Tracts in Mathematics Ser.: No. 76). Date not set. 45.00 (ISBN 0-521-23102-7). Cambridge U Pr.

Mahler, Kurt. Introduction to p-Adic Numbers & Their Function. (Tracts in Mathematics & Mathematical Physics: No. 64). 19.95 (ISBN 0-521-20001-6). Cambridge U Pr.

Mahler, Walter R. Diagnostic Studies. (Illus.). 224p. 1974. text ed. 16.95 (ISBN 0-201-04437-4). A-W.

Mahler, William F., ed. see Shinners, Lloyd H.

Mahlin, Everett, jt. auth. see Weitz, John.

Mahlstede, John P. & Haber, E. S. Plant Propagation. LC 57-5924. 1957. 23.50 (ISBN 0-471-56364-1). Wiley.

Mahmoud, Adel A. & Austen, K. Frank, eds. Eosinophil in Health & Disease. 1980. 39.50 (ISBN 0-8089-1274-7). Grune.

Mahmoudi, Jalil. A Concordance to the Hidden Words of Baha'u'llah. (Orig.). 1980. pap. 5.00 (ISBN 0-87743-148-5, 7-68-52). Baha'i.

--The Story As Told. rev. ed. LC 79-65925. (Illus.). 80p. (Orig.). 1980. pap. 5.50 (ISBN 0-933770-10-3). Kalimat.

Mahon, Denis. Studies in Seicento Art & Theory. LC 73-114544. (Illus.). 1971. Repr. of 1947 ed. lib. bdg. 25.00x (ISBN 0-8371-4743-3, MAST). Greenwood.

Mahon, Derek. Lives. 1972. pap. 3.50x o.p. (ISBN 0-19-211816-1). Oxford U Pr.

--Poems, Nineteen Sixty-Two to Nineteen Seventy-Eight. 128p. (Orig.). 1979. pap. 8.95x (ISBN 0-19-211897-8). Oxford U Pr.

Mahon, Harold P., et al. Efficient Energy Management. (Illus.). 496p. 1981. 24.95 (ISBN 0-13-791434-2). P-H.

Mahon, James J. The Marketing of Professional Accounting Services. LC 78-18221. 1978. 23.95 (ISBN 0-471-04480-6, Pub. by Wiley-Interscience). Wiley.

Mahon, John K. American Militia, Decade of Decision, 1789-1800. LC 60-63132. (Social Science Monographs: No. 6). 1960. pap. 3.25 (ISBN 0-8130-0153-6). U Presses Fla.

--The War of 1812. LC 79-137856. (Illus.). 391p. 1972. 12.50 o.p. (ISBN 0-8130-0318-0). U Presses Fla.

Mahon, Julia C. Mystery at Old Sturbridge Village. LC 64-16079. (Pilot Book Ser). (Illus.). (gr. 4-7). 1964. 6.95g (ISBN 0-8075-5360-3). A Whitman.

Mahon, Maureen. Thomas Hardy's Novels: A Study Guide. 1976. pap. text ed. 3.95x (ISBN 0-435-18552-7). Heinemann Ed.

Mahoney, Barry, jt. auth. see Westin, Alan P.

Mahoney, Bertha & Whitney, Elinor. Contemporary Illustrators of Children's Books. LC 79-185381. (Illus.). 1978. Repr. of 1930 ed. 34.00 (ISBN 0-8103-4308-8). Gale.

Mahoney, Edward P., ed. Philosophy & Humanism: Renaissance Essays in Honor of Paul Oskar Kristeller. LC 75-42285. 600p. 1976. 50.00x (ISBN 0-231-03904-2). Columbia U Pr.

Mahoney, John, ed. see Hungness, Carl, et al.

Mahoney, John L. The Logic of Passion: The Literary Criticism of William Hazlitt. (Salzburg Studies in English Literature Romantic Reassessment Ser.: No. 75). 1978. pap. text ed. 25.00x (ISBN 0-391-01468-4). Humanities.

Mahoney, John L., ed. see Dryden, John.

Mahoney, Michael. The Drawings of Salvator Rosa, 2 vols. LC 76-23637. (Outstanding Dissertations in the Fine Arts - 17th Century). (Illus.). 1977. Repr. of 1965 ed. Set. lib. bdg. 133.00 (ISBN 0-8240-2707-8). Garland Pub.

Mahoney, Michael J. Abnormal Psychology: Perspectives on Human Variance. 1980. text ed. 20.95 scp (ISBN 0-397-47410-5, HarpC); scp study guide 8.95 (ISBN 0-397-47411-3); instr's manual avail. (ISBN 0-397-47410-5). Har-Row.

--The Scientist As Subject: The Psychological Imperative. LC 76-5878. 192p. 1976. 16.50 (ISBN 0-88410-505-9); pap. text ed. 6.95 (ISBN 0-88410-514-8). Ballinger Pub.

Mahoney, R. Laboratory Techniques in Zoology. 2nd ed. LC 72-13645. 390p. 1973. 29.95 o.p. (ISBN 0-470-56375-3). Halsted Pr.

Mahoney, Susan & Gregorvich, Barbara. Math Word Problems. LC 79-730247. (Illus.). 1979. pap. text ed. 99.00 (ISBN 0-89290-130-6, A515-SATC). Soc for Visual.

Mahoney, Susan & Mills, Richard G. Metric Measurement. LC 76-731369. (Illus.). 1976. pap. text ed. 60.00 (ISBN 0-89290-128-4, 507-SAR-SATC). Soc for Visual.

Mahoney, Thomas A. Compensation & Reward Perspectives. 1979. pap. 12.95 (ISBN 0-256-02229-1). Irwin.

Mahoney, Thomas H., ed. see Burke, Edmund.

Mahoney, Tom & Sloane, Leonard. The Great Merchants. new & enl. ed. LC 73-14065. 384p. (YA) 1974. 12.95 o.s.i. (ISBN 0-06-012739-2, HarpT). Har-Row.

Mahony, Bertha E., et al, eds. Illustrators of Children's Books: 1744-1945, Vol. 1. (Illus.). 1947. 28.00x (ISBN 0-87675-015-3). Horn Bk.

Mahony, J. H., jt. ed. see Stokes, G. S.

Mahony, Sheila, et al. Keeping Pace with the New Television- Public Television & Changing Technology. 281p. 1980. pap. 3.25 (Pub Telecom). NAEB.

Mahood, Kenneth. Losing Willy. LC 77-6267. (Illus.). (ps-2). 1978. PLB 6.95 (ISBN 0-13-540583-1); pap. 2.95 (ISBN 0-13-540591-2). P-H.

Mahood, Ramona, jt. ed. see Lenz, Millicent.

Mahrer, Alvin R., ed. New Approaches to Personality Classification. LC 73-96313. 1970. 22.50x (ISBN 0-231-03296-X). Columbia U Pr.

Mahwin, Jean. Topolgical Degree Methods in Non-Linear Boundary Value Problems. LC 78-31906. (CBMS Regional Conference Ser. in Mathematics: No. 40). 1979. 7.60 (ISBN 0-8218-1690-X, CBMS-40). Am Math.

Mahy, B. W. & Barry, R. D., eds. Negative Strand Viruses: Proceedings, 2 vols, Vols. 1 & 2. 1975. Vol. 1. 87.00 (ISBN 0-12-465301-4); Vol. 2. 65.50 (ISBN 0-12-465302-2). Acad Pr.

Mahy, Margaret. The Boy Who Was Followed Home. LC 75-4866. 32p. (gr. k-3). 1975. PLB 5.90 o.p. (ISBN 0-531-02834-8). Watts.

--Leaf Magic. LC 76-3538. (Illus.). (gr. k-4). 1977. 5.95 o.s.i. (ISBN 0-8193-0889-7, Four Winds); PLB 5.41 o.s.i. (ISBN 0-8193-0890-0). Schol Bk Serv.

--Lion in the Meadow. (Illus.). (gr. k-3). 1969. PLB 4.90 o.p. (ISBN 0-531-00130-X). Watts.

--Rooms for Rent. LC 72-2882. (Illus.). (gr. k-3). 1974. PLB 4.90 o.p. (ISBN 0-531-02590-X). Watts.

--Ultra-Violet Catastrophe. LC 74-12445. (Illus.). (gr. k-3). 1975. 5.95 o.s.i. (ISBN 0-8193-0748-3, Four Winds); PLB 5.41 o.s.i. (ISBN 0-8193-0749-1); pap. 1.95 o.s.i. (ISBN 0-8193-0908-7). Schol Bk Serv.

--Witch in the Cherry Tree. LC 73-6738. (Illus.). 32p. (gr. k-3). 1974. 5.95 o.s.i. (ISBN 0-8193-0646-0, Four Winds); PLB 5.41 o.s.i. (ISBN 0-8193-0647-9). Schol Bk Serv.

Mai, Ludwig H. Approach to Economics. (Quality Paperback: No. 83). (Orig.). 1970. pap. 2.95 (ISBN 0-8226-0083-8). Littlefield.

--Men & Ideas in Economics: A Dictionary of World Economists Past & Present. (Quality Paperbacks Ser.: No. 284). 270p. (Orig.). 1977. pap. 4.95 (ISBN 0-8226-0284-9). Littlefield.

Mai, W. F. & Lyon, H. H. Pictorial Key to Genera of Plant-Parasitic Nematodes. 4th ed. LC 74-14082. (Illus.). 224p. 1975. 14.50x (ISBN 0-8014-0920-9). Comstock.

Maia, Ronaldo, jt. auth. see Otis, Denise.

Maibach, H. I., jt. ed. see Marzulli, F. N.

Mai Chan, Lois, jt. auth. see Immroth, John P.

Maichel, Karol. Guide to Russian Reference Books. Incl. Vol. 1. General Bibliographies & Reference Books. (Bibliographical Ser.: No. 10). 92p. 1962. 7.00 (ISBN 0-8179-2101-X); pap. 5.00 (ISBN 0-8179-2102-8); Vol. 2. History, Auxiliary Historical Sciences, Ethnography, & Geography. (Bibliographical Ser.: No. 18). 297p. 1964. 12.00 (ISBN 0-8179-2181-8); Vol. 5. Science, Technology & Medicine. (Bibliographical Ser.: No. 22). 384p. 1967. 17.50 (ISBN 0-8179-2321-7). LC 62-14067. Hoover Inst Pr.

--Soviet & Russian Newspapers at the Hoover Institution: A Catalog. LC 66-26281. (Bibliographical Ser.: No. 24). 235p. 1966. 8.00 (ISBN 0-8179-2241-5); pap. 6.00 (ISBN 0-8179-2242-3). Hoover Inst Pr.

Maid, Amy & Wallace, Roger. Not Just Schoolwork: New Directions in Written Expression. LC 76-9524. (Illus.). 201p. 1976. pap. 9.95 (ISBN 0-916250-15-6). Irvington.

Maiden, Cecil & Knight, Hilary. Beginning with Mrs. McBee. LC 60-15411. (Illus.). (gr. k-3). 1959. 5.95 (ISBN 0-8149-0356-8). Vanguard.

--Speaking of Mrs. McCluskie. LC 62-19862. (Illus.). (gr. 5-9). 1962. 5.95 (ISBN 0-8149-0355-X). Vanguard.

Maiden, R. L. British Racing Cars. pap. 2.00x (ISBN 0-392-07213-0, SpS). Soccer.

Maidens. Life, Death & the Government Regulating America's Health. 192p. 1981. lib. bdg. 19.95 (ISBN 0-87196-336-1). Facts on File.

Maidens, Melinda. America's Troubled Children. (Editorials on File Ser.). 220p. 1980. lib. bdg. 19.95 (ISBN 0-87196-369-8). Facts on File.

Maidment, Robert & Bronstein, Russell. Simulation Games: Design & Implementation. LC 73-75051. 1973. pap. text ed. 6.95 (ISBN 0-675-08968-9). Merrill.

Maidment, William R. Librarianship. LC 75-17. (Profession Ser). 144p. 1975. 11.95 o.p. (ISBN 0-7153-6897-4). David & Charles.

Maier, Barbara M., jt. auth. see Maier, Richard A.

Maier, Carol, tr. see Strand, Mark, et al.

Maier, Charles S. & White, Dan S., eds. Thirteenth of May: The Advent of De Gaulle's Republic. (Problems in European History Ser). (Orig.). 1968. pap. 4.95x (ISBN 0-19-500959-2). Oxford U Pr.

Maier, Eugene, ed. see Ashley, John P. & Harvey, E. R.

Maier, Eugene, ed. see Pappin, Charlene.

Maier, Franz G. Cyprus. 1968. 11.95 (ISBN 0-236-17602-1, Pub. by Paul Elek). Merrimack Bk Serv.

Maier, G., ed. see NATO Advanced Study Institute, University of Waterloo, Canada 2-12, August 1977.

Maier, Georg, jt. auth. see Bork, Albert W.

Maier, Joan M., jt. auth. see Dougherty, Richard M.

Maier, John & Tollers, Vincent, eds. The Bible in Its Literary Milieu. (Orig.). 1980. pap. 12.95 (ISBN 0-8028-1799-8). Eerdmans.

Maier, L., jt. ed. see Kosolapoff, G. M.

Maier, Manfred. Basic Principles of Design. 392p. 1981. pap. 35.00 (ISBN 0-442-21206-2). Van Nos Reinhold.

Maier, Norman R. Psychology in Industrial Organizations. 4th ed. LC 74-4797. 750p. 1973. text ed. 19.95 (ISBN 0-395-14046-3, 3-34269); instructor's manual pap. 2.50 (ISBN 0-395-15102-3, 3-34270). HM.

Maier, Norman R. F. The Appraisal Interview: Three Basic Approaches. LC 75-40984. 228p. 1976. pap. 15.00 (ISBN 0-88390-111-0). Univ Assocs.

Maier, Norman R. F., et al. The Role-Play Technique: A Handbook for Management & Leadership Practice. LC 74-30943. Orig. Title: Supervisory & Executive Development. 290p. 1975. pap. 14.50 (ISBN 0-88390-104-8). Univ Assocs.

Maier, Paul. The Flames of Rome. LC 80-2561. (Illus.). 384p. 1981. 12.95 (ISBN 0-385-17091-2, Galilee). Doubleday.

Maier, Paul L. The Best of Walter A. Maier. 1980. pap. 7.95 (ISBN 0-570-03823-5, 12-2786). Concordia.

--A Man Spoke, a World Listened. 1980. pap. 8.95 (ISBN 0-570-03822-7, 12-2762). Concordia.

Maier, Richard A. & Maier, Barbara M. Comparative Animal Behavior. LC 78-95056. (Core Bks. in Psychology Ser.). 1970. text ed. 14.95 o.p. (ISBN 0-685-07578-8). Brooks-Cole.

Maier, Siegfried, jt. auth. see Reiter, Toni.

Maier, Walter A. The Book of Nahum. (Thornapple Commentaries). 392p. 1980. pap. 6.95 (ISBN 0-8010-6098-2). Baker Bk.

Maigne, Robert. Orthopedic Medicine: A New Approach to Vertebral Manipulations. Liberson, W. T., tr. (Illus.). 456p. 1980. 30.50 (ISBN 0-398-02349-2). C C Thomas.

Maignet, Gerard, ed. Chanson de Roland: Edition bilingue. (Du texte a l'idee). (Old fr. & mod. fr.). 1969. pap. 5.50x o.p. (ISBN 0-685-13820-8, 3023). Larousse.

Maiken, Peter. Rip-off: How to Spot It, How to Avoid It. 1979. 12.95 o.p. (ISBN 0-8362-6203-4); pap. 5.95 o.p. (ISBN 0-8362-6204-2). Andrews & McMeel.

Maikowski, Stephen, jt. ed. see Hammerman, Susan.

Mail, Patricia D., jt. auth. see McDonald, David R.

Mailer, Norman. Advertisements for Myself. 540p. 1981. pap. 6.95 (ISBN 0-399-50538-5, Perigee). Putnam.

--Armies of the Night. 1971. pap. 2.50 (ISBN 0-451-09053-5, E9053, Sig). NAL.

--Barbary Shore. LC 79-26233. 312p. 1980. Repr. of 1951 ed. 15.95 (ISBN 0-86527-218-2). Fertig.

--The Deer Park. LC 79-20163. 375p. 1980. Repr. of 1955 ed. 15.95 (ISBN 0-86527-235-2). Fertig.

--The Deer Park. 384p. 1981. pap. 4.95 (ISBN 0-399-50531-8, Perigee). Putnam.

--The Executioner's Song. 1980. 3.95 (ISBN 0-686-68993-3). Warner Bks.

--Existential Errands. 320p. 1973. pap. 1.75 (ISBN 0-451-05422-9, E5422, Sig). NAL.

--Marilyn. (Illus.). 384p. 1975. pap. 3.50 (ISBN 0-446-96747-5). Warner Bks.

--The Naked & the Dead. 744p. 1980. pap. 7.95 (ISBN 0-03-059043-4, Owl Bks). HR&W.

--Of Women & Their Elegance. (Illus.). 1980. 29.95 (ISBN 0-671-24020-X). S&S.

--The Short Fiction of Norman Mailer. LC 79-20189. 285p. 1980. Repr. of 1967 ed. 15.95 (ISBN 0-86527-303-0). Fertig.

Mailey, Jean, jt. auth. see Dimand, M. S.

Mailick, Mildred, jt. ed. see Caroff, Phyllis.

Maillet, Pierre. The Construction of a European Community: Achievements & Prospects for the Future. LC 77-10605. (Praeger Special Studies). 1977. 22.95 (ISBN 0-03-022366-0). Praeger.

Maillol, Aristide, illus. Maillol Nudes: Thirty-Five Lithographs by Aristide Maillol. (Dover Art Library). Orig. Title: The Dialogues of the Courtesans. (Illus.). 1980. pap. 2.00 (ISBN 0-486-24000-2). Dover.

Maillot, Antoine L. La Musique au Theatre. LC 80-2288. 1981. Repr. of 1863 ed. 44.00 (ISBN 0-404-18856-7). AMS Pr.

Mailman, Leo. The Kid Comes Home. 1980. 2.00 (ISBN 0-916918-01-7, Pub. by Duck Down Press). Maelstrom.

Mails, Thomas E. Fool's Crow. 1980. pap. 3.50 (ISBN 0-686-69256-X, 52175, Discus). Avon.

--The Mystic Warriors of the Plains. LC 72-76191. 608p. 1972. 35.00 (ISBN 0-385-04741-X). Doubleday.

Maimonides. Commandments, 2 Vols. Set. 35.00x (ISBN 0-685-01042-2). Bloch.

Main, Barbara Y., jt. ed. see Shoate, Alec.

Main, I. G. Vibration & Waves in Physics. LC 77-5546. (Illus.). 1978. 68.50 (ISBN 0-521-21662-1); pap. 15.95x (ISBN 0-521-29220-4). Cambridge U Pr.

Main, Jody & Portugal, Nancy. Sprout Booklet & Stainless Steel Screen. 3nd ed. (Illus.). 1980. pap. 1.98 (ISBN 0-937148-01-6). Wild Horses Potted Plant.

Main, John. Word into Silence. 96p. 1981. pap. 3.95 (ISBN 0-8091-2369-X). Paulist Pr.

Main, John, jt. ed. see Archer, Clive.

Main, Mary. Evita: The Woman with the Whip. LC 79-27288. 286p. 1980. 8.95 (ISBN 0-396-07834-6). Dodd.

Main, William. Auckland Through a Victorian Lens. LC 78-670050. (Illus.). 1977. 22.50x (ISBN 0-908582-05-6). Intl Pubns Serv.

Mainardi, Patricia & Hoffman, Susan. Susan Hoffman's Quilted Tapestries. LC 79-92444. (Illus.). 80p. Date not set. pap. cancelled (ISBN 0-89659-106-9). Abbeville Pr.

Maine, Charles E. Thirst. 1978. pap. 1.95 (ISBN 0-441-80676-7). Charter Bks.

Maine, Henry S. Ancient Law: The Connection with the Early History of Society & Its Relation to Modern Ideas. 9.00 (ISBN 0-8446-0784-3). Peter Smith.

Maines, Clark. The Western Portal of Saint-Loup-De-Naud. LC 78-74373. (Fine Arts Dissertations, Fourth Ser.). (Illus.). 1980. lib. bdg. 44.00 (ISBN 0-8240-3960-2). Garland Pub.

Mainga, Mutumba. Bulozi Under the Luyana Kings: Political Evolution & State Formation in Pre-Colonial Zambia. LC 73-174757. (Illus.). 296p. (Orig.). 1973. pap. text ed. 7.95x (ISBN 0-582-64088-1). Longman.

Maingot. Abdominal Operations, 2 vols. 8th ed. 1980. 142.00 (ISBN 0-8385-0044-7). ACC.

Maingot, Rodney. Abdominal Operations, 2 vols. 7th ed. 2802p. 1979. Set. 142.00x (ISBN 0-8385-8779-8). ACC.

Maini, R. N., jt. ed. see Dumonde, D. C.

Mainiero, Lina, ed. American Women Writers: A Critical Reference Guide, Vol. 2, F-Le. LC 78-20945. 1980. 45.00 (ISBN 0-8044-3152-3). Ungar.

Mainkar, T. G. The Making of the Vedanta. 1980. 14.00x (ISBN 0-8364-0623-0, Pub. by Ajanta). South Asia Bks.

Mainkar, Trimbak G. Mysticism in the Rgveda. 1961. text ed. 3.25x (ISBN 0-391-02012-9). Humanities.

Mainland, W. F., ed. see Hoffmann, E. T.

Maino, Evelyn, jt. auth. see McMinn, Howard E.

Maino, Jeanette & Boer, Dena. Scenes of the Stanislaus. 1979. 7.95 o.p. (ISBN 0-914330-25-X). Pioneer Pub Co.

Mainord, James C. & Love, Harold D. Teaching Educable Mentally Retarded Children: Methods & Materials. (Illus.). 276p. 1975. 13.75 (ISBN 0-398-02646-7). C C Thomas.

Mainous, Frank. Melodies to Harmonize with. (Illus.). 1978. pap. 11.95 ref. ed. (ISBN 0-13-574277-3). P-H.

Mainous, Frank, jt. auth. see Ottman, Robert.

Mainous, Frank D., jt. auth. see Ottman, Robert W.

Mains, Karen B. Open Heart-Open Home. 1980. pap. 1.95 (ISBN 0-451-09530-8, J9530, Sig). NAL.

Mainstone, Madeleine. The Seventeenth Century. LC 80-40039. (Cambridge History of Art Ser.: No. 4). (Illus.). 100p. Date not set. 19.95 (ISBN 0-521-22162-5); pap. 6.95 (ISBN 0-521-29376-6). Cambridge U Pr.

Maio, Gerald De see Kushner, Harvey W. & De Maio, Gerald.

Maiorano, Robert. Francisco. LC 78-4574. (Illus.). (gr. k-3). 1978. 8.95 (ISBN 0-02-762170-7, 76217). Macmillan.

Mair, Charles. Dreamland & Other Poems & Tecumseh: A Drama. LC 73-82586. (Literature of Canada Ser). 1974. pap. 5.00 (ISBN 0-8020-6203-2). U of Toronto Pr.

Mair, Lucy. African Kingdoms. (Illus.). 1977. text ed. 22.50x (ISBN 0-19-821698-X); pap. text ed. 9.95x (ISBN 0-19-874075-1). Oxford U Pr.

--African Societies. LC 73-93398. (Illus.). 236p. 1974. 27.50 (ISBN 0-521-20442-9); pap. 8.95x (ISBN 0-521-09854-8). Cambridge U Pr.

--Anthropology & Social Change. (Monographs on Social Anthropology Ser: No. 38). 1969. text ed. 7.00x (ISBN 0-485-19538-0, Athlone Pr); pap. text ed. 9.50x (ISBN 0-391-00210-4). Humanities.

--An Introduction to Social Anthropology. 2nd ed. 576p. 1972. pap. text ed. 5.95x (ISBN 0-19-874011-5). Oxford U Pr.

--Primitive Government. 8.00 (ISBN 0-8446-2513-2). Peter Smith.

Mairani, Alvaro, tr. see Beers, Gilbert.

Maire, Susan S. How to Raise & Train an English Setter. (Illus.). pap. 2.00 (ISBN 0-87666-292-0, DS1074). TFH Pubns.

Mairet, Philip, tr. see Mounier, Emmanuel.

Mais, Roger. Brother Man. (Caribbean Writers Ser.). 1974. pap. text ed. 3.95x (ISBN 0-435-98585-X). Heinemann Ed.

Maisel, Edward. Tai Chi for Health. new ed. (Illus.). 224p. 1972. 6.95 o.p. (ISBN 0-03-001416-6); tchr's manual 1.00 o.p. (ISBN 0-03-085864-X). HR&W.

Maisel, Louis, ed. Changing Campaign Techniques: Elections & Values in Contemporary Democracies. LC 76-6311. (Sage Electoral Studies Yearbook: Vol. 2). 1976. 20.00x (ISBN 0-8039-0683-8); pap. 9.95x (ISBN 0-8039-0684-6). Sage.

Maisel, Louis & Sacks, Paul M., eds. The Future of Political Parties. LC 75-5016. (Sage Electoral Studies Yearbook: Vol. 1). 1975. 20.00x (ISBN 0-8039-0426-6); pap. 9.95x (ISBN 0-8039-0570-X). Sage.

Maisel, Sherman J. & Roulac, Stephen E. Real Estate Investment & Finance. (Illus.). 1976. text ed. 20.50x (ISBN 0-07-039730-9, C); instr's manual 4.95 (ISBN 0-07-039731-7). McGraw.

Maislen, Ruth, et al. Eat, Think & Be Thinner: The Weigh of Life Way. LC 76-19810. 1976. 8.95 (ISBN 0-8069-0150-0); lib. bdg. 8.29 (ISBN 0-8069-0151-9). Sterling.

Maissin, Eugene. French in Mexico & Texas, 1838-1839. Shepphard, J. L., tr. (Illus.). 1961. 35.00 (ISBN 0-685-05002-5). A Jones.

Maister, David H. Management of Owner-Operator Fleets. LC 79-5112. 256p. 1980. 23.95 (ISBN 0-669-03197-6). Lexington Bks.

Maister, David H., jt. auth. see Wyckoff, D. Daryl.

Maital, Schlomo & Meltz, Noah. Lagging Productivity Growth. 1980. 19.50 (ISBN 0-88410-689-6). Ballinger Pub.

Maiten, Bill, tr. Little Woodland Books. (10 books & 10 cassettes). 111.00 (ISBN 0-87827-322-0). Ency Brit Ed.

Maitland, Frederic W. Constitutional History of England. 1908. text ed. 59.95x (ISBN 0-521-05656-X); pap. text ed. 15.95x (ISBN 0-521-09137-3). Cambridge U Pr.

--Forms of Action at Common Law. 1936. text ed. 15.95x (ISBN 0-521-05657-8); pap. text ed. 7.95x (ISBN 0-521-09185-3). Cambridge U Pr.

--Selected Historical Essays. Cam, H. M., ed. 1957. 41.50 (ISBN 0-521-05659-4). Cambridge U Pr.

Maitland, Frederic W., jt. auth. see Pollock, Edward.

Maitland, Frederick W. Life & Letters of Leslie Stephen. LC 67-23873. 1968. Repr. of 1906 ed. 15.00 (ISBN 0-8103-3058-X). Gale.

Maitland, G. D. Vertebral Manipulation. 4th ed. 1977. pap. 24.95 (ISBN 0-407-43505-0). Butterworths.

Maitland, Margaret. The Channings of Everleigh. 1977. pap. 1.95 (ISBN 0-505-51199-1). Tower Bks.

--East Side West Side. 1977. pap. 1.75 (ISBN 0-505-51210-6). Tower Bks.

--Sacred & Profane. 1978. pap. 1.75 (ISBN 0-505-51241-6). Tower Bks.

Maitland, Peter S. Biology of Fresh Waters. (Tertiary Level Biology Ser.). 244p. 1980. pap. text ed. 24.95x (ISBN 0-470-26986-3). Halsted Pr.

Maitland, Sara. The Languages of Love. LC 80-943. 288p. 1981. 10.95 (ISBN 0-385-17203-6). Doubleday.

Maitland-Jones, J. F. Politics in Africa: The Former British Territories. (Comparative Modern Government Ser.). (Illus.). 236p. 1974. pap. 4.95x (ISBN 0-393-09305-0). Norton.

Maixner, Paul. Robert Louis Stevenson: The Critical Heritage. (Critical Heritage Ser.). 1981. write for info. (ISBN 0-7100-0505-9). Routledge & Kegan.

Maiyagawa, Yasue. Hare & the Bear & Other Stories. LC 74-158840. (Illus.). (gr. k-3). 1971. 5.95 o.s.i. (ISBN 0-8193-0517-0, Four Winds); PLB 5.41 o.s.i. (ISBN 0-8193-0518-9). Schol Bk Serv.

Maizel, Bruno. Food & Beverage Cost Controls. LC 77-142501. 1971. text ed. 13.95 (ISBN 0-672-96077-X); tchr's manual 6.67 (ISBN 0-672-96079-6); wkbk. 6.50 (ISBN 0-672-96078-8). Bobbs.

--Food & Beverage Purchasing. LC 77-142502. 1971. text ed. 14.95 (ISBN 0-672-96071-0); tchr's manual 5.90 (ISBN 0-672-96073-7); wkbk. 6.50 (ISBN 0-672-96072-9). Bobbs.

Maizelis, I., jt. auth. see Averbakh, Yuri.

Maizels, Alfred. Exports & Economic Growth of Developing Countries. LC 68-26987. (Publications of the National Institute of Economic & Social Research: No. 25). 1969. 42.50 (ISBN 0-521-06959-9). Cambridge U Pr.

--Industrial Growth & World Trade. 44.50 (ISBN 0-521-05662-4); pap. 11.95x (ISBN 0-521-09527-1). Cambridge U Pr.

Maizels, Joan, jt. auth. see Holme, Anthea.

Majarian, Haig H. Patterns in Medical Parasitology. 2nd ed. 160p. 1980. Repr. of 1975 ed. lib. bdg. write for info. (U Pr of Pacific). Intl Schol Bk Serv.

Majaro, S. International Marketing: A Strategic Approach to World Markets. LC 76-44628. 1977. 29.95 (ISBN 0-470-98936-X). Halsted Pr.

Majer, J. R. & Berry, M. The Mass Spectrometer. LC 77-15307. (Wykeham Science Ser.: No. 44). 1977. 16.95x (ISBN 0-8448-1171-8). Crane-Russak Co.

Majewski, Henry P. Preromantic Imagination of L. S. Mercier. LC 70-135985. 1971. text ed. 8.75x (ISBN 0-391-00122-1). Humanities.

Majid, A., jt. auth. see Gupta, S. C.

Majid, Kamal I. Optimum Design of Structures. LC 73-15015. 264p. 1974. text ed. 30.95 (ISBN 0-470-56533-0). Halsted Pr.

Majkowski, J. Epilepsy. (Monographs in Neural Sciences: Vol. 5). (Illus.). 1980. pap. 56.50 (ISBN 3-8055-0635-X). S Karger.

Majmudar, J. V., jt. auth. see Rachie, Kenneth O.

Majone, Giandomenico & Quade, Edward S. Pitfalls of Analysis. LC 79-41700. (Wiley IIASA International Series on Applied Systems Analysis). 224p. 1980. 34.90 (ISBN 0-471-27746-0, Pub. by Wiley-Interscience). Wiley.

Major, Alan. Maritime Antiques. 1981. 12.95 (ISBN 0-498-02496-2). A S Barnes.

Major, Charles. Bears of Blue River. (Illus.). (gr. 5-7). 1963. 4.75g o.s.i. (ISBN 0-02-762200-2). Macmillan.

Major, Clarence. The Dark & the Feeling. LC 73-83162. 5.95 (ISBN 0-89388-119-8). Okpaku Communications.

--Swallow the Lake. LC 79-120258. (Wesleyan Poetry Program: Vol. 54). (Orig.). 1970. 10.00x (ISBN 0-8195-2054-3, Pub. by Wesleyan U Pr); pap. 4.95 (ISBN 0-8195-1054-8). Columbia U Pr.

Major, David C. & Lenton, Roberto L. Applied Water Resource Systems Planning. (Environmental Sciences Ser.). (Illus.). 1979. text ed. 24.95 (ISBN 0-13-043364-0). P-H.

Major, Francis J., jt. auth. see Silverberg, Steven G.

Major, Henriette, jt. auth. see Bell, Ken.

Major, J. Kenneth & Watts, Martin. Victorian & Edwardian Windmills & Watermills. 1977. 17.95 (ISBN 0-7134-0621-6, Pub. by Batsford England). David & Charles.

Major, J. Russell. Representative Government in Early Modern France. LC 79-14711. (Illus.). 800p. 1980. text ed. 45.00x (ISBN 0-300-02300-6). Yale U Pr.

Major, John M., ed. Sir Thomas Elyot's: The Book Named the Governor. LC 75-108883. 1970. text ed. 9.75 (ISBN 0-8077-1796-7); pap. 4.25x (ISBN 0-8077-1795-9). Tchrs Coll.

Major, Kevin. Hold Fast. LC 79-17544. (YA) (gr. 9-12). 1980. 8.95 (ISBN 0-440-03506-6). Delacorte.

Major, Mabel, ed. see Duval, John C.

Major, R. H. The Bibliography of the First Letter of Christopher Columbus: Describing His Discovery of the New World. 1971. Repr. of 1872 ed. text ed. 13.00x (ISBN 90-6041-083-1). Humanities.

Major, R. H., tr. see Columbus, Christopher.

Major, Ralph H. Classic Descriptions of Disease: With Biographical Sketches of the Authors. 3rd ed. (Illus.). 712p. 1978. 16.50 (ISBN 0-398-01202-4). C C Thomas.

Majors, Gary. Who Would Want to Kill Hallie Panky's Cat? new ed. 160p. 1980. 6.95 (ISBN 0-8038-8094-4). Hastings.

Majumader, Robin & McLaurin, Allen, eds. Virginia Woolf: The Critical Heritage. (The Critical Heritage Ser.). 1975. 38.00x (ISBN 0-7100-8138-3). Routledge & Kegan.

Majumdar, A. K. N-Benzoylphenylhydroxylamine & Its Analogues. 224p. 1972. text ed. 50.00 (ISBN 0-08-016754-3). Pergamon.

Majumdar, D. N. & Madan, T. N. An Introduction to Social Anthropology. x, 304p. 1981. pap. text ed. 8.95x (ISBN 0-210-33687-0). Asia.

Majumdar, N. N. A Textbook of Histology. 450p. 1980. text ed. 35.00 (ISBN 0-7069-1012-5, Vikas India). Advent Bk.

Majumdar, R. C. Historiography in Modern India. 4.50x (ISBN 0-210-22273-5). Asia.

Majumdar, Rupendra G. Apu's Initiation. (Redbird Bk.). 45p. 1976. lib. bdg. 9.00 (ISBN 0-89253-090-1); flexible bdg 4.80 (ISBN 0-89253-130-4). Ind-US Inc.

--Blunderbuss. (Writers Workshop Redbird Ser.). 1975. 8.00 (ISBN 0-88253-510-2); pap. text ed. 4.80 (ISBN 0-88253-509-9). Ind-US Inc.

Majumdar, Sachindra K. Yoga for Physical & Mental Fitness. LC 68-31613. (Illus.). 1968. 7.95 (ISBN 0-87396-013-0); pap. 3.95 (ISBN 0-87396-014-9). Stravon.

Majumdar, Shyamal K., jt. auth. see Riley, Herbert P.

Maka, Henryk. Szczecin-Stettin: Yesterday, Today & Tomorrow. Brice-Wojciechowska, Susan, tr. from Polish. LC 79-320867. (Illus.). 1979. 13.50x (ISBN 0-8002-2288-1). Intl Pubns Serv.

Makaroff, Dmitri, jt. auth. see Duff, Charles.

Makaryk, Irene. Comic Justice in Shakespeare's Comedies, Vols. 1 & 2. (Jacobean Drama Ser.: No. 91). 1980. pap. text ed. 25.00x ea. (ISBN 0-391-02143-5). Humanities.

Makaryk, Irene R. Comic Justice in Shakespeare's Comedies, Vol. 2. (Jacobean Drama Studies: No.91). 259p. 1980. pap. text ed. 25.00 (ISBN 0-391-02197-4). Humanities.

Makdisi, Samir A. Financial Policy & Economic Growth. LC 78-31561. (Modern Middle East Ser.). 1979. 20.00x (ISBN 0-231-04614-6). Columbia U Pr.

Makely, William O. City Life: Writing from Experience. 256p. 1974. 7.95 (ISBN 0-312-14105-X). St Martin.

Makens, James C. Canoe Trails Directory. 1979. pap. 5.95 (ISBN 0-385-12428-7, Dolp). Doubleday.

Makepeace, John, et al. The Art of Making Furniture. LC 80-52623. (Illus.). 192p. 1981. 21.95 (ISBN 0-8069-5426-4); lib. bdg. 18.39 (ISBN 0-8069-5427-2). Sterling.

Maker, June. Curiculum Development for the Gifted. 375p. 1981. text ed. price not set (ISBN 0-89443-347-4). Aspen Systems.

Makgetla, Neva S., jt. auth. see Seidman, Ann.

Makhlis, F. A. Radiation Physics & Chemistry of Polymers. Weiss, M., ed. Thier, tr. from Rus. LC 74-13587. 287p. 1975. 44.95 (ISBN 0-470-56537-3). Halsted Pr.

Makhult, Mihaly. Machine Support Design Based on Vibration Calculus. Meszner, Seebestyen, tr. from Ger. & Hungarian. (Illus.). 136p. 1977. text ed. 32.50x (ISBN 0-569-08228-5, Pub. by Collets England). Scholium Intl.

Maki, A. W., et al, eds. Biotransformation & Fate of Chemicals in the Aquatic Environment. (Illus.). 1980. write for info. (ISBN 0-914826-28-X). Am Soc Microbio.

Maki, Daniel & Thompson, Maynard. Mathematical Models & Applications: With Emphasis on the Social,Life, & Management Sciences. (Illus.). 464p. 1973. ref. ed. 23.95 (ISBN 0-13-561670-0). P-H.

Maki, John M., ed. Japan's Commission on the Constitution: The Final Report. LC 80-50869. (Asian Law Ser.: No. 7). 352p. 1980. 25.00 (ISBN 0-295-95767-0). U of Wash Pr.

Maki, Lillian. Mother, God, & Mental Health. LC 79-92840. 1980. pap. 4.95 (ISBN 0-8323-0353-4). Binford.

Makielski, S. J., Jr. Beleaguered Minorities: Cultural Politics in America. LC 73-12290. (Illus.). 1973. text ed. 18.95x (ISBN 0-7167-0789-6); pap. text ed. 9.95x (ISBN 0-7167-0788-8). W H Freeman.

Makielski, Stanislaw J. Politics of Zoning: New York, 1916-1960. LC 65-25662. (Metropolitan Politics Ser.: No. 4). 1966. 17.50x (ISBN 0-231-02789-3). Columbia U Pr.

Makilmenaeus, Rolandus, tr. see La Ramee, Pierre de.

Makin, Irene. Wildcat. (gr. 4-6). 1969. PLB 6.00 o.p. (ISBN 0-688-51093-0). Lothrop.

Makin, Peter. Provence & Pound. LC 77-76186. 1979. 27.50x (ISBN 0-520-03488-0). U of Cal Pr.

Makinen, Gil. Money: The Price Level & Interest Rates - an Introduction to Monetary Theory. (Illus.). 1977. ref. ed. 20.95 (ISBN 0-13-600486-5). P-H.

Makinodan, T., et al, eds. Aging Phenomena: Relationships Among Different Levels of Organization. (Advances in Experimental Medicine & Biology: Vol. 129). 330p. 1980. 37.50 (ISBN 0-306-40460-5, Plenum Pr). Plenum Pub.

Makkai, Adam. A Dictionary of American Idioms in Chinese. Gates & Boatner, eds. 396p. 1981. pap. 10.95 (ISBN 0-8120-2386-2). Barron.

Makkai, Adam, ed. see Linguistic Association of Canada & the U.S.

Makkai, Valerie B., tr. see Hagege, Claude.

Makki, Valerie, ed. see Linguistic Association of Canada & the U.S.

Maklad, Nabil F. Ultrasonic Diagnosis of Ectopic Pregnancy. 260p. (Orig.). 1981. 27.50 (ISBN 0-87527-222-3). Green. Postponed.

Maklan, David M. The Four-Day Work Week: Blue Collar Adjustment to a Nonconventional Arrangement of Work & Leisure Time. LC 77-14308. (Prager Special Studies). 1977. 23.95 (ISBN 0-03-039916-5). Praeger.

Makrakis, Apostolos. The Bible & the World & Triluminal Science. Orthodox Christian Educational Society, ed. Cummings, Denver, tr. from Hellenic. 531p. 1950. 6.00x (ISBN 0-938366-18-1). Orthodox Chr.

--Catechesis of the Orthodox Church. rev. ed. Orthodox Christian Educational Society, ed. 239p. 1969. pap. text ed. 4.00x (ISBN 0-938366-14-9). Orthodox Chr.

--The City of Zion--the Human Society in Christ, i.e., the Church Built Upon a Rock. Orthodox Christian Educational Society, ed. Cummings, Denver, tr. from Hellenic. 109p. 1958. pap. 3.00x (ISBN 0-938366-16-5). Orthodox Chr.

--Commentary on the Psalms of David. Orthodox Christian Educational Society, ed. Cummings, Denver, tr. from Hellenic. 990p. 1950. 10.00x (ISBN 0-938366-19-X). Orthodox Chr.

--Concerning Our Duties to God. Orthodox Christian Educational Society, ed. 170p. 1958. pap. text ed. 2.00x (ISBN 0-938366-13-0). Orthodox Chr.

--Divine & Sacred Catechism. Orthodox Christian Educational Society, ed. 224p. 1946. 4.00x (ISBN 0-938366-15-7). Orthodox Chr.

--The Foundation of Philosophy--a Refutation of Skepticism, the True Jesus Christ, the Science of God & Man; the God of the Christians. Orthodox Christian Educational Society, ed. Lekatsos, Anthony & Cummings, Denver, trs. from Fr. 103p. 1955. 6.00x (ISBN 0-938366-07-6). Orthodox Chr.

--Freemasonry Known by the Masonic Diploma. Cummings, Denver, tr. 135p. (Orig.). 1956. pap. 3.00x (ISBN 0-938366-42-4). Orthodox Chr.

--Hellenism & the Unfinished Revolution. Orthodox Christian Educational Society, ed. Stephanou, Archimandrite E., tr. from Hellenic. 191p. (Orig.). 1968. pap. 3.00x (ISBN 0-938366-26-2). Orthodox Chr.

--The Holy Orthodox Church. Orthodox Christian Educational Society, ed. Lisney, M. I. & Krick, L., trs. from Hellenic. 298p. (Orig.). 1980. pap. 5.00x (ISBN 0-938366-34-3). Orthodox Chr.

--The Human Nature of Christ: Growth & Perfection. Orthodox Christian Educational Society, ed. Cummings, D., tr. from Hellenic. 52p. (Orig.). 1965. pap. 1.00x (ISBN 0-938366-28-9). Orthodox Chr.

--The Innovations of the Roman Church. 82p. (Orig.). 1966. pap. 1.50x (ISBN 0-938366-39-4). Orthodox Chr.

--Interpretation of the Book of Revelation. Orthodox Christian Educational Society, ed. Alexander, A. G., tr. from Hellenic. 564p. 1972. 8.00x (ISBN 0-938366-12-2). Orthodox Chr.

--Interpretation of the Entire New Testament (Revelation Not Included, 2 vols. Orthodox Christian Educational Society, ed. Alexander, Albert G., tr. from Hellenic. 2052p. (Vol. 1, 1127 pp.;vol. 2, 925 pp.). 1949. Set. 20.00x (ISBN 0-938366-08-4). Orthodox Chr.

--The Interpretation of the Gospel Law. Orthodox Christian Educational Society, ed. Cummings, Denver, tr. from Hellenic. 317p. 1955. 6.00x (ISBN 0-938366-10-6). Orthodox Chr.

--Kyriakodromion (Sunday Sermonary) Orthodox Christian Educational Society, ed. Cummings, D., tr. from Hellenic. 637p. 1951. 8.00x (ISBN 0-938366-20-3). Orthodox Chr.

--Logic: An Orthodox Christian Approach. Orthodox Christian Educational Society, ed. Cummings, Denver, tr. from Hellenic. (The Logos & Holy Spirit in the Unity of Christian Thought Ser.: Vol. 3). 200p. 1977. pap. 3.50x (ISBN 0-938366-04-1). Orthodox Chr.

--Memoir of the Nature of the Church of Christ. Orthodox Christian Educational Society, ed. Cummings, Denver, tr. from Hellenic. 175p. 1947. 3.00x (ISBN 0-938366-21-1). Orthodox Chr.

--A New Philosophy & the Philosophical Sciences, 2 vols. Orthodox Christian Educational Society, ed. Cummings, Denver, tr. from Hellenic. Incl. Vol. 1. Introduction to Philosophy, Psychology, Logic, & Theology. 888p; Vol. 2. Introduction to Ethics. 745p. 1940. Repr. of 1890 ed. Set. 20.00x (ISBN 0-938366-01-7). Orthodox Chr.

--The Orthodox Approach to Philosophy. Orthodox Christian Educational Society, ed. Cummings, Denver, tr. from Hellenic. (The Logos & Holy Spirit in the Unity of Christian Thought Ser.: Vol. 1). 82p. 1977. pap. 2.50x (ISBN 0-938366-06-8). Orthodox Chr.

--Orthodox Christian Meditations (Spiritual Discourses for the Orthodox Christians) Orthodox Christian Educational Society, ed. Cummings, Denver, tr. from Hellenic. 143p. (Orig.). 1965. pap. 2.00x (ISBN 0-938366-22-X). Orthodox Chr.

--The Orthodox Definition of Political Science. Orthodox Christian Educational Society, ed. Cummings, Denver, tr. from Hellenic. 163p. 1968. pap. 2.00x (ISBN 0-938366-31-9). Orthodox Chr.

--An Orthodox Protestant Debate. Cummings, Denver, tr. 1949. pap. 2.00x (ISBN 0-938366-37-8). Orthodox Chr.

--The Paramount Doctrines of Orthodoxy--the Tricompositeness of Man, Apology of A. Makrakis & the Trial of A. Makrakis. Orthodox Christian Educational Society, ed. Cummings, Denver, tr. from Hellenic. 380p. 1954. 10.00x (ISBN 0-938366-17-3). Orthodox Chr.

--Philosophy: An Orthodox Christian Understanding. Orthodox Christian Educational Society, ed. Cummings, Denver, tr. from Hellenic. (The Logos & Holy Spirit in the Unity of Christian Thought Ser.: Vol. 5). 279p. 1977. pap. 3.50x (ISBN 0-938366-02-5). Orthodox Chr.

--The Political Philosophy of the Orthodox Church. Orthodox Christian Educational Society, ed. Cummings, Denver, tr. from Hellenic. Orig. Title: The Orthodox Definition of Political Science. 163p. (Orig.). 1965. pap. 2.00x (ISBN 0-938366-11-4). Orthodox Chr.

--Psychology: An Orthodox Christian Perspective. Orthodox Christian Educational Society, ed. Cummings, Denver, tr. from Hellenic. (The Logos & Holy Spirit in the Unity of Christian Thought Ser.: Vol. 2). 151p. 1977. pap. 3.50x (ISBN 0-938366-05-X). Orthodox Chr.

--A Revelation of Treasure Hid--Concerning Freedom, Concerning the Motherland, Concerning Justice, Apostolical Canons Respecting Baptism. Orthodox Christian Educational Society, ed. Cummings, Denver, tr. from Hellenic. 80p. (Orig.). 1952. pap. 1.00x (ISBN 0-938366-23-8). Orthodox Chr.

--A Scriptural Refutation of the Pope's Primacy. Cummings, Denver, tr. from Hellenic. 171p. (Orig.). 1952. pap. 2.00x (ISBN 0-938366-40-8). Orthodox Chr.

--Theology: An Orthodox Standpoint. Orthodox Christian Educational Society, ed. Cummings, Denver, tr. from Hellenic. (The Logos & Holy Spirit in the Unity of Christian Thought Ser.: Vol. 4). 216p. 1977. pap. 3.50x (ISBN 0-938366-03-3). Orthodox Chr.

--Three Great Friday Sermons & Other Theological Discourses. Orthodox Christian Educational Society, ed. Cummings, Denver, tr. from Hellenic. 107p. (Orig.). 1952. pap. 2.00x (ISBN 0-938366-48-3). Orthodox Chr.

--The Two Contrariant Schools, Concerning the Establishment of a Christian University. Orthodox Christian Educational Society, ed. Cummings, Denver, tr. from Hellenic. 87p. (Orig.). 1949. pap. 2.00x (ISBN 0-938366-27-0). Orthodox Chr.

Makrakis, Apostolos, ed. see Agapius, et al.

Makridakis, Spyros & Wheelwright, Steven C. Forecasting: Methods & Applications. LC 77-18806. (Management & Administration Ser.). 1978. 31.95 (ISBN 0-471-93770-3); tchrs'. manual avail. (ISBN 0-471-03726-5). Wiley.

Makridakis, Spyros, jt. auth. see Wheelwright, Steven C.

Makris, Kallistos. The God-Inspired Orthodox Julian Calendar VS. the False Gregorian Papal Calendar. Vlesmas, Jerry, tr. from Hellenic. 118p. (Orig.). 1971. pap. 2.00x (ISBN 0-938366-36-X). Orthodox Chr.

Maksakovsky, V., ed. The Economic Geography of the World. (Illus.). 1978. 10.00 (ISBN 0-8285-0002-9). Progress Pubs.

Maksoudian, Krikor, ed. see Koriwn.

Maksymowych, R. Analysis of Leaf Development. LC 72-83585. (Developmental & Cell Biology Monographs: No. 1). (Illus.). 112p. 1973. 35.50 (ISBN 0-521-20017-2). Cambridge U Pr.

Maktari, A. M. Water Rights & Irrigation Practices in Lahj: A Study of the Application of Customary & Shri'ah Law in South-West Arabia. LC 76-145606. (Oriental Publications: No. 21). (Illus.). 1972. 44.50 (ISBN 0-521-07930-6). Cambridge U Pr.

Malabre, Alfred L., Jr. America's Dilemma: Jobs Vs. Prices. LC 78-18809. 1978. 9.95 (ISBN 0-396-07586-X). Dodd.

--Understanding the Economy: For Those Who Can't Stand Economics. LC 76-2465. 1976. 8.95 (ISBN 0-396-07309-3). Dodd.

Malagoda, Kirsiri. Buddhism in Sinhalese Society, 1750-1900: A Study of Religious Revival & Change. LC 74-22966. 1976. 28.50x (ISBN 0-520-02873-2). U of Cal Pr.

Malamed, Stanley F. Handbook of Local Anesthesia. LC 80-17546. (Illus.). 249p. 1980. pap. text ed. 17.95 (ISBN 0-8016-3072-X). Mosby.

--Handbook of Medical Emergencies in the Dental Office. LC 77-17870. (Illus.). 1978. pap. text ed. 19.95 (ISBN 0-8016-3077-0). Mosby.

Malament, Barbara C., ed. After the Reformation: Essays in Honor of J. H. Hexter. LC 79-5254. 256p. 1980. 30.00x (ISBN 0-8122-7774-0). U of Pa Pr.

Malamud, Bernard. Dubin's Lives. 432p. 1979. pap. 2.50 (ISBN 0-380-48413-7, 48413). Avon.

--The Fixer. 352p. 1966. 17.50 (ISBN 0-374-15572-0). FS&G.

--The Magic Barrel. 214p. 1958. 14.95 (ISBN 0-374-19576-5); pap. 4.95 (ISBN 0-374-50412-1). FS&G.

--The Magic Barrel. 1980. pap. 2.50 (ISBN 0-380-49973-8, 49973). Avon.

--A Malamud Reader. 528p. 1967. pap. 9.95 (ISBN 0-374-51513-1). FS&G.

--The Natural. 237p. 1961. 10.95 (ISBN 0-374-21960-5); pap. 5.95 (ISBN 0-374-50200-5). FS&G.

--A New Life. 352p. 1980. pap. 2.75 (ISBN 0-380-52530-5, 52530). Avon.

--The Tenants. 160p. 1981. pap. 2.25 (ISBN 0-380-53538-6, 53538). Avon.

Malamud, Daniel I. & Machover, Solomon. Toward Self-Understanding: Group Techniques in Self-Confrontation. (American Lecture Psychology Ser.). 288p. 1975. 15.50 (ISBN 0-398-01204-0). C C Thomas.

Malamud, Nathan & Hirano, Asao. Atlas of Neuropathology. (Illus.). 1975. 57.50x (ISBN 0-520-02221-1). U of Cal Pr.

Malan, David H. Individual Psychotherapy & the Science of Psychodynamics. LC 78-40691. (Postgraduate Psychiatic Ser.). 1979. 18.95 (ISBN 0-407-00088-7). Butterworths.

Maland, David. Culture & Society in Seventeenth Century France. 1970. 40.00 (ISBN 0-7134-1520-7, Pub. by Batsford England). David & Charles.

Malandrino, Carmen P. The Italian Textbook: Ci Divertiamo con la Famiglia Tatasure. LC 76-20046. (Illus.). 1977. text ed. 8.50 o.p. (ISBN 0-682-48608-6, University). Exposition.

Malanga, Gerard. Ten Years After. 160p. 1977. signed o.p. 15.00 (ISBN 0-87685-287-8); pap. 4.00 (ISBN 0-87685-286-X). Black Sparrow.

Malantschuk, Gregor. Kierkegaard's Thought. Hong, Howard V. & Hong, Edna H., trs. from Dan. LC 77-155000. 400p. (Eng.). 1974. 25.00x (ISBN 0-691-07166-7, 317); pap. 4.45 (ISBN 0-691-01982-7). Princeton U Pr.

Malasanos, Lois. Health Assessment. 2nd ed. (Illus.). 753p. 1981. text ed. 26.95 (ISBN 0-8016-3073-8). Mosby.

Malatesta, Li & Cenini, S. Zerovalent Compounds of Metals. 1975. 36.50 (ISBN 0-12-466350-8). Acad Pr.

Malawicki, Douglas J. & Schwenn, Donald C. Model Rockets from Design to Launch. 1976. pap. text ed. 8.00x (ISBN 0-912468-16-5); tchrs'. ed. 10.00 (ISBN 0-912468-15-7). Rockets.

Malbin, Michael J. Religion & Politics: The Intentions of the Athors of the First Amendment. 1978. pap. 3.25 (ISBN 0-8447-3302-4). Am Enterprise.

Malbin, Michael J., ed. Parties. Interest Groups & Campaign Finance Laws. 1980. 15.25 (ISBN 0-8447-2168-9); pap. 8.25 (ISBN 0-686-64314-3). Am Enterprise.

Malca, Edward, jt. auth. see Schwimmer, Martin J.

Malcolm, A. Treatise of Musick, Speculative, Practical & Historical. LC 69-16676. (Music Ser). 1970. Repr. of 1721 ed. lib. bdg. 49.50 (ISBN 0-306-71099-4). Da Capo.

Malcolm, Janet. Diana & Nikon: Essays on the Aesthetic of Photography. (Illus.). 176p. 1980. pap. 8.95 (ISBN 0-87923-387-7). Godine.

Malcolm, John. A Memoir of Central India, Including Malwa, & Adjoining Provinces: With the History, & Copious Illustrations, of the Past & Present Condition of That Country, 2 vols. 3rd ed. 1127p. 1980. Repr. 84.00x (ISBN 0-7165-2129-6, Pub. by Irish Academic Pr). Biblio Dist.

Malcolm, Norman. Dreaming. 1962. text ed. 10.00x (ISBN 0-7100-3836-4); pap. text ed. 6.25x (ISBN 0-7100-8434-X). Humanities.

Malcolmson, Anne, ed. A Taste of Chaucer: Selections from the Canterbury Tales. LC 64-11493. (Illus.). 184p. (gr. 7 up). 1964. 5.95 o.p. (ISBN 0-15-284270-5, HJ). HarBraceJ.

Malcolmson, E., jt. auth. see Ryder, A.

Malcolmson, R. W. Popular Recreations in English Society, 1700-1850. LC 72-91958. (Illus.). 300p. 1973. 29.95 (ISBN 0-521-20147-0). Cambridge U Pr.

Malcolmson, Robert W. Popular Recreations in English Society: Seventeen Hundred to Eighteen Fifty. LC 72-91958. (Illus.). 1980. pap. 10.50 (ISBN 0-521-29595-5). Cambridge U Pr.

Malcolm X. Autobiography of Malcolm X. 1977. pap. 2.75 (ISBN 0-345-29420-3). Ballantine.

Malcom, Aleen. Ride Out the Storm. (Orig.). Date not set. pap. 3.25 (ISBN 0-440-17399-X). Dell.

Malcombe-Lawes, David J. Introduction to Radiochemistry. LC 79-18096. 145p. 1980. 26.95x (ISBN 0-470-26783-6). Halsted Pr.

Malcome-Lawes, D. J. Programming ALGOL. 1969. 13.75 (ISBN 0-08-006385-3); pap. 6.25 (ISBN 0-08-006384-5). Pergamon.

Malcomson, A. P. John Foster: The Politics of the Anglo-Irish Ascendancy. 1978. 55.00x (ISBN 0-19-920087-4). Oxford U Pr.

Maldon, Leo D. How to Build with Stone, Brick, Concrete & Tile. (Illus.). 1977. 9.95 o.p. (ISBN 0-8306-7980-4); pap. 6.95x (ISBN 0-8306-6980-9, 980). TAB Bks.

Maldonado, Luis & Power, David, eds. Symbol & Art in Worship, Concilium 132. (New Concilium 1980). 128p. 1980. pap. 5.95 (ISBN 0-8164-4765-9). Crossroad NY.

Male, D. J. Russian Peasant Organisation Before Collectivisation. LC 70-123662. (Soviet & East European Studies). 1971. 33.50 (ISBN 0-521-07884-9). Cambridge U Pr.

Male, David A. Approaches to Drama. (Unwin Education Books). 1973. text ed. 25.00x (ISBN 0-04-372007-2); pap. text ed. 7.95x (ISBN 0-04-372008-0). Allen Unwin.

Male, Robert A. & Perrone, Philip. The Development Education & Guidance of Talented Learners. 350p. 1981. text ed. price not set (ISBN 0-89443-359-8). Aspen Systems.

Male, Roy R., ed. Money Talks: Language & Lucre in American Fiction. LC 80-5945. 160p. 1981. 14.95 (ISBN 0-8061-1754-0). U of Okla Pr.

Maleady, Antoinette. Record & Tape Reviews Index, 1971. LC 72-3355. 1972. 10.00 (ISBN 0-8108-0522-7). Scarecrow.

--Record & Tape Reviews Index, 1972. LC 72-3355. 1973. 16.50 (ISBN 0-8108-0672-X). Scarecrow.

--Record & Tape Reviews Index, 1973. LC 72-3355. 1974. 24.00 (ISBN 0-8108-0720-3). Scarecrow.

--Record & Tape Reviews Index, 1974. LC 72-3355. 580p. 1975. 22.50 (ISBN 0-8108-0817-X). Scarecrow.

Maleady, Antoinette O. Index to Record & Tape Reviews: A Classical Music Buying Guide for 1979. 1980. 52.50 (ISBN 0-917600-05-3). Chulainn Press.

Malecot, Gustave. The Mathematics of Heredity. Yermanos, D. M., tr. from Fr. LC 69-12603. (Illus.). 1969. text ed. 15.95x (ISBN 0-7167-0678-4). W H Freeman.

Maleh, Issac. Mechanics, Heat, & Sound. (Merrill Physical Science Library). pap. text ed. 3.75x (ISBN 0-675-09638-3). Merrill.

Malek, Emile A. Snail Transmitted Parasitic Diseases, 2 vols. 1980. Vol. 1, 352p. 79.95 (ISBN 0-8493-5269-X); Vol. 2, 336p. 77.95 (ISBN 0-8493-5270-3). CRC Pr.

Malek, James S. & Backscheider, Paula R., eds. The Plays of John Home. LC 78-66641. (Eighteenth-Century English Drama Ser.: Vol. 22). 1980. lib. bdg. 50.00 (ISBN 0-8240-3596-8). Garland Pub.

Malek, Jaromir, jt. auth. see Baines, John.

Maleka, Leo, jt. auth. see Moore, John B.

Maleska, Eugene. A Pleasure in Words. 1981. 15.95 (ISBN 0-671-24881-2). S&S.

--Take My Words. 1981. 14.95 (ISBN 0-671-24881-2). S&S.

Maleska, Eugene T., ed. Simon & Schuster Crossword Book of Quotations. (Series 12). (Orig.). 1980. pap. write for info. (ISBN 0-671-24090-0, Fireside). S&S.

Maleske, Herald. You Really Don't Have To! Natural Therapy Updated. 200p. 1980. 12.95 (ISBN 0-937792-00-4). Nat Therapy.

Malet, Michael. Nestor Makhno in the Russian Civil War. 1980. text ed. 37.50x (ISBN 0-333-25969-6). Humanities.

Maletsky, Evan, jt. auth. see Sobel, Max.

Maletta, Gabe J. & Pirozzolo, Francis J., eds. The Aging Nervous System. LC 79-21167. (Advances in Neurogerontology: Vol. 1). 344p. 1980. 28.95 (ISBN 0-03-052136-X). Praeger.

Maley, Donald. The Industrial Arts Teacher's Handbook: Techniques, Principles & Methods. 1978. text ed. 15.95 o.p. (ISBN 0-205-05952-X). Allyn.

Malfetti, James L., jt. auth. see Stewart, Ernest I.

Malfitano, Gilbert J. The Seven Steps on How to Become a Mystic & Enjoy the Most Exhilirating Pleasure Available to Man on This Earth. (Illus.). 1979. deluxe ed. 37.50 (ISBN 0-930582-37-3). Gloucester Art.

Malgonkar, Manohar. Combat of Shadows. 292p. 1968. pap. 2.50 (ISBN 0-88253-056-9). Ind-US Inc.

Malguire, Desmond, ed. Short Stories of Padriac Pearse. 117p. (Dual language Irish & Eng.). 1968. pap. 4.25 (ISBN 0-85342-117-X). Irish Bk Ctr.

Malherbe, Abraham J. The Cynic Epistles: A Study Edition. LC 77-21619. (Society of Biblical Literature. Sources for Biblical Studies: No. 12). 1977. pap. 9.00 (ISBN 0-89130-151-8, 060312). Scholars Pr Ca.

--Social Aspects of Early Christianity. LC 77-3876. 1977. 7.95x (ISBN 0-8071-0261-X). La State U Pr.

Malherbe, Francois De see De Malherbe, Francois.

Malherbe, H. H. Viral Cytopathology. 128p. 1980. 54.95 (ISBN 0-8493-5567-2). CRC Pr.

Malhotra, V. M. Testing Hardened Concrete: Nondestructive Methods. (Monograph: No. 9). 1976. 19.95 (ISBN 0-685-85144-3, M-9) (ISBN 0-685-85145-1). ACI.

Mali, J. W., ed. Electronic Microsurgery of Skin. (Current Problems in Dermatology: Vol. 9). (Illus.). 1981. soft cover 48.00 (ISBN 3-8055-3080-3). S Karger.

Mali, Jane L., jt. auth. see Herzig, Alison C.

Mali, Millicent S. Madame Campan: Educator of Women, Confidante of Queens. LC 78-65428. 1978. pap. text ed. 9.75 (ISBN 0-8191-0662-3). U Pr of Amer.

Mali, Paul. Improving Total Productivity: MBO Strategies for Business, Government & Not-for-Profit Organizations. LC 77-26191. 1978. 27.95 (ISBN 0-471-03404-5, Pub. by Wiley-Interscience). Wiley.

--Management Handbook Operating Guidelines & Techniques. LC 80-20514. 1440p. 1981. 37.50 (ISBN 0-471-05263-9). Wiley.

--Managing by Objectives: An Operating Guide to Faster & More Profitable Results. LC 72-1803. (Illus.). 314p. 1972. 24.95 (ISBN 0-471-56575-X, Pub. by Wiley-Interscience). Wiley.

Malian, Ida, jt. auth. see Charles, C. M.

Malickson, David L. & Nason, John W. Advertising: How to Write the Kind That Works. LC 76-18310. (Illus.). 320p. 1977. 12.50 (ISBN 0-684-14770-X, ScribT); pap. 7.95 (ISBN 0-684-14771-8, SL679, ScribT). Scribner.

Malik, Hafeez. Sir Sayyid Ahmad Khan & Muslim Modernization in India & Pakistan. LC 80-13905. (Illus.). 288p. 1980. 25.00x (ISBN 0-231-04970-6). Columbia U Pr.

Malik, Hafeez, ed. Iqbal: Poet-Philosopher of Pakistan. LC 75-135475. (Studies in Oriental Culture Ser.: No. 7). 1971. 20.00x (ISBN 0-231-03320-6). Columbia U Pr.

Malik, Henrick J. & Mullen, Kenneth. Applied Statistics for Business & Economics. LC 74-12800. (Illus.). 496p. 1975. text ed. 17.95 (ISBN 0-201-04410-2); instr's manual 4.00 (ISBN 0-201-04472-2). A-W.

--A First Course in Probability & Statistics. LC 72-1941. 1973. text ed. 16.95 (ISBN 0-201-04413-7). A-W.

Malik, Rex, jt. auth. see Fedida, Sam.

Malik, Rex, ed. Future Imperfect: Science Fact & Science Fiction. 219p. 1980. 25.00x (ISBN 0-903804-64-6). Nichols Pub.

Malikin, David, ed. Social Disability: Alcoholism, Drug Addiction, Crime, & Social Disadvantage. LC 72-96468. 256p. 1973. 12.00x (ISBN 0-8147-5361-2). NYU Pr.

Malikin, David & Rusalem, Herbert, eds. Vocational Rehabilitation of the Disabled: An Overview. LC 69-19258. 1969. 15.00x (ISBN 0-8147-0283-X). NYU Pr.

Malin, Irving. Isaac Bashevis Singer. LC 73-185350. (Modern Literature Ser.). 128p. 1972. 10.95 (ISBN 0-8044-2588-4). Ungar.

--New American Gothic. LC 62-15005. (Crosscurrents-Modern Critiques Ser.). 190p. 1962. 11.95 (ISBN 0-8093-0071-0). S Ill U Pr.

Malin, Nigel, et al. Services for the Mentally Handicapped in Britain. 266p. 1980. boards 30.00x (ISBN 0-85664-869-8, Pub. by Croom Helm Ltd England). Biblio Dist.

Malina, Bruce J. The New Testament World: Insights from Cultural Anthropology. (Illus.). 224p. 1981. pap. 8.95 (ISBN 0-8042-0423-3). John Knox.

Malina, F. J. Applied Sciences Research & Utilization of Lunar Resources. 1970. 50.00 (ISBN 0-08-015565-0). Pergamon.

Malina, Frank J., ed. Visual Art, Mathematics & Computers: Selections from the Journal Leonardo. 1979. text ed. 64.00 (ISBN 0-08-021854-7); pap. text ed. 20.00 o.p. (ISBN 0-08-021853-9). Pergamon.

Malinchak, Alan A. Crime & Gerontology. (Ser. in Criminal Justice). (Illus.). 1980. text ed. 15.95 (ISBN 0-13-192815-5); pap. text ed. 13.95 (ISBN 0-13-192807-4). P-H.

Maling, Arthur. From Thunder Bay. LC 80-8397. 1981. 10.95 (ISBN 0-06-014832-2, HarpT). Har-Row.

--Lucky Devil. LC 77-11782. (Harper Novel of Suspense). 1978. 8.95 o.s.i. (ISBN 0-06-012854-2, HarpT). Har-Row.

--The Snowman. LC 72-9172. (Harper Novel of Suspense). 1973. 6.95 o.s.i. (ISBN 0-06-012778-3, HarpT). Har-Row.

Maling, D. H. Coordinate Systems & Map Projections. LC 73-330722. (Illus.). 255p. 1973. 22.50x (ISBN 0-540-00974-1). Intl Pubns Serv.

Maling, T. M., ed. see Hodson, C. J., et al.

Malino, Emily. Super Living Rooms. 1976. 10.00 o.p. (ISBN 0-394-49901-8); pap. 4.95 o.p. (ISBN 0-394-73103-4). Random.

Malinovsky, Nikolai N. & Kozlov, Valery A. Anticoagulant & Thrombolytic Therapy in Surgery. LC 78-21077. (Illus.). 1979. 37.50 (ISBN 0-8016-3079-7). Mosby.

Malinowski, Bronislaw. Crime & Custom in Savage Society. (Quality Paperback: No. 210). 1976. pap. 3.50 (ISBN 0-8226-0210-5). Littlefield.

--The Ethnography of Malinowski: The Trobriand Islands, 1915-18. Young, Michael W., ed. (Illus.). 1979. 24.00x (ISBN 0-7100-0013-8); pap. 12.95 (ISBN 0-7100-0100-2). Routledge & Kegan.

--Magic, Science & Religion & Other Essays. LC 54-4389. 1954. pap. 2.95 o.p. (ISBN 0-385-09246-6, A23, Anch). Doubleday.

--Sex & Repression in Savage Society. 1955. pap. 3.95 o.p. (ISBN 0-452-00405-5, F405, Mer). NAL.

Malinowsky, H. R., et al. Science & Engineering Literature: A Guide to Reference Sources. 2nd ed. LC 76-17794. (Library Science Text Ser.). 1976. 18.50x (ISBN 0-87287-098-7). Libs Unl.

Malinowsky, H. Robert & Richardson, Jeanne M. Science & Engineering Literature: A Guide to Reference Sources. 3rd ed. (Library Science Text Ser.). 380p. 1980. lib. bdg. 22.50 (ISBN 0-87287-230-0); pap. text ed. 14.50 (ISBN 0-87287-245-9). Libs Unl.

Malins, D. C. & Sargent, J. R. Biochemical & Biophysical Perspectives in Marine Biology. Vol. 1 1975. 47.00 (ISBN 0-12-466601-9); Vol. 2 1975. 49.50 (ISBN 0-12-466602-7); Vol. 3 1976. 63.50 (ISBN 0-12-466603-5). Acad Pr.

Malins, Edward. A Preface to Yeats. (Preface Bks). (Illus.). 1977. pap. text ed. 5.95x (ISBN 0-582-35106-5). Longman.

Malinski, Mieczyslaw. Our Daily Bread. 142p. 1979. 7.95 (ISBN 0-8164-0439-9). Crossroad NY.

Malinsky, Martine, jt. auth. see Frederic, Helene.

Malinvaud, Edmond. The Theory of Unemployment Reconsidered. LC 77-1117. 1977. 13.95 o.p. (ISBN 0-470-99075-9). Halsted Pr.

--The Theory of Unemployment Reconsidered. LC 77-1117. 128p. 1980. pap. 13.95x (ISBN 0-470-26883-2). Halsted Pr.

Malinvaud, Edmond & Fitouss, Jean-Paul, eds. Unemployment in Western Countries. LC 79-29710. 560p. 1980. 40.00 (ISBN 0-312-83268-0). St Martin.

Malipiero, Antonio. The Book of What & How: An Illustrated Catalog of the Products & Inventions of the Modern World. LC 78-3965. (Illus.). 1978. 10.00 o.p. (ISBN 0-312-09198-2). St Martin.

Malits, Elena. The Solitary Explorer: Thomas Merton's Transforming Journey. LC 80-7744. 192p. (Orig.). 1980. pap. 6.95 (ISBN 0-06-065411-2, RD 331, HarpR). Har-Row.

Malitz, S., ed. L-DOPA & Behavior. LC 75-181306. (Illus.). 1972. 13.50 (ISBN 0-911216-22-7). Raven.

Malitza, M., jt. auth. see Guiasu, S.

Malka, Sora & Silverstein, Solomon. Everyday Poems for the Jewish Child. (Illus.). 44p. (Orig.). (ps-6). 1980. pap. 2.50 (ISBN 0-89655-050-8). BRuach HaTorah.

Malkemes, Fred & Pires, Deborah S. Looking at English: An ESL Text-Workbook for Beginners, Bk. 1. (English As a Second Language Ser.). (Illus.). 256p. 1981. pap. text ed. 7.95 (ISBN 0-13-540401-0). P-H.

Malkenes, Fred & Pires, Deborah S. Looking at English: An ESL Text-Workbook for Beginners, Bk. 2. (Illus.). 288p. 1981. pap. text ed. 8.95 (ISBN 0-13-540427-4). P-H.

Malkiel, Yakov. Essays on Linguistic Themes. LC 68-15588. 1968. 19.50x (ISBN 0-520-00798-0). U of Cal Pr.

--From Particular to General Linguistics. Selected Essays 1965 to 1978. (Studies in Language Companion: No. 3). 1980. text ed. 68.50x (ISBN 0-391-01268-1). Humanities.

--Patterns of Derivational Affixation in the Cabraniego Dialect of East-Central Asturian. (U. C. Publ. in Linguistics: Vol. 64). 1970. pap. 6.50x (ISBN 0-520-09261-9). U of Cal Pr.

Malkin, A. Y., jt. auth. see Vinogradov, G. V.

Malkin, Carole. The Journeys of David Toback. LC 80-22962. 224p. 1981. 10.95 (ISBN 0-8052-3756-9). Schocken.

Malkin, Michael R. Training the Young Actor. 166p. 1981. Repr. of 1979 ed. 9.95 (ISBN 0-498-01957-8). A S Barnes.

Malko, Nicolai, jt. auth. see Green, Elizabeth.

Malkoff, Karl. Crowell's Handbook of Contemporary American Poetry. LC 73-14787. 338p. 1973. 10.95 o.s.i. (ISBN 0-690-22625-X, TYC-T). T Y Crowell.

--Escape from the Self: A Study in Contemporary Poetry & Poetics. LC 77-22880. 1977. 15.00x (ISBN 0-231-03720-1). Columbia U Pr.

--Muriel Spark. LC 68-54456. (Columbia Essays on Modern Writers Ser.: No. 36). (Orig.). 1968. pap. 2.00 (ISBN 0-231-03063-0, MW36). Columbia U Pr.

--Theodore Rothke: An Introduction to the Poetry. LC 66-23967. 1971. pap. 6.00x (ISBN 0-231-08650-4). Columbia U Pr.

Mall, David & Watts, Walter F., eds. Psychological Aspects of Abortion. 1979. 15.00 (ISBN 0-89093-298-0); pap. 5.00 (ISBN 0-89093-274-3). U Pubns Amer.

Mall, David, jt. ed. see Horan, Dennis J.

Mallakh, Ragaei El. OPEC: Twenty Years & Beyond. 240p. 1981. lib. bdg. 25.00x (ISBN 0-86531-163-3). Westview.

Mallakh, Ragaei El see El Mallakh, Ragaei.

Mallard, Lou. Ocie Dixon's Miracles Through Faith. 1979. 4.50 o.p. (ISBN 0-8062-1211-X). Carlton.

Mallarme, Stephane. Stephane Mallarme. 159p. 1980. Repr. of 1927 ed. lib. bdg. 20.00 (ISBN 0-8492-6835-4). R West.

Mallen, Bruce. Principles of Marketing Channel Management. LC 76-27923. (Illus.). 1977. 23.95 (ISBN 0-669-00985-7). Lexington Bks.

Maller, Dick & Feinman, Jeffrey. Twenty-One Days to a Trained Dog. 1979. pap. 2.95 (ISBN 0-671-25193-7, Fireside). S&S.

Maller, Venktesh N., jt. auth. see Naidu, Motukuru S.

Mallery, David. The Strengths of a Good School Faculty. 1975. pap. 6.50 (ISBN 0-934338-31-0). NAIS.

Mallery, Richard D. Grammar, Rhetoric & Composition. 1967. pap. 3.95 (ISBN 0-06-463228-8, EH 228, EH). Har-Row.

Mallet, Paul H. Northern Antiquities; or, a Description of the Manners, Customs, Religion & Laws of the Ancient Danes, & Other Northern Nations, 2 vols. Feldman, Burton & Richardson, Robert, eds. LC 78-60889. (Myth & Romanticism Ser.: Vol. 16). 1980. Set. lib. bdg. 132.00 (ISBN 0-8240-3565-8); lib. bdg. 66.00 ea. Garland Pub.

Mallet, Serge. Essays on the New Working Class. Howard, Dick & Savage, Dean, eds. Howard, Dick, tr. from Fr. LC 75-34904. 240p. (Orig.). 1975. 12.90 (ISBN 0-914386-13-1); pap. 4.50 (ISBN 0-914386-14-X). Telos Pr.

Mallet Du Pan, Jacques. Considerations on the Nature of the French Revolution & on the Causes Which Prolong Its Duration. LC 74-13491. xxii, 114p. 1975. Repr. of 1793 ed. 13.50 (ISBN 0-86527-032-5). Fertig.

Mallet-Joris, Francoise. The Paper House. Coltman, D., tr. from Fr. 1971. 6.95 o.p. (ISBN 0-374-22978-3). FS&G.

--The Witches. Briffault, Herma, tr. from Fr. 1969. 6.95 o.p. (ISBN 0-374-29157-8). FS&G.

Mallett, Anne. Here Comes Tagalong. LC 78-153790. (Illus.). (gr. k-2). 1971. 5.95 o.s.i. (ISBN 0-8193-0496-4, Four Winds); PLB 5.41 o.s.i. (ISBN 0-8193-0497-2). Schol Bk Serv.

Mallett, Jerry J. Reading Skills Activity Puzzles, 6 bks. Incl. Brain-Twisters (ISBN 0-87628-738-0); Comprehension Challengers (ISBN 0-87628-735-6); Dynamite Decoding Puzzles (ISBN 0-87628-733-X); Puzzles for Super Sleuths (ISBN 0-87628-736-4); Thingumajigs for Thinking (ISBN 0-87628-737-2); Word Power (ISBN 0-87628-734-8). (gr. 2-6). 1980. pap. 6.95x ea. Ctr Appl Res.

Mallett, Richard. Watson's Revenge. (Illus.). 36p. 1974. pap. 4.00 o.p. (ISBN 0-915230-01-1). Rue Morgue.

Mallette, Richard. Spenser, Milton, & Renaissance Pastoral. LC 78-73154. 224p. 1980. 18.50 (ISBN 0-8387-2412-4). Bucknell U Pr.

Malley, I., ed. Educating the User. 1979. pap. 11.50x (ISBN 0-85365-761-0, Pub. by Lib Assn England). Oryx Pr.

Malley, Sarah H., jt. auth. see Lightbody, Nancy K.

Mallick, A. K., jt. auth. see Cherepin, Valentin T.

Mallin, Jay. Ernesto 'Che' Guevara: Modern Revolutionary, Guerilla Theorist. Rahmas, D. Steve, ed. (Outstanding Personalities Ser.: No. 53). 32p. (Orig.). (gr. 7-12). 1973. lib. bdg. 2.75 incl. catalog cards (ISBN 0-87157-556-6); pap. 1.50 vinyl laminated covers (ISBN 0-87157-056-4). SamHar Pr.

--The Great Managua Earthquake. Rahmas, D. Steve, ed. (Events of Our Times Ser.: No. 14). 32p. (Orig.). (gr. 7-12). 1974. lib. bdg. 2.45 incl. catalog cards (ISBN 0-686-07224-3); pap. 1.25 vinyl laminated covers (ISBN 0-686-07225-1). SamHar Pr.

Mallin, Jay & Brown, Robert K. Merc: American Soldiers of Fortune. 1980. pap. 2.50 (ISBN 0-451-09529-4, E9529, Sig). NAL.

Mallinson, G. G. A Summary of Research in Science Education, 1975. (ERIC Bibliography Ser.). 1977. 12.95 (ISBN 0-471-04359-1). Wiley.

Mallinson, Jeremy. Earning Your Living with Animals. LC 74-81067. 176p. 1975. 10.50 (ISBN 0-7153-6760-9). David & Charles.

Mallinson, V. The Western European Idea in Education. (Illus.). 34.00 (ISBN 0-08-025208-7). Pergamon.

Mallis, A. George, jt. auth. see VanAllen, Leroy C.

Mallis, Arnold. American Entomologists. LC 78-132316. (Illus.). 1971. 35.00 (ISBN 0-8135-0686-7). Rutgers U Pr.

Mallis, Jackie. How to Start a Bible Institute. 1978. pap. 2.75 (ISBN 0-89265-051-6). Randall Hse.

Mallo, Jeronimo. Espana: Sintesis De Su Civilizacion. rev. & enl. 2nd ed. Rodriguez-Castellano, Juan, ed. (Illus.). 1970. text ed. 10.95x o.p. (ISBN 0-684-41351-5, ScribC). Scribner.

Malloch, David. Moulds: Their Isolation, Cultivation, & Identification. 88p. 1981. 12.95x (ISBN 0-8020-2418-1). U of Toronto Pr.

Mallock, W. H. The Heart of Life. Wolff, Robert L., ed. LC 75-1538. (Victorian Fiction Ser.). 1975. Repr. of 1895 ed. lib. bdg. 66.00 (ISBN 0-8240-1610-6). Garland Pub.

--A Human Document, 1892. Wolff, Robert L., ed. LC 75-1537. (Victorian Fiction Ser.). 1975. lib. bdg. 66.00 (ISBN 0-8240-1609-2). Garland Pub.

--The Old Order Changes. Wolff, Robert L., ed. LC 75-1533. (Victorian Fiction Ser.). 1975. lib. bdg. 66.00 (ISBN 0-8240-1605-X). Garland Pub.

Mallock, W. H. see Gould, Frederick J.

Mallon, John. Bridge Bidding: Lessons & Quizzes on Goren's Point Count Method. 1963. pap. 2.95 (ISBN 0-02-029200-7, Collier). Macmillan.

--Opening Leads & Signals in Contract Bridge. 1969. pap. 2.95 (ISBN 0-02-029210-4, Collier). Macmillan.

Mallonee, Richard C. The Naked Flagpole: Battle for Bataan. Mallonee, Richard C., ed. LC 80-15538. (Illus.). 1980. 14.95 (ISBN 0-89141-094-5). Presidio Pr.

Mallory, Cynthia, ed. see Holland, Andy.

Mallory, George. Boswell the Biographer. LC 73-18423. 1971. Repr. of 1912 ed. 20.00 (ISBN 0-8103-3675-8). Gale.

Mallory, James D. & Baldwin, Stanley C. The Kink & I: A Psychiatrist's Guide to Untwisted Living. 244p. 1973. pap. 3.50 (ISBN 0-88207-237-4). Victor Bks.

Mallory, Michael. The Sienese Painter Paolo Di Giovanni Fei (c.1345-1411) LC 75-23802. (Outstanding Dissertations in the Fine Arts - 15th Century). (Illus.). 1976. lib. bdg. 41.00 (ISBN 0-8240-1997-0). Garland Pub.

Mallough, Don. You Can Manage Your Life: 16 Keys to Success. 96p. (Orig.). 1981. pap. 3.95 (ISBN 0-8010-6114-8). Baker Bk.

Mallow, Jeffry. Science Anxiety: Fear of Science & How to Overcome It. 256p. 1981. 9.95 (ISBN 0-444-00457-2, Thomond). Elsevier.

Mallows, D. F. & Pickering, W. J. Stress Analysis Problems in SI Units. LC 71-171465. 1972. 25.00 (ISBN 0-08-016293-2); pap. 11.75 o.p. (ISBN 0-08-016292-4). Pergamon.

Malloy, Charles. The Poems of Emerson: Selected Criticism from the Coming Age & the Arena, 1899-1905. LC 80-2539. 1981. 32.50 (ISBN 0-404-19265-3). AMS Pr.

Malloy, John F. Thermal Insulation Handbook. 2nd ed. LC 76-52962. 570p. 1981. lib. bdg. 54.50 (ISBN 0-88275-510-2). Krieger. Postponed.

Malloy, John F., jt. auth. see Turner, William C.
Malloy, Judy. Bad Thad. LC 80-11349. (Illus.). 32p. (ps-k). 1980. PLB 7.95 (ISBN 0-525-26148-6). Dutton.
Malloy, Merrit. Beware of Older Men. LC 79-6886. 168p. 1980. 10.95 (ISBN 0-385-15941-2, Dolp); pap. 4.95 (ISBN 0-385-15942-0). Doubleday.
--Things I Meant to Say to You When We Were Old. LC 76-26353. 144p. 1977. pap. 3.95 (ISBN 0-385-12326-4, Dolp). Doubleday.
Malloy, Ruth L. Travel Guide to the People's Republic of China. LC 80-16428. (Illus.). 416p. 1980. 17.50 (ISBN 0-688-03690-2); pap. 10.95 (ISBN 0-688-08690-X). Morrow.
--Travel Guide to the People's Republic of China. LC 75-8510. (Illus.). 224p. 1975. 7.95 o.p. (ISBN 0-688-02933-7). Morrow.
Malm, Lloyd E., jt. auth. see Frantz, Harper W.
Malm, William P. Music Cultures of the Pacific, the Near East & Asia. 2nd ed. (Illus.). 1977. text ed. 13.95 (ISBN 0-13-608000-6); pap. text ed. 10.95 (ISBN 0-13-607994-6). P-H.
Malm, William P. & Sweeney, Amin. Studies in Malaysian Oral & Musical Traditions: Music in Kelantan - Malaysia & Some of Its Cultural Implications. LC 74-83599. (Michigan Papers on South & Southeast Asia, No. 8). (Illus.). 100p. 1974. pap. 3.50x o.p. (ISBN 0-89148-008-0). Ctr S&SE Asian.
Malmberg, B. Structural Linguistics & Human Communication. LC 63-12931. (Kommunikation und Kybernetik in Einzeldarstellungen: Band 2). (Illus.). 1976. 33.10 o.p. (ISBN 0-387-03888-4). Springer-Verlag.
Malmberg, B., jt. auth. see Brosnahan, L. F.
Malmgren, Harald B. Trade for Development. LC 76-152712. (Monographs: No. 4). 88p. 1971. 1.00 (ISBN 0-686-28691-X). Overseas Dev Council.
Malmstadt, H. V. & Enke, C. G. Computer Logic, a Laboratory Workbook. 1970. pap. 10.95 (ISBN 0-8053-6901-5). Benjamin-Cummings.
Malmstadt, H. V., et al. Electronic Measurements for Scientists, 4 modules. Incl. Module 1. Electronic Analog Measurements & Transducers. pap. text ed. 8.95 with experiments (ISBN 0-8053-6903-1); with lab summaries 7.95 (ISBN 0-8053-6908-2); Module 2. Control of Electrical Quantities in Instrumentation. pap. text ed. 8.95 with experiments (ISBN 0-8053-6904-X); with lab summeries 7.95 (ISBN 0-8053-6909-0); Module 3. Digital & Analog Data Conversions. pap. text ed. 8.95 with experiments (ISBN 0-8053-6905-8); with lab summaries 7.95 (ISBN 0-8053-6910-4); Module 4. Optimization & Electronic Measurements. pap. text ed. 8.95 with experiments (ISBN 0-8053-6906-6); pap. text ed. 5.95 with summaries (ISBN 0-8053-6911-2). 1974. Benjamin-Cummings.
Malmstrom, Jean. Grammar Basics: A Reading-Writing Approach. (English Language Ser.). (gr. 10 up). 1977. pap. text ed. 6.75x (ISBN 0-8104-6025-4). Hayden.
Malmstrom, Jean & Weaver, Constance. Transgrammar: English Structure, Style, & Dialects. 1973. pap. 9.95x (ISBN 0-673-07802-7). Scott F.
Malmstrom, Ruth, jt. auth. see Malmstrom, Vincent.
Malmstrom, Vincent & Malmstrom, Ruth. British Isles. rev. ed. LC 77-83908. (World Cultures Ser). (Illus.). 164p. (gr. 6 up). 1978. text ed. 9.95 ea. 1-4 copies (ISBN 0-88296-173-X); text ed. 7.96 ea. 5 or more copies; tchrs'. guide 8.94 (ISBN 0-88296-369-4). Fideler.
Malmstrom, Vincent H., et al. British Isles & Germany. rev. ed. LC 77-83891. (World Cultures Ser.). (Illus.). 320p. (gr. 6 up). 1978. text ed. 12.43 ea. 1-4 copies (ISBN 0-88296-148-9); text ed. 9.94 ea. 5 or more copies; tchrs'. guide 8.94 (ISBN 0-88296-369-4). Fideler.
Malo, David. Hawaiian Antiquities. (Special Publication Ser: No. 2). 278p. 1971. Repr. 6.00 (ISBN 0-910240-15-9). Bishop Mus.
Malo, John. Fly Fishing for Panfish: A Beginner's Guide. LC 80-26788. (Illus.). 150p. 1981. 8.95 (ISBN 0-87518-208-9). Dillon.
Malo, John W. All-Terrain Adventure Vehicles. LC 70-187074. (Illus.). 192p. 1972. 7.95 o.s.i. (ISBN 0-686-66685-2). Macmillan.
--All-Terrain Adventure Vehicles. LC 70-187074. 1972. pap. 3.95 o.s.i. (ISBN 0-02-029230-9, Collier). Macmillan.
--The Complete Guide to Houseboating. LC 73-2122. (Illus.). 192p. 1974. 8.95 o.s.i. (ISBN 0-02-579300-4). Macmillan.
--Snowmobiling: The Guide. 1971. pap. 3.95 o.s.i. (ISBN 0-02-029250-3, Collier). Macmillan.
--Wilderness Canoeing. LC 71-140902. (Illus.). 1971. 7.95 o.s.i. (ISBN 0-02-579270-9). Macmillan.
Maloff, Deborah R., ed. see Committee on Substance Abuse & Habitual Behavior.
Malo-Juvera, Dolores, et al, eds. Obstetrical Nursing Continuing Education Review. 2nd ed. 1979. pap. 9.50 (ISBN 0-87488-350-4). Med Exam.
Malon, Benoit. La Troisieme Defaite Du Proletariat Francais. (Commune De Paris En 1871 Ser). 539p. (Fr.). 1977. lib. bdg. 28.75x o.p. (ISBN 0-8287-0565-8); pap. text ed. 18.75x o.p. (ISBN 0-685-75629-7). Clearwater Pub.
Malone & Guerry. Studies in Louisiana Tort Law. 1970. with 1975 suppl. 35.00 (ISBN 0-672-82448-5, Bobbs-Merrill Law); 1975 suppl. 12.50 (ISBN 0-672-82024-2). Michie.
Malone & Roeber. Montana's Past: Selected Essays. 1973. 5.95 o.p. (ISBN 0-686-23486-3). U of MT Pubns Hist.
Malone, Bill C. Southern Music American Music. Ronald, Charles P., ed. LC 79-4005. (New Perspectives on the South Ser.). (Illus.). 216p. 1979. 11.50 (ISBN 0-8131-0300-2). U Pr of Ky.
Malone, Carl. The Serpentine Track. LC 79-90666. 1980. 9.95 (ISBN 0-533-04459-6). Vantage.
Malone, D. & Rauch, B. Crisis of the Union, 1841-1877, Vol. 3. 1964. 14.95 (ISBN 0-13-193573-9). P-H.
Malone, Dumas, ed. see Jefferson, Thomas.
Malone, Dumas, et al. Empire for Liberty: The Genesis & Growth of the United States of America, 1865-1960, 2 vols. LC 60-5002. (Illus., Vol. 1 to 1865, vol. 2 since 1865). 1960. Boxed Set. 82.00x (ISBN 0-89197-532-2). Irvington.
Malone, H. E. The Determination of Hydrazine-Hydrazide Groups. 1970. 46.00 (ISBN 0-08-015871-4). Pergamon.
Malone, John. Album of the American Cowboy. LC 79-151886. (Picture Albums Ser). (Illus.). (gr. 4-6). 1971. PLB 5.90 o.p. (ISBN 0-531-01512-2). Watts.
--Straight Women-Gay Men: A Special Relationship. 1980. 8.95 (ISBN 0-8037-8174-1). Dial.
Malone, John, jt. auth. see Crone, Robert.
Malone, Joseph J. Arab Lands of Western Asia. LC 73-5948. (Illus.). 288p. 1973. ref. ed. 13.95x (ISBN 0-13-043968-1); pap. text ed. 9.95 (ISBN 0-13-043950-9). P-H.
Malone, Leo J. Basic Concepts of Chemistry. LC 80-19501. 480p. 1981. text ed. 16.95 (ISBN 0-471-06381-9). Wiley.
Malone, Maggie. Classic American Patchwork Quilt Patterns. LC 77-80195. (Illus.). pap. 6.95 (ISBN 0-8069-8212-8). Sterling.
Malone, Martin, jt. auth. see Levinson, David.
Malone, Michael. Dingley Falls. 1981. pap. price not set (ISBN 0-671-42264-2). PB.
Malone, Midas. How to Do Business-Tax Free. LC 75-45877. 1976. 14.95 o.p. (ISBN 0-913864-10-2). Enterprise Del.
Malone, P. Interferences with Development. 1981. 25.00 (ISBN 0-685-32525-3). Univ Park.
Malone, Thomas F., intro. by. Weather & Climate Modification: Problems & Progress. LC 79-22479. 1980. Repr. of 1973 ed. 28.00 (ISBN 0-8103-1017-1). Gale.
Malone, Thomas P., jt. auth. see Whitaker, Carl A.
Malone, Wex S., et al. Cases & Materials on Workers' Compensation & Employment Rights. 2nd ed. LC 80-11963. (American Casebook Ser.). Orig. Title: Cases & Materials on the Employment Relation. 1043p. 1980. text ed. 21.95 (ISBN 0-8299-2088-9). West Pub.
Malone, William F. Electrosurgery in Dentistry: Theory & Application in Clinical Practice. (American Lectures in Dentistry Ser.). (Illus.). 248p. 1974. pap. 24.75 photocopy ed. (ISBN 0-398-02917-2). C C Thomas.
Malone, William F., jt. auth. see Tylman, Stanley D.
Malone, William F., ed. Tissue Management in Restorative Dentistry. 230p. 1981. 22.50 (ISBN 0-88416-154-4). PSG Pub.
Maloney, Cecelia. The Box Book. (Illus.). (gr. k-2). 1978. PLB 5.38 (ISBN 0-307-68910-7, Golden Pr). Western Pub.
Maloney, Clarence, ed. The Evil Eye. LC 76-16861. (Illus.). 1976. 17.50x (ISBN 0-231-04006-7). Columbia U Pr.
Maloney, E. S., jt. auth. see Chapman, Charles F.
Maloney, Edward T. Luftwaffe Aircraft & Aces. (Illus.). 1969. pap. 5.95 (ISBN 0-911721-74-6, Pub. by WW). Aviation.
--The Messerschmitt Me-262. (Illus.). 56p. 1980. pap. 6.95 (ISBN 0-9600248-5-9, Pub. by WW Two). Aviation.
--Zero Sen: Japanese Fighter. (Illus.). 1978. pap. 3.00 (Pub. by WW II). Aviation.
Maloney, Elliott C. Semitic Interference in Marcan Syntax. LC 80-13016. (Society of Biblical Literature Dissertation Ser.: No. 51). 15.00x (06 01 51); pap. 10.50x (ISBN 0-89130-406-1). Scholars Pr CA.
Maloney, George A. Prayer of the Heart. LC 80-69095. 208p. (Orig.). 1981. pap. 3.95 (ISBN 0-87793-216-6). Ave Maria.
Maloney, George S. A Theology of Uncreated Energies of God. (Pere Marquette Lecture Ser.). 1978. 6.95 (ISBN 0-87462-516-5). Marquette.
Maloney, John. Vintage Cameras & Images, Ident. & Value Guide. (Illus.). pap. 9.95 (ISBN 0-87069-342-5). Wallace-Homestead.
Maloney, John P., jt. auth. see Loeb, Robert H., Jr.
Maloney, Lawrence D., jt. auth. see Diez, Roy L.
Maloney, Michael P. & Ward, Michael P. Mental Retardation & Modern Society. (Illus.). 1979. text ed. 12.95x (ISBN 0-19-502473-7). Oxford U Pr.
--Psychological Assessment: A Conceptual Approach. 450p. 1976. text ed. 16.95x (ISBN 0-19-502027-8). Oxford U Pr.
Maloney, Shirley A. Albi Angel. (gr. k-4). 1977. pap. 5.95 (ISBN 0-570-03466-3, 56-1298). Concordia.
Malony, H. Newton, jt. auth. see Gorsuch, Richard L.
Maloof, Katherine, jt. auth. see Rey, Marilyn B.
Malory, Thomas. Malory: Works. Vinaver, Eugene, ed. 1977. pap. 7.95 (ISBN 0-19-281217-3). Oxford U Pr.
--Le Morte d'Arthur, 2 vols. 1953. 8.00x ea. (Everyman). Vol. 1 (ISBN 0-460-00045-4). Vol. 2 (ISBN 0-460-00046-2). pap. 3.75 ea. (Everyman). Vol. 1 (ISBN 0-460-01045-X). Vol. 2 (ISBN 0-460-01046-8). Dutton.
--Morte D'arthur: King Arthur & the Knights of the Round Table. Baines, Keith, tr. (Orig.). 1962. pap. 2.95 (ISBN 0-451-61878-5, ME1878, Ment). NAL.
Malory, Sir Thomas. Morte Darthur. Field, P. J., ed. LC 77-22498. (London Medieval & Renaissance Ser.). 1978. text ed. 26.50x (ISBN 0-8419-0333-6). Holmes & Meier.
Malott, Richard. Contingency Management in Education & Other Equally Exciting Places. 2nd ed. (Illus.). 260p. 1972. pap. text ed. 10.00 (ISBN 0-914474-08-1); instr's. quiz manual avail. F Fournies.
Malott, Richard, jt. auth. see Whaley, Donald L.
Malott, Richard, et al. Behavior Analysis & Behavior Modification: An Introduction. LC 78-380. (Illus.). 442p. (Orig.). 1978. pap. 11.00 (ISBN 0-914474-20-0); tests avail. F Fournies.
Malott, Richard W. & Whaley, Donald L. Psychology. 1976. text ed. 24.50 scp o.p. (ISBN 0-06-168401-5, HarpC); test file avail. o.p. (ISBN 0-685-77067-2). Har-Row.
Malouf, David. First Things Last. 58p. 1981. text ed. 13.25 (ISBN 0-7022-1564-3); pap. text ed. 7.25 (ISBN 0-7022-1565-1). U of Queensland Pr.
Maloux, M. Dictionnaire des proverbes, sentences et maximes. (Fr). 23.50 (ISBN 2-03-020291-6, 3618). Larousse.
Malozemov, V. N., jt. auth. see Demyanov, V.
Malpas, J. S., jt. auth. see Hector, Winifred.
Malpass, Eric. The Wind Brings up the Rain. 266p. 1981. 10.95 (ISBN 0-312-88215-7). St Martin.
Malpede, Karen & Chaikin, Joseph. Three Works by the Open Theater. LC 74-13837. (Illus.). 1975. 12.50 (ISBN 0-910482-54-3). Drama Bk.
Malpede, Karen, ed. Women in Theatre: Compassion & Hope. 1981. 15.00 (ISBN 0-89676-054-5); pap. 10.00 (ISBN 0-89676-055-3). Drama Bk.
Malphurs, J. G. Bible Key Word Quizzes. (Quiz & Puzzle Bks.). 1971. pap. 1.95 (ISBN 0-8010-5924-0). Baker Bk.
Malraux, Andre. Lazarus. Kilmartin, Terence, tr. LC 76-58426. 1977. 7.95 o.p. (ISBN 0-03-015351-4). HR&W.
Malsch, Brownson. Indianola: The Mother of Western Texas. (Illus.). 300p. 1977. 15.00 (ISBN 0-88319-033-8). Shoal Creek Pub.
Malsky, Stanley J. Hospital Administration for Middle Management: A Practical Approach. 320p. 1981. 27.50 (ISBN 0-87527-170-7). Green.
Malstrom, Vincent H., ed. Geography of Europe: A Regional Analysis. LC 72-144099. (Foundations of World Regional Geography Ser). 1971. pap. text ed. 4.95 o.p. (ISBN 0-13-351460-9). P-H.
Malta, Demetrio Aguilera see Aguilera Malta, Demetrio.
Maltbaek, J. C. Further Engineering Dynamics. 177p. 1980. pap. 21.95x (ISBN 0-470-26943-X). Halsted Pr.
Maltby, A. Sayer's Manual of Classification. (Grafton Books on Library Science). 1977. lib. bdg. 26.50x (ISBN 0-233-96603-X). Westview.
Maltby, Arthur & McKenna, Brian. Irish Official Publications: A Guide to Republic of Ireland Papers, with a Breviate of Reports 1922-1972. (Guides to Official Publications Ser.: Vol. 7). 388p. 1981. 54.00 (ISBN 0-08-023703-7). Pergamon.
Maltby, Arthur & Maltby, Jean. Ireland in the Nineteenth Century: A Breviate of Official Publications. (Guides to Official Publications Ser.: Vol. 4). (Illus.). 1979. 55.00 (ISBN 0-08-023688-X). Pergamon.
Maltby, Jean, jt. auth. see Maltby, Arthur.
Malte, Paul, jt. auth. see Backus, William.
Malte, Paul R. & Saffen, Wayne. In Touch. pap. 1.95 (ISBN 0-933350-02-3). Morse Pr.
Malterner, Virginia M. Growing into Christ: A Workbook for Confirmation. (Illus.). 96p. (Orig.). (gr. 7). 1975. pap. 3.50x o.p. (ISBN 0-8192-4061-3); tchrs. ed. 4.75x o.p. (ISBN 0-8192-4062-1). Morehouse.
Maltin, Leonard. Movie Comedy Teams. 352p. (RL 10). 1974. pap. 1.75 o.p. (ISBN 0-451-06480-1, E6480, Sig). NAL.
--Of Mice & Magic: A History of American Animated Cartoons. LC 79-21923. (Illus.). 488p. 1980. 19.95 (ISBN 0-07-039835-6, P&RB). McGraw.
--Of Mice & Magic: A History of American Animated Cartoons. 1980. pap. 9.95 (ISBN 0-452-25240-7, 25240, Plume). NAL.
--TV Movies (Revised 1979 Edition) (RL 6). 1978. pap. 2.95 o.p. (ISBN 0-451-08293-1, E8293, Sig). NAL.
Maltin, Leonard, ed. Hollywood Kids. (Film Ser.). 1978. pap. 2.25 o.p. (ISBN 0-445-04194-3). Popular Lib.
--Hollywood: The Movie Factory. 288p. 1976. pap. 1.50 o.p. (ISBN 0-445-03132-8). Popular Lib.
Maltitz, Horst Von see Von Maltitz, Horst.
Malton, James. A Picturesque & Descriptive View of the City of Dublin. (Illus.). 1799. Repr. of 1799 ed. text ed. 23.00x (ISBN 0-85105-336-X, Dolmen Pr). Humanities.
Maltz, Albert. The Journey of Simon McKeever. 1979. pap. 2.25 (ISBN 0-380-45526-9, 45526). Avon.
Maltz, B. My Glimpse of Eternity. 2.50 (ISBN 0-8007-8363-8). Revell.
Maltz, Maxwell. Live & Be Free Through Psychocybernetics. rev. ed. 1978. pap. 2.25 (ISBN 0-446-92670-1). Warner Bks.
--Psycho-Cybernetics. pap. 2.95 (ISBN 0-671-43270-2). PB.
Maltz, Maxwell & Barker, Raymond C. The Conquest of Frustration. 1979. pap. 2.50 (ISBN 0-345-27995-6). Ballantine.
Maluccio, Anthony N. Learning from Clients: Interpersonal Helping As Viewed by Clients & Social Workers. LC 78-67753. 1979. 14.95 (ISBN 0-02-919820-8). Free Pr.
Maluccio, Anthony N., ed. Promoting Competence in Clients: A New-Old Approach to Social Work Intervention. LC 80-1056. (Illus.). 1981. 17.95 (ISBN 0-02-919830-5). Free Pr.
Maluccio, Anthony N. & Sinanoglu, Paula A., eds. The Challenge of Partnership: Working with Parents of Children in Foster Care. (Orig.). 1981. pap. text ed. price not set (ISBN 0-87868-181-7). Child Welfare.
Malushitsky, Yu N. Centrifugal Model Testing of Waste-Heap Embankment. Schofield, A. N., ed. LC 78-67431. (Illus.). Date not set. price not set (ISBN 0-521-22423-3). Cambridge U Pr.
Maluzemoff, Irene K., et al. Housing for the Elderly: Evaluation of the Effectiveness of Congregate Projects. 1978. lib. bdg. 30.00 o.p. (ISBN 0-89158-303-3). Westview.
Malvern, Gladys. Six Wives of Henry Eighth. LC 71-134678. (Illus.). (gr. 7 up). 1969. 7.95 (ISBN 0-8149-0665-6). Vanguard.
--World of Lady Jane Grey. LC 64-23320. (Illus.). (gr. 9 up). 1964. 7.95 (ISBN 0-8149-0357-6). Vanguard.
Malvern, Lawrence E. Engineering Mechanics, 2 vols. Incl. Vol. 1. Statics. ref. ed. 19.95x (ISBN 0-13-278663-X); Vol. 2. Dynamics. ref. ed. 19.95x (ISBN 0-13-278671-0). (Illus.). 352p. 1976. P-H.
--Introduction to the Mechanics of a Continuous Medium. 1969. ref. ed. 27.95 (ISBN 0-13-487603-2). P-H.
Malville, Kim. A Feather for Daedalus: Explorations in Science & Myth. LC 79-1955. (Physics Ser.). 152p. 1975. pap. text ed. 6.95 o.p. (ISBN 0-8465-4335-4, 54335). Benjamin-Cummings.
Maly, Eugene H. Romans. Harrington, Wilfrid & Senior, Donald, eds. (New Testament Message Ser.: Vol. 9). 160p. 1980. 9.00 (ISBN 0-89453-132-8); pap. 4.95 (ISBN 0-89453-197-2). M Glazier.
Maly, Kurt & Hanson, Allen R. Fundamentals of the Computing Sciences. (Illus.). 1978. ref. ed. 19.95 (ISBN 0-13-335240-4); supplementary vol. 11.95 (ISBN 0-13-335257-9). P-H.
Malynes, Gerard De. Consuetudo, Vel Lex Mercatoria, or the Ancient Law-Merchant. LC 79-84121. (English Experience Ser.: No. 940). 524p. 1979. Repr. of 1622 ed. lib. bdg. 78.00 (ISBN 90-221-0940-2). Walter J Johnson.
Malyusz, Csaszar, ed. Theater & National Awakening. 350p. 1981. pap. 19.50 (ISBN 0-934214-00-X). Carrollton Pr.

Malyusz, Edith C. The Theatre & National Awakening. Szendrey, Thomas, tr. LC 79-89134. 349p. 1980. write for info. (ISBN 0-914648-10-1). Hungarian Cultural.

Malz, Betty. My Glimpse into Eternity. 1980. pap. 1.95 (ISBN 0-425-04581-1). Berkley Pub.

--Prayers That Are Answered. 1980. 6.95 (ISBN 0-912376-50-3). Chosen Bks Pub.

Malzberg, Barry. Everything Happened to Susan. 1978. pap. 1.50 (ISBN 0-505-51221-1). Tower Bks.

Malzberg, Barry N. & Pronzini, Bill. Prose Bowl. LC 80-2423. 192p. 1981. 9.95 (ISBN 0-385-17027-0). Doubleday.

Malzberg, Barry N., jt. auth. see Pronzini, Bill.

Malzberg, Barry N. & Pronzini, Bill, eds. Dark Sins, Dark Dreams. LC 77-76247. 1978. 7.95 o.p. (ISBN 0-385-12832-0). Doubleday.

Mamak, A. & Ali, A., eds. Race, Class & Rebellion in the South Pacific. LC 78-74189. (Studies in Society: No. 4). 1979. text ed. 18.95x (ISBN 0-86861-009-7); pap. text ed. 8.50x (ISBN 0-86861-017-8). Allen Unwin.

Mamak, Alexander, ed. see Young Nations Conference, Sydney, 1976.

Mamak, Alexander F. Colour, Culture & Conflict: A Study of Pluralism in Fiji. (Illus.). 1979. 29.00 (ISBN 0-08-023354-6); pap. 13.25 (ISBN 0-08-023353-8). Pergamon.

Maman, Andre, et al. France: Ses Grandes Heures Litteraires. (Level 4 or 5). (gr. 9-12). 1968. text ed. 15.95 (ISBN 0-07-039851-8, C); inst. manual 4.95 (ISBN 0-07-039852-6); exercises 5.95 (ISBN 0-07-039853-4); tapes 150.00 (ISBN 0-07-097885-9). McGraw.

Mamatey, Victor, ed. Education in Florida Past & Present. (Florida State U. Studies: No. 15). 1954. pap. 2.50 o.p. (ISBN 0-8130-0463-2). U Presses Fla.

Mamatey, Victor S. Techniques Used to Improve Education. (Florida State U. Studies: No. 21). 1955. pap. 2.00 o.p. (ISBN 0-8130-0467-5). U Presses Fla.

Mamberg, Fern, jt. ed. see Shapiro, William E.

Mambert, W. A. Presenting Technical Ideas: A Guide to Audience Communication. LC 67-28335. (Wiley Series on Human Communication). 1968. 20.95 (ISBN 0-471-56629-2, Pub. by Wiley-Interscience). Wiley.

Mamet, David. Lakeboat. LC 80-8919. 128p. 1981. 8.95 (ISBN 0-394-51952-3, Ever); pap. 3.95 (ISBN 0-394-17925-0). Grove.

--A Life in the Theatre. LC 77-91884. 8.95 (ISBN 0-394-50158-6, GP806). Grove.

--Reunion & Dark Pony: Two Plays. LC 79-2319. 1979. pap. 2.95 (ISBN 0-394-17459-3, E728, Ever). Grove.

Mamm, Peter, ed. Robert Walser: Leben und Werk in Daten und Bildern. (Insel Taschenbuecher: No. 264). (Illus.). 317p. (Orig.). 1980. pap. text ed. 10.40 (ISBN 3-458-31964-6, Pub. by Insel Verlag Germany). Suhrkamp.

Mammen, et al, eds. Treatment of Bleeding Disorders with Blood Compounds. LC 80-80246. (Reviews of Hematology: Vol. I). 384p. 1980. 39.95. PJD Pubns.

Mammen, Edward W., jt. auth. see Gondin, William R.

Mamot, Patricio R. Foreign Medical Graduates in America. 196p. 1974. 12.75 (ISBN 0-398-02751-X). C C Thomas.

Mamula, Richard A. & Newman, Nate. Community Placement of the Mentally Retarded: A Handbook for Community Agencies and Social Work Practitioners. (Illus.). 156p. 1973. 10.75 (ISBN 0-398-02704-8); pap. 6.75 (ISBN 0-398-02761-7). C C Thomas.

Man, Paul De see Flaubert, Gustave.

Manach, Jorge. Frontiers in the Americas: A Global Perspective. Phenix, Philip H., tr. from Span. LC 74-34325. 125p. 1975. 10.25x (ISBN 0-8077-2481-5); pap. 5.75x (ISBN 0-8077-2480-7). Tchrs Coll.

Management Publications, Ltd., ed. Job Evaluation: A Practical Guide for Managers. 1970. 11.95x (ISBN 0-8464-0538-5). Beekman Pubs.

Manaka, Yoshio & Urquhart, Ian A. The Layman's Guide to Acupuncture. LC 72-78590. (Illus.). 144p. 1975. pap. 5.95 (ISBN 0-8348-0107-8). Weatherhill.

Manaker, George H. Maintaining Interior Plantscapes. (Illus.). 336p. 1981. text ed. 17.95 o.p. (ISBN 0-13-545459-X). P-H.

Manar, Al. English-Arabic Dictionary. 1971. 25.00x. Intl Bk Ctr.

Manard, jt. auth. see Kart.

Manard, Barbara, jt. ed. see Kart, Cary S.

Manas, Vincent T. National Plumbing Code Illustrated. LC 62-16324. (Illus.). 1968. pap. 10.75 (ISBN 0-911804-01-3). Manas.

Manashil, Gordon B. Clinical Sialography. (Illus.). 112p. 1978. 19.50 (ISBN 0-398-03770-1). C C Thomas.

Manassah, Jamal T., ed. Alternate Energy Sources. 1981. Pt. A. write for info. (ISBN 0-12-467101-2); Pt. B. write for info. (ISBN 0-12-467102-0). Acad Pr.

Manasse, Fred K. Semiconductor Electronics Design. LC 76-13638. (Illus.). 1977. text ed. 26.95 (ISBN 0-13-806273-0). P-H.

Manassewitsch, Vadim. Frequency Synthesizers: Theory & Design. 2nd ed. LC 80-13345. 544p. 1980. 36.00 (ISBN 0-471-07917-0, Pub. by Wiley Interscience). Wiley.

Manaster, Guy J. Adolescent Development & the Life Tasks. 1977. text ed. 17.50x (ISBN 0-205-05547-8); instructor's manual free (ISBN 0-205-05553-2). Allyn.

Manceron, Claude. The French Revolution: Their Gracious Pleasure, Vol. III. LC 80-36724. (Illus.). 480p. 1981. 19.95 (ISBN 0-394-50155-1). Knopf.

Manchard, Alan, jt. auth. see Lehr, R. E.

Manchel, Frank. An Album of Great Science Fiction Films. (Picture Albums Ser.). (gr. 5 up). 1976. PLB 7.90 (ISBN 0-531-00345-0). Watts.

--The Box-Office Clowns: Bob Hope, Jerry Lewis, Mel Brooks, Woody Allen. (Illus.). (gr. 7 up). 1979. PLB 7.90 s&l (ISBN 0-531-02881-X). Watts.

--Gangsters on the Screen. LC 78-5953. (Illus.). (gr. 6 up). 1978. PLB 7.90 s&l (ISBN 0-531-01471-1). Watts.

--The Talking Clowns: From Laurel & Hardy to the Marx Brothers. LC 75-37902. (Illus.). 144p. (gr. 7 up). 1976. PLB 6.90 o.p. (ISBN 0-531-01153-4). Watts.

--Women on the Hollywood Screen. (Illus.). (gr. 7 up). 1977. PLB 6.90 s&l o.p. (ISBN 0-531-00389-2). Watts.

Manchester, Charles. Papa Rooster & Baby Chick. LC 79-63000. 27p. 1980. 4.95 (ISBN 0-533-04207-0). Vantage.

Manchester, Frederick, jt. tr. see Prabhavananda, Swami.

Manchester, Paul T. Who Might Have Said What. 1981. 4.75 (ISBN 0-8062-1575-5). Carlton.

Manchester, Richard B. The Third Mammoth Book of Word Games. 512p. 1981. pap. 8.95 (ISBN 0-89104-202-4). A & W Pubs.

Manchester, Richard N. & Taylor, Joseph H. Pulsars. LC 77-4206. (Astronomy & Astrophysics Ser.). (Illus.). 1977. text ed. 29.95x (ISBN 0-7167-0358-0). W H Freeman.

Manchester, William. The Death of a President: November 20-25, 1963. 1977. pap. 4.95 o.p. (ISBN 0-14-004801-4). Penguin.

--Good-Bye, Darkness: A Memoir of the Pacific War. 384p. 1980. 14.95 (ISBN 0-316-54501-5). Little.

Manchip-White, John. Everyday Life of the North American Indian. 1979. 22.50 (ISBN 0-7134-0043-9, Pub. by Batsford England). David & Charles.

Mancini, Anthony. Minnie Santangelo & the Evil Eye. 1979. pap. 1.75 o.p. (ISBN 0-449-23967-5, Crest). Fawcett.

--Minnie Santangelo's Mortal Sin. 1976. pap. 1.50 o.p. (ISBN 0-449-23024-4, Crest). Fawcett.

Mancini, Francesco. Gl Amanti Generosi. Brown, Howard M., ed. LC 76-21035. (Italian Opera 1640-1770 Ser.). 1978. lib. bdg. 75.00 (ISBN 0-8240-2617-9). Garland Pub.

Mancini, Janet K. Strategic Styles: Coping in the Inner City. LC 79-56773. (Illus.). 320p. 1980. 15.95 (ISBN 0-87451-179-8). U Pr of New Eng.

Mancini, Janet K. & Robbins, Franklyn A. Encountering Society: Introductory Readings in Sociology. LC 80-8253. 219p. 1980. pap. text ed. 10.50 (ISBN 0-8191-1181-3). U Pr of Amer.

Mancini, R. E. & Martini, L. Male Fertility & Sterility. 1975. 74.00 (ISBN 0-12-467250-7). Acad Pr.

Mancke, Richard. The Failure of U.S. Energy Policy. 1974. 15.00x (ISBN 0-231-03787-2); pap. 6.00x (ISBN 0-231-03853-4). Columbia U Pr.

Mancke, Richard B. Mexican Oil & Natural Gas: Political, Strategic & Economic Implications. LC 78-65353. 1979. 22.95 (ISBN 0-03-048451-0). Praeger.

--Squeaking by: U.S. Energy Policy Since the Embargo. 1976. 15.00x (ISBN 0-231-03989-1). Columbia U Pr.

Mancure, Jane B. Caring. Buerger, Jane, ed. 1980. 4.95 (4928). Standard Pub.

Mancuso, Arlene, jt. ed. see Norman, Elaine.

Mancuso, James C., jt. auth. see Sarbin, Theodore R.

Mancuso, Joseph R. How to Start, Finance & Manage Your Own Small Business. LC 77-14303. (Illus.). 1978. 18.95 (ISBN 0-13-434928-8); pap. 8.95 (ISBN 0-13-434910-5). P-H.

Mancuso, Joseph R., jt. auth. see Baumback, Clifford M.

Mandahl-Barth, G. Woodland Life. (European Ecology Ser.). (Illus.). 1966. 9.95 (ISBN 0-7137-0417-9, Pub by Blandford Pr England). Sterling.

Mandal, Anil K. & Bohman, Sven-Olof, eds. The Renal Papilla and Hypertension. (Illus.). 230p. 1980. 27.50 (ISBN 0-306-40506-7, Plenum Med Bk). Plenum Pub.

Mandal, R. B. Introduction to Rural Settlements. 1979. text ed. 18.50x (ISBN 0-391-01817-5). Humanities.

Mandal, R. B. & Sinha, V. N., eds. Recent Trends & Concepts in Geography, 3 vols. Incl. Vol. 1. 1980 (ISBN 0-391-01820-5); Vol. 2. 1980 (ISBN 0-391-01821-3); Vol. 3. 1980 (ISBN 0-391-01822-1). text ed. 27.75x ea. Humanities.

Mandala Press Staff, ed. Stories with Holes. 1975. pap. 2.50 (ISBN 0-686-60090-8). Irvington.

Mande, C., jt. ed. see Bonnelle, C.

Mandel, Abby. Abby Mandel's Cuisinart Classroom. McElheny, Ruth, ed. (Illus.). 288p. (Orig.). 1980. pap. 12.50 (ISBN 0-936662-03-4). Cuisinart Cooking.

Mandel, Adrienne, ed. see De Marivaux, Pierre.

Mandel, B. J. Statistics for Management: A Simplified Introduction to Statistics. 4th ed. LC 76-39577. 1977. 12.50 (ISBN 0-685-81631-1, 0-910486). Dangary Pub.

Mandel, Barrett J., ed. Three Language-Arts Curriculum Models: Pre-Kindergarten Through College. 1980. pap. 8.50 (ISBN 0-8141-5458-1). NCTE.

Mandel, Elias, jt. auth. see Meilach, Dona Z.

Mandel, Evelyn. The Art of Aging. Frost, Miriam, ed. Orig. Title: The Gray Matter. (Illus.). 176p. (Orig.). 1981. 14.95 (ISBN 0-03-059063-9); pap. 8.95 (ISBN 0-03-059063-9). Winston Pr.

Mandel, Jerome & Rosenberg, Bruce A., eds. Medieval Literature & Folklore Studies. LC 70-127053. 1971. 27.50 (ISBN 0-8135-0676-X). Rutgers U Pr.

Mandel, Loring & Seskin, Jane. Breaking up. (Orig.). 1977. pap. 1.95 o.s.i. (ISBN 0-515-04361-3). Jove Pubns.

Mandel, Morris. Affronts, Insults, & Indignities. LC 74-6568. 180p. 1975. 8.95 o.p. (ISBN 0-685-50514-6, 0-8246-0180). Jonathan David.

Mandel, N., tr. see Shostakovskii, M. F.

Mandel, N., tr. see Vdovenko, V. M. & Dubasov, Yu V.

Mandel, Neville. The Arabs & Zionism Before World War One. LC 73-78545. 1977. 20.00 o.p. (ISBN 0-520-02466-4); pap. 4.95 (ISBN 0-520-03940-8). U of Cal Pr.

Mandel, Oscar, ed. Three Classic Don Juan Plays. LC 73-149071. 1971. pap. 2.45x (ISBN 0-8032-5739-2, BB 537, Bison). U of Nebr Pr.

Mandel, Oscar, ed. see De Marivaux, Pierre.

Mandel, Paul, jt. ed. see DeFeudis, Francis V.

Mandel, Robert. Perception, Decision Making & Conflict. LC 78-65350. 1978. pap. text ed. 8.50 (ISBN 0-8191-0652-6). U Pr of Amer.

Mandel, Ruth B. In the Running: The New Woman Candidate. LC 80-24190. 304p. 1981. 12.95 (ISBN 0-89919-027-8). Ticknor & Fields.

Mandel, Siegfried. Group Forty Seven: The Reflected Intellect. LC 73-8698. (Crosscurrents-Modern Critiques Ser.). 245p. 1973. 8.95 (ISBN 0-8093-0641-7). S Ill U Pr.

Mandel, To, ed. see Talmon, J. L.

Mandel, William J., ed. Cardiac Arrhythmias: Their Mechanisms, Diagnosis, & Management. (Illus.). 592p. 1980. text ed. 55.00 (ISBN 0-397-50473-X). Lippincott.

Mandel, William M. Soviet Women. LC 74-12732. 360p. 1975. pap. 3.50 o.p. (ISBN 0-385-03255-2, Anch). Doubleday.

Mandela, Nelson. No Easy Walk to Freedom. (African Writers Ser.). 1973. pap. text ed. 3.25x (ISBN 0-435-90123-0). Heinemann Ed.

Mandela, Z. Black As I Am. LC 77-87417. (Illus.). 1978. pap. 5.95 (ISBN 0-89615-001-1). Guild of Tutors.

Mandelbaum, Albert J. Fundamentals of Protective Systems: Planning, Evaluation, Selection. (Illus.). 288p. 1973. text ed. 15.75 (ISBN 0-398-02657-2). C C Thomas.

Mandelbaum, Allen, ed. see Yeshurun, Avoth.

Mandelbaum, David G. Human Fertility in India: Social Components & Policy Perspectives. 1974. 14.50x (ISBN 0-520-02551-2). U of Cal Pr.

Mandelbaum, David G., ed. see Sapir, Edward.

Mandelbaum, Maurice. The Anatomy of Historical Knowledge. LC 76-46945. (Illus.). 256p. 1977. 15.00x (ISBN 0-8018-1929-6); pap. 4.95 (ISBN 0-8018-2180-0). Johns Hopkins.

Mandelbaum, Michael. The Nuclear Revolution: International Politics Before & After Hiroshima. LC 80-24194. 256p. Date not set. price not set (ISBN 0-521-23819-6); pap. price not set (ISBN 0-521-28239-X). Cambridge U Pr.

Mandelbrot, Benoit B. Fractals: Form, Chance, & Dimension. LC 76-57947. (Mathematics Ser.). (Illus.). 1977. text ed. 22.95x (ISBN 0-7167-0473-0). W H Freeman.

Mandeles, Stanley. Nucleic Acid Sequence Analysis. LC 79-186389. (Molecular Biology Ser). 352p. 1972. 20.00x (ISBN 0-231-03130-0). Columbia U Pr.

Mandelker. Housing Subsidies in the United States & England. 1973. 13.50 (ISBN 0-672-81871-X, Bobbs-Merrill Law). Michie.

Mandelker, et al. Thirteen Perspectives on Regulatory Simplification. Kolis, Annette, ed. LC 79-65686. (ULI Research Report: No. 29). 144p. 1979. pap. text ed. 11.75 (ISBN 0-87420-329-5). Urban Land.

Mandelker, Daniel R. Environment & Equity: A Regulatory Challenge. (Regulation of American Business & Industry (RABI) Ser.). 240p. 1981. 24.95 (ISBN 0-07-039864-X, P&RB). McGraw.

--Environmental & Land Controls Legislation. 1976. 30.00 (ISBN 0-672-82486-8, Bobbs-Merrill Law); 1980 suppl. 10.00 (ISBN 0-672-84303-X). Michie.

Mandelker, Daniel R. & Montgomery, Roger. Housing in America: Problems & Perspectives. 2nd ed. 600p. pap. 19.50 (ISBN 0-672-83699-8). Bobbs.

Mandelker, Daniel R. & Netsch, Dawn C. State & Local Government in a Federal System, Cases & Materials. (Contemporary Legal Education Ser.). 1977. 25.00 (ISBN 0-672-83047-7, Bobbs-Merrill Law). Michie.

Mandelkorn, Philip, ed. To Know Yourself: The Essential Teachings of Swami Satchidananda. LC 77-80901. 1978. pap. 3.95 (ISBN 0-385-12613-1, Anch). Doubleday.

Mandell, Arnold J., ed. Neurobiological Mechanisms of Adaptation & Behavior. LC 74-14475. (Advances in Biochemical Psychopharmacology Ser.: Vol. 13). 1975. 27.00 (ISBN 0-89004-001-X). Raven.

Mandell, Betty R. Where Are the Children? 128p. 1973. 17.95 (ISBN 0-669-88963-6). Lexington Bks.

Mandell, Betty R., ed. Welfare in America: Controlling the "Dangerous Classes". 192p. 1975. pap. 3.95 o.p. (ISBN 0-13-949305-0, Spec). P-H.

Mandell, Colleen J. & Fiscus, Edward D. Understanding Exceptional Children. (Illus.). 550p. 1981. text ed. 12.76 (ISBN 0-8299-0394-1). West Pub.

Mandell, Dale. Early Feminine Development: Current Psychoanalytic Views. 1981. text ed. write for info. (ISBN 0-89335-135-0). Spectrum Pub.

Mandell, Ernest. The Long Waves of Capitalist Development. LC 80-16244. (Studies in Moderm Capitalism). 112p. 1980. 14.95 (ISBN 0-521-23000-4). Cambridge U Pr.

Mandell, G. L., et al. Principles & Practice of Infectious Diseases, 2 vols. LC 79-17984. 1979. Set. 95.00 (ISBN 0-471-03489-4, Pub. by Wiley Medical). Wiley.

Mandell, Judith J. Buffalo Blinkie & the Crazy Circus Caper. (Illus.). (gr. 3-5). 1977. 5.00 (ISBN 0-89039-196-3); tchr's ed. 4.00 (ISBN 0-686-68523-7). Ann Arbor Pubs.

Mandell, L., jt. auth. see Menger, F. M.

Mandell, Lewis. Consumer Economics. 448p. 1980. pap. text ed. 15.95 (ISBN 0-574-19290-5, 13-2290); instr's guide avail. (ISBN 0-574-19291-3, 13-2291). SRA.

--Economics from the Consumer's Perspective. LC 74-34343. (Illus.). 300p. 1975. text ed. 15.95 (ISBN 0-574-18205-5, 13-2205); instr's guide avail. (ISBN 0-574-18206-3, 13-2206). SRA.

Mandell, Lewis, et al. Surveys of Consumers 1971-72: Contributions to Behavioral Economics. LC 72-619718. 352p. 1973. cloth 11.00 (ISBN 0-87944-140-2); pap. 7.00 (ISBN 0-87944-139-9). U of Mich Soc Res.

Mandell, M. & Rosenberg, L. Marketing. 2nd ed. 1981. 21.00 (ISBN 0-13-556225-2); pap. 7.95 study guide (ISBN 0-13-556233-3). P-H.

Mandell, Marshall & Scanlon, Lynne W. Dr. Mandell's Five-Day Allergy Relief System. LC 78-3309. (Illus.). 1979. 10.95 (ISBN 0-690-01471-6, TYC-T). T Y Crowell.

Mandell, Maurice & Rosenberg, Larry J. Marketing. 2nd ed. (Illus.). 608p. 1981. text ed. 21.00 (ISBN 0-13-556225-2). P-H.

Mandell, Maurice I. Advertising. 2nd ed. 1974. 18.95 o.p. (ISBN 0-13-014472-X). P-H.

--Advertising. 3rd ed. (Illus.). 1980. text ed. 21.95 (ISBN 0-13-014449-5). P-H.

Mandell, Muriel. Games to Learn By: One Hundred One Best Educational Games. rev. ed. LC 58-12540. (Illus.). 128p. (gr. k-6). 1972. 5.95 o.p. (ISBN 0-8069-4520-6); PLB 5.89 o.p. (ISBN 0-8069-4521-4). Sterling.

Mandell, Muriel & Wood, Robert E. Make Your Own Musical Instruments. rev. ed. LC 57-11535. (Illus.). (gr. 3-8). 1959. 6.95 (ISBN 0-8069-5022-6); PLB 7.49 (ISBN 0-8069-5023-4). Sterling.

Mandell, Richard. The Bats. LC 80-83027. 170p. (Orig.). 1981. pap. 4.50 (ISBN 0-9605008-0-4). Hermes Hse.

Mandell, Richard R. Nazi Olympics. (Illus.). 1971. 7.95 o.s.i. (ISBN 0-02-579290-3). Macmillan.

Mandell, Robert B. Contact Lens Practice: Hard & Flexible Lenses. 2nd ed. (Illus.). 840p. 1980. text ed. 33.75 (ISBN 0-398-03059-6). C C Thomas.

Mandell, Robert W. Financing the Capital Requirements of the U. S. Airline Industry in the 1980's. LC 79-7747. 192p. 1979. 21.95 (ISBN 0-669-03215-8). Lexington Bks.

Mandell, Sally. Change of Heart. 1981. pap. 2.95 (ISBN 0-440-11355-5). Dell.

Mandell, Steven L. Computers & Data Processing: Concepts & Applications. (Data Processing & Information Systems Ser.). (Illus.). 1979. text ed. 17.95 (ISBN 0-8299-0198-1); study guide 6.95 (ISBN 0-8299-0254-6); study guide 6.95 (ISBN 0-8299-0254-6). West Pub.

--Computers & Data Processing: Concepts & Applications with BASIC Appendix. (Data Processing & Information System Ser.). (Illus.). 1979. text ed. 18.95 (ISBN 0-8299-0247-3); instrs.' manual avail. (ISBN 0-8299-0633-9). West Pub.

--Principles of Data Processing. 2nd ed. (West Series in Data Processing & Information Systems). (Illus.). 165p. 1981. pap. text ed. write for info. (ISBN 0-8299-0392-5). West Pub.

--Principles of Data Processing. (West Ser. in Mass Communication). (Illus.). 1978. pap. text ed. 7.95 (ISBN 0-8299-0212-0); instrs.' manual avail. (ISBN 0-8299-0554-5). West Pub.

Mandell, Steven L., jt. auth. see Clark, Ann L.

Mandell, Steven L., et al. Introduction to Business: Concepts & Applications. (Illus.). 580p. 1981. pap. text ed. 15.95 (ISBN 0-8299-0393-3). West Pub.

--Introduction to Business Concepts & Applications: Test Bank. 1980. write for info. (ISBN 0-8299-0527-8). West Pub.

Mandell, William, tr. see Kohl, Philip L.

Mandelstam, Dorothy, ed. Incontinence & Its Management. (Illus.). 233p. 1980. bds. 25.00x (ISBN 0-7099-0088-0, Pub. by Croom Helm Ltd England). Biblio Dist.

Mandelstam, J. & McQuillen, K., eds. Biochemistry of Bacterial Growth. 2nd ed. LC 72-12036. 1973. pap. text ed. 24.95 (ISBN 0-470-56655-8). Halsted Pr.

Mandelstam, Nadezhda. Hope Abandoned, Vol. 2. Hayward, Max, tr. from Rus. LC 76-871412. 1973. 13.95 (ISBN 0-689-10549-5); pap. 12.95 (ISBN 0-689-70608-1). Atheneum.

Mandelstam, Osip. Osip Mandelstam: Fifty Poems. Meares, Bernard, tr. LC 76-52274. 1977. 7.95 (ISBN 0-89255-005-8); pap. 4.95 (ISBN 0-89255-006-6). Persea Bks.

Mandelstam, Stanley, jt. auth. see Yourgrau, Wolfgang.

Mander, Anica V. Blood Ties: A Woman's Autobiography. 1976. 10.00 o.p. (ISBN 0-394-40766-0). Random.

Mander, Raymond & Mitchenson, Joe. Victorian & Edwardian Entertainment. 1978. 22.50 (ISBN 0-7134-1257-7, Pub. by Batsford England). David & Charles.

--The Wagner Companion. LC 78-52877. (Illus.). 1978. 12.95 o.p. (ISBN 0-8015-8356-X). Dutton.

Manderson, Lenore. Women, Politics, & Change: The Kaum Ibu UMNO Malaysia, 1945-1972. (East Asian Social Science Monographs). (Illus.). 260p. 1981. 34.50 (ISBN 0-19-580437-6). Oxford U Pr.

Mandevile. Good Samaritan. (Ladybird Ser.). 1979. 1.49 (ISBN 0-87508-837-6). Chr Lit.

Mandeville. Lost Sheep. (Ladybird Ser.). 1979. pap. 1.49 (ISBN 0-87508-849-X). Chr Lit.

--Sower. (Ladybird Ser.). 1979. 1.49 (ISBN 0-87508-865-1). Chr Lit.

--Two New Houses. (Ladybird Ser.). 1977. 1.49 (ISBN 0-87508-871-6). Chr Lit.

Mandeville, Bernard. Free Thoughts on Religion, the Church, & National Happiness. LC 77-17171. Date not set. Repr. of 1720 ed. lib. bdg. price not set (ISBN 0-8201-1300-X). Schol Facsimiles. Postponed.

Mandeville, Sylvia. Amigos De Dios. Gutierrez, Edna L., tr. from Eng. (Serie Apunta Contu Dedo). 1980. pap. 7.95 (ISBN 0-311-38532-X, Edit Mundo). Casa Bautista.

Mandeville, Sylvia & Pierson, Lance. Conoce a Jesus. Gutierrez, Edna L., tr. from Eng. (Pointing Out Bk.). 1980. pap. 7.95 (ISBN 0-311-38531-1, Edit Mundo). Casa Bautista.

Mandiargues, Andre P. de see De Mandiargues, Andre P.

Mandino, Og. The Christ Commission. 272p. 1981. pap. 2.75 (ISBN 0-553-14515-0). Bantam.

--The Greatest Gift in the World. LC 76-43508. 7.95 (ISBN 0-8119-0274-9). Fell.

--The Greatest Miracle in the World. LC 75-12823. 1975. 7.95 (ISBN 0-8119-0255-2). Fell.

--Greatest Salesman in the World. LC 68-10798. (gr. 9 up). 7.95 (ISBN 0-8119-0400-8); pap. 4.95 span. ed.. (ISBN 0-88391-020-9). Fell.

--The Greatest Secret in the World. LC 79-175423. 200p. 1972. 7.95 (ISBN 0-8119-0212-9). Fell.

Mandino, Og, jt. auth. see Dewey, Edward R.

Mandl, F. Statistical Physics. (Manchester Physics Ser). 1971. 14.25 (ISBN 0-471-56658-6, Pub. by Wiley-Interscience). Wiley.

Mandl, Matthew. Fundamentals of Electronic Computers: Digital & Analog. 1967. ref. ed. 17.95 (ISBN 0-13-337915-9). P-H.

--Solid-State Circuit Design User's Manual. (Illus.). 1977. 18.95 o.p. (ISBN 0-87909-784-1). Reston.

Mandlin, Harvey, photos by. Early Childhood Series, 28 vols, Vols. 1-24. large type ed. Incl. Apple Is Red. Curry, Nancy. LC 67-31186 (ISBN 0-8372-0252-3); Beautiful Day for a Picnic. Curry, Nancy. LC 67-31187 (ISBN 0-8372-0255-8); Benny's Four Hats. Jaynes, Ruth M. Curry, Nancy, ed. LC 67-26370 (ISBN 0-8372-0243-4); The Biggest House. Jaynes, Ruth M. Curry, Nancy, ed. LC 67-31188; Box Tied with a Red Ribbon. Jaynes, Ruth M. Curry, Nancy, ed. LC 68-17034 (ISBN 0-8372-0261-2); Colors. Radlauer, Ruth & Radlauer, Ed. Curry, Nancy, ed. LC 68-17026. o.p. (ISBN 0-8372-0259-0); Do You Know What. Jaynes, Ruth M. Curry, Nancy, ed. LC 67-31189 (ISBN 0-8372-0253-1); Do You Suppose Miss Riley Knows. Curry, Nancy. LC 67-31327 (ISBN 0-8372-0263-9); Evening. Radlauer, Ruth & Radlauer, Ed. Curry, Nancy, ed. LC 68-17033 (ISBN 0-8372-0269-8); Father Is Big. Radlauer, Ruth & Radlauer, Ed.; Follow the Leader. Crume, Marion W (ISBN 0-8372-0242-6); Friends, Friends, Friends. Jaynes, Ruth M. Curry, Nancy, ed. LC 67-26371 **(ISBN 0-8372-0245-0); Funny Mr. Clown. Crume, Marion W. Curry, Nancy, ed. LC 67-27124 (ISBN 0-8372-0248-5); Furry Boy. Crume, Marion W. Curry, Nancy, ed. LC 67-31474 (ISBN 0-8372-0264-7); I Like Cats. Crume, Marion W. Curry, Nancy, ed. LC 67-31475 (ISBN 0-8372-0260-4); Let Me See You Try. Crume, Marion W. Curry, Nancy, ed. LC 67-31185 (ISBN 0-8372-0256-6); Listen. Crume, Marion W. LC 68-54580 (ISBN 0-8372-0251-5); The Littlest House. Curry, Nancy. LC 68-17032 (ISBN 0-8372-0258-2); Melinda's Christmas Stocking. Jaynes, Ruth M. Curry, Nancy, ed. LC 68-17031. o.p. (ISBN 0-8372-0265-5); Morning. Crume, Marion W. Curry, Nancy, ed. LC 68-17030; My Friend Is Mrs. Jones. Curry, Nancy. LC 67-26369 (ISBN 0-8372-0244-2); My Tricycle & I. Jaynes, Ruth M (ISBN 0-8372-0266-3); Tell Me, Please, What's That. Jaynes, Ruth M. Curry, Nancy, ed. LC 68-17028 (ISBN 0-8372-0267-1); That's What It Is. Jaynes, Ruth M. Curry, Nancy, ed. LC 67-31543 (ISBN 0-8372-0250-7). (ps-3). 1967-68. 5.97 ea.; 7 inch records avail. 3.39 ea. Bowmar-Noble.**

M&MR Mars, Sweet Treat Cookery. LC 78-61008. (Illus.). 1978. pap. 4.95 (ISBN 0-89586-013-9). H P Bks.

Mandrigues, Debra. Introductory Functional Analysis with Applications. LC 77-2560. 1978. text ed. 30.95 (ISBN 0-471-50731-8); answer bklt. avail. (ISBN 0-471-02872-X). Wiley.

Mandrou, Robert. Introduction to Modern France. 1977. pap. 5.95x (ISBN 0-06-131627-X, TB1627, Torch). Har-Row.

Mandyczewski, Eusebius, ed. see Brahms, Johannes.

Mandyczewski, Euseblus, ed. see Schubert, Franz.

Manela, Roger & Lauffer, Armand. Health Needs of Children. LC 78-26373. (Sage Human Services Guides: Vol. 9). 1979. pap. 6.50x (ISBN 0-8039-1217-X). Sage.

Manela, Roger, jt. auth. see Ferman, Louis A.

Manella, Raymond L., jt. auth. see Amos, William E.

Manella, Raymond L., jt. ed. see Amos, William E.

Maner, Jerome H., jt. auth. see Pond, Wilson G.

Manes, Stephen. Slim Down Camp. 192p. (gr. 4-8). 1981. 7.95 (ISBN 0-395-30170-X, Clarion). HM.

Manet, Edouard, jt. auth. see Delacroix, Eugene.

Manette, Jan. The Working Girl in a Man's World. LC 66-22896. 223p. 1966. 6.00 (ISBN 0-915988-01-1, Pub. by Hawthorne Books). Reading Gems.

Maney, Ardith. Representing the Consumer Interest: Mayors, Political Parties, & Interest Groups in Bureaucratic Politics. LC 78-66417. 1978. pap. text ed. 12.50 (ISBN 0-8191-0427-2). U Pr of Amer.

Manfred, Frederick. Conquering Horse. (Western Fiction Ser.). 1980. lib. bdg. 15.95 (ISBN 0-8398-2590-0). Gregg.

--Riders of Judgment. (Western Fiction Ser.). 1980. lib. bdg. 15.95 (ISBN 0-8398-2593-5). Gregg.

Manfred, Frederick F. The Golden Bowl. LC 75-40838. 240p. 1976. pap. 5.95 (ISBN 0-8263-0407-9). U of NM Pr.

Manfred, Madge, jt. auth. see Strenski, Ellen.

Mang, Anna, jt. auth. see True, Herb.

Mangalam, J. J. Human Migration: A Guide to Migration Literature in English, 1955-1962. LC 67-23777. (Illus.). 200p. 1968. 18.50x (ISBN 0-8131-1170-6). U Pr of Ky.

Mangalo, Bhikkhu. The Practice of Recollection: A Guide to Buddhist Meditation. 32p. 1978. pap. 1.50 o.p. (ISBN 0-87773-704-5, Prajna). Great Eastern.

Mangan, Doreen & Fehr, Terry. How to Be a Super Camp Counselor. (Concise Guides Ser.). (Illus.). (gr. 7 up). 1979. PLB 6.45 s&l (ISBN 0-531-02893-3). Watts.

Mangan, Frances S. Arithmetic for Self-Study. 2nd ed. 1975. text ed. 15.95x (ISBN 0-534-00380-X). Wadsworth Pub.

--Elementary Algebra: A Self-Study Course. 1979. pap. text ed. 16.95 (ISBN 0-8403-1978-9, 40197800). Kendall-Hunt.

--Intermediate Algebra. new ed. (Mathematics Ser). (Illus.). 480p. 1975. pap. text ed. 16.95 (ISBN 0-675-08742-2); instructor's manual 3.95 (ISBN 0-686-67092-2). Merrill.

Mangan, Frank, ed. see Metz, Leon C. & McKinney, Millard G.

Mangan, Frank J. Bordertown Revisited. LC 73-86307. (Illus.). 1973. 6.00 (ISBN 0-930208-03-X, Pub by Guynes Pr). Mangan Bks.

Mangan, Gordon L. Review of Published Research on the Relationship of Some Personality Variables to ESP Scoring Level. (Parapsychological Monographs, No. 1). 1958. pap. 2.00 (ISBN 0-912328-03-7). Parapsych Foun.

Mangan, J. A. Athleticism in the Victorian & Edwardian Public School. (Illus.). 336p. Date not set. price not set (ISBN 0-521-23388-7). Cambridge U Pr.

Mangan, James C. The Autobiography of James Clarence Mangan. Kilroy, James, ed. (New Dolmen Chapbooks: No. 9). 40p. 1968. pap. text ed. 2.50x (ISBN 0-85105-138-3, Dolmen Pr). Humanities.

Mangan, Terry W. Colorado on Glass, Colorado's First Half Century As Seen by the Camera. Collman, Russ, ed. (Illus.). 1975. 47.00 (ISBN 0-913582-13-1). Sundance.

--Colorado on Glass: First 50 Years of Glass-Plate Photography in Colorado. (Illus.). 416p. 47.00 (ISBN 0-913582-13-1). Sundance.

Mangat Rai, E. N. Patterns of Administrative Development in Independent India. (Commonwealth Papers Ser.: No. 19). 182p. 1976. pap. text ed. 22.25x (ISBN 0-485-17619-X, Athlone). Humanities.

Mangel, Charles, jt. auth. see Gifford, Frank.

Mangel, Charles, jt. auth. see Heifetz, Milton D.

Mangeot, Andre. Violin Technique. (Student's Music Library Ser). 1953. 6.95 (ISBN 0-234-77242-5). Dufour.

Manges, Axel, jt. auth. see Danz, Ernst.

Mangham, Ian & Bate, Paul. Exploring Participation. 320p. 1981. 38.50 (ISBN 0-471-27921-8, Pub. by Wiley-Interscience). Wiley.

Mangin, Marie-France, jt. auth. see Lochak, Michele.

Mangione, Jerre. Mussolini's March on Rome: October 30, 1922. LC 74-9816. (World Focus Bks). (Illus.). 72p. (gr. 5-9). 1975. PLB 4.90 o.p. (ISBN 0-531-02782-1). Watts.

Mango, Andrew. Turkey. (Nations & Peoples Library). (Illus.). (YA) 1968. 8.50x o.s.i. (ISBN 0-8027-2119-2). Walker & Co.

--Turkey: A Delicately Poised Ally. LC 75-31332. (Policy Papers Ser.: The Washington Papers, No. 28). 1975. 3.50x (ISBN 0-8039-0578-5). Sage.

Mango, Cyril. Byzantine Architecture. LC 75-4805. (History of World Architecture). (Illus.). 1976. 45.00 (ISBN 0-8109-1004-7). Abrams.

Mango, Cyril A., jt. auth. see Jacobs, David.

Mango, Karin. Armor: Yesterday & Today. LC 80-18103. (Illus.). 128p. (gr. 4 up). 1980. PLB 8.29 (ISBN 0-671-34015-8). Messner.

Mangold, George B. The Labor Argument in the American Protective Tariff Discussion. Bd. with Daniel Raymond: An Early Chapter in the History of Economic Theory in the United States. Neill, C. P. (The Neglected American Economists Ser.). 1974. lib. bdg. 50.00 (ISBN 0-8240-1034-5). Garland Pub.

Mangold, Tom, jt. auth. see Summers, Anthony.

Mangone, Gerard J. Marine Policy for America: The United States at Sea. LC 77-243. 1977. 26.95 (ISBN 0-669-01432-X). Lexington Bks.

Mangrum, Charles T. & Forgan, Harry W. Developing Competencies in Teaching Reading: A Modular Program for Preservice & Inservice Elementary & Middle School Teachers. Heilman, Arthur W., ed. (Elementary Education Ser.). 1979. pap. text ed. 15.95 (ISBN 0-675-08367-2); instructor's manual 3.95 (ISBN 0-685-86834-6). Merrill.

Mangrum, Charles T., jt. auth. see Forgan, Harry W.

Mangrum, Claude T., Jr. The Professional Practitioner in Probation. 288p. 1975. 16.75 (ISBN 0-398-03396-X). C C Thomas.

Manguel, Alberto & Guadalupi, Gianni, eds. The Dictionary of Imaginary Places. (Illus.). 416p. 1980. 24.95 (ISBN 0-02-579310-1). Macmillan.

Mangurian, David. Lito the Shoeshine Boy. LC 74-26826. (Illus.). 64p. (gr. 3 up). 1975. 7.95 (ISBN 0-590-07382-6, Four Winds). Schol Bk Serv.

Mangus, A. R. Changing Aspects of Rural Relief. LC 74-165685. (FDR & the Era of the New Deal Ser.). 1971. Repr. of 1938 ed. lib. bdg. 25.00 (ISBN 0-306-70346-7). Da Capo.

Mangus, A. R., jt. auth. see Asch, Berta.

Manhas, Maghar S. Chemistry of Penicillins & Other Beta-Lactams. Ajay, Bose K., ed. LC 78-27100. 248p. 1981. Repr. of 1971 ed. write for info. (ISBN 0-88275-830-6). Krieger.

Manheim, Frank T., jt. auth. see Fanning, Kent A.

Manheim, Henry L. Sociological Research: Philosophy & Methods. 1977. 16.95x (ISBN 0-685-81641-9). Dorsey.

Manheim, Jarol B. The Politics Within: A Primer in Political Attitudes & Behavior. (Illus.). 176p. 1975. text ed. 6.95 (ISBN 0-13-685362-5); pap. text ed. 8.95 (ISBN 0-13-685354-4). P-H.

Manheim, R., tr. see Auerbach, Erich.

Manheim, R., tr. see Campbell, Joseph.

Manheim, R., tr. see Kerenyi, Carl.

Manheim, Ralph, tr. Grimm's Tales for Young & Old: The Complete Stories. LC 76-56318. 1977. 14.95 (ISBN 0-385-11005-7). Doubleday.

Manheim, Ralph, tr. see Auerbach, Erich.

Manheim, Ralph, tr. see Bachofen, J. J.

Manheim, Ralph, tr. see Campbell, Joseph.

Manheim, Ralph, tr. see Cassirer, Ernst.

Manheim, Ralph, tr. see Grass, Guenter.

Manheim, Ralph, tr. see Grass, Gunter.

Manheim, Ralph, tr. see Jaspers, Karl.

Manheim, Ralph, tr. see Maass, Joachim.

Manheim, Ralph, tr. see Neumann, Erich.

Manheim, Ralph, tr. see Nossack, Hans E.

Manheim, Werner. Martin Buber. (World Authors Ser.: Germany: No. 269). 1974. lib. bdg. 10.95 (ISBN 0-8057-2182-7). Twayne.

Manheimer, Martha L. OCLC: An Introduction to Searching & Input. LC 79-23985. 1980. text ed. 8.50x (ISBN 0-918212-38-3); text ed. 4.95x 5 or more (ISBN 0-686-66212-1). Neal-Schuman.

Manheimer, Ronald J. Kierkegaard As Educator. 1978. 15.75x (ISBN 0-520-03312-4). U of Cal Pr.

Mani, M. S. & Giddings, L. E. Ecology of Highlands. (Monographiae Biologicae: No. 40). (Illus.). 236p. 1980. lib. bdg. 58.00 (ISBN 90-6193-093-6, Pub. by Dr. W. Junk). Kluwer Boston.

Mani, V. S. International Adjudication: Procedural Aspects. 456p. 1980. text ed. 26.75x (ISBN 0-391-01952-X). Humanities.

Maniatis, T., et al, eds. Molecular Cloning Lab Manual. Sambrook, J. (Orig.). 1981. pap. text ed. 24.00 (ISBN 0-87969-136-0). Cold Spring Harbor.

Manibhai, ed. see Aurobindo, Sri.

Manilla, James, jt. auth. see Goodwin, Nancy.

Maniloff, Jack, et al, eds. Effects of Metals on Cells, Subcellular Elements, & Macromolecules. (Illus.). 416p. 1970. text ed. 28.75 (ISBN 0-398-01210-5). C C Thomas.

Manis, Jerome & Meltzer, Bernard. Symbolic Interaction: A Reader in Social Psychology. 3rd ed. 1978. pap. text ed. 12.95 (ISBN 0-205-06062-5, 8160627). Allyn.

Maniscalco, Joe. Jesus. (Bible Hero Stories). (Illus.). 48p. (Orig.). (gr. 3-6). 1975. pap. 2.00 o.p. (ISBN 0-87239-036-5, 2738). Standard Pub.

Manitto, P. Biosynthesis of Natural Products Polyketides Terpenoids Steroids & Phnylpropano Ds. 550p. 1981. 117.95 (ISBN 0-470-27100-0). Halsted Pr.

Mank, Gregory W. It's Alive: The Classic Cinema Saga of Frankenstein. LC 80-26625. (Illus.). 176p. 1981. 15.00 (ISBN 0-498-02473-3). A S Barnes.

Mankiewicz, Frank & Jones, Kirby, eds. With Fidel: A Portrait of Castro & Cuba. (Illus.). 240p. Date not set. pap. 1.95 (ISBN 0-345-28242-6). Ballantine.

Mankin, Don. Toward a Post-Industrial Psychology: Emerging Perspectives on Technology, Work, Education & Leisure. LC 78-5302. 1978. pap. text ed. 12.95x (ISBN 0-471-02086-9). Wiley.

Mankin, Paul & Szogyi, Alex. Anthologie d'humour Francais. 1970. pap. 6.95x (ISBN 0-673-05111-0). Scott F.

Mankoff, Milton, jt. auth. see Chambliss, William J.

Manley & Robinson. Nuevo Auxiliar Biblico. Flores, Jose, tr. 1977. pap. 8.25 (ISBN 0-311-03636-8). Casa Bautista.

Manley, Albert. Complete Fencing. LC 76-56319. 1979. 14.95 o.p. (ISBN 0-385-12075-3). Doubleday.

Manley, Deborah. All About Me. LC 78-21097. (Ready, Set, Look Ser.). (Illus.). (gr. k-3). 1979. PLB 9.65 (ISBN 0-8172-1304-X). Raintree Pubs.

--Animals All. LC 78-21029. (Ready, Set, Look Ser.). (Illus.). (gr. k-3). 1979. PLB 9.65 (ISBN 0-8172-1309-0). Raintree Pubs.

--Animals One to Ten. LC 78-26648. (Ready, Set, Look Ser.). (Illus.). (gr. k-3). 1979. PLB 9.65 (ISBN 0-8172-1302-3). Raintree Pubs.

--Around the House. LC 78-31854. (Ready, Set, Look Ser.). (Illus.). (gr. k-3). 1979. PLB 9.65 (ISBN 0-8172-1307-4). Raintree Pubs.

--Finding Out About Bible Times. 1980. write for info. (ISBN 0-89191-339-4). Cook.

--From A to Z. LC 78-21027. (Ready, Set, Look Ser.). (Illus.). (gr. k-3). 1979. PLB 9.65 (ISBN 0-8172-1303-1). Raintree Pubs.

--Let's Grow Things. LC 78-26879. (Ready, Set, Look Ser.). (Illus.). (gr. k-3). 1979. PLB 9.65 (ISBN 0-8172-1308-2). Raintree Pubs.

--A New House. LC 78-31914. (Ready, Set, Look Ser.). (Illus.). (gr. k-3). 1979. PLB 9.65 (ISBN 0-8172-1306-6). Raintree Pubs.

--The Other Side. LC 78-21018. (Ready, Set, Look Ser.). (Illus.). (gr. k-3). 1979. PLB 9.65 (ISBN 0-8172-1301-5). Raintree Pubs.

--What Color Is It? LC 78-26525. (Ready, Set, Look Ser.). (Illus.). (gr. k-3). 1979. PLB 9.65 (ISBN 0-8172-1300-7). Raintree Pubs.

--Where Are We Going? LC 78-31860. (Ready, Set, Look Ser.). (Illus.). (gr. k-3). 1979. PLB 9.65 (ISBN 0-8172-1305-8). Raintree Pubs.

Manley, Frank. Resultances: Poems by Frank Manley. LC 80-14241. 64p. 1981. text ed. 10.00x (ISBN 0-8262-0312-4). U of Mo Pr.

Manley, Frank, ed. see Chapman, George.

Manley, G. T. Nuevo Auxiliar Biblica. Flores, Jose, tr. from Eng. 572p. (Span.). 1958. pap. 8.50 (ISBN 0-89922-001-0). Edit Caribe.

Manley, Mary D. The Adventures of Rivella. Bd. with The Adventures & Surprizing Deliverances of James Dubourdieu & His Wife Who Were Taken by Pyrates. Evans, Ambrose. LC 73-170534. LC 70-170533. (Foundations of the Novel Ser.: Vol. 22). lib. bdg. 50.00 (ISBN 0-8240-0534-1). Garland Pub.

--The Secret History of Queen Zarah & the Zarazians. LC 79-170514. (Foundations of the Novel Ser.: Vol. 10). lib. bdg. 50.00 (ISBN 0-8240-0522-8). Garland Pub.

--Secret Memoirs & Manners of Several Persons of Quality of Both Sexes from the New Atalantis. LC 74-170520. (Foundations of the Novel Ser.: Vol. 15). lib. bdg. 50.00 (ISBN 0-8240-0527-9). Garland Pub.

Manley, Paula J., jt. auth. see Hanft, Ethel W.

Manley, Seon. Adventures in Making: Romance of Crafts Around the World. LC 59-12397. (Illus.). (gr. 7 up). 1959. 7.95 (ISBN 0-8149-0361-4). Vanguard.

--Dorothy & William Wordsworth: The Heart of a Circle of Friends. LC 70-188693. (gr. 6-12). 1974. 7.95 (ISBN 0-8149-0710-5). Vanguard.

--Nathaniel Hawthorne: Captain of the Imagination. LC 69-10907. (Illus.). (gr. 8-10). 1969. 7.95 (ISBN 0-8149-0358-4). Vanguard.

--Rudyard Kipling: Creative Adventurer. LC 65-10230. (Illus.). (gr. 7 up). 7.95 (ISBN 0-8149-0360-6). Vanguard.

Manley, Seon & Lewis, Gogo, eds. Masters of Shades & Shadows. LC 77-76255. (gr. k up). 1978. PLB 7.95 (ISBN 0-385-12744-8). Doubleday.

--Masters of the Macabre. LC 69-11002. 336p. (gr. 9 up). 1975. 6.95 o.p. (ISBN 0-385-03270-6). Doubleday.

Manley, Seon. Christmas Ghosts. LC 77-26517. (gr. k up). 1978. 8.95a (ISBN 0-385-14032-0); PLB (ISBN 0-385-14033-9). Doubleday.

Manley-Casimir, Michael, jt. ed. see Cochrane, Don.

Manlove, C. N. Modern Fantasy: Five Studies. LC 74-31798. 320p. 1975. 42.00 (ISBN 0-521-20746-0); pap. 9.95x (ISBN 0-521-29386-3). Cambridge U Pr.

Manly, John M. Specimens of the Pre-Shakespearean Drama, 2 Vols. LC 67-18432. 1897. 20.00x (ISBN 0-8196-0200-0). Biblo.

Manly, William L. Death Valley in '49. 1977. 13.95 (ISBN 0-686-60853-4); pap. 9.95x (ISBN 0-912494-23-9). Chalfant Pr.

Mann, jt. auth. see Weiss.

Mann, Abby. Tuesdays & Thursdays. LC 76-2809. 1978. 8.95 o.p. (ISBN 0-385-08764-0). Doubleday.

Mann, C. W., jt. auth. see Mulvaney, J. E.

Mann, Carol. Modigliani. LC 79-28336. (World of Art Ser.). (Illus.). 300p. 1980. 17.95 (ISBN 0-19-520198-1); pap. 9.95 (ISBN 0-19-520199-X). Oxford U Pr.

Mann, Charles K. Tobacco: The Ants & Elephants. LC 74-29660. 176p. 1976. 8.95 o.p. (ISBN 0-913420-49-2). Olympus Pub Co.

Mann, Dale. Policy Decision Making in Education: An Introduction to Calculation & Control. LC 74-13962. 1975. text ed. 11.95x (ISBN 0-8077-2440-8); pap. text ed. 8.50x (ISBN 0-8077-2468-8). Tchrs Coll.

Mann, Dale, ed. Making Change Happen? LC 78-21849. (Orig.). 1978. pap. text ed. 14.95x (ISBN 0-8077-2548-X). Tchrs Coll.

Mann, Dean, ed. Environmental Policy. (Orig.). 1980. pap. 5.00 (ISBN 0-918592-43-7). Policy Studies.

Mann, Dean E. & Doig, Jameson W. The Assistant Secretaries: Problems & Processes of Appointment. 1965. 12.95 (ISBN 0-8157-5452-3). Brookings.

Mann, Dean E., jt. ed. see Ingram, Helen M.

Mann, Denese B. The Woman in Judaism. 1979. pap. 4.50 (ISBN 0-9603348-0-7). Jonathan Pubns.

Mann, Felix. Acupuncture, the Ancient Chinese Art of Healing. (Illus.). 7.25 (ISBN 0-8446-4583-4). Peter Smith.

--Scientific Aspects of Acupuncture. 1978. 21.00x (ISBN 0-433-20309-9). Intl Ideas.

--Treatment of Disease by Acupuncture. 3rd ed. 1974. 24.00x (ISBN 0-433-20308-0). Intl Ideas.

Mann, Fritz A. Studies in International Law. 500p. 1973. 49.50x (ISBN 0-19-825316-8). Oxford U Pr.

Mann, H. K. Radiation Sterilisation of Plastic Medical Devices: Seminar Under the Auspices of the University of Lowell, Mass., March 1979. 128p. 1980. pap. 21.00 (ISBN 0-08-025067-X). Pergamon.

Mann, J. Secondary Metabolism. (Chemistry Ser.). (Illus.). 1978. text ed. 29.00 (ISBN 0-19-855506-7). Oxford U Pr.

Mann, J. Y. & Milligan, I. S., eds. Aircraft Fatigue: Design, Operational & Economic Aspects. LC 71-125094. 570p. 1972. 73.00 (ISBN 0-08-017526-0). Pergamon.

Mann, Jacob. The Bible As Read & Preached in the Old Synagogue, Vol. 2. 1968. 39.50 (ISBN 0-685-22512-7). Ktav.

Mann, James A. Cotton Trade of Great Britain. LC 72-354341. Repr. of 1860 ed. 21.00x (ISBN 0-678-05184-4). Kelley.

Mann, James H. Reducing Made Easy: The Elments of Microfilm. LC 76-25335. 12.00 (ISBN 0-87716-069-4). Moore Pub Co.

Mann, James K., ed. see American Association of Critical Care Nurses.

Mann, Jill. Chaucer & Medieval Estates Satire. LC 72-90490. 384p. 1972. 49.50 (ISBN 0-521-20058-X); pap. 13.95x (ISBN 0-521-09795-9). Cambridge U Pr.

Mann, John, jt. auth. see Richard, Michel P.

Mann, John, ed. Learning to Be: The Education of Human Potential. LC 73-143524. 1972. 8.95 (ISBN 0-02-919970-0); pap. text ed. 7.95 (ISBN 0-02-919910-7). Free Pr.

Mann, John A. Secrets of Life Extension. (Illus.). 256p. (Orig.). 1980. 12.95 (ISBN 0-936602-06-6). Harbor Pub CA.

--Secrets of Life Extension. LC 80-15479. 180p. 1980. pap. 7.95 (ISBN 0-915904-47-0). And-Or Pr.

Mann, Klaus. Mephisto. 1979. pap. 2.25 o.p. (ISBN 0-345-25393-0). Ballantine.

Mann, Lawrence. Maintenance Management. 1976. 24.95 (ISBN 0-669-00143-0). Lexington Bks.

Mann, Lawrence, Jr. Applied Engineering Statistics for Practicing Engineers. LC 76-129578. 1970. pap. 8.95 (ISBN 0-8436-0317-8). CBI Pub.

Mann, Leon, jt. auth. see Janis, Irving L.

Mann, Leonard W. God's East Wind: Sermons for the Easter Season, Ser. A. 64p. (Orig.). 1980. pap. text ed. 3.95 (ISBN 0-89536-449-2). CSS Pub.

Mann, Lester & Sabatino, David, eds. The Fourth Review of Special Education. 1980. 44.50 (ISBN 0-8089-1263-1). Grune.

Mann, Lester, et al. Teaching the Learning-Disabled Adolescent. LC 77-74377. (Illus.). 1977. pap. text ed. 16.75 (ISBN 0-395-25434-5). HM.

Mann, Martha. Nathan Hale, Patriot. LC 44-8683. (Illus.). (gr. 6-9). 1944. 5.00 (ISBN 0-396-02565-X). Dodd.

Mann, Marty. Marty Mann Answers Your Questions About Drinking & Alcoholism. 128p. 1981. 8.95 (ISBN 0-03-081857-5); pap. 3.95 (ISBN 0-686-69289-6). HR&W.

--Marty Mann's New Primer on Alcoholism. 256p. 1981. 10.95 (ISBN 0-03-029595-5); pap. 5.95 (ISBN 0-686-69290-X). HR&W.

Mann, Maybelle. Francis William Edmonds. LC 75-24834. (Illus.). 128p. 1975. pap. 6.00 (ISBN 0-88397-050-3). Intl Exhibit Foun.

--Francis William Edmonds: Mammon & Art. LC 76-23638. (Outstanding Dissertations in the Fine Arts - American). (Illus.). 1977. Repr. of 1972 ed. lib. bdg. 41.00 (ISBN 0-8240-2708-6). Garland Pub.

Mann, Michael. Consciousness & Action Among the Western Working Class. (Studies in Sociology). 80p. (Orig.). 1975. pap. 6.75x (ISBN 0-333-13773-6). Humanities.

Mann, Nancy R., et al. Methods for the Statistical Analysis of Reliability & Life Data. LC 73-20461. (Ser. in Probability & Mathematical Statistics). 576p. 1974. 35.50 (ISBN 0-471-56737-X, Pub. by Wiley-Interscience). Wiley.

Mann, Patrick. Steal Big. 208p. 1981. 9.95 (ISBN 0-312-76139-2). St Martin.

Mann, Peggy. Golda: The Life of Israel's Prime Minister. 1973. pap. 1.25 o.s.i. (ISBN 0-671-48132-0). WSP.

--My Dad Lives in a Downtown Hotel. 1974. pap. 1.25 (ISBN 0-380-00096-2, 50146, Camelot). Avon.

--Street of the Flower Boxes. (gr. 3-5). 1971. pap. 0.60 o.s.i. (ISBN 0-671-29322-2). Archway.

--The Telltale Line: The Secrets of Handwriting Analysis. LC 76-8436. (Illus.). 96p. (gr. 5 up). 1976. 8.95 (ISBN 0-02-762240-1, 76224). Macmillan.

--There Are Two Kinds of Terrible. LC 76-42372. (gr. 3-7). 1977. 6.95a (ISBN 0-385-09588-0); PLB (ISBN 0-385-08185-5). Doubleday.

Mann, Peggy & Siegal, Vivian. The Man Who Bought Himself: The Story of Peter Still. LC 75-15514. 224p. (gr. 5 up). 1975. 8.95 (ISBN 0-02-762220-7, 76222). Macmillan.

Mann, Peggy, jt. auth. see Hrsch, Giselle.

Mann, Peter H. Approach to Urban Sociology. (International Library of Sociology & Social Reconstruction). 1965. text ed. 8.00x (ISBN 0-7100-3453-9). Humanities.

--Students & Books. 1974. 16.95x (ISBN 0-7100-7850-1). Routledge & Kegan.

Mann, Philip. Bomba de Incendios. Kreps, Georgian, tr. from Eng. (Shape Board Play Book). Orig. Title: Fire Engines. (Illus., Span.). (ps-3). 1981. bds. 3.50 plastic comb bdg (ISBN 0-89828-202-0, 5006SP). Tuffy Bks.

--Contando Para Divirtirme. Kreps, Georgian, tr. from Eng. (Shape Board Play Books). Orig. Title: Counting for Fun. (Illus.). 14p. (Span.). (ps-3). 1981. bds. 3.50 plastic com bdg (ISBN 0-89828-203-9, 5003SP). Tuffy Bks.

--El Gran Passo en Tren. Kreps, Georgian, tr. from Span. (Shape Board Play Book). Orig. Title: The Great Train Ride. (Illus.). 14p. (Eng.). (ps-3). 1981. bds. 3.50 plastic comb bdg. (ISBN 0-89828-201-2, 5005SP). Tuffy Bks.

Mann, Philip, ed. Camiones. Kreps, Georgian, tr. from Eng. (Shape Board Play Book). Orig. Title: Trucks. (Illus.). 14p. (Span.). (ps-3). 1981. bds. 3.50 plastic comb bdg (ISBN 0-89828-200-4, 5004SP). Tuffy Bks.

Mann, Philip, ed. see Imbo, M.

Mann, Philip, ed. see Pearson, Bill.

Mann, Philip A. Community Psychology. LC 77-83164. 1978. text ed. 17.95 (ISBN 0-02-920000-8). Free Pr.

--Psychological Consultation with a Police Department: A Demonstration of Cooperative Training in Mental Health. 184p. 1973. text ed. 13.75 (ISBN 0-398-02695-5). C C Thomas.

Mann, Philip H. & Suiter, Patricia. Handbook in Diagnostic Teaching: A Learning Disabilities Approach. abr. 2nd ed. 200p. 1974. pap. text ed. 12.50 o.p. (ISBN 0-205-04416-6). Allyn.

Mann, Philip H. & Suiter, Patricia A. Teacher's Handbook of Diagnostic Inventories: Spelling, Reading, Handwriting, Arithmetic-a Practical Guide. 136p. 1975. text ed. 21.95x o.s.i. (ISBN 0-205-04758-0); duplicating masters incl. o.s.i. (ISBN 0-685-52904-5). Allyn.

--Teacher's Handbook of Diagnostic Screening: Auditory, Visual, Motor, Language-a Practical Guide. 117p. 1975. text ed. 21.95x o.p. (ISBN 0-205-04759-9); duplicating masters incl. o.p. (ISBN 0-685-52905-3). Allyn.

Mann, Philip H., et al. Handbook in Diagnostic-Prescriptive Teaching. 2nd ed. 1979. pap. text ed. 28.50 (ISBN 0-205-06611-9). Allyn.

--Teachers Handbook of Diagnostic Inventories: Spelling, Reading, Handwriting, Arithmetic -- a Practical Guide with Duplicator Masters. 2nd ed. 1979. pap. text ed. 29.95 (ISBN 0-205-06625-9). Allyn.

--Teacher's Handbook of Diagnostic Screening: Auditory, Visual, Motor, Language, Social-Emotional Developmental Skills -- a Practical Guide with Duplicator Masters. 2nd ed. 1979. pap. text ed. 29.95 (ISBN 0-205-06626-7). Allyn.

Mann, Richard. Elvis. 1977. pap. cancelled o.s.i. (ISBN 0-89728-027-X, 688974). Omega Pubns OR.

Mann, Richard A. Fortran Four Primer. LC 77-188187. 1972. pap. text ed. 11.50 scp (ISBN 0-7002-2412-2, HarpC); solutions manual avail. (ISBN 0-685-23390-1). Har-Row.

Mann, Robert, tr. see Rognoni, Luigi.

Mann, Robert W., jt. auth. see Taylor, Angus E.

Mann, Roderick. Foreign Body. 1975. 6.95 o.s.i. (ISBN 0-02-579420-5). Macmillan.

Mann, Roger A. DuVries' Surgery of the Foot. 4th ed. LC 78-10829. (Illus.). 1978. text ed. 44.50 (ISBN 0-8016-2333-2). Mosby.

Mann, Stanley C. One Against the Storm. (Illus.). 221p. (Orig.). pap. write for info. (ISBN 0-938662-00-7). Quest Utah.

Mann, Stella T. How to Use the Power of Your Word. 173p. 1975. pap. 2.95 o.p. (ISBN 0-87516-207-X). De Vorss.

Mann, T. K. Administration of Justice in India. 1979. text ed. 13.50x (ISBN 0-391-01854-X). Humanities.

Mann, Thomas. Der Tod in Venedig. Boyd, George & Rosenwald, Henry, eds. (Illus.). 175p. (Ger.). 1973. pap. text ed. 4.95x (ISBN 0-19-501688-2). Oxford U Pr.

--Tonio Kroger. 2nd ed. Wilkinson, Elizabeth M., ed. (Blackwell's German Texts Ser.). 1968. pap. 9.95x (ISBN 0-631-01810-7, Pub. by Basil Blackwell). Biblio Dist.

--Two Stories. Witte, W., ed. Incl. Unordnung und Fruhes Leid; Mario und der Zauberer. (Blackwell's German Text Ser.). 1971. pap. 4.50x o.p. (ISBN 0-631-01870-0, Pub. by Basil Blackwell). Biblio Dist.

Mann, Thomas, Jr., jt. ed. see Spyers-Duran, Peter.

Mann, W. B. & Ayres, R. L., eds. Radioactivity & Its Measurement. 2nd ed. (Illus.). 1980. 41.00 (ISBN 0-08-025028-9); pap. 14.50 (ISBN 0-08-025027-0). Pergamon.

Mann, W. B., jt. ed. see Hutchinson, J. M.

Mann, W. Edward & Hoffman, Edward. The Man Who Dreamed of Tomorrow: A Conceptual Biography of Wilhelm Reich. LC 80-50405. 304p. 1980. 12.95 (ISBN 0-87477-143-9). J P Tarcher.

Mann, Wesley P., intro. by. How to Collect Stamps. rev. ed. (Illus.). 187p. (gr. 4 up). 1980. pap. 2.50 (ISBN 0-937458-00-7). Harris & Co.

Mann, William, ed. see Mannn, William.

Mann, William E. The Language of Logic. LC 79-66151. 1979. pap. text ed. 9.50 (ISBN 0-8191-0795-6). U Pr of Amer.

Mannari, Hiroshi, jt. auth. see Marsh, Robert M.

Manne, Henry G., et al. Wall Street in Transition: The Emerging System & Its Impact on the Economy. LC 74-15255. (Moskowitz Lectures). 206p. 1974. 10.00x (ISBN 0-8147-5369-8). NYU Pr.

Mannello, George. Americans All, 2 vols. (Orig.). (gr. 11-12). 1973. Vol. 1. pap. text ed. 6.25 (ISBN 0-87720-611-2); Vol. 2. pap. text ed. 6.25 (ISBN 0-87720-613-9); self-study wkbk, 1974 4.92 (ISBN 0-87720-614-7). AMSCO Sch.

--Our Long Island. 2nd ed. 1981. lib. bdg. write for info. (ISBN 0-88275-968-X). Krieger.

Mannerberg, Donald & Roth, Jane. Aerobic Nutrition: The Long-Life Plan for Ageless Health & Vigor. 1981. 14.95 (ISBN 0-8015-0070-2). Dutton.

Manners, Alexandra. The Singing Swans. 1977. pap. 1.50 o.p. (ISBN 0-425-03290-6). Berkley Pub.

Manners, David. The Soundless Voice: A Discovery in Stillness. Date not set. pap. price not set (ISBN 0-916108-10-4). Seed Center. Postponed.

Manners, David X. Complete Book of Home Workshops. (Illus.). 1970. 12.95 o.p. (ISBN 0-06-012767-8, HarpT). Har-Row.

--How to Plan & Build Your Workshop. LC 77-76854. (Illus.). 1977. 4.95 (ISBN 0-668-04131-5); pap. 2.50 o. p. (ISBN 0-668-04142-0). Arco.

Manners, G., jt. ed. see Chisholm, M.

Manners, Gerald. Geography of Energy. 1966. pap. text ed. 3.25x (ISBN 0-09-110381-9, Hutchinson U Lib). Humanities.

Manners, Gerald, et al. Regional Development in Britain. 2nd ed. LC 79-42901. 1980. 49.50 (ISBN 0-471-27636-7, Pub. by Wiley-Interscience). Wiley.

Manners, Ian. Coastal Energy Impact Program in Texas. (Research Monograph: 1980-1). 1980. pap. 5.00 (ISBN 0-87755-241-X). U of Tex Busn Res.

Manners, John. Country Crafts Today. LC 74-4355. (Illus.). 208p. 1974. 26.00 (ISBN 0-8103-2013-4). Gale.

--Crafts of the Highlands & Islands. LC 77-91724. 1978. 11.95 (ISBN 0-7153-7485-0). David & Charles.

Manners, Robert, jt. auth. see Kaplan, David.

Manners, Robert A. Hualapai Indians, Vol. 2: An Ethnological Report on the Hualapai (Walapai) Indians of Arizona. (American Indian Ethnohistory Ser: Indians of the Southwest). (Illus.). lib. bdg. 42.00 (ISBN 0-8240-0723-9). Garland Pub.

--Paiute Indians, Vol. One: Southern Paiute & Chemehuevi: an Ethnohistorical Report. (American Indian Ethnohistory Ser: California & Basin - Plateau Indians). (Illus.). lib. bdg. 42.00 (ISBN 0-8240-0740-9). Garland Pub.

Manners, Robert A., et al. Havasupai Indians. Horr, David A., ed. (American Indian Ethnohistory Ser.). 1974. lib. bdg. 42.00 (ISBN 0-8240-0707-7). Garland Pub.

Manners, Ruth A. & Manners, William. The Quick & Easy Vegetarian Cookbook. 288p. 1979. pap. 4.95 o.p. (ISBN 0-87131-303-0). M Evans.

Manners, William, jt. auth. see Manners, Ruth A.

Mannes, David. Music Is My Faith: An Autobiography. (Music Reprint, 1978 Ser.). (Illus.). 1978. Repr. of 1938 ed. lib. bdg. 27.50 (ISBN 0-306-77595-6). Da Capo.

Mannes, Marya & Osborn, Robert. Subverse: Rhymes for Our Times. (Illus.). 1959. 4.50 o.s.i. (ISBN 0-8076-0072-5). Braziller.

Mannheim, Hermann. Comparative Criminology: A Text Book, 2 vols. (International Library of Sociology). 1970. Repr. of 1965 ed. 22.00x ea. Vol. 1 (ISBN 0-7100-3458-X). Vol. 2 (ISBN 0-7100-3483-0). Routledge & Kegan.

Mannheim, Karl. From Karl Mannheim. Wolff, Kurt H., ed. (Orig.). 1971. pap. 7.95 (ISBN 0-19-501394-8, GB). Oxford U Pr.

--Man & Society in an Age of Reconstruction. Shils, Edward, tr. from Ger. (Studies in Modern Social Structure). 490p. 40.00 (ISBN 0-7100-1788-X). Routledge & Kegan.

Mannheim, Karl & Stewart, W. A. Introduction to the Sociology of Education. (International Library of Sociology & Social Reconstruction). 1970. text ed. 10.50x (ISBN 0-7100-3416-4); pap. text ed. 3.75x (ISBN 0-7100-6897-2). Humanities.

Mannheim, Karl, ed. Essays on the Sociology of Culture. (International Library of Sociology). 1969. 17.50x o.s.i. (ISBN 0-7100-3349-4). Routledge & Kegan.

Mannheimer, Jeffrey S. & Lampe, Gerald N. Clinical Transcutaneous Electrical Nerve Stimulation. 1981. 22.50 (ISBN 0-8036-5832-X). Davis Co.

Mannheimer, Marc, jt. auth. see Ehrlich, Jeffrey.

Manniche, P. & Porter, J. F., eds. Rural Development & the Changing Countries of the World, Bks. 1 & 2. LC 65-14224. 1970. 34.00 (ISBN 0-08-011155-6). Pergamon.

Mannie, Phillip, jt. auth. see Simonton, Wesley.

Mannin, Ethel. Practitioners of Love. 1970. 5.95 o.p. (ISBN 0-8180-1900-X). Horizon.

Manning. Society & Food: The Third World. (Sicon Bks Ser). 1977. 3.95 (ISBN 0-408-71304-6). Butterworths.

Manning, Anne, et al. Mary Powell & Deborah's Diary. Rhys, Ernest, ed. 228p. 1980. Repr. lib. bdg. 20.00 (ISBN 0-8495-3796-7). Arden Lib.

Manning, Bayless. A Concise Textbook on Legal Capital. 2nd ed. (University Textbook Ser.). 180p. 1981. pap. text ed. write for info. (ISBN 0-88277-020-9). Foundation Pr.

--The Conduct of United States Foreign Policy in the Nation's Third Century. (Headline Ser.: 231). 1976. pap. 2.00 (ISBN 0-87124-036-X, 76-9573). Foreign Policy.

Manning, Beverley. Index to American Women Speakers, Eighteen Twenty-Eight to Nineteen Seventy-Eight. LC 79-26928. viii, 672p. 1980. lib. bdg. 30.00 (ISBN 0-8108-1282-7). Scarecrow.

Manning, C. A. The Nature of International Society. LC 75-23427. 220p. 1962. 28.95 (ISBN 0-470-56760-0). Halsted Pr.

Manning, D. Disaster Technology: An Annotated Bibliography. 300p. 1976. text ed. 40.00 (ISBN 0-08-019984-4); pap. text ed. 25.00 (ISBN 0-08-019983-6). Pergamon.

Manning, Daniel F. Traveling Light. (Illus., Orig.). 1979. pap. 5.00x (ISBN 0-933192-00-2). Dancin Bee.

Manning, David. Reynolds. (Oresko-Jupiter Art Bks). (Illus.). 96p. 1981. 17.95 (ISBN 0-933516-85-1, Pub. by Oresko-Jupiter England). Hippocrene Bks.

Manning, Frank V. Managerial Dilemmas & Executive Growth. 1981. text ed. 17.95 (ISBN 0-8359-4231-7). Reston.

Manning, Harvey, jt. auth. see Spring, Ira.

Manning, Henry. The Fourth Dimension Simply Explained. 7.50 (ISBN 0-8446-2522-1). Peter Smith.

Manning, Hiram. Manning on Decoupage. (Illus.). 256p. 1980. pap. 6.00 (ISBN 0-486-24028-2). Dover.

Manning, Jack. Taking Better Pictures with Your Thirty-Five mm Automatic Camera. Swartz, Ava, ed. LC 79-3540. (Illus., Orig.). pap. cancelled o.s.i. (ISBN 0-88225-291-7). Newsweek.

Manning, Jason. Killer Gray. (Orig.). 1980. pap. 1.95 (ISBN 0-532-23212-7). Manor Bks.

Manning, Laurence. The Man Who Awoke. 1979. pap. 1.75 (ISBN 0-345-27969-7, Del Rey Bks). Ballantine.

Manning, Leonard F. The Law of Church-State Relations in a Nutshell. LC 80-22991. (Nutshell Ser.). 314p. 1980. pap. text ed. 6.95 (ISBN 0-8299-2113-3). West Pub.

Manning, M. J. & Turner, R. J. Comparative Immunobiology. LC 75-42363. (Teritiary Level Biology Ser.). 1976. pap. 9.95 (ISBN 0-470-14995-7). Halsted Pr.

Manning, Mary L. Chance McGraw. (Orig.). 1980. pap. 2.75 (ISBN 0-440-11523-X). Dell.

Manning, Matthew. The Link. (Illus.). 192p. 1976. pap. 1.75 o.p. (ISBN 0-345-25050-8). Ballantine.

Manning, Michael. Pardon My Lenten Smile: Daily Homily-Meditation Themes for the Weekdays of Lent. 90p. 1976. pap. 3.95 (ISBN 0-8189-0325-2). Alba.

Manning, Nick, jt. auth. see George, Vic.

Manning, Nick, jt. ed. see Hinshelwood, R. D.

Manning, Olivia. The Sum of Things. LC 80-7924. 1981. 10.95 (ISBN 0-689-11096-0). Atheneum.

Manning, Paul. Martin Bormann: Nazi in Exile. (Illus.). 320p. 1981. 14.95 (ISBN 0-686-69395-7). Lyle Stuart.

Manning, Peter B., jt. auth. see Thorner, Marvin E.

Manning, Peter K. Police Work: The Social Organization of Policies. 1979. 23.00 (ISBN 0-262-13130-7); pap. 8.95 (ISBN 0-262-63070-2). MIT Pr.

Manning, Peter K. & Zucker, Martine. The Sociology of Mental Health & Illness. LC 76-16067. (Studies in Sociology). 1976. pap. text ed. 5.95 (ISBN 0-672-61265-8). Bobbs.

Manning, Peter K., jt. ed. see Smith, Robert B.

Manning, Robert T., jt. auth. see Delp, Mahlon H.

Manning, S. A. The Naturalist in South East England. (Regional Naturalist Ser.). (Illus.). 1973. 14.95 (ISBN 0-7153-6109-0). David & Charles.

Manning, Thomas G. Government in Science: The U. S. Geological Survey, 1867-1894. LC 67-17851. (Illus.). 272p. 1967. 11.00x (ISBN 0-8131-1142-0). U Pr of Ky.

Manning, W. H., jt. auth. see Holder, C.

Manning, W. R. & Labrow, S. High Pressure Engineering. 1972. text ed. 37.50x (ISBN 0-7114-3804-8); pap. text ed. 19.95x (ISBN 0-685-83587-1). Intl Ideas.

Manning, Wallace, ed. Instrument Rating Written Test Answer Book, with Explanations. 1978. pap. 6.95 o.p. (ISBN 0-911721-39-8, Pub. by AvTest). Aviation.

Manning, Wallace E., ed. Airline Transport Pilot, Airplane, Answer Book. (Aviation Test Prep Ser.). 1979. pap. 10.95 o.p. (ISBN 0-911721-42-8, Pub. by AvTest). Aviation.

--Flight Instructor, Airplane, Answer Book. (Aviation Test Prep Ser.). 1979. pap. 8.95 o.p. (ISBN 0-911721-16-9, Pub. by AvTest). Aviation.

Manning, Wallace E., Jr., ed. Private Pilot, Airplane, Question & Answer Book: For Ac 61-32c. 1979. pap. 7.95 o.p. (ISBN 0-685-95909-0, Pub. by AvTest). Aviation.

Manning, William J. & Feder, William A. Biomonitoring Air Pollutants with Plants. (Illus.). x, 142p. 1981. 26.00x (ISBN 0-85334-916-9). Burgess-Intl Ideas.

Manningham, John. The Diary of John Manningham of the Middle Temple, 1602-1603. Sorlien, Robert P., ed. LC 74-22553. 481p. 1976. text ed. 27.50x (ISBN 0-87451-113-5). U Pr of New Eng.

Manning-Sanders, Ruth. Book of Dragons. (Illus.). (gr. 2-6). 1965. PLB 7.95 o.p. (ISBN 0-525-26824-3). Dutton.

--Book of Ghosts & Goblins. (Illus.). (gr. 2-5). 1973. pap. 1.25 o.p. (ISBN 0-525-45014-9, Anytime Bks). Dutton.

--A Book of Kings & Queens. (Illus.). (gr. 2-6). 1978. PLB 7.95 o.p. (ISBN 0-525-26925-8). Dutton.

--Book of Witches. (gr. 2-6). 1966. PLB 7.95 o.p. (ISBN 0-525-27054-X). Dutton.

--Story of Hans Andersen: Swan of Denmark. (gr. 7 up). 1966. PLB 5.95 o.p. (ISBN 0-525-40262-4). Dutton.

Mannion, Michael. Colleen. 1978. pap. 1.75 (ISBN 0-505-51274-2). Tower Bks.

Mannix, Daniel P. Healer. 1971. 6.95 o.p. (ISBN 0-525-12235-4). Dutton.

Mann, William. Aida: Verdi. Mann, William & Parker, Roger, eds. Tracey, Edmund, tr. 1980. pap. 4.95 (ISBN 0-7145-3770-5). Riverrun NY.

Mannon, James M. Emergency Encounters: A Study of an Urban Ambulance Service. (National University Publications, Sociology of Medicine Ser.). 1981. 15.00 (ISBN 0-8046-9281-5). Kennikat.

Mano, M. Digital Logic & Computer Design. 1979. 27.95 (ISBN 0-13-214510-3). P-H.

Mano, M. Morris. Computer Logic Design. (Automatic Computation Ser.). (Illus.). 464p. 1972. 28.95 (ISBN 0-13-165472-1). P-H.

--Computer System Architecture. (Illus.). 528p. 1976. ref. ed. 24.95 (ISBN 0-13-166363-1). P-H.

Manocchio, Anthony J. & Dunn, Jimmy. The Time Game: Two Views of a Prison. LC 77-85238. 1977. pap. 8.95x (ISBN 0-8039-0920-9). Sage.

Manocchio, Tony & Petitt, William. Families Under Stress: A Psychological Interpretation. 1975. 18.00 (ISBN 0-7100-8176-6). Routledge & Kegan.

Manocha, S. L. Nutrition & Our Overpopulated Planet. (Illus.). 488p. 1975. 31.75 (ISBN 0-398-03180-0); pap. 22.50 (ISBN 0-398-03181-9). C C Thomas.

Manocha, Sohan L. Malnutrition & Retarded Human Development. (Illus.). 400p. 1972. 39.50 (ISBN 0-398-02548-7). C C Thomas.

Manoff, Tom. The Music Kit. 1976. pap. text ed. 16.95x (ISBN 0-393-09179-1); tchrs. manual avail. (ISBN 0-393-09157-0). Norton.

Manohar, M. & Krishnamachar, P. Fluid Mechanics. 500p. 1981. text ed. 25.00x (ISBN 0-7069-1188-1, Pub. by Vikas India). Advent Bk.

--Hydraulic Machinery & Advanced Hydraulics. 600p. Date not set. text ed. 37.50 (ISBN 0-7069-1194-6, Pub. by Vikas India). Advent Bk.

Manolakes, George, et al. Try: Experiences for Young Children, Tasks 1-3. (gr. k-1,RL 1-3). 1967. Tasks 1-3. activity bks 2.52 ea.; tchrs'. guides 2.70 ea.; spanish teacher's guide 4.50 (ISBN 0-8372-9800-8). Bowmar-Noble.

Manoni, Mary, et al. Champions in Sports Learning Module. LC 76-731377. 1976. pap. text ed. 175.00 (ISBN 0-89290-112-8, CM-36). Soc for Visual.

Manoni, Mary H. & Cienkus, Robert. Phonetic Rules in Reading. LC 78-730055. (Illus.). 1978. pap. text ed. 99.00 (ISBN 0-89290-103-9, A329-SATC). Soc for Visual.

Manoni, Mary H. & O'Donnell, Elizabeth L. Rhetoric in Effective Communication. LC 78-730061. (Illus.). 1977. pap. text ed. 99.00 (ISBN 0-89290-122-5, A321). Soc for Visual.

Manoni, Mary H., jt. auth. see Gregorvich, Barbara.

Manooch, Charles S., III. Spring Comes to the Roanoke. (Illus.). 140p. 1979. 7.95 (ISBN 0-9605270-0-1). Era Davidson.

Manor, J. Curtis. Bible Manhunt. (Quiz & Puzzle Book Ser.). 128p. (Orig.). 1980. pap. 2.45 (ISBN 0-8010-6097-4). Baker Bk.

Manor, Ruth see Rescher, Nicholas.

Manougian, Manoug, jt. auth. see Ratti, Jogindar.

Mano-Zissi, Djordje, jt. ed. see Wiseman, James.

Manpower Demonstration Research Group. Tenant Management: Findings from a Three-Year Experiment in Public Housing. 240p. 1981. write for info. (ISBN 0-88410-694-2). Ballinger Pub.

Manrique, Jose. Thermodinamica Para Ingenieros. 1976. pap. text ed. 9.00 (ISBN 0-06-315512-5, IntlDept). Har-Row.

--Transferencia De Calor. 1977. pap. text ed. 8.00 (ISBN 0-06-315511-7, IntlDept). Har-Row.

Manschreck, Clyde L. & Zikmund, Barbara B., eds. The American Religious Experiment: Piety & Practicality. LC 76-7199. (Studies in Ministry & Parish Life). 128p. 1976. 12.95x (ISBN 0-913552-06-2); pap. 5.50x (ISBN 0-913552-07-0). Exploration Pr.

Mansell, Gilbert. Working with the Computer. 156p. 1972. pap. text ed. 9.75 (ISBN 0-08-016014-X). Pergamon.

Mansfeld, J. Pseudo-Hippocratic Tract & Greek Philosophy. (Philosophy Texts & Studies: No. 20). 1970. text ed. 33.50x (ISBN 9-0232-0701-7). Humanities.

Mansfield, A., ed. see Kelly, F. M.

Mansfield, Alan. Ceremonial Costume: Court, Civil & Civic Costume from Sixteen Sixty to the Present Day. (Illus.). 304p. 1980. 36.00x (ISBN 0-389-20124-3). B&N.

Mansfield, Alan, jt. auth. see Cunnington, Phyllis.

Mansfield, Carmella E. & Bahniuk, Margaret H. Writing Business Letters & Reports. 1981. write for info. (ISBN 0-672-97374-X); tchrs. manual avail. (ISBN 0-672-97375-8). Bobbs.

Mansfield, E. A., jt. auth. see Hillhouse, Marion S.

Mansfield, Edwin. Microeconomics: Theory & Applications. 3rd ed. (Illus.). 1979. text ed. 16.95x (ISBN 0-393-95002-6); text ed. 16.50x shorter ed. (ISBN 0-393-95010-7); instrs'. manual 3.95x (ISBN 0-393-95044-1). Norton.

--Principles of Microeconomics. 2nd ed. (Illus.). 1977. pap. text ed. 9.95x (ISBN 0-393-09113-9); readings, issues & cases 4.95x (ISBN 0-393-09102-3); study guide 4.95x (ISBN 0-393-09109-0); test item file gratis (ISBN 0-393-09105-8); transparency masters gratis (ISBN 0-393-09099-X). Norton.

--Statistics for Business & Economics. 1980. text ed. 16.95x (ISBN 0-393-95057-3); May 1980. pap. 8.95x readings & cases (ISBN 0-393-95066-2); pap. 6.95x problems, exercises & case studies (ISBN 0-393-95062-X); solutions manual 1.95x (ISBN 0-393-95070-0). Norton.

Mansfield, Elizabeth. A Country Squire. 1980. pap. write for info. o.p. (ISBN 0-425-04677-X). Berkley Pub.

--A Regency Charade. 224p. 1981. pap. 2.25 (ISBN 0-425-04835-7). Berkley Pub.

--Regency Galatea. 1981. pap. 2.25 (ISBN 0-425-04739-3). Berkley Pub.

Mansfield, Evelyn A. & Lucas, Ethel G. Clothing Construction. 2nd ed. 454p. 1974. text ed. 18.95 (ISBN 0-395-16728-0). HM.

Mansfield, Harvey C., ed. Congress Against the President. LC 75-17154. (Special Studies). 208p. 1975. text ed. 24.95 (ISBN 0-275-56230-1); pap. text ed. 10.95 (ISBN 0-275-64420-0). Praeger.

Mansfield, Harvey C., Jr. Machiavelli's New Modes & Orders: A Study of the "Discourses on Livy". LC 79-12380. 1979. 27.50x (ISBN 0-8014-1182-3). Cornell U Pr.

Mansfield, James R. A History of Early Spotsylvania. LC 77-87193. (Illus.). 1977. 10.75x (ISBN 0-685-89825-3). Va Bk.

Mansfield, John M., jt. auth. see Hall, G. Stanley.

Mansfield, Joseph K. Mansfield on the Condition of the Western Forts, 1853-54. Frazer, Robert W., ed. (American Exploration & Travel Ser.: No. 41). (Illus.). 1963. pap. 5.95 (ISBN 0-8061-1083-X). U of Okla Pr.

Mansfield, Katherine. Journal of Katherine Mansfield. Murry, John M., ed. LC 74-14981. (Illus.). 292p. 1975. Repr. of 1927 ed. 24.00 (ISBN 0-86527-265-4). Fertig.

--The Letters of Katherine Mansfield, 2 vols. in 1. Murry, John M., ed. LC 74-16016. 528p. 1975. Repr. of 1929 ed. 27.50 (ISBN 0-86527-271-9). Fertig.

--The Scrapbook of Katherine Mansfield. LC 74-16042. 288p. 1975. Repr. of 1939 ed. 22.50 (ISBN 0-86527-299-9). Fertig.

--The Urewera Notebook. Gordon, Ian A., intro. by. (Illus.). 108p. 1978. pap. text ed. 12.95x (ISBN 0-19-558034-6). Oxford U Pr.

Mansfield, Kenneth. Coarse Fishing As a Pastime. 10.00x (ISBN 0-392-06496-0, SpS). Soccer.

--Trout & How to Catch Them. 1978. 4.95 o.p. (ISBN 0-214-20234-8, 8005, Dist. by Arco). Barrie & Jenkins.

Mansfield, Kenneth, ed. Coarse Fishing. (Angler's Library). 1978. 7.50 o.p. (ISBN 0-214-65253-X, 8001, Dist. by Arco). Barrie & Jenkins.

--Fly Tying, Rod & Tackle Making. (Angler's Library). 1978. 4.50 o.p. (ISBN 0-214-65306-4, 8002, Dist. by Arco). Barrie & Jenkins.

--Salmon & Sea Trout. 1979. 4.50 o.p. (ISBN 0-214-66837-1, ADON 8088-4, Dist by Arco). Barrie & Jenkins.

Mansfield, Mike. Charting a New Course: Mike Mansfield & U. S. Asian Policy, Four Reports. LC 77-83044. (Illus.). 1977. pap. 3.95 (ISBN 0-8048-1256-X). C E Tuttle.

Mansfield, Peter. The Middle East: A Political & Economic Survey. (Illus.). 1980. 29.95 (ISBN 0-19-215851-1). Oxford U Pr.

Mansfield, Roger, jt. auth. see Poole, Michael.

Mansfield, T. A., ed. Effects of Air Pollutants on Plants. LC 75-32449. (Society for Experimental Biology Seminar Ser.: No. 1). (Illus.). 180p. 1976. 39.50 (ISBN 0-521-21087-9); pap. 14.95x (ISBN 0-521-29039-2). Cambridge U Pr.

Manskaya, S. M. & Drozdova, T. V. Geochemistry of Organic Substances. 1968. 60.00 (ISBN 0-08-012404-6). Pergamon.

Manske, R. H., et al, eds. The Alkaloids: Chemistry & Physiology. Incl. Vol. 1. 1965. 62.00 (ISBN 0-12-469501-9); Vol. 2. 1952. 62.00 (ISBN 0-12-469502-7); Vol. 3. 1965. 55.25 (ISBN 0-12-469503-5); Vol. 4. 1965. 52.50 (ISBN 0-12-469504-3); Vol. 5. Pharmacology. 1965. 52.50 (ISBN 0-12-469505-1); Vol. 6. Supplement to Volumes 1 & 2. 1965. 52.50 (ISBN 0-12-469506-X); Vol. 7. Supplement to Volumes 2, 3, 4 & 5. 1960. 59.00 (ISBN 0-12-469507-8); Vol. 8. The Indole Alkaloids. 1965. 72.25 (ISBN 0-12-469508-6); Vol. 9. 1967. 64.25 (ISBN 0-12-469509-4); Vol. 10. 1968. 64.25 (ISBN 0-12-469510-8); Vol. 11. 1968. 64.25 (ISBN 0-12-469511-6); Vol. 12. 1970. 64.25 (ISBN 0-12-469512-4); Vol. 13. 1971. 55.25 (ISBN 0-12-469513-2); Vol. 14. 1973. 68.50 (ISBN 0-12-469514-0); Vol. 15. 1975. 55.25 (ISBN 0-12-469515-9); Vol. 16. 1977. 73.00 (ISBN 0-12-469516-7); Vol. 17. 1979. 58.00 (ISBN 0-12-469517-5). Acad Pr.

Manski, Charles F. & McFadden, Daniel, eds. Structural Analysis of Discrete Data. 600p. 1981. text ed. 29.95x (ISBN 0-262-13159-5). MIT Pr.

Manson, H. W. Plays. Van Heyningen, C., ed. Incl. The Festival. o.p. (ISBN 0-685-22958-0); Magnus (ISBN 0-8426-1375-7); The Counsellors (ISBN 0-8426-1376-5); Potluck (ISBN 0-8426-1377-3). 1971. 8.50x ea. o.p. (ISBN 0-8426-1374-9). Verry.

Manson, S. S. Thermal Stress & Low-Cycle Fatigue. 416p. 1981. lib. bdg. price not set (ISBN 0-89874-279-X). Krieger.

Manson, T. W. Only to the House of Israel? Jesus & the Non-Jews. Reumann, John, ed. LC 64-11860. (Facet Bks). 1964. pap. 1.00 (ISBN 0-8006-3005-X, 1-3005). Fortress.

Manson-Hing, L. R. Panoramic Dental Radiography. 2nd ed. (Illus.). 224p. 1980. 41.25 (ISBN 0-398-03976-3). C C Thomas.

Manson-Hing, Lincoln R. Panoramic Dental Radiography. (Illus.). 224p. 1976. 41.25 o.p. (ISBN 0-398-03976-3). C C Thomas.

Manson-Hing, Lincoln R., jt. auth. see Wuehrmann, Arthur H.

Mansoor, Menahem. Biblical Hebrew Step by Step: A Significant Breakthrough for Learning Biblical Hebrew. 1978. pap. 9.95 (ISBN 0-8010-6041-9). Baker Bk.

--The Dead Sea Scrolls. 1964. Repr. 4.95 o.p. (ISBN 0-8028-3181-8). Eerdmans.

Manstein, Christof H. Von see Von Manstein, Christof H.

Mansubi, Fereydun. Self-Assessment of Current Knowledge in Neonatology & Perinatal Medicine. 1976. spiral bdg. 14.50 (ISBN 0-87488-240-0). Med Exam.

Mansukhani, Gobin S., ed. & tr. from Punjabi. Hymns from the Holy Granth. 1976. pap. 2.75 (ISBN 0-89253-063-4). Ind-US Inc.

Mansukhani, H. L. Smugglers' Paradise & Foreign Exchange Law. 1977. text ed. 20.00 o.p. (ISBN 0-686-59597-1, Pub. by Vikas India). Advent Bk.

Mansvelt-Beck, Frederick W. & Wiig, Karl M. The Economics of Offshore Oil & Gas Supplies. LC 76-54558. (Illus.). 1977. 17.95 (ISBN 0-669-01306-4). Lexington Bks.

Mant, Richard. Verses to the Memory of Joseph Warton DD, Repr. Of 1800. Reiman, Donald H., ed. Bd. with The Slave & Other Poetical Pieces: Being an Appendix to Poems. Repr. of 1807 ed; Poems. Repr. of 1806 ed; The Simpliciad: a Satirico Didactic Poem (Dedicated to Wordsworth, Southey & Coleridge) Repr. of 1808 ed. LC 75-31229. (Romantic Context Ser: Poetry 1789-1830). 1979. lib. bdg. 47.00 (ISBN 0-8240-2178-9). Garland Pub.

Mante, Daisy R. & Mathisen, Bonnie W. Growing Better Brighter Children. 160p. (Orig.). Date not set. pap. price not set (ISBN 0-931310-02-4). Jifunza Educ.

Mantegazza, Paolo. The Legends of Flowers. Kennedy, Mrs. Alexander, tr. LC 73-180973. (Illus.). 190p. 1975. Repr. of 1927 ed. 15.00 (ISBN 0-8103-4051-8). Gale.

Mantell, Charles L. Solid Wastes: Origin, Collection, Processing & Disposal. LC 74-26930. 1152p. 1975. 74.95 (ISBN 0-471-56777-9, Pub by Wiley-Interscience). Wiley.

Mantell, Laurie. Murder or Three. LC 80-54378. 1981. 9.95 (ISBN 0-8027-5432-5). Walker & Co.

Mantell, Martin E. Johnson, Grant, & the Politics of Reconstruction. 225p. 1973. 15.00x (ISBN 0-231-03507-1). Columbia U Pr.

Mantell, Walter, et al. Short Treatise of the Laws of England. Berkowitz, David S. & Thorne, Samuel E., eds. LC 77-86578. (Classics of English Legal History in the Modern Era Ser.: Vol. 17). 351p. 1979. lib. bdg. 40.00 (ISBN 0-8240-3066-4). Garland Pub.

Mantey, J. R., jt. auth. see Dana, H. E.

Mantinbard, James H., jt. tr. see Passage, Charles E.

Manton, Thomas. An Exposition of the Epistle of Jude. 1978. 12.00 (ISBN 0-686-12957-1). Klock & Klock.

Manuel, David. The Gathering. LC 80-53855. 250p. (Orig.). 1980. pap. 4.95 (ISBN 0-932260-07-1). Rock Harbor.

--Like a Mighty River. LC 77-90948. (Illus.). 220p. 1977. 5.95 (ISBN 0-932260-02-0). Rock Harbor.

Manuel, David, jt. auth. see Basansky, Bill.

Manuel, David, jt. auth. see Wilkerson, Don.

Manuel, Dino. Paragraph of Life: Killer-Your Friend? 64p. 1981. 5.00 (ISBN 0-682-49724-X). Exposition.

Manuel, Don J. El Conde Lucanor. (Span.). 7.95 (ISBN 84-241-5615-3). E Torres & Sons.

--Libro de los Estados. Tate, R. B. & MacPherson, Ian, eds. 420p. (Sp.). 1974. 49.50x (ISBN 0-19-815713-4). Oxford U Pr.

Manuila, A., ed. Progress in Medical Terminology. (Illus.). vi, 118p. 1981. pap. 30.00 (ISBN 3-8055-2112-X). S Karger.

Manum, Svein B., jt. auth. see Bjaerke, Tor.

Manunder, W. F., ed. see Munby, Denys & Watson, A. H.

Manus, Willard. The Fighting Men. 200p. 1981. 12.95 (ISBN 0-915572-55-9); pap. 6.95 (ISBN 0-915572-54-0). Panjandrum.

Manus, Willard B. Mystery of the Flooded Mine. LC 64-13844. (gr. 6-9). 1964. 5.95 o.p. (ISBN 0-385-03991-3). Doubleday.

Manvell, Roger, jt. ed. see Bluem, A. William.

Manvell, Roger, intro. by. Masterworks of the German Cinema: The Golem, Nosferatu M, the Threepenny Opera. LC 73-13005. (Icon Editions). (Illus.). 300p. 1974. pap. 4.95 o.s.i. (ISBN 0-06-430047-1, IN-47, HarpT). Har-Row.

Manvell, Roger, et al, eds. The Penguin Film Review 1946-1949, 2 vols. (Illus.). 1978. Repr. of 1946 ed. Set. 49.50x (ISBN 0-8476-6029-X). Rowman.

Manville, Bill. Saloon Society. 192p. 1980. pap. 2.25 (ISBN 0-515-05490-9). Jove Pubns.

Manwaring, George E. & Dobree, Bonamy. Floating Republic. LC 67-72366. (Illus.). Repr. of 1935 ed. 23.00x (ISBN 0-678-05185-2). Kelley.

Manwell, A. P. Hodograph Equations: An Introduction to the Mathematical Theory of Plane Transonic Flow. (University Mathematical Monograph Ser: No. 8). 1970. 30.25 o.s.i. (ISBN 0-02-848780-X). Hafner.

Manwell, Roger. Art & Animation: The Story of the Halas & Batchelor Animation Studio. (Illus.). 128p. 1980. 26.50 (ISBN 0-8038-0494-6, Visual Communications). Hastings.

Manwood, John. A Brefe Collection of the Lawes of the Forest. Berkowitz, David & Thorne, Samuel, eds. LC 77-86654. (Classics of English Legal History in the Modern Era Ser.: Vol. 100). 1979. Repr. of 1598 ed. lib. bdg. 55.00 (ISBN 0-8240-3087-7). Garland Pub.

--A Treatise of the Lawes of the Forest. LC 76-57398. (English Experience Ser.: No. 814). 1977. Repr. of 1615 ed. lib. bdg. 51.00 (ISBN 90-221-0814-7). Walter J Johnson.

Manyoshu. Manyoshu: The Nippon Gakujutsu Shinkokai Translation of One Thousand Poems. LC 65-15376. (Records of Civilization Ser.: No. 70). 1969. pap. 10.00x (ISBN 0-231-08620-2). Columbia U Pr.

Manypenny, George Washington. Our Indian Wards. LC 68-54844. (The American Scene Ser). 1972. Repr. of 1880 ed. lib. bdg. 25.00 (ISBN 0-306-71140-0). Da Capo.

Manzer, Bruce M. The Abstract Journal, 1790-1920: Origin, Development & Diffusion. LC 77-24143. 1977. 15.00 (ISBN 0-8108-1047-6). Scarecrow.

Manzione, J. V., Jr., jt. auth. see Bodak-Gyovai, L. Z.

Manzo, L., ed. Advances in Neurotoxicology: Proceedings of the International Congress on Neurotoxicology, Varese, 27-30 September 1979. (Illus.). 404p. 1980. 69.00 (ISBN 0-08-024953-1). Pergamon.

Manzoni, Alessandro. Betrothed. Cloquhoun, Archibald, tr. 1956. 5.00x o.p. (ISBN 0-460-00999-0, Everyman). Dutton.

Mao, Nathan K. Pa Chin. (World Authors Ser.: No. 496 (China)). 1978. 13.50 (ISBN 0-8057-6337-6). Twayne.

Mao, Nathan K. & Ts'Un-Yan, Liu. Li Yu. (World Authors Ser.: No. 448). 1977. lib. bdg. 12.50 (ISBN 0-8057-6283-3). Twayne.

Mao, Nathan K., tr. see Chi'en Chung-shu.

Mao, Nathan K., tr. see Li Yu.

Mao Tse-Tung. Selected Military Writings, 1928-1949. 1967-1968. 6.95 (ISBN 0-8351-0321-8); red plastic 3.95 (ISBN 0-8351-0323-4); pap. 4.95 (ISBN 0-8351-0322-6). China Bks.

Mao Dun. Midnight. 1980. 100.95 (ISBN 0-8351-0614-4). China Bks.

Mao Tsetung. Mao Tsetung Poems. 1976. red silk 4.95 (ISBN 0-8351-0257-2). pap. 2.95 (ISBN 0-8351-0258-0). China Bks.

Mao Tse-Tung. Selected Readings. 504p. 1971. 6.95 (ISBN 0-8351-0324-2). China Bks.

--Selected Works, 4 vols. Incl. Vol. 1. 1924-37. 1965 (ISBN 0-8351-0328-5); Vol. 2. 1937-41. 1965 (ISBN 0-8351-0330-7); Vol. 3. 1941-45. 1965 (ISBN 0-8351-0332-3) (ISBN 0-8351-0333-1); Vol. 4. 1945-49. 1961 (ISBN 0-8351-0334-X) (ISBN 0-8351-0335-8). 7.95 ea.; pap. 5.95 ea. China Bks.

--Selected Works of Mao Tse-Tung, 5 vols. LC 77-30658. 1977. Set. text ed. 60.00 (ISBN 0-08-022262-5); text ed. 15.00 (ISBN 0-686-68045-6). Vol. I (ISBN 0-08-022980-8). Vol. II (ISBN 0-08-022981-6). Vol. III (ISBN 0-08-022982-4). Vol. IV (ISBN 0-08-022983-2). Vol. V (ISBN 0-08-022984-0). Pergamon.

Mao Tse Tung. Selected Works of Mao Tse-Tung, Vol. 5. 1977. 7.95 (ISBN 0-8351-0336-6); pap. 5.95 (ISBN 0-8351-0337-4). China Bks.

Mapes, Lynn G. & Travis, Anthony. A Pictorial History of Grand Rapids. LC 75-8015. 1976. 14.95 (ISBN 0-8254-3213-8). Kregel.

Mapes, Roy, ed. Prescribing, Practice & Drug Usage. 217p. 1980. 32.50x (ISBN 0-7099-0378-2, Pub. by Croom Helm Ltd England). Biblio Dist.

Maple, Eric. Ghosts, Witchcraft, & Demonology in England. LC 78-53668. (Illus.). 1981. 10.95 o.p. (ISBN 0-498-02249-8). A S Barnes.

Maple, Frank F. Shared Decision-Making. LC 77-12109. (Sage Human Service Guides Ser.: Vol. 4). 1977. pap. 6.00x (ISBN 0-8039-0883-0). Sage.

Maple, Frank F., jt. auth. see Bertcher, Harvey J.

Maples, Evelyn. Norman Learns About the Scriptures. LC 61-9685. (Illus.). 40p. (gr. 1-3). 1972. 3.00 o.p. (ISBN 0-8309-0060-8). Herald Hse.

Maplet, John. A Greene Forest, or a Naturall Historie. LC 79-84122. (English Experience Ser.: No.941). 244p. 1979. Repr. of 1567 ed. lib. bdg. 18.00 (ISBN 90-221-0941-0). Walter J Johnson.

Mapp, Alf J., Jr. The Virginia Experiment. rev. ed. 1974. 22.50 (ISBN 0-87548-309-7); pap. 8.95 (ISBN 0-87548-308-9). Open Court.

Mapp, Alfred J., Jr. The Golden Dragon: Alfred the Great & His Times. LC 74-8983. 1974. 10.95 o.p. (ISBN 0-87548-293-7). Open Court.

Mapp, Edward. Blacks in American Films: Today & Yesterday. LC 72-172946. (Illus.). 1972. 10.00 (ISBN 0-8108-0458-1). Scarecrow.

--Directory of Blacks in the Performing Arts. LC 78-2436. 1978. 21.00 (ISBN 0-8108-1126-X). Scarecrow.

Mapp, Edward, ed. Puerto Rican Perspectives. LC 73-20175. 1974. 10.00 (ISBN 0-8108-0691-6). Scarecrow.

Maquet, J., ed. On Linguistic Anthropology: Essays in Honor of Harry Hoijer, 1979. LC 80-50214. (Other Realities Ser.: Vol. 2). 140p. text ed. 12.00; pap. text ed. 9.00. Undena Pubns.

Maquet, Jacques. Africanity: The Cultural Unity of Black Africa. Rayfield, Joan, tr. 1972. 14.95 (ISBN 0-19-519701-1). Oxford U Pr.

--Civilizations of Black Africa. Rayfield, Joan, tr. 1972. pap. 5.95 (ISBN 0-19-501464-2, GB368, GB). Oxford U Pr.

Mar, W. Del see Pender, H. & Del Mar, W.

Mara, Duncan. Sewage Treatment in Hot Climates. LC 75-23421. 240p. 1976. 30.25 (ISBN 0-471-56784-1, Pub. by Wiley-Interscience). Wiley.

Mara, Maura. Cover Girls. (Illus.). 96p. (gr. 5 up). Date not set. PLB 9.55 (ISBN 0-688-51996-2); pap. 6.95 (ISBN 0-688-41996-8). Morrow. Postponed.

Mara, Thalia & Wyndham, Lee. First Steps in Ballet: Home Practice in Basic Exercises. LC 55-6550. 1955. 6.95 (ISBN 0-385-02432-0). Doubleday.

Maracotta, Lindsay. Caribe. (Orig.). 1980. pap. 2.25 (ISBN 0-515-04692-2). Jove Pubns.

Maraini, Fosco. Japan: Patterns of Continuity. LC 76-107610. (Illus.). 240p. 1971. 27.50 (ISBN 0-87011-106-X). Kodansha.

--Tokyo. (The Great Cities Ser.). (Illus.). (gr. 6 up). 1976. lib. bdg. 14.94 (ISBN 0-685-77696-4, Pub by Time-Life). Silver.

--Tokyo. (Great Cities Ser). 1976. 14.95 (ISBN 0-8094-2266-2). Time-Life.

Marais, G. V., jt. auth. see Loewenthal, R. E.

Marais, Marin. Pieces a une et a Deux Violes, 1686-89: The Instrumental Works, Vol. 1. Hsu, John, ed. xxvii, 191p. 1980. lib. bdg. 67.50x (ISBN 0-8450-7201-3). Broude.

Maraldo, John C., jt. ed. see Dumoulin, Heinrich.

Maraldo, John C., ed. see Heidegger, Martin.

Marambaud, Pierre L. William Byrd of Westover, 1674-1744. LC 70-151251. (Illus.). 300p. 1971. 17.50x (ISBN 0-8139-0346-7). U Pr of Va.

Maramorosch, K. see Arber, W., et al.

Maramorosch, K., jt. ed. see Harris, K.

Maramorosch, Karl & Harris, Kerry. Plant Diseases & Vectors: Ecology & Epidemiology. 1981. price not set (ISBN 0-12-470240-6). Acad Pr.

Maramorosh, Karl, ed. Advances in Cell Culture, Vol. I. (Serial Publication Ser.). 1981. write for info. (ISBN 0-12-007901-1). Acad Pr.

--Advances in Cell Culture, Vol. 2. (Serial Publication). 1981. price not set (ISBN 0-12-007902-X). Acad Pr.

Maramzin, Vladimir. Tianitolka: Povesti. 200p. (Rus.). 1981. 15.00 (ISBN 0-88233-510-3); pap. 7.00 (ISBN 0-88233-511-1). Ardis Pubs.

--Tianitolkai: Povesti. (Rus.). 1981. 15.00 (ISBN 0-88233-510-3); pap. 7.50 (ISBN 0-88233-511-1). Ardis Pubs.

Maran, A. G., jt. auth. see Stell, P. M.

Maran, Marie Y., jt. auth. see Egan, Patricia B.

Maran, Stephen P., jt. auth. see Brandt, John C.

Maran, Stephen P., jt. ed. see Brandt, John C.

Marandel, J. Patrice, intro. by. Gray Is the Color: An Exhibition of Grisaille Painting, 13th-20th Centuries. LC 73-92776. (Illus.). 1974. pap. 5.00 (ISBN 0-914412-08-6). Inst for the Arts.

Marandet, Leon, jt. auth. see Guitard, Lucien.

Maranjian, Lorig, jt. auth. see Boss, Richard W.

Marans, Robert W. & Wellman, John D. The Quality of Non Metropolitan Living: Evaluations, Behaviors, & Expectations of Northern Michigan Residents. LC 70-69913. (Illus.). 352p. 1978. 17.00 (ISBN 0-87944-226-3); pap. 12.00 (ISBN 0-87944-225-5). U of Mich Soc Res.

Marantette, Carter H., jt. auth. see Basehore, C. J.

Marat, Jean - Paul. Le Junius Francais, Journal Politique. 104p. (Fr.). 1977. lib. bdg. 22.50x o.p. (ISBN 0-8287-0569-0); pap. text ed. 12.50x o.p. (ISBN 0-685-75627-0). Clearwater Pub.

Marateck, Samuel L. Fortran. 1977. 13.95 (ISBN 0-12-470460-3); instr' manual 1978 3.00 (ISBN 0-12-470462-X). Acad Pr.

Maratek, Samuel. BASIC. 1975. 13.95 (ISBN 0-12-470450-6); answer bk. 3.00 (ISBN 0-12-470452-2). Acad Pr.

Maratsos, M. P. The Use of Definite & Indefinite Reference in Young Children. (Illus.). 160p. 1976. 24.50 (ISBN 0-521-20924-2). Cambridge U Pr.

Marazzi, Rich. The Stein & Day Baseball Date Book, 1981. (Illus.). 128p. 1980. 6.95 (ISBN 0-8128-2770-8). Stein & Day.

Marazzi, Rich & Fiorito, Len. Aaron to Zuverink: A Nostalgic Look at the Baseball Players of the Fifties. LC 80-5893. 352p. 1981. 14.95 (ISBN 0-8128-2775-9). Stein & Day.

Marazzi, Richard. The Rules & Lore of Baseball. LC 79-3895. 224p. 1980. 12.95 (ISBN 0-8128-2715-5); pap. 7.95 (ISBN 0-8128-6058-6). Stein & Day.

Marbe, Karl, jt. auth. see Thumb, Albert.

Marbecke, Roger. A Defence of Tabacco: With a Friendly Answer to Worke for Chimnysweepers. LC 68-54636. (English Experience Ser.: No. 33). 1968. Repr. of 1602 ed. 11.50 (ISBN 90-221-0033-2). Walter J Johnson.

Marberger, H., et al, eds. see American-European Symposium, Vienna, Nov. 3-5, 1975, Sponsored by Physicians Associated for Continuing Education, Johns Hopkins University, & the University of Vienna & the Univ. of Innesbruck.

Marble, Annie R. Pen Names & Personalities. 256p. 1980. Repr. of 1930 ed. lib. bdg. 30.00 (ISBN 0-89987-563-7). Century Bookbindery.

Marburger, Carl, jt. auth. see NCCE.

Marceau, Jane. Class & Status in France: Economic Change & Social Immobility, 1945-1975. 1977. 24.00x (ISBN 0-19-827217-0). Oxford U Pr.

Marcel, Gabriel. Homo Viator: Introduction to a Metaphysic of Hope. Crauford, Emma, tr. 7.50 (ISBN 0-8446-2529-9). Peter Smith.

Marcel, Raymond, et al. Builders & Humanists: The Renaissance Popes As Patrons of the Arts. (Illus.). 1966. pap. 8.00 (ISBN 0-914412-20-5). Inst for the Arts.

March, Daniel. Night Scenes in the Bible. LC 77-189204. 1972. 8.95 (ISBN 0-8254-3211-1). Kregel.

March, Edward. Sailing Drifters. 1977. 38.00 (ISBN 0-7153-4679-2). David & Charles.

--Sailing Trawlers. 1977. 38.00 (ISBN 0-7153-4711-X). David & Charles.

March, Edwin G. The Gift. 1981. 6.95 (ISBN 0-8062-1635-2). Carlton.

March, Francis, et al. March's Thesaurus & Dictionary. 2nd ed. LC 79-92443. 1360p. 1980. 19.95 (ISBN 0-89659-107-7); pap. 10.95 (ISBN 0-89659-161-1). Abbeville Pr.

March, J. G., jt. auth. see Cyert, Richard M.

March, James G. & Olsen, Johan P. Ambiguity & Choice in Organizations. 2nd ed. 420p. 1980. pap. 29.00x (ISBN 8-2000-1960-8). Universitet.

March, James G., ed. see Carnegie Commission on Higher Education.

March, Jessica. Embrace the Fury. 1978. pap. 1.95 o.p. (ISBN 0-449-13973-5, GM). Fawcett.

March, Joseph M. Wild Party, A Certain Wilderness, The Set-Up. LC 68-27623. (Illus.). 310p. 1968. ltd. autographed ed. 25.00 (ISBN 0-87027-104-0); 10.95 (ISBN 0-87027-103-2). Wheelwright.

March, L., ed. The Architecture of Form. LC 74-80354. (Cambridge Urban & Architectural Studies: No. 4). (Illus.). 552p. 1976. 78.00 (ISBN 0-521-20528-X). Cambridge U Pr.

March, L., jt. ed. see Martin, Leslie.

March, Marion & McEvers, Joan. The Only Way to Learn Astrology: Vol. 2, Math & Aftermath. 2nd, rev. ed. (Illus.). 320p. 1981. pap. 11.95 (ISBN 0-917086-26-0). Astro Comp Serv.

March, N. H. & Tosi, M. P. Atomic Dynamics in Liquids. LC 76-16040. 1977. 59.95 (ISBN 0-470-15145-5). Halsted Pr.

March, N. H., jt. auth. see Jones, W.

March, Norman H. Liquid Metals. 1968. 25.00 (ISBN 0-08-012331-7). Pergamon.

--Self-Consistent Fields in Atoms. 1975. text ed. 27.00 (ISBN 0-08-017819-7); pap. text ed. 14.50 (ISBN 0-08-017820-0). Pergamon.

March, Norman H., et al. Many-Body Problem in Quantum Mechanics. (Cambridge Monographs on Physics). 1968. 47.95 (ISBN 0-521-05671-3). Cambridge U Pr.

March, Rita N., jt. auth. see Shires, H. Bess.

March, W. Eugene, ed. Texts & Testaments: Critical Essays on the Bible & Early Church Fathers. 321p. 1980. 15.00 (ISBN 0-911536-80-9). Trinity U Pr.

Marchaj, C. A. Aero-Hydrodynamics of Sailing. LC 79-27724. (Illus.). 1980. 40.00 (ISBN 0-396-07739-0). Dodd.

Marchalonis, J. J., ed. Comparative Immunology. LC 76-18782. 1976. 49.95 (ISBN 0-470-15160-9). Halsted Pr.

Marchalonis, John J. & Cohen, Nicholas, eds. Contemporary Topics in Immunobiology, Vol. 9: Self-Non Self Discrimination. LC 79-179761. (Illus.). 309p. 1980. 29.50 (ISBN 0-306-40263-7, Plenum Pr). Plenum Pub.

Marchand, Donald A. The Politics of Privacy, Computers, & Criminal Justice Records: Controlling the Social Costs of Technological Change. LC 80-80675. xvi, 433p. 1980. text ed. 34.95 (ISBN 0-87815-030-7). Info Resources.

Marchand, James W., jt. ed. see Fink, Karl J.

Marchand, Leslie A. Prefaces to Byron. 131p. 1980. Repr. of 1979 ed. lib. bdg. 30.00 (ISBN 0-8414-5876-6). Folcroft.

Marchant. Design for Fire Safety. 1981. text ed. price not set (ISBN 0-408-00487-8). Butterworth.

Marchant, Anyda. Viscount Maua & the Empire of Brazil: A Biography of Irineu Evangelista De Sousa. 1965. 22.75x (ISBN 0-520-00807-3). U of Cal Pr.

Marchant, Catherine. The Fen Tiger. 1981. pap. 2.75 (ISBN 0-440-12502-2). Dell.

Marchant, Harold & Smith, Helen M. Adolescent Girls at Risk. 1977. text ed. 16.50 (ISBN 0-08-018914-8); pap. text ed. 7.00 (ISBN 0-08-020634-4). Pergamon.

Marchant, James. Anthology of Jesus. Wiersbe, Warren W., ed. LC 80-25038. 1981. Repr. of 1926 ed. 8.95 (ISBN 0-8254-4015-7). Kregel.

--The Master Problem. Winick, Charles, ed. LC 78-60869. (Prostitution Ser.: Vol. 12). 371p. 1979. lib. bdg. 36.00 (ISBN 0-8240-9716-5). Garland Pub.

--The Reunion of Christendom: A Survey of Present Position. 329p. 1980. Repr. of 1929 ed. lib. bdg. 30.00 (ISBN 0-8495-3771-1). Arden Lib.

Marchant, Maurice P. Participative Management in Academic Libraries. LC 76-8740. (Contributions in Librarianship & Information Science: No. 16). 320p. 1977. lib. bdg. 18.95 (ISBN 0-8371-8935-7, MPM/). Greenwood.

Marchant, R. A. Church Under the Law. LC 79-80819. (Illus.). 1969. 47.50 (ISBN 0-521-07460-6). Cambridge U Pr.

--Man & Beast. LC 68-21304. (Illus.). (gr. 7 up). 1968. 4.95g o.s.i. (ISBN 0-02-762390-4). Macmillan.

--Where Animals Live. LC 69-18240. (Illus.). (gr. 5-8). 1970. 7.95g (ISBN 0-02-762420-X). Macmillan.

Marchant, Roger, jt. auth. see Ryalls, Alan.

Marchant, W. T. In Praise of Ale, or Songs, Ballads, Epigrams & Anecdotes Relating to Beer Malt, & Hops. LC 68-22038. 1968. Repr. of 1888 ed. 24.00 (ISBN 0-8103-3511-5). Gale.

Marchbank, Pearce, jt. auth. see Farren, Mick.

Marchesani, O. & Sautter, H. Atlas of the Oscular Fundus. 1959. 80.00 (ISBN 0-02-848820-2). Hafner.

Marchesi, Blanche. Singer's Pilgrimage. LC 77-1941. (Music Reprint Ser.: 1978). (Illus.). 1978. Repr. of 1923 ed. lib. bdg. 27.50 (ISBN 0-306-70878-7). Da Capo.

Marchesi, Mathilde. Bel Canto: Theoretical & Practical Vocal Method. 1970. pap. text ed. 5.00 (ISBN 0-486-22315-9). Dover.

--Marchesi & Music: Passages from the Life of a Famous Singing-Teacher. LC 77-27354. (Music Reprint Ser., 1978). 1978. Repr. of 1898 ed. lib. bdg. 27.50 (ISBN 0-306-77577-8). Da Capo.

Marchesi, Vincent T., et al, eds. Cell Surface Carbohydrates & Biological Recognition: Proceedings of the ICN-UCLA Symposium Held at Keystone, Col., Feb. 1977. LC 78-417. 690p. 1978. 76.00 (ISBN 0-8451-0023-8). A R Liss.

Marchetti, Albert. Common Cures for Common Ailments: A Doctor's Guide to Nonprescription, Over-the-Counter Medicines & His Recommendations for Their Use. LC 77-16114. 368p. 1981. pap. 8.95 (ISBN 0-8128-6107-8). Stein & Day.

--Dr. Marchetti's Walking Book. LC 78-66258. 142p. 1981. pap. 6.95 (ISBN 0-8128-6114-0). Stein & Day.

Marchetti, Victor & Marks, John D. CIA: The Cult of Intelligence. 1980. pap. 2.95 (ISBN 0-440-11329-6). Dell.

Marchington, John. Shooting: A Complete Guide for Beginners. (Illus.). 1972. 12.95 (ISBN 0-571-09868-1, Pub. by Faber & Faber). Merrimack Bk Serv.

Marchione, Margherita. Clemente Rebora. (World Authors Ser.: No. 521). 1979. lib. bdg. 13.95 (ISBN 0-8057-6362-7). Twayne.

Marchiori, Guiseppe. Matisse: The Artist & His Time. (Illus.). 1967. 12.50 o.p. (ISBN 0-688-61064-1). Reynal.

Marchmont, Arthur W. By Right of Sword. 1976. lib. bdg. 15.30x (ISBN 0-89968-064-X). Lightyear.

--In the Name of a Woman. 1976. lib. bdg. 16.30x (ISBN 0-89968-065-8). Lightyear.

--Marlwych Mystery; or, Parson Thring's Secret. 1976. lib. bdg. 15.80x (ISBN 0-89968-066-6). Lightyear.

--Miser Hoadley's Secret: A Detective Story. 1976. lib. bdg. 14.85x (ISBN 0-89968-067-4). Lightyear.

--The Mystery of Mortimore Strange. 1976. lib. bdg. 16.70x (ISBN 0-89968-068-2). Lightyear.

Marcholonis. Cancer Biology Reviews, Vol. 1. 368p. 1980. 44.50 (ISBN 0-8247-6856-6). Dekker.

Marchuk, G. I. & Nisevich, N. I., eds. Mathematical Methods in Clinical Practice. (Illus.). 150p. 1981. 60.00 (ISBN 0-08-025493-4). Pergamon.

Marciano, John, jt. auth. see Griffen, William L.

Marcion Of Sinope. The Gospel of the Lord. Hill, James H., tr. LC 78-63171. (Heresies II Ser.). 80p. 1980. Repr. of 1891 ed. 13.50 (ISBN 0-404-16186-3). AMS Pr.

Marck, Louis, jt. auth. see Rechtschaffen, Bernard.

Marckwardt, Albert H. American English. 1958. pap. text ed. 4.95x o.p. (ISBN 0-19-500960-6). Oxford U Pr.

Marco. An Introduction to Polo. (Illus.). 26.25 (ISBN 0-85131-142-3, Dist. by Sporting Book Center). J A Allen.

Marco, Anton, ed. see Bakker, Jim, et al.

Marco, Guy, et al. Information on Music: A Handbook of Reference Sources in European Languages, Vol. 2, The Americas. LC 74-32132. 1977. lib. bdg. 22.50x (ISBN 0-87287-141-X). Libs Unl.

Marco, Guy A. Information on Music: A Handbook of Reference Sources in European Languages Vol. 1, Basic & Universal Sources. LC 74-32132. 1975. lib. bdg. 17.50x (ISBN 0-87287-096-0). Libs Unl.

Marcorelles, Louis. Living Cinema: New Directions in Contemporary Flim-Making. Quigley, Isabel, tr. (Illus.). 1973. pap. 5.50 (ISBN 0-04-791026-7). Allen Unwin.

Marcos, Rafael, tr. see Gatje, Charles T. & Gatje, John F.

Marcue-Roberts, Helen, jt. auth. see Pai, Anna C.

Marcum, John A. Angolan Revolution Vol. 1: The Anatomy of an Explosion, 1950-1962. (Studies in Communism, Revisionism & Revolution). 1969. 30.00x (ISBN 0-262-13048-3). MIT Pr.

--The Angolan Revolution Volume II: Exile Politics & Guerrilla Warfare, 1962-1976. LC 69-11310. 1978. 30.00x (ISBN 0-262-13136-6). MIT Pr.

Marcus, A. & Marcus, W. Basic Electricity. 4th ed. 1973. 19.96 (ISBN 0-13-060152-7). P-H.

Marcus, Abraham. Electronics for Technicians. LC 69-10789. 1969. ref. ed. 18.95x (ISBN 0-13-252387-6). P-H.

Marcus, Abraham & Lenk, John D. Computers for Technicians. (Illus.). 400p. 1973. ref. ed. 18.95 (ISBN 0-13-166181-7). P-H.

Marcus, Abraham & Thrower, James R. Introduction to Applied Physics. 450p. 1980. text ed. 17.95x (ISBN 0-534-00825-9, Breton Pubs). Wadsworth Pub.

Marcus, Abraham, jt. auth. see Thomson, Charles M.

Marcus, Adrianne. Faced with Love. (Illus., Orig.). 1978. pap. 4.50 (ISBN 0-914278-13-4). Copper Beech.

Marcus, Adrianne, et al. Smith Special Issue 20: Poetry. pap. 1.00 o.p. (ISBN 0-685-78412-6). The Smith.

Marcus, Audrey F. & Zwerin, Raymond A. Shabbat Can Be. Syme, Daniel B., ed. (Illus.). (gr. k-3). 1979. pap. text ed. 5.00 (ISBN 0-8074-0023-8, 102560); tchrs'. guide 3.00 (ISBN 0-8074-0024-6, 208025). UAHC.

Marcus, David. A Manual of Akkadian. LC 78-63068. 1978. pap. text ed. 9.00 (ISBN 0-8191-0608-9). U Pr of Amer.

--A Manual of Babylonian Jewish Aramaic. LC 80-6073. 104p. (Orig.). 1981. pap. text ed. 7.75 (ISBN 0-8191-1363-8). U Pr of Amer.

Marcus, David, tr. see Merriman, Brian.

Marcus, Donald M., ed. The Harvey Lectures: Nineteen Seventy-Nine. 1980. write for info. (ISBN 0-12-312075-6). Acad Pr.

Marcus, Edward & Marcus, Mildred R. Economics. 1978. pap. text ed. 12.95 (ISBN 0-8403-1892-8). Kendall-Hunt.

Marcus, G. J. The Conquest of the North Atlantic. (Illus.). 256p. 1981. 25.00 (ISBN 0-19-520252-X). Oxford U Pr.

Marcus, George E. The Nobility & the Chiefly Tradition in the Modern Kingdom of Tonga. 1980. pap. text ed. 15.00x (Pub. by Polynesian Soc). U Pr of Hawaii.

Marcus, Greil. Mystery Train: Images of America in Rock 'n' Roll Music. 1976. pap. 5.50 (ISBN 0-525-47422-6). Dutton.

Marcus, Harold G. The Life & Times of Menelik II: Ethiopia 1844-1913. (Oxford Studies in African Affairs). (Illus.). 1975. 29.95x (ISBN 0-19-821674-2). Oxford U Pr.

--The Modern History of Ethiopia & the Horn of Africa: A Select & Annotated Bibliography. LC 78-155298. (Bibliographical Ser.: No. 56). 1972. 30.00 (ISBN 0-8179-2561-9). Hoover Inst Pr.

Marcus, Irving H. Dictionary of Wine Terms. 19th ed. 72p. 1979. pap. 1.25 (ISBN 0-686-64866-8). Wine Pubns.

Marcus, Isabel. Dollars for Reform: The OEO Neighborhood Health Center Experience. LC 78-2198. 1981. 22.95x (ISBN 0-669-03092-9). Lexington Bks.

Marcus, Jacob R. Israel Jacobson: The Founder of the Reform Movement in Judaism. 10.00 (ISBN 0-685-31435-9, Pub. by Hebrew Union). Ktav.

Marcus, Karin, ed. see Bawa Muhaiyaddeen, M. R.

Marcus, Leonard C. Veterinary Biology & Medicine of Captive Amphibians & Reptiles. LC 80-24859. (Illus.). 236p. 1981. text ed. write for info. (ISBN 0-8121-0700-4). Lea & Febiger.

Marcus, Leslie F. The Bingara Fauna: A Pleistocene Vertebrate Fauna from Murchison County, New South Wales, Australia. (Publications in Geological Sciences: Vol. 114). 1976. pap. 12.50x (ISBN 0-520-09538-3). U of Cal Pr.

Marcus, Maeva. Truman & the Steel Seizure Case. LC 77-4095. (Contemporary American History Ser.). 1977. text ed. 17.50x (ISBN 0-231-04126-8). Columbia U Pr.

--Truman & the Steel Seizure Case: The Limits of Presidential Power. 1979. pap. 8.00x (ISBN 0-231-04553-0). Columbia U Pr.

Marcus, Marie. Diagnostic Teaching of the Language Arts. LC 76-52400. 1977. text ed. 21.95x (ISBN 0-471-56854-6). Wiley.

Marcus, Mildred R., jt. auth. see Marcus, Edward.

Marcus, Mitchell P. Switching Circuits for Engineers. 3rd ed. (Illus.). 336p. 1975. ref. ed. 23.95 (ISBN 0-13-879908-3). P-H.

Marcus, Morton. The Armies Encamped in the Fields Beyond the Unfinished Avenues. (Illus.). 56p. 1977. pap. 2.50 (ISBN 0-937310-07-7). Jazz Pr.

--Big Winds, Glass Mornings, Shadows Cast by Stars. 64p. (Orig.). 1980. pap. 4.95 (ISBN 0-937310-06-9). Jazz Pr.

Marcus, Rebecca. Survivors of the Stone Age: Nine Tribes Today. (Illus.). 160p. (gr. 7 up). 1975. PLB 7.95 (ISBN 0-8038-6726-3). Hastings.

Marcus, Robert. The Principles of Specification Design Workbook. Weinberg, Gerald, ed. (Illus.). 284p. 1979. pap. text ed. 19.95 (ISBN 0-87619-459-5). R J Brady.

Marcus, Robert & Burner, David. American Voices: A Historical Reader, 2 vols. 1979. pap. 8.95x ea. Vol. 1 (ISBN 0-673-15172-7). Vol. 2 (ISBN 0-673-15173-5). Scott F.

Marcus, Robert D. A Brief History of the United States Since 1945. LC 74-24978. 224p. (Orig.). 1975. 15.95x (ISBN 0-312-09555-4); pap. text ed. 8.95 (ISBN 0-312-09590-2). St Martin.

Marcus, Robert D., jt. auth. see Burner, David.

Marcus, Robert D. & Burner, David, eds. America Since 1945. 2nd ed. LC 76-52588. 1977. pap. text ed. 8.95 (ISBN 0-312-03115-7). St Martin.

--American Scene: Varieties of American History, 2 vols. LC 73-136426. (Orig.). 1971. Vol. 1 Colonial Period To 1877. pap. text ed. 5.95x (ISBN 0-89197-018-5); Vol. 2 Since 1865. pap. text ed. 5.95x (ISBN 0-685-03161-6); pap. text ed. 5.95x brief ed. (colonial period to present) (ISBN 0-89197-019-3); instructor's manual free (ISBN 0-89197-020-7). Irvington.

Marcus, Samuel H. Basics of Structural Steel Design. (Illus.). 464p. 1977. text ed. 20.95 (ISBN 0-87909-069-3); student manual avail. Reston.

Marcus, Sharon, ed. see Bawa Muhaiyaddeen, M. R.

Marcus, Sheldon & Vairo, Philip D. Urban Education: Crisis or Opportunity. LC 72-5467. 1972. 10.00 (ISBN 0-8108-0531-6). Scarecrow.

Marcus, Shlomo, jt. ed. see Leibowitz, J. O.

Marcus, W., jt. auth. see Marcus, A.

Marcus, Y., et al, eds. Equilibrium Constants of Liquid-Liquid Distribution Reactions, Pt. 3: Compound Forming Extractants, Solvating Solvents & Inert Solvents. 1977. pap. text ed. 12.25 (ISBN 0-08-022032-0). Pergamon.

Marcuse, D. Principles of Optical Fiber Measurement. LC 80-2339. 1981. write for info. (ISBN 0-12-470980-X). Acad Pr.

Marcuse, Herbert. Eros & Civilization. LC 66-3219. 320p. 1974. pap. 6.95 (ISBN 0-8070-1555-5, BP496). Beacon Pr.

--One Dimensional Man. 1964. 7.50 o.p. (ISBN 0-8070-1574-1); pap. 5.95 (ISBN 0-8070-1575-X, BP221). Beacon Pr.

Marcuvitz, Nathan & Felsen, L. B. Radiation & Scattering of Waves. LC 78-167786. 1973. ref. ed. 38.00 (ISBN 0-13-750364-4). P-H.

Marcy, Carl. Presidential Commissions. LC 72-8109. (Studies in American History & Government Ser.). 156p. 1973. Repr. of 1945 ed. lib. bdg. 19.50 (ISBN 0-306-70532-X). Da Capo.

Marcy, Janis, jt. auth. see Marcy, Steve.

Marcy, Steve & Marcy, Janis. Addition & Subtraction with a Happy Ending. (Illus.). (gr. 4-7). 1976. wkbk. 4.75 (ISBN 0-88488-051-6). Creative Pubns.

Marczenko, Zygmund. Spectrophotometric Determination of Elements. LC 74-33186. (Ser. in Analytical Chemistry). 643p. 1976. 68.95 (ISBN 0-470-56865-8). Halsted Pr.

Marczewski, Jan. Crisis in Socialist Planning: Eastern Europe & the USSR. Lindsay, Noel, tr. from Fr. LC 73-15190. (Special Studies). (Illus.). 365p. 1974. text ed. 29.95 (ISBN 0-275-08140-0). Praeger.

--Inflation & Unemployment in France: A Quantitative Analysis. LC 77-25490. (Praeger Special Studies). 1978. 23.95 (ISBN 0-03-040921-7). Praeger.

Marden, Brice. Suicide Notes. (Illus.). 1974. 4.95 o.p. (ISBN 0-685-67985-3). Minneapolis Inst Arts.

Marden, P. G. & Hodgson, D., eds. Population, Environment & the Quality of Life. LC 74-579. 328p. 1975. pap. 9.95 (ISBN 0-470-56868-2). Halsted Pr.

Marder, Arthur. Operation Menace: The Dakar Expedition & the Dudley North Affair. 1976. 24.95x (ISBN 0-19-215811-2). Oxford U Pr.

Marder, Arthur J. From the Dreadnought to Scapa Flow: The Royal Navy in the Fisher Era, 1904-1919, 5 vols. Incl. Vol. 1. The Road to War, 1904-1914. 1961. 28.50x (ISBN 0-19-215122-3); Vol. 3. Jutland & After. 2nd ed. 1978. 23.50x (ISBN 0-19-215841-4); Vol. 4. 1917: Year of Crisis. 1969. 24.00x (ISBN 0-19-215170-3); Vol. 5. Victory & Aftermath. 1970. 27.95x (ISBN 0-19-215187-8). Oxford U Pr.

Marder, L. Time & the Space-Traveller. LC 77-182498. (Illus.). 1974. 9.95x (ISBN 0-8122-7650-7); pap. 4.95x (ISBN 0-8122-1054-9). U of Pa Pr.

--Vector Analysis. (Unwin Studies in Physics & Applied Mathematics). 1970. text ed. 7.95x o.p. (ISBN 0-04-512010-2). Allen Unwin.

Mardin, Yusuf. Colloquial Turkish. (Trubner's Colloquial Manuals). 1961. pap. 8.95 (ISBN 0-7100-8415-3). Routledge & Kegan.

Mardock, Robert W., jt. ed. see Richmond, Robert W.

Mardon, D. K. An Illustrated History of the Rothschild Collection of Fleas (siphonaptera) in the British Museum (Natural History) Vol. Six. Pygiopsyllidae. (Illus.). 296p. 1981. 100.00x (ISBN 0-565-00820-X, Pub. by Brit Mus Nat Hist England). Sabbot-Natural Hist Bks.

Mare, Eric De see De Mare, Eric.

Mare, Walter De La see De La Mare, Walter.

Mare, Walter de la see De La Mare, Walter.

Marechal, Ernest, jt. auth. see Kennedy, Joseph P.

Marechal, Sylvain. Culte et Loix D'une Societe D'hommes Sans Dieu. 64p. (Fr.). 1977. lib. bdg. 16.25x o.p. (ISBN 0-8287-0577-1); pap. text ed. 6.25x o.p. (ISBN 0-685-75625-4). Clearwater Pub.

Mare de la, Walter see De La Mare, Walter.

Marek, George R. Beethoven: Biography of a Genius. LC 72-85745. (Funk & W Bk.). (Illus.). 1969. 17.50 o.s.i. (ISBN 0-308-70104-6, TYC-T). T Y Crowell.

--Cosima Wagner. LC 80-7591. (Illus.). 256p. 1981. 15.95 (ISBN 0-06-012704-X, HarpT). Har-Row.

Marek, Julius & Sten, Terje. Traffic Environment & the Driver: Driver Behavior & Training in International Perspective. (Illus.). 284p. 1977. 24.75 (ISBN 0-398-03508-3); pap. 17.75 (ISBN 0-398-03509-1). C C Thomas.

Marek, R., ed. see Rose, Howard.

Maren, Jacobus W. Van see Van Maren, Jacobus W.

Marenbon, J. From the Circle of Alcuin to the School of Auxerre. (Cambridge Studies in Medieval Life & Thought: Third Ser., Vol. 15). (Illus.). 248p. Date not set. price not set (ISBN 0-521-23428-X). Cambridge U Pr.

Marenco, Ethne K. Transformation of Sikh Society. 342p. pap. 10.95 (ISBN 0-913244-08-2). Hapi Pr.

Marenzio, Luca. Il Settimo Libro de, Madrigali a Cinque Voci 1595: Luca Marenzio, the Secular Works, 14. Myers, Patricia, tr. (Illus.). xxxv, 224p. 1980. 35.00x (ISBN 0-8450-7114-9). Broude.

--Madrigali a Quattr Cinque e Sei Vodi, Libro Primo 1588: Luca Marenzio, the Secular Works, No. 7. Ledbetter, Steven, ed. xxvi, 167p. 1977. lib. bdg. 25.00 (ISBN 0-8450-7107-6). Broude.

--Ten Madrigals for Mixed Voices. Arnold, Denis, ed. 1966. 6.50x (ISBN 0-19-343675-2). Oxford U Pr.

Marer, Paul. U. S. Financing of East-West Trade: Studies in East European & Soviet Planning, Development, & Trade. (No. 22). 1975. pap. text ed. 8.00 (ISBN 0-89249-030-6). Intl Development.

Marer, Paul & Montias, John M., eds. East European Integration & East-West Trade. LC 79-3181. 416p. 1980. 32.50x (ISBN 0-253-16865-1). Ind U Pr.

Mares, E. A. The Unicorn Poem. 30p. (Orig.). 1980. pap. 3.00 (ISBN 0-88235-045-5). San Marcos.

Maresca, Thomas E., tr. see Bernardus Silvestris.

Marese, M. A., ed. Advances in Electronic Circuit Packaging, Vol. 4. 490p. 1964. 25.00 (ISBN 0-306-37014-X, Plenum Pr). Plenum Pub.

Mareth. Opening the Channels: The Changing Control of Public T. V. cancelled (ISBN 0-8070-3214-X). Beacon Pr.

Marett, R. R. Psychology & Folklore. 284p. 1971. Repr. of 1920 ed. text ed. 14.75x (ISBN 9-0623-4028-8). Humanities.

Marett, Robert R. Psychology & Folk-Lore. LC 74-10825. 275p. Repr. of 1920 ed. 18.00 (ISBN 0-8103-4045-3). Gale.

Maretzek, Max. Crochets & Quavers: Or Revelations of an Opera Manager in America. 2nd ed. LC 65-23397. (Music Ser). 1966. Repr. of 1855 ed. lib. bdg. 27.50 (ISBN 0-306-70915-5). Da Capo.

Marevna. Life with the Painters of la Ruche. LC 73-10564. (Illus.). 240p. 1974. 6.95 o.s.i. (ISBN 0-02-579450-7). Macmillan.

Marfia, Jim, tr. see Nimzovich, Aron.

Margach, James. The Abuse of Power: The War Between Downing Street & the Media from Lloyd George to James Callaghan. (Illus.). 1978. 15.95 (ISBN 0-491-02044-9). Transatlantic.

Margah, Irish, jt. auth. see Monroe, Elvira.

Margalith, Pinhas. Flavor Microbiology. (Illus.). 336p. 1980. 31.50 (ISBN 0-398-04083-4). C C Thomas.

Margaretten, Selma, tr. see Castro, Americo.

Marge, M., jt. auth. see Irwin, J.

Margen, Sheldon, ed. Progress in Human Nutrition, Vol. 2. (Illus.). 1978. text ed. 23.50 (ISBN 0-87055-255-4). AVI.

--Symposium: Progress in Human Nutrition. (Illus.). 1971. text ed. 23.50 (ISBN 0-87055-101-9). AVI.

Margenau, H. & Kestner, N. Theory of Intermolecular Forces. 2nd ed. 1971. 52.00 (ISBN 0-08-016502-8). Pergamon.

Margenau, Henry & Bergamini, David. Scientist. LC 64-8795. (Life Science Library). (Illus.). (gr. 5 up). 1964. PLB 8.97 o.p. (ISBN 0-8094-0466-4, Pub. by Time-Life). Silver.

Marger, Martin. Elites & Masses: An Introduction to Political Sociology. 1980. text ed. 15.95 (ISBN 0-442-25410-5); instr's. manual 2.00 (ISBN 0-442-24628-5). D Van Nostrand.

Margerison, Charles. How to Assess Your Managerial Style. 167p. 1981. 12.95 (ISBN 0-8144-5632-4). Am Mgmt.

Margerison, D. & East, G. C. An Introduction to Polymer Chemistry. 1966. 25.00 (ISBN 0-08-011891-7); pap. 12.75 (ISBN 0-08-011890-9). Pergamon.

Margeson, John M., ed. see World Shakespeare Congress, Vancouver, August 1971.

Margetson, Stella. Fifty Years of Victorian London. Date not set. 5.95 o.p. (ISBN 0-8038-7737-4). Hastings.

--Victorian High Society. LC 80-7989. (Illus.). 216p. 1980. text ed. 29.50x (ISBN 0-8419-0643-2). Holmes & Meier.

--Victorian People. 1977. 16.95 (ISBN 0-7134-1010-8, Pub. by Batsford England). David & Charles.

Margie, Joyce D., et al. Living Better: Recipes for a Healthy Heart. LC 80-66979. 320p. Date not set. 14.95 (ISBN 0-8019-7018-0). Chilton.

Margiotta, Franklin D., ed. The Changing World of the American Military. (Westview Special Studies in Military Affairs). 1978. lib. bdg. 27.50x (ISBN 0-89158-331-9); pap. 12.00x (ISBN 0-89158-309-2). Westview.

Margison, G. P., jt. ed. see Canonico.

Margittai, Tom G. & Kovi, Paul. The Four Seasons: Splendid Recipes from the World-Famous Restaurant. 1980. 24.95 (ISBN 0-671-25022-1). S&S.

Marglin, Stephen A. Value & Price in the Labor-Surplus Economy. (Illus.). 296p. 1976. 29.95x (ISBN 0-19-828194-3). Oxford U Pr.

Margo. Growing New Hair! How to Keep What You Have & Fill in Where It's Thin, by Margo, for Men Only. LC 80-66699. (Illus.). 112p. 1980. 7.95 (ISBN 0-394-51417-3). Autumn Pr.

Margolies, Edward, ed. Native Sons Reader. LC 74-103596. 1970. 6.95 o.p. (ISBN 0-397-47183-1); pap. 3.25 o.p. (ISBN 0-685-14246-9). Lippincott.

Margolies, Edward & Bakish, David, eds. Afro-American Fiction, Eighteen Fifty-Three to Nineteen Seventy-Six: A Guide to Information Sources. LC 73-16976. (American Literature, English Literature, & World Literatures in English Information Guide Ser.: Vol. 25). 1979. 30.00 (ISBN 0-8103-1207-7). Gale.

Margolies, John. The End of the Road. Smith, C. Ray, ed. 96p. 1981. pap. 12.95 (ISBN 0-14-005840-0). Penguin.

--The End of the Road. Smith, C. Ray, ed. (Illus.). 96p. 1981. 22.95 (ISBN 0-670-29482-9, Studio). Viking Pr.

Margolies, Luise, jt. auth. see Gasparini, Graziano.

Margolin, David, jt. auth. see Wylie, Jonathan.

Margolin, Malcolm. How We Lived: Reminiscences, Stories, Speeches, & Songs of California Indians. 1981. 10.95 (ISBN 0-930588-03-7); pap. 5.95 (ISBN 0-930588-04-5). Heyday Bks.

Margolin, Phillip M. The Last Innocent Man. 252p. 1981. 11.95 (ISBN 0-316-54617-8). Little.

Margolin, Victor. The Golden Age of the American Poster: A Concise Edition of the American Poster Renaissance. 1976. pap. 6.95 o.p. (ISBN 0-345-25129-6). Ballantine.

Margolin, Victor, ed. Paper Bullets, Propaganda Posters of WW II. LC 77-79049. (Illus.). 64p. 1980. Repr. of 1977 ed. 15.00 (ISBN 0-87754-204-X). Chelsea Hse.

Margolin, Victor, ed. see Rhodes, Anthony.

Margoliouth, David S. Cairo, Jerusalem, & Damascus, Three Chief Cities of the Egyptian Sultans. LC 80-1918. (Illus.). 1981. Repr. of 1907 ed. 54.50 (ISBN 0-404-18980-6). AMS Pr.

Margolis. The Practice of Medicine: A Self Assessment Guide. 2nd ed. (Illus.). 1980. pap. 14.95 (ISBN 0-8385-7877-2). ACC.

Margolis, Art. The Master Handbook of Electrical Wiring. (Illus.). 1978. pap. 9.95 (ISBN 0-8306-1019-7, 1019). TAB Bks.

--One Hundred Twenty-Five Typical Electronic Circuits Analyzed & Repaired. LC 73-78197. (Illus.). 224p. 1973. 7.95 o.p. (ISBN 0-8306-3658-7); pap. 4.95 (ISBN 0-8306-2658-1, 658). TAB Bks.

Margolis, Bruce L. & Kroes, William H. The Human Side of Accident Prevention: Psychological Concepts & Principles Which Bear on Industrial Safety. (Illus.). 160p. 1975. 15.50 (ISBN 0-398-03253-X). C C Thomas.

Margolis, Carmi Z. & Shapiro, Donald L. Newborn Management: Decision Trees & Management Problems. (Illus., Orig., With work sheets). 1977. pap. 11.50 (ISBN 0-913178-60-8). Redgrave Pub Co.

Margolis, Clorinda & Shrier, Linda. A Manual of Stress Management. 1981. write for info. Franklin Inst Pr.

Margolis, Diane R. The Managers: Corporate Life in America. 312p. 1981. pap. 5.95 (ISBN 0-688-00351-6, Quill). Morrow.

Margolis, Joseph. Knowledge & Existence: An Introduction to Philosophical Problems. 304p. 1973. text ed. 8.95x (ISBN 0-19-501589-4). Oxford U Pr.

--Values & Conduct. (Orig.). 1971. text ed. 9.95x (ISBN 0-19-501327-1); pap. text ed. 4.95x (ISBN 0-19-501328-X). Oxford U Pr.

Margolis, Max & Marx, Alexander. History of the Jewish People. LC 70-90074. (Temple Books). 1969. pap. text ed. 7.95x (ISBN 0-689-70134-9, T8). Atheneum.

Margolis, Maxine L. & Carter, William E., eds. Brazil: Anthropological Perspectives. LC 79-11843. Orig. Title: Anthropology of Brazil. (Illus.). 1979. 21.50x (ISBN 0-231-04714-2). Columbia U Pr.

Margolis, Neal & Harmon, N. Paul. Accounting Essentials. LC 72-4756. (Self-Teaching Guides Ser.). 320p. 1972. pap. text ed. 7.95 (ISBN 0-471-56867-8). Wiley.

Margolis, Philip M. Patient Power. 176p. 1973. 12.75 (ISBN 0-398-02839-7). C C Thomas.

Margolis, Richard. Wish Again, Big Bear. LC 75-160070. (gr. k-2). 1972. 7.95g (ISBN 0-02-762410-2). Macmillan.

Margolis, Richard J. Homer the Hunter. LC 73-185220. (Illus.). (gr. k-3). 1972. 6.95 (ISBN 0-02-762290-8). Macmillan.

Margolius, Ivan. Cubism in Architecture & the Applied Arts. LC 79-56251. (Illus.). 128p. 1980. 28.00 (ISBN 0-7153-7673-X). David & Charles.

Margolius, Sidney. Health Foods: Facts & Fakes. 256p. 1973. 6.95 o.s.i. (ISBN 0-8027-0375-5). Walker & Co.

Margoliuth, D. S., tr. see Zaydan, Jirji.

Margoliuth, David S. Mohammed. LC 79-2875. 151p. 1981. Repr. of 1939 ed. 14.50 (ISBN 0-8305-0044-8). Hyperion Conn.

Margon, Lester. Construction of American Furniture Treasures. (Illus.). 168p. 1975. pap. 5.00 (ISBN 0-486-23056-2). Dover.

--Masterpieces of American Furniture. 1965. 15.00 o.s.i. (ISBN 0-8038-0150-5). Architectural.

--Masterpieces of European Furniture Thirteen Hundred to Eighteen Forty. Date not set. 16.50 (ISBN 0-8038-0151-3). Hastings.

--More American Furniture Treasures. Date not set. 16.50 (ISBN 0-8038-0163-7). Hastings.

Margoninski, Y., ed. see Israeli Vacuum Congress, Fifth, Israel, April 1978.

Margrie, Janet. Pictures & Patterns. LC 77-8005. (Beginning Crafts Ser.). (Illus.). (gr. k-3). 1977. PLB 9.30 (ISBN 0-8393-0117-0). Raintree Child.

Marguerre, K. Mechanics of Vibrations. Wolfel, H., ed. (Mechanics of Structural Systems Ser.: No. 2). 282p. 1979. 30.00x (ISBN 90-286-0086-8). Sijthoff & Noordhoff.

Marguilies, S., tr. see Pauli, Wolfgang.

Margulas, Jerrold. Scorpion East. 1981. 12.95 (ISBN 0-87223-653-6). Seaview Bks.

Margulies, Leo, ed. Worlds of Weird. 1978. pap. 1.50 o.p. (ISBN 0-515-04826-7). Jove Pubns.

Margulies, Sylvia R. Pilgrimage to Russia: The Soviet Union & the Treatment of Foreigners, 1924-1937. 1968. 22.50 (ISBN 0-299-04720-2). U of Wis Pr.

Margulis, Alexander R. & Burhenne, H. Joachim. Alimentary Tract Radiology: Abdominal Imaging, Vol. 3. LC 72-14444. (Illus.). 1979. text ed. 87.50 (ISBN 0-8016-3134-3). Mosby.

Margulis, Alexander R. & Burhenne, H. Joachim, eds. Alimentary Tract Roentgenology, Vols. 1 & 2. 2nd ed. LC 72-14444. 1689p. 1973. Set. 157.50 (ISBN 0-8016-3131-9); Vol.1. 74.75 (ISBN 0-8016-3149-1); Vol. 2. 74.75 (ISBN 0-8016-3150-5). Mosby.

Margulis, Alexander R. & Gooding, Charles A., eds. Diagnostic Radiology, 1979. (Illus.). 125p. 1979. 96.25 (ISBN 0-89352-056-X). Masson Pub.

Margulis, Lynn. Symbiosis in Cell Evolution: Life & Its Environment on the Early Earth. LC 80-26695. (Illus.). 1981. text ed. 27.95x (ISBN 0-7167-1255-5); pap. text ed. 13.95x (ISBN 0-7167-1256-3). W H Freeman.

Margulis, Lynn, jt. ed. see Ponnamperuma, Cyril.

Marhoefer, Barbara M. Witches, Whales, Petticoats, & Sails. LC 74-151807. (Empire State Historical Publications Ser). (Illus.). 1971. 12.95 (ISBN 0-8046-8092-2). Friedman.

Maria, Robert De see De Maria, Robert.

Mariategui, Jose C. Seven Interpretive Essays on Peruvian Reality. Urquidi, Marjory, tr. LC 73-156346. (Texas Pan American Ser.). xxxvi, 302p. 1971. pap. 5.95 (ISBN 0-292-70115-2); pap. 5.95 (ISBN 0-292-77517-2). U of Tex Pr.

Maricich, Connie, jt. auth. see Hemingway, Joan.

Marie, Geraldine. The Magic Box. (Illus.). 32p. (ps-3). 1981. 5.95 (ISBN 0-525-66721-0). Elsevier-Nelson.

Marie, Jean. Gramps & the Coon Dog. Kulikowski, M. Karl, ed. (Gusto Press Poetry Discovery Ser.). (Orig.). 1979. pap. 3.95 (ISBN 0-933906-08-0). Gusto Pr.

Mariechild, Diane. Mother Wit: A Feminist Guide to Psychic Development. (Illus.). 200p. 1981. 12.95 (ISBN 0-89594-050-7); pap. 5.95 (ISBN 0-89594-051-5). Crossing Pr.

Marie Eugene. I Am a Daughter of the Church. M Verda Clare, tr. 1981. pap. cancelled (ISBN 0-87061-050-3). Chr Classics.

--I Want to See God. M. Verda Clare, tr. 1981. pap. cancelled (ISBN 0-87061-051-1). Chr Classics.

Marienthal, Hal. Best Picture: The Academy Awards, 1927 to 1980. LC 80-67901. 1981. 19.95 (ISBN 0-89615-029-1); pap. 11.95 (ISBN 0-89615-030-5). Guild of Tutors.

Marier, Donald & Wallace, Dan. Wind Power for the Homeowner: A Guide to Selecting, Siting, & Installing an Electricity-Generating Wind Power System. (Illus.). 320p. 1981. 14.95 (ISBN 0-87857-334-8); pap. 10.95 (ISBN 0-87857-350-X). Rodale Pr Inc.

Marieskind, Helen T. Women in the Health System: Patients, Providers & Programs. LC 80-19961. (Illus.). 330p. 1980. pap. text ed. 13.95 (ISBN 0-8016-3106-8). Mosby.

Mariken, Gene & Scheimann, Eugene. A Doctor's Sensible Approach to Alcohol & Alcoholism. (Illus.). 1969. pap. 2.50 (ISBN 0-685-56948-9). Budlong.

Maril, Nadja. Me, Molly Midnight, the Artist's Cat. (Illus.). (gr. k up). 1977. 7.95 (ISBN 0-916144-15-1); pap. 3.95 (ISBN 0-916144-16-X). Stemmer Hse.

Maril, S. Nadja. Runaway Molly Midnight, the Artist's Cat. LC 80-17097. (Illus.). 40p. (gr. k up). 1980. 9.95 (ISBN 0-916144-62-3); pap. 5.95 (ISBN 0-916144-63-1). Stemmer Hse.

Marill, Alvin H. The Films of Anthony Quinn. 1977. pap. 6.95 (ISBN 0-8065-0570-2). Citadel Pr.

--Samuel Goldwyn Presents. LC 75-20598. (Illus.). 352p. 1976. 19.95 o.p. (ISBN 0-498-01658-7). A S Barnes.

Marill-Alberes, Rene. Jean-Paul Sartre: Philosopher Without Faith. LC 60-15950. 1960. 4.75 (ISBN 0-8022-0015-X). Philos Lib.

Marin, jt. auth. see Chong.

Marin, A. C. Rise with the Wind. 1978. pap. 1.75 o.p. (ISBN 0-523-40455-7, Dist. by Independent News Co.). Pinnacle Bks.

Marin, Gerard P., ed. see Munoz Martin, Luis.

Marin, Javier J., tr. see Barclay, William.

Marin, Louis & Chabrol, Claude. The Gospel Narrative. Johnson, Alfred M., Jr., tr. (Pittsburgh Theological Monographs: No. 30). 1980. pap. cancelled (ISBN 0-915138-33-6). Pickwick.

Marinacci, Barbara & Marinacci, Rudy. California's Spanish Place-Names: What They Mean & How They Got There. LC 80-11381. (Illus.). 1980. pap. 6.95 (ISBN 0-89141-102-X). Presidio Pr.

Marinacci, Barbara, jt. auth. see Huff, Charles.

Marinacci, Rudy, jt. auth. see Marinacci, Barbara.

Marinaccio, Anthony & Marinaccio, M. Maxine. Human Relations & Cooperative Planning in Education & Management. 1978. pap. text ed. 7.95 (ISBN 0-8403-0921-X). Kendall-Hunt.

Marinaccio, M. Maxine, jt. auth. see Marinaccio, Anthony.

Marincola, Paula. Photography: Made in Philadelphia 4. LC 80-84551. (Illus.). 1979. pap. 4.00 (ISBN 0-88454-059-6). U of Pa Contemp Art.

Marine Board. Responding to Casualties of Ships Bearing Hazardous Cargoes. 1979. pap. 8.25 (ISBN 0-309-02935-X). Natl Acad Pr.

--Toward Fulfillment of a National Ocean Commitment. LC 70-183067. (Illus.). 572p. 1972. 5.25 (ISBN 0-309-01936-2). Natl Acad Pr.

Marine Board, Assembly of Engineering, National Research Council. Mining in the Outer Continental Shelf & in the Deep Ocean. 152p. 1975. pap. 6.25 (ISBN 0-309-02405-6). Natl Acad Pr.

--Outer Continental Shelf Frontier Technology. LC 80-82152. 1980. pap. text ed. 8.50 (ISBN 0-309-03084-6). Natl Acad Pr.

Marine, William M. British Invasion of Maryland, Eighteen Twelve to Eighteen Fifteen. Dielman, Louis H., ed. LC 66-128. (Illus.). xx, 519p. Repr. of 1913 ed. 18.00 (ISBN 0-8103-5036-X). Gale.

Mariner, Elwyn E. The Massachusetts Constitution: A Citizen's Edition. 2nd ed. LC 72-166478. 1977. pap. 3.75 (ISBN 0-685-58338-4). Mariner.

--The Massachusetts Retirement Plan. 9th ed. 1977. pap. 2.50. Mariner.

Mariner, James L. Human Reproduction & Development. (Illus.). 155p. (Orig.). (gr. 9-12). 1979. pap. text ed. 3.95x (ISBN 0-88334-118-2). Ind Sch Pr.

--An Introduction to Genetics & Evolution. (Illus.). (gr. 10-12). 1977. pap. text ed. 4.25 (ISBN 0-88334-092-5). Ind Sch Pr.

--Understanding Ecology. 207p. (gr. 9-12). 1975. pap. text ed. 4.50x (ISBN 0-88334-070-4). Ind Sch Pr.

Marinetti, Filippo. Marinetti: Selected Writings. Flint, R. W., tr. 1973. 12.95 (ISBN 0-374-20290-7); pap. 4.95 (ISBN 0-686-66758-1). FS&G.

Maring, Ester G., jt. auth. see Maring, Joel M.

Maring, Joel M. & Maring, Ester G. Historical & Cultural Dictionary of Burma. LC 73-1477. (Historical & Cultural Dictionaries of Asia Ser.: No. 4). 1973. 10.00 (ISBN 0-8108-0596-0). Scarecrow.

Maring, Norman H. American Baptists: Whence & Whither. (Orig.). 1968. pap. 2.50 o.p. (ISBN 0-8170-0398-3). Judson.

Marino, Francis A., et al. Principles of Pharmaceutical Accounting. LC 79-20380. (Illus.). 241p. 1980. text ed. 19.50 (ISBN 0-8121-0634-2). Lea & Febiger.

Marino, John, et al. John Marino's Bicycling Book. (Illus.). 320p. 1981. 12.95 (ISBN 0-87477-131-5). J P Tarcher.

Marino, Joseph P., jt. auth. see Sanders, William T.

Marino, Raul, jt. ed. see Rasmussen, Theodore.

Marino, Vito, jt. auth. see Lonstein, Albert I.

Marinone, N. & Guala, F. Complete Handbook of Greek Verbs. 353p. (YA) 1972. 9.95 (ISBN 0-685-20228-3). Schoenhof.

Mario, Thomas. Quantity Cooking. (Illus.). 1978. lib. bdg. 25.50 o.p. (ISBN 0-87055-236-8); pap. text ed. 16.00 (ISBN 0-87055-308-9). AVI.

Marion, Bruce W., et al. The Food Retailing Industry: Market Structure, Profits, & Prices. LC 78-19751. 1979. 22.95 (ISBN 0-03-046106-5). Praeger.

Marion, Frances. Off with Their Heads: A Serio-Comic Tale of Hollywood. (Illus.). 320p. 1972. 8.95 o.s.i. (ISBN 0-02-579500-7). Macmillan.

Marion, Frieda. China Half-Figures Called Pincushion Dolls. LC 74-178257. (Illus.). 1977. Repr. 7.95 (ISBN 0-89145-058-0). J Palmer.

Marion, Jerry. Classical Dynamics of Particles & Systems. 2nd ed. 1970. text ed. 22.95 (ISBN 0-12-472252-0). Acad Pr.

--Instructor's Manual for Physics in the Modern World. 2nd ed. 1980. 2.00 (ISBN 0-12-472282-2). Acad Pr.

--Physics in the Modern World. 2nd ed. 1980. 20.95 (ISBN 0-12-472280-6). Acad Pr.

--Study Guide to Physics in the Modern World. 2nd ed. 1980. 5.95 (ISBN 0-12-472284-9). Acad Pr.

Marion, Jerry B. Classical Electromagnetic Radiation. 1965. text ed. 21.50 o.p. (ISBN 0-12-472256-3). Acad Pr.

--Energy in Perspective. 1974. 9.95 (ISBN 0-12-472275-X). Acad Pr.

--General Physics with Bioscience Essays. LC 78-4487. 1979. text ed. 23.95x (ISBN 0-471-56911-9); tchrs. manual avail. (ISBN 0-471-03672-2); study guide avail. (ISBN 0-471-03673-0). Wiley.

Marion, Jerry B. & Van Patter, Douglas M., eds. Nuclear Research with Low Energy Nuclear Accelerators. 1967. 48.50 (ISBN 0-12-472259-8). Acad Pr.

Marion, Marion C. Guidance of Young Children. (Illus.). 226p. 1981. pap. text ed. 7.95 (ISBN 0-8016-3108-4). Mosby.

Marion, Mildred F., et al. Pharmacology Learning Guide. (Illus.). 100p. 1981. pap. text ed. 7.95 (ISBN 0-8016-3109-2). Mosby.

Marion, Phyllis. A Manual of AACR 2 Examples for Legal Materials. McClaskey, Marilyn J. & Swanson, Edward, eds. 50p. 1980. pap. 6.00 (ISBN 0-936996-08-0). Soldier Creek.

Marion, Robert. Educators, Parents & Exceptional Children. (Illus.). 275p. 1980. text ed. write for info. (ISBN 0-89443-334-2). Aspen Systems.

Mariotti, F. A., tr. see Hunter, Emily.

Mariotti, Federico A., tr. see Bryant, Cyril E.

Maris, Humphrey J., ed. Phonon Scattering in Condensed Matter. 500p. 1980. 52.50 (ISBN 0-306-40355-2, Plenum Pr). Plenum Pub.

Maris, Ronald W. Pathways to Suicide: A Survey of Self-Destructive Behaviors. LC 80-24520. (Illus.). 512p. 1981. text ed. 26.50x (ISBN 0-8018-2437-0). Johns Hopkins.

Maris, Terry. Assessment Centers. 1981. text ed. cancelled (ISBN 0-89832-014-3). Brighton Pub Co.

Marishall, Jean. The History of Miss Clarinda Cathcart and Miss Fanny Renton, 1765, 2 vols. in 1. (The Flowering of the Novel, 1740-1775 Ser: Vol. 71). 1974. lib. bdg. 50.00 (ISBN 0-8240-1170-8). Garland Pub.

Marison, Fiscar, tr. The Passion of Our Lord. 302p. 1980. pap. 3.95 (ISBN 0-911988-37-8). AMI Pr.

Maritain, Jacques. Bersognian Philosophy & Thomism. 1955. 6.00 o.p. (ISBN 0-8022-1057-0). Philos Lib.

--Essay on Christian Philosophy. Flannery, Edward H., tr. 1955. 20.00x (ISBN 0-89197-150-5). Irvington.

--Integral Humanism: Temporal & Spiritual Problems of a New Christendom. Evans, Joseph W., tr. from Fr. LC 73-12509. Orig. Title: Humanisme Integral. 328p. (Eng. & Fr.). 1973. text ed. 10.95x (ISBN 0-268-00516-8); pap. text ed. 3.95x (ISBN 0-268-00510-9). U of Notre Dame Pr.

Mariti, Giovanni. Travels in the Island of Cyprus. Cobham, Claude D., et al, trs. from Gr. (Bibliotheca Historica Cyprica). 1971. text ed. 11.75x (ISBN 0-900834-20-X). Humanities.

Maritime Transportation Research Board, National Research Council. Critical Issues in Coal Transportation Systems. 1979. pap. text ed. 9.75 (ISBN 0-309-02869-8). Natl Acad Pr.

Maritime Transportation Research Board. Legal Impediments to International Intermodal Transportation. LC 72-170156. 1971. pap. text ed. 5.50 (ISBN 0-309-01924-9). Natl Acad Pr.

Maritime Transportation Research Board, National Research Council. Maritime Metrication: A Recommended Metric Conversion Plan for the U.S. Maritime Industry. LC 76-1348. 121p. 1976. pap. 5.25 (ISBN 0-309-02447-1). Natl Acad Pr.

--Port Development in the United States. LC 76-5180. xv, 244p. 1976. pap. 6.50 (ISBN 0-309-02448-X). Natl Acad Pr.

--Public Involvement in Maritime Facility Development. 1979. pap. text ed. 7.00 (ISBN 0-309-02868-X). Natl Acad Pr.

Marivaux, de Pierre see De Marivaux, Pierre.

Marivaux, Pierre. Pharsamond; or, the New Knight-Errant, 1750, 2 vols. in 1. LC 74-17039. (Novel in England, 1700-1775 Ser). 1974. lib. bdg. 50.00 (ISBN 0-8240-1129-5). Garland Pub.

Marivaux, Pierre C. De Chamblain De see De Chamblain De Marivaux, Pierre C.

Marjoram, D. T. Exercises in Modern Mathematics. 1965. text ed. 6.95 (ISBN 0-08-011004-5); pap. 5.40 (ISBN 0-08-011003-7). Pergamon.

--Further Exercises in Modern Mathematics. 1966. text ed. 6.95 (ISBN 0-08-011969-7); pap. 5.40 (ISBN 0-08-011968-9). Pergamon.

--Modern Mathematics in Secondary Schools. 1964. text ed. 6.95 (ISBN 0-08-010719-2); pap. 5.40 (ISBN 0-08-010718-4). Pergamon.

Marjoribanks, Kevin. Families & Their Learning Environments. 1979. 22.00x (ISBN 0-7100-0167-3). Routledge & Kegan.

Mark, Charles & Mark, Paula F., eds. Sociology of America: A Guide to Information Sources. LC 73-17560. (American Studies Information Guide Ser.: Vol. 1). 564p. 1976. 30.00 (ISBN 0-8103-1267-0). Gale.

Mark, H., jt. auth. see Overberger, C.

Mark, H., et al, eds. Chemical After Treatment of Textiles. LC 70-147234. 1971. 63.50 o.p. (ISBN 0-471-56989-5, Pub. by Wiley-Interscience). Wiley.

Mark, H. F., et al. Encyclopedia of Polymer Science & Technology, 16 vols. Incl. Vol. 1. 1964 (ISBN 0-470-56970-0); Vol. 2. 1965 (ISBN 0-470-56973-5); Vol. 3. 1965 (ISBN 0-470-56975-1); Vol. 4. 1966 (ISBN 0-470-56977-8); Vol. 5. 1966 (ISBN 0-470-56979-4); Vol. 6. 1967 (ISBN 0-470-56980-8); Vol. 7. 1967 (ISBN 0-470-56981-6); Vol. 8. 1968 (ISBN 0-470-56982-4); Vol. 9. 1968 (ISBN 0-470-56983-2); Vol. 10. 1969 (ISBN 0-471-56984-4); Vol. 11. 1969 (ISBN 0-471-56969-0); Vol. 12. 1970 (ISBN 0-471-56992-5); Vol. 13. 1970 (ISBN 0-471-56993-3); Vol. 14. 1971 (ISBN 0-471-56994-1); Vol. 15. 1971 (ISBN 0-471-56995-X); Vol. 16. Index. 1972 (ISBN 0-471-56996-8). LC 64-22188. 85.00 ea.; Set. write for info. (ISBN 0-471-04184-X); supplements for vols. 1-2 avail. Supplement, Vol. 1 (ISBN 0-471-56997-6). Supplement, Vol. 2 (ISBN 0-471-56998-4). Wiley.

--Man-Made Fibers. LC 67-13954. (Polymer Engineering & Technology Ser.). 1967-68. Vol. 1. 40.00 (ISBN 0-470-56985-9, Pub. by Wiley-Interscience); Vol. 2. 42.50 (ISBN 0-470-56986-7); 62.50 (ISBN 0-470-56987-5). Wiley.

Mark, Herman F. Giant Molecules. LC 66-19119. (Life Science Library). (Illus.). (gr. 5 up). 1966. PLB 8.97 o.p. (ISBN 0-8094-0474-5, Pub. by Time-Life). Silver.

Mark, Jeffrey. Saving & Spending. 1980. lib. bdg. 59.95 (ISBN 0-8490-3083-8). Gordon Pr.

Mark, Joan T. Four American Anthropologists. 1980. lib. bdg. write for info. (ISBN 0-88202-190-7). N Watson.

Mark, Mary E. Falkland Road: Prostitutes of Bombay. LC 80-11778. (Illus.). 96p. 1981. 25.00 (ISBN 0-394-50987-0); pap. 12.95 (ISBN 0-394-74000-9). Knopf.

Mark, Melvin & Foster, Arthur R. Thermodynamics: Principles & Applications. 1979. text ed. 23.50 (ISBN 0-205-06631-3, 3266311); solutions man. o.p. avail. (ISBN 0-205-06632-1). Allyn.

Mark, Paula F., jt. ed. see Mark, Charles.

Mark, Peter A. Africans in European Eyes-the Portrayal of Black Africans in Fourteenth & Fifteenth Century Europe. LC 74-25878. (Foreign & Comparative Studies-Eastern African Ser.: No. 16). 98p. 1975. pap. 4.50x (ISBN 0-915984-13-X). Syracuse U Foreign Comp.

Mark, Polly. Nurse Molly's Search. 1978. 5.95 (ISBN 0-685-86410-3, Avalon). Bouregy.

Mark, Robert, ed. Policing a Perplexed Society. 1977. pap. text ed. 8.95x o.p. (ISBN 0-04-363006-5). Allen Unwin.

Mark, Robert A., jt. auth. see Hamersma, Richard J.

Mark, Ted. The Man from O.R.G.Y. Thy Neighbor's Orgy. 272p. (Orig.). 1981. pap. 2.25 (ISBN 0-89083-701-5). Zebra.

Mark, Theonie. Greek Islands Cooking. 1979. 27.00 (ISBN 0-7134-1283-6, Pub. by Batsford England). David & Charles.

Mark, W. D., jt. auth. see Crandall, Stephen H.

Markandaya, Kamala. The Golden Honeycomb. LC 76-27642. 1977. 10.00 o.s.i. (ISBN 0-690-01208-X, TYC-T). T Y Crowell.

Markarian, Ohannes, jt. auth. see Daniels, George.

Marke, Julius J. & Bander, Edward J. Commercial Law Information Sources. LC 73-120909. (Management Information Guide Ser.: No. 17). 1970. 30.00 (ISBN 0-8103-0817-7). Gale.

Markel, J. D., jt. ed. see Schafer, R. W.

Markel, J. E. & Gray, A. H. Linear Prediction of Speech. (Communications & Cybernetics Ser.: Vol. 12). (Illus.). 305p. 1976. 43.10 (ISBN 0-387-07563-1). Springer-Verlag.

Markel, R., ed. see Marx, Joseph L.

Markel, Robert, ed. see Ginott, Haim G.

Markel, Robert, ed. see Jacobson, Dan.

Markel, Robert, ed. see Silverman, Jerry.

Markel, Robert, ed. see Stetson, Damon.

Markell, Edward K. & Voge, Marietta. Medical Parasitology. 5th ed. (Illus.). 400p. 1981. text ed. price not set (ISBN 0-7216-6082-7). Saunders.

Marken, Jack W. American Indian: Language & Literature. LC 76-4624. (Goldentree Bibliographies in Language & Literature). 1978. pap. text ed. 12.95x (ISBN 0-88295-553-5). AHM Pub.

Marken, Jack W. & Hoover, Herbert T. Bibliography of the Sioux. LC 80-20106. (Native American Bibliography Ser.: No. 1). 388p. 1980. 17.50 (ISBN 0-8108-1356-4). Scarecrow.

Marken, Richard. Methods in Experimental Psychology. LC 80-20320. 375p. (Orig.). 1981. pap. text ed. 12.95 (ISBN 0-8185-0431-5). Brooks-Cole.

Marker, Frederick J. Kjeld Abell. LC 76-6102. (World Authors Ser.: Denmark: No. 394). 1976. lib. bdg. 12.50 (ISBN 0-8057-6236-1). Twayne.

Marker, Frederick J. & Marker, Lise-Lone. Edward Gordon Craig & the Pretenders: A Production Revisited. (Special Issues Ser.). (Illus.). Date not set. price not set (ISBN 0-8093-0966-1). S Ill U Pr.

Marker, Lise-Lone, jt. auth. see Marker, Frederick J.

Markert, Christopher. Your Hidden Potential: A Dynamic New System for Discovering the Power Within You. LC 80-23848. 172p. 1980. Repr. of 1980 ed. lib. bdg. 14.95x (ISBN 0-89370-647-7). Borgo Pr.

Market Linkage Project for Special Education, ed. Educational Products for the Exceptional Child. 1981. 45.00x (ISBN 0-912700-84-X). Oryx Pr.

Markey, T. L. H. C. Branner. (World Authors Ser.: Denmark: No. 245). 1973. lib. bdg. 10.95 (ISBN 0-8057-2172-X). Twayne.

Markey, T. L., ed. & tr. from Swedish. On Dating Phonological Change: A Miscellany of Articles by Lennart Moberg, Axel Kock, and Ernst Wigforss. (Linguistica Extranea Ser.: Studia 1). 113p. 1978. lib. bdg. 8.25 (ISBN 0-89720-002-0); pap. 5.50 (ISBN 0-89720-000-4). Karoma.

Markey, T. L., ed. see Hesseling, Dirk C.

Markey, T. L., ed. & tr. see Schuchardt, Hugo.

Markey, Thomas L. Frisian. (Contributions to the Sociology of Language Ser.: No. 30). 1979. text ed. 40.00x (ISBN 90-279-3128-3). Mouton.

Markham, Gervase & Sampson, Willliam. The True Tragedy of Herod & Antipater. Ross, Gordon N. & Orgel, Stephen, eds. LC 78-66833. (Renaissance Drama Ser.). 1979. lib. bdg. 28.00 (ISBN 0-8240-9734-3). Garland Pub.

Markham, Hugh. Scale Model Aircraft from Vac-Form Kits. (Illus.). 48p. (Orig.). 1978. pap. 5.00x (ISBN 0-905418-34-4). Intl Pubns Serv.

Markham, Jesse W. & Teplitz, Paul V. Baseball Economics & Public Policy. LC 79-6032. 1981. write for info. (ISBN 0-669-03607-2). Lexington Bks.

Markham, Marion M. Escape from Velos. (Prime Time Adventures Ser.). (Illus.). 64p. (gr. 4 up). 1981. PLB 7.95 (ISBN 0-516-02106-0). Childrens.

Marki, Ivan. The Trial of the Poet: An Interpretation of the First Edition of Leaves of Grass. LC 76-18792. 1976. 20.00x (ISBN 0-231-03984-0). Columbia U Pr.

Markiewicz, Dana. Ejido Organization in Mexico Nineteen Thirty-Four to Nineteen Seventy-Six. LC 79-620057. (Special Studies: Vol. 1). 1980. pap. text ed. 6.50 (ISBN 0-87903-501-3). UCLA Lat Am Ctr.

Markin, Rom J. Marketing. LC 78-11242. (Wiley Series in Marketing). 1979. text ed. 21.95 (ISBN 0-471-01999-2); tchrs. manual avail. (ISBN 0-471-02001-X); study guide avail. (ISBN 0-471-02000-1); tests avail. (ISBN 0-471-04828-3). Wiley.

Markl, H. & Feldman, M., eds. Evolution of Social Behavior: Hypotheses & Empirical Tests. (Dahlem Workshop Reports,Life Sciences Research Report Ser.: No. 18). (Illus.). 261p. (Orig.). 1980. pap. text ed. 22.50 (ISBN 0-89573-033-2). Verlag Chemie.

Markland, P. R., jt. auth. see Harding, T. D.

Markland, Robert E. Topics in Management Science. LC 78-17932. (Management & Administration Ser.). 1979. text ed. 26.95 (ISBN 0-471-01745-0); tchrs. manual (ISBN 0-471-01746-9). Wiley.

Markle, A. The Law of Arrest & Search & Seizure. (Illus.). 320p. 1974. 19.75 (ISBN 0-398-03188-6). C C Thomas.

Markle, Allan, jt. auth. see Rinn, Roger C.

Markle, Arnold. Criminal Investigation & Presentation of Evidence. (Criminal Justice Ser.). 1976. 12.95; instrs.' manual avail. (ISBN 0-8299-0370-4); pap. write for info. West Pub.

Markle, Gerald E. & Petersen, James C., eds. The Laetrile Phenomenon: Politics, Science, & Cancer. LC 80-13466. 208p. 1980. 20.00 (ISBN 0-89158-854-X); pap. 9.75 (ISBN 0-86531-046-7). Westview.

Markle, Gerald E. & Peterson, James C., eds. Politics, Science, & Cancer: The Laetrile Phenomenon. (AAAS Selected Symposium: No. 46). 250p. 1980. lib. bdg. 20.00 (ISBN 0-89158-854-X); pap. 9.50 (ISBN 0-86531-046-7). Westview.

Markle, Joyce B. Fighters & Lovers: Theme in the Novels of John Updike. LC 72-96469. 1973. 12.00x (ISBN 0-8147-5362-0). NYU Pr.

Markle, Susan M. Good Frames & Bad: A Grammer of Frame Writing. 2nd ed. LC 71-91153. 1969. pap. 16.50 (ISBN 0-471-57013-3); tchrs'. manual avail. (ISBN 0-471-57014-1). Wiley.

Markley, Francis X. Mercy with Love. (Illus.). 128p. 1980. 7.95 (ISBN 0-89962-025-6). Todd & Honeywell.

Markley, J. Gerald, tr. Epic of the Cid. LC 61-14564. 1961. pap. 3.95 (ISBN 0-672-60259-8, LLA77). Bobbs.

Markley, R. W., jt. auth. see Sheeler, W. D.

Markley, Rayner W. Handwriting Workbook. (Welcome to English Ser.). 1977. pap. text ed. 2.50x (ISBN 0-19-520029-2). Oxford U Pr.

Markman, Sidney D. Horse in Greek Art. LC 72-88057. (Illus.). 1969. Repr. of 1943 ed. 17.50x (ISBN 0-8196-0247-7). Biblo.

Markmann, Charles Lam, tr. see Petacco, Arrigo.

Marko, Katherine D. How the Wind Blows. LC 80-22754. 32p. (gr. 2-4). 1981. 5.95g (ISBN 0-687-17680-8). Abingdon.

Markoe, Karen & Phillips, Louis. Nutty Nock-Nocks. (Funnybones Ser.). (Illus.). 64p. (gr. 3-7). 1981. pap. 1.50 (ISBN 0-671-42249-9). Wanderer Bks.

--Sneakers. (Funnybones Ser.). (Illus.). 64p. 1981. pap. 1.50 (ISBN 0-671-42117-4). Wanderer Bks.

Markoe, Karen, jt. auth. see Phillips, Louis.

Markoff, Annabelle M. Teaching Low Achieving Children Reading, Spelling & Handwriting: Developing Perceptual Skills with the Graphic Symbols of the Language. (Illus.). 320p. 1976. 22.75 (ISBN 0-398-03483-4). C C Thomas.

Markov, Vladimir. Russian Futurism: A History. (Illus.). 1968. 22.75x o.p. (ISBN 0-520-00811-1). U of Cal Pr.

Markovic, Mihailo. From Affluence to Praxis: Philosophy & Social Criticism. 1980. 5.95 (ISBN 0-472-64000-3). U of Mich Pr.

Markovitz, R. L. African Politics & Society. LC 79-88119. 1970. pap. text ed. 9.95 (ISBN 0-02-920070-9). Free Pr.

Markovskii, N. I. Paleogeographic Principles of Oil & Gas Prospecting. LC 75-12798. 256p. 1979. 54.95x (ISBN 0-470-57215-9). Halsted Pr.

Markow, Herbert L. Small Boat Law Nineteen Seventy-Eight Supplement. LC 79-88475. 1979. pap. 14.95 (ISBN 0-934108-01-3). H L Markow.

--Small Boat Law: Nineteen Seventy-Nine to Nineteen Eighty Supplement. 1981. pap. write for info. (ISBN 0-934108-02-1). H L Markow.

--Small Boat Law Supplement 1979-1980. (Orig.). 1981. pap. write for info. (ISBN 0-934108-02-1). H L Markow.

Markowicz, Leon. Latin Correspondence by Alberice Gentili & John Rainolds on Academic Drama. (Salzburgh Studies in English Literature: Elizabethan & Renaissance Studies: No. 68). 1977. pap. text ed. 25.00x (ISBN 0-391-01473-0). Humanities.

Markowitz, Arnold L., ed. Historic Preservation: A Guide to Information Sources. LC 80-14313. (Art & Architecture Information Guide Ser.: Vol. 13). 220p. 1980. 30.00 (ISBN 0-8103-1460-6). Gale.

Markowitz, Endel. The Encyclopedia Yiddishanica. LC 79-89973. (Illus.). 450p. 1980. 24.95 (ISBN 0-933910-03-7); pap. write for info. (ISBN 0-933910-04-5). Haymark.

Markowitz, Gerald, jt. auth. see Cooke, Blanche.

Markowitz, Hal, ed. Behavior of Captive Wild Animals. LC 77-18156. (Illus.). 1978. text ed. 18.95x (ISBN 0-88229-385-0). Nelson-Hall.

Markowitz, Irving L. Power & Class in Africa: An Introduction to Change & Conflict in African Politics. 1977. pap. text ed. 11.95 (ISBN 0-13-686642-5). P-H.

Markowitz, Milton & Gordis, Leon. Rheumatic Fever. 2nd ed. LC 72-82808. (Major Problems in Clinical Pediatrics Ser.: Vol. 2). (Illus.). 309p. 1972. 13.50 (ISBN 0-7216-6091-6). Saunders.

Markowitz, Norman D. The Rise & Fall of the People's Century: Henry A. Wallace & American Liberalism, 1941-1948. LC 72-86508. (Illus.). 1973. 8.95 o.s.i. (ISBN 0-02-920090-3). Free Pr.

Marks, Alan. The Antenna Syndrome. 1979. pap. 1.75 (ISBN 0-505-51343-9). Tower Bks.

--Bearknife Gold. 1980. pap. 1.75 (ISBN 0-505-51453-2). Tower Bks.

Marks, Alex. Oceanic Pipeline Computations. 560p. 1980. 75.00 (ISBN 0-87814-143-X). Pennwell Pub.

Marks, Alfred H., jt. auth. see Polster, Edythe.

Marks, Anne W., ed. N P T: Paradoxes & Problems. LC 75-826. 1975. pap. 1.50 (ISBN 0-87003-022-1). Carnegie Endow.

Marks, Anthony E. Preceramic Sites. Save-Soderbergh, Torgny, ed. (Scandinavian Joint Expedition to Sudanese Nubia). (Illus.). 1970. text ed. 13.50x (ISBN 0-8419-8801-3). Holmes & Meier.

Marks, Barry A. E. E. Cummings. (U. S. Authors Ser.: No. 46). 1963. lib. bdg. 9.95 (ISBN 0-8057-0176-1). Twayne.

Marks, Bernard H. Basic & Clinical Pharmacology of Digitalis. (Illus.). 344p. 1972. 27.75 (ISBN 0-398-02350-6). C C Thomas.
Marks, Burton & Golfarb, Gerald. Winning with Your Lawyer. (McGraw-Hill Paperbacks Ser.). 224p. (Orig.). 1980. pap. 6.95 (ISBN 0-07-040390-2, SB). McGraw.
Marks, Burton & Marks, Rita. Give a Magic Show! LC 77-5436. (gr. 2-6). 1977. 7.25 o.p. (ISBN 0-688-41819-8); PLB 6.96 (ISBN 0-688-51819-2). Lothrop.
--Kites for Kids. LC 79-22559. (Illus.). (gr. 3 up). 1980. 6.95 (ISBN 0-688-41930-5); PLB 6.67 (ISBN 0-688-51930-X). Lothrop.
Marks, Cara G. A Handbook of Hebrew Calligraphy: The ABC's of the Alef-Bet. (Illus.). 128p. 1981. 10.95 (ISBN 0-89961-010-2); pap. 5.95 (ISBN 0-89961-011-0). SBS Pub.
Marks, Celia. Come into My Kitchen. 1969. spiral bd. 7.95. Plum Nelly.
Marks, Charles. Portal Venous System. (Illus.). 160p. 1973. 17.75 (ISBN 0-398-02708-0). C C Thomas.
Marks, Charles E. Commissurotomy, Consciousness & Unity of Mind. (Bradford Monograph Series in Cognitive & Neuro-Sciences). (Illus.). 64p. (Orig.). 1980. pap. 4.00 (ISBN 0-89706-003-2). Bradford Bks.
Marks, Claude. Pilgrims, Heretics & Lovers: A Medieval Journey. (Illus.). 320p. 1975. 14.95 o.s.i. (ISBN 0-02-579770-0). Macmillan.
Marks, David & Kammann, Richard. The Psychology of the Psychic. LC 80-7458. (Critiques of the Paranormal Ser.). 232p. 1980. 16.95 (ISBN 0-87975-121-5); pap. 8.95 (ISBN 0-87975-122-3). Prometheus Bks.
Marks, Elaine. Simone de Beauvoir: Encounters with Death. 1973. 14.00 (ISBN 0-8135-0707-3). Rutgers U Pr.
Marks, Elaine & De Courtivron, Isabelle, eds. New French Feminisms. LC 79-4698. 1979. 13.95x (ISBN 0-87023-280-0). U of Mass Pr.
Marks, Elaine, jt. ed. see Stambolian, George.
Marks, Emerson R. Coleridge on the Language of Verse. (Princeton Essays in Literature). 116p. 1981. 9.50x (ISBN 0-691-06458-X). Princeton U Pr.
Marks, Fred M. Getting the Most from Radio Control Systems. Angle, Burr, ed. LC 80-81430. (Illus.). 88p. (Orig.). 1980. pap. 8.95 (ISBN 0-89024-550-9). Kalmbach.
Marks, Geoffrey & Beatty, William K. Epidemics. LC 76-2584. 1978. pap. 4.95 o.p. (ISBN 0-684-15893-0, ScribT). Scribner.
--The Story of Medicine in America. LC 73-1369. (Illus.). 416p. 1974. 10.00 o.p. (ISBN 0-684-13537-X, ScribT). Scribner.
--Women in White. LC 70-38381. (Illus.). 288p. 6.95 o.p. (ISBN 0-684-12843-8, ScribT). Scribner.
Marks, H. S. Sketches of the Tennessee Valley in Antebellum Days. pap. 5.95 (ISBN 0-915536-02-1). H S Marks.
Marks, H. S. & Riggs, Gene B. Rivers of Florida. 4.95 (ISBN 0-915536-00-5). H S Marks.
Marks, Isaac. Cure & Care of Neuroses: Theory & Practice of Behavioral Psychotherapy. 272p. 1981. 22.50 (ISBN 0-471-08808-0, Pub. by Wiley-Interscience). Wiley.
Marks, J., jt. auth. see Tilleard-Cole, R. R.
Marks, J. M. Border Kidnap. LC 77-12725. (gr. 6 up): 1977. 6.95 (ISBN 0-525-66551-X). Elsevier-Nelson.
--Hijacked. (Alpha Books). (Illus.). 96p. (Orig.). 1979. pap. 2.25x (ISBN 0-19-424212-9). Oxford U Pr.
Marks, James R., et al. Handbook of Educational Supervision: A Guide for the Practioner. 2nd ed. 1978. text ed. 27.95 (ISBN 0-205-06020-X). Allyn.
Marks, Janet. Home Help. 112p. 1975. pap. text ed. 7.50x (ISBN 0-7135-1842-1, Pub. by Bedford England). Renouf.
Marks, Janet, jt. auth. see Shuster, Sam.
Marks, John D., jt. auth. see Marchetti, Victor.
Marks, Joseph, et al, eds. New French-English Dictionary of Slang & Colloquialisms. 1971. 8.50 o.p. (ISBN 0-525-16555-X). Dutton.
Marks, Leonard M., ed. see Chitrabhanu, Gurudev S.
Marks, Lillian B. Reister's Desire: The Origin of Reisterstown... with a Genealigical History of the Reister Family. LC 75-18893. (Illus.). 1976. 15.00 (ISBN 0-938420-16-X). Md Hist.
Marks, Marlene A. The Suing of America. LC 80-52412. 256p. 1981. 11.95 (ISBN 0-87223-658-7). Seaview Bks.
Marks, Micky K. First You Like Me. LC 69-13125. (Illus.). (gr. 3-7). 1969. 5.95 o.s.i. (ISBN 0-8193-0255-4, Four Winds); PLB 5.41 o.s.i. (ISBN 0-8193-0256-2). Schol Bk Serv.
Marks, Nancy C. Cerebral Palsied & Learning Disabled Children: A Handbook Guide to Treatment, Rehabilitation & Education. (Illus.). 424p. 1974. 23.75 (ISBN 0-398-02911-3). C C Thomas.
Marks, Paul. Stained Glass Astrology & Tarot Card Designs. (Illus.). 64p. 1980. pap. 2.95 (ISBN 0-8256-3842-9, Hidden Hse-Flash). Music Sales.
Marks, Paul F. Bibliography of Literature Concerning Yemenite-Jewish Music. LC 72-90431. (Detroit Studies in Music Bibliography Ser.: No. 27). 1973. pap. 5.00 (ISBN 0-911772-57-X). Info Coord.
Marks, Percy. The Plastic Age: A Novel. LC 80-17959. (Lost American Fiction Ser.). 352p. 1980. Repr. of 1924 ed. 12.95 (ISBN 0-8093-0984-X). S Ill U Pr.
Marks, R., jt. auth. see Robinson, A. T.
Marks, Rita, jt. auth. see Marks, Burton.
Marks, Robert. Hamlet: Another Interpretation. LC 80-50694. 1980. 12.00 (ISBN 0-9605486-0-2). Raven Pub Co.
Marks, Robert W., jt. auth. see Fuller, R. Buckminster.
Marks, Ronald. Personal Selling. 576p. 1981. text ed. 17.95 (ISBN 0-205-07327-1); free (ISBN 0-205-07328-X). Allyn.
Marks, Sally. Innocent Abroad: Belgium at the Paris Peace Conference of 1919. LC 80-13698. (Illus.). 456p. 1980. 26.00x (ISBN 0-8078-1451-2). U of NC Pr.
Marks, Shula & Atmore, Anthony, eds. Economy & Society in Pre-Industrial South Africa. (Illus.). 385p. (Orig.). 1980. pap. 25.00; pap. text ed. 9.95 (ISBN 0-582-64656-1). Longman.
Marks, Thomas C., jt. auth. see Moore, Richter H., Jr.
Marks, Thomas J. Bible Study Puzzle Book. (gr. 9 up). 1981. pap. 2.50 saddlewire (ISBN 0-8054-9106-6). Broadman.
Marks, Vic. Cloudburst Two. (Illus.). 1975. lib. bdg. 11.95 (ISBN 0-88930-009-7, Pub. by Cloudburst Canada); pap. 5.95 (ISBN 0-88930-010-0). Madrona Pubs.
Markson, David. Springer's Progress. LC 76-43496. 1977. 8.95 o.p. (ISBN 0-03-020341-4). HR&W.
Markson, Elizabeth & Batra, Gretchen, eds. Public Policies for an Aging Population. LC 79-3249. (The Boston University Ser. in Gerontology). 1980. 14.95 (ISBN 0-669-03398-7). Lexington Bks.
Markstein, George. The Goering Testament. 256p. 1981. 8.95 o.p. (ISBN 0-345-28095-4); pap. text ed. 2.50 o.p. (ISBN 0-345-28047-4). Ballantine.
--Traitor. 192p. 1981. pap. 2.75 (ISBN 0-345-28609-X). Ballantine.
Markun, Maloney P. The Panama Canal. rev. ed. (First Bks.). (Illus.). (gr. 4 up). 1979. PLB 6.45 s&l (ISBN 0-531-04075-5). Watts.
Markun, Patricia M. First Book of Mining. (First Bks). (Illus.). (gr. 4-6). 1959. PLB 4.90 o.p. (ISBN 0-531-00584-4). Watts.
--First Book of Politics. LC 72-93221. (First Bks). (Illus.). (gr. 4-6). 1970. PLB 4.90 o.p. (ISBN 0-531-00692-1). Watts.
Markun, Patricia M., ed. Parenting. LC 73-87791. (Illus.). 64p. 1977. 2.50x o.p. (ISBN 0-87173-036-7). ACEI.
Markus, George. Marxism & "Anthropology". The Concept of Human Essence in the Philosophy of Marx. (Dialectic & Society Ser.: No. 4). 1978. pap. text ed. 10.00x (ISBN 90-232-1615-6). Humanities.
Markus, Gregory B. Analyzing Panel Data. LC 79-91899. (University Papers: No. 18). (Illus.). 1979. pap. 3.50x (ISBN 0-8039-1372-9). Sage.
Markus, John. Modern Electronic Circuits Reference Manual. (Illus.). 1980. 44.50 (ISBN 0-07-040446-1, P&RB). McGraw.
Markus, Julia. American Rose. 320p. 1981. 12.95 (ISBN 0-395-30229-3). HM.
Markus, Julia & Reid, Barbara. Two Novellas. 1977. lib. bdg. 17.50 o.s.i. (ISBN 0-918222-03-6); pap. 2.95 (ISBN 0-918222-04-4). Apple Wood.
--Two Novellas: A Patron of the Arts & the Tears of San Lorenzo. 2nd ed. 96p. 1981. pap. 4.95 (ISBN 0-918222-23-0). Apple Wood.
Markus, Julia, ed. see Browning, Elizabeth B.
Markus, L., jt. auth. see Lee, E. B.
Markus, Lawrence. Lectures in Differentiable Dynamics. LC 71-145637. (CBMS Regional Conference Series in Mathematics: No. 3). vi, 30p. 1971. 4.80 o.p. (ISBN 0-8218-1652-7, CBMS-3). Am Math.
Markus, R. A. Saeculum: History & Society in the Theology of St Augustine. LC 71-87136. 1970. 42.00 (ISBN 0-521-07621-8). Cambridge U Pr.
Markus, Rebecca. First Book of Glaciers. (First Bks). (Illus.). (gr. 4-6). 1962. PLB 4.90 o.p. (ISBN 0-531-00541-0). Watts.
--First Book of the Cliff Dwellers. LC 68-11138. (First Bks). (Illus.). (gr. 4-6). 1968. PLB 4.90 o.p. (ISBN 0-531-00501-1). Watts.
--William Harvey: Trailblazer of Scientific Medicine. (Biography Ser). (gr. 7 up). 1962. PLB 5.90 o.p. (ISBN 0-531-00882-7). Watts.
Markus, Rebecca B. First Book of Prehistoric Cave Paintings. LC 68-25724. (First Bks). (Illus.). (gr. 7 up). 1968. PLB 4.90 o.p. (ISBN 0-531-00614-X). Watts.
--First Book of Volcanoes & Earthquakes. rev ed. LC 72-2301. (First Bks). (Illus.). (gr. 4-6). 1972. PLB 4.90 o.p. (ISBN 0-531-00799-5). Watts.
--Moses Maimonides: Rabbi, Philosopher, & Physician. LC 69-12594. (Biography Ser). (Illus.). (gr. 7 up). 1969. PLB 6.90 (ISBN 0-531-00899-1). Watts.
Markus, Rixi. Bridge Table Tales. LC 80-67582. (Illus.). 64p. 1980. 11.95 (ISBN 0-7153-7947-X). David & Charles.
Markus, Thomas. Building Conversion & Rehabilitation. 1979. text ed. 42.95 (ISBN 0-408-00313-8). Butterworths.
Markus, Tom. The Professional Actor: From Audition to Performance. LC 79-16668. 1980. 10.00 (ISBN 0-910482-91-8); pap. 8.95 (ISBN 0-89676-009-X). Drama Bk.
Markve, Arthur. The Witnesses. Orig. Title: A New Harmony of the Gospels. 416p. 1957. kivar 5.95 (ISBN 0-87123-393-2, 210393). Bethany Fell.
Markwest, Samuel H. A Message to a Priest Who Has Abandoned the Catholic Church. (Illus.). 1980. 29.75 (ISBN 0-89266-227-1). Am Classical Coll Pr.
Marland, Michael. Language Across the Curriculum. 1977. text ed. 21.95x (ISBN 0-435-80578-9); pap. text ed. 12.95x (ISBN 0-435-80631-9). Heinemann Ed.
Marler, Charles D. Philosophy & Schooling. 1975. text ed. 17.95 (ISBN 0-205-04491-3, 2244918); student manual 5.95 (ISBN 0-205-04493-X, 2244934); instr's manual free (ISBN 0-205-04492-1, 2244926). Allyn.
Marler, E. E. Pharmacological & Chemical Synonyms. LC 73-161638. 1976. 87.50x (ISBN 0-8002-1789-6). Intl Pubns Serv.
Marlette, Douglas N. If You Can't Say Something Nice... Political Cartoons by Marlette. LC 78-73463. (Orig.). 1978. pap. 4.95 o.s.i. (ISBN 0-89284-002-1). Graphic Pr.
Marley, Diana de see De Marley, Diana.
Marlin, C. D. Coroutines. (Lecture Notes in Computer Science Ser.: Vol. 95). (Illus.). 246p. 1981. pap. 16.80 (ISBN 0-387-10256-6). Springer-Verlag.
Marlin, John T. Compliance with Revenue Sharing Auditing Requirements: The New York State Case. (Government Auditing Ser.). 67p. 1980. pap. 7.50 (ISBN 0-916450-31-7). Coun on Municipal.
--Revenue Sharing Renewal. (COMP Papers Ser.). 52p. pap. 7.50 (ISBN 0-916450-36-8). Coun on Municipal.
Marlow, A. W. The Early American Furniture Maker's Manual. (Illus.). 160p. 1973. 12.95 (ISBN 0-02-579810-3). Macmillan.
--Fine Furniture. LC 55-13928. 1977. pap. 8.95 (ISBN 0-8128-2250-1). Stein & Day.
Marlow, David. I Loved You Wednesday. 1976. pap. 1.75 o.p. (ISBN 0-345-24950-X). Ballantine.
Marlow, Edwina. Danger at Dahlkari. 256p. (YA) 1975. 7.95 o.p. (ISBN 0-399-11607-9, Dist. by Putnam). Berkley Pub.
--Danger at Dahlkari. 1977. pap. 1.95 o.p. (ISBN 0-425-03448-8). Berkley Pub.
Marlow, Eugene. Managing the Corporate Media Center. (The Video Bookshelf Ser.). (Illus.). 175p. 1981. text ed. 19.95 (ISBN 0-914236-68-7). Knowledge Indus.
Marlow, W. H. Mathematics for Operations Research. LC 78-534. 1978. 29.95 (ISBN 0-471-57233-0, Pub. by Wiley-Interscience). Wiley.
Marlow, W. H., ed. Aerosol Microphysics I: Particle Interactions. (Topics in Current Physics: Vol. 16). (Illus.). 180p. 1980. 31.90 (ISBN 0-387-09866-6). Springer-Verlag.
Marlowe, Ann. Thunder in the Kerk. LC 79-9803. 1979. 8.95 (ISBN 0-396-07672-6). Dodd.
--The Winnowing Winds. LC 77-3881. 1977. 7.95 (ISBN 0-396-07445-6). Dodd.
Marlowe, Christopher. Complete Plays of Christopher Marlowe. Ribner, Irving, ed. LC 63-12619. 1963. pap. 9.50 (ISBN 0-672-63020-6). Odyssey Pr.
--The Complete Works of Christopher Marlowe, 2 vols. Bowers, F., ed. 922p. 1973. Set. 144.00 (ISBN 0-521-07323-5); Vol. 1. 80.00 (ISBN 0-521-20031-8); Vol. 2. 84.00 (ISBN 0-521-20032-6). Cambridge U Pr.
--Doctor Faustus. Jump, John, ed. LC 72-127572. (Casebook Ser). 1970. pap. text ed. 2.50 o.s.i. (ISBN 0-87695-043-8). Aurora Pubs.
--Doctor Faustus: Text & Major Criticism. Ribner, Irving, ed. LC 65-26778. 1966. pap. 5.55 (ISBN 0-672-63058-3). Odyssey Pr.
--The Famous Tragedy of the Rich Jew of Malta. 1974. text ed. 12.00 (ISBN 0-8277-3901-X); pap. text ed. 5.95 (ISBN 0-8277-2388-1). British Bk Ctr.
--Jew of Malta. Van Fossen, Richard W., ed. LC 63-14699. (Regents Renaissance Drama Ser). 1964. 8.50x (ISBN 0-8032-0270-9); pap. 3.95x (ISBN 0-8032-5270-6, BB 203, Bison). U of Nebr Pr.
--Marlowe: Five Plays. Ellis, Havelock, ed. Incl. Pts. 1-2. Tamburlaine the Great; Doctor Faustus; The Jew of Malta; Edward the Second. 344p. (Orig.). 1956. pap. 5.95 (ISBN 0-8090-0701-0, Mermaid). Hill & Wang.
--The Massacre at Paris: With the Death of the Duke of Guise. LC 73-25759. (English Experience Ser.: No. 335). 1971. Repr. of 1600 ed. 8.00 (ISBN 90-221-0335-8). Walter J Johnson.
--Tamburlaine: Text & Major Criticism, Parts 1 & 2. Ribner, Irving, ed. LC 73-7938. 1974. 9.95 (ISBN 0-672-53061-9); pap. 6.95 (ISBN 0-672-63061-3). Odyssey Pr.
--Tamburlaine the Great, Parts I & II. Jump, John D., ed. LC 67-10666. (Regents Renaissance Drama Ser). xxvi, 205p. 1967. pap. 2.95x (ISBN 0-8032-5271-4, BB 222, Bison). U of Nebr Pr.
Marlowe, Delphine. Bonnaire. 688p. (Orig.). 1980. pap. 2.75 (ISBN 0-515-04764-3). Jove Pubns.
Marlowe, Olwen C. Outdoor Design: A Handbook for the Architect & Planner. 301p. 1977. text ed. 76.00x (ISBN 0-258-97017-0, Pub. by Granada England). Renouf.
Marlowe, Stephen. Come Over, Red Rover. 1968. 4.95 o.s.i. (ISBN 0-02-579790-5). Macmillan.
--The Valkyrie Encounter. 1978. pap. 1.95 (ISBN 0-515-04705-8). Jove Pubns.
Marlowe, Valerious. How to Write a Book Which the Millions Will Want to Read. (Illus.). 1977. 28.45 (ISBN 0-89266-027-9). Am Classical Coll Pr.
Marmasse, Claude. Microscopes & Their Uses. 329p. 1980. 20.00 (ISBN 0-677-05510-2). Gordon.
Marmier, Pierre & Sheldon, Eric. Physics of Nuclei & Particles, Vols. 1-2. 1969-70. 25.95 ea. Vol. 1 (ISBN 0-12-473101-5). Vol. 2 (ISBN 0-12-473102-3). Acad Pr.
Marmion, Shakerly. A Fine Companion. Sonnershein, Richard & Orgel, Stephen, eds. LC 78-66827. (Renaissance Drama Ser.). 1979. lib. bdg. 33.00 (ISBN 0-8240-9731-9). Garland Pub.
Marmontel, Jean Francois. Belisarius, 1767. Shugrue, Michael F., ed. (The Flowering of the Novel, 1740-1775 Ser: Vol. 81). 1974. lib. bdg. 50.00 (ISBN 0-8240-1180-5). Garland Pub.
Marmor, Judd. Psychiatrists & Their Patients: A National Study of Private Office Practice. 181p. 1975. pap. 9.00 (ISBN 0-685-63943-6, P210-0). Am Psychiatric.
Marmor, Judd & Woods, Sherwyn M., eds. The Interface Between the Psychodynamic & Behavioral Therapies. LC 79-9197. (Critical Issues in Psychiatry Ser.). 397p. 1980. 22.50 (ISBN 0-306-40251-3, Plenum Pr). Plenum Pub.
Marmor, Solomon. Experiments in Organic Chemistry. 1981. text ed. write for info. (ISBN 0-8087-3966-2). Burgess.
Marmor, Theodore R. The Politics of Medicare. LC 76-169517. 160p. 1973. 15.95x (ISBN 0-202-24036-3); pap. 5.95 (ISBN 0-202-24037-1). Aldine Pub.
Marmor, Theodore R., ed. Poverty Policy: A Compendium of Cash Transfer Proposals. LC 71-140011. 1971. 17.50x (ISBN 0-202-32004-9). Aldine Pub.
Marmorek, Jan. Over a Barrell: A Guide to the Canadian Energy Crisis. LC 80-1068. 224p. 1981. 12.95 (ISBN 0-385-17192-7); pap. 6.95 (ISBN 0-385-17195-1). Doubleday.
Marmorstein, Emil. The Murder of Jacob De Haan by the Zionists: A Martyr's Message. 1980. lib. bdg. 59.95 (ISBN 0-686-68747-7). Revisionist Pr.
Marmorstein, Emile, tr. see Rosenthal, Franz.
Marmur, Mildred, tr. see Flaubert, Gustave.
Marnell, William H. Light from the West: The Irish Mission & the Emergence of Modern Europe. 1978. 11.95 (ISBN 0-8164-0389-9). Crossroad NY.
Marney, John. Liang Chien-Wen Ti. LC 75-22198. (World Authors Ser.: China: No. 374). 1976. lib. bdg. 12.50 (ISBN 0-8057-6221-3). Twayne.
Marns, Edwin W., Jr., ed. The Letters of Charles & Mary Lamb, 3 vols. 40.00 ea. Vol. I, 1975 (ISBN 0-8014-0930-6). Vol. II-1976 (ISBN 0-8014-0977-2). Vol. III-1978 (ISBN 0-8014-1129-7). Cornell U Pr.
Marohn, Richard C., et al. Juvenile Delinquents: Psychodynamic Assessment & Hospital Treatment. LC 80-18398. 300p. 1980. 22.50 (ISBN 0-87630-239-8). Brunner-Mazel.
Marois, Maurice, ed. Biological Balance & Thermal Modification. (Towards a Plan of Actions for Mankind Ser: Vol. 3). 1977. text ed. 99.00 (ISBN 0-08-021447-9). Pergamon.

--Towards a Plan of Actions for Mankind, 5 vols. Incl. Vol. 1. Long Range Mineral Resources & Growth. text ed. 60.00 (ISBN 0-08-021445-2); Vol. 2. Long Range Energetic Resources & Growth. text ed. 40.00 (ISBN 0-08-021446-0); Vol. 3. Biological Balance & Thermal Modification. text ed. 60.00 (ISBN 0-08-021447-9); Vol. 4. Design of Global System Models & Their Limitations. text ed. 55.00 (ISBN 0-08-021448-7); Vol. 5. Conclusions & Perspectives. text ed. 100.00 (ISBN 0-08-021449-5). 1977. Set. 445.00 (ISBN 0-08-021850-4). Pergamon.

Marolles, Michel de. Tableaux Du Temple Des Muses, Repr. Of 1655 Ed. Bd. with Iconologia or Moral Problems. Ripa, Cesare. Repr. of 1709 ed. LC 75-27876. (Renaissance & the Gods Ser.: Vol. 31). (Illus.). 1976. lib. bdg. 73.00 (ISBN 0-8240-2080-4). Garland Pub.

Marosi, Esteban, ed. El Plan De Dios y los Vencedores. Flores, Rhode, tr. 112p. (Span.). 1980. pap. 1.40 (ISBN 0-8297-0605-4). Vida Pubs.

Marosi, Esteban & Whidden, Angela, eds. A Llave De Oro. Ballin, Karen, tr. 168p. (Span.). 1980. pap. 1.75 (ISBN 0-8297-0546-5). Vida Pubs.

Marosi, Esteban, ed. see Cho, Paul Y.

Marosi, Esteban, ed. see Mears, Henrietta C.

Marosi, Esteban, ed. see Winley, Jesse.

Maroto, Angel R., ed. see Ballesteros, Antonio M.

Maroto, Angel R., ed. see Diosdado, Ana.

Marotta, Michael. Space Colonization: An Annotated Bibliography. 1979. pap. 4.00 o.p. (ISBN 0-686-23957-1). Loompanics.

Marotta, Theodore, jt. auth. see Herubin, Charles.

Marotta, Toby. The Politics of Homosexuality. 384p. 1981. 15.00 (ISBN 0-686-69057-5). HM.

Marotta, Tom. For They Are My Friends. LC 76-43510. 1977. o.p. (ISBN 0-917806-00-X); pap. 8.95 (ISBN 0-917806-01-8). Morgan.

Marovic, D. & Susic, I. King Fianchetto Defences. 1977. 15.95 (ISBN 0-7134-0250-4); pap. 10.95 (ISBN 0-7134-0251-2). David & Charles.

--King Pawn Openings. 1975. 19.95 (ISBN 0-7134-2920-8). David & Charles.

Marowitz, Charles. Artaud at Rodez. 112p. 1981. pap. 5.95 (ISBN 0-7145-2632-0, Pub. by M. Boyars). Merrimack Bk Serv.

--Sex Wars: Free Adaptations of Ibsen & Strindberg. 192p. 1981. 15.00 (ISBN 0-7145-2721-1, Pub. by M Boyars); pap. 8.95 (ISBN 0-7145-2722-X). Merrimack Bk Serv.

Marowitz, Charles, jt. auth. see Lebel, J. J.

Marpie, Margery. Not Raptured...but Resurected. 1979. 4.00 o.p. (ISBN 0-8062-1109-1). Carlton.

Marples, William F. Actuarial Aspects of Pension Security. 1965. text ed. 8.50x o.p. (ISBN 0-256-00655-5). Irwin.

Marquand, David. Parliament for Europe. 1979. o.p. (ISBN 0-224-01716-0, Pub. by Chatto Bodley Jonathan); pap. 6.50 (ISBN 0-224-01717-9). Merrimack Bk Serv.

Marquand, David, jt. auth. see Butler, David.

Marquand, John P. Last Laugh, Mr. Moto. (Mr. Moto Ser.). 1977. pap. 1.25 o.p. (ISBN 0-445-04078-5). Popular Lib.

Marquardt, Charles E., jt. auth. see Swanson, Richard W.

Marquardt, Dorothy A., jt. auth. see Ward, Martha E.

Marquardt, J., jt. auth. see Peterson, H.

Marquardt, Merv. Song for Joseph. (Arch Bks.: No. 18). (gr. k-4). 1981. pap. 0.79 (ISBN 0-570-06146-6, 59-1263). Concordia.

Marquardt, R. A., et al. Retail Management. 2nd ed. LC 78-56199. 1979. text ed. 20.95 (ISBN 0-03-043686-9). Dryden Pr.

Marques, Antonio H. De Oliveira see De Olivera Marques, Antonia H.

Marquess, Harlan E., jt. ed. see Galler, Meyer.

Marquez, Esther T., jt. auth. see Decker, Robert.

Marquez, Gabriel G. The Autumn of the Patriarch. 1977. pap. 2.95 (ISBN 0-380-01774-1, 51300, Bard). Avon.

--In Evil Hour. 1980. pap. 2.75 (ISBN 0-686-69253-5, 52167, Bard). Avon.

--One Hundred Years of Solitude. 1977. pap. 2.95 o.s.i. (ISBN 0-380-01758-X, 45278, Bard). Avon.

Marquez, Gabriel Garcia see Marquez, Gabriel G.

Marquez, Olga, jt. auth. see Phillips, Robert.

Marquez, Robert, ed. see Guillen, Nicolas.

Marquez-Sterling, Manuel. Fernan Gonzalez, First Count of Castile: The Man & the Legend. LC 80-15095. (Romance Monographs: No. 40). (Illus.). 160p. 1980. write for info. Romance.

Marquis, Alice G. Marcel Duchamp: Eros, C'est la Vie. 429p. 1980. lib. bdg. 28.50 (ISBN 0-87875-187-4). Whitston Pub.

Marquis, Don. Archy & Mehitabel. LC 62-56573. 6.95 (ISBN 0-385-04572-7); pap. 1.95 (ISBN 0-385-09478-7). Doubleday.

Marquis, Thomas B. Keep the Last Bullet for Yourself: The True Story of Custer's Last Stand. new ed. Irvine, Keith & Faherty, Robert, eds. LC 75-39093. (Illus.). 192p. 1976. 12.50 (ISBN 0-917256-02-6); pap. 5.95 (ISBN 0-917256-14-X). Ref Pubns.

--Keep the Last Bullet for Yourself: The True Story of Custer's Last Stand. Irvine, Keith & Faherty, Robert, eds. LC 75-39093. (Illus.). 1980. pap. 5.95 (ISBN 0-917256-14-X). Ref Pubns.

Marquis, Thomas B. & Heil, Anne R. Custer on the Little Bighorn. (Illus.). 1967. pap. 3.50 (ISBN 0-686-51606-0); tchr's ed. 2.10 (ISBN 0-686-51607-9). Custer.

Marquis, Thomas B., narrated by see Leforge, Thomas H.

Marquis, Thomas B., tr. Wooden Leg: A Warrior Who Fought Custer. LC 31-10067. (Illus.). 1962. pap. 3.50 (ISBN 0-8032-5124-6, BB 126, Bison). U of Nebr Pr.

Marquit, Erwin, ed. see Hoerz, Herbert, et al.

Marr, David. Barwick. (Illus.). 336p. 1981. 19.50 (ISBN 0-86861-058-5, 2566). Allen Unwin.

Marr, David G. Vietnamese Anticolonialism, 1885-1925. (Center for South & Southeast Asia Studies, UC Berkeley). 1971. 16.50 o.p. (ISBN 0-520-01813-3); pap. 9.95x o.p. (ISBN 0-520-02046-4, CAMPUS59). U of Cal Pr.

--Vietnamese Tradition on Trial, Nineteen Twenty to Nineteen Forty-Five. (Illus.). 450p. 1981. 25.00 (ISBN 0-520-04180-1, CAMPUS 271); pap. 9.95 (ISBN 0-520-04277-8). U of Cal Pr.

Marr, Dean. From Liquor & Loneliness to Love & Laughter. 1978. 8.95 o.p. (ISBN 0-8362-6502-5); pap. 4.95 o.p. (ISBN 0-8362-6503-3). Andrews & McMeel.

Marr, G. W. & Layton, R. C. General Engineering Science in SI Units, 2 vols 2nd ed. 1971. Vol. 1. 11.25 (ISBN 0-08-015805-6); Vol. 2. 11.25 (ISBN 0-08-015807-2); Vol. 1. pap. 4.80 (ISBN 0-08-015804-8); Vol. 2. pap. 4.80 (ISBN 0-08-015806-4). Pergamon.

Marr, Harko Gerrit De see De Maar, Harko Gerrit.

Marr, Iain L., jt. auth. see Bock, Rudolf.

Marr, J. Joseph, jt. auth. see Boyd, Robert F.

Marr, John S. A Breath of Air & a Breath of Smoke. LC 70-161362. (Illus.). 48p. (gr. 3 up). 1971. 4.95 (ISBN 0-87131-038-4). M Evans.

Marraffino, Elizabeth. Blue Moon Ruby Tuesday. (Illus.). 60p. (Orig.). 1981. pap. 3.00 (ISBN 0-936556-02-1). Contact Two.

Marram, Gwen D. The Group Approach in Nursing Practice. 2nd ed. LC 77-14584. (Illus.). 1978. pap. text ed. 11.00 (ISBN 0-8016-3126-2). Mosby.

Marran, Ray J. Table Games. LC 75-22567. (Illus.). 160p. 1976. 7.95 o.p. (ISBN 0-498-01829-6). A S Barnes.

Marranca, Bonnie & Dasgupta, Gautam. American Playwrights: A Critical Survey, Vol. 1. LC 80-23745. 225p. 1981. text ed. 13.95x (ISBN 0-89676-047-2); pap. text ed. 10.00x (ISBN 0-89676-048-0). Drama Bk.

--American Playwrights: A Critical Survey, Vol. 2. Date not set. price not set (ISBN 0-89676-049-9); pap. price not set (ISBN 0-89676-050-2). Drama Bk. Postponed.

Marrero, J. Espada. Madre y Hogar. 50p. (Span.). 1980. pap. 1.05 (ISBN 0-311-07302-6). Casa Bautista.

Marriage, Ellen, tr. see Balzac, Honore De.

Marric, J. J. Gideon's Drive. (Gideon Detective Ser.). 1977. pap. 1.25 o.p. (ISBN 0-445-04123-4). Popular Lib.

--Gideon's Fog. (Harper Novel of Suspense). 188p. 1974. 7.95 o.s.i. (ISBN 0-06-012798-8, HarpT). Har-Row.

--Gideon's Fog. 1981. pap. 1.95 (ISBN 0-445-08530-4). Popular Lib.

--Gideon's Men. (Gideon Detective Ser.). 1979. pap. 1.75 o.p. (ISBN 0-445-04422-5). Popular Lib.

--Gideon's Night. (Gideon Detective Ser.). 1978. pap. 1.50 o.p. (ISBN 0-445-01429-6). Popular Lib.

--Gideon's Power. (Gideon Detective Ser.). 1977. pap. 1.25 o.p. (ISBN 0-445-00451-7). Popular Lib.

--Gideon's Press. LC 73-4154. (Harper Novel of Suspense). 192p. (YA) 1973. 7.95 o.s.i. (ISBN 0-06-012787-2, HarpT). Har-Row.

--Gideon's Press. (Gideon Detective Ser.). 192p. 1981. pap. 1.95 (ISBN 0-445-00426-6). Popular Lib.

--Gideon's Ride. (Gideon Detective Ser.). 1979. pap. 1.75 o.p. (ISBN 0-445-04493-4). Popular Lib.

--Gideon's River. (Gideon Detective Ser.). 1977. pap. 1.25 o.p. (ISBN 0-445-04060-2). Popular Lib.

--Gideon's Wrath. (Gideon Detective Ser.). 1977. pap. 1.25 o.p. (ISBN 0-445-00435-5). Popular Lib.

Marrie, Alain, jt. auth. see Hollender, Louis F.

Marrin, Albert. Nicholas Murray Butler. (World Leaders Ser.: No. 52). 1976. lib. bdg. 10.95 (ISBN 0-8057-7706-7). Twayne.

--Norman Angell. (World Leaders Ser.: No. 79). 1979. lib. bdg. 14.50 (ISBN 0-8057-7725-3). Twayne.

Marriner, Ann. Current Perspectives in Nursing Management, Vol. I. LC 78-31446. (Illus.). 1979. text ed. 12.50 (ISBN 0-8016-3119-X); pap. text ed. 9.50 (ISBN 0-8016-3120-3). Mosby.

--A Guide to Nursing Management. LC 79-24241. (Illus.). 1980. pap. 10.00 (ISBN 0-8016-3121-1). Mosby.

--The Nursing Process: A Scientific Approach to Nursing Care. 2nd ed. LC 78-21093. (Illus.). 1979. pap. 11.50 (ISBN 0-8016-3122-X). Mosby.

Marriott. The Interpretation of Multiple Observations. 1974. 17.00 (ISBN 0-12-473450-2). Acad Pr.

Marriott, Alice. Osage Indians, Vol. Two: Osage Research Report, & Bibliography of Basic Research References. (American Indian Ethnohistory Ser: Plains Indians). (Illus.). lib. bdg. 42.00 (ISBN 0-8240-0748-4). Garland Pub.

--Saynday's People: The Kiowa Indians & the Stories They Told. LC 63-10928. (Illus.). 1963. pap. 2.45 (ISBN 0-8032-5125-4, BB 174, Bison). U of Nebr Pr.

Marriott, Alice & Rachlin, Carol K. American Indian Mythology. LC 68-21613. (Apollo Eds.). (Illus.). 211p. 1972. pap. 4.95 (ISBN 0-8152-0335-7, A335, TYC-T). T Y Crowell.

--Dance Around the Sun: The Life of Mary Little Bear Inkanish: Cheyenne. LC 77-1859. (Illus.). 1977. 12.95 o.s.i. (ISBN 0-690-01450-3, TYC-T). T Y Crowell.

Marriott, D. L., jt. ed. see Garrett, G. G.

Marriott, F. H. Basic Mathematics for the Biological & Social Sciences. LC 73-99863. 1970. text ed. 17.25 (ISBN 0-08-006663-1); pap. 9.25 (ISBN 0-08-006664-X). Pergamon.

Marriott, John A. Eastern Question: An Historical Study in European Diplomacy. 4th ed. (Histories of Nations Ser). (Illus.). 1940. 37.50x (ISBN 0-19-821508-8). Oxford U Pr.

Marriott, Sir John A. Commonwealth or Anarchy: A Survey of Projects of Peace from the Sixteenth to the Twentieth Century. LC 79-1636. 1981. Repr. of 1937 ed. 19.50 (ISBN 0-88355-939-0). Hyperion Conn.

Marris, Robin, ed. The Corporate Society: Growth, Competition & Innovative Power. LC 73-14655. 1974. text ed. 32.95 (ISBN 0-470-57245-0). Halsted Pr.

Marrocco, W. Thomas & Gleason, Harold. Music in America: An Anthology from the Landing of the Pilgrims to the Close of the Civil War 1620-1865. (Illus.). 384p. 1974. pap. 12.95x (ISBN 0-393-09296-8). Norton.

Marrow, Alfred J. Practical Theorist: The Life & Work of Kurt Lewin. LC 77-1400. 1977. pap. text ed. 7.50x (ISBN 0-8077-2525-0). Tchrs Coll.

Marrow, James H. & Shestack, Alan, eds. Hans Baldung Grien: Prints & Drawings. LC 80-52733. (Illus.). xiv, 282p. 1981. lib. bdg. 19.95 (ISBN 0-89467-013-1). Yale Art Gallery.

Marrow, Stanley B. Christ in Jesus. LC 68-16666. (Orig.). 1968. pap. 1.95 (ISBN 0-8091-1521-2, Deus). Paulist Pr.

--The Words of Jesus in Our Gospel. LC 79-52105. 1979. pap. 4.95 (ISBN 0-8091-2215-4). Paulist Pr.

Marrus, Michael R. Politics of Assimilation: A Study of the French-Jewish Community at the Time of the Dreyfus Affair. (Illus.). 1971. text ed. 27.00x (ISBN 0-19-821482-0). Oxford U Pr.

Marryat. Settlers in Canada. 1956. 5.00x o.p. (ISBN 0-460-00370-4, Evman). Dutton.

Marryat, Frederick. Masterman Ready, 3 vols. LC 75-32160. (Classics of Children's Literature, 1621-1932: Vol. 25). 1976. Repr. of 1842 ed. Set. lib. bdg. 105.00 (ISBN 0-8240-2274-2); PLB 38.00 ea. Garland Pub.

Mars, G., et al. Manpower Problems in the Hotel & Catering Industry. 180p. 1979. text ed. 23.00x (ISBN 0-566-00214-0, Pub. by Gower Pub Co England). Renouf.

Marsal, Raul, jt. auth. see Wilson, Stanley D.

Marsan, Jean C. Montreal in Evolution: Historical Analysis of the Development of Montreal Architecture & Urban Environment. (Illus.). 488p. 1981. 27.50x (ISBN 0-7735-0339-0). McGill-Queens U Pr.

Marschak, Jacob. Economic Information, Decision, & Prediction, 3 vols. (Theory & Decision Library: No. 7). 1980. Vol. I, 389 Pp. pap. 14.95 (ISBN 90-277-1195-X, Pub. by D. Reidel); Vol. II, 362 Pp. pap. 14.95 (ISBN 90-277-1196-8); Vol. III, 399 Pp. pap. 14.95 (ISBN 90-277-1197-6). Kluwer Boston.

Marschall, Laurence A., jt. ed. see Crowner, David L.

Marschall, Richard, jt. auth. see Adams, John P.

Marschall, Richard E., jt. ed. see Horn, Maurice.

Marschall, Rick. Rembrandt of the Comic Strip. 1981. 6.95 (ISBN 0-918348-04-8). Green Hill.

Marsden, A. M., jt. ed. see Henderson, S. T.

Marsden, Barry M. The Early Barrow Diggers. LC 74-76137. (Illus.). 126p. 1974. 9.95 (ISBN 0-8155-5027-8, NP). Noyes.

Marsden, C. D., jt. ed. see Meldrum, B. S.

Marsden, Dennis, jt. auth. see Jackson, Brian.

Marsden, George M. Evangelical Mind & the New School Presbyterian Experience: A Case Study of Thought & Theology in Nineteenth-Century America. LC 75-118731. (Publications in American Studies: No. 20). 1970. 18.50x o.p. (ISBN 0-300-01343-4). Yale U Pr.

--Fundamentalism & American Culture: The Shaping of Twentieth Century Evangelicalism, 1870-1925. (Illus.). 320p. 1980. 19.95 (ISBN 0-19-502758-2). Oxford U Pr.

Marsden, H. B. & Steward, J. K. Tumours in Children. (Recent Results in Cancer Research: Vol. 13). (Illus.). 1968. 39.40 o.p. (ISBN 0-387-04304-7). Springer-Verlag.

Marsden, Hilda, ed. see Bronte, Emily.

Marsden, J. & Weinstein, A. Calculus Unlimited. 1980. pap. 6.95 (ISBN 0-8053-6932-5). A-W.

Marsden, Jerold E. & Tromba, Anthony J. Vector Calculus. LC 75-17864. (Illus.). 1976. 22.95x (ISBN 0-7167-0462-5). W H Freeman.

Marsden, Jerrold & Weinstein, Alan. Calculus. 1979. 26.95 (ISBN 0-8053-6930-9); study guide 6.95. Benjamin-Cummings.

--Calculus Unlimited. 1980. pap. text ed. 6.95 (ISBN 0-8053-6932-5). Benjamin-Cummings.

Marsden, Jerrold E. Basic Complex Analysis. LC 72-89894. (Illus.). 1973. text ed. 22.95x (ISBN 0-7167-0451-X). W H Freeman.

--Elementary Classical Analysis. LC 74-5764. (Illus.). 1974. text ed. 24.95x (ISBN 0-7167-0452-8). W H Freeman.

Marsden, Jerrold E. & Tromba, Anthony J. Vector Calculus. 2nd ed. LC 80-24663. (Illus.). 1981. text ed. 22.95x (ISBN 0-7167-1244-X). W H Freeman.

Marsden, K. The Poems of Thomas Hardy. 1969. text ed. 19.00x (Athlone Pr). Humanities.

Marsden, Peter. Roman London. (Illus.). 224p. 1981. 19.95 (ISBN 0-500-25073-1). Thames Hudson.

Marsden, Ralph W., ed. Politics, Minerals, & Survival. LC 74-27310. 1975. 10.00 (ISBN 0-299-06810-2); pap. 5.95 (ISBN 0-299-06814-5). U of Wis Pr.

Marsden, Victor E., tr. from Russian. The Protocols of the Meetings of the Learned Elders of Zion. 1978. pap. 4.00x (ISBN 0-911038-42-6). Noontide.

Marsden, W. E. North West England. 2nd ed. LC 78-67243. (Geography of the British Isles). 1979. pap. 5.95 (ISBN 0-521-22474-8). Cambridge U Pr.

Marsden, Walter. Lapland. (The World's Wild Places Ser.). (Illus.). 1976. 12.95 (ISBN 0-8094-2053-8). Time-Life.

--Lapland. (The World's Wild Places Ser.). (Illus.). 1979. lib. bdg. 11.97 (ISBN 0-686-51021-6). Silver.

--West Germany. 1978. 22.50 (ISBN 0-7134-1087-6). David & Charles.

Marsella, Anthony & Pedersen, Paul B. Cross-Cultural Counseling & Psychotherapy. (General Psychology Ser.). Date not set. price not set (ISBN 0-08-025545-0). Pergamon. Postponed.

Marsh. The Old Man. pap. 1.50 o.p. (ISBN 0-686-12917-2). Schmul Pub Co.

Marsh, jt. auth. see Olivo.

Marsh, A. I., ed. Concise Encyclopedia of Industrial Relations. 1979. text ed. 41.00x (ISBN 0-566-02095-5, Pub. by Gower Pub Co England). Renouf.

Marsh, Angela. Pirate Treasure. LC 78-26275. (Raintree Great Adventures). (Illus.). (gr. 3-6). 1979. PLB 8.95 (ISBN 0-8393-0155-3). Raintree Child.

Marsh, Arthur, jt. ed. see Kaye, Seymour P.

Marsh, Carole. The Missing Head Mystery. LC 79-55447. (HistoryMystery Ser.). (Illus.). 160p. (Orig.). 1980. pap. 3.95 (ISBN 0-935326-01-4). Gallopade Pub Group.

Marsh, Charles R. Share Your Faith with a Muslim. 1975. pap. 2.25 (ISBN 0-8024-7900-6). Moody.

Marsh, David C., ed. Introducing Social Policy. 1979. 20.00x (ISBN 0-7100-0132-0); pap. 9.95 (ISBN 0-7100-0133-9). Routledge & Kegan.

Marsh, Derick R., ed. The Recurring Miracle. 208p. 1980. pap. 14.00x (ISBN 0-424-00085-7, Pub. by Sydney U Pr Australia). Intl Schol Bk Serv.

Marsh, Elsie A., ed. see Hollander, Jacob H.

Marsh, F. E. Five Hundred Bible Study Outlines. LC 79-2549. 382p. 1980. Repr. of 1897 ed. 8.95 (ISBN 0-8254-3229-4). Kregel.

--Living God's Way. LC 80-8073. 224p. 1981. pap. 4.95 (ISBN 0-8254-3233-2). Kregel.

--Major Bible Truths. LC 79-2533. 1980. 9.95 (ISBN 0-8254-3232-4). Kregel.

--One Thousand Bible Study Outlines. LC 75-125115. 1970. 9.95 (ISBN 0-8254-3209-X). Kregel.

Marsh, Frank. Variation & Fixity in Nature. LC 75-36531. (Dimension Ser.). 1976. pap. 5.95 (ISBN 0-8163-0269-3, 22110-1). Pacific Pr Pub Assn.
Marsh, Frank H. The Emerging Rights of Children in Treatment for Mental & Catastrophic Illnesses. LC 79-66481. 1979. text ed. 13.75 (ISBN 0-8191-0829-4); pap. text ed. 7.50 (ISBN 0-8191-0830-8). U Pr of Amer.
Marsh, George E. Methods for Teaching the Mildly Handicapped Adolescent. LC 80-13396. (Illus.). 1980. pap. text ed. 13.95 (ISBN 0-8016-3115-7). Mosby.
Marsh, George E., et al. The Learning Disabled Adolescent: Program Alternatives in the Secondary School. new ed. LC 77-18050. (Illus.). 1978. text ed. 16.95 (ISBN 0-8016-3118-1). Mosby.
Marsh, Glenda, jt. auth. see Marsh, Roger.
Marsh, Heary. The Rebel Jew: Paul of Tarsus. 1980. cancelled (ISBN 0-7050-0078-8). Attic Pr.
Marsh, James B. Four Years in the Rockies: Or the Adventures of Isaac P. Rose... Giving His Experience As a Hunter & Trapper. LC 75-7120. (Indian Captivities Ser.: Vol. 94). 1976. Repr. of 1884 ed. lib. bdg. 44.00 (ISBN 0-8240-1718-8). Garland Pub.
Marsh, Jean. Loving Partnership. (Aston Hall Romances Ser.). 192p. (Orig.). 1981. pap. 1.75 (ISBN 0-523-41132-4). Pinnacle Bks.
Marsh, John, tr. see Bultmann, Rudolf.
Marsh, John S. European Economic Issues: Agriculture, Economic Security, Industrial Democracy, the OECD. LC 76-30359. (Special Studies). 1977. text ed. 28.95 (ISBN 0-275-24410-5). Praeger.
Marsh, John S. & Swanney, Pamela J. Agriculture & the European Community. (Studies on Contemporary Europe). (Illus.). 96p. (Orig.). 1980. text ed. 15.95x (ISBN 0-04-338092-1, 2525); pap. text ed. 6.95x (ISBN 0-04-338093-X, 2526). Allen Unwin.
Marsh, Judy & Dyer, Carole, eds. The Maine Way -- a Collection of Maine Fish & Game Recipes: A Collection of Marine Fish & Game Recipes. (Illus.). 96p. (Orig.). 1978. pap. 3.95 (ISBN 0-686-69324-8). DeLorme Pub.
Marsh, Leonard. Report on Social Security for Canada. LC 74-82286. (Social History of Canada Ser.). 1975. 17.50x o.p. (ISBN 0-8020-2168-9); pap. 6.50 o.p. (ISBN 0-8020-6250-4). U of Toronto Pr.
Marsh, Margaret. Anarchist Women: 1870-1920. Davis, Allen F., ed. (American Civilization Ser.). (Illus.). 250p. 1980. 19.50 (ISBN 0-87722-202-9). Temple U Pr.
Marsh, Matthew E. California Mechanics' Lien Law Handbook. 3rd ed. LC 72-83952. 1979. 46.00 (ISBN 0-911110-30-5); 1980 suppl. incl. (ISBN 0-685-44105-9). Parker & Son.
Marsh, Meredith. I Had Wild Jack for a Lover. 1978. pap. 1.95 o.p. (ISBN 0-449-23749-4, Crest). Fawcett.
Marsh, Michael. The Rudelstein Affair. LC 80-29323. 1981. 9.95 (ISBN 0-918056-02-0). Ariadne Pr.
Marsh, Moreton. Easy Expert in American Antiques: Knowing, Finding, Buying & Restoring Early American Furniture. rev. ed. LC 78-9050. Orig. Title: The Easy Expert in Collecting & Restoring American Antiques. 1978. 12.95 (ISBN 0-397-01287-X); pap. 7.95 (ISBN 0-397-01288-8). Lippincott.
Marsh, Ngaio. Artists in Crime. (Ngaio Marsh Mystery Ser.). pap. 1.95 (ISBN 0-515-05414-3). Jove Pubns.
--Black As He's Painted. (Mystery Ser.). 224p. 1981. pap. 2.25 (ISBN 0-515-05871-8). Jove Pubns.
--The Clutch of Constables. (Ngaio Marsh Mystery Ser.). 1981. pap. 2.25 (ISBN 0-515-06013-5). Jove Pubns.
--Death & the Dancing Footman. (Ngaio Marsh Mysteries Ser.). pap. 1.95 (ISBN 0-515-05409-7). Jove Pubns.
--Death at the Bar. 1979. pap. 1.75 o.p. (ISBN 0-425-04082-8). Berkley Pub.
--Death at the Bar. (Ngaio Marsh Mysteries Ser.). pap. 1.95 (ISBN 0-515-05641-3). Jove Pubns.
--Death in a White Tie. (Ngaio Marsh Mysteries Ser.). pap. 2.25 (ISBN 0-515-05896-3). Jove Pubns.
--Death in Ecstasy. 256p. 1980. pap. 1.95 (ISBN 0-515-05499-2). Jove Pubns.
--Death of a Fool. (Ngaio Marsh Mystery Ser.). 288p. 1981. pap. 1.95 (ISBN 0-515-05762-2). Jove Pubns.
--Death of a Fool. 1978. pap. 1.50 o.p. (ISBN 0-515-04478-4). Jove Pubns.
--Death of a Peer. pap. 1.95 (ISBN 0-515-05413-5). Jove Pubns.
--Enter a Murderer. (Mystery Ser.). 192p. 1981. pap. 2.25 (ISBN 0-515-05943-9). Jove Pubns.
--False Scent. 1978. pap. 1.75 o.p. (ISBN 0-425-03999-4, Dist. by Putnam). Berkley Pub.
--Final Curtain. 288p. 1980. pap. 1.95 (ISBN 0-515-05554-9). Jove Pubns.
--Grave Mistake. 1980. pap. 1.95 (ISBN 0-515-05369-4). Jove Pubns.
--Hand in Glove. 1978. pap. 1.95 (ISBN 0-515-05763-0). Jove Pubns.
--Killer Dolphin. (Ngaio Marsh Mystery Ser.). 256p. 1980. pap. 1.95 (ISBN 0-515-05435-6). Jove Pubns.
--A Man Lay Dead. 1976. Repr. of 1934 ed. lib. bdg. 9.70 (ISBN 0-88411-488-0). Amereon Ltd.
--New Zealand. (Illus.). (gr. 7 up). 1964. 5.95g (ISBN 0-02-762380-7). Macmillan.
--New Zealand. 1976. Repr. of 1942 ed. lib. bdg. 13.30 (ISBN 0-88411-489-9). Amereon Ltd.
--Night at the Vulcan. 1977. pap. 1.75 o.s.i. (ISBN 0-515-05293-0). Jove Pubns.
--Nursing Home Murder. 1978. pap. 1.50 (ISBN 0-515-04530-6). Jove Pubns.
--Overture to Death. (Ngaio Marsh Mysteries Ser.). 320p. 1981. pap. 2.25 (ISBN 0-515-05966-8). Jove Pubns.
--Overture to Death. 1978. pap. 1.75 o.s.i. (ISBN 0-515-04531-4). Jove Pubns.
--Photo Finish. 1981. lib. bdg. 14.95 (ISBN 0-8161-3149-X, Large Print Bks). G K Hall.
--Scales of Justice. 256p. 1980. pap. 1.95 (ISBN 0-515-05436-4). Jove Pubns.
--Singing in the Shrouds. 1978. pap. 1.50 (ISBN 0-515-04532-2). Jove Pubns.
--Spinsters in Jeopardy. 1978. pap. 1.75 o.p. (ISBN 0-425-03998-6, Dist. by Putnam). Berkley Pub.
--Spinsters in Jeopardy. (Ngaio Marsh Mystery Ser.). pap. 1.95 (ISBN 0-515-05716-9). Jove Pubns.
--Tied up in Tinsel. 1978. pap. 1.75 (ISBN 0-515-04533-0). Jove Pubns.
--Vintage Murder. 1978. pap. 1.75 (ISBN 0-515-04534-9). Jove Pubns.
--When in Rome. 224p. 1980. pap. 1.95 (ISBN 0-515-05627-8). Jove Pubns.
--A Wreath for Rivera. LC 75-44993. (Crime Fiction Ser). 1976. Repr. of 1949 ed. lib. bdg. 17.50 (ISBN 0-8240-2385-4). Garland Pub.
Marsh, Paul & Beckett, Derrick. Mechanical Fixing Devices in the Building Industry. 1978. text ed. 30.00x (ISBN 0-904406-12-1). Longman.
Marsh, Paul, jt. auth. see Beckett, Derrick.
Marsh, Peter, et al. The Rules of Disorder. (The Social Worlds of Childhood Ser.). (Illus.). 1978. 14.00x (ISBN 0-7100-8747-0). Routledge & Kegan.
Marsh, Philip M. Freneau's Published Prose: A Bibliography. (Author Bibliographies Ser.: No. 5). 1970. 10.00 (ISBN 0-8108-0289-9). Scarecrow.
Marsh, R. W., ed. Systemic Fungicides. LC 72-4058. 1972. pap. 21.95 (ISBN 0-470-57250-7). Halsted Pr.
--Systemic Fungicides. 2nd ed. LC 76-49542. (Illus.). 1977. text ed. 40.00x (ISBN 0-582-44167-6). Longman.
Marsh, Robert M. & Mannari, Hiroshi. Modernization & the Japanese Factory. LC 75-3466. 560p. 1976. 32.50 (ISBN 0-691-09365-2); pap. 12.50 ltd. ed. (ISBN 0-691-10037-3). Princeton U Pr.
Marsh, Robert W. Maclaren's Men. 1979. pap. 1.75 (ISBN 0-505-51435-4). Tower Bks.
Marsh, Roger. Monoprints for the Artist. (gr. 10 up). 1969. pap. 7.50 (ISBN 0-85458-549-4). Transatlantic.
Marsh, Roger & Marsh, Glenda. Imaginative Printmaking. (Illus.). 132p. 1975. 12.00x o.p. (ISBN 0-8464-0502-4). Beekman Pubs.
Marsh, Stanley P. LASL Shock Hugoniot Data. (Los Alamos Scientific Laboratory Series on Dynamic Material Properties). 1980. 40.00 (ISBN 0-520-04008-2). U. of Cal Pr.
Marsh, U. Grant. Salesmanship: Modern Principles & Practices. LC 74-160524. (Illus.). 1972. 15.95x (ISBN 0-13-789453-8). P-H.
Marsh, William & Dozier, Jeffrey. Landscape: An Introduction to Physical Geography. LC 80-68120. (Geography Ser.). (Illus.). 656p. 1981. text ed. 20.95 (ISBN 0-201-04101-4). A-W.
Marsh, Zoe & Kingsnorth, G. W. A History of East Africa. 4th ed. LC 72-171677. (Illus.). 1972. 19.95 (ISBN 0-521-08346-X); pap. 7.95x (ISBN 0-521-09677-4). Cambridge U Pr.
Marshak, R. E., et al. Theory of Weak Interaction of Particle Physics. LC 72-76058. (Interscience Monographs & Texts in Physics & Astronomy). 1969. 62.50 o.p. (ISBN 0-471-57290-X, Pub. by Wiley-Interscience). Wiley.
Marshall. Adventures in Prayer. 1976. 1.95 (ISBN 0-8007-8269-0). Revell.
--Dynamics of Health & Disease. 1972. 12.50 o.p. (ISBN 0-8385-1873-7). ACC.
Marshall, Alan G. Biophysical Chemistry: Principles, Techniques & Applications. LC 77-19136. 1978. text ed. 28.95 (ISBN 0-471-02718-9); students manual avail. (ISBN 0-471-03674-9). Wiley.
Marshall, Alexandra. Tender Offer. LC 80-23233. 256p. 1981. 10.95 (ISBN 0-394-50757-6). Knopf.
Marshall, Alfred. New Testament Greek Primer. 176p. (Orig.). 1981. pap. 5.95 (ISBN 0-310-20401-1). Zondervan.
--RSV Interlinear Greek, New Testament. 17.95 (ISBN 0-310-20410-0). Zondervan.
Marshall, Anthony D. The Malagasy Republic. LC 72-4337. (First Bks). (Illus.). 96p. (gr. 5-9). 1972. PLB 4.90 o.p. (ISBN 0-531-00780-4). Watts.
--Trinidad-Tobago. LC 75-5527. (First Bks.). (Illus.). (gr. 5-7). 1975. PLB 4.47 o.p. (ISBN 0-531-00835-5). Watts.
Marshall, Arthur. I Say! 1978. 14.95 (ISBN 0-241-89682-7, Pub. by Hamish Hamilton England). David & Charles.
Marshall, Arthur K. California Probate Procedure, 3 vols. 4th ed. 1979. looseleaf 135.00 (ISBN 0-911110-28-3). Parker & Son.
Marshall, Austin. How to Get a Better Job. rev. ed. 1977. pap. 4.95 (ISBN 0-8015-3775-4, Hawthorn). Dutton.
Marshall, Beverly. Smocks & Smocking. 1981. 14.95 (ISBN 0-442-28268-0). Van Nos Reinhold.
Marshall, Bill. Bukom. 118p. (Orig.). 1979. pap. 5.00 (ISBN 0-582-64223-X, Drum Deat). Three Continents.
Marshall, Bill & Marshall, Christina M. The Marriage Secret. 1980. 8.95 (ISBN 0-8437-3349-7). Hammond Inc.
Marshall, Bob. Diary of a Yankee-Hater. 256p. (Orig.). 1981. pap. 7.95 (ISBN 0-531-09945-8). Watts.
Marshall, Bryan E., ed. see Papers from the Second Annual Conference on Shock, Williamsburg, Va., June 1979.
Marshall, C. Edmund. The Physical Chemistry & Mineralogy of Soils: Soils in Place, Vol. II. LC 64-20074. 1977. 32.95 (ISBN 0-471-02957-2, Pub. by Wiley-Interscience). Wiley.
Marshall, Catherine. Beyond Our Selves. (Spire Bk). 1968. pap. 1.95 o.p. (ISBN 0-8007-8003-5). Revell.
--Christy. 1968. pap. 2.50 (ISBN 0-380-00141-1, 44032). Avon.
--Friends with God. (gr. 2-4). 1972. pap. 1.25 (ISBN 0-380-01199-9, 33647). Avon.
--A Man Called Peter. (Spire Bk). pap. 1.95 o.p. (ISBN 0-8007-8027-2). Revell.
--Meeting God at Every Turn. (Illus.). 250p. 1981. 9.95 (ISBN 0-912376-61-9). Chosen Bks Pub.
Marshall, Catherine, ed. Mister Jones, Meet the Master. 1966. pap. 1.50 o.s.i. (ISBN 0-515-04810-0). Jove Pubns.
Marshall Cavendish Editorial Board. History of the Sailing Ship. LC 74-32633. (Illus.). 1975. 12.95 o.p. (ISBN 0-668-03780-6). Arco.
Marshall, Christina M., jt. auth. see Marshall, Bill.
Marshall, Clifford W. Applied Graph Theory. 1971. 30.50 o.p. (ISBN 0-471-57300-0, Pub. by Wiley-Interscience). Wiley.
Marshall, Dale & Montgomery, Roger, eds. Housing Policy for the Eighties. 1979. pap. 5.00 (ISBN 0-918592-36-4). Policy Studies.
Marshall, Dale R. The Politics of Participation in Poverty: A Case Study of the Board of Economic & Youth Opportunities Agency of Greater Los Angeles. LC 79-121192. 1971. 20.00x (ISBN 0-520-01741-2). U of Cal Pr.
Marshall, Dale R., ed. Urban Policy Making. LC 79-19162. (Sage Yearbooks in Politics & Public Policy: Vol. 7). (Illus.). 1979. 20.00x (ISBN 0-8039-1367-2); pap. 9.95x (ISBN 0-8039-1368-0). Sage.
Marshall, Don. R. Successful Techniques for Solving Employee Compensation Problems. LC 77-17964. 1978. 26.95 (ISBN 0-471-57297-7, Pub. by Wiley-Interscience). Wiley.
Marshall, Dorothy. Eighteenth Century England Seventeen Fourteen to Seventeen Eighty-Four. 2nd ed. (A History of England Ser.). (Illus.). 572p. 1975. pap. text ed. 14.50 (ISBN 0-582-48316-6). Longman.
--English People in the Eighteenth Century. LC 80-16871. (Illus.). xvi, 288p. 1980. Repr. of 1956 ed. lib. bdg. 27.50x (ISBN 0-313-21080-2, MAENP). Greenwood.
--Fanny Kemble. LC 77-3854. (Illus.). 1978. 8.95 o.p. (ISBN 0-312-28162-5). St Martin.
Marshall, Edison. Caravan to Xanadu. 1972. pap. 1.75 (ISBN 0-380-00873-4, 31401). Avon.
Marshall, Edward. Dr. Marshall's Lifelong Weight Control Program. 132p. 1981. 7.95 (ISBN 0-395-29476-2). HM.
--How to Use ESP to Win the American Daily Lottery. LC 80-69615. (Illus.). 64p. (Orig.). 1981. price not set (ISBN 0-938284-00-2). Inner Circle.
--Three by the Sea. (Easy-to-Read Ser.). (Illus.). 48p. (ps-3). 1981. PLB 5.99 (ISBN 0-8037-8687-5); pap. 2.50 (ISBN 0-8037-8671-9). Dial.
--Troll Country. LC 79-19324. (Easy-to-Read Bk.). (Illus.). (ps-3). 1980. PLB 5.89 (ISBN 0-8037-6211-9); pap. 1.95 (ISBN 0-8037-6210-0). Dial.
Marshall, F. Ray, et al. Labor Economics: Wage, Employment, & Trade Unionism. 3rd ed. 1976. text ed. 16.95x o.p. (ISBN 0-256-01824-3). Irwin.
--Labor Economics: Wages, Employment & Trade Unionism. 4th ed. 1980. 19.95 (ISBN 0-256-02334-4). Irwin.
Marshall, G. I., jt. auth. see Hanneman, L. J.
Marshall, Geoffrey & Moodie, G. C. Some Problems of the Constitution. rev. ed. (Orig.). 1967. text ed. 6.00x (ISBN 0-09-053243-0, Hutchinson U Lib); pap. text ed. 3.25x (ISBN 0-09-053244-9, Hutchinson U Lib). Humanities.
Marshall, George. Facing Death & Grief. 250p. 1981. 15.95 (ISBN 0-87975-140-1). Prometheus Bks.
Marshall, George C. Marshall's Mission to China: The Report & Appended Documents. 1976. Set. 60.00 (ISBN 0-89093-115-1). U Pubns Amer.
--Selected Speeches & Statements of General of the Army George C. Marshall. DeWeerd, H. A., ed. LC 72-10365. (FDR & the Era of the New Deal Ser.). 1973. Repr. of 1945 ed. lib. bdg. 29.50 (ISBN 0-306-70556-7). Da Capo.
Marshall, Gerald W. Reaching Your Possibilities Through Commitment. LC 80-53140. 128p. 1981. pap. 3.95 (ISBN 0-8307-0777-8, 5414407). Regal.
Marshall, Gordon. Presbyteries & Profits: Calvinism & the Development of Capitalism in Scotland, 1560 - 1707. 400p. 1980. 54.00x (ISBN 0-19-827246-4). Oxford U Pr.
Marshall, H., ed. Yevgeny Yevtushenko: Bilingual Edition. 1967. text ed. 13.75 (ISBN 0-08-012464-X). Pergamon.
Marshall, H., tr. see Gjessing, Lieve.
Marshall, H. H. From Dependence to Statehood, Vol. 1. 1980. 50.00 (ISBN 0-379-20348-0). Oceana.
--From Dependence to Statehood in Commonwealth Africa: Selected Documents, World War I to Independence. LC 80-10407. 734p. 1980. lib. bdg. 50.00 (ISBN 0-379-20348-0). Oceana.
Marshall, Helen, tr. see Scharfetter, C.
Marshall, Helen Lowrie. Aim for a Star. 1966. 2.95 (ISBN 0-385-08258-4). Doubleday.
--Close to the Heart. 1958. 2.50 o.p. (ISBN 0-385-08261-4). Doubleday.
--Gift of Wonder. LC 67-28483. 1967. 1.95 o.p. (ISBN 0-385-09465-5). Doubleday.
--Leave a Touch of Glory. LC 76-6203. 1976. 2.95 o.p. (ISBN 0-385-12306-X). Doubleday.
--Walk the World Proudly. LC 69-15210. 1969. 2.95 o.p. (ISBN 0-385-08253-3). Doubleday.
Marshall, Hermine H. Positive Discipline & Classroom Interaction: A Part of the Teaching-Learning Process. (Illus.). 144p. 1972. pap. 14.75 (ISBN 0-398-02457-X). C C Thomas.
Marshall, I. Howard. Acts of the Apostles. (Tyndale New Testament Commentaries Ser.). (Orig.). 1980. pap. 6.95 (ISBN 0-8028-1423-9). Eerdmans.
--Kept by the Power of God. LC 74-23996. 288p. 1975. pap. 5.95 (ISBN 0-87123-304-5, 210304). Bethany Fell.
--Last Supper & Lord's Supper. (Orig.). 1981. pap. price not set (ISBN 0-8028-1854-4). Eerdmans.
Marshall, I. Howard, ed. see Travis, Stephen H.
Marshall, J. D., ed. A History of Lancashire County Council 1889-1974. 456p. 1977. bds. 36.00x (ISBN 0-85520-215-7, Pub. by Martin Robertson England). Biblio Dist.
Marshall, J. John, ed. Mechanisms of Saccharide Polymerization & Depolymerization. LC 80-16155. 1980. 32.00 (ISBN 0-12-474150-9). Acad Pr.
Marshall, James. George & Martha One Fine Day. (Illus.). (gr. k-3). 1978. reinforced bdg. 6.95 (ISBN 0-395-27154-1). HM.
--George & Martha Tons of Fun. (gr. k-3). 1980. reinforced bdg. 6.95 (ISBN 0-395-29524-6). HM.
--The Guest. (gr. k-3). 1981. pap. 3.45x (ISBN 0-395-31127-6). HM.
--A Summer in the South. (gr. k-6). 1980. pap. 1.50 (ISBN 0-440-48105-8, YB). Dell.
--What's the Matter with Carruthers? LC 72-75607. (Illus.). 32p. (gr. k-3). 1972. reinforced bdg. 6.95 (ISBN 0-395-13895-7). HM.
--Yummers! LC 72-5400. (Illus.). 32p. (gr. k-3). 1973. reinforced bdg. 6.95 (ISBN 0-395-14757-3). HM.
Marshall, James F., tr. De Stael - Du Pont Letters: Correspondence of Madame De Stael & Pierre Samuel Du Pont De Nemours, & of Other Members of the Necker & Du Pont Families. (Illus.). 1968. 35.00 (ISBN 0-299-05061-0). U of Wis Pr.
Marshall, Janet, et al. Common Birds in New Zealand, 2 vols. (Mobil New Zealand Nature Ser.). (Illus.). 1973. Vol. 1. pap. 7.50 (ISBN 0-589-00730-0, Pub. by Reed Bks Australia); Vol. 2. pap. 7.50 (ISBN 0-589-00759-9). C E Tuttle.

--Uncommon Birds in New Zealand. (Mobil New Zealand Nature Ser.). (Illus.). 96p. 1975. pap. 7.50 (ISBN 0-589-00941-9, Pub. by Reed Bks Australia). C E Tuttle.

Marshall, Jay, ed. How to Perform Instant Magic. LC 79-55634. (Illus.). 1980. cancelled (ISBN 0-89196-044-9, Domus Bks); pap. 8.95 (ISBN 0-89196-043-0). Quality Bks IL.

Marshall, Jeff. The Bicycle Rider's Bible. LC 79-6868. (Outdoor Bible Ser.). (Illus.). 176p. 1981. pap. 4.50 (ISBN 0-385-15134-9). Doubleday.

Marshall, Joan K., compiled by. Serials for Libraries. LC 78-31144. 494p. 1979. lib. bdg. 52.50 (ISBN 0-87436-280-6). ABC-Clio.

Marshall, John. An Autobiographical Sketch by John Marshall. Adams, John S., ed. LC 71-160849. (American Constitutional Legal History Ser.). (Illus.). 74p. 1973. Repr. of 1937 ed. lib. bdg. 15.00 (ISBN 0-306-70216-9). Da Capo.

--Biographical Dictionary of Railway Engineers. 1978. 15.95 (ISBN 0-7153-7489-3). David & Charles.

--Forgotten Railways: North-West England. LC 80-68899. (Illus.). 176p. 1981. 16.95 (ISBN 0-7153-8003-6). David & Charles.

--George Washington, 5 vols. LC 80-25082. (American Statesmen Ser.). 2400p. 1981. Set. pap. 19.95 (ISBN 0-87754-175-2). Chelsea Hse.

--Lancashire & Yorkshire Railway, Vol. 1. (Railway History Ser.). 1970. 14.95 (ISBN 0-7153-4352-1). David & Charles.

--The Lancashire & Yorkshire Railway, Vol. 2. (Railway History Ser.). (Illus.). 327p. 1970. 14.95 (ISBN 0-7153-4906-6). David & Charles.

--The Lancashire & Yorkshire Railway, Vol. 3. (Railway History Ser.). 288p. 1972. 14.95 (ISBN 0-7153-5320-9). David & Charles.

--The Lancashire & Yorkshire Railway in Pictures. 13.50 (ISBN 0-7153-7478-8). David & Charles.

--Mohenjodaro & the Indus Civilization: Being an Official Account of Archaeological Excavations at Mohenjodaro Carried Out by the Government of India Between the Years 1922-1927, 3 vols. LC 73-905649. (Illus.). 716p. 1973. Repr. Set. 100.00x o.p. (ISBN 0-8364-0437-8). South Asia Bks.

--Planning for a Family. 1969. pap. 5.95 (ISBN 0-571-06260-1, Pub. by Faber & Faber). Merrimack Bk Serv.

--Taxila, 3 vols. (Illus.). 1975. Repr. Set. 100.00 (ISBN 0-89684-327-0). Orient Bk Dist.

Marshall, John & Davies-Spiell, Michael. Victorian & Edwardian Lake District. 1976. pap. 11.95 (ISBN 0-7134-3417-1, Pub. by Batsford England). David & Charles.

Marshall, John A. American Bastille. LC 71-121115. (Civil Liberties in American History Ser). 1970. Repr. of 1869 ed. lib. bdg. 69.50 (ISBN 0-306-71963-0). Da Capo.

Marshall, John C. & Hales, Loyde W. Classroom Test Construction. LC 70-133892. (Education Ser). 1971. text ed. 14.95 (ISBN 0-201-04506-0). A-W.

--Essentials of Testing. LC 74-158875. (Education Ser). 1972. pap. text ed. 6.95 (ISBN 0-201-04508-7). A-W.

Marshall, John L. & Barbash, Heather. The Sports Doctor's Fitness Book for Women. 1981. 12.95 (ISBN 0-440-08201-3). Delacorte.

Marshall, Judi & Cooper, Cary L. Executives Under Pressure. LC 78-72594. (Praeger Special Studies Ser.). 1979. 20.95 (ISBN 0-03-049496-6). Praeger.

Marshall, Judi, jt. auth. see Cooper, Cary L.

Marshall, K. Eric, jt. ed. see Flannagan, John F.

Marshall, Kim. Opening Your Class with Learning Stations. LC 75-12462. (Learning Handbooks Ser.). 1975. pap. 3.95 (ISBN 0-8224-1909-2). Pitman Learning.

--The Story of Life: From the Big Bang to You. LC 79-27727. (Illus.). 160p. (gr. 4-7). 1981. 8.95 (ISBN 0-03-054071-2). HR&W.

Marshall, Larry G. Evolution of the Borhyaenidae, Extinct South American Predaceous Marsupials. (Publications in Geological Sciences: Vol. 117). 1978. pap. 11.00x (ISBN 0-520-09571-5). U of Cal Pr.

Marshall, Lillian B. Cooking Across the South: A Collection & Recollection of Favorite Regional Recipes. LC 80-80752. 280p. 1980. 12.95 (ISBN 0-8487-0505-X). Oxmoor Hse.

Marshall, M., jt. auth. see Early, J.

Marshall, Madeleine. The Singer's Manual of English Diction. 1953. pap. text ed. 7.95 (ISBN 0-02-871100-9). Schirmer Bks.

Marshall, Margaret. The Librarian & the Handicapped Child. LC 80-51349. (Grafton Books on Library & Information Science). 160p. 1981. lib. bdg. 25.00x (ISBN 0-86531-056-4, Pub. by Andre Deutsch). Westview.

Marshall, Mel. The Care & Repair of Fishing Tackle. 1976. 12.95 (ISBN 0-87691-183-1). Winchester Pr.

--Cooking Over Coals. 1971. 9.95 (ISBN 0-87691-033-9). Winchester Pr.

--How to Choose & Use Lumber, Plywood, Panelboards, & Laminates. LC 79-4710. 1980. pap. 4.95 (ISBN 0-06-090724-X, CN 724, CN). Har-Row.

--How to Fish: A Commonsense Approach. (Illus.). 1978. 11.95 (ISBN 0-87691-273-0). Winchester Pr.

--How to Make Your Own Lures & Flies. (Funk & W Bk.). (Illus.). 1977. 7.95 o.s.i. (ISBN 0-308-10290-8, TYC-T); pap. 4.50 (ISBN 0-308-10292-4, TYC-T). T Y Crowell.

--Steelhead. (Illus.). 1980. 10.95 (ISBN 0-87691-093-2). Winchester Pr.

--Yard Buildings. LC 80-1125. (Homeowner's Bible Ser.). (Illus.). 160p. 1981. pap. 4.95 (ISBN 0-385-15400-3). Doubleday.

Marshall, Michael. Top Hat & Tails: The Story of Jack Buchanan. (Illus.). 1978. 24.00 (ISBN 0-241-89602-9, Pub. by Hamish Hamilton England). David & Charles.

Marshall, Michael, ed. Stanley Holloway: More Monologues & Songs. (Illus.). 128p. 1980. pap. 5.95 (ISBN 0-241-10478-5, Pub. by Hamish Hamilton England). David & Charles.

Marshall, Norman. Pocket Encyclopedia of Ocean Life. (Illus.). (gr. 7 up). 1971. 8.95 (ISBN 0-02-580180-5). Macmillan.

Marshall, P. J. East Indian Fortunes: The British in Bengal in the Eighteenth Century. (Illus.). 1976. 37.50x (ISBN 0-19-821566-5). Oxford U Pr.

Marshall, P. T. & Hughes, G. M. Physiology of Mammals & Other Vertebrates. 2nd ed. LC 78-73810. (Illus.). 1981. 39.50 (ISBN 0-521-22633-3); pap. 16.95 (ISBN 0-521-29586-6). Cambridge U Pr.

Marshall, P. T., jt. auth. see Hughes, D. T.

Marshall, P. T., jt. auth. see Hughes, David T.

Marshall, Patricia. Wild Mammals of Hong Kong. (Illus.). 1967. pap. 1.40x o.p. (ISBN 0-19-638060-X). Oxford U Pr.

Marshall, Paul W., et al. Operations Management: Text & Cases. 1975. text ed. 20.95 (ISBN 0-256-01682-8). Irwin.

Marshall, Peter. Keepers of the Springs: And Other Messages from Mister Jones, Meet the Master. (Inspirational Classics Ser). 1962. 4.95 (ISBN 0-8007-1011-8). Revell.

Marshall, Prince. Trucks & Vans Before 1927. (Illus.). 150p. 1972. 8.95 (ISBN 0-02-580190-2). Macmillan.

Marshall, R., jt. auth. see Skitok, J.

Marshall, R. G., et al. Fuente Hispana. (Level 3). (gr. 10-12). 1971. text ed. 11.95 (ISBN 0-07-040575-1, C); instructors' manual 3.95 (ISBN 0-07-040579-4); tapes 250.00 (ISBN 0-07-098975-3). test pkg. replacement 25.00 (ISBN 0-07-040578-6). McGraw.

Marshall, Ray, et al. Employment Discrimination: The Impact of Legal & Administrative Remedies. LC 78-17333. 1978. 22.95 (ISBN 0-03-045356-9). Praeger.

Marshall, Robert E., jt. auth. see Kooi, Kenneth A.

Marshall, Robert H. & Swanson, Rodney B. The Monetary Process: Essentials of Money & Banking. 2nd ed. 450p. 1980. text ed. 17.95 (ISBN 0-395-26530-4); instructors' manual 0.65 (ISBN 0-395-26527-4). HM.

Marshall, Roderick. William Morris & His Earthly Paradises. (Illus.). 317p. 1980. 29.50x (ISBN 0-389-20085-9). B&N.

Marshall, Roger. Designed to Win. (Illus.). 1981. 28.50 (ISBN 0-393-03229-9). Norton.

--Race to Win. (Illus.). 1980. 15.95 (ISBN 0-393-03236-1). Norton.

Marshall, S. L. A., jt. auth. see Sears, Stephen W.

Marshall, Stanley J., jt. auth. see Frost, Reuben B.

Marshall, Stephen E., ed. Randax Education Guide, 1979. 8th ed. 1979. pap. 5.75 o.p. (ISBN 0-914880-09-8). Educ Guide.

Marshall, Sybil. Experiment in Education. (Illus.). 28.95 (ISBN 0-521-05680-2); pap. 9.95x (ISBN 0-521-09372-4). Cambridge U Pr.

Marshall, Sybil, ed. Fenland Chronicle. LC 66-21652. 1981. pap. 10.95 (ISBN 0-521-28043-5). Cambridge U Pr.

Marshall, T. J. & Holmes, J. W. Soil Physics. LC 78-73809. (Illus.). 1980. 77.50 (ISBN 0-521-22622-8); pap. 21.95x (ISBN 0-521-29579-3). Cambridge U Pr.

Marshall, T. M. History of the Western Boundary of the Louisiana Purchase, 1819-1841. LC 73-87411. (American Scene Ser). (Illus.). 1970. Repr. of 1914 ed. lib. bdg. 27.50 (ISBN 0-306-71554-6). Da Capo.

Marshall, Tony M., jt. auth. see Rose, Gordon.

Marshall, Victor W. Last Chapters: A Sociology of Aging & Dying. LC 79-26915. (Social Gerontology Ser.). (Orig.). 1980. pap. text ed. 8.95 (ISBN 0-8185-0399-8). Brooks-Cole.

Marshall, W. & Lovesey, S. W. Theory of Thermal Neutron Scattering: The Use of Neutrons for the Investigation of Condensed Matter. (International Series of Monographs on Physics). (Illus.). 624p. 1971. 55.00x o.p. (ISBN 0-19-851254-6). Oxford U Pr.

Marshall, William. Gelignite. 1978. pap. 1.75 o.p. (ISBN 0-445-04289-3). Popular Lib.

--The Hatchet Man. 1977. 6.95 o.p. (ISBN 0-03-016901-1). HR&W.

--The Hatchet Man. 1978. pap. 1.50 o.p. (ISBN 0-445-04146-3). Popular Lib.

--Thin Air. LC 77-20786. 1978. 6.95 o.p. (ISBN 0-03-021071-2). HR&W.

Marshall, William, jt. auth. see Williams, Allan.

Marshall, William, tr. see Constantine I.

Marshall, William H. & De Martin, Elena L. La Vida En Espana. 1977. pap. text ed. 3.25x (ISBN 0-88334-105-0). Ind Sch Pr.

Marshall, William L. Gelignite. LC 77-1402. 1977. 6.95 o.p. (ISBN 0-03-016906-2). HR&W.

Marshall-Hardy, Eric. Angling Ways. 1978. 10.95 o.p. (ISBN 0-214-66870-3, 8007, Dist. by Arco). Barrie & Jenkins.

Marshall Kaplan, Gans & Kahn. Children & the Urban Environment: Evaluation of the WGBH-TV Educational Project. LC 70-187397. (Special Studies in U. S. Economic, Social & Political Issues). 1973. 28.00x (ISBN 0-275-28687-8). Irvington.

Marshburn, Joseph H. & Velie, Alan R. Blood & Knavery: A Collection of English Renaissance Pamphlets & Ballads of Crime & Sin. LC 72-3523. (Illus.). 239p. 1973. 14.50 (ISBN 0-8386-1010-2). Fairleigh Dickinson.

Marshh, Henry. The Rebel Jew. 160p. 1980. 19.50x (ISBN 0-7050-0078-8, Pub. by Skilton & Shaw England). State Mutual Bk.

Marshner, William H. Annulment or Divorce? 96p. (Orig.). 1978. pap. 2.95 (ISBN 0-931888-00-X, Chris. Coll. Pr.). Christendom Pubns.

Marsilius Of Padua. Defensor Pacis. Gewirth, Alan, tr. (Medieval Academy Reprints for Teaching Ser.). 1980. pap. 6.00x (ISBN 0-8020-6412-4). U of Toronto Pr.

Marsland, Amy L., jt. auth. see Klin, George.

Marsmann, H., jt. auth. see Kintzinger, J. P.

Marston, Adrian, et al, eds. Contemporary Operative Surgery. (Illus.). 237p. 1979. text ed. 38.95x (ISBN 0-7198-2566-0). Intl Ideas.

Marston, Doris. Exploring Patchwork. 1972. 5.75 o.p. (ISBN 0-8231-5040-2). Branford.

Marston, Elsa. The Cliffs of Cairo. LC 80-26785. 160p. (gr. 7 up). 1981. 7.95 (ISBN 0-8253-0032-0). Beaufort Bks NY.

Marston, Frank S. The Peace Conference of Nineteen Nineteen: Organization & Procedure. LC 80-28997. xi, 276p. 1981. Repr. of 1944 ed. lib. bdg. 25.00x (ISBN 0-313-22910-4, MAPEC). Greenwood.

Marston, Hope I. Trucks, Trucking, & You. LC 78-7725. (Illus.). (gr. 5 up). 1978. 6.95 (ISBN 0-396-07602-5). Dodd.

Marston, John. Antonio's Revenge: The Second Part of Antonio & Mellida. Hunter, G. K., ed. LC 65-12161. (Regents Renaissance Drama Ser.). 1965. pap. 6.50x (ISBN 0-8032-0273-3). U of Nebr Pr.

--Dutch Courtesan. Wine, M. L., ed. LC 65-11519. (Regents Renaissance Drama Ser). 1965. 8.75x (ISBN 0-8032-0274-1); pap. 2.35x (ISBN 0-8032-5274-9, BB 210, Bison). U of Nebr Pr.

--Fawn. Smith, Gerald A., ed. LC 65-11518. (Regents Renaissance Drama Ser). 1965. 7.95x (ISBN 0-8032-0276-8); pap. 1.65x (ISBN 0-8032-5275-7, BB 209, Bison). U of Nebr Pr.

--Malcontent. Wine, M. L., ed. LC 64-17228. (Regents Renaissance Drama Ser). 1964. 8.50x (ISBN 0-8032-0277-6); pap. 3.95x (ISBN 0-8032-5276-5, BB 206, Bison). U of Nebr Pr.

Marston, R. M. One Hundred & Ten CMOS Digital IC Projects. 1976. pap. 7.15 (ISBN 0-8104-0856-2). Hayden.

--One Hundred & Ten Electronic Alarm Projects. (gr. 10 up). 1977. pap. 7.25 (ISBN 0-8104-5660-5). Hayden.

--One Hundred & Ten OP-AMP Projects. (Illus.). 128p. 1975. pap. 7.15 (ISBN 0-8104-0701-9). Hayden.

--One Hundred-Ten Thyristor Projects Using SCR's & TRIAC's. (Illus.). 1973. pap. 7.50 (ISBN 0-8104-5096-8). Hayden.

Marston, V. Paul. The Biblical Family. LC 80-68332. 208p. 1980. pap. 4.95 (ISBN 0-89107-192-X, Cornerstone Bks.). Good News.

Marstrander, Sverre, ed. Acts of the International Symposium on Rock Art. (Illus., Six articles are in German). 1978. 20.50x (ISBN 82-00-14194-2, Dist. by Columbia U Pr.). Universitet.

Marszal, Barbara, tr. see Lem, Stanislaw.

Mart, Donald S. The Carbo-Calorie Diet. LC 72-92396. 120p. 1973. pap. 1.95 (ISBN 0-385-00615-2, Dolp). Doubleday.

--The Carbo-Calorie Diet Cookbook. LC 75-36617. 160p. 1976. pap. 2.95 (ISBN 0-385-09908-8, Dolp). Doubleday.

Marteau, P., ed. see International AIRAPT Conference, Le Creuset, France, July 30-Aug. 3, 1979.

Martel, Aimee. Secrets Not Shared. 1981. pap. 2.25 (ISBN 0-8439-0874-2, Leisure Bks). Nordon Pubns.

Martel, Harry, jt. ed. see Selsam, Howard.

Martel, Leon C. Lend-Lease, Loans, & the Coming of the Cold War: A Study of the Implementation of Foreign Policy. (Special Studies in International Relations). 1979. lib. bdg. 28.50x (ISBN 0-89158-453-6). Westview.

Martel, Suzanne. The City Under Ground. (gr. 4-6). 1975. pap. 0.95 o.s.i. (ISBN 0-671-29730-9). Archway.

--City Underground. (Illus.). (gr. 4-6). 1975. pap. 0.95 (ISBN 0-671-29730-9). PB.

Martelet, Gustave. The Risen Christ & the Eucharistic World. 1977. 10.95 (ISBN 0-8164-0316-3). Crossroad NY.

Martell, Arthur E. Inorganic Chemistry in Biology & Medicine. LC 80-23248. (ACS Symposium Ser.: No. 140). 1980. 39.50 (ISBN 0-8412-0588-4). Am Chemical.

Martell, Arthur E., jt. auth. see Khan, M. M.

Martell, Arthur E. & Smith, Robert M., eds. Critical Stability Constants, Vols.1-4. Incl. Vol. 1. Amino Acids. 469p. 1974. 35.00 (ISBN 0-306-35211-7); Vol. 2. Amines. 415p. 1975. 45.00 (ISBN 0-306-35212-5); Vol. 3. Other Organic Ligands. 495p. 1977. 49.50 (ISBN 0-306-35213-3); Vol. 4. Inorganic Complexes. 257p. 1976. 35.00 (ISBN 0-306-35214-1). LC 74-10610. (Illus., Plenum Pr). Plenum Pub.

Martell, John. Twentieth Century World. 3rd ed. (Illus.). 1981. pap. 13.95x. Intl Ideas.

Martells, Jack. Beer Can Collectors Bible. Date not set. pap. 5.95 (ISBN 0-394-28918-8). Ballantine.

Marten, ed. see Symposium on Theory of Argumentation, Groningen, October 11-13, 1978.

Marten, Clement. The Artist's Airbrush Manual. (Illus.). 72p. 1980. 25.00 (ISBN 0-7153-7997-6). David & Charles.

Marten, Elizabeth. Work-a-Day: Your Classrookm Employment Agency. 59p. 1979. pap. 4.95 (ISBN 0-914634-73-9, 7919). DOK Pubs.

Marten, Elizabeth H., jt. auth. see Crosby, Nina E.

Marten, Jacqueline. Let the Crags Comb Out Her Dainty Hair. 256p. 1975. pap. 1.25 o.p. (ISBN 0-445-00302-2). Popular Lib.

Marten, Michael & Chesterman, John. The Radiant Universe: Electronic Images from Space. (Illus.). 128p. 1980. 17.95 (ISBN 0-02-580420-0). Macmillan.

Martens, B. Investment & Divestment Policies of Multinationals in Europe. (Praeger Special Studies). 1979. 22.95 (ISBN 0-03-046196-0). Praeger.

Martens, Elmer A. God's Design: Focusing an Old Testament Theology. 368p. 1981. 12.95 (ISBN 0-8010-6115-6). Baker Bk.

Martens, Frederick H. The Book of the Opera & the Ballet & the History of the Opera. LC 80-2289. 1981. Repr. of 1925 ed. 22.50 (ISBN 0-404-18857-5). AMS Pr.

Martens, Frederick H., tr. see Bachmann, Alberto.

Martens, Frederick K. A Thousand & One Nights of Opera. LC 77-25416. (Music Reprint Ser., 1978). 1978. Repr. of 1926 ed. lib. bdg. 32.50 (ISBN 0-306-77565-4). Da Capo.

Martens, Hinrich R., jt. auth. see Cadzow, James A.

Martens, Rainer, ed. Joy & Sadness in Children's Sports. 375p. 1978. pap. text ed. 9.95x (ISBN 0-931250-15-3). Human Kinetics.

--Joy & Sadness in Children's Sports. LC 78-107073. (Illus.). 1978. 11.95x o.s.i. (ISBN 0-931250-10-2). Human Kinetics.

Martens, Robert W., jt. auth. see Sisson, James E.

Martensson, Kerstin. It's Easy to Sew-Knit and Stretch Fabric. (Illus.). 1973. pap. text ed. 5.95 o.p. (ISBN 0-913212-03-2). Kwik Sew.

--It's Easy to Sew Swimwear. (Illus.). 1971. pap. 5.95 o.p. (ISBN 0-913212-04-0). Kwik Sew.

--Kwik-Sew Method for Easy Sewing. (Illus.). pap. 6.95 (ISBN 0-913212-09-1). Kwik Sew.

Marthas, Marya S., jt. auth. see Sampson, Edward E.

Marti, Berthe M. Spanish College at Bologna. LC 63-15014. 1966. 14.00x o.p. (ISBN 0-8122-7402-4). U of Pa Pr.

Marti, Fritz. Religion & Philosophy: Collected Papers. LC 78-68801. 1979. pap. text ed. 9.50 (ISBN 0-8191-0702-6). U Pr of Amer.

--The Unconditional in Human Knowledge: Four Early Essays (1794-1796) by F. W. J. Schelling. Schelling, F. W., tr. LC 77-74407. 1980. 18.50 (ISBN 0-8387-2020-X). Bucknell U Pr.

Marti, J. T., ed. see Proceedings of the Colloquium on Numerical Analysis, Lausanne, Oct. 11-13, 1976.

Marti, Jose. Discursos Selectos De Jose Marti. LC 77-90959. 1977. pap. 4.95 (ISBN 0-685-95270-3). Ediciones.

Marti, Judy. Patchworkbook. 100p. 1981. pap. 9.95 (ISBN 0-9602970-2-2). Moon Over Mntn.

Marti, Manuel, Jr. Space Operational Analysis. LC 80-81340. (Illus.). 216p. 1981. 19.95 (ISBN 0-914886-11-8). PDA Pubs.

Marti, Noelia, jt. auth. see Grad, Frank P.
Marti, Oscar R., tr. see Lipman, Matthew.
Martial & Pliny. Selections. Kennedy, E. C., ed. text ed. 5.75x (ISBN 0-521-05683-7). Cambridge U Pr.
Marti-Ibanez, Felix. Ariel: Essays on the Arts & the History & Philosophy of Medicine. LC 62-8490. (Illus.). 1962. 6.50 o.p. (ISBN 0-910922-16-0). MD Pubns.
--To Be a Doctor. Bd. with The Young Princes; The Race & the Runner. LC 68-27688. 1968. 4.95 (ISBN 0-910922-18-7). MD Pubns.
Marti-Ibanez, Felix, ed. Health & Travel. 1955. 3.00 o.p. (ISBN 0-910922-02-0). MD Pubns.
--History of American Medicine. 1959. 4.00 o.p. (ISBN 0-910922-12-8). MD Pubns.
--Medical Writing. 1956. 3.00 o.p. (ISBN 0-910922-03-9). MD Pubns.
--Patient's Progress. LC 67-26612. 1967. 5.95 o.p. (ISBN 0-910922-17-9). MD Pubns.
--Psychiatry & Religion. 1956. 3.00 o.p. (ISBN 0-910922-04-7). MD Pubns.
Martin. Prologue to Economic Understanding. 1966. pap. text ed. 4.95x (ISBN 0-675-09716-9). Merrill.
Martin, et al. Comprehensive Rehabilitation Nursing. (Illus.). 816p. 1980. text ed. 22.95 (ISBN 0-07-040611-1, HP). McGraw.
Martin, A. E., ed. Emission Control Technology for Industrial Boilers. LC 80-26046. (Pollution Tech. Rev. 74 Ser.: Energy Tech. Rev. 62). (Illus.). 405p. 1981. 48.00 (ISBN 0-8155-0833-6). Noyes.
Martin, A. G. Finishing Processes in Printing. (Library of Printing Technology). Date not set. 22.00 (ISBN 0-8038-2289-8). Hastings.
Martin, Alan & Harbison, Samuel A. An Introduction to Radiation Protection. 2nd ed. LC 79-42847. 1980. pap. text ed. 15.00x o.p. (ISBN 0-412-20960-8, Pub. by Chapman & Hall). Methuen Inc.
--An Introduction to Radiation Protection. 2nd ed. LC 79-42847. 1980. 22.95x o.p. (ISBN 0-470-26761-5); pap. 12.95x o.p. (ISBN 0-470-26877-8). Halsted Pr.
Martin, Albert. One Man, Hurt. 288p. 1975. 8.95 o.s.i. (ISBN 0-02-580470-7). Macmillan.
Martin, Albert N. Practical Implications of Calvinism. 1979. pap. 0.75 (ISBN 0-85151-296-8). Banner of Truth.
Martin, Albro. Enterprise Denied: Origins of the Decline of American Railroads, 1897-1917. LC 71-159673. 1971. 20.00x (ISBN 0-231-03508-X); pap. 10.00x (ISBN 0-231-08362-9). Columbia U Pr.
Martin, Alexander C. & Barkely, William D. Seed Identification Manual. 1973. 22.75x (ISBN 0-520-00814-6). U. of Cal Pr.
Martin, Alexander H., jt. auth. see Francis, Carl C.
Martin, Alfred W. Seven Great Bibles: The Sacred Scriptures of Hinduism, Buddhism, Zoroastrianism, Confucianism, (Taoism), Mohammedanism, Judism & Christianity. LC 74-11849. 277p. 1975. Repr. of 1930 ed. lib. bdg. 25.00x (ISBN 0-8154-0495-6). Cooper Sq.
Martin, Arlan S. Vivaldi Violin Concertos: A Handbook. LC 76-169698. 1972. 10.00 (ISBN 0-8108-0432-8). Scarecrow.
Martin, Augustine, ed. Exploring English: Anthology of Irish Short Stories. 367p. 1967. pap. 4.95 (ISBN 0-7171-0056-1). Irish Bk Ctr.
Martin, B. G. Muslim Brotherhoods in 19th Century Africa. LC 75-35451. (African Studies Ser.: No. 18). 1977. 31.95 (ISBN 0-521-21062-3). Cambridge U Pr.
Martin, Barclay. Anxiety & Neurotic Disorders. LC 76-151033. (Approaches to Behavior Pathology Ser). 1971. pap. text ed. 10.95 (ISBN 0-471-57353-1). Wiley.
Martin, Beatrice D. Teaching Young Children. LC 74-20267. 1975. pap. 7.80 (ISBN 0-8273-0577-X); instructor's guide 1.60 (ISBN 0-8273-0578-8). Delmar.
Martin, Ben. Shipmaster's Handbook on Ship's Business. LC 68-20976. 1969. 12.00x (ISBN 0-87033-098-5). Cornell Maritime.
Martin, Bernard, ed. Movements & Issues in American Judaism: An Analysis & Sourcebook of Developments Since 1945. LC 77-87971. 1978. lib. bdg. 22.50 (ISBN 0-313-20044-0, MCJ/). Greenwood.
--A Shestov Anthology. LC 74-81453. xvii, 328p. 1970. 15.00x (ISBN 0-8214-0070-3). Ohio U Pr.
Martin, Bernard, tr. see Bergelson, David.
Martin, Bernard, tr. see Shestov, Lev.
Martin, Betty & Carson, Ben. The Principal's Handbook on the School Media Center. 212p. 1981. pap. 12.50x (ISBN 0-208-01912-X, Lib Prof Pubns). Shoe String.
Martin, Betty & Sargent, Linda. The Teacher's Handbook on the School Library Media Center. 399p. 1980. 18.50 (ISBN 0-208-01854-9, Lib Prof Pubns); pap. text ed. 14.50x (ISBN 0-208-01847-6). Shoe String.
Martin, Bill, Jr. Bill Martin Freedom Book Series, 10 bks. Incl. Adam's Balm. Foreman, Michael, illus (ISBN 0-8372-2052-1); America, I Know You. Rand, Ted, illus (ISBN 0-8372-2048-3); Freedom's Apple Tree. Rambola, John, illus (ISBN 0-8372-2047-5); Gentle, Gentle Thursday. Maitin, Samuel, illus (ISBN 0-8372-2055-6); I Am Freedom's Child. Shimin, Symeon, illus (ISBN 0-8372-2046-7); I Reach Out to the Morning. Markowitz, Henry, illus (ISBN 0-8372-2054-8); It's America for Me. Glanzman, Lou, illus (ISBN 0-8372-2049-1); Once There Were Bluebirds. Martin, Bernard, illus. o.p. (ISBN 0-8372-0652-9); Poor Old Uncle Sam. Murdocca, Sal, illus (ISBN 0-8372-2051-3); Spoiled Tomatoes. Ells, Jay, illus (ISBN 0-8372-2050-5). (gr. 5-12). pap. 11.70 pkg. of 6 copies (ISBN 0-685-29088-3); tchrs' guide 4.35 (ISBN 0-8372-0708-8). 10 records 84.90 (ISBN 0-8372-0230-2). complete lab: 60 s-c, 50 activity cards & teacherhs guide 198.00 set (ISBN 0-8372-2449-7); bks., guide, activitycards, & cassettes 198.00 set **(ISBN 0-8372-2044-0); book pack, 6 copies of one title avail.; activity cards 21.36 (ISBN 0-8372-1949-3). Bowmar-Noble.**
--Little Nature Books. Incl. Poppies Afield; Frogs in a Pond; Butterflies Becoming; Germanation; Ants Underground; A Mushroom Is Growing; A Hydro Goes Walking; Moon Cycle; Messenger Bee; June Bugs. (Illus.). (gr. 1-6). 1975. 111.00 (ISBN 0-87827-196-1); tchr's guide incl. (ISBN 0-685-55948-3); recordings incl. Ency Brit Ed.
Martin, Billy. Number One. 1981. pap. 3.25 (ISBN 0-440-16229-7). Dell.
Martin, Billy & Golenbock, Peter. Number One. 1980. 11.95 (ISBN 0-440-06416-3). Delacorte.
Martin, Bischof. Sunsets into Sunrises. Ozols, Violet, tr. 560p. Date not set. 20.00 (ISBN 0-934616-14-0). Valkyrie Pr.
Martin, Bruce. Joints in Buildings. 1977. 54.95 (ISBN 0-470-99106-2). Halsted Pr.
Martin, Bruce K. Philip Larkin. (English Author Ser.: No. 234). 1978. 12.50 (ISBN 0-8057-6705-3). Twayne.
Martin, C. A., jt. auth. see Fuller, M. M.
Martin, Carol A. Law Enforcement & Community Relations: A Selected Bibliography. (Public Administration Ser.: Bibliography: P-634). 1980. pap. 7.50. Vance Biblios.
Martin, Charles, jt. auth. see Babb, Hugh W.
Martin, Charles E., illus. The Story of Jonah. (Look Look Bks). (Illus.). 24p. (ps). 1981. pap. 1.25 (ISBN 0-307-11863-0, Golden Pr). Western Pub.
Martin, Charles N. Role of Perception in Science. 1963. text ed. 4.50x (ISBN 0-391-02039-0). Humanities.
Martin, Chuck. Gunsmoke Bonanza. 1978. pap. 1.25 (ISBN 0-505-51276-9). Tower Bks.
--Law for Tombstone. 1978. pap. 1.25 (ISBN 0-505-51268-8). Tower Bks.
Martin, Claude R., Jr., jt. ed. see Leigh, James H.
Martin, Cliff & Scott, Frank, eds. Rhythm & Blues Records: An Encyclopedic Discography Nineteen Forty-Three to Seventy-Five. (Ethnic Music Ser.: Vol. 1). Date not set. pap. 19.95 (ISBN 0-936518-05-7). Nighthawk Pr.
Martin, Clyde F., ed. see NATO ASI & AMS Summer Seminar in Applied Mathematics Held at Harvard University, Cambridge, Ma., June 18-29, 1979.
Martin, Constance R. Textbook of Endocrine Physiology. (Illus.). 485p. 1976. 19.95x (ISBN 0-19-502295-5). Oxford U Pr.
Martin, Curtis H. & Leone, Robert. Local Economic Development. LC 76-55537. (Illus.). 1977. 16.95 (ISBN 0-669-01319-6). Lexington Bks.
Martin, Cy. The Marshal of Packersville. (YA) 1976. 5.95 (ISBN 0-685-68914-X, Avalon). Bouregy.
Martin, Cynthia. Beating the Adoption Game. LC 80-16883. 1980. 9.95 (ISBN 0-916392-60-0). Oak Tree Pubns.
Martin, D. La Vida Espanola. 3rd ed. (Span.). 1970. pap. 8.50 (ISBN 0-13-522458-6). P-H.
Martin, D. & Hauthal, H. Dimethyl Sulphoxide. LC 75-1600. 1976. 64.95 (ISBN 0-470-57362-7). Halsted Pr.
Martin, D., tr. see Oberman, H. A.
Martin, D. G. & Wood, W. G. Experimental Method: A Guide to the Art of Experiment for Students of Science & Engineering. (Illus.). 106p. (Orig.). 1974. pap. text ed. 4.75x (ISBN 0-485-12022-4, Athlone Pr). Humanities.
Martin, Darwin J. How to Raise & Train a Schipperke. (Orig.). pap. 2.00 (ISBN 0-87666-381-1, DS1114). TFH Pubns.
Martin, David. Patriot or Traitor: The Case of General Mihailovich. LC 77-83123. (Archival Documentary Publication Ser: No. 191). (Illus.). 520p. 1978. 19.00 (ISBN 0-8179-6911-X). Hoover Inst Pr.
Martin, David, jt. auth. see Lemarchand, Rene.
Martin, David, ed. Anarchy & Culture: The Problem of the Contemporary University. LC 74-80271. 1969. 20.00x (ISBN 0-231-03317-6). Columbia U Pr.
Martin, David, et al, eds. Sociology & Theology. 170p. 1980. 22.50x (ISBN 0-312-74007-7). St Martin.
Martin, David G. Introduction to Psychotherapy. LC 75-145969. (Orig.). 1971. pap. text ed. 6.95 o.p. (ISBN 0-8185-0010-7). Brooks-Cole.
Martin, David L. Alabama's State & Local Government. LC 75-1714. (Government Ser.). 1975. perfect bdg. 6.95 (ISBN 0-8403-1121-4). Kendall Hunt.
Martin, David L., jt. auth. see Morlan, Robert L.
Martin, Derald. Professional Industrial Photography. (Illus.). 176p. 1980. 19.95 (ISBN 0-8174-4008-9). Amphoto.
Martin, Dick. The Apple Book. (Illus.). 24p. (ps-4). 1964. PLB 5.38 (ISBN 0-307-68904-2, Golden Pr). Western Pub.
--Cut & Assemble the Emerald City of Oz. (Illus.). 48p. (Orig.). (gr. 1-5). 1981. pap. 3.95 (ISBN 0-486-24053-3). Dover.
--The Fish Book. (Illus.). 24p. (gr. k-1). 1976. PLB 5.38 (ISBN 0-307-68982-4, Golden Pr). Western Pub.
--The Sandpail Book. (Illus.). 24p. (ps-4). 1977. Repr. of 1964 ed. PLB 5.38 (ISBN 0-307-68920-4, Golden Pr). Western Pub.
Martin, Dick, jt. auth. see Greene, David L.
Martin, Dolores M., ed. Handbook of Latin American Studies: No. 42, Humanities. 720p. 1981. text ed. 55.00x (ISBN 0-292-73016-0). U of Tex Pr.
Martin, Don. Don Martin Cooks up More Tales. (Mad Ser.). (Illus.). 192p. 1976. pap. 1.75 (ISBN 0-446-94413-0). Warner Bks.
--Don Martin Drops 13 Stories. (Mad Ser.). (Illus.). 1973. pap. 1.75 (ISBN 0-446-94414-9). Warner Bks.
--Don Martin Forges Ahead. (Mad Ser.). (Illus., Orig.). 1977. pap. 1.75 (ISBN 0-446-94415-7). Warner Bks.
--Don Martin Steps Out. (Mad Ser.). (Illus.). 1975. pap. 1.75 (ISBN 0-446-94416-5). Warner Bks.
--Mad Adventures of Captain Klutz. (Mad Ser.). (Illus., Orig.). 1974. pap. 1.75 (ISBN 0-446-94417-3). Warner Bks.
--Mad's Don Martin Carries on. (Mad Ser.). (Illus.). 1973. pap. 1.75 (ISBN 0-446-94419-X). Warner Bks.
--Mad's Don Martin Digs Deeper. (Mad Ser.). (Illus., Orig.). 1979. pap. 1.75 (ISBN 0-446-94420-3). Warner Bks.
--Mad's Maddest Artist Don Martin Bounces Back. (Mad Ser.). (Illus.). 1976. pap. 1.75 (ISBN 0-446-94420-3). Warner Bks.
Martin, Donald L. An Ownership Theory of the Trade Union: A New Approach. 160p. 1981. 14.50x (ISBN 0-520-03884-3). U of Cal Pr.
--To the People: Prepare for War. 64p. 1981. 7.95 (ISBN 0-89962-043-4). Todd & Honeywell.
Martin, Donald L. & Schwartz, Warren C., eds. Deregulating American Industry: Legal & Economic Problems. LC 77-5273. (Illus.). 1977. 15.95 (ISBN 0-669-01603-9). Lexington Bks.
Martin, Dorothy. Light at the Top of the Stairs. 256p. 1974. pap. 2.50 (ISBN 0-8024-4748-1). Moody.
--The Mystery of the Empty House. (Vickie Ser.). 128p. (Orig.). (gr. 6-8). Date not set. pap. 1.95 (ISBN 0-8024-5703-7). Moody.
--Mystery of the Jade Earring. (Vickie Ser.). (Orig.). 1980. pap. 1.50 (ISBN 0-8024-5702-9). Moody.
--Mystery of the Missing Bracelets. (gr. 4-7). 1980. pap. 1.50 (ISBN 0-8024-5701-0). Moody.
--Mystery on the Fourteenth Floor. 128p. (Orig.). (gr. 6-9). 1980. pap. 1.50 (ISBN 0-8024-5700-2). Moody.
Martin, Dorothy, tr. Sextette: Translations from the French Symbolists. LC 80-10539. (Symbolists Ser.). 112p. 1980. Repr. of 1928 ed. 18.50 (ISBN 0-404-16331-9). AMS Pr.
Martin, Dwight. The Triad Imperative. 288p. 1980. 10.95 (ISBN 0-312-92829-7). Congdon & Lattes.
Martin, E. W., ed. Comparative Development in Social Welfare. 1972. text ed. 25.00x (ISBN 0-04-361014-5). Allen Unwin.
Martin, E. W., Jr. Mathematics for Decision Making: A Programmed Basic Text, 2 vols. 1969. text ed. 18.95x ea. Vol. 1 (ISBN 0-256-00354-8). Vol. 2 (ISBN 0-256-00371-8). Irwin.
Martin, E. W., Jr. & Perkins, William C. Computers & Information Systems: An Introduction. 1973. text ed. 18.95 (ISBN 0-256-01452-3). Irwin.
Martin, E. Wainwright, Jr. Plaid for Basic Algebra. 1970. pap. 5.50 (ISBN 0-256-01286-5, 15-0852-00). Learning Syst.
Martin, Edith, jt. auth. see Parker, Betty.
Martin, Edwin. Southeast Asia & China: The End of Containment. LC 76-53510. 1977. lib. bdg. 18.00x (ISBN 0-89158-219-3). Westview.
Martin, Edwin M., jt. auth. see Atlantic Council Working Group on the U.S. & the Developing Countries.
Martin, Eleanor J. Rene Marques. (World Authors Ser.: No. 516). 1979. lib. bdg. 14.50 (ISBN 0-8057-6357-0). Twayne.
Martin, Elizabeth, et al, eds. Sourcebook of Harris National Surveys: Repeated Questions, 1963-1976. (IRSS Technical Papers). (Illus.). 515p. 1981. pap. write for info. (ISBN 0-89143-091-1). U NC Inst Res Soc Sci.
Martin, Elmer P. & Martin, Joanne M. The Black Extended Family. LC 77-17058. 1980. pap. 4.50 (ISBN 0-226-50797-1, P872, Phoen). U of Chicago Pr.
Martin, Eric W., et al. Techniques of Medication: A Manual of the Administration of Drug Products. LC 69-14854. (Illus.). 1969. 20.00 o.p. (ISBN 0-397-50243-5). Lippincott.
Martin, Esmond B. Zanzibar: Tradition & Revolution. 1979. 19.95 (ISBN 0-241-89937-0, Pub. by Hamish Hamilton England). David & Charles.
Martin, Everett D. Liberty. 307p. 1981. Repr. of 1930 ed. lib. bdg. 20.00. Arden Lib.
Martin, F. David. Sculpture & Enlivened Space: Aesthetics & History. LC 79-4006. 344p. Date not set. 23.50x (ISBN 0-8131-1386-5). U Pr of Ky. Postponed.
Martin, F. X & Byrne. The Scholar Revolutionary: Eoin Macneill 1867-1945, & the Making of the New Ireland. (Illus.). 320p. 1973. 20.00x (ISBN 0-7165-0577-0, Pub. by Irish Academic Pr Ireland). Biblio Dist.
Martin, F. X., ed. see Tierney, Michael.
Martin, Fay C. Availing Prayer. 120p. pap. 1.00. Faith Pub Hse.
Martin, Florence. Observing National Holidays & Church Festivals: A Weekday Church School Unit in Christian Citizenship Series for Grades Three & Four. LC 76-174077. 1971. Repr. of 1940 ed. 24.00 (ISBN 0-8103-3804-1). Gale.
Martin, Frank. A Composer Reflects on His Art. Aprahamian, Felix, tr. from Fr. LC 79-89940. (Illus.). Date not set. cancelled (ISBN 0-89793-015-0). Hunter Hse.
Martin, Franklin W. & Ruberte, Ruth. Patiofarming: A Compendium of Useful Tables. (Studies in Tropical Agriculture). 1980. lib. bdg. 69.95 (ISBN 0-8490-3075-7). Gordon Pr.
--The Round Garden: Plans for a Small Intensive Vegetable Garden for Year Round Production in the Tropics. (Studies in Tropical Agriculture). 1980. lib. bdg. 59.95 (ISBN 0-8490-3073-0). Gordon Pr.
Martin, Franklin W., et al. Vegetables for the Hot, Humid Tropics. (Studies in Tropical Agriculture). 1980. lib. bdg. 59.95 (ISBN 0-8490-3071-4). Gordon Pr.
Martin, Fred, jt. ed. see Ibrahim, Hilmi M.
Martin, Fred W. Nineteen Hundred & One Album of Designs for Boats, Launches & Yachts. rev. ed. LC 80-69290. (Illus.). 80p. 1980. pap. 5.00. Altair Pub Co.
Martin, Frederick. Clinical Audiometry & Masking. LC 74-183115. (Studies in Communicative Disorders Ser). 1972. pap. 2.95 (ISBN 0-672-61282-8). Bobbs.
Martin, Frederick N. Introduction to Audiology. (Illus.). 496p. 1975. 19.95 (ISBN 0-13-478123-6). P-H.
--Introduction to Audiology. 2nd ed. (Illus.). 480p. 1981. text ed. 19.95 (ISBN 0-13-478131-7). P-H.
Martin, Frederick N., ed. Medical Audiology: Disorders of Hearing. (Illus.). 512p. 1981. text ed. 32.00 (ISBN 0-13-572677-8). P-H.
--Pediatric Audiology. (Illus.). 1978. ref. 29.95 (ISBN 0-13-655472-5). P-H.
Martin, G. D., ed. & tr. Anthology of Contemporary French Poetry. (Edinburgh Bilingual Library: No. 5). 216p. 1972. 10.95x (ISBN 0-292-71006-2); pap. 5.50x (ISBN 0-292-71004-6). U of Tex Pr.
Martin, G. H. & Macintyre, Sylvia, eds. A Bibliography of British & Irish Municipal History, Vol. 2. 1980. text ed. 20.00x (ISBN 0-391-01198-7, Leicester). Humanities.
--A Bibliography of British & Irish Municipal History: Vol. 1. General Works. 750p. 1972. text ed. 38.00x (ISBN 0-391-00265-1, Leicester). Humanities.
Martin, G. J., et al. N-NMR Spectroscopy. (NMR-Basic Principles & Progress Ser.: Vol. 18). (Illus.). 390p. 1981. 87.30 (ISBN 0-387-10459-3). Springer-Verlag.
Martin, Gary. Competitive Karting. LC 80-83189. (Illus.). 144p. 1980. pap. 9.95 (ISBN 0-9605068-0-2). Martin Motorsports.
Martin, Gary, jt. auth. see Pear, Joseph.
Martin, Gary L. & Osborne, J. Grayson, eds. Helping in the Community: Behavioral Applications. 430p. 1980. 22.50 (ISBN 0-306-40402-8, Plenum Pr). Plenum Pub.
Martin, Gary M. Basic Concepts in Music. 2nd ed. 288p. 1980. pap. text ed. 12.95x (ISBN 0-534-00761-9). Wadsworth Pub.

--Musical Beginnings: For Teachers & Their Students. 1975. pap. text ed. 12.95x (ISBN 0-534-00385-0). Wadsworth Pub.

Martin, Geoffrey. The Life & Thought of Isaiah Bowman. (Illus.). 272p. 1980. 22.50 (ISBN 0-208-01844-1, Archon). Shoe String.

Martin, Geoffrey J., jt. auth. see James, Preston E.

Martin, George. Verdi, His Music, Life & Times. (Music Reprint Ser.). 1979. Repr. of 1963 ed. 35.00 (ISBN 0-306-79549-3). Da Capo.

Martin, George A. The Family Horse. 12.50 (ISBN 0-88427-020-3). Green Hill.

--Microfilm of Marriage & Death. Abstracts from Washington Intelligence (Washington, D.C.) 1800-1850. 1976. of 3 rolls 61.00 set (ISBN 0-915156-02-4). Natl Genealogical.

Martin, George H. Kinematics & Dynamics of Machines. 2nd ed. (Illus.). 544p. 1982. text ed. 28.95x (ISBN 0-07-040657-X, C); write for info. solutions manual (ISBN 0-07-040658-8). McGraw.

Martin, George R. New Voices I: The Campbell Award Nominees. 1978. pap. 1.75 o.s.i. (ISBN 0-515-04507-1). Jove Pubns.

--Night Flyers. Bd. with True Names. Vinge, Vernor. (Binary Star: No. 5). (Orig.). 1981. pap. 2.50 (ISBN 0-440-10757-1). Dell.

Martin, George R., ed. Fourth New Voices Annual Volume: The John W. Campbell Award Nominees. (Orig.). 1981. pap. 2.25 (ISBN 0-425-05033-5). Berkley Pub.

Martin, George W. Let's Communicate: A Self-Help Program on Writing Letters & Memos. LC 71-109516. (Supervisory Management Ser). 1970. pap. text ed. 8.95 (ISBN 0-201-04500-1). A-W.

Martin, Gillian. A Passage of Time. LC 78-18479. 1978. 8.95 o.p. (ISBN 0-684-15819-1, ScribT). Scribner.

Martin, Gottfried. Platons Ideenlehre. LC 72-81562. 1973. 41.75x (ISBN 3-1100-4135-9). De Gruyter.

Martin, Graham. The Architecture of Experience. 256p. 1981. 26.50x (ISBN 0-85224-409-6, Pub. by Edinburgh U Pr Scotland). Columbia U Pr.

Martin, Graham, tr. see Campert, Remco.

Martin, Graham M. Giftwish. 1981. 8.95 (ISBN 0-395-30348-6). HM.

Martin, H. G. Mathematics for Engineering Technology & Computing. 1970. 19.50 (ISBN 0-08-013961-2); pap. 9.75 (ISBN 0-08-013960-4). Pergamon.

Martin, H. R., jt. auth. see McCloy, D.

Martin, Hansborg. Kein Schnaps Fur Tamara. (Easy Readers, B). (Illus.). 1977. pap. text ed. 3.75 (ISBN 0-88436-282-5). EMC.

Martin, Hardie St. see Donoso, Jose.

Martin, Harold C., ed. Style in Prose Fiction. LC 59-11178. (Essays from the English Institute Ser.). 1959. 12.50x (ISBN 0-231-02353-7). Columbia U Pr.

Martin, Helen P., jt. auth. see Sohner, Charles P.

Martin, Henri. L' Homme fossile de la Quina. LC 78-72703. (Illus.). Repr. of 1923 ed. 41.00 (ISBN 0-404-18272-0). AMS Pr.

Martin, Henry, jt. auth. see Glanvill, John.

Martin, Henry B. The Polynesian Journal of Henry Byam Martin. Dodd, Edward, ed. (Illus.). 200p. 1981. write for info. (ISBN 0-87577-060-6). Peabody Mus Salem.

Martin, Herbert W. The Forms of Silence. LC 79-88742. 1980. pap. 4.00 perf. bound (ISBN 0-916418-20-0). Lotus.

Martin, Howard N. Myths & Folktales of the Alabama-Coushatta Indians. (Illus.). 1976. 8.95 o.p. (ISBN 0-88426-052-6). Encino Pr.

Martin, Hubert, Jr. Alcaeus. (World Authors Ser.: Greece: No. 210). lib. bdg. 10.95 (ISBN 0-8057-2016-2). Twayne.

Martin, Hugh. Jonah. (Banner of Truth Geneva Series Commentaries). 1978. 10.95 (ISBN 0-85151-115-5). Banner of Truth.

Martin, Hugh, ed. see Bernard de Clairvaux, St.

Martin, Hugh, ed. see Bernard De Clairvaux, Saint.

Martin, I. & Levey, A. B. Genesis of the Classical Conditioned Response. 164p. 1968. 25.00 (ISBN 0-08-013360-6). Pergamon.

Martin, Ira. The Ins & Outs & Wins of Contract Bridge. 1977. 6.00 o.p. (ISBN 0-682-48900-X). Exposition.

Martin, Irvin. Gnome Named Goodwill. 59p. (gr. k-4). 1978. 3.95 (ISBN 0-8059-2619-4). Dorrance.

Martin, J. Computer Data Base Organization. 2nd ed. 1977. 29.95 (ISBN 0-13-165423-3). P-H.

--Design of Real Time Computer Systems. 1967. ref. ed. 25.95 (ISBN 0-13-201400-9). P-H.

--End User's Guide to Data Base. 1981. 21.50 (ISBN 0-13-277129-2). P-H.

--Telecommunications & the Computer. 2nd ed. 1976. 35.00 (ISBN 0-13-902494-8). P-H.

--Viewdata & Information Society. 1981. 29.95 (ISBN 0-13-941906-3). P-H.

Martin, J. A. & Astone, N. A. Criminal Justice Vocabulary. 312p. 1980. lexotone 29.50 (ISBN 0-398-03987-9). C C Thomas.

Martin, J. A., jt. auth. see Rutter, Michael.

Martin, J. P. Private Yankee Doodle. Scheer, George F., ed. Orig. Title: Being a Narrative of Some of the Adventures, Dangers, & Sufferings of a Revolutionary Soldier. 305p. 1979. pap. 2.95 (ISBN 0-89062-047-4, Pub. by Eastern Natl Par). Pub Ctr Cult Res.

Martin, J. S. E. M. Forster, the Endless Journey. LC 76-4755. (British Authors Ser). 1976. 26.50 (ISBN 0-521-21272-3); pap. 7.95x (ISBN 0-521-29082-1). Cambridge U Pr.

Martin, J. W. Micromechanisms in Particle-Hardened Alloys. LC 78-70411. (Cambridge Solid State Science Ser.). (Illus.). 1980. 57.50 (ISBN 0-521-22623-6); pap. 17.50 (ISBN 0-521-29580-7). Cambridge U Pr.

--Precipitation Hardening. LC 67-31505. 1968. text ed. 22.00 (ISBN 0-08-012731-2); pap. text ed. 10.75 (ISBN 0-08-012730-4). Pergamon.

Martin, J. W. & Doherty, P. D. Stability of Microstructure in Metallic Systems. LC 75-38189. (Cambridge Solid State Science Ser.). (Illus.). 180p. 1976. 57.50 (ISBN 0-521-20875-0). Cambridge U Pr.

Martin, J. W. & Doherty, R. D. Stability of Microstructure in Metallic Systems. LC 75-38179. (Cambridge Solid State Science Ser.). (Illus.). 298p. 1980. pap. 17.50x (ISBN 0-521-29883-0). Cambridge U Pr.

Martin, J. W. & Hull, R. A. Elementary Science of Metals. LC 73-75479. (Wykeham Science Ser.: No. 1). 1969. 9.95x (ISBN 0-8448-1103-3). Crane Russak Co.

--Strong Materials. LC 72-189452. (Wykeham Science Ser.: No. 21). 1972. 9.95x (ISBN 0-8448-1123-8). Crane Russak Co.

Martin, James. Computer Networks & Distributed Processing: Software, Techniques, & Architecture. (Illus.). 544p. 1981. text ed. 32.50 (ISBN 0-13-165258-3). P-H.

--Design & Strategy for Distributed Data Processing. (Illus.). 672p. 1981. text ed. 37.50 (ISBN 0-13-201657-5). P-H.

--Design of Man-Computer Dialogues. (Illus.). 496p. 1973. ref. ed. 29.00 (ISBN 0-13-201251-0). P-H.

--Introduction to Teleprocessing. (Illus.). 1972. ref. ed. 21.95 (ISBN 0-13-499814-6). P-H.

--Principles of Data Base Management. (Illus.). 320p. 1976. Ref. Ed. 25.00 (ISBN 0-13-708917-1). P-H.

--Systems Analysis for Data Transmission. (Automatic Computation Ser). 1972. ref. ed. 39.95 (ISBN 0-13-881300-0). P-H.

Martin, James A. Conflict of Laws: Cases & Materials. 1978. text ed. 22.50 (ISBN 0-316-54851-0); write for info. suppl. Little.

Martin, James A., jt. auth. see Landers, Jonathan M.

Martin, James D., tr. see Von Rad, Gerhard.

Martin, James G. & Franklin, Clyde W. Minority Group Relations. LC 72-97539. 1973. text ed. 14.95x (ISBN 0-675-08953-0). Merrill.

Martin, James J., jt. auth. see Dennis, Lawrence.

Martin, James K. Men in Rebellion: Higher Governmental Leaders & the Coming of the American Revolution. 1973. 16.00 (ISBN 0-8135-0750-2). Rutgers U Pr.

Martin, James K. & Lender, Mark. A Respectable Army: The War for Independence & America's Military Origins, 1763-1783. LC 77-86040. (American History Ser.). Date not set. pap. 4.95 (ISBN 0-88295-775-9). AHM Pub.

Martin, James M., ed. John Denver: Rocky Mountain Wonder Boy. (Illus., Orig.). 1977. pap. 1.50 o.p. (ISBN 0-523-40002-0). Pinnacle Bks.

Martin, Jane, ed. Milestones in Development: A Cumulative Index to Industrial Development, Site Selection Handbook & Related Publications Covering a Quarter-Century of Professional Contribution. 1981. 75.00x (ISBN 0-910436-16-9). Conway Pubns.

Martin, Jerry, jt. auth. see Lutzker, John.

Martin, Joanne M., jt. auth. see Martin, Elmer P.

Martin, John B. U.S. Policy in the Caribbean. LC 78-52883. (Illus.). 1978. lib. bdg. 27.00x (ISBN 0-89158-061-1). Westview.

Martin, John D., et al. Cases in Basic Financial Management. 1979. pap. text ed. 10.95 (ISBN 0-13-117556-4). P-H.

--Basic Financial Management. (Illus.). 1979. ref. 20.95 (ISBN 0-13-060541-7); study guide 8.95 (ISBN 0-13-060558-1). P-H.

Martin, John F. Civil Rights & the Crisis of Liberalism: The Democratic Party, 1945-1976. 1979. lib. bdg. 24.50x (ISBN 0-89158-454-4). Westview.

--In the Way of the Whale: The Whaling Journal of John F. Martin, 1841 to 1844. Martin, Kenneth R., ed. LC 80-66462. (Illus.). 224p. 1981. 15.00 (ISBN 0-87923-350-8). Godine.

Martin, Joseph. The Management of the Australian Economy. (Illus.). 1979. 20.50x (ISBN 0-7022-1358-6); pap. 9.75x (ISBN 0-7022-1359-4). U of Queensland Pr.

Martin, Joseph, jt. auth. see Sharp, William J.

Martin, Joseph H. & Jackson, William. New Jersey Supplement for Modern Real Estate Practice. 3rd ed. 130p. (Orig.). 1981. pap. 7.95 (ISBN 0-88462-281-9). Real Estate Ed Co.

Martin, Judith A., jt. auth. see Kadushin, Alfred.

Martin, Katherine F. Operation Dixie: The C.I.O. Organizing Committee Papers 1946-1953-a Guide to the Microfilm Edition. 154p. 1980. pap. 25.00 (ISBN 0-667-00584-6). Microfilming Corp.

Martin, Kathryn. A Question of Age: The Dorm & I. 224p. 1981. price not set (ISBN 0-936988-01-0). Tompson & Rutter.

Martin, Ken & Bennett, Bill. Practice of Teaching. 1980. text ed. 15.70 (ISBN 0-06-318116-9, IntlDept); pap. text ed. 7.80 (ISBN 0-06-318117-7). Har-Row.

Martin, Kenneth R., ed. see Martin, John F.

Martin, Kevin. Telling Fortunes with Cards. 1971. pap. 1.50 o.s.i. (ISBN 0-02-077340-4, Collier). Macmillan.

Martin, L. C., ed. see Herrick, Robert.

Martin, Laura. Papers in Mayan Linguistics. 6.00. Lucas.

Martin, Lawrence. Physical Geography of Wisconsin. 3rd ed. (Illus.). 1965. text ed. 27.50 (ISBN 0-299-03472-0); pap. text ed. 8.95 (ISBN 0-299-03475-5). U of Wis Pr.

Martin, Leda B. & Barbaresi, Sara M. How to Raise & Train a Miniature Schnauzer. (Orig.). pap. 2.00 (ISBN 0-87666-338-2, DS1026). TFH Pubns.

Martin, Lee J. & Kroitor, Harry P. The Five Hundred Word Theme. 3rd ed. (Illus.). 1979. pap. text ed. 8.50 (ISBN 0-13-321588-1). P-H.

Martin, Lee R., ed. Economics of Welfare, Rural Development, & Natural Resources in Agriculture, 1940s - 1970s. (A Survey of Agricultural Economics Literature: Vol. 3). 720p. 1981. 35.00x (ISBN 0-8166-0819-9). U of Minn Pr.

Martin, Leonard C., ed. see Browne, Thomas.

Martin, Les. Raiders of the Lost Ark Storybook. (Movie Storybooks Ser.). (Illus.). 64p. (gr. 5-9). 1981. PLB 6.99 (ISBN 0-394-94802-5); pap. 5.95 boards (ISBN 0-394-84802-0). Random.

Martin, Leslie & March, L., eds. Urban Space & Structures. (Studies in Architecture: Vol. 1). 1972. 29.95 (ISBN 0-521-08414-8); pap. 9.95x (ISBN 0-521-09934-X). Cambridge U Pr.

Martin, Linda. The Way We Wore: Fashion Illustrations of Children's Wear 1870-1970. LC 78-17243. (Illus.). 1978. 17.50 (ISBN 0-684-15655-5, ScribT). Scribner.

Martin, Linda B., jt. auth. see Weidman, Bette S.

Martin, Lionel. A Traveler's Guide to Cuba. LC 77-11536. (Illus.). Date not set. pap. cancelled (ISBN 0-06-090644-8, CN-644, CN). Har-Row. Postponed.

Martin, Lynne. The Orchid Family. LC 73-23001. (Illus.). 96p. (gr. 3-7). 1974. 6.75 o.p. (ISBN 0-688-21784-2); PLB 6.48 (ISBN 0-688-31784-7). Morrow.

--Puffin, Bird of the Open Seas. LC 76-3486. (Illus.). (gr. 3-7). 1976. 7.25 (ISBN 0-688-22074-6); PLB 6.96 (ISBN 0-688-32074-0). Morrow.

Martin, M. C. & Hewett, C. A. Elements of Classical Physics. LC 73-3450. 1975. text ed. 26.00 (ISBN 0-08-017098-6). Pergamon.

Martin, M. J. & Denison, R. A., eds. Case Exercises in Operations Research. LC 75-146548. 1971. 21.00 (ISBN 0-471-57355-8, Pub. by Wiley-Interscience). Wiley.

Martin, M. Kay & Voorhies, Barbara. Female of the Species. 448p. 1974. 22.50x (ISBN 0-231-03875-5); pap. 10.00x (ISBN 0-231-03876-3). Columbia U Pr.

Martin, M. W. Topical Stamp Collecting. LC 74-19793. (Illus.). 192p. 1975. lib. bdg. 8.95 o. p. o.p. (ISBN 0-668-03754-7); pap. 5.95 o.p. (ISBN 0-668-03662-1). Arco.

Martin, Malachi. Jesus Now. 320p. 1974. pap. 1.95 o.p. (ISBN 0-445-08309-3). Popular Lib.

--King of Kings: A Novel of the Life of David. 1981. 14.95 (ISBN 0-671-24707-7). S&S.

Martin, Margaret. Colleagues or Competitors. 103p. 1969. pap. text ed. 5.00x (ISBN 0-7135-1538-4, Pub. by Bedford England). Renouf.

Martin, Margaret J., et al. Cacti & Their Cultivation. 1975. pap. 5.95 o.p. (ISBN 0-684-14365-8, SL601, ScribT). Scribner.

Martin, Marie Louise. Kimbangu. Moore, D. M., tr. 224p. 1976. 8.95 o.p. (ISBN 0-8028-3483-3). Eerdmans.

Martin, Martha. O Rugged Land of Gold. 1967. 4.95 o.s.i. (ISBN 0-02-580460-X). Macmillan.

Martin, Marvin. Britannica Junior Encyclopaedia, 15 vols. (Illus.). 1980. Set. write for info. (ISBN 0-85229-379-8). Ency Brit Ed.

Martin, Mary. Mary Martin's Needlepoint. LC 70-79725. (Illus.). 1969. 15.95 o.p. (ISBN 0-688-02060-7); pap. 5.95 o.p. (ISBN 0-688-05207-X). Morrow.

Martin, Mary L., jt. auth. see Bowers, Q. David.

Martin, Maurice H., jt. auth. see Allaud, Louis.

Martin, Melody. Mrs. Kamali Would Like to Speak to You About Cloud: Notes from a California Classroom. 212p. 1980. 9.95 (ISBN 0-8037-6003-5). Dial.

Martin, Michael. Social Science & Philosophical Analysis: Essays in Philosophy of the Social Sciences. LC 78-51142. 1978. pap. text ed. 12.00 (ISBN 0-8191-0478-7). U Pr of Amer.

Martin, Michel L. Warriors to Managers: The French Military Establishment Since 1945. LC 79-28114. (Illus.). 424p. 1981. 21.00x (ISBN 0-8078-1421-0). U of NC Pr.

Martin, N., jt. auth. see Hardy, C.

Martin, Nancy. Search & Rescue: The Story of the Coast Guard Service. LC 74-81053. (David & Charles Children's Bks). (Illus.). 80p. (gr. 3-8). 1975. 5.95 (ISBN 0-7153-6501-0). David & Charles.

Martin P. Catherwood Library-Cornell University. Library Catalogue of the Martin P. Catherwood Library of the New York State School of Industrial & Labor Relations: Fourth Supplement. (Library Catalogs & Supplements Ser.). 1980. lib. bdg. 260.00 (ISBN 0-8161-0333-X). G K Hall.

Martin, P. G. Cosmic Dust. (Studies in Physics). (Illus.). 1979. 24.95x (ISBN 0-19-851458-1). Oxford U Pr.

Martin, Patricia M. Rice Bowl Pet. LC 62-7744. (Illus.). (gr. k-3). 1962. PLB 8.79 (ISBN 0-690-69969-7, TYC-J). T Y Crowell.

Martin, Patricia Miles. Indians: The First Americans. LC 70-99132. (Finding-Out Books for Science & Social Studies, Grades 1-4). (Illus.). (gr. 1-4). 1970. PLB 5.41 o.p. (ISBN 0-8193-0359-3). Enslow Pubs.

Martin, Paul. Island of Immunity: Health Secrets from the Andes. (Illus.). 176p. 1981. 10.00 (ISBN 0-8159-5828-5). Devin.

Martin, Paul, ed. see Redenbaugh, Al.

Martin, Peter. Landsmen. 1979. pap. 2.50 o.p. (ISBN 0-445-04338-5). Popular Lib.

Martin, Peter, jt. ed. see Toon, Peter.

Martin, Philip. Contemporary Labor Relations. 1979. pap. text ed. 8.95x (ISBN 0-534-00688-4). Wadsworth Pub.

--Shakespeare's Sonnets: Self, Love & Art. LC 73-189593. 160p. 1972. 26.50 (ISBN 0-521-08525-X). Cambridge U Pr.

Martin, Philip R. Auto Mechanics for the Complete Dummy. 2nd ed. Ritums, John & Guido, Dennis, eds. LC 74-14655. (Illus.). 1981. pap. write for info. (ISBN 0-930968-01-8). Motormatics.

Martin, Phyllis. Martin's Magic Formula for Getting the Right Job. 160p. 1981. 10.95 (ISBN 0-312-51702-5). St Martin.

--Word Watchers' Handbook: A Deletionary of the Most Abused & Misused Words. LC 76-12741. 1976. 7.95 o.p. (ISBN 0-679-20354-0); pap. 3.95 o.p. (ISBN 0-679-20369-9). McKay.

Martin, R. The Sociology of Power. (International Library of Sociology). 1977. 20.00x (ISBN 0-7100-8563-X). Routledge & Kegan.

Martin, R. C. The Deep Sea Diver: Yesterday, Today & Tomorrow. LC 77-19076. (Illus.). 1978. 10.00 (ISBN 0-87033-238-4). Cornell Maritime.

Martin, R. D. Breeding Endangered Species in Captivity. 1975. 57.50 (ISBN 0-12-474850-3). Acad Pr.

Martin, R. D., jt. auth. see Charles-Dominique, P.

Martin, R. D., tr. see Charles-Dominique, Pierre.

Martin, R. H., ed. Terence, the Adelphoe. LC 75-36173. (Cambridge Greek & Latin Classics Ser.). 250p. 1976. 42.50 (ISBN 0-521-20936-6); pap. 12.95x (ISBN 0-521-29001-5). Cambridge U Pr.

Martin, R. M. Peirce's Logic of Relations & Other Studies. (Studies in Semiotics: No. 12). (Orig.). 1980. pap. text ed. 10.50x (ISBN 90-316-0133-0). Humanities.

Martin, Ralph. Fire on the Earth. 1975. pap. 1.95 (ISBN 0-89283-021-2). Servant.

--Hungry for God. 1976. pap. 1.50 (ISBN 0-89129-040-0). Jove Pubns.

--Reconciliation: A Study of Paul's Theology. Toon, Peter, ed. LC 80-16340. (New Foundations Theological Library). 272p. 1981. 18.50 (ISBN 0-8042-3709-3); pap. 11.95 (ISBN 0-8042-3729-8). John Knox.

Martin, Ralph, ed. see Avis, Paul D.

Martin, Ralph, ed. see Carson, D. A.

Martin, Ralph P. Commentary on Philippians. Black, Matthew, ed. (New Century Bible Commentary Ser.). 192p. 1980. pap. 5.95 (ISBN 0-8028-1840-4). Eerdmans.

--Where the Action Is. LC 75-23515. 1976. pap. 2.25 (ISBN 0-8307-0361-6, S303-1-08). Regal.

Martin, Raymond. Syntactical Evidence of Semitic Sources in Greek Documents. LC 73-89038. (Society of Biblical Literature. Septuagint & Cognate Studies). 1974. pap. 7.50 (ISBN 0-89130-168-2, 060403). Scholars Pr Ca.

Martin, Rhona. Gallows Wedding. 1980. pap. 2.50 o.p. (ISBN 0-425-04299-5). Berkley Pub.

Martin, Richard M. Intention & Decision: A Philosophical Study. LC 63-19620. 1963. 24.00x (ISBN 0-89197-231-5). Irvington.

Martin, Richard M., jt. ed. see Eisele, Carolyn.

Martin, Robert B. Introduction to Biophysical Chemistry. 1964. text ed. 23.00 o.p. (ISBN 0-07-040629-4, C). McGraw.

Martin, Robert C., et al. Practical Speech for Modern Business. LC 63-7333. 1963. 24.50x (ISBN 0-89197-353-2); pap. text ed. 16.95x (ISBN 0-89197-899-2). Irvington.

Martin, Robert H., Jr. Nonlinear Operators & Differential Equations in Banach Spaces. LC 76-15279. (Pure & Applied Mathematics Ser.). 544p. 1976. 39.95 (ISBN 0-471-57363-9, Pub. by Wiley-Interscience). Wiley.

Martin, Robert J. Teaching Through Encouragement: Techniques to Help Students Learn. 208p. 1980. 10.95 (Spec); pap. 4.95. P-H.

Martin, Robert L., ed. The Paradox of the Liar. 1979. lib. bdg. 21.00 (ISBN 0-917930-30-4); pap. text ed. 6.00x (ISBN 0-917930-10-X). Ridgeview.

Martin, Roger. Essai Sur Thomas Gray. 458p. 1980. Repr. of 1934 ed. lib. bdg. 100.00 (ISBN 0-89984-335-2). Century Bookbindery.

Martin, Rollard A. Occupational Disability: Causes, Prediction, Prevention. (Illus.). 220p. 1975. 19.75 (ISBN 0-398-03224-6). C C Thomas.

Martin, Roscoe C. Water for New York: A Study in State Administration of Water Resources. LC 60-9946. 1960. 7.95x (ISBN 0-8156-2028-4). Syracuse U Pr.

Martin, Ross M. Tuc: The Growth of a Pressure Group Eighteen Sixty Eight to Nineteen Seventy Six. 408p. 1980. text ed. 42.00x (ISBN 0-19-822475-3). Oxford U Pr.

Martin, Rupert. Looking at Italy. LC 67-10032. (Looking at Other Countries Ser). (Illus.). (gr. 4-6). 1967. 8.95 o.p. (ISBN 0-397-30966-X). Lippincott.

--Looking at Spain. LC 73-78938. (Looking at Other Countries Ser). (Illus.). (gr. 4-6). 1970. 8.95 (ISBN 0-397-31137-0). Lippincott.

Martin, Russell. The Desecration of Susan Browning. LC 80-83567. 256p. 1981. pap. 2.50 (ISBN 0-87216-802-6). Playboy Pbks.

Martin, S. J. The Biochemistry of Viruses. LC 77-8231. (Texts in Chemistry & Biochemistry Ser.). (Illus.). 1978. 38.50 (ISBN 0-521-21678-8); pap. 11.50x (ISBN 0-521-29229-8). Cambridge U Pr.

Martin, Sadie E. The Life & Professional Career of Emma Abbott. LC 80-2290. 1981. Repr. of 1891 ed. 28.50 (ISBN 0-404-18858-3). AMS Pr.

Martin, Samuel E. & Lee, Young-Sook C. Beginning Korean. LC 69-15452. (Linguistic Ser.). 1969. pap. text ed. 17.50x (ISBN 0-300-00285-8). Yale U Pr.

Martin, Sandy, jt. auth. see Rosen, Theodore.

Martin, Sheila. Seatramps: Five Years of Ocean Life. (Illus.). 1978. 12.95 (ISBN 0-236-40090-8, Pub by Paul Elek). Merrimack Bk Serv.

Martin, Simon. The Other Titanic. LC 79-56252. (Illus.). 208p. 1980. 19.95 (ISBN 0-7153-7755-8). David & Charles.

Martin, Steve. Cruel Shoes. 1980. pap. 2.25 (ISBN 0-446-92070-3). Warner Bks.

--Jerk. (Illus., Orig.). 1979. pap. 2.25 (ISBN 0-446-92523-3). Warner Bks.

Martin, Susan K. Library Networks: 1980-1981. 4th ed. LC 78-10666. (Professional Librarian Ser.). 176p. 1980. text ed. 29.50x (ISBN 0-914236-55-5); pap. text ed. 24.50x (ISBN 0-914236-66-0). Knowledge Indus.

Martin, T. T. Dear Heavenly Father: Letters from an Adopted Son. 1978. 4.50 o.p. (ISBN 0-682-49049-0). Exposition.

Martin, Terence. Nathaniel Hawthorne. (U. S. Authors Ser.: No. 75). 1964. lib. bdg. 11.95 (ISBN 0-8057-0348-9). Twayne.

Martin, Thomas L., Jr. Malice in Blunderland. (McGraw-Hill Paperbacks Ser.). 156p. 1980. pap. 3.95 (ISBN 0-07-040634-0). McGraw.

Martin, Thomas M. Images & the Imageless: A Study in Religious Consciousness & Film. LC 79-57611. 200p. 1981. 20.00 (ISBN 0-8387-5005-2). Bucknell U Pr.

Martin, Toy. Netball Fundamentals. LC 80-66418. (Illus.). 96p. 1980. 11.95 (ISBN 0-7153-7984-4). David & Charles.

Martin, Vicky. The Windmill Years. LC 77-10290. 1978. 8.95 o.p. (ISBN 0-312-88222-X). St Martin.

Martin, W. & Macdonell, A. Canadian Education: A Sociological Analysis. 1978. pap. 11.25 (ISBN 0-13-113092-7). P-H.

Martin, W. C. & Hutchins, C. R. A Flora of New Mexico, 2 vols. (Illus.). 3000p. 1980. lib. bdg. 160.00x (ISBN 3-7682-1263-7, Pub. by Cramer Germany). Lubrecht & Cramer.

Martin, W. C. & Hutchins, R. Flora of New Mexico, 2 vols. (Illus.). 3000p. 1980. Set. lib. bdg. 160.00x (ISBN 3-7682-1263-7, Pub. by Cramer Germany); Vol. 1. lib. bdg. 80.00x (ISBN 3-7682-1283-1); Vol. 2. lib. bdg. 8.00x (ISBN 3-7682-1284-X). Lubrecht & Cramer.

Martin, Wainwright E., Jr. Plaid for Linear Programming. 1974. pap. 5.50 (ISBN 0-256-01594-5, 15-1086-00). Learning Syst.

Martin, Walter. Christian Science. 1957. pap. 1.25 (ISBN 0-87123-064-X, 210064). Bethany Fell.

--Essential Christianity. rev. ed. 128p. 1980. pap. 3.95 (ISBN 0-88449-043-2). Vision Hse.

--Herbert W. Armstrong. rev. ed. 1969. pap. 1.25 (ISBN 0-87123-213-8, 210213). Bethany Fell.

--Jehovah's Witnesses. 1969. pap. 1.50 (ISBN 0-87123-270-7, 210270). Bethany Fell.

--Mormonism. 1968. pap. 0.95 (ISBN 0-87123-367-3, 210367). Bethany Fell.

--The New Cults. (Orig.). 1980. pap. 7.95 (ISBN 0-88449-016-5). Vision Hse.

--Rise of the Cults. rev. ed. 138p. 1980. pap. 3.95 (ISBN 0-88449-044-0). Vision Hse.

Martin, Walter R. Kingdom of the Cults. rev. ed. LC 64-22840. 1968. 10.95 (ISBN 0-87123-300-2, 230300). Bethany Fell.

Martin, Warren B. Conformity: Standards & Change in Higher Education. LC 72-92894. (Higher Education Ser.). 1969. 13.95x o.p. (ISBN 0-87589-045-8). Jossey-Bass.

Martin, Wendy. Love's Journey. 192p. (YA) 1976. 5.95 (ISBN 0-685-66479-1, Avalon). Bouregy.

--Two Hearts Adrift. 192p. (YA) 1976. 5.95 (ISBN 0-685-62026-3, Avalon). Bouregy.

Martin, William. Back Bay. 1981. pap. 3.50 (ISBN 0-671-41504-2). PB.

--Switzerland. 1971. 11.95 (ISBN 0-236-15402-8, Pub. by Paul Elek). Merrimack Bk Serv.

Martin, William A. The Siege in Peking: China Against the World. (Illus.). 190p. 1972. Repr. of 1900 ed. 25.00x (ISBN 0-686-28322-8, Pub. by Irish Academic Pr). Biblio Dist.

Martin, William C., jt. auth. see Davidson, Jessica.

Martin, William T. Writing Psychological Reports. 192p. 1972. pap. 13.50 spiral (ISBN 0-398-02352-2). C C Thomas.

Martin, William T., et al. Elementary Differential Equations. 3rd ed. 1981. text ed. 22.95 (ISBN 0-8162-5435-4). Holden-Day. Postponed.

Martina, Susanna W. A Great Estate at Work. LC 79-51827. (Illus.). 308p. 1980. 54.50 (ISBN 0-521-22696-1). Cambridge U Pr.

Martindale, Andrew. Gothic Art. (World of Art Ser.). (Illus.). 1967. pap. 9.95 (ISBN 0-19-519924-3). Oxford U Pr.

Martindale, David. Earth Shelters: The New Way to Live. (Illus.). 160p. 1981. 18.95 (ISBN 0-525-93199-6); pap. 10.95 (ISBN 0-525-93200-3). Dutton.

Martindale, David E. The Human Figure As an Art Object. (Illus.). 1980. deluxe ed. 37.75 (ISBN 0-930582-52-7). Gloucester Art.

Martindale, Don. Community, Character & Civilization. LC 63-13540. 1963. 10.95 o.s.i. (ISBN 0-02-920140-3). Free Pr.

--Ideals & Realities of Academic Advising. (Intercontinental Series in Sociology: No. 3). 207p. 1980. lib. bdg. 14.95 (ISBN 0-933142-02-1). Intercont Press.

--Ideals & Realities of Ph.D Advising. (Intercontinental Series in Sociology: No. 3). 14.95 (ISBN 0-933142-02-1). Intercont Press.

--Nature & Types of Sociological Theory. LC 60-50843. 1960. text ed. 20.50 (ISBN 0-395-04843-5, 3-34640). HM.

Martindale, Don & Mohan, Raj P. Ideals & Realities: Some Problem Areas of Professional Social Science. (Intercontinental Series in Sociogy: No. 2). 250p. 1980. lib. bdg. 14.95 (ISBN 0-933142-01-3). Intercont Press.

Martindale, Don, et al, trs. see Weber, Max.

Martindale, Don A. The Nature & Types of Sociological Theory. 2nd ed. LC 80-68142. (Illus.). 640p. 1981. text ed. 20.50 (ISBN 0-395-29732-X). HM.

Martindale, J. R., ed. The Prosopography of the Later Roman Empire, Vol. 2, A.D. 395-527. LC 77-118859. (Illus.). 1980. 140.00 (ISBN 0-521-20159-4). Cambridge U Pr.

Martindale, J. S. Release from Isolation: How to Find Friendship, Love, & Happiness. LC 79-162932. 1971. 11.95 (ISBN 0-911012-08-7). Nelson-Hall.

Martin Du Gard, Roger, pseud. The Postman. Russell, John, tr. from Fr. LC 74-13052. 156p. 1975. Repr. of 1955 ed. 13.50 (ISBN 0-86527-333-2). Fertig.

Martine. The Only Astrology Book You'll Ever Need. LC 80-5403. 288p. 1981. 14.95 (ISBN 0-8128-2726-0). Stein & Day.

Martine, James J., ed. American Novelists Nineteen Ten to Nineteen Forty-Five, 2 vols. (Dictionary of Literary Biography Ser.). (Illus.). 800p. 1981. Set. 108.00 (ISBN 0-8103-0931-9). Gale.

Martineau, Gilbert. Napoleon's Last Journey. Partridge, Frances, tr. (Illus.). 1977. 15.00 (ISBN 0-7195-3293-0). Transatlantic.

Martineau, Harriet. A History of the Thirty Years' Peace 1816-1846, 4 vols. (The Development of Industrial Society Ser.). 2007p. 1980. Repr. 160.00x (ISBN 0-7165-1753-1, Pub. by Irish Academic Pr). Biblio Dist.

--Society in America. Lipset, Seymour M., ed. (Socialscience Classics). 357p. 1981. 18.95 (ISBN 0-87855-420-3); pap. 7.95 (ISBN 0-87855-853-5). Transaction Bks.

Martineau, Richard & Girolami, Anne-Marie. Vient De Paraitre. 1975. pap. text ed. 3.75 (ISBN 0-88436-174-8). EMC.

Martinell, Charles, ed. see Chilton's Automotive Editorial Department.

Martinelli, Pat. Public Enemy. (Pal Paperbacks, Pal Skills II Ser.). (Illus.). (gr. 5-12). 1980. pap. text ed. 1.25 (ISBN 0-8374-6811-6). Xerox Ed Pubns.

Martinello, Marian & Field, William T. Who Are the Chinese Texans? (Young Readers Ser.). (Illus.). 81p. (Orig.). (gr. 3-6). 8.95x (ISBN 0-933164-36-X); pap. 5.95 (ISBN 0-933164-46-7). U of Tex Inst Tex Culture.

Martinet, A. V., jt. auth. see Thomson, A. J.

Martinez, Alicia. The Hero & Heroine of Shelley's "the Revolt of Islam". (Salzburg Studies in English Literature: Romantic Reassessment: No. 63). 109p. 1976. pap. text ed. 25.00x (ISBN 0-391-01474-9). Humanities.

Martinez, Cecelia, jt. auth. see Geist, Harold.

Martinez, Elizabeth, ed. see Rivas, Gilberto L.

Martinez, J. L., Jr., ed. Chicano Psychology. 1978. 12.50 (ISBN 0-12-475650-6). Acad Pr.

Martinez, Jorge C., jt. auth. see Mills, Dorothy H.

Martinez, Joseph D., ed. Salt Dome Utilization & Environmental Considerations: Proceedings of a Symposium. 1977. pap. 17.50x (ISBN 0-8071-0380-2). La State U Pr.

Martinez, Julio A., compiled by. Chicano Scholars & Writers: A Bio-Bibliographical Directory. LC 78-32076. 589p. 1979. 29.00 (ISBN 0-8108-1205-3). Scarecrow.

Martinez, Pam. Sugarless Cooking. 5.95 (ISBN 0-934230-05-6). Green Hill.

Martinez, Raul C. Organizational Behavior Management: A Manual for Supervisors. (Illus.). 148p. (Orig.). 1980. pap. 8.50 (ISBN 0-937230-00-6). NPD Corp.

Martinez, Raymond J. Marie Laveau Voodoo Queen & Folk Tales Along the Mississippi. 96p. pap. 3.50 (ISBN 0-911116-83-4). Pelican.

Martinez, Raymond J., jt. auth. see Hardy, Helen H.

Martinez, Ricardo A., et al, eds. Hispanic Culture & Health Care: Fact, Fiction, Folklore. LC 77-26985. 1978. pap. text ed. 11.50 (ISBN 0-8016-3143-2). Mosby.

Martinez-Alier, Verena. Marriage, Class & Colour in Nineteenth Century Cuba. LC 73-82463. 224p. 1974. 30.95 (ISBN 0-521-20412-7); pap. 10.95x (ISBN 0-521-09846-7). Cambridge U Pr.

Martinez-Bonati, Felix. Fictive Discourse & the Structures of Literature: A Phenomenological Approach. rev. exp. ed. Silver, Philip W., tr. from Span. (Illus.). 200p. 1981. 15.00x (ISBN 0-8014-1308-7). Cornell U Pr.

Martinez-Brawley, Emilia E. Seven Decades of Rural Social Work: From Country Life Commission to Rural Caucus. 275p. 1981. 21.95 (ISBN 0-03-058027-7). Praeger.

Martinez Diaz, Jose Luis, tr. see Thomas, I. D., et al.

Martinez Estrada, Ezequiel. X-Ray of the Pampa. Swietlicki, Alain, tr. LC 70-165913. (Texas Pan American Ser). 415p. 1971. 17.50 (ISBN 0-292-70140-3); pap. 7.95 (ISBN 0-292-79500-9). U of Tex Pr.

Martinez-Juarez, Alberto. The Drawing. 1981. 5.95 (ISBN 0-8062-1590-9). Carlton.

Martinez-Lopez, Jorge I. A CME Casebook of Electrocardiographic Tracings. 1981. write for info. (ISBN 0-88416-307-5). PSG Pub.

Martinez-Maldonado, M., ed. Methods in Pharmacology: Vols. 4A & 4B: Renal Pharmacology. Incl. Vol. 4A. 387p. 1976. 45.00 (ISBN 0-306-35264-8); Vol. 4B. 413p. 1978. 39.50 (ISBN 0-306-35265-6). Plenum Pr). Plenum Pub.

Martinez-Maldonado, Manuel, jt. auth. see Kurtzman, Neil A.

Martini, L., jt. auth. see Mancini, R. E.

Martini, L. & Ganong, W. F., eds. Frontiers in Neuroendocrinology, Vol. 4. LC 77-82030. 350p. 1976. 29.50 (ISBN 0-89004-033-8). Raven.

Martini, L. & Meites, J., eds. Neurochemical Aspects of Hypothalmic Function. 1971. 25.00 (ISBN 0-12-475560-7). Acad Pr.

Martini, L. & Pecile, A., eds. Hormonal Steroids, Biochemistry, Pharmacology, Therapeutics, 2 Vols. 1965. Vol. 1. 55.50 (ISBN 0-12-475301-9); Vol. 2. 55.50 (ISBN 0-12-475302-7). Acad Pr.

Martini, L., et al, eds. Hypothalamus. 1971. 61.75 (ISBN 0-12-475550-X). Acad Pr.

Martini, Luciano & Ganong, William F., eds. Frontiers in Neuroendocrinology, Vol. 6. 430p. 1979. text ed. 42.50 (ISBN 0-89004-404-X). Raven.

Martini, Luciano & Motta, Marcella, eds. Androgens & Antiandrogens. LC 76-19853. 1977. 36.00 (ISBN 0-89004-141-5). Raven.

Martini, Luciano, jt. ed. see Ganong, William F.

Martini, Luciano, jt. ed. see Serio, Mario.

Martini, R., ed. Geometrical Approaches to Differential Equations: Proceedings. (Lecture Notes in Mathematics: Vol. 810). (Illus.). 339p. 1980. pap. 19.50 (ISBN 0-387-10018-0). Springer-Verlag.

Martinique, Edward. Traditional Chinese Bookbinding. (Asian Library: No. 19). (Illus.). xiii, 87p. 1980. write for info. (ISBN 0-89644-596-8). Chinese Materials.

Martinis, Gloria. The Two Carolines. (Orig.). 1976. pap. 1.50 o.p. (ISBN 0-685-64018-3, LB339DK, Leisure Bks). Nordon Pubns.

Martino, Mario. God, Why Me? 1981. 4.95 (ISBN 0-8062-1703-0). Carlton.

Martinotti, Guido, jt. ed. see Kloskowska, Antonia.

Martins, Elisio. Colonialism & Imperialism in Mozambique. 206p. 1974. pap. 4.95 (ISBN 0-88289-097-2). Pelican.

Martins, Jose M. English for the Foreign Physician. (Illus.). 136p. 1974. photocopy ed. 12.75 (ISBN 0-398-01227-X). C C Thomas.

Martinson, Ruth A., jt. auth. see Council for Exceptional Children.

Martinsson, Anders. Evolution & Morphology of the Trilobita, Trilobitoidea, & Merostomata. 1975. pap. 70.00x (ISBN 82-00-04963-9, Dist. by Columbia U Pr). Universitet.

Martius. Operative Obstetrics. 1980. 16.00. Thieme Stratton.

Martner, Knud, ed. see Mahler, Alma.

Marton, Beryl M. Coupon Savers Cookbook. 224p. 1980. pap. 5.95 (ISBN 0-517-54203-X). Crown.

Marton, C. & Harmuth, H. F., eds. Advances in Electronics & Electron Physics, Supplement 14: Nonsinusoidal Waves for Radar & Radio Communication. (Serial Publication Ser.). 1981. write for info. (ISBN 0-12-014575-8). Acad Pr.

Marton, Claire, ed. Methods of Experimental Physics: Fluid Dynamics, Vol. 18A. LC 79-26343. 1981. write for info. (ISBN 0-12-475960-2). Acad Pr.

--Methods of Experimental Physics: Fluid Dynamics, Vol. 18B. 1981. write for info. (ISBN 0-12-475956-4). Acad Pr.

Marton, Claire, jt. ed. see Marton, L.

Marton, Katherin, jt. auth. see Boddewyn, J. J.

Marton, L. Advances in Electronics & Electron Physics, Supplement 13A: Applied Charged Particle Optics. 1980. 41.00 (ISBN 0-12-014573-1). Acad Pr.

Marton, L. see Marton, L.

Marton, L., ed. Advances in Electronics & Electron Physics. Incl. Vols. 1-5. 1948-53. 49.50 ea. Vol. 1 (ISBN 0-12-014501-4). Vol. 2 (ISBN 0-12-014502-2). Vol. 3 (ISBN 0-12-014503-0). Vol. 4 (ISBN 0-12-014504-9). Vol. 5 (ISBN 0-12-014505-7); Vols. 6-8. 1954-56. 49.50 ea. Vol. 6 (ISBN 0-12-014506-5). Vol. 7 (ISBN 0-12-014507-3). Vol. 8 (ISBN 0-12-014508-1); Vols. 9-10. 1957-58. 49.50 ea. Vol. 9 (ISBN 0-12-014509-X). Vol. 10 (ISBN 0-12-014510-3); Vol. 11. 1959. 49.50 (ISBN 0-12-014511-1); Vol. 12. Proceedings. Symposium on Photo-Electronic Image Devices - 1st. McGee, J. D. & Wilcock, W. L., eds. 1960. 36.50 (ISBN 0-12-014512-X); Vols. 13-15. 1960-61. 49.50 ea. Vol. 13 (ISBN 0-12-014513-8). Vol. 14 (ISBN 0-12-014514-6). Vol. 15 (ISBN 0-12-014515-4); Vol. 16. Proceedings. Symposium on Photo-Electronic Image Devices - 2nd. McGee, J. D., et al, eds. 1962. 68.00 (ISBN 0-12-014516-2); Vol. 17. 1963. 49.50 (ISBN 0-12-014517-0); Vol. 18. 1963. 49.50 (ISBN 0-12-014518-9); Vol. 19. 1964. 49.50 (ISBN 0-12-014519-7); **Vols. 20-21. 1965-66. 49.50 ea. Vol. 20 (ISBN 0-12-014520-0). Vol. 21 (ISBN 0-12-014521-9); Vol. 22. Proceedings. Symposium on Photo-Electronic Image Devices - 3rd. McGee, J. D., et al, eds. 1966. Pt. A. 69.00 (ISBN 0-12-014522-7); Pt. B. 41.00 (ISBN 0-12-014542-1); Vol. 23. 1967. 49.50 (ISBN 0-12-014523-5); Vol. 24. 1968. 49.50 (ISBN 0-12-014524-3); Vol. 25. 1968. 49.50 (ISBN 0-12-014525-1); Vol. 26. 1969. 49.50 (ISBN 0-12-014526-X); Vol. 27. 1970. 49.50 (ISBN 0-12-014527-8); Vol. 28. Proceedings. Symposium on Photo-Electronic Image Devices - 4th. McGee, J. D., et al, eds. 1969. Pt. A. 76.00 (ISBN 0-12-014528-6); Pt. B, 1970. 77.50 (ISBN 0-12-014548-0); Vol. 29. 1970. 49.50 (ISBN 0-12-014529-4); Vol. 30. 1971. 49.50 (ISBN 0-12-014530-8); Vol. 31. 1972. 49.50 (ISBN 0-12-014531-6); Vol. 32. 1973. 49.50 (ISBN 0-12-014532-4); Vol. 33. Proceedings. Symposium on Photo-Electronic Image Devices - 5th. McGee, J. D., et al, eds. 1972. Pt. A, 1972. 58.00, o.s.i. (ISBN 0-12-014533-2); Pt. A. 84.00 (ISBN 0-12-014533-2). Pt. B, 1973. Acad Pr.**

--Advances in Electronics & Electron Physics, Vols. 34 & 35. Vol. 34, 1973. 51.50 (ISBN 0-12-014534-0); Vol. 35, 1974. 51.50 (ISBN 0-12-014535-9). Acad Pr.

--Advances in Electronics & Electron Physics: Supplements. Incl. Suppl. 1. Electroluminescence & Related Effects. Ivey, Henry F. 1963. 44.00 (ISBN 0-12-014561-8); Suppl. 2. Optical Masers. Birnbaum, George. 1964. 40.50 (ISBN 0-12-014562-6); Suppl. 3. Narrow Angle Electron Guns & Cathode Ray Tubes. Moss, Hilary. 1968. 33.00 (ISBN 0-12-014563-4); Suppl. 5. Linear Ferrite Devices for Microwave Applications. Von Aulock, W. H. & Fay, C. E. 1969. 41.00 (ISBN 0-12-014565-0); Suppl. 6. Electron Probe Microanalysis. Tousimis, A. J. & Marton, L. 1969. 52.75 (ISBN 0-12-014566-9); Suppl. 7. Quadruples in Electron Lens Design. Hawkes, P. W. 1970. 49.00 (ISBN 0-12-014567-7); Suppl. 9. Sequency Theory Foundations & Applications. Harmuth, Henning F., ed. 1977. 52.75 (ISBN 0-12-014569-3); Suppl. 11. Acoustic Imaging with Electronic Circuits. Harmuth, Henning F., ed. 1979. 32.00 (ISBN 0-12-014571-5). Acad Pr.

--Methods of Experimental Physics. Incl. Vol. 1. Classical Methods. Estermann, Immanuel, ed. 1959. 47.50 (ISBN 0-12-475901-7); Vol. 3. Molecular Physics. Williams, Dudley, ed. 1961. write for info. (ISBN 0-12-475903-3); Vol. 4. Atomic & Electron Physics, Pts. A-B. Hughes, Vernon W. & Schultz, Howard L., eds. 1967. Pt. A. 58.50 (ISBN 0-12-475904-1); Pt. B. 48.50 (ISBN 0-12-475944-0); Vol. 6. Solid State Physics. Lark-Horovitz, K. & Johnson, Vivian A., eds. 1959. Pt. A. 43.50 (ISBN 0-12-475906-8); Pt. B. 43.50 (ISBN 0-12-475946-7); Vol. 7. Atomic & Electron Physics: Atomic Interactions. Bederson, B. & Fite, W., eds. 1968. Pt. A. 61.75 (ISBN 0-12-475907-6); Pt. B. 53.00 (ISBN 0-12-475947-5); Vol. 8. Problems & Solutions for Students. Marton, L. & Hornyak, W. F., eds. 1969. 41.00 (ISBN 0-12-475908-4); Vol. 9. Plasma Physics. Griem, Hans R. & Lovberg, Ralph H., eds. 1970-71. Pt. A. 52.50 (ISBN 0-12-475909-2); Pt. B. 45.00 (ISBN 0-12-475949-1); Vol. 10. Physical Principles of Far-Infrared Radiation. Robinson, L. C. 1973. 52.50 (ISBN 0-12-475910-6). Acad Pr.

Marton, L. & Marton, Claire, eds. Advances in Electronic & Electron Physics, Vol. 55. (Serial Publication). 1981. 47.50 (ISBN 0-12-014655-X); lib. bdg. 62.00 (ISBN 0-12-014710-6); microfiche ed. 33.50 (ISBN 0-12-014711-4). Acad Pr.

Marton, L. & Richard, Patrick, eds. Methods of Experimental Physics: Vol. 17, Atomic Physics Accelerators. (Serial Pub.). 1980. 70.00 (ISBN 0-12-475959-9). Acad Pr.

Marton, Laurence J., jt. ed. see Kabra, Pokar.

Martos, Joseph. Doors to the Sacred. LC 80-626. 552p. 1981. 15.95 (ISBN 0-385-15738-X). Doubleday.

Martuza, Victor R. Applying Norm-Referenced & Criterion-Referenced Measurement in Education. 1977. text ed. 19.95x (ISBN 0-205-05871-X); test items avail. (ISBN 0-685-71780-1). Allyn.

Marty, Martin E. By Way of Response. LC 80-20042. (Journeys in Faith Ser.). 1981. 7.95 (ISBN 0-687-04477-4). Abingdon.

--Our Faiths. 1976. pap. 1.75 (ISBN 0-89129-113-X). Jove Pubns.

--The Public Church. 192p. 1981. 10.95 (ISBN 0-8245-0019-9). Crossroad NY.

Marty, Martin E. & Peerman, Dean G. Handbook of Christian Theologians. (Fount Paperback Ser). pap. 4.95 (ISBN 0-529-01988-4, M244, Pub. by Collins Pubs). Abingdon.

Marty, Martin E., ed. The Place of Bonhoeffer: Problems & Possibilities in His Thought. LC 79-8718. 224p. 1981. Repr. of 1962 ed. lib. bdg. 22.50x (ISBN 0-313-20812-3, MAPL). Greenwood.

Marty, Martin E. & Peerman, Dean G., eds. Handbook of Christian Theologians. 1967. pap. 3.95 o.p. (ISBN 0-452-00244-3, F244, Mer). NAL.

--A Handbook of Christian Theologians. 512p. 1980. pap. 6.95 (ISBN 0-687-16566-0). Abingdon.

Marty, Sid. Men for the Mountains. LC 78-71651. 1979. 12.95 (ISBN 0-8149-0812-8). Vanguard.

--Men for the Mountains. (Illus.). 272p. 1981. Repr. of 1978 ed. pap. 6.95 (ISBN 0-89886-027-X). Mountaineers.

Martyn, Howe. Multinational Business Management. LC 75-116682. 1970. 29.50x (ISBN 0-669-58818-0). Irvington.

Martyn, J. Louis, jt. auth. see Rice, Charles.

Martyn, J. Louis, jt. ed. see Keck, Leander E.

Martyn, Sean. How to Start & Run a Successful Mail Order Business. 1971. 12.95 (ISBN 0-679-50259-9). McKay.

Martz. Ecuador: Conflicting Political Culture & the Quest for Progress. 4.95x o.p. (ISBN 0-205-03569-8, 7635699). Allyn.

Martz, John D. & Schoultz, Lars. Latin America, the United States, & the Inter-American System. (Westview Special Studies on Latin America & the Caribbean). 272p. 1980. lib. bdg. 26.00x (ISBN 0-89158-874-4). Westview.

Martz, John D. & Myers, David J., eds. Venezuela: The Democratic Experience. LC 77-7509. (Praeger Special Studies). 1977. text ed. 29.95 (ISBN 0-03-021841-1); pap. 11.95 (ISBN 0-03-023061-6). Praeger.

Martz, Kathren V., et al. Management of the Patient-Ventilator System: A Team Approach. LC 78-31819. (Illus.). 1979. pap. text ed. 12.95 (ISBN 0-8016-3139-4). Mosby.

Martz, Louis L. Poet of Exile: A Study of Milton's Poetry. LC 79-64079. 1980. 22.50x (ISBN 0-300-02393-6). Yale U Pr.

Martz, William J. Beginnings in Poetry. 2nd ed. 320p. 1973. pap. 7.95x (ISBN 0-673-07713-6). Scott F.

Marulli, Luciana. Documentation of the United Nations System: Co-Ordination in Its Bibliographic Control. LC 79-17510. 235p. 1979. 16.50 (ISBN 0-8108-1233-9). Scarecrow.

Marulli, Luciana, tr. see Lunati, Rinaldo.

Maruskin. OCLC, Inc. Its Goverence, Function, Finance & Technique. 160p. 1980. 22.75 (ISBN 0-8247-1179-3). Dekker.

Marusyn, Walt, et al. Track & Field. LC 77-74306. (Sports Playbook). (Illus.). 1978. pap. 3.50 o.p. (ISBN 0-385-06109-9). Doubleday.

Maruyama, Masakazu. Radiologic Diagnosis of Polyps & Carcinoma of the Large Bowl. LC 77-95452. (Illus.). 1978. 63.00 (ISBN 0-89640-025-5). Igaku-Shoin.

Marvan, P., et al, eds. Algal Assays & Monitoring Eutrophication. (Illus.). 253p. (Orig.). 1979. pap. 35.00x (ISBN 3-510-65091-3). Intl Pubns Serv.

Marvel, Elliot N. Thermal Electrocyclic Reactions. (Organic Chemistry Ser.). 1981. 51.00 (ISBN 0-12-476250-6). Acad Pr.

Marvel, Evalyn, jt. auth. see Moss, Arthur.

Marver, Hanes D. Consultants Can Help: The Use of Outside Experts in the U.S. Office of Child Development. LC 79-1557. 1979. 22.95 (ISBN 0-669-02904-1). Lexington Bks.

Marvick, Dwaine, ed. see Lasswell, Harold D.

Marvin, Edgar. When the Movies Began: First Film Stars. LC 78-15167. (Famous Firsts Ser.). (Illus.). 1978. lib. bdg. 7.35 (ISBN 0-686-51118-2). Silver.

Marvin, Frederic R. Last Words (Real & Traditional) of Distinguished Men & Women. LC 72-140424. 1971. Repr. of 1910 ed. 18.00 (ISBN 0-8103-3187-X). Gale.

Marvin, Mark C. New Vitamin Cures. new ed. LC 80-81401. 284p. 1980. 10.95 (ISBN 0-9604336-1-9); pap. 5.95 (ISBN 0-9604336-0-0). Marvanco.

Marvin, Philip. Product Planning Simplified. LC 74-188844. 240p. 1972. 14.50 o.p. (ISBN 0-8144-5299-X). Am Mgmt.

Marvin, Stephen. Africa Below the Sahara. rev. ed. (World Studies Inquiry Ser.). (gr. 7-12). 1979. pap. text ed. 6.04 (ISBN 0-201-42665-X, Sch Div); tchr's ed. 2.76 (ISBN 0-201-42666-8). A-W.

Marwah, Onkar & Pollack, Jonathan D., eds. Military Power & Policy in Asian States: Toward the 1980's. (Special Studies in Military Affairs Ser.). 1979. lib. bdg. 21.50x (ISBN 0-89158-407-2). Westview.

Marwick, Arthur. Class: Image & Reality in Britain, France & the U. S. A. Since 1930. 1980. 19.95 (ISBN 0-19-520203-1). Oxford U Pr.

Marwick, Arthur, et al, eds. The Illustrated Dictionary of British History. (Illus.). 320p. 1981. 19.95 (ISBN 0-500-25072-3). Thames Hudson.

Marwick, Christine M. Litigation Under the Federal Freedom of Information Act & Privacy Act: 1981 Edition. LC 80-683. 400p. 1980. pap. 25.00 (ISBN 0-86566-019-0). Ctr Natl Security.

Marwick, M. G. Sorcery in Its Social Setting. 1970. text ed. 20.25x (ISBN 0-7190-0257-5). Humanities.

Marx. Civil War in France. 1977. 3.95 (ISBN 0-8351-0562-8); pap. 2.25 (ISBN 0-8351-0044-8). China Bks.

--Critique of the Gotha Program. pap. 1.25 (ISBN 0-8351-0059-6). China Bks.

--Eighteenth Brumaire of Louis Bonaparte. 1978. pap. 1.95 (ISBN 0-8351-0578-4). China Bks.

Marx, Alexander, jt. auth. see Margolis, Max.

Marx, Anne. Face Lifts for All Seasons. 1980. 7.00 (ISBN 0-8233-0322-5). Golden Quill.

Marx, Arthur. Goldwyn. 1977. pap. 1.95 o.p. (ISBN 0-345-25555-0). Ballantine.

Marx, Herbert L., ed. Religions in America. (Reference Shelf Ser.). 1977. 6.25 (ISBN 0-8242-0608-8). Wilson.

Marx, Herbert L., Jr., ed. The American Indian: A Rising Ethnic Force. (Reference Shelf Ser: Vol. 45, No. 5). 1973. 6.25 (ISBN 0-8242-0508-1). Wilson.

--State & Local Government. (Reference Shelf Ser: Vol. 34, No. 3). 1962. 6.25 (ISBN 0-8242-0071-3). Wilson.

--The World Food Crisis. (Reference Shelf Ser: Vol. 47, No. 6). 1975. 6.25 (ISBN 0-8242-0574-X). Wilson.

Marx, John H., jt. auth. see Holzner, Burkart.

Marx, Joseph L. Nagasaki: The Necessary Bomb. Markel, R., ed. (Illus.). 1971. 11.95 o.s.i. (ISBN 0-02-580400-6). Macmillan.

Marx, K. & Engels, F. Mega, Vol. 1, Pt.10. 1390p. 60.00 (Pub. by Dietz Germany). Imported Pubns.

--Mega, Vol. 1, Pt. 22. 1790p. 60.00 (Pub. by Dietz Germany). Imported Pubns.

--Mega, Vol. 2, Pt. 1.1. 464p. 60.00 (Pub. by Dietz Germany). Imported Pubns.

--Mega, Vol. 2,pt. 3.1. 499p. 60.00 (Pub. by Dietz Germany). Imported Pubns.

--Mega, Vol. 2,pt. 3.2. 800p. 60.00 (Pub. by Dietz Germany). Imported Pubns.

--Mega, Vol. 2,pt. 3.3. 930p. 60.00 (Pub. by Dietz Germany). Imported Pubns.

--Mega, Vol. 2,pt. 3.4. 479p. 60.00 (Pub. by Dietz Germany). Imported Pubns.

--Mega, Vol. 3,pt. 1. 479p. 60.00 (Pub. by Dietz Germany). Imported Pubns.

--Mega, Vol. 4,pt. 1. 1047p. 60.00 (Pub. by Dietz Germany). Imported Pubns.

Marx, Karl. Capital, 3 vols. Engels, Frederick, ed. Incl. Vol. 1. Process of Capitalist Production. 820p; Vol. 2. Process of Circulation of Capital. 558p; Vol. 3. Process of Capitalist Production As a Whole. 960p. LC 67-19754. 1967. 35.00 set (ISBN 0-7178-0019-9); pap. 15.00 set (ISBN 0-7178-0018-0). Intl Pub Co.

--Capital. Eden & Paul, Cedar, trs. 1979. 16.00x (ISBN 0-460-00848-X, Evman). Dutton.

--Capital: A Critical Analysis of Capitalistic Production. 1946. text ed. 12.50x o.p. (ISBN 0-04-331018-4). Allen Unwin.

--Class Struggles in France, 1848-1850. LC 64-19792. 1964. pap. 2.25 (ISBN 0-7178-0030-X). Intl Pub Co.

--Contribution to the Critique of Political Economy. Dobb, Maurice, ed. LC 69-20357. 1971. 7.50 o.p. (ISBN 0-7178-0042-3); pap. 3.25 (ISBN 0-7178-0041-5). Intl Pub Co.

--Critique of Hegel's "Philosophy of Right". O'Malley, J., ed. LC 74-112471. (Cambridge Studies in the History & Theory of Politics). 1970. 23.95 o.p. (ISBN 0-521-07836-9); pap. 8.50x (ISBN 0-521-29211-5). Cambridge U Pr.

--Early Writings. 1963. pap. 3.95 (ISBN 0-07-040671-5, SP). McGraw.

--The Ethnological Notebooks of Karl Marx: Studies of Morgan, Phear, Maine, Lubbock. Krader, Lawrence, ed. 448p. 1972. text ed. 52.00x (ISBN 9-0232-0924-9). Humanities.

--Pre-Capitalist Economic Formations. Hobsbawm, Eric J., ed. Cohen, Jack, tr. LC 65-16393. 1965. 4.50 o.p. (ISBN 0-7178-0166-7); pap. 2.25 (ISBN 0-7178-0165-9). Intl Pub Co.

--Preface & Introduction to a Contribution to the Critque of Political Economy. 1.25 (ISBN 0-8351-0263-7). China Bks.

--Value, Price & Profit. 1899. text ed. 2.95x o.p. (ISBN 0-04-331019-2). Allen Unwin.

--Wage, Labour & Capital. 1978. pap. 1.25 (ISBN 0-8351-0547-4). China Bks.

--Wages, Price & Profit. 1965. pap. 1.25 (ISBN 0-8351-0422-2). China Bks.

Marx, Karl & Engels, Frederick. Civil War in the United States. pap. 3.25 o.p. (ISBN 0-7178-0028-8). Intl Pub Co.

--Karl Marx & Frederick Engels on Literature & Art. Baxandall, Lee & Morawski, Stefan, eds. (Documents on Marxist Aesthetics: Vol.I). 192p. 1974. 10.00 (ISBN 0-88477-000-1); pap. 4.25 (ISBN 0-88477-001-X). Intl General.

--Manifesto of the Communist Party. 1965. 2.95 (ISBN 0-8351-0561-X); pap. 1.25 (ISBN 0-8351-0146-0). China Bks.

--The Revolution of Eighteen Forty Eight-Forty Nine: Articles from the Neue Rheinische Zeitung. LC 77-188755. 240p. 1973. 7.50 (ISBN 0-7178-0339-2); pap. 2.25 o.p. (ISBN 0-7178-0340-6). Intl Pub Co.

--Selected Works of Marx & Engels. (Orig.). 1968. pap. 5.75 (ISBN 0-7178-0184-5). Intl Pub Co.

Marx, Karl & Engels, Friedrich. Communist Manifesto. Katz, Joseph, ed. Moore, Samuel, tr. (YA) (gr. 9-12). pap. 2.25 (ISBN 0-671-42218-9). WSP.

Marx, Karl & Frederick, Engels. Marx & Engels on the Means of Communication. De La Haye, Yves, ed. 176p. (Orig.). 1980. pap. 5.00 (ISBN 0-88477-013-3). Intl General.

Marx, Karl, jt. auth. see Engels, Friedrich.

Marx, Leo. Machine in the Garden: Technology & the Pastoral Ideal in America. (Illus.). 1967. pap. 6.95 (ISBN 0-19-500738-7, GB). Oxford U Pr.

Marx, Leo, ed. see Twain, Mark.

Marx, M., jt. auth. see Larsen, R.

Marx, Maxine. Growing up with Chico. LC 80-15387. 1980. 9.95 (ISBN 0-13-367821-0). P-H.

Marx, Milton. The Enjoyment of Drama. 2nd ed. LC 61-15689. (Goldentree Books in English Literature). 1961. pap. text ed. 8.95x (ISBN 0-89197-609-4). Irvington.

Marx, Robert F. Spanish Treasure in Florida Waters: A Billion Dollar Graveyard. (Illus.). 1979. 12.50case (ISBN 0-913352-06-3). Mariners Boston.

Marx, Samuel. Mayer & Thalberg: The Make-Believe Saints. (Illus.). 336p. 1980. pap. 2.95 (ISBN 0-446-83987-6). Warner Bks.

Marx, Victor. The Betrayal of the State of Israel & the Foreign Policy of the United States: A Blueprint for Peace in the Middle East. new ed. (Illus.). 1977. 47.50 (ISBN 0-89266-059-7). Am Classical Coll Pr.

--Catholicism, Judaism & the Effort at World Domination, 2 vols. in one. (Institute for Economic & Political World Strategic Studies). (Illus.). 191p. 1975. Set. 65.00 (ISBN 0-913314-61-7). Am Classical Coll Pr.

--Catholicism, Judaism & the Effort at World Domination. (Illus.). 1980. 65.00 (ISBN 0-89266-216-6). Am Classical Coll Pr.

--The Incredibly Foolish & Tragic Foreign Policy of the United States in the Middle East. new ed. (Illus.). 1977. 39.15 (ISBN 0-89266-084-8). Am Classical Coll Pr.

Marx, Walter H. Claimed by Vesuvius. (Illus.). 164p. 1975. pap. text ed. 4.95x (ISBN 0-88334-069-0). Ind Sch Pr.

--Thus Spake the Kings. (Illus.). 1978. pap. text ed. 4.95x (ISBN 0-88334-106-9). Ind Sch Pr.

Marx, Werner. Nuevas Fuerzas. LC 77-243. 166p. (Orig., Span.). 1976. pap. 3.25 (ISBN 0-89922-068-1). Edit Caribe.

Marxer. Elements of Data Processing. LC 75-153725. 215p. 1974. pap. 8.80 (ISBN 0-8273-0410-2); tchr's manual 2.00 (ISBN 0-8273-0411-0). Delmar.

Marxer & Hartford. Computer Programming with Cobol. LC 73-2158. 216p. 1974. pap. 8.00 (ISBN 0-8273-0415-3); instrs'. guide 2.00 (ISBN 0-8273-0416-1). Delmar.

--Elements of Computer Programming (Fortran) LC 75-153725. (Illus.). 224p. 1973. 8.00 (ISBN 0-8273-0413-7); tchr's manual 2.00 (ISBN 0-8273-0414-5). Delmar.

Marxhausen, Evelyn. When God Laid Down the Law. LC 59-1259. (Arch Bk.). 1981. pap. 0.79 (ISBN 0-570-06142-3). Concordia.

Marxhausen, Joanne. Banners. (A Nice Place to Live Ser.). 1978. pap. 2.25 (ISBN 0-570-07750-8, 12-2709). Concordia.

--Posters. (A Nice Place to Live Ser.). 1978. pap. 2.25 (ISBN 0-570-07752-4, 12-2711). Concordia.

--See His Banners Go. (Illus.). 32p. 1975. pap. 2.75 (ISBN 0-570-03702-6, 12-2604). Concordia.

--Three in One: Picture of God. 48p. (gr. k-4). 1973. 6.95 (ISBN 0-570-03419-1, 56-1148). Concordia.

Marxhaussen, Joanne. Thank God for Circles. LC 75-159012. 32p. 1980. pap. 3.50 (ISBN 0-8066-1805-1, 10-6241). Augsburg.

Marxsen, Willi. The Beginnings of Christology, together with The Lord's Supper. Achtemeier, Paul J. & Nieting, Lorenz, trs. from Ger. LC 79-7384. 128p. 1979. pap. 4.95 (ISBN 0-8006-1372-4, 1-1372). Fortress.

--New Testament as the Church's Book. Mignard, James E., tr. from Ger. LC 70-164554. 160p. (Orig.). 1972. pap. 3.95 (ISBN 0-8006-0102-5, 1-102). Fortress.

Mary. How Does Your Garden Grow? (Illus.). 64p. 1980. 4.95 (ISBN 0-517-54027-4); ten copy pre-pack 49.50 (ISBN 0-517-54118-1). Potter.

Mary, jt. ed. see Vetterling-Braggin.

Mary, Donnis, et al. The San Francisco Bay Area People's Yellow Pages. 4th ed. Sampson, Diane & Zobel, Jan, eds. (Illus., Orig.). 1975. pap. 3.50 o.p. (ISBN 0-686-20765-3). SF Bay Area.

Maryanski, Alexandra, jt. auth. see Turner, Jonathan H.

Maryanski, Fred J. Digital Computer Simulation. 336p. 1980. 15.95 (ISBN 0-8104-5118-2). Hayden.

Mary da Bergamo, Cajetan. Humility of Heart. Vaughan, Herbert C., tr. 240p. 1978. pap. 3.00 (ISBN 0-89555-067-9, 117). Tan Bks Pubs.

Maryk, Michael & Monahan, Brent. Deathbite. 1979. 8.95 o.p. (ISBN 0-8362-6104-6). Andrews & McMeel.

Maryland Hospital Education Institute. Hospital-Sponsered Ambulatory Care: The Governing Board's Role. LC 80-18004. 116p. (Orig.). 1980. pap. 18.75 (ISBN 0-87258-308-2, 1077). Am Hospital.

Maryland Webb, David. The Little Seed... LC 79-67086. (Illus.). 39p. (Orig.). (gr. 3-8). 1979. pap. 4.95 (ISBN 0-935054-00-6). Webb-Newcomb.

Mary Redempta, Sr. Practical Nursing Examination Review. LC 74-76633. (Arco Nursing Review Ser.). 288p. 1976. pap. 5.00 o.p. (ISBN 0-668-03488-2). Arco.

Marzahl, Peter. Town in the Empire: Government, Politics, & Society in Seventeenth-Century Popayan. LC 77-620062. (Latin American Monographs: No. 45). 1979. text ed. 14.95x (ISBN 0-292-78028-1); pap. text ed. 6.95x (ISBN 0-292-78029-X). U of Tex Pr.

Marzani, Carl. Promise of Eurocommunism. 367p. (Orig.). 1980. 16.95 (ISBN 0-88208-110-1); pap. 8.95 (ISBN 0-88208-111-X). Lawrence Hill.

Marzetti, Salli L. Santa Spreads Love Through God. (Illus.). 1980. 4.50 (ISBN 0-533-03800-6). Vantage.

Marzio, Peter, ed. A Nation of Nations. LC 75-25051. (Illus.). 416p. (YA) 1976. 27.50 (ISBN 0-06-012834-8, HarpT); pap. 8.95 o.p. (ISBN 0-06-012836-4, TD-256, HarpT). Har-Row.

Marzio, Peter C. The Men & Machines of American Journalism: A Pictorial Essay. LC 73-5371. (Illus.). 144p. 1973. pap. 4.95 (ISBN 0-87474-629-9). Smithsonian.

--Rube Goldberg: His Life & Work. LC 73-4108. (Illus.). 336p. 1973. 12.50 o.s.i. (ISBN 0-06-012830-5, HarpT). Har-Row.

Marzo, Luigi Di see Di Marzo, Luigi.

Marzollo, Jean. Halfway Down Paddy Lane. LC 80-25854. 176p. (gr. 6 up). 1981. 9.75 (ISBN 0-8037-3329-1). Dial.

Marzulli, F. N. & Maibach, H. I., eds. Advances in Modern Toxicology: Vol. 4, Dermatoxicology & Pharmacology. 592p. 1977. 37.50x o.p. (ISBN 0-470-99063-5). Halsted Pr.

Mas, Janet. Better Brochures, Catalogs & Mailing Pieces. (Illus.). 128p. 1981. 9.95 (ISBN 0-312-07730-0). St Martin.

Masada, Yoshiro. Analysis of Essential Oils by Gas Chromatography & Mass Spectrometry. LC 75-46590. 1976. 59.95 (ISBN 0-470-15019-X). Halsted Pr.

Masamune, S. Organic Synthesis. (Organic Synthesis Ser.: Vol. 55). 1976. 16.95 (ISBN 0-471-57390-6, Pub. by Wiley-Interscience). Wiley.

Masarik, Al. Nonesuch Creek: Selected Poems 1969 to 79. Robertson, Kirk, ed. 112p. (Orig.). 1980. pap. 4.50 (ISBN 0-916918-12-2). Duck Down.

Masaryk, Thomas G. The Making of a State. 1970. Repr. of 1927 ed. 16.50 (ISBN 0-86527-119-4). Fertig.

Mascaro, Juan, tr. The Dhammapada. (Classics Ser.). 1973. pap. 2.25 (ISBN 0-14-044284-7). Penguin.

Mascetta, Joseph. How to Prepare for the College Board Achievement Tests -- Chemistry. LC 68-26713. (gr. 10-12). 1981. pap. text ed. 5.50 (ISBN 0-8120-0304-7). Barron.

Maschke, Ruby. Life of Christ Story-N-Puzzle Book. 48p. (Orig.). (gr. 4 up). 1981. pap. 1.25 (ISBN 0-87239-449-2, 2839). Standard Pub.

--Teachings of Christ Story-N-Puzzle Book. 48p. (Orig.). (gr. 4 up). 1981. pap. 1.25 (ISBN 0-87239-451-4, 2842). Standard Pub.

Maschler, Fay, jt. auth. see Lord, John V.

Mascia, Leno. The Role of Additives in Plastics. LC 73-14098. 172p. 1974. 17.95 (ISBN 0-470-57410-0). Halsted Pr.

Mascott, Trina. Bella Figura. LC 76-28045. 1977. 8.95 o.p. (ISBN 0-312-07455-7). St Martin.

Masefield, Geoffrey B. A History of the Colonial Agricultural Service. 187p. 1972. 19.50x (ISBN 0-19-822336-6). Oxford U Pr.

Masefield, John. Bird of Dawning. 1943. 4.95 o.s.i. (ISBN 0-02-580760-9). Macmillan.

--Poems. complete ed. 1953. 19.95 (ISBN 0-02-580940-7). Macmillan.

--Salt-Water Poems & Ballads. (gr. 7 up). 1953. 4.95 o.s.i. (ISBN 0-02-581000-6); pap. 1.25 (ISBN 0-02-069930-1). Macmillan.

--Selected Poems. 1978. 14.95 (ISBN 0-02-581010-3). Macmillan.

--Taking of the Gry. 1967. 4.95 o.s.i. (ISBN 0-02-581500-8). Macmillan.

--Victorious Troy or the Hurrying Angel. 1967. 5.95 o.s.i. (ISBN 0-02-581590-3). Macmillan.

Masegawa, Sam. Linebackers. LC 74-23365. (Stars of the NFL Ser.). (gr. 4-12). 1975. PLB 7.95 (ISBN 0-87191-419-0). Creative Ed.

--Quarterbacks. LC 74-23143. (Stars of the NFL Ser.). (gr. 4-12). 1975. PLB 7.95 (ISBN 0-87191-417-4). Creative Ed.

Masella, Aristede B. Leggere Con Piacere. (gr. 7 up). 1976. pap. text ed. 4.83 (ISBN 0-87720-591-4). AMSCO Sch.

Maser, Jack D. & Seligman, Martin E., eds. Psychopathology: Experimental Models. LC 77-5032. (Psychology Ser.). (Illus.). 1977. text ed. 23.95x (ISBN 0-7167-0368-8); pap. text ed. 14.95x (ISBN 0-7167-0367-X). W H Freeman.

Maser, Werner. Hitler: Legend, Myth & Reality. Ross, Peter & Ross, Betty, trs. from Ger. LC 72-9136. (Illus.). 448p. 1973. 12.50 o.s.i. (ISBN 0-06-012831-3, HarpT). Har-Row.

--Hitler's Letters & Notes. Pomerance, Arnold, tr. from Ger. LC 73-10677. (Illus.). 400p. 1974. 12.50 o.s.i. (ISBN 0-06-012832-1, HarpT). Har-Row.

Maseres, Francis, jt. auth. see Towers, Joseph.

Masha, illus. Three Little Kittens. (Illus.). (ps-1). 1942. PLB 7.62 (ISBN 0-307-60410-1, Golden Pr). Western Pub.

Mashaw, Jerry L., et al. Social Security Hearings & Appeals: A Study of the Social Security Administration Hearing System. LC 78-3129. 1978. 15.95 (ISBN 0-669-02316-7). Lexington Bks.

Mashkara, K. I., jt. auth. see Usoltseva, E. V.

Mashruwala, K. G. Gandhi & Marx. 119p. (Orig.). 1981. pap. 1.50 (ISBN 0-934676-30-5). Greenlf Bks.

Masi, Dale A. Organizing for Women: Issues, Strategies, & Services. LC 78-19577. (Illus.). 1981. 22.95 (ISBN 0-669-02577-1). Lexington Bks.

Masia, Seth, jt. auth. see Bennet, John.

Masih, I. K. Plays of Samuel Beckett. 236p. 1980. text ed. write for info. (ISBN 0-391-02074-9). Humanities.

Masih, Y. Critical History of Modern Philosophy, Bacon to Kant: Hegal to Bradley. 471p. 1976. text ed. 19.50x (ISBN 0-8426-0803-6). Verry.

Masini, Jean, et al. Multinationals in Africa: A Case Study of the Ivory Coast. LC 78-19462. (Praeger Special Studies). 1978. 23.95 (ISBN 0-03-046256-8). Praeger.

Masinton, Charles G. Christopher Marlowe's Tragic Vision: A Study in Damnation. LC 77-181683. x, 168p. 1972. 10.95x (ISBN 0-8214-0101-7). Ohio U Pr.

Maskaleris, Thanasis. Kostis Palamas. (World Authors Ser.: Greece: No. 197). lib. bdg. 10.95 (ISBN 0-8057-2666-7). Twayne.

Maskell, Arthur M., jt. auth. see Fein, Sherman E.

Maskell, David. The Historical Epic in France 1500-1700. (Oxford Modern Languages & Literature Monographs). 275p. 1974. 24.95x (ISBN 0-19-815525-5). Oxford U Pr.

Maskit, B., jt. ed. see Kra, I.

Maslach, Christina, jt. auth. see Pines, Ayala M.

Maslach, Christina, jt. auth. see Zimbardo, Philip.

Maslinski, C., ed. Histamine: Mechanisms of Regulation of the Biogenic Amines Level in the Tissues with Special Reference to Histamine. LC 72-95941. 370p. 1974. 32.00 (ISBN 0-12-787052-0). Acad Pr.

Maslove, A. & Swimmer, G. Wage Controls in Canada, 1975-78. 182p. 1980. pap. text ed. 11.95x (ISBN 0-920380-50-6, Pub. by Inst Res Pub Canada). Renouf.

Maslove, Allan M., jt. auth. see Doern, G. Bruce.

Maslow, Abraham H. Eupsychian Management. 1965. pap. text ed. 10.50 (ISBN 0-256-00353-X). Irwin.

--The Psychology of Science. 1966. 9.95 o.p. (ISBN 0-06-034145-9, HarpT). Har-Row.

Maslow, Abraham H., ed. New Knowledge in Human Values. 1959. 9.95 o.p. (ISBN 0-06-034140-8, HarpT). Har-Row.

Maslow, William C., et al. Practical Diagnosis: Hematologic Disease. 1980. kroydenflex bdg. 16.00 (ISBN 0-89289-203-X). HM Prof Med Div.

Maslowsky, Edward, Jr. Vibrational Spectra of Organometallic Compounds. LC 76-18694. 1977. 35.00 o.p. (ISBN 0-471-58026-0, Pub. by Wiley-Interscience). Wiley.

Masnata, Albert. East-West Economic Cooperation: Problems & Solution. 1974. 17.95 (ISBN 0-347-01036-9, 93534-4, Pub. by Saxon Hse England). Lexington Bks.

Masnick, George & Bane, Mary Jo. The Nation's Families: 1960-1990. LC 80-20531. (Illus.). 200p. (Orig.). 1980. 17.95 (ISBN 0-86569-050-2); pap. 10.00 (ISBN 0-86569-051-0). Auburn Hse.

Mason. Plaid for Business & Economic Statistics. rev. ed. 1978. 5.50 (ISBN 0-256-00119-7, 10-0506-02). Learning Syst.

Mason & Lange. Plaid for Using the Metric System. 1976. pap. 4.95 (ISBN 0-256-01772-7, 15-1178-00). Learning Syst.

Mason, et al. Plaid for Business & Consumer Mathematics. 1978. pap. 5.50 (ISBN 0-256-01272-5, 15-0599-01). Learning Syst.

Mason, A. E. W. The Four Feathers. 1977. pap. text ed. 1.50 (ISBN 0-505-51162-2, 51162). Tower Bks.

Mason, A. T. & Beaney, Wiliam M. American Constitutional Law: Introductory Essays & Selected Cases. 6th ed. 1978. text ed. 21.95 (ISBN 0-13-024778-2). P-H.

Mason, Aaron S. & Granacher, Robert P. Clinical Handbook of Antipsychotic Drug Therapy. LC 80-11235. 1980. 25.00 (ISBN 0-87630-215-0). Brunner Mazel.

Mason, Alexander. Losers Keepers. (Orig.). 1980. pap. 2.25 (ISBN 0-505-51505-9). Tower Bks.

Mason, Alpheus T. The States Rights Debate: Antifederalism & the Constitution. 2nd ed. 224p. 1972. pap. text ed. 3.95x (ISBN 0-19-501553-3). Oxford U Pr.

Mason, Alpheus T. & Leach, Richard H. In Quest of Freedom: American Political Thought & Practice. LC 80-5749. 432p. 1981. pap. text ed. 12.00 (ISBN 0-8191-1473-1). U Pr of Amer.

Mason, Alpheus T. & Stephenson, D. Grier, eds. American Constitutional Development. LC 74-32555. (Goldentree Bibliographies in American History Ser.). 1977. o. p. 12.95x; pap. text ed. 12.95x (ISBN 0-88295-545-4). AHM Pub.

Mason, Anita & Packer, Diane. An Illustrated Dictionary of Jewellery. LC 73-11590. (Illus.). 400p. 1974. 15.95 o.s.i. (ISBN 0-06-012818-6, HarpT). Har-Row.

Mason, Anne. Swiss Cooking. 12.00 (ISBN 0-233-96257-3). Transatlantic.

Mason, Bernard S. The Book of Indian Crafts & Costumes. (Illus.). 1946. 15.95 (ISBN 0-8260-5720-9). Wiley.

--Dances & Stories of the American Indian. (Illus.). 1944. 11.95 o.p. (ISBN 0-8260-5735-7). Wiley.

--Drums, Tomtoms & Rattles: Primitive Percussion Instruments for Modern Use. (Illus.). 7.50 (ISBN 0-8446-5063-3). Peter Smith.

--Primitive & Pioneer Sports for Recreation Today: Rope Spinning, Lariat Throwing, Tumblesticks, Whip Cracking, Boomerangs, Log Rolling, Boomabirds, Tomahawks, Darts, Blowguns, & Many Others. LC 76-162516. (Illus.). 342p. 1975. Repr. of 1937 ed. 20.00 (ISBN 0-8103-4029-1). Gale.

Mason, Bernard S. & Mitchell, Elmer D. Party Games. 1962. pap. 2.95 (ISBN 0-06-463216-4, EH 216, EH). Har-Row.

Mason, Bessie M. On the Hill, No. 17. (Vagrom Chap Book Ser.: No. 17). 42p. (Orig.). 1980. pap. 3.95 (ISBN 0-935552-01-4). Sparrow Pr.

Mason, Bill. Path of the Paddle: An Illustrated Guide to the Art of Canoeing. 192p. 1980. 24.95 (ISBN 0-442-29630-4). Van Nos Reinhold.

Mason, Billy. Dollar Making Tips for Survival in the Eighties. 50p. (Orig.). 1981. lib. bdg. 9.95 (ISBN 0-686-28909-9). Kelso.

Mason, Billy, ed. Directory of Recycable Waste, Bk. 2. (Orig.). 1981. pap. 9.95 (ISBN 0-686-28908-0). Kelso.

Mason, Brian. Treasures Underground. (Illus.). (gr. 4-6). 1960. PLB 6.95 (ISBN 0-87396-015-7). Stravon.

Mason, Brian & Berry, L. G. Elements of Mineralogy. LC 68-13311. (Geology Ser.). (Illus.). 1968. 25.95x (ISBN 0-7167-0235-5). W H Freeman.

Mason, Brian, jt. auth. see Berry, Leonard G.

Mason, C. W., jt. auth. see Chamot, E. M.

Mason, Charles W. The Value-Philosophy of Alfred Edward Taylor: A Study in Theistic Implication. LC 79-52512. 1979. pap. text ed. 13.75 (ISBN 0-8191-0772-7). U Pr of Amer.

Mason, Clifford. When Love Was Not Enough. LC 80-82853. 272p. (Orig.). 1981. pap. 2.50 (ISBN 0-87216-779-8). Playboy Pbks.

Mason, D., ed. see Meigs, Walter B. & Meigs, Robert F.

Mason, David. Thalidomide: My Fight. 1976. 10.95 o.p. (ISBN 0-04-920046-1). Allen Unwin.

Mason, David & Dyller, Fran. Bitter Pills. 224p. 1977. 10.00 (ISBN 0-8065-0531-1). Citadel Pr.

--Pharmaceutical Dictionary & Reference for Prescription Drugs. LC 80-82854. (Illus.). 256p. 1981. pap. 3.50 (ISBN 0-87216-783-6). Playboy Pbks.

Mason, David M, et al see Heat Transfer & Fluid Mechanics Institute.

Mason, Dean T., jt. auth. see Berman, Danieal S.

Mason, E. A. & Spurling, T. H. The Viral Equation of State. LC 69-17903. 1970. text ed. 44.00 (ISBN 0-08-013292-8); pap. text ed. 19.00 (ISBN 0-08-018988-1). Pergamon.

Mason, Edite. To Be a Writer: A Course in Creative Writing. 1971. pap. 4.95 (ISBN 0-7195-2059-2). Transatlantic.

Mason, Edward E. Surgical Treatment of Obesity. (Major Problems in Clinical Surgery Ser.: Vol. 26). (Illus.). 512p. 1981. text ed. 32.50 (ISBN 0-7216-6141-6). Saunders.

Mason, Edward S. & Asher, Robert E. The World Bank Since Bretton Woods. LC 73-1089. 1973. 21.95 (ISBN 0-8157-5492-2). Brookings.

Mason, Edward S., ed. Corporation in Modern Society. LC 60-5392. 1966. pap. text ed. 4.95x (ISBN 0-689-70136-5, 86). Atheneum.

Mason, Elliott, jt. auth. see Spence, Alexander.

Mason, Elliott B., jt. auth. see Spence, Alexander P.

Mason, Enid. Embroidery Design. (Illus.). 128p. 1969. 8.50 (ISBN 0-8231-4010-5). Branford.

Mason, Eudo C. Goethe's Faust: Its Genesis & Purport. 1967. 20.00x (ISBN 0-520-00821-9). U of Cal Pr.

--Rilke, Europe, & the English-Speaking World. 1961. 43.50 (ISBN 0-521-05687-X). Cambridge U Pr.

Mason, F. K., jt. auth. see Windrow, Martin.

Mason, F. Van Wyck. Maryland Colony. LC 69-10782. (Forge of Freedom Ser). (Illus.). (gr. 5 up). 1969. 8.95 (ISBN 0-02-762870-1, CCPr). Macmillan.

Mason, F. Van Wyck see Van Wyck Mason, F.

Mason, Francis, jt. auth. see Balanchine, George.

Mason, Francis K. Hawker Hunter: Biography of a Thoroughbred. (Illus.). 244p. 1981. 43.95 (ISBN 0-85059-476-6). Aztex.

Mason, Franklin. Four Roses in Three Acts. LC 80-68007. 1981. 9.95 (ISBN 0-914590-64-2); pap. 4.95 (ISBN 0-914590-65-0). Fiction Coll.

Mason, Geoffrey, jt. ed. see Cooperstein, Bruce.

Mason, George & Sheldon, William D. Full Count. (Breakthrough Ser.). (RL 1). 1973. pap. text ed. 5.12 (ISBN 0-205-03336-9, 5233364); tchrs'. guide 2.40 (ISBN 0-205-03102-1, 5231027). Allyn.

--On the Level. (Breakthrough Ser.). (RL 1). 1973. pap. text ed. 5.12 (ISBN 0-205-03101-3, 5231019); tchrs'. guide 2.40 (ISBN 0-205-03102-1, 5231027). Allyn.

Mason, George E. A Primer on Teaching Reading: Basic Concepts & Skills of the Early Elementary Years. LC 80-52458. 234p. 1981. pap. text ed. 7.50 (ISBN 0-87581-262-7). Peacock Pubs.

Mason, George E. & Blanchard, Jay. Computer Applications in Reading. 106p. (Orig.). 1979. pap. text ed. 4.50 (ISBN 0-87207-936-8, 936). Intl Reading.

Mason, George F. Animal Appetites. (Illus.). (gr. 3-7). 1966. 6.25 o.p. (ISBN 0-688-21030-9). Morrow.

--Animal Baggage. (Illus.). (gr. 5-9). 1961. 6.75 (ISBN 0-688-21031-7); PLB 5.52 o.p. (ISBN 0-688-31031-1). Morrow.

--Animal Habits. (Illus.). (gr. 5-9). 1959. PLB 6.48 (ISBN 0-688-31034-6). Morrow.

--Animal Sounds. (Illus.). (gr. 5-9). 1948. PLB 6.48 (ISBN 0-688-31036-2). Morrow.

--Animal Tracks. (Illus.). (gr. 5-9). 1943. PLB 6.00 o.p. (ISBN 0-688-31041-9). Morrow.

Mason, H. Lee. Sermon Outlines for Evangelism. (Sermon Outline Ser.). (Orig.). 1981. pap. 1.45 (ISBN 0-8010-6120-2). Baker Bk.

Mason, Herbert. Summer Light. 148p. 1980. 9.95 (ISBN 0-374-27176-3). FS&G.

Mason, Herbert L. A Flora of the Marshes of California. LC 57-7960. (Illus.). 1957. 30.00x (ISBN 0-520-01433-2). U of Cal Pr.

Mason, Howard S., jt. ed. see Florkin, Marcel.

Mason, J. Barry & Mayer, Morris L. Modern Retailing: Theory & Practice. 1978. 18.95x (ISBN 0-256-02072-8). Business Pubns.

Mason, James D. Combat Handgun Shooting. (Illus.). 272p. 1980. 14.95 (ISBN 0-398-03461-3). C C Thomas.

Mason, James D., ed. see Bianchi, John.

Mason, Jess. How to Succeed in Real Estate...in Ten Minutes...Twice a Day! (Illus.). 160p. 1981. 12.50 (ISBN 0-682-49728-2). Exposition.

Mason, John. The Turk. (Salzburg Studies in English Literature: Jacobean Drama Studies: No. 30). 1979. pap. text ed. 25.00x (ISBN 0-391-01580-X). Humanities.

Mason, John H. The Indispensable Rousseau. 352p. (Orig.). 1980. 17.50 (ISBN 0-7043-2190-4, Pub. by Quartet England); pap. 7.95 (ISBN 0-7043-3220-5). Horizon.

Mason, K. L. Advanced Spanish Course. 1967. text ed. 11.40 (ISBN 0-08-012272-8); pap. text ed. 8.00 (ISBN 0-08-012271-X). Pergamon.

Mason, K. L. & Sager, J. C. Spanish Oral Drill Book. 1969. text ed. 8.20 (ISBN 0-08-013363-0); pap. text ed. 7.80 (ISBN 0-08-013362-2). Pergamon.

Mason, K. L., jt. auth. see Lawrence, M. J.

Mason, L. C. Building a Small Lathe. (Illus.). 82p. 1979. 7.50x (ISBN 0-85242-687-9). Intl Pubns Serv.

Mason, L. F. Photographic Processing Chemistry. 2nd ed. LC 75-20098. 326p. 1975. 39.95 (ISBN 0-470-57535-2). Halsted Pr.

Mason, L. Ryder. California Family Law Handbook. LC 79-90704. 1980. 36.00 (ISBN 0-911110-31-3); 1980 suppl. incl. Parker & Son.

Mason, Lauris, jt. auth. see Shapiro, Cecile.

Mason, Lowell. Musical Letters from Abroad. 2nd ed. LC 67-13035. (Music Ser). 1967. Repr. of 1854 ed. lib. bdg. 25.00 (ISBN 0-306-70940-6). Da Capo.

Mason, Lowell & Webb, George J. The Boston Glee Book. LC 76-52481. (Music Reprint Ser., 1977). 1977. Repr. of 1844 ed. lib. bdg. 27.50 (ISBN 0-306-70860-4). Da Capo.

Mason, Lowell, ed. The Boston Handel & Haydn Society Collection of Church Music. LC 77-171078. (Earlier American Music Ser.: Vol. 15). 324p. 1973. Repr. of 1822 ed. lib. bdg. 25.00 (ISBN 0-306-77315-5). Da Capo.

Mason, Marion, et al. The Dynamics of Clinical Dietetics. LC 77-21936. 1977. pap. text ed. 15.95 (ISBN 0-471-02172-5, Pub. by Wiley Medical). Wiley.

Mason, Melody, jt. auth. see Kollmar, Kerry.

Mason, Michael & Currey, H. L., eds. Clinical Rheumatology. 2nd ed. LC 75-32623. (Illus.). 1975. 24.00 o.p. (ISBN 0-397-58186-6). Lippincott.

Mason, Miriam E. Becky & Her Brave Cat, Bluegrass. (Illus.). (gr. 3-5). 1960. 3.95 o.s.i. (ISBN 0-02-762950-3). Macmillan.

--Broomtail, Brother of Lightning. (Illus.). (gr. 3-5). 1952. 3.75 o.s.i. (ISBN 0-02-763180-X); PLB 3.64 o.s.i. (ISBN 0-02-763200-8). Macmillan.

--Caroline & Her Kettle Named Maud. (Illus.). (gr. 4-6). 1951. 3.95g o.s.i. (ISBN 0-02-763280-6). Macmillan.

--Caroline & the Seven Little Words. (gr. 2-4). 1967. 4.95 o.s.i. (ISBN 0-02-763330-6). Macmillan.

--Hominy & His Blunt-Nosed Arrow. (gr. 2-4). 1967. 3.95g o.s.i. (ISBN 0-02-763720-4). Macmillan.

--Matilda & Her Family. (gr. 2-4). 1967. 3.50g o.s.i. (ISBN 0-02-764390-5). Macmillan.

--Middle Sister. (Illus.). (gr. 4-6). 1947. 3.95 o.s.i. (ISBN 0-02-764500-2). Macmillan.

--Miney & the Blessing. (Illus.). (gr. 2-6). 1961. 2.95 o.s.i. (ISBN 0-02-764610-6). Macmillan.

--Pony Called Lightning. (gr. 2-4). 1948. 3.95g o.s.i. (ISBN 0-02-764820-6). Macmillan.

--Sara & the Winter Gift. (Illus.). (gr. 2-4). 1968. 4.50g o.s.i. (ISBN 0-02-763060-9). Macmillan.

--Susannah, the Pioneer Cow. (gr. k-3). 1941. 4.95g o.s.i. (ISBN 0-02-765150-9). Macmillan.

Mason, Penelope E. A Reconstruction of the Hogen-Heiji Monogatari Emaki. LC 76-23639. (Outstanding Dissertations in the Fine Arts). (Illus.). 1977. Repr. of 1970 ed. lib. bdg. 48.50 (ISBN 0-685-76431-1). Garland Pub.

Mason, Philip. Kipling: The Glass, the Shadow & the Fire. LC 74-29175. 336p. (YA) 1975. 10.00 o.s.i. (ISBN 0-06-012833-X, HarpT). Har-Row.

--A Shaft of Sunlight. (Illus.). 1978. 12.50 o.p. (ISBN 0-684-15920-1, ScribT). Scribner.

Mason, Polly C. Records of Colonial Gloucester County, Virginia. (Illus.). 146p. (Repr. of 1946-1948 eds.). 30.00x o.p. (ISBN 0-685-65079-0). Va Bk.

Mason Publishing Company Staff, ed. see McLean, Daniels.

Mason Publishing Company Staff, ed. see Roer, Kathleen.

Mason Publishing Staff, ed. see Miller, John M.

Mason Publishing Staff, ed. see Stoneking, Gary E.

Mason Publishing Staff, ed. see Wagner, Michael P.

Mason, R. Essentials of Statistics. 1976. pap. text ed. 13.95 (ISBN 0-13-289561-7). P-H.

--Petrology of the Metamorphic Rocks. (Textbook of Petrology Ser.). (Illus.). 1978. text ed. 27.50x (ISBN 0-04-552013-5); pap. text ed. 14.95x (ISBN 0-04-552014-3). Allen Unwin.

Mason, R. A., jt. auth. see Feuchtwanger, E. J.

Mason, R. E. & Rath, P. M. Marketing & Distribution. 1968. text ed. 12.96 o.p. (ISBN 0-07-040675-8, G); tchr's manual & key 4.00 o.p. (ISBN 0-07-040678-2); tests 2.24 o.p. (ISBN 0-07-040677-4). McGraw.

Mason, R. Elaine. Tennis. (Illus.). 160p. 1975. pap. text ed. 6.50x (ISBN 0-205-03844-1, 6238440). Allyn.

Mason, R. H. Japan's First General Election, Eighteen Ninety. LC 68-23915. (University of Cambridge Oriental Pubns.). 1969. 38.50 (ISBN 0-521-07147-X). Cambridge U Pr.

--Portraiture at Home. 1977. 14.95 o.p. (ISBN 0-85242-488-4, Pub. by Fountain). Morgan.

Mason, R. H., ed. see Gotze, Hans.

Mason, R. H., et al. The Economics of International Business. 464p. 1981. Repr. of 1975 ed. text ed. 23.50 (ISBN 0-89874-248-X). Krieger.

Mason, R. Hal, ed. International Business in the Pacific Basin. LC 78-346. 1978. 19.95 (ISBN 0-669-02189-X). Lexington Bks.

Mason, R. Hal, et al. The Economics of International Business. LC 74-18476. (Management & Administration Ser). 464p. 1975. text ed. 20.50 o.p. (ISBN 0-471-57528-3); instructor's manual avail. o.p. (ISBN 0-471-57529-1). Wiley.

--International Business. 2nd ed. (Management & Administration Ser.). 500p. 1981. text ed. 21.95 (ISBN 0-686-69162-8). Wiley.

Mason, Ralph E. & Haines, Peter G. Cooperative Occupational Education & Work Experience in the Curriculum. 3rd ed. (Illus.). 1981. text ed. 11.75x (ISBN 0-8134-2150-0, 2150). Interstate.

--Cooperative Occupational Education & Work Experience in the Curriculum. LC 72-76306. (Illus.). 1972. text ed. 11.75x o.p. (ISBN 0-8134-1779-1, 1779). Interstate.

Mason, Ralph E., et al. Marketing & Distribution. 2nd ed. LC 73-2826. (Illus.). 576p. (gr. 11-12). 1974. text ed. 12.96 (ISBN 0-07-040690-1, G); teachers manual & key 4.00 (ISBN 0-07-040692-8); project activity guide 5.96 (ISBN 0-07-040691-X). McGraw.

Mason, Richard & Caiger, John. A History of Japan. LC 73-13581. 1973. 10.95 (ISBN 0-02-920290-6). Free Pr.

Mason, Richard H. & Swanson, E. Burton. Measurement for Management Decision. (Computer Science: Decision Support). (Illus.). 448p. 1981. text ed. 15.95 (ISBN 0-201-04646-6). A-W.

Mason, Richard O. & Mitroff, Ian I. Challenging Strategic Planning Assumptions: Theory, Cases & Techniques. 300p. 1981. 24.95 (ISBN 0-471-08219-8, Pub. by Wiley-Interscience). Wiley.

Mason, Robert D. Plaid for College Mathematics: With Applications in Business & Economics. 1976. pap. 5.50 (ISBN 0-256-01267-9, 15-0498-00). Learning Syst.

--Problems Manual. 4th ed. (To Accompany Statistical Techniques In Business & Economics). 1978. pap. text ed. 6.95 (ISBN 0-256-02026-4). Irwin.

--Statistical Techniques in Business & Economics. 4th ed. 1978. text ed. 18.95x (ISBN 0-256-02025-6). Irwin.

Mason, Robert D., et al. Mathematics for Business & Consumers. rev. ed. 1980. pap. text ed. 13.95x (ISBN 0-256-02433-2). Business Pubns.

Mason, Robert L., et al. The Clergyman & the Psychiatrist: When to Refer. LC 77-22597. 1978. 15.95x (ISBN 0-88229-260-9). Nelson-Hall.

Mason, Robert L., Jr., et al. The Emotionally Troubled Child. 196p. 1976. 18.50 (ISBN 0-398-03557-1). C C Thomas.

Mason, Robert M. & Crepps, John E., eds. Information Services: Economics, Management, & Technology. (Westview Special Studies in Information Management). 200p. 1980. lib. bdg. 26.50x (ISBN 0-89158-938-4). Westview.

Mason, Roger D., jt. auth. see O'Brien, Michael J.

Mason, Ronald J. Great Lakes Archaeology. LC 80-2340. (New World Archaeological Record Ser.). 1981. price not set (ISBN 0-12-477850-X). Acad Pr.

Mason, Russell E. Anxiety, Resolution, Relaxation, & Systematic Flexible Hierachy, Tape Uses, Set-AH. 1975. pap. 50.00x (ISBN 0-89533-009-1); incl. tape-1a, t-9, t-5a, t-10, t-8, t-11, Notes, Clinical Applications & Substitution Training. F I Comm.

--Basic, Advanced Systematic Substitution Training, Set-AS. 1975. pap. 25.00 (ISBN 0-89533-017-2); incl. tape 12 (ISBN 0-89533-042-3); t-13 (ISBN 0-89533-043-1); t-14 (ISBN 0-89533-044-X); notes (ISBN 0-89533-025-3); tran-ascendance forms H.E.S.T-a set avail. F I Comm.

--Basic, Elementary Systematic Substitution Training, Set-ES. 1973. pap. 25.00 (ISBN 0-89533-015-6); Relaxation Training, Substitution Training incl.; tape-1 (ISBN 0-89533-030-X); t-4 (ISBN 0-686-67261-5); t-5 (ISBN 0-89533-035-0). F I Comm.

--Comprehensive Set: Purposeful Relaxation, Problem Solutions, Value Considerations & Communication, Set-A. rev. ed. 1975. pap. 140.00x (ISBN 0-89533-021-0); 18 cassettes, notes, clinical applications 1979, relaxation training, feeling training, H.E.S.T. set incl. F I Comm.

--Extended (Experiential) Awareness, Purposeful Relaxation, & Multiple (Differentiated Psychophysiological) Feeling States, Set-CA. 1975. pap. 50.00x (ISBN 0-89533-013-X); Notes, Feeling Training, Substitution & Goal Achievement Training incl.; tape-1a; t-2. t-3; t-4; t-5A (ISBN 0-89533-034-2); t-7. F I Comm.

--Informational Guides for Groups, Communication, Living & Change, Set-GL. rev. ed. 1975. pap. 25.00x (ISBN 0-89533-019-9); tape-2, t-16, t-17 incl., notes, clinical applications 1979, H.E.S.T-a, set. F I Comm.

--Life-Extension, Purposeful Relaxation, Differential (Multiple) "Feeling" (Psychophysiological) Awareness & Communication, Set-t-a. 1975. hardback, paper, & tape 50.00x (ISBN 0-89533-018-0); =tape-1a, t-3, t-4, t-16, t-17, notes, H.E.S.T-a, set incl., positive personalities: joy, significance, & sexual feelings & values. F I Comm.

--Multiple Uses: Positive Substitution, Problem Solutions, Relaxation, & Goal Achievements, Set-MS. rev. ed. 1975. pap. 50.00x (ISBN 0-89533-008-3); tape-1a, t-2, t-5a t-10,t-16, t-17 incl., notes, clinical applications 1979, h.e.s.t-a, set. F I Comm.

--Positive Awareness (Experiential Extension), Purposeful Relaxati0n, & (Differentiated Psychophysiological) "Feeling" States, Set-PA. 1975. pap. 25.00x (ISBN 0-89533-012-1); tape-1a, t-3, t-4 incl., notes, feeling training. F I Comm.

--Positive Personality Fulfillment, Set-PPF. 1975. 25.00x (ISBN 0-89533-048-2); tape-1a, 1-5a incl., positive personalities: joy significance & sexual feeling & values. F I Comm.

--Positive Substitution, Purposeful Relaxation, & Goal Achievement Training: A Beginning, Set-PS. rev. ed. 1975. pap. 50.00x (ISBN 0-89533-014-8); Clinical Applications 1979, Relaxation Training, Substitution Training incl.; tape-1A; t-2; t-4; t-5 (ISBN 0-89533-035-0); t-6 avail. (ISBN 0-89533-036-9); t-10. F I Comm.

--Relaxation & (Re-, or) De-Sensitization Training, Set-RD. rev. ed. 1975. pap. 50.00x (ISBN 0-89533-006-7); tape-1a, t-1, t-2, t-5a, t-6, t-9, relaxation training, clinical application 1979 & hierarchy incl. F I Comm.

--Set, H.E.S.T-a: Humanistic Endeavor & Surgent Train-Ascendance. 1975. pap. 3.00 (ISBN 0-89533-028-8). F I Comm.

--Simple Guides to Daily Growth: Problem Solving or Purposeful Relaxation for Comfort or Effectiveness, Set-SG. rev. ed. 1975. pap. 25.00x (ISBN 0-89533-001-6); tape-1a, t-2, t-5a, notes, clinical applications, differential criteria, implications for bioawareness 1979 incl. F I Comm.

--Simplified Behavior & "Feeling" State Change & Goal Accomplishment, Set-SB. 1975. pap. 50.00x (ISBN 0-89533-002-4); tape-1a, t-2, t-5a, t-3, t-16, t-17 incl., notes, clinical applications, substitution training. F I Comm.

--Simplified Extended, Deep, & or Meditative Relaxation, Set-R. 1975. pap. 25.00x (ISBN 0-89533-004-0); tape-1a, t-l, t-6, relaxation training, clinical applications incl. (ISBN 0-89533-026-1). F I Comm.

--Simplified Relaxatiбn, Problem Solutions & Substitutions, & Value Considerations, Set-S. 1975. pap. 75.00x (ISBN 0-89533-020-2); tape-1a, t-5a, t-10-11, t-12, t-13, t-14, notes incl., clinical applications, substitution training & goal archievements. F I Comm.

--Solutions, Relaxation, or Understanding for Tense, Anxious, Depressive, Hostile (Irritated), & Disgusted States & Problems, Set-ST. 1975. pap. 50.00x (ISBN 0-89533-010-5); tape-1a, t-5a, t-11, t-12, t-13, t-14 incl., notes, clinical applications, substitution training. F I Comm.

Mason, Sally W. The New Holistic Way to Lose Weight & Rejuvenate. rev. ed. (Illus.). 228p. 1980. Repr. of 1979 ed. 9.95 (ISBN 0-8119-0348-6). Fell.

Mason, Shirlene. Daniel Defoe & the Status of Women. LC 78-59369. 1978. 12.95 (ISBN 0-88831-025-0). EPWP.

Mason, Stephen F. History of the Sciences. Orig. Title: Main Currents of Scientific Thought. 1962. pap. 6.95 (ISBN 0-02-093400-9, Collier). Macmillan.

Mason, Stuart & Swash, Michael. Hutchinson's Clinical Methods. 17th ed. 495p. 1980. 14.50 (ISBN 0-397-58270-6). Lippincott.

--Hutchinson's Clinical Methods. 17th ed. (Illus.). 495p. 1980. 14.50 (ISBN 0-397-58270-6). Lippincott.

Mason, Theodore K. On the Ice in Antarctica. LC 77-16856. (gr. 7 up). 1978. 6.95 (ISBN 0-396-07535-5). Dodd.

Mason, Van Wyck. Winter at Valley Forge. (Landmark Ser: No. 33). (Illus.). (gr. 10-12). 1953. PLB 5.99 (ISBN 0-394-90333-1, BYR). Random.

Mason, Warren P. & Thurston, Robert N., eds. Physical Acoustics: Principles & Methods, Vol. 15. 1981. 48.50 (ISBN 0-12-477915-8). Acad Pr.

Masooduzzafar, Translated by see Nejand, Farghaneh.

Masoro, E. J., ed. Pharmacology of Lipid Transport & Atherosclerotic Processes. 1974. text ed. 105.00 (ISBN 0-08-017762-X). Pergamon.

Masotti, Louis H., jt. ed. see Linesberry, Robert L.

Maspero, Henri. Taoism & Chinese Religion. Kierman, Frank A., tr. from Fr. LC 80-13444. Orig. Title: Le Taoisme et les religions Chinoises. 656p. 1981. lib. bdg. 32.50x (ISBN 0-87023-308-4). U of Mass Pr.

Mass. Audubon Society. Bird Identification Engagement Book, 1981. (Desk Date Bk.). (Illus.). 1981. 9.95 (ISBN 0-8289-0384-0). Greene.

--Birds of Eastern North America: 1981. (Wallcalendars Ser.). (Illus.). 1980. pap. 6.95 (ISBN 0-8289-0381-6). Greene.

--Birds of Western North America: 1981. (Wallcalendars Ser.). (Illus.). 1980. pap. 6.95 (ISBN 0-8289-0382-4). Greene.

Mass, Jeffrey P. The Development of Kamakura Rule, 1180-1250: A History with Documents. LC 78-62271. 1979. 18.50x (ISBN 0-8047-1003-1). Stanford U Pr.

Massachusetts Constitutional Convention - 1820-21. Journal of Debates & Proceedings. LC 76-133169. (Law, Politics, & History Ser). 1970. Repr. of 1853 ed. lib. bdg. 69.50 (ISBN 0-306-70068-9). Da Capo.

Massachusetts General Hospital. Clinical Anesthesia Procedures of the Massachusetts General Hospital. Lebowitz, Philip W., ed. 1978. pap. text ed. 10.95 (ISBN 0-316-54957-6). Little.

--Massachusetts General Hospital Department of Nursing Operating Room Procedure Manual. 1981. text ed. 13.95 (ISBN 0-8359-4252-X). Reston.

Massachusetts General Hospital Department of Nursing, et al, eds. Manual of Nursing Procedures. 1980. text ed. write for info. (ISBN 0-316-54958-4); pap. text ed. price not set (ISBN 0-316-54958-4). Little.

Massachusetts General Hospital Pediatric Nursing Service. Manual of Pediatric Nursing Practice. Pikl, Barbara H., ed. (Little, Brown Spiral Manual Series). 1980. pap. write for info. (ISBN 0-316-54958-4). Little.

Massachussetts General Hospital. Dept. of Nursing Staff Education Manual. Stetler, Cheryl B., et al, eds. 1981. text ed. 34.95 (ISBN 0-8359-1281-7). Reston.

Massalski, T. B., jt. auth. see Barrett, C. S.

Massam, B. H. The Spatial Structure of Administrative Systems. LC 75-185557. (CCG Resource Papers Ser.: No. 12). (Illus.). 1972. pap. text ed. 4.00 (ISBN 0-89291-059-3). Assn Am Geographers.

Massam, Bryan. Location & Space in Social Administration. LC 74-26536. 192p. 1975. 24.95 (ISBN 0-470-57600-6). Halsted Pr.

Massam, Bryan H. Spatial Search: Applications to Planning Problems in the Public Sector. (Urban & Regional Planning: Vol. 23). (Illus.). 33.00 (ISBN 0-08-024286-3). Pergamon.

Massan, Alastair, jt. auth. see Hitchcock, Edward.

Massee, William E. Massee's Wine Almanac. LC 80-13391. 240p. 1980. 12.95 (ISBN 0-13-559658-0); pap. 6.95 (ISBN 0-13-559641-6). P-H.

Masselman, George. Cradle of Colonialism. 1963. 47.50x (ISBN 0-685-69840-8). Elliots Bks.

Massena, Robert A. Le see Le Massena, Robert A.

Massengale, John D. The Principles & Problems of Coaching. 392p. 1975. 19.75 (ISBN 0-398-03258-0); pap. 15.50 (ISBN 0-398-03259-9). C C Thomas.

Massengale, Martin A., jt. ed. see Bethel, James S.

Masserman, Jules H., ed. Current Psychiatric Therapies, Vol. XIX. 1980. 29.50 (ISBN 0-8089-1300-X). Grune.

Massey, A. G., jt. auth. see Holliday, A. K.

Massey, Craig. I Love You, I Hear You. 160p. 1980. text ed. 6.95 (ISBN 0-8024-3957-8). Moody.

--The Warm Summer. (A Hearth Classic Ser.). 192p. 1980. pap. 2.50 (ISBN 0-310-41772-4). Zondervan.

Massey, H. A Perspective of Physics: Volume 4, Selections from Nineteen Seventy-Nine Comments on Modern Physics. 1980. write for info. (ISBN 0-677-16190-5). Gordon.

Massey, H. S., jt. auth. see Mott, N. F.

Massey, Harrie. Atomic & Molecular Collisions. LC 79-11716. 1979. 39.95x (ISBN 0-470-26742-9). Halsted Pr.

--Negative Ions. 3rd ed. LC 74-31792. (Cambridge Monographs on Physics). (Illus.). 600p. 1976. 126.00 (ISBN 0-521-20775-4). Cambridge U Pr.

Massey, Harrie, et al. Electronic & Ionic Impact Phenomena: Slow Position & Muon Collisions - & Notes on Recent Advances, Vol. 5. (International Ser. of Monographs on Physics). (Illus.). 596p. 1974. 69.00x (ISBN 0-19-851283-X). Oxford U Pr.

Massey, Howard C. Plumbing Estimators Handbook. 256p. (Orig.). 1981. pap. 15.25 (ISBN 0-910460-82-5). Craftsman.

Massey, Irving. The Gaping Pig: Literature & Metamorphoses. LC 74-22967. 1976. 17.50 (ISBN 0-520-02887-2). U of Cal Pr.

Massey, J. Earl. America's Money: The Story of Our Coins & Currency. LC 68-31772. (Illus.). 1968. 6.95 o.s.i. (ISBN 0-690-08656-3, TYC-T). T Y Crowell.

Massey, James A., ed. see Schleiermacher, Friedrich.

Massey, James A., tr. see Feuerbach, Ludwig.

Massey, James E. Designing the Sermon: Order & Movement in Preaching. LC 80-17920. (Abingdon Preacher's Library). 128p. (Orig.). 1980. pap. 4.95 (ISBN 0-687-10490-4). Abingdon.

Massey, James O. Readiness for Kindergarten. 1975. pap. 1.25 (ISBN 0-89106-014-6, 1281). Consulting Psychol.

Massey, Jamila, jt. auth. see Massey, Reginald.

Massey, John B. Manual of Dosimetry in Radiotherapy. (Technical Reports Ser.: No. 110). (Illus., Orig.). 1970. pap. 9.75 (ISBN 92-0-115370-8, IDC 110, IAEA). Unipub.

Massey, Morris E. The People Puzzle: Understanding Yourself & Others. (Illus.). 1980. text ed. 13.95 (ISBN 0-8359-5477-3). Reston.

Massey, Reginald & Massey, Jamila. The Immigrants. (Orient Paperbacks Ser.). 172p. (Orig.). 1973. pap. 2.50 (ISBN 0-88253-243-X). Ind-US Inc.

Massey, Reginald & Singha, Rina. Indian Dances: Their History & Growth. LC 67-20736. 1967. 12.50 o.s.i. (ISBN 0-8076-0427-5). Braziller.

Massey, Robert. Personality Theories: Comparisons & Syntheses. 1981. text ed. write for info. (ISBN 0-442-23892-4). D Van Nostrand.

Massialas, Byron, et al. Social Issues Through Inquiry: Coping in an Age of Crisis. (Illus.). 288p. 1975. pap. text ed. 10.95 (ISBN 0-13-815852-5). P-H.

Massialas, Byron G. & Hurst, Joseph. Social Studies in a New Era: The Elementary School As a Laboratory for Real-Life Experiences. LC 77-17716. 1978. pap. 14.95x (ISBN 0-582-28043-5). Longman.

Massialas, Byron G., jt. auth. see Kazamias, Andreas M.

Massie, Diane R. Briar Rose & the Golden Eggs. LC 73-1249. (Illus.). 48p. (gr. k-3). 1973. 5.95 o.s.i. (ISBN 0-8193-0684-3, Four Winds). Schol Bk Serv.

--Chameleon Was a Spy. LC 78-19510. (Illus.). (gr. 2-6). 1979. 6.95 (ISBN 0-690-03909-3, TYC-J); PLB 7.89 (ISBN 0-690-03910-7). T Y Crowell.

--Magic Jim. LC 67-18462. (Illus.). (gr. 1-3). 1967. 5.95 o.s.i. (ISBN 0-8193-0177-9, Four Winds); PLB 5.41 o.s.i. (ISBN 0-8193-0178-7). Schol Bk Serv.

--Zigger Beans. LC 70-117564. (Illus.). (gr. k-2). 1971. 5.95 o.s.i. (ISBN 0-8193-0416-6, Four Winds); PLB 5.41 o.s.i. (ISBN 0-8193-0417-4). Schol Bk Serv.

Massie, Dianne R. Monstrous Glisson Glop. LC 71-93856. (Illus.). (gr. k-3). 1970. 5.95 o.s.i. (ISBN 0-8193-0380-1, Four Winds); PLB 5.41 o.s.i. (ISBN 0-8193-0381-X). Schol Bk Serv.

Massie, J. L. & Douglas, John. Managing: A Contemporary Introduction. 2nd ed. LC 76-22521. (Illus.). 1977. text ed. 19.95 (ISBN 0-13-548545-2); student resource manual 6.95 (ISBN 0-13-548149-X). P-H.

Massie, Joseph L. Blazer & Ashland Oil: A Study in Management. LC 60-8519. (Illus.). 272p. 1960. 11.00x (ISBN 0-8131-1051-3). U Pr of Ky.

--Essentials of Management. 3rd ed. (Essentials of Management Ser.). (Illus.). 1979. ref. 15.95 (ISBN 0-13-286351-0); pap. 9.95 ref. (ISBN 0-13-286344-8). P-H.

Massie, Joseph L. & Douglas, John. Managing: A Contemporary Introduction. 3rd ed. (Illus.). 544p. 1981. text ed. 17.95 (ISBN 0-13-550327-2); pap. 7.95 student manual (ISBN 0-13-550368-X). P-H.

Massie, Joseph L., et al. Management: Analysis, Concepts, Cases. 3rd ed. (Illus.). 800p. 1975. ref. ed. 21.00 (ISBN 0-13-548412-X). P-H.

Massie, Rebecca. The Sydney & Frances Lewis Contemporary Art Fund Collection. (Illus.). 112p. (Orig.). 1980. pap. 7.95x (ISBN 0-917046-09-9). VA Mus Fine Arts.

Massie, Robert K. Peter the Great: His Life & His World. LC 80-7635. (Illus.). 864p. 1980. 17.95 (ISBN 0-394-50032-6). Knopf.

Massie, Robert K, Jr., jt. ed. see Green, Mark.

Massie, Suzanne. Land of the Firebird. 1980. 22.50 (ISBN 0-686-62882-9, 23051). S&S.

Massimino, Sal T. How to Sell to the People's Republic of China. LC 80-18997. (Illus.). 176p. 1980. 16.95 (ISBN 0-444-00454-8, Thomond Pr). Elsevier.

Massimo, L. Physics of High Temperature Reactors. 1975. text ed. 37.00 (ISBN 0-08-019616-0). Pergamon.

Massine, Leonide. Massine on Choreography: Theory & Exercises in Composition. (Illus.). 1977. 45.00 (ISBN 0-571-09302-7, Pub. by Faber & Faber). Merrimack Bk Serv.

Massinger, Phillip. City Madam. Hoy, Cyrus, ed. LC 64-11357. (Regents Renaissance Drama Ser). 1964. 6.95x (ISBN 0-8032-0278-4); pap. 1.65x (ISBN 0-8032-5277-3, BB 204, Bison). U of Nebr Pr.

Massoglia, Elinor T. Early Childhood Education in the Home. LC 76-14091. (gr. 9-12). 1977. pap. text ed. 9.20 (ISBN 0-8273-0589-3); instructor's guide 1.60 (ISBN 0-8273-0590-7). Delmar.

Massola, Aldo. Bunjil's Cave: Myths, Legends & Superstitions of the Aborigines of South-East Australia. (Illus.). 1968. text ed. 14.25x (ISBN 0-391-01962-7). Humanities.

Masson, Charles. Nouveau Traite Des Regles Pour La Composition De la Musique. 2nd ed. LC 67-25446. (Music Ser). 1967. Repr. of 1699 ed. lib. bdg. 16.50 (ISBN 0-306-70941-4). Da Capo.

Masson, David. Drummond on Hawthornden: The Story of His Life & Writings. 490p. 1980. Repr. of 1873 ed. lib. bdg. 50.00 (ISBN 0-8492-6834-6). R West.

Masson, G. M., jt. auth. see Thurber, Kenneth J.

Masson, J. Moussaiff, jt. ed. see Merwin, W. S.

Masson, Madeleine. Christine: A Search for Christine Granville. 1978. 19.95 (ISBN 0-241-89274-0, Pub. by Hamish Hamilton England). David & Charles.

Masson, O. Carian Inscriptions from North Sacqara & Buhen. 120p. 1979. 75.00x (ISBN 0-686-61264-7, Pub. by Aris & Phillips). Intl Schol Bk Serv.

Masson, Paul Marie. L' Opera de Rameau. LC 70-168675. (Music Ser). (Illus.). 596p. 1972. Repr. of 1930 ed. lib. bdg. 55.00 (ISBN 0-306-70262-2). Da Capo.

Masson, Pierre. Human Tumors: Histology, Diagnosis, & Technique. Kobernick, Sidney D., tr. from Fr. LC 70-83489. (Illus.). 1970. text ed. 45.00x (ISBN 0-8143-1405-8). Wayne St U Pr.

Masson, VeNeta. International Nursing. 1981. text ed. price not set (ISBN 0-8261-3170-0); pap. text ed. price not set (ISBN 0-8261-3171-9). Springer Pub.

Massy, Robert. You Are What You Breathe. 1980. 1.00 (ISBN 0-916438-41-4). Univ of Trees.

Massy, William F., jt. auth. see Hopkins, David S.

Mast, Gerald. The Comic Mind: Comedy & the Movies. 2nd ed. LC 78-68546. (Illus.). 1979. lib. bdg. 24.00x (ISBN 0-226-50976-1); pap. 8.95 (ISBN 0-266-50978-9, P827, Phoen). U of Chicago Pr.

--Film-Cinema-Movie: A Theory of Experience. LC 75-34679. (Illus.). 256p. 1977. 17.50 o.p. (ISBN 0-06-012822-4, HarpT). Har-Row.

--A Short History of the Movies. 2nd ed. LC 75-14302. 1975. pap. 10.50 o.p. (ISBN 0-672-63719-7). Pegasus.

--A Short History of the Movies. LC 80-18024. (Illus.). 516p. 1980. pap. text ed. 13.95 (ISBN 0-672-61521-5). Bobbs.

Mast, Gerald & Cohen, Marshall, eds. Film Theory & Criticism: Introductory Readings. 2nd ed. (Illus.). 1979. 26.95x (ISBN 0-19-502503-2); pap. text ed. 9.95x (ISBN 0-19-502498-2). Oxford U Pr.

Mastalerz, John W. The Greenhouse Environment: The Effect of Environmental Factors on Flower Crops. LC 77-6793. 1977. 25.95 (ISBN 0-471-57606-9). Wiley.

Masten, Billie B., jt. auth. see Masten, Ric.

Masten, Ric & Masten, Billie B. His & Hers: A Passage Through Middle-Age Crazies. 1978. pap. 3.95 (ISBN 0-931104-01-7). Sunflower Ink.

Masten, Rick. Stark Naked. 1980. pap. 4.95 (ISBN 0-931104-04-1). Sunflower Ink.

Master, Richard Le see Le Master, Richard.

Master, Roshen S. Elementary Psychiatry for Medical Undergraduates. 1968. 10.00x (ISBN 0-210-22708-7). Asia.

Master Hua, Ch'An. Flower Adornment (Avatamsaka) Sutra: Chapter 26, The Ten Grounds. Bhiksuni Heng Hsien, tr. from Chinese. (Illus.). 1980. pap. 7.00 (ISBN 0-917512-29-4). Buddhist Text.

Masterman, C. F. From the Abyss. Of Its Inhabitants by One of Them, London, 1903. LC 79-56963. (The English Working Class Ser.). 1980. lib. bdg. 12.00 (ISBN 0-8240-0115-X). Garland Pub.

Masterman, J. C. The Double Cross System. 4.95 (ISBN 0-686-28851-3). Academy Chi Ltd.

Masterman, Len. Teaching About Television. (Illus.). 238p. 1980. text ed. 26.00x (ISBN 0-333-26676-5); pap. text ed. 13.00x (ISBN 0-333-26677-3). Humanities.

Masters, Brian. Now Barabbas Was a Rotter: The Extraordinary Life of Corelli. 1979. 22.50 (ISBN 0-241-89767-X, Pub. by Hamish Hamilton England). David & Charles.

--A Student's Guide to Moliere. 1970. pap. text ed. 4.95x (ISBN 0-435-37570-9). Heinemann Ed.

Masters, Charles O. The Encyclopedia of Live Foods. (Illus.). 336p. 1975. 9.95 (ISBN 0-87666-093-6, PS-730). TFH Pubns.

--Encyclopedia of the Water-Lily. (Illus.). 512p. 1974. text ed. 14.95 (ISBN 0-87666-168-1, H-944). TFH Pubns.

--Pond Life. pap. 2.95 o.p. (ISBN 0-87666-135-5, PS651). TFH Pubns.

Masters, Donald C. The Winnipeg General Strike. LC 51-5058. (Illus.). xv, 159p. 1950. 11.50 o.p. (ISBN 0-8020-7018-3); pap. 4.00 o.p. (ISBN 0-8020-6217-2). U of Toronto Pr.

Masters, Edgar L. Mark Twain: A Portrait. LC 66-15216. 1938. 10.50x (ISBN 0-8196-0171-3). Biblo.

--New Spoon River Anthology. 1968. 10.95 (ISBN 0-02-581720-5). Macmillan.

--Spoon River Anthology with Additional Poems. 1963. 12.95 (ISBN 0-02-581740-X); pap. text ed. 7.95x 1916 ed. (ISBN 0-02-581730-2). Macmillan.

--Vachel Lindsay: A Poet in America. LC 68-56452. (Illus.). 1969. Repr. of 1935 ed. 17.00x (ISBN 0-8196-0239-6). Biblo.

--Whitman. LC 68-22695. 1968. Repr. of 1937 ed. 15.00x (ISBN 0-8196-0210-8). Biblo.

Masters, John. Heart of War. LC 80-12491. (Loss of Eden Ser.). 608p. 1980. write for info. McGraw.

Masters, John C., jt. auth. see Rimm, David C.

Masters, Joseph G. Shadows Fall Across the Little Horn: Custer's Last Stand. 62p. 1951. 20.00. South Pass Pr.

Masters, K. Spray Drying Handbook. 3rd ed. 1979. 87.95x (ISBN 0-470-26549-3). Halsted Pr.

Masters, Lowell F., jt. auth. see Mori, Allen A.

Masters, Margaret. Australian House & Garden Book of Chrysanthemums. pap. 6.50x (ISBN 0-392-06885-0, ABC). Soccer.

Masters, Melissa. Barbary Bride. 1980. pap. 2.50 o.s.i. (ISBN 0-440-14645-3). Dell.

Masters, Roy. How to Conquer Suffering Without Doctors. LC 76-489. 222p. 1976. pap. 6.50 (ISBN 0-933900-04-X). Foun Human Under.

--How to Control Your Emotions. Tappan, Melrose H., ed. & pref. by. LC 75-15708. 1975. pap. 6.50 (ISBN 0-933900-01-5). Foun Human Under.

--How Your Mind Can Keep You Well. 4th ed. Baker, Dorothy, ed. Orig. Title: Your Mind Can Keep You Well. 1976. pap. 6.50 (ISBN 0-933900-08-2). Foun Human Under.

--How Your Mind Can Keep You Well. 1977. pap. 1.75 o.p. (ISBN 0-449-23079-1, Crest). Fawcett.

--No One Has to Die. LC 76-20023. 1977. pap. 6.50 (ISBN 0-933900-03-1). Foun Human Under.

--The Satin Principle. LC 78-78158. 1978. pap. 6.50 (ISBN 0-933900-05-8). Foun Human Under.

--Secret of Life. LC 77-9148. 1972. pap. 6.50 (ISBN 0-933900-02-3). Foun Human Under.

--Sex, Sin & Salvation. LC 77-78040. 267p. 1977. pap. 6.50 (ISBN 0-933900-06-6). Foun Human Under.

Masters, William H., et al, eds. Ethical Issues in Sex Therapy & Research, Vol. 2. 456p. 1980. text ed. 22.50 (ISBN 0-316-54989-4). Little.

Masters, Zeke. Bottom Deal. (Orig.). 1981. pap. price not set (ISBN 0-671-42618-4). PB.

--Diamond Flush. 192p. 1980. pap. 1.75 (ISBN 0-671-83435-5). PB.

--Four of a Kind. (Orig.). 1981. pap. 1.75 (ISBN 0-671-42617-6). PB.

Masterson, Amanda R., ed. Index to the Proceedings of the Lunar & Planetary Science Conferences, Houston, Texas, 1970-1978. LC 79-20109. (Illus.). 325p. 1979. 33.00 (ISBN 0-08-024620-6). Pergamon.

Masterson, Graham. The Manitou. 1977. pap. 1.95 o.p. (ISBN 0-523-40233-3). Pinnacle Bks.

Masterson, James F. Treatment of the Borderline Adolescent: A Developmental Approach. LC 78-39721. (Personality Processes Ser). 1972. 28.95 (ISBN 0-471-57615-8, Pub. by Wiley-Interscience). Wiley.

Masterson, James F. & Costello, Jacinta L. From Borderline Adolescent to Functioning Adult: The Test of Time. LC 80-14270. 300p. 1980. 19.50 (ISBN 0-87630-234-7). Brunner-Mazel.

Masterson, James F., ed. New Perspective on Psychotherapy of the Borderline Adult. LC 77-94736. 1978. 12.50 (ISBN 0-87630-175-8). Brunner-Mazel.

Masterson, James F., jt. ed. see Offer, Daniel.

Masterson, Thomas R. & Nunan, J. Carlton. Ethics in Business. 240p. 1969. text ed. 18.50x (ISBN 0-8290-0288-X). Irvington.

Masterson, V. V. The Katy Railroad & the Last Frontier. (Illus.). 312p. 1981. 12.95 (ISBN 0-8061-0255-1). U of Okla Pr.

Masterton, Graham. The Djinn. 192p. 1977. pap. 1.75 o.p. (ISBN 0-685-75677-7, 40-523-0). Pinnacle Bks.

--The Sphinx. 1978. pap. 1.95 o.p. (ISBN 0-523-40189-2). Pinnacle Bks.

--The Sweetman Curve. 1979. pap. 2.50 (ISBN 0-441-79133-6). Ace Bks.

Masterton, James R. & Eberly, Joyce E., eds. Writings on American History Nineteen Sixty-One, 2 vols. (Writings on American History Ser.). (Orig.). 1978. Set. lib. bdg. 55.00 (ISBN 0-527-98252-0). Kraus Intl.

Masterton, R. B., et al, eds. Evolution, Brain & Behavior in Vertebrates, 2 vols. Incl. Vol. 1. Modern Concepts. 29.95 (ISBN 0-470-15045-9); Vol. 2. Persistent Problems. 14.95 (ISBN 0-470-15046-7). LC 76-6499. 1976. Halsted Pr.

Masthay, Carl. Mahican-Language Hymns, Biblical Prose, & Vocabularies from Moravian Sources: With 11 Mohawk Hymns (Transcription & Translation) LC 80-82410. 1980. write for info. Cresset Pubs.

Mastny, Vojtech. Czechs Under Nazi Rule: The Failure of National Resistance, 1939-42. LC 72-132065. (East Central European Studies of the Russian Institute). 1971. 17.50x (ISBN 0-231-03303-6). Columbia U Pr.

--Russia's Road to the Cold War. 1979. 20.00 (ISBN 0-231-04360-0). Columbia U Pr.

--Russia's Road to the Cold War: Diplomacy, Strategy, & the Politics of Communism, 1941-1945. 384p. 1980. pap. 8.50x (ISBN 0-231-04361-9). Columbia U Pr.

Maston, T. B. Christianity & World Issues. 1957. 5.95 o.s.i. (ISBN 0-02-581790-6). Macmillan.

--Consejos a la Juventud. Duffer, H. F., Jr., tr. Orig. Title: Advice to Youth. 60p. (Span.). 1980. pap. 1.00 (ISBN 0-311-46005-4). Casa Bautista.

--El Mundo En Crisis. Adams, Bob, tr. from Eng. 224p. (Span.). 1981. pap. write for info. (ISBN 0-311-46084-4). Casa Bautista.

Maston, T. B. & Pinson, William M., Jr. Right or Wrong. rev. 14th ed. LC 75-143282. (gr. 8 up). 1971. 5.50 (ISBN 0-8054-6101-9); pap. 2.50 (ISBN 0-686-66307-1). Broadman.

Mastronarde, Donald. Contact & Discontinuity: Some Conventions of Speech & Action on the Greek Tragic Stage. (University of California Publications in Classical Studies: Vol. 21). 1979. pap. 14.50x (ISBN 0-520-09601-0). U of Cal Pr.

Masubuchi. Analysis of Design & Fabrication of Welded Structures. 1980. 120.00 (ISBN 0-08-022714-7). Pergamon.

Masunaga, Shizuto & Ohashi, Wataru. Zen Shiatsu: How to Harmonize Yin and Yang for Better Health. (Illus.). 176p. 1977. pap. 9.95 (ISBN 0-87040-394-X). Japan Pubns.

Mat, Peter, jt. auth. see Schele, Linda.

Mata, Maria D., jt. auth. see Mills, Dorothy H.

Matar, Sami, jt. auth. see Hatch, Lewis F.

Matare, Herbert F. Conscientious Evolution. 1981. 9.75 (ISBN 0-8062-1700-6). Carlton.

Matcalf, William K. Embryology Review. (Basic Science Review Bks.). 1974. spiral binding 8.50 (ISBN 0-87488-207-9). Med Exam.

Matchan, Don C. We Mind If You Smoke. 1977. pap. 1.95 (ISBN 0-515-03680-3). Jove Pubns.

Matchett, William H. Fireweed & Other Poems. LC 80-52963. (Illus.). 64p. (Orig.). 1980. 15.00 (ISBN 0-930954-14-9); pap. 9.00 (ISBN 0-930954-15-7). Tidal Pr.

Mate, Bruce R., jt. auth. see Leatherwood, Stephen.

Mate, Ferenc. From a Bare Hull. 1975. 19.95 (ISBN 0-920256-00-7). Norton.

--From a Bare Hull. (Illus.). 1978. 19.95 o.p. (ISBN 0-920256-00-7, ScribT). Scribner.

--Waterhouses, the Romantic Alternative. (Illus.). 1978. 14.95 o.p. (ISBN 0-920256-01-5, ScribT). Scribner.

Mateene, Kahombo C., jt. ed. see Biebuyck, Daniel.

Mateosian, Richard. Programming the Z-Eight Thousand. LC 80-80042. (C Ser.). (Illus.). 1980. pap. 15.95 (ISBN 0-89588-032-6). Sybex.

Matera, Richard A. Rose Garden. LC 79-56881. 79p. 1981. 4.95 (ISBN 0-533-04551-7). Vantage.

Materer, Timothy. Vortex: Pound, Eliot, & Lewis. LC 79-13009. (Illus.). 1979. 14.50x (ISBN 0-8014-1225-0). Cornell U Pr.

Materials Advisory Board. Ceramic Processing. (Illus.). 1968. 16.00 (ISBN 0-309-01576-6). Natl Acad Pr.

Materne, Yves, ed. Indian Awakening in Latin America. (Orig.). 1980. pap. 5.95 (ISBN 0-377-00097-3). Friend Pr.

Mates, Benson. Skeptical Essays. LC 80-19553. 1981. lib. bdg. 17.00x (ISBN 0-226-50986-9). U of Chicago Pr.

Mates, Julian. The American Musical Stage Before 1800. 1962. 20.00 (ISBN 0-8135-0393-0). Rutgers U Pr.

Matesky, Ralph & Rush, Ralph E. Playing & Teaching Stringed Instruments, Pt. I. (Orig.). 1963. pap. text ed. 12.95 (ISBN 0-13-683789-1). P-H.

Math, Irwin. Wires & Watts: Understanding & Using Electricity. (Illus.). 96p. (gr. 7 up). 1981. 8.95 (ISBN 0-686-69287-X). Scribner.

Mathai, A. M. & Pederzoli, G. Characterizations of the Normal Probability Law. LC 77-13038. 1978. 11.95 (ISBN 0-470-99322-7). Halsted Pr.

Mathai, A. M. & Saxena, R. K. The H-Function with Applications in Statistics & Other Disciplines. 1978. 12.95 (ISBN 0-470-26380-6). Halsted Pr.

Mathan, Don C., jt. auth. see Kaye, Anna.

Mathe, G. & Rappaport, A. Histological & Cytological Typing of Neoplastic Diseases of Haematopoietic & Lymphoid Tissues. (World Health Organization: International Histological Classification of Tumours Ser.). 1976. 49.50 (ISBN 92-4-176014-1, 70-0-014-20); incl. slides 132.00 (ISBN 92-4-176014-1, 70-1-014-00). Am Soc Clinical.

Mathe, G. & Muggia, F. M., eds. Cancer Chemo- & Immunopharmacology, Part I: Chemopharmacology. (Recent Results in Cancer Research Ser.: Vol. 74). (Illus.). 315p. 1981. 66.00 (ISBN 0-387-10162-4). Springer-Verlag.

--Cancer Chemo- & Immunopharmacology, Part II: Immunopharmacology, Relations, & General Problems. (Recent Results in Cancer Research Ser.: Vol. 75). (Illus.). 260p. 1981. 52.00 (ISBN 0-387-10163-2). Springer-Verlag.

Matheney, Ruth V., et al. Fundamentals of Patient-Centered Nursing. 3rd ed. LC 72-185524. (Illus.). viii, 288p. 1972. pap. text ed. 10.50 o.p. (ISBN 0-8016-3153-X). Mosby.

Mather, Anne. Edge of Temptation. (Harlequin Presents Ser.). 192p. (Orig.). 1981. pap. 1.50 (ISBN 0-373-10405-7, Pub. by Harlequin). PB.

--A Haunting Compulsion. (Harlequin Presents Ser.). 192p. 1981. pap. 1.50 (ISBN 0-373-10429-4, Pub. by Harlequin). PB.

--Images of Love. (Harlequin Presents Ser.). 192p. 1980. pap. 1.50 (ISBN 0-373-10402-2, Pub. by Harlequin). PB.

--Sandstorm. (Harlequin Presents Ser.). 192p. 1980. pap. 1.50 (ISBN 0-373-10382-4, Pub. by Harlequin). PB.

--The Smouldering Flame. (Alpha Books). 80p. (Orig.). 1979. pap. text ed. 2.25x (ISBN 0-19-424164-5). Oxford U Pr.

--Whisper of Darkness. (Harlequin Presents Ser.). 192p. 1980. pap. 1.50 (ISBN 0-373-10376-X, Pub. by Harlequin). PB.

Mather, Arthur. The Mindbreaker. 1980. 10.95 (ISBN 0-440-05294-7). Delacorte.

Mather, Cotten. Decennium Luctuosum. an History of...the Long War, Which New England Hath Had with the Indian Savages. LC 75-7022. (Indian Captivities Ser.: Vol. 3). 1976. Repr. of 1698 ed. lib. bdg. 44.00 (ISBN 0-8240-1627-0). Garland Pub.

Mather, Cotten see Dickinson, Jonathan.

Mather, Cotton. The Angel of Bethesda. Jones, Gordon W., ed. LC 72-185323. 384p. 1972. 19.95x (ISBN 0-8271-7220-6, Dist. by U Pr of Va). Am Antiquarian.

--Christian Philosopher: A Collection of the Best Discoveries in Nature, with Religious Improvements. LC 68-29082. 1968. Repr. of 1721 ed. 33.00x (ISBN 0-8201-1033-7). Schol Facsimiles.

--Day of Humiliation: Times of Affliction & Disaster. LC 68-24211. 1970. 41.00x (ISBN 0-8201-1067-1). Schol Facsimiles.

--Great Works of Christ in America, 2 vols. 1979. Set. 37.95; Vol. 1. (ISBN 0-85151-280-1); Vol. 2. (ISBN 0-85151-280-1). Banner of Truth.

Mather, F. C., ed. Chartism & Society. LC 80-15587. 488p. 1980. text ed. 45.00x (ISBN 0-8419-0625-4). Holmes & Meier.

Mather, Frank J., Jr., et al see Gabriel, Ralph H.

Mather, Frank L., ed. Who's Who of the Colored Race. LC 79-178669. 1976. Repr. of 1915 ed. 42.00 (ISBN 0-8103-4247-2). Gale.

Mather, Helen. Light Horsekeeping. 1970. 7.95 o.p. (ISBN 0-525-14620-2). Dutton.

Mather, Increase. An Essay for the Recording of Illustrious Providences. LC 77-17526. 1977. Repr. of 1684 ed. lib. bdg. 40.00 (ISBN 0-8201-1299-2). Schol Facsimiles.

Mather, John R. The Climate Water Budget in Environmental Analysis. LC 77-17726. (Illus.). 1978. 23.95 (ISBN 0-669-02087-7). Lexington Bks.

Mather, K. & Jinks, J. L. Introduction to Biomedical Genetics. LC 77-76809. 1978. 19.50x (ISBN 0-8014-1123-8). Cornell U Pr.

Mather, Maurice W. & Hewitt, Joseph. Xenophon's Anabasis, Bks. 1-4. (Illus.). (YA) 1976. pap. 9.95x (ISBN 0-8061-1347-2). U of Okla Pr.

Mather, Paul M. Computers in Geography: A Practical Approach. (Illus.). 1976. 21.95x (ISBN 0-631-16870-2, Pub. by Basil Blackwell). Biblio Dist.

Mather, Roger. The Art of Playing the Flute: Breath Control. LC 80-52140. (A Series of Workbooks: Vol. 1). (Illus.). 88p. (Orig.). 1980. pap. 6.95 (ISBN 0-9604640-0-X). Romney Pr.

Mathers, Ann. Astrology Love Book. 1969. pap. 1.50 (ISBN 0-451-08908-1, W8908, Sig). NAL.

Mathers, Michael. Portraits: Friends & Strangers. LC 79-336. (Illus.). 1979. 14.95 (ISBN 0-914842-36-6); pap. 9.95 (ISBN 0-914842-35-8). Madrona Pubs.

--Sheepherders. (Illus.). 1975. 4.95 (ISBN 0-395-20723-1, Pub. by Montana Bks). Madrona Pubs.

Mathers, Powys, tr. from Fr. The Book of a Thousand Nights & One Night, 4 vols. LC 77-188396. 1972. 60.00 o.p. (ISBN 0-312-09030-7, B50020). Vol. 1 (ISBN 0-312-09065-X). Vol. 2 (ISBN 0-312-09100-1). Vol. 3 (ISBN 0-312-09135-4). Vol. 4 (ISBN 0-312-09170-2). St Martin.

Mathes, J. C. & Stevenson, Dwight W. Designing Technical Reports: Writing for Audiences in Organizations. LC 75-44249. 1976. text ed. 19.95 (ISBN 0-672-61367-0); tchr's manual 2.50 (ISBN 0-672-61405-7). Bobbs.

Mathes, Stephen J. & Nahai, Foad. Clinical Atlas of Muscle & Musculocutaneous Flaps. LC 79-10739. (Illus.). 1979. text ed. 44.50 (ISBN 0-8016-3141-6). Mosby.

Matheson, D. M., tr. see Schuon, Frithjot.

Matheson, Peter. A Just Peace. (Orig.). 1981. pap. 5.95 (ISBN 0-377-00107-4). Friend Pr.

--The Third Reich & the Christian Churches. LC 80-26767. 112p. (Orig.). 1981. pap. 5.95 (ISBN 0-8028-1873-0). Eerdmans.

Matheson, R. People Development in Developing Countries. LC 77-28208. 1978. 29.95x (ISBN 0-470-99382-0). Halsted Pr.

Matheson, Richard. Shock I. 1979. pap. 1.75 o.p. (ISBN 0-425-04095-X). Berkley Pub.

--Shock Two. 1979. pap. 1.95 o.p. (ISBN 0-425-04158-1). Berkley Pub.

--Shock Waves. 1979. pap. 1.95 o.p. (ISBN 0-425-04218-9). Berkley Pub.

--A Stir of Echoes. 1979. pap. 1.95 o.p. (ISBN 0-425-04107-7). Berkley Pub.

Matheson, Sylvia A. Persia: An Archaeological Guide. new ed. (Illus.). 1976. pap. 13.95 (ISBN 0-571-04888-9, Pub. by Faber & Faber). Merrimack Bk Serv.

Mathew, Brian. Dwarf Bulbs. 1973. 30.00 (ISBN 0-7134-0403-5, Pub. by Batsford England). David & Charles.

--The Larger Bulbs. 1978. 30.00 (ISBN 0-7134-1246-1, Pub. by Batsford England). David & Charles.

Mathew, John, tr. see Janvier, Ludovic.

Mathews, Aidan C. Windfalls. 48p. 1978. pap. text ed. 5.00x (ISBN 0-85105-325-4, Dolmen Pr). Humanities.

Mathews, Anthony S. The Darker Reaches of Government: Access to Information About Public Administration in the United States, Britain & South Africa. LC 78-64475. (Perspectives on Southern Africa Ser.: No. 27). 1979. 27.50x (ISBN 0-520-03803-7). U of Cal Pr.

Mathews, Christopher K. Bacteriophage Biochemistry. LC 70-143542. (ACS Monograph: No. 166). 1971. 31.75 (ISBN 0-8412-0288-5). Am Chemical.

Mathews, Dorothy, jt. auth. see Schaffter, Dorothy.

Mathews, F. Neil & Smith, Linda H. Entomology: Investigative Activities for Could-Be Bug Buffs. 1978. pap. 3.95 (ISBN 0-936386-03-7). Creative Learning.

Mathews, G. Vinyl & Allied Polymers, Vol. 2. 1972. text ed. 39.95 (ISBN 0-592-05443-8). Butterworths.

Mathews, George B. Theory of Numbers. 2nd ed. LC 61-17958. 9.95 (ISBN 0-8284-0156-X). Chelsea Pub.

Mathews, Harry. Country Cooking & Other Stories. (Burning Deck Fiction Ser.). (Illus.). 90p. 1980. 12.50 (ISBN 0-930900-81-2); pap. 3.50 (ISBN 0-930900-82-0). Burning Deck.

--The Sinking of the Odradek Stadium & Other Novels. LC 74-15881. 1975. pap. 5.95 o.p. (ISBN 0-06-012841-0, TD-220, HarpT). Harrow.

Mathews, J. J. Life & Death of an Oilman. 1974. pap. 5.95 (ISBN 0-8061-1238-7). U of Okla Pr.

Mathews, Jackson, ed. see Baudelaire, Charles.

Mathews, John J. Osages: Children of the Middle Waters. (Civilization of the American Indian Ser.: No. 60). (Illus.). 1981. Repr. of 1961 ed. 24.95 (ISBN 0-8061-0498-8). U of Okla Pr.

--Talking to the Moon. LC 80-50704. (Illus.). 244p. 1980. text ed. 12.95 (ISBN 0-8061-1611-0). U of Okla Pr.

Mathews, John M. Legislative & Judicial History of the Fifteenth Amendment. LC 77-129081. (American Constitutional & Legal History Ser). 1971. Repr. of 1909 ed. lib. bdg. 17.50 (ISBN 0-306-70063-8). Da Capo.

Mathews, Jon & Walker, Robert L. Mathematical Methods of Physics. 2nd ed. 1970. text ed. 24.95 (ISBN 0-8053-7002-1). Benjamin-Cummings.

Mathews, Louise. Bunches & Bunches of Bunnies. LC 78-7625. (Illus.). (gr. k-3). 1978. 6.95 (ISBN 0-396-07601-7). Dodd.

--Bunches & Bunches of Bunnies. (Illus.). 32p. 1980. Repr. pap. 1.95 (ISBN 0-590-31536-6, Schol Pap). Schol Bk Serv.

--The Great Take-Away. LC 80-12961. (Illus.). 48p. (ps-3). 1980. PLB 7.95 (ISBN 0-396-07846-X). Dodd.

Mathews, Marthiel, ed. see Baudelaire, Charles.

Mathews, Shailer & Smith, Gerald B., eds. Dictionary of Religion & Ethics. LC 70-145713. 1971. Repr. of 1921 ed. 22.00 o.p. (ISBN 0-8103-3196-9). Gale.

Mathews, Zena P. The Relation of Seneca False Face Masks to Seneca & Ontario Archeology. LC 77-94707. (Outstanding Dissertations in the Fine Arts Ser.). 1978. lib. bdg. 36.00x (ISBN 0-8240-3239-X). Garland Pub.

Mathewson, Christopher C. Engineering Geology. (Illus.). 416p. 1981. text ed. 24.95 (ISBN 0-675-08032-0). Merrill.

Mathewson, Hugh S. Pharmacology for Respiratory Therapists. 2nd ed. (Illus.). 105p. 1981. pap. text ed. 10.95 (ISBN 0-8016-3161-0). Mosby.

--Respiratory Therapy in Critical Care. LC 76-13633. (Illus., Orig.). 1976. pap. 10.00 (ISBN 0-8016-3158-0). Mosby.

Mathewson, Joseph. Alicia's Trump. 224p. (Orig.). 1980. pap. 2.25 (ISBN 0-380-76521-7, 76521). Avon.

Mathewson, Kent & Neenan, William B., eds. Financing the Metropolis. 352p. 1980. 29.95 (ISBN 0-03-056886-2). Praeger.

Mathewson, Stephen W. The Manual for the Home & Farm Production of Alcohol Fuel. 1980. 12.95 (ISBN 0-89815-030-2); pap. 7.95 (ISBN 0-89815-029-9). Ten Speed Pr.

Mathey, Francois, jt. auth. see Belves, Pierre.

Mathias, Frank F. Albert D. Kirwan: A Man for All Seasons. LC 74-18936. (Illus.). 208p. 1975. 13.00x (ISBN 0-8131-1325-3). U Pr of Ky.

Mathias, Frank F., ed. see Parsons, Thomas W.

Mathias, Jim & Kennedy, Thomas L. Computers, Language Reform, & Lexicography in China. 1980. pap. 5.00 (ISBN 0-87422-015-7). Bellman.

Mathias, Michael & Hector, Derek. Glastonbury: Mecca of the Westcountry. LC 78-51083. (Illus.). 1979. 10.50 (ISBN 0-7153-7798-1). David & Charles.

Mathias, Mildred E. & Constance, Lincoln. A Revision of the Genus Bowlesia Ruiz & Pav (Umbelliferae-Hydrocotyloideae) & Its Relatives. (U. C. Publ. in Botany: Vol. 38). 1965. pap. 6.00x (ISBN 0-520-09010-1). U of Cal Pr.

Mathias, Peter. Brewing Industry in England, Seventeen Hundred to Eighteen Thirty. 1959. 71.95 (ISBN 0-521-05691-8). Cambridge U Pr.

--Living with the Neighbours: The Role of Economic History. (Inaugural Lectures Ser). 24p. 1971. pap. 1.00x o.p. (ISBN 0-19-951286-8). Oxford U Pr.

Mathias, Peter, ed. Science & Society, 1600-1900. (Illus.). 176p. 1972. 23.95 (ISBN 0-521-08375-3). Cambridge U Pr.

Mathies, Lorraine & Thomas, W. Overseas Opportunities for American Educators & Students. 2nd ed. 1973. 11.95 o.s.i. (ISBN 0-02-469370-7). Macmillan Info.

Mathiesen, Thomas. The Politics of Abolition: Scandanavian Studies in Criminology. LC 74-1601. 1974. 18.95x (ISBN 0-470-57627-8). Halsted Pr.

Mathieson, John A. The Advanced Developing Countries: Emerging Actors in the World Economy. LC 79-91996. (Development Papers: No. 28). 72p. 1979. pap. 3.00 (ISBN 0-686-28672-3). Overseas Dev Council.

Mathieson, Margaret. The Preachers of Culture: A Study of English & Its Teachers. (Unwin Education Bks.). 1975. text ed. 25.00x (ISBN 0-04-370067-5); pap. text ed. 10.95x (ISBN 0-04-370068-3). Allen Unwin.

Mathieson, Moira. Shepherds of the Delectable Mountains: The Story of the Washington County Mission. 1979. 2.00 (ISBN 0-686-28792-4). Forward Movement.

Mathieson, Moria B. The Complete Guide to Careers in the Catholic Church for Religious & Laity. 200p. (Orig.). 1980. pap. text ed. 15.00 (ISBN 0-8434-0759-X, Consortium). McGrath.

Mathieson, R. S. The Soviet Union: An Economic Geography. (Illus.). 342p. 1975. 20.00x (ISBN 0-06-494647-9). B&N.

Mathieson, Raymond S. Japan's Role in Soviet Economic Growth: Transfer of Technology Since 1965. LC 78-19790. 1979. 21.95 (ISBN 0-03-046481-1). Praeger.

Mathieu, Aron. The Book Market: How to Write, Publish & Market Your Book. LC 80-71059. 512p. 1981. 14.95 (ISBN 0-939014-00-9). Andover Pr.

Mathieu, G., ed. Advances in the Teaching of Modern Languages, Vol. 2. 1966. 23.00 (ISBN 0-08-011840-2). Pergamon.

Mathieu, Gustave B., jt. auth. see Haas, Werner.

Mathieu, Jean P., jt. auth. see Rousseau, M.

Mathieu, Joe. The Olden Days. (Pictureback Ser.). (Illus.). 32p. (ps-3). 1981. PLB 4.99 (ISBN 0-394-94085-7); pap. 1.25 (ISBN 0-394-84085-2). Random.

Mathiot, G. Nouveau Larousse gastronomique. (Illus., Fr.). 79.75x (ISBN 0-685-14004-0, 3905). Larousse.

Mathis, F. John, ed. Offshore Lending by U. S. Commercial Banks. 2nd ed. LC 80-83082. (Illus.). 344p. 1980. 18.00 (ISBN 0-936742-01-1). R Morris Assocs.

Mathis, Harry R. Along the Border: A History of Virgilina, Virginia & the Surrounding Area in Halifax & Mecklenburg Counties in Virginia & Person & Granville Counties in North Carolina. LC 64-7237. (Illus.). 344p. 1964. 9.00x (ISBN 0-685-65080-4). Va Bk.

Mathis, James L. Clear Thinking About Sexual Deviations: A New Look at an Old Problem. LC 72-80165. 1972. 11.95 (ISBN 0-911012-40-0). Nelson-Hall.

Mathis, James L., et al. Basic Psychiatry: A Primer of Concepts & Terminology. 2nd ed. 1972. pap. 10.75 o.p. (ISBN 0-8385-0623-2). ACC.

Mathis, Robert L. & Jackson, John H. Personnel: Contemporary Perspectives & Applications. 2nd ed. (Illus.). 1979. text ed. 17.95 (ISBN 0-8299-0199-X); readings & exercises by Sally Coltrin 6.95 (ISBN 0-686-67441-3); instrs.' manual avail. (ISBN 0-8299-0555-3); study guide 6.95 (ISBN 0-8299-0282-1). West Pub.

Mathis, Sharon B. Ray Charles. LC 72-7552. (Biography Ser.). (Illus.). (gr. 1-5). 1973. 7.95 (ISBN 0-690-67065-6, TYC-J); PLB 6.89 o.p. (ISBN 0-690-67066-4). T Y Crowell.

Mathisen, Bonnie W., jt. auth. see Mante, Daisy R.

Mathur, D. C. Naturalistic Philosophies of Experience. LC 79-117613. 192p. 1971. 12.00 (ISBN 0-87527-052-2). Fireside Bks.

Mathur, D. S. Mechanics. 1978. 20.00 (ISBN 0-7069-0623-3, Pub. by Vikas India). Advent Bk.

Mathur, Iqbal, jt. auth. see Jain, Subhash C.

Mathur, M. V. & Narain, I., eds. Panchayati Raj Planning & Democracy. 17.50x (ISBN 0-210-22548-3). Asia.

Mathur, Rita S., ed. Shifting Skies. 192p. 1980. text ed. 17.95 (ISBN 0-7069-1271-3, Pub by Vikas India). Advent Bk.

Mathur, S. M. New Textbook of Higher Plane Geometry. pap. 3.00x o.p. (ISBN 0-210-22652-8). Asia.

Matick, Richard E. Computer Storage Systems & Technology. LC 77-5812. 1977. 39.95 (ISBN 0-471-57629-8, Pub. by Wiley-Interscience). Wiley.

Matiegka, Jindrich. Homo Predmostensis, fosilni Clovek z Predmosti na Morave, 2 vols. LC 78-72704. Repr. of 1938 ed. Set. 72.50 (ISBN 0-404-18273-9). Vol. 1 (ISBN 0-404-18274-7). Vol. 3 (ISBN 0-404-18275-5). AMS Pr.

Matilda, E. & Neill, June E. Social Work in General Practice. (National Institute Social Services Library). 1972. text ed. 18.95x (ISBN 0-04-360025-5); pap. text ed. 8.95x o.p. (ISBN 0-04-360026-3). Allen Unwin.

Matile, G. A., tr. see List, Friedrich.

Matin, Philip. Handbook of Clinical Nuclear Medicine. 1977. cancelled (ISBN 0-87488-610-4). Med Exam.

Matisoff, James A. The Grammar of Lahu. (U. C. Publ. in Linguistics: Vol. 75). 1973. pap. 17.75x (ISBN 0-520-09467-0). U of Cal Pr.

Matisoff, Susan. The Legend of Semimaru: Blind Musician of Japan. LC 77-24601. (Studies in Oriental Cultures Ser.: No. 14). 1978. 17.50x (ISBN 0-231-03947-6). Columbia U Pr.

Matisse, Herni. Matisse Line Drawings & Prints. (Illus.). 1980. pap. 2.00 (ISBN 0-486-23877-6). Dover.

Matlack. Statistics for Public Policy & Management. LC 79-11886. 1980. text ed. 19.95 (ISBN 0-87872-226-2). Duxbury Pr.

Matlack, Helena, ed. Brand Name & Trademark Guide: 1896, 1904, 1915, 1922, 1943, 1950, 1965, 1969. 10th ed. (Illus.). 300p. 1978. 19.95 (ISBN 0-931744-03-2). Jewelers Circular.
Matlak, Raymond, jt. auth. see Burleigh, Robert.
Matlaw, Ralph E., ed. Belinsky, Chernyshevsky, & Dobrolyubov: Selected Criticism. LC 75-34729. (Midland Books: No. 200). 256p. 1976. 9.50x (ISBN 0-253-31155-1); pap. 2.95x (ISBN 0-253-20200-0). Ind U Pr.
Matlaw, Ralph E., ed. see Chekhov, Anton.
Matlaw, Ralph E., ed. see Turgenev, Ivan.
Matles, James J. & Higgins, James. Them & Us: Struggles of a Rank-&-File Union. LC 73-19656. 324p. 1974. 6.95 o.p. (ISBN 0-13-913079-9). P-H.
Matley, Ian M. The Geography of International Tourism. Natoli, Salvatore J., ed. LC 76-18390. (Resource Papers for College Geography Ser.). (Illus.). 1976. pap. text ed. 4.00 (ISBN 0-89291-110-7). Assn Am Geographers.
Matley, Jay & Chemical Engineering Magazine. Practical Process Instrumentation & Control. (Chemical Engineering Ser.). 512p. 1980. 29.50 (ISBN 0-07-010712-2). McGraw.
Matlin, Samuel, jt. auth. see Neimark, Paul.
Matlis, Eben. Cotorsion Modules. LC 52-42839. (Memoirs: No. 49). 1979. pap. 8.40 (ISBN 0-8218-1249-1, MEMO-49). Am Math.
Matlock, Bill, jt. auth. see Schell, Frank R.
Matlock, Bill J., jt. auth. see Schell, Frank R.
Matloff, Maurice, ed. The Civil War: A Concise History of the War Between the States. 1978. 6.95 o.p. (ISBN 0-679-50840-6). McKay.
Matney, William C., ed. Who's Who Among Black Americans, 1980-1981. 3rd ed. LC 76-643293. 1981. 49.95 (ISBN 0-915130-33-5). Who's Who Black Am.
Matore, G. Histoire des dictionnaires francais. (Langue Vivante Ser). (Fr). pap. 11.95 (ISBN 0-685-13937-9, 3625). Larousse.
Matos, Antonio. Guide to Reviews of Books from & About Hispanic America, 1978: Guia a las Resenas De Libros De y Sobre Hispanoamerica, 1978. LC 66-96537. 1980. 80.00 (ISBN 0-87917-073-5). Blaine Ethridge.
Matos, Luis Pales see Pales Matos, Luis.
Matossian, Mary A. The Impact of Soviet Policies in Armenia, Nineteen Twenty to Nineteen Thirty-Six: A Study of Planned Cultural Transformation. LC 79-2910. 239p. 1981. Repr. of 1962 ed. 21.50 (ISBN 0-8305-0080-4). Hyperion Conn.
Matousek, Clifford H., jt. auth. see Gray, Al.
Matrai, M., jt. auth. see Tarjan, I.
Matras, Judah. Introduction to Population Studies: A Sociological Approach. (Illus.). 1977. text ed. 18.95 (ISBN 0-13-493122-X). P-H.
--Social Inequality, Stratification, & Mobility. LC 74-18070. (Illus.). 448p. 1975. text ed. 18.95 (ISBN 0-13-815803-7). P-H.
Matrazzo, Donna. The Corporate Scriptwriting Book. LC 80-81823. (Illus.). 199p. (Orig.). 1980. pap. 14.95 (ISBN 0-935608-01-X). Media Concepts.
Matre, Joseph G. Van see Van Matre, Joseph G. & Gilbreath, Glenn H.
Matricardi, Paolo, jt. auth. see Angelucci, Enzo.
Matsagouras, E. The Early Church Fathers As Educators. 1977. pap. 3.95 (ISBN 0-937032-10-7). Light & Life Pub Co MN.
Matsch, Lee A., jt. auth. see Gross, William.
Matson, Carl E. Thirty Instruction Units in Basic Electricity. slow learner ed. (gr. 9-12). 1961. pap. 4.60 o.p. (ISBN 0-87345-254-2). McKnight.
Matson, Donald D. Neurosurgery of Infancy & Childhood. 2nd ed. (Illus.). 952p. 1969. pap. 49.00 spiral (ISBN 0-398-01236-9). C C Thomas.
Matson, Floyd W. The Broken Image. 1964. 6.95 o.s.i. (ISBN 0-8076-0256-6). Braziller.
--The Idea of Man. 1976. 8.95 (ISBN 0-440-04038-8). Delacorte.
Matson, John A. Dear Osborne. (Illus.). 1978. 17.95 (ISBN 0-241-89870-6, Pub. by Hamish Hamilton England). David & Charles.
Matson, T. M., et al. Traffic Engineering. 1955. text ed. 25.50 o.p. (ISBN 0-07-040910-2, C). McGraw.
Matson, Wallace I. Sentience. LC 75-3774. 160p. 1976. 13.75x (ISBN 0-520-02987-9). U of Cal Pr.
Matson, Wallace I., jt. auth. see Warren, Thomas B.
Matsubara, Saburo, jt. auth. see Akiyama, Terukazu.
Matsuda, R. Morphology & Evolution of the Insect Abdomen. Kerkut, ed. 568p. 1976. text ed. 90.00 (ISBN 0-08-018753-6). Pergamon.
Matsui, Masato, jt. ed. see Song, Minako I.
Matsui, Takayoshi & Hirano, Asao. An Atlas of the Human Brain for Computerized Tomography. LC 77-95453. (Illus.). 1978. 66.00 (ISBN 0-89640-027-1). Igaku-Shoin.
Matsumoto, Seicho. Points & Lines. LC 72-117385. 159p. 1970. 8.95x (ISBN 0-87011-126-4). Kodansha.
Matsumoto, Teruo. Acupuncture for Physicians. (Illus.). 224p. 1974. 19.75 (ISBN 0-398-02958-X). C C Thomas.
--Tissue Adhesives in Surgery. 1972. 30.00 o.p. (ISBN 0-87488-756-9). Med Exam.
Matsumoto, Teuro. Pre- & Postoperative Evaluation of Surgical Patients. 1979. pap. 15.50 (ISBN 0-87488-735-6). Med Exam.
Matsunaga, Alicia & Matsunaga, Daigan. Foundation of Japanese Buddhism: The Aristocratic Age, Vol. I. LC 74-83654. 1974. 13.75x (ISBN 0-914910-25-6); pap. 7.75x (ISBN 0-914910-26-4). Buddhist Bks.
Matsunaga, Alicia, jt. auth. see Matsunaga, Daigan L.
Matsunaga, Daigan, jt. auth. see Matsunaga, Alicia.
Matsunaga, Daigan L. & Matsunaga, Alicia. Buddhist Concept of Hell. LC 73-145466. (Illus.). 1971. 4.95 o.p. (ISBN 0-8022-2048-7). Philos Lib.
Matsunami, Kodo. Introducing Buddhism. LC 75-28970. (Illus.). 304p. 1976. pap. 7.50 (ISBN 0-8048-1192-X). C E Tuttle.
Matsunami, Niichiro. Japanese Constitution & Politics. (Studies in Japanese Law & Government). 577p. 1979. 38.75 (ISBN 0-89093-217-4). U Pubns Amer.
Matsuo, Shimegi. Screw-Retained Dental Prostheses. 140p. 1981. 42.00 (ISBN 0-931386-35-7). Quint Pub Co.
Matsushima, Seizo. Rice Cultivation for the Million. 350p. 1980. 35.00x (ISBN 0-89955-203-X, Pub. by JSSP Japan). Intl Schol Bk Serv.
Matsushita, Konosuke. Japan at the Brink. Terry, Charles, tr. from Japanese. LC 75-30180. 136p. 1975. 8.95 (ISBN 0-87011-270-8). Kodansha.
Matsushita, S. & Campbell, W. H., eds. Physics of Geomagnetic Phenomena, 2 Vols. (International Geophysics Ser.: Vol. 11). 1967. Vol. 1. 59.00 (ISBN 0-12-480301-6); Vol. 2, 1968. 68.50 (ISBN 0-12-480302-4). Acad Pr.
Matsutani, Miyoko. Witch's Magic Cloth. Tresselt, Alvin, tr. LC 79-77787. Orig. Title: Yamanbano Nishiki. (gr. k-3). 1969. 5.95 o.s.i. (ISBN 0-8193-0319-4, Four Winds); PLB 5.41 o.s.i. (ISBN 0-8193-0320-8). Schol Bk Serv.
Matsuyama, Takashi, jt. ed. see Nagao, Makoto.
Matt, Paul, jt. auth. see Rust, Kenn C.
Matt, Paul, et al. Historical Aviation Album, Vol. XVI. Rust, Kenn & Foxworth, Thomas, eds. (All American Ser.). (Illus.). 96p. (Orig.). 1980. pap. 10.00 (ISBN 0-911852-15-8). Hist Aviation.
Matt, Stephen R. Electricity & Basic Electronics. LC 79-6346. (Illus.). 1980. text ed. 11.96 (ISBN 0-87006-285-9). Goodheart.
Mattavi, James N. & Amann, Charles A., eds. Combustion Modeling in Reciprocating Engines. (General Motors Research Laboratories Ser.). 616p. 69.50 (ISBN 0-306-40431-1, Plenum Pr). Plenum Pub.
Matte, Jackie. Madam Says Keep the Lorry off the Grass. 138p. 1980. 7.95 (ISBN 0-533-04740-4). Vantage.
Matte, James A. The Art & Science of the Polygraph Technique. (Illus.). 296p. 1980. 29.50 (ISBN 0-398-04044-3). C C Thomas.
Matte, Robert, Jr. Asylum Picnic. Robertson, Kirk, ed. LC 77-73205. 1980. pap. 3.00 (ISBN 0-916918-07-6). Duck Down.
Mattel, E. & Mayan, B. Meaning in Children's Art. 1981. 15.95 (ISBN 0-13-567115-9); pap. 12.95 (ISBN 0-13-567107-8). P-H.
Mattelart, Armand. Mass Media, Ideologies & the Revolutionary Movement. (Marxist Theory & Contemporary Capitalism Ser.: No. 30). 288p. 1980. text ed. 32.50x (ISBN 0-391-01777-2). Humanities.
--Multinational Corporations & the Control of Culture: The Ideological Apparatuses of Imperialism. Chanan, Michael, tr. LC 79-221. (Marxist Theory & Contemporary Capitalism: No. 26). 1979. text ed. 29.50x (ISBN 0-391-00978-8). Humanities.
Mattelart, Armand, jt. auth. see Dorfman, Ariel.
Mattelart, Armand & Siegelaub, Seth, eds. Communications & Class Struggle: Capitalism, Imperialism, Vol. 1. 448p. 1979. pap. 16.95 (ISBN 0-88477-011-7). Intl General.
Matteo, Gino J. Shakespeare's Othello: The Study & the Stage, 1604-1904. (Salzburg Studies in English Literature, Poetic Drama & Poetic Theory: No. 11). 286p. 1974. pap. text ed. 25.00x (ISBN 0-391-01476-5). Humanities.
Matteotti, Giacomo. The Fascisti Exposed: A Year of Fascist Domination. LC 68-9637. 1969. Repr. of 1924 ed. 10.50 (ISBN 0-86527-064-3). Fertig.
Matter, Albert & Tucker, Maurice E., eds. Modern & Ancient Lake Sediments. (International Association of Sedimentologists & the Societas Internationalis Limnologiae Symposium Proceding Ser.). 1979. 34.95 (ISBN 0-470-26571-X). Halsted Pr.
Matter, Joseph A. Love, Altruism, & World Crisis: The Challenge of Pitirim Sorokin. LC 73-84209. 1974. 17.95 (ISBN 0-88229-114-9). Nelson-Hall.
Mattern, Carolyn J. Soldiers When They Go: The Story of Camp Randall, 1861-1865. LC 80-26238. (Illus.). 156p. 1981. 4.95x (ISBN 0-87020-206-5). State Hist Soc Wis.
Matterson, Alan. Polytechnics & Colleges. (Illus.). 320p. 1981. text ed. 34.00 (ISBN 0-582-49095-2). Longman.
Mattes, Merrill J. Missouri Valley. 1971. pap. 2.95 (ISBN 0-8077-1718-5). Tchrs Coll.
Matteson, David M. Organization of the Government Under the Constitution. LC 72-118201. (American Constitutional & Legal History Ser). 1970. Repr. of 1943 ed. lib. bdg. 37.50 (ISBN 0-306-71935-5). Da Capo.
Matteson, David R. Adolescence Today: Sex Roles & the Search for Identity. 1975. pap. text ed. 10.95x (ISBN 0-256-01731-X). Dorsey.
Matteson, Esther. The Piro (Arawakan) Language. (U. C. Publ. in Linguistics: Vol. 42). 1965. pap. 11.00x (ISBN 0-520-09237-6). U of Cal Pr.
Matteson, George. Draggermen: Fishing on Georges Bank. LC 78-21767. (Illus.). 144p. (gr. 5 up). 1979. 8.95 (ISBN 0-590-07534-9, Four Winds). Schol Bk Serv.
Matteson, Marilee, ed. Small Feasts: Soups, Salads, & Sandwiches. (Clarkson N. Potter Bks.). 1980. 17.95 (ISBN 0-517-54052-5). Crown.
Matteson, Michael & Ivancevich, John. Management Classics. 2nd ed. 1981. pap. text ed. write for info. (ISBN 0-8302-5469-2). Goodyear.
Matteson, Michael T., jt. auth. see Ivancevich, John M.
Matteson, Stephen R., et al. Dental Radiology. 3rd ed. (Dental Assisting Manuals: No. 5). 130p. 1980. 8.00 (ISBN 0-8078-1379-6). U of NC Pr.
Mattessich, Richard. Accounting & Analytical Methods. LC 64-22113. 1978. Repr. of 1964 ed. text ed. 20.00 (ISBN 0-914348-21-3). Scholars Bk.
--Instrumental Reasoning & Systems Methodology. (Theory & Decision Library: No. 15). xvii, 396p. 1980. lib. bdg. 44.75 (ISBN 90-277-0837-1); pap. 19.95 (ISBN 90-277-1081-3). Kluwer Boston.
Matthew, D. J., tr. see Rorig, Fritz.
Matthew, Eunice S. The Land & People of Thailand. LC 64-13808. (Portraits of the Nations Ser.). (Illus.). (gr. 7-9). 1964. 8.95 (ISBN 0-397-30766-7). Lippincott.
Matthew, Gary K., jt. auth. see Tesar, Delbert.
Matthew, H. C. The Liberal Imperialists: The Ideas & Politics of a Post-Gladstonian Elite. (Oxford Historical Monographs). 1973. 36.00x (ISBN 0-19-821842-7). Oxford U Pr.
Matthew, H. C., ed. see Gladstone, William E.
Matthew, Helen G., ed. Asia in the Modern World. (Illus.). 1963. pap. 1.25 o.p. (ISBN 0-451-61215-9, MY1215, Ment). NAL.
Matthew, James E. Literature of Music. LC 69-12688. (Music Ser). 1969. Repr. of 1896 ed. lib. bdg. 27.50 (ISBN 0-306-71227-X). Da Capo.
Matthew, Scott. The First Woman of Medicine: The Story of Elizabeth Blackwell. LC 78-16305. (Famous Firsts Ser.). (Illus.). 1978. lib. bdg. 7.35 (ISBN 0-686-51111-5). Silver.
Matthews, jt. auth. see Evans.
Matthews, A. Warren. Abraham Was Their Father. LC 81-146. vii, 266p. 1981. 19.50 (ISBN 0-86554-005-5). Mercer Univ Pr.
Matthews, Allen R. The Assault. LC 80-14926. (Great Classic Stories of World War II Ser.). 1980. 8.95 (ISBN 0-396-07874-5); pap. 5.95 (ISBN 0-396-07875-3). Dodd.
Matthews, Archibald M. Reminiscences of a Small County Lawyer. 1981. 5.75 (ISBN 0-8062-1689-1). Carlton.
Matthews, B., jt. auth. see Khan, M. A.
Matthews, B. E., jt. auth. see Croll, Neil A.
Matthews, Brander. Historical Novel & Other Essays. LC 68-30586. 1969. Repr. of 1901 ed. 15.00 (ISBN 0-8103-3218-3). Gale.
--Rip Van Winkle Goes to the Play. LC 67-27625. 1967. Repr. of 1926 ed. 12.00 (ISBN 0-8046-0303-0). Kennikat.
Matthews, Brander, ed. Ballads of Books. LC 70-141032. 1971. Repr. of 1887 ed. 15.00 (ISBN 0-8103-3384-8). Gale.
Matthews, Byron S. Local Government: How to Get into It, How to Administer It Effectively. LC 78-110451. 1970. 14.95 (ISBN 0-911012-04-4). Nelson-Hall.
Matthews, C. D., jt. auth. see Blaikie, W. G.
Matthews, Charles C., et al. Student-Structured Learning in Science: A Program for the Teacher. 3rd ed. 1977. pap. text ed. 7.95 o.p. (ISBN 0-8403-1651-8). Kendall-Hunt.
Matthews, Clayton. Dallas. pap. 2.50 (ISBN 0-686-68322-6). PB.
Matthews, Clyde. The Ides of March Conspiracy. LC 80-83593. 320p. 1981. pap. 2.75 (ISBN 0-87216-789-5). Playboy Pbks.
Matthews, Daryl B. Disposable Patients. LC 77-25778. 1980. 14.95 (ISBN 0-669-02164-4). Lexington Bks.
Matthews, Denis. Brahms Piano Music. LC 75-27955. (BBC Music Guides: No. 37). (Illus.). 64p. (Orig.). 1978. pap. 2.95 (ISBN 0-295-95480-9). U of Wash Pr.
Matthews, Donald R. U. S. Senators & Their World. LC 80-17163. (Illus.). xvi, 303p. 1980. Repr. of 1960 ed. lib. bdg. 25.00x (ISBN 0-313-22664-4, MASE). Greenwood.
Matthews, Donald R., jt. auth. see Keech, William R.
Matthews, Donald R., ed. Perspectives on Presidential Selection. (Studies in Presidential Selection). 1973. 14.95 (ISBN 0-8157-5508-2); pap. 5.95 (ISBN 0-8157-5507-4). Brookings.
Matthews, Douglas. Sue the B-st-rds: The Victim's Handbook. rev. ed. 1981. pap. 7.95 (ISBN 0-87795-288-4). Arbor Hse.
Matthews, E., tr. see Runciman, W. G.
Matthews, E. C. Joseph Pennell's Sketches of Old New Orleans. 64p. 1966. pap. 2.00 (ISBN 0-911116-85-0). Pelican.
Matthews, Edward. Celebrating Mass with Children: A Commentary on the Directory of Masses with Children. LC 78-58564. 1978. pap. 6.95 (ISBN 0-8091-2160-3). Paulist Pr.
Matthews, Ellen. Putting up with Sherwood. LC 80-17574. (Illus.). (gr. 3-5). 1980. PLB 9.95 (ISBN 0-664-32672-2). Westminster.
Matthews, F. Survey of the Graphic Arts. 1974. pap. 7.90x o.p. (ISBN 0-87563-067-7). Stipes.
Matthews, G. A. Pesticide Application Methods. new ed. LC 77-26033. (Illus.). 1979. text ed. 55.00 (ISBN 0-582-46054-9). Longman.
Matthews, G. M., ed. Keats: The Critical Heritage. 1971. 36.00x (ISBN 0-7100-7147-7). Routledge & Kegan.
Matthews, G. M., ed. see Shelley, Percy Bysshe.
Matthews, G. V. Bird Navigation. 3rd ed. LC 68-23181. (Cambridge Monographs in Experimental Biology). (Illus.). 1968. 27.50 (ISBN 0-521-07271-9); pap. 10.50x (ISBN 0-521-09541-7). Cambridge U Pr.
Matthews, Gwynneth. Plato's Epistemology & Related Logical Problems. (Selections from Philosophers Ser.). 263p. 1972. text ed. 15.00x (ISBN 0-391-00260-0); pap. text ed. 7.25x (ISBN 0-571-09909-2). Humanities.
Matthews, Harrison L. The Natural History of the Whale. (Illus.). 1978. 20.00x (ISBN 0-231-04588-3). Columbia U Pr.
Matthews, Herbert L. Cuba. (Illus.). (gr. 7 up). 1964. 6.95g (ISBN 0-02-765280-7). Macmillan.
Matthews, J. E., et al, eds. Automatic Turning Machines. 2nd ed. (Engineering Craftsmen: No. H30/3). (Illus.). 1978. spiral bdg. 21.00x (ISBN 0-85083-405-8). Intl Ideas.
Matthews, J. F. Andre Breton. LC 67-16892. (Columbia Essays on Modern Writers Ser.: No. 26). (Orig.). 1967. pap. 2.00 (ISBN 0-231-02910-1, MW26). Columbia U Pr.
Matthews, J. H. Benjamin Peret. LC 74-30229. (World Authors Ser.: France: No. 359). 1975. lib. bdg. 12.50 (ISBN 0-8057-2691-8). Twayne.
--Surrealism & American Feature Films. (Theatrical Arts Ser.). 1979. lib. bdg. 10.95 (ISBN 0-8057-9265-1). Twayne.
--Surrealism & Film. LC 75-163624. (Illus.). 1971. 8.50 o.p. (ISBN 0-472-64135-2). U of Mich Pr.
--Surrealism & the Novel. LC 66-17021. 1966. 5.95 o.p. (ISBN 0-472-64140-9). U of Mich Pr.
Matthews, J. W., ed. Epitaxial Growth, Pts. A & B. (Materials Science & Technology Ser). 1975. Pt. A. 52.75 (ISBN 0-12-480901-4); Pt. B. deluxe ed. 49.00 (ISBN 0-12-480902-2). Acad Pr.
Matthews, Jack. Charisma Campaigns. LC 71-174511. 1972. 5.95 o.p. (ISBN 0-15-116800-8). HarBraceJ.
Matthews, Jack, ed. Archetypal Themes in Modern Story. 256p. 1973. text ed. 7.95 (ISBN 0-312-04795-9). St Martin.
Matthews, Jacqueline D. Association System of the European Community. LC 76-12865. 1977. text ed. 22.95 (ISBN 0-275-23270-0). Praeger.
Matthews, James, jt. auth. see Judge, Ken.
Matthews, James M., ed. Kime's International Law Directory for 1980. 88th ed. 809p. 1981. 52.50x (ISBN 0-900503-12-2). Intl Pubns Serv.
Matthews, Janice R., jt. auth. see Matthews, Robert W.
Matthews, John. Western Aristocracies & Imperial Court A.D. Three Hundred Sixty-Four - Four Hundred Twenty-Five. 442p. 1975. 45.00x (ISBN 0-19-814817-8). Oxford U Pr.
Matthews, John, et al, eds. see Disraeli, Benjamin.

Matthews, John A. Quantitative & Statistical Approaches to Geography: A Practical Manual. (Pergamon Oxford Geographies). Date not set. 19.21 (ISBN 0-686-66169-9); pap. price not set (ISBN 0-08-024295-2). Pergamon.
Matthews, John B., Jr., jt. auth. see Smith, George A., Jr.
Matthews, John F. George Bernard Shaw. LC 72-92031. (Columbia Essays on Modern Writers Ser.: No. 45). (Orig.). 1969. pap. 2.00 (ISBN 0-231-03145-9, MW45). Columbia U Pr.
Matthews, Joseph R. Choosing an Automated Library System: A Planning Guide. LC 80-17882. 128p. 1980. 11.00 (ISBN 0-8389-0310-X). ALA.
Matthews, Kenneth & McDevitt, Robert. The Unlikely Legacy: The Story of John Ringling, the Circus & Sarasota. (Illus.). 64p. 1979. pap. 3.95 (ISBN 0-936076-00-3). Aaron Pubs.
--The Unlikely Legacy, the Story of John Ringling: The Circus & Sarasota. 2nd rev. ed. (Illus.). 64p. (Orig.). 1980. 5.95 (ISBN 0-936076-02-X); pap. 3.95 (ISBN 0-936076-00-3). Aaron Pubs.
Matthews, L. Harrison. The Natural History of the Whale. (Illus.). 1980. pap. 9.95 (ISBN 0-231-04589-1). Columbia U Pr.
Matthews, Laura. Aim of a Lady. (Orig.). 1980. pap. 1.75 (ISBN 0-446-94341-X). Warner Bks.
--The Seventh Suitor. 208p. (Orig.). 1979. pap. 1.75 (ISBN 0-446-94340-1). Warner Bks.
Matthews, Mervyn. Soviet Sociology, 1964-75: A Bibliography. LC 77-83454. (Praeger Special Studies). 1978. 37.95 (ISBN 0-03-022346-6). Praeger.
Matthews, Michael. The Marxist Theory of Schooling: A Study in Epistemology & Education. 1981. text ed. 30.00x (ISBN 0-391-01801-9). Humanities.
Matthews, Mollie, jt. auth. see Matthews, Patrick.
Matthews, Noel. Materials for West African History in the Archives of the United Kingdom. (Guides to Materials for West African History in European Archives Ser: No. 5). 225p. 1973. pap. text ed. 12.00x (ISBN 0-485-17205-4, Athlone Pr). Humanities.
Matthews, Noel & Wainwright, M. Doreen. A Guide to Manuscripts & Documents in the British Isles Relating to the Far East. Pearson, J. D., ed. 1977. text ed. 59.00x (ISBN 0-19-713591-9). Oxford U Pr.
Matthews, Noel & Wainwrights, Doreen M., eds. A Guide to Manuscrpits & Documents in the British Isles Relating to the Middle East & North Africa. 500p. 1980. 148.00x (ISBN 0-19-713598-6). Oxford U Pr.
Matthews, P. H. Inflectional Morphology: A Theoretical Study Based on Aspects of Latin Verb Conjugation. LC 76-171678. (Studies in Linguistics Ser., No. 6). (Illus.). 500p. 1972. 49.50 (ISBN 0-521-08372-9); pap. 14.95x (ISBN 0-521-29065-1). Cambridge U Pr.
--Morphology: An Introduction to the Theory of Word-Structure. LC 73-91817. (Cambridge Textbooks in Linguistics Ser.). 256p. 1974. 37.50 (ISBN 0-521-20448-8); pap. 9.95x (ISBN 0-521-09856-4). Cambridge U Pr.
Matthews, Patricia. Love Forever More. 1977. pap. 2.75 (ISBN 0-523-41203-7). Pinnacle Bks.
--Love's Magic Moment. 1979. pap. 2.75 (ISBN 0-523-41200-2). Pinnacle Bks.
Matthews, Patrick & Matthews, Mollie. Snowy Toes & the Magic Music Box. 1976. 3.95 (ISBN 0-7207-0813-3, Pub. by Michael Joseph). Merrimack Bk Serv.
Matthews, Paula, ed. see Mochon, Anne.
Matthews, R. E. Plant Virology. 2nd ed. 1981. write for info. (ISBN 0-12-480560-4). Acad Pr.
Matthews, R. E., ed. Classification & Nomenclature of Viruses: Report of the International Committee on Taxonomy of Viruses, 3rd. (Intervirology: Vol. 12, Nos. 3-5, 1979). 1980. pap. 6.00 (ISBN 3-8055-0523-X). S Karger.
Matthews, Ray A. Gospel Anchors Aweigh. LC 79-87732. (Destiny Ser.). 1980. pap. 4.95 (ISBN 0-8163-0382-7, 07690-1). Pacific Pr Pub.
Matthews, Robert J. Unto All Nations: A Guide to the Book of Acts & the Writings of Paul. 59p. (Orig.). 1975. pap. 1.50 o.p. (ISBN 0-87747-601-2). Deseret Bk.
Matthews, Robert T. Engraved Glass & Other Decorated Glass. LC 76-48555. (Illus.). 1978. soft bound 10.95 (ISBN 0-9601150-1-3). R T Matthews.
Matthews, Robert W. & Matthews, Janice R. Insect Behavior. LC 78-7869. 1978. 28.50 (ISBN 0-471-57685-9, Pub. by Wiley-Interscience). Wiley.
Matthews, Robley K. Dynamic Stratigraphy: An Introduction to Sedimentation & Stratigraphy. 1974. 20.95 (ISBN 0-13-222273-6). P-H.
Matthews, Rose, jt. auth. see Finnegan, Patrick.
Matthews, Sallie R. Interwoven: A Pioneer Chronicle. (M. K. Brown Range Life Ser: No. 13). (Illus.). 226p. 1973. Repr. 15.00 (ISBN 0-292-73800-5). U of Tex Pr.
Matthews, Sarah, tr. see Braudel, Fernand.
Matthews, Stephen F. & Levi, Donald R. Missouri Agricultural Law. 4th ed. (Lucas Text Ser). 1979. spiral bdg. 10.00x (ISBN 0-87543-132-1). Lucas.
Matthews, Thomas. Splendid Art: A History of the Opera. LC 78-93717. (Illus.). (gr. 7-12). 1970. 5.95g o.s.i. (ISBN 0-02-765290-4, CCPr). Macmillan.
Matthews, Velda. Basic Bible Dictionary: Simplified Descriptions of Bible People. (Illus.). (gr. 4 up). 1978. pap. 1.95 (ISBN 0-87239-250-3, 2781). Standard Pub.
--Basic Bible Dictionary: Simplified Descriptions of Bible Places. (Illus.). (gr. 4 up). 1978. pap. 1.95 (ISBN 0-87239-254-6, 2782). Standard Pub.
Matthews, Velda & Beard, Ray. Basic Bible Dictionary: Simplified Definitions of Bible Words. (Illus.). (gr. 4 up). 1977. pap. 1.95 (ISBN 0-87239-249-X, 2780). Standard Pub.
Matthews, W. H. The Geologic Story of Longhorn Cavern. 50p. 1963. 1.00 (GB 4). Bur Econ Geology.
--The Geologic Story of Palo Duro Canyon. (Illus.). 51p. 1969. 1.00 (GB 8). Bur Econ Geology.
--Mazes & Labyrinths. LC 70-75946. 1969. Repr. of 1922 ed. 18.00 (ISBN 0-8103-3839-4). Gale.
--Texas Fossils: An Amateur Collector's Handbook. (Illus.). 123p. 1960. Repr. 1.00 (GB 2). Bur Econ Geology.
Matthews, W. K. Russian Historical Grammar. (London East European: No. 1). 1960. text ed. 26.25x (ISBN 0-485-17509-6, Athlone Pr). Humanities.
Matthews, William. Charles II's Escape from Worcester: A Collection of Essays Assembled by Samuel Pepys. 1966. 16.50x (ISBN 0-520-00831-6). U of Cal Pr.
--Cockney Past & Present: A Short History of the Dialect of London. LC 68-30638. 1970. Repr. of 1938 ed. 15.00 (ISBN 0-8103-3609-X). Gale.
--Sleek for the Long Flight. 1972. pap. 1.95 o.p. (ISBN 0-394-70762-1). Random.
Matthews, William, ed. Later Medieval English Prose. LC 63-9439. (Goldentree Books in English Literature). (Orig.). 1963. pap. text ed. 8.95x (ISBN 0-89197-270-6). Irvington.
--Medieval Secular Literature: Four Essays. (UCLA Center for Medieval & Renaissance Studies). 1965. 16.50x (ISBN 0-520-00832-4). U of Cal Pr.
Matthews, William, ed. see Pepys, Samuel.
Matthews, William, tr. see Follain, Jean.
Matthews, William H. Fossils: An Introduction to Prehistoric Life. (Orig.). 1962. pap. 3.95 (ISBN 0-06-463280-6, EH 280, EH). Har-Row.
Matthews, William H., III. Geology Made Simple. LC 67-10378. 1967. pap. 2.50 o.p. (ISBN 0-385-01469-4, Made). Doubleday.
--Story of the Earth. LC 67-16904. (Story of Science Ser.). (Illus.). (gr. 5-10). 1968. PLB 7.29 (ISBN 0-8178-3932-1). Harvey.
Matthews, William H., III, compiled by. Helping Children Learn Earth-Space Science: A Selection of Articles Reprinted from "Science & Children". 1971. pap. 5.00 (ISBN 0-87355-000-5). Natl Sci Tchrs.
Matthews, William H., 3rd. Earth's Crust. LC 76-134367. (First Bks). (Illus.). (gr. 4-6). 1971. PLB 4.90 o.p. (ISBN 0-531-00724-3). Watts.
--First Book of Soils. LC 70-121921. (First Bks). (Illus.). (gr. 4-6). 1970. PLB 4.90 o.p. (ISBN 0-531-00716-2). Watts.
Matthiae, Paolo. EBLA: An Empire Rediscovered. LC 77-80898. (Illus.). 240p. 1981. 14.95 (ISBN 0-385-12904-1). Doubleday.
Matthias, John. Bucyrus. LC 75-132579. (New Poetry Ser.: No. 42). 102p. 1971. 7.95 (ISBN 0-8040-0522-2); pap. 3.95 (ISBN 0-8040-0523-0). Swallow.
--Turns. LC 75-535. 111p. 1975. 7.95 (ISBN 0-8040-0689-X). Swallow.
Matthias, John, ed. Introducing David Jones. 240p. 1980. 18.95 (ISBN 0-571-11526-8, Pub. by Faber & Faber); pap. 8.95 (ISBN 0-571-11525-X, Pub. by Faber & Faber). Merrimack Bk Serv.
--Twenty-Three Modern British Poets. LC 71-150757. 338p. 1971. 15.00x (ISBN 0-8040-0507-9); pap. 8.95x (ISBN 0-8214-0508-X). Swallow.
Matthias, John & Printz-Pahlson, Goran, trs. Contemporary Swedish Poetry. LC 79-9655. 136p. 1980. 16.95x (ISBN 0-8040-0811-6); pap. 7.95 (ISBN 0-8040-0812-4). Swallow.
Matthiasson, Carolyn J., ed. Many Sisters: Women in Cross-Cultural Perspectives. LC 74-2654. (Illus.). 1979. pap. text ed. 9.95 (ISBN 0-02-920320-1). Free Pr.
Matthies, Leslie H. The Management System: Systems Are for People. LC 76-4572. (Wiley Series on Systems & Controls for Financial Management). 240p. 1976. 26.50 (ISBN 0-471-57697-2, Pub. by Wiley-Interscience). Wiley.
Matthiessen, F. O. American Renaissance: Art & Expression in the Age of Emerson & Whitman. 1968. pap. 10.95 (ISBN 0-19-500759-X, 230, GB). Oxford U Pr.
Matthiessen, Peter. Sand Rivers. LC 80-36703. (Illus.). 240p. 1981. 19.95 (ISBN 0-670-61696-6, Studio). Viking Pr.
--The Wind Birds. (Illus.). 192p. 1973. 9.95 o.p. (ISBN 0-670-77096-5, Studio). Viking Pr.
Matthyse, S., ed. see Scottish Rite Schizophrenia Research Program, Conference, Rochester, 2-6 May 1976.
Matthysse, Steven & Kety, Seymour S. Catecholamines & Their Enzymes in the Neuropathology of Schizophrenia. LC 75-4093. (Illus.). 382p. 1975. text ed. 57.00 (ISBN 0-08-018242-9). Pergamon.
Mattick, Paul. Marx & Keynes: The Limits of the Mixed Economy. LC 69-15526. (Extending Horizons Ser.). 1973. pap. 3.45 (ISBN 0-87558-069-6). Porter Sargent.
Mattick, Paul, Sr. Economic Crisis & Crisis Theory. LC 80-5459. Orig. Title: Krisen und Krisentheorien. 228p. 1980. 22.50 (ISBN 0-87332-179-0). M E Sharpe.
Mattil, Edward L. Meaning in Crafts. 3rd ed. LC 73-123087. 1971. ref. ed. 16.50 (ISBN 0-13-567156-6). P-H.
Mattingly, H. Aes & Pecunia Records of Roman Currency Down to 269 B. C. Date not set. pap. 3.00 (ISBN 0-916710-51-3). Obol Intl.
Mattingly, Harold. The Imperial Civil Service of Rome. LC 79-1638. 1981. Repr. of 1910 ed. 16.50 (ISBN 0-88355-940-4). Hyperion Conn.
Mattingly, Hugh, tr. see Tacitus.
Mattingly, Paul H. The Classless Profession: American Schoolmen of the Nineteenth Century. LC 74-29126. (New York University Series in Education & Socialization in American History). 235p. 1975. 15.00x (ISBN 0-8147-5400-7); pap. 6.00x (ISBN 0-8147-5420-1). NYU Pr.
Mattingly, Paul H., jt. ed. see Katz, Michael B.
Mattingly, Richard F., jt. auth. see Te Linde, Richard W.
Mattinson, Janet & Sinclair, Ian. Mate & Stalemate: Working with Marital Problems in a Social Services Dept. (The Practice of Social Work: Vol. 1). 1979. 21.95x (ISBN 0-631-11821-7, Pub. by Basil Blackwell England). Biblio Dist.
Mattinson, Janet, jt. auth. see Guthrie, Lorna.
Mattis, George. Whitetail: Fundamentals & Fine Points for the Hunter. rev. ed. 290p. 1980. 15.95 (ISBN 0-442-23355-8). Van Nos Reinhold.
Mattison, Alice. Animals. LC 79-54884. 72p. 1979. pap. 4.95 (ISBN 0-914086-29-4). Alicejamesbooks.
Mattison, Charles W. & Alvarez, Joseph. Man & His Resources. LC 66-25119. (In Todays World Ser). (Illus.). (gr. 4-8). 1967. PLB 7.95 (ISBN 0-87191-001-2). Creative Ed.
Mattock, G., ed. New Processes of Waste Water Treatment & Recovery. 1978. 69.95x (ISBN 0-470-26341-5). Halsted Pr.
Mattoon, Mary Ann. Applied Dream Analysis: A Jungian Approach. 1978. 13.95x (ISBN 0-470-26418-7). Halsted Pr.
Mattox. Minnesota Legal Forms-Criminal Law. 1981. ring binder 15.00 (ISBN 0-917126-84-X). Mason Pub.
Mattox, Phil, jt. auth. see Giammatteo, Mike.
Matts, Abraham, tr. see Sperling, Abraham I.
Mattson, Dale E. Statistics: Difficult Concepts-Understandable Explanations. (Illus.). 402p. 1981. pap. text ed. 16.95 (ISBN 0-8016-3173-4). Mosby.
Mattson, Lloyd, jt. ed. see Graendorf, Werner.
Mattson, Paul R. Fifty-One Top Quarter Horses: A Pedigree Study. 1980. pap. 9.95 (ISBN 0-686-28067-9). PRESCOB.
Matulich, Serge, jt. auth. see Heitger, Lester E.
Matunas, Edward. American Ammunition & Ballistics. (Illus.). 1979. 13.95 (ISBN 0-87691-290-0). Winchester Pr.
--Handbook of Metallic Cartridge Reloading. (Illus.). 272p. 1981. 14.95 (ISBN 0-87691-320-6). Winchester Pr.
Maturin, Charles R. Melmoth the Wanderer: A Tale. LC 61-5561. 1961. pap. 4.50x (ISBN 0-8032-5127-0, BB 114, Bison). U of Nebr Pr.
--The Milesian Chief. Wolff, Robert L., ed. (Ireland-Nineteenth Century Fiction Ser. Two: Vol. 12). 1979. lib. bdg. 184.00 (ISBN 0-8240-3461-9); lib. bdg. 46.00 ea. Garland Pub.
--The Wild Irish Boy. Wolff, Robert L., ed. (Ireland-Nineteenth Century Fiction, Ser. Two: Vol. 11). 1979. lib. bdg. 126.00 (ISBN 0-8240-3460-0); lib. bdg. 46.00 ea. Garland Pub.
--Women; or, Pour et Contre: A Tale, 3 vols. Wolff, Robert L., ed. (Ireland Nineteenth Century Fiction, Ser. Two: Vol. 13). 1979. Set. lib. bdg. write for info. (ISBN 0-8240-3462-7); lib. bdg. 46.00 ea. Garland Pub.
Matyas, Antal. History of Modern Non-Marxian Economics. Veges, Istvan, tr. (Illus.). 598p. 1980. 50.00x (ISBN 963-05-1894-5). Intl Pubns Ser.
Matz, Samuel A. Bakery Technology & Engineering. 2nd ed. (Illus.). 1972. text ed. 41.50 (ISBN 0-87055-109-4). AVI.
--Cereal Technology. (Illus.). 1970. 26.50 o.p. (ISBN 0-87055-071-3). AVI.
--Snack Food Technology. (Illus.). 1976. text ed. 36.00 (ISBN 0-87055-193-0). AVI.
Matz, Samuel A. & Matz, Theresa D. Cookie & Cracker Technology. 2nd ed. (Illus.). 1978. lib. bdg. 36.50 (ISBN 0-87055-235-X). AVI.
Matz, Theresa D., jt. auth. see Matz, Samuel A.
Matza, D. Deliquency & Drift. LC 64-18135. 1964. pap. text ed. 8.95x (ISBN 0-471-57708-1). Wiley.
Matza, David. Becoming Deviant. 1969. pap. text ed. 10.95 (ISBN 0-13-073171-4). P-H.
Matzke, Gordon. Wildlife in Tanzanian Settlement Policy: The Case of the Selous. LC 77-18175. (Foreign & Comparative Studies Africa Ser.: No. 28). 1978. pap. 6.50x (ISBN 0-915984-50-4). Syracuse U Foreign Comp.
Maubrey, Pierre. Connaissance du francais. 1973. text ed. 10.95x o.p. (ISBN 0-673-05112-9). Scott F.
Maubrey, Pierre, jt. auth. see Parker, Clifford S.
Mauchline, John. A Key to the Exercises in the Introductory Hebrew Grammar. 146p. Repr. of 1967 ed. 10.95x (ISBN 0-567-01006-6). Attic Pr.
Mauchline, John, ed. see Davidson, A. B.
Mauck, JoAnn, jt. auth. see Pelstring, Linda.
Maud, Marjory V. Divide & Conquer or Life Among the Left Overs. (Illus.). 1981. 9.95 (ISBN 0-938562-00-2). Single Impressinons.
Maude, Aylmer, tr. see Tolstoy, Leo.
Maude, Barry. Leadership in Management. 240p. 1978. text ed. 29.50x (ISBN 0-220-66361-0, Pub. by Busn Bks England). Renouf.
Maudsley, Henry. Physiology & Pathology of the Mind. (Contributions to the History of Psychology Ser.: Medical Psychology). 1978. Repr. of 1867 ed. 30.00 (ISBN 0-89093-168-2). U Pubns Amer.
--Responsibility in Mental Disease. Bd. with Treatise on Insanity. (Contributions to the History of Psychology Ser., Vol. III, Pt. C: Medical Psychology). 1978. Repr. of 1876 ed. 30.00 (ISBN 0-89093-167-4). U Pubns Amer.
Maue, Wilma M., jt. auth. see Dickson, David R.
Mauer, George J., ed. Crises in Campus Management: Case Studies in the Administration of Colleges & Universities. LC 75-23981. (Special Studies). 1976. text ed. 19.95 o.p. (ISBN 0-275-55710-3). Praeger.
Mauet, Thomas A. Fundamentals of Trial Techniques. 1980. pap. text ed. 10.00 (ISBN 0-316-55082-5). Little.
Mauger, Emily M. Modern Display Techniques. LC 64-18578. 1964. 10.00 (ISBN 0-87005-045-1). Fairchild.
Mauger, G., et al. Le Francais commercial, 3 vols. Vol. 1. pap. text ed. 7.50 (ISBN 2-03-040404-7, 3760); Vol. 2. pap. text ed. 8.50 (ISBN 2-03-040405-5, 3761); Vol. 3. pap. text ed. 7.50 (ISBN 0-685-13927-1, 3762). Larousse.
Mauger, Gaston. Cours De Langue et De Civilization Francaises, 4 Vols. (Fr). Vol. 1. 7.00 (ISBN 0-685-20231-3); Vol. 2. 7.00 (ISBN 0-685-20232-1); Vol. 3. 7.50 (ISBN 0-685-20233-X); Vol. 4. 9.90 (ISBN 0-685-20234-8). Schoenhof.
Mauger, Juan & Oakes, Peter. Ivan Mauger's World Speedway Book. (Illus.). 1974. 9.95 (ISBN 0-7207-0725-0). Transatlantic.
Mauger, Peter. British People Nineteen Two - Nineteen Seventy-Five. 1976. pap. text ed. 13.95x (ISBN 0-435-31570-6). Heinemann Ed.
Maugham, Frederic H. U.N.O. & War Crimes. LC 74-27728. 143p. 1975. Repr. of 1951 ed. lib. bdg. 12.75x (ISBN 0-8371-7911-4, MAUN). Greenwood.
Maugham, W. Somerset. The Moon & Sixpence. 1977. pap. 2.95 (ISBN 0-14-000468-8). Penguin.
--Of Human Bondage. 685p. Date not set. pap. 3.95 (ISBN 0-394-70137-2, Vin). Random.
Maugham, W. Somerset see Salerno, Henry F.
Maughan, Jackie J. & Puddicombe, Ann. Hiking the Back Country. 224p. (Orig.). 1981. pap. 9.95 (ISBN 0-8117-2170-1). Stackpole.
Maughan, Ralph. Beyond the Tetons. (Illus.). 135p. (Orig.). 1981. pap. 5.95 (ISBN 0-87108-580-1). Pruett.
Mauksch, Ingeborg G. & Miller, Michael H. Implementing Change in Nursing. LC 80-16576. (Illus.). 195p. 1980. pap. text ed. 10.95 (ISBN 0-8016-3476-8). Mosby.
Maul, Terry, jt. auth. see Conrad, Eva.

Mauldin, Bill. I've Decided I Want My Seat Back. LC 63-20294. (Illus.). 1965. 10.00 o.s.i. (ISBN 0-06-012845-3, HarpT). Har-Row.
Maule, H. G. & Weiner, J. S., eds. Human Factors in Work Design & Production. 1977. 26.95 (ISBN 0-470-99074-0). Halsted Pr.
Maule, Tex. Bart Starr: Professional Quarterback. LC 72-7355. (Illus.). 128p. (gr. 5 up). 1973. PLB 5.90 o.p. (ISBN 0-531-02610-8). Watts.
Maull, H. Europe & World Energy. LC 80-40488. (Illus.). 1980. text ed. 43.95 (ISBN 0-408-10629-8). Butterworths.
Maull, Kimball I. & Griffen, Ward O., Jr. Trauma Surgery. (Medical Examination Review Book: Vol. 36). 1977. spiral bdg. 15.00 o.s.i. (ISBN 0-87488-179-X). Med Exam.
Maunder, A. H. & Hirsch, G. P. Farm Amalgamation in Western Europe. 132p. 1979. text ed. 21.00x (ISBN 0-566-00253-1, Pub. by Gower Pub Co England). Renouf.
Maunder, C. R. Algebraic Topology. LC 79-41610. (Illus.). 1980. 59.50 (ISBN 0-521-23161-2); pap. 22.95 (ISBN 0-521-29840-7). Cambridge U Pr.
Maunder, Elwood R., jt. auth. see Reed, William G.
Maunder, Peter, ed. Government Intervention in the Developed Economy. LC 78-72590. 1979. 25.95 (ISBN 0-03-049501-6). Praeger.
Maunder, W. F., ed. Health Surveys & Related Studies. LC 78-40963. (Reviews of United Kingdom Statistical Sources Ser.: Vol. IX). 1979. 55.00 (ISBN 0-08-022459-8). Pergamon.
Maunder, W. F. & Coppock, J. T., eds. Land Use & Town & Country Planning. 1978. text ed. 37.00 (ISBN 0-08-022451-2). Pergamon.
Maunder, W. F., ed. see Baxter, R. E. & Phillips, C.
Mauner, George. The Nabis: Their History & Their Art, 1888-1896. LC 77-94708. (Outstanding Dissertations in the Fine Arts Ser.). 1979. lib. bdg. 45.00 (ISBN 0-8240-3240-3). Garland Pub.
Mauntz, Alfred Von see Von Mauntz, Alfred.
Maupas, P., jt. ed. see Melnick, J. L.
Maupassant. Mon Oncle Jules. (Easy Reader, D). pap. 3.75 (ISBN 0-88436-044-X, FRA301052). EMC.
Maupassant, Guy De. Contes Choisis. Price, W. R., ed. 1930. 3.50 (ISBN 0-672-73238-6). Odyssey Pr.
Maupassant, Guy De see De Maupassant, Guy.
Maupassant, Guy De see Maupassant, Guy De.
Maupin, B. Blood Platelets in Man & Animals, 2 Vols. 1969. Set. 150.00 (ISBN 0-08-006405-1). Pergamon.
Maurer, A. E. see Dryden, John.
Maurer, David J., ed. United States Politics & Elections: A Guide to Information Sources. LC 78-13669. (American Government & History Information Guide Ser.: Vol. 3). 1978. 30.00 (ISBN 0-8103-1367-7). Gale.
Maurer, David W. The American Confidence Man. 316p. 1974. 16.75 (ISBN 0-398-02974-1); pap. 9.75 (ISBN 0-398-02976-8). C C Thomas.
--Language of the Underworld. LC 79-57574. 1981. price not set (ISBN 0-8131-1405-5). U Pr of Ky.
Maurer, David W. & Vogel, Victor H. Narcotics & Narcotic Addiction. 4th ed. (American Lectures in Public Protection). (Illus.). 496p. 1973. 24.75 (ISBN 0-398-02906-7). C C Thomas.
Maurer, Friedrich, ed. Gottfried Von Strassburg Tristan & Isolde. 4th ed. 1977. 6.25x (ISBN 3-11-006841-9). De Gruyter.
Maurer, H. A. & Williams, M. R. A Collection of Programming Problems & Techniques. (Illus.). 256p. 1972. pap. 17.95x ref. ed. (ISBN 0-13-139592-0). P-H.
Maurer, H. Rainer, jt. ed. see Allen, Robert.
Maurer, Harry. Not Working. 1981. pap. 6.95 (ISBN 0-452-25272-5, Z5272, Plume). NAL.
Maurer, Katharine, jt. auth. see Goodenough, Florence.
Maurer, W. C. Novel Drilling Techniques. 1968. 26.00 (ISBN 0-08-012734-7). Pergamon.
Maurer, Ward D. Programming: An Introduction to Computer Techniques. rev. 2nd ed. LC 70-188126. (Illus.). 1972. text ed. 23.95x (ISBN 0-8162-5453-2). Holden Day.
Maurer, William. Advanced Drilling Techniques. 576p. 1980. 45.00 (ISBN 0-87814-117-0). Pennwell Pub.
Mauriac, Claude. Conversations with Andre Gide. LC 65-23178. 1965. 5.00 o.s.i. (ISBN 0-8076-0320-1). Braziller.
--Dinner in Town. Howard, Richard, tr. 1980. pap. 4.95 (ISBN 0-7145-0199-9). Riverrun NY.
--Femmes Fatales. Wolff, Henry, tr. 1980. pap. 4.95 (ISBN 0-7145-0232-4). Riverrun NY.
--The Marquise Went Out at Five. Howard, Richard, tr. 1981. pap. 4.95 (ISBN 0-7145-0367-3). Riverrun NY.
Mauriac, Francois. Maltaverne. Stewart, Jean, tr. from Fr. 1970. 5.95 o.p. (ISBN 0-374-20112-9). FS&G.
--Memoires Interieurs. Hopkins, Gerard, tr. from Fr. 1961. 4.75 o.p. (ISBN 0-374-20644-9). FS&G.
--Mystere Frontenac. (Documentation thematique). (Illus., Fr.). pap. 2.95 (ISBN 0-685-13998-0, 178). Larousse.
Maurice & Follett, Ken. The Gentlemen of Sixteen July. 1980. 9.95 (ISBN 0-87795-298-1). Arbor Hse.
Maurice, Arthur B. & Cooper, Frederic T. History of the Nineteenth Century in Caricature. LC 79-136560. (Tower Bks). (Illus.). 1971. Repr. of 1904 ed. 28.00 (ISBN 0-8103-3909-9). Gale.
Maurice, Charles, jt. auth. see Ferguson, C. E.
Maurice, D. Convolution & Fourier Transforms for Communications Engineers. LC 75-34082. 1976. 24.95x (ISBN 0-470-57770-3). Halsted Pr.
Maurice, Frederick D. Theological Essays. 1980. Repr. of 1891 ed. cancelled (ISBN 0-87921-048-6). Attic Pr.
Maurice, Nelson R., compiled by. The Management of Public Enterprise: A Bibliography. (Miscellaneous Publications Ser.). (Orig.). 1975. pap. 7.50 (ISBN 0-86603-009-3). Bureau Busn Res U Wis.
Maurier, Daphne Du see Du Maurier, Daphne.
Maurier, George Du see Du Maurier, George.
Mauro, Alexander, ed. Muscle Regeneration. 1979. text ed. 59.50 (ISBN 0-89004-284-5). Raven.
Maurois, Andre. Illusions. LC 68-29043. 1968. 12.50x (ISBN 0-231-03171-8). Columbia U Pr.
--Lelia: The Life of George Sand. Hopkins, Gerard, tr. 1977. pap. 4.95 (ISBN 0-14-004354-3). Penguin.
Mauron, Charles. Introduction to the Psychoanalysis of Mallarme. McLendon, Will & Henderson, Archibald, Jr., trs. (Perspectives in Criticism: No. 10). 1963. 18.50x (ISBN 0-520-00833-2). U of Cal Pr.
Maurus, Walt. All About Bettas. (Orig.). 1976. pap. 5.95 (ISBN 0-87666-452-4, PS-654). TFH Pubns.
Maury, C. J. Recent Mollusks Gulf Coast. 1971. Repr. 5.00 (ISBN 0-87710-361-5). Paleo Res.
Maury, Curt. Folk Origins of Indian Art. LC 75-94909. (Illus.). 1969. 22.50x (ISBN 0-231-03198-X). Columbia U Pr.
Maury, E. A. Drainage in Homoeopathy. 1980. text ed. 4.00x (ISBN 0-8464-1007-9). Beekman Pubs.
Maury, Richard. Saga of Cimba. 1973. 7.50 (ISBN 0-8286-0063-5). De Graff.
Mauser, August & Lockavitch, Joseph. Lateral Awareness & Directionality Test. 64p. 1980. pap. text ed. 7.50 manual (ISBN 0-87879-250-3). Acad Therapy.
Mauser, August J., jt. auth. see Sabatino, David A.
Mauser, Pat R. How I Found Myself at the Fair. LC 80-12058. (Illus.). 64p. (gr. 2-5). 1980. 7.95 (ISBN 0-689-30780-2). Atheneum.
Maushart, R., jt. auth. see Kiefer, H.
Mauskopf, Seymour H. & McVaugh, Michael R. The Elusive Science: Origins of Experimental Psychical Research. LC 80-7991. (Illus.). 400p. 1981. text ed. 24.50x (ISBN 0-8018-2331-5). Johns Hopkins.
Mauskopf, Seymour H., ed. Reception of Unconventional Science by the Scientific Community. 1979. lib. bdg. 17.00x (ISBN 0-89158-297-5). Westview.
Mausner, Bernard. A Citizen's Guide to the Social Sciences. LC 78-16626. 1979. text ed. 16.95 (ISBN 0-88229-401-6); pap. 7.95 (ISBN 0-88229-650-7). Nelson-Hall.
Mausolf, F. The Anatomy of the Ocular Adnexa: Guide to Orbital Dissection. (Illus.). 66p. 1975. pap. 8.75 (ISBN 0-398-03172-X). C C Thomas.
Mauss, Marcel. Sociology & Psychology: Essays. Brewster, Ben, tr. from Fr. 1979. 18.50x (ISBN 0-7100-8877-9). Routledge & Kegan.
Maust, Don. Bottle & Glass Handbook. (Illus.). 5.95 o.p. (ISBN 0-685-21843-0). Warman.
Maust, Don, ed. American Woodenware & Other Primitives. (Illus.). 1974. 8.95 o.p. (ISBN 0-685-49052-1). Warman.
Mautz, R. K., et al. Internal Control in U. S. Corporations: The State of the Art. LC 80-66623. 1980. 6.50 (ISBN 0-910586-33-0). Finan Exec.
Mautz, Robert K. Fundamentals of Auditing. 2nd ed. LC 64-20075. 1964. text ed. 22.95x o.p. (ISBN 0-471-57785-5); solutions avail. o.p. (ISBN 0-471-57817-7). Wiley.
Mavalwala, Jamshed. Dermatoglypics: An International Perspective. (World Anthropology Ser.). 1978. text ed. 47.00x (ISBN 90-279-7590-6). Mouton.
Maves, Mary C., jt. auth. see Maves, Paul B.
Maves, Paul B. Older Volunteers in Church & Community. 96p. 1981. pap. 6.95 (ISBN 0-8170-0889-6). Judson.
Maves, Paul B. & Maves, Mary C. Exploring How the Bible Came to Be. (Getting to Know Your Bible Ser). 128p. (Orig.). (gr. 4 up). 1973. pap. 1.75 (ISBN 0-687-12428-X). Abingdon.
Mavissakalian, Matig & Barlow, David H., eds. Phobia: Psychological and Pharmacological Treatment. 260p. 1981. 20.00 (ISBN 0-89862-602-1). Guilford Pr.
Mavrakis, Kostas. On Trotskyism. 280p. (Orig.). 1976. pap. 16.00 (ISBN 0-7100-8277-0). Routledge & Kegan.
Mawardi, Betty H. Physicians & Their Careers. LC 79-25421. 524p. (Orig.). 1980. 38.25 (ISBN 0-8357-0497-1, SS-00130). Univ Microfilms.
Mawby, Janet. Writers & Politics in Modern Scandinavia. LC 78-18931. (Writers & Politics Ser.). 1979. 10.50x (ISBN 0-8419-0414-6); pap. text ed. 6.00x (ISBN 0-8419-0417-0). Holmes & Meier.
Mawby, Rob. Policing the City. 1979. text ed. 28.25x (ISBN 0-566-00277-9, Pub. by Gower Pub Co England). Renouf.
Mawdesley-Thomas, Lionel E., ed. see Zoological Society of London - 30th Symposium.
Mawson, C. O. Dictionary of Foreign Terms. rev. 2nd ed. Berlitz, Charles, ed. LC 74-12492. 384p. 1974. 9.95 o.s.i. (ISBN 0-690-00171-1, TYC-T). T Y Crowell.
Mawson, C. O., ed. see Roget, Peter M.
Max, Leslie. Barney's Picnic. (Play & Learn Shape Board Bks). 14p. (gr. k-3). 1981. bds. 2.95 comb bdg. (ISBN 0-89828-101-6, 6002, Ottenheimer Pubs Inc). Tuffy Bks.
--Dino's Happy & Sad Book. (Play & Learn Shape Board Bks). 14p. (gr. k-3). 1981. bds. 2.95 comb bdg. (ISBN 0-89828-103-2, 6004, Ottenheimer Pubs Inc). Tuffy Bks.
--Fred Flintstone's Counting Book. (Play & Learn Shape Board Bks). 14p. (gr. k-3). 1981. bds. 2.95 comb bdg. (ISBN 0-89828-100-8, 6001, Pub. by Ottenheimer Pubs Inc). Tuffy Bks.
--Huckleberry Hound Takes a Trip. (Play & Learn Shape Board Bks). 14p. (gr. k-3). 1981. bds. 2.95 comb-bdg. (ISBN 0-89828-105-9, 6006, Ottenheimer Pubs Inc). Tuffy Bks.
Max, Stefan. Dialogues et Situations. 2nd ed. 1979. cassettes 35.00 (ISBN 0-669-01788-4); cahier de travaux practiques 4.95 (ISBN 0-669-01788-4); cahier de travaux practiques 4.95 (ISBN 0-669-01907-0); cassettes 30.00 (ISBN 0-669-01908-9). Heath.
Maxcy, Spencer J. Educational Philosophy for the Future. LC 77-18479. 1978. pap. text ed. 10.00x (ISBN 0-8191-0420-5). U Pr of Amer.
Maxim, George. The Sourcebook: Activities to Enrich Programs for Infants & Young Children. 208p. 1980. pap. text ed. 11.95x (ISBN 0-534-00854-2). Wadsworth Pub.
--The Very Young: Guiding Children from Infancy Through the Early Years. 576p. 1980. text ed. 17.95x (ISBN 0-534-00820-8). Wadsworth Pub.
Maximoff, G. P., ed. see Bakunin, Mikhail A.
Maximov, Vladimir E., ed. Kontinent Three. LC 77-76282. 1978. pap. 3.95 o.p. (ISBN 0-385-12581-X, Anch). Doubleday.
Maxman, Jerrold S. A Good Night's Sleep: A Step-by-Step Program for Overcoming Insomnia & Other Sleep Problems. (Illus.). 1981. 14.95 (ISBN 0-393-01437-1). Norton.
Maxmen, Jerrold S. The Post-Physician Era: Medicine in the 21st Century. LC 76-2442. (Health, Medicine & Society Ser.). 1976. 24.50 (ISBN 0-471-57880-0, Pub. by Wiley-Interscience). Wiley.
Maxon, James C. Lake Mead-Hoover Dam: The Story Behind the Scenery. DenDooven, Gweneth R., ed. LC 79-87573. (Illus.). 1980. 7.95 (ISBN 0-916122-62-X); pap. 3.00 (ISBN 0-916122-61-1). K C Pubns.
Maxon, John, et al, eds. Museum Studies. (Museum Studies Ser.). (Orig.). pap. 5.00 ea.; No. 1. (ISBN 0-86559-006-0); No. 2. (ISBN 0-86559-007-9); No. 3. (ISBN 0-86559-009-5); No. 4. (ISBN 0-86559-010-9); No.5. (ISBN 0-86559-011-7); No. 6. (ISBN 0-86559-012-5); No. 7. (ISBN 0-86559-013-3). Art Inst Chi.
--Museum Studies, 1-9. (Museum Studies Ser.). (Orig.). pap. 5.00 ea; No. 8. (ISBN 0-86559-018-4); No. 9. (ISBN 0-86559-027-3). Art Inst Chi.
Maxson, Eva. Mountain to Climb. LC 75-30319. (Desting Ser.). 1976. pap. 4.95 (ISBN 0-8163-0223-5, 13685-3). Pacific Pr Pub Assn.
Maxson, J. Robin, jt. auth. see Friesen, Garry.
Maxton, Hugh. The Noise of the Fields. 1976. pap. text ed. 5.00x (ISBN 0-85105-294-0, Dolmen Pr). Humanities.
Maxtone-Graham, John. Dark Brown Is the River. LC 75-42365. 375p. 1976. 9.95 o.s.i. (ISBN 0-02-582360-4, 58236). Macmillan.
--The Only Way to Cross. (Illus.). 480p. 1972. 15.95 (ISBN 0-02-582350-7). Macmillan.
Maxwell. Reading Progress from Eight to Fifteen. 1977. pap. text ed. 18.75x (ISBN 0-85633-120-1, NFER). Humanities.
Maxwell, A., jt. auth. see Tinkle, L.
Maxwell, A. E. Multivariate Analysis in Behavioral Research. LC 76-25110. 164p. 1977. pap. text ed. 13.95x o.p. (ISBN 0-412-14300-3, Pub. by Chapman & Hall). Methuen Inc.
--Multivariate Analysis in Behavioral Research. LC 76-25110. 1977. pap. text ed. 13.95 o.p. (ISBN 0-470-98902-5). Halsted Pr.
Maxwell, A. E. & Ruud, Ivar. The Year-Long Day: One Man's Arctic. LC 75-40412. (Illus.). 1976. 8.95 o.p. (ISBN 0-397-01131-8). Lippincott.
Maxwell, A. Graham. Can God Be Trusted? LC 77-10550. 1977. pap. 1.95 (ISBN 0-8127-0155-0). Southern Pub.
Maxwell, A. K., et al. Faber's Anatomical Atlas for Nurses & Students. 1962. pap. text ed. 5.95 (ISBN 0-571-06461-2, Pub. by Faber & Faber). Merrimack Bk Serv.
Maxwell, Daphne, ed. see Reid, Tim.
Maxwell, David. The Exhibit Medium: Theory & Practice of Trade Show Participation. (Illus.). 144p. 1978. 24.95 (ISBN 0-89047-030-8). Herman Pub.
Maxwell, Desmond E. Poetry of T. S. Eliot. (Orig.). 1970. pap. text ed. 2.00x o.p. (ISBN 0-7100-4602-2). Humanities.
Maxwell, E. A. Geometry by Transformations. LC 74-76568. (School Mathematics Project Handbook Ser). (Illus.). 200p. 1974. 42.00 (ISBN 0-521-20405-4); pap. 13.95x (ISBN 0-521-29125-9). Cambridge U Pr.
Maxwell, Edith. Game of Truth. (YA) (gr. 7-9). 1977. pap. 1.75 (ISBN 0-671-56004-2). PB.
--Just Dial a Number. (gr. 7-9). 1972. pap. 1.95 (ISBN 0-671-42891-8). Archway.
--Just Dial a Number. (YA) (gr. 7-9). 1972. pap. 1.95 (ISBN 0-671-56103-0). PB.
Maxwell, Edwin A. Analytical Calculus, 4 vols. 1954. Vol. 1. 14.50x (ISBN 0-521-05696-9); Vol. 2. 21.50x (ISBN 0-521-05697-7); Vol. 3. 16.95x (ISBN 0-521-05698-5); Vol. 4. 21.95x (ISBN 0-521-05699-3). Cambridge U Pr.
--Fallacies in Mathematics. 1959. 12.95 (ISBN 0-521-05700-0). Cambridge U Pr.
--Gateway to Abstract Mathematics. 11.95 (ISBN 0-521-05701-9). Cambridge U Pr.
Maxwell, Harvey C. Bowls: The American Lawn Bowler's Guide. 4th rev. enl. ed. (Illus.). 1976. lib. bdg. 5.95 imitation leather (ISBN 0-685-64304-2). Am Lawn Bowlers.
Maxwell, J. C., ed. see Wordsworth, William.
Maxwell, J. R., jt. ed. see Douglas, A G.
Maxwell, James A. & Aronson, J. Richard. Financing State & Local Governments. 3rd ed. LC 76-54871. (Studies of Government Finance). 1977. 14.95 (ISBN 0-8157-5512-0); pap. 5.95 (ISBN 0-8157-5511-2). Brookings.
Maxwell, James C. Electricity & Magnetism, 2 Vols. (Illus.). 1891. pap. text ed. 6.50 ea.; Vol. 1. pap. text ed. (ISBN 0-486-60636-8); Vol. 2. pap. text ed. (ISBN 0-486-60637-6). Dover.
Maxwell, Jessica. The Eye-Body Connection. (Illus., Orig.). 1980. pap. 6.95 (ISBN 0-446-87950-9). Warner Bks.
Maxwell, John A. Rock & Mineral Analysis. LC 68-29396. (Chemical Analysis Ser: Vol. 27). 1968. 45.00 (ISBN 0-471-57900-9, Pub. by Wiley-Interscience). Wiley.
Maxwell, John A., jt. auth. see Johnson, Wesley M.
Maxwell, Joseph R., Sr. Pyramiding in the Futures Market. (Illus.). Date not set. pap. 13.25 cancelled (ISBN 0-917832-17-5). Speer Bks.
Maxwell, Lawrence. Mightiest Lover of All. (Uplook Ser.). 1978. pap. 0.75 (ISBN 0-8163-0090-9, 13494-0). Pacific Pr Pub Assn.
--Pathfinder Field Guide. rev. ed. 1980. 6.95 (ISBN 0-8280-0053-0, 16070-5); pap. 4.95 (ISBN 0-686-62242-1, 16071-3). Review & Herald.
Maxwell, Lee M. & Reed, Myril B. The Theory of Graphs: A Basis for Network Theory. LC 77-106387. 181p. 1975. 16.00 (ISBN 0-08-016321-1). Pergamon.
Maxwell, Leigh. My God! Maiwand. (Illus.). 1979. 15.00 (ISBN 0-85052-247-1, Cooper). Shoe String.
Maxwell, Margaret. Handbook for AACR2. 700p. 1980. pap. text ed. 20.00 (ISBN 0-8389-0301-0). ALA.
Maxwell, Mervyn. Tell It to the World. LC 76-6619. 1976. 7.95 (ISBN 0-8163-0217-0, 20077-4). Pacific Pr Pub Assn.
Maxwell, Morton H. & Kleeman, Charles R. Clinical Disorders of Fluid & Electrolyte Metabolism. 2nd ed. (Illus.). 1972. text ed. 60.00 o.p. (ISBN 0-07-040993-5, HP). McGraw.
Maxwell, Neal A. The Smallest Part. LC 73-87240. 104p. 1973. 4.95 o.p. (ISBN 0-87747-505-9). Deseret Bk.
Maxwell, Neville. China's Road to Development. 1976. pap. text ed. 20.00 o.p. (ISBN 0-08-019979-8). Pergamon.
--China's Road to Development. 2nd ed. 1979. text ed. 55.00 (ISBN 0-08-023140-3); pap. text ed. 12.75 (ISBN 0-08-023139-X). Pergamon.

--India & the Nagas. (Minority Rights Group: No. 17). 1973. pap. 2.50 (ISBN 0-89192-103-6). Interbk Inc.

Maxwell, Nicole. Witch Doctor's Apprentice. (Illus.). 288p. 1975. pap. 1.95 o.s.i. (ISBN 0-02-096020-4, Collier). Macmillan.

Maxwell, Patricia. Bride of a Stranger. 1978. pap. 1.50 o.p. (ISBN 0-449-13818-6, GM). Fawcett.

--How to Become a Christian & Stay One. LC 79-4603. (Waymark Ser.). 1979. pap. 1.25 (ISBN 0-8127-0221-2). Southern Pub.

--The Notorious Angel. 1977. pap. 1.95 o.p. (ISBN 0-449-13825-9, GM). Fawcett.

--Sweet Piracy. 1978. pap. 1.95 o.p. (ISBN 0-449-13990-5, GM). Fawcett.

Maxwell, R. A. The Big Bend of the Rio Grande: A Guide to the Rocks, Landscape, Geologic History & Settlers of the Area of Big Bend National Park. (Illus.). 138p. 1968. Repr. 3.00 (GB 7). Bur Econ Geology.

--Geologic & Historic Guide to the State Parks of Texas. (Illus.). 197p. 1973. Repr. of 1970 ed. 3.00 (GB 10). Bur Econ Geology.

--Mineral Resources of South Texas: Region Served Through the Port of Corpus Christi. (Illus.). 140p. 1962. 3.50 (RI 43). Bur Econ Geology.

Maxwell, Robert. Health & Wealth: An International Study of Health-Care Spending. LC 80-8472. 1981. 22.95 (ISBN 0-669-04109-2). Lexington Bks.

Maxwell, Stephen, jt. auth. see Archer, Clive.

Maxwell, W. & Unger. Printmaking: A Beginning Handbook. 1977. 18.95 (ISBN 0-13-710699-8, Spec); pap. 9.95 (ISBN 0-13-710681-5, Spec). P-H.

Maxwell, William. The Folded Leaf. LC 80-67031. 288p. 1980. pap. 7.50 (ISBN 0-87923-351-6, Nonpareil Bks). Godine.

--So Long, See You Tomorrow. 160p. 1981. pap. 2.95 (ISBN 0-345-29194-8). Ballantine.

--So Long, See You Tomorrow. 1980. lib. bdg. 10.95 (ISBN 0-8161-3093-0, Large Print Bks). G K Hall.

Maxwell, William, jt. auth. see Pratt, Charles.

Maxwell, William E. & Crain, Ernest. Texas Politics Today. 2nd ed. (Illus.). 585p. 1981. pap. text ed. 8.76 (ISBN 0-8299-0395-X). West Pub.

--Texas Politics Today. (Illus.). 1978. pap. text ed. 10.95 (ISBN 0-8299-0216-3); instrs.' manual avail. (ISBN 0-8299-0556-1). West Pub.

Maxwell, William H. Erin-Go-Bragh or Irish Life Pictures. Wolff, Robert L., ed. (Ireland Nineteenth Century Fiction Ser. Two: Vol. 52). 742p. 1979. lib. bdg. 32.00 (ISBN 0-8240-3501-1). Garland Pub.

--The Fortunes of Hector O'halloran & His Man, Mark Anthony O'toole. Wolff, Robert L., ed. (Ireland Nineteenth Century Fiction - Ser. Two: Vol. 51). 416p. 1979. lib. bdg. 32.00 (ISBN 0-8240-3500-3). Garland Pub.

--O'Hara - or Seventeen Ninety-Eight. Wolff, Robert E., ed. (Ireland Nineteenth Century Fiction - Ser. Two: Vol. 50). 610p. 1979. lib. bdg. 32.00 (ISBN 0-8240-3499-6). Garland Pub.

Maxwell-Cook, John C. Structural Notes & Details. (C & CA Viewpoint Publication Ser.). (Illus.). 1976. text ed. 20.00 (ISBN 0-7210-1006-7). Scholium Intl.

Maxwell-Lefroy, C. Land & People of Burma. (gr. 5-9). 1965. 3.95g o.s.i. (ISBN 0-02-765330-7). Macmillan.

May. Tropical Fish: Their Care & Breeding. (Illus.). 96p. 1981. 3.95 (ISBN 0-903264-23-4, 5216-3, Pub. by K & R Bks England). Arco.

May, jt. auth. see Bird.

May, Allan. A Voice in the Wilderness. LC 77-28519. (Illus.). 1978. 12.95 (ISBN 0-88229-309-5); pap. 6.95 (ISBN 0-88229-605-1). Nelson-Hall.

May, Arthur J. Passing of the Hapsburg Monarchy, 1914-1918, 2 Vols. LC 64-22874. 1966. 20.00 o.p. (ISBN 0-8122-7463-6). U of Pa Pr.

May, Brian. The Indonesian Tragedy. (Illus.). 1978. 27.50x (ISBN 0-7100-8834-5). Routledge & Kegan.

--The Third World Calamity. (Illus.). 272p. 1981. price not set (ISBN 0-7100-0764-7). Routledge & Kegan.

May, C. Lowell, jt. auth. see Hickler, Holly.

May, Charles E., ed. Short Story Theories. LC 75-36982. xiv, 251p. 1976. 13.00x (ISBN 0-8214-0189-0); pap. 5.95x (ISBN 0-8214-0221-8). Ohio U Pr.

May, Charles P. James Clerk Maxwell & Electromagnetism. (Biography Ser). (Illus.). (gr. 7 up). 1962. PLB 5.90 o.p. (ISBN 0-531-00902-5). Watts.

--Oceania: Polynesia, Melanesia, Micronesia. LC 72-13152. (World Neighbors Ser.). (Illus.). 224p. (gr. 6 up). 1973. 7.95 o.p. (ISBN 0-525-67068-8). Elsevier-Nelson.

--Publishing Careers: Books & Magazines. (Career Concise Guides Ser.). (Illus.). (gr. 7 up). 1978. PLB 6.45 s&l (ISBN 0-531-01422-3). Watts.

May, Cheryl. Cattle Management. 350p. 1981. text ed. 16.95 (ISBN 0-8359-0721-X); instr's. manual free. Reston.

May, Clayton A., ed. Resins for Aerospace. LC 80-15342. (ACS Symposium Ser.: No. 132). 1980. 48.00 (ISBN 0-8412-0567-1). Am Chemical.

May, Derwent. A Revenger's Comedy. 191p. 1981. 10.95 (ISBN 0-7011-2461-X, Pub. by Chatto-Bodley-Jonathan). Merrimack Bk Serv.

May, Elizabeth. T.S.K.H. Tickle, Snug, Kiss, Hug. LC 77-70643. 1977. 10.00 (ISBN 0-8091-0226-9); pap. 6.95 (ISBN 0-8091-2022-4). Paulist Pr.

May, Elizabeth, ed. Musics of Many Cultures: An Introduction. 1981. 50.00x (ISBN 0-520-03393-0). U of Cal Pr.

May, Elizabeth E., et al. Independent Living for the Handicapped & the Elderly. 1974. text ed. 17.95 (ISBN 0-395-18108-9). HM.

May, Ernest R. Boom & Bust, 1917-1932. LC 63-8572. (Life History of the United States). (Illus.). (gr. 5 up). 1974. PLB 9.96 (ISBN 0-8094-0559-8, Pub. by Time-Life). Silver.

--Lessons of the Past: The Use & Misuse of History in American Foreign Policy. 224p. 1973. 12.95 (ISBN 0-19-501698-X). Oxford U Pr.

--The Progressive Era, 1901-1917. LC 63-8572. (Life History of the United States). (Illus.). (gr. 5 up). 1974. PLB 9.96 (ISBN 0-8094-0558-X, Pub. by Time-Life). Silver.

May, Ernest R. & Fraser, Janet. Campaign Seventy-Two: The Managers Speak. LC 73-85182. 318p. 1974. 10.00 (ISBN 0-674-09141-8); pap. 4.95 (ISBN 0-674-09143-4). Harvard U Pr.

May, Eydie & Hunsberger, Arn. Diet the Natural Way. LC 77-75938. (Orig.). 1980. pap. cancelled (ISBN 0-89081-067-2). Harvest Hse.

May, Florence L. Hispanic Lace & Lacemaking. 1980. 12.00 (ISBN 0-87535-048-8). Hispanic Soc.

May, Frank B. To Help Children Communicate. (Elementary Education Ser.: No. C22). 472p. 1980. pap. text ed. 14.95 (ISBN 0-675-08197-1). Merrill.

May, Frank B. & Eliot, Susan B. To Help Children Read. 2nd ed. (Elementary Education Ser.). 1978. pap. text ed. 14.95 (ISBN 0-675-08370-2); instructor's manual 3.95 (ISBN 0-685-86843-5). Merrill.

May, Gary. China Scapegoat: The Diplomatic Ordeal of John Carter Vincent. LC 79-4129. (Illus.). 1979. 15.95 o.p. (ISBN 0-915220-49-0). New Republic.

May, George. Doctor's Secret Journal. (Illus.). 1960. pap. 1.50 (ISBN 0-911872-30-2). Mackinac Island.

--War Eighteen Twelve. (Illus.). 43p. (Orig.). 1962. pap. 1.50 (ISBN 0-911872-28-0). Mackinac Island.

May, George O. Financial Accounting: A Distillation of Experience. 1972. Repr. of 1943 ed. text ed. 13.00 (ISBN 0-914348-05-1). Scholars Bk.

--Twenty-Five Years of Accounting Responsibility 1911-1936, Vols. I & II. Hunt, Carleton, ed. 1971. Repr. of 1936 ed. text ed. 26.00 (ISBN 0-914348-03-5). Scholars Bk.

May, George W. Down Illinois Rivers. (Illus.). 400p. 1981. 16.00 (ISBN 0-9605566-5-6). G W May.

May, Georges. D'Ovid a Racine. (Yale Romanic Studies). 1949. pap. 27.50x (ISBN 0-685-69841-6). Elliots Bks.

May, Gita. Madame Rolland & the Age of Revolution. LC 70-108418. (Illus.). 1970. 20.00x (ISBN 0-231-03379-6). Columbia U Pr.

--Stendhal & the Age of Napoleon: An Interpretive Biography. LC 77-8379. 1977. 20.00x (ISBN 0-231-04344-9). Columbia U Pr.

May, Harriett J. Enterostomal Therapy. LC 76-19894. 1977. pap. 13.00 (ISBN 0-89004-144-X). Raven.

May, Harry S. Francisco Franco: The Jewish Connection. 1978. pap. text ed. 9.00x (ISBN 0-8191-0363-2). U Pr of Amer.

May, Henry F. The Enlightenment in America. LC 75-32349. 1976. 24.95 (ISBN 0-19-502018-9). Oxford U Pr.

--The Enlightenment in America. LC 75-32349. 1978. pap. 6.95 (ISBN 0-19-502367-6, GB529, GB). Oxford U Pr.

May, Irvin M., Jr. Marvin Jones: The Public Life of an Agrarian Advocate. LC 79-5282. (The Centennial Series of the Association of Former Students: No. 8). (Illus.). 312p. 1980. 22.95x (ISBN 0-89096-093-3). Tex A&M Univ Pr.

May, J. Peter. Classifying Spaces & Fibrations. (Memoirs: No. 155). 98p. 1980. pap. 5.60 (ISBN 0-8218-1855-4, MEMO-155). Am Math.

May, Jacques M. Ecology of Human Disease. LC 58-13432. 1958. 7.50 o.p. (ISBN 0-910922-11-X). MD Pubns.

May, James D. Avant-Garde Choral Music: An Annotated Selected Bibliography. LC 76-30577. 1977. 12.00 (ISBN 0-8108-1015-8). Scarecrow.

May, Janice C. The Texas Constitutional Revision Experience in the 70's. LC 75-26954. (Orig.). 1975. 8.95 o.p. (ISBN 0-88408-027-7). Sterling Swift.

May, Janis S. The Avenging Maid. (Orig.). 1980. pap. 1.50 o.s.i. (ISBN 0-440-10329-0). Dell.

May, John R. The Pruning Word: The Parables of Flannery O'Connor. LC 75-19878. 216p. 1976. text ed. 10.95x o.p. (ISBN 0-268-01518-X). U of Notre Dame Pr.

May, Judy G. Scuba Diver's Guide to Underwater Ventures. LC 73-9949. (Illus.). 192p. 1973. pap. 3.95 o.p. (ISBN 0-8117-2017-9). Stackpole.

May, Julian. A. J. Foyt: Championship Auto Racer. LC 75-28934. (Sports Close-up Ser.). (gr. 3-9). 1975. PLB 5.95 o.p. (ISBN 0-913940-33-X); pap. 2.95 o.p. (ISBN 0-913940-99-2). Crestwood Hse.

--Antarctic: Bottom of the World. Publication Associates, ed. LC 79-156054. (Investigating the Earth Ser). (Illus.). (gr. 4-6). 1972. PLB 5.95 o.p. (ISBN 0-87191-058-6). Creative Ed.

--Arctic: Top of the World. Publication Associates, ed. LC 75-156053. (Investigating the Earth Ser). (Illus.). (gr. 4-6). 1971. PLB 5.95 o.p. (ISBN 0-87191-057-8). Creative Ed.

--Arthur Ashe: World Tennis Champion. LC 75-28932. (Sports Close-up Ser.). (gr. 3-9). 1975. PLB 5.95 o.p. (ISBN 0-913940-31-3); pap. 2.95 o.p. (ISBN 0-913940-98-4). Crestwood Hse.

--Baltimore Colts. LC 74-988. (Superbowl Champions Ser). 48p. 1974. PLB 6.45 (ISBN 0-87191-331-3); pap. 2.95 (ISBN 0-89812-084-5). Creative Ed.

--The Baltimore Colts. (The NFL Today Ser.). (gr. 4-8). 1980. lib. bdg. 6.45 (ISBN 0-87191-728-9); pap. 2.95 (ISBN 0-89812-231-7). Creative Ed.

--Billie Jean King: Tennis Champion. LC 74-82744. (Sports Close-up Ser.). (gr. 3-5). 1974. PLB 5.95 o.p. (ISBN 0-913940-09-7); pap. 2.50 o.p. (ISBN 0-913940-97-6). Crestwood Hse.

--Boxing's Heavyweight Championship. LC 76-4861. (Sports Classics Ser.). (Illus.). (gr. 4-12). 1976. PLB 8.95 o.p. (ISBN 0-87191-503-0). Creative Ed.

--Chris Evert: Princess of Tennis. LC 75-28936. (Sports Close-up Ser.). (gr. 3-9). 1975. PLB 5.95 o.p. (ISBN 0-913940-35-6); pap. 2.50 o.p. (ISBN 0-89686-001-9). Crestwood Hse.

--The Cincinnati Bengals. (NFL Today Ser.). (gr. 4-8). 1980. PLB 6.45 (ISBN 0-87191-734-3); pap. 2.95 (ISBN 0-89812-237-6). Creative Ed.

--Cloud Book. Publication Associates, ed. LC 76-156056. (Investigating the Earth Ser). (Illus.). (gr. 4-6). 1972. PLB 5.95 o.p. (ISBN 0-87191-064-0). Creative Ed.

--Dallas Cowboys. LC 74-3241. (Superbowl Champions Ser). 48p. 1974. PLB 6.45 (ISBN 0-87191-327-5); pap. 2.95 (ISBN 0-89812-085-3). Creative Ed.

--The Dallas Cowboys. (NFL Today Ser.). (gr. 4-8). 1980. PLB 6.45 (ISBN 0-87191-730-0); pap. 2.95 (ISBN 0-89812-233-3). Creative Ed.

--The Daytona Five-Hundred. LC 76-8443. (Sports Classics Ser.). (Illus.). (gr. 4-12). 1976. PLB 8.95 o.p. (ISBN 0-87191-522-7). Creative Ed.

--The Denver Broncos. (The NFL Today Ser.). (gr. 4-8). 1980. lib. bdg. 6.45 (ISBN 0-87191-732-7); pap. 2.95 (ISBN 0-89812-235-X). Creative Ed.

--Deserts: Hot & Cold. Publication Associates, ed. LC 71-156052. (Investigating the Earth Ser). (Illus.). (gr. 4-6). 1971. PLB 5.95 o.p. (ISBN 0-87191-056-X). Creative Ed.

--Dodos & Dinosaurs Are Extinct. Publication Associates, ed. LC 73-104925. (gr. 2-4). 1970. PLB 6.95 o.p. (ISBN 0-87191-038-1). Creative Ed.

--The First Living Things. LC 79-119799. (Illus.). (gr. k-3). 1970. reinforced bdg. 4.50 o.p. (ISBN 0-8234-0177-4). Holiday.

--Fran Tarkenton: Scrambling Quarterback. LC 73-80423. (Sports Close-up Ser.). (gr. 3-9). 1973. PLB 5.95 o.p. (ISBN 0-913940-03-8); pap. 2.95 o.p. (ISBN 0-913940-96-8). Crestwood Hse.

--Frank Robinson: Slugging Toward Glory. LC 74-31949. (Sports Close-up Ser.). (gr. 3-9). 1975. PLB 5.95 o.p. (ISBN 0-913940-14-3); pap. 2.95 o.p. (ISBN 0-913940-21-6). Crestwood Hse.

--The Grand Prix World Championship. LC 76-5460. (Sports Classics Ser.). (Illus.). (gr. 4-12). 1976. PLB 8.95 o.p. (ISBN 0-87191-506-5). Creative Ed.

--Green Bay Packers. LC 74-905. (Superbowl Champions Ser). 48p. 1974. 6.45 (ISBN 0-87191-330-5); pap. 2.95 (ISBN 0-89812-086-1). Creative Ed.

--The Green Bay Packers. (The NFL Today Ser.). (gr. 4-8). 1980. lib. bdg. 6.45 (ISBN 0-87191-727-0); pap. 2.95 (ISBN 0-89812-230-9). Creative Ed.

--Hillary & Tenzing: Conquerors of Mt. Everest. LC 72-85045. 40p. (gr. 2-5). 1972. PLB 5.90 (ISBN 0-87191-219-8). Creative Ed.

--Indianapolis Five Hundred. LC 75-8502. (Sports Classics Ser.). (Illus.). 48p. (gr. 4-6). 1975. PLB 8.95 o.p. (ISBN 0-87191-441-7). Creative Ed.

--Joe Namath: High-Flying Quarterback. LC 74-31946. (Sports Close-up Ser.). (gr. 3-9). 1975. PLB 5.95 o.p. (ISBN 0-913940-17-8); pap. 2.50 o.p. (ISBN 0-913940-24-0). Crestwood Hse.

--Johnny Unitas: And the Long Pass. LC 72-77302. (Sports Close-Up Ser.). (gr. 3-9). 1972. PLB 5.95 o.p. (ISBN 0-87191-200-7); pap. 2.50 o.p. (ISBN 0-685-64985-7). Crestwood Hse.

--Kansas City Chiefs. LC 74-2301. (Superbowl Champions Ser). 48p. 1974. PLB 6.45 (ISBN 0-87191-353-4); pap. 2.95 (ISBN 0-89812-087-X). Creative Ed.

--The Kansas City Chiefs. (The NFL Today Ser.). (gr. 4-8). 1980. lib. bdg. 6.45 (ISBN 0-87191-729-7); pap. 2.95 (ISBN 0-89812-232-5). Creative Ed.

--Kentucky Derby. LC 75-6976. (Sports Classics Ser.). (Illus.). 48p. (gr. 4-6). 1975. PLB 8.95 o.p. (ISBN 0-87191-442-5). Creative Ed.

--Life Cycle of a Fox. LC 73-1224. (Illus.). (gr. 2-4). 1973. PLB 4.95 o.p. (ISBN 0-87191-238-4). Creative Ed.

--Life Cycle of a Moth. LC 73-1059. (Illus.). (gr. 2-4). 1973. PLB 4.95 o.p. (ISBN 0-87191-236-8). Creative Ed.

--Life Cycle of a Rabbit. LC 73-1185. (Illus.). (gr. 2-4). 1973. PLB 4.95 o.p. (ISBN 0-87191-237-6). Creative Ed.

--Life Cycle of a Raccoon. LC 73-1187. (Illus.). (gr. 2-4). 1973. PLB 4.95 o.p. (ISBN 0-87191-234-1). Creative Ed.

--Life Cycle of a Turtle. LC 73-1061. (Illus.). (gr. 2-4). 1973. PLB 4.95 o.p. (ISBN 0-87191-239-2). Creative Ed.

--Life Cycle of an Opossum. LC 73-1225. (Illus.). (gr. 2-4). 1973. PLB 4.95 o.p. (ISBN 0-87191-235-X). Creative Ed.

--Los Angeles Rams. (The NFL Today). (Illus.). (gr. 3-6). 1977. PLB 6.45 (ISBN 0-87191-596-0); pap. 2.95 (ISBN 0-686-67473-1). Creative Ed.

--The Many-Colored Land. (Saga of Pliocene Exile Ser.). 432p. 1981. 12.95 (ISBN 0-686-69053-2). HM.

--Matthew Henson: Co-Discoverer of the North Pole. LC 72-85038. 40p. (gr. 4-8). 1972. PLB 5.95 o.p. (ISBN 0-87191-218-X). Creative Ed.

--Miami Dolphins. LC 74-4139. (Superbowl Champions Ser). 48p. 1974. PLB 6.45 (ISBN 0-87191-328-3); pap. 2.95 (ISBN 0-89812-088-8). Creative Ed.

--The Miami Dolphins. (The NFL Today Ser.). (gr. 4-8). 1980. lib. bdg. 6.45 (ISBN 0-87191-725-4); pap. 2.95 (ISBN 0-89812-228-7). Creative Ed.

--Mickey Mantle: Slugs It Out. LC 72-77303. (Sports Close-up Ser.). (gr. 3-9). 1972. PLB 5.95 o.p. (ISBN 0-87191-202-3); pap. 2.95 o.p. (ISBN 0-686-67382-4). Crestwood Hse.

--Minnesota Vikings. (The NFL Today). (Illus.). (gr. 3-6). 1977. PLB 6.45 (ISBN 0-87191-594-4); pap. 2.95 (ISBN 0-686-67477-4). Creative Ed.

--Muhammad Ali: Boxing Superstar. LC 74-31948. (Sports Close-up Ser.). (gr. 3-9). 1975. PLB 5.95 o.p. (ISBN 0-913940-15-1); pap. 2.50 o.p. (ISBN 0-913940-22-4). Crestwood Hse.

--New York Giants. (The NFL Today). (Illus.). (gr. 3-6). 1977. PLB 6.45 (ISBN 0-87191-598-7); pap. 2.95 (ISBN 0-686-67476-6). Creative Ed.

--New York Jets. LC 74-908. (Superbowl Champions Ser). 48p. 1974. PLB 6.45 (ISBN 0-87191-329-1); pap. 2.95 (ISBN 0-89812-089-6). Creative Ed.

--The New York Jets. (The NFL Today Ser.). (gr. 4-8). 1980. PLB 6.45 (ISBN 0-87191-726-2); pap. 2.95 (ISBN 0-89812-229-5). Creative Ed.

--O. J. Simpson: Juice on the Gridiron. LC 74-82745. (Sports Close-up Ser.). (Illus.). (gr. 3-5). 1974. PLB 5.95 o.p. (ISBN 0-913940-10-0); pap. 2.50 o.p. (ISBN 0-913940-72-0). Crestwood Hse.

--Oakland Raiders. (The NFL Today). (Illus.). (gr. 3-6). 1977. PLB 6.45 (ISBN 0-87191-595-2); pap. 2.95 (ISBN 0-686-67475-8). Creative Ed.

--The Oakland Raiders Super Bowl Champions. (Super Bowl Champions Ser.). (Illus.). (gr. 3-9). 1978. PLB 6.45 (ISBN 0-87191-614-2); pap. 2.95 (ISBN 0-89812-091-8). Creative Ed.

--The Olympics. LC 75-8755. (Sports Classics Ser.). (Illus.). 48p. (gr. 4-6). 1975. PLB 8.95 o.p. (ISBN 0-87191-453-0). Creative Ed.

--Pele: World Soccer Star. LC 75-28935. (Sports Close-up Ser.). (gr. 3-9). 1975. PLB 5.95 o.p. (ISBN 0-913940-34-8); pap. 2.95 o.p. (ISBN 0-89686-000-0). Crestwood Hse.

--Phil Esposito: The Big Bruin. LC 74-31950. (Sports Close-up Ser.). (gr. 3-9). 1975. PLB 5.95 o.p. (ISBN 0-913940-13-5); pap. 2.50 o.p. (ISBN 0-913940-20-8). Crestwood Hse.

--The Pittsburgh Steelers. (NFL Today Ser.). (gr. 4-8). 1980. PLB 6.45 (ISBN 0-87191-731-9); pap. 2.95 (ISBN 0-89812-234-1). Creative Ed.

--Pittsburgh Steelers. (Super Bowl Champions Ser.). (Illus.). (gr. 3-8). 1977. PLB 6.45 (ISBN 0-87191-454-9); pap. 2.95 (ISBN 0-89812-090-X). Creative Ed.

--Prairie Has an Endless Sky. Publication Associates, ed. LC 75-156061. (Investigating the Earth Ser). (Illus.). (gr. 4-8). 1972. PLB 5.95 o.p. (ISBN 0-87191-062-4). Creative Ed.

--Quanah: Leader of the Comanche. LC 72-14173. 40p. (gr. 2-5). 1973. PLB 5.95 o.p. (ISBN 0-87191-227-9). Creative Ed.

--Rainbows, Frost & Foggy Dew. Publication Associates, ed. LC 73-156058. (Investigating the Earth Ser). (Illus.). (gr. 4-8). 1972. PLB 5.95 o.p. (ISBN 0-87191-066-7). Creative Ed.

--Reptiles We Know. LC 73-4908. (Illus.). (gr. 2-4). 1973. PLB 5.95 o.p. (ISBN 0-87191-245-7). Creative Ed.

--The Rose Bowl. LC 76-8459. (Sports Classics Ser.). (Illus.). (gr. 4-12). 1976. PLB 8.95 o.p. (ISBN 0-87191-521-9). Creative Ed.

--The San Diego Chargers. (The NFL Today Ser.). (gr. 4-8). 1980. PLB 6.45 (ISBN 0-87191-733-5); pap. 2.95 (ISBN 0-89812-236-8). Creative Ed.

--San Francisco Forty Nine'ers. (The NFL Today). (Illus.). (gr. 3-6). 1977. PLB 6.45 (ISBN 0-87191-599-5); pap. 2.95 (ISBN 0-686-67474-X). Creative Ed.

--Sitting Bull: War Chief of the Sioux. LC 72-89462. 40p. (gr. 2-5). 1972. PLB 5.95 (ISBN 0-87191-221-X). Creative Ed.

--Snowfall. LC 70-156057. (Investigating the Earth Ser). (Illus.). (gr. 4-8). 1972. PLB 5.95 o.p. (ISBN 0-87191-065-9). Creative Ed.

--Superbowl. LC 75-5855. (Sports Classics Ser.). (Illus.). 48p. (gr. 4-6). 1975. PLB 8.95 o.p. (ISBN 0-87191-446-8). Creative Ed.

--They Turned to Stone. (Illus.). 40p. (gr. k-3). 1965. reinforced bdg. 5.95 o.p. (ISBN 0-8234-0118-9). Holiday.

--Thor Heyerdahl: Modern Viking Adventurer. LC 72-85046. 40p. (gr. 2-5). 1973. PLB 5.75 o.p. (ISBN 0-87191-220-1). Creative Ed.

--Vince Lombardi: The Immortal Coach. LC 74-31947. (Sports Close-up Ser.). (gr. 3-9). 1975. PLB 5.95 o.p. (ISBN 0-913940-16-X); pap. 2.95 o.p. (ISBN 0-913940-23-2). Crestwood Hse.

--Washington Redskins. (The NFL Today). (Illus.). (gr. 3-6). 1977. PLB 6.45 (ISBN 0-87191-597-9); pap. 2.95 (ISBN 0-686-67472-3). Creative Ed.

--Weather. (Beginning Science Ser.). (Illus.). (gr. 2-4). 1966. PLB 5.97 o.p. (ISBN 0-695-89210-X). Follett.

--The Winter Olympics. LC 76-4860. (Sports Classics Ser.). (Illus.). (gr. 4-12). 1976. PLB 8.95 o.p. (ISBN 0-87191-504-9). Creative Ed.

--The World Series. LC 75-22387. (Sports Classics Ser.). (Illus.). 48p. (gr. 4-6). 1975. PLB 8.95 o.p. (ISBN 0-87191-447-6). Creative Ed.

May, Keith M. Aldous Huxley. 1972. text ed. 15.50x (ISBN 0-236-17682-X). Humanities.

May, Leland C. Parodies of the Gothic Novel. Varma, Devendra P., ed. LC 79-8464. (Gothic Studies & Dissertations Ser.). 1980. lib. bdg. 15.00x (ISBN 0-405-12654-9). Arno.

May, Lola J. Teaching Mathematics in the Elementary School. 2nd ed. LC 73-11694. (Illus.). 1974. 16.95 (ISBN 0-02-920380-5); pap. text ed. 10.95 (ISBN 0-02-920370-8). Free Pr.

May, Naomi. At Home. 1980. pap. 4.95. Riverrun NY.

--Troubles. 1979. 11.95 (ISBN 0-7145-3555-9); pap. 5.95 (ISBN 0-7145-3606-7). Riverrun NY.

May, Phil, jt. auth. see Brindle, Melbourne.

May, Phillip T. Programming Business Applications in Fortran IV. LC 72-7634. 1973. pap. text ed. 14.25 (ISBN 0-395-14047-1, 3-34905); solutions man. pap. 1.50 (ISBN 0-395-17159-8, 3-34906). HM.

May, Robert L. Rudolph the Red-Nosed Reindeer & Rudolph Shines Again. LC 64-21581. (Illus.). 1964. 5.95 o.p. (ISBN 0-695-87780-1). Follett.

May, Robert M., ed. see Cavalli-Sforza, L. L. & Feldman, M. W.

May, Rollo. Art of Counseling. (Series B). 1978. pap. 4.50 (ISBN 0-687-01766-1). Abingdon.

May, Rollo, ed. Symbolism in Religion & Literature. LC 59-8842. 6.95 o.s.i. (ISBN 0-8076-0115-2). Braziller.

May, Ron, jt. auth. see Barnes, Mark.

May, Thomas. The Tragoedy of Cleopatra Queene of Aegypt. Smith, Denzell S. & Orgel, Stephen, eds. LC 78-66784. (Renaissance Drama Ser.). 1979. lib. bdg. 35.00 (ISBN 0-8240-9732-7). Garland Pub.

May, William & Westley, Richard. The Right to Die. (Catholic Perspectives Ser.). 112p. 1980. pap. 3.95 (ISBN 0-88347-115-9). Thomas More.

Maya, Hugh B. The Irresistible Virgin: A Vision of Unrequited Love Within & Outside the Confines of a Closed World. (An Intimate Life of Man Library Book). (Illus.). 1979. 27.75 (ISBN 0-89266-199-2). Am Classical Coll Pr.

Mayakovsky, Vladimir. Bedbug & Selected Poetry. Blake, Patricia, ed. Hayward, Max & Reavey, George, trs. from Rus. LC 75-10805. (Midland Bks.: No. 189). 320p. 1975. 10.50x (ISBN 0-253-31130-6); pap. 3.95x (ISBN 0-253-20189-6). Ind U Pr.

--Wi the Haill Voice. Morgan, Edwin, tr. from Rus. (Translation Ser.). (Scots.). 1979. 6.95 o.s.i. (ISBN 0-902145-41-X, Pub. by Carcanet New Pr England). Persea Bks.

Mayakovsky, Vladimir & Brik, Lily. Enchained in Film. Segall, Helen, tr. (Illus.). 1981. 15.00x (ISBN 0-931556-01-5); pap. 6.50 (ISBN 0-931556-03-1). Translation Pr.

Mayall, J. & Navari, C., eds. The End of the Post-War Era: Documents on Great Power Relations, 1968-1975. LC 79-50512. 1980. 59.50 (ISBN 0-521-22698-8). Cambridge U Pr.

Mayall, M. W., jt. auth. see Mayall, R. N.

Mayall, R. N. & Mayall, M. W. Skyshooting: Photography for Amateur Astronomers. (Illus.). 7.50 (ISBN 0-8446-2553-1). Peter Smith.

Mayan, B., jt. auth. see Mattel, E.

Maybanks, Sheila & Bryce, Marvin. Home-Based Services for Children & Families: Policy, Practice, & Research. 384p. 1979. 22.50 (ISBN 0-398-03880-5). C C Thomas.

Maybaum, Ignaz. Happiness Outside the State. 128p. 1980. 25.00 (ISBN 0-85362-183-7). Routledge & Kegan.

Maybee, John & Greenberg, Harvey, eds. Computer-Assisted Analysis & Model Simplification. 1981. price not set (ISBN 0-12-480720-8). Acad Pr.

Mayberry, Claude, Jr., ed. Urban Education: The City As a Living Curriculum. LC 80-67288. (Orig.). 1980. pap. text ed. 6.50 (ISBN 0-87120-100-3, 611-80206). Assn Supervision.

Maybury, Anne. Falcon's Shadow. 1977. pap. 2.25 (ISBN 0-441-22583-7). Ace Bks.

Maybury, Barry. Creative Writing for Juniors. 1972. pap. 16.95 (ISBN 0-7134-3175-X, Pub. by Batsford England). David & Charles.

--Writer's Workshop: Techniques in Creative Writing. 1979. 17.95 (ISBN 0-7134-1557-6, Pub. by Batsford England). David & Charles.

Maybury-Lewis, David. Akwe-Shavante Society. (Illus.). 392p. 1974. pap. write for info. Oxford U Pr.

Maycock, Paul D. & Stirewalt, Edward N. Photovoltaics: Sunlight to Electricity in One Step. 224p. (Orig.). 1981. 19.95 (ISBN 0-931790-24-7); pap. 9.95 (ISBN 0-931790-17-4). Brick Hse Pub.

Mayeda, Wataru. Graph Theory. LC 70-37366. 704p. 1972. 43.50 (ISBN 0-471-57950-5, Pub. by Wiley-Interscience). Wiley.

Mayer. Capital Expenditure Analysis: For Managers & Engineers. LC 77-84052. 1978. text ed. 17.95x (ISBN 0-917974-12-3). Waveland Pr.

Mayer, A. M., et al. The Germination of Seeds. 2nd ed. Wareing, P. F. & Galston, A. W., eds. 160p. 1976. text ed. 30.00 (ISBN 0-08-018966-0); pap. text ed. 18.00 (ISBN 0-08-018965-2). Pergamon.

Mayer, Adrian C. Peasants in the Pacific: A Study of Fiji Indian Rural Society. 2nd, rev. ed. LC 72-91618. (Illus.). 1973. 18.50x (ISBN 0-520-02333-1). U of Cal Pr.

Mayer, Albert. Urgent Future: People, Housing, City Region. 1967. 27.50 o.p. (ISBN 0-07-040991-9, P&RB). McGraw.

Mayer, Albert I., Jr. Olympiad. LC 61-12875. (Illus.). (gr. 7-11). 1938. 8.50x (ISBN 0-8196-0115-2). Biblo.

Mayer, Ann M. Beatrix Potter. LC 74-2082. (People to Remember Ser.). 40p. 1974. 5.95 (ISBN 0-87191-324-0). Creative Ed.

--Dag Hammarskjold. LC 74-1498. (Personal Closeups Ser). 40p. 1974. 5.75 o.p. (ISBN 0-87191-322-4). Creative Ed.

--Sir Frederick Banting. LC 74-2048. (Personal Closeups Ser). 40p. (gr. 4-6). 1974. 5.75 o.p. (ISBN 0-87191-323-2). Creative Ed.

Mayer, Arno. The Persistence of the Old Regime: Europe to the Great War. 1981. 16.95 (ISBN 0-394-51141-7). Pantheon.

Mayer, Bernard W. Pediatric Anesthesia: A Guide to Its Administration. (Illus.). 192p. 1981. pap. text ed. 16.50 (ISBN 0-397-50478-0). Lippincott.

Mayer, Carl, jt. auth. see Meringer, Rudolf.

Mayer, D. H. The Ruelle-Araki Transfer Operator in Classical Statistical Mechanics. (Lecture Notes in Physics: Vol. 123). 154p. 1980. pap. 12.00 (ISBN 0-387-09990-5). Springer-Verlag.

Mayer, E. G. Diagnose und Differentialdiagnose in der Schaedelroentgenologie. (Ger, Eng, Span, Fr.). 1959. 147.50 (ISBN 0-387-80517-6). Springer-Verlag.

Mayer, Edward E., jt. auth. see Moore, Robin.

Mayer, Eve R. Let's Stay Lovers. 1981. 7.95 (ISBN 0-533-04917-2). Vantage.

Mayer, Gloria, jt. ed. see Ciske, Karen.

Mayer, Greta & Hoover, Mary. When Children Need Special Help with Emotional Problems. 55p. 1974. pap. 1.25 (ISBN 0-686-12281-X). Jewish Bd Family.

Mayer, Gustav. Friedrich Engels: A Biography. LC 68-9596. 1969. Repr. of 1936 ed. 22.00 (ISBN 0-86527-075-9). Fertig.

Mayer, Hans E. The Crusades. Gillingham, John, tr. from Ger. (Illus.). 336p. 1973. pap. text ed. 8.95x (ISBN 0-19-873016-0). Oxford U Pr.

Mayer, Harold M. & Wade, Richard C. Chicago: Growth of a Metropolis. LC 68-54054. (Illus.). 1969. 35.00 (ISBN 0-226-51273-8). U of Chicago Pr.

--Chicago: Growth of a Metropolis. LC 68-54054. (Illus.). 1973. pap. 12.50 (ISBN 0-226-51274-6, P546, Phoen). U of Chicago Pr.

Mayer, Harold M. & Kohn, Clyde F., eds. Readings in Urban Geography. LC 59-11973. (Illus.). 1959. 12.50x (ISBN 0-226-51270-3). U of Chicago Pr.

Mayer, Herbert. Books of the New Testament. LC 69-12766. 1981. pap. 3.95 (ISBN 0-570-03755-7, 12-2310). Concordia.

--C.O.M.E. Members Manual. pap. 12.50 (ISBN 0-933350-24-4). Morse Pr.

Mayer, Herbert A., jt. auth. see Meyer, Daniel P.

Mayer, J. P., ed. see De Tocqueville, Alexis C.

Mayer, J. P., ed. see Tocqueville, Alexis de.

Mayer, Jean. Human Nutrition: Its Physiological, Medical & Social Aspects,A Series of 82 Essays. (Illus.). 740p. 1979. 23.75 (ISBN 0-398-02359-X). C C Thomas.

Mayer, Jean, ed. U. S. Nutrition Policies in the Seventies. LC 72-6548. 1973. text ed. 17.95x (ISBN 0-7167-0599-0); pap. text ed. 9.95x (ISBN 0-7167-0596-6). W H Freeman.

Mayer, JoAnne C. & Sippl, Charles J. Essential Computer Dictionary & Speller for Secretaries, Managers, & Office Personnel. (Illus.). 256p. 1980. text ed. 14.95 (ISBN 0-13-284364-1, Spec); pap. 6.95 (ISBN 0-13-284356-0). P-H.

Mayer, John E. Jewish-Gentile Courtships: An Exploratory Study of a Social Process. LC 80-16130. x, 240p. 1980. Repr. of 1961 ed. lib. bdg. 22.50x (ISBN 0-313-22465-X, MAJG). Greenwood.

Mayer, John E. & Timms, Noel. The Client Speaks: Working Class Impressions of Casework. 1970. 16.00 (ISBN 0-7100-6906-5); pap. 9.50 (ISBN 0-7100-7673-8). Routledge & Kegan.

Mayer, K. & Greenwood, Ernest. The Design of Social Policy Research. (Illus.). 1980. text ed. 18.95 (ISBN 0-13-201558-7). P-H.

Mayer, Karl H. Mushroom Stones of Meso-America. (Illus.). 1977. pap. 4.95 (ISBN 0-916552-09-8). Acoma Bks.

Mayer, Kurt B. Economic Development & Population Growth in Rhode Island. LC 53-5994. 70p. 1953. pap. 2.00 (ISBN 0-87057-033-1, Pub. by Brown U Pr). Univ Pr of New England.

Mayer, Kurt B. & Goldstein, Sidney. Migration & Economic Development in Rhode Island. LC 58-10480. 1958. pap. 2.00 (ISBN 0-87057-051-X, Pub. by Brown U Pr). Univ Pr of New England.

Mayer, Lawrence C. & Burnett, John H. Politics in Industrial Societies: A Comparative Perspection. LC 76-54694. 1977. text ed. 19.95x (ISBN 0-471-57986-6). Wiley.

Mayer, Martin. The Bankers. 608p. 1976. pap. text ed. 3.50 (ISBN 0-345-29569-2). Ballantine.

--The Fate of the Dollar. 1981. Repr. pap. 3.50 (ISBN 0-451-09612-6, E9612, Sig). NAL.

Mayer, Mercer. Appelard & Liverwurst. LC 77-21233. (Illus.). 40p. (gr. k-3). 1978. 8.95 (ISBN 0-590-07506-3, Four Winds). Schol Bk Serv.

--Bubble Bubble. LC 80-16777. (Illus.). 40p. (ps-2). 1980. Repr. of 1973 ed. 7.95 (ISBN 0-590-07759-7, Four Winds). Schol Bk Serv.

--East of the Sun & West of the Moon. LC 80-11496. (Illus.). 48p. 1980. 10.95 (ISBN 0-590-07538-1, Four Winds). Schol Bk Serv.

--The Great Cat Chase. LC 74-13120. (Illus.). 32p. (gr. k-2). 1975. 3.95 (ISBN 0-590-07400-8, Four Winds). Schol Bk Serv.

--Herbert the Timid Dragon. (Illus.). (gr. 4-8). 3.95 (ISBN 0-307-13732-5, Golden Pr). Western Pub.

--Herbert, the Timid Dragon. (Illus.). (ps-3). 1980. PLB 9.15 (ISBN 0-307-63732-8, Golden Pr); pap. 3.95 (ISBN 0-307-13732-5). Western Pub.

--Just Me & My Dad. (Look-Look Ser.). (Illus.). 1977. PLB 5.38 (ISBN 0-307-66839-8, Golden Pr); pap. 0.95 (ISBN 0-307-11839-8). Western Pub.

--Little Monster's Bedtime Book. (Golden Look-Look Bks.). (ps-3). 1978. PLB 5.38 (ISBN 0-307-61848-X, Golden Pr); pap. 0.95 (ISBN 0-307-11848-7). Western Pub.

--Little Monster's Counting Book. (Golden Look-Look Bks.). (ps-3). 1978. PLB 5.38 (ISBN 0-307-61844-7, Golden Pr); pap. 0.95 (ISBN 0-307-11844-4). Western Pub.

--Little Monster's Neighborhood. (Golden Look-Look Bks.). (ps-3). 1978. PLB 5.38 (ISBN 0-307-61849-8, Golden Pr); pap. 0.95 (ISBN 0-307-11849-5). Western Pub.

--Little Monster's Scratch & Sniff Mystery. 32p. 1980. 4.95 (ISBN 0-307-13546-2). Western Pub.

--Little Monster's Scratch & Sniff Mystery. 32p. 1980. lib. bdg. 9.92 (ISBN 0-307-64546-0). Western Pub.

--Liza Lou & the Yeller Belly Swamp. LC 80-16605. (Illus.). 48p. (gr. k-5). 1980. Repr. of 1976 ed. 8.95 (ISBN 0-590-07771-6, Four Winds). Schol Bk Serv.

--Mrs. Beggs & the Wizard. LC 80-15279. (Illus.). 48p. (ps-3). 1980. Repr. of 1973 ed. 8.95 (ISBN 0-590-07773-2, Four Winds). Schol Bk Serv.

--Professor Wormbog's Crazy Cut-Ups. (Golden Book Ser.). (Illus.). 144p. (gr. 1-7). 1980. 3.95 (ISBN 0-307-15807-1, Golden Pr). Western Pub.

--A Silly Story. LC 80-16784. (Illus.). 48p. (ps-3). 1980. Repr. of 1972 ed. 7.95 (ISBN 0-590-07778-3, Four Winds). Schol Bk Serv.

--Terrible Troll. LC 68-28730. (Illus.). 32p. (ps-2). 1981. pap. 2.75 (ISBN 0-8037-8636-0, Pied Piper Bk). Dial.

--What Do You Do with a Kangaroo? LC 72-87073. (Illus.). 48p. (gr. k-3). 1974. 6.95 (ISBN 0-590-07286-2, Four Winds). Schol Bk Serv.

--What Do You Do with a Kangaroo? (Illus.). (gr. k-3). 1975. pap. 1.95 (ISBN 0-590-10007-6, Schol Pap); pap. 3.50 bk. & record (ISBN 0-590-20791-1). Schol Bk Serv.

--You're the Scaredy-Cat. LC 80-16859. (Illus.). 40p. (ps-3). 1980. Repr. of 1974 ed. 7.95 (ISBN 0-590-07783-X, Four Winds). Schol Bk Serv.

Mayer, Michael F. Divorce & Annulment in the Fifty States. rev. ed. LC 74-24800. (Know Your Law Bks.). 1975. pap. 1.45 o.p. (ISBN 0-668-01437-7). Arc Bks.

Mayer, Milton. They Thought They Were Free: The Germans 1933-45. 2nd ed. LC 55-5137. 1966. 13.50x o.s.i. (ISBN 0-226-51190-1). U of Chicago Pr.

Mayer, Morris L., jt. auth. see Mason, J. Barry.

Mayer, Nancy. Male Mid-Life Crisis. LC 73-79637. 1978. 8.95 o.p. (ISBN 0-385-01529-1). Doubleday.

Mayer, Ralph. Dictionary of Art Terms & Techniques. (Illus.). 1969. 12.95 (ISBN 0-690-23673-5, TYC-T). T Y Crowell.

--A Dictionary of Art Terms & Techniques. LC 69-15414. (Apollo Eds.). (Illus.). 464p. 1975. pap. 6.95 o.s.i. (ISBN 0-8152-0371-3, A-371, TYC-T). T Y Crowell.

--A Dictionary of Art Terms & Techniques. LC 80-8854. (Illus.). 464p. 1981. pap. 6.95 (ISBN 0-06-463531-7, EH 531, EH). Har-Row.

--The Painter's Craft: An Introduction to Artists' Methods & Materials. (Penguin Handbook Ser.). (Illus.). 1979. pap. 8.95 (ISBN 0-14-046369-0). Penguin.

Mayer, Richard E. The Promise of Cognitive Psychology. LC 80-39997. (Psychology Ser.). (Illus.). 1981. text ed. 10.95x (ISBN 0-7167-1275-X); pap. text ed. 5.95x (ISBN 0-7167-1276-8). W H Freeman.

Mayer, Richard E., jt. auth. see Tarpy, Roger M.

Mayer, Robert. The Execution. 1979. 8.95 o.p. (ISBN 0-670-30050-0). Viking Pr.

Mayer, Robert & Rohner, Traugott. Oboe Reeds: How to Make & Adjust Them. (Illus.). pap. 7.00 (ISBN 0-686-15900-4). Instrumentalist Co.

Mayer, Robert R. Social Planning & Social Change. LC 75-151511. (Foundations of Social Welfare Ser). 172p. 1972. 8.95 o.p. (ISBN 0-13-817270-6). P-H.

Mayer, Robert T., tr. Bernard of Clairvaux: The Irishman. LC 78-768. (Cistercian Fathers Ser.). 1978. 7.95 (ISBN 0-685-87078-2); pap. 4.00 (ISBN 0-87907-910-X). Cistercian Pubns.

Mayer, Rosemary. Pontormo's Diary. (Illus.). 200p. 1981. pap. price not set (ISBN 0-915570-17-3). Oolp Pr.

Mayer, Thomas, et al. Money, Banking, & the Economy. 1981. 16.95x (ISBN 0-393-95121-9). Norton.

Mayer, Victor. Stopwatch. 5.75 o.p. (ISBN 0-8062-1201-2). Carlton.

Mayer, William. Early Travelers in Mexico (1534 to 1816) (Illus.). 20.00 (ISBN 0-911268-31-6). Rogers Bk.

Mayer, William V. & Van Gelder, R. G., eds. Physiological Mammalogy, 2 vols. Incl. Vol. 1 (ISBN 0-12-481001-2); Vol. 2 (ISBN 0-12-481002-0). 1964. 46.00 ea. Acad Pr.

Mayer-Gurr, Alfred. Petroleum Engineering. LC 76-6449. (Geology of Petroleum Ser: Vol. 3). 208p. 1976. pap. text ed. 13.95x (ISBN 0-470-15082-3). Halsted Pr.

Mayers, Marvin. Christianity Confronts Culture. (Contemporary Evangelical Perspectives Ser.). 8.95 (ISBN 0-310-28891-6). Zondervan.

Mayers, Marvin K., jt. auth. see Grunlan, Stephen A.

Mayers, Patrick. Lost Bear, Found Bear. LC 72-13353. (Self Starter Ser.). (Illus.). 32p. (ps-1). 1973. 6.50g (ISBN 0-8075-4760-3). A Whitman.

Mayers, Ronald B. Religious Ministry in a Transcendentless Culture. LC 79-3424. 1980. pap. text ed. 8.50 (ISBN 0-8191-0889-8). U Pr of Amer.

Mayers, Ronald B., pref. by see Bancroft, Emery.

Mayers, William F. Chinese Reader's Manual. LC 68-30660. 1968. Repr. of 1910 ed. 20.00 (ISBN 0-8103-3335-X). Gale.

Mayerson. Shoptalk. 1979. 13.95 (ISBN 0-7216-6207-2). Dryden Pr.

Mayerson, Evelyn W. Sanjo. (gr. 10 up). 1980. pap. write for info. (ISBN 0-671-83397-9). PB.

Mayerson, Philip. Classical Mythology in Literature, Art, & Music. 1971. text ed. 20.95 (ISBN 0-471-00365-4). Wiley.

Mayes, A. D. Deuteronomy. Clements, Ronald E., ed. (New Century Bible Commentary Ser.). (Orig.). 1981. pap. 8.95 (ISBN 0-8028-1882-X). Eerdmans.

--Deuteronomy. (New Century Bible Ser.). 352p. Repr. of 1979 ed. 19.50x (ISBN 0-551-00804-0). Attic Pr.

Mayes, Anne C., jt. auth. see Mayes, David G.

Mayes, David G. The Property Boom: The Effects of Building Society Behaviour on House Prices. 146p. 1979. 30.50x (ISBN 0-85520-296-3, Pub by Martin Robertson England). Biblio Dist.

Mayes, David G. & Mayes, Anne C. Introductory Economic Statistics. LC 73-14378. 248p. 1976. 28.50 (ISBN 0-471-58031-7); pap. 15.95 (ISBN 0-471-58111-9, Pub. by Wiley-Interscience). Wiley.

Mayes, Edythe B. Is Sexual Reproduction Necessary? LC 79-92237. 1980. 15.00 (ISBN 0-89002-157-0); pap. 3.95 (ISBN 0-89002-156-2). Northwoods Pr.

Mayes, Herbert R. The Magazine Maze: A Prejudiced Perspective. LC 79-8028. 384p. 1980. 14.95 (ISBN 0-385-15322-8). Doubleday.

Mayes, LaSalle, et al. Writing Concepts. 1978. pap. text ed. 11.95 (ISBN 0-8403-1872-3). Kendall-Hunt.

Mayesky, et al. Creative Activities for Young Children. LC 78-52620. 1980. pap. 10.60 (ISBN 0-8273-1571-6); instructor's guide 1.50 (ISBN 0-8273-1572-4). Delmar.

Mayfair, Norman P. The Religious Practices of Primitive Peoples. (Illus.). 139p. 1980. deluxe ed. 47.75 (ISBN 0-89266-241-7). Am Classical Coll.

Mayfield, A., intro. by. Odhams Knitting Encyclopaedia. (Illus.). 1971. 8.95 (ISBN 0-600-72123-X). Transatlantic.

Mayfield, Chris, ed. Growing up Southern: Southern Exposure Looks at Childhood, Then & Now. (Illus.). 1981. 17.95 (ISBN 0-394-50913-7); pap. 7.95 (ISBN 0-394-74809-3). Pantheon.

Mayfield, Craig K. Reading Skills for Law Students. 199p. 1980. pap. 10.00 (ISBN 0-87215-313-4). Michie.

Mayfield, J. M. & Webber, B. M. Fundamentals of Senior Physics Textbook, 2 bks. 1973. pap. text ed. 12.95x; Bk. 1. pap. text ed. 13.95 (00510); Bk. 2. pap. text ed. 13.95 (000502). Heinemann Ed.

Mayfield, Jack. Loving Strangers. 1978. pap. 1.95 o.p. (ISBN 0-451-08216-8, J8216, Sig). NAL.

Mayfield, Janis B., ed. see Zuber, William P.

Mayfield, John. Rehearsal for Republicanism: Free Soil & the Politics of Antislavery. (National University Publications, Political Science Ser.). 1980. 17.50 (ISBN 0-8046-9253-X). Kennikat.

Mayfield, Robert C., jt. ed. see English, Paul W.

Mayhall, Carole. Del Corazon de una Mujer. Rojas, Juan, tr. from Eng. 111p. (Orig., Span.). 1978. pap. 2.25 (ISBN 0-89922-130-0). Edit Caribe.

--Lord of My Rocking Boat. (Orig.). 1981. price not set. NavPress.

Mayhall, Carole, jt. auth. see Mayhall, Jack.

Mayhall, Jack & Mayhall, Carole. Marriage Takes More Than Love. LC 77-85736. 1978. pap. 4.50 (ISBN 0-89109-426-1, 14266). NavPress.

Mayhall, Jane. Givers & Takers 2. LC 68-55445. 78p. 1973. pap. 1.95 (ISBN 0-87130-033-8). Eakins.

Mayhall, P. D. & Geary, D. P. Community Relations & the Administration of Justice. 2nd ed. LC 78-135200. 1979. text ed. 17.50x (ISBN 0-471-04135-1); tchrs. manual avail. (ISBN 0-471-05311-2); study guide avail. (ISBN 0-471-05314-7). Wiley.

Mayhall, Pamela D., jt. auth. see Schickedanz, H. Ruth.

Mayhead, Robin. John Keats. (British Authors Ser). (Orig.). 1967. 23.95 (ISBN 0-521-05706-X); pap. 7.95x (ISBN 0-521-09419-4). Cambridge U Pr.

--Understanding Literature. (Orig.). 1965. 32.50 (ISBN 0-521-05705-1); pap. 7.95x (ISBN 0-521-09282-5). Cambridge U Pr.

--Walter Scott. LC 72-88622. (British Authors Ser.). 128p. 1973. 27.50 (ISBN 0-521-20115-2); pap. 7.95x (ISBN 0-521-09781-9). Cambridge U Pr.

Mayhew, Catherine M. Genealogical Periodical Annual Index, Nineteen Seventy Eight, Vol.17. Towle, Laird C., ed. xii, 167p. 1980. 12.50 (ISBN 0-917890-23-X). Heritage Bk.

Mayhew, David R. Congress: The Electoral Connection. LC 74-78471. (Studies in Political Science: No. 26). (Illus.). 192p. 1974. 12.00x (ISBN 0-300-01777-4, Y-277); pap. 3.95x (ISBN 0-300-01809-6). Yale U Pr.

Mayhew, Edgar D. & Myer, Minor, Jr. American Interiors from Colonial Era to Nineteen Fifteen. (Illus.). 304p. 1980. 45.00 (ISBN 0-684-16293-8). Scribner.

Mayhew, Edgar D. & Myers, Minor. Documentary History of American Interiors. (Illus.). 1980. 45.00 (ISBN 0-684-16293-8, ScribT). Scribner.

Mayhew, George P., ed. Rage or Raillery: The Swift Manuscripts at the Huntington Library. LC 66-28200. 1967. 8.50 (ISBN 0-87328-029-6). Huntington Lib.

Mayhew, George P., ed. see Yeats, William B.

Mayhew, Henry. London Labour & the London Poor: A Cyclopedia of the Conditions & Earnings of Those That Will Work, Those That Cannot Work & Those That Will Not Work, 4 vols. LC 67-16357. 1981. Repr. of 1862 ed. 85.00x (ISBN 0-678-05073-2). Kelley.

Mayhew, Henry & Binny, J. Criminal Prisons of London. LC 68-18227. (Illus.). Repr. of 1862 ed. 22.50x (ISBN 0-678-05072-4). Kelley.

Mayhew, Jonathan. A Discourse Concerning Unlimited Submission. Tanis, Norman E., ed. (American Classics Facsimile Ser.: Pt. III). 1976. pap. 10.00 (ISBN 0-937048-02-X). CSUN.

Mayhew, Leonard F., tr. see Touraine, Alain.

Mayhew, Lewis B. Arrogance on Campus. LC 71-128699. (Higher Education Ser.). 1970. 11.95x o.p. (ISBN 0-87589-074-1). Jossey-Bass.

--Colleges Today & Tomorrow. LC 74-75939. (Higher Education Ser.). 1969. 13.95x o.p. (ISBN 0-87589-037-7). Jossey-Bass.

Mayhew, Lewis B., ed. Educational Leadership & Declining Enrollments. LC 74-12823. 1974. 15.50x (ISBN 0-8211-1214-7); text ed. 14.00x (ISBN 0-685-14293-0). McCutchan.

Mayhew, Y. R., jt. auth. see Rogers, G. F.

Maylam, Paul. Rhodes, the Tswana, & the British: Colonialism, Collaboration, & Conflict in the Bechuanaland Protectorate, 1885-1899. LC 79-8582. (Contributions in Comparative Colonial Studies: No. 4). (Illus.). x, 245p. 1980. lib. bdg. 29.25 (ISBN 0-313-20885-9, MTB/). Greenwood.

Maylem, John see Fleming, William.

Maynard, Christopher. All About Ghosts. LC 77-17613. (The World of the Unknown). (Illus.). (gr. 4-5). 1978. PLB 6.95 (ISBN 0-88436-469-0). EMC.

--Exploring the Great Ice Age. (Explorer Bks.). (Illus.). (gr. 3-5). 1979. 2.95 (ISBN 0-531-09128-7); PLB 6.45 s&l (ISBN 0-531-09113-9). Watts.

--Prehistoric Life. (Modern Knowledge Library). (Illus.). 48p. (gr. 5 up). 1976. 3.95 (ISBN 0-531-02446-6); PLB 6.90 (ISBN 0-531-01193-3). Watts.

--War Vehicles. (The Question & Answer Books Ser.). (Illus.). 36p. (gr. 3-8). 1980. PLB 5.95 (ISBN 0-8225-1185-1). Lerner Pubns.

--The Young Scientist Book of Stars & Planets. LC 78-17545. (Young Scientist Ser.). (Illus.). (gr. 3-5). 1978. text ed. 6.95 (ISBN 0-88436-528-X). EMC.

Maynard, Dave. Dave Maynard's Tried & True All-Night Radio Secret Family Recipe Cookbook. (Illus.). 256p. pap. 6.95 (ISBN 0-201-05008-0). A-W.

Maynard, Jim. Celestial Influences, 1981: Eastern Time. pap. 4.95 (ISBN 0-930356-24-1). Quicksilver Prod.

--Celestial Influences: 1981, Pacific Time. 1981. 4.95 (ISBN 0-930356-21-7). Quicksilver Prod.

Maynard, Joyce. Baby Love. LC 80-2707. 288p. 1981. 10.95 (ISBN 0-394-51802-0). Knopf.

Maynard, Leslie J. The Freedom Diet - Games Dieters Play. LC 76-47654. 1977. 9.95 (ISBN 0-8119-0275-7). Fell.

Maynard, Temple & Backscheider, Paula R., eds. The Plays of Robert Jephson. LC 78-66647. (Eighteenth-Century English Drama Ser.: Vol. 24). 1980. lib. bdg. 50.00 (ISBN 0-8240-3598-4). Garland Pub.

Maynard, Theodore. Orestes Brownson: Yankee, Radical, Catholic. 1971. Repr. of 1943 ed. 18.00 o.s.i. (ISBN 0-02-849030-4). Hafner.

Mayne, Roger, jt. auth. see Jellicoe, Ann.

Mayne, William. Earthfasts. (gr. 5 up). 1967. PLB 7.95 o.p. (ISBN 0-525-29008-7). Dutton.

--The Incline. (gr. 5 up). 1972. PLB 6.95 o.p. (ISBN 0-525-32550-6). Dutton.

--It. LC 78-1902. (gr. 5-9). 1978. 7.95 (ISBN 0-688-80173-0); PLB 7.63 (ISBN 0-688-84173-2). Greenwillow.

--Max's Dream. LC 77-12728. (Illus.). (gr. 5-9). 1978. 7.95 (ISBN 0-688-80131-5); PLB 7.63 (ISBN 0-688-84131-7). Greenwillow.

--The Mouse & the Egg. LC 80-15084. (Illus.). 32p. (gr. k-3). 1981. 9.95 (ISBN 0-688-80301-6); PLB 9.55 (ISBN 0-688-84301-8). Greenwillow.

--Salt River Times. LC 80-20806. 160p. (gr. 5-7). 1981. 7.95 (ISBN 0-688-80311-3). Greenwillow.

--A Year & a Day. 112p. (gr. 4-6). 1976. PLB 6.95 o.p. (ISBN 0-525-43450-X). Dutton.

--Yellow Airplane. 1974. 6.95 o.p. (ISBN 0-525-66395-9). Elsevier-Nelson.

Mayne, Zachary. Two Dissertations Concerning Sense, & the Immagination, with an Essay on Consciousness. Wellek, Rene, ed. LC 75-11234. (British Philosophers & Theologians of the 17th & 18th Centuries: Vol. 35). 1976. Repr. of 1728 ed. lib. bdg. 42.00 (ISBN 0-8240-1787-0). Garland Pub.

Mayneord, W. V. Some Applications of Nuclear Physics to Medicine. 1980. 15.00x (Pub. by Brit Inst Radiology). State Mutual Bk.

Mayneord, W. V. & Clark, R. H. Carcinogenesis & Radiation Risk: A Biomathematical Reconnaissance. 1980. 35.00x (Pub. by Brit Inst Radiology England). State Mutual Bk.

Mayo. Basic Finance. 1978. 19.95 (ISBN 0-7216-6209-9). Dryden Pr.

Mayo, A. History of Mexico: From Pre-Columbia to Present. 1978. 13.95 (ISBN 0-13-390203-X). P-H.

Mayo, Alzina. Tapestry of a Soul. (Illus.). 1980. pap. 4.00 (ISBN 0-933646-13-5). Aries Pr.

Mayo, B. Instructions to the British Ministers to the United States, 1791-1812. LC 70-75280. (Law, Politics & History Ser). 1971. lib. bdg. 42.50 (ISBN 0-306-71303-9). Da Capo.

Mayo, Bernard. Jefferson Himself. LC 70-87871. 7.50x o.p. (ISBN 0-8139-0284-3); pap. 5.95x (ISBN 0-8139-0310-6). U Pr of Va.

Mayo, Bernard, ed. Thomas Jefferson & His Unknown Brother. LC 80-25272. 1981. price not set (ISBN 0-8139-0890-6). U Pr of Va.

Mayo, E. L. The Collected Poems of E. L. Mayo. Ray, David, ed. LC 80-84519. (New Letters Bks.). 185p. (Orig.). 1981. pap. text ed. 6.00 (ISBN 0-938652-00-1). New Letters.

Mayo, Edward J. & Jarvis, Lance P. The Psychology of Leisure Travel: Effective Marketing & Selling of Travel Services. 448p. 1981. 9.95 (ISBN 0-8436-2204-0). CBI Pub.

Mayo, Frank R., ed. Oxidation of Organic Compounds, 3 vols. LC 67-7520. (Advances in Chemistry Ser: Nos. 75, 76, 77). 1968. Set. 72.00 (ISBN 0-8412-0618-X); Vol. 1. 29.25 (ISBN 0-8412-0076-9); Vol. 2. 33.50 (ISBN 0-8412-0077-7); Vol. 3. 25.75 (ISBN 0-8412-0078-5). Am Chemical.

Mayo, G. Douglas & Gilliland, Burl E., eds. Learning & Instructional Improvement Digest. LC 79-624710. (J. W. Brister Library Monographs: No. 8). 120p. (Orig.). 1979. pap. 6.95x (ISBN 0-87870-058-7). Memphis St Univ.

Mayo, Gene, jt. auth. see Luciano.

Mayo, Herbert B. Basic Investments. 544p. 1980. text ed. 19.95 (ISBN 0-03-054691-5). Dryden Pr.

Mayo, Margaret. Burning Desire. (Harlequin Romances Ser.). 192p. (Orig.). 1981. pap. 1.25 (ISBN 0-373-02385-5, Pub. by Harlequin). PB.

--Stormy Affair. (Harlequin Romance Ser.). (Orig.). 1980. pap. 1.25 o.p. (ISBN 0-373-02327-8, Pub. by Harlequin). PB.

--Valley of the Hawk. (Harlequin Romances Ser.). 192p. 1980. pap. 1.25 o.p. (ISBN 0-373-02360-X, Pub. by Harlequin). PB.

Mayo, R. Britton & Social Systems, Inc. Corporate Planning & Modeling with Simplan. 1978. pap. text ed. 10.95 (ISBN 0-201-05227-X). A-W.

Mayor, jt. auth. see Amin.

Mayor, A. H. Prints & People: A Social History of Printed Pictures. 1980. 37.50 (ISBN 0-691-03958-5); pap. 12.95 (ISBN 0-691-00326-2). Princeton U Pr.

Mayor, A Hyatt. Prints & People: A Social History of Printed Pictures. rev. ed. LC 80-7817. (Illus.). 496p. 1980. 37.50x; pap. 12.50. Princeton U Pr.

Mayor, A. Hyatt, intro. by. A Century of American Sculpture: Treasures from Brookgreen Gardens. (Illus.). 128p. 1981. 29.95 (ISBN 0-89659-185-9); pap. 16.95 (ISBN 0-89659-150-6). Abbeville Pr.

Mayor, Andreas, tr. see Gerard, Yves.

Mayor, Georges & Zingg, Ernst J. Urologic Surgery: Diagnosis, Techniques Postoperative Treatment. 1976. 132.50 (ISBN 0-471-01408-7, Pub. by Wiley Medical). Wiley.

Mayor, Joseph B. The Epistle of Saint James. 1977. 19.25 (ISBN 0-686-12971-7). Klock & Klock.

--The Epistle of St. Jude & the Second Epistle of Peter. 1978. 15.25 (ISBN 0-686-12945-8). Klock & Klock.

Mayor, Susan. Collecting Fans. (The Christies International Collectors Ser.). (Illus.). 128p. 1980. 14.95 (ISBN 0-8317-3199-0). Mayflower Bks.

Mayr, Ernst. Birds of the Southwest Pacific. (Illus.). 1968. pap. 16.80 (ISBN 3-7682-0533-9). Lubrecht & Cramer.

Mayr, Otto. Origins of Feedback Control. 1970. 8.95x o.p. (ISBN 0-262-13067-X); pap. 3.95 (ISBN 0-262-63056-7, 283). MIT Pr.

Mayr, Otto, ed. The Clockwork Universe. 1980. lib. bdg. 55.00 (ISBN 0-88202-188-5); N Watson.

Mayr, Roswitha & Hogg, James. The Concept of Love in Sidney & Spenser; John Leanerd's the Rambling Justice, or the Jealous Husbands: A Restoration Plagiarism of Thomas Middletown's More Dissemblers Besides Women? (Salzburg Studies in English Literature, Elizabethan & Renaissance Studies: No. 70). 1978. pap. text ed. 25.00x (ISBN 0-391-01477-3). Humanities.

Mayreder, Rosa. A Survey of the Woman Problem. Herman, Scheffauer, tr. from Ger. LC 79-2944. 275p. 1981. Repr. of 1913 ed. 21.50 (ISBN 0-8305-0108-8). Hyperion Conn.

Mayrose, V., jt. auth. see Battaglia, R. A.

Mays, Benjamin. Born to Rebel. LC 77-123857. (Illus.). 1972. pap. 3.95 o.p. (ISBN 0-684-12971-X, SL378, ScribT). Scribner.

Mays, Benjamin E. Lord, the People Have Driven Me on. 1981. 7.95 (ISBN 0-533-04503-7). Vantage.

Mays, Buddy. A Pilgrim's Notebook: Guide to Western Wildlife. LC 77-22043. (Illus., Orig.). 1977. pap. 5.95 (ISBN 0-87701-103-6). Chronicle Bks.

--Wildwaters. LC 76-58033. (Illus.). 1977. pap. 6.95 o.p. (ISBN 0-87701-089-7). Chronicle Bks.

Mays, James L., ed. Interpreting the Gospels. LC 80-8057. 320p. 1981. pap. 13.50 (ISBN 0-8006-1439-9, 1-1439). Fortress.

Mays, Maxine. Student Teaching in Special Classes for the Mentally Retarded. (Illus.). 108p. 1974. pap. 7.75 (ISBN 0-398-02861-3). C C Thomas.

Mays, Willie & Berger, Maxine. Willie Mays, "Play Ball!". LC 80-13352. (Illus.). 160p. (gr. 7 up). 1980. PLB 8.29 (ISBN 0-671-41314-7). Messner.

Mays, Wolfe, jt. ed. see Curtis, Bernard.

Mayshark, Cyrus & Foster, Roy A. Health Education in Secondary Schools. rev. ed. 3rd ed. LC 77-173431. (Illus.). 1972. text ed. 12.50 o.p. (ISBN 0-8016-3176-9). Mosby.

Maz, Veronica. The Stick-Carrier. 1975. 6.00 o.p. (ISBN 0-682-48423-7). Exposition.

Mazda, F. F. Integrated Circuits. LC 77-71418. (Illus.). 1978. 35.50 (ISBN 0-521-21658-3). Cambridge U Pr.

Mazel, David. Arizona Trails. Winnett, Thomas, ed. LC 80-53682. (Wilderness Press Trail Guide Ser.). (Illus.). 192p. (Orig.). 1981. pap. 7.95 (ISBN 0-89997-003-6). Wilderness Pr.

Mazel, Judy. The Beverly Hills Diet: Get As Slim As You Like for the Rest of Your Life. 192p. 1981. 9.95 (ISBN 0-02-582600-X). Macmillan.

Mazer, Bill & Fischler, Stan. The Amazing Bill Mazer's Baseball Trivia. 224p. (Orig.). 1981. pap. 2.50 (ISBN 0-446-91784-2). Warner Bks.

Mazer, Harry. Guy Lenny. LC 79-157839. (gr. 4-7). 1971. 4.95 (ISBN 0-440-03316-0); PLB 4.58 o.s.i. (ISBN 0-440-03313-6). Delacorte.

--The Island Keeper. LC 80-39762. 192p. (gr. 6 up). 1981. PLB 8.95 (ISBN 0-440-03976-2). Delacorte.

--The Last Mission. (gr. 7 up). 1981. pap. 1.50 (ISBN 0-440-94797-9, LE). Dell.

--The War on Villa Street: A Novel. LC 78-50454. (gr. 7 up). 1978. 7.95 (ISBN 0-440-09349-X). Delacorte.

Mazer, Norma F. Mrs. Fish, Ape, & Me the Dump Queen. LC 79-20262. 144p. (gr. 4-7). 1980. PLB 8.95 (ISBN 0-525-35380-1). Dutton.

Mazet, Horace S. Wild Ivory. 1971. 6.95 o.p. (ISBN 0-87874-003-1, Nautilus). Galloway.

Mazlish, Bruce, ed. see Smith, Adam.

Mazlish, Elaine, jt. auth. see Faber, Adele.

Mazmanian, Daniel & Sabatier, Paul, eds. Successful Policy Implementation. (Orig.). 1980. pap. 5.00 (ISBN 0-918592-37-2). Policy Studies.
Mazmanian, Daniel & Sabatier, Paul A., eds. Effective Policy Implementation. LC 79-3041. (Policy Study Organization Bks.). 1981. 23.95x (ISBN 0-669-03311-1). Lexington Bks.
Mazmanian, Daniel A. Third Parties in Presidential Elections. LC 74-281. (Studies in Presidential Selection). 140p. 1974. 11.95 (ISBN 0-8157-5522-8); pap. 4.95 (ISBN 0-8157-5521-X). Brookings.
Mazmanian, Daniel A. & Nienaber, Jeanne. Can Organizations Change? Environmental Protection, Citizen Participation, & the Army Corps of Engineers. 1979. 14.95 (ISBN 0-8157-5524-4); pap. 5.95 (ISBN 0-8157-5523-6). Brookings.
Mazo, Joseph H. Prime Movers: The Makers of Modern Dance in America. LC 76-15375. (Illus.). 1978. pap. 6.95 o.p. (ISBN 0-688-08078-2, Quill). Morrow.
--Prime Movers: The Makers of Modern Dance in America. 1977. 12.50 o.p. (ISBN 0-688-03078-5); pap. 6.95 o.p. (ISBN 0-686-67558-4). Morrow.
Mazo De La Roche. The Building of Jalna. 288p. 1977. pap. 1.50 o.p. (ISBN 0-449-23071-6, Crest). Fawcett.
--Finch's Fortune. 1976. pap. 1.50 o.p. (ISBN 0-449-23053-8, Crest). Fawcett.
--Young Renny. 1976. pap. 1.50 o.p. (ISBN 0-449-22842-8, Q2842, Crest). Fawcett.
Mazor, Emma S. Tears & Laughter in My Poetry. 192p. 1981. 7.50 (ISBN 0-682-49708-8). Exposition.
Mazor, L. Analytical Chemistry of Organic Halogen Compounds. LC 75-5934. 400p. 1975. text ed. 50.00 (ISBN 0-08-017903-7). Pergamon.
Mazrui, Ali. Soldiers & Kinsmen in Uganda: The Making of a Military Ethnocracy. LC 75-5017. (Armed Forces & Society Ser.: Vol. 5). 1975. 20.00x o.p. (ISBN 0-8039-0427-4). Sage.
Mazrui, Ali A. Africa's International Relations: The Diplomacy of Dependency & Change. LC 77-595. 1978. text ed. 13.50 (ISBN 0-89158-671-7). Westview.
--Political Values & the Educated Class in Africa. 1978. 24.00x (ISBN 0-520-03292-6). U of Cal Pr.
--Violence & Thought: Essays on Social Tensions in Africa. (Orig.). 1969. text ed. 6.00x (ISBN 0-391-00207-4). Humanities.
Mazrui, Ali A., ed. The Warrior Tradition in Modern Africa. (International Studies in Sociology & Social Anthropology Ser.: No. XXIII). 1977. text ed. 34.25x (ISBN 90-04-05646-7). Humanities.
Mazumdar, Dipak. Urban Labor Market & Income Distribution in Peninsular Malaysia. (World Bank Research Publications Ser.). (Illus.). 456p. 1981. 18.95 (ISBN 0-19-520213-9); pap. 7.95 (ISBN 0-19-520214-7). Oxford U Pr.
Mazumdar, Dwijendra L. Towards a Philosophy of the Modern Corporation. 1967. 8.50x (ISBN 0-210-26968-5). Asia.
Mazumdar, N. C. Indices of Heat Stress. 132p. 1980. 4.95x (ISBN 0-89955-318-4, Pub. by Interprint India). Intl Schol Bk Serv.
Mazur, Allan & Robertson, Leon S. Biology & Social Behavior. LC 72-169236. 1972. 12.95 (ISBN 0-02-920450-X); pap. text ed. 3.00 (ISBN 0-02-920410-0). Free Pr.
Mazur, Allan C. The Dynamics of Technical Controversy. (Illus.). 175p. 1981. text ed. 11.95x (ISBN 0-89461-033-3); pap. text ed. 5.95x (ISBN 0-89461-034-1). Comm Pr Inc.
Mazur, Mary Ann, jt. auth. see Katz, Sedelle.
Mazur, Michael P. Economic Growth & Development in Jordan. (Special Studies on the Middle East). 1979. lib. bdg. 29.50x (ISBN 0-89158-455-2). Westview.
Mazurkiewicz, B. K. Design & Consruction of Dry Docks. (Illus.). 500p. 68.00x (ISBN 0-87849-028-0); pap. 38.00x (ISBN 0-87849-036-1). Trans Tech.
Mazursky, Paul, jt. auth. see Greenfield, Josh.
Mazza, Eliane G., jt. auth. see Branch, Melville C.
Mazzaferri, Ernest L. & Skillman, Thomas G. Endocrinology Case Studies. 2nd ed. 1975. spiral bdg. 14.00 (ISBN 0-87488-008-4). Med Exam.
Mazzaferri, Ernest L., ed. Endocrinology: A Review of Clinical Endocrinology. LC 79-91978. (Medical Outline Ser). 1980. pap. 18.50 (ISBN 0-87488-614-7). Med Exam.
Mazzaoui, Maureen F. The Italian Cotton Industry in the Later Middle Ages: Eleven Hundred to Sixteen Hundred. LC 80-41023. (Illus.). 272p. Date not set. price not set (ISBN 0-521-23095-0). Cambridge U Pr.
Mazzara, Richard A., tr. see Rodrigues, Jose H.
Mazzaro, Jerome. Changing the Windows: Poems. LC 66-21764. 1966. 4.75 o.p. (ISBN 0-8214-0020-7). Ohio U Pr.
Mazze, Edward M., ed. Combined Proceedings: 1975, 2 vols. in 1. LC 75-30572. 1975. pap. 15.00 o.p. (ISBN 0-87757-067-1). Am Mktg.
Mazzei, George. Shaping up: The Complete Guide to a Customized Fitness Program. (Orig.). 1981. pap. 7.95 (ISBN 0-345-29471-8). Ballantine.
Mazzini, Joseph. The Duties of Man & Other Essays. 327p. 1980. lib. bdg. 15.00 (ISBN 0-89760-546-2). Telegraph Bks.
Mazzocco, Alexis, jt. auth. see Potter, Lance D.
Mazzolani, Lidia S. Empire Without End: Three Historians of Rome. McConnell, Joan & Pel, Mario, trs. LC 76-20672. (A Helen & Kurt Wolff Bk). 1976. Repr. of 1972 ed. 10.95 (ISBN 0-15-128780-5). HarBraceJ.
Mazzolini, R. Government Controlled Enterprises: International Strategic & Policy Decisions. LC 78-10961. 1979. 36.50 (ISBN 0-471-99727-7, Pub. by Wiley-Interscience). Wiley.
Mazzoni, Tim L., Jr., jt. auth. see Campbell, Roald F.
Mazzucchi, Lois E., jt. auth. see Torres, Hazel O.
Mbabuike, Chikeho M. Reflections on Senghor. 140p. 1981. 12.95 (ISBN 0-88254-504-3). Hippocrene Bks.
Mbodaher, David J. So You're Ready to Drive a Car. (Illus.). 128p. (gr. 8 up). 1981. write for info. (ISBN 0-671-32891-3). Messner.
Meaburn, John. Detection & Spectronomy of Faint Light. (Astrophysics & Space Science Library: No. 56). 270p. 1980. pap. 14.95 (ISBN 90-277-1198-4, Pub. by D. Reidel). Kluwer Boston.
Meacock, M. H. Refrigeration Processes: A Practical Handbook on the Physical Properties of Refrigerants & Their Applications. (International Series in Heating, Ventilation & Refrigeration: Vol. 12). 1979. 41.00 (ISBN 0-08-024211-1); pap. 18.75 (ISBN 0-08-024234-0). Pergamon.
Mead, Bernard, jt. ed. see Gay, Jeanne.
Mead, C. A. Symmetry & Chirality. LC 51-5497. (Topics in Current Chemistry: Vol. 49). (Illus.). 90p. 1974. 17.60 (ISBN 0-387-06705-1). Springer-Verlag.
Mead, Carver & Conway, Lynn. Introduction to VLSI Systems. LC 78-74688. 1979. text ed. 29.95 (ISBN 0-201-04358-0). A-W.
Mead, Daniel R., jt. auth. see Geddes, Robert N.
Mead, Eleanor T. Lay up Your Treasures in Heaven. 1977. pap. 3.95 o.p. (ISBN 0-88270-257-2). Logos.
Mead, Frank S. Encyclopedia of Religious Quotations. 1976. pap. 2.25 (ISBN 0-89129-194-6). Jove Pubns.
Mead, G. R., ed. & intro. by see Blavatsky, Helena P.
Mead, George H. The Philosophy of the Present. Murphy, Arthur E., ed. LC 80-16334. 240p. 1980. pap. 5.95 (ISBN 0-226-51670-9, P909, Phoen). U of Chicago Pr.
Mead, Gretchen, jt. auth. see Chioffi, Nancy.
Mead, Harry. Inside the North York Moors. 1978. 17.95 (ISBN 0-7153-7699-3). David & Charles.
Mead, Igor, jt. auth. see Sjeklocha, Paul.
Mead, James F. & Fulco, Armand J. Unsaturated & Polyunsaturated Fatty Acid in Health & Disease. (American Lectures in Living Chemistry Ser.). (Illus.). 208p. 1976. 22.75 (ISBN 0-398-03413-3). C C Thomas.
Mead, John T. Marine Refrigeration & Fish Preservation. rev. ed. LC 80-25359. (Illus.). 1980. 25.00 (ISBN 0-912524-19-7). Busn News.
--Marine Refrigeration & Fish Preservation. LC 73-78044. (Illus.). 256p. 1973. 21.00 o.p. (ISBN 0-912524-08-1). Busn News.
Mead, Lawrence M. Institutional Analysis: An Approach to Implemental Problems in Medicaid. (An Institute Paper). 190p. 1977. pap. 4.50 o.p. (ISBN 0-685-99530-5, 46000). Urban Inst.
Mead, Leon & Newell, Gilbert F. Manual of Forensic Quotations. LC 68-26591. 1968. Repr. of 1903 ed. 15.00 (ISBN 0-8103-3188-8). Gale.
Mead, Loren B., ed. Celebrations of Life. 1974. pap. 5.95 (ISBN 0-8164-2092-0). Crossroad NY.
Mead, Lucia A. Law or War? LC 70-147601. (Library of War & Peace; International Law). lib. bdg. 38.00 (ISBN 0-8240-0362-4). Garland Pub.
Mead, Margaret. Culture & Commitment. rev. ed. 1978. 12.50x (ISBN 0-231-04632-4). Columbia U Pr.
--Culture & Commitment-the New Relationships Between the Generations in the 1970s. 1978. pap. 2.95 (ISBN 0-385-13387-1, Anch). Doubleday.
--Growing up in New Guinea. 8.75 (ISBN 0-8446-2569-8). Peter Smith.
--Letters from the Field: Nineteen Twenty-Five to Nineteen Seventy-Five. Anshen, Ruth N., ed. LC 73-4110. (World Perspectives Ser.). (Illus.). 1978. 13.95 o.s.i. (ISBN 0-06-012961-1, HarpT). Har-Row.
--Ruth Benedict. (Illus.). 1974. 15.00x (ISBN 0-231-03519-5); pap. 6.00x (ISBN 0-231-03520-9). Columbia U Pr.
Mead, Margaret & Metraux, Rhoda. Aspects of the Present. 288p. 1981. pap. 6.95. Morrow.
Mead, Margaret & Metraux, Rhoda, eds. Study of Culture at a Distance. LC 53-13135. 1953. 20.00x (ISBN 0-226-51508-7). U of Chicago Pr.
Mead, Margaret, et al, eds. Science & the Concept of Race. LC 68-19754. 1969. 15.00x (ISBN 0-231-03101-7); pap. 5.00x (ISBN 0-231-08594-X). Columbia U Pr.
Mead, Marj, jt. ed. see Kilby, Clyde.
Mead, Matthew, tr. see Bobrowski, Johannes.
Mead, Robert D. Literature of the American Nation: From Independence to the Gilded Age. 1976. pap. 1.95 o.p. (ISBN 0-451-61470-4, MJ1470, Ment). NAL.
Mead, Robert Douglas. The Canoer's Bible. LC 74-33610. 176p. 1976. pap. 3.50 (ISBN 0-385-07276-7). Doubleday.
--Journeys Down the Line: Building the Trans-Alaska Pipeline. LC 77-92226. 1978. 12.95 o.p. (ISBN 0-385-11578-4). Doubleday.
--Ultimate North: Canoeing Mackenzie's Arctic Great River. LC 75-35418. 356p. 1976. 10.00 o.p. (ISBN 0-385-07252-X). Doubleday.
Mead, Robert G., Jr; see Bree, Germaine.
Mead, Robert G., Jr., ed. Language Teaching: Broader Contexts. Incl. Coordination of Foreign Language Teaching. Blew, Genevieve S; Research & Language Learning. Sullivan, Edward D; Wider Uses for Foreign Languages. Corrin, Brownlee S. 104p. 1966. pap. 7.95x (ISBN 0-915432-66-8). NE Conf Teach Foreign.
Mead, Robin. Crete. (Illus.). 144p. 1980. 24.00 (ISBN 0-7134-1331-X, Pub. by Batsford England). David & Charles.
--Greece. 1976. 24.00 (ISBN 0-7134-3080-X). David & Charles.
--The Greek Islands. LC 79-56491. (Illus.). 160p. 1980. 22.50 (ISBN 0-7134-0625-9, Pub. by Batsford England). David & Charles.
Mead, Ruth, tr. see Bobrowski, Johannes.
Mead, Shepherd. How to Succeed in Tennis Without Really Trying. 1977. 8.95 o.p. (ISBN 0-679-50749-3). McKay.
Mead, Sidney. The Old Religion in the Brave New World: Reflections on the Relation Between Christendom & the Republic. (Jafferson Memorial Lecture). 1977. 11.95 (ISBN 0-520-03322-1). U of Cal Pr.
Mead, Sidney E. History & Identity. LC 78-26543. (American Academy of Religion. Studies in Religion: No. 19). 1979. 12.00 (ISBN 0-89130-274-3, 010019); pap. 7.50 (ISBN 0-89130-297-2). Scholars Pr Ca.
--Lively Experiment: The Shaping of Christianity in America. 1963. pap. 4.95x (ISBN 0-06-065545-3, RD-194, HarpR). Har-Row.
Mead, Taylor. On Amphetamine and in Europe: Excerpts from the Anonymous Diary of a New York Youth, Vol. 3. 1968. pap. 7.95 (ISBN 0-932430-01-5). Boss Bks.
Mead, W. R. & Brown, E. H. United States & Canada: A Regional Geography. 1964. text ed. 7.25x (ISBN 0-09-103750-6, Hutchinson U Pr). Humanities.
Mead, W. R. & Hall, Wendy. Scandinavia. (Nations & Peoples Library). 1972. 8.50x o.s.i. (ISBN 0-8027-2125-7). Walker & Co.
Mead, W. R., ed. The American Environment. (Institute of U. S. Studies Monographs Ser: No. 1). (Illus.). 72p. (Orig.). 1974. pap. text ed. 7.00x (ISBN 0-485-12901-9, Athlone Pr). Humanities.
Mead, Walter J. Competition & Oligopsony in the Douglas-Fir Lumber Industry. (Institute of Business & Economic Research, UC Berkeley). 1966. 21.50x (ISBN 0-520-00848-0). U of Cal Pr.
Mead, William B., jt. auth. see Feinsilber, Mike.
Meade, C. Wade. Ruins of Rome: A Guide to the Classical Antiquities. LC 80-81128. (Illus.). 1980. 16.95 (ISBN 0-936638-00-1); pap. 10.95 (ISBN 0-936638-01-X). Palatine Pubns.
Meade, Eston. Old Abe Dead & Other Stories. 1981. 6.95 (ISBN 0-533-04800-1). Vantage.
Meade, George P. & Chen, James C. Cane Sugar Handbook: A Manual for Cane Sugar Maufacturers & Their Chemists. 10th ed. LC 76-51046. 1977. 70.00 (ISBN 0-471-58995-0, Pub. by Wiley-Interscience). Wiley.
Meade, J. E. The Growing Economy: The Principles of Political Economy, Vol.2. 1968. pap. text ed. 14.95x (ISBN 0-04-330122-3). Allen Unwin.
--A Neo-Classical Theory of Economic Growth. 1964. pap. text ed. 7.95x o.p. (ISBN 0-04-330062-6). Allen Unwin.
Meade, James. The Structure & Reform of Direct Taxation. (Illus.). 1978. text ed. 50.00x (ISBN 0-04-336064-5); pap. text ed. 19.95x (ISBN 0-04-336065-3). Allen Unwin.
Meade, James P., Jr. Making Reality: Coping with Limitations Successfully. 1981. 7.50 (ISBN 0-8062-1652-2). Carlton.
Meade, Marion. Eleanor of Aquitaine: A Biography. (Illus.). 1980. pap. 6.95 (ISBN 0-8015-2232-3). Dutton.
--Eleanor of Aquitaine: A Biography. Orig. Title: Eagle in the Court of Love: the Life of Eleanor of Aquitaine. (Illus.). 1977. 13.95 o.p. (ISBN 0-8015-2231-5). Dutton.
Meade, Richard. Gaylord's Badge. 1976. pap. 1.25 o.p. (ISBN 0-505-50974-1, BT50974). Tower Bks.
--Swimming the Channel. LC 80-26545. 80p. 1981. 7.95 (ISBN 0-686-69065-6); pap. 3.95 (ISBN 0-931704-06-5). Story Pr.
Meade, Richard H. History of Thoracic Surgery. (Illus.). 960p. 1961. 89.75 (ISBN 0-398-01271-7). C C Thomas.
Meade, Robert D. Patrick Henry: Practical Revolutionary, Vol. 2. LC 69-16162. 1969. 10.00 o.s.i. (ISBN 0-397-00596-2). Lippincott.
Meaden, Frank. A Manual of European Bird Keeping. (Illus.). 1979. 17.95 (ISBN 0-7137-0935-9, Pub by Blandford Pr England). Sterling.
Meader, Robert F., compiled by. Catalogue of the Emma B. King Library of the Shaker Museum. (Illus.). 63p. 1970. pap. 1.75 (ISBN 0-937942-00-6). Shaker Mus.
Meader, Stephen W. Buckboard Stranger. LC 54-8574. (Illus.). (gr. 7 up). 1954. 4.95 o.p. (ISBN 0-15-212851-4, HJ). HarBraceJ.
--Clear for Action. LC 40-27736. (Illus.). (gr. 7 up). 1940. 4.95 o.p. (ISBN 0-15-218937-8, HJ). HarBraceJ.
--Keep 'em Rolling. LC 67-17155. (Illus.). (gr. 7 up). 1967. 4.95 o.p. (ISBN 0-15-242195-5, HJ). HarBraceJ.
--Lumberjack. LC 34-31292. (Illus.). (gr. 7-9). 1934. 4.95 o.p. (ISBN 0-15-249904-0, HJ). HarBraceJ.
--Red Horse Hill. LC 30-23594. (Illus.). (gr. 6 up). 6.95 o.p. (ISBN 0-15-266193-X, HJ). HarBraceJ.
Meador, C. Lawrence, jt. ed. see Davidson, Frank P.
Meador, Douglas. Trail Dust. 7.95 (ISBN 0-685-48784-9). Nortex Pr.
Meador, Prentice A., Jr. Who Rules Your Life? LC 79-64089. (Journey Bks.). 1979. pap. 2.60 (ISBN 0-8344-0107-X). Sweet.
Meadow. Help for Bedwetting. Date not set. pap. text ed. 2.75 (ISBN 0-443-02236-4). Churchill.
Meadow, Charles. The Analysis of Information Systems. 2nd ed. LC 72-11518. (Information Sciences Ser.). 416p. 1973. 27.50 (ISBN 0-471-59002-9, Pub. by Wiley-Interscience). Wiley.
Meadow, Charles T. Story of Computers. LC 70-89781. (Story of Science Ser). (gr. 5-8). 1970. PLB 7.29 (ISBN 0-8178-4572-0). Harvey.
Meadow, Charles T. & Atherton, Pauline. Basics of Online Searching. (Information Science Ser.). 200p. 1981. 14.95 (ISBN 0-471-05283-3, Pub. by Wiley-Interscience). Wiley.
Meadow, Kathryn P. Deafness & Child Development. LC 74-81435. 1980. 12.95 (ISBN 0-520-02819-8). U of Cal Pr.
Meadow, Pauline M., jt. ed. see Bull, Alan T.
Meadow, Richard H. & Zeder, Melinda A., eds. Approaches to Faunal Analysis in the Middle East. LC 78-50908. (Peabody Museum Bulletin). 1978. pap. text ed. 10.00 (ISBN 0-87365-951-1). Peabody Harvard.
Meadow, Robert G. Politics As Communications. LC 79-25176. (Communication & Information Sciences Ser.). 1980. text ed. 24.95 (ISBN 0-89391-031-7). Ablex Pub.
Meadow, Robert G. see Bishop, George F., et al.
Meadowcroft, Enid L. First Year. LC 46-22591. (Illus.). (gr. 5 up). 1946. 8.95 (ISBN 0-690-30349-1, TYC-J). T Y Crowell.
--Scarab for Luck. LC 63-18417. (Illus.). (gr. 3-7). 1964. 7.95 o.p. (ISBN 0-690-72027-0, TYC-J). T Y Crowell.
Meadowcroft, James, II. Beginning Algebra for Mature Students. 1971. pap. text ed. 13.95 (ISBN 0-13-073726-7). P-H.
Meadowes, Alicia. Tender Torment. (Orig.). 1980. pap. 2.25 (ISBN 0-446-92179-3). Warner Bks.
Meadows, A. J. Early Solar Physics. LC 74-103021. 1970. 35.00 (ISBN 0-08-006653-4); pap. 11.75 (ISBN 0-08-006654-2). Pergamon.
--Stellar Evolution. 1967. 9.90 (ISBN 0-08-012693-6); pap. 4.95 (ISBN 0-08-012224-8). Pergamon.
--Stellar Evolution. 2nd ed. 1978. text ed. 23.00 (ISBN 0-08-021668-4); pap. text ed. 7.00 (ISBN 0-08-021669-2). Pergamon.
Meadows, A. J., tr. see Kirzhnits, D. A.
Meadows, D. H., jt. auth. see Meadows, D. L.
Meadows, D. L. & Meadows, D. H. Limits to Growth. pap. 1.95 (ISBN 0-451-08985-5, J8985, Sig). NAL.

Meadows, Don. Historic Place Names of Orange County. (Illus.). 1966. 9.50 (ISBN 0-685-59751-2). Acoma Bks.

Meadows, Faye. Fifty New Creative Poodle Grooming Styles. LC 79-25786. (Illus.). 1980. spiral 9.95 (ISBN 0-668-04857-3). Arco.

Meadows, P. S. & Campbell, J. I. An Introduction to Marine Science. LC 78-6738. (Tertiary Level Biology Ser.). 1978. pap. text ed. 19.95x (ISBN 0-470-26379-2). Halsted Pr.

Meadows, Paul & Mizruchi, Ephraim H. Urbanism, Urbanization, & Change: Comparative Perspectives. 2nd ed. LC 75-28723. (Illus.). 448p. 1976. pap. text ed. 11.95 (ISBN 0-201-04616-4). A-W.

Meadows, Robert. Pocket Atlas of Human Histology. (Illus.). 465p. 1981. text ed. 29.50x (ISBN 0-19-261248-4); pap. text ed. 16.95x (ISBN 0-19-261177-1). Oxford U Pr.

Meadows, T. T. The Chinese & Their Rebellions. (Illus.). 716p. 1972. Repr. of 1856 ed. 55.00x (ISBN 0-7165-2038-9, Pub. by Irish Academic Pr Ireland). Biblio Dist.

Meadway, Clifford, jt. auth. see Nock, O. S.

Meagher, John. The Gathering of the Ungifted: Toward a Dialogue on Christian Identity. 168p. 1972. 5.95 (ISBN 0-8164-1034-8). Crossroad NY.

--The Way of the Word. 250p. 1975. 9.50 (ISBN 0-8164-0270-1). Crossroad NY.

Meagher, John A. The Huntingdon Plays: A Critical Edition with Introduction and Notes, of "The Downfall & The Death of Robert Earl of Huntington. Orgel, Stephen, ed. LC 79-54352. (Renaissance Drama Second Ser.). 583p. 1980. lib. bdg. 55.00 (ISBN 0-8240-4469-X). Garland Pub.

Meagher, Robert. An Introduction to Augustine. LC 77-99085. 1978. 17.50x (ISBN 0-8147-5423-6). NYU Pr.

Meagher, Robert F. An International Redistribution of Wealth & Power: A Study of the Charter of Economic Rights & Duties of States. (Pergamon Policy Studies). 1979. text ed. 29.50 (ISBN 0-08-022478-4). Pergamon.

Meagher, Sylvia & Owens, Gary. Master Index to the J. F. K. Assassination Investigation: The Reports & Supporting Volumes of the House Select Committee on Assassinations & the Warren Commission. LC 80-17494. xii, 435p. 1980. 20.00 (ISBN 0-8108-1331-9). Scarecrow.

Mealey, Barbara, ed. see Indiana University School of Medicine Faculty Women's Club.

Meals, Roy & Lesavoy, Malcolm A. Hand Surgery Review. 184p. 1980. softcover 14.95 (ISBN 0-683-05899-1). Williams & Wilkins.

Meanley, Brooke. Birds & Marshes of the Chesapeake Bay Country: Including the Chincoteague Salt Marshes. LC 75-17558. (Illus.). 168p. 1975. pap. 6.50 (ISBN 0-87033-207-4, Pub. by Tidewater). Cornell Maritime.

Means, Evan & Tennessee Trails Association. Tennessee Trails. LC 79-11566. (Illus.). 192p. (Orig.). 1979. pap. 6.95 (ISBN 0-914788-11-6). East Woods.

Means, L. Intramurals: Their Organization & Administration. 2nd ed. 1973. ref. ed. 16.95 (ISBN 0-13-477216-4). P-H.

Means, Louis E. & Applequist, Harry A. Dynamic Movement Experiences for Elementary School Children: Combining the Traditional Approach with Movement Education to Produce a Physical Education That Enhances & Complements Intellectual Growth. (Illus.). 536p. 1974. 29.75 (ISBN 0-398-03148-7); pap. 21.75 (ISBN 0-398-03151-7). C C Thomas.

Means, Philip A. Biblioteca Andina: Essays on the Lives & Works of the Chroniclers. LC 72-97615. (Illus.). 257p. 1973. Repr. of 1928 ed. 14.50x o.p. (ISBN 0-87917-025-5). Blaine Ethridge.

Meares, Bernard, tr. see Mandelstam, Osip.

Mearns, Andrew, et al. Bitter Cry of Outcast London. Wohl, Anthony S., ed. (Victorian Library). 1970. Repr. of 1883 ed. text ed. 8.00x (ISBN 0-7185-5003-X, Leicester). Humanities.

Mears, Dana C. External Skeletal Fixation. (Illus.). 584p. 1981. write for info. (5900-9). Williams & Wilkins.

Mears, Henrietta C. Lo Que Nos Dice la Biblia. Marosi, Esteban, ed. Powell, David, tr. from Eng. 624p. (Span.). 1979. pap. text ed. 6.95 (ISBN 0-8297-0485-X). Vida Pubs.

--What the Bible Is All About. LC 79-92452. 12.95 (ISBN 0-8307-0512-0, 5102421); pap. 7.95 (ISBN 0-8307-0473-6, 54-047-03). Regal.

--What the Bible Is All About. 698p. 1980. pap. 7.95 (ISBN 0-89066-024-7). World Wide Pubs.

--What the New Testament Is All About. pap. 3.95 (ISBN 0-8307-0525-2, 5015618). Regal.

--What the Old Testament Is All About. LC 76-51196. (Illus.). 1977. pap. 1.95 (ISBN 0-8307-0466-3, S111-1-28). Regal.

Mears, Henrrieta, tr. Ha Poder Em Suas Palavras. (Portugese Bks.). (Port.). 1979. write for info. (ISBN 0-8297-0659-3). Life Pubs Intl.

--Lo Que Dices Recibes. (Spanish Bks.). (Span.). 1978. 1.90 (ISBN 0-8297-0808-1). Life Pubs Intl.

Measeles, Evelyn B. Lee's Ferry: A Crossing on the Colorado. (Illus.). 150p. 1981. 12.95 (ISBN 0-87108-576-3). Pruett.

Meats, Stephen, ed. see Perry, Benjamin F.

Mebane, John. Collecting Nostalgia. 1973. pap. 1.50 o.p. (ISBN 0-445-03008-9). Popular Lib.

Mebane, Mary E. Mary: An Autobiography. LC 80-51999. 256p. 1981. 12.95 (ISBN 0-670-45938-0). Viking Pr.

Mecca, Stephen J. & Robertshaw, Joseph E. Home Energy Management: Principles & Practices. (Illus.). 160p. 1981. 12.00 (ISBN 0-89433-146-9). Petrocelli.

Mecca, Stephen J., jt. auth. see Robertshaw, Joseph E.

Mech, Doris. Joy with Honey. 135p. 1979. 3.95 (ISBN 0-930756-46-0, 4230-JH). Women's Aglow.

Mech, L. David. The Wolf: The Ecology & Behavior of an Endangered Species. LC 80-27364. (Illus.). 385p. 1981. pap. 8.95 (ISBN 0-8166-1026-6). U of Minn Pr.

Mechanic, David. The Growth of Bureaucratic Medicine: An Inquiry into the Dynamics of Patient Behavior & the Organization of Medical Care. LC 75-29347. (Health, Medicine & Society Ser.). 368p. 1976. 19.95 o.p. (ISBN 0-471-59021-5, Pub. by Wiley-Interscience). Wiley.

--Medical Sociology. 2nd ed. LC 77-3850. 1978. text ed. 16.95 (ISBN 0-02-920720-7). Free Pr.

--Mental Health & Social Policy. 2nd ed. (Ser. in Social Policy). 1980. pap. text ed. 10.95 (ISBN 0-13-576025-9). P-H.

--Politics, Medicine & Social Science. 306p. 1974. 21.00 (ISBN 0-471-59008-8, Pub. by Wiley-Interscience). Wiley.

--Students Under Stress: A Study in the Social Psychology of Adaptation. LC 77-91058. 1978. 20.00 (ISBN 0-299-07470-6); pap. text ed. 6.95 (ISBN 0-299-07474-9). U of Wis Pr.

Mechanix Illustrated Editors. Mechanix Illustrated Fix-It Home Repairs Handbook. rev. ed. LC 72-95382. (Illus.). 112p. 1973. Repr. of 1970 ed. lib. bdg. 3.95 o.p. (ISBN 0-668-02937-4). Arco.

Mecher, Daniel. Planning for Better Imposition. LC 76-102070. 1977. 26.95 (ISBN 0-912920-55-6). North Am Pub Co.

Mechlenburg, Roy, jt. auth. see Davidson, Harold.

Mechling, Jay, ed. Church State & Public Policy. 1979. 10.25 (ISBN 0-8447-2159-X); pap. 5.25 (ISBN 0-8447-2160-3). Am Enterprise.

Meck, Charles R., ed. The Great Outdoors Book. LC 81-65103. (Illus.). 256p. (Orig.). 1981. pap. 8.95 (ISBN 0-910676-24-0, 7706). DBI.

Meck, H. R. Scientific Analysis for Programmable Calculators. (Illus.). 160p. 1981. 13.95 (ISBN 0-13-796417-X, Spec); pap. 6.95 (ISBN 0-13-796409-9). P-H.

Meckfennel, D. Your Via Dolorosa & Victory. 4.50 o.p. (ISBN 0-8062-1126-1). Carlton.

Mecking, P. R. Confessions of a Late Bloomer: Or, Wear Enough Eye Make-up & No One Will Notice Your Hips. Donnelly, K., ed. (Illus., Orig.). 1979. pap. 4.95 (ISBN 0-935282-00-9). Quinn-Gallagher.

Mecklenburg, Robert S. Endocrine Emergencies. LC 79-26132. 60p. (Orig.). 1978. pap. 5.00x (ISBN 0-9601944-2-8). MARC.

Mecklenburgh, J. C. Plant Layout for Chemical Engineers. 1974. 18.95x (ISBN 0-249-44125-X). Intl Ideas.

Meckler, Alan, jt. auth. see Shenton, James P.

Medawar, Charles. The Social Audit Consumer Handbook: A Guide to the Social Responsibilities of Business to the Consumer. (Illus.). 1978. text ed. 23.00x (ISBN 0-333-21665-2); pap. text ed. 10.25x (ISBN 0-333-21666-0). Humanities.

Medawar, Jean. Lifeclass. (Illus.). 80p. (gr. 3-6). 1981. 13.50 (ISBN 0-686-69427-9, Pub. by Hamish Hamilton England). David & Charles.

Medawar, P. B. Advice to a Young Scientist. LC 79-1676. 128p. 1981. pap. 3.95 (ISBN 0-06-090810-6, CN 810, CN). Har-Row.

Medawar, Peter B. The Uniqueness of the Individual. 192p. 1981. pap. write for info. (ISBN 0-486-24042-8). Dover.

Medcalf, G. Marketing & the Brand Manager. 1967. 23.00 (ISBN 0-08-012602-2); pap. 11.25 (ISBN 0-08-012601-4). Pergamon.

Meddaugh, Susan. Beast. (gr. k-3). 1981. 8.95 (ISBN 0-395-30349-4). HM.

--Maude & Claude Go Abroad. (Illus.). (gr. k-3). 1980. reinforced bdg. 7.95 (ISBN 0-395-29162-3). HM.

Meddis, R. Elementary Analysis of Variance for the Behavioral Sciences. LC 72-12493. (Illus.). 129p. 1973. pap. text ed. 10.50x (ISBN 0-470-59007-6). Halsted Pr.

--The Sleep Instinct. 1977. 15.00 (ISBN 0-7100-8545-1). Routledge & Kegan.

Medearis, Kenneth G., jt. ed. see American Society of Civil Engineers.

Medeiros, Huberto C. Thy Kingdom Come. 1980. write for info. (ISBN 0-8198-7307-1); pap. write for info. (ISBN 0-8198-7308-X). Dghtrs St Paul.

Meder, Albert E., Jr., ed. see Buchanan, O. Lexton, Jr.

Meder, J. & Handbuck, Ein. Durer-Katalog. LC 75-87642. (Graphic Art Ser.: Vol. 12). (Illus.). 358p. 1971. Repr. of 1932 ed. lib. bdg. 59.50 (ISBN 0-306-71788-3). Da Capo.

Meder, Marylouise D., ed. Library School Review, Vol. 18. 1979. pap. 2.00. Sch Lib Sci.

Medes, Elizabeth. Exciting River Running in the U.S. 1979. 9.95 o.p. (ISBN 0-8092-7508-2); pap. 5.95 o.p. (ISBN 0-8092-7507-4). Contemp Bks.

Medgyessy, Pal. Decomposition of Superpositions of Density Functions & Discrete Distributions. LC 75-46231. 1977. 39.95x (ISBN 0-470-15017-3). Halsted Pr.

Medhi, J. P. An Introduction to Stochastic Processes. 320p. 1981. 19.95 (ISBN 0-470-27000-4). Halsted Pr.

Medhurst, Kenneth. The Basques. (Minority Rights Group: No. 9). 1972. pap. 2.50 (ISBN 0-89192-098-6). Interbk Inc.

Medhurst, Kenneth, ed. Allende's Chile. LC 73-81735. 212p. 1973. 17.95 (ISBN 0-312-02100-3). St Martin.

Medhurst, Kenneth M. Government in Spain: The Executive at Work. 1973. text ed. 16.50 (ISBN 0-08-016940-6). Pergamon.

Media Institute, ed. see Bethell, Tom.

Medical Economics Company. Medical-Surgical Tips-Techniques. (Illus.). 1975. pap. 12.50 (ISBN 0-87489-089-6). Med Economics.

--Antidepressants. 1972. 6.95 (ISBN 0-87489-026-8). Med Economics.

--Cartoon Classics, 2 bks. (Illus.). 1963. 29.50 set (ISBN 0-87489-028-4). Med Economics.

--Pediatrics. (Illus.). 1974. pap. 5.95 (ISBN 0-87489-052-7). Med Economics.

Medical Sciences Division. Chromium. LC 74-3493. (Medical & Biologic Effects of Environmental Pollutants Ser). 168p. 1974. pap. 9.00 (ISBN 0-309-02217-7). Natl Acad Pr.

--Manganese. LC 73-18174. (Medical & Biologic Effects of Environmental Pollutants Ser.). 192p. 1973. pap. 9.00 (ISBN 0-309-02143-X). Natl Acad Pr.

--Vanadium. LC 74-7131. (Medical & Biologic Effects of Environmental Pollutants Ser.). (Illus.). 128p. 1974. pap. 7.50 o.p. (ISBN 0-309-02218-5). Natl Acad Pr.

Medicinal Chemistry Symposium, 20th, New York, May 1979. Drug Action & Design. Mechanism Based on Enzyme Inhibitors: Proceedings. Kalman, T. I., ed. LC 79-17370. (Developments in Biochemistry: Vol. 6). 1979. 40.00 (ISBN 0-444-00345-2, North Holland). Elsevier.

Medina, Angel. Reflection, Time & the Novel. (International Library of Phenomenology & Moral Sciences). 1979. 20.00x (ISBN 0-7100-0273-4). Routledge & Kegan.

Medina, Barbara F. A Mathematical Approach to Evaluating Systems. 250p. 1981. price not set (ISBN 0-677-05570-6). Gordon.

--Structured System Analysis: A New Technique. 1981. write for info. (ISBN 0-677-05570-6). Gordon.

Medina, Gwen, jt. auth. see Morris, Myrle.

Medina, H. R. & Association of the Bar of the City of New York. Freedom of the Press & Fair Trial: Final Report with Recommendations. LC 67-15897. 1967. 12.50x (ISBN 0-231-03054-1). Columbia U Pr.

Medina, Jose T. Medallas De Proclamaciones y Juras De los Reyes De Espana En America. LC 72-85123. (Illus.). 356p. (Span.). 1973. Repr. of 1917 ed. 35.00x (ISBN 0-88000-017-1). Quarterman.

Medinnus, Gene R., jt. auth. see Johnson, Ronald C.

Medler, John T. Insects of Nigeria. (Memoir Ser.: No. 30). 919p. 1980. 68.00 (ISBN 0-686-27978-6). Am Entom Inst.

Medley, Donald B., ed. see National Computer Conference, 1980.

Medley, Margaret. Yuan Porcelain & Stoneware. 1974. 48.00 (ISBN 0-571-10512-2, Pub. by Faber & Faber). Merrimack Bk Serv.

Medley, Morris L. & Conyers, James E., eds. Sociology for the Seventies: A Contemporary Perspective. LC 70-168640. 1972. pap. text ed. 9.95x o.p. (ISBN 0-471-59015-0). Wiley.

Medlicott, W. N. Contemporary England: 1914-1964. LC 67-26796. (Social & Economic History of England Ser.). 1976. pap. text ed. 12.95x (ISBN 0-582-48487-1). Longman.

Medlicott, W. N. & Coveney, D. Bismarck & Europe. 1972. 18.95 (ISBN 0-312-08225-8). St Martin.

Medlin, William K., jt. auth. see Jensen, Gale E.

Medlin, William K., et al. Images of the U.S.A. A High School History Reader from Textbooks in Other Lands. 203p. (gr. 10-12). 1969. pap. text ed. 3.50x o.p. (ISBN 0-89039-101-7). Ann Arbor Pubs.

Mednick, M. S., et al, eds. Women & Achievement: Social & Motivational Analyses. LC 75-22047. 447p. 1975. 19.95 (ISBN 0-470-59025-4); pap. 11.95 (ISBN 0-470-99150-X). Halsted Pr.

Mednick, Sarnoff A. & Baert, Andre E., eds. Prospective Longitudinal Research in Europe: An Empirical Basis for the Primary Prevention of Psychosocial Disorders. (Illus.). 450p. 1981. text ed. 99.50 (ISBN 0-19-261184-4). Oxford U Pr.

Mednick, Sarnoff A. & Shoham, Shlomo, eds. New Paths in Criminology. LC 77-25739. 1979. 21.95 (ISBN 0-669-01510-5). Lexington Bks.

Medoff, Mark. Children of a Lesser God. LC 80-24379. xxii, 91p. 1980. 8.98 (ISBN 0-88371-032-3); pap. 4.95 (ISBN 0-88371-034-X). J T White.

Medrano, A., ed. see Gonzalez-Mena, Frank & Gonzalez-Mena, Janet.

Medsger, Betty. Women at Work. (Illus.). 224p. 1975. 14.95 o.p. (ISBN 0-685-52958-4); pap. 7.95 o.p. (ISBN 0-8362-0614-2). Andrews & McMeel.

Medved, Eva. Food in Theory & Practice. LC 77-76340. (Illus.). 1978. text ed. 15.95x (ISBN 0-916434-24-9). Plycon Pr.

Medvedev, R. A. Problems in the Literary Biography of Mikhail Sholokhov. Briggs, A. D., tr. LC 76-14032. 1977. 32.50 (ISBN 0-521-21333-9). Cambridge U Pr.

Medvedev, Roy. The October Revolution. Saunders, George, tr. from Rus. LC 79-9854. 1979. 15.00 (ISBN 0-231-04590-5). Columbia U Pr.

--On Soviet Dissent: Interviews with Piero Ostellino. Packer, William A., tr. from Italian. LC 79-27877. 1980. 10.95 (ISBN 0-231-04812-2). Columbia U Pr.

Medvedev, Roy, ed. Samizdat Reigister Two. 1981. 19.95 (ISBN 0-393-01419-3). Norton.

Medvedev, Roy A. & Medvedev, Zhores A. Khrushchev: The Years in Power. LC 76-19104. 240p. 1976. 15.00x (ISBN 0-231-03939-5). Columbia U Pr.

Medvedev, Roy A., ed. The Samizdat Register. 1977. pap. 24.95 (ISBN 0-393-05652-X); pap. write for info. (ISBN 0-393-09081-7). Norton.

Medvedev, Zhores A. Protein Biosynthesis: And Problems of Heredity, Development, & Aging. LC 66-28598. 584p. 1966. 49.50 (ISBN 0-306-30284-5, Plenum Pr). Plenum Pub.

--Ten Years After Ivan Denisovich. LC 74-3433. 1974. pap. 1.95 o.p. (ISBN 0-394-71112-2, Vin). Random.

Medvedev, Zhores A., jt. auth. see Medvedev, Roy A.

Medwin, Herman, jt. auth. see Clay, Clarence S.

Medwin, Thomas. Thomas Medwin (Seventeen Eighty-Eight to Eighteen Sixty-Nine) Reiman, Donald H., ed. LC 75-31230. (Romantic Context Ser.: Poetry 1789-1830). 1978. lib. bdg. 47.00 (ISBN 0-8240-2179-7). Garland Pub.

Mee, A. J., et al. Science for the Seventies, 2 bks. pap. text ed. 4.95x ea.; Bk. 1. pap. text ed. (ISBN 0-435-57574-0); Bk. 2. pap. text ed. (ISBN 0-435-57576-7); Bk. 1. tchrs'. ed. 7.95x (ISBN 0-435-57575-9); Bk. 2. tchrs'. ed. 9.95 (ISBN 0-435-57577-5). Heinemann Ed.

Mee, Charles L., Jr. The End of Order: Versailles, Nineteen Nineteen. 410p. 1980. 15.95 (ISBN 0-525-09810-0). Dutton.

--The Ohio Gang: The World of Warren G. Harding. Katz, Herbert M., ed. 250p. 1981. 12.95 (ISBN 0-87131-340-5). M Evans.

--Seizure. 1979. pap. 2.25 (ISBN 0-515-05424-0). Jove Pubns.

Mee, Charles L., Jr. & Walker, John. Lorenzo De'Medici & the Renaissance. (Horizon Caravel Bks). (Illus.). 153p. (gr. 6 up). 1969. 9.95 (ISBN 0-8281-0000-4, J036-0, Dist. by Har-Row); PLB 12.89 (ISBN 0-06-024173-X, Dist. by Har-Row). Am Heritage.

Mee, Charles L., Jr; see Corrigan, Robert W.

Mee, Graham. Organisation for Education. 114p. 1980. pap. text ed. 25.00 (ISBN 0-582-78300-3). Longman.

Meebelo, Henry S. Reaction to Colonialism: A Prelude to the Politics of Independence in Northern Zambia, 1893-1939. 1971. text ed. 9.00x (ISBN 0-7190-1028-4); pap. text ed. 4.75x (ISBN 0-7190-1029-2). Humanities.

Meech, Sanford B., ed. see Kempe, Margery B.

Meehan, Eugene J. Reasoned Argument in Social Science: Linking Research to Policy Ser. LC 80-1198. (Illus.). 248p. 1981. lib. bdg. 27.50 (ISBN 0-313-22481-1, MRE). Greenwood.

Meek, B. L., jt. auth. see Hill, I. D.

Meek, Brian & Heath, Patricia, eds. Guide to Good Programming Practice. 181p. 1979. 29.95 (ISBN 0-470-26869-7). Wiley.

Meek, Christine. Lucca, Thirteen Sixty-Nine to Fourteen Hundred: Politics & Society in an Early Renaissance City-State. (Oxford Historical Monographs). 438p. 1978. text ed. 45.00x (ISBN 0-19-821866-4). Oxford U Pr.

Meek, Forrest B. Michigan's Heartland. Date not set. 14.50 (ISBN 0-9602472-0-3). Edgewood.

--Michigan's Timber Battleground. 2nd ed. 483p. lib. bdg. 9.95 softcover sewn binding (ISBN 0-9602472-1-1). Edgewood.

Meek, G. A. & Elder, H. Y., eds. Analytical & Quantitative Methods in Microscopy. LC 76-22983. (Society for Experimental Biology Seminar Ser: No. 3). (Illus.). 1977. 42.50 (ISBN 0-521-21404-1); pap. 15.95x (ISBN 0-521-29141-0). Cambridge U Pr.

Meek, J. M. & Craggs, J. D. Electrical Breakdown of Gases. 878p. 1978. 139.50 (ISBN 0-471-99553-3). Wiley.

Meek, Jay. Drawing on the Walls. LC 79-51607. (Poetry Ser.). 1980. 9.95 (ISBN 0-915604-31-0); pap. 4.95 (ISBN 0-915604-32-9). Carnegie-Mellon.

Meek, Mary E., jt. auth. see David, Alfred.

Meek, R. L. Social Science & the Ignoble Savage. LC 75-22985. (Cambridge Studies in the History & Theory of Politics). 262p. 1976. 32.95 (ISBN 0-521-20969-2). Cambridge U Pr.

Meek, R. L., ed. see Smith, Adam.

Meek, Wilbur T. The Exchange Media of Colonial Mexico. (Perspectives in Latin American History Ser.: No. 5). vi, 114p. 1980. Repr. of 1948 ed. lib. bdg. 13.50x (ISBN 0-87991-070-4). Porcupine Pr.

Meeker, Barbara F., jt. auth. see Leik, Robert K.

Meeker, Charles A. Chinese Acupuncture: Do-It Yourself, a Text Book for Practitioners. 4th ed. LC 60-972. (Illus.). 210p. Date not set. 15.50 (ISBN 0-935068-07-4). Meeker Pub.

Meeker, Joseph W. Comedy of Survival. LC 79-54815. 1980. pap. 7.95 (ISBN 0-89615-048-8). Guild of Tutors.

Meeker, Joseph W., ed. The New Natural Philosophy Reader. LC 80-67899. 1981. pap. 8.95 (ISBN 0-89615-026-7). Guild of Tutors.

Meeker, Josephine see Dawson, Thomas F.

Meeker, Mary. Structure of Intellect: Its Interpretation & Uses. LC 69-17296. 1969. text ed. 17.95 (ISBN 0-675-09516-6). Merrill.

Meeks, Carol B. Housing. (Illus.). 1980. text ed. 15.95 (ISBN 0-13-394981-8). P-H.

Meeks, Dorothy R., et al. Practical Nursing: A Textbook for Students & Graduates. 5th ed. LC 73-20244. 1974. text ed. 15.95 (ISBN 0-8016-3390-7). Mosby.

Meeks, Esther & Bagwell, Elizabeth. How New Life Begins. (gr. 4-6). 1969. lib. ed. 3.48 o.p. (ISBN 0-695-43855-7). Follett.

Meeks, G. Disappointing Marriage: A Study of the Gains from Merger. LC 77-73287. (Department of Applied Economics, Occasional Paper: No. 51). (Illus.). 1977. 14.95 o.p. (ISBN 0-521-21691-5); pap. 15.95x (ISBN 0-521-29234-4). Cambridge U Pr.

Meeks, Howard D., jt. auth. see Randolph, Paul H.

Meeks, Linda B., et al. Teaching Health Science in Middle & Secondary Schools. 400p. write for info (ISBN 0-697-07392-0). Wm C Brown.

Meeks, Wayne A. & Wilken, Robert L. Jews & Christians in Antioch in the First Four Centuries of the Common Era. LC 78-3760. 1978. pap. 6.00 (ISBN 0-89130-331-6). Scholars Pr Ca.

Meenaghan, Thomas M. & Washington, Robert O. Social Policy & Social Welfare: Structure & Applications. LC 79-54669. (Illus.). 1980. text ed. 12.95 (ISBN 0-02-920750-9). Free Pr.

Meer, Atie Van Der see Van Der Meer, Ron & Van Der Meer, Atie.

Meer, Ron Van Der see Van Der Meer, Ron & Van Der Meer, Atie.

Meer, Van Der Wybe J. see Van Der Meer, Wybe J., et al.

Meer, Wybe J. van Der see Van Der Meer, Wybe J.

Meer Atie, Van Der see Van Der Meer, Ron & Van Der Meer, Atie.

Meerhaeghe, M. A. Van see Van Meerhaeghe, M. A.

Meerhaeghe, M. A. van see Van Meerhaeghe, M. A.

Meerhaeghe, M. A. Van see Van Meerhaeghe, M. A.

Meerhaghe, Marcel A. Van see Van Meerhaeghe, Marcel A.

Meerloo, Joost A. Hidden Communion. LC 64-24910. 1964. 4.75 o.p. (ISBN 0-912326-12-3). Garrett-Helix.

Meerman, Jacob P. Public Expenditure in Malaysia: Who Benefits & Why. (World Bank Research Publications Ser.). (Illus.). 1979. 14.95x (ISBN 0-19-520096-9); pap. 6.95x (ISBN 0-19-520097-7). Oxford U Pr.

Meer Ron, Van Der see Van Der Meer, Ron & Van Der Meer, Atie.

Meers, Gary, et al. Handbook of Special Vocational Needs Education. LC 80-17759. 383p. 1980. 26.95 (ISBN 0-89443-288-5). Aspen Systems.

Mees, A. I. Dynamics of Feedback Systems. LC 80-40501. 212p. 1981. 35.75 (ISBN 0-471-27822-X, Pub. by Wiley-Interscience). Wiley.

Meeter, John. He Took Bread & Broke It. 1981. 6.95 (ISBN 0-533-04729-3). Vantage.

Meetham, A. R. Atmospheric Pollution. 3rd rev. ed. 1964. 15.15 (ISBN 0-08-010143-7). Pergamon.

--Encyclopedia of Linguistics, Information & Control. 1969. 115.00 (ISBN 0-08-012337-6). Pergamon.

Meetham, A. R., et al. Atmospheric Pollution: Its History, Origins & Prevention. 4th ed. (Illus.). 288p. 1980. 38.00 (ISBN 0-08-024003-8); pap. 15.00 (ISBN 0-08-024002-X). Pergamon.

Meeting of the American Orthopsychiatric Assoc., 47th. On the Urban Scene: Proceedings. Levitt, Morton & Rubenstein, Ben, eds. LC 72-1440. 1972. 13.50x (ISBN 0-8143-1478-3). Wayne St U Pr.

Meeting of the Midwest Autumn Immunology Conference, 7th, Michigan, Nov. 1978. Immunologic Tolerance & Macrophage Function: Proceedings. Baram, R., et al, eds. LC 79-243. (Developments in Immunology Ser.: Vol. 4). 1979. 40.00 (ISBN 0-444-00316-9, North Holland). Elsevier.

Meeuse, B. J. The Story of Pollination. (Illus.). 1961. 14.50 o.p. (ISBN 0-8260-5960-0). Ronald Pr.

Mefford, W. H. The Games of 'Eighty. (Orig.). 1980. pap. 1.95 (ISBN 0-505-51494-X). Tower Bks.

Meftah, Michael. Smoking & Chemical Abuse. 1981. 5.75 (ISBN 0-8062-1616-6). Carlton.

Megargee, Edwin I. & Bohn, Martin J., Jr. Classifying Criminal Offenders: A New System Based on the MMPI. LC 79-11677. (Sage Library of Social Research: Vol. 82). 288p. 1979. 18.00 (ISBN 0-8039-1168-8); pap. 8.95 (ISBN 0-8039-1167-X). Sage.

Megargee, Edwin I., jt. auth. see Rosenquist, Carl M.

Megateli, Abderrahmane. Investment Policies of National Oil Companies: A Comparative Study of Sonatrach, Nioc & Pemex. LC 80-12841. 344p. 1980. 31.95 (ISBN 0-03-052736-8). Praeger.

Megaw, J. V., ed. Hunters, Gatherers & First Farmers Beyond Europe: An Archaeological Survey. (Illus.). 250p. 1976. pap. text ed. 15.00x (ISBN 0-7185-1136-0, Leicester). Humanities.

Megaw, J. V. & Simpson, D. D., eds. Introduction to British Prehistory. 1979. text ed. 47.50x (ISBN 0-7185-1122-0, Leicester). Humanities.

Megaw, Vincent, jt. ed. see Greenhalgh, Michael.

Megged, Aharon. The Short Life: A Novel. Arad, Miriam, tr. from Hebrew. LC 80-13001. Orig. Title: Ha-Hayim ha-Ketsarim. 288p. 1980. 10.95 (ISBN 0-8008-7180-4). Taplinger.

Meggendorfer, Lothar. The International Circus: A Reproduction of the Antique Pop-up Book. LC 79-67737. (Illus.). (gr. k-3). 1980. 7.95 (ISBN 0-670-40011-4, Co-Pub. by Kestral Books). Viking Pr.

Meggers, Betty J. Amazonia: Man & Culture in a Counterfeit Paradise. LC 74-141427. (Worlds of Man Ser). 1971. 11.00x (ISBN 0-88295-608-6); pap. 5.75x (ISBN 0-88295-609-4). AHM Pub.

--Prehistoric America: An Ecological Perspective. 2nd ed. LC 78-169504. 1979. text ed. 15.95 (ISBN 0-202-33078-8); pap. 8.50 (ISBN 0-202-33079-6). Aldine Pub.

Meggett, Joan M. Music Periodical Literature: An Annotated Bibliography of Indexes & Bibliographies. LC 77-19120. 1978. 10.00 (ISBN 0-8108-1109-X). Scarecrow.

Megginson, Leon C. Personnel & Human Resources Administration. 3rd. ed. 1977. text ed. 18.95 (ISBN 0-256-01909-6). Irwin.

Meggitt, M. J., jt. ed. see Lawrence, P.

Meggs, Brown. The Matter of Paradise. 1975. 6.95 o.p. (ISBN 0-394-49627-2). Random.

--War Train. LC 79-55612. 1981. 13.95 (ISBN 0-689-11052-9). Atheneum.

Meggyesy, Dave. Out of Their League. (Illus.). 1971. pap. 1.75 o.s.i. (ISBN 0-446-59950-6). Warner Bks.

Meghdessian, Samira R. The Status of the Arab Woman: A Select Bibliography. LC 80-1028. 176p. 1980. lib. bdg. 32.50 (ISBN 0-313-22548-6, MEA/). Greenwood.

Megill, K. A. New Democratic Theory. LC 71-122277. 1971. 7.95 o.s.i. (ISBN 0-02-920780-0); pap. text ed. 4.50 o.s.i. (ISBN 0-02-920790-8). Free Pr.

Megill, R. E. How to Be a More Productive Employee. LC 72-9445. 120p. 1973. 15.00 (ISBN 0-87814-140-5). Pennwell Pub.

--An Introduction to Exploration Economics. 2nd ed. LC 75-153985. 160p. 1979. 23.00 (ISBN 0-87814-004-2). Pennwell Pub.

Meglin, Nick. Mad Stew. (Mad Ser.). (Illus., Orig.). 1978. pap. 1.75 (ISBN 0-446-94437-8). Warner Bks.

Meglin, Nick & Woodbridge, George. Sound of Mad. (Mad Ser.). (Illus., Orig.). 1980. pap. 1.50 (ISBN 0-446-88844-3). Warner Bks.

Mehaffy, Robert E. Writing for the Real World. 1980. pap. text ed. 9.95x (ISBN 0-673-15244-8). Scott F.

Mehaffy, Robert E. & Goodban, Dale F. Building a Vocabulary. 96p. (Orig.). (gr. 9-12). 1981. pap. text ed. 4.95 (ISBN 0-917962-68-0). Peek Pubns.

Mehan, Hugh & Wood, Houston. The Reality of Ethnomethodology. LC 75-1190. 259p. 1975. 21.50 (ISBN 0-471-59060-6, Pub. by Wiley-Interscience). Wiley.

Mehata, K. M., jt. auth. see Srinivasan, S. K.

Mehden, Fred R. Von Der see Von Der Mehden, Fred R.

Mehdi, M. T. Peace in Palestine. LC 75-43266. 1976. pap. 3.00 (ISBN 0-911026-08-8). New World Press NY.

Mehdi, M. T., ed. Palestine & the Bible. LC 71-114557. 1971. pap. 2.00 (ISBN 0-911026-06-1). New World Press NY.

Mehdi, Mohammad. Nation of Lions...Chained. LC 62-17245. 1963. pap. 5.00 (ISBN 0-911026-05-3). New World Press NY.

Mehdi, Mohammad T. Kennedy & Sirhan, Why. LC 68-57262. (Illus., Orig.). pap. 3.00 (ISBN 0-911026-04-5, KSW). New World Press NY.

--Peace in the Middle East. (Illus.). 1967. pap. 3.00 o.p. (ISBN 0-911026-09-6). New World Press NY.

Mehl, Dieter. Essays & Studies, Vol. 32, 1979. (New Series of Essays & Studies). 1979. text ed. 18.00x (ISBN 0-391-01035-2). Humanities.

--The Middle English Romances of the Thirteenth & Fourteenth Centuries. 1969. 28.00x (ISBN 0-7100-6240-0). Routledge & Kegan.

Mehlberg, Henry. Time, Causality & the Quantum Theory, 2 vols. Benecerraf, Paul, tr. from Fr. Incl. Vol. 1. Essay on the Causal Theory of Time. 299p. lib. bdg. 39.50 (ISBN 90-277-0721-9); pap. 17.00 (ISBN 90-277-1074-0); Vol. 2. Time in a Quantized Universe. 296p. lib. bdg. 34.20 (ISBN 90-277-1075-9); pap. 16.00 (ISBN 90-277-1076-7). (Boston Studies in the Philosophy of Science: No. 19). 1980. Kluwer Boston.

Mehlinger, Howard & Davis, O. L., Jr., eds. The Social Studies. LC 80-83744. (National Society for the Study of Education 80th Yearbooks: Pt. II). 300p. 1981. lib. bdg. 16.00x. U of Chicago Pr.

Mehlman, Jeffrey. Revolution & Repetition: Marx-Hugo-Balzac. (Quantum Ser.). 1977. 11.95x (ISBN 0-520-03111-3); pap. 2.45 (ISBN 0-520-03531-3). U of Cal Pr.

Mehlman, M. A. & Shapiro, R. Advances in Modern Toxicology: New Concepts in Safety Evaluation, 2 pts, Vol. 1. LC 76-27277. 1976. Pt. 1. 24.50x (ISBN 0-470-98919-X); Pt. 2. 24.50x (ISBN 0-470-26382-2). Halsted Pr.

Mehlman, M. A., jt. ed. see Demopoulos, H. B.

Mehlman, Myron A., et al. Carcinogenesis & Mutagenesis. (Journal of Environmental Pathology & Toxicology: Vol. 1, No. 2, Nov.-Dec. 1977). (Illus.). 388p. (Orig.). 1978. text ed. 23.00x (ISBN 0-930376-02-1); pap. 18.50x (ISBN 0-686-64026-8). Pathotox Pubs.

Mehlmann, Marilyn. When People Use Computers: An Approach to Developing an Interface. (Ser. in Software). (Illus.). 160p. 1981. text ed. 15.00 (ISBN 0-13-956219-2). P-H.

Mehnert, Klaus. Moscow & the New Left. Fischer, Helmut, tr. LC 73-90660. 1975. 20.00x (ISBN 0-520-02652-7). U of Cal Pr.

--Youth in Soviet Russia. Davidson, Michael, tr. LC 79-2914. 270p. 1981. Repr. of 1933 ed. 22.00 (ISBN 0-8305-0083-9). Hyperion Conn.

Mehr. Human Services: Concepts & Intervention Strategies. 1979. text ed. 15.95 (ISBN 0-205-06807-3). Allyn.

--Plaid for Life Insurance. 1979. pap. 5.50 (ISBN 0-256-02101-5, 03-1293-01). Learning Syst.

--Plaid for Principles of Insurance. rev. ed. 1978. 5.50 (ISBN 0-256-02097-3, 03-0859-02). Learning Syst.

Mehr, Linda, ed. Motion Pictures, Television & Radio. (Reference Publications Ser.). 1977. lib. bdg. 27.00 (ISBN 0-8161-8089-X). G K Hall.

Mehr, Robert I. Life Insurance: Theory & Practice. rev. ed. 1977. 19.95x (ISBN 0-256-01938-X). Business Pubns.

Mehr, Robert I. & Cammack, Emerson. Principles of Insurance. 7th ed. 1980. 18.95x (ISBN 0-256-02321-2). Irwin.

--Principles of Insurance. 6th ed. 1976. text ed. 16.95x o.p. (ISBN 0-256-01833-2). Irwin.

Mehr, Robert I. & Hedges, Bob A. Risk Management: Concepts & Applications. 1974. text ed. 18.50 (ISBN 0-256-01614-3). Irwin.

Mehra, Parshotam. The North-East Frontier: A Documentary Study of the Internecine Rivalry Between India, Tibet & China, Vol. 1, 1906-14. 270p. 1979. text ed. 9.95x (ISBN 0-19-561158-6). Oxford U Pr.

Mehrabi, Jacqueline. Stories for Children. (Illus.). (gr. 1-5). 1970. pap. 2.00 o.p. (ISBN 0-900125-05-5, 7-52-65). Baha'i.

Mehrabian, Albert. Basic Behavior Modification. LC 77-85582. (New Vistas in Counseling Ser.: Vol. 9). 1978. 10.95 (ISBN 0-87705-322-7). Human Sci Pr.

--Nonverbal Communication. LC 72-172859. 336p. 1972. 19.95x (ISBN 0-202-25091-1). Aldine Pub.

--Silent Messages. 1971. pap. 8.95x (ISBN 0-534-00059-2). Wadsworth Pub.

--Silent Messages: Implicit Communication of Emotions & Attitudes. 2nd ed. 208p. 1980. pap. text ed. 8.95x (ISBN 0-534-00910-7). Wadsworth Pub.

--Tactics of Social Influence. 1970. pap. text ed. 9.95 (ISBN 0-13-882159-3). P-H.

Mehrabian, Albert & Russell, James A. An Approach to Environmental Psychology. 266p. 1980. pap. 8.95x o.p. (ISBN 0-262-63071-0). MIT Pr.

Mehrabian, Albert & Russsell, James A. An Approach to Environmental Psychology. 240p. 1974. 15.00x (ISBN 0-262-13090-4); pap. 8.95x (ISBN 0-262-63071-0). MIT Pr.

Mehrabian, Albert, jt. auth. see Wiener, Morton.

Mehrkam, Deborah, ed. see Conway, Martin.

Mehrotra, S. R. Towards India's Freedom & Partition. LC 79-108398. 322p. 1979. 13.50x (ISBN 0-7069-0712-4). Intl Pubns Serv.

Mehrtens, Herbert & Richter, Steffen, eds. Naturwissenschaft, Technik und NS-Ideologie. (Suhrkamp Taschenbuecher Wissenschaft: Vol. 303). 288p. (Orig.). 1980. pap. text ed. 8.45 (ISBN 3-518-07903-4, Pub. by Insel Verlag Germany). Suhrkamp.

Mehta, D. S. Mass Communication & Journalism in India. 1979. 15.00x o.p. (ISBN 0-8364-0450-5). South Asia Bks.

Mehta, Gita. Karma Kola. 1981. pap. 5.95 (ISBN 0-671-25084-1, Touchstone). S&S.

Mehta, Jamshed K. Economics of Growth. 2nd ed. 1970. pap. 6.50x (ISBN 0-210-31183-5). Asia.

Mehta, Jawahar & Mehta, Paulette, eds. Platelets & Prostaglandins in Cardiovascular Disease. 300p. 1981. write for info. (ISBN 0-87993-089-6). Futura Pub.

Mehta, Jeroo. One Hundred & One Parsi Recipes. (Illus.). 146p. 1975. comb. bound 4.95 (ISBN 0-88253-438-6). Ind-US Inc.

Mehta, L. A., jt. auth. see Kothari, M. L.

Mehta, M. L., jt. auth. see Harkness, E. L.

Mehta, Nitin H. & Maher, Donald J. Hospital Accounting Systems & Controls. 272p. 1977. 32.95 (ISBN 0-686-68586-5, 14919). Hospital Finan.

Mehta, Paulette, jt. ed. see Mehta, Jawahar.

Mehta, Rohit. Science of Meditation. 1978. 7.50 (ISBN 0-89684-007-7, Pub. by Motilal Banarsidass India); pap. 4.50 (ISBN 0-89684-008-5). Orient Bk Dist.

Mehta, S. S. Productivity, Production Function & Technical Change. 1980. text ed. 9.00x (ISBN 0-391-01830-2). Humanities.

Mehta, Ved. Daddyji. 224p. 1972. 6.95 o.p. (ISBN 0-374-13438-3). FS&G.

--Face to Face. LC 57-9323. 1978. pap. 4.95 (ISBN 0-19-520014-4, GB537, GB). Oxford U Pr.

--John Is Easy to Please: Encounters with the Written & Spoken Word. 256p. 1971. 7.50 (ISBN 0-374-17986-7). FS&G.

--The Photographs of Chachaji: The Making of a Documentary Film. (Illus.). 300p. 1980. 15.95 (ISBN 0-19-502792-2). Oxford U Pr.

Mehul, Etienne. Ariodant. Gossett, Philip & Rosen, Charles, eds. LC 76-49220. (Early Romantic Opera Ser.). 1979. lib. bdg. 82.00 (ISBN 0-8240-2938-0). Garland Pub.

--Uthal. Gossett, Philip & Rosen, Charles, eds. LC 76-49222. (Early Romantic Opera Ser.: Vol. 40). 1979. lib. bdg. 82.00 (ISBN 0-8240-2939-9). Garland Pub.

Mehul, Etienne N. Euphrosine et Coradin Ou le Tyran Corrige. Gossett, Phillip & Rosen, Charles, eds. LC 76-49224. (Early Romantic Opera Ser.: No. 38). 1980. lib. bdg. 82.00 (ISBN 0-8240-2937-2). Garland Pub.

Meid, Louise B. Van Der see Van Der Meid, Louise B.

Meiden, Walter, jt. auth. see Moore, Olin H.

Meidl, J. H. Explosive & Toxic Hazardous Materials. 2nd ed. Date not set. cancelled (ISBN 0-685-48939-6, 47658). Macmillan.

Meidl, James. Explosive & Toxic Hazardous Materials. Gruber, Harvey, ed. (Glencoe Press Fire Science Ser). 1970. text ed. 14.95x (ISBN 0-02-476380-2, 47638). Macmillan.

--Hazardous Materials Handbook. (Fire Science Ser). 1972. pap. text ed. 7.95x (ISBN 0-02-476370-5, 47637). Macmillan.

Meidl, James H. Flammable Hazardous Materials. 2nd ed. 1978. text ed. 14.95x (ISBN 0-02-476570-8). Macmillan.

Meidner, Hans & Sheriff, D. W. Water & Plants. LC 75-41425. (Tertiary Level Biology Ser). 148p. 1976. pap. 13.95 (ISBN 0-470-14996-5). Halsted Pr.

Meienhofer, Johannes, jt. ed. see Goodman, Murray.

Meienhofer, Johannes, jt. ed. see Gross, Erhard.

Meier. Facilitating Children's Development: A Systematic Guide to Open Learning, 2 vols. Incl. Vol. I. Infant & Toddler Learning Episodes. 22.95 (ISBN 0-8391-1261-0); Vol. II. Learning Episodes for Older Preschoolers. 24.50 (ISBN 0-8391-1339-0). 1979. Univ Park.

Meier & Brudney. Applied Statistics & Analytic Techniques for Public Administrators. 1981. 15.95. Duxbury Pr.

Meier, A., ed. see Mestwerdt.

Meier, August. Negro Thought in America, 1880-1915: Racial Ideologies in the Age of Booker T. Washington. 1963. pap. 4.95 (ISBN 0-472-06118-6, 118, AA). U of Mich Pr.

Meier, August & Rudick, Elliott. CORE: A Study in the Civil Rights Movement, 1942-1968. 448p. 1973. 24.95 (ISBN 0-19-501627-0). Oxford U Pr.

Meier, August & Rudwick, Elliott. Along the Color Line: Explorations in the Black Experience. LC 76-27293. (Blacks in the New World Ser.). 1977. 17.50 (ISBN 0-252-00636-4). U of Ill Pr.

--Black Detroit & the Rise of the UAW. (Illus.). 1979. 17.95 (ISBN 0-19-502561-X). Oxford U Pr.

--Black Detroit & the Rise of the Uaw. (Illus.). 304p. 1981. pap. 6.95 (ISBN 0-19-502895-3, GB 632, OPB). Oxford U Pr.

Meier, August, jt. auth. see Meltzer, Milton.

Meier, Blanche G., jt. auth. see McClinton, Barbara S.

Meier, Carl L., jt. auth. see Klotter, John C.

Meier, D., ed. Block Copolymers. (Mmi Press Symposium Ser.: Vol. 2). 350p. 1981. lib. bdg. 44.00 lib. bdg. (ISBN 0-686-65733-0). Harwood Academic.

Meier, Dagmar M. David & His Alien Friend, Bks. I & II. (Illus.). Date not set. 8.00 (ISBN 0-682-49505-0). Exposition.

Meier, Gerald M. International Trade & Development. LC 73-13405. 208p. 1975. Repr. of 1963 ed. lib. bdg. 19.50x (ISBN 0-8371-7061-3, MEIT). Greenwood.

--Problems of Cooperation for Development. 272p. 1974. pap. text ed. 5.95x (ISBN 0-19-501867-2). Oxford U Pr.

Meier, Joel F., et al. High Adventure Outdoor Pursuits: Organization & Leadership. (Brighton Ser. in Recreation & Leisure). (Illus.). 240p. (Orig.). 1980. pap. 9.95 (ISBN 0-89832-019-4). Brighton Pub.

Meier, John P. Matthew. (New Testament Message Ser.). 12.95 (ISBN 0-89453-126-3); pap. 7.95 (ISBN 0-89453-191-3). M Glazier.

--The Vision of Matthew: Christ, Church & Morality in the First Gospel. LC 78-70820. 1979. pap. 5.95 (ISBN 0-8091-2171-9). Paulist Pr.

Meier, Paul & Meier, Richard. Family Foundations. 96p. (Orig.). 1981. 8.95 (ISBN 0-8010-6117-2); pap. 4.95 (ISBN 0-8010-6122-9). Baker Bk.

Meier, Paul, jt. auth. see Korem, Danny.

Meier, R. C. & Archer, S. H. Introduction to Mathematics for Business Analysis. 1960. text ed. 15.95 o.p. (ISBN 0-07-041332-0, C); answers 4.95 o.p. (ISBN 0-07-041333-9). McGraw.

Meier, Richard, jt. auth. see Meier, Paul.

Meier, Richard L. Urban Futures Observed: In the Asian Third World. LC 79-28624. (Pergamon Policy Studies on International Development). 256p. 1980. 29.50 (ISBN 0-08-025954-5). Pergamon.

Meier, Robert F., ed. Theory in Criminology: Contemporary Views. LC 77-81151. (Sage Research Progress Series in Criminology: Vol. 1). 1977. 12.95x (ISBN 0-8039-0915-2); pap. 6.50x (ISBN 0-8039-0910-1). Sage.

Meier, Robert S., jt. auth. see Geis, Gilbert.

Meier, W., jt. ed. see Schrader, B.

Meiggs, Russell & Lewis, David, eds. Selection of Greek Historical Inscriptions to the End of the 5th Century, B. C. 1969. 34.00x (ISBN 0-19-814266-8). Oxford U Pr.

Meighan, Clement & True, D. L., eds. Prehistoric Trails of Atacama. (Monumenta Archaeologica: No. 7). (Illus.). 258p. 1980. 32.65 (ISBN 0-917956-10-9). UCLA Arch.

Meighen, J. Van see Landsberg, H. E.

Meigs & Meigs. Plaid for Auditing. 1975. pap. 5.50 (ISBN 0-256-01758-1, 01-1172-00). Learning Syst.

Meigs, et al. Plaid for Auditing. rev. ed. 1981. write for info. (ISBN 0-256-02399-9, 01-1172-02). Learning Syst.

Meigs, Cornelia. Fair Wind to Virginia. (Illus.). (gr. 4-6). 1964. 7.95g (ISBN 0-02-765700-0). Macmillan.

--Willow Whistle. (Illus.). (gr. 4-6). 1931. 4.95g o.s.i. (ISBN 0-02-766470-8). Macmillan.

Meigs, Cornelia, et al. Critical History of Children's Literature. rev. ed. LC 67-10271. (Illus.). 1969. 17.95 (ISBN 0-02-583900-4). Macmillan.

Meigs, R. F. Computers & the Accounting Process. 1973. 6.95 o.p. (ISBN 0-07-041418-1, C). McGraw.

Meigs, Robert F., jt. auth. see Meigs, Walter B.

Meigs, W. M. Relation of the Judiciary to the Constitution. LC 73-124896. (American Constitutional & Legal History Ser). 1971. Repr. of 1919 ed. lib. bdg. 29.50 (ISBN 0-306-71988-6). Da Capo.

Meigs, Walter B. & Meigs, Robert F. Accounting: The Basis for Business Decisions. 5th ed. Singer, M. & Mason, D., eds. (Illus.). 1216p. 1980. text ed. 20.95 (ISBN 0-07-041551-X, C); study guide 7.50 (ISBN 0-07-041552-8); Learning Objectives avail. (ISBN 0-07-041565-X); practice set 1 6.50 (ISBN 0-07-041558-7); practice set 2 6.50 (ISBN 0-07-041559-5); comp. exam guide free (ISBN 0-07-041557-9); overhead transparencies 375.00 (ISBN 0-07-074714-8); Chapters 1-28. wksheets A 6.95 ea. (ISBN 0-07-041560-9); Chapters 1-28. wksheets B 6.95 ea. McGraw.

Meigs, Walter B., et al. Principles of Auditing. 6th ed. 1977. text ed. 20.95x (ISBN 0-256-01902-9). Irwin.

--Principles of Auditing. canadian ed. 1978. 21.90x (ISBN 0-256-02092-2). Irwin.

Meigs, William M. Life of Charles Jared Ingersoll. LC 71-127194. (American Scene Ser). 1970. Repr. of 1897 ed. lib. bdg. 35.00 (ISBN 0-306-70041-7). Da Capo.

--Life of John Caldwell Calhoun, Vol 1. LC 75-127195. (American Scene Ser). 1970. Repr. of 1917 ed. lib. bdg. 69.50 (ISBN 0-306-70042-5). Da Capo.

--Life of Thomas Hart Benton. LC 71-126599. (American Scene Ser). 1970. Repr. of 1904 ed. lib. bdg. 49.50 (ISBN 0-306-70043-3). Da Capo.

Meij, J. L. Mechanization in Agriculture. 1960. 47.50x (ISBN 0-686-50048-2). Elliots Bks.

Meijer, Marinus J. Introduction to Modern Criminal Law in China. (Studies in Chinese Government & Law). 1977. Repr. of 1950 ed. 20.00 (ISBN 0-89093-057-0). U Pubns Amer.

Meijer, Reinder P. Literature of the Low Countries: A Short History of Dutch Literature in the Netherlands & Belgium. 1971. text ed. 34.50x (ISBN 0-8057-3431-7); pap. text ed. 18.50x (ISBN 0-89197-825-9). Irvington.

Meijers, Daniel, jt. auth. see Schoffeleers, Matthews.

Meijers, J. J. Problem-Solving Therapy with Socially Anxious Children. 290p. 1978. pap. text ed. 22.75 (ISBN 90-265-0282-6, Pub. by Swets Pub Serv Holland). Swets North Am.

Meijlink, Jane, ed. see De Waal, M.

Meilach, Dona, jt. auth. see Davis, M. Edward.

Meilach, Dona Z. Ethnic Jewelry: Design & Inspiration for Craftsmen & Collectors. Aymar, Brant, ed. 1981. price not set. Crown.

--Ethnic Jewelry: Design & Inspiration for Craftsmen & Collectors. Aymar, Brandt, ed. (Illus.). 192p. 1981. pap. 19.95 (ISBN 0-517-52974-2, Harmony). Crown.

Meilach, Dona Z. & Mandel, Elias. Doctor Talks to Five to Eight Year Olds. (Illus.). 1980. pap. 2.50 (ISBN 0-910304-14-9). Budlong.

Meilach, Dona Z., jt. auth. see Birch, William G.

Meilakh, M., ed. see Vvendenskii, Aleksandr.

Meiland, Jack. First Time in London. LC 78-21547. 1979. pap. 5.95 (ISBN 0-684-16505-8, ScribT). Scribner.

Meiland, Jack W. Talking About Particulars. (International Library of Philosophy & Scientific Method). 1970. text ed. 8.00x (ISBN 0-391-00056-X). Humanities.

Meilicke, Carl A. & Storch, Janet L. Perspectives on Canadian Health & Social Services Policy: History & Emerging Trends. (Illus.). 522p. text ed. 38.95 (ISBN 0-914904-42-6). Health Admin Pr.

Meillassoux, C., ed. Maidens, Meal & Money. Edholm, Felicity, tr. from French. LC 79-52834. (Themes in the Social Sciences Ser.). 200p. write for info. (ISBN 0-521-22902-2); pap. write for info. (ISBN 0-521-29708-7). Cambridge U Pr.

Meillet, Antoine. Altarmenisches Elementarbuch. 1980. Repr. of 1913 ed. 25.00x (ISBN 0-88206-043-0). Caravan Bks.

Mei Mei Alicia Chu Polido, ed. see Gitman, Lawrence J.

Meinardi, H. & Rowan, A. J., eds. Advances in Epileptology, 1977: Psychology, Pharmacotherapy & New Diagnostic Approaches. 468p. 1978. pap. text ed. 37.75 (ISBN 90-265-0273-7, Pub. by Swets Pub Serv Holland). Swets North Am.

Meinardus, Guenter. Approximation of Functions: Theory & Numerical Methods. Schumaker, L. L., tr. LC 67-21464. (Springer Tracts in Natural Philosophy: Vol. 13). (Illus.). 1967. 41.30 (ISBN 0-387-03985-6). Springer-Verlag.

Meinecke, Friedrich. The Age of German Liberation, 1795-1815. Paret, Peter & Fischer, Helmut, trs. from Ger. LC 74-79767. Orig. Title: Das Zeitalter der Deutschen Erhebung. 1977. 20.00x (ISBN 0-520-02792-2); pap. 4.95x (ISBN 0-520-03454-6). U of Cal Pr.

Meinel, Aden B. & Meinel, Marjorie P. Applied Solar Energy: An Introduction. 400p. 1976. text ed. 25.95 (ISBN 0-201-04719-5). A-W.

Meinel, Marjorie P., jt. auth. see Meinel, Aden B.

Meiners, H. F., et al. Laboratory Physics. 1972. 14.95x (ISBN 0-471-59159-9). Wiley.

Meiners, Harry F., ed. Physics Demonstration Experiments, 2 Vols. (Illus.). 1400p. 1970. Set. 59.95 (ISBN 0-8260-5990-2, 66923, Pub. by Wiley-Interscience). Wiley.

Meiners, Roger E. Victim Compensation. LC 77-80772. 1978. 15.95 (ISBN 0-669-01667-5). Lexington Bks.

Meinhard, Heinrich. German Wines. (Illus.). 1971. 7.95 (ISBN 0-85362-107-1, Oriel). Routledge & Kegan.

Meinhardt, F. Untersuchungen Zur Genetik Des Fortpflanzungsverhaltens und der Fruchtkoerper- und Antibiotikabbildung Des Basidiomyceten Agrocybe Aegerita. (Bibliotheca Mycologica: No. 75). (Illus.). 128p. (Ger.). 1981. pap. text ed. 20.00x (ISBN 3-7682-1275-0). Lubrecht & Cramer.

Meinig, D. W. Southwest: Three Peoples in Geographical Change, 1600-1970. (Historical Geography of North America Ser). (Orig.). 1971. text ed. 10.95x (ISBN 0-19-501288-7); pap. text ed. 4.95x (ISBN 0-19-501289-5). Oxford U Pr.

Meinig, D. W., ed. The Interpretation of Ordinary Landscapes. (Illus.). 1979. pap. text ed. 5.95 (ISBN 0-19-502536-9). Oxford U Pr.

Meinke, Peter. Trying to Surprise God. LC 80-54062. (Pitt Poetry Ser). x, 78p. 1981. 9.95 (ISBN 0-8229-3434-5); pap. 4.50 (ISBN 0-8229-5326-9). U of Pittsburgh Pr.

Meirovitch, Leonard. Computational Methods in Structural Dynamics. (Mechanics: Dynamical Systems Ser.: No. 4). 450p. 1980. 35.00x (ISBN 90-286-0580-0). Sijthoff & Noordhoff.

Meisami, Esmail & Brazier, Mary A. Neural Growth & Differentiation. (International Brain Research Organization Monographs: Vol. 5). 1979. text ed. 52.00 (ISBN 0-89004-378-7). Raven.

Meise, Norman R. Conceptual Design of an Automated National Library System. (Illus.). 1969. 10.00 (ISBN 0-8108-0050-0). Scarecrow.

Meisel, Anthony C. & Del Mastro, M. L., trs. The Rule of St. Benedict. LC 74-33611. 120p. 1975. pap. 2.45 (ISBN 0-385-00948-8, Im). Doubleday.

Meisel, David J. Attorney Malpractice: Law & Procedure, Vol.1. LC 79-89562. 1980. 47.50. Lawyers Co-Op.

Meisel, Janet. Barons of the Welsh Frontier: The Corbet, Pantulf, & Fitz Warin Families, 1066 - 1272. LC 80-10273. xx, 231p. 1980. 19.95x (ISBN 0-8032-3064-8). U of Nebr Pr.

Meisel, Jurgen & Pam, Martin, eds. Linear Order & Generative Theory. (Current Issues in Linguistic Theory: No. 7). 1978. text ed. 57.00x (ISBN 90-272-0908-1). Humanities.

Meisel, Louis K. Photorealism. (Illus.). 528p. 1980. 125.00 (ISBN 0-686-62703-2, 1464-6). Abrams.

Meisel, Perry. Freud: A Collection of Critical Essays. (Twentieth Century Views Ser.). 256p. 1981. 13.95 (ISBN 0-13-331405-7, Spec); pap. 5.95 (ISBN 0-13-331397-2). P-H.

Meisel, Tony. A Manual of Singlehanded Sailing. LC 80-22856. (Illus.). 224p. 1981. lib. bdg. 12.95 (ISBN 0-668-04998-7, 4998). Arco.

Meiselas, Susan. Nicaragua-June Nineteen Seventy-Eight to July Nineteen Seventy-Nine. (Illus.). 1981. 20.00 (ISBN 0-394-51265-0); pap. 11.95 (ISBN 0-394-73931-0). Pantheon.

Meiselman, David M., ed. Varieties of Monetary Experience. LC 70-116027. (Economic Research Center Ser). 1971. 20.00x (ISBN 0-226-51930-9). U of Chicago Pr.

Meisenholder, Robert, jt. auth. see Broun, Kenneth S.

Meislin, Harvey W. Priorities in Multiple Trauma. 176p. 1980. text ed. 21.95 (ISBN 0-89443-287-7). Aspen Systems.

Meislin, Harvey W. & Dresnick, Stephen J. Skills & Procedures of Emergency & General Medicine. 250p. 1982. text ed. 29.95 (ISBN 0-8359-7009-4). Reston.

Meislin, Jack. Rehabilitation Medicine & Psychiatry. (Illus.). 564p. 1976. 32.75 (ISBN 0-398-03432-X). C C Thomas.

Meisner, Maurice. Mao's China: A History of the People's Republic. LC 76-51566. (The Transformation of Modern China Ser.). 1979. pap. text ed. 8.95 (ISBN 0-02-920810-6). Free Pr.

Meisner, Maurice & Murphy, Rhoads. The Mozartian Historian: Essays on the Works of Joseph R. Levenson. LC 74-82849. 250p. 1976. 15.75x (ISBN 0-520-02826-0). U of Cal Pr.

Meiss, Harriet & Jaeger, Doris, eds. Information to Authors: Editorial Guidelines Reprinted from 200 Medical Journals. LC 80-19712. 1980. pap. 26.00 (ISBN 0-8067-1251-1). Urban & S.

Meiss, Millard. The De Levis Hours & the Bedford Workshop. 73p. 1981. text ed. 10.00x (ISBN 0-300-03507-1). Yale U Pr.

--Giotto & Assisi. (Illus.). 12.95x (ISBN 0-912158-42-5). Hennessey.

Meiss, Millard & Beatson, Elizabeth H.commentaries by. The Belles Heures of Jean, Duke of Berry. LC 74-75688. (Illus.). 268p. 1974. slip-cased ed. 70.00 (ISBN 0-8076-0750-9); leatherbound 150.00 (ISBN 0-685-49198-6). Braziller.

Meiss, Millard, intro. by. The Visconti Hours. LC 75-75371. (Illus.). 264p. 1972. slipcase 70.00 (ISBN 0-8076-0651-0). Braziller.

--The Rohan Master. LC 73-77880. (Illus.). 248p. 1973. slipcase 65.00 (ISBN 0-8076-0690-1). Braziller.

Meissner, Hans-Oho. Magda Goebbels: The First Lady of the Third Reich. (Illus.). 288p. 1981. 14.95 (ISBN 0-686-69087-7). Dial.

Meissner, Loren P. & Organick, Elliot I. FORTRAN Seventy-Seven: Featuring Structured Programming. 3rd ed. LC 78-74689. 1980. pap. text ed. 13.95 (ISBN 0-201-05499-X). A-W.

Meissner, Loren P., jt. auth. see Organick, Elliot I.

Meissner, William. Learning to Breathe Underwater. LC 79-18881. 66p. 1980. 8.95 (ISBN 0-8214-0418-0); pap. 5.95 (ISBN 0-8214-0426-1). Ohio U Pr.

Meissner, William W. The Assault on Authority: Dialogue or Dilemma? LC 70-152878. 1971. 7.95x o.p. (ISBN 0-88344-018-0). Orbis Bks.

Meister, Alton. Advances in Enzymology & Related Areas of Molecular Biology, Vol. 52. 350p. 1981. 27.50 (ISBN 0-471-08120-5, Pub. by Wiley-Interscience). Wiley.

Meister, Alton, ed. Advances in Enzymology & Related Areas of Molecular Biology. Incl. Vol. 36, 1972 (ISBN 0-471-59171-8). Vol. 37, 1973 (ISBN 0-471-59172-6). Vol. 38, 1973 (ISBN 0-471-59173-4). Vol. 39, 1973 (ISBN 0-471-59174-2). Vol. 40, 1974 (ISBN 0-471-59175-0). Vol. 41, 1974 (ISBN 0-471-59176-9); Vol. 42, 1975 (ISBN 0-471-59177-7). Vol. 43, 1975 (ISBN 0-471-59178-5). LC 41-9213. (Pub. by Wiley-Interscience). Wiley.

--Advances in Enzymology & Related Areas of Molecular Biology. Vol. 45, 1977. 36.50 (ISBN 0-471-02726-X, Pub. by Wiley-Interscience); Vol. 46, 1978. 41.50 (ISBN 0-471-02993-9); Vol. 47, 1978. 42.50 (ISBN 0-471-04116-5); Vol. 51, 1980, 225p. 29.50 (ISBN 0-471-05653-7). Wiley.

Meister, Barbara. An Introduction to the Art Song. LC 79-66640. 1980. 11.95 (ISBN 0-8008-4203-0, Crescendo). Taplinger.

Meister, David. Behavioral Foundations of System Development. LC 76-1834. (Human Factors Ser.). 464p. 1976. 37.50 (ISBN 0-471-59195-5). Wiley.

--Behavioral Science: Research & Public Policy. (Pergamon Policy Studies). 350p. Date not set. price not set (ISBN 0-08-024659-1). Pergamon.

--Human Factors: Theory & Practice. LC 77-148505. (Human Factors Ser). 1971. 36.95 (ISBN 0-471-59190-4, Pub. by Wiley-Interscience). Wiley.

Meister, Jurg. Soviet Warships of the Second World War. LC 76-28690. (Illus.). 1977. 19.95 o.p. (ISBN 0-668-04086-6). Arco.

Meister, Richard & Loftis, Anne. A Long Time Coming: The Struggle to Unionize America's Farm Workers. LC 76-54510. 1977. 17.95 (ISBN 0-02-583920-9, 58392). Macmillan.

Meister, Robert. Fathers: Daughters, Sons, Fathers Reveal Their Deepest Feelings. 224p. 1981. 12.95 (ISBN 0-399-90107-8). Marek.

Meistrell, Lois & Barbaresi, Sara M. How to Raise & Train a Dachshund. pap. 2.00 (ISBN 0-87666-276-9, DS1011). TFH Pubns.

Meites, J., jt. ed. see Martini, L.

Meites, L. An Introduction to Chemical Equilibrium & Kinetics. (Pergamon Ser. on Analytical Chemistry: Vol. 2). 1981. 75.00 (ISBN 0-08-023802-5); pap. 19.95 (ISBN 0-08-023803-3). Pergamon.

Meites, L. & Zuman, P. Electrochemical Data, Vol. A: Organic, Organometallic, & Biochemical Substances, Pt. 1, LC 74-14958. 727p. 1974. 60.00 (ISBN 0-471-59200-5, Pub. by Wiley-Interscience). Wiley.

Meites, Louis. Polarographic Techniques. 2nd ed. LC 65-19735. (Electrochemical Data Ser.). (Illus.). 1965. 50.00 (ISBN 0-470-59205-2, Pub. by Wiley-Interscience). Wiley.

Meites, Louis, et al. Crc Handbook Series in Inorganic Electrochemistry. 350p. 1980. 64.95 (ISBN 0-8493-0361-3). CRC Pr.

Meites, S. see Reiner, Miriam, et al.

Meites, Samuel, ed. Pediatric Clinical Chemistry. rev. ed. LC 80-66259. 400p. 1981. 35.00 (ISBN 0-915274-12-4). Am Assn Clinical Chem.

Meites, Samuel, jt. ed. see Faulkner, Willard R.

Meixner, A. Chemische Farbreaktion von Pilzen. 1975. 14.75 o.p. (ISBN 3-7682-0956-3). Lubrecht & Cramer.

Mejia, Alfonso, et al. Foreign Medical Graduates: The Case of the United States. LC 80-7576. 1980. 18.95 (ISBN 0-669-03760-5). Lexington Bks.

Mekeel, Arhtur J. The Relation of the Quakers to the American Revolution. LC 79-66173. 1979. pap. text ed. 12.50 (ISBN 0-8191-0792-1). U Pr of Amer.

Mekeirle, Joseph O. The Arab World: A Guide to Business, Economics & Industrial Information Sources. LC 79-91352. 1980. 75.00 (ISBN 0-916400-07-7). Inter Crescent.

--Multinational Corporations: The ECISM Guide to Information Sources. 71.95 (ISBN 0-03-046261-4). Praeger.

Meketa, Charles & Meketa, Jacqueline. One Blanket & Ten Days Rations. Jackson, Earl & Dodson, Carolyn, eds. LC 79-67811. (Popular Ser.: No. 27). (Illus.). 100p. (Orig.). pap. 4.50x (ISBN 0-911408-54-1). SW Pks Mnmts.

Meketa, Jacqueline, jt. auth. see Meketa, Charles.

Mekler, Eva, jt. ed. see Schulman, Michael.

Mela, Leena M., ed. see Papers from the First Annual Conference on Shock, Airlie, Va., June 1978.

Melady, Margaret, jt. auth. see Melady, Thomas.

Melady, Thomas & Melady, Margaret. Uganda: The Asian Exiles. LC 76-10321. 1976. 6.95x o.p. (ISBN 0-88344-506-9). Orbis Bks.

Melady, Thomas P. Burundi: The Tragic Years. LC 73-89357. (Illus.). 126p. 1974. 4.95x o.p. (ISBN 0-88344-045-8). Orbis Bks.

Melamed, Barbara G. & Siegel, Lawrence J. Behavioral Medicine: Practical Applications in Health Care. LC 80-13418. (Springer Series on Behavior Therapy & Behavioral Medicine: Vol. 6). (Illus.). 1980. text ed. 22.95 (ISBN 0-8261-2170-5). Springer Pub.

Melamed, Myron, et al. The Adult Postoperative Chest. (Illus.). 396p. 1977. 41.75 (ISBN 0-398-03476-1). C C Thomas.

Melanchthon, Philip. A Very Godly Defense, Defending the Mariage of Preists. Beuchame, L., tr. LC 76-25643. (English Experience Ser.: No. 199). 1969. Repr. of 1541 ed. 8.00 (ISBN 90-221-0199-1). Walter J Johnson.

Melanchthon, Philipp. The Justification of Man by Faith Only. Lesse, Nicholas, tr. LC 79-84123. (English Experience Ser.: No. 942). 204p. 1979. Repr. of 1548 ed. lib. bdg. 15.00 (ISBN 90-221-0942-9). Walter J Johnson.

Melander, Goran & Nobel, Peter, eds. African Refugees & the Law. (Scandinavian Institute of African Studies, Uppsala). 1978. text ed. 11.50 (ISBN 0-8419-9736-5). Holmes & Meier.

Melaniphy, John C., Jr. Commercial & Industrial Condominiums. LC 76-27171. (Illus.). 80p. 1976. pap. text ed. 14.50 (ISBN 0-87420-572-7). Urban Land.

Melaro, Constance. Bitter Harvest: The Odyssey of a Teacher. 1969. 8.95 (ISBN 0-8392-1148-1). Astor-Honor.

Melberg, Edith. Let's Cook It & Edith. (Illus.). 196p. Date not set. pap. 7.95 o.s.i. (ISBN 0-89716-054-1). Peanut Butter.

Melby, Edward C., Jr. & Altman, Norman H., eds. Handbook of Laboratory Animal Science, CRC, 2 vols. LC 74-19795. (Handbook Ser.). Vol. 2, 1974, 523p. 59.95 (ISBN 0-8493-0341-9); Vol. 2. 64.95 (ISBN 0-8493-0342-7). CRC Pr.

Melcher, Arlyn J. Structure & Process of Organization: A Systems Approach. (Illus.). 480p. 1976. 19.95 (ISBN 0-13-855254-1). P-H.

Melcher, James R. Continuum Electromechanics. (Illus.). 700p. 1981. text ed. 37.50x (ISBN 0-262-13165-X). MIT Pr.

Melcher, Joan. Watering Hole: A User's Guide to Montana Bars. 128p. 1980. pap. text ed. 6.95 (ISBN 0-938314-00-9). MT Mag.

Melcher, Marguerite F. Shaker Adventure. 1980. pap. 6.00 (ISBN 0-937942-08-1). Shaker Mus.

--The Shaker Adventure. 1975. pap. 7.50 o.p. (ISBN 0-686-11180-X). Shaker Mus.

Melcher, Robert A. & Warch, Willard F. Music for Advanced Study. (Orig.). 1964. pap. text ed. 13.95 (ISBN 0-13-607317-4). P-H.

--Music for Keyboard Harmony. 1966. pap. text ed. 13.95 (ISBN 0-13-607432-4). P-H.

--Music for Score Reading. LC 78-119859. (Music Ser). 1971. pap. text ed. 12.95 (ISBN 0-13-607507-X). P-H.

Melchers, F., et al, eds. Lymphocyte Hybridomas: Second Workshop. (Illus.). 1979. 16.40 (ISBN 0-387-09670-1). Springer-Verlag.

Melchior, Ib. Sleeper Agent. LC 74-15882. 312p. (YA) 1975. 8.95 o.p. (ISBN 0-06-012942-5, HarpT). Har-Row.

Melcuk, Igor A. Studies in Dependency Syntax. Roberge, Paul T., ed. Stern, Lev, tr. from Russian. (Linguistica Extranea: Studia 2). 172p. 1979. pap. 7.25 (ISBN 0-89720-001-2). Karoma.

Melden, A. I. Ethical Theories: A Book of Readings with Revisions. 2nd ed. 1967. text ed. 18.95 (ISBN 0-13-290122-6). P-H.

--Human Rights. 1970. pap. 7.95x (ISBN 0-534-00220-X). Wadsworth Pub.

--Rights & Persons. 1978. 20.00x (ISBN 0-520-03528-3); pap. 5.95 (ISBN 0-520-03839-8). U of Cal Pr.

Melder, Keith. Life & Times in Shoe City: The Shoe Workers of Lynn, An Exhibition at the Essex Institute, Salem. (Illus.). 56p. 1979. pap. 2.00 (ISBN 0-88389-101-8). Essex Inst.

Meldman, Monte J. The Problem-Oriented Psychiatric Index & Treatment Plans. 1st ed. Johnson, Edith, ed. LC 76-200. (Illus.). 1976. pap. text ed. 10.50 (ISBN 0-8016-3393-1). Mosby.

Meldrum, B. S. & Marsden, C. D., eds. Primate Models of Neurological Disorders. LC 74-21980. (Advances in Neurology: Vol. 10). 378p. 1975. 36.00 (ISBN 0-89004-002-8). Raven.

Meldrum, B. S., jt. ed. see Brierly, J. B.

Mele, Joan F., tr. see Baudelaire, Charles.

Mele, Pietro P. Tibet. (Illus.). 1969. text ed. 30.00 (ISBN 0-685-12304-9, Oxford & IBH Pub Co). Paragon.

Meleager. The Poems of Meleager. Whigham, Peter, tr. LC 75-7196. 128p. 1976. 14.50x (ISBN 0-520-03003-6). U of Cal Pr.

Melegari, Vezio. Hidden Treasures. (International Library). (Illus.). 128p. (gr. 7 up). 1972. PLB 6.90 o.p. (ISBN 0-531-02109-2). Watts.

Melekhin, V. N., jt. auth. see Kapitza, S. P.

Melendy, H. Brett. Asians in America. (American Immigrant Ser.). 340p. 1981. pap. 6.95 (ISBN 0-88254-513-2). Hippocrene Bks.

--Asians in America: Filipinos, Koreans, & East Indians. (Immigrant Heritage of America Ser.). 1977. lib. bdg. 10.95 (ISBN 0-8057-8414-4). Twayne.

--The Oriental Americans. LC 73-187154. (Immigrant Heritage of America Ser.). 1972. lib. bdg. 9.95 (ISBN 0-8057-3254-3). Twayne.

Melet-Sanson, J. Fouquet. (Illus.). (gr. 10-12). 1978. 10.95 (ISBN 0-8120-5280-3, Screpel). Barron.

Melhorn, W. N. & Flemal, R. C., eds. Theories of Landform Development. (Binghamton Symposia in Geomorphology: International Ser.: No. 6). (Illus.). 312p. 1980. text ed. 20.00x (ISBN 0-04-551039-3, 2507). Allen Unwin.

Melhuish, A. Executive Health. 190p. 1978. text ed. 24.50x (ISBN 0-220-66351-3, Pub. by Busn Bks England). Renouf.

Melhuish, K. J., jt. ed. see Bramsted, E. K.

Melick, George F., Jr. John Mark & the Origin of the Gospels: A Foundation Document Hypohasis. LC 79-52095. 69p. 1979. 4.95 (ISBN 0-8059-2650-X). Dorrance.

Melillo, G., et al, eds. Respiratory Allergy. 214p. 26.50. Masson Pub.

Melissinos, Adrian. Experiments in Modern Physics. 1966. text ed. 23.95 (ISBN 0-12-489850-5). Acad Pr.

Melitz, Leo L. The Opera Goers' Complete Guide. Hackney, Louise W., rev. by. Salinger, Richard, tr. LC 80-2293. 1981. Repr. of 1936 ed. 54.50 (ISBN 0-404-18859-1). AMS Pr.

Melkman, Alan V. How to Handle Major Customers Profitably. 1979. text ed. 34.50x (ISBN 0-566-02097-1, Pub. by Gower Pub Co England). Renouf.

Melko, Matthew & Weigel, Richard D. Peace in the Ancient World. LC 80-20434. 225p. 1981. lib. bdg. 15.95x (ISBN 0-89950-020-X). McFarland & Co.

Mell, Donald C. A Poetics of Augustan Elegy: Studies of Poems by Dryden, Pope, Prior, Swift, Gray & Johnson. 116p. (Orig.). 1974. pap. text ed. 11.50x (ISBN 90-6203-278-8). Humanities.

Mell, Donald C., et al, eds. Contemporary Studies of Swift's Poetry. LC 79-21610. (Illus.). 216p. 1980. 18.50 (ISBN 0-87413-173-1, 173). U Delaware Pr.

Mellado De Hunter, Elena. Anglicimos Profesionales De Puerto Rico. LC 80-17935. (Coleccion Mente y Palabra). 241p. (Span.). 1980. 6.25 (ISBN 0-8477-0578-1); pap. 5.00 (ISBN 0-8477-0579-X). U of PR Pr.

Mellafe, Rolando. Negro Slavery in Latin America. 1975. 20.00x (ISBN 0-520-02106-1). U of Cal Pr.

Mellanby, Kenneth. Human Guinea Pigs. 1973. pap. 3.00 o.p. (ISBN 0-686-23495-2, Merlin Pr). Carrier Pigeon.

Mellard, James M. The Exploded Form: The Modernist Novel in America. LC 79-25993. 224p. 1980. 15.00 (ISBN 0-252-00801-4). U of Ill Pr.

--Quaternion: Stories, Poems, Plays, Essays. 1978. pap. 9.95x (ISBN 0-673-15102-6). Scott F.

Mellard, Rudolph. Pony Express, Carry My Message. (Illus.). 1979. 15.00. A Jones.

Mellen, Joan. Natural Tendencies. 256p. 1981. 11.95 (ISBN 0-686-69088-5). Dial.

Mellen, Kathleen D. The Gods Depart: The Hawaiian Kingdom, 1832-1873. new ed. (Kathleen Dickenson Mellen's Epic Saga of the Hawaiian Kingdom Ser.). 300p. 1980. pap. 7.95 o.p. (ISBN 0-8038-2708-3). Hastings.

--Island Kingdom Passes. 1958. 7.95 (ISBN 0-8038-3357-1). Hastings.

--The Lonely Warrior: Kamehameha the Great of Hawaii. (Kathleene Dickenson Mellen's Epic Saga of of the Hawaiian Kingdom Ser.). (Illus.). 177p. 1980. pap. 6.95 o.p. (ISBN 0-8038-4334-8). Hastings.

--The Magnificent Matriarch: Kaahumanu, Queen of Hawaii, 1772-1838. new ed. (Illus.). 302p. 1980. pap. 7.95 o.p. (ISBN 0-8038-4732-7). Hastings.

Mellen, Sydney L. The Evolution of Love. LC 80-18028. 1981. text ed. 15.95x (ISBN 0-7167-1271-7); pap. text ed. 8.95x (ISBN 0-7167-1272-5). W H Freeman.

Meller, Helen, ed. see Barnett, Canon.

Meller, Walter C. Old Times. LC 68-26592. (Illus.). 1968. Repr. of 1925 ed. 15.00 (ISBN 0-8103-3453-4). Gale.

Mellerio, Andre. Odilon Redon. LC 67-27461. (Graphic Art Ser). (Fr). 1968. Repr. of 1913 ed. lib. bdg. 55.00 (ISBN 0-306-70975-9). Da Capo.

Mellerowicz, H. Der Kreislauf des Jugendlichen bei Arbeit und Sport. 2nd ed. (Illus.). viii, 60p. 1980. pap. 11.50 (ISBN 3-8055-1140-X). S Karger.

Mellerowicz, Harald. Ergometry: Basics of Medical Exercise Testing. Smodlaka, Vojin N., ed. Rice, Allan L., tr. from Ger. 1981. text ed. write for info. (ISBN 0-8067-1241-4). Urban & S.

Mellers, Wilfrid. Bach & the Dance of God. 1981. 39.95 (ISBN 0-19-520232-5). Oxford U Pr.

--Caliban Reborn: Renewal in Twentieth-Century Music. (Music Reprint Ser.). 1979. Repr. of 1967 ed. lib. bdg. 22.50 (ISBN 0-306-79569-8). Da Capo.

--The Twilight of the Gods: The Music of the Beatles. LC 73-3508. (Illus.). 1975. pap. 5.95 (ISBN 0-02-871390-7). Schirmer Bks.

Mellert, Robert B. What Is Process Theology? LC 74-28933. 1975. pap. 2.95 (ISBN 0-8091-1867-X). Paulist Pr.

Mellett, P., jt. auth. see Annual Conference of the Society of Psychosomatic Research, 21st, Royal College of Physicians, London, November 21-22 1977.

Mellgren, L. & Walker, M. New Horizons in English: English As a Second Language, 6 bks. (gr. 10-12). 1973-74. Bks.1-2. pap. 3.72 ea.; Bks. 3-6. pap. 3.84 ea.; Bks. 1-2, 5-6. tchr's guides 3.96 ea.; Bks. 3-4. tchr's guides 5.32 ea. Bk. 1 (ISBN 0-201-04415-3). Bk. 2 (ISBN 0-201-04418-8). Bk. 3 (ISBN 0-201-04421-8). Bk. 4 (ISBN 0-201-04424-2). Bk. 5 (ISBN 0-201-04427-7). A-W.

Melliar, Margaret. Pattern Cutting. 1977. 17.95 (ISBN 0-7134-2897-X, Pub. by Batsford England). David & Charles.

Mellin, Jeanne. The Morgan Horse Handbook. LC 72-91799. 256p. 1980. pap. 8.95 (ISBN 0-8289-0390-5). Greene.

Mellin, Laurel. Shapedown: Weight Management Program for Adolescents. LC 80-67385. (Illus.). 186p. (Orig.). (gr. 7-12). 1980. tchr's ed. 10.00 (ISBN 0-935902-02-3); wkbk. 10.00 (ISBN 0-935902-01-5). Balboa Pub.

Mellini, Peter. Sir Eldon Gorst: The Overshadowed Proconsul. LC 76-51878. (Publication Ser: No. 178). (Illus.). 1977. 10.95 (ISBN 0-8179-6781-8). Hoover Inst Pr.

Mellinkoff, Ruth. The Horned Moses in Medieval Art & Thought. LC 77-85450. (California Studies in the History of Art: No. XIV). (Illus.). 1970. 22.50x (ISBN 0-520-01705-6). U of Cal Pr.

--The Mark of Cain. (A Quantum Bk.). 128p. 1981. 12.50x (ISBN 0-520-03969-6). U of Cal Pr.

Mellish, Michael. The Docks After Devlin. Clegg, Hugh & Bain, George, eds. 1972. pap. text ed. 6.95x o.p. (ISBN 0-435-85605-7). Heinemann Ed.

Mello, Fernando de see De Mello, Fernando.

Mellon, DeForest, Jr. The Physiology of Sense Organs. (Illus.). 1968. 8.95x (ISBN 0-7167-0669-5). W H Freeman.

Mellon, Susan, jt. auth. see Crawford, Tad.

Mellon, W. Giles, jt. auth. see Bernstein, Samuel J.

Melloni, B. J., et al. Anatomy & Physiology, 4 bks. 1971. 375.00 set o.p. (ISBN 0-07-076420-4, HP); 100.00 ea. o.p. Bk. 1 (ISBN 0-07-076421-2). Bk. 2 (ISBN 0-07-076422-0). Bk. 3 (ISBN 0-07-076423-9). Bk. 4 (ISBN 0-07-076424-7). McGraw.

Mellor. Geography of Two Germanies. 1978. 20.40 (ISBN 0-06-318066-9, IntlDept). Har-Row.

--Mellor's Comprehensive Treatise on Inorganic & Theoretical Chemistry: Pt. 5 Boron. (Illus.). 825p. 1980. lib. bdg. 170.00 (ISBN 0-582-46277-0). Longman.

Mellor, Anne K. Blake's Human Form Divine. LC 72-161995. (Illus.). 1974. 31.50x (ISBN 0-520-02065-0). U of Cal Pr.

Mellor, Constance. How to Be Healthy, Wealthy & Wise. 112p. 1976. pap. 6.00x (ISBN 0-8464-1023-0). Beekman Pubs.

Mellor, D. H., ed. Prospects for Pragmatism. 270p. 1981. 29.50 (ISBN 0-521-22548-5). Cambridge U Pr.

Mellor, David H. Matter of Chance. LC 70-152629. (Illus.). 1971. 29.95 (ISBN 0-521-08194-7). Cambridge U Pr.

Mellor, Helen. The Imperishable. 1979. 8.95 o.p. (ISBN 0-533-03962-2). Vantage.

Mellor, Isha. Honey. (Illus.). 80p. 1981. 6.95 (ISBN 0-312-92306-6). St Martin.

--Honey: A Consideration. (Illus.). 80p. 1981. 6.95 (ISBN 0-312-92306-6). Congdon & Lattes.

Mellor, J. R. Urban Sociology in an Urbanized Society. (International Library of Sociology). 1977. 24.00 (ISBN 0-7100-8683-0). Routledge & Kegan.

Mellor, J. W. & Parkes, G. D. A Comprehensive Treatise on Inorganic & Theoretical Chemistry. Incl. Vol. 1. 1922. o.p. (ISBN 0-471-59295-1); Vol. 3. 1922. o.p. (ISBN 0-471-59297-8); Vol. 4. 1923. o.p. (ISBN 0-471-59298-6); Vol. 5. 1924. o.p. (ISBN 0-471-59303-6); Vol. 6. 1929. o.p. (ISBN 0-471-59304-4); Vol. 7. 1930. o.p. (ISBN 0-471-59305-2); Vol. 8. 1930. o.p. (ISBN 0-471-59306-0); Vol. 9. 1930. 64.95 (ISBN 0-471-59307-9); Vol. 10. 1930. o.p. (ISBN 0-471-59308-7); Vol. 11. 1931. 69.95 (ISBN 0-471-59309-5); Vol. 12. 1932. o.p. (ISBN 0-471-59310-9); Vol. 13. 1934. o.p. (ISBN 0-471-59311-7); Vol. 14. 1935. o.p. (ISBN 0-471-59312-5); Vol. 15. 1936. o.p. (ISBN 0-471-59313-3); Vol. 16. 1937. o.p. (ISBN 0-471-59314-1). Halsted Pr.

--Comprehensive Treatise on Inorganic & Theoretical Chemistry, Vol. 8. 1972. Suppl. 2. 69.95 o.p. (ISBN 0-471-59321-4); Suppl. 3. 114.95 o.p. (ISBN 0-471-59325-7). Halsted Pr.

Mellor, John W. Economics of Agricultural Development. LC 66-19491. (Illus.). 1966. 25.00x (ISBN 0-8014-0297-2); pap. 7.95 (ISBN 0-8014-9102-9, CP102). Cornell U Pr.

--India: A Rising Middle Power. (Special Studies on South & Southeast Asia). 1979. lib. bdg. 27.50x (ISBN 0-89158-298-3). Westview.

--The New Economics of Growth: A Strategy for India & the Developing World. (A Twentieth Century Fund Study). 1980. 14.50 o.p. (ISBN 0-8014-1000-2); pap. 7.95 o.p. Cornell U Pr.

--The New Economics of Growth: A Strategy for India & the Developing World. LC 75-38430. (Illus.). 384p. 1976. 18.50x (ISBN 0-8014-0999-3); pap. 7.95 (ISBN 0-8014-9188-6). Cornell U Pr.

Mellor, Kathleen, jt. ed. see Schaefer, Charles E.

Mellor, Roy & Smith, E. Alistair. Europe: A Geographical Survey of the Continent. LC 78-10171. 1979. 15.00x (ISBN 0-231-04708-8). Columbia U Pr.

Mellor, Roy E. Eastern Europe: A Geography of the Comecon Countries. 1975. 20.00x (ISBN 0-231-03940-9); pap. 12.50x (ISBN 0-231-03945-X). Columbia U Pr.

--The Two Germanies: A Modern Geography. 1978. text ed. 15.70 (ISBN 0-06-318066-9, IntlDept, IntlDept). Har-Row.

Mellor, Roy E. H. The Two Germanies: A Modern Geography. (Illus.). 1978. text ed. 19.50x (ISBN 0-06-494778-5); pap. 9.95x (ISBN 0-06-494779-3). B&N.

Mellors, Colin. The British MP: A Socio-Economic Study of the House of Commons. (Illus.). 1978. 18.95 (ISBN 0-566-00138-1, 00708-0, Pub. by Saxon Hse England). Lexington Bks.

Mellors, Samaatha. The Orphan. 224p. (Orig.). 1980. pap. 2.25 (ISBN 0-515-05402-X). Jove Pubns.

Mellott, Douglas W., Jr. Marketing: Application & Cases. (Illus.). 1978. 8.95 (ISBN 0-8359-4253-8). Reston.

--Marketing: Principles & Practices. (Illus.). 1978. ref. ed. 15.95 (ISBN 0-87909-455-9); instrs'. manual avail. Reston.

Mellow, James R. Nathaniel Hawthorne in His Time. 672p. 1980. 19.95 (ISBN 0-395-27602-0). HM.

Mellown, Elgin W. Edwin Muir. (English Authors Ser.: No. 248). 1979. lib. bdg. 12.95 (ISBN 0-8057-6687-1). Twayne.

Mellows, Joan. A Different Face. (Regency Romance Ser.). 1979. pap. 1.75 o.p. (ISBN 0-449-24046-0, Crest). Fawcett.

--Friends at Knoll House. (A Fawcett Regency Novel Ser.). 224p. 1976. pap. 1.25 o.p. (ISBN 0-449-22530-5, P2530, Crest). Fawcett.

--Harriet. 1977. pap. 1.50 o.p. (ISBN 0-449-23209-3, Crest). Fawcett.

Melluish, J. W., jt. ed. see Kinchin, F.

Melluzzo, Paul J. & Nealon, Eleanor. Living with Surgery: Before & After. rev. ed. LC 80-53188. 304p. 1980. pap. 6.95 (ISBN 0-7216-6261-7). Saunders.

--Living with Surgery: Before & After. LC 80-51388. 320p. (Orig.). 1981. pap. 6.95 (ISBN 0-03-059081-7). HR&W.

Melly, George & Glaves-Smith, J. R. A Child of Six Could Do It! Cartoons About Modern Art. (Tate Gallery Art Ser.). (Illus.). 1977. pap. 1.95 (ISBN 0-8120-0854-5). Barron.
Melmouth, W. see Cicero.
Melnechuk, Theodore, jt. ed. see Baxter, Claude.
Melnick, J. L., ed. Progress in Medical Virology, Vol. 26. (Illus.). viii, 240p. 1980. 89.95 (ISBN 3-8055-0702-X). S Karger.
Melnick, J. L. & Maupas, P., eds. Hepatitis B Virus & Primary Liver Cancer. (Progress in Medical Virology Ser.: Vol. 27). (Illus.). 250p. 1981. 90.00 (ISBN 3-8055-1784-X). S Karger.
Melnick, Michael, ed. Clinical Dysmorphology of Oral-Facial Structures. Shields, Edward D. & Burzynski, Norbert J. (Post Graduate Dental Handbook Ser.: Vol. 12). 1981. 49.50 (ISBN 0-88416-169-2). PSG Pub.
Melnick, Michael & Bixler, David, eds. Etiology of Cleft Lip & Cleft Palate. (Progress in Clinical & Biological Research: Vol. 46). 566p. 1980. 40.00 (ISBN 0-8451-0046-7). A R Liss.
Melnick, Michael & Jorgenson, Ronald, eds. Developmental Aspects of Craniofacial Dysmorphology. LC 79-2487. (Alan R. Liss Ser.: Vol. 15, No. 8). 1979. 16.00 (ISBN 0-8451-1033-0). March of Dimes.
Melnicoe, William & Mennig, Jan. Elements of Police Supervision. (Criminal Justice Ser). (Illus.). 1969. text ed. 10.95x (ISBN 0-02-476400-0, 47640). Macmillan.
Melnicoe, William B. & Mennig, Jan. Elements of Police Supervision. 2nd ed. 1978. text ed. 11.95 (ISBN 0-02-476000-5). Macmillan.
Melnitz, W., jt. auth. see MacGowan, Kenneth.
Melnitz, William W., ed. Theatre Arts Publications in the U. S., 1947-52. 188p. 1959. 5.00, ATA members 3.00 (ISBN 0-686-05078-9). Am Theatre Assoc.
Melnychyn, P., jt. auth. see DeMan, J. M.
Melnyk, Myron. Principles of Applied Statistics. LC 73-7943. 1974. text ed. 23.00 (ISBN 0-08-017108-7). Pergamon.
Meloan, Clifton & Pomeranz, Y. Food Analysis Laboratory Experiments. 2nd ed. (Illus.). 1980. pap. 10.50 (ISBN 0-87055-351-8). AVI.
Meloan, Clifton E. & Pomeranz, Y. Food Analysis Laboratory Experiments. (Illus.). 143p. 1973. pap. text ed. 10.50 o.p. (ISBN 0-87055-149-3). AVI.
Meloan, Clifton E., jt. auth. see Pomeranz, Y.
Melody, Michael E. Apaches: A Critical Bibliography. LC 77-6918. (Newberry Library Center for the History of the American Indian Bibliographical Ser.). 96p. 1977. pap. 3.95x (ISBN 0-253-30764-3). Ind U Pr.
Melody, William H., et al. Culture, Communication, & Dependency: The Tradition of H. A. Innis. 288p. 1980. text ed. write for info. (ISBN 0-89391-065-1). Ablex Pub.
Melon, jt. auth. see Rosa-Nieves.
Meloon, Will. We've Been Robbed: A Baptist Minister Explores the Fundamentalist's Dilemma. LC 70-166500. 87p. 1971. pap. 2.95 o.p. (ISBN 0-912106-19-0). Logos.
Melrose, John. Bucomco: A Business Communication Simulation. LC 76-30752. 1977. text ed. 6.95 (ISBN 0-574-20025-8, 13-3025); instr's guide avail. (ISBN 0-574-20026-6, 13-3026). SRA.
Melsa, James L. & Sage, Andrew P. An Introduction to Probability & Stochastic Processes. (Illus.). 448p. 1973. ref. ed. 26.95 (ISBN 0-13-034850-3). P-H.
Melsa, James L., jt. auth. see Cohn, David L.
Melton, David. Harry S. Truman: The Man Who Walked with Giants. (Illus.). 128p. (gr. 5 up). 1980. 20.00 (ISBN 0-8309-0293-7). Independence Pr.
Melton, James E. Your Right to Fly. LC 80-82961. (Illus.). 217p. pap. 6.95 (ISBN 0-9604752-0-6). Global Pubns WI.
Melton, Richard S. Statistical Methods for the Behavioral Science: An Introduction. 380p. 1981. pap. text ed. write for info. (ISBN 0-697-06549-9); instr's manual avail. (ISBN 0-697-06550-2). Wm C Brown.
Meltrecht, K. H. Machine Shop Practice, 2 vols. (Illus.). 1971. 14.00ea. o.p. (ISBN 0-686-57944-5); Vol. 1. (ISBN 0-8311-1069-4); Vol. 2. (ISBN 0-8311-1070-8). Indus Pr.
Meltsner, Arnold J. The Politics of City Revenue. LC 70-129610. (Oakland Project). 1971. 18.50x (ISBN 0-520-01812-5); pap. 5.95x (ISBN 0-520-02773-6). U of Cal Pr.
Meltsner, Arnold J., ed. Towards Presidential Governance. 300p. (Orig.). 1981. pap. write for info. (ISBN 0-917616-40-5). Inst Contemporary.
Meltz, Noah, jt. auth. see Maital, Schlomo.
Meltz, Noah, et al. Sharing the Work: An Analysis of the Issues of Worksharing & Jobsharing. 100p. 1981. 7.50 (ISBN 0-8020-2383-5). U of Toronto Pr.
Meltzer, A. C., et al. Principles of Digital Computer Design, Vol. 1. (Illus.). 624p. 1976. 26.95 (ISBN 0-13-701524-0). P-H.
Meltzer, B. & Michie, D. Machine Intelligence, Vols. 4-7. Vol. 4, 1969. 18.95x o.p. (ISBN 0-470-59336-9); Vol. 5, 1970. 27.95x o.p. (ISBN 0-470-59337-7); Vol. 6, 1971. 41.95x (ISBN 0-470-59339-3); Vol. 7. 1973 o.p. 41.00x (ISBN 0-470-60110-8). Halsted Pr.
Meltzer, B. N., et al. Symbolic Interactionism: Genesis, Varieties & Criticsms. (Monographs in Social Theory). 1977. pap. 6.95 (ISBN 0-7100-8056-5). Routledge & Kegan.
Meltzer, Bernard, jt. auth. see Manis, Jerome.
Meltzer, David. Six. (Illus.). 130p. (Orig.). 1976. ltd. signed o.p. 15.00 (ISBN 0-87685-271-1); pap. 4.00 (ISBN 0-87685-270-3). Black Sparrow.
Meltzer, E. & Dunning, J. Textbook of Coronary Care. LC 72-91695. (Illus.). 820p. 1972. text ed. 24.95 (ISBN 0-913486-11-6). Charles.
Meltzer, Herbert L. Chemistry of Human Behavior. LC 77-19195. (Illus.). 1978. 18.95 (ISBN 0-88229-177-7). Nelson-Hall.
Meltzer, L. E., et al. Concepts & Practices of Intensive Care for Nurse Specialists. 2nd ed. LC 75-27692. 1976. 21.95 (ISBN 0-913486-48-5). Charles.
--Intensive Coronary Care: A Manual for Nurses. 3rd ed. LC 77-12120. (Illus.). 230p. 1977. 15.95 (ISBN 0-913486-79-5). Charles.
Meltzer, Michael. The World of the Small Commercial Fishermen: Their Lives & Their Boats. (Illus.). 1980. pap. 4.95 (ISBN 0-486-23945-4). Dover.
Meltzer, Milton. Brother Can You Spare a Dime? The Great Depression, 1929-1933. (Sundial Paperbks.). 1972. pap. 1.95 (ISBN 0-394-70806-7, VS-6, Vin). Random.
--The Human Rights Book. LC 79-13017. 272p. (gr. 6 up). 1979. 9.95 (ISBN 0-374-33514-1). FS&G.
--In Their Own Words: A History of the American Negro. Incl. 1619-1865. LC 64-22541. 1964. 2.95 (ISBN 0-8152-0348-9); 1865-1916. LC 65-23778. 1965. 1.65 (ISBN 0-8152-0349-7); 1916-1966. LC 66-1439. 1967. 1.65 (ISBN 0-8152-0350-0). (Illus.). (gr. 5 up). pap. (AE-J). Apollo Eds.
--Remember the Days: A Short History of the Jewish American. LC 74-5531. 128p. 1974. 4.95 (ISBN 0-385-05946-9, Zenith); pap. 2.50 (ISBN 0-385-07676-2). Doubleday.
Meltzer, Milton & Harding, Walter A. A Thoreau Profile. (Illus.). 8.50 (ISBN 0-8446-0797-5). Peter Smith.
Meltzer, Milton & Meier, August. Time of Trial, Time of Hope: The Negro in America, 1919-1941. LC 66-20917. (Illus.). pap. 2.50 o.p. (ISBN 0-385-05978-7, Z8, Zenith). Doubleday.
Meltzer, Milton, ed. see Block, Irvin.
Meltzer, Sol. Herb Gardening in the South. LC 76-52240. (Illus.). 1977. pap. 3.95 (ISBN 0-88415-366-5). Pacesetter Pr.
Meltzer, Y. Water-Soluble Polymers: Recent Developments. LC 78-68940. (Chemical Technology Review Ser.: No. 126). (Illus.). 1979. 48.00 o.p. (ISBN 0-8155-0742-9). Noyes.
Meltzer, Yale L. Water-Soluble Polymers: Developments Since 1978. LC 80-26174. (Chemical Technology Rev. Ser.: 181). (Illus.). 608p. 1981. 54.00 (ISBN 0-8155-0834-4). Noyes.
Meluch, R. M. Wind Dancers. (Orig.). 1981. pap. 1.95 (ISBN 0-451-09786-6, J9786, Sig). NAL.
Melvasia, Carlo C. The Life of Guido Reni. Enggass, Catherine & Enggass, Robert, trs. from Ital. LC 80-11650. (Illus.). 150p. 1981. 11.95x (ISBN 0-271-00264-6). Pa St U Pr.
Melvil, Dewey. Dewey Decimal Classification & Relative Index, 3 vols. 19th ed. LC 77-27967. 1979. Set. 90.00x (ISBN 0-910608-23-7); Vol 1, Introduction & Tables. 30.00x (ISBN 0-910608-19-9); Vol. 2, Schedules. 30.00x (ISBN 0-910608-20-2); Vol. 3, Index. 30.00x (ISBN 0-910608-21-0). Forest Pr.
Melvil, Dewey, jt. auth. see Winslade, B. A. J.
Melvill, Harry, tr. see Bakst, Leon.
Melville, Annabelle M. Elizabeth Bayley Seton. 1976. lib. rep. ed. 20.00x (ISBN 0-684-14735-1, ScribT). Scribner.
--Elizabeth Bayley Seton. 1976. pap. 2.25 (ISBN 0-89129-218-7). Jove Pubns.
Melville, Anne. Blaize. 528p. 1981. 15.95 (ISBN 0-385-14832-1). Doubleday.
Melville, Chuck. The Harlem Globetrotters. (Illus.). 1978. 12.95 o.p. (ISBN 0-679-50803-1); pap. 6.95 o.p. (ISBN 0-679-50812-0). McKay.
Melville, Dorothy Sutherland. Tyler-Browns of Brattleboro. 1973. 10.00 o.p. (ISBN 0-682-47687-0). Exposition.
Melville, Herman. Billy Budd. (Literature Ser). (gr. 7-12). 1969. pap. text ed. 3.25 (ISBN 0-87720-703-8). AMSCO Sch.
--Billy Budd. Stern, Milton, ed. LC 73-8967. (LL Ser: No. 43). 244p. 1975. 10.50 (ISBN 0-672-51466-4); pap. 6.50 (ISBN 0-672-61040-X). Bobbs.
--Billy Budd. (Now Age Illustrated V Ser.). (Illus.). 64p. (gr. 4-12). 1979. text ed. 4.50 (ISBN 0-88301-397-5); pap. text ed. 1.45 (ISBN 0-88301-385-1); student activity bk. 0.95 (ISBN 0-88301-409-2). Pendulum Pr.
--Billy Budd & Other Stories. pap. 1.75. Bantam.
--Billy Budd with Reader's Guide. (Amsco Literature Program). (gr. 10-12). 1971. pap. text ed. 3.92 (ISBN 0-87720-810-7); tchr's ed. 2.60 (ISBN 0-87720-910-3). AMSCO Sch.
--Confidence Man. pap. 1.75 (ISBN 0-451-51367-3, CE1367, Sig Classics). NAL.
--Confidence-Man: His Masquerade. Franklin, H. Bruce, ed. LC 66-30445. 1967. pap. 5.95 (ISBN 0-672-60986-X, LL13). Bobbs.
--Moby Dick. pap. 1.95. Bantam.
--Moby Dick. 1954. 11.50x (ISBN 0-460-00179-5, Evman); pap. 4.95 (ISBN 0-460-01179-0). Dutton.
--Moby Dick. (Illus.). (gr. 7 up). 1962. 5.95 o.s.i. (ISBN 0-02-766830-4). Macmillan.
--Moby Dick. (Literature Ser). pap. text ed. 4.17 (ISBN 0-87720-710-0). AMSCO Sch.
--Moby-Dick. Beaver, Harold, ed. (English Library). 1975. pap. 3.95 (ISBN 0-14-043082-2). Penguin.
--Moby Dick or, The Whale. Feidelson, Charles, Jr., ed. LC 64-16178. 1964. pap. 6.95 (ISBN 0-672-60971-1, LL5). Bobbs.
--Moby Dick with Reader's Guide. (Amsco Literature Program Ser.). 1970. pap. 4.67 (ISBN 0-87720-806-9); tchr's ed. 3.00 (ISBN 0-87720-906-5). AMSCO Sch.
--On the Slain Collegians. Frasconi, Antonio, ed. (Illus.). 48p. 1971. 5.95 o.p. (ISBN 0-374-22637-7); pap. 1.95 o.p. (ISBN 0-374-50954-9). FS&G.
--Redburn: His First Voyage. 1957. pap. 2.95 (ISBN 0-385-09321-7, A118, Anch). Doubleday.
Melville, Jennie. Nun's Castle. 224p. 1975. pap. 1.25 o.p. (ISBN 0-685-51457-9, P2412-125, Crest). Fawcett.
--Tarot's Tower. 1979. pap. 1.75 o.p. (ISBN 0-449-24001-0, Crest). Fawcett.
Melville, Joy. First Aid in Mental Health. 192p. 1981. text ed. cancelled o.s.i. (ISBN 0-04-362033-7, 2563); pap. 11.50 o.s.i. (ISBN 0-04-362034-5, 2564). Allen Unwin.
Melville, Keith. Marriage & Family Today. 1977. text ed. 14.95x o.p. (ISBN 0-394-31072-1). Random.
Melville, Leslie W. Forms & Agreements on Intellectual Property & International Licensing. 3rd ed. LC 78-17576. 1979. looseleaf with 1979 rev. pages 67.50 (ISBN 0-686-57648-9). Boardman.
Melville, Lewis & Hargreaves, Reginald. Famous Duels & Assassinations. LC 72-178619. (Illus.). 288p. 1974. Repr. of 1929 ed. 18.00 (ISBN 0-8103-3973-0). Gale.
Melville, Margarita B. Twice a Minority: Mexican-American Woman. LC 80-11177. (Illus.). 1980. pap. text ed. 11.95 (ISBN 0-8016-3386-9). Mosby.
Melville, T. H. & Russell, Conrad. Microbiology for Dental Students. 2nd ed. (Illus.). 1975. pap. text ed. 18.95x (ISBN 0-433-21149-0). Intl Ideas.
Melvin, Betsy & Melvin, Tom. Robert Frost Country. LC 76-2806. (Illus.). 1977. 17.95 (ISBN 0-385-12180-6). Doubleday.
Melvin, Bruce L. Rural Youth on Relief. LC 78-165686. (FDR & the Era of the New Deal Ser). 1971. Repr. of 1937 ed. lib. bdg. 15.00 (ISBN 0-306-70343-2). Da Capo.
Melvin, Bruce L. & Smith, Elna N. Youth in Agricultural Villages. LC 79-165603. (FDR & the Era of the New Deal Ser). 1971. Repr. of 1940 ed. lib. bdg. 15.00 (ISBN 0-306-70353-X). Da Capo.
Melvin, Julia, ed. see Nelson, John.
Melvin, Kenneth B., et al, eds. Psy Fi One: An Anthology of Psychology in Science Fiction. 1977. pap. text ed. 5.95x (ISBN 0-394-30576-0). Random.
Melvin, Tom, jt. auth. see Melvin, Betsy.
Melwani, Murli D. Critical Essays on Indo-Anglian Themes. (Greybird Bk.). 1976. 9.00 (ISBN 0-89253-595-4); flexible bdg. 5.00 (ISBN 0-89253-128-2). Ind-US Inc.
--Deep Roots. (Writers Workshop Bluebird Ser.). 56p. 1975. 8.00 (ISBN 0-88253-524-2); pap. text ed. 4.80 (ISBN 0-88253-523-4). Ind-US Inc.
--Stories of a Salesman. 1976. lib. bdg. 8.00 (ISBN 0-89253-084-7); flexible bdg. 6.75 (ISBN 0-89253-268-8). Ind-US Inc.
Melwani, Murli D. see Melwani, Murli D.
Melwood, Mary. Nettlewood. LC 74-19426. 352p. (gr. 6 up). 1975. 8.95 (ISBN 0-395-28919-X, Clarion). HM.
Melyan, Gary G. & Chu, Wen-Kaung. I-Ching: The Hexagrams Revealed. LC 76-6029. 1976. 8.75 (ISBN 0-8048-1182-2). C E Tuttle.
Melzer, Annabelle. Latest Rage the Big Drum: Dada & Surrealist Performance. (Studies in Fine Arts: The Avant-Garde, No. 7). 1980. 27.95 (ISBN 0-8357-1081-5). Univ Microfilms.
Melzi, Kay. Art in the Primary School. 1967. text ed. 7.50x (ISBN 0-631-11880-2). Humanities.
Melzi, Robert C. The New College Italian & English Dictionary. (Orig.). (gr. 7-12). 1976. pap. text ed. 8.50 (ISBN 0-87720-592-2). AMSCO Sch.
Members & Friends of the Fashiion Group Inc. The Last Word: Exploring Careers in Contemporary Communication. Ovesy, Regina, ed. 128p. (gr. 7-12). 1980. lib. bdg. 5.97 (ISBN 0-8239-0526-8). Rosen Pr.
Members of English Dept. of University of Michigan. Essays & Studies in English. 231p. 1980. Repr. of 1932 ed. lib. bdg. 40.00 (ISBN 0-686-65606-7). Century Bookbindery.
Members of the American Academy of Podiatric Sports Medicine. Sports Medicine Nineteen Eighty: A Review by the Members of the American Academy of Podiatric Sports Medicine, Pt. 1. Rinaldi, Robert R. & Sabia, Michael L., eds. LC 80-66360. (Archives of Podiatric Medicine & Foot Surgery: Supplement III). (Illus.). 224p. 1980. pap. 15.00 (ISBN 0-87993-141-8). Futura Pub.
Members of the American Dietetic Assoc. Your Future As a Dietician. (Careers in Depth Ser.). (gr. 7-12). 1976. PLB 4.98 o.p. (ISBN 0-8239-0321-4). Rosen Pr.
—Your Future As a Dietitian. rev ed. 140p. 1980. lib. bdg. 5.97 (ISBN 0-8239-0521-7). Rosen Pr.
Members of the Development Assistance Committee. Development Co-Operation, 1976 Review: Efforts & Policies. 1976. 16.25 o.p. (ISBN 92-64-11589-7). OECD.
Membership of the Society. The Lake Trout & Legend Society Cookbook. Davis, Charlie, ed. (Illus.). 64p. 1980. softcover 2.00 (ISBN 0-930000-08-0). Mathom.
Membrane Processes for Industry, Symposium, May 19-20,1966. Proceedings. Feazel, Charles E. & Lacey, Robert E., eds. LC 66-30620. (Illus.). 268p. 1966. pap. 5.00 (ISBN 0-686-27919-0). S Res Inst.
Memlimg, Carl. Riddles, Riddles from A to Z. (ps-3). 1962. PLB 5.00 (ISBN 0-307-60940-5, Golden Pr). Western Pub.
Memling, Carl. A B C Rhymes. (Illus.). (ps-3). 1970. PLB 4.57 o.p. (ISBN 0-307-60543-4, Golden Pr). Western Pub.
—Hi, All You Rabbits. LC 78-117558. (Illus.). (ps-2). 1970. 5.95 o.s.i. (ISBN 0-8193-0430-1, Four Winds); PLB 5.41 o.s.i. (ISBN 0-8193-0431-X). Schol Bk Serv.
—Ride, Willy Ride. new ed. LC 78-85950. (Beginning-to-Read Bks). (Illus.). (gr. 1-3). 1970. 2.50 o.p. (ISBN 0-695-80087-6); PLB 3.39 o.p. (ISBN 0-695-40087-8); pap. 1.50 o.p. (ISBN 0-695-30087-3). Follett.
—Ten Little Animals. (Illus.). (ps-1). 1961. PLB 5.00 (ISBN 0-307-60541-8, Golden Pr). Western Pub.
Memorial Hospital Junior Auxiliary Easton Maryland. A Cook's Tour of the Easton Shore. LC 59-15724. (Illus.). 1959. pap. 8.50 (ISBN 0-87033-001-2, Pub. by Tidewater). Cornell Maritime.
Mena, Janet Gonzalez see Gonzalez-Mena, Janet & Eyer, Dianne W.
Menage, Ronald H. The Unheated Greenhouse: How to Maximize Its Potential. LC 80-52346. (Illus.). 128p. 1980. pap. 5.95 (ISBN 0-8069-8954-8). Sterling.
Menake, George T. Policy-Making in the American System: The Case of the Manpower, Development & Training Program. LC 77-18584. 1978. pap. text ed. 11.50x (ISBN 0-8191-0409-4). U Pr of Amer.
Menaker, Lewis. Biological Basis of Dental Caries: An Oral Biology Textbook. (Illus.). 532p. 1980. 45.00 (ISBN 0-06-141726-2, Harper Medical). Har-Row.
Menander. The Girl from Samos. Turner, E. G., tr. from Gr. 64p. 1972. pap. text ed. 5.75x (ISBN 0-485-12019-4, Athlone Pr). Humanities.
—The Rape of the Locks. Murray, Gilbert, tr. 1942. pap. text ed. 3.95x (ISBN 0-04-882046-6). Allen Unwin.
Menard, H. W. Geology, Resources & Society: An Introduction to Earth Science. LC 73-17151. (Geology Ser.). (Illus.). 1974. text ed. 21.95x (ISBN 0-7167-0260-6); instructor's guide avail. W H Freeman.
Menard, H. W., intro. by. Ocean Science: Readings from Scientific American. LC 77-23465. (Illus.). 1977. text ed. 19.95x (ISBN 0-7167-0014-X); pap. text ed. 9.95x (ISBN 0-7167-0013-1). W H Freeman.
Mencher, A. G., ed. Management & Technology: An Anglo-American Exchange of Views. 96p. 1972. 23.00 (ISBN 0-08-018748-X). Pergamon.
Mencher, George T. & Gerber, Sanford. Early Management of Hearing Loss. 1980. write for info. (ISBN 0-8089-1346-8). Grune.
Mencher, George T., jt. auth. see Gerber, Sanford E.

Mencher, Melvin. News Reporting & Writing. 2nd ed. 500p. 1980. pap. text ed. write for info. (ISBN 0-697-04338-X); write for info. wkbk. (ISBN 0-697-04343-6); write for info. instr's. manual (ISBN 0-697-04339-8). Wm C Brown.

Mencher, Samuel. Private Practice in Britain. 95p. 1967. pap. text ed. 5.00x (Pub. by Bedford England). Renouf.

Mencken, H. L. Happy Days. Repr. of 1955 ed. 6.95 o.p. (ISBN 0-394-42767-X). Knopf.

--Heathen Days. Repr. of 1955 ed. 8.95 o.p. (ISBN 0-394-42810-2). Knopf.

--Newspaper Days. 1955. Repr. 8.95 o.p. (ISBN 0-394-43831-0). Knopf.

Mendel, Arthur, jt. auth. see Ellis, Alexander J.

Mendel, Arthur, tr. see Bekker, Paul.

Mendel Centennial Symposium - Fort Collins - 1965. Heritage from Mendel. Brink, R. Alexander & Styles, E. Derek, eds. (Illus., Orig.). 1967. 27.50 (ISBN 0-299-04270-7); pap. 10.95 (ISBN 0-299-04274-X). U of Wis Pr.

Mendel, Douglas. The Politics of Formosan Nationalism. LC 78-94982. (Illus.). 1970. 21.50x (ISBN 0-520-01557-6). U of Cal Pr.

Mendel, Roberta. Epigrams to Live & Die by. (Sketchbook Ser.). (Illus., Orig.). 1981. pap. 4.00 (ISBN 0-936424-08-7, 008). Pin Prick.

--The First Book of Whimsy: Bits of Almost-Haiku & Other Things. (Books for Browsers Ser.). (Illus.). 24p. (Orig.). 1978. pap. 3.00x o.p. (ISBN 0-936424-00-1, 001). Pin Prick.

--A Survival Manual for the Independent Woman Traveler. (Orig.). 1981. pap. write for info. (ISBN 0-936424-06-0, 007). Pin Prick. Postponed.

Mendel, Roberta, ed. The Pin Prick Press Annual Index of Serial & Chapbook Publications, 1980. (Orig.). 1981. pap. 3.00 (ISBN 0-936424-07-9, 007). Pin Prick.

Mendelievich, Elias, ed. see International Labour Office, Geneva.

Mendelowitz, Daniel M. Drawing. LC 80-50905. (Illus.). xvi, 464p. 1980. Repr. of 1967 ed. 29.50 (ISBN 0-8047-1089-9). Stanford U Pr.

Mendels, J., ed. Psychobiology of Affective Disorders. (Illus.). 192p. 1980. pap. 24.00 (ISBN 3-8055-1400-X). S Karger.

Mendelsohn, Allan R., jt. auth. see Richan, Willard C.

Mendelsohn, Erich. Amerika: Bilderbuch Tines Architekten. LC 76-40319. (Architecture & Decorative Art Ser.). (Ger.). 1977. Repr. of 1926 ed. lib. bdg. 45.00 (ISBN 0-306-70830-2). Da Capo.

Mendelsohn, Ezra. Class Struggle in the Pale. LC 71-96097. 1970. 23.50 (ISBN 0-521-07730-3). Cambridge U Pr.

Mendelsohn, H., jt. auth. see Bayley, D. H.

Mendelsohn, Harold & O'Keefe, Garrett J. The People Choose a President: Influences on Voter Decision Making. LC 75-23983. (Special Studies). 1976. text ed. 24.95 (ISBN 0-275-56110-0). Praeger.

Mendelsohn, M. The Guide to Franchising. 2nd ed. LC 78-40961. 1978. 27.50 (ISBN 0-08-022466-0). Pergamon.

Mendelsohn, Martin. Castaways, One Hundred Thousand Dollar Nineteen Seventy-Nine Pro Football Handicapping Championship. 64p. (Orig.). 1980. pap. 2.95 (ISBN 0-89650-644-4). Gamblers.

Mendelsohn, Robert O. Towards Efficient Regulation of Air Pollution from Coal-Fired Power Plants. LC 78-75020. (Outstanding Dissertations in Economics Ser.). 1979. lib. bdg. 24.00 (ISBN 0-8240-4055-4). Garland Pub.

Mendelson, Bert. Introduction to Topology. 3rd ed. 1975. text ed. 15.95x o.s.i. (ISBN 0-205-04495-6, 564495X). Allyn.

Mendelson, Danuta. Metaphor in the Works of Isaac Babel. 1981. 17.50 (ISBN 0-88233-702-5). Ardis Pubs.

Mendelson, Drew. Pilgrimage. 1981. pap. 2.25 (ISBN 0-87997-612-8, UE1612). DAW Bks.

Mendelson, Edward. Early Auden. 1981. 16.95 (ISBN 0-670-28712-1). Viking Pr.

--W. H. Auden: Nineteen Hundred Seven to Nineteen Hundred Seventy-Three. (Illus.). 64p. 1980. 11.00 (ISBN 0-87104-264-9). NY Pub Lib.

Mendelson, Edward, ed. see Auden, W. H.

Mendelson, Elliot. Number Systems & the Foundations of Analysis. 1973. text ed. 19.95 (ISBN 0-12-490850-0). Acad Pr.

Mendelson, Maurice. Life & Work of Walt Whitman: A Soviet View. Bromfield, Andrew, tr. from Rus. 1976. 10.00x o.p. (ISBN 0-8464-0569-5). Beekman Pubs.

Mendelson, Phyllis C., jt. ed. see Hall, Sharon.

Mendelson, R. M. Interrelated Intergrated Electronics Circuits for the Radio Amateur, Technicians, Hobbyist & CB'er. 128p. 1979. pap. 7.70 (ISBN 0-8104-0760-4). Hayden.

Mendelson, Robert E. & Quinn, Michael A., eds. The Politics of Housing in Older Urban Areas. LC 75-23984. (Special Studies). 1976. text ed. 32.50 (ISBN 0-275-56120-8). Praeger.

Mendelson, Robert S. Male Practice: How Doctors Manipulate Women. 1981. 10.95 (ISBN 0-8092-5974-5). Contemp Bks.

Mendelssohn, Felix. Complete Works for Pianoforte Solo, 2 vols. 416p. 1975. pap. 6.00 ea. (ISBN 0-486-23136-4). Vol. 1. Vol. 2 (ISBN 0-486-23137-2). Dover.

Mendenhall & Ott. Understanding Statistics. 3rd ed. LC 79-20914. (Illus.). 1980. text ed. 15.95 (ISBN 0-87872-241-6); study guide 7.95 (ISBN 0-686-65952-X). Duxbury Pr.

Mendenhall, Charles A. Deadly Duo: The B25-B26 in World War Two. (Illus.). 200p. 1981. write for info. (ISBN 0-933424-22-1). Specialty Pr.

Mendenhall, Kitty. Moon of the Lost Frenchman. 192p. (YA) 1976. 4.95 o.p. (ISBN 0-685-64249-6, Avalon). Bouregy.

Mendenhall, Thomas. A Short History of American Rowing. (Illus., Orig.). 1980. 14.95 (ISBN 0-89182-019-1); pap. 7.95 (ISBN 0-89182-026-4). Charles River Bks.

Mendenhall, William & Schaeffer, Richard L. Mathematical Statistics with Applications. 2nd ed. 500p. 1981. text ed. 22.95 (ISBN 0-87872-279-3). Duxbury Pr.

Mendes, Helen. African Heritage Cookbook. (Illus.). 1970. 7.95 o.s.i. (ISBN 0-02-584210-2). Macmillan.

Mendes-Flohr, Paul R. & Reinharz, Jehuda. The Jew in the Modern World: A Documentary History. 1980. pap. text ed. 11.95x (ISBN 0-19-502632-2). Oxford U Pr.

Mendez, M., jt. auth. see Crottel, L.

Mendez, Pepe. Complete Course in Stained Glass. 1977. 4.95 (ISBN 0-672-23287-1). Bobbs.

Mendilow, A. A. Time & the Novel. 244p. 1972. Repr. of 1952 ed. text ed. 15.00x (ISBN 0-391-00220-1). Humanities.

Mendis, G. C., ed. Colebrooke-Cameron Papers: Documents of British Colonial Policy in Ceylon, 1796-1833, 2 Vols. 1956. 22.85x o.p. (ISBN 0-19-635027-1). Oxford U Pr.

Mendl, James, ed. see Skirvanek, John J.

Mendler, Allen, jt. auth. see Curwin, Richard.

Mendlewicz, J., ed. Psychoneuroendocrinology & Abnormal Behaviour. (Advances in Biological Psychiatry: Vol. 5). (Illus.). vi, 130p. 1980. pap. 34.75 (ISBN 3-8055-0599-X). S Karger.

Mendlovitz, Saul H., ed. On the Creation of a Just World Order: Preferred Worlds for the 1990's. LC 74-28937. (Preferred Worlds for the 1990's Ser.). 1977. pap. text ed. 7.95 (ISBN 0-02-920910-2). Free Pr.

Mendlowitz, Edward. Successful Tax Planning. LC 79-25586. 1980. flexible bdg. 50.00 (ISBN 0-932648-07-X). Boardroom.

Mendlowitz, Milton. Systemic Arterial Hypertension. (Illus.). 208p. 1974. 16.75 (ISBN 0-398-02884-2). C C Thomas.

Mendoza, E., jt. auth. see Flowers, B. H.

Mendoza, Ester F. Juana De Ibarbourou: Oficio De Poesia. LC 80-20020. (Mente y Palabra Ser.). (Illus.). xi, 370p. (Span.). 1980. 6.25 (ISBN 0-8477-0572-2); pap. 5.00 (ISBN 0-8477-0573-0). U of PR Pr.

Mendoza, George. Fearsome Brat. LC 73-133625. (Illus.). (gr. k-3). 1971. 6.75 (ISBN 0-688-41306-4); PLB 6.48 o.p. (ISBN 0-688-51306-9). Lothrop.

--Norman Rockwell's Diary for a Young Girl. (Illus.). 1978. 17.95 (ISBN 0-89659-013-5). Abbeville Pr.

--Norman Rockwell's Scrapebook for a Young Boy. (Illus.) 180p. 1979. 17.95 (ISBN 0-89659-026-7); pap. 12.95 (ISBN 0-89659-162-X). Abbeville Pr.

Mendoza, Gunnar, ed. see Arzans de Orsua y Vela, Bartolome.

Mendoza, Jose A, jt. auth. see Papalia, Anthony.

Mendoza, Jose A., jt. auth. see Papalia, Anthony.

Mendoza De Mann, Wilma, tr. see Hunter, Emily.

Menduina, Claudio Sanchez-Albornoz y see Sanchez-Albornoz y Menduina, Claudio.

Menefee, Selden C. Vocational Training & Employment of Youth. LC 70-166953. (FDR & the Era of the New Deal Ser). 1971. Repr. of 1942 ed. lib. bdg. 17.50 (ISBN 0-306-70357-2). Da Capo.

Meneker, Jerry S. Essays on Deviance & Marginality. LC 79-66577. 1979. pap. text ed. 7.75 (ISBN 0-8191-0844-8). U Pr of Amer.

Menell, Zoe, jt. ed. see Musgrave, Beatrice.

Menen, Aubrey. Art & Money: An Irreverent History. LC 79-18359. 226p. 1980. 11.95 (ISBN 0-07-041483-1). McGraw.

--The Artist & His Money. LC 79-18359. (Illus.). 1980. 12.95 (ISBN 0-07-041483-1). McGraw.

--London. (Great Cities Ser.). (Illus.). 1976. 14.95 (ISBN 0-8094-2254-9). Time-Life.

--London. (The Great Cities Ser.). (Illus.). (gr. 6 up). 1976. FLB 14.94 (ISBN 0-8094-2255-7, Pub by Time-Life). Silver.

--Venice. (Great Cities Ser.). (Illus.). 1976. 14.95 (ISBN 0-8094-2262-X). Time-Life.

--Venice. (The Great Cities Ser.). (Illus.). (gr. 6 up). 1976. FLB 14.94 (ISBN 0-8094-2263-8, Pub by Time-Life). Silver.

Menendez, Josefa. The Way of Divine Love. LC 79-112493. 1977. pap. 7.50 (ISBN 0-89555-030-X, 104). TAN Bks Pubs.

Menendez Menendez, Emilio. Lecciones de teoria general del derecho. LC 79-16559. (Sp.). 1980. pap. text ed. write for info. (ISBN 0-8477-3017-4). U of PR Pr.

Menering, Dean & O'Hare, Frank. The Writer's Work: Guide to Effective Composition. (Illus.). 1980. text ed. 12.95 (ISBN 0-13-969865-5); diagnostic test 29.95. P-H.

Menestrier, Claude. L' Art Des Emblemes, Ou S'enseigne la Morale Par les Figures De la Fable, De L'Histoire et De la Nature. Orgel, Stephen, ed. LC 78-68190. (Philosophy of Images Ser.: Vol. 18). (Illus.). 1980. lib. bdg. 66.00 (ISBN 0-8240-3692-1). Garland Pub.

--La Philosophie des Images, 2 vols. Orgel, Stephen, ed. LC 78-68189. (The Renaissance & the Gods: the Philosophy of Images Ser.). 1980. lib. bdg. 66.00 (ISBN 0-8240-3691-3). Garland Pub.

--Traite De Tournois, Joustes, Carrousels et Autres Spectacles Publics. Orgel, Stephen, ed. LC 78-68198. (Philosophy of Images Ser.: Vol. 16). (Illus.). 1980. Repr. of 1669 ed. lib. bdg. 66.00 (ISBN 0-8240-3690-5). Garland Pub.

Menestrier, Claude F. L' Art Des Emblemes. Orgel, Stephen, ed. LC 78-68185. (Philosophy of Images Ser.: Vol. 15). (Illus.). 1979. lib. bdg. 66.00 (ISBN 0-8240-3689-1). Garland Pub.

Menez, Joseph F., jt. auth. see Bartholomew, Paul C.

Menezes, M. N. British Policy Towards the Amerindians in British Guiana, 1803-1973. (Illus.). 1977. 39.50x (ISBN 0-19-821567-3). Oxford U Pr.

Meng, Heinz, jt. auth. see Kaufmann, John.

Mengden, V. & Just, eds. Medical Data Transmission by Public Telephone Systems. 1979. pap. text ed. 24.00 (ISBN 0-8067-0961-8). Urban & S.

Mengelatte, Pierre, et alcompiled by. Buffets and Receptions. Fuller, John & Small, Michael, eds. (Illus.). 1978. 89.95 (ISBN 0-685-90325-7, Virtue & Co.). CBI Pub.

Menger, Carl. Principles of Economics. Dingwall, James & Hoselitz, Bert F., trs. (The Institute for Humane Studies Ser. in Economic Theory). 328p. 1981. text ed. 20.00x (ISBN 0-8147-5380-9); pap. text ed. 7.00x (ISBN 0-8147-5381-7). NYU Pr.

Menger, F. M. & Mandell, L. Electronic Interpretation of Organic Chemistry: A Problems-Oriented Text. 215p. 1980. text ed. 27.50 (ISBN 0-306-40379-X, Plenum Pr); pap. text ed. 12.50 (ISBN 0-306-40391-9, Plenum Pr). Plenum Pub.

Menger, Frederic M., et al. Organic Chemistry: A Concise Approach. 2nd ed. 1975. 19.95 (ISBN 0-8053-3281-2, 33281). Benjamin-Cummings.

Menger, Karl. Kurventheorie. 2nd, rev. ed. LC 63-11314. (Ger). 1968. 22.50 (ISBN 0-8284-0172-1). Chelsea Pub.

Menger, Karl, jt. auth. see Blumenthal, Leonard M.

Menges, Constantine C. Spain: The Struggle for Democracy Today. LC 78-62797. (The Washington Papers: No. 58). 1978. 3.50x (ISBN 0-8039-1123-8). Sage.

Mengin, Robert. No Laurels for De Gaulle: An Appraisal of the London Years. 1966. 6.95 o.p. (ISBN 0-374-22296-7). FS&G.

Menhennet, Alan. Romantic Movement. (The Literary History of Germany Ser.: Vol. 6). 276p. 1981. 28.50x (ISBN 0-389-20104-9). B&N.

Menil, Dominique De see Hess, Thomas B. & Feldman, Morton.

Menil, Dominique de see De Menil, Dominique.

Menil, Dominique De see Lemagny, J. C.

Menke, A. S., jt. auth. see Bohart, R. M.

Menke, Arnold, ed. The Semi-Aquatic & Aquatic Hemiptera of California (Herteroptera: Hemiptera) (California Insect Survey Ser.: Vol. 21). 1979. pap. 19.50x (ISBN 0-520-09592-8). U of Cal Pr.

Menke, Frank G. The Encyclopedia of Sports. 1977. pap. 8.95 (ISBN 0-385-12262-4, Dolp). Doubleday.

Menkveld, H. Dutch Baking & Pastry. (Illus.). viii, 156p. 1980. 15.00x (ISBN 0-85334-839-1, Pub. by Applied Science). Burgess-Intl Ideas.

Menlove, Coleen K. Ready, Set, Go: How to Give Your Children a Head Start Before They Go to School. 1978. 10.95 (ISBN 0-13-762286-4, Spec); pap. 5.95 (ISBN 0-13-762278-3). P-H.

Menna, F., ed. Therapeutic Effects in Ocular Lesions Obtained by Systemic & Topical Administration of an Activator of the Oxygen Metabolism. (Journal: Ophthalmologica: Vol. 180, Suppl. 1). (Illus.). vi, 92p. 1980. 19.75 (ISBN 3-8055-1686-X). S Karger.

Mennel, Robert M. Thorns & Thistles: Juvenile Delinquents in the United States, 1825-1940. LC 72-95187. 259p. 1973. pap. text ed. 15.00x (ISBN 0-87451-070-8). U Pr of New Eng.

Mennell, John M., jt. auth. see Zohn, David A.

Mennell, William. The British Economy. 64p. 1964. pap. 2.95x o.p. (ISBN 0-8464-0211-4). Beekman Pubs.

Mennick, Simon, jt. auth. see Briazack, Norman J.

Mennicke, J. L., ed. Burnside Groups. (Lecture Notes in Mathematics: Vol. 806). 274p. 1980. pap. 16.80 (ISBN 0-387-10006-7). Springer-Verlag.

Mennig, Jan, jt. auth. see Melnicoe, William.

Mennig, Jan, jt. auth. see Melnicoe, William B.

Menning, Edgar. Yosemite Waterfalls. (Illus., Orig.). 1970. pap. 1.25 o.p. (ISBN 0-913832-11-1). Mus Graphics.

Menning, J. H., et al. Communicating Through Letters & Reports. 6th ed. 1976. text ed. 16.50x o.p. (ISBN 0-256-01819-7). Irwin.

Menninger, Jeanetta L., jt. auth. see Menninger, Karl A.

Menninger, Karl. Whatever Became of Sin? 1973. 8.95 (ISBN 0-8015-8556-2, Hawthorn); pap. 4.95 (ISBN 0-8015-8554-6, Hawthorn). Dutton.

Menninger, Karl A. Love Against Hate. LC 42-50183. 1959. pap. 3.50 (ISBN 0-15-653892-X, HB28, Harv). HarBraceJ.

Menninger, Karl A. & Menninger, Jeanetta L. Love Against Hate. LC 42-50183. 1959. 10.75 o.p. (ISBN 0-15-153891-3). HarBraceJ.

Menninger, Karl A., 2nd, jt. auth. see Haavik, Sarah F.

Menolascino, Frank J. Challenges in Mental Retardation: Progressive Ideology & Services. LC 76-6947. 1977. text ed. 24.95 (ISBN 0-87705-295-6). Human Sci Pr.

Menon, B. P. Bridges Across the South: Technical Cooperation Among Developing Countries. (Pergamon Policy Studies). 1980. 21.00 (ISBN 0-08-024645-1); pap. 6.95 (ISBN 0-08-024646-X). Pergamon.

Menon, Bhashkar P. Global Dialogue: The New International Economic Order. 1977. text ed. 21.00 (ISBN 0-08-021498-3); pap. text ed. 8.50 (ISBN 0-08-021499-1). Pergamon.

Menon, K. M. & Reel, Jerry R., eds. Steroid Hormone Action & Cancer. LC 76-25873. (Current Topics in Molecular Endocrinology Ser.: Vol. 4). 182p. 1976. 29.50 (ISBN 0-306-34004-6, Plenum Pr). Plenum Pub.

Menon, K. P. Lamp & the Lampstand. 1967. pap. 2.65x o.p. (ISBN 0-19-635248-7). Oxford U Pr.

Menon, Narayana, tr. see Pillai, Thakazhi S.

Menon, R. R., tr. see Kuttykrishnan, P. C.

Menon, R. Rabindranath. Dasavatara & Other Poems. (Redbird Bk.). 1976. lib. bdg. 5.00 (ISBN 0-89253-118-5); flexible bdg. 4.00 (ISBN 0-89253-148-7). Ind-US Inc.

--Seventy Seven. (Writers Workshop Redbird Ser.). 78p. 1975. 14.00 (ISBN 0-88253-630-3); pap. text ed. 4.80 (ISBN 0-88253-629-X). Ind-US Inc.

--Shadows in the Sun. 1976. 8.00 (ISBN 0-89253-813-9); flexible cloth 4.80 (ISBN 0-89253-814-7). Ind-US Inc.

--Straws in the Wind. (Writers Workshop Redbird Ser.). 1975. 12.00 (ISBN 0-88253-650-8); pap. text ed. 4.80 (ISBN 0-88253-649-4). Ind-US Inc.

Menpes, Mortimer. China. 139p. 1980. Repr. of 1909 ed. lib. bdg. 35.00 (ISBN 0-89987-562-9). Darby Bks.

Mensendieck, Bess M. Look Better, Feel Better. (Illus.). 1954. 8.95 o.s.i. (ISBN 0-06-111140-6, HarpT). Har-Row.

Mensh, Ivan N., jt. auth. see Schwartz, Arthur N.

Mensing, Raymond C. Toleration & Parliament, 1660-1719. LC 79-63260. 1979. pap. text ed. 9.00 (ISBN 0-8191-0723-9). U Pr of Amer.

Men'sov, D. E. Limits of Indeterminancy in Measure of T-Means of Subseries of a Trigonometric Series. (Trudy Steklov Ser.: No. 149). Date not set. cancelled (ISBN 0-8218-3044-9). Am Math.

Mente, Boye De see De Mente, Boye.

Mente, Boye De see Longo, Peter.

Mente, Boye De see Whitlach, John.

Mentelle, Harold W. Consistent Profits in Tape Reading. (The New Stock Market Library Books). (Illus.). 1979. 37.50 (ISBN 0-89266-180-1); spiral bdg. 12.35 (ISBN 0-685-91838-6). Am Classical Coll Pr.

Menten, Ted. The Illuminated Alphabet. (Illus.). 1978. pap. 1.50 (ISBN 0-486-22745-6). Dover.

Menten, Theodore. Art Nouveau Decorative Ironwork: One Hundred & Fifty Photographic Illustrations. (Illus.). 144p. 1981. pap. write for info. (ISBN 0-486-23986-1). Dover.

--The Victorian Parlor: A Cut & Color Book. (Illus.). 32p. (Orig.). (ps-1). 1975. pap. 1.95 (ISBN 0-486-23115-1). Dover.

Menten, Theodore, ed. Ancient Egyptian Cut & Use Stencils. (Illus.). 1978. pap. 3.25 (ISBN 0-486-23626-9). Dover.

--The Art Deco Style in Household Objects, Architecture, Sculpture, Graphics, Jewelry. (Illus.). 192p. (Orig.). 1972. pap. 6.00 (ISBN 0-486-22824-X). Dover.

--Japanese Border Designs. LC 75-13124. (Pictorial Archive Ser). Orig. Title: Kodal Moshiki Zuko. (Illus.). 93p. 1975. pap. 2.50 (ISBN 0-486-23180-1). Dover.

Menting, J. P., jt. ed. see Van Essen, A. J.

Menton, Seymour. Prose Fiction of the Cuban Revolution. LC 75-5993. (Latin American Monographs: No. 37). 344p. 1975. 16.50x (ISBN 0-292-76421-9). U of Tex Pr.

Menuhin, Moshe. Decadence of Judaism in Our Time. 7.00 o.p. (ISBN 0-911026-00-2); pap. 5.00 o.p. (ISBN 0-685-18877-9). New World Press NY.

--The Decadence of Judaism in Our Time. 585p. 1969. 13.00x (ISBN 0-911038-88-4, Inst Hist Rev). Noontide.

Menuhin, Yehudi. The Violin & Viola. Primrose, William & Stevens, Denis, eds. LC 76-328. (The Yehudi Menuhin Music Guide Ser). 1976. 12.95 (ISBN 0-02-871410-5); pap. 6.95 (ISBN 0-02-871350-8). Schirmer Bks.

Menveille, Douglas, ed. see Lindsay, David.

Menville, Douglas, ed. see Arnold, Edwin L.

Menville, Douglas, ed. see Barringer, Leslie.

Menville, Douglas, ed. see Coblentz, Stanton A.

Menville, Douglas, ed. see Dunsany, Lord Edward.

Menville, Douglas, ed. see Haggard, H. Rider.

Menville, Douglas, ed. see Morris, Kenneth.

Menville, Douglas, ed. see Morris, William.

Menville, Douglas, ed. see Newbolt, Henry.

Menville, Douglas, jt. ed. see Reginald, R.

Menville, Douglas, ed. see Stoker, Bram.

Menyuk, Paula. Acquisition & Development of Language. LC 79-135023. (Current Research in Developmental Psychology Ser). 1971. 16.95x (ISBN 0-13-003087-2). P-H.

--The Development of Speech. LC 74-173981. (Studies in Communicative Disorders Ser). 1972. pap. text ed. 2.15 o.p. (ISBN 0-672-61276-3). Bobbs.

Menze, Arnold E. Regulation of Cell Membrane Activities in Plants. 1977. 39.00 (ISBN 0-7204-0615-3, North-Holland). Elsevier.

Menze, Ernest A., ed. Totalitarianism Reconsidered. (National University Publications, Political Science Ser.). 1981. 20.00 (ISBN 0-8046-9268-8). Kennikat.

Menze, Ernest A., tr. see Glaser, Herman.

Menzel, Donald H. Fundamental Formulas of Physics, 2 Vols. 2nd ed. (Illus.). 1960. Vol. 1. pap. text ed. 5.00 (ISBN 0-486-60595-7); Vol. 2. pap. text ed. 5.00 (ISBN 0-486-60596-5). Dover.

--Mathematical Physics. Orig. Title: Theoretical Physics. 1953. pap. text ed. 6.00 (ISBN 0-486-60056-4). Dover.

Menzel, Donald H., ed. Selected Papers on Physical Processes in Ionized Plasmas. (Orig.). 1962. pap. text ed. 5.00 (ISBN 0-486-60060-2). Dover.

Menzel, Dorothy. Pottery Style & Society in Ancient Peru: Art As a Mirror of History in the Ica Valley, 1350-1570. LC 74-29797. 1976. 36.50x (ISBN 0-520-02970-4). U of Cal Pr.

Menzel, Harold H. How to Deal with Lawyers. LC 76-27568. 1977. 15.00 o.p. (ISBN 0-931204-00-3). Caroline Hse.

Menzel, Viktor. Die Entstehung Des Lehnswesens. LC 80-2015. 1981. Repr. of 1890 ed. 18.50 (ISBN 0-404-18579-7). AMS Pr.

Menzies, jt. auth. see Simons.

Menzies, Ken. Talcott Parsons & the Social Image of Man. (International Library of Sociology). 1976. 17.95x (ISBN 0-7100-8369-6). Routledge & Kegan.

Menzies, Robert. The Riches of His Grace. 175p. Repr. of 1956 ed. 7.95 (ISBN 0-227-67583-5). Attic Pr.

Menzies, William W. Anointed to Serve: The Story of the Assemblies of God. LC 79-146707. (Illus.). 1971. 10.95 (ISBN 0-88243-465-9, 02-0465). Gospel Pub.

Meo, Leila. Lebanon, Improbable Nation: A Study in Political Development. LC 75-46621. 246p. 1976. Repr. of 1965 ed. lib. bdg. 20.25x (ISBN 0-8371-8727-3, MELE). Greenwood.

Mepham, John, ed. see Bettelheim, Charles.

Mepham, John, et al, trs. see Gorz, Andre.

Mera, H. P. Pueblo Indian Embroidery. LC 74-31607. (Illus.). 80p. 1975. 15.00 (ISBN 0-88307-512-1); pap. 4.95 (ISBN 0-88307-513-X). Gannon.

Mercado, A., tr. see Dubinin, N. P. & Gol'dfarb, D. M.

Mercado, A., tr. see Strogonov, B. P., et al.

Mercado, A., tr. see Zaika, V. E.

Mercado, Ben, ed. see Eareckson, Joni & Estes, Stephen.

Mercado, Benjamin, ed. El Testimonio De Dios. Flores, Rhode, tr. 148p. (Span.). 1980. pap. 1.60. Vida Pubs.

Mercado, Benjamin, ed. see Barrett, Ethel.

Mercado, Benjamin, ed. see Neimark, Paul.

Mercatante, Anthony S. Good & Evil: Mythology & Folklore. LC 77-11809. (Illus.). 1978. 10.95 o.s.i. (ISBN 0-06-012968-9, HarpT). Har-Row.

Mercer, A., et al. Operational Distribution Research: Innovative Case Studies. (ORASA Text Ser.: No. 2). 1978. pap. 19.95x (ISBN 0-470-26537-X). Halsted Pr.

Mercer, Ann, jt. auth. see Mercer, Cecil.

Mercer, Cecil & Mercer, Ann. Teaching Students with Learning Problems. (Orig.). 1981. pap. text ed. 14.95 (ISBN 0-675-08040-1). Merrill.

Mercer, Cecil D. Children & Adolescents with Learning Disabilities. (Special Education Ser.). 1979. text ed. 18.50 (ISBN 0-675-08272-2). Merrill.

Mercer, Charles. Murray Hill. 1981. pap. 2.95 (ISBN 0-440-16124-X). Dell.

--Pacific. 1981. 12.95 (ISBN 0-671-25587-8). S&S.

Mercer, E. H. The Foundations of Biological Theory. 290p. 1981. 30.00 (ISBN 0-471-08797-1, Pub. by Wiley Interscience). Wiley.

Mercer, E. I., jt. auth. see Goodwin, T. W.

Mercer, G. The Employment of Nurses: Nursing Labour Turnover in the NHS. 185p. 1979. 37.00x (ISBN 0-7099-0015-5, Pub. by Croom Helm Ltd England). Biblio Dist.

Mercer, H., jt. auth. see Davey, H.

Mercer, H. Glenn, jt. auth. see Davey, Homer C.

Mercer, Henry C. Ancient Carpenters' Tools. 5th ed. (Illus.). 339p. 1975. 12.95 (ISBN 0-8180-0818-0). Bucks Co Hist.

--The Hill-Caves of Yucatan: A Search for Evidence of Man's Antiquity in the Caverns of Central America. LC 75-12599. (Speleologia Ser). (Illus.). 256p. 1975. 11.95 (ISBN 0-914264-04-4); pap. 5.50 o.p. (ISBN 0-914264-05-2). Zephyrus Pr.

Mercer, James L. & Koester, Edwin H. Public Management Systems. LC 77-16392. 1978. 24.95 (ISBN 0-8144-5456-9). Am Mgmt.

Mercer, James L. & Philips, Ronald J., eds. Public Technology: Key to Improved Government Productivity. 451p. 1981. 24.95 (ISBN 0-8144-5546-8). Am Mgmt.

Mercer, Jean. Guided Observations in Child Development. LC 79-88267. 1979. pap. text ed. 9.00 (ISBN 0-8191-0768-9). U Pr of Amer.

--Small People: How Children Develop & What You Can Do About It. LC 78-27345. 1979. 12.95 (ISBN 0-88229-318-4); pap. 6.95 (ISBN 0-88229-664-7). Nelson-Hall.

Mercer, John. The Canary Islanders: Their Prehistory Conquest & Survival. (Illus.). 285p. 1980. 32.50x (ISBN 0-389-20213-4). B&N.

Mercer, John D. & Mercer, Patricia. Island of the Pelicans. LC 75-39153. (Illus.). 1976. 6.00 (ISBN 0-916480-01-1). Creative Eye.

Mercer, John E. Alchemy, Its Science & Romance. LC 79-8617. (Illus.). Repr. of 1921 ed. 27.50 (ISBN 0-404-18481-2). AMS Pr.

Mercer, Patricia, jt. auth. see Mercer, John D.

Mercer, Philip. Sympathy & Ethics: A Study of the Relationship Between Sympathy & Morality with Special Reference to Hume's Treatise. 1972. 9.95x o.p. (ISBN 0-19-824363-4). Oxford U Pr.

Mercer, R. Jack. The Band Director's Brain Bank. pap. 9.50 (ISBN 0-686-15897-0). Instrumentalist Co.

Merchant & Sturgul. Applied Fortran Program W Standard Fortan, Watfor, Watfiv & Structured Watfiv. 1977. 15.95x (ISBN 0-534-00497-0). Wadsworth Pub.

Merchant, Jane. The Greatest of These. (Orig.). pap. 1.25 (ISBN 0-89129-175-X). Jove Pubns.

Merchant, M. J., jt. auth. see Sturgul, John R.

Merchant, Michael J. ABC's of FORTRAN Programming. 1979. pap. text ed. 14.95x (ISBN 0-534-00634-5). Wadsworth Pub.

Mercier, B. Lectures on Topics in Finite Element Solution of Elliptic Problems. (Tata Institute Lectures on Mathematics). (Illus.). 191p. 1980. pap. 8.00 (ISBN 0-387-09543-8). Springer-Verlag.

Mercier, Charles. Criminal Responsibility. (Historical Foundations of Forensic Psychiatry & Psychology Ser.). 256p. 1980. Repr. of 1931 ed. lib. bdg. 25.00 (ISBN 0-306-76064-9). Da Capo.

Mercier, J., ed. Anticonvulsant Drugs, Vols. 1-2. LC 72-8044. 1974. Vol. 1. text ed. 64.00 (ISBN 0-08-016840-X); Vol. 2. text ed. 50.00 (ISBN 0-08-017245-8). Pergamon.

Mercier, J. P. & Legras, R. Recent Advances in the Field of Crystallization & Fusion of Polymers. (Journal of Polymer Science Symposia). 1977. 14.95 (ISBN 0-471-04425-3, Pub. by Wiley-Interscience). Wiley.

Mercier, Sebastien. Memoirs of the Year Two Thousand Five Hundred, 1772, 2 vols. in 1. LC 74-16201. (Novel in England, 1700-1775 Ser). 1974. lib. bdg. 50.00 (ISBN 0-8240-1199-6). Garland Pub.

Mercier, Vivian. Irish Comic Tradition. 1969. pap. 4.95 (ISBN 0-19-500297-0, 284, GB). Oxford U Pr.

Meredith. Refrigeration Technician's Pocketbook. 1981. text ed. price not set (ISBN 0-408-00545-9). Butterworth.

Meredith, Bronwen. The Vogue Body & Beauty Book. (Illus.). 360p. 1981. pap. 6.95 (ISBN 0-89104-199-0). A & W Pubs.

Meredith, Dale D., et al. Design & Planning of Engineering Systems. (Civil Engineering & Engineering Mechanics Ser). (Illus.). 384p. 1973. ref. ed. 26.95 (ISBN 0-13-200196-9). P-H.

Meredith, Dennis, jt. auth. see Biller, Henry, Ph.D.

Meredith, Dennis L., ed. Nuclear Power Plant Siting: A Handbook for the Layman. rev. ed. (Marine Bulletin Ser.: No. 6). 1972. pap. 1.00 (ISBN 0-938412-11-6). URI MAS.

Meredith, George. Letters of George Meredith, 3 Vols. Cline, C. L., ed. 1970. 98.00x (ISBN 0-19-811473-7). Oxford U Pr.

--Ordeal of Richard Feverel. 1956. 5.00x o.p. (ISBN 0-460-00916-8, Evman). Dutton.

Meredith, Grace E. Girl Captives of the Cheyennes: A True Story of the Capture & Rescue of 4 Pioneer Girls, 1874, Repr. Of 1927 Ed. Bd. with Narrative of the Captivity of Mrs. Jane Frazier: In: Thomas' History of Allegheny County, Pennsylvania. Frazier, Jane. Repr. of 1930 ed; History of the Capture & Captivity of David Boyd from Cumberland County, Pennsylvania, in 1756. Davis, Marion M., ed. Repr. of 1931 ed; The Means Massacre, Molly Finney, the Canadian Captive. Illsley, Charles P. Repr. of 1932 ed; Narrative of Titus King of Northampton, Mass., a Prisoner of the Indians in Canada, 1755-1758. Repr. of 1938 ed. LC 75-7137. (Indian Captivities Ser.: Vol. 109). 1977. lib. bdg. 44.00 (ISBN 0-8240-1733-1). Garland Pub.

Meredith, Jack, jt. auth. see Turban, Efraim.

Meredith, Nancy, jt. auth. see Eldridge, Evelyn.

Meredith, P. Instruments of Communication. 1966. 56.00 (ISBN 0-08-010663-3). Pergamon.

--Learning, Remembering & Knowing. (Teach Yourself Ser.). 1974. pap. 2.95 o.p. (ISBN 0-679-10434-8). McKay.

Meredith, Richard C. Run, Come See Jerusalem. 256p. (Orig.). 1976. pap. 1.50 o.p. (ISBN 0-345-25066-4). Ballantine.

--Vestiges of Time. LC 77-76255. 1978. 6.95 o.p. (ISBN 0-385-13174-7). Doubleday.

Meredith, Robert C. & Fitzgerald, John D. Structuring Your Novel. 1972. pap. 4.50 (ISBN 0-06-463325-X, EH 325, EH). Har-Row.

Meredith, Roy. Mr. Lincoln's Camera Man: Matthew B. Brady. 2nd, rev. ed. (Illus.). 14.00 (ISBN 0-8446-5224-5). Peter Smith.

Meredith, Ruby F., jt. ed. see O'Kunewick, James P.

Meredith, T. The Eye: Disease, Diagnosis, Treatment. (Illus.). 1975. pap. 7.95 (ISBN 0-87618-068-3). R J Brady.

Meredith, T. J., jt. ed. see Vale, J. A.

Meredith, Ted. Northeast Wine. LC 80-80917. (Illus.). 160p. (Orig.). 1980. pap. 6.95 (ISBN 0-936666-00-5). Nexus Pr.

--Northwest Wine. LC 80-80917. (Illus.). 180p. 1980. pap. 6.95 (ISBN 0-936666-00-5). Nexus Pr.

Merenda, Merilyn & Polichak, C. W. Speech Communication & Theatre Arts: A Classified Bibliography of Theses & Dissertations, 1937-1978. LC 79-9373. 340p. 1979. 75.00 (ISBN 0-306-65182-3). IFI Plenum.

Merenda, Peter F., jt. auth. see Lindeman, Richard H.

Mereness, Dorothy A. & Taylor, Cecelia M. Essentials of Psychiatric Nursing. 10th ed. LC 77-10817. (Illus.). 1978. text ed. 17.95 (ISBN 0-8016-3399-0). Mosby.

Meres, Francis. Palladis Tamia. LC 73-170413. (The English Stage Ser.: Vol. 10). lib. bdg. 50.00 (ISBN 0-8240-0593-7). Garland Pub.

Meresco, Donald. New Light on the Rapture. LC 80-67028. (Orig.). 1980. pap. 9.95 (ISBN 0-937078-00-X). Bible Light.

Merewether, H. A. & Stephens, J. A. The History of the Boroughs & Municipal Corporations of the United Kingdom: From the Earliest to the Present Time, 3 vols. 1972. Repr. of 1835 ed. Set. text ed. 150.00x (ISBN 0-85527-402-6). Humanities.

Mergault, J., jt. auth. see Chaffurin, L.

Mergener, Robert J. Functions: An Approach to Algebra & Trigonometry. 2nd ed. 1978. pap. text ed. 18.50 (ISBN 0-8403-2339-5). Kendall-Hunt.

Merha, Lester. Cheyenne Manhunt. (Orig.). 1980. pap. 1.75 (ISBN 0-8439-0742-8, Leisure Bks). Nordon Pubns.

Merha, Lester W. Return to Elkhorne. (YA) 1977. 4.95 o.p. (ISBN 0-685-73813-2, Avalon). Bouregy.

Merhaut, Josef. Theory of Electroacoustics. (Illus.). 336p. 1981. 44.95 (ISBN 0-07-041478-5, C). McGraw.

Merhav, M. Technological Dependence, Monopoly & Growth. 1968. 18.00 (ISBN 0-08-012754-1). Pergamon.

Merhav, Peretz. The Israeli Left: History, Problems, Documents. LC 77-84578. 1980. 15.00 (ISBN 0-498-02184-X). A S Barnes.

Merhige. The Richmond School Decision. LC 72-83394. pap. 6.00 (ISBN 0-912008-02-4). Integrated Ed Assoc.

Meriam, J. L. Dynamics. 2nd ed. LC 74-30017. 480p. (SI version). 1975. text ed. 20.95x (ISBN 0-471-59607-8); solutions manual avail. (ISBN 0-471-59610-8). Wiley.

--Engineering Mechanics: Statics & Dynamics Combined. LC 78-518. 1978. text ed. 28.95x (ISBN 0-471-01979-8); tchrs'. manual avail. (ISBN 0-471-02753-7). Wiley.

--Statics. 2nd ed. SI Version, ed. LC 74-11459. 381p. 1975. text ed. 20.95x (ISBN 0-471-59604-3). Wiley.

Meriam, James L. Dynamics. 2nd ed. LC 71-142138. 1971. text ed. 20.95x (ISBN 0-471-59601-9). Wiley.

--Statics. 2nd ed. LC 71-136719. (Illus.). 1971. text ed. 20.95x (ISBN 0-471-59595-0). Wiley.

Merigan, William & Weiss, Bernard, eds. Neurotoxicity of the Visual System. 1980. text ed. 34.50 (ISBN 0-89004-400-7). Raven.

Merikangas, James R. Brain-Behavior Relationships. LC 79-2075. 240p. 1981. 23.95x (ISBN 0-669-03082-1). Lexington Bks.

--Preventing Neurologic Syndromes. 250p. 1981. 22.50 (ISBN 0-87527-224-X). Green. Postponed.

Merimee, Prosper. A Slight Misunderstanding. Parmee, Douglas, tr. 1980. pap. 2.95 (ISBN 0-7145-0529-3). Riverrun NY.

Merin, S., ed. see Jerusalem Conference on Impaired Vision in Childhood, May 1977.

Meringer, Rudolf & Mayer, Carl. Versprechen und Verlessen: Eine Psychologisch Linguistische Studie. (Classics in Psycholinguistics Ser.: No. 2). 1979. text ed. 40.00x (ISBN 90-272-0971-5). Humanities.

Merino, Barabara D., jt. auth. see Previts, Gary J.

Merino, Hugo Zemelman see Petras, James & Zemelman Merino, Hugo.

Merino Manon, Jose, jt. auth. see Macon, Jorge.

Meritt, Benjamin D. Athenian Year. (Sather Classical Lectures: No. 32). 1961. 12.50x o.p. (ISBN 0-520-00851-0). U of Cal Pr.

Meritt, Lucy S. History of the American School of Classical Studies at Athens, Nineteen Thirty-Nine to Nineteen Eighty. 1981. price not set (ISBN 0-87661-942-1). Am Sch Athens.

Merivale, C., ed. see Sallust.

Merivale, John H. Orlando in Roncevalles: A Poem. Reiman, Donald H., ed. LC 75-29781. (Romantic Context Ser.: Poetry 1789-1830: Vol. 81). 1978. Repr. of 1814 ed. lib. bdg. 47.00 (ISBN 0-8240-2180-0). Garland Pub.

Meriwether, Elizabeth A. Recollections of Ninety-Two Years 1824-1916. (Illus.). 262p. 1958. 8.50x o.p. (ISBN 0-87402-011-5). U of Tenn Pr.

Meriwether, James B. Studies in The Sound & the Fury. LC 70-126048. 1970. pap. text ed. 2.95x (ISBN 0-675-09300-7). Merrill.

Meriwether, James B. & Millgate, Michael, eds. Lion in the Garden: Interviews with William Faulkner, 1926-1962. LC 80-17080. xvi, 299p. 1980. 17.50x (ISBN 0-8032-3068-0); pap. 5.95 (ISBN 0-8032-8108-0, BB 749, Bison). U of Nebr Pr.

Meriwether, Louise. Daddy Was a Numbers Runner. 1976. pap. 1.95 (ISBN 0-515-05456-9). Jove Pubns.

Merk, Frederick. The Monroe Doctrine & American Expansionism 1843-1849. 320p. 1972. pap. 1.95 o.p. (ISBN 0-394-71760-0, V760, Vin). Random.

Merkel, Fred. The Descent of Man. 36p. 1975. pap. 1.00 o.p. (ISBN 0-686-20749-1). Samisdat.

Merkel, James A. Basic Engineering Principles. (Illus.). 1974. pap. 15.00 (ISBN 0-87055-301-1). AVI.

--Managing Livestock Wastes. (Illus.). 1981. text ed. 22.50 (ISBN 0-87055-373-9). AVI.

Merkin, Donald H. Pregnancy As a Disease: The Pill in Society. 1976. 12.95 (ISBN 0-8046-9138-X, Natl U). Kennikat.

Merkl, Peter, ed. see Mugomba, Agrippah I.

Merkl, Peter H. Political Continuity & Change. rev ed. 1972. pap. text ed. 15.50 scp o.p. (ISBN 0-685-03002-4, 06-044413-4, HarpC); instructors' manual. avail. o.p. (ISBN 0-06-364406-1). Har-Row.

Merkl, Peter H., ed. see Cassinelli, C. W.

Merkle, Judith A. Management & Ideology: The Legacy of the International Scientific Management Movement. 300p. 1980. 18.50x (ISBN 0-520-03737-5). U of Cal Pr.

Merklein, Helmut & Murchison, William. Those Gasoline Lines & How They Got There. 150p. 1980. lib. bdg. 10.95x (ISBN 0-933028-10-5); pap. 5.95x (ISBN 0-933028-09-1). Fisher Inst.

Merklein, Helmut A. Macro Economics. 1972. 14.95x (ISBN 0-534-00175-0). Wadsworth Pub.

Merklin, Lewis, Jr. They Chose Honor: The Problem of Conscience in Custody. LC 74-5794. 352p. (YA) 1974. 8.95 o.s.i. (ISBN 0-06-012939-5, HarpT). Har-Row.

Merle, Robert. Day of the Dolphin. 1977. pap. 1.95 o.p. (ISBN 0-449-23240-9, Crest). Fawcett.

Merleau-Ponty, Maurice. Humanism & Terror. LC 71-84797. 1969. pap. 5.95x (ISBN 0-8070-0277-1, BP342). Beacon Pr.

--Humanism & Terror: An Essay on the Communist Problem. O'Neill, John, tr. from Fr. LC 80-21672. xlvii, 189p. 1980. Repr. of 1969 ed. lib. bdg. 25.00x (ISBN 0-313-22748-9, MEHU). Greenwood.

--Phenomenology of Perception. Smith, Colin, tr. 1962. text ed. 26.00x (ISBN 0-391-00070-5). Humanities.

Merlen, R. H. De Canibus: Dog & Hound in Antiquity. (Illus.). 8.75 (ISBN 0-85131-054-0, Dist. by Sporting Book Center). J A Allen.

Merli, Frank J. & Wilson, Theodore A. Makers of American Diplomacy. LC 73-1321. (Illus.). 672p. (Paper text edition in two vols.). 1974. Vol. 1. pap. 9.95x o.p. (ISBN 0-684-13797-6, ScribC); Vol. 2. pap. 9.95x o.p. (ISBN 0-684-13798-4, ScribC). Scribner.

Merlin, Rene. De Canibus: Dog & Hound in Antiquity. 1972. 10.95 o.p. (ISBN 0-8277-1033-X). British Bk Ctr.

Merlonghi, Ferdinando, et al. Oggi in Italia: A First Course in Italian. LC 77-83330. 1978. text ed. 16.50 (ISBN 0-395-26244-5); tchrs'. ed. 17.60 (ISBN 0-395-26243-7); wkbk. 5.50 (ISBN 0-395-26242-9); tapes 148.20 (ISBN 0-395-26245-3). HM.

Merlonghi, Franca, jt. auth. see Valencia, Pablo.

Mermelstein, David & Alcaly, Roger. The Fiscal Crisis of American Cities: Essays on the Political Economy of Urban America with Special Reference to New York. 1977. pap. 5.95 (ISBN 0-394-72193-4, V-193, Vin). Random.

Mernier, G. & Spingler, M., eds. Nouvelles et Recits Du XXIeme Siecle. 1971. pap. 7.95 o.p. (ISBN 0-13-625335-0). P-H.

Mernissi, Fatima. Beyond the Veil: Male-Female Dynamics in a Modern Muslim Society. 2nd ed. 132p. 1981. pap. text ed. 6.95x (ISBN 0-87073-267-6). Schenkman.

Merory, Joseph. Food Flavorings: Composition, Manufacture & Use. 2nd, rev. ed. 1968. 37.50 o.p. (ISBN 0-87055-024-1). AVI.

Merrell, David J. Ecological Genetics. (Illus.). 570p. 1981. 25.00x (ISBN 0-8166-1019-3). U of Minn Pr.

Merrell, James L. The Power of One. new ed. 128p. 1976. pap. text ed. 1.25 (ISBN 0-8272-2925-9). Bethany Pr.

Merrell, Jo A. The Tree of Life. (Orig.). 1980. 3.50 (ISBN 0-87123-564-1, 210564). Bethany Fell.

Merrett, A. J., et al. Capital Budgeting & Company Finance. 2nd ed. LC 73-86116. 1974. pap. text ed. 6.00x o.p. (ISBN 0-582-45058-6). Longman.

Merrett, C. E. A Selected Bibliography of Natal Maps. 1979. lib. bdg. 42.50 (ISBN 0-8161-8276-0). G K Hall.

Merrett, Stephen. State Housing in Britain. (Illus.). 1979. 34.00x (ISBN 0-7100-0264-5). Routledge & Kegan.

Merriam, Alan P. Bibliography of Jazz. LC 75-127282. (The Roots of Jazz). 1970. Repr. of 1954 ed. lib. bdg. 18.50 (ISBN 0-306-70036-0). Da Capo.

--Congo, Background of Conflict. (African Studies Ser.: No. 6). (Illus.). 1961. 14.95x o.s.i. (ISBN 0-8101-0169-6). Northwestern U Pr.

Merriam, Allen H. Gandhi & Jinnah. 1980. 16.00x (ISBN 0-8364-0039-9). South Asia Bks.

Merriam, C. W., 3rd. Fortran Computer Programs. LC 77-14792. 1978. 24.95 (ISBN 0-669-01995-X). Lexington Bks.

Merriam Company. Webster's Biographical Dictionary. 1976. 15.00 (ISBN 0-87779-443-X). Merriam.

Merriam Company, ed. Liberty's Women. 1980. 15.00 (ISBN 0-87779-064-7). Merriam.

--Webster's Big Seven Collegiate Dictionary. rev. ed. 1976. 14.95 (ISBN 0-87779-314-X). Merriam.

Merriam, D. F., ed. Capture, Management & Display of Geological Data: With Special Emphasis on Energy & Mineral Resources. LC 76-56893. 1977. pap. text ed. 41.25 (ISBN 0-08-021422-3). Pergamon.

--Computer Software for the Geosciences: Proceedings of the Fifth Geochautauqua, 1976. LC 77-30468. 1977. pap. text ed. 41.25 (ISBN 0-08-022090-8). Pergamon.

--Quantitative Stratigraphic Correlation: Proceedings of the 6th Geochautauqua, Syracuse University, October 1977, Vol. 4, No. 3. (Illus.). 112p. 1979. pap. 41.25 (ISBN 0-08-023979-X). Pergamon.

--Recent Advances in Geomathematics: An International Symposium. 1978. text ed. 45.00 (ISBN 0-08-022095-9). Pergamon.

Merriam, Daniel F., jt. auth. see Gill, Dan.

Merriam, Eve. Do You Want to See Something? (Illus.). (gr. 2-3). 1969. pap. 1.25 o.p. (ISBN 0-590-00103-5, Schol Pap). Schol Bk Serv.

--A Husband's Notes About Her. LC 75-25973. 96p. 1976. 9.95 o.s.i. (ISBN 0-02-584350-8, 58435). Macmillan.

--A Husband's Notes About Her. LC 75-25970. 104p. 1976. pap. 2.95 o.s.i. (ISBN 0-02-070120-9, Collier). Macmillan.

--It Doesn't Always Have to Rhyme. (Illus.). (gr. 5 up). 1964. PLB 5.95 o.p. (ISBN 0-689-20671-2). Atheneum.

--There Is No Rhyme for Silver. (Illus.). (gr. 2-6). 1962. PLB 3.07 o.p. (ISBN 0-689-20272-5). Atheneum.

--Unhurry Harry. LC 78-1302. (Illus.). 32p. (gr. k-3). 1978. 5.95 (ISBN 0-590-07480-6, Four Winds). Schol Bk Serv.

Merriam, Eve, jt. ed. see Larrick, Nancy.

Merriam, George S., ed. see Bowles, Samuel.

Merriam, H. G., ed. Frontier Woman: The Story of Mary Ronan. (Illus.). 1975. pap. 4.50 o.p. (ISBN 0-686-15662-5). U of MT Pubns Hist.

Merriam, H. G., ed. see Linderman, Frank B.

Merriam, Sharan B. Coping with Male Mid-Life: A Systematic Analysis Using Literature As a Data Source. LC 80-5124. 137p. 1980. pap. text ed. 7.50 (ISBN 0-8191-1051-5). U Pr of Amer.

Merriam-Webster Editorial Staff. Webster's American Military Biographies. 1978. 12.95 o.p. (ISBN 0-87779-063-9). Merriam.

--Webster's New Collegiate Dictionary. 8th ed. 1568p. 1980. gray lexotone 11.95 (ISBN 0-87779-398-0); thumb-indexed red linen 12.95 (ISBN 0-87779-399-9); thumb-indexed brown skivertex 13.95 (ISBN 0-87779-400-6). Merriam.

--Webster's New Geographical Dictionary. rev. ed. (Illus.). 1568p. 1977. 14.95 (ISBN 0-87779-446-4). Merriam.

--Webster's School Thesaurus. 1978. 7.95 (ISBN 0-87779-178-3). Merriam.

--Webster's Secretarial Handbook. 1976. 9.95 (ISBN 0-87779-036-1). Merriam.

Merriam Webster Editorial Staff, ed. Webster's Collegiate Thesaurus. 1976. 10.95 (ISBN 0-87779-069-8); brown skivertex 11.95 (ISBN 0-87779-070-1). Merriam.

Merriam-Webster Reference Editor, ed. Webster's Instant Word Guide. 384p. 1972. 2.95 (ISBN 0-87779-273-9). Merriam.

Merrick, Franck. Practicing the Piano. 1978. lib. bdg. 9.95 o.p. (ISBN 0-214-15726-1, 8025, Dist. by Arco). Barrie & Jenkins.

Merrick, Gordon. An Idol for Others. 1977. pap. 2.50 (ISBN 0-380-00971-4, 44842). Avon.

--The Lord Won't Mind. 1971. pap. 2.25 (ISBN 0-380-01404-1, 36772). Avon.

Merrick, Helen H. Sweden. LC 71-151884. (First Bks). (Illus.). (gr. 4-6). 1971. PLB 4.90 o.p. (ISBN 0-531-00751-0). Watts.

Merrifield, Edward see Washburn, Wilcomb E.

Merrifield, M. Practical Directions for Portrait Painting. (Library of the Arts Ser.). (Illus.). 1977. 27.35 (ISBN 0-89266-069-4). Am Classical Coll Pr.

Merrigan, John J., jt. auth. see Guy, Edward T.

Merrigan, Joseph A. Sunlight to Electricity: Prospects for Solar Energy Conversion by Photovoltaics. LC 75-6933. 192p. (Orig.). 1975. 15.00x (ISBN 0-262-13116-1); pap. 5.95 (ISBN 0-262-63072-9). MIT Pr.

Merril, Judith. The Best of Judith Merril. 1976. pap. 1.25 o.s.i. (ISBN 0-446-86058-1). Warner Bks.

Merrill, Boynton. Jefferson's Nephews: A Frontier Tragedy. 1977. pap. 2.95 (ISBN 0-380-01837-3, 36277, Discus). Avon.

Merrill, Boynton, Jr. A Bestiary. LC 75-3549. (Illus.). 72p. 1976. 8.00x (ISBN 0-8131-1329-6). U Pr of Ky.

Merrill, Dean. How to Really Love Your Wife. 196p. 1980. pap. 4.95 (ISBN 0-310-35321-1, 10685). Zondervan.

Merrill, Dean, tr. Magnificos Tres. (Spanish Bks.). (Span.). 1979. 1.50 (ISBN 0-8297-0733-6). Life Pubs Intl.

--Manual Del Esposo. (Spanish Bks.). (Span.). 1979. 1.90 (ISBN 0-8297-0891-X). Life Pubs Intl.

--Tres Magnificos, Os. (Portugese Bks.). (Port.). 1979. 2.20 (ISBN 0-8297-0892-8). Life Pubs Intl.

Merrill, Edward A. For the Sake of the Trust: Sherlock Holmes & the Musgrave Ritual. LC 80-67700. (Sherlock Holmes Monograph). (Illus.). 112p. 1981. 10.95 (ISBN 0-934468-05-2). Gaslight.

Merrill, Elmer D. Plant Life of the Pacific World. LC 80-51195. (Illus.). 312p. 1981. Repr. of 1945 ed. 13.50 (ISBN 0-8048-1370-1). C E Tuttle.

--Plant Life of the Pacific World. (Illus.). 1945. 12.50x (ISBN 0-686-51288-X). Elliots Bks.

Merrill, George D., jt. ed. see Hillesheim, James W.

Merrill, H. W. Merrill's Guide to Computer Performance Evaluation: Analysis of Smf-Rmf Data with SAS. (Illus.). 352p. 1980. 395.00 (ISBN 0-686-65590-7). SAS Inst.

Merrill, Horace S. & Merrill, Marion G. The Republican Command, Eighteen Ninety-Seven to Nineteen Thirteen. LC 76-147852. (Illus.). 376p. 1971. 17.00x (ISBN 0-8131-1245-1). U Pr of Ky.

Merrill, James. Fire Screen. LC 71-86549. 1969. pap. 6.95 (ISBN 0-689-10185-6). Atheneum.

--Mirabell: Books of Number. LC 78-4350. 1979. 10.95 (ISBN 0-689-10901-6); pap. 7.95 (ISBN 0-689-11167-3). Atheneum.

--Scripts for the Pageant. LC 79-55588. 1980. 12.95 (ISBN 0-689-11053-7); pap. 8.95 (ISBN 0-689-11065-0). Atheneum.

Merrill, James M. A Sailor's Admiral: A Biography of William F. Halsey. LC 76-8880. (Illus.). 1976. 9.95 o.s.i. (ISBN 0-690-01163-6, TYC-T). T Y Crowell.

Merrill, Jean. Seraphina. 224p. (Orig.). 1980. pap. 1.75 (ISBN 0-449-50124-8, Coventry). Fawcett.

--The Superlative Horse. (gr. 4-7). 1961. PLB 5.95 o.p. (ISBN 0-685-21701-9, A-W Childrens). A-W.

Merrill, John C. & Lowenstein, Ralph L. Media, Messages & Men. 2nd ed. 1979. pap. text ed. 9.95 (ISBN 0-582-29008-2). Longman.

Merrill, John N. Legends of Derbyshire. 2nd ed. (Illus.). 71p. (Orig.). (gr. 6 up). 1975. pap. 3.00 (ISBN 0-913714-15-1). Legacy Bks.

Merrill, John R. Using Computers in Physics. LC 75-25012. (Illus.). 384p. 1976. pap. text ed. 9.25 o.p. (ISBN 0-395-21411-4). HM.

Merrill, Kathleen K., jt. auth. see Feldman, Shirley C.

Merrill, Marion G., jt. auth. see Merrill, Horace S.

Merrill, Mary A. Chemistry: Process & Prospect. LC 72-90998. (gr. 9-12). 1973. text ed. 17.95x (ISBN 0-675-09023-7); wkbk. 9.95 (ISBN 0-675-09026-1). Merrill.

Merrill, Melissa. Polygamist's Wife. LC 74-29659. (Illus.). 168p. (Orig.). 1975. 5.95 o.p. (ISBN 0-913420-52-2). Olympus Pub Co.

Merrill, Richard, ed. Radical Agriculture. LC 76-23504. 1976. 17.50x (ISBN 0-8147-5414-7). NYU Pr.

Merrill, Richard A. & Hutt, Peter B. Food & Drug Law, Cases & Materials. LC 80-23167. (University Casebook Ser.). 959p. 1980. text ed. write for info. (ISBN 0-88277-016-0). Foundation Pr.

Merrill, Robert. Norman Mailer. (United States Authors Ser.: No. 322). 1978. 12.50 (ISBN 0-8057-7254-5). Twayne.

Merrill, Samuel W. Fluid Power for Aircraft: Modern Hydraulic Technology. 3rd ed. 1974. pap. 10.00 (ISBN 0-914680-01-3). Intermtn Air.

Merrill, Samuel W., compiled by. Regulations for Aircraft Maintenance. rev. ed. 1975. pap. 8.75 (ISBN 0-685-69727-4). Intermtn Air.

Merrill, Susan. Washday. LC 77-12621. (Illus.). (ps-4). 1978. 6.95 (ISBN 0-395-28817-7, Clarion). HM.

Merrill, Toni. Activities for the Aged & Infirm: A Handbook for the Untrained Worker. (Illus.). 392p. 1979. 16.50 (ISBN 0-398-01294-6). C C Thomas.

--Discussion Topics for Oldsters in Nursing Homes: 365 Things to Talk About. 256p. 1974. pap. 24.75 (ISBN 0-398-03129-0). C C Thomas.

--Party Packets: For Hospitals & Homes Shortcuts for a Single Activity Worker. (Illus.). 196p. 1970. pap. 17.50 photocopy ed. (ISBN 0-398-01295-4). C C Thomas.

--Social Clubs for the Aging. (Illus.). 320p. 1973. 13.75 (ISBN 0-398-02644-0). C C Thomas.

Merrill, Vic. Can You Hear Me, God? 96p. 1981. 6.00 (ISBN 0-682-49740-1). Exposition.

Merrill, Virginia & Richardson, Susan M. Reproducing Period Furniture & Accessories in Miniature. Aymar, Brant, ed. 1981. 25.00 (ISBN 0-517-53816-4). Crown.

Merrill, W. K. The Survival Handbook. (Illus.). 1972. 10.95 (ISBN 0-87691-068-1). Winchester Pr.

Merrill, William K. Hunter's Bible. 1968. 3.50 (ISBN 0-385-01533-X). Doubleday.

Merriman, Brian. The Midnight Court. 3rd ed. Marcus, David, tr. 1975. pap. text ed. 1.75x (ISBN 0-85105-273-8, Dolmen Pr). Humanities.

Merriman, D., jt. ed. see Sears, M.

Merriman, Henry S. Young Mistley. Van Thal, Herbert, ed. 1888-1966. 5.00 (ISBN 0-304-93090-3); pap. 2.95 (ISBN 0-685-09212-7). Dufour.

Merriman, John, ed. Consciousness & Class Experience in 19th Century Europe. LC 79-16032. 1980. text ed. 24.50x (ISBN 0-8419-0444-8); pap. 9.85x (ISBN 0-8419-0610-6). Holmes & Meier.

--French Cities in the Nineteenth Century. 256p. 1981. text ed. 28.50x (ISBN 0-8419-0464-2). Holmes & Meier.

Merriman, Lyle, jt. auth. see Voxman, Himie.

Merriman, Roger B. Life & Letters of Thomas Cromwell, 2 vols. Incl. Vol. 1. Life, Letters of 1535; Vol. 2- Letters from 1536, Notes, Index. 1902. 59.00x (ISBN 0-19-822305-6). Oxford U Pr.

Merriss, B. L., et al. Stainless Steel Piping, Fittings & Accessories for the Pulp & Paper Industry. 3rd rev. ed. (TAPPI PRESS Reports). (Illus.). 1979. pap. 19.85 (ISBN 0-89852-330-3, 01-01-R030). TAPPI.

Merrit, Walter. History for the League for Industrial Rights. LC 76-120852. (Civil Liberties in Americana History Ser.). 1970. Repr. of 1925 ed. lib. bdg. 17.50 (ISBN 0-306-71961-4). Da Capo.

Merritt & McEwen. Mass Spectronomy, Pt. B. 416p. 1980. 49.75 (ISBN 0-8247-6947-3). Dekker.

Merritt, A. The Metal Monster. (Orig.). 1976. pap. 1.50 o.p. (ISBN 0-380-00862-9, 31294). Avon.

Merritt Company Staff. OSHA Reference Manual. 1981. 197.00 (ISBN 0-930868-03-X). Merritt Co.

Merritt, F. S. Modern Mathematical Methods in Engineering. 1970. 28.50 o.p. (ISBN 0-07-041512-9, P&RB). McGraw.

Merritt, Frederick S., rev. by see Dalzell, J. Ralph.

Merritt, Herbert E. Hydraulic Control Systems. LC 66-28759. 1967. 39.00 (ISBN 0-471-59617-5, Pub. by Wiley-Interscience). Wiley.

Merritt, Richard L., ed. Foreign Policy Analysis. LC 75-27808. (Policy Studies Organization Study). 176p. 1975. 17.95 (ISBN 0-669-00251-8). Lexington Bks.

Merritt, Richard W. & James, Maurice T. The Micropezidae of California (Diptera) (Bulletin of the California Insect Survey: Vol. 14). 1973. 8.00x (ISBN 0-520-09435-2). U of Cal Pr.

Merry, Henry J. Constitutional Function of Presidential-Administrative Separation. LC 78-53415. 1978. pap. text ed. 7.50x (ISBN 0-8191-0497-3). U Pr of Amer.

--Five-Branch Government: The Full Measure of Constitutional Checks & Balances. LC 79-22499. 290p. 1980. 17.50 (ISBN 0-252-00797-2). U of Ill Pr.

Merry, Uri & Allerhand, Melvin E. Developing Teams & Organizations: A Practical Handbook for Managers & Consultants. LC 76-17719. (Illus.). 1977. text ed. 18.95 (ISBN 0-201-04531-1). A-W.

Merryman, J. H. Law & Social Change in Mediterranean Europe & Latin America: A Handbook of Legal & Social Indicators for Comparative Study. 1980. 47.50 (ISBN 0-379-20700-1). Oceana.

Mersand, Joseph. The English Teacher: Basic Traditions & Successful Innovations. 1977. 15.00 (ISBN 0-8046-9170-3); pap. text ed. 8.95 (ISBN 0-8046-9175-4). Kennikat.

Merschel, Sylvia, jt. auth. see Perry, Donald.

Merserve, Bruce E. & Sobel, Max A. Introduction to Mathematics. 4th ed. (Illus.). 1978. text ed. 17.95 (ISBN 0-13-487553-2). P-H.

Mersky, Roy M. & Jacobstein, J. Myron, eds. Ten Year Index to Periodical Articles Related to Law (1958-1968) LC 65-29677. 1970. 35.00 (ISBN 0-87802-050-0). Glanville.

Mersky, Roy M., et al, eds. Index to Periodical Articles Related to Law: Five Year Cumulation,(1969-1973) LC 65-29677. 428p. 1974. lib. bdg. 35.00 (ISBN 0-87802-051-9). Glanville.

Mertens, John R. Attic White-Ground: Its Development on Shapes Other Than Lekythoi. LC 76-23641. (Outstanding Dissertations in the Fine Arts - 2nd Series - Ancient). (Illus.). 1977. Repr. of 1972 ed. lib. bdg. 48.00x (ISBN 0-8240-2711-6). Garland Pub.

Mertens, Thomas & Bennett, Alice S. Laboratory Investigations in the Principles of Biology. 3rd ed. 1973. spiral bdg. 8.95 (ISBN 0-8087-1360-4). Burgess.

Mertens, Thomas R. Human Genetics: Readings on the Implications of Genetic Engineering. LC 74-30471. 320p. 1975. text ed. 10.95x (ISBN 0-471-59628-0). Wiley.

Mertens, Thomas R., jt. auth. see Allamong, Betty D.

Mertens, Thomas R., jt. auth. see Gardner, Elton J.

Mertens, Thomas R., jt. auth. see Parker, Gary E.

Mertes, Harald, jt. auth. see Hollander, Neil.

Merton, Henry. Your Gold & Silver. (Illus.). 96p. 1981. 4.95 (ISBN 0-02-077410-9, Collier). Macmillan.

Merton, R. Science, Technology & Society in Seventeenth Century England. LC 79-82308. 1970. 19.50 (ISBN 0-86527-178-X). Fertig.

Merton, Robert K. Mass Persuasion: The Social Psychology of a War Bond Drive. LC 77-136076. 1971. Repr. of 1946 ed. lib. bdg. 19.75x (ISBN 0-8371-5226-7, MEMP). Greenwood.

--On Theoretical Sociology: Five Essays, Old & New. 1967. pap. text ed. 3.95 (ISBN 0-02-921150-6). Free Pr.
--Science, Technology & Society in Seventeenth Century England. 1978. pap. text ed. 6.95x (ISBN 0-685-41725-5). Humanities.
--Social Theory & Social Structure. LC 68-28789. 1968. text ed. 17.95 (ISBN 0-02-921130-1). Free Pr.
Merton, Robert K. & Gaston, Jerry, eds. The Sociology of Science in Europe. LC 77-2996. (Perspectives in Sociology). 397p. 1977. 22.95x (ISBN 0-8093-0633-6). S Ill U Pr.
Merton, Robert K. & Riley, Matilda W., eds. Sociological Traditions from Generation to Generation: Glimpses of the American Experience. LC 79-26693. (Modern Sociology: Series of Monographs, Treatises, & Texts). (Illus.). 1980. text ed. 14.95 (ISBN 0-89391-034-1); tchrs' ed. 9.95 (ISBN 0-89391-061-9). Ablex Pub.
Merton, Robert K., et al, eds. Reader in Bureaucracy. 1965. pap. text ed. 10.95 (ISBN 0-02-921070-4). Free Pr.
Merton, Stephen. Mark Rutherford (William H. White) (English Authors Ser.: No. 53). lib. bdg. 10.95 (ISBN 0-8057-1468-5). Twayne.
Merton, Thomas. The Ascent to Truth. 1981. 5.95 (ISBN 0-15-608682-4, Harv). HarBraceJ.
--The Asian Journal of Thomas Merton. Stone, Naomi B., et al, eds. LC 71-103370. (Illus.). 448p. 1973. 12.50 (ISBN 0-8112-0464-2); pap. 6.95 (ISBN 0-8112-0570-3, NDP394). New Directions.
--The Collected Poems of Thomas Merton. LC 77-9902. 1088p. 1980. pap. 17.00 (ISBN 0-8112-0769-2, NDP504). New Directions.
--Conjectures of a Guilty Bystander. LC 66-24311. pap. 3.95 (ISBN 0-385-01018-4, Im). Doubleday.
--Contemplation in a World of Action. 400p. 1973. pap. 3.95 (ISBN 0-385-02550-5, Im). Doubleday.
--Contemplative Prayer. 1971. pap. 1.95 (ISBN 0-385-09219-9, Im). Doubleday.
--Geography of Lograire. LC 78-88727. (Orig.). 1969. pap. 2.75 (ISBN 0-8112-0098-1). New Directions.
--Introductions East & West. (Illus.). 175p. 1981. 19.95 (ISBN 0-87775-139-0); pap. 9.95 (ISBN 0-87775-140-4). Unicorn Pr.
--Life & Holiness. pap. 1.95 (ISBN 0-385-06277-X, D183, Im). Doubleday.
--The Living Bread. 157p. 1956. 12.95 (ISBN 0-374-14613-6); pap. 5.95 (ISBN 0-374-51520-4). FS&G.
--Love & Living. Stone, Naomi B. & Hart, Bro. Paterick, eds. 240p. 1979. 10.00 (ISBN 0-374-19237-5). FS&G.
--The Monastic Journey. Hart, Patrick, Bro., ed. LC 77-27714. 1978. pap. 2.95 (ISBN 0-385-14094-0, Im). Doubleday.
--The Monastic Journey. Hart, Patrick, ed. 1977. 8.95 o.p. (ISBN 0-8362-0665-7). Andrews & McMeel.
--My Argument with the Gestapo: A Macaronic Journal. LC 69-20082. 256p. 1975. pap. 3.75 (ISBN 0-8112-0586-X, NDP403). New Directions.
--The New Man. 256p. 1962. pap. 4.95 (ISBN 0-374-51444-5). FS&G.
--No Man Is an Island. LC 78-7108. 1978. pap. 4.50 (ISBN 0-15-665962-X, Harv). HarBraceJ.
--The Nonviolent Alternative. Date not set. 12.95 (ISBN 0-374-22312-2); pap. 6.95 (ISBN 0-374-51575-1). FS&G.
--The Seven Storey Mountain. LC 78-7109. 1978. pap. 5.95 (ISBN 0-15-680679-7, Harv). HarBraceJ.
--The Sign of Jonas. pap. 3.95 (ISBN 0-385-07898-6, Im). Doubleday.
--The Silent Life. 178p. 1975. pap. 4.50 (ISBN 0-374-51281-7). FS&G.
--Wisdom of the Desert. LC 59-15021. 1970. 6.50 (ISBN 0-8112-0313-1); pap. 2.95 (ISBN 0-8112-0102-3, NDP295). New Directions.
Merton, Thomas, ed. see Gandhi, Mohandas.
Mertz, Barbara. Red Land, Black Land: Daily Life in Ancient Egypt. LC 78-9552. (Illus.). 1978. 12.95 (ISBN 0-396-07575-4); pap. 7.95 (ISBN 0-396-07640-8). Dodd.
--Temples, Tombs & Hieroglyphs: A Popular History of Ancient Egypt. LC 78-9806. (Illus.). 1978. 12.95 (ISBN 0-396-07576-2); pap. 7.95 (ISBN 0-396-07641-6). Dodd.
Merva, George E. Physioengineering Principles. (Illus.). 1975. pap. text ed. 20.50 (ISBN 0-87055-304-6). AVI.
Mervine, Kathryn E. & Cawley, Rebecca E. NSTA Energy-Environment Materials Guide. 80p. 1975. pap. text ed. 2.00 o.p. (ISBN 0-685-55989-0, 471-14694). Natl Sci Tchrs.
Mervyn, Len. Minerals & Your Health. LC 80-84442. 144p. 1981. Repr. 9.95 (ISBN 0-686-69376-0). Keats.
Merwe, Alwyn Van Der, jt. ed. see Yourgrau, Wolfgang.
Merwe, Hendrik Van der see Van der Merwe, Hendrik & Schrire, Robert A.
Merwe, Hendrik W. Van Der see Van Der Merwe, Hendrik W., et al.
Merwe, Henrik van Der see Van der Merwe, Henrik.
Merwin, Henry C. Life of Bret Harte, with Some Account of the California Pioneers. LC 67-23887. 1967. Repr. of 1911 ed. 20.00 (ISBN 0-8103-3042-3). Gale.
Merwin, John. Stillwater Trout. LC 80-492. 1980. 15.95 (ISBN 0-385-17140-4, NLB). Doubleday.
Merwin, Richard E., ed. see National Computer Conference, 1979.
Merwin, W. S. Carrier of Ladders. LC 72-124964. 1970. pap. 5.95 (ISBN 0-689-10343-3). Atheneum.
--The Compass Flower. LC 76-27345. 1977. pap. 5.95 (ISBN 0-689-10768-4). Atheneum.
--Writings to an Unfinished Accompaniment. LC 72-92616. 128p. 1973. pap. 5.95 (ISBN 0-689-10556-8). Atheneum.
Merwin, W. S. & Masson, J. Moussaiff, eds. Classical Sanskrit Love Poetry. LC 77-13407. 1977. 17.50x (ISBN 0-231-04282-5). Columbia U Pr.
Merwin, W. S., tr. Asian Figures. LC 72-92617. 64p. 1973. pap. 6.95 (ISBN 0-689-10557-6). Atheneum.
Merwin, W. S., tr. see Euripides.
Meryman, Richard. Hope: A Loss Survived. 1980. 10.95 (ISBN 0-316-56786-8). Little.
--Louis Armstrong - a Self Portrait. LC 70-152507. 1971. 6.95x o.s.i. (ISBN 0-87130-026-5); pap. 3.95 (ISBN 0-87130-027-3). Eakins.
Merz, Florian. Pop Art in School. 1970. 16.95 (ISBN 0-7134-2288-2, Pub. by Batsford England). David & Charles.
Merzer, Meridee. Winning the Diet Wars. LC 79-2765. 1980. 9.95 (ISBN 0-15-196378-9). HarBraceJ.
Merzlyakov, N. S., jt. auth. see Yaroslavskii, L. P.
Mesa-Lago, Carmelo. The Economy of Socialist Cuba: A Two-Decade Appraisal. 296p. 1981. price not set (ISBN 0-8263-0578-4); pap. price not set (ISBN 0-8263-0585-7). U of NM Pr.
Mesarovic, M. D. & Takahara, Y. General Systems Theory: Mathematical Foundations. 1975. 37.50 (ISBN 0-12-491540-X); lib ed. 48.00 (ISBN 0-12-491541-8); microfiche 27.50 (ISBN 0-12-491542-6). Acad Pr.
Mesarovic, M. D., ed. see Systems Symposium - 4th - Case Western Reserve University, Institute of Technology.
Mesarovic, Mihajlo & Pestel, Eduard. Mankind at the Turning Point: The Second Report to the Club of Rome. 224p. 1974. 12.95 o.p. (ISBN 0-525-15230-X); pap. 4.95 o.p. (ISBN 0-525-03945-7). Dutton.
Meschan, Isadore. Synopsis of Analysis of Roentgen Signs in General Radiology. LC 75-8181. (Illus.). 655p. 1976. 32.00 (ISBN 0-7216-6301-X). Saunders.
Meschia, Giacomo, ed. see Battagila, Frederick C. & Hagerman, Dwain D.
Mescon, Michael H. & Bramlette, Carl A., Jr., eds. Individual & the Future of Organizations, Vol. 9. (Franklin Foundation Lecture Ser.). 1980. pap. 3.75 (ISBN 0-88406-139-6). GA St U Busn Pub.
--Individual & the Future of Organizations, Vol. 10. (Franklin Foundation Lecture Ser.). 1981. pap. 3.75 (ISBN 0-88406-144-2). GA St U Busn Pub.
--Individual & the Future of Organizations, Vol. 11. (Franklin Foundation Lecture Ser.). 1981. pap. 3.75 (ISBN 0-88406-145-0). GA St U Busn Pub.
Mescon, Michael M. & Rachman, David J. Business Today. 1976. text ed. 13.95 o.p. (ISBN 0-394-31948-6). Random.
Meserole, Harrison T., compiled by. MLA International Bibliography of Books & Articles on the Modern Languages & Literatures, 1970. 1972. 150.00x (ISBN 0-87352-202-8). Modern Lang.
Meserole, Harrison T., ed. Seventeenth-Century American Poetry. LC 68-29435. (Stuart Editions). 1968. 22.50x (ISBN 0-8147-0301-1). NYU Pr.
Meserole, Harrison T., compiled by. MLA International Bibliography of Books & Articles on the Modern Languages & Literatures, 1971. 1973. 150.00x (ISBN 0-87352-213-3). Modern Lang.
--MLA International Bibliography of Books & Articles on the Modern Languages & Literatures, 1972. 1974. 150.00x (ISBN 0-87352-221-4). Modern Lang.
--MLA International Bibliography of Books & Articles on the Modern Languages & Literatures, 1973. 1975. 150.00x (ISBN 0-87352-233-8). Modern Lang.
--MLA International Bibliography of Books & Articles on the Modern Languages & Literatures, 1969. 1970. 150.00x (ISBN 0-87352-409-8). Modern Lang.
--MLA International Bibliography of Books & Articles on the Modern Languages & Literatures, 1974. 1976. 150.00x (ISBN 0-87352-241-9). Modern Lang.
Meserole, Harrison T., et al. American Literature: Tradition & Innovation, 4 vols. Incl. Vol. 1. From the Beginnings to William Cullen Bryant. 12.95x o.p. (ISBN 0-669-95943-X); Vol. 2. Ralph Waldo Emerson to Sidney Lanier. 11.95x o.p. (ISBN 0-669-95950-2); Vol. 3. Walt Whitman to Stephen Crane. 11.95x o.p. (ISBN 0-669-95968-5); Vol. 4. Henry Adams to the Present. 11.95x o.p. (ISBN 0-669-95976-6). 1969. Heath.
Meserve, B. E. & Sobel, Max A. Contemporary Mathematics. 2nd ed. (Illus.). 1977. text ed. 18.95 (ISBN 0-13-170092-8). P-H.
Meservé, Bruce E. & Sobel, Max A. Contemporary Mathematics. 3rd ed. (Illus.). 688p. 1981. text ed. 18.95 (ISBN 0-13-170076-6). P-H.
Meserve, Walter. Studies in Death of a Salesman. LC 79-171570. 1972. pap. text ed. 2.95x (ISBN 0-675-09259-0). Merrill.
Meserve, Walter J. Emerging Entertainment: The Drama of the American People to 1828. LC 77-74444. 352p. 1977. 17.50x (ISBN 0-253-37007-8). Ind U Pr.
Meserve, Walter J., ed. American Drama to Nineteen Hundred: A Guide to Information Sources. (American Literature, English Literature, & World Literature in English Information Guide Ser.: Vol. 28). 1980. 30.00 (ISBN 0-8103-1365-0). Gale.
Meservy, Jay A. & Alonzo, J. The Terrible, Awful, Deplorable, Loveable Little Troll. (gr. 1-5). Date not set. cancelled (ISBN 0-8197-0464-4). Bloch.
Meshelany, C. Infection Control Manual. 2nd ed. 1979. 49.95 (ISBN 0-87489-232-5). Med Economics.
Meshenberg, Michael J., ed. Environmental Planning: A Guide to Information Sources. LC 73-17538. (Man & the Environment Information Guide Ser.: Vol. 3). 480p. 1976. 30.00 (ISBN 0-8103-1340-5). Gale.
Mesirow, Kip. The Care & Use of Japanese Woodworking Tools. LC 78-60055. (Illus.). 1980. pap. 8.95 (ISBN 0-918036-08-9). Woodcraft Supply.
Meskill, John, ed. An Introduction to Chinese Civilization. LC 72-9410. 650p. 1973. 27.50x (ISBN 0-231-03649-3). Columbia U Pr.
Meslee, Edmond La see La Meslee, Edmond M.
Mesmer, Franz A. Mesmerism: A Translation of the Original Medical & Scientific Writings of F. A. Mesmer, M.D. Bloch, George, tr. from Lat., Fr. & Ger. LC 80-14736. 180p. 1980. 11.50 (ISBN 0-913232-88-2). W Kaufmann.
Messance. Nouvelles Recherches Sur la Population De la France. (Principal French Demographic Works of the 18th Century Ser.). (Fr.). 1976. lib. bdg. 40.00x o.p. (ISBN 0-8287-0608-5); pap. text ed. 30.00x o.p. (ISBN 0-685-71501-9). Clearwater Pub.
--Recherches Sur la Population Des Generalities D'auvergne, De Lyon, De Rouen et De Queleques Provinces et Villes Du Royaume. (Principal French Demographic Works of the 18th Century Ser.). (Fr.). 1976. lib. bdg. 60.00x o.p. (ISBN 0-8287-0609-3); pap. text ed. 50.00x o.p. (ISBN 0-685-71503-5). Clearwater Pub.
Messec, Jerry L., jt. auth. see Kranich, Roger E.
Messec, Jerry L., jt. auth. see Kranich, Rogert E.
Messegue, Maurice. Maurice Messegue's Way to Natural Health & Beauty. Winston, Clara, tr. from Fr. LC 74-8944. 324p. 1974. 6.95 o.s.i. (ISBN 0-02-584370-2). Macmillan.
--Of Men & Plants. LC 72-81079. 384p. 1973. 6.95 o.s.i. (ISBN 0-02-584380-X). Macmillan.
Messel, H. & Crawford, D. F. Electron-Photon Shower Distribution Function: Tables for Lead, Copper & Air Absorbers. LC 69-16049. 1970. 180.00 (ISBN 0-08-013374-6). Pergamon.
Messel, H., ed. Surveys of Tidal River Systems in the Northern Territory & Their Crocodile Populations, 7 vols. Incl. Tidal Waterways of Castlereagh Bay & Hutchinson & Cadell Straits: Bennett, Darbitla, Djigaglia Djabura, Ngandadauda Creeks & the Glyde & Woolen Rivers. (Monograph: No. 9). 23.25 (ISBN 0-08-024801-2); Tidal Waterways of Buckingham & Ulundurwi Bays: Buckingham, Kalarwoi, Warawuruwoi & Kurala Rivers & Slippery Creek. (Monograph: No. 10). 18.00 (ISBN 0-08-024802-0); Tidal Waterways of Arnhem Bay: Darwarunga, Habgood, Baralminer, Gobalpa, Coromuro, Cato, Peter John & Burungbirinung Rivers. (Monograph: No. 11). 21.50 (ISBN 0-08-024803-9); Tidal Waterways on the South-Western Coast of the Gulf of Carpentaria: Limmen Bight Towns, Roper, Phelp & Wilson Rivers; Nayarnpi, Wungguliyanga, Painnyilatya, Mangkurdurrungku & Yiwapa Creeks. (Monograph: No. 12). 17.00 (ISBN 0-08-024804-7); Tidal Waterways on the Southern Coast of the Gulf of Carpentaria: Calvert, Robinson, Wearyan & McArthur Rivers & **Some Intervening Creeks. (Monograph: No. 13). 19.00 (ISBN 0-08-024805-5); Tidal Waterways of the Van Diemen Gulf: Ilamary; River, Iwalg, Saltwater & Minimini: Creeks & Coastal Arms on Cobourg Peninsula. Resurveys of the Alligator Region Rivers. (Monograph: No. 14). 20.00 (ISBN 0-08-024806-3); Some River & Creek Systems on the West Coast of Cape York Peninsula in the Gulf of Carpentaria: Nassau, Staaten & Gilbert Rivers & Duck Creek. (Monograph: No. 16). write for info. (ISBN 0-08-024807-1). (Illus.). 1980. Pergamon.**
Messel, H. & Butler, S. T., eds. Solar Energy. LC 75-15144. 350p. 1975. text ed. 25.00 (ISBN 0-08-019817-1); pap. text ed. 13.25 (ISBN 0-08-019781-7). Pergamon.
Messel, H., et al. Survey of Tidal River Systems in the Northern Territory & Their Crocodile Populations: Monographs, Nos. 2-8. Incl. No. 2. The Victoria & Fitzmaurice River Systems. 52p (ISBN 0-08-023098-9); No. 3. The Adelaide, Daly & Moyle Rivers. 58p (ISBN 0-08-023099-7); No. 4. The Alligator Region River System: Murgenella & Cooper's Creeks; East, South & West Alligator Rivers & Wildman River. 70p (ISBN 0-08-024789-X); No. 5. The Goodmadeer & King River Systems: Majarie, Wurugoij & All Night Creeks. 62p (ISBN 0-08-024790-3); No. 6. Some River & Creek Systems on Melville & Grant Islands: North & South Creeks on Grant Island. 64p (ISBN 0-08-024784-9); No. 7. The Liverpool-Tomkinson River Systems & Nungbulgarri Creek. 84p (ISBN 0-08-024785-7); No. 8. Some Rivers & Creeks on the Western Shore of the Gulf of Carpentaria: Rose River, Muntak Creek; Hart, Walker & Koolatong Rivers. 40p (ISBN 0-08-024786-5). (Illus.). 1979. pap. 16.00 ea. Pergamon.
Messel, Harry, ed. Energy for Survival. (Illus.). 368p. 1979. 38.00 (ISBN 0-08-024794-6); pap. 15.00 (ISBN 0-08-024791-1). Pergamon.
Messenger, Charles. The Blitzkrieg Story. LC 76-18633. (Encore Edition). (Illus.). 272p. 1976. 3.95 o.p. (ISBN 0-684-15712-8, ScribT). Scribner.
Messenger, E. C., tr. see Guiraud, Jean.
Messenger, Robert C., jt. auth. see Andrews, Frank M.
Messent, Jan. Designing for Needlepoint & Embroidery from Ancient & Primitive Sources. LC 76-7589. 128p. 1976. 14.95 o.s.i. (ISBN 0-02-584431-8, 58443). Macmillan.
--Embroidery & Nature. (Illus.). 168p. 1980. 22.75 (ISBN 0-8231-4258-2). Branford.
Messent, Peter. Understanding Your Dog: The Intelligent Person's Guide to a Lifelong Relationship with Another Species. LC 80-51643. (Illus.). 160p. 1980. 12.95 (ISBN 0-8128-2746-5). Stein & Day.
Messent, Peter B., ed. Literature of the Occult: A Collection of Critical Essays. (Twentieth Century Views Ser.). 224p. 1981. text ed. 12.95 (ISBN 0-13-537712-9, Spec); pap. text ed. 4.95 (ISBN 0-13-537704-8, Spec). P-H.
Messer, Andrew C., jt. auth. see Alexander, Daniel E.
Messer, Thomas M. Edward Munch. LC 70-142783. (Library of Great Painters Ser.). (Illus.). 168p. 1973. 35.00 (ISBN 0-8109-0333-4). Abrams.
Messerli, Douglas & Fox, Howard N., eds. Index to Periodical Fiction in English, 1965-69. LC 76-42288. 1977. 35.00 (ISBN 0-8108-0952-4). Scarecrow.
Messiah, A. Quantum Mechanics. Vol. 1, 1961. pap. 16.95x (ISBN 0-471-59766-X); Vol. 2 1962. pap. 14.95x (ISBN 0-471-59768-6). Halsted Pr.
Messick, Hank & Goldblatt, Burt. The Only Game in Town: An Illustrated History of Gambling. LC 75-26583. (Illus.). 224p. 1976. 12.50 o.s.i. (ISBN 0-690-01061-3, TYC-T). T Y Crowell.

Messier, Charles. The Messier Catalogue. Niles, P. H., ed. LC 80-70586. 52p. (Orig.). 1981. pap. 1.50 (ISBN 0-9602738-2-4). Auriga.

Messimer, Dwight R. No Margin for Error: The U. S. Navy's Transpacific Flight of 1925. 176p. 1981. 15.95 (ISBN 0-87021-497-7). Naval Inst Pr.

Messina, Edmund J. Cytology. LC 74-79836. (Allied Health Ser). 1975. pap. 7.65 (ISBN 0-672-61382-4). Bobbs.

Messing, Shep & Hirshey, David. The Education of an American Soccer Player. LC 78-8099. (Illus.). 1978. 8.95 (ISBN 0-396-07568-1). Dodd.

Messinger, Sheldon L., jt. ed. see Bittner, Egon.

Messmer, K., ed. see Advances in Diagnosis & Therapy, Muenchen, November 1980.

Messnen, Stephen D., jt. auth. see Kinnard, William N.

Messner, F., ed. see International Conference on Marketing Systems for Developing Countries.

Messner, Gerald & Messner, Nancy S. Collection: Literature of the Seventies. LC 79-162644. 915p. 1972. pap. text ed. 11.95x (ISBN 0-669-63636-3); tchrs. manual avail. (ISBN 0-669-75390-4). Heath.

Messner, Nancy S., jt. auth. see Messner, Gerald.

Messner, Reinhold. Everest: Expedition to the Ultimate. (Illus.). 1979. 18.95 (ISBN 0-19-520135-3). Oxford U Pr.

--K Two: Mountain of Mountains. (Illus.). 176p. 1981. 35.00 (ISBN 0-19-520253-8). Oxford U Pr.

--Solo: Nanga Parbat. (Illus.). 1981. 19.95 (ISBN 0-19-520196-5). Oxford U Pr.

Messner, Yvonne. Campfire Cooking. LC 73-90003. (Illus.). 128p. (Orig.). 1973. pap. 1.95 o.p. (ISBN 0-912692-29-4). Cook.

Messora, L. Start Sailing. (Orig.). 1980. pap. 8.95x (ISBN 0-8464-1051-6). Beekman Pubs.

Mesters, Carlos. God, Where Are You? Meditations on the Old Testament. Drury, John, tr. from Port. LC 76-41356. 1977. 6.95x o.p. (ISBN 0-88344-162-4). Orbis Bks.

Mesthene, Emmanuel. Technology & Social Change. LC 67-23043. (Orig.). 1967. pap. 2.50 (ISBN 0-672-60900-2, CR14). Bobbs.

Mestinsek, Erma. Discoveries of the Hidden Things of God. 64p. 1980. 12.50 (ISBN 0-682-49635-9). Exposition.

Mestwerdt. Atlas of Colposcopy. Meier, A., ed. 1981. text ed. price not set (ISBN 0-7216-6268-4). Saunders.

Meszaros, I. Lukacs' Concept of Dialectic: With Biography, Bibliography & Documents. (Illus.). 211p. 1972. text ed. 8.25x (ISBN 0-85036-159-1). Humanities.

--Marx's Theory of Alienation. 356p. 1973. text ed. 13.00x (ISBN 0-85036-144-3). Humanities.

--The Necessity of Social Control. 1971. text ed. 3.00x (ISBN 0-85036-154-0). Humanities.

Meszaros, Istvan. Lukacs' Concept of Dialect. (Illus.). pap. 4.95 (ISBN 0-686-23497-9, Merlin Pr). Carrier Pigeon.

--Marx's Theory of Alienation. 1970. pap. 10.95 (ISBN 0-686-23498-7, Merlin Pr). Carrier Pigeon.

--Necessity of Social Control. 1971. pap. 2.95 (ISBN 0-686-23499-5, Merlin Pr). Carrier Pigeon.

Meszaros, Julia, jt. ed. see Enyedi, Gyorgy.

Meszaros, William. Cardiac Roentgenology: Plain Films & Angiographic Findings. (Amer. Lec. Roentgen Diagnosis Ser.). 600p. 1969. pap. 65.00 spiral (ISBN 0-398-01297-0). C C Thomas.

Meszner, Seebestyen, tr. see Makhult, Mihaly.

Metall, R. A., jt. ed. see Engel, Salo.

Metastasio, Pietro. Three Melodramas: Dido Abandoned, Demetrius, the Olimpiad. Fucilla, Joseph G., tr. LC 80-51017. (Studies in Romance Languages: No. 24). 164p. 1981. 11.00x (ISBN 0-8131-1400-4). U Pr of Ky.

Metaxas, B. N. The Economics of Tramp Shipping. (Illus.). 304p. 1971. text ed. 27.50x (ISBN 0-485-11127-6, Athlone Pr). Humanities.

Metayer, Maurice, ed. & tr. Tales from the Igloo. LC 76-54253. (Illus.). 1977. pap. 4.95 o.p. (ISBN 0-312-78418-X). St Martin.

Metcalf, Alan A. Chicano English. (Language in Education Ser.: No. 21). 1979. 2.95 (ISBN 0-87281-107-7). Ctr Appl Ling.

Metcalf & Eddy, Inc. & Tchobanoglous, George. Pumping & Collection of Wastewater. (Water Resources & Engineering Ser.). (Illus.). 400p. 1981. text ed. 28.95 (ISBN 0-07-041680-X, C); student's manual 4.95 (ISBN 0-07-041681-8). McGraw.

Metcalf, Deborah. Mouth to Mouth. 1980. 10.95 (ISBN 0-399-90086-1). Marek.

Metcalf, E. W., Jr. Paul Laurence Dunbar: A Bibliography. LC 75-14466. (Author Bibliographies Ser.: No. 23). 202p. 1975. 10.00 (ISBN 0-8108-0849-8). Scarecrow.

Metcalf, Frank J. American Psalmody. 2nd ed. LC 68-13274. (Music Reprint Ser). (Illus.). 1968. Repr. of 1917 ed. lib. bdg. 12.50 (ISBN 0-306-71132-X). Da Capo.

Metcalf, Harold J. Air Track Physics: A First Semester Laboratory Manual. 49p. 1980. pap. text ed. 4.95 (ISBN 0-8403-2286-0). Kendall-Hunt.

Metcalf, Kenneth N., ed. Transportation Information Sources. LC 65-24657. (Management Information Guide Ser.: No. 8). 1965. 30.00 (ISBN 0-8103-0808-8). Gale.

Metcalf, P., jt. auth. see Huntington, R.

Metcalf, Paul. U. S. Dept. of the Interior. LC 80-66485. (Illus.). 88p. (Orig.). 1980. pap. 5.00 (ISBN 0-917788-23-0). Gnomon Pr.

Metcalf, Pricilla. James Knowles: Victorian Editor & Architect. (Illus.). 414p. 1980. 44.00x (ISBN 0-19-812626-3). Oxford U Pr.

Metcalf, Robert, jt. auth. see Rose, Tom.

Metcalf, Robert L., jt. ed. see Pitts, James N., Jr.

Metcalf, Samuel L. A Collection of Some of the Most Interesting Narratives of Indian Warfare in the West. LC 75-7060. (Indian Captivities Ser.: Vol. 38). 1977. Repr. of 1821 ed. lib. bdg. 44.00 (ISBN 0-8240-1662-9). Garland Pub.

Metcalf, Thomas R. Land, Landlords, & the British Raj: Northern India in the Nineteenth Century. (Center for South & Southeast Asia Studies, UC Berkeley). 1979. 25.00x (ISBN 0-520-03575-5). U of Cal Pr.

Metcalf, William K., jt. auth. see Earle, Alvin M.

Metcalf, William K., et al. Gross Anatomy Review. (Basic Science Review Bks.). 1975. spiral bdg. 8.00 o.s.i. (ISBN 0-87488-220-6). Med Exam.

Metcalfe, C. R., ed. Anatomy of the Monocotyledons, 4 vols. Incl. Vol. 1. Gramineae. 1960. o.p. (ISBN 0-19-854339-5); Vol. 2. Palmae. Tomlinson, P. B. 1961. 49.00x (ISBN 0-19-854344-1); Vol. 3. Commelinales-Zingiberales. Tomlinson, P. B. 1969. 48.00x (ISBN 0-19-854365-4); Vol. 4. Juncales. Cutler, D. F. 1969. 42.00x (ISBN 0-19-854369-7); Vol. 5. Cyperaceae. Metcalfe, C. R. (Illus.). 610p. 1971. 62.00x (ISBN 0-19-854372-7); Vol. 6. Dioscoreales. Ayensu, E. S. (Illus.). 226p. 1972. 49.00x (ISBN 0-19-854376-X). Oxford U Pr.

Metcalfe, C. R. & Chalk, L., eds. Anatomy of the Dicotyledons, 2 vols. 2nd ed. (Illus.). 1979. Set. 55.00x (ISBN 0-19-854383-2). Oxford U Pr.

Metcalfe, Edna, ed. Trees of Christmas. (Illus.). (gr. 3 up). 1969. 8.95 o.p. (ISBN 0-687-42590-5). Abingdon.

Metcalfe, James J. Poem Portraits for All Occasions. LC 61-9537. 5.95 o.p. (ISBN 0-385-08938-4). Doubleday.

Metcalfe, T. J. Weighing Machines: Non-Self-Indicating Mechanisms, Vol. 1. 192p. 1969. 42.50x (ISBN 0-85264-095-1, Pub. by Griffin England). State Mutual Bk.

--Weighing Machines: Semi-Self-Indicating & Self-Indicating Mechanisms, Vol. 2. 178p. 1969. 44.95x (ISBN 0-686-68843-0, Pub. by Griffin England). State Mutual Bk.

Metchnikoff, Elias. Optimism & Pessimism in Goethe's Life. (Illus.). 113p. 1981. Repr. of 1908 ed. 41.85 (ISBN 0-89901-025-3). Found Class Reprints.

Metelka, Charles J., ed. The Dictionary of Tourism. 1981. 14.95 (ISBN 0-916032-10-8). Merton Hse.

Meteyard, Peter. Stanley, the Tale of the Lizard. (Illus.). (gr. k-3). 1979. PLB 7.95 (ISBN 0-233-97071-1). Andre Deutsch.

Metge, Joan. The Maoris of New Zealand. 1976. 26.00x (ISBN 0-7100-8352-1); pap. 12.50 (ISBN 0-7100-8381-5). Routledge & Kegan.

Metgler, K. Newsgathering. pap. 14.50 (ISBN 0-13-621037-6). P-H.

Metheny, Burton R. How to Develop the Power of Transcendental Experience. (Illus.). 117p. 1980. 39.45 (ISBN 0-89920-014-1). Am Inst Psych.

Metherell, A. F., ed. Acoustical Imaging, Vol. 8. 1980. 59.50. (ISBN 0-306-40171-1, Plenum Pr). Plenum Pub.

Metherell, A. J., jt. auth. see Landshoff, P. V.

Methold, K. & Waters, D. D. Understanding Technical English, 3 bks. (Illus.). 1975. pap. text ed. 3.75x ea. (ISBN 0-582-69032-3); Bk. 1. pap. text ed. 3.75x student's bk. 2 (ISBN 0-582-69032-3); Bk. 2. pap. text ed. 3.75 student's bk 3 (ISBN 0-582-69035-8). Bk. 3 (ISBN 0-582-69036-6). Longman.

Methold, Kenneth. English Conversation Practice. 1975. pap. text ed. 3.00x (ISBN 0-582-55221-4). Longman.

--Practice in Medical English. 1975. pap. text ed. 4.75x (ISBN 0-582-55057-2). Longman.

Methvin, John J. Andele, or the Mexican - Kiowa Captive. a Story of Real Life Among the Indians, Repr. Of 1899 Ed. Bd. with Grandfather's Captivity & Escape. Benton, Mrs. L. G. Repr; Stirring Adventures of the Joseph R. Brown Family. Their Captivity During the Indian Uprising of 1862 & Description of Their Old Home Near Sacred Heart-Destroyed by the Indians. Allanson, George G. Repr. LC 75-7131. (Indian Captivities Ser.: Vol. 103). 1976. lib. bdg. 44.00 (ISBN 0-8240-1727-7). Garland Pub.

Metken, Gunter. Herbert List: Metaphysical Photographs, 1930-1970. LC 80-51597. (Illus.). 168p. 1981. pap. 32.50 (ISBN 0-8478-0344-9). Rizzoli Intl.

Metos, Thomas H. Robots A Two Z. LC 80-21004. (Illus.). 80p. (gr. 4 up). 1980. PLB 7.79 (ISBN 0-671-34027-1). Messner.

Metraux, Guy P. Western Greek Land: Use & City-Planning in the Archaic Period. LC 77-94709. (Outstanding Dissertations in the Fine Arts Ser.). 1978. lib. bdg. 21.00x (ISBN 0-8240-3241-1). Garland Pub.

Metraux, Rhoda, jt. auth. see Mead, Margaret.

Metraux, Rhoda, jt. ed. see Mead, Margaret.

Metress, James F., jt. ed. see Brace, C. Loring.

Metropolis, N., et al, eds. A History of Computing in the Twentieth Century. LC 79-51683. 1980. 29.50 (ISBN 0-12-491650-3). Acad Pr.

Metropolitan Museum of Art. Treasures from the Bronze Age of China: An Exhibition from the People's Republic of China. (Illus.). 192p. 12.95 (ISBN 0-345-29051-8). Ballantine.

Metropolitan Museum of Art, jt. auth. see British Museum.

Metropolitan Museum of Art (New York) Library Catalog of the Metropolitan Museum of Art. 2nd ed. 1980. lib. bdg. 4650.00 (ISBN 0-8161-0295-3). G K Hall.

Metropolitan Philaret. On the Law of God: To the Young People of the Church. 1975. pap. 5.00 (ISBN 0-913026-76-X, Synaxis Pr). St Nectarios.

Mets, David R. NATO: Alliance for Peace. (Illus.). 190p. (gr. 9-12). 1981. PLB price not set (ISBN 0-671-34065-4). Messner.

--Nato: An Alliance for Peace. (Illus.). 1981. write for info. Messner.

Metternich, Clemens V. Memoirs of Prince Metternich, 1773-1835, 5 Vols. LC 68-9611. 1970. Repr. of 1881 ed. Set. 85.00 (ISBN 0-86527-128-3). Fertig.

Mettler, Barbara & Warner, June, eds. Materials of Dance As a Creative Art Activity. 4th ed. 1974. 15.00x o.p. (ISBN 0-912536-02-0). Mettler Studio.

Mettler, George. Down Home. 352p. (Orig.). 1981. pap. 2.95 (ISBN 0-449-14403-8, GM). Fawcett.

Mettler, George B. Criminal Investigation. 1977. text ed. 16.50 (ISBN 0-205-05761-6, 825761-2); instructor's manual free (ISBN 0-205-05762-4, 825762-0). Allyn.

Mettler, Lawrence E. & Gregg, Thomas G. Population Genetics & Evolution. LC 69-16809. (Foundations of Modern Genetics Ser). (Illus.). 1969. pap. 10.95x ref. ed. (ISBN 0-13-685289-0). P-H.

Mettlin, Curtis, ed. see Symposium at Roswell Park Memorial Institute, Buffalo, May 1980.

Metts, Wally. Home Sweet Hassle. LC 79-53293. (Orig.). 1981. pap. 2.95 (ISBN 0-89636-036-9). Accent Bks.

Metwalli, S. M., jt. ed. see Shawki, G. S. A.

Metz, Charles B. & Monroy, Alberto, eds. Fertilization: Comparative Morphology, Biochemistry & Immunology, 2 vols. Incl. Vol 1. 1967. 55.50 (ISBN 0-12-492650-9); Vol. 2. 1969. 63.50 (ISBN 0-12-492651-7). Set. 96.50 (ISBN 0-685-23219-0). Acad Pr.

Metz, David. Specimen Questions & Answers for Master, Mate, Pilot & Certified Tankerman on the Central Western Rivers. LC 63-23041. 1963. pap. 6.50x (ISBN 0-87033-116-7). Cornell Maritime.

Metz, Ferdinand. Culinary Olympics Cookbook. LC 78-23567. 1979. 24.95 (ISBN 0-8436-2151-6). CBI Pub.

Metz, J. B. & Jossua, J. P. Christianity & Socialism. (Conciliums Ser.: Vol. 105). 1978. pap. 4.95 (ISBN 0-8164-2148-X). Crossroad NY.

Metz, J. B., jt. auth. see Jossua, J. P.

Metz, J. B. & Jossua, J. P., eds. The Crisis of Religious Language. (Concilium Ser.: Religion in the Seventies: Vol. 85). 156p. 1973. pap. 4.95 (ISBN 0-8164-2541-8). Crossroad NY.

Metz, J. C. The Two Merry Milkmaids. Orgel, Stephen, ed. LC 78-66811. (Renaissance Drama Ser.). 1979. lib. bdg. 33.00 (ISBN 0-8240-9740-8). Garland Pub.

Metz, Johann B. The Emergent Church: The Future of Christianity in a Post-Bourgeois World. 160p. (Ger.). 1981. 10.95 (ISBN 0-8245-0036-9). Crossroad NY.

--Faith in History & Society: Toward a Practical Fundamental Theology. 1979. 12.95 (ISBN 0-8164-0426-7). Crossroad NY.

Metz, Johann B., jt. auth. see Rahner, Karl.

Metz, Johann B., jt. ed. see Schillebeeckx, Edward.

Metz, Johannes B. Followers of Christ: Perspectives on the Religious Life. LC 78-70817. 1979. pap. 3.95 (ISBN 0-8091-2138-7). Paulist Pr.

--New Questions on God. LC 73-185752. (Concilium Ser.: Religion in the Seventies: Vol. 76). 1972. pap. 4.95 (ISBN 0-8164-2532-9). Crossroad NY.

--Theology of Joy. (Concilium Ser.: Religion in the Seventies: Vol. 95). pap. 4.95 (ISBN 0-8164-2579-5). Crossroad NY.

--Theology of the World. 1969. pap. 3.95 (ISBN 0-8164-2568-X). Crossroad NY.

Metz, Johannes B., ed. Moral Evil Under Challenge. (Concilium Ser.: Religion in the Seventies: Vol. 56). 1969. pap. 4.95 (ISBN 0-8164-2512-4). Crossroad NY.

--Perspectives of a Political Ecclesiology. LC 79-150306. (Concilium Ser.: Religion in the Seventies: Vol. 66). 1971. pap. 4.95 (ISBN 0-8164-2522-1). Crossroad NY.

Metz, Joseph G. The Politics of People-Power: Interest Groups & Lobbies in New York State. new ed. Dillon, Mary E., ed. LC 76-184891. (Politics of Government Ser.). 110p. (Orig.). 1972. pap. 2.50 o.p. (ISBN 0-8120-0453-1). Barron.

Metz, Leon C. Pat Garrett: The Story of a Western Lawmen. (Illus.). 305p. 1974. 14.95 (ISBN 0-8061-1067-8). U of Okla Pr.

Metz, Leon C. & McKinney, Millard G. Fort Bliss, a Pictorial History. Mangan, Frank, ed. Date not set. 30.00 (ISBN 0-930208-10-2). Mangan Bks. Postponed.

Metz, Mary H. Classrooms & Corridors: The Crisis of Authority in Desegregated Secondary Schools. 1978. 17.95x (ISBN 0-520-03396-5); pap. 4.95 (ISBN 0-520-03941-6). U of Cal Pr.

Metz, Richard. The Graduated Swing Method. (Illus.). 128p. 1981. 12.95 (ISBN 0-684-16868-5, ScribT). Scribner.

Metz, Robert, et al. Geology Laboratory Manual: Geology from New Jersey. LC 79-55477. (Illus.). 1979. 7.80 (ISBN 0-93443-00-X). RA Corp.

Metz, W. New Writing: From Lead to 30, with Revisions. 1979. 12.95 o.p. (ISBN 0-686-52159-5); pap. 11.95 o.p. (ISBN 0-13-617514-7). P-H.

Metzbower, Edward A., ed. Applications of Lasers in Materials Processing. 1979. 32.00 (ISBN 0-87170-084-0). ASM.

Metzger, Barbara. Bething's Folly. LC 80-54483. 192p. 1981. 9.95 (ISBN 0-8027-0677-0). Walker & Co.

Metzger, Bruce M. Introduction to the Apocrypha. 1957. pap. 5.95 (ISBN 0-19-502340-4). Oxford U Pr.

--Lexical Aids for Students of New Testament Greek. 3rd ed. 1969. pap. 4.95x (ISBN 0-8401-1618-7). Allenson.

--New Testament: Its Background, Growth & Content. 1965. 9.95 (ISBN 0-687-27913-5). Abingdon.

--Text of the New Testament: Its Transmission, Corruption, & Restoration. 2nd ed. 1968. 9.95 (ISBN 0-19-500391-8). Oxford U Pr.

Metzger, Bruce M., ed. A Textual Commentary on the Greek New Testament. 1978. 6.45 (ISBN 3-438-06010-8, 08515). United Bible.

Metzger, D. Electric Components, Instruments & Troubleshooting. 1981. 28.95 (ISBN 0-13-250266-6). P-H.

Metzger, Deena. The Axis Mundi Poems. (Illus.). 52p. (Orig.). 1981. pap. 4.95 (ISBN 0-937310-09-3). Jazz Pr.

--The Woman Who Slept with Men to Take the War Out of Them & Tree. LC 80-83933. 192p. 1981. 12.95 (ISBN 0-915238-42-X); pap. 8.95 (ISBN 0-915238-43-8). Peace Pr.

Metzger, Deena, et al. Children of the Moon. (Valhalla Ser., No. 2). (300 copies on pearl paper). 1973. 2.00 o.p. (ISBN 0-686-09147-7). Merging Media.

Metzger, Mendel, jt. auth. see Metzger, Therese.

Metzger, Nancy J., jt. auth. see Phillips, Gerald M.

Metzger, Norman. The Health Care Supervisor's Handbook. LC 78-12513. 1978. text ed. 21.50 (ISBN 0-89443-078-5). Aspen Systems.

Metzger, Norman & Munn, Harry. Communication in Health Care. 150p. 1981. text ed. price not set (ISBN 0-89443-356-3). Aspen Systems.

Metzger, Philip. Managing a Programming Project. 2nd ed. (Illus.). 288p. 1981. text ed. 21.50 (ISBN 0-13-550772-3). P-H.

Metzger, Therese & Metzger, Mendel. Jewish Life in the Middle Ages: Illuminated Hebrew Manuscripts. Watson, Rowan, tr. from Hebrew. (Illus.). 1981. 75.00 (ISBN 0-19-520168-X). Oxford U Pr.

Metzger, Thomas A. Escape from Predicament: Neo-Confucianism and China's Evolving Political Culture. LC 76-25445. 208p. 1977. 17.50x (ISBN 0-231-03979-4). Columbia U Pr.

Metzger, Walter P. Academic Freedom in the Age of the University. LC 61-2328. 1955. pap. 6.00x (ISBN 0-231-08512-5). Columbia U Pr.

Metzger, Will. Tell the Truth. 220p. (Orig.). 1981. pap. 5.95 (ISBN 0-87784-464-X). Inter Varsity.

Metzing, Dieter, ed. Frame Conceptions & Text Understanding. (Research in Text Theory: No. 5). 167p. 1980. text ed. 42.50x (ISBN 3-11-008006-0). De Gruyter.

Metzker, Isaac & Golden, Harry. A Bintel Brief. 1977. pap. 1.25 (ISBN 0-345-22903-7). Ballantine.

Metzler, David. Biochemistry: The Chemical Reactions of Living Cells. 1129p. 1977. 29.50 (ISBN 0-12-492550-2); instr's manual 3.00 (ISBN 0-12-492552-9). Acad Pr.

Metzler, K. Creative Interviewing: The Writer's Guide to Gathering Information by Asking Questions. 1977. 12.95 (ISBN 0-13-189720-9); pap. 7.95 (ISBN 0-13-189712-8). P-H.

Metzler, Ken. Newswriting Exercises. (Illus.). 288p. 1981. pap. text ed. 11.95 (ISBN 0-13-617803-0). P-H.

Metzler, P. Tennis: Styles & Stylists. 1970. 7.95 o.s.i. (ISBN 0-02-584480-6). Macmillan.

Metzler, Paul. Advanced Tennis. rev ed. LC 68-18790. (Illus.). 192p. (gr. 5 up). 1972. 8.95 (ISBN 0-8069-4000-X); PLB 8.29 (ISBN 0-8069-4001-8). Sterling.

--Fine Points of Tennis. LC 77-93309. (Illus.). 1978. 8.95 (ISBN 0-8069-4118-9); lib. bdg. 8.29 (ISBN 0-8069-4119-7). Sterling.

--Getting Started in Tennis. LC 70-180467. (Illus.). 160p. (gr. 7 up). 1972. 7.95 o.p. (ISBN 0-8069-4050-6); PLB 7.49 o.p. (ISBN 0-8069-4051-4). Sterling.

Metzner, H. Die Ascorbinsaeure in der Pflanzenzelle. Bd. with Vitamin C in the Animal Cell. Bourne, G. H. (Protoplasmatologia: Vol. 2B, Pt. 2b). (Illus.). iv, 159p. (Eng., Ger.). 1957. pap. 44.30 o.p. (ISBN 0-387-80453-6). Springer-Verlag.

Meulen, Jan van Der see Van der Meulen, Jan & Price, Nancy W.

Meulenbelt-Nieuwburg, Albarta. Embroidery Motifs from Dutch Samplers. 1975. 24.00 (ISBN 0-7134-2875-9, Pub. by Batsford England). David & Charles.

Meuller, Francis J. Elements of Algebra. 3rd ed. (Illus.). 496p. 1981. text ed. 16.95 (ISBN 0-13-262469-9). P-H.

Meun, Jean De see De Lorris, Guillaume & De Meun, Jean.

Mevburg, Arnim H., jt. ed. see Stopher, Peter R.

Mew, James. Traditional Aspects of Hell. LC 73-140321. 1971. Repr. of 1903 ed. 24.00 (ISBN 0-8103-3693-6). Gale.

Mew, James & Ashton, John. Drinks of the World. LC 70-78207. (Illus.). 1971. Repr. of 1892 ed. 20.00 (ISBN 0-8103-3772-X). Gale.

Mewees, Tim. Treehouse Gang to the Rescue. (Better Living Ser.). 32p. (ps). 1981. write for info. (ISBN 0-8127-0311-1). Southern Pub.

Mews, Hazel. Frail Vessels: Woman's Role in Women's Novels from Fanny Burney to George Eliot. 1969. text ed. 18.75x (ISBN 0-485-11105-5, Athlone Pr). Humanities.

Mews, Webster, jt. auth. see Frankel, Sandor.

Mewshaw, Michael. Man in Motion. 1970. 5.95 o.p. (ISBN 0-394-43481-1). Random.

Mey, Marx De. The Cognitive Paradigm. (Harvester Studies in Cognitive Science). 1980. text ed. write for info. (ISBN 0-391-01062-X). Humanities.

Meyberg, Arnim, jt. auth. see Stopher, Peter R.

Meyen, Edward L. Developing Instructional Units: For the Regular & Special Teacher. 3rd ed. 325p. 1981. pap. text ed. 7.95x (ISBN 0-697-06245-7); instructor's manual avail. (ISBN 0-697-06228-7). Wm C Brown.

Meyendorff, Alexander F., jt. auth. see Kohn, S.

Meyendorff, Elizabeth, tr. see Stremooukhoff, D.

Meyendorff, John. Byzantium & the Rise of Russia. LC 80-40110. 340p. Date not set. 69.50 (ISBN 0-521-23183-3). Cambridge U Pr.

--Christ in Eastern Christian Thought. LC 75-31977. Orig. Title: Le Christ Dans la Theologie Byzantine. 248p. 1975. pap. 6.95 (ISBN 0-913836-27-3). St Vladimirs.

--The Orthodox Church: Its Past & Its Role in the World Today. 258p. 1981. pap. write for info. (ISBN 0-913836-81-8). St Vladimirs.

Meyer, jt. auth. see Madrigal.

Meyer, Alfred G., ed. see Casals, Felipe G.

Meyer, Balthasar Henry. A History of the Northern Securities Case. LC 70-124898. (American Constitutional & Legal History Ser). 136p. 1972. Repr. of 1906 ed. lib. bdg. 19.50 (ISBN 0-306-71989-4). Da Capo.

Meyer, Bernadine & Kolasa, Blair. Legal Systems. (Illus.). 1978. 18.95 (ISBN 0-13-529404-5). P-H.

Meyer, C. A., et al. ASME Steam Tables. 4th ed. 1979. pap. text ed. 22.50 (G00038). ASME.

Meyer, Carl D., Jr., jt. auth. see Sagan, Hans.

Meyer, Carol H. Social Work Practice. 2nd ed. LC 75-20949. (Illus.). 15.95 (ISBN 0-02-921140-9); pap. text ed. 8.95 (ISBN 0-02-921160-3). Free Pr.

--Staff Development in Public Welfare Agencies. LC 66-10730. 1966. 17.50x (ISBN 0-231-02722-2). Columbia U Pr.

Meyer, Carol H., ed. Social Work with the Aging. LC 75-27193. (NASW Modular Ser.). 140p. 1975. Set. pap. text ed. 8.00x (ISBN 0-87101-002-X, CAB-001-I). Natl Assn Soc Wkrs.

Meyer, Carol H., ed. see National Association of Social Workers.

Meyer, Carolyn. Being Beautiful: The Story of Cosmetics from Ancient Art to Modern Science. 1977. 7.25 (ISBN 0-688-22125-4); lib. bdg. 6.96 (ISBN 0-688-32125-9). Morrow.

--Coconut, the Tree of Life. LC 76-22673. (Illus.). 96p. (gr. 5-9). 1976. 7.25 (ISBN 0-688-22084-3); PLB 6.96 (ISBN 0-688-32084-8). Morrow.

--Milk, Butter, & Cheese: The Story of Dairy Products. LC 73-13574. (Illus.). 96p. (gr. 5-9). 1974. PLB 6.96 (ISBN 0-688-30100-2). Morrow.

--The Needlework Book of Bible Stories. LC 75-10135. (Illus.). 96p. (gr. 5 up). 1975. 6.95 o.p. (ISBN 0-15-256793-3, HJ). HarBraceJ.

--Rock Band: Big Men in a Great Big Town. LC 80-13349. 168p. (gr. 9 up). 1980. 8.95 (ISBN 0-689-50181-1, McElderry Bk). Atheneum.

--Saw, Hammer & Paint: Woodworking & Finishing for Beginners. (Illus.). 128p. (gr. 7 up). 1973. 7.25 o.p. (ISBN 0-688-20069-9); PLB 6.96 o.p. (ISBN 0-688-30069-3). Morrow.

--Stitch by Stitch: Needlework for Beginners. LC 77-117618. (gr. 4-6). 1970. 5.50 o.p. (ISBN 0-15-280350-5, HJ). HarBraceJ.

Meyer, Charles W. Social Security Disability Insurance: Problems of Unexpected Growth. 1979. pap. 4.25 (ISBN 0-8447-3365-2). Am Enterprise.

Meyer, Clarence. Fifty Years of the Herbalist Almanac: An Anthology. Meyer, David C., ed. (Illus.). 1977. pap. 6.95 (ISBN 0-916638-02-2). Meyerbooks.

--Vegetarian Medicines. Meyer, David C., ed. (Illus.). 96p. (Orig.). 1981. pap. 5.95 (ISBN 0-916638-06-5). Meyerbooks.

Meyer, Clarence, jt. auth. see Meyer, Joseph E.

Meyer, Conrad F. Der Heilige: Novelle. Coupe, W. A., ed. (Blackwell's German Texts Ser.). 1965. pap. 4.50x o.p. (ISBN 0-631-01700-3, Pub. by Basil Blackwell). Biblio Dist.

--The Saint. Hauch, E. F., tr. from Ger. 1976. Repr. of 1930 ed. 12.00 (ISBN 0-86527-298-0). Fertig.

--The Saint. Twaddell, W. F., tr. LC 77-7038. 129p. 1977. 7.50 (ISBN 0-87057-149-4, Pub. by Brown U Pr). Univ Pr of New England.

--The Tempting of Pescara. Bell, C., tr. LC 75-4902. 184p. 1975. Repr. of 1890 ed. 11.50 (ISBN 0-86527-313-8). Fertig.

Meyer, D. Eugene. The Student Teacher on the Firing Line. LC 80-69236. 135p. 1981. perfect bdg. 11.95 (ISBN 0-86548-048-6). Century Twenty One.

Meyer, D. K., jt. auth. see Platner, W. S.

Meyer, Daniel P. & Mayer, Herbert A. Radar Target Detection: Handbook of Theory & Practice. (Electrical Science Series). 1973. 48.50 (ISBN 0-12-492850-1). Acad Pr.

Meyer, David C., ed. see Meyer, Clarence.

Meyer, Duane. Highland Scots of North Carolina. (Illus.). 1968. pap. 1.00 (ISBN 0-86526-081-8). NC Archives.

Meyer, E. Y. Die Rueckfahrt. (Suhrkamp Taschenbuecher: 578). 448p. (Ger.). 1980. pap. text ed. 6.50 (ISBN 3-518-37078-2, Pub. by Insel Verlag Germany). Suhrkamp.

Meyer, Edith M. Enjoying Food on a Diabetic Diet. LC 73-16511. 240p. 1974. pap. 4.95 (ISBN 0-385-01344-2, Dolp). Doubleday.

Meyer, Edith P. Not Charity, but Justice: The Story of Jacob Riis. LC 73-83032. (gr. 6-10). 1974. 7.95 (ISBN 0-8149-0736-9). Vanguard.

--Petticoat Patriots of the Revolution. LC 75-25139. (Illus.). 1978. 7.95 (ISBN 0-8149-0771-7). Vanguard.

Meyer, Erika. German Graded Readers, 3 bks. Incl. Bk. 1. Auf Dem Dorfe. 2nd ed. 1964. pap. text ed. 3.90 (ISBN 0-395-04887-7, 3-37456); Bk. 2. In der Stadt. 2nd ed. 1964. pap. text ed. o.p. (ISBN 0-685-23334-0, 3-37461); Bk. 3. Genialische Jugend: Zwei Erzahlungen. 1949. pap. text ed. o.p. (ISBN 0-685-23335-9, 3-37465). LC 49-4261. HM.

--German Graded Readers: Alternate Series, 3 bks. Incl. Bk. 1. Ein Briefwechsel. pap. text ed. 3.90 (ISBN 0-395-04890-7, 3-37470); Bk. 2. Akademische Freiheit. pap. text ed. o.p. (ISBN 0-685-23336-7, 3-37475); Bk. 3. Goslar. pap. text ed. o.p. (ISBN 0-685-23337-5, 3-37480). 1954. HM.

Meyer, Ernst. English Chamber Music. LC 71-127181. (Music Ser). (Illus.). 1970. Repr. of 1946 ed. lib. bdg. 27.50 (ISBN 0-306-70037-9). Da Capo.

Meyer, Eugene. Introduction to Modern Chemistry. (Illus.). 1979. text ed. 19.95 (ISBN 0-13-488320-9); student manual 6.95 (ISBN 0-13-488338-1). P-H.

Meyer, F. B. Devotional Commentary on Exodus. LC 78-9530. 1978. 10.95 (ISBN 0-8254-3225-1). Kregel.

--Our Daily Walk. 1970. Repr. 7.95 (ISBN 0-310-29140-2, 10213). Zondervan.

--The Secret of Guidance. LC 77-93177. 1978. pap. 1.95 (ISBN 0-87123-501-3, 200501). Bethany Fell.

Meyer, F. B., et al. Funeral Sermons & Outlines. (Ministers Handbook Ser). pap. 2.50 o.p. (ISBN 0-8010-5873-2). Baker Bk.

Meyer, Franz S. Handbook of Ornament. 4th ed. (Illus.). 1892. pap. 6.00 (ISBN 0-486-20302-6). Dover.

Meyer, Fred & Baker, Ralph, eds. Determinants of Law Enforcement Policies. LC 79-1540. (Policy Studies Organization Bk.). 240p. 1979. 19.95 (ISBN 0-669-02900-9). Lexington Bks.

Meyer, Fred, jt. ed. see Baker, Ralph.

Meyer, Fred, Jr., jt. auth. see Baker, Ralph.

Meyer, Frederick B. Secret of Guidance. pap. 1.50 (ISBN 0-8024-7682-1, 33-32, MG). Moody.

Meyer, George G., et al. Folk Medicine & Herbal Healing. write for info. (ISBN 0-398-04470-8). C C Thomas.

Meyer, Harvey K. Historical Dictionary of Honduras. LC 76-4539. (Latin American Historical Dictionaries Ser.: No. 13). 413p. 1976. 18.00 (ISBN 0-8108-0921-4). Scarecrow.

--Historical Dictionary of Nicaragua. LC 72-2441. (Latin American Historical Dictionaries Ser.: No. 6). (Illus.). 1972. 16.50 (ISBN 0-8108-0488-3). Scarecrow.

Meyer, Hazel. Complete Book of Home Freezing. rev. ed. (Illus.). 1970. 10.00 o.p. (ISBN 0-397-00639-X). Lippincott.

Meyer, Henry, jt. auth. see Litwak, Eugene.

Meyer, Henry, jt. auth. see Foote, Caleb.

Meyer, Henry I. Corporate Financial Planning Models. LC 77-24881. (Ser. on Systems & Controls for Financial Management). 1977. 29.95 (ISBN 0-471-59996-4, Pub. by Wiley-Interscience). Wiley.

Meyer, Iain & Huggett, Richard. Geography, Bk. 1. 1979. pap. text ed. 9.50 (ISBN 0-06-318096-0, IntlDept). Har-Row.

--Geography Theory in Practice: Book Three. 1981. pap. text ed. 13.10 (ISBN 0-06-318164-9, IntlDept). Har-Row.

--Geography Theory in Practice: Book Two. 1980. pap. text ed. 13.10 (ISBN 0-06-318166-5, IntlDept). Har-Row.

Meyer, Iain R. Geography: Theory in Practice, Bk. 1, Settlements. 201p. (Orig.). pap. text ed. 9.50 (ISBN 0-06-318096-0, Pub. by Har-Row Ltd England). Har-Row.

Meyer, J. A. The Cristero Rebellion. LC 75-35455. (Cambridge Latin American Studies: No. 24). (Illus.). 1976. 32.95 (ISBN 0-521-21031-3). Cambridge U Pr.

Meyer, Jack, Sr. The Preacher & His Work. 6.50 (ISBN 0-89315-207-2). Lambert Bk.

Meyer, Jerome. The Big Book of Family Games. (Illus.). 208p. 1980. pap. 4.95 (ISBN 0-8015-0624-7, Hawthorn). Dutton.

Meyer, John S. Outlines for Christmas Sermons. (Sermon Outline Ser.). 48p. 1980. pap. 1.95 (ISBN 0-8010-6107-5). Baker Bk.

--Review of Pathology. LC 74-8558. 1974. pap. 13.95 o.p. (ISBN 0-8016-3420-2). Mosby.

Meyer, Joseph E. The Herbalist. (Illus.). 304p. 1981. 10.95 (ISBN 0-8069-3902-8); lib. bdg. 9.89 (ISBN 0-8069-3903-6). Sterling.

Meyer, Joseph E. & Meyer, Clarence. The Herbalist. rev. & updated ed. (Illus.). 1979. 9.95 (ISBN 0-916638-01-4). Meyerbooks.

Meyer, Judy A. Sewing Dictionary. LC 77-84579. (Illus.). 1979. cloth 12.00 (ISBN 0-498-02306-0); pap. 5.95 (ISBN 0-498-02306-0). A S Barnes.

Meyer, Karl. Hell's Ransom. (Orig.). 1980. pap. 2.25 (ISBN 0-532-23183-X). Manor Bks.

--Return of the Native. (Orig.). 1980. pap. 1.75 (ISBN 0-532-23184-8). Manor Bks.

Meyer, Karl E. The Art Museum: Power, Money & Ethics. (Illus.). 352p. 1981. pap. 8.95. Morrow.

Meyer, Kathleen. The Time to Sleep Book. (Illus.). (gr. k-2). 1978. PLB 5.38 (ISBN 0-307-68889-5, Golden Pr). Western Pub.

Meyer, Leonard B. Music, the Arts, & Ideas. LC 67-25515. 1969. pap. 6.95 (ISBN 0-226-52141-9, P336, Phoen). U of Chicago Pr.

Meyer, Lillian Hoagland. Food Chemistry. 3rd, rev. ed. (Illus.). 1978. Repr. soft cover 13.50 (ISBN 0-87055-171-X). AVI.

Meyer, Linda C., jt. auth. see McCahill, Thomas W.

Meyer, Linda D. The Cesarean (R) Evolution: A Handbook for Parents & Professionals. rev., 2nd ed. (Illus.). 150p. 1981. pap. 5.95 (ISBN 0-9603516-1-2). C Franklin Pr.

--The Cesarean Revolution: A Handbook for Parents & Professionals. rev. & expanded ed. (Illus.). 1979. pap. 5.95 (ISBN 0-9603516-0-4). C Franklin Pr.

Meyer, Lois & Moyer, Ruth. Machine Transcription in Modern Business. LC 77-25874. 1978. pap. text ed. 14.95 (ISBN 0-471-02735-9); scripts 3.75 (ISBN 0-471-03800-8). Wiley.

Meyer, Luc. The Best of the Left Bank: A Very Special Cookbook. 1980. pap. write for info. (ISBN 0-89716-064-9). Peanut Butter.

Meyer, M. W. Change in Public Bureaucracies. LC 76-47193. (Illus.). 1979. 22.50 (ISBN 0-521-22670-8). Cambridge U Pr.

Meyer, Manfred & Nissen, Ursula, eds. Effects & Functions of Television: Children & Adolescents. 1979. pap. 14.80 (ISBN 0-89664-171-6, Pub. by K G Saur). Shoe String.

Meyer, Marshall W. Theory of Organizational Structure. LC 76-56415. (Studies in Sociology Ser.). 1977. pap. text ed. 3.95 (ISBN 0-672-61193-7). Bobbs.

Meyer, Marshall W., et al. Environments & Organizations: Theoretical & Empirical Perspectives. LC 76-50706. (Social & Behavioral Science Ser.). (Illus.). 1978. text ed. 16.95x (ISBN 0-87589-374-0). Jossey-Bass.

Meyer, Martin J. Don't Bank on It! LC 79-3156. 1979. 9.95 (ISBN 0-87863-174-7). Farnswth Pub.

--Don't Bank on It. 240p. pap. 2.50 (ISBN 0-671-41606-5). PB.

Meyer, Marvin W. The Mithras Liturgy. LC 76-18288. (Society of Biblical Literature. Texts & Translation - Graeco-Roman Religion Ser.). 1976. pap. 4.50 (ISBN 0-89130-113-5, 060210). Scholars Pr Ca.

Meyer, Mary. Ornamental Grasses. LC 75-11720. (Encore Editions). (Illus.). 1975. 2.95 o.p. (ISBN 0-684-15259-2, ScribT). Scribner.

Meyer, Mary Jane. Bits of Faith & Love & Fun. 1977. 4.50 o.p. (ISBN 0-682-48975-1). Exposition.

Meyer, Mary K., ed. Genealogical Research in Maryland: A Guide. 2nd ed. LC 72-91197. 1976. 6.00 (ISBN 0-938420-05-4). Md Hist.

Meyer, Matthew. Speaking in Tongues. pap. 1.95 (ISBN 0-87178-809-8). Brethren.

Meyer, Merle, ed. Foundations of Contemporary Psychology. (Illus.). 1979. text ed. 17.95x (ISBN 0-19-502327-7). Oxford U Pr.

Meyer, Michael. Several More Lives to Live: Thoreau's Political Reputation in America. LC 76-56622. (Contributions in American Studies: No. 29). 1977. lib. bdg. 16.95 (ISBN 0-8371-9477-6, MES/). Greenwood.

Meyer, Michael, ed. Henrik Ibsen, Vol. 1: The Making of a Dramatist, 1864-1882. 260p. 1980. text ed. 9.25x (ISBN 0-246-64457-5). Humanities.

--Henrik Ibsen, Vol. 2: The Farewell to Poetry, 1864-1882. 344p. 1980. text ed. 13.00x (ISBN 0-246-64001-4). Humanities.

--Henrik Ibsen, Vol. 3: The Top of a Cold Mountain 1883-1906. 368p. 1980. text ed. 14.50x (ISBN 0-246-64040-5). Humanities.

Meyer, Michael A. The Origins of the Modern Jew: Jewish Identity & European Culture in Germany, 1749-1824. LC 67-12384. (Waynebooks Ser: No. 32). 250p. 1972. 9.95x (ISBN 0-8143-1315-9); pap. 4.95x (ISBN 0-8143-1470-8). Wayne St U Pr.

Meyer, Michael C. & Sherman, William L. The Course of Mexican History. (Illus.). 1979. 29.95 (ISBN 0-19-502413-3); pap. text ed. 12.95x (ISBN 0-19-502414-1). Oxford U Pr.

Meyer, Michael C., jt. ed. see Greenleaf, Richard E.

Meyer, Michael R. The Astrology of Relationship: A Humanistic Approach to the Practice of Synastry. LC 75-44528. 280p. 1976. pap. 3.95 (ISBN 0-385-11556-3, Anch). Doubleday.

--Handbook for the Humanistic Astrologer. LC 73-83657. 456p. 1974. pap. 5.95 (ISBN 0-385-05729-6, Anch). Doubleday.

Meyer, Miriam W. The Blind Guards of Easter Island. LC 77-14529. (Great Unsolved Mysteries Ser.). (Illus.). (gr. 4-5). 1977. PLB 9.65 (ISBN 0-8172-1048-2). Raintree Pubs.

Meyer, Monica, jt. auth. see Chekenian, Jane.

Meyer, Nicholas. The West End Horror. Date not set. pap. 2.50 (ISBN 0-345-28481-X). Ballantine.

Meyer, Niels I., et al. Revolt from the Centre. Hauch, Christine, tr. LC 79-56838. (Open Forum Ser.). 192p. 1980. 14.00 (ISBN 0-7145-2701-7, Pub. by M Boyars). Merrimack Bk Serv.

Meyer, Owen. Basic Beekeeping. 1979. pap. 3.95 o.s.i. (ISBN 0-7225-0477-2). Newcastle Pub.

Meyer, Pauline. Keep Your Face to the Sunshine: A Lost Chapter in the History of Woman Suffrage. LC 80-68583. (Illus.). 64p. 1980. pap. 6.95 (ISBN 0-936998-00-8). Alcott Pr.

Meyer, Peter. James Earl Carter: The Man & the Myth. (Illus.). 1978. 9.95 o.p. (ISBN 0-8362-6605-6). Andrews & McMeel.

Meyer, Peter B. Drug Experiments on Prisoners. LC 75-13307. 144p. 1976. 16.95 (ISBN 0-669-00047-7). Lexington Bks.

Meyer, Philip E. Applied Accounting Theory: A Financial Reporting Perspective. 1980. 20.95x (ISBN 0-256-02360-3). Irwin.
Meyer, Pirmin, ed. see Schneider, Reinhold.
Meyer, R., jt. auth. see Denecke, H. J.
Meyer, R. W. Leibniz & the Seventeenth Century Revolution. Stern, J. P., tr. 1952. text ed. 6.75x (ISBN 0-391-02000-5). Humanities.
Meyer, Ray. Baha'i: Follower of the Light. rev ed. (Illus.). 1979. pap. 3.00 (ISBN 0-909991-01-4, 7-31-96). Baha'i.
Meyer, Richard & Parter, Seymour, eds. Singular Perturbations & Syasymptotics. LC 80-24946. 1980. lib ed 22.00 (ISBN 0-12-493260-6). Acad Pr.
Meyer, Richard E. Introduction to Mathematical Fluid Dynamics. LC 75-158527. (Pure & Applied Mathematics Ser.: No. 24). 1971. 25.95 o.p. (ISBN 0-471-60050-4, Pub. by Wiley-Interscience). Wiley.
Meyer, Richard H. Bankers' Diplomacy: Monetary Stabilization in the Twenties. LC 79-111120. (Columbia Studies in Economics Ser.: No. 4). 1970. 20.00x (ISBN 0-231-03325-7). Columbia U Pr.
Meyer, Robert H. Anatomy of a Theme. 128p. 1969. pap. text ed. 3.95x (ISBN 0-02-476430-2, 47643). Macmillan.
Meyer, Ronald E., jt. auth. see Cushenbery, Donald C.
Meyer, Roy W. History of the Santee Sioux: United States Indian Policy on Trial. LC 80-11810. xviii, 434p. 1979. pap. 7.95 (ISBN 0-8032-8109-9, BB 751, Bison). U of Nebr Pr.
--The Middle Western Farm Novel in the Twentieth Century. LC 64-17221. viii, 265p. 1974. pap. 3.45x (ISBN 0-8032-5793-8, BB 587, Bison). U of Nebr Pr.
Meyer, Samuel. The Deacon & the Jewess: Adventures in Heresy. LC 80-84734. 1981. 10.00 (ISBN 0-8022-2379-6). Philos Lib.
Meyer, Stuart L. Data Analysis for Scientists & Engineers. LC 74-8873. (Illus.). 448p. 1975. text ed. 28.95 (ISBN 0-471-59995-6). Wiley.
Meyer, Susan, ed. see Craig, James.
Meyer, Susan E., jt. auth. see Green, Floyd.
Meyer, Susan E., ed. see Craig, James.
Meyer, Ursula & Wolfson, Alice. Workbook in Everyday German. (gr. 9-10). 1976. pap. text ed. 3.75 (ISBN 0-88345-277-4). Regents Pub.
Meyer, Verna E. Verna Meyer's Menu Cookbook: Dining at Home in Style. LC 80-19120. 206p. 1980. 12.95 (ISBN 0-87518-199-6). Dillon.
Meyer, Verne, jt. auth. see Sebranek, Patrick.
Meyer, Victor C. & Chesser, Edward S. Behavior Therapy in Clinical Psychiatry. LC 71-159480. 1971. 20.00x (ISBN 0-87668-043-0). Aronson.
Meyer, Warren G., jt. auth. see Crawford, Lucy C.
Meyer, Warren G., et al. Retailing Principles & Practices. 7th ed. LC 80-24885. (Illus.). 560p. (gr. 11-12). text ed. 13.48 (ISBN 0-07-041693-1, G). McGraw.
Meyer, William F. Life & Health: Insurance Law. LC 72-76891. (Insurance Law Library). 1972. 47.50 (ISBN 0-686-14516-X). Lawyers Co-Op.
Meyer, William J. The Political Experience: A Preface to the Study of Politics. LC 76-17254. 286p. 1978. Repr. of 1977 ed. lib. bdg. 12.95 o.p. (ISBN 0-88275-716-4). Krieger.
Meyer, William J. & Dusek, Jerome B. Child Psychology: A Developmental Perspective. 1979. text ed. 16.95x (ISBN 0-669-88971-7). Heath.
Meyer, Zoe. Stories from The Dawn-Breakers. (Illus.). (gr. 3-5). 1955. 6.00 (ISBN 0-87743-035-7, 7-52-58). Baha'i.
Meyer-Arendt, Jurgen. Introduction to Classical & Modern Optics. LC 71-157723. (Illus.). 1972. ref. ed. 23.95 (ISBN 0-13-479436-2). P-H.
Meyerbeer, Giacomo. Il Crociato in Egitto, 2 vols. Gossett, Philip & Rosen, Charles, eds. LC 76-49193. (Early Romantic Opera Ser.: Vol. 18). 1980. Set. lib. bdg. 164.00 (ISBN 0-8240-2917-8). Garland Pub.
--L' Etoile du Nord. LC 76-49198. (Early Romantic Opera Ser.: Vol. 22). 1980. lib. bdg. 82.00 (ISBN 0-8240-2921-6). Garland Pub.
--Les Huguenots, 2 vols. Rosen, Charles & Gossett, Philip, eds. LC 76-49196. (Early Romantic Opera Ser.: Vol. 20). 1980. lib. bdg. 82.00 (ISBN 0-8240-2919-4). Garland Pub.
--L'africaine, 2 vols. Grossett, Philip & Rosen, Charles, eds. LC 76-49200. (Early Romantic Opera Ser.: Vol. 24). 944p. 1980. lib. bdg. 82.00 (ISBN 0-8240-2923-2). Garland Pub.
--Le Pardon De Ploermel. Gossett, Phillip & Rosen, Charles, eds. LC 76-49199. (Early Romantic Opera Ser.: No. 23). 1981. lib. bdg. 82.00 (ISBN 0-8240-2922-4). Garland Pub.
--Le Prophete. Gossett, Philip & Rosen, Charles, eds. LC 76-49197. (Early Romantic Opera Ser.: Vol. 21). 1978. lib. bdg. 82.00 (ISBN 0-8240-2920-8). Garland Pub.
--Robert le Diable, 2 vols. Gossett, Phillip & Rosen, Charles, eds. LC 76-49194. (Early Romantic Opera Ser.: No. 19). 1980. Set. lib. bdg. 82.00 (ISBN 0-8240-2918-6). Garland Pub.
Meyerhoff, Barbara G., jt. ed. see Moore, Sally F.
Meyerhoff, Hans. Time in Literature. (Library Reprint Ser: No. 6). 1974. 15.75x (ISBN 0-520-00856-1). U of Cal Pr.
Meyerowitz, Joel. St. Louis & the Arch. 112p. 1981. pap. 29.95 (ISBN 0-8212-1105-6). NYGS.
Meyerriecks, Andrew J. Man & Birds: Evolution & Behavior. LC 79-175222. (Topics in Biological Science Ser). 1972. pap. 4.95 (ISBN 0-672-63558-5). Pegasus.
Meyers. Coal Handbook. Date not set. price not set (ISBN 0-8247-1270-6). Dekker.
Meyers, A. I. Heterocycles in Organic Synthesis. (General Heterocyclic Chemistry Ser.). 336p. 1974. 36.95 (ISBN 0-471-60065-2). Wiley.
Meyers, Alan, jt. auth. see Carlson, Karen.
Meyers, Bernice. Not This Bear. (Illus.). (gr. k-3). 1971. pap. 1.25 (ISBN 0-590-01556-7, Schol Pap); pap. 3.50 bk. & record (ISBN 0-590-20741-5). Schol Bk Serv.
Meyers, Beth. The Steady Flame. (YA) 1972. 5.95 (ISBN 0-685-25149-7, Avalon). Bouregy.
Meyers, Bill. Dr. Luke Examines Jesus. 1979. pap. 2.50 (ISBN 0-88207-768-6). Victor Bks.
Meyers, Carlton R. Measurement in Physical Education. 2nd ed. (Illus.). 642p. 1974. 21.50 (ISBN 0-8260-6051-X). Wiley.
Meyers, Carole T. Getting in the Spirit: Annual Bay Area Christmas Events. LC 79-19253. (Illus., Orig.). 1979. pap. write for info. (ISBN 0-917120-05-1). Carousel Pr.
--Weekend Adventures for City-Weary People: A Guide to Overnight Trips in Northern California. rev. ed. LC 80-24121. (Weekend Adventures for City-Weary People, a Guide to Overnight Trips in the U.S.A. Ser.). Orig. Title: Weekend Adventures for City-Weary Families, a Guide to Overnight Trips in Northern California, 1976. (Illus.). 1980. pap. 5.95 (ISBN 0-917120-06-X). Carousel Pr.
Meyers, Donald L. Modern Roofing: Care & Repair. Horowitz, Shirley M., ed. (Illus.). 144p. (Orig.). 1981. pap. 6.95 (ISBN 0-686-69553-4). Creative Homeowner.
Meyers, Eric M. & Strange, James F. Archaeology, the Rabbis, & Early Christianity. LC 80-24208. 208p. 1981. pap. 7.95 (ISBN 0-687-01680-0). Abingdon.
Meyers, Frederick H., et al. Review of Medical Pharmacology. 7th, rev. ed. LC 80-82744. (Illus.). 747p. 1980. lexotone cover 17.50 (ISBN 0-87041-153-5). Lange.
Meyers, Gail & Myers, Michele. The Dynamics of Human Communication. 3rd ed. (Illus.). 1980. pap. text ed. 13.95 (ISBN 0-07-044218-5); instrs'. manual 4.95 (ISBN 0-07-044219-3). McGraw.
Meyers, Harvey. Hariyana: Part One,"the Yoga of Dejection". LC 79-84779. (Illus.). 256p. (Orig.). 1979. pap. 6.00 (ISBN 0-934094-01-2). Omkara Pr.
Meyers, Jack F., jt. ed. see Murdick, Olin J.
Meyers, Jeff. One of a Kind: The Legend of Carl Joseph. 200p. 1980. pap. 6.95 (ISBN 0-86629-028-1); 11.95 (ISBN 0-86629-025-7). Sunrise MO.
Meyers, Jeffrey, ed. George Orwell: The Critical Heritage. (Critical Heritage Ser.). 432p. 1975. 30.00x (ISBN 0-7100-8255-X). Routledge & Kegan.
Meyers, Joan, jt. auth. see Whitaker, George O.
Meyers, Joel, et al. School Consultation: Readings about Preventive Techniques for Pupil Personnel Workers. (Illus.). 368p. 1977. pap. 16.75 (ISBN 0-398-03485-0). C C Thomas.
Meyers, L. D. Chilton's Complete Home Wiring & Lighting Guide. LC 80-971. Date not set. 14.95 (ISBN 0-8019-6790-2); pap. 10.95 (ISBN 0-8019-6791-0). Chilton.
Meyers, Lawrence S. & Grossen, Neal E. Behavioral Research: Theory, Procedure, & Design. 2nd ed. LC 78-2212. (Psychology Ser.). (Illus.). 1978. text ed. 17.95x (ISBN 0-7167-0049-2). W H Freeman.
Meyers, Manny. The Last Mystery of Edgar Allan Poe: The Troy Dossier. 1978. 8.95 o.p. (ISBN 0-397-01315-9). Lippincott.
Meyers, Martin. Hung Up to Die. (Hardy Ser.: No. 4). 192p. 1976. pap. 1.25 o.p. (ISBN 0-445-00378-2). Popular Lib.
--Kiss & Kill. (Hardy Ser.: No. 1). 176p. 1975. pap. 1.25 o.p. (ISBN 0-445-08408-1). Popular Lib.
Meyers, Marvin. The Mind of the Founder: Sources of the Political Thought of James Madison. rev. ed. 400p. 1981. 12.50 (ISBN 0-87451-201-8). U Pr of New Eng.
Meyers, Marvin, ed. The Mind of the Founder: Sources of the Political Thought of James Madison. LC 72-158723. (American Heritage Ser: No. 39). 1973. pap. 10.95 (ISBN 0-672-60054-4). Bobbs.
Meyers, Michael. Goodbye, Columbus, Hello M. LC 76-15403. 1976. 8.95 o.p. (ISBN 0-688-03090-4). Morrow.
Meyers, Stanna, ed. see Wentworth, Frank L.
Meyers, Susan. Pearson, a Harbor Seal Pub. LC 80-13041. (Illus.). 64p. (gr. 3-7). 1980. 9.95 (ISBN 0-525-36845-0). Dutton.
--The Truth About Gorillas. LC 79-19393. 40p. (gr. 1-4). 1980. PLB 7.95 (ISBN 0-525-41564-5, Smart Cat). Dutton.
Meyers, Walter D. The Young Landlords. 1980. pap. 1.95 (ISBN 0-686-69271-3, 52191). Avon.
Meyers, Warren B. Who Is That? (Illus.). 1976. pap. 3.95 (ISBN 0-8065-0535-4). Citadel Pr.
Meyersohn, Maxwell. Memorable Quotations of John F. Kennedy. LC 65-21411. 1965. 6.95 o.s.i. (ISBN 0-690-53070-6, TYC-T). T Y Crowell.
Meyerson, Martin & Banfield, Edward C. Politics, Planning & the Public Interest. LC 55-7335. 1964. pap. text ed. 5.95 (ISBN 0-02-921230-8). Free Pr.
Meyerson, Paul G., jt. auth. see Adler, Gerald.
Meyerson, Simon, ed. Adolescence & Breakdown. (Tavistock Clinic of Human Relations Studies). 1975. text ed. 17.95x (ISBN 0-04-150053-9); pap. text ed. 11.50x (ISBN 0-04-150054-7). Allen Unwin.
--Adolescence: The Crises of Adjustment. (Tavistock Clinic of Human Relations Studies). 1975. text ed. 12.50x o.p. (ISBN 0-04-150051-2); pap. text ed. 11.50x (ISBN 0-04-150052-0). Allen Unwin.
Meyler, Ruth, jt. auth. see Sillar, F. C.
Meyn, Rodney E. & Withers, H. R., eds. Radiation Biology in Cancer Research. (M. D. Anderson Symposia on Fundamental Cancer Research Ser.). 1980. text ed. 61.50 (ISBN 0-89004-402-3). Raven.
Meynaud, J. Technocracy. LC 69-11976. 1969. 10.95 o.s.i. (ISBN 0-02-921210-3). Free Pr.
Meynell, Elinor, jt. auth. see Meynell, G. G.
Meynell, G. G. Drug-Resistance Factors & Other Bacterial Plasmids. 1973. 18.00 (ISBN 0-262-13085-8). MIT Pr.
Meynell, G. G. & Meynell, Elinor. Theory & Practice in Experimental Bacteriology. 2nd ed. LC 72-85729. (Illus.). 1970. 49.50 (ISBN 0-521-07682-X). Cambridge U Pr.
Meynell, Hugh. Freud, Marx & Morals. 1981. 23.00x (ISBN 0-389-20045-X). B&N.
Meynen, Emil. Bibliography on German Settlements in Colonial North America. LC 66-25870. 1966. Repr. of 1937 ed. 36.00 (ISBN 0-8103-3336-8). Gale.
Meyst, Lucille. Tyler Lane & the Gold Nugget Mystery. 128p. (Orig.). (gr. 4-6). 1976. pap. 1.50 (ISBN 0-8024-3849-0). Moody.
Meza, David de see De Meza, David & Osborne, Michael.
Mezerik, A. G., ed. Thirty Arab Refugees in the Middle East. 94p. 1980. 20.00. Intl Review.
Mezerik, Avrahm, ed. Goa: Indian Takeover. 15.00 (ISBN 0-685-40641-5, 70). Intl Review.
--Rhodesia & the U. N. 1966. 15.00 (ISBN 0-685-40642-3, 89). Intl Review.
Mezerik, Avrahm G., ed. Arab-Israel Conflict & U N. 1962. pap. 25.00 (ISBN 0-685-13185-8, 73). Intl Review.
--Common Market: Political Impacts. 1962. pap. 15.00 (ISBN 0-685-13191-2, 72). Intl Review.
--Malaysia-Indonesia Conflict. 1965. pap. 15.00 (ISBN 0-685-13205-6, 86). Intl Review.
Mezey, Robert, ed. Poems from the Hebrew. LC 75-132299. (Poems of the World Ser.). (Illus.). 156p. (gr. 9-12). 1973. 8.95 (ISBN 0-690-63685-7, TYC-J). T Y Crowell.
Mezey, Robert, jt. ed. see Berg, Stephen.
Mezezers, Valdis. Sirds Ko Dzili Iemileja, II. 2nd ed. LC 79-53071. 106p. 1980. Repr. of 1977 ed. 9.00 (ISBN 0-936302-01-1). Pub Vaidava.
Mezirow, Jack, et al. Last Gamble on Education: Dynamics of Adult Basic Education - New Dimensions in Program Analysis. 206p. 1975. 11.00 (ISBN 0-685-63817-0). Adult Ed.
Mezirow, Jack D. Dynamics of Community Development. LC 63-7458. 1963. 10.00 (ISBN 0-8108-0038-1). Scarecrow.
Mezo, Francine. The Fall of Worlds. 320p. (Orig.). 1980. pap. 2.50 (ISBN 0-380-75564-5, 75564). Avon.
--No Earthly Shore. 256p. (Orig.). 1981. pap. 2.50 (ISBN 0-380-77347-3, 77347). Avon.
--Unless She Burn. 176p. 1981. pap. 2.25 (ISBN 0-380-76968-9, 76968). Avon.
Miall, A. B. Nocturnes & Pastorals. Fletcher, Ian & Stokes, John, eds. LC 76-20104. (Decadent Consciousness Ser.: Vol. 28). 1977. Repr. of 1896 ed. lib. bdg. 38.00 (ISBN 0-8240-2777-9). Garland Pub.
Miall, Anthony, jt. auth. see Colt, C. F.
Miall, Bernard, tr. see Eyck, Erich.
Miall, Bernard, tr. see Hamburger, Max.
Miall, Bernard, tr. see Pirenne, Henri.
Miami International Conference on Alternative Energy Sources, 2nd. Alternative Energy Sources: Proceedings, 9 vols. Veziroglu, T. Nejat, ed. LC 80-25788. (Illus.). 4300p. 1981. Set. text ed. 595.00 (ISBN 0-89116-208-9). Hemisphere Pub.
Micali, Paul. The Lacy Techniques of Salesmanship. 1973. pap. 5.50 (ISBN 0-8015-4368-1, Hawthorn). Dutton.
Micali, Paul J. Survival Handbook for Salespeople. 160p. 1981. pap. 8.95 (ISBN 0-8436-0853-6). CBI Pub.
Micallef, Benjamin A. Keypunching: A Basic Office Skill. LC 74-75692. (Data Processing Ser.). 160p. 1974. pap. 8.95 o.p. (ISBN 0-8465-4734-1, 54734). Benjamin-Cummings.
Micarelli, Charles N. Manual & Identification Guide to the United States Regular Issues 1847 Through 1934. (Illus., Orig.). 1979. pap. text ed. write for info. o.p. (ISBN 0-9603474-0-2). Adriatic Stamp.
Miceli, Vincent B. Antichrist. LC 80-66294. 1981. 12.95 (ISBN 0-8158-0395-8). Chris Mass.
Michael, A. M. Irrigation: Theory & Practice. 1978. text ed. 30.00 (ISBN 0-7069-0613-6, Pub. by Vikas India). Advent Bk.
Michael, Albert D. British Tyroglyphicae, 2 Vols. Repr. of 1903 ed. Set. 69.50 (ISBN 0-384-38875-2). Johnson Repr.
Michael, Aloysius. Radhakrishnan on Hindu Moral Life & Action. 1979. text ed. 14.50x (ISBN 0-391-01857-4). Humanities.
Michael, Ernest D., et al. Laboratory Experiences in Exercise Physiology. 1979. lab manual 4.95 (ISBN 0-932392-05-9). Mouvement Pubns.
Michael, Franz & Chang, Chung-Li. The Taiping Rebellion: Documents & Comments. Incl. Vol. 2. 756p (ISBN 0-295-73959-2); Vol. 3. 1107p (ISBN 0-295-73958-4). LC 66-13538. (Publications on Asia of the Institute for Foreign & Area Studies: No. 14, Pt. 2). 1971. 30.00 ea. U of Wash Pr.
--The Taiping Rebellion: History, Vol. 1. (Publications on Asia of the Institute for Foreign & Area Studies: No. 14, Pt. 1). 256p. 1966. 10.00 (ISBN 0-295-73958-4); pap. 5.95 (ISBN 0-295-95244-X). U of Wash Pr.
Michael, George. The Basic Book of Antiques. LC 74-77072. (Illus.). 1979. pap. 5.95 (ISBN 0-668-04712-7). Arco.
Michael, George & Lindsay, Ray. George Michael's Secrets for Beautiful Hair. LC 79-7693. (Illus.). 256p. 1981. 19.95 (ISBN 0-385-15465-8). Doubleday.
Michael, Jerome & Adler, Mortimer J. Crime, Law & Social Science. (Social Science Classics Ser.). 440p. 1982. 19.95 (ISBN 0-87855-362-2); text ed. 19.95 (ISBN 0-686-68056-1); pap. 7.95 (ISBN 0-87855-786-5); pap. text ed. 7.95 (ISBN 0-686-68057-X). Transaction Bks. Postponed.
Michael, Paul, jt. auth. see Sataloff, Joseph.
Michael, S. T., jt. auth. see Langner, T. S.
Michael, Stephen R., et al. Techniques of Organizational Change. (Illus.). 363p. 1981. 16.95 (ISBN 0-07-041775-X). McGraw.
Michael, William B., jt. auth. see Isaac, Stephen.
Michaelis, Bill, jt. auth. see Michaelis, Dolores.
Michaelis, Carol T. Home & School Partnerships in Exceptional Education. 375p. 1980. text ed. 27.95 (ISBN 0-89443-330-X). Aspen Systems.
Michaelis, Dolores & Michaelis, Bill. Learning Through Noncompetitive Activities & Play. LC 77-89123. (Learning Handbooks Ser.). 1977. pap. 3.95 (ISBN 0-8224-1906-8). Pitman Learning.
Michaelis, J. U. Social Studies for Children in a Democracy: Recent Trends & Developments. 6th ed. (Illus.). 1976. 17.95 (ISBN 0-13-818872-6). P-H.
Michaelis, John. Social Studies for Children: A Guide to Basic Instruction. 7th ed. (Illus.). 1980. text ed. 17.95 (ISBN 0-13-813880-7). P-H.
Michaelis, John U. & Nelson, J. Secondary Social Studies Introduction, Curriculum, Evaluation. (Illus.). 1980. text ed. 17.95 (ISBN 0-13-797753-0). P-H.
Michaelis, John U., jt. auth. see Hannah, Larry S.
Michaelis, Michael, ed. see A.D. Little, Inc.
Michaelis-Jena, Ruth, tr. see Hobusch, Erich.
Michaelis-Jena, Ruth, tr. see Loschburg, Winfried.
Michaelle. Yoga & Prayer. Cumming, Diane, tr. pap. 6.50 (ISBN 0-87061-059-5). Chr Classics.
Michaelman, Herbert, ed. see Appleman, Phillip.
Michaelman, Herbert, ed. see Lesburg, Sandy.
Michaelman, Herbert, ed. see Murphy, Edward.
Michaelman, Herbert, ed. see Roberts, David.
Michaelman, Herbert, ed. see Sann, Paul.
Michaelman, Herbert, ed. see Shuldner, Herbert.
Michaels, Allen. Backdoor Guide to Entering a Profession. 60p. (Orig.). 1981. pap. 10.00. Sunrise PA.
Michaels, Barbara. Greygallows. LC 72-3149. 320p. 1972. 6.95 o.p. (ISBN 0-396-06635-6). Dodd.
--Greygallows. 1977. pap. 1.75 o.p. (ISBN 0-449-23052-X, Crest). Fawcett.
--House of Many Shadows. 1978. pap. 1.75 o.p. (ISBN 0-449-23720-6, Crest). Fawcett.
--Patriot's Dream. LC 76-20500. 1976. 8.95 (ISBN 0-396-07337-9). Dodd.

--The Patriot's Dream. 1977. pap. 1.75 o.p. (ISBN 0-449-23342-1, Crest). Fawcett.
--The Sea King's Daughter. LC 75-28200. 1975. 7.95 (ISBN 0-396-07208-9). Dodd.
--Wait for What Will Come. LC 78-18319. 1978. 8.95 (ISBN 0-396-07577-0). Dodd.
--Wings of the Falcon. LC 77-24927. 1977. 8.95 (ISBN 0-396-07458-8). Dodd.
--The Wizard's Daughter. LC 80-15157. 352p. 1980. 9.95 (ISBN 0-396-07899-0). Dodd.
Michaels, Claire F. & Carello, Claudia A. Direct Perception. (Illus.). 224p. 1981. text ed. 18.00 (ISBN 0-13-214791-2). P-H.
Michaels, David D. Visual Optics & Refraction: A Clinical Approach. 2nd ed. LC 80-15472. (Illus.). 748p. 1980. text ed. 59.50 (ISBN 0-8016-3414-8). Mosby.
--Visual Optics & Refraction: A Clinical Approach. (Illus.). 518p. 1975. 29.50 o.p. (ISBN 0-8016-3424-5). Mosby.
Michaels, Fern. Captive Passions. LC 76-56142. 1977. pap. 2.50 (ISBN 0-345-29081-X). Ballantine.
--Captive Splendors. 1980. pap. 2.50 (ISBN 0-345-28847-5). Ballantine.
--The Delta Ladies. 1980. pap. 2.75 (ISBN 0-671-83337-5). PB.
--Golden Lasso. 192p. (Orig.). 1980. pap. 1.50 (ISBN 0-671-57032-3). S&S.
--Sea Gypsy. 192p. (Orig.). 1980. pap. 1.50 (ISBN 0-671-57015-3). S&S.
--Valentina. 1981. pap. 2.75 (ISBN 0-345-29580-3). Ballantine.
--Vixen in Velvet. 224p. Date not set. pap. 2.25 (ISBN 0-345-29611-7). Ballantine.
--Whisper My Name. 192p. 1981. pap. 1.50 (ISBN 0-671-57061-7). S&S.
Michaels, Irene. Frenchman's Mistress. (Orig.). 1980. pap. 2.75 (ISBN 0-440-12545-6). Dell.
Michaels, J. Ramsey. Servant & Son: Jesus in Parable & Gospel. LC 80-8465. 1981. pap. 8.95 (ISBN 0-8042-0409-8). John Knox.
Michaels, Joe. Prime of Your Life. 288p. 1981. 17.50 (ISBN 0-87196-478-3). Facts on File.
Michaels, Kirstin. A Special Kind of Love. Bd. with Enchanted Journey. 1981. pap. 1.95 (ISBN 0-451-09619-3, J9619, Sig). NAL.
Michaels, Kristin. Design for Love. (Orig.). 1981. pap. price not set (Signet Bks). NAL.
--Enchanted Twilight. Bd. with Song of the Heart. 1980. pap. 2.25 (ISBN 0-451-09536-7, 9536, Sig). NAL.
--Love's Pilgrimage. (Orig.). 1981. pap. 1.75 (ISBN 0-451-09681-9, E9681, Sig). NAL.
Michaels, Leonard. The Men's Club. 1981. 9.95 (ISBN 0-374-20782-8). FS&G.
Michaels, Marjorie. The Bargain Shopper's Guide to Europe. (Illus., Orig.). 1980. pap. 5.95 (ISBN 0-8037-0502-6). Dial.
--Stay Healthy with Wine: Natural Cures & Beauty Secrets from the Vineyards. 256p. 1981. 11.95 (ISBN 0-686-69092-3). Dial.
Michaels, Norman, jt. auth. see Steinbrunner, Chris.
Michaels, Richard M. Transportation Planning & Policy Decision Making: Behavioral Science Contributions. 264p. 1980. 24.95 (ISBN 0-03-055786-0). Praeger.
Michaels, Robert M. Four Poached & Oatmeal. LC 80-81367. (Illus.). 50p. (Orig.). 1980. pap. 3.50 (ISBN 0-9604292-0-4). KaChunk Pr.
Michaelsen, Hila, jt. auth. see Camiel, Reva.
Michaelsen, Katherine J. Archipenko: A Study of the Early Works, 1908-1920. LC 76-23644. (Outstanding Dissertations in the Fine Arts - 2nd Series - 20th Century). (Illus.). 1977. Repr. of 1975 ed. lib. bdg. 60.00 (ISBN 0-8240-2712-4). Garland Pub.
Michaelson, Arthur M. Income Taxation of Estates & Trusts. 11th ed. LC 80-83758. 220p. 1980. text ed. 35.00 (ISBN 0-686-69169-5, J1-1434). PLI.
--Income Taxation of Estates & Trusts. 10th ed. 1978. text ed. 25.00 o.p. (ISBN 0-685-86796-X, J1-1422). PLI.
Michaelson, I. C. & Berman, Elaine R., eds. Causes & Prevention of Blindness. 1973. 25.00 (ISBN 0-12-493650-4). Acad Pr.
Michaelson, Isaac C., ed. Ballantyne's Textbook of the Fundus of the Eye. 3rd ed. (Illus.). 912p. 1981. text ed. 1.62 (ISBN 0-443-01782-4). Churchill.
Michaelson, Robert. Piety in the Public School: Trends & Issues in the Relationship Between Religion & the Public School in the United States. LC 72-87896. 1970. 6.95 o.s.i. (ISBN 0-02-584460-1). Macmillan.
Michael X. Amazing Visions of the Endtime. 1970. pap. 5.95 (ISBN 0-685-00408-2). Saucerian.
--D-Day Seers Speak. 1969. pap. 5.95 (ISBN 0-685-20195-3). Saucerian.
--Flying Saucer Revelations. 1969. pap. 5.95 (ISBN 0-685-20196-1). Saucerian.
--Rainbow City & the Inner Earth People. 1969. pap. 5.95 (ISBN 0-685-20200-3). Saucerian.
--Release Your Cosmic Powers. 1969. pap. 5.95 (ISBN 0-685-20201-1). Saucerian.
--Secrets of Higher Contact. 1969. pap. 5.95 (ISBN 0-685-20202-X). Saucerian.
--Venusian Health Magic. 1972. pap. 12.95 (ISBN 0-685-37600-1). Saucerian.
--We Want You - Is Hitler Alive? 1969. pap. 5.95 (ISBN 0-685-20205-4). Saucerian.
--Your Part in the Great Plan. 1972. pap. 3.95 o.p. (ISBN 0-685-37601-X). Saucerian.
Michailoff, Helen. Mikhail Lermontov: Magic & Mystery. 1981. 20.00. Ardis Pubs.
Michalak, Donald F. & Yager, Edwin G. Making the Training Process Work. LC 78-17907. (Continuing Management Education Ser.). 1979. text ed. 13.95 scp (ISBN 0-06-044429-0, HarpC). Har-Row.
Michalec, George W. Precision Gearing: Theory & Practice. LC 66-21045. 1966. 46.95 (ISBN 0-471-60142-X, Pub. by Wiley-Interscience). Wiley.
Michalopoulos, Andre. Homer. (World Authors Ser.: Greece: No. 4). 1966. lib. bdg. 9.95 (ISBN 0-8057-2432-X). Twayne.
Michal-Smith, Harold, jt. auth. see Morgenstern, Murry.
Michalson, G. E. The Historical Dimensions of Rational Faith: The Role of History in Kant's Religious Thought. 1977. 9.50 (ISBN 0-8191-0308-X). U Pr of Amer.
Michard, L., jt. auth. see Lagarde, A.
Michas, jt. auth. see Reynolds.
Michaud, Roland & Michaud, Sabrina. Caravans to Tartary. (Illus.). 1978. 37.50 o.p. (ISBN 0-670-20384-X, Studio). Viking Pr.
Michaud, Roland & Michaud, Sabrina, photos by. Afghanistan. LC 80-51192. (Illus.). 144p. 1980. 45.00 (ISBN 0-86565-009-8). Vendome.
Michaud, Sabrina, jt. auth. see Michaud, Roland.
Michaux, Henri. Au Pays De la Magie. Broome, Peter, ed. (Athlone French Poets Ser). 1977. text ed. 20.75x (ISBN 0-485-14711-4, Athlone Pr); pap. text ed. 10.75x (ISBN 0-485-12711-3). Humanities.
--Infinite Turbulence. 1980. 12.95 (ISBN 0-7145-1018-1). Riverrun NY.
Michaux, Jean-Pierre, ed. George Gissing: Critical Essays. (Critical Studies). 208p. 1981. 25.00x (ISBN 0-389-20061-1). B&N.
Michel. Little Wild Chimpanzee. (gr. 3). 1980. pap. 1.25 (ISBN 0-590-30151-9, Schol Pap). Schol Bk Serv.
Michel, A. & Herget, C. Mathematical Foundations in Engineering & Science: Algebra & Analysis. 1981. 27.95 (ISBN 0-13-561035-4). P-H.
Michel, Aime. Flying Saucers & the Straight-Line Mystery. LC 58-8787. (Illus.). 1958. 12.95 (ISBN 0-87599-077-0). S G Phillips.
Michel, Andree, ed. Family Issues of Employed Women in Europe & America. (International Studies in Sociology & Social Anthropology: Vol. 11). (Illus.). 166p. 1971. text ed. 24.00x (ISBN 90-040-2633-9). Humanities.
Michel, Anna. Little Wild Chimpanzee. LC 77-20986. (An I AM READING Bk.). (Illus.). (gr. 1-4). 1978. 3.95 (ISBN 0-394-83716-9); PLB 5.99 (ISBN 0-394-93716-3). Pantheon.
--Little Wild Elephant. LC 78-18407. (I Am Reading Bk.). (Illus.). (gr. 1-4). 1979. 4.95 (ISBN 0-394-83884-X); PLB 5.99 (ISBN 0-394-93884-4). Pantheon.
--Little Wild Lion Club. LC 79-17509. (I Am Reading Book Ser.). (Illus.). 48p. (gr. 1-4). 1980. 4.95 (ISBN 0-394-84352-5); PLB 5.99 (ISBN 0-394-94352-X). Pantheon.
Michel, Charles, jt. auth. see Waters, Ethel.
Michel, Donald E. Music Therapy: An Introduction to Therapy & Special Education Through Music. (Illus.). 152p. 1979. 12.75 (ISBN 0-398-03518-0). C C Thomas.
Michel, Freda. Price of Vengeance. 1977. pap. 1.50 o.p. (ISBN 0-449-23211-5, Crest). Fawcett.
Michel, Henri. World War II. (Saxon House Bks.). 1974. 4.95 o.p. (ISBN 0-347-00001-0). Gordon-Cremonesi.
Michel, Jean-Pierre & Fairbridge, Rhodes W. Dictionary of Earth Science: French-English & English-French. 340p. 1980. 14.50 (ISBN 0-89352-076-4). Masson Pub.
Michel, Pierre. James Gould Cozzens. (U. S. Authors Ser.: No. 237). 1974. 10.95 (ISBN 0-8057-0163-X). Twayne.
Michel, Walter. Wyndham Lewis: Paintings & Drawings. LC 69-11616. (Illus.). 1970. 58.50x (ISBN 0-520-01612-2). U of Cal Pr.
Michelangelo. Life Drawings of Michelangelo. (Dover Art Library). (Illus.). 1980. pap. 2.00 (ISBN 0-486-23876-8). Dover.
--Michelangelo. Hartt, Frederick, ed. (Library of Great Painters Ser). 1965. 35.00 (ISBN 0-8109-0299-0). Abrams.
Michelant, H., ed. Guillaume De Palerne. 1876. 25.25 (ISBN 0-384-20400-7); pap. 23.00 (ISBN 0-685-13449-0). Johnson Repr.
Michelin. Michelin Green Guide London. 2nd ed. 1980. pap. 7.95 (ISBN 2-06-015431-6). Michelin.
--Michelin Green Guide Rome. 2nd ed. (Fr.). 1979. pap. 7.95 (ISBN 2-06-005580-6). Michelin.
--Michelin Green Guide to Hollande. 1979. pap. 7.95 (ISBN 2-06-005530-X). Michelin.
--Michelin Green Guide to Provence Eng. (Avail. Fr. & Ger.). 1980. pap. 7.95 (ISBN 2-06-013640-7). Michelin.
Michelin Guides & Maps. Dictionnaire des Communes de France (Guide to French Townships) 1979. 45.00 (ISBN 2-06-007500-9). Michelin.
--Michelin Green Guide Belgique et Grand Duche du Luxembourg. 1978. pap. 7.95 (ISBN 2-06-005100-2). Michelin.
--Michelin Green Guide to Alpes. (Green Guide Ser.). (Fr.). pap. 7.95 (ISBN 2-06-003000-5). Michelin.
--Michelin Green Guide to Auvergne. 1st ed. (Green Guide Ser.). (Fr.). 1978. pap. 7.95 (ISBN 2-06-003030-7). Michelin.
--Michelin Green Guide to Bourgogne. 16th ed. (Fr.). 1980. pap. 7.95 (ISBN 2-06-003060-9). Michelin.
--Michelin Green Guide to Brittany. 16th ed. (Green Guide Ser.). (Avail. in Fr). 1980. pap. 7.95 (ISBN 2-06-013120-0). Michelin.
--Michelin Green Guide to Causses-Cevennes. 2nd ed. (Green Guide Ser.). (Fr.). 1979. pap. 7.95 (ISBN 2-06-003150-8). Michelin.
--Michelin Green Guide to Corse. 3rd ed. (Green Guide Ser.). (Fr.). 1979. pap. 7.95 (ISBN 2-06-003251-2). Michelin.
--Michelin Green Guide to Cote De L'atlantique. 9th ed. (Green Guide Ser.). (Fr.). 1978. pap. 7.95 (ISBN 2-06-003330-6). Michelin.
--Michelin Green Guide to Environs De Paris. 19th ed. (Green Guide Ser.). (Fr.). 1979. pap. 7.95 (ISBN 2-06-100351-6). Michelin.
--Michelin Green Guide to Jura. 2nd ed. (Green Guide Ser.). (Fr.). 1979. pap. 7.95 (ISBN 2-06-003391-8). Michelin.
--Michelin Green Guide to Londres. 2nd ed. (Green Guide Ser.). (Fr.). 1976. pap. 7.95 (ISBN 2-06-005420-6). Michelin.
--Michelin Green Guide to Maroc. 3rd ed. (Green Guide Ser.). (Fr.). 1979. pap. 7.95 (ISBN 2-06-005450-8). Michelin.
--Michelin Green Guide to New York City. 5th ed. (Green Guide Ser.). (Avail. in fr.). 1979. pap. 7.95 (ISBN 2-06-015510-X). Michelin.
--Michelin Green Guide to Nord De la France. 4th ed. (Green Guide Ser.). (Fr.). 1977. pap. 7.95 (ISBN 2-06-003420-5). Michelin.
--Michelin Green Guide to Provence. (Green Guide Ser.). (Fr.). 1979. pap. 6.95 o.p. (ISBN 2-06-003630-5). Michelin.
--Michelin Green Guide to Pyrenees. (Green Guide Ser.). (Fr.). 1978. pap. 7.95 (ISBN 2-06-003660-7). Michelin.
--Michelin Green Guide to Spain. rev. 1st ed. (Green Guide Ser.). (Avail. in Fr. & Span.). pap. 7.95 (ISBN 2-06-121900-4). Michelin.
--Michelin Green Guide to Switzerland. 6th ed. (Green Guide Ser.). (Avail. in Fr., Ger.). pap. 7.95 (ISBN 2-06-121801-6). Michelin.
--Michelin Green Guide to Vallee Du Rhone. 4th ed. (Green Guide Ser.). (Fr.). 1979. pap. 7.95 (ISBN 2-06-003690-9). Michelin.
--Michelin Green Guide to Vosges. 2nd ed. (Green Guide Ser.). 1980. pap. 7.95 (ISBN 2-06-003720-4). Michelin.
--Michelin Red Guide to Benelux: Belgium, Luxembourg, Netherlands. (Red Guide Ser.). 1980. 12.95 (ISBN 2-06-006001-X). Michelin.
--Michelin Red Guide to Germany. (Red Guide Ser.). 1981. 14.95 (ISBN 3-92-107801-6). Michelin.
--Michelin Red Guide to Great Britain & Ireland. (Red Guide Ser.). 1981. 12.95 (ISBN 2-06-006501-1). Michelin.
--Michelin Red Guide to Italy. (Red Guide Ser.). 1981. 14.95 (ISBN 2-06-006701-4). Michelin.
--Michelin Red Guide to London. (Red Guide Ser.). 1981. pap. 3.95 (ISBN 2-06-006601-8). Michelin.
--Michelin Red Guide to Paris: Paris Hotels & Restaurants. (Red Guide Ser.). 1981. Avail. In Fr. & Eng. pap. 3.25 (ISBN 2-06-006901-7). Michelin.
--Michelin Red Guide to Spain & Portugal. (Red Guide Ser.). 1981. 12.95 (ISBN 2-06-006301-9). Michelin.
--Paris Index & Map. 4th ed. 1980. pap. 7.95 (ISBN 2-06-000112-9). Michelin.
Michelin Guides & Maps Dept. Michelin Green Guide to French Riviera. 7th ed. (Green Guide Ser.). (Avail. in Fr.). pap. 7.95 (ISBN 2-06-013300-9). Michelin.
--Michelin Green Guide to Germany. 4th ed. (Green Guide Ser.). (Avail. in Fr., Ger.). pap. 7.95 (ISBN 2-06-015030-2). Michelin.
--Michelin Green Guide to Italy. 8th ed. (Green Guide Ser.). (Avail. in Fr., Ger., Ital.). pap. 7.95 (ISBN 2-06-121401-0). Michelin.
--Michelin Green Guide to Normandy. 5th ed. (Green Guide Ser.). (Avail. in Fr.). pap. 7.95 (ISBN 2-06-013480-3). Michelin.
--Michelin Green Guide to Paris. 3rd ed. (Green Guide Ser.). (Avail. in Fr., Ger.). pap. 7.95 (ISBN 2-06-013540-0). Michelin.
--Michelin Green Guide to Portugal. 2nd ed. (Green Guide Ser.). (Avail. in Fr.). pap. 7.95 (ISBN 2-06-015570-3). Michelin.
Michelin Guides & Maps Division. Camping Caravanning in France. (Annual Ser.). 1980. pap. 7.95 (ISBN 2-06-006101-6). Michelin.
--France Motorway Atlas. 4th ed. pap. 3.95 (ISBN 0-686-10140-5). Michelin.
--Michelin Green Guide to Austria. 5th ed. (Green Guide Ser.). (Avail. in Ger., Fr.). pap. 7.95 (ISBN 2-06-015120-1). Michelin.
--Michelin Green Guide to Chateaux Loire. 6th ed. (Green Guide Ser.). (Avail. in Fr., Ger.). pap. 7.95 (ISBN 2-06-013210-X). Michelin.
Micheline, Jack. Skinny Dynamite & Other Short Stories. Winans, A. D., ed. LC 79-63969. 96p. (Orig.). 1980. pap. 4.95x (ISBN 0-915016-27-3). Second Coming.
Michell, Ewan. The Businessman's Guide to Letter-Writing & to the Law on Letters. 2nd ed. 222p. 1979. text ed. 23.50x (ISBN 0-220-66326-2, Pub. by Busn Bks England). Renouf.
Michell, John. City of Revelation. 1977. pap. 1.75 o.p. (ISBN 0-345-25875-4). Ballantine.
--Natural Likeness: Faces & Figures in Nature. LC 79-84214. (Illus.). 1979. pap. 7.95 o.p. (ISBN 0-525-47584-2). Dutton.
Michell, S. J. Introduction to Fluid & Particle Mechanics. 1970. 41.00 (ISBN 0-08-013313-4); pap. 14.00 (ISBN 0-08-013312-6). Pergamon.
Michelman, Herber, ed. see Chinoy, Helen K. & Jenkins, Linda W.
Michelman, Herbert, ed. see David, Carl.
Michelman, Herbert, ed. see Gowland, Peter.
Michelman, Herbert, ed. see Kalich, Robert.
Michelmann, Hans J. Organisational Effectiveness in a Multinational Bureaucracy. LC 78-60532. 1979. 26.95 (ISBN 0-03-047211-3). Praeger.
Michelsen, Neil F. American Ephemeris for the 20th Century: Noon. (The American Ephemeris Ser.). 620p. (Orig.). 1980. pap. 15.95 (ISBN 0-917086-20-1, Pub. by Astro Computing Serv). Para Res.
--American Ephemeris for the 20th Century: Midnight. (The American Ephemeris Ser.). 620p. (Orig.). 1980. pap. 15.95 (ISBN 0-917086-19-8, Pub. by Astro Computing Serv). Para Res.
--The American Ephemeris: Nineteen Eighty-One. 1980. pap. 1.00 (ISBN 0-917086-24-4). Para Res.
--The American Ephemeris 1901 to 1930. (The American Ephemeris Ser). 17.50 o.p. (ISBN 0-917086-11-2, Pub. by Astro Computing Serv.); pap. 14.95 o.p. (ISBN 0-917086-12-0). Para Res.
--The American Ephemeris: 1991 to 2000. 1980. pap. 5.00 (ISBN 0-917086-21-X). Para Res.
Michelsen, Odd B. Analysis & Application of Rare Earth Materials. 374p. 1973. 57.00x (ISBN 8-200-04780-6, Dist. by Columbia U Pr). Universitet.
Michelson, Annette, ed. see Bresson, Robert.
Michelson, Herb, jt. auth. see Freed, Alvyn M.
Michelson, M. J. & Ziemel, E. V. Acetylcholine: An Approach to the Molecular Mechanism of Action. LC 73-11271. 252p. 1974. text ed. 49.00 (ISBN 0-08-017159-1). Pergamon.
Michelson, M. J., ed. Comparative Pharmacology, 2 vols. 1008p. 1974. Set. text ed. 150.00 (ISBN 0-08-016389-0). Pergamon.
Michelson, Michael, jt. auth. see Villadsen, John.
Michelson, Peter. The Eater. LC 78-189187. (New Poetry Ser.: No. 45). 119p. 1972. 7.95 (ISBN 0-8040-0586-9). Swallow.
Michelson, William H. Man & His Urban Environment: A Sociological Approach. rev. ed. 1976. 8.95 (ISBN 0-201-04726-8). A-W.
Michener, Dorothy & Muschlitz, Beverly. Day in Day Out. LC 80-82304. (Illus.). 160p. 1980. pap. text ed. 8.95 (ISBN 0-913916-71-4). Incentive Pubns.
Michener, James. Caravans. 1979. pap. 2.75 (ISBN 0-449-23959-4, Crest). Fawcett.
--A Michener Miscellany, 1950-1970. 384p. 1975. pap. 1.95 o.p. (ISBN 0-449-22526-7, C2526, Crest). Fawcett.
Michener, James A. The Covenant. LC 80-5315. 1980. 35.00 (ISBN 0-394-50505-0); Limited Ed. 35.00 (ISBN 0-394-51400-9). Random.
--Hawaii. 1978. pap. 3.50 (ISBN 0-449-23761-3, Crest). Fawcett.
--Return to Paradise. 416p. 1978. pap. 2.75 (ISBN 0-449-23831-8, Crest). Fawcett.
--Sayonara. 1978. pap. 2.50 (ISBN 0-449-23857-1, Crest). Fawcett.
--Tales of the South Pacific. 192p. 1978. pap. 2.50 (ISBN 0-449-23852-0, Crest). Fawcett.
Michener, James A., ed. & intro. by. Firstfruits: A Harvest of 25 Years of Israeli Writing. 432p. 1974. pap. 1.75 o.p. (ISBN 0-449-30641-0, X641, Prem). Fawcett.
Michener, Leslie & Donaldson, Gerald. The Exercise Book. LC 78-7096. (Illus.). 1978. 15.00 o.p. (ISBN 0-03-045521-9); pap. 8.95 o.p. (ISBN 0-685-27620-1). HR&W.
Michie, D., jt. auth. see Meltzer, B.
Michie, D., jt. ed. see Collins, N. L.
Michie, D., jt. ed. see Elcock, E. W.

Michie, Donald. Essays on Machine Intelligence & Other Topics. 250p. 1981. write for info. (ISBN 0-677-05560-9). Gordon.
--Essays on Machine Intelligence & Other Topics. 250p. 1981. price not set (ISBN 0-677-05560-9). Gordon.
--Expert Systems in a Microelectronic Age. 200p. 1980. 22.50x (ISBN 0-85224-381-2, Pub by Edinburgh U Pr Scotland). Columbia U Pr.
Michie Editorial Staff. Code of Alabama 1975, 27 vols. 1980. write for info. with 1979 cum suppl (ISBN 0-87215-126-3); write for info. 1980 cum. suppl (ISBN 0-87215-341-X). Michie.
--Code of Virginia, 1950, 23 vols. with 1980 cum. suppl. Set. write for info. (ISBN 0-87215-137-9); write for info. 1980 suppl. (ISBN 0-87215-342-8). Michie.
--General Statutes of North Carolina, Annotated with 1979 Cum. Suppl, 17 vols. Set. write for info. (ISBN 0-87215-132-8); write for info. 1979 suppl. & index (ISBN 0-87215-308-8); 1980 interim suppl. avail. (ISBN 0-87215-347-9). Michie.
--Michie on Banks & Banking, 11 vols. with 1980 cum. suppl. Set. with 1980 cum. suppl. 400.00 (ISBN 0-87215-034-8); 1980 cum. suppl. 97.50 (ISBN 0-87215-345-2). Michie.
--Michie's Jurisprudence of Virginia & West Virginia, 40 vols., with 1979 cum. suppl. rev. ed. 1948. 975.00 set (ISBN 0-87215-128-X); 1979 cum. suppl. only 145.00 (ISBN 0-87215-350-9). Michie.
Michie Editorial Staff, ed. Maryland Rules of Procedure Annotated (Red Book) 1979. 1352p. pap. 30.00 o.p. (ISBN 0-87215-242-1). Michie.
Michie Staff. Virginia Rules Annotated. 470p. 1979. pap. 25.00 o.p. (ISBN 0-87215-317-7). Michie.
Michie Staff, ed. Rules of the U. S. Bankruptcy Court for the Eastern District of Virginia. 156p. 1980. pap. text ed. 15.00 (ISBN 0-87215-328-2). Michie.
Michiels, J. L., jt. ed. see Desirant, M.
Michigan United Conservation Clubs. Great Lakes Nature Guide. rev. ed. 1978. pap. 1.75 (ISBN 0-933112-05-X). Mich United Conserv.
--Michigan County Maps & Outdoor Guide. 1977. pap. 8.00 (ISBN 0-933112-04-1). Mich United Conserv.
Michman, Ronald. Marketing Channels. LC 75-11303. (Marketing Ser.). 1974. pap. text ed. 9.95 o.p. (ISBN 0-88244-058-6). Grid Pub.
Michman, Ronald D. & Jugenheimer, Donald W. Strategic Advertising Decisions: Selected Readings. LC 75-28535. (Advertising & Journalism Ser.). 1976. pap. text ed. 9.95 o.p. (ISBN 0-88244-091-8). Grid Pub.
Michman, Ronald D. & Sibley, Stanley D. Marketing Channels & Strategies. 2nd ed. LC 78-4987. (Marketing Ser.). 1980. text ed. 20.95 (ISBN 0-88244-176-0). Grid Pub.
Michon, Georges. The Franco Russian Alliance, 1891-1917. LC 68-9610. 1969. Repr. of 1929 ed. 17.50 (ISBN 0-86527-072-4). Fertig.
Michon, Jacques, jt. auth. see Vilain, Raymond.
Mick, Beverly J. Holiday Graphs. (Illus.). 64p. (For tchrs. of gr. 6-9). 1978. 5.95 (ISBN 0-932786-00-6). Bellefontaine.
--Multiplication Facts & Basic Fractions. (gr. 5-12). 1981. Set. price not set (ISBN 0-932786-04-9); Bk. 1. 4.25 (ISBN 0-932786-05-7); Bk. 2. 4.25 (ISBN 0-932786-06-5). Bellefontaine.
--Multiplication Facts, Decimals, & Percents, 2 bks. (gr. 5-12). 1981. Set. price not set (ISBN 0-932786-04-9); Bk. 1. 4.25 (ISBN 0-932786-05-7); Bk. 2. 4.25 (ISBN 0-932786-06-5). Bellefontaine.
Mickadeit, Robert E., jt. auth. see Huntington, Whitney C.
Mickaharic, Draja. Spiritual Cleansing. 128p. 1981. pap. 6.95 (ISBN 0-87728-531-4). Weiser.
Mickel, Emanuel J., Jr., ed. see Myers, Geoffrey M.
Mickelsen, Alvera & Mickelsen, Berkley. Family Bible Encyclopedia, 2 vols. Incl. Volume I (A-K (ISBN 0-89191-100-6); Volume II (L-Z (ISBN 0-89191-127-8). LC 78-55384. (Illus.). 1978. 9.95 ea.; Set. 16.95 (ISBN 0-89191-201-0). Cook.
Mickelsen, Berkley, jt. auth. see Mickelsen, Alvera.
Mickelsen, William C., ed. & tr. Hugo Riemann's Theory of Harmony. Bd. with History of Music Theory, Book III. LC 76-15366. 1977. 15.00x (ISBN 0-8032-0891-X). U of Nebr Pr.
Mickelson, Alvera, jt. auth. see Karo, Nancy.
Mickelson, Anne Z. Reaching Out: Sensitivity & Order in Recent American Fiction by Women. LC 78-26164. 1979. lib. bdg. 12.00 (ISBN 0-8108-1194-4). Scarecrow.
--Thomas Hardy's Women & Men: The Defeat of Nature. LC 76-28366. 1976. 10.00 (ISBN 0-8108-0985-0). Scarecrow.
Mickelson, B. Seventy-Two Hours at the Crap Table. new ed. (Gamblers Book Shelf). (Illus.). 64p. (Orig.). 1972. pap. 2.95 (ISBN 0-89650-529-4). Gamblers.
Mickelson, Joel C. Images of the American City in the Arts. 1978. pap. text ed. 8.95 (ISBN 0-8403-1858-8). Kendall-Hunt.
Mickelwait, Donald R., et al, eds. New Directions in Development: Study of U. S. Aid. Sweet, Charles F. & Morse, Elliott R. 1979. lib. bdg. 22.00x (ISBN 0-89158-266-5). Westview.
Mickens, Ronald E. An Introduction to Nonlinear Oscillations. LC 80-13169. (Illus.). 320p. Date not set. text ed. price not set (ISBN 0-521-22208-7). Cambridge U Pr.
Mickey, Paul. Essentials of Wesleyan Theology: A Contemporary Affirmation. 160p. 1980. pap. 4.95 (ISBN 0-310-39151-2). Zondervan.
Mickiewicz, Ellen. Media & the Russian Public. 170p. 1981. 19.95 (ISBN 0-03-057681-4); pap. 8.95 (ISBN 0-03-057679-2). Praeger.
Mickiewicz, Ellen, ed. Handbook of Soviet Social Science Data. LC 72-86510. (Illus.). 1973. 25.00 (ISBN 0-02-921190-5). Free Pr.
Mickish, Verle. Creative Art: Junior High Grades. (Illus.). 1962. pap. 4.95x o.p. (ISBN 0-87108-133-4). Pruett.
Micklem, Nathaniel, jt. ed. see Fanchiotti, Margherita.
Micklish, Rita. Sugar Bee. LC 78-176034. (gr. 3-7). 1972. 5.95 o.s.i. (ISBN 0-440-08358-3); PLB 5.47 o.s.i. (ISBN 0-440-08350-8). Delacorte.
Mickolus, Edward F. Transnational Terrorism: A Chronology of Events, 1968-1979. LC 79-6829. xxxviii, 967p. 1980. lib. bdg. 75.00 (ISBN 0-313-22206-1, MTT/). Greenwood.
Mickolus, Edward F., compiled by. The Literature of Terrorism: A Selectively Annotated Bibliography. LC 80-541. xi, 553p. 1980. lib. bdg. 55.00 (ISBN 0-313-22265-7, MLT/). Greenwood.
Micks, Marianne H. Future Present: The Phenomenon of Christian Worship. LC 75-103844. 1970. pap. 4.95 (ISBN 0-8164-2109-9). Crossroad NY.
--Introduction to Theology. 1967. pap. 3.95 (ISBN 0-8164-2036-X, SP40). Crossroad NY.
Micks, Marianne H. & Ridenhour, Thomas E. Lent. Achtemeier, Elizabeth, et al, eds. LC 79-7377. (Proclamation 2: Aids for Interpreting the Lessons of the Church Year Ser. C). 64p. 1979. pap. 2.50 (ISBN 0-8006-4082-9, 1-4082). Fortress.
Mico, Paul, jt. auth. see Ross, Helen S.
Micoleau, T., jt. auth. see Canham, Don.
Micoleau, T., jt. auth. see Moore, Jim.
Micro Ink, Inc. The Best of Micro: June 1979 to May 1980, Vol. 3. Tripp, Robert M., ed. (The Best of Micro Ser.). (Illus.). 320p. (Orig.). 1980. pap. 10.00 (ISBN 0-938222-03-1). Computerist.
--The Best of Micro: June 1980 to May 1981, Vol.4. Tripp, Robert M., ed. (The Best of Micro Ser.). (Illus.). Date not set. pap. price not set (ISBN 0-938222-04-X). Computerist.
--The Best of Micro: Vol. 2, Oct-Nov 78 to May 79. Tripp, Robert M., ed. (Illus.). 224p. (Orig.). pap. 8.00 (ISBN 0-938222-02-3). Computerist.
Microfilming Corporation of America. Columbia University Oral History Collection: An Index to the Memoirs in Part 1 of the Microform Edition. 162p. 1979. 95.00 (ISBN 0-667-00612-5). Arno.
Middendorff, Wolf. Effectiveness of Punishment, Especially in Relation to Traffic Offenses. LC 68-9171. (New York University Criminal Law Education & Research Center Pubns. Ser.: Vol. 5). 1968. 12.50x (ISBN 0-8377-0826-5). Rothman.
Middle East Market Research Bureau Ltd. Marketing to Middle East Consumers. 220p. 1980. 55.00x (ISBN 0-86010-198-3, Pub. by Graham & Trotman England). State Mutual Bk.
Middle, P., tr. see Schmidt, W. J. & Keil, A.
Middlebrook, Martin, ed. The Diaries of Private Horace Bruckshaw, Royal Marine Light Infantry, Nineteen Fifteen to Nineteen Sixteen. (Illus.). xxiii, 229p. 1980. 18.50 (ISBN 0-208-01879-4, Archon). Shoe String.
Middlebrooks, E. J. Industrial Pollution Control: Vol. 1, Agro-Industries. LC 79-10573. (Environmental Science & Technology: Texts & Monographs: Vol. 1). 1979. 27.00 (ISBN 0-471-04779-1, Pub. by Wiley-Interscience). Wiley.
Middlebrooks, E. Joe. Water Reuse: State-of-the-Art. 1981. text ed. 40.00 (ISBN 0-250-40359-5). Ann Arbor Science.
Middlehurst, Barbara M., jt. ed. see Kuiper, Gerard P.
Middlekauff, Woodrow W. The Cephid Stem Borers of California (Hymenoptera: Cephidae) (Bulletin of the California Insect Survey: Vol. 11). 1969. pap. 5.00x (ISBN 0-520-09036-5). U of Cal Pr.
Middlekauff, Woodrow W. & Lane, Robert S. Adult & Immature Tabanidae (Diptera) of California. (Bulletin of the California Insect Survey Ser.: Vol. 22). 1980. pap. 10.50 (ISBN 0-520-09604-5). U of Cal Pr.
Middleman, R. & Goldberg, Gale. Social Service Delivery: A Structural Approach to Social Work Practice. LC 74-3304. 248p. 1974. 13.00x (ISBN 0-231-03730-9). Columbia U Pr.
Middleman, Stanley. Flow of High Polymers: Continuum & Molecular Rheology. LC 67-29460. 1968. 27.95 (ISBN 0-470-60235-X, Pub. by Wiley-Interscience). Wiley.
Middlemas, Keith. Politics in Industrial Society: The Experience of the British System Since 1911. 512p. 1979. 37.50x (ISBN 0-8476-6872-X). Rowman.
Middlemas, Keith & Barnes, John. Baldwin. LC 70-87902. 1970. 14.95 o.s.i. (ISBN 0-02-507370-2). Macmillan.
Middlemass, Tom. Irish Standard Guage Railways. LC 80-68690. (Illus.). 96p. 1981. 16.50 (ISBN 0-7153-8007-9). David & Charles.
Middlemiss, F. A. British Stratigraphy. (Introducing Geology Ser.). 1975. pap. text ed. 5.95x (ISBN 0-04-550023-1). Allen Unwin.
--Fossils. (Introducing Geology Ser.). 1976. pap. text ed. 4.95x (ISBN 0-04-560005-8). Allen Unwin.
--Guide to Invertebrate Fossils. rev. ed. (Illus.). 128p. 1972. pap. text ed. 3.75x (ISBN 0-09-108401-6, Hutchinson U Lib). Humanities.
Middlemiss, F. A., et al. Faunal Provinces in Space & the Time: Geological Journal Special Issue, No. 4. (Liverpool Geological Society & the Manchester Geological Association). 1980. 32.50 (ISBN 0-471-27751-7, Pub. by Wiley-Interscience). Wiley.
Middlemist, R. Dennis & Hitt, Michael A. Organizational Behavior. 512p. 1981. text ed. 18.95 (ISBN 0-574-19390-1, 13-2390); instr's. guide avail. (ISBN 0-574-19391-X, 13-2391). SRA.
Middleton, Christopher. Bolshevism in Art & Other Expository Writings. 1978. pap. text ed. 15.75x (ISBN 0-85635-155-5). Humanities.
Middleton, Conyers. A Free Enquiry into the Miraculous Powers, Which Are Supposed to Have Subsisted in the Christian Church. Wellek, Rene, ed. LC 75-11235. (British Philosophers & Theologians of the 17th & 18th Centuries: Vol. 36). 1977. Repr. of 1749 ed. lib. bdg. 42.00 (ISBN 0-8240-1788-9). Garland Pub.
Middleton, E. D. Cruise of the Kate. (Mariners Library). 1953. Repr. of 1870 ed. text ed. 4.75x o.p. (ISBN 0-246-63543-6). Humanities.
Middleton, Elliott, et al. Allergy: Principles & Practice. LC 77-9311. (Illus.). 1978. 99.50 (ISBN 0-8016-3419-9). Mosby.
Middleton, Sir Henry. The Last East Indian Voyage. LC 74-25700. (English Experience Ser.: No. 307). 1971. Repr. of 1606 ed. 11.50 (ISBN 90-221-0307-2). Walter J Johnson.
Middleton, Herman A. Hayden's Complete Tube Caddy, Tube Substitution Guidebook. 24th ed. 1979. pap. 5.50 (ISBN 0-8104-0809-0). Hayden.
Middleton, Jenkins B., jt. auth. see McKitterick, Nathaniel.
Middleton, John. Cooperative School Television & Educational Change. 135p. 1979. pap. 6.95. NAEB.
Middleton, John, ed. From Child to Adult: Studies in the Anthropology of Education. LC 75-44039. (Texas Press Sourcebooks in Anthropology: No. 9). 1976. pap. 7.95x (ISBN 0-292-72416-0). U of Tex Pr.
--Gods & Rituals: Readings in Religious Beliefs & Practices. LC 75-44032. (Texas Press Sourcebooks in Anthropology: No. 6). 1976. pap. 7.95x (ISBN 0-292-72708-9). U of Tex Pr.
--Myths & Cosmos: Readings in Mythology & Symbolism. LC 75-43817. (Texas Press Sourcebooks in Anthropology: No. 5). 1976. pap. 7.95x (ISBN 0-292-75030-7). U of Tex Pr.
Middleton, John & Tait, David, eds. Tribes Without Rulers: Studies in African Segmentary Systems. 1970. pap. text ed. 7.75x (ISBN 0-391-00090-X). Humanities.
Middleton, Karen P. & Jussawalla, Meheroo. The Economics of Communication: A Selected Bibliography with Asbstracts. LC 80-50505. (Pergamon Policy Studies on Internatioanl Development). 250p. 1981. 25.00 (ISBN 0-08-026325-9). Pergamon.
--The Economics of Communication: A Selected Bibliography with Abstracts Published in Cooperation with the East-West Center, Hawaii. LC 80-20505. (Pergamon Policy Studies on International Development). 1981. 25.000 (ISBN 0-08-026325-9). Pergamon.
Middleton, Katherine & Hess, Mary A. The Art of Cooking for the Diabetic. 1979. pap. 2.75 (ISBN 0-451-08719-4, E8719, Sig). NAL.
Middleton, L. Tito & His Family. 4.00 o.p. (ISBN 0-8062-1055-9). Carlton.
Middleton, Neil, ed. Catholics & the Left: The Slant Manifesto. Date not set. pap. cancelled (ISBN 0-87243-018-9). Templegate.
Middleton, O. E. Confessions of an Ocelot. Bd. with Not for a Seagull. LC 79-670341. (Orig.). 1979. pap. 8.50x (ISBN 0-908565-86-0). Intl Pubns Serv.
Middleton, Robert. Practical Electricity. 3rd ed. LC 73-94187. (Illus.). 1974. 10.95 (ISBN 0-672-23218-9). Audel.
--Radiomans Guide. 4th ed. LC 76-45882. (Illus.). 1977. 11.95 (ISBN 0-672-23259-6, 23259). Audel.
--Television Service Manual. 4th ed. LC 76-24074. 1977. 11.95 (ISBN 0-672-23247-2, 23247). Audel.
Middleton, Robert G. Know Your Oscilloscope. 4th ed. LC 80-52230. 1980. pap. 8.95. Sams.
--One Hundred & One Ways to Use Your Oscilloscope. 3rd ed. 1980. pap. 6.95 (ISBN 0-672-21794-5). Sams.
--One Hundred & One Ways to Use Your Oscilloscope. 2nd ed. LC 66-24122. (Illus.). 1966. pap. 5.50 o.p. (ISBN 0-672-20416-9, 20416). Sams.
--One Hundred & One Ways to Use Your VOM, TVM, DVM. 3rd ed. LC 80-52934. 1980. pap. 9.95 (ISBN 0-672-21756-2). Sams.
--One Hundred & One Ways to Use Your VOM & VTVM. 2nd ed. LC 66-29409. (Illus., Orig.). 1966. pap. 4.95 o.p. (ISBN 0-672-20510-6, 20510). Sams.
--Privilege & Burden. 1969. 4.95 o.p. (ISBN 0-8170-0440-8). Judson.
--Troubleshooting with the Oscilloscope. 4th ed. LC 80-51719. 1980. 9.95 (ISBN 0-672-21738-4). Sams.
--Troubleshooting with the Oscilloscope. 3rd ed. LC 74-15456. (Illus.). 1975. 5.95 o.p. (ISBN 0-672-21103-3). Sams.
Middleton, Robert G., ed. see Smith, Paul C.
Middleton, Robin & Watkin, David. Neoclassical & Nineteenth Century Architecture. (History of World Architecture Ser.). (Illus.). 492p. 1980. 45.00 (ISBN 0-8109-1014-4). Abrams.
Middleton, Sallie & Sibley, Celestine. The Magical Realm of Sallie Middleton. LC 80-80974. 112p. 1980. 19.95 (ISBN 0-8487-0503-3). Oxmoor Hse.
Middleton, Thomas. A Game of Chess. 1980. pap. text ed. 25.00x (ISBN 0-391-02145-1). Humanities.
--Mad World, My Masters. Henning, Standish, ed. LC 65-10544. (Regents Renaissance Drama Ser). 1965. 7.50x (ISBN 0-8032-0279-2); pap. 1.85x (ISBN 0-8032-5278-1, BB 211, Bison). U of Nebr Pr.
--Michaelmas Term. Levin, Richard, ed. LC 66-17765. (Regents Renaissance Drama Ser). 1967. 9.25x (ISBN 0-8032-0280-6); pap. 1.65x (ISBN 0-8032-5280-3, BB 220, Bison). U of Nebr Pr.
--The Widow: A Critical Edition. Levine, Robert T., ed. (Salzburg Studies in English Literature, Jacobean Studies Drama Ser.: No. 56). 260p. 1975. pap. text ed. 25.00x (ISBN 0-391-01482-X). Humanities.
Middleton, Thomas & Rowley, William. Changeling. Williams, George W., ed. LC 65-15340. (Regents Renaissance Drama Ser). 1966. 7.50x (ISBN 0-8032-0281-4); pap. 2.25x (ISBN 0-8032-5281-1, BB 214, Bison). U of Nebr Pr.
Middleton, William. South Shore: America's Last Interurban. LC 70-131244. 18.95 (ISBN 0-87095-003-7). Golden West.
Middleton, William D. North Shore. LC 64-16408. (Illus.). 1963. 15.95 (ISBN 0-87095-016-9). Golden West.
--Railroad Scene. LC 69-20446. (Illus.). 1969. 15.95 (ISBN 0-87095-000-2). Golden West.
Midgaard, J., ed. Norway-Brief History. 7th ed. (Tanum of Norway Tokens Ser.). 1979. pap. 12.50x (ISBN 82-518-0053-6, N-441). Vanous.
Midgaard, John. Brief History of Norway. 7th ed. LC 67-7814. (Norwegian Guides Ser). (Illus., Orig.). 1979. pap. 9.50x (ISBN 82-518-0053-6). Intl Pubns Serv.
Midgalski, Edward C. How to Make Fish Mounts & Other Fish Trophies. 2nd ed. 288p. 1981. 15.95 (ISBN 0-471-07990-1, Pub. by Wiley-Interscience). Wiley.
Midgely, Charles, tr. see Sollertinsky, Dmitri & Sollertinsky, Ludmilla.
Midgley, A. Rees & Sadler, William A., eds. Ovarian Follicular Development & Function. LC 77-17750. 1978. 30.00 (ISBN 0-89004-186-5). Raven.
Midgley, David. Innovation & New Product Marketing. LC 76-50052. 1978. pap. 17.95x o.p. (ISBN 0-470-26517-5). Halsted Pr.
Midgley, David A. American History: Pre-Colonial to the Present Day. rev. ed. LC 77-4648. (gr. 9-12). 1977. pap. text ed. 5.50 (ISBN 0-8120-0787-5). Barron.
Midgley, Graham. The Life of Orator Henley. (Illus.). 1973. text ed. 19.25x o.p. (ISBN 0-19-812032-X). Oxford U Pr.
Midgley, W., jt. auth. see Lilley, A. E.
Midkiff, Pat. Colonial Furniture for Doll Houses & Miniature Rooms. LC 76-27807. 1977. pap. 5.95 o.p. (ISBN 0-8069-8220-9). Sterling.

Midlarsky, Manus I. On War: Political Violence in the International System. LC 74-9195. (Illus.). 1975. 19.95 (ISBN 0-02-921200-6). Free Pr.

Midwest Plan Service. Midwest Plan Service Structures & Environment Handbook. 9th ed. LC 77-24236. 1977. spiral bdg. 8.00 o.p. (ISBN 0-89373-030-0, MWPS-1). Midwest Plan Serv.

--Professional Design Supplement to the MWPS Structures & Environment Handbook. 5th ed. LC 77-24229. (Illus.). 1978. pap. text ed. 9.50 (ISBN 0-89373-037-8, MWPS-17). Midwest Plan Serv.

Midwest Plan Service Engineers. Designs for Glued Trusses. 4th ed. Midwest Plan Service Staff, ed. LC 80-39547. (Illus., 4#80). 1981. pap. 3.00 (ISBN 0-89373-051-3, MWPS-9). Midwest Plan Serv.

--Structures & Environment Handbook. 10th, rev. ed. Midwest Plan Service Staff, ed. LC 76-27983. (Illus.). 490p. 1980. pap. 10.00 (ISBN 0-686-68276-9, MWPS-1). Midwest Plan Serv.

Midwest Plan Service Personnel. Designs for Glued Trusses. 3rd ed. LC 78-4488. (Illus.). 1978. pap. 2.50 o.p. (ISBN 0-89373-033-5, MWPS-9). Midwest Plan Serv.

--Planning Grain-Feed Handling for Live-Stock & Cash-Grain Farms. (Illus.). 1974. pap. 2.50 (ISBN 0-89373-007-6, MWPS-13). Midwest Plan Serv.

Midwest Plan Service Staff, ed. see Midwest Plan Service Engineers.

Midwinter, Eric. Education & the Community. LC 75-20256. 163p. 1976. 12.95 (ISBN 0-470-60239-2). Halsted Pr.

--Education for Sale. (Classroom Close-Ups Ser.). 1977. text ed. 12.50x o.p. (ISBN 0-04-371049-2); pap. text ed. 4.95x o.p. (ISBN 0-04-371050-6). Allen Unwin.

Mieczkowski, Bogdan. Transportation in Eastern Europe. (Eastern European Monographs: No. 38). 1978. 14.50x (ISBN 0-914710-31-1, Dist. by Columbia U Pr). East Eur Quarterly.

Mieczkowski, Bogdan, ed. Eastern European Transportation: Systems & Modes. (Developments in Transportation Studies: No. 2). 366p. 1980. lib. bdg. 44.75 (ISBN 90-247-2390-6). Kluwer Boston.

Mields, Hugh, Jr. Federally Assisted New Communities: New Dimensions in Urban Development. LC 73-78874. (Special Report Ser.). (Illus.). 1973. pap. 4.75 (ISBN 0-87420-557-3). Urban Land.

Miele, Philip, jt. auth. see Silva, Jose.

Mieli, Aldo. Science Arabe & Son Role Dans l'Evolution Scientifique Mondiale. (Medieval Studies Reprint Ser.). (Fr.). Repr. of 1938 ed. lib. bdg. 29.50x (ISBN 0-697-00044-3). Irvington.

Mielke, James H. & Crawford, Michael H., eds. Current Developments in Anthropological Genetics: Vol. 1, Theory & Methods, Vol. 1. 450p. 1980. 45.00 (ISBN 0-306-40390-0, Plenum Pr). Plenum Pub.

Mierow, Dorothy, jt. auth. see Mishra, Hemant R.

Miers, Earl J. Blood of Freedom. LC 58-13521. (Williamsburg in America Ser.: Vol. 3). (Illus.). 4.95 o.p. (ISBN 0-910412-49-9). Williamsburg.

Miers, Suzanne & Kopytoff, Igor, eds. Slavery in Africa: Historical & Anthropological Perspectives. LC 76-53653. 1977. 25.00 (ISBN 0-299-07330-0); pap. 9.95 (ISBN 0-299-07334-3). U of Wis Pr.

Mies, Maria. Indian Women & Patriarchy. 311p. 1980. text ed. 17.00x (ISBN 0-391-02126-5). Humanities.

Miesel, Victor H., ed. Voices of German Expressionism. LC 71-90968. 1974. 5.95 o.s.i. (ISBN 0-13-943712-6). Brown Bk.

Mieszlowski, Peter & Oakland, William, eds. Fiscal Federalism & Grants-in-Aid. (Papers on Public Economics Ser.: Vol.1). 166p. (Orig.). 1979. pap. text ed. 5.50 (26300). Urban Inst.

Mieth, Dietmar & Pohier, Jacques, eds. Christian Ethics & Economics: The North South Conflict, Concilium 140. (New Concilium 1980). 128p. 1980. pap. 5.95 (ISBN 0-8245-4773-X). Crossroad NY.

Mieth, Dietmar, jt. ed. see Pohier, Jacques.

Miethe, Terry L. & Bourke, Vernon J., eds. Thomistic Bibliography, 1940-1978. LC 80-1195. xxii, 318p. 1980. lib. bdg. 39.95 (ISBN 0-313-21991-5, MTH/). Greenwood.

Mietus, Norbert J. & West, Bill W. Personal Law. LC 74-34192. (Consumer Education Ser). (Illus.). 464p. 1975. text ed. 16.95 (ISBN 0-574-18215-2, 13-2215); instr's guide avail. (ISBN 0-574-18216-0, 13-2216). SRA.

--Personal Law. 2nd ed. 512p. 1981. text ed. 16.95 (ISBN 0-574-19505-X, 13-2505); instr's. guide avail. (ISBN 0-574-19506-8, 13-2506). Sci Res Assoc Coll.

Mifflin, Lawrie, jt. auth. see Rush, Cathy.

Mifflin, R., jt. ed. see Lemarechale, C.

Migaki, George, jt. ed. see Montali, Richard J.

Migaki, George, jt. ed. see Ribelin, William E.

Migdail, Sherry R. & Vail, Priscilla L. Supplement to a Teacher's Notebook: Alternatives for Children with Learning Problems. 1978. pap. 4.25 (ISBN 0-934338-10-8). NAIS.

Migdalski, Edward C. Angler's Guide to the Salt Water Game Fishes: Atlantic & Pacific. (Illus.). 1958. 12.95 o.p. (ISBN 0-8260-6080-3). Ronald Pr.

--Clay Target Games. (Illus.). 1978. pap. 8.95 (ISBN 0-87691-277-3). Winchester Pr.

--How to Make Fish Mounts & Other Fish Trophies. (Illus.). 1960. 17.50 (ISBN 0-8260-6095-1). Ronald Pr.

Migel, J. Michael, ed. The Masters on the Dry Fly. (Illus.). 1977. 12.00 o.p. (ISBN 0-397-01188-1). Lippincott.

Migel, Michael J. & Wright, Leonard M., Jr. Masters on the Nymph. LC 78-20638. (Illus.). 1979. 14.95 (ISBN 0-385-15151-9, NLB). Doubleday.

Migeon, G., jt. auth. see Saladin, H.

Mignard, James E., tr. see Marxsen, Willi.

Migne, Jacques P. Patrologiae Cursus Completus. Incl. Patrologia Latina, 146 vols. Repr. of 1844 ed. pap. write for info.; Patrologia Graeco Latina, 60 vols. Repr. of 1857 ed. pap. write for info.. 1965-71. Adler.

Migone, L., ed. Urinary Proteins. (Contributions to Nephrology Ser.: Vol. 26). (Illus.). vi, 150p. 1981. pap. 54.00 (ISBN 3-8055-1848-X). S Karger.

Migraine Symposium, 5th, London, 1972. Background to Migraine: Proceedings. Cumings, J. N., ed. 1973. 23.00 (ISBN 0-387-91115-4). Springer Verlag.

Mihailescu, V., ed. One Hundred Years of Geosciences in Romania. 1976. pap. text ed. 28.00 (ISBN 0-08-019969-0). Pergamon.

Mihailhov, V. P., ed. see Steklov Institute of Mathematics, No. 126.

Mihajlov, Mihajlo. Russian Themes. LC 68-20172. 373p. 1968. 6.95 (ISBN 0-374-25292-0); pap. 2.45 o.p. (ISBN 0-374-50700-7). FS&G.

Mihalas, Dimitri. Stellar Atmospheres. 2nd ed. LC 77-13211. (Astronomy & Astrophysics Ser.). (Illus.). 1978. text ed. 33.95x (ISBN 0-7167-0359-9). W H Freeman.

Mihalek, R. J. Projective Geometry & Algebraic Structures. 1972. text ed. 18.95 (ISBN 0-12-495550-9). Acad Pr.

Mihalich, Joseph C. Existentialism & Thomism. (Quality Paperback: No. 170). 1969. pap. 2.50 (ISBN 0-8226-0170-2). Littlefield.

Mihalyi, Elemer. Application of Proteolytic Enzymes to Protein Structure Studies, Vol. 2. 2nd ed. 1978. 59.95 (ISBN 0-8493-5190-1). CRC Pr.

Mihalyka, Jean M., compiled by. Gravestone Inscriptions in Northampton County Virginia. 6.00 (ISBN 0-686-69510-0). Va State Lib.

Mihich, Enrico. New Leads in Cancer Chemotherapeutics. 1981. lib. bdg. 27.50 (ISBN 0-8161-2148-6, Hall Medical). G K Hall.

Miisuhashi, S., et al, eds. Antibiotic Resistance: Proceedings. (Illus.). 410p. 1981. 55.50 (ISBN 0-387-10322-8). Springer-Verlag.

Mika, J. & Torok, T. Analytical Emission Spectroscopy. LC 73-75866. 260p. 1974. 42.50x (ISBN 0-8448-0203-4). Crane-Russak Co.

Mikael'An, Galina, jt. auth. see Akhmanova, Olga.

Mikami, Y. The Development of Mathematics in China & Japan. 2nd ed. LC 74-6716. 383p. 1974. text ed. 12.95 (ISBN 0-8284-0149-7). Chelsea Pub.

Mikellides, Byron, ed. Architecture for People. LC 79-48067. (Illus.). 196p. 1980. 18.95 (ISBN 0-03-057491-9); pap. 9.95 (ISBN 0-03-057489-7). HR&W.

Mikes, George. Charlie: A Novel. 1977. 10.00 (ISBN 0-233-96842-3). Transatlantic.

--How to Be an Alien: England. (Illus.). 1946. 9.75 (ISBN 0-233-95500-3). Transatlantic.

--How to Run a Stately Home. (Illus.). 125p. 1972. 6.95 (ISBN 0-233-95848-7). Transatlantic.

Mikes, O. Laboratory Handbook of Chromatigraphic & Allied Methods. (Analytical Chemistry Ser.). 1979. 149.95x (ISBN 0-470-26399-7). Halsted Pr.

Mikesell, jt. auth. see Bitter.

Mikesell, John, jt. ed. see McCaffery, Jerry.

Mikesell, R. M., jt. auth. see Hay, Leon E.

Mikesell, Raymond. World Copper Industry: Structure & Economic Analysis. LC 79-4581. (Resources for the Future Ser.). 1979. 25.00x (ISBN 0-8018-2257-2); pap. 10.95 (ISBN 0-8018-2270-X). Johns Hopkins.

Mikesell, Raymond, jt. auth. see Behrman, Jack.

Mikesell, Raymond F. & Farah, Mark G. U. S. Export Competitiveness in Manufactures in Third World Countries, Vol. II. LC 80-67711. (Significant Issues Ser.: No. 9). 144p. 1980. 5.95 (ISBN 0-89206-026-3). CSI Studies.

Mikesh, Robert C. The Albatros D.Va: German World War I Fighter. LC 80-36711. (Famous Aircraft of the National Air & Space Museum Ser.: No. 4). (Illus.). 115p. (Orig.). 1980. pap. 7.95 (ISBN 0-87474-633-7). Smithsonian.

--Excalibur III: Story of a P-51 Mustang. LC 78-606028. (Famous Aircraft of the National Air & Space Museum Ser.: No. 1). (Illus.). 76p. 1978. pap. 5.95 (ISBN 0-87474-635-3). Smithsonian.

--Japanese Cockpit Interiors, Pt.2. (Monogram Aircraft Close-up: No. 15). (Illus.). 1978. pap. 5.95 (ISBN 0-914144-15-4, Pub by Monogram). Aviation.

--Japanese Cockpit Interiors: Pt. 1. LC 76-6214. (Monogram Close-up: No. 14). (Illus.). 1976. pap. 5.95 (ISBN 0-914144-14-6, Pub. by Monogram). Aviation.

Mikhail, E. H. An Annotated Bibliography of Modern Anglo-Irish Drama. LC 80-51874. 306p. 1981. 20.00x (ISBN 0-87875-201-3). Whitston Pub.

--Bibliography of Modern Irish Drama, 1899-1970. LC 72-1373. 63p. 1972. 10.50 (ISBN 0-295-95229-6). U of Wash Pr.

--Brendan Behan: An Annotated Bibliography of Criticism. 1980. text ed. 23.50x (ISBN 0-06-494826-9). B&N.

--Comedy & Tragedy: A Bibliography of Critical Studies. LC 75-183299. 1972. pap. 5.00x o.p. (ISBN 0-87875-019-3). Whitston Pub.

--English Drama, Nineteen Hundred-Nineteen Fifty: A Guide to Information Sources. LC 74-11523. (American Literature, English Literature & World Literatures in English Information Guide Ser.: Vol. 11). 1977. 30.00 (ISBN 0-8103-1216-6). Gale.

Mikhail, Edward M. & Gracie, Gordon. Analysis & Adjustment of Survey Measurements. 368p. 1980. text ed. 28.50 (ISBN 0-442-25369-9). Van Nos Reinhold.

Mikhailov, V. A. Analytical Chemistry of Neptunium. LC 72-4103. (Analytical Chemistry of the Elements Ser.). 235p. 1973. 39.95x (ISBN 0-470-60300-3). Halsted Pr.

Mikhailov, Z. K., jt. ed. see Kopel, Zdenek.

Miklos, Mary O. Mathematical Ideas. LC 80-5871. 344p. 1980. pap. text ed. 11.50 (ISBN 0-8191-1099-X). U Pr of Amer.

--Preparation for Criterion-Referenced Tests: A Brief Review of Mathamatical Competencies for Teachers of Early Childhood. LC 80-5430. 88p. 1980. pap. text ed. 6.25 (ISBN 0-8191-1092-2). U Pr of Amer.

Miklosich, Franz. Monumenta Linguae Palaeoslovenicae e Codice Supraliensi. LC 80-2361. 1981. Repr. of 1851 ed. 57.00 (ISBN 0-404-18909-1). AMS Pr.

Miklowitz, Gloria. Unwed Mother. rev. ed. (Easy to Read Edition Ser.). (gr. 4 up). 1981. pap. 1.95 (ISBN 0-448-17248-8, Tempo). G&D.

Miklowitz, Gloria D. Did You Hear What Happened to Andrea? (YA) (gr. 7-12). pap. 1.75 (ISBN 0-440-91853-7, LE). Dell.

--Movie Stunts & the People Who Do Them. LC 80-7984. (Illus.). 64p. (gr. 4-6). 1980. pap. 3.95 (ISBN 0-15-256039-4, VoyB). HarBraceJ.

Miklowitz, Gloria D. & Yates, Madelein. The Young Tycoons. LC 80-8803. (Illus.). 128p. (gr. 7 up). 1981. 9.95 (ISBN 0-15-299879-9, HJ). HarBraceJ.

Mikola, Peitsa, ed. Tropical Mycorrhiza Research. 288p. 1980. 45.00x (ISBN 0-19-854553-3). Oxford U Pr.

Mikolowski, Ken. Little Mysteries. LC 79-15299. (Illus., Orig.). 1979. pap. 3.00 (ISBN 0-915124-31-9, Bookslinger). Toothpaste.

Miksa, Francis, ed. Charles Ammi Cutter: Library Systematizer. LC 76-58870. (Heritage of Librarianship: No. 3). 1977. lib. bdg. 20.00x (ISBN 0-87287-112-6). Libs Unl.

Mikulas, William L., ed. Psychology of Learning: Readings. LC 77-8234. 1977. text ed. 23.95 (ISBN 0-88229-226-9); pap. 11.95 (ISBN 0-88229-519-5). Nelson-Hall.

Mikulecky, Thomas J., ed. Small Cities Management Training Program. LC 75-27076. 1975. text ed. 40.00 (ISBN 0-87326-011-2). Intl City Mgt.

Mikusinski, Jan. Operational Calculus, Vol. 1. 2nd ed. (International Series in Pure & Applied Mathematics: Vol. 109). (Illus.). 320p. 1981. 27.00 (ISBN 0-08-025071-8). Pergamon.

Mikusinskii, J. Operational Calculus. 1969. 46.00 (ISBN 0-08-006367-5). Pergamon.

Milam, Edward E., jt. auth. see Sellers, James H.

Milan, Albert R. Breast Self-Examination. LC 79-56529. (Illus.). 128p. 1980. pap. 3.50 (ISBN 0-89480-124-4). Liberty Pub.

Milan, F. A., ed. The Human Biology of Circumpolar Populations. LC 79-322. (International Biological Programme Ser.: No. 21). (Illus.). 1980. 90.00 (ISBN 0-521-22213-3). Cambridge U Pr.

Milani, Lucille. Tailoring the Easy Way. (Illus.). 192p. 1976. 11.95x o.p. (ISBN 0-13-882183-6, Spec); pap. 4.95x o.p. (ISBN 0-13-882175-5). P-H.

Milano, Dominic, ed. see Traum, Happy.

Milanovic, Petar. Karst Hydrogeology. 1981. 29.00 (ISBN 0-918334-36-5). WRP.

Milar, Melissa. Photographer's Market Nineteen Eighty. 3rd ed. (Illus.). 1979. 12.95 o.p. (ISBN 0-89879-001-8). Writers Digest.

Milash, Nikodim. Das Kirchenrecht der Morgenlandischen Kirche. 2nd ed. LC 80-2360. 1981. Repr. of 1905 ed. 83.00 (ISBN 0-404-18910-5). AMS Pr.

Milazzo, G., ed. Topics in Bioelectrochemistry & Bioenergetics, 3 vols. LC 76-18231. (Topics in Bioelectrochemistry & Bioenergetics Ser.). Vol. 1, 1978. 65.00 (ISBN 0-471-01356-0, Pub. by Wiley-Interscience); Vol. 2, 1978. 45.50 (ISBN 0-471-99533-9); Vol. 3, 1980. 96.95 (ISBN 0-471-99744-7, Pub. by Wiley-Interscience). Wiley.

Milazzo, Richard, ed. see Gillespie, Abraham L.

Milazzo, Richard, tr. see Ballerini, Luigi.

Milbauer, B. & Jacobson, K. K. Come to Your Senses. (Getting in Touch Ser: Bk. 4). (gr. 5-8). 0.95 o.p. (ISBN 0-531-02090-8, Q28). Watts.

--Feeling Alive. (Getting in Touch Ser: Bk. 2). (gr. 5-8). 0.95 o.p. (ISBN 0-531-02093-2, Q26). Watts.

--Life-Read All About It. (Getting in Touch Ser: Bk. 3). (gr. 5-8). 0.95 o.p. (ISBN 0-531-02089-4, P43). Watts.

Milbauer, Barbara. Suppose You Were a Dinka: Teens in Other Societies. (gr. 7 up). 1981. PLB price not set (ISBN 0-671-32891-3). Messner. Postponed.

--Teenagers in Other Societies. 192p. (gr. 7 up). 1981. write for info. (ISBN 0-671-32891-3). Messner.

Milbrath, Lester W. & Inscho, Frederick R., eds. The Politics of Environmental Policy. LC 75-27013. (Contemporary Social Science Issues Ser.: Vol. 18). 1975. 4.95x (ISBN 0-8039-0567-X). Sage.

Milbrath, Mona A. Credentials: A Guide to Business Designations. LC 80-66740. 221p. (Orig.). 1980. pap. 9.95 (ISBN 0-936324-01-5). Blue River.

Milbrath, Susan. Study of Olmec Sculptural Chronology. LC 79-89248. (Studies in Pre-Columbian Art & Archaeology: No. 23). (Illus.). 75p. 1979. pap. 5.00 (ISBN 0-88402-093-2, Ctr Pre-Columbian). Dumbarton Oaks.

Milburn, J. A. Water Flow in Plants. LC 77-30743. (Integrated Themes in Biology Ser.). (Illus.). 1979. pap. text ed. 17.50 (ISBN 0-582-44387-3). Longman.

Milburn, Josephine & Shuck, Victoria, eds. New England Politics. LC 80-14530. 320p. 1981. text ed. 27.00x (ISBN 0-87073-356-7); pap. text ed. 10.50x (ISBN 0-87073-357-5). Schenkman.

Milburn, Joyce & Smith, Lynette. The Natural Childbirth Book. 224p. (Orig.). 1981. pap. 5.95 (ISBN 0-87123-399-1, 210339). Bethany Fell.

Milburn, Thomas W., jt. ed. see Hermann, Margaret G.

Milbury-Steen, Sarah L. European & African Stereotypes in Twentieth-Century African Fiction. (The Gotham Library). 208p. 1981. 24.50x (ISBN 0-8147-5378-7); pap. 12.00 (ISBN 0-8147-5379-5). NYU Pr.

Milby, Robert V. Plastics Technology. (Illus.). 576p. 1973. text ed. 22.95x (ISBN 0-07-041918-3, G); instructor's manual 3.00 (ISBN 0-07-041919-1). McGraw.

Milch, H. Osteotomy at the Upper End of Femur. 177p. 1965. 12.50 o.p. (ISBN 0-683-05988-2, Pub. by Williams & Wilkins). Krieger.

Mildren, K. W., ed. Use of Engineering Literature. 608p. 1976. 64.95 (ISBN 0-408-70714-3). Butterworths.

Mileaf, Harry. Electricity Seven. rev., 2nd ed. (gr. 10 up). 1978. pap. 6.60 (ISBN 0-8104-5951-5). Hayden.

--Electricity Three. rev., 2nd ed. (gr. 10 up). 1977. pap. 6.60 (ISBN 0-8104-5947-7). Hayden.

--Electronics Five. rev., 2nd ed. 1978. pap. 6.60 (ISBN 0-8104-5958-2). Hayden.

--Electronics Four. 2nd rev. ed. (gr. 10 up). 1977. pap. 7.25 (ISBN 0-8104-5957-4). Hayden.

--Electronics Seven. rev., 2nd ed. (gr. 10 up). 1978. pap. 6.60 (ISBN 0-8104-5960-4). Hayden.

Mileaf, Harry, ed. Electricity One. rev., 2nd ed. (Illus.). (gr. 10-12). 1976. pap. 6.60 (ISBN 0-8104-5945-0). Hayden.

--Electricity One-Four. rev., 2nd, combined ed. (Illus.). (gr. 10-12). 1976. 16.60x (ISBN 0-8104-5919-1). Hayden.

--Electricity One-Seven. Incl. Electricity Two. rev., 2nd ed. pap. (ISBN 0-8104-5946-9); Electricity Four. 2nd ed. pap. (ISBN 0-8104-5948-5); Electricity Five. pap. (ISBN 0-8104-5949-3); Electricity Six. rev., 2nd ed. pap. (ISBN 0-8104-5950-7); Electricity Seven. pap. o.p. (ISBN 0-8104-5550-1). (Illus.). (gr. 10-12). 1978. pap. 6.60 ea.; ea 2.15, transparencies; exam sets, vols. 1-7 0.50 ea.; transparency set 1252.00 (ISBN 0-685-46436-9). Hayden.

--Electricity One-Seven. combined, rev., 2nd ed. (Illus.). (gr. 10-12). 1976. 25.95x (ISBN 0-8104-5952-3). Hayden.

--Electricity One-Seven, 7 vols. rev., 2nd ed. (Illus.). (gr. 10-12). 1976. pap. 46.20 set (ISBN 0-8104-5944-2). Hayden.

--Electronics One. rev., 2nd ed. (Illus.). (gr. 10-12). 1976. pap. 6.60 (ISBN 0-8104-5954-X). Hayden.

--Electronics One-Seven, 7 vols. rev. 2nd ed. (Illus.). (gr. 10-12). 1976. Set. pap. 46.85 (ISBN 0-8104-5953-1). Hayden.

--Electronics Six. rev., 2nd ed. (Illus.). (gr. 10-12). 1976. pap. 6.60 (ISBN 0-8104-5959-0). Hayden.

--Electronics Three. rev., 2nd ed. (Illus.). (gr. 10-12). 1976. pap. 6.60 (ISBN 0-8104-5956-6). Hayden.

--Electronics Two. rev., 2nd ed. (Illus.). (gr. 10-12). 1976. pap. 6.60 (ISBN 0-8104-5955-8). Hayden.

Mileaf, Henry, ed. Electronics One-Seven. rev. 2nd ed. (Illus.). (gr. 10-12). 1976. 27.50x (ISBN 0-8104-5961-2); exam sets, vols. 1-7 0.50 ea.; transparencies 1270.45 (ISBN 0-685-70978-7). Hayden.

Mileck, Joseph. Herman Hesse: Biography & Bibliography, 2 vols. 1977. 70.00 (ISBN 0-520-02756-6). U of Cal Pr.

--Hermann Hesse: Life & Art. 1978. 16.95 (ISBN 0-520-03351-5); pap. 5.95 (ISBN 0-520-04152-6). U of Cal Pr.

Milenky, Edward S. Argentina's Foreign Policies. LC 77-90536. 1978. lib. bdg. 28.00x (ISBN 0-89158-427-7). Westview.

Milepost Staff, ed. The Milepost: All-the-North Travel Guide. 33rd ed. 1981. pap. 7.95 (ISBN 0-88240-151-3). Alaska Northwest.

Miles & Lane. Business & Personal Taxes Nineteen Eighty-One. 400p. 1980. text ed. 19.95 (ISBN 0-205-07163-5, 1071637). Allyn.

Miles, jt. auth. see Laffer.

Miles, compiled by. The Beatles in Their Own Words. 1979. pap. 5.95 (ISBN 0-8256-3925-5, Quick Fox). Music Sales.

Miles, A. J. Rio De Janeiro Interzonals 1979. 1979. 9.95 (ISBN 0-7134-3427-9, Pub. by Batsford England). David & Charles.

Miles, A. J. & Spearman. Riga Interzonals 1979. 1979. 9.95 (ISBN 0-7134-3429-5, Pub. by Batsford England). David & Charles.

Miles, A. Marie. Bible: Chain of Truth. 168p. pap. 1.25. Faith Pub Hse.

Miles, A. R. Introduccion Popular Al Estudio De las Sagradas Escrituras. Orig. Title: Introduction to the Bible. 234p. (Span.). 1970. pap. write for info o.p. (ISBN 0-89922-007-X). Edit Caribe.

Miles, Austin. The Real Ringmaster. Boneck, John & Dudley, Cliff, eds. LC 80-83458. 150p. 1980. 8.95 (ISBN 0-89221-079-6). New Leaf.

Miles, Betty. Just the Beginning. 1978. pap. 1.75 (ISBN 0-380-01913-2, 55004, Camelot). Avon.

--The Trouble with Thirteen. (gr. 3-7). 1980. pap. 1.95 (ISBN 0-380-51136-3, 51136, Camelot). Avon.

Miles, Bob, jt. auth. see Phizacklea, Annie.

Miles, Catherine C., jt. auth. see Terman, Lewis M.

Miles, Catherine E. & Lane, Joseph E., Jr. Business & Personal Taxes. 4th rev. ed. 1977. text ed. 14.95x o.p. (ISBN 0-205-05808-6); instructor's manual avail. o.p. (ISBN 0-205-05809-4). Allyn.

Miles, Cecile. Making & Designing Clothes. (Illus.). 160p. 1975. 9.95x o.p. (ISBN 0-8464-0584-9). Beekman Pubs.

Miles, Clement A. Christmas Customs & Traditions: Their History and Significance. LC 76-9183. Orig. Title: Christmas in Ritual and Tradition. (Illus.). 1976. pap. 5.00 (ISBN 0-486-23354-5). Dover.

--Christmas in Ritual & Tradition, Christian & Pagan. LC 68-54858. 1968. Repr. of 1912 ed. 20.00 (ISBN 0-8103-3354-6). Gale.

Miles, Delos. Church Growth - a Mighty River. 1981. pap. 5.95 (ISBN 0-8054-6227-9). Broadman.

Miles, Dick. The Game of Table Tennis. (Illus.). 1971. 7.95 o.s.i. (ISBN 0-397-00527-X); pap. 2.95 (ISBN 0-397-00878-3, LP-59). Lippincott.

--Sports Illustrated Table Tennis. LC 74-5313. 1974. 5.95 (ISBN 0-397-01024-9); pap. 2.95 (ISBN 0-397-01036-2). Lippincott.

Miles, Donald. Boast. 256p. 1980. 11.95 (ISBN 0-312-08722-5). St Martin.

Miles, Edwin A. Jacksonian Democracy in Mississippi. LC 78-107415. (American Scene Ser). 1970. Repr. of 1960 ed. lib. bdg. 25.00 (ISBN 0-306-71884-7). Da Capo.

Miles, Edwin A., jt. ed. see Remini, Robert V.

Miles, Fern H., jt. auth. see Miles, Herbert J.

Miles, Gary B. Virgil's Georgics: A New Interpretation. 1980. 17.50x (ISBN 0-520-03789-8). U of Cal Pr.

Miles, H., tr. see Bunin, Ivan.

Miles, Herbert J. Sexual Understanding Before Marriage. 224p. 1972. pap. 2.95 (ISBN 0-310-29212-3). Zondervan.

Miles, Herbert J. & Miles, Fern H. Husband-Wife Equality. 1978. 7.95 o.p. (ISBN 0-8007-0906-3). Revell.

Miles International Symposium, 12th. Polypeptide Hormones: Proceedings. Beers, Roland F. & Bassett, Edward, eds. 544p. 1980. text ed. 49.00 (ISBN 0-89004-462-7). Raven.

Miles, J. Vegetation Dynamics. LC 78-13070. (Outline Studies in Ecology). 80p. 1979. pap. text ed. 4.95x o.p. (ISBN 0-470-26504-3). Halsted Pr.

Miles, J. Todd. A Vegetable Growers Primer. 2nd ed. 58p. 1980. 11.95x (ISBN 0-9605070-0-0); soft cover 6.95x (ISBN 0-9605070-1-9). Foto Res.

Miles, James, et al. Technical Communication. 416p. Date not set. text ed. 10.95t (ISBN 0-686-63006-8). SRA. Postponed.

Miles, John G., Jr., et al. The Law Officer's Pocket Manual: 1980-81 Edition. 128p. 1980. 5.00 (ISBN 0-686-68899-6). BNA.

Miles, Josephine. Kinds of Affection. LC 67-24108. (Wesleyan Poetry Program: Vol. 36). (Orig.). 1967. 10.00x (ISBN 0-8195-2036-5, Pub. by Wesleyan U Pr). Columbia U Pr.

--Poetry & Change: Donne, Milton, Wordsworth, & the Equilibrium of the Present. 1974. 16.75 (ISBN 0-520-02554-7). U of Cal Pr.

--The Primary Language of Poetry in the 1640's. LC 78-11614. (Univ. of California Publications in English: Vol. 19, No. 1). (Illus.). 160p. 1979. Repr. of 1948 ed. lib. bdg. 16.50x (ISBN 0-313-20661-9, MIPP). Greenwood.

--The Ways of the Poem. rev. ed. LC 78-146676. (English Literature Ser). 448p. 1972. pap. text ed. 9.50x (ISBN 0-13-946319-4). P-H.

Miles, Joyce C. House Names Around the World. LC 72-12695. 135p. 1973. 14.00 (ISBN 0-8103-2009-6). Gale.

Miles, Judith. The Feminine Principle. LC 75-5828. 160p. 1975. kivar 3.50 (ISBN 0-87123-159-X, 210159). Bethany Fell.

--The Feminine Principle. LC 75-5828. 160p. 1976. pap. 2.50 (ISBN 0-87123-160-3, 200160). Bethany Fell.

--Journal from an Obscure Place. LC 78-60279. 1978. pap. 1.95 (ISBN 0-87123-273-1, 200273). Bethany Fell.

Miles, L., jt. auth. see Craft, M.

Miles, Laughton E. & Dement, William C. Sleep & Aging. (Sleep Ser.: Vol. 3, No. 2). 108p. 1981. text ed. 20.00 (ISBN 0-89004-651-4). Raven.

Miles, Margaret R. Augustine on the Body. LC 79-14226. (American Academy of Religion, Dissertation Ser.: No. 31). 1979. 12.00x (ISBN 0-89130-288-3, 010131); pap. 7.50 (ISBN 0-89130-289-1). Scholars Pr Ca.

Miles, Marshall. How to Win at Duplicate Bridge. rev. ed. 1962. pap. 1.95 o.s.i. (ISBN 0-02-029280-5, Collier). Macmillan.

Miles, Matthew B. Learning to Work in Groups. 2nd ed. 360p. 1981. pap. text ed. 12.95x (ISBN 0-8077-2586-2). Tchrs Coll.

Miles, Matthew B., ed. Innovation in Education. LC 64-15445. 1964. text ed. 16.50x (ISBN 0-8077-1803-3). Tchrs Coll.

Miles, Mildred L. Index to Playboy: Belles-Lettres, Articles & Humor, December, 1953 to December, 1969. LC 68-25183. 1970. 10.00 (ISBN 0-8108-0327-5). Scarecrow.

Miles, Miska. Apricot ABC. LC 68-22072. (Illus.). (gr. k-3). 1969. 8.95 (ISBN 0-316-57030-3, Pub. by Atlantic Monthly Pr). Little.

--Jenny's Cat. LC 79-11501. (Illus.). (gr. 1-4). 1979. PLB 7.50 (ISBN 0-525-32746-0, Unicorn Bk.). Dutton.

Miles, Nelson A. Personal Recollections & Observations of General Nelson A. Miles. rev. ed. LC 68-23812. (American Scene Ser). (Illus.). Repr. of 1896 ed. lib. bdg. 55.00 (ISBN 0-306-71020-X). Da Capo.

Miles, Patricia H., jt. auth. see Bracegirdle, Brian.

Miles, Robert & Bertonasco, Marc F. Prose Style for the Modern Writer. 1977. pap. text ed. 8.95 (ISBN 0-13-731521-X). P-H.

Miles, Robert & Phizacklea, Annie, eds. Racism & Political Action in Britain. 1978. 23.50x (ISBN 0-7100-0035-9); pap. 10.00 (ISBN 0-7100-0036-7). Routledge & Kegan.

Miles, Sylva. Shadow Over Beauclaire. 192p. (YA) 1975. 5.95 (ISBN 0-685-51237-1, Avalon). Bouregy.

Miles, T. R., jt. auth. see Harzem, P.

Miles, Timothy R., jt. auth. see Pavlidis, George.

Miles, Tony & Moskow, Erik. Sicilian Dragon: Yugoslav Attack. 1979. 18.95 (ISBN 0-7134-2029-4, Pub. by Batsford England); pap. 13.50 (ISBN 0-7134-2030-8). David & Charles.

Miles, V. C. Thermostatic Control: Principles & Practice. (Illus.). 213p. 1974. 22.50x (ISBN 0-408-00131-3). Transatlantic.

Miles, William. The Image Makers: A Bibliography of American Presidential Campaign Biographies. LC 79-19472. 272p. 1979. 13.50 (ISBN 0-8108-1252-5). Scarecrow.

--Journal of the Sufferings & Hardships of Capt. Parker H. French's Overland Expedition to California. 8.50 (ISBN 0-8363-0057-2); pap. 4.50 wrappers (ISBN 0-685-13276-5). Jenkins.

Miles-Brown, John. Directing Drama. (Illus.). 176p. 1980. text ed. 24.75x (ISBN 0-7206-0557-1). Humanities.

Mileti, Dennis S., jt. auth. see Gillespie, David F.

Miletich, John J. Corporate Power, Leadership, & Success: A Selective Bibliography to 1977. (Public Administration Ser.: Bibliography P-518). 49p. 1980. pap. 5.50. Vance Biblios.

--Employee Absenteeism in Both the Public & Private Sectors: An Annotated Bibliography to 1979. (Public Administration Ser.: Bibliographies: P-639). 53p. 1981. pap. 8.25. Vance Biblios.

Milewski, Robert J., et al. Jack Kerouac: An Annotated Bibliography of Secondary Sources, 1944-1979. LC 80-24477. (Author Bibliographies Ser.: No. 52). 237p. 1981. 12.50 (ISBN 0-8108-1378-5). Scarecrow.

Milford, Humphrey, ed. see Browning, Robert.

Milford, Nancy. Zelda. 1971. pap. 2.50 (ISBN 0-380-00784-3, 40014). Avon.

Milgate, W., ed. see Donne, John.

Milgram, R. J., ed. Algebraic & Geometric Topology, 2 pts. LC 78-14304. (Proceedings of Symposia in Pure Mathematics: Vol. 32). 1980. Repr. of 1978 ed. Set. 34.00 (ISBN 0-8218-1432-X, PSPUM 32.1); 20.00 (32.2); 20.00 (ISBN 0-8218-1433-8). Am Math.

Milgram, Stanley. The Individual in a Social World: Essays & Experiments. (Social Psychology Ser.). (Illus.). text ed. 9.95 (ISBN 0-201-04382-3). A-W.

Milgrom, Harry. ABC of Ecology. LC 74-20654. (Illus.). 32p. (gr. k-3). 1976. pap. 1.95 o.s.i. (ISBN 0-02-044740-X, 04474, Collier). Macmillan.

--ABC Science Experiments. LC 75-116788. (Illus.). (gr. k-3). 1970. 5.95g o.s.i. (ISBN 0-02-766980-7). Macmillan.

--Adventures with a Straw. (Illus.). (ps-2). 1967. lib. bdg. 7.95 o.p. (ISBN 0-525-25229-0). Dutton.

--Understanding Weather. (Illus.). (gr. 4-8). 1970. 4.95g o.s.i. (ISBN 0-02-766940-8, CCPr). Macmillan.

Milgrom, Jacob. Studies in Levitical Terminology, 1: The Encroacher & the Levite, the Term Aboda. (U. C. Publ. in Near Eastern Studies: Vol. 14). 1970. pap. 9.00x (ISBN 0-520-09308-9). U of Cal Pr.

Milgrom, Peter. Regulation & the Quality of Dental Care. LC 78-1922. 1978. text ed. 28.00 (ISBN 0-89443-034-3). Aspen Systems.

Milhaud, Darius. Notes Without Music. LC 72-87419. (Music Ser). (Illus.). 1970. Repr. of 1953 ed. lib. bdg. 35.00 (ISBN 0-306-71565-1). Da Capo.

Milhaven, John Giles. Toward a New Catholic Morality. LC 77-116235. 1972. pap. 1.95 (ISBN 0-385-03000-2, Im). Doubleday.

Milhollen, Hirst D. & Johnson, James R. Best Photos of the Civil War. LC 61-16881. (Illus.). 1961. lib. bdg. 3.95 o.p. (ISBN 0-668-00782-6). Arco.

Milhous, Judith. Thomas Betterton & the Management of Lincoln's Inn Fields, 1695-1708. LC 78-21017. 304p. 1979. 18.95x (ISBN 0-8093-0906-8). S Ill U Pr.

Milhous, Katherine. The Egg Tree. (Illus.). 32p. (gr. k-3). pap. 2.95 (ISBN 0-689-70492-5, A-119, Aladdin). Atheneum.

--Through These Arches. LC 64-13810. (Illus.). (gr. 4-9). 1964. 6.50 o.p. (ISBN 0-397-30785-3). Lippincott.

Mili, Gjon. Gjon Mili: Photographs & Recollections. 1980. 40.00 (ISBN 0-8212-1116-1, 315001). NYGS.

Miliband & Saville. Socialist Register Nineteen Seventy Nine. 346p. 1979. text ed. 15.75x (ISBN 0-85036-252-0). Humanities.

Miliband, Ralph. Parliamentary Socialism. pap. 9.95 (ISBN 0-686-23500-2, Merlin Pr). Carrier Pigeon.

Miliband, Ralph & Saville, John. Socialist Register 1971: A Survey of Various Movements up to Current Bangladesh. 15.00 (ISBN 0-87556-440-2). Saifer.

Miliband, Ralph & Saville, John, eds. The Socialist Register Nineteen Seventy Five. 372p. 1977. text ed. 15.75x (ISBN 0-85036-224-5). Humanities.

--The Socialist Register Nineteen Seventy Six. 1976. text ed. 13.50x (ISBN 0-85036-217-2). Humanities.

--The Socialist Register Nineteen Seventy Two. 306p. 1972. text ed. 11.00x (ISBN 0-85036-163-X). Humanities.

Milic, Louis T., ed. see Gerlach, John & Gerlach, Lana.

Milinowski, Marta. Teresa Carreno "by the Grace of God". LC 76-58931. (Music Reprint Ser.). 1977. Repr. of 1940 ed. lib. bdg. 25.00 (ISBN 0-306-70870-1). Da Capo.

Milio, Nancy. Ninety Two Ninety Six Kercheval: The Storefront That Did Not Burn. 1971. pap. 4.50 (ISBN 0-472-06180-1, 180, AA). U of Mich Pr.

--Promoting Health Through Public Policy. 320p. 1981. text ed. 25.00 (ISBN 0-8036-6177-0, 6177-0). Davis Co.

Military of Justice, Japan. Constitution of Japan & Criminal Statutes. (Studies in Japanese Law & Government). 1979. Repr. of 1957 ed. 38.00 (ISBN 0-89093-221-2). U Pubns Amer.

Militineos, Peter, tr. see Jannacone, Pasquale.

Miliukov, Paul N. Russian Revolution, Vol. 1. (Russian Ser.: Vol. 44, Pt. 1). 18.50 (ISBN 0-87569-027-0). Academic Intl.

Miliukov, Pavel N. Bolshevism: An International Danger; Its Doctrine & Its Practice Through War & Revolution. LC 79-2915. 303p. 1981. Repr. of 1920 ed. 23.75 (ISBN 0-8305-0084-7). Hyperion Conn.

Miljan, Toivo, et al. Food & Agriculture in Global Perspective: Discussions in the Committee of the Whole of the United States. (Illus.). 260p. 28.00 (ISBN 0-08-025550-7). Pergamon.

Milkman, Raymond, et al. Alleviating Economic Distress: Evaluating a Federal Effort. LC 71-174597. (Illus.). 320p. 1972. 20.00 o.p. (ISBN 0-669-81216-1). Lexington Bks.

Mill, Cyril R. Activities for Trainers: Fifty Useful Designs. LC 80-50465. 240p. 1980. pap. 16.50 (ISBN 0-88390-159-5). Univ Assocs.

Mill, James. Essay on Government. Shields, Currin V., ed. (gr. 9 up). 1955. pap. 2.95 (ISBN 0-672-60215-6, LLA47). Bobbs.

Mill, John S. Autobiography. LC 57-14630. 1957. pap. 5.50 (ISBN 0-672-6028 -4, LLA91). Bobbs.

--Considerations on Representative Government. Shields, Currin V., ed. LC 57-14632. 1958. pap. 6.25 o.p. (ISBN 0-672-60249-0, LLA71). Bobbs.

--Essays on Politics & Culture. Himmelfarb, Gertrude, ed. 8.00 (ISBN 0-8446-0801-7). Peter Smith.

--Essays on Some Unsettled Questions of Political Economy. 2nd ed. LC 68-25642. Repr. of 1874 ed. 15.00x (ISBN 0-578-00390-4). Kelley.

--John Stuart Mill: A Selection of His Works. Robson, John M., ed. LC 66-19868. (College Classics in English Ser). 1966. pap. 7.50 (ISBN 0-672-63062-1). Odyssey Pr.

--On Liberty. Shields, Currin V., ed. 1956. pap. 3.95 (ISBN 0-672-60234-2, LLA61). Bobbs.

--Theism. Taylor, Richard, ed. 1957. pap. 2.25 o.p. (ISBN 0-672-60238-5, LLA64). Bobbs.

--Utilitarianism. Gorovitz, Samuel, ed. LC 74-132935. (Text & Critical Essays Ser). (Orig.). 1971. pap. 10.95 (ISBN 0-672-61120-1, TC7). Bobbs.

--Utilitarianism. Piest, Oskar, ed. 1957. pap. 2.95 (ISBN 0-672-60164-8, LLA1). Bobbs.

Mill, John S., jt. auth. see Bentham, Jeremy.

Mill, John S; see Bentham, Jeremy & Mill, John S.

Mill, John S; see Carlyle, Thomas.

Millan, W. H., jt. auth. see Rogers, J. W.

Millar, Annie, et al. Monitoring the Outcome of Social Services, 2 vols. Incl. Vol. 1. Preliminary Suggestions (ISBN 0-87766-194-4, 19100); Vol. 2. A Review of Past Research & Test Activities (ISBN 0-87766-200-2, 19200). (An Institute Paper). 1977. Set. pap. 7.00 (ISBN 0-686-53140-X, 20600); pap. 4.00 ea. Urban Inst.

Millar, Dan & Millar, Frank. Messages & Myths: Understanding Interpersonal Communication. LC 75-33811. 250p. 1976. pap. text ed. 7.95x (ISBN 0-88284-022-3). Alfred Pub.

Millar, Frank, jt. auth. see Millar, Dan.

Millar, George. Road to Resistance: An Autobiography. (Illus.). 432p. 1980. 13.95 (ISBN 0-316-57143-1). Little.

Millar, J. H. Multiple Sclerosis: A Disease Acquired in Childhood. (American Lecture Living Chemistry Ser.). (Illus.). 120p. 1971. text ed. 10.75 (ISBN 0-398-01307-). C C Thomas.

Millar, James A., jt. auth. see Eply, Donald R.

Millar, Jean A. British Management German Management. text ed. 15.75x (ISBN 0-566-00289-2, Pub. by Gower Pub Co England). Renouf.

Millar, Jeff. Private Sector. 288p. 198 . pap. 2.95 (ISBN 0-449-24368-0, Crest). Fawcett.

Millar, Margaret. Ask for Me Tomorrow. 1977. pap. 1.50 (ISBN 0-380-01805-5, 35518). Avon.

--Ask Me for Tomorrow. 1976. 6.95 o.p. (ISBN 0-394-40883-7). Random.

--Birds & the Beasts Were There. LC 66-12002. (Illus.). 1971. 10.00 o.p. (ISBN 0-394-42289-9). Random.

Millar, Perry S. & Baar, Carl. Judicial Administration in Canada. (Institute of Public Administration of Canada, Ipac Ser). (Illus.). 550p. 1981. 35.95x (ISBN 0-7735-0367-6); pap. 18.95x (ISBN 0-7735-0368-4). McGill-Queens U Pr.

Millar, R. P., ed. Neuropeptides: Biochemical & Physiological Studies. (Illus.). 368p. 1981. lib. bdg. 55.90 (ISBN 0-443-02265-8). Churchill.
Millar, Robert, jt. auth. see Brown, T. M.
Millar, William R. Isaiah Twenty-Four to Twenty-Seven & the Origin of Apocalyptic. LC 76-3561. (Harvard Semetic Museum Ser.). 1976. 7.50 (ISBN 0-89130-102-X, 040011). Scholars Pr Ca.
Millard. Flaming Star. (gr. 3-5). pap. 1.50 (ISBN 0-590-11923-0, Schol Pap). Schol Bk Serv.
--Symposium, Vol. 13. LC 76-16519. (Illus.). 432p. 1976. 45.00 (ISBN 0-8016-3413-X). Mosby.
Millard, Adele. Cats - in Fact & Legend. LC 76-1173. (Illus.). 128p. 1976. 5.95 o.p. (ISBN 0-8069-3728-9); PLB 5.89 o.p. (ISBN 0-8069-3729-7). Sterling.
--Dogs - in Fact & Legend. (gr. 5 up). 1977. 5.95 o.p. (ISBN 0-8069-3736-X); PLB 5.89 o.p. (ISBN 0-8069-3737-8). Sterling.
--Plants for Kids to Grow Indoors. LC 75-14509. 128p. 1975. 6.95 o.p. (ISBN 0-8069-3070-5); PLB 6.69 o.p. (ISBN 0-8069-3071-3). Sterling.
Millard, Anne. The Incas. (Warwick Press Ser.). (gr. 5 up). 1980. PLB 6.90 (ISBN 0-531-09171-6, F23). Watts.
Millard, Anne, et al. The Egyptians. LC 77-86182. (Peoples of the Past Ser.). (Illus.). 1977. lib. bdg. 7.95 (ISBN 0-686-51156-5). Silver.
Millard, B. J. Stocks & Shares Simplified. 1980. write for info. (ISBN 0-85501-083-5). Heyden.
Millard, Charles W. Miro: Selected Paintings. LC 79-9662. (Illus.). 94p. 1980. 20.00 (ISBN 0-87474-638-8). Smithsonian.
Millard, D. Ralph, Jr. Cleft Craft: Alveolar & Palatal Deformities, Vol. III. 1980. 125.00 (ISBN 0-316-57139-3). Little.
--Cleft Craft: the Evolution of Its Surgery, Vol. 1: The Unilateral Deformity. 1976. text ed. 95.00 (ISBN 0-316-57137-7). Little.
Millard, J., jt. auth. see Gilliland, Ken.
Millard, M. Troy. 4.50 o.p. (ISBN 0-8062-1074-5). Carlton.
Millard, Margaret. Casenotes of a Medical Astrologer. 1980. pap. 7.95 (ISBN 0-87728-484-9). Weiser.
Millard, W. F., jt. auth. see Barker, Eric J.
Millay, Edna St. Vincent. Collected Lyrics. LC 43-51349. 1943. 10.95 o.p. (ISBN 0-06-012930-1, HarpT). Har-Row.
Mille, Agnes de see De Mille, Agnes.
Mille, Richard de see De Mille, Richard.
Mille, Richard De see De Mille, Richard.
Millea, Thomas V. Ghetto Fever. 1968. 3.95 (ISBN 0-685-07639-3, 80530). Macmillan.
Miller. Basic Electricity. (gr. 9-12). 1978. 6.00 (ISBN 0-87002-288-1); pap. 4.32 (ISBN 0-87002-276-8). Bennett IL.
--Fury, Stallion of Broken Wheel Ranch. (gr. 3-5). 1980. pap. 1.50 (ISBN 0-590-31260-X, Schol Pap). Schol Bk Serv.
--Industrial Electricity. (gr. 9-12). 1978. text ed. 15.00 (ISBN 0-87002-200-8); student guide 2.60 (ISBN 0-87002-244-X). Bennett IL.
--Servomechanisms: Devices & Fundamentals. 1977. text ed. 17.95 (ISBN 0-87909-760-4); instrs'. manual avail. Reston.
Miller, jt. auth. see Hofstader.
Miller, jt. auth. see Nelson.
Miller, et al. Illustrators of Children's Books: 1946-1956, Vol. 2. LC 57-31264. (Illus.). 1958. 28.00 (ISBN 0-87675-016-1). Horn Bk.
--Exploring Careers in Industry. LC 74-14422. (gr. 7-9). 1975. text ed. 14.64 (ISBN 0-87345-108-2). McKnight.
Miller, A. G. Social Psychology of Psychological Research. LC 76-143522. 1972. 14.95 (ISBN 0-02-921510-2). Free Pr.
Miller, A. L. Hearing Loss, Hearing Aids & Your Child. (Illus.). 112p. 1980. lexotone 7.50 (ISBN 0-398-03979-8). C C Thomas.
Miller, A. T. The Principles & Techniques of Stock Market Manipulation. (The New Stock Market Reference Library Ser.). (Illus.). 117p. 1981. 39.85 (ISBN 0-918968-95-X). Inst Econ Finan.
Miller, A. T., jt. auth. see Durand, John.
Miller, A. V., tr. see Hegel, G. W.
Miller, A. W. The Destroyers. (Orig.). 1980. pap. 1.75 (ISBN 0-8439-0738-X, Leisure Bks). Nordon Pubns.
Miller, Aaron. In the Eye. 8.00 (ISBN 0-89253-700-0); flexible cloth 4.80 (ISBN 0-89253-701-9). Ind-US Inc.
Miller, Agnes P. Sand Design for Aquariums and Terrariums. (Illus.). 1975. pap. 0.50 (ISBN 0-87666-625-X, P-901). TFH Pubns.
Miller, Alan R. Eighty-Eighty - ZEighty Assembly Language: Techniques for Improved Programming. 224p. 1980. pap. text ed. 8.95 (ISBN 0-471-08124-8). Wiley.
Miller, Alan S. A Planet to Choose. 192p. (Orig.). 1978. pap. 6.95 (ISBN 0-8298-0348-3). Pilgrim NY.
Miller, Albert & Thompson, Jack. Elements of Meteorology. 3rd ed. 1979. text ed. 18.95 (ISBN 0-675-08293-5); instructor's manual 3.95 (ISBN 0-686-67289-5). Merrill.
Miller, Albert G. Backward Beasts. (ABC Serendipity Ser). (gr. 2-6). 1973. pap. 4.35 o.p. (ISBN 0-8372-0819-X). Bowmar-Noble.
--Mark Twain in Love. LC 73-5243. (gr. 7-9). 1973. 5.95 o.p. (ISBN 0-15-230295-6, HJ). HarBraceJ.
--Our Friends the ABC's. (ABC Serendipity Ser). (gr. 2-6). 1973. 4.35 o.p. (ISBN 0-8372-0820-3). Bowmar-Noble.
--Talking Letters. (ABC Serendipity Ser). (Illus.). (gr. 2-6). 1973. 6.57 o.p. (ISBN 0-8372-0824-6); pap. 4.35 o.p. (ISBN 0-685-28631-2). Bowmar-Noble.
--Twenty-Six Riddles from A to Z. (ABC Serendipity Ser). (gr. 2-6). 1973. 6.57 o.p. (ISBN 0-8372-0821-1); pap. 4.35 o.p. (ISBN 0-686-66687-9). Bowmar-Noble.
--Where Did That Word Come from. (ABC Serendipity Ser). (Illus.). (gr. 2-6). 1973. 6.57 o.p. (ISBN 0-8372-1815-2); pap. 4.35 o.p. (ISBN 0-8372-0823-8). Bowmar-Noble.
Miller, Albert G., ed. Pop-up Aladdin & the Wonderful Lamp. (Pop-up Classics Ser.: No. 7). (Illus.). 1970. 3.95 o.p. (ISBN 0-394-81105-4, BYR). Random.
--Pop-up Hide & Seek: A Child's First Counting Book. (Pop-up Books Ser). (Illus.). (ps). 1966. 4.95 o.p. (ISBN 0-394-81590-4, BYR). Random.
--Pop-up Story of the Nativity. (Pop-up Books Ser). (Illus.). 1970. 3.95 o.p. (ISBN 0-394-80498-8, BYR). Random.
Miller, Albert J. Confrontation, Conflict & Dissent: A Bibliography of a Decade of Controversy, Nineteen Sixty to Nineteen Seventy. LC 78-189440. 1972. 20.50 (ISBN 0-8108-0490-5). Scarecrow.
Miller, Albert J. & Acri, Michael J. Death: A Bibliographical Guide. LC 77-1205. 1977. 19.50 (ISBN 0-8108-1025-5). Scarecrow.
Miller, Alfred E. Challenges & Strategies in Health: The Coming of Post-Clinical Medicine. (Health, Medicine, & Society Ser.). 504p. 1981. 27.50 (ISBN 0-471-60409-7, Pub. by Wiley-Interscience). Wiley.
Miller, Alfred E. & Miller, Maria G. Options in Health & Health Care. (Health Medicine & Society Ser.). 512p. 1981. 27.50 (ISBN 0-471-60409-7, Pub. by Wiley-Interscience). Wiley.
Miller, Alfred J. West of Alfred Jacob Miller. rev. & enl. ed. Ross, Marvin C., ed. (Illus.). 1968. 37.50 o.p. (ISBN 0-8061-0229-2). U of Okla Pr.
Miller, Alice. Prisoners of Childhood. LC 80-50535. 1981. 11.95 (ISBN 0-465-06347-0). Basic.
Miller, Alice P. Little Store on the Corner. (Illus.). (gr. k-3). 1974. pap. 1.25 (ISBN 0-590-04839-2, Schol Pap); pap. 3.50 bk. & record (ISBN 0-590-20740-7). Schol Bk Serv.
Miller, Alice V. Homespun Yarns of a Country Schoolmaster. 3.50 o.p. (ISBN 0-685-48821-7). Nortex Pr.
Miller, Allan. Beginning Piano for Adults. 1970. 5.95 o.s.i. (ISBN 0-02-584810-0). Macmillan.
Miller, Allan L., jt. auth. see Ferguson, Robert J., Jr.
Miller, Allan L., jt. auth. see Ferguson, Robert T., Jr.
Miller, Allen O. & Osterhaven, M. Eugene, trs. Heidelberg Catechism. LC 62-20891. 1963. 2.25 (ISBN 0-8298-0059-X); pap. 2.00 (ISBN 0-8298-0060-3). Pilgrim NY.
Miller, Amos. Abraham: Friend of God. LC 73-6406. 1973. 7.95x o.p. (ISBN 0-685-32288-2). Jonathan David.
Miller, Amos C. Sir Richard Grenville of the Civil War. (Illus.). 215p. 1979. 16.50x (ISBN 0-8476-6160-1). Rowman.
Miller, Amy B. & Fuller, Persis. Best of Shaker Cooking. (Illus.). 1970. 10.00 o.s.i. (ISBN 0-02-584820-8). Macmillan.
--The Best of Shaker Cooking. (Illus.). 480p. 1976. pap. 9.95 (ISBN 0-02-009810-3, Collier). Macmillan.
Miller, Andrew S. Marital Expectations: What to Do When They Go Unmet. 125p. (Orig.). 1980. pap. 3.50 (ISBN 0-937442-00-3). Bibl Based Develop.
Miller, Anita, ed. see Equal Rights Amendment Project.
Miller, Ann, jt. auth. see Cooke, R. Gordon.
Miller, Ann F., ed. College in Dispersion: Women at Bryn Mawr, 1896-1975. LC 76-2735. (Special Studies in Higher Education Ser). 1976. 23.50x (ISBN 0-89158-040-9). Westview.
Miller, Anne. Finding Career Alternatives for Teachers: A Step-by-Step Guide. 84p. (Orig.). 1979. pap. 9.95 (ISBN 0-9604134-0-5). Apple Pub Co.
Miller, Arthur. After the Fall. (Plays Ser). 1968. pap. 2.50 o.p. (ISBN 0-670-00231-3). Penguin.
--The American Clock: A Mural for Theatre. 144p. 1981. 10.95 (ISBN 0-670-11728-5). Viking Pr.
--Arthur Miller's Collected Plays, Vol. II. LC 80-52008. 704p. 1981. 17.95 (ISBN 0-670-13598-4). Viking Pr.
--Crucible: Text & Criticism. Weales, Gerald, ed. LC 73-119776. (Critical Library: No. 7). 1977. pap. 5.50 (ISBN 0-14-015507-4). Penguin.
--Death of a Salesman. (Illus.). 1949. 10.00 (ISBN 0-670-26154-8). Viking Pr.
--Death of a Salesman: Special Illustrated Edition. LC 80-53290. (Illus.). 144p. 1981. 15.00 (ISBN 0-670-26156-4) (ISBN 0-670-26157-2). Viking Pr.
--Final Edition. 384p. (Orig.). 1981. pap. 2.75 (ISBN 0-523-41170-7). Pinnacle Bks.
--Portable Arthur Miller. Clurman, Harold, ed. LC 77-119777. (Viking Portable Library: No. 71). 1977. pap. 5.95 (ISBN 0-14-015071-4). Penguin.
--A View from the Bridge. (Plays Ser.). 1977. pap. 2.95 (ISBN 0-14-048135-4). Penguin.
Miller, Arthur & Morath, Inge. Chinese Encounters. (Illus.). 256p. 1981. pap. 9.95 (ISBN 0-14-005781-1). Penguin.
Miller, Arthur see Watson, E. Bradlee & Pressey, Benfield.
Miller, Arthur C., jt. auth. see Balshofer, Fred J.
Miller, Arthur G., et al. Physical Education: Teaching Human Movement in the Elementary Schools. (Illus.). 420p. 1974. 16.95 (ISBN 0-13-668301-0). P-H.
Miller, Arthur S. Democratic Dictatorship: The Emergent Constitution of Control. LC 80-25424. (Contributions in American Studies: No. 54). 312p. 1981. lib. bdg. 29.95 (ISBN 0-313-22836-1, MDD/). Greenwood.
--The Modern Corporate State: Private Governments & the American Constitution. LC 75-35350. (Contributions in American Studies: No. 23). 320p. 1976. lib. bdg. 17.95 (ISBN 0-8371-8589-0, MCS/). Greenwood.
Miller, Augustus T., jt. auth. see Morehouse, Laurence E.
Miller, B. Drifters. 1972. pap. 1.95 o.s.i. (ISBN 0-02-061320-2, Collier). Macmillan.
--Organic Chemistry: The Basis of Life. 1980. 19.95 (ISBN 0-8053-7071-4); instrs guide with test items 3.95 (ISBN 0-8053-7072-2); write for info. study guide (ISBN 0-8053-7073-0). A-W.
Miller, Barbara, jt. auth. see Conn, Charles P.
Miller, Barbara S., jt. auth. see Gordon, Leonard A.
Miller, Barbara S., tr. Bhartrihari: Poems. (Bilingual, Orig). 1967. 15.00x (ISBN 0-231-02999-3). Columbia U Pr.
Miller, Barbara S., tr. from Sanskrit. The Hermit & the Love-Thief. 1978. 15.00 (ISBN 0-231-04644-8); pap. 6.00x (ISBN 0-231-04645-6). Columbia U Pr.
Miller, Barbara S., tr. Phantasies of a Love-Thief: The Caurapancasika Attributed to Bilhana. LC 77-122947. (Studies in Oriental Culture: No. 6). 1971. 17.50x (ISBN 0-231-03451-2). Columbia U Pr.
Miller, Barbara S., tr. see Pizarro, Agueda.
Miller, Barry. Alphabet World. LC 77-127470. (Illus.). (gr. k-1). 1971. 6.95 o.s.i. (ISBN 0-02-766970-X). Macmillan.
Miller, Basil. Charles G. Finney. 1969. pap. 1.95 (ISBN 0-87123-061-5, 200061). Bethany Fell.
--George Mueller: Man of Faith. 160p. 1972. pap. 2.25 (ISBN 0-87123-182-4, 200182). Bethany Fell.
--John Wesley. 1969. pap. 2.25 (ISBN 0-87123-272-3, 200272). Bethany Fell.
Miller, Bernard. Organic Chemistry. 1980. 16.95 (ISBN 0-8053-7071-4); study guide 6.95 (ISBN 0-8053-7073-0). Benjamin Cummings.
Miller, Bertha M. & Field, Elinor W., eds. Caldecott Medal Books, 1938-1957. LC 57-11582. (Illus.). 1957. 17.00 (ISBN 0-87675-001-3). Horn Bk.
--Newbery Medal Books, 1922-1955. LC 55-13968. (Illus.). 1955. 17.00 (ISBN 0-87675-000-5). Horn Bk.
Miller, Bonnie N. Look What I Wrote. LC 79-67864. 1980. 8.95 (ISBN 0-934588-01-5). Ranger Assocs.
Miller, Brown. Hiroshima Flows Through Us. LC 77-22290. 1977. pap. 2.50x o.p. (ISBN 0-916156-23-0); pap. 12.50x signed ed (ISBN 0-916156-29-X). Cherry Valley.
Miller, Bruce E. Teaching the Art of Literature. (Orig.). 1980. pap. 5.50 (ISBN 0-8141-5192-2, 51922). NCTE.
Miller, Bruce R. The Philosophy of Schopenhauer in Dramatic Representational Expressions. (Illus.). 101p. 1981. 19.75 (ISBN 0-89266-279-4). Am Classical Coll Pr.
Miller, C. George, et al. Cerre Colorade: A Case Study of the Role of Canadian Crown Corporations in Foreign Mineral Development. 60p. (Orig.). 1978. pap. text ed. 3.00x (ISBN 0-686-63142-0, Pub. by Ctr Resource Stud Canada). Renouf.
Miller, C. J. Evangelism & Your Church. 1980. pap. 2.95 (ISBN 0-87552-290-4). Presby & Reformed.
Miller, C. John. Repentance & Twentieth-Century Man. (Orig.). 1980. pap. 1.95 (ISBN 0-87508-334-X). Chr Lit.
Miller, C. Leslie. All About Angels. 1976. pap. 1.25 (ISBN 0-89129-233-0). Jove Pubns.
Miller, Calvin. Once Upon a Tree. 1978. pap. 3.95 (ISBN 0-8010-6050-8). Baker Bk.
Miller, Carey. All About Monsters. LC 77-17933. (World of the Unknown). (Illus.). (gr. 4-5). 1978. PLB 6.95 (ISBN 0-88436-467-4). EMC.
Miller, Carl, jt. auth. see Bobri, Vladimir.
Miller, Carl, compiled by. Rockabye Baby: Lullabies from Many Nations & Peoples. (gr. k-8). 1975. pap. 3.50 (ISBN 0-935738-04-5, 5035). US Comm Unicef.
Miller, Carl, ed. Sing Children Sing. (gr. k up). 1972. pap. 3.50 (ISBN 0-935738-05-3, 5027). US Comm UNICEF.
Miller, Carol L., et al. Self-Assessment of Current Knowledge in Maternity Nursing. 1975. spiral bdg. 8.00 o.p. (ISBN 0-87488-299-0). Med Exam.
Miller, Carolyn H. Illustrated T.V. Dictionary. LC 78-73761. (Illustrated Dictionaries Ser.). (Illus.). (gr. 4 up). 1980. PLB 6.79 (ISBN 0-8178-6220-X). Harvey.
Miller, Charles. Battle for the Bundu: The First World War in East Africa. LC 73-14013. (Illus.). 380p. 1974. 9.95 o.s.i. (ISBN 0-02-584930-1). Macmillan.
--Khyber: The Story of an Imperial Migraine. LC 77-6382. (Illus.). 1977. 12.95 o.s.i. (ISBN 0-02-584860-7). Macmillan.
Miller, Charles A. The Official & Political Manual of the State of Tennessee. LC 73-22440. (Illus.). 380p. 1974. Repr. of 1890 ed. 18.00 (ISBN 0-87152-162-8). Reprint.
Miller, Charles B. How to Organize & Maintain an Efficient Hospital Housekeeping Department. (Illus.). 142p. (Orig.). 1980. pap. 18.75 (ISBN 0-87258-290-6, 1440). Am Hospital.
Miller, Charles D. & Heeren, Vern E. Mathematical Ideas. 3rd ed. 1978. 16.59x (ISBN 0-673-15090-9). Scott F.
--Mathematics: An Everyday Experience. 2nd ed. 1980. text ed. 16.95x (ISBN 0-673-15279-0). Scott F.
Miller, Charles D. & Lial, Margaret L. Intermediate Algebra: A Text-Workbook. 1980. pap. text ed. 14.95x (ISBN 0-673-15271-5). Scott F.
Miller, Charles D. & Salzman, Stanley A. Arithmetic: A Text-Workbook. 1981. pap. text ed. 13.95x (ISBN 0-673-15274-X). Scott F.
--Business Mathematics: A Programmed Approach, Book 1. 1980. pap. text ed. 9.95x (ISBN 0-673-15347-9). Scott F.
Miller, Charles D., jt. auth. see Lial, Margaret A.
Miller, Charles D., jt. auth. see Lial, Margaret L.
Miller, Charles D., jt. auth. see Salzman, Stanley A.
Miller, Christian. Daisy, Daisy: A Journey Across America on a Bicycle. LC 80-2946. 192p. 1981. 11.95 (ISBN 0-385-17475-6). Doubleday.
Miller, Christopher R. Stroke of Luck. (Sportellers Ser.). (Illus.). 64p. (gr. 5 up). 1981. PLB 7.95 (ISBN 0-516-02268-7). Childrens.
Miller, Chuck. Now That I'm a Christian, Vol. 1. (Orig.). 1974. pap. 3.95 (ISBN 0-8307-0326-8, 52-019-18). Regal.
--Now That I'm a Christian, Vol. 2. (Orig.). 1976. pap. 2.75 (ISBN 0-8307-0327-6, 52-015-00). Regal.
Miller, Chuck, jt. ed. see Underhill, Tim.
Miller, Clara B. Crying Heart. 1965. pap. 3.50 (ISBN 0-8024-3813-X). Moody.
--Katie. 288p. 1974. pap. 2.95 (ISBN 0-8024-4524-1). Moody.
Miller, Constance. Technical & Cultural Prerequisites for the Invention of Printing in China & the West. (Asian Library Ser.: No. 21). 1980. write for info. (ISBN 0-89644-622-0). Chinese Materials.
Miller, D. A. Narrative & Its Discontents: Problems of Closure in the Traditional Novel. LC 80-8565. 320p. 1981. 20.00x (ISBN 0-691-06459-8). Princeton U Pr.
Miller, D. L., jt. auth. see Farmer, R. D.
Miller, D. N. Motorcycles. (Illus.). text ed. 9.95x o.p. (ISBN 0-8464-0646-2). Beekman Pubs.
Miller, Dallas. Passage West. 1980. pap. 2.75 (ISBN 0-380-50278-X, 50278). Avon.
Miller, Dana, jt. auth. see Liebers, Arthur.
Miller, David. Ophthalmology: The Essentials. (Illus.). 1979. 16.00x (ISBN 0-89289-325-7). HM Prof Med Div.
--A Song of Love. Date not set. 5.95 (ISBN 0-533-04741-2). Vantage.
Miller, David & Benedek, George. Intraocular Light Scattering: Theory & Clinical Application. (Illus.). 132p. 1973. text ed. 11.75 (ISBN 0-398-02665-3). C C Thomas.
Miller, David H. The Alaska Treaty. (Materials for the Study of Alaska History Ser.: No. 18). (Illus.). 1981. 16.50x (ISBN 0-919642-94-2). Limestone Pr.
--Energy at the Surface of the Earth. 1981. 49.50 (ISBN 0-12-497150-4). Acad Pr.
Miller, David M. Frank Herbert. (Starmont Reader's Guide: No. 5). 80p. 1981. Repr. lib. bdg. 9.95x (ISBN 0-89370-036-3). Borgo Pr.

--John Milton: Poetry. (English Authors Ser.: No. 242). 1978. 12.50 (ISBN 0-8057-6724-X). Twayne.

--Reader's Guide to Frank Herbert. Schlobin, Roger C., ed. LC 80-20880. (Reader's Guides to Contemporary Science Fiction & Fantasy Author Ser.: Vol. 5). (Illus., Orig.). 1980. pap. text ed. 3.95 (ISBN 0-916732-07-X). Starmont Hse.

--Understanding the Metric System: A Programed Text. new ed. (gr. 9-12). 1979. pap. text ed. 4.80 (ISBN 0-205-06581-3, 566581-7); tchrs'. guide 2.40 (ISBN 0-205-06582-1, 566582-5). Allyn.

Miller, David W. Waste Disposal Effects on Ground Water. LC 78-65680. (Illus.). 512p. 1980. pap. 16.00x (ISBN 0-912722-01-0). Prem Press.

Miller, David W. & Starr, Martin K. Executive Decisions & Operations Research. 2nd ed. 1969. ref. ed. 21.00 (ISBN 0-13-294538-X). P-H.

--Structure of Human Decisions. (Orig.). 1967. pap. text ed. 10.95 (ISBN 0-13-854687-8). P-H.

Miller, Delbert C. Handbook of Research Design & Social Measurement. 3rd ed. LC 77-128. 1977. pap. 12.95x (ISBN 0-582-29007-4, Pub. by MacKay). Longman.

Miller, Delmas F., jt. auth. see Trump, J. Lloyd.

Miller, Denis R. & Pearson, Howard A. Smith's Blood Diseases of Infancy & Childhood. 4th ed. LC 78-7023. 1978. pap. text ed. 57.50 (ISBN 0-8016-4691-X). Mosby.

Miller, Dick. Triumphant Journey. LC 80-10834. (Illus.). 272p. 1980. 13.95 (ISBN 0-03-045331-3). HR&W.

Miller, Don C., jt. auth. see Cohen, Stan B.

Miller, Donald B. Careers, Eighty - Eighty-One: A Human Resource Consultants' Views of Career Management & a Guide to 600 Current Books & Articles. (Orig.). 1980. pap. 11.95 (ISBN 0-930918-02-9). Vitality Assocs.

--Careers Nineteen Seventy-Nine: A Guide to Books & Information About Career Management & Planning. 1978. pap. 5.00 o.p. (ISBN 0-930918-01-0). Vitality Assocs.

--Personal Vitality. LC 76-55638. (Illus.). 1977. text ed. 12.95 (ISBN 0-201-04739-X); wkbk. 4.50 (ISBN 0-201-04738-1). A-W.

--Twice Turned Tales. LC 77-88730. (Illus.). 1977. pap. 3.50 o.p. (ISBN 0-930918-00-2). Vitality Assocs.

--Working with People: Human Resource Management in Action. LC 79-16914. 1979. pap. 11.95 (ISBN 0-8436-0776-9). CBI Pub.

Miller, Donald C. Ghost Towns of the Southwest: Arizona, New Mexico & Utah. (Western Ghost Town Ser.). 1980. 14.95 (ISBN 0-87108-565-8). Pruett.

Miller, Donald E. Awareness & Flexibility: The Keys to Successful Credit Judgment. 32p. 1974. pap. 1.50 (ISBN 0-934914-14-1). NACM.

--The Case for Liberal Christianity. LC 80-8355. 160p. 1980. 9.95 (ISBN 0-06-065753-7). Har-Row.

Miller, Donald E. & Relkin, Donald B. Improving Credit Practice. LC 70-119384. 1971. 24.95 o.p. (ISBN 0-8144-5222-1). Am Mgmt.

Miller, Donald E., et al. Using Biblical Simulations, Vol. 2. 224p. (Orig.). 1975. pap. 6.95 (ISBN 0-8170-0668-0). Judson.

--Using Biblical Simulations. LC 72-9569. 224p. (Orig.). 1973. pap. 6.95 (ISBN 0-8170-0580-3). Judson.

Miller, Dorcas S. The Maine Coast: A Nature Lover's Guide. LC 79-10290. (Illus.). 192p. 1978. lib. bdg. 10.25 o.p. (ISBN 0-914788-12-4). East Woods.

--The New Healthy Trail Food Book. rev. ed. LC 79-28172. (Orig.). 1980. lib. bdg. 7.25 o.p. (ISBN 0-914788-25-6). East Woods.

Miller, Dorothy. Runaways, Illegal Aliens in Their Own Land: Implications for Service. LC 79-11682. (Praeger Special Studies Ser.). 224p. 1980. 22.95 (ISBN 0-03-051051-1). Praeger.

Miller, Douglas T. Birth of Modern America, 1820-1850. LC 79-114173. (Illus.). 1970. pap. 7.50 (ISBN 0-672-63509-7). Pegasus.

Miller, Dulcy B. & Barry, Jane T. Nursing Home Organization & Operation. LC 79-183. (Illus.). 1979. text ed. 19.95 (ISBN 0-8436-0782-3). CBI Pub.

Miller, E. Introduction to Cultural Anthropology. 1979. pap. 13.95 (ISBN 0-13-480236-5); study guide & wkbk. 5.95 (ISBN 0-13-480244-6). P-H.

Miller, E. & Coffey, P. Wild Blue U. 1972. 7.95 o.s.i. (ISBN 0-02-584840-2). Macmillan.

--Wild Blue U: The Story of the United States Air Force Academy. 192p. 1972. pap. 3.95 o.s.i. (ISBN 0-02-035100-3, Collier). Macmillan.

Miller, E. & Weitz, C. Introduction to Anthropology. 1979. 17.95 (ISBN 0-13-478008-6); study guide 6.95 (ISBN 0-13-478016-7). P-H.

Miller, E., ed. Foundations of Child Psychiatry. 1968. 82.00 (ISBN 0-08-011826-7). Pergamon.

Miller, E. Eugene. Jail Management. LC 76-43590. 1978. 18.95 (ISBN 0-669-00959-8). Lexington Bks.

Miller, E. Eugene & Montilla, Robert. Corrections in the Community: Success Models in Correctional Reform. 1977. text ed. 14.95 (ISBN 0-87909-174-6); pap. text ed. 10.95 (ISBN 0-87909-173-8). Reston.

Miller, E. J. & Gwynne, G. V. Life Apart. LC 72-304977. xii, 240p. 1972. 9.75 o.p. (ISBN 0-422-73910-3). Lippincott.

Miller, Edgar G., Jr. American Antique Furntire, 2 vols. (Illus.). Set. 32.50 (ISBN 0-8446-2589-2). Peter Smith.

Miller, Edmund. Drudgerie Divine: The Rhetoric of God & Man in George Herbert. (SSEL Elizabethan Studies: No. 84). 1980. pap. text ed. 25.00x (ISBN 0-391-01904-X). Humanities.

--Exercises in Style. 68p. 1980. pap. 4.00x (ISBN 0-9600486-3-4). Edmund Miller.

Miller, Edna. Mousekin Takes a Trip. (Illus.). (gr. k-3). 1976. 5.95 (ISBN 0-13-604363-1); pap. 1.95 (ISBN 0-13-604348-8). P-H.

--Mousekin's ABC's. (gr. 1-4). 1972. PLB 6.95 (ISBN 0-13-604389-5). P-H.

--Mousekin's Christmas Eve. (Illus.). (gr. k-3). 1965. PLB 6.95 (ISBN 0-13-604454-9); pap. 1.95 (ISBN 0-13-604447-6). P-H.

--Mousekin's Close Call. LC 77-27571. (Illus.). (ps-2). 1978. 6.95g (ISBN 0-13-604207-4); pap. 1.95 (ISBN 0-13-604207-4). P-H.

--Mousekin's Family. (Illus.). (gr. k-3). 1969. PLB 6.95 (ISBN 0-13-604462-X); pap. 1.95 (ISBN 0-13-604157-4). P-H.

--Mousekin's Golden House. (gr. k-3). 1964. PLB 6.95 (ISBN 0-13-604421-2); pap. 1.95 (ISBN 0-13-604439-5). P-H.

Miller, Edward. Prince of Librarians: The Life & Times of Antonio Panizzi of the British Museum. LC 67-26123. (Illus.). 356p. 1967. 15.00x (ISBN 0-8214-0030-4). Ohio U Pr.

--That Noble Cabinet: A History of the British Museum. LC 73-85452. (Illus.). 400p. 1974. 18.00x (ISBN 0-8214-0139-4). Ohio U Pr.

Miller, Edward & Hatcher, John. Medieval England: Rural Society & Economic Change 1086-1348. LC 77-21445. (A Social & Economic History of England Ser.). 1979. text ed. 26.00x (ISBN 0-582-48218-6); pap. text ed. 13.95 (ISBN 0-582-48547-9). Longman.

Miller, Edward B. An Administrative Appraisal of the NLRB. 3rd ed. 165p. 1980. pap. 10.50 (ISBN 0-89546-013-0). Indus Res Unit-Wharton.

Miller, Edward J., jt. ed. see Wolensky, Robert P.

Miller, Edwin. Seventeen Interviews: Film Stars & Superstars. (Illus.). (gr. 7 up). 1970. 6.95 o.s.i. (ISBN 0-02-584830-5). Macmillan.

Miller, Edwin, et al. Management of Human Resources: Newer Approaches. (Illus.). 1980. pap. text ed. 13.95 (ISBN 0-13-549410-9). P-H.

Miller, Edwin H., ed. see Whitman, Walt.

Miller, Elizabeth & Cohen, Jane. Cat & Dog & the Mixed-up Week. (ps). 1980. 2.95 (ISBN 0-531-03529-8); PLB 5.95 (ISBN 0-531-04123-9). Watts.

--Cat & Dog Give a Party. (ps). 1980. 2.95 (ISBN 0-531-03527-1); PLB 5.95 (ISBN 0-531-04126-3). Watts.

--Cat & Dog Have a Contest. (ps). 1980. 2.95 (ISBN 0-531-03528-X); PLB 5.95 (ISBN 0-531-04125-5). Watts.

--Cat & Dog Raise the Roof. (ps). 1980. 2.95 (ISBN 0-531-03530-1); PLB 5.95 (ISBN 0-531-04124-7). Watts.

--Cat & Dog Take a Trip. (ps). 2.95 (ISBN 0-531-03531-X); PLB 5.95 (ISBN 0-531-04127-1). Watts.

Miller, Ella M. I Am a Woman. (Orig.). 1967. pap. 1.50 (ISBN 0-8024-3925-X). Moody.

Miller, Ellen, jt. auth. see Kellar, Jane C.

Miller, Elwood L. Accounting Problems of Multinational Enterprises. LC 78-20273. (Illus.). 1979. 21.00 (ISBN 0-669-02712-X). Lexington Bks.

Miller, Emery P. & Taft, David D., eds. Fundamentals of Powder Coating. new ed. (Illus.). 287p. 1974. 10.00x (ISBN 0-87263-033-1). SME.

Miller, Eric J., ed. Task & Organization. LC 75-12606. (Wiley Series Individuals, Groups & Organizations). 480p. 1976. 41.25 (ISBN 0-471-60605-7, Pub. by Wiley-Interscience). Wiley.

Miller, Ernest C. This Was Early Oil: Contemporary Accounts of the Growing Petroleum Industry, 1848-1885. 211p. (Orig.). 1968. 7.00 (ISBN 0-911124-15-2); pap. 4.00 (ISBN 0-911124-14-4). Pa Hist & Mus.

Miller, Ernest L. Removable Partial Prosthodontics. 21.00 o.p. (ISBN 0-683-05989-0). Williams & Wilkins.

Miller, Ernest L. & Grasso, Joseph E. Removable Partial Prosthodontics. 2nd ed. 440p. 1981. write for info. (5990-4). Williams & Wilkins.

Miller, Ernestine. The Art of Advertising. (Illus.). 64p. 1980. pap. 10.95 (ISBN 0-312-05416-5). St Martin.

Miller, Ethel B., tr. see Institut Francais De Pertrole.

Miller, Eugene. Barron's Guide to Graduate Business Schools: Eastern Edition. rev. ed. LC 80-12843. 1980. pap. text ed. 5.95 (ISBN 0-8120-2068-5). Barron.

Miller, Evelyn. How to Raise & Train a Boston Terrier. (Illus.). pap. 2.00 (ISBN 0-87666-251-3, DS1005). TFH Pubns.

--How to Raise & Train a Bulldog. (Illus.). pap. 2.00 (ISBN 0-87666-259-9, DS1007). TFH Pubns.

--How to Raise & Train a Cocker Spaniel. pap. 2.00 (ISBN 0-87666-269-6, DS1009). TFH Pubns.

--How to Raise & Train a Fox Terrier. (Illus.). pap. 2.00 (ISBN 0-87666-294-7, DS1038). TFH Pubns.

--How to Raise & Train a Golden Retriever. (Illus.). pap. 2.00 (ISBN 0-87666-306-4, DS1018). TFH Pubns.

--How to Raise & Train a Miniature Pinscher. (Illus.). pap. 2.00 (ISBN 0-87666-337-4, DS1039). TFH Pubns.

--How to Raise & Train a Poodle. pap. 2.00 (ISBN 0-87666-355-2, DS1030). TFH Pubns.

--How to Raise & Train a Pug. (Illus.). pap. 2.00 (ISBN 0-87666-364-1, DS1031). TFH Pubns.

--How to Raise & Train a Shetland Sheepdog. (Illus.). pap. 2.00 (ISBN 0-87666-386-2, DS1033). TFH Pubns.

--How to Raise & Train an Airedale. (Illus.). pap. 2.00 (ISBN 0-87666-233-5, DS1002). TFH Pubns.

Miller, F. & Berman, P. Multi-Hull Racing: The Hobie Cats & Other Catamarans. 3rd rev. ed. (Illus.). 1981. pap. 14.95 (ISBN 0-89404-036-7). Aztex.

Miller, Frank O. Minobe Tatsukichi: Interpreter of Constitutionalism in Japan. (Center for Japanese & Korean Studies, UC Berkeley). 1965. 23.50x (ISBN 0-520-00865-0). U of Cal Pr.

Miller, Frank W. Prosecution: The Decision to Charge a Suspect with a Crime. 366p. 1970. pap. 6.95 (ISBN 0-316-57346-9). Little.

Miller, Frank W., et al. Guidance: Principles & Services. 3rd ed. (Guidance Ser.). 1977. text ed. 18.95 (ISBN 0-675-08461-X). Merrill.

Miller, Fred. Passport to Better Health Through Eating. Date not set. pap. 3.95 (ISBN 0-89404-028-6). Aztex. Postponed.

Miller, Fred D. & Smith, Nicholas D., eds. Thought Probes: Philosophy Through Science Fiction. (Illus.). 368p. 1981. text ed. 11.95 (ISBN 0-13-920041-X). P-H.

Miller Freeman Publications, Inc. Maintenance Methods for the Pulp & Paper Industry. Coleman, Matthew, ed. LC 80-82934. (Pulp & Paper Focus Bk.). (Illus.). 192p. 1980. pap. 29.50 (ISBN 0-87930-088-4). Miller Freeman.

Miller, G. A., jt. auth. see Grusky, O.

Miller, G. R. & Nicholson, H. E. Communication Inquiry: A Perspective on a Process or, From Questions to Answers. 1976. 6.50 (ISBN 0-201-04746-2). A-W.

Miller, G. Tyler. Chemistry: A Basic Introduction. 1978. text ed. 18.95x o.p. (ISBN 0-534-00527-6); study guide 6.95x o.p. (ISBN 0-534-00623-X); lab manual 8.95x o.p. (ISBN 0-534-00529-2). Wadsworth Pub.

Miller, G. Tyler, Jr. Chemistry: A Basic Introduction. 2nd ed. 560p. 1980. text ed. 18.95x (ISBN 0-534-00878-X). Wadsworth Pub.

--Chemistry: A Contemporary Approach. 1976. text ed. 19.95x (ISBN 0-534-00456-3). Wadsworth Pub.

--Energy & Environment: The Four Energy Crises. 2nd ed. 208p. 1980. pap. text ed. 7.95x (ISBN 0-534-00836-4). Wadsworth Pub.

--Energy & Environment: The Four Energy Crises. 1975. pap. text ed. 5.95x o.p. (ISBN 0-534-00407-5). Wadsworth Pub.

--Living in the Environment. 2nd ed. 1979. text ed. 19.95x (ISBN 0-534-00684-1). Wadsworth Pub.

Miller, Gabriel. Daniel Fuchs. (United States Authors Ser.: No. 333). 1979. lib. bdg. 14.95 (ISBN 0-8057-7240-5). Twayne.

Miller, Gail & Tompkins, Sandra. Kidnapped at Chowchilla. 1977. pap. 1.95 o.p. (ISBN 0-88270-217-3). Logos.

Miller, Gary. Linear Circuits for Electronics Technology. (Illus.). 368p. 1974. ref. ed. 19.95 (ISBN 0-13-536698-4). P-H.

Miller, Gary A. & Borgen, C. Winston. Professional Selling-Inside & Out. LC 77-83518. 1979. pap. text ed. 8.80 (ISBN 0-8273-1638-0); instructor's guide 1.60 (ISBN 0-8273-1639-9). Delmar.

Miller, Gary J. Cities by Contract: The Politics of Municipal Incorporation. 256p. 1981. text ed. 22.50x (ISBN 0-262-13164-1). MIT Pr.

Miller, Gene E. The Art of Gun Collecting. 1981. 8.95 (ISBN 0-8062-1599-2). Carlton.

Miller, Geoffrey. The Black Glove. LC 80-54087. 276p. 1981. 12.95 (ISBN 0-670-17166-2). Viking Pr.

Miller, George A. Language & Speech. LC 80-27018. (Illus.). 1981. text ed. price not set (ISBN 0-7167-1297-0); pap. text ed. price not set (ISBN 0-7167-1298-9). W H Freeman.

Miller, George A., jt. ed. see Grusky, Oscar.

Miller, George B., Jr., et al, eds. Property Library: An Annotated Bibliography Based on the Batchelder-McPharlin Collection at the University of New Mexico. LC 80-23474. 200p. 1981. lib. bdg. 29.95 (ISBN 0-313-21359-3, HPL). Greenwood.

--Puppetry Library: An Annotated Bibliography Based on the Batchelder-McPharlin Collection at the University of New Mexico. Hannaford, William E. Jr. LC 80-23474, 200p. 1981. lib. bdg. 29.95 (ISBN 0-313-21359-3, HPL/). Greenwood.

Miller, George H. Railroads & the Granger Laws. LC 75-138059. 1971. 25.00x (ISBN 0-299-05870-0). U of Wis Pr.

Miller, George H. & Gidbeau, Kenneth W. Residential Real Estate Appraisal: An Introduction to Real Estate Appraising. (Illus.). 1980. text ed. 18.95 (ISBN 0-13-774521-4). P-H.

Miller, George H., et al. California Real Estate Appraisal: Residential Properties. 2nd ed. LC 77-5121. (Illus.). 1977. ref. ed. 18.95 (ISBN 0-13-112599-0). P-H.

Miller, George L. Primarily BASIC. 160p. (Orig.). pap. text ed. 9.95 (ISBN 0-8403-2177-5). Kendall-Hunt.

Miller, George W. Moral & Ethical Implications of Human Organ Transplants. (Illus.). 164p. 1971. 12.75 (ISBN 0-398-01311-X). C C Thomas.

Miller, Gerald R. An Introduction to Speech Communication. 2nd ed. LC 78-173982. 1972. pap. text ed. 3.95 (ISBN 0-672-61298-4, SC7). Bobbs.

Miller, Gerald R. & Fontes, Norman E. Videotape on Trial: A View from the Jury Box. LC 79-18774. (People & Communication Ser.: Vol. 7). (Illus.). 1979. 20.00x (ISBN 0-8039-0967-5); pap. 9.95x (ISBN 0-8039-0968-3). Sage.

Miller, Gerald R. & Simons, Herbert W., eds. Perspectives on Communication in Social Conflict. LC 74-3263. (Speech Communication Ser.). 1974. 16.95 (ISBN 0-13-660389-8). P-H.

Miller, Gerald R., jt. ed. see Roloff, Michael E.

Miller, Glenn. Quimica Elemental. (Span.). 1978. pap. text ed. 6.80 (ISBN 0-06-315625-3, IntlDept). Har-Row.

Miller, Glenn E., ed. Chicago Psychoanalytic Literature Index Nineteen Seventy-Five. 1975. write for info. Chicago Psych.

--Chicago Psychoanalytic Literature Index 1980: Chicago Institute for Psychoanalysis. 1981. lib. bdg. 50.00 (ISBN 0-918568-07-2). Chicago Psych.

Miller, Glenn E., ed. see Chicago Institute for Psychoanalysis.

Miller, Gordon. How to Choose a Career After College. 128p. 1981. 4.95 (ISBN 0-346-12443-3). Cornerstone.

--Life Choices. 176p. 1981. pap. 2.50 (ISBN 0-553-14154-6). Bantam.

Miller, Gordon W. Educational Opportunity & the Home. (Sociology of Education Ser). 1971. text ed. 3.50x (ISBN 0-582-32453-X); pap. text ed. 3.00x (ISBN 0-582-32454-8). Humanities.

Miller, Grady, jt. auth. see Cambanis, S.

Miller, Hannah E. Films in the Classroom: A Practical Guide. LC 78-21941. 1979. lib. bdg. 13.50 (ISBN 0-8108-1184-7). Scarecrow.

Miller, Harlan B. Arguments, Arrows, Trees, & Truth. 2nd ed. Schumway, Dwight, ed. (Illus.). 242p. (Orig.). 1980. pap. text ed. 8.65x (ISBN 0-89894-036-2). Advocate Pub Group.

Miller, Harry, jt. auth. see Howell, Yvonne.

Miller, Harry H. Speaking of Pets. 1962. pap. 0.95 o.s.i. (ISBN 0-02-063410-2, Collier). Macmillan.

Miller, Helen H. Historic Places Around the Outer Banks. (Illus., Orig.). 1974. pap. 2.95 o.p. (ISBN 0-685-52518-X). McNally.

Miller, Henry. Black Spring. 1964. pap. 2.95 (ISBN 0-394-17471-2, B61, BC). Grove.

--Cosmological Eye. LC 75-88729. 1969. 10.95 (ISBN 0-8112-0319-0); pap. 7.95 (ISBN 0-8112-0110-4, NDP109). New Directions.

--Joey: A Loving Portrait of Alfred Perles Together with Some Bizarre Episodes Relating to the Other Sex. (Book of Friends Ser.: Vol. 3). 1979. 8.95 (ISBN 0-88496-136-2); pap. 3.95 (ISBN 0-88496-137-0). Capra Pr.

--Medicine & Society. (Science & Engineering Policy Ser). 100p. 1973. text ed. 8.95x o.p. (ISBN 0-19-858321-4); pap. text ed. 3.00x o.p. (ISBN 0-19-858322-2). Oxford U Pr.

--The Rosy Crucifixion. Incl. Sexus; Plexus; Nexus. LC 80-8064. 1600p. 1980. box set 11.95 (ISBN 0-394-17774-6, B 449, BC). Grove.

--The Rosy Crucifixion: Sexus, Plexus, & Nexus, 3 vols. boxed set. LC 80-8064. 1600p. 1980. 10.95 (ISBN 0-394-17774-6). Grove.
--Stand Still Like the Hummingbird. LC 62-10408. 1967. pap. 4.95 (ISBN 0-8112-0322-0, NDP236). New Directions.
Miller, Henry, jt. auth. see Briar, Scott.
Miller, Henry A. Practical Wiring, 2 vols. 1969. Vol. 1. pap. 4.40 (ISBN 0-08-013288-X); Vol. 2. pap. 4.40 (ISBN 0-08-013403-3). Pergamon.
--Practical Wiring in SI Units, Vols. 1 & 2. rev. ed. LC 68-57882. (Pergamon International Library, Electrical Engineering Division). 108p. 1975. Vol. 1. 1975. pap. text ed. 5.75 (ISBN 0-08-019754-X); Vol. 2. 1976. pap. text ed. 5.75 (ISBN 0-08-020573-9). Pergamon.
Miller, Henry K., ed. see Fielding, Henry.
Miller, Herman P. Rich Man, Poor Man. LC 75-127609. (Apollo Eds.). (Illus.). 1971. pap. 3.95 o.s.i. (ISBN 0-8152-0289-X, A289-G, TYC-T). T Y Crowell.
Miller, Holly, jt. auth. see Ashpaugh, Bill.
Miller, Hope, jt. auth. see Miller, Orson.
Miller, Howard L. & Siegel, Paul S. Loving: A Psychological Approach. LC 72-3770. 224p. 1972. pap. 9.95x (ISBN 0-471-60390-2). Wiley.
Miller, Hugh M. Introduction to Music. (Illus., Orig.). 1978. pap. 4.50 (ISBN 0-06-460177-3, CO 177, COS). Har-Row.
Miller, I. & Freund, J. Probability & Statistics for Engineers. 2nd ed. (Illus.). 1977. 23.95 (ISBN 0-13-711945-3). P-H.
Miller, Ian. The Secret Art of Ian Miller. (Illus.). 96p. 1980. pap. 9.95 (ISBN 0-8256-9551-1, Quick Fox). Music Sales.
Miller, Irving. Israel: The Eternal Idea. 1955. 17.50x (ISBN 0-686-50046-6). Elliots Bks.
Miller, Isobel, jt. auth. see Hall, Kenneth.
Miller, J. Popery & Politics in England, 1660-1688. LC 73-79306. (Illus.). 278p. 1973. 41.50 (ISBN 0-521-20236-1). Cambridge U Pr.
Miller, J., jt. auth. see Riegel, R.
Miller, J. D. The World of States: Connected Essays. 1981. price not set (ISBN 0-312-89240-3). St Martin.
Miller, J. E., jt. auth. see Brown, E. K.
Miller, J. H., ed. Topics in Numerical Analysis III. 1978. 65.50 (ISBN 0-12-496953-4). Acad Pr.
Miller, J. H. & Reznikoff, W. S., eds. The Operon. 2nd ed. LC 80-15490. (Monograph Ser.: No. 7). (Illus.). 469p. (Orig.). 1980. pap. text ed. 18.00x (ISBN 0-87969-133-6). Cold Spring Harbor.
Miller, J. Hillis. The Disappearance of God: Five Nineteenth Century Writers. 392p. 1976. text ed. 17.50x (ISBN 0-674-21101-4). Harvard U Pr.
Miller, J. Lane, jt. auth. see Miller, Madeleine S.
Miller, J. P. Big & Little. LC 75-36464. (Illus.). 14p. (ps-1). 1975. 2.50 (ISBN 0-394-83239-6, BYR). Random.
--Tales from Aesop. LC 74-2539. (Picturebacks Ser). (Illus.). 32p. (ps-1). 1976. pap. 1.25 (ISBN 0-394-82812-7, BYR). Random.
Miller, J. Q., jt. auth. see Hartshorne, Hugh.
Miller, Jack E. Cooperative Education Workbook for Foodservice Hospitality. LC 78-23193. (Illus.). (gr. 11-12). 1978. 9.95 (ISBN 0-8436-2117-6). CBI Pub.
--Menu Pricing & Strategy. LC 79-25932. (Illus.). 1980. pap. 13.95 (ISBN 0-8436-2144-3). CBI Pub.
Miller, Jack S. The Healing Power of Grief. 1978. 7.95 (ISBN 0-8164-0402-X). Crossroad NY.
Miller, Jake C. The Black Presence in American Foreign Affairs. LC 78-69860. 1978. pap. text ed. 11.00 (ISBN 0-8191-0584-8). U Pr of Amer.
Miller, Jama. Theory of Finance. 1972. 21.95 (ISBN 0-03-086732-0). Dryden Pr.
Miller, James. Caithness. 112p. 1980. 14.75x (ISBN 0-7050-0068-0, Pub. by Skilton & Shaw England). State Mutual Bk.
--History & Human Existence: From Marx to Merleau-Ponty. LC 78-51747. 1979. 20.00x (ISBN 0-520-03667-0). U of Cal Pr.
Miller, James A. see Heat Transfer & Fluid Mechanics Institute.
Miller, James D., ed. Media Canada: Guidelines for Educators. 2nd rev. ed. 1970. 4.50 (ISBN 0-08-016508-7). Pergamon.
Miller, James E., Jr. F. Scott Fitzgerald: His Art & His Technique. LC 64-16900. (Gotham Library). 1964. pap. 5.00 (ISBN 0-8147-0309-7). NYU Pr.
--Walt Whitman. (U. S. Authors Ser.: No. 20). lib. bdg. 9.95 (ISBN 0-8057-0792-1). Twayne.
Miller, James E., Jr. & Slote, Bernice. The Dimensions of the Short Story: A Critical Anthology. 2nd ed. 598p. 1980. pap. text ed. 8.95 scp (ISBN 0-06-044457-6, HarpC); avail. Har-Row.
Miller, James E., Jr., ed. Myth & Method: Modern Theories of Fiction. LC 60-12941. 1960. pap. 2.45x (ISBN 0-8032-5134-3, BB 105, Bison). U of Nebr Pr.
Miller, James E., Jr., ed. see James, Henry.
Miller, James E., Jr., et al. Start with the Sun: Studies in the Whitman Traditon. LC 60-5493. 1963. pap. 1.95x (ISBN 0-8032-5135-1, BB 165, Bison). U of Nebr Pr.
Miller, James M. Separation Methods in Chemical Analysis. LC 74-13781. 320p. 1975. 26.00 (ISBN 0-471-60490-9, Pub. by Wiley-Interscience). Wiley.
Miller, James N. Spirochetes in Body Fluids & Tissues: Manual of Investigative Methods. (Illus.). 86p. 1971. pap. 7.75 (ISBN 0-398-01312-8). C C Thomas.
Miller, James W. Logic Workbook. 1958. 4.95x (ISBN 0-19-500988-6); pap. 3.95x teacher's key (ISBN 0-19-500989-4). Oxford U Pr.
Miller, James W., ed. Essays in Chinese Poetry. 1981. text ed. 18.00 (ISBN 0-89581-452-8, Asian Humanities). Lancaster-Miller.
Miller, James W., jt. ed. see Wagner, Marsha.
Miller, Jane. Many Junipers, Heartbeats. (Illus., Orig.). 1980. pap. 4.50 (ISBN 0-914278-29-0). Copper Beech.
Miller, Janeen, jt. auth. see Kueter, Roger A.
Miller, Jason. That Championship Season. LC 72-87905. 1972. pap. 3.95 o.p. (ISBN 0-689-10538-X). Atheneum.
Miller, Jeffrey, ed. see Burroughs, William.
Miller, Jeffrey, ed. see Clark, Tom.
Miller, Jeffrey, ed. see Dorn, Edward.
Miller, Jeffrey, ed. see Tinker, Carol.
Miller, Jeffrey C., jt. auth. see Lindley, Dennis V.
Miller, Jeffrey G., jt. auth. see Buffa, Elwood S.
Miller, Jeffrey H. Experiments in Molecular Genetics. LC 72-78914. (Illus.). 466p. 1972. 32.00 (ISBN 0-87969-106-9). Cold Spring Harbor.
Miller, Jerome K. U. S. Copyright Documents: An Annotated Collection for Use by Educators & Librarians. LC 80-24768. 360p. 1980. lib. bdg. 25.00x (ISBN 0-87287-239-4). Libs Unl.
Miller, Jim, ed. see Rolling Stone Press.
Miller, Joan. Cookery for Today. 1974. pap. text ed. 4.95x o.p. (ISBN 0-435-42602-8). Heinemann Ed.
--More Cookery for Today. 1974. pap. text ed. 4.95x0 o.p. (ISBN 0-435-42601-X). Heinemann Ed.
Miller, Joanne L., jt. ed. see Eimas, Peter D.
Miller, Jody G., et al, eds. Penjerdel Location & Market Guide. LC 77-78304. (Illus.). 1981. pap. 20.00 (ISBN 0-918964-00-8). Greater Phila.
Miller, John. The Workingman's Paradise. Wilding, Michael, ed. 272p. 1980. 18.50x (ISBN 0-424-00057-1, Pub.by Sydney U Pr Australia). Intl Schol Bk Serv.
Miller, John, jt. auth. see Hersh, Richard.
Miller, John & Gakenheimer, Ralph A., eds. Latin American Urban Policies & the Social Sciences. LC 70-103481. 1971. 20.00x o.p. (ISBN 0-8039-0056-2). Sage.
Miller, John C. The Emergence of the Nation, 1783-1815. 190p. 1972. pap. 7.95x (ISBN 0-673-05764-X). Scott F.
--Federalist Era, Seventeen Eighty Nine to Eighteen-One. (New American Nation Ser.). (Illus.). pap. 6.95x (ISBN 0-06-133027-2, TB 3027, Torch). Har-Row.
--The Wolf by the Ears: Thomas Jefferson & Slavery. LC 76-51590. 1977. 15.95 (ISBN 0-02-921500-5). Free Pr.
Miller, John C., ed. The Colonial Image. LC 62-9930. (American Epochs Ser). 10.00 (ISBN 0-8076-0168-3); pap. 4.95 o.s.i. (ISBN 0-8076-0392-9). Braziller.
Miller, John M. Minnesota Legal Forms-Commercial Real Estate. Mason Publishing Staff, ed. 150p. 1981. ring binder 15.00 (ISBN 0-917126-89-0). Mason Pub.
Miller, John R., ed. see Saint-Exupery, Antoine De.
Miller, John W. The Paradox of Cause & Other Essays. 192p. 1981. pap. 5.95 (ISBN 0-393-00032-X). Norton.
--Step by Step Through the Parables. 192p. (Orig.). 1981. pap. 6.95 (ISBN 0-8091-2379-7). Paulist Pr.
Miller, John W., tr. see Goldoni, Carlo.
Miller, Jolanda. You Can Become Whole Again: A Guide to Healing for Christians in Grief. LC 80-84652. 1981. pap. 5.00 (ISBN 0-8042-1156-6). John Knox.
Miller, Jon D., et al. Citizenship in an Age of Science: A Public Opinion Survey of Young Adults. (Pergamon Policy Studies). 1980. 39.00 (ISBN 0-08-024662-1). Pergamon.
Miller, Jonathan. The Body in Question. (Illus.). 1979. 15.95 (ISBN 0-394-50280-9). Random.
Miller, Joseph. Republican Chaos: Campaigns from Truman Through Nixon. (Illus.). 1980. 9.00 (ISBN 0-912472-24-3). Miller Bks.
Miller, Joseph, ed. Arizona Cavalcade. (Illus.). 1962. 7.95 (ISBN 0-8038-0320-6). Hastings.
Miller, Joseph B. Food Allergy: Provocative Testing & Injection Therapy. 160p. 1972. pap. 15.25 spiral (ISBN 0-398-02601-7). C C Thomas.
Miller, Joseph C. Kings & Kingsman: Early Mbundu States in Angola. (Oxford Studies in African Affairs Ser.). (Illus.). 1976. 45.00x (ISBN 0-19-822704-3). Oxford U Pr.
Miller, Judi. Save the Last Dance for Me. 1981. pap. 2.75 (ISBN 0-671-83650-1). PB.
Miller, Julian A. Breaking Through: Freeing Yourself from Fear, Helplessness & Depression - Before It's Too Late. LC 78-3310. 1979. 9.95 o.s.i. (ISBN 0-690-01771-5, TYC-T). T Y Crowell.
Miller, K. M. Psychological Testing in Personnel Assessment. LC 75-18451. 1976. 29.95 (ISBN 0-470-60392-5). Halsted Pr.
Miller, Karl, ed. Memoirs of a Modern Scotland. (Illus.). 1970. 7.95 (ISBN 0-571-08750-7, Pub. by Faber & Faber). Merrimack Bk Serv.
Miller, Keith. Habitation of Dragons. 1976. pap. 1.75 (ISBN 0-89129-209-8). Jove Pubns.
--Second Touch. 1976. pap. 1.75 (ISBN 0-89129-133-4). Jove Pubns.
Miller, Keith & Larson, Bruce. The Passionate People: Carriers of the Spirit. 1979. pap. 5.95 (ISBN 0-8499-2832-X). Word Bks.
Miller, Ken. Mormonism: A Happy Way to Live! (Illus.). 1977. 6.95 o.p. (ISBN 0-88290-085-4). Horizon Utah.
Miller, Kenneth S. Partial Differential Equations in Engineering Problems. 1953. ref. ed. 19.95 (ISBN 0-13-650408-6). P-H.
Miller, L. Keith. Principles of Everyday Behavior Analysis. 2nd ed. LC 79-27797. 1980. pap. text ed. 15.95 (ISBN 0-8185-0373-4). Brooks-Cole.
Miller, L. S., ed. see Carnegie Commission on Higher Educaion.
Miller, LaMar P., ed. The Testing of Black Students. LC 74-6237. 128p. 1974. 15.95 (ISBN 0-13-911966-3). P-H.
Miller, Lani & Rodgers, Diane. We Love Your Body. LC 80-81842. 1980. pap. 9.95 (ISBN 0-933350-32-5). Morse Pr.
Miller, Larry. Selling in Agribusiness. Lee, Jasper S., ed. (Career Preparation for Agriculture-Agribusiness Ser.). (Illus.). 1979. pap. text ed. 5.80x (ISBN 0-07-041962-0, G); activity guide 3.60x (ISBN 0-07-041963-9); tchr's manual & key 2.75x (ISBN 0-07-041964-7). McGraw.
Miller, Lawrence M. Behavior Management: The New Science of Managing People at Work. LC 77-28602. 1978. 19.95 (ISBN 0-471-02947-5, Pub. by Wiley-Interscience). Wiley.
Miller, Lee O. Assignment: Burma. (Orig.). 1980. pap. 1.75 (ISBN 0-505-51498-2). Tower Bks.
Miller, Leslie H. College Geometry. LC 57-5574. (Century Mathematics Ser.). (Illus.). 1957. text ed. 14.95x (ISBN 0-89197-088-6). Irvington.
Miller, Leslie W., ed. see Washington University Dept. of Medicine.
Miller, Leta E., jt. auth. see Cohn, Albert.
Miller, Liam. The Dun Emer Press Later the Cuala Press. (New Yeats Papers Ser.: Vol. 7). 1973. pap. text ed. 7.50x (ISBN 0-85105-246-0, Dolmen Pr). Humanities.
--The Noble Drama of W. B. Yeats. (New Yeats Papers: No. 13). (Illus.). 500p. 1977. text ed. 52.00x (ISBN 0-391-00633-9, Dolmen Pr). Humanities.
Miller, Liam, compiled by. The Dolmen Press XXV Years: Illustrated Bibliography of the Dolmen Press 1951-1976. (Dolmen Editions Ser.: No. XxV). 1976. text ed. 39.00x (ISBN 0-85105-309-2, Dolmen Pr). Humanities.
Miller, Liam, jt. ed. see Hanley, Mary.
Miller, Lillian B., ed. see Library of Congress.
Miller, Linda A., jt. ed. see Davis, Richard C.
Miller, Lyle H., et al. Neuropeptide Influences on the Brain & Behavior. LC 76-5663. (Advances in Biochemical Psychopharmacology: Vol. 17). 1977. 31.50 (ISBN 0-89004-130-X). Raven.
Miller, Lynn, jt. auth. see Lieberman, Ann.
Miller, Lynn F., jt. auth. see Comtois, M. F.
Miller, Lynne G. & Brammer, Miriam, eds. Poster Packet & Teaching Guide for Elementary Classrooms. (Illus.). 1975. pap. text ed. 9.95 (ISBN 0-590-09597-8, Citation). Schol Bk Serv.
Miller, M. Clinton & Knapp, Rebecca G. Evaluating Quality of Care: Analytic Procedures, Monitoring Techniques. LC 79-4482. 1979. 30.95 (ISBN 0-89443-091-2). Aspen Systems.
Miller, Madeleine S. & Miller, J. Lane. Harper's Encyclopedia of Bible Life. rev ed. Bennett, Boyce M., Jr. & Scott, David H., eds. LC 78-4752. (Illus.). 1978. 16.95 (ISBN 0-06-065676-X, HarpR). Har-Row.
Miller, Mara. Where to Go for What: How to Research, Organize & Present Your Information. (Illus.). 240p. 1981. 11.95 (ISBN 0-13-957217-1, Spec); pap. 5.95 (ISBN 0-13-957209-0). P-H.
Miller, Marc S., ed. Working Lives: The "Southern Exposure" History of Labor in the South. (Illus.). 1981. 17.95 (ISBN 0-394-50912-9); pap. 7.95 (ISBN 0-394-73965-5). Pantheon.
Miller, Marcia. Deadly Pursuit. 192p. (YA) 1976. 5.95 (ISBN 0-685-66477-5, Avalon). Bouregy.
Miller, Marcia M. Post Card Views & Other Souvenirs. (Illus.). 64p. 1973. pap. 2.95 (ISBN 0-913270-24-5). Sunstone Pr.
Miller, Margaret M. & Aarseth, Sigmund. Norwegian Rosemaling: Decorative Painting on Wood. (Illus.). 1973. pap. 12.95 (ISBN 0-684-16743-3, ScribT). Scribner.
Miller, Margaret S. Economic Development of Russia, 1905-1914. 2nd ed. LC 67-3033. Repr. of 1926 ed. 24.00x (ISBN 0-678-05074-0). Kelley.
Miller, Maria B., jt. auth. see Ferguson, Jeanne.
Miller, Maria G., jt. auth. see Miller, Alfred E.
Miller, Marian E. & Sachs, Marvin L. About Bedsores. LC 74-3385. 1974. text ed. 8.50 (ISBN 0-397-54186-4); pap. text ed. 7.50 (ISBN 0-397-54156-2). Lippincott.
Miller, Marion M. Great Debates in American History. 1970. Repr. of 1913 ed. 140.00 (ISBN 0-8108-0386-0). Scarecrow.
Miller, Mark E., ed. Amish Cooking. 320p. 1981. Repr. 14.95 (ISBN 0-8361-1958-4). Herald Pr.
Miller, Marshall L., ed. Occupational Health & Safety Regulation. LC 78-60849. 154p. 1980. pap. text ed. 22.50 (ISBN 0-86587-078-0). Gov Insts.
Miller, Martin A. Miller Comprehensive Solutions to the Uniform CPA Examination. Incl. Solutions to the May 1978 Examination. 224p. pap. (ISBN 0-15-003951-4); Solutions to the November 1978 Examination. 202p. pap. (ISBN 0-15-003953-0); Solutions to the May 1979 Examination. 203p. pap. (ISBN 0-15-003956-5); Solutions to the November 1979 Examination. 200p. pap. text ed. 15.00 ea. (HC). HarBraceJ.
Miller, Mary Anne & Brooten, Dorothy. The Childbearing Family: A Nursing Perspective. 1977. text ed. 16.95 (ISBN 0-316-57146-6, Little Med Div). Little.
Miller, Mary K. Mathematics for Nurses with Clinical Applications. LC 80-26040. 385p. (Orig.). 1981. pap. text ed. 14.95 (ISBN 0-8185-0429-3). Brooks-Cole.
Miller, Mary R. Thomas Campbell. (English Authors Ser.: No. 227). 1978. 12.50 (ISBN 0-8057-6728-2). Twayne.
Miller, Mary S. Bringing Learning Home: How Parents Can Play a More Active & Effective Role in Their Children's Education. LC 80-7856. 256p. 1981. 9.95 (ISBN 0-690-01952-1). Har-Row.
Miller, Mary S. & Schiller, Patricia. A Teacher's Round Table on Sex Education. (Illus.). 1977. pap. 8.00 (ISBN 0-934338-21-3). NAIS.
Miller, Maureen. Family Communication: Keeping Connected in Changing Times. LC 80-80226. 1980. pap. 7.95 (ISBN 0-8091-2220-0). Paulist Pr.
Miller, Maurice. Hearing Aids. LC 72-190707. (Studies in Communicative Disorders Ser). 1972. pap. 2.50 (ISBN 0-672-61284-4). Bobbs.
Miller, Maurice H. & Polisar, Ira A. Audiological Evaluation of the Pediatric Patient. (Amer. Lec. in Speech & Hearing Ser.). (Illus.). 132p. 1971. 9.50 (ISBN 0-398-02160-0). C C Thomas.
Miller, Max D., jt. auth. see Dyken, Paul D.
Miller, Max D., jt. auth. see Rao, P. Syamasundar.
Miller, May. The Clearing & Beyond. LC 73-93070. 1974. 7.50 (ISBN 0-685-41659-3). Charioteer.
Miller, Merl, jt. auth. see Townsend, Carl.
Miller, Merl, jt. auth. see Warren, Carl.
Miller, Merl, jt. auth. see Willis, Jerry.
Miller, Merl K. & Sippl, Charles J. Home Computers: A Beginners Glossary & Guide. 1978. pap. 8.95 (ISBN 0-918398-02-9). Dilithium Pr.
Miller, Merle. Lyndon: An Oral Biography. 1980. 17.95 (ISBN 0-399-12357-1). Putnam.
--Plain Speaking: An Oral Biography of Harry S. Truman. (Illus.). 288p. (YA) 1974. 8.95 o.p. (ISBN 0-399-11261-8, Dist. by Putnam). Berkley Pub.
Miller, Merton H. & Upton, Charles W. Macroeconomics: A Neoclassical Introduction. 1974. text ed. 16.00x o.p. (ISBN 0-256-01550-3). Irwin.
Miller, Michael B. Current Issues in Clinical Geriatrics. LC 77-95435. 1979. casebound 13.50 (ISBN 0-685-85789-1). Tiresias Pr.
Miller, Michael C. The Guide to Home Renovation: For Those Without the Time or Inclination to Do It Themselves. LC 80-70390. (Illus.). 136p. (Orig.). 1981. pap. 7.95 (ISBN 0-686-69518-6). Chilton.
Miller, Michael C., jt. auth. see Wasserman, Fred W.
Miller, Michael H., jt. auth. see Mauksch, Ingeborg G.
Miller, Michael H. & Flynn, Beverly, eds. Current Perspectives in Nursing: Social Issues & Trends. LC 76-57746. (Current Perspectives Ser.). (Illus.). 1979. 12.50 (ISBN 0-8016-3461-X); pap. 9.50 (ISBN 0-8016-3464-4). Mosby.

Miller, Mike & Wayburn, Peggy. Alaska: The Great Land. (Illus.). 128p. 1975. pap. 7.95 o.p. (ISBN 0-684-14125-6, SL576, ScribT). Scribner.

Miller, Mildred & Snyder, Bascha. The Kosher Gourmet Cookbook. LC 74-80926. (Illus.). 1976. 10.00 (ISBN 0-8397-4830-2); pap. 7.50 (ISBN 0-8397-4831-0). Eriksson.

Miller, Millie. Kinnikinnick: The Mountain Flower Book. Date not set. pap. 3.95 (ISBN 0-933472-09-9). Johnson Colo.

Miller, Milton G. & Schwartzman, Sylvan D. Our Religion & Our Neighbors. rev. ed. LC 63-14742. (Illus.). (gr. 9). 1971. text ed. 7.50 (ISBN 0-8074-0145-5, 141513); tchrs'. guide 3.50 (ISBN 0-8074-0146-3, 204280). UAHC.

Miller, Minnie M., et al. Precis de Civilisation Francaise. (Fr.). (gr. 10 up). 1979. pap. text ed. 8.95x o.p. (ISBN 0-89197-354-0). Irvington.

Miller, Molly. The Saints of Gwynedd. (Studies in Celtic History). 132p. 1979. 19.50x (ISBN 0-8476-6186-5). Rowman.

Miller, Morris & Janis, Arthur. Modern Bookkeeping & Accounting. 2nd ed. LC 72-109961. Orig. Title: Fundamentals of Modern Bookkeeping. (gr. 10-12). 1973. text ed. 13.28 (ISBN 0-8224-2011-2); tchrs'. manual 4.80 (ISBN 0-8224-2070-8); solutions 8.00 (ISBN 0-8224-2072-4); Workbook I (units 1-26) 5.32 (ISBN 0-8224-2068-6); Workbook II (units 27-45) 5.32 (ISBN 0-8224-2069-4); tests 40.00 (ISBN 0-8224-2071-6). Pitman Learning.

Miller, Morton W. & Clarkson, Thomas W. Mercury, Mercurials & Mercaptans. (Illus.). 404p. 1973. 27.50 (ISBN 0-398-02600-9). C C Thomas.

Miller, Myron, jt. auth. see Houck, Carter.

Miller, N. & Aya, R. National Liberation. LC 65-11900. 1971. 12.95 (ISBN 0-02-921520-X); pap. text ed. 4.50 (ISBN 0-02-921360-6). Free Pr.

Miller, N., jt. auth. see Aya, R.

Miller, Nancy & Cohen, Gene D., eds. Clinical Aspects of Alzheimer's Disease & Senile Dementia. (Aging Ser.: Vol. 15). 350p. 1981. text ed. 33.00 (ISBN 0-89004-326-4). Raven.

Miller, Nancy F., jt. auth. see Kurtz, Rosemary B.

Miller, Naomi. French Renaissance Fountains. LC 76-23645. (Outstanding Dissertations in the Fine Arts - 16th Century). (Illus.). 1977. Repr. of 1966 ed. lib. bdg. 63.00 (ISBN 0-8240-2713-2). Garland Pub.

Miller, Nathan. The Child in Primitive Society. LC 76-167074. 1975. Repr. of 1928 ed. 21.00 (ISBN 0-8103-3995-1). Gale.

--The U. S. Navy: An Illustrated History. LC 77-24139. (Illus.). 416p. 1977. 12.95 (ISBN 0-8281-0204-X, Dist. by Scribner); deluxe ed. 39.95 slipcased (ISBN 0-8281-0205-8, Dist. by Scribner). Am Heritage.

Miller, Neal E., et al, eds. Biofeedback & Self Control, 1973: An Aldine Annual on the Regulation of Bodily Processes & Consciousness. LC 74-151109. 512p. 1974. text ed. 34.95 (ISBN 0-202-25108-X). Aldine Pub.

Miller, Ned A. The Complete Guide to Employee Benefit Plans. LC 79-88343. 1977. 29.95 (ISBN 0-87863-149-6). Farnswth Pub.

Miller, Neil. Conversation in Portuguese: Points of Departure. rev 2nd ed. LC 80-83025. (Illus.). 1980. pap. text ed. 5.95x (ISBN 0-9601444-2-0). N Miller.

Miller, Nicholas, jt. ed. see Scott, John.

Miller, Nick. Battered Spouses. 69p. 1975. pap. text ed. 5.00x (ISBN 0-7135-1936-3, Pub. by Bedford England). Renouf.

Miller, Nyle H. & Snell, Joseph W. Great Gunfighters of the Kansas Cowtowns, 1867-1886. LC 63-63480. (Illus.). 1967. 16.95x (ISBN 0-8032-0123-0); pap. 4.50 (ISBN 0-8032-5137-8, BB 333, Bison). U of Nebr Pr.

Miller, Olga K., ed. Genealogical Research for Czech & Slovak Americans. LC 78-13086. (Genealogy & Local History Ser.: Vol. 2). (Illus.). 1978. 30.00 (ISBN 0-8103-1404-5). Gale.

Miller, Orson & Miller, Hope. Mudhrooms in Color: How to Know Them, Where to Find Them, & What to Avoid. 11.95 (ISBN 0-686-69507-0, Hawthorn). Dutton.

Miller, Owen J., jt. ed. see Valdes, Mario J.

Miller, P. J., jt. auth. see Cowd, M. A.

Miller, P. M. Behavioral Treatment of Alcoholism. 1976. 27.00 (ISBN 0-08-019519-9); pap. 10.75 (ISBN 0-08-019518-0). Pergamon.

Miller, Patrick D., Jr. Genesis One Through Eleven: Studies in Structure & Theme. (JSOT Supplement Ser.: No. 8). 50p. 1978. pap. text ed. 4.95x (ISBN 0-905774-07-8, Pub. by JSOT Pr England). Eisenbrauns.

Miller, Paul E. Esquire's Jazz Books, 3 vols. Incl. 1944 Jazz Book (ISBN 0-306-79525-6); 1945 Jazz Book (ISBN 0-306-79526-4); 1946 Jazz Book (ISBN 0-306-79527-2). (The Roots of Jazz Ser.). (Repr. of 1944-46 ed.). 1979. Set. 50.00 (ISBN 0-306-79528-0); 19.50 ea. Da Capo.

Miller, Paul M. Leading the Family of God. 216p. 1981. pap. 7.95 (ISBN 0-8361-1950-9). Herald Pr.

Miller, Paul S. Business Math. (Illus.). 1980. pap. text ed. 13.95x (ISBN 0-07-042157-9); instructor's manual 8.50 (ISBN 0-07-042158-7). McGraw.

Miller, Paul W., ed. see Whitlock, Brand.

Miller, Peggy Jean, jt. auth. see Miller, Ron.

Miller, Percival A. At Summer's End: Southpoems. 66p. 1980. pap. 4.95 (ISBN 0-8059-2739-5). Dorrance.

Miller, Perry. Orthodoxy in Massachusetts 1630-1650. 8.00 (ISBN 0-8446-1312-6). Peter Smith.

Miller, Perry, ed. American Puritans. LC 56-7536. 1956. pap. 2.95 (ISBN 0-385-09204-0, A80, Anch). Doubleday.

--American Transcendentalists. LC 57-11433. 1957. pap. 3.50 (ISBN 0-385-09326-8, A119, Anch). Doubleday.

Miller, Perry & Johnson, Thomas H., eds. Puritans: A Sourcebook of Their Writings, 2 vols. (Orig.). Vol. 1. pap. 5.95x (ISBN 0-06-131093-X, TB1093, Torch); Vol. 2. pap. 7.95x (ISBN 0-06-131094-8, TB1094, Torch). Har-Row.

Miller, Perry, jt. ed. see Heimert, Alan.

Miller, Perry, jt. ed. see Heimert, Alan E.

Miller, Perry G. Errand into the Wilderness. LC 56-11285. 1956. 10.00x (ISBN 0-674-26151-8, Belknap Pr); pap. 4.95 (ISBN 0-674-26155-0). Harvard U Pr.

Miller, Peter. Peter Miller's Ski Almanac. LC 79-7660. (Nick Lyons Bk.). (Illus.). 1979. pap. 9.95 (ISBN 0-385-15713-4, NLB). Doubleday.

Miller, Philip B., ed. An Abyss Deep Enough: The Letters of Heinrich Von Kleist with a Selection of Essays & Anecdotes. 288p. 1981. 16.95 (ISBN 0-525-05479-0). Dutton.

Miller, Philip B., ed. & tr. see Kleist, Heinrich von.

Miller, Phyllis, jt. auth. see Norton, Andre.

Miller, Pierre. Captivity of Father Peter Milet: Among the Oneida Indians. His Own Narrative with Supplementary Documents, Repr. Of 1888 Ed. Bd. with Captivity Among the Oneidas in 1690-91 of Father Pierre Milet of the Society of Jesus. Repr. of 1897 ed; Lost & Found: Or 3 Months with the Wild Indians; a Brief Sketch of the Life of Ole T. Nystel, Embracing His Experience While in Captivity to the Comanches & Subsequent Liberation from Them. Repr. of 1888 ed; Wehman's Book on the Scalping Knife: Or the Log Cabin in Flames. Wehman, Henry J. Repr. of 1890 ed; Left by the Indians. Story of My Life. Fuller, Emeline L. Repr. of 1892 ed. LC 75-7123. (Indian Captivities Ser.: Vol. 96). 1976. lib. bdg. 44.00 (ISBN 0-8240-1720-X). Garland Pub.

Miller, R. The Resistance. (World War II Ser.). (Illus.). 1979. lib. bdg. 14.94 (ISBN 0-8094-2523-8); kivar bdg. 9.93 (ISBN 0-8094-2524-6). Silver.

--Space Art. 1978. pap. 8.95 (ISBN 0-931064-04-X). Starlog Pr.

Miller, R. Bryan, jt. ed. see McMurry, John.

Miller, R. C. This We Can Believe. 1976. 6.95 (ISBN 0-8164-0376-7). Crossroad NY.

Miller, Ralph, tr. see Bornstein, Harry.

Miller, Randall J. Regional Impact of Monetary Policy in the United States. LC 78-59750. (Illus.). 1978. 19.95 (ISBN 0-669-02373-6). Lexington Bks.

Miller, Randall M., ed. The Afro-American Slaves: Community or Chaos? 128p. (Orig.). 1981. pap. 5.50 (ISBN 0-89874-078-9). Krieger.

Miller, Randolph C. The Theory of Christian Education Practice: How Theology Affects Christian Education. LC 80-15886. 312p. (Orig.). 1980. pap. 10.95 (ISBN 0-89135-049-7). Religious Educ.

Miller, Ray. Camaro! Chevy's Classy Chassis. (Illus.). 320p. 1981. write for info. (ISBN 0-913056-10-3). Evergreen Pr.

Miller, Raymond W. A Conservative Looks at Cooperatives. LC 64-15585. 245p. 1964. 11.95 (ISBN 0-8214-0000-2). Ohio U Pr.

Miller, Rex. Machinists Library, 3 vols. Incl. Vol. 1. Basic Machine Shop (ISBN 0-672-23301-0); Vol. 2. Machine Shop (ISBN 0-672-23302-9); Vol. 3. Toolmakers Handy Book (ISBN 0-672-23303-7). LC 78-57172. 1978. 10.95 ea. (ISBN 0-672-23300-2); 29.95 set (ISBN 0-685-92871-3). Audel.

--Residential Wiring. (Illus.). 300p. 1981. text ed. 10.64 (ISBN 0-87002-331-4); price not set student guide (ISBN 0-87002-332-2). Bennett IL.

Miller, Rex & Anderson, Edwin P. Electric Motors. 3rd ed. LC 77-71584. 1977. 10.95 (ISBN 0-672-23264-2). Audel.

Miller, Rex & Morrisey, Thomas J. Metal Technology. LC 74-77817. 1976. 16.50 (ISBN 0-672-21079-7); tchr's guide 3.33 (ISBN 0-672-21107-6); lab bk. 3.95 (ISBN 0-672-21106-8). Bobbs.

Miller, Rex, jt. auth. see Baker, Glenn E.

Miller, Rex, jt. auth. see Fuller, Nelson.

Miller, Richard. Bohemia: The Protoculture Then & Now. LC 77-14073. (Illus.). 1978. 17.95 (ISBN 0-88229-293-5); pap. 9.95 (ISBN 0-88229-518-7). Nelson-Hall.

--English, French, German & Italian Techniques of Singing: A Study in National Tonal Preferences & How They Relate to Functional Efficiency. LC 76-58554. (Illus.). 1977. 12.00 (ISBN 0-8108-1020-4). Scarecrow.

Miller, Richard & Henry, Patricia. Plane Trigonometry. LC 80-18403. 275p. 1981. text ed. 15.95 (ISBN 0-8185-0421-8). Brooks-Cole.

Miller, Richard, tr. see Barthes, Roland.

Miller, Richard J. Ancient Japanese Nobility: The Kabane Ranking System. (Publications in Occasional Papers, Vol. 7). 1974. pap. 14.50x (ISBN 0-520-09494-8). U of Cal Pr.

Miller, Richard K. & Sell, George R. Volterra Integral Equations & Topological Dynamics. LC 52-42839. (Memoirs: No. 102). 1979. pap. 7.60 (ISBN 0-8218-1802-3, MEMO-102). Am Math.

Miller, Richard L., jt. auth. see Suls, Jerry.

Miller, Richard U. Hospital Labor Relations. (Wisconsin Business Monographs: No. 11). (Illus.). 104p. 1980. 7.50 (ISBN 0-86603-003-4). Bureau Busn Res U Wis.

Miller, Richard V., et al. The Impact of Collective Bargaining on Hospitals. 1979. 26.50 (ISBN 0-03-051346-4). Praeger.

Miller, Richards T., jt. auth. see Henry, Robert G.

Miller, Rita S., ed. Brooklyn, U. S. A. (Brooklyn College Studies on Society in Change Ser.). (Illus.). 1979. 20.00 (ISBN 0-930888-02-2). Brooklyn Coll Pr.

Miller, Robert C. Sea. (Illus.). 1966. 20.00 o.p. (ISBN 0-394-44400-0). Random.

Miller, Robert D., jt. auth. see Hershey, Nathan.

Miller, Robert E. Agni. (Writers Workshop Redbird Ser.). 1975. 8.00 (ISBN 0-88253-492-0); pap. text ed. 4.80 (ISBN 0-88253-491-2). Ind-US Inc.

Miller, Robert H. Graham Greene: A Descriptive Catalogue. LC 77-92925. 88p. 1979. 12.50x (ISBN 0-8131-1383-0). U Pr of Ky.

--Textbook of Basic Emergency Medicine. 2nd ed. LC 79-27337. (Illus.). 1980. pap. text ed. 12.95 (ISBN 0-8016-3449-0). Mosby.

Miller, Robert H. & Cantrell, James R. Textbook of Basic Emergency Medicine. LC 75-9765. (Illus.). 272p. 1975. pap. text ed. 13.95 o.p. (ISBN 0-8016-3448-2). Mosby.

Miller, Robert R., jt. auth. see Bannon, John F.

Miller, Robert W. Clock Guide: Identification with Prices. rev. & enl. ed. (Illus.). 1978. 8.95 o.p. (ISBN 0-87069-251-8). Wallace-Homestead.

--Flea Market Price Guide. 2nd ed. (Illus.). 6.95 o.p. (ISBN 0-87069-268-2). Wallace-Homestead.

--Western Horse Behavior & Training. 336p. 1975. 6.95 (ISBN 0-385-08181-2, Dolp). Doubleday.

Miller, Robert W., ed. Price Guide to Antiques & Pattern Glass. 6th ed. (Illus.). 9.95 o.p. (ISBN 0-87069-281-X). Wallace-Homestead.

--Wallace-Homestead Price Guide to Antiques & Pattern Glass. 7th ed. (Illus.). 592p. 1980. pap. 10.95 (ISBN 0-87069-305-0). Wallace-Homestead.

Miller, Roberta. Chipmunk's ABC. (Illus.). 24p. (gr. k-1). 1976. PLB 4.57 o.p. (ISBN 0-307-60512-4, Golden Pr). Western Pub.

Miller, Roger L. Economic Issues for Consumers. 3rd ed. (Illus.). 600p. 1980. text ed. 19.95 (ISBN 0-8299-0396-8). West Pub.

--Economic Issues for Consumers. 2nd ed. (Illus.). 1978. text ed. 17.50 (ISBN 0-8299-0151-5); pap. text ed. 6.50 study guide (ISBN 0-8299-0217-1); instrs.' manual avail. (ISBN 0-8299-0560-X). West Pub.

--Personal Finance Today. (Illus.). 1979. text ed. 18.50 (ISBN 0-8299-0233-3); pap. study guide & wkbk. by Grant J. Wells 7.50 (ISBN 0-8299-0256-2); instrs.' manual avail. (ISBN 0-8299-0561-8). West Pub.

Miller, Roger L., jt. auth. see Rao, Potluri M.

Miller, Roger L., jt. auth. see West, Edwin G.

Miller, Ron. Space Art. Reed, Jon-Michael, ed. (gr. 3 up). 1978. pap. 13.00 slip case (ISBN 0-931064-06-6); pap. 8.95 (ISBN 0-931064-04-X). Starlog.

Miller, Ron & Miller, Peggy Jean. The Chemehuevi Indians of Southern California. 1973. 1.00 (ISBN 0-686-25507-0). Malki Mus Pr.

Miller, Ron, compiled by. Space Art Poster Book. (Illus.). 48p. (Orig.). 1979. pap. 10.95 (ISBN 0-8117-2077-2). Stackpole.

Miller, Ron, et al. Planet Tours. LC 80-54620. (Illus.). 192p. 19.95 (ISBN 0-89480-147-3); pap. 9.95 (ISBN 0-89480-146-5). Workman Pub.

Miller, Ronald. Orkney. 1976. 19.95 o.p. (ISBN 0-7134-3131-8, Pub. by Batsford England). David & Charles.

Miller, Ronald B., ed. Black American Literature & Humanism. LC 80-5179. 122p. 1981. price not set (ISBN 0-8131-1436-5). U Pr of Ky.

Miller, Ronald D., ed. Anesthesia. (Illus.). 1500p. 1981. lib. bdg. 65.00 (ISBN 0-443-08082-8). Churchill.

Miller, Ronald E. Dynamic Optimization & Economic Applications. (Illus.). 1980. text ed. 32.95 (ISBN 0-07-042180-3); solutions manual 3.95 (ISBN 0-07-042181-1). McGraw.

Miller, Roy A. Japanese Language. LC 67-16777. (History & Structure of Language Ser.). 1967. 17.50x o.s.i. (ISBN 0-226-52717-4). U of Chicago Pr.

--The Japanese Language. LC 67-16777. (History & Structure of Languages Ser.). 496p. 1980. pap. 16.00x (ISBN 0-226-52718-2, Midway). U of Chicago Pr.

--Origins of the Japanese Language. LC 80-50871. (Publications on Asia of the School for International Studies: No. 34). (Illus.). 192p. 1980. 17.50 (ISBN 0-295-95766-2). U of Wash Pr.

--Studies in the Grammatical Tradition in Tibet. (Studies in the History of Linguistics: No. 6). 1976. text ed. 23.00x (ISBN 0-391-01651-2). Humanities.

Miller, Russell. The East Indiamen. Time-Life Books, ed. (The Seafarers Ser.). (Illus.). 176p. 1981. 14.95 (ISBN 0-8094-2689-7). Time-Life.

Miller, Russell R. & Greenblatt, David J. Drug Effects in Hospitalized Patients: Experiences of the Boston Collaborative Drug Surveillance Program, 1966-1975. LC 75-28124. 368p. 1976. 35.95 (ISBN 0-471-60372-4, Pub. by Wiley Medical). Wiley.

--Drug Therapy Reviews. LC 76-54569. 272p. 1977. 33.00 (ISBN 0-89352-001-2). Masson Pub.

Miller, Ruth. Black American Literature: 1760 to the Present. 1971. pap. text ed. 12.95x (ISBN 0-02-476420-5, 47642). Macmillan.

--High School Hookers. 1979. pap. 1.75 (ISBN 0-505-51417-6). Tower Bks.

Miller, Ruth H. Autumn Leaves. LC 80-82931. 54p. 1981. 9.95 (ISBN 0-686-28764-9). R J Pub.

Miller, Ryle, tr. see Institut Francais De Pertrole.

Miller, S. J. Eyes. 3rd ed. (Operative Surgery Ser.). 1976. 49.95 (ISBN 0-407-00609-5). Butterworths.

Miller, Sally M. The Radical Immigrant. (Immigrant Heritage of America Ser.). 1974. lib. bdg. 9.95 (ISBN 0-8057-3266-7). Twayne.

Miller, Sally M., ed. Flawed Liberation: Socialism & Feminism. LC 80-1050. (Contributions to Women's Studies Ser.: No. 19). 240p. 1981. lib. bdg. 27.50 (ISBN 0-313-21401-8, MFL/). Greenwood.

Miller, Sammy. Sammy Miller on Trials. (Illus.). 1971. 5.95 (ISBN 0-87880-002-6). Norton.

Miller, Samuel F. Lectures on the Constitution of the United States. xxi, 765p. 1981. Repr. of 1893 ed. lib. bdg. 45.00x (ISBN 0-8377-0836-2). Rothman.

Miller, Samuel I., jt. auth. see Rock, Sidney.

Miller, Sarah W. Quintet: Five One-Act Plays. 1981. pap. 3.95 (ISBN 0-8054-7520-6). Broadman.

Miller, Saunders. The Economics of Nuclear & Coal Power. LC 76-24361. (Illus.). 1976. text ed. 24.95 (ISBN 0-275-23710-9). Praeger.

Miller, Sharon. Colby Moves West. 132p. (gr. 6-12). 1981. pap. 2.25 (ISBN 0-88207-489-X). Victor Bks.

Miller, Sherod, ed. Marriage & Families: Enrichment Through Communication. LC 75-27012. (Sage Contemporary Social Science Issues Ser.: Vol. 20). 1975. 4.95x (ISBN 0-8039-0569-6). Sage.

Miller, Sherod, et al. Alive & Aware: Improving Communications in Relationships. LC 75-27948. (Illus.). 1975. 8.95 o.p. (ISBN 0-917340-01-9); pap. text ed. 7.95 (ISBN 0-917340-02-7); tchrs. manual o.p. 3.95 (ISBN 0-917340-03-5); couple workbook o.p. 3.95 (ISBN 0-917340-04-3); student workbook o.p. 3.95 (ISBN 0-917340-05-1). Interpersonal Comm.

--Couple Communication I: Talking Together. (Couple Communication Ser.). 1979. pap. 8.95 (ISBN 0-917340-09-4). Interpersonal Comm.

--Straight Talk: How to Improve Your Relationships Through Better Communication. LC 80-51251. 1980. 12.95 (ISBN 0-89256-143-2). Rawson Wade.

--Working Together: Improving Communication on Your Job. (Illus.). 200p. 1980. pap. 49.95 (ISBN 0-917340-11-6). Interpersonal Comm.

Miller, Shirley. The Vertical File & Its Satellites: A Handbook of Acquisition, Processing, & Organization. 2nd ed. LC 79-13773. (Library Science Text Ser.). 1979. lib. bdg. 17.50x (ISBN 0-87287-164-9). Libs Unl.
Miller, Shirley, ed. see Miller, Tom.
Miller, Stanley. The Mary Celeste. 182p. 1981. 9.95 (ISBN 0-312-51862-5). St Martin.
Miller, Stanley L. & Orgel, Leslie E. The Origins of Life on the Earth. (Concepts of Modern Biology Ser). (Illus.). 208p. 1974. pap. 11.95x ref. ed. (ISBN 0-13-642074-5). P-H.
Miller, Stella. Two Groups of Thessalian Gold. LC 77-80473. (UC Publications in Classical Studies: Vol. 18). 1979. pap. 13.00x (ISBN 0-520-09580-4). U of Cal Pr.
Miller, Stephen G. The Prytaneion: Its Function & Architectural Form. LC 76-24590. 1978. 20.00x (ISBN 0-520-03316-7). U of Cal Pr.
Miller, Stephen H., et al. Practical Points in Plastic Surgery. LC 79-91201. 1980. pap. 20.00 (ISBN 0-87488-719-4). Med Exam.
Miller, Stephen W., ed. Memory & Storage Technolgy, Vol II. (The Information Technology Ser.). (Illus.). 182p. 1977. pap. 20.00 (ISBN 0-88283-015-5). AFIPS Pr.
Miller, Steven B. The Midnight Son. LC 79-10759. (Illus.). 128p. (gr. 5 up). 1981. 14.95 (ISBN 0-590-07582-9, Four Winds); pap. 9.95 (ISBN 0-590-07811-9, Four Winds). Schol Bk Serv.
--The Midnignt Son. LC 79-10759. (Illus.). 128p. 1981. 14.95 (ISBN 0-590-07582-9, Four Winds); pap. 9.95 (ISBN 0-686-69196-2). Schol Bk Serv.
Miller, Stuart C. The Unwelcome Immigrant: The American Image of the Chinese, 1785-1882. 1969. 17.50x (ISBN 0-520-01380-8); pap. 3.25 (ISBN 0-520-02620-9). U of Cal Pr.
Miller, Stuart J., jt. auth. see Bartollas, Clemens.
Miller, Sylvia R. A Pictoral Memoir. LC 80-81146. (Illus.). 120p. 1980. 20.00 (ISBN 0-913504-57-2). Lowell Pr.
Miller, T. A. Cuticle Techniques in Arthropods. (Springer Series in Experimental Entomology). (Illus.). 410p. 1981. 59.80 (ISBN 0-387-90475-1). Springer-Verlag.
Miller, Teresa L. Remnants of Glory. LC 80-52413. 352p. 1981. 12.95 (ISBN 0-87223-657-9). Seaview Bks.
Miller, Theodore K. & Prince, Judith S. The Future of Student Affairs: A Guide to Student Development for Tomorrow's Higher Education. LC 76-19496. (Higher Education Ser.). 1976. 13.95x (ISBN 0-87589-298-1). Jossey-Bass.
Miller, Thomas. History of World War 1 First Day Bombardment Group. 1970. pap. 1.95x o.p. (ISBN 0-685-55084-2, Pub. by WW). Aviation.
Miller, Thomas A., jt. ed. see Dudrick, Stanley J.
Miller, Thomas E. & Sher, Lisa, eds. Findex: The Dictionary of Market Research Reports, Studies & Surveys. 1981. 125.00 (ISBN 0-931634-07-5). Info Clearing House.
Miller, Thomas G., Jr. The Cactus Air Force. 256p. 1981. pap. 2.50 (ISBN 0-553-14766-8). Bantam.
Miller, Thomas L. Public Lands of Texas, 1519-1970. LC 75-160500. (Illus.). 1972. 18.95 (ISBN 0-8061-0972-6); pap. 8.95 (ISBN 0-8061-1302-2). U of Okla Pr.
Miller, Tice L. Bohemians & Critics: American Theatre Criticism in the Nineteenth Century. LC 80-24430. x, 190p. 1981. 12.00 (ISBN 0-8108-1377-7). Scarecrow.
Miller, Tom. Angler's Guide to Baja California. Miller, Shirley, ed. (Illus.). 1979. pap. 5.95x (ISBN 0-914622-04-8). Baja Trail.
--The Assassination Please Almanac. LC 76-55654. (Illus.). 1977. pap. 5.95 o.p. (ISBN 0-8092-7903-7). Contemp Bks.
--On the Border: Portraits of America's Southwestern Frontier. LC 79-2631. 224p. 1981. 10.95 (ISBN 0-06-013039-3, HarpT). Har-Row.
--World of the California Gray Whale. (Illus.). 1975. pap. 4.00 (ISBN 0-914622-02-1). Baja Trail.
Miller, Tron. Gold Rocker Handbook. 1980. pap. 4.00 (ISBN 0-89316-619-7); plastic bdg. 6.00. Exanimo Pr.
Miller, Vassar. My Bones Being Wiser. LC 60-13157. (Wesleyan Poetry Program: Vol. 19). (Orig.). 1960. 10.00x (ISBN 0-8195-2019-5, Pub. by Wesleyan U Pr); pap. 4.95 (ISBN 0-8195-1019-X). Columbia U Pr.
--Onions & Roses. LC 68-27544. (Wesleyan Poetry Program: Vol. 42). 1968. 10.00x (ISBN 0-8195-2042-X, Pub. by Wesleyan U Pr); pap. 4.95 (ISBN 0-8195-1042-4). Columbia U Pr.
--Selected & New Poems: 1950-1980. 1980. write for info.; pap. write for info. Latitudes Pr.
--Wage War on Silence. LC 63-17793. (Wesleyan Poetry Program: Vol. 8). (Orig.). 1963. 10.00x (ISBN 0-8195-2008-X, Pub. by Wesleyan U Pr); pap. 2.45 o.p. (ISBN 0-8195-1008-4). Columbia U Pr.
Miller, Victor. Toga Party. 1979. pap. 1.95 o.p. (ISBN 0-449-14261-2, GM). Fawcett.
Miller, W., jt. auth. see Sattler, William M.
Miller, W. R. Acoma Grammar & Texts. (U. C. Publ. in Linguistics: Vol. 40). 1965. pap. 9.00x (ISBN 0-520-09234-1). U of Cal Pr.
--Uto-Aztecan Cognate Sets. (U. C. Publ. in Linguistics: Vol. 48). 1967. pap. 4.50x o.p. (ISBN 0-520-09243-0). U of Cal Pr.
Miller, W. R. & Boyd, T. Gardner. Teaching Elementary Industrial Arts. LC 70-117395. (Illus.). 1970. text ed. 9.28 (ISBN 0-87006-115-1). Goodheart.
Miller, W. R. & Munoz, Ricardo F. How to Control Your Drinking. (Illus.). 1976. 9.95 o.p. (ISBN 0-13-404392-8); pap. 3.95 o.p. (ISBN 0-13-404384-7). P-H.
Miller, Walter J., ed. see Verne, Jules.
Miller, Walter J., tr. see Verne, Jules.
Miller, Walter M., Jr. A Canticle for Leibowitz. (Science Fiction Ser). 336p. 1975. Repr. of 1959 ed. lib. bdg. 14.50 (ISBN 0-8398-2309-6). Gregg.
Miller, Wanda, et al. Reading Faster & Understanding More Book III. (Illus.). 416p. 1981. pap. text ed. 12.95 (ISBN 0-87626-733-9). Winthrop.
Miller, Warren. The Cool World. 1975. pap. 1.25 o.p. (ISBN 0-449-30751-4, P751, Prem). Fawcett.
Miller, Warren & Sorel, Edward. King Carlo of Capri. LC 58-1749. (Illus.). (gr. 1-4). 1958. 2.95 o.p. (ISBN 0-15-242744-9, HJ). HarBraceJ.
Miller, Warren C. Chronic Obstructive Pulmonary Disease. LC 79-91977. (Discussions in Pateint Managemenrt Ser.). 1980. pap. 12.00 (ISBN 0-87488-872-7). Med Exam.
--A Small Town Is Best for Waiting & Other Stories. 1979. 2.50 (ISBN 0-686-28279-5). Climate Bks.
Miller, Warren E., et al. American National Election Study, 1974. LC 75-12906. 1975. codebook 24.00 (ISBN 0-89138-111-2). ICPSR.
Miller, Wayne Charles. An Armed America: Its Face in Fiction: A History of the American Military Novel. LC 75-111521. 294p. 1970. 12.00x (ISBN 0-8147-0473-5). NYU Pr.
Miller, Wayne Charles, compiled by. A Comprehensive Bibliography for the Study of American Minorities, 2 vols. LC 74-21636. 1400p. 1976. 100.00x (ISBN 0-8147-5373-6). NYU Pr.
Miller, Webb & Wrathall, Celia. Software for Roundoff Analysis of Matrix Algorithms. LC 80-12662. (Computer Science & Applied Mathematics Ser.). 1980. 18.50 (ISBN 0-12-497250-0). Acad Pr.
Miller, Wilbur R. Drafting. LC 78-53388. (Basic Industrial Arts Ser.). (Illus.). 1978. 6.00 (ISBN 0-87345-793-5); softbound 4.48 (ISBN 0-87345-785-4). McKnight.
Miller, Wilbur R., jt. auth. see McKnight Staff Members.
Miller, William, Jr. The Great Luxury Liners, 1927-1952: A Photographic Record. (Illus.). 160p. Date not set. pap. 6.95 (ISBN 0-486-24056-8). Dover.
Miller, William, jt. auth. see Hof, Larry.
Miller, William, ed. Recent Advances in Addictions Research: Selected Proceedings from the Taos International Conference on Treatment of Addictive Disorders Held in the University of New Mexico 1979. 100p. 1980. 24.50 (ISBN 0-08-025771-2). Pergamon.
Miller, William & Rockwood, D. Stephen, eds. College Librarianship. LC 80-25546. 290p. 1981. 15.00 (ISBN 0-8108-1383-1). Scarecrow.
Miller, William A. Conservations. 96p. 1980. pap. 2.95 (ISBN 0-934104-04-2). Woodland.
--Conversations. LC 80-54283. 96p. 1980. pap. 3.95 (ISBN 0-934104-04-2). Woodland.
Miller, William C. Educator's Fact Book on School Organization. LC 72-95011. 1973. pap. 3.60 (ISBN 0-8224-2610-2). Pitman Learning.
--Feeding Ponies. (Illus.). pap. 4.35 (ISBN 0-85131-211-X, Dist. by Sporting Book Center). J A Allen.
Miller, William D. Memphis During the Progressive Era, 1900-1917. (Illus.). 242p. 1957. 10.00 (ISBN 0-87057-043-9, Pub. by Brown U Pr). Univ Pr of New England.
Miller, William G. The Data of Jurisprudence. xiv, 477p. 1980. Repr. of 1903 ed. lib. bdg. 42.50x (ISBN 0-8377-0835-4). Rothman.
Miller, William M. Tales of Persia: A Book for Children. LC 79-51273. (Illus.). 145p. (gr. 2-8). 1979. 5.00 (ISBN 0-8059-2635-6). Dorrance.
Miller, William R. The Addictive Behaviors: Treatment of Alcoholism, Drug Abuse, Smoking & Obesity. (Illus.). 275p. 1980. 36.00 (ISBN 0-08-025203-6). Pergamon.
Miller, Wilma H. The Reading Activities Handbook. 476p. 1980. pap. 15.95 (ISBN 0-03-051371-5). HR&W.
--Teaching Reading in the Secondary School. (Illus.). 532p. 1974. 18.75 (ISBN 0-398-03026-X). C C Thomas.
Miller, Wright. Russians As People. 1961. pap. 2.95 o.p. (ISBN 0-525-47085-9). Dutton.
Miller, Zane L. Suburb: Neighborhood & Community in Forest Park, Ohio, 1935-1976. LC 80-21828. (Twentieth-Century America Ser.). 256p. 1981. 18.50x (ISBN 0-87049-289-6). U of Tenn Pr.
Miller, Zane L., ed. see Drake, Daniel.
Miller, Zane L., jt. ed. see Dubeck, Paula J.
Millerd, Clara E. On the Interpretation of Empedocles. LC 78-66600. (Ancient Philosopy Ser.). 98p. 1980. lib. bdg. 13.00 (ISBN 0-8240-9591-X). Garland Pub.
Millerson, Gerald. Basic TV Staging. Date not set. pap. 7.95 o.p. (ISBN 0-8038-0747-3). Hastings.
Milles, George. Health Careers & Medical Sciences. LC 74-79837. (Allied Health Ser). 1975. pap. 5.50 (ISBN 0-672-61384-0). Bobbs.
Millet, Jean. La Belle Methode Ou l'Art De Bien Chanter. LC 71-126600. (Music Ser). 76p. 1973. Repr. of 1666 ed. lib. bdg. 18.50 (ISBN 0-306-70044-1). Da Capo.
Millett, Allan R. Semper Fidelis: The History of the United States Marine Corps. LC 80-1059. (The Macmillan Wars of the United States Ser.). (Illus.). 1980. 29.95 (ISBN 0-02-921590-0). Free Pr.
Millett, Allan R., ed. Short History of the Vietnam War. LC 77-23623. (Midland Bks: No. 210). 224p. 1978. 12.50x (ISBN 0-253-35215-0); pap. 3.95x (ISBN 0-253-20210-8). Ind U Pr.
Millett, Fred B. & Bentley, Gerald E. Art of the Drama. (Illus.). 1947. 29.00x (ISBN 0-89197-034-7). Irvington.
Millett, John David. The Process & Organization of Government Planning. LC 76-38753. (FDR & the Era of the New Deal Ser). 188p. 1972. Repr. of 1947 ed. lib. bdg. 22.50 (ISBN 0-306-70444-7). Da Capo.
Millett, Kate. Sita. 1977. 10.00 o.p. (ISBN 0-374-26546-1). FS&G.
Millett, Richard & Will, W. Marvin, eds. The Restless Caribbean: Changing Patterns of International Relations. LC 78-19764. 1979. 24.95 (ISBN 0-03-041806-2). Praeger.
Millett, Stephen M., ed. A Selected Bibliography of American Constitutional History. LC 75-8677. 116p. 1975. 4.50 (ISBN 0-87436-204-0). ABC-Clio.
Milley, John. Treasures of Independence. (Illus.). 224p. 1980. 25.00 (ISBN 0-8317-8593-4). Mayflower Bks.
Millgate, Jane. Macaulay. (Routledge Author Guides Ser.). 1973. cased 14.50 (ISBN 0-7100-7663-0); pap. 6.95 (ISBN 0-7100-7685-1). Routledge & Kegan.
Millgate, Jane, ed. Editing Nineteenth-Century Fiction, Vol. 13. LC 78-3393. (Conference on Editorial Problems Ser.). 1978. lib. bdg. 16.50 (ISBN 0-8240-2428-1). Garland Pub.
Millgate, Michael. The Achievement of William Faulkner. LC 78-16318. 1978. 15.00x (ISBN 0-8032-3054-0); pap. 4.95 (ISBN 0-8032-8102-1, BB 680, Bison). U of Nebr Pr.
--Thomas Hardy. 1971. 10.00 o.p. (ISBN 0-394-46121-5). Random.
Millgate, Michael, jt. ed. see Meriwether, James B.
Millgate, Michael, jt. ed. see Purdy, Richard Little.
Millham, Spencer, et al. Locking up Children: Secure Provision Within the Child-Care System. (Illus.). 1978. 21.95 (ISBN 0-566-00170-5, 01320-X, Pub. by Saxon Hse). Lexington Bks.
Millhiser, Marlys. Michael's Wife. 1976. pap. 1.50 o.p. (ISBN 0-449-22903-3, Crest). Fawcett.
--Nightmare Country. 384p. 1981. 12.95 (ISBN 0-399-12595-7). Putnam.
--Willing Hostage. 1977. pap. 1.50 o.p. (ISBN 0-449-23226-3, Crest). Fawcett.
Millichap, Joseph R. Hamilton Basso. (United States Authors Ser.: No. 331). 1979. lib. bdg. 13.95 (ISBN 0-8057-7225-1). Twayne.
Milligan, C., jt. auth. see Alves, Ronald.
Milligan, Charles & Higgs, Jim. The Wizard's Eye. Vandenburgh, Jane, ed. LC 78-13507. (Illus.). 1978. pap. 8.95 o.p. (ISBN 0-87701-119-2, Prism Editions). Chronicle Bks.
Milligan, Charles, jt. auth. see Alves, Ron.
Milligan, David. Reasoning & the Explanation of Action. 1980. text ed. 42.50x (ISBN 0-391-01802-7). Humanities.
Milligan, I. S., jt. ed. see Mann, J. Y.
Milligan, Jerry L. Reading Difficulties: Their Analysis & Treatment. 1981. pap. 7.50 (ISBN 0-87562-069-8). Spec Child.
Milligan, Spike. The Milligan Book of Records. 1980. 7.95 (ISBN 0-7181-1377-2, Pub. by Michael Joseph). Merrimack Bk Serv.
--Puckoon. 2nd ed. (Illus.). 1978. 9.95 (ISBN 0-7181-1271-7, Pub. by Michael Joseph). Merrimack Bk Serv.
--Small Dreams of a Scorpion. 1972. 6.95 (ISBN 0-7181-1049-8, Pub. by Michael Joseph). Merrimack Bk Serv.
Milligan, W. D., jt. auth. see Bowman, Arthur G.
Milligan, William. The Acension of Christ. Date not set. 12.50 (ISBN 0-86524-061-2). Klock & Klock.
Millikan, Max F., ed. Income Stabilization for a Developing Democracy. 1953. 75.00x (ISBN 0-685-69843-2). Elliots Bks.
Millikan, Robert A. Evolution in Science & Religion. 1935. 42.50x (ISBN 0-686-51381-9). Elliots Bks.
Milliken, Mary E. Understanding Human Behavior. 224p. pap. 6.00 o.p. (ISBN 0-8273-0338-6). Delmar.
--Understanding Human Behavior. LC 80-51266. (Practical Nursing Ser.). 256p. 1981. 9.20 (ISBN 0-8273-1968-1); pap. 6.80 (ISBN 0-8273-1439-6); instr's. guide 1.70 (ISBN 0-8273-1445-0). Delmar.
Milliken, Stephen F., jt. auth. see Fellows, Otis E.
Millimaki, Robert H. Fingerprint Detective. (gr. 4-7). 1973. 10.95 (ISBN 0-397-31484-1). Lippincott.
--The Making of a Detective. LC 76-8519. (gr. 4-6). 1976. 10.95 (ISBN 0-397-31694-1). Lippincott.
Millingen, J. G. Curiosities of Medical Experience. LC 72-83373. 1969. Repr. of 1839 ed. 20.00 (ISBN 0-8103-3487-9). Gale.
Millington, Roger. Crossword Puzzles: Their History & Their Cult. LC 75-9505. (Illus.). 190p. (gr. 7 up). 1975. 7.95 o.p. (ISBN 0-525-66471-8). Elsevier-Nelson.
Millington, T. Alaric, jt. auth. see Millington, William.
Millington, William & Millington, T. Alaric. Dictionary of Mathematics. 1971. pap. 3.95 (ISBN 0-06-463311-X, EH 311, EH). Har-Row.
Millington, William G. Law & the College Student: Justice in Evolution. LC 79-14211. 629p. 1979. text ed. 15.95 (ISBN 0-8299-2047-1). West Pub.
Millis, Walter. Road to War: America, 1914-1917. LC 68-9614. 1970. Repr. 27.50 (ISBN 0-86527-173-9). Fertig.
Millison, Martin B. Teenage Behavior in Shopping Centers. 1976. 12.00 (ISBN 0-685-82622-8). Intl Coun Shop.
Miller, R. Bryan & Wade, L. G., Jr., eds. Annual Reports in Organic Synthesis 1976, Vol. 7. 1977. 25.50 (ISBN 0-12-040807-4). Acad Pr.
Millman, Dan. Way of the Peaceful Warrior: A Basically True Story. LC 79-66725. 210p. 1980. 8.95 (ISBN 0-87477-121-8). J P Tarcher.
Millman, Howard L., jt. auth. see Huber, Jack T.
Millman, Howard L., jt. auth. see Schaefer, Charles E.
Millman, Howard L., et al. Therapies for School Behavior Problems. LC 80-8318. (Social & Behavioral Science Ser.). 1980. text ed. 18.95x (ISBN 0-87589-483-6). Jossey-Bass.
Millman, J., jt. auth. see Pauk, W.
Millman, Jason & Gowin, D. Appraising Educational Research: A Case Study Approach. LC 73-18004. (Educational Movement, Research & Statistics Ser.). (Illus.). 224p. 1974. pap. 10.95 ref. ed. (ISBN 0-13-043638-0). P-H.
Millman, Joan & Behrmann, Polly. Parents As Playmates: A Games Approach to the Pre-School Years. LC 79-4547. 1979. pap. 9.95 (ISBN 0-87705-404-5). Human Sci Pr.
Millman, Marcia. Such a Pretty Face: Being Fat in America. 1981. pap. 2.75 (ISBN 0-425-04849-7). Berkley Pub.
--The Unkindest Cut: Life in the Backrooms of Medicine. LC 76-18726. 1977. 8.95 o.p. (ISBN 0-688-03120-X); pap. 4.95 o.p. (ISBN 0-688-08120-7). Morrow.
Millman, Marcia & Kanter, Rosabeth Moss, eds. Another Voice. LC 75-8206. 400p. 1975. pap. 3.50 o.p. (ISBN 0-385-04032-6, Anch). Doubleday.
Millman, Michael L. Politics & the Expanding Physician Supply. LC 78-73591. (Conservation of Human Resources: No. 11). (Illus.). 176p. 1980. text ed. 22.50 (ISBN 0-916672-84-0). Allanheld.
Millman, Paul, jt. auth. see Millman, Ted.
Millman, Richard. Britain & the Eastern Question 1875-1878. (Illus.). 1979. 65.00x (ISBN 0-19-822379-X). Oxford U Pr.
Millman, Ted & Millman, Paul. Squash. (Illus.). 93p. 1980. 10.95 (ISBN 0-7136-1857-4). Transatlantic.
Millner, Darrell. Minority Teachers As Change Agents: A Case Study. 1977. pap. text ed. 7.50x (ISBN 0-8191-0136-2). U Pr of Amer.
Millon, Henry A. & Nochlin, Linda, eds. Art & Architecture in the Service of Politics. 1978. 37.50x (ISBN 0-262-13137-4). MIT Pr.
Millon, Judith. St. Pauls Within-the-Walls: Rome, a History. 1981. 8.95 (ISBN 0-87233-058-3). Bauhan.

Millon, T. & Diessenhaus, H. I. Research Methods in Psychopathology. (Approaches to Behavior Pathology Ser.). 1972. pap. 10.95x (ISBN 0-471-60626-X). Wiley.
Millon, Theodore. Disorders of Personality: DSMIII; AXIS II. 352p. 1981. 27.50 (ISBN 0-471-06403-3, Pub. by Wiley-Interscience). Wiley.
Millon, Theodore, ed. Medical Behavioral Science. LC 74-4581. (Illus.). 545p. 1975. text ed. 19.95 o.p. (ISBN 0-7216-6387-7). Saunders.
Millonzi, Joel C. Citizenship in Africa: The Role of Adult Education in the Political Socialization of Tanganyikans, 1891-1961. LC 75-30644. (Foreign and Comparative Studies Eastern African Series XIX). 119p. 1975. pap. text ed. 4.50x (ISBN 0-915984-16-4). Syracuse U Foreign Comp.
Millot, N., ed. see Zoological Society Of London - 20th Symposium.
Mills. Trauma, Vol. 1. 1981. pap. text ed. 25.00 (ISBN 0-443-02018-3). Churchill.
Mills & Broughton. Class J. (Bliss Education Classification Ser.). 1977. text ed. 19.95 (ISBN 0-408-70829-8). Butterworths.
--Class P: Religion, the Occult, Morals & Ethics. (Bliss Bibliographic Classification Ser.). 1977. 19.95 (ISBN 0-408-70832-8). Butterworths.
--Social Welfare, Political Science, Public Administration, Law. (Bliss Bibliographic Classification Ser.). 1977. 19.95 (ISBN 0-408-70833-6). Butterworths.
Mills, tr. see Mueller, F. Max.
Mills, Adelbert P., et al. Materials of Construction. 6th ed. LC 55-7368. 1955. text ed. 31.95x (ISBN 0-471-60654-5). Wiley.
Mills, Alice S., jt. auth. see Joseph, Lou.
Mills, C. Wright. Power Elite. 1956. 17.50 (ISBN 0-19-500020-X). Oxford U Pr.
--Power Elite. 1959. pap. 5.95 (ISBN 0-19-500680-1, GB). Oxford U Pr.
--Power, Politics, & People. Horowitz, Irving L., ed. 1963. 22.50 (ISBN 0-19-500021-8). Oxford U Pr.
--Power, Politics & People: The Collected Essays of C. Wright Mills. Horowitz, Irving L., ed. (YA) (gr. 9 up). 1967. pap. 6.95 (ISBN 0-19-500752-2, GB). Oxford U Pr.
--Sociological Imagination. 1967. pap. 4.95 (ISBN 0-19-500751-4, GB). Oxford U Pr.
--White Collar: American Middle Classes. 1956. pap. 6.95 (ISBN 0-19-500677-1, GB). Oxford U Pr.
Mills, C. Wright, ed. Images of Man. LC 60-8989. 1960. 10.00 o.p. (ISBN 0-8076-0114-4). Braziller.
Mills, Claudia. Luisa's American Dream. LC 80-69997. 160p. (gr. 7 up). 1981. 8.95 (ISBN 0-590-07684-1, Four Winds). Schol Bk Serv.
Mills, D. E. Collection of Tales from Uji. LC 72-114604. (Cambridge Oriental Publications: No. 15). (Illus.). 1970. 49.50 (ISBN 0-521-07754-0). Cambridge U Pr.
Mills, Daniel Q., jt. auth. see Lange, Julian E.
Mills, David. Overcoming Religion. 1980. pap. 3.95 (ISBN 0-8065-0742-X). Lyle Stuart.
Mills, David H., jt. auth. see Fretz, Bruce R.
Mills, Dennis R. Lord & Peasant in Nineteenth Century Britain. (Illus.). 232p. 1980. 31.50x (ISBN 0-8476-6806-1). Rowman.
Mills, Dick. Aquarium Fishes. LC 80-80742. (Arco Fact Guides in Color Ser.). (Illus.). 128p. 1980. 7.95 (ISBN 0-668-04944-8, 4944-8). Arco.
Mills, Dick, jt. auth. see Singleton, Val.
Mills, Dorothy H. & Martinez, Jorge C. Dictionary for the Health Professional: English-Spanish-Spanish-English. LC 79-90820. (Illus.). 250p. 1981. pap. 21.20 (ISBN 0-935356-03-7). Mills Pub Co.
Mills, Dorothy H. & Mata, Maria D. Survival Spanish: Book One. LC 80-66641. (Illus.). 180p. (Orig., Eng. & Span.). 1981. pap. text ed. 16.96 (ISBN 0-935356-01-0). Mills Pub Co.
Mills, E. Design for Industry. (Illus.). Date not set. text ed. cancelled (ISBN 0-408-00342-1). Butterworths.
Mills, Edmund J. The Secret Petrarch. 219p. 1980. Repr. lib. bdg. 45.00 (ISBN 0-89984-336-0). Century Bookbindery.
Mills, Edward D. Changing Workplace: Modern Technology & the Working Environment. 1972. text ed. 15.95x (ISBN 0-7114-3304-6). Intl Ideas.
Mills, Edward D., ed. Building Maintenance & Preservation: A Guide for Design & Management. (Illus.). 192p. 1980. pap. text ed. 39.95 (ISBN 0-408-00470-3). Butterworths.
Mills, Edwin S. The Economics of Environmental Quality. (Illus.). 1978. 12.95 (ISBN 0-393-09043-4). Norton.
--Urban Economics. 1972. 13.95x o.p. (ISBN 0-673-07716-0). Scott F.
Mills, Edwin S. & Oates, Wallace E. Fiscal Zoning & Land Use Controls. LC 74-21877. 224p. 1975. 19.95 (ISBN 0-669-96685-1). Lexington Bks.
Mills, Edwin S., ed. Economic Analysis of Environmental Problems. (Universities-National Bureau Conference Ser.: No. 26). 1975. 17.50 (ISBN 0-87014-267-4). Columbia U Pr.
Mills, Frederick V., Sr. Bishops by Ballot: An Eighteenth-Century Ecclesiastical Revolution. 1978. 16.95 (ISBN 0-19-502411-7). Oxford U Pr.
Mills, Gary B. The Forgotten People: Cane River's Creoles of Color. LC 77-452. (Illus.). 1977. 20.00x (ISBN 0-8071-0279-2); pap. 8.95 (ISBN 0-8071-0287-3). La State U Pr.
Mills, Glen E. Putting a Message Together. 2nd ed. LC 78-179367. Orig. Title: Message Preparation: Analysis & Structure. 1972. pap. 3.95 (ISBN 0-672-61299-2, SC8). Bobbs.
Mills, Gordon. Introduction to Linear Algebra for Social Scientists. 1969. text ed. 18.95x o.p. (ISBN 0-04-512008-0); pap. text ed. 8.95x o.p. (ISBN 0-04-512009-9). Allen Unwin.
Mills, H. R. Teaching & Training: A Handbook for Students. 3rd ed. 1978. pap. 12.95 (ISBN 0-470-99317-0). Halsted Pr.
Mills, Helen. Commanding Paragraphs. 2nd ed. 1981. pap. text ed. 9.95x (ISBN 0-673-15442-4). Scott F.
Mills, Howard W. Peacock, His Circle & His Age. LC 68-23183. (Illus.). 1969. 49.50 (ISBN 0-521-07262-X). Cambridge U Pr.
Mills, Howard W., ed. see Crabbe, George.
Mills, J. & Broughton, V., eds. Bliss Bibliographic Classification: Part T: Economics, Enterprise, Management. 2nd ed. Date not set. text ed. price not set (ISBN 0-408-70834-4). Butterworths.
Mills, J. W. Head & Figure Modelling. 1977. 24.00 (ISBN 0-7134-3258-6, Pub. by Batsford England). David & Charles.
Mills, James. The Prosecutor. 256p. 1969. 5.95 (ISBN 0-374-23836-7). FS&G.
--The Seventh Power. 1977. pap. 1.95 o.s.i. (ISBN 0-515-04415-6). Jove Pubns.
Mills, Jeannie. Six Years with God. (Illus.). 1979. 12.95 (ISBN 0-89479-046-3). A & W Pubs.
Mills, Jerry L. & Mitchell, Roy E. General Chemistry Experiments. (Illus.). 1979. lab manual 8.95 (ISBN 0-89582-012-9). Morton Pub.
Mills, Jerry L., jt. auth. see Hardison, O. B., Jr.
Mills, John. Low-Cost Car Repairs. (Illus.). 1967. 7.95 (ISBN 0-571-08052-9, Pub. by Faber & Faber); pap. 4.95 (ISBN 0-571-08982-8). Merrimack Bk Serv.
--The Technique of Sculpture. (Illus.). 160p. 1976. 16.95 o.p. (ISBN 0-8230-5210-9). Watson-Guptill.
--Up in the Clouds, Gentlemen Please. LC 80-22002. (Illus.). 320p. 1981. 14.95 (ISBN 0-89919-024-3). Ticknor & Fields.
Mills, John A. Arthritis: Diseases & Treatment, 3 vols. 3rd ed. Incl. Bk. 1. Inflammation (ISBN 0-89147-049-2); Bk. 2. Arthritis (ISBN 0-89147-050-6); Bk. 3. Anti-Inflammatory Therapy. (Illus) (ISBN 0-89147-051-4). 1977. Set. pap. text ed. 45.00 (ISBN 0-89147-048-4). pap. text ed. 16.50 ea. CAS.
Mills, John F. Peacock Festival: Selected Color Woodcuts. LC 64-8130. (Illus.). 1964. pap. 8.00 (ISBN 0-933652-00-3). Domjan Studio.
Mills, Joshua E., jt. auth. see Fornatale, Peter.
Mills, K. & Paul, J. Successful Retail Sales. 1979. pap. 12.95 (ISBN 0-13-869602-0). P-H.
Mills, K. L., ed. Guide to Orthopaedics, Vol. 1: Trauma. (Illus.). 280p. Date not set. text ed. 25.00x (ISBN 0-443-02018-3). Churchill.
Mills, Kenneth G. Surprises. 1980. 10.95 (ISBN 0-919842-06-2). Sun-Scape Pubns.
--A Word Fitly Spoken. 1980. 14.95 (ISBN 0-686-64679-7); pap. 7.95 (ISBN 0-919842-05-4). Sun-Scape Pubns.
Mills, Nick D., Jr., tr. see Hurtado, Osvaldo.
Mills, Nicolaus. Comparisons: A Short Story Anthology. 432p. 1972. text ed. 9.95 o.p. (ISBN 0-07-042370-9, C). McGraw.
--The New Journalism: An Historical Anthology. (Illus.). 512p. 1974. pap. text ed. 12.95 o.p. (ISBN 0-07-042349-0, C); pap. text ed. 9.95 o.p. (ISBN 0-07-042350-4). McGraw.
Mills, Nicolaus, ed. Busing U.S.A. LC 78-31327. 1979. text ed. 15.95x (ISBN 0-8077-2554-4). Tchrs Coll.
--The Great School Bus Controversy. LC 73-16469. 356p. 1973. 15.00x (ISBN 0-8077-2430-0); pap. 8.75x (ISBN 0-8077-2431-9). Tchrs Coll.
Mills, Patrick. Rape Intervention Resource Manual. (Illus.). 300p. 1977. 19.75 (ISBN 0-398-03594-6). C C Thomas.
Mills, Queenie B. & Mower, Rosalie. Picture Stories. (ps-k). 1973. pap. text ed. 3.92 (ISBN 0-205-03510-8, 5235103); tchrs'. guide 8.20 (ISBN 0-205-03511-6, 5235111). Allyn.
Mills, Randall V. Stern-Wheelers up Columbia: A Century of Steamboating in the Oregon Country. LC 77-7161. (Illus.). 1977. 10.95x (ISBN 0-8032-0937-1); pap. 3.75 (ISBN 0-8032-5874-7, BB 650, Bison). U of Nebr Pr.
Mills, Richard G. & Weiss, John M. Doctor Discusses Care of the Skin. (A Doctor Discusses...Ser.). (Illus.). 112p. pap. cancelled o.s.i. (ISBN 0-686-63407-1). Budlong.
Mills, Richard G., jt. auth. see Mahoney, Susan.
Mills, Richard G., jt. auth. see Quinn, Daniel.
Mills, Richard W. Classroom Observation of Primary School Children: All in a Day. (Unwin Education Bks). (Illus.). 248p. (Orig.). 1980. text ed. 22.50x (ISBN 0-04-372028-5); pap. text ed. 9.95x (ISBN 0-04-372029-3). Allen Unwin.
Mills, Robert E. Red Apache Sun. (Kansan Ser.: No. 3). 1981. pap. 1.95 (ISBN 0-8439-0877-7, Leisure Bks). Nordon Pubns.
Mills, Roger. Badminton. (Sports Library). (Illus.). 1979. 12.95 (ISBN 0-8069-9104-6); pap. 6.95 (ISBN 0-8069-9106-2). Sterling.
Mills, Roger F., ed. see Wojowasito, Soewojo.
Mills, Sonya, ed. The Book of Presents: Easy-to-Make Gifts for Every Occasion. LC 79-2187. 1979. 14.95 o.p. (ISBN 0-394-50782-7). Pantheon.
Mills, W. Jay, ed. see Paterson, William.
Mills, Willis N., Jr., jt. auth. see Lushington, Nolan.
Millsaps, Daniel & Washington International Arts Letter Editors. National Directory of Arts Support by Private Foundations, Vol. 4. (Arts Patronage Ser.: No. 9). 214p. 1980. pap. 65.00 (ISBN 0-912072-10-5). Wash Intl Arts.
Millsaps, Daniel, et al. The National Directory of Arts Support by Private Foundations. LC 77-79730. (Arts Patronage Ser.: No. 6, Vol. 3). 1978. pap. 65.00 (ISBN 0-912072-07-5). Wash Intl Arts.
Millspaugh, Arthur. Americans in Persia. LC 76-9837. (Politics & Strategy of World War II Ser.). 1976. Repr. of 1946 ed. lib. bdg. 27.50 (ISBN 0-306-70764-0). Da Capo.
Millspaugh, Arthur Chester. Crime Control by the National Government. LC 70-168678. (American Constitutional Legal History Ser). 306p. 1972. Repr. of 1937 ed. lib. bdg. 29.50 (ISBN 0-306-70418-8). Da Capo.
Millstein, Beth & Bodin, Jeanne. We, the American Women. (Illus.). 331p. 1977. lib. bdg. 17.20 (ISBN 0-574-42003-7, 11-1003); pap. text ed. 10.00 (ISBN 0-574-42000-2, 11-1002); tchrs'. guide 2.14 (ISBN 0-574-42001-0, 11-1001); student activity bk. 2.73 (ISBN 0-686-67300-X, 11-1002). SRA.
Millstein, Ira M. & Katsh, Salem M. The Limits of Corporate Power: Existing Constraints on the Exercise of Corporate Discretion. LC 80-69280. (Studies of the Modern Corporation). (Illus.). 1981. 15.95 (ISBN 0-02-921490-4). Free Pr.
Millward, R. & Robinson, A. Upland Britain. LC 79-56047. (Illus.). 192p. 1980. 25.00 (ISBN 0-7153-7823-6). David & Charles.
Millward, Roy & Robinson, Adrian. Landscapes of Britain. 1977. 14.95 (ISBN 0-7153-7181-9). David & Charles.
--Landscapes of North Wales. LC 78-6690. (Illus.). 1978. 22.50 (ISBN 0-7153-7713-2). David & Charles.
Milly, Jean. La Phrase de Proust. (Collection L). (Orig., Fr.). 1976. pap. text ed. 19.95 (ISBN 0-685-66286-1). Larousse.
Millyard, Anne W., jt. auth. see Wilks, Rick J.
Milman, Donald S. & Goldman, George D., eds. Group Process Today: Evaluation & Perspective. 336p. 1974. 19.75 (ISBN 0-685-50187-6). C C Thomas.
Milman, Donald S., jt. ed. see Goldman, George D.
Milman, Henry. History of Christianity from the Birth of Christ to the Abolition of Paganism in the Roman Empire, 3 vols. Repr. Set. 85.00 o.p. (ISBN 0-686-12344-1). Church History.
Milman, Henry H. The Belvidere Apollo: A Prize Poem, Repr. Of 1812 Ed. Bd. with Fazio: A Tragedy. Repr. of 1815 ed; Samor, Lord of the Bright City: An Heroic Poem. Repr. of 1818 ed. LC 75-31232. (Romantic Context: Poetry 1789-1830 Ser.: Vol. 83). 1977. lib. bdg. 47.00 (ISBN 0-8240-2182-7). Garland Pub.
--The Fall of Jerusalem: A Dramatic Poem, Repr. Of 1820 Ed. Bd. with Belshazzar: A Dramatic Poem. Repr. of 1822 ed. LC 75-31233. (Romantic Context: Poetry 1789-1830 Ser.: Vol. 84). 1977. lib. bdg. 47.00 (ISBN 0-8240-2183-5). Garland Pub.
--The Martyr of Antioch: A Dramatic Poem, Repr. Of 1822 Ed. Bd. with Anne Boleyn: A Dramatic Poem. Repr. of 1826 ed. LC 75-31234. (Romantic Context: Poetry 1789-1830 Ser.: Vol. 85). 1976. lib. bdg. 47.00 (ISBN 0-8240-2184-3). Garland Pub.
Milne, A. A. Gallery of Children. reissue ed. (Illus.). 1976. 4.95 o.p. (ISBN 0-679-50689-6). McKay.
--Walt Disney's Winnie-the-Pooh: A Tight Squeeze. (Illus.). (ps-3). 1962. 1.95 (ISBN 0-307-10859-7, Golden Pr); PLB 7.62 (ISBN 0-307-60859-X). Western Pub.
--Walt Disney's Winnie-the-Pooh & Eeyore's Birthday. 1964. 1.95 (ISBN 0-307-10861-9, Golden Pr); PLB 7.62 (ISBN 0-307-60861-1). Western Pub.
--When We Were Very Young. (gr. 1-5). 1961. 6.95 (ISBN 0-525-42580-2). Dutton.
--Winnie Ille Pu: A Latin Edition of Winnie-the-Pooh. Lenard, Alexander, tr. (Illus.). (gr. 7 up). 1962. 6.95 o.p. (ISBN 0-525-43007-5). Dutton.
--Winnie the Pooh. (Illus.). (gr. 1-5). 6.95 (ISBN 0-525-43035-0). Dutton.
--Winnie-the-Pooh & Eeyore's House. (Tell-a-Tale Reader). (Illus.). (gr. k-3). 1976. PLB 4.77 (ISBN 0-307-68620-5, Whitman). Western Pub.
--Winnie-the-Pooh & the Blustery Day. (Tell-a-Tale Readers). (Illus.). (gr. k-3). 1979. PLB 4.77 (ISBN 0-307-68577-2, Whitman). Western Pub.
--Winnie-the-Pooh & Tigger. (Illus.). (gr. k-3). 1976. PLB 5.00 (ISBN 0-307-60121-8, Golden Pr). Western Pub.
--Winnie-the-Pooh Meets Gopher. (Illus.). 24p. (gr. k-3). 1976. PLB 5.00 (ISBN 0-307-60017-3, Golden Pr). Western Pub.
--Winnie-the-Pooh: Unbouncing of Tigger. (Tell-a-Tale Readers). (Illus.). (gr. k-3). 1978. PLB 4.77 (ISBN 0-307-10504-0, Whitman); pap. 1.95 (ISBN 0-307-10504-0). Western Pub.
--Winnie the Pooh's Calendar Book: 1981. (Illus.). 1980. 3.95 o.p. (ISBN 0-525-43049-0). Dutton.
--Winnie-the-Pooh's Calendar Book 1982. 32p. (ps up). 1981. spiral 4.50 (ISBN 0-525-43050-4). Dutton.
Milne, A. J. Freedom & Rights. 1968. text ed. 10.75x (ISBN 0-04-170021-X). Humanities.
Milne, A. T., ed. Librarianship & Literature. 1970. text ed. 17.00x (ISBN 0-485-11117-9, Athlone Pr). Humanities.
Milne, Andrew. Metternich. 189p. 1975. 12.00x o.p. (ISBN 0-87471-591-1). Rowman.
Milne, Antony. Noise Pollution: Impact & Countermeasures. 1979. 17.95 (ISBN 0-7153-7701-9). David & Charles.
Milne, C., jt. auth. see Singer, R. N.
Milne, Christopher. Enchanted Places. (Illus.). (gr. 9 up). 1975. 8.25 o.p. (ISBN 0-525-29293-4). Dutton.
Milne, F. A. see Gomme, George L., et al.
Milne, Gordon. Stephen Crane at Brede: An Anglo-American Literary Circle of the Eighteen Nineties. LC 80-8126. 69p. 1980. lib. bdg. 12.75 (ISBN 0-8191-1139-2); pap. text ed. 6.25 (ISBN 0-8191-1140-6). U Pr of Amer.
Milne, J. G. Greek & Roman Coins & the Study of History. (Illus.). 128p. 1980. 30.00. Obol Intl.
--Greek & Roman Coins & the Study of History. (Illus.). 1977. 15.00 (ISBN 0-916710-80-7). Obol Intl.
Milne, John, ed. Heinemann Guided Readers. Incl. Beginner Level. Rich Man, Poor Man. Jupp, T. C. 1976. pap. text ed. 1.25x (ISBN 0-435-27022-2); Beginner Level. Death of a Soldier. Prowse, Philip. 1976. pap. text ed. 1.25x (ISBN 0-435-27036-2); Beginner Level. Marco. Espien, Mike. 1976. pap. text ed. 1.25x (ISBN 0-435-27023-0); Dangerous Journey. Cox, Alwyn. 1976. pap. text ed. 1.25x (ISBN 0-435-27021-4); Beginner Level. Money for a Motorbike. Milne, John. 1976. pap. text ed. 1.25x (ISBN 0-435-27035-4); Beginner Level. The Truth Machine. Whitney, Norman. 1976. pap. text ed. 1.25x (ISBN 0-435-27037-0); Elementary Level. Road to Nowhere. Milne, John. 1975. pap. text ed. 1.50x (ISBN 0-435-27013-3); Elementary Level. The Black Cat. Milne, John. 1975. pap. text ed. 1.50x (ISBN 0-435-27012-5); Elementary Level. Star for a Day. Prowse, Philip. 1976. pap. text ed. 1.50x (ISBN 0-435-27034-6); Intermediate Level. Bristol Murder. Prowse, Philip. pap. text ed. 1.75x (ISBN 0-435-27003-6); Intermediate Level. **The Smuggler. Plowright, Piers. pap. text ed. 1.75x (ISBN 0-435-27005-2); Intermediate Level. Football. Forbes, Duncan. pap. text ed. 1.75x (ISBN 0-435-27004-4); Intermediate Level. The Woman Who Disappeared. Prowse, Philip. 1975. pap. text ed. 1.75x (ISBN 0-435-27011-7); Intermediate Level. The Raid. Frewer, Glyn. 1976. pap. text ed. 1.75x (ISBN 0-435-27017-6); Upper Level. Money for Sale. Hardcastle, Michael. 1975. pap. text ed. 1.95x (ISBN 0-435-27020-6); Upper Level. The Story of Pop. Byrne, John. 1975. pap. text ed. 1.95x (ISBN 0-435-27025-7); Upper Level. The Olympic Games. Tulloh, Bruce. 1976. pap. text ed. 1.95x (ISBN 0-435-27027-3). pap. text ed. 2.25x 1977 handbook (ISBN 0-435-27039-7). Heinemann Ed.**
Milne, Lorus & Milne, Margery. The Audubon Society Field Guide to North American Insects & Spiders. LC 80-7620. (Illus.). 1008p. 1980. 9.95 (ISBN 0-394-50763-0). Knopf.

--Gadabouts & Stick-at-Homes: Wild Animals & Their Habitats. (Sierra Club-Scribner's Juvenile Ser.). (Illus.). 128p. (gr. 4 up). 1980. 8.95 (ISBN 0-684-16473-6). Sierra.
--Living Plants of the World. 1967. 20.00 o.p. (ISBN 0-394-43343-2). Random.
Milne, Lorus, et al. The Secret Life of Animals: Pioneering Discoveries in Animal Behavior. LC 75-10073. 200p. 1975. 29.95 o.p. (ISBN 0-525-19932-2). Dutton.
Milne, Lorus J. & Milne, Margery. Behavior in the Insect World. (Illus.). 192p. 1980. cancelled o.p. (ISBN 0-684-16627-5, ScribT). Scribner.
--Mountains. rev. ed. LC 62-11577. (Life Nature Library). (Illus.). (gr. 5 up). 1970. PLB 8.97 o.p. (ISBN 0-8094-0616-0, Pub. by Time-Life). Silver.
Milne, Lururus J. & Milne, Margery J. The World of Night. (Nature Library Ser.). (Illus.). 248p. (Orig.). 1981. pap. 5.95 (ISBN 0-06-090839-4, CN 839, CN). Har-Row.
Milne, Margery, jt. auth. see Milne, Lorus.
Milne, Margery, jt. auth. see Milne, Lorus J.
Milne, Margery J., jt. auth. see Milne, Lururus J.
Milne, Marvis J., jt. auth. see Andrews, John T.
Milne, P. H. Fish & Shellfish Farming in Coastal Waters. (Illus.). 208p. 24.75 (ISBN 0-85238-022-4, FN). Unipub.
Milne, Roseleen. The Major's Lady. 1980. pap. write for info. (ISBN 0-671-83652-8). PB.
Milne, Terry. The Ultimate Bay Book: A Guide to the Pleasures of the San Francisco Bay. Ratner, Elaine & Stewart, Jay, eds. LC 78-52509. (Illus.). 1979. pap. 9.95 (ISBN 0-89395-010-6). Cal Living Bks.
Milne, William E. Numerical Solution of Differential Equations. 1970. pap. text ed. 5.00 (ISBN 0-486-62437-4). Dover.
Milner, Alfred. England in Egypt. 13th ed. LC 68-9624. 1971. Repr. of 1920 ed. 17.00 (ISBN 0-86527-331-6). Fertig.
Milner, Andrew. John Milton & the English Revolution: A Study in the Sociology of Literature. 224p. 1981. 29.50x (ISBN 0-389-20123-5). B&N.
Milner, Anita C. Newspaper Indexes: A Location & Subject Guide for Researchers, Vol. II. LC 77-7130. 303p. 1979. 11.00 (ISBN 0-8108-1244-4). Scarecrow.
--Newspaper Indexes: A Location & Subject Guide for Researchers. LC 77-7130. 1977. 10.00 (ISBN 0-8108-1066-2). Scarecrow.
Milner, D. R. & Apps, R. L. Introduction to Welding & Brazing. 1968. text ed. 19.50 (ISBN 0-08-012306-6); pap. text ed. 8.50 (ISBN 0-08-013342-8). Pergamon.
Milner, G. W. & Phillips, G. Coulometry in Analytical Chemistry. 1967. text ed. 23.00 (ISBN 0-08-012439-9); pap. text ed. 11.25 (ISBN 0-08-012438-0). Pergamon.
Milner, John. Russian Revolutionary Art. (Oresko-Jupiter Art Bks). (Illus.). 96p. 1980. 17.95 (ISBN 0-905368-22-3, Pub. by Oresko-Jupiter England). Hippocrene Bks.
--Symbolism. (Oresko-Jupiter Art Bks). (Illus.). 96p. 1981. 17.95 (ISBN 0-933516-87-8, Pub. by Oresko-Jupiter England). Hippocrene Bks.
Milner, Max, et al, eds. Protein Resources & Technology. (Illus.). 1978. text ed. 45.00 (ISBN 0-87055-249-X). AVI.
Milner, Murray, Jr. Unequal Care: A Case Study of Interorganizational Relations. (Illus.). 224p. 1980. 22.50x (ISBN 0-231-05006-2). Columbia U Pr.
Milner, Neal, jt. auth. see Hottois, James W.
Milner, R. A Calculus of Communicating Systems. (Lecture Notes in Computer Science Ser.: Vol. 92). 260p. 1981. pap. 11.80 (ISBN 0-387-10235-3). Springer-Verlag.
Milner, Ron, jt. ed. see King, Woodie.
Milner-Gulland, R. R., ed. Yevgeny Yevtushenko: Selected Poetry. 1963. 6.70 (ISBN 0-08-009808-8); pap. 5.15 (ISBN 0-08-009807-X). Pergamon.
Milnes, John, et al. The Magic Flute: Mozart. Beasch, Anthony & Besch, Anthony, trs. 1980. pap. 4.95 (ISBN 0-7145-3768-3). Riverrun NY.
Milne-Thomson, L. M. The Calculus of Finite Difference. 2nd ed. LC 80-65906. xxiii, 558p. 1980. text ed. 22.50 (ISBN 0-8284-0308-2). Chelsea Pub.
--Russian-English Mathematical Dictionary. (Mathematical Research Center Pubns., No. 7). 1962. 40.00x (ISBN 0-299-02600-0). U of Wis Pr.
Milo, Mary. A Bird in a Box. 335p. (Orig.). 1980. pap. 2.50 (ISBN 0-345-28673-1). Ballantine.
Milofsky, David. Playing from Memory. 1981. 12.95 (ISBN 0-671-25252-6). S&S.
Milonas, Rolf. Fantasex. 1977. pap. 1.50 o.p. (ISBN 0-345-25657-3). Ballantine.
Miloradovich, Milo, jt. auth. see LoPinto, Maria.
Milosz, Czeslaw. Bells in Winter. Milosz, Czeslaw & Vallee, Lillian, trs. from Polish. LC 78-5617. (gr. 10-12). 1978. 9.95 (ISBN 0-912946-56-3). Ecco Pr.
--Emperor of the Earth: Modes of Eccentric Vision. LC 76-20005. 1977. 14.95 (ISBN 0-520-03302-7). U of Cal Pr.
--History of Polish Literature. LC 69-10189. (Illus.). 1969. 14.95 o.s.i. (ISBN 0-02-585010-5). Macmillan.
--The Issa Valley. Iribarne, Louis, tr. 1981. 12.95 (ISBN 0-374-17798-8). FS&G.
--Native Realm: A Search for Self-Definition. 304p. 1981. 12.95 (ISBN 0-385-17596-5). Doubleday.
--Selected Poems. LC 73-6424. 144p. 1973. 8.95 (ISBN 0-8264-0049-3). Continuum.
--Selected Poems. rev. ed. LC 80-21470. 129p. 1981. pap. 8.95 (ISBN 0-912946-76-8). Ecco Pr.
Milroy, James. The Language of Gerard Manley Hopkins. 1978. lib. bdg. 28.50 o.p. (ISBN 0-233-96916-0). Westview.
Milsark, Gary L. Existential Sentences in English. Hankamer, Jorge, ed. LC 78-66570. (Outstanding Dissertations in Linguistics Ser.). 1979. lib. bdg. 30.00 (ISBN 0-8240-9678-9). Garland Pub.
Milsom, S. F. The Legal Framework of English Feudalism. LC 75-23531. (Cambridge Studies in English Legal History). 1976. 33.95 (ISBN 0-521-20947-1). Cambridge U Pr.
Milson, A. & Kirk, D. Principles of Design & Operation of Catering Equipment. american ed. (Illus.). 1980. pap. text ed. 30.00 (ISBN 0-87055-357-7). AVI.
Milson, Fred. An Introduction to Community Work. 168p. 1974. 14.00x (ISBN 0-7100-7840-4); pap. 5.25 (ISBN 0-7100-7841-2). Routledge & Kegan.
Milstein, Jeffrey, jt. auth. see Walker, Les.
Milstein, Mike M. Impact & Response: Federal Education Programs & State Agencies. LC 76-14887. 1976. text ed. 13.95 (ISBN 0-8077-2502-1); pap. 8.25x (ISBN 0-8077-2501-3). Tchrs Coll.
Milstein, Mike M. & Jennings, Robert E. Educational Policy-Making & the State Legislature: The New York Experience. LC 78-185780. (Special Studies in U.S. Economic, Social & Political Issues). 1973. 28.00x (ISBN 0-275-28719-X). Irvington.
Milstein, Mike M., ed. Schools, Conflict & Change. LC 79-30327. 1980. 19.95x (ISBN 0-8077-2571-4). Tchrs Coll.
Milt, Harry. Alcholism: Its Causes & Cure. LC 76-8476. 192p. 1976. 8.95 o.p. (ISBN 0-684-14667-3, ScribT). Scribner.
--Basic Handbook of Mental Illness. rev. ed. LC 73-19278. 128p. 1974. 5.95 o.p. (ISBN 0-684-13738-0, ScribT); pap. 2.95 o.p. (ISBN 0-684-13753-4, SL513, ScribT). Scribner.
Milthorpe, F. L. & Moorby, J. Introduction to Crop Physiology. 2nd ed. LC 78-26380. (Illus.). 1980. 42.50 (ISBN 0-521-22624-4); pap. 12.50x (ISBN 0-521-29581-5). Cambridge U Pr.
Milton, Charles R. Human Behavior in Organizations. (Illus.). 432p. 1981. text ed. 18.95x (ISBN 0-13-444596-1). P-H.
Milton, David. The Politics of U. S. Labor: From the Great Depression to the New Deal. LC 80-8934. 352p. 1981. 18.00 (ISBN 0-85345-569-4). Monthly Rev.
Milton, David & Milton, Nancy D. The Wind Will Not Subside: Years in Revolutionary China,1964-1969. LC 75-10370. 1976. pap. 7.95 (ISBN 0-394-70936-5). Pantheon.
Milton, David, jt. auth. see Bradley, D.
Milton, David S. Kabbalah. LC 79-3360. 360p. 1980. 13.95 (ISBN 0-15-146608-4). HarBraceJ.
Milton, Donald, jt. auth. see Baggelaar, Kristin.
Milton, Hilary. The Brats & Mr. Jack. LC 80-23144. 160p. (gr. 5 up). 1980. 8.95 (ISBN 0-8253-0004-5). Beaufort Bks NY.
--Emergency: Ten Thirty-Three. (gr. 5 up). 1977. PLB 7.90 s&l (ISBN 0-531-02905-0). Watts.
--The Gitaway Box. (gr. 4-9). 1980. pap. 2.95 (ISBN 0-89191-243-6). Cook.
--The Longest Highway. LC 78-74526. 1979. pap. 2.50 (ISBN 0-89191-138-3). Cook.
--Mayday! Mayday! (gr. 5 up). 1979. PLB 7.90 s&l (ISBN 0-531-02890-9). Watts.
--Nowhere to Run. LC 78-2798. (gr. 7 up). 1978. PLB 7.90 s&l (ISBN 0-531-02247-1). Watts.
Milton, J. Paradise Lost, Bks. 7 & 8. Aers, D. & Radzinowics, Mary Ann, eds. LC 77-181884. (Milton for Schools & Colleges Ser). 200p. 1974. pap. text ed. 6.95x (ISBN 0-521-20457-7). Cambridge U Pr.
Milton, J. H. & Leach, R. M. Marine Steam Boilers. 4th ed. (Illus.). 700p. 1980. text ed. 33.75 (ISBN 0-408-00416-9). Butterworths.
Milton, John. Areopagitica. 80p. 1972. Repr. of 1644 ed. 7.50x (ISBN 0-87556-219-1). Saifer.
--English Poems. Skeat, W. W., ed. (World's Classics Ser). 7.95 o.p. (ISBN 0-19-250182-8). Oxford U Pr.
--John Milton: Complete Poems & Major Prose. Hughes, Merritt Y., ed. 1957. 18.95 (ISBN 0-672-63178-4). Odyssey Pr.
--Odes, Pastorals, Masques. Broadbent, et al, eds. LC 73-94355. (Milton for Schools & Colleges). 300p. 1975. pap. text ed. 8.50x (ISBN 0-521-20456-9). Cambridge U Pr.
--Paradise Lost. Elledge, Scott, ed. (Critical Editions Ser). 546p. 1975. 19.95 (ISBN 0-393-04406-8); pap. 6.95x (ISBN 0-393-09230-5). Norton.
--Paradise Lost, Bks. 5 & 6. Hodge, R. I. & MacCaffrey, I., eds. LC 75-8314. (Milton for Schools & Colleges Ser). (Illus.). 176p. 1975. pap. text ed. 6.95x (ISBN 0-521-20796-7). Cambridge U Pr.
--Paradise Lost, a New Edition: A Poem in Twelve Books. Hughes, Merritt Y., ed. LC 62-11937. (Orig.). 1962. pap. 3.95 (ISBN 0-672-63080-X). Odyssey Pr.
--Paradise Lost & Other Poems. pap. 2.25 (ISBN 0-451-61881-5, ME1881, Ment). NAL.
--Poems. Wright, B. A., ed. 1956. 6.00x (ISBN 0-460-00384-4, Evman); pap. 9.25 (ISBN 0-460-01384-X). Dutton.
--Poems of John Milton. Darbishire, Helen, ed. 1961. 29.00x o.p. (ISBN 0-19-811421-4). Oxford U Pr.
--The Poetical Works, 2 vols. Darbishire, Helen, ed. Incl. Vol. 1. Paradise Lost. 1952. 42.00x (ISBN 0-19-811819-8); Vol. 2. Paradise Regained, Samson Agonistes, Poems Upon Several Occasions. 1955. 39.00x (ISBN 0-19-811820-1). (Oxford English Texts Ser). Oxford U Pr.
--Samson Agonistes. Prince, F. T., ed. 1957. pap. 5.95x (ISBN 0-19-831910-X). Oxford U Pr.
Milton, John, ed. & intro. by. Conversations with Frank Waters. LC 78-189195. 90p. 1971. 5.00 o.s.i. (ISBN 0-8040-0575-3); pap. 3.50 (ISBN 0-8040-0576-1). Swallow.
Milton, John R. The Novel of the American West. LC 79-17713. xviii, 341p. 1980. 17.95 (ISBN 0-8032-0980-0). U of Nebr Pr.
--South Dakota. (States & the Nation Ser.). (Illus.). 1977. 12.95 (ISBN 0-393-05627-9, Co-Pub by AASLH). Norton.
Milton, Joyce. A Friend of China. (Books for Young Readers Ser.). (Illus.). 128p. (gr. 7 up). 1980. PLB 8.95 (ISBN 0-8038-2388-6). Hastings.
Milton, Mary Lee. The Poetry of Samual Traylor Coleridge: An Annotated Bibliography of Criticism, 1935 to 1970. LC 80-83650. 250p. 1981. lib. bdg. 30.00 (ISBN 0-8240-9451-4). Garland Pub.
Milton, Nancy D., jt. auth. see Milton, David.
Milton, Octavia. Assist Three: For Consonant Blends of L, R, & S. 50p. 1981. pap. text ed. 13.00 (ISBN 0-88450-729-7). Communication Skill.
Milton, Ohmer & Shoben, Edward J., Jr., eds. Learning & the Professors. LC 67-22230. xvii, 216p. 1968. 12.00x (ISBN 0-8214-0036-3); pap. 5.95x (ISBN 0-8214-0105-X). Ohio U Pr.
Milts, Michael H. & Larsen, Carl. Only a Gringo Would Die for an Anteater: The Adventures of a Veterinarian. (McGraw-Hill Paperbacks Ser.). 240p. 1980. pap. 3.95 (ISBN 0-07-042391-1). McGraw.
Miluck, Michael, ed. The Genoa-Carson Valley Book, 1981-82. (Illus.). 96p. 1981. pap. 3.00 (ISBN 0-686-28841-6). Dragon Ent.
Miluck, Nancy C. Nevada: This Is Our Land. (Illus.). 148p. 1978. pap. 6.50 (ISBN 0-686-27941-7). Dragon Ent.
Milunsky, Aubrey. Know Your Genes. 1978. pap. 1.95 (ISBN 0-380-40899-6, 40899). Avon.
--The Prenatal Diagnosis of Hereditary Disorders. (Illus.). 276p. 1973. text ed. 16.75 (ISBN 0-398-02747-1). C C Thomas.
--Prevention of Genetic Disease & Mental Retardation. LC 74-21015. (Illus.). 450p. 1975. 29.00 (ISBN 0-7216-6395-8). Saunders.
Milunsky, Aubrey, et al, eds. Advances in Perinatal Medicine, Vol. 1. 450p. 1981. 35.00 (ISBN 0-306-40482-6, Plenum Pr). Plenum Pub.
Milutnovic, Barbara, jt. auth. see Broadwell, Lucile.
Milverstedt, F. M. In This Corner: Muhammad Ali. LC 75-42338. (Sports Profiles Ser.). (Illus.). 48p. (gr. 4-11). 1976. 7.49 o.p. (ISBN 0-8172-0130-0). Raintree Pubs.
--The Quiet Legend: Henry Aaron. LC 75-19277. (Sports Profiles Ser.). (Illus.). 48p. (gr. 4-11). 1975. PLB 8.50 (ISBN 0-8172-0102-5). Raintree Pubs.
Milverstedt, Van & Sanders, Peter. On the Boards. LC 75-1128. (The Venture Ser, a Reading Incentive Program). (Illus.). 80p. (gr. 7-12,RL 4.5-6.5). 1975. In Packs Of 5. text ed. 23.25 ea. pack (ISBN 0-8172-0210-2). Follett.
Milward, Alan S. The German Economy at War. 1965. text ed. 14.00x (ISBN 0-485-11075-X, Athlone Pr). Humanities.
--War, Economy & Society: 1939-1945. 1977. 21.50x (ISBN 0-520-03338-8, CAL432); pap. 6.95 (ISBN 0-520-03942-4). U of Cal Pr.
Milward, Alan S. & Saul, S. B. The Economic Development of Continental Europe 1780-1870. 2nd ed. (Illus.). 1973. text ed. 39.95x (ISBN 0-04-330229-7); pap. text ed. 15.95x (ISBN 0-04-330299-8). Allen Unwin.
Milward, Peter. Oddities in Modern Japan: Observations of an Outsider. (Illus.). viii, 187p. 1980. pap. 11.50 (ISBN 0-89346-183-0, Pub. by Hokuseido Pr). Heian Intl.
Milwidski, B. M., jt. auth. see Davidsohn, A.
Mimistry of Finance, Japan. Guide to the Economic Laws of Japan, 2 vols. (Studies in Japanese Law & Government). 1979. Repr. of 1950 ed. Set. 62.50 (ISBN 0-89093-220-4). U Pubns Amer.
Mims, Charles W., jt. auth. see Alexopoulos, Constantine J.
Mims, Edwin, Jr. see Gabriel, Ralph H.
Mims, George L., ed. The Minority Administrator in Higher Education: Progress, Experiences, & Perspectives. 220p. 1981. text ed. 22.50x (ISBN 0-87073-161-0); pap. text ed. 8.95x (ISBN 0-87073-162-9). Schenkman.
Mims, W. B. The Linear Electric Field Effect in Paramagnetic Resonance. (Illus.). 1976. 24.95x (ISBN 0-19-851944-3). Oxford U Pr.
Minahan, Anne, jt. auth. see Pincus, Allen.
Minahan, John. The Complete American Graffiti: The Novel. 1979. pap. 2.25 o.p. (ISBN 0-425-04249-9). Berkley Pub.
--Eyewitness. 176p. (Orig.). 1981. pap. 2.25 (ISBN 0-380-77388-0, 77388). Avon.
--Nine-Thirty-Fifty-Five. pap. 1.75 o.p. (ISBN 0-380-00970-6, 32474). Avon.
Minahan, John, jt. auth. see Tress, Arthur.
Minai, Naila. Women in Islam. LC 80-52405. 320p. 1981. 11.95 (ISBN 0-87223-666-8). Seaview Bks.
Minar, William M. Greenhouse Gardening in the South. LC 76-1685. (Illus.). 96p. 1976. pap. 3.95 (ISBN 0-88415-327-4). Pacesetter Pr.
Minc, Alain, jt. auth. see Nora, Simon.
Mincu, Julian. Diabetic Macro- & Microahgiopathy. LC 73-82434. 1975. 73.00x (ISBN 3-11-004533-8). De Gruyter.
Mindszenty, Cardinal Jozsef. Mindszenty. (Illus.). 480p. 1974. 10.00 o.s.i. (ISBN 0-02-585050-4). Macmillan.
Mine Advisory Committee, ed. see Symposium On Underwater Physiology - 2nd - Feb. 25-26 - Washington D.C. - 1963.
Minear, Beulah F., ed. & illus. see Minear, Larry M.
Minear, Larry M. Air Travel Answers. Minear, Beulah F., ed. & illus. LC 79-52955. (Illus.). 1979. 2.10 (ISBN 0-934268-00-2). Aerofacts.
Minear, Paul S. To Die & to Live: Christ's Resurrection & Christian Vocation. 1977. 8.95 (ISBN 0-8164-0340-6). Crossroad NY.
--To Heal & to Reveal: The Prophetic Vocation According to Luke. 1976. 8.95 (ISBN 0-8164-0295-7). Crossroad NY.
Minear, Paul S. & Adams, Harry B. Pentecost 2. Achtemeier, Elizabeth, et al, eds. LC 79-7377. (Proclamation 2: Aids for Interpreting the Lessons of the Church Year, Ser. A). 64p. (Orig.). 1981. pap. 2.50 (ISBN 0-8006-4097-7, 1-4097). Fortress.
Minear, Ralph E., jt. auth. see Reinisch, Edith H.
Minehan, Thomas. Boy & Girl Tramps of America. LC 76-7792. (Americana Library: No.29). 280p. 1976. Repr. of 1934 ed. 16.00 (ISBN 0-295-95450-7). U of Wash Pr.
Miner, Caroline E. & Kimball, Edward L. Camilla. LC 80-69723. (Illus.). 1980. 5.95 (ISBN 0-87747-845-7). Deseret Bk.
Miner, Earl, ed. Illustrious Evidence: Approaches to Early Seventeenth-Century Literature. 1975. 15.75x (ISBN 0-520-02782-5). U of Cal Pr.
--Seventeenth Century Imagery: Essays on Uses of Figurative Language from Donne to Farquhar. LC 76-132417. (Seventeenth & Eighteenth Centuries Studies Group, UCLA: No. 1). 1971. 18.50x (ISBN 0-520-01825-7). U of Cal Pr.
--Stuart & Georgian Moments: Clark Library Seminar Papers on Seventeeth & Eighteenth Century Literature. (Seventeenth & Eighteenth Centuries Studies Group, UCLA: No. 3). 308p. 1972. 18.50x (ISBN 0-520-01641-6). U of Cal Pr.
--Writers & Their Background: John Dryden. LC 72-95818. (Writers & Their Background Ser.). xxvi, 363p. 1972. 15.00x (ISBN 0-8214-0119-X); pap. 6.95x (ISBN 0-8214-0120-3). Ohio U Pr.
Miner, Earl see Dryden, John.
Miner, Earl, tr. Japanese Poetic Diaries. (Center for Japanese & Korean Studies, UC Berkeley). (Illus.). 1969. 18.50x (ISBN 0-520-01466-9); pap. 3.95 (ISBN 0-520-03047-8). U of Cal Pr.
Miner, Lynn E., jt. auth. see Griffith, Jerry.
Mineralogical Society Geochemistry Group, November 1 & 2, 1978. The Evidence of Chemical Heterogeneity in the Earth's Mantle. Bailey, D. K., et al, eds. (Illus.). 357p. 1980. text ed. 100.00x (ISBN 0-85403-144-8, Pub. by Royal Soc London). Scholium Intl.

Mines, Allan. Respiratory Physiology. (Raven Press Ser. in Physiology). 180p. 1981. 12.50 (ISBN 0-89004-634-4). Raven.
Mingay, G. E. The Gentry: The Rise & Fall of a Ruling Class. LC 76-13576. (Themes in British Social History). (Illus.). 1976. pap. text ed. 10.95x (ISBN 0-582-48403-0). Longman.
--Georgian London. (Illus.). 164p. 1976. 18.50 o.s.i. (ISBN 0-7134-3045-1). Hippocrene Bks.
--Georgian London. 1975. 33.00 (ISBN 0-7134-3045-1, Pub. by Batsford England). David & Charles.
Mingay, G. E., jt. auth. see Chambers, J. D.
Mingay, G. E., ed. The Agricultural Revolution: Changes in Agriculure Sixteen Fifty to Eighteen Eighty. (Documents in Economic History). 1977. text ed. 18.25x (ISBN 0-7136-1703-9). Humanities.
--The Victorian Countryside, 2 vols. (Illus.). 370p. 1981. 45.00 (ISBN 0-7100-0734-5); 45.00 (ISBN 0-7100-0735-3); Set. price not set (ISBN 0-7100-0736-1). Routledge & Kegan.
Mingay, Gordon E., ed. see Hammond, J. L. & Hammond, B.
Mingilton, Jesse, jt. auth. see Dowall, David E.
Mingle, James R. Fact Book on Higher Education in the South: 1977 & 1978. rev. ed. 1978. pap. 3.00 o.p. (ISBN 0-686-23906-7). S Regional Ed.
Mingot, Tomas De Galiana. Pequeno Larousse de ciencias y tecnicas. new ed. 1056p. 1975. 23.00 (ISBN 0-685-55467-8, 21115). Larousse.
Ming-tse Li, Lillian. China's Silk Trade: A Traditional Industry & the International Market, 1842-1937. (Harvard East Asian Monograph: No. 97). 1981. text ed. 15.00x (ISBN 0-674-11962-2). Harvard U Pr.
Mingus, Charles. Beneath the Underdog. 1980. pap. 3.95 (ISBN 0-14-003880-9). Penguin.
Minifie, Bernard W. Chocolate Cocoa and Confectionery: Science & Technology. 1970. 29.00 o.p. (ISBN 0-87055-097-7). AVI.
--Chocolate, Cocoa & Confectionery: Science & Technology. 2nd ed. (Illus.). 1980. lib. bdg. 45.00 (ISBN 0-87055-330-5). AVI.
Minikin, R. R. Winds, Waves & Maritime Structures. 295p. 1963. 29.75x (ISBN 0-85264-091-9, Pub. by Griffin England). State Mutual Bk.
Mining Information Services. Mining Methods & Equipment. 224p. 1980. 16.50 (ISBN 0-07-039794-5). McGraw.
Mining Journal Books Ltd. Negotiation & Drafting of Mining Development Agreements. 236p. 1980. 19.00x (ISBN 0-900117-11-7, Pub. by Mining Journal England). State Mutual Bk.
--Tungsten. 190p. 1980. 28.00x (ISBN 0-900117-21-4, Pub. by Mining Journal England). State Mutual Bk.
--Uranium & Nuclear Energy. 326p. 1980. 36.00x (ISBN 0-900117-20-6, Pub. by Mining Journal England). State Mutual Bk.
--Uranium: Balance of Supply & Demand Nineteen Seventy Eight to Nineteen Ninety. 60p. 1980. 20.00x1311 (ISBN 0-900117-19-2, Pub. by Mining Journal England). State Mutual Bk.
Mining Journal Editors. Mining Annual Review 1980. 200p. 1980. 60.00x (Pub. by Mining Journal England). State Mutual Bk.
Minio, Robert, jt. auth. see Dummett, Michael.
Minio-Paluello, L., ed. see Aristotle.
Minirth, Frank, et al. The Workaholic & His Family: An Inside Look. 144p. (Orig.). 1981. 8.95 (ISBN 0-8010-6111-3). Baker Bk.
Minis, Cola, ed. see Gentry, Francis G.
Minish & Lidvall. Fundamentals of Meat Animal Evaluation. 1981. text ed. 15.95 (ISBN 0-8359-2137-9); instr's. manual free (ISBN 0-8359-2138-7). Reston.
Minish, Gary L. & Fox, Danny G. Beef Production & Management. (Illus.). 1979. text ed. 16.95 (ISBN 0-8359-0445-8); instrs'. manual avail. Reston.
Ministers of Foreign Affairs of the American Republics-5th-Santiago-Chile 1959. Final Act: Meeting of Consultation. (Port. & Fr.). pap. 1.00 ea. o.p. OAS.
Ministers of Foreign Affairs of the American Republics-6th-San Jose-Costa Rica-1960. Final Act: Meeting of Consultation. (Sp.). pap. 1.00 (ISBN 0-8270-1675-1). OAS.
Ministers of Foreign Affairs of the American Republics-7th-San Jose-Costa Rica-1960. Final Act: Meeting of Consultation. (Sp.). pap. 1.00 (ISBN 0-8270-1700-6). OAS.
Ministers of Foreign Affairs of the American Republic-8th-Punta Del Este-Uruguay-1962. Final Act: Meeting of Consultation. (Eng., Span. & Port.). pap. 1.00 ea. o.p. OAS.
Ministers of Foreign Affairs of the American Republics-12th-Washington D. C.-1968. Final Act: Meeting of Consultation. (Span. & Eng.). pap. 1.00 Eng. ed. (ISBN 0-8270-1735-9); pap. 1.00 Span ed. (ISBN 0-8270-1740-5). OAS.
Ministers of Foreign Affairs of the American Republics-15th Quito, Ecuador. Final Act: Meeting of Consultation. (Eng., Span., Fr.). 1974. pap. 1.00 Eng. ed. (ISBN 0-8270-1745-6); pap. 1.00 Span. ed. (ISBN 0-8270-1750-2); pap. 1.00 French ed. (ISBN 0-8270-1755-3). OAS.
Ministry of Labor, Japan. Japan Labor Code, 2 vols. (Studies in Japanese Law & Government). 1979. Repr. of 1953 ed. Set. 56.00 (ISBN 0-89093-217-4). U Pubns Amer.
Minium, E. W. Statistical Reasoning in Psychology & Education. 2nd ed. 1978. text ed. 22.95x (ISBN 0-471-60828-9); wkbk (ISBN 0-471-03633-1); instructors' manual avail. (ISBN 0-471-04055-X). Wiley.
Mink, B. Washburn, jt. auth. see Roueche, N. E.
Mink, Louis O. Finnegans Wake Gazetteer. LC 77-74443. 600p. 1978. 25.00x (ISBN 0-253-32210-3). Ind U Pr.
Mink, Oscar G. Developing & Managing Open Organizations. LC 79-10195. 1979. text ed. 17.95 (ISBN 0-89384-045-9). Learning Concepts.
Mink, Oscar G., jt. ed. see Smith, C. E.
Minke, Karl A. & Carlson, John G. Mastering the Essentials of Psychology & Life. 10th ed. 1980. pap. text ed. 5.95x (ISBN 0-673-15170-0). Scott F.
Minkkinen, Arno R., ed. New American Nudes. (Illus.). 128p. 1981. pap. 19.95 (ISBN 0-87100-178-0). Morgan.
Minkoff, Eli. C. A Laboratory Guide to Frog Anatomy. LC 74-22206. 176p. 1975. pap. text ed. 7.75 (ISBN 0-08-018315-8). Pergamon.
Minkow, Howard, jt. auth. see Minkow, Rosalie.
Minkow, Rosalie. Money Management for Women. LC 80-84373. 256p. (Orig.). 1981. pap. 2.50 (ISBN 0-87216-816-6). Playboy Pbks.
Minkow, Rosalie & Minkow, Howard. The Complete List of IRS Tax Deductions. LC 80-82660. 272p. (Orig.). 1981. pap. 2.50 (ISBN 0-87216-775-5). Playboy Pbks.
Minkowich, Avram. Success & Failure in Israeli Elementary Education. 400p. 1981. 29.95 (ISBN 0-87855-370-3). Transaction Bks.
Minkowski, A. & Monset-Couchard, M., eds. Physiological & Biochemical Basis for Perinatal Medicine. (Illus.). x, 370p. 1981. 72.00 (ISBN 3-8055-1283-X). S Karger.
Minkowski, Hermann. Diophantische Approximationen. LC 56-13056. (Ger). 11.95 (ISBN 0-8284-0118-7). Chelsea Pub.
--Gesammelte Abhandlungen, 2 Vols. in 1. LC 66-28570. (Ger). 35.00 (ISBN 0-8284-0208-6). Chelsea Pub.
Minnaert, M. Nature of Light & Colour in the Open Air. 1948. pap. text ed. 4.00 (ISBN 0-486-20196-1). Dover.
Minneapolis Institute of Arts. Arakawa. (Illus.). 1979. 8.00. Minneapolis Inst Arts.
Minneapolis Institute of Arts, jt. auth. see Walker Art Center.
Minnear, Festus L. & Grimes, Ruby M. Review of Mathematics, for Beginning Science & Engineering Students. LC 60-5903. (Illus.). 1960. pap. text ed. 6.75x o.p. (ISBN 0-7167-0404-8). W H Freeman.
Minnery, John. How to Kill, Vol. III. (Illus.). 92p. (Orig.). 1979. pap. 6.00 (ISBN 0-87364-156-6). Paladin Ent.
--How to Kill, Vol. IV. (Illus.). 92p. (Orig.). 1979. pap. 6.00 (ISBN 0-87364-162-0). Paladin Ent.
--How to Kill, Vol. V. (Illus.). 86p. 1980. pap. 5.00 (ISBN 0-87364-201-5). Paladin Ent.
Minnery, John, jt. auth. see Truby, J. David.
Minnesota Historical Society. Chippewa & Dakota Indians: A Subject Catalog of Books, Pamphlets, Periodical Articles & Manuscripts in the Minnesota Historical Society. LC 70-102272. 131p. 1969. pap. 7.50 (ISBN 0-87351-056-9). Minn Hist.
--A Complete Index to the Gopher Historian, 1946-1972. LC 68-51880. 73p. 1977. pap. 7.50 (ISBN 0-87351-113-1). Minn Hist.
Minnesota Hospital Association, compiled by. The Changing Role of the Hospital: Options for the Future. 336p. (Orig.). 1980. pap. 35.00 (ISBN 0-87258-310-4, 1186). Am Hospital.
Minney, R. J., jt. auth. see Laden, Alice.
Minnich, Harvey C. Williams Holmes McGuffey & His Readers. LC 74-19214. (Illus.). xii, 203p. 1975. Repr. of 1936 ed. 18.00 (ISBN 0-8103-4104-2). Gale.
Minnich, Harvey C., ed. see McGuffey, William H.
Minnick, John & Strauss, Raymond. Beginning Algebra. 2nd ed. (Illus.). 288p. 1976. text ed. 15.95 (ISBN 0-13-073791-7). P-H.
Minnick, John H. Intermediate Algebra. 2nd ed. (Illus.). 1978. ref. ed. 16.95 (ISBN 0-13-469569-0). P-H.
Minnick, Sally. Dear World: A Collection of Form Letters for You to Use & Enjoy. 1981. 7.95. Green Hill.
Minno, Frances P., jt. ed. see Levine, Harriet.
Minns, Ellis H. Scythians & Greeks. LC 65-15248. (Illus.). 1913. 50.00x (ISBN 0-8196-0277-9). Biblo.
Minns, Richard & Thornley, Jennifer. State Shareholding: The Role of Local & Regional Authorities. 1979. text ed. 35.00x (ISBN 0-333-23739-0). Verry.
Minogue, Kenneth, jt. ed. see De Crespigny, Anthony.
Minogue, Kenneth R. The Concept of the University. 1973. 16.50x (ISBN 0-520-02390-0, CAL 287). U of Cal Pr.
Minogue, M. & Molloy, J., eds. African Aims & Attitudes: Selected Documents. LC 74-76567. 404p. 1974. 39.50 (ISBN 0-521-20426-7); pap. text ed. 12.95x (ISBN 0-521-09851-3). Cambridge U Pr.
Minogue, Valerie. Nathalie Sarraute: The War of the Words. 156p. 1981. 21.00x (ISBN 0-85224-405-3, Pub. by Edinburgh U Pr Sctland). Columbia U Pr.
Minor, Andrew C. & Mitchell, M. Bonner, eds. Renaissance Entertainment: Festivities for the Marriage of Cosimo I, Duke of Florence, in 1539. LC 68-11348. (Illus.). 1968. 15.00x (ISBN 0-8262-8522-8). U of Mo Pr.
Minor, Harold D., ed. Creative Procedures for Adult Groups. LC 68-17624. (Orig.). 1968. pap. 2.50 o.p. (ISBN 0-687-09833-5). Abingdon.
Minor, Lewis J., jt. auth. see Smith, Laura L.
Minor, M. Three in a Hill. 5.95 o.p. (ISBN 0-8062-1114-8). Carlton.
Minor, Marz & Minor, Nono. The American Indian Craft Book. LC 77-14075. (Illus.). 1978. 15.00 (ISBN 0-8032-0974-6); pap. 5.50 (ISBN 0-8032-5891-7, BB 661, Bison). U of Nebr Pr.
Minor, Nono, jt. auth. see Minor, Marz.
Minor, Robert, jt. auth. see Fetridge, Clark.
Minor, William S. Creativity in Henry Nelson Wieman. LC 77-8087. (ATLA Monograph Ser.: No. 11). 250p. 1977. lib. bdg. 12.00 (ISBN 0-8108-1041-7). Scarecrow.
Minorsky, V. Studies in Caucasian History. (Cambridge Oriental Ser). 44.00 (ISBN 0-521-05735-3). Cambridge U Pr.
Minorsky, Vladimir. The Turks, Iran & the Caucasus in the Middle Ages. 368p. 1980. 69.00x (ISBN 0-86078-028-7, Pub. by Variorum England). State Mutual Bk.
Minot, G. R. History of the Insurrections in Massachusetts in 1786. LC 76-148912. (Era of the American Revolution Ser). 1971. Repr. of 1788 ed. lib. bdg. 22.50 (ISBN 0-306-70100-6). Da Capo.
Minovi, Ramin. Early Reading & Writing. (Classroom Close-Ups Ser.). 1976. text ed. 10.50x o.p. (ISBN 0-04-372016-1); pap. text ed. 4.95x o.p. (ISBN 0-04-372017-X). Allen Unwin.
Mins, Henry F., tr. see Horvat, Branko.
Minshall, G. N. The New Europe, an Economic Geography of the EEC. 2nd ed. LC 78-6581. 288p. 1981. pap. text ed. 17.50x (ISBN 0-8419-6221-9). Holmes & Meier.
Minshall, Herbert L. Window on the Sea. Pourade, Richard F., ed. LC 80-52787. (Illus.). 190p. 1980. 18.50 (ISBN 0-913938-22-X). Copley Bks.
Minsheu, John. Ductor in Linguas: The Guide into Tongues. LC 78-14754. 600p. 1978. Repr. of 1617 ed. lib. bdg. 120.00x (ISBN 0-8201-1321-2). Schol Facsimiles.
Minshull, Roger. The Changing Nature of Geography. 1970. pap. text ed. 7.25x (ISBN 0-09-102711-X, Hutchinson U Lib). Humanities.
--Regional Geography. 168p. 1967. text ed. 4.50x (ISBN 0-09-082772-4, Hutchinson U Pr); pap. text ed. 2.00x (ISBN 0-09-082773-2). Humanities.
Minski, L. & Shepperd, M. J. Non-Communicating Children. (Illus.). 1970. 10.95 (ISBN 0-407-33200-6). Butterworths.
Minsky, Betty J. Gimmicks Make Money in Retailing. 2nd ed. LC 71-153566. (Illus.). 200p. 1972. 8.95 (ISBN 0-87005-095-8). Fairchild.
Minsky, Hyman P. John Maynard Keynes. (Essays on the Great Economists). 192p. 1975. 17.50x (ISBN 0-231-03616-7); pap. 4.00x (ISBN 0-231-03917-4). Columbia U Pr.
Minsky, Marvin. Computation: Finite & Infinite Machines. 1967. ref. ed. 23.95 (ISBN 0-13-165563-9). P-H.
Minsky, Marvin L. & Papert, Seymour. Perceptrons: An Introduction to Computational Geometry. 1969. pap. 8.95x (ISBN 0-262-63022-7). MIT Pr.
Minteer, Catherine. Words & What They Do to You: Beginning Lessons in General Semantics for Junior & Senior High School. (gr. 7-12). text ed. 4.00x (ISBN 0-910780-06-4). Inst Gen Semantics.
Minter, Charles R. A Processor Design for the Efficient Implementation of APL. LC 79-7305. (Outstanding Dissertations in the Computer Sciences Ser.: Vol. 11). 285p. 1980. lib. bdg. 28.00 (ISBN 0-8240-4421-5). Garland Pub.
Minter, David. William Faulkner: His Life & Work. LC 80-13089. 325p. 1980. text ed. 16.95x (ISBN 0-8018-2347-1). Johns Hopkins.
Minter, James F. Pencil Pastimes, No. 9. 128p. 1981. pap. 2.50 (ISBN 0-89104-172-9). A & W Pubs.
Minter, Phyllis V., jt. auth. see Rogers, Ferial.
Minters, Frances C., jt. auth. see Sands, Harry.
Minto, C. S. Victorian & Edwardian Edinburgh. 1976. pap. 11.95 (ISBN 0-7134-0333-0, Pub. by Batsford England). David & Charles.
Minton, Arthur J. & Shipka, Thomas A. Philosophy: Paradox & Discovery. 2nd ed. 496p. 1982. pap. text ed. 11.95 (ISBN 0-07-042413-6, C). McGraw.
Minton, Madge R., jt. auth. see Minton, Sherman A.
Minton, Robert. Forest Hills: An Illustrated History. LC 75-14461. (Illus.). 268p. 1975. 17.95 o.p. (ISBN 0-397-01094-X). Lippincott.
Minton, S. A. Venom Diseases. (American Lectures in Living Chemistry Ser.). (Illus.). 256p. 1974. 16.75 (ISBN 0-398-03051-0). C C Thomas.
Minton, Sherman A. & Minton, Madge R. Venomous Reptiles. rev. ed. (Illus.). 320p. 1980. 12.95 (ISBN 0-684-16626-7, ScribT). Scribner.
Mintonye, Grace, jt. auth. see Seidelman, James E.
Minty, Judith. In the Presence of Mothers. LC 80-5259. (Pitt Poetry Ser.). 1981. 9.95 (ISBN 0-8229-3427-2); pap. 4.50 (ISBN 0-8229-5321-8). U of Pittsburgh Pr.
--Letters to My Daughters. 24p. (Orig.). 1981. pap. 4.00 (ISBN 0-932412-03-3). Mayapple Pr.
Mintz, Elizabeth E. Marathon Groups: Reality & Symbol. LC 73-157796. (Century Psychology Ser.). 1971. 24.00x (ISBN 0-89197-293-5); pap. text ed. 6.95x (ISBN 0-89197-294-3). Irvington.
Mintz, Grafton K., ed. see Han, Woo-Keun.
Mintz, Jerome R., jt. ed. see Ben-Amos, Dan.
Mintz, Jerome R., tr. see Ben-Amos, Dan & Mintz, Jerome R.
Mintz, Leigh W. Historical Geology. 2nd ed. (Physical Science Ser.). 1977. text ed. 20.95 (ISBN 0-675-08603-5). Merrill.
--Historical Geology: The Science of a Dynamic Earth. 3rd ed. (Illus.). 576p. 1981. text ed. 20.95 (ISBN 0-675-08028-2); tchr's. ed. 3.95 (ISBN 0-686-69492-9). Merrill.
Mintz, Lorelie, jt. auth. see Mintz, Thomas.
Mintz, Marilyn D. The Martial Arts Film. 9.95 o.p. (ISBN 0-498-01775-3). A S Barnes.
Mintz, Samuel I. Hunting of Leviathan. 1962. 35.50 (ISBN 0-521-05736-1). Cambridge U Pr.
Mintz, Samuel I., et al, eds. From Smollett to James: Studies in the Novel & Other Essays Presented to Edgar Johnson. LC 79-25865. 1981. 27.50x (ISBN 0-8139-0663-6). U Pr of Va.
Mintz, Sidney W. Caribbean Transformations. LC 74-82602. 360p. 1974. lib. bdg. 23.95x (ISBN 0-202-01125-9). Aldine Pub.
Mintz, Sidney W., ed. Slavery, Colonialism, & Racism. 213p. 1975. text ed. 10.95x 1975 (ISBN 0-393-01115-1); pap. text ed. 3.95x 1974 (ISBN 0-393-09234-8). Norton.
Mintz, Thomas & Mintz, Lorelie. Threshold: A Doctor Gives Straightforward Answers to Teenagers' Most Often Asked Questions About Sex. LC 77-78991. (Illus.). (gr. 5-9). 1978. 7.95 o.s.i. (ISBN 0-8027-6307-3); PLB 7.85 (ISBN 0-8027-6308-1). Walker & Co.
Mintzberg, Henry. Structuring of Organizations. (Theory of Management Policy Ser.). (Illus.). 1979. ref. ed. 22.95 (ISBN 0-13-855270-3). P-H.
Minault, Gail. The Khilafat Movement: Religious Symbolism & Political Mobilization in India. 1981. text ed. 22.50x (ISBN 0-231-05072-0). Columbia U Pr.
Mi-pham, Lama. Calm & Clear. LC 73-79058. (Tibetan Translation Ser., Vol. 1). (Illus.). 128p. 1973. pap. 4.95 (ISBN 0-913546-02-X). Dharma Pub.
MIR Publishers, tr. see Glinka, N.
MIR Publishers, tr. see Kompaneyets, Alexander.
Mira, C., jt. auth. see Gumowski, I.
Mira, C., jt. auth. see Gumowski, Igor.
Mira, Giuseppe M. Bibliografia Siciliana, Ovvero Gran Dizionario Bibliografico Delle Opere Editi E Inedite, Antiche E Moderne Di Autori Siciliani O Di Argomento Siciliano Stampate in Sicilia, 3 vols. 1873-1881. 82.50 (ISBN 0-8337-2400-2); inc. supplement by giuseppe salvo-cozzo (ISBN 0-685-06732-7). B Franklin.
Mira, Julio A. Arithmetic Clear & Simple. (Orig.). 1965. pap. 2.95 (ISBN 0-06-463270-9, EH 270, EH). Har-Row.
--Mathematical Teasers. LC 74-101122. (Orig.). 1970. pap. 2.95 (ISBN 0-06-463230-X, EH 230, EH). Har-Row.
Mirabeau see Bentley, Eric.
Mirabella, Lauren, jt. ed. see Konsler, Runelle.

Miracle, Marvin P. Maize in Tropical Africa. (Illus.). 1966. 25.00 (ISBN 0-299-03850-5). U of Wis Pr.
Miranda, J. B., Jr., jt. auth. see Hallauer, Arnel R.
Miranda, Miguel Dario Cardinal Foreword by see Abeloe, William N.
Mirande, Alfredo & Enriquez, Evangelina. La Chicana: The Mexican-American Woman. LC 79-13536. (Illus.). x, 284p. 1981. pap. 6.95 (ISBN 0-226-53160-0). U of Chicago Pr.
Mirandola, Giovanni Pico Della see Pico Della Mirandola, Giovanni.
Miranker, Willard L. Numerical Methods for Stiff Equations & Singular Perturbation Problems. (Mathematics & Its Applications Ser.: No. 5). 216p. 1980. lib. bdg. 29.95 (ISBN 90-277-1107-0, Pub. by D. Reidel). Kluwer Boston.
Miranker, Willard L., jt. auth. see Kulisch, Ulrich W.
Mirchandani, G. G. State Assembly Elections. 240p. 1980. text ed. 22.50x (ISBN 0-7069-1288-8, Pub. by Vikas India). Advent Bk.
Mireaux, Emile. Daily Life in the Time of Homer. Sells, Iris, tr. 1959. 9.95 (ISBN 0-02-585090-3). Macmillan.
Mirenda, Rose, et al. Nutrition & Diet Therapy. 2nd ed. (Nursing Examination Review Book: Vol. 8). 1972. spiral bdg. 6.00 (ISBN 0-87488-508-6). Med Exam.
Mirengoff, William & Rindler, Lester. CETA: Manpower Programs Under Local Control. 1978. pap. text ed. 10.50x (ISBN 0-309-02792-6). Natl Acad Pr.
--The Comprehensive Employment & Training Act: Impact on People, Places, & Programs: an Interim Report. LC 75-42971. 175p. 1976. pap. 6.00 (ISBN 0-309-02443-9). Natl Acad Pr.
Mirengoff, William, et al. Ceta: Assessment of Public Service Employment Programs. xxl, 197p. 1980. pap. text ed. 10.50 (ISBN 0-309-02925-2). Natl Acad Pr.
Mirin, Susan R. The Nurses Guide to Writing for Publication. LC 80-84085. (Nursing Dimension Administrative Ser & Nursing Dimension Administrative Ser.). 180p. 1981. text ed. 14.50 (ISBN 0-913654-71-X). Nursing Res.
Mirkovic, Irene. The Greedy Shopkeeper. LC 80-13034. (Illus.). 32p. (gr. k-3). 1980. pap. 2.95 (ISBN 0-15-232552-2, VoyB). HarBraceJ.
Miroff, Bruce. Pragmatic Illusions: The Presidential Politics of John F. Kennedy. LC 76-7554. 1976. 10.95x (ISBN 0-679-30298-0, Pub. by MacKay); pap. 8.95x (ISBN 0-582-28130-X). Longman.
Miroff, Franklin I., jt. auth. see Smith, Jerome.
Mirollo, James V., jt. ed. see Gibaldi, Joseph.
Miron, Murray S. & Goldstein, Arnold P. Hostage. rev. ed. LC 77-16554. (Pergamon General Psychology Ser.: No. 79). 170p. 1979. 22.00 (ISBN 0-08-023875-0); pap. 8.75 (ISBN 0-08-023876-9). Pergamon.
Mirov, Nicholas T. The Genus Pinus. (Illus.). 1967. 26.50 (ISBN 0-8260-6140-0, Pub. by Wiley-Interscience). Wiley.
Mirov, Nicholas T. & Hasbrouck, Jean. Story of Pines. LC 74-30899. (Illus.). 160p. 1976. 7.95x (ISBN 0-253-35462-5). Ind U Pr.
Mirow, Gregory. Treasury of Design for Artists & Craftsmen. LC 69-18877. (Pictoral Archive Ser). 1969. pap. 4.00 (ISBN 0-486-22002-8). Dover.
Mirra, Joseph M. Bone Tumors: Diagnosis & Treatment. (Illus.). 1980. text ed. 69.50 (ISBN 0-397-50428-4). Lippincott.
Mirrlees, Hope. Lud-in-the-Mist. (Del Rey Bks). 1977. pap. 1.95 o.p. (ISBN 0-345-25848-7). Ballantine.
Mirsky, A. E., jt. ed. see Brachet, Jean.
Mirvis, Philip H. & Berg, David N. Failures in Organization Development & Change: Cases & Essays for Learning. LC 77-21625. 1977. 29.95 (ISBN 0-471-02405-8). Ronald Pr.
Mirza, A. I., tr. from Urdu. Modern Urdu Stories. (Writers Workshop Saffronbird Bk Ser.). 1977. flexible bdg. 4.80 (ISBN 0-89253-643-8); text ed. 10.00 (ISBN 0-89253-642-X). Ind-US Inc.
Mirza, Sarah M, jt. auth. see Hinnebusch, Thomas J.
Misa, Ted. Baseball Quiz Book, No. 2. 1975. pap. 3.50 o.p. (ISBN 0-8015-0523-2). Dutton.
--Baseball Quiz Book (or Who's on First?, No. 1. 128p. 1974. pap. 3.50 (ISBN 0-8015-0524-0, Hawthorn). Dutton.
Misch, Robert Jay. Quick Guide to the Wines of All the Americas. LC 76-23783. 1977. 4.95 o.p. (ISBN 0-385-06469-1). Doubleday.
Mischa, Helen, ed. see Morris, Ben.
Mische, Bernard & Mische, Fridolin. Spreading the Word: Daily Homily-Meditation Themes for the Weekdays of the Year. pap. 4.75 o.p. (ISBN 0-685-61282-1). Alba.
Mische, Fridolin, jt. auth. see Mische, Bernard.
Mische, Gerald & Mische, Patricia. Toward a Human World Order: Beyond the National Security Straitjacket. LC 76-41440. 1977. 9.95 (ISBN 0-8091-0216-1); pap. 2.95 (ISBN 0-8091-1977-3). Paulist Pr.
Mische, Patricia, jt. auth. see Mische, Gerald.
Mischel, Florence, jt. auth. see Jacobson, Helen.
Mischel, Harriet N., jt. auth. see Mischel, Walter.
Mischel, Theodore, ed. The Self: Psychological & Philosophical Issues. 359p. 1977. pap. 12.00x (ISBN 0-8476-6946-7). Rowman.
--The Self: Psychological & Philosophical Issues. 1977. 23.50x o.p. (ISBN 0-87471-969-0). Rowman.
Mischel, W. Personality & Assessment. LC 67-31183. 1968. 23.95 (ISBN 0-471-60925-0). Wiley.
Mischel, Walter & Mischel, Harriet N. Essentials of Psychology. 1977. text ed. 14.95 o.p. (ISBN 0-394-31860-9). Random.
Mischke, Bernard C. & Mischke, Fritz. Pray Today's Gospel: Reflections on the Day's Good News. LC 80-14186. 358p. (Orig.). 1980. pap. 9.95 (ISBN 0-8189-0403-8). Alba.
Mischke, Fritz, jt. auth. see Mischke, Bernard C.
Miscia, Vincent F., jt. auth. see Holsinger, James W., Jr.
Mise, Raymond W. The Gothic Heroine & the Nature of the Gothic Novel. Varma, Devendra P., ed. LC 79-8465. (Gothic Studies & Dissertations Ser.). 1980. lib. bdg. 25.00x (ISBN 0-405-12675-1). Arno.
Misenheimer, Helen E. Rousseau on the Education of Women. LC 80-5857. 109p. 1981. lib. bdg. 15.75 (ISBN 0-8191-1404-9); pap. text ed. 7.50 (ISBN 0-8191-1405-7). U Pr of Amer.
Mises, Ludwig Von. Liberlaism: A Socio-Economic Exposition. 1978. write for info. NYU Pr.
--The Ulitmate Foundation of Economic Science: An Essay on Method. 1978. wrtie for info. NYU Pr.
--The Ultimate Foundation of Economic Science: An Essay on Method. LC 77-20127. (Studies in Economic Theory Ser.). 148p. 1978. Repr. of 1962 ed. 15.00x; pap. 4.95x. NYU Pr.
Mises, Ludwig Von see Von Mises, Ludwig.
Mises, Ludwig von see Von Misis, Ludwig.
Mises, Margit Von see Von Mises, Margit.
Mises, Richard Von see Von Mises, Richard & Von Karman, Theodore.
Mishan, E. J. Cost Benefit Analysis. revised ed. LC 76-1988. (Praeger Special Studies Ser.). 454p. 1976. text ed. 32.50 (ISBN 0-275-56530-0); pap. text ed. 11.95 (ISBN 0-275-85690-9). Praeger.
--Elements of Cost-Benefit Analysis. 1976. pap. text ed. 7.50x (ISBN 0-04-300066-5). Allen Unwin.
--An Introduction to Normative Economics. (Illus.). 576p. (Orig.). 1981. pap. text ed. 14.95x (ISBN 0-19-502791-4). Oxford U Pr.
--Pornography, Psychedelics & Technology: Essays on the Limits to Freedom. 184p. 1980. text ed. 22.50x (ISBN 0-04-300081-9, 2547). Allen Unwin.
Mishchenko, E. F. & Rozov, B. Kh. Differential Equations with Small Parameters & Relaxation Oscillations. (Mathematical Concepts & Methods in Science & Engineering Ser.: Vol. 13). (Illus.). 251p. 1980. 29.50 (ISBN 0-306-39253-4, Plenum Pr). Plenum Pub.
Mishell, Barbara B. & Shiigi, Stanley M., eds. Selected Methods in Cellular Immunology. LC 79-19990. (Illus.). 1980. text ed. 31.95x (ISBN 0-7167-1106-0). W H Freeman.
Mishima, Sumie. My Narrow Isle: The Story of a Modern Woman in Japan. LC 79-2945. (Illus.). 280p. 1981. Repr. of 1941 ed. 22.50 (ISBN 0-8305-0109-6). Hyperion Conn.
Mishima, Yukio. Five Modern No Plays. Keene, Donald, tr. from Japanese. (Illus.). 206p. 1957. pap. 6.50 (ISBN 0-8048-1380-9). C E Tuttle.
--Five Modern No Plays. Keene, Donald, tr. 198p. Date not set. pap. 1.95 (ISBN 0-394-71883-6, Vin). Random.
--Sun & Steel. Bester, John, tr. from Japanese. 176p. 1972. pap. 4.95 (ISBN 0-394-17765-7, E583, Ever). Grove.
Mishler, Clifford, jt. auth. see Krause, Chester L.
Mishler, Clifford, jt. auth. see Wilhite, Robert.
Mishler, Elliot G. Social Contexts of Health, Illness, & Patient Care. LC 80-22604. 256p. Date not set. price not set (ISBN 0-521-23559-6); pap. price not set (ISBN 0-521-28034-6). Cambridge U Pr.
Mishne, Judith, ed. Psychotherapy & Training in Clinical Social Work. LC 78-57616. (Clinical Social Work Ser.). 1978. 22.95x (ISBN 0-470-26387-3). Halsted Pr.
Mishra, Bhawani. Astrology for All. (Illus.). 200p. (Orig.). 1974. pap. 2.95 (ISBN 0-88253-299-5). Ind-US Inc.
Mishra, C. B. Hydraulic Machines Through Theory & Examples. x, 318p. (Orig.). 1980. pap. text ed. 10.00x (ISBN 0-210-33860-1). Asia.
Mishra, C. B., jt. auth. see Arwikar, J. S.
Mishra, Hemant R. & Mierow, Dorothy. Wild Animals of Nepal. (Illus.). 6.95x (ISBN 0-685-89511-4). Himalaya Hse.
Mishra, Rammurti S. Fundamentals of Yoga: A Handbook of Theory, Practice & Application. 240p. 1974. pap. 2.50 (ISBN 0-385-00952-6, Anch). Doubleday.
--Yoga Sutras: The Textbook of Yoga Psychology. 440p. 1973. pap. 3.50 o.p. (ISBN 0-385-08358-0, Anch). Doubleday.
Mishra, S. K., jt. auth. see Udupa, K. N.
Mishra, S. N. Politics & Leadership in Municipal Government. 1979. text ed. 9.00x (ISBN 0-391-01845-0). Humanities.
--Politics & Society in Rural India: A Case Study of Darauli Gram Panchayat, Siwan District, Bihar. 184p. 1980. text ed. 11.25x (ISBN 0-391-02123-0). Humanities.
Mishra, Sachida N. Political Socialization in India. (Illus.). 156p. 1980. pap. text ed. 8.75x (ISBN 0-391-02207-5). Humanities.
Mishra, V. Growth Multiplier & a General Theory of Economic Growth. 5.00x o.p. (ISBN 0-210-33999-3). Asia.
Misiak, Henryk, jt. ed. see Sexton, Virginia S.
Miskawayh, Ali. Refinement of Character. Zurayk, Constantine, tr. 1977. pap. 14.00x (ISBN 0-8156-6051-0, Am U Beirut). Syracuse U Pr.
Miskell, Jack T. Energy Transmission & Transportation E-018. 1979. 675.00 o.p. (ISBN 0-89336-190-9). BCC.
--Solar Hardware Supplies: A Review Analysis, E-036. 1980. 875.00 (ISBN 0-89336-192-5). BCC.
Miskimin, A. The Economy of the Later Renaissance Europe: 1460-1600. LC 75-17120. (Illus.). 1977. pap. 26.95 (ISBN 0-521-21608-7); pap. 7.95x (ISBN 0-521-29208-5). Cambridge U Pr.
Miskimin, Alice S. The Renaissance Chaucer. LC 74-79174. 328p. 1975. 18.50x o.p. (ISBN 0-300-01768-5). Yale U Pr.
Miskimin, H. A. Economy of Early Renaissance Europe. LC 75-15607. (Illus.). 204p. 1975. 21.50 (ISBN 0-521-21017-8); pap. 7.95x (ISBN 0-521-29021-X). Cambridge U Pr.
Miskovits, Christine. Echocardiography - A Manual for Technicians. 1977. spiral bdg. 15.00 (ISBN 0-87488-987-1). Med Exam.
Misner, Arthur J., jt. auth. see Dvorin, Eugene P.
Misner, Charles W., et al. Gravitation. LC 78-156043. (Physics Ser.). (Illus.). 1279p. 1973. pap. text ed. 38.95x (ISBN 0-7167-0344-0). W H Freeman.
Misner, Gordon E. Criminal Justice: Its Transdisciplinary Nature. 1981. pap. text ed. 14.95 (ISBN 0-8016-3457-1). Mosby.
Misner, Gordon E. & Crim, D. Criminal Justice Studies: Their Trans-Disciplinary Nature. (Illus.). 350p. 1981. pap. text ed. 14.95 (ISBN 0-8016-3457-1). Mosby.
Misra, Atmanand. Educational Finance in India. 1962. 18.50 o.p. (ISBN 0-210-34001-0). Asia.
--Financing of Indian Education. 1968. 7.50x o.p. (ISBN 0-210-31188-6). Asia.
Misra, Bhabagrahi. Verrier Elwin: A Pioneer Indian Anthropologist. 1974. lib. bdg. 8.95x (ISBN 0-210-40556-2). Asia.
Misra, K. P. Afghanistan in Crisis. 1981. 20.00x (ISBN 0-7069-1305-1, Pub. by Vikas India). Advent Bk.
--Foreign Policy & Its Planning. 1971. 5.50x (ISBN 0-210-22333-2). Asia.
Misra, K. P. & Beal, Richard S., eds. International Relations Theory: Western & Non-Western Perspectives. 272p. 1980. text ed. 27.50 (ISBN 0-7069-1087-7, Pub. by Vikas India). Advent Bk.
Misra, K. P., jt. ed. see Narayanan, K. R.
Misra, K. S. Plays of J. M. Synge: A Critical Study. 1978. 10.00x (ISBN 0-210-40622-4). Asia.
Misra, R. P., ed. Habitat Asia: Issues & Responses, 3 vols. Incl. Vol. 1. India (ISBN 0-391-01824-8); Vol. 2. Indonesia & the Philippines (ISBN 0-391-01825-6); Vol. 3. Japan & Singapore (ISBN 0-391-01827-2). 1979. text ed. 15.50 ea. Humanities.
Misra, R. P., et al, eds. Regional Planning & Nation Development. 1979. 34.00x (ISBN 0-7069-0555-5, Pub. by Croom Helm Ltd. England). Biblio Dist.
Misra, R. R., jt. auth. see Rastogi, R. P.
Misra, Shital P., jt. auth. see Shukla, Ashok C.
Misrock, Henry. Mischianza. 1967. 4.95 o.s.i. (ISBN 0-02-585150-0). Macmillan.
Misselwitz, Henry F. The Dragon Stirs: An Intimate Sketchbook of China's Kuomintang Revolution. LC 79-2835. (Illus.). 296p. 1981. Repr. of 1941 ed. 22.50 (ISBN 0-8305-0012-X). Hyperion Conn.
Misses, Ludwig Von see Von Misses, Ludwig.
Missildine, Fred & Karas, Nicholas. Score Better at Trap. (Illus.). 1970. 7.95 (ISBN 0-87691-025-8); pap. 5.95 (ISBN 0-87691-153-X). Winchester Pr.
Missildine, Fred & Karas, Nick. Score Better at Skeet. (Illus.). 1972. 7.95 (ISBN 0-87691-049-5); pap. 5.95 (ISBN 0-87691-050-9). Winchester Pr.
Missner, Marshall. Ethics of the Business System. LC 79-22806. 1980. pap. 8.95 (ISBN 0-88284-100-9). Alfred Pub.
Miss Piggy. Miss Piggy's Guide to Life. LC 80-2708. (Illus.). 192p. 1981. 12.95 (ISBN 0-394-51912-4). Knopf.
Mistral, Gabriela. Cartas De Gabriela Mistral a Juan Ramon Jimnez. pap. 0.50 o.p. (ISBN 0-8477-3139-1). U of PR Pr.
Mital, K. V. Optimization Methods in Operations Research & Systems Analysis. LC 76-56846. 1977. 14.95 (ISBN 0-470-99056-2). Halsted Pr.
--Optimization Methods in Operations Research & Systems Analysis. 259p. 1980. pap. 8.95 (ISBN 0-470-27081-0). Halsted Pr.
Mitau, G. Theodore. A Selected Bibliography of Minnesota Government, Politics, & Public Finance Since 1900. (Studies in Minn. Govt. & Politics). 94p. 1960. pap. 2.50 (ISBN 0-685-47099-7). Minn Hist.
Mitch, Miami. The Blues Brothers. (Orig.). 1980. pap. 2.50 (ISBN 0-515-05630-8). Jove Pubns.
Mitcham, Samual W., Jr. Rommel's Desert War: The Life & Death of the Afrika Korps. LC 80-6153. 228p. 1981. 13.95 (ISBN 0-8128-2784-8). Stein & Day.
Mitchel, Kevin M., jt. auth. see Berenson, Bernard G.
Mitchell, A. C., jt. auth. see Kellington, S. H.
Mitchell, Alan, jt. auth. see Lambert, Terence.
Mitchell, Allan. Bismarck & the French Nation: 1848-1890. LC 72-167692. 1971. 24.50x (ISBN 0-672-53510-6). Irvington.
Mitchell, Arthur. Labour in Irish Politics: Eighteen Ninty to Nineteen Thirty. (Illus.). 317p. 1974. 20.00x (ISBN 0-686-28343-0, Pub. by Irish Academic Pr). Biblio Dist.
Mitchell, Audrey, ed. Compton's Encyclopedia, 1980, 26 vols. 1980. write for info. (ISBN 0-85229-380-1). Ency Brit Ed.
Mitchell, B. R. & Jones, H. G. Second Abstract of British Historical Statistics. LC 72-128502. (Department of Applied Economics Monographs: No. 18). (Illus.). 1971. 45.00 (ISBN 0-521-08001-0). Cambridge U Pr.
Mitchell, Basil. The Justification of Religious Belief. LC 73-17904. 1974. 8.95 (ISBN 0-8164-1152-2). Crossroad NY.
--Morality-Religious & Secular: The Dilemma of the Traditional Conscience. 180p. 1980. 22.50 (ISBN 0-19-824537-8). Oxford U Pr.
Mitchell, Bob. Amphoto Pocket Companion: Konica TC & FS-I. (Illus.). 128p. 1980. pap. 4.95 spiral bdg. (ISBN 0-8174-5525-6). Amphoto.
--Color Printing. LC 75-8142. (Photography How-to Ser.). (Illus.). 1975. pap. 4.95 (ISBN 0-8227-0101-4). Petersen Pub.
Mitchell, Breon. James Joyce & the German Novel - 1922-1933. LC 75-36980. xvi, 194p. 1976. 12.95x (ISBN 0-8214-0192-0). Ohio U Pr.
Mitchell, Brian. Running to Keep Fit. 96p. 1980. pap. 2.95 o.p. (ISBN 0-679-12428-4). McKay.
Mitchell, Brian R. & Deane, P. Abstract of British Historical Statistics. (Department of Applied Economics Monographs: No. 17). 1962. 68.50 (ISBN 0-521-05738-8). Cambridge U Pr.
Mitchell, Broadus. Alexander Hamilton: A Concise Biography. LC 75-16899. (Illus.). 384p. 1976. 17.95x (ISBN 0-19-501979-2). Oxford U Pr.
--Rise of Cotton Mills in the South. 2nd ed. LC 68-8128. (American Scene Ser). 1968. Repr. of 1921 ed. lib. bdg. 27.50 (ISBN 0-306-71141-9). Da Capo.
Mitchell, Bruce, jt. auth. see Crossley-Holland, Kevin.
Mitchell, Bruce M., et al. Planning for Creative Learning. 2nd ed. 176p. 1981. pap. text ed. 9.95 (ISBN 0-8403-2302-6). Kendall-Hunt.
Mitchell, Charity. Speech Index: An Index to Collections of World Famous Orations & Speeches for Various Occasions; Supplement, 1971-1975. 4th ed. LC 66-13749. 1977. 10.00 (ISBN 0-8108-1000-X). Scarecrow.
Mitchell, Charity, jt. auth. see Sutton, Roberta B.
Mitchell, Christopher. The Legacy of Populism in Bolivia: From the MNR to Military Rule. LC 77-83461. (Praeger Special Studies). 1978. 23.95 (ISBN 0-03-039671-9). Praeger.
Mitchell, Colin. Terrain Evaluation. Houston, J., ed. LC 74-158517. (Illus.). 224p. 1974. pap. text ed. 10.95x (ISBN 0-582-48426-X). Longman.
Mitchell, Curtis C. Let's Live! 160p. 1975. 6.95 (ISBN 0-8007-0716-8). Revell.
Mitchell, Daniel J. B. Unions, Wages & Inflation. 1980. 16.95 (ISBN 0-8157-5752-2); pap. 6.50 (ISBN 0-8157-5751-4). Brookings.
Mitchell, Daniel J. B., jt. auth. see Weber, Arnold R.

Mitchell, David. Introduction to Logic. 1967. text ed. 9.00x (ISBN 0-09-064633-9, Hutchinson U Lib); pap. text ed. 6.25x (ISBN 0-09-064634-7, Hutchinson U Lib). Humanities.
--The Jesuits. (Illus.). 320p. 1981. 17.50 (ISBN 0-531-09947-4). Watts.
Mitchell, Denis, jt. ed. see Hawkins, Neil M.
Mitchell, Don & Grimm, Gary. Cemetery Box. (gr. 3-8). 1976. 10.95 (ISBN 0-916456-01-3, GA62). Good Apple.
Mitchell, Don & Wayman, Joe. Ballad of Lucy Lum. (gr. k-8). 1977. 5.95 (ISBN 0-916456-10-2, GA56). Good Apple.
Mitchell, Don, jt. auth. see Grimm, Gary.
Mitchell, Don, jt. auth. see Wayman, Joe.
Mitchell, Don G. Top Man. 192p. 1980. 12.95 o.p. (ISBN 0-8144-5205-1). Am Mgmt.
Mitchell, Donald. Benjamin Britten, Nineteen Thirteen to Nineteen Seventy-Six: Pictures from A Life. (Encore Edition). (Illus.). 1979. 8.95 (ISBN 0-684-16550-3, ScribT). Scribner.
--Britten & Auden in the Thirties: The Year 1936. LC 80-25980. (Illus.). 174p. 1981. 15.00 (ISBN 0-295-95814-6). U of Wash Pr.
--Gustav Mahler: The Wunderhorn Years. 1980. pap. 10.95 (ISBN 0-520-04220-4, CAL 442). U of Cal Pr.
--A History of Russian & Soviet Sea Power. (Illus.). 400p. 1974. 19.95 (ISBN 0-02-585290-6). Macmillan.
Mitchell, Donald, ed. see Mahler, Alma.
Mitchell, Donald G. About Old Story-Tellers. LC 75-159859. 1971. Repr. of 1877 ed. 20.00 (ISBN 0-8103-3732-0). Gale.
Mitchell, Douglas D. Amaeru: The Expression of Reciprocal Dependency in Japanese Politics & Law. new ed. LC 76-43354. 1977. 22.00 o.p. (ISBN 0-89158-710-1). Westview.
Mitchell, E. F. Cooperative Vocational Education: Principles - Methods - Problems. new ed. 1977. text ed. 18.95 (ISBN 0-205-05768-3). Allyn.
Mitchell, Edward. The Miocene Pinniped Allodesmus. (U. C. Publ. in Geological Sciences: Vol. 61). 1966. pap. 5.00x (ISBN 0-520-09162-0). U of Cal Pr.
Mitchell, Edward & Schulte, Rainer, eds. Continental Short Stories. 1969. 4.95x (ISBN 0-393-09797-8); study questions free (ISBN 0-393-09854-0). Norton.
Mitchell, Edward J. U. S. Energy Policy: A Primer. 103p. 1974. pap. 5.25 (ISBN 0-8447-3131-5). Am Enterprise.
Mitchell, Edward J., ed. Oil Pipelines & Public Policy: Analysis of Proposals for Industry Reform & Reorganization. 1979. 15.25 (ISBN 0-8447-2157-3); pap. text ed. 8.25 (ISBN 0-8447-2158-1). Am Enterprise.
--Perspectives on U. S. Energy Policy: A Critique of Regulation. LC 76-23093. (American Enterprise Institute Perspectives: Vol. 3). (Illus.). 1976. 24.95 (ISBN 0-275-23640-4). Praeger.
Mitchell, Edwin V. Horse & Buggy Age in New England. LC 74-7066. 1974. Repr. of 1937 ed. 15.00 (ISBN 0-8103-3657-X). Gale.
--It's an Old State of Maine Custom. LC 78-8102. 1978. lib. bdg. 11.50 o.p. (ISBN 0-89621-007-3); pap. 4.95x (ISBN 0-89621-006-5). Thorndike Pr.
Mitchell, Edwin V., ed. The Pleasures of Walking. LC 48-11993. (Illus.). 1979. 8.95 (ISBN 0-8149-0825-X). Vanguard.
Mitchell, Eli. After Hard Guns. 272p. (Orig.). 1980. pap. 1.95 (ISBN 0-89083-699-X). Zebra.
Mitchell, Elmer D., jt. auth. see Mason, Bernard S.
Mitchell, Emerson B. & Allen, T. D. Miracle Hill: The Story of a Navaho Boy. 230p. 1967. 10.95 o.p. (ISBN 0-8061-0743-X); pap. 5.95 (ISBN 0-8061-1616-1). U of Okla Pr.
Mitchell, Ethel, jt. auth. see Cotton, E. J.
Mitchell, Eugene. American Victoriana: Floor Plans & Renderings from the Gilded Age. LC 79-20404. (Illus., Orig.). 1979. 19.95 (ISBN 0-87701-147-8, Prism Editions). Chronicle Bks.
Mitchell, Ewan. The Director's & Company Secretary's Handbook of Draft Legal Letters. 2nd ed. 596p. 1979. text ed. 43.00x (ISBN 0-220-67001-3, Pub. by Busn Bks England). Renouf.
--The Director's Lawyer & the Company Secretary's Legal Guide. 4th ed. 645p. 1978. text ed. 43.00x (ISBN 0-220-66346-7, Pub. by Busn Bks England). Renouf.
--The Employer's Guide to the Law on Health, Safety & Welfare at Work. 2nd ed. 471p. 1977. text ed. 36.75x (ISBN 0-220-66341-6, Pub. by Busn Bks England). Renouf.
Mitchell, F. H. & Mitchell, F. H., Jr. Essentials of Electronics. (Physics Ser). 1970. text ed. 17.95 (ISBN 0-201-04761-6). A-W.
Mitchell, G. Duncan, ed. Dictionary of Sociology. LC 67-30870. 1967. 15.95x (ISBN 0-202-30079-X). Aldine Pub.
--Sociology: An Outline for the Intending Student. (Outlines Ser). 1970. 14.00x (ISBN 0-7100-6842-5). Routledge & Kegan.
Mitchell, Gladys. Watson's Choice. 1981. pap. 2.25 o.s.i. (ISBN 0-440-19501-2). Dell.
--Winking at the Brim. 1981. pap. 2.25 (ISBN 0-440-19326-5). Dell.
Mitchell, H. Retail Floral Shop Management. 1982. text ed. 16.95 (ISBN 0-8359-6676-3); instr's. manual free (ISBN 0-8359-6677-1). Reston.
Mitchell, H. G., et al. Haggai, Zechariah, Malachi, & Jonah. LC 12-22008. (International Critical Commentary Ser.). 544p. Repr. of 1912 ed. 23.00x (ISBN 0-567-05020-3). Attic Pr.
Mitchell, H. L. Mean Things Happening in This Land: The Life & Times of H. L. Mitchell. LC 78-65660. 372p. 1979. text ed. 10.95 (ISBN 0-916672-25-5). Allanheld.
Mitchell, Hobart. We Would Not Kill. 1980. write for info (ISBN 0-913408-63-8). Friends United.
Mitchell, Howard, ed. The University & the Urban Crisis. LC 74-6113. (Community Psychology Ser: Vol. 2). 1974. text ed. 19.95 (ISBN 0-87705-139-9). Human Sci Pr.
Mitchell, Hugh. Codification in Manufacturing & Materials Management. 1973. 13.95x o.p. (ISBN 0-8464-0252-1). Beekman Pubs.
Mitchell, Ian. Job Hunting Blueprint: How to Get the Job You Want. (Orig.). 1981. pap. 5.95 (ISBN 0-938306-00-6). Shoreline Pub.
Mitchell, Ingrid. Breastfeeding Together. (Illus.). 1978. 7.95 (ISBN 0-8164-9351-0). Continuum.
Mitchell, J. How to Write Reports. 1975. pap. 1.50 o.p. (ISBN 0-531-06068-3, Fontana Pap). Watts.
Mitchell, J. Clyde. The Yao Village: A Study in the Social Structure of a Malawian Tribe. (Institute of African Studies Ser). (Illus.). 238p. 1971. pap. text ed. 17.50x (ISBN 0-7190-1034-9). Humanities.
Mitchell, J. Clyde, ed. Numerical Techniques in Social Anthropology. LC 80-11082. (ASA Essays in Social Anthropology Ser.: Vol. 3). (Illus.). 1981. text ed. 22.00x (ISBN 0-915980-93-2); pap. text ed. 9.95x (ISBN 0-89727-013-4). Inst Study Human.
--Social Networks in Urban Situations: Analyses of Personal Relationships in Central African Towns. (Illus.). 378p. 1969. pap. text ed. 17.50x (ISBN 0-7190-1035-7). Humanities.
Mitchell, J. Clyde, jt. ed. see Boissevain, Jeremy.
Mitchell, J. M. Petronius Leader of Fashion. 364p. 1981. Repr. of 1922 ed. lib. bdg. 35.00 (ISBN 0-89987-565-3). Darby Bks.
Mitchell, J. R., jt. auth. see Blanshard, J. M.
Mitchell, J. R. & Domenet, J. G., eds. Thromboembolism: A New Approach to Therapy. 1978. 25.00 (ISBN 0-12-500050-2). Acad Pr.
Mitchell, Jack. The Gun Digest Book of Pistolsmithing. 288p. 1980. pap. 8.95 (ISBN 0-695-81429-X). Follett.
Mitchell, Jack, jt. auth. see Lewis, Jack.
Mitchell, James G. The Design & Construction of Flexible & Efficent Interactive Programming Systems. LC 79-50563. (Outstanding Dissertations in the Computer Sciences Ser.: Vol.12). 1980. lib. bdg. 15.50 (ISBN 0-8240-4414-2). Garland Pub.
Mitchell, James K. Fundamentals of Soil Behavior. LC 75-28096. (Soil Engineering Ser). 384p. 1976. text ed. 35.95 (ISBN 0-471-61168-9). Wiley.
Mitchell, James R., ed. Antique Metalware. LC 77-70771. (Antiques Magazine Library). (Illus.). 1977. 12.95x o.s.i. (ISBN 0-87663-298-3, Main Street); pap. 7.95 (ISBN 0-87663-970-8). Universe.
Mitchell, James W., jt. auth. see Zief, Morris.
Mitchell, Jane F., tr. see Caesar, Julius.
Mitchell, Jean B. Great Britain: Geographical Essays. 1962. 48.00 (ISBN 0-521-05739-6); pap. 19.95x (ISBN 0-521-09986-2). Cambridge U Pr.
Mitchell, Jeffrey & Resnik, H. L. Emergency Response to Crisis. (Illus.). 256p. 1981. text ed. 15.95 (ISBN 0-87619-856-6); pap. 12.95 (ISBN 0-87619-828-0). R J Brady.
Mitchell, Joan. Price Determination & Prices Policy. (Economic & Society Ser.). 1977. text ed. 19.95x (ISBN 0-04-338084-0); pap. text ed. 8.95x (ISBN 0-04-338085-9). Allen Unwin.
Mitchell, John. Better Fishing: Freshwater. rev. ed. LC 68-108518. (Illus.). 1978. 8.50x (ISBN 0-7182-1455-2). Intl Pubns Serv.
--On the Line. 9.50x (ISBN 0-392-06594-0, SpS). Soccer.
Mitchell, John G. Fellowship: Three Letters from John. LC 77-18501. (Orig.). 1974. pap. text ed. 3.95 (ISBN 0-930014-06-5). Multnomah.
--The Hunt. LC 80-7621. 320p. 1980. 11.95 (ISBN 0-394-50684-7). Knopf.
Mitchell, John H. Court of the Connectable: A Study of a French Administrative Tribunal During the Reign of Henry Iv. 1947. 34.50x (ISBN 0-686-51365-7). Elliots Bks.
--Writing for Technical & Professional Journals. LC 67-31374. (Wiley Ser. on Human Communications). 1968. 19.95 (ISBN 0-471-61170-0, Pub. by Wiley-Interscience). Wiley.
Mitchell, John H. & Griswold, Whit. Hiking Cape Cod. LC 77-93759. (Illus.). 192p. 1978. lib. bdg. 9.25 o.p. (ISBN 0-914788-04-3). East Woods.
Mitchell, John J., jt. auth. see Nightingale, Demetra S.
Mitchell, John, Jr. & Smith, Donald M. Aquametry: A Treatise on Methods for the Determination of Water, Part 1. 2nd ed. LC 77-518. (Chemical Analysis Ser: Vol. 5). 1977. 46.50 (ISBN 0-471-02264-0). Wiley.
--Aquametry: A Treatise on Methods for the Determination of Water, Pt. 3. 2nd ed. LC 77-518. (Chemical Analysis Ser.). 1980. 80.00 (ISBN 0-471-02266-7, Pub. by Wiley-Interscience). Wiley.
Mitchell, Johnny. Energy & How We Lost It. LC 78-62621. 128p. 1979. 9.95 (ISBN 0-88415-431-9). Pacesetter Pr.
--Secret War of Captain Johnny Mitchell. LC 76-2963. 103p. 1976. 5.95 (ISBN 0-685-66076-1). Pacesetter Pr.
Mitchell, Joseph. Reminiscences of My Life in the Highlands, 1884: Containing Notices of the Changes in the Country During the Present Century, Vol. 2. 288p. 1971. 11.00 (ISBN 0-7153-5300-4). David & Charles.
Mitchell, Joseph B. Decisive Battles of the American Revolution. 1976. pap. 2.25 (ISBN 0-449-30745-X, Q745, Prem). Fawcett.
Mitchell, Joyce S. Be a Mother & More. 224p. (Orig.). 1980. pap. 2.95 (ISBN 0-553-13926-6). Bantam.
--Other Choices for Becoming a Woman: A Handbook to Help High School Women Make Decisions. LC 76-5588. (gr. 7 up). 1976. 7.95 o.s.i. (ISBN 0-440-06795-2). Delacorte.
--The Work Book: A Guide to Skilled Jobs. LC 78-62196. (Illus.). 1978. 9.95 (ISBN 0-8069-3108-6); lib. bdg. 9.29 (ISBN 0-8069-3109-4). Sterling.
Mitchell, Kathleen & Nason, Marty. Cesarean Birth: A Couple's Guide for Decision & Preparation. 208p. 1981. pap. 7.95 (ISBN 0-936602-17-1). Harbor Pub CA.
Mitchell, Kenneth. The Flavour of Montreal. (Illus.). 1977. 8.95 o.s.i. (ISBN 0-7715-9338-4). Vanguard.
Mitchell, L. G. Charles James Fox & the Disintegration of the Whig Party, 1782-1794. (Oxford Historical Monographs). 1971. 29.95x (ISBN 0-19-821838-9). Oxford U Pr.
Mitchell, Lee C. Witnesses to a Vanishing America: The Nineteenth-Century Response. LC 80-8567. (Illus.). 288p. 1981. 16.50x (ISBN 0-691-06461-X). Princeton U Pr.
Mitchell, Leonel. Liturgical Change: How Much Do We Need. 96p. 1975. pap. 3.50 (ISBN 0-8164-2113-7). Crossroad NY.
Mitchell, Leslie. Holland House. (Illus.). 320p. 1980. 32.00x (ISBN 0-7156-1116-X, Pub. by Duckworth England). Biblio Dist.
Mitchell, Lillias. Irish Spinning Dyeing & Weaving. (Illus.). 1978. 12.95 (ISBN 0-85221-101-5). Dufour.
Mitchell, Lizzie R. History of Pike County, Georgia, 1822-1932. LC 80-23352. x, 162p. 1980. Repr. 15.00 (ISBN 0-87152-345-0). Reprint.
Mitchell, Lloyd A. How to Make Money in Wall Street Through the Intelligent Use of Price-Earnings Ratios. (The New Stock Market Reference Library). (Illus.). 112p. 1981. 39.45 (ISBN 0-918968-93-3). Inst Econ Fina.
Mitchell, Loren. Beautiful San Diego. Shangle, Robert D., ed. LC 79-17663. (Illus.). 80p. 1979. 14.95 (ISBN 0-89802-060-3); pap. 7.95 (ISBN 0-89802-059-X). Beautiful Am.
Mitchell, Louise K., jt. auth. see Liban, Felicia.
Mitchell, M. Bonner, jt. ed. see Minor, Andrew C.
Mitchell, Margaret. Gone with the Wind. (gr. 9 up). 1936. 12.95 (ISBN 0-02-585390-2); 2 vol. lg. print ed. 13.95 (ISBN 0-02-489440-0); anniversary ed. 19.96 (ISBN 0-02-585350-3). Macmillan.
--Gone with the Wind. 1974. pap. 3.50 (ISBN 0-380-00109-8, 49841). Avon.
--Gone with the Wind. 1974. pap. 4.95 (ISBN 0-380-00759-2, 30445). Avon.
Mitchell, Marge & Sedgwick, Joan. Bakery Lane Soup Bowl. 1977. pap. 6.95 (ISBN 0-394-73375-4). Random.
Mitchell, Memory F. Legal Aspects of Conscription & Exemption in North Carolina, 1861-1865. (James Sprunt Study in History & Political Science: Vol. 47). (Orig.). 1965. pap. text ed. 3.50x (ISBN 0-8078-5047-0). U of NC Pr.
--North Carolina's Signers: Brief Sketches of the Men Who Signed the Declaration of Independence & the Constitution. (Illus.). 1969. pap. 0.25 o.p. (ISBN 0-86526-097-4). NC Archives.
Mitchell, P. Concepts Basic to Nursing. 3rd ed. (Illus.). 720p. text ed. 18.95 (ISBN 0-07-042582-5). McGraw.
Mitchell, P. M. Henrik Pontoppidan. (World Authors Ser.: No. 524). 1979. lib. bdg. 14.95 (ISBN 0-8057-6366-X). Twayne.
--Vilhelm Gronbech. (World Authors Ser.: No. 397). 1978. lib. bdg. 11.95 (ISBN 0-8057-6306-6). Twayne.
Mitchell, P. M., jt. ed. see Billeskov-Jansen, F. J.
Mitchell, P. M., tr. see Gronbech, Vilhelm.
Mitchell, Paige. Sundark. 552p. 1981. 14.95 (ISBN 0-385-14368-0). Doubleday.
Mitchell, Peggy. Country Crafts. Pringle, P., ed. LC 70-468023. (Pegasus Bks.: No. 19). (Illus.). 1968. 10.50x (ISBN 0-234-77157-7). Intl Pubns Serv.
Mitchell, Ralph. Introduction to Environmental Microbiology. (Illus.). 400p. 1974. ref. ed. 26.95x (ISBN 0-13-482489-X). P-H.
Mitchell, Ralph, ed. Water Pollution Microbiology. LC 73-168641. 1972. Vol. 1. 20.50 (ISBN 0-471-61100-X, Pub. by Wiley-Interscience); Vol. 2 1978. 33.00 (ISBN 0-471-01902-X). Wiley.
Mitchell, Richard H. The Korean Minority in Japan. (Center for Japanese & Korean Studies, UC Berkeley). 1967. 18.50x (ISBN 0-520-00870-7). U of Cal Pr.
Mitchell, Richard S. Variation in the Polygonum Amphibium Complex & Its Taxonomic Significance. (U. C. Publ. in Botany: Vol. 45). 1968. pap. 6.50x (ISBN 0-520-09018-7). U of Cal Pr.
Mitchell, Robert L. Engineering Economics. 1980. 29.50 (ISBN 0-471-27640-5, Pub. by Wiley-Interscience); pap. text ed. 16.00 o.p. (ISBN 0-686-65932-5). Wiley.
--Tristan Corbiere. (World Authors Ser.: No. 511). 1979. lib. bdg. 13.50 (ISBN 0-8057-6352-X). Twayne.
Mitchell, Robert L., ed. Pre-Text, Text, Context: Essays on Nineteenth-Century French Literature. 302p. 1980. 29.00 (ISBN 0-8142-0305-1). Ohio St U Pr.
Mitchell, Robert M. Calvin's & the Puritan's View of the Protestant Ethic. LC 79-66537. 1979. pap. text ed. 7.00 (ISBN 0-8191-0842-1). U Pr of Amer.
Mitchell, Robert W., jt. auth. see Pittard, Kay.
Mitchell, Robert W. & Reddell, James R., eds. Studies on the Cavernicole Fauna of Mexico & Adjacent Regions. (Association for Mexican Cave Studies: Bulletin 5). 201p. 1973. 13.00. Speleo Pr.
Mitchell, Robert W., jt. ed. see Reddell, James R.
Mitchell, Rodger. The Analysis of Indian Agro-Ecosystems. (Environmental Science Ser.). 180p. 1980. 6.50x (ISBN 0-89955-329-X, Pub. by Interprint India). Intl Schol Bk Serv.
Mitchell, Roger. Letters from Siberia & Other Poems. LC 79-151102. (Illus.). 80p. 1970. 5.00 (ISBN 0-685-23806-7, Pub. by New Rivers Pr); signed ed. 10.00 (ISBN 0-685-23807-5); pap. 2.50 (ISBN 0-685-23808-3). SBD.
Mitchell, Roger S. Synopsis of Clinical Pulmonary Diseases. 2nd ed. LC 77-11024. (Illus.). 1978. pap. text ed. 15.95 (ISBN 0-8016-3430-X). Mosby.
Mitchell, Ronald. Opera-Dead or Alive: Production, Performance, & Enjoyment of Musical Theatre. LC 73-121772. (Illus.). 1970. 25.00 (ISBN 0-299-05811-5); pap. 7.95 (ISBN 0-299-05814-X). U of Wis Pr.
Mitchell, Rose G. & Mackenzie, James, eds. Child Health in the Community. 2nd ed. (Illus.). 352p. 1980. text ed. 37.50 (ISBN 0-443-02195-3). Churchill.
Mitchell, Roy E., jt. auth. see Mills, Jerry L.
Mitchell, Sally. The Fallen Angel. 1981. write for info. (ISBN 0-87972-155-3); pap. write for info. (ISBN 0-87972-156-1). Bowling Green Univ.
Mitchell, Sandra, jt. auth. see Bee, Helen.
Mitchell, Scott C. SuperStudent! The Student's High School Handbook. rev. ed. LC 80-84049. (Illus.). 112p. (gr. 9-12). 1981. pap. text ed. 4.95 (ISBN 0-938494-00-7). Kingsfield.
Mitchell, Simon. The Logic of Poverty: The Case of the Brazilian Northeast. (Direct Edition Ser.). 200p. (Orig.). 1981. pap. 18.95 (ISBN 0-7100-0637-3). Routledge & Kegan.
Mitchell, Stanley, tr. see Lukacs, Georg.
Mitchell, Steve. More How to Speak Southern. 64p. (Orig.). 1980. pap. 1.95 (ISBN 0-553-14351-4). Bantam.
Mitchell, Stewart. Horatio Seymour of New York. LC 69-19475. (American Scene Ser). 1970. Repr. of 1938 ed. lib. bdg. 59.50 (ISBN 0-306-71252-0). Da Capo.
Mitchell, T. F. Principles of Firthian Linguistics. (Illus.). 232p. 1975. text ed. 19.50x (ISBN 0-582-52455-5). Longman.
Mitchell, T. R., jt. auth. see Ebert, R. J.
Mitchell, Terence, jt. auth. see Scott, William G.
Mitchell, Victor, illus. God's Wonderful World of Fish. (gr. 2-6). 1978. pap. 0.79 o.p. (ISBN 0-8307-0627-5, 56-059-03). Regal.
Mitchell, W. H., jt. auth. see Sawyer, L. A.
Mitchell, W. J. Beethoven - Opus Sixty-Nine First Movement: Pinaforte & Violoncello. LC 74-120289. 6.00x (ISBN 0-231-03417-2). Columbia U Pr.

Mitchell, W. J., ed. The Language of Images. LC 80-5225. 1980. pap. 6.95 (ISBN 0-226-53215-1, P887, Phoen). U of Chicago Pr.
Mitchell, W. M., jt. auth. see Greer, Frances A.
Mitchell, Wesley C. Business Cycles & Their Causes. (California Library Reprint Series: No. 29). 1971. 15.00x (ISBN 0-520-02071-5). U of Cal Pr.
Mitchell, William E. Mishpokhe: A Study of New York City Jewish Family Clubs. 262p. 1980. text ed. 19.95 (ISBN 90-27976-95-3); pap. text ed. 5.95 (ISBN 0-202-01166-6). Aldine Pub.
Mitchell, William E., jt. auth. see Leichter, Hope J.
Mitchell, William J. Elementary Harmony. 3rd ed. 1965. 17.50x (ISBN 0-13-257279-6). P-H.
Mitchell, William J. & Salzer, Felix, eds. Music Forum, 3 vols. LC 67-16204. 1967-73. Vol. 1. 20.00 o.p. (ISBN 0-231-02806-7); Vol. 2. 20.00x o.p. (ISBN 0-231-03153-X); Vol. 3. 22.50x (ISBN 0-231-03522-5). Columbia U Pr.
Mitchell, William J., ed. see Bach, Carl P.
Mitchell, William L. & Girdler, Allan, eds. Corvette: A Piece of the Action. LC 77-83506. 1977. 38.95 (ISBN 0-915038-11-0); leather ed. 58.95 (ISBN 0-915038-23-4). Princeton Pub.
Mitchell, William S. East Sussex: A Shell Guide. 1978. 14.95 (ISBN 0-571-10751-6, Pub. by Faber & Faber). Merrimack Bk Serv.
Mitchell, William S., jt. ed. see Blake, Michael P.
Mitchell-Thome, Raoul C. Geology of the South Atlantic Islands. (Beitraege zur regionalen Geologie der Erde: Vol. 10). (Illus.). 366p. 1970. lib. bdg. 90.05x (ISBN 3-443-11010-X, Pub by Gebrueder Borntraeger Germany). Lubrecht & Cramer.
Mitchelmore, Peter. The Pigkeeper's Guide. LC 80-68686. (Illus.). 136p. 1981. 14.95 (ISBN 0-7153-7995-X). David & Charles.
Mitchelson, Marvin. Living Together. 1981. 10.95 (ISBN 0-671-24981-9). S&S.
Mitcheltree, Tom. Terror in Room Two-O-One. (Orig.). 1980. pap. 1.75 (ISBN 0-505-51475-3). Tower Bks.
Mitchenson, Joe, jt. auth. see Mander, Raymond.
Mitcheson, Rosalind. Life in Scotland. 1978. 25.00 (ISBN 0-7134-1559-2, Pub. by Batsford England). David & Charles.
Mitchinson, J. M. Biology of the Cell Cycle. LC 72-160100. (Illus.). 1972. 49.50 (ISBN 0-521-08251-X); pap. 14.50x (ISBN 0-521-09671-5). Cambridge U Pr.
Mitchison, Naomi. Conquered. 1959. 14.95 (ISBN 0-224-60496-1). Dufour.
--A Life for Africa: The Story of Bram Fischer. 1973. 8.95 (ISBN 0-85036-170-2). Dufour.
Mitchison, Rosalind. The Roots of Nationalism: Studies in Northern Europe. 175p. 1980. text ed. 31.25x (ISBN 0-85976-058-8). Humanities.
Mitchison, Rosiland. British Population Change Since 1860. (Studies in Economic & Social History). 1977. pap. text ed. 4.75x (ISBN 0-333-13585-7). Humanities.
Mitford, Nancy. Love in a Cold Climate. Bd. with The Pursuit of Love. 1975. pap. 1.95 o.p. (ISBN 0-445-08405-7). Popular Lib.
Mitgang, Herbert. The Montauk Fault. LC 80-70744. 320p. 1981. 12.95 (ISBN 0-87795-320-1). Arbor Hse.
Mitgutsch, Ali. The Busy Book. (Illus.). 1976. 2.95 o.p. (ISBN 0-307-13768-6, Golden Pr); PLB 7.62 o.p. (ISBN 0-307-63768-9). Western Pub.
--World on Wheels: Rolling Along from Ancient to Modern Times. (Illus.). 48p. (gr. 1-6). 1975. 3.95 o.p. (ISBN 0-307-15795-4, Golden Pr); PLB 10.69 o.p. (ISBN 0-307-65795-7). Western Pub.
Mitgutsch, Waltraud, jt. auth. see Hogg, James.
Mithang, Dennis E. Prevocational Training for Retarded Students. (Illus.). 304p. 1981. text ed. 29.50 (ISBN 0-398-04111-3). C C Thomas.
Mitman, John L. C. Premarital Counseling: A Manual for Clergy & Counselors. 144p. 1980. 9.95 (ISBN 0-8164-0467-4). Seabury.
Mitnick, Harold. How to Handle Your Divorce Step by Step. LC 80-80875. 177p. 1981. 21.95; pap. 14.95 (ISBN 0-936550-00-7). Lone Oak.
Mitra, A. P., ed. see COSPAR, Twenty-Second Plenary Meeting, Bangalore, India, 1979.
Mitra, Ashok, tr. see Tagore, Rabindranath.
Mitra, Sanjit K. Active Inductorless Filters. LC 70-179914. (IEEE Press Selected Reprint Ser). 1971. 15.95 (ISBN 0-471-61177-8, Pub. by Wiley-Interscience); pap. text ed. 7.95 o.p. (ISBN 0-471-61176-X). Wiley.
Mitra, Sujit K., jt. auth. see Rao, C. R.
Mitrany, David. Effect of the War in Southeastern Europe. LC 75-114590. 1973. Repr. 16.50 (ISBN 0-86527-055-4). Fertig.
Mitroff, Ian I., jt. auth. see Mason, Richard O.
Mitruka, Brij M. Gas Chromatographic Applications in Microbiology & Medicine. LC 74-18002. (Techniques in Pure & Applied Microbiology Ser). 496p. 1975. 55.50 (ISBN 0-471-61183-2, Pub. by Wiley Medical). Wiley.
Mitruka, Brij M. & Rawnsley, Howard M. Clinical Biochemical & Hematological Reference Values in Normal Experimental Animals. LC 77-84608. (Illus.). 286p. 1977. 28.75 (ISBN 0-89352-006-3). Masson Pub.
Mitscher, Lester A., jt. auth. see Lednicer, Daniel.
Mitson, Betty E., jt. ed. see Hansen, Arthur A.
Mitsumasa, Anno. Anno's Magical ABC: An Anamorphic Alphabet. (Illus.). 64p. 1981. 15.95 (ISBN 0-399-20788-0). Philomel.
Mitsuo, Shimizu, jt. auth. see Stubel, Hans.
Mittal, K. L., ed. Micellization, Solubilization, & Microemulsions, 2 vols. 1977. Vol. 1. 487p. 45.00 (ISBN 0-306-31023-6, Plenum Pr); Vol. 2. 945p. 45.00 (ISBN 0-306-31024-4). Plenum Pub.
Mittelbach, Frank G., jt. auth. see Grebler, Leo.
Mittelholzer, Edgar. The Old Blood. 1977. pap. 1.95 o.p. (ISBN 0-449-23355-3, Crest). Fawcett.
Mittelman, Arnold, jt. auth. see Murphy, Gerald P.
Mittelman, James H. Underdevelopment & the Transition to Socialism: Mozambique & Tanzania. (Studies in Social Discontinuity Ser.). 1981. price not set (ISBN 0-12-500660-8). Acad Pr.
Mittemeyer, B. T., jt. auth. see McLeod, D. G.
Mitter, Partha. Much Maligned Monsters: History of European Reactions to Indian Art. (Illus.). 1978. 44.00x (ISBN 0-19-817336-9). Oxford U Pr.
Mitter, Wolfgang. Secondary School Graduation: University Entrance Qualification in Socialist Countries. new ed. LC 77-30471. 1978. text ed. 23.00 (ISBN 0-08-022237-4); pap. text ed. 15.00 (ISBN 0-08-022238-2). Pergamon.
--The Use of Tests & Interviews for Admission to Higher Education: A European Symposium (Published for the Council of Europe) (Orig.). 1979. pap. text ed. 27.50x (ISBN 0-85633-183-X, NFER). Humanities.
Mitterhauser, Klaus, jt. auth. see Waldner, George K.
Mitterling, Philip I., ed. United States Cultural History: A Guide to Information Sources. LC 79-24061. (American Government & History Information Guide Ser.: Vol. 5). 1980. 30.00 (ISBN 0-8103-1369-3). Gale.
Mittleider, Jacob R. Gardening by the Foot. LC 80-84564. 150p. 1981. pap. 4.95 (ISBN 0-88290-175-3, 4026). Horizon Utah.
--Let's Grow Tomatoes. LC 80-84563. (Illus.). 150p. 1981. pap. 4.95 (ISBN 0-88290-176-1, 4027). Horizon Utah.
Mittler, Abe, jt. ed. see Doyle, Edwin S.
Mittler, P., ed. Research to Practice in Mental Retardation: IASSMD Proceedings, 3 vols. 1977. Vol. 1. 29.50 (ISBN 0-8391-1122-3); Vol. 2. 29.50 (ISBN 0-8391-1123-1); Vol. 3. 29.50 (ISBN 0-8391-1124-X). Univ Park.
Mittler, T. E., et al, eds. Annual Review of Entomology, Vol. 26. LC 56-5750. (Illus.). 1981. text ed. 20.00 (ISBN 0-8243-0126-9). Annual Reviews.
Mittman, Benjamin & Borman, Lorraine. Personalized Data Base Systems. 326p. 1981. Repr. of 1975 ed. lib. bdg. price not set (ISBN 0-89874-298-6). Krieger.
Mitton, S., jt. ed. see Hazard, C.
Mitton, Simon. The Crab Nebula. (Illus.). 1979. 16.95 (ISBN 0-684-16077-3, ScribT). Scribner.
--Daytime Star: The Story of Our Sun. (Illus.). 192p. 1981. 14.95 (ISBN 0-684-16840-5, ScribT). Scribner.
--Exploring the Galaxies. LC 76-42913. (Encore Edition). (Illus.). 1978. pap. 1.95 (ISBN 0-684-16912-6, ScribT). Scribner.
Mittra, R. A. J., ed. Computer Techniques for Electromagnetics. 416p. 1973. text ed. 75.00 (ISBN 0-08-016888-4). Pergamon.
Mittra, Sid. New Horizon in Central Banking. 1968. 14.50x o.p. (ISBN 0-210-31161-4). Asia.
Mittwer, Marie, jt. auth. see Doyle, Marvyl.
Mitzman, Max E. George Baxter & the Baxter Prints. LC 78-52165. (Illus.). 1978. 32.00 (ISBN 0-7153-7629-2). David & Charles.
Mitzner, D. T., et al. Constitutional Problems in Church-State Relations: A Symposium. LC 75-155825. (Symposia on Law & Society Ser). 1971. Repr. of 1966 ed. lib. bdg. 14.50 (ISBN 0-306-70131-6). Da Capo.
Mitzner, Seymour, jt. auth. see Sharp, Richard M.
Miura, Lydia, ed. see Graphic Arts Trade Journal Intl Inc.
Mix, Floyd M. House Wiring Simplified. LC 80-2122. (Illus.). 384p. 1981. 8.00 (ISBN 0-87006-309-X). Goodheart.
--Housewiring Simplified. LC 80-21122. (Illus.). 176p. 1981. text ed. 8.00 (ISBN 0-87006-309-X). Goodheart.
Mixter, Richard W., ed. see Heller, Lois J. & Mohrman, David E.
Miyakawa, T. Scott, jt. ed. see Conroy, Hilary.
Miyamoto, Shoson. The Buddhist Philosophy of the Middle Way. 1981. 9.95 (ISBN 0-914910-07-8); pap. 6.95 (ISBN 0-914910-08-6). Buddhist Bks.
Miyashiro, A. Metamorphism & Metamorphic Belts. LC 72-13983. 1978. pap. 29.95 (ISBN 0-470-99390-1). Halsted Pr.
Miyashita, Tadao. The Currency & Financial System of Mainland China. (China in the 20th Century Ser.). 1976. Repr. of 1966 ed. lib. bdg. 22.50 (ISBN 0-306-70758-6). Da Capo.
Miyazaki, Ichisada. China's Examination Hell: The Civil Service Examinations of Imperial China. Schirokauer, Conrad, tr. from Chinese. LC 80-54223. 142p. 1981. pap. 4.95 (ISBN 0-300-02639-0). Yale U Pr.
Miyoshi, Sekiya, illus. Singing David. LC 74-110722. (Illus.). (gr. k-3). 1971. PLB 4.90 o.p. (ISBN 0-531-01936-5). Watts.
Mize, C. J. Watch Out for the Wind. (Orig.). 1980. pap. 2.25 (ISBN 0-505-51555-5). Tower Bks.
Mizener, Arthur, ed. Modern Short Stories. 4th ed. 1979. pap. text ed. 8.95x (ISBN 0-393-95025-5); handbk. 2.95x (ISBN 0-393-95032-8). Norton.
Mizener, Artur, ed. The Fitzgerald Reader. LC 62-9632. 1963. pap. text ed. 7.95 (ISBN 0-684-15871-X, ScribC). Scribner.
Mizrahi, Abe & Sullivan, Michael. Calculus with Applications to Business & the Life Sciences. LC 75-17964. 384p. 1976. text ed. 19.95x (ISBN 0-471-61192-1); solutions manual avail. (ISBN 0-471-01607-1). Wiley.
--Finite Mathematics with Applications for Business & Social Sciences. 3rd ed. LC 78-12522. 1979. text ed. 19.95 (ISBN 0-471-03336-7); tchrs. manual avail. (ISBN 0-471-05507-7); study guide avail. (ISBN 0-471-05499-2). Wiley.
Mizruchi, Ephraim H., jt. auth. see Meadows, Paul.
Mizumura, Kazue. Blue Whale. LC 70-139107. (A Let's-Read-and-Find-Out Science Bk). (Illus.). (gr. k-3). 1971. PLB 7.89 (ISBN 0-690-14994-8, TYC-J). T Y Crowell.
--Emperor Penquins. LC 69-10486. (A Let's Read & Find Out Science Bk). (Illus.). (gr. k-3). 1969. PLB 7.89 (ISBN 0-690-26088-1, TYC-J). T Y Crowell.
--If I Built a Village... LC 77-140645. (Illus.). (gr. k-3). 1971. 7.95 (ISBN 0-690-42903-7, TYC-J); PLB 7.89 o.p. (ISBN 0-690-42904-5). T Y Crowell.
--If I Were a Mother... LC 67-23668. (Illus.). (gr. k-3). 1968. PLB 7.89 o.p. (ISBN 0-690-42917-7, TYC-J). T Y Crowell.
--Way of an Ant. LC 72-87155. (Illus.). (gr. 1-5). 1970. 7.95 (ISBN 0-690-87044-2, TYC-J); PLB 8.79 (ISBN 0-690-87045-0). T Y Crowell.
Mizuno, Soji. Early Foundations for Japan's Twentieth Century Economic Emergence. Date not set. 8.95 (ISBN 0-533-04541-X). Vantage.
Mlambo, Eshmael. Rhodesia: The Struggle for a Birthright. 1972. pap. text ed. 9.50x (ISBN 0-900966-72-6). Humanities.
Mlynar, Zdenek. Nightfrost in Prague: The End of Humane Socialism. Wilson, Paul, tr. from Czech. Orig. Title: Mraz Prichazi Z Kremlu. 1980. 16.95x (ISBN 0-918294-08-8). Karz Pub.
Mmarzio, Peter C. Democratic Art: An Exhibition on the History of Chromolithography in America, 1840-1900. 1979. pap. 9.95 (ISBN 0-88360-034-X). Amon Carter.
Mnookin, Robert. Child, Family & State, Cases & Materials on Children & the Law. 857p. (Orig.). 1978. text ed. 23.25 (ISBN 0-316-57650-6). Little.
Mo, Sam. Why Heart Attack? 1981. 6.95 (ISBN 0-8062-1546-1). Carlton.
Mo, Timothy. The Monkey King. LC 79-7875. 288p. 1980. 10.95 (ISBN 0-385-15621-9). Doubleday.
Moak, Helen, tr. see Fortini, Arnaldo.
Moates, Bob. Selected Poems. 3.50 o.p. (ISBN 0-685-48831-4). Nortex Pr.
Moates, Danny R. & Schumacher, Gary M. Introduction to Cognitive Psychology. 1979. text ed. 19.95x (ISBN 0-534-00724-4). Wadsworth Pub.
Moats, Alice-Leone. The Million Dollar Studs. 1977. 8.95 o.p. (ISBN 0-440-05683-7). Delacorte.
Moberg. The Upper Limb on Tetraplegia. 1979. 18.00. Thieme Stratton.
Moberg, Dennis G., jt. auth. see Brown, Warrren B.
Moberg, Verne, tr. see Janssen-Jurreit, Marielouise.
Moberg, Vilhelm. Emigrants. (Emigrants Saga: No. 1). 1971. pap. 2.75 (ISBN 0-445-08561-4). Popular Lib.
Moberly, Walter. Legal Responsibility & Moral Responsibility. Sherman, Franklin, ed. LC 65-21820. (Facet Bks). 64p. (Orig.). 1965. pap. 1.00 (ISBN 0-8006-3020-3, 1-3020). Fortress.
Mobley, Jane, ed. Phantasmagoria: Tales of Fantasy & the Supernatural. LC 76-52007. 1977. pap. 3.50 (ISBN 0-385-12329-9, Anch). Doubleday.
Mobley, Jonathan H. The Elusive Peace: The Middle East, Oil & the Economic & Political Future of the World. (The Major Currents in Contemprary World History Lib.). (Illus.). 122p. 1981. 46.55 (ISBN 0-930008-79-0). Inst Econ Pol.
Mobley, Tony A., jt. auth. see Brightbill, Charles K.
Moche. The Star Wars Question & Answer Book About Space. (Illus.). (gr. 4). Date not set. pap. cancelled (ISBN 0-590-30065-2, Schol Pap). Schol Bk Serv.
Moche, Diane L. What's up There? (gr. 4-6). 1976. pap. 1.25 (ISBN 0-590-04850-3, Schol Pap). Schol Bk Serv.
Moche, Dinah. Mars. LC 78-2762. (Easy-Read-Fact Bks.). (Illus.). (gr. 2-4). 1978. PLB 6.45 s&l (ISBN 0-531-01374-X). Watts.
--My First Airplane Trip. (Look Look Bk). (Illus.). 24p. 1981. pap. 1.25 (ISBN 0-307-11869-X, Golden Pr). Western Pub.
--Radiation: Benefits-Dangers. (Impact Ser.). (Illus.). (gr. 7 up). 1979. PLB 6.90 s&l (ISBN 0-531-02860-7). Watts.
--Search for Life Beyond Earth. (Impact Bks.). (Illus.). (gr. 7 up). 1978. lib. bdg. 6.90 (ISBN 0-531-02204-8). Watts.
Moche, Dinah L. Astronomy. LC 77-27367. (Self-Teaching Guides Ser.). 1978. pap. text ed. 7.95 (ISBN 0-471-01764-7). Wiley.
--The Star Wars Question & Answer Book About Space. LC 78-19684. (Illus.). (gr. 3-6). 1979. PLB 5.99 (ISBN 0-394-84053-4, BYR); 5.99g (ISBN 0-394-94053-9). Random.
Mochi, Ugo & Carter, T. Donald. Hoofed Mammals of the World. LC 75-169790. (Illus.). 1971. 9.95 o.p. (ISBN 0-684-12382-7, Scribt). Scribner.
Mochon, Anne. Gabriele Muunter: Between Munich & Murnau. Walsh, Peter & Matthews, Paula, eds. LC 80-21810. (Illus.). 65p. 1980. pap. 9.95 (ISBN 0-916724-19-0). Fogg Art.
Mock, James R. Censorship Nineteen Seventeen. LC 74-37864. (Civil Liberties in American History Ser). 250p. 1972. Repr. of 1941 ed. lib. bdg. 25.00 (ISBN 0-306-70436-6). Da Capo.
Mock, Theodore J. & Grove, Hugh D. Measurement, Accounting, & Organizational Information. LC 78-10536. (Accounting & Information Systems Ser.). 1979. text ed. 21.95x (ISBN 0-471-61202-2). Wiley.
Mock, Valerie E. A.S.M.D. Multi-Graded Arithmetic Practice & Drill Sheets. (Makemaster Bk.). (gr. 1-8). 1977. pap. 14.95 (ISBN 0-8224-0462-1). Pitman Learning.
Mocker, Donald W. & Spear, George E., eds. Urban Education: A Guide to Information Sources. LC 78-13627. (Urban Studies Information Guide Ser.: Vol. 3). 1978. 30.00 (ISBN 0-8103-1431-2). Gale.
Mockler, Anthony. Our Enemies the French: Being an Account of the War Fought Between the French & the British - Syria 1941. (Illus.). xix, 252p. 1976. 18.00 (ISBN 0-85052-194-7). Shoe String.
Moczarski, Kazimierz. Conversations with an Executioner. (Illus.). 256p. 1981. 12.95 (ISBN 0-13-171918-1). P-H.
Modayil, Sujatha. Crucifixions. (Redbird Ser). 1975. 8.00 (ISBN 0-88253-725-3); flexible bdg. 4.80 (ISBN 0-89253-543-1). Ind-US Inc.
--We the Unreconciled. (Redbird Ser.). 52p. 1975. 10.00 (ISBN 0-88253-672-9); pap. text ed. 4.80 (ISBN 0-88253-671-0). Ind-US Inc.
Moddie, A. D. Brahmanical Culture & Modernity. 6.50x (ISBN 0-210-98130-X). Asia.
Modell, Frank. Seen Any Cats? LC 79-11607. (Illus.). (gr. k-3). 1979. 6.95 (ISBN 0-688-80229-X); PLB 6.67 (ISBN 0-688-84229-1). Greenwillow.
--Stop Trying to Cheer Me up! LC 78-17557. 1978. 8.95 (ISBN 0-396-07627-0). Dodd.
--Tooley! Tooley! LC 76-49645. (Illus.). (gr. k-3). 1979. 7.50 (ISBN 0-688-80092-0); PLB 7.20 (ISBN 0-688-84092-2). Greenwillow.
Modell, Jerome H. Pathophysiology & Treatment of Drowning & Near-Drowning. (Illus.). 136p. 1971. 12.75 (ISBN 0-398-02361-1). C C Thomas.
Modell, Michael & Reid, Robert C. Thermodynamics & Its Applications. (Physical & Chemical Engr. Sciences Intl Ser.). (Illus.). 528p. 1974. 27.95 (ISBN 0-13-914861-2). P-H.
Modell, Walter. Drugs of Choice, Nineteen Eighty to Nineteen Eighty-One. LC 58-6889. (Illus.). 1980. text ed. 44.50 (ISBN 0-8016-3444-X). Mosby.
Modell, Walter & Lansing, Alfred. Drugs. LC 67-25859. (Life Science Library). (Illus.). (gr. 5 up). 1967. PLB 8.97 o.p. (ISBN 0-8094-0482-6, Pub. by Time-Life). Silver.
Modell, Walter, ed. Drugs in Current Use & New Drugs 1981. 1981. pap. text ed. 8.95 (ISBN 0-8261-0159-3). Springer Pub.
Modell, Walter, et al. Applied Pharmacology. LC 75-21148. (Illus.). 975p. 1976. 25.00 (ISBN 0-7216-6425-3). Saunders.

Modelski, George. Principles of World Politics. LC 70-163237. 1972. 16.95 (ISBN 0-02-921440-8). Free Pr.

Modelski, George, ed. Transnational Corporations & World Order: Readings in International Political Economy. LC 78-12964. (Illus.). 1979. text ed. 21.95x (ISBN 0-7167-1026-9); pap. text ed. 10.95x (ISBN 0-7167-1025-0). W H Freeman.

Modenov, P. S. & Parkhomenko, A. S. Projective Transformations. 1966. 22.50 o.p. (ISBN 0-12-503102-5); pap. 9.00 o.p. (ISBN 0-12-503162-9). Acad Pr.

Moder, Joseph J. & Elmaghraby, Salah E., eds. Handbook of Operations Research, 2 vols. 1978. Vols. 1 & 2. 32.50 ea. Vol. 1 (ISBN 0-442-24595-5). Vol. 2 (ISBN 0-442-24596-3). Vol. 3. 59.50 (ISBN 0-442-24597-1). Van Nos Reinhold.

Modgil, Celia, jt. auth. see Modgil, Sohan.

Modgil, Celia & Modgil, Sahan, eds. Toward a Theory of Psychological Development. 814p. 1980. text ed. 47.50x (ISBN 0-85633-185-6, NFER). Humanities.

Modgil, Sahan, jt. ed. see Modgil, Celia.

Modgil, Sohan. Piagetian Research: A Handbook of Recent Studies. 476p. 1974. text ed. 30.25x (ISBN 0-85633-030-2, NFER). Humanities.

--Piagetian Research-Compilation & Commentary, No. 7: Training Techniques. (Orig.). 1976. pap. text ed. 16.00x (ISBN 0-85633-107-4, NFER). Humanities.

Modgil, Sohan & Modgil, Celia. Piagetian Research, Compilation & Commentary, No. 1: Jean Piaget, Theory of Cognitive Development & Sensorimotor Intelligence. (Orig.). 1976. pap. text ed. 12.50x (ISBN 0-85633-089-2, NFER). Humanities.

--Piagetian Research, Compilation & Commentary, No. 4: School Curriculum & Test Development. (Orig.). 1976. pap. text ed. 18.75x (ISBN 0-85633-103-1, NFER). Humanities.

--Piagetian Research, Compilation & Commentary, No. 5: Personality, Socialization & Emotionality Reasoning Among Handicapped Children. 1976. pap. text ed. 25.75 (ISBN 0-85633-098-1, NFER). Humanities.

--Piagetian Research, Compilation & Commentary, No. 6: The Cognitive-Development Approach to Morality. (Piagetian Research). 1976. pap. text ed. 15.75x (ISBN 0-85633-106-6, NFER). Humanities.

--Piagetian Research, Compilation & Commentary, No. 8: Cross-Cultural Studies. (Piagetian Research Ser.). 1976. pap. text ed. 16.00x (ISBN 0-85633-108-2, NFER). Humanities.

--Piagetian Research: Compilation & Commentary, Nos. 2 & 3. Incl. Experimental Validation of Conservation. pap. text ed. 15.75x (ISBN 0-685-92662-1); Early Growth of Logic. pap. text ed. 20.75x (ISBN 0-85633-098-1). 1976 (NFER). Humanities.

Modi, Jivanji J. The Religious Ceremonies & Customs of the Parsees: Bombay, 1922. LC 78-74280. (Oriental Religions Ser.: Vol. 7). 563p. 1980. lib. bdg. 60.50 (ISBN 0-8240-3913-0). Garland Pub.

Modica, Alfred J. Franchising. (Illus.). 192p. 1981. pap. 7.95 (ISBN 0-8256-3203-X, Quick Fox). Music Sales.

Modica, Alfred J., Jr., jt. auth. see Seltz, David D.

Modica, Christee. Poems for Today. 1981. 4.50 (ISBN 0-8062-1666-2). Carlton.

Modisett, Noah F. & Luter, James G. Speaking Clearly: The Basics of Voice & Diction. 1979. 9.95 (ISBN 0-8087-3949-2). Burgess.

Modjeska, Helena. Letters to Emilia: Record of a Friendship. Coleman, Marion M., ed. Kwapiszewski, Michael, tr. (Illus.). 1967. pap. 2.00 (ISBN 0-910366-05-5). Alliance Coll.

Modjeska, Lee. Handling Employment Discrimination Cases, Vol. 1. LC 78-70830. 1980. 47.50. Lawyers Co-Op.

Modular Mathematics Organization. Modular Mathematics: Modules 1-18 Teachers Pack. 65.00 o.p. (ISBN 0-435-50899-7). Heinemann Ed.

--Modular Mathematics: Modules 19-36 Teachers Pack. 80.00 o.p. (ISBN 0-435-50900-4). Heinemann Ed.

Mody, Homi. Sir Pherozeshah Mehta: A Political Biography. 10.00x (ISBN 0-210-33946-2). Asia.

Moe, Alden J., jt. auth. see Woods, Mary L.

Moe, Christian, jt. auth. see McCalmon, George.

Moe, John H., et al. Scoliosis & Other Spinal Deformities. LC 76-50153. (Illus.). 1978. text ed. 49.00 (ISBN 0-7216-6427-X). Saunders.

Moe, Jorgen, jt. auth. see Asbjornsen, P. Chr.

Moe, Jorgen E., jt. auth. see Asbjornsen, P. C.

Moe, Phyllis, jt. ed. see Benardete, Jane.

Moehle, Natalia R. The Dimensions of Evil & Transcendence: A Sociological Perspective. LC 78-59124. 1978. pap. text ed. 10.50 (ISBN 0-8191-0550-3). U Pr of Amer.

Moeller, Beverley B. Phil Swing & Boulder Dam. LC 71-633550. (Illus.). 1971. 18.50x (ISBN 0-520-01932-6). U of Cal Pr.

Moeller, F. H. Fungi of the Faeros, 2 pts. Incl. Pt. 1. Basidiomycetes. 1945; Pt. 2. Myxomycetes, Archimycetes, Phycomycetes, Asomycetes, & Fungi Imperfecti (with Appendix to Pt. 1) 1958. (Illus.). 15.00 set (ISBN 0-934454-42-6). Lubrecht & Cramer.

Moeller, Jack & Liedloff, Helmut. Deutsch Heute: Grundstufe. 2nd ed. LC 78-52718. (Illus.). 1979. text ed. 17.15 (ISBN 0-395-27175-4); inst. annot. ed. 18.25 (ISBN 0-395-27174-6); wkbk. 5.50 (ISBN 0-395-27173-8); recordings 114.68 (ISBN 0-395-27171-1). HM.

Moeller, Jack R., et al. Blickpunkt Deutschland. LC 76-190308. 416p. 1973. text ed. 16.76 (ISBN 0-395-13690-3, 2-37474); instr. ed. 16.52 (ISBN 0-395-14218-0, 2-37475); workbook 4.24 (ISBN 0-395-14212-1). HM.

Moeller, T. The Chemistry of the Lanthanides. (Pergamon Texts in Inorganic Chemistry: Vol. 26). 104p. 1975. text ed. 23.00 (ISBN 0-08-018878-8); pap. text ed. 13.25 (ISBN 0-08-018877-X). Pergamon.

Moellering, H. A. & Bartling, V. Pastoral Epistles & Philemon. (Concordia Commentary Ser). 1970. 10.95 (ISBN 0-570-06285-3, 15-2067). Concordia.

Moeller Van Den Bruck, Arthur. Germany's Third Empire. 1972. 16.00 (ISBN 0-86527-085-6). Fertig.

Moelwyn-Hughes, E. A. Physical Chemistry. 2nd rev. ed. 1964. 60.00 (ISBN 0-08-010846-6). Pergamon.

Moen, Aaron N. Wildlife Ecology: An Analytical Approach. LC 73-6833. (Animal Science Ser.). (Illus.). 1973. text ed. 35.95x (ISBN 0-7167-0826-4). W H Freeman.

Moenkemeyer, Heinz. Francois Hemsterhuis. (World Authors Ser.: Netherlands: No. 277). 1975. lib. bdg. 12.50 (ISBN 0-8057-2419-2). Twayne.

Moenssens, Andre A., et al. Cases & Comments on Criminal Procedure. (Contemporary Legal Education Ser.). 900p. 1979. text ed. 21.00 (ISBN 0-672-83683-1). Bobbs.

Moerchen, Barbara D., jt. auth. see Blankenship, Martha L.

Moeri. A Horse for X.Y.Z. (gr. 4-6). 1980. pap. 1.25 (ISBN 0-590-30039-3, Schol Pap). Schol Bk Serv.

Moeri, Louise. The Girl Who Lived on the Ferris Wheel. 112p. 1980. pap. 1.75 (ISBN 0-380-52506-2, 52506). Avon.

--A Horse for X.Y.Z. (Illus.). (gr. 3-6). 1977. PLB 7.50 (ISBN 0-525-32220-5). Dutton.

--Save Queen of Sheba. LC 80-23019. (gr. 4-7). 1981. PLB 8.95 (ISBN 0-525-33202-2). Dutton.

--Star Mother's Youngest Child. (Illus.). (ps-3). 1980. pap. 2.50 (ISBN 0-395-29929-2, Sandpiper). HM.

Moerikke, Eduard. Mozart's Journey to Prague. Loewenberg, tr. 1981. pap. 3.95 (ISBN 0-7145-0389-4). Riverrun NY.

Moers, Ellen. The Dandy: Brummell to Beerbohm. LC 78-8915. (Illus.). 1978. 15.00x (ISBN 0-8032-3052-4); pap. 4.95 (ISBN 0-8032-8101-3, BB 674, Bison). U of Nebr Pr.

--Literary Women. LC 74-33686. 336p. 1976. 10.00 o.p. (ISBN 0-385-07427-1). Doubleday.

Moertono, Soemarsaid. State & Statecraft in Old Java: A Study of the Later Mataram Period, 16th to 19th Centruy. (Monograph Ser.). 1974. pap. 3.00 o.p. (ISBN 0-685-41682-8). Cornell Mod Indo.

Moeschberger, Melvin L., jt. auth. see Madsen, Richard W.

Moeschlin, O. & Pallaschke, D., eds. Game Theory & Related Topics. LC 79-15339. 399p. 1979. 53.75 (ISBN 0-444-85342-1, North Holland). Elsevier.

Moeschlin, O., ed. see Symposium on Game Theory & Related Topics, Hagen & Bonn, Sept. 1978.

Moffat, Abbot L. Mongkut, the King of Siam. (Illus.). 254p. (YA) (gr. 9-12). 1968. pap. 3.95 (ISBN 0-8014-9069-3, CP69). Cornell U Pr.

Moffat, Alex W. & Porter, C. Burnham. The Galley Guide - Updated. LC 77-22546. 1977. 7.95 (ISBN 0-396-07427-8). Dodd.

Moffat, Anne & Schiller, Marc. Landscape Design That Saves Energy. (Illus.). 224p. 1981. 17.95 (ISBN 0-688-00031-2, Quill); pap. 9.95 (ISBN 0-688-00395-8). Morrow.

Moffat, Bobby. Intermediate Soccer Guide. (Illus.). 160p. (Orig.). 1981. pap. write for info. (ISBN 0-89037-181-4). Anderson World.

Moffat, D. B. The Mammalian Kidney. LC 74-82590. (Biological Structure & Function Ser.: No. 5). (Illus.). 272p. 1975. 53.50 (ISBN 0-521-20599-9). Cambridge U Pr.

Moffat, Derry, ed. The Lady & the Tramp. (Disney Classics Ser.). (Illus.). (gr. k-4). 1980. pap. 0.95 (ISBN 0-448-16109-5). G&D.

Moffat, Gene H., jt. auth. see Williams, Richard L.

Moffat, George B. Winning on the Wind: Championship Soaring Techniques, Sailplanes & History. LC 74-82783. (Illus.). 244p. 1974. pap. 5.95 (ISBN 0-930514-00-9, Pub. by Soaring). Aviation.

Moffat, Gwen. Hard Road West: Alone on the California Trail. 1981. 12.95 (ISBN 0-670-36145-3). Viking Pr.

Moffatt, G. W., et al see Wulff, J.

Moffatt, James. An Introduction to the Literature of the New Testament. 3rd ed. (International Theological Library). 704p. Repr. of 1918 ed. 13.95x (ISBN 0-567-07213-4). Attic Pr.

--James, Hebrews. LC 24-21703. (International Critical Commentary Ser.). 336p. Repr. of 1924 ed. text ed. 17.50 (ISBN 0-567-05034-3). Attic Pr.

Moffatt, Thomas L. Selection Interviewing for Managers. LC 78-9302. (Continuing Management Education Ser.). 1979. text ed. 13.95 scp (ISBN 0-06-044573-4, HarpC). Har-Row.

Moffet, Hugh L. Clinical Microbiology. 2nd ed. 1980. text ed. 17.75 (ISBN 0-397-50450-0). Lippincott.

Moffett, James. Teaching the Universe of Discourse. (Orig.). 1968. pap. text ed. 10.95 (ISBN 0-395-04928-8, 3-38140). HM.

Moffett, James & Wagner, Betty J. Student Centered Language Arts & Reading, K-13: A Handbook for Teachers. 2nd ed. LC 76-11920. (Illus.). 640p. 1976. 19.50 (ISBN 0-395-20630-8). HM.

Moffett, James & McElheny, Kenneth R., eds. Points of View: An Anthology of Short Stories. pap. 2.95 (ISBN 0-451-61880-7, ME1880, Ment). NAL.

Moffett, Joseph O. Some Beekeepers & Associates, Pt. I. (Illus.). 140p. lib. bdg. 19.90; pap. 9.90 (ISBN 0-686-28741-X). Moffett.

Moffett, Kenworth. Michael Steiner. (Illus.). 1974. pap. 1.50 (ISBN 0-87846-079-9). Mus Fine Arts Boston.

--Morris Louis in the Museum of Fine Arts, Boston. LC 79-6360. (Illus.). 1979. pap. 6.95 (ISBN 0-87846-135-3). Mus Fine Arts Boston.

--The New Generation: A Curator's Choice. LC 80-52831. (Illus.). 96p. (Orig., Eng., Fr., & Ger.). 1980. pap. 10.00 (ISBN 0-9604746-0-9). Rhineburgh Pr.

Moffett, Martha & Moffett, Robert. Dolphins. LC 76-134497. (First Bks). (Illus.). (gr. 4-6). 1971. PLB 4.90 o.p. (ISBN 0-531-00723-5). Watts.

Moffett, Robert, jt. auth. see Moffett, Martha.

Moffett, Samuel. Americanization of Canada. LC 79-189601. (Social History of Canada Ser.). 128p. 1972. pap. 3.50 (ISBN 0-8020-6143-5). U of Toronto Pr.

Moffit, Ian. The Australian Outback. (The World's Wild Places Ser.). (Illus.). 1976. lib. bdg. 11.97 (ISBN 0-686-51016-X). Silver.

Moffitt, Donald, ed. The Wall Street Journal Views America Tomorrow. LC 76-52501. 1977. 11.95 (ISBN 0-8144-5438-0). Am Mgmt.

Moffitt, Frederick J. Tales from Ancient Greece. LC 78-56059. (The World Folktale Library). (Illus.). 1979. lib. bdg. 7.65 (ISBN 0-686-50008-3). Silver.

Moffitt, Ian. Australian Outback. (The World's Wild Places Ser.). (Illus.). 1976. 12.95 (ISBN 0-8094-2059-7). Time-Life.

Mogel, Leonard. The Magazine: Everything You Need to Know to Make It in the Magazine Business. (Illus.). 1979. text ed. 16.95 (ISBN 0-13-543710-5, Spec); pap. 7.95 (ISBN 0-13-543702-4). P-H.

Mogen, David. Wilderness Visions: Science Fiction Westerns, Vol. 1. LC 80-8673. (I. O. Evans Studies in the Philosophy & Criticism of Literature: No. 1). 64p. 1981. lib. bdg. 8.95x (ISBN 0-89370-152-1); pap. text ed. 2.95x (ISBN 0-89370-252-8). Borgo Pr.

Mogenson, Gordon J. The Neurobiology of Behavior: An Introduction. LC 77-18283. 1977. 14.95 (ISBN 0-470-99341-3). Halsted Pr.

Moger, Allen W. Virginia: Bourbonism to Byrd, 1870-1925. LC 68-8538. (Illus.). 400p. 1968. 10.95 (ISBN 0-8139-0182-0). U Pr of Va.

Moger, Victoria. The Favour of Your Company: Invitations to London Social Events, 1750 to 1850. (Illus.). 48p. 1980. pap. 14.00 (ISBN 0-913720-09-7). Sandstone.

Moges, Marquis De see De Moges, Marquis.

Mogey, John, jt. auth. see Morris, R. N.

Mogey, John, ed. Family & Marriage. (International Studies in Sociological & Social Anthropology). 1963. pap. text ed. 12.50x (ISBN 90-040-1046-7). Humanities.

Mogey, John H., ed. see Howard, Ronald L.

Mogey, John H., ed. see Howard, Ronald L., et al.

Moggridge, D., ed. see Keynes, John M.

Moggridge, D. E. British Monetary Policy, Nineteen Twenty-Four to Nineteen Thirty-One. LC 76-169576. (Department of Applied Economics Monographs: No. 21). 1972. 42.50 (ISBN 0-521-08225-0). Cambridge U Pr.

Moghissi, A. A., ed. Oil Spills. 80p. 1980. pap. 12.80 (ISBN 0-08-026237-6). Pergamon.

Moghissi, Kamran S. Birth Defects & Fetal Development: Endocrine & Metabolic Factors. (Illus.). 352p. 1974. text ed. 32.75 (ISBN 0-398-02784-6). C C Thomas.

Moghissi, Kamran S. & Hafez, E. S., eds. Biology of Mammalian Fertilization & Implantation. (Illus.). 520p. 1972. 42.50 (ISBN 0-398-02362-X). C C Thomas.

--The Placenta: Biological & Clinical Aspects. (Illus.). 412p. 1974. text ed. 38.75 (ISBN 0-398-02999-7). C C Thomas.

Mogulof, Melvin B. Citizen Participation: The Local Perspective. 1970. pap. 3.00 o.p. (ISBN 0-87766-065-4, 80002). Urban Inst.

--Five Metropolitan Governments. 1972. pap. 3.50 o.p. (ISBN 0-87766-033-6, 12000). Urban Inst.

Mohammad, Ali. Dynamics of Agricultural Development in India. 1978. 24.00x o.p. (ISBN 0-8364-0314-2). South Asia Bks.

Mohammad, Ali, ed. Dynamics of Agricultural Development in India. 1979. text ed. 19.50x (ISBN 0-391-01859-0). Humanities.

Mohammed, Abbas Ahmed. White Nile Arabs: Political Leadership & Economic Change. (Monographs on Social Anthropology: No. 53). 1980. text ed. 37.50x (ISBN 0-391-00969-9, Athlone Pr). Humanities.

Mohammed, M. J., jt. auth. see Lambert, E. N.

Mohammed, Rasheed & Mohammed, Tinamarie. My First Trip to the Library. 66p. 1980. 5.95 (ISBN 0-533-04357-3). Vantage.

Mohammed, Tinamarie, jt. auth. see Mohammed, Rasheed.

Mohan, John, et al. Freestyle Skiing. 1976. 11.95 (ISBN 0-87691-185-8). Winchester Pr.

--Freestyle Skiing. 1978. pap. 8.95 (ISBN 0-87691-265-X). Winchester Pr.

Mohan, Kshitij. Ashes of Gold. (Writers Workshop Redbird Ser.). 39p. 1975. 8.00 (ISBN 0-88253-502-1); pap. text ed. 4.80 (ISBN 0-88253-501-3). Ind-US Inc.

Mohan, Madan, jt. ed. see Hull, Ronald E.

Mohan, Maden & Risko, Victoria. Perception Stimulators. (Illus.). 64p. (Orig.). 1980. tchr's ed. 2.50 (ISBN 0-914634-80-1, 6932). DOK Pubs.

Mohan, Raj P., jt. auth. see Martindale, Don.

Mohanty, J. B., tr. see Satpathi, Nandini.

Mohanty, Jitendra N. The Concept of Intentionality. LC 70-176186. 213p. 1971. 12.50 (ISBN 0-87527-115-4). Fireside Bks.

Mohiddin, Ahmed. African Socialism in Two Countries. 231p. 1981. 25.00x (ISBN 0-389-20170-7). Barron.

Mohl, Raymond A. Poverty in New York, 1783-1825. (Urban Life in America Ser). 1971. 15.95 (ISBN 0-19-501367-0). Oxford U Pr.

Mohlenbrock, Robert H. Flowering Plants: Flowering Rush to Rushes. LC 69-16117. (Illustrated Flora of Illinois Ser.). (Illus.). 286p. 1970. 22.95x (ISBN 0-8093-0407-4). S Ill U Pr.

--Flowering Plants: Lilies to Orchids. LC 69-16118. (Illustrated Flora of Illinois Ser.). (Illus.). 304p. 1970. 22.95x (ISBN 0-8093-0408-2). S Ill U Pr.

--Flowering Plants: Magnolias to Pitcher Plants. LC 80-18529. (Illustrated Flora of Illinois Ser.). (Illus.). 256p. 1981. 18.95x (ISBN 0-8093-0920-3). S Ill U Pr.

--Flowering Plants: Willows to Mustards. LC 79-10981. (Illustrated Flora of Illinois Ser.). (Illus.). 302p. 1980. 22.95x (ISBN 0-8093-0922-X). S Ill U Pr.

--Grasses: Bromus to Paspalum. LC 71-156793. (Illustrated Flora of Illinois Ser.). (Illus.). 352p. 1972. 22.95x (ISBN 0-8093-0520-8). S Ill U Pr.

--Grasses: Panicum to Danthonia. LC 73-6807. (Illustrated Flora of Illinois Ser). (Illus.). 398p. 1973. 22.95x (ISBN 0-8093-0521-6). S Ill U Pr.

--Guide to the Vascular Flora of Illinois. LC 75-22414. 506p. 1975. lib. bdg. 22.95x (ISBN 0-8093-0704-9); pap. 10.95x (ISBN 0-8093-0756-1). S Ill U Pr.

--Sedges: Cyperus to Scleria. LC 76-15267. (Illustrated Flora of Illinois Ser.). (Illus.). 208p. 1976. 22.95x (ISBN 0-8093-0604-2). S Ill U Pr.

Mohlenbrock, Robert H., jt. auth. see Voigt, John W.

Mohler, Irvin C., jt. ed. see Rogers, Senta S.

Mohn, Peter B. Naval Special Warfare Teams. LC 80-26004. (Illus.). 48p. (gr. 4-8). 1981. PLB 9.25 (ISBN 0-686-69420-1). Childrens.

Mohney, Nell. The Inside Story: Personal Experiences of Faith. LC 79-67135. 1979. pap. 3.50x (ISBN 0-8358-0377-5). Upper Room.

Mohney, Russ. Why Wild Edibles? The Joys of Finding, Fixing, & Tasting - West of the Rockies. LC 75-12071. (Illus.). 320p. 1975. pap. 7.95 o.s.i. (ISBN 0-914718-07-X). Pacific Search.

Mohr, Charles E. The World of the Bat. LC 76-7355. (Living World Ser.). (Illus.). 1976. 10.95 (ISBN 0-397-00800-7). Lippincott.

Mohr, Dolores V., tr. see Akhmanova, O. S., et al.

Mohr, James C. Abortion in America: The Origins & Evolution of National Policy. 1978. 15.95 (ISBN 0-19-502249-1). Oxford U Pr.

Mohr, Lillian H. Frances Perkins: That Woman in FDR's Cabinet. 14.95 (ISBN 0-88427-019-X). Green Hill.

Mohr, Victor. The Advent of Christ. 116p. Date not set. pap. 4.95 (ISBN 0-934616-16-7). Valkyrie Pr.

--A Spiritual View of Life. Ozols, Violet, tr. from Ger. (Victor Mohr Ser.). 364p. Date not set. pap. 15.00 (ISBN 0-934616-15-9). Valkyrie Pr.

Mohrman, David E., jt. auth. see Heller, Lois J.

Mohs, Frederic E. Chemosurgery: Microscopically Controlled Surgery for Skin Cancer. (Illus.). 400p. 1978. 49.75 (ISBN 0-398-03725-6). C C Thomas.

Mohs, Mayo, jt. auth. see Heald, Tim.

Mohsenin, Nuri N. Physical Properties of Food & Agricultural Materials: A Teachin Manual. 1981. price not set (ISBN 0-677-05630-3). Gordon.

Mohtadi, M. F., ed. Man & His Environment, Vol. 2: Proceedings of the Second Banff Conference. 216p. 1975. text ed. 37.00 (ISBN 0-08-019922-4). Pergamon.

Moikobu, Josephine. Blood & Flesh: Black American & African Identifications. LC 80-1706. (Contributions in African American Studies: No. 59). (Illus.). 224p. 1981. lib. bdg. 25.00 (ISBN 0-313-22549-4, MBF/). Greenwood.

Moir, G., ed. Into Television. LC 68-8870. 1969. pap. 7.50 (ISBN 0-08-013032-1). Pergamon.

--Teaching & Television: ETV Explained. 1967. 22.00 (ISBN 0-08-012355-4); pap. 10.75 (ISBN 0-08-012354-6). Pergamon.

Moir, John. Just in Case: Disaster Preparedness & Emergency Self-Help. LC 79-28435. (Orig.). 1980. pap. 4.95 (ISBN 0-87701-200-8). Chronicle Bks.

Moir, May A., jt. auth. see Moir, W. W.

Moir, W. W. & Moir, May A. Breeding Variegata Oncidiums. LC 80-15946. (Illus.). 136p. 1980. pap. text ed. 12.00x (ISBN 0-8248-0712-X). U Pr of Hawaii.

Moise, Edwin E. Calculus. 2nd ed. LC 76-150576. (Mathematics Ser). 1972. text ed. 19.95 (ISBN 0-201-04810-8). A-W.

--Elementary Geometry from an Advanced Standpoint. 2nd ed. LC 73-2347. 1974. text ed. 17.95 (ISBN 0-201-04793-4). A-W.

Moiseiwitsch, Benjamin L. Integral Equations. LC 76-10282. (Longman Mathematical Texts). (Illus.). 1977. pap. text ed. 11.95x (ISBN 0-582-44288-5). Longman.

Moiser, Jeremy, tr. see Boecker, Hans J.

Moiser, Jeremy, tr. see Carretto, Carlo.

Moiser, Jeremy, tr. see Rahner, Karl.

Moiser, Jeremy, tr. see Wiedekehr, Dietrich.

Moises, Rosalio, et al. A Yaqui Life: The Personal Chronicle of a Yaqui Indian. LC 76-56789. Orig. Title: The Tall Candle: the Personal Chronicle of a Yaqui Indian. (Illus.). 1977. 13.95x (ISBN 0-8032-0944-4); pap. 3.95 (ISBN 0-8032-5857-7, BB 637, Bison). U of Nebr Pr.

Moison, Lawrence G. Home Windmills. (Illus.). 60p. (Orig.). 1980. pap. text ed. 2.95. Mod Handcraft.

Moitessier, Bernard. The Long Way. 1979. 17.95x (ISBN 0-8464-0075-8). Beekman Pubs.

Moivre, Abraham De see De Moivre, Abraham.

Mojena, Richard, jt. auth. see Ageloff, Roy.

Mojica Sandoz, Luis, jt. auth. see Rivera Cianchini, Osvaldo.

Mojumder, Atindra, tr. from Bengali. The Caryapadas: Tantric Poems of the Eighty-Four Mahasiddhas (Siddhacaryas) 2nd rev. ed. 225p. 1980. text ed. 13.95x (ISBN 0-935548-03-3). Santarasa Pubns.

Mojzer, Miklos. Dutch Genre Paintings. 2nd rev ed. Racz, Evz, tr. from Hungarian. (Illus.). 1977. 25.00 (ISBN 0-8283-1727-5). Branden.

Mok, Charles. Practical Hors d'oeuvre & Canape Art. LC 78-1066. (Illus.). 1978. spiral bdg. 22.95 (ISBN 0-8436-2159-1). CBI Pub.

--Practical Salad & Dessert Art. 1973. spiral bdg. 22.95 (ISBN 0-8436-0570-7). CBI Pub.

Mok, Ellie M. & Jofen, Jean. Chinese for Advanced Beginners. LC 80-5492. 110p. (Orig.). 1980. pap. 6.95 (ISBN 0-8044-6506-1). Ungar.

--Chinese for Beginners. LC 80-5492. 110p. (Orig.). 1980. pap. 6.95 (ISBN 0-8044-6505-3). Ungar.

Mokanski, jt. auth. see Cunsolo.

Mokashi-Punekar, S. An Epistle to Professor David McCutchion. (Writers Workshop Redbird Book Ser.). 19p. 1975. 4.80 (ISBN 0-88253-534-X); pap. text ed. 4.00 (ISBN 0-88253-533-1). Ind-US Inc.

--The Indo-Anglian Creed. (Writers Workshop Greybird Ser.). 72p. 1975. 14.00 (ISBN 0-88253-566-8); pap. text ed. 4.80 (ISBN 0-88253-565-X). Ind-US Inc.

--P. Lal: An Appreciation. (Greybird Ser). 1975. 5.00 (ISBN 0-88253-721-0); flexible bdg. 4.00 (ISBN 0-89253-790-6). Ind-US Inc.

--The Pretender. 6.75 (ISBN 0-89253-702-7); flexible cloth 4.00 (ISBN 0-89253-703-5). Ind-US Inc.

Mokri, M. Al-Hadiyati 'l-Hamidiyah: Kurdish-Arabic Dictionary. 1975. 18.00x. Intl Bk Ctr.

Mokwa, Michael P. & Dawson, William M. Marketing the Arts: Praeger Series in Public & Nonprofit Sector Marketing. Permut, S., ed. LC 79-26603. (Praeger Special Studies Ser.). 304p. 1980. 22.95 (ISBN 0-03-052141-6). Praeger.

Mol, Hans J. Indentity & the Sacred. LC 76-27153. 1977. 19.95 (ISBN 0-02-921600-1). Free Pr.

Molander, David W., ed. Lymphoproliferative Diseases. (Illus.). 592p. 1975. text ed. 52.75 (ISBN 0-398-03025-1). C C Thomas.

Molander, Earl A. Responsive Capitalism: Case Studies in Corporate Social Conduct. (Management Ser.). (Illus.). 432p. 1980. text ed. 10.00x (ISBN 0-07-042658-9, C); pap. text ed. 5.95 (ISBN 0-07-042659-7); instructor's manual 4.95 (ISBN 0-07-042659-7). McGraw.

Molarsky. Take It or Leave It. (gr. 3-5). 1980. pap. 1.25 (ISBN 0-590-30072-5, Schol Pap). Schol Bk Serv.

Molarsky, Osmond. The Fearless Leroy. (Illus.). (gr. 4-7). 1977. 6.95 o.p. (ISBN 0-8098-0008-X). Walck.

--The Peasant & the Fly. LC 80-11609. (Illus.). 48p. (gr. k-3). 1980. pap. 3.95 (ISBN 0-15-260153-8, VoyB). HarBraceJ.

Moldafsky, Annie. The Good Buy Book -- South. 228p. (Orig.). 1981. pap. 4.95 (ISBN 0-528-88046-2). Rand.

--The New Good Buy Book: Illinois, Wisconsin, Ohio, Michigan & Indiana. LC 76-3129. 224p. 1977. pap. 3.25 (ISBN 0-8040-0705-5). Swallow.

Moldaver, J. & Conley, J. The Facial Palsies. (Illus.). 272p. 1980. 35.75 (ISBN 0-398-03988-7). C C Thomas.

Moldenhauer, Hans & Irvine, Demar, eds. Anton Von Webern: Perspectives. LC 77-9523. (Music Reprint Ser., 1978). (Illus.). 1978. Repr. of 1966 ed. lib. bdg. 22.50 (ISBN 0-306-77518-2). Da Capo.

Moldenhauer, William C., pref. by. Soil Conservation Policies: An Assessment. LC 80-406. 154p. (Orig.). 1980. pap. 6.50 (ISBN 0-935734-04-X). Soil Conservation.

Moldenke, A. L., jt. auth. see Moldenke, H. N.

Moldenke, H. N. & Moldenke, A. L. Plants of the Bible. (Illus.). 1952. 15.50 o.p. (ISBN 0-8260-6170-2, Pub. by Wiley-Interscience). Wiley.

Moldovsky, Joel & DeWolf, Rose. The Best Defense. 288p. 1975. 8.95 o.s.i. (ISBN 0-02-585590-5). Macmillan.

Moldrup, William, jt. auth. see Frates, Jeffrey.

Moldvay, Al & Fabian, Erica. Amphoto Travel Guides. 1980. 5.95 ea. Watson-Guptill.

Moldvay, Albert & Fabian, Erika. Photographing Mexico City & Acapulco. (Amphoto Travel Guide Ser.). Orig. Title: Photographer's Guide to Mexico City & Alcapulco. (Illus.). 1980. pap. 5.95 (ISBN 0-8174-2122-X). Amphoto.

Mole, Michaela M., ed. Away We Go! A Guidebook of Family Trips to Places of Interest in New Jersey, Nearby Pennsylvania & New York. 4th ed. 1976. pap. 3.50 o.p. (ISBN 0-8135-0817-7). Rutgers U Pr.

Molek, Ivan. Two Worlds. Molek, Mary, tr. from Slovene. LC 77-88259. Orig. Title: Dva svetova. 166p. softcover 3.45 (ISBN 0-9603142-2-9). M Molek Inc.

Molek, Mary, compiled by. Comprehensive Bibliography of the Literary Works of Ivan (John) Molek. LC 76-50170. (Illus.). 82p. 1976. 3.50 (ISBN 0-9603142-0-2). M Molek Inc.

Molek, Mary, tr. see Molek, Ivan.

Molella, Arthur P., et al. A Scientist in American Life: The Essays & Lectures of Joseph Henry. LC 80-19367. (Illus.). 145p. 1981. pap. 6.95 (ISBN 0-87474-641-8). Smithsonian.

Moler, C., jt. auth. see Forsythe, George E.

Moles, Ian N., tr. see Vacalopoulos, Apostolos E.

Moles, John. French Defence: Main Line Winawer. 1975. 20.95 (ISBN 0-7134-2921-6, Pub. by Batsford England). David & Charles.

Moles, John & Wicker, Kevin. French Winawer: Modern & Auxiliary Lines. 1979. 25.50 (ISBN 0-7134-2037-5, Pub. by Batsford England). David & Charles.

Molesworth, G. N. Curfew on Olympus: The Last Days of British Rule in India. 12.50x (ISBN 0-210-27143-4). Asia.

Molesworth, James T. Molesworth's Marathi-English Dictionary. 1978. Repr. 32.00x o.p. (ISBN 0-8364-0233-2). South Asia Bks.

Molesworth, Mary L. The Cuckoo Clock, Repr. Of 1877 Ed. Bd. with The Tapestry Room. Repr. of 1879 ed. LC 75-32182. (Classics of Children's Literature, 1621-1932: Vol. 45). (Illus.). 1976. PLB 38.00 (ISBN 0-8240-2294-7). Garland Pub.

--Four Winds Farm, Repr. Of 1887 Ed. Bd. with The Children of the Castle. Repr. of 1890 ed. LC 75-32192. (Classics of Children's Literature, 1621-1932: Vol. 54). (Illus.). 1976. PLB 38.00 (ISBN 0-8240-2303-X). Garland Pub.

Moley, Raymond. After Seven Years. LC 71-168390. (FDR & the Era of the New Deal Ser.). 446p. 1972. Repr. of 1939 ed. lib. bdg. 42.50 (ISBN 0-306-70327-0). Da Capo.

--First New Deal. LC 66-22282. (Illus.). 1966. 12.50 o.p. (ISBN 0-15-131290-7). HarBraceJ.

--Realities & Illusions Eighteen Eighty-Six to Nineteen Thirty-Two. Freidel, Frank, ed. LC 78-13887. (The History of the United States 1876-1976: Vol. 13). 1980. lib. bdg. 20.00 (ISBN 0-8240-9692-4). Garland Pub.

Molica, Jim & Nellor, Bill. Funny Fizzles. (Orig.). 1978. pap. 1.25 o.p. (ISBN 0-451-07973-6, Y7973, Sig). NAL.

Moliere. Amphitryon. (Documentation thematique). (Fr.). pap. 2.95 (ISBN 0-685-92173-5, 203). Larousse.

--Dom Juan Ou le Festin De Pierre. Howarth, W. D., ed. (French Texts Ser.). 1975. pap. text ed. 9.95x (ISBN 0-631-00580-3, Pub. by Basil Blackwell). Biblio Dist.

--L' Ecole des Femmes & la Critique de L'ecole des Femmes. Howarth, W. D., ed. (Blackwell's French Text Ser.). 1968. pap. text ed. 9.95x (ISBN 0-631-00630-3, Pub. by Basil Blackwell). Biblio Dist.

--Le Misanthrope. Rudler, G., ed. (French Texts Ser.). 1947. pap. text ed. 9.95x (ISBN 0-631-00520-X, Pub. by Basil Blackwell). Biblio Dist.

Moliere, Jean B. Miser & Other Plays. Wood, John, tr. Incl. Would-Be Gentleman; That Scoundrel Scapin; Don Juan; Love's the Best Doctor. (Classics Ser.). (Orig.). (YA) (gr. 9 up). 1953. pap. 2.75 (ISBN 0-14-044036-4). Penguin.

--Reluctant Doctor. Hannan, W., tr. (Orig.). 1963. pap. 2.25x (ISBN 0-87830-535-1). Theatre Arts.

--Tartuffe. Hartle, Robert W., tr. LC 60-12946. (Orig.). 1965. pap. 3.95 (ISBN 0-672-60275-X, LLA87). Bobbs.

--Tartuffe. Block, Haskell M., ed. LC 58-13149. (Crofts Classics Ser.). 1958. pap. text ed. 2.75x (ISBN 0-88295-059-2). AHM Pub.

Molin, Y. N., et al. Spin Exchange: Principles & Applications in Chemistry & Biology. (Springer Series in Chemical Physics: Vol. 8). (Illus.). 242p. 1980. 39.00 (ISBN 0-387-10095-4). Springer-Verlag.

Molina, S. P., tr. see Dobbins, G. S.

Molinard, P., illus. Dreams of Paris. LC 75-465802. (Illus.). 1967. 13.50x (ISBN 0-8002-0754-8). Intl Pubns Serv.

Molinaro, Ursule. Nightschool for Saints. 128p. 1981. 10.95 (ISBN 0-89097-021-1); pap. 5.95 (ISBN 0-89097-022-X). Archer Edns.

Molinaro, Ursule, tr. see Best, Otto F.

Molinaro, Ursule, tr. see Wolf, Christa.

Moline, Mary. The Best of Ford. (Illus.). 1973. 10.00 (ISBN 0-913444-01-4, Pub. by Rumbleseat Press). Motorbooks Intl.

--Mimi: A Norman Rockwell Character Story. LC 80-52873. 1980. 12.00 (ISBN 0-913444-05-7). Rumbleseat.

--Model A Miseries & Cures. (Illus.). 1972. pap. 6.00 (ISBN 0-913444-00-6, Pub. by Rumbleseat Press). Motorbooks Intl.

--Norman Rockwell Collectibles Value Guide. 3rd ed. LC 80-66161. 1980. pap. 9.95 (ISBN 0-913444-06-5). Rumbleseat.

--Norman Rockwell Encylopedia. LC 79-90498. (Illus.). 1979. 15.95 (ISBN 0-89387-032-3). Sat Eve Post.

Molinsky, Steven J. & Bliss, Bill. Side by Side: English Grammar Through Guided Conversations, Bk. I. 1980. pap. text ed. 7.95 (ISBN 0-13-809848-4); tapes 129.95 (ISBN 0-13-809830-1). P-H.

Molitch, Mark E. Management of Medical Problems in Surgical Patients. 1981. 30.00 (ISBN 0-8036-6286-6). Davis Co.

Molitor, Joseph W. Architectural Photography. LC 76-6537. 180p. 1976. 34.50 (ISBN 0-471-61312-6, Pub. by Wiley-Interscience). Wiley.

Moliver, Donald M. & Abbondante, Paul J. The Economy of Saudi Arabia. 200p. 1980. 21.95 (ISBN 0-03-057004-2). Praeger.

Moll, Aristides A. Aesculapius in Latin America. LC 76-101589. (Illus.). 1969. Repr. of 1944 ed. 17.50. Argosy.

Moll, J. H. Ankylosing Spondylitis. (Illus.). 320p. 1980. text ed. 75.00x (ISBN 0-443-01830-8). Churchill.

Molle, W., et al. Regional Disparity & Economic Development in the European Community. LC 79-91668. 428p. 1980. text ed. 37.50 (ISBN 0-916672-50-6). Allanheld.

Mollen, Art, Dr. Run for Your Life. LC 77-78517. 1978. pap. 4.95 (ISBN 0-385-13257-3, Dolp). Doubleday.

Mollenkott, Virginia R. Speech, Silence, Action! The Cycle of Faith. LC 80-15812. (Journey in Faith Ser.). 144p. 1980. 7.95 (ISBN 0-687-39169-5). Abingdon.

Mollenkott, Virginia R., jt. auth. see Scanzoni, Letha.

Moller, James H. & Neal, William A. Heart Disease in Infancy. 522p. 1980. 36.50x (ISBN 0-8385-3671-9). ACC.

Moller, Mary L., jt. ed. see Hefferren, John J.

Molli, Jeanne, jt. auth. see Avedon, Luciana.

Mollo, Andrew. Naval, Marine & Air Force Uniforms of World War 2. LC 75-28336. (Macmillan Color Ser.). (Illus.). 232p. 1976. 9.95 (ISBN 0-02-579391-8, 57939). Macmillan.

Mollo, Andrew & McGregor, Malcolm. Army Uniforms of World War II. (Illus.). 183p. 1980. 9.95 (ISBN 0-7137-0611-2, Pub. by Blandford Pr England). Sterling.

Mollo, Andrew, et al. World Army Uniforms: Nineteen Thirty-Nine to the Present. (Illus.). 360p. 1981. 24.95 (ISBN 0-7137-1189-2, Pub. by Blandford Pr England). Sterling.

Mollo, Boris. Uniforms of the Imperial Russian Army. (Illus.). 1979. 13.95 (ISBN 0-7137-0893-X, Pub by Blandford Pr England). Sterling.

Mollo, John. Uniforms of the American Revolution. LC 74-23543. (Illus.). 208p. 1975. 8.95 (ISBN 0-02-585580-8, 58558). Macmillan.

Mollo, Terry, ed. U. S. Book Publishing Yearbook & Directory: 1980-1981. 2nd ed. LC 79-649219. (Communications Library). 225p. 1980. pap. 35.00 (ISBN 0-914236-63-6). Knowledge Indus.

Mollo, Victor. Bridge in the Fourth Dimension. 1974. 11.95 (ISBN 0-571-10634-X, Pub. by Faber & Faber). Merrimack Bk Serv.

--Bridge in the Fourth Dimension: Further Adventures of the Hideous Hog. 192p. 1981. pap. 6.95 (ISBN 0-571-11675-2, Pub. by Faber & Faber). Merrimack Bd Serv.

--Instant Bridge. (Illus.). 1975. 12.95 (ISBN 0-571-10871-7, Pub. by Faber & Faber). Merrimack Bk Serv.

--Victor Mollo's Winning Double. 2nd ed. 1973. 5.95 o.p. (ISBN 0-571-04827-7, Pub. by Faber & Faber). Merrimack Bk Serv.

Mollo, Victor & Gardener, Nico. Card Play Technique. rev. ed. 1971. 10.95 (ISBN 0-571-09744-8, Pub. by Faber & Faber). Merrimack Bk Serv.

Mollo, Victor & Nielson, Aksel J. Defense at Bridge. 1976. 15.95 (ISBN 0-571-10891-1, Pub. by Faber & Faber). Merrimack Bk Serv.

Molloy, Anne. Wampum. (Illus.). (gr. 3 up). 1977. 7.95 (ISBN 0-8038-8079-0). Hastings.

Molloy, Edmond S., jt. auth. see Cummings, Thomas G.

Molloy, J., jt. ed. see Minogue, M.

Molloy, J. Fitzgerald. Court Life Below Stairs: or London Under the Last Georges. 427p. 1980. Repr. of 1897 ed. lib. bdg. 50.00 (ISBN 0-89984-337-9). Century Bookbindery.

Molloy, John T. Dress for Success. (Illus.). 1978. pap. 3.95 (ISBN 0-446-97529-X). Warner Bks.

--Dress for Success. (Illus.). 248p. 1976. pap. 2.50 (ISBN 0-446-93706-1). Warner Bks.

--Molloy's Live for Success. LC 80-2279. (Illus.). 288p. 1981. 11.95 (ISBN 0-688-00412-1). Morrow.

--The Woman's Dress for Success Book. (Illus.). 1978. pap. 4.95 (ISBN 0-446-97572-9). Warner Bks.

Molloy, Julia S. Performance Goals Record. (John Day Bk.). 1972. 2.50 o.s.i. (ISBN 0-381-97073-6, TYC-T). T Y Crowell.

--Trainable Children. rev. ed. LC 70-155017. (John Day Bk.). 256p. 1972. text ed. 18.00 (ISBN 0-381-97028-0, A82402, TYC-T); pap. 13.95 o.s.i. (ISBN 0-381-97027-2, A82401, JD-T). T Y Crowell.

Molloy, Paul. Where Did Everybody Go? LC 79-6605. 192p. 1981. 11.95 (ISBN 0-385-04997-8). Doubleday.

Molnar, Gail, jt. auth. see Kennedy, Maureen O.

Molnar, Joe. Elizabeth: A Puerto Rican-American Child Tells Her Story. LC 74-10713. (Illus.). (gr. 4-6). 1975. PLB 5.90 (ISBN 0-531-02795-3). Watts.

--Graciela: A Mexican-American Child Tells Her Story. LC 77-182297. (Illus.). 48p. (gr. 4-7). 1972. PLB 4.90 o.p. (ISBN 0-531-02023-1). Watts.

Molnar, John E. Author-Title Index to Joseph Sabin's Dictionary of Books Relating to America, 3 vols. LC 74-6291. 1974. Set. 135.00 (ISBN 0-8108-0652-5). Scarecrow.

Molnar, Mikos. A Short History of the Hungarian Communist Party. LC 77-27898. (Special Studies on the Soviet Union & Eastern Europe Ser.). 1978. lib. bdg. 21.00 o.p. (ISBN 0-89158-032-7). Westview.

Molnar, P., jt. ed. see Grastyan, E.

Molnar, Paul, jt. auth. see Fried, Jacob.

Molnar, Thomas. Theist & Atheist: A Typology of Non-Belief. 1979. text ed. 33.50x (ISBN 90-279-7788-7). Mouton.

Molner, J. Stay Well Every Year of Your Life: Dr. Molners Guide to Total Health. 1964. 6.95 o.p. (ISBN 0-13-846345-X). P-H.

Molner, Stephen. Races, Types & Ethnic Groups: The Problem of Human Variation. LC 74-23935. (Illus.). 224p. 1975. pap. 9.95 (ISBN 0-13-750240-0). P-H.
Molodenkov, M. N., jt. auth. see Lopukhin, Y. M.
Moloney, F. J. Disciples & Prophets. 240p. 1981. 9.95 (ISBN 0-8245-0049-0). Crossroad NY.
Moloney, Joan. Making Puppets & Puppet Theatres. LC 74-78175. (Illus.). 1974. 9.95 (ISBN 0-8119-0242-0). Fell.
Molotch, Harvey L. Managed Integration: Dilemmas of Doing Good in the City. LC 74-142049. 280p. 1973. 18.50x (ISBN 0-520-01889-3). U of Cal Pr.
Molow, Paul. Your Life Is What You Make It. 192p. 1981. 10.00 (ISBN 0-682-49739-8). Exposition.
Molseed, Elwood. The Genus Tigridia (Iridaceae) of Mexico & Central America. (U. C. Publ. in Botany: Vol. 54). 1970. pap. 7.50x (ISBN 0-520-09028-4). U of Cal Pr.
Moltmann, Jurgen. The Crucified God. LC 73-18694. 352p. 1974. 15.95 (ISBN 0-06-065901-7, HarpR). Har-Row.
--Experiences of God. Kohl, Margaret, tr. from Ger. LC 80-8046. 96p. 1980. pap. 3.95 (ISBN 0-8006-1406-2, 1-1406). Fortress.
--The Trinity & the Kingdom. LC 80-8352. 320p. 1981. 15.00 (ISBN 0-06-065906-8, HarpR). Har-Row.
Moltmann, Jurgen, jt. auth. see Lapide, Pinchas.
Moltmann, Jurgen, jt. ed. see Kung, Hans.
Moltrecht, K. H. Machine Shop Practice. 2nd ed. (Illus.). 1981. Vol. 1, 512 Pp. 19.95 (ISBN 0-8311-1126-7); Vol. 2, 528 Pp. 19.95 (ISBN 0-8311-1132-1). Indus Pr.
Momaday, N. Scott. The Gourd Dancer. LC 75-30338. (Illus.). 96p. (YA) 1976. 9.95 o.s.i. (ISBN 0-06-012982-4, HarpT); pap. 2.95 o.s.i. (ISBN 0-06-012983-2, TD-250, HarpT). Har-Row.
Momatiuk, Yva & Eastcott, John. High Country. (Illus.). 128p. 1980. 25.00 (ISBN 0-589-01321-1, Pub. by Reed Bks Australia). C E Tuttle.
Momboisse, Raymond M. Blueprint of Revolution: The Rebel, the Party, the Techniques of Revolt. 360p. 1970. 14.75 (ISBN 0-398-01323-3). C C Thomas.
--Community Relations & Riot Prevention. (Illus.). 272p. 1974. 13.75 (ISBN 0-398-01324-1). C C Thomas.
--Industrial Security for Strikes, Riots & Disasters. 516p. 1977. 24.75 (ISBN 0-398-01325-X). C C Thomas.
--Riots, Revolts, & Insurrections. (Illus.). 544p. 1977. 17.50 (ISBN 0-398-01326-8). C C Thomas.
Momen, Moojan. Dr. John Ebenezer Esslemont. (Illus.). 1979. pap. 2.50 (ISBN 0-900125-30-6, 7-31-06). Baha'i.
Momigliano, A. D. Alien Wisdom: The Limits of Hellenization. LC 75-10237. 140p. 1976. 23.95 (ISBN 0-521-20876-9). Cambridge U Pr.
Momigliano, Arnaldo. Claudius, the Emperor & His Achievement. rev. ed. Hogarth, W. D., tr. from Ital. LC 80-26158. xv, 143p. 1981. Repr. of 1961 ed. lib. bdg. 17.50x (ISBN 0-313-20813-1, MOCE). Greenwood.
--Essays in Ancient & Modern Historiography. LC 76-41484. 1977. lib. bdg. 22.50x (ISBN 0-8195-5010-8, Pub. by Wesleyan U Pr). Columbia U Pr.
Mommsen, Wolfgang J. Age of Bureaucracy. 1977. pap. 3.95x o.p. (ISBN 0-06-131862-0, TB 1862, Torch). Har-Row.
--Theories of Imperialism. Falla, P. S., tr. LC 80-5279. 156p. 1981. 9.95 (ISBN 0-394-50932-3). Random.
Mommsen, Wolfgang J., ed. The Emergence of the Welfare State in Britain & Germany. 350p. 1981. 31.00x (ISBN 0-7099-1710-4, Pub. by Croom Helm LTD England). Biblio Dist.
Momose, K. J. Functional Approach to the Interpretation of the Skull in Infancy & Childhood. LC 70-111805. (Illus.). 250p. 1981. 17.50 (ISBN 0-87527-225-8). Green.
Monaco, James. Alain Resnais. (Illus.). 1979. pap. 6.95 (ISBN 0-19-520038-1, GB540, GB). Oxford U Pr.
--How to Read a Film: The Art, Technology, Language, History & Theory of Film & Television. (Illus.). 1977. 17.95 (ISBN 0-19-502227-0); pap. text ed. 9.95x (ISBN 0-19-502178-9). Oxford U Pr.
--How to Read a Film: The Art, Technology, Language, History, & Theory of Film & Media. rev. ed. (Illus.). 576p. 1981. 25.00 (ISBN 0-19-502802-3); pap. 11.95 (ISBN 0-19-502806-6). Oxford U Pr.
Monaco, Paul, jt. ed. see Graff, Harvey J.
Monaco, Richard. Parsival: Or a Knight's Tale. (Illus.). 1977. 12.95 (ISBN 0-02-585540-9). Macmillan.
Monad, Adolphe. Adolphe Monad's Farewell. 1962. pap. 1.95 (ISBN 0-686-12506-1). Banner of Truth.
Monaghan, David, ed. Jane Austen in a Social Context. 176p. 1981. 22.50x (ISBN 0-389-20007-7). B&N.
Monaghan, Jay. Custer: The Life of General George Armstrong Custer. LC 59-5937. (Illus.). 1971. 16.95x (ISBN 0-8032-3056-7); pap. 5.25 (ISBN 0-8032-5732-5, BB 530, Bison). U of Nebr Pr.
Monaghan, Patricia. The Book of Goddesses & Heroines. 1981. pap. 9.95 (ISBN 0-525-47664-4). Dutton.
Monaghan, William & Louis, Louise. Walking into Time. (Illus.). 1971. Repr. of 1969 ed. text ed. 3.98. Pen-Art.
Monahan, Brent, jt. auth. see Maryk, Michael.
Monahan, Brent J. The Art of Singing: A Compendium of Thoughts on Singing Published Between 1777 & 1927. LC 78-16630. 1978. 15.00 (ISBN 0-8108-1155-3). Scarecrow.
Monahan, Evelyn & Bakken, Terry. Put Your Psychic Powers to Work: A Practical Guide to Parapsychology. LC 73-84208. 1973. 10.95 (ISBN 0-88229-132-7). Nelson-Hall.
Monahan, John, jt. auth. see Heller, Kenneth.
Monahan, John, ed. Community Mental Health & the Criminal Justice System. 350p. 1976. pap. text ed. 12.75 (ISBN 0-08-018758-7). Pergamon.
--Who Is the Client? The Ethics of Psychological Intervention in the Criminal Justice System. LC 80-14101. 1980. 7.50 (ISBN 0-912704-14-4). Am Psychol.
Monahan, John, jt. ed. see Chappell, Duncan.
Monahan, Lynn H & Farmer, Richard E. Stress & the Police: A Manual for Prevention. LC 80-83671. 1981. pap. 7.95 (ISBN 0-913530-23-9). Palisades Pubs.
Monahan, Valerie. Collecting Postcards in Color 1914-1930. (Illus.). 176p. 1980. 12.95 (ISBN 0-7137-1002-0, Pub. by Blandford Pr England); pap. 6.95 (ISBN 0-7137-1080-2). Sterling.
Monahan, Valerie, jt. auth. see Duval, William.
Monat, Alan & Lazarus, Richard S., eds. Stress & Coping: An Anthology. LC 77-3264. 1977. 25.00x (ISBN 0-231-08358-0); pap. 10.00x (ISBN 0-685-75645-9). Columbia U Pr.
Monath, Thomas P., ed. St Louis Encephalitis. LC 79-53721. (Illus.). 700p. 1980. text ed. 20.00x (ISBN 0-87553-090-7). Am Pub Health.
Monbeck, Michael E. Meaning of Blindness: Attitudes Toward Blindness & Blind People. LC 73-77853. 224p. 1973. 8.50x (ISBN 0-253-33727-5). Ind U Pr.
Monchick, Randolph B., jt. auth. see Nash, Bruce M.
Moncrief & Jones. Elements of Physical Chemistry. 1976. 20.95 (ISBN 0-201-04897-3). A-W.
Moncrieff, A. R. Romance of Chivalry. LC 80-23872. (Newcastle Mythology Library: Vol. 2). 439p. 1980. Repr. of 1976 ed. lib. bdg. 11.95x (ISBN 0-89370-638-8). Borgo Pr.
--The Romance of Chivalry. (Newcastle Mythology Library: Vol. 2). Orig. Title: Romance & Legend of Chivalry. (Illus.). 439p. 1976. pap. 4.95 (ISBN 0-87877-038-0, M-38). Newcastle Pub.
Moncrieff, C. K., tr. see Pirandello, Luigi.
Moncrieff, C. Scott, tr. see Roland.
Moncure, Jane. Kindness. (What Does the Bible Say? Ser.). (Illus.). 32p. 4.95 (ISBN 0-89565-167-X, 4929). Standard Pub.
Moncure, Jane B. About Me. LC 76-16556. (Illus.). (ps-2). 1976. 5.50 (ISBN 0-913778-52-4). Childs World.
--All by Myself. LC 76-5487. (Illus.). (ps-3). 1976. 5.95 (ISBN 0-913778-40-0). Childs World.
--Animal, Animal, Where Do You Live? LC 75-29237. (Illus.). (ps-3). 1975. 5.95 (ISBN 0-913778-14-1). Childs World.
--Barbara's Pony, Buttercup. LC 76-52921. (Illus.). (ps-3). 1977. 5.50 (ISBN 0-913778-74-5). Childs World.
--A Beach in My Bedroom. LC 77-12960. (Creative Dramatics Ser.). (Illus.). (ps-3). 1978. PLB 5.50 (ISBN 0-89565-005-3); pap. 2.50 (ISBN 0-89565-038-X). Childs World.
--Caring. LC 80-14200. (What Does the Bible Say? Ser.). (Illus.). 32p. (ps-2). 1980. PLB 4.95. Childs World.
--Caring. rev. ed. LC 80-27506. (What Is It? Ser.). (Illus.). (gr. k-3). 1981. PLB 5.50 (ISBN 0-89565-201-3). Childs World.
--Christmas Is a Happy Time. Buerger, Jane, ed. 1980. 4.95 (ISBN 0-89565-171-8, 4922). Standard Pub.
--Courage. LC 80-14201. (What Does the Bible Say? Ser.). (Illus.). 32p. (ps-2). 1980. PLB 4.95 (ISBN 0-89565-168-8, 4930). Standard Pub.
--Courage. rev. ed. LC 80-39515. (What Is It? Ser.). (Illus.). 32p. (gr. k-3). 1981. PLB 5.50 (ISBN 0-89565-202-1). Childs World.
--Fall Is Here! LC 75-14019. (Illus.). (ps-2). 1975. 5.50 (ISBN 0-913778-13-3). Childs World.
--The Gift of Christmas. LC 79-10279. (Bible Story Books). (Illus.). (ps-3). 1979. PLB 5.50 (ISBN 0-89565-083-5). Childs World.
--Hi, Word Bird. LC 80-15919. (Early-Bird Reader Ser.). (Illus.). 32p. (ps-2). 1980. PLB 5.50 (ISBN 0-89565-159-9). Childs World.
--Honesty. rev. ed. LC 80-39571. (What Is It? Ser.). (Illus.). 32p. (gr. k-3). 1981. PLB 5.50 (ISBN 0-89565-203-X). Childs World.
--How Beautiful God's Gifts. Buerger, Jane, ed. (Illus.). 1980. 4.95 (ISBN 0-89565-172-6, 4923). Standard Pub.
--How Beautiful God's Gifts. LC 80-1544. (Illus.). 32p. (ps-2). 1980. PLB 4.95 (ISBN 0-89565-172-6). Childs World.
--I Never Say I'm Thankful, but I Am. LC 78-21577. (Illus.). (ps-3). 1979. PLB 5.95 (ISBN 0-89565-023-1). Childs World.
--If a Dinosaur Came to Dinner. LC 77-12957. (Creative Dramatics Ser.). (Illus.). (ps-3). 1978. PLB 5.50 (ISBN 0-89565-008-8); pap. 2.50 (ISBN 0-89565-041-X). Childs World.
--Jobs People Do. LC 76-5452. (Illus.). (ps-3). 1976. 5.95 (ISBN 0-913778-37-0). Childs World.
--Just the Right Place! LC 75-34176. (Illus.). (ps-3). 1976. 5.50 (ISBN 0-913778-36-2). Childs World.
--Kindness. rev. ed. LC 80-39535. (What Is It? Ser.). (Illus.). 32p. (gr. k-3). 1981. PLB 5.50 (ISBN 0-89565-204-8). Childs World.
--The Little Boy Samuel. LC 79-12174. (Bible Story Bks.). (Illus.). (ps-3). PLB 5.50 (ISBN 0-89565-084-3). Childs World.
--Love. Buerger, Jane, ed. (Illus.). 1980. 4.95 (ISBN 0-89565-165-3, 4927). Standard Pub.
--Love. rev. ed. LC 80-27479. (What Is It? Ser.). (Illus.). 32p. (gr. k-3). 1981. PLB 5.50 (ISBN 0-89565-205-6). Childs World.
--My Baby Brother Needs a Friend. LC 78-21935. (Illus.). (ps-3). 1979. PLB 5.95 (ISBN 0-89565-019-3). Childs World.
--No! No! Word Bird. LC 80-29491. (Word Birds for Early Birds Ser.). (Illus.). 32p. (gr. k-2). 1981. PLB 5.50 (ISBN 0-89565-161-0). Childs World.
--One Little World. LC 75-35975. (Illus.). (ps-3). 1975. 5.50 (ISBN 0-913778-31-1). Childs World.
--People Who Help People. LC 75-29225. (Illus.). (ps-3). 1975. 5.95 (ISBN 0-913778-16-8). Childs World.
--Pets Are Smart. LC 76-4834. (Illus.). (ps-3). 1976. 5.95 (ISBN 0-913778-39-7). Childs World.
--Plants Give Us Many Kinds of Food. LC 75-29268. (Illus.). (ps-3). 1975. 5.95 (ISBN 0-913778-17-6). Childs World.
--Play with A & T. LC 73-4740. (Alphabet Books). (Illus.). (gr. k-2). 1973. PLB 4.95 (ISBN 0-913778-02-8); pap. 2.75 (ISBN 0-89565-135-1). Childs World.
--Play with E & D. LC 73-4743. (Alphabet Books). (Illus.). (ps-2). 1973. PLB 4.95 (ISBN 0-913778-03-6); pap. 2.75 (ISBN 0-89565-133-5). Childs World.
--Play with I & G. LC 73-4739. (Alphabet Books). (Illus.). (ps-2). 1973. PLB 4.95 (ISBN 0-913778-04-4); pap. 2.75 (ISBN 0-89565-134-3). Childs World.
--Play with O & G. LC 73-4742. (Alphabet Books). (Illus.). (ps-2). 1973. PLB 4.95 (ISBN 0-913778-05-2); pap. 2.75 (ISBN 0-89565-131-9). Childs World.
--Play with U & G. LC 73-4741. (Alphabet Books). (Illus.). (ps-2). 1973. PLB 4.95 (ISBN 0-913778-06-0); pap. 2.75 (ISBN 0-89565-132-7). Childs World.
--A Rabbit Has a Habit. LC 75-35608. (Illus.). (ps-3). 1976. 5.50 (ISBN 0-913778-35-4). Childs World.
--See My Garden Grow. LC 76-4512. (Illus.). (ps-3). 1976. 5.95 (ISBN 0-913778-38-9). Childs World.
--Skip Aboard a Space Ship. LC 77-12958. (Creative Dramatics Ser.). (Illus.). (ps-3). 1978. PLB 5.50 (ISBN 0-89565-009-6); pap. 2.50 (ISBN 0-89565-042-8). Childs World.
--Spring Is Here! LC 75-14202. (Illus.). (ps-2). 1975. 5.50 (ISBN 0-913778-11-7). Childs World.
--Stop! Go! Word Bird. LC 80-16273. (Early Bird Reader Ser.). (Illus.). 32p. (ps-2). 1980. PLB 5.50 (ISBN 0-89565-160-2). Childs World.
--Summer Is Here! LC 75-12945. (Illus.). (ps-2). 1975. 5.50 (ISBN 0-913778-12-5). Childs World.
--Thank You, Animal Friends. LC 75-29241. (Illus.). (ps-3). 1975. 5.95 (ISBN 0-913778-15-X). Childs World.
--Try on a Shoe. LC 73-4738. (Illus.). (ps-2). 1973. 5.95 (ISBN 0-913778-00-1). Childs World.
--What Do the Animals Do in the Zoo. LC 75-33954. (Illus.). (ps-4). 1976. 5.50 (ISBN 0-913778-31-1). Childs World.
--What Does a Koala Bear Need? LC 75-33956. (Illus.). (ps-3). 1976. 5.50 (ISBN 0-913778-34-6). Childs World.
--What Will It Be? LC 75-35542. (Illus.). (ps-3). 1976. PLB 5.50 (ISBN 0-913778-24-9); pap. 2.75 (ISBN 0-89565-066-5). Childs World.
--What Will It Rain? A Book About Fall. LC 76-46295. (Illus.). (ps-3). 1977. 5.50 (ISBN 0-913778-69-9). Childs World.
--Winter Is Here! LC 75-14201. (ps-2). 1975. 5.50 (ISBN 0-913778-10-9). Childs World.
--Wishes, Whispers & Secrets. LC 78-31295. (Illus.). (ps-3). 1979. PLB 5.95 (ISBN 0-89565-024-X). Childs World.
--Word Bird's Circus Surprise. LC 80-29528. (Word Birds for Early Birds Ser.). (Illus.). 32p. (gr. k-2). 1981. PLB 5.50 (ISBN 0-89565-162-9). Childs World.
Mond, Alan Le see Spitz, Mark & LeMond, Alan.
Mondale, Joan, intro. by. Carter on the Arts. 1977. pap. 2.50 o.p. (ISBN 0-686-67828-1). Interbk Inc.
Mondelli, R. J. & Ponterotto, Italo L. Conversational Spanish Review Grammar. (gr. 9-12). 1961. text ed. 5.25 o.p. (ISBN 0-8260-6185-0, Pub. by Ronald Pr). Wiley.
Mondello, Salvatore, jt. auth. see Iorizzo, Luciano J.
Mondy & Noe. Personnel: The Management of Human Resources. 750p. 1980. text ed. 20.95 (ISBN 0-205-07217-8, 0872172); free tchr's ed. (ISBN 0-205-07218-6). Allyn.
Mondy, et al. Management: Concepts & Practices. 704p. 1980. text ed. 18.95 (ISBN 0-205-06859-6, 0868590); study guide 6.95 (ISBN 0-205-06861-8, 0868612). Allyn.
Mondy, Nell I. Experimental Food Chemistry. (Illus.). 1980. pap. text ed. 15.50 (ISBN 0-87055-343-7). AVI.
Mondy, Robert W. Pioneers & Preachers: Stories of the Old Frontier. (Illus.). 1980. 21.95 (ISBN 0-88229-619-1); pap. 11.95 (ISBN 0-88229-722-8). Nelson-Hall.
Monegal, Emir & Reid, Alistair. The Borges Reader: Luis Borges. 320p. 1980. 12.95 (ISBN 0-525-06998-4); pap. 7.95 (ISBN 0-525-47654-7). Dutton.
Moneli, Susanna & Moneli, illus. Sing Through the Seasons: Ninety-Nine Songs for Children. LC 70-164916. (Illus.). 190p. 9.75 (ISBN 0-87486-006-7); l.p. record 5.25 (ISBN 0-87486-040-7); with record 15.00 (ISBN 0-686-66591-0). Plough.
Monette. Nosferatu: Vampyre. 1979. pap. 2.25 (ISBN 0-380-44107-1, 44107). Avon.
Monette, Paul. The Long Shot. pap. 5.95. Avon.
Money, John. Love & Love Sickness: The Science of Sex; Gender. Difference & Pair Bonding. LC 79-3679. 1980. 16.95x (ISBN 0-8018-2317-X); pap. text ed. 5.95 (ISBN 0-8018-2318-8). Johns Hopkins.
Money, John, jt. auth. see Wolman, Benjamon B.
Money, John, jt. ed. see Green, Richard.
Money, Keith. Fonteyn: The Making of a Legend. LC 74-3578. (Illus.). 320p. 1974. 25.00 o.p. (ISBN 0-688-61163-X). Morrow.
Money, L. C. Chiozza. Riches & Poverty: London Nineteen Six. LC 79-56955. (The English Working Class Ser.). 1980. lib. bdg. 30.00. Garland Pub.
Money, Metta K. de see De Money, Netta K.
Money, Netta D. De see De Money, Netta D.
Monfort, Platt. Styro-Flyers: How to Build Super Model Airplanes from Hamburger Boxes & Other Fast-Food Containers. (Illus.). 32p. (gr. 5 up). 1981. pap. 3.95 (ISBN 0-394-84715-6). Random.
Monga, G. S. Mathematics & Statistics for Economics. 3rd ed. 1979. 18.95 (ISBN 0-7069-0588-1, Pub. by Vikas India). Advent Bk.
Monga, Mohinder. Through the Night Raptly. 8.00 (ISBN 0-89253-778-7); flexible cloth 4.80 (ISBN 0-89253-779-5). Ind-US Inc.
Monge, Jose Trias see Trias Monge, Jose.
Monge, Peter R. & Capella, Joseph N., eds. Multivariate Techniques in Human Communications Research. LC 79-28430. (Human Communication Research Ser.). 1980. 45.00 (ISBN 0-12-504450-X). Acad Pr.
Mongia, J. N. Economics for Administrators. 600p. 1981. text ed. 40.00x (ISBN 0-7069-1293-4, Pub by Vikas India). Advent Bk.
Mongillo, John F., et al. Reading About Science, Skills & Concepts. Kane, Joanne E., ed. (Reading About Science, Skills & Concepts Ser.). (Illus.). 128p. (gr. 4-6). 1980. Bk. C. pap. text ed. 4.84 (ISBN 0-07-002423-5, W); Bk. E. pap. text ed. 5.04 (ISBN 0-07-002425-1); Bk. F. pap. text ed. 5.28 (ISBN 0-07-002426-X); tchr's. guide 3.24 (ISBN 0-07-002428-6). McGraw.
Monicard, R. Properties of Reservoir Rocks: Core Analysis. 204p. 1980. 24.95 (ISBN 0-87201-765-6). Gulf Pub.
Monich, Timothy, jt. auth. see Skinner, Edith.
Monie, J & Wise, A. Social Policy & It's Administration. 1977. 48.00 (ISBN 0-08-021943-8). Pergamon.
Monie, Willis J., ed. see Davenport, Robert.
Moniere, Denis. The Development of Ideologies in Quebec. Howard, Richard, tr. from Fr. Orig. Title: Le Developpement Des Ideologies Du Quebec. 320p. 1981. 27.50x (ISBN 0-8020-5452-8); pap. 10.00 (ISBN 0-8020-6358-6). U of Toronto Pr.

Monier-Williams. Sanskrit-English Dictionary. 1973. 37.00x (ISBN 0-8364-0464-5). South Asia Bks.

Monier-Williams, Monier, et al. Sanskrit-English Dictionary. rev. ed. 1899. 89.00x (ISBN 0-19-864308-X). Oxford U Pr.

Monif, Gilles R., ed. Infectious Diseases in Obstetrics & Gynecology. (Illus.). 1974. text ed. 37.00x (ISBN 0-06-141795-5, Harper Medical). Har-Row.

Monin, A. S., et al. Variability of the Oceans. LC 77-826. 1977. 34.50 (ISBN 0-471-61328-2, Pub. by Wiley-Interscience). Wiley.

Monjo, F. N. The House at Stink Alley. (gr. k-6). 1980. pap. 1.25 (ISBN 0-440-43376-2, YB). Dell.

Monk, Edwin. Modern Boat Building. rev. ed. LC 72-1220. (Encore Edition). (Illus.). 6.95 o.p. (ISBN 0-684-15257-6, ScribT). Scribner.

Monk, J. Donald. Introduction to Set Theory. LC 79-21279. 206p. 1980. Repr. lib. bdg. 14.50 (ISBN 0-89874-006-1). Krieger.

Monk, K. Fun with Fabric Printing. 8.00 o.p. (ISBN 0-87245-231-X). Textile Bk.

Monk, Robert, et al. Exploring Religious Meaning. 2nd ed. (Illus.). 1980. text ed. 13.95 (ISBN 0-13-297515-7). P-H.

Monk, Samuel A. see Dryden, John.

Monk, Samuel H., ed. see Defoe, Daniel.

Monkhouse, Donald C., ed. Animal Health Products Design & Evaluation. LC 78-69826. 1978. softcover 18.00 (ISBN 0-917330-23-4). Am Pharm Assn.

Monkhouse, F. Dictionary of Natural Environment with English-Arabic Glossary. 16.00x (ISBN 0-686-65472-2). Intl Bk Ctr.

Monkhouse, F. J. A Dictionary of the Natural Environment. rev. ed. Small, John, ed. 1977. 29.95 (ISBN 0-470-99333-2); pap. 9.95 (ISBN 0-470-99334-0). Halsted Pr.

--Landscape from the Air. 2nd ed. LC 70-134621. (Illus.). 1971. text ed. 5.75x (ISBN 0-521-08000-2). Cambridge U Pr.

Monkhouse, F. J. & Hardy, A. V. The Man-Made Landscape. (Illus.). 96p. 1974. text ed. 5.75x (ISBN 0-521-20365-1). Cambridge U Pr.

Monkhouse, F. J., jt. auth. see Hardy, Albert V.

Monkhouse, Frank & Williams, Joe. Climber & Fellwaker in Lakeland. (Climbing & Walking). (Illus.). 216p. 1971. 13.50 (ISBN 0-7153-5459-0). David & Charles.

Monkkonen, Eric. Police in Urban America, Eighteen Hundred Sixty to Nineteen Twenty. LC 80-16762. (Interdisciplinary Perspectives on Modern History Ser.). (Illus.). 256p. Date not set. price not set (ISBN 0-521-23454-9). Cambridge U Pr.

Monkman, Marjorie M. A Milieu Therapy Program for Behaviorally Disturbed Children. (Illus.). 312p. 1972. 19.75 (ISBN 0-398-02363-8). C C Thomas.

Monks, T. G., ed. Comprehensive Education in England & Wales. (Research Reports Ser.). 1968. pap. text ed. 16.25x (ISBN 0-901225-28-2, NFER). Humanities.

Monkshood, G., tr. see De Goncourt, Edmond.

Monmonier, Mark S. Maps, Distortion, & Meaning. Natoli, Salvatore, ed. LC 76-44640. (Resource Papers for College Geography Ser). 48p. 1977. pap. text ed. 4.00 (ISBN 0-89291-120-4). Assn Am Geographers.

Monna, M. C. The Gathas of Zarathustra: A Reconstruction of the Text. 1978. pap. text ed. 34.25x (ISBN 90-6203-582-5). Humanities.

Monnickendam, Marjorie, jt. ed. see Balls, M.

Mono, Madeleine. Making Eyes with Madeleine Mono. LC 80-7892. (Illus.). 128p. 1981. 10.95 (ISBN 0-690-01945-9, HarpT). Har-Row.

Monod, Jacques & Borek, Ernest, eds. Of Microbes & Life. LC 71-133382. (Molecular Biology Ser). (Illus.). 1971. 20.00x (ISBN 0-231-03431-8). Columbia U Pr.

Monod-Fontaine, Isabelle, jt. ed. see Tabart, Marielle.

Monoghan, Frank J. Hypnosis in Criminal Investigation. (Orig.). 1980. pap. text ed. 6.95 (ISBN 0-8403-2132-5). Kendall-Hunt.

Monopoli, Richard, jt. ed. see Narendra, Kumpati.

Monro, Alexander. Three Treatises: On the Brain, the Eye, & the Ear. Bd. with Croonian Lectures on Cerebral Localization. Ferrier, D. (Contributions to the History of Psychology Ser., Vol. VII, Pt. E: Psysiological Psychology). 1980. Repr. of 1797 ed. 30.00 (ISBN 0-89093-326-X). U Pubns Amer.

Monro, D. B., ed. see Homer.

Monro, David H. Empiricism & Ethics. 1967. pap. 32.95 (ISBN 0-521-05752-3). Cambridge U Pr.

Monro, I. S., jt. auth. see Monro, K. M.

Monro, K. M. & Monro, I. S. Clubwoman's Manual. 1957. 5.95 o.s.i. (ISBN 0-02-585570-0). Macmillan.

Monroe, Alex. Barnacle & His Friends. (Illus.). 42p. (Orig.). (gr. 1-6). 1980. pap. 2.75 (ISBN 0-933614-07-1). Peregrine Pr.

Monroe, Arthur E. Monetary Theory Before Adam Smith. 1923. 8.50 (ISBN 0-8446-1314-2). Peter Smith.

Monroe City County Fine Arts Council. Brighten the Corner. Little, Elsie & Gibson, Catherine, eds. (Illus.). 188p. 1977. pap. 7.00x (ISBN 0-686-28490-9). Monroe County Lib.

Monroe, Debbie, jt. auth. see Kuhle, Leo.

Monroe, Doris, ed. Adventures in Christian Living & Learning: A Resource Book for Use with Retarded Persons, Pt. 2. (Cooperative Ser: Curriculum Materials for the Mentally Retarded). (Illus., Orig.). (gr. 6-10). 1970. pap. 1.25 ea. o.p. (ISBN 0-8042-1140-X); tchrs' ed. 2.50 ea. o.p. (ISBN 0-8042-1141-8). John Knox.

Monroe, Elizabeth, jt. auth. see Jones, Arnold H.

Monroe, Elvira. Say Cheesecake - & Smile. 220p. 1981. pap. 5.95 (ISBN 0-933174-11-X). Wide World.

Monroe, Elvira & Margah, Irish. Hawaii: Cooking with Aloha. LC 80-52928. 120p. 1981. pap. 5.95 (ISBN 0-933174-10-1). Wide World.

Monroe, James T. Hispano-Arabic Poetry: A Student Anthology. LC 72-103925. 1975. 30.00x (ISBN 0-520-01692-0). U of Cal Pr.

--Shu'Ubiyya in Al'Andalus: The Risala of Ibn Garcia & Five Refutations. (U. C. Publ. in Near Eastern Studies: Vol. 13). 1970. pap. 7.50x (ISBN 0-520-09307-0). U of Cal Pr.

Monroe, James T., ed. & tr. Risalat at-Tawabic Wa Z-Zawabi (the Treatise of Familiar Spirits - Demons) by Abu a Mir Ibn Shuhaid Al-Ashja I, Al-Andalusi. (U. C. Publ. in Near Eastern Studies: Vol. 15). 1971. pap. 8.00x (ISBN 0-520-09382-8). U of Cal Pr.

Monroe, Jane A., jt. auth. see Twaite, James A.

Monroe, Jane B. Birds, Baboons, & Barefoot Bears. LC 77-13025. (Creative Dramatics Ser.). (Illus.). (ps-3). 1978. PLB 5.50 (ISBN 0-89565-006-1); pap. 2.50 (ISBN 0-89565-039-8). Childs World.

--The Four Magic Boxes. LC 77-12959. (Creative Dramatics Ser.). (Illus.). (ps-3). 1978. PLB 5.50 (ISBN 0-89565-007-X); pap. 2.50 (ISBN 0-89565-040-1). Childs World.

--Tick, Tock, the Popcorn Clock. LC 77-13120. (Creative Dramatics Ser.). (Illus.). (ps-3). 1978. PLB 5.50 (ISBN 0-89565-010-X); pap. 2.50 (ISBN 0-89565-043-6). Childs World.

Monroe, Judson, et al. The Science of Scientific Writing. LC 76-46822. 1976. pap. text ed. 5.95 (ISBN 0-8403-1645-3). Kendall-Hunt.

Monroe, Keith, jt. auth. see Harman, Bob.

Monroe, Lee S., jt. auth. see Spencer, Francis M.

Monroe, Paul, ed. Cyclopedia of Education, 5 vols. LC 68-56361. (Illus.). 1968. Repr. of 1911 ed. Set. 260.00 (ISBN 0-8103-3537-9). Gale.

Monroe, R. E., et al, eds. Psychiatric Epidemiology & Mental Health Planning. 400p. 1967. pap. 5.00 (ISBN 0-685-24861-5, P022-0). Am Psychiatric.

Monroe, Robert A. Journeys Out of the Body. LC 72-157612. 288p. 1977. pap. 6.50 (ISBN 0-385-00861-9, Anch). Doubleday.

Monroe, Russell R. Brain Dysfunction in Aggressive Criminals. LC 78-4402. (Illus.). 1978. 19.95 (ISBN 0-669-02349-3). Lexington Bks.

Monroe, S. Approach Interview to Owners of a Closely Held Corp. 1981. 24.95 (ISBN 0-87863-209-3). Farnswth Pub. Postponed.

Monroe, Tom. How to Rebuild Your Ford V-8. (Orig.). 1980. pap. 7.95 (ISBN 0-89586-036-8). H P Bks.

--How to Rebuild Your Small-Block Ford. LC 78-74545. (Illus.). 1979. pap. 7.95 (ISBN 0-912656-89-1). H P Bks.

Monroe, Wendall L. Mastering the Itimate Life of Man. (Illus.). 153p. 1980. deluxe ed. 37.85 (ISBN 0-89266-243-3). Am Classical Coll Pr.

Monroe, Wilbur F. The New Internationalism: Strategy & Initiatives for U.S. Foreign Economic Policy. LC 75-36989. 1976. 18.95 (ISBN 0-669-00391-3). Lexington Bks.

Monroe, Will S. Bibliography of Education. LC 68-30661. 1968. Repr. of 1897 ed. 15.00 (ISBN 0-8103-3337-6). Gale.

Monroy, Alberto & Moscona, A. A., eds. Current Topics in Developmental Biology, Vols. 1-12. Incl. Vol. 1. 1966. 38.50 (ISBN 0-12-153101-5); Vol. 2. 1967. 38.50 (ISBN 0-12-153102-3); Vol. 3. 1968. 38.50 (ISBN 0-12-153103-1); Vol. 4. 1969. 38.50 (ISBN 0-12-153104-X); Vol. 5. 1970. 44.50 (ISBN 0-12-153105-8); Vol. 6. 1971. 38.50 (ISBN 0-12-153106-6); Vol. 7. 1972. 38.50 (ISBN 0-12-153107-4); Vol. 8. 1974. 38.50 (ISBN 0-12-153108-2); Vol. 9. 1975. 33.00 (ISBN 0-12-153109-0); Vol. 10. 1975. 33.00 (ISBN 0-12-153110-4); Vol. 11. 1977. 30.50 (ISBN 0-12-153111-2); Vol. 12. 1978. 30.50 (ISBN 0-12-153112-0). Acad Pr.

Monroy, Alberto, jt. ed. see Metz, Charles B.

Monsarrat, Ann. An Uneasy Victorian: Thackery the Man 1811-1863. LC 80-20640. (Illus.). 480p. 1980. 15.00 (ISBN 0-396-07866-4). Dodd.

Monsarrat, Nicholas. The Kappillan of Malta. 1974. 8.95 o.p. (ISBN 0-688-00243-9). Morrow.

--The Master Mariner: Darken Ship. LC 80-20222. (Illus.). 192p. 1981. 9.95 (ISBN 0-688-00017-7). Morrow.

Monsell, Helen A. Her Own Way, the Story of Lottie Moon. LC 58-9919. (gr. 4-8). 1958. 4.50 (ISBN 0-8054-4303-7). Broadman.

Monsen, Erling, tr. see Snorri.

Monsen, Harry, tr. see Lopez-Antunez, Luis.

Monsen, Harry, tr. see Pernkopf, Eduard.

Monsen, Harry, tr. see Pernkoph, Eduard.

Monset-Couchard, M., jt. ed. see Minkowski, A.

Monsma, Hester. Bobby Keeps Watch. (Voyager Ser.). 128p. (Orig.). (gr. 6-10). 1981. pap. 2.45 (ISBN 0-8010-6088-5). Baker Bk.

Monsman, Gerald. Walter Pater. (English Authors Ser.: No. 207). 1977. lib. bdg. 10.95 (ISBN 0-8057-6676-6). Twayne.

Monson, Gale & Sumner, Lowell, eds. The Desert Bighorn: Its Life History, Ecology, & Management. LC 80-18889. 1980. text ed. 27.50x (ISBN 0-8165-0689-2); pap. 14.95 (ISBN 0-8165-0713-9). U of Ariz Pr.

Monson, J., et al, eds. see Cleeve, Richard.

Monson, Richard R. Occupational Epidemiology. 256p. 1980. 59.95 (ISBN 0-8493-5793-4). CRC Pr.

Monson, Thomas S. Behold Thy Mother. 1976. pap. 0.50 o.p. (ISBN 0-87747-586-5). Deseret Bk.

Monsted, Mette & Walii, Parve. A Demographic Analysis of East Africa: A Sociological Interpretation. (Scandinavian Institute of African Studies, Uppsala). 1978. pap. text ed. 14.50x (ISBN 0-8419-9728-4). Holmes & Meier.

Montadori Editors, ed. The Simon & Schuster Book of the Ballet. (Illus.). 1980. 24.95 (ISBN 0-671-25099-X). S&S.

Montag, Mildred L. Evaluation of Graduates of Associate Degree Nursing Programs. LC 72-84012. 1972. pap. text ed. 4.50x (ISBN 0-8077-1828-9). Tchrs Coll.

Montag, Mildred L. & Rines, Alice R. Handbook of Fundamental Nursing Techniques. LC 76-5246. 200p. 1976. 13.95 (ISBN 0-471-01475-3, Pub. by Wiley Medical); Arabic Translation avail. (ISBN 0-471-04525-X). Wiley.

Montag, Mildred L., jt. auth. see Rines, Alice R.

Montag, Tom. Concerns: Essays & Reviews 1972-76. LC 75-1956. (Orig.). 1977. 18.50x (ISBN 0-915316-34-X); pap. 6.50x (ISBN 0-915316-09-9). Pentagram.

--Ninety Notes Toward Partial Images & Lovers Prints. 1976. pap. 2.50x (ISBN 0-915316-37-4); signed 7.50x (ISBN 0-915316-38-2). Pentagram.

Montagna, Paul D. Certified Public Accounting: A Sociological View of a Profession in Change. LC 73-90140. 1975. text ed. 13.00 (ISBN 0-914348-14-0). Scholars Bk.

--Occupations & Society: Toward a Sociology of the Labor Market. LC 76-40121. 1977. text ed. 18.95x (ISBN 0-471-61383-5). Wiley.

Montagne. Atlas of Foot Radiology. 1981. price not set (ISBN 0-89352-097-7). Masson Pub.

Montagu. On Being Human. (gr. 9-12). 1967. 4.95 (ISBN 0-8015-5508-6, Hawthorn); pap. 3.50 (ISBN 0-8015-5514-0, Hawthorn). Dutton.

Montagu, Ashley. Culture & the Evolution of Man. (Illus., Orig.). 1962. pap. 4.95 (ISBN 0-19-500701-8, GB88, GB). Oxford U Pr.

--Natural Superiority of Women. rev. ed. 1968. 7.95 o.s.i. (ISBN 0-02-585620-0). Macmillan.

Montagu, Ashley & Rowe, David N. Great Issues 76: A Forum on Important Questions Facing the American Public, Vol. 8. LC 77-85525. 11.95 (ISBN 0-916624-11-0). Troy State Univ.

Montagu, Ashley, jt. auth. see Levitan, Max.

Montagu, Ashley, ed. The Concept of Race. LC 80-21682. xviii, 270p. 1980. Repr. of 1964 ed. lib. bdg. 27.50x (ISBN 0-313-22721-7, MOCR). Greenwood.

Montagu, Ivor, tr. see Leonov, Leonid M.

Montagu, Jeremy. The World of Baroque & Classical Musical Instruments. LC 78-65227. (Instrument Ser.). (Illus.). 1979. 23.95 (ISBN 0-87951-089-7). Overlook Pr.

--The World of Medieval & Renaissance Musical Instruments. LC 76-5987. (Illus.). 1976. 27.95 (ISBN 0-87951-045-5). Overlook Pr.

--The World of Romantic & Modern Musical Instruments. LC 80-26106. (Musical Instruments Ser.). (Illus.). 136p. 1981. pap. 27.95 (ISBN 0-87951-126-5). Overlook Pr.

Montagu, Mary W. The Complete Letters of Lady Mary Wortley Montagu, 2 vols. Halsbard, Robert, ed. Incl. Vol. 1. 1708-1720. 1965. 26.50x o.p. (ISBN 0-19-811446-X); Vol. 2. 1721-1751. 1966. 49.50x (ISBN 0-19-811455-9); Vol. 3. 1752-1762. 1967. 49.50x (ISBN 0-19-811456-7). Oxford U Pr.

Montagu, Richard. A Gagg for the New Gospell? No: A New Gagg for an Old Goose. LC 74-28872. (English Experience Ser.: No. 751). 1975. Repr. of 1624 ed. 26.00 (ISBN 90-221-0751-5). Walter J Johnson.

Montague, Albert C., jt. auth. see Lewison, Edward F.

Montague, Andrew A. Successful Shotgun Shooting. LC 70-150384. (Illus.). 1971. 8.95 (ISBN 0-87691-034-7). Winchester Pr.

Montague, Arens. American Dimension. 2nd ed. 1981. 8.95 (ISBN 0-88284-119-X). Alfred Pub.

Montague, Arthur, jt. auth. see Klein, John F.

Montague, Gene. Poetry & a Principle. LC 76-37397. 280p. 1972. pap. text ed. 3.95 o.p. (ISBN 0-397-47216-1). Lippincott.

Montague, Gene, et al. Experience of Literature. 2nd ed. 1970. pap. text ed. 12.95x (ISBN 0-13-294728-5). P-H.

Montague, George T. Mark: Good News for Hard Times: A Popular Commentary on the the Earliest Gospel. 200p. (Orig.). 1981. pap. 5.95 (ISBN 0-89283-096-4). Servant.

--Riding the Wind. 1977. pap. 1.25 (ISBN 0-89129-256-X). Jove Pubns.

Montague, John. Chosen Light. LC 71-81498. 69p. 1970. 6.50 (ISBN 0-8040-0040-9). Swallow.

--Poisoned Lands. new ed. 1977. pap. text ed. 6.00x (ISBN 0-85105-319-X, Dolmen Pr). Humanities.

--Tides. LC 73-135384. 63p. 1971. 6.50 (ISBN 0-8040-0526-5); pap. 3.75 (ISBN 0-8040-0825-6). Swallow.

Montague, John, ed. Book of Irish Verse. 400p. 1977. 14.95 (ISBN 0-02-585630-8, 58563). Macmillan.

Montague, Sarah. Pas De Deux: Great Partnerships in Dance. LC 80-54502. (Illus.). 112p. 1981. text ed. 12.50x (ISBN 0-87663-346-7); pap. 7.95x (ISBN 0-87663-553-2). Universe.

Montague, Susan, jt. auth. see Arens, W.

Montague, W. J., tr. see Kasemann, Ernst.

Montague-Smith, Patrick, ed. Debrett's Peerage & Baronetage Nineteen Eighty: Comprises Information Concerning the Royal Family, the Peerage, Privy Counsellors, Scottish Lords of Session, Baronets, & Chiefs of Names & Clans in Scotland. (Illus.). 1979. 135.00 (ISBN 0-8103-0949-1, Debretts Peerage Ltd). Gale.

Montagu-Nathan, M. History of Russian Music. LC 76-82815. 1918. 12.00x (ISBN 0-8196-0251-5). Biblo.

Montaigne, Michel De. In Defense of Raymond Sebond. Beattie, Arthur H., tr. LC 59-15521. (Milestones of Thought Ser.). 1959. 6.50 (ISBN 0-8044-5694-1); pap. 2.45 (ISBN 0-8044-6519-3). Ungar.

--Montaigne: Selections from the Essays. Frame, Donald M., ed. & tr. LC 72-96557. (Crofts Classics Ser.). 1973. pap. text ed. 2.95x (ISBN 0-88295-105-X). AHM Pub.

Montaigne, Sanford H. Blood Over Texas: The Unpopular Truth About Mexico's War with the United States. 1976. 8.95 o.p. (ISBN 0-87000-342-9). Arlington Hse.

Montaigne-Smith, Patrick, ed. Debrett's Peerage & Baronetage. LC 42-17925. 2336p. 1980. 112.50x (ISBN 0-905649-20-6). Intl Pubns Serv.

Montalbano, Mike. Decision Tables: Program Structure, Data Structure. LC 73-92630. (Illus.). 210p. 1974. pap. text ed. 10.95 (ISBN 0-574-19040-6, 13-2040). SRA.

Montale, Eugenio. The Butterfly of Dinard. Singh, G., tr. LC 78-550605. 1971. 9.00x (ISBN 0-8131-1252-4). U Pr of Ky.

--It Depends: A Poet's Notebook. Singh, G., tr. from Ital. LC 80-16629. 192p. 1980. 12.95 (ISBN 0-8112-0773-0); pap. 4.95 (ISBN 0-8112-0774-9, NDP507). New Directions.

Montali, Richard J., ed. Mycobacterial Infections of Zoo Animals. LC 77-60860. (Symposia of the National Zoological Park Ser.: No. 1). (Illus.). 275p. 1979. text ed. 19.95x (ISBN 0-87474-644-2); pap. text ed. 9.95x (ISBN 0-87474-645-0). Smithsonian.

Montali, Richard J. & Migaki, George, eds. The Comparative Pathology of Zoo Animals. LC 79-24354. (Symposia of the National Zoological Park Ser.: No. 6). (Illus.). 684p. 1980. text ed. 45.00x (ISBN 0-87474-642-6); pap. text ed. 25.00x (ISBN 0-87474-643-4). Smithsonian.

Montana, Patrick H. & Borst, Diane, eds. Managing Non-Profit Organizations. 1979. pap. 6.95 (ISBN 0-8144-7512-4). Am Mgmt.

Montanare, John S. Chinese-English Phrase Book for Travellers. 200p. 1981. pap. text ed. 4.95 (ISBN 0-471-08298-8). Wiley.

Montanaro, John S. Chinese-English Phrase Book for Travellers. 200p. 1981. pap. text ed. 4.95 (ISBN 0-471-08298-8). Wiley.

Montandon, Pat. Intruders. 1977. pap. 1.95 o.p. (ISBN 0-449-22963-7, Crest). Fawcett.

Montaner, Carlos A. Secret Report on the Cuban Revolution. Zayas-Bazan, Eduardo, tr. from Span. LC 79-66693. 292p. (Orig.). 1981. 14.95 (ISBN 0-87855-300-2); pap. 6.95 (ISBN 0-87855-720-2). Transaction Bks.

Montavon, Remy, et al. The Role of Multinational Companies in Latin America: A Case Study in Mexico. 124p. 1980. 27.50 (ISBN 0-03-057973-2). Praeger.

Montbrial, Thierry de see De Montbrial, Thierry.

Monte, Evelyn, jt. ed. see Pisano, Beverly.

Monte, John R. De see De Monte, John R.

Monte, Provindencia C., ed. Learning Modules for the Basic Course in English, Vol. 1. LC 79-22332. 304p. 1980. pap. 8.00 (ISBN 0-8477-3324-6). U of PR Pr.

Monteath, C. D. Applications of the Electromagnetic Reciprocity Principle. 1973. 27.00 (ISBN 0-08-016895-7). Pergamon.

Montefiore, A., ed. Neutrality & Impartiality. 320p. 1975. 38.50 (ISBN 0-521-20664-2); pap. 9.95x (ISBN 0-521-09923-4). Cambridge U Pr.

Monteiro, George. Henry James & John Hay: The Record of a Friendship. LC 65-24094. 205p. 1965. 8.50x (ISBN 0-87057-091-9, Pub. by Brown U Pr). Univ Pr of New England.

Monteiro, George & Murphy, Brenda, eds. John Hay-Howells Letters: The Correspondence of John Milton Hay & William Dean Howells 1861-1905. (American Literary Manuscripts Ser.). 1981. lib. bdg. 14.95 (ISBN 0-8057-9652-5). Twayne.

Monteith, Lesley, jt. auth. see Dickinson, Francis.

Montel, Paul. Familles Normales. LC 73-14649. xiii, 301p. 1974. text ed. 12.00 (ISBN 0-8284-0271-X). Chelsea Pub.

Monteleone, Tom. Dark Stars & Other Illuminations. LC 79-6872. (Double D Science Fiction Ser.). 192p. 1981. 9.95 (ISBN 0-385-15769-X). Doubleday.

Montell, William L. Ghosts Along the Cumberland: Deathlore in the Kentucky Foothills. LC 74-32241. (Illus.). 283p. 1975. 13.50x (ISBN 0-87049-165-2). U of Tenn Pr.

--Saga of Coe Ridge: A Study in Oral History. LC 74-77846. (Illus.). 1970. 13.50x (ISBN 0-87049-096-6). U of Tenn Pr.

Montemurro, Donald G. & Bruni, J. Edward. The Human Brain in Dissection. 1981. text ed. price not set (ISBN 0-7216-6438-5). Saunders.

Monter, Barbara H., tr. see Pavlova, Karolina.

Monter, E. William, ed. European Witchcraft. LC 76-89682. 1969. pap. text ed. 10.95x (ISBN 0-471-61402-5). Wiley.

Montero, Darell & Weber, Marsha I. Vietnamese Americans: Patterns of Resettlement & Socioeconomic Adaption in the United States. 1979. lib. bdg. 22.50x (ISBN 0-89158-264-9). Westview.

Montero, Lidia D., tr. see Goetze, Joan.

Montes-Huidobro, Matias. Ojos Para No Ver. LC 79-52160. (Coleccion Teatro Ser.). (Illus.). 59p. (Span.). 1980. pap. 5.95 (ISBN 0-89729-229-4). Ediciones.

Montesquieu. The Spirit of Laws: A Compendium of the First English Editon with an English Translation of "an Essay on Causes Affecting Mind & Characters", 1737-1743. Carrithers, David W., ed. (No. 192). 1978. 30.00x (ISBN 0-520-02566-0); pap. 6.95x (ISBN 0-520-03455-4, CAMPUS SER., NO. 192). U of Cal Pr.

Montesquieu, Charles D. Persian Letters, Pt. 1. LC 73-170550. (Novel in England, 1700-1775 Ser). lib. bdg. 50.00 (ISBN 0-8240-0549-X). Garland Pub.

--Persian Letters, Pt. 2. LC 73-170550. (Novel in England, 1700-1775 Ser). lib. bdg. 50.00 (ISBN 0-8240-0550-3). Garland Pub.

Montessori, Maria. The Discovery of the Child. 1972. pap. 2.75 (ISBN 0-345-29390-8). Ballantine.

--The Secret of Childhood. 1972. pap. 1.50 o.p. (ISBN 0-345-22554-6). Ballantine.

Montfaucon, Bernard de. Antiquity Explained & Represented in Sculptures, 2 vols. Humphreys, David, tr. LC 75-27881. (Renaissance & the Gods Ser.: Vol. 36). (Illus.). 1977. Repr. of 1722 ed. Set. lib. bdg. 146.00 (ISBN 0-8240-2085-5); lib. bdg. 73.00 ea. Garland Pub.

Montfaucon, Bernard De see De Montfaucon, Bernard.

Montford, Alison, jt. auth. see Doig, William B.

Montfort, Guy. Saving the Tiger. LC 80-5363. 120p. 1981. 16.95 (ISBN 0-670-61999-X, Studio). Viking Pr.

Montgomery. Vermont School Bus Ride. (Easy Reading Ser.: No. 1). 1974. 5.95 (ISBN 0-915248-00-X). Vermont Crossroads.

Montgomery, A. Daniel. LC 27-14200. (International Critical Commentary Ser.). 520p. Repr. of 1927 ed. 23.00x (ISBN 0-567-05017-3). Attic Pr.

Montgomery, A. T. Financial Accounting Information: An Introduction to Its Preparation & Use. LC 77-83023. 1978. text ed. 17.95 (ISBN 0-201-04924-4); instr's man. avail. (ISBN 0-201-04923-6). A-W.

Montgomery, A. Thompson. Managerial Accounting Information: An Introduction to Its Content & Usefulness. LC 78-67943. 1979. text ed. 18.95 (ISBN 0-201-04927-9). A-W.

Montgomery, Bobbie. The Donkey-Cart Kids. LC 80-15656. (Orion Ser.). 128p. (gr. 1-6). 1980. pap. 2.50 (ISBN 0-8127-0286-7). Southern Pub.

Montgomery, Chandler. Art for Teachers of Children. 2nd ed. LC 72-97008. 1973. text ed. 17.95 (ISBN 0-675-08962-X). Merrill.

Montgomery, Clarence. The Book of Beautiful Homes with Building Instructions. (A Promotion of the Arts Library Bk.). (Illus.). 1979. 39.75 (ISBN 0-89266-194-1). Am Classical Coll Pr.

Montgomery, David. Beyond Equality. 544p. 1972. pap. 2.95 o.p. (ISBN 0-394-71744-9, V744, Vin). Random.

--Beyond Equality: Labor & the Radical Republicans, 1862-1872. LC 80-24434. 550p. 1981. pap. 9.95 (ISBN 0-252-00869-3). U of Ill Pr.

--Mountain Man Crafts & Skills. LC 80-82706. (Illus.). 1981. 6.95 (ISBN 0-88290-156-7, 4024). Horizon Utah.

--Workers' Control in America. LC 78-32001. (Illus.). 1979. 16.95 (ISBN 0-521-22580-9). Cambridge U Pr.

--Workers' Control in America: Studies in History of Work, Technology, & Labor Struggles. 1980. 5.95 (ISBN 0-521-28006-0). Cambridge U Pr.

Montgomery, Douglas C. Design & Analysis of Experiments. 1976. text ed. 25.95x (ISBN 0-471-61421-1). Wiley.

Montgomery, Douglas C., jt. auth. see Hines, William W.

Montgomery, Eleanor M. Tantra Today. 200p. 1980. 35.00 (ISBN 0-89975-001-X). World Authors.

Montgomery, Elizabeth R. Story Behind Modern Books. LC 49-7920. (gr. 4-6). 1949. 5.95 (ISBN 0-396-03046-7). Dodd.

Montgomery, Florence M. Printed Textiles: English & American Cottons & Linens, 1700-1850. (Illus.). 1970. 16.95 o.p. (ISBN 0-670-57722-7). Viking Pr.

Montgomery, G. Gene, ed. The Ecology of Arboreal Folivores. LC 78-3103. (Symposia of the National Zoological Park Ser.: No. 3). (Illus.). 574p. 1978. 35.00x (ISBN 0-87474-646-9); pap. 15.00x (ISBN 0-87474-647-7). Smithsonian.

Montgomery, Gerald W. The Selling of You: A Practical Guide to Job Hunting. new ed. 103p. 1980. 12.95 (ISBN 0-937096-01-6); pap. 9.95 (ISBN 0-937096-00-8). Montgomery Comm.

Montgomery, Herb, jt. auth. see Delbene, Ron.

Montgomery, Hugh. Dictionary of Political Phrases & Allusions with a Short Bibliography. LC 68-28333. 1968. Repr. of 1906 ed. 18.00 (ISBN 0-8103-3092-X). Gale.

Montgomery, J. A. & Gehman, H. S. Kings I & II. LC 52-8522. (International Critical Commentary Ser.). 624p. Repr. of 1951 ed. 23.00x (ISBN 0-567-05006-8). Attic Pr.

Montgomery, J. W., tr. A Seventeenth-Century View of European Libraries: Lomeier's De Bibliothecis Chapter X. (U. C. Publ. in Librarianship: Vol. 3). 1962. pap. 7.50x (ISBN 0-520-09206-6). U of Cal Pr.

Montgomery, James. The West Indies, Repr. Of 1810 Ed. Reiman, Donald H., ed. Bd. with The World Before the Flood; a Poem, in Ten Cantos. with Other Occasional Pieces. Repr. of 1813 ed. LC 75-31239. (Romantic Context Ser.: Poetry 1789-1830). 1979. lib. bdg. 47.00 (ISBN 0-8240-2187-8). Garland Pub.

Montgomery, Jo. Quiet Miracle. LC 62-10500. 1962. 6.00 o.p. (ISBN 0-8309-0251-1). Herald Hse.

Montgomery, John. Kerouac West Coast: A Bohemian Pilot, Detailed Navigational Instructions. LC 76-40359. 1976. bds. 5.95 (ISBN 0-918704-02-2); pap. 1.95 (ISBN 0-918704-01-4). Fels & Firn.

Montgomery, John W. Crisis in Lutheran Theology, 2 vols. in one. 1973. pap. 6.95 (ISBN 0-87123-050-X, 210050). Bethany Fell.

--Damned Through the Church. 1970. 1.25 (ISBN 0-87123-090-9, 200090). Bethany Fell.

--Demon Possession. LC 75-19313. 1967. pap. 6.95 (ISBN 0-87123-102-6, 210102). Bethany Fell.

--How Do We Know There Is a God? LC 73-16882. 96p. 1973. pap. 2.25 (ISBN 0-87123-221-9, 200221). Bethany Fell.

--Law Above the Law. LC 75-31395. 1975. pap. 2.25 (ISBN 0-87123-329-0, 200329). Bethany Fell.

--Principalities & Powers. LC 74-29081. 256p. 1973. pap. 1.75 (ISBN 0-87123-460-2, 200460). Bethany Fell.

--Quest for Noah's Ark. rev. ed. LC 74-21993. (Illus.). 1972. pap. 3.95 (ISBN 0-87123-477-7, 200477). Bethany Fell.

--The Shape of the Past. LC 75-26651. 400p. 1975. pap. 5.95 (ISBN 0-87123-535-8, 210535). Bethany Fell.

--Slaughter of the Innocents. (Orig.). 1981. pap. 3.95 (ISBN 0-89107-216-0). Good News.

--Suicide of Christian Theology. LC 70-270170. 1970. 6.95 (ISBN 0-87123-521-8, 210521). Bethany Fell.

--Where Is History Going? LC 69-11659. 1969. 5.95 (ISBN 0-87123-640-0, 210640). Bethany Fell.

Montgomery, John W., ed. & intro. by. Christianity for the Tough-Minded. LC 73-4842. 300p. 1973. kivar 5.95 (ISBN 0-87123-076-3, 210079). Bethany Fell.

Montgomery, John W., ed. God's Inerrant Word: An International Symposium on the Trustworthiness of Scripture. LC 74-4100. 288p. 1974. 7.95 (ISBN 0-87123-179-4, 230179). Bethany Fell.

--Myth, Allegory, & Gospel. LC 74-1358. Orig. Title: Names & Titles of Christ. 160p. 1974. pap. 4.95 (ISBN 0-87123-358-4, 210358). Bethany Fell.

Montgomery, John Warwick. The Shaping of America. LC 76-15682. 1976. 6.95 (ISBN 0-87123-227-8, 230227). Bethany Fell.

Montgomery, L. M. Anne's House of Dreams, No. 5. 240p. (gr. 7-9). 1981. pap. 2.25 (ISBN 0-553-14995-4). Bantam.

Montgomery, Michael. All Out for Everest. 1975. 12.95 (ISBN 0-236-40012-6, Pub. by Paul Elek). Merrimack Bk Serv.

Montgomery, Michael & Stratton, John. The Writer's Hotline Handbook. (Orig.). 1981. pap. 3.95 (ISBN 0-451-61972-2, MF 1972, Mentor Bks). NAL.

Montgomery Museum of Fine Arts. American Fashion Designs by Wilson Folmar. Campbell, Katherine, ed. LC 78-61234. (Illus.). 48p. 1978. pap. 5.00 o.p. (ISBN 0-89280-011-9). Montgomery Mus.

Montgomery, Nancy S., jt. auth. see Hamilton, Michael P.

Montgomery, Paula K., jt. auth. see Walker, H. Thomas.

Montgomery, R. H. The Solar Decision Book: Your Guide to Making a Sound Investment. LC 79-762. 1978. pap. text ed. 15.95 (ISBN 0-471-05652-9); tchrs. manual avail. (ISBN 0-471-06319-3). Wiley.

Montgomery, Raymond A. The Mystery of the Maya, No. 11. 128p. (Orig.). 1981. pap. 1.50 (ISBN 0-553-14600-9). Bantam.

Montgomery, Rex & Swenson, Charles A. Quantitative Problems in Biochemical Sciences. 2nd ed. LC 75-42234. (Illus.). 1976. text ed. 10.95x (ISBN 0-7167-0178-2); answer bk. avail. W H Freeman.

Montgomery, Rex, et al. Biochemistry: A Case Oriented Approach. 3rd ed. (Illus.). 1980. pap. text ed. 19.95 (ISBN 0-8016-3470-9). Mosby.

Montgomery, Robert L. Memory Made Easy: The Complete Book of Memory Training. (Illus.). 1979. 10.95 (ISBN 0-8144-5523-9). Am Mgmt.

--The Reader's Eye: Studies in Didactic Literary Theory from Dante to Tasso. 1979. 15.75x (ISBN 0-520-03700-6). U of Cal Pr.

Montgomery, Robert M., ed. The Best Critical Studies Issued by the American Institute for Management & Inventiveness, 2 vols. 1979. Set. deluxe ed. 67.45 (ISBN 0-918968-25-9). Inst Econ Finan.

Montgomery, Robin. The History of Montgomery County. (Illus.). 333p. 1975. 12.50 o.p. (ISBN 0-8363-0129-3). Jenkins.

Montgomery, Roger, jt. auth. see Mandelker, Daniel R.

Montgomery, Roger, jt. auth. see Woodbridge, Sally B.

Montgomery, Roger, jt. ed. see Marshall, Dale.

Montgomery, Royce L. Basic Anatomy for the Allied Health Professions. LC 79-19131. (Illus.). 1980. text ed. 22.75 (ISBN 0-8067-1231-7). Urban & S.

Montgomery, Royce L., et al, eds. Nervous System Basic Sciences. 2nd ed. 1977. spiral bdg. 11.75 (ISBN 0-87488-210-9). Med Exam.

Montgomery, Ruth. Born to Heal. 224p. 1976. pap. 2.25 (ISBN 0-445-08450-2). Popular Lib.

--Here & Hereafter. 1978. pap. 2.25 (ISBN 0-449-24166-1, Crest). Fawcett.

--World Beyond. 1978. pap. 2.25 (ISBN 0-449-24085-1, Crest). Fawcett.

Montgomery, S. Fixed Rings of Finite Automorphism Groups of Associative Rings. (Lectures Notes in Mathematics Ser.: Vol. 818). 126p. 1981. pap. 9.80 (ISBN 0-387-10232-9). Springer-Verlag.

Montgomery, Walter, ed. American Art & American Art Collections, 2 vols. LC 75-28883. (Art Experience in Late 19th Century America Ser.: Vol. 17). (Illus.). 1976. Repr. of 1889 ed. Set. lib. bdg. 178.00 (ISBN 0-8240-2241-6). Garland Pub.

Montgomery, Wayne, jt. auth. see Breihan, Carl W.

Montherlant, Henry de. Port-Royal. Griffiths, Richard, ed. (French Texts Ser.). 1976. pap. text ed. 11.25x (ISBN 0-631-00730-X, Pub. by Basil Blackwel). Biblio Dist.

Montias, John M., jt. ed. see Marer, Paul.

Montier, David. Atlas of Breeding Birds: London. 1977. 60.00 (ISBN 0-7134-0876-6, Pub. by Batsford England). David & Charles.

Montilla, M. Robert & Harlow, Nora, eds. Correctional Facilities Planning. LC 78-19930. 1979. 19.95 (ISBN 0-669-02437-6). Lexington Bks.

Montilla, Robert, jt. auth. see Miller, E. Eugene.

Montlyard, I. de, tr. see Valeriano Bolzani, Giovanni P.

Montoye, Henry, jt. auth. see Nagle, Francis.

Montoye, Henry J. An Introduction to Measurement in Physical Education. 1978. text ed. 19.95 (ISBN 0-205-05787-X, 6257879); instr's man. avail. (ISBN 0-205-05789-6); lab manual avail. (ISBN 0-205-05796-9). Allyn.

--Physical Activity & Health: An Epidemiologic Study of an Entire Community. (Intl. Physical Education Research Monograph). (Illus.). 209p. 1975. ref. ed. 13.50 (ISBN 0-13-665604-8). P-H.

Montrose, J. L. Precedent in English Law & Other Essays. 374p. 1968. 25.00x (ISBN 0-7165-0503-7, Pub. by Irish Academic Pr Ireland). Biblio Dist.

Montrose, Louis A. Curious Knotted Garden: The Form, Themes & Contexts of Shakespeare's Love's Labour's Lost. (Salzburg Studies in English Literature: Elizabethan & Renaissance Studies: No. 56). (Orig.). 1977. pap. text ed. 25.00x (ISBN 0-391-01483-8). Humanities.

Montross, Lynn. War Through the Ages. new & enl. ed. LC 60-7533. (Illus.). 1960. 22.95 o.s.i. (ISBN 0-06-013000-8, HarpT). Har-Row.

Montville, John B. The Packard Truck: Ask the Man Who Owns One. (Illus.). 128p. 1981. pap. 14.95 (ISBN 0-89404-052-9). Aztex.

Monty, C., ed. Phanerozoic Stromatolites: Case Histories. (Illus.). 260p. 1981. 52.60 (ISBN 0-387-10474-7). Springer-Verlag.

Monvel, Maurice Boutet de see Boutet de Monvel, Maurice.

Mooberry, F. M. & Scott, Jane H. Grow Native Shrubs in Your Garden. LC 80-69807. 1980. 5.95x. Brandywine Conserv.

Moock, Joyce L. & Moock, Peter R. Higher Education & Rural Development in Africa. 42p. 1977. pap. 1.75 (ISBN 0-89192-228-8). Interbk Inc.

Moock, Peter R., jt. auth. see Moock, Joyce L.

Mood, Alexander, ed. see Carnegie Commission on Higher Education.

Mood, Dale P. Numbers in Motion: A Balanced Approach to Measurement & Evaluation in Physical Education. LC 79-91835. (Illus.). 396p. 1980. text ed. 15.95 (ISBN 0-87484-503-3). Mayfield Pub.

Mood, John, ed. see Rilke, Ravier M.

Moodie, G. C., jt. auth. see Marshall, Geoffrey.

Moodie, Michael. Sovereignty, Security & Arms. LC 79-88220. (The Washington Papers: No. 67). 1979. pap. 3.50 (ISBN 0-8039-1320-6). Sage.

Moodie, Michael, jt. auth. see Bray, Frank T.

Moodie, T. Dunbar. The Rise of Afrikanerdom: Power, Apartheid, & the Afrikaner Civil Religion. LC 72-85512. (Perspectives on Southern Africa Ser). 1975. 19.50x (ISBN 0-520-02310-2); pap. 5.95 (ISBN 0-520-03943-2). U of Cal Pr.

Moodle, Graeme C. & Studdert-Kennedy, Gerald. Opinions, Publics & Pressure Groups: An Essay on "Vox Populi" & Representative Government. (Studies in Political Science). 1970. pap. text ed. 10.95x (ISBN 0-04-322002-9). Allen Unwin.

Moody, A. D. Thomas Stearns Eliot: Poet. LC 78-54719. 376p. 1980. pap. 14.95 (ISBN 0-521-29968-3). Cambridge U Pr.

--Thomas Stearns Eliot: Poet. LC 78-54719. (Illus.). 1979. 29.95 (ISBN 0-521-22065-3). Cambridge U Pr.

Moody, Alton B. Navigation Afloat: A Manual for the Seaman. 768p. 1981. 35.00 (ISBN 0-442-25488-1). Van Nos Reinhold.

Moody, B. I. What the Catholic Bible Teaches: Home Study. pap. 3.00x o.p. (ISBN 0-686-12325-5). Christs Mission.

Moody, C., ed. Ilya Ehrenburg: Selections from People, Years & Life. LC 73-128339. 312p. 1972. pap. text ed. 12.75 (ISBN 0-08-006354-3). Pergamon.

Moody, D. L. Day by Day with D. L. Moody. 1977. pap. 2.25 (ISBN 0-8024-1759-0). Moody.

Moody, Dale. The Word of Truth. 624p. 1981. 24.95 (ISBN 0-8028-3533-3). Eerdmans.

Moody, Dwight L. Prevailing Prayer. pap. 1.50 (ISBN 0-8024-6814-4). Moody.

Moody, Ernest. Studies in Medieval Philosophy, Science & Logic: Collected Papers, 1933-1969. LC 73-91661. 1975. 28.50 (ISBN 0-520-02668-3). U of Cal Pr.

Moody, F., jt. ed. see Baron, J. H.

Moody, H. L. The Teaching of Literature. 1974. pap. text ed. 5.50x (ISBN 0-582-52602-7). Longman.

Moody, John see Johnson, Allen & Nevins, Allan.

Moody, Michael E., jt. ed. see Cole, C. Robert.

Moody, P. Writing Today: A Rhetoric Handbook. 1981. 10.95 (ISBN 0-13-971556-8); pap. 9.95 wkbk & key (ISBN 0-13-971572-X). P-H.

Moody, Patricia. Writing Today: A Rhetoric & Handbook. (Illus.). 512p. 1981. pap. text ed. 12.95 (ISBN 0-13-971556-8). P-H.

Moody, Paul A. Genetics of Man. 2nd ed. (Illus.). 525p. 1975. text ed. 11.95x o.p. (ISBN 0-393-09228-3); answer bk. avail. o.p. (ISBN 0-393-09221-6). Norton.

Moody, Peter R. The Three Hundred & Sixty-Seventh Fighter Group in World War II. 1980. pap. 13.00 (ISBN 0-89126-080-3). Military Aff Aero.

Moody, Peter R., Jr. Opposition & Dissent in Contemporary China. LC 77-72054. (Publication Ser: No. 177). (Illus.). 360p. 1977. 14.95 (ISBN 0-685-80269-8). Hoover Inst Pr.

Moody, Raymond A., Jr. Life After Life. LC 75-37963. 1976. 5.95 o.p. (ISBN 0-8117-0946-9). Stackpole.

Moody, Richard. Fossils. (Illus.). 128p. 1979. 8.95 (ISBN 0-600-36313-9). Transatlantic.

--Ned Harrigan: From Corlear's Hook to Herald Square. LC 80-221. (Illus.). 288p. 1980. 20.95 (ISBN 0-88229-674-4); pap. 10.95 (ISBN 0-88229-755-4). Nelson-Hall.

Moody, Robert. The First Book of Microcomputers: The Home Computer Owner's Best Friend. 1978. pap. 5.95 (ISBN 0-8104-5121-2). Hayden.

Moody, Robert E., ed. Papers of Leverett Saltonstall, 1816-1845. (Collections of the Massachusetts Historical Society Ser.). (Illus.). Vol. 1, 1978. 25.00 ea. Vol. 2, 1981. Mass Hist Soc.

Moody, Ronald, jt. tr. see Kell, Gulla.

Moody, Sophy. What Is Your Name: A Popular Account of the Meaning & Derivations of Christian Names. LC 73-5523. 1975. Repr. of 1863 ed. 26.00 (ISBN 0-8103-4250-2). Gale.

Moody, William J. How to Probate an Estate. new rev. ed. 1981. pap. 3.95 (ISBN 0-346-12350-X). Cornerstone.

Moody-Stuart, K. Brownlow North: His Life & Work. 1961. 1.95 (ISBN 0-686-12509-6). Banner of Truth.

Mooers, Robert L., Jr. Finding Your Way in the Outdoors. (Illus.). 1972. 6.95 o.p. (ISBN 0-525-10505-0). Dutton.

Mook, Dean T., jt. auth. see Nayfeh, Ali H.

Mookerjee, S. Buddhist Philosophy of Universal Flux. 1975. Repr. 25.00 (ISBN 0-8426-0852-4). Orient Bk Dist.

Mookerji, Tapati. The Golden Road to Samarkand. 5.00 (ISBN 0-89253-526-1). Ind-US Inc.

Moon, E. L. Experiences with My Cockatiels. rev. ed. 1976. 4.95 (ISBN 0-87666-759-0, AP-1280). TFH Pubns.

Moon, F. C., ed. Mechanics of Superconducting Structures. (AMD: No. 41). 148p. 1980. 24.00 (G00174). ASME.

Moon, Harold K. Alejandro Casona, Playwright. (Charles E. Merrill Monograph Series in the Humanities & Social Sciences: Vol. 2, No. 1). 1970. pap. 1.50 o.p. (ISBN 0-8425-0216-5). Brigham.

Moon, Helen M. The Lyfe of Soule: An Edition with Commentary. (Salzburg Studies in English Literature, Elizabethan & Renaissance Studies: No. 75). pap. text ed. 25.00x (ISBN 0-391-01484-6). Humanities.

Moon, Jan. Living with Nature in Hawaii. rev. ed. 136p. 1979. pap. 5.50 (ISBN 0-912180-06-4). Petroglyph.

Moon, John C. An Instructor for the Drum. (Musick of the Fifes & the Drum: Vol. Iv). (Illus.). 56p. (Orig.). 1981. pap. 3.95 (ISBN 0-87935-059-8); record 5.95 (ISBN 0-686-69569-0); Set. pap. 8.95 (ISBN 0-87935-060-1). Williamsburg.

Moon, Lawrence D. God's Fool. 12.95 (ISBN 0-531-09946-6). Watts.

Moon, Parry & Spencer, Donna E. The Photic Field. 272p. 1981. text ed. 25.00x (ISBN 0-262-13166-8). MIT Pr.

Moon, Richard G. Understanding Elementary Algebra. (Mathematics Ser.). 1978. text ed. 15.95 (ISBN 0-675-08406-7); instructor's manual 3.95 (ISBN 0-686-67994-6). Merrill.

Moon, Robert. Applied Mathematics for Technical Programs: Arithmetic & Geometry. LC 72-96904. 1973. pap. text ed. 16.95 (ISBN 0-675-08983-2); media: audiocassettes 140.00, 2-5 sets, 95.00 ea., 6 or more sets, 70.00 ea. (ISBN 0-675-08918-2); instructor's manual 3.95 (ISBN 0-686-66869-3); test 3.95 (ISBN 0-686-66870-7). Merrill.

--Basic Arithmetic. 2nd ed. (Mathematics Ser.). 1977. pap. text ed. 15.95 (ISBN 0-675-08627-2); cassettes 160.00 (ISBN 0-675-08515-2); 2-6 sets 100.00, 7 or more sets 75.00 (ISBN 0-686-57848-1); instructor's manual 3.95 (ISBN 0-686-67518-5); tests 1 & 2 3.95 ea. Merrill.

Moon, Robert, et al. Basic Arithmetic. LC 78-144087. 1971. pap. text ed. 14.95 (ISBN 0-675-09230-2); instructor's manual 3.95 (ISBN 0-686-66280-6); test 3.95 (ISBN 0-686-66281-4). Merrill.

Moon, Robert A. & Davis, Robert D. Elementary Algebra. 3rd ed. (Mathematics Ser.). 528p. 1980. pap. text ed. 14.95 (ISBN 0-675-08158-0); instructor's manual 3.95 (ISBN 0-686-63339-3). Merrill.

Moon, Robert G. Applied Mathematics for Technical Programs: Algebra. LC 73-75638. 1973. pap. text ed. 16.95 (ISBN 0-675-08943-3); media: audiocassettes 140.00, 2-5 sets, 95.00 ea., 6 or more sets, 70.00 ea. (ISBN 0-675-08910-7); instructor's manual 3.95 (ISBN 0-686-66867-7); test 3.95 (ISBN 0-686-66868-5). Merrill.

--Applied Mathematics for Technical Programs: Trigonometry. LC 73-77913. 1973. pap. text ed. 17.95 (ISBN 0-675-08923-9); media: audiocassettes 140.00, 2-5 sets, 95.00 ea., 6 or more sets, 70.00 ea. (ISBN 0-675-08900-X); instructor's manual 3.95 (ISBN 0-686-66871-5). Merrill.

Moon, Sheila. A Magic Dwells: A Poetic & Psychological Study of the Navaho Emergence Myth. LC 72-105501. 1970. 12.50x (ISBN 0-8195-4018-8, Pub. by Wesleyan U Pr); pap. 5.95 (ISBN 0-8195-6036-7). Columbia U Pr.

Moon, Terrence. The Deadly Frost. 1980. pap. 2.75 (ISBN 0-345-28947-1). Ballantine.

Moon, Warren G. Greek Vase-Painting in Midwestern Collections. Prokopoff-Giannini, Paula & Wegner, Susan, eds. LC 79-56832. (Illus.). 231p. (Orig.). 1979. pap. 12.50x (ISBN 0-86559-041-9). Art Inst Chi.

Mooney, Chase C. William H. Crawford, 1772-1834. LC 70-147853. 376p. 1974. 18.00x (ISBN 0-8131-1246-X). U Pr of Ky.

Mooney, David A. Introduction to Thermodynamics & Heat Transfer. 1955. text ed. 26.95 (ISBN 0-13-499681-X). P-H.

Mooney, E., jt. auth. see Oettinger, K.

Mooney, E. F., ed. Annual Reports on NMR Spectroscopy. Incl. Vol. 1. 1968. 49.00 (ISBN 0-12-505350-9); Vol. 5B. 1974. 62.00 (ISBN 0-12-505345-2); Vol. 6, 2 pts. 1976-78. Pt. B. 34.00 (ISBN 0-12-505346-0); Pt. C. 90.00 (ISBN 0-12-505347-9); Vol. 7. 1978. 43.50 (ISBN 0-12-505307-X); Vol. 8. 1978. 71.00 (ISBN 0-12-505308-8); Vol. 9. 1978. 57.50 (ISBN 0-12-505309-6). Acad Pr.

Mooney, Elizabeth. Alone: Surviving As a Widow. 320p. 1981. 10.95 (ISBN 0-399-12601-5). Putnam.

--In the Shadow of the White Plague: A Memoir. LC 78-3311. 1979. 9.95 o.s.i. (ISBN 0-690-01696-4, TYC-T). T Y Crowell.

Mooney, Frank V. & Thomas, Cleveland A. Basic English Usage: The Parts of Speech. (Illus.). (gr. 7-12). 1962. pap. text ed. 37.80 (ISBN 0-89290-116-0, A133-SA). Soc for Visual.

--Basic English Usage: The Sentence. (Illus.). (gr. 7-12). 1964. pap. text ed. 49.50 (ISBN 0-89290-117-9, A133SB). Soc for Visual.

Mooney, James. Historical Sketch of the Cherokee. LC 75-20706. (Illus.). 265p. 1975. 12.50x o.p. (ISBN 0-87474-652-3); pap. 5.95x o.p. (ISBN 0-87474-653-1). Smithsonian.

Mooney, James E., jt. ed. see Shipton, Clifford K.

Mooney, Jean F., jt. auth. see Savage, John F.

Mooney, Michael & Stuber, Florian, eds. Small Comforts for Hard Times. LC 77-5851. 1977. 22.50x (ISBN 0-231-04042-3). Columbia U Pr.

Mooney, Michael, ed. see Kristeller, Paul O.

Mooney, Michael M. The Ministry of Culture: Politics in Art. 1980. 14.95 (ISBN 0-671-61021-X, Wyndham). S&S.

Mooney, Richard E. Colony: Earth. 320p. 1977. pap. 1.95 o.p. (ISBN 0-449-23243-3, Crest). Fawcett.

Mooney, Sean & Green, George. Sean Mooney's Practical Guide to Running a Pub. LC 78-27436. 1979. 14.95 (ISBN 0-88229-400-8); pap. 8.95 (ISBN 0-88229-681-7). Nelson-Hall.

Mooney, Thomas, ed. Race for Glory. (Pal Paperbacks Kit B Ser.). (Illus., Orig.). (gr. 7-12). 1973. pap. text ed. 1.25 (ISBN 0-8374-3521-8). Xerox Ed Pubns.

--Varoom. (Pal Paperbacks Kit A Ser.). (Illus., Orig.). (gr. 7-12). 1973. pap. text ed. 1.25 (ISBN 0-8374-3483-1). Xerox Ed Pubns.

Mooney, Thomas, ed. see Lane, Ken.

Mooney, Thomas, ed. see McCarthy, Pat.

Mooney, Thomas, ed. see Verdick, Mary.

Mooney, Thomas J. Sports for All. Verdick, Mary, ed. (Beginning Pal Paperbacks Ser.). (Illus., Orig.). (gr. 7-12). 1977. pap. text ed. 1.25 (ISBN 0-8374-3456-4). Xerox Ed Pubns.

Mooney, Thomas J., ed. The Big Freeze. (Pal Paperbacks Ser., Kit A). (Illus., Orig.). (gr. 7-12). 1976. pap. text ed. 1.25 (ISBN 0-8374-3493-9). Xerox Ed Pubns.

--Old Yellow Eyes. (Pal Paperbacks - Kit A Ser.). (Illus., Orig.). (gr. 7-12). 1976. pap. text ed. 1.25 (ISBN 0-8374-3494-7). Xerox Ed Pubns.

--One Cool Sister. (Pal Paperbacks Kit A Ser.). (Illus., Orig.). (gr. 7-12). 1976. pap. text ed. 1.25 (ISBN 0-8374-3501-3). Xerox Ed Pubns.

--Speed Kings. (Pal Paperbacks Kit B Ser.). (Illus., Orig.). (gr. 7-12). 1973. pap. text ed. 1.25 (ISBN 0-8374-3517-X). Xerox Ed Pubns.

Mooney, Thomas J., ed. see Algieri, Shirley.

Mooney, Thomas J., ed. see Carlson, Gordon.

Mooney, Thomas J., ed. see Conan, Pierre.

Mooney, Thomas J., ed. see Doyle, Tim.

Mooney, Thomas J., ed. see Lefkowitz, William.

Mooney, Thomas J., ed. see Olfson, Lewy.

Mooney, Thomas J., ed. see Otfinoski, Steven.

Mooney, Thomas J., ed. see Schleifer, Jay.

Mooney, Thomas J., ed. see Verdick, Mary.

Mooney, Tom, ed. see Oldham, Neild.

Mooney, Will C. Your Shih Tzu. rev. ed. LC 72-80628. (Your Dog Bk.). (Illus.). 128p. 1981. price not set (ISBN 0-87714-073-1). Denlingers.

Moonman, Jane, ed. Zionist Year Book 1980. 29th ed. LC 52-65547. (Illus.). 384p. 1980. pap. 15.00 (ISBN 0-8002-2413-2). Intl Pubns Serv.

Moor, Christine H. From School to Work: Effective Counselling & Guidance. LC 74-31569. (Sage Studies in Social & Educational Change: Vol. 3). (Illus.). 1976. 18.00x (ISBN 0-8039-9947-X); pap. 9.95x (ISBN 0-8039-9856-2). Sage.

Moor, Fred B., et al. Manual of Hydrotherapy & Massage. LC 64-23214. 169p. 1964. 4.95 (ISBN 0-8163-0023-2, 13160-7). Pacific Pr Pub Assn.

Moor, George. Fox Gold. 1980. 12.95 (ISBN 0-7145-3615-6). Riverrun NY.

Moorby, J., jt. auth. see Milthorpe, F. L.

Moorcock, Michael. The Black Corridor. Bd. with Adventures of una Persson & Catherine Cornelius in the Twentieth Century. 52p. 1980. pap. 4.95 (ISBN 0-8037-1343-6). Dial.

--Breakfast in the Ruins. 1980. pap. 1.95 (ISBN 0-380-49148-6, 49148). Avon.

--The Champion of Garathoram. 1981. pap. 2.25 (ISBN 0-440-11173-0). Dell.

--Chinese Agent. Sandum, Howard, ed. LC 79-96746. (Cock Robin Mystery). 1970. 4.50 o.s.i. (ISBN 0-02-585790-8). Macmillan.

--The Eternal Champion: A Fantastic Romance. LC 77-3797. 1978. Repr. 10.95 o.s.i. (ISBN 0-06-013014-8, HarpT). Har-Row.

--The Ice Schooner. 1978. pap. 1.75 o.s.i. (ISBN 0-440-14445-0). Dell.

--The Ice Schooner. LC 76-47249. 1977. 9.95 o.p. (ISBN 0-06-013006-7, HarpT). Har-Row.

--The Jewel in the Skull. (Science Fiction Ser.). 1977. pap. 1.75 (ISBN 0-87997-419-2, UE1547). DAW Bks.

--The Quest for Tanelorn. 1981. pap. 2.25 (ISBN 0-440-17193-8). Dell.

--The Vanishing Tower. (Elric of Melnibone Ser.). (Illus.). 224p. 1980. 20.00slipcase (ISBN 0-915822-38-5). Archival Pr.

Moorcock, Michael J. The Silver Warriors. 1977. pap. 1.75 o.s.i. (ISBN 0-440-17994-7). Dell.

Moore. Buy & Bust. LC 73-11665. (Illus.). 1977. 15.95 (ISBN 0-669-88179-1). Lexington Bks.

--Fighting Ships Nineteen Eighty to Nineteen Eighty-One. 1980. 135.00 (ISBN 0-531-03937-4). Watts.

--Fighting Ships Nineteen Seventy-Nine to Nineteen Eighty. 1980. 99.50 (ISBN 0-531-03913-7). Watts.

--Principles of Chemical Metallurgy. 1981. text ed. price not set (ISBN 0-408-00567-X); pap. text ed. price not set (ISBN 0-408-00430-4). Butterworth.

Moore, jt. auth. see Elliott.

Moore, Aimee, jt. auth. see Hoover, Loretta.

Moore, Albert B. Conscription & Conflict in the Confederacy. 1963. text ed. 15.00x (ISBN 0-391-00459-X). Humanities.

Moore, Albert C. Iconography of Religions: An Introduction. LC 76-62598. 344p. 1977. 25.00 (ISBN 0-8006-0488-1, 1-489). Fortress.

Moore, Alex. Ballroom Dancing. 8th ed. (Illus.). 324p. (gr. 9 up). 1980. Repr. of 1974 ed. text ed. 17.95x (ISBN 0-273-00381-X, LTB). Soccer.

--The Revised Techniques of Ballroom Dancing. 9th ed. 108p. 1980. pap. text ed. 12.50x (ISBN 0-392-07521-0, LTB). Soccer.

Moore, Arthur. The Proud. (River of Fortune Ser.). 400p. (Orig.). 1980. pap. 2.50 (ISBN 0-89083-665-5). Zebra.

--The Strong Americans: The Raging Heart. 384p. (Orig.). 1981. pap. 2.75 (ISBN 0-523-41144-8). Pinnacle Bks.

--Trackdown. (Orig.). 1980. pap. 1.75 (ISBN 0-505-51501-6). Tower Bks.

Moore, Arthur, jt. auth. see Dowson, Ernest.

Moore, Austin L. Knight Errant in Africa: A Journal. 143p. 1966. 4.95 (ISBN 0-8040-0177-4). Swallow.

Moore, B. C., et al. A Dictionary of Special Education Terms. 128p. 1980. lexotone 12.75 (ISBN 0-398-04009-5). C C Thomas.

Moore, B. M. Block or Day Release? A Comparative Study of Engineering Apprentices. (Research Reports Ser.). (Illus.). 198p. 1972. Repr. of 1969 ed. text ed. 13.75x (ISBN 0-901225-01-0, NFER). Humanities.

Moore, Ballard J. & Henderson, Thomas E. Shuttlecock Action. (Illus.). 1977. pap. text ed. 4.50 (ISBN 0-8403-1773-5). Kendall-Hunt.

Moore, Barbara. Hard on the Road. LC 73-13091. 312p. 1974. 6.95 o.p. (ISBN 0-385-08191-X). Doubleday.

Moore, Barbara, ed. see Rutter, Laurence.

Moore, Barbara N. A Manual of AACR for Cartographic Materials. McClaskey, Marilyn J. & Swanson, Edward, eds. 50p. 1980. pap. 6.00 (ISBN 0-936996-07-2). Soldier Creek.

Moore, Basil J. An Introduction to Modern Economic Theory. LC 77-96708. 1973. text ed. 16.95 (ISBN 0-02-921960-4). Free Pr.

--Introduction to the Theory of Finance: Asset Holder Behaviour Under Uncertainty. LC 68-12033. (Orig.). 1968. pap. text ed. 7.95 (ISBN 0-02-921950-7). Free Pr.

Moore, Bernice M. & Holtzman, W. H. Tomorrow's Parents: A Study of Youth & Their Families. (Hogg Foundation Research Series). 1965. 13.50x (ISBN 0-292-73409-3). U of Tex Pr.

Moore, Bobbie, jt. auth. see Bowerman, Bill.

Moore, Brian. The Mangan Inheritance. 1980. pap. 2.95 (ISBN 0-14-005671-8). Penguin.

--Two Stories. (Santa Susana Press Ser.). 1979. numbered 35.00 (ISBN 0-937048-22-4); lettered 60.00 (ISBN 0-937048-29-1). CSUN.

Moore, C. B. Meteorites. (Earth Science Curriculum Project Pamphlet Ser). 1971. pap. 3.20 (ISBN 0-395-02624-5, 2-14610). HM.

Moore, C. Bradley, ed. Chemical & Biochemical Applications of Lasers, Vol. 5. 1980. 23.00 (ISBN 0-12-505405-X). Acad Pr.

Moore, C. L. The Best of C. L. Moore. 384p. (Orig.). 1976. pap. 2.25 (ISBN 0-345-28952-8). Ballantine.

--Judgement Night. 1979. pap. 2.25 o.s.i. (ISBN 0-440-14442-6). Dell.

Moore, Cecil, tr. see Schwartz, Federico.

Moore, Cecil A. Restoration Literature: Poetry & Prose, 1660-1700. 1981. 38.50x (ISBN 0-89197-383-4); pap. text ed. 18.50x (ISBN 0-89197-919-0). Irvington.

Moore, Charles. Daniel H. Burnham: Architect Planner of Cities. LC 68-27726. (Architecture & Decorative Art Ser). (Illus.). 1968. Repr. of 1921 ed. lib. bdg. 45.00 (ISBN 0-306-71151-6). Da Capo.

--Life & Times of Charles Follen McKim. LC 70-99857. (Architecture & Decorative Art Ser). (Illus.). 1969. Repr. of 1929 ed. lib. bdg. 32.50 (ISBN 0-306-71324-1). Da Capo.

Moore, Charles, ed. see Burnham, Daniel H. & Bennett, Edward H.

Moore, Charles L. Incense & Iconoclasm. 343p. 1980. Repr. of 1915 ed. lib. bdg. 30.00 (ISBN 0-89987-573-4). Century Bookbindery.

Moore, Clement. Night Before Christmas. LC 79-165390. (Illus.). 1971. pap. 1.50 (ISBN 0-486-22797-9). Dover.

--The Night Before Christmas. LC 80-11758. (Illus.). 32p. (ps up). 1980. PLB 10.95 (ISBN 0-8234-0414-5); pap. 4.95 (ISBN 0-8234-0417-X). Holiday.

Moore, Clement C. The Night Before Christmas. LC 78-72136. (Illus.). (gr. k-5). Date not set. price not set (ISBN 0-89799-143-5); pap. price not set (ISBN 0-89799-061-7). Dandelion Pr. Postponed.

--The Night Before Christmas. (Golden Storytime Bk.). (Illus.). 1981. 1.95 (ISBN 0-307-11956-4, Golden Pr). Western Pub.

--A Visit from St. Nicholas. (Illus.). 1980. pap. 1.95 (ISBN 0-671-95528-4). Wanderer Bks.

Moore, Clifford H. Ancient Beliefs in the Immortality of the Soul. LC 63-10283. (Our Debt to Greece & Rome Ser). 183p. Repr. of 1930 ed. 18.50x (ISBN 0-8154-0154-X). Cooper Sq.

Moore, D. B. The Poetry of Louis MacNeice. 272p. 1972. text ed. 11.50x (ISBN 0-7185-1105-0, Leicester). Humanities.

Moore, D. F. Friction & Lubrication of Elastomers. 305p. 1972. text ed. 42.00 (ISBN 0-08-016749-7); pap. text ed. 24.00 (ISBN 0-08-019002-2). Pergamon.

--Principles & Applications of Tribology. 1974. text ed. 44.00 (ISBN 0-08-017902-9); pap. text ed. 18.50 (ISBN 0-08-019007-3). Pergamon.

Moore, D. M., tr. see Martin, Marie Louise.

Moore, Daniel C. Regional Block: A Handbook for Use in the Clinical Practice of Medicine & Surgery. 4th ed. (Illus.). 1979. 23.75 (ISBN 0-398-01337-3). C C Thomas.

Moore, Daphne. The Book of the Foxhound. (Illus.). 17.50 (ISBN 0-85131-209-8, Dist. by Sporting Book Center). J A Allen.

Moore, David S. Statistics: Concepts & Controversies. LC 78-12740. (Illus.). 1979. text ed. 18.95x (ISBN 0-7167-1022-6); pap. text ed. 8.95x (ISBN 0-7167-1021-8). W H Freeman.

Moore, David S. & Yackel, James W. Applicable Finite Mathematics. 432p. 1974. text ed. 20.50 (ISBN 0-395-17771-5); instructors' manual 2.15 (ISBN 0-395-17813-4). HM.

Moore, Dewey J. Preventing Misbehavior in Children. 184p. 1972. 13.50 (ISBN 0-398-02364-6); pap. 6.75 (ISBN 0-398-02487-1). C C Thomas.

Moore, Donna M. Battered Women. LC 79-982. (Focus Editions Ser.: Vol. 9). (Illus.). 232p. 1979. 18.95 (ISBN 0-8039-1162-9); pap. 9.95 (ISBN 0-8039-1163-7). Sage.

Moore, Doris L. The Late Lord Byron. LC 76-22934. (Illus.). 1977. Repr. of 1961 ed. 25.00 o.p. (ISBN 0-06-013013-X, HarpT). Har-Row.
Moore, Dorothy, jt. auth. see Moore, Raymond.
Moore, E., jt. auth. see Gysbers, N.
Moore, Ed. Fresh Water Fishing. (Illus., Orig.). 1965. pap. 0.95 o.s.i. (ISBN 0-02-029320-8, Collier). Macmillan.
Moore, Elaine B. God's Day, Today, & Everyday. 1980. pap. 2.95 (ISBN 0-570-03497-3, 56-1348). Concordia.
Moore, Eliakim H., et al. The New Haven Mathematical Colloquium. 1910. 75.00x (ISBN 0-686-51424-6). Elliots Bks.
Moore, Elisabeth. Bend with the Wind. LC 78-31664. Date not set. 12.95 (ISBN 0-87949-142-6). Ashley Bks.
Moore, Elizabeth A., jt. auth. see Moore, John W.
Moore, Elizabeth C. An Almanac for Music Lovers. LC 70-167078. (Tower Bks). xiv, 382p. 1972. Repr. of 1940 ed. 24.00 (ISBN 0-8103-3940-4). Gale.
Moore, Emily. Something to Count on. LC 79-23277. 112p. (gr. 5 up). 1980. 7.95 (ISBN 0-525-39595-4). Dutton.
Moore, Eric G., jt. ed. see Clark, W. A. V.
Moore, Eric V. Rhythm of the Zodiac & the Wisdom Dinner. LC 80-51680. (Illus.). 80p. (Orig.). 1980. pap. 4.00 (ISBN 0-937236-00-4, 4W). Sonrise Prods.
Moore, Ethel, ed. Contemporary Art Nineteen Forty-Two to Seventy-Two: Collection of the Albright-Knox Art Gallery. LC 70-189296. (Illus.). 1972. 18.00 (ISBN 0-914782-28-2, Pub. by Albright-Knox Art Gallery). C E Tuttle.
Moore, Eva. Clarion Cook Book for Boys & Girls. LC 79-129210. (Illus.). (gr. 1-4). 1971. 5.95 (ISBN 0-395-28818-5, Clarion). HM.
--The Cookie Book. LC 76-190381. (gr. 1-4). 6.95 (ISBN 0-395-28866-5, Clarion). HM.
Moore, F. C., jt. ed. see Ahmed Al Shahi.
Moore, F. C., tr. see Degerando, Joseph-Marie.
Moore, Frances S. Blue Locket. (YA) 1972. 5.95 (ISBN 0-685-28625-8, Avalon). Bouregy.
--Fair Is My Love. (YA) 1971. 5.95 (ISBN 0-685-23395-2, Avalon). Bouregy.
--The Storm. 256p. (YA) 1973. 5.95 (ISBN 0-685-27998-7, Avalon). Bouregy.
Moore, Frank. The Magic Moving Alphabet. (Illus.). 1978. pap. 2.50 (ISBN 0-486-23593-9). Dover.
Moore, Frank G. The Roman's World. LC 65-23486. (Illus.). 502p. (gr. 7 up). 1936. 15.00x (ISBN 0-8196-0155-1). Biblo.
Moore, Franklin G. & Hendrick, Thomas. Production-Operations Management. 7th ed. 1977. text ed. 17.50x o.p. (ISBN 0-256-01921-5). Irwin.
--Production-Operations Management. 8th ed. 1980. 21.95x (ISBN 0-256-02286-0). Irwin.
Moore, G. F. History of Religions: China, Japan, Egypt, Babylonia, Assyria, India, Persia, Greece, Rome, Vol. I. (International Theological Library). 654p. 1914. text ed. 13.95x (ISBN 0-567-07202-9). Attic Pr.
--History of Religions: Judaism, Christianity, Mohammedanism, Vol. II. (International Theological Library). 568p. 1920. text ed. 13.95x (ISBN 0-567-07203-7). Attic Pr.
--Judges. LC 25-19368. (International Critical Commentary Ser.). 528p. 1895. text ed. 23.00x (ISBN 0-567-05004-1). Attic Pr.
Moore, Gary T., ed. Emerging Methods in Environmental Design & Planning. 1970. 20.50x o.p. (ISBN 0-262-13057-2); pap. 6.95 (ISBN 0-262-63048-6). MIT Pr.
Moore, Gay M. Seaport in Virginia: George Washington's Alexandria. rev. ed. LC 73-188711. 274p. 1972. Repr. 12.95 (ISBN 0-8139-0183-9). U Pr of Va.
Moore, Gaylen, jt. auth. see Gilbert, Lynn.
Moore, Geoffrey. Business Cycles, Inflation & Forecasting. 1980. 40.00 (ISBN 0-88410-685-3). Ballinger Pub.
Moore, George. Brook Kerith. new ed. LC 74-92700. 1969. 7.95 o.p. (ISBN 0-87140-507-5). Liveright.
--Esther Waters. (World's Classics). 1968. 14.95 (ISBN 0-19-250594-7). Oxford U Pr.
--Evelyn Innes, Repr. Of 1898 Ed. Wolff, Robert L., ed. Bd. with Sister Teresa. Repr. of 1901 ed. LC 75-464. (Victorian Fiction Ser). 1975. lib. bdg. 66.00 (ISBN 0-8240-1542-8). Garland Pub.
--Flowers of Passion. Fletcher, Ian & Stokes, John, eds. Bd. with Pagan Poems. LC 76-20138. (Decadent Consciousness Ser.). 1978. lib. bdg. 38.00 (ISBN 0-8240-2778-7). Garland Pub.
--Hail & Farewell. Cave, Richard, ed. (Illus.). 774p. 1980. text ed. 35.00x (ISBN 0-7705-1467-7). Humanities.
--Heloise & Abelard, 2 Vols. in One. (Black & Gold Lib). 1945. 7.95 o.p. (ISBN 0-87140-871-6). Liveright.
--Letters of George Moore (Eighteen Fifty-Two to Nineteen Thirty-Three) to His Brother Col. M. Moore National Library of Ireland Mss 2646-7. 1980. text ed. write for info. (ISBN 0-391-01200-2). Humanities.
--Literature at Nurse. Fletcher, Ian & Stokes, John, eds. Bd. with A Mere Accident. LC 76-20110. (Decadent Consciousness Ser.). 1978. lib. bdg. 38.00 (ISBN 0-8240-2769-8). Garland Pub.
--Literature at Nurse, or, Circulating Morals: A Polemic on Victorian Censorship. (Society & the Victorians). 96p. 1976. Repr. of 1885 ed. text ed. 5.25x (ISBN 0-391-00588-X). Humanities.
--Mike Fletcher. Fletcher, Ian & Stokes, John, eds. LC 76-20121. (Decadent Consciousness Ser.). 1977. Repr. of 1889 ed. lib. bdg. 38.00 (ISBN 0-8240-2770-1). Garland Pub.
--Modern Painting. 288p. 1980. cancelled (ISBN 0-8180-0130-5). Horizon.
Moore, George F. The Birth & Growth of Religion. 188p. Repr. of 1927 ed. 2.95 (ISBN 0-567-02199-8). Attic Pr.
Moore, Gerald. Am I Too Loud? (Illus.). 1979. 22.50 (ISBN 0-241-90019-0, Pub. by Hamish Hamilton England). David & Charles.
--The Schubert Song Cycles: With Thoughts on Performance. 240p. 1979. 22.50 (ISBN 0-241-89082-9, Pub. by Hamish Hamilton England). David & Charles.
--Singer & Accompanist: The Performance of Fifty Songs. LC 73-11859. (Illus.). xi, 232p. 1973. Repr. of 1953 ed. lib. bdg. 18.00x (ISBN 0-8371-7090-7, MOSC). Greenwood.
--Twelve African Writers. LC 80-7988. (Illus.). 320p. 1980. 22.50x (ISBN 0-253-19619-1). Ind U Pr.
Moore, Gerald E. Algebra. rev. ed. 1970. pap. 3.95 (ISBN 0-06-460038-6, CO 38, COS). Har-Row.
Moore, Glover. The Missouri Controversy, 1819-1821. LC 53-5518. (Illus.). 392p. 1966. pap. 5.50x (ISBN 0-8131-0106-9). U Pr of Ky.
Moore, H., jt. auth. see Town, H. C.
Moore, H. Frazier & Canfield, Bertrand R. Public Relations: Principles, Cases, & Problems. 1977. 18.95 (ISBN 0-256-01927-4). Irwin.
Moore, Hal G. Pre-Calculus Mathematics. 2nd ed. LC 76-18678. 1977. text ed. 20.95x (ISBN 0-471-61454-8). Wiley.
Moore, Hal G., jt. auth. see Yaqub, Adil.
Moore, Harriet L. Soviet Far Eastern Policy, 1931-1945. 16.00 (ISBN 0-86527-187-9). Fertig.
Moore, Harris W. Chip Carving. LC 75-19755. (Illus.). 48p. 1976. pap. 1.75 (ISBN 0-486-23256-5). Dover.
Moore, Harry T. Contemporary American Novelists. LC 64-20254. (Crosscurrents-Modern Critiques Ser.). 1966. pap. 7.95 (ISBN 0-8093-0195-4). S Ill U Pr.
--D. H. Lawrence: His Life & Works. (Illus.). 330p. 1964. 24.50x (ISBN 0-8290-0164-6). Irvington.
--The Priest of Love: A Life of D. H. Lawrence. rev ed. LC 77-5714. (Illus.). 516p. 1977. pap. 12.95 (ISBN 0-8093-0839-8). S Ill U Pr.
Moore, Harry T., ed. Contemporary American Novelists. LC 64-20254. (Crosscurrents-Modern Critiques Ser.). 252p. 1964. 10.95 (ISBN 0-8093-0141-5). S Ill U Pr.
Moore, Harry T., ed. see Luhan, Mabel L., et al.
Moore, Harry T., jt. ed. see MacNiven, Ian S.
Moore, Harvey D. Little Threads & Other Object Lessons for Children. LC 73-21959. 80p. 1974. 3.95 o.p. (ISBN 0-687-22169-2). Abingdon.
Moore, Harvey D. & Moore, Patsie S. The Mysterious Marvelous Snowflake. LC 80-20996. 128p. (Orig.). 1981. pap. 4.95 (ISBN 0-687-27640-3). Abingdon.
Moore, Honor. Poem in Four Movements. (Out & Out Pamphlet Ser.). pap. 1.00 (ISBN 0-918314-11-9). Out & Out.
Moore, Ian & Legner, E. F. An Illustrated Guide to the Genera of the Staphylinidae of America North of Mexico. (Illus.). 1979. pap. 10.00x (ISBN 0-931876-31-1, 4093). Ag Sci Pubns.
Moore, Inga. Aktil's Big Swim. (Illus.). 32p. (ps-3). 1980. 10.95 (ISBN 0-19-554250-9). Oxford U Pr.
Moore, J. WATFIV. 1975. pap. 13.95 (ISBN 0-87909-876-7). Reston.
Moore, J. E. Design for Good Acoustics & Noise Control. 1979. text ed. 26.50x (ISBN 0-333-24292-0); pap. 15.95x (ISBN 0-333-24293-9). Scholium Intl.
Moore, J. M. Manuscript Tradition of Polybius. (Cambridge Classical Studies). 1966. 17.95 (ISBN 0-521-05755-8). Cambridge U Pr.
Moore, J. M., ed. see Augustus.
Moore, J. R. Principal of Oral Surgery. (Pergamon Series on Dentistry: Vol. 3). 11.00 o.p. (ISBN 0-08-011395-8). Pergamon.
Moore, J. T. Introduction to Abstract Algebra. 1975. text ed. 20.95 (ISBN 0-12-505750-4). Acad Pr.
Moore, James. Gurdjieff & Mansfield. (Illus.). 304p. 1980. 25.00 (ISBN 0-7100-0488-5). Routledge & Kegan.
Moore, James & Turvey, Alan. Starting Sailing. 11.95 (ISBN 0-7153-6095-7). David & Charles.
Moore, James E. Everybody's Virgin Islands. 1979. pap. 8.95 (ISBN 0-397-01324-8). Lippincott.
Moore, James H. Vespers at St. Mark's: Music of Alessandro Grandi, Giovanni Rovetta & Francesco Cavalli, 2 vols. Buelow, George, ed. (Studies in Musicology). 1981. Set. 59.95 (ISBN 0-8357-1143-9, Pub. by UMI Res Pr); Vol. 1. (ISBN 0-8357-1144-7); Vol. 2. (ISBN 0-8357-1145-5). Univ Microfilms.
Moore, Jane. Cityward Migration: Swedish Data. 1938. 32.50x (ISBN 0-686-51354-1). Elliots Bks.
Moore, Jerry R., jt. ed. see Williams, Paul L.
Moore, Jim. Flip Line. 300p. (Orig.). 1981. pap. 2.95. Tuppence.
Moore, Jim & Micoleau, T. Football Techniques Illustrated. rev. ed. (Illus.). 1962. 11.50 (ISBN 0-8260-6215-6). Ronald Pr.
Moore, John. Zeluco: Various Views of Human Nature Taken from Life and Manners, Foreign and Domestic, 2 vols. in 1. LC 80-2492. 1981. Repr. of 1789 ed. 89.50 (ISBN 0-404-19126-6). AMS Pr.
Moore, John, jt. auth. see Corlett, William.
Moore, John, tr. see Stevenson, William.
Moore, John A. Fray Luis De Granada. (World Authors Ser.: No. 438). 1977. lib. bdg. 12.50 (ISBN 0-8057-6276-0). Twayne.
--Heredity & Development. rev. 2nd ed. (Illus.). 1972. pap. text ed. 5.95x (ISBN 0-19-501478-2). Oxford U Pr.
--Ramon de la Cruz. (World Authors Ser.: Spain: No. 179). lib. bdg. 10.95 (ISBN 0-8057-2252-1). Twayne.
--Wonder of Life. (Illus.). (gr. 4-6). 1960. PLB 6.95 (ISBN 0-87396-016-5). Stravon.
--Write for the Religion Market. LC 80-25607. 128p. 1981. 9.95 (ISBN 0-88280-084-1). ETC Pubns.
Moore, John B. Four Phases of American Development: Federalism, Democracy, Imperialism, Expansion. LC 72-109551. (Law, Politics & History Ser). 1970. Repr. of 1912 ed. lib. bdg. 25.00 (ISBN 0-306-71905-3). Da Capo.
Moore, John B. & Maleka, Leo. Structured FORTRAN. 2nd ed. 567p. 1981. text ed. 19.95 (ISBN 0-8359-7104-X); pap. text ed. 13.95 (ISBN 0-8359-7103-1); soln. manual avail. (ISBN 0-8359-7105-8). Reston.
Moore, John B., jt. auth. see Anderson, Brian.
Moore, John C. Love in Twelfth Century France. LC 75-170268. (Orig.). 1972. 10.00x (ISBN 0-8122-7648-5); pap. 4.95x (ISBN 0-8122-1027-1, Pa Paperbks). U of Pa Pr.
Moore, John H. Growth with Self-Management: Yugoslav Industrialization 1952-1975. LC 79-2464. (Publication Ser.: No. 220). (Illus.). 350p. 1980. 17.95 (ISBN 0-8179-7201-3). Hoover Inst Pr.
--Your Book of Photography. (Your Book Ser.). (Illus.). 1967. 5.95 (ISBN 0-571-08127-4, Pub. by Faber & Faber). Merrimack Bk Serv.
Moore, John M. Aristotle & Xenophon on Democracy & Oligarchy. LC 74-16713. 1975. 19.50x (ISBN 0-520-02863-5); pap. 5.95x (ISBN 0-520-02909-7). U of Cal Pr.
Moore, John R., ed. Economic Impact of TVA. LC 67-12217. 1967. 10.50x (ISBN 0-87049-072-9). U of Tenn Pr.
Moore, John Travers. Story of Silent Night. LC 65-19252. (gr. 2-3). 1965. 5.50 (ISBN 0-570-03430-2, 56-1056). Concordia.
Moore, John W. Moore's Historical, Biographical, & Miscellaneous Gatherings. LC 68-17977. 1968. Repr. of 1886 ed. 30.00 (ISBN 0-8103-3312-0). Gale.
Moore, John W. & Moore, Elizabeth A. Environmental Chemistry. 1976. 21.95 (ISBN 0-12-505050-X). Acad Pr.
Moore, Joseph, jt. auth. see Moore, Roberta.
Moore, K. E., jt. ed. see Rech, R.
Moore, Karen. The House on E Street. 1979. pap. 1.75 (ISBN 0-505-51446-X). Tower Bks.
Moore, Kay, jt. auth. see Conger, Shirley.
Moore, Keith L. Clinically Oriented Anatomy. (Illus.). 950p. 1980. lib. bdg. 26.95 (ISBN 0-683-06146-1). Williams & Wilkins.
Moore, Kenneth C. Airport, Aircraft & Airline Security. LC 76-45104. (Illus.). 1976. 19.95 (ISBN 0-913708-26-7). Butterworths.
Moore, Kristin A., et al. Teenage Motherhood: Social & Economic Consequences. (An Institute Paper). 50p. 1979. pap. 4.00 (ISBN 0-87766-243-6, 24300). Urban Inst.
Moore, L. Hugh & Knight, Karl F. A Concise Handbook of English Composition. (Illus.). 144p. 1972. pap. text ed. 5.95 (ISBN 0-13-166959-1). P-H.
Moore, Lawrie. Foundations of Programming with Pascal. (Series of Computers & Their Applications). 238p. 1980. 47.95 (ISBN 0-470-27022-5, Pub. by Halsted Pr). Wiley.
Moore, Lenard D. Poems of Love & Understanding. 1981. 4.50 (ISBN 0-8062-1549-6). Carlton.
Moore, Lettie W. My Son Dan. LC 77-94241. (Destiny Ser.). 1978. pap. 4.95 (ISBN 0-8163-0007-0, 13875-0). Pacific Pr Pub Assn.
Moore, Lilian. Think of Shadows. LC 80-13496. (Illus.). 40p. (gr. 2 up). 1980. 8.95 (ISBN 0-689-30782-9). Atheneum.
Moore, Lilian, jt. auth. see Charlip, Remy.
Moore, Lloyd. The Jury: History of the Trial Jury. 1973. 12.00 (ISBN 0-87084-576-4). Anderson Pub C.
Moore, Lorna G., et al. Biocultural Basis of Health: Expanding Views of Medical Anthropology. LC 80-11554. (Illus.). 1980. pap. text ed. 11.95 (ISBN 0-8016-3481-4). Mosby.
Moore, Lou. I Live in the City: A B C. (Tell-a-Tale Readers). (Illus.). (ps-1). 1969. PLB 4.77 (ISBN 0-307-68554-3, Whitman). Western Pub.
Moore, Lou, ed. TCG Survey Nineteen Seventy-Eight. 54p. 1979. 5.00 o.p. (ISBN 0-930452-12-7, Pub. by Theatre Comm). Pub Ctr Cult Res.
--TCG Survey 1979. (Illus.). 64p. 1980. 5.00x (ISBN 0-930452-10-0, Pub by Theatre Comm). Pub Ctr Cult Es.
Moore, M. H., tr. see Cournot, Antoine A.
Moore, M. J. & Sieverding, C. H. Two-Phase Steam Flow in Turbines & Separators: Theory, Instrumentation, Engineering. LC 76-9125. 1976. text ed. 34.50 (ISBN 0-07-042992-8, C). McGraw.
Moore, Malcolm T., jt. auth. see Fox, Edward J.
Moore, Malcolm T., jt. auth. see Fox, Edward J., Jr.
Moore, Marcia & Douglas, Mark. Astrology, the Divine Science. rev. ed. LC 77-82609. (Illus.). 1978. 20.00 (ISBN 0-912240-04-0). Arcane Pubns.
--Reincarnation, Key to Immortality. LC 67-19603. 1968. 10.00 (ISBN 0-912240-02-4). Arcane Pubns.
--Yoga, Science of the Self. rev. ed. LC 67-19602. (Illus.). 1979. 10.00 (ISBN 0-912240-01-6). Arcane Pubns.
Moore, Marianne. Collected Poems. 1951. 8.95 (ISBN 0-02-586170-0). Macmillan.
--The Complete Poems of Marianne Moore. (Illus.). 320p. 1981. 16.95 (ISBN 0-670-23505-9). Viking Pr.
Moore, Marie A. How to Raise & Train a Mastiff. (Orig.). pap. 2.00 (ISBN 0-87666-336-6, DS1099). TFH Pubns.
--The Mastiff. LC 77-87765. (Other Dog Bk.). (Illus.). 112p. 1978. 14.95 (ISBN 0-87714-059-6). Denlingers.
Moore, Mark. Together with Daddy. (Illus.). 1977. bds. 3.95 (ISBN 0-8054-4153-0, 4241-53). Broadman.
Moore, Marvin. Conquering High Mountains. LC 79-84604. (Destiny Ser). 1979. pap. 4.95 (ISBN 0-8163-0327-4, 03514-7). Pacific Pr Pub Assn.
--How to Handle Your Imagination. LC 78-13660. (Flame Ser.). 1979. pap. 0.95 (ISBN 0-8127-0195-X). Southern Pub.
--Sacrifice. LC 78-21712. (Flame Ser.). 1979. pap. 0.95 (ISBN 0-8127-0214-X). Southern Pub.
Moore, Marvin H. How to Handle Competition. LC 77-17494. (Better Living Ser.). 1977. pap. 0.95 (ISBN 0-8127-0145-3). Southern Pub.
Moore, Marvin L. Witnesses Through Trial. LC 78-24294. (Orion Ser). 1979. pap. 1.95 (ISBN 0-8127-0216-6). Southern Pub.
Moore, Mary. Man of the High Country. (Harlequin Romances Ser.). 192p. 1980. pap. 1.25 o.p. (ISBN 0-373-02349-9, Pub. by Harlequin). PB.
Moore, Mary E. Robin Williams: Jr. Bio. O'Hehir, Kathy, ed. (Junior Bio Ser.). (Illus.). 1980. pap. 1.95 (ISBN 0-448-17128-7, Tempo). G&D.
Moore, Mary H. Parent Partnership Training Program, 8 bks. Incl. Bk. 1. Introductory Guide. LC 78-68013. 128p. pap. text ed. 12.90 (ISBN 0-8027-9053-4); Bk. 2. Parent's Manual. 192p. pap. text ed. 17.80 (ISBN 0-8027-9054-2); Bk. 3. Basic Communications Skills. LC 78-68015. 288p. pap. text ed. 39.10 (ISBN 0-8027-9055-0); Bk. 4. Developing Social Acceptability. LC 78-62918. 216p. pap. text ed. 29.70 (ISBN 0-8027-9056-9); Bk. 5. Developing Responsible Sexuality. LC 78-62919. 160p. pap. text ed. 19.50 (ISBN 0-8027-9057-7); Bk. 6. Light Housekeeping & In-Home Assistance. LC 78-61387. 272p. pap. text ed. 32.60 (ISBN 0-8027-9058-5); Bk. 7. Heavy Duty Cleaning & Yards & Ground Care. LC 78-62939. 240p. pap. text ed. 32.60 (ISBN 0-8027-9059-3); Bk. 8. Skills of Daily Living. LC 78-62940. 304p. pap. text ed. 29.80 (ISBN 0-8027-9060-7). (For use with K-12 handicapped). 1979. Walker Educ.
--A Yorkshire Cookbook. LC 79-56056. (Illus.). 96p. 1980. 11.95 (ISBN 0-7153-7892-9). David & Charles.

Moore, Mary L. The Newborn & the Nurse. 2nd ed. (Illus.). 450p. 1981. text ed. price not set (ISBN 0-7216-6491-1). Saunders.

Moore, Micahel A., jt. auth. see Buckalew, Vardaman M.

Moore, N. Manpower Planning in Libraries. Wilson, A., ed. (A Library Association Management Pamphlet Ser.). 1980. pap. 8.95x (ISBN 0-85365-532-4, Lib Assn England). Oryx Pr.

Moore, Nancy & Leight, Edward. Ermintrude. LC 60-9730. (Illus.). (ps). 1960. 4.95 (ISBN 0-8149-0370-3). Vanguard.

--Miss Harriet Hippopotamus & the Most Wonderful. LC 63-11499. (Illus.). (gr. k-2). 5.95 (ISBN 0-8149-0369-X). Vanguard.

--Sandman Who Lost His Sand. LC 59-7769. (Illus.). (ps-3). 5.95 (ISBN 0-8149-0371-1). Vanguard.

Moore, Olin H. & Meiden, Walter. Onze Contes. LC 57-674. (Fr). 1957. pap. text ed. 7.70 (ISBN 0-395-04941-5, 3-38350). HM.

Moore, P. D. & Webb, J. A. An Illustrated Guide to Pollen Analysis. LC 77-8822. 1978. 24.95x (ISBN 0-470-99218-2). Halsted Pr.

Moore, P. G. Principles of Statistical Techniques. LC 75-85731. (Illus.). 280p. 1976. 29.95 (ISBN 0-521-07631-5); pap. 12.50x (ISBN 0-521-29055-4). Cambridge U Pr.

--Risk in Business Decision. LC 72-11307. 365p. 1972. 26.95x (ISBN 0-470-61440-4). Halsted Pr.

Moore, Patrick. The A-Z of Astronomy. (Encore Edition). (Illus.). 1977. pap. 1.95 (ISBN 0-684-16913-4, SL700, ScribT). Scribner.

--Naked-Eye Astronomy. (Illus.). 1966. 8.95 o.p. (ISBN 0-393-06303-8). Norton.

--The New Concise Atlas of the Universe. 1978. 35.00 (ISBN 0-528-83031-7). Rand.

--Your Book of Astronomy. 4th ed. (Illus.). (gr. 6 up). 1979. 6.95 (ISBN 0-571-04951-6, Pub. by Faber & Faber). Merrimack Bk Serv.

Moore, Patrick & Brinton, Henry. Exploring Weather. (gr. 4 up). 4.50 (ISBN 0-685-20579-7). Transatlantic.

Moore, Patrick & Tombaugh, Clyde. Out of the Darkness: The Planet Pluto. (Illus.). 224p. 1980. 14.95 (ISBN 0-8117-1163-3). Stackpole.

Moore, Patrick, ed. Yearbook of Astronomy, 1981. (Illus.). 1981. 14.95 (ISBN 0-393-01415-0). Norton.

Moore, Patrick, ed. see Jolley, E. H.

Moore, Patsie S., jt. auth. see Moore, Harvey D.

Moore, Paula. This Golden Rapture. 1980. pap. 2.50 (ISBN 0-671-41266-3). PB.

Moore, Peter. God Made the Stars. (Illus.). 32p. (Orig.). (gr. k-2). 1981. pap. write for info. (ISBN 0-933770-18-9). Kalimat.

Moore, Preston L. Drilling Practices Manual. LC 74-80812. 600p. 1974. 37.50 (ISBN 0-87814-057-3). Pennwell Pub.

Moore, R. Pit-Men, Preachers & Politics. LC 73-88307. 39.50x (ISBN 0-521-20356-2, 1974); pap. 12.95x (ISBN 0-521-29752-4, 1979). Cambridge U Pr.

Moore, R., ed. see Hillison, John & Crunkilton, John.

Moore, R. I., ed. The Birth of Popular Heresy. LC 75-32934. (Documents of Medieval History Ser.). 176p. 1976. text ed. 22.95 (ISBN 0-312-08190-1). St Martin.

Moore, R. J. Churchill, Cripps, & India, Nineteen Thirty-Nine to Nineteen Forty-Five. 1979. 29.50x (ISBN 0-19-822485-0). Oxford U Pr.

--The Crisis of Indian Unity, 1917-1940. 280p. 1974. 24.95x (ISBN 0-19-821560-6). Oxford U Pr.

Moore, R. Keith, compiled by. How to Make Big Improvements in the Small PR Shop. (Orig.). 1979. pap. text ed. 8.00 (ISBN 0-89964-046-X). CASE.

Moore, Ramon E., jt. auth. see Daniel, James W.

Moore, Rayburn S. Paul Hamilton Hayne. (U. S. Authors Ser.: No. 202). lib. bdg. 10.95 (ISBN 0-8057-0352-7). Twayne.

Moore, Raymond & Moore, Dorothy. Home Grown Kids. 1981. 9.95 (ISBN 0-8499-0270-3). Word Bks.

Moore, Raymond C. & Teichert, Curt, eds. Treatise on Invertebrate Paleontology: Part T: Echinodermata 2 (Crinoidea, 3 vols. LC 53-12913. (Treatise on Invertebrate Paleontology). (Illus.). 1978. Set. 55.00x (ISBN 0-8137-3021-X); Vol. 1. 27.00x (ISBN 0-686-52382-2); Vol. 2. 26.00x (ISBN 0-686-52383-0); Vol. 3. 13.00x (ISBN 0-686-52384-9). Geol Soc.

Moore, Raymond S. Adventist Education at the Crossroads. LC 76-1147. (Dimension Ser.). 1976. pap. 5.95 (ISBN 0-8163-0230-8, 01104-9). Pacific Pr Pub Assn.

Moore, Raymond S., et al. School Can Wait. LC 78-19198. 1979. 12.95 o.p. (ISBN 0-8425-1283-7); pap. 7.95 (ISBN 0-8425-1314-0). Brigham.

Moore, Richard E. Historical Dictionary of Guatemala. rev. ed. LC 73-2828. (Latin American Historical Dictionaries Ser.: No. 1). 1973. 10.00 (ISBN 0-8108-0604-5). Scarecrow.

Moore, Richard R. West Texas After the Discovery of Oil: A Modern Interpretation. (Illus.). 1971. 8.50 o.p. (ISBN 0-8363-0100-5). Jenkins.

Moore, Richter H., Jr. & Marks, Thomas C. Readings in Criminal Justice. LC 75-38727. 1976. pap. 10.95 (ISBN 0-672-61371-9). Bobbs.

Moore, Robert. The Bright Blue Plymouth Station Wagon. 192p. 1972. pap. text ed. 5.95x (ISBN 0-87835-034-9). Boyd & Fraser.

--Sports & Mental Health. 128p. 1966. pap. 7.50 spiral (ISBN 0-398-01340-3). C C Thomas.

Moore, Robert & Wallace, Tina. Slamming the Door: The Administration of Immigration Control. 126p. 1975. 23.25x (ISBN 0-85520-107-X, Pub by Martin Robertson England); pap. 8.95x (ISBN 0-85520-106-1). Biblio Dist.

Moore, Robert, jt. auth. see Ellis, Joseph.

Moore, Robert E. Henry Purcell & the Restoration Theatre. LC 73-15057. (Illus.). 223p. 1974. Repr. of 1961 ed. lib. bdg. 19.75x (ISBN 0-8371-7155-5, MOHQ). Greenwood.

Moore, Robert L. Economic Principles in Action. (Illus.). 1979. pap. text ed. 8.95 (ISBN 0-13-226845-0). P-H.

--John Wesley & Authority: A Psychological Perspective. LC 79-13709. (American Academy of Religion. Dissertation Ser.: No. 29). 1979. 12.00 (ISBN 0-89130-290-5, 010129); pap. 7.50 (ISBN 0-89130-291-3). Scholars Pr Ca.

--They Know Not What They Do: Baseball. (Illus.). 112p. (Orig.). 1971. pap. 2.00 (ISBN 0-912178-03-5). Mor-Mac.

Moore, Robert L., ed. Sources of Vitality in American Church Life. LC 78-71065. (Studies in Ministry & Parish Life). 1978. text ed. 12.95x (ISBN 0-913552-14-3); pap. text ed. 5.50x (ISBN 0-913552-15-1). Exploration Pr.

Moore, Roberta & Moore, Joseph. The Problem of War: A Global Issue. 144p. (gr. 10 up). 1980. pap. text ed. 6.19x (ISBN 0-8104-6073-4). Hayden.

Moore, Roberta, jt. auth. see Herr, Edwin L.

Moore, Robin. Compulsion: The True Story of an Addictive Gambler. LC 78-20028. 384p. 1981. 12.95 (ISBN 0-385-13322-7). Doubleday.

--The Crippled Eagles. Harris, A. Bradley, ed. 375p. 13.95 (ISBN 0-89975-005-2, Hippocrene Book Co). World Authors.

--Fiedler: The Colorful Mr. Pops. (Music Reprint Ser.). (Illus.). 1980. Repr. of 1968 ed. lib. bdg. 27.50 (ISBN 0-306-76008-8). Da Capo.

--Search & Destroy. 352p. 1980. pap. 2.50 (ISBN 0-441-75691-3). Charter Bks.

Moore, Robin & Mayer, Edward E. The Cobra Team. 352p. 1981. pap. 2.75 (ISBN 0-441-11289-7). Charter Bks.

Moore, Ruth. Evolution. rev. ed. LC 62-20276. (Life Nature Library). (gr. 5 up). 1969. PLB 8.97 o.p. (ISBN 0-8094-0620-9, Pub. by Time-Life). Silver.

--Evolution. (Young Readers Library). (Illus.). 1977. lib. bdg. 7.95 (ISBN 0-686-51089-5). Silver.

Moore, Ruth, jt. auth. see Washburn, S. L.

Moore, Ruth N. Mystery at Indian Rocks. LC 80-25803. (Illus.). 192p. (gr. 5-10). 1981. pap. 4.95 (ISBN 0-8361-1944-4). Herald Pr.

--Mystery of the Lost Treasure. LC 78-11748. (Illus.). (gr. 4-8). 1978. 4.95 o.p. (ISBN 0-8361-1870-7); pap. 3.50 (ISBN 0-8361-1871-5). Herald Pr.

Moore, S. E. Secret Island. LC 77-7331. (Illus.). 224p. (gr. 5 up). 1977. 8.95 (ISBN 0-590-07479-2, Four Winds). Schol Bk Serv.

Moore, Sally F. Law As Process: An Anthopological Approach. 1978. 22.00x (ISBN 0-7100-8758-6). Routledge & Kegan.

Moore, Sally F. & Meyerhoff, Barbara G., eds. Secular Ritual. 1977. text ed. 37.00x (ISBN 90-232-1457-9). Humanities.

Moore, Samuel, tr. see Marx, Karl & Engels, Friedrich.

Moore, Sebastian. The Crucified Jesus Is No Stranger. 1977. 6.95 (ISBN 0-8164-0341-4). Crossroad NY.

--The Fire & the Rose Are One. 176p. 1980. 9.95 (ISBN 0-8164-0468-2). Seabury.

Moore, Shelia J., jt. ed. see Coveney, James.

Moore, Stanley B. Ornamental Horticulture As a Vocation. (gr. 11 up). 1969. text ed. 8.00x (ISBN 0-912178-01-9). Mor-Mac.

Moore, Susie. The Terrible Ordeal of Daniyell Moore. 1981. 4.50 (ISBN 0-8062-1713-8). Carlton.

Moore, Suzanne, jt. auth. see Benmaman, Virginia.

Moore, Suzanne T. Coffee. 144p. 1974. pap. 3.95 (ISBN 0-686-09052-7). MTM Pub Co.

--Coffee Too. 64p. (Orig.). 1975. pap. 1.95 (ISBN 0-686-10980-5). MTM Pub Co.

--Palestina. Date not set. 6.95 (ISBN 0-686-10451-X). MTM Pub Co. Postponed.

Moore, T. Inglis. Social Patterns in Australian Literature. LC 71-133027. 1971. 22.50x (ISBN 0-520-01828-1). U of Cal Pr.

Moore, T. V. Haggai-Malachi. (Geneva Commentaries Ser.). 1974. 7.95 (ISBN 0-85151-079-5). Banner of Truth.

--Haggi, Malachi, & Zechariah. (Banner of Truth Geneva Series Commentaries). 1979. 10.95 (ISBN 0-85151-288-7). Banner of Truth.

--Zechariah. (Geneva Commentaries Ser.). 1974. 7.95 (ISBN 0-85151-078-7). Banner of Truth.

Moore, T. W. Educational Theory: An Introduction. (Students Library of Education Ser.). 1974. 11.00x (ISBN 0-7100-7918-4); pap. 6.00 (ISBN 0-7100-8463-3). Routledge & Kegan.

Moore, Terris. Mt. McKinley: The Pioneer Climbs. (Illus.). 224p. 1981. pap. 8.95 (ISBN 0-89886-021-0). Mountaineers.

Moore, Thomas. The Poetical Works of Thomas Moore, 10 vols. 1980. Repr. of 1840 ed. lib. bdg. 300.00 (ISBN 0-89987-599-8). Century Bookbindery.

Moore, Thomas G. Uranium Enrichment & Public Policy. 1978. pap. 4.25 (ISBN 0-8447-3286-9). Am Enterprise.

Moore, Timothy E., ed. Cognitive Development & the Acquisition of Language. 1973. 29.00 (ISBN 0-12-505850-0). Acad Pr.

Moore, Vardine. Mice Are Rather Nice. LC 80-23121. 112p. (gr. 3-7). 1981. PLB 7.95 (ISBN 0-689-30819-1). Atheneum.

--Pre-School Story Hour. 2nd ed. LC 78-188549. 1972. 10.00 (ISBN 0-8108-0474-3). Scarecrow.

Moore, W. American Negro Slavery & Abolition. LC 73-148362. 1971. 10.00 (ISBN 0-89388-000-0); pap. 5.95. Okpaku Communications.

Moore, W. C. British Parasitic Fungi. 1959. 68.50 (ISBN 0-521-05758-2). Cambridge U Pr.

Moore, W. G. The Tutorial System & Its Future. 1968. text ed. 11.25 (ISBN 0-08-012659-6); pap. text ed. 6.25 (ISBN 0-08-012658-8). Pergamon.

Moore, W. J. The Mammalian Skull. (Biological Structure & Function Ser.: No. 8). (Illus.). 400p. Date not set. 85.00 (ISBN 0-521-23318-6). Cambridge U Pr.

Moore, W. S. & Penner, Rudolph G., eds. Constitution & the Budget. 1980. 13.25 (ISBN 0-8447-2179-4); pap. 7.25 (ISBN 0-8447-2180-8). Am Enterprise.

Moore, Ward. Caduceus Wild. (Futorian Science Fiction Ser.). 1978. pap. 1.75 o.p. (ISBN 0-523-40246-5). Pinnacle Bks.

Moore, Willard B. Molokan Oral Tradition: Legends & Memorates of an Ethnic Sect. (U. C. Publ. in Folklore Studies: Vol. 28). 1974. pap. 9.00x (ISBN 0-520-09483-2). U of Cal Pr.

Moore, William. Bayonets in the Sun. LC 77-76645. 1978. 7.95 o.p. (ISBN 0-312-07016-0). St Martin.

Moore, William & Berlitz, Charles. The Philadelphia Experiment. 224p. 1980. pap. 2.50 (ISBN 0-449-24280-3, Crest). Fawcett.

Moore, William G. The Adjunct to Understanding Data Processing: The Course on Modern Data Processing & Accounting Procedures. 1979. pap. text ed. 2.99 (ISBN 0-934488-01-0). Williams Ent.

--The Use of the Magnetic Ink Character Reader. 1979. pap. text ed. 1.99 (ISBN 0-934488-00-2). Williams Ent.

Moore, William G., Sr. Basic Business Facts: Evaluating Money Resources. 1980. pap. text ed. 1.99 (ISBN 0-934488-02-9). Williams Ent.

Moore, William L., jt. auth. see Berlitz, Charles.

Moorehead, ed. Theory Practice & Application of Prevention in Personal Health Services: Quality Control & Evaluation of Preventive Health Services. LC 76-15083. 1976. pap. text ed. 4.95x o.p. (ISBN 0-88202-105-2). N Watson.

Moorehead, Alan. Darwin & the Beagle. LC 69-17879. (Illus.). 1969. 20.00 o.p. (ISBN 0-06-013016-4, HarpT); pap. 8.95 o.s.i. (ISBN 0-06-013017-2, TD-120, HarpT). Har-Row.

--White Nile. LC 78-160663. (Illus.). 1971. deluxe ed. 20.00 o.s.i. (ISBN 0-06-013049-0, HarpT). Har-Row.

Moorehouse, Geoffrey, jt. auth. see Time-Life Books Editors.

Moore-Landecker, Elizabeth. Fundamentals of the Fungi. (Biological Ser). (Illus.). 1972. ref. ed. 23.95x (ISBN 0-13-339267-8). P-H.

Moorer, Thomas H., jt. auth. see Cottrell, Alvin J.

Moorer, Thomas H., jt. auth. see Tate, William.

Moores, Donald F. Educating the Deaf: Psychology, Principles & Practices. LC 77-72896. (Illus.). 1977. text ed. 18.50 (ISBN 0-395-24486-2). HM.

Moorey, P. R. Ancient Persian Bronzes in the Adam Collection. 1974. 36.00 (ISBN 0-571-10216-6, Pub. by Faber & Faber). Merrimack Bk Serv.

--Kish Excavations 1923-1933: With a Microfiche Catalogue of the Objects of the Ashmolean Museum. (Illus.). 1978. 49.50x (ISBN 0-19-813191-7). Oxford U Pr.

Moorhead, Jack, ed. Numerical Control Applications. LC 80-52613. (Manufacturing Update Ser.). (Illus.). 260p. 1980. 29.00 (ISBN 0-87263-058-7). SME.

--Numerical Control Fundamentals. LC 80-52723. (Manufacturing Update Ser.). (Illus.). 242p. 1980. 29.00 (ISBN 0-87263-057-9). SME.

Moorhouse, C. San Francisco. (The Great Cities Ser.). (Illus.). 1979. lib. bdg. 14.94 (ISBN 0-686-51010-0). Silver.

Moorhouse, Earl. Wake up, It's a Crash: A Survivor's Account. (Illus.). 184p. 1981. 17.95 (ISBN 0-7153-8093-1). David & Charles.

Moorhouse, Geoffrey. The Fearful Void. LC 73-19977. (Illus.). 1974. 10.00 o.p. (ISBN 0-397-01019-2). Lippincott.

--San Francisco. Time-Life Books, ed. (The Great Cities). (Illus.). 1979. 14.95 (ISBN 0-8094-2347-2). Time-Life.

Moorman, Charles. Kings & Captains: Variations on a Heroic Theme. LC 78-147858. 208p. 1971. 10.00x (ISBN 0-8131-1248-6). U Pr of Ky.

--A Knyght There Was: The Evolution of the Knight in Literature. LC 67-17846. 180p. 1967. 9.00x (ISBN 0-8131-1133-1). U Pr of Ky.

Moorman, John R. A History of the Church in England. 3rd rev ed. 485p. 1973. 24.95 (ISBN 0-8192-1282-2). Morehouse.

Moorman, Mary. William Wordsworth: A Biography, 2 vols. (Vol. 1, Early Years, 1770-1803; vol. 2, Later Years, 1803-1850). Vol. 1. 39.00x (ISBN 0-19-811565-2); Vol. 2. pap. 5.95x (ISBN 0-19-881146-2, OPB). Oxford U Pr.

Moorman, Mary, ed. see Wordsworth, Dorothy.

Moorman, R. B., jt. auth. see Parcel, John I.

Moorman, Ruth & Williams, Lalla. A Salad a Day. (Illus.). 80p. 1980. pap. 4.95 (ISBN 0-937552-02-X). Quail Ridge.

--Seven Chocolate Sins. (Illus.). 80p. 1979. pap. 4.95 (ISBN 0-937552-01-1). Quail Ridge.

--Twelve Days of Christmas Cookbook. (Illus.). 80p. 1978. pap. 4.95 (ISBN 0-937552-00-3). Quail Ridge.

Moorthy, K. Krishna. After Tito What? (Illus.). 225p. 1980. text ed. 12.50x (ISBN 0-391-02063-3). Humanities.

Moorty, D. N. The Feel of Feel. (Redbird Bk.). 1976. lib. bdg. 8.00 (ISBN 0-89253-097-9); flexible bdg. 4.80 (ISBN 0-89253-133-9). Ind-US Inc.

Moos, Felix, jt. ed. see Goodman, Grant K.

Moos, N. H. How to Acquire a Million. pap. 1.25 (ISBN 0-912576-08-1). R Collier.

Moos, Rudolf H. Evaluating Correctional & Community Settings. LC 73-17450. 400p. 1975. 23.95 (ISBN 0-471-61502-1, Pub. by Wiley-Interscience). Wiley.

--Evaluating Treatment Environments: A Social Ecological Approach. LC 73-17450. (Wiley-Interscience Ser. Health, Medicine, & Society). 304p. 1974. 27.50 (ISBN 0-471-61503-X, Pub. by Wiley-Interscience). Wiley.

--The Human Context: Environmental Determinants of Behavior. LC 75-26870. 444p. 1976. 28.95 (ISBN 0-471-61504-8, Pub. by Wiley-Interscience). Wiley.

Moos, Rudolf H., ed. Human Adaption: Coping with Life Stresses. 464p. 1976. 19.95 (ISBN 0-669-00390-5). Lexington Bks.

Moosbrugger, Bernhard & Weigner, Gladys. A Voice of the Third World: Dom Helder Camara. LC 80-82008. (Illus.). 1972. pap. 1.95 (ISBN 0-8091-1738-X). Paulist Pr.

Moose, J. W. The Application of Comparative Morphology in the Identification of Intestinal Parasites. (American Lectures in Clinical Microbiology Ser.). (Illus.). 56p. 1973. 10.75 (ISBN 0-398-02874-5). C C Thomas.

Moose, Mary E., jt. auth. see St. Pierre, Brian.

Mooser, Stephen. The Ghost with the Halloween Hiccups. (Illus.). (gr. k-3). 1978. pap. 1.75 (ISBN 0-380-40287-4, 51953, Camelot). Avon.

Moossa, A. R. Tumors of the Pancreas. (Illus.). 576p. 1980. lib. bdg. 62.00 (ISBN 0-683-06147-X). Williams & Wilkins.

Moots, Philip R., jt. auth. see Gaffney, Edward M.

Mopsik, Stanley I. & Agard, Judith A. An Education Handbook for Parents of Handicapped Children. LC 78-67848. 1980. 22.50 (ISBN 0-89011-511-7). Abt Assoc.

Moquin, Wayne, ed. Makers of America, 10 Vols. (Illus.). (gr. 7-12). 1971. Set. 129.00 (ISBN 0-87827-000-0). Ency Brit Ed.

Mor, Carlo G. L' Eta Feudale, 2 vols. LC 80-2016. 1981. Repr. of 1952 ed. Set. 110.00 (ISBN 0-404-18609-2). AMS Pr.

Mor, Vincent, jt. auth. see Sherwood, Sylvia.

Mora, Abdias A., tr. see Copeland, E. L.

Mora, Jaime & Palacios, Rafael, eds. Glutamine: Metabolism, Enzymology & Regulation. 1980. 28.00 (ISBN 0-12-506040-8). Acad Pr.

Mora, Jose Ferrater see Ferrater Mora, Jose.

Mora, Magdalena & Del Castillo, Adelaida, eds. Mexican Women in the United States: Struggles Past & Present. LC 80-10682. (Occasional Papers Ser.: No. 2). (Illus.). 214p. (Orig.). 1980. pap. 12.95 (ISBN 0-89551-022-7). UCLA Chicano Stud.

Moraes, Dom. Indira Gandhi. 340p. 1980. 14.95 (ISBN 0-316-58191-7). Little.

Moraes, Frank. India Today. 1960. 4.50 o.s.i. (ISBN 0-02-586350-9). Macmillan.

--Sir Purshotamdas Thakurdas. Repr. 10.00x (ISBN 0-210-33748-6). Asia.

Moragne, Lenora & Moragne, Rudolph. Baby's Early Years: A Record Book. (Illus.). 1975. spiral bdg. 4.45 o.p. (ISBN 0-917230-02-7). LenChamps Pubs.

Moragne, Rudolph, jt. auth. see Moragne, Lenora.

Morain, Genelle G. Kinesics & Cross-Cultural Understanding. (Language in Education Ser.: No. 7). 1978. pap. 2.95 (ISBN 0-87281-089-5). Ctr Appl Ling.

Morais, J. Victor, ed. Who's Who in Malaysia & Singapore 1979-80. 13th ed. (Illus.). 761p. 1980. 60.00x (ISBN 0-8002-2469-8). Intl Pubns Serv.

Morais, Victor J., ed. Who's Who in Malaysia: 1978-79. 12th ed. LC 72-940164. (Illus.). 1978. 50.00x o.p. (ISBN 0-8002-0411-5). Intl Pubns Serv.

Morales, Armando & Sheafor, Bradford. Social Work: A Profession of Many Faces. 2nd ed. 1980. text ed. 16.95 o.p.; instr's manual free o.p. Allyn.

Morales, Jorge Luis. Alfonso Reyes y la Literatural Espanola. (Mante y Palabra Ser.). 193p. (Span.). 1980. 6.25 (ISBN 0-8477-0558-7); pap. 5.00 (ISBN 0-8477-0559-5). U of PR Pr.

Morales, Juan-Antonio. Bayesian Full Information Structural Analysis. LC 70-155592. (Lecture Notes in Operation Research: Vol. 43). 1971. pap. 10.70 o.p. (ISBN 0-387-05417-0). Springer-Verlag.

Morales, Mahi, ed. see Campbell, Sid.

Morales, Sebastian. The Gun Runners. 160p. (Orig.). 1975. pap. 0.95 o.p. (ISBN 0-445-00684-6). Popular Lib.

Morales-Carrione, Arturo. Auge y Decadencia De la Trata Negrera En Puerto Rico (1820-1860) LC 77-11193. (Illus.). 1978. pap. cancelled o.p. (ISBN 0-8477-0850-0). U of PR Pr.

Moran & Aubuchon. Applied Business Mathematics. 2nd ed. 368p. 1976. pap. text ed. 15.95 (ISBN 0-205-04889-7, 174889-0); instr's manual avail. (ISBN 0-205-04920-6, 174920-X); test manual avail. (ISBN 0-205-05548-6, 175548-X). Allyn.

Moran, Barbara K., jt. auth. see Gornick, Vivian.

Moran, Deborah, et al. GED Mathematics Test Preparation Guide: High School Equivalency Examination. (Cliffs Test Preparation Ser.). 182p. (gr. 10 up). 1981. pap. 3.95 (ISBN 0-8220-2016-5). Cliffs.

Morán, Gabriel. Catechesis of Revelation. 1968. pap. 3.95 (ISBN 0-8164-2502-7). Crossroad NY.

--Design for Religion - Toward Ecumenical Education. LC 78-130860. 1971. pap. 1.95 (ISBN 0-8164-2544-2). Crossroad NY.

--Interplay: A Theory of Religion & Education. LC 80-53203. 125p. (Orig.). 1981. pap. 5.95 (ISBN 0-88489-125-9). St Mary's.

--The Present Revelation: In Quest of Religious Foundations. 204p. 1972. 8.95 (ISBN 0-8164-1105-0). Crossroad NY.

--Religious Body: Design for a New Reformation. 1974. 8.95 (ISBN 0-8164-1176-X). Crossroad NY.

--Theology of Revelation. 1968. pap. 3.95 (ISBN 0-8164-2567-1). Crossroad NY.

Moran, Goerge, jt. auth. see Erskine, Jim.

Moran, Hugh, ed. Words to Live by: Chiara Lubich & Christians from All Over the World. Dauphinais, Raymond & Moran, Hugh, trs. from Fr. & Ital. LC 80-82419. 1980. pap. 4.50 (ISBN 0-911782-08-7). New City.

Moran, Hugh, ed. see Lubich, Chiara.

Moran, Hugh, ed. see Silvan, Matthew.

Moran, Hugh, tr. see Lorit, Sergius C.

Moran, Hugh, tr. see Moran, Hugh.

Moran, James. The Double Crown Club. (Illus.). 128p. 1980. 85.00 (ISBN 0-913720-16-X). Sandstone.

--Fit to Be Styled a Typographer. (Illus.). 66p. 1980. 32.00 (ISBN 0-913720-10-0); pap. 18.50 (ISBN 0-913720-11-9). Sandstone.

--Printing Presses: History & Development from the Fifteenth Century to Modern Times. (Illus.). 1973. 30.00x (ISBN 0-520-02245-9); pap. 7.95 (ISBN 0-520-02904-6). U of Cal Pr.

--Wynkyn de Worde: Father of Fleet Street. (Illus.). pap. 10.00 (ISBN 0-913720-15-1). Sandstone.

Moran, John C. An F. Marion Crawford Companion. LC 80-1707. (Illus.). 608p. 1981. lib. bdg. 45.00 (ISBN 0-313-20926-X, MCC/). Greenwood.

Moran, Joseph M., et al. Introduction to Environmental Science. LC 79-19007. (Illus.). 1980. text ed. 19.95x (ISBN 0-7167-1020-X); instr's manual & transparency masters avail. W H Freeman.

Moran, Lois, ed. see American Craft Council.

Moran, Marguerite K., jt. auth. see Lowenheim, Frederick A.

Moran, Michael. Standards Relating to Appeals & Collateral Review. (Juvenile Justice Standards Project Ser.). 1980. softcover 5.95 (ISBN 0-88410-815-5); casebound 12.50. Ballinger Pub.

--Standards Relating to Appeals & Collateral Review. LC 77-3982. (Juvenile Justice Standards Project Ser.). 1977. softcover 5.95 o.p. (ISBN 0-88410-776-0); 12.50, casebound o.p. (ISBN 0-88410-239-4). Ballinger Pub.

Moran, Robert D. How to Avoid OSHA. (Illus.). 256p. 1981. 49.95 (ISBN 0-87201-652-8). Gulf Pub.

Moran, S. F. Notes on Japanese Sword Fittings. pap. 5.00 o.p. (ISBN 0-686-65148-0). Hawley.

Moran, Tom. Roller Skating Is for Me. (Sports for Me Bks.). (Illus.). (gr. 2-5). 1981. PLB 5.95 (ISBN 0-8225-1097-9). Lerner Pubns.

Morante, Elsa. History, a Novel. 1978. pap. 2.95 (ISBN 0-380-41889-4, 41889, Bard). Avon.

Morariu, Mircea A. Major Neurological Syndromes. (Illus.). 368p. 1979. text ed. 25.75 (ISBN 0-398-03831-7). C C Thomas.

Moraski, Art. Complete Guide to Walleye Fishing. 1980. pap. 9.95 (ISBN 0-932558-12-7). Willow Creek.

Morasky, jt. auth. see Johnson.

Morath, Inge, jt. auth. see Miller, Arthur.

Morauta, Louise. Beyond the Village: Local Politics in Madang, Papua New Guinea. (Monographs on Social Anthropology: No. 49). 208p. 1974. text ed. 19.50x (ISBN 0-391-00327-5, Athlone Pr). Humanities.

Moraux, Paul. Le Commentaire D'alexandre D'aphrodise Aux "Seconds Analytiques" D'aristote. (Peripatoi Ser.). 1979. text ed. 43.50x (ISBN 3-11-007805-8). De Gruyter.

Moravcsik, Michael J. How to Grow Science. LC 80-17469. (Illus.). 224p. (Orig.). 1980. text ed. 12.50x (ISBN 0-87663-344-0). Universe.

Moravetz, Bruno. The Big Book of Mountaineering. (Illus.). 1980. 49.95 (ISBN 0-8120-5332-X). Barron.

Moravia. Sette Racconti. (Easy Reader, C). pap. 3.75 (ISBN 0-88436-060-1, ITA301051). EMC.

Moravia, Alberto. Which Tribe Do You Belong to? Davidson, Angus, tr. from Ital. 1974. 7.95 o.p. (ISBN 0-374-28922-0). FS&G.

Moravisin, Sylvester. Why Our Universities Are Turning Out Ordinary Barbarians. (American Culture Library). (Illus.). 105p. 1981. 47.85 (ISBN 0-89266-299-9). Am Classical Coll Pr.

Morawetz, David. The Andean Group: A Case Study in Economic Integration Among Developing Countries. LC 74-3070. 216p. 1974. 23.00x (ISBN 0-262-13109-9). MIT Pr.

Morawski, Stefan, jt. ed. see Baxandall, Lee.

Morawski, Stefan, ed. see Marx, Karl & Engels, Frederick.

Morbidoni, Barbara. Stars & Stoves: An Astrological Cookbook. (Illus., Orig.). 1979. pap. 5.00 (ISBN 0-933646-07-0). Aries Pr.

Morcombe, Michael. Birds of Australia. (Encore Editions). (Illus.). 1977. 3.95 o.p. (ISBN 0-684-14991-5, ScribT). Scribner.

Mordecai, John. Federation of the West Indies. LC 67-24014. 1968. 16.75x o.s.i. (ISBN 0-8101-0172-6). Northwestern U Pr.

Mordike, Janet, tr. see Haasen, Peter.

Mordue, W., et al. Insect Physiology. LC 79-27743. 1981. pap. 16.95x (ISBN 0-470-26931-6). Halsted Pr.

More, Hannah. Strictures on the Modern System of Female Education, 2 vols. Luria, Gina, ed. (The Feminist Controversy in England, 1788-1810 Ser.). 1974. Set. lib. bdg. 100.00 (ISBN 0-8240-0873-1); lib. bdg. 50.00 ea. Garland Pub.

More, Hannah see Barbauld, Anna L.

More, Harry, ed. Critical Issues in Law Enforcement. 3d ed. LC 79-55205. 352p. 1981. pap. text ed. price not set (ISBN 0-87084-582-9). Anderson Pub Co.

More, Harry W. Criminal Justice Management: A Text & Readings. (Criminal Justice Ser.). 1977. pap. text ed. 12.95; pap. write for info. (ISBN 0-8299-0625-8). West Pub.

More, Harry W., Jr., jt. auth. see Kenney, John P.

More, Henry. Henry More: A Collections of Several Philosophical Writings, 2 vols. Wellek, Rene, ed. LC 75-11238. (British Philosophers & Theologians of the 17th & 18th Centuries Ser.). 1978. lib. bdg. 42.00 (ISBN 0-8240-1790-0). Garland Pub.

More, Jasper. The Land of Egypt. (Illus.). 192p. 1980. 24.00 (ISBN 0-7134-1635-1, Pub. by Batsford England). David & Charles.

More, Paul E., ed. Shelburne Essays, 11 vols. Incl. Vol. 1. 1904. 253p. (ISBN 0-685-22556-9); Vol. 2. 1905. 253p. (ISBN 0-685-22557-7); Vol. 3. 1906. 265p. (ISBN 0-685-22558-5); Vol. 4. 1906. 286p. (ISBN 0-685-22559-3); Vol. 5. 1908. 216p. (ISBN 0-685-22560-7); Vol. 6. Studies in Religious Dualism, 1909. 355p. (ISBN 0-685-22561-5); Vol. 7. 1910. 272p. (ISBN 0-685-22562-3); Vol. 8. Drift of Romanticism, 1913. 316p. (ISBN 0-685-22563-1); Vol. 9. Aristocracy & Justice, 1915. 253p. (ISBN 0-685-22564-X); Vol. 10. With the Wits, 1919. 323p. (ISBN 0-685-22565-8); Vol. 11. A New England Group & Others, 1921. 300p. (ISBN 0-685-22566-6). LC 67-17764. 1967. Repr. of 1921 ed. 8.00 ea.; Set. 85.00 (ISBN 0-87753-028-9). Phaeton.

More, Thomas. Utopia. Incl. Dialogue of Comfort Against Tribulation. 1955. 10.50x (ISBN 0-460-00461-1, Evman); pap. 2.95 (ISBN 0-460-01461-7, Evman). Dutton.

More, Sir Thomas. A Dyaloge of Syr T. More...Wherein Be Treatyd Dyvers Maters, As of the Veneration & Worshyp of Ymagys. LC 74-28873. (English Experience Ser.: No. 752). 1975. Repr. of 1529 ed. 26.50 (ISBN 90-221-0752-3). Walter J Johnson.

More, William S. Emotions & Adult Learning. 1974. 19.95 (ISBN 0-347-01050-4, 93633-2, Pub. by Saxon Hse England). Lexington Bks.

Morea, Andre. Surrounded by Angels. LC 76-22930. 1976. pap. 1.95 (ISBN 0-87123-503-X, 200503). Bethany Fell.

Morea, Deborah. A Realistic Approach to Any Philosophy. 1981. pap. 7.95 (ISBN 0-9603022-2-0). Davida Pubns.

--Through the Doors of Truth, Find Thyself. 1978. 5.50 (ISBN 0-9603022-0-4). Davida Pubns.

--The Transmutation of Attitudes. 1979. pap. 6.50 (ISBN 0-9603022-1-2). Davida Pubns.

Moreau, Celestin. Bibliographie Des Mazarinades, 4 vols. (Societe De L'histoire De France: Nos. 61, 63, & 67). Repr. of 1850 ed. Set. 79.50 (ISBN 0-8337-2454-1); 4 supplements in 1 vol. incl. (ISBN 0-685-06734-3). B Franklin.

Moreau, Daniel, ed. L' Espagne. (Collection monde et voyages). (Illus.). 159p. (Fr.). 1973. 21.00x (ISBN 2-03-053101-4). Larousse.

--Les Etats Unis. (Collection monde et voyages). (Illus.). 159p. (Fr.). 1973. 21.00x (ISBN 2-03-053106-5, 3895). Larousse.

--La Grece. new ed. (Collection monde et voyages). 159p. (Fr.). 1973. 21.00x (ISBN 2-03-053105-7, 3897). Larousse.

--L' Inde. (Collection monde et voyages). 159p. (Fr.). 1973. 21.00x (ISBN 2-03-053119-7). Larousse.

--L' Israel. (Collection monde et voyages). 159p. (Fr.). 1973. 21.00x (ISBN 2-03-053120-0). Larousse.

--L' Italie. (Collection monde et voyages). (Illus.). 159p. (Fr.). 1973. 21.00x (ISBN 2-03-053102-2, 3898). Larousse.

--Le Japon. new ed. (Collection monde et voyages). 159p. (Fr.). 1973. 21.00 (ISBN 2-03-053115-4, 2720). Larousse.

--Le Maroc. new ed. (Collection monde et voyages). (Illus.). 159p. (Fr.). 1973. 21.00x (ISBN 2-03-053111-1). Larousse.

--Le Mexique. new ed. (Collection monde et voyages). (Illus.). 159p. (Fr.). 1973. 21.00x (ISBN 2-03-053108-1, 3900). Larousse.

--Le Monde autour de l'an 33. new ed. (Collection monde et histoire). (Illus.). 160p. (Fr.). 1973. 14.50x o.p. (ISBN 0-685-39577-4). Larousse.

--Le Monde autour de 1492. new ed. (Collection monde et histoire). (Illus.). 160p. (Fr.). 1973. 15.00x (ISBN 2-03-053201-0). Larousse.

--Le Monde autour de 1793. new ed. (Collection monde et histoire). (Illus.). 160p. (Fr.). 1973. 15.00x (ISBN 2-03-053205-3). Larousse.

--Le Monde autour de 1871. new ed. (Collection monde et histoire). (Illus.). 160p. (Fr.). 1973. 15.00x (ISBN 2-03-053203-7). Larousse.

--Le Monde autour de 1938. new ed. (Collection monde et histoire). (Illus.). 160p. (Fr.). 1973. 15.00x (ISBN 2-03-053204-5). Larousse.

--Le Portugal. new ed. (Collection monde et voyages). (Illus.). 159p. (Fr.). 1973. 21.00x (ISBN 2-03-053113-8). Larousse.

--La Russie. new ed. (Collection monde et voyages). (Illus.). 159p. (Fr.). 1973. 21.00 (ISBN 2-03-053112-X, 3902). Larousse.

--La Scandinavie. new ed. (Collecion monde et voyages). 159p. (Fr.). 1973. 21.00 (ISBN 2-03-053116-2, 5164). Larousse.

--La Suisse. new ed. (Collection monde et voyages). (Illus.). 159p. (Fr.). 1973. 21.00 (ISBN 2-03-053103-0). Larousse.

--La Turquie. new ed. (Collection monde et voyages). (Illus.). 159p. (Fr.). 1973. 21.00 (ISBN 2-03-053110-3). Larousse.

Moreau, J. J., et al. Hashish & Mental Illness. Peters, H. & Nahas, G., eds. Barnett, G. J., tr. from Fr. LC 76-107227. Orig. Title: Du Haschish et De l'Alienation Mentale. 1973. pap. 18.00 (ISBN 0-911216-14-6). Raven.

Moreau, Jules L., tr. see Boman, Thorleif.

Moreau, Marcel. The Selves of Quinte. LC 65-14604. 1965. 5.00 o.s.i. (ISBN 0-8076-0298-1). Braziller.

Moreau, R. E. Bird Faunas of Africa & Its Islands. 1967. 58.50 (ISBN 0-12-506650-3). Acad Pr.

Moreby, D. H. Personnel Management in Merchant Ships. 1968. 27.00 (ISBN 0-08-012993-5); pap. 14.00 (ISBN 0-08-012992-7). Pergamon.

Morehead, et al, eds. Hoyles Rules of Games. (RL 7). 1973. pap. 2.25 (ISBN 0-451-09001-2, E9001, Sig). NAL.

Morehead, Joe. Introduction to U. S. Public Documents. 2nd ed. LC 78-16866. (Library Science Text). (Illus.). 1978. lib. bdg. 22.50x (ISBN 0-87287-186-X); pap. text ed. 13.50x (ISBN 0-87287-190-8). Libs Unl.

--Theory & Practice in Library Education: The Teaching-Learning Process. LC 80-17431. (Research Studies in Library Science: No. 16). 1980. lib. bdg. 25.00x (ISBN 0-87287-215-7). Libs Unl.

Morehouse, Kathleen M. Rain on the Just: A Novel. LC 79-18762. (Lost American Fiction Ser.). 333p. 1980. Repr. of 1936 ed. 13.95 (ISBN 0-8093-0945-9). S Ill U Pr.

Morehouse, Laurence E. & Miller, Augustus T. Physiology of Exercise. 7th ed. LC 75-22186. (Illus.). 320p. 1976. text ed. 15.95 (ISBN 0-8016-3485-7). Mosby.

Morehouse, Thomas A. & Harrison, Gordon S. An Electoral Profile of Alaska. LC 73-620227. (Joint Institute of Social & Economic Research Ser.: No. 37). 104p. 1973. pap. 3.00 (ISBN 0-295-95336-5). U of Wash Pr.

Morehouse, Thomas A., jt. auth. see McBeath, Gerald A.

Morehouse, Ward. Separate, Unequal, but More Autonomous. (Working Papers in the World Order Models Project Ser.). 50p. (Orig.). 1981. pap. 1.50 (ISBN 0-686-28913-7). Transaction Bks.

--Understanding Science & Technology in India & Pakistan. (Occasional Publication). 78p. 1967. pap. 2.00 (ISBN 0-89192-136-2). Interbk Inc.

Morehouse, Ward, III. The Waldorf: The Story Behind America's Grandest Hotel. (Illus.). 320p. 1981. 11.95 (ISBN 0-399-12541-8). Putnam.

Morel, Alice & Wise, Gilbert J. Urologic Endoscopic Procedures. 2nd ed. LC 78-31423. (Illus.). 1979. text ed. 17.95 (ISBN 0-8016-3491-1). Mosby.

Morel, Alice, jt. auth. see Winter, C. Chester.

Morel, E. D. Great Britain & the Congo: The Pillage of the Congo Basin. LC 68-9619. 1969. Repr. of 1909 ed. 15.50 (ISBN 0-86527-088-0). Fertig.

Morel, Edmund D. Truth & the War. LC 70-147478. (Library of War & Peace; the Character & Causes of War). lib. bdg. 38.00 (ISBN 0-8240-0270-9). Garland Pub.

Morel, Juliette. Lingerie Parisienne. LC 76-44581. (Illus.). 1977. pap. 3.95 o.p. (ISBN 0-312-48702-9). St Martin.

Moreland, Floyd L & Fleischer, Rita M. Latin: An Intensive Course. LC 75-36500. (Campus Ser.: No. 186). (gr. 10 up). 1977. 12.95x (ISBN 0-520-03183-0). U of Cal Pr.

Morell, Jonathan A. Program Evaluation in Social Research. LC 78-11949. (Pergamon Series in General Psychology). 1980. 22.00 (ISBN 0-08-023360-0); pap. 9.95 (ISBN 0-08-023359-7). Pergamon.

Morell, R. W. & Henry, M. Daniel. The Practice of Management. LC 80-8136. 510p. 1981. lib. bdg. 26.00 (ISBN 0-8191-1489-8); pap. text ed. 16.75 (ISBN 0-8191-1490-1). U Pr of Amer.

Morella, Joseph, jt. auth. see Epstein, Edward.

Morelly. Le Prince: Les Delices Des Coeurs Ou Trait Des Qualites D'un Grand Roi et Systeme General D'un Sage Gouvernement. 390p. (Fr.). 1977. Repr. of 1751 ed. lib. bdg. 47.50x o.p. (ISBN 0-8287-0639-5). Clearwater Pub.

Morely, Jim & Foley, Doris, eds. Gold Cities: Grass Valley & Nevada City. 2nd ed. (Illus.). 96p. 1980. 9.95 (ISBN 0-8310-7136-2); pap. 3.50 (ISBN 0-8310-7135-4). Howell-North.

Moreno, Cesar F. & Schulman, Ivan A., eds. Latin America in Its Literature. Berg, Mary G., tr. from Span. LC 79-26626. (Latin America in Its Culture). Orig. Title: America Latina En Su Cultura. 350p. 1980. text ed. 44.50x (ISBN 0-8419-0530-4). Holmes & Meier.

Moreno, Francisco Jose. Between Faith & Reason: An Approach to Individual & Social Psychology. LC 76-56926. 1977. 10.00x (ISBN 0-8147-5416-3). NYU Pr.

Moreno, Harriet N., et al. Test of English As a Foreign Language: TOEFL. 2nd ed. LC 77-13180. 1978. lib. bdg. 12.00 (ISBN 0-668-04446-2); pap. text ed. 8.95 (ISBN 0-668-04450-0). Arco.

Moreno, Judith W., jt. auth. see Morgan, Arthur J.

Morentz, James W., jt. auth. see Chartrand, Robert L.

Morentz, James W., Jr., jt. ed. see Chartrand, Robert Lee.

Moret, P. R., et al, eds. Lactate: Physiologic, Methodologic & Pathologic Approach. (Illus.). 270p. 1980. pap. 24.00 (ISBN 0-387-09829-1). Springer-Verlag.

Moreton, N. Edwina. East Germany & the Warsaw Alliance: The Politics of Detente. (A Westview Replica Edition). 1978. lib. bdg. 24.50x (ISBN 0-89158-265-7). Westview.

Moretz, Judy, ed. see Glubetich, Dave.

Morevski, Abraham. Shylock & Shakespeare. LC 67-19382. 112p. 1967. 3.95 (ISBN 0-87529-056-6). Fireside Bks.

Morewedge, Parviz, ed. Islamic Philosophy & Mysticism. LC 80-14364. 1980. write for info. (ISBN 0-88206-302-2). Caravan Bks.

Morewood, William H. Building the Raritan. LC 77-89451. (Illus.). 82p. 1977. 17.00 (ISBN 0-914104-04-7); pap. 14.50 (ISBN 0-914104-03-9). Wildwood Pubns MI.

Morey, Adrian & Brooke, C. N. Gilbert Foliot & His Letters. (Cambridge Studies in Medieval Life & Thought). 1966. 44.95 (ISBN 0-521-05764-7). Cambridge U Pr.

Morey, G. B. & Hanson, Gilbert N., eds. Selected Studies of Archean Gneisses & Lower Proterozoic Rocks: Southern Canadian Shield. LC 80-67113. (Special Paper Ser.: No. 182). (Illus., Orig.). 1980. pap. write for info. (ISBN 0-8137-2182-2). Geol Soc.

Morey, G. B., jt. ed. see Sims, P. K.

Morey, George. Soviet Union. LC 75-44865. (Macdonald Countries). (Illus.). (gr. 6 up). 1976. PLB 7.95 (ISBN 0-382-06103-9, Pub. by Macdonald Ed). Silver.

--West Germany. LC 75-44866. (Macdonald Countries). (Illus.). (gr. 7 up). 1976. lib. bdg. 7.95 (ISBN 0-685-73288-6, Pub. by Macdonald Ed). Silver.

Morey, Joan. Let's Look at Houses & Homes. LC 78-85228. (Let's Look Ser). (Illus.). (gr. 4-8). 1969. 4.95g o.p. (ISBN 0-8075-4477-9). A Whitman.

Morey, Robert A. Reincarnation & Christianity. 64p. 1980. pap. 1.95 (ISBN 0-87123-493-9, 210493). Bethany Fell.

Morey, Sylvester M., ed. Can the Red Man Help the White Man. LC 80-83370. (Illus.). 130p. 1970. pap. 3.50 (ISBN 0-913098-35-3). Myrin Institute.

Morey, Sylvester M. & Gilliam, Olivia L., eds. Respect for Life: The Traditional Upbringing of American Indian Children. LC 80-83371. (Illus.). 202p. 1980. pap. text ed. 4.95 (ISBN 0-913098-34-5). Myrin Institute.

Morey, Walt. Canyon Winter. (gr. 4 up). 1972. PLB 10.95 (ISBN 0-525-27410-3). Dutton.

--Gentle Ben. 1976. pap. 1.75 (ISBN 0-380-00743-6, 48884, Camelot). Avon.

--The Lemon Meringue Dog. LC 80-171. 176p. (gr. 4-7). 1980. 9.95 (ISBN 0-525-33455-6). Dutton.

--Scrub Dog of Alaska. (gr. 4 up). 1971. PLB 8.95 (ISBN 0-525-38908-3). Dutton.

Morford, Mark P. & Lenardon, Robert J. Classical Mythology. 2nd ed. 1977. pap. 11.95x (ISBN 0-582-28004-4). Longman.

Morgagni, John B. The Seats & Causes of Disease Investigated by Anatomy, 3 vols. Alexander, Benjamin, tr. LC 60-13365. (History of Medicine Ser.). 1980. Repr. of 1960 ed. Set. monograph 85.00 (ISBN 0-87993-148-5). Futura Pub.

Morgan, Albert. Airborne for Pleasure: A Guide to Flying, Gliding, Ballooning & Parachuting. LC 74-20449. (Illus.). 128p. 1975. 9.95 o.p. (ISBN 0-7153-6477-4). David & Charles.

Morgan, Alfred. The Boy's Second Book of Radio & Electronics. LC 57-6078. (Illus.). 288p. (gr. 7-9). 1977. 6.95 (ISBN 0-684-13154-4). Scribner.

Morgan, Alice P. If You Ask Me...! LC 78-62901. (Illus.). 1978. 7.95 (ISBN 0-916624-23-4). TSU Pr.

Morgan, Alison. At Willy Tucker's Place. LC 76-41183. (Illus.). (gr. 4-12). 1976. 5.95 o.p. (ISBN 0-525-66515-3). Elsevier-Nelson.

Morgan, Alyssa. The Beckoning Heart. 1981. pap. 1.50 o.s.i. (ISBN 0-440-10749-0). Dell.

Morgan, Anne H., jt. auth. see Morgan, H. Morgan.

Morgan, Arlene. Starfire. large print ed. 1981. Repr. of 1974 ed. 9.95 (ISBN 0-89621-271-8). Thorndike Pr.

Morgan, Arthur J. & Moreno, Judith W. The Practice of Mental Health Nursing: A Community Approach. 1st ed. 225p. 1973. 8.50 o.p. (ISBN 0-397-54142-2); pap. 7.50 (ISBN 0-397-54148-1). Lippincott.

Morgan, Arthur N., jt. auth. see La Farge, Oliver.

Morgan, Augustus De see Smith, David E. & De Morgan, Augustus.

Morgan, B. Men & Discoveries in Chemistry. (Illus.). (gr. 9 up). 1962. 7.50 (ISBN 0-7195-0944-0). Transatlantic.

--Men & Discoveries in Electricity. (Illus.). (gr. 9 up). 6.95 (ISBN 0-7195-0943-2). Transatlantic.

Morgan, Barbara. Martha Graham: Sixteen Dances in Photographs. rev. ed. LC 80-81766. (Illus.). 168p. 1980. Repr. of 1941 ed. 35.00 (ISBN 0-87100-176-4). Morgan.

Morgan, Barbara, ed. Photomontage: Barbara Morgan. LC 80-81142. 64p. (Orig.). pap. 9.95 (ISBN 0-87100-171-3). Morgan.

Morgan, Bayard Q. A Critical Bibliography of German Literature in English Translation, 1481-1927. 2nd ed. LC 65-13549. 1965. Repr. of 1938 ed. 13.50 (ISBN 0-8108-0032-2). Scarecrow.

Morgan, Brian. Monetarists & Keynesians: Their Contributions to Monetary Theory. 1980. pap. text ed. 10.95x (ISBN 0-470-26885-9). Halsted Pr.

--Osteomalacia, Renal Osteodystrophy & Osteoporosis. (American Lectures in Living Chemistry Ser.). (Illus.). 440p. 1973. 27.75 (ISBN 0-398-02602-5). C C Thomas.

Morgan, Bryan. Men & Discoveries in Mathematics. 235p. 1980. 15.00x (ISBN 0-7195-2587-X, Pub. by Murray Pubs England). State Mutual Bk.

--Men & Discoveries in Mathematics. 1972. 10.95 (ISBN 0-7195-2587-X). Transatlantic.

Morgan, C., jt. auth. see Jackson, J.

Morgan, C. Lloyd. Introduction to Comparative Psychology. (Contributions to the History of Psychology D, II Comparative Psychology Ser.). 1978. Repr. of 1894 ed. 30.00 (ISBN 0-89093-171-2). U Pubns Amer.

Morgan, Charlie. How to Raise, Store & Sell Nighcrawlers. 1975. pap. 2.50 (ISBN 0-686-65538-9). Shields WI.

Morgan, Chris. Future Man. (Future Studies Series). (Illus.). 208p. 1979. 16.00 (ISBN 0-8290-0144-1). Irvington.

--Future Man: An Optimistic Look at What the Future Holds for Mankind. 208p. 1981. pap. 6.95 (ISBN 0-686-28897-1). Lewis Pub Co.

Morgan, D., jt. auth. see Cox, H.

Morgan, D. H. Social Theory & the Family. (International Library of Sociology). 320p. 1975. 22.50x (ISBN 0-7100-8179-0); pap. 10.00 (ISBN 0-7100-8180-4). Routledge & Kegan.

Morgan, D. J. Changes in British Aid Policy: 1951-1970, Vol. 4. 1980. text ed. cancelled (ISBN 0-391-01687-3). Humanities.

--Developing British Colonial Resources Nineteen Forty-Five to Nineteen Fifty-One, Vol. 2. 1980. text ed. cancelled (ISBN 0-391-01685-7). Humanities.

--Guidance Towards Self-Government in British Colonies: 1941-1971, Vol. 5. (Official History of Colonial Development Ser.). 1980. text ed. cancelled (ISBN 0-391-01688-1). Humanities.

--The Official History of Colonial Development, 5 vols. Incl. Vol. 1. The Origins of British Aid Policy 1924-1945. 253p (ISBN 0-391-01684-9); Vol. 2. Developing British Colonial Resources 1945-1951. 398p (ISBN 0-391-01685-7); Vol. 3. Reassessment of British Aid Policy 1951-1965. 334p (ISBN 0-391-01686-5); Vol. 4. Changes in British Aid Policy 1951-1970. 275p (ISBN 0-391-01687-3); Vol. 5. Guidance Towards Self-Government on British Colonies 1941-1971. 382p (ISBN 0-391-01688-1). 1980. text ed. 37.50x ea. Humanities.

--The Origins of British Aid Policy Nineteen Twenty-Four to Nineteen Forty-Five. (Official History of Colonial Development Ser.). 1980. text ed. cancelled (ISBN 0-391-01684-9). Humanities.

--A Reassessment of British Aid Policy: 1951-1970, Vol. 3. (Official History of Colonial Development Ser.). 1980. text ed. cancelled (ISBN 0-391-01686-5). Humanities.

Morgan, D. V., jt. auth. see Howes, M. J.

Morgan, D. V., jt. ed. see Howes, M. J.

Morgan, D. V., et al. Solid State Electronic Devices. (Wykeham Science Ser.: No. 20). 1972. 6.50x o.p. (ISBN 0-8448-1122-X). Crane Russak Co.

Morgan, D. W. Whips & Whipmaking: With a Practical Introduction to Braiding. LC 72-78240. (Illus.). 1972. pap. 6.00 (ISBN 0-87033-270-8). Cornell Maritime.

Morgan, Dale L. Jedediah Smith & the Opening of the West. LC 53-10550. (Illus.). 1964. pap. 4.50 (ISBN 0-8032-5138-6, BB 184, Bison). U of Nebr Pr.

Morgan, David. The Capitol Press Corps: Newsmen & the Governing of New York State. LC 77-84771. (Contributions in Political Science: No. 2). 1978. lib. bdg. 16.95 (ISBN 0-8371-9883-6, MCP/). Greenwood.

Morgan, David P., ed. I Like Trains: Great Reading from THE Magazine of Railroading. LC 80-84023. (Illus.). 104p. (Orig.). 1981. 6.50 (ISBN 0-89024-553-3). Kalmbach.

Morgan, David R. & Kirkpatrick, Samuel A. Urban Political Analysis. LC 74-156838. 1972. 15.95 (ISBN 0-02-922060-2). Free Pr.

Morgan, Don, jt. auth. see Lacy, Madison S.

Morgan, Donn F. Wisdom in the Old Testament Tradition. LC 80-84653. 17.50 (ISBN 0-8042-0188-9); pap. 8.95 (ISBN 0-8042-0189-7). John Knox.

Morgan, Douglas & Hall, William. Disease of the Temporomandibular Apparatus: A Multidisciplinary Approach. LC 77-3904. (Illus.). 1977. 49.50 (ISBN 0-8016-3487-3). Mosby.

Morgan, E. Philip, jt. ed. see Carter, Gwendolen.

Morgan, E. Philip, jt. ed. see Carter, Gwendolen M.

Morgan, E. S., tr. see Schelling, Friedrich.

Morgan, E. V. First Approach to Economics. pap. 26.00x (ISBN 0-392-07843-0, SpS). Soccer.

Morgan, E. Victor. Theory & Practice of Central Banking 1797-1913. LC 67-24754. Repr. of 1943 ed. 22.50x (ISBN 0-678-05189-5). Kelley.

Morgan, E. Victor & Harrington, Richard. Capital Markets in the E.E.C. LC 76-27854. 1977. lib. bdg. 47.50x (ISBN 0-89158-700-4). Westview.

Morgan, E. Victor & Thomas, W. A. Stock Exchange. 1970. 39.95 o.p. (ISBN 0-236-30952-8, Pub. by Paul Elek). Merrimack Bk Serv.

Morgan, Edmund M., jt. auth. see Joughin, Louis.

Morgan, Edmund S. American Slavery - American Freedom: The Ordeal of Colonial Virginia. 454p. 1975. 11.95 (ISBN 0-393-05554-X); pap. text ed. 5.95x (ISBN 0-393-09156-2). Norton.

--The Genius of George Washington. 1981. 12.95 (ISBN 0-393-01440-1). Norton.

Morgan, Edmund S., ed. Prologue to Revolution: Sources & Documents on the Stamp Act Crisis, 1764-1766. (Documentary Problems in Early American History Ser.). 164p. 1972. pap. text ed. 3.95x (ISBN 0-393-09424-3). Norton.

--Puritan Political Ideas 1558-1794. LC 65-22347. (Orig.). 1965. pap. 7.35 o.p. (ISBN 0-672-60042-0, AHS33). Bobbs.

Morgan, Edward. John Elias: Life & Letters. 1973. 11.95 (ISBN 0-85151-174-0). Banner of Truth.

Morgan, Edward P. Inequality in Classroom Learning: Schooling & Democratic Citizenship. LC 77-5577. (Special Studies). 1977. text ed. 26.50 (ISBN 0-275-24510-1). Praeger.

Morgan, Edwin. From Glasgow to Saturn. (Poetry Ser.). 1979. 6.95 o.s.i. (ISBN 0-85635-040-0, Pub. by Carcanet New Pr England). Persea Bks.

Morgan, Edwin, tr. see Mayakovsky, Vladimir.

Morgan, Ernest. Manual of Death Education & Simple Burial. 8th ed. 1977. pap. 2.00 o.p. (ISBN 0-914064-05-3). Celo Pr.

Morgan, Frederick. The Tarot of Cornelius Agrippa. (Illus.). 1978. pap. 4.50 (ISBN 0-915298-11-2). Sagarin Pr.

Morgan, G. Life in a Medieval Village. LC 74-12981. (Introduction to the History of Mankind Ser). 48p. (gr. 6-11). 1975. text ed. 3.95 (ISBN 0-521-20404-6). Cambridge U Pr.

Morgan, G. Campbell. Discipleship. (Morgan Library). 1973. pap. 3.45 (ISBN 0-8010-5920-8). Baker Bk.

--God's Perfect Will. (Morgan Library). 1978. pap. 3.95 (ISBN 0-8010-6055-9). Baker Bk.

--Hosea: The Heart & Holiness of God. (Morgan Library). 1974. pap. 3.95 (ISBN 0-8010-5952-6). Baker Bk.

--The Parable of the Father's Heart. (Morgan Library). 96p. 1981. pap. 2.95 (ISBN 0-8010-6118-0). Baker Bk.

--Parables & Metaphors of Our Lord. 1956. 10.95 (ISBN 0-8007-0245-X). Revell.

--Practice of Prayer. (Morgan Library). pap. 3.45 (ISBN 0-8010-5896-1). Baker Bk.

--Preaching. (Morgan Library). 1974. pap. 2.95 (ISBN 0-8010-5953-4). Baker Bk.

--The Spirit of God. (Morgan Library). 240p. 1981. pap. 3.95 (ISBN 0-8010-6119-9). Baker Bk.

--Studies of the Four Gospels, 4 vols. Incl. The Gospel According to Matthew. 320p (ISBN 0-8007-0122-4); The Gospel According to Mark. 352p (ISBN 0-8007-0121-6); The Gospel According to Luke. 288p (ISBN 0-8007-0120-8); The Gospel According to John. 336p (ISBN 0-8007-0119-4). Set. 34.95 (ISBN 0-8007-0373-1). Revell.

--Voice of the Devil. (Morgan Library). 1978. pap. 2.45 (ISBN 0-8010-6058-3). Baker Bk.

Morgan, G. Campbell, ed. Gospel According to John. 8.95 (ISBN 0-8007-0119-4). Revell.

--Gospel According to Luke. 8.95 (ISBN 0-8007-0120-8). Revell.

--Gospel According to Mark. 8.95 (ISBN 0-8007-0121-6). Revell.

--Gospel According to Matthew. 8.95 (ISBN 0-8007-0122-4). Revell.

Morgan, G. Christopher. The Rich & the Lonely. LC 80-27486. 256p. 1981. 10.95 (ISBN 0-8253-0043-6). Beaufort Bks NY.

Morgan, G. G., jt. ed. see Boim, L.

Morgan, Geoffrey, jt. auth. see Eron, Judy.

Morgan, George W. Human Predicament: Dissolution & Wholeness. LC 68-23791. 348p. 1971. Repr. of 1968 ed. 12.50 (ISBN 0-87057-111-7, Pub. by Brown U Pr). Univ Pr of New England.

Morgan, Gerald, ed. The Franklin's Tale from the Canterbury Tales. (London Medieval & Renaissance Ser.). 144p. 1981. pap. text ed. 11.75x (ISBN 0-8419-0653-X). Holmes & Meier.

Morgan, Glebe. The Rail Rogues. (Orig.). 1980. pap. 1.75 (ISBN 0-505-51490-7). Tower Bks.

Morgan, Gordon D. Introductory Sociology: Lectures, Readings & Exercises. LC 80-65606. 145p. 1981. perfect bdg. 10.50 (ISBN 0-86548-049-4). Century Twenty One.

Morgan, H. G. Death Wishes? The Understanding & Management of Deliberate Self-Harm. LC 79-1044. 1980. 36.00 (ISBN 0-471-27591-3, Pub. by Wiley-Interscience). Wiley.

Morgan, H. G., jt. auth. see Cooper, Brian.

Morgan, H. Morgan & Morgan, Anne H. Oklahoma: A History. (The States & the Nation Ser.). (Illus.). 1977. 12.95 (ISBN 0-393-05642-2). Norton.

Morgan, H. Wayne, ed. Victorian Culture in America, 1865-1914. LC 72-89722. (AHM Primary Sources in American History Ser.). 1973. pap. text ed. 4.95x (ISBN 0-88295-787-2). AHM Pub.

Morgan, Hal. Big Time. (Illus.). 80p. 1981. pap. 6.95 (ISBN 0-312-07852-8). St Martin.

Morgan, Harry T. Chinese Symbols & Superstitions. LC 74-167079. (Illus.). 192p. 1972. Repr. of 1942 ed. 22.00 (ISBN 0-8103-3069-5). Gale.

Morgan, Harvey. The Complete Money-Saving Book of Appliance Repairs. (Illus.). 1980. 14.95 (ISBN 0-684-15290-8, ScribT). Scribner.

Morgan, Helen. Mrs. Pinny & the Salty Sea Day. (Illus.). (ps-5). 1972. 7.95 (ISBN 0-571-09863-0, Pub. by Faber & Faber). Merrimack Bk Serv.

Morgan, Henry J. Bibliotheca Canadensis: A Bio-Bibliographical Manual of Canadian Literature. LC 68-27177. 1968. Repr. of 1867 ed. 30.00 (ISBN 0-8103-3151-9). Gale.

Morgan, Howard W. America's Road to Empire: The War with Spain & Overseas Expansion. LC 64-8714. (America in Crisis Ser.). 124p. 1965. pap. text ed. 7.95 (ISBN 0-471-61520-X). Wiley.

Morgan, J. B., jt. auth. see Snell, K. S.

Morgan, J. Q., tr. see Von Goethe, Johann W.

Morgan, James. Our Presidents. 2nd, enl. ed. (Illus.). (gr. 9 up). 1958. 6.50 o.s.i. (ISBN 0-02-586950-7); 1969 updated ed 8.95 o.s.i. (ISBN 0-02-586960-4). Macmillan.

Morgan, James J., jt. auth. see Stumm, Werner.

Morgan, James N., jt. auth. see Lansing, John B.

Morgan, Jane. Louis. 1979. pap. 1.95 o.p. (ISBN 0-425-04151-4). Berkley Pub.

Morgan, Jane, et al. Nicknames: Their Origins & Social Consequences. (Social Worlds of Childhood Ser.). 1979. 16.00x (ISBN 0-7100-0139-8). Routledge & Kegan.

Morgan, Janet, ed. The Backbench Diaries of Richard Crossman. 1072p. 1981. text ed. 35.00 (ISBN 0-8419-0686-6). Holmes & Meier.

Morgan, Janet P. The House of Lords & the Labour Government, 1964-1970. (Illus.). 270p. 1975. text ed. 37.50x (ISBN 0-19-827191-3). Oxford U Pr.

Morgan, Jean, jt. ed. see Wasserman, Paul.

Morgan, Jefferson, jt. auth. see Baugh, Jack W.

Morgan, Jefferson, jt. auth. see Lunde, Donald T.

Morgan, Jimmy. How the World Looks to a Georgian. 1978. 5.50 o.p. (ISBN 0-682-49062-8). Exposition.

Morgan, Joan, ed. see Conference on Recombinant DNA, Committee on Genetic Experimentation (COGENE) & the Royal Society of London, Wye College, Kent, UK, April, 1979.

Morgan, Joe W. Cataracts & Their Treatment. 144p. 1981. 6.95 (ISBN 0-8059-2775-1). Dorrance.

Morgan, John. Golf. (Sports Library). (Illus.). 1979. 12.95 (ISBN 0-8069-9116-X); pap. 6.95 (ISBN 0-8069-9118-6). Sterling.

--The Life & Adventures of William Buckley. 1979. Repr. of 1852 ed. text ed. 19.50x (ISBN 0-904573-12-5). Humanities.

Morgan, John H. Gilbert Stuart & His Pupils. LC 72-96440. (Library of American Art Ser). 1969. Repr. of 1939 ed. lib. bdg. 18.50 (ISBN 0-306-71827-8). Da Capo.

--In Search of Meaning: From Freud to Teilhard De Chardin (an Analysis of the Classic Statements) 1977. 7.50 (ISBN 0-8191-0251-2). U Pr of Amer.

Morgan, John H., ed. Understanding Religion & Culture: Anthropological & Theological Perspectives. LC 79-66684. 1979. pap. text ed. 9.50 (ISBN 0-8191-0848-0). U Pr of Amer.

Morgan, John S. British Independent Light Railways. LC 79-56060. 96p. 1980. 17.95 (ISBN 0-7153-7933-X). David & Charles.

Morgan, Jonnie. History of Wichita Falls. 9.95 (ISBN 0-685-48810-1). Nortex Pr.

Morgan, Joseph. Introduction to University Physics, 2 vols. LC 77-12757. 1978. Repr. of 1969 ed. Set. 30.00 (ISBN 0-88275-617-6); Vol. 1 560p. lib. bdg. 17.50 (ISBN 0-88275-617-6); Vol. 2 512p. lib. bdg. 17.00 (ISBN 0-88275-874-8). Krieger.
Morgan, K., jt. auth. see Essery, R. J.
Morgan, K., jt. auth. see Lewis, R. W.
Morgan, K., jt. ed. see Taylor, C.
Morgan, Kathryn L. Children of Strangers: The Stories of a Black Family. (Illus.). 160p. 1980. 9.95 (ISBN 0-87722-203-7). Temple U Pr.
Morgan, Keith, jt. auth. see Lewis, Arnold.
Morgan, Keith, jt. ed. see Lewis, Arnold.
Morgan, Kenneth. Consensus & Disunity: The Lloyd George Coalition Government, 1918 to 1922. 448p. 1979. text ed. 45.00x (ISBN 0-19-822497-4). Oxford U Pr.
Morgan, Kenneth O. Rebirth of a Nation: Wales 1880-1980. (History of Wales Ser.: Vol. VI). 1981. 25.00 (ISBN 0-19-821736-6). Oxford U Pr.
Morgan, Kenneth W., ed. The Religion of the Hindus: Interpreted by Hindus. 1953. 21.50 (ISBN 0-8260-6260-1). Wiley.
Morgan, L. H. League of the Iroquois. (Illus.). 11.50 (ISBN 0-8446-2612-0). Peter Smith.
Morgan, Lael. Tatting: A New Look at the Old Art of Making Lace. LC 76-2808. 1977. pap. text ed. 5.50 o.p. (ISBN 0-385-07707-6). Doubleday.
Morgan, Lane & Morgan, Murray C. Seattle: A Pictorial History. (Illus.). 205p. 1981. pap. price not set (ISBN 0-89865-091-7). Donning Co.
Morgan, Lane, ed. The Northwest Experience Two. 192p. 1981. lib. bdg. 10.00 (ISBN 0-686-62337-1); pap. 4.95 (ISBN 0-686-62338-X). Madrona Pubs.
Morgan, Len. The Douglas DC-3. LC 64-7851. 1980. pap. 4.95 (ISBN 0-8168-5650-8). Aero.
--The P-Fifty-One Mustang. LC 63-14945. (Famous Aircraft Ser.). (Illus.). 1979. pap. 4.95 (ISBN 0-8168-5647-8). Aero.
--P-Forty Seven Thunderbolt. LC 63-22711. (Famous Aircraft Ser). (Illus.). 1963. pap. 4.95 (ISBN 0-668-01297-8). Arco.
--The P-Forty-Seven Thunderbolt. LC 63-22711. (Illus.). 1979. pap. 4.95 (ISBN 0-8168-5648-6). Aero.
Morgan, Len & Morgan, Terry. Seven-Twenty-Seven Scrapbook. LC 78-72164. 1978. 12.00 (ISBN 0-8168-8344-0); pap. 7.95 (ISBN 0-8168-8349-1). Aero.
Morgan, Lewis H. see Seaver, James E.
Morgan Library Curators, compiled by. The Pierpont Morgan Library: A Review of Acquisitions, 1949-1968. (Illus.). 1969. 22.50 (ISBN 0-87598-022-8); pap. 10.00 (ISBN 0-87598-005-8). Pierpont Morgan.
Morgan, Lorraine L., et al. Beyond the Open Classroom: Toward Informal Education. LC 80-69235. 140p. 1981. perfect bdg. 9.50 (ISBN 0-86548-050-8). Century Twenty One.
Morgan, Lyndon, ed. see National Computing Centre.
Morgan, M. R. The Chronicle of Ernoul & the Continuations of William of Tyre. (Oxford Historical Monographs). 214p. 1974. 22.50x (ISBN 0-19-821851-6). Oxford U Pr.
Morgan, Majorie. English Lands of the Abbey of Bec. 1946. 8.00x o.p. (ISBN 0-19-822302-1). Oxford U Pr.
Morgan, Malcolm. Treasure Island. pap. text ed. 2.50x o.p. (ISBN 0-435-21001-7). Heinemann Ed.
Morgan, Marabel. Total Joy. 1977. pap. 2.25 (ISBN 0-8007-8326-3, Spire). Revell.
--The Total Woman. 192p. 1973. 8.95 (ISBN 0-8007-0608-0). Revell.
Morgan, Margaret K. & Irby, David M. Evaluating Clinical Competence in the Health Profession. LC 77-26935. (Illus.). 1978. text ed. 18.95 (ISBN 0-8016-3493-8). Mosby.
Morgan, Margaret K., jt. auth. see Ford, Charles W.
Morgan, Margery M., ed. see Shaw, George B.
Morgan, Mary H. How to Dress an Old-Fashioned Doll. LC 72-93612. Orig. Title: How to Dress a Doll. (Illus.). 96p. (gr. 5-8). 1973. pap. 1.75 (ISBN 0-486-22912-2). Dover.
Morgan, Michael. Lenin. LC 74-158177. 226p. 1971. 9.50x o.p. (ISBN 0-8214-0094-0). Ohio U Pr.
--Lenin. LC 74-158177. 1973. pap. 2.95 o.s.i. (ISBN 0-02-922040-8). Free Pr.
--Lenin. 1972. 12.95 (ISBN 0-8214-0094-0). Lib Soc Sci.
Morgan, Michael & Briggs, D., eds. Historical Sources in Geography. (Sources & Methods in Geography Ser.). 1979. pap. 6.95 (ISBN 0-408-10609-3). Butterworths.
Morgan, Michael, et al, eds. see Shaw, Stephen M.
Morgan, Michael J. Molyneux's Question: Vision, Touch, & the Philosophy of Perception. LC 76-54066. 1977. 27.50 (ISBN 0-521-21558-7). Cambridge U Pr.
Morgan, Michaela. Zanzara. 1978. pap. 2.25 o.p. (ISBN 0-523-40388-7, Dist. by Independent News Co.). Pinnacle Bks.
Morgan, Morris H., tr. see Vitruvius.
Morgan, Murray. The Last Wilderness. LC 76-41. 290p. 1976. pap. 5.95 (ISBN 0-295-95319-5). U of Wash Pr.
--One Man's Gold Rush: A Klondike Album. rev. ed. LC 67-13109. (Illus.). 224p. 1976. Repr. of 1967 ed. pap. 12.50 (ISBN 0-295-95187-7). U of Wash Pr.
--Puget's Sound: A Narrative of Early Tacoma & the Southern Sound. LC 79-4844. (Illus.). 370p. 1979. 14.95 (ISBN 0-295-95680-1). U of Wash Pr.
Morgan, Murray C., jt. auth. see Morgan, Lane.
Morgan, Patricia. Delinquent Fantasies. LC 78-309292. 1979. 18.50 (ISBN 0-85117-116-8). Transatlantic.
Morgan, Patrick M. Theories & Approaches to International Politics. 3rd ed. 302p. 1981. 24.95 (ISBN 0-87855-350-9); text ed. 24.95 (ISBN 0-686-68062-6); pap. 9.95 (ISBN 0-87855-791-1); pap. text ed. 9.95 (ISBN 0-686-68063-4). Transaction Bks.
Morgan, Paula. Say Yes! 144p. pap. 2.25 (ISBN 0-523-41408-0). Pinnacle Bks.
Morgan, Peter. Designs & Pattern Cutting for Children's Clothes. 1977. 24.00 (ISBN 0-7134-2712-4, Pub. by Batsford England). David & Charles.
--Making Hats. 1978. 11.95 (ISBN 0-7134-1078-7, Pub. by Batsford England). David & Charles.
Morgan, Philip, ed. Berkshire. (Domesday Bk.: Vol. 5). (Illus.). 160p. 1979. 15.00x (ISBN 0-8476-3143-5). Rowman.
Morgan, R., jt. auth. see Alden, J.
Morgan, R. E., jt. ed. see Potholm, C. P.
Morgan, R. P. C. Soil Erosion. (Topics in Applied Geography). (Illus.). 1979. pap. text ed. 11.50x (ISBN 0-582-48692-0). Longman.
Morgan, Richard, ed. see Patchen, Kenneth.
Morgan, Richard E. Domestic Intelligence: Monitoring Dissent in America. LC 80-13254. 204p. 1980. text ed. 13.95x (ISBN 0-292-76463-4); pap. 6.95x (ISBN 0-292-71529-3). U of Tex Pr.
--The Politics of Religious Conflict: Church & State in America. 2nd ed. LC 79-48094. 118p. 1980. text ed. 15.50 (ISBN 0-8191-1007-8); pap. text ed. 7.25 (ISBN 0-8191-1008-6). U Pr of Amer.
--The Supreme Court & Religion. LC 72-80077. 1972. 12.95 (ISBN 0-02-921970-1). Free Pr.
--The Supreme Court & Religion. LC 72-80077. 1974. pap. text ed. 3.95 (ISBN 0-02-922070-X). Free Pr.
Morgan, Richard E., et al. American Politics: Directions of Change, Dynamics of Choice. LC 78-18644. (Political Science Ser.). (Illus.). 1979. text ed. 15.95 (ISBN 0-201-01434-3); inst. manual avail. 4.00. A-W.
Morgan, Robert P. & Iceman, Larry J. Renewable Resource Utilization for Development. (PPS on International Development Ser.). 325p. 1981. 35.00 (ISBN 0-08-026338-0). Pergamon.
Morgan, Robert P., et al. Science & Technology for Development: The Role of U. S. Universities. (Policy Studies). (Illus.). 1979. 47.00 (ISBN 0-08-025107-2). Pergamon.
Morgan, Robert W., jt. auth. see Kenaga, E. E.
Morgan, Robin, ed. Going Too Far: The Personal Chronicle of a Feminist. 348p. Date not set. pap. 4.95 (ISBN 0-394-72612-X, Vin). Random.
Morgan, Roger P. High Politics, Low Politics: Toward a Foreign Policy for Western Europe. LC 73-86712. (The Washington Papers: No. 11). 1973. 3.50x (ISBN 0-8039-0284-0). Sage.
Morgan, Roseann. The Writer's Work Workbook. 248p. 1981. pap. text ed. 6.95 (ISBN 0-13-969840-X). P-H.
Morgan, S. W. Zinc & Its Alloys. (Illus.). 224p. 1977. pap. 13.95x (ISBN 0-7121-0945-5, Pub. by Macdonald & Evans England). Intl Ideas.
Morgan, Sam B. The Unreachable Child: An Introduction to Early Childhood Autism. 208p. 1981. text ed. 15.95 (ISBN 0-87870-202-4); pap. text ed. 7.95 (ISBN 0-87870-201-6). Memphis St Univ.
Morgan, Speer. Belle Starr. 1980. pap. write for info. (ISBN 0-671-83227-1). PB.
Morgan, Sydney O. Missionary: An Indian Tale, 3 vols. in 1. LC 80-20308. 1980. Repr. of 1811 ed. 35.00x (ISBN 0-8201-1358-1). Schol Facsimilies.
Morgan, T. L. Bomber Aircraft of the United States. LC 66-28699. (Illus., Orig.). 1967. lib. bdg. 5.95 o.p. (ISBN 0-668-01596-9); pap. 2.95 (ISBN 0-668-01597-7). Arco.
Morgan, Ted. Maugham. 1981. pap. 9.95 (ISBN 0-671-42811-X, Touchstone). S&S.
--Rowing Toward Eden. 256p. 1981. 10.95 (ISBN 0-395-29714-1). HM.
Morgan, Terry, jt. auth. see Morgan, Len.
Morgan, Theodore & Spoelstra, Nyle, eds. Economic Interdependence in Southeast Asia. LC 68-9021. 1969. 27.50x (ISBN 0-299-05150-1). U of Wis Pr.
Morgan, Thomas. The Moral Philosopher in a Dialogue Between Philalethes, a Christian Deist, & Theophanes, a Christian Jew. LC 75-11239. (British Philosophers & Theologians of the 17th & 18th Centuries: Vol. 39). 1977. Repr. of 1737 ed. lib. bdg. 42.00 (ISBN 0-8240-1791-9). Garland Pub.
Morgan, Thomas H. Theory of the Gene. 1964. pap. 18.50 o.s.i. (ISBN 0-02-849280-3). Hafner.
Morgan, W. B. Agriculture in the Third World: A Spatial Analysis. LC 77-24064. (Advanced Economic Geopraphies Ser.). (Illus.). 1978. lib. bdg. 32.50x (ISBN 0-89158-820-5). Westview.
Morgan, W. B. & Munton, R. J. Agricultural Geography. 165p. 1972. 13.95 (ISBN 0-312-01470-8). St Martin.
Morgan, W. K., et al. Pulmonary Diseases. 2nd ed. (Medical Examination Review Book: Vol. 24). 1977. spiral bdg. 16.50 (ISBN 0-87488-143-9). Med Exam.
Morgan, W. L., Jr., jt. auth. see Engel, George L.
Morgan, Willard D. & Lester, Henry M. Graphic Graflex Photography: The Master Book for the Larger Camera. facsimile ed. LC 70-167717. (Illus.). 424p. 1971. text ed. 16.00 o.p. (ISBN 0-87100-018-0). Morgan.
Morgan, William. Portals & Photographs. 1981. pap. 5.95 (ISBN 0-87233-057-5). Bauhan.
Morgan, William, jt. auth. see Young, Robert W.
Morgan, William J., Jr. Hospitality Personnel Management. LC 78-22031. 1979. text ed. 14.95 (ISBN 0-8436-2138-9). CBI Pub.
--Supervision & Management of Quantity Food Preparation - Principles & Procedures. LC 73-7239. 1974. 24.00x (ISBN 0-8211-1225-2); text ed. 19.50x (ISBN 0-685-72314-3). McCutchan.
--Supervision & Management of Quantity Preparation. 2nd, rev ed. LC 80-83876. (Illus.). 1981. price not set (ISBN 0-8211-1254-6); text ed. price not set. McCutchan.
Morgan, Wm. T. English Political Parties & Leaders in the Reign of Queen Anne, 1702-1710. (Yale Historical Studies, Miscellany: No. VII). 1920. 47.50x (ISBN 0-685-69845-9). Elliots Bks.
Morgane & Panksepp. Handbook of the Hypothalmus, Vol. 3, Pt. A. 472p. 1980. 145.00 (ISBN 0-8247-6904-X). Dekker.
--Physiology of the Hypothalmus, Vol. 2. 672p. 1980. 145.00 (ISBN 0-8247-6904-X). Dekker.
Morgane, P. & Panksepp, J. Handbook of the Hypothalmus, Vol. 1. 1979. 95.00 (ISBN 0-8247-6834-5). Dekker.
Morgane, Panksepp. Behavioral Studies of the Hypothalmus. 480p. Date not set. 93.50. Dekker.
Morgans, W. M. Outlines of Paint Technology, Vol. 1. 1981. 75.00x (ISBN 0-686-68842-2, Pub. by Griffin England). State Mutual Bk.
Morgan-Witts, Max, jt. auth. see Thomas, Gordon.
Morgenbesser, Mel & Nehls, Nadine. Joint Custody: An Alternative for Divorcing Families. LC 80-22182. (Illus.). 176p. 1981. 13.95 (ISBN 0-88229-620-5). Nelson-Hall.
Morgenbesser, Sidney, ed. Dewey & His Critics. LC 77-94488. 1977. lib. bdg. 30.00 (ISBN 0-931206-00-6); pap. text ed. 12.50 (ISBN 0-931206-01-4). Hackett Pub.
Morgenroth, Barbara. Demons at My Door. LC 80-12053. 168p. (gr. 5-10). 1980. 8.95 (ISBN 0-689-30781-0). Atheneum.
--Ride a Proud Horse. LC 77-21111. (gr. 6-9). 1978. 8.95 (ISBN 0-689-30624-5). Atheneum.
--Will the Real Renie Lake Please Stand up. LC 80-21904. 168p. (gr. 6 up). 1981. PLB 9.95 (ISBN 0-689-30820-5). Atheneum.
Morgenstern, Carol, jt. auth. see Hines, Henry.
Morgenstern, Christian. Christian Morgenstern's Galgenlieder (Gallows Songs) bilingual ed. Knight, Max, tr. & intro. by. (Illus.). (gr. 9 up). 1963. 12.95x (ISBN 0-520-00883-9, CAL 101); pap. 4.95 (ISBN 0-520-00884-7). U of Cal Pr.
--The Rabbit Book. Barthold, Helga & Theobald, John, trs. from Ger. (Illus.). 1980. text ed. 8.95 (ISBN 0-914676-43-1); pap. 5.95 (ISBN 0-914676-38-5). Green Tiger.
Morgenstern, Jay. The Dandelion. 1980. 6.95 o.p. (ISBN 0-934256-00-4). Caroline Hse.
Morgenstern, Murry & Michal-Smith, Harold. Psychology in the Vocational Rehabilitation of the Mentally Retarded. 100p. 1973. text ed. 8.75 (ISBN 0-398-02696-3). C C Thomas.
Morgenstern, Oskar. National Income Statistics: A Critique of Macroeconomic Aggregation. (Cato Papers Ser.: No.5). 64p. 1979. pap. 2.00 (ISBN 0-932790-04-6). Cato Inst.
Morgenstern, Oskar & Thompson, G. L. Mathematical Theory of Expanding & Contracting Economies. LC 75-18399. 288p. 1976. 22.95 (ISBN 0-669-00089-2). Lexington Bks.
Morgenstern, Steve. Metric Puzzles, Tricks & Games. (gr. 3 up). 1978. 6.95 (ISBN 0-8069-4588-5); PLB 6.69 (ISBN 0-8069-4589-3). Sterling.
Morgenstern, William W. How the Secrets of Economic Psychology May Double, Triple & Even Quadruple the Profits of Your Business. (The International Council for Excellence in Management Library). (Illus.). 115p. 1980. 28.95 (ISBN 0-89266-248-4). Am Classical Coll Pr.
Morgenthaler, G. W. & Hollstein, M., eds. Space Shuttle & Spacelab Utilization: Near-Term & Long-Term Benefits for Mankind, Pt. II. LC 57-43769. (Advances in the Astronautical Sciences: Vol. 37, Pt. II). 1978. lib. bdg. 45.00 (ISBN 0-87703-097-9). Univelt Inc.
Morgenthaler, George W. & Morra, Robert, eds. Planning Challenges of the Seventies in Space. LC 57-43769. (Advances in the Astronautical Sciences Ser.: Vol. 26). (Illus.). 1970. lib. bdg. 35.00 (ISBN 0-87703-053-7); microfiche suppl. 15.00 (ISBN 0-87703-130-4). Am Astronaut.
Morgenthau, Hans J. Human Rights & Foreign Policy. LC 79-53084. (First Distinguished CRIA Lecture on Morality & Foreign Policy Ser.). 1979. pap. 4.00 (ISBN 0-87641-216-9). Coun Rel & Intl.
--In Defence of the National Interest. rev. ed. 354p. 1980. cancelled (ISBN 0-935764-04-6). Ark Hse NY.
Morgenthau, Hans J., ed. Germany & the Future of Europe. (Midway Reprint Ser.). (Illus.). viii, 180p. 1975. pap. text ed. 7.00x o.s.i. (ISBN 0-226-53831-1). U of Chicago Pr.
--The Purpose of American Politics. rev. 2nd ed. 384p. cancelled (ISBN 0-935764-05-4). Ark Hse NY.
Morgenthau, Ruth S. Political Parties in French-Speaking West Africa. (Oxford Studies in African Affairs Ser). 1964. 37.50x (ISBN 0-19-821624-6). Oxford U Pr.
Mori, Allen A. & Masters, Lowell F. Teaching the Severely Mentally Retarded: Adaptive Skills Training. LC 79-27489. 407p. 1980. text ed. 26.50 (ISBN 0-89443-173-0). Aspen Systems.
Mori, Allen A. & Olive, Jane E. Handbook of Preschool Special Education: Programming, Curriculum, Training. LC 80-14199. 528p. 1980. 34.95 (ISBN 0-89443-276-1). Aspen Systems.
Mori, Hisashi. Japanese Portrait Sculpture. Ishibashi, W. Chie, tr. LC 76-9353. (Japanese Arts Library: Vol. 2). 1977. 16.95 (ISBN 0-87011-286-4). Kodansha.
Mori, K., et al. Synthetic Chemistry of Insect Phermones & Juvenile Hormones. (Recent Developments in the Chemistry of Natural Carbon Compounds: Vol. 9). (Illus.). 420p. 1979. 40.00x (ISBN 963-05-1632-2). Intl Pubns Serv.
Mori, Ogai. Vita Sexualis. Ninomiya, Kazuji & Goldstein, Sanford, trs. LC 72-79020. 1972. pap. 4.95 (ISBN 0-8048-1048-6). C E Tuttle.
Mori, Scott A., jt. auth. see Prance, Ghillean T.
Moriarty, Charles P. Adopt Your Way to Inheritance & Gift Tax Savings. LC 80-23202. 1980. 12.95 (ISBN 0-916076-31-8). Writing.
Moriarty, David M. The Loss of Loved Ones. 288p. 1981. 18.50 (ISBN 0-87527-198-7). Green.
Moriarty, Larry. The Traveling Salesman: How to Find Answers for Lots of Things for Lots of People Especially Salesman. LC 81-50012. (Illus.). 200p. 1981. 14.95 (ISBN 0-939102-13-7). MLM Pubs.
Moriarty, Tim & Bereswell, Joe. The Dynamic Islanders: From Cellar to Stanley Cup. (Illus.). 144p. 1981. pap. 9.95 (ISBN 0-385-17489-6). Doubleday.
Morice, Anne. Death of a Wedding Guest. LC 75-26187. 1976. 7.95 o.p. (ISBN 0-312-18830-7). St Martin.
--The Men in Her Death. 224p. 1981. 9.95 (ISBN 0-312-52939-2). St Martin.
Morice, Dave. Dot Town. (Illus.). 36p. (Orig.). (gr. 2-4). 1981. pap. 5.00 (ISBN 0-915124-38-6). Toothpaste.
--A Visit from St. Alphabet. (Illus.). 20p. (Orig.). (gr. 3 up). 1980. pap. 5.00 (ISBN 0-915124-47-5). Toothpaste.
Morice, G. P., ed. David Hume: Bicentenary Papers. LC 77-81915. 1978. 12.50 (ISBN 0-292-71515-3). U of Tex Pr.
Morick, Harold. Challenges to Empiricism. LC 72-806552. 329p. 18.50 (ISBN 0-915144-89-1); pap. text ed. 7.95 (ISBN 0-915144-90-5). Hackett Pub.
--Challenges to Empiricism. 320p. 1972. pap. 10.95x o.p. (ISBN 0-534-00187-4). Wadsworth Pub.
--Introduction to the Philosophy of Mind: Readings from Descartes to Strawson. 1970. 12.95x o.p. (ISBN 0-673-05973-1); pap. 9.95x o.p. (ISBN 0-673-05193-5). Scott F.
Morift, H. Mason & Ratzer, Erick R. Surgical Oncology Case Studies. 1977. 18.50 (ISBN 0-87488-063-7). Med Exam.

Morike, Eduard. Poems. Thomas, Lionel, ed. (Blackwell's German Text Ser.). 1970. pap. 9.95x (ISBN 0-631-01660-0, Pub. by Basil Blackwell). Biblio Dist.

Morike, K, jt. auth. see Schmidt, H.

Morillo, Marvin, ed. see Shirley, James.

Morimando, Patricia. The Neptune Effect. 1979. pap. 3.95 (ISBN 0-87728-487-3). Weiser.

Morin, Claude. Braided Cord Animals You Can Make. LC 76-19816. (Easy Craft Ser.). (Illus.). (gr. 4 up). 1976. 5.95 o.p. (ISBN 0-8069-5400-0); PLB 5.89 o.p. (ISBN 0-8069-5401-9). Sterling.

Morin, Joseph F., jt. auth. see Morris, Paul C.

Morin, Thomas D. Mariano Picon Salas. (World Authors Ser.: No. 545). 1979. lib. bdg. 14.50 (ISBN 0-8057-6388-0). Twayne.

Morine, L. A., ed. Guidance & Control 1980. LC 57-43769. (Advances in the Astronautical Sciences: Vol. 42). (Illus.). 738p. 1980. lib. bdg. 60.00x (ISBN 0-87703-137-1); pap. 45.00x (ISBN 0-87703-138-X). Univelt Inc.

Morini, Simona. Body Sculpture: Plastic Surgery from Head to Toe. 1972. 10.00 o.s.i. (ISBN 0-440-00740-2). Delacorte.

--Encyclopedia of Health & Beauty. 1977. pap. 2.50 o.p. (ISBN 0-445-04095-5). Popular Lib.

Moris, Jon R. Managing Induced Rural Development. 1981. pap. 8.00 (ISBN 0-89249-033-0). Intl Development.

Morisawa, Marie. Geomorphology Laboratory Manual with Report Forms. LC 76-13456. 1976. pap. text ed. 13.95x (ISBN 0-471-01847-3). Wiley.

Morishima, M. The Economic Theory of Modern Society. Anthony, D. W., tr. from Japanese. LC 75-39375. (Illus.). 332p. 1976. 49.50 (ISBN 0-521-21088-7); pap. 15.95x (ISBN 0-521-29168-2). Cambridge U Pr.

--Marx's Economics: A Dual Theory of Value & Growth. LC 72-83591. (Illus.). 224p. 1973. 32.95 (ISBN 0-521-08747-3); pap. 14.95x (ISBN 0-521-29303-0). Cambridge U Pr.

--Walras's Economics. LC 76-40833. 1977. 29.95 (ISBN 0-521-21487-4). Cambridge U Pr.

Morishima, M., et al. The Working of Econometric Models. LC 79-184901. (Illus.). 300p. 1972. 44.50 (ISBN 0-521-08502-0). Cambridge U Pr.

Morishima, Michio. Equilibrium, Stability, & Growth: A Multi-Sectoral Analysis. 1964. 27.00x (ISBN 0-19-828145-5). Oxford U Pr.

--Theory of Demand: Real & Monetary. (Illus.). 326p. 1973. 29.95x (ISBN 0-19-828180-3). Oxford U Pr.

--Theory of Economic Growth. 1969. 29.95x (ISBN 0-19-828164-1). Oxford U Pr.

Morison, Bradley L. Sunlight on Your Doorstep. 3.95 (ISBN 0-87018-044-4); pap. 1.95 (ISBN 0-87018-073-8). Ross.

Morison, Elizabeth F., jt. auth. see Morison, Elting E.

Morison, Elting E. & Morison, Elizabeth F. New Hampshire. (States & the Nation Ser). (Illus.). 1976. 12.95 (ISBN 0-393-05583-3, Co-Pub by AASLH). Norton.

Morison, Frank. Quien Movio la Piedra? Ward, Rhode, tr. from Eng. LC 77-11752. 206p. (Orig., Span.). 1977. pap. 3.95 (ISBN 0-89922-100-9). Edit Caribe.

Morison, Margaret P., jt. auth. see White, John.

Morison, Robert S. Scientist. 1964. 4.95 o.s.i. (ISBN 0-02-586980-9). Macmillan.

Morison, Samuel E. The Oxford History of the American People. 1965. text ed. 18.95x (ISBN 0-19-500997-5). Oxford U Pr.

--Oxford History of the American People, Vol. 1. pap. 2.25 ea. (Ment). Vol. 1 (ISBN 0-451-61653-7, ME1653). Vol. 2 (ME1890). Vol. 3 (ISBN 0-451-61655-3, ME1891). NAL.

Morison, Stanley. John Bell Seventeen Forty-Five to Eighteen Thirty-One, Bookseller, Printer, Publisher, Typefounder, Journalist, &C. LC 78-74416. (Nineteenth-Century Book Arts & Printing History Ser.: Vol. 13). 245p. 1980. lib. bdg. 44.00 (ISBN 0-8240-3887-8). Garland Pub.

--John Fell, the University Press & the Fell Types. LC 78-74401. (Nineteenth-Century Book Arts & Printing History Ser.: Vol. 14). 315p. 1980. lib. bdg. 83.00 (ISBN 0-8240-3888-6). Garland Pub.

--Tally of Types. Crutchley, B., ed. LC 72-90486. 144p. 1973. 49.50 (ISBN 0-521-20043-1); pap. 14.95 (ISBN 0-521-09786-X). Cambridge U Pr.

Morisson, A. Management of Sensorineural Deafness. 1975. 48.95 (ISBN 0-407-00024-0). Butterworths.

Moritsch, Andreas, jt. auth. see Barker, Thomas M.

Moritz, C., jt. auth. see Cohn, Frederick.

Moritz, Karl P. ABC-Buch Kinderlogik, 2 vols. Guenther, Horst, ed. (Ger.). Repr. of 1793 ed. text ed. 50.70 (ISBN 3-458-04938-X, Pub. by Insel Verlag Germany). Suhrkamp.

Moritz, Theresa A., jt. auth. see Allen, Judson B.

Morize, Andre. Problems & Methods of Literary History. LC 66-13475. 1922. 12.00x (ISBN 0-8196-0168-3). Biblo.

Morizot, Carol A. Child of Scorn: A Mind Play in Three Parts & Numerous Voices. LC 78-52256. (Orig.). 1978. pap. 3.95 o.p. (ISBN 0-930138-02-3). Harold Hse.

--Just This Side of Madness: Creativity & the Drive to Create. LC 78-55258. (Illus.). 1978. pap. 6.95 o.p. (ISBN 0-930138-04-X). Harold Hse.

--Survivors & Other Poems. LC 77-80488. (Illus., Orig.). 1977. pap. 3.95 o.p. (ISBN 0-930138-00-7). Harold Hse.

Morizot, Donald C., jt. auth. see Chakravarti, Aravinda.

Mork, Gordon R. Modern Western Civilization: A Concise History. 1976. pap. text ed. 8.50 o.p. (ISBN 0-256-01804-9). Dorsey.

--Modern Western Civilization: A Concise History. LC 80-6198. 253p. (Orig.). 1981. lib. bdg. 19.25 (ISBN 0-8191-1434-0); pap. text ed. 10.00 (ISBN 0-8191-1435-9). U Pr of Amer.

Mork, Knut A., ed. Energy Prices, Inflation, & Economic Activity. 1980. reference 22.50 (ISBN 0-88410-691-8). Ballinger Pub.

Morlan, Don M. & Tuttle, Goerge E., Jr. Specific Situations in Effective Oral Communication. (gr. 12). 1977. pap. 9.50 (ISBN 0-672-61410-3); tchr's manual 2.50 (ISBN 0-672-61411-1). Bobbs.

Morlan, Robert L. American Government: Policy & Process. 3rd ed. LC 78-69574. (Illus.). 1979. pap. text ed. 12.50 (ISBN 0-395-26631-9); inst. manual 0.70 (ISBN 0-395-26632-7). HM.

--Capitol, Courthouse & City Hall. 5th ed. LC 76-13093. (Illus.). 384p. 1977. pap. text ed. 10.95 (ISBN 0-395-24331-9). HM.

Morlan, Robert L. & Martin, David L. Capitol, Courthouse, & City Hall. 6th ed. LC 80-82016. (Illus.). 480p. 1981. pap. text ed. 11.50 (ISBN 0-395-29186-0). HM.

Morley. Inflation & Unemployment. 2nd ed. 1979. pap. 6.95 (ISBN 0-03-041016-9). Dryden Pr.

Morley, Alexander F. The Harrap Opera Guide. 320p. 1971. 15.00 (ISBN 0-245-50509-1). Dufour.

Morley, Christopher. Parnassus on Wheels. (Illus.). 1955. 6.50 o.p. (ISBN 0-397-00065-0). Lippincott.

Morley, D. Pediatric Priorities in the Developing World. 1976. 9.95 (ISBN 0-407-35113-2). Butterworths.

Morley, D. A. Mathematical Modelling in Water & Wastewater Treatment. (Illus.). 1979. 62.10x (ISBN 0-85334-842-1). Intl Ideas.

Morley, David, et al, eds. Making Cities Work: The Dynamics of Urban Innovation. LC 79-5489. 288p. 1980. lib. bdg. 30.00x (ISBN 0-89158-656-3, Pub. by Croom Helm England). Westview.

Morley, Felix. The Power in the People. LC 72-81839. 293p. 1972. 10.00x o.p. (ISBN 0-8402-1296-8); pap. 5.95x o.p. (ISBN 0-686-65431-5). Nash Pub.

--The Power in the People. 3rd ed. LC 72-81839. 1976. 10.00x o.p. (ISBN 0-916054-37-3, Caroline Hse Inc). Green Hill.

Morley, Frank. Literary Britain: A Reader's Guide to Its Writers & Landmarks. LC 78-2147. (Illus.). 482p. 1980. 19.95 (ISBN 0-06-013056-3, HarpT). Har-Row.

Morley, Henry. Journal of a London Playgoer. (Victorian Library Ser.). 348p. 1974. Repr. of 1866 ed. text ed. 13.50x (ISBN 0-7185-5031-5, Leicester). Humanities.

--Memoirs of Bartholomew Fair. LC 67-24348. 1968. Repr. of 1880 ed. 20.00 (ISBN 0-8103-3495-X). Gale.

Morley, Ian & Stephenson, G. M. The Social Psychology of Bargaining. 1977. text ed. 35.00x (ISBN 0-04-301081-4). Allen Unwin.

Morley, J., jt. auth. see Watling, T.

Morley, James W., ed. Deterrent Diplomacy: Japan, Germany, & the USSR, 1935-1940. LC 75-25524. (Japan's Road to the Pacific War Ser.). 376p. 1976. 20.00x (ISBN 0-231-08969-4). Columbia U Pr.

--A Guide to Japanese Foreign Policy. (Studies of the East Asian Institute). 624p. 1973. 27.50x (ISBN 0-231-08966-X). Columbia U Pr.

Morley, Joan. Improving Spoken English. LC 76-49151. 1979. pap. text ed. 9.95x (ISBN 0-472-08660-X). U of Mich Pr.

Morley, John. Diderot & the Encyclopaedists, 2 vols. LC 74-145521. 1971. Repr. of 1923 ed. 24.00 (ISBN 0-8103-3987-0). Gale.

Morley, John, ed. see Colvin, Sidney.

Morley, Malcolm. Margate & Its Theatres. 8.95 (ISBN 0-392-08118-0, SpS). Soccer.

Morley, Robert. Worry! How to Kick the Serenity Habit in Ninety Eight Easy Steps. (Illus.). 176p. 1981. 10.00 (ISBN 0-399-12596-5). Putnam.

Morley, Sheridan. Oscar Wilde. LC 76-4727. 1976. 14.95 o.p. (ISBN 0-03-017586-0). HR&W.

Morling, K. Geometric & Engineering Drawing. 2nd ed. (Illus.). 1974. pap. 15.95x (ISBN 0-7131-3319-8). Intl Ideas.

Morman, Jean M. Art: Of Wonder & a World. rev. ed. (Illus.). 1978. text ed. 11.90x (ISBN 0-912242-12-4); pap. 8.15x o.p. (ISBN 0-912242-11-6); tchr's manual 3.15 (ISBN 0-685-62930-9). Art Educ.

Morman, Jean M. & Laliberte, Norman. Limits of Defiance: Strikes, Rights, & Government. LC 73-149012. (Illus.). (gr. 10-12). 1971. PLB 6.90 (ISBN 0-531-01980-2). Watts.

Mornand, Pierre. Color Woodcuts. Intrator, Mira, tr. from Fr. (Illus.). 1972. pap. 6.00x (ISBN 0-933652-02-X). Domjan Studio.

--In the Forest of the Golden Dragon. LC 73-76776. (Fr. & Eng.). 1973. 20.00 (ISBN 0-933652-04-6). Domjan Studio.

Morneau, Robert F. Discovering God's Presence. 175p. (Orig.). 1980. pap. 5.95 (ISBN 0-8146-1197-4). Liturgical Pr.

--Mantras for the Morning: An Introduction to Holistic Prayer. (Illus.). 120p. 1981. pap. 4.25 (ISBN 0-8146-1210-5). Liturgical Pr.

Morneau, Robert H., Jr. & Rockwell, Robert R. Sex, Motivation, & the Criminal Offender. (Illus.). 416p. 1980. text ed. 29.75 (ISBN 0-398-03933-X). C C Thomas.

Morner, Magnus, ed. Race & Class in Latin America. (Institute for Latin American Studies). 1970. 17.50x (ISBN 0-231-03295-1); pap. 5.00x (ISBN 0-231-08661-X). Columbia U Pr.

Morningstar, Jim. Spiritual Psychology: A New Age Course for Body, Mind & Spirit. 2nd ed. (Illus.). 119p. Date not set. pap. 8.00 (ISBN 0-9604856-0-0). Morningstar.

Morningstar, Ramon S. Zero Weather. Edwards, Una, ed. LC 80-20072. 320p. (Orig.). 1980. pap. 6.95 (ISBN 0-937770-00-0). Family Pub CA.

Morones, Gregorio. Practicas de Laboratorio de Fisica. (Span.). 1979. pap. text ed. 4.20 (ISBN 0-06-315700-4, Pub. by HarLA Mexico). Har-Row.

Moroney, John R. Income Inequality: Trends & International Comparisons. LC 79-4726. 192p. 1979. 20.95 (ISBN 0-669-03058-9). Lexington Bks.

Moroney, R. M. The Family & the State: Considerations for Social Policy. LC 75-45230. (Illus.). 1976. pap. text ed. 8.50x (ISBN 0-582-48493-6). Longman.

Moroni, J. Alfred & Lahey, Francis J. An Accounting Manual for Catholic Elementary & Secondary Schools. rev. ed. 86p. 1969. 4.00. Natl Cath Educ.

Morowitz, Harold J. The Wine of Life & Other Essays on Societies, Energy & Living Things. 240p. 1981. pap. 2.95 (ISBN 0-553-14353-0). Bantam.

Morowitz, Harold J. & Morowitz, Lucille S. Life on the Planet Earth. new ed. (Illus.). 400p. 1974. text ed. 14.95x (ISBN 0-393-09269-0). Norton.

Morowitz, Lucille S., jt. auth. see Morowitz, Harold J.

Morozov, G. V. & Kalashnik, Ia. M., eds. Forensic Psychiatry. LC 76-77458. 1970. 22.50 o.p. (ISBN 0-87332-024-7). M E Sharpe.

Morpeth, Robert S., jt. auth. see Donaldson, Gordon.

Morphet, jt. auth. see Green.

Morphet, Edgar L., jt. auth. see Johns, Roe L.

Morphet, Edgar L., et al. Educational Organization & Administration. 3rd ed. LC 73-18138. (Illus.). 432p. 1974. ref. ed. 18.95 (ISBN 0-13-236711-4). P-H.

Morphet, Richard. Warhol. (Tate Gallery Art Ser.). (Illus.). 1977. 6.95 o.p. (ISBN 0-8120-5140-8). Barron.

Morpurgo, Michael & Simmons, Clifford, eds. Living Poets. (Orig.). 1975. pap. 6.50 (ISBN 0-7195-3000-8). Transatlantic.

Morr, Mary L. & Irmiter, Theodore F. Introductory Foods: A Laboratory Manual of Food Preparation & Evaluation. 3rd ed. (Illus.). 1980. pap. text ed. 8.95 (ISBN 0-02-384120-6). Macmillan.

Morra, Robert, jt ed. see Morgenthaler, George W.

Morrcock, Michael. Count Brass. 1981. pap. 2.25 (ISBN 0-440-11541-8). Dell.

Morreall, John S. Analogy & Talking About God: A Critique of the Thomistic Approach. LC 77-18494. 1978. pap. text ed. 7.75 (ISBN 0-8191-0423-X). U Pr of Amer.

Morrell. The Future of Dollar & World Reserve System. 1981. text ed. price not set (ISBN 0-408-10674-3); pap. text ed. price not set (ISBN 0-408-10675-1). Butterworth.

Morrell, David. First Blood. 256p. 1976. pap. 1.75 o.p. (ISBN 0-449-22976-9, Crest). Fawcett.

--The Last Reveille. 1978. pap. 1.95 o.p. (ISBN 0-449-23527-0, Crest). Fawcett.

--Testament. 1976. pap. 1.95 o.p. (ISBN 0-449-23033-3, Crest). Fawcett.

Morrell, George, et al, eds. Drug Monitoring & Pharmacokinetic Date. LC 79-90657. 1980. 19.50 (ISBN 0-930376-10-2). Pathotox Pubs.

Morressey, John. Ironbrand. LC 80-80999. 320p. (Orig.). 1980. pap. 2.25 (ISBN 0-87216-689-9). Playboy Pbks.

Morressy. The Humans of Ziax II: The Drought on Ziax II. (gr. 3-5). 1980. pap. 1.25 (ISBN 0-590-30382-1, Schol Pap). Schol Bk Serv.

Morressy, John. Displaced Persons. 224p. 1976. pap. 1.50 o.p. (ISBN 0-445-03130-1). Popular Lib.

Morrey, Charles B., Jr., jt. auth. see Protter, Murray H.

Morrice, A. Fundamentals of Economics. 1972. pap. text ed. 13.95x (ISBN 0-685-83783-1). Intl Ideas.

Morrice, J. K. Crisis Intervention: Case Histories. Kahn, J. H., ed. 117p. 1976. text ed. 16.50 (ISBN 0-08-019742-6); pap. text ed. 7.75 (ISBN 0-08-019741-8). Pergamon.

Morrill, Bernard. An Introduction to Equilibrium Thermodynamics. 1973. text ed. 32.00 (ISBN 0-08-016891-4); pap. text ed. 17.60 (ISBN 0-08-019003-0); manual 0.50 (ISBN 0-686-67231-3). Pergamon.

Morrill, Chester, Jr. Computers & Data Processing Information Sources. LC 70-85486. (Management Information Guide Ser.: No. 15). 1969. 30.00 (ISBN 0-8103-0815-0). Gale.

Morrill, Chester, Jr., ed. Systems & Procedures Including Office Management Information Sources. LC 67-31261. (Management Information Ser.: No. 12). 1967. 30.00 (ISBN 0-8103-0812-6). Gale.

Morrill, George P. Snow, Stars & Wild Honey. 1975. 8.95 o.p. (ISBN 0-397-01029-X). Lippincott.

Morrill, J. S. The Cheshire Grand Jury, 1625-1959: A Social & Administrative Study. (Occasional Papers in English Local History, Third Series: No. 1). (Illus., Orig.). 1976. pap. text ed. 6.75x (ISBN 0-7185-2031-9, Leicester). Humanities.

--Cheshire Sixteen Thirty to Sixteen Sixty: County Government & Society During the English Revolution. (Oxford Historical Monographs Ser). 367p. 1974. 37.50x (ISBN 0-19-821855-9). Oxford U Pr.

--The Revolt of the Provinces: Conservatives & Radicals in the English Civil War, 1630-1650. (Historical Problems: Studies & Documents). 1976. pap. text ed. 8.95x o.p. (ISBN 0-04-942159-X). Allen Unwin.

Morrill, Richard L. Teaching Values in College: Facilitating Development of Ethical, Moral & Value Awareness in Students. LC 80-8003. (Higher Education Ser.). 1980. text ed. 13.95x (ISBN 0-87589-475-5). Jossey-Bass.

Morrill, Terence C., ed. see Silverstein, Robert M. & Bassler, G. Clayton.

Morrill, W. T., jt. ed. see Dyke, B.

Morrill, Weston H. & Hurst, James C., eds. Dimensions of Intervention for Student Development. Oetting, E. R., tr. LC 80-16939. (Counseling & Human Development Ser.). 360p. 1980. text ed. 26.50 (ISBN 0-471-05249-3, Pub. by Wiley-Interscience). Wiley.

Morrin, Helen C. Communication for Nurses. (Quality Paperback: No. 302). (Orig.). 1965. pap. 2.95 (ISBN 0-8226-0302-0). Littlefield.

Morris. Dolphin. (Illus.). (gr. 2-3). Date not set. pap. cancelled (ISBN 0-590-30026-1, Schol Pap). Schol Bk Serv.

Morris, A. E. History of Urban Form: Before the Industrial Revolutions. 2nd ed. 1979. 46.95x (ISBN 0-470-26614-7); pap. 18.95 (ISBN 0-470-26612-0). Halsted Pr.

Morris, A. J. C. P. Trevelyan, Eighteen Seventy - Nineteen Fifty Eight: Portrait of a Radical. 1979. 19.95 (ISBN 0-312-11242-4). St Martin.

--Edwardian Radicalism 1900-1914. 288p. 1974. 22.00 (ISBN 0-7100-7866-8). Routledge & Kegan.

Morris, Alison, et al. Justice for Children. 176p. 1980. text ed. 26.00x (ISBN 0-333-27486-5); pap. text ed. 9.95x (ISBN 0-686-64581-2). Humanities.

Morris, Alvin L., ed. Dental Specialties in General Practice. Bohannan, Harry M. LC 68-23689. (Illus.). 1969. 26.50 o.p. (ISBN 0-7216-6560-8). Saunders.

Morris, Anne C., ed. see Morris, Gouverneur.

Morris, Arthur S. South America. LC 79-13729. (Illus.). 1979. text ed. 17.50x (ISBN 0-06-494981-8); pap. text ed. 14.50x (ISBN 0-06-494982-6). B&N.

Morris, Arval A. The Constitution & American Education. 2nd ed. LC 79-28177. (American Casebook Ser.). 1034p. 1980. text ed. 19.95 (ISBN 0-8299-2080-3). West Pub.

Morris, Audrey S. One Thousand Inspirational Things. (Library of Beautiful Things: Vol. 2). (YA) (gr. 9-12). 1956. 9.95 (ISBN 0-8015-5568-X, Hawthorn). Dutton.

Morris, Barbara. Victorian Table Glass & Ornaments. 1979. 17.95 o.p. (ISBN 0-214-20551-7, 8055, Dist. by Arco). Barrie & Jenkins.

Morris, Ben. Marketing Mass Transit. Mischa, Helen, ed. 150p. (Orig.). 1980. pap. 11.00x (ISBN 0-89894-034-6); pap. text ed. 11.50x (ISBN 0-686-64262-7). Advocate Pub Group.

--Objectives & Perspectives in Education: Studies in Educational Theory, 1955-70. 284p. 1972. 22.00x (ISBN 0-7100-7247-3). Routledge & Kegan.

Morris, Berenice R. American Popular Music: The Twentieth Century. LC 74-2461. (American Popular Music Ser). (Illus.). 72p. (gr. 4-6). 1974. PLB 4.33 o.p. (ISBN 0-531-02729-5). Watts.

Morris, Bernard S. Imperialism & Revolution: An Essay for Radicals. LC 73-81164. (Midland Bks.: No. 170). 96p. 1973. pap. 1.95x (ISBN 0-253-20170-5). Ind U Pr.

Morris, Brian, jt. auth. see Boehm, Klaus.

Morris, Brian, ed. Christopher Marlowe: Five Plays. LC 77-7525. 1969. pap. 4.50 o.p. (ISBN 0-8090-0701-0). Hill & Wang.

Morris, Brian, ed. see Cleveland, John.

Morris, C. Psychology: An Introduction. 3rd ed. 1979. 18.95 (ISBN 0-13-734194-6); study guide & wkbk. 6.95 (ISBN 0-13-734202-0); psi-unit mastery wkbk. 7.95 (ISBN 0-13-734269-1). P-H.

Morris, C., ed. Literature & the Social Worker: A Selected Reading List for Use in Bibliotherapy. (Library Association Book Ser.). 1975. 3.30x (ISBN 0-85365-078-0, Pub. by Lib Assn England). Oryx Pr.

Morris, C. B. Generation of Spanish Poets, Nineteen Twenty - Nineteen Thirty-Six. LC 69-11270. (Illus.). 1969. 48.00 (ISBN 0-521-07381-2); pap. 11.50x (ISBN 0-521-29481-9). Cambridge U Pr.

--This Loving Darkness: Silent Films & Spanish Writers 1920 - 1936. 240p. 1980. 39.50 (ISBN 0-19-713440-8). Oxford U Pr.

Morris, C. J. & Morris, P. Separation Methods in Biochemistry. 2nd ed. LC 73-9380. 1976. 92.95x (ISBN 0-470-61579-6). Halsted Pr.

Morris, C. Robert, jt. auth. see Morris, Clarence.

Morris, Carl & Rolph, John. Introduction to Data Analysis & Statistical Inference. (Illus.). 416p. 1981. pap. text ed. 13.95. P-H.

Morris, Charles. Festival. LC 66-12904. 1966. 4.00 o.s.i. (ISBN 0-8076-0346-5). Braziller.

--The Pragmatic Movement in American Philosophy. LC 79-119642. 1970. 6.50 o.s.i. (ISBN 0-8076-0564-6); pap. 3.25 (ISBN 0-8076-0563-8). Braziller.

Morris, Charles F. Origins, Orient & Oriana. LC 79-28664. (Illus.). xx, 491p. 1980. 56.00 (ISBN 0-935786-00-7). McCartan & Root.

Morris, Charles W. Varieties of Human Value. LC 56-6641. (Midway Reprint Ser). 1973. Repr. of 1956 ed. pap. 9.00x o.s.i. (ISBN 0-226-53883-4). U of Chicago Pr.

Morris, Christopher. Political Thought in England: Tyndale to Hooker. LC 79-1638. 1981. Repr. of 1953 ed. 19.50 (ISBN 0-88355-941-2). Hyperion Conn.

Morris, Clarence. Justification of the Law. LC 77-153424. 1971-72. 15.00 (ISBN 0-8122-7639-6); pap. 4.95x (ISBN 0-8122-1030-1, Pa Paperbacks). U of Pa Pr.

Morris, Clarence & Bodde, Derk. Law in Imperial China. (Pennsylvania Paperbacks Ser). 620p. 1973. pap. 6.95x o.p. (ISBN 0-8122-1060-3). U of Pa Pr.

Morris, Clarence & Morris, C. Robert. Morris on Torts. 2nd ed. LC 80-170. (University Textbook Ser.). 457p. 1980. write for info. (ISBN 0-88277-002-0). Foundation Pr.

Morris, Clarence, ed. Great Legal Philosophers: Selected Readings in Jurisprudence. LC 57-11955. 1971. pap. 8.95x (ISBN 0-8122-1008-5, Pa Paperbks). U of Pa Pr.

Morris, Colin. The Discovery of the Individual, 1050-1200. LC 72-84235. 208p. 1973. 4.50x (ISBN 0-06-131718-7, TB1718, Torch). Har-Row.

--History of Hants & Dorset Motor Services. 1973. 12.95 (ISBN 0-7153-6051-5). David & Charles.

Morris, Dan & Morris, Inez. The Complete Outdoor Cookbook. 1979. pap. 6.95 (ISBN 0-8015-1627-7, Hawthorn). Dutton.

Morris, Dan & Strung, Norman. Fisherman's Almanac. LC 70-93179. (Illus.). 1970. 5.95 o.s.i. (ISBN 0-02-587120-X). Macmillan.

Morris, Danny. Discovery Our Family Covenant. 1981. pap. 2.25x (ISBN 0-8358-0419-4). Upper Room.

Morris, Danny E. Any Miracle God Wants to Give. (Prayer in My Life Ser.: Ser. I). 1974. pap. 1.00x (ISBN 0-8358-0314-7). Upper Room.

Morris, David B. The Religious Sublime: Christian Poetry & Critical Tradition in Eighteenth-Century England. LC 70-190534. 272p. 1972. 12.00x (ISBN 0-8131-1270-2). U Pr of Ky.

Morris, David J. Introduction to Communication Command & Control Systems. 1977. text ed. 45.00 (ISBN 0-08-020378-7). Pergamon.

Morris, Dean. Animals That Burrow. LC 77-8114. (Read About Animals Ser.). (Illus.). (gr. k-3). 1977. PLB 9.95 (ISBN 0-8393-0012-3). Raintree Child.

--Animals That Live in Shells. LC 77-7911. (Read About Animals Ser.). (Illus.). (gr. k-3). 1977. PLB 9.95 (ISBN 0-8393-0013-1). Raintree Child.

--Birds. LC 77-8302. (Read About Animals Ser.). (Illus.). (gr. k-3). 1977. PLB 9.95 (ISBN 0-8393-0006-9). Raintree Child.

--Butterflies & Moths. LC 77-7912. (Read About Animals Ser.). (Illus.). (gr. k-3). 1977. PLB 9.95 (ISBN 0-8393-0010-7). Raintree Child.

--Cats. LC 77-8118. (Read Animals Ser.). (Illus.). (gr. k-3). 1977. PLB 9.95 (ISBN 0-8393-0002-6). Raintree Child.

--Dinosaurs & Other First Animals. LC 77-23398. (Read About Animals Ser.). (Illus.). (gr. k-3). 1977. PLB 9.95 (ISBN 0-8393-0000-X). Raintree Child.

--Endangered Animals. LC 77-8365. (Read About Animals Ser.). (Illus.). (gr. k-3). 1977. PLB 9.95 (ISBN 0-8393-0011-5). Raintree Child.

--Horses. LC 77-8243. (Read About Animals Ser.). (Illus.). (gr. k-3). 1977. PLB 9.95 (ISBN 0-8393-0008-5). Raintree Child.

--Insects That Live in Families. LC 77-8254. (Read About Animals Ser.). (Illus.). (gr. k-3). 1977. PLB 9.95 (ISBN 0-8393-0001-8). Raintree Child.

--Monkeys & Apes. LC 77-8148. (Read About Animals Ser.). (Illus.). (gr. k-3). 1977. PLB 9.95 (ISBN 0-8393-0005-0). Raintree Child.

--Snakes & Lizards. LC 77-8147. (Read About Animals Ser.). (Illus.). (gr. k-3). 1977. PLB 9.65 (ISBN 0-8393-0007-7). Raintree Child.

--Spiders. LC 77-8115. (Read About Animals Ser.). (gr. k-3). 1977. PLB 9.95 (ISBN 0-8393-0004-2). Raintree Child.

--Underwater Life: The Oceans. LC 77-23051. (Read About Animals Ser.). (Illus.). (gr. k-3). 1977. PLB 9.95 (ISBN 0-8393-0009-3). Raintree Child.

Morris, Demond. Patterns of Reproductive Behavior. (Illus.). 528p. 1980. 12.95 (ISBN 0-224-61795-8, Pub. by Chatto Bodley Jonathan). Merrimack Bk Serv.

Morris, Derek, ed. The Economic System in the United Kingdom. 2nd ed. 1977. 34.95x (ISBN 0-19-877141-X). Oxford U Pr.

Morris, Don. Elementary School Physical Education: Toward Inclusion. (Brighton Ser. in Health & Physical Education). (Illus.). 1980. text ed. 15.95 (ISBN 0-89832-012-7). Brighton Pub Co.

Morris, Dwight A. & Morris, Lynne D., eds. Health Care Administration: A Guide to Information Sources. LC 78-53431. (Health Affairs Information Guide Ser.: Vol. 1). 1978. 30.00 (ISBN 0-8103-1378-2). Gale.

Morris, Earl W. & Winter, Mary. Housing, Family, & Society. LC 77-24772. 1978. text ed. 16.95x (ISBN 0-471-61570-6); tchrs. manual 4.00 (ISBN 0-471-03939-X). Wiley.

Morris, Edita. Dear Me. LC 67-27522. 1967. 5.00 o.s.i. (ISBN 0-8076-0425-9). Braziller.

Morris, Edmund. The Rise of Theodore Roosevelt. 1980. pap 8.95 (ISBN 0-345-28707-X). Ballantine.

Morris, Edward E. Austral English. LC 68-18003. 1968. Repr. of 1898 ed. 34.00 (ISBN 0-8103-3287-6). Gale.

Morris, Fern. You Wouldn't Believe It. 1981. 5.75 (ISBN 0-8062-1634-4). Carlton.

Morris, Frank T. Field Guide to Birds of Prey of Australia. 124p. 29.95 (ISBN 0-686-62178-6). Eastview.

--Finches of Australia: A Folio. (Illus.). 124p. 65.00 (ISBN 0-7018-1000-9). Eastview.

Morris, Freda. Hypnosis with Friends & Lovers. LC 78-360. (Orig.). 1979. pap. 5.95 (ISBN 0-06-250600-5, RD 286, HarpR). Har-Row.

Morris, George E. Engineering: A Decision Making Process. LC 76-13090. (Illus.). 1977. pap. text ed. 8.95 (ISBN 0-395-24546-X). HM.

--Technical Illustrating. 250p. 1975. 17.95 (ISBN 0-13-898155-8). P-H.

Morris, Gouverneur. Diary & Letters of Gouverneur Morris, 2 Vols. Morris, Anne C., ed. LC 70-98691. (American Public Figures Ser). 1969. Repr. of 1888 ed. lib. bdg. 95.00 (ISBN 0-306-71835-9). Da Capo.

Morris, Greggory. Basketball Basics. LC 75-34142. (Illus.). (gr. 2-6). 1976. 6.95 (ISBN 0-13-072256-1); pap. 1.50 (ISBN 0-13-072223-5). P-H.

Morris, Helen. Where's That Poem? rev & enl ed. 287p. 1980. pap. 10.50x (ISBN 0-631-11791-1, Pub. by Basil Blackwell). Biblio Dist.

Morris, Henry. Bible & Modern Science. 1956. pap. 1.50 (ISBN 0-8024-0572-X). Moody.

Morris, Henry M. Biblical Cosmology & Modern Science. pap. 3.95 (ISBN 0-87552-349-8). Presby & Reformed.

--The Remarkable Birth of Planet Earth. new ed. 112p. 1972. pap. 1.50 (ISBN 0-87123-485-8, 200485). Bethany Fell.

--Twilight of Evolution. 1963. pap. 2.95 (ISBN 0-8010-5862-7). Baker Bk.

Morris, Dr. Henry M. That You Might Believe. LC 78-68398. pap. 4.95 (ISBN 0-89107-157-1). Good News.

Morris, Herbert. On Guilt & Innocence: Essays in Legal Philosophy & Moral Psychology. LC 72-89789. 1976. 11.50x o.p. (ISBN 0-520-02349-8); pap. 3.95 (ISBN 0-520-03944-0). U of Cal Pr.

Morris, Hugh. The Art of Kissing. LC 76-40626. 1977. pap. 1.95 (ISBN 0-385-12630-1, Dolp). Doubleday.

Morris, Ian. Introduction to the Algae. (Orig.). 1967. pap. text ed. 7.50x (ISBN 0-09-080713-8, Hutchinson U Lib). Humanities.

Morris, Inez, jt. auth. see Morris, Dan.

Morris, Ivan. Tale of Genji Scroll. LC 77-128695. (Illus.). 1971. ltd. ed. 350.00 (ISBN 0-87011-131-0). Kodansha.

Morris, Ivan, ed. Madly Singing in the Mountains: An Appreciation & Anthology of Arthur Waley. 400p. 1981. pap. 7.95 (ISBN 0-916870-35-9). Creative Arts Bk.

--Modern Japanese Stories: An Anthology. LC 61-11971. (Illus.). 1977. pap. 8.50 (ISBN 0-8048-1226-8). C E Tuttle.

Morris, Ivan, tr. see Ooka, Shohei.

Morris, J., jt. auth. see Kish, Joseph L., Jr.

Morris, J. A., ed. Growth of Industrial Britain: A Work Book & Study Guide in Social & Economic History. (Illus.). 1971. text ed. 16.95x (ISBN 0-245-50324-2). Intl Ideas.

Morris, J. D., ed. see Parapsychological Association.

Morris, J. D., et al, eds. see Parapsychological Association.

Morris, Jack. The Deadly Routine. LC 80-82429. (Illus.). 210p. 1980. wkbk 8.95 (ISBN 0-686-28036-9). Palmer Pub CA.

Morris, Jacquelyn M. & Elkins, Elizabeth A. Library Searching: Resources & Strategies with Examples from the Environmental Sciences. (Library Resources Ser.). 1978. text ed. 8.95x o.p. (ISBN 0-88432-004-9); pap. text ed. 5.95x (ISBN 0-88432-005-7). J Norton Pubs.

Morris, James. Coronation Everest. (Illus.). 1958. 1.95 o.p. (ISBN 0-571-09649-2, Pub. by Faber & Faber). Merrimack Bk Serv.

--The World of Venice. rev. ed. LC 73-18461. (Helen & Kurt Wolff Bk). (Illus.). 1973. 8.95 (ISBN 0-15-199086-7). HarBraceJ.

Morris, James M. Our Maritime Heritage: Maritime Developments & Their Impact on American Life. 1979. pap. text ed. 10.75 (ISBN 0-8191-0700-X). U Pr of Amer.

Morris, Jan. Spain: With Illustrations by the Author. (Illus.). 1979. 12.95 (ISBN 0-19-520169-8). Oxford U Pr.

--Travels. LC 76-2531. (Helen & Kurt Wolff Book). (Illus.). 160p. 1976. 7.95 o.p. (ISBN 0-15-191075-8). HarBraceJ.

--The Venetian Empire. LC 80-14046. (Helen & Kurt Wolff Bk). (Illus.). 208p. 1980. 19.95 (ISBN 0-15-193504-1). HarBraceJ.

Morris, Janet. Dream Dancer. 312p. 1981. 12.95 (ISBN 0-399-12591-4). Putnam.

--High Couch of Silistra. 256p. (Orig.). 1981. pap. 2.50 (ISBN 0-553-14532-0). Bantam.

Morris, Janet E. The Carnelian Throne. 256p. (Orig.). 1981. pap. 2.50 (ISBN 0-553-14924-5). Bantam.

--The Golden Sword. 384p. 1981. pap. 2.50 (ISBN 0-553-14846-X). Bantam.

--Wind from the Abyss. (New Age Ser.). 352p. (Orig.). 1981. pap. 2.50 (ISBN 0-553-14343-3). Bantam.

Morris, Jeffrey B., jt. ed. see Morris, Richard B.

Morris, Joan. The Lady Was a Bishop: The Hidden History of Women with Clerical Ordination & the Jurisdiction of Bishops. LC 72-89049. 192p. 1973. 6.95 o.s.i. (ISBN 0-02-587130-7). Macmillan.

Morris, Joan, jt. auth. see Fotheringham, John.

Morris, John. How Mad Tulloch Was Taken Away. 1976. pap. 4.95 (ISBN 0-571-11020-7, Pub. by Faber & Faber). Merrimack Bk Serv.

Morris, John, ed. Nennius: British History & the Welsh Annals. (History from the Sources Ser.). 100p. 1980. 13.00x (ISBN 0-8476-6264-0). Rowman.

--Oxfordshire. (Domesday Bk.). (Illus.). 154p. 1978. 18.00x (ISBN 0-8476-2286-X). Rowman.

Morris, John E. Welsh Wars of Edward First. 1901. 15.95x o.p. (ISBN 0-19-822304-8). Oxford U Pr.

Morris, John G., ed. see Third Colloquy for Directors of National Research Institutions in Education, Hamburg, 12-14 September 1978, Educational Research in Europe.

Morris, John W. Ghost Towns of Oklahoma. (Illus.). 1978. 15.95 (ISBN 0-8061-1358-8); pap. 7.95 (ISBN 0-8061-1420-7). U of Okla Pr.

Morris, John W., jt. auth. see Goins, Charles R.

Morris, Johnny, ed. The Faber Book of Animal Stories. 1978. 9.95 (ISBN 0-571-11221-8, Pub. by Faber & Faber). Merrimack Bk Serv.

Morris, Kenneth. The Fates of the Princes of Dyfed. Reginald, R. & Menville, Douglas, eds. LC 80-19430. (Newcastle Forgotten Fantasy Library: Vol. 15). 362p. 1980. Repr. of 1978 ed. lib. bdg. 10.95x (ISBN 0-89370-514-4). Borgo Pr.

Morris, Kenneth T. & Cinnamon, Kenneth M. Controversial Issues in Human Relations Training Groups. 168p. 1975. 13.75 (ISBN 0-398-03456-7); pap. 8.50 (ISBN 0-398-03458-3). C C Thomas.

Morris, L. W. Critical Path: Construction & Analysis. 1967. text ed. 25.00 (ISBN 0-08-012472-0); pap. text ed. 12.75 (ISBN 0-08-012471-2). Pergamon.

Morris, Larry A. Hiking the Grand Canyon & Havasupai. (Illus.). 96p. 1981. pap. 4.95 (ISBN 0-89404-053-7). Aztex.

Morris, Leavitt F. An Editor at Large. 160p. 1981. 12.50 (ISBN 0-682-49705-3). Exposition.

Morris, Leon. Creo en la Revalacion. Blanch, Miguel, tr. from Eng. (Serie Creo). 223p. (Orig., Span.). 1979. pap. 3.95 (ISBN 0-89922-140-8). Edit Caribe.

--Studies in the Fourth Gospel. LC 68-12790. 1969. 8.95 (ISBN 0-8028-1818-8). Eerdmans.

--Testaments of Love: A Study of Love in the Bible. (Orig.). 1981. pap. price not set (ISBN 0-8028-1874-9). Eerdmans.

Morris, Louis, et al, eds. Product Labeling. LC 80-22728. (Banbury Report Ser.: Report 6). 325p. 1980. 45.00x (ISBN 0-87969-205-7). Cold Spring Harbor.

Morris, Lynn L. & Fitz-Gibbon, Carol T. How to Deal with Goals & Objectives. rev. ed. LC 78-57012. (Program Evaluation Kit Ser.: Vol. 2). (Illus.). 78p. 1978. pap. 4.50 (ISBN 0-8039-1065-7). Sage.

--How to Measure Achievement. rev. ed. LC 78-58656. (Program Evaluation Kit Ser.: Vol. 6). (Illus.). 159p. 1978. pap. 7.50 (ISBN 0-8039-1067-3). Sage.

--How to Measure Program Implementation. LC 78-58655. (Program Evaluation Kit Ser.: Vol. 4). (Illus.). 140p. 1978. pap. 6.95 (ISBN 0-8039-1066-5). Sage.

Morris, Lynn L., jt. auth. see Fitz-Gibbon, Carol T.

Morris, Lynn L., et al. Program Evaluation Kit. rev. ed. LC 78-59613. (Illus.). 1080p. 1978. pap. 49.95 (ISBN 0-8039-1073-8). Sage.

Morris, Lynne D., jt. ed. see Morris, Dwight A.

Morris, Madeleine C. The Amazing Power of Solar-Kinetics. 1977. 8.95 o.p. (ISBN 0-13-023697-7). P-H.

Morris, Mair. Creative Thread Design. LC 73-17334. (Illus.). 88p. 1974. 9.95 (ISBN 0-8231-7033-0). Branford.

Morris, Margaret F., ed. Essays on the Gilded Age. LC 72-8266. (Walter Prescott Webb Memorial Lectures Ser: No. 7). 110p. 1973. 8.95 (ISBN 0-292-72004-1). U of Tex Pr.

Morris, Margaret F. & Myres, Sandra L., eds. Essays on American Foreign Policy. LC 73-19500. (Walter Prescott Webb Memorial Lectures Ser.: No. 8). 120p. 1974. 8.95x (ISBN 0-292-72009-2). U of Tex Pr.

Morris, Margaret F. & West, Elliott, eds. Essays on Urban America. LC 74-31058. (Walter Prescott Webb Memorial Lectures: No. 9). 128p. 1975. 8.95x (ISBN 0-292-72011-4). U of Tex Pr.

Morris, Marshall. Saying & Meaning in Puerto Rico: Some Problems in the Ethnography of Discourse. (Language & Communication Library: Vol. 1). 186p. 1980. 19.50 (ISBN 0-08-025822-0). Pergamon.

Morris, Mary. Vanishing Animals & Other Stories. (Illus.). 192p. 1980. pap. 7.95 (ISBN 0-87923-388-5). Godine.

Morris, Merle E., jt. auth. see Braham, Raymond L.

Morris, Michael A. International Politics & the Sea: The Case of Brazil. (Westview Replica Edition). 1979. lib. bdg. 27.00x (ISBN 0-89158-456-0). Westview.

Morris, Monica B. An Excursion into Creative Sociology. LC 76-19023. 1977. 15.00x (ISBN 0-231-03987-5); pap. 7.00x (ISBN 0-686-67485-5). Columbia U Pr.

Morris, Morris D. Measuring the Condition of the World's Poor: The Physical Quality of Life Index. LC 79-16613. 190p. 1979. pap. 5.95 (ISBN 0-08-023889-0). Overseas Dev Council.

Morris, Myrle & Medina, Gwen. You, Too, Can Be Forgiven! 1978. pap. 1.95 (ISBN 0-88368-082-3). Whitaker Hse.

Morris, Noel M. Digital Electronics for Works Electricians. (Illus.). 148p. 1980. pap. 14.50 (ISBN 0-07-084523-9). McGraw.

Morris, Norma A. How to Set up a Business Office: The Complete Guide to Locating, Outfitting & Staffing. (Illus.). 210p. 1981. 14.95 (ISBN 0-913864-62-5). Enterprise Del.

Morris, Norval. Crime & Justice: An Annual Review of Criminal Justice Research, Vol. II. Tonry, Michael, ed. 1981. lib. bdg. 19.50x (ISBN 0-226-53957-1). U of Chicago Pr.

Morris, Norval & Hawkins, Gordon. The Honest Politican's Guide to Crime Control. LC 76-101467. 272p. 1972. pap. text ed. 4.50 (ISBN 0-226-53902-4, P460, Phoen). U of Chicago Pr.
Morris, Norval & Tonry, Michael. Crime & Justice: An Annual Review of Research. (Vol. II). 480p. 1981. pap. 7.95 (ISBN 0-226-53959-8). U of Chicago Pr.
Morris, Norval & Tonry, Michael, eds. Crime & Justice: An Annual Review of Research. (Vol. 1). xii, 348p. 1980. pap. 6.95 (ISBN 0-226-53956-3, P903, Phoen). U of Chicago Pr.
Morris, P., jt. auth. see Morris, C. J.
Morris, Paul C. & Morin, Joseph F. The Island Steamers: A Chronology of Steam Transportation to & from the Offshore Islands of Martha's Vineyard & Nantucket. 2nd ed. Towne, Sumner A., Jr., ed. LC 77-79090. (Illus.). 196p. 1977. pap. 11.95 (ISBN 0-686-28900-5). Nantucket Nautical.
Morris, Percy A. Boy's Book of Snakes: How to Recognize & Understand Them. (Illus.). (gr. 6-12). 1948. 12.95 (ISBN 0-8260-6335-7). Ronald Pr.
Morris, Peter, tr. see Bunge, Hans.
Morris, Peter, tr. see Sadoul, Georges.
Morris, R. J. Class & Class Consciousness in the Industrial Revolution, 1780-1850. (Studies in Economic & Social History). 80p. 1979. pap. text ed. 4.75x (ISBN 0-333-15454-1). Humanities.
Morris, R. N. & Mogey, John. The Sociology of Housing: Studies at Berinsfield. 1965. text ed. 8.25x o.p. (ISBN 0-7100-3454-7). Humanities.
Morris, R. W. The Prehistoric Rock Art of Argyll. 1978. 9.95 o.p. (ISBN 0-85642-043-3, Pub. by Blandford Pr England); pap. 3.50 o.p. (ISBN 0-85642-059-X). Sterling.
Morris, R. Winston, ed. Tuba Music Guide. pap. 7.00 (ISBN 0-686-15895-4). Instrumentalist Co.
Morris, Ralph. Computer Basics for Managers. 241p. 1980. text ed. 23.50x (ISBN 0-09-141570-5, Pub. by Busn Bks England). Renouf.
Morris, Reginald O. Foundations of Practical Harmony & Counterpoint. 2nd ed. LC 79-10541. (Illus.). xii, 148p. 1980. Repr. of 1931 ed. lib. bdg. 15.75x (ISBN 0-313-21465-4, MOPH). Greenwood.
Morris, Richard B. First Book of the American Revolution. (First Bks). (Illus.). (gr. 4-6). 1956. PLB 4.90 o.p. (ISBN 0-531-00459-7); pap. 1.25 o.p. (ISBN 0-531-02307-9). Watts.
--First Book of the Constitution. (First Bks). (Illus.). (gr. 4-6). 1958. PLB 4.90 o.p. (ISBN 0-531-00511-9); pap. 1.25 o.p. (ISBN 0-531-02310-9). Watts.
--First Book of the Founding of the Republic. LC 68-10728. (First Bks). (Illus.). (gr. 4-6). 1968. PLB 4.90 o.p. (ISBN 0-531-02313-3); pap. 1.25 o.p. (ISBN 0-685-21864-3). Watts.
--First Book of the Indian Wars. (First Bks). (Illus.). (gr. 4-6). 1959. PLB 4.90 o.p. (ISBN 0-531-00560-7). Watts.
--First Book of the War of 1812. (First Bks). (Illus.). (gr. 4-6). 1961. PLB 4.90 o.p. (ISBN 0-531-00662-X). Watts.
--John Jay: The Nation & the Court. LC 67-25933. 1967. 7.00x (ISBN 0-8419-8713-0, Pub. by Boston U Pr). Holmes & Meier.
--The Making of a Nation, 1775-1789. LC 63-8572. (Life History of the United States). (Illus.). (gr. 5 up). 1974. PLB 9.96 (ISBN 0-8094-0551-2, Pub. by Time-Life). Silver.
--The New World: Before 1775. LC 63-8572. (Life History of the United States). (Illus.). (gr. 5 up). 1974. PLB 9.96 (ISBN 0-8094-0550-4, Pub. by Time-Life). Silver.
--Seven Who Shaped Our Destiny: The Founding Fathers As Revolutionaries. LC 73-4111. (Illus.). 348p. (YA) 1973. 11.95 o.s.i. (ISBN 0-06-013078-4, HarpT). Har-Row.
Morris, Richard B. & Graff, Henry F. America at Two Hundred. (Headline Ser.: 227). (Illus.). 1979. pap. 2.00 (ISBN 0-87124-032-7, 75-26057). Foreign Policy.
Morris, Richard B., jt. auth. see Cunliffe, Marcus.
Morris, Richard B. & Morris, Jeffrey B., eds. Encyclopedia of American History. bicentennial, 5th ed. LC 74-15840. (Illus.). 1260p. (YA) 1976. 29.95 o.s.i. (ISBN 0-06-013081-4, HarpT); lib. bdg. 26.79 (ISBN 0-06-013083-0). Har-Row.
Morris, Richard B., jt. ed. see Commager, Henry S.
Morris, Richard B., ed. see Thomas, Emory M.
Morris, Richard J., ed. Perspectives in Abnormal Behavior. 570p. 1976. text ed. 26.00 (ISBN 0-08-017738-7); pap. text ed. 10.50 (ISBN 0-08-017739-5); test items 0.50 (ISBN 0-686-67339-5). Pergamon.
Morris, Richard K. John P. Holland: 1841-1914. LC 79-6120. (Navies & Men Ser.). (Illus.). 1980. Repr. of 1966 ed. lib. bdg. 18.00x (ISBN 0-405-13048-1). Arno.
Morris, Richard S. Bum Rap on America's Cities: The Real Cause of Urban Decay. 204p. 1980. pap. text ed. 8.50 (ISBN 0-13-089219-X). P-H.
--Bum Rap on America's Cities: The Real Causes of Urban Decay. LC 77-17196. 1978. 8.95 o.p. (ISBN 0-13-089227-0). P-H.
Morris, Richard S., ed. see Smelser, Marshal L.
Morris, Richard T., jt. auth. see Sherlock, Basil J.
Morris, Robert. Allocating Health Resources for the Aged & Disabled: Technology Versus Politics. 1981. price not set (ISBN 0-669-04329-X). Lexington Bks.
--Country Inns of the Great Lakes: A Guide to Inns, Lodges, & Historic Hostelries of the Upper Midwest. 180p. (Orig.). 1981. pap. 4.95 (ISBN 0-89286-165-7). One Hund One Prods.
--Select Architecture. LC 72-87427. (Architecture & Decorative Art Ser.). 102p. 1973. Repr. of 1757 ed. lib. bdg. 25.00 (ISBN 0-306-71573-2). Da Capo.
--Self-Destruct: Dismantling America's Internal Security. 1979. 12.95 o.p. (ISBN 0-87000-437-9). Arlington Hse.
Morris, Robert & Binstock, Robert H. Feasible Planning for Social Change. LC 66-15763. 1966. 15.00x (ISBN 0-231-02746-X). Columbia U Pr.
Morris, Robert & King County Arts Commision, eds. Earthworks: Land Reclamation As Sculture. 71p. 1980. pap. text ed. 5.95 (ISBN 0-932216-04-8). Seattle Art.
Morris, Robert C. Reading, 'Writing, & Reconstruction: The Education of Freedmen in the South, 1861-1870. LC 80-25370. (Illus.). 1981. lib. bdg. price not set (ISBN 0-226-53928-8). U of Chicago Pr.
Morris, Robert H., et al. Intertidal Invertebrates of California. LC 77-92946. (Illus.). 904p. 1980. 30.00x (ISBN 0-8047-1045-7). Stanford U Pr.
Morris, Roger. The Genie in the Bottle: Unravelling the Myths About Wine. (Illus.). 204p. 1981. 12.95 (ISBN 0-89104-213-X); pap. 5.95 (ISBN 0-89104-198-2). A & W Pubs.
Morris, Roger, jt. auth. see Sheets, Hal.
Morris, Ronald W. The Prehistoric Rock Art of Galloway & the Isle of Man. (Illus.). 1979. 25.00 (ISBN 0-7137-0974-X, Pub by Blandford Pr England); pap. 19.95 (ISBN 0-7137-0975-8). Sterling.
Morris, S. A. Pontryagin Duality & the Structure of Locally Compact Abelian Groups. LC 76-53519. (London Mathematical Society Lecture Note Ser.: No. 29). 1977. 16.95x (ISBN 0-521-21543-9). Cambridge U Pr.
Morris, S. F. Catalogue of Type & Figured Fossil Crustacea (Exc. Ostracoda), Chelicerata & Myriapoda in the British Museum (Natural History) (Illus.). 56p. 1980. pap. 13.00x (ISBN 0-565-00828-5). Sabbot-Natural Hist Bks.
Morris, Scot. The Book of Strange Facts & Useless Information. LC 73-9040. 1979. pap. 5.95 (ISBN 0-385-00618-7, Dolp). Doubleday.
Morris, Shirley. The Pelican Guide to Virginia. (Pelican Guide Ser.). 1981. pap. 4.95 (ISBN 0-88289-206-1). Pelican.
Morris, Terence. Deviance & Control. 1980. pap. text ed. 9.25x (ISBN 0-09-126871-0, Hutchinson U Lib). Humanities.
Morris, Terry. Just Sixteen. 176p. (Orig.). (gr. 7 up). 1980. pap. 1.50 (ISBN 0-590-31341-X, Schol Pap). Schol Bk Serv.
Morris, Terry N. Goodnight, Dear Monster. LC 79-26904. (Illus.). 32p. 1980. bds. 1.95 (ISBN 0-394-84221-9). Knopf.
Morris, Thomas see Bleecker, Ann E.
Morris, Tina, et al. New Writers Seven: Special Volume on Dreams. (New Writing & Writers Ser.). 1969. text ed. 13.00x (ISBN 0-7145-0012-7). Humanities.
--New Writers Seven. 1980. pap. 6.00 (ISBN 0-7145-0013-5). Riverrun NY.
Morris, V. J., jt. auth. see Jennings, B. R.
Morris, Van C. & Pai, Young. Philosophy & the American School. 2nd ed. LC 75-26083. (Illus.). 544p. 1976. text ed. 17.50 (ISBN 0-395-18620-X). HM.
Morris, Vera. Distributional Effects of Public Expenditure. 176p. 1980. 21.50x (ISBN 0-86003-030-X, Pub. by Allan Pubs England); pap. 10.50x (ISBN 0-86003-129-2). State Mutual Bk.
Morris, Victoria S. Birds-Poems, Prints & Projects. (Orig.). 1980. pap. 4.50 (ISBN 0-914318-13-6). V S Morris.
--The Hand Puppet Show: Methods & Plays. rev ed. (gr. 1-8). 1976. pap. 4.50 o.p. (ISBN 0-914318-01-2). V S Morris.
--Let's Make a Mobile. (Mobiles Ser.: Vol. 1). (gr. 1-8). 1972. pap. 2.00 o.p. (ISBN 0-914318-02-0). V S Morris.
--More Mobiles: Math Shapes & Forms. (Mobiles Ser.: Vol. 2). (gr. 1-8). 1977. pap. 3.00 (ISBN 0-914318-03-9). V S Morris.
Morris, W. A Note by Wlliam Morris on...the Kelmscott Press. 76p. Repr. of 1829 ed. 15.00x (ISBN 0-7165-0620-3, Pub by Irish Academic Pr). Biblio Dist.
Morris, William. Architecture, Industry & Wealth: Collected Papers by William Morris. Freedberg, Sydney J., ed. LC 77-25760. (Connoisseurship, Criticism & Art History Ser.: Vol. 13). 163p. 1979. lib. bdg. 21.00 (ISBN 0-8240-3271-3). Garland Pub.
--Child Christopher & Goldilind the Fair. Reginald, R. & Menville, Douglas, eds. LC 80-19163. (Newcastle Forgotten Fantasy Library: Vol. 12). 219p. 1980. Repr. of 1977 ed. lib. bdg. 10.95x (ISBN 0-89370-511-X). Borgo Pr.
--A Choice of William Morris' Verse. Grigson, Geoffrey, ed. 1969. 7.50 (ISBN 0-686-16375-3, Pub. by Faber & Faber); pap. 3.95 (ISBN 0-571-08980-1). Merrimack Bk Serv.
--Golden Wings, & Other Stories. Reginald, R. & Menville, Douglas, eds. LC 80-19101. (Newcastle Forgotten Fantasy Library: Vol. 8). 169p. 1980. Repr. of 1976 ed. lib. bdg. 9.95x (ISBN 0-89370-507-1). Borgo Pr.
--Hopes & Fears for Art. Freedberg, Sydney J., ed. LC 77-19374. (Connoisseurship Criticism & Art History Ser.: Vol. 12). 217p. 1979. lib. bdg. 23.00 (ISBN 0-8240-3270-5). Garland Pub.
--News from Nowhere. Redmond, James, ed. (Routledge English Texts). 1970. pap. 6.95 (ISBN 0-7100-6799-2). Routledge & Kegan.
--A Note by William Morris on His Aims in Founding the Kelmscott Press. 1968. Repr. of 1898 ed. 15.00x o.p. (ISBN 0-7165-0024-8, Pub. by Irish Academic Pr Ireland). Biblio Dist.
--The Roots of the Mountains: Wherein Is Told Somewhat of the Lives of the Men of Burgdale, Their Friends, Their Neighbours, Their Foeman & Their Fellows in Arms. Reginald, R. & Menville, Douglas, eds. LC 80-19676. (Newcastle Forgotten Fantasy Library Ser.: Vol. 19). 424p. 1980. Repr. of 1979 ed. lib. bdg. 11.95x (ISBN 0-89370-518-7). Borgo Pr.
--The Story of the Glittering Plain, Which Has Been Also Called the Land of Living Men, or the Acre of the Undying. Reginald, R. & Menville, Douglas, eds. LC 80-19460. (Newcastle Forgotten Fantasy Library Ser.: Vol. 1). 174p. 1980. Repr. of 1973 ed. lib. bdg. 9.95x (ISBN 0-89370-500-4). Borgo Pr.
--A Tale of the House of the Wolfings & All the Kindreds of the Mark. Reginald, R. & Menville, Douglas, eds. LC 80-19670. (Newcastle Forgotten Fantasy Library Ser.: Vol. 16). 199p. 1980. Repr. of 1978 ed. lib. bdg. 10.95x (ISBN 0-89370-515-2). Borgo Pr.
--The Wood Beyond the World. (Facsimile of the Kelmscott Press Edition). Repr. of 1894 ed. 9.00 (ISBN 0-8446-4589-3). Peter Smith.
Morris, William, ed. see Ruskin, John.
Morris, William, et al. Arts & Crafts Essays. LC 76-17783. (Arts & Crafts Movement Ser.: Vol. 34). 1977. Repr. of 1893 ed. lib. bdg. 44.00x (ISBN 0-8240-2483-4). Garland Pub.
Morris, William C. & Sashkin, Marshal. Organization Behavior in Action: Skill Building Experiences. LC 76-490. (Illus.). 288p. 1976. pap. text ed. 11.95 (ISBN 0-8299-0080-2); instrs.' manual avail. (ISBN 0-8299-0562-6). West Pub.
Morris, William T. Decision Analysis. LC 76-15720. 1977. pap. 10.95 (ISBN 0-88244-131-0). Grid Pub.
Morris, Willie. The Ghosts of Old Miss, & Other Essays on Home. 165p. 1981. 9.95. Yoknapatawpha.
--Good Old Boy. LC 80-52627. 144p. 1980. Repr. 9.95. Yoknapatawpha.
--A Southern Album. Glusker, Irwin, ed. LC 76-49690. 8.95 o.p. (ISBN 0-89104-058-7). A & W Pubs.
Morris, Willie, ed. The South Today: 100 Years After Appomattox. 8.00 (ISBN 0-8446-4010-7). Peter Smith.
Morris, Wright. A Bill of Rites, a Bill of Wrongs, a Bill of Goods. LC 80-389. x, 177p. 1980. 13.50x (ISBN 0-8032-3065-6); pap. 4.25 (ISBN 0-8032-8107-2, BB 738, Bison). U of Nebr Pr.
--Cause for Wonder. LC 77-14594. 1978. 12.50x (ISBN 0-8032-0966-5); pap. 3.95 (ISBN 0-8032-5885-2, BB 656, Bison). U of Nebr Pr.
--Ceremony in Lone Tree. LC 60-7775. viii, 308p. 1973. pap. 3.25 (ISBN 0-8032-5782-1, BB 560, Bison). U of Nebr Pr.
--The Field of Vision. LC 56-8525. 251p. 1974. 11.50x (ISBN 0-8032-3060-5); pap. 3.50 (ISBN 0-8032-5789-9, BB 577, Bison). U of Nebr Pr.
--The Fork River Space Project. LC 77-3798. 1977. 8.95 o.s.i. (ISBN 0-06-013106-3, HarpT). Har-Row.
--God's Country & My People. LC 80-23155. (Illus.). 176p. 1981. pap. 15.95 (ISBN 0-8032-3067-2, BB 752, Bison). U of Nebr Pr.
--The Home Place. LC 48-1792. (Illus.). xii, 178p. 1968. pap. 4.50 (ISBN 0-8032-5139-4, BB 386, Bison). U of Nebr Pr.
--The Huge Season. LC 54-10858. viii, 306p. 1975. pap. 2.95 (ISBN 0-8032-5805-4, BB 590, Bison). U of Nebr Pr.
--In Orbit. LC 75-14359. 153p. 1976. 8.50x (ISBN 0-8032-0882-0); pap. 2.45 (ISBN 0-8032-5830-5, BB 612, Bison). U of Nebr Pr.
--Love Among the Cannibals. LC 76-16574. 1977. 12.50x (ISBN 0-8032-0880-4); pap. 3.25 (ISBN 0-8032-5842-9, BB 620, Bison). U of Nebr Pr.
--Man & Boy. LC 51-2263. viii, 212p. 1974. pap. 2.25 (ISBN 0-8032-5787-2, BB 575, Bison). U of Nebr Pr.
--The Man Who Was There. LC 76-16590. 1977. 11.95x (ISBN 0-8032-0881-2); pap. 3.25 (ISBN 0-8032-5813-5, BB 598, Bison). U of Nebr Pr.
--My Uncle Dudley. LC 75-5696. viii, 210p. 1975. pap. 2.95 (ISBN 0-8032-5804-6, BB 589, Bison). U of Nebr Pr.
--One Day. LC 76-3766. 1976. 15.95x (ISBN 0-8032-0879-0); pap. 4.95 (ISBN 0-8032-5841-0, BB 619, Bison). U of Nebr Pr.
--Plains Song. (Contemporary American Fiction Ser.). 241p. 1981. pap. 3.95 (ISBN 0-14-005778-1). Penguin.
--Will's Boy: A Memoir. LC 80-8708. 192p. 1981. 11.95 (ISBN 0-06-014856-X, HarpT). Har-Row.
--The Works of Love. LC 51-11978. x, 269p. 1972. pap. 2.45 (ISBN 0-8032-5767-8, BB 558, Bison). U of Nebr Pr.
--World in the Attic. LC 49-5058. 1971. 10.95x (ISBN 0-8032-3053-2); pap. 3.50 (ISBN 0-8032-5729-5, BB 528, Bison). U of Nebr Pr.
--Wright Morris: A Reader. LC 77-83614. 1970. 12.95 o.s.i. (ISBN 0-06-013089-X, HarpT). Har-Row.
Morrisey, G. L. Performance Appraisal: Keys to Effective Supervision. 1981. pap. write for info. (ISBN 0-201-04831-0). A-W.
Morrisey, George L. Appraisal & Development Through Objectives & Results. (Illus.). 1972. pap. text ed. 8.95 (ISBN 0-201-04834-5). A-W.
--Effective Business & Technical Presentations. 2nd ed. LC 74-24920. 224p. 1975. pap. text ed. 8.95 (ISBN 0-201-04828-0). A-W.
--Getting Your Act Together: Goal Setting for Fun, Health & Profit. (Wiley Self-Teaching Guide Ser.). 1980. pap. text ed. 7.95 (ISBN 0-471-08185-X). Wiley.
--Management by Objectives & Results for Business & Industry. 2nd ed. (Illus.). 260p. 1977. pap. text ed. 8.95 (ISBN 0-201-04906-6); inst. guide 1.00 (ISBN 0-201-04907-4). A-W.
--Management by Objectives & Results in the Public Sector. LC 76-1746. (Illus.). 204p. 1976. pap. text ed. 8.95 (ISBN 0-201-04825-6); instr's guide 1.00 (ISBN 0-201-04813-2). A-W.
Morrisey, Thomas. Twenty American Peaks & Crags. 1978. 11.95 o.p. (ISBN 0-8092-7569-4); pap. 6.95 o.p. (ISBN 0-8092-7568-6). Contemp Bks.
Morrisey, Thomas J., jt. auth. see Miller, Rex.
Morrish, George. Concordance of the Septuagint. 14.95 (ISBN 0-310-20300-7). Zondervan.
Morrish, Ivor. The Background of Immigrant Children. (Unwin Education Books). 1971. text ed. 18.95x o.p. (ISBN 0-04-301034-2). Allen Unwin.
--Education Since Eighteen Hundred. (Unwin Education Books). 1970. pap. text ed. 10.95x (ISBN 0-04-370030-6). Allen Unwin.
Morris-Jones, W. H., ed. From Rhodesia to Zimbabwe: Behind & Beyond Lancaster House. (Studies in Commonwealth Politics & History: No. 9). (Illus.). 123p. 1980. 22.50x (ISBN 0-7146-3167-1, F Cass Co). Biblio Dist.
--The Making of Politicians: Studies from Africa & Asia. (Commonwealth Papers: No. 20). 272p. 1976. pap. text ed. 26.00x (ISBN 0-485-17620-3, Athlone Pr). Humanities.
Morris-Jones, W. H. & Fischer, Georges, eds. Decolonisation & After: The British & French Experience. (Studies in Commonwealth Politics & History: No. 7). 369p. 1980. 29.50x (ISBN 0-7146-3095-0, F Cass Co). Biblio Dist.
Morris-Jones, W. H., jt. ed. see Madden, A. F.
Morrison, Alex. Early Man in Britain & Ireland. 1980. write for info. (ISBN 0-312-22463-X). St Martin.
--Photofinish. 144p. 1981. 16.95 (ISBN 0-442-21262-3). Van Nos Reinhold.
Morrison, Bonnie M., jt. auth. see Nattrass, Karen.
Morrison, Brysson N. Haworth Harvest: The Story of the Brontes. LC 78-89661. (Illus.). 1969. 8.95 (ISBN 0-8149-0670-2). Vanguard.
Morrison, C. L., ed. Pithy Sayings from FORMAT Interviews, Vol. II. 1980. pap. 2.50 (ISBN 0-932508-07-3). Seven Oaks.
Morrison, Carl & Morrison, Dorothy V. Can I Help How I Feel? LC 76-4931. (Illus.). (gr. 5-9). 1976. 7.95 (ISBN 0-689-30542-7). Atheneum.
Morrison, D. L., jt. tr. see Filesi, Teobaldo.
Morrison, Delmont, et al. Sensory-Motor Dysfunction & Therapy in Infancy & Early Childhood. (Illus.). 288p. 1978. 17.50 (ISBN 0-398-03766-3). C C Thomas.

Morrison, Donald G., et al. Black Africa. LC 72-143505. 1972. 45.00 (ISBN 0-02-921450-5). Free Pr.
Morrison, Dorothy N. Chief Sarah. LC 79-22545. (Illus.). (gr. 6-7). 1980. 9.95 (ISBN 0-689-30752-7). Atheneum.
Morrison, Dorothy V., jt. auth. see Morrison, Carl.
Morrison, Frances S., et al, eds. Self-Assessment of Current Knowledge in Hematology, Part 2: Literature Review. 1975. spiral bdg. 13.00 (ISBN 0-87488-283-4). Med Exam.
Morrison, Frank. Adventure Stories for Boys. (Upper Grade Bk.). (Illus.). (gr. 4-6). PLB 4.50 o.p. (ISBN 0-513-00485-8). Denison.
Morrison, G. C. Emergencies in Child Psychiatry: Emotional Crises of Children, Youth and Their Families. 516p. 1975. 32.75 (ISBN 0-398-03229-7). C C Thomas.
Morrison, George, jt. auth. see Fitzgibbon, Constantine.
Morrison, George, ed. & tr. from Persian. Vis & Ramin. LC 70-169960. (Persian Heritage Ser). 492p. 1972. 22.50x (ISBN 0-231-03408-3). Columbia U Pr.
Morrison, George S. Early Childhood Education Today. 2nd ed. (Early Childhood Education Ser.: No. C24). 456p. 1980. text ed. 16.95 (ISBN 0-675-08133-5); instructor's manual 3.95 (ISBN 0-686-63337-7). Merrill.
Morrison, Godfrey. The Southern Sudan & Eritrea: Aspects of Wider African Problems. (Minority Rights Group: No. 5). 1973. pap. 2.50 (ISBN 0-89192-094-3). Interbk Inc.
Morrison, Herbert S. British Parliamentary Democracy. pap. 3.50x (ISBN 0-210-34064-9). Asia.
Morrison, Hugh. Early American Architecture: From the First Colonial Settlement to the National Period. 1952. text ed. 19.95x (ISBN 0-19-500999-1). Oxford U Pr.
Morrison, Ivan G., jt. auth. see Brown, Arlen D.
Morrison, J. D., jt. auth. see Morrow, D. F.
Morrison, Jack, ed. see Carnegie Commission on Higher Education.
Morrison, James. Cruising Yacht Maintenance. (Illus.). 144p. Date not set. 10.95 (ISBN 0-668-04993-6, 4993-6). Arco.
Morrison, James D. Masterpieces of Religious Verse. 1977. pap. 9.95 (ISBN 0-8010-6038-9). Baker Bk.
--Organic Chemistry. 1979. text ed. 18.95x (ISBN 0-534-00605-1); study guide 7.95x (ISBN 0-534-00720-1); lab manual 8.95x (ISBN 0-534-00690-6). Wadsworth Pub.
Morrison, James H. The Human Side of Management. (Business Ser). (Illus.). 1971. pap. text ed. 8.95 (ISBN 0-201-04839-6). A-W.
Morrison, James H. & O'Hearne, John. Practical Transactional Analysis in Management. (Illus.). 168p. 1977. pap. text ed. 7.95 (ISBN 0-201-04898-1). A-W.
Morrison, James K. A Consumer Approach to Community Psychology. LC 79-1172. 1979. 18.95 (ISBN 0-88229-458-X). Nelson-Hall.
Morrison, James R. Your Brother's Keeper: A Guide for Families of the Mentall Ill. LC 79-27810. 352p. 1981. 20.95 (ISBN 0-88229-563-2). Nelson-Hall.
Morrison, James W. Bon Voyage: The Cruise Guide to the Caribbean. LC 80-26848. 192p. 1980. 9.95 (ISBN 0-668-04865-4); pap. 6.95 (ISBN 0-668-04851-4). Arco.
--Certificate in Data Processing Examination. rev. ed. LC 80-16390. 368p. 1980. pap. 12.00 (ISBN 0-668-04922-7, 4922-7). Arco.
--The Complete Coalburning Stove & Furnace Guide. (Illus.). 288p. 1981. 11.95 (ISBN 0-668-05097-7, 5097-7). Arco.
--The Complete Energy-Saving Home Improvement Guide. 4th ed. LC 80-23996. (Illus.). 1981. pap. 2.50 (ISBN 0-668-05085-3, 5085-3). Arco.
--Economics: Advanced Test for the G.R.E. 3rd ed. LC 78-5776. 1980. pap. 5.95 (ISBN 0-668-04548-5, 4548). Arco.
--The Florida Literacy Test: Statewide Assessment Program of Basic Skills & Functional Literacy. LC 78-6863. 1978. pap. 4.95 o.p. (ISBN 0-668-04669-4). Arco.
--Solid Mechanics: Strength of Material & Structural Design. LC 77-18555. (Professional Career Exam Ser.). (Illus.). 1978. pap. 10.00 o.p. (ISBN 0-668-04409-8, 4409). Arco.
Morrison, James W. & Hall, James. Environmental Studies: A Field & Laboratory Approach. LC 77-5372. 1978. lib. bdg. 11.95 o.p. (ISBN 0-668-04458-6, 4144); pap. text ed. 7.95 o.p. (ISBN 0-668-04144-7). Arco.
Morrison, Joel see Espenshade, Edward B., Jr.
Morrison, Joel L., jt. ed. see Espenshade, Edward B., Jr.
Morrison, John. The Media Men. (Today's World Ser.). 1978. 16.95 (ISBN 0-7134-0047-1, Pub. by Batsford England). David & Charles.
Morrison, John A. The Deacon of Dobbinsville. 64p. pap. 0.60. Faith Pub Hse.
Morrison, John S. & Williams, R. T. Greek Oared Ships, Nine Hundred - Three Hundred Twenty-Two B.C. LC 67-19504. (Illus.). 1968. 72.00 (ISBN 0-521-05770-1). Cambridge U Pr.
Morrison, Karl F. Europe's Middle Ages: Five Sixty-Five to Fifteen Hundred. 1970. pap. 7.95x (ISBN 0-673-05792-5). Scott F.
Morrison, Kristin. In Black & White. LC 70-171568. 1972. pap. text ed. 4.50 o.s.i. (ISBN 0-02-921980-9). Free Pr.
Morrison, L. M. & Schjeide, O. A. Coronary Heart Disease & the Mucopolysaccharides (Glycosaminoglycans) (Illus.). 288p. 1974. 22.50 (ISBN 0-398-02903-2). C C Thomas.
Morrison, L. Robert, jt. auth. see Eckhouse, Richard H., Jr.
Morrison, Leger R. Typewriting for Business. rev. ed. LC 74-23629. (Illus.). 1981. pap. text ed. 9.00 (ISBN 0-913310-05-0). PAR Inc.
Morrison, Leona. Island of Eden. LC 76-41021. 1977. 8.95 o.p. (ISBN 0-688-03151-X). Morrow.
Morrison, Leonard A. & Sharples, Stephen P. History of the Kimball Family in America from Sixteen Thirty-Four to Eighteen Ninety-Seven. 1978. Repr. of 1897 ed. 30.00x o.s.i. (ISBN 0-932334-02-4). Heart of the Lakes.
Morrison, Lillian. Overheard in a Bubble Chamber & Other Sciencepoems. (Illus.). 64p. (gr. 7 up). 1981. 7.95 (ISBN 0-688-00490-3); PLB 7.63 (ISBN 0-688-00493-8). Morrow.
Morrison, Lillian, ed. Diller, a Dollar: Rhymes & Sayings for the Ten O'Clock Scholar. LC 55-9213. (Illus.). (gr. 4 up). 1955. 8.95 (ISBN 0-690-23957-2, TYC-J). T Y Crowell.
--Remember Me When This You See. LC 60-11536. (Illus.). (gr. 4 up). 1961. 8.95 (ISBN 0-690-69613-2, TYC-J). T Y Crowell.
--Touch Blue. LC 57-10284. (Illus.). (gr. 4 up). 1958. 8.95 (ISBN 0-690-83316-4, TYC-J). T Y Crowell.
Morrison, Louis. Monarch Notes on Tolkein's Fellowship of the Ring. 1976. pap. 1.95 (ISBN 0-671-00971-0). Monarch Pr.
Morrison, M. A., et al. Quantum States of Atoms, Molecules, & Solids. 204p. 1976. 28.95 (ISBN 0-13-747980-8). P-H.
Morrison, Mary C. Jesus: Sketches for a Portrait. rev. & enl. ed. 1979. 2.00 (ISBN 0-686-28782-7). Forward Movement.
Morrison, Mary G., ed. see Garnier, Robert.
Morrison, Minion K. Ethnicity & Political Integration: Ashanti, Ghana. (Foreign & Comparative Studies Program African Ser.: No. XXXVI). 1981. pap. text ed. price not set (ISBN 0-915984-59-8). Syracuse U Foreign Comp.
Morrison, N. Brysson. Private Life of Henry the Eighth. LC 63-13796. (Illus.). 1964. 8.95 (ISBN 0-8149-0162-X). Vanguard.
Morrison, Nan. Katherine Tree. (YA) 5.95 (ISBN 0-685-07440-4, Avalon). Bouregy.
Morrison, R., tr. see Annensky, Innokenty.
Morrison, R. H. Divorce Dirty Tricks. 248p. 1980. 9.95 (ISBN 0-8119-0408-3, Pegasus Rex). Fell.
--Divorce Dirty Tricks. 265p. 1980. 9.95 (ISBN 0-937484-03-2). Pegasus Rex NJ.
Morrison, Robert T. & Boyd, Robert N. Organic Chemistry. 3rd ed. 1280p. 1973. text ed. 28.95 (ISBN 0-205-03239-7, 6832393); study guide 15.95 (ISBN 0-205-04466-2, 6844669). Allyn.
Morrison, Samuel E. Oxfod History of the American People. Incl. Vol. 2 (ISBN 0-451-61890-4, M*E 1890); Vol. 3 (ISBN 0-451-61891-2, ME1891). Date not set. pap. 2.50 (Ment). NAL.
Morrison, Stanley, jt. auth. see Bott, Raymond.
Morrison, Stanley, jt. auth. see Fairman, Charles.
Morrison, T. A. Cornwall's Central Mines: The Northern District, 1810-1895. 400p. 1980. 40.00x (ISBN 0-906720-10-9, Pub. by Hodge England). State Mutual Bk.
Morrison, T. I., jt. auth. see Johnstone, A. H.
Morrison, Theodore. Leave of Absence: A Novel. 1981. 12.95 (ISBN 0-393-01439-8). Norton.
Morrison, Thomas K. Manufactured Exports from Developing Countries. LC 76-25353. (Illus.). 1976. text ed. 17.95 o.p. (ISBN 0-275-56880-6). Praeger.
Morrison, Toni. Song of Solomon. (RL 7). 1978. pap. 2.75 (ISBN 0-451-09443-3, E9443, Sig). NAL.
--Tar Baby. LC 80-22821. 320p. 1981. 11.95 (ISBN 0-394-42329-1). Knopf.
Morrison, Velma F. Going on a Dig. LC 80-2776. (Illus.). 128p. (gr. 5 up). 1981. PLB 6.95 (ISBN 0-396-07915-6). Dodd.
Morrison, Wilbur H. The Incredible 305th. 1977. pap. 1.50 (ISBN 0-505-51154-1). Tower Bks.
--Point of No Return. LC 80-81000. (World War II Ser.). (Illus.). 272p. (Orig.). 1980. pap. 2.50 (ISBN 0-87216-716-X). Playboy Pbks.
--Wings Over the Seven Seas. LC 73-22597. (Illus.). 1976. 20.00 o.p. (ISBN 0-498-01485-1). A S Barnes.
Morrison, Winifrede. Drying & Preserving Flowers. 1973. 17.95 (ISBN 0-7134-2324-2, Pub. by Batsford England). David & Charles.
--Flower Arrangements for Special Occasions. (Illus.). 88p. 1976. 8.95 o.s.i. (ISBN 0-7134-3088-5). Hippocrene Bks.
Morriss, James E., jt. auth. see Freedman, Russell.
Morrissett, Irving, ed. International Perspectives on Social-Political Education. 1980. pap. write for info (ISBN 0-89994-253-9). Soc Sci Ed.
Morrissette, Bruce A. Alain Robbe-Grillet. LC 65-26337. (Columbia Essays on Modern Writers Ser.: No. 11). (Orig.). pap. 2.00 (ISBN 0-231-02682-X, MW11). Columbia U Pr.
Morrissey, Charles T. Vermont: The States & the Nation. (Illus.). 240p. 1981. 12.95 (ISBN 0-393-05625-2). Norton.
Morrissey, Dianne J. A Gossamered View with a Special Section on the Legends of Christmas. LC 80-68777. (Illus.). 92p. (Orig.). 1980. pap. 3.95 (ISBN 0-9604664-0-1). Artemis Pr.
Morrissey, Joseph P., et al, eds. The Enduring Asylum: Cycles of Institutional Reform at Worcester State Hospital. 1980. 31.50 (ISBN 0-8089-1291-7). Grune.
Morrissey, Kathleen M. Speech Bingo, Set 1. (Illus.). 1980. pap. 7.95x (ISBN 0-8134-2144-6). Interstate.
Morrissy, Lois E., jt. auth. see Burns, Margaret A.
Morrow, et al. Dental Laboratory Procedures, Complete Dentures, Vol. 1. LC 79-16785. (Illus.). 1979. text ed. 37.50 (ISBN 0-8016-3513-6). Mosby.
Morrow, Bradford & Cooney, Seamus. Bibliography of the Black Sparrow Press Nineteen Sixty-Six to Nineteen Seventy-Eight. (Illus.). 375p. 1980. 40.00 (ISBN 0-87685-465-X); ltd. ed. 75.00 (ISBN 0-87685-466-8). Black Sparrow.
Morrow, C. Paul & Townsend, Duane E. Synopsis of Gynecologic Oncology. 500p. 1981. 29.50 (ISBN 0-471-06504-8, Pub. by Wiley-Med). Wiley.
Morrow, Carol K. Health Care Guidance: Commercial Health Insurance & National Health Policy. LC 76-14415. 1976. text ed. 21.50 (ISBN 0-275-56950-0). Praeger.
Morrow, Carolyn C. & Schoenly, Steven B. A Conservation Bibliography for Librarian, Archivists, & Admimistrators. LC 79-64847. 271p. 1979. 18.50x (ISBN 0-87875-170-X). Whitston Pub.
Morrow, D. F. & Morrison, J. D. Anaesthesia for Eye, Ear, Nose & Throat Surgery. (Illus.). 160p. 1975. text ed. 18.95 o.s.i. (ISBN 0-443-01187-7). Churchill.
Morrow, David A. Current Therapy in Theriogenology: Diagnosis, Treatment & Prevention of Reproductive Diseases in Animal. LC 77-84675. (Illus.). 1287p. 1980. text ed. 69.50 (ISBN 0-7216-6564-0). Saunders.
Morrow, E. Frederic. Way Down South, Up North. LC 72-13451. 1973. 6.95 (ISBN 0-8298-0246-0). Pilgrim NY.
Morrow, Honore. On to Oregon. (Illus.). (gr. 5-9). 1946. Repr. of 1926 ed. 8.95 (ISBN 0-688-21639-0). Morrow.
--Seven Alone. (gr. 7-12). 1977. pap. 1.50 (ISBN 0-590-10291-5, Schol Pap). Schol Bk Serv.
Morrow, James & Suid, Murray. Media & Kids: Real-World Learning in the Schools. 1977. pap. text ed. 10.75x (ISBN 0-8104-5798-9). Hayden.
Morrow, James, jt. auth. see Suid, Murray.
Morrow, James E. The Freshwater Fishes of Alaska. LC 80-1116. (Illus.). 272p. (Orig.). 1980. pap. 24.95 (ISBN 0-88240-134-3). Alaska Northwest.
Morrow, John, ed. see Rivkin, Arnold.
Morrow, K. & Johnson, K. Communicate One. (Cambridge English Language Learning Ser.). 1980. students' ed. 7.95 (ISBN 0-521-21850-0); tchr's. ed. 5.95 (ISBN 0-521-21849-7); cassette 13.95 (ISBN 0-521-21848-9). Cambridge U Pr.
Morrow, Linda & Morrow, Ray. Go Fly a Sailplane. LC 80-65995. (Illus.). 192p. 1981. 10.95 (ISBN 0-689-11080-4). Atheneum.
Morrow, Ray, jt. auth. see Morrow, Linda.
Morrow, Robert M. Handbook of Immediate Overdentures. LC 78-16585. (Illus.). 1978. pap. text ed. 17.95 (ISBN 0-8016-3543-8). Mosby.
Morrow, Robert M., jt. auth. see Brewer, Allen A.
Morrris, Lynn L. & Fitz-Gibbon, Carol T. How to Present an Evaluation Report. rev. ed. LC 78-58657. (Program Evaluation Kit Ser.: Vol. 8). (Illus.). 80p. 1978. pap. 4.50 (ISBN 0-8039-1069-X). Sage.
Morsberger, Katherine M., jt. auth. see Morsberger, Robert E.
Morsberger, Robert & Thompson, Tracy, eds. American Screenwriters One & Two, 2 vols. (Dictionary of Literary Biography Ser.). (Illus.). 1981. Set. 108.00 (ISBN 0-8103-0917-3, Bruccoli Clark Book). Gale.
Morsberger, Robert E. Commonsense Grammar & Style. rev ed. LC 78-78273. (Apollo Eds.). 400p. 1975. pap. 3.95 o.s.i. (ISBN 0-8152-0375-6, A-375, TYC-T). T Y Crowell.
--James Thurber. (U. S. Authors Ser.: No. 62). 1964. lib. bdg. 10.95 (ISBN 0-8057-0728-X). Twayne.
--Swordplay & the Elizabethan & Jacobean Stage. (Salzburg Studies in English Literature, Jacobean Drama Studies: No. 37). (Illus.). 129p. 1974. pap. text ed. 25.00x (ISBN 0-391-01485-4). Humanities.
Morsberger, Robert E. & Morsberger, Katherine M. Lew Wallace: Militant Romantic. (Illus.). 384p. 1980. 17.95 (ISBN 0-07-043305-4). McGraw.
Morse, Ann. Barry Manilow. (Rock 'n Pop Stars Ser.). (Illus.). (gr. 4-12). 1978. PLB 5.95 (ISBN 0-87191-617-7); pap. 2.95 (ISBN 0-89812-122-1). Creative Ed.
--Olivia Newton-John. (Rock 'n Pop Stars Ser.). (Illus.). (gr. 3-6). 1976. PLB 5.95 (ISBN -087191-475-1); pap. 2.75 o. p. (ISBN 0-89812-117-5). Creative Ed.
--Tony Orlando. (Rock 'n Pop Stars Ser.). (Illus.). (gr. 4-12). 1978. PLB 5.95 (ISBN 0-87191-616-9); pap. 2.95 (ISBN 0-89812-123-X). Creative Ed.
Morse, Ann & Morse, Charles. Margaret Mead. LC 75-1343. (People to Remember Ser.). (Illus.). 32p. (gr. 3-6). 1975. PLB 5.95 (ISBN 0-87191-425-5). Creative Ed.
Morse, Ann, jt. auth. see Morse, Charles.
Morse, Ben W. & Phelps, Lynn A. Interpersonal Communication: A Relational Perspective. 1979. 15.95 (ISBN 0-8087-3963-8). Burgess.
Morse, Bruce. How to Negotiate the Labor Agreement. 8th ed. 1979. 8.85 (ISBN 0-9602426-0-0). Trends Pub.
Morse, C. A. Running Backs. LC 74-23176. (Stars of the NFL Ser.). (gr. 4-12). 1975. PLB 7.95 (ISBN 0-87191-416-6). Creative Ed.
Morse, Charles. Peggy Fleming. LC 74-18429. (Sports Superstars Ser). (Illus.). 32p. (gr. 3-6). 1974. PLB 5.95 o.p. (ISBN 0-87191-380-1); pap. 2.75 o.p. (ISBN 0-89812-192-2). Creative Ed.
Morse, Charles & Morse, Ann. Arthur Ashe. LC 74-954. (Creative's Superstars Ser). 32p. 1974. 5.50 o.p. (ISBN 0-87191-340-2). Creative Ed.
--Bob Griese. LC 74-4426. (Creative's Superstars Ser). 32p. 1974. 5.50 o.p. (ISBN 0-87191-345-3). Creative Ed.
--Carly Simon. LC 74-14550. (Rock'n Pop Stars Ser.). 32p. (gr. 4-12). 1974. PLB 5.95 (ISBN 0-87191-393-3); pap. 2.95 (ISBN 0-89812-101-9). Creative Ed.
--Evonne Goolagong. LC 74-796. (Creative's Superstars Ser). 32p. 1974. 5.50 o.p. (ISBN 0-87191-339-9). Creative Ed.
--Jackson Five. LC 74-12248. (Rock 'n Pop Stars Ser.). (Illus.). 32p. (gr. 3-6). 1974. PLB 5.95 (ISBN 0-87191-389-5); pap. 2.95 (ISBN 0-89812-098-5). Creative Ed.
--John Denver. LC 74-14551. (Rock'n Pop Stars Ser.). (Illus.). 32p. (gr. 3-6). 1974. PLB 5.95 (ISBN 0-87191-392-5); pap. 2.95 (ISBN 0-89812-104-3). Creative Ed.
--Lee Trevino. LC 74-2420. (Creative's Superstars Ser). 32p. 1974. 5.95 (ISBN 0-87191-342-9). Creative Ed.
--Roberta Flack. LC 74-13938. (Rock'n Pop Stars Ser.). (Illus.). 32p. (gr. 3-6). 1974. PLB 5.95 (ISBN 0-87191-396-8); pap. 2.75 o. p. (ISBN 0-89812-105-1). Creative Ed.
Morse, Charles, jt. auth. see Morse, Ann.
Morse, D. Motown. 1972. 5.95 o.s.i. (ISBN 0-02-587200-1). Macmillan.
--Motown. 1972. pap. 1.95 o.s.i. (ISBN 0-02-061340-7, Collier). Macmillan.
Morse, David. Grandfather Rock: The New Poetry & the Old. LC 76-156048. (gr. 7 up). 1972. 6.95 o.s.i. (ISBN 0-440-03016-1). Delacorte.
--Perspectives on Romanticism: A Transformational Analysis. 362p. 1981. 29.50x (ISBN 0-389-20164-2). B&N.
--Romanticism: A Structural Analysis. 252p. 1981. 29.50x (ISBN 0-389-20165-0). B&N.
Morse, Dean. Peripheral Worker. LC 73-76251. 1969. 20.00x (ISBN 0-231-03278-1). Columbia U Pr.
Morse, Dean & Gray, Susan. Early Retirement: Boon or Bane. LC 79-54970. (Conservation of Human Resources Ser.: No. 14). (Illus.). 180p. 1980. text ed. 23.00 (ISBN 0-916672-44-1). Allanheld.
Morse, Dean & Warner, Aaron W., eds. Technological Innovation & Society. LC 66-18342. (Seminar on Technology & Social Change Ser.). 1966. 20.00x (ISBN 0-231-02927-6). Columbia U Pr.
Morse, Dean W. Pride Against Prejudice: Work in the Lives of Older Blacks & Young Puerto Ricans. LC 78-65534. (Conservation of Human Resources Ser.: No. 9). 260p. 1980. text ed. 21.00 (ISBN 0-916672-67-0). Allanheld.
Morse, Dean W., jt. auth. see Hiestand, Dale L.

Morse, Donald R. Clinical Endodontology: A Comprehensive Guide to Diagnosis, Treatment & Prevention. (Illus.). 664p. 1974. 39.75 (ISBN 0-398-03121-5). C C Thomas.

Morse, Donald R. & Furst, Merrick L. Stress & Relaxation: Application to Dentistry. (Illus.). 284p. 1978. 17.75 (ISBN 0-398-03816-3). C C Thomas.

Morse, Dorothea B. Across the Pastures. 1981. 8.95 (ISBN 0-8062-1592-5). Carlton.

Morse, Douglas H. Behavioral Mechanisms in Ecology. LC 80-12130. 1980. text ed. 25.00x (ISBN 0-674-06460-7). Harvard U Pr.

Morse, Edward L. Foreign Policy & Interdependence in Gaullist France. LC 72-5391. (Center of International Studies). 388p. 1973. 21.50x (ISBN 0-691-05209-3). Princeton U Pr.

Morse, Edward L., ed. Samuel F.B. Morse: His Letters & Journals, 2 vols. 440p. 1980. Repr. of 1914 ed. lib. bdg. 65.00 (ISBN 0-89984-331-X). Century Bookbindery.

Morse, Elisabeth, jt. ed. see Hollingsworth, Dorothy.

Morse, Elliott R. see Mickelwait, Donald R., et al.

Morse, Flo. How Does It Feel to Be a Tree? LC 75-19177. (Illus.). 40p. (ps-3). 1976. 5.95 o.s.i. (ISBN 0-8193-0829-3, Four Winds); PLB 5.41 o.s.i. (ISBN 0-8193-0830-7). Schol Bk Serv.

Morse, John T., Jr. John Quincy Adams. LC 80-20125. (American Statesmen Ser.). 335p. 1981. pap. 5.95 (ISBN 0-87754-182-5). Chelsea Hse.

--Oliver Wendell Holmes, 2 vols. LC 80-21475. (American Men & Women of Letters Ser.). 700p. 1981. Set. pap. 10.95 (ISBN 0-87754-171-X). Chelsea Hse.

--Thomas Jefferson. LC 80-23357. (American Statesmen Ser.). 330p. 1981. pap. 5.95 (ISBN 0-87754-183-3). Chelsea Hse.

Morse, Joyce. Peter Sinks in the Water. (Books I Can Read). 32p. (Orig.). (gr. 2). 1980. pap. 1.25 (ISBN 0-8127-0281-6). Southern Pub.

--Where Is Jesus? (Books I Can Read). 32p. (gr. 2). 1980. pap. 1.25 (ISBN 0-8127-0280-8). Southern Pub.

Morse, L. A. The Flesh Eaters. 1979. pap. 2.25 (ISBN 0-446-82633-2). Warner Bks.

Morse, L. E. & Henifin, M. S., eds. Rare Plant Conservation: Geographical Data Organization. 1981. pap. 25.00 (ISBN 0-89327-223-X). NY Botanical.

Morse, Lawrence. Writing the Economics Paper. 1981. pap. text ed. 3.75 (ISBN 0-8120-2113-4). Barron.

Morse, Leon W. Practical Handbook of Industrial Traffic Management. 6th ed. LC 77-9240. 552p. 1980. text ed. write for info. (ISBN 0-87408-020-7). Traffic Serv.

Morse, M. Selected Papers. (Illus.). 710p. 1981. 35.00 (ISBN 0-387-90532-4). Springer-Verlag.

Morse, Marston. Variational Analysis: Critical Extremals & Sturmian Extensions. LC 72-8368. (Pure & Applied Mathematics Ser). 304p. 1973. 34.50 (ISBN 0-471-61700-8, Pub. by Wiley-Interscience). Wiley.

Morse, P. & Brand, T. Home-Style Learning: Activities for Young Children & Their Parents. 1981. pap. 5.95 (ISBN 0-13-392944-2); 10.95 (ISBN 0-13-392951-5). P-H.

Morse, Philip M. & Kimball, George E. Methods of Operations Research. (Illus.). 179p. 1980. pap. 14.95 (ISBN 0-932146-03-1). Peninsula.

Morse, Philip M., et al. Nuclear, Particle & Many Body Physics, 2 vols. 1972. Vol. 1. 53.50 (ISBN 0-12-508201-0); Vol. 2. 50.50 (ISBN 0-12-508202-9); Set. 84.50 (ISBN 0-685-27233-8). Acad Pr.

Morse, Robert L., ed. Exercise & the Heart: Guidelines for Exercise Programs. (Illus.). 292p. 1974. 28.75 (ISBN 0-398-02365-4). C C Thomas.

Morse, Roger A. Bees & Beekeeping. LC 74-14082. (Illus.). 320p. 1975. 17.50x (ISBN 0-8014-0920-9). Comstock.

Morse, Roger A., ed. Honey Bee Pests, Predators & Diseases. LC 78-58027. (Illus.). 1978. 32.50x (ISBN 0-8014-0975-6). Comstock.

Morse, S. A. Basalts & Phase Diagrams: An Introduction to the Quantitative Use of Phase Diagrams in Igneous Petrology. (Illus.). 400p. 1980. 29.80 o.p. (ISBN 0-387-90477-8). Springer-Verlag.

Morse, Samuel C., tr. see Fujioka, Ryoichi.

Morse, Samuel F. Changes. LC 64-25346. 91p. 1964. 5.95 (ISBN 0-8040-0034-4). Swallow.

Morse, Samuel F., et al. Wallace Stevens Checklist & Bibliography of Stevens Criticism. LC 63-21871. 98p. 1963. 7.95x (ISBN 0-8040-0316-5). Swallow.

Morse, Stearns A., jt. auth. see Stoiber, Richard E.

Morse, Stephen P. The Eighty Eighty-Six Primer: An Introduction to Its Architecture, System Design & Programming. 224p. 1980. pap. 9.95 (ISBN 0-8104-5165-4). Hayden.

Morse, W. J., jt. auth. see Piper, Charles V.

Morse, Wayne J. Cost Accounting: Processing, Evaluating, & Using Cost Data. (Illus.). 752p. 1981. text ed. 18.95 (ISBN 0-201-04677-6). A-W.

Morse, Whit, jt. auth. see Firestone, Linda.

Morse, Willard S. & Brinckle, Gertrude. Howard Pyle. LC 68-31099. 1969. Repr. of 1921 ed. 15.00 (ISBN 0-8103-3493-3). Gale.

Morse, William C., ed. Humanistic Teaching for Exceptional Children: An Introduction to Special Education. (Illus.). 344p. 1979. 18.00x (ISBN 0-8156-2199-X); pap. 8.95x (ISBN 0-8156-2215-5). Syracuse U Pr.

Morse, William C., et al, eds. Affective Education for Special Children & Youth. LC 80-65499. 128p. (Orig.). pap. 6.75 (ISBN 0-86586-104-8). Coun Exc Child.

Morselli, P. L., et al, eds. Basic & Therapeutic Aspects of Perinatal Pharmacology. LC 74-21981. (Monograph of the Mario Negri Institute of Pharmacological Research). 1975. 37.50 (ISBN 0-89004-016-8). Raven.

--Drug Interactions. LC 74-77802. (Monograph of the Mario Negri Institute for Pharmacological Research). 1974. 37.50 (ISBN 0-911216-59-6). Raven.

Morshead, O. F., ed. see Pepys, Samuel.

Morsicato, Helen G. Currency Translation & Performance Evaluation in Multinationals. Dufey, Gunter, ed. (Research for Business Decisions). 176p. 1980. 24.95 (ISBN 0-8357-1104-8, Pub. by UMI Res Pr). Univ Microfilms.

Morson, B. C. Histological Typing of Intestinal Tumours. LC 70-101520. (International Histological Classification of Tumours (World Health Organization) Ser.). (Illus.). 69p. 1976. text ed. 53.00 (ISBN 92-4-176015-X); text & slides 142.00. Am Soc Clinical.

Morson, Basil C., jt. ed. see Yardley, John H.

Morson, Gary S. The Boundaries of Genre: Dostoevsky's "Diary of a Writer" & the Traditions of Literary Utopia. 272p. 1981. text ed. 25.00x (ISBN 0-292-70732-0). U of Tex Pr.

Morson, John. Christ the Way: The Christology of Guerric of Igny. (Cistercian Studies: N0.25). 1978. 11.95 (ISBN 0-87907-825-1). Cistercian Pubns.

Morss, Elliott R. & Rich, Robert F. Government Information Management: A Counter-Report to the Commission on Federal Paperwork. (Westview Special Studies in Information Management). 225p. 1980. lib. bdg. 26.50x (ISBN 0-89158-596-6). Westview.

Mort, Terry A. Systematic Selling: How to Influence the Buying Decision Process. new ed. LC 77-5937. (Illus.). 1977. 14.95 (ISBN 0-8144-5439-9). Am Mgmt.

Mortell, Arthur. Anatomy of a Successful Salesman. LC 72-97792. 1973. 9.95 (ISBN 0-87863-041-4). Farnswth Pub.

Mortensen, A. Russell, jt. ed. see Mulder, William.

Mortensen, Donald & Schmuller, Alan. Guidance in Today's Schools. 3rd ed. LC 75-35989. 1976. text ed. 24.95 (ISBN 0-471-61779-2). Wiley.

Mortensen, Eric S. The Essence & the Vocation of Man. (Illus.). 1980. deluxe ed. 37.55 (ISBN 0-89266-231-X). Am Classical Coll Pr.

Mortensen, Ralph, tr. see Yeh Ch'ing.

Mortenson, William P. Modern Marketing of Farm Products. 3rd ed. LC 76-14650. (Illus.). (gr. 9-12). 1977. 15.35 (ISBN 0-8134-1816-X); text ed. 11.50x (ISBN 0-685-77710-3). Interstate.

Mortenson, William P., jt. auth. see Brickbauer, Elwood A.

Mortenson, William P., jt. auth. see Juergenson, Elwood M.

Morth, H. T., tr. see Breuer, Georg.

Mortier, Agnes. The Soul of the World. 1977. 5.95 o.p. (ISBN 0-533-02767-5). Vantage.

Mortimer, Carole. Brand of Possession. (Harlequin Presents Ser.). 192p. (Orig.). 1981. pap. 1.50 (ISBN 0-373-10406-5, Pub. by Harlequin). PB.

--Devil Lover. (Harlequin Presents Ser.). 192p. 1981. pap. 1.50 (ISBN 0-373-10430-8, Pub. by Harlequin). PB.

--Engaged to Jarrod Stone. (Harlequin Presents Ser.). 192p. pap. 1.50 (ISBN 0-373-10388-3, Pub. by Harlequin). PB.

--Fear of Love. (Harlequin Presents Ser.). 192p. 1980. pap. 1.50 (ISBN 0-373-10377-8, Pub. by Harlequin). PB.

--The Flame of Desire. (Harlequin Presents Ser.). 192p. 1981. pap. 1.50 (ISBN 0-373-10418-9, Pub. by Harlequin). PB.

--Living Together. (Harlequin Presents Ser.). 192p. 1981. pap. 1.50 (ISBN 0-373-10423-5, Pub. by Harlequin). PB.

--Yesterday's Scars. (Harlequin Presents Ser.). 192p. 1980. pap. 1.50 (ISBN 0-373-10383-2, Pub. by Harlequin). PB.

Mortimer, G., et al, eds. Coach Trimming: Part One, 2 vols. (Engineering Craftsmen: No. E3). (Illus.). 1969. Set. spiral bdg. 36.50x set (ISBN 0-85083-041-9). Intl Ideas.

--Coach Trimming: Part Two. (Engineering Craftsmen: No. E23). (Illus.). 1970. spiral bdg. 26.00x (ISBN 0-85083-124-5). Intl Ideas.

Mortimer, Hilda & George, Dan. You Call Me Chief: Impressions of the Life of Chief Dan George. LC 78-60297. (Illus.). 192p. 1981. 11.95 (ISBN 0-385-04806-8). Doubleday.

Mortimer, J. E. The Professional Union. 432p. 1980. text ed. 37.50x (ISBN 0-04-331076-1). Allen Unwin.

Mortimer, J. E., jt. auth. see Jenkins, C.

Mortimer, James A. & Schuman, Leonard M., eds. The Epidemiology of Dementia. (Illus.). 200p. 1981. text ed. 18.95x (ISBN 0-19-502906-2). Oxford U Pr.

Mortimer, John. The Trials of Rumpole. 206p. 1981. pap. 2.95 (ISBN 0-14-005162-7). Penguin.

--Will Shakespeare. 1978. 8.95 o.s.i. (ISBN 0-440-09792-4). Delacorte.

Mortimer, Mildred P., ed. Contes Africains. LC 71-168855. (Illus., Orig.). 1972. pap. text ed. 7.20 (ISBN 0-395-12078-0, 3-39210). HM.

Mortimer, Raymond, jt. auth. see Todd, Dorothy.

Mortimer, Robert A. The Third World Coalition in International Politics. LC 79-23208. 160p. 1980. 19.95 (ISBN 0-03-055286-9). Praeger.

Mortlock, A. J. & Hueneke, K. Beyond the Cotter. LC 79-53837. (Canberra Companions Ser.). (Illus.). 66p. (Orig.). 1980. pap. 3.95 (ISBN 0-7081-1581-0, 0541). Bks Australia.

Morton. China: Its History & Culture. 1981. 10.95 (ISBN 0-690-01863-0). Lippincott & Crowell.

--Use of Medical Literature. 2nd ed. 1978. 64.95 (ISBN 0-408-70916-2). Butterworths.

Morton & Morton, Desmond. Rebellions in Canada. (gr. 6-10). 1980. PLB 6.90 (ISBN 0-531-00449-X). Watts.

Morton, A. L. People's History of England. (Illus.). 1980. pap. 2.95 (ISBN 0-7178-0150-0). Intl Pub Co.

--World of Ranters-Religious Radicalism in the English Revolution. 1979. pap. 6.75x (ISBN 0-85315-497-X). Humanities.

Morton, A. L., tr. see Sperber, D.

Morton, Adam. Frames of Mind: Constraints of the Common-Sense Conception of the Mental. (Illus.). 180p. 1980. text ed. 22.00x (ISBN 0-19-824607-2). Oxford U Pr.

--A Guide Through the Theory of Knowledge. 1977. pap. 9.95x (ISBN 0-8221-0195-5). Dickenson.

Morton, Alexander C. Airline Guide to Stewardess & Steward Careers: 1979-1980. (Illus.). 1979. lib. bdg. 9.00 o.p. (ISBN 0-668-04346-6); pap. 6.95 o.p. (ISBN 0-668-04350-4). Arco.

--Official Nineteen Seventy Nine-Eighty Guide to Airline Careers: 1979-1980. rev. ed. (Illus.). 1979. lib. bdg. 9.00 o. p. (ISBN 0-668-04353-9); pap. 6.95 (ISBN 0-668-03955-8). Arco.

Morton, B. R. Numerical Approximation. (Library of Mathematics). 1969. pap. 5.00 (ISBN 0-7100-4354-6). Routledge & Kegan.

Morton, Brian N. & Morton, Jacqueline. Presse Deux. 2nd ed. 1977. pap. text ed. 7.95x (ISBN 0-669-01636-5). Heath.

Morton, Bruce L., jt. auth. see Jicks, John M.

Morton, Craig & Burger, Bob. Courage to Believe. 1981. 9.95 (ISBN 0-13-184416-4). P-H.

Morton, David. The Traditional Music of Thailand. LC 70-142048. 1976. 28.50x (ISBN 0-520-01876-1). U of Cal Pr.

Morton, David L. Traveller's Guide to the Art Museums of Europe. LC 80-67766. 175p. Date not set. pap. price not set (ISBN 0-912944-62-5). Berkshire Traveller. Postponed.

Morton, Desmond. The Queen Vs Louis Riel. LC 73-91562. (Social History of Canada Ser.). (Illus.). 1974. pap. 7.50 (ISBN 0-8020-6232-6). U of Toronto Pr.

Morton, Desmond, jt. auth. see Morton.

Morton, Don, jt. auth. see Stack, Louise.

Morton, Donald E. Vladimir Nabokov. LC 74-76128. (Modern Literature Ser.). 176p. 1974. 10.95 (ISBN 0-8044-2638-4). Ungar.

Morton, Eugene S., jt. ed. see Keast, Allen.

Morton, Frederic. A Nervous Splendor: Vienna 1888-1889. 1980. pap. 4.95 (ISBN 0-14-005667-X). Penguin.

--The Rothschilds. 1977. pap. 1.75 o.p. (ISBN 0-449-23242-5, Crest). Fawcett.

Morton, Harry. And Now New Zealand. 3rd ed. LC 77-353297. 1976. pap. 5.00x (ISBN 0-908565-07-0). Intl Pubns Serv.

Morton, Henry W. & Tokes, Rudolf L. Soviet Politics & Society in the 1970's. LC 73-10575. (Illus.). 1974. 17.95 (ISBN 0-02-922090-4). Free Pr.

Morton, J. E. Molluscs. (Hutchinson Biological Sciences Ser.). (Illus.). 244p. 1979. pap. text ed. 11.25 (ISBN 0-09-134161-2, Hutchinson U Lib). Humanities.

Morton, Jacqueline. English Grammar for Students of French. LC 79-87578. 1979. pap. 4.50 (ISBN 0-934034-00-1). Olivia & Hill.

Morton, Jacqueline, jt. auth. see Morton, Brian N.

Morton, James. In the Sea of Sterile Mountains: The Chinese in British Columbia. (Illus.). 294p. 1980. pap. 7.95 (ISBN 0-295-95724-7). U of Wash Pr.

Morton, Jane & Morton, Richard J. Innovation Without Renovation in the Elementary School. LC 74-79466. 192p. 1974. pap. text ed. 3.95 (ISBN 0-590-09582-X, Citation). Schol Bk Serv.

Morton, Jean S. Science in the Bible. 1978. pap. 14.95 (ISBN 0-8024-7629-5). Moody.

Morton, John H., ed. Principles of Surgery Patient Management Problems Pretest Self-Assessment & Review. (Illus., Orig.). 1981. pap. 25.00 (ISBN 0-07-050968-9). McGraw-PreTest.

Morton, Joyce. Edge of Fear. (YA) 1978. 5.95 (ISBN 0-685-84747-0, Avalon). Bouregy.

Morton, Judy C., et al. Dental Teamwork Strategies: Interpersonal & Organizational Approaches. LC 79-20229. 1979. pap. 11.95 (ISBN 0-8016-0979-8). Mosby.

--Building Assertive Skills: A Practical Guide to Professional Development for Allied Dental Health Providers. (Illus.). 283p. 1980. pap. text ed. 11.95 (ISBN 0-8016-3520-9). Mosby.

Morton, Julia. Atlas of Medicinal Plants of Middle America: Bahamas to Yucatan. (Illus.). 1400p. 1981. 147.50 (ISBN 0-398-04036-2). C C Thomas.

Morton, K. & Tulloch, P. Trade & Developing Countries. LC 76-30567. 1977. 24.95 (ISBN 0-470-99054-6). Halsted Pr.

Morton, K. W., jt. auth. see Richtmyer, Robert D.

Morton, Kathryn. Aid & Dependence: British Aid to Malawi. 188p. 1975. 21.00x o.p. (ISBN 0-8419-5501-8). Holmes & Meier.

Morton, Louis, ed. see Trask, David F.

Morton, Lucie, tr. see Galet, Pierre.

Morton, Lynne, jt. auth. see Schneider, Stephen H.

Morton, Malvin, ed. Can Public Welfare Keep Pace. LC 76-89859. 1969. 20.00x (ISBN 0-231-03324-9). Columbia U Pr.

Morton, Miriam. The Arts & the Soviet Child: The Esthetic Education of Children in the U.S.S.R. LC 72-156840. 1972. 10.95 o.s.i. (ISBN 0-02-921990-6). Free Pr.

Morton, Miriam, ed. A Harvest of Russian Children's Literature. (Illus.). (ps up). 1967. 27.50x (ISBN 0-520-00886-3); pap. 5.95 (ISBN 0-520-01745-5, CAL199). U of Cal Pr.

Morton, Miriam, ed. & tr. see Chukovsky, Kornei.

Morton, N. E. Outline of Genetic Epidemiology. (Illus.). x, 250p. 1981. pap. 25.75 (ISBN 3-8055-2269-X). S Karger.

Morton, Nancy A. Picnics with Pizzazz. (Orig.). 1981. pap. 5.95 (ISBN 0-8092-5922-2). Contemp Bks.

Morton, R. S. Sexual Freedom & Venereal Disease. (Contemporary Issues Ser: No. 5). 1971. text ed. 17.00x (ISBN 0-7206-0411-7). Humanities.

Morton, Richard, jt. ed. see Browning, John.

Morton, Richard J., jt. auth. see Morton, Jane.

Morton, Richard R., jt. auth. see Anderson, C. L.

Morton, Robert. Robert Morton: The Collected Works. Atlas, Allan, ed. (Masters & Monuments of the Renaissance Ser.: Vol. 2). xxxvi, 105p. 1981. 30.00x (ISBN 0-8450-7302-8). Broude.

Morton, Robin, compiled by. Come Day, Go Day, God Send Sunday: The Songs & Life Story, Told in His Own Words, of John Maguire, Traditional Singer & Farmer from County Fermanagh, N. Ireland. (Illus.). 202p. 1973. 13.00 (ISBN 0-7100-7634-7). Routledge & Kegan.

--Come Day, Go Day, God Send Sunday: The Songs & Life Story, Told in His Own Words, of John Maguire, Traditional Singer & Farmer from County Fermanagh, N. Ireland. (Illus.). 1976. pap. 6.95 (ISBN 0-7100-8388-2). Routledge & Kegan.

Morton, S. Fiona, ed. A Bibliography of Arnold J. Toynbee. 300p. 1980. 74.00 (ISBN 0-19-215261-0). Oxford U Pr.

Morton, Terry B., ed. Monumentum. (Illus.). 128p. (Orig.). 1976. pap. 10.00 (ISBN 0-89133-087-9). Preservation Pr.

Morton, Virgil L., jt. auth. see Ellfeldt, Lois.

Morton, W. E. & Hearle, J. W. Physical Properties of Textile Fibres. 2nd ed. LC 74-30834. 660p. 1975. 68.95x (ISBN 0-470-61850-7). Halsted Pr.

Morton, W. L. Henry Youle Hind, Eighteen Twenty-Three to Nineteen Eight. (Canadian Biographical Stud.). 1980. 7.50 (ISBN 0-8020-3278-8). U of Toronto Pr.

--The Progressive Party in Canada. (Scholarly Reprint Ser.). 1980. Repr. 35.00x (ISBN 0-8020-7096-5). U of Toronto Pr.

Morton, W. Scott. China: It's History & Culture. (Illus.). 1980. 16.95 (ISBN 0-690-01863-0). Lippincott.

Morton, Walter A. Housing Taxation. 1955. 20.00x (ISBN 0-299-01240-9). U of Wis Pr.

Morton, William L. Canadian Identity. 2nd ed. (Orig.). 1972. 17.50x (ISBN 0-299-06130-2); pap. 6.95 (ISBN 0-299-06134-5). U of Wis Pr.

Moruzzi, V. L., et al. Calculated Electronic Properties of Metals: Designing Our Career Machines. LC 79-14183. 1978. 37.00 (ISBN 0-08-022705-8). Pergamon.

Moryadas, S., jt. auth. see Lowe, John C.

Mos, L. P., jt. ed. see Royce, J. R.

Mosbacher, Eric, tr. see Ferenczi, Sandor.

Mosby, Dewey F. Alexandre-Gabriel Decamps (1803-1860, 2 vols. LC 76-23651. (Outstanding Dissertations in the Fine Arts - 2nd Series - 19th Century). (Illus.). 1977. Repr. of 1973 ed. Set. lib. bdg. 128.00 (ISBN 0-8240-2714-0). Garland Pub.

Mosby, Robert. The Degeneration in the Leadership in the United States As the Primary Cause for the Moral, Economic & Political Collapse of the World. (Illus.). 243p. 1976. 25.00 (ISBN 0-913314-67-6); lib. bdg. 39.50 (ISBN 0-685-66467-8). Am Classical Coll Pr.

Mosca, Gaetano. The Ruling Class. Livingston, Arthur, ed. Kahn, Hannah D., tr. from Italian. LC 80-17230. xli, 514p. 1980. Repr. of 1939 ed. lib. bdg. 37.50x (ISBN 0-313-22617-2, MORU). Greenwood.

Moscarello, Louis C., et al. Retail Accounting & Financial Control. 4th ed. LC 76-24550. 1976. 32.50 (ISBN 0-8260-6402-7). Ronald Pr.

Moscati, Sabatino. Face of the Ancient Orient. pap. 2.95 (ISBN 0-385-01397-3, A289, Anch). Doubleday.

Moscato, Donald R. Building Financial Decision-Making Models: An Introduction to Principles & Procedures. 144p. 1980. 17.95 (ISBN 0-8144-5609-X). Am Mgmt.

Moscheles, Ignatz. Recent Music & Musicians As Described in the Diaries & Correspondence of Ignatz Moscheles. LC 73-125057. (Music Ser). 1970. Repr. of 1873 ed. lib. bdg. 32.50 (ISBN 0-306-70022-0). Da Capo.

Moschini, Francesco, ed. Massimo Scolari. LC 80-50657. (Illus.). 240p. 1980. pap. 17.50 (ISBN 0-8478-0317-1). Rizzoli Intl.

Moschovakis, Y. N. Descriptive Set Theory. (Studies in Logic & the Foundations of Mathematics: Vol. 100). 640p. 1979. 73.25 (ISBN 0-444-85305-7, North Holland). Elsevier.

Moschytz, G. S. Active Filter Design Handbook: For Use with Programmable Pocket Calculators & Minicomputers. 296p. 1981. 49.95 (ISBN 0-471-27850-5, Pub. by Wiley-Interscience). Wiley.

Moschytz, G. S. & Neirynck, J., eds. Circuit Theory & Design. 1978. text ed. 84.00x (ISBN 2-604-00033-4). Renouf.

Moschytz, G. S., ed. see Brayton, R. K., et al.

Moschzisker, R. Von see Von Moschzisker, R.

Mosco, Maisie. Almonds & Raisins. 384p. (Orig.). 1981. pap. cancelled (ISBN 0-553-13913-4). Bantam.

Moscona, A. A., jt. ed. see Monroy, Alberto.

Moscona, Aron, ed. The Cell Surface in Development. LC 74-7308. 1974. 48.95 (ISBN 0-471-61855-1, Pub. by Wiley Medical). Wiley.

Moscove, Stephen. Accounting Fundamentals: A Self-Instructional Approach. 2nd ed. 1980. pap. text ed. 10.95 (ISBN 0-8359-0061-4); wkbk. 7.95 (ISBN 0-8359-0070-3); instr's. manual avail. (ISBN 0-8359-0062-2). Reston.

Moscove, Stephen A. & Simkin, Mark G. Accounting Information Systems: Concepts & Practice for Effective Decision Making Systems. LC 80-15445. (Wiley Ser. in Accounting & Information Systems). 560p. 1981. 23.95 (ISBN 0-471-03369-3); tchr's manual avail. (ISBN 0-471-03371-5). Wiley.

Moscovici, Serge. Society Against Nature. Rabinowitz, Sacha, tr. from Fr. (European Ideas Ser.). 1976. text ed. 17.00x (ISBN 0-391-00523-5). Humanities.

Moscovitch, Allan & Drover, Glenn, eds. Inequality: Essays on the Political Economy of Social Welfare. (Studies in the Political Economy of Canada). 408p. 1981. 30.00x (ISBN 0-8020-2403-3); pap. 10.00 (ISBN 0-8020-6426-4). U of Toronto Pr.

Moscow, Henry. Thomas Jefferson & His World. LC 60-11827. (American Heritage Junior Library). (Illus.). 153p. (gr. 6 up). 1960. 9.95 (ISBN 0-8281-0386-0, J003-0); PLB 12.89 (ISBN 0-06-024346-5, Dist. by Har-Row). Am Heritage.

Moseley, Caroline & Moseley, David. Language & Reading Among Underachievers: A Practical Review. (General Ser.). 1977. pap. text ed. 10.50x (ISBN 0-85633-136-8, NFER). Humanities.

Moseley, David, jt. auth. see Moseley, Caroline.

Moseley, David V. Special Provision for Reading: When Will They Ever Learn ? (General Ser). 240p. 1975. pap. text ed. 20.00x (ISBN 0-85633-063-9, NFER). Humanities.

Moseley, F., jt. auth. see Wright, A. E.

Moseley, Frank. Advanced Geological Map Interpretation. LC 79-11243. 1979. pap. 10.95x (ISBN 0-470-26708-9). Halsted Pr.

Moseley, George V., 3rd. Consolidation of the South China Frontier. (Center for Chinese Studies, UC Berkeley). 1973. 19.50x (ISBN 0-520-02102-9). U of Cal Pr.

Moseley, H. F. Shoulder Lesions. 3rd ed. 1969. 57.00x o.p. (ISBN 0-443-00634-2). Churchill.

Moseley, James G., ed. A Complex Inheritance. LC 75-8955. (American Academy of Religion. Dissertation Ser.). ix, 169p. 1975. pap. 7.50 (ISBN 0-89130-000-7, 010104). Scholars Pr Ca.

Moseley, L. G. Research for Social Welfare: Six Case Studies in Cyprus. 143p. 1979. pap. text ed. 9.90x (ISBN 0-7199-0948-1, Pub. by Bedford England). Renouf.

Moseley, M. E. The Maritime Foundations of Andean Civilization. LC 74-84816. 138p. 1975. text ed. 5.50 o p. (ISBN 0-8465-4800-3, 54800). Benjamin-Cummings.

Moseley, Malcolm. Growth Centres in Spatial Planning. LC 74-9962. 1974. text ed. 19.00 (ISBN 0-08-018055-8). Pergamon.

Moseley, Michael E. & Mackey, Carol. Twenty-Four Architectural Plans of Chan Chan, Peru. LC 73-92493. 1974. maps 30.00 (ISBN 0-87365-778-0). Peabody Harvard.

Moseley, Micheal E. & Day, Kent C., eds. Chan Chan: Andean Desert City. (School of American Research Advanced Seminar Ser.). (Illus.). 440p. 1981. 29.95x (ISBN 0-8263-0575-X). U of NM Pr.

Moseley, Spencer & Reed, Gervais. Walter F. Isaacs: An Artist in America, Eighteen Eighty-Six to Nineteen Sixty-Four. (Index of Art in the Pacific Northwest Ser: No. 8). (Illus.). Date not set. price not set o.p. (ISBN 0-295-95389-6); pap. price not set o.p. (ISBN 0-295-95396-9). U of Wash Pr. Postponed.

Moselle, Gary. Building Cost Manual Nineteen Eighty-One. 240p. (Orig.). 1980. pap. 10.00 (ISBN 0-910460-77-9). Craftsman.

--Installing Solar Heating Systems. 224p. (Orig.). 1981. pap. 13.50 (ISBN 0-910460-83-3). Craftsman.

--National Construction Estimator Nineteen Eighty-One. (Illus.). 304p. (Orig.). 1980. pap. 10.75 (ISBN 0-910460-29-9). Craftsman.

Mosely, ed. see Cowles, Julia.

Mosely, Jane, ed. see Lynch, Daniel.

Moser, et al. Better Living & Breathing: A Manual for Patients. 2nd ed. LC 80-17943. (Illus.). 94p. 1980. pap. text ed. 4.95 (ISBN 0-8016-3565-9). Mosby.

Moser, Charles. Dimitrov of Bulgaria. 14.95. Green Hill.

Moser, Charles A. Denis Fonvizin. (World Authors Ser.: No. 560). 1979. lib. bdg. 14.95 (ISBN 0-8057-6402-X). Twayne.

Moser, Don. The Central American Jungles. (The American Wilderness Ser.). (Illus.). 1975. 12.95 (ISBN 0-8094-1342-6). Time-Life.

--Central American Jungles. LC 75-14284. (American Wilderness). (Illus.). (gr. 6 up). 1975. PLB 11.97 (ISBN 0-8094-1343-4, Pub. by Time-Life). Silver.

--China-Burma-India. Time Life Books, ed. (World War II Ser.). 1978. 12.95 (ISBN 0-8094-2482-7). Time-Life.

--The Snake River Country. (The American Wilderness Ser.). (Illus.). 1974. 12.95 (ISBN 0-8094-1241-1). Time-Life.

--The Snake River Country. LC 74-80283. (American Wilderness). (Illus.). (gr. 6 up). 1974. PLB 11.97 (ISBN 0-8094-1242-X, Pub. by Time-Life). Silver.

Moser, Harold D., ed. see Webster, Daniel.

Moser, J. Dynamical Systems, Theory & Applications. LC 75-14488. (Lecture Notes in Physics Ser.). vi, 624p. 1975. pap. 23.90 o.p. (ISBN 0-387-07171-7). Springer-Verlag.

Moser, Jurgen & Kyner, Walter T. Lectures on Hamiltonian Systems, & Rigorous & Formal Stability of Orbits About an Oblate Planet. LC 52-42839. (Memoirs: No. 81). 1979. pap. 8.40 (ISBN 0-8218-1281-5, MEMO-81). Am Math.

Moser, Kenneth M., jt. auth. see Shibel, Elaine.

Moser, Leo J. The Technology Trap. LC 78-26034. 1979. 14.95 (ISBN 0-88229-419-9); pap. 8.95 (ISBN 0-88229-669-8). Nelson-Hall.

Moser, Lida. Amphoto Guide to Special Effects. (Illus.). 168p. 1980. 10.95 (ISBN 0-8174-3523-9); pap. 6.95 (ISBN 0-8174-3524-7). Amphoto.

Moser, Norman. I Live in the South of My Heart. Herron, Bill, ed. 60p. 1980. 2.00. Illuminations Pr.

--Open Season. 32p. 1980. 3.00. Illuminations Pr.

Moser, Thomas. How to Build Shaker Furniture. LC 76-46809. (Illus.). 1979. 14.95 (ISBN 0-8069-8394-9); PLB 12.49 (ISBN 0-8069-8395-7). Sterling.

Moser, Thomas, ed. see Conrad, Joseph.

Moser, Thomas C. The Life in the Fiction of Ford Madox Ford. LC 80-7548. 360p. 1981. 22.50 (ISBN 0-691-06445-8); pap. 8.95 (ISBN 0-691-10102-7). Princeton U Pr.

Moser, Tilmann. Gottesvergiftung. (Suhrkamp Taschenbuecher: No. 533). 112p. 1980. pap. text ed. 3.25 (ISBN 3-518-37033-2, Pub. by Insel Verlag Germany). Suhrkamp.

Moser, W. O., jt. auth. see Coxeter, H. S.

Moses, jt. auth. see McBride.

Moses, A. J. Handbook of Electronic Materials, Vol. 1: Optical Materials Properties. LC 76-147312. 104p. 1971. 37.50 (ISBN 0-306-67101-8). IFI Plenum.

--Nuclear Techniques in Analytical Chemistry. LC 64-15736. (International Series on Analytical Chemistry: Vol. 20). 1965. 11.30 o.p. (ISBN 0-08-010695-1). Pergamon.

Moses, Alice E. Identity Management in Lesbian Women. (Praeger Special Studies). 1978. 21.95 (ISBN 0-03-047641-0). Praeger.

Moses, Edward A., jt. auth. see Gitman, Larry.

Moses, Harold A., ed. Student Personnel Work in General Education: A Humanistic Approach. (Illus.). 408p. 1974. 22.75 (ISBN 0-398-03128-2). C C Thomas.

Moses, J. L. & Byham, C. Applying the Assessment Center Method. LC 76-30476. 1978. text ed. 24.00 (ISBN 0-08-019581-4). Pergamon.

Moses, James A., jt. auth. see Strickland, Winifred G.

Moses, John. German Trade Unionism from Bismarck to Hitler: 1869-1933, 2 vols. Incl. Vol. 1. Bismarck to 1918. 400p (ISBN 0-389-20072-7); Vol. 2. 1919-1933. 400p (ISBN 0-389-20073-5). 1981. 25.00x ea. B&N.

Moses, John, ed. Historical Disciplines & Culture in Australasia. 1980. 23.50x (ISBN 0-7022-1295-4). U of Queensland Pr.

Moses, John A. Germany, Eighteen Forty-Eight to Eighteen Seventy-Nine. (History Monographs). 1973. pap. text ed. 4.50x (ISBN 0-435-31620-6). Heinemann Ed.

Moses, L. E., jt. auth. see Chernoff, Herman.

Moses, Larry W. The Political Role of Mongol Buddhism. (Indiana University Uralic & Altaic Ser.: Vol. 133). x, 299p. 1977. 14.95 (ISBN 0-933070-01-2). Ind U Res Inst.

Moses, Michael A., jt. auth. see Doktor, Robert H.

Moses, Montrose J. Children's Books & Reading. LC 74-23680. 1975. Repr. of 1907 ed. 20.00 (ISBN 0-8103-3767-3). Gale.

Moses, Robert A. Adler's Physiology of the Eye. 7th ed. LC 80-16862. (Illus.). 747p. 1980. text ed. 41.00 (ISBN 0-8016-3541-1). Mosby.

--Adler's Physiology of the Eye: Clinical Application. 6th ed. LC 74-28483. 800p. 1975. text ed. 36.50 (ISBN 0-8016-3540-3). Mosby.

Moses, Sam & Sanders, Peter. Gearing Down. LC 74-34463. (The Venture Ser, a Reading Incentive Program). (Illus.). 80p. (gr. 7-12,RL 4.5-6.5). 1975. In Packs Of 5. text ed. 23.25 ea. pack (ISBN 0-8172-0218-8). Follett.

Moses, W. R. Identities. LC 65-14051. (Wesleyan Poetry Program: Vol. 26). (Orig.). 1965. 10.00x (ISBN 0-8195-2026-8, Pub. by Wesleyan U Pr); pap. 4.95 (ISBN 0-8195-1026-2). Columbia U Pr.

--Passage. LC 75-33361. (Wesleyan Poetry Program: Vol. 81). 1976. text ed. 10.00x (ISBN 0-8195-2081-0, Pub. by Wesleyan U Pr); pap. 4.95 (ISBN 0-8195-1081-5). Columbia U Pr.

Moses Of Chorene. Patmowtiwn Hayots. Date not set. Repr. of 1913 ed. cancelled (ISBN 0-88206-032-5). Caravan Bks.

--Patmowtiwn Hayots: History of the Armenians. Thomson, Robert W., ed. 1980. write for info. (ISBN 0-88206-032-5). Caravan Bks.

Mosesson. The Perfect Put-Down. (Illus.). (gr. 7-12). 1975. pap. 1.25 (ISBN 0-590-09940-X, Schol Pap). Schol Bk Serv.

Mosey, Anne C. Activities Therapy. LC 73-79286. 193p. 1973. 12.50 (ISBN 0-911216-41-3). Raven.

Moshansky, Mozelle. Mendelssohn: His Life & Times. LC 78-53224. (Life & Times of the Composer Ser.). (Illus.). 1981. 16.95 (ISBN 0-8467-0488-9, Pub by Midas Bks); pap. 7.95 (ISBN 0-8467-0461-7). Hippocrene Bks.

Mosher, Edith K. & Wagoner, Jennings L., Jr., eds. The Changing Politics of Education Prospects for the 1980's. LC 77-75609. (Education Ser.). 1978. 19.00 (ISBN 0-8211-1252-X); text ed. 17.00 ten copies (ISBN 0-685-04968-X). McCutchan.

Mosher, Frederick C. Democracy & the Public Service. (Public Administration & Democracy Ser). (Orig.). 1968. 12.95 (ISBN 0-19-500031-5); pap. 5.95x (ISBN 0-19-501000-0). Oxford U Pr.

Mosher, Frederick C. & Harr, John E. Programming Systems & Foreign Affairs Leadership: An Attempted Innovation. (Orig.). 1970. text ed. 9.95x (ISBN 0-19-501324-7); pap. text ed. 4.95x (ISBN 0-19-501325-5). Oxford U Pr.

Mosher, Frederick C., ed. Basic Literature of American Public Administration, 1787-1950. LC 79-28553. 1980. text ed. 18.00x (ISBN 0-8419-0574-6); pap. text ed. 9.50x (ISBN 0-8419-0575-4). Holmes & Meier.

Mosher, Frederick D. The GAO: The Quest for Accountability in American Government. 1979. pap. text ed. 13.25x (ISBN 0-89158-459-5). Westview.

Mosher, John A. The Shooter's Workbench. (Illus.). 1977. 12.95 (ISBN 0-87691-199-8). Winchester Pr.

Mosher, R. H. & Davis, D. S., eds. Industrial & Specialty Papers: Their Technology, Manufacture, & Use, 2 vols. (Illus.). 16.50 ea. (ISBN 0-8206-0222-1). Vol. 1. Vol. 4 (ISBN 0-8206-0223-X). Chem Pub.

Mosher, Ralph, ed. Moral Education: A First Generation of Research & Development. LC 80-18607. 450p. 1980. 29.95 (ISBN 0-03-053961-7). Praeger.

Mosher, Robert E. Trigonometry for Today. 336p. 1976. text ed. 16.95 scp o.p. (ISBN 0-06-044630-7, HarpC); scp study guide 7.50 o.p. (ISBN 0-06-044631-5); instructor's manual free o.p. (ISBN 0-06-364583-1). Har-Row.

Moshimer, Joan. The Complete Rug Hooker: A Guide to the Craft. LC 74-25357. (Illus.). 176p. 1975. 15.95 (ISBN 0-8212-0647-8, 152730); pap. 8.95 (ISBN 0-8212-0747-4, 152854). NYGS.

Moshinsky, Julius. A Grammar of Southeastern Pomo. (Publications in Linguistics Vol. 72). 1974. pap. 11.50x (ISBN 0-520-09450-6). U of Cal Pr.

Mosier, Alice & Pace, Frank J. Medical Records Technology. LC 74-18676. (Allied Health Ser). 1975. pap. 8.35 (ISBN 0-672-61396-4). Bobbs.

Mosier, John, jt. auth. see Gaillard, Dawson.

Mosimann, E. A., jt. ed. see Callery, Bernadette G.

Mosimann, Elizabeth, compiled by see Callery, Bernadette, et al.

Moskalenko, Yu E., ed. Biophysical Aspects of Cerebral Circulation. LC 78-41243. (Illus.). 174p. 1980. 48.00 (ISBN 0-08-022672-8). Pergamon.

Moskin. Day of the Blizzard. (gr. 5). Date not set. pap. cancelled (ISBN 0-590-30092-X, Schol Pap). Schol Bk Serv.

Moskin, Marietta. Paper Dragon. LC 68-11310. (gr. 7 up). 1968. 8.95 (ISBN 0-381-99749-9, A59200, JD-J). John Day.

Moskin, Marietta D. Dream Lake. LC 80-18999. 156p. (gr. 5-9). 1981. PLB 8.95 (ISBN 0-689-30821-3). Atheneum.

--In the Name of God. LC 80-12319. (Illus.). 192p. (gr. 5 up). 1980. 10.95 (ISBN 0-689-30783-7). Atheneum.

Moskof, Martin S., jt. auth. see Hefter, Richard.

Moskoff, William. Comparative National Economic Policies: A Reader for Introductory Economics. 1973. pap. text ed. 7.95x o.p. (ISBN 0-669-83188-3). Heath.

Moskos, Charles C., Jr. Greek Americans: Struggle & Success. 1980. text ed. 10.95 (ISBN 0-13-365106-1); pap. text ed. 7.95 (ISBN 0-13-365098-7). P-H.

Moskos, Charles C., Jr., ed. Public Opinion & the Military Establishment. LC 70-151672. (Sage Research Progress Series on War, Revolution & Peacekeeping: Vol. 1). 1971. 20.00x o.p. (ISBN 0-8039-0115-1); pap. 9.95x (ISBN 0-8039-0116-X). Sage.

Moskow, Erik, jt. auth. see Miles, Tony.

Moskow, M., jt. auth. see Lowenberg, J.

Moskowitz, et al. Shiel in Diverse Hands: A Series of Essays. Date not set. price not set. Reynolds Morse.

Moskowitz, Gertrude see Dodge, James W.

Moskowitz, H. & Wright, G. Operations Research Techniques for Management. 1979. 21.00 (ISBN 0-13-637389-5). P-H.

Moskowitz, H. R. & Warren, Craig, eds. Odor Quality & Chemical Structure. (ACS Symposium Ser.: No. 148). 1981. price not set (ISBN 0-8412-0607-4). Am Chemical.

Moskowitz, Ira, ed. Great Drawings of All Time, 4 vols. LC 75-19869. (Illus.). 2250p. 1976. Repr. of 1962 ed. Set. 375.00 (ISBN 0-87011-294-5). Kodansha.

Moskowitz, Lester R. Permanent Magnet Design & Application Handbook. LC 75-28109. 1976. 45.00 (ISBN 0-8436-1800-0). CBI Pub.

Moskowitz, Louis. Dun & Bradstreet's Handbook of Modern Factoring & Commercial Finance. LC 76-26628. 1977. 18.95 o.s.i. (ISBN 0-690-01203-9, TYC-T). T Y Crowell.

Moskowitz, Milton, et al, eds. Everybody's Business: An Almanac. Katz, Michael. LC 80-7736. (Illus.). 008p. 1980. 21.00 (ISBN 0-06-250620-X, HarpR); pap. 9.95 (ISBN 0-06-250621-8). Har-Row.

Moskowitz, Moses. The Roots & Reaches of United Nations Actions & Decisions. LC 80-51741. 220p. 1980. 28.50x (ISBN 90-286-0140-6). Sijthoff & Noordhoff.

Moskowitz, Robert. How to Organize Your Work & Your Life. LC 80-1815. (Illus.). 312p. 1981. 12.95 (ISBN 0-385-17011-4). Doubleday.

--How to Organize Your Work & Your Life. LC 80-1815. (Illus.). 312p. 1981. pap. 6.95 (ISBN 0-385-17011-4, Dolp). Doubleday.

Moskowitz, Sam. Strange Horizons: The Spectrum of Science Fiction. LC 76-17088. 1976. 8.95 o.p. (ISBN 0-684-14774-2). Scribner.

Moskowitz, Sam, ed. Exploring Other Worlds. (Orig.). 1963. pap. 0.95 o.s.i. (ISBN 0-02-023110-5, Collier). Macmillan.

Moskvitin, Jurij. Essay on the Origin of Thought. LC 72-85540. 297p. 1974. 15.00x (ISBN 0-8214-0156-4). Ohio U Pr.

Moslemi, A. A. Particleboard, Vol. 1: Materials. LC 74-2071. 256p. 1974. 18.95x (ISBN 0-8093-0655-7). S Ill U Pr.

--Particleboard, Vol. 2: Technology. LC 74-2071. 252p. 1974. 18.95x (ISBN 0-8093-0656-5). S Ill U Pr.

Mosler Anti-Crime Bureau. Security Risk Management: A Practitioners Guide to Building Security. Rosberg, Robert, ed. (Illus.). 192p. 1980. 10.95 (ISBN 0-916752-42-9). Dorison Hse.

Mosler, Gerard. Puzzle Fun. (gr. 4-6). pap. 1.25 (ISBN 0-590-03203-8, Schol Pap). Schol Bk Serv.

Mosler, Hermann. The International Society As a Legal Community. LC 80-50454. (Collected Courses, the Hague Academy of International Law: Vol. 140, 1974-IV). 327p. 1980. pap. 27.50x (ISBN 90-286-0080-9). Sijthoff & Noordhoff.

Mosley, Diana. The Duchess of Windsor. LC 80-20793. (Illus.). 224p. 1980. 14.95 (ISBN 0-8128-2759-7). Stein & Day.

Mosley, Donald C. & Pietri, Paul H., Jr. Management: The Art of Working with & Through People. 1974. pap. 12.95x o.p. (ISBN 0-8221-0137-8). Dickenson.

Mosley, L. Battle of Britain. LC 76-45540. (World War II Ser.). (Illus.). (gr. 6 up). 1977. PLB 14.94 (ISBN 0-8094-2459-2, Pub. by Time-Life). Silver.

Mosley, Leonard. Blood Relations. LC 79-55584. (Illus.). 1980. 17.50 (ISBN 0-689-11055-3). Atheneum.

--Druid. LC 80-69367. 1981. 12.95 (ISBN 0-689-11106-1). Atheneum.

Mosley, Leonard, ed. The Battle of Britain. (World War II Ser.). 1977. 12.95 (ISBN 0-8094-2458-4). Time-Life.

Mosley, Philip. Ingmar Bergman: The Cinema As Mistress. 192p. 1981. 15.00 (ISBN 0-7145-2644-4, Pub. by M. Boyars). Merrimack Bk Serv.

Mosley, R. K. Story of the Cabinet Office. (Library of Political Studies). 1969. text ed. 6.00x (ISBN 0-7100-6600-7). Humanities.

--Westminster Workshop: A Student's Guide to the British Government. 4th ed. LC 78-41284. (Illus.). 1979. pap. 9.50 (ISBN 0-08-020636-0); pap. 9.50 (ISBN 0-08-020635-2); pap. 6.75 (ISBN 0-08-024316-9). Pergamon.

Mosmann, Charles, jt. auth. see Rothman, Stanley.

Moss, Abigail J. Blood Donor Characteristics & Types of Blood Donations, U. S., 1973. LC 75-35546. (Ser. 10: No.106). 51p. 1976. pap. text ed. 1.50 (ISBN 0-8406-0056-9). Natl Ctr Health Stats.

Moss, Albert A., ed. Computed Tomography, Ultrasound & X-Ray: An Integrated Approach. 1979. Goldberg, Henry I. (Illus.). 574p. 1979. 65.50 (ISBN 0-89352-055-1). Masson Pub.

Moss, Alfred A., Jr. The American Negro Academy. LC 80-18026. 400p. 1981. 30.00 (ISBN 0-8071-0699-2); pap. 12.95 (ISBN 0-8071-0782-4). La State U Pr.

Moss, Arthur & Marvel, Evalyn. Cancan & Barcarolle: The Life & Times of Jacques Offenbach. LC 75-2629. (Illus.). 280p. 1975. Repr. of 1954 ed. lib. bdg. 19.75x (ISBN 0-8371-8045-7, MOCB). Greenwood.

Moss, Arthur J. & Patton, Robert D. Antiarrhythmic Agents. (Illus.). 176p. 1973. 14.75 (ISBN 0-398-02622-X). C C Thomas.

Moss, Bernard H. The Origins of the French Labor Movement. LC 75-3775. 1976. 16.00x (ISBN 0-520-02982-8). U of Cal Pr.

Moss, Brian. The Ecology of Fresh Waters. 360p. 1980. pap. 29.95x (ISBN 0-470-26942-1). Halsted Pr.

Moss, David, jt. auth. see Moss, Rosalyn.

Moss, Elaine. Polar. (Illus.). (ps-1). 1979. PLB 8.95 (ISBN 0-233-96695-1). Andre Deutsch.

Moss, Elaine & Sherrard-Smith, Barbara. Children's Books of the Year: 1979. 1980. 10.95 (ISBN 0-531-04178-6). Watts.

Moss, Frank E. & Halamandaris, Val J. Too Old, Too Sick, Too Bad: Nursing Homes in America. LC 77-72515. 1977. 22.00 (ISBN 0-912862-43-2). Aspen Systems.

Moss, Frank T. Modern Saltwater Fishing Tackle. LC 76-8780. (Illus.). 1977. 22.50 (ISBN 0-87742-068-8). Intl Marine.

--Successful Striped Bass Fishing. LC 73-93527. (Illus.). 192p. 1974. 15.00 (ISBN 0-87742-040-8). Intl Marine.

Moss, G. L. Ordinary Level Practical Physics. 1971. pap. text ed. 5.50x o.p. (ISBN 0-435-67604-0). Heinemann Ed.

Moss, Gordon E. Illness, Immunity & Social Interaction. 298p. 1981. Repr. of 1973 ed. text ed. price not set (ISBN 0-89874-266-8). Krieger.

--Illness, Immunity & Social Interaction: The Dynamics of Biosocial Resonation. LC 72-11782. 352p. 1973. 24.50 o.p. (ISBN 0-471-61925-6, Pub. by Wiley-Interscience). Wiley.

Moss, Henry S. The Birth of the Middle Ages, Three Ninety-Five to Eight Fourteen. LC 80-24038. (Illus.). xvi, 291p. 1980. Repr. of 1964 ed. lib. bdg. 29.75x (ISBN 0-313-22708-X, MOBM). Greenwood.

Moss, Hilary see Marton, L.

Moss, Howard. Notes from the Castle. LC 79-52417. 1979. 10.00 (ISBN 0-689-11014-6); pap. 5.95 (ISBN 0-689-11021-9). Atheneum.

--Selected Poems. LC 70-139321. 1971. pap. 3.95 (ISBN 0-689-10561-4). Atheneum.

Moss, Howard, ed. The Poet's Story. 352p. 1973. 7.95 o.s.i. (ISBN 0-02-587560-4). Macmillan.

Moss, James E. Providence: Ye Lost Towne at Severn in Maryland. LC 76-5575. (Illus.). 1976. lib. bdg. 16.50x (ISBN 0-938420-14-3). Md Hist.

Moss, Jeffrey. Oscar-the-Grouch's Alphabet of Trash. (Sesame Street Shape Bks.). (Illus.). (ps-2). 1977. PLB 5.38 (ISBN 0-307-68880-1, Golden Pr). Western Pub.

--People in My Family. (Illus.). 24p. (gr. k-2). 1976. PLB 5.38 (ISBN 0-307-68968-9, Golden Pr). Western Pub.

--People in Your Neighborhood. (Illus.). (ps-2). 1971. PLB 5.38 (ISBN 0-307-68969-7, Golden Pr). Western Pub.

Moss, Jeffry. Oscar's Book. (Illus.). (ps-3). 1975. PLB 5.00 (ISBN 0-307-60120-X, Golden Pr). Western Pub.

Moss, John. How to Win at Poker. LC 55-7025. 1955. pap. 2.95 (ISBN 0-385-00094-4, Dolp). Doubleday.

Moss, John Lawrence. The Morphology & Phylogenetic Relationships of the Lower Permian Tetrapod Tseajaia campi Vaughn (Amphibia: Seymouriamorpha) (U. C. Publ. in Geological Sciences: Vol. 98). 1973. pap. 8.00x (ISBN 0-520-09439-5). U of Cal Pr.

Moss, Keith. Heating & Hot Water Services for Technicians. 1978. 20.00 (ISBN 0-408-00300-6). Transatlantic.

Moss, Laurence S. The Economics of Ludwig Von Mises: Toward a Critical Reappraisal. LC 75-41380. (Studies in Economic Theory). 129p. 1976. 12.00; pap. 3.95. NYU Pr.

Moss, Leonard. Arthur Miller. rev. ed. (United States Author Ser.: No. 115). (gr. 10-12). 1980. lib. bdg. 8.95 (ISBN 0-8057-7311-8). Twayne.

--Management Stress. (Occupational Stress Ser.). 224p. 1981. pap. text ed. 6.50 (ISBN 0-201-05050-1). A-W.

Moss, M., ed. see Riviere, J.

Moss, M., tr. see Riviere, J.

Moss, Michael & Forrester, Andrew. Britain from Waterloo to the Great Exhibition. (History Broadsheets Ser.). 1976. pap. text ed. 6.95x o.p. (ISBN 0-435-31640-0). Heinemann Ed.

Moss, Michael & Forrester, Andrew, eds. Changing Life in Scotland 1760 - 1820. (History Broadsheets Ser.). (Illus.). 1977. pap. text ed. 6.95x o.p. (ISBN 0-435-31641-9). Heinemann Ed.

Moss, Michael S., jt. auth. see Hume, John R.

Moss, Mitchell L. Telecommunications & Productivity. 416p. 1980. text ed. 37.50 (ISBN 0-201-04649-0). A-W.

Moss, R. P., ed. see African Studies Association of the United Kingdom, 1972.

Moss, Ralph W. The Cancer Syndrome. LC 79-2300. 320p. 1981. pap. 7.95 (ISBN 0-394-17896-3, BC). Grove.

Moss, Ralph W., jt. auth. see Randolph, Theron G.

Moss, Robert. Chile's Marxist Experiment. LC 74-558. 225p. 1973. 13.95 (ISBN 0-470-61910-4). Halsted Pr.

--The Collapse of Democracy. 1976. 9.95 o.p. (ISBN 0-87000-359-3). Arlington Hse.

Moss, Robert, jt. auth. see Bauer, Barbara.

Moss, Robert, jt. auth. see De Borchgrave, Arnaud.

Moss, Robert A. & Jones, Maitland, Jr. Carbenes, Vol. 2. LC 80-11836. (Reactive Intermediates in Organic Chemistry Ser.). 390p. 1981. Repr. of 1975 ed. lib. bdg. write for info. (ISBN 0-89874-160-2). Krieger.

Moss, Robert A., jt. auth. see Jones, Maitland.

Moss, Robert A., jt. ed. see Jones, Maitland, Jr.

Moss, Rosalyn & Moss, David. An Invitation to Shabbat. (Illus.). 160p. 1981. 12.95 (ISBN 0-89961-013-7); pap. 6.95 (ISBN 0-89961-014-5). SBS Pub.

Moss, Stanley. Skull of Adam. 1980. 7.95 (ISBN 0-8180-1578-0); pap. 3.95 (ISBN 0-686-64570-7). Horizon.

Moss, Sylvia, jt. auth. see Tubbs, Stewart L.

Moss, T. S., jt. ed. see Schultz, G.

Moss, Thelma. The Body Electric. 1979. 10.00 o.p. (ISBN 0-312-90437-1). St Martin.

Moss, William T., et al. Radiation Oncology: Rationale, Technique, Results. 5th ed. LC 79-14367. (Illus.). 1979. text ed. 49.50 (ISBN 0-8016-3556-X). Mosby.

Moss, William W. Oral History Program Manual. LC 73-19446. (Special Studies). 122p. 1974. text ed. 24.95 (ISBN 0-275-08370-5). Praeger.

Mossa, Matti, tr. & intro. by see Huwayyik, Yusaf.

Mossavar-Rahmane, Bijan. Energy Policy in Iran: Domestic Choices & International Implications. LC 80-27995. (PPS on Science & Technnology Ser.). (Illus.). 160p. 1981. 15.00 (ISBN 0-08-026293-7). Pergamon.

Mossberg, Howard E., jt. auth. see Rosser, James M.

Mosse, Claude. Athens in Decline 404-86 B. C. Stewart, Jean, tr. (Illus.). 1973. 21.50 (ISBN 0-7100-7649-5). Routledge & Kegan.

Mosse, George L. The Crisis of German Ideology: Intellectual Origins of the Third Reich. 1979. Repr. 22.50 o.p. (ISBN 0-86527-036-8). Fertig.

--The Crisis of German Ideology: Intellectual Origins of the Third Reich. LC 78-19126. viii, 373p. 1981. Repr. of 1964 ed. 27.50x (ISBN 0-86527-036-8). Fertig.

--The Crisis of Germany Ideology: Intellectual Origins of the Third Reich. 384p. 1981. Repr. of 1964 ed. pap. text ed. 7.95 (ISBN 0-8052-0669-8). Schocken.

--The Holy Pretence. LC 68-14552. 1968. 14.25 (ISBN 0-86527-099-6). Fertig.

--Masses & Man: Nationalist & Fascist Perceptions of Reality. LC 80-15399. xi, 362p. 1980. 25.00 (ISBN 0-86527-334-0). Fertig.

--Nazi Culture. LC 80-26608. 432p. 1981. pap. 8.95 (ISBN 0-8052-0668-X). Schocken.

Mosse, George L., jt. auth. see Koenigsberger, H. G.

Mosse, W. E. Liberal Europe: The Age of Bourgeois Realism 1848-1875. (Library of European Civilization). (Illus.). 180p. 1974. 10.00 (ISBN 0-500-32032-2). Transatlantic.

Mossi, John. Bread Blessed & Broken. LC 74-16844. 1975. pap. 7.95 (ISBN 0-8091-1855-6). Paulist Pr.

Mossien, Herbert J., jt. auth. see Fram, Eugene H.

Mossin, Jan. The Economic Efficiency of Financial Markets. 1977. 18.95 (ISBN 0-669-01004-9). Lexington Bks.

Mossman, Frank H., et al. Financial Dimensions of Marketing Management. LC 77-14990. (Wiley Series on Marketing Management). 1978. 22.95 (ISBN 0-471-03376-6). Wiley.

Mossman, Harland W. & Duke, Kenneth L. Comparative Morphology of the Mammalian Ovary. LC 72-143765. 320p. 1972. 35.00 (ISBN 0-299-05930-8, 593); pap. 12.50 (ISBN 0-299-05934-0). U of Wis Pr.

Mossman, Jennifer. New Pseudonyms & Nicknames--Supplements: Supplements to Pseudonyms & Nicknames Dictionary. 1981. softbound 45.00 (ISBN 0-8103-0548-8). Gale.

Mossman, Jennifer, ed. Pseudonyms & Nicknames Dictionary. LC 80-13274. 700p. 1980. 55.00 (ISBN 0-8103-0549-6). Gale.

Mossman, Philip L. A Problem-Oriented Approach to Stroke Rehabilitation. 480p. 1976. pap. 44.00 spiral (ISBN 0-398-03427-3). C C Thomas.

Mossman, Tam. Gardens That Care for Themselves: How to Grow Neater, Healthier Plants, Cut Your Outdoor Chores in Half. LC 77-76254. 1978. 10.95 o.p. (ISBN 0-385-11171-1). Doubleday.

Mossner, Ernest C., ed. see Smith, Adam.

Moss-Salentijn, Letty & Klyvert, Marlene. Dental & Oral Tissues: An Introduction for Paraprofessionals in Dentistry. LC 80-10516. (Illus.). 326p. 1980. text ed. 16.50 (ISBN 0-8121-0701-2). Lea & Febiger.

Mosston, Muska. Teaching: From Command to Discovery. 300p. 1972. pap. 8.95x (ISBN 0-534-00165-3). Wadsworth Pub.

--Teaching Physical Education. 2nd ed. (Illus.). 256p. 1981. pap. text ed. 12.95 (ISBN 0-675-08036-3). Merrill.

Most, Bernard. There's an Ape Behind the Drape. LC 80-24280. (Illus.). 32p. (gr. k-3). 1981. 6.95 (ISBN 0-688-00380-X); PLB 6.67 (ISBN 0-688-00381-8). Morrow.

Most, Kenneth S. Accounting Theory. LC 76-41424. (Accounting Ser.). 1977. text ed. 19.50 (ISBN 0-88244-142-6). Grid Pub.

Most, William G. The Consciousness of Christ. (Orig.). 1980. pap. text ed. 5.95 (ISBN 0-931888-03-4). Christendom Pubns.

Mosteller, F. R. & Rourke, Robert E. Sturdy Statistics: Nonparametrics & Order Statistics. LC 70-184162. 1973. text ed. 18.95 (ISBN 0-201-04868-X). A-W.

Mosteller, Frederick, jt. auth. see Fairley, William B.

Mosti, Francisco H. Suppression. 64p. 1981. 9.00 (ISBN 0-682-49691-X). Exposition.

Mostofi, F. K. Histological Typing of Testis Tumours. (World Health Organization: International Histological Classification of Tumours Ser.). (Illus.). 1976. pap. text ed. 59.50 (ISBN 92-4-176016-8, 70-1-016-20); with slides 188.00 (ISBN 92-4-176016-8, 70-1-015-00). Am Soc Clinical.

Mostofi, F. K., jt. ed. see Gall, Edward A.

Mostofsky, D. Behavior Control & Modification of Physiological Activity. 1976. text ed. 25.95 (ISBN 0-13-073908-1). P-H.

Mostowski, Andrej. Thirty Years of Foundational Studies: Lectures on the Development of Mathematical Logic & the Study of the Foundations of Mathematics in 1930-1964. 1966. 10.50x o.p. (ISBN 0-631-09550-0, Pub. by Basil Blackwell). Biblio Dist.

Mostowski, J. & Stark, M. Introduction to Higher Algebra. 1964. 25.00 (ISBN 0-08-010152-6). Pergamon.

Mostwin, Danuta. Social Dimension of Family Treatment. LC 79-92201. (Illus.). 264p. 1980. pap. 12.50x (ISBN 0-87101-083-6, CBF-083-C). Natl Assn Soc Wkrs.

Motani, Nizar. On His Majesty's Service in Uganda: The Origins of Uganda's African Civil Service, 1912-1940. (Foreign & Comparative Studies-African Ser.: No. 29). 72p. 1978. pap. text ed. 5.00x (ISBN 0-915984-51-2). Syracuse U Foreign Comp.

Mother Earth News Staff. How to Convert Your Vehicle to Propane. Hoffman, Robert, ed. 50p. (Orig.). 1981. pap. 7.50 (ISBN 0-938432-01-X). Mother Earth.

Mother Earth News Staff, jt. ed. see Kerley, Michael R.

Mother Ant, Henry de see De Montherlant, Henry.

Mother Martha. Papa Nicholas Planas. Holy Transfiguration Monastery, ed. & tr. from Greek. (Orig.). 1981. pap. price not set (ISBN 0-913026-18-2). St Nectarios.

Mothersole, Megan, tr. see Etienne, Gilbert.

Motherwell, Robert, ed. The Dada Painters & Poets: An Anthology. LC 79-91825. (Documents of Modern Art Ser.). (Illus.). 388p. 1981. Repr. of 1951 ed. lib. bdg. 40.00 (ISBN 0-87817-266-1). Hacker. Postponed.

Motherwell, William. Minstrelsy Ancient & Modern. LC 68-24477. 1968. Repr. of 1873 ed. 20.00 (ISBN 0-8103-3415-1). Gale.

Mothner, Ira. Woodrow Wilson, Champion of Peace. LC 69-10888. (Biography Ser). (Illus.). (gr. 7 up). 1969. PLB 5.90 o.p. (ISBN 0-531-00932-7). Watts.

Mothudi, Namus. Black, No Sugar. 1981. 5.95 (ISBN 0-533-04824-9). Vantage.

Motion, Andrew. The Poetry of Edward Thomas. 192p. 1981. 27.50 (ISBN 0-7100-0471-0). Routledge & Kegan.

Motley. Theatre Props. LC 75-6786. 1976. 12.50x (ISBN 0-910482-66-7). Drama Bk.

Motley, Annette. The Sins of the Lion. 448p. 1981. pap. 2.75 (ISBN 0-445-04647-3). Popular Lib.

Motley, Marion B. A. E.'s Paintings. (Collected Edition of the Writings of G. W. Russell Ser.: No. 8). 1980. text ed. write for info. (ISBN 0-391-01201-0). Humanities.

Motley, Robert J., jt. auth. see Leaming, Majorie P.

Motor Cycle Magazine, ed. Motorcycles & How to Manage Them: A Nineteen Twenty-Six Handbook. 1975. Repr. of 1926 ed. 14.95x o.p. (ISBN 0-8464-0647-0). Beekman Pubs.

Mott, Frank L. Women, Work, & Family. LC 77-18329. (Illus.). 1978. 16.95 (ISBN 0-669-02092-3). Lexington Bks.

Mott, Frank L., ed. Missouri Reader. LC 64-14412. 1964. 15.00 (ISBN 0-8262-0024-9). U of Mo Pr.

Mott, Jacolyn. Creativity & Imagination. LC 73-610. (Illus.). (gr. 5-12). 1973. PLB 7.50 o.p. (ISBN 0-87191-249-X). Creative Ed.

Mott, L. C. Engineering Drawing & Construction. 2nd ed. (Illus.). 1976. pap. 12.50x (ISBN 0-19-859114-4). Oxford U Pr.

Mott, Mary. Teaching the Pre-Academic Child: Activities for Children Displaying Difficulties of Processing Information. 188p. 1974. text ed. 13.75 (ISBN 0-398-03083-9). C C Thomas.

Mott, Michael. The Blind Cross: A Novel of Children's Crusade. LC 68-27739. (gr. 7 up). 1970. 3.95 o.s.i. (ISBN 0-440-00646-5). Delacorte.

--Counting the Grasses. LC 80-67430. (Illus., Orig.). 1980. signed & numbered 25.00 (ISBN 0-938078-13-5); pap. 5.00 perfect bdg. (ISBN 0-938078-12-7). Anhinga Pr.

Mott, N. F. & Massey, H. S. Theory of Atomic Collisions. 3rd ed. (International Series of Monographs on Physics). (Illus.). 1965. 65.00x (ISBN 0-19-851242-2). Oxford U Pr.

Mott, Nevill & Berry, M. Elementary Quantum Mechanics. LC 76-189453. (Wykeham Science Ser.: No. 22). 1972. 9.95x (ISBN 0-8448-1124-6). Crane Russak Co.

Mott, Nevill, ed. The Beginnings of Solid State Physics. (Royal Society Ser.). 177p. 1980. lib. bdg. 30.00x (ISBN 0-85403-143-X, Pub. by Royal Soc London). Scholium Intl.
Mott, Nevill F. & Jones, H. Theory of the Properties of Metals & Alloys. 1936. pap. 6.00 (ISBN 0-486-60456-X). Dover.
Mott, Paul E., et al. Shift Work. LC 65-11466. (Illus.). 1965. 8.50x o.p. (ISBN 0-472-08675-8). U of Mich Pr.
Mott, Robert L. Applied Fluid Mechanics. 2nd ed. (Mechanical Technology Ser.). 1979. text ed. 19.95 (ISBN 0-675-08305-2); instructor's manual 3.95 (ISBN 0-686-67359-X). Merrill.
Mott, Rodney L. Due Process of Law. LC 72-165604. (American Constitutional & Legal History Ser.). 702p. 1973. Repr. of 1926 ed. lib. bdg. 65.00 (ISBN 0-306-70225-8). Da Capo.
Mott, Thomas H., Jr., et al. Introduction to PL-1 Programming for Library & Information Science. (Library & Information Science Ser.). 239p. 1972. text ed. 19.95 (ISBN 0-12-508750-0). Acad Pr.
Mott, Vincent, jt. auth. see Chirovsky, Nicholas.
Motta, Dick, jt. auth. see Isaacs, Neil D.
Motta, Giuseppe. Dizionario Commerciale Inglese-Italiano--Italiano-Inglese: Economia, Legge, Finanza, Banca, Etc. 1051p. 1978. 40.00x (ISBN 0-913298-50-6). S F Vanni.
Motta, Marcella, ed. Endocrine Functions of the Brain. (Comprehensive Endocrinology Ser.). 493p. 1980. text ed. 42.50 (ISBN 0-89004-343-4). Raven.
Motta, Marcella, jt. ed. see Martini, Luciano.
Motta, Marcelo R., jt. auth. see Crowley, Aleister.
Motta, P. M. & Hafez, E. S., eds. Biology of the Ovary. (Developments in Obstetrics & Gynecology Ser.: No. 2). 345p. 1980. lib. bdg. 86.85 (ISBN 90-247-2316-7). Kluwer Boston.
Motta, Pietro, et al. The Liver: An Atlas of Scanning Electron Microscopy. LC 77-95454. (Illus.). 1978. 46.00 (ISBN 0-89640-026-3). Igaku-Shoin.
Motte, Andrew, tr. see Newton, Sir Isaac.
Motte, G. A. & Iitaka, Y. Evaluation of Trawl Performance by Statistical Inference of the Catch. (Marine Technical Report Ser.: No. 36). 1975. pap. 2.00 (ISBN 0-938412-08-6). URI MAS.
Motter, T. H., ed. see Allen, F. Sturges.
Mottershead, D. N. see Bowen, D. Q.
Motto, Sytha. More Than Conquerers: Makers of History. (Illus.). 228p. 1980. 15.00 (ISBN 0-913270-88-1); ltd. signed 22.50 (ISBN 0-913270-94-6). Sunstone Pr.
Mottram, Tony. Play Better Tennis. LC 70-161216. (Illus.). 127p. 1972. pap. 1.65 o.p. (ISBN 0-668-02494-1). Arc Bks.
--Play Better Tennis. LC 70-161213. (Illus.). 1971. 4.50 o.p. (ISBN 0-668-02502-6). Arco.
Motulsky, Arno G., jt. ed. see Goodman, Richard M.
Motyer, J. A. Tests of Faith. LC 76-134726. (Orig.). 1970. pap. 1.50 o.p. (ISBN 0-87784-066-0). Inter-Varsity.
Motyer, J. A., ed. see Lucas, R. J.
Motyer, J. A., ed. see Stott, John R.
Motyer, J. A., ed. see Wilcock, Michael.
Motyl, Alexander J. The Turn to the Right: The Ideological Origins & the Development of Ukrainina Nationalism, 1919-1929. (East European Monographs: No. 65). 1980. 15.00x (ISBN 0-914710-58-3). East Eur Quarterly.
Motylewski, Leo F. Essene Plan. LC 76-14499. 1976. 8.75 (ISBN 0-8022-2183-1). Philos Lib.
Motz, Annabelle B., jt. auth. see Finsterbusch, Kurt.
Motz, Lloyd. This Is Astronomy. LC 56-12016. (Illus., Orig.). 1958. pap. 5.00 (ISBN 0-231-08549-4). Columbia U Pr.
--The Universe - Its Beginning & End. LC 75-6635. (Illus.). 416p. 1976. 14.95 o.p. (ISBN 0-684-14239-2); pap. 4.95 (ISBN 0-684-15062-X, SL726, ScribT). Scribner.
Motz, Lloyd & Duveen, Anneta. Essentials of Astronomy. 2nd ed. LC 76-19068. 1977. 20.00x (ISBN 0-231-04009-1). Columbia U Pr.
Mouck, N. G., jt. auth. see Bear, H. S.
Mouffe, Chantal. Gramsci & Marxist Theory. 1979. 26.00x (ISBN 0-7100-0357-9); pap. 14.50 (ISBN 0-7100-0358-7). Routledge & Kegan.
Mouhy, Charles. The Virtuous Villager; or, Virgin's Victory, 1742, 2 vols. in 1. Shugrue, Michael F., ed. Haywood, Eliza, tr. from Fr. (The Flowering of the Novel, 1740-1775 Ser: Vol. 7). 1974. lib. bdg. 50.00 (ISBN 0-8240-1106-6). Garland Pub.
Mouillaud, G. Le Rouge et le noir de Stendhal: Le Roman possible. new ed. (Collection themes et textes). 240p. (Orig., Fr.). 1973. pap. 6.75 (ISBN 2-03-035014-1, 2658). Larousse.
Moul, Edward W. Stations Along the Reading Company's Philadelphia to Williamsport Line (Pa) (RSHS Monograph: No. 5). (Illus.). 1974. softcover 2.50 o.p. (ISBN 0-686-12300-X). Jove Pubns.
Mould, Daphne Pochin see Pochin-Mould, Daphne.
Mould, J. Albert & Geffner, Saul L. Review Text in General Science. 2nd ed. (gr. 10-12). 1974. pap. text ed. 5.92 (ISBN 0-87720-001-7). AMSCO Sch.
Mould, P. R., jt. auth. see Cotterill, P.
Mould, Richard F. Radiotherapy Treatment Planning. (Medical Physics Handbook: No. 7). 192p. 1981. 31.00 (ISBN 0-9960020-6-5, Pub. by a Hilger England). Heyden.
Moulder, F. V. Japan, China & the Modern World Economy. LC 76-2230. (Illus.). 1977. 24.95 (ISBN 0-521-21174-3); pap. 7.95x (ISBN 0-521-29736-2). Cambridge U Pr.
Moulder, Michael B. The Creative Use of Clay: In First & Middle Schools. (Practical Guides for Teachers Ser.). (Illus.). 1973. pap. 3.50x o.p. (ISBN 0-631-14060-3, Pub. by Basil Blackwell). Biblio Dist.
Moule, C. F. Meaning of Hope: A Biblical Exposition with Concordance. Reumann, John, ed. LC 63-17881. (Facet Bks). 80p. (Orig.). 1963. pap. 1.00 (ISBN 0-8006-3001-7, 1-3001). Fortress.
--The Origin of Christology. LC 76-11087. 1977. 23.95 (ISBN 0-521-21290-1); pap. 7.50x (ISBN 0-521-29363-4). Cambridge U Pr.
Moule, Charles F. Idiom Book of New Testament Greek. 2nd ed. 1959. 36.00 (ISBN 0-521-05774-4); pap. text ed. 9.95x (ISBN 0-521-09237-X). Cambridge U Pr.
Moule, H. C. Moule Popular Commentary Series, 6 vols. 1980. 15.00 (ISBN 0-8254-3224-3). Kregel.
Moule, H. C. & Orr, J. The Resurrection of Christ. Date not set. 16.95 (ISBN 0-86524-062-0). Klock & Klock.
Moule, H. C. G. Colossian & Philemon Studies. Date not set. 10.50 (ISBN 0-86524-052-3). Klock & Klock.
Moulik, Moni. Twilight. 1976. 9.00 (ISBN 0-89253-829-5); flexible cloth 6.75 (ISBN 0-89253-830-9). Ind-US Inc.
Moulin, Tom & DeNevi, Don. Inside Bohemian Grove: The Most Exclusive Men's Gathering in the World. LC 78-75157. (Illus.). 1979. cancelled (ISBN 0-89395-017-3); pap. cancelled (ISBN 0-89395-018-1). Cal Living Bks.
Moult, Thomas, ed. Best Poems of 1925. LC 79-51986. (Granger Poetry Library). (Illus.). 1981. Repr. of 1926 ed. 15.00x (ISBN 0-89609-180-5). Granger Bk.
--Best Poems of 1927. LC 79-51986. (Granger Poetry Library). 1981. Repr. of 1928 ed. 15.00x (ISBN 0-89609-185-6). Granger Bk.
--Best Poems of 1928. LC 79-51986. (Granger Poetry Library). (Illus.). 1981. Repr. of 1929 ed. 15.00x (ISBN 0-89609-192-9). Granger Bk.
--Best Poems of 1929. LC 79-51986. (Granger Poetry Library). (Illus.). 1981. Repr. of 1929 ed. 15.00x (ISBN 0-89609-194-5). Granger Bk.
--Best Poems of 1933. LC 79-51986. (Granger Poetry Library). (Illus.). 1981. Repr. of 1933 ed. 15.00x (ISBN 0-89609-187-2). Granger Bk.
--Best Poems of 1934. LC 79-51986. (Granger Poetry Library). (Illus.). 1981. Repr. of 1934 ed. 15.00x (ISBN 0-89609-188-0). Granger Bk.
--Best Poems of 1935. LC 79-51986. (Granger Poetry Library). (Illus.). 1981. Repr. of 1935 ed. 15.00x (ISBN 0-89609-189-9). Granger Bk.
--Best Poems of 1936. LC 79-51986. (Granger Poetry Library). (Illus.). 1981. Repr. of 1936 ed. 15.00x (ISBN 0-89609-190-2). Granger Bk.
--Best Poems of 1937. LC 79-51986. (Granger Poetry Library). (Illus.). 1981. Repr. of 1937 ed. 15.00x (ISBN 0-89609-191-0). Granger Bk.
Moulton, Betty L., tr. see Lappe, Marc & McCurdy, John C.
Moulton, Charles W. The Library of Literary Criticism of English & American Authors, 8 vols. Set. 108.00 (ISBN 0-8446-1318-5); 13.50 ea. Peter Smith.
Moulton, Forest R. & Schifferes, Justus J., eds. The Autobiography of Science. 748p. 1980. 25.00x (ISBN 0-7195-0979-3, Pub. by Murray Pubs England). State Mutual Bk.
Moulton, Harold G., et al. The Recovery Problem in the United States. LC 73-176337. (FDR & the Era of the New Deal Ser.). (Illus.). Repr. lib. bdg. 65.00 (ISBN 0-306-70421-8). Da Capo.
Moulton, J. H., et al. A Grammar of New Testament Greek: Accidence & Word Formation, Vol. 2. 572p. 1979. text ed. 17.50x (ISBN 0-567-01012-0). Attic Pr.
--A Grammar of New Testament Greek: Syntax, Vol. 3. 438p. 1963. text ed. 17.50x (ISBN 0-567-01013-9). Attic Pr.
--A Grammar of New Testament Greek: The Prolegomena, Vol. I. 3rd ed. 320p. 1978. write for info. (ISBN 0-567-01011-2). Attic Pr.
--A Grammar of the New Testament Greek: Style, Vol. 4. LC 7-13420. 1976. text ed. 15.00x (ISBN 0-567-01018-X). Attic Pr.
Moulton, Jack, ed. Tumors in Domestic Animals. 2nd ed. 1978. 36.75 (ISBN 0-520-02386-2). U of Cal Pr.
Moulton, Janice & Robinson, George M. Organization of Language. LC 80-19052. 400p. Date not set. 42.50 (ISBN 0-521-23129-9); pap. 14.95 (ISBN 0-521-29851-2). Cambridge U Pr.
Moulton, Jenni K. & Moulton, William G. Spoken German. Incl. Book, Units 1-30. viii, 582p. pap. o.p. (ISBN 0-87950-090-5); Units 1-12. viii, 328p. pap. 8.00x (ISBN 0-87950-091-3); Records, Six 12-Inch Lp (33.3 Rpm) 40.00x (ISBN 0-87950-094-8); Record Course-Bk. & Records. pap. 45.00x (ISBN 0-87950-095-6); Cassettes, Six Dual Track. 60.00x (ISBN 0-87950-096-4); Cassette Course-Bk. & Cassettes. pap. text ed. 65.00x (ISBN 0-87950-097-2). LC 74-176091. (Spoken Language Ser.). (Prog. Bk.). 1976. Spoken Lang Serv.
Moulton, LeArta. Nature's Medicine Chest, Sets 1-6. (Illus.). Sets 1&2. 3.50 ea. o.p.; Sets 3-6. 4.50 ea. o.p.; file box 1.25 o.p. (ISBN 0-685-85405-1). Bi World Indus.
Moulton, Peter. Foundation of Programming Through Basic. LC 78-21569. 1979. text ed. 14.95 (ISBN 0-471-03311-1); tchrs. manual avail. (ISBN 0-471-05414-3). Wiley.
Moulton, R. G. Modern Aeromodelling. 3rd ed. 1974. 9.95 (ISBN 0-571-04852-8, Pub. by Faber & Faber). Merrimack Bk Serv.
Moulton, Richard G., ed. Modern Reader's Bible. 1943. 9.95 o.s.i. (ISBN 0-02-587860-3). Macmillan.
Moulton, W. F., et al. A Concordance to the Greek Testament: According to the Texts of Westcott & Hort, Tischendorf & the English Revisers. 5th ed. 1120p. 1978. text ed. 45.00x (ISBN 0-567-01021-X). Attic Pr.
Moulton, William G; see Bird, Thomas E.
Moulton, William G., jt. auth. see Moulton, Jenni K.
Mouly, George J. Educational Research: The Art & Science of Investigation. 1978. text ed. 18.50 (ISBN 0-205-05812-4); instr's manual (ISBN 0-205-05813-2). Allyn.
Mouly, J. & Costa, E. Employment Policies in Developing Countries. 1975. text ed. 35.00x (ISBN 0-04-330245-9). Allen Unwin.
Mounce, Earl W., jt. auth. see Dawson, Townes L.
Mound, L. A., ed. see Royal Entomological Society of London, Ninth.
Mounier, Emmanuel. Personalism. Mairet, Philip, tr. LC 75-122050. 1970. pap. 3.95 (ISBN 0-268-00434-X). U of Notre Dame Pr.
Mounin, G. Les Semiologies Des Litteraires. (Casal Bequest Lecture Ser). 1977. text ed. 3.75x (ISBN 0-485-16107-9, Athlone Pr). Humanities.
Mounsey, Augustus H. Satsuma Rebellion: An Episode of Modern Japanese History. (Studies in Japanese History & Civilization). 1979p. Repr. of 1879 ed. 24.00 (ISBN 0-89093-259-X). U Pubns Amer.
Mount, Ellis. University Science & Engineering Libraries. LC 74-34562. (Contributions in Librarianship & Information Science: No. 15). (Illus.). 214p. 1975. lib. bdg. 17.95 (ISBN 0-8371-7955-6, MSE/). Greenwood.
Mount, Ellis, ed. Guide to Basic Information Sources in Engineering. LC 75-43261. (Information Resources Ser.). 1976. 13.95x (ISBN 0-470-15013-0). Halsted Pr.
--Science & Technical Libraries of the Seventies: A Guide to Information Sources. (Books, Publishing & Libraries Information Guide Ser.: Vol. 4). 300p. 1980. 30.00 (ISBN 0-8103-1483-5). Gale.
Mount, James L. The Food & Health of Western Man. LC 75-11989. 270p. 1975. 19.95x (ISBN 0-470-61957-0). Halsted Pr.
Mount, Laurence E. Energy Metabolism. LC 80-40265. (Studies in the Agricultural & Food Sciences). (Illus.). 416p. 1980. text ed. 79.95 (ISBN 0-408-10641-7). Butterworths.
Mount, Robert H. The Reptiles & Amphibians of Alabama. (Illus.). 354p. 1975. pap. 9.95 (ISBN 0-8173-0054-6, Pub. by Ag Experiment). U of Ala Pr.
Mount, Tom & Ikehara, Akira J. Practical Diving: A Complete Manual for Compressed Air Divers. LC 75-1059. (Illus.). 192p. 1975. pap. 5.95 o.p. (ISBN 0-87024-299-7). U of Miami Pr.
Mountain, Lee. Dragon Don & John: Dragon Donaldo y Juan. Gunning, Monica, tr. (Storybooks for Beginners Ser.). (Illus.). 15p. (Eng. & Span.). 1980. pap. 12.50 set (ISBN 0-89061-213-7). Jamestown Pubs.
--Dragon Don: Dragon Donaldo, Bk. 1. Gunning, Monica, tr. (Storybooks for Beginners Ser.). (Illus.). 15p. 1980. pap. 12.50 set (ISBN 0-89061-212-9). Jamestown Pubs.
--Sports Trip. (Attention Span Stories Ser). (Illus., Orig.). (gr. 6-10). 1978. pap. text ed. 3.20x (ISBN 0-89061-147-5, 583). Jamestown Pubs.
--Star Trip. (Attention Span Stories Ser). (Illus., Orig.). (gr. 6-10). 1978. pap. text ed. 3.20x (ISBN 0-89061-149-1, 585). Jamestown Pubs.
--Survival Trip. (Attention Span Stories Ser). (Illus., Orig.). (gr. 6-10). 1978. pap. text ed. 3.20x (ISBN 0-89061-146-7, 582). Jamestown Pubs.
--Time Trip. (Attention Span Ser). (Illus., Orig.). (gr. 6-10). 1978. pap. text ed. 3.20x (ISBN 0-89061-145-9, 581). Jamestown Pubs.
Mountain, Lee, ed. Jungle Trip. (Attention Span Stories Ser). (Illus., Orig.). (gr. 6-10). 1978. pap. text ed. 3.20x (ISBN 0-89061-148-3, 584). Jamestown Pubs.
Mountain, Marian. The Zen Environment: The Impact of Zen Meditation. 288p. 1981. 10.95 (ISBN 0-688-00350-8). Morrow.
Mountain States Telephone & Telegraph Company. Pricing in Regulated Industries Theory & Application Two. Wenders, John T., ed. LC 79-83623. (Illus.). 1979. 5.00 o.p. (ISBN 0-9602580-1-9). Mountain St Tel.
Mountcastle, Vernon B. Medical Physiology, 2 vols. 14th ed. LC 79-25943. (Illus.). 1980. Set. 54.50 (ISBN 0-8016-3560-8); Vol. 1. 42.50 (ISBN 0-8016-3562-4); Vol. 2. 37.00 (ISBN 0-8016-3566-7). Mosby.
Mountford, A., jt. auth. see MacKay, R.
Mountford, Alan. English in Agriculture. (English in Focus Ser.). (Illus.). 1978. pap. text ed. 6.95x (ISBN 0-19-437514-5); tchr's ed. 9.25x (ISBN 0-19-437506-4). Oxford U Pr.
--English in Workshop Practice. (English in Focus Ser.). 1975. pap. text ed. 6.95x (ISBN 0-19-437511-0); tchrs'. ed. 9.25x (ISBN 0-19-437502-1). Oxford U Pr.
Mountjoy, Alan B. Industrialization & Developing Countries. 4th rev. ed. 1975. text ed. 11.75x (ISBN 0-09-123620-7, Hutchinson U Lib); pap. text ed. 6.50x (ISBN 0-09-123621-5, Hutchinson U Lib). Humanities.
Mountjoy, M. E. Agent Secret. (Illus., Fr.). (gr. 7-9). 1969. pap. 4.95 (ISBN 0-312-01400-7). St Martin.
--Gehoert, Geschrieben, Gelernt! 1973. pap. text ed. 2.95x o.p. (ISBN 0-435-38602-6). Heinemann Ed.
--Hoert Zu! 1971. pap. text ed. 2.95x o.p. (ISBN 0-435-38600-X); tape 24.00x o.p. (ISBN 0-435-38601-8). Heinemann Ed.
--Ingrid und Maria. (German Through Reading Ser.: Stage 1). (Illus.). 1977. pap. text ed. 2.50x (ISBN 0-435-38608-5). Heinemann Ed.
--Patrice. 1970. pap. text ed. 2.95x o.p. (ISBN 0-435-37621-7). Heinemann Ed.
--Das Stimmt! 1975. pap. text ed. 2.95x o.p. (ISBN 0-435-38605-0); tape 20.00x o.p. (ISBN 0-686-67894-X). Heinemann Ed.
Mountney, George J. Poultry Products Technology. 2nd ed. (Illus.). 1976. text ed. 29.00 (ISBN 0-87055-199-X). AVI.
Mourad, Leona A. Nursing Care of Adults with Orthopedic Conditions. LC 79-26251. 1980. 17.95 (ISBN 0-471-04677-9, Pub. by Wiley Med). Wiley.
Mouras, Belton P. I Care About Animals. LC 76-58590. (Illus.). 1977. cloth 9.95 (ISBN 0-498-02195-5); pap. 5.95 (ISBN 0-498-02195-5). A S Barnes.
Moure, J. S., jt. auth. see Hurd, P. D., Jr.
Moure, Nancy. Painting & Sculpture in Los Angeles, 1900-1945. (Illus.). 112p. (Orig.). 1980. pap. 14.95 (ISBN 0-87587-098-8). La Co Art Mus.
Moure, Nancy D., jt. auth. see Smith, Lyn W.
Moureau, Magdaleine & Brace, Gerald, eds. Dictionary of Petroleum Technology-Dictionnaire Dechnique Du Petrol: English-French - French-English. rev. ed. LC 64-56944. (Collection Des Dictionnaires Techniques: No. 1). 975p. 1979. 100.00x (ISBN 2-7108-0361-5). Intl Pubns Serv.
Mourelatos, Alexander P. D., ed. The Pre-Socratics: A Collection of Critical Essays. LC 73-11729. 576p. 1974. pap. 5.95 (ISBN 0-385-05480-7, Anch). Doubleday.
Mouret, Francois J., jt. ed. see Chapman, Carol J.
Mourgue, Jacques-Antoine. Essai de Statistique. (Principal French Demographic Works of the 18th Century Ser.). (Fr.). 1977. lib. bdg. 25.00x o.p. (ISBN 0-8287-0647-6); pap. text ed. 15.00x o.p. (ISBN 0-685-75746-3). Clearwater Pub.
Mourgues, Odette De see De Mourgues, Odette.
Mouridsen, H. T. & Palshof, T., eds. Breast Cancer - Experimental & Clinical Aspects: Proceedings of the Second E.O.R.T.C. (European Organization for Research on Treatment of Cancer) Breast Cancer Working Conference, Held in Copenhagen, May 30 to June 2, 1979. LC 79-41496. (Illus.). 475p. 1980. 78.00 (ISBN 0-08-025886-7). Pergamon.
Mouritsen, Maren, ed. Blueprints for Living: Perspectives for Latter-day Saint Women, 2 vols. 128p. 1980. pap. 5.95 ea. Vol. 1 (ISBN 0-8425-1812-6). Vol. 2 (ISBN 0-8425-1814-2). Brigham.
Mourlot, Fernand, jt. auth. see Leiris, Michael.
Moursund, David. Calculators in the Classroom. 192p. 1980. pap. text ed. 8.95 (ISBN 0-471-08113-2). Wiley.
Moursund, David, jt. auth. see Billings, Karen.

Moursund, Janet P. Learning & the Learner. LC 76-7717. 1976. pap. text ed. 11.95 (ISBN 0-8185-0197-9). Brooks-Cole.
Mouser, Bruce L., ed. Guinea Journals: Journeys into Guinea-Conakry During the Sierra Leone Phase, 1800-1821. LC 79-62896. 1979. pap. text ed. 10.25 (ISBN 0-8191-0713-1). U Pr of Amer.
Moussa-Mahmoud, Fatma, tr. see Mahfouz, Naguib.
Mousset-Jones, Pierre, ed. see International Mine Ventilation Congress, 2nd.
Mousset-Jones, Pierre F. Geostatistics. 180p. 1980. 15.50 (ISBN 0-07-043568-5). McGraw.
Moustakas, Clark. Authentic Teacher. LC 80-67902. 1981. pap. 8.95 (ISBN 0-89615-031-3). Guild of Tutors.
--Child's Discovery of Himself. 1975. pap. 1.75 o.p. (ISBN 0-345-24892-9). Ballantine.
Moustakas, Clark E. Alive & Growing Teacher. 1959. 4.00 o.p. (ISBN 0-685-77550-X). Philos Lib.
--Psychotherapy with Children. 1973. pap. 1.65 o.p. (ISBN 0-345-23174-0, Walden). Ballantine.
Moustakas, Clark E., ed. Self: Explorations in Personal Growth. 1956. 9.95x o.p. (ISBN 0-06-034530-6, HarpT). Har-Row.
Mouthany, J. R. English Without Teacher & Dictionary: English-Arabic. 7.95x. Intl Bk Ctr.
Mouton, Claude. The Montreal Canadians. 256p. 1981. 19.95 (ISBN 0-442-29634-7). Van Nos Reinhold.
Mouton, Jane S., jt. auth. see Blake, Robert R.
Mouton, Jean, jt. ed. see Arland, Marcel.
Moutsopoulos, Evanghelos. Petros Brailas-Armenis. (World Authors Ser.: Greece: No. 261). 1974. lib. bdg. 10.95 (ISBN 0-8057-2170-3). Twayne.
Mouw, Richard. Politics & the Biblical Drama. 1976. pap. 2.95 o.p. (ISBN 0-8028-1657-6). Eerdmans.
Mouw, Richard J. Called to Holy Worldliness. Gibbs, Mark, ed. LC 80-8047. (Laity Exchange). 160p. (Orig.). 1980. pap. 5.50 (ISBN 0-8006-1397-X, 1-1397). Fortress.
--Called to World: Called to Holy Worldliness. 1980. pap. 5.95 (ISBN 0-529-05741-7, Pub. by Collins Pubs). Fortress.
Mouzaki, Rozanna. Greek Dances for Americans. Dallas-Damis, Athena, tr. LC 77-25604. (Illus.). 192p. 1981. pap. 9.95 (ISBN 0-385-14041-X). Doubleday.
Mouzakis. Investigative Guidelines & Procedures, No. 1. 1981. text ed. 43.95 (ISBN 0-409-95016-5). Butterworth.
Mouzelis, Nicos P. Organisation & Bureaucracy: An Analysis of Modern Theories. LC 68-11361. 1968. 15.95x (ISBN 0-202-30072-2); pap. 6.95x (ISBN 0-202-30078-1). Aldine Pub.
Movius, Hallam L., Jr. Excavation of Abri Pataud, Les Eyzies (Dordoane) Stratigraphy. LC 76-52630. (American School of Prehistoric Bulletins Ser.: No. 31). (Illus.). 1977. pap. 30.00 (ISBN 0-87365-534-6). Peabody Harvard.
Movius, Hallam L., Jr., ed. Excavation of the Abri Pataud, Les Eyzies (Dordogne) LC 74-77559. (American School of Prehistoric Research Bullentins Ser.: No. 30). (Illus.). 1975. pap. 30.00 (ISBN 0-87365-533-8). Peabody Harvard.
Movius, Hallam L., Jr., et al. The Analysis of Certain Major Classes of Upper Palaeolitic Tools. LC 68-55995. (ASPR Bulletin: No. 26). 1969. pap. text ed. 10.00 (ISBN 0-87365-527-3). Peabody Harvard.
Mow, Anna B. Secret of Married Love. 1976. pap. 1.50 (ISBN 0-89129-190-3). Jove Pubns.
Mowat, Charles L. East Florida As a British Province, 1763-1784. LC 64-66326. (Floridia Facsimile && Reprint Ser.). 1964. Repr. of 1943 ed. 9.50 (ISBN 0-8130-0167-6). U Presses Fla.
Mowat, Farley. And No Birds Sang. LC 79-23231. 1980. 10.95 (ISBN 0-316-58695-1, Pub. by Atlantic-Little Brown). Little.
--The Boat Who Wouldn't Float. 1970. 10.95 (ISBN 0-316-58650-1, Pub. by Atlantic Monthly Pr). Little.
--The Boat Who Wouldn't Float. 208p. 1981. pap. 2.50 (ISBN 0-553-14355-7). Bantam.
--Dog Who Wouldn't Be. (gr. 6-10). 1970. pap. 1.50 (ISBN 0-515-05617-0, N2333). Jove Pubns.
--The Dog Who Wouldn't Be. 208p. 1981. pap. 1.95 (ISBN 0-553-14354-9). Bantam.
--Never Cry Wolf. 1963. 9.95 (ISBN 0-316-58639-0, Pub. by Atlantic Monthly Pr). Little.
--Owls in the Family. (Skylark Ser.). 96p. 1981. pap. 1.50 (ISBN 0-553-15094-4). Bantam.
--People of the Deer. (Orig.). pap. 1.95 (ISBN 0-515-05131-4). Jove Pubns.
--Serpent's Coil. 1976. pap. 1.75 o.p. (ISBN 0-345-25029-X). Ballantine.
--A Whale for the Killing. 224p. 1981. pap. 2.25 (ISBN 0-553-14702-1). Bantam.
Mowat, R. B. Gibbon. 282p. 1980. Repr. of 1936 ed. lib. bdg. 30.00 (ISBN 0-8495-3827-0). Arden Lib.
Mower, David. Gaudi. (Illus.). 1977. 15.95 (ISBN 0-8467-0248-7, Pub. by Two Continents); pap. 9.95 (ISBN 0-8467-0247-9). Hippocrene Bks.
Mower, Rosalie, jt. auth. see Mills, Queenie B.
Mowhan, ed. Crystal Structure at High Pressure. pap. 5.00 (ISBN 0-686-60376-1). Polycrystal Bk Serv.
Mowle, Frederic J. Systematic Approach to Digital Logic Design. LC 75-18156. (A-W Series in Electrical Engineering). 500p. 1976. text ed. 25.95 (ISBN 0-201-04920-1); solution manual 5.95 (ISBN 0-201-04921-X). A-W.
Mowoe, Isaac J., ed. The Performance of Soldiers As Governors: African Politics & the African Military. LC 79-5511. 1980. text ed. 23.00 (ISBN 0-8191-0903-7); pap. text ed. 13.50 (ISBN 0-8191-0904-5). U Pr of Amer.
Mowrer, Donald E. Methods of Modifying Speech Behaviors: Learning Theory in Speech Pathology. (Special Education Ser.). 1978. text ed. 16.95 (ISBN 0-675-08438-5). Merrill.
--A Program to Establish Speech Fluency. 1979. pap. text ed. 5.95 (ISBN 0-675-08271-4); cassettes 60.00, 2 or more sets 40.00 (ISBN 0-675-08270-6). Merrill.
Mowrer, O. Hobart. Psychology of Language & Learning. (Cognition & Language Ser.). (Illus.). 275p. 1980. 27.50 (ISBN 0-306-40371-4, Plenum Pr). Plenum Pub.
Mowry, Arthur M. see Friedman, Leon.
Mowry, George E. Era of Theodore Roosevelt: 1900-1912. (New American Nation Ser). 1958. 15.00x o.s.i. (ISBN 0-06-013095-4, HarpT). Har-Row.
Mowry, George E. & Brownell, Blaine E. The Urban Nation: Nineteen Twenty to Nineteen Eighty. Donald, David H., ed. 1981. 12.50 (ISBN 0-8090-9541-6); pap. 5.95 (ISBN 0-8090-0148-9). Hill & Wang.
Moxey, Keith P. Pieter Aertsen, Joachim Beuckelaer & the Rise of Secular Painting in the Context of the Reformation. LC 76-23656. (Outstanding Dissertations in the Fine Arts - 16th Century). (Illus.). 1977. Repr. of 1974 ed. lib. bdg. 48.00 (ISBN 0-8240-2715-9). Garland Pub.
Moxley, R. T., jt. ed. see Griggs, Robert C.
Moxon, Peter. Gundogs: Questions & Answers. (Illus.). 96p. (Orig.). 1980. pap. 7.50x (ISBN 0-85242-734-4). Intl Pubns Serv.
Moy, Susan L. Chinese in Chicago: The First Hundred Years. 1980. pap. write for info. (ISBN 0-934584-12-5). Pacific-Asian.
Moya, Eddy D. An Art Quaderno of Nineteenth Century Steel Engravings of Ancient Landscapes. (Illus.). 1979. 179.80 (ISBN 0-930582-49-7). Gloucester Art.
Moya, Frank. Fundamentals of Management for the Physician. (Illus.). 208p. 1974. 14.75 (ISBN 0-398-02945-8). C C Thomas.
Moyar, Gerald J. & Pilkey, Walter D., eds. Advanced Techniques, Proceedings of a Conference Held in Chicago, Sept. 27-28, 1978: Advanced Techniques, Proceedings of the Conference Held in Chicago, Sept. 27-28, 1977. LC 78-1678. 484p. 55.00 (ISBN 0-08-022153-X). Pergamon.
Moyer, Anne, ed. see Organic Gardening & Farming Editors.
Moyer, Carolyn. The Secret of Bourke's Mansion. (YA) 1977. 4.95 o.p. (ISBN 0-685-75642-4, Avalon). Bouregy.
Moyer, Charles R. & Kretlow, William. Contemporary Financial Management. (Illus.). 700p. 1981. text ed. 19.95 (ISBN 0-8299-0400-X). West Pub.
Moyer, Elizabeth A. Self-Assessment of Current Knowledge in Occupational Therapy. 1976. spiral bdg. 9.50 (ISBN 0-87488-249-4). Med Exam.
Moyer, Frank A. Police Guide to Bomb Search Techniques. (Illus.). 198p. (Orig.). 1980. pap. text ed. 12.95 (ISBN 0-87364-196-5). Paladin Ent.
Moyer, Frank A. & Scroggie, Robert J. Special Forces Combat Firing Techniques. new ed. Brown, Robert K., ed. LC 72-180974. (Illus.). 120p. 1971. 15.95 (ISBN 0-87364-010-1). Paladin Ent.
Moyer, John W. Famous Frontiersmen. LC 76-13740. (Illus.). (gr. 4-8). 1972. 6.95 o.p. (ISBN 0-528-82807-X). Rand.
--Famous Indian Chiefs. LC 76-13741. (Illus.). (gr. 4-8). 1957. 6.95 o.p. (ISBN 0-528-82808-8). Rand.
Moyer, K. E. You & Your Child: A Primer for Parents. LC 74-17316. 230p. 1974. 12.95 (ISBN 0-88229-156-4). Nelson-Hall.
Moyer, Kenneth E., ed. Physiology of Aggression & Implications for Control: An Anthology of Readings. LC 74-14476. 1976. pap. 15.50 (ISBN 0-89004-003-6). Raven.
Moyer, Kenneth E., jt. ed. see Crabtree, J. Michael.
Moyer, R. Charles, jt. auth. see McGuigan, James R.
Moyer, R. Charles, et al. Managerial Economics: Readings, Cases & Exercises. 1979. pap. text ed. 11.95 (ISBN 0-8299-0157-4); pap. text ed. solutions manual avail. (ISBN 0-8299-0632-0). West Pub.
Moyer, Reed & Hutt, Michael D. Macro Marketing: A Social Perspective. 2nd ed. LC 77-26816. (Wiley Ser. in Marketing). 1978. text ed. 10.50 (ISBN 0-471-02699-9); teacher's manual (ISBN 0-471-02768-5). Wiley.
Moyer, Ruth. Business English Basics. LC 80-64. 1980. text ed. 13.95x (ISBN 0-471-04337-0); tchr's manual avail. (ISBN 0-471-08249-X). Wiley.
Moyer, Ruth, jt. auth. see Meyer, Lois.
Moyers, R. E. & Krogman, W. M. Cranio Facial Growth in Man. 1971. 55.00 (ISBN 0-08-016331-9). Pergamon.
Moyes, Elizabeth, ed. Manual of Law Librarianship: The Use & Organization of Legal Literature. LC 76-25099. 1976. lib. bdg. 50.00x (ISBN 0-89158-637-7). Westview.
Moyes, Patricia. The Curious Affair of the Third Dog. 208p. 1976. pap. 1.95 o.p. (ISBN 0-14-004027-7). Penguin.
--Many Deadly Returns. 1981. pap. 2.25 o.s.i. (ISBN 0-440-16172-X). Dell.
Moyes, Philip J. see Taylor, John W.
Moyles, R. G., ed. English-Canadian Literature to 1900: A Guide to Information Sources. LC 73-16986. (American Literature, English Literature, & World Literatures in English Information Guide Ser.: Vol. 6). 208p. 1976. 30.00 (ISBN 0-8103-1222-0). Gale.
Moynahan, Brian. Airport Confidential. LC 79-24395. 1980. 15.95 (ISBN 0-671-40111-4); pap. 6.95 (ISBN 0-671-40119-X). Summit Bks.
Moynahan, J. McCauslin, Jr. Police Ju Jitsu. (Illus.). 132p. 1962. 8.75 (ISBN 0-398-01366-7). C C Thomas.
Moynahan, Michael E. How the Word Became Flesh: Story Dramas for Education & Worship. 1981. pap. 9.95 (ISBN 0-89390-029-X). Resource Pubns.
Moyne, Claudia W., jt. auth. see Pierre, Andrew J.
Moynihan, Cornelius T., jt. auth. see Goldwhite, Harold.
Moynihan, Daniel P. Maximum Feasible Misunderstanding. LC 69-18005. 1970. 5.95 o.s.i. (ISBN 0-02-922000-9); pap. text ed. 5.95 (ISBN 0-02-922010-6). Free Pr.
Moynihan, Daniel P., jt. auth. see Glazer, Nathan.
Moynihan, Fergus & Moynihan, Liz. The Positive Way to Good Health. 1977. 8.95 (ISBN 0-236-40030-4, Pub. by Paul Elek). Merrimack Bk Serv.
Moynihan, Liz, jt. auth. see Moynihan, Fergus.
Moynihan, William T., et al. Reading, Writing & Rewriting. rev. ed. LC 69-15533. 1969. pap. text ed. 4.75x o.p. (ISBN 0-397-47161-0). Lippincott.
Mozan. Mozan's Racing Numerology. (Gambler's Book Shelf). 102p. 1972. pap. 2.95 (ISBN 0-89650-536-7). Gamblers.
Mozans, H. J. Women in Science. 1974. 17.50x o.p. (ISBN 0-262-13113-7); pap. 5.95 (ISBN 0-262-63054-0). MIT Pr.
Mozart, Leopold. Treatise on the Fundamental Principles of Violin Playing. 2nd ed. Knocher, Editha, tr. (Illus.). 1951. 27.00x (ISBN 0-19-318502-4). Oxford U Pr.
Mozart, Wolfgang A. Complete String Quintets. 181p. 1978. pap. 6.00 (ISBN 0-486-23603-X). Dover.
--Symphony Number 35 in D. K. 385: The Haffner Symphony. facsimile ed. 1968. Set. boxed 22.50 (ISBN 0-19-393180-X); pap. 5.00 (ISBN 0-19-385289-6). Oxford U Pr.
Mozeen, Thomas. Young Scarron. (The Flowering of the Novel, 1740-1775 Ser: Vol. 37). 1974. Repr. of 1752 ed. lib. bdg. 50.00 (ISBN 0-8240-1136-8). Garland Pub.
Mozeson, Isaac E. The Watcher. 48p. (Orig.). 1980. pap. 2.50 (ISBN 0-917402-17-0). Downtown Poets.
Mozley, John K. Doctrine of the Atonement. (Studies in Theology: No. 19). 1915. 6.00x o.p. (ISBN 0-8401-6019-4). Allenson.
Mozsi, F., ed. Szivarvany (Rainbow, No. 1. (Illus.). 96p. (Orig.). 1980. pap. 6.50 (ISBN 0-936398-00-0). Framo Pub.
Mozsik, Gy., et al, eds. Gastrointestinal Defence Mechanisms: Proceedings of a Satellite Symposium of the 28th International Congress of Physiological Sciences, Budapest, 1980. LC 80-41883. (Advances in Physiological Sciences: Vol. 29). (Illus.). 590p. 1981. 70.00 (ISBN 0-08-027350-5). Pergamon.
Mphahlele, Ezekiel. Down Second Avenue: Growing up in a South African Ghetto. 7.50 (ISBN 0-8446-4451-X). Peter Smith.
--Voices in the Whirlwind & Other Essays. LC 70-163568. 1972. 6.95 o.p. (ISBN 0-8090-9627-7); pap. 2.65 o.p. (ISBN 0-8090-1361-4). Hill & Wang.
Mphalele, Ezekiel. Modern African Stories. Komey, Ellis A., ed. (Orig.). 1966. pap. 5.95 (ISBN 0-571-11217-X, Pub. by Faber & Faber). Merrimack Bk Serv.
Mrachek, L. & Kromschlies, C. Technical-Vocational Mathematics. LC 76-48917. 1978. pap. 14.95 (ISBN 0-13-898569-3). P-H.
Mrak, E. M. & Stewart, G. F., eds. Advances in Food Research: Supplements. Incl. Suppl. 1. Phenolic Substances in Grapes & Wine & Their Significance. Singleton, V. L. & Esau, P. 1969. 37.50 (ISBN 0-12-016461-2); Suppl. 2. The Chemical Constituents of Citrus Fruits. Kefford, J. F. & Chandler, B. V. 1970. 31.50 (ISBN 0-12-016462-0); Suppl. 3. Advances in the Chemistry of Plant Pigments. Chichester, O., ed. 1972. 31.50 (ISBN 0-12-016463-9). Acad Pr.
Mrak, E. M., et al, eds. Advances in Food Research, Vols. 1-24. Incl. Vol. 1. 1948 (ISBN 0-12-016401-9); Vol. 2. 1949 (ISBN 0-12-016402-7); Vols. 3-5. 1951-54. Vol. 3 (ISBN 0-12-016403-5). Vol. 4 (ISBN 0-12-016404-3). Vol. 5 (ISBN 0-12-016405-1); Vol. 6. 1955 (ISBN 0-12-016406-X); Vols. 7-8. 1957-58. Vol. 7 (ISBN 0-12-016407-8). Vol. 8 (ISBN 0-12-016408-6); Vol. 9. Chichester, C. O., et al, eds. 1960 (ISBN 0-12-016409-4); Vols. 11-13. 1963-64. Vol. 10. o.s.i (ISBN 0-12-016410-8). Vol. 11 (ISBN 0-12-016411-6). Vol. 12 (ISBN 0-12-016412-4). Vol. 13 (ISBN 0-12-016413-2); Vol. 14. 1965 (ISBN 0-12-016414-0); Vol. 15. 1967 (ISBN 0-12-016415-9); Vol. 16. 1968. o.s.i (ISBN 0-12-016416-7); Vol. 17. 1969 (ISBN 0-12-016417-5); Vol. 18. 1970 (ISBN 0-12-016418-3); Vol. 19. 1971 (ISBN 0-12-016419-1); Vol. 20. 1973 (ISBN 0-12-016420-5); Vol. 21. 1975 (ISBN 0-12-016421-3). lib ed. 59.50 (ISBN 0-686-66766-2); microfiche 33.50 (ISBN 0-12-016485-X); Vol. 22. 1976 (ISBN 0-12-016422-1). lib ed. 59.50 (ISBN 0-686-66767-0); **microfiche 33.50 (ISBN 0-12-016487-6); Vol. 23. 1977. 43.50 (ISBN 0-12-016423-X); lib ed. 46.50 (ISBN 0-12-016488-4); microfiche 27.00 (ISBN 0-12-016489-2); Vol. 24. 1978. 40.00 (ISBN 0-12-016424-8). Vols. 1-22. 46.50 ea. Acad Pr.**
Mrazek, James. Hang Gliding. rev. ed. (Illus.). 160p. 1981. 17.95 (ISBN 0-312-35912-8). St Martin.
Mrazek, James E. Sailplanes & Soaring. (Illus.). pap. 2.95 o.p. (ISBN 0-8015-6512-X). Dutton.
Mrazek, Patricia B. & Kempe, C. H. Sexually Abused Children & Their Families. 300p. 1981. 72.01 (ISBN 0-08-026796-3). Pergamon.
Mr. J. More of the World's Dirty Jokes. 1980. pap. 3.95 (ISBN 0-8065-0689-X). Lyle Stuart.
Mrosovsky, Nicholas. Hibernation & the Hypothalamus. 287p. 1971. 22.50 (ISBN 0-306-50058-2, Plenum Pr). Plenum Pub.
Mroz, John E. Beyond Security: Private Perceptions Among Arabs & Israelis. (Illus.). 230p. 1981. 20.00 (ISBN 0-08-027517-6); pap. 9.95 (ISBN 0-08-027516-8). Pergamon.
Ms. Magazine Editors. The First Ms. Reader. 228p. (Orig.). 1973. pap. 1.95 o.s.i. (ISBN 0-446-89027-8). Warner Bks.
Mtewa, Mekki. Consultant Connexion: Evaluation of the Federal Consulting Service. LC 80-8141. 238p. 1980. lib. bdg. 18.50 (ISBN 0-8191-1161-9); pap. text ed. 9.50 (ISBN 0-8191-1162-7). U Pr of Amer.
--Public Policy & Development Politics: The Politics of Technical Expertise in Africa. LC 79-48041. 364p. 1980. text ed. 20.75 (ISBN 0-8191-1003-5); pap. text ed. 12.00 (ISBN 0-8191-1004-3). U Pr of Amer.
Mubarak, Scott J., et al. Compartment Snydromes & Volkmann's Contracture. (Saunder's Monographs in Clinical Orthopedics: Vol. 3). (Illus.). 200p. 1981. text ed. price not set (ISBN 0-7216-6604-3). Saunders.
Muccigrosso, Robert. American Gothic: The Mind & Art of Ralph Adams Cram. LC 79-5436. 1980. pap. text ed. 11.25 (ISBN 0-8191-0884-7). U Pr of Amer.
Mucciolo, Louis. Small Business: Look Before You Leap; a Catalog of Sources of Information to Help You Start & Manage Your Own Small Business. 256p. 1981. pap. 7.95 (ISBN 0-668-05173-6, 5173). Arco.
Mucha, Alphonse. The Art Nouveau Style Book of Alphonse Mucha. (Illus.). 80p. 1980. pap. 7.95 (ISBN 0-486-24044-4). Dover.
Mucha, Jiri & Henderson, Marina. Alphonse Mucha. rev. & enl. ed. LC 73-90408. (Illus.). 1974. 25.00 (ISBN 0-312-55160-6). St Martin.
Muchmore, John M., jt. auth. see Nadeau, Ray E.
Muchnick, David M. Urban Renewal in Liverpool. 120p. 1970. pap. text ed. 6.25x (Pub. by Bedford England). Renouf.
Muchnick, Steven S. & Jones, Neil D. Program Flow Analysis: Theory & Application. (Software Ser.). (Illus.). 448p. 1981. 21.50 (ISBN 0-13-729681-9). P-H.
Muchnik, Michoel. The Cuckoo Clock Castle of Shir. LC 79-55560. (Illus.). (ps-3). 1980. 5.95 (ISBN 0-8197-0476-8). Bloch.

Muchow, Kenneth & Deem, Bill. Microprocessor Principles, Programming & Interfacing. 1982. text ed. 18.95 (ISBN 0-8359-4383-6); instrs.' manual avail. (ISBN 0-8359-4384-4). Reston.
Muckelroy, K. Maritime Archaeology. LC 78-5693. (New Studies in Archaeology). 1979. 49.50 (ISBN 0-521-22079-3); pap. 14.50x (ISBN 0-521-29348-0). Cambridge U Pr.
Muckelroy, Keith, ed. Archaeology Under Water: An Atlas of the World's Submerged Sites. LC 79-18380. (Illus.). 1980. 24.95 (ISBN 0-07-043951-6). McGraw.
Muckersie, John R., jt. auth. see Wilson, James M.
Muckle, D. S. Femoral Neck Fractures & Hip Joint Injuries. LC 77-82681. 1977. 29.50 o.p. (ISBN 0-471-03799-0, Pub. by Wiley Medical). Wiley.
Muckle, David S. Sports Injuries. rev. ed. 1978. pap. 7.95 (ISBN 0-85362-173-X, Oriel). Routledge & Kegan.
Mucnik, jt. auth. see Humbaraci.
Mudge, Lewis S., ed. see Ricoeur, Paul.
Mudie-Smith, Richard, ed. Handbook of the Daily News Sweated Industries Exhibition: Nineteen Six. LC 79-56964. (The English Working Class Ser.). 1980. lib. bdg. 16.00 (ISBN 0-8240-0116-8). Garland Pub.
Muehlbacher, J., ed. G I-Five Jahrestagung. (Lecture Notes in Computer Science: Vol. 34). 755p. 1975. pap. 29.30 (ISBN 0-387-07410-4). Springer-Verlag.
Muehlbock, O., ed. see International Pigment Cell Conference - 6th.
Muehrcke, P. Thematic Cartography. LC 72-77214. (CCG Resource Papers Ser.: No. 19). (Illus.). 1972. pap. text ed. 4.00 (ISBN 0-89291-066-6). Assn Am Geographers.
Muehrcke, Phillip C. Map Use: Reading, Analysis & Interpretation. rev. ed. LC 78-70573. (Illus.). xi, 469p. 1980. pap. text ed. 16.25 (ISBN 0-9602978-1-2). JP Pubns WI.
Muehsam, Gerd. Guide to Basic Information Sources in the Visual Arts. LC 77-17430. 289p. 1980. 27.50 (ISBN 0-87436-278-4). ABC-Clio.
--Guide to Basic Information Sources in the Visual Arts: Where to Find the Facts in Every Art Field. 276p. 1980. pap. 9.95 (ISBN 0-442-21200-3). Van Nos Reinhold.
Mueller, jt. auth. see Heitzman.
Mueller, A. C. Bible Heroes. LC 56-1128. (Bible Story Booklet Ser). (Illus.). (gr. 3-5). 1981. pap. 0.69 (ISBN 0-570-06700-6, 56-1128). Concordia.
--Our Savior Lives. (Bible Story Booklets Ser). (Illus.). (gr. 3-5). 1971. pap. 0.69 (ISBN 0-570-06705-7, 56-1133). Concordia.
--People God Chose. LC 56-1129. (Bible Story Booklets Ser). (Illus.). (gr. 3-5). 1971. pap. 0.69 (ISBN 0-570-06701-4, 56-1129). Concordia.
Mueller, Alois, jt. ed. see Greinacher, Norbert.
Mueller, C., jt. auth. see DePaula, H.
Mueller, Carolyn J., jt. auth. see Grubb, Reba D.
Mueller, Charles, jt. auth. see Kim, Jae-On.
Mueller, Charles W., jt. auth. see Price, James L.
Mueller, Christopher B., jt. auth. see Louisell, David W.
Mueller, Claus. The Politics of Communication: A Study in the Political Sociology of Language, Socialization, & Legitimation. LC 73-83937. 256p. 1975. pap. 4.95 (ISBN 0-19-501961-X, 443, GB). Oxford U Pr.
Mueller, D. C. Public Choice. LC 78-11197. (Surveys in Economic Literature). 1979. 35.50 (ISBN 0-521-22550-7); pap. 7.95x (ISBN 0-521-29548-3). Cambridge U Pr.
Mueller, Dale M. J. The Peristome of Fissidens limbatus Sullivant. (U. C. Publ. in Botany: Vol. 63). 1973. pap. 9.50x (ISBN 0-520-09446-8). U of Cal Pr.
Mueller, Dennis C., ed. The Determinants & Effects of Mergers: An International Comparison. 416p. 1980. text ed. 27.50 (ISBN 0-89946-045-3). Oelgeschlager.
Mueller, F. M., ed. Sacred Books of the East: Index Volume, Vol. 50. 1979. 15.00 (ISBN 0-8426-1603-9). Verry.
Mueller, F. Max, ed. Bhagavadita, Vol. 8. Telang, K. T., tr. (Sacred Books of the East Ser.). 15.00x (ISBN 0-8426-1394-3). Verry.
--Buddhist Mahayana Texts, Vol. 49. Muller & Fausboll, trs. (Sacred Books of the East Ser.). 15.00x (ISBN 0-8426-1395-1). Verry.
--Buddhist Suttas, Vol. 11. Beal, tr. (Sacred Books of the East Ser.). 15.00x (ISBN 0-8426-1396-X). Verry.
--Dhammapada & Sutta-Nipata, Vol. 10. Davids, Rhys, tr. (Sacred Books of the East Ser.). 15.00x (ISBN 0-8426-1397-8). Verry.
--Fo-Sho-Hing-Tsan-King, Vol. 19. Beal, tr. (Sacred Books of the East Ser.). 15.00x (ISBN 0-8426-1398-6). Verry.
--Grihya-Sutras, Rules of Vedic Domestic Ceremonies, Vols. 29 & 30. Oldenburg & Muller, trs. (Sacred Books of the East Ser.). 15.00x ea.; Vol. 29. (ISBN 0-8426-1399-4); Vol. 30. (ISBN 0-8426-1400-1). Verry.
--Hymns of the Atharva-Veda, Vol. 42. Bloomfield, tr. (Sacred Books of the East Ser.). 15.00x (ISBN 0-8426-1401-X). Verry.
--Institutes of Vishnu, Vol. 7. Jolly, tr. (Sacred Books of the East Ser.). 15.00x (ISBN 0-8426-1402-8). Verry.
--Laws of Manu, Vol. 25. Buhler, tr. (Sacred Books of the East Ser.). 15.00x (ISBN 0-8426-1403-6). Verry.
--Minor Law-Books, Vol. 33. Jolly, tr. (Sacred Books of the East Ser.). 15.00x (ISBN 0-8426-1404-4). Verry.
--Pahlavi Texts, Vols. 5, 18, 24, 37, 47. Darmesteter & Mills, trs. (Sacred Books of the East Ser.). 15.00 ea.; Vol. 5. (ISBN 0-8426-1405-2); Vol. 18. (ISBN 0-8426-1406-0); Vol. 24. (ISBN 0-8426-1407-9); Vol. 37. (ISBN 0-8426-1408-7); Vol. 47. (ISBN 0-8426-1409-5). Verry.
--Questions of King Melinda, 2 Vols, Vols. 35 & 36. David & Oldenberg, trs. (Sacred Books of the East Ser.). 15.00x ea.; Vol. 35. (ISBN 0-8426-1410-9); Vol. 36. (ISBN 0-8426-1411-7). Verry.
--Qur'an, Vols. 6 & 9. Winternitz, tr. (Sacred Books of the East Ser.). 15.00x ea.; Vol. 6. (ISBN 0-8426-1412-5); Vol. 9. (ISBN 0-8426-1413-3). Verry.
--Sacred Books of China, Vols. 3, 16, 27, 28, 39, & 40. Palmer, tr. (Sacred Books of the East Ser.). 15.00x ea.; Vol. 3. (ISBN 0-8426-1414-1); Vol. 16. (ISBN 0-8426-1415-X); Vol. 27. (ISBN 0-8426-1416-8); Vol. 28. (ISBN 0-8426-1417-6); Vol. 39. (ISBN 0-8426-1418-4); Vol. 40. (ISBN 0-8426-1419-2). Verry.
--Sacred Books of the East, 50 Vols. Set. 700.00x (ISBN 0-8426-1420-6); 12.00x ea. Verry.
--Sacred Laws of the Aryas, Vols. 2 & 14. Buhler, tr. (Sacred Books of the East Ser.). 15.00x ea.; Vol. 2. (ISBN 0-8426-1421-4); Vol. 14. (ISBN 0-8426-1422-2). Verry.
--Saddharma-Pundarika or the Lotus of the True Law, Vol. 21. Davids & Oldenberg, trs. (Sacred Books of the East Ser.). 15.00x (ISBN 0-8426-1423-0). Verry.
--Satapatha-Brahmana, Vols. 12, 26, 41, 43 & 44. Eggeling, tr. (Sacred Books of the East Ser.). 15.00x ea.; Vol. 12. (ISBN 0-8426-1424-9); Vol. 26. (ISBN 0-8426-1425-7); Vol. 41. (ISBN 0-8426-1426-5); Vol. 43. (ISBN 0-8426-1427-3); Vol. 44. (ISBN 0-8426-1428-1). Verry.
--Vedanta-Sutras, Vols. 34 & 38. Thibaut, tr. (Sacred Books of the East Ser.). 15.00x ea.; Vol. 34. (ISBN 0-8426-1429-X); Vol. 38. (ISBN 0-8426-1430-3). Verry.
--Vedanta Sutras, Vol. 48. (Sacred Books of the East Ser.). 15.00x (ISBN 0-8426-1431-1). Verry.
--Vedic Hymns, Vols. 32 & 46. Oldenburg, tr. (Sacred Books of the East Ser.). 15.00x ea.; Vol. 32. (ISBN 0-8426-1432-X); Vol. 46. (ISBN 0-8426-1433-8). Verry.
--Vinaya Texts, Vols. 13, 17, & 20. West, tr. (Sacred Books of the East Ser.). 15.00x ea.; Vol. 13. (ISBN 0-8426-1434-6); Vol. 17. (ISBN 0-8426-1435-4); Vol. 20. (ISBN 0-8426-1436-2). Verry.
--Zend-Avesta, Vols. 4, 23 & 31. Legge, tr. (Sacred Books of the East Ser.). 15.00x ea.; Vol. 4. (ISBN 0-8426-1273-4); Vol. 23. (ISBN 0-8426-1274-2); Vol. 31. (ISBN 0-8426-1275-0). Verry.
Mueller, F. Max, ed. see Cowell, E. B., et al.
Mueller, F. Max, tr. Upanishads, 2 vols. (Sacred Books of the East: Vols. 1, 15). 15.00x ea.; Vol. 1. (ISBN 0-8426-1437-0); Vol. 15. (ISBN 0-8426-1438-9). Verry.
Mueller, Ferdinand Von. Fragmenta Phytographicae Australiae, Vols.1-11 & Suppl. 1974. 240.00 (ISBN 90-6123-311-9). Lubrecht & Cramer.
Mueller, Filip. Eyewitness Auschwitz. LC 78-66257. (Illus.). 192p. 1981. pap. 6.95 (ISBN 0-8128-6084-5). Stein & Day.
Mueller, Francis J. Essential Mathematics for College Students. 3rd ed. (Illus.). 320p. 1976. pap. 13.95 (ISBN 0-13-286518-1). P-H.
--Intermediate Algebra. (Illus.). 1979. pap. 16.95 ref. (ISBN 0-13-469452-X). P-H.
Mueller, G. Mikroradiographische Untersuchungen Zur Mineralisation der Knochen Fruehgeborener und Junger Saeuglinge, 1980. (Journal: Acta Anatomica: Vol. 108, Suppl. 64). (Illus.). iv, 44p. 1980. pap. 27.00 (ISBN 3-8055-1719-X). S Karger.
--Plating on Plastics. rev. 2nd ed. (Illus.). 206p. 1971. 27.50x (ISBN 0-85218-038-1). Intl Pubns Serv.
Mueller, G. O., jt. auth. see Wise, E. M.
Mueller, Geo. God Answers Prayer. pap. 2.95 (ISBN 0-686-27009-6). Schmul Pub Co.
Mueller, Georgiana. How to Raise & Train a Greyhound. (Illus.). 1965. pap. 2.00 (ISBN 0-87666-312-9, DS1083). TFH Pubns.
Mueller, Gerhard. Accounting Book of Readings. 2nd ed. LC 73-115174. 1977. pap. 10.95 (ISBN 0-03-089908-7). Dryden Pr.
Mueller, Gerhard O. Comparative Criminal Law in the United States. (New York University Criminal Law Education Research Center Monograph: No. 4). (Illus.). 72p. 1970. pap. text ed. 8.50x (ISBN 0-8377-0827-3). Rothman.
--Essays in Criminal Science. (New York University Criminal Law Education & Research Center Pubns: Vol. 1). 1960. 17.50x (ISBN 0-8377-0828-1). Rothman.
--Sentencing: Process & Purpose. (Criminal Law Education & Research Center Ser.). 228p. 1977. 19.75 (ISBN 0-398-03591-1). C C Thomas.
Mueller, Gerhard O. & Wise, E. M. International Criminal Law. (New York University Criminal Law Education & Research Center Pubns: Vol. 2). 1965. 20.00x o.p. (ISBN 0-8377-0829-X). Rothman.
Mueller, Gerhard O., et al. Delinquency & Puberty Examination of a Juvenile Delinquency Fad. (New York University Criminal Law Education & Research Center Monograph: No. 5). (Illus.). 123p. (Orig.). 1971. pap. text ed. 8.50x (ISBN 0-8377-0830-3). Rothman.
Mueller, Herbert C. Learning to Teach Through Playing: A Brass Method. (Music Series). (Illus., Orig.). 1968. pap. 16.50 (ISBN 0-201-04890-6). A-W.
Mueller, J. Gesammelte Lichenologische Schriften, 2 vols. Incl. Vol. 1. Lichenologische Beitraege 1-XXXV. o.p. (ISBN 0-686-22233-4). 1967. 220.00 set (ISBN 3-7682-0440-5). Lubrecht & Cramer.
Mueller, Jerome F. Standard Mechanical & Electrical Details. (Illus.). 1980. 24.50 (ISBN 0-07-043960-5). McGraw.
Mueller, Jerry E. Restless River. LC 74-80107. 1975. 8.00 o.p. (ISBN 0-87404-050-7); pap. 5.00 o.p. (ISBN 0-685-56283-2). Tex Western.
Mueller, John E. War, Presidents & Public Opinion. LC 72-8072. 288p. 1973. pap. text ed. 11.95x (ISBN 0-471-62300-8). Wiley.
Mueller, John H., et al. Statistical Reasoning in Sociology. 3rd ed. LC 76-13097. (Illus.). 1977. text ed. 19.95 (ISBN 0-395-24417-X); solutions manual 2.30 (ISBN 0-395-24416-1). HM.
Mueller, Kimberly J. The Nuclear Power Issue: A Guide to Who's Doing What in the U. S. & Abroad. LC 79-52430. (Who's Doing What Ser.: No. 8). (Illus., Orig.). 1981. pap. 12.00x (ISBN 0-912102-44-6). Cal Inst Public.
Mueller, Klaus A. & Hoppmann-Liecty, Susanne. Die Presse: A Reader & Workbook. 192p. 1976. pap. text ed. 7.95x (ISBN 0-669-92536-5). Heath.
Mueller, L., ed. see CISM (International Center for Mechanical Sciences) Dept. of Mechanics of Solids.
Mueller, Larry. Successful Home Electrical Wiring. Case, Virginia, ed. LC 80-18678. (Successful Ser.). (Illus.). 144p. 1980. 15.95 (ISBN 0-89999-008-8); pap. 6.95 (ISBN 0-89999-009-6). Structures Pub.
--Successful Reviving the Older Home. rev. ed. Case, Virginia, ed. (Successful Ser.). (Illus.). 164p. Date not set. price not set (ISBN 0-89999-012-6); pap. price not set (ISBN 0-89999-013-4). Structures Pub.
Mueller, Lisel, et al. Primavera, IV. Heller, Janet R., et al, eds. LC 76-647540. (Illus.). 1978. pap. 4.00 (ISBN 0-916980-04-9). Primavera.
Mueller, M. E., et al. Manual of Internal Fixation: Technique Recommended by the AO-Group. Schatzker, J., et al, trs. from Ger. LC 76-138812. (Illus.). 1970. 95.00 o.p. (ISBN 0-387-05219-4); slides 210.70 o.p. (ISBN 0-387-92101-X). Springer-Verlag.
Mueller, Martin. Children of Oedipus & Other Essays on the Imitation of Greek Tragedy Fifteen Fifty to Eighteen Hundred. 1980. 25.00x (ISBN 0-8020-5478-1); pap. 12.50 (ISBN 0-8020-6381-0). U of Toronto Pr.
Mueller, Melinda. Asleep in Another Country. 1979. 4.00 (ISBN 0-918116-17-1). Jawbone Pr.
Mueller, Myrl R. Lost in the Annals: The Story of the New Madrid Earthquake, Eighteen Eleven to Eighteen Twelve. (Orig.). 1980. pap. 4.95 (ISBN 0-917200-29-2). ESPress.
Mueller, Pat & Reznik, John W. Intramural-Recreational Sports: Programming & Administration. 5th ed. LC 78-10122. 1979. text ed. 18.95 (ISBN 0-471-04911-5). Wiley.
Mueller, Peter G. & Ross, Douglas A. China & Japan: Emerging Global Powers. LC 74-33039. (Special Studies). (Illus.). 240p. 1975. text ed. 24.95 (ISBN 0-275-05400-4); pap. text ed. 9.95 (ISBN 0-275-89390-1). Praeger.
Mueller, Ralph & Turk, Jerry. Report After Action: The Story of the 103rd Infantry Division. (Divisional Ser.: No. 1). (Illus.). 1978. pap. 15.00 o.p. (ISBN 0-89839-010-9). Battery Pr.
Mueller, Robert K. Board Compass: What It Means to Be a Director in a Changing World. (Arthur D. Little Books). (Illus.). 1979. 21.95 (ISBN 0-669-02903-3). Lexington Bks.
--Career Conflict: Management's Inelegant Dysfunction. LC 78-19240. (Arthur D. Little Books). 1978. 15.95 (ISBN 0-669-02471-6). Lexington Bks.
--The Incompleat Board: The Unfolding of Corporate Governance. LC 80-8639. 1981. 29.95 (ISBN 0-669-04339-7). Lexington Bks.
Mueller, Robert Kirk. New Directions for Directors: Behind the by-Laws. LC 77-10216. 1978. 18.95 (ISBN 0-669-01889-9). Lexington Bks.
Mueller, Virginia. La Invitacion del Rey. Villalobos, Fernando, tr. from Eng. (Libros Arco). (Illus.). 32p. (Orig., Span.). (gr. 1-3). 1970. pap. 0.95 o.s.i. (ISBN 0-89922-039-8). Edit Caribe.
Mueller, Virginia, jt. auth. see Pape, Donna L.
Mueller, W. Avenues to Understanding: Dynamics of Therapeutic Interactions. 1973. text ed. 12.95 (ISBN 0-13-055012-4). P-H.
Mueller, W. & Wagenhaeuser, F. J., eds. Die Lumoischialgie. (Fortibildungskurse Fuer Rhermatologie Ser.: Vol. 6). (Illus.). viii, 240p. 1981. pap. 54.00 (ISBN 3-8055-2207-X). S Karger.
Mueller, W. M., et al, eds. Metal Hydrides. 1969. 55.75 o.p. (ISBN 0-12-509550-3). Acad Pr.
Mueller, Willard F. Primer on Monopoly & Competition. 1970. pap. text ed. 3.95 (ISBN 0-394-30738-0). Random.
Mueller, William J., jt. auth. see Kell, Bill L.
Mueller, Wolfgang D. Man Among the Stars. (Illus.). 1956. 10.95 (ISBN 0-87599-079-7). S G Phillips.
Mueller-Dombois, Dieter & Ellenberg, Heinz. Aims & Methods of Vegetation Ecology. LC 74-5492. 432p. 1974. text ed. 25.95 (ISBN 0-471-62290-7). Wiley.
Mueller-Schwefe, Hans-Ulrich. Von Nun an Neue Deutsche Erzaehler. (Edition Suhrkamp). 300p. (Orig.). 1980. pap. text ed. 5.20 (ISBN 3-518-11003-9, Pub. by Insel Verlag Germany). Suhrkamp.
Muench, David, jt. auth. see Pike, Donald.
Muenchow, Charles A., tr. see Westermann, Claus.
Muenscher, Minnie W. Minnie Muenscher's Herb Cookbook. LC 77-90908. (Illus.). 224p. 1978. 11.50 (ISBN 0-8014-1166-1). Comstock.
Muenscher, Walter C. Weeds. 2nd ed. LC 79-48017. (Illus.). 560p. 1980. 29.50x (ISBN 0-8014-1266-8). Comstock.
Muenscher, Walter C. & Rice, Myron A. Garden Spice & Wild Pot-Herbs: An American Herbal. LC 78-56899. (Illus.). 218p. 1978. pap. 7.95 (ISBN 0-8014-9174-6). Comstock.
Muentzig, Arne. Triticale: Results & Problems. (Advances in Plant Breeding Ser.: Vol. 10). (Illus.). 103p. (Orig.). 1979. pap. text ed. 35.00 (ISBN 3-489-76210-X). Parey Sci Pubs.
Mueser, Anne M. The Picture Story of Rod Carew. LC 80-420. (Illus.). 64p. (gr. 4-6). 1980. PLB 6.97 (ISBN 0-671-33049-7). Messner.
Mueser, Annie. Bugs, Snakes & Creepy Things. (Pal Paperbacks, - Pal Skills II Ser.). (Illus.). (gr. 5-12). 1980. pap. 1.25 (ISBN 0-8374-6803-5). Xerox Ed Pubns.
--Cobra in the Tub. (Pal Paperbacks, - Pal Skills II Ser.). (Illus.). (gr. 5-12). 1980. pap. 1.25 (ISBN 0-8374-6810-8). Xerox Ed Pubns.
--Face at the Window. (Pal Paperbacks, - Pal Skills II Ser.). (Illus.). (gr. 5-12). 1980. pap. text ed. 1.25 (ISBN 0-8374-6808-6). Xerox Ed Pubns.
Muessen, H. J. How the World Cooks Chicken. LC 80-51608. 350p. 1980. 17.95 (ISBN 0-8128-2740-6). Stein & Day.
Muessig, Raymond H., jt. auth. see Commager, Henry S.
Muessig, Raymond H., jt. auth. see Kitchens, James A.
Muessig, Raymond H., jt. auth. see Pelto, Pertti J.
Muessig, Raymond H., jt. auth. see Straayer, John A.
Muff, Rolf. The Antimony Deposits in the Murchison Range of the Northeastern Transvaal Republic of South Africa. LC 78-321157. (Monograph Series on Mineral Deposits: Vol. 16). (Illus.). 90p. (Orig.). 1978. pap. 40.00x (ISBN 3-443-12016-4). Intl Pubns Serv.
Muffett, D. J. Empire Builder Extraordinary Sir George Goldie: His Philosophy of Government & Empire. (Illus.). 1978. text ed. 22.50x (ISBN 0-904980-18-9). Humanities.
Muffler, L. J., jt. ed. see Rybach, L.
Mufti, I. H. Computational Methods in Optimal Control Problems. LC 77-121990. (Lecture Notes in Operations Research & Mathematical Systems: Vol. 27). 1970. pap. 10.70 o.p. (ISBN 0-387-04951-7). Springer-Verlag.
Mufti, Shawkat. Heroes & Emperors in Circassian History. (Arab Background Ser.). 1972. 14.00x (ISBN 0-685-77100-8). Intl Bk Ctr.
Mugar, Jayson, jt. auth. see Boarman, Patrick M.
Mugford, E., jt. auth. see Legge, K.
Muggenberg, James see O'Neal, William B.

Muggenthaler, August K. German Raiders of World War II. LC 76-30612. 1977. 14.95 o.p. (ISBN 0-13-354027-8). P-H.

Muggerbridge, Malcolm. The Thirties, Nineteen Thirty to Nineteen Forty. 327p. 1980. Repr. of 1940 ed. lib. bdg. 30.00 (ISBN 0-89987-574-2). Darby Bks.

Muggeridge, Malcolm. Something Beautiful for God. LC 77-155106. (Illus.). 1971. 10.95 (ISBN 0-06-066041-4, HarpR). Har-Row.

--Something Beautiful for God: Mother Teresa of Calcutta. 1977. pap. 2.45 (ISBN 0-385-12639-5, Im). Doubleday.

Muggeridge, Malcolm, et al. Christian Married Love: Five Contributions. Englund, Sergia & Leiva, Erasmo, trs. 150p. (Orig.). 1981. pap. price not set (ISBN 0-89870-008-6). Ignatius Pr.

Muggia, F. M., jt. ed. see Mathe, G.

Muggia, Franco & Rozencweig, Marcel, eds. Lung Cancer: Progress in Therapeutic Research. LC 77-84552. (Progress in Cancer Research & Therapy Ser.: Vol. 11). 1978. 52.00 (ISBN 0-89004-223-3). Raven.

Mugglestone, Patricia. Planning & Using the Blackboard. (Practical Language Teaching Ser.). (Illus.). 96p. (Orig.). 1980. pap. text ed. 6.95x (ISBN 0-04-371062-X, 2368). Allen Unwin.

Muggleton-Harris, Audrey L., jt. ed. see Bourne, G. H.

Mughisuddin, Mohammed, ed. Conflict & Cooperation in the Persian Gulf. LC 77-11124. (Praeger Special Studies). 1977. 24.50 (ISBN 0-03-021851-9). Praeger.

Mugno, John F., jt. auth. see Rustow, Dankwart A.

Mugomba, Agrippah I., ed. Independence Without Freedom. Nyaggah, Mougo. Merkl, Peter, ed. LC 80-154. (International & Comparative Politics Ser.: No. 13). 289p. 1980. 27.50 (ISBN 0-87436-293-8). ABC Clio.

Muhaiyaddeen, M. R. Bawa see Bawa Muhaiyaddeen, M. R.

Muhammad Ibn Zakariya. Practical Chemistry in the Twelfth Century. Steele, Robert R., ed. Gerard Of Cremona, tr. LC 79-8590. Repr. of 1929 ed. 12.50 (ISBN 0-404-18444-8). AMS Pr.

Muhl, Anita M. Automatic Writing. (Illus.). 1964. 4.50 o.p. (ISBN 0-912326-08-5). Garrett-Helix.

Muhlbauer, K. C. Statics: An Individualized Approach. 1972. pap. 13.95 (ISBN 0-201-04888-4). A-W.

Muhlemann, Hans R. Introduction to Oral Preventive Medicine. (Illus.). 253p. 1976. 22.00. Quint Pub Co.

Muhlschlegel, Peter. Auguste Forel & the Baha'i Faith. Neri, Helene, tr. from Ger. 1979. pap. 1.85 (ISBN 0-85398-076-4, 7-32-35, Pub by G Ronald England). Baha'i.

Muileman, Kathryn S., jt. auth. see Saltzman, Marvin L.

Muir, jt. auth. see Sharp.

Muir, Alex, ed. see Goldschmidt, Victor M.

Muir, Bernice L. Pathophysiology: An Introduction to Mechanisms of Disease. LC 79-27791. 1980. 18.95 (ISBN 0-471-03202-6, Pub. by Wiley Med). Wiley.

Muir, D. C., ed. Clinical Aspects of Inhaled Particles. (Illus.). 1972. 17.95x (ISBN 0-433-22700-1). Intl Ideas.

Muir, Dorothy T. General Washington's Headquarters: Seventeen Seventy-Five to Seventeen Eighty-Three. LC 76-45927. (Illus.). 1977. 19.95 (ISBN 0-916624-06-4). TSU Pr.

Muir, Edward. Civic Ritual in Renaissance Venice. LC 80-8568. (Illus.). 368p. 1981. 17.50x (ISBN 0-691-05325-1). Princeton U Pr.

Muir, Edwin. Selected Poems. 1965. pap. 4.95 (ISBN 0-571-06342-X, Pub. by Faber & Faber). Merrimack Bk Serv.

Muir, J., ed. Virgil: Selections from Aeneid, Vol. 4. (Latin Texts Ser.). 1977. limp bdg 3.25x (ISBN 0-521-21581-1). Cambridge U Pr.

Muir, J. V., ed. Virgil: Selection from Aeneid Four Handbook. LC 76-52324. (Cambridge Latin Texts Ser.). 1977. 6.95x (ISBN 0-521-21645-1). Cambridge U Pr.

Muir, James. A Modern Approach to English Grammar: An Introduction to Systemic English Grammar. 148p. 1972. pap. text ed. 10.25x (ISBN 0-7134-2008-1). Humanities.

Muir, James F. & Roberts, Ronald J., eds. Recent Advances in Aquaculture. 320p. 1980. 50.00x (Pub. by Croom Helm England). State Mutual Bk.

Muir, John. Como Mantener Tu Volkswagen Vivo. rev. ed. Holt, Virginia, tr. from Eng. LC 75-21414. (Illus.). 1980. pap. 9.00 (ISBN 0-912528-21-4). John Muir.

--Our Yosemite National Park. Jones, William R., ed. (Illus.). 96p. (Orig.). pap. 4.95 (ISBN 0-89646-061-4). Outbooks.

--Sierra Big Trees. abr. ed. Jones, William R., ed. (Illus.). 80p. 1981. pap. 3.95 (ISBN 0-89646-069-X). Outbooks.

--Stickeen: The Story of a Dog. LC 73-10825. pap. 2.95 o.p. (ISBN 0-385-08624-5). Doubleday.

--Story of My Boyhood & Youth. (Illus.). 1965. 10.00 (ISBN 0-299-03650-2); pap. 5.00 (ISBN 0-299-03654-5). U of Wis Pr.

--The Velvet Monkey Wrench. rev. ed. LC 72-96736. (Illus.). 247p. 1980. pap. 6.00 (ISBN 0-912528-02-8). John Muir.

Muir, K. Shakespeare's Jacobean Tragedies. LC 72-97884. (Shakespeare Survey Ser.: No. 26). (Illus.). 200p. 1973. 32.50 (ISBN 0-521-20216-7). Cambridge U Pr.

Muir, K. & Schoenbaum, S. New Companion to Shakespeare Studies. LC 78-118066. (Illus.). 1971. 47.50 (ISBN 0-521-07941-1); pap. 10.95 (ISBN 0-521-09645-6). Cambridge U Pr.

Muir, K., ed. Shakespeare Survey, Vols. 1-18, 25 & 28-31. Incl. Vols. 1-18. Nicoll, Allardyce, ed; Vol. 25. Shakespeare's Problem Plays. 200p. 1972 (ISBN 0-521-08528-4); Vol. 28. 200p. 1975 (ISBN 0-521-20837-8); Vol. 29. 1976 (ISBN 0-521-21227-8); Vol. 30. 1977 (ISBN 0-521-21636-2); Vol. 31. 1979 (ISBN 0-521-22011-4). LC 49-1639. 32.50 ea. Cambridge U Pr.

--Shakespeare Survey: King Lear, No. 33. LC 49-1639. (Shakespeare Surveys Ser.). (Illus.). 230p. Date not set. 39.50 (ISBN 0-521-23249-X). Cambridge U Pr.

--Shakespeare's Early Tragedies. LC 49-1639. (Shakespeare Survey Ser.: No. 27). (Illus.). 200p. 1974. 32.50 (ISBN 0-521-20468-2). Cambridge U Pr.

Muir, K. & Edwards, P., eds. Aspects of Macbeth: Articles Reprinted from Shakespeare Survey. LC 76-56239. (Reprint Offshoot Ser. from Shakespeare Survey). (Illus.). 1977. 26.50 (ISBN 0-521-21500-5); pap. 8.95x (ISBN 0-521-29176-3). Cambridge U Pr.

--Aspects of Othello. LC 76-57095. (Articles Reprinted from Shakespeare Survey Ser.). (Illus.). 1977. 26.50 (ISBN 0-521-21499-8); pap. 7.95x (ISBN 0-521-29175-5). Cambridge U Pr.

Muir, K. & Wells, S., eds. Aspects of Hamlet. LC 78-18100. (Illus.). 1979. 26.50 (ISBN 0-521-22228-1); pap. 8.95x (ISBN 0-521-29400-2). Cambridge U Pr.

Muir, Kenneth. Comedy of Manners. 1970. pap. text ed. 2.50x (ISBN 0-09-100481-0, Hutchinson U Lib). Humanities.

--Sir Philip Sidney. Dobree, Bonamy, et al, eds. Bd. with Sir Thomas Wyatt. Baldi, Sergio; Edmund Spenser. Freeman, Rosemary. LC 63-63096. (British Writers & Their Work Ser: Vol. 8). 1965. pap. 1.60x (ISBN 0-8032-5658-2, BB 457, Bison). U of Nebr Pr.

Muir, Kenneth, intro. by. The Romantic Period. 140p. 1981. pap. 5.95 (ISBN 0-312-69174-2). St Martin.

Muir, Kenneth, tr. see Calderon de la Barca, Pedro.

Muir, Kenneth, tr. & intro. by see Racine, Jean.

Muir, Matthew M. The Story of Alchemy & the Beginnings of Chemistry. LC 79-8618. Repr. of 1903 ed. 24.50 (ISBN 0-404-18482-0). AMS Pr.

Muir, Percival N. A Bibliography of the First Editions of Books by George Eliot (Mary Ann Evans) (1819-1880) 52p. 1980. Repr. of 1927 ed. lib. bdg. 10.00 (ISBN 0-8492-6833-8). R West.

Muir, Percy. English Children's Books. 1979. 53.00 (ISBN 0-7134-2246-7, Pub. by Batsford England). David & Charles.

Muir, Percy H., ed. see National Book League.

Muir, Ramsey. Medieval & Modern: Including Ancient & Classical, 6th Ed. & Medieval & Modern, 11th Ed. Ancient, Medieval & Modern. 10th ed. Fullard, Harold & Treharne, R. E., eds. (Illus.). 1964. Repr. of 1911 ed. 19.50x (ISBN 0-06-495016-6). B&N.

Muir, Richard. The English Village. (Illus.). 208p. 1980. 19.95 (ISBN 0-500-24106-6). Thames Hudson.

--Modern Political Geography. 262p. 1975. 19.95 (ISBN 0-470-62356-X); pap. 14.95 (ISBN 0-470-99194-1). Halsted Pr.

--Riddles in the British Landscape. (Illus.). 200p. 1981. 17.95 (ISBN 0-500-24108-2). Thames Hudson.

Muir, Richard & Paddison, Ronan, eds. Politics, Geography & Behavior. (Illus.). 196p. 1980. lib. bdg. cancelled (ISBN 0-86531-058-0). Westview.

Muir, Walter, jt. auth. see Boersma, Frederic J.

Muir, William E., jt. ed. see Sinha, R. N.

Muirden, James. The Amateur Astronomer's Handbook. rev. ed. LC 74-5411. (Illus.). 384p. 1974. 12.95 (ISBN 0-690-00505-9, TYC-T). T Y Crowell.

--Astronomy with Binoculars. LC 77-11568. (Illus.). 1979. 9.95 (ISBN 0-690-01723-5, TYC-T). T Y Crowell.

Muirden, James, jt. auth. see Robinson, J. Hedley.

Muirhead, H. Notes on Elementary Particle Physics. 264p. 1972. text ed. 29.00 (ISBN 0-08-016550-8). Pergamon.

Muirhead, J. H., jt. ed. see Radhakrishnan, Sarvepelli.

Muirhead, James F. America the Land of Contrasts: A Briton's View of His American Kin. LC 74-87430. (American Scene Ser). Orig. Title: Bodley Head. 1970. Repr. of 1902 ed. lib. bdg. 32.50 (ISBN 0-306-71576-7). Da Capo.

Muirhead, John H. Coleridge As Philosopher. (Muirhead Library of Philosophy). 1970. Repr. of 1930 ed. text ed. 9.25x o.p. (ISBN 0-04-192025-2). Humanities.

Muirhead, John H., ed. Contemporary British Philosophy Series One & Two, 2 Vols. in 1. (Muirhead Library of Philosophy). 1924. text ed. 41.75x (ISBN 0-04-192011-2). Humanities.

Muirhead, L. A. The Times of Christ. (Handbooks for Bible Classes). 179p. 1907. text ed. 3.50 (ISBN 0-567-08133-8). Attic Pr.

Muir-Wood, Helen M. Malayan Lower Carboniferous Fossils & Their Bearing on the Visean Palaeogeography of Asia. (Illus.). 118p. 1948. 11.50x (ISBN 0-565-00374-7, Pub. by Brit Mus Nat Hist England). Sabbot-Natural Hist Bks.

Mujeeb, M. Akbar. (gr. 6-9). 1969. pap. 1.00 (ISBN 0-88253-350-9). Ind-US Inc.

Mujeeb-Ur Rahman, Mohammed, ed. The Freudian Paradigm: Psychoanalysis & Scientific Thought. LC 73-89486. 1977. 23.95 (ISBN 0-911012-89-3); pap. 11.95 (ISBN 0-88229-461-X). Nelson-Hall.

Mujica, Francisco. History of the Skyscraper. LC 76-57764. (Architecture & Decorative Art Ser.). 1977. Repr. of 1929 ed. lib. bdg. 85.00 (ISBN 0-306-70862-0). Da Capo.

Mujtaba, Ghazala S. The Burning Bud. 1981. 5.95 (ISBN 0-533-04532-0). Vantage.

Mujumdar, A. S. Advances in Transport Processes, Vol. I. 263p. 1980. 27.95x (ISBN 0-470-26957-X). Halsted Pr.

Mujumdar, Arun S., ed. Advances in Drying, Vol. 1. LC 80-10432. (Illus.). 301p. 1980. text ed. 55.00 (ISBN 0-89116-185-6). Hemisphere Pub.

Mukerjee. The Song of the Self Supreme. Date not set. pap. 7.95 (ISBN 0-913922-14-5). Dawn Horse Pr. Postponed.

Mukerjee, Gitanjali, jt. ed. see Smith, Donald A.

Mukerjee, Himangshir B. Education for Fullness. 20.00x (ISBN 0-210-33845-8). Asia.

Mukerjee, Radhakamal. Destiny of Civilization. 1964. 10.00x (ISBN 0-210-31185-1). Asia.

Mukerjee, Radhakamal, ed. Social Sciences & Planning in India. 1974. 7.95x o.p. (ISBN 0-210-22677-3). Asia.

Mukerjee, Radhakamal, tr. The Song of the Self Supreme: Astavakra Gita. LC 74-24308. 1980. 7.95 (ISBN 0-913922-14-5). Dawn Horse Pr.

Mukerji, A. B. The Chamars of Uttar Pradesh: A Study in Social Geography. 155p. 1980. text ed. 11.25x (ISBN 0-391-02124-9). Humanities.

Mukerji, Dhan G. Kari, the Elephant. (Illus.). (gr. 5-7). 1922. PLB 7.95 o.p. (ISBN 0-525-33008-9). Dutton.

Mukerji, Rose, jt. auth. see Lasky, Lila.

Mukherjee, J. N. Forward with Nature: An Integrated Approach to World Problems of Technology, Energy & Agriculture. 188p. 1979. text ed. 18.00x (ISBN 0-8426-1676-4). Verry.

Mukherjee, Kanai L. Introductory Mathematics for the Clinical Laboratory. LC 78-10915. (Illus.). 1979. pap. text ed. 20.00 (ISBN 0-89189-069-6, 45-9-006-00). Am Soc Clinical.

Mukherjee, Kanai Lai. Review of Clinical Laboratory Methods: A Key Word Index System. LC 79-15463. (Illus.). 1979. pap. text ed. 13.95 (ISBN 0-8016-3589-6). Mosby.

Mukherjee, Meenakshi, tr. see Bhattacharya, Lokenath.

Mukherjee, Meenakshi, tr. see Chakrabarti, Nirendranath.

Mukherjee, Prabhat K. Life of Rabindranath Tagore. 1976. lib. bdg. 10.00 (ISBN 0-89253-024-3). Ind-US Inc.

Mukherjee, Ramkrishna. The Rise & Fall of the East India Company: A Sociological Appraisal. LC 73-90082. (Illus.). 464p. 1974. 15.00x o.p. (ISBN 0-85345-315-2, CL-3152); pap. 6.50 (ISBN 0-85345-407-8). Monthly Rev.

Mukherjee, S. N., ed. South Asian Affairs Two, the Movement for National Freedom in India. (St. Anthony's Papers Ser). 1966. 5.00x o.p. (ISBN 0-19-827502-1). Oxford U Pr.

Mukherjee, Sujit, tr. see Chakrabarti, Nirendranath.

Mukherji, A. K. Analytical Chemistry of Zirconium & Hafnium. LC 71-109236. 1970. 49.00 (ISBN 0-08-006886-3). Pergamon.

Mukherji, Purna C. Report on a Tour of Exploration of the Antiquities of Kapilavastu, Tarai of Nepal During February & March 1899. (Illus.). 1969. 13.00x o.p. (ISBN 0-8426-0004-3). Verry.

Mukherji, S. M. Pericyclic Reactions: A Mechanistic Study. 1980. 16.00x (ISBN 0-8364-0637-0, Pub. by Macmillan India). South Asia Bks.

Mukhopadhyay, Arun. Agricultural Extension: A Field Study. 1971. 10.00 o.p. (ISBN 0-88386-197-6). South Asia Bks.

Mukhyopadhyaya, Pramatha N. see Woodroffe, John.

Mukoh, Takao, tr. see Tsunetomo, Yamamoto.

Muktananda. I Love You. (Illus.). 22p. (Orig.). 1975. pap. text ed. 1.25 (ISBN 0-914602-58-6). SYDA Found.

Muktananda, Swami. A Book for the Mind. (Illus., Orig.). 1976. pap. 1.25 (ISBN 0-685-99448-1). SYDA Found.

--God Is with You. (Illus., Orig.). 1978. pap. 1.25 (ISBN 0-914602-57-8). SYDA Found.

--I Am That: The Science of Hamsa from Vijnana Bhairava, Vol. 24. (Illus., Orig.). 1978. pap. 3.50 (ISBN 0-914602-27-6). SYDA Found.

--I Welcome You All with Love. (Illus., Orig.). 1978. pap. 1.25 (ISBN 0-914602-59-4). SYDA Found.

--Satsang with Baba, 2 vols. LC 76-1384. Vol. 1 1974. pap. 5.95 (ISBN 0-914602-30-6); Vol. 2 1976. pap. 5.95 (ISBN 0-914602-31-4). SYDA Found.

--Satsang with Baba, Vol. 4. (Illus.). 319p. 1978. pap. text ed. 5.95 (ISBN 0-914602-32-2). SYDA Found.

--Siddha Meditation. pap. 2.95 (ISBN 0-914602-22-5). SYDA Found.

--Understanding Siddha Yoga, Vol. 1. (Orig.). 1979. pap. text ed. 7.95 (ISBN 0-686-53153-1). SYDA Found.

Mulac, Jim, jt. ed. see Sklar, Morty.

Mulaik, Stanley. The Foundations of Factor Analysis. (McGraw-Hill Paperbacks). (Illus.). 480p. 1972. text ed. 30.00 o.p. (ISBN 0-07-043980-X, C). McGraw.

Mular, A. L. & Bhappu, R. B., eds. Mineral Processing Plant Design. 2nd ed. LC 79-57345. (Illus.). 958p. 1980. text ed. 27.00x (ISBN 0-89520-269-7). Soc Mining Eng.

Mulay, L. N., jt. auth. see Boudreaux, E. A.

Mulbauer, jt. auth. see Keller.

Mulcahy, E. W. The Pickling of Steels. LC 74-154842. (Illus.). 95p. 1973. 13.50x (ISBN 0-901994-20-0). Intl Pubns Serv.

Mulcahy, Kevin, jt. auth. see Swaim, C. Richard.

Mulcahy, Kevin V. & Katz, Richard S. America Votes: What You Should Know About Elections Today. LC 76-15592. 1976. pap. text ed. 4.95 (ISBN 0-13-023788-4, Spec). P-H.

Mulcahy, Michael. Conversational BASIC: A Dialogue Approach to Programming. LC 80-16705. 1980. pap. 11.95 (ISBN 0-8436-1600-8). CBI Pub.

Mulcahy, Risteard. Beat Heart Disease! LC 78-24490. (Positive Health Guide Ser.). (Illus.). 1979. 8.95 (ISBN 0-668-04678-3, 4678-3); pap. 4.95 (ISBN 0-668-04685-6, 4685-6). Arco.

Mulcoon, Paul. Why Brownlee Left. LC 80-50846. 48p. 1981. pap. 4.95 (ISBN 0-916390-13-6). Wake Forest.

Mulder, J. W. Sets & Relations in Phonology: An Axiomatic Approach to the Description of Speech. 1968. 13.75x o.p. (ISBN 0-19-811932-1). Oxford U Pr.

Mulder, John M., jt. auth. see Wilson, John F.

Mulder, John R. Temple of the Mind: Education & Literary Taste in Seventeenth-Century England. LC 79-79059. 1969. 23.50x (ISBN 0-672-53602-1). Irvington.

Mulder, Karen, jt. auth. see Jurries, Ginger.

Mulder, Robert L., jt. auth. see Luper, Harold L.

Mulder, Ronald A. The Insurgent Progressives in the United States Senate & the New Deal, 1933-1939. Freidel, Frank, ed. LC 78-62389. (Modern American History Ser.: Vol. 14). 1979. lib. bdg. 30.00 (ISBN 0-8240-3637-9). Garland Pub.

Mulder, William & Mortensen, A. Russell, eds. Among the Mormons: Historic Accounts by Contemporary Observers. LC 58-5825. xiv, 496p. 1973. 8.50 (ISBN 0-8032-5778-3, BB 568, Bison). U of Nebr Pr.

Muldoon, James, ed. The Expansion of Europe: The First Phase. LC 77-81455. (Middle Ages Ser). 1977. 16.00x (ISBN 0-8122-7729-5); pap. 7.95x (ISBN 0-8122-1091-3). U of Pa Pr.

Muldoon, Joseph A. & Berdie, Mitchell. Effective Employee Assistance: A Comprehensive Guide for the Employer. 1980. 49.95 (ISBN 0-89638-048-3). CompCare.

Muldoon, Maureen, ed. Abortion: An Annotated Indexed Bibliography. (Studies in Women & Religion: Vol. 3). 1980. 39.95x (ISBN 0-88946-972-5). E Mellen.

Muldoon, Sylvan. The Case for Astral Projection. 1936. 3.00 (ISBN 0-933646-05-4). Aries Pr.

Mule, Marty & Remy, Bob. Louisiana Athletes: The Top Twenty. (Illus.). (gr. 6 up). 1981. 8.95 (ISBN 0-88289-282-7). Pelican.

Mules, Helen B., jt. auth. see Denison, Cara D.

Mulford, A. C. Boundaries & Landmarks. 1977. pap. 8.50 (ISBN 0-686-18920-5, 611). CARBEN Survey.

Mulford, David C. Northern Rhodesia General Election, 1962. 1964. 5.00x o.p. (ISBN 0-19-690287-8); pap. 2.65x o.p. (ISBN 0-19-519606-6). Oxford U Pr.

Mulgrave, Dorothy. Speech: A Handbook of Voice Training, Diction & Public Speaking. (Orig.). 1954. pap. 3.95 (ISBN 0-06-460089-0, CO 89, COS). Har-Row.
Mulhall, M. G. Fifty Years of National Progress, 1837-1887. 126p. 1971. Repr. of 1887 ed. 17.00x (ISBN 0-7165-1584-9, Pub. by Irish Academic Pr Ireland). Biblio Dist.
Mulhall, Michael G. Dictionary of Statistics. LC 68-18013. 1969. Repr. of 1899 ed. 44.00 (ISBN 0-8103-3887-4). Gale.
--The Progress of the World: In Arts, Agriculture, Century. (The Development of Industrial Society Ser.). 569p. 1980. Repr. 50.00x (ISBN 0-7165-1584-9, Pub. by Irish Academic Pr). Biblio Dist.
Mulhauser, Ruth E. Maurice Sceve. LC 76-28722. (World Authors Ser: France: No. 424). 1977. lib. bdg. 12.50 (ISBN 0-8057-6264-7). Twayne.
Mulhern, Chieko. Koda Rohan. (World Authors Ser.: No. 432). 1977. lib. bdg. 12.50 (ISBN 0-8057-6272-8). Twayne.
Mulholland, John. Book of Magic. LC 63-9766. (Encore Edition). 1963. pap. 1.95 (ISBN 0-684-16914-2, SL379, ScribT). Scribner.
Mulholland, Mary E., ed. see American Foundation for the Blind.
Mulier, Eco O. & Haitsma, G. The Myth of Venice & Dutch Republican Thought in the Seventeenth Century. 250p. 1980. pap. text ed. 20.00x (ISBN 90-232-1781-0). Humanities.
Mulisch, Harry. Two Women. Early, Els, tr. 1981. 11.95 (ISBN 0-7145-3810-8); pap. 5.95 (ISBN 0-7145-3839-6). Riverrun NY.
--What Poetry Is. Barkan, Stanley H., ed. White, Claire Nicolas, tr. (Cross-Cultural Review Chapbook 9). 40p. (Dutch & Eng.). 1980. pap. 3.50 (ISBN 0-89304-808-9). Cross Cult.
Mulkerin, Larry E. Practical Points in Radiation Oncology. 1979. spiral bdg. 17.00 (ISBN 0-87488-726-7). Med Exam.
Mulkerne, Donald, J.D. & Kahn, Gilbert. The Term Paper Step by Step. LC 76-40631. 5.95 (ISBN 0-385-12775-8, Anchor Pr); pap. 2.95 (ISBN 0-385-12380-9, Anch). Doubleday.
Mullan, Fitzhugh. White Coat, Clenched Fist: The Political Education of an American Physician. 1976. 12.95 (ISBN 0-02-587910-3). Macmillan.
Mullany, Peter. Monarch Notes on Marlowe's Dr. Faustus & Other Writings. (Orig.). pap. 1.95 (ISBN 0-671-00717-3). Monarch Pr.
Mullany, Peter F. Religion & the Artifice of Jacobean & Caroline Drama. (Salzburg Studies in English Literature: Jacobean Drama Studies: No. 41). 1977. pap. text ed. 25.00x (ISBN 0-391-01486-2). Humanities.
Mullen, Dore. All We Know of Heaven. (Orig.). 1980. pap. 2.50 (ISBN 0-440-10178-6). Dell.
Mullen, E. Theodore, Jr. The Assembly of the Gods: The Divine Council in Canaanite & Hebrew Literature. LC 80-10128. (Harvard Semitic Museum Monographs: No. 24). 10.50x (ISBN 0-89130-380-4, 04 00 24). Scholars Pr CA.
Mullen, Edward J. Carlos Pellicer. (World Authors Ser.: Noo. 451). 1977. 12.50 (ISBN 0-8057-6288-4). Twayne.
--Poems by a Slave in the Island of Cuba. 1981. 25.00 (ISBN 0-208-01900-6, Archon). Shoe String.
Mullen, J., jt. auth. see Harrison, William.
Mullen, James C., jt. auth. see Drees, Jack.
Mullen, John D. Kierkegaard's Philosophy: Self-Deception & Cowardice in the Present Age. (Orig.). 1981. pap. 2.95 (ISBN 0-451-61945-5, ME1945, Ment). NAL.
Mullen, Kenneth, jt. auth. see Malik, Henrick J.
Mullen, Tom. Mountaintops & Molehills. 1981. 6.95 (ISBN 0-8499-0193-6). Word Bks.
Muller, jt. auth. see Cowell.
Muller, tr. see Mueller, F. Max.
Muller, A., jt. ed. see Rouiller, C.
Muller, Alexander V., tr. see Solovier, S. M.
Muller, Alois. Catechetics for the Future. (Concilium Ser.: Religion in the Seventies: Vol. 53). 1970. pap. 4.95 (ISBN 0-8164-2509-4). Crossroad NY.
--Democratization of the Church. LC 73-147026. (Concilium Ser.: Religion in the Seventies: Vol. 63). 1971. pap. 4.95 (ISBN 0-8164-2519-1). Crossroad NY.
--Experience of Dying. (Concilium Ser.: Religion in the Seventies: Vol. 94). pap. 4.95 (ISBN 0-8164-2578-7). Crossroad NY.
--Ongoing Reform of the Church. (Concilium Ser.: Religion in the Seventies: Vol. 73). 1972. pap. 4.95 (ISBN 0-8164-2529-9). Crossroad NY.
Muller, Alois, ed. see Greinacher, Norbert.
Muller, Alois, jt. ed. see Greinacher, Norbert.
Muller, Antal. Quantum Mechanics: A Physical World Picture. LC 73-18062. 1974. text ed. 28.00 (ISBN 0-08-017936-3). Pergamon.
Muller, E. Reading Architectural Working Drawings. 2nd ed. 1981. 19.95 (ISBN 0-13-753939-8). P-H.
Muller, Edward J. Reading Architectural Working Drawings. (Illus.). 1971. pap. text ed. 19.95 (ISBN 0-13-753913-4). P-H.
Muller, Eugenio E., et al. Neurotransmitters & Anterior Pituitary. 1978. 50.00 (ISBN 0-12-510550-9). Acad Pr.
Muller, F. M., ed. see Scherer, W., et al.
Muller, F. Max. Upanishads, 2 Vols. 1963. Repr. of 1890 ed. text ed. 5.00 ea. Vol. 1 (ISBN 0-486-20992-X) (ISBN 0-486-20993-8). Dover.
Muller, F. Max see Kant, Immanuel.
Muller, F. Max, ed. see Cowell & Muller.
Muller, Fred. America's Coming Nightmare Inflation, Economic Collapse & Crime Revolution. 120p. 1980. 10.00 (ISBN 0-686-68648-9). State Ptg.
Muller, G., jt. auth. see Fuchtbauer, Hans.
Muller, George. Autobiography of George Muller. Wayland, H. Lincoln, ed. (Giant Summit Books Ser.). 490p. 1981. pap. 8.95 (ISBN 0-8010-6105-9). Baker Bk.
Muller, H. G. An Introduction to Food Rheology. LC 72-81532. 260p. 1973. 19.50x (ISBN 0-8448-0013-9). Crane-Russak Co.
Muller, H. G. & Tobin, G. Nutrition & Food Processing. 240p. 1980. 35.00x (ISBN 0-85664-540-0, Pub. by Croom Helm England). State Mutual Bk.
--Nutrition & Food Processing. american ed. 1980. pap. 30.00 (ISBN 0-87055-363-1). AVI.
Muller, Heinrich. Panzer Grenadiers. 288p. (Orig.). 1980. pap. 2.25 (ISBN 0-89083-697-3). Zebra.
Muller, Herbert J. Uses of the Past: Profiles of Former Societies. 1952. 17.95 (ISBN 0-19-500032-3). Oxford U Pr.
Muller, J. P. My System. 5.00x o.p. (ISBN 0-392-07048-0, SpS). Soccer.
Muller, Jacobus J. Epistles of Paul to the Philippians & Philemon. (New International Commentary on the New Testament). 1955. 10.95 (ISBN 0-8028-2188-X). Eerdmans.
Muller, James E., ed. see Vikhert, Anatolii M. & Zhdanov, Valentin S.
Muller, Joseph. The Star Spangled Banner: Words & Music Issued Between 1814-1864. LC 79-169653. (Music Ser). (Illus.). 1973. Repr. of 1935 ed. lib. bdg. 25.00 (ISBN 0-306-70263-0). Da Capo.
Muller, Joseph E. & Elgar, Frank. Modern Painters. (Illus.). 172p. 1980. pap. 7.95 (ISBN 0-8120-2285-8). Barron.
Muller, Katherine K., et al. Trees of Santa Barbara. (Illus.). 1974. 10.00 (ISBN 0-916436-00-4). Santa Barb Botanic.
Muller, L., et al. The Coinage of Ancient Africa: (Numismatique De L'Ancienne Afrique) (Illus.). 1977. 80.00 (ISBN 0-916710-35-1). Obol Intl.
Muller, Leone, tr. see Schmidt, K. O.
Muller, Max, ed. Sacred Books of the East, 50 vols. 1977-1980. Repr. of 1975 ed. 11.50 ea. Orient Bk Dist.
Muller, P. Economy & Ecological Equilibrium. 100p. 1975. pap. text ed. 24.00 (ISBN 0-08-019681-0). Pergamon.
Muller, Peter O. Contemporary Suburban America. (Illus.). 240p. 1981. pap. 9.95 (ISBN 0-13-170647-0). P-H.
--The Outer City: Geographical Consequences of the Urbanization of the Suburbs. Natoli, Salvatore J., ed. LC 76-29264. (Resource Papers for College Geography Ser.). (Illus.). 1976. pap. text ed. 4.00 (ISBN 0-89291-114-X). Assn Am Geographers.
Muller, Peter O., jt. auth. see Wheeler, James O.
Muller, R., jt. auth. see Gray, W. A.
Muller, Ralph. Worms & Disease: A Manual of Medical Helminthology. (Illus.). 1975. 36.95x (ISBN 0-433-17580-X). Intl Ideas.
Muller, Ralph, jt. ed. see Taylor, Angela E.
Muller, Robert. Most of All They Taught Me Happiness. LC 78-52110. 1978. 8.95 (ISBN 0-385-14310-9). Doubleday.
Muller, Robert, jt. auth. see Hogg, James.
Muller, Robert see Hogg, James & Muller, Robert.
Muller, Ronald E. Revitalizing America. 1980. 13.95 (ISBN 0-671-24889-8). S&S.
Muller, Thomas. Economic Impacts of Land Development: Employment, Housing & Property Values. (Land Development Impact Ser.). 148p. 1976. pap. 3.95 (ISBN 0-87766-173-1, 15800). Urban Inst.
--Growing & Declining Urban Areas: A Fiscal Comparison. (An Institute Paper). 121p. 1975. pap. 3.50 (ISBN 0-87766-154-5, 13400). Urban Inst.
Muller, Thomas & Dawson, Grace. The Economic Effects of Annexation: A Second Case Study in Richmond, Virginia. (An Institute Paper). 91p. 1976. pap. 2.50 (ISBN 0-87766-165-0, 14400). Urban Inst.
--The Fiscal Impact of Residential & Commercial Development: A Case Study. 140p. 1972. pap. 3.00 o.p. (ISBN 0-87766-074-3, 22000). Urban Inst.
--The Impact of Annexation on City Finances: A Case Study in Richmond, Virginia. 1973. pap. 1.75 o.p. (ISBN 0-685-40588-5, 41000). Urban Inst.
Muller, Thomas, et al. The Impact of Beltways on Central Business Districts: A Case Study of Richmond. 101p. 1978. pap. 5.50 (ISBN 0-87766-216-9, 21500). Urban Inst.
Muller, Vladimir K. English-Russian Dictionary. 6th ed. 17.50 (ISBN 0-685-20186-4, 067-4). Saphrograph.
Muller, Wilhelm. Customs Dictionary: German-English-French-Italian. LC 72-311634. 277p. 1971. 17.50x (ISBN 3-8029-8565-6). Intl Pubns Serv.
Muller, William D. The Kept Men? The First Century of Trade Union Representation in the British House of Commons, 1874-1975. (Illus.). 1977. text ed. 39.75x (ISBN 0-85527-184-1). Humanities.
Muller-Brockmann, Josef. Graphic Artist & His Design Problems. (Visual Communication Bks.). 1961. 29.00 o.p. (ISBN 0-8038-2618-4). Hastings.
--Grid Systems in Graphic Design: A Visual Communications Manual. (Visual Communications Bks.). (Illus.). 176p. (Eng. & Ger.). 1981. 45.00 (ISBN 0-8038-2711-3). Hastings.
--A History of Visual Communication. 2nd ed. (Illus.). 334p. 1981. pap. 29.50 (ISBN 0-8038-3059-9, Visual Communication). Hastings.
Muller-Pfeiffer, Erich. Spectralk Theory of Ordinary Differential Equations. LC 80-42097. (Mathematics & Its Application Ser.). 260p. 1981. 51.95 (ISBN 0-470-27103-5). Halsted Pr.
Muller-Reuter, Theodor. Lexikon der Deutschen Konzertliteratur, 2 Vols. LC 70-171079. (Music Ser). 1972. Repr. of 1921 ed. lib. bdg. 95.00 (ISBN 0-306-70274-6). Da Capo.
Muller-Schwarz. Introduction to Electrical Engineering. 1980. write for info. (ISBN 0-85501-259-5). Heyden.
Muller-Schwarze, D. & Silverstein, R. M., eds. Chemical Signals: Vertebrates & Aquatic Invertebrates. 450p. 1980. 39.50 (ISBN 0-306-40339-0, Plenum Pr). Plenum Pub.
Muller-Vollmer, Kurt. Hermeneutics Reader. 1981. 20.00 (ISBN 0-916354-88-1); pap. 8.95 (ISBN 0-916354-89-X). Urizen Bks.
Mullet, Rosa M. God's Marvelous Work, Bk. 1. 1975. Repr. of 1980 ed. write to pub. for info. (ISBN 0-686-11149-4); tchrs. ed avail. (ISBN 0-686-11150-8). Rod & Staff.
--God's Marvelous Work, Bk. 2. 1979. write for info. (ISBN 0-686-25256-X); tchr's ed. avail. (ISBN 0-686-25257-8). Rod & Staff.
Mullett, G. M. Spider Woman Stories. LC 78-11556. 1979. 11.95 o.s.i. (ISBN 0-8165-0669-8); pap. 4.95 (ISBN 0-8165-0621-3). U of Ariz Pr.
Mulligan. Integrating Music with Other Studies. write for info. (ISBN 0-87628-218-4). Ctr Appl Res.
Mulligan, Elizabeth. Hoodlum's Priest. 174p. 1979. 9.95 (ISBN 0-86629-000-1). Sunrise MO.
Mulligan, Fergus, compiled By. A Pocket Book of Daily Prayer. 128p. 1980. pap. 3.50 (ISBN 0-03-057848-5). Winston Pr.
Mulligan, Raymond A., jt. auth. see Fredericksen, Hazel.
Mulliken, Robert S., ed. Ab Initio Calculations on Diatomic Molecules. Ermler, W. C. 1977. 28.50 (ISBN 0-12-510750-1). Acad Pr.
Mullin, Arthur, ed. The Questing Mind: Readings for Background & Comprehension. LC 68-22410. (Orig.). 1968. pap. 7.50 (ISBN 0-672-63095-8). Odyssey Pr.
Mullin, Donald C. The Development of the Playhouse: A Survey of Theatre Architecture from the Renaissance to the Present. LC 77-84532. (Illus.). 1970. 25.00x (ISBN 0-520-01391-3). U of Cal Pr.
Mullin, Gerald W. Flight & Rebellion: Slave Resistence in Eighteenth Century Virginia. 224p. 1972. 15.95 (ISBN 0-19-501514-2). Oxford U Pr.
Mullin, Michael, ed. American Negro Slavery: A Documentary History. (Documentary History of the U.S. Ser.). (Orig.). 1975. pap. 5.95x o.p. (ISBN 0-06-131806-X, TB1806, Torch). Har-Row.
Mullin, Ray C. Electrical Wiring-Residential. LC 77-90331. 1978. pap. 10.56 (ISBN 0-8273-1410-8); instructor's guide 1.60 (ISBN 0-8273-1411-6). Delmar.
--Electrical Wiring Residential: Based on 1981 National Electrial Code. 7th ed. 288p. 1981. 14.95. Van Nos Reinhold.
Mullin, Ray C. & Smith, Robert L. Electrical Wiring - Commercial. 4th rev. ed. LC 80-65467. (Electrical Trades Ser.). (Illus.). 208p. 1981. pap. text ed. 10.00 (ISBN 0-8273-1953-3); price not set instr's. guide (ISBN 0-8273-1954-1). Delmar.
--Electrical Wiring-Commercial. LC 77-92084. 1978. pap. 10.56 (ISBN 0-8273-1412-4); instructor's guide 1.60 (ISBN 0-8273-1413-2). Delmar.
Mullin, Richard. Christmas Party Games. (Standard Ideas Ser.). 1978. pap. 1.75 (ISBN 0-87239-216-3, 2817). Standard Pub.
--Don't Tell Me. 1976. pap. 1.50 (ISBN 0-8024-1781-7). Moody.
Mullin, Timothy J. Training the Gunfighter. (Illus.). 1981. 24.95 (ISBN 0-87364-185-X). Paladin Ent.
Mullin, William F. ABC's of Capacitors. 3rd ed. LC 77-90500. 1978. pap. 5.60 (ISBN 0-672-21498-9). Sams.
Mullins, B. P., ed. see Shtern, V. Y.
Mullins, Carolyn J. A Guide to Writing & Publishing in the Social & Behavioral Sciences. LC 77-1153. 1977. pap. 13.50 (ISBN 0-471-02708-1, Pub. by Wiley-Interscience). Wiley.
Mullins, David W., Jr., jt. auth. see Homonoff, Richard B.
Mullins, E. L. Guide to the Historical & Archaeological Publications of Societies in England & Wales, 1901-1933. 1968. text ed. 47.50x (ISBN 0-485-11094-6, Athlone Pr). Humanities.
Mullins, Edgar Y. Christian Religion in Its Doctrinal Expression. 7.95 o.p. (ISBN 0-8170-0042-9). Judson.
--La Religion Cristiana En Su Expresion Doctrinal. Hale, Sara A., tr. Orig. Title: The Christian Religion in Its Doctrinal Expression. 522p. 1980. pap. 8.95 (ISBN 0-311-09042-7). Casa Bautista.
Mullins, Hugh A. & Buglass, Leslie J. Marine Insurance Digest. 2nd ed. LC 59-15426. 1959. 7.00x (ISBN 0-87033-046-2). Cornell Maritime.
Mullins, L. J. Ion Transport in Heart. 125p. 1981. 15.00 (ISBN 0-89004-645-X). Raven.
Mullins, L. J., et al, eds. Annual Review of Biophysics & Bioengineering, Vol. 10. LC 79-188446. (Illus.). 1981. text ed. 20.00 (ISBN 0-8243-1810-2). Annual Reviews.
Mullins, Nicholas. Science: Some Sociological Perspectives. LC 72-12826. (Studies in Sociology Ser.). 42p. 1973. pap. text ed. 2.50 (ISBN 0-672-61205-4). Bobbs.
Mullins, Phil, et al, eds. Political Reform in California: Evaluation & Perspective. LC 77-26850. (Research Report 78-3). 1978. pap. 6.50x (ISBN 0-87772-252-8). Inst Gov Stud Berk.
Mullins, R. N., jt. auth. see Hutchinson, W. H.
Mullish, Henry. Modern Programming: Fortran 4. 1968. pap. 12.95x o.p. (ISBN 0-471-00388-3). Wiley.
Mullish, Henry & Kochan, Stephen. Programmable Pocket Calculators. 264p. 1980. pap. 9.95 (ISBN 0-8104-5175-1). Hayden.
Mulliss, Christine. Goodness! Eating Healthily. 64p. 1977. pap. 4.00x (ISBN 0-8464-1014-1). Beekman Pubs.
Mulloy, Teresa A., ed. Guide to Graduate Departments of Geography in the United States & Canada, 1980-1981. 13th ed. LC 68-59269. 1980. pap. 6.00 (ISBN 0-89291-152-2). Assn Am Geographers.
Mulock, Dinah M. The Adventures of a Brownie, Repr. Of 1872 Ed. Bd. with The Little Lame Prince. Repr. of 1875 ed. LC 75-32175. (Classics of Children's Literature, 1621-1932: Vol. 38). (Illus.). 1977. PLB 38.00 (ISBN 0-8240-2287-4). Garland Pub.
Mulryne, J. R., ed. see Webster, John.
Mulvaney, J. E. & Mann, C. W. Practical Business Models. LC 75-33219. 1976. 13.95 o.p. (ISBN 0-470-62386-1). Halsted Pr.
Mulvaney, Robert J. & Zeltner, Philip M., eds. Pragmatism: Its Sources & Prospects. LC 80-26475. 1981. text ed. 9.95 (ISBN 0-87249-404-7). U of SC Pr.
Mulvany, Mollie. All About Obedience Training for Dogs. 1973. 9.95 (ISBN 0-7207-0616-5, Pub. by Michael Joseph). Merrimack Bk Serv.
Mulvey, C., jt. auth. see Trevithick, J. A.
Mulvey, John M., jt. auth. see Glover, Fred.
Mulvey, T. & Webster, R. K., eds. Modern Physical Techniques in Materials Technology. (Harwell Ser.). (Illus.). 336p. 1974. text ed. 45.00x (ISBN 0-19-851708-4). Oxford U Pr.
Mulvihill, Edward R., ed. see Laforet, Carmen.
Mulvihill, John J. & Riccardi, Vincent M., eds. Neurofibromatosis (von Recklinghausen's Disease) (Advances in Neurology Ser.: Vol. 29). 225p. 1981. text ed. 22.50 (ISBN 0-686-64310-0). Raven.
Mulvihill, John J., et al, eds. Genetics of Human Cancer. LC 75-44924. (Progress in Cancer Research & Therapy: Vol. 3). 1977. 28.00 (ISBN 0-89004-110-5). Raven.
Mulvihill, Mary L. Human Diseases: A Systemic Approach. LC 79-23053. (Illus.). 399p. 1980. pap. text ed. 13.95 (ISBN 0-87619-623-7). R J Brady.

Mulville, Frank. The Death of Schooner Integrity. Campbell, Dennis, ed. (Illus.). 169p. Date not set. 12.95 (ISBN 0-89182-032-9); pap. 7.95 (ISBN 0-89182-033-7). Charles River Bks.

Mulvoy, Mark. Sports Illustrated Golf. LC 80-8692. (Illus.). 192p. 1981. 8.95 (ISBN 0-06-014871-3, HarpT); pap. 5.95 (ISBN 0-06-090868-8, CN868). Har-Row.

Muma, John R. Language Handbook: Concepts, Assessment, Intervention. (Illus.). 1978. 19.95 (ISBN 0-13-522755-0). P-H.

Mumey, Glen A. Canadian Business Finance. 1977. 17.50 (ISBN 0-256-01787-5). Irwin.

Mumey, Nolie. Professor Oscar J. Goldrick & His Denver. LC 59-11065. 1959. pap. 1.25 (ISBN 0-8040-0080-8). Swallow.

Mumford, Alan. Manager & Training. (Times Management Library). 1971. 12.00x o.p. (ISBN 0-8464-0594-6, 0-273-3155-2). Beekman Pubs.

Mumford, Amy R. It Only Hurts Between Paydays. 2nd ed. 160p. 1981. pap. 2.25 (ISBN 0-89636-067-9). Accent Bks.

Mumford, Bob. Living Happily Ever After. 64p. 1973. 2.95 o.p. (ISBN 0-8007-0596-3). Revell.

Mumford, Clive. Portrait of the Isles of Scilly. LC 67-98842. (Portrait Bks.). (Illus.). 1967. 10.50x (ISBN 0-7091-1718-3). Intl Pubns Serv.

Mumford, D. Algerbraic Geometry I: Complex Projective Varieties, I. (Grundlehren der Mathematischen Wissenschaften: Vol. 221). (Illus.). 200p. 1981. 18.90 (ISBN 0-387-07603-4). Springer-Verlag.

--Geometric Invariant Theory. (Ergebnisse der Mathematik und Ihrer Grenzgebiete: Vol. 34). (Illus.). 1965. 22.50 o.p. (ISBN 0-387-03284-3). Springer-Verlag.

Mumford, David. Curves & Their Jacobians. LC 75-14899. (The Ziwet Lectures Ser: 1974). 1975. pap. 6.95x (ISBN 0-472-66000-4). U of Mich Pr.

Mumford, Enid & Henshall, Don. Participative Approach to Computer Systems Design: A Case Study of the Introduction of a New Computer System. LC 78-23831. 1978. 21.95 (ISBN 0-470-26581-7). Halsted Pr.

Mumford, Enid & Weir, Mary. Computer Systems in Work Design: The Ethnics Method: Effective Technical & Human Implementation of Computer Systems. LC 78-32068. 1979. 34.95 (ISBN 0-470-26656-2). Halsted Pr.

Mumford, James G. How to Cut Your Children's Medical Costs. LC 79-67043. 54p. 1980. 5.95 (ISBN 0-533-04430-8). Vantage.

Mumford, Janice H., jt. auth. see Granowsky, Alvin.

Mumford, Lewis. Art & Technics. LC 52-1930. (Bampton Lecture Ser. in American: No. 4). 1952. 12.50x (ISBN 0-231-01903-3); pap. 2.45 (ISBN 0-231-08509-5, 9). Columbia U Pr.

--The Culture of Cities. LC 80-23130. (Illus.). xviii, 586p. 1981. Repr. of 1970 ed. lib. bdg. 45.00x (ISBN 0-313-22746-2, MUCC). Greenwood.

--The Highway & the City. LC 80-22641. viii, 246p. 1981. Repr. of 1953 ed. lib. bdg. 25.00x (ISBN 0-313-22747-0, MUHC). Greenwood.

--Myth of the Machine, 2 vols. Incl. Vol. 1. Technics & Human Development. LC 67-16088. 1971. Repr. of 1967 ed. pap. 5.95 (ISBN 0-15-662341-2, HB208); Vol. 2. Pentagon of Power. LC 73-13626. 1974. Repr. of 1970 ed. pap. 5.95 (ISBN 0-15-671610-0, HB274). (Illus., Harv). HarBraceJ.

--Roots of Contemporary American Architecture. LC 75-171490. 1972. pap. text ed. 6.00 (ISBN 0-486-22072-9). Dover.

--South in Architecture. LC 67-27462. (Architecture & Decorative Art Ser). 1967. Repr. of 1941 ed. lib. bdg. 19.50 (ISBN 0-306-70972-4). Da Capo.

--The Story of Utopias. 8.25 (ISBN 0-8446-1319-3). Peter Smith.

--Technics & Civilization. LC 63-19641. (Illus.). 1963. pap. 6.95 (ISBN 0-15-688254-X, H030, Hbgr). HarBraceJ.

--Technics & Human Development: The Myth of the Machine, Vol. 1. LC 67-16088. (Illus.). 342p. 12.00 o.p. (ISBN 0-15-163975-2). HarBraceJ.

--Works & Days. LC 78-14077. 545p. 1979. 13.95 (ISBN 0-15-164087-4). HarBraceJ.

Mummah, Hazel & Smith, Marsella. The Geriatric Assistant. (Illus.). 320p. 1980. pap. text ed. 11.95 (ISBN 0-07-044015-8, HP). McGraw.

Mumpton, F. A., jt. ed. see Sand, L. B.

MUNA. The Arab Executive. LC 80-13711. 1980. write for info. (ISBN 0-312-04697-9). St Martin.

Munakata, Toshinori. Matrices & Linear Programming with Business Applications. 1979. text ed. 18.95x (ISBN 0-8162-6166-0); solutions manual 5.95x (ISBN 0-8162-6167-9). Holden-Day.

Munat, Charles, jt. auth. see Munat, Florence.

Munat, Florence & Munat, Charles. Would You Believe? McCarthy, Patricia, ed. (Pal Paperbacks Kit B Ser.). (Illus., Orig.). (gr. 7-12). 1974. pap. text ed. 1.25 (ISBN 0-8374-3505-6). Xerox Ed Pubns.

Munby, D. L. Inland Transport Statistics Great Britain, 1900-1970. Watson, A. H., ed. LC 78-40311. (Railways, Public Road Passenger Transport, London's Transport: Vol. I). (Illus.). 1978. 65.00x (ISBN 0-19-828409-8). Oxford U Pr.

Munby, Denys & Watson, A. H. Road Passenger Transport & Road Goods Transport. Manunder, W. F., ed. LC 77-30558. 1978. text ed. 37.00 (ISBN 0-08-022449-0). Pergamon.

Muncey, R. W. Heat Transfer Calculations for Buildings. (Illus.). 1979. 23.20x (ISBN 0-85334-852-9, Pub. by Applied Science). Burgess-Intl Ideas.

Munch. Life Insurance in Estate Planning. 1981. text ed. price not set (ISBN 0-316-58930-6). Little.

Munch, Peter A. & Olsen, Magnus, eds. Norse Mythology: Legends of Gods & Heroes. rev. ed. Hustuedt, Sigurd B., tr. LC 68-31092. (Illus.). 1968. Repr. of 1926 ed. 18.00 (ISBN 0-8103-3454-2). Gale.

Munck, Eckehard. Biology of the Future. LC 73-15300. (International Library). (Illus.). 128p. (gr. 7 up). 1974. PLB 6.90 o.p. (ISBN 0-531-02118-1). Watts.

Munck, Johannes. Paul & the Salvation of Mankind. LC 60-5412. 1977. pap. 6.95 (ISBN 0-8042-0373-3). John Knox.

Muncy, Lysbeth W. The Junker in the Prussian Administration Under William Second, 1888-1914. LC 70-80574. 1970. Repr. of 1944 ed. 15.75 (ISBN 0-86527-112-7). Fertig.

Mund, Vernon A., jt. auth. see Wolf, Ronald H.

Munda, Ramdayal, tr. see Bhattacarya, Jagadishvhra.

Munday, A., tr. from Fr. The Defence of Contraries. LC 72-188. (English Experience Ser.: No. 175). 1969. Repr. of 1593 ed. 13.00 (ISBN 90-221-0175-4). Walter J Johnson.

Munday, Anthony. The English Roman Life. Ayres, Phillip J., ed. (Studies in Tudor & Stewart Literature Ser.). (Illus.). 142p. 1980. 22.00 (ISBN 0-19-812635-2). Oxford U Pr.

Munday, C. W., ed. see IFAC Symposium, 8th, Oxford, England, 2-6 July 1979.

Munday, J. G., jt. auth. see Dhir, R. K.

Mundel, Marvin E. Motion & Time Study. 5th ed. (P-H Industrial Engineering Ser.). (Illus.). 1978. ref. 24.95 (ISBN 0-13-602987-6). P-H.

Mundell, Robert A. Man & Economics. LC 68-13522. (Illus.). 1968. pap. 2.95 o.p. (ISBN 0-07-044038-7, SP). McGraw.

Mundell, Robert A. & Polak, Jacques J., eds. The New International Monetary System. LC 77-10485. 1977. 15.00x (ISBN 0-231-04368-6). Columbia U Pr.

Mundell, Robert A. & Swoboda, Alexander K., eds. Monetary Problems of the International Economy. pap. write for info. (ISBN 0-226-55066-4). U of Chicago Pr.

Munden, D. L. & Dorkin, C. M. Developments in the Clothing Industry. 56p. 1973. 70.00x (ISBN 0-686-63760-7). State Mutual Bk.

Mundhenk, Robert T. & Siebenschuh, William R. Contact: A Guide to Writing Skills. LC 77-73468. (Illus.). 1977. pap. text ed. 10.50 (ISBN 0-395-25110-9); inst. manual 0.25 (ISBN 0-395-25111-7). HM.

Mundinger, Mary O. Autonomy in Nursing. LC 79-25630. (Illus.). 222p. 1980. text ed. 22.00 (ISBN 0-89443-171-4). Aspen Systems.

Mundis, Hester. No He's Not a Monkey, He's an Ape & He's My Son. 1978. pap. 1.75 o.s.i. (ISBN 0-515-04748-1). Jove Pubns.

Mundo, Laura. The Mundo Ufo Report. 1981. 9.95 (ISBN 0-533-04735-8). Vantage.

Mundt, J. Carl, ed. Limited Entry into the Commercial Fisheries. Institute for Marine Studies. 154p. 1976. pap. 5.50 (ISBN 0-295-95496-5). U of Wash Pr.

Mundus, Frank & Wisner, Bill. Sport Fishing for Sharks. 392p. 1976. pap. 4.95 o.s.i. (ISBN 0-02-029540-5, Collier). Macmillan.

Mundy, Anthony. A Second & Third Blast of Retrait from Plaies & Theaters. LC 77-170405. (The English Stage Ser.: Vol. 4). lib. bdg. 45.00 (ISBN 0-8240-0587-2). Garland Pub.

Mundy, Jean & Odum, Linda. Leisure Education: Theory & Practice. LC 78-12434. 1979. text ed. 18.50 (ISBN 0-471-01347-1). Wiley.

Mundy, John H., et al. Essays in Medieval Life & Thought. LC 65-25472. 1955. 12.00x (ISBN 0-8196-0159-4). Biblo.

Mundy, Mary-Ruth. A Writer's Effort: Trial & Error. (Orig.). 1979. pap. 3.00x o.p. (ISBN 0-918342-08-2). Cambric.

Mundy, Mary-Ruth C. Peacocks, Vultures & Nightingales. Lawrence, Joseph, ed. 56p. (Orig.). 1980. pap. write for info. (ISBN 0-89144-113-1). Crescent Pubns.

Munem, Mustafa & Foulis, David. Calculus. LC 79-770818. (Illus.). 1978. text ed. 27.95 (ISBN 0-87901-087-8); Pt. 1, LC79-64155. 18.95x (ISBN 0-87901-105-X); Pt. 2, LC79-64155. 18.95x (ISBN 0-87901-106-8); study guide 4.95 (ISBN 0-686-68021-9). Worth.

Munem, Mustafa & Tschirhart, William. Beginning Algebra. 2nd ed. LC 76-27110. (Illus.). 1977. 15.95x (ISBN 0-87901-063-0); study guide 6.95x (ISBN 0-685-34683-8). Worth.

--College Trigonometry. 1974. text ed. 16.95x (ISBN 0-87901-028-2); study guide 6.95x (ISBN 0-87901-029-0). Worth.

--Intermediate Algebra. 2nd ed. LC 76-27388. (Illus.). 1977. text ed. 15.95x (ISBN 0-87901-064-9); study guide 6.95x (ISBN 0-87901-067-3). Worth.

Munem, Mustafa & Yizze, James P. Precalculus. 3rd ed. LC 77-81759. (Illus.). 1978. text ed. 17.95x (ISBN 0-87901-086-X); study guide 6.95x (ISBN 0-87901-092-4). Worth.

Munem, Mustafa, et al. College Algebra. 2nd ed. LC 78-65417. 1979. text ed. 16.95x (ISBN 0-87901-098-3); study guide 6.95x (ISBN 0-87901-099-1). Worth.

Munford, Clarence J. Production Relations, Class & Black Liberation: A Marxist Perspective in Afro-American Studies. (Philosophical Currents Ser. 24: No. 24). 1978. pap. text ed. 25.75x (ISBN 90-6032-107-3). Humanities.

Mungall, William S., jt. auth. see Doyle, Michael P.

Munger, Bryce L. & Baird, Irwin L. Anatomy Px: A Practical Introduction to Anatomical Correlates of the Physical Examination. (Illus.). 80p. 1980. pap. 6.95 (ISBN 0-683-06151-8). Williams & Wilkins.

Mungham, Geoff & Bankowski, Zenon, eds. Essays in Law & Society. 216p. (Orig.). 1980. pap. 18.00 (ISBN 0-7100-0489-3). Routledge & Kegan.

Mungham, Geoff & Pearson, Geoff, eds. Working Class Youth Culture. (Routledge Direct Editions Ser.). (Orig.). 1976. pap. 9.95 (ISBN 0-7100-8374-2). Routledge & Kegan.

Mungo, Raymond. Between Two Moons. 1972. 3.95 (ISBN 0-8070-6402-5, Pub. by Montana Bks); pap. 1.95 (ISBN 0-8070-6405-X). Madrona Pubs.

--Famous Long Ago. 1970. 3.95 (ISBN 0-8070-6182-4, Pub. by Montana Bks); pap. 1.95 (ISBN 0-8070-6183-2). Madrona Pubs.

--Living on the Moon. 1979. pap. cancelled (ISBN 0-9601428-7-8). Entwhistle Bks.

--Return to Sender. 1975. 3.95 (ISBN 0-685-59658-3, Pub. by Montana Bks). Madrona Pubs.

--Total Loss Farm: A Year in the Life. LC 73-125905. 1977. pap. 4.95 (ISBN 0-914842-16-1). Madrona Pubs.

Munini, Diane J. Developmental Arts...Hands-on Enrichment Activities for Young Children. 2nd rev. ed. LC 80-70128. 68p. 1980. pap. 6.50 (ISBN 0-9605372-0-1). Developmental Arts.

Munitz, Milton K. The Mystery of Existence: An Essay in Philosophical Cosmology. LC 65-14242. 270p. 1974. 13.00x (ISBN 0-8147-5419-8). NYU Pr.

Munitz, Milton K., ed. Identity & Individuation. LC 73-124530. (Studies in Contemporary Philosophy). 1971. 15.00x o.p. (ISBN 0-8147-5352-3); pap. 7.00x (ISBN 0-8147-5375-2). NYU Pr.

--Logic & Ontology. LC 72-96480. (Studies in Contemporary Philosophy). 320p. 1973. 17.50x (ISBN 0-8147-5363-9); pap. 7.00x (ISBN 0-8147-5377-9). NYU Pr.

--Theories of the Universe: From Babylonian Myth to Modern Science. LC 57-6746. 1965. pap. 6.95 (ISBN 0-02-922270-2). Free Pr.

Munitz, Milton K. & Unger, Peter K., eds. Semantics & Philosophy. LC 74-15427. 291p. 1974. 18.00x (ISBN 0-8147-5366-3); pap. 7.00x (ISBN 0-8147-5376-0). NYU Pr.

Munjack, Dennis J. & Oziel, L. Jerome. Sexual Medicine & Counseling in Office Practice. 1980. text ed. 15.95 (ISBN 0-316-58940-3). Little.

Munk, L. R. Thames: An Eating, Drinking & Cruising Guide. (Illus.). 4.50 o.p. (ISBN 0-8038-7058-2). Hastings.

Munk, W. H. The Rotation of the Earth. LC 73-130911. (Monographs in Mechanics & Applied Mathematics). (Illus.). 323p. 1975. 29.95 (ISBN 0-521-20778-9). Cambridge U Pr.

Munkres, James. Topology: A First Course. (Illus.). 448p. 1975. ref. ed. 21.95 (ISBN 0-13-925495-1). P-H.

Munksgaard, Elisabeth. Denmark: An Archaeological Guide. (Illus.). 1974. 5.50 (ISBN 0-571-09196-2, Pub. by Faber & Faber). Merrimack Bk Serv.

Munn, H. Warner. Merlin's Godson. 320p. 1976. pap. 2.25 (ISBN 0-345-28982-X). Ballantine.

Munn, Harry, jt. auth. see Metzger, Norman.

Munn, Henry, tr. see Estrada, Alvaro.

Munn, Norman L. Evolution of the Human Mind. LC 75-146722. (Illus., Orig.). 1971. pap. text ed. 8.95 (ISBN 0-395-11149-8, 3-39665). HM.

--The Growth of Human Behavior. 3rd ed. 512p. 1974. text ed. 20.95 (ISBN 0-395-17017-6). HM.

Munn, R. E. Biometeorological Methods. LC 71-97488. (Environmental Science Ser). 1970. 15.50 (ISBN 0-12-510250-X); pap. 8.95 (ISBN 0-12-510256-9). Acad Pr.

Munn, R. E. see Landsberg, H. E.

Munn, Vella. Rodeo Riders. LC 80-81792. (Illus.). 96p. (gr. 4-9). 1981. PLB 6.59 (ISBN 0-8178-0013-1). Harvey.

Munnell, Alicia H. The Future of Social Security. LC 76-51883. (Studies in Social Economics). 1977. 11.95 (ISBN 0-8157-5896-0); pap. 4.95 (ISBN 0-8157-5895-2). Brookings.

Munnz, Ludwig & Haak, B. Rembrandt. (Library of Great Painters Ser). 1966. 35.00 (ISBN 0-8109-0437-3). Abrams.

Munoz. La Musica En Puerto Rico. 1966. 12.95 (ISBN 0-87751-012-1, Pub by Troutman Press). E Torres & Sons.

Munoz, A. Lopez. Programas Para Dias Especiales Tomo II. 64p. 1980. Repr. of 1977 ed. pap. 1.60 (ISBN 0-311-07006-X). Casa Bautista.

Munoz, Heraldo, ed. From Dependency to Development: Strategies to Overcome Underdevelopment & Inequality. (Westview Special Studies in Social, Political, & Economic Development). 300p. 1981. lib. bdg. 26.50x (ISBN 0-89158-902-3); pap. text ed. 12.50 (ISBN 0-86531-079-3). Westview.

Munoz, Lopez A. Programas Para Dias Especiales Tomo I. 107p. 1980. pap. 1.60 (ISBN 0-311-07005-1). Casa Bautista.

Munoz, Olivia, jt. auth. see Lipton, Gladys.

Munoz, Ricardo F., jt. auth. see Miller, W. R.

Munoz Martin, Luis. Mensajes al Pueblo Puertorriqueno: Pronunciados Ante las Camaras Legislativas, 1949-1964. Marin, Gerard P. & Rios, Louis J., eds. 358p. 1980. 15.00 (ISBN 0-913480-47-9); pap. 6.95 (ISBN 0-913480-48-7); Rack Size. 4.95 (ISBN 0-913480-49-5). Inter Am U Pr.

Munro, A. & McCullough, W. Psychiatry for Social Workers. LC 75-80842. 1970. 17.25 (ISBN 0-08-006366-7); pap. 9.75 (ISBN 0-08-006365-9). Pergamon.

Munro, Andrew K. Autobiography of a Thief. 155p. 1973. 8.50 (ISBN 0-7181-0944-9). Transatlantic.

Munro, Colin, jt. auth. see Teff, Harvey.

Munro, Dana C. The Kingdom of the Crusaders. LC 65-20472. 1966. Repr. of 1935 ed. 11.50 (ISBN 0-8046-0326-X). Kennikat.

Munro, Dana G. Intervention & Dollar Diplomacy in the Carribean, Nineteen Hundred - Nineteen Hundred Twenty-One. LC 80-14089. (Illus.). ix, 553p. 1980. Repr. of 1964 ed. lib. bdg. 42.25x (ISBN 0-313-22510-9, MUIN). Greenwood.

Munro, H. A. T. Lucreti Cari De Rerum Natura Libri Sex, 3 vols. 4th ed. LC 77-70833. (Latin Poetry Ser.: Vol. 8). 1978. Repr. of 1886 ed. Set. lib. bdg. 97.00 (ISBN 0-8240-2957-7). Garland Pub.

Munro, Ian S. Island of Bute. (Islands Ser). (Illus.). 208p. 1973. 16.95 (ISBN 0-7153-6081-7). David & Charles.

Munro, James. The Money That Money Can't Buy. 288p. 1981. pap. 2.50 (ISBN 0-441-53698-0). Charter Bks.

Munro, John F., jt. auth. see Ford, Michael J.

Munro, John M. James Elroy Flecker. LC 75-46531. (English Authors Ser.: No. 185). 1976. lib. bdg. 10.95 (ISBN 0-8057-6656-1). Twayne.

--Nairn Way: Desert Bus to Baghdad. LC 80-11875. 1980. 22.00x (ISBN 0-88206-035-X). Caravan Bks.

Munro, John M., ed. Decadent Poetry of the Eighteen Nineties. (Illus.). 1967. 10.00x (ISBN 0-8156-6018-9, Am U Beirut). Syracuse U Pr.

Munro, Kathleen D. Teach Yourself French Revision. (Teach Yourself Ser). 1965. pap. 2.95 o.p. (ISBN 0-679-10216-7). McKay.

Munro, Mary. This Girl Is Mine. (Aston Hall Ser.: No. 118). 192p. (Orig.). 1981. pap. 1.75 (ISBN 0-523-41134-0). Pinnacle Bks.

Munro, Pamela E. Topics in Mojave Syntax. LC 75-25120. (American Indian Linguistics Ser.). 1976. lib. bdg. 42.00 (ISBN 0-8240-1970-9). Garland Pub.

Munro, Sandra H., jt. auth. see Shelly, Mary V.

Munro, Stanley, ed. & tr. from Chinese. Genesis of a Revolution. (Writing in Asia Ser.). 1978. pap. text ed. 5.95x (ISBN 0-686-58245-4, 00206). Heinemann Ed.

Munro, William. Scottish Lighthouses. (Illus.). 240p. 1980. 22.50 (ISBN 0-906191-32-7, Pub. by Thule Pr England). Intl Schol Bk Serv.

Munroe, C. J. The Smallholder's Guide. LC 78-74077. 1979. 14.95 (ISBN 0-7153-7652-7). David & Charles.

Munroe, John A. Louis McLane: Federalist & Jacksonian. (Illus.). 768p. 1974. 45.00 (ISBN 0-8135-0757-X). Rutgers U Pr.

Munroe, M. Evans. Language of Mathematics. LC 63-14015. (Ann Arbor Science Library Ser). (Illus.). 1963. 4.00 o.p. (ISBN 0-472-00113-2). U of Mich Pr.
Munroe, Marshall E. Introductory Real Analysis. 1965. 17.95 (ISBN 0-201-04905-8). A-W.
Munroe, Robert, jt. auth. see Browne, Corinne.
Munroe, Ruth H., et al. Handbook of Cross-Cultural Human Development. LC 79-12028. 900p. 1980. lib. bdg. 75.00 (ISBN 0-8240-7045-3). Garland Pub.
Muns, George F. Chemical Analysis of Ores & Minerals for Copper, Silver, Gold, & the Platinum Metals. (Illus.). 53p. (Orig.). 1980. pap. 6.50 (ISBN 0-9604924-0-2). Muns.
Munsell, Joel. Chronology of the Origin & Progress of Paper & Paper-Making. Bidwell, John, ed. LC 78-74389. (Nineteenth-Century Book Arts & Printing History Ser.: Vol. 4). 1980. lib. bdg. 27.50 (ISBN 0-8240-3878-9). Garland Pub.
Munsen, Sylvia. Cooking the Norwegian Way. (Easy Menu Ethnic Cookbooks). (Illus.). (YA) (gr. 5 up). 1981. PLB 4.95g (ISBN 0-8225-0901-6). Lerner Pubns.
Munsey, Cecil. The Illustrated Guide to Collecting Bottles. 1977. pap. 10.95 (ISBN 0-8015-3940-4, Hawthorn). Dutton.
Munsey, D. T. Tachometric Tables for the Metric User. 1971. 14.95x (ISBN 0-291-39336-5). Intl Ideas.
Munshaw, Nancy, jt. ed. see Nagel, Stuart.
Munshi, Vijay. Silences. (Redbird Book Ser). 24p. 1975. 8.00 (ISBN 0-88253-846-2); pap. text ed. 4.80 (ISBN 0-88253-715-6). Ind-US Inc.
Munson, Eric M., ed. see Bone, Hugh A. & Ranney, Austin.
Munson, Eric M., ed. see Brieland, Donald, et al.
Munson, Eric M., ed. see Faunce, William.
Munson, Eric M., ed. see Ferguson, John H. & McHenry, Dean E.
Munson, Eric M., ed. see Palen, J. John.
Munson, Eric M., ed. see Pritchett, C. H.
Munson, Fred C., et al. Nursing Assignment Patterns: User's Manual. (Illus.). 300p. (Orig.). 1980. pap. text ed. 32.50 (ISBN 0-914904-40-X). Health Admin Pr.
Munson, K. Airliners Since Nineteen Forty-Six. 2nd. rev. ed. 1975. 9.95 (ISBN 0-02-588180-9). Macmillan.
Munson, Kenneth. Airliners Between the Wars Nineteen Nineteen to Nineteen Thirty Nine, Vol. 14. LC 76-160081. (Pocket Encyclopedia of World Aircraft in Color Ser.). (Illus.). 176p. 1972. 8.95 (ISBN 0-02-588000-4). Macmillan.
--Airliners Since Nineteen Forty-Six. rev. ed. LC 76-186444. (Pocket Encyclopedia of World Aircraft in Color Ser.). (Illus.). 192p. 1972. 5.95 o.s.i. (ISBN 0-02-588160-4). Macmillan.
--Bombers in Service: Patrol & Transport Aircraft Since 1960. rev. ed. LC 75-14214. (Illus.). 156p. 1976. 6.95 o.s.i. (ISBN 0-02-587940-5, 58794). Macmillan.
--Bombers: Patrol & Reconnaissance Aircraft 1914-1919. LC 68-20156. (Illus.). (YA) 1968. 8.95 (ISBN 0-02-588060-8). Macmillan.
--Bombers: World War Two. 1969. 8.95 (ISBN 0-02-588020-9). Macmillan.
--Fighters: Attack & Training Aircraft, 1914-1919. (Illus.). 1968. 8.95 (ISBN 0-02-588070-5). Macmillan.
--Fighters in Service: Attack & Training Aircraft Since 1960. rev. ed. LC 75-12742. (Illus.). 168p. 1975. 8.95 (ISBN 0-02-587960-X, 58796). Macmillan.
--Fighters, Nineteen Thirty-Nine to Nineteen Forty-Five: World War Two. (Illus.). 1969. 8.95 (ISBN 0-02-588010-1). Macmillan.
--Pocket Encyclopedia of Seaplanes & Flying Boats. Wood, John W., ed. (World Aircraft in Color Ser). (Illus.). 1971. 8.95 (ISBN 0-02-587990-1). Macmillan.
Munson, P. L., et al, eds. Vitamins & Hormones, Vol. 38. (Serial Publication Ser.). 1981. write for info. (ISBN 0-12-709838-0). Acad Pr.
Munson, Paul L. see Harris, Robert S., et al.
Munson, Paul L., et al, eds. Vitamins & Hormones: Advances in Research & Applications, Vol. 37. LC 43-10535. 1980. 35.00 (ISBN 0-12-709837-2). Acad Pr.
Munson, Paul L., et al see Harris, Robert S., et al.
Munson, Richard, jt. ed. see Courrier, Kathleen.
Munson, Ron. Intervention & Reflection: Basic Issues in Medical Ethics. 1979. text ed. 19.95x (ISBN 0-534-00608-6). Wadsworth Pub.
Munson, Ronald. The Way of Words: An Informal Logic. LC 75-31028. (Illus.). 448p. 1976. 15.75 (ISBN 0-395-20625-1); answer bk. 2.00 (ISBN 0-395-24229-0). HM.
Munster, A. Statistical Thermodynamics, 2 vols. Vol. 1, 1969. 72.00 (ISBN 0-12-510901-6); Vol. 2, 1974. 90.00 (ISBN 0-12-510902-4). Acad Pr.
Munster, Andrew. Burn Care for the House Officer. (House Officer Ser.). (Illus.). 185p. 1980. softcover 9.95 (ISBN 0-683-06157-7). Williams & Wilkins.
Munster, Andrew M. & Thomas, George J. Surgical Anatomy for Clinical Examination. (Illus.). 144p. 1973. text ed. 14.75 (ISBN 0-398-02715-3). C C Thomas.
Munsterberg, Hugo. Arts of China. LC 70-188012. 1972. 29.50 (ISBN 0-8048-0039-1). C E Tuttle.
Muntean, Michaela. I Like School. (Sesame Street Early Bird Bks). (Illus.). 32p. (ps). 1981. 3.50 (ISBN 0-307-11602-6, Golden Pr). Western Pub.
Munteanu, Voichita. The Cycle of Frescoes of the Chapel of Le Liget. LC 77-94712. (Outstanding Dissertations in the Fine Arts Ser.). 1978. lib. bdg. 31.00x (ISBN 0-8240-3244-6). Garland Pub.
Munter, Preston K., jt. auth. see Greiff, Barrie S.
Munter, R. L. History of the Irish Newspaper, Sixteen Eighty-Five - Seventeen Sixty. 49.50 (ISBN 0-521-05786-8). Cambridge U Pr.
Munthe, Adam. Anna & the Echo-Catcher. (Illus.). 32p. (gr. k-3). 1981. 9.95 (ISBN 0-7011-2498-9, Pub. by Chatto-Bodley-Jonathan). Merrimack Bk Serv.
Munton, Alan, ed. see Lewis, Wyndham.
Munton, Don, jt. ed. see Stairs, Denis.
Munton, R. & Stott, J. R. Refrigeration at Sea. 2nd ed. (Illus.). 1978. text ed. 51.30x (ISBN 0-85334-766-2, Pub. by Applied Science). Burgess-Intl Ideas.
Munton, R. J., jt. auth. see Morgan, W. B.
Munts, Raymond. Bargaining for Health: Labor Unions, Health Insurance, & Medical Care. 1967. 25.00 (ISBN 0-299-04320-7). U of Wis Pr.
Muntz, Carrie, tr. see Graham, Billy.
Muntz, E. Phillip, jt. auth. see Logan, Wende W.
Muntz, Hope. The Golden Warrior. 1978. pap. 1.95 o.p. (ISBN 0-445-04315-6). Popular Lib.
Muntzing, L. Manning, ed. Nuclear Power & Its Regulation in the United States. (Illus.). 125p. 1980. pap. 30.00 (ISBN 0-08-027139-1). Pergamon.
Munves, James. The Treasure of Diogenes Sampuez. LC 78-21768. 192p. (gr. 5-9). 1979. 7.95 (ISBN 0-590-07384-2, Four Winds). Schol Bk Serv.
Munz, Lucille T. & Slauson, Nedra. Index to Illustrations of the Natural World Outside of North America. 1980. write for info. (ISBN 0-208-01857-3, Archon). Shoe String.
Munz, Peter. The Shapes of Time. LC 77-2459. 1977. lib. bdg. 20.00x (ISBN 0-8195-5017-5, Pub. by Wesleyan U Pr). Columbia U Pr.
Munz, Philip A. California Desert Wildflowers. (Illus., Orig.). 1962. 14.50 (ISBN 0-520-00898-7); pap. 3.95 (ISBN 0-520-00899-5). U of Cal Pr.
--California Spring Wildflowers: From the Base of the Sierra Nevada & Southern Mountains to the Sea. (Orig.). 1961. 6.50x o.p. (ISBN 0-520-00895-2); pap. 4.95 (ISBN 0-520-00896-0). U of Cal Pr.
--Shore Wildflowers of California, Oregon, & Washington. (Illus., Orig.). 1965. 6.50x o.p. (ISBN 0-520-00902-9); pap. 4.95 (ISBN 0-520-00903-7). U of Cal Pr.
--Supplement to a California Flora. 1968. 11.50x (ISBN 0-520-00904-5). U of Cal Pr.
Munzert, Alfred. National Directory of External Degree Programs. 1977. 8.95 o.p. (ISBN 0-9991729-2-1); pap. 4.95 (ISBN 0-9991729-3-X). Dutton.
Munzert, Alfred W. Analyze Your Personality Through Color. (Test Yourself Ser.). 1980. pap. 3.95 (ISBN 0-671-34036-0). Monarch Pr.
--Test Your Compatibility. (Test Yourself Ser.). 1980. pap. 3.95 (ISBN 0-671-34037-9). Monarch Pr.
--Test Your E.S.P. (Test Yourself Ser.). 1980. pap. 3.95 (ISBN 0-671-34039-5). Monarch Pr.
--Test Your I.Q. (Test Yourself Ser.). 1980. pap. 3.95 (ISBN 0-671-34035-2). Monarch Pr.
Munzert, Alfred W., jt. auth. see Elskamp, Karen E.
Mur, L., jt. ed. see Barica, J.
Murach, Mike. Business Data Processing. 3rd ed. 432p. 1980. 15.95 (ISBN 0-574-21275-2, 13-4275); instr's. guide avail. (ISBN 0-574-21276-0, 13-4276); study guide 4.95 (ISBN 0-574-21277-9, 13-4277); transparency masters 3.95 (ISBN 0-574-21278-7, 13-4278); FORTRAN suppl 5.95 (ISBN 0-574-21285-X, 13-4279); BASIC suppl. 5.95 (ISBN 0-574-21290-6, 13-4280); COBOL suppl. 6.95 (ISBN 0-574-21280-9, 13-4281). SRA.
--Standard COBOL. 2nd ed. LC 74-34184. (Illus.). 400p. 1975. pap. text ed. 15.95 (ISBN 0-574-18401-5, 13-4010); instr's guide avail. (ISBN 0-574-18402-3, 13-4011). SRA.
--Structured COBOL. 1980. pap. text ed. 13.95 (ISBN 0-574-21260-4, 13-4260); instr's guide avail. (ISBN 0-574-21261-2, 13-4261); oS supplement 4.50 (ISBN 0-574-21263-9, 13-4263); dOS supplement 4.50 (ISBN 0-574-21264-7, 13-4264). SRA.
--System-Three-Sixty RPG. LC 70-178830. (Illus.). 297p. 1972. pap. text ed. 14.95 (ISBN 0-574-16097-3, 13-1415); instr's guide avail. (ISBN 0-574-16128-7, 13-1416); transparency masters 29.95 (ISBN 0-574-16129-5, 13-1417). SRA.
Murad, Anatol. Franz Joseph I of Austria & His Empire. LC 68-17233. (Illus.). 259p. 1968. text ed. 22.50x (ISBN 0-8290-0172-7). Irvington.
Murad, Orlene. The English Comedians at the Habsburg Court in Graz 1607-1608. (Salzburg Studies in Elizabethan & Renaissance Ser.: No. 81). 1978. pap. text ed. 25.00x (ISBN 0-391-01487-0). Humanities.
Murahashi, S., jt. ed. see Imahori, K.
Murai, Harold M., jt. auth. see Bradford, Ann L.
Murakami, Hyoe & Seidensticker, E. G., eds. Guide to Japanese Culture. 224p. 1977. 16.50 (ISBN 0-87040-403-2). Japan Pubns.
Murakami, Hyoye & Harper, Thomas J., eds. Great Historical Figures of Japan. (Illus., Orig.). 1978. 18.50 (ISBN 0-87040-431-8). Japan Pubns.
Murakami, Ryu. Almost Transparent Blue. Andrew, Nancy, tr. from Japanese. LC 77-75959. 126p. 1977. 9.95x (ISBN 0-87011-305-4). Kodansha.
Muralidhar, A., jt. ed. see Patanjali, V.
Muralidhar, A., tr. see Patanjali, V. & Muralidhar, A.
Murari, Timeri. Lovers & Not People. 1979. pap. 2.25 o.s.i. (ISBN 0-515-04763-5). Jove Pubns.
Murarka, Dev. Soviet Union. (Nations & Peoples Library). 1971. 8.50x o.s.i. (ISBN 0-8027-2123-0). Walker & Co.
Muraro, Michelangelo, jt. auth. see Rosand, David.
Murasaki, Lady. The Tale of Genji-One. LC 50-47132. pap. 2.95 (ISBN 0-385-09275-X, Anch). Doubleday.
Muraskin, William A. Middle-Class Blacks in a White Society. 1975. 22.75x (ISBN 0-520-02705-1). U of Cal Pr.
Murata, Alice K. & Farguhar, Judith, eds. Issues in Pacific-Asian American Health & Mental Health. (Occasional Paper Ser.). (Orig.). 1981. pap. write for info. (ISBN 0-934584-12-5). Pacific-Asian.
Murata, Kenji. Practical Bonsai for Beginners. LC 64-7611. (Illus.). 1977. pap. 7.95 (ISBN 0-87040-230-7). Japan Pubns.
Murata, Kyuzo. Bonsai: Miniature Potted Trees. 116p. 1980. pap. 7.50 (ISBN 0-87040-241-2, Pub. by Shufunotomo Japan). Intl Schol Bk Serv.
Murav'Yov, Nikolay. Journey to Khiva Through the Turkoman Country. 1977. text ed. 25.50x (ISBN 0-905820-00-2). Humanities.
Murayama, Misako. Cross Stitch Patterns Two. new ed. (Ondori Needlework Ser.). (Illus.). 1978. pap. 4.50 (ISBN 0-87040-427-X). Japan Pubns.
Murayama, Misako, jt. auth. see Ondori Publishing Co. Staff.
Murch, Alma E., tr. see Giono, Jean.
Murch, Gerald M. Visual & Auditory Perception. LC 74-172349. (Illus.). 1973. pap. 14.95 (ISBN 0-672-60779-4). Bobbs.
Murch, Gerald M., ed. Studies in Perception. LC 74-8398. 1976. pap. text ed. 9.50 (ISBN 0-672-61189-9). Bobbs.
Murchison, D. E. Surveying & Photogrammetry, Computation for Civil Engineers. 1977. 16.00 (ISBN 0-408-00293-X). Transatlantic.
Murchison, Irene, et al. Legal Accountability in the Nursing Process. 1978. pap. text ed. 10.50 (ISBN 0-8016-3603-5). Mosby.
Murchison, Thomas M., ed. Prose Writings of Donald Lamont, 1874-1958. 1958. 15.00x (ISBN 0-7073-0038-X, Pub. by Scottish Academic Pr Scotland). Columbia U Pr.
Murchison, William, jt. auth. see Merklein, Helmut.
Murcray, David G., ed. Handbook of High Resolution Infrared Spectra of Gases of Atmospheric Interest. 304p. 1981. 49.95 (ISBN 0-8493-2950-7). CRC Pr.
Murdeshwar, M. G. General Topology. LC 80-18434. 480p. 1981. 19.95 (ISBN 0-470-26916-2). Halsted Pr.
Murdick, Olin J. & Meyers, Jack F., eds. Boards of Education-a Primer. 78p. 1972. 2.00. Natl Cath Educ.
Murdick, Robert C. & Ross, Joel E. Introduction to Management Information Systems. (Illus.). 1977. 18.95 (ISBN 0-13-486233-3). P-H.
Murdick, Robert G. Business Research: Concept & Practice. 226p. 1969. pap. text ed. 8.50 scp o.p. (ISBN 0-7002-2232-4, HarpC). Har-Row.
--MIS: Concepts & Design. 1980. text ed. 21.00 (ISBN 0-13-585331-1). P-H.
Murdick, Robert G. & Ross, Joel E. Information Systems for Modern Management. 2nd ed. (Illus.). 640p. 1975. ref. ed. 21.95 (ISBN 0-13-464602-9). P-H.
Murdick, Robert G., jt. auth. see Karger, Delmar W.
Murdick, Robert G., et al. Business Policy: A Framework for Analysis. 3rd ed. LC 79-20129. (Management Ser.). 1980. pap. text ed. 10.50 (ISBN 0-88244-204-X). Grid Pub.
Murdocca, Sal. The Hero of Hamblett. LC 80-11346. (Illus.). 48p. (gr. 3 up). 1980. PLB 8.44 (ISBN 0-440-04458-8); pap. 4.95 (ISBN 0-440-04457-X). Delacorte.
--Take Me to the Moon! LC 76-6113. (Fun-To-Read Bk.). (Illus.). 64p. (gr. 1-4). 1976. 6.95 (ISBN 0-688-41766-3); PLB 6.67 (ISBN 0-688-51766-8). Lothrop.
--Tuttle's Shell. (Illus.). 64p. (gr. 1-4). 1976. PLB 6.67 (ISBN 0-688-51724-2). Lothrop.
Murdocca, Sol. Grover's Own Alphabet. (Illus.). (ps-1). 1978. PLB 4.77 (ISBN 0-307-68654-X, Whitman). Western Pub.
Murdoch, Beamish. Epitome of the Laws of Nova Scotia, 4 vols. LC 73-26626. 1034p. Repr. of 1833 ed. Set. 90.00x (ISBN 0-912004-04-5). W W Gaunt.
Murdoch, Brian & Read, Malcolm. Siegfried Lenz. (Modern German Authors Ser.: No. 6). 1978. text ed. 10.50x (ISBN 0-85496-068-6). Humanities.
Murdoch, Brian O. The Recapitulated Fall: A Comparative Study in Medieval Literature. LC 73-91188. (Amsterdamer Publikationen Zur Sprache und Literatur: No. 11). 207p. (Orig.). 1974. pap. text ed. 20.00x (ISBN 90-6203-021-1). Humanities.
Murdoch, David C. Linear Algebra. LC 72-121911. 1970. text ed. 21.95x o.p. (ISBN 0-471-62500-0). Wiley.
Murdoch, Iris. Nuns & Soldiers. LC 80-16935. 512p. 1981. 14.95 (ISBN 0-670-51826-3). Viking Pr.
--Sartre: Romantic Realist. 78p. 1980. Repr. of 1953 ed. 15.00x (ISBN 0-06-495034-4). B&N.
--A Severed Head. 1976. pap. 2.50 (ISBN 0-14-002003-9). Penguin.
Murdoch, J. & Barnes, J. Statistics: Problems & Solutions. LC 72-8592. 352p. 1973. pap. 11.95x (ISBN 0-470-62510-4). Halsted Pr.
Murdoch, Joseph, ed. Library of Golf 1743-1966: A Bibliography of Golf Books. LC 67-29083. (Illus.). 1968. 30.00 (ISBN 0-8103-0961-0). Gale.
Murdoch, Joseph S. & Seagle, Janet, eds. Golf: A Guide to Information Sources. LC 79-23270. (Sports, Games & Pastimes Information Guide Ser.: Vol. 7). 1979. 30.00 (ISBN 0-8103-1457-6). Gale.
Murdoch, Nancy & Fassett, Linda. Life-God's Way. 1976. pap. 1.95 (ISBN 0-87123-327-4, 210327). Bethany Fell.
Murdock, Carol V. & Lawson, Kenneth. The Rainbow Generation: Over Fifty-Five & Living Forward. 176p. pap. cancelled (ISBN 0-88421-098-7). Butterick Pub.
Murdock, Dick, ed. see Murdock, Jayne M.
Murdock, Eugene C. One Million Men: The Civil War Draft in the North. LC 80-14431. (Illus.). xi, 366p. 1980. Repr. of 1971 ed. lib. bdg. 29.75x (ISBN 0-313-22502-8, MUOM). Greenwood.
Murdock, George P. Atlas of World Cultures. LC 80-53030. (Illus.). 152p. 1981. 9.95x (ISBN 0-8229-3432-9). U of Pittsburgh Pr.
--Social Structure. 1965. pap. text ed. 8.95 (ISBN 0-02-922290-7). Free Pr.
--Theories of Illness: A World Survey. LC 80-5257. (Illus.). 160p. 1980. 9.95 (ISBN 0-8229-3428-0). U of Pittsburgh Pr.
Murdock, George P. & O'Leary, Timothy. Ethnographic Bibliography of North America, 5 vols. 4th ed. Incl. Vol. 1. 492p (ISBN 0-87536-205-2); Vol. 2. 294p (ISBN 0-87536-207-9); Vol. 3. 304p (ISBN 0-87536-209-5); Vol. 4. 292p (ISBN 0-87536-211-7); Vol. 5. 444p (ISBN 0-87536-213-3). LC 75-17091. (Behavior Science Bibliographies Ser.). 1975. text ed. 35.00 ea. HRAFP.
Murdock, George P., et al. Outline of Cultural Materials. 5th, rev. ed. LC 80-81130. (Bibliography Ser.). Date not set. cancelled (ISBN 0-87536-652-X). HRAFP.
Murdock, James. Fluid Mechanics & Its Applications. LC 75-31024. (Illus.). 384p. 1976. text ed. 23.95 (ISBN 0-395-20626-X); solutions manual 2.50 (ISBN 0-395-24216-9). HM.
Murdock, Jayne M. Brief Infinity: A Love Story in Haiku. Murdock, Dick, ed. LC 80-83998. (Illus.). 64p. (Orig.). 1981. pap. 6.00 (ISBN 0-932916-06-6). May Murdock.
Murdock, L. J. & Brook, K. M. Concrete Materials & Practices. 5th ed. LC 78-27476. 1979. 54.95x (ISBN 0-470-26639-2). Halsted Pr.
Murdock, Robert, jt. ed. see Chassman, Neil A.
Murdock, Steven H. & Leistritz, F. Larry. Energy Development in the Western United States: Impact on Rural Areas. LC 79-18478. 384p. 1979. 32.95 (ISBN 0-03-051351-0). Praeger.
Murdock, Steven H., jt. auth. see Leistritz, F. Larry.
Murdoff, Ron, jt. auth. see Evans, Idella M.

Mure, G. R. Aristotle. LC 75-17199. 282p. 1975. Repr. of 1932 ed. lib. bdg. 22.25x (ISBN 0-8371-8298-0, MUAR). Greenwood.

Murfin, Marjorie E. & Wynar, Lubomyr R. Reference Service: An Annotated Bibliographic Guide. LC 76-54879. 1977. lib. bdg. 18.50x (ISBN 0-87287-132-0). Libs Unl.

Murfree, Mary N. In the Tennessee Mountains. LC 78-100406. (Tennesseana Editions Ser.). (Illus.). 1970. 9.50 (ISBN 0-87049-105-9). U of Tenn Pr.

Murgatroyd, Stephen, ed. Helping the Troubled Child. 1980. text ed. 18.35 (ISBN 0-06-318067-7, IntlDept); pap. text ed. 9.25 (ISBN 0-06-318068-5, IntlDept). Har-Row.

Murgia, Charles E. Prolegomena to Servius 5-the Manuscripts. (Publications in Classical Studies: Vol. 2). 1975. pap. 14.50x (ISBN 0-520-09466-2). U of Cal Pr.

Murie, Alan, jt. auth. see Birrell, Derek.

Murie, Olaus J. Elk of North America. LC 79-83649. (Illus.). 376p. (gr. 7-12). 1979. 13.50 (ISBN 0-933160-02-X); pap. 9.95 (ISBN 0-933160-03-8). Teton Bkshop.

Muriell, Christopher. An Answer Unto the Catholiques Supplication, Presented Unto the Kings Maiestie, for a Tolleration of Popish Religion in England...Annexed the Supplication of the Papists. LC 74-28874. (English Experience Ser.: No. 753). 1975. Repr. of 1603 ed. 3.50 (ISBN 90-221-0753-1). Walter J Johnson.

Murle, Alan, et al. Housing Policy & the Housing System. (Urban & Regional Studies). 1976. text ed. 25.00x o.p. (ISBN 0-04-350051-X); pap. text ed. 10.95x o.p. (ISBN 0-04-350053-6). Allen Unwin.

Murlless, Dick & Stallings, Constance. Hikers' Guide to the Smokies. LC 72-83981. (Totebook Ser.). (Illus.). 374p. 1973. pap. 7.95 (ISBN 0-87156-068-2); Hiker's Map of the Smokies 1.95 (ISBN 0-87156-095-X). Sierra.

Murnane, Richard J. The Impact of School Resources on the Learning of Inner City Children. LC 75-4663. 144p. 1975. text ed. 16.50 o.p. (ISBN 0-88410-161-4). Ballinger Pub.

Muro, James J., jt. auth. see Dinkmeyer, Don C.

Muroga, Saburo. Logic Design & Switching Theory. LC 78-12407. 1979. 35.00 (ISBN 0-471-04418-0, Pub. by Wiley-Interscience). Wiley.

Murph, Roxane C. Richard III: The Making of a Legend. LC 77-4021. 1977. 10.00 (ISBN 0-8108-1034-4). Scarecrow.

Murphey, Cecil. Comforting Those Who Grieve. LC 78-71052. 64p. 1979. pap. 2.50 (ISBN 0-8042-1099-3). John Knox.

--Prayerobics: Getting Started & Staying Going. 1979. 7.95 (ISBN 0-8499-0146-4). Word Bks.

Murphey, Rhoads. The Outsiders: The Western Experience in India & China. LC 76-27279. (Michigan Studies on China Ser.). 1976. 16.50x (ISBN 0-472-08679-0). U of Mich Pr.

Murphey, Sara. Animal Hat Shop. (Beginning-to-Read Ser.). (Illus.). (gr. 1-3). 1964. 2.50 o.p. (ISBN 0-695-80425-1). Follett.

Murphey, Wayne K. & Jorgensen, Richard. Wood As an Industrial Arts Material. 1974. text ed. 21.00 (ISBN 0-08-017906-1); pap. text ed. 12.75 (ISBN 0-08-017907-X). Pergamon.

Murphree, M. W. Christianity & the Shona. LC 68-18053. (Monographs on Social Anthropology Ser: No. 36). 1969. text ed. 12.50x (ISBN 0-485-19536-4, Athlone Pr). Humanities.

Murphy. Infinite Power for Richer Living. pap. 3.95 (ISBN 0-13-464396-8, Parker). P-H.

--The Language of Agriculture in English. (English for Careers Ser.). (gr. 10 up). 1981. pap. text ed. 3.25 o.p. (ISBN 0-88345-350-9, 18524). Regents Pub.

Murphy, jt. auth. see Carlo.

Murphy, Agnes. Melba: A Biography. LC 77-8029. (Music Reprint Ser.). (Illus.). 1977. Repr. of 1909 ed. lib. bdg. 32.50 (ISBN 0-306-77428-3). Da Capo.

Murphy, Albert T. Families of Hearing-Impaired Children. 1979. pap. 4.50 (ISBN 0-88200-128-0). Bell Assn Deaf.

Murphy, Allan H. & Katz, Richard W., eds. Probability, Statistics, & Decision Making in Meterology. 450p. (Orig.). 1981. lib. bdg. 28.50x (ISBN 0-86531-152-8); pap. text ed. 15.00x (ISBN 0-86531-153-6). Westview.

Murphy, Angeline. Mother Florence: Biographical History. (Biblio. Index Notes Ser.). (Illus.). 64p. 1980. 15.00 (ISBN 0-682-49625-1). Exposition.

Murphy, Arthur. Lives of Henry Fielding & Samuel Johnson, with Essays from Gray's Inn Journal, 1752-1792. LC 68-24212. 1968. 49.00x (ISBN 0-8201-1035-3). Schol Facsimiles.

Murphy, Arthur E., ed. see Mead, George H.

Murphy, Arthur W., ed. The Nuclear Power Controversy. (Illus.). 1976. pap. 3.95 (ISBN 0-13-625574-4, Spec). P-H.

Murphy, Bernadette, jt. auth. see Murphy, Lawrence.

Murphy, Brenda, jt. ed. see Monteiro, George.

Murphy, Brian. Teach Yourself Management Accounting. (Teach Yourself Ser.). 1978. pap. 2.50 (ISBN 0-679-10477-1). McKay.

Murphy, Bruce. Lampmaking. LC 76-16360. (Illus.). 192p. 1976. 14.95 (ISBN 0-8069-5420-5); lib. bdg. 13.29 (ISBN 0-8069-5421-3). Sterling.

Murphy, Bruce & Lopo, Ana. Lampmaking. rev. ed. LC 76-16360. (Illus.). 192p. 1980. pap. 7.95 (ISBN 0-8069-8462-7). Sterling.

Murphy, Bruce, jt. auth. see Lopo, Ana G.

Murphy, Catharine A. Thomas Morley: Editions of Italian Canzonets & Madrigals, 1597-98. LC 64-64160. (Florida State U. Studies: No. 42). 1964. 12.00 (ISBN 0-8130-0480-2). U Presses Fla.

Murphy Center for Liturgical Research, ed. Made, Not Born: New Perspectives on Christian Initiation & the Catechumenate. 200p. 1976. 9.95x o.p. (ISBN 0-268-00708-X). U of Notre Dame Pr.

Murphy, Charles, jt. auth. see Bryan, James.

Murphy, Charles F. Working Plans for Working Decoys. (Illus.). 1979. 14.95 (ISBN 0-87691-286-2). Winchester Pr.

Murphy, D. W., et al, eds. Materials for Advanced Batteries. (NATO Conference Ser. (Series VI--Materials Science): Vol. 2). 355p. 1981. 39.50 (ISBN 0-306-40564-4, Plenum Pr). Plenum Pub.

Murphy, Daniel. Queen Elizabeth Park & the Bloedel Conservatory. Campbell, M., ed. (Illus.). 50p. (Orig.). 1981. pap. 4.95 (ISBN 0-88839-088-2). Hancock Hse.

Murphy, Daniel, jt. auth. see Ehrlich, Eugene H.

Murphy, Daniel B. & Rousseau, Viateur. Foundations of College Chemistry. 3rd ed. LC 79-17521. 1980. text ed. 21.95x (ISBN 0-471-04621-3); tchrs. manual avail. (ISBN 0-471-05916-1); study guide avail. (ISBN 0-471-05605-7). Wiley.

Murphy, Dennis D. Directory of Conservative & Libertarian Serials, Publishers, & Freelance Markets. LC 78-65733. 1979. pap. 4.95x o.p. (ISBN 0-918788-02-1). D D Murphy.

Murphy, Dennis G. The Materials of Interior Design. Murphy, Gladys N., ed. (Interior Furnishings & Products Ser.). (Illus.). 208p. (Orig.). 1978. 10.50 (ISBN 0-938614-00-2, 211-196). Stratford Hse.

Murphy, Dervla. In Ethiopia with a Mule. 1970. 9.95 (ISBN 0-7195-1830-X). Transatlantic.

--On a Shoestring to Coorg. 1977. 18.50 (ISBN 0-7195-3284-1). Transatlantic.

--Tibetan Foothold. 1967. 8.95 (ISBN 0-7195-0989-0). Transatlantic.

--Waiting Land: A Spell in Nepal. (Illus.). 1969. 8.95 (ISBN 0-7195-1745-1). Transatlantic.

--Wheels Within Wheels. LC 79-27095. 240p. 1980. 10.95 (ISBN 0-89919-006-5). Ticknor & Fields.

Murphy, E. Jefferson. The Bantu Civilization of Southern Africa. LC 73-17194. (Illus.). 256p. (gr. 7 up). 1974. 12.95 (ISBN 0-690-00399-4, TYC-J). T Y Crowell.

--Creative Philanthropy: Carnegie Corporation in Africa, 1953-74. LC 76-14886. 1976. text ed. 19.90 (ISBN 0-8077-2473-4); pap. text ed. 9.95 (ISBN 0-8077-2479-3). Tchrs Coll.

--History of African Civilization. (Illus.). 448p. 1972. 12.50 o.s.i. (ISBN 0-690-38194-8, TYC-T). T Y Crowell.

--Understanding Africa. rev. ed. LC 77-11560. (Illus.). (gr. 7 up). 1978. 8.95 (ISBN 0-690-03834-8, TYC-J); PLB 9.79 (ISBN 0-690-03846-1). T Y Crowell.

Murphy, Earl F. Energy & Environmental Balance. (Pergamon Policy Studies). 1980. 36.00 (ISBN 0-08-025082-3). Pergamon.

--Governing Nature. 1970. pap. 2.95 o.p. (ISBN 0-531-06464-6). Watts.

Murphy, Edmond A. Skepsis, Dogma, & Belief: Uses & Abuses in Medicine. LC 80-8870. 176p. 1981. text ed. 14.95x (ISBN 0-8018-2510-5). Johns Hopkins.

Murphy, Edward. Two Thousand Five Hundred One Line Quotations for Speakers, Writers & Raconteurs. Michaelman, Herbert, ed. 1981. 12.95 (ISBN 0-517-54281-1, Michaelman Books). Crown.

Murphy, Elspeth & Hanna, Wayne. My First Books About Jesus, 4 bks. Incl. Bk. 1. Jesus Does Good Things (ISBN 0-89191-334-3); Bk. 2. Jesus Is God's Son (ISBN 0-89191-332-7); Bk. 3. Jesus Loves Chilren (ISBN 0-89191-333-5); Bk. 4. Jesus Tells Us About God (ISBN 0-89191-335-1). (Illus.). 1981. write for info. board bks. Cook.

Murphy, Francis, ed. Yvor Winters: The Uncollected Essays & Reviews. LC 72-91915. 320p. 1972. 12.95 (ISBN 0-8040-0604-0). Swallow.

Murphy, Francis X. The Papacy Today. 256p. 1981. lib. bdg. 10.95 (ISBN 0-02-588240-6). Macmillan.

--This Church, These Times: The Roman Catholic Church Since Vatican II. (Illus.). 128p. 1981. cancelled (ISBN 0-695-81446-X, Assn Pr). Follett.

Murphy, Frank D. Model & Department Policy Statement with Job Descriptions for Hospitals. (Medical Bks.). 1980. lib. bdg. 64.95 (ISBN 0-8161-2199-0, Hall Medical). G K Hall.

Murphy, G. J. Transport & Distribution. 2nd ed. 300p. 1978. text ed. 24.50x (ISBN 0-220-66321-1, Pub. by Busn Bks England). Renouf.

--The Transport Operators Guide to Professional Competence. 314p. 1980. pap. 21.00x (ISBN 0-09-141591-8, Pub. by Busn Bks England). Renouf.

Murphy, Gardner. Psychological Thought from Pythagoras to Freud: An Informal Introduction. LC 68-25371. (Orig.). 1968. pap. 3.65 o.p. (ISBN 0-15-674701-4, H068, Hbgr). HarBraceJ.

Murphy, Gene & Driscoll, Tim. An Album of Irish Americans. LC 73-13994. (Picture Albums Ser.). (Illus.). 96p. (gr. 5-8). 1974. PLB 5.90 o.p. (ISBN 0-531-01519-X). Watts.

Murphy, George E., Jr., ed. The Poet's Choice: One Hundred American Poets' Favorite Poems. 176p. 1980. 10.95 (ISBN 0-937504-01-7); pap. 5.95 (ISBN 0-937504-00-9). Tendril.

Murphy, Gerald. Ossianic Lore & Romantic Tales of Medieval Ireland. rev. ed. (Life & Cult Ser.). 69p. 1971. pap. 1.50 o.p. (ISBN 0-85342-267-2). Irish Bk Ctr.

Murphy, Gerald D., ed. Cancer: Signals & Safeguards. (Illus.). 364p. 1981. text ed. 27.50 (ISBN 0-88416-229-X). PSG Pub.

Murphy, Gerald P. & Mittelman, Arnold. Chemotherapy of Urogenital Tumors. (Illus.). 288p. 1975. 32.75 (ISBN 0-398-03319-6). C C Thomas.

Murphy, Gerald P., ed. International Advances in Surgical Oncology, Vol. 4. LC 78-51119. 365p. 1981. 46.00x (ISBN 0-8451-0503-5). A R Liss.

Murphy, Gerald P., ed. see Symposium at Roswell Park Memorial Institute, Buffalo, May 1980.

Murphy, Gerard, ed. Early Irish Lyrics: Eighth to Twelfth Century. 1956. 24.00x (ISBN 0-19-815207-8). Oxford U Pr.

Murphy, Gladys N., ed. see Murphy, Dennis G.

Murphy, Gretchen, jt. auth. see Waters, Kathleen.

Murphy, Hank. Tang Soo Do. (Illus.). 112p. (Orig.). 1980. pap. 8.00 (ISBN 0-87364-202-3). Paladin Ent.

Murphy, Henry T., jt. ed. see Kerker, Ann E.

Murphy, Herta & Peck, Charles. Effective Business Communication. 2nd ed. Kane, William J., ed. (Illus.). 1976. pap. text ed. 15.95 o.p. (ISBN 0-07-044061-1, C). ans. to test questions 4.95 o.p. (ISBN 0-07-044067-0). McGraw.

Murphy, Howard A. & Stringham, E. J. Creative Harmony & Musicianship: An Introduction to the Structure of Music. 1951. pap. 16.95 (ISBN 0-13-189704-7). P-H.

Murphy, Howard A., et al. Music for Study: A Sourcebook of Excerpts. 2nd ed. 192p. 1973. pap. text ed. 13.95 (ISBN 0-13-607515-0). P-H.

Murphy, J. Carter. International Monetary System: Beyond the First Stage of Reform. 1979. pap. 7.25 (ISBN 0-8447-3362-8). Am Enterprise.

Murphy, J. L., jt. auth. see Harnett, D. L.

Murphy, James B., jt. auth. see Armstrong, Barry L.

Murphy, James E. & Murphy, Sharon M. Let My People Know: American Indian Journalism, 1828-1978. LC 80-5941. 300p. 1981. 14.95 (ISBN 0-8061-1623-4). U of Okla Pr.

Murphy, James F. Concepts of Leisure. 2nd ed. (Illus.). 192p. 1981. text ed. 13.95 (ISBN 0-13-166512-X). P-H.

Murphy, James F., Jr. The Mill. 320p. 1981. pap. 2.95 (ISBN 0-380-77198-5). Avon.

Murphy, James J. Medieval Eloquence: Studies in the Theory & Practice of Medieval Rhetoric. 1978. 22.75x (ISBN 0-520-03345-0). U of Cal Pr.

--Renaissance Rhetoric: A Short Title Catalogue. LC 80-8501. 400p. 1981. lib. bdg. 50.00 (ISBN 0-8240-9487-5). Garland Pub.

--Rhetoric in the Middle Ages: A History of Rhetorical Theory from Saint Augustine to the Renaissance. 1981. pap. 7.95x (ISBN 0-520-04406-1, CAMPUS 277). U of Cal Pr.

--Rhetoric in the Middle Ages, A.D. 400-1500, the Renaissance. 1974. 23.75x (ISBN 0-520-02439-7). U of Cal Pr.

Murphy, James J. & Ericson, Jon M. Debater's Guide. LC 61-17897. (Orig.). 1961. pap. 3.95 (ISBN 0-685-07188-X). Bobbs.

Murphy, James J., ed. Three Medieval Rhetorical Arts. LC 72-132416. 1971. 18.75x (ISBN 0-520-01820-6). U of Cal Pr.

Murphy, James K. Will N. Harben. (United States Authors Ser.: No. 330). 1979. lib. bdg. 13.50 (ISBN 0-8057-7245-6). Twayne.

Murphy, James L. An Archeological History of the Hocking Valley. LC 73-92906. (Illus.). xi, 360p. 1975. 20.00 (ISBN 0-8214-0151-3). Ohio U Pr.

Murphy, Jeffrie G. The Philosophy of Law. (Philosophy & Society Ser.). 1981. 18.50x (ISBN 0-8476-6277-2); pap. 9.95x (ISBN 0-8476-6278-0). Rowman. Postponed.

--Punishment & Rehabilitation. 1973. pap. 7.95x (ISBN 0-534-00335-4). Wadsworth Pub.

Murphy, John. The El Greco Puzzle. 288p. 1976. pap. 1.50 o.p. (ISBN 0-345-25053-2). Ballantine.

--Irish Shop Prints. (Illus.). 72p. 1981. pap. cancelled (ISBN 0-312-43623-8). St Martin.

Murphy, John A. The Homeowner's Energy Guide: How to Beat the Heating Game. LC 77-106. (Illus.). 1977. 9.95 o.s.i. (ISBN 0-690-01486-4, TYC-T); pap. 6.95 o.s.i. (ISBN 0-690-01487-2). T Y Crowell.

Murphy, John F. The Pinnacle: The Contemporary American Presidency. LC 74-3164. 1974. pap. text ed. 2.95 o.p. (ISBN 0-397-47312-5). Lippincott.

Murphy, John F., jt. ed. see Evans, Alona E.

Murphy, John S. Basics of Digital Computers, 3 Vols. rev. 2nd ed. (Illus.). (gr. 10-12). 1970. Set. pap. 15.95x o.p. (ISBN 0-8104-0737-X). Vol. 1. pap. 5.35 (ISBN 0-8104-0738-8); Vol. 2. pap. 6.45 o.p. (ISBN 0-8104-0739-6); Vol. 3. pap. 6.45 (ISBN 0-8104-0740-X); transparencies 255.30 (ISBN 0-685-03720-7); exam set, vol. 1 0.40 (ISBN 0-8104-0742-6); exam set vol. 2 0.40 (ISBN 0-8104-0743-4); exam set vol. 3 0.40 (ISBN 0-8104-0744-2). Hayden.

Murphy, Joseph. Miracle Power for Infinite Riches. 1972. 8.95 (ISBN 0-13-585638-8, Parker); pap. 3.45. P-H.

Murphy, Judith & Florio, Carol. Never Too Old to Teach. 116p. 1978. pap. 5.00 (ISBN 0-89192-243-1). Interbk Inc.

Murphy, Keith. Battle of the Alamo. LC 78-26292. (Raintree Great Adventures). (Illus.). (gr. 3-6). 1979. PLB 8.95 (ISBN 0-8393-0154-5). Raintree Child.

Murphy, Kenneth H., jt. auth. see Feinstein, Irwin K.

Murphy, Lawrence & Murphy, Bernadette. Field Guide to New Mexico Birds. Ratkevich, Ronald P., ed. (Illus.). 1979. pap. 3.95 (ISBN 0-932680-02-X). Dinograph SW.

Murphy, Leonard J. History of Urology. (Illus.). 548p. 1972. 44.75 (ISBN 0-398-02366-2). C C Thomas.

Murphy, Louise. My Garden: A Journal for Gardening Around the Year. LC 79-29650. (Illus.). (gr. 1-7). 1980. 8.95 (ISBN 0-684-16486-8). Scribner.

Murphy, M. A. Aptian & Albian Tetragonitidae (Ammonoidea) from Northern California. (U. C. Publ. in Geological Sciences: Vol. 70). 1967. pap. 5.50x (ISBN 0-520-09173-6). U of Cal Pr.

--The Aptian Cenomanian Members of the Ammonite Genus Tetragonites. (U. C. Publ. in Geological Sciences: Vol. 69). 1967. pap. 7.00x (ISBN 0-520-09172-8). U of Cal Pr.

Murphy, M. A., jt. auth. see Berry, W. B.

Murphy, M. A., jt. auth. see Klapper, Gilbert.

Murphy, M. J., Jr., ed. In Vitro Aspects of Erythropoiesis. LC 78-16104. (Illus.). 1978. 37.30 (ISBN 0-387-90320-8). Springer-Verlag.

Murphy, Margaret. Meat Makes the Meal. (Berkley-Dorison House Bks). (Illus.). (YA) 1978. 7.95 o.p. (ISBN 0-916752-11-9, Dist. by Putnam). Berkley Pub.

Murphy, Margaret D. The Faberware Convection Turbo-Oven Cookbook. Kostick, Marilyn, ed. LC 80-68017. (Illus.). 144p. 1980. 8.95 (ISBN 0-916752-44-5). Dorison Hse.

--The Farberware Convection Turbo Oven Cookbook. 1981. 8.95 (ISBN 0-916752-44-5). Green Hill.

--Freezer Cookery. 7.95 (ISBN 0-916752-02-X). Green Hill.

--Meat Makes the Meal. 7.95 (ISBN 0-916752-11-9). Green Hill.

Murphy, Marion F., jt. auth. see Murphy, Raymond E.

Murphy, Mary A., jt. auth. see Brown, Marie.

Murphy, Mary A., jt. auth. see Brown, Marie S.

Murphy, Mary E. I'm Gonna Right a Book: Teaching for Successful Living & Learning. 1981. pap. write for info (ISBN 0-914562-06-1). Merriam Eddy.

Murphy, Michael A. Paleontology & Stratigraphy of the Lower Chickabally Mudstone (Berremain-Aptian) in the Ono Quadrangle, Northern California. (Publcations in Geological Sciences Ser.: Vol. 113). 1975. pap. 9.00x (ISBN 0-520-09536-7). U of Cal Pr.

Murphy, Michael C. How to Buy a Home While You Can Still Afford to. LC 79-91390. (Illus.). 160p. 1981. 12.95 (ISBN 0-8069-7154-1); lib. bdg. 9.89 (ISBN 0-8069-7155-X); pap. 6.95 (ISBN 0-8069-8912-2). Sterling.

--How to Buy a Home While You Can Still Afford One. LC 79-91390. (Illus.). 160p. 1981. 10.95 o.p. (ISBN 0-8069-7154-1); lib. bdg. 9.89 o.p. (ISBN 0-8069-7155-X); pap. 5.95 o.p. (ISBN 0-8069-8912-2). Sterling.

Murphy, Michael J., jt. auth. see Abels, Paul.

Murphy, Michael J., jt. ed. see Cresswell, Anthony M.

Murphy, Murtagh. Asia Pacific Stories. (Oxford Progressive English Readers Ser.). (Illus.). 1974. pap. text ed. 2.95x (ISBN 0-19-580718-9). Oxford U Pr.

Murphy, Nonie C. Mutual Arrangements. 1978. pap. 1.95 o.p. (ISBN 0-425-03864-5, Dist. by Putnam). Berkley Pub.

Murphy, P. Teaching for Employability. 1973. pap. 1.00 (ISBN 0-686-14994-7, 261-08414). Home Econ Educ.

--Writings by & About Georg Lukacs: A Bibliography. 1976. 1.00 (ISBN 0-89977-032-0). Am Inst Marxist.

Murphy, Patricia & Taylor-Gordon, Elaine. The Business-Woman's Guide to Thirty American Cities. 400p. 1981. 19.95 (ISBN 0-312-92072-5); pap. 9.95 (ISBN 0-312-92073-3). St Martin.

--Businesswoman's Guide to Thirty American Cities. 400p. 1980. 17.95 (ISBN 0-312-92072-5); pap. 9.95 (ISBN 0-312-92073-3). St Martin.

--The Businesswoman's Guide to Thirty American Cities: Vital Information for Women Who Travel in Their Work. 400p. 1981. 19.95 (ISBN 0-312-92072-5); pap. 9.95 (ISBN 0-312-92073-3). Congdon & Lattes.

Murphy, Paul J. Brezhnev: Soviet Politician. LC 80-15901. (Illus.). 371p. 1981. lib. bdg. 24.95x (ISBN 0-89950-002-1). McFarland & Co.

Murphy, Paul L. Constitution in Crisis Times, 1918-1969. LC 70-156570. (New American Nation Ser). (Illus.). 1972. 15.00x o.s.i. (ISBN 0-06-013118-7, HarpT). Har-Row.

Murphy, Paul R., tr. see Herbert, George.

Murphy, R. & Van Iersel, B., eds. Office & Ministry in the Church. LC 72-3946. (Concilium Ser.: Vol. 80 Religion in the Seventies: Scripture). 156p. 1972. pap. 4.95 (ISBN 0-8164-2536-1, 73610). Crossroad NY.

Murphy, Raymond E. & Murphy, Marion F. Pennsylvania Landscapes: A Geography of the Commonwealth. LC 73-77560. (gr. 8-10). 1974. 7.95 (ISBN 0-931992-19-2); teachers guide 1.00 (ISBN 0-931992-20-6). Penns Valley.

Murphy, Rhoads, jt. auth. see Meisner, Maurice.

Murphy, Richard. The Battle of Aughrim & the God Who Eats Corn. 1968. 4.95 o.p. (ISBN 0-571-08724-8, Pub. by Faber & Faber). Merrimack Bk Serv.

--High Island: New & Selected Poems. LC 74-1838. 128p. 1975. pap. 2.95 o.s.i. (ISBN 0-06-013121-7, TD-205, HarpT). Har-Row.

--Sailing to an Island. 1968. pap. 4.95 (ISBN 0-571-08354-4, Pub. by Faber & Faber). Merrimack Bk Serv.

--Status & Conformity. LC 76-11334. (Human Behavior). (Illus.). (gr. 5 up). 1976. PLB 9.99 o.p. (ISBN 0-8094-1955-6, Pub. by Time-Life). Silver.

Murphy, Richard W. Status & Conformity. (Human Behavior Ser.). 9.95 (ISBN 0-8094-1954-8). Time-Life.

--World of Cezanne. (Library of Art). (Illus.). 1968. 15.95 (ISBN 0-8094-0243-2). Time-Life.

--World of Cezanne. LC 68-17688. (Library of Art Ser.). (Illus.). (gr. 6 up). 1968. 12.96 (ISBN 0-8094-0272-6, Pub. by Time-Life). Silver.

Murphy, Robert. The Dialectics of Social Life: Alarms & Escursions in Anthropological Theory. (A Morningside Book). 272p. 1980. pap. 6.00x (ISBN 0-231-05069-0). Columbia U Pr.

--Heritage Restored: America's Wildlife Refuges. (Illus.). (gr. 7 up). 1969. PLB 9.95 o.p. (ISBN 0-525-31765-1). Dutton.

Murphy, Robert, et al. Women of the Forest. (Illus.). 256p. 1974. 12.50x (ISBN 0-231-03682-5); pap. 5.00x (ISBN 0-231-03881-X). Columbia U Pr.

Murphy, Robert C., et al. Canton Island. (Museum Pictorial Ser.: No. 10). 1954. pap. 1.10 o.p. (ISBN 0-916278-39-5). Denver Mus Natl Hist.

Murphy, Robert F. Robert Lowie. LC 72-1969. (Leaders of Modern Anthropology Ser). (Illus.). 200p. 1972. 15.00x (ISBN 0-231-03375-3); pap. 6.00x (ISBN 0-231-03397-4). Columbia U Pr.

Murphy, Roland, ed. Theology, Exegesis, & Proclamation. LC 74-168652. (Concilium Ser.: Religion in the Seventies: Vol. 70). 1971. pap. 4.95 (ISBN 0-8164-2526-4). Crossroad NY.

Murphy, Roland, jt. ed. see Benoit, Pierre.

Murphy, Roland E. Wisdom Literature: Ruth, Esther, Job, Proverbs, Ecclesiastes, Canticles. (The Forms of the Old Testament Literature Ser.). (Orig.). 1981. pap. write for info. (ISBN 0-8028-1877-3). Eerdmans.

Murphy, Seamus. Stone Mad: A Sculptor's Life & Craft. (Illus.). 1976. pap. 7.50 (ISBN 0-7100-8542-7). Routledge & Kegan.

Murphy, Sharon M., jt. auth. see Murphy, James E.

Murphy, Shirley R. Caves of Fire & Ice. LC 80-12887. 180p. (gr. 6 up). 1980. 9.95 (ISBN 0-689-30784-5, Argo). Atheneum.

Murphy, Thomas, et al. Inside the Bureaucracy: The View from the Assistant Secretary's Desk. (Westview Special Studies in Public Policy & Public Systems Management). 1979. lib. bdg. 24.00x (ISBN 0-89158-154-5). Westview.

Murphy, Thomas P. Government Management Internships & Executive Development. (Illus.). 1973. 19.00 o.p. (ISBN 0-669-86363-7). Lexington Bks.

Murphy, Thomas P. & Rehfuss, John. Urban Politics in the Suburban Era. 1976. pap. 10.95x (ISBN 0-256-01848-0). Dorsey.

Murphy, Thomas P., ed. Urban Indicators: A Guide to Information Sources. LC 80-13333. (Urban Studies Information Guide Ser.: Vol. 10). 1980. 30.00 (ISBN 0-8103-1451-7). Gale.

--Urban Politics: A Guide to Information Sources. LC 78-54117. (Urban Studies Information Guide: Vol. 1). 1978. 30.00 (ISBN 0-8103-1395-2). Gale.

Murphy, Thomas P. & Kline, Robert D., eds. Urban Law: A Guide to Information Sources. (Urban Studies Information Guide Ser.: Vol. 11). 1980. 30.00 (ISBN 0-8103-1409-6). Gale.

Murphy, Thomas P., et al. Contemporary Public Administration: A Study in Emerging Realities. LC 80-83377. 517p. 1981. text ed. 14.95 (ISBN 0-87581-269-4). Peacock Pubs.

Murphy, Tom. Auction. (Orig.). 1980. pap. 2.95 (ISBN 0-451-09478-6, Sig). NAL.

Murphy, Vreni, jt. auth. see Baker, Joseph T.

Murphy, Walter F. The Vicar of Christ. 1980. pap. 2.95 (ISBN 0-345-29346-0). Ballantine.

Murphy, Walter F. & Pritchett, Herman C., eds. Courts, Judges & Politics: An Introduction to the Judicial Process. 3rd ed. LC 78-24033. 1979. text ed. 17.95x (ISBN 0-394-32117-0). Random.

--Courts, Judges & Politics: An Introduction to the Judicial Process. 2nd ed. 1974. 13.95 o.p. (ISBN 0-394-31809-9). Random.

Murphy, Warren. Assassins Play-off. (Destroyer Ser.: No. 20). 192p. (Orig.). 1975. pap. 1.50 (ISBN 0-523-40294-5). Pinnacle Bks.

--Brain Drain. (Destroyer Ser.: No. 22). 192p. (Orig.). 1976. pap. 1.75 (ISBN 0-523-40898-6). Pinnacle Bks.

--Chained Reaction. (Destroyer Ser.: No. 34). 1978. pap. 1.50 (ISBN 0-523-40156-6, Dist. by Independent News Co.). Pinnacle Bks.

--Child's Play. (Destroyer No. 23). 192p. 1976. pap. 1.95 (ISBN 0-523-41238-X). Pinnacle Bks.

--Created, the Destroyer. (Destroyer Ser.: No. 1). 1976. pap. 1.95 (ISBN 0-523-41216-9). Pinnacle Bks.

--Deadly Seeds. (Destroyer Ser.: No. 21). 192p. (Orig.). 1975. pap. 1.50 (ISBN 0-523-40295-3). Pinnacle Bks.

--Death Check. (Destroyer Ser.: No. 2). 192p. 1980. pap. 1.95 (ISBN 0-523-41217-7). Pinnacle Bks.

--Destroyer: Midnight Man, No. 43. 192p. (Orig.). 1981. pap. 1.95 (ISBN 0-523-40717-3). Pinnacle Bks.

--Destroyer, No. 10: Terror Squad. (Orig.). 1974. pap. 1.50 (ISBN 0-523-40284-8). Pinnacle Bks.

--The Destroyer, No. 12: Slave Safari. 1974. pap. 1.75 (ISBN 0-523-40888-9). Pinnacle Bks.

--The Destroyer, No. 13: Acid Rock. (Orig.). 1973. pap. 1.50 (ISBN 0-523-40287-2). Pinnacle Bks.

--The Destroyer, No. 14: Judgement Day. 192p. (Orig.). 1974. pap. 1.75 (ISBN 0-523-40890-0). Pinnacle Bks.

--Destroyer, No. 16: Oil Slick. 192p. (Orig.). 1974. pap. 1.50 (ISBN 0-523-40290-2). Pinnacle Bks.

--The Destroyer, No. 17: Last War Dance. 192p. (Orig.). 1974. pap. 1.50 (ISBN 0-523-40291-0). Pinnacle Bks.

--Destroyer, No. 18: Funny Money. 192p. (Orig.). 1975. pap. 1.75 (ISBN 0-523-40894-3). Pinnacle Bks.

--Destroyer, No. 19: Holy Terror. 192p. (Orig.). 1975. pap. 1.75 (ISBN 0-523-40895-1). Pinnacle Bks.

--Destroyer, No. 2: Death Check. (The Destroyer Ser.). 1977. pap. 1.95 (ISBN 0-523-41217-7). Pinnacle Bks.

--Destroyer, No. 27: The Last Temple. (The Destroyer Ser.). (Orig.). 1977. pap. 1.95 (ISBN 0-523-41242-8). Pinnacle Bks.

--Destroyer, No. 28: Ship of Death. (The Destroyer Ser.). 192p. 1977. pap. 1.95 (ISBN 0-523-41243-6). Pinnacle Bks.

--The Destroyer, No. 3: Chinese Puzzle. (Orig.). 1974. pap. 1.75 (ISBN 0-523-40879-X). Pinnacle Bks.

--Destroyer: No. 37, Bottom Line. 1979. pap. 1.95 (ISBN 0-523-41252-5). Pinnacle Bks.

--The Destroyer, No. 4: Mafia Fix. (Orig.). 1974. pap. 1.75 (ISBN 0-523-40880-3). Pinnacle Bks.

--The Destroyer, No. 5: Dr. Quake. (Orig.). 1974. pap. 1.75 (ISBN 0-523-40881-1). Pinnacle Bks.

--The Destroyer, No. 6: Death Therapy. (Orig.). 1974. pap. 1.75 (ISBN 0-523-40882-X). Pinnacle Bks.

--The Destroyer, No. 7: Union Bust. (Orig.). 1974. pap. 1.95 (ISBN 0-523-41222-3). Pinnacle Bks.

--The Destroyer No. 8: Summit Chase. (Orig.). 1974. pap. 1.75 (ISBN 0-523-40884-6). Pinnacle Bks.

--The Destroyer, No. 9: Murder's Shield. (Orig.). 1974. pap. 1.95 (ISBN 0-523-41224-X). Pinnacle Bks.

--Destroyer, Number Forty-Four: Balance of Power. 192p. (Orig.). 1981. pap. 1.95 (ISBN 0-523-40718-1). Pinnacle Bks.

--The Final Death, No. 29. (Destroyer Ser.). 1977. pap. 1.75 (ISBN 0-523-40885-4). Pinnacle Bks.

--The Head Men: Destroyer No. 31. (Destroyer Ser.). 1977. pap. 1.75 (ISBN 0-523-40905-2). Pinnacle Bks.

--In Enemy Hands: The Destroyer No. 26. (The Destroyer Ser.). 1977. pap. 1.75 (ISBN 0-523-40251-1). Pinnacle Bks.

--Killer Chromosomes. (The Destroyer Ser.: No. 32). 1978. pap. 1.75 (ISBN 0-523-40908-7). Pinnacle Bks.

--King's Curse. (Destroyer Ser.: No. 24). 1976. pap. 1.95 (ISBN 0-523-41239-8). Pinnacle Bks.

--Last Call. (Destroyer: No. 35). 1978. pap. 1.50 (ISBN 0-523-40157-4). Pinnacle Bks.

--The Missing Link. (Destroyer Ser.: No. 39). (Orig.). 1980. pap. 1.95 (ISBN 0-523-41254-1). Pinnacle Bks.

--Muggers Blood: Destroyer No. 30. LC 76-42891. (Destroyer Ser.). 1977. pap. 1.50 (ISBN 0-523-40110-8). Pinnacle Bks.

--Murder Ward. (The Destroyer Ser., No. 15). (Orig.). 1974. pap. 1.50 (ISBN 0-523-40289-9). Pinnacle Bks.

--Power Play. (Destroyer: No. 36). 1979. pap. 1.75 (ISBN 0-523-40912-5). Pinnacle Bks.

--Sweet Dreams. (Destroyer Ser.: No. 25). 1976. pap. 1.75 (ISBN 0-523-40901-X). Pinnacle Bks.

--Voodoo Die. (Destroyer Ser.: No. 33). (Orig.). 1978. pap. 1.75 (ISBN 0-523-40909-5). Pinnacle Bks.

Murphy, Warren, jt. auth. see Sapir, Richard.

Murphy, Wendy B., jt. auth. see Crockett, James U.

Murphy, William M. The Yeats Family & the Pollexfens of Sligo. (New Yeats Papers Ser.: Vol. 1). (Illus.). 88p. 1971. pap. text ed. 3.75x (ISBN 0-85105-196-0, Dolmen Pr). Humanities.

Murphy, William M., ed. see Yeats, J. B.

Murphy-O'Connor, Jerome. First Corinthians. (New Testament Message Ser.: Vol. 10). 172p. 1980. 9.95 (ISBN 0-89453-133-6); pap. 4.95 (ISBN 0-89453-198-0). M Glazier.

--The Holy Land: An Archaeological Guide from Earliest Times to 1700. (Illus.). 1352p. 1980. 19.95 (ISBN 0-19-217689-7); pap. 9.95 (ISBN 0-19-285088-1). Oxford U Pr.

Murr, Alfred. Export-Import Traffic Management & Forwarding. 6th ed. LC 79-18987. 1979. 22.50x (ISBN 0-87033-261-9). Cornell Maritime.

Murr, Lawrence E., ed. Solar Materials Science. LC 80-18959. 1980. 35.00 (ISBN 0-12-511160-6). Acad Pr.

Murra, John V., ed. see American Ethnological Society, 1974.

Murrah, Charles R. Don't Talk to Me About Death. LC 77-75935. 1977. text ed. 3.95 (ISBN 0-87863-147-X). Farnswth Pub.

Murrah, David J. C. C. Slaughter: Rancher, Banker, Baptist. (Illus.). 184p. 1981. 14.95 (ISBN 0-292-71067-4). U of Tex Pr.

Murray. Murray on Contracts. 877p. 1974. 25.00 (ISBN 0-672-81775-6, Bobbs-Merrill Law). Michie.

Murray, A. A. Anybody's Spring. LC 60-9717. 1960. 3.95 (ISBN 0-8149-0165-4). Vanguard.

Murray, A. D., ed. The Autobiography of John Ludlow, Christian Socialist. 1980. 30.00x (ISBN 0-7146-3085-3, F Cass Co). Biblio Dist.

Murray, A. R. An Introduction to Political Philosophy. 1968. Repr. of 1953 ed. 18.50 (ISBN 0-7100-1873-8). Routledge & Kegan.

Murray, Alexander. Reason & Society. 1978. 49.50x (ISBN 0-19-822540-7). Oxford U Pr.

Murray, Andrew. Absolute Surrender. pap. 1.50 (ISBN 0-8024-0560-6). Moody.

--Absolute Surrender. 128p. 1981. pap. 2.50 (ISBN 0-88368-093-9). Whitaker Hse.

--Believer's Daily Renewal. 144p. 1981. pap. 2.95 (ISBN 0-87123-147-6, 210147). Bethany Fell.

--The Blood of the Cross. 128p. 1981. pap. 2.50 (ISBN 0-88368-103-X). Whitaker Hse.

--Confession & Forgiveness. pap. 2.50 (ISBN 0-310-29732-X). Zondervan.

--Daily Secrets of Christian Living. LC 77-17187. 1978. pap. 4.95 (ISBN 0-87123-500-5, 210500). Bethany Fell.

--Day by Day. 1969. pap. 2.25 (ISBN 0-87123-092-5, 200092). Bethany Fell.

--Holy in Christ. 1969. pap. 3.95 (ISBN 0-87123-216-2, 210216). Bethany Fell.

--How to Raise Your Children for Christ. LC 75-29344. 1975. pap. 3.95 (ISBN 0-87123-224-3, 210224). Bethany Fell.

--Jesus Christ: Prophet-Priest. 64p. 1967. pap. 1.75 (ISBN 0-87123-271-5, 200271). Bethany Fell.

--Like Christ. 240p. 1981. pap. 2.50 (ISBN 0-88368-099-8). Whitaker Hse.

--Like Christ. 240p. 1974. pap. 2.25 (ISBN 0-87123-337-1, 200337). Bethany Fell.

--The Master's Indwelling. LC 76-23363. 1977. pap. 2.25 (ISBN 0-87123-355-X, 200355). Bethany Fell.

--Money: Christ's Perspective on the Use & Abuse of Money. 1978. pap. 1.50 (ISBN 0-87123-382-7, 200382). Bethany Fell.

--New Life. rev. ed. LC 80-7531. 1965. pap. 2.95 (ISBN 0-87123-395-9, 200395). Bethany Fell.

--The Prayer Life. 160p. 1981. pap. 2.50 (ISBN 0-88368-102-1). Whitaker Hse.

--Prayer Life. pap. 1.95 (ISBN 0-8024-6806-3). Moody.

--School of Obedience. pap. 1.50 (ISBN 0-8024-7627-9). Moody.

--The Secret of Believing Prayer. 96p. 1980. pap. 2.50 (ISBN 0-87123-528-5, 210528). Bethany Fell.

--The Spirit of Christ. 2nd ed. LC 79-51335. 1979. pap. 3.50 (ISBN 0-87123-495-5, 200495). Bethany Fell.

--Thy Will Be Done. (Summit Bks). 200p. 1981. pap. 3.45 (ISBN 0-8010-6109-1). Baker Bk.

--True Vine. pap. 1.50 (ISBN 0-8024-8798-X). Moody.

--Waiting on God. 160p. 1981. pap. 2.50 (ISBN 0-88368-101-3). Whitaker Hse.

--With Christ in the School of Prayer. (Spire Bk). pap. 1.95 (ISBN 0-8007-8046-9). Revell.

Murray, Andrew, ed. see Law, William.

Murray, Andrew, tr. La Palabra Irresistible. (Spanish Bks.). (Span.). 1979. 1.95 (ISBN 0-8297-0520-1). Life Pubs Intl.

Murray, Bruce, et al. Earthlike Planets: Surfaces of Mercury, Venus, Earth, Moon, Mars. LC 80-19608. (Illus.). 1981. text ed. 24.95x (ISBN 0-7167-1148-6); pap. text ed. 14.95x (ISBN 0-7167-1149-4). W H Freeman.

Murray, Bruce C. & Burgess, Eric. Flight to Mercury. LC 76-25017. (Illus.). 1976. 17.50 (ISBN 0-231-03996-4). Columbia U Pr.

Murray, Bruce C., jt. auth. see Davies, Merton.

Murray, Bruce K. The People's Budget Nineteen Hundred & Nine to Nineteen Hundred & Ten: Lloyd George & Liberal Politics. 360p. 1980. 49.95 (ISBN 0-19-822626-8). Oxford U Pr.

Murray, Charles A. A Behavioral Study of Rural Modernization: Social & Economic Change in Thai Villages. LC 77-7827. (Praeger Special Studies). 1977. 21.95 (ISBN 0-03-022856-5). Praeger.

--Travels in North America, Including a Summer with the Pawnees. 2nd ed. LC 68-54845. (American Scene Ser.). 878p. 1974. Repr. of 1839 ed. lib. bdg. 69.50 (ISBN 0-306-71021-8). Da Capo.

Murray, Charles A. & Cox, Louis A., Jr. Beyond Probation: Juvenile Corrections & the Chronic Delinquent. LC 79-17859. (Sage Library of Social Research: Vol. 94). (Illus.). 1979. 18.00x (ISBN 0-8039-1336-2); pap. 8.95x (ISBN 0-8039-1337-0). Sage.

Murray, Chris. Youth in Contemporary Society: Theoretical & Research Perspectives. (General Ser.). 1979. pap. text ed. 17.00x (ISBN 0-85633-170-8, NFER). Humanities.

--Youth Unemployment. (General Ser.). 1979. pap. text ed. 15.00x (ISBN 0-85633-172-4, NFER). Humanities.

Murray, Christopher, ed. St. Stephen's Green or the Generous Lovers. (Dolmen Texts Ser.: No. 6). (Illus.). 112p. 1980. text ed. 15.00x (ISBN 0-85105-367-X, Dolmen Pr). Humanities.

Murray, Colin. Families Divided: The Impact of Migrant Labour in Lesotho. (African Studies: No. 29). (Illus.). 236p. Date not set. price not set (ISBN 0-521-23501-4). Cambridge U Pr.

Murray, Colin, jt. auth. see Lye, William F.

Murray, D. A., ed. see International Symposium on Chironomidae, 7th, Dublin, August 1979.

Murray, D. D., jt. auth. see Burke, D. C.

Murray, D. J. Studies in Nigerian Administration. 342p. 1978. pap. text ed. 13.75x (ISBN 0-8419-6602-8). Holmes & Meier.

--Work of Administration in Nigeria: Case Studies. (Illus.). 1970. text ed. 6.75x (ISBN 0-09-099610-0, Hutchinson U Lib); pap. text ed. 3.25x (ISBN 0-09-099611-9, Hutchinson U Lib). Humanities.

Murray, David R. Odious Commerce: Britain, Spain & the Abolition of the Cuban Slave Trade. LC 79-52835. (Cambridge Latin American Studies: No. 37). 435p. Date not set. 44.50 (ISBN 0-521-22867-0). Cambridge U Pr.

Murray, Diane & Conte, William. Bones & Muscles of the Human Form. (Illus.). 1980. pap. 2.95 (ISBN 0-88284-107-6). Alfred Pub.

Murray, Donald M. Writer Teaches Writing. LC 68-6986. (Illus.). 1968. pap. text ed. 10.75 (ISBN 0-395-04989-X, 3-40075). HM.
Murray, E. C. Side-Lights on English Society: Sketches from Life, Social & Satirical. rev ed. LC 75-83371. (Illus.). xii, 436p. 1969. Repr. of 1885 ed. 20.00 (ISBN 0-8103-3285-X). Gale.
Murray, Edward. Fellini the Artist. LC 75-25423. (Illus.). 1976. 12.00 (ISBN 0-8044-2648-1). Ungar.
Murray, Elwood, et al. Speech: Science-Art. LC 79-77823. 1969. text ed. 11.50 (ISBN 0-672-60863-4). Bobbs.
Murray, Emily, jt. auth. see Murray, J. B.
Murray, Frances. Castaway. 208p. 1981. pap. 1.95 (ISBN 0-345-28684-7). Ballantine.
--Castaway. LC 78-12633. 1979. 8.95 o.p. (ISBN 0-684-16064-1, ScribT). Scribner.
--The Heroine's Sister. 208p. 1976. pap. 1.25 o.p. (ISBN 0-345-25004-4). Ballantine.
--Red Rowan Berry. 1978. pap. 1.95 o.p. (ISBN 0-345-25956-4). Ballantine.
Murray, Francis X. Energy: A National Issue. LC 76-52878. (Illus.). 1976. pap. text ed. 3.95 (ISBN 0-89206-001-8). CSI Studies.
Murray, Frank. Program Your Heart for Health. 368p. (Orig.). 1977. pap. 2.95 (ISBN 0-915962-20-9). Larchmont Bks.
Murray, Frank, jt. auth. see Adams, Ruth.
Murray, George B., jt. ed. see Fisher, Alden L.
Murray, Gilbert, tr. see Aeschylus.
Murray, Gilbert, tr. see Aristophanes.
Murray, Gilbert, tr. see Euripides.
Murray, Gilbert, tr. see Menander.
Murray, Gilbert, tr. see Sophocles.
Murray, Grace A. Personalities of the Eighteenth Century: (Samuel Foote, Christopher Smart, William Hazlitt) 230p. 1980. Repr. of 1927 ed. lib. bdg. 25.00 (ISBN 0-8495-3772-X). Arden Lib.
Murray, Henry. The Art of Painting & Drawing with Colored Crayons. (Illus.). Repr. of 1865 ed. deluxe ed. 27.45 (ISBN 0-930582-35-7). Gloucester Art.
Murray, Henry A. Endeavors in Psychology: Selections from the Personology of Henry A. Murray. Shneidman, Edwin S., ed. LC 80-7598. 656p. 1981. 30.00 (ISBN 0-06-014039-9, HarpT). Har-Row.
Murray, I. G. Victorian & Edwardian Middlesex. 1977. 22.50 (ISBN 0-7134-0181-8, Pub. by Batsford England). David & Charles.
Murray, I. MacKay, M.D. Human Anatomy Made Simple: A Comprehensive Course for Self-Study & Review. LC 68-22473. 1969. pap. 3.50 (ISBN 0-385-01116-4, Made). Doubleday.
Murray, Iain. The Invitation System. 1973. pap. 0.50 (ISBN 0-85151-171-6). Banner of Truth.
--John Knox. 1976. pap. 0.50. Banner of Truth.
--El Obstaculo Al Evangelismo. (Span.). Date not set. pap. 0.60 (ISBN 0-686-28950-1). Banner of Truth.
Murray, Iain H. The Forgotton Spurgeon. 1978. pap. 3.95 (ISBN 0-85151-156-2). Banner of Truth.
--The Puritan Hope. 1975. pap. 5.45 (ISBN 0-686-12534-7). Banner of Truth.
Murray, Iain H., ed. Diary of Kenneth Macrae. (Illus.). 535p. 1980. 16.95 (ISBN 0-85151-297-6). Banner of Truth.
Murray, Isobel M., ed. see Wilde, Oscar.
Murray, J. & Karpovick, P. Weight Training in Athletics. 1956. 8.95 (ISBN 0-13-947986-4). P-H.
Murray, J. A. An Introduction to a Christian Psycho-Therapy. 2nd ed. 291p. 1947. text ed. 4.95 (ISBN 0-567-02202-1). Attic Pr.
Murray, J. B. & Murray, Emily. And Say What He Is: The Life of a Special Child. LC 75-5810. 304p. 1975. 12.00x (ISBN 0-262-13115-3); pap. 4.95 (ISBN 0-262-63069-9). MIT Pr.
Murray, J. D. Asymptotic Analysis. Orig. Title: Introduction to Asymptotic Analysis. 160p. 1974. 17.95x (ISBN 0-19-853153-2). Oxford U Pr.
--Lectures on Nonlinear-Differential-Equation Models in Biology. (Illus.). 1978. 39.95x (ISBN 0-19-853350-0). Oxford U Pr.
Murray, Jack, et al. Poems from Prison. 1973. 6.25x (ISBN 0-7022-0875-2). U of Queensland Pr.
Murray, James. Continuous National Survey: A Compendium of Questionnaire Items, Articles 1 Through 12. (Report Ser: No. 125). 1974. (ISBN 0-932132-18-9). NORC.
Murray, James G. Henry Adams. (World Leaders Ser.: No. 31). 1974. lib. bdg. 10.95 (ISBN 0-8057-3651-4). Twayne.
--Henry David Thoreau. (World Leaders Ser). lib. bdg. 9.95 (ISBN 0-8057-3723-5). Twayne.
Murray, Jan. Dance Now. 1979. pap. 3.95 o.p. (ISBN 0-14-005307-7). Penguin.
Murray, Janet H. & Stark, Myra, eds. The Englishwoman's Review of Social & Industrial Questions, Vols. 13 & 14. 1979. lib. bdg. 44.00 ea. Garland Pub.
Murray, Janice L., ed. Canadian Cultural Nationalism: The Fourth Lester B. Pearson Conference on the Canada-United States Relationship. LC 77-15362. 1977. pap. 5.00x (ISBN 0-8147-5421-X). NYU Pr.
Murray, Jerry. Mo-Ped: The Wonder Vehicle. (Illus.). (YA) (gr. 7-9). 1978. pap. 1.25 (ISBN 0-671-29882-8). PB.
--Moped: The Wonder Vehicle. (gr. 7-9). 1978. pap. 1.25 (ISBN 0-671-29882-8). Archway.
Murray, Jim. Weight Lifting & Progressive Resistance Exercise. (Illus.). 1954. 11.50 (ISBN 0-8260-6560-0). Ronald Pr.
Murray, Joan. A CB Picture Dictionary. LC 80-1725. (Illus.). 64p. (gr. 5 up). 8.95a (ISBN 0-385-14782-1); PLB (ISBN 0-385-14783-X). Doubleday.
Murray, Johhn F., jt. auth. see Hinshaw, H. Corwin.
Murray, John. Christian Baptism. pap. 2.50 (ISBN 0-87552-343-9). Presby & Reformed.
--The Collected Writings of John Murray: Lectures in Systematic Theology, Vol. 2. 1978. 11.95 (ISBN 0-85151-242-9). Banner of Truth.
--The Collected Writings of John Murray: The Claims of Truth, Vol. 1. 1976. 18.95 (ISBN 0-85151-241-0). Banner of Truth.
--The Media Law Dictionary. LC 78-63257. 1978. pap. text ed. 7.50 (ISBN 0-8191-0616-X). U Pr of Amer.
--Murray's Handbook for Travellers in Switzerland. (Victorian Library). 1970. Repr. of 1838 ed. text ed. 10.00x (ISBN 0-391-00111-6, Leicester). Humanities.
Murray, John J. Amsterdam in the Age of Rembrandt. (Centers of Civilization Ser.: No. 21). 5.95x o.p. (ISBN 0-8061-0746-4). U of Okla Pr.
Murray, John L. Infaquatics: A Parents Guide to Swimmimg. LC 80-82072. (Illus.). 248p. (Orig.). 1980. pap. text ed. 6.95 (ISBN 0-918438-59-4). Leisure Pr.
--Infaquatics: Teaching Kids to Swim. (Illus.). 224p. 1981. Repr. of 1980 ed. pap. 6.95 (ISBN 0-688-00476-8, Quill). Morrow.
Murray, John P. Television & Youth: Twenty-Five Years of Research & Controversy. 278p. (Orig.). 1980. pap. text ed. 10.00 (ISBN 0-938510-00-2, 010-TV). Boys Town Ctr.
Murray, John V. & Van Der Embse, Thomas J. Organizational Behavior: Incidents & Analysis. LC 72-95928. 1973. pap. text ed. 13.95 (ISBN 0-675-08963-8). Merrill.
Murray, Jon G. An Atheist's Bertrand Russell. 1980. pap. 3.29 (ISBN 0-911826-14-9). Am Atheist.
--Essays of an Atheist Activist. 1980. pap. 3.29. Am Atheist.
Murray, Joseph A. Police Officer. 8th ed. LC 80-24919. 352p. 1981. lib. bdg. 10.00 (ISBN 0-668-05128-0); pap. 6.00 (ISBN 0-668-05130-2). Arco.
Murray, Joseph N. Developing Assessment Programs for the Multi-Handicapped Child. (Illus.). 304p. 1980. 17.50 (ISBN 0-398-04052-4); pap. 11.75 (ISBN 0-398-04076-1). C C Thomas.
Murray, K. M. Caught in the Web of Words: James A. H. Murray & the "Oxford English Dictionary". LC 77-76309. (Illus.). 1977. 20.00x (ISBN 0-300-02131-3). Yale U Pr.
Murray, Katharine, jt. auth. see Bourdeaux, Michael.
Murray, Ken. Golden Days of San Simeon. LC 73-130962. 1971. 14.95 (ISBN 0-385-04632-4). Doubleday.
Murray, Linda. The Dark Fire. LC 76-58848. 1977. 11.95 o.p. (ISBN 0-688-03198-6). Morrow.
--The High Renaissance & Mannerism: Italy, the North, & Spain, 1500-1600. (World of Art Ser.). (Illus.). 1978. pap. text ed. 9.95 (ISBN 0-19-519990-1). Oxford U Pr.
Murray, Linda, jt. auth. see Murray, Peter.
Murray, M. Fundamentals of Nursing. 1976. text ed. 20.95x (ISBN 0-13-341354-3); student wkbk. study guide 6.95 (ISBN 0-13-341370-5). P-H.
Murray, Malinda. Fundamentals of Nursing. 2nd ed. (Illus.). 1980. text ed. 20.95 (ISBN 0-13-341313-6); pap. text ed. 8.95 study guide (ISBN 0-13-341347-0). P-H.
Murray, Margaret. God of the Witches. (Illus.). 1970. pap. 4.95 (ISBN 0-19-501270-4, GB). Oxford U Pr.
Murray, Margaret, tr see Haselbach, Barbara.
Murray, Marian. Circus: From Rome to Ringling. LC 74-171420. (Illus.). 354p. 1956. Repr. of 1956 ed. lib. bdg. 29.75x (ISBN 0-8371-6259-9, MUCI). Greenwood.
--Hunting for Fossils. 1967. 11.95 (ISBN 0-02-588150-7). Macmillan.
--Plant Wizard: The Life of Lue Gim Gong. LC 77-119131. (Illus.). (gr. 4 up). 1970. 3.95g o.s.i. (ISBN 0-02-767750-8, CCPr). Macmillan.
Murray, Martin J. The Development of Capitalism in Colonial Indochina. 1981. 29.50x (ISBN 0-520-04000-7). U of Cal Pr.
Murray, Melba W. Engineered Report Writing. LC 68-26960. 138p. 1969. 12.95 (ISBN 0-87814-006-9). Pennwell Pub.
Murray, Meredith. Ways to High Consciousness. 136p. 1978. pap. 2.50 (ISBN 0-8334-1706-1). Multimedia.
Murray, Merrill G., jt. auth. see Haber, William.
Murray, Michele. The Crystal Nights. LC 72-93807. 320p. (gr. 6 up). 1973. 7.95 (ISBN 0-395-28920-3, Clarion). HM.
--Nellie Cameron. LC 75-133060. (gr. 3-6). 1971. 6.95 (ISBN 0-395-28867-3, Clarion). HM.
Murray, Mimi. Women's Gymnastics: Coach, Participant, Spectator. 1979. text ed. 18.95x (ISBN 0-205-06162-1, 6261620). Allyn.
Murray, Patrick. Literary Criticism: A Glossary of Major Terms. 208p. 1978. pap. text ed. 7.95 (ISBN 0-582-35247-9). Longman.
Murray, Patrick, tr. see Hobusch, Erich.
Murray, Patrick, tr. see Loschburg, Winfried.
Murray, Peter. The Dulwich Picture Gallery: A Catalogue. (Illus.). 312p. 1980. 85.00x (ISBN 0-85667-071-5, Pub. by Sotheby Parke Bernet England). Biblio Dist.
--Renaissance Architeture. LC 70-149850. (History of World Architecture). (Illus.). 1971. 45.00 (ISBN 0-8109-1000-4). Abrams.
Murray, Peter & Murray, Linda. The Art of the Renaissance. (World of Art Ser.). (Illus.). 1963. pap. 9.95 (ISBN 0-19-519928-6). Oxford U Pr.
Murray, Peter R. Principles of Organic Chemistry. 1977. pap. text ed. 12.95x (ISBN 0-435-65643-0). Heinemann Ed.
Murray, Philip. Poems After Martial. LC 67-24109. 1967. 10.00x (ISBN 0-8195-3083-2, Pub. by Wesleyan U Pr). Columbia U Pr.
Murray, R. Symbols of Church & Kingdom. LC 74-80363. 430p. 1975. 49.95 (ISBN 0-521-20553-0). Cambridge U Pr.
--Trade Preferences for Developing Countries. LC 76-58546. (Problems of Economic Integration Ser.). 1977. 22.95 (ISBN 0-470-99080-5). Halsted Pr.
Murray, R., Jr., jt. auth. see Grant, H.
Murray, Raymond L. Nuclear Energy. LC 74-8685. 296p. 1975. text ed. 24.00 o.p. (ISBN 0-08-018164-3); pap. text ed. 14.25 o.p. (ISBN 0-08-018163-5). Pergamon.
Murray, Robb. Batter My Heart. (Orion Ser.). 192p. 1980. pap. write for info. (ISBN 0-8127-0301-4). Southern Pub.
Murray, Robert F., Jr., et al, eds. The Genetic, Metabolic & Developmental Aspects of Mental Retardation. (Illus.). 366p. 1972. 23.50 (ISBN 0-398-02531-2). C C Thomas.
Murray, Ronald C. Provincial Mineral Policies: Saskatchewan 1944-75. 65p. (Orig.). 1978. pap. text ed. 3.50x (ISBN 0-686-63139-0, Pub. by Ctr Resource Stud Canada). Renouf.
Murray, Rosemary & Kijek, Jean C. Current Perspectives in Rehabilitation Nursing. (Illus.). 1979. text ed. 12.50 (ISBN 0-8016-3605-1); pap. text ed. 10.50 (ISBN 0-8016-3606-X). Mosby.
Murray, Ruth B. & Zentner, Judith P. Nursing Assessment & Health Promotion Through the Life Span. 2nd ed. (Illus.). 1979. ref. 15.95 (ISBN 0-13-627588-5); pap. 12.95 (ISBN 0-13-627596-6). P-H.
--Nursing Concepts for Health Promotion. 2nd ed. (Illus.). 1979. ref. 15.95 (ISBN 0-13-627638-5); pap. text ed. 12.95 (ISBN 0-13-627620-2). P-H.
Murray, Sheila. Potters in Ireland. Beesley, Alan, ed. 80p. 1974. pap. text ed. 3.95 (ISBN 0-8277-2529-9). British Bk Ctr.
Murray, Sonja J. Seashell Collector's Handbook & Identifier. LC 73-93592. (Illus.). 240p. 1975. 8.95 o.p. (ISBN 0-8069-3064-0); lib. bdg. 8.29 o.p. (ISBN 0-8069-3065-9). Sterling.
Murray, Spence. Complete Book of Pickup and Vans. 2nd ed. LC 76-1545. (Petersen's Enthusiasts Ser.). (Illus.). 176p. 1976. pap. 3.95 o.p. (ISBN 0-8227-0667-9). Petersen Pub.
Murray, Spence, ed. Basic Carburetion & Fuel Systems. 6th, rev. ed. LC 68-6315. (Petersen's Basic Repair & Maintenance Manuals Ser.). (Illus.). (gr. 9-12). 1977. pap. 6.95 (ISBN 0-8227-5013-9). Petersen Pub.
--Basic Engine Hot Rodding. 2nd ed. LC 75-181330. (Petersen's Enthusiasts Ser.). (Illus.). 1975. pap. 4.95 o.p. (ISBN 0-8227-0097-2). Petersen Pub.
--Creative Customizing. LC 78-50827. (Illus.). 176p. (Orig.). 1978. pap. 6.95 (ISBN 0-8227-5026-0). Petersen Pub.
--Ford Tune-Up & Repair. LC 78-65687. (Tune-up & Repair Ser.). (gr. 9-12). 1979. pap. 4.95 (ISBN 0-8227-5041-4). Petersen Pub.
Murray, Spencer, ed. Basic Chassis, Suspension & Brakes. 4th rev. ed. LC 74-78893. (Petersen's Basic Repair & Maintenance Manuals Ser.). 1978. pap. 6.95 (ISBN 0-8227-5021-X). Petersen Pub.
Murray, T. J., jt. auth. see Pryse-Phillips, William.
Murray, Thomas C. & Barnes, Valerie. The Seven Wonders of New Jersey--& Then Some. (Illus.). 128p. 1980. 7.95 o.p. (ISBN 0-89490-016-1). Enslow Pubs.
--The Seven Wonders of New Jersey--& Then Some. LC 80-16424. (Illus.). 128p. 1981. pap. 6.95 (ISBN 0-89490-017-X). Enslow Pubs.
Murray, Thomas J., jt. auth. see Bryson, Reid A.
Murray, Tom. Sport's Magazine All-Time All-Stars. 1977. pap. 2.50 (ISBN 0-451-09169-8, E9169, Sig). NAL.
Murray, W. H. Beautiful Scotland. 1978. pap. 5.95 (ISBN 0-7134-3217-9, Pub. by Batsford England). David & Charles.
Murray, W. J., jt. ed. see Gilchrist, W.
Murray, William. Horse Fever. LC 76-12532. 1976. 7.95 (ISBN 0-396-07336-0). Dodd.
Murray, William D. & Rigney, Francis J. Paperfolding for Beginners. Orig. Title: Introduction to Paperfolding. (Illus.). (gr. 1 up). pap. 1.75 (ISBN 0-486-20713-7). Dover.
Murray, William G., ed. see Lee, Warren F., et al.
Murray, William M., Jr. Thomas W. Martin: A Biography. LC 77-85483. (Illus.). 276p. 1978. 6.50 (ISBN 0-686-27918-2). S Res Inst.
Murray-Aynsley, Harriet G. Symbolism of the East & West. LC 77-141748. (Illus.). 1971. Repr. of 1900 ed. 20.00 (ISBN 0-8103-3395-3). Gale.
Murray-Brown, Jeremy. Kenyatta. 1973. 12.50 o.p. (ISBN 0-525-13855-2). Dutton.
Murrell, John. Athletics, Sports & Games. (Greek & Roman Topics Ser.). 1975. pap. text ed. 3.95x (ISBN 0-04-930006-7). Allen Unwin.
Murrell, Sandra & Olsen, Paul. Mathematics for the Health Sciences. (Developmental & Precalculus Math Ser.). (Illus.). 432p. 1981. pap. text ed. 13.95 (ISBN 0-201-04647-4). A-W.
Murrell, Stanley. Community Psychology & Social Systems. LC 73-8504. 228p. 1973. text ed. 14.95 (ISBN 0-87705-108-9). Human Sci Pr.
Murrells, Joseph. The Book of Golden Discs. (Illus.). 1979. 21.95 o.p. (ISBN 0-214-20480-4, ADON 8086-8, Dist by Arco); pap. 11.95 o.p. (ISBN 0-214-20512-6, ADON 8081-7). Barrie & Jenkins.
Murrill, Paul W. & Smith, Cecil L. Fortran Four Programming for Engineers & Scientists. 2nd ed. LC 73-1689. (Illus.). 322p. 1973. pap. text ed. 14.95 scp (ISBN 0-7002-2419-X, HarpC); solution manual avail. (ISBN 0-685-28248-1). Har-Row.
Murrison, Wayne G. Buy or Sell Your Own Home, Lot, or Farm. Orig. Title: Homeowner Sell Your House Yourself. (Illus.). 92p. 1980. pap. text ed. 20.00. Murrison Co.
Murry, John, jt. ed. see Murry, Thomas.
Murry, John M. The Problem of Style. LC 80-21463. x, 133p. 1980. Repr. of 1960 ed. lib. bdg. 19.50x (ISBN 0-313-22523-0, MUPR). Greenwood.
--The Scientific Diet Management for Business Executives: How to Eat All You Want & Still Lose One Pound a Day. (The International Council for Excellence in Management Library). (Illus.). 99p. 1980. plastic spiral bdg. 29.95 (ISBN 0-89266-246-8). Am Classical Coll Pr.
Murry, John M., ed. see Mansfield, Katherine.
Murry, Thomas & Murry, John, eds. Infant Communication: Cry & Early Speech. (Illus.). 342p. 1980. text ed. 28.95 (ISBN 0-933014-62-7). College-Hill.
Murthy, S. N., ed. see Project Squid Workshop on Turbulence in Internal Flows: Turbomachinery & Other Applications, Airlie House, Warrenton, Va., June 14-15, 1976.
Murty, K. S. Revelation & Reason in Advaita Vedanta. 1974. Repr. 9.95 (ISBN 0-8426-0662-9). Orient Bk Dist.
Murty, K. Satchidananda. Nagarjuna. (National Biography Ser.). 1979. pap. 2.00 o.p. (ISBN 0-89744-199-0). Auromere.
Murty, Katta G. Linear & Combinatorial Programming. LC 76-7047. 560p. 1976. 30.95 (ISBN 0-471-57370-1). Wiley.
Murtz, Harold A., ed. Guns Illustrated. (Illus.). 288p. 1979. pap. 7.95 (ISBN 0-695-81310-2). Follett.
--Guns Illustrated 1981. 13th ed. 288p. 1980. pap. 8.95 (ISBN 0-910676-12-7). DBI.
Musa, Mark, ed. see Boccaccio, Giovanni.
Musa, Mark, tr. see Dante Alighieri.
Musashi, Miyamoto. A Book of Five Rings: A Guide to Strategy. Harris, Victor, tr. from Japanese. LC 73-83986. (Illus.). 96p. 1974. 10.95 (ISBN 0-87951-018-8). Overlook Pr.
Muscatine, Charles. Chaucer & the French Tradition: A Study in Style & Meaning. 1957. 15.75x (ISBN 0-520-01434-0); pap. 4.95 (ISBN 0-520-00908-8, CAL104). U of Cal Pr.
Muscatine, Charles C. Education at Berkeley: Report of the Select Committee on Education. rev. ed. 1968. 15.00x o.p. (ISBN 0-520-00909-6); pap. 1.95 o.p. (ISBN 0-520-00912-6, CAL149). U of Cal Pr.

Muschalek, Christian, jt. auth. see Kirchenmann, Jorg C.

Muschalek, Georg. Power & Impotence of Certitude. 150p. (Orig.). 1981. pap. text ed. price not set (ISBN 0-935780-01-7). Herbert Pubs.

Muschenheim, William. Why Architecture? 13.50 (ISBN 0-89720-033-0). Green Hill.

Muschlitz, Beverly, jt. auth. see Michener, Dorothy.

Musciano, Walter. Building & Flying Model Airplanes. LC 71-146441. (Funk & W Bk.). (Illus.). 192p. 1974. pap. 2.95 o.p. (ISBN 0-308-10136-7, F102, TYC-T). T Y Crowell.

Muse, Bill & White, Dan. We Can Teach You to Play Soccer. 160p. 1976. pap. 3.95 o.p. (ISBN 0-8015-6911-7). Dutton.

Muse, Charles B. The Catholic Sex Manual for Teenagers. (Illus.). 1980. 21.50 (ISBN 0-89266-217-4). Am Classical Coll Pr.

Muse, Ivan D. & Squires, David A. Activities & Games for Successful Teaching. (Illus.). 1977. pap. 14.95x o.p. (ISBN 0-8425-0635-7). Brigham.

Muse, Ken. Photo One: Basic Photo Text. (Illus.). 240p. 1973. pap. text ed. 11.95 (ISBN 0-13-665331-6). P-H.

Muser, Curt, compiled by. Facts & Artifacts of Ancient Middle America: A Glossary of Terms & Words Used in the Archaeology & Art History of Pre-Columbian Mexico & Central America. 1978. 16.95 o.p. (ISBN 0-525-10215-9); pap. 9.95 o.p. (ISBN 0-525-47489-7). Dutton.

Museum of Concord Antiquarian Society. An Olde Concorde Christmas. (Illus.). 104p. 1980. 12.95 (ISBN 0-312-58421-0). St Martin.

Museum of Fine Arts, Boston, ed. Art & Commerce: American Prints of the Nineteenth Century. LC 78-13848. (Illus.). 1978. 15.00 (ISBN 0-87846-130-2). Mus Fine Arts Boston.

Museum of Fine Arts, Boston, Department of Fine Arts. A. C. Goodwin. (Illus.). 1974. pap. 2.00 o.p. (ISBN 0-87846-084-5). Mus Fine Arts Boston.

Museum of International Folk Art. Spanish Textile Tradition of New Mexico & Colorado. (Ser. in Southwestern Culture). 1979. 25.95 o.p. (ISBN 0-89013-112-0); pap. 14.95 (ISBN 0-89013-113-9). Museum Nm Pr.

Museum Staff. Los Angeles County Museum of Art Report, July 1, 1977-June 30, 1978. D'Andrea, Jeanne & Hirsch, Alison, eds. LC 80-641019. (Illus.). 84p. (Orig.). 1980. pap. 2.00 (ISBN 0-87587-093-7). La Co Art Mus.

Musgrave, Beatrice & Menell, Zoe, eds. Change & Choice: Women & Middle Age. 186p. 1980. text ed. 18.50x (ISBN 0-7206-0539-3). Humanities.

Musgrave, Clifford. Regency Furniture, Eighteen Hundred to Eighteen Thirty. 2nd ed. 1970. 26.00 o.p. (ISBN 0-571-04694-0, Pub. by Faber & Faber). Merrimack Bk Serv.

Musgrave, Florence. Like a Red, Red Rose. (Illus.). (gr. 6-9). 1958. 4.95 o.p. (ISBN 0-8038-4236-8). Hastings.

Musgrave, Frank W., ed. Health Economics & Health Care: Irreconcilable Gap? LC 78-59166. 1978. pap. text ed. 9.25 (ISBN 0-8191-0546-5). U Pr of Amer.

Musgrave, G. Ray. Individualized Instruction: Teaching Strategies Focusing on the Learner. 189p. 1975. text ed. 11.95 o.p. (ISBN 0-205-04709-2); pap. 7.95x o.p. (ISBN 0-205-04779-3, 2247798). Allyn.

Musgrave, Gerald L., jt. auth. see Ramsey, James B.

Musgrave, Gerald L., ed. The Galbraith Viewpoint in Perspective: Critical Commentary on "The Age of Uncertainty" Television Series. LC 77-92085. (Hoover Special Project Ser). 1978. pap. 3.00 (ISBN 0-8179-4212-2). Hoover Inst Pr.

Musgrave, J. H., jt. auth. see Frankcom, G.

Musgrave, Peter. The Economic Structure. (Aspects of Modern Sociology Ser). 1969. text ed. 4.00x (ISBN 0-582-48804-4); pap. text ed. 2.50x (ISBN 0-582-48805-2). Humanities.

Musgrave, Richard A. Fiscal Reform in Bolivia: Final Report of the Bolivian Mission on Tax Reform. LC 80-14943. (Illus.). 1981. pap. text ed. 15.00 (ISBN 0-915506-22-X). Harvard Law Intl Tax.

--The Theory of Public Finance: A Study in Public Economy. 646p. 1981. Repr. of 1959 ed. lib. bdg. 32.50 (ISBN 0-89874-110-6). Krieger.

Musgraves, Don & Balsiger, Dave. One More Time. LC 74-1395. 224p. 1974. pap. 2.45 (ISBN 0-87123-419-X, 210419). Bethany Fell.

Musgrove, Bill & Blair, Gerry. Fur Trapping. (Illus.). 1979. 11.95 (ISBN 0-87691-284-6). Winchester Pr.

Musgrove, Frank. School & the Social Order. LC 79-40738. 1980. 34.00 (ISBN 0-471-27651-0, Pub. by Wiley-Interscience); pap. 15.00 (ISBN 0-471-27653-7, Pub. by Wiley-Interscience). Wiley.

Musgrove, Frank & Taylor, Philip H. Society & the Teacher's Role. 1969. text ed. 4.00x (ISBN 0-7100-6447-0). Humanities.

Musgrove, Philip. Consumer Behavior in Latin America: Income & Spending of Families in Ten Andean Cities. LC 77-1108. 1978. 18.95 (ISBN 0-8157-5914-2). Brookings.

Mushakoji, Kinhide, jt. auth. see Kaplan, Morton A.

Musheno, Elizabeth J. The Home Decorating Sewing Book. 1978. 16.95 (ISBN 0-02-588190-6); pap. 7.95 (ISBN 0-02-011890-2). Macmillan.

Mushinsky, Henry R. A Laboratory Manual for General Zoology, Pt. 1. 1978. pap. text ed. 6.95 (ISBN 0-8403-1213-X). Kendall-Hunt.

Mushkat, Jerome. The Reconstructiom of the New York Democracy, 1861-1874. LC 79-16826. 328p. 1981. 25.00 (ISBN 0-8386-3002-2). Fairleigh Dickinson.

--The Reconstruction of the New York Democracy, 1861-1874. LC 78-16826. 328p. 1981. 25.00 (ISBN 0-8386-3002-2, 3002). Fairleigh Dickinson.

Mushkin, Selma J. & Sandifer, Frank H. Personnel Management & Productivity in City Government. (Illus.). 1979. 19.95 (ISBN 0-669-02805-3). Lexington Bks.

Mushkin, Selma J., ed. Public Prices for Public Products. Orig. Title: Property, Taxation, Housing & Urban Growth. 1972. 10.95 (ISBN 0-87766-010-7, 90010); pap. 6.50 (ISBN 0-87766-018-2, 90009). Urban Inst.

Mushkin, Selma J. & Dunlop, David W., eds. Health: What Is It Worth? Measures of Health Benefits. (Pergamon Policy Studies). 1979. 19.25 (ISBN 0-08-023898-X). Pergamon.

Musicant, Elke & Musicant, Ted. The Night Vegetable Eater. LC 80-22389. (Illus.). 48p. (gr. k-3). 1981. PLB 7.95 (ISBN 0-396-07923-7). Dodd.

Musicant, Ted, jt. auth. see Musicant, Elke.

Musick, Phil. Hank Aaron: The Man Who Beat the Babe - from Mobile to Immortality. 192p. (Orig.). 1974. pap. 1.25 o.p. (ISBN 0-445-08258-5). Popular Lib.

Musick, Ruth A. The Telltale Lilac Bush & Other West Virginia Ghost Tales. LC 64-14000. (Illus.). 208p. 1976. pap. 5.50 (ISBN 0-8131-0136-0). U Pr of Ky.

Musielak, Julian, ed. Commentationes Mathematicae: Tomus Specialis in Honorem Ladislai Orlicz, 2 vols, Vol. I & Vol. II. LC 78-326610. 1979. 27.50x ea. Vol. 1, 384 P (ISBN 0-8002-2271-7). Vol. 2, 347 P (ISBN 0-8002-2272-5). Intl Pubns Serv.

Musiker, Reuben. South Africa. (World Bibliographical Ser.: No. 7). 194p. 1980. 25.25 (ISBN 0-903450-16-X). ABC-Clio.

--Special Libraries: A General Survey with Particular Reference to South Africa. 1970. 10.00 (ISBN 0-8108-0310-0). Scarecrow.

Musil, George. Urbanization in Socialist Countries. Orig. Title: Urbanizace v socialistickych zemich. (Illus.). 192p. 1980. 20.00 (ISBN 0-87332-180-4). M E Sharpe.

Musil, Robert. Three Short Stories. Sacker, Hugh, ed. (Clarendon German Ser). 1970. pap. 5.95x (ISBN 0-19-832467-7). Oxford U Pr.

Musk, George. Canadian Pacific: The Story of the Famous Shipping Line. (Illus.). 272p. 1981. 45.00 (ISBN 0-7153-7968-2). David & Charles.

Muske, Carol. Skylight. LC 80-712. 96p. 1981. pap. 5.95 (ISBN 0-385-17087-4). Doubleday.

Musker, Frank F., jt. auth. see Armbruster, David A., Sr.

Muskett, Netta. Blue Haze. (Orig.). 1978. pap. 1.75 o.s.i. (ISBN 0-515-04539-X). Jove Pubns.

--Cast the Spear. 1978. pap. 1.50 o.s.i. (ISBN 0-515-04537-3). Jove Pubns.

--Silver Gilt. 1978. pap. 1.75 o.s.i. (ISBN 0-515-04538-1). Jove Pubns.

Muskie, Edmund S. & Brock, Bill. What Price Defense? LC 74-21550. 1974. 5.75 (ISBN 0-8447-2054-2); pap. text ed. 2.50 o. p. (ISBN 0-8447-2053-4). Am Enterprise.

Muskie, Edmund S., jt. auth. see Bundy, McGeorge.

Muslin, H. L., et al. Evaluative Methods in Psychiatric Education. 220p. 1974. pap. 10.00 (ISBN 0-685-65574-1, P182-0). Am Psychiatric.

Musolf, Lloyd D. & Springer, J. Frederick. Malaysia's Parliamentary System: Representative Politics & Policymaking in a Divided Society. (Westview Relica Edition). 1979. lib. bdg. 20.00x (ISBN 0-89158-460-9). Westview.

Mussa, Michael L. & Kormendi, Roger G. Taxation of Municipal Bonds: An Economic Appraisal. 1979. pap. 7.25 (ISBN 0-8447-3331-8). Am Enterprise.

Musselman, Donald L., jt. auth. see Musselman, Vernon A.

Musselman, Vernon. Introduction to Modern Business: Issues and Environment: Issues & Environment. 7th ed. (Illus.). 1977. text ed. 18.95 (ISBN 0-13-488148-6); study guide & wkbk. 7.95 (ISBN 0-13-488130-3). P-H.

Musselman, Vernon A. & Hughes, Eugene. Introduction to Modern Business: Issues & Environment. 8th ed. (Illus.). 640p. 1981. text ed. 17.95 (ISBN 0-13-488072-2); pap. 7.95 study guide (ISBN 0-13-488080-3). P-H.

Musselman, Vernon A. & Musselman, Donald L. Methods in Teaching Basic Business Subjects. 4th ed. 332p. 1980. pap. text ed. 6.95x- (ISBN 0-8134-2107-1). Interstate.

Musselman, Vernon L. & Hughes, Eugene H. Study Guide & Applied Readings to Introduction to Modern Business: Issues & Environment. 8th ed. 272p. 1981. pap. text ed. 7.95 (ISBN 0-13-488080-3). P-H.

Mussen, P. H. Carmichael's Manual of Child Psychology, 2 vols. 3rd ed. LC 69-16127. 1970. Set. 99.95 (ISBN 0-471-62697-X); Vol. 1. 69.95 (ISBN 0-471-62695-3); Vol. 2. 45.95 (ISBN 0-471-62696-1). Wiley.

Mussen, Paul. Psychological Development of the Child. 3rd ed. (Foundations of Modern Psychology). (Illus.). 1979. text ed. 12.95 (ISBN 0-13-732420-0); pap. text ed. 6.95 (ISBN 0-13-732412-X). P-H.

Mussen, Paul & Eisenberg-Berg, Nancy. Roots of Caring, Sharing, & Helping: The Development of Prosocial Behavior in Children. LC 77-22750. (Psychology Ser.). (Illus.). 1977. text ed. 16.95x (ISBN 0-7167-0045-X); pap. text ed. 7.95x (ISBN 0-7167-0044-1). W H Freeman.

Mussen, Paul & Rosenzweig, Mark. Psychology: An Introduction. 2nd ed. 1976. text ed. 17.95x (ISBN 0-669-00497-9); instructor's manual free (ISBN 0-669-00521-5); study guide 5.95x (ISBN 0-669-00505-3); individualized prog. 5.95x (ISBN 0-669-00513-4); test item file to adopters free (ISBN 0-669-00539-8). Heath.

Mussen, Paul H., et al. Essentials of Child Development & Personality. 480p. 1980. text ed. 19.50 scp (ISBN 0-06-044693-5, HarpC); study guide by ray v. peters 6.50 (ISBN 0-06-045141-6). Har-Row.

--Readings in Child & Adolescent Psychology. 280p. 1980. pap. text ed. 8.50 scp (ISBN 0-06-041888-5, HarpC). Har-Row.

Musser, Harlan C. Sex -- Our Myth Theology? 196p. 1981. pap. 7.95 (ISBN 0-8059-2768-9). Dorrance.

Musser, Joe. The Coming World Earthquake. 1981. pap. 2.25 (ISBN 0-8423-0405-3). Tyndale.

Musser, Joe, jt. auth. see Eareckson, Joni.

Musser, Sandra K. I Would Have Searched Forever. (Orig.). 1980. pap. 4.95 (ISBN 0-88270-487-7). Logos.

Musset, Alfred De see De Musset, Alfred.

Musset, Anthony, jt. auth. see Stone, Janet.

Mussett, A. E., jt. auth. see Brown, G. C.

Mussolini, Benito. Memoirs, 1942-1943. Klibanksy, Raymond, ed. Lobb, Frances, tr. from It. xxviii, 320p. 1975. Repr. of 1949 ed. 20.00 (ISBN 0-86527-126-7). Fertig.

--Mussolini As Revealed in His Political Speeches: November 1914-August 1923. Quaranta Di San Severino, B., ed. LC 75-16288. xxviii, 375p. 1977. Repr. of 1923 ed. 22.50 (ISBN 0-86527-134-8). Fertig.

Mussulman, Joseph A. The Uses of Music: An Introduction to Music in Contemporary American Life. LC 73-21801. (Illus.). 256p. 1974. pap. 7.95x o.p. (ISBN 0-13-939413-3); records 10.95 o.p. (ISBN 0-13-939439-7). P-H.

Muste, A. J. Of Holy Disobedience. 23p. 1952-1964. pap. 0.75 (ISBN 0-934676-09-7). Greenlf Bks.

Musulin, Stella. Vienna in the Age of Metternich: From Napoleon to Revolution, 1805-48. LC 75-19264. (Illus.). 320p. 1975. 23.75x (ISBN 0-89158-501-X). Westview.

Mutananda, Swami. Sadhana. 1976. pap. 7.95 (ISBN 0-914602-63-2). SYDA Found.

Muter, W. Grant. The Buildings of an Industrial Community: Coalbrookdale & Ironbridge. (Illus.). 69p. 1979. 22.50x (ISBN 0-8476-3039-0). Rowman.

Muth, Eginhard J. Transform Methods with Applications to Engineering & Operations Research. (Illus.). 1977. ref. ed. 25.95 (ISBN 0-13-928861-9). P-H.

Muth, Stephen, jt. auth. see Rust, Kenn C.

Mutharika, A. Peter. The Alien Under American Law. LC 80-18236. 575p. 1980. looseleaf 85.00 (ISBN 0-379-20341-3). Oceana.

Muther, Richard. Systematic Layout Planning. 2nd ed. LC 72-91983. 1973. 23.50 (ISBN 0-8436-0814-5); text ed. 16.50 o.p. (ISBN 0-8436-0817-X). CBI Pub.

Muther, Richard & Haganas, Knut. Systematic Handling Analysis. LC 73-90920. 1969. spiral bdg. 22.95 (ISBN 0-8436-1002-6). CBI Pub.

Muther, Richard & Hales, Lee. Systematic Planning of Industrial Facilities, Vol. II. LC 79-84256. 1980. write for info. (ISBN 0-933684-02-9). Mgmt & Indus Res Pubns.

Muthesius, Stefan, jt. auth. see Dixon, Roger.

Mutibwa, Phares M. The Malagasy & the Europeans. (Ibadan History Ser). (Illus.). 395p. 1974. text ed. 18.00x (ISBN 0-391-00348-8). Humanities.

Mutkoski, Stephen A. & Schurer, Marcia L. Meat & Fish Management for Food Service. 1981. text ed. 17.95 (ISBN 0-534-00907-7, Breton Pubs). Wadsworth Pub.

Mutt, V., jt. ed. see Jorpes, T. E.

Muttalib, M. A. Democracy, Bureaucracy & Technocracy. 144p. 1980. text ed. 11.25x (ISBN 0-391-02120-6). Humanities.

Mutton, Alice F. Western Europe in Color. (Illus.). 279p. 1972. 12.75 (ISBN 0-7137-0546-9); pap. 7.50 (ISBN 0-7137-0555-8). Transatlantic.

Mutwa, Credo V. My People, My Africa. (John Day Bk.). (Illus.). 1969. 7.95 o.s.i. (ISBN 0-381-98161-4, A52400, TYC-T). T Y Crowell.

Mutwa, Vusamazulu C. Indaba My Children. 1971. pap. text ed. 18.25x (ISBN 0-900707-07-0). Humanities.

Muuss, Rolfe. Theories of Adolescence. 2nd ed. 9.00 (ISBN 0-8446-2635-X). Peter Smith.

Muybridge, Eadweard. Human Figure in Motion. (Illus.). 1955. 13.95 (ISBN 0-486-20204-6). Dover.

--Muybridge's Complete Human & Animal Locomotion: All 781 Plates from the 1887 Animal Locomotion, 3 vols. Incl. Vol. 1 (ISBN 0-486-23792-3); Vol. 2 (ISBN 0-486-23793-1); Vol. 3 (ISBN 0-486-23794-X). (Illus.). 1979. Repr. of 1887 ed. Set. 28.33 ea. (ISBN 0-685-92659-1). Dover.

Muzaffer, Sheikh. The Unveiling of Love. Holland, Muhtar, tr. from Turk. 1981. 10.95 (ISBN 0-89281-023-8); pap. 8.95 (ISBN 0-89281-017-3). Inner Tradit.

Muzzarelli, Riccardo A. Chitin. LC 76-52421. 365p. 1977. text ed. 57.00 (ISBN 0-08-020367-1). Pergamon.

--Natural Chelating Polymers. 260p. 1974. text ed. 40.00 (ISBN 0-08-017235-0). Pergamon.

Muzzey, Artemas B. Reminiscences & Memorials of Men of the Revolution. LC 70-142542. 1971. Repr. of 1883 ed. 26.00 (ISBN 0-8103-3629-4). Gale.

M. Verda Clare, tr. see Marie Eugene.

M Verda Clare, tr. see Marie Eugene.

Mwansasu, Bismarck & Pratt, Cranford, eds. Towards Socialism in Tanzania. LC 78-10350. 1979. 20.00x (ISBN 0-8020-2330-4); pap. 7.50 (ISBN 0-8020-6433-7). U of Toronto Pr.

Myasoedov, B. I., et al. Analytical Chemistry of Transplutonium Elements. Slutzkin, D., ed. Kaner, N., tr. from Rus. LC 73-17086. (Analytical Chemistry of the Elements Ser.). 404p. 1974. 41.95 (ISBN 0-470-62715-8). Halsted Pr.

Myatt, Frederick. Peninsular General: Sir Thomas Picton, Seventeen Fifty-Eight to Eighteen Fifteen. LC 79-56256. (Illus.). 224p. 1980. 28.00 (ISBN 0-7153-7923-2). David & Charles.

Myatt, L. J. Symmetrical Components. 1968. text ed. 19.50 (ISBN 0-08-012979-X); pap. text ed. 9.75 (ISBN 0-08-012978-1). Pergamon.

Myer, Donna. Answers to Your Mushroom Questions Plus Recipes. LC 77-87780. (Illus.). 1977. pap. 3.95x (ISBN 0-9601516-1-3). Mushroom Cave.

Myer, John. Cost Accounting for Non-Accountants. 1971. 7.95 o.p. (ISBN 0-8015-1776-1). Dutton.

Myer, Minor, Jr., jt. auth. see Mayhew, Edgar D.

Myerhoff, Barbara, jt. auth. see Tufte, Virginia.

Myerhoff, Barbara, jt. ed. see Tufte, Virginia.

Myerhoff, Barbara G. Peyote Hunt: The Sacred Journey of Huichol Indians. LC 73-16923. (Symbol, Myth & Ritual Ser.). (Illus.). 288p. 1974. 22.50x (ISBN 0-8014-0817-2); pap. 5.95 1976 ed. (ISBN 0-8014-9137-1). Cornell U Pr.

Myerhoff, Barbara G. & Simic, Andrei, eds. Life's Career--Aging: Cultural Variations on Growing Old. LC 77-14268. (Sage Series Cross Cultural Research & Methodology: Vol. 4). 1978. 20.00x (ISBN 0-8039-0867-9); pap. 9.95 (ISBN 0-8039-1346-X). Sage.

Myers. Bernice Myers' Book of Giggles. (ps-3). 1980. pap. 1.25 (ISBN 0-590-30067-9, Schol Pap). Schol Bk Serv.

--Fast Sam, Cool Clyde, & Stuff. (YA) (gr. 7 up). 1978. pap. 1.50 (ISBN 0-380-01943-4, 45294). Avon.

Myers, A. & Seider, W. Introduction to Chemical Engineering Computer Calculations. 1976. 27.95 (ISBN 0-13-479238-6). P-H.

Myers, Albert C., jt. auth. see Penn, William.

Myers, Alfred S. Letters for All Occasions. (Orig.). 1952. pap. 2.95 (ISBN 0-06-463237-7, EH 237, EH). Har-Row.

Myers, Alpha & Temkin, Sara. Your Future in Library Careers. LC 75-29605. (Career Guidance Ser.). 160p. 1976. pap. 3.50 (ISBN 0-668-03913-2). Arco.

Myers, Arthur. The Ghost Hunters. LC 80-19668. (Illus.). 160p. (gr. 7 up). 1980. PLB 9.29 (ISBN 0-671-33076-4). Messner.

Myers, Barbara. The Chinese Restaurant Cookbook. LC 80-6229. 348p. 1981. 14.95 (ISBN 0-8128-2803-8). Stein & Day.

--Christmas Entertaining. LC 80-51252. 256p. 1980. 13.95 (ISBN 0-686-62320-7). Rawson Wade.
--Woman's Day Old-Fashioned Desserts. 1978. 10.95 o.s.i. (ISBN 0-397-01314-0). Lippincott.
Myers, Bernard. Supermazes: No. 1. 1977. pap. 2.95 (ISBN 0-385-11467-2, Dolp). Doubleday.
Myers, Bernice. The Apple War. LC 72-8191. (Illus.). 48p. (gr. k-3). 1973. 5.95 o.s.i. (ISBN 0-8193-0650-9, Four Winds); PLB 5.41 o.s.i. (ISBN 0-8193-0651-7). Schol Bk Serv.
--Herman & the Bears Again. (Illus.). (gr. k-3). 1979. pap. 1.25 (ISBN 0-590-10243-5, Schol Pap); pap. 3.50 bk. & record (ISBN 0-590-20803-9). Schol Bk Serv.
--Little John Bear in the Big City. LC 78-15595. (Illus.). 32p. (gr. k-3). 1979. 5.95 (ISBN 0-590-07601-9, Four Winds). Schol Bk Serv.
--My Mother Is Lost. (gr. k-3). 1971. pap. 1.25 (ISBN 0-590-04478-8, Schol Pap); pap. 3.50 bk. & record (ISBN 0-590-20694-X). Schol Bk Serv.
--Not at Home. (Illus.). (gr. 6-9). 6.95 (ISBN 0-688-41974-7). Lothrop.
--Not at Home? LC 80-16288. (Illus.). 48p. (gr. 1-3). 1981. 6.95 (ISBN 0-688-41974-7); PLB 6.67 (ISBN 0-688-51974-1). Morrow.
--Sally's Secret. (gr. k-3). 1977. pap. 1.25 (ISBN 0-590-10418-7, Schol Pap). Schol Bk Serv.
Myers, Betsy. How to Protect Your Home & Family. 110p. 1981. pap. cancelled (ISBN 0-686-68067-7). Cornerstone.
Myers, Buddy L. & Enrick, Norbert L. Statistical Functions & Formulas: A Source of Simplified Derivations Based on Elementary Mathematics. 174p. 1981. Repr. of 1970 ed. text ed. price not set (ISBN 0-89874-286-2). Krieger.
Myers, Carol F. Women in Literature: Criticism of the Seventies. LC 75-35757. 1976. 12.00 (ISBN 0-8108-0885-4). Scarecrow.
Myers, Charles A., jt. auth. see Pigors, Paul.
Myers, D. A., et al. Geology of the Late Paleozoic Horseshoe Atoll in West Texas. (Illus.). 113p. 1956. 2.00 (PUB 5607). Bur Econ Geology.
Myers, David G. The Inflated Self: Human Illusions and the Biblical Call to Hope. 176p. 1980. 9.95 (ISBN 0-8164-0459-3). Seabury.
Myers, David J., jt. ed. see Martz, John D.
Myers, David V., jt. auth. see Cochrane, Carmie T.
Myers, Desaix. Labor Practices of U. S. Corporations in South Africa. LC 77-3020. (Special Studies). 1977. text ed. 21.95 (ISBN 0-275-24520-9). Praeger.
--The Nuclear Power Debate: Moral, Economic, Technical, & Political Issues. LC 75-25022. (Special Studies). 1977. text ed. 23.95 (ISBN 0-275-56440-1). Praeger.
Myers, Earl & Hacker, Rich. Track & Field. (Creative Sports Ser). (Illus.). (gr. 4 up). 1962. PLB 7.95 o.p. (ISBN 0-87191-022-5). Creative Ed.
Myers, Elisabeth P. Langston Hughes. (gr. k-6). Date not set. pap. price not set (ISBN 0-440-44723-2, YB). Dell.
Myers, Ernest R. The Community Psychology Concept: Integrating Theory, Education & Practice in Psychology, Social Work & Public Administration. 1977. pap. text ed. 9.00x (ISBN 0-8191-0291-1). U Pr of Amer.
Myers, Eugene N., jt. ed. see Suen, James Y.
Myers, Gail E. & Myers, Michele T. The Dynamics of Human Communication: A Laboratory Approach. 2nd ed. (Illus.). 416p. 1975. pap. text ed. 11.95 o.p. (ISBN 0-07-044212-6, C); instructor's manual 3.95 o.p. (ISBN 0-07-044213-4). McGraw.
Myers, Gary, et al. A Guide for Helping the Child with Spina Bifida. (Illus.). 352p. 1981. text ed. 19.75 (ISBN 0-398-04113-X). C C Thomas.
Myers, Geoffrey M. Les Chetifs. Nelson, Jan A. & Mickel, Emanuel J., Jr., eds. (Old French Crusade Cycle Ser.: Vol. V). 352p. Date not set. 25.00 (ISBN 0-8173-0023-6). U of Ala Pr.
Myers, George. Piranhas. pap. 4.95 (ISBN 0-87666-133-9, M539). TFH Pubns.
Myers, Glenford J. The Art of Software Testing. LC 78-12923. (Business Data Processing Ser.). 1979. 18.95 (ISBN 0-471-04328-1, Pub. by Wiley-Interscience). Wiley.
--Software Reliability: Principles & Practices. LC 76-22202. (Business Data Processing Ser.). 1976. 25.95 (ISBN 0-471-62765-8, Pub. by Wiley-Interscience). Wiley.
Myers, Gustavus. History of Canadian Wealth. LC 68-9159. 1968. Repr. of 1914 ed. 15.00 (ISBN 0-87266-024-9). Argosy.
Myers, Harold. Table Tennis. (Illus.). 1977. pap. 4.95 (ISBN 0-571-11001-0, Pub. by Faber & Faber). Merrimack Bk Serv.
Myers, Henry, ed. Reduce Your Tax Bite. LC 79-21653. (Orig.). 1980. pap. 5.95 (ISBN 0-87128-583-5, Pub. by Dow Jones). Dow Jones-Irwin.
Myers, Henry Allen, jt. auth. see Holbik, Karel.
Myers, Howard. Cloud Chamber. 1977. pap. 1.50 o.p. (ISBN 0-445-03215-4). Popular Lib.
Myers, Iris H. Rompecabezas y actividades espanoles. (gr. 7-12). 1976. dup. masters 28.00 (ISBN 0-205-05458-7, 4254589). Allyn.
Myers, Isabel B. Introduction to Type. 3rd ed. 18p. 1980. Repr. of 1970 ed. pap. 0.75 (ISBN 0-935652-06-X). Ctr Applications Psych.
Myers, Isabel B. & Myers, Peter B. Gifts Differing. (Orig.). 1980. 21.50 (ISBN 0-89106-015-4); pap. 12.00 (ISBN 0-89106-011-1). Consulting Psychol.
Myers, J. Jay. Red Chiefs & White Challengers. (gr. 7-12). 1972. pap. 1.25 o.s.i. (ISBN 0-671-48125-8). WSP.
Myers, J. M. Grace & Torah. LC 74-26343. 96p. 1975. pap. 2.95 (ISBN 0-8006-1099-7, 1-1099). Fortress.
Myers, James E. Jones. 256p. 1981. 9.95 (ISBN 0-916392-77-5). Oak Tree Pubns.
Myers, James H. & Reynolds, William H. Consumer Behavior & Marketing Management. LC 68-1942. (Illus., Orig.). 1967. pap. 10.75 (ISBN 0-395-04987-3, 3-39771). HM.
Myers, Jerome L. Fundamentals of Experimental Design. 3rd ed. 1979. text ed. 21.95x (ISBN 0-205-06615-1). Allyn.
Myers, John G., et al. Energy Consumption in Manufacturing. LC 74-8111. (Ford Foundation Energy Policy Project Ser.). 736p. 1974. text ed. 40.00 (ISBN 0-88410-307-2); pap. text ed. 25.00 o.s.i. (ISBN 0-88410-323-4). Ballinger Pub.
--Marketing Research & Knowledge Development: An Assessment for Marketing Management. (Illus.). 1980. text ed. 19.95 (ISBN 0-13-557686-5). P-H.
Myers, John M. The Alamo. LC 48-5208. (Illus.). 240p. 1973. 10.95x (ISBN 0-8032-0884-7); pap. 3.25 (ISBN 0-8032-5779-1, BB 566, Bison). U of Nebr Pr.
--Doc Holliday. LC 55-5528. 224p. 1973. pap. 3.95 (ISBN 0-8032-5781-3, BB 570, Bison). U of Nebr Pr.
--The Last Chance: Tombstone's Early Years. LC 50-5638. (Illus.). 260p. 1973. pap. 2.45 (ISBN 0-8032-5780-5, BB 569, Bison). U of Nebr Pr.
--The Saga of Hugh Glass: Pirate, Pawnee, & Mountain Man. LC 75-38613. viii, 237p. 1976. 14.50x (ISBN 0-8032-0867-7); pap. 3.25 (ISBN 0-8032-5834-8, BB 614, Bison). U of Nebr Pr.
Myers, Kenneth A. North Atlantic Security: The Forgotten Flank? LC 78-66209. (The Washington Papers: No. 62). 1979. pap. 3.50x (ISBN 0-8039-1231-5). Sage.
Myers, Kent E., jt. auth. see Shirts, Morris A.
Myers, Larry. Training with Cerutty. LC 77-85323. (Illus.). 174p. 1977. pap. 4.95 (ISBN 0-89037-081-8); handbk. 6.95 (ISBN 0-89037-080-X). Anderson World.
Myers, Laura G., jt. auth. see Burrows, Lois M.
Myers, Lonny & Leggitt, Hunter. Adultery & Other Private Matters: Your Right to Personal Freedom in Marriage. LC 75-4701. (Illus.). 224p. 1975. 13.95 (ISBN 0-911012-51-6). Nelson-Hall.
Myers, M. Bert, jt. ed. see Grabb, William C.
Myers, M. Scott. Every Employee a Manager. Newton, William R., ed. (Illus.). 1981. 16.50 (ISBN 0-07-044269-X, P&RB). McGraw.
Myers, Margaret G. Financial History of the United States. LC 70-104900. 1970. 22.50x (ISBN 0-231-02442-8); pap. 7.50x (ISBN 0-231-08309-2). Columbia U Pr.
Myers, Mary R. Captain's Pleasure. (Orig.). 1981. pap. 2.75 (ISBN 0-449-14399-6, GM). Fawcett.
Myers, Michele, jt. auth. see Meyers, Gail.
Myers, Michele T., jt. auth. see Myers, Gail E.
Myers, Minor, jt. auth. see Mayhew, Edgar D.
Myers, Nancy. Algebra & Trigonometry for College Students. 650p. 1980. pap. text ed. 16.95 (ISBN 0-442-25758-9); instr's. manual avail. (ISBN 0-442-25701-5). Van Nos Reinhold.
--Algebra for College Students. 446p. 1979. pap. text ed. 13.95 (ISBN 0-442-25625-6). Van Nos Reinhold.
Myers, Norma & Scobey, Joan. Gifts from the Kitchen. LC 79-8914. 320p. 1980. pap. 9.95 (ISBN 0-672-52631-X). Bobbs.
Myers, Norman. The Long African Day. LC 71-182022. (Illus.). 400p. 1972. 25.00 o.s.i. (ISBN 0-02-588200-7). Macmillan.
Myers, Patricia, tr. see Marenzio, Luca.
Myers, Patricia A. An Introduction to Radiographic Technique. 1980. 12.95 (ISBN 0-03-056654-1). Praeger.
Myers, Patricia L. & Hammill, Donald D. Methods for Learning Disorders. 2nd ed. LC 75-37504. 1976. text ed. 21.95 (ISBN 0-471-62751-8). Wiley.
Myers, Peter B., jt. auth. see Myers, Isabel B.
Myers, Philip. Patterns of Reproduction of Four Species of Vespertiliohia Bats in Paraguay. (Publ. in Zoology Ser: Vol. 107). 1977. pap. 9.75x (ISBN 0-520-09554-5). U of Cal Pr.
Myers, R. E., jt. auth. see Torrance, E. Paul.
Myers, Ramon H., jt. auth. see Arnold, Julean.
Myers, Ramon H., jt. auth. see Fortune, Robert.
Myers, Ramon H., ed. Selected Essays in Chinese Economic Development. LC 78-74360. (The Modern Chinese Economy Ser.). 251p. 1980. 33.00 (ISBN 0-8240-4277-8). Garland Pub.
Myers, Robert J. Cambodia: The Struggle for Survival. 1980. 10.00 o.p. (ISBN 0-531-09914-8). Watts.
--Indexation of Pension & Other Benefits. 1979. 11.00 (ISBN 0-256-02118-X). Irwin.
--Systems of Demographic Measurement the Dual Record System. LC 77-71086. (Scientific Report Ser.: No. 26). (Illus.). 1976. pap. text ed. 3.50 (ISBN 0-89383-032-1). Intl Program Labs.
Myers, Robin. Dictionary of Literature in the English Language, 2 vols. LC 68-18529. Vol. 1. 52.50 (ISBN 0-08-012079-2); Vol. 2. 37.50 (ISBN 0-08-016142-1); Set. 85.00 (ISBN 0-08-016143-X). Pergamon.
--A Dictionary of Literature in the English Language. 1978. 85.00 (ISBN 0-08-018050-7). Pergamon.
Myers, Rollo, ed. Richard Strauss & Romain Rolland: Correspondence, Diary, & Essays. 1968. 20.00x (ISBN 0-520-00913-4). U of Cal Pr.
Myers, Rollo, tr. see Chailley, Jacques.
Myers, Russell. Life Begins at One Thousand Five Hundred. 128p. 1981. pap. 1.50 (ISBN 0-449-14378-3, GM). Fawcett.
Myers, Stanley. RPG Two with Business Applications. (Illus.). 544p. 1980. text ed. 19.95 (ISBN 0-8359-6303-9). Reston.
Myers, Stanley & Figiel, Richard. Creative Home Remodeling. (Illus.). 240p. 1981. text ed. 16.95 (ISBN 0-13-189613-X, Spec); pap. text ed. 7.95 (ISBN 0-13-189605-9, Spec). P-H.
Myers, Stewart C., jt. auth. see Robichek, Alexander A.
Myers, Walter D. Black Pearl & the Ghost. LC 79-20268. (Illus.). (gr. 1-5). 1980. 6.95 (ISBN 0-670-17284-7). Viking Pr.
--Brainstorm. (Triumph Books Ser.). (Illus.). 1977. PLB 6.90 (ISBN 0-531-01325-1). Watts.
--The Golden Serpent. (Illus.). 40p. (gr. 1-4). 1980. 9.95 (ISBN 0-670-34445-1). Viking Pr.
--The Legend of Tarik. (Illus.). 192p. (gr. 7 up). 1981. 9.95 (ISBN 0-670-42312-2). Viking Pr.
--Mojo & the Russians. (gr. 5 up). 1978. pap. 1.50 (ISBN 0-380-41814-2, 41814). Avon.
Myers, William. Dryden. 1973. text ed. 9.00x (ISBN 0-09-116540-7, Hutchinson U Lib); pap. text ed. 5.50x (ISBN 0-09-116451-6). Humanities.
Myers, William & Swett, Ira. Trolleys to the Surf. LC 76-9685. (Special Ser.: No. 63). (Illus.). 1976. 13.75 (ISBN 0-916374-22-X). Interurban.
Myers, William S. The Foreign Policies of Herbert Hoover, 1929-1933. Freidel, Frank, ed. LC 78-66558. (The History of the United States Ser.: Vol. 14). 272p. 1979. lib. bdg. 20.00 (ISBN 0-8240-9699-1). Garland Pub.
--The Mexican War Diary of General George B. McClellan. LC 71-87641. (The American Scene Ser). 98p. 1972. Repr. of 1917 ed. lib. bdg. 17.50 (ISBN 0-306-71789-1). Da Capo.
--The Republican Party: A History. (Government & Political Science Ser). 1968. Repr. of 1928 ed. 25.50 (ISBN 0-384-40741-2); with Democratic Party by Kent 46.00 (ISBN 0-685-13576-4). Johnson Repr.
Myerscough, John, jt. auth. see Lowerson, John.
Myerson, Joel, ed. The American Renaissance in New England. LC 77-82803. (Dictionary of Literary Biography Ser.: Vol. 1). (Illus.). 1978. 54.00 (ISBN 0-8103-0913-0, Bruccoli Clark Bk). Gale.
--Antebellum Writers in New York & the South. LC 79-15481. (Dictionary of Literary Biography Ser.: Vol 3.). (Illus.). 1979. 54.00 (ISBN 0-8103-0915-7, Bruccoli Clark Bk). Gale.
Myhill, Henry. Portugal. (Illus.). 1972. 14.00 (ISBN 0-571-09640-9). Transatlantic.
Myhra, David. Energy Plant Sites: Community Planning for Large Projects. Conway, McKinley & Liston, L. L., eds. LC 79-54253. (Illus.). 1980. pap. 35.00x (ISBN 0-910436-13-4). Conway Pubns.
Myhrman, David W. Sumerian Administrative Documents from the Second Dynasty of Ur. (Publications of the Babylonian Section, Ser.A: Vol. 3). (Illus.). 146p. 1910. soft bound 8.00 o.p. (ISBN 0-686-11912-6). Univ Mus of U PA.
Myint, H. The Economics of the Developing Countries. rev. 4th ed. Parkin, Michael, ed. 160p. 1973. pap. text ed. 9.25x (ISBN 0-09-118261-1, Hutchinson U Lib). Humanities.
Mykel. Windchime Legacy. 419p. 1980. 12.95 (ISBN 0-312-88219-X). St Martin.
Myklebust, Helmer R. The Pupil Rating Scale: Screening for Learning Disabilities. 1971. pap. 18.00 (ISBN 0-8089-0684-4); record forms, pkg. of 50 11.75 (ISBN 0-8089-0794-8); specimen set, 1 record form 11.75 (ISBN 0-8089-0752-2); computer scoring from, 50 scoring forms, 2 class header sheets, school report form 27.25 (ISBN 0-8089-0989-4). Grune.
--Your Deaf Child: A Guide for Parents. (Amer. Lec. in Otolaryngology Ser.). (Illus.). 150p. 1979. pap. 6.75 (ISBN 0-398-03127-4). C C Thomas.
Myler, Charles E., Jr. Arizona Supplement to Modern Real Estate Practice. 3rd ed. 200p. (Orig.). 1980. pap. 7.95 (ISBN 0-88462-295-9). Real Estate Ed Co.
Myles, Colette G., ed. The Butterflies Carried Him Home: And Other Indian Tales. LC 80-70506. (Illus.). 65p. (Orig.). 1981. pap. 4.95 (ISBN 0-9605468-1-2). Artmans Pr.
--The Butterflies Carried Him Home & Other Indian Tales. (Illus.). 65p. 1981. 5.00 (ISBN 0-686-28917-X). Artmans Pr.
Myles, Glenn. Down & Country. (Bebop Drawing Club Book). (Illus.). 58p. 1974. pap. 2.00 (ISBN 0-9605468-0-4). Artmans Pr.
Myller, Rolf. Mazes: 60 Beautiful & Beastly Labyrinths with Solutions. (Illus.). 160p. (gr. 1 up). 1976. pap. 3.95 (ISBN 0-394-83254-X). Pantheon.
Mylonas, Anastassios D. Perception of Police Power: A Study in Four Cities. (New York University Criminal Law Education & Research Center Monograph: No. 8). (Illus.). x, 131p. (Orig.). 1974. pap. text ed. 8.50x (ISBN 0-8377-0418-9). Rothman.
Mylonas, George E. Eleusis & the Eleusinian Mysteries. 1961. 22.50x (ISBN 0-691-03513-X); pap. 8.95 (ISBN 0-691-00205-3). Princeton U Pr.
Mynors, R. A., ed. see Virgil.
Mynors, R. A., tr. see Erasmus.
Mynors, R. A., tr. see Erasmus, Desiderius.
Mynors, Roger A., ed. see Pliny.
Myra, Donald. Headliners: Billy Joel. 192p. (Orig.). 1981. pap. 2.25 (ISBN 0-448-17175-9, Tempo). G&D.
Myra, Harold. The Choice. 1980. 9.95 (ISBN 0-8423-0249-2). Tyndale.
--Love Notes to Jeanette. 1979. pap. 3.95 (ISBN 0-88207-638-8). Victor Bks.
--The New You. (gr. 9-12). 1980. pap. 2.25 (ISBN 0-88207-581-0). Victor Bks.
Myrdal, Alva & Klein, Viola. Women's Two Roles: At Home & Work. rev. ed. (International Library of Sociology & Social Reconstruction). (Illus.). 1970. pap. text ed. 6.50x (ISBN 0-7100-2894-6). Humanities.
Myrdal, Gunnar. Value in Social Theory: A Selection of Essays on Methodology. (International Library of Sociology). 1968. Repr. of 1958 ed. 25.00x (ISBN 0-7100-3370-2). Routledge & Kegan.
Myrdal, Jan. China Notebook, Nineteen Seventy-Five to Nineteen Seventy-Eight. Von Dorp, Rolf, tr. from Swedish. LC 79-88412. (Illus.). lib. bdg. 8.95 (ISBN 0-930720-59-8); pap. 3.95 (ISBN 0-930720-58-X). Liberator Pr.
--Report from a Chinese Village. (Illus.). 1981. pap. 6.95 (ISBN 0-394-74802-6). Pantheon.
Myrer, Anton. The Big War. 1981. pap. 3.25 (ISBN 0-425-04672-9). Berkley Pub.
Myres, J. N., jt. auth. see Collingwood, Robin G.
Myres, Sandra L., ed. Ho for California: Women's Overland Diaries from the Huntington Library. LC 79-28115. (Illus.). 1980. 20.00 (ISBN 0-87328-103-9). Huntington Lib.
Myres, Sandra L., jt. ed. see Morris, Margaret F.
Myrianthopoulos, Ntinos C. & Bergsma, Daniel, eds. Recent Advances in the Developmental Biology of Central Nervous System Malformations. LC 79-4947. (Alan R. Liss Ser.: Vol. 15, No. 3). 1979. 16.00 (ISBN 0-8451-1026-8). March of Dimes.
Myrick, Bismarck & Easterbrook, David L. Three Aspects of Crisis in Colonial Kenya. LC 75-30552. (Foreign and Comparative Studies Eastern Africa Series XXI). 91p. 1975. pap. text ed. 4.50x (ISBN 0-915984-18-0). Syracuse U Foreign Comp.
Myrick, David. Railroads of Arizona, Vol. 2. LC 75-27787. (Illus.). 480p. 30.00 (ISBN 0-8310-7118-4). Howell-North.
Myrick, David F. Railroads of Arizona, Vol. 1. (Illus.). 480p. Date not set. Repr. of 1975 ed. 30.00 (ISBN 0-8310-7111-7). Howell-North.
Myrick, Kenneth. Sir Philip Sidney As a Literary Craftsman. LC 35-13065. 1966. pap. 3.95x (ISBN 0-8032-5140-8, BB 312, Bison). U of Nebr Pr.
Myrick, William J., Jr. Coordination: Concept or Reality? A Study of Libraries in a University System. LC 74-22456. 1975. 10.00 (ISBN 0-8108-0776-9). Scarecrow.

Myrivilis, Stratis. Life in the Tomb. Bien, Peter, tr. from Greek. LC 76-50678. (Illus.). 345p. 1977. text ed. 17.50x (ISBN 0-87451-134-8). U Pr of New Eng.
Myron, Robert & Sundell, Abner. Art in America: From Colonial Days Through the Nineteenth Century. LC 69-10347. (Illus.). (gr. 7-10). 1969. 4.95g o.s.i. (ISBN 0-02-767770-2, CCPr). Macmillan.
Myrsiades, Kostas. Takis Papatsonis. LC 74-6370. (World Authors Ser.: Greece: No. 313). 168p. 1974. lib. bdg. 12.50 (ISBN 0-8057-2669-1). Twayne.
Myrus, Don. Dog Catalog. 1978. 19.95 (ISBN 0-02-588230-9). Macmillan.
Myrus, Donald. Ballads, Blues, & the Big Beat. (gr. 7 up). 1966. 5.95g o.s.i. (ISBN 0-02-768060-6). Macmillan.
--I Like Jazz. (gr. 7 up). 1964. 3.95g o.s.i. (ISBN 0-02-768020-7). Macmillan.
Mysak, Edward D. Neurospeech Therapy for Cerebral Palsied: 2nd. 1980. text ed. 22.50x (ISBN 0-8077-2612-5). Tchrs Coll.
--Speech Pathology & Feedback Theory. (Illus.). 124p. 1971. 9.75 (ISBN 0-398-01379-9). C C Thomas.
Myshlyaeva, L. V. & Krasnoshchekov, V. V. Analytical Chemistry of Silicon. Schmorak, J., tr. from Rus. LC 73-20490. 230p. 1974. 37.50 o.p. (ISBN 0-470-62785-9). Halsted Pr.
Mystic Seaport Museum, Inc. International Congress of Maritime Museums, 3rd Conference: Proceedings, 1978. LC 79-26650. 306p. (Orig.). 1979. pap. 20.00 (ISBN 0-913372-22-6, IS-00103, Pub. by Mystic Seaport). Univ Microfilms.
Mytton-Davies, Peter. Canoeing for Beginners. 1971. 5.95 (ISBN 0-236-17613-7, Pub. by Paul Elek). Merrimack Bk Serv.

N

N. Y. Board of Trade & Rickles, Robert, eds. Energy in the City Environment. LC 72-96106. 200p. 1973. 12.50 o.p. (ISBN 0-8155-5019-7, NP). Noyes.
Naamani, Israel T. The State of Israel. LC 79-12757. (Illus.). 1980. pap. 5.95x (ISBN 0-87441-278-1). Behrman.
Nabakov. Nabokovs Quartet. 1968. pap. 1.75 o.s.i. (ISBN 0-515-01882-1, V1882). Jove Pubns.
Nabakov, Vladmir. Glory: A Novel. 1971. 6.95 (ISBN 0-07-045733-6, GB). McGraw.
Nabarro, Gerald. Steam Nostalgia: Locomotive & Railway Preservation in Great Britain. (Illus.). 286p. 1972. 22.00 (ISBN 0-7100-7391-7); pap. 7.50 (ISBN 0-7100-8386-6). Routledge & Kegan.
Nabavi, C. D. The Engineering of Microprocessor Systems: Guidelines on System Development. LC 79-40952. 1979. 21.00 (ISBN 0-08-025435-7); pap. 7.25 (ISBN 0-08-025434-9). Pergamon.
Naber, Gregory L. Methods of Topology in Euclidean Spaces. LC 79-7225. (Illus.). 1980. 23.95x (ISBN 0-521-22746-1). Cambridge U Pr.
Nabholtz, John R., ed. see Hazlitt, William.
Nabholtz, John R., ed. see Lamb, Charles.
Nabil-i-A'zam. The Dawn-Breakers. Effendi, Shoghi, ed. & tr. LC 32-8946. (Illus.). 1932. 18.00 (ISBN 0-87743-010-1, 7-31-53); pap. 8.00 (ISBN 0-87743-092-6, 7-31-54). Baha'i.
Nabokov, Dmitri, tr. see Nabokov, Vladimir.
Nabokov, Peter. Indian Running. (Illus.). 160p. (Orig.). 1981. pap. 7.95 (ISBN 0-88496-162-1). Capra Pr.
Nabokov, Vladimir. Ada or Ardor: A Family Chronicle. (McGraw-Hill Paperback Ser.). 612p. 1980. pap. 6.95 (ISBN 0-07-045723-9, GB). McGraw.
--Annotated Lolita. Appel, Alfred, Jr., ed. 1970. pap. 6.95 (ISBN 0-07-045730-1). McGraw.
--Blednii Ogon' Tsvetkov, Alexei, tr. (Rus.). 1981. 19.00 (ISBN 0-88233-602-9); pap. 12.50 (ISBN 0-88233-603-7). Ardis Pubs.
--Details of a Sunset & Other Stories. (McGraw-Hill Paperback Ser.). 180p. 1980. pap. 4.95 (ISBN 0-07-045721-2). McGraw.
--King, Queen, Knave. 288p. 1980. pap. 5.95 (ISBN 0-07-045722-0, GB). McGraw.
--Look at the Harlequins! 264p. 1981. pap. 5.95 (ISBN 0-07-045717-4). McGraw.
--Mashenka. (Rus.). 1979. 15.00 (ISBN 0-88233-092-6); pap. 6.00 (ISBN 0-88233-093-4). Ardis Pubs.
--Nikolai Gogol. LC 44-8135. 1961. pap. 4.95 (ISBN 0-8112-0120-1, NDP78). New Directions.
--A Russian Beauty & Other Stories. Nabokov, Dmitri & Karlinsky, Simon, trs. from Rus. LC 72-10094. 224p. 1974. pap. 4.95 (ISBN 0-07-045711-5, SP). McGraw.
--Strong Opinions. 348p. 1981. pap. 6.95 (ISBN 0-07-045725-5). McGraw.
--Tyrants Destroyed & Other Stories. 252p. 1981. pap. 5.95 (ISBN 0-07-045718-2). McGraw.
--Vozvrashchenie Chorba. (Sobranie Rasskazov I Povestei: Vol. 1). (Rus.). 1976. pap. 7.00 (ISBN 0-88233-226-0). Ardis Pubs.
Nabokov, Vladimir, tr. see Carroll, Lewis.
Nabokov, Vladimir, tr. see Pushkin, Aleksandr.
Nabseth, L. & Ray, G. F. Diffusion of New Technology. (National Institute of Economic & Social Research Economic & Social Studies: No. 29). (Illus.). 300p. 1974. 35.50 (ISBN 0-521-20430-5). Cambridge U Pr.
Nabudere, Dan W. Imperialism in East Africa: Vol. II: Imperialism & Exploitation. 240p. (Orig.). 1981. 18.95 (ISBN 0-905762-05-3, Pub. by Zed Pr); pap. 7.95 o.p. (ISBN 0-905762-06-1). Lawrence Hill.
--Imperialism in East Africa: Vol. 1: Imperialism & Integration. 240p. (Orig.). 1981. 18.95 (ISBN 0-905762-99-1, Pub. by Zed Pr); pap. 7.95 o.p. (ISBN 0-905762-86-X). Lawrence Hill.
Nabudere, Wadada D. Essays on the Theory & Practice of Imperialism. 192p. 1980. text ed. 22.25x (ISBN 0-906383-02-1); pap. text ed. 9.25x (ISBN 0-906383-03-X). Humanities.
Nacci, Chris N. Ignacio Manuel Altamirano. (World Authors Ser.: Mexico: No. 124). lib. bdg. 12.50 (ISBN 0-8057-2040-5). Twayne.
Nachant, Frances G. Song of Peace. 1969. 4.00 o.p. (ISBN 0-8233-0126-5). Golden Quill.
Nachazel, Delbert P., jt. auth. see Smith, Joan F.
Nachbar, J. Western: Focus on. 7.95 (ISBN 0-13-950634-9); pap. 3.25 (ISBN 0-13-950626-8). P-H.
Nachbin. An Introduction to Functional Analysis. 200p. 1981. 19.75 (ISBN 0-8247-6984-8). Dekker.
Nachbin, Leopoldo, ed. Mathematical Analysis & Applications. (Advances in Mathematics Supplementary Studies: Vol. 7). 1981. Pt. A. write for info. (ISBN 0-12-512801-0); Pt. B. write for info. (ISBN 0-12-512802-9). Acad Pr.
Nachman, Gerald. Playing House. LC 76-56323. 1978. 6.95 o.p. (ISBN 0-385-12341-8). Doubleday.
Nachman, L. J. Fundamental Mathematics. 657p. 1978. 20.95 (ISBN 0-471-62815-8). Wiley.
Nachman, Paul, jt. auth. see Smil, Vaclav.
Nachmanpohn, David. Chemical & Molecular Basis of Nerve Activity. 2nd & rev. ed. 1975. 31.50 (ISBN 0-12-512757-X). Acad Pr.
Nachmias, David & Rosenbloom, David H. Bureaucratic Culture: Citizens & Administrators in Israel. LC 78-17638. 1978. 17.95x (ISBN 0-312-10808-7). St Martin.
Nachtigal, Gustav. Sahara & Sudan: Bornu, Kanem, Borku, Ennedi, Vol. II. Fisher, Allan G. & Fisher, Humphrey J., trs. from Ger. (Illus.). 1980. text ed. 60.00x (ISBN 0-8419-5752-5). Holmes & Meier.
--Sahara & Sudan, Vol. IV: Wadai & Darfur. 1971. 38.75x (ISBN 0-520-01789-7). U of Cal Pr.
Nachtmann, Francis W. Exercises in French Phonics. 1970. spiral bdg. 5.95x (ISBN 0-673-05988-X). Scott F.
Nacker, Marilyn. Taking Notice. LC 79-28166. 128p. 1980. 9.95 (ISBN 0-394-51223-5); pap. 5.95 (ISBN 0-394-73917-5). Knopf.
Nackman, Mark E. A Nation Within a Nation: The Rise of Texas Nationalism. (American Studies Ser.). 183p. 1975. 15.00 (ISBN 0-8046-9131-2, Natl U). Kennikat.
NACM, ed. Bonds on Public Works. 1981. pap. 4.75 (ISBN 0-934914-38-9). NACM.
--Credit & Collection Letters. 2nd ed. 324p. 1971. loose-leaf 23.00 (ISBN 0-934914-01-X). NACM.
--Credit Clues in Financial Statements. 1975. pap. 3.95 (ISBN 0-934914-20-6). NACM.
--Mechanics Lien Laws & Federal Tax Lien Law. 1981. pap. 4.50 (ISBN 0-686-69391-4). NACM.
--Practical Guide to Creditors' Committees. 29p. 1968. pap. 3.50 (ISBN 0-934914-12-5). NACM.
NACM Publications, ed. Credit Manual of Commercial Laws. 1980. 30.00 o.p. (ISBN 0-934914-33-8). NACM.
NACM Publications Editors. Bonds on Public Works. 130p. 1980. pap. 4.50 o.p. (ISBN 0-934914-34-6). NACM.
--Mechanic's Lien Laws & Federal Tax Lien Law. 1980. pap. 4.25 o.p. (ISBN 0-934914-35-4). NACM.
Naczi, Frances D. Without Bombast & Blunders: An Executive's Guide to Effective Writing. LC 80-17857. 1980. 5.95 (ISBN 0-87863-007-4). Farnswth Pub.
Nadal, R. M., tr. see Calderon De La Barca, Pedro.
Naddor, Eliezer. Inventory Systems. LC 65-26850. 1966. 25.95 (ISBN 0-471-62830-1). Wiley.
Nadeau, Claude, et al, eds. Psychology of Motor Behavior & Sport: 1979. LC 78-641529. (Illus.). 1980. text ed. 24.95x (ISBN 0-686-64327-5). Human Kinetics.
Nadeau, Ray E. & Muchmore, John M. Speech Communication: A Career Education Approach. 2nd ed. LC 78-18640. (Speech Ser.). 1979. text ed. 12.50 (ISBN 0-201-05007-2). A-W.
Nadeau, Raymond E. A Modern Rhetoric of Speech-Communication. 2nd ed. LC 74-167994. (Speech Ser). 1972. text ed. 11.95 (ISBN 0-201-04999-6). A-W.
--Speech Communication: A Career Education Approach. 2nd ed. 1979. text ed. 12.50 (ISBN 0-201-05007-2). A-W.
Nadeau, Roland & Tesson, William. Listen: A Guide to the Pleasures of Music. 3rd ed. 544p. 1980. pap. text ed. 14.95 (ISBN 0-8403-2332-8). Kendall-Hunt.
Nadeau, Roland L. Debussy & the Crisis of Tonality. 1981. cancelled (ISBN 0-930350-11-1). NE U Pr.
Nadel & Sherrer. How to Prepare for the CLEP Subject Examination: Analysis & Interpretation of Literature. 1981. pap. 4.95 (ISBN 0-8120-0619-4). Barron.
Nadel, Ira B. & Oberlander, Cornelia H. Trees in the City. LC 77-1713. 1978. text ed. 15.00 (ISBN 0-08-021489-4); pap. text ed. 7.75 (ISBN 0-08-021488-6). Pergamon.
Nadel, Ira B., ed. Jewish Writers of North America: A Guide to Information Sources. (American Studies Information Guide Ser.: Vol. 8). 500p. 1980. 30.00 (ISBN 0-8103-1484-3). Gale.
Nadel, Mark. Politics of Consumer Protection. LC 78-170712. (Policy Analysis Ser). 1971. pap. 6.25 (ISBN 0-672-61223-2). Bobbs.
Nadel, Max & Sherrer, Arthur. English: Advance Placement Exam. 320p. (gr. 9-12). 1980. pap. text ed. 4.95 (ISBN 0-8120-2070-7). Barron.
Nadel, Max & Sherrer, Arthur, Jr. How to Prepare for Advanced Placement Examinations: English. rev. ed. LC 80-15687. (gr. 11-12). 1980. pap. text ed. 4.95 (ISBN 0-8120-2070-7). Barron.
Nadel, S. F. The Theory of Social Structure. 1969. Repr. of 1957 ed. 16.50x (ISBN 0-7100-1881-9). Routledge & Kegan.
Naden, C. J., adapted by. Pegasus, the Winged Horse. new ed. LC 80-50069. (gr. 3-5). 1980. PLB 5.89 (ISBN 0-89375-361-0); pap. 2.50 (ISBN 0-89375-365-3). Troll Assocs.
Naden, Corinne. Triangle Shirtwaist Fire, March 25, 1911: The Blaze That Changed an Industry. LC 70-137153. (Focus Bks). (Illus.). (gr. 7 up). 1971. PLB 4.47 o.p. (ISBN 0-531-01023-6); pap. 1.25 o.p. (ISBN 0-531-02334-6). Watts.
Naden, Corinne J. The Colony of New Jersey. LC 74-872. (First Bks). (Illus.). 96p. (gr. 4-7). 1974. PLB 4.90 o.p. (ISBN 0-531-02722-8). Watts.
--First Book of Grasslands Around the World. LC 72-117184. (First Bks). (Illus.). (gr. 7 up). 1970. PLB 6.90 (ISBN 0-531-00714-6). Watts.
--Haymarket Affair, Chicago, 1886: The Great Anarchist Riot & Trial. (Focus Bks). (Illus.). (gr. 7 up). 1968. PLB 4.90 o.p. (ISBN 0-531-01001-5); pap. 1.25 o.p. (ISBN 0-531-02332-X). Watts.
--Let's Find Out About Frogs. LC 79-189120. (Let's Find Out Bks). (Illus.). 48p. (gr. 3-4). 1972. PLB 4.47 o.p. (ISBN 0-531-00081-8). Watts.
--The Mississippi: America's Great River System. LC 73-14702. (First Bks). (Illus.). 72p. (gr. 4-6). 1974. PLB 4.90 o.p. (ISBN 0-531-00819-3). Watts.
--Woodlands Around the World. LC 72-12712. (First Bks). (Illus.). 72p. (gr. 4-8). 1973. PLB 6.45 (ISBN 0-531-00802-9). Watts.
Nader, George. Chrome. 1979. pap. 1.75 (ISBN 0-515-04846-1). Jove Pubns.
Nader, Helen. The Mendoza Family in the Spanish Renaissance, 1350-1550. 1979. 21.00 (ISBN 0-8135-0876-2). Rutgers U Pr.
Nader, Laura, ed. No Access to Law: Alternatives to the American Judicial System. LC 80-526. 1980. 27.50 (ISBN 0-12-513560-2); pap. 12.95 (ISBN 0-12-513562-9). Acad Pr.
Nader, Laura & Todd, Harry F., Jr., eds. The Disputing Process in Ten Societies. 1978. 22.50x (ISBN 0-231-04536-0); pap. 10.00x (ISBN 0-231-04537-9). Columbia U Pr.
Nader, Philip R. Options for School Health: Meeting Community Needs. LC 78-9628. 1978. text ed. 21.95 (ISBN 0-89443-038-6). Aspen Systems.
Nader, Ralph & Green, Mark. Verdicts on Lawyers. LC 75-23292. 1977. 10.00 o.p. (ISBN 0-690-01006-0, TYC-T); pap. 4.95 (ISBN 0-690-01667-0, TYC-T). T Y Crowell.
Nader, Ralph, et al. The Lemon Book. (Illus.). 300p. (Orig.). 1980. pap. 7.95 (ISBN 0-89803-039-0). Caroline Hse.
Nader, Ralph, et al, eds. Who's Poisoning America: Corporate Polluters & Their Victims in the Chemical Age. 320p. 1981. 12.95 (ISBN 0-87156-276-6). Sierra.
Nadich, Judah. Eisenhower & the Jews. (Return to Zion Ser.). (Illus.). 271p. 1980. Repr. of 1953 ed. lib. bdg. 20.00x (ISBN 0-87991-122-0). Porcupine Pr.
Nadien, Margot B. The Child's Psychosocial Development: From Birth to Early Adolescence. 160p. (Orig.). 1980. pap. 6.95 (ISBN 0-89529-115-0). Avery Pub.
Nadler, David A. Feedback & Organization Development: Using Data-Based Methods. (Illus.). 1977. pap. text ed. 7.50 (ISBN 0-201-05006-4). A-W.
Nadler, Leonard. Developing Human Resources. 2nd ed. LC 79-4147. 1979. text ed. 17.95 (ISBN 0-89384-044-0). Learning Concepts.
Nadler, Leonard, ed. see Human Resource Development Press.
Nadler, Myra, ed. How to Start an Audiovisual Collection. LC 78-1993. 1978. 10.00 (ISBN 0-8108-1124-3). Scarecrow.
Nadler, Paul. Commercial Banking in the Economy. rev. ed. 1973. pap. text ed. 3.95 o.p. (ISBN 0-394-31776-9). Random.
Nadler, Samuel, jt. auth. see Greenberg, Harold I.
Naef, Hans. Die Bildniszeichnungen Von J.A.D. Ingres, 5 vols. only vols. 1-4 are available. (Illus.). 1980. 175.00x ea. (Pub. by Sotheby Parke Bernet England). Vol. 1 (ISBN 3-7165-0087-9). Vol. 2 (ISBN 3-7165-0249-9). Vol. 3.1979 (ISBN 3-7165-0250-2). Vol. 4 (ISBN 3-7165-0122-0). Biblio Dist.
Naef, Weston J., jt. auth. see Ferrez, Gilberto.
Naegeli, Bruce A., jt. auth. see Gara, Otta G.
Naerssen, F. H. & Jongh, R. C. The Economic & Administrative History of Early Indonesia. 1977. text ed. 43.50x (ISBN 90-04-04918-5). Humanities.
Naess, Arne. Communication & Argument: Elements of Applied Semantics. 1966. text ed. 17.00x (ISBN 8-200-02073-8, Dist. by Columbia U Pr). Universitet.
--Freedom, Emotion & Self-Substance: The Structure of a Central Part of Spinoza's Ethics. 1975. pap. text ed. 11.00x (ISBN 8-200-01459-2, Dist. by Columbia U Pr). Universitet.
--The Pluralist & Possibilist Aspect of the Scientific Enterprise. 1972. text ed. 30.00x (ISBN 8-200-04609-5, Dist. by Columbia U Pr). Universitet.
--Scepticism. LC 68-22775. (International Library of Philosophy & Scientific Method). 1968. text ed. 11.25x (ISBN 0-7100-3639-6). Humanities.
Naess, Arne & Hannay, Alistair, eds. Invitation to Chinese Philosophy. 1972. pap. 19.00x (ISBN 82-00-02264-1, Dist. by Columbia U Pr). Universitet.
Naeye, Richard L., et al. Perinatal Diseases. (The International Academy of Pathology Monograph: No. 22). (Illus.). 300p. 1981. write for info. (6301-4). Williams & Wilkins.
Naff, Thomas & Owen, Roger, eds. Studies in 18th Century Islamic History. LC 77-22012. 462p. 1977. 24.95x (ISBN 0-8093-0819-3). S Ill U Pr.
Naffziger, Frederick J., jt. auth. see Wolfe, Arthur D.
Naftolin, Frederick & Stubblefield, Phillip G., eds. Dilation of the Uterine Cervix: Connective Tissue Biology & Clinical Management. 1979. text ed. 38.50 (ISBN 0-89004-300-0). Raven.
Nafzinger, E. Wayne. African Capitalism: A Case Study in Nigerian Entrepreneurship. LC 76-48484. (Publication Ser: No. 169). (Illus.). 1977. 8.95 (ISBN 0-8179-6691-9). Hoover Inst Pr.
Nag, B. R. Theory of Electrical Transport in Semi-Conductors. 238p. 1973. text ed. 34.00 (ISBN 0-08-016802-7). Pergamon.
Nagai, Haruka. Makko-Ho: Five Minutes' Physical Fitness. LC 72-84812. (Illus.). 80p. 1972. pap. 4.95 o.p. (ISBN 0-87040-170-X). Japan Pubns.
Nagami, Keio. Dimension Theory. (Pure & Applied Mathematics Ser.: Vol. 37). 1970. 38.00 (ISBN 0-12-513650-1). Acad Pr.
Nagan, Peter. Fail Safe Investing: How to Make Money with Less Than Ten Thousand Dollars...Without Losing Sleep. 192p. 1981. 9.95 (ISBN 0-399-12616-3). Putnam.
Nagao, Makoto & Matsuyama, Takashi, eds. A Structural Analysis of Complex Aerial Photographs. (Advanced Applications in Pattern Recognition Ser.). 200p. 1980. 32.50 (ISBN 0-306-40571-7, Plenum Pr). Plenum Pub.
Nagarajan, K. Chronicles of Kedaram. 8.00x (ISBN 0-210-33818-0). Asia.
Nagarjuna. The Precious Garland & the Song of the Four Mindfulnesses. Hopkins, Jeffrey & Rimpoche, Lati, trs. (Wisdom of Tibet Ser.). (Illus.). 1975. pap. 6.95 (ISBN 0-04-294089-3). Allen Unwin.

Nagarkar, Kiran. Seven Sixes Are Forty-Three. Slee, Shubha, tr. from Marathi. (Asian & Pacific Writing Ser.: No. 14). 213p. 1981. text ed. 15.75 (ISBN 0-7022-1503-1); pap. 8.50 (ISBN 0-7022-1502-3). U of Queensland Pr.

Nagarwalla, Arati. The Bait. (Writers Workshop Bluebird Ser.). 33p. 1975. 5.00 (ISBN 0-88253-506-4); pap. text ed. 4.00 (ISBN 0-88253-505-6). Ind-US Inc.

Nagashima, Kei, jt. auth. see Watanabe, Masahiro.

Nagata, M. Polynomial Rings & Affine Spaces. LC 78-8264. (Conference Board of the Mathematical Sciences Ser.: No. 37). 1980. Repr. of 1978 ed. 7.40 (ISBN 0-8218-1687-X, CBMS 37). Am Math.

Nagata, Shinji. Mixing: Principals & Applications. LC 75-2056. 1975. 64.95 (ISBN 0-470-62863-4). Halsted Pr.

Nagatsuka, Ruyji. I Was a Kamikaze. LC 72-11281. (Illus.). 224p. 1974. 6.95 o.s.i. (ISBN 0-02-588280-5). Macmillan.

Nagel, Charles. Children Learning by Doing. (Illus.). (gr. k-3). 1973. 3.25x (ISBN 0-933892-01-2). Child Focus Co.

Nagel, Ernest. The Structure of Science. LC 60-15504. 1979. lib. bdg. 25.00 (ISBN 0-915144-72-7); pap. text ed. 12.50 (ISBN 0-915144-71-9). Hackett Pub.

--Teleology Revisited & Other Essays in the Philosophy & History of Science. 1979. 22.50x (ISBN 0-231-04504-2). Columbia U Pr.

Nagel, Ernest & Newman, James R. Godel's Proof. LC 58-5610. 1958. 9.50 (ISBN 0-8147-0324-0); pap. 4.50x (ISBN 0-8147-0325-9). NYU Pr.

Nagel, Fritz. Fritz: The World War I Memoirs of a German Lieutenant. Baumgartner, Richard A., ed. (Illus.). 160p. (Orig.). 1980. pap. 6.95 (ISBN 0-9604770-0-4). Der Angriff.

Nagel, G. A., jt. ed. see Burkert, H.

Nagel, H. T., et al. An Introduction to Computer Logic. (Illus.). 544p. 1975. ref. ed. 27.95 (ISBN 0-13-480012-5). P-H.

Nagel, Harry, jt. auth. see Bosworth, Bruce.

Nagel, Hildegard, tr. see Jung, Emma.

Nagel, James. American Fiction: Historical & Critical Essays. (United States Author Ser.). 1978. lib. bdg. 16.95 (ISBN 0-8057-9006-3). Twayne.

--Stephen Crane & Literary Impressionism. LC 80-16051. 200p. 1980. 16.50x (ISBN 0-271-00267-0). Pa St U Pr.

Nagel, James & Astro, Richard, eds. American Literature: The New England Heritage. LC 80-8517. 250p. 1981. lib. bdg. 30.00 (ISBN 0-8240-9467-0). Garland Pub.

Nagel, Paul C. Missouri: A History. (States & the Nation Ser.). (Illus.). 1977. 12.95 (ISBN 0-393-05633-3, Co-Pub. by AASLH). Norton.

Nagel, Shirley. Tree Boy. (Sierra Club-Scribner's Juvenile Ser.). (Illus.). 96p. (gr. 5 up). 1978. 6.95 (ISBN 0-684-15722-5). Sierra.

Nagel, Stuart & Munshaw, Nancy, eds. Policy Studies Personnel Directory. 1979. pap. 5.00 (ISBN 0-918592-33-X). Policy Studies.

Nagel, Stuart S. Law & Social Change. LC 73-89941. (Contemporary Social Science Issues Ser.: No. 3). 1973. 4.95x o.p. (ISBN 0-8039-0334-0). Sage.

--Legal Process from a Behavorial Perspective. 1969. text ed. 14.50 o.p. (ISBN 0-256-01151-6). Dorsey.

--Policy Studies & the Social Sciences. LC 75-2292. (Policy Studies Organization Policy Study Ser.). 192p. 1975. 22.95 (ISBN 0-669-99531-2). Lexington Bks.

--Policy Studies in America & Elsewhere. (Policy Studies Organization Ser.). 256p. 1975. 19.95 (ISBN 0-669-99549-5). Lexington Bks.

Nagel, Stuart S. & Neef, Marian. Legal Policy Analysis. LC 76-14046. 1977. 23.95 (ISBN 0-669-00731-5). Lexington Bks.

--Operations Research Methods. LC 76-25693. (University Papers Ser.: Quantitative Applications in the Social Sciences, No. 2). 1976. pap. 3.50x (ISBN 0-8039-0651-X). Sage.

--Policy Analysis in Social Science Research. LC 78-11463. (Sage Library of Social Research: Vol. 72). 1979. 18.00x (ISBN 0-8039-1156-4); pap. 8.95x (ISBN 0-8039-1157-2). Sage.

Nagel, Stuart S. & Neef, Marion. Decision Theory & the Legal Process. LC 78-20348. 1979. 24.95 (ISBN 0-669-02742-1). Lexington Bks.

Nagel, Stuart S., ed. Environmental Politics. LC 74-3138. (Special Studies). 250p. 1974. 34.95 (ISBN 0-275-09030-2). Praeger.

--Improving Policy Analysis. LC 79-23019. (Sage Focus Editions: Vol. 16). (Illus.). 1980. 18.95x (ISBN 0-8039-1390-7); pap. 9.95x (ISBN 0-8039-1391-5). Sage.

Nagel, T. Mortal Questions. LC 78-58797. 1979. 29.95 (ISBN 0-521-22360-1); pap. 7.95x (ISBN 0-521-29460-6). Cambridge U Pr.

Nagell, John R. van see Van Nagell, John R., Jr. & Barber, Hugh R.

Nagell, Trygve. Introduction to Number Theory. 309p. 1981. 14.95 (ISBN 0-8284-0163-2). Chelsea Pub.

Nagell, Trygve, et al, eds. Selected Mathematicae Papers of Axel Thue. 1977. 40.00x (ISBN 82-00-01649-8, Dist. by Columbia U Pr). Universitet.

Nagera, Humberto. Developmental Understanding of the Child. LC 80-69668. 378p. 1981. 30.00 (ISBN 0-87668-432-0). Aronson.

Nagera, Humberto, ed. Basic Psychoanalytic Concepts, 4 vols. (The Hampstead Clinic Psychoanalytic Library). 1977. pap. text ed. 4.95x ea.; Vol. 1. o.p. (ISBN 0-04-150059-8); Vol. 2. o.p. (ISBN 0-04-150060-1); Vol. 3. o.p. (ISBN 0-04-150061-X); Vol. 4. (ISBN 0-04-150062-8). Allen Unwin.

Nagi, Saad & Corwin, Ronald, eds. The Social Contexts of Research. LC 78-18770. 422p. 1979. Repr. of 1972 ed. lib. bdg. 19.50 o.p. (ISBN 0-88275-701-6). Krieger.

Nagi, Saad Z. Child Maltreatment in the United States. LC 77-22121. 1977. 15.00x (ISBN 0-231-04394-5). Columbia U Pr.

Nagin, Paul & Ledgard, Henry F. BASIC with Style: Programming Proverbs. (gr. 10 up). 1978. pap. text ed. 7.15 (ISBN 0-8104-5115-8). Hayden.

Nagle, Barbara T., jt. auth. see Hitner, Henry.

Nagle, Francis & Montoye, Henry. Exercise in Health & Disease. (Illus.). 440p. 1981. write for info. (ISBN 0-398-04120-2). C C Thomas.

Nagle, James J. Heredity & Human Affairs. 2nd ed. LC 78-27066. (Illus.). 1979. pap. text ed. 15.95 (ISBN 0-8016-3621-3). Mosby.

Nagle, John D. The National Democratic Party: Right-Radicalism in the Federal Republic of Germany. LC 78-101340. 1970. 20.00x (ISBN 0-520-01649-1). U of Cal Pr.

Nagle, John N., jt. auth. see Hummel, Raymond C.

Nagle, Judy. The Responsive Arts. 1980. pap. 15.95 (ISBN 0-88284-101-7). Alfred Pub.

Nagler, A. M. Misdirection: Opera Production in the Twentieth Century. 134p. 1981. 15.00 (ISBN 0-208-01899-9, Archon). Shoe String.

--Theatre Festivals of the Medici, 1539-1637. LC 76-8447. 1976. Repr. of 1964 ed. lib. bdg. 25.00 (ISBN 0-306-70779-9). Da Capo.

Nagler, Alois M. Source Book in Theatrical History. Orig. Title: Sources of Theatrical History. (Illus.). 1952. pap. 6.95 (ISBN 0-486-20515-0). Dover.

Nagler, Michael. Spontaneity & Tradition: A Study in the Oral Art of Homer. 1975. 18.75x (ISBN 0-520-02244-0). U of Cal Pr.

Nagpaul, Hans, jt. auth. see Cousins, Albert N.

Nagrath, I. J. & Gopal, M. Control Systems Engineering. 1977. pap. 12.95x (ISBN 0-470-99281-6). Halsted Pr.

Nagreine, Donall. A Bottle of Psychology. (Illus.). 64p. 1981. 5.00 (ISBN 0-682-49679-0). Exposition.

Nagro, C. F. Christopher Columbus: Man of Destiny & Vision. 1981. 9.50 (ISBN 0-533-04809-5). Vantage.

Nagy, Charles J., Jr. Political Parties & System Flexibility. LC 80-5846. 196p. 1981. lib. bdg. 18.00 (ISBN 0-8191-1453-7); pap. text ed. 9.00 (ISBN 0-8191-1454-5). U Pr of Amer.

Nagy, D. Radiological Anatomy. 1966. 75.00 (ISBN 0-08-010675-7). Pergamon.

Nagy, G. A. & Szilagyi, M. Introduction to the Theory of Space-Charge Optics. LC 76-39107. 1974. 31.95 o.p. (ISBN 0-471-62867-0). Halsted Pr.

Nagy, Steven & Attaway, John, eds. Citrus Nutrition & Quality. LC 80-22562. (ACS Symposium Ser.: No. 143). 1980. 36.25 (ISBN 0-8412-0595-7). Am Chemical.

Nagy, Steven & Shaw, Philip E., eds. Tropical & Subtropical Fruits. (Illus.). 1980. lib. bdg. 45.00 (ISBN 0-87055-350-X). AVI.

Nagy, Steven, et al. Citrus Science & Technology, Vol. 1. (Illus.). 1977. lib. bdg. 39.50 (ISBN 0-87055-221-X). AVI.

--Citrus Science & Technology, Vol. 2. (Illus.). 1977. lib. bdg. 42.50 (ISBN 0-87055-222-8). AVI.

Naha, E. Aliens. 1977. pap. 7.95 (ISBN 0-931064-03-1). Starlog Pr.

Naha, Ed. The Paradise Plot. 352p. (Orig.). 1980. pap. 2.25 (ISBN 0-553-13979-7). Bantam.

--Science Fiction Aliens. Reed, Jon-Michael & Zimmerman, Howard, eds. (Illus.). (gr. 3 up). 1977. pap. 7.95 (ISBN 0-931064-01-5). Starlog.

Nahai, Foad, jt. auth. see Mathes, Stephen J.

Nahal, Chaman. D. H. Lawrence: An Eastern View. LC 72-120066. 1970. 12.00 o.p. (ISBN 0-498-07720-9). A S Barnes.

Nahas, G., ed. see Moreau, J. J., et al.

Nahas, Gabriel G. Keep off the Grass: A Scientific Enquiry into the Biological Effects of Marijuana. (Illus.). 1979. 16.50 (ISBN 0-08-023779-7); pap. 9.95 (ISBN 0-08-023780-0). Pergamon.

--Marijuana-the Deceptive Weed. rev. ed. LC 72-76743. 1975. 19.00 (ISBN 0-911216-39-1). Raven.

Nahas, Gabriel G. & Frick, Henry C., II, eds. Drug Abuse in the Modern World: a Perspective for the Eighties: Proceedings of a Symposium Held at the College of Physicians & Surgeons of Columbia University, New York, N.Y. (Illus.). 320p. 40.00 (ISBN 0-08-026300-3). Pergamon.

Nahas, Gabriel G., ed. see International Congress of Pharmacology, 7th, Reims, 1978. Satellite Symposium.

Nahem, Joseph. Psychology & Psychiatry Today: A Marxist View. 1981. 15.00 (ISBN 0-7178-0581-6); pap. 5.50 (ISBN 0-7178-0579-4). Intl Pub Co.

Nahm, M. Readings in Philosophy of Art & Aesthetics. 1975. 19.95 (ISBN 0-13-760892-6). P-H.

Nahm, Milton C., ed. Selections from Early Greek Philosophy. 4th ed. (Orig.). 1964. pap. text ed. 10.95 (ISBN 0-13-800508-7). P-H.

Nahm, Milton C., ed. see Aristotle.

Nahmias, Andre J. & O'Reilly, Richard, eds. Immunology of Human Infection. Incl. Pt. 1, Bacteria, Mycoplasmae, Chlamydiae, & Fungi. 49.50 (ISBN 0-306-40257-2); Pt. 2, Viruses & Parasites Immunodiagnosis & Presentation of Infectious Disease. 45.00 (ISBN 0-306-40258-0). (Comprehensive Immunology Ser.: Vols. 8 & 9). 1981 (Plenum Pr). Plenum Pub.

Nahum, Henri & Fekete, Francois. Radiology of the Postoperative Digestive Tract. Oestreich, Alan E., tr. from Fr. LC 79-837338. (Illus.). 160p. 1979. 32.50 (ISBN 0-89352-027-6). Masson Pub.

Naib, Zuther M. & Willis, Dean, eds. Cytology Examination Review Book, Vol. 1. 2nd ed. 1978. spiral bdg. 9.50 (ISBN 0-87488-454-3). Med Exam.

Naidich, Arnold. Do-It-Yourself Safety Inspective Manual. rev. ed. 1978. 59.95 (ISBN 0-686-26874-1). Busn Res Pubns.

--Protect Your Company from A-Z. 1976. 49.95. Busn Res Pubns.

Naidich, Arnold, jt. auth. see Heyel, Carl.

Naidu, D. S. Engineering Materials & Their Testing, Pt. 1. 7.50x (ISBN 0-210-27000-4). Asia.

Naidu, M. V. Alliances & Balance of Power. LC 74-82531. 256p. 1975. 17.95x (ISBN 0-312-02135-6). St Martin.

Naidu, Motukuru S. & Maller, Venktesh N. Advances in High Voltage Insulation & Arc Interruption in SF & Vacuum. Date not set. 35.00 (ISBN 0-08-024726-1). Pergamon.

Naidu, Ratna. The Communal Edge to Plural Societies: India & Malaysia. 1978. text ed. 14.00x (ISBN 0-7069-0922-4). Humanities.

Naierman, Naomi, et al. Community Mental Health Centers: A Decade Later. LC 78-67184. 1978. 15.00x (ISBN 0-89011-510-9). Abt Assoc.

Naifeh & Smith. Moving up: The Successful Man's Guide to Impeccable Taste. 1980. 10.95 (ISBN 0-312-55070-7). St Martin.

Naifeh, Steven W. & Smith, Gregory W. Moving up in Style: The Successful Man's Guide to Impeccable Taste. 1980. 10.95 (ISBN 0-312-55070-7). St Martin.

Naik, J. A. Russia & the Communist Countries. 1980. text ed. 49.25x (ISBN 0-391-01792-6). Humanities.

--Russia & the Western World. 227p. 1980. text ed. 25.00x (ISBN 0-391-01745-4). Humanities.

Naik, J. P. Elementary Education in India: The Unfinished Business. 1966. 6.50x (ISBN 0-210-22509-2). Asia.

Naik, M. K. Aspects of Indian Writing in English. 319p. (Orig.). 1979. pap. text ed. 4.50x (ISBN 0-333-90301-3). Humanities.

--Mulk Raj Anand. (Indian Writers Ser.). 1976. 8.50 (ISBN 0-89253-507-5). Ind-US Inc.

Naik, M. K., ed. Aspects of Indian Writing in English. 319p. (Orig.). 1980. pap. text ed. 5.50x (ISBN 0-333-90301-3). Humanities.

Naik, M. N. Mighty Voices: Studies in T. S. Eliot. 128p. 1980. text ed. 9.50x (ISBN 0-391-01788-8). Humanities.

Naik, Sandra, jt. auth. see Pennington, G. W.

Naim, C. M., ed. Iqbal, Jinnah, & Pakistan: The Vision & the Reality. LC 79-25477. (Foreign & Comparative Studies-South Asian Ser: No. 5). 216p. (Orig.). 1979. pap. text ed. 6.50x (ISBN 0-915984-81-4). Syracuse U Foreign Comp.

Naiman, Doris. Education for Severely Handicapped Hearing Impaired Students. 84p. 1981. pap. text ed. 6.95x (ISBN 0-913072-34-6). Natl Assn Deaf.

Naiman, Robert J. & Solt, David L. Fishes in North American Deserts. 360p. 1981. 35.00 (ISBN 0-471-08523-5, Pub. by Wiley-Interscience). Wiley.

Naimpally, S. A. & Warrack, B. D. Proximity Spaces. LC 73-118858. (Tracts in Mathematics & Mathematical Physics: No. 59). 1971. 20.50 (ISBN 0-521-07935-7). Cambridge U Pr.

Naipaul, V. S. In a Free State. 1977. pap. 2.95 (ISBN 0-14-003711-X). Penguin.

--Miguel Street. 1977. pap. 2.95 (ISBN 0-14-003302-5). Penguin.

--The Mystic Masseur. 1977. pap. 2.95 (ISBN 0-14-002156-6). Penguin.

Nair, K. K., pseud. A Profile of Indian Culture. (The India Library Ser., Vol. 1). 202p. 1975. 8.95 (ISBN 0-88253-774-1). Ind-US Inc.

Nair, P. K. Glimpses in Plant Research: Botanical Lectures & Essays, Vol. V. 400p. 1980. text ed. 50.00 (ISBN 0-7069-0827-9, Pub. by Vikas India). Advent Bk.

--Intensive Multiple Cropping with Coconuts in India: Principles, Programmes & Prospects. (Advances in Agronomy & Crop Science Ser.: Vol. 6). (Illus.). 148p. (Orig.). 1979. pap. text ed. 28.00 (ISBN 3-489-71210-2). Parey Sci Pubs.

Nair, P. K., ed. Glimpses in Plant Research. 300p. 1980. 35.00x (Pub. by Croom Helm England). State Mutual Bk.

Nair, P. Krishnan. Essential of Palynology. 1966. 5.00x (ISBN 0-210-26918-9). Asia.

Nair, Sreedhar, et al, eds. Computers in Critical Care & Pulmonary Medicine. (Computers in Biology & Medicine Ser.). 418p. 1980. 39.50 (ISBN 0-306-40449-4, Plenum Pr). Plenum Pub.

Nairn, Alan E., et al, eds. The Ocean Basins & Margins, Vol. 5: The Arctic Ocean. 610p. 1981. 55.00 (ISBN 0-686-63459-4, Plenum Pr). Plenum Pub.

NAIS Admission & Minority Affairs Committees. Recruiting Minority Students. 1979. pap. 3.25 (ISBN 0-934338-41-8). NAIS.

Nais Committee for International & World Education, ed. Internationalize Your School. 1977. pap. 3.25 (ISBN 0-934338-22-1). NAIS.

Nais School Administration & Trustee Committees. Evaluating Our Performance: An Advisory for Boards of Trustees & School Heads. 1978. pap. 6.50 (ISBN 0-934338-30-2). NAIS.

NAIS Spanish Committee. A Teacher's Notebook: Spanish. 45p. 1973. pap. 3.25 (ISBN 0-934338-01-9). NAIS.

NAIS Task Force on Secondary Mathematics. Graphing, Factoring Quadratic Trinomials. (Occasional Papers Ser.: No. 2). (Illus.). 1978. pap. 3.25 (ISBN 0-934338-14-0). NAIS.

--Quadratic Functions & Equivalence. (Occasional Papers Ser.: No. 3). (Illus.). 1979. pap. 3.25 (ISBN 0-934338-15-9). NAIS.

--Signed Numbers, Linear Functions, Surface Area Blocks. (Occasional Papers Ser.: No. 1). (Illus.). 21p. 1977. pap. 3.25 (ISBN 0-934338-13-2). NAIS.

NAIS Teacher Services Committee. Interdependence: A Handbook for Environmental Education. 1979. pap. 4.75 (ISBN 0-934338-23-X). NAIS.

Naismith, A. Twelve Hundred Scripture Outlines. (Source Book for Ministers). 1978. pap. 3.95 (ISBN 0-8010-6692-1). Baker Bk.

Naismith, Helen. One Hundred Famous American Festivals & Their Food. LC 75-30398. (Illus.). 1979. 10.00 (ISBN 0-933718-30-6). Browning Pubns.

Naito, Akira. Katsura: A Princely Retreat. Terry, Charles S., tr. from Jap. LC 75-30183. 182p. 1977. 55.00 (ISBN 0-87011-271-6). Kodansha.

Naito, H., ed. Nutrition & Heart Disease. (Monographs of the American College of Nutrition: Vol. 5). 1981. text ed. 25.00 (ISBN 0-89335-119-9). Spectrum Pub.

Naito, Herbert K., jt. ed. see Brewster, Marge A.

Najaka. City Cat. 110p. Date not set. 2.95 (ISBN 0-07-045858-8). McGraw.

--Country Cat. 111p. Date not set. 2.95 (ISBN 0-07-045859-6). McGraw.

Najean, Yves, ed. Medullary Aplasia. LC 80-80966. (Illus.). 312p. 1980. 39.50 (ISBN 0-89352-064-0). Masson Pub.

Najim, M & Abdel-Fettah, Y. M., eds. System Approach for Developement: Proceedings of the Third IFAC-IFIP-IFORS Conference, Rabat, Morocco, 24-27 November 1980. LC 80-41530. 600p. 1981. 105.00 (ISBN 0-08-025670-8); pap. 80.00 (ISBN 0-08-027283-5). Pergamon.

Najor, Julia. Babylonian Cuisine: Chaldean Cookbook from the Middle East. 1981. 10.00 (ISBN 0-533-04628-9). Vantage.

Najors, Julie. Babylon Cookbook. (Arabic.). pap. 12.00x (ISBN 0-686-63566-3). Intl Bk Ctr.

Nakabayashi, Sadaki, et al. Judo. LC 58-10422. (Athletic Institute Ser). (Illus.). 128p. (gr. 7 up). 1974. 6.95 (ISBN 0-8069-4316-5); PLB 7.49 (ISBN 0-8069-4317-3). Sterling.

Nakagawa, Rieko. A Blue Seed. (Illus.). Date not set. 4.95 (ISBN 0-8038-0690-6). Hastings.

Nakagawa, Sensaka. Kutani Ware. Bester, John, tr. LC 77-86501. (Japanese Art Library: Vol. 7). 181p. 1979. 16.95 (ISBN 0-87011-322-4). Kodansha.

Nakajima, A., jt. auth. see Goldberg, E. P.

Nakamura, Eiji. Flying Origami. LC 70-188761. (Illus.). 64p. 1972. pap. 6.50 (ISBN 0-87040-023-1). Japan Pubns.

Nakamura, Hajime. Gotama Buddha. LC 77-8589. 1977. 8.95x (ISBN 0-914910-05-1); pap. 5.95x (ISBN 0-914910-06-X). Buddhist Bks.

--Parallel Developments: A Comparative History of Ideas. LC 75-24947. 567p. 1975. 34.50x (ISBN 0-87011-272-4). Kodansha.

--Ways of Thinking of Eastern Peoples: India, China, Tibet, Japan. rev. ed. Wiener, Philip P., ed. 1964. 15.00x o.p. (ISBN 0-8248-0010-9, Eastwest Ctr); pap. text ed. 7.95x (ISBN 0-8248-0078-8). U Pr of Hawaii.

Nakamura, Hiroshi. Tuna: Distribution & Migration. (Illus.). 84p. 8.25 (ISBN 0-85238-002-X, FN). Unipub.

Nakamura, R., et al, eds. Immunoassays: Clinical Laboratory Techniques for the 1980's. LC 80-21230. (Laboratory & Research Methods in Biology & Medicine: Vol. 4). 482p. 1980. 58.00 (ISBN 0-8451-1653-3). A R Liss.

Nakamura, Robert M. & Deodhar, Sharad. Laboratory Tests in the Diagnosis of Autoimmune Disorders. LC 75-27329. (Illus.). 206p. 1975. pap. text ed. 22.00 (ISBN 0-89189-002-5, 45-A-003-00). Am Soc Clinical.

Nakamura, Robert M., jt. auth. see Deodhar, Sharad.

Nakamura, Robert M., et al. Autoantibodies to Nuclear Antigens: Immunochemical Specificities & Significance in Systemic Rheumatic Diseases. LC 78-18282. (Illus.). 1978. pap. text ed. 18.00 (ISBN 0-89189-061-0, 45-A-004-00). Am Soc Clinical.

Nakane, Chie. Japanese Society. LC 71-100021. (Center for Japanese & Korean Studies, UC Berkeley). 1970. 15.75x (ISBN 0-520-01642-4); pap. 4.50x (ISBN 0-520-02154-1, CAMPUS74). U of Cal Pr.

--Kinship & Economic Organization in Rural Japan. (Monographs on Social Anthropology: No. 32). 1967. text ed. 9.50x (ISBN 0-485-19532-1, Athlone Pr). Humanities.

Nakanishi, Akira. Writing Systems of the World: Alphabets, Syllabaries, Pictograms. LC 79-64826. (Illus.). 1981. 19.50 (ISBN 0-8048-1293-4). C E Tuttle.

Nakanishi, Koji & Solomon, Philippa H. Infrared Absorption Spectroscopy. 2nd ed. LC 76-27393. 1977. pap. 15.95x (ISBN 0-8162-6251-9). Holden-Day.

Nakano, Kenneth K. Neurology of Musculoskeletal & Rheumatic Disorders. (Illus.). 1979. 40.00x (ISBN 0-89289-401-6). HM Prof Med Div.

Nakano, Leatrice, jt. auth. see Nakano, Takeo U.

Nakano, Takeo U. & Nakano, Leatrice. Within the Barbed Wire Fence: A Japanese Man's Account of His Internment in Canada. (Illus.). 136p. 1981. 10.00 (ISBN 0-295-95789-1). U of Wash Pr.

Nakayama, M. Dynamic Karate. Kauz, Herman, tr. LC 66-28954. (Illus.). 308p. 1966. 22.50 (ISBN 0-87011-037-3). Kodansha.

Nakayama, Masatoshi. Best Karate: Seven Kata: 7 Katta: Jutte, Hangstsu, Empi. LC 77-74829. (Best Karate Ser.: Vol. 7). (Illus.). 144p. 1980. pap. 6.95 (ISBN 0-87011-390-9). Kodansha.

--Best Karate: 8 Kata: Gankaku, Jion. LC 77-74829. (Best Karate Ser.: Vol. 8). (Illus.). 144p. (Orig.). 1981. pap. 6.95 (ISBN 0-87011-402-6). Kodansha.

Nakayama, Masatoshi & Draeger, Donn F. Karate Pratique, Vol. 2. (Illus., Orig., Fr.). 1965. pap. 2.75 o.p. (ISBN 0-8048-0338-2). C E Tuttle.

Nakhimovsky, A. D. & Paperno, V. A. An English-Russian Dictionary of Nabokov's "Lolita". (Rus. & Eng.). 1981. 16.50x (ISBN 0-88233-443-3); pap. 7.50x (ISBN 0-88233-444-1). Ardis Pubs.

Nakhimovsky, Alexander, tr. see Strugatsky, Arkady & Strugatsky, Boris.

Nakhjavani, Bahiyyih. When We Grow up. 1979. 6.50 (ISBN 0-85398-085-3, 7-32-38, Pub. by G Ronald England); pap. 2.25 (ISBN 0-85398-086-1, 7-32-39, Pub. by G Ronald England). Baha'i.

Nakhleh, Emile A. Bahrain: Political Development in a Modernizing Society. LC 75-37274. (Illus.). 208p. 1976. 18.95 (ISBN 0-669-00454-5). Lexington Bks.

--West Bank & Gaza: Toward the Making of a Palestinian State. 1979. pap. 4.25 (ISBN 0-8447-3335-0). Am Enterprise.

Nakhleh, Emile A., jt. ed. see Koury, Enver M.

Nakhshabi, Ziya'U'D-Din. Cleveland Museum of Art's Tuti-Nama. Simsar, Muhammed A., tr. from Persian. LC 76-55714. (Illus.). 362p. 1979. 45.00x (ISBN 0-910386-29-3, Pub. by Cleveland Mus Art). Ind U Pr.

Nakmura, Zeko. Bonsai: Miniatures. (Illus.). 60p. 1980. pap. 4.50 (ISBN 0-87040-244-7, Pub. by Shufunotomo Japan). Intl Schol Bk Serv.

Nakon, Robert. Chemical Problem Solving Using Dimensional Analysis. (Illus.). 1978. pap. 9.95 (ISBN 0-13-128645-5). P-H.

Nalanda Translation Committee, tr. see Trungpa, Chogyam.

Nalbandian, Louise Z. The Armenian Revolutionary Movement: The Development of Armenian Political Parties Through the Nineteenth Century. (Near Eastern Center, UCLA). 1963. 15.75 (ISBN 0-520-00914-2). U of Cal Pr.

Nalbandov, A. V. Reproductive Physiology of Mammals & Birds: The Comparative Physiology of Domestic & Laboratory Animals & Man. 3rd ed. LC 75-25890. (Animal Science Ser.). (Illus.). 1976. 24.95x (ISBN 0-7167-0843-4). W H Freeman.

Nalbandoy, Sergei, tr. see Leonov, Leonid M.

Nalbantian, Suzanne. The Symbol of the Soul from Holderlin to Yeats: A Study in Metonymy. LC 76-25550. 1976. 17.50x (ISBN 0-231-04148-9). Columbia U Pr.

Nalder, Lanny J. Traveler's Health Guide: A Nutritional, Medical & Fitness Handbook for Travelers & People Away from Home. LC 80-82454. 120p. (Orig.). 1981. pap. 4.95 (ISBN 0-88290-094-3, 4025). Horizon Utah.

Nale, Nell. Sand Dollar Shuffle. (Kindergarten Keys Ser). (Illus.). 1975. pap. text ed. 2.49 (ISBN 0-87892-658-5); tchr's manual 2.49 (ISBN 0-87892-659-3). Economy Co.

Nale, Nell, et al. Kindergarten Keys. rev. ed. 1975. tchr's guidebk. 85.50 (ISBN 0-87892-655-0). Economy Co.

--The Caterpillar Caper. (Kindergarten Keys Ser.). (Illus.). 1975. pap. text ed. 2.49 (ISBN 0-87892-656-9); 2.49 (ISBN 0-87892-657-7); prereading skills test 7.29 (ISBN 0-87892-664-X). Economy Co.

Nalimov, V. V. In the Labyrinths of Language: A Mathematician's Journey. Colodny, Robert G., ed. (Illus.). 246p. 1981. 22.50 (ISBN 0-89495-007-X). ISI Pr.

Nall, G. H., ed. see Cicero.

Nall, T. Otto. Builder of Bridges. LC 80-50241. 222p. 1980. text ed. 6.95x (ISBN 0-8358-0400-3). Upper Room.

Nalmanoff, George, jt. ed. see Friedman, Wolfgang.

Nalty, Bernard C., jt. ed. see MacGregor, Morris J.

Nam, Charles B. & Gustavus, Susan O. Population: The Dynamics of Change. LC 75-31031. (Illus.). 352p. 1976. text ed. 16.75 (ISBN 0-395-20627-8). HM.

Nambiar, O. K. Kunjalis, Admirals of Calicut. 1963. 7.00x o.p. (ISBN 0-210-34057-6). Asia.

Nameri, Dorothy. Three Versions of the Story of King Lear: Anonymous Ca. 1594-1605; William Shakespeare 1607-1608; Nahum Tate 1681, 2 vols. (Salzburg Studies in English Literature, Elizabethan & Renaissance Studies: Nos. 50 & 51). (Illus.). 1976. Set. pap. text ed. 50.25x (ISBN 0-391-01489-7). Humanities.

Namias. Study Guide in Physics, 2 vols. Incl. Vol. 1. Mechanics. 8.95x o.p. (ISBN 0-205-04009-8, 7340095); Vol. 2. Fluid Mechanics, Waves & Thermodynamics. 7.95x o.p. (ISBN 0-205-04210-4, 7342101). Allyn.

Namias, Victor. Study Guide in Physics: Electricity, Magnetism, Geometrical Optics, & Wave Optics, Vol. 3. 1976. pap. text ed. 6.95x o.p. (ISBN 0-205-05719-5). Allyn.

Namier, L. B. Diplomatic Prelude, 1938-1939. 19.50 o.p. (ISBN 0-86527-044-9). Fertig.

Namikawa, Y. Toroidal Compactification of Siegel Spaces. (Lecture Notes in Mathematics: Vol. 812). 162p. 1980. pap. 11.80 (ISBN 0-387-10021-0). Springer-Verlag.

Namikoshi, Tokujiro. Shiatsu: Japanese Finger-Pressure Therapy. LC 68-19983. (Illus.). 84p. 1972. pap. 6.95 (ISBN 0-87040-169-6). Japan Pubns.

Namikoshi, Toru. Complete Book of Shiatsu Therapy. LC 79-1963. (Illus.). 1980. pap. 9.95 (ISBN 0-87040-461-X). Japan Pubns.

--Shiatsu Therapy: Its Theory & Practice. (Illus.). 1977. pap. 7.95 (ISBN 0-87040-270-6). Japan Pubns.

Namioka, Lensey. Japan: A Traveller's Companion. LC 78-63639. (Illus.). 1979. 12.95 (ISBN 0-8149-0810-1); pap. 7.95 (ISBN 0-8149-0816-0). Vanguard.

--Village of the Vampire Cat: A Novel. LC 80-68737. 218p. (YA) (gr. 8-12). 1981. 8.95 (ISBN 0-440-09377-5). Delacorte.

--Who's Hu? LC 80-20062. 124p. (gr. 4 up). 1981. 8.95 (ISBN 0-8149-0843-8). Vanguard.

Namjoshi, Sarojini, tr. see Govindagraj.

Namjoshi, Suniti. More Poems. 8.00 (ISBN 0-89253-706-X); flexible cloth 4.00 (ISBN 0-89253-707-8). Ind-US Inc.

--Poems. 5.00 (ISBN 0-89253-704-3); flexible cloth 4.00 (ISBN 0-89253-705-1). Ind-US Inc.

Namjoshi, Suniti, tr. see Govindagraj.

Nammack, Georgiana C. Fraud, Politics & the Disposition of the Indians: The Iroquois Land Frontier in the Colonial Period. (Civilization of the American Indian Ser.: Vol. 97). (Illus.). 128p. 1969. 8.95x (ISBN 0-8061-0854-1). U of Okla Pr.

Namon, Richard, jt. auth. see Richey, E. T.

Namrick, Alma W. The Call of San Saba: A History of San Saba Country. 12.50 (ISBN 0-685-64413-8). Jenkins.

Namuth, Hans. Pollock Painting. new ed. Rose, Barbara, ed. LC 79-57621. (Illus.). 112p. 1980. 25.00 (ISBN 0-9601068-6-3); pap. 14.95 (ISBN 0-9601068-5-5). Agrinde Bks.

Namuth, Hans, intro. by. Fifty-Two Artists: Photographs by Hans Namuth. (Illus., Exhibit portfolio). 12.00 (ISBN 0-89062-012-1, Pub. by Comm Visual). Pub Ctr Cult Res.

Nanak, Guru. Adi-Granth: The Japji. Singh, Sangat, tr. from Punjabi. 128p. (Orig.). 1974. pap. 2.25 (ISBN 0-88253-317-7). Ind-US Inc.

Nanassay, Louis C., et al. Personal Typing. (gr. 9-12). 1970. pap. 8.20 (ISBN 0-8224-0272-6); tchrs'. manual 3.80 (ISBN 0-8224-2001-5). Pitman Learning.

Nanassy, Louis C., ed. Readings in Teaching Business Subjects. LC 78-72079. 1979. pap. 16.00 (ISBN 0-8224-5828-4). Pitman Learning.

Nanassy, Louis C., et al. Principles & Trends in Business Education. LC 76-57995. 1977. text ed. 19.50 (ISBN 0-672-97092-9). Bobbs.

Nancarrow, P. Early China & the Wall. LC 76-51411. (Cambridge Introduction to the History of Mankind). 1978. pap. 3.95 (ISBN 0-521-20880-7). Cambridge U Pr.

Nance, Guinevera, jt. auth. see Jones, Judith.

Nance, H. W. & Nolan, R. E. Office Work Measurement. 1971. 23.50 o.p. (ISBN 0-07-045880-4, P&RB). McGraw.

Nance, Joseph M. After San Jacinto: The Texas-Mexican Frontier, 1836-1841. (Illus.). 1962. 25.00x (ISBN 0-292-73156-6). U of Tex Pr.

Nance, Walter E., et al, eds. see International Congress on Twin Studies, 2nd.

Nanda, B. R., et al. Gandhi & Nehru. 76p. 1979. pap. text ed. 4.50x (ISBN 0-19-561148-9). Oxford U Pr.

Nanda, Krish, jt. auth. see Sarkesian, Sam C.

Nanda, Navin. Two Dimensional Echocardiography. 1981. write for info. (ISBN 0-87993-134-5). Futura Pub.

Nanda, Navin C. & Gramiak, Raymond. Clinical Echocardiography. LC 78-4116. 1978. text ed. 41.50 (ISBN 0-8016-3622-1). Mosby.

Nanda, Ned P., et al, eds. Developing Human Rights. (Westview Special Study Ser.). 285p. 1981. lib. bdg. 28.50x (ISBN 0-89158-858-2). Westview.

Nanda, Ved P., jt. auth. see Bassiouni, M. Cherif.

Nanda, Ved P., jt. ed. see Bassiouni, M. Cherif.

Nandakumar, Prema. The Mother of Sri Aurobindo Ashram. (National Biography Ser.). 1979. pap. 2.25 (ISBN 0-89744-198-2). Auromere.

Nandan, Yash, ed. Emile Durkheim: Contributions to L'Annee Sociologique. LC 79-54670. 1980. 27.50 (ISBN 0-02-907980-2). Free Pr.

Nandedkar, V. G. Local Government: Its Role in Development Administration. 1979. text ed. 12.50x (ISBN 0-686-61444-5). Humanities.

Nandi, Proshanta & Yu, Elena, eds. Asian Americans: Identity, Adaptation & Survival. (Monograph Ser.). (Orig.). 1981. cancelled (ISBN 0-934584-13-3). Pacific-Asian. Postponed.

Nandris. Handbook of Old Church Slavonic, Pt. 1: Old Church Slavonic Grammar. 1959. text ed. 26.25x (ISBN 0-485-17507-X, Athlone Pr). Humanities.

Nandris, Grigore. Colloquial Rumanian: Grammar, Exercises, Reader & Vocabulary. (Tribner's Colloquial Manuals). 1967. 9.95 (ISBN 0-7100-4334-1). Routledge & Kegan.

Nandy, Ashis. At the Edge of Psychology: Essays on Politics & Culture. 152p. 1981. 9.95 (ISBN 0-19-561205-1). Oxford U Pr.

Nandy, Dipak. The Politics of Race Relations. (Political Issues of Modern Britain Ser.). 1980. text ed. write for info. o.p. (ISBN 0-391-01147-2). Humanities.

Nandy, Pritish. On Either Side of Arrogance. (Redbird Ser.). 1975. 4.80 (ISBN 0-88253-596-X); pap. text ed. 4.00 (ISBN 0-88253-595-1). Ind-US Inc.

--Riding the Midnight River: Selected Poems of Pritish Nandy. (Indian Poetry Ser.). 144p. 1975. 9.00 (ISBN 0-89253-013-8). Ind-US Inc.

--Rites for a Plebian Statue. 8.00 (ISBN 0-89253-654-3); flexible cloth 4.80 (ISBN 0-89253-655-1). Ind-US Inc.

Nandy, Pritish, ed. Indian Poetry in English Today. (Indian Poetry Ser.). 140p. (Orig.). 1974. 2.00 (ISBN 0-88253-312-6). Ind-US Inc.

Nandy, Pritish, tr. see Sen, Samar.

Nanes, Allan, jt. ed. see Alexander, Yonah.

Nangle, Benjamin. The Gentleman's Magazine Biographical & Obituary Notices, 1781-1819: An Index. LC 80-907. (Garland Reference Library of Humanities). 450p. 1980. 55.00 (ISBN 0-8240-9510-3). Garland Pub.

Nanjio, Bunyiu, tr. from Japanese. Short History of the Twelve Buddhist Sects. (Studies in Japanese History & Civilization). 1979. Repr. of 1886 ed. 19.75 (ISBN 0-89093-252-2). U Pubns Amer.

Nankin, Howard, jt. ed. see Troen, Philip.

Nanney & Cable. Algebra & Trigonometry: A Skills Approach. 600p. 1980. text ed. 17.80 (ISBN 0-205-06917-7, 5669170); study guide avail. (ISBN 0-205-06919-3, 5669197). Allyn.

--College Algebra: A Skills Approach. 1978. pap. text ed. 16.75 (ISBN 0-205-05913-9); instr's manual (ISBN 0-205-05914-7). Allyn.

--College Algebra: A Skills Approach, Lecture Version. 320p. 1980. text ed. 16.75 (ISBN 0-205-06914-2, 5669146). Allyn.

Nanney & Calbe. Trigonometry: A Skills Approach, Lecture Version. 301p. 1980. text ed. 14.65 (ISBN 0-205-06920-7, 5669200); study goide 5.95 (ISBN 0-205-06922-3, 5669200). Allyn.

Nanney, J. L. & Shaffer, R. D. Arithmetic: A Review. text ed. 15.95x (ISBN 0-471-62990-1). Wiley.

Nanney, J. Louis & Cable, John L. Trigonometry: A Skills Approach. 1979. pap. text ed. 15.25 (ISBN 0-205-06603-8, 5666031); instr's man. o.p. avail. (ISBN 0-205-06608-9). Allyn.

Nanney, Louis & Cable, John. Developing Skills in Algebra: A Lecture Worktext, 2 vols. 2nd ed. 1976. Vol. 1. pap. text ed. 8.50x o.p. (ISBN 0-205-05417-X); Vol. 2. pap. text ed. 9.50x o.p. (ISBN 0-205-05472-2); pap. text ed. 14.95x combined ed. o.p. (ISBN 0-205-05493-5). Allyn.

--Developing Skills in Algebra: A Lecture Worktext, 2 vols. 3rd ed. 1978. pap. text ed. 17.80 set; Vol. I. 13.25 (ISBN 0-205-06507-4); Vol. II. 12.55 (ISBN 0-205-06508-2); Combined Ed. pap. text ed. 15.95x (ISBN 0-205-06509-0); instr's. manual avail. (ISBN 0-205-06534-1). Allyn.

Nanney, T. Ray. Computing: A Problem-Solving Approach Using FORTRAN Seventy-Seven. (Illus.). 432p. 1981. text ed. 17.95 (ISBN 0-13-165209-5). P-H.

Nansen, Fridtjof. Armenia & the Near East. LC 76-25120. (Middle East in the Twentieth Century Ser.). 1977. Repr. of 1928 ed. lib. bdg. 29.50 (ISBN 0-306-70760-8). Da Capo.

Nanyenya-Takirambudde, Peter. Technology Transfer & International Law. LC 79-23571. 190p. 1980. 22.95 (ISBN 0-03-047531-7). Praeger.

Napear, Peggy. Brain Child: A Mother's Diary. LC 72-9141. (Illus.). 576p. 1974. 10.00 o.p. (ISBN 0-06-013156-X, HarpT). Har-Row.

Napier, Augustus Y. & Whitaker, Carl A. The Family Crucible. 320p. 1980. pap. 3.95 (ISBN 0-553-13576-7). Bantam.

Napier, B. Davie. Come Sweet Death. rev. ed. 64p. 1981. pap. 4.95 (ISBN 0-8298-0422-6). Pilgrim NY.

Napier, Davie. Song of the Vineyard: A Guide Through the Old Testament. rev. ed. LC 78-14672. 360p. 1981. pap. 11.95 (ISBN 0-8006-1352-X, 1-1352). Fortress.

Napier, Davie, jt. auth. see Borsch, Frederick H.

Napier, Elizabeth R., tr. see Kandinsky, Wassily.

Napier, John. Big Foot: The Yeti & Sasquatch in Myth & Reality. 1973. 9.95 o.p. (ISBN 0-525-06658-6). Dutton.

--Bigfoot. pap. 1.50 o.p. (ISBN 0-425-03381-3). Berkley Pub.

Napier, John T. Selected Poetry & Prose of John T. Napier. Rubin, David, ed. 73p. pap. 1.00. Pikeville Coll.

Napier, Mary. The Waiting. 240p. (Orig.). 1980. pap. 2.25 (ISBN 0-553-13477-9). Bantam.

Napier, Miles. Blood Will Tell. pap. 8.75 (ISBN 0-85131-254-3, Dist. by Sporting Book Center). J A Allen.

--The Racing Men of TV. new ed. 1978. pap. 8.75 (ISBN 0-85131-301-9, Dist. by Sporting Book Center). J A Allen.

--Thoroughbred Pedigrees Simplified. 11.37 (ISBN 0-85131-191-1, Dist. by Sporting Book Center). J A Allen.

Napier, P. H. Catalogue of Primates in the British Museum (Natural History) & Elsewhere in the British Isles, Part 2: Family Cercopithecidae, Subfamily Cercopthecinae. 120p. 1980. pap. 25.00x (ISBN 0-565-00815-3). Sabbot-Natural Hist Bks.

Napier, Rodney & Gershenfeld, Matti. Groups: Theory & Experience. 2nd ed. (Illus.). 448p. 1981. text ed. write for info. (ISBN 0-395-29703-6). HM.

Napier, Rodney W. & Gershenfeld, Matti K. Groups: Theory & Experience. LC 72-7925. 325p. 1973. text ed. 17.95 (ISBN 0-395-12658-4, 3-40200); instructors' manual pap. 4.50 (ISBN 0-395-14048-X, 3-40201). HM.

Napier, Tel L. Outdoor Recreation Planning, Perspectives & Research. 288p. 1981. pap. text ed. 12.95 (ISBN 0-8403-2309-3). Kendall-Hunt.

Napier, William, et al. Pacific Voyages. 480p. 1973. 7.95 o.p. (ISBN 0-385-04335-X). Doubleday.

Napleton, Lewis. Guide to Microwave Catering. 3rd ed. (Illus.). 1976. pap. 11.95x (ISBN 0-7198-2523-7). Intl Ideas.

Napoleoni, Claudio. Economic Thought of the Twentieth Century. Cigno, Alessandro, tr. 174p. 1981. pap. 12.50x (ISBN 0-85520-009-X, Pub. by Martin Robertson England). Biblio Dist.

--Smith, Ricardo, Marx. Gee, J. M., tr. from It. LC 75-15962. 198p. 1975. lib. bdg. 19.95 (ISBN 0-470-63011-6). Halsted Pr.

Napoli, Donald S. The Architects of Adjustment: The History of the Psychological Profession in America. (National University Publications, American Studies Ser.). 185p. 1981. 20.00 (ISBN 0-8046-9269-6). Kennikat.

Napoli, Donna J., jt. ed. see Cressey, William W.

Napolitano, L. G., ed. see International Astronautical Congress, 29th, Dubrovnik, 1-8 October 1978.

Napolitano, Luigi G. & International Astronautical Congress, 27th, Anaheim, Ca., Oct. 1976. Proceedings. 1977. text ed. 64.00 (ISBN 0-08-021732-X). Pergamon.

Napolitano, Luigi G. & International Astronautical Congress, 28th, Prague, 1977. Using Space--Today & Tomorrow: Proceedings, Vol. 1. 1978. text ed. 60.00 (ISBN 0-08-023231-0). Pergamon.

Napolski, Max von. Leben und Werke Des Trobadors Ponz De Capduoill. LC 80-2183. 1981. Repr. of 1879 ed. 26.50 (ISBN 0-404-19009-X). AMS Pr.

Nappi, Carmine. Commodity Market Controls. LC 78-24715. (Illus.). 224p. 1979. 23.95 (ISBN 0-669-02812-6). Lexington Bks.

Narahashi, Toshio. Cellular Pharmacology of Excitable Tissues. (Illus.). 552p. 1975. 47.50 (ISBN 0-398-03358-7). C C Thomas.

Narahashi, Toshio & Bianchi, C. Paul, eds. Advances in General & Cellular Pharmacology. Incl. Vol. 1. 252p. 1976. 29.50 (ISBN 0-306-35071-8); Vol. 2. 195p. 1977. 24.50 (ISBN 0-306-35072-6). Plenum Pr). Plenum Pub.

Narain, A. K. Studies in History of Buddhism: Papers Presented at the International Conference on the History of Buddhism at the University of Wisconsin, Madison August 19-21,1976. 421p. 1980. text ed. 40.50 (ISBN 0-391-02212-1). Humanities.

Narain, I., jt. ed. see Mathur, M. V.

Narasimaiah, C. D. Raja Rao. (Indian Writers Ser.). 8.50 (ISBN 0-89253-511-3). Ind-US Inc.

Narasimhaiah, C. D., ed. see Kohli, Devindra.

Narasimhaiah, C. D., ed. see Sastri, P. S.

Narasimhamurty, T. S. Photoelastic & Electro-Optic Properties of Crystals. (Illus.). 490p. 1981. 37.50 (ISBN 0-306-31101-1, Plenum Pr). Plenum Pub.

Narasimhan, Chakravarthi V., tr. The Mahabharata. LC 64-10347. 254p. (English version based on selected verses). 1973. pap. 6.00 (ISBN 0-231-08321-1). Columbia U Pr.

Narasimhan, Raji. The Heart of Standing Is You Cannot Fly. (Writers Workshop Greenbird Book Ser.). 131p. 1975. 14.00 (ISBN 0-88253-558-7); pap. text ed. 6.75 (ISBN 0-88253-557-9). Ind-US Inc.

Naravane, V. S. Elephant & the Lotus Essays in Philosophy & Culture. 1964. 15.00x (ISBN 0-210-26853-0). Asia.

--Premchand: His Life & Work. 280p. 1980. text ed. 18.95x (ISBN 0-7069-1091-5, Pub. by Vikas India). Advent Bk.

Naravane, Vishwanath S. Ananda K. Coomaraswamy. (World Leaders Ser.: No. 75). 1978. 12.50 (ISBN 0-8057-7722-9). Twayne.

Narayan, B. K. Mohammed: The Prophet of Islam, a Flame in the Desert. 250p. 1980. text ed. 27.50x (ISBN 0-8426-1662-4). Verry.

--Oman & Gulf-Security. 300p. 1980. text ed. 24.00x (ISBN 0-8426-1660-8). Verry.

Narayan, R. K. The Bachelor of Arts. 1980. pap. 3.95 (ISBN 0-686-69041-9). U of Chicago Pr.

--The Dark Room. iv, 210p. 1981. lib. bdg. 15.00x (ISBN 0-226-56836-9); pap. 4.95 (ISBN 0-226-56837-7). U of Chicago Pr.

--Lawley Road & Other Stories. 159p. 1969. pap. 1.95 o.p. (ISBN 0-88253-062-3). Ind-US Inc.

--Mr Sampath: The Printer of Malgudi. LC 80-27352. 220p. 1981. lib. bdg. 15.00x (ISBN 0-226-56838-5); pap. 4.95 (ISBN 0-226-56839-3). U of Chicago Pr.

--Reluctant Guru. 173p. 1975. pap. 2.50 (ISBN 0-88253-729-6). Ind-US Inc.

--Swami & Friends. LC 80-16119. 192p. 1980. lib. bdg. 13.00x (ISBN 0-226-56829-6); pap. 3.95 (ISBN 0-226-56831-8). U of Chicago Pr.

Narayan, S. A. Sudhin N. Ghose. (Indian Writers Ser.). 8.50 (ISBN 0-89253-557-1). Ind-US Inc.

Narayanan, K. R. & Misra, K. P., eds. Nonalignment in Contemporary International Relations. 275p. 1981. text ed. 27.50x (ISBN 0-7069-1286-1, Pub by Vikas India). Advent Bk.

Narayana Rao, K. V. The Emergence of Andhra Pradesh. 350p. 1974. lib. bdg. 12.50 (ISBN 0-88253-472-6). Ind-US Inc.

Narayanaswamy, K. R. Unreal Past & Other Poems. 6.75 (ISBN 0-89253-710-8); flexible cloth 3.00 (ISBN 0-89253-711-6). Ind-US Inc.

Narbeth, Colin, et al. Collecting Paper Money & Bonds. (The Christies International Collectors Ser.). (Illus.). 128p. 1980. 14.95 (ISBN 0-8317-0940-5). Mayflower Bks.

Narcisco, John, jt. auth. see Burkett, David.

Nardi, George, tr. see Valdoni, Pietro.

Nardine, Elisabeth. Daydreams & Night. LC 76-15240. (Moods & Emotions Ser.). (Illus.). 32p. (gr. k-3). 1976. PLB 8.95 (ISBN 0-8172-0014-2). Raintree Pubs.

Nardini, William, ed. see Caldwell, Robert G.

Nardo, Anna K. Milton's Sonnets & the Ideal Community. LC 79-17221. 1979. 15.95x (ISBN 0-8032-3302-7). U of Nebr Pr.

Nardulli, Peter F. & Stonecash, Jeffrey M. Politics, Rationality, & the Urban Services: The Police. LC 80-27169. 228p. 1981. lib. bdg. 20.00 (ISBN 0-89946-076-3). Oelgeschlager.

Narell, Irena. Joshua: Fighter for Bar Kochba. LC 78-55959. (gr. 6-12). 1979. pap. 8.95 (ISBN 0-934764-01-8). Akiba Pr.

Narendra, Kumpati & Monopoli, Richard, eds. Applications of Adaptive Control. 1980. 39.50 (ISBN 0-12-514060-6). Acad Pr.

Nares, George S. Nares Seamanship Eighteen Sixty-Two. 2nd ed. (Illus.). 239p. 1979. 15.00x (ISBN 0-905418-37-9). Intl Pubns Serv.

Nares, Robert. Glossary of Words, Phrases, Names & Allusions in the Works of English Authors. LC 66-25635. 1966. Repr. of 1905 ed. 34.00 (ISBN 0-8103-3219-1). Gale.

Narici, Lawrence, jt. auth. see Bachman, George.

Narita, Katsuya. Systems of Higher Education: Japan. (Design & Management of Systems of Higher Education Ser.). 154p. (Orig.). 1978. pap. text ed. 5.50 (ISBN 0-89192-202-4). Interbk Inc.

Narita, Shigehisa, tr. see Kawamoto, Shigeo & Nishiwaki, Junzaburo.

Narkiewicz, Olga A. Making of the Soviet State Apparatus. 1970. text ed. 11.00x (ISBN 0-7190-0401-2). Humanities.

Narkiss, B., ed. The Journal of Jewish Art, Vol. 7. (Illus.). 90p. 1981. pap. 15.00 (ISBN 0-8390-0271-8). Allanheld & Schram.

Narkiss, Bezalel. Hebrew Illuminated Manuscripts in the British Isles: A Catalogue Raisonne, Vol. I; Spanish & Portugese Manuscripts. (Illus.). 492p. 1981. 125.00 (ISBN 0-686-69114-8) (ISBN 0-19-725977-4). Oxford U Pr.

Narlikar, J. V., jt. auth. see Hoyle, Fred.

Narlikar, Jayant V., jt. auth. see Hoyle, Fred.

Narmour, Eugene. Beyond Schenkerism: The Need for Alternatives in Music Analysis. LC 76-25632. xii, 238p. 1980. pap. 7.50 (ISBN 0-226-56848-2, P893, Phoen). U of Chicago Pr.

Naroll, Raoul & Cohen, Ronald, eds. A Handbook of Method in Cultural Anthropology. 1973. 47.50x (ISBN 0-231-03731-7); pap. 20.00x (ISBN 0-231-03749-X). Columbia U Pr.

Narramore, Bruce. Why Children Misbehave. 176p. 1980. 8.95 (ISBN 0-310-30360-5). Zondervan.

Narramore, Clyde & Narramore, Ruth. Como Dominar la Tension Nerviosa. Ward, Rhode, tr. from Eng. 216p. (Orig., Span.). 1978. pap. 3.95 (ISBN 0-89922-129-7). Edit Caribe.

Narramore, Clyde M. Counseling Youth. new ed. 128p. (Orig.). 1974. pap. 3.95 (ISBN 0-310-29891-1). Zondervan.

--Life & Love: A Christian View of Sex. (gr. 6 up). pap. 2.25 (ISBN 0-310-29922-5). Zondervan.

--Psychology of Counseling. 9.95 (ISBN 0-310-29930-6). Zondervan.

--This Way to Happiness. (gr. 8 up). pap. 2.95 (ISBN 0-310-29942-X). Zondervan.

--Woman's World. pap. 2.95 (ISBN 0-310-29962-4). Zondervan.

--Young Children & Their Problems. (Christian Psychology Ser). 1961. pap. 0.75 o.p. (ISBN 0-310-30222-6). Zondervan.

--Young Only Once. (gr. 8 up). pap. 2.95 (ISBN 0-310-29972-1). Zondervan.

Narramore, Ruth, jt. auth. see Narramore, Clyde.

Narrell, Irena. Our City: The Jews of San Francisco. LC 80-21216. 1980. 15.00 (ISBN 0-8310-7122-2). Howell-North.

Narvaez, Leon. Ambientes Hispanicos One: No. 1. LC 79-15478. (Illus.). 1979. 8.95 (ISBN 0-88436-544-1); pap. text ed. 5.95 (ISBN 0-88436-543-3). EMC.

--Ambientes Hispanicos Two. LC 80-12977. (Illus.). 1980. text ed. 9.50 (ISBN 0-88436-547-6); pap. text ed. 6.50 (ISBN 0-88436-546-8). EMC.

Narver, John C. Conglomerate Mergers & Market Competition. (Institute of Business & Economic Research, UC Berkeley). 1967. 20.00x (ISBN 0-520-00915-0). U of Cal Pr.

Nasar, Syed A. Schaum's Outline of Electric Machines & Electromechanics. (Schaum's Outline Ser.). (Illus.). 208p. 1981. pap. 6.95 (ISBN 0-07-045886-3, SP): McGraw.

Nasatir, Abraham P., jt. auth. see Bailey, Helen M.

Nasatir, David. Data Archives for the Social Sciences: Purposes, Operations, & Problems. LC 72-96443. 126p. (Orig.). 1973. pap. 4.75 (ISBN 92-3-101052-2, U150, UNESCO). Unipub.

Nasaw, David. Schooled to Order: A Social History of Public Schooling in the United States. 316p. 1981. pap. 5.95 (ISBN 0-19-502892-9, GB 626, OPB). Oxford U Pr.

Nasciemento, Abdiasdo. Sortilego. 1980. pap. 2.95 (ISBN 0-88378-086-0). Third World.

Nascimento, Edson Arantes do. Learning Soccer with Pele. LC 78-1334. (Illus.). 1978. 8.95 o.s.i. (ISBN 0-397-01280-2); pap. 4.95 o.s.i. (ISBN 0-397-01281-0). Lippincott.

Nasedkin, John N., jt. auth. see Celenza, Frank V.

Nash. Science of Psi: ESP & PK. 308p. 1978. 19.75 (ISBN 0-398-03803-1). C C Thomas.

Nash, jt. auth. see Gurti.

Nash, Al. Ruskin College: A Challenge to Adult & Labor Education. 1981. pap. price not set (ISBN 0-87546-084-4). NY Sch Indus Rel.

--Union Steward: Duties, Rights, & Status. (Key Issues Ser.: No. 22). 1977. pap. 3.00 (ISBN 0-87546-235-9). NY Sch Indus Rel.

Nash, Allan N. & Carroll, Stephen J. The Management of Compensation. LC 74-18922. (Behavioral Science in Industry Ser.). (Illus.). 1975. text ed. 11.95x (ISBN 0-8185-0135-9); pap. text ed. 8.95 (ISBN 0-8185-0135-9). Brooks-Cole.

Nash, Andrew J. Statistical Techniques in Forestry. 2nd ed. 6.00x (ISBN 0-685-52947-9). Lucas.

Nash, Bruce M. & Monchick, Randolph B. The Book of Tests: The Ultimate Collection of Quizzes to Help You Find Out What You're Really Like. LC 79-6611. 384p. 1980. pap. 8.95 (ISBN 0-385-15471-2, Dolp). Doubleday.

Nash, Christopher, jt. auth. see Pearce, David.

Nash, Constance & Oakey, Virginia. The Screenwriter's Handbook: What to Write, How to Write It, Where to Sell It. LC 77-76031. 1978. 10.95 o.p. (ISBN 0-06-013162-4, HarpT). Har-Row.

Nash, David T. Coronary: Prediction & Prevention. LC 78-13099. (Illus.). 1979. 12.50 o.p. (ISBN 0-684-15820-5, ScribT). Scribner.

Nash, Dephne, jt. auth. see Allen, Derek.

Nash, Donald J. Individual Identification & the Law Enforcement Officer. (Illus.). 176p. 1978. 16.75 (ISBN 0-398-03708-6). C C Thomas.

Nash, Eric, ed. Behavioral Assessment Childhood Disorders. Terdal, Leif. (Behavioral Assessment Ser.). 750p. 1981. 27.50 (ISBN 0-89862-141-0). Guilford Pr.

Nash, Ernest. Pictorial Dictionary of Ancient Rome, 2 vols. LC 79-91827. (Illus.). 1076p. 1980. Repr. of 1968 ed. Set. lib. bdg. 150.00 (ISBN 0-87817-265-3). Hacker.

Nash, Gary B. Class & Society in Early America. (Interdisciplinary Approaches to History). (Illus.). 1970. ref. ed. 11.95 (ISBN 0-13-135111-7); pap. text ed. 9.95 o.p. (ISBN 0-13-135103-6). P-H.

--Red, White, & Black: The Peoples of Early America. (Illus.). 320p. 1974. pap. text ed. 10.95 (ISBN 0-13-769802-X). P-H.

Nash, Gary B. & Weiss, Richard, eds. Great Fear: Race in the Mind of America. LC 77-118970. 1970. 5.95 o.p. (ISBN 0-03-085270-6). HR&W.

Nash, Gary B., jt. ed. see Sweet, David G.

Nash, George. Old Houses: A Rebuilder's Manual. (Illus.). 1980. 22.95 (ISBN 0-13-633875-5, Spec); pap. 12.95 (ISBN 0-13-633883-6). P-H.

Nash, George, ed. see Carnegie Commission on Higher Education.

Nash, Gerald B. As You Think. (Uplook Ser.). 1978. pap. 0.75 (ISBN 0-8163-0193-X, 0176507). Pacific Pr Pub Assn.

Nash, Gerald R. Why God Allows Trials & Disappointments. (Uplook Ser.). 31p. 1972. pap. 0.75 (ISBN 0-8163-0082-8, 23618-2). Pacific Pr Pub Assn.

Nash, Henry T. American Foreign Policy: Changing Perspectives on National Security. rev. ed. 1978. pap. text ed. 12.95x (ISBN 0-256-02055-8). Dorsey.

Nash, Howard P., Jr. A Naval History of the Civil War. LC 76-146768. (Illus.). 288p. 1972. 12.00 o.p. (ISBN 0-498-07841-8). A S Barnes.

Nash, J. Cubism, Futurism & Constructivism. LC 77-76770. (Modern Movements in Art Ser.). 1978. pap. 1.95 (ISBN 0-8120-0881-2). Barron.

Nash, J. P., et al. Road Building Materials in Texas. (Illus.). 159p. 1918. 0.50 (BULL 1839). Bur Econ Geology.

Nash, J. Robert. Bloodletters & Badmen, Vol. 1. (Illus.). 1975. pap. 2.75 (ISBN 0-446-95531-0). Warner Bks.

--Bloodletters & Badmen, Vol. 2. (Illus.). 1975. pap. 2.75 (ISBN 0-446-95532-9). Warner Bks.

--Bloodletters & Badmen, Vol. 3. (Illus.). 1975. pap. 2.75 (ISBN 0-446-95533-7). Warner Bks.

Nash, Jay R. Bloodletters & Badmen: A Narrative Encyclopedia of American Criminals from the Pilgrims to the Present. LC 72-95977. (Illus.). 640p. 1973. 16.95 o.p. (ISBN 0-87131-113-5); pap. 9.95 (ISBN 0-87131-200-X). M Evans.

--Citizen Hoover: A Critical Study of the Life & Times of J. Edgar Hoover & His FBI. LC 72-76266. (Illus.). 240p. 1972. 14.95 (ISBN 0-911012-60-5). Nelson-Hall.

--A Crime Story. 1981. 10.95 (ISBN 0-440-01534-0). Delacorte.

--Darkest Hours: A Narrative Encyclopedia of World Wide Disasters from Ancient Times to the Present. LC 76-7390. (Illus.). 1976. 49.95 (ISBN 0-88229-140-8). Nelson-Hall.

--Look for the Woman. De Kay, George C., ed. (Illus.). 320p. 1981. 14.95 (ISBN 0-87131-336-7). M Evans.

Nash, Jay R., ed. Almanac of World Crime. LC 79-6871. (Illus.). 432p. 1981. 19.95 (ISBN 0-385-15003-2). Doubleday.

Nash, Jean. The Golden Thread. (Orig.). 1980. pap. 2.25 (ISBN 0-505-51483-4). Tower Bks.

--The Silver Web. (Orig.). 1980. pap. 2.25 (ISBN 0-505-51473-7). Tower Bks.

Nash, John. Developmental Psychology: A Psychobiological Approach. 2nd ed. LC 77-27813. (Illus.). 1978. ref. ed. 19.95 (ISBN 0-13-208272-1). P-H.

Nash, June. We Eat the Mines & the Mines Eat Us: Dependency & Exploitation in Bolivian Tin Mines. LC 79-11623. 1979. 25.00 (ISBN 0-231-04710-X). Columbia U Pr.

Nash, June & Safa, Helen I., eds. Sex & Class in Latin America. new ed. (Illus.). 352p. 1980. lib. bdg. 19.95x (ISBN 0-89789-002-7); pap. text ed. 9.95x (ISBN 0-89789-003-5). J F Bergin.

Nash, Leonard K. ChemThermo: A Statistical Approach to Thermodynamics. 1972. pap. text ed. 6.95 (ISBN 0-201-05237-7). A-W.

--Elements of Chemical Thermodynamics. 2nd ed. LC 79-87040. 1970. pap. text ed. 6.95 (ISBN 0-201-05236-9). A-W.

--Elements of Statistical Thermodynamics. 2nd ed. 1974. 6.95 (ISBN 0-201-05229-6). A-W.

--Stoichiometry. LC 66-21269. (Chemistry Ser). (Orig.). 1966. pap. 6.95 (ISBN 0-201-05234-2). A-W.

Nash, Linda & Nash, Steve. Chicago & Beyond: Twenty-Six Bike Tours. 224p. 1981. pap. 6.95 (ISBN 0-695-81561-X). Follett.

Nash, Manning. Machine Age Maya: The Industrialization of a Guatemalan Community. LC 67-20810. 1967. pap. 3.95x (ISBN 0-226-56863-6, P262, Phoen). U of Chicago Pr.

Nash, Margaret A., ed. Christians: World Citizens. 1965. pap. 0.75 o.p. (ISBN 0-377-82551-4). Friend Pr.

Nash, N. Richard. Aphrodite's Cave. LC 80-1069. 480p. 1980. 13.95 (ISBN 0-385-14294-3). Doubleday.

--Cry Macho. 1975. 7.95 o.p. (ISBN 0-440-04996-2). Delacorte.

Nash, Ogden. Custard & Company. (Illus.). 128p. 1980. 8.95 (ISBN 0-316-59834-8). Little.

Nash, Paul. Fertile Image. 1975. 6.95 (ISBN 0-571-10636-6, Pub. by Faber & Faber). Merrimack Bk Serv.

Nash, Paul, et al. Models of Man: Explorations in the Western Educational Tradition. LC 67-29011. 1968. pap. text ed. 16.95x (ISBN 0-471-63043-8). Wiley.

Nash, Paul J. Land Hermit Crabs. (Illus., Orig.). 1976. text ed. 0.98 (ISBN 0-87666-907-0, A-325). TFH Pubns.

Nash, Ray. American Penmanship Eighteen Hundred to Eighteen Fifty: A History of Writing & a Bibliography of Copybooks from Jenkins to Spencer. LC 78-106556. 303p. 1969. 15.95x (ISBN 0-912296-10-0, Dist. by U Pr of Va). Am Antiquarian.

Nash, Roderick. American Environment: Readings in the History of Conservation. 2nd ed. LC 75-10913. 384p. 1976. pap. text ed. 9.50 (ISBN 0-201-05239-3). A-W.

Nash, Ronald H. The Light of the Mind: St. Augustine's Theory of Knowledge. LC 69-19765. 1969. 11.00 o.p. (ISBN 0-8131-1175-7). U Pr of Ky.

Nash, Rose. Comparing English & Spanish: Patterns in Phonology & Orthography. 1977. pap. text ed. 8.95 (ISBN 0-88345-297-9); cassettes 25.00 (ISBN 0-685-79303-6). Regents Pub.

Nash, Roy. Classrooms Observed: The Teacher's Perception & the Pupil's Performance. (Students Library of Education). 1973. cased 8.75x (ISBN 0-7100-7679-7); pap. 6.95 (ISBN 0-7100-7694-0). Routledge & Kegan.

--Conquest of Brazil. LC 67-29550. 1926. 14.00x (ISBN 0-8196-0207-8). Biblo.

Nash, Steve, jt. auth. see Nash, Linda.

Nash, Thomas. Description & First Procreation & Increase of the Towne of Great Yarmouth. Incl. Of the Praise of the Red Herring. 1975. text ed. 8.50 (ISBN 0-8277-3928-1); pap. text ed. 4.95 (ISBN 0-8277-2390-3). British Bk Ctr.

Nashe, Thomas. The Unfortunate Traveler: Or the Life of Jack Wilton. 194p. 1980. Repr. of 1926 ed. 30.00 (ISBN 0-89760-605-1). Telegraph Bks.

Nashe, Thomas see Rankins, William.

Nashelsky, L., jt. auth. see Boylestad, R.

Nashelsky, L., jt. auth. see Boylestad, Robert L.
Nashelsky, Louis. Introduction to Digital Computer Technology. 2nd ed. LC 76-42245. 1977. text ed. 22.95 (ISBN 0-471-02094-X). Wiley.
Nasir, Sari J. The Arabs & the English. 2nd ed. (Illus.). 1980. pap. 9.50 (ISBN 0-582-78306-2). Longman.
Nasiruddin, Al-Amir. Ar-Rafed: Arabic-Arabic Dictionary. 1971. 16.00x (ISBN 0-685-72028-4). Intl Bk Ctr.
Nasiruddin, Emir. Characteristics & Peculiarities of the Arabic Language. (Arabic.). 1968. 13.00x (ISBN 0-685-72031-4). Intl Bk Ctr.
Naske, Claus M. & Rowinski, Ludwig J. Anchorage: A Pictorial History. Friedman, Donna R., ed. (Illus.). 208p. 1981. pap. price not set (ISBN 0-89865-106-9). Donning Co.
--Fairbanks: A Pictorial History. Friedman, Donna R., ed. (Illus.). 208p. 1981. pap. price not set (ISBN 0-89865-108-5). Donning Co.
Nasmith, David. Institutes of English Adjective Law (Procedure in Court) Embracing an Outline of the Law of Evidence & Measure of Damages. xxii, 355p. 1980. Repr. of 1879 ed. lib. bdg. 30.00x (ISBN 0-8377-0904-0). Rothman.
--Institutes of English Private Law: Embracing an Outline of the Substantive Branch of the Law of the Persons & Things, 2 vols. 720p. 1980. Repr. of 1875 ed. Set. lib. bdg. 57.50x (ISBN 0-8377-0903-2). Rothman.
--Institutes of English Public Law: Embracing an Outline of General Jurisprudence, the Development of the British Constitution, Public International Law, & the Public Municipal Law of England. vi, 455p. 1980. Repr. of 1873 ed. lib. bdg. 35.00x (ISBN 0-8377-0905-9). Rothman.
Nason, Alvin & DeHaan, Robert L. The Biological World. LC 72-8573. 672p. 1973. text ed. 21.95x o.p. (ISBN 0-471-63045-4). Wiley.
Nason, Alvin & Goldstein, Philip. Biology: Introduction to Life. 337p. (gr. 10-12). 1969. text ed. 17.56 o.p. (ISBN 0-201-05240-7, Sch Div). lab. manual 5.36 o.p. (ISBN 0-201-05242-3). A-W.
Nason, Donna, jt. auth. see Nason, Michael.
Nason, Janet. Dolls of the Nineteen Thirties Paper Dolls. 8p. (gr. 8-12). 1978. pap. 3.50 (ISBN 0-914510-08-8). Evergreen.
Nason, John W., jt. auth. see Malickson, David L.
Nason, Marty, jt. auth. see Mitchell, Kathleen.
Nason, Michael & Nason, Donna. Tara: The Dramatic Story of a Brain Injured Child's Courageous Fight to Get Well. 1976. pap. 3.50 o.p. (ISBN 0-8015-7455-2). Dutton.
Nason, Richard. A Modern Dunciad. pap. 4.00 (ISBN 0-912292-49-0). The Smith.
Nason, Robert W., jt. ed. see Fisk, George.
Nason, T. No Golden Cities. 1971. 3.95 o.s.i. (ISBN 0-02-768100-9, CCPr). Macmillan.
Nason, Thelma. Our Statue of Liberty. LC 69-10260. (Beginning-To-Read Ser). (Illus.). (gr. 2-4). 1969. 2.50 o.p. (ISBN 0-695-86700-8); PLB 3.39 o.p. (ISBN 0-685-10945-3). Follett.
Nasr, Mohammed. Arabic Standard Atlas. (Arabic.). pap. 10.00x. Intl Bk Ctr.
Nasr, Raja. Colloquial Arabic: An Oral Approach. 1968. 10.95 (ISBN 0-685-77111-3). Intl Bk Ctr.
--English Colloquial Arabic Dict. 1972. 18.00x (ISBN 0-685-77122-9). Intl Bk Ctr.
--Intermediate Colloquial Arabic Course. 1974. 12.00x (ISBN 0-685-72047-0). Intl Bk Ctr.
--Learn to Read Arabic. 1977. pap. 5.00x (ISBN 0-917062-02-7); with cassette 20.00x (ISBN 0-685-77769-3). Intl Bk Ctr.
--Structure of Arabic: From Sound to Sentence. 1968. 12.00x (ISBN 0-685-77112-1). Intl Bk Ctr.
--Teaching of Arabic As a Foreign Language. 12.00x (ISBN 0-685-89880-6). Intl Bk Ctr.
Nasr, Seyyed H. Islam & the Plight of Modern Man. LC 75-29014. (World of Islam Ser.). 1976. text ed. 24.00x (ISBN 0-582-78053-5). Longman.
--Sadr al-Din Shirazi & His Transcendent Theosophy. LC 78-62006. 1979. 9.50 (ISBN 0-87773-734-7). Great Eastern.
Nasr, Seyyed H., ed. Ismaili Contributions to Islamic Culture. 1978. 15.00 (ISBN 0-87773-731-2). Great Eastern.
--Nasir-I Khusraw: Forty Poems from the Divan. Wilson, Peter L. & Aavani, Gholam R., trs. 1978. 12.50 (ISBN 0-87773-730-4). Great Eastern.
Nass, et al. Sexual Choices: An Introduction to Human Sexuality. (Illus.). 550p. 1981. text ed. 17.95 (ISBN 0-87872-285-8). Duxbury Pr.
Nass, Gilbert D. Marriage & the Family. (Illus.). 1978. text ed. 16.95 (ISBN 0-201-02500-0); instr's man 3.00 (ISBN 0-201-02502-7); study guide 4.95 (ISBN 0-201-02501-9); tests 2.00 (ISBN 0-201-02503-5). A-W.
Nass, Stanley & Weidhorn, Manfred. Turn Your Life Around: Self-Knowledge for Self Improvement. LC 78-15360. 1978. 11.95 (ISBN 0-13-933069-0, Spec); pap. 4.95 (ISBN 0-13-933051-8). P-H.
Nass, Ulla. Weaves of the Incas. (Illus.). 108p. soft cover 16.95. Nass.
Nassar Foundation for Lebanese Std. Cultural Resources in Lebanon. (Arab Background Ser.). 12.00x (ISBN 0-685-72034-9). Intl Bk Ctr.
Nasser, Munir K. Press, Politics, & Power: Egypt's Heikal & Al-Ahram. 1979. text ed. 15.50 (ISBN 0-8138-0955-X); pap. text ed. 9.50 (ISBN 0-8138-1290-9). Iowa St U Pr.
Nassi, Robert & Bernstein, Bernard. Spanish Workbook 2. 1977. wkbk. 6.25 (ISBN 0-87720-988-X). AMSCO Sch.
Nassi, Robert, et al. Spanish Workbook 3. 1977. wkbk. 6.25 (ISBN 0-87720-989-8). AMSCO Sch.
Nassi, Robert J. Workbook in Spanish First Year. (Illus., Orig.). (gr. 8-11). 1964. wkbk 5.58 (ISBN 0-87720-503-5). AMSCO Sch.
Nassi, Robert J. & Bernstein, Bernard. Review Text in Spanish First Year. 2nd ed. (Illus., Orig.). (gr. 7-12). 1972. pap. text ed. 5.33 (ISBN 0-87720-500-0). AMSCO Sch.
--Review Text in Spanish Two Years. 2nd ed. (Illus., Orig.). (gr. 7-12). 1969. pap. text ed. 5.33 (ISBN 0-87720-505-1). AMSCO Sch.
--Spanish Workbook: Book 1. 1976. pap. text ed. 6.25 (ISBN 0-87720-987-1). AMSCO Sch.
--Workbook in Spanish First Year. 2nd ed. (gr. 9-12). 1973. wkbk 6.25 (ISBN 0-87720-519-1). AMSCO Sch.
--Workbook in Spanish Two Years. 2nd ed. (Illus., Orig.). (gr. 9-12). 1969. wkbk 6.25 (ISBN 0-87720-506-X). AMSCO Sch.
Nassi, Robert J., et al. Review Text in Spanish Three Years. (Illus., Orig.). (gr. 7-12). 1965. pap. text ed. 5.33 (ISBN 0-87720-508-6). AMSCO Sch.
--Workbook in Spanish Three Years. (Orig.). (gr. 10-12). 1966. wkbk 6.25 (ISBN 0-87720-509-4). AMSCO Sch.
Nassif, Janet Z. Health Professions in Medicine's New Technology. LC 80-22030. (Illus.). 256p. 1981. pap. 5.95 (ISBN 0-668-04436-5, 4436). Arco.
Nassif, Ricardo. Methods of Teaching Librarianship. 1969. pap. 6.00 (ISBN 92-3-100758-0, U384, UNESCO). Unipub.
NASSP. Voter Education Curriculum Guide. Bruce, Carol, ed. 78p. (Orig.). 1980. pap. text ed. 10.00 (ISBN 0-88210-114-5). Natl Assn Principals.
Natale, S. An Experiment in Empathy. (General Ser). 99p. (Orig.). 1972. pap. text ed. 10.00x (ISBN 0-901225-86-X, NFER). Humanities.
Natan, Alex, ed. German Men of Letters: Twelve Literary Essays. Vol. 1. 15.95 (ISBN 0-85496-001-5); pap. 8.95 (ISBN 0-85496-002-3); Vol. 2. pap. 15.95 (ISBN 0-85496-004-X); Vol. 3. pap. 10.95 (ISBN 0-85496-006-6). Dufour.
--Swiss Men of Letters. 1970. 15.95 (ISBN 0-85496-064-3). Dufour.
Natan, Alex & Keith-Smith, Brian, eds. German Man of Letters: Twelve Literary Essays, Vols. 5 & 6. LC 66-28772. 318p. 1973. Vol. 5. 15.95 (ISBN 0-8023-1175-X); Vol. 6. 15.95 (ISBN 0-8023-1239-X). Dufour.
Natanson, ed. see Celms, Theodor.
Natanson, Maurice. The Journeying Self: A Study in Philosophy & Social Role. (Philosophy Ser). 1970. pap. text ed. 9.95 (ISBN 0-201-05249-0). A-W.
--Phenomenology, Role, & Reason: Essays on the Coherence & Deformation of Social Reality. (Amer. Lec. in Philosophy Ser.). 368p. 1974. 27.95 (ISBN 0-398-02904-0). C C Thomas.
Natanson, Maurice, ed. see Berger, Gaston.
Natanson, Maurice, ed. see Lotze, Hermann.
Natanson, Maurice, ed. see Stavenhagen, Kurt.
Natanson, Maurice, ed. see Sternberger, Adolf.
Natelson, Ethan A., jt. auth. see Natelson, Samuel.
Natelson, Ethan A., jt. ed. see Natelson, Samuel.
Natelson, Robert G. Condos. (Orig.). 1981. price not set. Cornerstone.
--How to Buy & Sell a Condominium. 160p. (Orig.). 1981. pap. 4.95 (ISBN 0-346-12537-5). Cornerstone.
Natelson, Samuel. Techniques of Clinical Chemistry. 3rd ed. (Illus.). 980p. 1971. 49.75 (ISBN 0-398-01384-5). C C Thomas.
Natelson, Samuel & Natelson, Ethan A. Principles of Applied Clinical Chemistry: Plasma Protein, Vol. 3. (Illus.). 575p. 1980. 42.50 (ISBN 0-306-40276-9, Plenum Pr). Plenum Pub.
Natelson, Samuel & Natelson, Ethan A., eds. Principles of Applied Clinical Chemistry. Incl. Vol. 1, Maintenance of Fluid & Electrolyte Balance. LC 75-4798. 393p. 1975. 22.50 (ISBN 0-306-35231-1); Vol. 2, the Erythrocyte. 584p. 1978. 39.50 (ISBN 0-306-35232-X). (Illus., Plenum Pr). Plenum Pub.
Natelson, Samuel, et al. Amniotic Fluid: Physiology, Biochemistry, & Clinical Chemistry. LC 74-4444. (Current Topics in Clinical Chemistry Ser.). 416p. 1974. 48.95 (ISBN 0-471-63063-2, Pub. by Wiley Medical). Wiley.
Natesh, R., ed. Nondestructive Evaluation in the Nuclear Industry. 1978. 42.00 (ISBN 0-87170-029-8). ASM.
Nath, B. Fundamentals of Finite Elements for Engineers. (Illus.). 256p. 1974. text ed. 25.00x (ISBN 0-485-11148-9, Athlone Pr). Humanities.
Nath, R. The Art of Khajuraho. 1980. 90.00x (ISBN 0-8364-0608-7, Pub. by Abhina India). South Asia Bks.
Nath, Rakhal. New Hindu Movement, Eighteen Sixty-Six to Nineteen Eleven. 1981. 14.50x (ISBN 0-685-59382-7). South Asia Bks.
Nath, Vishwa. Animal Gametes, Vol. 1. Male. (Illus.). 1966. 25.00x (ISBN 0-210-31158-4). Asia.
--Animal Gametes, Vol. 2. Female. (Illus.). 1971. 25.00x (ISBN 0-210-98197-0). Asia.
Nathan & Oliver. U. S. Foreign Policy & World Order. 2nd ed. 475p. (Orig.). 1981. pap. text ed. 10.95 (ISBN 0-316-59851-8). Little.
Nathan, Andrew. Peking Politics, 1918-1923: Factionalism & the Failure of Constitutionalism. LC 74-79769. 1976. 22.75x (ISBN 0-520-02784-1). U of Cal Pr.
Nathan, Dorothy. Women of Courage. (Landmark Ser: No. 107). (Illus.). (gr. 5-9). 1964. PLB 5.99 (ISBN 0-394-90407-9, BYR); pap. 0.75 (ISBN 0-394-82186-6). Random.
Nathan, Ernest D. Starting Right in Real Estate. LC 79-20780. (Illus.). 1980. pap. text ed. 10.95 (ISBN 0-201-05224-5). A-W.
--Twenty-Four Questions in Group Leadership. 2nd ed. 1979. pap. 8.95 (ISBN 0-201-05263-6). A-W.
Nathan, Hans. Dan Emmett & the Rise of Early Negro Minstrelsy. (Illus.). 1962. 22.50 (ISBN 0-8061-0540-2); pap. 9.95 (ISBN 0-8061-1423-1). U of Okla Pr.
Nathan, Isaac. Memoirs of Madame Malibran De Beriot. LC 80-2291. 1981. Repr. of 1836 ed. 18.50 (ISBN 0-404-18860-5). AMS Pr.
Nathan, Joan. The Larosa International Pasta Cookbook. 7.95 (ISBN 0-916752-25-9). Green Hill.
Nathan, John, tr. from Japane see Oe, Kenzaburo.
Nathan, Kurt C., jt. auth. see Gallagher, James J.
Nathan, Larry C. Laboratory Project in Modern Coordination Chemistry. LC 80-25233. 93p. (Orig.). 1981. pap. text ed. 8.95 (ISBN 0-8185-0433-1). Brooks-Cole.
Nathan, Leonard. The Day the Perfect Speakers Left. LC 69-17791. (Wesleyan Poetry Program: Vol. 45). 1969. 10.00x (ISBN 0-8195-2045-4, Pub. by Wesleyan U Pr); pap. 4.95 (ISBN 0-8195-1045-9). Columbia U Pr.
--Western Reaches. 1963. 2.25 o.p. (ISBN 0-934612-06-4). Talisman.
Nathan, Leonard, tr. The Transport of Love: The Meghaduta of Kalidasa. 1976. 11.95x (ISBN 0-520-03031-1); pap. 2.95 (ISBN 0-520-03271-3, CAL348). U of Cal Pr.
Nathan, Leonard E. Tragic Drama of William Butler Yeats: Figures in a Dance. LC 65-16513. 1965. 17.50x (ISBN 0-231-02765-6). Columbia U Pr.
Nathan, N. M. The Concept of Justice. (New Studies in Practical Philosophy). (Illus.). 79p. 1972. text ed. 8.25x (ISBN 0-333-12398-0). Humanities.
--Evidence & Assurance. LC 79-50505. (Cambridge Studies in Philosophy). 1980. 29.50 (ISBN 0-521-22517-5). Cambridge U Pr.
Nathan, Raymond, jt. auth. see Ruder, William.
Nathan, Richard P. The Plot That Failed: Nixon & the Administrative Presidency. LC 74-30272. 176p. 1975. pap. text ed. 8.95x (ISBN 0-471-63065-9). Wiley.
Nathan, Richard P. & Webman, Jerry A., eds. The Urban Development Action Grant Program: Papers & Conference Proceedings on Its First Two Years of Operation. LC 80-84901. (Illus.). 124p. 1980. pap. 5.00 (ISBN 0-938882-00-7). PURRC.
Nathan, Richard P., et al. Monitoring Revenue Sharing. 394p. 1975. 14.95 (ISBN 0-8157-5984-3); pap. 5.95 (ISBN 0-8157-5983-5). Brookings.
Nathan, Robert. Heaven & Hell & the Megus Factor. 128p. 1975. 6.95 o.p. (ISBN 0-440-04328-X). Delacorte.
--The Summer Meadows. 128p. 1973. 5.95 o.p. (ISBN 0-440-08444-X). Delacorte.
Nathan, Robert L. Coal Mine, Number Seven. 320p. 1981. 12.95 (ISBN 0-312-14499-7). St Martin.
Nathan, Robert S. Rising Higher. 312p. 1981. 11.95 (ISBN 0-686-69091-5). Dial.
Nathan, Ronald G. & Charlesworth, Edward A. Stress Management: A Conceptual & Procedural Guide. (Illus.). 223p. (Orig.). 1980. pap. text ed. 19.95 (ISBN 0-938176-01-3). Biobehavioral Pr.
--Stress Management: A Conceptual & Procedural Guide. LC 80-70400. (Illus.). 223p. (Orig.). 1980. 19.95 (ISBN 0-938176-01-3). Wendover.
Nathan, Simon. In Focus: A Rated Guide to the Best in Photographic Equipment. LC 80-7600. (Illus.). 224p. 1980. 9.95 (ISBN 0-06-014028-3, HarpT). Har-Row.
Nathan, Stella. Porky Pig & Bugs Bunny - Just Like Magic. (Illus.). (ps-3). PLB 5.00 (ISBN 0-307-60146-3, Golden Pr). Western Pub.
--Things That Go! (Word Bird Books). (Illus.). 24p. (ps-2). 1977. PLB 5.22 o.p. (ISBN 0-307-66255-1, Golden Pr). Western Pub.
--Toys & Games. (Word Bird Books). (Illus.). 24p. (ps-2). 1977. PLB 5.22 o.p. (ISBN 0-307-66253-5, Golden Pr). Western Pub.
--Wild Animals. (Word Bird Bks.). (Illus.). 24p. (ps-2). 1977. PLB 5.22 o.p. (ISBN 0-307-66252-7, Golden Pr). Western Pub.
Nathan, Stella W. Jack & the Beanstalk. (Illus.). 24p. (gr. k-3). 1976. PLB 5.00 (ISBN 0-307-60454-3, Golden Pr). Western Pub.
Nathanielsz, P. W., jt. auth. see Beard, R. W.
Nathanson, Jerome. John Dewey: The Reconstruction of the Democratic Life. LC 66-26511. (Orig.). (gr. 11-12). 1967. text ed. 5.50 o.p. (ISBN 0-8044-6580-0); pap. 2.45 (ISBN 0-686-66560-0). Ungar.
Nathanson, Maurice, jt. auth. see Hodgson, Shadworth H.
Nathanson, Melvyn B., ed. & tr. see Freiman, Grigori.
Nathanson, Neal, jt. ed. see Sartwell, Philip E.
Nation, Terry. Rebecca's World. Learmonth, Larry, tr. LC 76-39725. (Illus.). 114p. (gr. 3-5). 1977. 7.95 (ISBN 0-8149-0779-2). Vanguard.
National Academy of Arbitrators, Annual Meeting. Arbitration of Subcontracting & Wage Incentive Disputes: Proceedings. Stern, James L. & Dennis, Barbara D., eds. LC 79-24133. 1980. 20.00 (ISBN 0-87179-318-0). BNA.
National Academy of Engineering. Application of Technology to Improve Productivity in the Service Sector of the National Economy. LC 72-85833. Orig. Title: Productivity in the Service Sector of the Economy. (Illus.). 344p. 1973. pap. 10.50 (ISBN 0-309-02041-7). Natl Acad Pr.
--Costs of Health Care Facilities. 1968. pap. 7.75 (ISBN 0-309-01592-8). Natl Acad Pr.
--The Engineer and the City. 1969. 7.00 (ISBN 0-309-00125-0). Natl Acad Pr.
--Engineering & Medicine. LC 74-606277. (Illus., Orig.). 1970. pap. 7.25 (ISBN 0-309-01768-8). Natl Acad Pr.
--National Academy of Engineering Memorial Tributes. 1979. 10.00 (ISBN 0-309-02889-2). Natl Acad Pr.
--Process of Technological Innovation. LC 72-601240. (Illus., Orig.). 1969. pap. 4.75 (ISBN 0-309-01726-2). Natl Acad Pr.
--Product Quality, Performance & Cost. LC 72-81092. (Illus.). 160p. 1972. pap. 8.75 (ISBN 0-309-02036-0). Natl Acad Pr.
--Public Safety: A Growing Factor in Modern Design. (Orig.). 1970. pap. 5.50 (ISBN 0-309-01752-1). Natl Acad Pr.
--Science, Engineering, & the City. 1967. pap. 5.75 (ISBN 0-309-01498-0). Natl Acad Pr.
--State of the Nation's Air Transportation System. LC 76-47852. 1976. pap. 5.50 (ISBN 0-309-02534-6). Natl Acad Pr.
--Transportation & the Prospects for Improved Efficiency. (Illus.). 1973. pap. 9.75 (ISBN 0-309-02120-0). Natl Acad Pr.
--U. S. Energy Prospects: An Engineering Viewpoint. 1974. 8.00 o.p. (ISBN 0-309-02237-1). Natl Acad Pr.
National Academy of Sciences. Biographical Memoirs, Vol. 44. xii, 370p. 1974. 10.00 (ISBN 0-309-02238-X). Natl Acad Pr.
--Biographical Memoirs, Vol. 45. vii, 465p. 1974. 10.00 (ISBN 0-309-02239-8). Natl Acad Pr.
--Biographical Memoirs, Vol. 46, 47. 1975. Vol. 46. 10.00 (ISBN 0-309-02240-1); Vol. 47. 10.00 (ISBN 0-309-02245-2). Natl Acad Pr.
--Biographical Memoirs, Vol. 49. 1978. Vol. 49. 10.00 (ISBN 0-309-02449-8). Natl Acad Pr.
--Current Status of Modular Coordination. 1960. 2.50 o.p. (ISBN 0-309-00782-8). Natl Acad Pr.
--Documentation of Building Science Literature. 1960. pap. 2.00 (ISBN 0-309-00791-7). Natl Acad Pr.
--Effect of Genetic Variance on Nutritional Requirements of Animals. 1975. 6.50 (ISBN 0-309-02342-4). Natl Acad Pr.
--Energy Systems of Extended Endurance in the 1-100 Kilowatt Range for Undersea Applications. 1968. 5.75 (ISBN 0-309-01702-5). Natl Acad Pr.

--Feasibility of a Global Observation & Analysis Experiment. 1966. pap. 5.00 (ISBN 0-309-01290-2). Natl Acad Pr.
--Index to the Literature of Semiconductor Detectors. 1969. pap. 5.00 (ISBN 0-309-00093-9). Natl Acad Pr.
--Insulated Masonry Cavity Walls. 1960. pap. 4.00 o.p. (ISBN 0-309-00793-3). Natl Acad Pr.
--Marine Chemistry. LC 71-177418. 1971. pap. 2.75 (ISBN 0-309-01928-1). Natl Acad Pr.
--Mechanical Fasteners for Industrial Curtain Walls. 1961. 3.00 o.p. (ISBN 0-309-00916-2). Natl Acad Pr.
--Nutrient Requirements of Sheep. 1975. pap. 5.25 (ISBN 0-309-02212-6). Natl Acad Pr.
--Plastics in Building Illumination. 1958. pap. 3.00 o.p. (ISBN 0-309-00114-5). Natl Acad Pr.
--Potential of Lignocellulosic Materials for the Production of Chemicals, Fuels, & Energy. 1979. pap. 14.95 (ISBN 0-930978-92-7). Solar Energy Info.
--Prefinishing of Exterior Building Components. 1962. 6.00 o.p. (ISBN 0-309-00993-6). Natl Acad Pr.
--Principles of Plant & Animal Pest Control, Vol. 5, Vertebrate Pests. 1970. pap. 6.00 (ISBN 0-309-01697-5). Natl Acad Pr.
--Prospects of the World Food Supply. 1966. pap. 1.50 (ISBN 0-685-17308-9). Natl Acad Pr.
--Public Entrance Doors. 1961. pap. 6.00 (ISBN 0-309-00948-0). Natl Acad Pr.
--Reform of Medical Education. 1970. 8.75 (ISBN 0-309-01757-2). Natl Acad Pr.
National Academy of Sciences, jt. auth. see Committee on Nuclear & Alternative Energy Systems, National Research Council.
National Academy of Sciences Agricultural Board. Genetic Vulnerability of Major Crops. 304p. 1972. pap. 10.50 o.p. (ISBN 0-309-02030-1). Natl Acad Pr.
National Academy of Sciences, Division of Earth Sciences. Beneficial Modifications of the Marine Environment. (Illus.). 128p. 1972. pap. 4.75 (ISBN 0-309-02034-4). Natl Acad Pr.
National Academy Of Sciences - Division Of Mathematics Committee On Support Of Research In Mathematical Sciences. Mathematical Sciences: Undergraduate Education. 1968. pap. 5.50 (ISBN 0-309-01682-7). Natl Acad Pr.
National Academy Of Sciences Division Of Physical Sciences. Semiconductor Nuclear-Particle Detectors & Circuits. 1969. 26.00 (ISBN 0-309-01593-6). Natl Acad Pr.
National Academy Of Sciences Office Of Scientific Personnel. Careers of PhD's. 1968. 7.25 o.p. (ISBN 0-309-01577-4). Natl Acad Pr.
National Accreditation Council. Section D-9, Low Vision Services. (Self-Study & Evaluation Guide). 1981. 1.50. NACASBVH.
National Aeronautics & Space Administration. The Search for Extraterrestrial Intelligence. (Illus.). 190p. 1980. pap. 3.00 (ISBN 0-486-23890-3). Dover.
National Archives of the United States Office of Education. Washington: Design for the Federal City. 1981. pap. 9.95 (ISBN 0-87491-417-5). Acropolis.
National Art Education Association. American Artist Art School Directory: 1976-77. 1977. pap. 1.75 (ISBN 0-686-10436-6). Natl Art Ed.
--Black Art: A Bibliography. 1970. pap. 1.00 (ISBN 0-686-00140-0, 061-02180). Natl Art Ed.
--Careers in Art. rev. ed. 1971. pap. 1.00 (ISBN 0-686-00141-9, 061-25834). Natl Art Ed.
--Teaching Art As a Career. rev. ed. 1971. pap. 1.00 (ISBN 0-686-00143-5, 061-25836). Natl Art Ed.
National Association for Bilingual Education. Proceedings of the Eighth Annual International Bilingual Bicultural Education Conference. (Orig.). 1981. pap. write for info. (ISBN 0-89763-054-8). Natl Clearinghse Bilingual Ed.
National Association for Women Deans, Administration & Counselors. Women in Administration: A Book of Readings. 1979. pap. 8.50 (ISBN 0-686-27727-9). Natl Assn Women.
National Association of Broadcasters Engineering Conference, 1973. Technical Papers. LC 73-86770. 1973. vinyl 10.00 o.p. (ISBN 0-8306-3173-9, 173). TAB Bks.
National Association of College & University Food Services. Guide to Food Service Management. Cloyd, Frances, ed. LC 72-75293. 188p. 1972. pap. 9.95 o.p. (ISBN 0-8436-0554-5). CBI Pub.
National Association of College & University Business Officers, et al. A Planning Manual for Colleges. rev. ed. 73p. 1980. pap. text ed. 15.00 (ISBN 0-915164-09-4). Natl Assn Coll.
National Association of Independent Schools. A Teacher's Notebook: English 5-9, Vol. II. 1977. pap. 5.75 (ISBN 0-934338-06-X). NAIS.
--A Teacher's Notebook: English 5-9, Vol. 1. 1975. pap. 4.75 (ISBN 0-934338-05-1). NAIS.
--A Teacher's Notebook: French. 1974. pap. 4.75 (ISBN 0-934338-03-5). NAIS.
--A Teacher's Notebook: German. 1973. pap. 3.25 (ISBN 0-934338-02-7). NAIS.
--A Teacher's Notebook: Language Arts, K-4. 1972. pap. 3.25 (ISBN 0-934338-00-0). NAIS.
--A Teacher's Notebook: Mathematics, K-9. (Illus.). 1975. pap. 5.75 (ISBN 0-934338-08-6). NAIS.
National Association of Purchasing Management. Purchasing Handbook. 4th ed. Farrell, Paul V., ed. 1152p. Date not set. price not set (ISBN 0-07-045899-5, P&RB). McGraw. Postponed.
National Association of Secondary School Principals. Student Learning Styles: Diagnosing & Prescribing Programs. Koerner, Thomas F., ed. (Orig.). 1979. pap. text ed. 5.00 (ISBN 0-88210-103-X). Natl Assn Principals.
National Association of Social Workers. Preventive Intervention in Social Work. Meyer, Carol H., ed. LC 74-83318. (NASW Modulr Ser.). 128p. 1974. Set. pap. text ed. 6.00x (ISBN 0-87101-001-1, CAO-001-I). Natl Assn Soc Wkrs.
National Board on Graduate Education. Graduate School Adjustments to the New Depression in Higher Education. 1975. pap. 6.50 (ISBN 0-309-02328-9). Natl Acad Pr.
--Minority Group Participation in Graduate Education. LC 76-16850. 1976. pap. 7.00 (ISBN 0-309-02502-8). Natl Acad Pr.
--Science Development: An Evaluation Study. 1975. pap. 8.00 (ISBN 0-309-02329-7). Natl Acad Pr.
National Book League. Children's Books of Yesterday. Muir, Percy H., ed. LC 76-89280. 1970. Repr. of 1946 ed. 15.00 (ISBN 0-8103-3550-6). Gale.
National Broiler Council, jt. auth. see National Chicken Cooking Contest.
National Cancer Foundation, Inc., jt. auth. see Cancer Care, Inc.
National Catholic News Serv., ed. John Paul II, Pilgrimage of Faith: The First Year of the New Pope & the Story of His Visit to the United States. LC 79-23105. (Illus.). 278p. 1979. 17.50 (ISBN 0-8164-0109-8); pap. 8.95 (ISBN 0-8164-2014-9). Crossroad NY.
National Center for State Courts. Managing to Reduce Delay. (Orig.). 1980. pap. 5.50 (ISBN 0-89656-041-4, R0049). Natl Ctr St Courts.
--Pretrial Delay: A Review & Bibliography. 1978. pap. 4.00 (ISBN 0-89656-024-4, R0036). Natl Ctr St Courts.
--State Courts: Options for the Future. 1980. pap. 4.00 (ISBN 0-89656-037-6, R0045). Natl Ctr St Courts.
--Structural Responses to the Problems of Volume & Delay in Appellate Courts. Date not set. pap. price not set (ISBN 0-89656-048-1, R-0055). Natl Ctr St Courts.
--Workload Measures in the Court. 1980. pap. 8.00 (ISBN 0-89656-043-0, R0051). Natl Ctr St Courts.
National Chicken Cooking Contest & National Broiler Council. The Chicken Cookbook. 128p. 1975. pap. 1.25 o.p. (ISBN 0-445-08367-0). Popular Lib.
National Clearinghouse for Bilingual Education. Resources in Bilingual Education: A Preliminary Guide to Government Agency Programs of Interest to Minority Language Groups. 1978. pap. 3.50 o.p. (ISBN 0-89763-010-6). Natl Clearinghse Bilingual Ed.
--Sources of Materials for Minority Languages: A Preliminary List. LC 79-103423. 1978. pap. 2.75 o.p. (ISBN 0-89763-003-3). Natl Clearinghse Bilingual Ed.
National Collection of Fine Arts. Rauschenberg. LC 76-58522. (Illus.). 216p. 1976. 27.50 (ISBN 0-87474-170-X); pap. 15.50 (ISBN 0-87474-171-8). Smithsonian.
National Committee Against Discrimination in Housing. Fair Housing & Exclusionary Land Use. LC 74-13552. (Research Report Ser.: No. 23). 1974. pap. text ed. free o.p. (ISBN 0-87420-323-6). Urban Land.
National Committee for Citizens in Education. Public Testimony on Public Schools. LC 75-20297. 304p. 1975. 17.75x (ISBN 0-685-57430-X); text ed. 16.00x (ISBN 0-8211-1016-0). McCutchan.
National Committee on Careers for Older Americans. Older Americans: An Untapped Resource. LC 79-51560. 63p. (Orig.). 1979. pap. 8.50 (ISBN 0-89492-006-5). Acad Educ Dev.
National Computer Conference, 1977. AFIPS Proceedings, Vol. 46. Korfhage, Robert R., ed. LC 55-44701. (Illus.). xiv, 1026p. 1977. 60.00 (ISBN 0-88283-007-4). AFIPS Pr.
National Computer Conference, 1978. AFIPS Proceedings, Vol. 47. Ghosh, Sakti P. & Liu, Leonard Y., eds. LC 55-44701. (Illus.). xxxiv, 1300p. 1978. 60.00 (ISBN 0-88283-006-6). AFIPS Pr.
National Computer Conference, 1979. AFIPS Proceedings, Vol. 48. Merwin, Richard E., ed. LC 55-44701. (Illus.). xi, 1114p. 1979. 60.00 (ISBN 0-88283-005-8). AFIPS Pr.
National Computer Conference, 1980. AFIPS Proceedings, Vol. 49. Medley, Donald B., ed. LC 80-66206. (Illus.). 1980. 60.00 (ISBN 0-88283-003-1). AFIPS Pr.
National Computing Centre. Control of DP Production. Walker, G. S., ed. LC 80-483613. (Illus.). 121p. 1980. pap. 27.50x (ISBN 0-85012-227-9). Intl Pubns Serv.
--High-Level Languages for Microprocessor Projects. Taylor, David & Morgan, Lyndon, eds. (Illus.). 279p. (Orig.). 1980. pap. 37.50x (ISBN 0-85012-233-3). Intl Pubns Serv.
--Impact of Microprocessors on British Business. LC 80-478324. 72p. (Orig.). 1979. pap. 15.00x (ISBN 0-85012-232-5). Intl Pubns Serv.
--Planning for Standby. Waring, L. P., ed. LC 77-361948. 1976. pap. 16.50x (ISBN 0-85012-183-3). Intl Pubns Serv.
National Computing Centre Ltd, ed. Computer Appreciation for the Majority. LC 72-97128. 220p. 1973. pap. 27.50x (ISBN 0-85012-153-1). Intl Pubns Serv.
National Conference Bar Exam. Multistate Bar Exam IV. 1978. text ed. 2.50x (ISBN 0-87543-144-5). Lucas.
National Conference on Rational Psychotherapy, 2nd, June 1977. The Many Facets of Rational-Emotive Therapy: Proceedings. Di Giuseppe, Raymond, ed. LC 78-71033. Date not set. pap. cancelled (ISBN 0-917476-17-4). Rational Living.
National Conference on Social Welfare. Developing Social Policies in Conditions of Rapid Change. 1973. 20.00x (ISBN 0-231-03790-2). Columbia U Pr.
--National Conference on Social Welfare: Social Welfare Forum 1976. Swart, Dorothy M., ed. LC 8-8537. 1977. 20.00x (ISBN 0-231-04268-X). Columbia U Pr.
--The Social Welfare Forum: Official Proceedings. Incl. 94th Annual Forum. 1967 (ISBN 0-231-03136-X); 95th Annual Forum. 1968 (ISBN 0-231-03232-3); 96th Annual Forum. 1969 (ISBN 0-231-03390-7); 97th Annual Forum. 1970 (ISBN 0-231-03473-3); 98th Annual Forum. 1971 (ISBN 0-231-03587-X). LC 8-85377. 20.00x ea. Columbia U Pr.
--The Social Welfare Forum, 1972: 99th Annual Forum. 376p. 1974. 20.00x (ISBN 0-231-03722-8). Columbia U Pr.
--The Social Welfare Forum, 1974: 101st Annual Forum 1974. 1975. 20.00x (ISBN 0-231-03948-4). Columbia U Pr.
National Conference on Social Welfare, May 1975. Social Welfare Forum, 1975: 102nd Annual Forum. 256p. 1976. 20.00x (ISBN 0-231-04048-2). Columbia U Pr.
National Conference on Social Welfare. The Social Welfare Forum 1977: 104th Annual Forum. 1978. 20.00x (ISBN 0-231-04500-X). Columbia U Pr.
National Conference on Social Welfare, ed. The Social Welfare Forum 1979. 1980. 25.00x (ISBN 0-231-04990-0). Columbia U Pr.
--The Social Welfare Forum, 1980. 288p. 1981. 27.50 (ISBN 0-231-05290-1). Columbia U Pr.
National Conference on Social Welfare. Social Work Practice: Proceedings. Incl. Ninety-Third Annual Meeting. 1966 (ISBN 0-231-03032-0); Ninety-Fourth Annual Meeting. 1967 (ISBN 0-231-03154-8); Ninety-Fifth Annual Meeting. 1968 (ISBN 0-231-03247-1); Ninety-Sixth Annual Meeting. 1969 (ISBN 0-231-03389-3); Ninety-Seventh Annual Meeting. 1970 (ISBN 0-231-03474-1); Ninety-Eighth Annual Meeting. 1971 (ISBN 0-231-03588-8). LC 8-85377. 20.00x ea. Columbia U Pr.
National Council for Cooperation in Aquatics. The New Science of Skin & Skuba Diving. 5th rev. ed. 320p. 1980. pap. 7.95 (ISBN 0-695-81424-9); min. purchase of 10 copies, 32p. 9.95 (ISBN 0-695-81516-4). Follett.
National Council of Social Service. The Right to Know- a Review of Advice Services in Rural Areas. 71p. 1978. pap. text ed. 1.90x (ISBN 0-7199-0954-6, Pub. by Bedford England). Renouf.
National Council of Teachers of Mathematics see Shumway, Richard.
National Council of Teachers of Mathematics. Directory of NCTM Individual Members. 1980. 20.00 (ISBN 0-87353-168-X). NCTM.
--Organizing Data & Dealing with Uncertainty. 1979. pap. 6.25 (ISBN 0-87353-141-8). NCTM.
--Problem Solving in School Mathematics, 1980 Yearbook. 1980. 12.00 (ISBN 0-87353-162-0). NCTM.
--The Rhind Mathematical Papyrus. 1979. Repr. 15.00 (ISBN 0-87353-133-7). NCTM.
National Data Processing Institute, Inc. Computer Concepts, 2 vols. Incl. 1969. 3rd ed. Vol. 1 (ISBN 0-672-26021-2). Vol. 2 (ISBN 0-672-26023-9). pap. text ed. 13.95 ea.; tchr's manual 5.00 ea. (ISBN 0-672-96023-0). Bobbs.
National Federation of Community Assoc. Creative Living. 76p. 1974. pap. text ed. 3.75x (ISBN 0-7199-0896-5, Pub. by Bedford England). Renouf.
National Fire Protection Association. Danger! Fire Fighters at Work Safety One. LC 79-720640. (Illus.). 1979. pap. text ed. 60.00 (ISBN 0-87765-163-9, SL-53). Natl Fire Prot.
--The Fire Department Safety Program: Safety Two. LC 79-720641. (Illus.). 1979. pap. text ed. 60.00 (ISBN 0-87765-164-7, SL-54). Natl Fire Prot.
--Hydraulics for the Fire Service: Hydraulic Field Equations, Vol. VI. Lyons, Paul R., ed. LC 78-50007. (Illus.). 72p. (Orig.). 1980. pap. text ed. 42.50 (ISBN 0-87765-171-X, SL-60). Natl Fire Prot.
National Fisherman International Marine Publishing Company. The Mariner's Catalog. (Funk & W Bk.). 192p. 1974. pap. 4.95 o.s.i. (ISBN 0-308-10134-0, F110, TYC-T). T Y Crowell.
National Flightshops. All Those Cessna 150's: Owners Manuals 1959-1977. Date not set. pap. 12.95 (Pub. by National Flightshops). Aviation.
National Food Processors Association, ed. Laboratory Manual for Food Canners & Processors, Vol. 1 Microbiology & Processing. 3rd ed. (Illus.). 1968. 28.50 (ISBN 0-87055-027-6). AVI.
--Laboratory Manual for Food Canners & Processors, Vol. 2. Analysis, Sanitation & Statistics. 3rd ed. (Illus.). 1968. 39.00 (ISBN 0-87055-028-4). AVI.
National Foundation for Educational Research in England & Wales. Register of Educational Research in the United Kingdom, 1973-76, Vol. 1. (General Ser.). 450p. (Orig.). 1976. pap. text ed. 45.00x (ISBN 0-85633-117-1, NFER). Humanities.
--Register of Educational Research in the UK: 1976-1977, Vol. 2. (General Ser.). 1978. pap. text ed. 49.50x (ISBN 0-85633-145-7, NFER). Humanities.
--The Register of Research in the United Kingdom: 1977-78, Vol. 3. (Orig.). 1979. pap. text ed. 77.00x (ISBN 0-85633-187-2). Humanities.
National Information Center for Educational Media. Index to Educational Overhead Transparencies. 6th ed. LC 79-89661. 1980. pap. 61.00 (ISBN 0-89320-032-8). Univ SC Natl Info.
--Index to Educational Records. 5th ed. LC 79-89688. 1980. pap. 54.00 (ISBN 0-89320-034-4). Univ SC Natl Info.
--Index to Educational Slides. 4th ed. LC 79-66599. 1980. pap. 49.00 (ISBN 0-89320-035-2). Univ SC Natl Info.
--Index to Educational Video Tapes. 5th ed. LC 79-89686. 1980. pap. 34.00 (ISBN 0-89320-036-0). Univ SC Natl Info.
--Index to Eight-mm Motion Cartridges. 6th ed. LC 79-89662. 1980. pap. 54.00 (ISBN 0-89320-031-X). Univ SC Natl Info.
--Index to Environmental Studies - Multimedia. 2nd ed. LC 79-66630. 1980. pap. 40.00 (ISBN 0-89320-041-7). Univ SC Natl Info.
National Information Center for Education Media. Index to Health & Safety Education - Multimedia. 4th ed. LC 79-66629. 1980. pap. 55.00 (ISBN 0-89320-040-9). Univ SC Natl Info.
National Information Center for Educational Media. Index to Producers & Distributors. 5th ed. LC 79-66600. 1980. pap. 24.00 (ISBN 0-89320-037-9). Univ SC Natl Info.
--Index to Psychology - Multimedia. 4th ed. LC 79-66627. 1980. pap. 55.00 (ISBN 0-89320-038-7). Univ SC Natl Info.
--Index to Sixteen-mm Educational Films. 7th ed. LC 79-89659. 1980. pap. 126.00 (ISBN 0-89320-029-8). Univ SC Natl Info.
--Index to Thirty-Five-mm Filmstrips. 7th ed. LC 79-89660. 1980. pap. 99.00 (ISBN 0-89320-030-1). Univ SC Natl Info.
--Index to Vocational & Technical Education - Multimedia. 4th ed. LC 79-66628. 1980. pap. 55.00 (ISBN 0-89320-039-5). Univ SC Natl Info.
--NICSEM Special Education Thesaurus. 2nd ed. LC 80-83509. 1980. pap. 16.00 (ISBN 0-89320-028-X). Univ SC Natl Info.
--Special Education Index to Learner Materials. LC 79-84454. 462p. 1979. pap. 60.00 (ISBN 0-89320-024-7). Univ SC Natl Info.
National Information Center for Special Education Materials (NICSEM) NICSEM Master Index to Special Education Materials, 3 vols. LC 80-83854. 1980. Set. pap. 106.00 (ISBN 0-89320-049-2). Univ SC Natl Info.

--NICSEM Mini-index to Special Education Materials: Functional Communication Skills. LC 80-82540. 1980. pap. 16.00 (ISBN 0-89320-045-X). Univ SC Natl Info.
--NICSEM Mini-Index to Special Education Materials: Family Life & Sex Education. LC 80-82540. 1980. pap. 16.00 (ISBN 0-89320-043-3). Univ SC Natl Info.
--NICSEM Mini-index to Special Education Materials: High Interests, Controlled Vocabulary Supplementary Reading Materials for Adolescents & Young Adults. LC 80-82901. 1980. pap. 16.00 (ISBN 0-89320-047-6). Univ. SC Natl Info.
--NICSEM Mini-index to Special Education Materials: Independent Living Skills for Moderately & Severely Handicapped Students. LC 80-82530. 1980. pap. 16.00 (ISBN 0-89320-044-1). Univ SC Natl Info.
--NICSEM Mini-index to Special Education Materials: Personal & Social Developments for Moderately & Severely Handicapped Students. LC 80-82541. 1980. pap. 16.00 (ISBN 0-89320-046-8). Univ SC Natl Info.
--NICSEM Source Directory. LC 80-83757. 1980. pap. 12.50 (ISBN 0-89320-050-6). Univ SC Natl Info.
--Special Education Index to Assessment Devices. LC 79-84457. (Orig.). 1980. pap. 21.00 (ISBN 0-89320-026-3). Univ. SC Natl Info.
--Special Education Index to Inservice Training Materials. LC 79-84458. (Orig.). 1980. pap. 12.00 (ISBN 0-89320-027-1). Univ. SC Natl Info.
National Information Center for Special Education Materials (NISCEM) Special Education Index to Parent Materials. LC 79-84456. (Orig.). 1979. pap. 21.00 (ISBN 0-89320-025-5). Univ SC Natl Info.
National Institute for Burn Medicine. International Bibliogrphy on Burns: 1980 Supplement. Feller, I., ed. LC 71-94573. 144p. 1980. 12.00 (ISBN 0-917478-11-8). Natl Inst Burn.
--NIBM: A Decade of Progress in Burn Medicine. LC 80-82419. (Illus.). pap. write for info. Natl Inst Burn.
National Institute for Foodservice Industry. Applied Foodservice Sanitation. 2nd ed. 1978. text ed. 12.95x (ISBN 0-669-00792-7); coursebook 4.25 (ISBN 0-669-02106-7); instructor's manual free (ISBN 0-669-02730-8). Heath.
National Journal. The Carter Presidency. 1979. 2.35 o.s.i. (ISBN 0-89234-004-5). Natl Journal.
--Politics & Parties Between Elections. Polsby, Nelson W., ed. (National Journal Reprints Ser). 1977. pap. text ed. 2.35 o.p. (ISBN 0-685-59296-0). Natl Journal.
--Politics, Parties & 1980. Polsby, Nelson W., ed. (National Journal Reprints). 56p. (Orig.). 1979. pap. 3.95 o.p. (ISBN 0-89234-023-1). Natl Journal.
National Judicial College. Significant State Appellate Decisions. (Ser. 1850). 1980. pap. 7.50 (ISBN 0-686-08770-4). Natl Judicial Coll.
National Lampoon Editors, ed. The Job of Sex. (Illus.). 1974. pap. 2.25 (ISBN 0-446-92837-2). Warner Bks.
National Lawyers Guild. Immigration & Defense. 2nd ed. LC 79-9735. 1979. 60.00 (ISBN 0-87632-109-0). Boardman.
--Representation of Witnesses Before Federal Grand Juries. LC 76-20443. 1976. looseleaf with 1979 rev. pages 55.00 (ISBN 0-87632-107-4). Boardman.
National Library of Australia. Australian National Bibliography, 1976. 16th ed. LC 63-33739. 1464p. 1977. 67.50x (ISBN 0-8002-1048-4). Intl Pubns Serv.
National Materials Advisory Board. Fundamentals of Amorphous Semiconductors. LC 75-188496. 128p. 1972. pap. 6.00 (ISBN 0-309-01944-3). Natl Acad Pr.
--High-Temperature Oxidation Resistant Coatings for Superalloys,Refractory Metals, & Graphite. LC 78-606278. (Orig.). 1971. pap. text ed. 13.25 (ISBN 0-309-01769-6). Natl Acad Pr.
--Materials & Processes for Electron Devices. LC 72-84753. (Illus.). 240p. 1972. pap. 9.75 (ISBN 0-309-02040-9). Natl Acad Pr.
--National Materials Policy. LC 74-23549. 1975. pap. 11.50 (ISBN 0-309-02247-9). Natl Acad Pr.
--Yield of Electronic Materials & Devices. 96p. 1972. pap. 5.25 (ISBN 0-309-02108-1). Natl Acad Pr.
National Materials Advisory Board, National Research Council. Electroslag Remelting & Plasma Arc Melting. LC 76-13351. (Illus.). 1976. pap. 7.25 (ISBN 0-309-02505-2). Natl Acad Pr.
--Materials of Construction for Shipboard Waste Incinerators. 1977. pap. 8.75 (ISBN 0-309-02606-7). Natl Acad Pr.
--Rapid Inexpensive Tests for Determining Fracture Toughness. LC 76-39632. 1976. pap. 8.25 (ISBN 0-309-02537-0). Natl Acad Pr.
National Micrographics Assn. Document Mark (Blip) Used in Image Mark Retrieval Systems: ANSI-NMA MS8-1979. 1980. 4.50 (ISBN 0-89258-060-7). Natl Micrograph.
--Format & Coding for Computer Output Microfilm: ANSI-NMA MS2-1978. 1978. 6.00 (ISBN 0-89258-054-2). Natl Micrograph.
--Guide to Micrographic Equipment: RS15-1979. 7th ed. 1979. 30.00 (ISBN 0-89258-053-4). Natl Micrograph.
--Identification of Microforms: ANSI-NMA MS19-1978. 1978. 4.50 (ISBN 0-89258-051-8). Natl Micrograph.
--Measuring COM Recording Speeds: MS21-1979. 1979. 3.50 (ISBN 0-89258-058-5). Natl Micrograph.
--Microfilm Readers: ANSI-NMA MS20-1979. 1980. 4.50 (ISBN 0-89258-061-5). Natl Micrograph.
--Microfilming Newspapers: ANSI-NMA MS111-1977. 1978. 4.50 (ISBN 0-89258-050-X). Natl Micrograph.
--Practice for Uniform Product Disclosure for Unitized Microform Readers (Microfiche, Jackets & Image Cards) NMA MS22-1979. 1980. 3.00 (ISBN 0-89258-057-7). Natl Micrograph.
National Opinion Research Center. General Social Survey, 1976. 1977. codebk. 12.00 (ISBN 0-89138-158-9). ICPSR.
National Powder Metallurgy Conferenes, Los Angeles & Cincinnati, 1978 & 1979. Progress in Powder Metallurgy: Proceedings, Vols. 34 & 35. Cebulak, W., et al, eds. (Illus., Orig.). 1980. pap. text ed. 56.00 (ISBN 0-918404-49-5). Metal Powder.
National Press Photographers & the University of Missouri, School of Journalism. Best of Photojournalism Two. LC 77-81586. (Illus.). 1978. 16.95 o.p. (ISBN 0-88225-253-4); pap. 9.95 o.p. (ISBN 0-88225-252-6). Newsweek.
National Press Photographers Association. The Best of Photojournalism, Vol. 5. LC 77-81586. (National Press Photographers Association, University of Missouri Journalism School Ser.). (Illus.). 256p. 1980. 24.95 (ISBN 0-8262-0321-3). U of Mo Pr.
National Press Photographers Association & the University of Missouri School of Journalism & Bayrd, Edwin. The Best of Photojournalism: Three. LC 77-8156. (Illus.). 1979. 16.95 o.p. (ISBN 0-88225-263-1). Newsweek.
National Quantum Electronics Conference, 4th, Heriot-Watt University Edinburgh, 1979. Laser Advances & Applications Proceedings. Wherrett, B. S., ed. LC 80-40119. 278p. 1980. 45.00 (ISBN 0-471-27792-4). Wiley.
National Radio Institute Staff. Mathematics for Electronic-Electricity. (Illus.). 1963. 8.25 (ISBN 0-8104-0465-6). Hayden.
National Register Publishing Co. Directory of Corporate Affiliations. LC 67-22770. 1981. 140.00 (ISBN 0-87217-002-0). Natl Register.
--Standard Directory of Advertisers: Classified Edition. LC 5-21147. 1981. 109.00 (ISBN 0-87217-000-4). Natl Register.
--Standard Directory of Advertisers: Geographical Edition. LC 15-21147. 1981. 109.00 (ISBN 0-87217-001-2). Natl Register.
--Standard Directory of Advertising Agencies, 3 vols. 1981. 52.00 (ISBN 0-87217-003-9); 127.00 set (ISBN 0-686-52432-2). Natl Register.
National Research & Appraisal Co., compiled By. Machine Tool Value Guide, Vol. 1. 1980. pap. 50.00 (ISBN 0-89692-102-6). Equipment Guide.
National Research & Appraisal Co. & Sharninghouse, Jane, eds. OSHA for Machine Tools. 1000p. 1980. write for info. (ISBN 0-89692-101-8). Equipment Guide.
National Research Center of the Arts. Americans & the Arts. LC 80-28923. (Illus., Orig.). Date not set. pap. 10.00 (ISBN 0-915400-27-8). Am Council Arts.
--Americans & the Arts: A Survey of Public Opinion. LC 74-33144. (Illus., Orig.). 1974. pap. text ed. 5.00 (ISBN 0-915400-00-6). Am Council Arts.
--Americans & the Arts: Highlights. (Orig.). pap. 3.00 (ISBN 0-915400-28-6). Am Council Arts.
National Research Center of the Arts, Inc. A Second Look: The Nonprofit Arts & Cultural Industry of New York State 1975-76. 308p. 1978. pap. 8.50x (ISBN 0-89062-097-0, Pub. by NY Found Arts). Pub Ctr Cult Res.
National Research Council. Invisible University: Postdoctoral Education in the United States. LC 70-601489. (Illus., Orig.). 1969. pap. 13.75 (ISBN 0-309-01730-0). Natl Acad Pr.
--Mineral Resources & the Environment. 1975. pap. 8.25 (ISBN 0-309-02343-2). Natl Acad Pr.
--World Food & Nutrition Study: Potential Contributions of Research, Commission on International Relations. 1977. pap. 10.50 (ISBN 0-309-02628-8). Natl Acad Pr.
National Research Council, Commission on Sociotechnical Systems. Materials Technology in the Near-Term Energy Program. xiii, 122p. 1974. pap. 7.00 (ISBN 0-309-02322-X). Natl Acad Pr.
National Research Council - Committee On Animal Nutrition. Biological Energy Interrelationships & Glossary of Energy Tables. (Illus.). 1966. pap. 3.00 o.p. (ISBN 0-309-01411-5). Natl Acad Pr.
National Research Council - Committee For The Survey Of Chemistry. Nuclear Chemistry: A Current Review. 1966. pap. 3.00 (ISBN 0-309-01292-9). Natl Acad Pr.
National Research Council, Committee on Animal Nutrition. Nutrients & Toxic Substances in Water for Livestock & Poultry. LC 74-2836. (Illus.). v, 93p. 1974. pap. 4.75 (ISBN 0-309-02312-2). Natl Acad Pr.
National Research Council, Division of Medical Sciences, Medical & Biologic Effects of Environmental Pollutants, ed. Ozone & Other Photochemical Oxidants. LC 77-1293. 1977. pap. text ed. 18.00 (ISBN 0-309-02531-1). Natl Acad Pr.
National Research Council, Food & Nutrition Board. Proposed Fortification Policy for Cereal-Grain Products. LC 74-10542. 44p. 1974. pap. 3.75 (ISBN 0-309-02232-0). Natl Acad Pr.
National Research Council, Maritime Transportation Research Board. Nuclear Merchant Ships. (Illus.). xi, 125p. 1974. pap. 9.25 (ISBN 0-309-02318-1). Natl Acad Pr.
National Research Council, U. S. National Committee for Geochemistry. Geochemistry & the Environment: The Relation of Selected Trace Elements to Health & Disease, Vol. 1. LC 74-13309. (Illus.). ix, 113p. 1974. pap. 10.00 (ISBN 0-309-02223-1). Natl Acad Pr.
National Retail Merchants Assn. Manual for Reducing Transportation Costs. 1981. pap. text ed. 25.25 (ISBN 0-685-74622-4, T90576). Natl Ret Merch.
--OCR-A Implementation Handbook. 1979. pap. text ed. 50.00 (ISBN 0-685-95732-2, U1679). Natl Ret Merch.
National Retail Merchants Association, ed. Voluntary Standard for the Electronic Purchase Order and Invoice. 1980. 18.75. Natl Ret Merch.
National School of Mines. Federal Mine Electrical Certification: Surface & Underground. LC 79-87486. 1979. text ed. 35.00 (ISBN 0-930206-02-9). M-A Pr.
National School Public Relations Association, jt. auth. see **Jones, J. William.**
National Science Foundation Research Applications Directorate. Alternatives in Energy Conservation: The Use of Earth Covered Buildings. 1979. pap. cancelled (ISBN 0-930978-90-0). Solar Energy Info.
National Science Teachers Association. Metric Is Coming. 1973. pap. 0.75 o.p. (ISBN 0-685-42400-6, 471-14662). Natl Sci Tchrs.
National Society of Patient Representatives of the American Hospital Association. Assessing the Patient Representative Program in Hospitals. LC 80-28949. (Illus., Orig.). 1981. pap. 8.00 (ISBN 0-87258-334-1, 1082). Am Hospital.
National Society of the Colonial Dames of America. American War Songs. LC 73-156922. 1974. Repr. of 1925 ed. 18.00 (ISBN 0-8103-3722-3). Gale.
--Catalogue of the Genealogical & Historical Library of the Colonial Dames of the State of New York. LC 76-149778. 1971. Repr. of 1912 ed. 34.00 (ISBN 0-8103-3713-4). Gale.
National Telecommunications & Information Administration, ed. The Nixon Administration Public Broadcasting Papers. 124p. 1979. pap. 5.00. NAEB.
National Trust for Historic Preservation. American Landmarks: Properties of the National Trust for Historic Preservation. (Illus.). 72p. (Orig.). 1980. pap. 5.95 (ISBN 0-89133-093-3). Preservation Pr.
--Conserve Neighborhoods Notebook. (Illus.). 154p. 1980. 12.95 (ISBN 0-89133-092-5). Preservation Pr.
National Trust for Historic Preservation, ed. Information: A Preservation Sourcebook. 1979. ring binder 15.00 (ISBN 0-89133-084-4). Preservation Pr.
National Trust for Historic Preservation. Preservation: Reusing America's Energy. (Illus.). 128p. (Orig.). 1981. pap. 9.95 (ISBN 0-89133-095-X). Preservation Pr.
National Union Of Christian Schools. Hymns for Youth. (Illus.). 1966. pap. 3.95 o.p. (ISBN 0-8028-9002-4, Pub. by NUCS). Eerdmans.
--New Christian Hymnal. PLB 2.95 o.p. (ISBN 0-8028-9004-0). Eerdmans.
--The Pilot Series in Literature. pap. 5.00 ea. Bk. 1, Gr. 7b (ISBN 0-8028-1720-3). Bk. 2, Gr. 8 (ISBN 0-8028-1721-1). Bk. 3, Gr. 9 (ISBN 0-8028-1722-X). Eerdmans.
National Zoological Park. Zoobook. LC 76-9653. (Illus.). 80p. 1976. 9.95 (ISBN 0-87474-846-1); pap. 4.50 (ISBN 0-87474-845-3). Smithsonian.
National Zoological Park, Office of Education. Zoobook. LC 76-9653. (Illus.). 80p. 1978. pap. 4.50 (ISBN 0-87474-845-3). Smithsonian.
Nations, D. The Record of Geologic Time: A Vicarious Trip. (McGraw-Hill Concepts in Introductory Geology). (Illus.). 80p. 1975. text ed. 7.95x (ISBN 0-07-012326-8, C); slides 50.00 (ISBN 0-07-074427-0). McGraw.
Nations, Opal L. The Marvels of Professor Pettingruel. (Illus.). 1978. sewn in wrappers 5.00 (ISBN 0-685-50395-X). Black Stone.
Nat'l Foundation-March of Dimes Symposium, April, 1976, New York City. Diabetes & Other Endocrine Disorders During Pregnancy & in the Newborn: Proceedings. New, Maria I. & Fiser, Robert H., Jr., eds. LC 76-21204. (Progress in Clinical & Biological Research: Vol. 10). 262p. 1976. 30.00x (ISBN 0-8451-0010-6). A R Liss.
Natland, M. L., et al. A System of Stages for Correlation of Magallanes Basin Sediments. LC 74-75964. (Memoir: No. 139). (Illus.). 1974. 15.50x (ISBN 0-8137-1139-8). Geol Soc.
NATO. Economic Reforms in Eastern Europe & Prospects for the 1980s. (NATO Colloquim, 16-18 April 1980, Brussels, Belgium). (Illus.). 325p. 1980. 60.00 (ISBN 0-08-026801-3). Pergamon.
NATO Advanced Study Institute on Two-Phase Flows & Heat Transfer, Istanbul, Aug. 1976. Two-Phase Flows & Heat Transfer: Proceedings, 3 vols. new ed. Kakac, S., et al, eds. LC 77-8801. 1977. Set. text ed. 155.00 (ISBN 0-89116-167-8). Hemisphere Pub.
NATO Advanced Study Institute, University of Waterloo, Canada 2-12, August 1977. Engineering Plasticity by Mathematical Programming: Proceedings. Cohn, M. Z. & Maier, G., eds. LC 78-8474. (Illus.). 1979. 55.00 (ISBN 0-08-022735-X); pap. 34.00 (ISBN 0-08-022736-8). Pergamon.
Nato Advanced Study Institution, et al. Cytopharmacology of Secretion: Proceedings. Ceccarelli, B., et al, eds. LC 74-76090. (Advances in Cytopharmacology Ser: Vol. 2). 400p. 1974. 58.50 (ISBN 0-911216-58-8). Raven.
NATO ASI & AMS Summer Seminar in Applied Mathematics Held at Harvard University, Cambridge, Ma., June 18-29, 1979. Geometrical Methods for Th Theory of Linear Systems: Proceedings. Byrnes, Christopher I. & Martin, Clyde F., eds. (NATO Advanced Study Institutes Series C: Mathematical & Physical Sciences, 62). 313p. 1980. lib. bdg. 39.50 (ISBN 90-277-1154-2, Pub. by D. Reidel). Kluwer Boston.
Natoli, Salvatore, ed. see **Georges, Daniel E.**
Natoli, Salvatore, ed. see **Lakshmanan, T. R. & Chatterjee, Lata.**
Natoli, Salvatore, ed. see **Monmonier, Mark S.**
Natoli, Salvatore J., ed. see **Baumann, Duane & Dworkin, Daniel.**
Natoli, Salvatore J., ed. see **Cook, Earl.**
Natoli, Salvatore J., ed. see **Greenberg, Michael, et al.**
Natoli, Salvatore J., ed. see **Knight, C. Gregory & Wilcox, R. Paul.**
Natoli, Salvatore J., ed. see **Lord, J. Dennis.**
Natoli, Salvatore J., ed. see **Matley, Ian M.**
Natoli, Salvatore J., ed. see **Muller, Peter O.**
Natoli, Salvatore J., ed. see **Platt, Rutherford H.**
Natoli, Salvatore J., ed. see **Roseman, Curtis C.**
Natoli, Salvatore J., ed. see **Salter, Christopher & Lloyd, William.**
Natoli, Salvatore J., ed. see **Smith, Christopher J.**
Natoli, Salvatore J., ed. see **Stutz, Frederick P.**
Natoli, Salvatore J., ed. see **Wiseman, Robert.**
Natow, Annette B., et al. Geriatric Nutrition. LC 80-12282. 1980. text ed. 16.95 (ISBN 0-8436-2184-2). CBI Pub.
Natow, Annette B., jt. auth. see **Heslin, Jo-Ann.**
Natowitz, J. B., jt. ed. see **Tamura, T.**
Natterer, F., jt. ed. see **Herman, G. T.**
Nattrass, Karen & Morrison, Bonnie M. Human Needs in Housing: An Ecological Approach. 1977. pap. text ed. 9.00x (ISBN 0-8191-0094-3). U Pr of Amer.
Natu, Waman R. Regulation of Forward Markets. 8.95x (ISBN 0-210-34069-X). Asia.
Naturalization, jt. auth. see **President's Commission On Immigration.**
Nau, Erika S. Self-Awareness Through Huna-Hawaii's Ancient Wisdom. Grunwald, Stefan, ed. (Orig.). 1981. pap. write for info. (ISBN 0-89865-099-2, Unilaw). Donning Co.
Nau, Henry R. Technology Transfer & U.S. Foreign Policy. LC 76-2908. (Illus.). 1976. text ed. 32.50 (ISBN 0-275-56790-7). Praeger.
Nau, Robert H. Basic Electrical Engineering. LC 58-5633. 1958. 16.95 (ISBN 0-471-07212-5); instr's manual avail. (ISBN 0-471-07582-5). Wiley.

Naudascher, E. & Rockwell, D., eds. Practical Experiences with Flow-Induced Vibrations: Symposium Proceedings. (International Association for Hydraulic Research - International Union of Theoretical & Applied Mechanics). (Illus.). 850p. 1980. 82.60 (ISBN 0-387-10314-7). Springer-Verlag.
Nauer, Barbara. Rise up & Remember. LC 76-54011. 120p. 1977. pap. 2.95 o.p. (ISBN 0-385-12955-6). Doubleday.
Naughton, K. S. The Gentry of Bedfordshire in the 13th & 14th Centuries. (Occasional Papers in English Local History, Third Series: No. 2). (Illus., Orig.). 1976. pap. text ed. 8.50x (ISBN 0-7185-2032-7, Leicester). Humanities.
Naughton, Maria A. Coarticulation Manual for the Remediation of -S- LC 78-61748. 1979. pap. 2.95x (ISBN 0-8134-2051-2, 2051). Interstate.
Nault, Andy. Staying Alive in Alaska's Wild. Loftin, Tee, ed. (Illus.). 224p. (Orig.). (gr. 6-12). 1980. pap. 8.00 (ISBN 0-934812-01-2). Loftin Pubs.
Nauman, Eileen. American Book of Medical Astrology. (Illus.). 368p. (Orig.). 1981. pap. 14.95 (ISBN 0-917086-28-7). Astro Comp Serv.
Naumann, Jens, jt. auth. see Hufner, Klaus.
Naumann, Jens see Hufner, Klaus.
Naumann, Jens, jt. ed. see Hufner, Klaus.
Naumann, Manfred, et al, eds. Society, Literature, Reading: The Reception of Literature Considered in Its Theoretical Context. (Linguistic & Literary Studies in Eastern Europe). 550p. 1980. text ed. 85.50x (ISBN 90-272-1509-X). Humanities.
Naumann, Marina Turkevich. Blue Evenings in Berlin: Nabokov's Short Stories of the 1920s. LC 77-82751. (New York University Studies in Comparative Literature: Vol. 9). 254p. 1978. 15.00x (ISBN 0-8147-5753-7). NYU Pr.
Naumburg, Margaret. An Introduction to Art Therapy: Studies of the "Free" Art Expression of Behavior Problem Children & Adolescents As a Means of Diagnosis & Therapy. rev. ed. LC 73-78074. (Illus.). 225p. 1973. text ed. 9.40 (ISBN 0-8077-2412-2); pap. text ed. 9.75x (ISBN 0-8077-2425-4). Tchrs Coll.
Naumes. Case Organizational Strategy Policy. 1978. pap. 12.95 (ISBN 0-7216-6662-0). Dryden Pr.
Naumes, William. Entrepreneurial Manager in the Small Business: Text Readings & Cases. LC 77-83029. (Illus.). 1978. text ed. 17.95 (ISBN 0-201-05201-6). A-W.
Naus, Joseph I., jt. auth. see Neff, Norman D.
Nauta, W. J., jt. auth. see Brady, J.
Navajata. Sri Aurobindo. (National Biography Ser.). 1979. pap. 2.00 o.p. (ISBN 0-89744-201-6). Auromere.
Naval Science Dept., U. S. Naval Academy, ed. Naval Operations Analysis. 2nd ed. LC 77-73342. 1977. 16.95x (ISBN 0-87021-440-3). Naval Inst Pr.
Navaretta, Cynthia. Guide to Women's Art Organizations. LC 79-83876. (Illus., Orig.). 1979. pap. text ed. 5.00 (ISBN 0-9602476-0-2, Pub. by Women's Artist News). Midmarch Assocs.
Navaretta, Cynthia, ed. Voices of Women: Three Critics on Three Poets on Three Heroines. LC 80-80281. (Illus.). 1980. pap. 4.50. Midmarch Assocs.
Navarette, Vincent H. The Two Most Miraculous Words in the English Language & How to Use Them Successfully. (Essential Knowledge Library Bk.). (Illus.). 1979. 6.00 (ISBN 0-89266-159-3). Am Classical Coll Pr.
Navari, C., jt. ed. see Mayall, J.
Navarra, John G. Earth, Space, & Time: An Introduction to Earth Science. LC 79-14000. 1980. text ed. 22.95x (ISBN 0-471-63061-6). Wiley.
--Earthquake. LC 79-8938. (Illus.). 96p. (gr. 6-7). 1980. 7.95a (ISBN 0-385-15080-6); PLB (ISBN 0-385-15081-4). Doubleday.
Navarra, John G. & Zafforoni, Joseph. Science in the Elementary School: Content & Methods. LC 74-83046. (Elementary Education Ser). 640p. 1975. text ed. 18.95 (ISBN 0-675-08772-4). Merrill.
Navarra, John Gabriel. Supercars. LC 73-10949. (gr. 1-5). 1975. PLB 7.95 (ISBN 0-385-06827-1). Doubleday.
--Superplanes. LC 77-16936. (gr. 3-7). 1979. 7.95a (ISBN 0-385-12561-5); PLB (ISBN 0-385-12562-3). Doubleday.
--Supertrains. LC 74-18820. 80p. (gr. 1-5). 1976. 7.95 (ISBN 0-385-02024-4). Doubleday.
--Wheels for Kids. LC 73-76448. 64p. (gr. k-3). 1973. 5.95 o.p. (ISBN 0-385-02693-5); PLB write for info. o.p. (ISBN 0-385-04630-8). Doubleday.
Navarre, Marguerite de see De Navarre, Marguerite.
Navarre, Monte, ed. see Airguide Publications.
Navarre, Yves. Sweet Tooth. Watson, Donald, tr. 1980. 8.95 (ISBN 0-7145-3522-2). Riverrun NY.
Navarro, Antonio. Tocayo: The True Story of a Resistance Leader in Castro's Cuba. 288p. 1981. 14.95 (ISBN 0-87000-508-1). Arlington Hse.
Navarro, J. Cervos, jt. auth. see Weller, R. O.
Navarro, Marysa, jt. auth. see Fraser, Nicholas.
Navarro, Vincente. Social Security & Medicine in the USSR: A Marxist Critique. LC 77-227. (Illus.). 1977. 17.95 (ISBN 0-669-01452-4). Lexington Bks.
Navas, Gerardo, ed. Cambio y Desarrollo En Puerto Rico: La Transformacion Ideologica Del Partido Popular Democratico. LC 77-4483. (Planning Ser: G-2). 1978. pap. 10.00 (ISBN 0-8477-2435-2). U of PR Pr.
Navascues, Miguel. Lecturas Modernas De Hispanoamerica: An Intermediate Spanish Reader. (Illus.). 1980. pap. text ed. 8.95 (ISBN 0-13-527804-X). P-H.
Navasky, Victor. Naming Names. LC 80-15044. 468p. 1980. 15.95 (ISBN 0-670-50393-2). Viking Pr.
Nave, Orville J. Nave's Topical Bible. 1979. 16.95 (ISBN 0-8407-4992-9). Nelson.
Nave, Patricia S., ed. see Hetherington-Parke.
Naveh, Zev, jt. ed. see Bakshi, Trilochan S.
Navia, Luis E. & Kelly, Eugene, eds. Ethics & the Search for Values. LC 80-82123. 1980. pap. text ed. 12.95 (ISBN 0-87975-139-8). Prometheus Bks.
Navon, David H. Electronic Materials & Devices. 1975. text ed. 23.95 (ISBN 0-395-18917-9); solutions manual 5.20 (ISBN 0-395-19374-5). HM.
Navon, Yitzhak. The Six Days & the Seven Gates. 1980. 6.00 (ISBN 0-930832-57-4); pap. 4.00. Herzl Pr.
Navy Times Editors, jt. ed. see Slinkman, John.
Nawakowski, T. The Radziwills. (Illus.). 352p. 1974. 12.50 o.p. (ISBN 0-440-07340-5, Sey Lawr). Delacorte.
Nawrath, Alfred. The Aegean World. (Illus.). 1978. 25.00 o.p. (ISBN 0-88331-097-X, Joseph Binns Bk). McKay.
Nawratzki, I., ed. see Jerusalem Conference on Impaired Vision in Childhood, May 1977.
Nawrocki, Dennis A. & Holleman, Thomas J. Art in Detroit Public Places. (Illus.). 160p. 1980. 9.95 (ISBN 0-8143-1653-0); pap. 4.95 (ISBN 0-8143-1649-2). Wayne St U Pr.
Nay, W. Robert. Behavioral Intervention: Contemporary Strategies. LC 76-7510. 384p. 1976. 19.95 (ISBN 0-470-15088-2). Halsted Pr.
Nayagam, S. X. Thani see Thani Nayagam, S. X.
Nayagam, Xavier T. Tamil Culture & Civilisation: Readings, the Classical Period. 1971. 8.95x (ISBN 0-210-98163-6). Asia.
Nayfeh, Ali H. Introduction to Perturbation Techniques. LC 80-15233. 475p. 1980. 24.95 (ISBN 0-471-08033-0, Pub. by Wiley Interscience). Wiley.
Nayfeh, Ali H. & Mook, Dean T. Nonlinear Oscillations. LC 78-27102. (Pure & Applied Mathematics Texts, Monographs & Tracts). 1979. 39.50 (ISBN 0-471-03555-6, Pub. by Wiley-Interscience). Wiley.
Nayfeh, Ali-Hasan. Perturbation Methods. LC 72-8068. (Pure & Applied Mathematics Ser). 496p. 1973. 29.95 (ISBN 0-471-63059-4, Pub. by Wiley-Interscience). Wiley.
Naylor, Bernard, et al, eds. Directory of Libraries & Special Collections on Latin America & the West Indies. (Institute of Latin American Studies Monographs: No. 5). 100p. 1975. text ed. 16.25x (ISBN 0-485-17705-6, Athlone Pr). Humanities.
Naylor, Brenda. Technique of Fashion Design. 1975. 24.00 (ISBN 0-7134-3009-5, Pub. by Batsford England). David & Charles.
Naylor, C. W. The Redemption of Howard Gray. 72p. pap. 0.50. Faith Pub Hse.
Naylor, D., jt. auth. see Duff, George F.
Naylor, E. & Hartnoll, E. G., eds. Cyclic Phenomena in Marine Plants & Animals. 1979. 6.80 (ISBN 0-08-023217-5). Pergamon.
Naylor, E. W. An Elizabethan Virginal Book. LC 70-87638. (Music Ser). 1970. Repr. of 1905 ed. lib. bdg. 25.00 (ISBN 0-306-71792-1). Da Capo.
Naylor, Edward W. Shakespeare & Music. LC 65-16244. (Music Ser). 1965. Repr. of 1931 ed. lib. bdg. 18.50 (ISBN 0-306-70908-2). Da Capo.
--Shakespeare Music. LC 75-171080. 68p. 1973. Repr. of 1927 ed. lib. bdg. 14.95 (ISBN 0-306-70275-4). Da Capo.
Naylor, Gillian. Arts & Crafts Movement: A Study of Its Sources, Ideals & Influence on Design Theory. 1980. pap. 10.95 (ISBN 0-262-64018-X). MIT Pr.
Naylor, Henry D. Horace, Odes & Epodes: A Study in Poetic Word-Order. (Latin Poetry Ser.: Vol. 9). (LC 77-070832). 1977. Repr. of 1922 ed. lib. bdg. 33.00 (ISBN 0-8240-2958-5). Garland Pub.
Naylor, James C., jt. auth. see Blum, Milton L.
Naylor, John & Wood, Alan. Practical Marketing Audits: A Guide to Increased Profitability. LC 78-2948. 1978. 24.95x (ISBN 0-470-26327-X). Halsted Pr.
Naylor, Maria, ed. Authentic Indian Designs. LC 74-17711. (Illus.). 256p. 1975. pap. 6.50 (ISBN 0-486-23170-4). Dover.
Naylor, Natalie A., jt. auth. see Kniker, Charles R.
Naylor, Paz B., ed. Austronesian Studies: Papers from the Second Eastern Conference on Austronesian Languages. LC 79-87814. (Michigan Papers on South & Southeast Asia: No. 15). 314p. (Orig.). 1980. pap. 8.00x (ISBN 0-89148-015-3). Ctr S&SE Asian.
Naylor, Penelope. The Woman's Guide to Business Travel. 288p. (Orig.). Date not set. pap. 4.95 (ISBN 0-346-12441-7). Cornerstone. Postponed.
Naylor, Phyllis. All Because I'm Older. LC 80-18586. (Illus.). 32p. (ps-4). 1981. PLB 8.95 (ISBN 0-689-30824-8). Atheneum.
--Faces in the Water. LC 80-24057. 180p. (gr. 6 up). 1981. PLB 9.95 (ISBN 0-689-30823-X). Atheneum.
--Jennifer Jean, the Cross-Eyed Queen. LC 67-15701. (General Juvenile Bks). (Illus.). (gr. k-5). 1967. PLB 3.95 o.p. (ISBN 0-8225-0263-1). Lerner Pubns.
--Revelations. 1981. pap. 2.95 o.s.i. (ISBN 0-440-16923-2). Dell.
--Revelations. 1980. 10.95 (ISBN 0-312-67928-9). St Martin.
Naylor, Phyllis R. Getting Along with Your Teachers. LC 80-22319. 96p. (gr. 4-6). 1981. 7.50g (ISBN 0-687-14123-0). Abingdon.
--Shadows on the Wall. LC 80-12967. (gr. 6 up). 1980. 8.95 (ISBN 0-689-30785-3). Atheneum.
--Witch's Sister. 1980. pap. 1.95 (ISBN 0-689-70471-2, Aladdin). Atheneum.
Naylor, Thomas H. Corporate Planning Models. LC 77-93329. 1978. text ed. 20.50 (ISBN 0-201-05226-1). A-W.
--Simulation Models in Corporate Planning. LC 78-31258. (Praeger Special Studies). 1979. 24.95 (ISBN 0-03-047061-7). Praeger.
Naylor, Thomas H., et al. Computer Simulation Techniques. LC 66-17622. 1966. 26.95 (ISBN 0-471-63060-8). Wiley.
Nayrayana. Combinatorics, Representation Theory & Statistical Methods in Groups: Young Day Proceedings. 192p. 1980. 25.00 (ISBN 0-686-68601-2). Dekker.
Naysmith, Brian & Hill, Terry. Basketball. 1978. 10.50 (ISBN 0-7153-7509-1). David & Charles.
Nayyar, Deepak, ed. Economic Relations Between Socialist Countries & the Third World. LC 77-84409. 294p. 1978. text ed. 25.50x (ISBN 0-86598-000-4). Allanheld.
Nazarian, Barry. Blood Rites. (Orig.). 1980. pap. 2.25 (ISBN 0-451-09203-1, E9203, Sig). NAL.
--The Circe Factor. LC 80-52407. 320p. 1981. 11.95 (ISBN 0-87223-664-1). Seaview Bks.
Nazaroff, Alexander. The Land & People of Russia. rev. ed. LC 70-37860. (Portraits of the Nations Ser.). (Illus.). (gr. 6 up). 1972. 8.95 (ISBN 0-397-31514-7). Lippincott.
Nazim. Babus, Brahmans & Bureaucrats: A Critique of the Administrative System in Pakistan. LC 73-936432. 144p. 1973. 5.75x o.p. (ISBN 0-88386-281-6). South Asia Bks.
Nazzaro, Anthony M., ed. see Simenon, Georges.
NCCE & Marburger, Carl. Who Controls the Schools. 1978. pap. 3.50 (ISBN 0-934460-06-X). NCCE.
NCCE, jt. auth. see Fernandez, Happy.
NCCE, ed. see Fernandez, Happy.
NCCE, ed. see Fernandez, Happy & NCCE.
NCR Corporation. NCR Basic Electronics Course, with Experiments. LC 78-56596. 1978. pap. 11.95 (ISBN 0-672-21549-7). Sams.
--NCR Data Communications Concepts. LC 78-56590. 1971. pap. 6.95 (ISBN 0-672-21548-9). Sams.
NCTE Committee on the Junior High School Book List. Your Reading: A Booklist for Junior High Students. LC 75-21358. 448p. 1975. pap. 2.95 (ISBN 0-590-09608-7, Citation). Schol Bk Serv.
NE Conf Teach Foreign, ed. Nineteen Eighty-Our Profession: Present Status & Future Directions. 1980. 7.95x (ISBN 0-915432-80-3). NE Conf Teach Foreign.
Neagley, Ross L. & Evans, D. Handbook for Effective Curriculum Development. 1967. 14.95 o.p. (ISBN 0-13-372607-X). P-H.
Neagley, Ross L. & Evans, N. Dean. Handbook for Effective Supervision of Instruction. 3rd ed. 1980. text ed. 18.95 (ISBN 0-13-372672-X). P-H.
Neal, Arminta, jt. auth. see Wormington, H. M.
Neal, Arthur G., et al. Violence in Animal Human Societies. LC 76-21241. (Illus.). 1976. 17.95 (ISBN 0-88229-249-8). Nelson-Hall.
Neal, B. G. Structural Theorems & Their Applications. 1964. 19.50 (ISBN 0-08-010872-5); pap. 9.75 (ISBN 0-08-010871-7). Pergamon.
Neal, B. G., ed. see Cheung, Y. K.
Neal, Bill. History of Hardeman County: The Last Frontier. 17.95 (ISBN 0-685-48798-9). Nortex Pr.
Neal, Charles D. Do-It-Yourself Housebuilding Step-by-Step. LC 72-91256. 1977. pap. 10.95 (ISBN 0-8128-2188-2). Stein & Day.
Neal, Emily G. The Healing Power of Christ. 1972. pap. 4.50 (ISBN 0-8015-3348-1, Hawthorn). Dutton.
--In the Midst of Life. 1974. pap. 2.95 (ISBN 0-8015-3980-3, Hawthorn). Dutton.
Neal, Ernest. Badgers. (Illus.). 1978. 19.95 (ISBN 0-7137-0816-6, Pub. by Blandford Pr England). Sterling.
Neal, Harry E. Story of the Kite. LC 52-11121. (Illus.). (gr. 4-9). 1954. 6.95 (ISBN 0-8149-0373-8). Vanguard.
Neal, Helen. Better Communications for Better Health. LC 62-15058. 1962. 20.00x (ISBN 0-231-02584-X). Columbia U Pr.
Neal, J. W., Jr. A Manual for Determining Small Dosage Calculations of Pesticides & Conversion Tables. 1976. 6.25 (ISBN 0-686-18863-2). Entomol Soc.
Neal, John. Log of the Mahina. (Illus.). 288p. 4.95 o.p. (ISBN 0-918074-00-2). Western Marine Ent.
Neal, L. F. & Robertson, Andrew. The Manager's Guide to Industrial Relations. (Studies in Management). 1977. write for info o.p. (ISBN 0-04-658023-9). Allen Unwin.
Neal, Larry. Hoodoo Hollerin Bebop Ghosts. LC 73-88972. 144p. 1974. 6.95x (ISBN 0-88258-011-6). Howard U Pr.
Neal, Lois S. Abstracts of Vital Records from Raleigh, North Carolina, Newspapers 1820-1829, Vol. 2. LC 79-13328. (Abstracts of Vital Records from Raleigh, North Carolina, Newspapers 1799-1915 Ser.). (Illus.). 940p. 1980. 50.00 (ISBN 0-87152-296-9). Reprint.
Neal, Margo C. & Cohen, Patricia F. Nursing Care Planning Guides, Set 2. 2nd ed. 1980. pap. 11.95 (ISBN 0-935236-16-3). Nurseco.
--Nursing Care Planning Guides for Psychiatric & Mental Health. 1980. pap. 15.95 (ISBN 0-935236-15-5). Nurseco.
Neal, Margo C. & Cooper, Signe S., eds. Perspectives on Continuing Education in Nursing. 1980. pap. text ed. 11.95 (ISBN 0-935236-12-0). Nurseco.
Neal, Patsy. Coaching Methods for Women. 2nd ed. LC 77-77737. (Physical Education Ser.). (Illus.). 1978. text ed. 14.95 (ISBN 0-201-05228-8). A-W.
Neal, Patsy & Tutko, Thomas A. Coaching Girls & Women: Psychological Perspectives. 224p. 1975. text ed. 12.95x o.p. (ISBN 0-205-04693-2). Allyn.
Neal, Patsy E. Basketball Techniques for Women. (Illus.). 1966. 15.50 (ISBN 0-8260-6620-8). Wiley.
Neal, Richard G. & Felts, Frances I. Bargaining Tactics: A Reference Manual for Public Sector Labor Negotiations. LC 80-83023. 275p. 1981. 30.00 (ISBN 0-686-28742-8); pap. 25.00 (ISBN 0-686-28743-6). Neal Assoc.
Neal, Timothy R., jt. ed. see Mader, Charles L.
Neal, W. D., ed. Education in Western Australia. 324p. 1980. 22.50x (ISBN 0-85564-147-9, Pub. by U of West Australia Pr Australia). Intl Schol Bk Serv.
Neal, William A., jt. auth. see Moller, James H.
Neale, et al. Programs for School Improvement: Cooperative Planning & Organization Development. 300p. 1980. text ed. 16.95 (ISBN 0-205-06950-9, 2369508). Allyn.
Neale, A. D. & Goyder, D. G. Antitrust Laws of the U. S. A. 3rd ed. (Economic & Social Research Ser.: No. 19). 525p. 1981. 42.50 (ISBN 0-521-23569-3); pap. 14.95 (ISBN 0-521-28044-3). Cambridge U Pr.
Neale, Allan D. Anti-Trust Laws of the U. S. A. 2nd ed. LC 73-92251. (National Institute of Economic & Social Research Economic & Social Studies: No. 19). 1970. 13.95x (ISBN 0-521-09528-X). Cambridge U Pr.
Neale, Charles M. An Index to Pickwick. 75p. 1980. Repr. of 1897 ed. lib. bdg. 12.50 (ISBN 0-89987-603-X). Darby Bks.
Neale, Donald. Common Foot Disorders. (Illus.). 224p. 1981. lib. bdg. 24.00 (ISBN 0-443-01938-X). Churchill.
Neale, J. E. The Age of Catherine de Medici. 1978. pap. 6.50 (ISBN 0-224-60566-6, Pub. by Chatto Bodley Jonathan). Merrimack Bk Serv.
--Queen Elizabeth First: A Biography. 1957. pap. 3.95 (ISBN 0-385-09312-8, A105, Anch). Doubleday.
Neale, John M. & Liebert, Robert M. Science & Behavior: An Introduction to the Methods of Research. 2nd ed. (Ser. in Social Learning Theory). (Illus.). 1980. text ed. 17.95 (ISBN 0-13-795195-7). P-H.
Neale, John M. & Oltmanns, Thomas F. Schizophrenia. LC 80-10169. 1980. text ed. 23.95 (ISBN 0-471-63086-1). Wiley.
Neale, John M., jt. auth. see Davison, Gerald C.

Neale, R. S. Bath Sixteen Eighty to Eighteen Fifty: A Social History. (Illus.). 400p. 1981. price not set (ISBN 0-7100-0639-X). Routledge & Kegan.

--Class in English History: 1680-1850. 1981. 28.50x (ISBN 0-389-20177-4). B&N.

Neale, Robert E. The Art of Dying. LC 72-11361. 160p. 1973. 5.95 (ISBN 0-06-066087-2, HarpR); pap. 4.95 (ISBN 0-06-066085-6, RD-200). Har-Row.

Neale, Walter C. The British Economy: Toward a Decent Society. LC 79-16553. (Economics Ser.). 1980. pap. text ed. 7.95 (ISBN 0-88244-194-9); 12.95 (ISBN 0-686-65968-6). Grid Pub.

Neale-Silva, Eduardo & Nicholas, Robert L. Adelante! A Cultural Approach to Intermediate Spanish. 2nd ed. 1980. text ed. 15.95x (ISBN 0-673-15412-2); pap. text ed. 5.95x wkbk. (ISBN 0-673-15440-8). Scott F.

--En Camino! A Cultural Approach to Beginning Spanish. 2nd ed. 1980. text ed. 15.95x (ISBN 0-673-15411-4); pap. text ed. 5.95x wkbk. (ISBN 0-673-15441-6). Scott F.

Nealon, Eleanor, jt. auth. see Melluzzo, Paul J.

Neame, Alan, jt. auth. see Stanley, Richard.

Neame, K. D. & Homewood, C. A. Liquid Scintillation Counting. LC 74-11613. 180p. 1974. 17.95 o.p. (ISBN 0-470-63085-X). Halsted Pr.

Neame, K. D. & Richards, T. G. Elementary Kinetics of Membrane Carrier Transport. LC 72-2047. (Illus.). 120p. 1972. pap. 14.95 (ISBN 0-470-63078-7). Halsted Pr.

Nearing, Helen. Simple Food for the Good Life: An Alternative Cook Book. 1980. 12.95 (ISBN 0-440-08479-2). Delacorte.

Neary, Peter & O'Flaherty, Patrick, eds. By Great Waters: A Newfoundland & Labrador Anthology. LC 73-91561. (Social History of Canada Ser.). 1974. pap. 5.95 (ISBN 0-8020-6233-4). U of Toronto Pr.

Neary, Peter, jt. ed. see Hiller, James.

Neat, K. P., ed. see Lifshitz, A.

Neat, K. P., tr. see Botvinnik, M. M.

Neat, K. P., tr. see Polugayevsky, Lyev.

Neat, K. P., tr. see Tal, M., et al.

Neatby, L. H. Discovery in Russian & Siberian Waters. LC 72-85535. (Illus.). 226p. 1973. 12.95x (ISBN 0-8214-0124-6). Ohio U Pr.

Neate, W. R. Mountaineering & Its Literature. LC 80-7785. 1980. pap. 9.95 (ISBN 0-89886-004-0). Mountaineers.

Neave, Guy. How They Fared: The Impact of the Comprehensive School Upon the University. 1975. 26.00x (ISBN 0-7100-7967-2). Routledge & Kegan.

--Patterns of Equality: New Structures in European Higher Education. (General Ser.). 1976. pap. text ed. 16.50x (ISBN 0-85633-114-7, NFER). Humanities.

Neave, Guy, jt. auth. see McPherson, Andrew.

Neave, Guy, ed. Research Perspectives on the Transition from School to Work: Report of a European Contact Workshop Organised by the Institute of Education (ECF) Under the Auspices of the Commission of the European Communities, Bruges, July 1977. 144p. 1978. pap. text ed. 12.75 (ISBN 90-265-0278-8, Pub. by Swets Pub Serv Holland). Swets North Am.

Nebeker, Helen. Jean Rhys: Woman in Passage. 250p. 1981. price not set (ISBN 0-920792-04-9). Eden Women.

Nebel, Bernard J. Environmental Science: The Way the World Works. (Illus.). 1980. text ed. 18.95 (ISBN 0-13-283002-7). P-H.

Nebel, Henry M., Jr., tr. see Karamzin, N. M.

Nebergall, William H., et al. College Chemistry with Qualitative Analysis. 6th ed. 1980. text ed. 21.95x (ISBN 0-669-02217-9); instrs.' manual avail. (ISBN 0-669-02475-9); study guide 7.95 (ISBN 0-669-02474-0); basic laboratory studies 8.95 (ISBN 0-669-02473-2); problems & solutions manual 6.95 (ISBN 0-669-02472-4). Heath.

--General Chemistry. 6th ed. 1980. text ed. 21.95x (ISBN 0-669-02218-7); instrs'. manual avail. (ISBN 0-669-02475-9); study guide 7.95 (ISBN 0-669-02474-0); basic lab. studies 8.95 (ISBN 0-669-02473-2); problems & solutions manual 6.95 (ISBN 0-669-02472-4). Heath.

Neblekopf, Ethan. The Herbal Connection. 1980. 12.95 (ISBN 0-89557-048-3). Bi World Indus.

Neblett, Lucy Ann, tr. see Wampler, Joseph.

Nebraska Curriculum Development Center. Nebraska Curriculum for English: Grade 12, Unit 114, Rhetoric. (Nebraska Curriculum for English Ser). (Orig.). 1974. pap. 3.25x student manual (ISBN 0-8032-7546-3). U of Nebr Pr.

--Nebraska Curriculum for English: Grade 12, Units 109-110, Man, Society, Nature & Moral Law. (Nebraska Curriculum for English Ser). (Orig.). 1973. pap. 3.95x teacher manual (ISBN 0-8032-7542-0); pap. 2.75x student manual (ISBN 0-8032-7543-9). U of Nebr Pr.

--Nebraska Curriculum for English, Grade 10: Units 97-98, Man & Nature. (Nebraska Curriculum for English Ser). (Orig.). 1970. pap. 4.95x student manual (ISBN 0-8032-7530-7); pap. 3.00x tch. manual (ISBN 0-8032-7529-3). U of Nebr Pr.

--Nebraska Curriculum for English: Grade 7, Units 71-72, the Rhetoric of Literature. (Nebraska Curriculum for English Ser). 1967. pap. 2.00x teacher manual (ISBN 0-8032-7509-9); pap. 2.75x student manual (ISBN 0-8032-7510-2). U of Nebr Pr.

--Nebraska Curriculum for English, Grade 8: Units 82-84, the Hero. (Nebraska Curriculum for English Ser). 1968. pap. 6.95x, student's manual (ISBN 0-8032-7519-6); 3.00x, teachers' manual (ISBN 0-8032-7518-8). U of Nebr Pr.

--Nebraska Curriculum for English, Grade 9: Units 89-90, the Rhetoric of Literature. (Nebraska Curriculum for English Ser). 1969. pap. 3.20x student's manual (ISBN 0-8032-7524-2); 2.00x, teachers manual (ISBN 0-8032-7523-4). U of Nebr Pr.

Nebraska Symposium on Motivation, 1979. Nebraska Symposium on Motivation, 1979: Attitudes, Values, & Beliefs. Howe, Herbert E., Jr. & Page, Monte M., eds. LC 53-11655. (Nebraska Symposium on Motivation Ser.: Vol. 27). xii, 365p. 1980. 19.95x (ISBN 0-8032-2313-7); pap. 9.95x (ISBN 0-8032-7207-3). U of Nebr Pr.

Nebreda, E. Bibliographia Augustiniana Seu Operum Collectio Quae, Divi Augustini Vitam et Doctrinam Quadantenus exponunt. (Classical Studies Ser.). (Lat.). Repr. of 1928 ed. lib. bdg. 28.00x (ISBN 0-697-00013-3). Irvington.

Necheles. An Introduction to the Morphology of the Cellular Elements of the Blood. 1975. pap. 17.95 o.p. (ISBN 0-8385-4350-2). ACC.

Necheles, Thomas F. The Acute Leukemias. (Clinical Monographs in Hematology: Vol. 1). (Illus.). 1979. pap. 14.75 (ISBN 0-913258-57-1). Thieme-Stratton.

Necker, Claire. The Cat's Got Our Tongue. 1973. 10.00 (ISBN 0-8108-0545-6). Scarecrow.

--Four Centuries of Cat Books: A Bibliography, 1570-1970. LC 72-363. 1972. 20.50 (ISBN 0-8108-0480-8). Scarecrow.

Neckers, D. C., jt. ed. see Blossey, E. C.

Nedderman, R. M., jt. auth. see Kay, J. M.

Nedelec, C., ed. FAO Catalogue of Small Scale Fishing Gear. (Illus.). 192p. 24.25 (ISBN 0-85238-077-1, FN). Unipub.

Nederhood, Joel. Promises, Promises, Promises. LC 79-18889. (Orig.). 1979. pap. text ed. 2.45 (ISBN 0-933140-09-6). Bd of Pubns CRC.

Nedler, Shari & McAfee, Oralie. Working with Parents: Guidelines for Early Childhood & Elementary Teachers. 1979. pap. text ed. 9.95x (ISBN 0-534-00622-1). Wadsworth Pub.

Nee, Brett De B., jt. auth. see Nee, Victor G.

Nee, John G. Jig & Fixture Design & Detailing. LC 78-71562. (Illus.). 1979. pap. 14.90x (ISBN 0-911168-41-9). Prakken.

--Mechanism Drafting & Design: A Workbook. LC 80-80861. (Illus.). 1980. pap. text ed. 14.95x (ISBN 0-911168-45-1). Prakken.

Nee, Robert H., jt. ed. see Roberts, Robert W.

Nee, T. S. Autoridade Espirituale. Balthazar, Vera, ed. Caruso, Luiz A., tr. from Eng. 240p. (Portuguese.). 1979. pap. 1.85 (ISBN 0-8297-0922-3). Vida Pubs.

Nee, Victor G. & Nee, Brett De B. Lontime Californ' A Documentary Study of an American Chinatown. (Pantheon Village Ser.). 1981. pap. 6.95 (ISBN 0-394-73846-2). Pantheon.

Nee, Watchman. Changed into His Likeness. 1969. 3.00 (ISBN 0-87508-411-7); pap. 2.50 (ISBN 0-87508-410-9). Chr Lit.

--Full of Grace & Truth, Vol. 1. Kaung, Stephen, tr. 1980. 2.95 (ISBN 0-935008-49-7). Christian Fellow Pubs.

--The Messenger of the Cross. Kaung, Stephen, tr. (Orig.). 1980. pap. text ed. write for info. (ISBN 0-935008-50-0); pap. 2.95 (ISBN 0-935008-50-0). Christian Fellow Pubs.

--Normal Christian Life. 1961-1963. pap. 2.95 (ISBN 0-87508-414-1). Chr Lit.

--Normal Christian Life Study Guide. Foster, ed. 1978. pap. 1.25. Chr Lit.

--Song of Songs. 1965-1967. 3.00 o.p. (ISBN 0-87508-421-4); pap. 1.75 (ISBN 0-87508-420-6). Chr Lit.

Nee, Watchman, tr. Autoridad Espiritual. (Spanish Bks.). (Span.). 1978. 1.75 (ISBN 0-8297-0805-7). Life Pubs Intl.

--L' Autorite Spirituelle. (French Bks.). (Fr.). 1979. 1.75 (ISBN 0-686-28817-3). Life Pubs Intl.

Needham, Barrie. Guidelines for a Local Employment Study. 1978. text ed. 23.00x (ISBN 0-566-00241-8, Pub. by Gower Pub Co England). Renouf.

Needham, Charles W. Cerebral Logic: Solving the Problem of Mind & Brain. (Illus.). 232p. 1978. 23.50 (ISBN 0-398-03754-X). C C Thomas.

Needham, D. E. Iron Age to Independence: A History of Central Africa. (Illus.). 208p. 1974. pap. text ed. 5.95x (ISBN 0-582-60298-X). Longman.

Needham, Dorothy M. Machina Carnis: The Biochemistry of Muscular Contraction in Its Historical Development. (Illus.). 1972. 99.50 (ISBN 0-521-07974-8). Cambridge U Pr.

Needham, George H. The Practical Use of the Microscope. (Illus.). 520p. 1977. 28.75 (ISBN 0-398-03645-4). C C Thomas.

Needham, J. Development of Iron & Steel Technology in China. LC 75-22549. (Illus.). 76p. 1975. 19.95 (ISBN 0-521-21045-3). Cambridge U Pr.

--Science & Civilisation in China: Vol. 5, Pt. 4, Spagyrical Discovery & Invention: Apparatus, Theories & Gifts. 1980. 105.00 (ISBN 0-521-08573-X). Cambridge U Pr.

Needham, J., jt. auth. see Lu, Gwei-Djen.

Needham, J., jt. auth. see Ronan, Colin A.

Needham, James G. & Needham, Paul R. Guide to the Study of Freshwater Biology. 5th ed. LC 62-20742. (Illus.). 1962. pap. 5.95x (ISBN 0-8162-6310-8). Holden-Day.

Needham, James G. & Westfall, Minter J. Manual of Dragonflies of North America (Anisoptera) Including the Greater Antilles & the Provinces of the Mexican Border. (Lbrary Reprint Ser.: No. 65). 1981. Repr. of 1975 ed. 42.50x (ISBN 0-520-02913-5). U of Cal Pr.

Needham, Joseph. Biochemistry & Morphogenesis. 1942. 99.50 (ISBN 0-521-05797-3). Cambridge U Pr.

--Chemistry of Life: Eight Lectures on the History of Biochemistry. LC 78-85733. (Illus.). 1970. 32.95 (ISBN 0-521-07379-0). Cambridge U Pr.

--Clerks & Craftsmen in China & the West: Lectures & Addresses on the History of Science & Technology. (Illus.). 1970. 65.00 (ISBN 0-521-07235-2). Cambridge U Pr.

--The Grand Titration: Science & Society in East & West. LC 76-483302. 1979. pap. 7.50 (ISBN 0-8020-6359-4). U of Toronto Pr.

--Science & Civilization in China, 5 vols. Incl. Vol. 1. Introductory Orientations. 1954. 50.00 (ISBN 0-521-05799-X); Vol. 2. History of Scientific Thought. 85.00 (ISBN 0-521-05800-7); Vol. 3. Mathematics & the Sciences of the Heavens & the Earth. 125.00 (ISBN 0-521-05801-5); Vol. 4. Physics & Physical Technology, 3 pts; Pt. 1. Physics. 1962. 65.00 (ISBN 0-521-05802-3); Pt. 2. Mechanical Engineering. 105.00 (ISBN 0-521-05803-1); Pt. 3. Engineering & Nautics. 1970. 125.00 (ISBN 0-521-07060-0); Pt. 4. Spagyrical Discovery & Invention. 500p. 105.00 (ISBN 0-521-08573-X). Cambridge U Pr.

Needham, Paul. Twelve Centuries of Bookbindings: Four Hundred to Sixteen Hundred. LC 79-52345. (Illus.). 368p. 1979. 75.00 (ISBN 0-19-211580-4); pap. 39.95 (ISBN 0-686-68488-5). Pierpont Morgan.

--Twelve Centuries of Bookbindings: Four Hundred to Sixteen Hundred. (Illus.). 1979. 75.00x (ISBN 0-19-211580-4). Oxford U Pr.

Needham, Paul R., jt. auth. see Needham, James G.

Needham, R. M., jt. auth. see Wilkes, M. V.

Needham, Rodney, ed. see Starcke, Carl N.

Needle, Jan. Rottenteeth. (Illus.). (gr. k-3). 1980. 8.95 (ISBN 0-233-97205-6). Andre Deutsch.

Needleman, Carolyn E., jt. auth. see Needleman, Martin L.

Needleman, Herbert L., ed. Low Level Lead Exposure: The Clinical Implications of Current Research. 336p. 1980. text ed. 36.50 (ISBN 0-89004-455-4). Raven.

Needleman, Jacob. A Sense of the Cosmos: The Encounter of Modern Science & Ancient Truth. 1977. pap. 4.50 (ISBN 0-525-47446-3). Dutton.

Needleman, Jacob, ed. Speaking of My Life: The Art of Living in the Cultural Revolution. LC 78-19502. (Illus., Orig.). 1979. pap. 4.95 (ISBN 0-06-250643-9, RD 216, HarpR). Har-Row.

Needleman, Jacob & Baker, George, eds. Understanding the New Religions. 1978. 17.50 (ISBN 0-8164-0403-8); pap. 6.95 (ISBN 0-8164-2188-9). Crossroad NY.

Needleman, Martin L. & Needleman, Carolyn E. Guerrillas in the Bureaucracy: The Community Planning Experiment in the United States. LC 73-19806. (Urban Research Ser.). 384p. 1974. 22.95 (ISBN 0-471-63099-3, Pub. by Wiley-Interscience). Wiley.

Needler, Martin C. An Introduction to Latin American Politics: The Structure of Conflict. LC 77-23222. 1977. text ed. 16.95 (ISBN 0-13-486043-8). P-H.

Needles, Belverd E., et al. Principles of Accounting. LC 80-80503. (Illus.). 1008p. 1981. text ed. 20.95 (ISBN 0-395-29527-0); study guide 6.95 (ISBN 0-395-29529-7); price not set test bank (ISBN 0-395-29538-6); practice set 1 5.95 (ISBN 0-395-29534-3); price not set achievement tests 1-14A (ISBN 0-395-29539-4); price not set achievement tests 1-14B (ISBN 0-395-29540-8); price not set achievement tests 14-28A (ISBN 0-395-29541-6); price not set achievement tests 14-28B (ISBN 0-395-29542-4). HM.

Needles, Belverd E., Jr. & Williams, Doyle Z., eds. The CPA Examination: A Complete Review, Vol. II. (Illus.). 768p. 1980. pap. text ed. 20.95 (ISBN 0-13-187815-8). P-H.

--CPA Examination: A Complete Review, Vol. 1. (Illus.). 1000p. 1980. text ed. 22.95 (ISBN 0-13-187807-7). P-H.

Needles, Howard L. Handbook of Textile Fibers, Dyes, and Finishes. LC 79-23188. 175p. 1980. lib. bdg. 27.50 (ISBN 0-8240-7046-1). Garland Pub.

Neef, Marian, jt. auth. see Nagel, Stuart S.

Neef, Marion, jt. auth. see Nagel, Stuart S.

Neelameghan, A. Presentation of Ideas in Technical Writing. 1975. 12.50 (ISBN 0-7069-0340-4, Pub. by Vikas India). Advent Bk.

Neels, Betty. Caroline's Waterloo. (Harlequin Romances). 192p. 1981. pap. 1.25 (ISBN 0-373-02393-6, Pub. by Harlequin). PB.

--Hannah. (Harlequin Romances Ser.). 192p. 1981. pap. 1.25 (ISBN 0-373-02403-7, Pub. by Harlequin). PB.

--The Silver Thaw. (Harlequin Romances Ser.). 192p. (Orig.). 1981. pap. 1.25 (ISBN 0-373-02386-3, Pub. by Harlequin). PB.

--Winter Wedding. (Harlequin Romances Ser.). (Orig.). 1980. pap. text ed. 1.25 o.p. (ISBN 0-373-02338-3, Pub. by Harlequin). PB.

Neely. Organic Chemicals in the Environment. 424p. 1980. 37.50 (ISBN 0-8247-6975-9). Dekker.

Neely, Esther L. Chateau Laurens. (Orig.). 1980. pap. 1.95 (ISBN 0-505-51515-6). Tower Bks.

Neely, Mark E., Jr. The Abraham Lincoln Encyclopedia. (Illus.). 448p. 1981. write for info (ISBN 0-07-046145-7, P&RB). McGraw.

Neely, Martina & Neely, William. The International Chili Society Official Chili Cookbook. (Illus.). 224p. 1981. 10.95 (ISBN 0-312-41988-0). St Martin.

Neely, Richard. The Japanese Mistress. 1979. pap. 1.75 (ISBN 0-515-05164-0). Jove Pubns.

--Lies. 1979. pap. 1.75 o.s.i. (ISBN 0-515-04879-8). Jove Pubns.

--No Certain Life. 1978. pap. 1.50 o.s.i. (ISBN 0-685-86780-3, 4548). Jove Pubns.

Neely, William, jt. auth. see Neely, Martina.

Ne'eman, Nira, jt. auth. see Bartal, Lee.

Ne'Emann, Yuval, ed. Jerusalem Einstein Centennial Symposium. (Illus.). 528p. 1980. text ed. 39.50 (ISBN 0-201-05289-X). A-W.

Neenan. Urban Public Economics. 1981. text ed. write for info. Duxbury Pr.

Neenan, William B., jt. ed. see Mathewson, Kent.

Neeper, Cary. A Place Beyond Man. 1977. pap. 1.50 o.s.i. (ISBN 0-440-16931-3). Dell.

Neer, C. S. Shoulder Reconstruction. (Illus.). 1981. text ed. write for info. Churchill.

Neese, Harvey, ed. Gold Mining for Recreation. (Illus., Orig.). 1981. pap. 4.95 (ISBN 0-87701-182-6). Chronicle Bks.

Neese, Harvey C. The Almanac of Rural Living. 1979. 14.95 (ISBN 0-688-03411-X); pap. 8.95 (ISBN 0-688-08411-7). Morrow.

Neese, Martha & Neese, Marvin. Fun with Flowers. LC 68-27867. (Illus.). 72p. 1980. pap. 8.95 (ISBN 0-8348-0152-3). Weatherhill.

Neese, Martha, jt. auth. see Neese, Marvin.

Neese, Marvin & Neese, Martha. Fun with Flowers. LC 68-57453. (Illus.). 112p. 1980. pap. 8.95 (ISBN 0-8348-0153-1, Pub. by John Weatherhill Inc Japan). C E Tuttle.

Neese, Marvin, jt. auth. see Neese, Martha.

Neeson, Jean D. & Stockdale, Connie R. The Practitioners Handbook of Ambulatory OB-GYN. 400p. 1981. 17.95 (ISBN 0-471-05670-7, Pub. by Wiley Medical). Wiley.

Neevel, Walter G., Jr. Yamuna's Vedanta & Pancaratra: Integrating the Classical & the Popular. LC 77-4048. (Harvard Theological Review. Dissertation Ser.). 1977. pap. 9.00 (ISBN 0-89130-136-4, 020110). Scholars Pr Ca.

Neff, Emery E. The Poetry of History: The Contribution of Literature & Literary Scholarship to the Writing of History Since Voltaire. LC 47-30933. 1947. pap. 6.00x (ISBN 0-231-08525-7). Columbia U Pr.

Neff, Herbert & Pilch, Judith. Teaching Handicapped Children Easily: A Manual for the Average Classroom Teacher Without Specialized Training. (Illus.). 264p. 1976. 16.50 (ISBN 0-398-03439-7). C C Thomas.

Neff, Herbert P., Jr. Basic Electromagnetic Fields. (Illus.). 608p. Date not set. text ed. 28.50 scp (ISBN 0-06-044785-0, HarpC). Har-Row.

Neff, Jerry M. Polycyclic Aromatic Hydrocarbons in the Aquatic Environment. (Illus.). 1979. 51.80x (ISBN 0-85334-832-4). Intl Ideas.

Neff, Norman D. & Naus, Joseph I. The Distribution of the Size of the Maximum Cluster of Points on a Line. LC 74-6283. (Selected Tables in Mathematical Statistics: Vol. 6). 1980. 12.80 (ISBN 0-8218-1906-2). Am Math.

Neff, Paula E., jt. auth. see Wojniechowski, William V.

Neff, Thomas L. The Social Costs of Solar Energy: A Study of Photovoltaic Energy Systems. LC 80-23732. (Pergamon Policy Studies on Science & Technology). (Illus.). 110p. Date not set. price not set (ISBN 0-08-026315-1). Pergamon.

Neff, William D., ed. Contributions to Sensory Physiology, 5 vols. Incl. Vol. 1. 1965. 38.50 (ISBN 0-12-151801-9); Vol. 2. 1967 (ISBN 0-12-151802-7); Vol. 3. 1969 (ISBN 0-12-151803-5); Vol. 4. 1970 (ISBN 0-12-151804-3); Vol. 5. 1971 (ISBN 0-12-151805-1). 38.50 ea. Acad Pr.

Negandhi, Anant R. Quest for Survival & Growth: A Comparative Study of American, European, & Japanese Multinationals. LC 78-71603. 1979. 29.95 (ISBN 0-03-046416-1). Praeger.

Negoita, C. V. & Ralescu, D. A. Applications of Fuzzy Sets to Systems Analysis. LC 75-35789. 1976. 27.95 (ISBN 0-470-63105-8). Halsted Pr.

Negoita, Constantin. Management Applications of System Theory. (Interdisciplinary Systems Research: No. 57). 1979. 19.50 (ISBN 3-7643-1032-4). Birkhauser.

Negri, Antonio. Marx Beyond Marx: Notebooks on the Grundrisse. Orig. Title: Marx Oltre Marx. 232p. 1981. 21.95x (ISBN 0-89789-018-3). J F Bergin.

Negri, Renata. Matisse & the Fauves. (Illus.). 1975. Repr. 5.95 o.p. (ISBN 0-88308-013-3). Lamplight Pub.

Negrini, Sergio, ed. The Uffizi of Florence. LC 72-94912. (Great Galleries of the World Ser.). (Illus.). 104p. 1974. 6.95 o.p. (ISBN 0-668-02923-4). Arco.

Negroponte, Nicholas. The Architecture Machine. (Illus.). 164p. 1970. 7.95 o.p. (ISBN 0-262-14008-X); pap. 4.95 (ISBN 0-262-64010-4). MIT Pr.

Negus, Kenneth. H. J. C. Von Grimmelshausen. (World Authors Ser.: No. 291). 1974. lib. bdg. 10.95 (ISBN 0-8057-2405-2). Twayne.

Negus, R. W. Fundamentals of Finite Mathematics. LC 73-17469. 448p. 1974. text ed. 19.95x o.p. (ISBN 0-471-63121-3). Wiley.

Negus, Robert W. Fundamentals of Finite Mathematics. 416p. 1981. Repr. of 1974 ed. text ed. price not set (ISBN 0-89874-270-6). Krieger.

Nehari, Zeev. Conformal Mapping. LC 74-27513. (Illus.). 416p. 1975. pap. text ed. 5.50 (ISBN 0-486-61137-X). Dover.

Neher, Andre. The Exile of the World: From the Silence of the Bible to the Silence of Auschwitz. 224p. 1980. 16.95 (ISBN 0-8276-0176-X, 465). Jewish Pubn.

Neher, Andrew. The Psychology of Transendence. (Transpersonal Ser.). (Illus.). 320p. 1980. text ed. 13.95 (ISBN 0-13-736652-3, Spec); pap. text ed. 6.95 (ISBN 0-13-736645-0). P-H.

Nehls, Edward H., ed. D. H. Lawrence: A Composite Biography, 3 vols. 1957-59. 30.00 ea.; Vol. 1. (ISBN 0-299-81501-3); Vol. 2. (ISBN 0-299-81502-1); Vol. 3. (ISBN 0-299-81503-X). U of Wis Pr.

Nehls, Nadine, jt. auth. see Morgenbesser, Mel.

Nehmer, Kathleen S., ed. Elementary Teachers Guide to Free Curriculum Materials. 37th rev. ed. LC 44-52255. 1980. pap. 15.00 (ISBN 0-87708-104-2). Ed Prog.

Nehmer, Kathleen S., et al, eds. Educators Grade Guide to Free Teaching Aids. 26th rev. ed. LC 56-2444. 1980. looseleaf 33.25 (ISBN 0-87708-105-0). Ed Prog.

Nehrling, Arno & Nehrling, Irene. The Picture Book of Annuals. LC 76-45745. (Illus.). 1977. pap. 3.95 o.p. (ISBN 0-668-04158-7). Arco.

--The Picture Book of Perennials. LC 76-46317. (Illus.). 1977. pap. 3.95 o.p. (ISBN 0-668-04163-3). Arco.

Nehrling, Irene, jt. auth. see Nehrling, Arno.

Nehrt, Lee C. International Marketing of Nuclear Power Plants. LC 65-24596. (Social Science Ser: No. 22). 1966. pap. 15.00x o.p. (ISBN 0-253-38422-2). Ind U Pr.

Nehru, Jawajarial. India's Freedom. (Unwin Bks.). 1962. pap. 2.95 o.p. (ISBN 0-04-320028-1). Allen Unwin.

Neiburger, Morris, et al. Understanding Our Atmospheric Environment. LC 72-4753. (Illus.). 1973. text ed. 20.95x (ISBN 0-7167-0257-6). W H Freeman.

Neidecker, Elizabeth. School Programs in Speech-Language: Organization & Management. (Illus.). 1980. text ed. 17.95 (ISBN 0-13-794321-0). P-H.

Neider, Charles. Beyond Cape Horn: Travels in the Antarctic. LC 80-13220. (Illus.). 400p. 1980. 16.95 (ISBN 0-87156-233-2). Sierra.

--Beyond Cape Horn: Travels in the Antarctic. (Illus.). 424p. 1980. 18.95 o.p. (ISBN 0-87156-233-2). Sierra.

Neider, Charles see Twain, Mark.

Neider, Charles, ed. see Twain, Mark.

Neiderman, Andrew. Pin. 1981. pap. 2.50 (ISBN 0-671-41501-8). PB.

Neidig, Kenneth L. Music Director's Complete Handbook of Forms. 1973. 14.95 o.p. (ISBN 0-13-607135-X). P-H.

Neidle, Cecyle S. America's Immigrant Women. LC 75-12738. (Immigrant Heritage of America Ser.). 1975. lib. bdg. 10.95 (ISBN 0-8057-8400-4). Twayne.

--Great Immigrants. (Immigrant Heritage of America Ser). 1972. lib. bdg. 9.95 (ISBN 0-8057-3222-5). Twayne.

--The New Americans. (Immigrant Heritage of American Ser.). lib. bdg. 9.95 (ISBN 0-8057-3247-0). Twayne.

Neidle, Enid A. Pharmacology & Therapeutics for Dentistry. LC 80-10522. (Illus.). 736p. 1980. text ed. 29.50 (ISBN 0-8016-3635-3). Mosby.

Neighbour, Oliver. The Music of William Byrd, Vol. 3: Consort & Keyboard Music. 1979. 38.50x (ISBN 0-520-03486-4). U of Cal Pr.

Neighbours, Kenneth F. Indian Exodus: Texas Indian Affairs. 6.95 (ISBN 0-685-48786-5). Nortex Pr.

Neigoff, Mike. Best in Camp. LC 78-79545. (Pilot Book Ser). (Illus.). (gr. 4-7). 1969. 6.95g (ISBN 0-8075-0660-5). A Whitman.

--Dive In. LC 65-23885. (Pilot Book Ser). (Illus.). (gr. 3-5). 1965. 6.95g (ISBN 0-8075-1644-9). A Whitman.

--Goal to Go. LC 70-115898. (Pilot Book Ser). (Illus.). (gr. 3-5). 1970. 6.95g (ISBN 0-8075-2974-5). A Whitman.

--Playmaker. LC 73-7314. (Pilot Book Ser.). (Illus.). 128p. (gr. 4-7). 1973. 6.95g (ISBN 0-8075-6543-1). A Whitman.

--Runner-up. LC 75-1089. (Pilot Book Ser.). (Illus.). (gr. 4-8). 1975. 6.95g (ISBN 0-8075-7181-4). A Whitman.

--Ski Run. LC 70-188433. (Pilot Books Ser.). (Illus.). 128p. (gr. 4-7). 1972. 6.95g (ISBN 0-8075-7396-5). A Whitman.

--Soccer Hero. Rubin, Caroline, ed. LC 76-18750. (Pilot Bks). (Illus.). 128p. (gr. 4-8). 1976. 6.95g (ISBN 0-8075-7529-1). A Whitman.

--Terror on the Ice. LC 74-3405. (Pilot Book Ser.). (Illus.). 128p. (gr. 4-7). 1974. 6.95g (ISBN 0-8075-7808-8). A Whitman.

--Two on First. LC 67-17419. (Pilot Book Ser). (Illus.). (gr. 3-5). 1967. 6.95g (ISBN 0-8075-8161-5). A Whitman.

--Up Sails. LC 66-16080. (Pilot Book Ser). (Illus.). (gr. 3-5). 1966. 6.95g (ISBN 0-8075-8331-6). A Whitman.

Neihardt, John C. Black Elk Speaks. (gr. 10-12). pap. 2.95 (ISBN 0-671-43268-0). PB.

Neihardt, John G. Lyric & Dramatic Poems. LC 65-22374. 1965. pap. 3.50 (ISBN 0-8032-5143-2, BB 322, Bison). U of Nebr Pr.

--Mountain Men. LC 70-134770. Orig. Title: A Cycle of the West, (Illus.). 1971. pap. 5.95 (ISBN 0-8032-5733-3, BB 531, Bison). U of Nebr Pr.

--River & I. LC 68-13650. (Illus.). 1968. pap. 4.95 (ISBN 0-8032-5144-0, BB 378, Bison). U of Nebr Pr.

--Splendid Wayfaring: The Exploits & Adventures of Jedediah Smith & the Ashley-Henry Men, 1822-1831. LC 71-116054. (Illus.). 1970. pap. 5.25 (ISBN 0-8032-5723-6, BB 525, Bison). U of Nebr Pr.

--Twilight of the Sioux. LC 74-134771. Orig. Title: A Cycle of the West. 1971. pap. 4.50 (ISBN 0-8032-5734-1, BB 532, Bison). U of Nebr Pr.

--When the Tree Flowered: The Fictional Autobiography of Eagle Voice, a Sioux Indian. LC 75-116055. 1970. pap. 4.95 (ISBN 0-8032-5724-4, BB 526, Bison). U of Nebr Pr.

Neihouse, Leon. The Theory of Business Relativity. 112p. 1981. 6.50 (ISBN 0-682-49707-X). Exposition.

Neil, Charles, jt. ed. see Wright, Charles.

Neil, E. H. An Analysis of Color Changes & Social Behavior of Tilapia Mossambica. (U. C. Publ. in Zoology: Vol. 75.1). 1964. pap. 5.50x (ISBN 0-520-09330-5). U of Cal Pr.

Neil, Grant. The German-Soviet Pact, August 23, 1939: A Nonagression Pact. LC 75-8512. (World Focus Bks). (Illus.). 72p. (gr. 7 up). 1975. PLB 6.45 (ISBN 0-531-02174-2). Watts.

Neil, J. Meredith see O'Neal, William B.

Neil, William. The Bible Story. (Fount Religious Paperbacks Ser). 1977. pap. 1.95 (ISBN 0-00-623184-5, FA3184, Pub. by Collins Pubs). World Bible.

--Can We Trust the Old Testament? 1979. 6.95 (ISBN 0-8164-0435-6). Crossroad NY.

--The Message of the Bible: A Concise Introduction to the Old & New Testament. LC 79-3602. 224p. (Orig.). 1980. pap. 3.95 (ISBN 0-06-066092-9, RD 322, HarpR, HarpR). Har-Row.

--Why Listen? The Difficult Sayings of Jesus. (Orig.). pap. 1.50 (ISBN 0-89129-227-6). Jove Pubns.

Neil, William, tr. see Keller, Werner.

Neill, C. P; see Mangold, George B.

Neill, Ian. Trout from the Hills. 10.00x (ISBN 0-392-06403-0, SpS). Soccer.

Neill, June E., jt. auth. see Matilda, E.

Neill, Kenneth. The Age of Steam & Steel. (Illus.). 1976. pap. 4.95x o.p. (ISBN 0-7171-0786-8). Irish Bk Ctr.

--Our Changing Times: Ireland, Europe & the Modern World Since 1890. (Illus.). 1976. pap. text ed. 5.95 large format limp bdg. o.p. (ISBN 0-7171-0761-2). Irish Bk Ctr.

Neill, Mary, jt. auth. see Chervin, Ronda.

Neill, Robin. New Theory of Value: The Canadian Economics of Harold Adams Innis. LC 77-185867. 184p. 1972. pap. 3.50 (ISBN 0-8020-6152-4). U of Toronto Pr.

Neill, Shirley B. Suspensions & Expulsions. 1976. pap. 8.00 (ISBN 0-87545-004-0). Natl Sch Pr.

Neill, Stephen. Christian Faith & Other Faiths: The Christian Dialogue with Other Religions. 2nd ed. 1970. 10.95 (ISBN 0-19-213305-5); pap. 6.95x (ISBN 0-19-283011-2, OPB196). Oxford U Pr.

--The Christians' God. 1980. 1.25 (ISBN 0-686-28774-6). Forward Movement.

--Interpretation of the New Testament, 1861-1961. 1964. pap. 8.95x (ISBN 0-19-283005-8, OPB). Oxford U Pr.

--Salvation Tomorrow. 1976. pap. 3.95 o.p. (ISBN 0-687-36799-9). Abingdon.

Neill, Wilfred T. Archeology & a Science of Man. LC 77-11038. 1977. 28.50x (ISBN 0-231-03661-2). Columbia U Pr.

--Geography of Life. LC 68-8877. (Illus.). 1969. 22.50x (ISBN 0-231-02876-8). Columbia U Pr.

--Reptiles & Amphibians in the Service of Man. LC 73-8745. (Biological Science Ser). 1974. pap. 5.95 (ISBN 0-672-53687-0). Pegasus.

--Twentieth-Century Indonesia. (Illus.). 413p. 1973. 25.00 (ISBN 0-231-03547-0); pap. 10.00x (ISBN 0-231-08316-5). Columbia U Pr.

Neilson, Frances, jt. auth. see Neilson, Winthrop.

Neilson, W. A. & MacPherson, J. C. The Legislative Process in Canada: The Need for Reform. 328p. 1978. pap. text ed. 12.95x (ISBN 0-920380-11-5, Pub. by Inst Res Pub Canada). Renouf.

Neilson, Winthrop & Neilson, Frances. Letter to Philemon. 1973. pap. 1.25 o.s.i. (ISBN 0-515-03216-6). Jove Pubns.

Neiman, Fraser. Matthew Arnold. LC 68-24283. (English Authors Ser.: No. 69). 1969. lib. bdg. 10.95 (ISBN 0-8057-1012-4). Twayne.

Neiman, Harvey L. & Yao, James S. Angiography in Vascular Disease. (Illus.). 700p. 1981. text ed. write for info. (ISBN 0-443-08030-5). Churchill. Postponed.

Neiman, Leroy. LeRoy Neiman Posters. (Illus.). 64p. 1980. pap. 12.95 (ISBN 0-686-62713-X, 84911-3); signed, lim. ed. o.p. 150.00 (ISBN 0-686-62714-8, 2237-1). Abrams.

--The Prints of LeRoy Neiman. (Illus.). 364p. 1980. 100.00. Control Data.

Neiman, Richard S., jt. auth. see Enriquez, Pablo.

Neimark, Anne. With This Gift: The Story of Edgar Cayce. (Illus.). (gr. 7 up). 1978. 7.95 (ISBN 0-688-22147-5); PLB 7.63 (ISBN 0-688-32147-X). Morrow.

Neimark, Paul. Camping & Ecology. (Wilderness World Ser.). (Illus.). 64p. (gr. 3 up). 1981. PLB 9.25 (ISBN 0-516-02451-5). Childrens.

--Fishing. (Wilderness World Ser.). (Illus.). 64p. (gr. 3 up). 1981. PLB 9.25 (ISBN 0-516-02452-3). Childrens.

--Hiking & Exploring. (Wilderness World Ser.). (Illus.). 64p. (gr. 3 up). 1981. PLB 9.25 (ISBN 0-516-02453-1). Childrens.

--Survival. (Wilderness World Ser.). (Illus.). 64p. (gr. 3 up). 1981. PLB 9.25 (ISBN 0-516-02454-X). Childrens.

Neimark, Paul & Berkowitz, Gerald. A Doctor Discusses Care of the Back. 1980. pap. 2.50 (ISBN 0-910304-04-1). Budlong.

Neimark, Paul & Matlin, Samuel. Doctor Discusses Female Surgery. (Illus.). 1979. pap. 2.50 (ISBN 0-686-65550-8). Budlong.

Neimark, Paul, jt. auth. see Glieberman, Herbert A.

Neimark, Paul, jt. auth. see Owens, Jesse.

Neimark, Paul, jt. auth. see Scheimann, Eugene.

Neimark, Paul, jt. auth. see Schmidt, Jay H.

Neimark, Paul, ed. Jesse. Neimark, Pul. Mercado, Benjamin, ed. Flores, Rhode, tr. from Eng. 192p. (Span.). 1979. pap. 1.95 (ISBN 0-8297-0677-1). Vida Pubs.

Neimark, Paul, et al. A Doctor Discusses Your New Baby & Your New Life. (Illus.). 1980. pap. 2.50 (ISBN 0-685-46338-9). Budlong.

Neimark, Paul G. & Schmidt, Jay. A Doctor Discusses How to Stay Young & Live Longer. (Illus.). 1977. pap. 2.50 (ISBN 0-685-46340-0). Budlong.

Neimark, Pul see Neimark, Paul.

Neinstein & Kornbluh. Business Law. (High School Exams & Answer Ser.). 1980. pap. 3.95 (ISBN 0-8120-0192-3). Barron.

--Business Mathematics. (High School Exams & Answers Ser.). 1980. pap. 3.95 (ISBN 0-8120-0108-7). Barron.

Neinstein, Murray & Kornbluh, Elaine. Bookkeeping. LC 58-32560. (High School Exams & Answer Ser). (gr. 9-12). 1977. pap. 3.95 (ISBN 0-8120-0107-9). Barron.

Neiomark, Joseph, jt. auth. see Lake, Frances.

Neirynck, J., ed. see Brayton, R. K., et al.

Neirynck, J., jt. ed. see Moschytz, G. S.

Neisendorfer, Joseph. Primary Homotopy Theory. LC 80-12109. (Memoirs of the American Mathematical Society Ser.). 1980. 4.00 (ISBN 0-8218-2232-2, MEMO-232). Am Math.

Neisser, Edith G. Mothers & Daughters: A Lifelong Relationship. rev. ed. LC 73-4113. 412p. 1973. 11.95 o.s.i. (ISBN 0-06-013171-3, HarpT). Har-Row.

Neisser, Ulric. Cognition & Reality: Principles & Implications of Cognitive Psychology. LC 76-24813. (Psychology Ser.). (Illus.). 1976. text ed. 16.00x o.p. (ISBN 0-7167-0478-1); pap. text ed. 8.95x (ISBN 0-7167-0477-3). W H Freeman.

Neisworth, John. Individualized Education for Preschool Exceptional Children. LC 80-12722. 250p. 1980. text ed. 22.95 (ISBN 0-89443-285-0). Aspen Systems.

Neisworth, John T. & Smith, Robert M. Modifying Retarded Behavior. (Illus.). 200p. 1973. text ed. 18.50 (ISBN 0-395-14049-8, 3-40420). HM.

Neithammer, Carolyn. American Indian Food & Lore. LC 73-7681. (Illus.). 256p. 1974. pap. 7.95 (ISBN 0-02-010000-0, Collier). Macmillan.

Neitzel, James, ed. Our Social Security System: How Can We Make It Sound, Successful, & Solvent. 94p. (Orig.). 1977. pap. 7.50 (ISBN 0-89154-123-3). Intl Found Employ.

Neitzel, James J., ed. Canadian Conference of the International Foundation of Employee Benifit Plans, Oct. 31-Nov. 3, 1976: Proceedings. 1977. spiral bdg 8.75 (ISBN 0-89154-057-1). Intl Found Employ.

--Canadian Conference, 10th Annual, Sept. 10-14, 1977: Proceedings. 1978. spiral bdg. 8.75 (ISBN 0-89154-071-7). Intl Found Employ.

--Investments Institute, April 1976, Palm Springs, California: Proceedings. 1976. spiral bdg. 10.50 (ISBN 0-89154-051-2). Intl Found Employ.

--Investments Institute, New Orleans, May, 1977: Proceedings. 1977. spiral bdg. 12.50 (ISBN 0-89154-066-0). Intl Found Employ.

--Our Social Security System: How We Make It Sound, Solvent & Successful? 1977. spiral bdg. 7.50 o.p. (ISBN 0-89154-068-7). Intl Found Employ.

--Public Conference, Tahoe Nevada, Oct. 2-5, 1977: Proceedings. spiral bdg. 7.50 (ISBN 0-89154-074-1). Intl Found Employ.

--Public Employees Conference, Sept. 12-15, San Francisco: Proceedings. 1977. spiral bdg 3.75 (ISBN 0-89154-055-5). Intl Found Employ.

--Public Employees Conference, 1974: Proceedings. (Civil Service Pensions). 82p. 1975. spiral bdg 3.75 (ISBN 0-89154-035-0). Intl Found Employ.

Nejand, Farghaneh. If a Black Were President of the USA. 1977. 4.00 o.p. (ISBN 0-682-48853-4). Exposition.

Nekhom, Lisa M., jt. auth. see Wright, Ione S.

Nekrasov, V. Kira Georgievna. Greene, M. & Blair, H., eds. (Rus). text ed. 17.50x (ISBN 0-521-05806-6). Cambridge U Pr.

Nelder, J. A. & Kime, R. D. Computers in Biology. (Wykeham Science Ser.: No. 32). 1974. 9.95x (ISBN 0-8448-1159-9). Crane Russak Co.

Nelkin, Dorothy. Controversy: Politics of Technical Decisions. LC 78-21339. (Focus Editions Ser.: Vol. 8). 256p. 1979. 18.95 (ISBN 0-8039-1209-9); pap. 9.95 (ISBN 0-8039-1210-2). Sage.

--Methadone Maintenance: A Technological Fix. LC 72-96071. (Science, Technology & Society Ser). 192p. 1973. 6.95 o.s.i. (ISBN 0-8076-0681-2); pap. 1.95 (ISBN 0-8076-0680-4). Braziller.

--Nuclear Power & Its Critics: Moral Politics at M.I.T. LC 70-147316. 6.50 (ISBN 0-8076-0722-3, Orig. Pub. by Cornell U. Press); pap. 1.75 o.s.i. (ISBN 0-8076-0723-1). Braziller.

--The University & Military Research: The Cayuga Lake Controversy. LC 74-38285. 7.95 o.s.i. (ISBN 0-8076-0718-5, Orig. Pub. by Cornell U. Press); pap. 1.95 (ISBN 0-8076-0719-3). Braziller.

Nelkin, Dorothy & Pollack, Michael. The Atom Besieged: Nuclear Dissent in France & Germany. 352p. 1980. text ed. 17.50 (ISBN 0-262-14034-9). MIT Pr.

Nelkin, Dorothy, ed. Controversy: Politics of Technical Decisions. LC 78-21339. (Sage Focus Editions: Vol. 8). 256p. 1979. 18.95 (ISBN 0-8039-1209-9); pap. 9.95 (ISBN 0-8039-1210-2). Sage.

Nelkon, M. Graded Exercises & Worked Examples in Physics. 5th ed. 1977. pap. text ed. 5.95x o.p. (ISBN 0-435-68657-7). Heinemann Ed.

--Mechanics & Properties of Matter. 1969. text ed. 7.95 o.p. (ISBN 0-435-68633-X). Heinemann Ed.

--New Test Papers in Physics. 1974. pap. text ed. 3.95x o.p. (ISBN 0-435-68654-2). Heinemann Ed.

--Optics, Waves & Sound. 1973. pap. text ed. 11.95x (ISBN 0-435-68662-3). Heinemann Ed.

--Principles of Atomic Physics & Electronics. 1976. text ed. 9.95x o.p. (ISBN 0-435-68656-9). Heinemann Ed.

--Revision Book in Ordinary Level Physics. 3rd ed. 1973. pap. text ed. 5.95x o.p. (ISBN 0-435-67661-X). Heinemann Ed.

--Revision Notes in Physics, 2 bks. 4th ed. Incl. Bk. 1. Mechanics, Electricity, Atomic Physics. 1979. pap. text ed. 3.50x o.p. (ISBN 0-435-68640-2); Bk. 2. Optics, Waves, Sound, Heat, Properties of Matter. 1977. pap. text ed. 6.50x o.p. (ISBN 0-435-68658-5). Heinemann Ed.

--Scholarship Physics. 4th ed. 1971. text ed. 12.95x o.p. (ISBN 0-435-68646-1). Heinemann Ed.

--Solutions to Advanced Level Physics Questions. 7th ed. 1975. pap. text ed. 5.50x o.p. (ISBN 0-435-68336-5). Heinemann Ed.

Nelkon, M. & Humphreys, H. I. Electronics & Radio: An Introduction. 1975. pap. text ed. 11.95x (ISBN 0-435-68335-7). Heinemann Ed.

Nelkon, M., jt. auth. see Abbott, A. F.

Nell, Edward J., jt. auth. see Hollis, Martin I.

Nell, Edward J., ed. Growth, Profits & Property. LC 79-47192. (Illus.). 352p. 1980. 39.50 (ISBN 0-521-22396-2). Cambridge U Pr.

Nell, Onora. Acting on Principle: An Essay in Kantian Ethics. LC 74-20647. 192p. 1975. 15.00x (ISBN 0-231-03848-8). Columbia U Pr.

Nelli, Humbert S. The Business of Crime: Italians & Syndicate Crime in the United States. LC 75-32350. (Illus.). 304p. 1976. 17.95 (ISBN 0-19-502010-3). Oxford U Pr.

--The Business of Crime: Italians & Syndicate Crime in the United States. LC 80-27196. xiv, 314p. 1981. pap. 6.95 (ISBN 0-226-57132-7). U of Chicago Pr.

--The Italians in Chicago, 1880-1930: A Study in Ethnic Mobility. (Urban Life in America Ser.). (Illus.). 300p. 1973. 15.95 (ISBN 0-19-501283-6); pap. text ed. 4.50x (ISBN 0-19-501674-2). Oxford U Pr.

Nellor, Bill, jt. auth. see Molica, Jim.

Nelms, Henning. Play Production. rev. ed. 1958. pap. 3.95 (ISBN 0-06-460073-4, CO 73, COS). Har-Row.

--Scene Design: A Guide to the Stage. LC 74-25249. (Illus.). 96p. 1975. pap. 3.50 (ISBN 0-486-23153-4). Dover.

Nelms, Mrs. Henning & Pym, Mrs. Michael. How to Raise & Train a Cardigan Welsh Corgi. (Orig.). pap. 2.00 (ISBN 0-87666-263-7, DS1067). TFH Pubns.

Nelsen, Anne K., jt. auth. see Nelsen, Hart M.

Nelsen, Donald. Sam & Emma. LC 72-136998. (Illus.). (gr. k-3). 1971. 5.95 o.s.i. (ISBN 0-8193-0467-0, Four Winds); PLB 5.41 o.s.i. (ISBN 0-8193-0468-9). Schol Bk Serv.

--The Spotted Cow. LC 73-5738. (Illus.). 48p. (gr. k-3). 1973. 5.95 o.s.i. (ISBN 0-8193-0694-0, Four Winds); PLB 5.41 o.s.i. (ISBN 0-8193-0695-9). Schol Bk Serv.

Nelsen, Hart M. & Nelsen, Anne K. Black Church in the Sixties. LC 74-18937. 184p. 1976. pap. 5.50x (ISBN 0-8131-0137-9). U Pr of Ky.

Nelsen, Harvey W. The Chinese Military System: An Organizational Study of the Chinese People's Liberation Army. (Special Studies on China & East Asia). (Illus.). 266p. (Orig.). 1981. lib. bdg. 25.00x (ISBN 0-86531-069-6); pap. text ed. 15.00x (ISBN 0-86531-192-7). Westview.

Nelson & Miller. Modern Management Accounting. 2nd ed. 640p. 1981. write for info. (ISBN 0-8302-5904-X). Goodyear.

Nelson, jt. ed. see Daphne.

Nelson, et al. BASIC: A Simplified Structural Approach. 1980. pap. text ed. 12.95 (ISBN 0-8359-0338-9); soln. manual avail. (ISBN 0-8359-0339-7). Reston.

Nelson, A. C. The Homeopathic Handbook. (Orig.). Date not set. 9.95 (ISBN 0-87983-239-8); pap. 6.95 (ISBN 0-87983-240-1). Keats. Postponed.

Nelson, A. T. & Smith, Howard. Car Clouting: The Crime, the Criminal & the Police. 180p. 1958. pap. 6.00 spiral (ISBN 0-398-01390-X). C C Thomas.

Nelson, Aaron G., ed. see Lee, Warren F., et al.

Nelson, Aaron G., et al. Agricultural Finance. 6th ed. (Illus.). 1973. text ed. 12.50x o.p. (ISBN 0-8138-0050-1). Iowa St U Pr.

Nelson, Al P., jt. auth. see Keating, Lawrence A.

Nelson, Alan H., ed. The Plays of Henry Medwall. (Tudor Interludes Ser.). (Illus.). 237p. 1980. 33.50x (ISBN 0-8476-6243-8). Rowman.

Nelson, Alice D. People & Music. new ed. (gr. 9-12). 1973. text ed. 14.80 (ISBN 0-205-03292-3, 5832926); tchrs'. guide 2.40 (ISBN 0-205-03646-5, 5836468). Allyn.

Nelson, Allen H., jt. auth. see Kruegar, Janelle C.

Nelson, Alvar. Responses to Crime: An Introduction to Swedish Criminal Law & Administration. Getz, Jerome L., tr. from Swedish. (New York University Criminal Law Education & Research Center Monograph: No. 6). vi, 90p. 1972. pap. text ed. 8.50x (ISBN 0-8377-0900-8). Rothman.

Nelson, Andrew. Modern Reader's Japanese-English Character Dictionary. LC 61-11973. 1962. 35.00 (ISBN 0-8048-0408-7). C E Tuttle.

Nelson, Ann H., jt. auth. see Wertheimer, Barbara M.

Nelson, Anna K., ed. The Records of Federal Officials: A Selection of Materials from the National Study Commission on Records & Documents of Federal Officials. LC 78-9907. (History of the United States 1876-1976 Ser.: Vol. 15). 1979. lib. bdg. 38.00 (ISBN 0-8240-3672-7). Garland Pub.

Nelson, Anson & Nelson, Fanny. Memorials of Sarah Childress Polk: Wife of the Eleventh President of the United States. LC 73-22435. (Illus.). 322p. 1974. Repr. of 1892 ed. 16.75 (ISBN 0-87152-163-6). Reprint.

Nelson, Benjamin. Monarch Notes on Tennessee Williams' Major Plays. (Orig.). pap. 1.95 (ISBN 0-671-00650-9). Monarch Pr.

--On the Roads to Modernity--Conscience, Science, & Civilization: Selected Writings. Huff, Toby E., ed. 1981. 27.50x (ISBN 0-8476-6209-8). Rowman.

Nelson, Bernard C. A Revision of the New World Species of Ricinus (Mallophaga) Occuring on Passeriformes (Aves) (U. C. Publ. in Entomology: Vol. 68). 1973. pap. 10.50x (ISBN 0-520-09412-3). U of Cal Pr.

Nelson, Bobby J. Brothers. LC 74-30378. 223p. 1975. 7.95 o.s.i. (ISBN 0-02-588590-1, 58859). Macmillan.

Nelson, Brian A. Hustle Won't Bring the Kingdom of God: Jesus' Parables Interpreted for Today. 1978. pap. 2.95 (ISBN 0-8272-1417-0). Bethany Pr.

Nelson, Bruce. Land of the Dacotahs. LC 65-108129. (Illus.). 1964. pap. 3.95 (ISBN 0-8032-5145-9, BB 176, Bison). U of Nebr Pr.

Nelson, Bruce A., jt. auth. see Bromage, Mary C.

Nelson, Byron & Dennis, Larry. Shape Your Swing the Modern Way. new ed. LC 76-264. (Illus.). 1979. pap. 5.95 o.p. (ISBN 0-914178-25-3, 24920). Golf Digest.

Nelson, Byron C. Deluge Story in Stone. (Illus.). 1968. Repr. of 1931 ed. 4.95 (ISBN 0-87123-095-X, 210095). Bethany Fell.

Nelson, C. Ellis. Where Faith Begins. LC 67-22004. 1967. pap. 4.50 o.s.i. (ISBN 0-8042-1471-9). John Knox.

Nelson, Carl A. Mechanical Trades Pocket Manual. LC 73-91639. 208p. (Orig.). 1974. pap. 8.95 (ISBN 0-672-23215-4). Audel.

--Millwrights & Mechanics Guide. 2nd ed. LC 72-75119. (Illus.). 800p. 1972. 14.95 (ISBN 0-672-23201-4). Audel.

Nelson, Carol. Dear Angie: Your Family Is Getting a Divorce. LC 79-57210. (gr. 5-8). 1980. pap. 2.50 (ISBN 0-89191-246-0). Cook.

Nelson, Cathryn A., ed. A Critical Edition of Wit's Triumvirate, or the Philosopher, 2 vols. (Salzburg Studies in English Literature, Jacobean Drama Studies Ser.: Nos. 57-58). 422p. 1975. Set. pap. text ed. 50.25x (ISBN 0-391-01490-0). Humanities.

Nelson, Charles & Wilentz, Joan S. You Can Speak Again. (Funk & W Bk.). 1976. 8.95 o.s.i. (ISBN 0-308-10257-6, TYC-T); pap. 4.95 o.s.i. (ISBN 0-308-10260-6, TYC-T). T Y Crowell.

Nelson, Charles A. & Turk, Frederick J. Financial Management for the Arts: A Guidebook for Arts Organizations. LC 75-43360. (Illus.). 52p. (Orig.). 1975. pap. text ed. 5.95 (ISBN 0-915400-01-4). Am Council Arts.

Nelson, Charles R. Applied Time Series Analysis for Managerial Forecasting. LC 72-88942. 350p. 1973. text ed. 23.95x (ISBN 0-8162-6366-3). Holden-Day.

Nelson, Charles W., jt. auth. see Keedy, Mervin L.

Nelson, Clemens A., jt. auth. see Zumberge, James H.

Nelson, Clifford A., jt. ed. see Hammarberg, Melvin A.

Nelson, Cy, ed. see Chanticleer Press.

Nelson, Cyril I. The Quilt Engagement Calendar 1982. (Illus.). 114p. 1981. spiral 6.95 (ISBN 0-525-93179-1). Dutton.

Nelson, Cyril L., ed. see Friedland, Edward P.

Nelson, Cyril T., ed. see Woodard, Thomas K. & Greenstein, Blanche.

Nelson, Dalmas H., ed. see Wormuth, Francis D.

Nelson, Daniel. Managers & Workers: Origins of the New Factory System in the United States, 1880-1920. 1979. pap. 6.95 (ISBN 0-299-06904-4). U of Wis Pr.

--Unemployment Insurance: The American Experience, 1915-1935. (Illus.). 1969. 25.00x (ISBN 0-299-05200-1). U of Wis Pr.

Nelson, Daniel N., ed. Local Politics in Communist Countries. LC 78-58121. 240p. 1981. 17.50 (ISBN 0-8131-1398-9). U Pr of Ky.

--Romania in the Nineteen Eighties. (Westview Special Studies on the Soviet Union & Eastern Europe). 250p. 1981. lib. bdg. 22.50x (ISBN 0-86531-027-0). Westview.

Nelson, David, tr. see Bhattacarya, Jagadishvhra.

Nelson, Dawn & Nelson, Douglas. Diner's Dictionary: French Regional & Specialty Dishes. (The Diner's Dictionaries Ser.). (Illus.). 128p. 1981. 4.95 (ISBN 0-906071-52-6). Proteus Pub NY.

--Diner's Dictionary: German & Austrian. (The Diner's Dictionaries Ser.). (Illus.). 128p. 1981. 4.95 (ISBN 0-906071-44-5). Proteus Pub NY.

--Diner's Dictionary: Italian. (Illus.). 128p. 1981. 4.95 (ISBN 0-906071-33-X). Proteus Pub NY.

Nelson, Dick & Nelson, Sharon. Easy Field Guide to Interesting Birds of Glacier National Park. (Illus.). 32p. (Orig.). (gr. 1-12). 1978. pap. 1.00 (ISBN 0-915030-17-9). Tecolote Pr.

--Easy Field Guide to Mammals of Glacier National Park. (Illus.). 32p. (Orig.). (gr. 1-12). 1978. pap. 1.00 (ISBN 0-915030-15-2). Tecolote Pr.

--Easy Field Guide to Trees of Glacier National Park. (Illus.). 32p. (Orig.). (gr. 1-12). 1978. pap. 1.00 (ISBN 0-915030-16-0). Tecolote Pr.

--Hiker's Guide to Glacier National Park. (Illus.). 112p. (Orig.). 1978. pap. 5.95 (ISBN 0-915030-24-1). Tecolote Pr.

--Short Hikes & Strolls in Glacier National Park. (Illus.). 48p. (Orig.). (gr. 7-12). 1978. pap. 2.95 (ISBN 0-915030-23-3). Tecolote Pr.

Nelson, Don H. The Adrenal Cortex: Physiological Function & Disease. LC 79-64776. (MPIM Ser.: Vol. 18). (Illus.). 281p. 1980. text ed. 29.00 (ISBN 0-7216-6733-3). Saunders.

Nelson, Donald F. Electric, Optic, & Acoustic Interactions in Dielectrics. LC 78-25964. 1979. 36.95 (ISBN 0-471-05199-3, Pub. by Wiley-Interscience). Wiley.

Nelson, Donald M. Arsenal of Democracy: The Story of American War Production. LC 72-2378. (FDR & the Era of the New Deal Ser.). 439p. 1973. Repr. of 1946 ed. lib. bdg. 39.50 (ISBN 0-685-27840-9). Da Capo.

Nelson, Douglas, jt. auth. see Nelson, Dawn.

Nelson, E. Clifford, ed. Lutherans in North America. rev. ed. LC 74-26337. (Illus.). 576p. 1980. o. p. 22.50x (ISBN 0-8006-0409-1); pap. 14.95 (ISBN 0-8006-1409-7, 1-1409). Fortress.

Nelson, Edward B., jt. auth. see Henry, Dennis C.

Nelson, Elizabeth R. Monarch Notes on Hardy's Far from the Madding Crowd. (Orig.). pap. 1.95 (ISBN 0-671-00890-0). Monarch Pr.

Nelson, Erland, ed. see Princeton Conference on Cerebrovascular Disease, 11th., Mar. 1978.

Nelson, Esther L. Dancing Games for Children of All Ages. LC 78-83456. (Illus.). 72p. (gr. 2 up). 1973. 8.95 (ISBN 0-8069-4522-2); PLB 8.29 (ISBN 0-8069-4523-0). Sterling.

--Movement Games for Children of All Ages. LC 74-31710. (Illus.). 96p. (gr. 1 up). 1975. 7.95 (ISBN 0-8069-4530-3); PLB 7.49 (ISBN 0-8069-4531-1). Sterling.

--Musical Games for Children of All Ages. LC 76-19804. (Illus.). (gr. 3 up). 1976. 8.95 (ISBN 0-8069-4540-0); PLB 8.29 (ISBN 0-8069-4541-9). Sterling.

--Singing & Dancing Games for the Very Young. LC 77-79513. (Illus.). 1977. 8.95 (ISBN 0-8069-4568-0); lib. bdg. 8.29 (ISBN 0-8069-4569-9). Sterling.

Nelson, Fanny, jt. auth. see Nelson, Anson.

Nelson, Gareth & Platnick, Norman I. Systematics & Biogeography: Cladistics & Vicariance. LC 80-20828. (Illus.). 592p. 1981. text ed. 35.00x (ISBN 0-231-04574-3). Columbia U Pr.

Nelson, Gareth & Rosen, Donn E., eds. Vicariance Biogeography: A Critique. LC 80-15351. (Illus.). 616p. 1981. 30.00x (ISBN 0-231-04808-4). Columbia U Pr.

Nelson, Gayle L. & Winters, Thomas A. ESL Operations: Techniques for Learning While Doing. (Orig.). 1980. pap. text ed. 4.95 (ISBN 0-88377-149-7). Newbury Hse.

Nelson, Gordon K., jt. auth. see Costa, Joseph H.

Nelson, Harold A. Sociology in Bondage: An Introduction to Graduate Study. LC 80-65605. 145p. 1981. perfect bdg. 9.95 (ISBN 0-86548-051-6). Century Twenty One.

Nelson, Harry & Jurmain, Robert. Introduction to Physical Anthropology. (Illus.). 1979. pap. text ed. 16.50 (ISBN 0-8299-0240-6); study guide 4.95 (ISBN 0-8299-0285-6); instrs.' manual avail. (ISBN 0-8299-0563-4). West Pub.

Nelson, Harry W. Command Performance & Other Poems. LC 80-67066. (Illus.). 1980. pap. 3.95 (ISBN 0-915206-80-3). Blue Leaf.

Nelson, Herbert B. English Essentials: With Self-Scoring Exercises. (Quality Paperback: No. 52). (Orig.). 1977. pap. 3.95 (ISBN 0-8226-0052-8). Littlefield.

Nelson, Hilda. Charles Nodier. (World Authors Ser.: France: No. 242). lib. bdg. 10.95 (ISBN 0-8057-2654-3). Twayne.

Nelson, Hugh. Make Your Own Backpack & Other Wilderness Camp Gear. (Illus.). 131p. (Orig.). 1981. pap. 12.95 (ISBN 0-8040-0355-6). Swallow.

Nelson, J., jt. auth. see Michaelis, John U.

Nelson, J. C., jt. auth. see Lind, L. F.

Nelson, J. Craig, ed. Psychiatry: PreTest Self-Assessment & Review. LC 77-78729. (Clinical Sciences: PreTest Self-Assessment & Review Ser.). 1977. pap. 9.95 (ISBN 0-07-051604-9). McGraw-Pretest.

Nelson, J. Robert. Science & Our Troubled Conscience. LC 80-8045. 192p. (Orig.). 1980. pap. 6.95 (ISBN 0-8006-1398-8, 1-1398). Fortress.

Nelson, James A. How to Handle Life's Hurts. LC 80-65056. 160p. (Orig.). 1980. pap. 3.95 (ISBN 0-89636-046-6). Accent Bks.

Nelson, James R., ed. Criteria for Transport Pricing. LC 73-4373. 1973. pap. 10.00x (ISBN 0-87033-176-0). Cornell Maritime.

Nelson, Jan, et al, eds. see De Troyes, Chretien.

Nelson, Jan A., ed. see Myers, Geoffrey M.

Nelson, John. The History of Islington. Melvin, Julia, ed. (Illus.). 417p. 1980. Repr. of 1811 ed. 80.00x (ISBN 0-85667-104-5, Pub. by Sotheby Parke Bernet England). Biblio Dist.

--Preliminary Investigation & Police Reporting: A Complete Guide to Police Written Communication. (Criminal Justice Ser.). 1970. text ed. 14.95x (ISBN 0-02-476530-9, 47653). Macmillan.

Nelson, John see McCarthy, Charlotte.

Nelson, John A. Handbook of Drafting Technology. 368p. 1981. text ed. 22.95 (ISBN 0-442-28661-9); pap. text ed. 14.95 (ISBN 0-442-28662-7). Van Nos Reinhold.

Nelson, John D., ed. see International Congress of Chemotherapy, 11th & Interscience Conference on Antimicrobial Agents & Chemotherapy, 19th.

Nelson, Kay S. Complete International Breakfast - Brunch Cookbook. LC 80-5714. 296p. 1981. 14.95 (ISBN 0-8128-2786-4). Stein & Day.

--The Complete International Salad Book. 304p. 1981. pap. 2.50 (ISBN 0-553-13557-0). Bantam.

--The Delectable Vegetable. (John Day Bk.). 1976. 8.95 o.p. (ISBN 0-381-98292-0, TYC-T). T Y Crowell.

--The Yogurt Cookbook. LC 76-11508. (Cookbook Ser). (Illus.). 220p. 1976. pap. 3.00 (ISBN 0-486-23416-9). Dover.

Nelson, Keith. Behavior & Morphology in the Glandulocaudine Fishes (Ostariophysi, Characidae) (U. C. Publ. in Zoology: Vol. 75.2). 1964. pap. 6.50x (ISBN 0-520-09331-3). U of Cal Pr.

Nelson, Keith, ed. see Grattan, C. H.

Nelson, Keith E., ed. Children's Language. LC 77-26226. (Children's Language Ser.: Vols. 1 & 2). Vol. 1, 1978. 24.95 (ISBN 0-470-99385-5); Vol. 2, 1979. 29.95 (ISBN 0-470-26716-X). Halsted Pr.

Nelson, Keith L. Victors Divided: America & the Allies in Germany, 1918-1923. (Illus.). 424p. 1975. 28.50x (ISBN 0-520-02315-3). U of Cal Pr.

Nelson, Kennard S. Flower & Plant Production in the Greenhouse. 3rd ed. LC 77-79741. (Illus.). (gr. 9-12). 1978. 15.35 (ISBN 0-8134-1965-4); text ed. 11.50x (ISBN 0-685-03893-9). Interstate.

--Greenhouse Grower. LC 76-1113. 1977. 15.35 (ISBN 0-8134-1811-9, 1811); text ed. 11.50x (ISBN 0-685-77708-1). Interstate.

--Greenhouse Management for Flower & Plant Production. 4th ed. 1980. 15.35 (ISBN 0-8134-2070-9, 2070); text ed. 11.50x (ISBN 0-8134-2070-9). Interstate.

Nelson, Kent. Cold Wind River. LC 80-20013. 233p. 1981. 8.95 (ISBN 0-396-07835-4). Dodd.

Nelson, Klayton E. Harvesting & Handling California Table Grapes for Market. LC 79-51948. (Illus.). 1979. pap. 6.00x (ISBN 0-931876-33-8, 4095). Ag Sci Pubns.

Nelson, Larry C. The Hills Aren't Black: Poetry of the Black Hills. (Illus.). 48p. (Orig.). 1980. pap. 3.00 (ISBN 0-917624-20-3). Lame Johnny.

Nelson, Larry E. Bullets, Ballots, & Rhetoric: Confederate Policy for the United States Presidential Contest of Eighteen Sixty-Four. LC 79-27869. 256p. 1980. 17.50x (ISBN 0-8173-0037-6). U of Ala Pr.

Nelson, Leonard. Progress & Regress in Philosophy: From Hume & Kant to Hegel & Fries, 2 vols. Kraft, Julius, ed. Palmer, Humphrey, tr. Vol. 1, 1970. 17.50x o.p. (ISBN 0-631-12520-5, Pub. by Basil Blackwell); Vol. 2, 1971. 17.50x o.p. (ISBN 0-631-13850-1). Biblio Dist.

--System of Ethics. 1956. 42.50x (ISBN 0-685-69846-7). Elliots Bks.

Nelson, Leonard T., jt. auth. see Bennett, Albert B.

Nelson, M. Janice, ed. Clinical Perspectives in Nursing Research: Relevance, Suffering, Recovery. LC 78-18242. 1978. pap. text ed. 5.75x (ISBN 0-8077-2549-8). Tchrs Coll.

Nelson, Malcolm A. The Robin Hood Tradition in the English Renaissance. (Salzburg Studies in English Literature, Elizabethan & Renaissance Studies: No. 14). 269p. 1973. pap. text ed. 25.00x (ISBN 0-391-01491-9). Humanities.

Nelson, Marie. The Narcissistic Condition: A Fact of Our Lives & Times, Vol. 1. LC 76-20724. (Self in Process Ser.). 1977. text ed. 22.95 (ISBN 0-87705-250-6). Human Sci Pr.

Nelson, Martha. On Being a Deacon's Wife: Study Guide. LC 72-96150. 1977. saddlewire 1.35 (ISBN 0-8054-3507-7). Broadman.

Nelson, Michael. Nobs & Snobs. 1976. 13.95 o.p. (ISBN 0-86033-028-1). Gordon-Cremonesi.

Nelson, Nathan. Workshops for the Handicapped in the United States: An Historical & Developmental Perspective. 480p. 1971. pap. 20.25 spiral (ISBN 0-398-02168-6). C C Thomas.

Nelson, Nicholas M., jt. ed. see Smith, Clement A.

Nelson, Nicholas R. Paradox: A Round Trip Through the Bermuda Triangle. 112p. 1980. 5.95 (ISBN 0-8059-2707-7). Dorrance.

Nelson, Nici. Why Has Development Neglected Rural Women? A Review of the South Asian Literature. LC 79-40235. (Women in Development Ser.: Vol. 1). (Illus.). 1979. 28.00 (ISBN 0-08-023377-5); pap. 10.50 (ISBN 0-08-023376-7). Pergamon.

Nelson, Nina. Canada. (Illus.). 160p. 1980. 24.00 (ISBN 0-7134-1841-9, Pub. by Batsford England). David & Charles.

--Egypt. 1978. 22.50 (ISBN 0-7134-3181-4). David & Charles.

--Malta. 1978. 22.50 (ISBN 0-7134-0941-X). David & Charles.

Nelson, Norton & Hinkle, Lawrence E., Jr., eds. Theory, Practice & Application of Prevention in Environmental Health & Social Determinants of Human Health. LC 76-15142. 1976. pap. text ed. 4.50 o.p. (ISBN 0-88202-107-9). N Watson.

Nelson, P. Greenhouse Operation & Management. 1978. 18.95 (ISBN 0-87909-319-6); instrs'. manual avail. Reston.

Nelson, P. C., tr. Doctrinas Biblicas. (Spanish Bks.). (Span.). 1979. pap. 1.75 (ISBN 0-8297-0539-2). Life Pubs Intl.

--Doutrinas Biblicas. (Portuguese Bks.). 1979. 1.25 (ISBN 0-8297-0658-5). Life Pubs Intl.

Nelson, Paul. Greenhouse Operation & Management. 2nd ed. 520p. 1981. text ed. 16.95 (ISBN 0-8359-2576-5); instr's. manual free (ISBN 0-8359-2577-3). Reston.

--Rod Stewart: A Biography. LC 80-8063. (Illus.). 160p. 1980. pap. 8.95 cancelled (ISBN 0-394-17745-2, E 770, BC). Grove.

Nelson, Paul E. & Pearson, Judy C. Confidence in Public Speaking. 300p. 1981. pap. text ed. write for info. (ISBN 0-697-04179-4); instructor's manual avail. (ISBN 0-697-04183-2). Wm C Brown.

Nelson, Philip E. & Tressler, Donald K. Fruit & Vegetable Juice Processing Technology. 3rd ed. (Illus.). 1980. text ed. 36.00 (ISBN 0-87055-362-3). AVI.

Nelson, R. H. An Introduction to Feeding Farm Livestock. 2nd ed. 1979. text ed. 28.00 (ISBN 0-08-023757-6); pap. text ed. 9.75 (ISBN 0-08-023756-8). Pergamon.

Nelson, R. J. Play Within a Play. LC 72-87356. (Theater, Film & the Performing Arts Ser.). 182p. 1971. Repr. of 1958 ed. lib. bdg. 22.50 (ISBN 0-306-71580-5). Da Capo.

Nelson, Ralph, jt. auth. see Preston, Paul.

Nelson, Randy F. Almanac of American Letters. 350p. (Orig.). 1981. 16.95 (ISBN 0-86576-018-7); pap. 9.95 (ISBN 0-86576-008-X). W Kaufmann.

Nelson, Raymond. Philippines. LC 66-22509. (Nations & Peoples Library). (Illus.). (YA) 1968. 8.50x o.s.i. (ISBN 0-8027-2115-X). Walker & Co.

Nelson, Richard & Berger, H. Handball. (Prentice-Hall Sports Ser). 1971. pap. 4.95 ref. ed. (ISBN 0-13-372433-6). P-H.

Nelson, Richard K. Hunters of the Northern Forest: Designs for Survival Among the Alaskan Kutchin. 1973. 10.50x (ISBN 0-226-57177-7). U of Chicago Pr.

--Shadow of the Hunter: Stories of Eskimo Life. LC 80-11091. 272p. 1980. lib. bdg. 12.50 (ISBN 0-226-57179-3). U of Chicago Pr.

Nelson, Richard L. Soccer for Men. 4th ed. (Physical Education Activities Ser.). 1981. pap. text ed. 3.25x (ISBN 0-697-07094-8). Wm C Brown.

Nelson, Richard R. & Yates, Douglas T. Innovation & Implementation in Public Organizations. LC 74-16938. 1977. 21.95 (ISBN 0-669-95596-5). Lexington Bks.

Nelson, Robert J. Corneille: His Heroes & Their Worlds. LC 63-7859. 1963. 8.50x o.p. (ISBN 0-8122-7384-2). U of Pa Pr.

Nelson, Robert J. & Oxenhandler, Neal, eds. Aspects of French Literature. LC 61-5992. (Fr.). 1961. 29.50x (ISBN 0-89197-037-1); pap. text ed. 12.95x (ISBN 0-89197-038-X). Irvington.

Nelson, Robert L. Downhill to Uphill. LC 79-6756. 76p. 1980. pap. text ed. 5.75 (ISBN 0-8191-0946-0). U Pr of Amer.

Nelson, Robert V. Coal: The New Energy Source. Ide, Arthur F., ed. LC 79-9940. (E Equals M C Squared Ser.). (Illus.). 70p. (Orig.). 1981. 12.00 (ISBN 0-86663-804-0); pap. 7.50 (ISBN 0-86663-805-9). Ide Hse.

--Hydro-Electric Energy: Past - or Future? Ide, Arthur F., ed. & illus. (E Equals MC Squared Ser.: Vol. 14). (Illus.). 60p. 1980. 10.00 (ISBN 0-86663-802-4); pap. 6.95 (ISBN 0-86663-803-2). Ide Hse.

--Understanding Basic Energy Terms. Ide, Arthur F., ed. LC 79-9940. (E Equals MC Squared Ser.). (Illus.). 60p. 1980. 9.00 (ISBN 0-86663-806-7); pap. 6.25 (ISBN 0-86663-807-5). Ide Hse.

Nelson, Robert V. & Nelson, Rosalie K. E Equals M C Squared: Energy - Management, Conservation & Communication, 17 vols. Ide, Arthur F., ed. (Illus., Orig.). 1981. write for info. (ISBN 0-86663-800-8); pap. write for info. (ISBN 0-86663-801-6). Ide Hse.

Nelson, Roberta. Creating Community Acceptance for Handicapped People. (Illus.). 240p. 1978. 17.50 (ISBN 0-398-03788-4). C C Thomas.

Nelson, Roger H. Personal Money Management: An Objectives & Systems Approach. LC 77-190163. 1973. text ed. 16.95 (ISBN 0-201-05255-5). A-W.

Nelson, Roland H., Jr., jt. auth. see Brubaker, Dale L.

Nelson, Rosalie K., jt. auth. see Nelson, Robert V.

Nelson, Roy P. Articles & Features. LC 77-85340. (Illus.). 1978. text ed. 14.95 (ISBN 0-395-25517-1). HM.

--Comic Art & Caricature. 1978. 12.95 o.p. (ISBN 0-8092-7848-0); pap. 6.95 o.p. (ISBN 0-685-25108-X). Contemp Bks.

--The Design of Advertising. 4th ed. 1980. text ed. 16.95x (ISBN 0-697-04348-7). Wm C Brown.

--Fell's Guide to the Art of Cartooning. pap. 4.95 o.s.i. (ISBN 0-88391-022-5, Aim-High). Fell.

Nelson, Roy P. & Ferris, Byron. Fell's Guide to Commercial Art. LC 66-14801. (gr. 10 up). 8.95 (ISBN 0-8119-0041-X). Fell.

Nelson, Ruth A. Plants of Rocky Mountain National Park. rev. ed. LC 80-522. 1981. pap. 6.95 (ISBN 0-87081-092-8). Colo Assoc.

Nelson, Ruth Y. God's Song in My Heart: Daily Devotions. LC 56-11912. 432p. 1957. 7.50 (ISBN 0-8006-0254-4, 1-254). Fortress.

Nelson, S. A. The ABC of Stock Speculation & the Anticipation of the Wave Theory. (The New Stock Market Library Ser.). 1978. Repr. of 1903 ed. 57.50 (ISBN 0-89266-097-X). Am Classical Coll Pr.

Nelson, Sharlene & LeMieux, Joan. Cruising the Columbia & Snake Rivers: Eleven Cruises in the Inland Waterway. 192p. 1981. pap. 8.95 (ISBN 0-914718-57-6). Pacific Search.

Nelson, Sharon, jt. auth. see Nelson, Dick.

Nelson, Stanley. Idlewild: Special Issue 4. pap. 1.00 (ISBN 0-912292-21-0). The Smith.

Nelson, W. L. Guide to Refinery Operating Costs. 3rd ed. LC 74-125557. 126p. 1976. 30.00 (ISBN 0-87814-002-6). Pennwell Pub.

Nelson, Walter R., jt. auth. see Kase, Kenneth R.

Nelson, Walter R. & Jenkins, T. M., eds. Computer Techniques in Radiation Transport & Dosimetry. (Ettore Majorana International Science Ser., Physical Sciences: Vol. 3). 530p. 1980. 55.00 (ISBN 0-306-40307-2, Plenum Pr). Plenum Pub.

Nelson, William. Lex Testamentaria. Berkowits, David S. & Thorne, Samuel E., eds. LC 77-89254. (Classics of English Legal History in the Modern Era Ser.: Vol. 81). 552p. 1979. lib. bdg. 40.00 (ISBN 0-8240-3180-6). Garland Pub.

Nelson, William, ed. Form & Convention in the Poetry of Edmund Spenser. LC 61-16780. (Papers of the English Institute Ser.). 1961. 15.00x (ISBN 0-231-02502-5). Columbia U Pr.

Nelson, William E. Dispute & Conflict Resolution in Plymouth County, Massachusetts, 1725 - 1825. LC 80-17403. (Studies in Legal History). 240p. 1980. 19.50x (ISBN 0-8078-1454-7). U of NC Pr.

Nelson, William R. Interference Handbook. (Illus.). 240p. 1981. 8.95 (ISBN 0-933616-01-5). Radio Pubns.

Nelson, Wilton M., ed. Diccionario Ilustrado de la Biblia. (Illus.). 735p. (Span.). 1974. 24.95 (ISBN 0-89922-033-9); pap. 15.95 (ISBN 0-89922-099-1). Edit Caribe.

Nelson-Erichsen, Jean & Erichsen, Heino R. Gamines: How to Adopt from Latin America. LC 79-26965. (Illus.). 1981. 12.95 (ISBN 0-87518-197-X). Dillon.

--Gamins: How to Adopt from Latin America. (Illus.). 1979. pap. 9.95x (ISBN 0-686-25160-1); pap. text ed. 9.95x (ISBN 0-686-25159-8). Dillon.

Nelson-Rees, Walter A. Lillie May Nicholson: 1884-1964 an Artist Rediscovered. LC 80-53867. (Illus.). 88p. 1981. 38.50 (ISBN 0-938842-00-5). WIM Oakland.

Nemati, Parviz. Rugs As an Investment. (Illus.). 212p. Date not set. 60.00 (ISBN 0-937266-01-9). Agate Pr.

Nemat-Nasser, S. Variational Methods in the Mechanics of Solids: Proceedings of the UUTAM Symposium, Sept. 11-13, 1978. LC 80-41529. (Illus.). 426p. 1981. 100.00 (ISBN 0-08-024728-8). Pergamon.

Nemat-Nasser, S., ed. Mechanics Today, Vol. 6. LC 80-41699. (Illus.). 225p. 1981. 50.00 (ISBN 0-08-024749-0); pap. 40.00 (ISBN 0-08-027318-1). Pergamon.

Nemcova, Jeanne, tr. see Lustig, Arnost.

Nemec, David. The Even More Challenging Baseball Quiz Book. 1978. pap. 1.95 o.s.i. (ISBN 0-02-023200-4, Collier). Macmillan.

Nemenyi, R. Protective & Carbonizing Atmospheres. 1977. text ed. 48.01 (ISBN 0-08-019883-X). Pergamon.

Nemerov, Howard. Gnomes & Occasions. 1974. pap. 1.95 o.s.i. (ISBN 0-226-57255-2, PP15, Phoen). U of Chicago Pr.

--Journal of the Fictive Life. 1965. 12.00 o.p. (ISBN 0-8135-0493-7). Rutgers U Pr.

--Next Room of the Dream: Poems & Two Plays. LC 62-22328. 1962. 5.75x o.s.i. (ISBN 0-226-57249-8). U of Chicago Pr.

--Poetry & Fiction: Essays. 1963. 22.00 (ISBN 0-8135-0438-4). Rutgers U Pr.

--Reflexions on Poetry & Poetics. LC 74-185396. 1972. 17.50 (ISBN 0-8135-0727-8). Rutgers U Pr.

--Sentences. LC 80-17702. 76p. 1980. 8.95 (ISBN 0-226-57260-9). U of Chicago Pr.

Nemerow, Nelson L. Industrial Water Pollution: Origins, Characteristics & Treatment. LC 76-46612. 1978. text ed. 28.95 (ISBN 0-201-05246-6). A-W.

Nemerowicz, Gloria M. Children's Perceptions of Gender & Work Roles. LC 79-11783. 1979. 24.95 (ISBN 0-03-049811-2). Praeger.

Nemet, Roslyn. Cook to Your Heart's Content. 1981. pap. 1.75 (ISBN 0-8439-0870-X, Leisure Bks). Nordon Pubns.

Nemeth, Bela A. Chemical Tables. LC 75-19223. 1975. 37.95 (ISBN 0-470-63161-9). Halsted Pr.

Nemeth, Doris I. & Kenzie, Peggy, eds. The Poet. new ed. (Illus.). 446p. (gr. 5 up). 1980. pap. 9.50 (ISBN 0-932192-02-5). Fine Arts Soc.

Nemetz, Peter N. Energy Policy: The Global Challenge. 1979. pap. text ed. 20.50x (ISBN 0-920380-30-1, Pub. by Inst Res Pub Canada). Renouf.

Nemhauser, George L. Introduction to Dynamic Programming. (Series in Decision & Control). 1966. 23.95 o.p. (ISBN 0-471-63150-7, Pub. by Wiley-Interscience). Wiley.

Nemhauser, George L., jt. auth. see Garfinkel, Robert.

Nemiro, Beverly & Von Allman, Marie. Lunchbox Cookbook. LC 65-25794. 127p. 1965. 4.95 (ISBN 0-8040-0192-8, SB). Swallow.

Nemiro, Beverly A., jt. auth. see Hamilton, Donna M.

Nemirovitch-Dantchenko, Vladimir. My Life in the Russian Theatre. LC 67-18053. (Illus.). 1968. pap. 3.45 (ISBN 0-87830-520-3). Theatre Arts.

Nemirovskii, P. E. Contemporary Models of the Atomic Nucleus. 1963. 37.00 (ISBN 0-08-009840-1); pap. 22.00 (ISBN 0-08-013582-X). Pergamon.

Nemmers, Erwin E. & Grunewald, Alan E. Basic Managerial Finance. 2nd ed. LC 74-17164. 750p. 1975. text ed. 19.95 (ISBN 0-8299-0025-X); 7.95 (ISBN 0-8299-0027-6); study guide avail. (ISBN 0-8299-0564-2); instrs.' manual avail. West Pub.

Nemo, John. Back in the World: An Annotated Bibliography of American Imaginative Responses to the War in Viet Nam, 1960-1980. 208p. 1981. 29.95x (ISBN 0-933180-15-2). Ellis Pr.

--Patrick Kavanagh. (English Authors Ser.: No. 267). 1979. lib. bdg. 14.50 (ISBN 0-8057-6770-3). Twayne.

Nemo, John, ed. see Kavanaugh, Patrick & O'Connor, P. J.

Nemodruk, A. A. & Karalova, Z. K. Analytical Chemistry of Boron. (Analytical Chemistry of the Elements Ser.). 1971. 29.95 (ISBN 0-470-63168-6). Halsted Pr.

Nemoianu, Anca M. The Boat's Gonna Leave: A Study of Children Learning a Second Language from Conversations with Other Children. (Pragmatics & Beyond: No.13). 122p. 1980. pap. text ed. 17.25x (ISBN 90-272-2507-9). Humanities.

Nenadovic, Proto M. Memoirs of Prota Matija Nenadovic. Edwards, Lovett F., ed. 1969. 10.25x o.p. (ISBN 0-19-821476-6). Oxford U Pr.

Nenninger, Timothy K. The Leavenworth Schools & the Old Army: Education, Professionalism, & the Officer Corps of the United States Army, 1881-1918. LC 77-91105. (Contributions in Military History: No. 15). 1978. lib. bdg. 17.95x (ISBN 0-313-20047-5, NFL/). Greenwood.

Nenno, Robert, jt. auth. see Gilligan, Lawrence.

Nentl, Jerolyn. Disco Dancing. Schroeder, Howard, ed. LC 79-27801. (Funseekers Ser.). (Illus.). (gr. 3-5). 1980. lib. bdg. 5.95 (ISBN 0-89686-073-6); pap. 2.95 (ISBN 0-89686-077-9). Crestwood Hse.

--Marathon Running. Schroeder, Howard, ed. LC 79-27799. (Funseekers Ser.). (Illus.). (gr. 3-5). 1980. lib. bdg. 5.95 (ISBN 0-89686-074-4); pap. 2.95 (ISBN 0-89686-078-7). Crestwood Hse.

--Mountain Climbing. Schroeder, Howard, ed. LC 80-415. (Funseekers Ser.). (Illus.). (gr. 3-5). 1979. lib. bdg. 5.95 (ISBN 0-89686-075-2); pap. 2.95 (ISBN 0-89686-079-5). Crestwood Hse.

--Roller Skating. Schroeder, Howard, ed. LC 80-10475. (Funseekers Ser.). (Illus.). (gr. 3-5). 1980. lib. bdg. 5.95 (ISBN 0-89686-072-8); pap. 2.95 (ISBN 0-89686-076-0). Crestwood Hse.

Nentl, Jerolyn & Schroeder, Howard. Fishing. LC 80-10490. (Back to Nature Ser.). (Illus.). (gr. 3-5). 1980. lib. bdg. 5.95 (ISBN 0-89686-070-1). Crestwood Hse.

Nentl, Jerolyn, jt. auth. see East, Ben.

Nentle, Jerolyn. The Celsius Thermometer. LC 76-24205. (Metrics America Ser.). (gr. 4). 1976. 5.95 (ISBN 0-913940-48-8). Crestwood Hse.

Nepos, Cornelius. Vitae. Winstedt, E. O., ed. (Oxford Classical Texts Ser). 1904. 14.95x (ISBN 0-19-814617-5). Oxford U Pr.

Nerbonne, T. Confucius: Moments in His Life. (Illus.). 20.00 (ISBN 0-685-58449-6). Rogers Bk.

Nere, J. Foreign Policy of France. (Foreign Policies of the Great Powers). 1975. 26.00x (ISBN 0-7100-7968-0). Routledge & Kegan.

Neri, Helene, tr. see Muhlschlegel, Peter.

Neri, Helene M., tr. see Schaefer, Udo.

Nerlich, G. The Shape of Space. 260p. 1976. 33.95 (ISBN 0-521-21101-8). Cambridge U Pr.

Nernst, W. New Heat Theorem. Barr, Guy, tr. LC 69-15365. (Illus.). 1969. pap. text ed. 3.00 (ISBN 0-486-62252-5). Dover.

Nero, Anthony V., Jr. A Guidebook to Nuclear Reactors. (Cal. Ser.: No. 393). 1979. 27.50x (ISBN 0-520-03482-1); pap. 9.95 (ISBN 0-520-03661-1). U of Cal Pr.

Nero, Robert W. The Great Gray Owl: Phantom of the Nortern Forest. LC 80-607110. (Illus.). 168p. 1980. 17.50 (ISBN 0-87474-672-8). Smithsonian.

Neruda, Pablo. A Call for the Destruction of Nixon & Praise for the Chilean Revolution. Anderson, Teresa, tr. LC 80-53809. (Illus.). 80p. (Orig.). 1980. pap. 3.25 (ISBN 0-931122-22-8). West End

--Incitement to Nixonicide & Praise for the Chilean Revolution. 2nd ed. Kowit, Steve, tr. from Spanish. (Illus.). 82p. 1980. pap. 5.00 (ISBN 0-686-68219-X). Quixote.

--Isla Negra. Reid, Alastair, tr. (Span. & Eng.). 1981. 12.95 (ISBN 0-374-17759-7). FS&G.

--Passions & Impressions. Peden, Margaret S., tr. from Span. 1981. 17.95 (ISBN 0-374-22994-5). FS&G.

--Song of Protest. 1976. 5.95 o.p. (ISBN 0-688-03043-2); pap. 2.95 (ISBN 0-688-08043-X). Morrow.

--Twenty Love Poems & a Song of Despair. LC 70-481699. (Cape Editions Ser). 1976. pap. 2.95 (ISBN 0-14-042205-6, Grossman). Penguin.

Nesbit, E. The Complete Book of Dragons. LC 72-165245. (Illus.). 208p. (gr. 3 up). 1973. 5.95g o.s.i. (ISBN 0-02-768120-3). Macmillan.

--The Last of the Dragons. LC 79-28584. (Illus.). 32p. (gr. k-4). 1980. 6.95 (ISBN 0-07-046285-2). McGraw.

Nesbit, Paul W. Longs Peak: Its Story & a Climbing Guide. 8th rev. ed. LC 72-86007. (Illus.). 1972. pap. 2.50x o.p. (ISBN 0-911746-02-1). Nesbit.

Nesbit, Robert C. Wisconsin: A History. LC 72-9990. (Illus.). 620p. 1973. 15.004 (ISBN 0-299-06370-4). U of Wis Pr.

Nesbitt, Alexander. Two Hundred Decorative Title Pages. (Illus., Orig.). 1964. pap. 6.00 (ISBN 0-486-21264-5). Dover.

Nesbitt, Cathleen. Little Love & Good Company. LC 76-43369. (Illus.). 1977. 8.95 (ISBN 0-916144-10-0). Stemmer Hse.

Nesbitt, Mark. If the South Won Gettysburg. LC 80-52561. (Illus.). 200p. (Orig.). 1980. pap. 2.50 (ISBN 0-937740-01-2). Reliance Pub.

Nesbitt, Rosemary S. The Great Rope. 1980. Repr. lib. bdg. 5.95x (ISBN 0-686-68699-3). Mathom.

Nesheim, Asbjorn, jt. ed. see Nielsen, Konrad.

Nesheim, Margaret. Wet Landing-Dry Landing. (Illus.). 192p. 1981. 10.00 (ISBN 0-682-49673-1). Exposition.

Nesi, Ruth, jt. auth. see Stalberg, Roberta.

Neskora, Teanna W., jt. auth. see Langenbach, Michael.

Neslan, J. M. All About Canaries. (Illus.). 1979. 9.95 o.p. (ISBN 0-686-01017-5, 8051, Dist. by Arco). Barrie & Jenkins.

Nesman, Edgar G. Peasant Mobilization & Rural Development. 160p. 1981. text ed. 14.50x (ISBN 0-87073-717-1); pap. text ed. 8.95x (ISBN 0-87073-718-X). Schenkman.

Nesmeyanov, A. N. Selected Works in Organic Chemistry. 1964. 105.00 (ISBN 0-08-010158-5). Pergamon.

Nesmit, Hayden R. Poetical Memories from the Pen of Hayden R. Nesmith. 5.75 (ISBN 0-8062-1630-1). Carlton.

Nesmith, Robert I., jt. auth. see Cochran, Hamilton.

Nespojohn, Katherine. Worms. (First Bks). (Illus.). 72p. (gr. 4-6). 1972. PLB 4.47 o.p. (ISBN 0-531-00766-9). Watts.

Ness, Bethann Van see Van Ness, Bethann.

Ness, Evaline. Do You Have the Time Lydia. (Illus.). (gr. k-3). 1971. 7.95 o.p. (ISBN 0-525-28790-6). Dutton.

--Do You Have the Time Lydia? (gr. k-3). 1974. pap. 1.25 o.p. (ISBN 0-525-45024-6, Anytime Bks). Dutton.

--Old Mother Hubbard & Her Dog. LC 74-182788. (Illus.). 40p. (ps-3). 1972. reinfoced bdg. 4.95 (ISBN 0-03-088369-5); pap. 1.45 (owlet bk.) o.p. (ISBN 0-03-005721-3). HR&W.

--A Victorian Paper House: To Cut Out & Color. (Illus.). (gr. 4 up). 1978. spiral bdg. 8.95 o.p. (ISBN 0-684-15177-4, ScribJ). Scribner.

Ness, Evaline, illus. Fierce the Lion. LC 80-10172. (Illus.). 32p. (ps-3). 1980. PLB 8.95 (ISBN 0-8234-0412-9). Holiday.

Ness, Frederic W. An Uncertain Glory: Letters of Cautious but Sound Advice. LC 74-152812. (Higher Education Ser.). 1971. 10.95x o.p. (ISBN 0-87589-098-9). Jossey-Bass.

Ness, Gayl D. Bureaucracy & Rural Development in Malaysia. 1967. 20.00x (ISBN 0-520-00922-3). U of Cal Pr.

Ness, John R. Van see Kutsche, Paul & Van Ness, John R.

Ness, Pamela M. Assissi Embroidery. (Illus.). 1978. pap. 1.75 (ISBN 0-486-23743-5). Dover.

Ness, Thomas E. Marketing in Action: A Decision Game Student's Manual. 4th ed. Day, Ralph L., tr. 1978. pap. text ed. 8.95x (ISBN 0-256-01924-X). Irwin.

Nessel, Denise D. & Jones, Margaret B. Language-Experience Approach to Reading: A Handbook for Teachers of Reading. (Orig.). 1981. pap. 8.95. Tchrs Coll.

Nessen, Robert L. The Real Estate Book: A Complete Guide to Acquiring, Financing, & Investing in a Home or Commercial Property. 272p. 1981. 12.95 (ISBN 0-686-69140-7). Little.

Nestell, Merlynd, tr. see Plesner, A. I.

Nestle, E. & Aland, K., eds. Novum Testamentum Graece. 26th ed. 1979. 8.65 (ISBN 3-438-05100-1, 57902). United Bible.

Nestorides, E. J., ed. Handbook on Torsional Vibration. 1958. 86.50 (ISBN 0-521-04326-3). Cambridge U Pr.

Netanyahu, Benjamin & Netanyahu, Iddo, eds. Self-Portrait of a Hero: The Letters of Jonathan Netanyahu (1963-1976) 1981. 12.95 (ISBN 0-394-51376-2). Random.

Netanyahu, Iddo, jt. ed. see Netanyahu, Benjamin.

Netboy, Anthony. The Columbia River Salmon & Steelhead Trout: Their Fight for Survival. LC 80-50866. (Illus.). 192p. 1980. 13.95 (ISBN 0-295-95768-9). U of Wash Pr.

Netcher, Jack. A Management Model for Competency-Based Hper Programs. LC 76-57884. (Illus.). 1977. pap. 7.95 o.p. (ISBN 0-8016-3630-2). Mosby.

Neter, John & Wasserman, William. Applied Linear Statistical Models. 1974. text ed. 21.95x (ISBN 0-256-01498-1). Irwin.

Neter, John, et al. Applied Statistics. 1978. text ed. 20.95 (ISBN 0-205-05982-1); instr's man. avail. (ISBN 0-205-05983-X); solutions man. avail. (ISBN 0-205-06038-2). Allyn.

--Fundamental Statistics for Business & Economics. 4th abr. ed. 514p. 1975. text ed. 16.95x (ISBN 0-205-04547-2); instr's manual free (ISBN 0-205-04548-0); ans. bk. 3.95 (ISBN 0-205-04567-7). Allyn.

Nethercot, A. H., et al, eds. Stuart Plays. rev. ed. LC 72-161203. 1971. 49.50x (ISBN 0-03-083029-X). Irvington.

Nethercot, D. A., jt. auth. see Kirby, P. A.

Netherlands State Archives Service, ed. Guide to the Sources of the History of Africa South of the Sahara in the Netherlands, Vol. 9. (Guides to the Sources for the History of Nations Ser. II: Africa South of the Sahara). 241p. 1978. 36.00 (ISBN 0-89664-007-8, Pub. by K G Saur). Gale.

Netherton, Morris & Shiffrin, Nancy. Past Lives Therapy. LC 77-29262. 1978. 8.95 o.p. (ISBN 0-688-03298-2). Morrow.

Netsch, Dawn C., jt. auth. see Mandelker, Daniel R.

Netsky, Martin G., jt. auth. see Sarnat, Harvey B.

Nett, Louise M., jt. auth. see Petty, Thomas L.

Nettels, Curtis P. Roots of American Civilization: A History of American Colonial Life. 2nd ed. LC 63-8707. (Illus.). 1963. 34.50x (ISBN 0-89197-386-9); pap. text ed. 18.50x (ISBN 0-89197-925-5). Irvington.

Nettels, Elsa. James & Conrad. LC 76-2897. (SAMLA Studies Award Ser.). 289p. 1977. 17.50x (ISBN 0-8203-0408-5). U of Ga Pr.

Netter, Frank, illus. Respiratory System, Vol. 7. (Medical Illustrations Ser.). (Illus.). 1979. 47.00x (ISBN 0-914168-09-6). C I B A Pharm.

Netter, Frank H., illus. The C I B A Collection of Medical Illustrations, 7 vols. Incl. Vol. 1. Nervous System. 24.50x (ISBN 0-914168-01-0); Vol. 2. Reproductive System. 34.00x (ISBN 0-914168-02-9); Vol. 3, Pt. 1. Digestive System: Upper Digestive Tract. 27.00x (ISBN 0-914168-03-7); Vol. 3, Pt. 2. Digestive System: Lower Digestive Tract. 29.50x (ISBN 0-914168-04-5); Vol. 3, Pt. 3. Digestive System: Liver, Biliary Tract & Pancreas. 25.00x (ISBN 0-914168-05-3); Vol. 4. Endocrine System & Selected Metabolic Diseases. 34.00x (ISBN 0-914168-06-1); Vol. 5. Heart. 42.00x (ISBN 0-914168-07-X); Vol. 6. Kidneys, Ureters & Urinary Bladder. 44.00x (ISBN 0-914168-08-8). LC 53-2151. (Illus.). 1974. Set. 288.00x (ISBN 0-914168-00-2). C I B A Pharm.

Nettind, Dwayne, jt. auth. see Blalock, Jane.

Nettl, Bruno. Folk & Traditional Music of the Western Continents. 2nd ed. (Illus.). 272p. 1973. pap. 10.95 (ISBN 0-13-322933-5). P-H.

--Theory & Method in Ethnomusicology. LC 64-16964. (Illus.). 1964. text ed. 15.95 (ISBN 0-02-922860-3). Free Pr.

Nettl, Bruno, et al. Contemporary Music & Music Cultures. 304p. 1974. 14.95 (ISBN 0-13-170175-4). P-H.

Nettl, J. P. Political Mobilization. (Society Today & Tomorrow Ser.). (Illus.). 1967. 9.95 o.p. (ISBN 0-571-08053-7, Pub. by Faber & Faber). Merrimack Bk Serv.

Nettl, Paul. Mozart & Masonry. LC 78-114564. (Music Ser). 1957. Repr. of 1957 ed. lib. bdg. 17.50 (ISBN 0-306-71922-3). Da Capo.

Nettleford, Rex. Carribean Cultural Identity: The Case of Jamaica. Hill, Robert A. & Wilbert, Johannes, eds. LC 79-54305. (Afro-American Culture & Society Monograph: No. 1). Orig. Title: Cultural Action & Social Change: the Case of Jamaica. (Illus.). 239p. 1980. 13.95x (ISBN 0-934934-00-2, Co-Pub by UCLA Lat Am Ctr); pap. 8.00x (ISBN 0-934934-02-9, Co-Pub by UCLA Lat Am Ctr). Ctr Afro-Am Stud.

Nettles, Tom, jt. auth. see Bush, Russ.

Nettleship, Richard L. Theory of Education in the Republic of Plato. LC 68-54676. 1968. text ed. 8.75 (ISBN 0-8077-1850-5); pap. text ed. 3.50x (ISBN 0-8077-1849-1). Tchrs Coll.

Nettleton, David. Our Infallible Bible. LC 77-15540. 1978. pap. 1.75 (ISBN 0-87227-055-6); tchr's guide 4.50 (ISBN 0-87227-056-4). Reg Baptist.

Netzer, Aharon, ed. see Symposium on Advanced Ozone Technology, Toronto Canada, May 1978.

Netzer, Corinne T. Brand Name Calorie Counter. (Orig.). 1981. pap. 2.75 (ISBN 0-440-10676-1). Dell.

--Brand Name Carbohydrate Gram Counter. (Orig.). 1981. pap. 2.75 (ISBN 0-440-10658-3). Dell.

Netzer, D. The Subsidized Muse. LC 77-25441. (Illus.). 289p. 1980. pap. 9.95 (ISBN 0-521-29796-6). Cambridge U Pr.

--The Subsidized Muse. LC 77-25441. (Illus.). 1978. 24.95 (ISBN 0-521-21966-3). Cambridge U Pr.

Netzer, Dick. Economics of the Property Tax. (Studies of Government Finance). 326p. 1966. pap. 5.95 (ISBN 0-8157-6039-6). Brookings.

Netzer, Lanore A., et al. Strategies for Instructional Management. 1979. text ed. 18.95 (ISBN 0-205-06448-5). Allyn.

Neu, H. C. & Caldwell, A. D., eds. Problems of Antibiotic Therapy. (Royal Society of Medicine International Congress & Symposium Ser.: No. 13). 1979. 11.50 (ISBN 0-8089-1218-6). Grune.

Neu, Jerome. Emotion, Thought,& Therapy: A Study of Hume & Spinoza & the Relationship of Philosophical Theories of the Emotions to Psychological Theories of Therapy. LC 76-20010. 1977. 18.50x (ISBN 0-520-03288-8). U of Cal Pr.

Neu, John, jt. auth. see Lindsay, Robert O.

Neu, John, jt. ed. see Lindsay, Robert O.

Neu, John, et al, eds. Chemical, Medical, & Pharmaceutical Books Printed Before 1800: In the Collections of the University of Wisconsin Libraries. 1965. 27.50x (ISBN 0-299-03680-4). U of Wis Pr.

Neubeck, Deborah K. Guide to the Microfilm Edition of The Frank B. Kellogg Papers. LC 78-63612. 56p. 1978. pap. 2.00 (ISBN 0-87351-126-3). Minn Hist.

Neubecker, Ottfried. A Guide to Heraldry. LC 79-13611. (Illus.). 1980. 9.95 (ISBN 0-07-046312-3). McGraw.

Neuber, Keith A., et al. Needs Assessment: A Model for Community Planning. LC 79-27929. (Sage Human Services Guides: Vol. 14). 107p. 1980. pap. 6.50x (ISBN 0-8039-1396-6). Sage.

Neuberg, Hans. Conceptions of International Exhibitions. Date not set. 37.50 o.p. (ISBN 0-8038-1138-1). Hastings.

Neuberg, Paul. The Hero's Children: A Report on the Post-War Generation in Eastern Europe. 1973. 10.00 o.p. (ISBN 0-688-00138-6). Morrow.

Neuberg, Victor, ed. Nineteenth Century Education: Selected Sources. (Social History of Education, Second Ser.: No. 6). 285p. 1981. 27.50x (ISBN 0-7130-0015-5, Pub. by Woburn Pr England). Biblio Dist.

Neuberg, Victor E., ed. Eighteenth Century Education: Selected Sources. (Social History of Education Second Ser.: No. 2). 1981. 25.00x (ISBN 0-7130-0011-2, Pub. by Woburn Pr England). Biblio Dist.

Neuberger, Egon & Duffy, William J. Comparative Economic Systems: A Decision-Making Approach. 384p. 1976. text ed. 20.95x (ISBN 0-205-04850-1). Allyn.

Neuberger, Egon & Tyson, Laura D., eds. The Impact of International Economic Disturbances on the Soviet Union & Eastern Europe. (Pergamon Policy Studies). 60.00 (ISBN 0-08-025102-1). Pergamon.

Neuberger, Egon, jt. ed. see Brown, Alan A.

Neuberger, Richard L. & Loe, Kelley. An Army of the Aged. LC 72-2379. (FDR & the New Deal Ser). 332p. 1973. Repr. of 1936 ed. lib. bdg. 32.50 (ISBN 0-306-70518-4). Da Capo.

Neubert, Christopher & Withiam, Jack, Jr. How to Handle Your Own Contracts. rev. ed. (Illus.). 1979. pap. 7.95 (ISBN 0-8069-8868-1). Sterling.

Neubert, Gunter, ed. Technical Dictionary of Hydraulics & Pneumatics. 1973. text ed. 37.00 (ISBN 0-08-016958-9). Pergamon.

Neubert, Hermann K. Instrument Transducers: An Introduction to Their Performance & Design. 2nd ed. (Illus.). 1976. 69.00x (ISBN 0-19-856320-5). Oxford U Pr.

Neuburg, Victor E., ed. Thomas Frognall Dibdin: Selections. LC 77-18012. (The Great Bibliographers Ser.: No. 3). 1978. 12.00 (ISBN 0-8108-1077-8). Scarecrow.

Neuder, Gustav F. & Ullrich, Heinz M. Dictionary of Radiological Engineering. 1979. pap. text ed. 36.50 (ISBN 3-11-007807-4). De Gruyter.

Neudorfer, Giovanna. Vermont Stone Chambers: An Inquiry into Their Past. 1980. pap. 4.50 (ISBN 0-934720-22-3). VT Hist Soc.

Neuenschwander, John A. Middle Colonies & the Coming of the American Revolution. LC 73-83267. (National University Pubns.). 288p. 1974. 17.50 (ISBN 0-8046-9054-5). Kennikat.

Neufeld, John. Edgar Allan. LC 68-31175. (Illus.). (gr. 5-8). 1968. 9.95 (ISBN 0-87599-149-1). S G Phillips.

--Freddy's Book. (gr. 2-7). 1975. pap. 1.75 (ISBN 0-380-00203-5, 53298, Camelot). Avon.

--Lisa, Bright & Dark. (gr. 7 up). 1969. 9.95 (ISBN 0-87599-153-X). S G Phillips.

--Touching. LC 76-125867. (gr. 8 up). 1970. 9.95 (ISBN 0-87599-174-2). S G Phillips.

Neufeldt, Ronald. F. Max Muller & the Rg-Veda. 1980. 16.00x (ISBN 0-8364-0040-2). South Asia Bks.

Neufeldt, Victor A. see Pratt, John C.

Neufert, E. Architect's Data: The Handbook of Building Types, 2nd (International) English Edition. 420p. 1980. 69.95x (ISBN 0-470-26947-2). Halsted Pr.

Neufert, Ernst. Architects' Data. Herz, Rudolf, ed. (Illus.). 1978. text ed. 34.95x o.s.i. (ISBN 0-8464-0145-2). Beekman Pubs.

Neuffer, Claude H. Names in South Carolina, 1954-65: Vols. I-XII. LC 76-29026. 1976. Repr. 25.00 (ISBN 0-87152-248-9). C H Neuffer.

Neuffer, Mark, jt. auth. see Amigo, Eleanor.

Neugarten, Bernice L., jt. auth. see Havighurst, Robert J.

Neugebauer, O. Exact Sciences in Antiquity. 2nd ed. LC 57-12342. (Illus.). 240p. 1970. Repr. of 1957 ed. 10.00 (ISBN 0-87057-044-7, Pub. by Brown U Pr). Univ Pr of New England.

Neugebauer, O. & Sachs, A. Mathematical Cuneiform Texts. (American Oriental Ser.: Vol. 29). 1945. 10.00x (ISBN 0-686-00013-7). Am Orient Soc.

Neugebauer, Wilbert. Marine Aquarium Fish Identifier. LC 74-82341. (Identifier Ser). (Illus.). 256p. 1975. 6.95 (ISBN 0-8069-3724-6); PLB 6.69 (ISBN 0-8069-3725-4). Sterling.

Neugeboren, Jay. Corky's Brother. LC 78-87214. 1969. 5.95 o.p. (ISBN 0-374-12968-1). FS&G.

--An Orphan's Tale. LC 75-24989. 1976. 8.95 o.p. (ISBN 0-03-015271-2). HR&W.

--The Stolen Jew. 336p. 1981. 14.95 (ISBN 0-03-056223-6). HR&W.

Neugroschel, Joachim, ed. Yenne Velt: The Great Works of Jewish Fantasy & Occult, 2 vols. 736p. 1976. 25.00 (ISBN 0-88373-025-1). Stonehill Pub Co.

Neugroschel, Joachim, tr. see Hamburger, Jean.

Neugroschel, Joachim, tr. see Vogt, Paul, et al.

Neugrosschel, Joachim, tr. see Speer, Albert.

Neuhaus, Edmund C. & Astwood, William. Practicing Psychotherapy. LC 79-25464. 208p. text ed. 18.95 (ISBN 0-87705-467-3). Human Sci Pr.

Neuhaus, Heinrich. The Art of Piano Playing. Leibovitch, D. A., tr. 1978. 10.95 o.p. (ISBN 0-214-65364-1, 8020, Dist. by Arco). Barrie & Jenkins.

Neuhaus, O. W. & Halver, J. E., eds. Fish in Research. LC 74-107020. 1969. 32.50 (ISBN 0-12-515850-5). Acad Pr.

Neuhaus, Otto W., jt. auth. see Orten, James M.

Neuhaus, Richard. Time Toward Home: The American Experience As Revelation. 250p. 1975. 9.50 (ISBN 0-8164-0272-8). Crossroad NY.

Neuhaus, Richard J. In Defense of People. 1971. 6.95 o.s.i. (ISBN 0-02-588830-7). Macmillan.

--In Defense of People. 1971. pap. 1.95 o.s.i. (ISBN 0-02-088730-2, Collier). Macmillan.

Neuhaus, Richard J., jt. auth. see Berger, Peter.

Neuhaus, Robert & Neuhaus, Ruby. Family Crises. LC 73-85104. 1974. pap. 12.95 (ISBN 0-675-08890-9). Merrill.

Neuhaus, Ruby, jt. auth. see Neuhaus, Robert.

Neuhauser, Duncan, jt. auth. see Wilson, Florence.

Neuhauser, Duncan, ed. Quest for Excellence in Health Care Delivery. (Illus.). 180p. 1981. text ed. price not set (ISBN 0-914904-70-1). Health Admin Pr.

Neuhauser, Duncan, jt. ed. see Kovner, Anthony R.

Neujahr, James. The Individualized Instruction Game. LC 75-22491. 1976. text ed. 8.00x (ISBN 0-8077-2485-8). Tchrs Coll.

Neulinger, John. To Leisure: An Introduction. 276p. 1980. text ed. 16.95 (ISBN 0-205-06936-3, 8469369). Allyn.

Neumaier, J. J., ed. see Durrenmatt, Friedrich.

Neuman, Daniel M. The Life of Music in North India: The Organization of an Artistic Tradition. LC 79-16889. (Illus.). 1979. 16.95x (ISBN 0-8143-1632-8). Wayne St U Pr.

Neuman, Donald B. Experiences in Science for Young Children. LC 76-53185. 1978. pap. text ed. 8.80 (ISBN 0-8273-1642-9); instructor's guide 1.75 (ISBN 0-8273-1643-7). Delmar.

Neuman, F. Questions & Problems in Auditing. 1980. 9.20x (ISBN 0-87563-157-6). Stipes.

Neuman, Fred G. Irvin S. Cobb. (American Newspapermen 1790-1933 Ser.). (Illus.). 275p. 1974. Repr. of 1934 ed. 16.50x o.s.i. (ISBN 0-8464-0011-1). Beekman Pubs.

Neuman, Fredric. Caring: Home Treatment for the Emotionally Disturbed. 245p. 1980. 10.95 (ISBN 0-8037-0969-2). Dial.

--The Seclusion Room. 1979. pap. 1.95 o.p. (ISBN 0-449-24152-1, Crest). Fawcett.

Neuman, Michael R., et al, eds. Physical Sensors for Biomedical Applications. 160p. 1980. 49.95 (ISBN 0-8493-5975-9). CRC Pr.

Neuman, Patricia O. Moving: The What, When, Where, & How of It. (Illus.). 128p. 1981. pap. 5.95 (ISBN 0-89651-450-1). Icarus.

Neuman, Pearl. High Action Reading for Comprehension, C. Incl. Study Skills. Hansen, Merrily. pap. text ed. 2.40 (ISBN 0-87895-325-6); Vocabulary. Christensen, Barbara. pap. text ed. 2.40 (ISBN 0-87895-323-X). (Skillbooster Ser.). (gr. 3). 1979. pap. text ed. 2.40 (ISBN 0-87895-324-8). Modern Curr.

Neuman, Robert W. Caddoan Indians Two. Horr, David A., ed. (American Indian Ethnohistory Ser.). 1978. lib. bdg. 42.00 (ISBN 0-8240-0764-6). Garland Pub.

Neuman, Shirley. Some One Myth: Yeats's Autobiographies. (New Yeats's Papers: No. XIX). (Illus.). 112p. 1980. pap. text ed. 16.50x (ISBN 0-85105-369-6, Dolmen Pr). Humanities.

Neuman, Stephanie G., ed. Small States & Segmented Societies: National Political Integration Environment. LC 75-23986. (Special Studies). 200p. 1976. text ed. 23.95 (ISBN 0-275-55730-8). Praeger.

Neuman, Stephanie G. & Harkavy, Robert E., eds. Arms Transfers in the Modern World. LC 78-19778. (Praeger Special Studies Ser.). 400p. 1980. 31.95 (ISBN 0-03-045361-5); student ed. 11.95 (ISBN 0-03-051171-2). Praeger.

Neumann, A. L. Beef Cattle. 7th ed. LC 76-46616. 1977. 28.95 (ISBN 0-471-63236-8). Wiley.

Neumann, Angelo. Personal Recollections of Wagner. (Music Reprint Ser.). 329p. 1976. Repr. of 1906 ed. 25.00. Da Capo.

Neumann, B. H., ed. see International Conference on the Theory of Groups, 1969.

Neumann, Bonnie R. Robert Smith Surtees. (English Authors Ser.: No. 220). 1978. 12.50 (ISBN 0-8057-6722-3). Twayne.

Neumann, E., jt. ed. see Schoffeniels, E.

Neumann, Erich. Depth Psychology & the New Ethic. Rolfe, Eugene, tr. from Ger. 160p. 1973. pap. 3.95 (ISBN 0-06-131777-2, TB1777, Torch). Har-Row.

--The Great Mother: An Analysis of the Archetype. Manheim, Ralph, tr. (Bollingen Ser.: Vol. 47). 628p. 1972. 25.00x (ISBN 0-691-09742-9); pap. 6.95 (ISBN 0-691-01780-8). Princeton U Pr.

Neumann, Gerhard & Pierson, W. J. Principles of Physical Oceanography. (Illus.). 1966. 35.95 (ISBN 0-13-709741-7). P-H.

Neumann, Hans. Foreign Travel & Immunization Guide. 10th ed. 1981. pap. 5.50 (ISBN 0-87489-254-6). Med Economics.

Neumann, I. Biotaxonomische Untersuchungen an Einigen Hefen der Gattung Saccharomyces. 1972. 20.00 (ISBN 3-7682-5440-2). Lubrecht & Cramer.

Neumann, Inge S. European War Crimes Trials: A Bibliography. Rosebaum, Robert A., ed. LC 77-18934. (Additional material furnished by the Wiener Library, London). 1978. Repr. of 1951 ed. lib. bdg. 17.50x (ISBN 0-313-20210-9, NEEW). Greenwood.

Neumann, Phyllis L. Sonoma County Bike Trails. (Illus.). 112p. (Orig.). pap. 3.95 (ISBN 0-686-28739-8). Sonoma County.

Neumann, Ronald D., ed. Pathology. 2nd ed. LC 79-83716. (Basic Sciences PreTest Self-Assessment & Review Ser.). (Illus.). 1979. 9.95 (ISBN 0-07-050964-6). McGraw-Pretest.

Neumann, Rudolf. Bad Bear. Prelutsky, Jack, tr. (Illus.). (gr. k-3). 1967. 3.95g o.s.i. (ISBN 0-02-768090-8). Macmillan.

Neumeyer, E. S., jt. auth. see Neumeyer, Martin H.

Neumeyer, Martin H. & Neumeyer, E. S. Leisure & Recreation: A Study of Leisure & Recreation in Their Sociological Aspects. 3rd ed. 1958. 9.95 o.p. (ISBN 0-8260-6695-X). Wiley.

Neuner, John J. & Deakin, Edward B. Cost Accounting: Principles & Practice. 9th ed. 1977. pap. text ed. 18.95 (ISBN 0-256-01903-7); job order cost practice set 5.95x (ISBN 0-256-00377-7); study guide 4.95 (ISBN 0-256-01960-6). Irwin.

Neunhoeffer, Hans & Wiley, Paul F. Chemistry of One, Two, Three-Triazines & One, Two, Four-Triazines, Tetrazines & Pentazines. LC 77-18932. (Chemistry of Heterocyclic Compounds Ser.: Vol. 33). 1978. Vol. 33. 132.95 (ISBN 0-471-03129-1, Pub. by Wiley-Interscience). Wiley.

Neunier, John, ed. Proceedings of the Sixty-Eighth A.C.S.A. Annual Meeting. 300p. 1981. pap. 17.50 (ISBN 0-8408-0506-3). Carrollton Pr.

Neurath, Hans & Hill, Robert L. The Proteins, Vol. 1. 3rd ed. 1975. 54.75 (ISBN 0-12-516301-0); by subscription 47.00 (ISBN 0-12-516301-0). Acad Pr.

Neurath, Marie. They Lived Like This in Ancient China. LC 67-10000. (They Lived Like This Ser). (Illus.). (gr. 4-6). 1967. PLB 3.90 o.p. (ISBN 0-531-01377-4). Watts.

--They Lived Like This in Ancient Crete. LC 66-14736. (They Lived Like This Ser). (Illus.). (gr. 4-6). 1966. PLB 3.90 o.p. (ISBN 0-531-01378-2). Watts.

--They Lived Like This in Ancient Mesopotamia. LC 65-10066. (They Lived Like This Ser). (Illus.). (gr. 4-6). 1965. PLB 3.90 o.p. (ISBN 0-531-01383-9). Watts.

--They Lived Like This in Ancient Rome. LC 68-14093. (They Lived Like This Ser). (Illus.). (gr. 4-6). 1969. PLB 3.90 o.p. (ISBN 0-531-01386-3). Watts.

--They Lived Like This in Chaucer's England. LC 68-10837. (They Lived Like This Ser). (Illus.). (gr. 4-6). 1967. PLB 5.90 (ISBN 0-531-01388-X). Watts.

--They Lived Like This in Old Japan. (They Lived Like This Ser). (Illus.). (gr. 4-6). 1967. PLB 3.90 o.p. (ISBN 0-531-01387-1). Watts.

--They Lived Like This in the Old Stone Age. LC 74-91876. (They Lived Like This Ser). (gr. 4-6). 1971. PLB 3.90 o.p. (ISBN 0-531-01393-6). Watts.

--They Lived Like This: The Ancient Maya. LC 67-10095. (They Lived Like This Ser). (Illus.). (gr. 4-6). 1967. PLB 3.90 o.p. (ISBN 0-531-01382-0). Watts.

Neuringer, Charles, ed. Psychological Assessment of Suicidal Risk. (Illus.). 256p. 1974. text ed. 16.50 (ISBN 0-398-03008-1). C C Thomas.

Neuse, Erna K. Deutsch Fur Anfanger. LC 77-135899. (Orig., Ger.). 1971. text ed. 13.95 (ISBN 0-13-203356-9); audiotape 150.00 (ISBN 0-13-203372-0). P-H.

Neuse, Erna K., ed. Neue Deutsche Prosa. LC 68-30796. (Illus., Orig., Ger.). 1968. pap. text ed. 5.95x (ISBN 0-89197-315-X). Irvington.

Neusner, J., et al, eds. see Vermes, Pamela.

Neusner, Jacob. Between Time & Eternity: The Essentials of Judaism. 1975. pap. 7.95x (ISBN 0-8221-0160-2). Dickenson.

--First-Century Judaism in Crisis: Yohanan Ben Zakkai & the Renaissance of Torah. LC 74-14799. 208p. 1975. pap. 4.50 o.p. (ISBN 0-687-13120-0). Abingdon.

--Form-Analysis & Exegesis: A Fresh Approach to the Interpretation of Mishnah. 224p. 1981. 22.50x (ISBN 0-8166-0984-5); pap. 9.95x (ISBN 0-8166-0985-3). U of Minn Pr.

--The Life of Torah: Readings in the Jewish Religious Experience. 1974. pap. text ed. 7.95x (ISBN 0-8221-0124-6). Dickenson.

--Meet Our Sages. LC 80-12771. (Illus.). 128p. (gr. 5-8). 1980. pap. text ed. 4.95x (ISBN 0-87441-327-3). Behrman.

--Strangers at Home: Essays on "The Holocaust", Zionism, & American Judaism. LC 80-19455. 1981. 15.00 (ISBN 0-226-57628-0). U of Chicago Pr.

--Understanding Rabbinic Judaism: From Talmudic to Modern Times. 1974. pap. 8.95x (ISBN 0-685-56200-X). Ktav.

Neustadt, Egon. The Lamps of Tiffany. LC 78-142102. (Illus.). 224p. 1970. 165.00 (ISBN 0-913158-01-1); Museum Edition. 205.00 (ISBN 0-685-26779-2). Fairfield.

Neustadt, Richard E. Alliance Politics. LC 77-120855. 1970. 15.00x (ISBN 0-231-03066-5); pap. 6.00x (ISBN 0-231-08307-6). Columbia U Pr.

--Presidential Power: The Politics of Leadership from FDR to Carter. LC 79-19474. 1979. pap. text ed. 8.95 (ISBN 0-471-05988-9). Wiley.

Neuwirth, L. P., ed. Knots, Groups, & 3-Manifolds. LC 75-5619. (Annals of Mathematics Studies: No. 84). 345p. 1975. 21.00 o.p. (ISBN 0-691-08170-0); pap. 7.50 (ISBN 0-691-08167-0). Princeton U Pr.

Nevai, Paul G. Orthogonal Polynomials. LC 78-32112. (Memoirs: No. 213). 1980. Repr. of 1979 ed. 7.80 (ISBN 0-8218-2213-6). Am Math.

Nevakivi, Jukka. Britain, France & the Arab Middle East 1914-1920. (Univ. of London Historical Studies: No. 23). 1969. text ed. 25.00x (ISBN 0-485-13123-4, Athlone Pr). Humanities.

Nevanlinna, R. Le Theoreme de Picard-Borel. LC 73-14779. 179p. 1974. Repr. of 1970 ed. text ed. 9.95 (ISBN 0-8284-0272-8). Chelsea Pub.

Nevdeck, Gerold W., jt. auth. see Hayt, William H.

Nevers, Noel De see De Nevers, Noel.

Nevill, John C. Thomas Chatterton. 261p. 1980. Repr. of 1948 ed. lib. bdg. 30.00 (ISBN 0-8495-4020-8). Arden Lib.

Neville, A. M. High Alumina Cement Concrete. LC 75-14379. 1975. 28.95 (ISBN 0-470-63280-1). Halsted Pr.

Neville, A. M. & Chatterton, M., eds. New Concrete Technologies & Building Design. 134p. 1980. 44.95x (ISBN 0-470-26944-8). Halsted Pr.

Neville, Anne. Gold in Her Hair, No. 2. (Starlight Romance Ser.). 144p. 1981. pap. 1.75 (ISBN 0-553-14364-6). Bantam.

--Voices of Loving. (Starlight Romance Ser.). 144p. 1981. pap. 1.75 (ISBN 0-553-14363-8). Bantam.

Neville, Eric H. Elliptic Functions: A Primer. Langford, W. J., ed. 211p. 1972. text ed. 25.00 (ISBN 0-08-016369-6). Pergamon.

Neville, Giles. Incidents in the Life of Joseph Grimaldi. (Illus.). 64p. 1981. 10.95 (ISBN 0-224-01869-8, Pub. by Chatto-Bodley-Jonathan). Merrimack Bk Serv.

Neville, Gwen K., jt. auth. see Westerhoff, John H.

Neville, Joyce. How to Share Your Faith Without Being Offensive. (Orig.). 1979. pap. 4.95 (ISBN 0-8164-2228-1). Crossroad NY.

Neville, Mary, ed. If a Poem Bothers You. (Illus.). 64p. (Orig.). 1980. pap. 3.75x (ISBN 0-913678-14-7). New Day Pr.

Neville, Robert C. Creativity & God: A Challenge to Process Theology. 192p. 1980. 9.95 (ISBN 0-8164-0120-9). Crossroad NY.

Nevin, Bruce E. Astrology Inside Out. (Illus.). 288p. (Orig.). 1981. pap. 9.95 (ISBN 0-914918-19-2). Para Res.

Nevin, D. The Soldiers. LC 73-79475. (Old West Ser). (Illus.). (gr. 5 up). 1973. kivar 12.96 (ISBN 0-8094-1463-5, Pub. by Time-Life). Silver.

Nevin, David. The American Touch in Micronesia. 1977. 9.95 o.p. (ISBN 0-393-05617-1). Norton.

--The Expressman. (The Old West Ser.). (Illus.). 1974. 12.95 (ISBN 0-8094-1484-8). Time-Life.

--The Expressmen. LC 74-12941. (The Old West). (Illus.). (gr. 5 up). 1974. kivar 12.96 (ISBN 0-8094-1486-4, Pub. by Time-Life). Silver.

--The Mexican War. LC 77-95212. (The Old West Ser.). (Illus.). 1978. lib. bdg. 12.96 (ISBN 0-686-51079-8). Silver.

--Mexican War. Time-Life Books, ed. (Old West). (Illus.). 1978. 12.95 (ISBN 0-8094-2300-6). Time-Life.

--The Soldiers. (The Old West Ser.). (Illus.). 1973. 12.95 (ISBN 0-8094-1462-7). Time-Life.

--The Texans. (Old West Ser.). (Illus.). 1976. 12.95 (ISBN 0-8094-1500-3). Time-Life.

--The Texans. LC 75-15450. (The Old West). (Illus.). (gr. 5 up). 1975. kivar 12.96 (ISBN 0-8094-1502-X, Pub. by Time-Life). Silver.

Nevin, Edward. Introduction to Microeconomics. 300p. 1974. text ed. 10.00x o.p. (ISBN 0-85665-018-8). Verry.

Nevin, Edward & Davis, E. W. The London Clearing Banks. 1970. 24.95 (ISBN 0-236-17654-4, Pub. by Paul Elek). Merrimack Bk Serv.

Nevin, George R., Jr. Homegrown. (Orig.). 1980. pap. 2.50 (ISBN 0-532-23140-6). Manor Bks.

Nevin, John A., jt. auth. see Commons, Michael L.

Nevin, John A., jt. ed. see Commons, Michael.

Nevin, John W. My Own Life: The Earlier Years. LC 64-57065. 1964. pap. 5.00 (ISBN 0-685-09356-5). Evang & Ref.

--Mystical Presence & Other Writings on the Eucharist. abr. ed. Thompson, Bard & Bricker, George M., eds. LC 66-16193. 1966. 9.95 (ISBN 0-8298-0093-X). Pilgrim NY.

Nevins, Albert J. A Saint for Your Name: Saints for Boys. LC 79-92504. (Illus.). 120p. (YA) (gr. 7 up). 1980. 7.95 (ISBN 0-87973-330-6, 330); pap. 4.95 (ISBN 0-87973-320-9, 320). Our Sunday Visitor.

--A Saint for Your Name: Saints for Girls. LC 79-92502. (Illus.). 104p. (YA) (gr. 7 up). 1980. 7.95 (ISBN 0-87973-331-4, 331); pap. 4.95 (ISBN 0-87973-321-7, 321). Our Sunday Visitor.

Nevins, Allan. Ordeal of the Union, 8 vols. Incl. Vol. 1. Ordeal of the Union: Fruits of Manifest Destiny, 1847-1852. 1947 (ISBN 0-684-10423-7); Vol. 2. Ordeal of the Union: A House Dividing, 1852-1857. 1947 (ISBN 0-684-10424-5); Vol. 3. The Emergence of Lincoln: Douglas, Buchanan, & Party Chaos, 1857-1859. 1950 (ISBN 0-684-10415-6). pap. o.p. Lyceum Ed. (ISBN 0-684-71851-0, 169, SL); Vol. 4. The Emergence of Lincoln: Prologue to Civil War, 1859-1861. 1950 (ISBN 0-684-10416-4). pap. o.p. Lyceum Ed. (ISBN 0-684-71852-9, 170, SL); Vol. 5. The War for the Union: The Improvised War, 1861-1862. LC 47-11072. 1959 (ISBN 0-684-10426-1); Vol. 6. The War for the Union: War Becomes Revolution, 1862-1863. LC 59-3690. 1960 (ISBN 0-684-10427-X); Vol. 7. The War for the Union: The Organized War, 1863-1864. LC 47-11072. 1971 (ISBN 0-684-10428-8); Vol. 8. The War for the Union: The Organized War to Victory, 1864-1865. LC 47-11072. 1971 (ISBN 0-684-10429-6). (Illus.). 25.00 ea. Scribner.

--Place of Franklin D. Roosevelt in History. (Sir George Watson Lectures). (Orig.). 1965. pap. text ed. 1.75x (ISBN 0-7185-1046-1, Leicester). Humanities.

Nevins, Allan & Commager, Henry S. A Pocket History of the United States. 2nd, rev. ed. 1981. pap. write for info. PB.

Nevins, Allan see Johnson, Allen & Nevins, Allan.

Nevins, Allan, jt. auth. see Weisberger, Bernard A.

Nevins, Allan, ed. Letters of Grover Cleveland. LC 70-123752. (American Public Figures Ser). 1970. Repr. of 1933 ed. lib. bdg. 59.50 (ISBN 0-306-71982-7). Da Capo.

Nevins, Allan, jt. ed. see Hyman, Harold.

Nevins, Allan, jt. ed. see Johnson, Allen.

Nevins, Allan, ed. see Kennedy, John F.

Nevinson, Henry W. Essays in Freedom & Rebellion. 1921. 13.50x (ISBN 0-686-51378-9). Elliots Bks.

--Essays in Rebellion. 241p. 1980. Repr. of 1913 ed. lib. bdg. 30.00 (ISBN 0-8495-4018-6). Arden Lib.

Nevison, J. M. Executive Computing. 1981. pap. text ed. 8.95 (ISBN 0-201-05248-2). A-W.

Nevitte, Neil, jt. auth. see Feldman, Elliot J.

Nevius, Blake. Cooper's Landscapes: An Essay on the Picturesque Vision. LC 74-77730. (Quantum Bks). 1976. 14.50x (ISBN 0-520-02751-5). U of Cal Pr.

--Edith Wharton: A Study of Her Fiction. (California Library Reprint Ser). 1976. 18.50x (ISBN 0-520-03180-6). U of Cal Pr.

--Ivy Compton-Burnett. LC 74-110600. (Columbia Essays on Modern Writers Ser.: No. 47). (Orig.). 1970. pap. 2.00 (ISBN 0-231-02988-8, MW47). Columbia U Pr.

Nevius, Blake, jt. ed. see Nisbet, Ada.

Nevo, David, jt. auth. see Lewy, Arieh.

Nevo, David, jt. auth. see Smilansky, Moshe.

New, jt. auth. see Wright.

New, Anthony S. The Observer's Book of Cathedrals. (The Observer Bks). (Illus.). 1979. 4.95 (ISBN 0-684-16026-9, ScribT). Scribner.

New, Bill D., jt. auth. see Wright, D. Franklin.

New, C. C. Managing the Manufacture of Complex Products. 379p. 1977. text ed. 29.50x (ISBN 0-220-66318-1, Pub. by Busn Bks England). Renouf.

New, Earl H. The New Look in Home Landscaping. 1975. pap. 12.00 (ISBN 0-686-19191-9). Thomson Pub CA.

New England Deaconess Hospital. A Guide to I. V. Admixture Compatibility. 3rd ed. 1980. pap. 6.95 (ISBN 0-87489-248-1). Med Economics.

New Eye Photography. Star Trek Maps. 1980. pap. 8.95 (ISBN 0-553-01202-9). Bantam.

New Games Foundation. The New Games Book. Fluegelman, Andrew, ed. 4.95 (ISBN 0-385-12516-X, Dolp). Doubleday.

New Inc.-Fourth World Movement, ed. Children of Our Time. (Symposium Ser.: Vol. 7). (Illus., Orig.). 1981. soft cover 9.95x (ISBN 0-88946-911-3). E Mellen.

New Individualist Review Journal. New Individualist Review. LC 65-35281. 1024p. 1981. 12.00 (ISBN 0-913966-90-8). Liberty Fund.

New Jersey Supreme Court. In the Matter of Karen Quinlan, Vol. 1: The Complete Legal Briefs, Court Proceedings, & Decision in the Superior Court of New Jersey. 575p. 1975. 29.50 (ISBN 0-89093-100-3). U Pubns Amer.

New Jersey Supreme Court, et al. In the Matter of Karen Quinlan: Volume 2, The Complete Briefs, Oral Agruments, & Opinion in the New Jersey Supreme Court. 1976. 22.50 (ISBN 0-89093-114-3). U Pubns Amer.

New, Maria & Levine, Lenore, eds. Juvenile Hypertension. LC 76-51556. 1977. 20.00 (ISBN 0-89004-145-8). Raven.

New, Maria I., ed. see Nat'l Foundation-March of Dimes Symposium, April, 1976, New York City.

New Mexico State Poetry Society, ed. Turquoise Land: Anthology of New Mexico Poetry. 115p. 1974. 4.95 o.p. (ISBN 0-89015-067-2). Nortex Pr.

New, Michael. The Year of the Apple. LC 80-15933. (Illus.). 128p. (gr. 3-7). 1980. PLB 7.95 (ISBN 0-201-05220-2, 5220, A-W Childrens). A-W.

New Orleans Academy of Ophthalmology Symposium on Surgery of the Orbit & Adnexa. Surgery of the Orbit & Adnexa: Proceedings. LC 73-14508. 1974. 38.50 o.p. (ISBN 0-8016-3677-9). Mosby.

New Orleans Academy of Ophthalmology. Symposium on Cataracts. 1st ed. LC 79-4489. (Illus.). 1979. text ed. 43.50 (ISBN 0-8016-3674-4). Mosby.

--Symposium on Glaucoma. (Illus.). 536p. 1981. text ed. 57.95 (ISBN 0-8016-3667-1). Mosby.

--Symposium on Strabismus: Transactions of the New Orleans Academy of Ophthalmology. (Illus.). 1978. 49.50 (ISBN 0-8016-3687-6). Mosby.

New Orleans Academy of Opthalmology Symposium of 1975-76. Proceedings: Symposium on Neuro-Opthalmology. LC 75-43983. (Illus.). 448p. 1976. text ed. 42.50 o.p. (ISBN 0-8016-3681-7). Mosby.

New Orleans Academy of Opthalmology. Symposium on Glaucoma: Transactions of the New Orleans Academy of Opthalmology. LC 75-2075. 1975. 39.50 o.p. (ISBN 0-8016-3679-5). Mosby.

--Symposium on Medical & Surgical Diseases of the Cornea. LC 80-13693. (Illus.). 1980. text ed. 72.50 (ISBN 0-8016-3666-3). Mosby.
New, Peter G. Book Production. (Outlines of Modern Librarianship Ser.). 152p. 1979. text ed. 12.00 (ISBN 0-89664-411-1, Pub. by K G Saur). Shoe String.
New York Academy of Medicine. Author Catalog of the Library of the New York Academy of Medicine, Second Supplement. 1979. lib. bdg. 500.00 (ISBN 0-8161-1181-2). G K Hall.
--Subject Catalog of the Library of the New York Academy of Medicine, Second Supplement. 1979. lib. bdg. 500.00 (ISBN 0-8161-1182-0). G K Hall.
New York Assn. of Realtors & Harwood, Bruce. New York Real Estate. 1981. text ed. 16.95 (ISBN 0-8359-4894-3). Reston.
New York Botanical Garden Library. Catalog of the Manuscript & Archival Collections & Index to the Correspondence of John Torrey. 1973. 50.00 (ISBN 0-8161-1018-2). G K Hall.
New York Community Trust. Heritage of New York: Historic-Landmark Plaques of the New York Community Trust. LC 69-13762. 1970. 25.00 o.p. (ISBN 0-8232-0825-7). Fordham.
New York Constitutional Convention, 1821. Reports of the Proceedings & Debates. LC 72-133168. (Law, Politics & History Ser.). 1970. Repr. of 1821 ed. lib. bdg. 65.00 (ISBN 0-306-70069-7). Da Capo.
New York Heart Association. Nomenclature & Criteria for Diagnosis of Diseases of the Heart & Great Vessels. 8th ed. LC 78-71219. 349p. 1979. text ed. 14.95 (ISBN 0-316-60536-0); pap. text ed. 11.95 (ISBN 0-316-60537-9). Little.
New York Personnel & Guidance Assn. Tips (to Improve Personal Study Skills) LC 68-8175. (Illus.). 60p. 1968. pap. 2.40 (ISBN 0-8273-0370-X). Delmar.
New York Public Library. The Eno Collection of New York City Views. Weitenkampf, Frank, ed. LC 79-162522. (Illus.). 1971. Repr. of 1925 ed. 20.00 (ISBN 0-8103-3744-4). Gale.
New York Public Library Research Library & Library of Congress Research Library. Bibliographic Guide to Black Studies. 1979. lib. bdg. 60.00 (ISBN 0-8161-6864-4). G K Hall.
--Bibliographic Guide to Business & Economics. 1979. lib. bdg. 205.00 (ISBN 0-8161-6865-2). G K Hall.
--Bibliographic Guide to Conference Publications. 1979. lib. bdg. 130.00 (ISBN 0-8161-6866-0). G K Hall.
--Bibliographic Guide to Government Publications. 1979. 180.00 (ISBN 0-8161-6870-9). G K Hall.
--Bibliographic Guide to Music. 1979. lib. bdg. 85.00 (ISBN 0-8161-6875-X). G K Hall.
New York Public Library, Research Libraries & Library of Congress. Bibliographic Guide to Soviet & East European Studies, 1980. (Library Catalogs - Bibliographic Guides Ser.). 1981. lib. bdg. 195.00 (ISBN 0-8161-6894-6). G K Hall.
New York Public Library Research Library. Bibliographic Guide to Technology. Library of Congress, ed. 1979. lib. bdg. 125.00 (ISBN 0-8161-6861-X). G K Hall.
New York Times. The Complete Book of Baseball. LC 79-92320. (Sports Ser.). (Illus.). 224p. 1980. 14.95 (ISBN 0-686-61137-3). Bobbs.
--The Complete Book of Football: A New York Times Scrapbook History. LC 79-92321. (Sports Ser.). (Illus.). 224p. 1980. 14.95 (ISBN 0-672-52637-9). Bobbs.
--The Complete Book of Golf. LC 79-92319. (Sports Ser.). (Illus.). 224p. 1980. 14.95 (ISBN 0-672-52636-0). Bobbs.
--The Complete Book of Tennis: A New York Times Scrapbook History. LC 79-56751. (Sports Ser.). (Illus.). 224p. 1980. 14.95 (ISBN 0-672-52638-7). Bobbs.
New York University. Library Catalog of the Conservation Center of the Institute of Fine Arts. 1980. lib. bdg. 95.00 (ISBN 0-8161-0303-8). G K Hall.
New York University, Division of General Education. Conference on Practice & Procedure Under the Immigration & Nationality Act (McCarran-Walter Act) Held on June 13, 1953: Proceedings. Sellin, Henry, ed. LC 54-7877. xii, 145p. Repr. of 1954 ed. lib. bdg. 11.75x (ISBN 0-8371-7684-0, NYUP). Greenwood.
Newall, A. B., jt. auth. see Wilson, James G.
Newall, Edward T. Coinage of the Western Seleucid Mints. (Illus.). 1977. pap. 35.00 o.p. (ISBN 0-89192-230-X). Interbk Inc.
Newall, Venetia J., ed. Folklore Studies in the Twentieth Century: Proceedings of the Centenary Conference of the Folklore Society. 1981. 85.00x (ISBN 0-8476-3638-0). Rowman.
Newberg, Paula R., ed. The Politics of Human Rights. LC 79-1998. (A UNA-USA Bk.). 1981. 22.50x (ISBN 0-8147-5754-5); pap. 9.00x (ISBN 0-8147-5755-3). NYU Pr.
Newberger, Eli, ed. see Tutela, Dawn.
Newberger, Eli H., jt. ed. see Bourne, Richard.
Newbery, F. Cries of London. Lurie, Alison & Schiller, Justin G., eds. Incl. Cries of New York. Wood, Samuel. LC 75-32142. (Classics of Children's Literature 1621-1932 Ser.). PLB 38.00 (ISBN 0-8240-2258-0). Garland Pub.
Newbery, John. The History of Little Goody Two-Shoes, Repr. Of 1765 Ed. Bd. with The Fairing or a Golden Toy for Children. Alderson, Brian, pref. by. Repr. of 1768 ed. LC 75-32141. (Classics of Children's Literature, 1621-1932: Vol. 8). 1976. PLB 38.00 (ISBN 0-8240-2257-2). Garland Pub.
Newbery, John, et al, eds. Original Mother Goose's Melody. LC 68-31093. 1969. Repr. of 1892 ed. 15.00 (ISBN 0-8103-3485-2). Gale.
Newbigging, Thomas. Fables & Fabulists, Ancient & Modern. LC 70-78212. 1971. Repr. of 1895 ed. 18.00 (ISBN 0-8103-3770-3). Gale.
Newbigin, Lesslie. Sign of the Kingdom. 48p. (Orig.). 1981. pap. 1.95 (ISBN 0-8028-1878-1). Eerdmans.
Newbold, David. Ability Grouping: The Banbury Enquiry. (General Ser.). (Illus.). 1977. pap. text ed. 16.00x (ISBN 0-85633-142-2, NFER). Humanities.
Newbold, G., jt. auth. see Ambrose, G.
Newbold, H. L. The Psychiatric Programming of People: Neo-Behavioral Orthomolecular Psychiatry. 170p. 1972. 17.25 (ISBN 0-08-016791-8). Pergamon.
--Vitamin C Against Cancer. LC 79-5301. (Illus.). 384p. 1981. pap. 7.95 (ISBN 0-8128-6098-5). Stein & Day.
Newbolt, Henry. Aladore. Reginald, R. & Menville, Douglas, eds. LC 80-19114. (Newcastle Forgotten Fantasy Library: Vol. 5). 363p. 1980. Repr. of 1975 ed. lib. bdg. 10.95x (ISBN 0-89370-504-7). Borgo Pr.
Newborn, Sasha, ed. Brasi! Contemporary Brazilian Writing. LC 77-642342. (Rockbottom Specials Ser.). (Illus., Eng. & Port.). Date not set. 12.00 o.p. (ISBN 0-930012-21-6); pap. 5.00 o.p. (ISBN 0-930012-20-8). Mudborn. Postponed.
Newbould, Gerald D. & Luffman, George A. Successful Business Policies. LC 78-70561. 1979. 25.95 (ISBN 0-03-049386-2). Praeger.
Newbould, Gerald D., et al. Going International: The Experience of Smaller Companies Overseas. LC 78-15729. 1978. 27.95 (ISBN 0-470-26493-4). Halsted Pr.
Newbound, Betty, jt. auth. see Newbound, Bill.
Newbound, Bill & Newbound, Betty. Blue Ridge Dinnerware. (Illus.). 1980. pap. 8.95 (ISBN 0-89145-129-3). Collector Bks.
Newbrun, Ernest, ed. Fluorides & Dental Caries. 2nd ed. (Illus.). 208p. 1978. 15.75 (ISBN 0-398-03448-6). C C Thomas.
Newbury, P. A. R. A Geography of Agriculture. (Illus.). 336p. 1980. pap. text ed. 18.95x (ISBN 0-7121-0733-9). Intl Ideas.
Newby, Cliff. Canaries for Pleasure & Profit. (Orig.). 1965. pap. 2.00 (ISBN 0-87666-418-4, AP270). TFH Pubns.
Newby, Eric, ed. A Short Walk in the Hindu Kush. 1981. pap. 4.95 (ISBN 0-14-002663-0). Penguin.
Newby, F. How to Find Out About Patents. 1967. 22.00 (ISBN 0-08-012333-3); pap. 10.75 (ISBN 0-08-012332-5). Pergamon.
Newby, H. International Perspectives in Rural Sociology. 220p. 1978. 38.25 (ISBN 0-471-99606-8). Wiley.
Newby, Hayes A. Audiology. 4th ed. LC 78-14797. (Illus.). 1979. ref. 19.95 (ISBN 0-13-050856-X). P-H.
Newby, Howard, jt. ed. see Bell, Colin.
Newby, Howard, jt. ed. see Buttel, Frederick H.
Newby, Howard, et al. Property, Paternalism, & Power: A Study of East Anglian Farmers. LC 78-2030. (Illus.). 1979. Repr. 27.50 (ISBN 0-299-07870-1). U of Wis Pr.
Newby, I. A., ed. Civil War & Reconstruction, 1850-1877. (Literature of History Ser). (Orig.). 1971. 18.95x (ISBN 0-89197-080-0); pap. text ed. 7.95x (ISBN 0-89197-081-9). Irvington.
Newby, J. C. Mathematics for the Biological Sciences: From Graph Through Calculus to Differential Equations. (Illus.). 250p. 1980. 59.00 (ISBN 0-19-859623-5); pap. 27.00 (ISBN 0-19-859624-3). Oxford U Pr.
Newby, James E. Black Authors & Education: An Annotated Bibliography of Books. LC 79-9677. 113p. 1980. text ed. 15.00 (ISBN 0-8191-0974-6); pap. text ed. 7.50 (ISBN 0-8191-0975-4). U Pr of Amer.
Newcity, Michael A. Copyright Law in the Soviet Union. LC 76-12867. (Praeger Special Studies). 1978. 24.95 (ISBN 0-275-56450-9). Praeger.
Newcomb, Charles K. Journals of Charles King Newcomb. Johnson, Judith K., ed. (Brown University Studies: No. 10). (Illus.). 299p. 1946. 10.00x (ISBN 0-87057-025-0, Pub. by Brown U Pr). Univ Pr of New England.
Newcomb, Duane. Growing Vegetables the Big Yield-Small Space Way. (Illus.). 272p. 1981. pap. 7.95 (ISBN 0-87477-170-6). J P Tarcher.
--The Owner-Built Adobe. (Illus.). 224p. 1980. 14.95 (ISBN 0-684-16609-7, ScribT). Scribner.
Newcomb, Duane, jt. auth. see Clark, Georgie W.
Newcomb, Franc J. Navaho Neighbors. (Illus.). 1966. 12.95 (ISBN 0-8061-0704-9); pap. 5.95 (ISBN 0-8061-1040-6). U of Okla Pr.
Newcomb, Horace. TV the Most Popular Art. LC 74-3559. 280p. 1974. pap. 2.50 (ISBN 0-385-03602-7, Anch). Doubleday.
Newcomb, Horace, ed. Television: The Critical View. 2nd ed. LC 78-13290. 1979. pap. 7.95 (ISBN 0-19-502501-6). Oxford U Pr.
Newcomb, Joan I. John F. Kennedy: An Annotated Bibliography. LC 77-7568. 1977. 10.00 (ISBN 0-8108-1042-5). Scarecrow.
Newcomb, Loda, jt. auth. see Knapper, Arno.
Newcomb, Simon. A Critical Examination of Our Financial Policy During the Southern Rebellion. (The Neglected American Economists Ser.). 1974. lib. bdg. 50.00 (ISBN 0-8240-1016-7). Garland Pub.
Newcomb, Stanley, jt. auth. see Wright, Al G.
Newcomb, T. P. & Spurr, R. T. Commercial Vehicle Braking. (Illus.). 1979. text ed. 15.95 (ISBN 0-408-00362-6). Butterworths.
Newcomb, Wilburn W. Wood Stove Handbook. LC 78-57170. 1978. pap. 7.95 (ISBN 0-672-23319-3). Audel.
Newcombe, Josephine M. Leonid Andreyev. LC 72-79938. (Modern Literature Ser.). 1973. 10.95 (ISBN 0-8044-2657-0). Ungar.
Newcombe, R. J., jt. auth. see Wilson, J. M.
Newcombe, R. J. see Wilson, J. R., et al.
Newcomer. Understanding & Teaching Emotionally Disturbed Children. new ed. 456p. 1979. text ed. 17.95 (ISBN 0-205-06843-X, 2468433). Allyn.
Newcomer, Kenneth, jt. auth. see Shufeldt, H. H.
Newell, A. Donald. Gunstock Finishing & Care. (Illus.). 512p. 1949. 19.95 (ISBN 0-8117-0780-6). Stackpole.
Newell, Adnah C. Coloring, Finishing & Painting Wood. Holtrop, ed. (gr. 9-12). 1972. text ed. 18.00 (ISBN 0-87002-124-9). Bennett IL.
Newell, Allen & Simon, Herbert. Human Problem Solving. LC 79-152528. (Illus.). 1972. 28.95 (ISBN 0-13-445403-0). P-H.
Newell, Charldean, jt. auth. see Kraemer, Richard.
Newell, Clarence A. Human Behavior in Educational Administration: A Behavioral Science Interpretation. (Illus.). 1978. ref. ed. 16.95 (ISBN 0-13-444638-0). P-H.
Newell, Edward F. The Pre-Imperial Coinage of Roman Antioch. 45p. 1980. pap. 5.00 (ISBN 0-916710-66-1). Obol Intl.
Newell, Edythe W. Rescue of the Sun & Other Tales from the Far North. LC 76-91741. (Folklore Ser). (Illus.). (gr. 3 up). 1970. 5.95g o.p. (ISBN 0-8075-6948-8). A Whitman.
Newell, Frank W. Ophthalmology: Principles & Concepts. 4th ed. 1978. 34.50 (ISBN 0-8016-3640-X). Mosby.
Newell, Frank W., ed. Hereditary Disorders of the Eye & Ocular Adnexa. (Illus.). 288p. 1980. text ed. 14.95 (ISBN 0-936820-00-4). Ophthalmic.
Newell, G. E. & Newell, R. C. Marine Plankton: Practical Guide. 1966. pap. text ed. 10.00x (ISBN 0-09-110541-2, Hutchinson U Lib). Humanities.
Newell, G. F. Traffic Flow on Transportation Networks. (MIT Press Series Intransportation Studies: No. 5). (Illus.). 288p. 1980. 30.00x (ISBN 0-262-14032-2). MIT Pr.
Newell, Gilbert F., jt. auth. see Mead, Leon.
Newell, Gordon & Sherwood, Don. Totem Tales of Seattle. 1974. pap. 1.50 (ISBN 0-345-24141-X). Ballantine.
Newell, Gordon & Williamson, J. Pacific Tugboats. (Illus.). 1975. Repr. encore ed. 9.95 o.s.i. (ISBN 0-87564-221-7). Superior Pub.
Newell, Guy R. & Ellison, Neil M., eds. Cancer & Nutrition: Etiology & Treatment. 475p. 1981. 45.00 (ISBN 0-89004-631-X). Raven.
Newell, Henry H., jt. auth. see Schwerin, Horace S.
Newell, Jack E. Laboratory Management. LC 76-155040. (Series in Laboratory Medicine). 250p. 1972. 19.95 (ISBN 0-316-60451-8). Little.
Newell, James E. Builder's Guide to Government Loans. (Orig.). 1981. pap. 13.75 (ISBN 0-910460-74-4). Craftsman.
Newell, Neil K. The Reluctant Wizard. (Orig.). 1980. pap. 1.95 (ISBN 0-532-23315-8). Manor Bks.
Newell, Pete & Benington, John. Basketball Methods. (Illus.). 1962. 14.95 (ISBN 0-8260-6710-7). Wiley.
Newell, R. C., jt. auth. see Newell, G. E.
Newell, William R. Romans Verse by Verse. 1938. 12.95 (ISBN 0-8024-7385-7). Moody.
Newendorp, Paul D. Decision Analysis for Petroleum Exploration. LC 75-10936. 1976. 39.50 (ISBN 0-87814-064-6). Pennwell Pub.
Newey, Bob. East Bay Trails. 4th, rev. ed. LC 80-69075. (Illus.). 144p. 1981. pap. 4.95 (ISBN 0-9605186-0-6). Footloose Pr.
--East Bay Trails - a Hiker's Guide. 3rd ed. (Illus.). 1976. pap. 3.50 o.p. (ISBN 0-686-21246-0). Footloose Pr.
Newey, Vincent, ed. The Pilgrim's Progress: Critical & Historical Views. (English Texts & Studies). 302p. 1980. 30.00x (ISBN 0-389-20016-6). B&N.
Newfield, Jack. Bread & Roses Too. 1971. pap. 3.95 o.p. (ISBN 0-525-03100-6). Dutton.
Newfield, Marcia. Six Rags Apiece. LC 76-6776. (Illus.). (ps-3). 1976. 6.95 o.p. (ISBN 0-7232-6132-6). Warne.
Newhall, Beaumont. The Daguerreotype in America. (Illus.). 176p. 1976. pap. 7.95 (ISBN 0-486-23322-7). Dover.
--The Daguerreotype in America. 3rd rev. ed. (Illus.). 12.50 (ISBN 0-8446-5461-2). Peter Smith.
Newhall, Beaumont & Edkins, Diana. William H. Jackson. LC 73-89076. (Morgan & Morgan Monograph). 160p. 1974. 14.00 o.p. (ISBN 0-87100-045-8). Morgan.
Newhall, Beaumont, ed. Photography: Essays & Images; Illustrated Readings in the History of Photography. 1981. 29.95 (ISBN 0-87070-387-0, 706949); pap. 14.95 (ISBN 0-87070-385-4, 706957). NYGS.
Newhall, Esther M. Sandy, the Talking Cat. (Illus.). 1977. 5.00 o.p. (ISBN 0-682-48932-8). Exposition.
Newhall, Nancy. The Eloquent Light. (Illus.). 200p. 1980. 47.50, after june 30, 1981 60.00 (ISBN 0-89381-066-5); after June 31, 1981 60.00 (ISBN 0-686-65238-X). Aperture.
--P. H. Emerson: The Fight for Photography As a Fine Art. LC 74-76911. (An Aperture Monograph). (Illus.). 30.00 (ISBN 0-912334-58-4); pap. 15.00 (ISBN 0-912334-59-2). Aperture.
Newhall, Nancy, ed. Time in New England. 1980. 35.00 (ISBN 0-89381-060-6); after dec. 31, 1980 40.00 (ISBN 0-686-65241-X); ltd. ed., 450 copies 175.00 (ISBN 0-89381-061-4). Aperture.
Newhall, Richard A. Muster & Review: A Problem of English Military Administration, Fourteen Twenty to Fourteen Forty. 1940. 27.50x (ISBN 0-686-51420-3). Elliots Bks.
Newhall, T. The Crusades. 146p. 1963. pap. 6.50 (ISBN 0-03-082837-6, Pub. by HR&W). Krieger.
Newham, A. T., jt. auth. see Fayle, H.
Newhouse, Dora. The Encyclopedia of Homonyms-Sound Alikes: Condensed & Abridged Edition. LC 76-50944. (gr. 4-12). 1978. text ed. 9.95 (ISBN 0-918050-02-2); pap. 6.95 (ISBN 0-918050-00-6). Newhouse Pr.
Newhouse, Flower A. Disciplines of the Holy Quest. 4th ed. LC 59-15553. (Illus.). 1959. 9.00 (ISBN 0-910378-05-3). Christward.
--Drama of Incarnation. 3rd ed. 1948. 6.50 (ISBN 0-910378-04-5). Christward.
--Gateways into Light. LC 74-75517. 160p. 1974. pap. 6.50 (ISBN 0-910378-09-6). Christward.
--The Journey Upward. Bengtson, Athene, ed. LC 78-74955. 1978. pap. 6.00 (ISBN 0-910378-15-0). Christward.
--Kingdom of the Shining Ones. 5th ed. 1955. 8.50 (ISBN 0-910378-03-7). Christward.
--The Meaning & Value of the Sacraments. LC 77-186123. 123p. 1971. 5.50 (ISBN 0-910378-07-X). Christward.
--Rediscovering the Angels & Natives of Eternity. 6th ed. (Illus.). 8.50 (ISBN 0-910378-02-9). Christward.
--The Sacred Heart of Christmas. Bengtson, Athene, ed. LC 78-74956. (Illus.). 1978. pap. 5.00 (ISBN 0-910378-14-2). Christward.
--Songs of Deliverance. LC 72-94582. 250p. 1972. 8.00 (ISBN 0-910378-08-8). Christward.
--These, Too, Shall Be Loved. LC 76-49246. 1976. pap. 4.50 (ISBN 0-910378-11-8). Christward.
--Through Lent to Resurrection. Bengtson, Melodie N., ed. LC 77-77088. (Illus.). 1977. pap. 4.00 (ISBN 0-910378-13-4). Christward.
Newhouse, Flower A., et al. Insights into Reality. LC 75-36869. 1975. pap. 6.50 (ISBN 0-910378-10-X). Christward.
Newhouse, John. Cold Dawn: The Story of SALT. LC 72-91556. 288p. 1973. 7.95 o.p. (ISBN 0-03-001631-2). HR&W.
Newhouse, John, et al. U. S. Troops in Europe: Issues, Costs & Choices. LC 71-179325. 1971. 11.95 (ISBN 0-8157-6046-9); pap. 4.95 (ISBN 0-8157-6045-0). Brookings.
Newhouse, Neville H. Joseph Conrad. LC 69-16157. (Literary Critiques Ser.). (Illus.). 1969. Repr. lib. bdg. 4.95 o.p. (ISBN 0-668-01887-9). Arco.
New House, Vernon. Applied Superconductivity, 2 vols. 1975. Vol. 1. 60.00 (ISBN 0-12-517701-1); Vol. 2. 48.50 (ISBN 0-12-517702-X); Set. 88.25. Acad Pr.
Newiger, Hans-Joachim. Untersuchungen zu Gorgias' Schrift Ueber das Nichtseiende. 1973. 44.75x (ISBN 3-11-003432-8). De Gruyter.

Newitt, Jane. Future Trends in Education Policy. LC 78-19672. 1979. 16.95 (ISBN 0-669-02713-8). Lexington Bks.

Newland, Kathleen. City Limits: Emerging Constraints on Urban Growth. LC 80-52951. (Worldwatch Papers). 1980. pap. 2.00 (ISBN 0-916468-37-2). Worldwatch Inst.

--Women, Men & the Division of Labor. LC 80-51662. (Worldwatch Papers). 1980. pap. 2.00 (ISBN 0-916468-36-4). Worldwatch Inst.

Newland, Mary & Walklin, Carol. Printing & Embroidery. 1977. 19.95 (ISBN 0-7134-0136-2, Pub. by Batsford England). David & Charles.

Newland, Mary R. Good King Wenceslas: With Illustrations & Musical Settings. (Illus.). 32p. 1980. 7.95 (ISBN 0-8164-0474-7). Seabury.

Newland, Mary R., jt. ed. see Hill, Brennan.

Newland, T. Ernest. Gifted in Socio-Educational Perspective. (Special Education Ser.). (Illus.). 448p. 1976. 18.95 (ISBN 0-13-356287-5). P-H.

Newlander, John A., jt. auth. see Atherton, Henry V.

Newlands, George. Theology of the Love of God. LC 80-22547. 224p. 1981. 12.50 (ISBN 0-8042-0726-7); pap. 6.95 (ISBN 0-8042-0727-5). John Knox.

Newlin, Algie. Charity Cook. 1981. write for info. (ISBN 0-913408-66-2). Friends United.

Newlin, D., tr. see Bauer-Lechner, Natalie.

Newlin, Dika, tr. see Leibowitz, Rene.

Newlin, Margaret. The Book of Mourning. 1981. 10.00 (ISBN 0-88233-677-0); pap. 4.00 (ISBN 0-88233-678-9). Ardis Pubs.

Newlon, Clarke. The Middle East & Why. LC 76-53443. (gr. 7 up). 1977. 6.95 (ISBN 0-396-07425-1). Dodd.

--Southern Africa, The Critical Land. LC 78-7734. (Illus.). 1978. 6.95 (ISBN 0-396-07589-4). Dodd.

Newlove, Donald. Leo & Theodore. LC 74-154265. 1973. 7.95 o.p. (ISBN 0-8415-0175-0). Dutton.

--Those Drinking Days: Myself & Other Writers. 150p. 1981. 8.95 (ISBN 0-8180-0250-6). Horizon.

Newlyn, W. The Financing of Economic Development. (Illus.). 1978. 37.50x (ISBN 0-19-828402-0). Oxford U Pr.

Newlyn, Walter T. Theory of Money. 3rd. ed. (Illus.). 1978. pap. 24.95x (ISBN 0-19-877099-5); pap. 9.95 (ISBN 0-19-877100-2). Oxford U Pr.

Newman. Ecological Effects of Agricultural Chemistry. 1981. text ed. price not set. Butterworth.

Newman & Boulanger. Sunflakes & Snowshine. (ps-3). pap. 1.25 (ISBN 0-590-05412-0, Schol Pap). Schol Bk Serv.

Newman, jt. auth. see Buffa.

Newman, A. A., ed. Photographic Techniques in Scientific Research, Vol. 3. 1979. 89.00 (ISBN 0-12-517963-4). Acad Pr.

Newman, Alan B., ed. New England Reflections, Eighteen Eighty-Two to Nineteen Seven: Photographs by the Howes Brothers. (Illus.). 1981. 25.00 (ISBN 0-394-51375-4); pap. 12.95 (ISBN 0-394-74912-X). Pantheon.

Newman, Albert H. Manual of Church History, 2 vols. 7.50 ea. o.p.; Vol. 1. (ISBN 0-8170-0097-6); Vol. 2. (ISBN 0-8170-0098-4). Judson.

Newman, Arnold. Artists: Portraits from Four Decades. 180p. 1980. 49.95 (ISBN 0-8212-1099-8, 052779). NYGS.

Newman, Arthur J., ed. In Defense of the American Public School. LC 78-19570. 1979. 16.60 (ISBN 0-8211-1307-0); text ed. 15.00 ten or more copies (ISBN 0-685-59769-5). McCutchan.

Newman, Aubrey. The United Synagogue, 1870-1970. 1976. 21.00 (ISBN 0-7100-8456-0). Routledge & Kegan.

Newman, Aubrey, ed. The Parliamentary Lists of the Early Eighteenth Century: Their Compilation & Use. 96p. 1973. text ed. 6.75x (ISBN 0-7185-1112-3, Leicester). Humanities.

Newman, B. M. & Nida, E. A. Translators Handbook on the Gospel of John. (Helps for Translators Ser.). 1980. softcover 4.85 (ISBN 0-8267-0137-X, 08620). United Bible.

Newman, B. M., Jr. & Nida, E. A. Translators Handbook on Paul's Letter to the Romans. (Helps for Translators Ser.). 1979. Repr. of 1973 ed. soft cover 2.95 (ISBN 0-8267-0139-6, 08517). United Bible.

--Translators Handbook on the Acts of the Apostles. (Helps for Translators Ser.). 1979. Repr. of 1972 ed. 3.85 (ISBN 0-8267-0138-8, 08514). United Bible.

Newman, Barbara M. & Newman, Philip R. Development Through Life: A Psychosocial Approach, Revised Edition: Study Guide. 1979. pap. text ed. 4.00x (ISBN 0-256-02240-2). Dorsey.

--Development Through Life: A Psychosocial Approach. rev. ed. 1979. pap. text ed. 18.95x (ISBN 0-256-02198-8). Dorsey.

--Infancy & Childhood Development & Its Contexts. LC 78-10455. 1978. text ed. 21.95x (ISBN 0-471-02212-8); tchrs. manual avail. (ISBN 0-471-03802-4). Wiley.

--Personality Development Through the Lifespan. LC 80-14291. (Life-Span Human Development Ser.). 150p. 1980. pap. text ed. 6.95 (ISBN 0-8185-0380-7). Brooks-Cole.

Newman, Barbara M. & Newman, Phillip R., eds. Development Through Life: A Case Study Approach. 1976. pap. 9.50x (ISBN 0-256-01779-4). Dorsey.

Newman, Barbara W. & Newman, Philip R. An Introduction to the Psychology of Adolescence. 1979. 17.95x (ISBN 0-256-02188-0). Dorsey.

Newman, Barclay M. A Concise Greek-English Dictionary of the New Testament. 1971. 3.50 (ISBN 3-438-06008-6, 56493). United Bible.

Newman, Benjamin. Forms Manual for the CPA: For Audit, Review, & Compilation of Financial Statements. LC 80-17271. 450p. 1980. 39.95 (ISBN 0-471-05762-2, Pub. by Ronald). Wiley.

Newman, Carol, ed. see Hildebrand, Verna.

Newman, Carole, jt. auth. see Newman, Isadore.

Newman, Charles. A Child's History of America: Some Ribs & Riffs for the Sixties. LC 73-5951. 307p. 1973. 13.95 (ISBN 0-8040-0644-X). Swallow.

--There Must Be More to Love Than Death: Three Novellas. LC 76-17743. 217p. 1976. 11.95 (ISBN 0-8040-0748-9). Swallow.

Newman, Charles, jt. ed. see Appel, Alfred, Jr.

Newman, Charles L. Sourcebook on Probation, Parole & Pardons. 3rd ed. 488p. 1977. 22.75 (ISBN 0-398-01396-9). C C Thomas.

Newman, Claire M., jt. auth. see Fass, Arnold L.

Newman, Daisy. A Procession of Friends. 1980. pap. 10.95 (ISBN 0-913408-59-X). Friends United.

Newman, Danny. Subscribe Now! Building Arts Audiences Through Dynamic Subscription Promotion. LC 77-81452. (Illus.). 1977. text ed. 12.95x (ISBN 0-930452-00-3, Pub. by Theatre Comm); pap. text ed. 7.95x (ISBN 0-930452-01-1). Pub Ctr Cult Res.

--Subscribe Now! Building Arts Audiences Through Dynamic Subscription Promotion. LC 77-81452. (Illus.). 276p. 1977. 12.95x (ISBN 0-930452-00-3, Pub. by Theatre Comm); pap. 7.95x (ISBN 0-930452-01-1). Pub Ctr Cult Res.

Newman, Derek. Organization Design. 1973. 16.50x (ISBN 0-7131-3292-2). Intl Ideas.

Newman, E. The Life of Richard Wagner, 4 vols. 1976. pap. 14.50 ea.; Vol. 1. pap. (ISBN 0-521-08786-4); Vol. 2. pap. (ISBN 0-521-29095-3); Vol. 3. pap. (ISBN 0-521-29096-1); Vol. 4. pap. (ISBN 0-521-29097-X); pap. 44.50 set (ISBN 0-521-29149-6). Cambridge U Pr.

Newman, Edwin. A Civil Tongue. LC 76-11607. 1976. 9.95 (ISBN 0-672-52267-5). Bobbs.

--A Civil Tongue. 1977. pap. 2.75 (ISBN 0-446-95954-5). Warner Bks.

--Edwin Newman on Language: Strictly Speaking & a Civil Tongue. 1980. pap. 6.95 (ISBN 0-446-97459-5). Warner Bks.

--Strictly Speaking. 1975. pap. 2.75 (ISBN 0-446-95945-6). Warner Bks.

--Strictly Speaking: Will America Be the Death of English? LC 74-6525. 224p. 1974. 9.95 (ISBN 0-672-51990-9). Bobbs.

Newman, Ernest. Essays from the World of Music. LC 77-17326. (Music Reprint Ser.: 1978). (Illus.). 1978. Repr. of 1956 ed. lib. bdg. 22.50 (ISBN 0-306-77519-0). Da Capo.

--More Essays from the World of Music. LC 77-17332. (Music Reprint Ser.: 1978). (Illus.). 1978. Repr. of 1958 ed. lib. bdg. 27.50 (ISBN 0-306-77520-4). Da Capo.

--A Musical Motley. LC 76-10332. (Music Reprint Ser.). 1976. lib. bdg. 22.50 (ISBN 0-306-70784-5). Da Capo.

Newman, Ernest, tr. see Schweitzer, Albert.

Newman, Frances. The Hard Boiled Virgin. LC 80-16376. (Brown Thrasher Ser.). 300p. 1980. pap. 5.95 (ISBN 0-8203-0526-X). U of Ga Pr.

Newman, Francis. Phases of Faith. (Victorian Library). 1970. Repr. of 1860 ed. text ed. 5.75x (ISBN 0-391-00109-4, Leicester). Humanities.

Newman, G. B., jt. auth. see Franklin, D. A.

Newman, Georgiana C. & Dawson, Mildred A. Baker's Dozen. rev. ed. (Cornerstone Ser.). (gr. 2-3). 1978. pap. text ed. 4.52 (ISBN 0-201-41024-9, Sch Div); tchr's ed. 5.56 (ISBN 0-201-41025-7). A-W.

Newman, Gerald. The Changing Eskimos. LC 78-15956. (Easy-Read Fact Book). (Illus.). (gr. 2-4). 1979. PLB 6.45 s&l (ISBN 0-531-02271-4). Watts.

--How to Write a Report. (gr. 7 up). 1980. PLB 6.45 (ISBN 0-531-04135-2). Watts.

--Lebanon. (First Bks). (Illus.). (gr. 4-6). 1978. PLB 6.45 s&l (ISBN 0-531-02237-4). Watts.

Newman, Gerry, compiled by. Encyclopedia of Health & the Human Body. (Illus.). (gr. 7 up). 1977. PLB 16.90 s&l (ISBN 0-531-01331-6). Watts.

Newman, Graeme R, ed. Crime & Deviance: A Comparative Perspective. LC 80-11629. (Sage Annual Reviews of Studies in Deviance: Vol. 4). (Illus.). 335p. 1980. 20.00x (ISBN 0-8039-1076-2); pap. 9.95x (ISBN 0-8039-1077-0). Sage.

Newman, Harold. Reading Disabilities: Selections on Identification & Treatment. LC 70-80026. 1969. pap. 11.95 (ISBN 0-672-63098-2). Odyssey Pr.

Newman, Harry R., jt. auth. see Fruchtman, Bernard.

Newman, Isadore & Newman, Carole. Conceptual Statistics for Beginners. LC 79-64100. 1979. pap. text ed. 10.25 (ISBN 0-8191-0752-2). U Pr of Amer.

Newman, J., jt. auth. see Knight, C.

Newman, James. Ecological Basis for Subsistence Change Among the Sandawe of Tanzania. LC 75-607171. (Foreign Field Research Program Ser). (Illus., Orig.). 1970. pap. 11.75 (ISBN 0-309-01851-X). Natl Acad Pr.

Newman, James L., ed. Drought, Famine & Population Movement in Africa. LC 74-25877. (Foreign & Comparative Studies-Eastern African Ser.: No. 17). 144p. 1975. pap. 4.50x (ISBN 0-915984-14-8). Syracuse U Foreign Comp.

Newman, James R., jt. auth. see Nagel, Ernest.

Newman, James W. Release Your Brakes! 1978. pap. 2.95 (ISBN 0-446-93889-0). Warner Bks.

Newman, Joan, ed. see Kulvinskas, Viktoras.

Newman, Joel. Dead Man's Tears. LC 80-27171. 192p. 1981. 9.95 (ISBN 0-8253-0035-5). Beaufort Bks NY.

Newman, John, jt. auth. see Colvin, Howard.

Newman, John H. Discourses Mixed Congregations. 1966. 10.50 o.p. (ISBN 0-87061-029-5). Chr Classics.

--Idea of a University. 1979. pap. 10.50 o.p. (ISBN 0-87061-023-6). Chr Classics.

--The Letters & Diaries of John Henry Newman. Dessain, Charles S. & Dessain, Charles S., eds. Incl. Vol. 11. Littemore to Rome, October 1845 to December 1846. 1961. o.p. (ISBN 0-19-920044-0); Vol. 19. Consulting the Laity, January 1859 to June 1861. 1969. 34.95x (ISBN 0-19-920051-3); Vol. 20. Standing Firm Amid Trials, July 1861 to December 1863. 1970. 34.95x (ISBN 0-19-920052-1); Vol. 21. The Apologia, January 1864 to June 1865. Kelly, Edward E., ed. 1971. 36.00x (ISBN 0-19-920053-X); Vol. 22. Between Pussey & the Extremists, July 1865 to December 1866. 1972. 34.95x (ISBN 0-19-920054-8). Oxford U Pr.

--Loss & Gain: The Story of a Convert, 1848. Wolff, Robert L., ed. Bd. with Callista: A Sketch of the Third Century, 1856. (Victorian Fiction Ser.). 1975. lib. bdg. 66.00 (ISBN 0-8240-1530-4). Garland Pub.

--Meditations & Devotions. 10.50 o.p. (ISBN 0-87061-037-6). Chr Classics.

--Parochial & Plain Sermons, 8 Vols. 1966-1968. Set. 10.50 o.p. (ISBN 0-87061-016-3). Vol. 1 (ISBN 0-87061-008-2). Vol. 2 (ISBN 0-87061-009-0). Vol. 3 (ISBN 0-87061-010-4). Vol. 4 (ISBN 0-87061-011-2). Vol. 5 (ISBN 0-87061-012-0). Vol. 6 (ISBN 0-87061-013-9). Vol. 7 (ISBN 0-87061-014-7). Vol. 8 (ISBN 0-87061-015-5). Chr Classics.

--Sermons on Subjects of the Day. 1968. 10.50 o.p. (ISBN 0-87061-020-1). Chr Classics.

--Sermons Preached on Various Occasions. 1968. 10.50 o.p. (ISBN 0-87061-021-X). Chr Classics.

--The Theological Papers of John Henry Newman: On Biblical Inspiration & on Infallibility. Holmes, J. Derek, ed. 1979. text ed. 19.95x (ISBN 0-19-920081-5). Oxford U Pr.

--The Theological Papers of John Henry Newman: On Faith & Certainty, Vol. 1. Holmes, Derek, ed. 1976. 19.95x (ISBN 0-19-920071-8). Oxford U Pr.

--The Uses of Knowledge: Selections from the Idea of the University. Ward, Leo L., ed. LC 48-8929. (Crofts Classics Ser.). 1948. pap. text ed. 2.75x (ISBN 0-88295-063-0). AHM Pub.

Newman, John Henry Cardinal. Apologia Pro Vita Sua. 1977. pap. 3.50 (ISBN 0-385-12646-8, Im). Doubleday.

Newman, Jon O., jt. auth. see Ribicoff, Abraham.

Newman, Laura. Make Your Juicer Your Drug Store. LC 66-125414. (Illus.). 192p. 1978. pap. 2.50 (ISBN 0-87904-001-7). Lust.

Newman, Lawrence W., ed. The Comprehensive Russian Grammar of A.A. Barsov. lxxxvi, 382p. (Rus. & Eng.). 1980. 24.95 (ISBN 0-89357-072-9). Slavica.

Newman, M. Haskell, et al, eds. Handbook of Ear, Nose & Throat Emergencies. 2nd ed. 1973. spiral bdg. 11.00 (ISBN 0-87488-639-2). Med Exam.

Newman, Mary T., jt. auth. see Grasty, William K.

Newman, Matt & Lemay, Nita K. The Human Reproductive System. (Illus.). (gr. 5-8). 1980. pap. text ed. 88.00 (ISBN 0-89290-101-2, A794-SATC). Soc for Visual.

Newman, Matt H., ed. Goldilocks & the Three Bears. (Children's Stories Bk). (Illus.). 18p. (ps). 1980. pap. 22.00 ten bks & one cass. (ISBN 0-89290-085-7, BC13-2). Soc for Visual.

--Little Red Riding Hood. (Children's Stories Bk). (Illus.). 18p. (ps). 1980. pap. 22.00 ten bks & one cass. (ISBN 0-89290-084-9, BC13-1). Soc for Visual.

--Rumpelstiltskin. (Children's Stories Bk). (Illus.). 18p. (ps). 1980. pap. 22.00 ten bks & one cass. (ISBN 0-89290-086-5, BC13-3). Soc for Visual.

Newman, Maurice S. Financial Accounting Estimates Through Statistical Sampling by Computer. LC 76-23400. (Systems & Controls for Financial Management Ser.). 27.95 (ISBN 0-471-01567-9). Ronald Pr.

Newman, Michael, jt. auth. see Beryl.

Newman, Mike. Dealer's Special. 1979. pap. 2.95 (ISBN 0-89650-672-X, Gambler's Book Shelf). Gamblers.

Newman, Mildred & Berkowitz, Bernard. How to Be Your Own Best Friend. 96p. 1974. pap. 1.95 (ISBN 0-345-28379-1). Ballantine.

Newman, Nate, jt. auth. see Mamula, Richard A.

Newman, Oscar. Community of Interest. (Illus.). 368p. 1981. pap. 8.95 (ISBN 0-385-11124-X, Anch). Doubleday.

--Unmasking of a King. 192p. 1981. 10.95 (ISBN 0-02-588890-0). Macmillan.

Newman, Patty. Do It up Brown. pap. 3.95 (ISBN 0-686-05784-8). Prod Hse.

Newman, Paul. A Grammar of Tera: Transformational Syntax & Texts. (U. C. Publ. in Linguistics: Vol. 57). 1970. pap. 9.50x (ISBN 0-520-09254-6). U of Cal Pr.

--The Hill of the Dragon: An Enquiry into the Nature of Dragon Legends. (Illus.). 275p. 1980. 18.50x (ISBN 0-8476-6228-4). Rowman.

Newman, Paul, ed. Journal of African Languages & Linguistics 1979, Vol. 1, No. 1. 1979. pap. text ed. 14.25x (ISBN 0-686-59702-8). Humanities.

Newman, Paul & Newman, Roxanna M., eds. Modern Hausa-English Dictionary. 168p. 1979. pap. text ed. 6.95x (ISBN 0-19-575303-8). Oxford U Pr.

Newman, Philip R., jt. auth. see Newman, Barbara M.

Newman, Philip R., jt. auth. see Newman, Barbara W.

Newman, Phillip R., jt. ed. see Newman, Barbara M.

Newman, Phyllis, jt. ed. see Davis, John G.

Newman, Phyllis, ed. see Group-Effort.

Newman, R. G. Methadone Treatment in Narcotic Addiction: Program Management,Findings, & Prospects for the Future. 1977. 29.00 (ISBN 0-12-517050-5). Acad Pr.

Newman, Richard. Black Index: Afro-Americana in Selected Periodicals. LC 80-835. (Garland Reference Library of Social Science; Critical Studies in Black Life & Culture). 280p. 1981. 35.00 (ISBN 0-8240-9513-8). Garland Pub.

Newman, Robert. The Boy Who Could Fly. 1976. pap. 1.75 (ISBN 0-686-68377-3, 53306, Camelot). Avon.

--The Case of the Baker Street Irregular. 176p. 1981. pap. 1.75 (ISBN 0-553-14272-0). Bantam.

--The Case of the Somerville Secret. LC 80-18584. 192p. (gr. 4-6). 1981. PLB 9.95 (ISBN 0-689-30825-6). Atheneum.

--The Twelve Labors of Hercules. LC 75-132300. (Hero Tales Ser.). (Illus.). 150p. (gr. 3-5). 1972. 8.95 (ISBN 0-690-83920-0, TYC-J). T Y Crowell.

Newman, Roxanna M., jt. ed. see Newman, Paul.

Newman, Ruby A. Layle Jonathan, of Mountain Springs. 140p. (Orig.). 1981. pap. 3.50 (ISBN 0-932964-07-9). MN Pubs.

--Thorns & Roses. LC 79-92510. 1980. pap. 3.50 (ISBN 0-932964-05-2). MN Pubs.

Newman, S. J. Dickens at Play. 1981. 14.95 (ISBN 0-312-19980-5). St Martin.

Newman, Samuel, ed. see Institute of Internal Auditors, Inc.

Newman, Seymour, jt. ed. see Paul, D. R.

Newman, Sharan. Guinevere. 256p. 1981. 10.95 (ISBN 0-312-35318-9). St Martin.

Newman, Sharon. The Dagda's Harp. LC 76-10559. (YA) 1977. 7.50 o.p. (ISBN 0-312-18200-7). St Martin.

Newman, Sidney H. & Klein, Zanvel E., eds. Behavioral Social Aspects of Contraceptive Sterilization. LC 77-94. 1978. 18.95 (ISBN 0-669-01442-7). Lexington Bks.

Newman, Simon K. March Nineteen Thirty-Nine: A Study in the Continuity of British Foreign Policy. 1976. 36.00x (ISBN 0-19-822532-6). Oxford U Pr.

Newman, Stephen A., ed. Thermodynamics of Aqueous Systems: With Industrial Applications. LC 80-16044. (ACS Symposium Ser.: No. 133). 1980. 58.00 (ISBN 0-8412-0569-8). Am Chemical.

Newman, Steven L. & Christopher, Mark S. Get Oppenheimer! 288p. 1980. 14.95 (ISBN 0-8129-0927-5). Times Bks.
Newman, Vicky, jt. auth. see Cumming, Candy.
Newman, Virginia H. Teaching an Infant to Swim. LC 67-11972. (Illus.). 1967. 5.95 o.p. (ISBN 0-15-188110-3). HarBraceJ.
Newman, W. H. Management of Expanding Enterprise. LC 55-7927. 1955. 20.00x (ISBN 0-231-02102-X). Columbia U Pr.
Newman, William H. Administrative Action: The Techniques of Organization & Management. 2nd ed. 1963. ref. ed. 19.95x (ISBN 0-13-007195-1). P-H.
--Managers for the Year Two Thousand. (Illus.). 1978. ref. ed. 15.95 (ISBN 0-13-549378-1); pap. 8.95 o.p. P-H.
--Process of Management: The Concepts, Behavior & Practice. 4th ed. 1977. pap. 21.00 (ISBN 0-13-723429-5); study guide casebook 7.95 (ISBN 0-13-723411-2). P-H.
Newman, William J. Liberalism & the Retreat from Politics. LC 64-10787. 1964. 5.00 o.s.i. (ISBN 0-8076-0252-3). Braziller.
Newman, William M. Le Domaine Royal Sous les Premiers Capetiens (987-1180) LC 80-2014. 1981. Repr. of 1937 ed. 36.00 (ISBN 0-404-18581-9). AMS Pr.
--The Kings, the Court & Royal Power in France in the Eleventh Century. LC 80-2030. 1981. Repr. of 1929 ed. 24.50 (ISBN 0-404-18582-7). AMS Pr.
Newman, Winifred B. The Secret in the Garden. (Illus.). 32p. (Orig.). (gr. k-5). 1980. 5.00 (ISBN 0-87743-151-5); pap. 2.50 (ISBN 0-87743-159-0). Baha'i.
Newmann, Dana. Teacher's Almanack: Practical Ideas for Every Day of the School Year. 1973. 12.95x o.p. (ISBN 0-87628-797-6). Ctr Appl Res.
Newmann, Fred M. Education for Citizen Action: Challenge for the Secondary Curriculum. LC 74-30963. 250p. 1975. 15.00 (ISBN 0-8211-1305-4); text ed. 14.00 (ISBN 0-685-52139-7). McCutchan.
Newmarch, Rosa. The Music of Czechoslovakia. LC 77-26269. (Music Reprint Ser., 1978). 1978. Repr. of 1942 ed. lib. bdg. 22.50 (ISBN 0-306-77563-8). Da Capo.
Newmark, Charles S., jt. auth. see Faschingbauer, Thomas R.
Newmark, Charles S., ed. MMPI: Clinical & Research Trends. LC 79-17777. (Praeger Special Studies). 464p. 1979. 35.95 (ISBN 0-03-048926-1). Praeger.
Newmark, Leonard, et al. Spoken Albanian, Bk.2. LC 79-56549. 348p. 1980. Bk. 2 & Cassettes. pap. 65.00x (ISBN 0-87950-008-5); pap. 10.00x (ISBN 0-87950-005-0); 6 dual track cassettes 60.00x (ISBN 0-87950-007-7). Spoken Lang Serv.
Newmark, M. & Penry, J. K., eds. Photosensitivity & Epilepsy. 1979. 19.50 (ISBN 0-89004-393-0). Raven.
Newmark, M. E., ed. Genetics of Epilepsy: A Review. Penry, J. K. 1979. 16.00 (ISBN 0-89004-394-9). Raven.
Newmark, Maxim & Kendris, Christopher. French Level Three: Forty Classroom Tests. LC 58-47141. (High School Regents Exams & Answer Ser.). (gr. 9-12). 1977. pap. 3.50 (ISBN 0-8120-0198-2). Barron.
--Spanish Level Three: Forty Classroom Tests. LC 58-31609. (Regents Exams & Answers Ser.). (gr. 9-12). 1977. pap. 3.50 (ISBN 0-8120-0120-6). Barron.
Newmark, Maxim & Walz, Rosemary. How to Prepare for College Board Achievement Tests: German. rev. ed. LC 61-18358. (gr. 11-12). 1980. pap. 4.50 (ISBN 0-8120-0977-0). Barron.
Newmark, N. M. & Rosenblueth, E. Fundamentals of Earthquake Engineering. (Civil Engineering & Engineering Mechanics Ser). (Illus.). 1972. ref. ed. 33.95 (ISBN 0-13-336206-X). P-H.
Newmark, Peter. Approaches to Translation: Aspects of Translation. LC 80-41008. (MFLP Ser.). 160p. 1980. 23.95 (ISBN 0-08-024603-6); pap. 11.95 (ISBN 0-08-024602-8). Pergamon.
Newmyer, Joseph & Klentos, Gus. Intermediate Algebra. LC 74-106504. 1970. text ed. 14.95 (ISBN 0-675-09352-X). Merrill.
Newmyer, Joseph, Jr. & Klentos, Gus. Intermediate Algebra. 2nd ed. Kleinfeld, ed. (Mathematics Ser). (Illus.). 416p. 1975. pap. text ed. 15.95 (ISBN 0-675-08744-9); instructors manual 3.95 (ISBN 0-685-50980-X); audio cassettes 140.00 (ISBN 0-685-50981-8); 2-6 90.00 ea. (ISBN 0-675-08717-1); 7 or more 60.00 (ISBN 0-686-67093-0). Merrill.
Newmyer, Joseph, Jr., jt. auth. see Klentos, Gus.
Newnan, C. Dean. Engineer-in-Training License Review. 8th ed. LC 76-27234. 1976. pap. 11.95 o.p. (ISBN 0-910554-22-6). Eng Pr.
Newnan, Donald G. Engineering Economic Analysis. rev. ed. LC 79-13237. 470p. 1980. text ed. 21.95 (ISBN 0-910554-31-5). Eng Pr.
Newport. Demons, Demons, Demons. LC 78-189503. 4.95 (ISBN 0-8054-5518-3). Broadman.
Newport, M. G., jt. auth. see Robinson, G. E.
Newport, M. Gene. Labor Relations & the Supervisor. LC 68-19343. (Orig.). 1968. text ed. 8.95 (ISBN 0-201-05270-9). A-W.
--The Tools of Managing: Functions, Techniques & Skills. (Illus.). 1972. pap. text ed. 8.95 (ISBN 0-201-05271-7). A-W.
Newport, M. Gene, jt. auth. see Trewatha, Robert L.
Newsom, Barbara, ed. The Art Museum As Educator. 1978. 40.00x (ISBN 0-520-03248-9); pap. 14.95 (ISBN 0-520-03249-7). U of Cal Pr.
Newsom, D. E. The Newspaper: Everything You Need to Know to Make It in the Newspaper Business. (Illus.). 256p. 1981. 19.95 (ISBN 0-13-616045-X, Spectrum); pap. 10.95 (ISBN 0-13-616037-9). P-H.
Newsom, David. David Newsom, the Western Observer, 1805-1882. LC 72-92062. (Illus.). 1972. pap. 7.95 (ISBN 0-87595-040-X). Oreg Hist Soc.
Newsom, Doug & Scott, Alan. This Is PR: The Realities of Public Relations. 1976. text ed. 19.95x (ISBN 0-534-00421-0). Wadsworth Pub.
Newsom, Ed. Brannigan. 208p. (Orig.). 1981. pap. 1.95 (ISBN 0-89083-713-9). Zebra.
Newsom, Robert. Dickens on the Romantic Side of Familiar Things: Bleak House & the Novel Tradition. LC 77-23476. 1977. 20.00x (ISBN 0-231-04244-2). Columbia U Pr.
Newsom, Robert S., jt. auth. see Glick, Rush G.
Newsome, Arden. Cork & Wood Crafts. LC 72-112370. (Illus.). 64p. (gr. k-3). 1971. PLB 7.21 (ISBN 0-87460-229-7). Lion.
Newsome, David. Godliness & Good Learning: Four Studies on a Victorian Ideal. (Illus.). 1961. 10.95 (ISBN 0-7195-1015-5). Transatlantic.
--On the Edge of Paradise: A. C. Benson; the Diarist. LC 80-12747. (Illus.). 416p. 1980. lib. bdg. 25.00x (ISBN 0-226-57742-2). U of Chicago Pr.
Newsome, Walter L. Government Reference Books 78-79: A Biennial Guide to U. S. Government Publications, 6th Biennial Volume. 450p. 1980. lib. bdg. 25.00x (ISBN 0-87287-192-4). Libs Unl.
--New Guide to Popular Government Publications: For Libraries & Home Reference. LC 78-12412. 1978. lib. bdg. 20.00 (ISBN 0-87287-174-6). Libs Unl.
Newson, E. F. Management Science & the Manager: A Casebook. (Illus.). 1980. pap. text ed. 11.95 (ISBN 0-13-549444-3). P-H.
Newson, Elizabeth, jt. auth. see Newson, John.
Newson, John & Newson, Elizabeth. Perspectives on School at Seven Years Old. 1977. text ed. 25.00x (ISBN 0-04-136017-6). Allen Unwin.
--Seven Years Old in the Home Environment. LC 75-17184. 1976. 35.95 (ISBN 0-470-63855-1). Halsted Pr.
Newspaper Enterprise Ass'n. The Ballantine Find-a-Quote Puzzle Book. 128p. (Orig.). 1975. pap. 1.95 o.p. (ISBN 0-345-24543-1). Ballantine.
Newspaper Enterprise Assn., ed. The Ballantine Diagramless Puzzle Book. 128p. (Orig.). 1975. pap. 1.95 o.p. (ISBN 0-345-24542-3). Ballantine.
Newspaper Enterprise Assoc. The World Almanac Guide to Metrics. 1977. pap. 1.75 o.p. (ISBN 0-449-13828-3, GM). Fawcett.
Newspaper Enterprise Inc., ed. World Almanac & Book of Facts, 1980. 1979. 7.95 (ISBN 0-385-15711-8). Doubleday.
Newstead, Martin S., jt. auth. see Coullery, Marie-Therese.
Newstrom, John, jt. auth. see Davis, Keith.
Newsweek Books Editors, ed. see Jefferson, Thomas.
Newth, D. R. & Balls, M., eds. Maternal Effects in Development. LC 78-73812. (British Society for Developmental Biology Symposium: No. 4). (Illus.). 1980. 92.00 (ISBN 0-521-22685-6). Cambridge U Pr.
Newth, D. R. & Usherwood, P. N., eds. Simple Nervous Systems. LC 75-7810. 1975. 47.50x (ISBN 0-8448-0713-3). Crane-Russak Co.
Newton. Motor Vehicle. 10th ed. 1981. text ed. price not set. Butterworth.
Newton, A. Edward. Greatest Book in the World & Other Papers. LC 78-86572. (Essay & General Literature Index Reprint Ser). (Illus.). 1969. Repr. 19.50 (ISBN 0-8046-0579-3). Kennikat.
Newton, Alice S. A Bowl of Remembering. (Illus.). 1980. 5.50 (ISBN 0-8233-0312-8). Golden Quill.
Newton, B. The Generative Interpretation of Dialect: A Study of Modern Greek Phonology. LC 72-187080. (Studies in Linguistics: No. 8). (Illus.). 240p. 1973. 35.00 (ISBN 0-521-08497-0); pap. 11.95x (ISBN 0-521-29062-7). Cambridge U Pr.
Newton, Charles H. The Reasons Why Place Names in Arizona Are So Named. 48p. pap. 1.95 (ISBN 0-915030-25-X). Tecolote Pr.
Newton, D. B. The Land Grabbers. (Johnny Logan Ser.: No. 3). 144p. 1975. pap. 0.95 o.p. (ISBN 0-445-00665-X). Popular Lib.
Newton, David F. Elements of Environmental Health. LC 93-91307. (Public Service Technology Ser.). 362p. 1974. text ed. 16.95 (ISBN 0-675-08832-1). Merrill.
Newton, F. B. & Ender, K. L. Student Development Practices. (Illus.). 348p. 1980. 22.75 (ISBN 0-398-03997-6). C C Thomas.
Newton, Francis. The Jazz Scene. LC 75-4748. (Roots of Jazz Ser). 303p. 1975. Repr. of 1960 ed. lib. bdg. 25.00 (ISBN 0-306-70685-7). Da Capo.
Newton, G. W. Bankruptcy & Insolvency Accounting: Practice & Procedure. 1975. 29.95 (ISBN 0-8260-6715-8). Ronald Pr.
Newton, Gerald. The Netherlands: An Historical & Cultural Survey 1795-1977. LC 77-16100. (Nations of the Modern World Ser.). 1978. lib. bdg. 28.50x (ISBN 0-89158-802-7). Westview.
Newton, Grant W. Bankruptcy & Insolvency Accounting. 2nd ed. 500p. 1981. 29.95 (ISBN 0-471-07992-8). Ronald Pr.
--Certificate in Management Accounting Review, 6 vols. 1979. scp package set 89.50 (ISBN 0-06-453735-8, HarpC). Har-Row.
--CMA, 6 vols. Incl. Vol. 1. Economics & Business. 177p. pap. text ed. 18.50 scp (ISBN 0-06-453723-4); Vol. 2. Organization & Behavior, Including Ethical Considerations. 123p. pap. text ed. 14.95 scp (ISBN 0-06-453729-3); Vol. 3. Public Reporting Standards & Auditing. 201p. pap. text ed. 18.50 scp (ISBN 0-06-453730-7); Vol. 4. Periodic Reporting for Internal & External Purposes. 260p. pap. text ed. 18.50 scp (ISBN 0-06-453731-5); Vol. 5. Decision Analysis, Including Modeling & Information Systems. 246p. pap. text ed. 19.50 scp (ISBN 0-06-453732-3); Vol. 6. Taxes Current Pronouncements, & Updated CMA Questions. 1980. pap. text ed. 18.50 scp (ISBN 0-06-453742-0). pap. (HarpC). Har-Row.
Newton, Harry. The Escalating Corporate Telephone Bill: Remedies & Opportunities. 1980. 25.00 (ISBN 0-686-12129-5). Telecom Lib.
--Professional Managemant Via Telecommunications. 1980. softcover 7.50 (ISBN 0-936648-03-1). Telecom Lib.
Newton, Isaac. Correspondence of Isaac Newton, 4 vols. Turnbull, H. W. & Scott, J. F., eds. 1961. 72.50 ea.; Vol. 1. (ISBN 0-521-05812-0); Vol. 2. (ISBN 0-521-05813-9); Vol. 3. (ISBN 0-521-05814-7); Vol. 4. (ISBN 0-521-05815-5). Cambridge U Pr.
--The Correspondence, Seventeen Hundred Nine to Seventeen Thirteen, Vol. 5. Hall, A. R. & Tilling, Laura, eds. 1975. 95.00 (ISBN 0-521-08721-X). Cambridge U Pr.
--The Correspondence, 1713-1718, Vols. 6 & 7. Hall, A. R. & Tilling, Laura, eds. (Correspondence of Isaac Newton Ser.). (Illus.). 500p. 1976. Vol. 6. 95.00 ea. (ISBN 0-521-08722-8). Vol. 7 (ISBN 0-521-08723-6). Cambridge U Pr.
--Mathematical Papers of Isaac Newton, Vol. 5. Whiteside, D. T., et al, eds. LC 65-11203. (Illus.). 600p. 1972. 150.00 (ISBN 0-521-08262-5). Cambridge U Pr.
--Mathematical Papers of Isaac Newton, Vol. 1, 1664-1666. Whiteside, D. T. & Hoskin, M. A., eds. 150.00 (ISBN 0-521-05817-1). Cambridge U Pr.
--Mathematical Papers of Isaac Newton, Vol. 3, 1670-1673. Whiteside, D. T. & Hoskin, M. A., eds. LC 65-11203. (Illus.). 150.00 (ISBN 0-521-07119-4). Cambridge U Pr.
--Mathematical Papers of Isaac Newton, Vol. 6: 1684-1691. Whiteside, D. T. & Hoskin, M. A., eds. LC 73-86046. (Illus.). 6000p. 1975. 150.00 (ISBN 0-521-08719-8). Cambridge U Pr.
--The Mathematical Papers of Isaac Newton: Vol. 8, 1697-1722. Whiteside, D. T., ed. LC 65-11203. (Illus.). 750p. Date not set. price not set (ISBN 0-521-20103-9). Cambridge U Pr.
--Optics. 1952. pap. text ed. 5.50 (ISBN 0-486-60205-2). Dover.
Newton, Sir Isaac. Mathematical Principles of Natural Philosophy and His System of the World. (Principia) Cajori, Florian, rev. by. Motte, Andrew, tr. Incl. Vol. I. The Motions of Bodies. pap. 5.95x (ISBN 0-520-00928-2, CAMPUS70); Vol. II. The System of the World. pap. 5.95 (ISBN 0-520-00929-0, CAMPUS71). 1962. Set. pap. 5.95x (ISBN 0-520-00927-4). U of Cal Pr.
Newton, J. R., et al. Workshop on Fertility Control. (Royal Society of Medicine International Congress & Symposium Ser.: No. 31). 1980. 17.50 (ISBN 0-8089-1297-6). Grune.
Newton, James R. The March of the Lemmings. LC 75-42491. (A Lets-Read-&-Find-Out Bk). (Illus.). 40p. (gr. k-3). 1976. PLB 7.89 (ISBN 0-690-01085-0, TYC-J). T Y Crowell.
Newton, Jan, jt. auth. see Young, John.
Newton, John. Letters of John Newton. 1976. pap. 2.45 (ISBN 0-85151-120-1). Banner of Truth.
--Out of the Depths. (Shepherd Illustrated Classics). (Illus.). 144p. 1981. pap. 5.95 (ISBN 0-87983-243-6). Keats.
Newton, K. M. George Eliot: Romantic Humanist--A Study of the Philosophical Structure of Her Novels. 215p. 1981. 26.50x (ISBN 0-389-20081-6). B&N.
Newton, Kathleen & Looney, Gerald. Doctor Discussses Making the Mid-Years the Prime of Life. (Illus.). 1978. pap. 2.50 (ISBN 0-685-46333-8). Budlong.
Newton, Kenneth. Second City Politics: Democratic Processes & Decision-Making in Birmingham. (Illus.). 1976. pap. 22.50x (ISBN 0-19-827197-2). Oxford U Pr.
Newton, Michael. Chemicals in the Forest. 160p. 1980. pap. 10.95 (ISBN 0-917304-25-X, Pub. by Timber Pr). Intl Schol Bk Serv.
--Handbook of Weed & Insect Control Chemicals for Forest Resource Management. 160p. 1980. pap. 24.95x (ISBN 0-917304-25-X, Pub. by Timber Pr). Intl Schol Bk Serv.
Newton, Norman. Thomas Gage in Spanish America. (Great Travellers Ser.). (Illus.). 1969. 4.95 o.p. (ISBN 0-571-08799-X, Pub. by Faber & Faber). Merrimack Bk Serv.
Newton, R., jt. auth. see Jenkins, G. Curtis.
Newton, Robert. Moon's Acceleration & Its Physical Origins: Vol. 1, As Deduced from Solar Eclipses. LC 78-2059. 1979. 32.50x (ISBN 0-8018-2216-5). Johns Hopkins.
--Panzer Fort. (Orig.). 1980. pap. 1.95. Manor Bks.
Newton, Robert R. Ancient Astronomical Observations & the Accelerations of the Earth & Moon. LC 70-122011. (Illus.). 309p. 1970. 19.50x o.p. (ISBN 0-8018-1180-5). Johns Hopkins.
--Medieval Chronicles & the Rotation of the Earth. LC 78-39780. 848p. 1972. 30.00x o.p. (ISBN 0-8018-1402-2). Johns Hopkins.
Newton, Roger G. Scattering Theory of Waves & Particles. 1966. text ed. 29.95 o.p. (ISBN 0-07-046409-X, C). McGraw.
Newton, Stella M. Fashion in the Age of the Black Prince: A Study of the Years 1340-1365. (Illus.). 151p. 1980. 37.50x (ISBN 0-8476-6939-4). Rowman.
--Renaissance Theatre Costume. (Illus.). 1975. 29.95 (ISBN 0-87830-108-9). Theatre Arts.
Newton, Thomas H. Radiology of the Skull & Brain, Vol. 5: Technical Aspects of Computed Tomography. (Illus.). 616p. 1980. text ed. 79.50 (ISBN 0-8016-3662-0). Mosby.
Newton, Thomas H. & Potts, D. Gordon. Radiology of the Skull & Brain: Angiography, 4 pts, Vol. 2. LC 74-12407. 1974. text ed. 285.00 set (ISBN 0-8016-3647-7); text ed. 99.75 ea. part; Pt. 1. (ISBN 0-8016-3641-8); Pt. 2. (ISBN 0-8016-3642-6); Pt. 3. (ISBN 0-8016-3644-2); Pt. 4. (ISBN 0-8016-3649-3). Mosby.
Newton, Thomas H. & Potts, Gordon. Ventricles & Cisterns: Radiology of the Skull & Brain, Vol. 4. LC 78-173600. 1978. text ed. 67.50 (ISBN 0-8016-3661-2). Mosby.
Newton, Thomas H. & Potts, D. Gordon, eds. Radiology of the Skull & Brain: Anatomy & Pathology, Vol. III. LC 78-173600. 1977. 60.00 (ISBN 0-8016-3648-5). Mosby.
Newton, Trevor. Cost-Benefit Analysis in Administration. (Royal Institute of Public Administration). 1972. text ed. 21.00x o.p. (ISBN 0-04-336043-2). Allen Unwin.
Newton, Violette. The Proxy. 4.50 o.p. (ISBN 0-685-48832-2). Nortex Pr.
Newton, William E. & Otsuka, Sei, eds. Molybdenum Chemistry of Biological Significance. 435p. 1980. 39.50 (ISBN 0-306-40352-8, Plenum Pr). Plenum Pub.
Newton, William R., ed. see Arnold, John.
Newton, William R., ed. see Kitzing, Donald.
Newton, William R., ed. see Myers, M. Scott.
Newton, William R., ed. see Zand, Dale.
Newton, William T. & Donati, Robert M. Radioassay in Clinical Medicine. (Illus.). 200p. 1974. 16.50 (ISBN 0-398-03012-X). C C Thomas.
Newton-De Molina, David, ed. The Literary Criticism of T. S. Eliot: New Essays. 1977. text ed. 26.00x (ISBN 0-485-11167-5, Athlone Pr). Humanities.
Neyman, Jerzy & Pearson, E. S. The Selected Papers of Jerzy Neyman & E. S. Pearson, 3 vols. Incl. Vol. 1. The Selected Papers of E. S. Pearson. 1966. 17.00 o.p. (ISBN 0-520-00990-8); Vol. 2. Joint Statistical Papers. 1967. 25.00x (ISBN 0-520-00991-6); Vol. 3. A Selection of Early Statistical Papers of J. Neyman. 1967. 28.50x (ISBN 0-520-00992-4). U of Cal Pr.

NFL Public Relations Dept. NFL Nineteen Eighty-One Media Information Book. (Illus.). 130p. 1981. pap. 7.95 (ISBN 0-89480-148-1). Workman Pub.

Ng, David & Thomas, Virginia. Children in the Worshipping Community. LC 80-84653. (Illus.). 128p. (Orig.). 1981. pap. 6.50 (ISBN 0-8042-1688-6). John Knox.

Ng, Kung-Fu, jt. auth. see Wong, Yau-Chuen.

Ng, Lorenz K. & Davis, Devra, eds. Strategies for Public Health: Promoting Health & Preventing Disease. 384p. 1980. text ed. 21.95 (ISBN 0-442-24428-2). Van Nos Reinhold.

Ng, Yew-Kwang. Welfare Economics: Introduction & Development of Basic Concepts. LC 79-22797. 332p. 1980. text ed. 24.95x (ISBN 0-470-26886-7). Halsted Pr.

Ngafua, Zizwe. Nommo (the Word) (Illus.). 56p. (Orig.). 1978. pap. 4.00 (ISBN 0-917886-04-6). Shamal Bks.

Ngcobo, Lauretta J. Crown of Gold. (Sun-Lit Ser.). 250p. (Orig.). 1981. 10.00x (ISBN 0-89410-170-6); pap. 6.00x (ISBN 0-89410-171-4). Three Continents.

Ngo, Bach & Zimmerman, Gloria. Classic Cuisine of Vietnam. LC 79-20323. (Illus.). 1979. 17.95 (ISBN 0-8120-5309-5). Barron.

Nguyen-Dinh-Hoa. Easy Vietnamese. rev. ed. LC 66-17558. (Orig.). (gr. 7 up). 1966. pap. 3.75 (ISBN 0-8048-0160-6). C E Tuttle.

Nguyen Dinh-Hoa. Colloquial Vietnamese. rev ed. LC 74-5132. 400p. 1974. text ed. 14.95x (ISBN 0-8093-0685-9); pap. text ed. 10.95x (ISBN 0-8093-0686-7). S Ill U Pr.

Nguyen-Dinh-Hoa. English Phrase Book for Vietnamese Speakers: Useful & Practical Phrases & Expressions Needed by Vietnamese. LC 75-34842. 1975. pap. 3.25 (ISBN 0-8048-1193-8). C E Tuttle.

--Read Vietnamese. LC 66-18965. 189p. 1980. pap. 9.50 (ISBN 0-8048-1355-8). C E Tuttle.

--Speak Vietnamese. LC 66-17774. 381p. 1980. pap. 12.50 (ISBN 0-8048-1356-6). C E Tuttle.

Nguyen Hy Quang. English-Vietnamese Phrase Book with Useful Word List: For Vietnamese Speakers. LC 75-24856. (Vietnamese Refugee Education Ser.: No. 1). 1975. pap. text ed. 4.00x (ISBN 0-87281-043-7). Ctr Appl Ling.

Nguyen-The-Ank. Bibliographie Critique Sur les Relations Entre le Viet-Nam et l'Occident: Ouvrages et Articles En Langues Occidentales. (Illus.). 310p. 1970. 18.00x o.p. (ISBN 0-8002-0693-2). Intl Pubns Serv.

Niall, Ian see Scowen, Kenneth.

Nias, David, jt. auth. see Wilson, Glenn.

Niatum, Duane. Songs for the Harvester of Dreams. LC 80-50864. 64p. 1980. 7.95 (ISBN 0-295-95758-1). U of Wash Pr.

Niblett, Brian, ed. Computer Science & Law. LC 80-40071. 256p. 1980. 32.95 (ISBN 0-521-23451-4). Cambridge U Pr.

Niblett, R., ed. The Sciences, the Humanities, & the Technological Threat. LC 74-11838. 1975. 18.95 (ISBN 0-470-63655-6). Halsted Pr.

Niblett, Rosalind, jt. auth. see Ferri, Elsa.

Niblett, W. R. Education & the Modern Mind. (Orig.). 1967. pap. 4.50 (ISBN 0-686-24604-7, Pub. by Faber & Faber). Merrimack Bk Serv.

--Moral Education in a Changing Society. (Orig.). 1970. pap. 3.95 (ISBN 0-571-09411-2, Pub. by Faber & Faber). Merrimack Bk Serv.

Niblett, W. R., et al. The University Connection. (General Ser). 300p. (Orig.). 1975. pap. text ed. 20.75x (ISBN 0-85633-064-7, NFER). Humanities.

Niblett, W. Roy, ed. Higher Education: Demand & Response. LC 71-110637. (Higher Education Ser.). 1970. 14.95x o.p. (ISBN 0-87589-064-4). Jossey-Bass.

Niblett, W. Roy & Butts, R. Freeman, eds. Universities Facing the Future: An International Perspective. LC 70-186577. (Higher Education Ser.). 1972. 16.95x o.p. (ISBN 0-87589-133-0). Jossey-Bass.

Nibley, Hugh C. Since Cumorah. 7.95 o.p. (ISBN 0-87747-240-8). Deseret Bk.

Niblock, Margaret. The Afghan Hound: A Definitive Study. LC 79-57391. (Illus.). 448p. 1980. 49.95 (ISBN 0-668-04934-0, 4934-0). Arco.

Niccolai, Giulia, tr. see Higgins, Dick.

Niccoli, Ria. How to Raise & Train a Pembroke Welsh Corgi. (Illus.). pap. 2.00 (ISBN 0-87666-349-8, DS1106). TFH Pubns.

Nice, Robert L. Van see Van Nice, Robert L.

Nice, Stephen D., jt. auth. see Hunter, Edna.

Nicely, Tom. Adam & His Work: A Bibliography of Sources by & About Paul Goodman (Nineteen Eleven to Nineteen Seventy-Two) LC 79-11662. (Scarecrow Author Bibliographies: No. 42). 362p. 1979. 19.00 (ISBN 0-8108-1219-3). Scarecrow.

Nichol, tr. see Durer, Albrecht.

Nichol, B. P. Translating Translating Apollinaire. 1979. pap. 4.00 (ISBN 0-87924-031-8). Membrane Pr.

Nichol, Gladys. Malaysia & Singapore. (Batsford Travel Ser.). (Illus.). 1978. 12.95 o.s.i. (ISBN 0-7134-0839-1). Hippocrene Bks.

Nichol, Lawrence, jt. auth. see Frieden, Carl.

Nichol, R. T., tr. see Durer, Albrecht.

Nicholas, jt. auth. see Will.

Nicholas, Anna K. & Brearley, Joan M. The Book of the Pekingese. (Illus.). 352p. 1975. 12.95 (ISBN 0-87666-348-X, H-953). TFH Pubns.

Nicholas, B., ed. see Jolowicz, H. F.

Nicholas, Charles. The Elephant Book. (Illus.). 24p. (gr. k-1). 1976. PLB 5.38 (ISBN 0-307-68980-8, Golden Pr). Western Pub.

Nicholas, Charles, illus. Star Wars. (Contemporary Motivators Ser.). (Illus.). (gr. 4-12). 1978. pap. text ed. 1.25 o.p. (ISBN 0-88301-307-X); spirit masters 15.00 o.p. (ISBN 0-685-90747-3). Pendulum Pr.

Nicholas, David. The Middle East: Its Oil, Economics, & Investment Policies: A Guide to Sources of Financial Information. LC 80-28555. xxiv, 201p. 1981. lib. bdg. 40.00 (ISBN 0-313-22986-4, NME/). Greenwood.

Nicholas, H. G. The Nature of American Politics. 142p. 1980. 12.95 (ISBN 0-19-219121-7). Oxford U Pr.

--The United Nations As a Political Institution. 5th ed. 270p. 1975. pap. 5.95 (ISBN 0-19-519826-3, 105, GB). Oxford U Pr.

Nicholas, H. G., ed. Dispatches from Washington, 1941 to 1945: Weekly Political Reports from the British Embassy. 748p. 1981. 40.00 (ISBN 0-226-58004-0). U of Chicago Pr.

Nicholas, J. E. Chemical Kinetics: A Modern Survey of Gas Reactions. LC 75-17433. 1976. 24.95 (ISBN 0-470-63686-6). Halsted Pr.

Nicholas, J. Karl. Writing & Revising: A Workbook. 250p. 1981. pap. 7.95 (ISBN 0-13-971499-5). P-H.

Nicholas, J. W. Psience: A General Theory of Existence. LC 77-11135. pap. 3.95 (ISBN 0-915520-09-5). Ross-Erikson.

Nicholas, Jeanne L., jt. auth. see Mc Dermott, Irene E.

Nicholas, Leslie. Sexually Transmitted Diseases. (Illus.). 264p. 1973. 19.75 (ISBN 0-398-02697-1). C C Thomas.

Nicholas, Robert L., jt. auth. see Neale-Silva, Eduardo.

Nicholas, Susan C., et al. Rights & Wrongs: Women's Struggle for Legal Equality. (Women's Lives-Women's Work Ser). (Illus.). 1979. pap. 3.95 (ISBN 0-912670-58-4, Co-Pub. by McGraw). Feminist Pr.

Nicholas, Ted. The Complete Book of Corporate Forms. LC 80-67502. 1980. 49.95 (ISBN 0-913864-54-4). Enterprise Del.

--How to Get Out If You're in Over Your Head. LC 75-45878. 1977. 12.95 o.p. (ISBN 0-913864-22-6). Enterprise Del.

--How to Get Out of Debt. (Illus.). 146p. 1980. 14.95 (ISBN 0-913864-60-9). Enterprise Del.

--How to Self-Publish Your Own Book & Make It a Best Seller. 2nd ed. LC 75-33601. 1976. 14.95 o.p. (ISBN 0-913864-11-0). Enterprise Del.

--The Ted Nicholas Small Business Course. 500p. (Orig.). 1981. pap. 14.95 (ISBN 0-913864-65-X). Enterprise Del.

Nicholas, Tim & Touchton, Ken. More Than Just Talk. Furlow, Elaine S., ed. (Human Touch Photo-Text Ser.). (Illus.). 1977. 6.95g (ISBN 0-937170-16-X). Home Mission.

Nicholas, Tracy. Rastafari: A Way of Life. LC 77-76285. (Illus.). 1979. pap. 7.95 (ISBN 0-385-11575-X, Anch). Doubleday.

Nicholas, Warwick L. The Biology of Free-Living Nematodes. (Illus.). 224p. 1975. 42.00x (ISBN 0-19-854379-4). Oxford U Pr.

Nicholds, Elizabeth. In-Service Casework Training. LC 65-20775. 1966. 20.00x (ISBN 0-231-02741-9). Columbia U Pr.

--Primer of Social Casework. LC 60-12810. 1960. 17.50x (ISBN 0-231-02406-1). Columbia U Pr.

Nicholes, Paul S., jt. auth. see Gebhardt, Louis P.

Nicholl, Ann, jt. auth. see Hudson, Kenneth.

Nicholl, David S. Advertising. 2nd ed. LC 74-152834. (Illus.). 196p. 1978. 13.50x (ISBN 0-7121-0166-7). Intl Pubns Serv.

Nicholls, Andrew. Clocks in Color. LC 75-17890. (Illus.). 176p. 1976. 6.95 o.s.i. (ISBN 0-02-589460-9, 58946). Macmillan.

Nicholls, Audrey & Nicholls, Howard. Creative Teaching. (Unwin Education Books). 1975. text ed. 13.50x (ISBN 0-04-371039-5); pap. text ed. 6.95x (ISBN 0-04-371040-9). Allen Unwin.

Nicholls, D. The Chemistry of Iron, Cobalt & Nickel. (Pergamon Texts in Inorganic Chemistry: Vol. 24). 184p. 1975. text ed. 32.00 (ISBN 0-08-018874-5); pap. text ed. 17.50 (ISBN 0-08-018873-7). Pergamon.

Nicholls, David. From Dessalines to Duvalier: Race, Colour & National Independence in Haiti. LC 78-56817. (Cambridge Latin American Studies: No. 34). 1979. 39.95 (ISBN 0-521-22177-3). Cambridge U Pr.

Nicholls, Howard, jt. auth. see Nicholls, Audrey.

Nicholls, John E. Structure & Design of Programming Languages. LC 74-12801. (IBM Systems Programming). (Illus.). 592p. 1975. text ed. 21.95 (ISBN 0-201-14454-9). A-W.

Nicholls, John G., jt. auth. see Kuffler, Stephen W.

Nicholls, R. W., jt. auth. see Armstrong, B. H.

Nicholls, Richard. Beginning Hydroponics. 224p. 1979. pap. 1.95 o.p. (ISBN 0-441-05340-8). Charter Bks.

Nichols & Pachard. Maine One Hundred Years Ago. (Sun Historical Ser.). (Illus.). pap. 3.50 (ISBN 0-89540-049-9). Sun Pub.

Nichols & Woolson. Old Florida. (Sun Historical Ser.). (Illus.). pap. 3.50 (ISBN 0-89540-054-5). Sun Pub.

Nichols, Aidan. The Art of God Incarnate: Theology & Image in Christian Tradition. LC 80-81443. 192p. 1980. pap. 7.95 (ISBN 0-8091-2300-2). Paulist Pr.

Nichols, Bill, ed. Movies & Methods. LC 74-22968. 1977. 32.50x (ISBN 0-520-02890-2); pap. 8.95 (ISBN 0-520-03151-2, CAL 339). U of Cal Pr.

Nichols, C. Maynard, ed. Webster's New World Crossword Treasury, Vols. 2-3. 1972. pap. 2.50 ea. o.s.i. (TYC-T); Vol. 2. pap. (ISBN 0-690-00374-9); Vol. 3. pap. (ISBN 0-690-00375-7). T Y Crowell.

Nichols, C. William. Shake up Your Faith. 1978. pap. 2.95 (ISBN 0-8272-3416-3). Bethany Pr.

Nichols, Carol & Derven, Ronald. How to Cut Your Energy Bills. LC 76-28727. (Illus.). 1976. 12.00 o.p. (ISBN 0-912336-28-5); pap. 5.95 o.p. (ISBN 0-912336-29-3). Structures Pub.

Nichols, Carol, jt. auth. see Derven, Ronald.

Nichols, Charles H., ed. Arna Bontemps-Langston Hughes Letters (1925-1967) LC 79-17341. 1980. 17.95 (ISBN 0-396-07687-4). Dodd.

Nichols, David. Echinoderms. (Orig.). 1966. text ed. 5.25x (ISBN 0-09-065994-5, Hutchinson U Lib); pap. text ed. 5.00x (ISBN 0-09-065993-7, Hutchinson U Lib). Humanities.

Nichols, David, ed. Monitoring the Marine Environment. LC 78-71806. 220p. 1979. 27.95 (ISBN 0-03-050746-4). Praeger.

Nichols, David, et al. Motor Activities for the Underachiever. (Illus.). 150p. 1980. 13.75 (ISBN 0-398-04090-7). C C Thomas.

Nichols, E. & Jocelyn, S. Selection of Data Communications Equipment. (Illus.). 239p. (Orig.). 1979. pap. 37.50x (ISBN 0-85012-217-1). Intl Pubns Serv.

Nichols, Frederick D. & Bear, James A., Jr. Monticello: A Guide Book. (Orig.). 1967. pap. 2.95x (ISBN 0-8139-0329-7). U Pr of Va.

Nichols, Frederick D. & Griswold, Ralph E. Thomas Jefferson, Landscape Architect. LC 77-10601. (Illus.). ix, 196p. 1981. pap. 4.95x (ISBN 0-8139-0899-X). U Pr of Va.

--Thomas Jefferson Landscape Architect. LC 77-10601. (Illus.). 1977. 10.95x (ISBN 0-8139-0603-2). U Pr of Va.

Nichols, Frederick D; see O'Neal, William B.

Nichols, Frederick D., ed. Thomas Jefferson's Architectural Drawings. 2nd ed. LC 76-163982. (Orig.). 1961. pap. 2.95 (ISBN 0-8139-0328-9). U Pr of Va.

Nichols, Gerald E. Programmed Cost Accounting: A Participative Approach. 1973. text ed. 18.95 (ISBN 0-256-01446-9). Irwin.

Nichols, Geraldine C. Miguel Hernandez. (World Authors Ser.: No. 464). 1978. lib. bdg. 12.50 (ISBN 0-8057-6301-5). Twayne.

Nichols, Harold. The Work of the Deacon & Deaconess. (Orig.). pap. 2.95 (ISBN 0-8170-0328-2). Judson.

Nichols, Herbert L., Jr. Heavy Equipment Repair. LC 64-22821. (Illus.). 1964. 15.00 o.p. (ISBN 0-911040-06-4). North Castle.

Nichols, J. G. The Poetry of Ben Jonson. 1969. 18.00x (ISBN 0-7100-6448-9). Routledge & Kegan.

Nichols, Jack. Men's Liberation: A New Definition of Masculinity. (Orig.). 1975. pap. 3.95 (ISBN 0-14-004036-6). Penguin.

Nichols, James H. History of Christianity, 1650-1950: Secularization of the West. 1956. 17.50 o.p. (ISBN 0-8260-6725-5). Wiley.

Nichols, James L. Confederate Quartermaster in the Trans-Mississippi. 1964. 9.95 (ISBN 0-292-73198-1). U of Tex Pr.

Nichols, John Treadwell. The Milagro Beanfield War. 652p. 1976. pap. 3.50 (ISBN 0-345-29533-1). Ballantine.

Nichols, Joseph C., et al. Z-Eighty Microprocessor Programming & Interfacing, 2 bks. LC 79-63822. 1979. Bk. 1. pap. 11.95 (ISBN 0-672-21609-4); Bk. 2. pap. 14.95 (ISBN 0-672-21610-8, 21610); Set. pap. 24.95 (ISBN 0-672-21611-6). Sams.

Nichols, K. G. Microprocessors: Theory & Practice. (Computer Systems Engineering Ser.). 1981. text ed. price not set (ISBN 0-8448-1384-2). Crane-Russak Co.

Nichols, Lawrence T., jt. auth. see Alper, Benedict S.

Nichols, Lew, jt. auth. see Proulx, Annie.

Nichols, Marion. Encyclopedia of Embroidery Stitches, Including Crewel. LC 72-97816. (Illus.). 224p. (Orig.). 1974. pap. 5.95 (ISBN 0-486-22929-7). Dover.

Nichols, Maynard. Webster's New World Crossword Treasury, Vol. 1. LC 75-13672. (Funk & W Bk.). 1974. pap. 2.50 o.s.i. (ISBN 0-308-10216-9, TYC-T). T Y Crowell.

--Webster's New World Crossword Treasury, Vol. 4. LC 75-785. (Funk & W Bk.). 64p. 1974. pap. 2.50 o.s.i. (ISBN 0-308-10106-5, F89, TYC-T). T Y Crowell.

Nichols, Mel. Ferrari Berlinetta Boxer. (Autohistory Ser.). (Illus.). 1979. 12.95 (ISBN 0-85045-326-7, Pub. by Osprey Pubns. England). Motorbooks Intl.

Nichols, Mosezelle, ed. see John, Yvonne A.

Nichols, Nell B., jt. auth. see Farm Journal, Editors Of.

Nichols, P. J. Rehabilitation Medicine. 2nd ed. LC 79-42891. 1980. text ed. 39.95 (ISBN 0-407-00175-1). Butterworths.

Nichols, Paul L. & Chen, Ta-Chuan. Minimal Brain Dysfunction: A Prospective Study. LC 80-18739. 356p. 1981. text ed. 24.95 (ISBN 0-89859-074-4). L Erlbaum Assocs.

Nichols, Peter. Born in the Gardens. 1980. pap. 6.95 (ISBN 0-571-11476-8, Pub. by Faber & Faber). Merrimack Bk Serv.

--Chez Nous: A Domestic Comedy in Two Acts. 1974. 8.50 (ISBN 0-571-10583-1, Pub. by Faber & Faber); pap. 4.95 (ISBN 0-571-10602-1). Merrimack Bk Serv.

--Forget-Me-Not Lane. 1971. 8.95 (ISBN 0-571-09855-X, Pub. by Faber & Faber); pap. 5.50 (ISBN 0-571-09857-6). Merrimack Bk Serv.

--The Freeway. 1975. pap. 4.95 (ISBN 0-571-10744-3, Pub. by Faber & Faber). Merrimack Bk Serv.

Nichols, Phyllis. A Thousand Errors. (Orig.). 1980. pap. 1.95 (ISBN 0-532-23121-X). Manor Bks.

Nichols, R. & McLeish, K. Through Roman Eyes. LC 75-10043. (Illus.). 128p. 1976. 18.95 (ISBN 0-521-20345-7); pap. 6.95 (ISBN 0-521-20944-7). Cambridge U Pr.

Nichols, R. & Nichols, S. Greek Everyday Life. (Aspects of Greek Life Ser.). (Illus.). 1978. pap. text ed. 2.95x (ISBN 0-582-20672-3). Longman.

Nichols, R. & McLeish, K., eds. Through Greek Eyes. LC 74-80353. (Illus.). 144p. (gr. 7-12). 1975. 17.95 (ISBN 0-521-20632-4); pap. 6.50 (ISBN 0-521-08560-8). Cambridge U Pr.

Nichols, R. Eugene. Picture Yourself a Winner. 1978. pap. 4.95 (ISBN 0-87707-206-X). CSA Pr.

Nichols, R. W., ed. Acoustic Emission. (Illus.). 1976. text ed. 33.60x (ISBN 0-85334-681-X, Pub. by Applied Science). Burgess-Intl Ideas.

--Developments in Pressure Vessel Technology: Materials & Fabrication, No. 3. (Illus.). xii, 364p. 1981. 68.00x (ISBN 0-686-69032-X). Intl Ideas.

--Developments in Pressure Vessel Technology Vol. 1: Flaw Analysis. (Illus.). 1979. 46.70x (ISBN 0-85334-802-2, Pub. by Applied Science). Burgess-Intl Ideas.

--Developments in Pressure Vessel Technology, Vol. 2: Inspection & Testing. (Illus.). 1979. 37.50x (ISBN 0-85334-806-5, Pub. by Applied Science). Burgess-Intl Ideas.

--Developments in Stress Analysis for Pressured Components. (Illus.). 1977. 49.70x (ISBN 0-85334-724-7, Pub. by Applied Science). Burgess-Intl Ideas.

--Non-Destructive Examination in Relation to Structural Integrity. (Illus.). x, 286p. 1980. 60.00x (ISBN 0-85334-908-8). Burgess-Intl Ideas.

--Pressure Vessel Engineering Technology. (Illus.). 1970. 89.50x (ISBN 0-444-20061-4). Intl Ideas.

Nichols, Rodney W., jt. auth. see Seitz, Frederick.

Nichols, Roger. Debussy. (Oxford Studies of Composers Ser: No. 10). (Illus.). 86p. 1973. pap. 7.95x (ISBN 0-19-315426-9). Oxford U Pr.

Nichols, Roger & Halley, Patrick L. Stephen Long & America Frontier Expedition. LC 78-68878. (Illus.). 280p. 1980. 19.50 (ISBN 0-87413-149-9). U Delaware Pr.

Nichols, Roger L. The American Indian: Past & Present. 2nd ed. LC 80-20436. 283p. 1980. text ed. 9.95 (ISBN 0-471-06321-5). Wiley.

Nichols, Roy, jt. auth. see Corley, Monte.

Nichols, Roy F. Franklin Pierce. LC 58-7750. 1964. 12.50x o.p. (ISBN 0-8122-7044-4). U of Pa Pr.

Nichols, Roy F., ed. Battles & Leaders of the Civil War, 4 vols. Incl. Vol. 1. From Sumter to Shiloh; Vol. 2. North to Antientam. 5.95 o.p. (ISBN 0-686-66596-1); Vol. 3. Retreat from Gettysburg; Vol. 4. Way to Appomatox. 1957. boxed set 50.00 o.p. (ISBN 0-498-07014-X, Yoseloff). A S Barnes.

Nichols, S., jt. auth. see Nichols, R.

Nichols, Sallie. Jung & Tarot: An Archetypal Journey. 1980. 25.00 (ISBN 0-87728-480-6); pap. 9.95 (ISBN 0-87728-515-2). Weiser.

Nichols, Sally. Do You Not See: Sixteen Chinese Poems. LC 79-3833. (Illus., Orig.). 1980. pap. 6.95 (ISBN 0-06-090772-X, CN 772, CN). Har-Row.

Nichols, Sarah. Fleur. (The Wyndham Saga: No. 3). 1977. pap. 1.50 o.p. (ISBN 0-445-03216-2). Popular Lib.

--Grave's Company. 256p. (Orig.). 1975. pap. 1.25 o.p. (ISBN 0-445-00252-2). Popular Lib.

Nichols, Sue. Words on Target: For Better Christian Communication. LC 63-16410. (Illus., Orig.). 1963. pap. 3.95 (ISBN 0-8042-1476-X). John Knox.

Nichols, T. L. Streak of Sunshine. 4.00 o.p. (ISBN 0-8062-1012-5). Carlton.

Nichols, Talmage & Stiles, Harold. Woodworking Workbook. rev. ed. (gr. 9-12). 1971. pap. 3.40 (ISBN 0-87002-105-2); ans sheet avail. (ISBN 0-685-00121-0). Bennett IL.

Nichols, Theo. Ownership, Control & Ideology. (Studies in Management Ser.). (Illus.). 272p. 1970. text ed. 8.95x (ISBN 0-04-338042-5). Allen Unwin.

Nichols, Theo & Beynon, Huw. Living with Capitalism: Class Relations & the Modern Factory. 1977. 18.00x (ISBN 0-7100-8594-X); pap. 10.00 (ISBN 0-7100-8595-8). Routledge & Kegan.

Nichols, Virginia. Show Your Own Dog. 1970. 9.95 (ISBN 0-87666-661-6, PS607). TFH Pubns.

Nicholsen, Margaret, ed. People in Books. LC 69-15811. 1969. 16.00 (ISBN 0-8242-0394-1). Wilson.

Nicholson. The Autonomous House. 4.25 (ISBN 0-915248-31-X). Vermont Crossroads.

--Microeconomic Theory. 2nd ed. 1978. 21.95 (ISBN 0-03-020831-9). Dryden Pr.

--Pediatric Ocular Tumors. 1981. price not set (ISBN 0-89352-125-6). Masson Pub.

Nicholson, Alasdair. The Cold War. Yapp, Malcolm, et al, eds. (World History Ser.). (Illus.). 32p. (gr. 10). 1980. Repr. of 1977 ed. 5.95 (ISBN 0-89908-236-X); pap. text ed. 1.95 (ISBN 0-89908-211-4). Greenhaven.

Nicholson, B. E., ed. see Brightman, Frank H.

Nicholson, Charles L. & Alcorn, Charles L. Educational Applications of the WISC-R: A Handbook of Interpretive Strategies & Remedial Recommendations. LC 79-66967. 104p. 1980. pap. text ed. 9.70x (ISBN 0-87424-160-X). Western Psych.

Nicholson, Don H., ed. Ocular Pathology Update. LC 80-80967. (Illus.). 304p. 1980. 59.50 (ISBN 0-89352-051-9). Masson Pub.

Nicholson, E. W., jt. ed. see Baker, J.

Nicholson, Edward A., et al. Business Responsibility & Social Issues. new ed. 416p. 1974. text ed. 15.95 (ISBN 0-675-08826-7). Merrill.

Nicholson, H., ed. Modelling of Dynamic Systems, Vol. 1, Vol. 2. (IEE Control Engineering Ser.). (Illus.). 256p. 1981. 62.00 (ISBN 0-906048-38-9, Pub. by Peregrinus England). Inst Elect Eng.

Nicholson, H. B. & Cordy-Collins, Alana. Pre-Columbian Art from the Land Collection. Land, L. K., ed. LC 78-78330. (Illus.). 280p. (Orig.). 1981. pap. 24.95 (ISBN 0-295-95809-X, Pub. by Calif Acad Sci). U of Wash Pr.

Nicholson, H. E., jt. auth. see Miller, G. R.

Nicholson, Heather J. & Nicholson, Ralph L. Distant Hunger: Agriculture, Food & Human Values. LC 78-60761. (Science & Society: a Purdue University Series in Science Technology, & Human Values: Vol. 3.). (Illus.). 240p. 1979. pap. 3.95 (ISBN 0-931682-00-2). Purdue Univ Bks.

Nicholson, J. B. The Gurkha Rifles. LC 74-76623. (Men-at-Arms Ser). (Illus.). 40p. (Orig.). 1974. pap. 7.95 (ISBN 0-88254-235-4). Hippocrene Bks.

Nicholson, J. P., ed. Scientific Aids in Hospital Diagnosis. 288p. 1976. 35.00 (ISBN 0-306-30938-6, Plenum Pr). Plenum Pub.

Nicholson, James B. A Manual of the Art of Bookbinding Containing Full Instructions in the Different Branches of Forwarding, Gilding & Finishing. Bidwell, John, ed. LC 78-74391. (Nineteenth-Century Book Arts & Printing History Ser.: Vol. 6). (Illus.). 1980. lib. bdg. 33.00 (ISBN 0-8240-3880-0). Garland Pub.

Nicholson, James R. Shetland. new, rev. ed. LC 79-52367. (Illus.). 1979. 17.95 (ISBN 0-7153-7808-2). David & Charles.

Nicholson, Joan. Embroidery for Schools. 1977. 16.95 (ISBN 0-7134-0241-5, Pub. by Batsford England). David & Charles.

--Needleworks Projects for All: Canvas Work Simplified. LC 73-79196. (Illus.). 96p. 1973. 5.95 o.p. (ISBN 0-668-03320-7). Arco.

Nicholson, John. Folk-Lore of East Yorkshire. 168p. 1980. Repr. of 1972 ed. lib. bdg. 20.00 (ISBN 0-8492-1984-1). R West.

Nicholson, Loren. Rails Across the Ranchos. (Illus.). 160p. 1980. 18.95 (ISBN 0-913548-72-3, Valley Calif). Western Tanager.

Nicholson, Luree & Torbet, Laura. How to Fight Fair with Your Kids...& Win. LC 79-1837. 1980. 12.95 o.p. (ISBN 0-15-142191-9); pap. 7.95 o.p. (ISBN 0-15-642191-7). HarBraceJ.

Nicholson, Lynda, tr. see Brenan, G.

Nicholson, N. L. & Sebert, L. M. Maps of Canada: A Guide to Official Canadian Maps, Charts, Atlases & Gazetteers. (Illus.). 200p. 1981. 32.50 (ISBN 0-208-01782-8, Archon). Shoe String.

Nicholson, Nigel, ed. see Woolf.

Nicholson, Norman. A Local Habituation. 1973. pap. 8.95 (ISBN 0-571-10425-8, Pub. by Faber & Faber). Merrimack Bk Serv.

--A Local Habituation. 1972. pap. 3.95 (ISBN 0-571-09982-3, Pub. by Faber & Faber). Merrimack Bk Serv.

--Portrait of the Lakes. LC 64-4949. (Portrait Bks.). (Illus.). 1964. 10.50x (ISBN 0-7091-2897-5). Intl Pubns Serv.

--Selected Poems. 1966. pap. 4.95 (ISBN 0-571-06733-6, Pub. by Faber & Faber). Merrimack Bk Serv.

--William Cowper. 167p. 1980. Repr. of 1951 ed. text ed. 25.00 (ISBN 0-8492-1973-6). R West.

Nicholson Publications. Nicholson's Complete London. 1978. pap. 5.95 (ISBN 0-684-15640-7, SL794, ScribT). Scribner.

Nicholson, R., jt. ed. see Kelly, A.

Nicholson, R. A. Mystics of Islam. 1975. pap. 6.50 (ISBN 0-7100-8015-8). Routledge & Kegan.

--Studies in Islamic Mysticism. LC 78-73958. 1979. 42.00 (ISBN 0-521-05836-8); pap. 12.50x (ISBN 0-521-29546-7). Cambridge U Pr.

Nicholson, Ralph L., jt. auth. see Nicholson, Heather J.

Nicholson, Reynold A. Literary History of the Arabs. 2nd ed. 1969. 78.00 (ISBN 0-521-05823-6); pap. 21.50x (ISBN 0-521-09572-7). Cambridge U Pr.

Nicholson, Reynold A., ed. Rumi: Poet & Mystics 1207-1273. (Ethical & Religious Classics of East & West Ser.: No. 1). 1950. text ed. 8.75x o.p. (ISBN 0-04-891021-X). Humanities.

--Selected Poems from the Divani Shamsi Tabriz. LC 77-1340. 1977. pap. text ed. 47.50 (ISBN 0-521-21646-X); pap. 15.95x (ISBN 0-521-29217-4). Cambridge U Pr.

Nicholson, Robert, ed. The Shell Weekend Guide to London & the South East. (Illus.). 1979. 15.00 o.p. (ISBN 0-905522-12-5, ADON 8111-2, Pub. by R Nicholson). Barrie & Jenkins.

Nicholson, Robin. A Passion for Treason. 384p. (Orig.). 1981. pap. 2.75 (ISBN 0-515-05663-4). Jove Pubns.

Nicholson, Sam. The Light-Bearer. 1980. pap. 1.95 (ISBN 0-425-04587-0). Berkley Pub.

Nicholson, Susan M. Catalogue of the Prehistoric Metalwork in Merseyside County Museum, No. 2. (Worknotes Ser.). (Illus.). 148p. (Orig.). 1981. pap. 12.50x (ISBN 0-87474-675-2). Smithsonian.

Nicholson, T. R. Passenger Cars, 1863-1904. LC 75-115303. (Cars of the World in Color Ser.: No. 2). (Illus.). 1970. 9.95 (ISBN 0-02-589380-7). Macmillan.

--Passenger Cars, 1905-1912. Bartholomew, Alick, ed. (Cars of the World in Color Ser). (Illus.). 1971. 9.95 (ISBN 0-02-589420-X). Macmillan.

--Racing Cars, 1898-1921. (Cars of the World in Color Ser.: No. 5). (Illus.). 1972. 3.95 o.s.i. (ISBN 0-02-589410-2). Macmillan.

--Sports Cars, 1907-1927. 1970. 9.95 (ISBN 0-02-589390-4). Macmillan.

--Sprint: Speed Hillclimbs & Speed Trials in Britain, 1889-1925. 9.95 o.p. (ISBN 0-685-42130-9). David & Charles.

Nicholson, W. L., jt. auth. see Dixon, W. J.

Nicholson, W. R. Colossians. LC 73-81742. 1969. 6.95 (ISBN 0-8254-3301-0); pap. 4.95 (ISBN 0-8254-3300-2). Kregel.

Nicholson, Walter. Intermediate Microeconomics & Application. 2nd ed. LC 78-56197. 1979. text ed. 20.95 (ISBN 0-03-041481-4). Dryden Pr.

Nicholson, William. The Seventh Level. 1980. pap. 2.75 (ISBN 0-451-09479-4, E9479, Sig). NAL.

Nick, Dagmar. Summons & Sign. Barnes, Jim, tr. from Ger. LC 80-18367. Orig. Title: Zeugnis & Zeichen. (Illus.). 124p. (Orig.). 1980. pap. 3.00 (ISBN 0-933428-02-2). Chariton Review.

Nickel, Gerhard, ed. Papers in Contrastive Linguistics. LC 78-149434. (Illus.). 1971. 19.95 (ISBN 0-521-08091-6). Cambridge U Pr.

Nickel, Karl L. Interval Mathematics: 1980. LC 80-25009. 1980. lib ed 29.50 (ISBN 0-12-518850-1). Acad Pr.

Nickel, Mildred L. Let's Find Out About a Book. LC 79-131146. (Let's Find Out Bks). (Illus.). (gr. 3 up). 1971. PLB 4.47 o.p. (ISBN 0-531-00066-4). Watts.

Nickel, R., et al. The Viscera of the Domestic Mammals. LC 72-95370. (Illus.). 1973. 54.60 o.p. (ISBN 0-387-91107-3). Springer-Verlag.

Nickel, Vernon M. Orthopaedic Rehabilitation. (Illus.). 500p. 1981. text ed. price not set (ISBN 0-443-08060-7). Churchill. Postponed.

Nickell, S. J. The Investment Decision of Firms. LC 78-73957. (Economic Handbooks Ser.). 1975. 42.50 (ISBN 0-521-22465-9); pap. 13.95x (ISBN 0-521-29511-4). Cambridge U Pr.

Nickels, Steven. The Gypsy Season. Date not set. 10.95 (ISBN 0-87949-187-6). Ashley Bks.

Nickels, Sylvia. The Travellers' Guide to Yugoslavia. LC 79-427483. (Travellers' Guide Ser.). (Illus.). 1979. 9.95 (ISBN 0-224-61593-9, Pub. by Chatto Bodley Jonathan). Merrimack Bk Serv.

Nickels, Sylvie. The Vikings. (Jackdaw Ser: No. 133). (gr. 7 up). 1976. 5.95 o.p. (ISBN 0-670-74683-5). Viking Pr.

Nickels, William G. Marketing Communications & Promotion. 2nd ed. LC 79-17114. (Grid Ser. in Marketing). 1980. text ed. 20.50 (ISBN 0-88244-197-3). Grid Pub.

Nickels, Williams G. Marketing Principles: A Broadened Concept of Marketing. LC 77-24308. 1978. text ed. 18.95 (ISBN 0-13-558205-9); study guide 5.95 (ISBN 0-13-558213-X). P-H.

Nickelsburg, George, ed. Studies on the Testament of Moses. LC 73-89039. (Society of Biblical Literature. Septuagint & Cognate Studies). 1973. pap. 7.50 (ISBN 0-89130-167-4, 060404). Scholars Pr Ca.

Nickelsburg, George W. Jewish Literature Between the Bible & the Mishnah: A Historical & Literary Introduction. LC 80-16176. 352p. 1981. 19.95 (ISBN 0-8006-0649-3, 1-649). Fortress.

Nickelsburg, George W., Jr., ed. Studies on the Testament of Abraham. LC 76-44205. (Society of Biblical Literature. Septuagint & Cognate Studies). 1976. pap. 9.00 (ISBN 0-89130-117-8, 060406). Scholars Pr Ca.

Nickelsen, John R. Romeo & Juliet: A Study Text. LC 79-26683. (Illus.). 1980. pap. text ed. 5.25 (ISBN 0-684-16497-3, SSP 46, ScribC). Scribner.

Nickens, John M., et al. Research Methods for Needs Assessment. LC 80-5126. 98p. 1980. pap. text ed. 6.75 (ISBN 0-8191-1047-7). U Pr of Amer.

Nickerson, Charles A. & Nickerson, Ingeborg A. Business Mathematics: A Consumer Approach. (Illus.). 256p. 1981. pap. text ed. 13.95 (ISBN 0-675-08071-1); tchr's. manual avail. Merrill.

--Consumer Mathematics. (General Business Ser.). 325p. 1981. pap. text ed. 13.95 (ISBN 0-675-08071-1). Merrill.

--Statistical Analysis for Decision Making. (Illus.). 1979. text ed. 23.00 (ISBN 0-89433-001-2). Petrocelli.

Nickerson, Clarence B. Accounting Handbook for Non-Accountants. 2nd ed. LC 79-1368. 1979. 27.50 (ISBN 0-8436-0765-3). CBI Pub.

Nickerson, Doyne. Three Hundred Sixty Five Ways to Cook Hamburger. LC 60-13551. 1960. 4.95 o.p. (ISBN 0-385-00847-3). Doubleday.

Nickerson, Eileen T., et al, eds. Helping Women: Readings in the Psychology & Counseling of Women. LC 78-64371. 1978. pap. text ed. 11.00 o.p. (ISBN 0-8191-0631-3). U Pr of Amer.

Nickerson, Ingeborg A., jt. auth. see Nickerson, Charles A.

Nickerson, Jane S. Homage to Malthus. 1975. 12.95 (ISBN 0-8046-9105-3, Natl U). Kennikat.

--Short History of North Africa. LC 68-54233. 1961. 9.00x (ISBN 0-8196-0219-1). Biblo.

Nickerson, John T. & Ronsivall, Louis J. Elementary Food Science. 2nd ed. 1980. pap. text ed. 19.00 (ISBN 0-87055-318-6). AVI.

Nickerson, Ohla E. Blossom Where You Are Planted. (Orig.). 1980. pap. 1.95 (ISBN 0-532-23200-3). Manor Bks.

Nickerson, Raymond S., ed. Attention & Performance VIII. LC 80-23850. 864p. 1980. 49.95 (ISBN 0-89859-038-8). L Erlbaum Assocs.

Nickerson, Robert L., jt. auth. see Whalen, Harold B.

Nickerson, Roy. Brother Whale. LC 76-30828. (Illus.). 1977. pap. 5.95 (ISBN 0-87701-087-0). Chronicle Bks.

Nickes, Ruth, ed. see Northwest Regional Educational Laboratory.

Nicklaus, Carol. Drawing Pets. (gr. 1-3). 1980. PLB 7.90 (ISBN 0-531-04138-7). Watts.

--Drawing Your Family & Friends. (gr. 1-3). 1980. PLB 7.90 (ISBN 0-531-04139-5). Watts.

--Harry the Hider. (Illus.). (gr. k-3). 1980. pap. 1.50 (ISBN 0-380-49189-3, 49189, Camelot). Avon.

--Harry the Hider. LC 78-10250. (Easy-Read Story Bks.). (Illus.). (gr. k-3). 1979. 3.95 (ISBN 0-531-02381-8); PLB 6.45 s&l (ISBN 0-531-02298-6). Watts.

Nicklaus, Jack. Play Better Golf. (Orig.). 1981. pap. price not set (ISBN 0-671-83624-2). PB.

Nicklaus, Jack & Bowden, Ken. Jack Nicklaus' Lesson Tee. LC 76-46733. (Illus.). 160p. 1977. 10.95 (ISBN 0-914178-11-3). Golf Digest Bks.

--Jack Nicklaus' Playing Lessons. (Illus.). 144p. 1981. 12.95 (ISBN 0-914178-42-3, 42901-9). Golf Digest Bks.

Nickle, Keith F. The Synoptic Gospels: An Introduction. LC 79-92069. (Orig.). 1980. pap. 6.95 (ISBN 0-8042-0422-5). John Knox.

Nickles, Elizabeth & Ashcraft, Laura. The Coming Matriarchy: How Women Will Gain the Balance of Power. (Illus.). 352p. 1981. 13.95 (ISBN 0-87223-686-2). Seaview Bks.

Nickles, Harry G. Middle Eastern Cooking. LC 70-85530. (Foods of the World Ser). (Illus.). (gr. 6 up). 1969. PLB 14.94 (ISBN 0-8094-0068-5, Pub. by Time-Life). Silver.

--Middle Eastern Cooking. (Foods of the World Ser). (Illus.). 1969. 14.95 (ISBN 0-8094-0041-3). Time-Life.

Nickles, Steve H., jt. auth. see Epstin, David G.

Nickles, Thomas, ed. Scientific Discovery: Case Studies. (Boston Studies in the Philosophy of Science: No. 60). 386p. 1980. lib. bdg. 36.50 (ISBN 90-277-1092-9); pap. 15.95 (ISBN 90-277-1093-7). Kluwer Boston.

Nicklesburg, George, ed. Studies on the Testament of Joseph. LC 75-26923. (Society of Biblical Literature. Septurgint & Cognate Studies). 153p. 1975. pap. 7.50 (ISBN 0-89130-027-9, 060405). Scholars Pr Ca.

Nickse, Ruth S. Assessing Life Skills Competence: The New York State External High School Diploma Program. LC 80-82712. (CBE Forum Ser.: Bk. 3). 1980. pap. 8.95 (ISBN 0-8224-0515-6). Pitman Learning.

Nicksic, Esther. The Plus & Minus of Fluids & Electrolytes. 1981. text ed. 14.95 (ISBN 0-8359-5561-3); pap. text ed. 12.95 (ISBN 0-8359-5560-5). Reston.

Nickum, James E., ed. Water Management Organization in China. 1981. 22.50 (ISBN 0-87332-140-5). M E Sharpe.

Nicod, Jean. Geometry & Induction: Containing Geometry in the Sensible World & the Logical Problem of Induction. Bell, J. & Wood, M., trs. LC 70-107149. 1970. 14.50x (ISBN 0-520-01689-0). U of Cal Pr.

Nicol, Abioseh. Two African Tales. 1965. text ed. 3.95x (ISBN 0-521-05826-0). Cambridge U Pr.

Nicol, C., jt. auth. see King, A.

Nicol, D. M. Church & Society in the Last Centuries of Byzantium. LC 78-72092. (The Birkbeck Lectures, 1977). 1979. 23.95 (ISBN 0-521-22438-1). Cambridge U Pr.

--The End of the Byzantine Empire. 109p. 1980. text ed. 17.50x (ISBN 0-8419-5826-2). Holmes & Meier.

Nicol, Davidson & D'Onofrio-Flores, Pamela, eds. Scientific-Technological Change & the Role of Women in Development. (Special Studies in Social, Political, & Economic Development). 200p. 1981. lib. bdg. 25.00x (ISBN 0-86531-145-5). Westview.

Nicol, Donald. The Last Centuries of Byzantium. 462p. 1980. text ed. 17.00x (ISBN 0-246-10559-3). Humanities.

Nicol, Donald M. Byzantium: Its Ecclesiastical History & Relations with the Western World. 336p. 1980. 60.00x (ISBN 0-902089-35-8, Pub. by Variorum England). State Mutual Bk.

--The Last Centuries of Byzantium. 1979. 19.95x (ISBN 0-8464-0103-7). Beekman Pubs.

Nicol, Dr. Davidson Foreword by see Kagwa, Benjamin N. H.

Nicol, Gladys. Athens. 1978. 24.00 (ISBN 0-7134-0627-5). David & Charles.

Nicol, J. C., ed. see Cicero.

Nicol, Malcom, et al. Experimental Studies for General Chemistry. 2nd ed. 1974. lab manual 9.95x (ISBN 0-8162-6441-4). Holden-Day.

Nicol, W. B. De Bear see Jones, Thora B. & De Bear, Nicol.

Nicola, P. De see De Nicola, P., et al.

Nicolai, Jurgen. Bird Keeping. Bleher, Petra, tr. from Ger. (Illus.). 96p. 1980. 2.95 (ISBN 0-87666-997-6, KW034). TFH Pubns.

Nicolaides, A., jt. auth. see Lynch, P.

Nicolaides, A. N. & Yao, James T. Investigation of Vascular Disorders. (Illus.). 1981. text ed. 40.00 (ISBN 0-443-08020-8). Churchill. Postponed.

Nicolaisen, Age. Pocket Encyclopedia of Indoor Plants in Color. Goren, Richard, ed. LC 77-91385. 1970. 9.95 (ISBN 0-02-589500-1). Macmillan.

Nicolaisen, Jay. Italian Opera in Transition, Eighteen Seventy-One to Eighteen Ninety-Three. Buelow, George, ed. (Studies in Musicology). 273p. 1980. 34.95 (ISBN 0-8357-1121-8, Pub. by UMI Res Pr). Univ Microfilms.

Nicolas, Jean F., jt. auth. see Sonnenschmidt, Fredric H.

Nicolas, John F. The Complete Book of American Fish & Shellfish. LC 80-16534. (Illus.). 384p. 1980. 29.95 (ISBN 0-8436-2191-5). CBI Pub.

Nicole, Christopher. Black Dawn. LC 77-76648. 1977. 10.95 o.p. (ISBN 0-312-08307-6). St Martin.
--The Inheritors. (Haggard Ser.: No. 2). (Orig.). 1981. pap. 2.95 (ISBN 0-451-09763-7, E9763, Sig). NAL.
--The Secret Memoirs of Lord Byron. 1978. 10.95 o.p. (ISBN 0-397-01290-X). Lippincott.
Nicoletta, Peter. The Old Time Radio Hour. 1977. 2.50 (ISBN 0-918116-08-2). Jawbone Pr.
Nicoletti, Sally. Japanese Motifs for Needlepoint. LC 80-22650. (Illus.). 136p. 1981. 14.95 (ISBN 0-688-00163-7). Morrow.
Nicoliasen, W. F. Scottish Place-Names. 1976. 19.95 (ISBN 0-7134-3253-5). David & Charles.
Nicolich, Lorraine, jt. auth. see Woolfolk, Anita.
Nicolini, Claudio, ed. Chromatin Structure & Function, Pt. B: Levels of Organization & Cell Function. (NATO Advanced Study Institutes Ser., Series A, Life Sciences: Vol. 21B). 502p. 1979. 42.50 (ISBN 0-306-40076-6, Plenum Pr). Plenum Pub.
Nicolini, Gerard. The Ancient Spaniards. (Illus.). 312p. 1975. 15.95 o.p. (ISBN 0-347-00023-1). Saxon.
Nicolis, G. & Lefever, R., eds. Membranes, Dissipative Structures & Evolution. LC 74-23611. (Advances in Chemical Physics Ser: Vol. 29). 390p. 1975. 43.50 (ISBN 0-471-63792-0, Pub. by Wiley-Interscience). Wiley.
Nicolis, G., et al. Order & Fluctuations in Equilibrium & Nonequilibrium Statistical Mechanics: XVIIth International Solvay Conference on Physics. LC 80-13215. 416p. 1981. 35.00 (ISBN 0-471-05927-7, Pub. by Wiley Interscience). Wiley.
Nicoll, A. The World of Harlequin. LC 76-18411. (Illus.). 1976. 58.00 (ISBN 0-521-05834-1); pap. 18.95 (ISBN 0-521-29132-1). Cambridge U Pr.
Nicoll, Allardyce. English Drama: The Beginnings of the Modern Period, 1900-1930. 115.00 (ISBN 0-521-08416-4). Cambridge U Pr.
--The Garrick Stage: Theatres & Audiences in the Eighteenth Century. LC 79-9667. (Illus.). 192p. 1980. 25.00 (ISBN 0-8203-0510-3). U of Ga Pr.
--History of English Drama, 1660-1900, 6 vols. Incl. Vol. 1. Restoration Drama. 62.00 (ISBN 0-521-05827-9); Vol. 2. Early Eighteenth Century Drama. 59.50 (ISBN 0-521-05828-7); Vol. 3. Late Eighteenth Century Drama. 57.50 (ISBN 0-521-05829-5); Vol. 4. Early Nineteenth Century Drama, 1800-1850. 72.00 (ISBN 0-521-05830-9); Vol. 5. Late Nineteenth Century Drama. 77.00 (ISBN 0-521-05831-7); Vol. 6. Alphabetical Catalogue of the Plays. 57.50 (ISBN 0-521-05832-5). 1959. 340.00 set (ISBN 0-521-08777-5). Cambridge U Pr.
Nicoll, Allardyce see Muir, K.
Nicoll, Helen & Pienkowski, Jan. Meg's Eggs. (Picture Puffin Bks.). (Illus.). (ps-2). 1976. pap. 1.95 (ISBN 0-14-050118-5, Puffin). Penguin.
Nicoll, John. Rossetti. LC 75-23267. (Illus.). 176p. 1976. 22.95 o.s.i. (ISBN 0-02-589340-8, 58934). Macmillan.
Nicoll, Josephine, tr. see Von Boehn, Max.
Nicoll, M. Living Time. 5.95 o.p. (ISBN 0-685-01077-5). Weiser.
Nicoll, Maurice. Dream Psychology. 1979. pap. 4.95 (ISBN 0-87728-475-X). Weiser.
Nicollier, Alain, ed. European Universities, Nineteen Seventy-Five to Eighty-Five: Proceedings of the 5th General Assembly of the Standing Conference of Rectors & Vice-Chancellors of the European Universities, Bologna, 1974. LC 75-4331. 1975. pap. text ed. 28.00 (ISBN 0-08-019710-8); French Ed. pap. text ed. 34.00 (ISBN 0-08-019711-6). Pergamon.
Nicoloff, Philip L. Emerson on Race & History: An Examination of English Traits. LC 80-2540. 1981. Repr. of 1961 ed. 33.50 (ISBN 0-404-19266-1). AMS Pr.
Nicolson, Garth L., et al, eds. see ICN-UCLA Conference, Squaw Valley, Calif., March 2-7, 1975.
Nicolson, Harold. The Congress of Vienna: A Study in Allied Unity Eighteen Twelve to Eighteen Twenty-Two. 8.00 (ISBN 0-8446-4053-0). Peter Smith.
--Development of English Biography. 1928. text ed. 3.50x (ISBN 0-7012-0176-2). Humanities.
--Good Behavior: Being a Study of Certain Types of Civility. 7.50 (ISBN 0-8446-0822-X). Peter Smith.
Nicolson, Ian. Surveying Small Craft. LC 73-90687. (Illus.). 224p. 1974. 12.50 o.p. (ISBN 0-87742-039-4). Intl Marine.
Nicolson, James R. Beyond the Great Glen. LC 74-81071. (British Topographical Ser). (Illus.). 1975. 7.50 (ISBN 0-7153-6778-1). David & Charles.
Nicolson, James R., rev. by see Linklater, Eric.
Nicolson, M. H., ed. see Conway, Anne.
Nicolson, Marjorie H., ed. see Shadwell, Thomas.
Nicolson, Nigel. The Himalayas. (The World's Wild Places Ser.). (Illus.). 1975. 13.95 (ISBN 0-8094-2021-X). Time-Life.
--The Himalayas. (The World's Wild Places Ser.). (Illus.). 1978. lib. bdg. 11.97 (ISBN 0-686-51019-4). Silver.
--Portrait of a Marriage. LC 79-25497. 1973. 10.00 (ISBN 0-689-10574-6); pap. 6.95 (ISBN 0-689-70597-2). Atheneum.
Nida, E. A. Bible Translating. 2nd ed. 1961. 1.75 (ISBN 0-8267-0016-0, 08628). United Bible.
Nida, E. A., jt. auth. see Arichea, D. C.
Nida, E. A., jt. auth. see Arichea, D. C., Jr.
Nida, E. A., jt. auth. see Bratcher, R. G.
Nida, E. A., jt. auth. see De Waard, J.
Nida, E. A., jt. auth. see Ellingworth, P.
Nida, E. A., jt. auth. see Loh, I.
Nida, E. A., jt. auth. see Newman, B. M.
Nida, E. A., jt. auth. see Newman, B. M., Jr.
Nida, Eugene A. Customs & Cultures: Anthropology for Christian Missions. 2nd ed. LC 54-8976. (Applied Cultural Anthropology Ser.). 306p. 1975. Repr. of 1954 ed. 5.95x (ISBN 0-87808-723-0). William Carey Lib.
--Learning a Foreign Language. (Orig.). 1957. pap. 4.50 o.p. (ISBN 0-377-29041-6). Friend Pr.
--Morphology: The Descriptive Analysis of Words. 2nd ed. 1949. pap. 7.95x (ISBN 0-472-08684-7). U of Mich Pr.
Nida, Eugene A., jt. auth. see Bratcher, Robert G.
Nida, Eugene A., jt. auth. see Price, Brynmor F.
Nida, Eugene A. & Taber, C. R., eds. The Theory & Practice of Translation. 1969. 5.50 (ISBN 90-04-03857-4, 08510). United Bible.
Nidditch, P. H., ed. see Hume, David.
Nidetch, Jean. Weight Watchers New Program Cookbook. 1979. 9.95 o.p. (ISBN 0-453-01003-2, TE3, Sig). NAL.
Nie, et al. SCSS: A User's Guide to the SCSS Conversational System. (Illus.). 592p. 1980. text ed. 22.95 (ISBN 0-07-046538-X, C); pap. text ed. 14.95 (ISBN 0-07-046533-9). McGraw.
Nie, Norman, jt. ed. see Sackman, Harold.
Nie, Norman H., jt. auth. see Hull, C. Hadlai.
Niebel, Benjamin W. Motion & Time Study. 6th ed. 1976. 20.50x (ISBN 0-256-01775-1). Irwin.
Niebel, Benjamin W. & Gjesdahl, Maurice S. Production Engineering. LC 72-190969. (Illus.). 148p. 1975. 15.00 (ISBN 92-833-1003-9, APO57, APO). Unipub.
Niebelschuetz, Wolf Von. Der Blaue Kammerherr. 1070p. (Ger.). 1980. Repr. 20.80 (ISBN 3-518-03736-6, Pub. by Insel Verlag Germany). Suhrkamp.
Niebuhr, C. Travels Thru Arabia & Other Countries in the East, 2 vol. (Arab Background Ser.). 30.00x (ISBN 0-685-77101-6). Intl Bk Ctr.
Niebuhr, H. Richard. The Purpose of the Church & Its Ministry. LC 76-62925. (Orig.). 1977. pap. 4.95 (ISBN 0-06-066174-7, RD 211, HarpR). Har-Row.
--Radical Monotheism in Western Culture. pap. 3.50x (ISBN 0-06-131491-9, TB1491, Torch). Har-Row.
Niebuhr, H. Richard, jt. ed. see Beach, Waldo.
Niebuhr, Reinhold. Beyond Tragedy: Essays on the Christian Interpretation of History. 1937. pap. 4.95 o.p. (ISBN 0-684-71853-7, SL38, ScribT). Scribner.
--Faith & History: A Comparison of Christian & Modern Views of History. (Lib. Rep. Ed.). 1949. 17.50x (ISBN 0-684-15318-1, ScribT). Scribner.
--Faith & Politics. Stone, Ronald H., ed. & intro. by. LC 68-29097. 1968. 6.50 o.p. (ISBN 0-8076-0459-3). Braziller.
--An Interpretation of Christian Ethics. (Library of Contemporary Theology). 1979. pap. 6.95 (ISBN 0-8164-2206-0). Crossroad NY.
--Leaves from the Notebook of a Tamed Cynic: Prelude to Depression. LC 76-27833. (Prelude to Depression Ser.). 1976. Repr. of 1929 ed. lib. bdg. 19.50 (ISBN 0-306-70852-3). Da Capo.
--Nature & Destiny of Man, Two Vols. Vol. 1, Human Nature, Vol. 2, Human Destiny. 1949. Vol. 1. pap. 5.95 o.p. (ISBN 0-684-71858-8, SL97, ScribT); Vol. 2. pap. 5.95 o.p. (ISBN 0-684-71859-6, SL98, ScribT). Scribner.
Nieckels, Lars. Transfer Pricing in Multinational Firms: A Heuristic Programming Approach & Case Studies. LC 76-6174. 1976. 21.95 (ISBN 0-470-15084-X). Halsted Pr.
Niedenthal, Morris & Lacocque, Andre. Pentecost 1. LC 74-76929. (Proclamation 1: Aids for Interpreting the Lessons of the Church Year, Ser. A). 64p. 1975. pap. 1.95 (ISBN 0-8006-4066-7, 1-4066). Fortress.
Niederhoffer, Arthur. Behind the Shield: The Police in Urban Society. LC 67-16896. 1969. pap. 2.95 (ISBN 0-385-06128-5, A653, Anch). Doubleday.
Niederhoffer, Arthur & Niederhoffer, Elaine. The Police Family. LC 73-11678. 1978. 16.95 (ISBN 0-669-90498-8). Lexington Bks.
Niederhoffer, Arthur, jt. auth. see Bloch, Herbert.
Niederhoffer, Elaine, jt. auth. see Niederhoffer, Arthur.
Niederland, William G. Folgen der Verfolgung: Das Ueberlebenden-Syndrom. (Edition Suhrkamp. Neue Folge: esNF 15). 280p. (Orig., Ger.). 1980. pap. text ed. 7.80 (ISBN 3-518-11015-2, Pub. by Insel Verlag Germany). Suhrkamp.
Niedermayer, Franz. Jose Ortega y Gasset. Tirner, Peter, tr. from Ger. LC 71-163150. (Modern Literature Ser.). 1973. 10.95 (ISBN 0-8044-2659-7). Ungar.
Niedermeyer, Ernest & Da Silva, F. H. Textbook of Electroencephalography. 700p. 1981. 45.00 (ISBN 0-8067-1301-1). Urban & S.
Niedermeyer, Ernst. Compendium of the Epilepsies. (Illus.). 352p. 1974. 19.75 (ISBN 0-398-02878-8). C C Thomas.
Niederreiter, H., jt. auth. see Kuipers, L.
Niedrach, Robert J. & Rockwell, Robert B. Birds of Denver & Mountain Parks. 2nd rev. ed. (Popular Ser.: No. 5). 1959. 3.95 (ISBN 0-916278-13-1); pap. 2.20 o.p. (ISBN 0-916278-12-3). Denver Mus Natl Hist.
Niedrach, Robert J., jt. auth. see Bailey, Afred M.
Nieh, Hua-ling. Shen Ts'Ung-Wen. (World Authors Ser.: China: No. 237). lib. bdg. 10.95 (ISBN 0-8057-2818-X). Twayne.
Nieh, Hualing. Literature of the Hundred Flowers, 2 vols. LC 80-36748. 1981. Vol. 1, 288p. 27.50 (ISBN 0-231-05074-7); Vol. 2, 560p. 42.50 (ISBN 0-231-05076-3). Columbia U Pr.
Niehaus, John F., jt. auth. see Thierauf, Robert J.
Niehaus, Richard J. Computer-Assisted Human Resources Planning. LC 78-27708. 338p. 1979. 29.95 (ISBN 0-471-04081-9, Pub. by Wiley-Interscience). Wiley.
Niehaus, Sandy I. A Wise Man's Guide to Fine Spirits Through the Coming Financial Hard Times. rev. ed. Stollo, Toni, ed. (Illus.). 56p. 1980. 3.85 (ISBN 0-938452-00-2). Santam.
Niehaus, Theodore F. A Biosystematic Study of the Genus Brodiaea (Amaryllidaceae) (U. C. Publ. in Botany: Vol. 60). 1971. 7.00x (ISBN 0-520-09390-9). U of Cal Pr.
Niehoff, Arthur H., jt. auth. see Arensberg, Conrad M.
Nielsen. Direct Integrel Theory. 184p. 1980. 23.50 (ISBN 0-8247-6971-6). Dekker.
Nielsen, D. R. Nitrogen in the Environment, Vol. 1. 1978. 32.00 (ISBN 0-12-518401-8). Acad Pr.
Nielsen, Gary. Helping Children Behave: A Handbook of Applied Learning Principles. LC 73-94303. 224p. 1974. 14.95 (ISBN 0-911012-90-7). Nelson-Hall.
Nielsen, Greg, jt. auth. see Polansky, Joseph.
Nielsen, Greg, jt. auth. see Toth, Max.
Nielsen, Jens & Nielson, Jackie. How to Save or Make Thousands When You Buy or Sell Your House. LC 78-62635. 1979. Repr. of 1971 ed. 6.95 (ISBN 0-385-13522-X, Dolp). Doubleday.
Nielsen, Joyce M. Sex in Society: Perspectives on Stratification. 1978. pap. 7.95x (ISBN 0-534-00573-X). Wadsworth Pub.
Nielsen, Kai. Contemporary Critiques of Religion. Hick, John, ed. LC 72-170200. (Philosophy of Religion Ser). 1972. 6.95 (ISBN 0-8164-1021-6). Crossroad NY.
Nielsen, Kaj L. Algebra: A Modern Approach. LC 68-26403. (Illus., Orig.). 1969. pap. 4.50 (ISBN 0-06-460064-5, CO 64, COS). Har-Row.
--College Mathematics. (Orig.). 1958. pap. 3.95 (ISBN 0-06-460105-6, CO 105, COS). Har-Row.
--Differential Equations. 2nd ed. (Orig.). 1969. pap. 4.95 (ISBN 0-06-460072-6, CO 72, COS). Har-Row.
--Logarithmic & Trigonometric Tables to Five Places, rev. ed. (Orig.). 1971. pap. 2.95 (ISBN 0-06-460044-0, CO 44, COS). Har-Row.
--Mathematics for Practical Use. (Orig.). 1962. pap. 2.95 (ISBN 0-06-463212-1, EH 212, EH). Har-Row.
--Modern Trigonometry. (Illus., Orig.). 1966. pap. 4.95 (ISBN 0-06-460047-5, CO 47, COS). Har-Row.
Nielsen, Kaj L. & Gemmel, Charlotte M. Algebra. LC 69-18677. (Rapid Reviews Ser.). pap. text ed. 3.95 (ISBN 0-8220-1760-1). Cliffs.
Nielsen, Kaj L. & Vanlonkhuyzen, John H. Plane & Spherical Trigonometry. rev. ed. (Orig.). 1954. pap. 4.95 (ISBN 0-06-460045-9, CO 45, COS). Har-Row.
Nielsen, Kaj L., jt. auth. see Horblit, Marcus.
Nielsen, Kirsten. Yahweh As Prosecutor & Judge: An Investigation of the Prophetic Lawsuit (Rib Pattern) (JSOT Supplement Ser.: No. 9). 104p. 1978. text ed. 25.95x (ISBN 0-905774-13-2, Pub. by JSOT Pr England); pap. text ed. 12.95x (ISBN 0-905774-08-6, Pub. by JSOT Pr England). Eisenbrauns.
Nielsen, Konrad & Nesheim, Asbjorn, eds. Lapp Dictionary, 5 vols. 3221p. 1980. 250.00x set (ISBN 82-00-14201-9). Universitet.
Nielsen, Louis S. Standard Plumbing Engineering Design. (Illus.). 384p. 1981. 21.50 (ISBN 0-07-046541-X). McGraw.
Nielsen, Niels. Die Gammafunktion, 2 vols. in 1. Incl. Integrallogarithmus. LC 64-13785. (Ger.). 1965. 16.50 (ISBN 0-8284-0188-8). Chelsea Pub.
Nielsen, Niels C., Jr. The Crisis of Human Rights. LC 78-4056. 1978. pap. 3.95 o.p. (ISBN 0-8407-5644-5). Nelson.
Nielsen, Patricia H. & Sucher, Floyd. Mockingbird Flight: Music Book & Records. (Kindergarten Keys Ser.). (Illus.). 1975. pap. text ed. 10.80 (ISBN 0-87892-660-7); record set 49.50 (ISBN 0-87892-666-6). Economy Co.
Nielsen, Sally E., ed. Insulating the Old House: A Handbook for the Owner. (Illus.). 1979. pap. 1.95 (ISBN 0-9600612-7-4). Greater Portland.
--Investing in Old Buildings. (Illus.). 1980. pap. 3.95. Greater Portland.
Nielsen, Swen C. General Organizational & Administrative Concepts for University Police. 96p. 1971. 9.75 (ISBN 0-398-02164-3). C C Thomas.
Nielsen, Virginia. Yankee Lover. 1978. pap. 1.75 o.p. (ISBN 0-449-14020-2, GM). Fawcett.
Nielsen, Waldemar. The Big Foundations. LC 72-3676. (A Twentieth Century Fund Study). 475p. 1972. 17.50x (ISBN 0-231-03665-5); pap. 9.00x (ISBN 0-231-03666-3). Columbia U Pr.
Nielsen, Waldemar A. The Endangered Sector. LC 79-15772. 1979. 15.00x (ISBN 0-231-04688-X). Columbia U Pr.
Nielsen, Y., jt. auth. see Rabinowitz, D.
Nielson, Aksel J., jt. auth. see Mollo, Victor.
Nielson, Jackie, jt. auth. see Nielsen, Jens.
Nielson, Larry. How Would You Like to See the Slides of My Mission. LC 80-82708. (Illus.). 80p. (Orig.). 1980. pap. 4.95 (ISBN 0-88290-153-2, 2040). Horizon Utah.
Nielson, Niels C., Jr. Solzhenitsyn's Religion. 1976. pap. 1.75 (ISBN 0-89129-141-5). Jove Pubns.
Niemand, Jasper, ed. & intro. by see Judge, William Q.
Niemeyer, Carl, ed. see Carlyle, Thomas.
Niemeyer, E. V., Jr. Revolution at Queretaro: The Mexican Constitutional Convention of 1916-1917. LC 73-20203. (Latin American Monographs: No. 33). (Illus.). 326p. 1974. 14.95 (ISBN 0-292-77005-7). U of Tex Pr.
Niemi, A., et al, eds. see International Federation of Automatic Control, 7th Triennial World Congress, Helsinki, Finland, June 1978.
Niemi, John A., jt. auth. see Ilsley, Paul.
Niemi, Richard G., jt. auth. see Jennings, M. Kent.
Niemi, Richard G. & Weisberg, Herbert F., eds. Controversies in American Voting Behavior. LC 76-13564. (Illus.). 1976. text ed. 21.95x (ISBN 0-7167-0536-2); pap. text ed. 10.95x (ISBN 0-7167-0535-4). W H Freeman.
Nieminsky, Arthur C., jt. auth. see Partington, A. M.
Nienaber, Jeanne, jt. auth. see Mazmanian, Daniel A.
Niendorf, Robert M., jt. auth. see Ward, David J.
Niendorff, John S. Listen to the Light. 96p. 1980. pap. 2.50 (ISBN 0-911336-84-2). Sci of Mind.
Nienhauser, William H., Jr. P'I Jih-Hsiu. (World Authors Ser.: No. 530). 1979. lib. bdg. 14.95 (ISBN 0-8057-6372-4). Twayne.
Nienhauser, William H., Jr., et al. Liu Tsung-Yuan. (World Authors Ser.: China: No. 255). 1971. lib. bdg. 10.95 (ISBN 0-8057-2538-5). Twayne.
Nienhuis, A., jt. ed. see Stamatoyannopoulos, G.
Nier, Charles J. Dynamics of Classroom Structure. LC 80-69330. 140p. 1981. perfect bdg. 11.50 (ISBN 0-86548-052-4). Century Twenty One.
Nierenberg, Gerard I. Art of Negotiating. (Illus.). 1971. pap. 3.95 (ISBN 0-346-12272-4). Cornerstone.
--Art of Negotiating. LC 68-30720. 1968. 9.95 (ISBN 0-8015-0408-2, Hawthorn). Dutton.
--Fundamentals of Negotiating. new ed. 1977. 14.95 (ISBN 0-8015-2868-2, Hawthorn); pap. 6.50 (ISBN 0-8015-2869-0, Hawthorn). Dutton.
Nierenberg, Gerard I. & Calero, Henry H. How to Read a Person Like a Book. 180p. 1972. pap. 3.95 (ISBN 0-346-12283-X). Cornerstone.
Nierenberg, Judith & Janovic, Florence. The Hospital Experience: A Complete Guide to Understanding & Participating in Your Own Care. LC 78-55658. (Illus.). 1978. 12.95 (ISBN 0-672-52372-8); pap. 9.95 (ISBN 0-672-52373-6). Bobbs.
Nies, Richard C. The Security of Salvation. LC 78-17523. (Waymark Ser.). 1978. pap. 1.25 (ISBN 0-8127-0187-9). Southern Pub.

Niese, Gerhard. Physics Is Fun. LC 60-7489. (Illus.). 1960. 5.00 (ISBN 0-910172-01-3). Astro Comp Serv.
Nieshtadt, Yakov, ed. Catastrophe in the Opening. (Pergamon Chess Ser.). (Illus.). 1980. 17.25 (ISBN 0-08-023121-7); pap. 9.60 (ISBN 0-08-024097-6). Pergamon.
Niess, Alfred D. Monkeyshines for a Laughing Lunacy. 1978. pap. 4.95 (ISBN 0-686-15529-7). S&S Co OR.
Nieting, Lorenz. Lesser Festivals 4: Saints' Days & Special Occasions. Achtemeier, Elizabeth, et al, eds. LC 79-7377. (Proclamation Two Ser.: Aids for Interpreting the Lessons of the Church Year). 64p. (Orig.). 1981. pap. 2.50 (ISBN 0-8006-1396-1, 1-1396). Fortress.
Nieting, Lorenz, tr. see Marxsen, Willi.
Nieto, M. The Titius-Bode Law of Planetary Distance. 173p. 1972. text ed. 25.00 (ISBN 0-08-016784-5). Pergamon.
Nietzel, Michael. Crime & Its Modification: A Social Learning Perspective. LC 78-23984. (Pergamon General Psychology Ser.: Vol. 77). (Illus.). 1979. 33.00 (ISBN 0-08-023878-5); pap. 10.95 (ISBN 0-08-023877-7). Pergamon.
Nietzsche, F. The Portable Nietzsche. Kaufman, Walter, ed. (Viking Portable Library: No. 62). 1980. 14.95 (ISBN 0-670-51119-6). Viking Pr.
Nietzsche, Friedrich. On the Advantage & Disadvantage of History for Life. Preuss, Peter, tr. from Ger. LC 80-16686. (Philosophical Classics Ser.). 80p. 1980. lib. bdg. 12.50 (ISBN 0-915144-95-6); pap. text ed. 1.95 (ISBN 0-915144-94-8). Hackett Pub.
Nietzsche, Friedrich W. Use & Abuse of History. 2nd ed. Collins, Adrian, tr. LC 57-4499. 1957. pap. 2.50 (ISBN 0-672-60172-9, LLA11). Bobbs.
Nieuwenhuijze, C. Van see Van Nieuwenhuijze, C.
Nieuwenhuysen, J. P., jt. auth. see Altman, J. C.
Niewyk, Donald L., tr. see Stoldt, Hans-Herbert.
Niezing, Johan. Sociology, War & Disarmament: Studies in Peace Research. (Publications of the Polemological Centre of the Free University of Brussles: Vol. 1). 144p. pap. text ed. 13.50 (ISBN 90-237-6223-1, Pub. by Swets Pub Serv Holland). Swets North Am.
Niezing, Johan, ed. Urban Guerilla: Studies on the Theory, Strategy & Practice of Political Violence in Modern Societies. (Publications of the Polemological Centre of the Free University of Brussels: Vol. 4). 156p. 1974. pap. text ed. 17.75 (ISBN 90-237-6245-2, Pub. by Swets Pub Serv Holland). Swets North Am.
Nigam, R. C. Law of Crimes in India, Vol. 1. 1965. 25.00x (ISBN 0-210-27046-2). Asia.
Nightingale, Demetra S. & Mitchell, John J. A Data Book for Welfare-Employment Programs. (An Institute Paper). 187p. 1978. pap. 9.50 (ISBN 0-87766-239-8, 24200). Urban Inst.
Nightingale, Earl. This Is Earl Nightingale. LC 67-12840. 1969. 8.95 o.p. (ISBN 0-385-08501-X). Doubleday.
Nightingale, J. D., jt. auth. see Foster, J.
Nightingale, R. H. Crossing Jordan at Flood Tide. LC 75-16541. 1975. pap. 2.95 o.p. (ISBN 0-8163-0172-7, 03648-3). Pacific Pr Pub Assn.
Nigra, Gene, jt. ed. see Gerry De La Ree.
Nigrini, Catherine. Radiolaria in Pelagic Sediments from the Indian & Atlantic Oceans. (Bulletin of the Scripps Institution of Oceanography: Vol. 11). 1967. pap. 8.00x (ISBN 0-520-09315-1). U of Cal Pr.
Nigro, Felix A. & Nigro, Lloyd G. The New Public Personnel Administration. 2nd ed. LC 80-83098. 420p. 1981. text ed. 14.95 (ISBN 0-87581-265-1). Peacock Pubs.
Nigro, Lloyd G., jt. auth. see Nigro, Felix A.
Ni Hua-Ching, Master & Hua-Ching. The Complete Works of Lao Tzu: Tao Teh Ching & Hua Hu Ching. LC 79-88745. 219p. 1979. pap. text ed. 7.50x (ISBN 0-937064-00-9). Wisdom Garden.
--Tao-the Subtle Universal Law & the Integral Way of Life. LC 79-91720. 166p. 1980. pap. text ed. 7.50 (ISBN 0-937064-01-7). Wisdom Garden.
--The Taoist Inner View of the Universe & the Immortal Realm. LC 79-91720. 218p. 1980. pap. text ed. 12.50x (ISBN 0-937064-02-5). Wisdom Garden.
Nijholt, A. Context-Free Grammars: Covers, Normal Forms, & Parsing. (Lecture Notes in Computer Science Ser.: Vol. 93). 253p. 1981. pap. 16.80 (ISBN 0-387-10245-0). Springer-Verlag.
Nijinsky, Romola. Nijinsky & the Last Days of Nijinsky. 1980. 16.95 (ISBN 0-671-41123-3). S&S.
Nijjar, B. S. Punjab Under the British Rule: 1849-1947. Incl. Vol. 1. 1849-1902. o.p.; Vol. 2. 1903-1926. 8.50x o.p.. LC 75-901549. 200p. 1974. South Asia Bks.
Nijkamp, P. see Lakshmanan, T. R.
Nijkamp, Peter. Environmental Policy Analysis: Operational Methods & Models. LC 79-41778. 283p. 1980. 44.00 (ISBN 0-471-27763-0, Pub. by Wiley-Interscience). Wiley.
--Multidimensional Spatial Data & Decision Analysis. LC 79-40518. 322p. 1980. 46.95 (ISBN 0-471-27603-0, Pub. by Wiley-Interscience). Wiley.
Nijkamp, Peter, jt. auth. see Paelinck, Jean H.
Nikam, Narayanrao A. Sense, Understanding & Reason: A Digest of Kant's First Critique. 1966. 4.00 o.p. (ISBN 0-210-22654-4). Asia.
Nikas. Critical Neurological Assessment & Management. 1981. text ed. price not set. Churchill.
Nikas, Diana L. Critical Neurological Surgical Assessment & Management: Contemporary Issues in Critical Care Nursing. (Vol. 2). (Illus.). 224p. 1981. lib. bdg. 20.00 (ISBN 0-443-08158-1). Churchill.
Nikel, Casimir M., jt. auth. see Pfeiffer, Guy O.
Nikelly, Arthur G., ed. Techniques for Behavior Change: Applications of Adlerian Theory. 224p. 1979. 18.75 (ISBN 0-398-01401-9). C C Thomas.
Nikhilananda, Swami, tr. Bhagavad Gita. LC 44-33674. 404p. with notes 7.00 (ISBN 0-911206-09-4); without notes, 256p. 3.00 (ISBN 0-911206-10-8). Ramakrishna.
--Gospel of Sri Ramakrishna. LC 58-8948. (Illus.). 1106p. 15.00 (ISBN 0-911206-01-9); abridged ed., with index, 640p. 7.00 (ISBN 0-911206-02-7). Ramakrishna.
--Self-Knowledge: Sankara's "Atmabodha". LC 50-36440. 248p. with notes 6.00 (ISBN 0-911206-11-6). Ramakrishna.
--Upanishads, 4 Vols. LC 49-9558. Set. with notes 28.00 (ISBN 0-911206-14-0); 7.50 ea.; Vol. 1, 333p. (ISBN 0-911206-15-9); Vol. II, 400p. (ISBN 0-911206-16-7); Vol. III, 408p. (ISBN 0-911206-17-5); Vol. IV, 422p. (ISBN 0-911206-18-3). Ramakrishna.
Nikitin, E. E. Theory of Elementary Atomic & Molecular Processes in Gases. Kearsley, M. J., tr. (Illus.). 486p. 1974. 55.00x (ISBN 0-19-851928-1). Oxford U Pr.
Nikitin, E. E., jt. auth. see Kondratiev, V. N.
Nikkel, Stan R., jt. auth. see Larson, Calvin J.
Niklas, Gerald R. The Making of a Pastoral Person. 159p. (Orig.). 1981. pap. 5.95 (ISBN 0-8189-0409-7). Alba.
Niklaus, Thelma. Harlequin. 1960. 7.50 o.p. (ISBN 0-8076-0036-9). Braziller.
Niklewiczowa, Maria. Sparrow's Magic. Tresselt, Alvin, tr. LC 73-99583. Orig. Title: Suzume No Mahou. (Illus., Japanese). (gr. k-3). 1970. 5.95 o.s.i. (ISBN 0-8193-0412-3, Four Winds); PLB 5.41 o.s.i. (ISBN 0-8193-0413-1). Schol Bk Serv.
Nikolaev, N. S., et al. Analytical Chemistry of Fluorine. LC 72-4101. (Analytical Chemistry of the Elements Ser.). 222p. 1973. 38.95 (ISBN 0-470-63860-5). Halsted Pr.
Nikolai, Loren A., et al. Intermediate Accounting. 1120p. 1980. text ed. 22.95x (ISBN 0-534-00786-4, Kent Pub.); guide 7.95xstudy (ISBN 0-534-00821-6); papers 9.95xworking (ISBN 0-534-00830-5). Kent Pub Co.
Nikolaieff, George A. Computers & Society. (Reference Shelf Ser: Vol. 41, No. 6). 1970. 6.25 (ISBN 0-8242-0111-6). Wilson.
Nikolaieff, George A., ed. President & the Constitution. (Reference Shelf Ser: Vol. 46, No. 4). 1974. 6.25 (ISBN 0-8242-0523-5). Wilson.
--Stabilizing America's Economy. (Reference Shelf Ser: Vol. 44, No. 2). 256p. 1972. 6.25 (ISBN 0-8242-0465-4). Wilson.
--Water Crisis. (Reference Shelf Ser: Vol. 38, No. 6). 1967. 6.25 (ISBN 0-8242-0093-4). Wilson.
Nikol'ski, S. M., ed. Theory & Applications of Differentiable Functions of Several Variables, Vol. 4. LC 68-1677. (Proceedings of the Steklov Institute). 1974. 43.60 (ISBN 0-8218-3017-1, STEKLO-117). Am Math.
Nikolskii, G. V. Theory of Fish Population Dynamics As the Biological Background for Rational Exploitation & Management of Fishery Resources. Jones, R., ed. Bradley, J. E., tr. from Rus. (Illus.). 323p. 1980. Repr. of 1969 ed. lib. bdg. 43.25x (ISBN 3-87429-171-5). Lubrecht & Cramer.
Nikol'Skii, S. M., ed. Theory & Applications of Differentiable Functions of Several Variables, VII. (Trudy Steklov: No. 150). Date not set. cancelled (ISBN 0-8218-3047-3). Am Math.
Nikolsky, G. V. The Ecology of Fishes. rev ed. Orig. Title: The Biology of Fishes. (Illus.). 1978. pap. 4.95 (ISBN 0-87666-505-9, H-999). TFH Pubns.
Nikolsky, S. M., ed. see Steklov Institute of Mathematics, No. 117.
Nilakantha. The Elephant-Lore of the Hindus: The Elephant-Sport (Matanga-Lila) of Nilakantha. Edgerton, Franklin, ed. 1931. 32.50x (ISBN 0-686-50042-3). Elliots Bks.
Niles, John D., ed. Old English Literature in Context: Ten Essays. (Illus.). 184p. 1980. 42.50x (ISBN 0-8476-6770-7). Rowman.
Niles, John J. Singing Soldiers. LC 68-26595. 1968. Repr. of 1927 ed. 15.00 (ISBN 0-8103-3416-X). Gale.
Niles, Kathryn B. Food Preparation Recipes. 1955. text ed. 19.50x (ISBN 0-471-63888-9). Wiley.
Niles, Nathan O. Plane Trigonometry. 3rd ed. LC 75-28337. 394p. 1976. text ed. 18.95x (ISBN 0-471-64025-5); solutions manual avail. (ISBN 0-471-01716-7). Wiley.
Niles, P. H., ed. see Messier, Charles.
Nilles, Jack M., et al. The Telecommunications--Transportation Tradeoff: Options for Tomorrow. LC 76-18107. 196p. 1976. 34.95 (ISBN 0-471-01507-5, Pub. by Wiley-Interscience). Wiley.
Nilsen, Alleen P., jt. auth. see Nilsen, Don L.
Nilsen, Don L. & Nilsen, Alleen P. Pronunciation Contrasts in English. 1973. text ed. 4.50 o.p. (ISBN 0-88345-133-6, 17417); pap. text ed. 3.95 (ISBN 0-88345-134-4, 17416). Regents Pub.
Nilsen, Helge N. Hart Crane's Divided Vision: An Analysis of "The Bridge". 192p. 1980. pap. 20.00x (ISBN 82-00-01938-1). Universitet.
Nilsen, O, jt. auth. see Guezou, J.
Nilsen, Thomas R. Ethics of Speech Communication. 2nd ed. LC 72-86834. 1974. pap. 3.50 (ISBN 0-672-61300-X, SC10). Bobbs.
Nilson, Bee. Making Ice-Cream & Other Cold Sweets. 1973. 7.95 (ISBN 0-7207-0612-2, Pub. by Michael Joseph). Merrimack Bk Serv.
Nilsson, B. H. Competing in Cross-Country Skiing. LC 74-82340. (Illus.). 160p. (gr. 10 up). 1974. 9.95 (ISBN 0-8069-4076-X); PLB 9.29 (ISBN 0-8069-4077-8); pap. 4.95 (ISBN 0-8069-8866-5). Sterling.
Nilsson, Birgit. My Memoirs in Pictures. Teal, Thomas, tr. from Swedish. LC 78-22343. (Illus.). 128p. 1981. 19.95 (ISBN 0-385-14835-6). Doubleday.
Nilsson, Great, et al. Facts About Furs. rev. ed. Animal Welfare Institute, tr. LC 80-65265. (Illus.). 257p. 1980. pap. text ed. 3.00 (ISBN 0-938414-02-X). Animal Welfare.
Nilsson, Martin P. Greek Folk Religion. (Illus.). 8.50 (ISBN 0-8446-0218-3). Peter Smith.
--Greek Folk Religion. 1972. pap. 4.95x (ISBN 0-8122-1034-4, Pa. Paperbacks). U of Pa Pr.
--Homer & Mycenae. (Illus.). 1972. pap. 5.95x (ISBN 0-8122-1033-6, Pa. Paperbacks). U of Pa Pr.
--The Mycenaean Origin of Greek Mythology. enl ed. LC 70-181440. (Sather Classical Lectures: Vol. 8). 258p. 1973. 17.50x (ISBN 0-520-01951-2); pap. 3.65 o.p. (ISBN 0-520-02163-0, CAMPUS76). U of Cal Pr.
Nilsson, Nils A. Art, Society, Revolution: Russia 1917-1921. 272p. 1980. text ed. 25.00x (ISBN 0-391-01939-2). Humanities.
Nilsson, Nils A., ed. Russian Romanticism: Studies in the Poetic Codes. (Stockholm Studies in Russian Literature: No. 10). 226p. 1980. pap. 29.50x (ISBN 91-22-00281-2). Humanities.
Nilsson, Nils J. Principles of Artificial Intelligence. LC 79-67584. (Illus.). 1980. text ed. 27.50 (ISBN 0-935382-01-1). Tioga Pub Co.
Nilsson, Sam. The State of the Planet: A Report Prepared by the International Federation of Institutes for Advanced Study, Stockholm. (Illus.). 1980. 27.00 (ISBN 0-08-024717-2); pap. 12.00 (ISBN 0-08-024716-4). Pergamon.
Nilsson, W. D. & Hicks, Philip. Orientation to Professional Practice. (Illus.). 400p. 1980. text ed. 19.95 (ISBN 0-07-046571-1, C). McGraw.
Nilsson-Cantell, Carl A. Cirripedia Thoracica & Acrothoracica. (Illus.). 1978. pap. 16.50 (ISBN 82-00-01670-6, Dist. by Columbia U Pr). Universitet.
Nimbark, Jai. The Lotus Leaves. 12.00 (ISBN 0-89253-628-4); flexible cloth 4.80 (ISBN 0-89253-629-2). Ind-US Inc.
Nimley, Anthony J. The Liberian Bureaucracy: An Analysis & Evaluation of the Environment, Structures & Functions. LC 79-63561. 1979. pap. text ed. 11.25 (ISBN 0-8191-0732-8). U Pr of Amer.
Nimmer, Melville B. Cases & Materials on Copyright & Other Aspects of Law Pertaining to Literary, Musical & Artistic Works. 2nd ed. LC 79-13515. (American Casebook Ser.). (Illus.). 1023p. 1979. text ed. 21.95 (ISBN 0-8299-2038-2). West Pub.
Nimmer, Raymond T. The Nature of System Change: Reform Impact in the Criminal Courts. Sikes, Bette, ed. 1978. 10.00 (ISBN 0-910058-93-8); pap. 5.00 (ISBN 0-685-65361-7). Am Bar Foun.
Nimmo, D. & Combs, J. Subliminal Politics: Myths & Mythmakers in America. 1980. 10.95 (ISBN 0-13-859116-4); pap. 4.95 (ISBN 0-13-859108-3). P-H.
Nimmo, Dan & Ungs, Thomas. Political Patterns in America: Conflict Representation & Resolution. LC 78-11419. (Illus.). 1979. text ed. 16.95x (ISBN 0-7167-1009-9). W H Freeman.
Nimmo, Dan & Rivers, William L., eds. Watching American Politics. LC 80-23788. (Illus.). 336p. (Orig.). 1981. pap. text ed. 9.95 (ISBN 0-582-28197-0). Longman.
Nimmo, Ian. Portrait of Edinburgh. LC 71-401261. (Portrait Bks.). (Illus.). 1969. 10.50x (ISBN 0-7091-5350-3). Intl Pubns Serv.
Nimmo, W. S., ed. see International Conference on Drug Absorption, Edinburgh, 1979.
Nimocks, Patricia E. Decoupage. LC 68-11372. (Encore Ed.). (Illus.). 1968. 3.95 o.p. (ISBN 0-684-15430-7, ScribT). Scribner.
Nims, C. F. Thebes of the Pharaohs. 1965. 19.95 o.p. (ISBN 0-236-31027-5, Pub. by Paul Elek). Merrimack Bk Serv.
Nims, John F. The Harper Anthology of Poetry. (Illus.). 864p. 1980. text ed. write for info. (ISBN 0-06-044846-6, 0-06-44874, HarpC); pap. text ed. 10.50 scp (ISBN 0-06-044846-6). Har-Row.
Nims, John F., tr. The Poems of St. John of the Cross. 3rd ed. LC 79-12943. 1979. lib. bdg. 15.50x (ISBN 0-226-40108-1); pap. 4.50 (ISBN 0-226-40110-3, P845). U of Chicago Pr.
Nims, John Frederick. Western Wind. 1974. pap. text ed. 8.85 (ISBN 0-394-31231-7). Random.
Nimtz, August H., Jr. Islam & Politics in East Africa: The Sufi Order in Tanzania. LC 80-429. (Illus.). 1980. 20.00x (ISBN 0-8166-0963-2). U of Minn Pr.
Nimuendaju, Curt. Apinaye. Lowie, Robert H., tr. (Illus.). 1967. pap. text ed. 9.50x (ISBN 9-0623-4032-6). Humanities.
Nimzovich, Aron. Selected Games from the Carlsbad International Chess Tournament 1929. Marfia, Jim, tr. from Rus. 143p. (Orig.). 1981. pap. price not set (ISBN 0-486-24115-7). Dover.
Nin, Anais. Cities of the Interior, 5 vols. in 1. Incl. Ladders to Fire; Children of the Albatross; The Four-Chambered Heart; A Spy in the House of Love; Seduction of the Minotaur. LC 74-21884. (Illus.). xx, 589p. 1975. 19.95 (ISBN 0-8040-0665-2); pap. 12.95 (ISBN 0-8040-0666-0). Swallow.
--D. H. Lawrence: An Unprofessional Study. LC 64-16109. 110p. (Orig.). 1964. pap. 4.95 (ISBN 0-8040-0067-0, 58). Swallow.
--Diary of Anais Nin, 7 vols. 1978. Set. pap. 22.50 (ISBN 0-15-626034-4, Harv). HarBraceJ.
--House of Incest. LC 61-65487. 72p. 1958. pap. 3.95 (ISBN 0-8040-0148-0, 31). Swallow.
--Ladders to Fire. LC 61-66834. 152p. 1959. pap. 5.95 (ISBN 0-8040-0181-2, 79, 79). Swallow.
--Linotte: The Early Diary of Anais Nin 1914-1920, Vol. 1. Sherman, Jean, tr. LC 77-20314. (Illus.). 1978. 14.95 o.p. (ISBN 0-15-152488-2). HarBraceJ.
--Novel of the Future. 1970. pap. 2.95 o.s.i. (ISBN 0-02-053100-1, Collier). Macmillan.
--A Photographic Supplement to the Diary of Anais Nin. LC 77-2085. 80p. (Orig.). 1974. pap. 2.95 (ISBN 0-15-626024-7, HB293, Harv). HarBraceJ.
--Seduction of the Minotaur. LC 61-17529. (Orig.). 1961. pap. 5.95 (ISBN 0-8040-0268-1, 28). Swallow.
--Spy in the House of Love. LC 66-6833. 140p. 1959. pap. 5.95 (ISBN 0-8040-0280-0, 82). Swallow.
--Under a Glass Bell. LC 61-65444. 101p. 1948. pap. 3.95 (ISBN 0-8040-0302-5, 30). Swallow.
--Waste of Timelessness: And Other Early Stories. LC 74-28648. 105p. 1980. 7.95 (ISBN 0-8027-0569-3). Ohio U Pr.
--Waste of Timelessness & Other Early Stories. 1977. 7.95 o.s.i. (ISBN 0-8027-0569-3). Walker & Co.
--Winter of Artifice. LC 61-17530. 175p. (Orig.). 1961. pap. 5.95 (ISBN 0-8040-0322-X, 29). Swallow.
Nineham, D. E. Saint Mark. LC 77-81621. (Westminster Pelican Commentaries Ser.). 1978. 12.95 (ISBN 0-664-21344-8). Westminster.
Nineham, D. E., ed. see Henderson, Ian.
Nineham, D. E., ed. see Thomas, J. Heywood.
Nineham, D. E., ed. see Towers, Bernard.
Nineham, Dennis E., ed. see Perkins, Robert L.
Ninkovich, F. A. The Diplomacy of Ideas: U. S. Foreign Policy & Cultural Relations, 1938-1950. 256p. Date not set. 24.95 (ISBN 0-521-23241-4). Cambridge U Pr.
Ninomiya, Kazuji, tr. see Mori, Ogai.
Niobey, G. Dictionnaire analogique. (Fr). 26.50 (ISBN 0-685-13850-X, 3608). Larousse.
Nipp, Susan, jt. auth. see Beall, Pamela.
Nirenberg, Jesse S. Breaking Through to Each Other: Creative Persuasion on the Job & in the Home. LC 74-1841. 192p. 1976. 9.95 o.s.i. (ISBN 0-06-013207-8, HarpT). Har-Row.
Nirenberg, Louis. Lectures on Linear Partial Differential Equations. LC 74-4400. (CBMS Regional Conference Series in Mathematics: No. 17). 1979. pap. 5.60 (ISBN 0-8218-1667-5, CBMS-17). Am Math.

Niro-Sey, K., ed. see Internaional Numismatic Symposium, Warsaw & Budapest, 1976.
Nisbet, Ada. Dickens & Ellen Ternan. 1952. 15.00x (ISBN 0-520-00946-0). U of Cal Pr.
Nisbet, Ada & Nevius, Blake, eds. Dickens Centennial Essays. 1971. 18.50x (ISBN 0-520-01874-5). U of Cal Pr.
Nisbet, H. B. Goethe's Die Wahlverwandtschaften. Reiss, Hans, ed. (Blackwell's German Text Ser.). 1971. pap. 6.00x o.p. (ISBN 0-631-01840-9, Pub. by Basil Blackwell). Biblio Dist.
Nisbet, H. B., ed. see Hegel, Georg W.
Nisbet, J., jt. auth. see Watts, L.
Nisbet, James D. The Dow Is Dead: How to Profit in Uncommon Stocks. Folts, Betty, ed. LC 79-54885. (Illus.). 1979. 14.95 (ISBN 0-686-26329-4). Capital Tech.
--The Entrepreneur. Folts, Betty, ed. (Illus.). 1976. 10.00 (ISBN 0-686-63615-5). Capital Tech.
Nisbet, John, et al. Towards Community Education: An Evaluation of Community Schools. 144p. 1980. 20.25 (ISBN 0-08-025735-6). Pergamon.
Nisbet, R. G., ed. see Cicero.
Nisbet, Robert. Sociology As an Art Form. LC 76-9278. 1976. 12.95 (ISBN 0-19-502102-9). Oxford U Pr.
--Sociology of Emile Durkheim. 320p. 1973. 17.95 (ISBN 0-19-501733-1); pap. 4.95x (ISBN 0-19-501734-X). Oxford U Pr.
--Twilight of Authority. 272p. 1975. 14.95x (ISBN 0-19-501942-3). Oxford U Pr.
--Twilight of Authority. LC 75-7357. 1977. pap. 5.95 (ISBN 0-19-502177-0, 485, GB). Oxford U Pr.
Nisbet, Robert, jt. ed. see Bottomore, Tom.
Nisbet, Robert A. Quest for Community. 1962. pap. 5.95 (ISBN 0-19-500703-4, GB91, GB). Oxford U Pr.
--Social Change & History: Aspects of the Western Theory of Development. LC 69-17772. 1970. pap. 5.95 (ISBN 0-19-500805-7, 313, GB). Oxford U Pr.
Nisbet, Robin G. & Hubbard, Margaret. Commentary on Horace: Odes. Bk. 1 1970. 55.00x (ISBN 0-19-814439-3); Bk. 2 1978. 39.00x (ISBN 0-19-814452-0). Oxford U Pr.
Nisbet, T. S. Rolling Bearings. (Engineering Design Guides Ser.). (Illus.). 1974. pap. 12.50x (ISBN 0-19-859135-7). Oxford U Pr.
Nisbett, Alec. Technique of the Sound Studio. 3rd ed. (Library of Communication Techniques). Date not set. 12.50 (ISBN 0-8038-7122-8). Hastings.
Nisbett, Richard & Ross, Lee. Human Inference: Strategies & Shortcomings in Social Judgement. (Century Psychology Ser.). (Illus.). 1980. text ed. 15.95 (ISBN 0-13-445130-9). P-H.
Nisevich, N. I., jt. ed. see Marchuk, G. I.
Nish, Dale L. Artistic Woodturning. LC 80-21302. (Illus.). 288p. 1980. 17.95 (ISBN 0-8425-1842-8); pap. 12.95 (ISBN 0-8425-1826-6). Brigham.
Nish, I & Steeds, D. China, Japan, & Nineteenth Century Britain. (Government & Society in Nineteenth Century Britain Ser.). 1977. 20.00x (ISBN 0-7165-2225-X, Pub. by Irish Academic Pr Ireland). Biblio Dist.
Nish, Ian. Japanese Foreign Policy, 1869-1942: Kasumigaseki to Miyakezaka. (Foreign Policies of the Great Powers Ser.). 1976. 22.00 (ISBN 0-7100-8421-8). Routledge & Kegan.
--The Story of Japan. (Story Ser.). (Illus.). 1968. 6.95 (ISBN 0-571-08440-0, Pub. by Faber & Faber). Merrimack Bk Serv.
Nish, Ian H. Alliance in Decline: A Study in Anglo-Japanese Relations 1908-23. (University of London Historical Studies: No. 33). (Illus.). 472p. (Orig.). 1972. text ed. 47.00x (ISBN 0-485-13133-1, Athlone Pr). Humanities.
Nishi, Toshio. The American Experiment: Japan 1945-1952. (Publication Ser.: No. 244). 380p. 1981. 19.95 (ISBN 0-8179-7441-5). Hoover Inst Pr.
--The American Experiment: Japan 1945-1952, No. 244. 380p. 1981. 19.95 (ISBN 0-8179-7441-5). Hoover Inst Pr.
Nishida, Kitaro. Intelligibility & the Philosophy of Nothingness. Schinzinger, Robert, tr. from Japanese. LC 72-12319. (Illus.). 251p. 1973. Repr. of 1958 ed. lib. bdg. 24.75x (ISBN 0-8371-6689-6, NIIP). Greenwood.
Nishikawa, Kyotaro. Bugaku Masks. Bethe, Monica, tr. LC 77-75971. (Japanese Arts Library: Vol. 5). (Illus.). 1978. 16.75 (ISBN 0-87011-312-7). Kodansha.
Nishimoto, Richard, jt. auth. see Thomas, Dorothy S.
Nishimura, Shizuya. Decline of Inland Bills of Exchange in the London Money Market, 1855-1913. LC 70-134613. (Illus.). 1971. 41.00 (ISBN 0-521-08055-X). Cambridge U Pr.
Nishio, T., jt. auth. see Osaki, S.
Nishisato, Shizuhiko. Analysis of Categorical Data: Dual Scaling & Its Applications. (Mathematical Expositions Ser.). 148p. 1980. 25.00x (ISBN 0-8020-5489-7). U of Toronto Pr.
Nishiwaki, Junzaburo, jt. ed. see Kawamoto, Shigeo.
Nishiyama, Hidetaka & Brown, Richard C. Karate: Art of Empty Hand Fighting. LC 59-10409. (Illus.). (gr. 9 up). 1960. 22.50 (ISBN 0-8048-0340-4). C E Tuttle.
Niss, James F. & Smith, Melvin H. Consumer Economics. (Illus.). 224p. 1974. pap. 9.95 ref. ed. (ISBN 0-13-169441-3). P-H.
Niss, Mogens, jt. auth. see Booss, Bernhelm.
Nissen, M., jt. auth. see Steimann, I.
Nissen, Ursula, jt. ed. see Meyer, Manfred.
Nissenbaum, Stephen, jt. ed. see Boyer, Paul.
Nissiotis, M. Interpeting Orthodoxy. 1980. pap. 2.45 (ISBN 0-937032-23-9). Light&Life Pub Co MN.
Nissman, Blossom S., jt. auth. see Stamm, Martin L.
Nissman, David M., et al. Beating the Insanity Defense: Denying the License to Kill. LC 80-8028. 1980. 18.95 (ISBN 0-669-03943-8). Lexington Bks.
Nist, Al, jt. auth. see Jameson, Mack.
Nist, John. Love Songs for Marisa. 1978. 10.95 (ISBN 0-89002-116-3); pap. 3.50 (ISBN 0-89002-115-5). Northwoods Pr.
--Phonological Aspects of Modern English. LC 78-53426. 1978. pap. text ed. 8.25x (ISBN 0-8191-0495-7). U Pr of Amer.
Nister, Ernest. Animal Tales. (Illus.). 7.95 (ISBN 0-529-05612-7). Philomel.
--Golden Tales from Long Ago, 3 vols. LC 80-7614. (Illus., 24p. ea.). (gr. 3-12). 1980. Set. 5.95 (ISBN 0-440-03015-3). Delacorte.
--Magic Windows: An Antique Revolving Picture Book. (Illus.). 14p. (ps up). 1981. 6.95 (ISBN 0-399-20773-2). Philomel.
Niswander, Kenneth R. Obstetrics: Essentials of Clinical Practice. 2nd ed. 1981. pap. text ed. price not set. Little.
Nitchie, Edward. How to Read Lips for Fun & Profit. 1979. pap. 3.95 (ISBN 0-8015-3740-1, Hawthorn). Dutton.
Nitchie, George W. Marianne Moore: An Introduction to the Poetry. LC 79-96998. 1969. 15.00x (ISBN 0-231-03119-X); pap. 5.00 (ISBN 0-231-08312-2, CP148). Columbia U Pr.
Nite, Norm N. Rock on: The Illustrated Encyclopedia of Rock 'n Roll: the Solid Gold Years. LC 74-12247. (Illus.). 448p. 1974. 16.95 (ISBN 0-690-00583-0, TYC-T). T Y Crowell.
Nitecki, Matthew H. Biotic Crises in Ecological & Evolutionary Time. LC 80-70597. 1981. 25.00 (ISBN 0-12-519640-7). Acad Pr.
Nitecki, Z. & Robinson, C., eds. Global Theory of Dynamical Systems: Proceedings. (Lecture Notes in Mathematics Ser.: Vol. 819). 499p. 1981. pap. 29.50 (ISBN 0-387-10236-1). Springer-Verlag.
Nitecki, Zbigniew. Differentiable Dynamics: An Introduction to the Orbit Structure of Diffeomorphisms. 1971. pap. 10.00x (ISBN 0-262-64011-2). MIT Pr.
Nitka, Louis. Ski with Nitka. LC 72-82134. (Illus.). 64p. 1972. pap. 1.25 o.p. (ISBN 0-88208-006-7). Lawrence Hill.
Nitsch, Friedrich A. A General & Introductory View of Professor Kant's Principles. Wellek, Rene, ed. LC 75-11240. (British & Theologians of the 17th & 18th Centuries: Vol. 40). 1977. Repr. of 1796 ed. lib. bdg. 42.00 (ISBN 0-8240-1792-7). Garland Pub.
Nitske, W. Robert & Wilson, Charles M. Rudolph Diesel: Pioneer in the Age of Power. (Illus.). 318p. (Orig.). 1965. pap. 7.95 (ISBN 0-8061-1164-X). U of Okla Pr.
Nitske, W. Robert, tr. see Wilhelm, Paul.
Nitti, John J. Aragonese Version of the Libro De Marco Polo. 1980. write for info. Hispanic Seminary.
Nittler, Alan. Health Questions & Answers. 1976. pap. 1.75 o.s.i. (ISBN 0-515-03723-0). Jove Pubns.
Nitz, Paul H., et al. Securing the Seas: The Soviet Naval Challenge & Western Alliance Options. (Illus.). 1979. lib. bdg. 29.50x (ISBN 0-89158-359-9); pap. text ed. 14.50x (ISBN 0-89158-360-2). Westview.
Nitze, William A. & Wilkins, Ernest H. A Handbook of French Phonetics. 1945. pap. text ed. 12.95x (ISBN 0-89197-781-3). Irvington.
Nitzsche, Jane C. The Genius Figure in Antiquity & the Middle Ages. LC 74-17206. 1975. 15.00x (ISBN 0-231-03852-6). Columbia U Pr.
Nitzsche, Werner & Wenzel, Gerhard. Haploids in Plant Breeding. (Advances in Plant Breeding Ser.). (Illus.). 101p. 1977. pap. text ed. 28.00 (ISBN 3-489-75010-1). Parey Sci Pubs.
Nivardus, Magister. Ysengrimus. Sypher, F. J. & Sypher, Eleanor, trs. from Lat. (Illus.). 280p. 1980. 95.00x (ISBN 0-8386-3005-7). F Sypher.
Nivedita, Sr. Complete Works of Sister Nivedita, 4 vols. Incl. Vol. 1. Our Master & His Message, the Master As I Saw Him, Kali the Mother, Lectures & Articles (ISBN 0-87481-112-0); Vol. 2. The Web of Indian Life, an Indian Study on Love & Death, Studies from an Eastern Home, Lectures & Articles (ISBN 0-87481-113-9); Vol. 3. Indian Art, Cradle Tales of Hinduism, Religion & Dharma (ISBN 0-87481-114-7); Vol. 4. Footfalls of Indian History, Bodh-Gaya, Civic Ideal & Indian Nationality, Hints on National Education in India (ISBN 0-87481-115-5). 32.00x set (ISBN 0-87481-150-3). Vedanta Pr.
--Cradle Tales of Hinduism. (Illus.). 329p. (gr. 3-12). 1972. 5.75 o.s.i. (ISBN 0-87481-170-8); pap. 3.95 (ISBN 0-87481-131-7). Vedanta Pr.
--Footfalls of Indian History. (Illus.). pap. 2.95 o.p. (ISBN 0-87481-127-9). Vedanta Pr.
--Master As I Saw Him. 6.50 (ISBN 0-87481-088-4). Vedanta Pr.
Nivelle, Armand. Fruehromantische Dichtungstheorie. (Ger). 1970. 35.90x (ISBN 3-11-002703-8). De Gruyter.
Niven. D. H. Lawrence. 1980. 9.95 (ISBN 0-684-16666-6, ScribT). Scribner.
Niven, A. D. H. Lawrence: The Novels. LC 77-8475. (British Authors Ser.). 1978. 26.50 (ISBN 0-521-21744-X); pap. 7.95 (ISBN 0-521-29272-7). Cambridge U Pr.
Niven, Alexander C. A Brief History of Russia to 1689. LC 78-54603. 1978. pap. text ed. 6.75x (ISBN 0-8191-0511-2). U Pr of Amer.
Niven, Douglas. The Development of Housing in Scotland. (Illus.). 136p. 1979. 19.00x (ISBN 0-7099-0159-3, Pub. by Croom Helm Lgtd England). Biblio Dist.
Niven, Ivan & Zuckerman, Herbert S. An Introduction to the Theory of Numbers. 4th ed. LC 79-24869. 355p. 1980. text ed. 19.95 (ISBN 0-471-02851-7); solutions manual avail. (ISBN 0-471-06394-0). Wiley.
Niven, John. Gideon Welles. (Illus.). 500p. 1973. 27.50 (ISBN 0-19-501693-9). Oxford U Pr.
Niven, Larry. The Flight of the Horse. 1976. pap. 1.95 (ISBN 0-345-27549-7). Ballantine.
--A Gift from Earth. 256p. 1975. pap. 1.50 o.p. (ISBN 0-345-24509-1). Ballantine.
--Hole in Space. (Orig.). 1976. pap. 1.95 (ISBN 0-345-29225-1). Ballantine.
--Long Arm of Gil Hamilton. 1976. pap. 1.95 (ISBN 0-345-28922-6). Ballantine.
--Protector. 224p. (Orig.). 1981. pap. 2.25 (ISBN 0-345-29302-9, Del Rey). Ballantine.
--Ringworld. 352p. (Orig.). 1981. pap. 2.50 (ISBN 0-345-29301-0, Del Rey). Ballantine.
--The Ringworld Engineers. 368p. 1981. pap. 2.50 (ISBN 0-345-26009-0, Del Rey). Ballantine.
--World of Ptavvs. 192p. Date not set. pap. 1.95 (ISBN 0-345-28619-7). Ballantine.
--A World Out of Time. 1976. 7.95 o.p. (ISBN 0-03-017776-6). HR&W.
Niven, Larry, jt. auth. see Gerrold, David.
Niver, Kemp R. D. W. Griffith: His Biograph Films in Perspective. LC 74-81838. (Illus.). 1974. 15.00 (ISBN 0-913986-06-2). Locare.
--D. W. Griffith's "the Battle at Elderbush Gulch". LC 72-85599. (Illus.). 1972. 7.50 (ISBN 0-913986-04-6). Locare.
--Klaw & Erlanger: Famous Plays in Pictures. LC 75-44556. (Illus.). 1976. 15.00 (ISBN 0-913986-07-0). Locare.
--Motion Pictures from the Library of Congress Paper Print Collection, 1894-1912. 1967. 57.50x (ISBN 0-520-00947-9). U of Cal Pr.
Nivison, Davdi, ed. A Concordance to Chu Hsi, "Ta Hsieh Chang Chu". And a Concordance to Chu Hsi, Chung Yung Chang Chu, Vol. 1. (Stanford Chinese Concordance Ser.). 1979. 20.00x (ISBN 0-89644-575-5, SCCS-1). Chinese Materials.
Nivison, David S., ed. A Concordance to Tai Chen, "Yuan Shan". Bd. with A Concordance to Tai Chen, "Meng Tzu I Shu Cheng". (No. 6, Vol. 4). vi, 496p. (Stanford Chinese Concordance Ser.: No. 5, Vol. 4). xxviii, 152p. 1979. 35.00x. Chinese Materials.
--A Concordance to Wang Yang-Ming, "Ch'uan Hsi Lu.". Concordance. Bd. with Concordance to Wang Yang-Ming, "Ta Hsueh Wen". (No. 4, Vol. 3). iv, 42p. (Stanford Chinese Concordance Ser.: No. 3.2, Vol. 3). xxvi, 510p. 1979. 30.00x (ISBN 0-89644-577-1). Chinese Materials.
Nivola, Pietro S. The Urban Service Problem: A Study of Housing Inspection. LC 78-21444. 192p. 1979. 19.95 (ISBN 0-669-02801-0). Lexington Bks.
Niwano, Nikkyo. Buddhism for Today. 476p. 1980. pap. 10.95 (ISBN 0-8348-0147-7, Pub. by John Weathehill Inc Japan). C E Tuttle.
Niwayama, Gen, jt. auth. see Resnick, Donald.
Nix, J. S., jt. auth. see Barnard, C. S.
Nix, Sam. Salt-Water Fly-Fishing Handbook. LC 71-180095. 168p. 1973. 3.95 o.p. (ISBN 0-385-04033-4). Doubleday.
Nix, William E., jt. auth. see Geisler, Norman L.
Nixon. Muffie & the Birthday Party. (ps-3). 1980. pap. 1.25 (ISBN 0-590-30064-4, Schol Pap). Schol Bk Serv.
--Surgical Conditions in Pediatrics. Apley, M. J., ed. (Operative Surgery Ser.). 1978. 68.95 (ISBN 0-407-00090-9). Butterworths.
Nixon, A. U., jt. ed. see Fisher, K. D.
Nixon, H. C., jt. auth. see Grant, Daniel R.
Nixon, H. H. Pediatric Surgery. 3rd ed. Rob & Smith, eds. (Operative Surgery Ser.). 1978. 125.00 (ISBN 0-407-00634-6). Butterworths.
Nixon, Harold, jt. auth. see Charles-Edwards, Imelda.
Nixon, Hershell H. & Lowery, Joan. Oil & Gas: From Fossils to Fuel. LC 77-1671. (Let Me Read Bk.). (Illus.). 64p. (gr. 1-4). 1977. 5.95 (ISBN 0-15-257700-9, HJ). HarBraceJ.
Nixon, Hershell H. & Nixon, Joan L. Volcanoes: Nature's Fireworks. LC 77-16873. (Illus.). (gr. 2-5). 1978. 4.95 (ISBN 0-396-07559-2). Dodd.
Nixon, Howard L. The Small Group. LC 78-13207. (P-H Ser. in Sociology). (Illus.). 1979. ref. ed. 17.95 (ISBN 0-13-814244-0). P-H.
Nixon, Howard L., III. Sport & Social Organization. LC 75-31742. (Studies in Sociology). 64p. 1976. pap. text ed. 4.50 (ISBN 0-672-61337-9). Bobbs.
Nixon, Howard M. Five Centuries of English Bookbinding. (Illus.). 244p. 1978. 35.00 (ISBN 0-85967-411-8, Pub. by Scolar Pr England). Biblio Dist.
Nixon, Joan L. Before You Were Born. LC 79-91741. (Illus.). 32p. (ps up). 1980. 5.95 (ISBN 0-87973-353-5); pap. 3.95 (ISBN 0-87973-343-8). Our Sunday Visitor.
--Casey & the Great Idea. (Illus.). (gr. 4-6). 1980. PLB 9.95 (ISBN 0-525-27525-8). Dutton.
--The Christmas Eve Mystery. Fay, Ann, ed. (First Read-Alone Mysteries Ser.). (Illus.). 32p. (gr. 1-3). 1981. 5.50 (ISBN 0-8075-1150-1). A Whitman.
--The Halloween Mystery. Pacini, Kathy, ed. LC 79-166. (First Read-Alone Mysteries). (Illus.). (gr. 1-3). 1979. 5.50g (ISBN 0-8075-3136-7). A Whitman.
--The Happy Birthday Mystery. Ann, Fay, ed. LC 79-18362. (First Read-Alone Mysteries). (Illus.). (gr. 1-3). 1980. 5.50g (ISBN 0-8075-3150-2). A Whitman.
--The Kidnapping of Christina Lattimore. (gr. 7-12). 1980. pap. 1.50 (ISBN 0-440-94520-8, LFL). Dell.
--Muffie Mouse & the Busy Birthday. LC 77-28866. (ps-3). 1978. 6.95 (ISBN 0-395-28868-1, Clarion). HM.
--The New Year's Mystery. Pacini, Kathy, ed. LC 79-172. (First Read-Alone Mysteries Ser.). (Illus.). (gr. 1-3). 1979. 5.50g (ISBN 0-8075-5592-4). A Whitman.
--The Thanksgiving Mystery. Fay, Ann, ed. LC 79-27346. (A First Read-Alone Mystery Bk.). (Illus.). (gr. 1-3). 1980. PLB 5.50 (ISBN 0-8075-7820-7). A Whitman.
--The Valentine Mystery. Tucker, Kathleen, ed. LC 79-7055. (First Read-Alone Mysteries). (Illus.). (gr. 1-3). 1979. 5.50g (ISBN 0-8075-8450-9). A Whitman.
Nixon, Joan L. & Fay, Ann. The April Fool Mystery. LC 80-18809. (First Read-Alone Mysteries Ser.). (Illus.). 32p. (gr. 1-3). 1980. 5.50g (ISBN 0-8075-0406-8). A Whitman.
Nixon, Joan L., jt. auth. see Nixon, Hershell H.
Nixon, Lucille M. & Tana, Tomoe, trs. Sounds from the Unknown: A Collection of Japanese-American Tanka. LC 64-16108. 133p. (Orig.). 1963. 3.75 o.p. (ISBN 0-8040-0278-9); pap. 2.95 (ISBN 0-8040-0279-7, 60). Swallow.
Nixon, Richard. The Memoirs of Richard Nixon, Vol. 1. 736p. 1981. pap. 2.95 (ISBN 0-446-93259-0). Warner Bks.
--The Memoirs of Richard Nixon, Vol. 2. 728p. 1981. pap. 2.95 (ISBN 0-446-93260-4). Warner Bks.
--The Real War. 400p. 1981. pap. 3.50 (ISBN 0-446-96136-1). Warner Bks.
--The Real War. LC 79-28358. 320p. 1980. 12.50 (ISBN 0-446-51201-X). Warner Bks.
--RN: The Memoirs of Richard Nixon, 2 vols. (Illus.). 1979. pap. 2.95 ea. Vol. 1, 736p (ISBN 0-446-93259-0). Vol. 3, 728p (ISBN 0-446-93260-4). Warner Bks.
Nixon, Richard M. Six Crises. 576p. 1981. pap. 2.95 (ISBN 0-446-93101-2). Warner Bks.
Nixon, Tom. Fly Tying & Fly Fishing for Bass & Panfish. 2nd rev. ed. LC 75-20613. 14.50 (ISBN 0-498-01826-1). A S Barnes.
Nixon, W. M. The Sailing Cruiser. LC 77-28372. (Illus.). 1978. 12.95 (ISBN 0-396-07573-8). Dodd.
Nixson, Fred, jt. auth. see Colman, David.
Nizami, Azra, ed. & tr. see Husaini, Khwaza K.
Nizan, Paul. Antoine Bloye. Stevens, Edmund, tr. from Fr. LC 72-92034. 256p. (YA) 1973. 6.95 o.p. (ISBN 0-85345-277-6, CL2776). Monthly Rev.
--The Trojan Horse. 1975. Repr. 15.50 (ISBN 0-86527-317-0). Fertig.
Nizer, Louis. My Life in Court. 1978. pap. 1.95 o.s.i. (ISBN 0-515-04570-5). Jove Pubns.

Njoku, John E. Analyzing Nigerian-Americans Under a New Economic Order. LC 80-5916. 128p. (Orig.). 1981. pap. text ed. 7.50 (ISBN 0-8191-1448-0). U Pr of Amer.

--The World of the African Woman. LC 80-23832. 132p. 1980. 10.00 (ISBN 0-8108-1350-5). Scarecrow.

Nkrumah, Kwame. Africa Must Unite. LC 70-140209. 1970. 6.95 (ISBN 0-7178-0295-7); pap. 2.95 (ISBN 0-7178-0296-5). Intl Pub Co.

--Handbook of Revolutionary Warfare. (Orig.). 1969. pap. 1.95 (ISBN 0-7178-0226-4). Intl Pub Co.

--Revolutionary Path. LC 73-78905. 1973. 12.50 (ISBN 0-7178-0400-3); pap. 4.95 (ISBN 0-7178-0401-1). Intl Pub Co.

Noad, Frederick M. The Guitar Songbook. LC 69-16492. 1969. pap. 6.95 (ISBN 0-02-871730-9). Schirmer Bks.

--Playing the Guitar. 3rd ed. LC 80-5494. (Illus.). 1981. pap. 7.95 (ISBN 0-02-871990-5). Schirmer Bks.

--Solo Guitar Playing, Book 1. 2nd ed. LC 76-12833. 1976. pap. 7.95 (ISBN 0-02-871680-9). Schirmer Bks.

Noah, Harold J. Financing Soviet Schools. LC 66-29416. (Orig.). 1967. text ed. 9.25x (ISBN 0-8077-1857-2); pap. text ed. 7.00x (ISBN 0-8077-1854-8). Tchrs Coll.

Noakes, Ann M., jt. ed. see Hranitz, John R.

Noakes, D., jt. ed. see Bergens, A.

Noakes, David, tr. see Hodeir, Andre.

Noakes, G. R., jt. auth. see Bacon, G. E.

Noakes, G. R., jt. auth. see Taylor, A. W.

Noakes, G. R., ed. Sources of Physics Teaching: Atomic Energy. Holography. Electrostatics, Vol. 4. 1970. pap. text ed. 12.95x (ISBN 0-85066-038-6). Intl Ideas.

--Sources of Physics Teaching: Gravity. Liquids. Gases, Vol. 5. 1970. pap. text ed. 12.95x (ISBN 0-85066-040-8). Intl Ideas.

Noakes, G. R., et al, eds. Sources of Physics Teaching: Electrolysis, X-Ray Analysis. Electron Diffraction, Vol. 3. 1969. pap. 11.95x (ISBN 0-85066-031-9). Intl Ideas.

Noakes, Ingrid, tr. see Kaelble, Hartmut.

Noakes, Jeremy. The Nazi Party in Lower Saxony 1921-1933. (Oxford Historical Monographs). (Illus.). 312p. 1971. 29.50x (ISBN 0-19-821839-7). Oxford U Pr.

Noar, Gertrude. Every Child a Winner: Individualized Instruction. 150p. 1981. pap. price not set (ISBN 0-89874-340-0). Krieger.

--Individualized Instruction: Every Child a Winner. LC 71-179420. 1972. pap. text ed. 7.50x o.p. (ISBN 0-471-64157-X). Wiley.

Noback, Charles & Demarest, Robert. The Human Nervous System: Basic Principles of Neurobiology. 3rd ed. (Illus.). 1980. text ed. 24.00 (ISBN 0-07-046851-6, HP). McGraw.

Nobay, A. R. see Artis, M. J.

Nobay, A. R., ed. see Association of University Teachers of Economics, Edinburgh, 1976.

Nobay, A. R., jt. ed. see Parkin, J. M.

Nobbs, Douglas. England & Scotland, 1560-1707. LC 80-25749. xxi, 173p. 1981. Repr. of 1952 ed. lib. bdg. 19.75x (ISBN 0-313-22773-X, NOES). Greenwood.

Nobecourt, Jacques. Hitler's Last Gamble. 1980. pap. 2.25 (ISBN 0-505-51474-5). Tower Bks.

Nobel, Park S. Introduction to Biophysical Plant Physiology. LC 73-13696. (Illus.). 1974. text ed. 27.95x (ISBN 0-7167-0592-3). W H Freeman.

Nobel, Pat. Bloodbath Hill. (Orig.). 1980. pap. 2.25 (ISBN 0-532-23187-2). Manor Bks.

--One on One. (Orig.). 1980. pap. 2.25 (ISBN 0-532-23186-4). Manor Bks.

Nobel, Peter, jt. ed. see Melander, Goran.

Nobes, Chris. Introduction to Financial Accounting. (Illus.). 272p. 1980. text ed. 27.50x (ISBN 0-04-332071-6, 2363); pap. text ed. 11.50x (ISBN 0-04-332072-4, 2364). Allen Unwin.

Nobes, Christopher, jt. auth. see James, Simon.

Nobile, Philip, ed. Favorite Movies: Critics' Choice. 320p. 1973. 8.95 o.s.i. (ISBN 0-02-589800-0). Macmillan.

Nobile, Philip, jt. ed. see Deedy, John.

Noble, Andrew, ed. Selected Literary Criticism of Edwin Muir. (Barnes & Noble Critical Studies). 208p. 1981. 27.50x (ISBN 0-389-20202-9). B&N.

Noble, Ben & Daniel, James W. Applied Linear Algebra. 2nd ed. (Illus.). 1977. ref. ed. 20.95 (ISBN 0-13-041343-7). P-H.

Noble, D. Progress in Biophysics & Molecular Biology, Vol. 34. 1979. 62.50 (ISBN 0-08-024858-6). Pergamon.

Noble, D. & Blundell, T. L., eds. Progress in Biophysics & Molecular Biology, Vol. 35. (Illus.). 206p. 1981. 62.50 (ISBN 0-08-027122-7). Pergamon.

Noble, Daniel. Brain & Its Physiology. (Contributions to the History of Pcychology E. V, Physiological Psychology Ser.). 1980. Repr. of 1846 ed. 30.00 (ISBN 0-89093-324-3). U Pubns Amer.

Noble, David. Ancient Ruins of the Southwest: An Archaeological Guide. LC 80-83016. (Illus.). 128p. 1981. pap. 8.95 (ISBN 0-87358-274-8). Northland.

--Facts & Observations Relative to the Influence on Manufactures Upon Health & Life. 81p. 1971. Repr. of 1843 ed. 13.00x (ISBN 0-686-28333-3, Pub. by Irish Academic Pr). Biblio Dist.

Noble, David F. America by Design: Science, Technology, & the Rise of Corporate Capitalism. (Galaxy Books). 410p. (Orig.). 1979. pap. 5.95 (ISBN 0-19-502618-7, GB 588, GB). Oxford U Pr.

Noble, Denis. The Initiation of the Heartbeat. 2nd ed. 1977. 19.95x (ISBN 0-19-857177-1); pap. text ed. 9.95x (ISBN 0-19-857178-X). Oxford U Pr.

Noble, Enrique, ed. Literatura Afro-Hispano Americana: Poesia y prosa de ficcion. LC 77-189125. 216p. 1973. pap. text ed. 8.95x (ISBN 0-471-00757-9). Wiley.

Noble, Frances. Destiny's Daughter. 1980. pap. 2.25 (ISBN 0-505-51462-1). Tower Bks.

Noble, Gil. Black Is the Color of My TV Tube. (Illus.). 1981. 10.00 (ISBN 0-8184-0297-0). Lyle Stuart.

Noble, Iris. Susan B. Anthony. LC 74-30230. (Biography Ser). 192p. (gr. 7 up). 1975. PLB 5.29 o.p. (ISBN 0-671-32715-1). Messner.

--Treasure of the Caves: The Story of the Dead Sea Scrolls. LC 69-11303. (Illus.). (gr. 7 up). 1971. 5.95 o.s.i. (ISBN 0-02-768130-0). Macmillan.

Noble, J. K. Bowmar-Noble Handwriting, 9 bks. Incl. Bk. A (ISBN 0-8372-3752-1). tchr's ed. (ISBN 0-8372-3761-0); Bk. B (ISBN 0-8372-3753-X). tchr's ed. (ISBN 0-8372-3761-0); Bk. C (ISBN 0-8372-3754-8). tchr's ed. (ISBN 0-8372-3761-0); Bk. D (ISBN 0-8372-3755-6). tchr's ed. (ISBN 0-8372-3761-0); Bk. E (ISBN 0-8372-3756-4). tchr's ed. (ISBN 0-8372-3762-9); Bk. F (ISBN 0-8372-3757-2). tchr's ed. (ISBN 0-8372-3762-9); Bk. G (ISBN 0-8372-3758-0). tchr's ed. (ISBN 0-8372-3762-9); Bk. H (ISBN 0-8372-3759-9). tchr's ed. (ISBN 0-8372-3762-9); Bk. I (ISBN 0-8372-3760-2). tchr's ed. (ISBN 0-8372-3762-9). (80p. ea.). (gr. k-8). Date not set. pap. 1.95 ea.; tchr's eds. 2.52 ea. Bowmar-Noble.

Noble, Judith & Lacosa, Jaime. Handbook of Spanish Verbs. (gr. 9-12). 1980. pap. text ed. 18.95 (ISBN 0-8138-1095-7). Iowa St U Pr.

Noble, June. Where Do I Fit In? LC 79-1073. (Illus.). 32p. (gr. k-2). 1981. 6.95 (ISBN 0-03-046181-2). HR&W.

Noble, June & Noble, William. The Custody Trap: Helping Children of Divorce. LC 78-64642. Date not set. pap. 4.50 cancelled (ISBN 0-931328-03-9). Timely Bks.

Noble, Lela G., jt. auth. see Suhrke, Astri.

Noble, Margaret see Nivedita, Sr.

Noble, Marguerite. Filaree. 272p. 1980. pap. 2.50 (ISBN 0-345-28709-6). Ballantine.

Noble, Pat. Resource Based Learning in Post-Compulsory Education. 200p. 1980. 25.00x (ISBN 0-89397-091-3). Nichols Pub.

Noble, Phyllis, ed. Book of Bread. (Orig.). 1975. pap. 3.95 (ISBN 0-8164-1175-1). Crossroad NY.

Noble, R. Joe & Rothbaum, Donald A. Geriatric Cardiology. (Cardiovascular Clinics Ser.: Vol. 12, No. 1). 1981. 40.00 (ISBN 0-8036-6565-2). Davis Co.

Noble, Robert C. Sexually Transmitted Diseases. LC 78-71163. (Discussions in Patient Management Ser.). 1979. pap. 9.50 (ISBN 0-87488-881-6). Med Exam.

Noble, Rudolf E. A Chicken for Every Pot: San Francisco's Famous Chicken Diet. 124p. 1980. pap. 4.95 (ISBN 0-930306-35-X). Delphi Info.

Noble, Trevor. Modern Britain: Structure & Change. 1975. 38.00 (ISBN 0-7134-2987-9, Pub. by Batsford England); pap. 15.95 (ISBN 0-7134-2988-7). David & Charles.

Noble, Valerie, compiled by. A Librarians Guide to Personal Development: An Annotated Bibliography. (Bibliography Ser.: No. 7). 1980. pap. 4.50 (ISBN 0-87111-272-8). SLA.

Noble, William, jt. auth. see Noble, June.

Noblitt, James S. Nouveau Point De Vue. 1978. text ed. 16.95x (ISBN 0-669-96545-6); inst. manual free (ISBN 0-669-00335-2); wkbk. 5.95 (ISBN 0-669-96552-9); Sets. reels 60.00 (ISBN 0-669-96560-X); cassettes 60.00 (ISBN 0-669-00250-X). Heath.

Noblitt, Thomas, ed. Music East & West: Essays in Honor of Walter Kaufman. (Festschrift Ser.: No. 3). (Illus.). x, 386p. 1981. lib. bdg. 36.00 (ISBN 0-918728-15-0). Pendragon NY.

Nochlin, L. Impressionism & Post-Impressionism, 1874-1904: Sources in Documents. 1966. pap. 10.95 (ISBN 0-13-452003-3). P-H.

Nochlin, Linda. Gustave Courbet: a Study of Style & Society. LC 75-23803. (Outstanding Dissertations in the Fine Arts - 19th Century). (Illus.). 1976. lib. bdg. 41.00 (ISBN 0-8240-1998-9). Garland Pub.

--Realism & Tradition in Art, Eighteen Forty-Eight - Nineteen Hundred: Sources & Documents. (Orig.). 1966. pap. 10.95 ref. ed. (ISBN 0-13-766584-9). P-H.

Nochlin, Linda, jt. ed. see Millon, Henry A.

Nochumson, David H. Models for the Long Distance Transport of Atmospheric Sulfur Oxides. LC 78-74994. (Outstanding Dissertations on Energy). 1980. lib. bdg. 38.00 (ISBN 0-8240-3992-0). Garland Pub.

Nock, O. S. British Steam Railway Locomotive: Volume 2, 1925-1965. 31.50x (ISBN 0-392-07700-0, SpS). Soccer.

--The Gresley Pacifics: Part 1 1922-1935. (Locomotive Monographs). 1973. 14.95 (ISBN 0-7153-6336-0). David & Charles.

--The Gresley Pacifics, Part 2: 1935-1974. LC 74-157265. 1975. 14.95 (ISBN 0-7153-6718-8). David & Charles.

--GWR Stars Castle & Kings. LC 80-66419. (Illus.). 304p. 1980. 32.00 (ISBN 0-7153-7977-1). David & Charles.

--The GWR Stars, Castles & Kings. LC 80-66419. (Illus.). 304p. 1980. 29.95. Darby Bks.

--The GWR Stars, Castles & Kings: Part 1 1906-1930. LC 74-78254. (Locomotive Monographs). (Illus.). 1975. 16.95 (ISBN 0-7153-6681-5). David & Charles.

--The Last Years of British Railways Steam: Reflections Ten Years After. 1978. 14.95 (ISBN 0-7153-7583-0). David & Charles.

--Locomotion: A World Survey of Railway Traction. LC 75-27489. (Encore Edition). (Illus.). 1976. 6.95 o.p. (ISBN 0-684-15431-5, ScribT). Scribner.

--One Hundred & Fifty Years of Main Line Railways. LC 79-56455. (Illus.). 1980. 17.95 (ISBN 0-7153-7881-3). David & Charles.

--Railway Archaeology. (Illus.). 160p. 1981. 35.95 (ISBN 0-85059-451-0). Aztex.

--Railways at the Zenith of Steam, 1920-1940. LC 71-115302. (Railways of the World in Color Ser.: Vol. 2). 1970. 8.95 (ISBN 0-02-589710-1). Macmillan.

--Railways at Their Pre Eminence. (Railways of the World in Color Ser). (Illus.). 1971. 8.95 (ISBN 0-02-589720-9). Macmillan.

--Railways in the Formative Years, 1851-1895. LC 72-12449. (Railways of the World in Color Ser.: Vol. 5). (Illus.). 80p. 1973. 8.95 (ISBN 0-02-589740-3). Macmillan.

--Railways in the Years of Transition: 1940-1963. (Railways of the World in Color Ser.: Vol. 6). (Illus.). 170p. 1975. 5.95 o.s.i. (ISBN 0-02-589750-0). Macmillan.

--Railways of the Modern Age Since 1963. LC 75-28489. (Macmillan Color Ser. Railways of the World in Color). (Illus.). 160p. 1976. 6.95 o.s.i. (ISBN 0-02-589760-8, 58976). Macmillan.

--Railways of Western Europe. (Illus.). 1978. 20.00 (ISBN 0-7136-1686-5). Transatlantic.

--Royal Scots & Patriots of the LMS. 1978. 14.95 (ISBN 0-7153-7480-X). David & Charles.

--The Southern King Arthur Family. LC 76-2885. (Illus.). 96p. 1976. 13.50 (ISBN 0-7153-7156-8). David & Charles.

--Standard Gauge Great Western Four-Four-Zero's, Vol. 1. 1977. 16.95 (ISBN 0-7153-7411-7). David & Charles.

--Standard Gauge Great Western Four-Four-Zero's: 1904-1965, Vol. 2. LC 78-62486. (Illus.). 1978. 16.95 (ISBN 0-7153-7684-5). David & Charles.

Nock, O. S. & Meadway, Clifford. Dawn of World Railways 1800-1850. LC 76-152282. (Illus.). 192p. 1972. 8.95 (ISBN 0-02-589730-6). Macmillan.

Nockels, David. Animal Acrobats. LC 80-25703. (Animal Pop-Up Ser.). (Illus.). 12p. (ps-3). 1981. 3.50 (ISBN 0-8037-0088-1). Dial.

--Animal Athletes. LC 80-25008. (Animal Pop-Up Ser.). (Illus.). 12p. (ps-3). 1981. 3.50 (ISBN 0-8037-0106-3). Dial.

--Animal Builders. LC 80-26316. (Animal Pop-Up Ser.). (Illus.). 12p. (ps-3). 1981. 3.50 (ISBN 0-8037-0113-6). Dial.

--Animal Marvels. LC 80-25443. (Animal Pop-Up Ser.). (Illus.). 12p. (ps-3). 1981. 3.50 (ISBN 0-8037-0085-7). Dial.

Nockolds, Harold. Lucas, Vol. 2. 1978. 35.00 (ISBN 0-7153-7316-1). David & Charles.

--Lucas: The First Hundred Years, Vol. 1. 1976. 35.00 (ISBN 0-7153-7306-4). David & Charles.

--Rescue from Disaster: The Story of the RFD Group. LC 80-66422. (Illus.). 224p. (Orig.). 1980. 32.00 (ISBN 0-7153-7969-0). David & Charles.

Nockolds, Harold, ed. The Coachmakers. (Illus.). 26.25 (ISBN 0-85131-270-5, Dist. by Sporting Book Center). J A Allen.

Nockolds, S. T., et al. Petrology for Students. 8th ed. LC 76-52186. (Illus.). 1978. 67.50 (ISBN 0-521-21553-6); pap. 16.95x (ISBN 0-521-29184-4). Cambridge U Pr.

Noda, Barbara. Strawberries. (Illus.). 1980. pap. 2.95 (ISBN 0-915288-40-0). Shameless Hussy.

Noddings, Thomas C. Advanced Investment Strategies. LC 78-62631. 1978. 17.50 (ISBN 0-87094-170-4). Dow Jones-Irwin.

Nodier, Charles. Contes choisis. (Classiques Larousse). (Illus., Fr.). pap. 1.50 o.p. (ISBN 0-685-13841-0, 229). Larousse.

--History of the Secret Societies of the Army, & of the Military Conspiracies Which Had As Their Object the Destruction of the Government of Bonaparte. LC 78-14740. 1978. Repr. of 1815 ed. 26.00x (ISBN 0-8201-1318-2). Schol Facsimiles.

Nodine, Calvin F. & Fisher, Dennis, eds. Perception & Pictorial Representation. LC 79-4613. (Praeger Special Studies Ser.). 448p. 1979. 39.95 (ISBN 0-03-049816-3). Praeger.

Nodset, Joan L. & Siebel, Fritz. Who Took the Farmer's Hat? (gr. k-3). 1970. pap. 1.50 (ISBN 0-590-02950-9, Schol Pap). Schol Bk Serv.

Nodtuedt, Magnus. Rebirth of Norway's Peasantry: Folk Leader Hans Nielsen Hauge. 305p. 1965. octavo 5.95. Holmes.

Noe, jt. auth. see Mondy.

Noe, Lee, ed. Foundation Grants Index 1978. 1979. write for info. o.p. (ISBN 0-87954-020-6, Dist. by Foundation Ctr). Columbia U Pr.

Noe, Randolph. Kentucky Probate Methods with 1979 Supplement. 1976. 35.00 (ISBN 0-672-82532-5, Bobbs-Merrill Law); 1979 suppl 7.50 (ISBN 0-672-83978-4). Michie.

Noe, Sydney P. The Silver Coinage of Massachusetts. LC 72-77024. 300p. 1974. Repr. 35.00x (ISBN 0-88000-005-8). Quarterman.

Noe, Tom. The Sixth Day. LC 79-55296. (Illus.). 80p. (Orig.). (gr. 3-7). 1979. pap. 2.95 (ISBN 0-87793-190-9). Ave Maria.

Noel, Daniel C., ed. Echoes of the Wordless "Word". LC 73-88582. (American Academy of Religion & Society of Biblical Literature. Religion & the Arts Ser.). 1973. 9.00 (ISBN 0-88414-033-4, 090102). Scholars Pr Ca.

Noel, Diana. Five to Seven. (Illus.). 144p. 1980. pap. 2.95 (ISBN 0-86072-032-2, Pub. by Quartet England). Horizon.

Noel, Dix & Phillips, Jerry J. Products Liability in a Nutshell. 2nd ed. (Nutshell Ser.). 353p. 1981. pap. text ed. 6.95 (ISBN 0-8299-2121-4). West Pub.

Noel, John V. The Boating Dictionary: Sail & Power. 304p. 1981. text ed. 16.95 (ISBN 0-442-26048-2). Van Nos Reinhold.

Noel, John V., Jr. Division Officer's Guide. 7th ed. LC 75-39931. 224p. 1976. 9.95x (ISBN 0-87021-160-9). Naval Inst Pr.

--The VNR Dictionary of Ships & the Sea. 400p. 1980. text ed. 19.95 (ISBN 0-442-25631-0). Van Nos Reinhold.

Noel, S. J. Politics in Newfoundland. LC 73-151382. 1971. pap. 5.50 (ISBN 0-8020-6187-7). U of Toronto Pr.

Noel, Spike. Fish & the Sea. (Junior Reference Ser.). (Illus.). 64p. (gr. 7 up). 1972. 7.95 (ISBN 0-7136-1239-8). Dufour.

Noel, Thomas. Denver: Rocky Mountain Gold. Blakey, Ellen S. & Silvey, Larry P., eds. LC 80-66339. (American Portrait Ser.). (Illus.). 240p. 1980. 24.95 (ISBN 0-932986-12-9). Continent Herit.

--Theories of the Fable in the Eighteenth Century. 176p. 1975. 20.00x (ISBN 0-231-03858-5). Columbia U Pr.

Noel-Baker, Lord. The First World Disarmament: And Why It Failed. 1979. 19.00 (ISBN 0-08-023365-1). Pergamon.

Noel-Hume, Audrey, jt. auth. see Noel-Hume, Ivor.

Noel-Hume, Ivor. All the Best Rubbish. LC 73-4093. (Illus.). 320p. 1974. 10.00 o.p. (ISBN 0-06-011997-7, HarpT). Har-Row.

Noel-Hume, Ivor & Noel-Hume, Audrey. Tortoises. Foyles, Christina, ed. (Foyle's Handbks). (Illus.). 1973. 3.95 (ISBN 0-685-55798-7). Palmetto Pub.

Noella. Decedent Hair Styling: Desairology Manual. LC 82-330. (Illus.). 100p. 1980. 17.95x (ISBN 0-9604610-0-0); pap. 11.95x (ISBN 0-9604610-1-9). JJ Pub FL.

Noer, David. How to Beat the Employment Game. Date not set. pap. 4.95 (ISBN 0-913668-96-6). Ten Speed Pr.

Noerlund, Niels H. Differenzenrechung. LC 56-1592. (Ger). 19.50 (ISBN 0-8284-0100-4). Chelsea Pub.

Noether, Gottfried E. Introduction to Statistics: A Nonparametric Approach. 2nd ed. LC 75-19532. (Illus.). 336p. 1976. text ed. 18.25 (ISBN 0-395-18578-5); solutions manual 1.50 (ISBN 0-395-18789-3). HM.

Noffke, Suzanne, ed. Catherine of Sienna: The Dialogue. (Classics of Western Spirituality Ser.). 398p. 1980. 11.95 (ISBN 0-8091-0295-1); pap. 7.95 (ISBN 0-8091-2233-2). Paulist Pr.

Noffsinger, Ella M., jt. auth. see Allen, M. W.

Nofker The Stammerer, jt. auth. see Einhard.

Noflew, A. G., jt. ed. see Warren, Thomas B.

Nogales, Manuel C. Heroes & Beasts of Spain. Harding, D. C., ed. De Baeza, Luis, tr. from Span. LC 79-53465. (Short Story Index Reprint Ser.). Date not set. Repr. of 1937 ed. 24.50x (ISBN 0-8486-5006-9). Core Collection. Postponed.

Nogee, Joe, jt. ed. see Spanier, John.

Nogee, Joseph L. & Donaldson, Robert H. Soviet Foreign Policy Since World War II. (Pergamon Policy Studies on International Politics). 300p. Date not set. 35.00 (ISBN 0-08-025997-9); pap. 10.95 (ISBN 0-08-025996-0). Pergamon.

Noggle, Burl. Teapot Dome: Oil & Politics in the 1920's. LC 80-15396. (Illus.). ix, 234p. 1980. Repr. of 1962 ed. lib. bdg. 22.50x (ISBN 0-313-22601-6, NOTD). Greenwood.

Noggle, Fritz. Introductory Plant Physiology. (Illus.). 592p. 1976. ref. ed. 23.95 (ISBN 0-13-502187-1). P-H.

Nogotov, E. F. Applications of Numerical Methods to Heat Transfer. (Illus.). 1978. pap. text ed. 28.50 (ISBN 0-07-046852-4, C). McGraw.

Nohel, J. A., jt. auth. see Brauer, F.

Nohl, Johannes. The Black Death: A Chronicle of the Plague Compiled from Contemporary Sources. (Unwin Bks.). (Illus.). 248p. 1961. pap. 3.95 o.p. (ISBN 0-04-942058-5, 9023). Allen Unwin.

Nohl, Johannes, ed. Black Death: A Chronicle of the Plague Compiled from Contemporary Sources. 1961. pap. text ed. 3.25x (ISBN 0-04-942058-5). Humanities.

Nohl, Louis. Life of Liszt. LC 70-140402. 1970. Repr. of 1889 ed. 18.00 (ISBN 0-8103-3610-3). Gale.

Noiseux, Ronald A., jt. auth. see Glass, Robert L.

Nokleby, Berit, jt. auth. see Riste, Olav.

Nolan, D. Big Pig. 1976. 5.95 (ISBN 0-13-076158-3). P-H.

Nolan, David, ed. Dante Commentaries: Eight Studies of the Divine Comedy. 184p. 1977. 21.50x (ISBN 0-87471-966-6). Rowman.

--Dante Soundings. 1981. 22.50x (ISBN 0-8476-3633-X). Rowman.

Nolan, Dennis. Monster Bubbles: A Counting Book. LC 76-10167. 1976. PLB 5.95 (ISBN 0-13-600635-3); pap. 1.95 (ISBN 0-13-600643-4). P-H.

--Wizard McBean & His Flying Machine. LC 77-3472. (Illus.). (ps-2). 1977. PLB 7.95 (ISBN 0-13-961607-1); pap. 2.50 (ISBN 0-13-961599-7). P-H.

Nolan, Frederick. Brass Target. 1979. pap. 1.75 o.s.i. (ISBN 0-685-54627-6, 04849-6). Jove Pubns.

--White Nights, Red Dawn. 416p. 1980. 13.95 (ISBN 0-02-589850-7). Macmillan.

Nolan, Frederick, ed. see Armes, Jay J.

Nolan, Fredrick. Carver's Kingdom. 1980. pap. 2.50 (ISBN 0-446-81201-3). Warner Bks.

Nolan, James. What Moves Is Not the Wind. 72p. 1980. 10.00 (ISBN 0-8195-2099-3, Pub. by Wesleyan U Pr); pap. 4.95 (ISBN 0-8195-1099-8). Columbia U Pr.

--Why I Live in the Forest. LC 74-5967. (Wesleyan Poetry Program: Vol. 74). 1974. 10.00x (ISBN 0-8195-2074-8, Pub. by Wesleyan U Pr); pap. 4.95 (ISBN 0-8195-1074-2). Columbia U Pr.

Nolan, Jeannette C. Story of Clara Barton of the Red Cross. (Biography Ser.). (gr. 7up). 1941. 4.64 o.p. (ISBN 0-671-32606-6). Messner.

Nolan, Joellen, jt. auth. see Block, Gloria.

Nolan, Joseph R. Cases & Materials on Trial Practice. (American Casebook Ser.). 514p. 1981. text ed. 17.95 (ISBN 0-686-69319-1). West Pub.

Nolan, Joseph R., ed. see Black, Henry C.

Nolan, Joseph T. Welcome Christian: What Baptism Means Today. (Illus.). 40p. 1977. pap. 1.50 o.p. (ISBN 0-89570-105-7). Claretian Pubns.

Nolan, Kenneth. Masonry Contractors Handbook. 256p. (Orig.). 1981. pap. 13.50 (ISBN 0-910460-81-7). Craftsman.

Nolan, Madeena S. The Gift. (Orig.). 1981. pap. 2.50 (ISBN 0-440-12875-7). Dell.

Nolan, Michael. A Treatise of the Laws for the Relief & Settlement of the Poor, 2 vols. Berkowitz, David & Thorne, Samuel, eds. LC 77-89221. (Classics of English Legal History in the Modern Era Ser.: Vol. 130). 1979. Repr. of 1805 ed. Set. lib. bdg. 55.00 ea. (ISBN 0-8240-3167-9). Garland Pub.

Nolan, Paul T. Marc Connelly. (U. S. Authors Ser.: No. 149). 1969. lib. bdg. 10.95 (ISBN 0-8057-0152-4). Twayne.

Nolan, Peter J. & Bigliani, Raymond E. Experiments in Physics. 1981. pap. text ed. price not set (ISBN 0-8087-1446-5). Burgess.

Nolan, R. E., jt. auth. see Nance, H. W.

Nolan, Richard see Bernard, Dan, et al.

Nolan, Robert, jt. ed. see Deal, Terrence.

Nolan, Robert L. & Schwartz, Jerome L., eds. Rural & Appalachian Health. 272p. 1973. 16.75 (ISBN 0-398-02605-X). C C Thomas.

Nolan, Walter I. Facts of Baccarat. rev. ed. 1976. pap. 1.50 (ISBN 0-89650-018-7). Gamblers.

--Facts of Blackjack. rev. ed. 1976. pap. 1.50 (ISBN 0-89650-019-5). Gamblers.

--Facts of Craps. rev. ed. 1976. pap. 1.50 (ISBN 0-89650-020-9). Gamblers.

--Facts of Roulette. 1970. pap. 1.50 (ISBN 0-89650-022-5). Gamblers.

--Facts of Slots. 1970. pap. 1.50 (ISBN 0-89650-023-3). Gamblers.

Nolan, William F., ed. Ray Bradbury Companion: A Life & Career History, Photolog, & Comprehensive Checklist of Writings, with Facsimiles from Ray Bradbury's Unpublished & Uncollected Works in All Media. LC 74-10397. (A Bruccoli Clark Book). (Illus.). 339p. 1974. 48.00 (ISBN 0-8103-0930-0). Gale.

Nolan, William Fl & Greenberg, Martin H., eds. Science Fiction Origins. 1980. 2.25 (ISBN 0-445-04626-0). Popular Lib.

Noland, Aaron. The Founding of the French Socialist Party, 1893-1905. 14.25 (ISBN 0-86527-070-8). Fertig.

Noland, George B. General Biology. 10th ed. LC 78-27065. (Illus.). 1979. text ed. 19.95 (ISBN 0-8016-3673-6). Mosby.

Noland, George B. & Beaver, William C. Laboratory Manual in General Biology. 9th ed. 1975. pap. text ed. 8.95 (ISBN 0-8016-3685-X). Mosby.

Noland, Robert L. Counseling Parents of the Mentally Retarded: A Sourcebook. (Illus.). 420p. 1978. 16.75 (ISBN 0-398-01405-1). C C Thomas.

--Research & Report Writing in the Behavioral Sciences: Psychiatry, Psychology, Sociology, Educational Psychology, Cultural Anthropology, Managerial Psychology. 108p. 1970. pap. 10.75 (ISBN 0-398-01406-X). C C Thomas.

Noland, Robert L., ed. Counseling Parents of the Ill & the Handicapped. (Illus.). 628p. 1979. pap. 12.95 (ISBN 0-398-01404-3). C C Thomas.

Nolane, Richard D., ed. Terra SF. 1981. pap. 2.25 (ISBN 0-87997-595-4, UE1595). Daw Bks.

Nolen, Barbara. Ethiopia. LC 70-131149. (First Bks). (Illus.). (gr. 4-6). 1971. PLB 4.90 o.p. (ISBN 0-531-00733-2). Watts.

Nolen, Jerry A. & Benenson, Walter, eds. Atomic Masses & Fundamental Constants 6. 585p. 1980. 59.50 (ISBN 0-306-40441-9, Plenum Pr). Plenum Pub.

Nolfi, George J., ed. Experiences of Recent High School Graduates. new ed. LC 78-2075. 1978. 19.95 (ISBN 0-669-02264-0). Lexington Bks.

Nolin, Bertil. George Brandes. LC 76-2718. (World Authors Ser.: Denmark: No. 390). 1976. lib. bdg. 12.50 (ISBN 0-8057-6232-9). Twayne.

Noll, Edward M. Broadcast & Two-Way Radio Operators Permit Handbook. 5th ed. LC 79-65743. 1979. pap. 6.50 (ISBN 0-672-21627-2). Sams.

--Commercial Radiotelephone License: Question & Answer Study Guide. 3rd ed. LC 75-16859. 1976. pap. 8.50 (ISBN 0-672-24033-5, 24033). Editors.

--Commercial Radiotelephone License Question & Answer Study Guide. 3rd ed. LC 75-16859. 1976. pap. 8.50 (ISBN 0-672-24033-5). Sams.

--First Class Radiotelephone License Handbook. 5th ed. LC 80-52936. 1980. pap. 11.95 (ISBN 0-672-21757-0). Sams.

--First-Class Radiotelephone License Handbook. 4th ed. LC 74-15459. (Illus.). 416p. 1974. pap. 8.50 o.p. (ISBN 0-672-21144-0). Sams.

--Second Class Radiotelephone License Handbook. 6th ed. LC 80-51713. (Illus.). 1980. pap. 12.50 (ISBN 0-672-21722-8). SAMS.

Noll, Roger G., ed. Government & the Sports Business. LC 74-279. (Studies in the Regulation of Economic Activity). 1974. 14.95 (ISBN 0-8157-6106-6); pap. 6.95 (ISBN 0-8157-6105-8). Brookings.

Nollen, Stanley D., et al. Permanent Part-Time Employment: The Manager's Perspective. LC 78-17767. 1978. 23.95 (ISBN 0-03-043071-2). Praeger.

Noller, Ruth B., et al. Guide to Creative Action. rev. ed. LC 76-44541. 1977. pap. text ed. 12.95x (ISBN 0-684-14888-9, ScribC). Scribner.

Nollson, John. Washington in Pieces. LC 80-713. 264p. 1981. 11.95 (ISBN 0-385-15413-5). Doubleday.

Nolte, Dietrich. Speaking of: Asthma. Heyden, Francoise, tr. from Ger. LC 80-68766. (Medical Adviser Ser.). Orig. Title: Sprechstunde: Asthma. 128p. (Orig.). 1980. pap. 3.95 (ISBN 0-8326-2250-8, 7460). Delair.

Nolte, John. Neuroanatomy. (Illus.). 382p. 1981. pap. text ed. 13.50 (ISBN 0-8016-3702-3). Mosby.

Nolte, Lawrence W. & Wilcox, Dennis L., eds. Fundamentals of Public Relations: Professional Guidelines, Concepts & Integrations. 2nd ed. 1979. 16.45 (ISBN 0-08-022470-9). Pergamon.

Nolte, William A. Oral Microbiology. 3rd ed. LC 77-1945. (Illus.). 1977. text ed. 31.95 (ISBN 0-8016-3688-4). Mosby.

Nolte, William H. H. L. Mencken, Literary Critic. LC 66-18117. 1966. lib. bdg. 17.50x (ISBN 0-8195-3063-8, Pub. by Wesleyan U Pr). Columbia U Pr.

Nolte-Heuritsch, Ilse. Aqua - Rhythmics: Exercises for the Swimmimg Pool. LC 78-57782. (Illus.). 1978. 7.95 (ISBN 0-8069-4130-8); lib. bdg. 7.49 (ISBN 0-8069-4131-6); pap. 4.95 o.p. (ISBN 0-8069-4132-4). Sterling.

Noma, Elliot, jt. auth. see Baird, John C.

Noma, Seiroku. Arts of Japan, 2 vols. Rosenfield, John, tr. LC 65-19186. Orig. Title: Nihon Bijutsu. (Illus.). 1978. 22.50 ea. Vol. I (ISBN 0-87011-335-6). Vol. II (ISBN 0-87011-336-4). Kodansha.

--Arts of Japan Vol. 1: Ancient & Medieval. LC 65-19186. (Arts of Japan Ser.: Vol. 1). (Illus.). 1967. 85.00 (ISBN 0-87011-018-7). Kodansha.

--Arts of Japan Vol. 2: Late Medieval to Modern. LC 65-19186. (Arts of Japan Ser.: Vol. 2). (Illus.). 1967. 85.00 (ISBN 0-87011-050-0). Kodansha.

Nomad, Max. Apostles of Revolution. rev. & enl. ed. 1961. pap. 1.50 o.s.i. (ISBN 0-02-074560-5, Collier). Macmillan.

Nommensen, B. P. Comfort for the Sick. rev. ed. 1976. pap. 5.00 (ISBN 0-8100-0011-3, 06N0553). Northwest Pub.

Nomura Research Institute. Investing in Japan. (Illus.). 208p. 1980. 25.00x (ISBN 0-85941-067-6). Herman Pub.

Nonas, Richard. Boiling Coffee. 168p. 1980. 15.95 (ISBN 0-934378-12-6); pap. 8.95 (ISBN 0-934378-11-8). Tanam Pr.

Nonet, Phillippe & Selznick, Philip. Law & Society in Transition. (Orig.). 1978. pap. 4.95x (ISBN 0-06-131954-6, TB 1954, Torch). Har-Row.

Nonhebel, D. C. & Tedder, J. M. Radicals. LC 78-54721. (Cambridge Texts in Chemistry & Biochemistry Ser.). (Illus.). 1979. 38.50 (ISBN 0-521-22004-1); pap. 15.95x (ISBN 0-521-29332-4). Cambridge U Pr.

Nonhebel, D. C. & Walton, J. C. Free-Radical Chemistry. LC 73-97887. (Illus.). 600p. 1973. 99.00 (ISBN 0-521-20149-7). Cambridge U Pr.

Nonhebel, G. & Berry, M. Chemical Engineering in Practice. LC 73-77793. (Wykeham Science Ser.: No. 28). 1973. pap. 6.25x (ISBN 0-8448-1155-6). Crane-Russak Co.

Nonte, George. Firearms Encyclopedia. (An Outdoor Life Bk.). 1973. 19.95 o.s.i. (ISBN 0-06-013213-2, HarpT). Har-Row.

--The Home Guide to Cartridge Conversions. rev. ed. 15.00 (ISBN 0-88227-005-2). Gun Room.

--Modern Handloading. (Illus.). 1972. 10.00 o.p. (ISBN 0-87691-046-0). Winchester Pr.

Nonte, George C. Handgun Competition. (Illus.). 1978. 14.95 (ISBN 0-87691-253-6). Winchester Pr.

--The Pistol Guide. 256p. 1980. pap. 7.95 (ISBN 0-695-81122-3). Follett.

Nonte, George C., Jr. Combat Handguns. Jurras, Lee F., ed. (Illus.). 354p. 1980. 19.95 (ISBN 0-8117-0409-2). Stackpole.

--Pistolsmithing. LC 74-10783. (Illus.). 560p. 1974. 19.95 (ISBN 0-8117-1265-6). Stackpole.

Nonte, George C., Jr. & Jurras, Lee E. Handgun Hunting. (Illus.). 1975. 10.95 (ISBN 0-87691-211-0). Winchester Pr.

Noojin, Ray O. Dermatology for Students. (Illus.). 320p. 1961. 13.75 (ISBN 0-398-01407-8). C C Thomas.

Noojin, Ray O., et al. Dermatology - a Practitioner's Guide. 1977. spiral bdg. 14.50 (ISBN 0-87488-720-8). Med Exam.

Noonan, John T., Jr. The Antelope: The Ordeal of the Recaptured Africans in the Administrations of James Monroe & John Quincy Adams. 1977. 15.75 (ISBN 0-520-03319-1). U of Cal Pr.

--A Private Choice: Abortion in America in the Seventies. LC 78-67752. 1979. 14.95 (ISBN 0-02-923160-4). Free Pr.

Noonan, K. Emotional Adjustment to Illness. LC 73-13485. 168p. 1975. pap. 6.60 (ISBN 0-8273-0347-5); instructor's guide 1.60 (ISBN 0-8273-0348-3). Delmar.

Noonan, Karen A. Coping with Illness. 2nd ed. LC 80-67825. (Practical Nursing Ser.). (Illus.). 288p. 1981. pap. text ed. 8.00 (ISBN 0-8273-1438-8); instr's. guide 1.25 (ISBN 0-8273-1922-3). Delmar.

Noonan, R. D. School Resources, Social Class, & Student Achievement. LC 76-7957. (IEA Monograph Studies: No. 5). 1976. pap. 14.95 (ISBN 0-470-15091-2). Halsted Pr.

Noonan, Thomas E., jt. ed. see Rockwell, Jeanne.

Noonberg, A., jt. auth. see Olton, D.

Noone, Edwinna. The Craghold Curse. 1977. pap. 1.25 (ISBN 0-505-51156-8). Tower Bks.

Noor, A. K. & McComb, H. G., eds. Computational Methods in Nonlinear Structural & Solid Mechanics: Papers Presented at the Symposium on Computational Methods in Nonlinear Structural & Solid Mechanics, 6-8 October 1980. LC 80-41608. 70.00 (ISBN 0-08-027299-1). Pergamon.

Noorbergen, Rene. Death Cry of an Eagle: The Rise and Fall of Christian Values in the United States. 192p. 1980. pap. 5.95 (ISBN 0-310-30431-8). Zondervan.

--Secrets of the Lost Races. (Illus.). 1978. pap. 4.50 (ISBN 0-06-464025-6, CO 32, BN). Har-Row.

Noord, Glenn Van, jt. auth. see Hendricks, William.

Nooten, Barend A. see Van Nooten, Barend A.

Nopany, Nandini & Lal, P., eds. Twenty-Four Stories by Premchand. 208p. 1981. text ed. 17.95 (ISBN 0-7069-1199-7, Pub by Vikas India). Advent Bk.

Nora, Audrey H., jt. auth. see Nora, James J.

Nora, James J. & Nora, Audrey H. Genetics & Counseling in Cardiovascular Diseases. (Illus.). 240p. 1978. 21.75 (ISBN 0-398-03755-8). C C Thomas.

Nora, Simon & Minc, Alain. The Computerization of Society. 1980. text ed. 12.50 (ISBN 0-262-14031-4). MIT Pr.

Norback, C. T. & Norback, P. The Health Care Directory. 1977. 49.95 o.p. (ISBN 0-87489-079-9). Med Economics.

Norback, Craig. Check Yourself Out. 256p. 1981. 8.95 (ISBN 0-8129-0935-6). Times Bks.

--The Complete Book of American Surveys. (Orig.). 1981. pap. 3.50 (ISBN 0-451-09571-5, E9571, Sig). NAL.

Norback, Craig, jt. auth. see Norback, Peter.

Norback, Craig T. The Computer Invasion. 304p. 1981. text ed. 18.95 (ISBN 0-442-26121-7). Van Nos Reinhold.

--U. S. Publicity Directory, 5 vols. Incl. Vol. 1. Radio-TV (ISBN 0-471-06372-X); Vol. 2. Newspapers (ISBN 0-471-06375-4); Vol. 3. Magazines (ISBN 0-471-06373-8); Vol. 4. Business & Finance (ISBN 0-471-06371-1); Vol. 5. Communication Services (ISBN 0-471-06374-6). 1980. 65.00 ea. (Pub. by Wiley-Interscience); Set. write for info. (ISBN 0-471-06369-X). Wiley.

Norback, Craig T., ed. Careers Encyclopedia. 360p. 1980. 27.50 (ISBN 0-87094-203-4). Dow Jones-Irwin.

Norback, Craig T., jt. ed. see Asthma & Allergy Foundation of America.

Norback, Judith. Signet Book of World Winners. 1980. pap. 2.95 (ISBN 0-451-09585-5, E9585, Sig). NAL.

Norback, P., jt. auth. see Norback, C. T.

Norback, Peter & Norback, Craig. The Consumer's Energy Handbook. 272p. 1981. 19.95 (ISBN 0-442-26066-0); pap. 14.95 (ISBN 0-442-26067-9). Van Nos Reinhold.

Norbelle, Bernard, tr. see Hedin, Sven.

Norberg-Schulz, Christian. Baroque Architecture. LC 74-149851. (History of World Architecture Ser). (Illus.). 1971. 45.00 (ISBN 0-8109-1002-0). Abrams.

--Late Baroque & Rococo Architecture. LC 73-980. (History of World Architecture Ser.). (Illus.). 400p. 1975. 45.00 (ISBN 0-8109-1012-8). Abrams.

Norbie, D. R. Early Church. 1981. pap. 10.00 (ISBN 0-937396-13-3). Walterick Pubs.

Norbie, Don. Your New Life. 66p. pap. 0.10. Walterick Pubs.

Norbom, Mary Ann. Richard Dawson & Family Feud. (Illus., Orig.). 1981. pap. 1.95 (ISBN 0-451-09773-4, J9773, Sig). NAL.

Norbu, Tenzin, tr. see Gyatso, Geshe.

Norbury, James. Traditional Knitting Patterns from Scandinavia, the British Isles, France, Italy & Other European Countries. LC 73-79490. (Illus.). 240p. 1973. pap. 4.50 (ISBN 0-486-21013-8). Dover.

Norbury, Paul & Bownas, G. Business in Japan: A Guide to Japanese Business Practice & Procedure. LC 74-18421. 351p. 1974. 19.95 (ISBN 0-470-64225-4). Halsted Pr.

Norbury, Paul & Bownas, Geoffrey, eds. Business in Japan: A Guide to Japanese Business Practice & Procedure. (Illus.). 210p. 1980. lib. bdg. 25.00 (ISBN 0-86531-059-9). Westview.

Norbye, Jan. Modern Diesel Cars. (Modern Automotive Ser.). (Illus.). 1978. 9.95 (ISBN 0-8306-9899-X); pap. 7.95 (ISBN 0-8306-2046-X, 2046). TAB Bks.

Norbye, Jan P. & Dunne, Jim. Pontiac: The Postwar Years. LC 79-17430. (Illus.). 205p. 1980. 18.95 (ISBN 0-87938-060-8). Motorbooks Intl.

Norcliffe, G. B. Inferential Statistics for Geographers: An Introduction. LC 77-9427. 1977. 24.95 (ISBN 0-470-99206-9). Halsted Pr.

Norcliffe, Glen, ed. Planning African Development: The Kenya Experience. Pinfold, Tom. 224p. 1981. lib. bdg. 25.00x (ISBN 0-86531-161-7). Westview.

Norcross, C. & Hysom, J. Apartment Communities: The Next Big Market. LC 68-57114. 1968. pap. 4.75 (ISBN 0-87420-061-X, TB61). Urban Land.

Norcross, Carl. Townhouses & Condominiums: Residents' Likes & Dislikes. LC 73-82886. (Special Report Ser.). (Illus.). 1973. pap. 14.50 (ISBN 0-87420-558-1). Urban Land.

Norcross, Lisabet. The Lady & the Rogue. 1978. pap. 1.50 o.s.i. (ISBN 0-515-04449-0). Jove Pubns.

--Reluctant Heiress. 1978. pap. 1.50 o.s.i. (ISBN 0-515-04463-6). Jove Pubns.

Nord. Etching of Glass & Sandblasting. (Illus.). 80p. 1980. 6.95 (ISBN 0-935656-01-4, 101 B). Chrome Yellow.

Nord, Barry & Nord, Elaine. The Child's Book of Glass. (Illus.). 64p. (Orig.). (gr. 7-9). Date not set. pap. price not set (101E). Chrome Yellow.

--Glass Etching-Pattern Book I: Fruit, Flowers, & Birds. (Illus.). 50p. (Orig.). 1980. pap. 3.95 (ISBN 0-935656-02-2, 101C). Chrome Yellow.

--Glass Etching-Pattern Book II: Wildlife, Alphabets, Geometrics. (Illus.). 50p. (Orig.). 1980. pap. 3.95 (ISBN 0-935656-03-0, 101D). Chrome Yellow.

Nord, Elaine, jt. auth. see Nord, Barry.

Nord, F. F. Advances in Enzymology. Incl. Vol. 14. 1953. 28.50 (ISBN 0-470-64647-0); Vol. 15. 1954. 31.50 (ISBN 0-470-64680-2); Vol. 23. 1961. 34.00 (ISBN 0-470-64944-5); Vol. 25. 1963. 34.00 (ISBN 0-470-64948-8). LC 41-9213 (Pub. by Wiley-Interscience). Wiley.

Nordberg, H. O., et al. Free to Choose: A Guide to Effective Communication. rev. ed. LC 74-84819. 1975. 8.95 (ISBN 0-8465-4850-X, 51958). Benjamin-Cummings.

--World of Words: A Guide to Effective Communication. 1970. pap. 8.95 (ISBN 0-201-43007-X); tchr's guide 4.00 (ISBN 0-201-43008-8). A-W.

Nordberg, H. Orville, et al. World of Words: A Guide to Effective Communication. 1970. text ed. 8.95 (ISBN 0-8464-3007-X). Benjamin-Cummings.

Nordby, Vernon J. & Hall, Calvin S. A Guide to Psychologists & Their Concepts. LC 74-11165. (Psychology Ser.). (Illus.). 1974. pap. text ed. 6.95x (ISBN 0-7167-0759-4). W H Freeman.

Nordby, Vernon J., jt. auth. see Hall, Calvin S.

Norden, Carroll R. Deserts. LC 77-27090. (Read About Sciences Ser.). (Illus.). (gr. k-3). 1978. PLB 9.95 (ISBN 0-8393-0082-4). Raintree Child.

--The Jungle. LC 77-27590. (Read About Animals Ser.). (Illus.). (gr. k-3). 1978. PLB 9.95 (ISBN 0-8393-0078-6). Raintree Child.

Norden, Heinz, tr. see Goethe, Johann W.

Norden, John. England: An Intended Guyde, for English Travailers. LC 79-84125. (English Experience Ser.: No. 944). 84p. 1979. Repr. of 1625 ed. lib. bdg. 14.00 (ISBN 90-221-0944-5). Walter J Johnson.

--The Surveiors Dialogue...for All Men to Peruse, That Have to Do with the Revenues of Land, or the Manurance, Use or Occupation. Third Time Imprinted & Enlarged. LC 79-84126. (English Experience Ser.: No. 945). 280p. 1979. Repr. of 1618 ed. lib. bdg. 26.00 (ISBN 90-221-0945-3). Walter J Johnson.

Norden, Peter. Madam Kitty. 1977. pap. 1.50 (ISBN 0-345-24228-9). Ballantine.

Norden, Rudolph F. Radiant Faith. Feucht, Oscar E., ed. 1966. pap. 0.85 study guide (ISBN 0-570-03527-9, 14-1330); pap. 1.15 leader's manual (ISBN 0-570-03528-7, 14-1331). Concordia.

Nordenfalk, Carl. Celtic & Anglo-Saxon Painting: Book Illumination in the British Isles 600-800. 1977. 19.95 (ISBN 0-8076-0825-4); pap. 9.95 (ISBN 0-8076-0826-2). Braziller.

Nordenskiold, Adolf E. Facsimile Atlas to the Early History of Cartography: Reproductions of the Most Important Maps Printed in the Fifteenth & Sixteenth Centuries. (Illus.). 256p. 1973. pap. text ed. 12.95 (ISBN 0-486-22964-5). Dover.

Nordenstreng, Kaarle & Varis, Tapio. Television Traffic - a One-Way Street? A Survey & Analysis of the International Flow of Television Programme Material. (Reports & Papers on Mass Communication, No. 70). (Illus.). 62p. (Orig.). 1974. pap. 2.50 (ISBN 92-3-101135-9, U669, UNESCO). Unipub.

Nordhaus, George, et al, eds. Insurance Is a Funny Business. (Illus.). 139p. 1971. 9.95 o.p. (ISBN 0-88245-003-4). Merritt Co.

Nordhaus, George W. Insurance Agency Advertising & Public Relations. (Illus.). 228p. 1964. 4.95 o.p. (ISBN 0-88245-002-6). Merritt Co.

Nordhauser, Norman. The Quest for Stability. Freidel, Frank, ed. LC 78-62510. (Modern American History Ser.: Vol. 15). 1979. lib. bdg. 24.00 (ISBN 0-8240-3638-7). Garland Pub.

Nordheimer, Stuart. Beginner's Photography Simplified. 1975. 10.95 o.p. (ISBN 0-13-074070-5, Spec). P-H.

Nordic, Rolla. The Tarot Shows the Path. 1979. pap. 3.95 (ISBN 0-87728-477-6). Weiser.

Nordin, Albert A., jt. auth. see Alder, William H.

Nordin, Margareta, jt. ed. see Frankel, Victor H.

Nordin, Virginia D., jt. auth. see Edwards, Harry T.

Nordland, Rod. Names & Numbers: A Journalist's Guide to the Most Needed Information Sources & Contacts. LC 78-18903. 560p. 1978. 28.95 (ISBN 0-471-03994-2, Pub. by Wiley-Interscience). Wiley.

Nordlinger, Eric. Soldiers in Politics: Military Coups & Government. (Illus.). 1977. pap. text ed. 10.95 (ISBN 0-13-822163-4). P-H.

Nordloh, David J., ed. see Howells, W. D.

Nordlund, Donald A., et al, eds. Semiochemicals: Their Role in Pest Control. 400p. 1981. 27.50 (ISBN 0-471-05803-3, Pub. by Wiley-Interscience). Wiley.

Nordlund, James, ed. Internal Medicine Patient Management Cases: PreTest Self-Assessment & Review. LC 77-78730. (PreTest Self-Assessment & Review Ser.). (Illus.). 1977. pap. 20.00 o.p. (ISBN 0-07-079145-7). McGraw-Pretest.

--Internal Medicine PreTest Self-Assessment & Review. (PreTest Self-Assessment & Review Ser.). (Illus.). 1977. pap. 20.00 o.p. (ISBN 0-07-050798-8). McGraw-Pretest.

Nordlund, Willis J. & Robson, R. Thayne. Energy & Employment. LC 79-22133. 1980. 20.95 (ISBN 0-03-055291-5). Praeger.

Nordmann, Jean J., jt. auth. see Maddrell, Simon H.

Nordner, William. How to Build Model Ships. (Illus.). (gr. 4-6). 1969. 2.95 o.p. (ISBN 0-8015-5112-9, 7561). Dutton.

Nordquist, Joan. Audiovisuals for Women. LC 80-14691. 153p. 1980. lib. bdg. 10.95x (ISBN 0-89950-011-0); pap. 8.95x (ISBN 0-89950-012-9). McFarland & Co.

Nordquist, M. New Directions in the Law of the Sea, Vol. 7. 1980. 45.00 (ISBN 0-379-00532-8). Oceana.

Nordstrom, Carl. Frontier Elements in a Hudson River Village. new ed. LC 72-91175. (National University Publications). 1973. 13.95 (ISBN 0-8046-9033-2). Kennikat.

Nordstrom, Hans-Ake & Haland, Randi. Neolithic & A-Group Sites, 2 vols. LC 73-851683. (Scandinavian Joint Expedition to Sudanese Nubia Ser). (Illus.). 420p. 1973. Set. text ed. 65.00x (ISBN 0-8419-8802-1, Africana). Holmes & Meier.

Nordtvedt, Matilda. Living Beyond Depression. LC 78-58082. 1978. pap. 2.25 (ISBN 0-87123-339-8, 200339). Bethany Fell.

Nordtvedt, Matilda & Steinkuehler, Pearl. Something Old, Something New. (Orig.). 1981. pap. 1.95 (ISBN 0-8024-0927-X). Moody.

Nordvedt, Matilda. No Longer a Nobody. (Illus.). 32p. (Orig.). (gr. 1-3). 1976. pap. 1.95 (ISBN 0-8024-5938-2). Moody.

Nordvedt, Matilda, tr. Por el Tunel De la Depresion. (Spanish Bks.). (Span.). 1979. 1.60 (ISBN 0-8297-0796-4). Life Pubs Intl.

Nore, Petter, jt. ed. see Green, Francis.

Norel, K. Stand by, Boys! Schoolland, Marian, tr. from Dutch. (Children's Summit Ser.). (Orig.). 1980. pap. 1.65 (ISBN 0-8010-6734-0). Baker Bk.

Norelli-Bachelet, Patrizia. The Gnostic Circle. 1978. pap. 7.95 (ISBN 0-87728-411-3). Weiser.

Noren, Catherine. Photography: How to Improve Your Technique. LC 73-5687. (Career Concise Guides Ser.). (gr. 5 up). 1973. PLB 4.90 o.p. (ISBN 0-531-02640-X). Watts.

Norenberg, W. & Weidenmuller, H. A. Introduction to the Theory of Heavy-Ion Collisions. (Lecture Notes in Physics: Vol. 51). (Illus.). 1976. soft cover 13.10 o.p. (ISBN 0-387-07801-0). Springer-Verlag.

Noreng, Oystein. The Oil Industry & Government Strategy in the North Sea. 268p. 1980. 35.00x (ISBN 0-85664-850-7, Pub. by Croom Helm Ltd England). Biblio Dist.

Norfleet, Barbara. The Champion Pig: Great Moments in Everyday Life. (Illus.). 123p. 1980. pap. 8.95 (ISBN 0-14-005551-7). Penguin.

Norgren, Paul H. & Hill, Samuel E. Toward Fair Employment. LC 64-17756. 1964. 20.00x (ISBN 0-231-02716-8). Columbia U Pr.

Norgrove, Ross. The Charter Game: How to Make Money Sailing Your Own Boat. LC 78-55784. (Illus.). 1979. 17.50 (ISBN 0-87742-092-0). Intl Marine.

--The Cruising Life. LC 79-53764. (Illus.). 1980. pap. 19.95 (ISBN 0-87742-114-5). Intl Marine.

Noriega, L. A. De see De Noriega, L. A. & Leach, F.

Norkin, S. B., jt. auth. see Elsgolts, L. E.

Norland, Howard B., ed. see Beaumont, Francis & Fletcher, John.

Norland, Howard B., ed. see Swinburne, Algernon C.

Norlen, Urban. Simulation Model Building: A Statistical Approach to Modelling in the Social Sciences with the Simulation Methods. LC 75-4935. 1976. pap. 21.95 (ISBN 0-470-65090-7). Halsted Pr.

Norlev, E. & Koefoed, H. Danish Languague: Way to. 3rd ed. 1979. text ed. 20.00x (ISBN 8-7160-0998-3, D-727). Vanous.

Norling, Rita. Rituals & Magic for Perfect Living. 1974. 7.95 o.p. (ISBN 0-13-781328-7). P-H.

Norman. Vitamin D. Molecular Biology & Clinical Nutrition. 760p. 1980. 85.00 (ISBN 0-8247-6891-4). Dekker.

Norman, jt. auth. see Burrows.

Norman, A. V. & Pottinger, Don. A History of War & Weapons: 449 to 1660 (English Warfare from the Anglo-Saxons to Cromwell) 1967. 7.95 o.p. (ISBN 0-690-39366-0, TYC-T). T Y Crowell.

Norman, A. W., et al, eds. Vitamin D: Biochemical & Clinical Aspects Related to Calcium Metabolism. 973p. 1977. text ed. 109.50x (ISBN 3-11006-918-0). De Gruyter.

Norman, Barbara. Glass Engraving. LC 80-18031. (Illus.). 208p. 1981. 25.00 (ISBN 0-668-05081-0, 5081). Arco.

Norman, Barry. The Hollywood Greats. 1980. 12.95 (ISBN 0-531-09917-2, C22). Watts.

Norman, Cecilia. The Crepe & Pancake Cookbook. (Illus.). 1979. 9.95 o.p. (ISBN 0-214-20577-0, ADON 8074-4, Dist by Arco). Barrie & Jenkins.

Norman, Claude E. & Livingstone, Elizabeth. Dental Assistant's Manual. (Illus.). 1971. 16.95x (ISBN 0-685-83745-9). Intl Ideas.

Norman, Colin. Microelectronics at Work: Productivity & Jobs in the World Economy. LC 80-53425. (Worldwatch Papers). 1980. pap. 2.00 (ISBN 0-916468-38-0). Worldwatch Inst.

Norman, David. Silver City. (Frontier Rakers: No. 4). (Orig.). 1980. pap. 2.75 (ISBN 0-89083-681-7, Kable News Co). Zebra.

Norman, Donald A. & Rumelhart, David E. Explorations in Cognition. LC 74-32244. (Psychology Ser.). (Illus.). 1975. text ed. 27.95x (ISBN 0-7167-0736-5). W H Freeman.

Norman, Donald A., jt. auth. see Lindsay, Peter H.

Norman, Donald A., ed. Perspectives on Cognitive Science. 320p. 1981. 19.95 (ISBN 0-89391-071-6). Ablex Pub.

Norman, E. Herbert. Ando Shoeki & the Anatomy of Japanese Feudalism. (Studies in Japanese History & Civilization). 254p. 1979. Repr. of 1949 ed. 26.25 (ISBN 0-89093-224-7). U Pubns Amer.

Norman, E. R. Christianity & the World Order. 1979. 9.95 (ISBN 0-19-215510-5); pap. 4.95 (ISBN 0-19-283019-8). Oxford U Pr.

--Church & Society in England, 1770-1970: A Historical Survey. 1976. 54.00x (ISBN 0-19-826435-6). Oxford U Pr.

Norman, Elaine, jt. auth. see Jenkins, Shirley.

Norman, Elaine & Mancuso, Arlene, eds. Women's Issues & Social Work Practice. LC 79-91106. 276p. 1980. pap. text ed. 7.95 (ISBN 0-87581-249-X). Peacock Pubs.

Norman, Elizabeth. Sleep My Love. 1979. pap. 2.50 (ISBN 0-380-48694-6, 48694). Avon.

Norman, Ernest L. The Little Red Box. 1968. 3.95 (ISBN 0-932642-47-0); pap. 2.95 (ISBN 0-685-62826-4). Unarius.

Norman, Geoffrey A., ed. Soybean Physiology, Agronomy, & Utilization. 1978. 30.50 (ISBN 0-12-521160-0). Acad Pr.

Norman, Geraldine. Nineteenth Century Painters & Painting: A Dictionary. (Illus.). 1978. 42.50 (ISBN 0-520-03328-0). U of Cal Pr.

Norman, H. John, jt. auth. see Norman, Herbert.

Norman, Herbert & Norman, H. John. The Organ Today. (Illus.). 224p. 1981. 25.00 (ISBN 0-7153-8053-2). David & Charles.

Norman, Howard, ed. & tr. The Wishing Bone Cycle: Narrative Poems from the Swampy Cree Indians. 192p. 1976. 9.95 (ISBN 0-88373-045-6); pap. 3.45 (ISBN 0-88373-046-4). Stonehill Pub Co.

Norman, Howard, tr. see Barton, Paule.

Norman, J. R., jt. auth. see Greenwood, P. H.

Norman, Jack. Skillbook in Reading. (gr. 6-12). 1975. wkbk 5.08 (ISBN 0-87720-322-9). AMSCO Sch.

--Stories to Teach & Delight. (gr. 9-10). 1977. pap. text ed. 5.17 (ISBN 0-87720-304-0). AMSCO Sch.

Norman, James. Terry's Guide to Mexico. rev. ed. LC 70-171308. 1972. 9.95 o.p. (ISBN 0-385-04181-0). Doubleday.

Norman, James & Schmidt, Margaret Fox. A Shopper's Guide to Mexico: What, Where & How to Buy. rev. ed. LC 72-85363. 280p. 1973. pap. 2.50 (ISBN 0-385-02055-4, Dolp). Doubleday.

Norman, Jane, jt. auth. see Harris, Myron.

Norman, Jerry. A Concise Manchu-English Lexicon. LC 77-14307. (Publications on Asia of the School for International Studies: No. 32). 336p. 1979. 22.50 (ISBN 0-295-95574-0). U of Wash Pr.

Norman, John. Gor Promotion. Incl. Tarnsman of Gor. pap. 1.75 o. p. (ISBN 0-345-27135-1); Outlaw of Gor. pap. 1.75 o. p. (ISBN 0-345-27136-X); Priest Kings of Gor. pap. 1.75 o. p. (ISBN 0-345-27199-8); Nomad of Gor. pap. 1.75 o. p. (ISBN 0-345-27346-X); Assassin of Gor. pap. 1.75 o. p. (ISBN 0-345-27347-8); Raiders of Gor. pap. 1.75 o. p. (ISBN 0-345-27200-5); Captive of Gor. pap. 2.50 (ISBN 0-345-29414-9). 1973. Ballantine.

--Imaginative Sex. (Orig.). 1975. pap. 2.25 (ISBN 0-87997-146-0, UE1546). DAW Bks.

--Rogue of Gor. 1981. pap. 2.50 (ISBN 0-87997-602-0, UE1602). Daw Bks.

--Slave Girl of Gor. (Science Fiction Ser). 1977. pap. 2.25 (ISBN 0-87997-474-5, UE1474). DAW Bks.

Norman, John W. Elementary Dynamic Programming. LC 75-13746. (Illus.). 110p. 1975. pap. 11.50x (ISBN 0-8448-0719-2). Crane-Russak Co.

Norman, M. J. Annual Cropping Systems in the Tropics. LC 79-10625. (Illus.). x, 276p. 1980. text ed. 20.00 (ISBN 0-8130-0632-5). U Presses Fla.

Norman, Marc. Fool's Errand. 1979. pap. 2.25 o.p. (ISBN 0-345-28060-1). Ballantine.

--Fool's Errand. 1978. 8.95 o.p. (ISBN 0-03-019301-X). HR&W.

Norman, Marsha. Getting Out. 1979. pap. 2.50 (ISBN 0-380-75184-4, 75184, Bard). Avon.

Norman, Michael, jt. auth. see Scott, Beth.

Norman, Nicole. The Heather Song. 1980. pap. 2.50 (ISBN 0-671-41463-1). PB.

Norman, Philip. London Signs & Inscriptions. LC 68-22039. (Camden Library Ser). (Illus.). 1968. Repr. of 1893 ed. 15.00 (ISBN 0-8103-3496-8). Gale.

--The Skater's Waltz. 320p. 1980. 17.95 (ISBN 0-241-10255-3, Pub. by Hamish Hamilton England). David & Charles.

Norman, R. G. & Bahiri, S. Productivity Measurements & Incentives. 20.00x (ISBN 0-408-70308-3). Transatlantic.

Norman, Richard. Hegel's Phenomenology: A Philosophical Introduction. (Philosophy Now). 1980. text ed. write for info. (ISBN 0-391-01720-9); pap. text ed. 4.50x (ISBN 0-391-01721-7). Humanities.

Norman, Richard W. Van see Van Norman, Richard W.

Norman, Ruth E. Countdown to Space Fleet Landing. (Tesla Speaks Ser.: Vol. VII). (Illus.). 1974. pap. 4.95 (ISBN 0-932642-28-4). Unarius.

--Twenty-Five Planets Speak to Planet Earth. (Tesla Speaks Ser.: Vol. V). (Illus.). 1975. 7.95 (ISBN 0-932642-26-8); pap. 5.95 (ISBN 0-932642-27-6). Unarius.

Norman, Thelma. A Nurse Called Tommie. LC 59-13496. (Destiny Ser.). 1959. 4.95 (ISBN 0-8163-0140-9, 14600-1). Pacific Pr Pub Assn.

--Wife Called Tommie. LC 74-78317. (Destiny Ser.). 1975. pap. 4.95 (ISBN 0-8163-0170-0, 23680-2). Pacific Pr Pub Assn.

Norman, Ursel. Pasta! Pasta! Pasta! LC 75-510. (Illus.). 64p. 1975. 7.95 o.p. (ISBN 0-688-02922-1). Morrow.

Norman, V. D., jt. auth. see Dixit, A.

Norman, Victor D. Education, Learning & Productivity. 1976. pap. text ed. 12.50x (ISBN 8-200-02344-3, Dist. by Columbia U Pr). Universitet.

Norman, W. H., tr. see Akutagawa, Ryunosuke.

Norman, Yvonne. Leaves on the Wind. (YA) 1978. 5.95 (ISBN 0-685-85778-6, Avalon). Bouregy.

Normann, D. Recursion on the Countable Functionals. (Lecture Notes in Mathematics: Vol. 811). 191p. 1980. pap. 11.80 (ISBN 0-387-10019-9). Springer-Verlag.

Normano, Joao F. Brazil: A Study of Economic Types. LC 67-29551. 1935. 12.00x (ISBN 0-8196-0208-6). Biblo.

Norona, Delf, ed. Cyclopedia of United States Postmarks & Postal History. LC 75-1788. (Illus.). 416p. 1975. Repr. 35.00x (ISBN 0-88000-063-5). Quarterman.

Noronha, Leslie De. The Mango & Tamarind Tree. 12.00 (ISBN 0-89253-632-2); flexible cloth 6.75 (ISBN 0-89253-633-0). Ind-US Inc.

--Poems. (Redbird). 1976. lib. bdg. 5.00 (ISBN 0-89253-127-4); flexible bdg. 4.80 (ISBN 0-89253-141-X). Ind-US Inc.

--Stories. 8.00 (ISBN 0-89253-630-6); flexible cloth 4.80 (ISBN 0-89253-631-4). Ind-US Inc.

Noronha, Leslie de see Noronha, Leslie De.

Norpoth, Helmut, jt. auth. see Iversen, Gudmund R.

Norquay, Karen, jt. auth. see Bernard, Carl.

Norquist, Marilyn. The Beatitudes: Jesus' Pattern for a Happy Life. 112p. 1981. pap. 2.95 (ISBN 0-89243-136-9). Liguori Pubns.

--Como Leer Y Orar los Evangelios. McPhee, John, ed. Diaz, Olimpia, tr. from Eng. (Handbook of the Bible Ser.). Orig. Title: Hand. 64p. 1980. pap. 1.50 (ISBN 0-89243-127-X). Liguori Pubns.

--How to Read & Pray Saint Paul. (Handbook of the Bible Ser.). 1979. pap. 1.50 (ISBN 0-89243-110-5). Liguori Pubns.

Norregard, Georg. Danish Settlements in West Africa, 1658-1850. LC 66-21611. (Pub. by Boston U Pr). 1966. 11.50x (ISBN 0-8419-8708-4, Africana). Holmes & Meier.

Norris, Carolyn. Island of Silence. 1976. pap. 1.25 o.p. (ISBN 0-445-00411-8). Popular Lib.

Norris, Charles, jt. auth. see Rubin, Wallace.

Norris, Charles G. Salt or the Education of Griffith Adams: A Novel. (Lost American Fiction Ser.). 400p. 1981. Repr. of 1918 ed. price not set (ISBN 0-8093-1011-2). S Ill U Pr.

Norris, Christopher. William Empson & the Philosophy of Literary Criticism. 1978. text ed. 25.75x (ISBN 0-485-11175-6, Athlone Pr). Humanities.

Norris, Chuck. Winning Tournament Karate. Cocoran, John, ed. LC 75-5497. (Ser. 121). (Illus.). 1975. pap. text ed. 5.95 (ISBN 0-89750-016-4). Ohara Pubns.

Norris, David O. Vertebrate Endocrinology. LC 80-10332. (Illus.). 524p. 1980. text ed. 29.50 (ISBN 0-8121-0699-7). Lea & Febiger.

Norris, Dorothy E. & Shiner, Reva P. Keynotes to Modern Dance. 3rd ed. LC 69-15426. 1969. pap. 8.95 o.p. (ISBN 0-8087-1411-2). Burgess.

Norris, Frank. McTeague. 1977. pap. 2.25 (ISBN 0-449-30810-3, Prem). Fawcett.

--McTeague. 1976. lib. bdg. 18.95x (ISBN 0-89968-071-2). Lightyear.

--McTeague. Pizer, Donald, ed. LC 77-479. (Norton Critical Editions). 1977 12.95 (ISBN 0-393-04460-2); pap. text ed. 6.95x 1978 (ISBN 0-393-09136-8). Norton.

--McTeague: A Story of California. LC 72-184736. 1971. lib. bdg. 12.50x (ISBN 0-8376-0406-0). Bentley.

--McTeague: A Story of San Francisco. 9.00 (ISBN 0-8446-2663-5). Peter Smith.

--The Octopus. 1976. lib. bdg. 19.50x (ISBN 0-89968-070-4). Lightyear.

--The Octopus: A Story of California. LC 76-184737. 464p. 1971. Repr. lib. bdg. 12.50x (ISBN 0-8376-0405-2). Bentley.

--Pit. (Literature Ser). (gr. 10-12). 1970. pap. text ed. 3.67 (ISBN 0-87720-735-6). AMSCO Sch.

--The Pit. 1976. lib. bdg. 18.25x (ISBN 0-89968-069-0). Lightyear.

--The Pit: A Story of Chicago. LC 70-184738. 432p. 1971. Repr. of 1903 ed. lib. bdg. 12.50x (ISBN 0-8376-0407-9). Bentley.

Norris, G. & Ewart, W. Choosing & Managing Information Systems for Public Administration. 1979. text ed. 19.25x (ISBN 0-566-00244-2, Pub. by Gower Pub Co England). Renouf.

Norris, Gerald. Stanford, Cambridge Jubilee & Tchaikovsky. LC 80-66085. (Illus.). 576p. 1980. 75.00 (ISBN 0-7153-7856-2). David & Charles.

Norris, Graeme. The Effective University: A Management by Objectives Approach. 1978. text ed. 23.00x (ISBN 0-566-00242-6, Pub. by Gower Pub Co England). Renouf.

--Justifying Research & Teaching Objectives in Universities. 1979. text ed. 26.50x (ISBN 0-566-00243-4, Pub. by Gower Pub Co England). Renouf.

Norris, Gunilla B. The Friendship Hedge. (Illus.). 48p. (gr. 2-4). 1973. PLB 6.95 o.p. (ISBN 0-525-30210-7). Dutton.

Norris, Henry D. The Plans Book. LC 77-86203. 1977. pap. 12.50 (ISBN 0-930560-01-9, Pub. by Two Continents). Hippocrene Bks.

Norris, J. E. History of the Lower Shenandoah Valley Counties of Frederick, Berkeley, Jefferson, & Clarke. (Illus.). 925p. Repr. of 1890 ed. 32.50 (ISBN 0-685-65082-0). Va Bk.

Norris, J. R. & Bergen, T., eds. Methods in Microbiology, Vols. 10 & 11. 1978-79. Vol. 10. 52.00 (ISBN 0-12-521510-X); Vol. 11. 40.50 (ISBN 0-12-521511-8). Acad Pr.

Norris, James A. First Afghan War: 1838-42. LC 67-21962. 1967. 65.00 (ISBN 0-521-05838-4). Cambridge U Pr.

Norris, James D. R. G. Dun & Co., Eighteen Forty-One to Nineteen Hundred: The Development of Credit-Reporting in the Nineteenth Century. LC 77-95359. (Contributions in Economics & Economic History: No. 20). (Illus.). 1978. lib. bdg. 18.95x (ISBN 0-313-20326-1, NDC/). Greenwood.

Norris, Jeanne L., jt. auth. see McDermott, Irene E.

Norris, John. Christian Blessedness (with) Reflections Upon a Late Essay Concerning Human Understanding. Wellek, Rene, ed. LC 75-11241. (British Philosophers & Theologians of the 17th & 18th Centuries Ser.). 1978. Repr. of 1690 ed. lib. bdg. 42.00 (ISBN 0-8240-1793-5). Garland Pub.

--A Collection of Miscellanies. Wellek, Rene, ed. LC 75-11242. (British Philosophers & Theologians of the 17th & 18th Centuries Ser.). 1978. Repr. of 1687 ed. lib. bdg. 42.00 (ISBN 0-8240-1794-3). Garland Pub.

--An Essay Towards the Theory of the Ideal or Intelligible World, 2 Vols., 1701 & 1704. Wellek, Rene, ed. LC 75-11243. (British Philosophers & Theologians of the 17th & 18th Centuries Ser.). 1978. Set. lib. bdg. 42.00 (ISBN 0-8240-1795-1). Garland Pub.

--Treatises Upon Several Subjects. Wellek, Rene, ed. LC 75-11244. (British Philosophers & Theologians of the 17th & 18th Centuries Ser.). 1978. Repr. of 1698 ed. lib. bdg. 42.00 (ISBN 0-8240-1796-X). Garland Pub.

Norris, K. A., jt. ed. see Rutgers, A.

Norris, Keith & Valzey, John. The Economics of Research & Technology. (Studies in Economics Ser.). 1973. text ed. 18.95 o.p. (ISBN 0-04-330227-0); pap. text ed. 10.95x (ISBN 0-04-330228-9). Allen Unwin.

Norris, Kenneth S., ed. Whales, Dolphins, & Porpoises. (Library Reprint Ser.). 1978. 42.50x (ISBN 0-520-03283-7). U of Cal Pr.

Norris, Leslie. Islands off Maine. (Illus., Ltd. ed. 50 boxed, 500 trade). 1977. boxed Gray Parrot Deluxe ed. 50.00 (ISBN 0-930954-16-5); pap. 8.50 o.p. (ISBN 0-930954-00-9); deluxe ed. avail. (ISBN 0-930954-16-5). Tidal Pr.

Norris, Louis W. Values & the Credibility of the Professor. LC 80-5501. 171p. 1980. lib. bdg. 16.75 (ISBN 0-8191-1114-7); pap. text ed. 8.75 (ISBN 0-8191-1115-5). U Pr of Amer.

Norris, M. W. Local Government in Peninsular Malaysia. 121p. 1980. text ed. 27.00x (ISBN 0-566-00283-3, Pub. by Gower Pr England). Renouf.

Norris, Malcolm. Monumental Brasses: The Craft. (Illus.). 1978. 58.00 (ISBN 0-571-09891-6, Pub. by Faber & Faber). Merrimack Bk Serv.

Norris, Martin J. The Law of Maritime Personal Injuries, 2 vols. 3rd ed. LC 75-4186. 1975. Set. 110.00 (ISBN 0-686-14495-3). Lawyers Co-Op.

--The Law of Seamen, 3 vols. 3rd ed. LC 74-112518. 1970. Set. 144.00 (ISBN 0-686-14494-5). Lawyers Co-Op.

Norris, P. About Honey: Nature's Elixir for Health. 1980. pap. 1.95 (ISBN 0-87904-043-2). Lust.

Norris, Patrick, tr. see Ferriz, David.

Norris, R. M. & Webb, R. W. Geology of California. 379p. 1976. 21.95 (ISBN 0-471-61566-8). Wiley.

Norris, Richard A., tr. see Norris, Richard A., Jr. & Rusch, William G.

Norris, Richard A., Jr. & Rusch, William G., eds. The Christological Controversy. Norris, Richard A., tr. LC 79-8890. (Sources of Early Christian Thought). 176p. 1980. pap. 6.95 (ISBN 0-8006-1411-9, 1-1411). Fortress.

Norris, Robert E. & Haring, L. Lloyd. Political Geography. (Geography Ser.). 328p. 1980. text ed. 21.95 (ISBN 0-675-08223-4). Merrill.

Norris, Rosalie N., ed. & tr. see Salomone-Marino, Salvatore.

Norris, William C., et al. The Spinal Injury Learning Series. LC 80-26576. (Illus.). 1981. price not set (ISBN 0-87805-131-7). U Pr of Miss.

Norse, Harold. Hotel Nirvana: Selected Poems. LC 73-93942. (Pocket Poets Ser.: No. 32). (Orig.). 1974. pap. 2.00 o.p. (ISBN 0-87286-078-7). City Lights.

Norse, Harold, tr. from It. & see Belli, Giuseppe G.

Norster, E. R. Combustion & Heat Transfer in Gas Turbine Systems. (Cranfield International Symposium Ser: Vol. 11). (Illus.). 1971. 58.00 o.p. (ISBN 0-08-016524-9). Pergamon.

North & North. Simeon North: First Official Pistol Maker of the United States. Repr. 9.95 (ISBN 0-88227-001-X). Gun Room.

North, Arthur A. Supreme Court: Judicial Process & Judicial Politics. LC 66-17855. (Orig.). 1966. pap. text ed. 5.95x (ISBN 0-89197-435-0). Irvington.

North, Barbara & Crittenden, Penelope. Anti-Stress Workbook. (Illus.). 79p. (Orig.). 1980. pap. 4.95 (ISBN 0-938480-00-6). Healthworks.

North, Brownlow. The Rich Man & Lazarus. 1979. pap. 2.45 (ISBN 0-85151-121-X). Banner of Truth.

--Wilt Thou Go with This Man? 1966. pap. 1.95 (ISBN 0-686-12545-2). Banner of Truth.

North, C. Plant Breeding & Genetics in Horticulture. LC 79-10436. 1980. pap. 16.95 (ISBN 0-470-26661-9). Halsted Pr.

North Carolina Writers Conference, jt. auth. see Chowan College Creative Writing Group.

North, Christopher R. Second Isaiah Introduction, Translation & Commentary to Chapters 15-55. 1964. 22.95x (ISBN 0-19-826154-3). Oxford U Pr.

North, D. C. & Thomas, R. P. The Rise of the Western World: A New Economic History. LC 73-77258. (Illus.). 192p. 1973. 23.95 (ISBN 0-521-20171-3); pap. 6.95x (ISBN 0-521-29099-6). Cambridge U Pr.

North, Douglass, jt. auth. see Davis, Lance.

North, Eric M. The Book of a Thousand Tongues. LC 73-174087. (Tower Bks). 386p. 1972. Repr. of 1938 ed. 22.00 (ISBN 0-8103-3948-X). Gale.

North, Ernest D. The Wit & Wisdom of Charles Lamb. 267p. 1980. Repr. of 1892 ed. lib. bdg. 25.00 (ISBN 0-8495-4109-3). Arden Lib.

North, Gloria. Twentieth Century Man. 16p. 1979. pap. 1.00 (ISBN 0-686-27736-8). Samisdat.

North, Hallie B. Commercial Food Patents, U. S. Nineteen Seventy-Nine. (Illus.). 1980. lib. bdg. 30.00 (ISBN 0-87055-358-5). AVI.

--Commercial Food Patents, U.S. Nineteen-Eighty. (Illus.). 1981. lib. bdg. 30.00 (ISBN 0-87055-371-2). AVI.

North, Helen. From the Myth to Icon: Reflections of Greek Ethical Doctrine in Literature & Art. LC 79-7619. (Cornell Studies in Classical Philology). (Illus.). 1979. 19.50x (ISBN 0-8014-1135-1). Cornell U Pr.

North, Helen F., ed. Interpretations of Plato: A Swarthmore Symposium. (Supplement Mnemosyne: No. 50). viii, 112p. 1980. text ed. 21.75x (ISBN 0-391-01138-3). Humanities.

North, Henry, jt. auth. see De Bartolo, Dick.

North, Ira. You Can March for the Master. 6.50 (ISBN 0-89225-186-7); pap. 4.00 (ISBN 0-89225-187-5). Gospel Advocate.

North, Jessica. Mask of the Jaguar. 288p. 1981. 10.95 (ISBN 0-698-11050-1). Coward.

North, Joseph, ed. The New Masses: An Anthology of the Rebel Thirties. (Illus.). 1980. pap. 2.25 (ISBN 0-7178-0355-4). Intl Pub Co.

North, M. A. & Hillard, A. E. Latin Prose Composition. 320p. (gr. 8-12). 1979. 20.00x (ISBN 0-7156-1321-9, Pub. by Duckworth England); pap. 10.95x (ISBN 0-7156-1322-7, Pub. by Duckworth England). Biblio Dist.

North, Mack O. Commercial Chicken Production Manual. 2nd ed. (Illus.). 1978. lib. bdg. 38.50 (ISBN 0-87055-259-7). AVI.

North, Rachel. Flower of Love. (Orig.). 1980. pap. 2.50 (ISBN 0-505-51525-3). Tower Bks.

North, Robert, jt. auth. see Choucri, Nazli.

North, Robert C. Chinese Communism. (Illus., Orig.). (gr. 9-12). 1966. pap. 2.95 o.p. (ISBN 0-07-047450-8, SP). McGraw.

--The World That Could Be. (Illus.). 1978. 8.95 (ISBN 0-393-05677-5); pap. 4.95 (ISBN 0-393-00882-7). Norton.

North, Sterling. Rascal. (gr. 5 up). 1976. pap. 1.75 (ISBN 0-380-01518-8, 44800). Avon.

--Young Thomas Edison. (North Star Bks). (Illus.). (gr. 7-11). 1958. 2.95 o.p. (ISBN 0-395-07252-2). HM.

North Texas State University Guidance & Counseling Staff, ed. Preparation of Guidance Associates & Professional Counselors Within the Framework of a Competency Based Program. (ACES Monograph: No. 1). 1973. 6.50 (ISBN 0-686-05522-5, 051). Am Personnel.

Northall, G. F. English Folk-Rhymes: A Collection of Traditional Verses Relating to Places & Persons, Customs, Superstitions, Etc. LC 67-23918. 1967. Repr. of 1892 ed. 22.00 (ISBN 0-8103-3455-0). Gale.

Northam, J. Ibsen: A Critical Study. LC 72-80297. (Major European Authors Ser.). 240p. 1973. 38.50 (ISBN 0-521-08682-5); pap. 11.50x (ISBN 0-521-09733-9). Cambridge U Pr.

Northampton Craft Conference 1976. Design Education in Crafts & Technology: Proceedings. 1976. pap. 13.50 (ISBN 0-7134-3177-6, Pub. by Batsford England). David & Charles.

Northbrooke, John. A Treatise Wherein Dicing, Dauncing, Vaine Playes or Enterluds Are Reproved. LC 72-170401. (English Stage Ser.: Vol. 1). lib. bdg. 50.00 (ISBN 0-8240-0584-8). Garland Pub.

Northcott, Cecil. South Seas Sailor (John Williams) 1965. 1.95 (ISBN 0-87508-622-5). Chr Lit.

Northcott, D. G. Affine Sets & Affine Groups. LC 79-41595. (London Mathematical Society Lecture Note Ser.: No. 39). 1980. pap. 26.95x (ISBN 0-521-22909-X). Cambridge U Pr.

--Finite Free Resolutions. LC 75-31397. (Tracts in Mathematics Ser.: No. 71). 250p. 1976. 49.50 (ISBN 0-521-21155-7). Cambridge U Pr.

--A First Course of Homological Algebra. LC 72-97873. 250p. 1973. 29.95 (ISBN 0-521-20196-9). Cambridge U Pr.

--A First Course of Homological Algebra. LC 72-87873. 217p. 1980. pap. 12.50x (ISBN 0-521-29976-4). Cambridge U Pr.

Northcott, Douglas G. Ideal Theory. (Cambridge Tracts in Mathematics & Mathematical Physics: No. 42). 1953. 20.50 (ISBN 0-521-05840-6). Cambridge U Pr.

--Lessons on Rings, Modules & Multiplicities. LC 68-21397. 1968. 48.00 (ISBN 0-521-07151-8). Cambridge U Pr.

Northcut, Allan, ed. see Knauff, Thomas.

Northcut, Debbie, ed. see Knauff, Thomas.

Northeast Drama Institute. Full-Color Designs from Chinese Opera Costumes. (Illus.). 1980. pap. 6.00 (ISBN 0-486-23979-9). Dover.

Northedge, F. S. The Foreign Policies of the Powers. 2nd ed. 1974. 14.95 o.p. (ISBN 0-571-04837-4, Pub. by Faber & Faber). Merrimack Bk Serv.

--International Political System. 1976. 15.95 o.p. (ISBN 0-571-11008-8, Pub. by Faber & Faber); pap. 9.95 (ISBN 0-571-11009-6). Merrimack Bk Serv.

Northedge, F. S., ed. The Foreign Policies of the Powers. LC 75-3762. 1975. 17.95 (ISBN 0-02-923170-1); pap. text ed. 8.95 (ISBN 0-02-923180-9). Free Pr.

--The Use of Force in International Relations. LC 74-10140. 1974. 17.95 (ISBN 0-02-923210-4). Free Pr.

Northen, Helen. Social Work with Groups. LC 69-19462. 1969. 15.00x (ISBN 0-231-02965-9). Columbia U Pr.

Northen, Helen, jt. auth. see Roberts, Robert W.

Northen, Henry T. Introductory Plant Science. 3rd ed. (Illus.). 586p. 1968. 28.95 (ISBN 0-8260-6770-0); instr's manual avail. (ISBN 0-471-07522-1). Wiley.

Northington, David K. Systematic Studies of the Genus Pyrrhopappus (Compositae, Cichorieae) (Special Publications: No. 6). 38p. 1974. pap. 2.00 (ISBN 0-89672-031-4). Tex Tech Pr.

Northman, John E., jt. auth. see Baker, Frank.

Northrop, Stuart A. Turquois & Spanish Mines in New Mexico. LC 75-7474. (Illus.). 96p. 1975. pap. 3.45 o.p. (ISBN 0-8263-0371-4). U of NM Pr.

Northrup. Compulsory Arbitration & Government Intervention in Labor Disputes. LC 66-22184. 7.00 (ISBN 0-910294-18-6). Brown Bk.

Northrup, David. Trade Without Rulers: Pre-Colonial Economic Development in South-Eastern Nigeria. (Studies in African Affairs). (Illus.). 1978. 36.00x (ISBN 0-19-822712-4). Oxford U Pr.

Northrup, F. S. Taming of the Nations: A Study of the Cultural Bases of International Policy. 1971. Repr. of 1952 ed. 16.25 o.s.i. (ISBN 0-02-849740-6). Hafner.

Northrup, Herbert R., jt. auth. see Bloom, Gordon F.

Northrup, James P. Old Age, Handicapped & Vietnam-Era Antidiscrimination Legislation. rev. ed. 1980. pap. 15.00 (ISBN 0-89546-020-3). Indus Res Unit-Wharton.

Northrup, Melvin. Toby's Gift. (Books I Can Read). 32p. (Orig.). (gr. 2). 1980. pap. 1.25 (ISBN 0-8127-0291-3). Southern Pub.

Northup, Solomon. Twelve Years a Slave. Eakin, Sue & Logsdon, Joseph, eds. LC 68-13454. (Library of Southern Civilization: No. 1). (Illus.). 1968. 14.95x (ISBN 0-8071-0633-X); pap. text ed. 5.95 (ISBN 0-8071-0150-8). La State U Pr.

Northwest Regional Educational Laboratory. Comparison Shopping & Caring for Your Personal Possessions. (Lifeworks Ser.). (Illus.). 1980. pap. text ed. 4.00 (ISBN 0-07-047309-9). McGraw.

--Competency-Based Education: Beyond Minimum Competency Testing. Nickes, Ruth, ed. Date not set. pap. price not set (ISBN 0-8077-2606-0). Tchrs Coll.

--Ordering from Catalogs & Dining Out. (Lifeworks Ser.). (Illus.). 1980. pap. text ed. 4.00 (ISBN 0-07-047305-6). McGraw.

Northwestern University. Joint Acquisitions List of Africana: 1978. 1980. lib. bdg. 90.00 (ISBN 0-8161-0329-1). G K Hall.

Northwood, Arthur, Jr., jt. auth. see Rapport, Leonard.

Northwood Publications,London, ed. Consulting Engineer's Who's Who & Yearbook 1979 (British Edition) 1979. 25.00x (ISBN 0-7198-2780-9). Intl Ideas.

Nortman, Dorothy & Hofstatter, Ellen. Population & Family Planning Programs. 10th ed. LC 80-52443. (Illus.). 96p. (Orig.). 1980. pap. 4.50 (ISBN 0-87834-041-6). Population Coun.

Norton, A. V., tr. see Blume, Helmut.

Norton, Alice, ed. Public Relations Information Sources. LC 77-137574. (Management Information Guide Ser.: No. 22). 1970. 30.00 (ISBN 0-8103-0822-3). Gale.

Norton, Aloysius A. Theodore Roosevelt. (United States Authors Ser.). 1980. lib. bdg. 8.95 (ISBN 0-8057-7309-6). Twayne.

Norton, Andre. The Beast Master. 1978. pap. 1.95 (ISBN 0-449-23637-4, Crest). Fawcett.

--The Forerunner. 288p. (Orig.). 1981. pap. 2.50 (ISBN 0-523-41481-1). Pinnacle Bks.

--Forerunner Foray. 1975. pap. 2.25 (ISBN 0-441-24621-4). Ace Bks.

--Fur Magic. (gr. 4-6). 1978. pap. 1.75 (ISBN 0-671-41403-8). Archway.

--Fur Magic. (Illus.). (gr. 4-6). 1978. pap. 1.75 (ISBN 0-671-41403-8). PB.
--Gryphon in Glory. LC 80-24835. 132p. (gr. 7 up). 1981. 9.95 (ISBN 0-689-50195-1, McElderry Book). Atheneum.
--Horn Crown. 1981. pap. 2.50 (ISBN 0-87997-635-7, UE1635). DAW Bks.
--Iron Cage. 1976. pap. 1.954 (ISBN 0-441-37291-0). Ace Bks.
--Judgment on Janus. 1979. pap. 1.95 o.p. (ISBN 0-449-24214-5, Crest). Fawcett.
--Lore of the Witch World. (Science Fiction Ser.). 1980. pap. 1.95 (ISBN 0-87997-560-1, UE1560). Daw Bks.
--Octagon Magic. (Illus.). (gr. 4-6). 1978. pap. 1.75 (ISBN 0-671-56074-3). PB.
--The Opal-Eyed Fan. (gr. 7 up). 1977. 7.95 o.p. (ISBN 0-525-36440-4). Dutton.
--Operation Time Search. 224p. 1981. pap. 2.25 (ISBN 0-449-24370-2, Crest). Fawcett.
--Outside. LC 73-92454. (Illus.). 128p. (gr. 2-5). 1974. 5.95 o.s.i. (ISBN 0-8027-6185-2). Walker & Co.
--Outside. (gr. 4-7). 1975. pap. 1.75 (ISBN 0-380-00435-6, 52720, Camelot). Avon.
--Plague Ship. 1976. pap. 1.95 (ISBN 0-441-66835-6). Ace Bks.
--Shadow Hawk. 1979. pap. 1.95 o.p. (ISBN 0-449-24186-6, Crest). Fawcett.
--Sorceress of the Witchworld. 224p. 1977. pap. 1.95 (ISBN 0-441-77555-1). Ace Bks.
--Star Guard. 1978. pap. 1.95 (ISBN 0-449-23646-3, Crest). Fawcett.
--Star Rangers. 1979. pap. 1.95 (ISBN 0-449-24076-2, Crest). Fawcett.
--Steel Magic. (Illus.). (gr. 4-6). 1978. pap. 1.75 (ISBN 0-671-56094-8). PB.
--Velvet Shadows. 1978. pap. 1.95 (ISBN 0-449-23135-6, Crest). Fawcett.
--Web of the Witch World. 192p. 1976. pap. 1.95 (ISBN 0-441-87875-X). Ace Bks.
--The White Jade Fox. 1979. pap. 1.95 (ISBN 0-449-24005-3, Crest). Fawcett.
--Witch World. 224p. 1977. pap. 1.95 (ISBN 0-441-89705-3). Ace Bks.
--The X Factor. 224p. 1981. pap. 2.25 (ISBN 0-449-24395-8, Crest). Fawcett.
--Year of the Unicorn. 224p. 1976. pap. 1.95 (ISBN 0-441-94254-7). Ace Bks.

Norton, Andre & Gilbert, Michael. The Day of the Ness. LC 74-78111. (Illus.). 128p. (gr. 3-7). 1975. 5.95 o.s.i. (ISBN 0-8027-6195-X). Walker & Co.

Norton, Andre & Madlee, Dorothy. Star Ka'at World. LC 75-36018. (Illus.). 128p. 1976. 6.95 (ISBN 0-8027-6300-6); PLB 6.85 (ISBN 0-8027-6301-4). Walker & Co.
--Star Ka'ats & the Plant People. (Illus.). (gr. 3-5). 1980. pap. 1.75 (ISBN 0-671-56045-X). PB.
--Star Ka'ats & the Winged Warriors. (Star Ka'ats Ser.). (Illus.). 128p. (gr. 2-6). 1981. 8.95 (ISBN 0-8027-6416-9); PLB 9.85 (ISBN 0-8027-6417-7). Walker & Co.

Norton, Andre & Miller, Phyllis. Seven Spells to Sunday. (gr. 4-7). 1980. pap. write for info. (ISBN 0-671-56086-7). PB.

Norton, Caroline. English Laws for Women in the Nineteenth Century. LC 79-2948. 188p. 1981. Repr. of 1854 ed. 17.00 (ISBN 0-8305-0111-8). Hyperion Conn.

Norton, Caroline S. Selected Writings of Caroline Norton. LC 78-18828. 1978. 85.00x (ISBN 0-8201-1312-3). Schol Facsimiles.

Norton, Charles E., ed. see Carlyle, Thomas.

Norton, Cynthia, jt. auth. see Brooks, Stewart.

Norton, Cynthia F. Microbiology. LC 80-23350. (Life Sciences Ser.). (Illus.). 850p. 1981. text ed. 19.95 (ISBN 0-201-05304-7). A-W.

Norton, D. Hospitals & the Long-Stay Patient. 1967. 21.00 (ISBN 0-08-011053-3); pap. 9.75 (ISBN 0-08-011052-5). Pergamon.

Norton, Elliott, tr. see Dante Alighieri.

Norton, Eloise S. Folk Literature of the British Isles: Readings for Librarians, Teachers, & Those Who Work with Children & Young Adults. LC 78-10324. 1978. lib. bdg. 14.00 (ISBN 0-8108-1177-4). Scarecrow.

Norton, F. G., jt. auth. see Clarke, L. Harwood.

Norton, F. J. Descriptive Catalogue of Printing in Spain & Portugal, 1501-1520. LC 76-11062. 1978. 240.00 (ISBN 0-521-21136-0). Cambridge U Pr.

Norton, F. J. & Wilson, E. M. Two Spanish Chap-Books. facsimile ed. 1969. 58.00 (ISBN 0-521-05843-0). Cambridge U Pr.

Norton, Frederick H. Ceramics for the Artist Potter. 1956. 18.95 (ISBN 0-201-05300-4). A-W.
--Elements of Ceramics. 2nd ed. LC 72-9316. 1974. text ed. 19.95 (ISBN 0-201-05306-3). A-W.
--Refractories. 4th ed. 1968. text ed. 37.50 o.p. (ISBN 0-07-047538-5, P&RB). McGraw.

Norton, Frederick J. Printing in Spain, 1501-20. 1966. 84.00 (ISBN 0-521-05842-2). Cambridge U Pr.

Norton, G. A. & Hollings, C. S., eds. Pest Management: Proceedings of an International Conference, 25-29 October 1976, Laxenburg, Austria. LC 78-40825. 1979. text ed. 60.00 (ISBN 0-08-023427-5). Pergamon.

Norton, G. Ron. Parenting. 1977. 12.95 (ISBN 0-13-650077-3, Spec); pap. 3.95 (ISBN 0-13-650069-2). P-H.

Norton, Henry K. The Far Eastern Republic of Siberia. LC 79-2917. (Illus.). 1981. Repr. of 1923 ed. 25.00 (ISBN 0-8305-0086-3). Hyperion Conn.

Norton, Howard. Rosalynn. 1977. pap. 2.95 o.p. (ISBN 0-88270-260-2). Logos.

Norton, Howard, jt. auth. see Swieson, Eddy.

Norton, John. Abel Being Dead, Yet Speaketh. LC 78-8184. 1978. Repr. of 1658 ed. 20.00 (ISBN 0-8201-1310-7). Schol Facsimiles.

Norton, Lucy. First Lady of Versailles: Marie Adelaide of Savoy, Dauphine of France. (Illus.). 1978. 15.00 o.s.i. (ISBN 0-397-01051-6). Lippincott.

Norton, Maggie Jo. Crochet Designs from Simple Motifs. 1978. 19.95 (ISBN 0-7134-1238-0). David & Charles.

Norton, Margaret. Infant Crafts for School & Home. (Illus.). 1975. 8.50 (ISBN 0-7137-0671-6, Pub by Blandford Pr England). Sterling.

Norton, Mary. The Complete Adventures of the Borrowers, 4 bks. Bd. with Bk 1. The Borrowers; Bk. 2. The Borrowers Afield; Bk. 3. The Borrowers Afloat; Bk. 4. The Borrowers Aloft. (Illus.). (gr. 8 up). 1975. pap. 7.25 boxed set (ISBN 0-15-613605-8, VoyB). HarBraceJ.

Norton, Mary B. Liberty's Daughters: The Revolutionary Experience of American Women. 1980. 15.00 (ISBN 0-316-61251-0); pap. 7.95 (ISBN 0-316-61252-9). Little.

Norton, Mary B., jt. auth. see Berkin, Carol.

Norton, Paul F. Latrobe, Jefferson, & the National Capitol. LC 76-23662. (Outstanding Dissertations in the Fine Arts Ser.). 1977. lib. bdg. 56.00x (ISBN 0-8240-2716-7). Garland Pub.

Norton, Paul F. see O'Neal, William B.

Norton, Philip. Dissension in the House of Commons: Nineteen Seventy-Four to Nineteen Seventy-Nine. (Illus.). 560p. 1980. text ed. 79.00x (ISBN 0-19-827430-0). Oxford U Pr.

Norton, Thomas, jt. auth. see Sackville, Thomas.

Norton, Thomas E. & Frank, Robert. The Fur Trade in Colonial New York, 1686-1776. LC 73-2047. 272p. 1974. 25.00x (ISBN 0-299-06420-4). U of Wis Pr.

Norton, Thomas W. Solar Energy Experiments. LC 77-4918. 1977. 8.95 (ISBN 0-87857-179-5). Rodale Pr Inc.

Norton, Wilbert H., jt. auth. see Engel, James F.

Norton, William, jt. auth. see Holmgren, Rod.

Norton-Griffiths, M., jt. auth. see Sinclair, A. R.

Norton-Kyshe, James W. Dictionary of Legal Quotations. LC 68-30648. 1968. Repr. of 1904 ed. 18.00 (ISBN 0-8103-3189-6). Gale.

Norton-Smith, John. Geoffrey Chaucer. (Medieval Authors Ser.). 1974. 25.00 (ISBN 0-7100-7801-3). Routledge & Kegan.

Norvedt, Matilda. Daddy Isn't Coming Home. (Pathfinder Ser.). 96p. (Orig.). (gr. 3-6). 1981. pap. 2.95 (ISBN 0-310-45941-8). Zondervan.

Norvedt, Matilda, tr. Derrotando O Desespero E Depressao. (Portuguese Bks.). 1979. 1.25 (ISBN 0-8297-0828-6). Life Pubs Intl.

Norvell. The Million Dollar Secret Hidden in Your Mind. 223p. 1973. pap. 2.95 (ISBN 0-06-463345-4, EH 345, EH). Har-Row.
--Universal Secrets of Telecosmic Power. 1975. pap. 1.50 o.p. (ISBN 0-451-06810-6, W6810, Sig). NAL.

Norvell, Anthony. The Mystical Power of Pyramid Astrology. LC 78-18405. 1978. 9.95 (ISBN 0-8119-0289-7). Fell.

Norvell, Theodore J. The Meaning & the Objective of History. (Illus.). 123p. 1980. deluxe ed. 37.65 (ISBN 0-89266-238-7). Am Classical Coll Pr.

Norville, Mary F. Drug Dosage & Solutions Workbook. (Illus.). 128p. (Orig.). 1981. pap. text ed. 9.95 (ISBN 0-87619-920-1). R J Brady.

Norville, Warren. Death Tide. 1979. pap. 1.95 o.s.i. (ISBN 0-515-05146-2). Jove Pubns.

Norwak, Mary. Beginner's Guide to Home Freezing. (Beginners Guide Ser.). 1973. 12.95 (ISBN 0-7207-0660-2, Pub. by Michael Joseph). Merrimack Bk Serv.
--Cooking with Fruit. 1960. 6.50 (ISBN 0-685-20569-X). Transatlantic.
--From Garden to Table. (Illus.). 1978. 16.95 (ISBN 0-241-89593-6, Pub. by Hamish Hamilton England). David & Charles.
--The Poultry Cookbook. 1979. 19.95 (ISBN 0-241-89807-2, Pub. by Hamish Hamilton England). David & Charles.
--Self-Sufficiency for Children. (Illus.). 96p. (gr. 8 up). 1981. 10.95 (ISBN 0-7207-1095-2). Merrimack Bk Serv.
--Toffees, Fudges, Chocolates & Sweets. 1977. 14.50 (ISBN 0-7207-0956-3). Transatlantic.

Norweb, Emery M. English Gold Coins: Ancient to Modern Times. LC 68-9275. (Illus.). 96p. 1968. pap. text ed. 10.00x (ISBN 0-910386-44-7, Pub. by Cleveland Mus Art). Ind U Pr.

Norwegian Institute of Rock Schach Blasting Techniques. Rock Bolting: A Practical Handbook Describing All Aspects of Rock Bolts & Their Application in Rock Engineering. 1979. 13.75 (ISBN 0-08-022503-9). Pergamon.

Norwegian Petroleum Society. Contracts & Taxation in the Norwegian North Sea. 130p. 1980. 75.00x (Pub. by Norwegian Info Norway). State Mutual Bk.
--Corrosion Problems Related to Electrical, Instrumentation & Automation Components Offshore. 152p. 1980. 75.00x (ISBN 82-7270-007-7, Pub. by Norwegian Info Norway). State Mutual Bk.
--Development Through Cooperation Between the Scandinavian & Oapec Countries. 296p. 1980. 75.00x (Pub. by Norwegian Info Norway). State Mutual Bk.
--Engineering & Construction of an Oil Production Platform. 1980. 70.00x (ISBN 82-7270-015-8, Pub. by Norwegian Info Norway). State Mutual Bk.
--European Petroleum Related Industries. 109p. 1980. 75.00x (ISBN 82-7270-016-6, Pub. by Norwegian Info Norway). State Mutual Bk.
--Large Scale Flow Measurement of Hydrocarbon Fluids. 173p. 1980. 75.00x (ISBN 82-7270-003-4, Pub. by Norwegian Info Norway). State Mutual Bk.
--Marginal Fields-Criteria for Development. 197p. 1980. 60.00x (ISBN 82-7270-006-9, Pub. by Norwegian Info Norway). State Mutual Bk.
--Measuring Accuracy of Parameters Used in Formation Evaluation in the North Sea. 193p. 1980. 75.00x (ISBN 82-7270-002-6, Pub. by Norwegian Info Norway). State Mutual Bk.
--North Sea Field Development: Experiences & Challenges. 314p. 1980. 95.00x (ISBN 82-7270-012-3, Pub. by Norwegian Info Norway). State Mutual Bk.
--Offshore North Sea 1978, 2 vols. 1980. 165.00x (Pub. by Norwegian Info Norway). State Mutual Bk.
--Offshore Seismic Data Acquisition & Quality Control. 287p. 1980. 100.00x (ISBN 82-7270-001-8, Pub. by Norwegian Info Norway). State Mutual Bk.
--Quality Assurance Related to Offshore Activities. 336p. 1980. 95.00x (ISBN 82-7270-009-3, Pub. by Norwegian Info Norway). State Mutual Bk.

Norwegina Petroleum Society. Contingency Planning. 223p. 1980. 75.00x (ISBN 8-27270-010-7, Pub. by Norwegian Info Norway). State Mutual Bk.

Norwick, Kenneth H. Molecular Dynamics in Biosystems. 1977. 66.00 (ISBN 0-08-020420-1). Pergamon.

Norwood, Christopher. At Highest Risk: Protecting Children from Environmental Pollution. 1981. pap. 4.95 (ISBN 0-14-005830-3). Penguin.

Norwood, Frederick A. The Story of American Methodism. LC 74-10621. 448p. 1974. pap. 14.95 (ISBN 0-687-39640-9); pap. 10.95 (ISBN 0-687-39641-7). Abingdon.

Norwood, Gilbert. Pindar. (Sather Classical Lectures: Vol. 19). 1974. 20.00x (ISBN 0-520-01952-0). U of Cal Pr.

Norwood, J. Twentieth Century Physics. 1976. 22.95 (ISBN 0-13-935155-8). P-H.

Norwood, James E. & Angerman, David. Battle Songs of the Second American Revolution. LC 79-50654. 1979. pap. 12.00 (ISBN 0-915854-20-1). Friend Freedom.

Norwood, James Ervin, ed. A Nation of Crusaders: The General Plan for the Second American Revolution. LC 75-14729. 1975. 30.00 (ISBN 0-915854-01-5). Friend Freedom.

Norwood, Joe, et al. Joe Norwood's Golf-O-Metrics. LC 75-21238. 1978. 7.95 o.p. (ISBN 0-385-01823-1). Doubleday.

Norwood, Joseph, Jr. High Speed Sailing: A Study of High-Performance Multihull Yacht Design. LC 79-87640. (Illus.). 1979. 14.95 (ISBN 0-396-07738-2). Dodd.
--Intermediate Classical Mechanics. (Illus.). 1979. ref. 25.95 (ISBN 0-13-469635-2). P-H.

Norwood, O'Tar T. Hair Transplant Surgery. (Illus.). 148p. 1973. 14.75 (ISBN 0-398-02892-3). C C Thomas.

Norwood, Richard. The Sea-Mans Practice. LC 74-28877. (English Experience Ser.: No. 755). 1975. Repr. of 1637 ed. 13.00 (ISBN 90-221-0755-8). Walter J Johnson.

Norwood, W. Daggett. Health Protection of Radiation Workers. (Illus.). 468p. 1975. 37.50 (ISBN 0-398-03291-2). C C Thomas.

Noseda, Giorgio, et al, eds. Diet & Drug in Atherosclerosis. 352p. 1980. text ed. 26.00 (ISBN 0-89004-491-0). Raven.

Noshay, Allen & McGrath, James E. Block Polymers. 1977. 61.00 (ISBN 0-12-521750-1). Acad Pr.

Noss, Richard B. & Purtle, Dale. Spoken Cambodian, Bk. II. 363p. 1980. pap. 10.00x (ISBN 0-87950-667-9); cassettes i 145.00x (ISBN 0-87950-669-5); book il & cassettes il 150.00x (ISBN 0-87950-671-7); book i & book il & cassettes i & il 240.00x (ISBN 0-87950-672-5). Spoken Lang Serv.

Noss, Richard B., et al. Spoken Cambodian, Bk. I. 449p. 1980. pap. 10.00x (ISBN 0-87950-666-0); cassettes i 19 dual track 95.00x (ISBN 0-87950-668-7); book i & cassettes i 100.00x (ISBN 0-87950-670-9); books i & il & cassettes i & il 240.00 (ISBN 0-87950-672-5). Spoken Lang Serv.

Nossack, Hans E. The Impossible Proof. Lebeck, M., tr. 1968. 5.95 o.p. (ISBN 0-374-17532-2). FS&G.
--To the Unknown Hero. Manheim, Ralph, tr. 1974. 6.95 o.p. (ISBN 0-374-27838-5). FS&G.

Nostlinger, Christine. Fly Away Home. Bell, Anthea, tr. 144p. (gr. 7 up). 1975. 5.88 o.p. (ISBN 0-531-01096-1). Watts.
--Girl Missing. Bell, Anthea, tr. from Ger. LC 76-13893. 144p. (gr. 6 up). 1976. PLB 5.90 o.p. (ISBN 0-531-00346-9). Watts.
--Konrad. (Illus.). (gr. 4-6). 1977. lib. bdg. 7.90 s&l (ISBN 0-531-01341-3). Watts.
--Luke & Angela. Bell, Anthea, tr. LC 80-8804. 144p. (gr. 7 up). 1981. 8.95 (ISBN 0-15-249902-4, HJ). HarBraceJ.

Nostrand, A. D. Van see Van Nostrand, A. D., et al.

Notarianni, Frederick. The Making of a Don. 176p. 1981. 9.00 (ISBN 0-682-49685-5). Exposition.

Notarianni, Philip F., jt. auth. see Haglund, Karl T.

Notaro, Thom. Van Til & the Use of Evidence. 1980. pap. 3.75 (ISBN 0-87552-353-6). Presby & Reformed.

Note, Gene Van see Van Note, Gene.

Notehelfer, F. G. Kotoku Shusui: Portrait of a Japanese Radical. (Illus.). 1971. 42.50 (ISBN 0-521-07989-6). Cambridge U Pr.

Notestein, Wallace. English People on the Eve of Colonization, 1603-1630. (New American Nation Ser). 1954. 15.00x o.s.i. (ISBN 0-06-013220-5, HarpT). Har-Row.

Noth, Martin. The Deuteronomic History. (Journal for the Study of the Old Testament, Supplement Ser.: No. 15). 1980. 19.95 (ISBN 0-905774-25-6, Pub. by JSOT Pr England). Eisenbrauns.

Nothaft, Anne. Breeding Cockatoos. (Illus.). 96p. 1979. 2.95 (ISBN 0-87666-877-5, KW-059). TFH Pubns.

Nothdurft, K. H. The Complete Guide to Successful Business Negotiation. LC 73-77703. 224p. 1972. 9.00x (ISBN 0-900537-16-7, Dist. by Hippocrene Books Inc.). Leviathan Hse.

Notley, Alice. How Spring Comes. 56p. 1981. 25.00 (ISBN 0-915124-41-6, Bookslinger); pap. 6.00 (ISBN 0-915124-42-4). Toothpaste.

Notman, Larry. Advertising Layout Basics: Ad Kit 4. 220p. 1981. pap. 4.00x (ISBN 0-918488-09-5). Newspaper Serv.
--Community Newspaper: Front Office Worker. (Illus.). 1978. pap. 4.00x (ISBN 0-918488-07-9). Newspaper Serv.
--Community Newspaper Management: Starting Out. 1981. pap. 10.00x (ISBN 0-918488-10-9). Newspaper Serv.

Noton, A. R. Introduction to Variational Methods in Control Engineering. 1965. text ed. 11.75 o.p. (ISBN 0-08-011365-6); pap. text ed. 7.50 o.p. (ISBN 0-08-013584-6). Pergamon.

Noton, M. Modern Control Engineering. LC 72-181056. 288p. 1972. text ed. 28.00 (ISBN 0-08-016820-5). Pergamon.

Noton, T. A. Thieves. LC 78-67232. 264p. 1980. pap. 3.95 (ISBN 0-914850-48-2). Impact Tenn.

Nott, Kathleen. A Soul in the Quad: The Use of Language in Philosophy & Literature. 1969. 25.00 (ISBN 0-7100-6502-7). Routledge & Kegan.

Nott, Stanley C. Chinese Jade Throughout the Ages: A Review of Its Characteristics, Decoration, Folklore & Symbolism. LC 62-8839. (Illus.). 1962. 47.50 (ISBN 0-8048-0100-2). C E Tuttle.

Notter, Lucille, jt. auth. see Robinson, Alice M.

Notter, Lucille E. & Spalding, Eugenia K. Professional Nursing: Foundations, Perspectives & Relationships. 9th ed. LC 76-2653. 1976. 16.95 o.p. (ISBN 0-397-54192-9); pap. 12.75 (ISBN 0-397-54182-1). Lippincott.

Notter, Lucille E., jt. auth. see Spalding, Eugenia K.

Nottingham, Pamela. Technique of Bobbin Lace. 1976. 27.00 (ISBN 0-7134-3230-6, Pub. by Batsford England). David & Charles.
--The Technique of Torchon Lace. 1979. 22.50 o.p. (ISBN 0-7134-0268-7, Pub. by Batsford England). David & Charles.

Nottingham, Ronald M. The Fairy Tales of Ronald M. Nottingham Sr. 1979. 4.95 (ISBN 0-533-03888-X). Vantage.

Nouaille-Rouault, Genevieve, jt. auth. see George, Waldemar.

Nourse, Alan. The Giant Planets. LC 73-14515. (First Bks). (Illus.). 96p. (gr. 5 up). 1974. PLB 6.45 (ISBN 0-531-00816-9). Watts.
--Menstruation: Just Plain Talk. (gr. 4 up). PLB 6.45 (ISBN 0-686-65171-5). Watts.
Nourse, Alan E. Asteroids. LC 74-12020. (Illus.). (gr. 4-8). 1975. PLB 6.45 (ISBN 0-531-00822-3). Watts.
--Clear Skin, Healthy Skin. LC 76-12640. (Career Concise Guides Ser.). (Illus.). 72p. (gr. 7 up). 1976. PLB 6.45 (ISBN 0-531-00343-4). Watts.
--Fractures, Dislocations & Sprains. LC 78-6855. (First Bks). (Illus.). (gr. 4 up). 1978. PLB 6.45 s&l (ISBN 0-531-01494-0). Watts.
--Hormones. (Impact Ser.). (Illus.). (gr. 7 up). 1979. PLB 6.90 s&l (ISBN 0-531-02892-5). Watts.
--Lumps, Bumps & Rashes: A Look at Kid's Diseases. LC 75-34276. (First Bks. Ser.). (Illus.). 72p. (gr. 4 up). 1976. PLB 6.45 (ISBN 0-531-00845-2). Watts.
--The Practice. LC 75-25094. 1978. 10.95 o.p. (ISBN 0-06-013194-2, HarpT). Har-Row.
--Universe Between. (gr. 7 up). 1965. 4.95 o.p. (ISBN 0-679-20226-9); PLB 4.19 o.p. (ISBN 0-685-14519-0). McKay.
--Universe, Earth & Atom: The Story of Physics. LC 69-13493. (Illus.). 1969. 15.00 o.s.i. (ISBN 0-06-004972-3, HarpT). Har-Row.
--Venus & Mercury. LC 73-182900. (First Bks). (Illus.). 72p. (gr. 7 up). 1972. PLB 4.90 o.p. (ISBN 0-531-00765-0). Watts.
--Viruses. LC 75-19142. (First Bks.). (Illus.). 72p. (gr. 5 up). 1976. PLB 6.45 (ISBN 0-531-00839-8). Watts.
--Vitamins. (Career Concise Guides Ser.). (Illus.). (gr. 6 up). 1977. PLB 6.45 (ISBN 0-531-00096-6). Watts.
Nourse, Alan E. & Halliday, Eleanore. So You Want to Be a Nurse. LC 61-6189. (So You Want Series). 1961. lib. bdg. 6.79 o.s.i. (ISBN 0-06-005101-9, HarpT). Har-Row.
Nourse, E., et al. Three Years of the Agricultural Adjustment Administration. LC 79-173654. (FDR & the Era of the New Deal Ser.). 600p. 1971. Repr. of 1937 ed. lib. bdg. 59.00 (ISBN 0-306-70365-3). Da Capo.
Nourse, Edwin G. & Drury, Horace B. Industrial Price Policies & Economic Progress. (Brookings Institution Reprint Ser). (Illus.). Repr. of 1938 ed. lib. bdg. 29.50x (ISBN 0-697-00177-6). Irvington.
Nourse, Edwin G., et al. America's Capacity to Produce. (Brookings Institution Reprint Ser.). (Illus.). Repr. of 1934 ed. lib. bdg. 29.00x (ISBN 0-697-00176-8). Irvington.
Nourse, Joan T. Monarch Notes on Miller's Death of a Salesman. (Orig.). pap. 1.95 (ISBN 0-671-00688-6). Monarch Pr.
Nouwen, Henri J. A Cry for Mercy: Prayers from the Genesee. LC 80-2563. 144p. 1981. 9.95 (ISBN 0-385-17507-8). Doubleday.
--The Genesee Diary: Report from a Trappist Monastery. 192p. 1981. pap. 3.95 (ISBN 0-385-17446-2, Im). Doubleday.
--Intimacy: Pastoral Psychological Essays. rev. ed. LC 79-79241. 1977. pap. 2.95 o.p. (ISBN 0-8190-0614-9). Fides Claretian.
--The Living Reminder: Service & Prayer in Memory of Jesus Christ. 1977. 5.95 (ISBN 0-8164-1219-7). Crossroad NY.
--Making All Things New: An Invitation to Life in the Spirit. LC 80-8897. 96p. 1981. 6.95 (ISBN 0-06-066326-X). (Illus.). Har-Row.
--Pray to Live: Thomas Merton: a Contemplative Critic. LC 72-10395. 1972. pap. 2.95 o.p. (ISBN 0-8190-0620-3). Fides Claretian.
--Thomas Merton: Contemplative Critic. LC 80-8898. 176p. 1981. pap. 3.95 (ISBN 0-06-066324-3, HarpR). Har-Row.
--The Wounded Healer: Ministry in Contemporary Society. LC 72-186312. 120p. 1972. 6.95 (ISBN 0-385-02856-3). Doubleday.
Nouwen, Henri J. M. The Genesee Diary: Report from a Trappist Monastery. LC 75-38169. 192p. 1976. 8.95 (ISBN 0-385-11368-4). Doubleday.
--Intimacy. LC 80-8906. 160p. 1981. pap. 3.95 (ISBN 0-06-066323-5, HarpR). Har-Row.
--Reaching Out: The Three Movements of Spiritual Life. LC 74-9460. 120p. 1975. 7.95 (ISBN 0-385-03212-9). Doubleday.
Nouwen, Henri J. M. & Gaffney, Walter J. Aging: The Fulfillment of Life. LC 74-1773. 160p. 1974. 2.45 (ISBN 0-385-00918-6, Im). Doubleday.
Nova, Craig. The Geek. LC 74-15884. (Illus.). 208p. 1975. 8.95 o.p. (ISBN 0-06-013209-4, HarpT). Har-Row.
Novack, David E., ed. see Rozen, Marvin E.
Novak, jt. auth. see Evans.
Novak, Angela R. & Heal, Laird W., eds. Integration of Developmentally Disabled Individuals into the Community. LC 80-21082. (Illus.). 262p. 1980. pap. text ed. 12.95 (ISBN 0-933716-10-9). P H Brookes.
Novak, Barbara. Nature & Culture: American Landscape & Painting Eighteen Twenty-Five to Eighteen Seventy-Five. (Illus.). 1980. 35.00 (ISBN 0-19-502606-3). Oxford U Pr.
--Nature & Culture: American Landscape & Painting 1825-1875. (Illus.). 336p. 1981. pap. 18.95 (ISBN 0-19-502935-6, OPB). Oxford U Pr.
Novak, Daniel A. The Wheel of Servitude: Black Forced Labor After Slavery. LC 77-76334. 144p. 1978. 10.50x (ISBN 0-8131-1371-7). U Pr of Ky.
Novak, Franc. Surgical Gynecological Techniques. LC 77-92099. 421p. 1978. 100.00 (ISBN 0-471-04276-5, Pub. by Wiley Medical). Wiley.
Novak, M., ed. see IFAC-IFIP Symposium on Software for Computer Control, 2nd, Prague, Czechoslovakia, 11-15, June 1979.
Novak, Maximillan E. see Dryden, John.
Novak, Maximillian E., ed. English Literature in the Age of Disguise. 1977. 15.00x o.p. (ISBN 0-520-03342-6). U of Cal Pr.
Novak, Michael. American Vision: Essay on the Future of Democratic Capitalism. 1978. pap. 4.25 (ISBN 0-8447-3324-5). Am Enterprise.
--Ascent of the Mountain, Flight of the Dove: An Invitation to Religious Studies. rev. ed. LC 77-20463. 1978. pap. 5.95 (ISBN 0-06-066322-7, RD 232, HarpR). Har-Row.
--Belief & Unbelief. 1965. 4.95 o.s.i. (ISBN 0-02-590750-6). Macmillan.
--Experience of Nothingness. 1971. pap. 3.95x (ISBN 0-06-131938-4, TB 1938, Torch). Har-Row.
--Rise of the Unmeltable Ethnics. LC 70-185143. 1972. 7.95 o.s.i. (ISBN 0-02-590780-8). Macmillan.
Novak, Michael, ed. Capitalism &Socialism: A Theological Inquiry. 1979. 12.25 (ISBN 0-8447-2153-0); pap. 6.25 (ISBN 0-8447-2154-9). Am Enterprise.
--Democracy & Mediating Structures: A Theological Inquiry. 1980. 13.25 (ISBN 0-8447-2175-1); pap. 7.25 (ISBN 0-8447-2176-X). Am Enterprise.
--Denigration of Capitalism. 1979. pap. 4.25 (ISBN 0-8447-3364-4). Am Enterprise.
Novak, Michael, et al. Values in an American Government Textbook: Three Appraisals. Lefever, Ernest W., ed. 57p. 1978. pap. 3.00. Ethics & Public Policy.
Novakovic, L. The Pseudo-Spin Method in Magnetism & Ferroelectricity. 200p. 1976. text ed. 34.00 (ISBN 0-08-018060-4). Pergamon.
Novalis. Hymns to the Night & Other Writings. Passage, Charles, tr. LC 60-9556. 1960. pap. 2.95 (ISBN 0-672-60316-0, LLA115). Bobbs.
Nove, Alec. Political Economy & Soviet Socialism. 1979. text ed. 27.50x (ISBN 0-04-335037-2). Allen Unwin.
--The Soviet Economic System. 1977. text ed. 29.50 (ISBN 0-04-335035-6); pap. text ed. 12.50x (ISBN 0-04-335036-4). Allen Unwin.
--Stalinism & After. (Illus.). 1975. text ed. 7.50x (ISBN 0-04-320105-9, 2203). Allen Unwin.
Novello, Don. The Lazlo Letters. LC 77-5811. (Illus.). 1977. 3.95 (ISBN 0-911104-96-8). Workman Pub.
Novello, Eugenio V. Portentous Signs Which Indicate That the World Has Entered into One of the Last Phases of Its Existence. (Illus.). 149p. 1980. deluxe ed. 73.45 (ISBN 0-930008-71-5). Inst Econ Pol.
Novello, Joseph R., ed. A Practical Handbook of Psychiatry. (Amer. Lec. in Clinical Psychiatry Ser.). (Illus.). 648p. 1974. 24.75 (ISBN 0-398-02868-0). C C Thomas.
Nover, Arno & Blodi, Frederick C. The Ocular Fundus: Methods of Examination & Typical Findings. 4th ed. (Illus.). 212p. 1981. text ed. write for info. (ISBN 0-8121-0709-8). Lea & Febiger.
Noverr, Douglas A., jt. ed. see Huddleston, Eugene L.
Novich, Max & Kaufman, Ted. The High-Energy Diet for Dynamic Living. 1977. pap. 1.95 o.p. (ISBN 0-345-25153-9). Ballantine.
Novick, Allan, ed. see Seyer, Philip & Harmon, Paul.
Novick, David. A World of Scarcities: Critical Issues in Public Policy. LC 75-42278. 1976. 27.95 (ISBN 0-470-15002-5). Halsted Pr.
Novick, David, et al. Wartime Production Controls. LC 76-5795. (FDR & the Era of the New Deal Ser). 1976. Repr. of 1949 ed. lib. bdg. 35.00 (ISBN 0-306-70818-3). Da Capo.
Novick, Julius, ed. see Shaw, George B.
Novick, Lloyd F. & Al-Ibrahim, Mohamed S. Health Problems in the Prison Setting. (Illus.). 244p. 1977. 19.75 (ISBN 0-398-03664-0). C C Thomas.
Novick, Melvin R., jt. auth. see Lord, Frederic M.
Novick, Oscar, jt. auth. see Joseph, Lou.
Novicow, Jacques. War & Its Alleged Benefits. LC 75-147482. (Library of War & Peace; the Character & Causes of War). lib. bdg. 38.00 (ISBN 0-8240-0274-1). Garland Pub.
Novik, Jack, jt. auth. see Hayden, Trudy.
Novikov, S. O., ed. Mathematical Physics Review, Vol.i. (Soviet Scietific Reviews Ser.). 218p. 1980. 44.50 (ISBN 3-7186-0019-6). Harwood Academic.
Novin, D., et al, eds. Hunger: Basic Mechanisms & Clinical Implications. LC 75-14563. 510p. 1976. 39.00 (ISBN 0-89004-059-1). Raven.
Novit, Mitchell S. Essentials of Personnel Management. (Essentials of Management Ser.). (Illus.). 1979. ref. 14.95 (ISBN 0-13-286617-X); pap. 6.95 ref. (ISBN 0-13-286609-9). P-H.
Novitski, Edward. Human Genetics. (Illus.). 1977. text ed. 16.95 (ISBN 0-02-388550-5). Macmillan.
Novograd, Nancy, ed. see Gardner, Martin.
Novotney, Jerrold M., jt. auth. see Tye, Kenneth A.
Novotny, Ann & Smith, Carter. Images of Healing. (Illus.). 144p. 1980. 16.95 (ISBN 0-02-590820-0). Macmillan.
Novotny, Eva. Introduction to Stellar Atmospheres & Interiors. 680p. 1973. text ed. 22.95x (ISBN 0-19-501588-6). Oxford U Pr.
Novotny, Fritz. Painting & Sculpture in Europe: 1780-1880. (Pelican History of Art Ser: No. 20). (Illus.). 1978. pap. 17.95 (ISBN 0-14-056120-X, Pelican). Penguin.
Novotny, Vladimir, jt. auth. see Krenkel, Peter A.
Novozhilov, Yuri V. Introduction to Elementary Particle Theory. Rosner, Jonathon L., tr. 1974. text ed. 64.00 (ISBN 0-08-017954-1). Pergamon.
Nowacki, Perry, ed. Health Hazards & Pollution Control in Synthetic Liquid Fuel Conversion. LC 80-16694. (Pollution Tech. Review, No. 68; Environmental Health Review, No. 2; Chemical Tech. Review, No. 165; Energy Tech. Review: No. 57). 511p. (Orig.). 1980. 54.00 (ISBN 0-8155-0810-7). Noyes.
--Lignite Technology. LC 79-26051. (Energy Technology Review Ser. No. 53; Chemical Technology Review Ser.: No. 146). (Illus.). 1980. 42.00 (ISBN 0-8155-0783-6). Noyes.
--Oil Shale Technical Data Handbook. LC 80-27547. (Energy Tech. Rev. 63 Ser.: Chemical Tech. Rev. 182). (Illus.). 309p. 1981. 48.00 (ISBN 0-8155-0835-2). Noyes.
Nowak, Mariette. Eve's Rib. 272p. 1981. pap. 5.95 (ISBN 0-312-27240-5). St Martin.
Nowak, Ronald M. North American Quarternary Canis. Wiley, E. O., ed. (U of KS Museum of Nat. Hist. Monograph: No. 6). (Illus.). 154p. 1979. pap. 10.00 (ISBN 0-89338-007-5). U of KS Mus Nat Hist.
Nowak, Stefan. Understanding & Prediction. (Synthese Library: No. 94). 482p. 1980. pap. 15.95 (ISBN 90-277-1199-2, Pub. by D. Reidel). Kluwer Boston.
Nowak, W. S. The Marketing of Shellfish. (Illus.). 280p. 15.25 (ISBN 0-85238-010-0, FN). Unipub.
Nowarra, Heinz J. Focke Wulf 190, a Famous German Fighter. LC 65-15546. (Harleyford Ser). (Illus.). 1965. 18.95 (ISBN 0-8168-6365-2). Aero.
--Messerschmitt 109, a Famous German Fighter. LC 63-14331. (Harleyford Ser). (Illus.). 1963. 18.95 (ISBN 0-8168-6375-X). Aero.
Nowell, Iris. The Dog Crisis. LC 78-221402. 1979. 8.95 o.p. (ISBN 0-312-21613-0). St Martin.
Nowell, Robert. A Passion for Truth: Hans Kung & His Theology. 376p. 1981. 17.50 (ISBN 0-8245-0039-3). Crossroad NY.
Nowell-Smith, H. Ethics. 1958. 7.50 o.p. (ISBN 0-8022-1232-8). Philos Lib.
Nowinski, Ira, photos by. Cafe Society: Photographs & Poetry from San Francisco's North Beach. LC 78-63332. 1978. pap. 8.95 (ISBN 0-916860-05-1). Bean Pub.
Nowinson, Marie. Winds of Change. 1979. pap. 2.25 o.p. (ISBN 0-345-27587-X). Ballantine.
Nowlan, P. IPS Notebook. rev. ed. (Illus.). 128p. 1980. pap. 3.52 (ISBN 0-913688-02-9). Pawnee Pub.
Nowlan, Phil, jt. auth. see Calkins, Dick.
Nowlis, Elizabeth, jt. auth. see Ellis, Janice.
Nowlis, Elizabeth A., jt. auth. see Ellis, Janice R.
Nowotny, A. Basic Exercises in Immunochemistry: A Laboratory Manual. (Illus.). 1969. 22.60 o.p. (ISBN 0-387-04666-6). Springer-Verlag.
Nowottny, Winifred. The Language Poets Use. 1962. pap. text ed. 8.25x (ISBN 0-485-12009-7, Athlone Pr). Humanities.
Noy, William. The Principal Grounds & Maxims with an Analysis of the Laws of England. 3rd ed. xxviii, 219p. 1980. Repr. of 1845 ed. lib. bdg. 25.00x (ISBN 0-8377-0906-7). Rothman.
Noyce, John. The Directory of British Alternative Periodicals Nineteen Sixty-Five to Nineteen Seventy-Four. 1978. text ed. 52.00x (ISBN 0-391-00898-6). Humanities.
Noyes. Figure Skating. 1979. pap. 3.95 (ISBN 0-8015-2626-4, Hawthorn). Dutton.
Noyes, Charles R. Economic Man in Relation to His Natural Environment, 2 Vols. LC 48-7550. 1948. 27.50x (ISBN 0-231-01646-8). Columbia U Pr.
Noyes, Ethel J. Women of the Mayflower & Women of Plymouth Colony. LC 73-12780. Repr. of 1921 ed. 18.00 (ISBN 0-8103-3668-5). Gale.
Noyes, James H. The Clouded Lens: Persian Gulf Security & U.S. Policy. Staar, Richard F., ed. LC 78-70390. 1979. pap. 6.95 (ISBN 0-8179-7062-2). Hoover Inst Pr.
Noyes, Robert, ed. Small & Micro Hydroelectric Power Plants: Technology & Feasibility. LC 80-19099. (Energy Tech. Rev. 60). (Illus.). 457p. 1981. 42.00 (ISBN 0-8155-0819-0). Noyes.
Noyes, Russell. William Wordsworth. (English Authors Ser.: No. 118). lib. bdg. 9.95 (ISBN 0-8057-1580-0). Twayne.
Noyes, Russell, ed. English Romantic Poetry & Prose. 1956. 19.95x (ISBN 0-19-501007-8). Oxford U Pr.
Noyes, Stanley. Western. 32p. (Orig.). 1980. pap. 3.00 (ISBN 0-88235-044-7). San Marcos.
Noyle, Ken. The Geisha Diary. (YA) 1976. 7.95 o.p. (ISBN 0-399-11795-4, Dist. by Putnam). Berkley Pub.
--The Most Holy Man. Grunwald, Stefan, ed. (Orig.). 1981. pap. price not set (ISBN 0-89865-127-1, Unilaw). Donning Co.
Nozhko, K. G. Methods of Estimating the Demand for Specialists & of Planning Specialized Training Within the U. S. S. R. 1964. pap. 2.50 (ISBN 92-3-100559-6, U382, UNESCO). Unipub.
Nozick, Martin. Miguel de Unamuno. (World Authors Ser.: Spain: No. 175). lib. bdg. 9.95 (ISBN 0-8057-2906-2). Twayne.
Nozick, Martin, ed. see Unamuno, Miguel De.
Nozik, Art J., ed. Photoeffects at Semiconductor-Electrolyte Interfaces. LC 80-27773. (Symposium Ser.: No. 146). 1981. 39.00 (ISBN 0-8412-0604-X). Am Chemical.
NPA Center for Economic & Demographic Projections Staff. Basic Maps of the U.S. Economy, Nineteen Hundred Sixty-Seven to Nineteen Hundred Ninety. 304p. 1979. 25.00 (ISBN 0-686-28102-0). Natl Planning.
Nriagu, Jerome O. Cadmium in the Environment: Ecological Cycling, Pt. I. LC 79-25087. (Environmental Science & Technology: a Wiley-Interscience Series of Texts & Monographs). 1980. 70.00 (ISBN 0-471-06455-6, Pub. by Wiley-Interscience). Wiley.
--Nickel in the Environment. LC 80-16600. (Environmental Science & Technology: a Wiley Interscience Ser. of Texts & Monographs). 833p. 1980. 65.00 (ISBN 0-471-05885-8, Pub. by Wiley Interscience). Wiley.
--Sulfur in the Environment: Atmospheric Cycle, Pt. 1. LC 78-6807. (Environmental Science & Technology Ser.). 464p. 1978. 46.50 (ISBN 0-471-02942-4, Pub. by Wiley-Interscience). Wiley.
--Zinc in the Environment, 2 pts. Incl. Pt. I. Ecological Cycling (ISBN 0-471-05888-2); Pt. II. Health Effects (ISBN 0-471-05889-0). LC 79-19257. (Environmental Science & Technology: a Wiley-Interscience Ser. of Texts & Monographs). 1980. 47.50 ea. (Pub. by Wiley-Interscience). Wiley.
Ntuk-Idem, Moses. Compensatory Education. 164p. 1978. text ed. 19.00x (ISBN 0-566-00226-4, Pub. by Gower Pub Co England). Renouf.
Nuckolls, James L. Interior Lighting for Environmental Designers. LC 75-40413. 371p. 1976. 32.50 (ISBN 0-471-65163-X, Pub. by Wiley-Interscience). Wiley.
Nuclear Energy Agency & Organization for Economic Cooperation & Development. Plate Inspection Programme, PISC: November, 1979. (Illus.). 78p. (Orig.). 1980. pap. text ed. 7.50x (ISBN 92-64-12028-9, 66 80 02 1). OECD.
Nuclear Track Detection Conference, Neuherberg Munich, Sept. 30 to Oct. 6, 1976. Solid State Nuclear Track Detectors: Proceedings, 2 vols. Granzer, F., et al, eds. 1978. Set. text ed. write for info. (ISBN 0-08-021659-5). Pergamon.
Nudelman, J., jt. auth. see Troyka, Lynn Q.
Nudelman, Jerrold, jt. auth. see Troyka, Lynn Q.
Nudelman, Sol & Patton, Dennis D., eds. Imaging for Medicine: Volume 1, Nuclear Medicine, Ultrasonics & Thermography. (Illus.). 494p. 1980. 49.50 (ISBN 0-306-40384-6, Plenum Pr). Plenum Pub.
Nueces County Historical Society. The History of Neuces County. 224p. 1974. 9.50 o.p. (ISBN 0-8363-0122-6). Jenkins.
--Nueces County, Texas. (Illus.). 9.50 o.p. (ISBN 0-8363-0122-6). Jenkins.

Nuechterlein, Donald E. National Interests & Presidential Leadership: The Setting of Priorities. LC 78-2764. (Westview Special Studies in International Relations & U.S. Foreign Policy). (Illus.). 1978. lib. bdg. 24.00 o.p. (ISBN 0-89158-169-3); pap. text ed. 9.75x (ISBN 0-89158-170-7). Westview.

--United States National Interests in a Changing World. LC 73-77255. (Illus.). 216p. 1973. 10.00x (ISBN 0-8131-1287-7). U Pr of Ky.

Nuelle, Helen. The Treacherous Heart. (Orig.). 1981. pap. 1.50 (ISBN 0-440-18561-0). Dell.

Nuernberger, Phil. Freedom from Stress: A Holistic Method. (Illus., Orig.). 1981. 10.00 (ISBN 0-89389-071-5); pap. 6.95 (ISBN 0-89389-064-2). Himalayan Intl Inst.

Nuffield Foundation. Mathematics Project Series, 24 bks. Incl. Beginnings. LC 68-21009. 1968. pap. 7.50 (ISBN 0-471-65169-9); Checking Up One. LC 77-39607. 1970. pap. 3.95 (ISBN 0-471-65181-8); Checking Up Two. 1972. pap. 5.50 (ISBN 0-471-65205-9); Computation & Structure. LC 68-21012. 1968. Cir. 2. pap. 5.95 (ISBN 0-471-65175-3); Cir. 3. pap. 5.95 (ISBN 0-471-65214-8); Cir. 4. pap. 5.95 (ISBN 0-471-65217-2); Cir. 5. pap. 4.95 (ISBN 0-471-65218-0); Computers & Young Children. LC 75-39285. 1972. pap. 6.95 (ISBN 0-471-65179-6); Graphs Heading to Algebra: Square Two. LC 70-88358. 1969. pap. 5.95 (ISBN 0-471-65213-X); Guides to the Guides. 1975. pap. 3.50 (ISBN 0-471-65207-5); How to Build a Pond. pap. 4.50 (ISBN 0-471-65177-X); I Do & I Understand. LC 67-25008. 1967. pap. 3.95 (ISBN 0-471-65171-0); Into Secondary School. LC 72-126926. 1970. pap. 3.95 (ISBN 0-471-65182-6); The Later Primary Years. LC 70-39605. 1972. pap. 9.50 (ISBN 0-686-65751-9); Logic. LC 73-39606. 1972. pap. 7.50 (ISBN 0-471-65199-0); **Mathematics: The First Three Years. LC 73-168554. 1970. pap. 7.50 (ISBN 0-471-65189-3); Maths with Everything. 1971. pap. 3.95 (ISBN 0-471-65187-7); Module on Angles, Courses & Bearings. 1973. pap. 6.50 (ISBN 0-471-65194-X); Module on Decimals One. 1973. pap. 6.50 (ISBN 0-471-65201-6); Module on Number Patterns One. 1973. pap. 6.50 (ISBN 0-471-65202-4); Module on Speed & Gradient One. 1973. pap. 5.95 (ISBN 0-471-65193-1); Module on Symmetry. 1973. pap. 6.50 (ISBN 0-471-65195-8); The Primary Years. 1972. pap. 9.50 (ISBN 0-686-65752-7); Probability & Statistics. 1969. pap. 5.95 (ISBN 0-471-65219-9); Shape & Size, 3 pts. LC 68-21011. 1968-1971. Tri. 2. pap. 5.95 (ISBN 0-471-65178-8); Tri. 3. pap. 4.50 (ISBN 0-471-65212-1); Tri. 4. pap. 4.50 (ISBN 0-471-65186-9); Story So Far. LC 69-88360. 1969. pap. 4.95 (ISBN 0-471-65220-2); Your Child & Mathematics. 1968. pap. 3.95 (ISBN 0-471-65210-5). Wiley.**

Nugent, Frank A. Professional Counseling: An Overview. LC 80-25726. 310p. 1981. text ed. 14.95 (ISBN 0-8185-0424-2). Brooks-Cole.

Nugent, N. & King, R., eds. The British Right: Conservative & Right-Wing Politics in Britian. (Illus.). 1977. 23.95 (ISBN 0-566-00156-X, 00989-X, Pub by Saxon Hse England). Lexington Bks.

Nugent, Nancy. How to Get Along with Your Stomach: A Complete Guide to the Prevention & Treatment of Stomach Distress. 1979. pap. 3.95 (ISBN 0-385-14947-6, Anch). Doubleday.

Nugent, Patricia M. see Saxton, Dolores F., et al.

Nugent, Robert. Paul Eluard. LC 74-4132. (World Authors Ser.: France: No. 322). 152p. 1974. lib. bdg. 10.95 (ISBN 0-8057-2299-8). Twayne.

Nugent, Thomas, tr. see Condillac, Etienne Bonnot de.

Nugent, Walter T. K. From Centennial to World War: American Society, 1876-1917. LC 76-15164. (History of American Society Ser.). 1976. pap. text ed. 7.95 (ISBN 0-672-60932-0). Bobbs.

Nuitter, C. & Thoinan, E. Les Origines De L'opera Francais. LC 77-4106. (Music Reprint Ser., 1977). 1977. Repr. of 1886 ed. lib. bdg. 32.50 (ISBN 0-306-70895-7). Da Capo.

Nuke, Susan. Processes of the Earth's Surface. 96p. 1980. lab manual 6.95. Mountain Pr.

Nukunya, G. K. Kinship & Marriage Among the Anlo Ewe. LC 68-18054. (Monographs on Social Anthropology Ser: No. 37). 1969. text ed. 23.50x (ISBN 0-485-19537-2, Athlone Pr). Humanities.

Nulcany, B. To Speak True: A Study of Poetry As a Spoken Art. 4.40 o.p. (ISBN 0-08-006444-2). Pergamon.

Null, Gary. Biofeedback, Fasting & Meditation. (Orig.). 1974. pap. 1.50 o.s.i. (ISBN 0-515-03400-2, A3400). Jove Pubns.

--Handbook of Skin & Hair. 1976. pap. 1.75 (ISBN 0-515-03619-6). Jove Pubns.

--Man & His Whole Earth. LC 75-29260. 160p. 1976. 6.95 o.p. (ISBN 0-8117-0969-8). Stackpole.

--Protein for Vegetarians. rev. ed. 1975. pap. 2.25 o.p. (ISBN 0-515-05692-8). Jove Pubns.

--Successful Pregnancy. (Orig.). 1976. pap. 1.50 (ISBN 0-515-03622-6). Jove Pubns.

Null, Gary & Null, Steve. Why Your Stomach Hurts. LC 78-23507. 1979. 8.95 (ISBN 0-396-07630-0). Dodd.

Null, Gary & Null, Steven. Man & His Whole Earth. 1977. pap. 1.50 o.s.i. (ISBN 0-515-03620-X). Jove Pubns.

Null, Gary, et al. Food Combining Handbook. 1973. pap. 1.75 (ISBN 0-515-05779-7, V3202). Jove Pubns.

Null, Steve, jt. auth. see Null, Gary.

Null, Steven, jt. auth. see Null, Gary.

Nulsen, David. Mobile Home Park Plans & Specifications. Date not set. 69.50 o.s.i. (ISBN 0-87593-009-3). Trail-R. Postponed.

Nulsen, David & Nulsen, Robert H. ABC's of Mobile Home & Recreation Vehicle Park Investments. 1980. 24.95 o.s.i. (ISBN 0-87593-040-9). Trail-R.

--Mobile Home & Recreation Vehicle Park Operation Manual: (Two Looseleaf Volumes) 1978. 129.50 (ISBN 0-87593-126-X). Trail-R.

Nulsen, Robert H., jt. auth. see Nulsen, David.

Nultsch, Wilhelm. General Botany. (Ger). 1971. text ed. 19.50 (ISBN 0-12-522850-3). Acad Pr.

Nulty, Leslie. The Green Revolution in West Pakistan: Implications of Technological Change. LC 73-170471. (Special Studies in International Economics & Development). 1972. 26.50x (ISBN 0-89197-779-1). Irvington.

Numbers, Ronald L., ed. The Education of American Physicians: Historical Essays. 1980. 35.00x (ISBN 0-520-03611-5). U of Cal Pr.

Numbers, Ronald L., jt. ed. see Leavitt, Judith W.

Numeroff, Laura J. Amy for Short. LC 76-8842. (Ready to Read Ser.). (Illus.). 48p. (gr. 1-4). 1976. 7.95 (ISBN 0-02-768180-7, 76818). Macmillan.

--Phoebe Dexter Has Harriet Peterson's Sniffles. LC 76-54661. (Illus.). (ps-3). 1977. 7.25 (ISBN 0-688-80091-2); PLB 6.96 (ISBN 0-688-84091-4). Greenwillow.

Numeroff, Laura J. & Richter, Alice N. Emily's Bunch. LC 78-2637. (Illus.). (gr. k-3). 1978. 8.95 (ISBN 0-02-768430-X, 76843). Macmillan.

Nun, Jose. Latin America: The Hegemonic Crisis & the Military Coup. (Politics of Modernization Ser.: No. 7). 1969. pap. 2.00x o.p. (ISBN 0-87725-207-6). U of Cal Intl St.

Nunan, J. Carlton, jt. auth. see Masterson, Thomas R.

Nunez, Benjamin. Dictionary of Afro-Latin American Civilization. LC 79-7731. (Illus.). xxxv, 525p. 1980. lib. bdg. 45.00 (ISBN 0-313-21138-8, NAL/). Greenwood.

Nunez, Paul L. Electric Fields of the B. (Illus.). 500p. 1981. text ed. 35.00x (ISBN 0-19-502796-5). Oxford U Pr.

Nunk, Arthur W. A Synoptic Approach to the Riddle of Existence. LC 77-818. 336p. 1977. 15.00 (ISBN 0-87527-165-0). Fireside Bks.

Nunn, C. F. Foreign Immigrants in Early Bourbon Mexico: Seventeen Hundred to Seventeen Sixty. LC 78-1159. (Cambridge Latin American Studies: No. 31). 1979. 35.50 (ISBN 0-521-22051-3). Cambridge U Pr.

Nunn, G. Raymond. Asian Libraries & Librarianship: An Annotated Bibliography of Selected Books & Periodicals & a Draft Syllabus. LC 73-6629. 1973. 10.00 (ISBN 0-8108-0633-9). Scarecrow.

Nunn, Henry P. Short Syntax of New Testament Greek. 5th ed. 1931. text ed. 7.50x (ISBN 0-521-09941-2). Cambridge U Pr.

Nunn, J., jt. auth. see Gray, T. C.

Nunn, J. F. Applied Respiratory Physiology. 2nd ed. 1977. 59.95 (ISBN 0-407-00060-7). Butterworths.

Nunn, John. The Pirc for the Tournament Player. (Algebraic Chess Openings Ser.). (Illus.). 128p. 1980. 17.95 (ISBN 0-7134-3588-7, Pub. by Batsford England); pap. 10.50 (ISBN 0-7134-3589-5). David & Charles.

Nunn, Marshall. Sports. LC 75-33869. (Spare Time Guides Ser.: No. 10). 1976. 22.50 (ISBN 0-87287-124-X). Libs Unl.

Nunn, Richard V. Home Improvement, Home Repair. Horowitz, Shirley M., ed. LC 80-66637. (Illus.). 256p. 1980. 14.95 (ISBN 0-932944-17-5). Creative Homeowner.

--Home Improvement-Home Repair. Horowitz, Shirley M., ed. LC 80-66637. (Illus.). 256p. (Orig.). 1980. pap. 7.95 (ISBN 0-932944-18-3). Creative Homeowner.

--Home Storage. LC 75-12122. (Family Guidebooks Ser.). (Illus.). 96p. 1975. pap. 2.95 (ISBN 0-8487-0386-3). Oxmoor Hse.

Nunnally, David A. & Bogitsh, Burton J. Introductory Zoology. LC 72-7415. 441p. 1973. 18.00 (ISBN 0-471-65188-5, Pub. by Wiley). Krieger.

Nunnery, Gene. The Old Pro Turkey Hunter. LC 80-80630. (Illus.). 1980. 12.50 (ISBN 0-916620-48-4). Portals Pr.

Nunnery, Michael Y., jt. auth. see Kimbrough, Ralph B.

Nunney. Engineering Technology One. 1981. text ed. price not set (ISBN 0-408-00511-4). Butterworth.

Nunny, M. J. The Automotive Engine. (Illus.). 280p. 1976. 20.00 (ISBN 0-408-00178-X). Transatlantic.

Nunz, Gregory J. Electronics in Our World: A Survey. LC 70-146682. (Illus.). 1972. ref. ed. 19.95 (ISBN 0-13-252288-8). P-H.

Nunzio, Pasquale J. Come Walk with Me & Listen to the Wind. (Illus.). 1978. pap. cancelled (ISBN 0-914090-51-8). Chicago Review.

Nurbaksh, Javad. Divani Nurbakhsh: Sufi Poetry. Rothschild, Jeffrey & Weber, Paul, eds. Godlas, Alan & Lewisohn, Leonard, trs. from Persian. 280p. 1980. 9.95 (ISBN 0-933546-04-1). Khaniqahi-Nimatullahi.

Nurenberg, Thelma. New York Colony. LC 77-77966. (Forge of Freedom Ser). (Illus.). (gr. 5-8). 1969. 7.95 (ISBN 0-02-768400-8, CCPr). Macmillan.

Nurge, Ethel, ed. The Modern Sioux: Social Systems & Reservation Culture. LC 71-88089. (Illus.). xvi, 352p. 1970. 15.00x (ISBN 0-8032-0715-8); pap. 4.50 (ISBN 0-8032-5812-7, BB 596, Bison). U of Nebr Pr.

Nurnberg, Maxwell. I Always Look up the Word "Egregious". 196p. 1981. 10.00 (ISBN 0-13-448720-6). P-H.

Nurnberg, Maxwell & Rosenblum, Morris. All About Words: An Adult Approach to Vocabulary Building. (RL 7). 1971. pap. 2.25 (ISBN 0-451-61681-2, ME1879, Ment). NAL.

--How to Build a Better Vocabulary. 1977. pap. 1.95 (ISBN 0-445-08386-7). Popular Lib.

Nurnberger, John I., ed. Biological & Environmental Determinants of Early Development. (ARNMD Research Publications Ser: Vol. 51). 1973. 34.50 (ISBN 0-683-00245-7). Raven.

Nurock, Max, jt. ed. see Boasson, Charles.

Nursing Development Conference Group. Concept Formalization in Nursing: Process & Product. 2nd ed. LC 79-88164. 313p. 1979. text ed. 12.95 (ISBN 0-316-61421-1). Little.

Nursing Theories Conference Group. Nursing Theories: The Base for Professional Nursing Practice. (Illus.). 1980. pap. text ed. 11.95 (ISBN 0-13-627703-9). P-H.

Nursten, H. E., jt. ed. see Land, D. G.

Nursten, J. P., jt. auth. see Kahn, J. H.

Nursten, Jean, ed. see Gore, Elizabeth.

Nusbacher, Jacob, jt. ed. see Sandler, S. Gerald.

Nusbaum, Rosemary. Tierra Dulce: The Jesse Nusbaum Papers. (Illus.). 128p. 1980. pap. 7.95 (ISBN 0-913270-83-0). Sunstone Pr.

Nuss, A. Export Marketing French. 1979. pap. text ed. 7.95 (ISBN 0-582-35157-X); casettes 30.00 (ISBN 0-582-37361-1). Longman.

Nussbaum, A. & Phillips, R. Contemporary Optics for Scientists & Engineers. 1976. 27.95 (ISBN 0-13-170183-5). P-H.

Nussbaum, Al. Gypsy. (Pacesetters Ser.). (Illus.). 64p. (gr. 4 up). 1978. PLB 7.95 (ISBN 0-516-02170-2). Childrens.

Nussbaum, Felicity & Backscheider, Paula R., eds. The Plays of David Mallet. LC 78-66605. (Eighteenth-Century English Drama Ser.: Vol. 28). 1980. lib. bdg. 50.00 (ISBN 0-8240-3602-6). Garland Pub.

Nussbaum, Hedda. Animals Build Amazing Homes. LC 79-11326. (Step-up Bks.: No. 29). (Illus.). (gr. 2-5). 1979. 3.95 (ISBN 0-394-83850-5, BYR); PLB 4.99 (ISBN 0-394-93850-X). Random.

Nussbaum, Murray. Understanding Hematology. 1973. 12.00 (ISBN 0-87488-977-4). Med Exam.

Nussbaum, Roger D. Differential-Delay Equations with Two Time Lags. LC 78-16320. (Memoirs: No. 205). 1978. 6.80 (ISBN 0-8218-2205-5, MEMO-205). Am Math.

Nussbaumer, H. Fast Fourier Transform & Convoution Algorithms. (Springer Series in Information Sciences: Vol. 2). (Illus.). 330p. 1981. 36.60 (ISBN 0-387-10159-4). Springer-Verlag.

Nussdorf, Maggie & Nussdorf, Steve. Dress for Health: The New Clothes Consciousness. (Illus.). 224p. 1980. 14.95 (ISBN 0-8117-0524-2). Stackpole.

Nussdorf, Steve, jt. auth. see Nussdorf, Maggie.

Nute, Grace L. & Ackermann, Gertrudecompiled by. Guide to the Personal Papers in the Manuscripts Collections of the Minnesota Historical Society, Guide No. 1. LC 35-27911. 146p. 1935. pap. 2.00 (ISBN 0-87351-004-6). Minn Hist.

Nutman, P. S., ed. Symbiotic Nitrogen Fixation in Plants. LC 75-2732. (International Biological Programme Ser.: No. 7). (Illus.). 652p. 1976. 105.00 (ISBN 0-521-20645-6). Cambridge U Pr.

Nutt, Alfred T. The Fairy Mythology of Shakespeare. 49p. 1980. Repr. of 1900 ed. lib. bdg. 10.00 (ISBN 0-8495-4019-4). Arden Lib.

Nutt, Grady. Being Me. LC 71-145984. (gr. 7 up). 1971. pap. 2.75 (ISBN 0-8054-6909-5). Broadman.

--So Good, So Far. LC 79-90248. 152p. 1981. pap. 4.95 (ISBN 0-914850-68-7). Impact Tenn.

--So Good, So Far. Edwards, frwd. by. LC 79-90248. 1979. 5.95 (ISBN 0-914850-53-9). Impact Tenn.

Nutt, Merle C. Meeting the Challenge of Supervision. LC 70-179468. 1972. text ed. 10.00 o.p. (ISBN 0-682-47408-8, University). Exposition.

--Metallurgy & Plastics for Engineers. LC 76-19249. 1977. text ed. 35.00 (ISBN 0-08-021684-6). Pergamon.

Nutt, Paul C. Evaluation Concepts & Methods: Shaping Policy for the Health Administrator. (Health Care Administration: Vol. 14). (Illus.). 364p. 1981. text ed. 29.95 (ISBN 0-89335-094-X). Spectrum Pub.

Nuttall, A. D. Dostoevsky's Crime & Punishment: Murder As Philosonic Experiment. (Text & Context Ser.). 1978. pap. 9.25x (ISBN 0-85621-071-4). Humanities.

Nuttall, Clayton L. The Conflict: The Separation of the Church & State. LC 80-21267. 144p. 1980. pap. 4.95 (ISBN 0-87227-076-9, RBP5088). Reg Baptist.

Nuttall, D. L. & Willmott, A. S. British Examinations: Techniques of Analysis. (General Ser.). 1972. text ed. 13.25x (ISBN 0-901225-79-7, NFER). Humanities.

Nuttall, G. Christian Pacifism & History. pap. 1.25 (ISBN 0-8164-9235-2). Crossroad NY.

--Christian Pacifism in History. pap. 1.25 (ISBN 0-8164-9235-2). Continuum.

Nuttall, Jeff. Performance Art Memoirs, Vol. I. 1981. 13.95 (ISBN 0-7145-3788-8); pap. 6.95 (ISBN 0-7145-3711-X). Riverrun NY.

--Performance Art Scripts, Vol. II. 1981. 13.95 (ISBN 0-7145-3789-6); pap. 6.95 (ISBN 0-7145-3712-8). Riverrun NY.

Nuttall, Kenneth. Your Book of Acting. (Illus.). 84p. (gr. 4-9). 1972. 7.95 (ISBN 0-571-04668-1). Transatlantic.

Nuttall, Thomas. A Journal of Travels into the Arkansas Territory During the Year 1819. Lottinville, Savoie, ed. LC 79-4742. 1980. 25.00 (ISBN 0-8061-1598-X). U of Okla Pr.

Nuttall, William. The Miraculous Lunacy of War. 1981. 8.95 (ISBN 0-533-04665-3). Vantage.

Nutter, G. Warren. The Strange World of Ivan Ivanov. LC 68-54124. (Principles of Freedom Ser.). 1976. Repr. of 1969 ed. 9.95x o.p. (ISBN 0-916054-25-X, Caroline Hse Inc). Green Hill.

Nutter, G. Warren & Einhorn, Henry. Enterprise Monopoly in the United States, 1899-1958. LC 69-15570. 1969. 20.00x (ISBN 0-231-02974-8). Columbia U Pr.

Nuttgens, Patrick. York: The Continuing City. 1976. 25.00 (ISBN 0-571-09733-2, Pub. by Faber & Faber). Merrimack Bk Serv.

Nutting, George. Resurrection Is Not a Fairy Tale. 1981. 5.75 (ISBN 0-8062-1649-2). Carlton.

Nutting, Wallace. The Clock Book. LC 70-178648. (Illus.). 1975. Repr. of 1924 ed. 28.00 (ISBN 0-8103-4145-X). Gale.

--Furniture Treasury, 3 Vols. (Illus.). Vols. 1 & 2 In 1. 29.95 (ISBN 0-02-590980-0); Vol. 3. 24.95 (ISBN 0-02-591040-X). Macmillan.

--Windsor Handbook. LC 73-77579. (Illus.). 1973. pap. 4.95 (ISBN 0-8048-1105-9). C E Tuttle.

Nuwer, Hank, jt. auth. see Boyles, Tiny.

Nuzzolo, Luccio & Vellucci, Augusto. Tissue Culture Techniques. LC 67-26015. (Illus.). 284p. 1981. 22.50 (ISBN 0-87527-117-0). Green.

Nwabara. Iboland: A Century of Conflict with Britain 1860-1960. (Illus.). 1978. pap. text ed. 14.50x (ISBN 0-391-00552-9). Humanities.

Nwanko, G. O. The Nigerian Financial System. 400p. 1980. text ed. 43.50x (ISBN 0-8419-5076-8). Holmes & Meier.

Nwankwo, Nkem. Danda. (African Writers Ser.). 1970. pap. text ed. 5.25 (ISBN 0-435-90067-6). Heinemann Ed.

Nwoga, Donatus I., ed. West African Verse: An Anthology. (Orig.). 1967. pap. text ed. 3.00x (ISBN 0-582-60100-2). Humanities.

Nwulia, Moses D. The History of Slavery in Mauritius & the Seychelles, 1810-1875. LC 79-15363. 280p. 1981. 18.50 (ISBN 0-8386-2398-0). Fairleigh Dickinson.

Nyaggah, Mougo see Mugomba, Agrippah I.

Nybakken, Elizabeth I., ed. The Centinel: Warnings of a Revolution. LC 77-92570. 240p. 1980. 19.50 (ISBN 0-87413-141-3). U Delaware Pr.

Nybakken, James W., jt. auth. see McDonald, Gary R.

Nyberg-Hansen, R. Functional Organization of Descending Supraspinal Fibre Systems to the Spinal Cord: Anatomical Observations & Physiological Correlations. (Advances in Anatomy, Embryology & Cell Biology: Vol. 39, Pt. 2). (Illus.). 1966. pap. 11.30 o.p. (ISBN 0-387-03494-3). Springer-Verlag.

Nyborg, Philip S. & McCarter, Pender M., eds. Information Processing in the United States: A Quantitative Summary. (Illus.). vii, 55p. 1977. saddle-stitch 6.00 (ISBN 0-686-68785-X). AFIPS Pr.

Nyce, Vera. A Jolly Christmas at the Patterprints. LC 76-153795. (Illus.). (gr. k-3). 1971. 5.95 o.s.i. (ISBN 0-8193-0521-9, Four Winds); PLB 5.41 o.s.i. (ISBN 0-8193-0522-7). Schol Bk Serv.

Nydahl, John, jt. auth. see Silver, Howard.

Nye, ed. see Schachenmayr.

Nye, Bill. Bill Nye's Western Humor. Larson, T. A., ed. LC 67-20599. (Illus.). 1968. 12.95x (ISBN 0-8032-0133-8); pap. 3.95 (ISBN 0-8032-5821-6, BB 605, Bison). U of Nebr Pr.

Nye, David E. Henry Ford: Ignorant Idealist. (National University Publications, American Studies). 1979. 12.50 (ISBN 0-8046-9242-4). Kennikat.

Nye, Doug. Motor Racing in Color. (Illus.). 1978. 12.95 (ISBN 0-7137-0904-9, Pub. by Blandford Pr England). Sterling.

--Motor Racing in Color. (Illus.). 214p. 1980. pap. 6.95 (ISBN 0-7137-0904-9). Sterling.

--The U.S. Grand Prix. LC 77-11393. 1978. 10.95 o.p. (ISBN 0-385-14203-X). Doubleday.

Nye, F. Ivan & Berardo, Felix M., eds. Emerging Conceptual Frameworks in Family Analyses. (Special Studies on the Family). 356p. 1981. 13.95 (ISBN 0-03-057043-3). Praeger.

Nye, I. W., ed. see Watson, A., et al.

Nye, J. F. Physical Properties of Crystals: Their Representation by Tensors & Matrices. 1957. 37.50x (ISBN 0-19-851105-1). Oxford U Pr.

Nye, Joseph, jt. auth. see Deese, David.

Nye, Nelson. Gun Feud at Tiedown: Rogues Rendezvous. 160p. (Orig.). 1976. pap. 2.25 (ISBN 0-441-30798-1). Ace Bks.

--Gunsmoke. 1979. pap. 1.25 (ISBN 0-505-51377-3). Tower Bks.

--Hellbound for Ballarat: Trouble at Quinn's Crossing. 160p. (Orig.). 1976. pap. 2.25 (ISBN 0-441-32727-3). Ace Bks.

--Quick Fire Hombre. 1977. pap. 1.25 (ISBN 0-505-51177-0). Tower Bks.

--Saddle Bow Slim. 1979. pap. 1.25 (ISBN 0-505-51378-1). Tower Bks.

--The Texas Gun. 160p. (Orig.). 1976. pap. 1.75 (ISBN 0-441-80402-0). Ace Bks.

Nye, O. B. Generic Revision & Skeletal Morphology of Some Cerioporid Cyclostomes, No. 291. (Bulletins of American Paleontology: Vol. 71). pap. 25.00 (ISBN 0-87710-229-5). Paleo Res.

Nye, Robert. Darker Ends, Poems by Robert Nye. LC 69-16840. 1969. pap. 1.75 o.p. (ISBN 0-8090-1348-7). Hill & Wang.

--Doubtfire. 1968. 4.95 o.p. (ISBN 0-8090-3960-5). Hill & Wang.

--Faust. 290p. 1981. 12.95 (ISBN 0-399-12606-6). Putnam.

--Tales I Told My Mother. LC 72-86821. 1969. 4.95 o.p. (ISBN 0-8090-9106-2). Hill & Wang.

--Taliesin. (Illus.). (gr. 5 up). 1967. 3.95 o.p. (ISBN 0-8090-9110-0). Hill & Wang.

Nye, Robert, ed. A Choice of Swinburne's Verse. Swinburne, Algernon C. 1973. 7.50 (ISBN 0-571-09260-8, Pub. by Faber & Faber); pap. 2.95 o.p. (ISBN 0-571-09261-6). Merrimack Bk Serv.

Nye, Robert, ed. see Raleigh, Walter.

Nye, Robert D. Three Psychologies: Perspectives from Freud, Skinner & Rogers. 2nd ed. LC 80-25716. 170p. (Orig.). 1981. pap. text ed. 7.95 (ISBN 0-8185-0438-2). Brooks-Cole.

--What Is B. F. Skinner Really Saying? 1979. 11.95 (ISBN 0-13-952192-5, Spec); pap. 4.95 (ISBN 0-13-952184-4). P-H.

Nye, Robert E. & Bergethon, Bjorner. Basic Music: Functional Musicianship for the Non-Music Major. 5th ed. (Illus.). 240p. 1981. pap. text ed. 11.95 (ISBN 0-13-065672-0). P-H.

Nye, Robert E. & Nye, Vernice T. Essentials of Teaching Elementary School Music. (Illus.). 288p. 1974. 15.95 (ISBN 0-13-289280-4); pap. 11.95 (ISBN 0-13-289272-3). P-H.

Nye, Roger, jt. auth. see Le Vine, Victor T.

Nye, Russel B. Midwestern Progressive Politics: 1870-1958. rev. ed. 1963. 6.50 o.p. (ISBN 0-87013-042-0). Mich St U Pr.

--Society & Culture in America: 1830-1860. (New American Nation Ser.). 1974. pap. 7.95x (ISBN 0-06-131826-4, TB1826, Torch). Harper-Row.

Nye, Vernice T., jt. auth. see Nye, Robert E.

Nye, Wilbur S. Bad Medicine & Good: Tales of the Kiowas. (Illus.). 1969. Repr. of 1962 ed. 13.95 o.p. (ISBN 0-8061-0521-6). U of Okla Pr.

--Carbine & Lance: The Story of Old Fort Sill. rev. centennial ed. 1937. 14.95 (ISBN 0-8061-0856-8). U of Okla Pr.

--Plains Indian Raiders: The Final Phases of Warfare from the Arkansas to the Red River. LC 67-24624. (Illus.). 1974. 22.50 (ISBN 0-8061-0803-7); pap. 8.95 o.p. (ISBN 0-8061-1175-5). U of Okla Pr.

Nyenhuis, Jacob E., jt. ed. see Cutt, Thomas.

Nyerere, Julius K. Freedom & Development - Uhuru Na Maendeleo. (Illus.). 420p. 1974. pap. 4.95x (ISBN 0-19-519772-0, GB412, GB). Oxford U Pr.

--Freedom & Socialism: A Selection from Writings & Speeches 1965-1967. 1970. pap. 6.95 (ISBN 0-19-501241-0, GB). Oxford U Pr.

--Man & Development - Binadamu Na Maendeleo. 128p. 1974. pap. text ed. 4.95x (ISBN 0-19-519785-2). Oxford U Pr.

--Ujamaa: Essays on Socialism. 1971. pap. 3.95 (ISBN 0-19-501474-X, GB359, GB). Oxford U Pr.

Nyerges, Anton N. Babits & Psychoanalysis Christiana. 100p. (Orig.). 1981. pap. price not set (ISBN 0-9600954-2-X). Nyerges.

--Gyula Juhasz the Beard Sunner. 117p. 1980. pap. 12.00 (ISBN 0-9600954-0-3). Nyerges.

Nygaard, Gary. Law & Sport. (Brighton Ser. in Recreation & Leisure Studies). 1981. pap. text ed. 9.95x o.p. (ISBN 0-89832-013-5); 14.95. Brighton Pub Co.

Nygard, Roald. Personality, Situation & Persistence. 1977. pap. 22.50x (ISBN 82-00-01563-7, Dist. by Columbia U Pr). Universitet.

Nygren, Anders. Commentary on Romans. Rasmussen, Carl, tr. LC 49-48317. 472p. 1949. pap. 5.50 (ISBN 0-8006-1684-7, 1-1684). Fortress.

Nygren, Bill. Gnomes Color & Story Album. (Illus.). 32p. 1980. pap. 3.50 (ISBN 0-89844-019-X). Troubador Pr.

Nygren, Birgitta, jt. auth. see Anell, Lars.

Nygren, Carolyn J., jt. auth. see Withrow, Frank B.

Nyhan, Michael J., jt. ed. see Cater, Douglass.

Nyhart, Nina & Lockwood, Margo. Openers & Temper. LC 78-74232. 88p. 1979. pap. 4.95 (ISBN 0-914086-26-X). Alicejamesbooks.

Nyhus. Surgery Annual: 1973, Vol. 5. (Illus.). 1973. 21.00 o.p. (ISBN 0-8385-8705-4). ACC.

--Surgery Annual: 1974, Vol. 6. (Illus.). 1974. 25.50 o.p. (ISBN 0-8385-8706-2). ACC.

--Surgery Annual: 1975, Vol. 7. (Illus.). 1975. 25.50 o.p. (ISBN 0-8385-8707-0). ACC.

--Surgery Annual: 1976, Vol. 8. (Illus.). 1976. 27.50 o.p. (ISBN 0-8385-8708-9). ACC.

--Surgery Annual: 1977, Vol. 9. (Illus.). 1977. 28.50 o.p. (ISBN 0-8385-8710-0). ACC.

Nyhus, Lloyd M. Surgery Annual, 1981. (Surgery Annual Series). 1981. 27.00 (ISBN 0-8385-8715-1). ACC.

Nyhus, Lloyd M., ed. Surgery Annual 1980. (Surgery Annual Ser.). 512p. 1980. 33.50x (ISBN 0-8385-8713-5). ACC.

Nyiroe, L., ed. Literature & Its Interpretation. (De Proprietatibus Litteraruum, Series Minor: No. 24). 1979. pap. text ed. 41.25x (ISBN 90-279-3387-1). Mouton.

Nykoruk, Barbara, ed. Authors in the News, 2 vols. LC 75-13541. (Illus.). 502p. 42.00 ea.; Vol. 1 1975. (ISBN 0-8103-0043-5); Vol. 2 1976. (ISBN 0-8103-0045-1). Gale.

Nylander, Jane C. Fabrics for Historic Buildings. 2nd ed. LC 80-18918. (Illus.). 68p. 1980. pap. 6.95 (ISBN 0-89133-081-X). Preservation Pr.

Nylander, W. Collected Lichenological Papers: Collected Lichenological Papers. Incl. Vol. 4. Papers 1888-1900; Vol. 5. Synopsis Lichenum et Supplementum 1858-1869. (Illus.); Vol. 6. Prodromus Licherographiae Galliae et Algeriae 1857. Lichens Scandinaviae sive Prodomus... 1861. Supplementum: Lichens Lapponicae orientalis 1866. (Illus.). Date not set. 75.00 ea. Lubrecht & Cramer. Postponed.

Nyman, C. J., et al. Problems for General Chemistry & Qualitative Analysis. 4th ed. LC 79-24489. 342p. 1980. pap. text ed. 9.95 (ISBN 0-471-05299-X). Wiley.

Nyman, Heikki, ed. see Wittgenstein, Ludwig.

Nyrop, Christopher. Kiss & Its History. Harvey, William F., tr. LC 68-22040. 1968. Repr. of 1901 ed. 15.00 (ISBN 0-8103-3512-3). Gale.

Nystrom, Carolyn. Lord, I Want to Have a Quiet Time. LC 80-69305. 224p. (gr. 7-12). 1981. pap. 5.95 (ISBN 0-915684-77-2). Christian Herald.

--Romans: Christianity on Trial. (Young Fisherman Bible Studyguides). (Illus.). 124p. 1980. tchr's ed 4.95 (ISBN 0-87788-899-X); student wkbk. 3.95 (ISBN 0-87788-898-1). Shaw Pubs.

--A Woman's Workshop on Romans-Leader's Manual. 112p. (Orig.). 1981. pap. 1.95 (ISBN 0-310-41911-5). Zondervan.

--A Woman's Workshop on Romans-Student's Manual. 144p. (Orig.). 1981. pap. 2.95 (ISBN 0-310-41921-2). Zondervan.

Nystrom, Carolyn, jt. auth. see Fromer, Margaret.

Nystrom, Dennis, jt. auth. see Stadt, Ronald.

Nystrom, Dennis C. & Bayne, Keith G. Instructional Methods in Occupational Education. LC 76-43204. 1977. 13.50 (ISBN 0-672-97111-9). Bobbs.

Nyvall, Robert F. Field Crop Disease Handbook. (Illus.). 1979. lib. bdg. 45.00 (ISBN 0-87055-336-4); pap. text ed. 25.00 (ISBN 0-87055-344-5). AVI.

O

Oakes. Willy Wong: American. (gr. 4-6). pap. 0.95 o.s.i. (ISBN 0-686-68478-8, 29725). Archway.

Oakes, Annalee, ed. see American Assoc. of Critical-Care Nurses.

Oakes, Annalee R, ed. see American Association of Critical Care Nurses.

Oakes, George & Chapman, Alexandra. Turn Right at the Fountain. 3rd ed. 1971. 5.95 o.p. (ISBN 0-03-086006-7). HR&W.

Oakes, George W. & Chapman, Alexandra. Turn Right at the Fountain. 4th, rev. ed. LC 80-17568. (Illus.). 352p. 1981. 14.95 (ISBN 0-03-047171-0); pap. 7.95 (ISBN 0-686-69129-6). HR&W.

Oakes, Guy, tr. & intro. by see Weber, Max.

Oakes, Maud, jt. auth. see Henderson, Joseph L.

Oakes, Peter, jt. auth. see Mauger, Juan.

Oakes, R., jt. auth. see Harrison, C.

Oakeshott, Ewart. European Weapons & Armour. (Illus.). 277p. 1980. 29.95 (ISBN 0-686-68855-4). Beinfeld Pub.

Oakeshott, M. Experience & Its Modes. LC 77-85696. 1978. 38.50 (ISBN 0-521-05852-X). Cambridge U Pr.

Oakeshott, Michael. On Human Conduct. 350p. 1975. 34.00x (ISBN 0-19-827195-6). Oxford U Pr.

--The Social & Political Doctrines of Contemporary Europe. 241p. 1980. Repr. of 1947 ed. lib. bdg. 35.00 (ISBN 0-89987-625-0). Darby Bks.

Oakey, Virginia, jt. auth. see Nash, Constance.

Oakford, Robert V. Capital Budgeting: A Quantitative Evaluation of Investment Alternatives. 1970. 19.95 o.p. (ISBN 0-8260-6815-4). Wiley.

Oakland, Thomas & Phillips, Beeman N., eds. Assessing Minority Group Children. LC 68-52341. 128p. 1973. text ed. 12.95 (ISBN 0-87705-154-2). Human Sci Pr.

Oakland, William, jt. ed. see Mieszlowski, Peter.

Oakley, Barry. The Great God Mogadon & Other Plays. 119p. 1980. pap. 10.95x (ISBN 0-7022-1437-X); pap. 6.00x (ISBN 0-7022-1437-X). U of Queensland Pr.

Oakley, Cletus O. Analytic Geometry. (Illus., Orig.). 1957. pap. 3.95 (ISBN 0-06-460068-8, CO 68, COS). Har-Row.

--Calculus. rev. ed. (Orig.). 1957. pap. 3.95 (ISBN 0-06-460048-3, CO 48, COS). Har-Row.

--Calculus: A Modern Approach. (Illus., Orig.). 1971. pap. 4.50 (ISBN 0-06-460134-X, CO 134, COS). Har-Row.

Oakley, D. The Phenomenon of Architecture in Cultures in Change. 1971. 32.00 (ISBN 0-08-016075-1). Pergamon.

Oakley, Francis. The Medieval Experience: Foundations of Western Culture Singularity. LC 73-19356. 250p. 1974. pap. text ed. 6.95x o.p. (ISBN 0-684-13737-2, ScribC). Scribner.

--Political Thought of Pierre D'Ailly. (Yale Historical Pubs. Miscellany Ser.: No. 81). 1964. 42.50x (ISBN 0-685-69849-1). Elliots Bks.

--The Western Church in the Later Middle Ages. LC 79-7621. 1979. 19.50x (ISBN 0-8014-1208-0). Cornell U Pr.

Oakley, Gilbert. Self Hypnosis Explained. 1978. pap. 4.95 (ISBN 0-8119-0396-6). Fell.

Oakley, Graham. The Church Cat Abroad. 1980. pap. 2.95 (ISBN 0-689-70472-0, Aladdin). Atheneum.

--Church Mice at Christmas. LC 80-14518. (Illus.). 40p. (gr. k up). 1980. 10.95 (ISBN 0-689-30797-7). Atheneum.

Oakley, Janet & Parkin, S. F. A Textbook for Dental Surgery Assistants. (Illus., Orig.). 1963. pap. 8.95 (ISBN 0-571-10253-0, Pub. by Faber & Faber). Merrimack Bk Serv.

Oakley, John B. & Thompson, Robert S. Law Clerks & the Judicial Process: Perceptions of the Qualities & Functions of Law Clerks in American Courts. 150p. 1981. 10.00x (ISBN 0-520-04046-5). U of Cal Pr.

Oakley, K. & Richmond, W. A Systematic Approach to Commercial & Clerical Training. 1970. pap. 6.25 (ISBN 0-08-015722-X). Pergamon.

Oakley, Kenneth & Campbell, Bernard, eds. Catalogue of Fossil Hominids: Nineteen Eighty, 3 vols. Incl. Pt. 1. Africa. 223p. pap. 27.50 (ISBN 0-87474-700-7); Pt. 2. Europe. 379p. pap. 42.50 (ISBN 0-87474-701-5); Pt. 3. Americas, Asia, Australia. 226p. pap. 30.00 (ISBN 0-87474-702-3). (Illus.). 1980. Set. pap. 87.50 (ISBN 0-87474-699-X, Pub. by Trustees Brit. Mus. Nat. Hist.). Smithsonian.

Oakman, Barbara F. Countdown to Successful Reading. (Illus., Orig.). (gr. 5-9). 1971. pap. text ed. 11.95 (ISBN 0-13-183616-1). P-H.

Oakshott, Walter. The Two Winchester Bibles. (Illus.). 260p. 1981. 395.00 (ISBN 0-19-818235-X). Oxford U Pr.

Oana, Robert G. Pillow Face & Other Stories. (Illus.). (ps-7). 1978. pap. 2.95 (ISBN 0-8100-0067-9, 17-1619). Northwest Pub.

OAO Corp. Biomass Energy Systems Program Summary Nineteen Eighty. 220p. 1981. pap. 24.50 (ISBN 0-89934-103-9). Solar Energy Info.

OAS Department of Publication, ed. Actas y Documentos: Resoluciones Aprobadas. Septimo Periodo Extraordinario de Sesiones. Washington, D.C. 22 de Mayo de 1979. 266p. 1980. pap. text ed. 15.00 (ISBN 0-8270-1171-7). OAS.

OAS General Secretariat. Actas y Documentos Segunda Conferencia Especializada Interamericana Sobre Derecho Internacional Privado, 3 vols. (CIDIP-II Ser.: Vols. 1-3). 1980. Vol. 1, 455p. pap. text ed. 25.00 (ISBN 0-8270-1113-X); Vol. 2, 547p. pap. text ed. 25.00 (ISBN 0-8270-1114-8); Vol. 3, 469p. pap. text ed. 25.00 (ISBN 0-8270-1115-6). OAS.

--Aplicacoes Da Teoria De Grupos Na Espectroscopia De Raman E Do Infravermelho. (Fisica Monografia: No. 14). 102p. 1980. pap. text ed. 2.00 (ISBN 0-8270-1126-1). OAS.

--Decima Primeira Reunino Do Conselho Interamericano De Educacao, Ciencia E Cultura: Relatorio Final. 206p. (Port., 27 de julho a 2 de agosto de 1980, Bogota, Colombia). 1980. pap. text ed. 19.00 (ISBN 0-8270-1199-7). OAS.

--Guia De las Fuentes En Hispanoamerica Para el Estudio De la Administracion Virreinal Espanola En Mexico y En el Peru 1535-1700. 523p. 1980. pap. 15.00 (ISBN 0-8270-1091-5). OAS.

--Manual De Normas Vigentes En Materia De Direitos Humanos: Actualizado Em Julho De 1980. (Human Rights Ser.). 149p. (Port.). 1980. pap. text ed. 4.00 (ISBN 0-8270-1203-9). OAS.

--Onzieme Reunion Du Conseil Interamericain Pour L'education, la Science et la Culture: Rapport Final. 236p. (Fr.). 1980. pap. text ed. 19.00 (ISBN 0-8270-1198-9). OAS.

--Revista Interamericana De Bibliografia: (Inter-American Review of Bibliography) (Vol. XXX, No. 3). 116p. (Engl. & Span.). 1980. pap. text ed. 2.00. OAS.

--Short-Term Economic Reports: Colombia, Vol. 1. 2nd ed. (Short Term Economic Reports Ser.). 77p. 1980. pap. text ed. 5.00 (ISBN 0-8270-1261-6). OAS.

--Sintesis De las Decisiones Tomadas En las Sesiones y Textos De las Resoluciones Aprobadas. (Vol. XXXI Enero-Diciembre De 1978). 174p. 1980. pap. text ed. 3.00 (ISBN 0-8270-6300-8). OAS.

--Trabajos Realizados Por el Comite Juridico Interamericano Durante el Periodo Ordinario De Sesiones. (International Law Ser.). 147p. 1980. text ed. 10.00 (ISBN 0-8270-1156-3). OAS.

--Trabajos Realizados Por el Comite Juridico Interamericano Durante el Periodo Ordinario De Sesiones: Celebrado Del 4 Al 29 De Agosto De 1980. (Comite Juridico Interamericano). 155p. (Span.). 1980. pap. text ed. 10.00 (ISBN 0-8270-1267-5). OAS.

--Trabalhos Realizados Pela Comissao Juridica Interamericana Durante Seu Periodo Ordinario De Sessoes: 30 de Julho a 16 de Agosto de 1979. 165p. (Port.). 1980. pap. text ed. 7.00 (ISBN 0-8270-1146-6). OAS.

--Tratados y Convenciones Interamerianos. (Serie Sobre Tratados: No. 9). 303p. 1980. pap. text ed. 15.00 (ISBN 0-8270-1159-8). OAS.

--Los Virus. (Serie De Biologia: No. 8). 72p. (Orig.). 1980. pap. text ed. 2.00 (ISBN 0-8270-1169-5). OAS.

--Work Accomplished by the Inter-American Juridical Committee During Its Regular Meeting: Held from January 14 to February 9, 1980. 127p. 1980. pap. text ed. 11.00 (ISBN 0-8270-1223-3). OAS.

OAS General Secretariat, ed. Boletin Estadistico de la OEA: Enero-Junio 1980, Vol. 2, Nos. 1-2. 221p. 1980. pap. text ed. 4.00. OAS.

OAS General Secretariat Bureau of Legal Affairs, ed. Status of Inter-American Treaties & Conventions. rev. ed. (Treaty Ser.: No. 5). 53p. text ed. 5.00 (ISBN 0-8270-1147-4). OAS.

OAS General Secretariat Bureau of Legal Affairs. Tratados Sobre el Canal De Panama Suscritos Entre la Republica De Panama y los Estados Unidos De America. (Serie Sobre Tratados: No. 57 & 57a). 157p. 1979. text ed. 9.00 (ISBN 0-8270-0715-9). OAS.

OAS General Secretariat Deparment of Scientific & Technological Affairs. A Vida Da Celula. (Serie De Biologia: No. 5). (Illus.). 117p. (Orig.). Repr. of 1968 ed. 2.00 (ISBN 0-8270-1141-5). OAS.

OAS General Secretariat Department of Publications, ed. Boletin Estadistico De la OEA. (Periodical-Quarterly Ser.). 207p. 4.00 (ISBN 0-686-68291-2). OAS.

OAS General Secretariat Department of Scientific & Technological Affairs. Semiconductors. 2nd ed. (Serie De Fisica (Monograph on Physics): No. 6). 63p. 1980. Repr. text ed. 2.00 (ISBN 0-8270-1068-0). OAS.

OAS General Secretariat, Dept. of Publications. Sexto Curso de Derecho Internationsl Organizado Por el Comite Juridico Interamericano: Julio-Agosto de 1979, Conferencias e Informes. 630p. (Span.). 1979. pap. text ed. 25.00 (ISBN 0-8270-1144-X). OAS.

OAS General Secretariat Dept. of Scientific Affairs. Fisica Cuantica. rev. ed. (Monografias Cientificas (Scientific Monographs)). 62p. (Orig.). 1980. Repr. of 1971 ed. 2.00 (ISBN 0-8270-1100-8). OAS.

OAS General Secretariat Inter-American Commission of Women. Informe De la Comision Interamericana De Mujeres A la Conferenci A Mundial Del Decenio De las Naciones Unidas Para la Mujer: Iqualdad, Desarrollo Y Paz. (Inter-American Commission of Women). 40p. 1980. 2.00 o.p. (ISBN 0-8270-1163-6). OAS.

OAS General Secretariat Inter-American Commision of Human Rights. Informe Sobre la Situacion De los Derechos Humanos En Haiti. (Human Rights Ser.). 77p. 1980. text ed. 5.00 (ISBN 0-8270-1095-8). OAS.

OAS General Secretariat Inter-American Commission of Human Rights. Manual De Normas Wicentes En Materia De Derechos Humanos. (Human Rights Ser.). 153p. 1980. text ed. 6.00 (ISBN 0-8270-1153-9). OAS.

OAS General Secretariat Inter-American Commission of Human Rights, ed. Rapport Sur la Situation Des Droits De L'homme En Haiti. (Human Rights Ser.). 76p. 1980. 5.00 (ISBN 0-8270-1098-2). OAS.

OAS General Secretariat Inter-American Commission of Human Rights. Report on the Situation of Human Rights in Haiti. (Human Rights Ser.). 81p. 1980. lib. bdg. 5.00 (ISBN 0-8270-1094-X). OAS.

--Report on the Situation of Human Rights in Argentina. (Human Rights Ser.). 266p. (Orig.). 1980. 12.00 (ISBN 0-8270-1099-0). OAS.

OAS General Secretariat International Trade & Export Development Program. Sistema Generalizado De Preferencial De Estados Unidos: Cobertura Y Procedimientos Administrativos Vignetes En 1980. (International Trade Ser.). 58p. pap. text ed. 5.00 (ISBN 0-8270-1125-3). OAS.

--The United States Generalized System of Preferences: Coverage & Administrative Procedures in Force in 1980. (International Trade Ser.). 58p. 1980. text ed. 5.00 (ISBN 0-8270-1101-6). OAS.

OAS General Secretariat Office of Development & Codification of International Law. Actas Y Documentos Segunda Conferencia Especializada Interamerica Sobre Derecho Internacional Privado, Vol. 1. (International Law). 455p. 1980. lib. bdg. 25.00 (ISBN 0-8270-1113-X). OAS.

OAS General Secretariat Office of Development & Codification of Inernational Law. Actas Y Documentos Segunda Conferencia Especializada Interamericana Sobre Derecho Internacional Privado, Vol. 3. (International Law Ser.). 469p. 1980. text ed. 25.00 (ISBN 0-8270-1115-6). OAS.

OAS General Secretariat Planning & Statistics. Synthesis Fo Economic Performance in Latin America During 1979. (Statistics Ser.). 40p. 1979. pap. 3.00 (ISBN 0-686-68295-5). OAS.

OAS General Secretariat Technical Unit of Performing Arts. Compositores De America, No. 8. rev. ed. (Composers of the Americas Ser.). (Illus.). 157p. (Eng.-Span.). 1980. Repr. of 1962 ed. 7.00 (ISBN 0-8270-1085-0). OAS.

OAS General Secretariat, Dept. of Educational Affairs. Glosario de Technologia Educativa. (Illus.). 83p. (Span.). 1978. pap. text ed. 3.00 (ISBN 0-8270-1060-5). OAS.

OAS General Secretatiat Office of Development & Codification of International Law. Actas Y Documentos Segunda Conferencia Especializada Interamericana Sobre Derecho Internacional Privado, Vol. 2. (International Law Ser.). 450p. 1980. text ed. 25.00 (ISBN 0-8270-1114-8). OAS.

OAS Gerneral Secretariat Department of Scientific & Technological Affairs. Principios Generales De Microbiologia: Serie De Biologia No. 7. 2nd ed. (Biology Ser.: No. 7). 143p. 1980. text ed. 2.00 (ISBN 0-8270-1097-4). OAS.

Oastler, John. Concept Analysis: From Socrates to Wittgenstein. LC 78-52288. 1978. pap. text ed. 16.75x o.p. (ISBN 0-8191-0491-4). U Pr of Amer.

Oates, Bob, Jr. The Winner's Edge. Date not set. 12.95 (ISBN 0-686-68762-0). Mayflower Bks.

Oates, John, ed. Early Cognitive Development. LC 78-17694. 1979. 24.95 (ISBN 0-470-26431-4). Halsted Pr.

Oates, John A. The Unknown Philosophy of Sex. (An Intimate Life of Man Library Book). (Illus.). 1979. 51.45 (ISBN 0-89266-175-5). Am Classical Coll Pr.

Oates, John F., et al. Checklist of Editions of Greek Papyri & Ostraca. LC 78-26003. (Bulletin of the American Society of Papyrologists Supplements: No. 1). 1978. pap. 6.00 (ISBN 0-89130-272-7, 311101). Scholars Pr Ca.

Oates, Joyce C. Angel of Light. 480p. 1981. 14.95 (ISBN 0-525-05483-9). Dutton.

--The Assassins. LC 75-25141. 576p. 1975. 10.95 (ISBN 0-8149-0767-9). Vanguard.

--Bellefleur. 1980. 13.95 (ISBN 0-525-06302-1, Henry Robbins Book). Dutton.

--By the North Gate. LC 63-13790. 1963. 10.95 (ISBN 0-8149-0174-3). Vanguard.

--By the North Gate. 1978. pap. 1.50 o.p. (ISBN 0-449-22979-3, P2302, Crest). Fawcett.

--Childwold. LC 76-42086. 380p. 1976. 10.95 (ISBN 0-8149-0777-6). Vanguard.

--Contraries: Essays. 192p. 1981. 15.00 (ISBN 0-19-502884-8). Oxford U Pr.

--Crossing the Border. LC 76-7148. 256p. 1976. 10.95 (ISBN 0-8149-0774-1). Vanguard.

--Do with Me What You Will. LC 73-83039. 579p. 1973. 10.95 (ISBN 0-8149-0751-2). Vanguard.

--Do With Me What You Will. 544p. 1978. pap. 2.95 (ISBN 0-449-23610-2, Crest). Fawcett.

--Expensive People. LC 68-8084. 1968. 10.95 (ISBN 0-8149-0170-0). Vanguard.

--Garden of Earthly Delights. LC 67-19288. 1967. 10.95 (ISBN 0-8149-0171-9). Vanguard.

--A Garden of Earthly Delights. 384p. 1977. pap. 1.95 o.p. (ISBN 0-449-23194-1, Crest). Fawcett.

--The Goddess & Other Women. LC 74-81808. 512p. 1974. 10.95 (ISBN 0-8149-0745-8). Vanguard.

--The Goddess & Other Women. 464p. 1976. pap. 1.95 o.p. (ISBN 0-449-22774-X, C2774, Crest). Fawcett.

--Love & Its Derangements & Other Poems. 192p. 1977. pap. 1.75 o.p. (ISBN 0-449-30811-1, Prem). Fawcett.

--Marriages & Infidelities. LC 72-83348. 416p. 1972. 10.95 (ISBN 0-8149-0718-0). Vanguard.

--Marriages & Infidelities. 416p. 1978. pap. 2.50 o.p. (ISBN 0-449-23724-9, Crest). Fawcett.

--New Heaven, New Earth: The Visionary Experience in Literature. LC 74-76438. 308p. 1974. 10.00 (ISBN 0-8149-0743-1). Vanguard.

--Night-Side. LC 77-77416. 1977. 10.95 (ISBN 0-8149-0793-8). Vanguard.

--The Poisoned Kiss & Other Portuguese Stories. LC 75-385. 196p. 1975. 10.95 (ISBN 0-685-52407-8). Vanguard.

--Scenes from American Life: Contemporary Short Fiction. 256p. 1972. pap. text ed. 6.95 (ISBN 0-394-31683-5). Random.

--A Sentimental Education: Stories. 192p. 1981. 12.95 (ISBN 0-525-19950-0). Dutton.

--Son of the Morning. LC 78-56428. 1978. 10.95 (ISBN 0-8149-0800-4). Vanguard.

--Them. LC 74-89660. 1969. 10.95 (ISBN 0-8149-0668-0). Vanguard.

--Unholy Loves. LC 79-64396. 1979. 11.95 (ISBN 0-8149-0813-6). Vanguard.

--Upon the Sweeping Flood. LC 66-16632. 10.95 (ISBN 0-8149-0172-7). Vanguard.

--Wheel of Love & Other Stories. LC 79-134661. 1970. 10.95 (ISBN 0-8149-0676-1). Vanguard.

--With Shuddering Fall. LC 64-23317. 1964. 10.95 (ISBN 0-8149-0173-5). Vanguard.

--With Shuddering Fall. 1976. pap. 1.75 (ISBN 0-449-24930-1, X2930, Crest). Fawcett.

--Wonderland. LC 72-155669. 10.95 (ISBN 0-8149-0659-1). Vanguard.

--Wonderland. 1979. pap. 1.95 o.p. (ISBN 0-449-22951-3, Crest). Fawcett.

Oates, Joyce Carol. All the Good People I've Left Behind. 250p. 1978. 14.00 o.p. (ISBN 0-87685-394-7); pap. 5.00 (ISBN 0-87685-393-9). Black Sparrow.

--Cybele. 200p. 1979. 14.00 (ISBN 0-87685-425-0); pap. 5.00 (ISBN 0-87685-424-2). Black Sparrow.

--The Edge of Impossibility: Tragic Forms in Literature. LC 77-188692. 1972. 10.95 (ISBN 0-8149-0675-3). Vanguard.

--The Hungry Ghosts: Seven Allusive Comedies. 200p. (Orig.). 1978. 14.00 (ISBN 0-87685-204-5); pap. 5.00 (ISBN 0-87685-203-7). Black Sparrow.

--The Poisoned Kiss. 1977. pap. 1.95 o.p. (ISBN 0-449-23299-9, Crest). Fawcett.

--Three Plays. LC 80-20210. 160p. 1980. 10.95 (ISBN 0-86538-001-5); pap. 5.95 (ISBN 0-86538-002-3). Ontario Rev NJ.

Oates, Stephen B. To Purge This Land with Blood: A Biography of John Brown. 1972. pap. 7.95x (ISBN 0-06-131655-5, TB1655, Torch). Har-Row.

Oates, Wallace, jt. ed. see Ashenfelter, Orley C.

Oates, Wallace E., jt. auth. see Baumol, William J.

Oates, Wallace E., jt. auth. see Kelejian, Harry H.

Oates, Wallace E., jt. auth. see Mills, Edwin S.

Oates, Wayne E. Pastoral Care & Counseling in Grief & Separation. Clinevell, Howard J. & Stone, Howard W., eds. LC 75-13048. (Creative Pastoral Care & Counseling Ser.). 96p. 1976. pap. 3.25 (ISBN 0-8006-0554-3, 1-554). Fortress.

--Workaholics: Make Laziness Work for You. LC 77-80906. 1978. 5.95 o.p. (ISBN 0-385-12977-7). Doubleday.

Oathout, John D. Trademarks in the Marketplace. (Illus.). 192p. 1981. 12.95 (ISBN 0-684-16844-8, ScribT). Scribner.

Oatley, C. W. The Scanning Electron Microscope. LC 70-190413. (Physics Monographs). (Illus.). 200p. 1972. 32.95 (ISBN 0-521-08531-4). Cambridge U Pr.

Oatman, Eric. Energy. 1980. 5.75 o.p. (ISBN 0-8242-0646-0). Wilson.

Oatman, Eric F., ed. Crime & Society. (Reference Shelf Ser.). 1979. 6.25 (ISBN 0-8242-0632-0). Wilson.

--Medical Care in the United States. (Reference Shelf Ser.: Vol. 50, No. 1). 1978. 6.25 (ISBN 0-8242-0622-3). Wilson.

Obach, Robert E. & Kirk, Albert. A Commentary on the Gospel of John. 288p. 1981. pap. 6.95 (ISBN 0-8091-2346-0). Paulist Pr.

Obach, Robert E., jt. auth. see Kirk, Albert.

Obal, F. & Benedek, G., eds. Environmental Physiology: Proceedings of the 28th International Congress of Physiological Sciences, Budapest, 1980 (Including the Satellite Symposium on Sports Physiology) LC 80-42102. (Advances in Physiological Sciences: Vol. 18). (Illus.). 375p. 1981. 40.00 (ISBN 0-08-027339-4). Pergamon.

O'Ballance, Edgar. The Arab-Israeli War, Nineteen Forty-Eight. LC 79-2877. (Illus.). 220p. 1981. Repr. of 1957 ed. 19.75 (ISBN 0-8305-0045-6). Hyperion Conn.

--Terror in Ireland: The Heritage of Hate. (Illus.). 280p. 1981. 14.95 (ISBN 0-89141-100-3). Presidio Pr.

Obanda, Dave L. The Witch Can Fly. Date not set. 6.95 (ISBN 0-533-04836-2). Vantage.

O'Banion, Dan R. An Ecological & Nutritional Approach to Behavioral Medicine. (Illus.). 248p. 1981. price not set (ISBN 0-398-04457-0). C C Thomas.

O'Banion, Daniel & Whaley, Donald L. Behavior Contracting: Arranging Contingencies of Reinforcement. LC 80-20231. 1980. text ed. 18.95 (ISBN 0-8261-3150-6); pap. 11.95 (ISBN 0-8261-3151-4). Springer Pub.

O'Bannon, Dan R. The Ecological & Nutritional Treatment of Health Disorders. (Illus.). 240p. 1981. price not set (ISBN 0-398-04455-4). C C Thomas.

O'Bannon, Freda V., jt. auth. see Gerald, Michael C.

Obbo, Christine. African Women: Their Struggle for Economic Independence. 240p. 1980. text ed. 18.95 (ISBN 0-905762-33-9, Pub. by Zed Pr); pap. 7.95. Lawrence Hill.

Obear, Katharine T. Through the Years in Old Winnsboro. LC 80-23314. xx, 258p. 1980. Repr. of 1940 ed. write for info. (ISBN 0-87152-344-2). Reprint.

Obeck, Victor, jt. auth. see Rossman, Isadore.

O'Beirne, T. H., ed. see Schuh, Fred.

Obele, Norma, jt. auth. see McNeely, Harold E.

Obelkevich, James. Religion & Rural Society: South Lindsey, 1825-1875. (Illus.). 1976. 42.00x (ISBN 0-19-822426-5). Oxford U Pr.

Obenzinger, Hilton. This Passover or the Next I Will Never Be in Jerusalem. LC 80-20986. 1980. lib. bdg. 12.50 (ISBN 0-917672-13-5); pap. 4.95 (ISBN 0-917672-12-7). Momos.

Ober, Kenneth H. Meir Goldschmidt. (World Author Ser: Denmark: No. 414). 1976. lib. bdg. 12.50 (ISBN 0-8057-6253-1). Twayne.

Ober, William B. Boswell's Clap & Other Essays: Medical Analyses of Literary Men's Afflictions. LC 78-16018. (Illus.). 320p. 1979. 19.95 (ISBN 0-8093-0889-4). S Ill U Pr.

Oberer, Walter E., et al. Cases & Materials on Labor Law: Collective Bargaining in a Free Society. 2nd ed. LC 78-20988. (American Casebook Ser.). 1168p. 1979. text ed. 23.95 (ISBN 0-8299-2024-2). West Pub.

Oberfirst, Robert. Al Jolson: You Ain't Heard Nothing Yet. LC 80-16736. 1980. 8.95 (ISBN 0-498-02500-4). A S Barnes.

Oberg, Arthur. Anna's Song. Webber, Joan M. & Blessing, Richard, eds. LC 79-4847. 112p. 1980. 8.95 (ISBN 0-295-95681-X). U of Wash Pr.

--Modern American Lyric: Lowell, Berryman, Creeley, & Plath. 1978. 13.00 (ISBN 0-8135-0826-6). Rutgers U Pr.

Oberg, Erik, et al. Machinery's Handbook. 21st rev. ed. Schubert, Paul B., ed. (Illus.). 2482p. 1979. 34.00 (ISBN 0-8311-1129-1); text ed. 19.00 o.p. (ISBN 0-8311-1108-9). Indus Pr.

Oberhelman, Harley D. The Presence of Faulkner in the Writings of Garcia Marquez. (Graduate Studies, Texas Tech Univ.: No. 22). (Illus.). 1980. pap. 7.00 (ISBN 0-89672-080-2). Tex Tech Pr.

Oberholtzer, Ellis P. Literary History of Philadelphia. LC 72-81510. 1969. Repr. of 1906 ed. 24.00 (ISBN 0-8103-3563-8). Gale.

--The Referendum in America. LC 70-153370. (American Constitutional & Legal History Ser). 1971. Repr. of 1912 ed. lib. bdg. 49.50 (ISBN 0-306-70149-9). Da Capo.

Oberhuber, Konrad & Jacoby, Beverly S., eds. French Drawings from a Private Collection: Louis XIII to Louis XVI. LC 80-65383. 182p. 1980. pap. 7.50 (ISBN 0-916724-42-5). Fogg Art.

Oberlander, Cornelia H., jt. auth. see Nadel, Ira B.

Oberley, Edith T. & Oberley, Terry D. Understanding Your New Life with Dialysis: Patient Guide for Physical & Psychological Adjustment to Maintenance Dialysis. 2nd ed. (Illus.). 168p. 1979. 16.75 (ISBN 0-398-03797-3); pap. 11.75 (ISBN 0-398-03798-1). C C Thomas.

Oberley, Terry D., jt. auth. see Oberley, Edith T.

Oberli-Turner, Maureen, tr. see Gidal, Tim N.

Oberli-Turner, Maureen, tr. see Jammes, Andre.

Obermair, Gilbert. Matchstick Puzzles, Tricks & Games. LC 77-79510. (Illus.). 128p. (gr. 4 up). 1980. pap. 3.50 (ISBN 0-8069-8934-3). Sterling.

--Matchstick Puzzles, Tricks & Games. LC 77-79510. (Illus.). (gr. 4 up). 1977. 5.95 (ISBN 0-8069-4564-8); PLB 5.89 (ISBN 0-8069-4565-6). Sterling.

Oberman, H. A. Masters of the Reformation: Rival Roads to a New Ideology. Martin, D., tr. from German. 432p. Date not set. price not set (ISBN 0-521-23098-5). Cambridge U Pr.

Oberman, R. M. Counting & Counters. 192p. 1981. 29.95 (ISBN 0-470-27118-3). Halsted Pr.

--Digital Circuits for Binary Arithmetic. 340p. 1979. 39.95x (ISBN 0-470-26373-3). Halsted Pr.

Obermann, Julian. Discoveries at Karatepe: A Phoenician Royal Inscription from Cilicia. (Supplements: 9). (Illus.). 1948. pap. 1.00 (ISBN 0-686-00045-5). Am Orient Soc.

Obermeyer, Henry. Successful Advertising Management. LC 69-18719. 1969. 18.50 o.p. (ISBN 0-07-047591-1, P&RB). McGraw.

Obermeyer, William G., Jr. & Jue-Obermeyer, Pauline M. Earthquake: Are You Prepared? LC 80-50463. (Illus.). 68p. (Orig.). 1980. pap. 2.95 (ISBN 0-936706-01-5). CERA.

Oberrecht, Kenn. The Apartment Workshop. 1980. 12.95 (ISBN 0-87691-313-3). Winchester Pr.

--The Practical Angler's Guide to Successful Fishing. (Illus.). 1978. 12.95 (ISBN 0-87691-250-1). Winchester Pr.

Oberschall, Anthony. Social Conflict & Social Movements. 1973. text ed. 17.95 (ISBN 0-13-815761-8). P-H.

Oberschall, Anthony R., jt. auth. see Beveridge, Andrew A.

Oberst, Bruce. Deuteronomy. LC 70-1070. (The Bible Study Textbook Ser.). 1968. 13.50 (ISBN 0-89900-009-6). College Pr Pub.

Oberst, Byron B. Practical Guidance for Office Pediatric & Adolescent Practice. (Illus.). 280p. 1973. 18.75 (ISBN 0-398-02552-5); pap. 12.75 (ISBN 0-398-02553-3). C C Thomas.

Obert, John C., jt. auth. see McIntyre, Thomas J.

Obert, Leonard & Duvall, W. L. Rock Mechanics & the Design of Structures in Rock. LC 66-26753. 650p. 1967. 49.95 (ISBN 0-471-65235-0, Pub. by Wiley-Interscience). Wiley.

Oberto, Martino. Anaphilosophia. Salamone, Rosa Maria, tr. from Ital. LC 78-58984. (Illus.). 1981. pap. 17.95 (ISBN 0-915570-10-6). Oolp Pr.

Obey see Bentley, Eric.

Obeyesekere, Ranjini & Fernando, Chitra, eds. An Anthology of Modern Writing from Sri Lanka. (Monographs of the Association for Asian Studies: No. XXXVIII). 1981. text ed. 12.95x (ISBN 0-8165-0702-3); pap. text ed. 6.50x (ISBN 0-8165-0703-1). U of Ariz Pr.

Obichere, Boniface I. Studies in Southern Nigerian History. 276p. 1981. 28.50x (ISBN 0-7146-3106-X, F Cass Co). Biblio Dist.

Obichere, Boniface I., ed. African States & the Military: Past & Present. 1980. 27.50x (ISBN 0-7146-3135-3, F Cass Co). Biblio Dist.

Obiechina, E. An African Popular Literature. 28.50 (ISBN 0-521-20015-6); pap. 11.50x (ISBN 0-521-09744-4). Cambridge U Pr.

--Culture, Tradition & Society in the West African Novel. LC 74-80358. (African Studies: No. 14). 300p. 1975. 45.00 (ISBN 0-521-20525-5); pap. 12.50x (ISBN 0-521-09876-9). Cambridge U Pr.

Obiechina, Emmanual. Onitsha Market Literature. (African Writers Ser.). 1972. pap. text ed. 6.50x (ISBN 0-435-90109-5). Heinemann Ed.

Obiols, J., et al, eds. Biologlical Psychiatry Today, Vols: A & B. (Developments in Psychiatry: Vol. 2). 1979. 151.25 (ISBN 0-444-80117-0, North Holland). Elsevier.

Obladen, Michael, jt. auth. see Wille, Lutz.

Oblander, Ruth. Dresses Cut-to-Fit. Leppert, Mary, ed. LC 76-53237. 1976. 3.80 (ISBN 0-933956-02-9); tchrs ed. 3.04. Sew-Fit.

--Sewing Without Pins. LC 76-53269. 1977. 3.80 (ISBN 0-933956-01-0); tchrs ed. 3.04 (ISBN 0-686-23591-6). Sew-Fit.

--Survival Sewing for Men. (Illus.). 56p. 1980. pap. 3.50 cancelled (ISBN 0-933956-06-1). Sew-Fit.

Oblander, Ruth, et al. The Sew-Fit Manual. Plum, Judy, ed. LC 77-84538. (Illus.). 1978. 24.00 (ISBN 0-933956-03-7); tchrs. ed 19.20. Sew-Fit.

Obler, Loraine K. & Albert, Martin L. Language & Communication in the Elderly: Clinical, Therapeutic, & Experimental Issues. LC 80-5348. 1980. 22.95x (ISBN 0-669-03868-7). Lexington Bks.

Obligado, Lilian, illus. Goldilocks & the Three Bears. (Golden Storytime Bk. for Learning). 24p. (gr. 3-6). 1980. 1.50 (ISBN 0-307-11980-7); PLB 6.08 s&l (ISBN 0-307-61980-X). Western Pub.

Obligado, Lillian, illus. The Story of the Three Bears. (Illus.). 24p. (ps). 1980. PLB 6.08 s&l o.p. (ISBN 0-307-61980-X, Golden Pr). Western Pub.

Oblinger, Carl. Interviewing the People of Pennsylvania: A Conceptual Guide to Oral History. pap. 3.00 (ISBN 0-911124-94-2). Pa Hist & Mus.

Oblitas, M. M. Certificate Chemistry: Multiple Choice Questions. 1976. pap. text ed. 3.95x o.p. (ISBN 0-435-64650-8). Heinemann Ed.

O'Block, Robert L. Security & Crime Prevention. c ed. (Illus.). 378p. 1981. pap. text ed. 13.95 (ISBN 0-8016-3738-4). Mosby.

Obojski, Robert. Bush League: A History of Minor League Baseball. LC 74-16345. (Illus.). 320p. 1975. 12.95 o.s.i. (ISBN 0-02-591300-X). Macmillan.

Obolensky, A. & James, T. Backgammon. 1969. pap. 4.95 (ISBN 0-02-081030-X, Collier). Macmillan.

Obolensky, Chloe & Hayward, Max. The Russian Empire: A Portrait in Photographs. LC 78-21800. 1979. 20.00 (ISBN 0-394-41029-7). Random.

Obolensky, D., jt. ed. see Auty, R.

Obolensky, S., et al. Spoken Amharic, Bk. 1 Units 1-50. 500p. 1980. pap. text ed. 10.00x (ISBN 0-87950-650-4); cassettes 1, 26 dual track 130.00x (ISBN 0-87950-652-0); Books & cassettes 1, 135.00x (ISBN 0-87950-654-7). Spoken Lang Serv.

--Spoken Amharic, Book 2, Units Fifty-One to Sixty-Eight. (Spoken Language Ser.). 500p. (Amharic.). 1980. pap. text ed. 10.00x (ISBN 0-87950-651-2); 2 cassettes, 5 dual track 30.00x (ISBN 0-87950-653-9); book 2 & cassettes 2 35.00x (ISBN 0-87950-655-5); books 1 & 2 & cassettes 1 & 2 160.00 (ISBN 0-87950-656-3). Spoken Lang Serv.

Oboler, Eli. The Fear of the Word: Censorship & Sex. LC 74-6492. 1974. 12.00 (ISBN 0-8108-0724-6). Scarecrow.

Oboler, Eli M. Defending Intellectual Freedom: The Library & the Censor. LC 79-8585. (Contributions in Librarianship & Information Science: No. 32). xix, 246p. 1980. lib. bdg. 22.95 (ISBN 0-313-21472-7, ODF/). Greenwood.

Obreanu, P. E., jt. ed. see Gould, S. H.

O'Brian, Henry. Atlantis in Ireland: Round Towers of Ireland. (Illus.). 544p. 1977. pap. 9.50 (ISBN 0-8334-1758-4, Steinerbooks). Multimedia.

O'Brian, Patrick, tr. see Daniel-Rops, Henri -.

O'Briant, R. G., et al. Recovery from Alcoholism: A Social Treatment Model. 112p. 1973. 10.50 (ISBN 0-398-02830-3). C C Thomas.

O'Brien, Aline & Rasmussen, Chrys, eds. Womanblood: Portraits of Women in Poetry & Prose. LC 80-69814. 200p. (Orig.). 1981. pap. 5.95 (ISBN 0-939140-00-4). Continuing SAGA.

O'Brien, B. P., ed. J. R. McCulloch (1789-1864) Treatise or Taxation? 1974. 30.00x (ISBN 0-7073-0189-0, Pub. by Scottish Academic Pr Scotland). Columbia U Pr.

O'Brien, Bonne B. So Great the Journey. LC 79-52332. (Illus.). 1980. 5.95 (ISBN 0-8054-5593-0). Broadman.

O'Brien, Brian J., ed. Environment & Science. (Way '79 Ser.). 1979. 18.95x (ISBN 0-85564-148-7, Pub. by U of W Austral Pr). Intl Schol Bk Serv.

O'Brien, Charles W. A Taxonomic Revision of the Genus Dorytomus in North America (Coleoptera: Curculionidae) (U. C. Publ. in Entomology: Vol. 60). 1970. pap. 7.00x (ISBN 0-520-09133-7). U of Cal Pr.

O'Brien, Conor C. Parnell & His Party: 1880-90. 1957. 36.00x (ISBN 0-19-821237-2). Oxford U Pr.

O'Brien, D. B. Saints & Politicians. LC 74-82221. (African Studies: No. 15). (Illus.). 224p. 1975. 24.95 (ISBN 0-521-20572-7). Cambridge U Pr.

O'Brien, D. P., ed. Correspondence of Lord Overstone, 3 vols. 1971. Vol. 1. 49.95 (ISBN 0-521-08097-5); Vol. 2. 49.95 (ISBN 0-521-08098-3); Vol. 3. 49.95 (ISBN 0-521-08099-1). Cambridge U Pr.

O'Brien, D. P. & Presley, John R., eds. Pioneers of Modern Economics in Britain. LC 79-55496. (Illus.). 392p. 1981. text ed. 26.50x (ISBN 0-06-495230-4). B&N.

O'Brien, Darcy. The Silver Spooner. 1981. 13.95 (ISBN 0-671-25264-X). S&S.

O'Brien, David J. The Renewal of American Catholicism. 320p. 1972. 11.95 (ISBN 0-19-501601-7). Oxford U Pr.

O'Brien, David J. & Shannon, Thomas A., eds. Renewing the Earth: Catholic Documents on Peace, Justice & Liberation. LC 76-52008. 1977. pap. 3.95 (ISBN 0-385-12954-8, Im). Doubleday.

O'Brien, David M. Privacy, Law & Public Policy. LC 79-14131. (Praeger Special Studies Ser.). 278p. 1979. 25.95 (ISBN 0-03-050406-6). Praeger.

O'Brien, Denise, jt. ed. see Cook, Edwin A.

O'Brien, Edna. I Hardly Knew You. 1979. pap. 1.95 (ISBN 0-380-45138-7, 45138). Avon.

--James & Nora: A Portrait of Joyce's Marraige. 50p. 1981. limited signed edition 35.00 (ISBN 0-935716-09-2). Lord John.

--Mother Ireland. 1976. 12.95 o.p. (ISBN 0-15-162587-5). HarBraceJ.

--A Pagan Place: A Play. 1973. 8.50 (ISBN 0-571-10336-7, Pub. by Faber & Faber); pap. 4.95 (ISBN 0-571-10316-2). Merrimack Bk Serv.

--A Rose in the Heart. 1980. pap. 2.75 (ISBN 0-380-50021-3, 50021). Avon.

--A Scandalous Woman & Other Stories. 144p. 1976. pap. 1.75 o.p. (ISBN 0-345-24805-8). Ballantine.

O'Brien, Edward L. & Fisher, Margaret E. Practical Law for Correctional Personnel: A Resource Manual & a Training Curriculum (by the National Street Law Institute) Austern, David T., ed. (Illus.). 205p. 1980. pap. text ed. write for info. (ISBN 0-8299-1034-4). West Pub.

O'Brien, Elinor. The Land & People of Ireland. rev. ed. LC 76-38335. (Portraits of the Nations Ser.). (Illus.). (gr. 6 up). 1972. 8.79 (ISBN 0-397-31299-7). Lippincott.

O'Brien, Flann. The Poor Mouth: A Bad Story About the Hard Life. Power, Patrick, tr. from Gaelic. LC 80-54558. (Illus.). 128p. 1981. pap. 4.95 (ISBN 0-394-17849-1). Seaver Bks.

O'Brien, Gary. One Hundred Twenty-Seven Sales Closes That Work. 192p. 1980. pap. 4.95 (ISBN 0-8015-5517-5, Hawthorn). Dutton.

O'Brien, James. Computers in Business Management: An Introduction. rev ed. 1979. text ed. 18.50 (ISBN 0-256-02121-X). Irwin.

O'Brien, James J. Construction Delay: Responsibilities, Risks, and Litigation. LC 76-19110. 1976. 19.50 o.p. (ISBN 0-8436-0162-0). CBI Pub.

O'Brien, John. Elves, Gnomes & Other Little People: A Coloring Book. (Illus.). 48p. 1980. pap. 2.00 (ISBN 0-486-24049-5). Dover.

O'Brien, John A. The Inquisition: A Tragic Mistake. LC 73-1962. 192p. 1973. 6.95 o.s.i. (ISBN 0-02-591400-6). Macmillan.

O'Brien, John T., ed. Crime & Justice in America. LC 79-182. (Pergamon Policy Studies). (Illus.). 1979. 39.00 (ISBN 0-08-023857-2). Pergamon.

O'Brien, Joseph V. William O'Brien & the Course of Irish Politics, 1881-1918. LC 74-22970. 350p. 1976. 22.75x (ISBN 0-520-02886-4). U of Cal Pr.

O'Brien, Kate C. A Gift Horse & Other Stories. 1981. 8.95 (ISBN 0-8076-0976-5). Braziller.

O'Brien, Katherine L., et al. Advanced French. 365p. 1965. 18.50x (ISBN 0-471-00400-6). Wiley.

O'Brien, Kevin, tr. see Guro, Elena.

O'Brien, Linda. Computers. (First Bks.). (Illus.). (gr. 4-6). 1978. PLB 6.45 s&l (ISBN 0-531-01486-X). Watts.

O'Brien, Linda, ed. see Poole, Frederick K.

O'Brien, Lois B. The Systematics of the Tribe Plectoderini in America North of Mexico (Homoptera: Fulgoroidea, Achilidae) (U. C. Publ. in Entomology: Vol. 64). 1971. pap. 7.00x (ISBN 0-520-09377-1). U of Cal Pr.

O'Brien, M., ed. Twentieth Century Interpretations of Oedipus Rex. 1968. 8.95 (ISBN 0-13-630467-2, Spec). P-H.

O'Brien, M. A. New Russian-English & English-Russian Dictionary. pap. 6.00 (ISBN 0-486-20208-9). Dover.

O'Brien, Marian M. The Collector's Guide to Dollhouses & Dollhouse Miniatures. 1974. 16.95 (ISBN 0-8015-1404-5, Hawthorn); pap. 12.95 (ISBN 0-8015-1405-3, Hawthorn). Dutton.

--Make & Furnish Your Own Miniature Rooms. 1976. 16.95 o.p. (Hawthorn); pap. 9.95 (ISBN 0-8015-4811-X, Hawthorn). Dutton.

--Make Your Own Dollhouses & Dollhouse Miniatures. 224p. 1977. 16.95 o.p. (Hawthorn); pap. 9.95 (ISBN 0-8015-4799-7, Hawthorn). Dutton.

O'Brien, Mark S., ed. Pediatric Neurological Surgery. LC 78-3005. (Seminars in Neurological Surgery Ser.). 1978. 26.00 (ISBN 0-89004-178-4). Raven.

O'Brien, Maureen. Communications & Relationships in Nursing. 2nd ed. LC 77-26260. (Illus.). 1978. pap. text ed. 9.50 (ISBN 0-8016-3700-7). Mosby.

O'Brien, Michael. Blue Springs: Poems. LC 74-34538. 1976. pap. 4.00 (ISBN 0-915342-06-5). SUN.

O'Brien, Michael J. & Mason, Roger D. A Late Formative Irrigation Settlement Below Monte Alban: Survey & Excavation on the Xoxocotlan Piedmont, Oaxaca, Mexico. (Institute of Latin American Studies Special Publications). (Illus.). 266p. 1980. pap. 16.95x (ISBN 0-292-74628-8). U of Tex Pr.

O'Brien, Patrick & Keyder, Caglar. Economic Growth in Britain & France 1780-1914: Two Paths to the Twentieth Century. 1978. text ed. 27.50x (ISBN 0-04-330288-2). Allen Unwin.

O'Brien, Rae A., jt. auth. see Rowan, Richard L.

O'Brien, Raymond J. American Sublime: Landscape & Scenery of the Lower Hudson Valley. (Illus.). 336p. 1981. 19.95 (ISBN 0-686-69182-2). Columbia U Pr.

O'Brien, Richard. The Golden Age of Comic Books, 1937-1945. (Orig.). 1977. pap. 6.95 o.p. (ISBN 0-345-25535-6). Ballantine.

O'Brien, Richard J. & Drizd, Terence A. Basic Data on Spirometry in Adults Twenty-Five to Seventy-Four Years of Age: United States 1971-75. Cox, Klaudia, ed. (Ser. 11, No. 222). 50p. Date not set. pap. text ed. 1.75 (ISBN 0-8406-0205-7). Natl Ctr Health Stats.

O'Brien, Richard J., ed. Georgetown University Papers on Languages & Linguistics. Incl. No. 1. 127p. 1970 (ISBN 0-87840-051-6); No. 2. 95p. 1971 (ISBN 0-87840-052-4); No. 4. 1972. pap. (ISBN 0-87840-054-0); No. 5. 1972. pap. (ISBN 0-87840-055-9); No. 6. 1972. pap. (ISBN 0-87840-056-7); No. 7. 1973. pap. (ISBN 0-87840-057-5); No. 9. 1975. pap. (ISBN 0-87840-059-1); No. 11. 1975. pap. (ISBN 0-87840-061-3); No. 12. 1976. pap. (ISBN 0-87840-062-1); No. 13. 1976. pap. (ISBN 0-87840-063-X); No. 14. 1978. pap. (ISBN 0-87840-064-8). pap. 2.25 ea. o.p. Georgetown U Pr.

O'Brien, Richard M., jt. auth. see Simek, Thomas C.

O'Brien, Richard M., et al, eds. Industrial Behavior Modification: A Learning Based Approach to Industrial-Organizational Problems. (Pergamon General Psychology Ser.). 300p. Date not set. price not set (ISBN 0-08-025558-2). Pergamon.

O'Brien, Robert, jt. auth. see Lewis, Edward V.

O'Brien, Robert, jt. auth. see Thompson, Philip D.

O'Brien, Saliee. Night of the Scorpion. large type ed. pap. 1.50 o.p. (ISBN 0-425-03238-8). Berkley Pub.

O'Brien, Shirley. Child Abuse: A Crying Shame. LC 80-23708. 184p. 1980. 15.95x (ISBN 0-8425-1829-0). Brigham.

O'Brien, Tim. Going After Cacciato. 1979. pap. 2.25 o.s.i. (ISBN 0-440-12966-4). Dell.

O'Brien, W. D., Jr., jt. ed. see Dunn, F.

O'Brien, William. When We Were Boys. (Nineteenth Century Fiction Ser.: Ireland: Vol. 76). 556p. 1979. lib. bdg. 46.00 (ISBN 0-8240-3525-9). Garland Pub.

O'Brien-ffrench, Conrad. Delicate Mission. 250p. 1980. 29.75x (ISBN 0-7050-0062-1, Pub. by Skilton & Shaw England). State Mutual Bk.

O'Brine, Manning. No Earth for Foxes. 288p. 1975. 7.95 o.p. (ISBN 0-440-06208-X). Delacorte.

Obrink, Ulla. Hala Sultan Tekke Five. (Studies in Mediterranean Archaeology XLV: No. 5). (Orig.). 1979. pap. text ed. 42.00x (ISBN 91-85058-91-2). Humanities.

Obrist, Jurg. Fluffy: The Story of a Cat. LC 79-10446. (Illus.). 32p. (ps-3). 1981. PLB 11.95 (ISBN 0-689-30722-5). Atheneum.

Obrist, Paul A., et al, eds. Cardiovascular Psychophysiology: Current Issues in Response Mechanisms, Biofeedback & Methodology. LC 73-89517. 624p. (Orig.). 1974. 29.95x (ISBN 0-202-25116-0). Aldine Pub.

O'Broin, Leon. Dublin Castle & the 1916 Rising. LC 78-138554. 1971. 12.00 (ISBN 0-8147-6150-X). NYU Pr.

--Michael Collins. (Gill's Irish Lives Ser.). 156p. 1980. 20.00 (ISBN 0-7171-1076-1, Pub. by Gill & Macmillan Ireland); pap. 6.50 (ISBN 0-7171-0968-2). Irish Bk Ctr.

Obstfeld, Raymond. Dead Heat. 224p. (Orig.). 1981. pap. 2.25 (ISBN 0-441-14110-2). Charter Bks.

O'Buachalla, Seamas, ed. see Pearse, P. H.

O'Buachalla, Seamus, ed. see Pearse, Patrick.

Obudho, R. A. & El-Shakhs, Salah S., eds. Development of Urban Systems in Africa. LC 78-19766. 432p. 1979. 32.50 (ISBN 0-03-047066-8). Praeger.

Obudho, R. A., jt. ed. see Taylor, D. R.

Obukhova, Lydia. Daughter of Night: A Tale of Three Worlds. Ginsburg, Mirra, tr. from Rus. LC 73-22621. 176p. (gr. 9 up). 1974. 5.95g o.s.i. (ISBN 0-02-768500-4, 76850). Macmillan.

O'Byrne, Robert. Senior Golf. 1977. 10.95 (ISBN 0-87691-231-5). Winchester Pr.

O'Cain, Raymond K., jt. ed. see Davis, Boyd H.

O'Callaghan, Dorothy. Circles of Friends: Two Hundred New Ways to Make Friends in Washington D. C. LC 76-25316. 1981. pap. 4.00 (ISBN 0-914694-02-2). Mail Order.

--The Job Catalog: Where to Find That Creative Job in Washington D. C./Baltimore. 2nd ed. LC 80-83443. 1980. pap. 6.00 (ISBN 0-914694-05-7). Mail Order.

--Mail Order U. S. A. A Consumer's Guide to Over 2,000 Top Mail Order Catalogs in the United States & Canada. 3rd ed. LC 78-51830. 1981. pap. 7.00 (ISBN 0-914694-03-0). Mail Order.

O'Callaghan, Edmund B. List of Editions of the Holy Scriptures & Parts Thereof Printed in American Previous to 1860. LC 66-25690. 1966. Repr. of 1861 ed. 20.00 (ISBN 0-8103-3313-9). Gale.

O'Callaghan, J. C. History of the Irish Brigades in the Service of France. 674p. 1969. Repr. of 1870 ed. 35.00x (ISBN 0-7165-0068-X, Pub. by Irish Academic Pr Ireland). Biblio Dist.

O'Callaghan, Michael C. Unity in Theology: Lonergan's Framework for Theology in Its New Context. LC 80-8177. 596p. 1980. lib. bdg. 24.50 (ISBN 0-8191-1151-1); pap. text ed. 16.75 (ISBN 0-8191-1152-X). U Pr of Amer.

O'Callaghan, P. W. Building for Energy Conservation. 1978. text ed. 31.00 (ISBN 0-08-022120-3). Pergamon.

O'Callaghan, P. W., ed. Energy for Industry. LC 78-41102. (Illus.). 1979. text ed. 75.00 (ISBN 0-08-022704-X). Pergamon.

O Canainn, Tomas. Traditional Music in Ireland. (Illus.). 1978. pap. 10.00 (ISBN 0-7100-0021-9). Routledge & Kegan.

O'Case, Thomas. The Coward & the Hero of the Blue Dandenongs & Sonetone. 4.50 o.p. (ISBN 0-685-58657-X). Vantage.

O'Casey, Sean see Watson, E. Bradlee & Pressey, Benfield.

Occupational Therapy Dept. Christchurch Hospital. Managing with Arthritis: Aids & Advice for Coping with the Activities of Daily Living. 55p. 1980. 12.00x (ISBN 0-7233-0598-6, Pub. by Whitcoulls New Zealand). State Mutual Bk.

Ocean Affairs Board. Assessing Potential Ocean Pollutants. 1975. pap. 9.25 (ISBN 0-309-02325-4). Natl Acad Pr.

--International Marine Science Affairs. LC 74-183584. 104p. (Orig.). 1972. pap. text ed. 5.00 (ISBN 0-309-01937-0). Natl Acad Pr.

--Numerical Models of Ocean Circulation. LC 74-28404. vii, 364p. 1975. 25.50 o.p. (ISBN 0-309-02225-8). Natl Acad Pr.

--Petroleum in the Marine Environment. LC 74-18572. 1975. pap. 9.00 (ISBN 0-309-02311-4). Natl Acad Pr.

Ocean Affairs Board, National Research Council. U. S. Directory of Marine Scientists 1975. vii, 325p. 1975. pap. 6.50 (ISBN 0-309-02408-0). Natl Acad Pr.

Ocean Affairs Board, Natl. Research Council. Disposal in the Marine Environment: An Oceanographic Assessment. LC 76-1319. 1976. pap. 5.00 (ISBN 0-309-02446-3). Natl Acad Pr.

Ocean Science Board. Tropospheric Transport of Pollutants & Natural Substances to the Ocean. 1978. pap. 11.75 (ISBN 0-309-02735-7). Natl Acad Pr.

Ocean Sciences Board, National Research Council. Continental Margins: Geological & Geophysical Research Needs. pap. 16.25x (ISBN 0-309-02793-4). Natl Acad Pr.

--The Continuing Quest: Large Scale Ocean Science for the Future. (Orig.). 1979. pap. text ed. 7.25x (ISBN 0-309-02798-5). Natl Acad Pr.

Ochberg, Frank, ed. Victims of Terrorism. (Special Studies in National & International Terrorism). 1981. lib. bdg. 18.75x (ISBN 0-89158-463-3). Westview.

OCHE & Madnick, Myra E. Consumer Health Education: A Guide to Hospital-Based Programs. LC 79-90381. 1980. text ed. 17.95 (ISBN 0-913654-61-2). Nursing Res.

Ochia, Ei-Ichiro. Bioinorganic Chemistry: An Introduction. 1977. text ed. 25.95x o.p. (ISBN 0-205-05508-7). Allyn.

Ochiai, Hidy. The Essence of Self-Defense. 1979. 14.95 o.p. (ISBN 0-8092-7378-0); pap. 7.95 (ISBN 0-8092-7377-2). Contemp Bks.

Ochoa, Anna S. & Shuster, Susan K. Social Studies in the Mainstreamed Classroom, K-6. LC 80-12323. 1980. pap. 11.95 (ISBN 0-89994-242-3). Soc Sci Ed.

Ochs, Phil. War Is Over. 1971. pap. 3.95 o.s.i. (ISBN 0-02-074570-2, Collier). Macmillan.

Ochse, Orpha. History of the Organ in the United States. LC 73-22644. (Illus.). 512p. 1975. 22.50x (ISBN 0-253-32830-6). Ind U Pr.

Ochsenwald, William. The Hijaz Railroad. LC 80-10505. 1980. 14.95x (ISBN 0-8139-0825-6). U Pr of Va.

Ochsner, et al. Tobacco & Marijuana. 1976. perfect bdg. 6.95 (ISBN 0-88252-048-2). Paladin Hse.

Ockendon, J. R. & Hodgkins, W. R., eds. Moving Boundary Problems in Heat Flow & Diffusion: University of Oxford, Conference, March 25-27, 1974. (Illus.). 308p. 1975. 24.50x o.p. (ISBN 0-19-853345-4). Oxford U Pr.

Ockenga, Harold J. Women Who Made Bible History. 1971. pap. 5.95 (ISBN 0-310-30461-X). Zondervan.

Ockerman, Herbert W. Source Book for Food Scientists. (Illus.). 1978. lib. bdg. 79.50 (ISBN 0-87055-228-7). AVI.

O'Clery, Helen. Atlantis. (Pegasus Books: No. 29). (Illus.). 192p. 1971. 10.50x (ISBN 0-234-77358-8). Intl Pubns Serv.

--East Africa. (Pegasus Books: No. 32). (Illus.). 184p. 1972. 10.50x (ISBN 0-234-77680-3). Intl Pubns Serv.

--Egypt. LC 79-436011. (Pegasus Books: No. 17). (Illus.). 185p. 1968. 7.50x (ISBN 0-234-77155-0). Intl Pubns Serv.

--Nile. LC 76-512551. (Pegasus Books: No. 30). (Illus.). 1970. 7.50x (ISBN 0-234-77483-5). Intl Pubns Serv.

O'Collins, Gerald. Fundamental Theology. LC 80-82809. 288p. (Orig.). 1981. pap. 6.95 (ISBN 0-8091-2347-9). Paulist Pr.

--What Are They Saying About Jesus? LC 77-70640. 1977. pap. 2.45 (ISBN 0-8091-2017-8). Paulist Pr.

--What Are They Saying About the Resurrection? LC 78-51594. 1978. pap. 2.45 (ISBN 0-8091-2109-3). Paulist Pr.

O'Connell, A., jt. auth. see O'Connell, V.

O'Connell, April & O'Connell, Vincent. Choice & Change: Psychology of Adjustment, Growth & Creativity. rev. ed. (Illus.). 1980. pap. text ed. 14.95 (ISBN 0-13-133066-7); study guide & wrk bk 5.95 (ISBN 0-13-133082-9). P-H.

O'Connell, C. B. Home Furnishing Self Help. LC 68-12618. 1968. 10.00 (ISBN 0-8108-0180-9). Scarecrow.

O'Connell, Cornelius J., ed. Laboratory Diagnosis of Infectious Disease: A Guide for Clinicians. 1980 ed. LC 80-16360. 1980. pap. 12.50 (ISBN 0-87488-965-0). Med Exam.

O'Connell, D. P. The Influence of Law on Sea Power. LC 75-21922. 1976. 15.50x (ISBN 0-87021-834-4). Naval Inst Pr.

O'Connell, Daniel P. State Succession in Municipal Law & International Law, 2 Vols. (Cambridge Studies in International & Comparative Law). 1967. Vol. 1. 85.00 (ISBN 0-521-05857-0); Vol. 2. 75.00 (ISBN 0-521-05858-9). Cambridge U Pr.

O'Connell, David. The Instructions of Saint Louis: A Critical Text. (Romance Language Ser.). 104p. 1980. pap. 8.00 (ISBN 0-8078-9216-5). U of NC Pr.

--Louis-Ferdinand Celine. LC 76-26059. (World Author Ser: France: No. 416). 1976. lib. bdg. 12.50 (ISBN 0-8057-6256-6). Twayne.

O'Connell, Desmond H. Aim for a Job in the Bakery Industry. LC 71-114139. (Career Guidance Ser). 1971. pap. 3.50 (ISBN 0-668-02227-2). Arco.

O'Connell, Edward J., et al. Self-Assessment of Current Knowledge in Pediatric Allergy. LC 79-91200. 1980. pap. 18.00 (ISBN 0-87488-238-9). Med Exam.

O'Connell, F. J. Batsford Fide Chess Yearbook, 1975-1976. 159p. 1976. 16.95 (ISBN 0-7134-1223-2). David & Charles.

O'Connell, Jeffrey & Simon, Rita J. Payment for Pain & Suffering: Who Wants What, When & Why? 1972. 10.00 o.p. (ISBN 0-88245-013-1). Merritt Co.

O'Connell, John J., jt. auth. see Soderman, Harry.

O'Connell, Julie, jt. ed. see Acheson, Sam.

O'Connell, K. J. Batsford Fide Chess Yearbook, 1976-1977. 1977. 16.95 (ISBN 0-7134-0675-5). David & Charles.

--Batsford Fide Chess Yearbook, 1977-1978. 1978. 16.95 (ISBN 0-7134-1223-2). David & Charles.

--Spanish (Ruy Lopez) Open. 1978. pap. 15.95 (ISBN 0-7134-0248-2, Pub. by Batsford England). David & Charles.

O'Connell, K. J. & Adams, J. B. Games of Anatoly Karpov. 1974. 19.95 (ISBN 0-7134-2849-X). David & Charles.

O'Connell, K. J. & Levy, David. Anatoly Karpov's Games As World Champion Nineteen Seventy-Five to Nineteen Seventy-Seven. 1978. pap. 16.95 (ISBN 0-7134-0227-X, Pub. by Batsford England). David & Charles.

O'Connell, K. J., jt. auth. see Wade, Robert.

O'Connell, K. J., et al. Complete Games of World Champion Karpov. 1976. pap. 18.95 (ISBN 0-7134-3141-5, Pub. by Batsford England). David & Charles.

O'Connell, Kevin J., jt. auth. see Fraenkel, Heinrich.

O'Connell, Lily H., et al. Nutrition in a Changing World. (Illus.). 152p. (Orig.). (gr. 5). 1981. pap. text ed. 11.95 (ISBN 0-8425-1916-5). Brigham.

O'Connell, M. R. Thomas Stapleton & the Counter Reformation. 1964. 29.50x (ISBN 0-685-69850-5). Elliots Bks.

O'Connell, Margaret. The Magic Cauldron: Witchcraft for Good & Evil. LC 75-26757. (Illus.). 256p. (gr. 9-12). 1975. 10.95 (ISBN 0-87599-187-4). S G Phillips.

O'Connell, Marie H. Helping the Child to Use Foster Family Care. 39p. 1953. pap. 2.45 o.p. (ISBN 0-87868-046-2, E-10). Child Welfare.

O'Connell, Marvin R. Counter Reformation: Fifteen Fifty-Nine to Sixteen Ten. Langer, William L., ed. LC 73-14278. (The Rise of Modern Europe Ser.). (Illus.). 408p. (YA) 1974. 15.00x o.s.i. (ISBN 0-06-013233-7, HarpT). Har-Row.

O'Connell, Matthew, tr. see Belo, Fernando.

O'Connell, Matthew J., tr. see Hamelin, Leonce.

O'Connell, Matthew J., tr. see Von Allmen, et al.

O'Connell, Matthew J., et al, trs. see Horkheimer, Max.

O'Connell, Merrilyn, jt. ed. see Rath, Frederick L., Jr.

O'Connell, Merrilyn R., jt. auth. see Rath, Frederick L.

O'Connell, Peadar. Proud Island. 2nd ed. 1975. 3.95 o.p. (ISBN 0-686-23687-4); pap. 3.95 o.p. (ISBN 0-905140-28-1). Irish Bk Ctr.

O'Connell, Robert F. The Marine Aquarium. 1973. 4.95 o.p. (ISBN 0-8200-0110-4, SL488, ScribT). Scribner.

O'Connell, Robert J. Saint Augustine's Early Theory of Man, A. D. 386-391. LC 68-21981. 1968. text ed. 16.50x (ISBN 0-674-78520-7, Belknap Pr). Harvard U Pr.

O'Connell, Sandra E. The Manager As Communicator. 1980. text ed. 13.95 (ISBN 0-06-044881-4, HarpC). Har-Row.

O'Connell, Timothy E. Principles for a Catholic Morality. 1978. 11.95 (ISBN 0-8164-0404-6). Crossroad NY.

--Principles for a Catholic Morality. 256p. 1980. pap. 7.95 (ISBN 0-8164-2031-9). Crossroad NY.

O'Connell, V. & O'Connell, A. Choice & Change: An Introduction to the Psychology of Growth. 1974. pap. 12.95 o.p. (ISBN 0-13-133165-5); wkbk. 5.95 o.p. (ISBN 0-13-133140-X). P-H.

O'Connell, Vincent, jt. auth. see O'Connell, April.

O'Conner, J. Paul, jt. auth. see Batalden, Paul B.

O'Conner, John. Introducing Relief Printing. LC 72-2115. 128p. 1973. 9.95 o.p. (ISBN 0-8230-6299-6). Watson-Guptill.

O'Conner, William E. An Introduction to Airline Economics. LC 77-7809. (Praeger Special Studies). 1978. 18.95 (ISBN 0-03-022416-0). Praeger.

O'Connor, tr. see Chukovsky, Kornei.

O'Connor, A. M. An Economic Geography of East Africa. (Advanced Economic Geography Ser.). 1971. lib. bdg. 24.00x (ISBN 0-7135-1626-7). Westview.

--Urbanization in Tropical Africa, Nineteen Sixty to Nineteen Seventy-Nine: An Annotated Bibliography. (Reference Bks.). 1981. lib. bdg. 48.00 (ISBN 0-8161-8262-0). G K Hall.

O'Connor, Anne, jt. ed. see Clarke, D. V.

O'Connor, Anthony M. The Geography of Tropical African Development: A Study of Spatial Patterns of Economic Change Since Independence. 2nd ed. LC 77-30470. 1978. text ed. 30.00 (ISBN 0-08-021847-4); pap. text ed. 11.25 (ISBN 0-08-021848-2). Pergamon.

O'Connor, B. A., jt. auth. see McDowell, D. M.

O'Connor, Brian. The One-Shot War. 1981. 9.95 (ISBN 0-8129-0939-9). Times Bks.

O'Connor, D. J., jt. ed. see Langford, Glenn.

O'Connor, Daniel & Jimenez, Jacques. The Images of Jesus: Exploring the Metaphors in Matthew's Gospel. (Orig.). 1977. pap. 6.95 o.p. (ISBN 0-03-021326-6). Winston Pr.

O'Connor, Daniel J. Aquinas & Natural Law. (New Studies in Ethics Series). (Orig.). 1969. pap. 4.95 (ISBN 0-312-04690-1). St Martin.

O'Connor, Daniel J., ed. Critical History of Western Philosophy. LC 64-13242. 1964. text ed. 19.95 (ISBN 0-02-923260-0). Free Pr.

O'Connor, Daniel J. One Hundred One Patented Solar Energy Uses. 96p. 1980. pap. 8.95 (ISBN 0-442-24432-0). Van Nos Reinhold.

O'Connor, Del, jt. ed. see DeMaroo, Cettie.

O'Connor, Dennis J. & Bueso, Alberto T. Managerial Finance: Theory & Techniques. (Illus.). 528p. 1981. text ed. 21.00 (ISBN 0-13-550269-1); pap. 8.95 study guide (ISBN 0-13-550293-4). P-H.

--A Self-Correcting Approach to Managerial Finance: Theory & Techniques. (Illus.). 320p. 1981. pap. text ed. 9.95 (ISBN 0-13-803189-4). P-H.

O'Connor, Dick. Foul Play. (Sportellers Ser.). (Illus.). 64p. (gr. 5 up). 1981. PLB 7.95 (ISBN 0-516-02263-6). Childrens.

--Reggie Jackson: Yankee Superstar. (gr. 4-6). 1978. pap. 1.25 (ISBN 0-590-05396-5, Schol Pap). Schol Bk Serv.

O'Connor, Edmund. Darwin. Yapp, Malcolm, et al, eds. (World History Ser.). (Illus.). 32p. (gr. 10). 1980. Repr. of 1977 ed. lib. bdg. 5.95 (ISBN 0-89908-047-2); pap. text ed. 1.95 (ISBN 0-89908-022-7). Greenhaven.

--Education. Yapp, Malcolm & O'Connor, Edmund, eds. (World History Ser.). (Illus.). 32p. (gr. 10). 1980. Repr. of 1977 ed. lib. bdg. 5.95 (ISBN 0-89908-147-9); pap. text ed. 1.95 (ISBN 0-89908-122-3). Greenhaven.

--Japan's Modernization. Yapp, Malcolm & Killingray, Marget, eds. (World History Ser.). (Illus.). (gr. 10). 1980. Repr. of 1977 ed. lib. bdg. 5.95 (ISBN 0-89908-232-7); pap. text ed. 1.95 (ISBN 0-89908-207-6). Greenhaven.

--Roosevelt. Yapp, Malcolm & Killingray, Margaret, eds. (World History Ser.). (Illus.). 32p. (gr. 10). 1980. lib. bdg. 5.95 (ISBN 0-89908-125-8); pap. text ed. 1.95 (ISBN 0-89908-100-2). Greenhaven.

--The Wealth of Japan. Yapp, Malcolm, et al, eds. (World History Ser.). (Illus.). 32p. (gr. 10). 1980. Repr. of 1977 ed. lib. bdg. 5.95 (ISBN 0-89908-237-8); pap. text ed. 1.95 (ISBN 0-89908-212-2). Greenhaven.

O'Connor, Edmund, ed. see Doncaster, Islay.

O'Connor, Edmund, ed. see Killingray, David.

O'Connor, Edmund, ed. see Killingray, Margaret.

O'Connor, Edmund, ed. see O'Connor, Edmund.

O'Connor, Edmund, ed. see Read, James & Yapp, Malcolm.

O'Connor, Edmund, ed. see Yapp, Malcolm.

O'Connor, Edward D. Pentecostal Movement in the Catholic Church. LC 70-153878. (Illus.). 304p. 1971. pap. 2.45 (ISBN 0-87793-035-X). Ave Maria.

O'Connor, Finbarr W., jt. ed. see Klockars, Carl B.

O'Connor, Flannery. The Complete Stories. 555p. 1971. 17.50 (ISBN 0-374-12752-2); pap. 6.95 (ISBN 0-374-51536-0). FS&G.

--Everything That Rises Must Converge. 269p. 1965. 10.00 (ISBN 0-374-15012-5); pap. 4.95 (ISBN 0-374-50464-4, N287). FS&G.

--Three by Flannery O'Connor: Wise Blood, the Violent Bear It Away, a Good Man Is Hard to Find. 1980. pap. 2.50 (ISBN 0-451-09251-1, E9251, Sig). NAL.

--Wise Blood. 232p. 1962. 10.95 (ISBN 0-374-29128-4); pap. 5.95 (ISBN 0-374-50584-5). FS&G.

O'Connor, Francine M. & Boswell, Kathryn. The ABC's of Faith, 2 bks. (gr. 1-4). 1979. Bk. 1. pap. 1.50 (ISBN 0-89243-113-X); Bk. 2. pap. 1.50 (ISBN 0-89243-114-8). Liguori Pubns.

O'Connor, Frank. The Little Monasteries. 48p. 1976. pap. text ed. 2.75x (ISBN 0-85105-296-7, Dolmen Pr). Humanities.

--Stories of Frank O'Connor. (YA) 1952. 10.00 o.p. (ISBN 0-394-44732-8). Knopf.

O'Connor, Frank & Hunt, Hugh. The Invincibles. (Abbey Theatre Ser.). pap. 2.95 (ISBN 0-912262-67-2). Proscenium.

O'Connor, G. Richard, jt. auth. see Silverstein, Arthur M.

O'Connor, Hyla. Miracle Microwave Cookbook. (Illus.). 160p. 1976. pap. 4.95 o.p. (ISBN 0-89104-044-7). A & W Pubs.

O'Connor, J. F. The Banking Crisis & Recovery Under the Roosevelt Administration. LC 73-171696. (FDR & the Era of the New Deal Ser.). 168p. 1971. Repr. of 1938 ed. lib. bdg. 20.00 (ISBN 0-306-70366-1). Da Capo.

O'Connor, Jack. Complete Book of Rifles & Shotguns. rev. ed. LC 61-6454. (Illus.). 1966. 12.50 o.p. (ISBN 0-06-071351-8, HarpT). Har-Row.

--Hunting Rifle. (Illus.). 1970. 12.95 (ISBN 0-87691-007-X). Winchester Pr.

--Sheep & Sheep Hunting. 1974. 12.95 (ISBN 0-87691-145-9). Winchester Pr.

O'Connor, James & Hart, Norman A., eds. Practice of Advertising. 1978. pap. 16.50x (ISBN 0-434-90362-0). Intl Ideas.

O'Connor, John & Brown, Lorraine. Free, Adult, Uncensored: The Living History of the Federal Theatre Project. LC 78-9292. (Illus.). 1978. 24.95 o.p. (ISBN 0-915220-37-7); pap. 11.95 o.p. (ISBN 0-915220-38-5). New Republic.

O'Connor, John E. William Paterson: Lawyer & Statesman, 1745-1806. 1979. 23.50 (ISBN 0-8135-0880-0). Rutgers U Pr.

O'Connor, John J. Amadis De Gaule & Its Influence on Elizabethan Literature. LC 76-96031. 1970. 21.00 (ISBN 0-8135-0622-0). Rutgers U Pr.

O'Connor, John T. Negotiator Out of Season: The Career of Wilhelm Egon von Furstenberg (1629-1704) LC 77-23872. 272p. 1978. 20.00x (ISBN 0-8203-0436-0). U of Ga Pr.

O'Connor, Katherine H. The Dot Book for Visual Perception Training. (Illus.). 28p. (gr. k-2). 1972. wkbk 0.60 (ISBN 0-910812-08-X). Johnny Reads.

--My First Writing Book: Manuscript Writing. rev ed. (Illus.). 57p. (gr. k-3). 1972. wkbk 1.00 (ISBN 0-910812-07-1). Johnny Reads.

--Read & Do: Learning to Follow Written Directions. rev. & enl. ed. (Illus.). 51p. (gr. 1-2). 1973. wkbk 1.00 (ISBN 0-910812-09-8). Johnny Reads.

--Removing Roadblocks in Reading. new ed. LC 72-96305. (Illus.). 200p. 1976. text ed. 12.95 (ISBN 0-910812-10-1); pap. text ed. 8.75 (ISBN 0-910812-11-X). Johnny Reads.

O'Connor, Len. Requiem: The Decline & Demise of Mayor Daley & His Era. 1978. pap. 3.95 o.p. (ISBN 0-8092-7409-4). Contemp Bks.

O'Connor, Maeve. The Scientist As Editor: Guidelines for Editors of Books & Journals. LC 78-60428. 218p. 1979. 14.50 (ISBN 0-471-04932-8, Pub. by Wiley Medical). Wiley.

O'Connor, Mariell. Born to Be Hurt. Date not set. 6.95 (ISBN 0-8062-1685-9). Carlton.

O'Connor, Maureen. First Steps in the Kitchen. (Illus.). 1971. 3.95 o.p. (ISBN 0-571-09338-8, Pub. by Faber & Faber). Merrimack Bk Serv.

O'Connor, Michael J. Origins of Academic Economics in the United States. (The Neglected American Economists Ser.). 1974. lib. bdg. 50.00 (ISBN 0-8240-1036-1). Garland Pub.

O'Connor, N. Language, Cognitive Deficits, and Retardation. 376p. 1975. 33.95 (ISBN 0-407-00007-0). Butterworths.

O'Connor, N., jt. auth. see Hermelin, B.

O'Connor, N., ed. Present Day Russian Psychology. 1967. 25.00 (ISBN 0-08-012099-7); pap. 12.75 (ISBN 0-08-012098-9). Pergamon.

O'Connor, P. J., jt. auth. see Kavanaugh, Patrick.

Oconnor, Patricia W. Gregorio & Maria Martinez Sierra. (World Authors Ser.: Spain: No. 412). 1977. lib. bdg. 12.50 (ISBN 0-8057-6252-3). Twayne.

O'Connor, Patricia W., ed. see Buero Vallejo, A.

O'Connor, Patrick. Black Tiger at Le Mans. (gr. 5-8). 1967. pap. 0.95 o.p. (ISBN 0-425-03513-1, Highland). Berkley Pub.

--Into the Strong City. 1979. 16.95 (ISBN 0-241-10065-8, Pub. by Hamish Hamilton England). David & Charles.

O'Connor, Patrick J. Retailing. LC 79-54049. (Marketing Distribution Ser.). 352p. 1981. pap. 9.20 (ISBN 0-8273-1777-8); instr's. guide 1.45 (ISBN 0-8273-1778-6). Delmar.

O'Connor, Peter D., jt. auth. see Wyne, Marvin D.

O'Connor, Philip F. Stealing Home. 288p. 1981. pap. 2.75 (ISBN 0-345-28478-X). Ballantine.

O'Connor, Raymond G. War, Diplomacy, & History: Papers & Reviews. LC 79-88951. 1979. pap. text ed. 11.25 (ISBN 0-8191-0790-5). U Pr of Amer.

O'Connor, Richard C., ed. Immunologic Diseases of the Mucous Membranes: Pathology, Diagnosis, & Treatment. LC 80-82050. (Illus.). 176p. 1980. 29.50 (ISBN 0-89352-102-7). Masson Pub.

O'Connor, Rochelle. Company Planning Meetings, Report No. 788. (Illus.). v, 50p. (Orig.). 1980. pap. 15.00 (ISBN 0-8237-0224-3). Conference Bd.

O'Connor, Rod. La Quimica. 1976. text ed. 12.00 (ISBN 0-06-316600-3, IntlDept). Har-Row.

O'Connor, Rod, jt. ed. see Birdwhistell, Ralph K.

O'Connor, Ulick. Life Styles. 1973. pap. text ed. 3.00x (ISBN 0-85105-250-9, Dolmen Pr). Humanities.

O'Connor, Vincent F. Mathematics at the Farm. LC 77-19169. (Raintree Mathematics Ser.). (Illus.). (gr. k-3). 1978. PLB 8.95 (ISBN 0-8393-0055-7). Raintree Child.

--Mathematics in Buildings. LC 77-19158. (Raintree Mathematics Ser.). (Illus.). (gr. k-3). 1978. PLB 8.95 (ISBN 0-8393-0053-0). Raintree Child.

--Mathematics in the Circus Ring. LC 77-19168. (Raintree Mathematics Ser.). (Illus.). (gr. k-3). 1978. PLB 8.95 (ISBN 0-8393-0056-5). Raintree Child.

--Mathematics in the Kitchen. LC 77-19160. (Raintree Mathematics Ser.). (Illus.). (gr. k-3). 1978. PLB 8.95 (ISBN 0-8393-0054-9). Raintree Child.

--Mathematics in the Toy Store. LC 77-19155. (Raintree Mathematics Ser.). (Illus.). (gr. k-3). 1978. PLB 8.95 (ISBN 0-8393-0052-2). Raintree Child.

--Mathematics on the Playground. LC 77-19180. (Raintree Mathematics Ser.). (Illus.). (gr. k-3). 1978. PLB 8.95 (ISBN 0-8393-0051-4). Raintree Child.

O'Connor, William V. Joyce Cary. LC 66-19552. (Columbia Essays on Modern Writers Ser.: No. 16). (Orig.). 1966. pap. 2.00 (ISBN 0-231-02680-3, MW16). Columbia U Pr.

O'Connor, William V., ed. Seven Modern American Novelists: An Introduction. LC 64-18175. (Library on American Writers: No. 1). 1964. 15.00x (ISBN 0-8166-0327-8). U of Minn Pr.

O'Cork, Shannon. Sports Freak. 1980. 8.95 (ISBN 0-312-75331-4). St Martin.

O'Corrain, Donncha. Ireland Before the Normans. (Gill History of Ireland: Vol. 2). (Illus.). 222p. 1972. pap. 6.95 (ISBN 0-7171-0559-8). Irish Bk Ctr.

Ocran, A. K. Politics of the Sword: A Personal Memoir on Military Involvement in Ghana & of Problems of Military Government. 167p. 1977. 16.50x (ISBN 0-8476-3101-X). Rowman.

Ocran, Emanuel B. Ocran's Acronyms: A Dictionary of Abbreviations & Acronyms Used in Scientific & Technical Writing. 1978. 25.00 (ISBN 0-7100-8869-8). Routledge & Kegan.

--Scientific & Technical Series: A Select Bibliography. LC 72-10880. 1973. 20.50 (ISBN 0-8108-0566-9). Scarecrow.

Ocvirk, Fred W., jt. auth. see Mabie, Hamilton H.

Ocvirk, Otto G. & Bone, Robert O. Art Fundamentals: Theory & Practice. 4th ed. 225p. 1981. pap. text ed. write for info. (ISBN 0-697-03232-9). Wm C Brown.

Oda, Mayumi. Goddesses: Silkscreen Prints by Mayumi Oda. (Lancaster-Miller Art Ser.). (Illus.). 100p. 1981. 9.95 (ISBN 0-89581-010-7). Lancaster-Miller.

Oda, S. International Law of the Resources of the Sea. 144p. 1980. Repr. 17.50 (ISBN 90-286-0399-9). Sijthoff & Noordhoff.

Odabasi, H., jt. auth. see Condon, E. U.

O'Daffer, P. & Clemens, S. Geometry: An Investigative Approach. new ed. (Grades 10-11). 1976. pap. text ed. 19.25 (ISBN 0-201-05420-5, Sch Div); tchrs. ed. 5.80 (ISBN 0-201-05421-3); wkbk. 2.75 (ISBN 0-201-05422-1). A-W.

O'Daffer, Phares G., jt. auth. see Eicholz, Robert E.

O'Daffer, Phares G. see Eicholz, Robert E., et al.

Odagiri, Hiroyuki. The Theory of Growth in a Corporate Economy: Management Preference, Research & Development & Economic Growth. LC 80-23494. (Illus.). 256p. Date not set. price not set (ISBN 0-521-23132-9). Cambridge U Pr.

Odajnyk, Volodymyr Walter. Jung & Politics: The Political & Social Ideas of C. G. Jung. LC 76-55153. 1976. 12.00x (ISBN 0-8147-6154-2). NYU Pr.

O'Day, Anita & Eells, George. High Times, Hard Times. 320p. 1981. 12.95 (ISBN 0-399-12505-1). Putnam.

O'Day, D. H. & Horgen, P. A., eds. Sexual Interactions in Eukaryotic Microbes. LC 80-39593. (Cell Biology Ser.). 1981. 45.00 (ISBN 0-12-524160-7). Acad Pr.

O'Day, Rosemary. The English Clergy: The Emergence & Consolidation of a Profession, 1558-1642. 1979. text ed. 31.25x (ISBN 0-7185-1167-0, Leicester). Humanities.

O'Day, Rosemary & Heal, Felicity. Princes & Paupers in the English Church. 1981. 27.50x (ISBN 0-389-20200-2). B&N.

O'Day, Rosemary & Heal, Felicity, eds. Continuity & Change: Personnel & Administration of the Church in England, 1500-1642. 300p. 1976. text ed. 21.00x (ISBN 0-7185-1138-7, Leicester). Humanities.

Odd, Gilbert. Ali, the Fighting Prophet. 1975. 8.95 o.p. (ISBN 0-7207-0845-1, Pub. by Michael Joseph). Merrimack Bk Serv.

Oddo, Vincent. Playing & Teaching the Strings. 208p. 1979. pap. text ed. 14.95x (ISBN 0-534-00614-0). Wadsworth Pub.

Oddy, Ray, et al, eds. World Energy Book: A-Z Atlas & Statistical Source Book. LC 78-50805. 1978. 27.50x (ISBN 0-89397-032-8). Nichols Pub.

O'Dea, Barbara. The Once & Future Church. LC 80-82554. 96p. (Orig.). 1980. pap. 4.95 (ISBN 0-934134-08-1, Celebration Bks). Natl Cath Reporter.

O'Dea, D. J. Cyclical Indicators for the Post War British Economy. LC 75-2738. (National Institute of Economic & Social Research, Occasional Papers Ser.: No. 28). (Illus.). 180p. 1975. 19.95x (ISBN 0-521-09963-3). Cambridge U Pr.

Odegaard, Charles E. Area Health Education Centers: The Pioneering Years, 1972-1978. LC 79-56245. (Carnegie Council on Policy Studies in Higher Education). 124p. 1980. pap. 5.00 (ISBN 0-295-95787-5). U of Wash Pr.

--Eleven Area Health Education Centers: The View from the Grass Roots. LC 80-50250. (Carnegie Council on Policy Studies in Higher Education). (Illus.). 808p. (Orig.). 1980. pap. 20.00 (ISBN 0-295-95748-4, Pub. by Carnegie Coun Policy). U of Wash Pr.

Odegard, Holtan P. The Planning Audit: A Framework with Special References to River Basin Planning. 1974. 9.00 o.p. (ISBN 0-9600524-2-9). Advance Planning.

--Sin & Science: Reinhold Niebuhr As Political Theologian. 245p. 1956. 13.00 (ISBN 0-9600524-1-0). Advance Planning.

Odegard, Warren W., jt. auth. see Bender, Roger J.

Odel, T. H. Ferromagnetodynamics: The Dynamics of Magnetic Bubbles Domains & Domain Walls. 232p. 1981. 54.95 (ISBN 0-470-27084-5). Halsted Pr.

O'Dell, Andrew C. & Richards, Peter S. Railways & Geography. 2nd rev. ed. 1971. pap. text ed. 6.25x (ISBN 0-09-106801-0, Hutchinson U Lib). Humanities.

O'Dell, Bob. Aerobatics Today. (Illus.). 224p. 1980. 12.95 (ISBN 0-312-00759-0). St Martin.

O'Dell, Marie W. Charles & Mary Stories. 1981. 4.95 (ISBN 0-8062-1582-8). Carlton.

Odell, P. R. & Van Der Knapp, Bert. Economic Geography of Western Europe. 1980. write for info. (ISBN 0-06-318087-1, IntlDept). Har-Row.

Odell, Patrick, jt. auth. see Gray, Henry L.

Odell, Peter R. British Oil Policy: A Radical Alternative. 75p. 1980. 35.00x (ISBN 0-85038-316-1). Nichols Pub.

Odell, Peter R. & Rosing, Kenneth E. Future of Oil: A Simulation Study of the Interrelationships of Resources, Reserves, & Use 1980-2080. 300p. 1980. 47.50x (ISBN 0-89397-097-2). Nichols Pub.

O'Dell, Scott. Carlota. LC 77-9468. (gr. 5-9). 1977. 10.95 (ISBN 0-395-25487-6). HM.

--Island of the Blue Dolphins. (gr. 7 up). 1960. 7.95 (ISBN 0-395-06962-9). HM.

--Kathleen, Please Come Home. (gr. 6-12). 1980. pap. 1.50 (ISBN 0-440-94283-7, LFL). Dell.

--Sing Down the Moon. LC 71-98513. (gr. 5 up). 1970. 9.95 (ISBN 0-395-10919-1). HM.

O'Dell, T. H. Magnetic Bubbles. LC 74-12048. 159p. 1974. 34.95 (ISBN 0-470-65259-4). Halsted Pr.

Oden, Chet & MacDonald, W. Scott. Moose: A Very Special Person. 1978. pap. 3.95 o.p. (ISBN 0-03-043936-1). Winston Pr.

Oden, Clifford. Thank God I Have Cancer! LC 76-9824. 1976. 7.95 o.p. (ISBN 0-87000-362-3). Arlington Hse.

Oden, J. T. & Reddy, J. N. An Introduction to the Mathematical Theory of Finite Elements. LC 76-6953. (Pure & Applied Mathematics Ser.). 429p. 1976. 35.00 (ISBN 0-471-65261-X, Pub. by Wiley-Interscience). Wiley.

Oden, J. T., ed. see International Conference on Computational Methods in Nonlinear Mechanics, 2nd, Univ. of Texas at Austin.

Oden, Robert A., Jr. Studies in Lucian's De Syria Dea. LC 76-54988. (Harvard Semitic Monograph). (Illus.). 1977. pap. 7.50 (ISBN 0-89130-123-2, 040015). Scholars Pr Ca.

Oden, Thomas C., et al. After Therapy What? (Illus.). 224p. 1974. text ed. 16.75 (ISBN 0-398-03105-3). C C Thomas.

Oderman, Stuart, jt. auth. see Diamond, Bernard.

Odian, George. Principles of Poly Merization. 2nd ed. 700p. 1981. 27.50 (ISBN 0-471-05146-2, Pub. by Wiley-Interscience). Wiley.

--Principles of Polymerization. LC 78-78958. (Illus.). 1970. 42.50 o.p. (ISBN 0-07-047585-7, P&RB). McGraw.

Odievre, Michel, jt. auth. see Alagille, Daniel.

Odin, Dexter, jt. auth. see Odin, Paula.

Odin, Paula & Odin, Dexter. Yachtsman's Legal Guide to Co-Ownership. 1981. 10.00 (ISBN 0-686-69463-5). De Graff.

Odinga, Oginga. Not Yet Uhuru. (African Writers Ser.). 1968. pap. text ed. 7.95x (ISBN 0-435-90038-2). Heinemann Ed.

Odiorne, George S. The Change Resisters: How They Prevent Progress & What Managers Can Do About Them. (Illus.). 304p. 1981. 16.95 (ISBN 0-13-127902-5, Spec); pap. 7.95 (ISBN 0-13-127894-0). P-H.

Odiorne, George S. Green Power: The Corporation & the Urban Crisis. 208p. text ed. 22.50 (ISBN 0-8290-0290-1); pap. text ed. 12.95 (ISBN 0-8290-0291-X). Irvington.

--MBO II: A System of Managerial Leadership for the 80's. LC 78-72336. 1979. 16.95 (ISBN 0-8224-0977-1). Pitman Learning.

--Plaid for Personnel Administration. 1973. pap. 5.50 (ISBN 0-256-01287-3, 08-0864-00). Learning Syst.

Odlozilik, Otakar. The Hussite King: Bohemia in European Affairs, 1440-1471. 1965. 22.00 (ISBN 0-8135-0497-X). Rutgers U Pr.

Odmark, John. Language, Literature & Meaning Two: Literary Theory & Criticism in Poland, Hungary & Czechoslovakia II: Current Trends in Literary Research. (Linguistic & Literary Studies in Eastern Europe: No. 2). 1980. text ed. 51.50x (ISBN 0-391-01281-9). Humanities.

Odo of Deuil. De Profectione Ludovici VII in Orienteni: The Journey of Louis the Seventh to the East. Berry, Virginia G., ed. & tr. 1965. pap. 5.95x (ISBN 0-393-09662-9). Norton.

O'Doherty, Brian, ed. Museums in Crisis. LC 79-183186. (Illus.). 192p. 1972. 6.95 o.s.i. (ISBN 0-8076-0629-4). Braziller.

O'Doherty, E. F. The Religious Formation of the Adolescent. LC 73-12969. 109p. 1973. pap. 2.95 o.p. (ISBN 0-8189-0280-9). Alba.

O'Doherty, Neil. Atlas of the Newborn. LC 78-70614. (Illus.). 1979. text ed. 34.00 (ISBN 0-685-99716-2). Lippincott.

Odom, Clark, jt. auth. see Gregorich, Barbara.

Odom, Keith C. Henry Green. (English Authors Ser.: No. 235). 1978. lib. bdg. 9.95 (ISBN 0-8057-6706-1). Twayne.

O'Donaill. Foclair Gaeilge Bearla (Irish-English Dictionary) 30.00x (ISBN 0-686-28280-9). Colton Bk.

Odoni, A., jt. auth. see Larson, R.

O'Donnell. Practice of Real Estate. 1978. 17.95 (ISBN 0-7216-6913-1). Dryden Pr.

--Principles of Real Estate. 576p. 1975. 19.95 (ISBN 0-7216-6911-5). Dryden Pr.

O'Donnell, C. P., jt. ed. see Roche, Thomas P., Jr.

O'Donnell, Elizabeth L., jt. auth. see Manoni, Mary H.

O'Donnell, Harold K. & Weihrich, Heinz. Management: A Book of Readings. 5th ed. (Illus.). 736p. text ed. 18.95x (ISBN 0-07-035418-9); pap. 14.95x (ISBN 0-07-035417-0). McGraw.

O'Donnell, James H., 3rd. Southern Indians in the American Revolution. LC 76-146662. 176p. 1973. 10.50x (ISBN 0-87049-131-8). U of Tenn Pr.

O'Donnell, James J. Cassiodorus. LC 77-93470. 1979. 20.00x (ISBN 0-520-03646-8). U of Cal Pr.

--Fire: Its Many Faces & Moods. LC 80-10123. 192p. (gr. 7 up). 1980. PLB 7.79 (ISBN 0-671-33021-7). Messner.

O'Donnell, James J. & Hall, Bryan D., eds. Penetrance & Variability in Malformation Syndromes. LC 79-5115. (Alan R. Liss Ser.: Vol. 15, No. 5b). 1979. 42.00 (ISBN 0-8451-1029-2). March of Dimes.

O'Donnell, Kevin, Jr. Caverns: The Journeys of McGill Feighan, Bk. I. (Orig.). 1981. pap. 2.25 (ISBN 0-425-04730-X). Berkley Pub.

O'Donnell, Mabel. From Near & Far. (Design for Reading Ser). (Illus.). (gr. 3). 1972. text ed. 10.36 (ISBN 0-06-516006-1, SchDept); tchr's ed. 14.28 (ISBN 0-06-516204-8); wkbk. 3.20, (ISBN 0-06-516305-2)tchr's ed. 6.36 (ISBN 0-06-516405-9); phonics wkbk. & tchr's ed. 2.68 5.36 (ISBN 0-06-516314-1); dupl masters a-b with ans. key 23.20 ea.; mastery test pkg. 14.48 (ISBN 0-06-516614-0); transition papbks. 2.52 ea.; tchrs' ed. 14.20 (ISBN 0-685-02883-6); wkbk. 2.52, tchr's wkbk. for Transition Bks. 5.04 (ISBN 0-685-02884-4). Har-Row.

--Fun for You. (Design for Reading Ser). (Illus.). (preprimer 3). 1972. pap. 2.92 (ISBN 0-06-516002-9, SchDept). Har-Row.

--In Sunshine & Shadows. 2nd ed. (Design for Reading Ser). (Illus.). (gr. 2-1). 1972. text ed. 8.56 (ISBN 0-06-516005-3, SchDept); tchr's ed. 14.28 (ISBN 0-06-516203-X); wkbk. 3.20, (ISBN 0-06-506304-4) tchr's ed. 6.36 (ISBN 0-06-516404-0); phonics wkbk. 2.68, (ISBN 0-06-516313-3) tchr's ed 5.36 (ISBN 0-06-516413-X); cupl. masters a & b with ans. key 22.52 ea.; mastery test pkg. of 30 14.48 (ISBN 0-06-516613-2); 5 Transition paperbacks 2.52 ea.; tchrs' ed. of Transition bks 14.20 (ISBN 0-685-02892-5); wkbk. 2.56, tchrs' wkbk. for Transition bks. 4.88 (ISBN 0-685-02893-3). Har-Row.

--It Happened This Way. (Design for Reading Ser). (Illus.). (gr. 1). 1972. text ed. 7.96 (ISBN 0-06-516004-5, SchDept); tchrs' ed. 13.24 (ISBN 0-06-516202-1); wkbk. 2.92, (ISBN 0-06-516303-6) tchr's ed. 5.76 (ISBN 0-06-516403-2); phonics wkbk. 2.68, (ISBN 0-06-516312-5) tchr's ed 5.36 (ISBN 0-06-516412-1); dupl. masters a & b with ans. key 22.52 ea.; mastery test pkg. of 30 14.48 (ISBN 0-06-516612-4). Har-Row.

--Something to Tell. (Design for Reading Ser). (Illus.). (primer). 1972. text ed. 7.12 (ISBN 0-06-516003-7, SchDept); tchr's ed. 12.20 (ISBN 0-06-516201-3); wkbk. 2.92, (IsBN 0-06-516302-8) tchr's wkbk. 5.76 (ISBN 0-06-516402-4); phonics wkbk. 2.52, (0-06-516311-7) tchr's ed. 5.00 (ISBN 0-06-516411-3); dupl. masters a & b 16.68 ea.; mastery test 14.48 (ISBN 0-06-516611-6); select-a-card for primer & 1st reader 80.92 (ISBN. 0-06-516812-7). Har-Row.

O'Donnell, Mabel, et al. From Stars to Sculptures. (Design for Reading Ser). (Subj. matter reading). (gr. 8). text ed. 12.20 (ISBN 0-06-511028-5, SchDept); tchr's manual 11.56 (ISBN 0-06-511218-0). Har-Row.

--Readiness Transition: Level Two. (Design for Reading). alphabet bk. 2.52 (ISBN 0-06-516322-2, SchDept); tchr's ed. 5.00 (ISBN 0-06-516421-0); readiness tests 14.28 (ISBN 0-06-516600-0); Alphabet cards 10.76 (ISBN 0-06-510503-6). Har-Row.

O'Donnell, Martin J., jt. ed. see Wade, L. G., Jr.

O'Donnell, Patrick A., jt. auth. see Bigge, June L.

O'Donnell, Peter. The Silver Mistress. (Modesty Blaise Ser.). (Illus.). 256p. 1980. 9.95 (ISBN 0-915822-51-2). Archival Pr.

O'Donnell, Pierce, et al. Toward a Just & Effective Sentencing System: Agenda for Legislative Reform. LC 76-24362. (Special Studies). 1977. text ed. 21.95 (ISBN 0-275-23990-X). Praeger.

O'Donnell, T. A. The Chemistry of Fluorine. (Pergamon Texts in Inorganic Chemistry: Vol. 5). 98p. 1975. text ed. 18.75 (ISBN 0-08-018784-6); pap. text ed. 10.75 (ISBN 0-08-018783-8). Pergamon.

O'Donnell, Terence & Vaugham, Thomas. Portland: A Historical Sketch & Guide. LC 72-251. (Illus.). 161p. 1976. pap. 2.95 o.p. (ISBN 0-87595-051-5). Oreg Hist Soc.

O'Donnell, W. R. & Todd, Loreto. Variety in Contemporary English. (Illus.). 176p. (Orig.). 1980. 25.00x (ISBN 0-04-421005-1, 2560); pap. 8.50 (ISBN 0-04-421006-X, 2561). Allen Unwin.

O'Donoghue, David J. Poets of Ireland. LC 68-30622. 1968. Repr. of 1912 ed. 28.00 (ISBN 0-8103-3152-7). Gale.

O'Donoghue, Patrick. Decision-Related Research on the Organization of Service Delivery Systems in Metropolitan Areas: Public Health. LC 79-83820. 1979. codebook 14.00 (ISBN 0-89138-984-9). ICPSR.

O'Donoghue, Patrick & Roberts, Tanya. Microsets: Putting Economic Theory to Work. 1980. text ed. 6.95x (ISBN 0-393-95141-3). Norton.

O'Donohue, Niall F. Epilepsies of Childhood. Apley, J., ed. LC 79-40722. (Postgraduate Pediatric Ser.). 1979. text ed. 46.95 (ISBN 0-407-00138-7). Butterworths.

O'Donovan, Daniel, tr. Bernard of Clairvaux, Treatises III: On Grace & Free Choice, in Praise of the New Knighthood. (Cistercian Studies Ser.: No. 3). 1977. 10.95 (ISBN 0-87907-119-2); pap. 4.95 (ISBN 0-87907-719-0). Cistercian Pubns.

O'Donovan, L. J. A World of Grace. 1980. 14.95 (ISBN 0-8164-0212-4); pap. 7.95 (ISBN 0-8164-2006-8). Crossroad NY.

O'Donovan, Michael. The Art of the Theatre. 50p. 1980. Repr. of 1947 ed. lib. bdg. 10.00 (ISBN 0-8492-7308-0). R West.

O'Donovan, Thomas R., ed. Ambulatory Surgical Centers: Development & Management. LC 76-15767. 1976. 27.00 (ISBN 0-912862-21-1). Aspen Systems.

Odor, Ruth. Moods & Emotions. Buerger, Jane, ed. 1980. 5.95 (ISBN 0-89565-177-7, 4934). Standard Pub.

--Thank You God, for Quiet Things. LC 80-15099. (Illus.). 32p. (ps-2). 1980. PLB 4.95 (ISBN 0-89565-169-6). Childs World.

--Thank You God, for the Quiet Things. Buerger, Jane, ed. (Illus.). 1980. 4.95 (ISBN 0-89565-169-6, 4920). Standard Pub.

--Thank You God, for Wonderful Things. Buerger, Jane, ed. (Illus.). 1980. write for info. (ISBN 0-89565-170-X, 4921). Standard Pub.

--Thank You, God, for Wonderful Things. LC 80-16106. (Illus.). 32p. (Orig.). (ps-2). 1980. PLB 4.95 (ISBN 0-89565-170-X). Childs World.

--What's a Body to Do? Buerger, Jane, ed. (Illus.). 1980. 5.95 (ISBN 0-89565-176-9, 4933). Standard Pub.

Odor, Ruth S. Baby in a Basket. LC 79-12092. (Bible Story Books). (Illus.). (ps-3). 1979. PLB 5.50 (ISBN 0-89565-086-X). Childs World.

--Bible Heroes. (Basic Bible Readers Ser.). (Illus.). (gr. 4). 1963. pap. 4.50 (ISBN 0-87239-261-9, 2758). Standard Pub.

--Happiest Day. LC 79-12184. (Bible Story Bks.). (Illus.). (ps-3). 1979. PLB 5.50 (ISBN 0-89565-085-1). Childs World.

--The Little Lost Lamb. LC 79-13155. (Bible Story Books). (Illus.). (ps-3). 1979. 5.50 (ISBN 0-89565-088-6). Childs World.

O'Dowd, Liam, et al. Northern Ireland: Between Civil Rights & Civil War. 224p. 1980. text ed. 26.00x (ISBN 0-906336-18-X); pap. text ed. 19.50x (ISBN 0-906336-19-8). Humanities.

O'Driscoll, Gerald P., Jr. Economics As a Coordination Problem: The Contributions of Friecrich A. Hayek. LC 77-23382. (Studies in Economic Theory). 171p. 1978. 15.00; pap. 4.95. NYU Pr.

O'Driscoll, Herbert. A Certain Life: Contemporary Meditations on the Way of Christ. 96p. (Orig.). 1980. pap. 3.95 (ISBN 0-8164-2040-8). Crossroad NY.

O'Driscoll, Robert. Symbolism & Some Implications of the Symbolic Approach: W. B. Yeats During the Eighteen Nineties. (New Yeats Papers Ser.: No. 9). 84p. 1975. pap. text ed. 8.00x (ISBN 0-85105-270-3, Dolmen Pr). Humanities.

O'Driscoll, Robert & Reynolds, Lorna, eds. Yeats Studies. Incl. Vol. 1. Yeats & the 1890's. (Illus.). 1971; Vol. 2. Theatre & the Visual Arts: a Centenary Celebration of Jack Yeats & John Synge. (Illus.). 1972. pap. 8.40x ea. (Pub. by Irish Academic Pr). Biblio Dist.

Odum, Elisabeth C., jt. auth. see Odum, Howard T.

Odum, Howard T. & Odum, Elisabeth C. Energy Basis for Man & Nature. 2nd ed. (Illus.). 352p. 1981. text ed. 19.50 (ISBN 0-07-047511-3, C); pap. text ed. 12.95 (ISBN 0-07-047510-5, C); instrs'. manual avail. McGraw.

Odum, Linda, jt. auth. see Mundy, Jean.

O'Dunn, Shannon, jt. auth. see Bassett, Allen M.

O'Dwyer, John J. College Physics. 752p. 1980. text ed. 22.95x (ISBN 0-534-00827-5). Wadsworth Pub.

Odysseus Elytis. Maria Nephele. Anagnostopoulos, Athan, tr. from Greek. 64p. 1981. 10.00 (ISBN 0-395-29465-7). HM.

Oe, Kenzaburo. The Silent Cry. Bester, John, tr. from Japanese. LC 74-77961. Orig. Title: Man'en Gannen No Football. 274p. 1974. 10.00x (ISBN 0-87011-232-5). Kodansha.

--Teach Us to Outgrow Our Madness. Nathan, John, tr. from Japanese. & intro. by. LC 76-54582. 1977. pap. 4.95 (ISBN 0-394-17002-4, E687, Ever). Grove.

OECD. Accounting Practices in OECD Member Countris. (International Investment & Multinational Enterprises). (Illus.). 250p. (Orig.). 1980. pap. text ed. 13.50x (ISBN 92-64-12076-9). OECD.

--Bargain Price Offers & Similar Marketing Practices. (Illus., Orig.). 1980. pap. text ed. 6.00 (ISBN 92-64-12033-5, 24-80-01-1). OECD.

--Collective Bargaining & Government Policies in Ten OECD Countries: Austria, Canada, France, Germany, Italy, Japan, N. Zealand, Sweden, UK & US. (Illus.). 151p. (Orig.). 1980. pap. 9.00x (ISBN 92-64-12011-4). OECD.

--Financial Support to the Fishing Industry. (Illus.). 161p. (Orig.). 1980. pap. 6.50x (ISBN 92-64-12087-4, 53-80-01-1). OECD.

--Information Computer Communications Policy (ICCP) 4. 233p. (Orig.). 1980. pap. 14.50 (ISBN 92-64-12035-1, 93-80-01-1). OECD.

--The Instability of Agricultural Commodity Markets. (Agricultural Products & Markets Ser.). (Illus.). 237p. 1980. pap. text ed. 9.95x (ISBN 92-64-12041-6, 51-80-03-1). OECD.

--Maritime Transport Nineteen Seventy-Nine. (Illus.). 151p. (Orig.). 1980. pap. text ed. 10.50x (ISBN 92-64-12122-6). OECD.

--Milk, Milk Products & Egg Balances in OECD Member Countries, 1973-1978. May 1980. (Illus.). 140p. (Orig., Eng. & Fr.). 1980. pap. 11.50x (ISBN 92-64-02093-4). OECD.

--National Accounts of OECD Countries, Vol. II (Illus.). 284p. 1980. pap. 18.00x (ISBN 92-64-02094-2, 30-80-03-3). OECD.

--Policy Implications of Data Network Developments in the OECD Area. (Information Computer Communications Policy: No. 3). (Illus.). 206p. (Orig., Fr.). 1980. pap. 12.50 (ISBN 92-64-12005-X, 93-79-02-1). OECD.

--Published Offical Sources of Financial Statistics. (Illus.). 132p. (Orig.). 1980. pap. 11.00x (ISBN 92-64-02095-0). OECD.

--Register of Development Research Projects in Asia. (Liason Bulletin Ser.). 350p. (Orig.). 1980. pap. text ed. 17.50x (ISBN 92-64-02096-9, 40-80-01-3). OECD.

--Review of Fisheries in OECD Member Countries Nineteen Seventy-Nine. (Illus.). 253p. (Orig.). 1980. pap. 12.00 (ISBN 92-64-12103-X). OECD.

--School & Community, Vol. II. (Illus.). 129p. 1980. pap. 8.00x (ISBN 92-64-12082-3, 96-80-01-1). OECD.

--Siting Procedures for Major Energy Facilities: Some National Cases. (Illus.). 142p. (Orig.). 1980. pap. text ed. 8.00x (ISBN 92-64-11986-8). OECD.

--Strategies for Change & Reform in Public Management. (Public Management Ser.: No. 1). 242p. (Orig.). 1980. pap. text ed. 16.00x (ISBN 92-64-12121-8). OECD.

--Tourism Policy & International Tourism in OECD Member Countries, 1980. (Illus.). 189p. (Orig.). 1980. pap. text ed. 19.50x (ISBN 92-64-12123-4). OECD.

OECD, jt. auth. see Imboden, Nicolas.

OECD, ed. Multilingual Dictionary of Fish & Fish Products. 2nd ed. 446p. 1978. 42.50x (ISBN 0-85238-086-0). Intl Pubns Serv.

--Urban Public Transport: Evaluation of Performance. (Road Research Ser.). (Illus.). 76p. 1980. pap. 5.50 (ISBN 9-2641-2127-7, 77-80-04-1). OECD.

OECD & IEA, eds. A Group Strategy for Energy Research, Development & Demonstration. 97p. (Orig.). 1980. pap. 8.00 (ISBN 9-2641-2124-2). OECD.

OECD Deveopment Centre, ed. see Conde, Julien, et al.

OECD-IEA. Energy Research, Development, & Demonstration in the IEA Countries: 1979 Review of National Programmes. (Illus.). 153p. (Orig.). 1980. pap. text ed. 12.00x (ISBN 92-64-12067-X, 61-80-03-1). OECD.

OECD-NEA. Radiological Significance & Management of Tritium, Carbon-14, Krypton-85, Iodine-129, Arising from the Nuclear Fuel Cycle. (Illus.). 222p. (Orig.). 1980. pap. text ed. 19.00x (ISBN 0-686-27701-5, 66-80-06-1) (ISBN 92-64-12083-1). OECD.

--Reference Seismic Grond Motions in Nuclear Safety Assessments. (Illus.). 171p. (Orig.). 1980. pap. text ed. 16.00x (ISBN 92-64-12100-5). OECD.

OECD Staff. Education & Regional Development, Vol. II. 460p. (Orig., Bi-lingual-English & French). 1980. pap. 20.00 (ISBN 92-64-01996-0). OECD.

--OECD Economic Survey: Austria. (OECD Economic Surveys 1980 Ser.). (Illus.). 62p. (Orig.). 1980. pap. 3.50x (ISBN 92-64-12029-7). OECD.

Oechsle, Robert. Ducky, Ucky & Mucky. (Illus.). 40p. (ps). 1975. pap. 4.25 (ISBN 0-9603376-0-1). Flourtown Pub.

Oehlbeck, J. Tracy. The Consumer's Guide to Life Insurance. (Orig.). 1975. pap. 1.75 o.s.i. (ISBN 0-515-03836-9). Jove Pubns.

Oehler, Gustave. Theology of the Old Testament. 1978. 20.00 (ISBN 0-686-12952-0). Klock & Klock.

Oehler, Mike. One Mexican Sunday. LC 80-82949. (Illus.). 112p. 1980. 8.50 (ISBN 0-9604464-1-9). Mole Pub Co.

Oehling, A., et al, eds. see International Congress of Allergology, 10th, Jerusalem, Israel, Nov. 1979.

Oehlke, Waldemar. Bettina Von Arnims Briefromane. 29.00 (ISBN 0-384-42980-7); pap. 26.00 (ISBN 0-685-02117-3). Johnson Repr.

Oehman, R. L. & Axelsson, R. A. Prolactin Responses to Neuroleptics. (Journal of Neural Transmission Supplementum: Vol. 17). (Illus.). 75p. 1981. pap. 16.00 (ISBN 0-387-81605-4). Springer-Verlag.

Oelhaf, Robert C. Organic Agriculture: Economic & Ecological Comparisons with Conventional Methods. 1979. 24.95 (ISBN 0-470-26427-6). Halsted Pr.

Oerke, jt. auth. see Gawne, Eleanor.

Oestereich, James & Pennington, Earl. Improving & Arranging on the Keyboard. (Illus.). 208p. 1981. 16.95 (ISBN 0-13-453563-4, Spec); pap. 7.95 (ISBN 0-13-453555-3). P-H.

Oesterreicher, John M. & Sinai, Anne. Jerusalem. (Illus., Orig.). 1974. text ed. 5.95 o.p. (ISBN 0-381-98266-1). John Day.

Oestreich, Alan E. Pediatric Radiology. 2nd ed. (Medical Outline Ser.). 1980. pap. 16.50 (ISBN 0-87488-658-9). Med Exam.

Oestreich, Alan E., tr. see Nahum, Henri & Fekete, Francois.

Oettgen, Herbert see Burchenal, Joseph.

Oettgen, Herbert, jt. auth. see Burchenal, Joseph.

Oetting, E. R., tr. see Morrill, Weston H. & Hurst, James C.

Oettinger, G. Run, Computer, Run: The Mythology of Educational Innovation. 1971. pap. 1.95 o.s.i. (ISBN 0-02-015040-7, Collier). Macmillan.

Oettinger, K. & Mooney, E. Not My Daughter: Facing up to Adolescent Pregnancy. 1979. 9.95 (ISBN 0-13-623850-5). P-H.

O'Farrell, P. J. England & Ireland Since 1800. 189p. 1975. text ed. 7.75x o.p. (ISBN 0-19-215814-7); pap. text ed. 3.95x (ISBN 0-19-289045-X). Oxford U Pr.

O'Farrell, R. C. Seafood Fishing for Amateur & Professional. (Illus.). 196p. 10.00 (ISBN 0-85238-097-6, FN). Unipub.

Offen, Carol. Country Music: The Poetry. (Orig.). 1977. pap. 1.50 o.p. (ISBN 0-345-25606-9). Ballantine.

Offen, Neil, jt. auth. see Horowitz, Steve.

Offenbach, Jacques. Jacques Offenbach. 1981. 29.95 (ISBN 0-7145-3512-5); pap. 11.95 (ISBN 0-7145-3841-8). Riverrun NY.

Offer, Avner. Property & Politics Eighteen-Seventy to Nineteen-Fourteen: Landownership, Law, Ideology & Urban Development in England. LC 80-41010. (Illus.). 480p. Date not set. price not set (ISBN 0-521-22414-4). Cambridge U Pr.

Offer, Daniel & Masterson, James F., eds. Teaching & Learning Adolescent Psychiatry. 180p. 1971. pap. 17.50 photocopy ed. (ISBN 0-398-01414-0). C C Thomas.

Office for Science & Technology. Science, Technology & Global Problems: The United Nations Advisory Committee on the Application of Science & Technology to Development. 62p. 1979. 16.00 (ISBN 0-08-025131-5). Pergamon.

Office of Adult Services. No Crystal Stair: A Bibliography of Black Literature. 63p. 1971. pap. 2.00 o.p. (ISBN 0-87104-600-8, Branch Lib). NY Pub Lib.

Office of Children's Services. Children's Book & Recordings, Nineteen Seventy-Eight. annual 1978. pap. 2.00 o.p. (ISBN 0-87104-632-6, Branch Lib). NY Pub Lib.

Office of Information, Gov't of Papua New Guinea. Papua New Guinea. LC 75-23775. (Illus.). 68p. 1976. text ed. 9.95x (ISBN 0-8248-0400-7, Eastwest Ctr). U Pr of Hawaii.

Office of Military Leadership, United States Military Academy Associates, ed. A Study of Organizational Leadership. LC 76-25242. 600p. 1976. pap. 12.95 (ISBN 0-8117-2059-4). Stackpole.

Office Of Scientific Personnel. Doctorate Production in United States Universities, 1920-1962, with Baccalaureate Origins of Doctorates in Sciences, Arts & Professions. (Illus.). 1963. pap. 6.00 (ISBN 0-309-01142-6). Natl Acad Pr.

--Doctorate Recipients from United States Universities, 1958-1966. 1967. pap. 9.75 (ISBN 0-309-01489-1). Natl Acad Pr.

--Mobility of PhD's: Before & After the Doctorate. LC 72-611001. (Orig.). 1971. pap. text ed. 6.75 (ISBN 0-309-01874-9). Natl Acad Pr.

--Profiles of PhD's in the Sciences. 1965. pap. 3.75 (ISBN 0-309-01293-7). Natl Acad Pr.

Office of Technology Assessment. Application of Solar Technology to Today's Energy Needs: Executive Summary. 1980. pap. 14.95 (ISBN 0-89934-004-0). Solar Energy Info.

--Energy from Biological Processes. 205p. 1981. lib. bdg. 34.50 (ISBN 0-89934-090-3); pap. 22.50 (ISBN 0-89934-107-1). Solar Energy Info.

--Energy from Biological Processes, Vol. 2. Date not set. lib. bdg. price not set (ISBN 0-89934-119-5); pap. price not set (ISBN 0-89934-120-9). Solar Energy Info.

Office of Technology Assessment, Congress of the U.S. The Effects of Nuclear War. LC 79-8544. 160p. text ed. 9.95 (ISBN 0-916672-36-0). Allanheld.

Office of Technology Assessment, Congress of the United States. Residential Energy Conservation. LC 79-55053. 342p. 1980. text ed. 15.00 (ISBN 0-916672-38-7). Allanheld.

Office of Technology Assessment Congress of the United States, ed. Technology & East West Trade. LC 80-26121. 312p. 1981. text ed. 25.00 (ISBN 0-86598-041-1). Allanheld.

Office of Technology Assessment, U.S. Congress. Energy from Biological Processes. 200p. 1981. lib. bdg. 20.00x (ISBN 0-86531-171-4). Westview.

Office Of The Foreign Secretary. Eastern European Academies of Sciences: A Directory. 1963. pap. 3.50 (ISBN 0-309-01090-X). Natl Acad Pr.

Office of the Foreign Secretary, National Research Council Commission on International Relations. In Search of Population Policy: Views from the Developing World. LC 74-10125. ix, 108p. 1974. pap. 5.75 (ISBN 0-309-02242-8). Natl Acad Pr.

Officer, Lawrence H. & Willett, Thomas D. International Monetary System. 4.50x (ISBN 0-87543-096-1). Lucas.

Offit, Avodah. The Laughing Orgasm & Other Perspectives for Erotic Love. LC 79-2589. 1980. cancelled o.p. (ISBN 0-397-01261-6). Lippincott.

--Night Thoughts: Reflections of a Sex Therapist. 284p. 1981. 11.95 (ISBN 0-312-92575-1). Congdon & Lattes.

Offit, Sidney. What Kind of Guy Do You Think I Am? (YA) (gr. 8 up). 1979. pap. 1.50 (ISBN 0-440-99455-1, LFL). Dell.

Offner, Hazel. Moses: A Man Changed by God. 72p. (Orig.). 1981. pap. 2.95 (ISBN 0-87784-617-0). Inter-Varsity.

Offner, Richard. Italian Primitives at Yale University. (Illus.). 1927. 75.00x (ISBN 0-685-89760-5). Elliots Bks.

Offord, R., jt. auth. see Yudkin, M.

Offord, R. E. Semisynthetic Proteins. LC 79-40521. 235p. 1980. 58.95 (ISBN 0-471-27615-4, Pub. by Wiley-Interscience). Wiley.

Offord, Robin, jt. auth. see Yudkin, Michael.

Offut, Andrew J. & Lyon, Richard K. The Eyes of Sarsis. (Orig.). 1980. pap. write for info. (ISBN 0-671-82679-4). PB.

Offutt, Andrew J. The Iron Lords. 1979. pap. 1.75 (ISBN 0-515-04600-0). Jove Pubns.

--My Lord Barbarian. (A Del Rey Bk.). 1978. pap. 1.50 o.p. (ISBN 0-685-75023-X, 345-25713-8-150). Ballantine.

Offutt, Nelson T. More Than a Cookbook. LC 79-93281. 1981. pap. 5.95 (ISBN 0-89709-019-5). Liberty Pub.

O'Flaherty, C. A. & Cross, I. Hovercraft & Hoverports. (Illus.). 1975. 16.00x o.p. (ISBN 0-8464-0490-7). Beekman Pubs.

O'Flaherty, Ellen. Toxicants & Drugs: Kinetics & Synamics. 320p. 1981. 27.50 (ISBN 0-471-06047-X, Pub. by Wiley-Interscience). Wiley.

O'Flaherty, Liam. Informer. pap. 1.25 o.p. (ISBN 0-451-50949-8, CY949, Sig Classics). NAL.

O'Flaherty, Patrick, jt. ed. see Neary, Peter.

O'Flaherty, Wendy, tr. Hindu Myths. (Classics Ser). 360p. 1975. pap. 3.50 (ISBN 0-14-044306-1). Penguin.

O'Flaherty, Wendy D. Asceticism & Eroticism in the Mythology of Siva. (Illus.). 401p. 1973. 36.00x (ISBN 0-19-713573-0). Oxford U Pr.

--Karma & Rebirth in Classical Indian Traditions. 400p. 1980. 27.50x (ISBN 0-520-03923-8). U of Cal Pr.

--The Origins of Evil in Hindu Mythology. 1977. 20.00x (ISBN 0-520-03163-6); pap. 8.95 (ISBN 0-520-04098-8). U of Cal Pr.

O'Flaherty, Wendy D., ed. The Critical Study of Sacred Texts. 1980. 16.00 (ISBN 0-89581-101-4). Lancaster-Miller.

O'Flanagan, J. Roderick. Lives of the Lord Chancellors & Keepers of the Great Seal of Ireland, 2 Vols. 1971. Repr. of 1870 ed. 60.00x (ISBN 0-8377-2500-3). Rothman.

Ofoegbu, Ray. A Foundation Course in International Relations for African Students. 224p. (Orig.). 1980. pap. text ed. 10.50x (ISBN 0-04-327058-1, AU448). Allen Unwin.

Ofshe, Lynne & Ofshe, Richard. Utility & Choice in Social Interaction. LC 70-101539. (Illus.). 1970. 24.50x (ISBN 0-13-939645-4). Irvington.

Ofshe, Richard. Interpersonal Behavior in Small Groups. (Illus.). 816p. 1973. text ed. 21.95x (ISBN 0-13-475020-9). P-H.

Ofshe, Richard, jt. auth. see Ofshe, Lynne.

Ofshe, Richard J. Sociology of the Possible. 2nd ed. 1977. pap. text ed. 10.95 (ISBN 0-13-821595-2). P-H.

Ogali, Ogali. Veronica My Daughter & Other Onitsha Plays & Stories. Sander, Reinhard W. & Ayers, Peter K., eds. LC 80-886. 376p. (Orig.). 1980. 18.00x (ISBN 0-914478-61-3); pap. 7.00x (ISBN 0-914478-62-1). Three Continents.

Ogan, George, jt. auth. see Ogan, Margaret.

Ogan, Margaret & Ogan, George. Smashing: Jimmy Connors. LC 76-10356. (Sports Profiles Ser.). (Illus.). 48p. (gr. 4-11). 1976. PLB 8.50 (ISBN 0-8172-0140-8). Raintree Pubs.

Ogander, M. Project Planning by Network Techniques, Third International Congress, 3 vols. LC 72-4802. 1972. Set. 94.95 (ISBN 0-470-65280-2). Halsted Pr.

Ogata, Katshuiko. System Dynamics. LC 77-20180. (Illus.). 1978. 29.95 (ISBN 0-13-880385-4). P-H.

Ogata, Katsuhiko. Modern Control Engineering. LC 72-84843. (Electrical Engineering Ser). 1970. ref. ed. 27.95 (ISBN 0-13-590232-0). P-H.

Ogburn, Charlton, Jr. The Forging of Our Continent. LC 68-22959. (Illus.). 160p. 1968. 4.95 (ISBN 0-8281-0343-7, JO411-0, Co-Pub. by Smithsonian). Am Heritage.

Ogburn, William F., ed. American Society in Wartime. LC 72-2380. (FDR & the Era of the New Deal Ser.). 237p. 1972. Repr. of 1943 ed. lib. bdg. 25.00 (ISBN 0-306-70484-6). Da Capo.

--Social Changes During Depression & Recovery. LC 72-2381. (FDR & the Era of the New Deal Ser.). 117p. 1974. Repr. of 1935 ed. lib. bdg. 17.50 (ISBN 0-306-70483-8). Da Capo.

Ogden, C. G. An Atlas of Freshwater Testate Amoebae. (Illus.). 228p. 1980. text ed. 49.50x (ISBN 0-19-858502-0). Oxford U Pr.

Ogden, Daniel M., Jr. & Bone, Hugh A. Washington Politics: Published Under the Auspices of the Citizenship Clearing House. LC 80-25647. (Illus.). vi, 77p. 1981. Repr. of 1960 ed. lib. bdg. 19.75x (ISBN 0-313-22803-5, OGWP). Greenwood.

Ogden, Dunbar H., tr. The Italian Baroque Stage: Documents by Giulio Troili, Andrea Pozzo, Ferdinando Galli-Bibiena, & Baldassare Orsini. LC 75-7197. 1978. 25.75x (ISBN 0-520-03006-0). U of Cal Pr.

Ogden, J. T. Applied Functional Analysis: A First Course for Students of Mechanics & Engineering Science. LC 78-541. (Illus.). 1979. ref. 27.95 (ISBN 0-13-040162-5). P-H.

Ogden, John B. & Pannwitt, Barbara. Inward Vision: Imaginative Writing. (gr. 9-11). 1971. pap. text ed. 4.50x (ISBN 0-88334-038-0). Ind Sch Pr.

Ogden, Lawrence, jt. auth. see Lounsbury, John F.

Ogden, Richard E. Green Knight & Red Mourning. (Orig.). 1980. pap. 1.95 (ISBN 0-532-23218-6). Manor Bks.

Ogden, Richard W. Manage Your Plant for Profit & Your Promotion. 1978. 14.95 (ISBN 0-8144-5466-6). Am Mgmt.

Ogden, Roland. Imaginative Management Control. (British Library of Business Studies). (Orig.). 1969. text ed. 12.75x (ISBN 0-7100-6584-1). Humanities.

Ogden, Sheila J., jt. auth. see Radcliff, Ruth K.

Ogden, Shelia J., jt. auth. see Radcliff, Ruth K.

Ogdin, Carol A. Microcomputer Design. (Illus.). 1978. ref. 16.95 (ISBN 0-13-580977-0); pap. 12.95 (ISBN 0-13-580985-1). P-H.

--Microcomputer Management & Programming. (Illus.). 1980. text ed. 21.95 (ISBN 0-13-580936-3). P-H.

--Software Design for Microcomputers. (Illus.). 1978. ref. ed. 16.95 (ISBN 0-13-821744-0); pap. 12.95 (ISBN 0-13-821801-3). P-H.

Ogdon, Donald P. Psychodiagnostics & Personality Assessment: A Handbook. 2nd ed. LC 66-29866. (Professional Handbook Ser.). 144p. 1977. pap. 9.75x (ISBN 0-87424-095-6). Western Psych.

Ogelsby, Mac, et al. Pet Games & Recreation. 1981. text ed. 14.95 (ISBN 0-8359-5530-3); pap. 9.95 (ISBN 0-8359-5529-X). Reston.

Ogg, David. Louis the Fourteenth of France: 2nd ed. (Oxford Paperbacks University Ser). pap. 4.95x (ISBN 0-19-888021-9). Oxford U Pr.

--William Third. 1968. pap. 1.25 o.s.i. (ISBN 0-02-035610-2, Collier). Macmillan.

Ogg, Frederic A. & Ray, P. Orman. Ogg & Ray's Essentials of American State & Local Government. 10th ed. Young, William H., ed. (Illus.). 1969. pap. text ed. 9.95 (ISBN 0-13-633644-2). P-H.

Ogg, Frederic A see Gabriel, Ralph H.

Oggel, Terry, ed. see Bibliographic Society of Northern Illinois.

Ogibalov, P. M., et al. Structural Polymers: Testing Methods, 2 vols. Pelz, T., tr. LC 73-16434. 612p. 1974. 83.95 (ISBN 0-470-65284-5). Halsted Pr.

Ogilive, R. M., ed. see Tacitus.

Ogilvie. Beautiful Girl. (gr. 7-12). 1980. pap. 1.50 (ISBN 0-590-31277-4, Schol Pap). Schol Bk Serv.

Ogilvie, Elisabeth. The Dreaming Swimmer. 1979. pap. 1.75 (ISBN 0-380-01878-0, 37051). Avon.

Ogilvie, Gordon. Jamie Reid. 448p. (Orig.). 1981. pap. 2.75 (ISBN 0-380-76737-6, 76737). Avon.

Ogilvie, Lloyd. Congratulations - God Believes in You. 128p. 1980. 5.95 (ISBN 0-8499-0197-9). Word Bks.

Ogilvie, Lloyd J. The Beauty of Caring. LC 80-80464. 1981. pap. 4.95 (ISBN 0-89081-244-6). Harvest Hse.

--The Beauty of Friendship. LC 80-80463. 1980. pap. 4.95 (ISBN 0-89081-243-8). Harvest Hse.

--The Beauty of Love. LC 80-80465. (Orig.). 1980. pap. 4.95 (ISBN 0-89081-245-4). Harvest Hse.

--The Beauty of Sharing. LC 80-8880. (Orig.). 1981. pap. 4.95 (ISBN 0-89081-246-2). Harvest Hse.

--How to Know God's Will. LC 80-84824. 1981. pap. 4.95 (ISBN 0-89081-282-9). Harvest Hse.

--Loved & Forgiven. LC 76-29889. 1977. pap. 2.50 (ISBN 0-8307-0442-6, S313-1-03). Regal.

--Radiance of the Inner Splendor. LC 80-51524. 144p. 1980. pap. text ed. 4.95x (ISBN 0-8358-0405-4). Upper Room.

Ogilvie, R. M. Roman Literature & Society. 303p. 1980. 23.50x (ISBN 0-389-20069-7). B&N.

--Roman Literature & Society. 1980. text ed. 19.50x (ISBN 0-391-01679-2). Humanities.

--Romans & Their Gods in the Age of Augustus. (Ancient Culture & Society Ser). (Illus.). 1970. 5.00x (ISBN 0-393-05399-7); pap. 4.95 (ISBN 0-393-00543-7). Norton,

Ogilvie, R. M., et al see Livy.

Ogilvie, R. M., et al, eds. see Tacitus.

Ogilvie, Robert M. Commentary on Livy, Bks 1-5. 1965. 59.00x (ISBN 0-19-814432-6). Oxford U Pr.

Ogilvie, Robert S. Basic Ice Skating Skills. LC 68-54414. (Illus.). (gr. 7-9). 1968. 10.95 (ISBN 0-397-00518-0); pap. 7.95 (ISBN 0-397-00519-9, LP10). Lippincott.

Ogilvie, Sheila A., tr. see Folz, Robert.

Ogilvy, David. Confessions of an Advertising Man. LC 79-25505. 172p. 1980. pap. 5.95 (ISBN 0-689-70601-4, 260). Atheneum.

--Confessions of an Advertising Man. LC 63-17855. 1963. 10.00 o.p. (ISBN 0-689-10215-1). Atheneum.

--Flying Light Aircraft. 2nd ed. (Illus.). 224p. 1979. 20.00 (ISBN 0-7136-1854-X). Transatlantic.

Ogilvy, James A. Many Dimensional Man: Decentralizing Self, Society & the Sacred. LC 76-57273. 1977. 17.95x (ISBN 0-19-502231-9). Oxford U Pr.

Ogilvy, Susan. Curds & Whey. LC 79-56445. (Illus.). 120p. 1980. 19.95 (ISBN 0-7134-1990-3, Pub. by Batsford England). David & Charles.

Ogle, Jane. The Stop Smoking Diet. De Kay, George C., ed. 192p. 1981. 8.95 (ISBN 0-87131-337-5). M Evans.

Ogle, Kenneth N. Optics: An Introduction for Ophthalmologists. 2nd ed. (Illus.). 288p. 1979. 13.75 (ISBN 0-398-01417-5). C C Thomas.

Ogle, Lucille & Thoburn, Tina. The Golden Picture Dictionary: A Beginning Dictionary of More Than 2500 Words. (Illus.). (gr. k-3). 1976. PLB 12.23 o.p. (ISBN 0-307-67861-X, Golden Pr); pap. 3.95 o.p. (ISBN 0-307-15991-4); 5.95 (ISBN 0-307-17861-7). Western Pub.

Ogle, Mary S. China Nurse. LC 74-79164. (Destiny Ser.). 1975. pap. 4.95 (ISBN 0-8163-0168-9, 03195-5). Pacific Pr Pub Assn.

Ogle, Nina M., jt. auth. see Johnson, Kenneth F.

Ogle, T. P., tr. see Andenaes, Johannes.

Ogler, Hertha. Alfred Adler: The Man & His Work. 1972. pap. 1.75 o.p. (ISBN 0-451-61165-9, ME1165, Ment). NAL.

Oglesby, Carl & Shaull, Richard. Containment & Change: Two Dissenting Views of American Society & Foreign Policy in the New Revolutionary Age. Orig. Title: Third World Revolution, Orig. 1967. cloth o.p. 5.95 o.s.i. (ISBN 0-02-592610-1); pap. 1.45 o.s.i. (ISBN 0-02-088090-1). Macmillan.

Oglesby, Enoch H. Ethics & Theology from the Other Side: Sounds of Moral Struggle. LC 79-62897. 1979. pap. text ed. 9.00 (ISBN 0-8191-0706-9). U Pr of Amer.

Ogletree, Earl J. & Garcia, David. Education of the Spanish-Speaking Urban Child: A Book of Readings. (Illus.). 504p. 1975. 34.50 (ISBN 0-398-03335-8). C C Thomas.

Ogletree, Earl J., ed. Introduction to Waldorf Education: Curriculum & Methods. LC 78-65425. 1978. pap. text ed. 16.25 (ISBN 0-8191-0665-8). U Pr of Amer.

Ogletree, Earl J., et al. The Unit Plan: A Plan for Curriculum Organizing & Teaching. LC 79-48018. 499p. 1980. pap. text ed. 13.75 (ISBN 0-8191-0996-7). U Pr of Amer.

Ogletree, Herbert H. Revelations: Forerunner of Christ. 1977. 6.50 o.p. (ISBN 0-682-48934-4). Exposition.

Oglivie, Lloyd J. Life As It Was Meant to Be: The Authentic Life from I & II Thessalonians. LC 80-50541. 160p. 1980. text ed. 8.95 (ISBN 0-8307-0740-9, 5108705). Regal.

O'Gorman, Frank. The Rise of Party in England: The Rockingham Whigs, 1760-1782. 1975. text ed. 32.50x o.p. (ISBN 0-04-942135-2). Allen Unwin.

O'Gorman, James F., intro. by. Portrait of a Place, Some American Landscape Painters in Gloucester. (Illus.). 1973. 7.50 (ISBN 0-930352-03-3). Nelson B Robinson.

O'Gorman, Ned. Night of the Hammer. LC 59-6419. 1959. 4.50 o.p. (ISBN 0-15-165621-5). HarBraceJ.

O'Gorman, Patricia W. Patios & Gardens of Mexico. (Illus.). Date not set. 22.95 (ISBN 0-8038-0210-2). Hastings.

Ogorodnikov, K. F. Dynamics of Stellar Systems. 1965. 46.00 (ISBN 0-08-010163-1); pap. 26.00 (ISBN 0-08-013772-5). Pergamon.

Ogot, B. A. & Kieran, J. A., eds. Zamani: A Survey of East African History. LC 68-26079. (Illus.). 1971. pap. text ed. 7.25x (ISBN 0-582-60293-9). Humanities.

Ogot, Bethwell A., ed. War & Society in Africa. 276p. 1972. 28.50x (ISBN 0-7146-2129-3, F Cass Co). Biblio Dist.

Ogra, P. L. & Dayton, Delbert H., eds. The Immunology of Breast Milk. LC 79-64434. 1979. 30.00 (ISBN 0-89004-387-6). Raven.

O'Grady, Desmond. The Gododdin. (Dolmen Editions Ser.: No. 26). (Illus.). 1977. text ed. 56.25x (ISBN 0-85105-310-6, Dolmen Pr). Humanities.

O'Grady, John F. Models of Jesus. LC 80-1726. 192p. 1981. 10.95 (ISBN 0-385-17320-2). Doubleday.

O'Grady, John M., jt. ed. see Lewis, Peter J.

O'Grady, Joseph P. How the Irish Became Americans. (The Immigrant Heritage of America Ser). lib. bdg. 11.95 (ISBN 0-8057-3229-2). Twayne.

O'Grady, Joseph P., ed. The Immigrants' Influence on Wilson's Peace Policies. LC 67-23776. 340p. 1967. 12.50x (ISBN 0-8131-1140-4). U Pr of Ky.

Ogren, Sylvia. Bake Breads from Frozen Dough. 2nd ed. LC 76-25064. (Illus.). 1979. pap. 6.95 (ISBN 0-87518-137-6). Dillon.

--Shape It & Bake It: Quick & Simple Ideas for Children from Frozen Bread Dough. LC 79-23923. (Doing & Learning Bks.). (Illus.). 128p. (gr. 5 up). 1981. PLB 7.95 (ISBN 0-87518-193-7). Dillon.

Ogul, Morris, jt. auth. see Keefe, William J.

Ogul, Morris S., jt. auth. see Keefe, William J.

Ogyu Sorai. Political Writings. McEwan, J. R., ed. 1962. 29.95 (ISBN 0-521-05627-6). Cambridge U Pr.

Oh, C. Y. Production Techniques for Instructional Graphic Materials. (Elementary Education Ser.). 1976. pap. text ed. 13.95 (ISBN 0-675-08462-8); instructor's manual 3.95 (ISBN 0-686-67618-1). Merrill.

Oh, T. Intensive Care Manual. (Illus.). 200p. 1980. text ed. 29.95 (ISBN 0-409-31380-7). Butterworths.

O'Hagan. Woman Who Got on at Jaspar Station & Other Stories. 1963. 1.65 o.p. (ISBN 0-8040-0326-2). Swallow.

O'Hagan, Caroline, ed. It's Easy to Have a Snail Visit You. LC 79-3457. (Illus.). 24p. (gr. 1-4). 1980. 4.95 (ISBN 0-688-41948-8); PLB 4.76 (ISBN 0-688-51948-2). Lothrop.

--It's Easy to Have a Worm Visit You. LC 79-3454. (Illus.). 24p. (gr. 1-4). 1980. 4.95 (ISBN 0-688-41946-1); PLB 4.76 (ISBN 0-688-51946-6). Lothrop.

O'Hair, Madalyn M. The American Atheist Radio Series of Ingersoll the Magnificent. 1977. pap. 3.00. Am Atheist.

--An Atheist Primer. 1980. pap. 3.00. Am Atheist.

--Women & Atheism: The Ultimate Liberation. 1979. pap. 3.00. Am Atheist.

Ohanian, Hans C. Gravitation & Space Time. new ed. (Illus.). 400p. 1976. text ed. 19.95x (ISBN 0-393-09198-8). Norton.

O'Hanlon, Thomas J. The Irish: Sinners, Saints, Gamblers, Gentry, Priests, Maoists, Rebels, Tories, Orangemen, Dippers, Heroes, Villains & Other Proud Natives of the Fabled Isle. LC 74-1843. (Illus.). 334p. (YA) 1975. 13.95 o.p. (ISBN 0-06-013238-8, HarpT). Har-Row.

Ohannessian, Sirarpi, et al, eds. Language Surveys in Developing Nations: Papers and Reports on Sociolinguistic Surveys. LC 75-7584. 1975. pap. text ed. 6.00 (ISBN 0-87281-037-2). Ctr Appl Ling.

O'Hara, Alan J. The A.G.E. of Planets. 1981. 8.95 (ISBN 0-533-04638-6). Vantage.

O'Hara, Betsy. Japan Nineteen Forty-Eight to Nineteen Fifty-Four Through One American's Eyes. Scott, Donald M., ed. Yamakawa, Reiko, tr. 72p. (Orig., English-Japanese.). 16.95x (ISBN 0-9604188-0-6); pap. 12.95x (ISBN 0-9604188-1-4). B O'Hara.

O'Hara, Charles E. & O'Hara, Gregory L. Fundamentals of Criminal Investigation. 5th ed. (Illus.). 928p. 1980. 26.75 (ISBN 0-398-04000-1). C C Thomas.

O'Hara, Charles E. & Osterburg, James W. Introduction to Criminalistics: The Application of the Physical Sciences to the Detection of Crime. rev. ed. LC 49-11434. 736p. 1972. Repr. of 1949 ed. 17.50x (ISBN 0-253-33103-X). Ind U Pr.

O'Hara, Charles E., ed. see Soderman, Harry & O'Connell, John J.

O'Hara, D. M., jt. auth. see Chisolm, J. J.

O'Hara, Daniel T. Tragic Knowledge: Yeat's Autobiography & Hermeneutics. LC 80-26825. 224p. 1981. 20.00x (ISBN 0-231-05204-9). Columbia U Pr.

O'Hara, Deborah, ed. The Micropublishers' Trade List Annual, 1980. 14000p. 1980. 98.50 (ISBN 0-913672-38-6). Microform Rev.

--Publishers Catalogs Annual 1980-81. 30000p. 1981. 147.50 (ISBN 0-930466-19-5). Meckler Bks.

O'Hara, Edgar, jt. ed. see Ramos-Garcia, Luis A.

O'Hara, Frank. Early Writing, 1946-1951. Allen, Donald, ed. LC 77-652. 1977. 12.00 (ISBN 0-912516-16-X); pap. 4.00 (ISBN 0-912516-17-8). Grey Fox.

--Poems Retrieved. Allen, Donald, ed. LC 77-554. 250p. 1977. 12.00 (ISBN 0-912516-18-6); pap. 5.00 (ISBN 0-912516-19-4). Grey Fox.

--Selected Plays. LC 78-9658. 1978. 14.95 (ISBN 0-916190-08-0); pap. 6.00 (ISBN 0-916190-09-9). Full Court NY.

--Selected Poems. Allen, Donald, ed. 1974. pap. 4.95 (ISBN 0-394-71973-5, V-973, Vin). Random.

O'Hara, Gerald J. Malsum. 320p. 1981. pap. 2.50 (ISBN 0-380-77289-2, 77289). Avon.

O'Hara, Gregory L., jt. auth. see O'Hara, Charles E.

O'Hara, James E., Jr. The Rhetoric of Love in Lyly's Euthues & His England & Sidney's Arcadia (1590) (Salzburg Studies in English Literature, Elizabethan & Renaissance Studies: No. 76). (Orig.). 1978. pap. text ed. 25.00x (ISBN 0-391-01243-6). Humanities.

O'Hara, Jean, jt. auth. see Rebert, Jo.

O'Hara, John. Appointment in Samarra. 1934. 3.00 o.p. (ISBN 0-394-41542-6). Random.

--Elizabeth Appleton. 312p. 1974. pap. 1.50 o.p. (ISBN 0-445-03039-9). Popular Lib.

--The Ewings. 352p. 1972. pap. 1.25 o.p. (ISBN 0-445-00136-4). Popular Lib.

--The Farmers Hotel. 128p. 1973. pap. 1.25 o.p. (ISBN 0-445-00161-5). Popular Lib.

--From the Terrace. 1974. pap. 2.25 o.p. (ISBN 0-445-08247-X). Popular Lib.

--The Hat on the Bed. 416p. 1975. pap. 1.50 o.p. (ISBN 0-445-03068-2). Popular Lib.

--Hellbox. 176p. 1975. pap. 1.25 o.p. (ISBN 0-445-00233-6). Popular Lib.

--Hope of Heaven. 176p. 1973. pap. 1.25 o.p. (ISBN 0-445-00149-6). Popular Lib.

--The Horse Knows the Way. 384p. 1975. pap. 1.50 o.p. (ISBN 0-445-03057-7). Popular Lib.

--The Lockwood Concern. 1977. pap. 1.95 o.p. (ISBN 0-445-08564-9). Popular Lib.

O'Hara, Sr. Kevin, jt. auth. see Walters, Sr. Annette.

O'Hara, Mary. Green Grass of Wyoming. (gr. 7-9). 1946. 10.95 (ISBN 0-397-00011-1). Lippincott.

--My Friend Flicka. new ed. LC 73-6611. (Illus.). 272p. (gr. 7-9). 1973. 9.95 (ISBN 0-397-00981-X); text ed. 3.40 (ISBN 0-397-00008-1). Lippincott.

--Thunderhead. (gr. 7-9). 1943. 10.95 (ISBN 0-397-00007-3). Lippincott.

O'Hara, Monica. New Hope Through Hypnotherapy: The Joe Keeton Phenomenon. 150p. 1980. 13.50x (ISBN 0-85626-194-7, Pub. by Abacus Pr England); pap. 7.95x (ISBN 0-85626-194-7). Intl Schol Bk Serv.

Ohara Publications. Dear Bruce Lee. (Series 407). pap. 7.95 (ISBN 0-89750-069-5). Ohara Pubns.

O'Hara, R. Philip, et al, trs. see Bultmann, Rudolf.

O'Hara, William T. & Hill, John G., Jr. The Student - the College - the Law. LC 72-87116. 1972. pap. 6.50x (ISBN 0-8077-2378-9). Tchrs Coll.

O'Hara-Deveraux, Mary, et al, eds. Eldercare: A Practical Guide to Clinical Geriatrics. 1980. write for info. (ISBN 0-8089-1285-2). Grune.

O'Hare, Frank, jt. auth. see Menering, Dean.

Ohashi, Wataru, jt. auth. see Masunaga, Shizuto.

O'Hear, Anthony. Education, Society & Human Nature: An Introduction to the Philosophy of Education. 192p. 1981. price not set (ISBN 0-7100-0747-7); pap. price not set (ISBN 0-7100-0748-5). Routledge & Kegan.

O'Hearn, George. Oikos, the Environment & Education. LC 74-33808. (Fastback Ser.: No. 52). (Illus.). 54p. (Orig.). 1975. pap. 0.75 (ISBN 0-87367-052-3). Phi Delta Kappa.

O'Hearne, John, jt. auth. see Morrison, James H.

O Hehir, Brendan. Expans'd Hieroglyphicks: A Study of Sir John Denham's Coopers Hill, with a Critical Edition of the Poem. LC 68-27163. 1968. 20.00x (ISBN 0-520-01496-0). U of Cal Pr.

--A Gaelic Lexicon for Finnegans Wake & Glossary for Joyce's Other Works. 1968. 22.75x (ISBN 0-520-00952-5). U of Cal Pr.

--Harmony from Discords: A Life of Sir John Denham. LC 68-27162. 1968. 20.00x (ISBN 0-520-00953-3). U of Cal Pr.

O'Hehir, Brendan & Dillon, John M. A Classical Lexicon for Finnegans Wake: A Glossary of the Greek & Latin in Major Works of Joyce. 1977. 30.00x (ISBN 0-520-03082-6). U of Cal Pr.

O'Hehir, Kathy, ed. see Moore, Mary E.

O Heithir, Breandan. Lead Us into Temptation. 1978. 12.00 (ISBN 0-7100-0030-8). Routledge & Kegan.

O'Henry. Alias Jimmy Valentine. Pauk, Walter & Harris, Raymond, eds. (Jamestown Classics Ser.). (Illus.). 37p. (gr. 6-12). 1979. pap. text ed. 1.60x (ISBN 0-89061-192-0, 409); tchrs. ed. 3.00 (ISBN 0-89061-194-7). Jamestown Pubs.

O. Henry. The Gift of the Magi. Pauk, Walter & Harris, Raymond, eds. (Jamestown Classics Ser.). (Illus.). 35p. (gr. 6-12). 1979. pap. text ed. 1.60x (ISBN 0-89061-186-6, 401); tchrs. ed. 2.50x (ISBN 0-89061-188-2, 403). Jamestown Pubs.

O'Henry. The Last Leaf. Pauk, Walter & Harris, Raymond, eds. (Jamestown Classics Ser.). (Illus.). 35p. (Orig.). (gr. 6-12). 1979. pap. text ed. 1.60x (ISBN 0-89061-195-5, 413); tchrs. ed. 3.00 (ISBN 0-89061-197-1, 415). Jamestown Pubs.

--The Ransom of Red Chief. Pauk, Walter & Harris, Raymond, eds. (Jamestown Classics Ser.). (Illus.). 40p. (Orig.). (gr. 6-12). 1979. pap. text ed. 1.60x (ISBN 0-89061-189-0, 405); tchrs. ed. 3.00 (ISBN 0-89061-191-2, 407). Jamestown Pubs.

Ohgel, Doris. The Devil in Vienna. (gr. 7-12). 1980. pap. 1.50 (ISBN 0-440-91777-8, LFL). Dell.

Ohio Family Historians. Eighteen Thirty Federal Population Census Index of Ohio, 2 vols. 1976. Repr. of 1964 ed. 42.50 set (ISBN 0-911060-06-5). Vol. 1 (ISBN 0-911060-04-9). Vol. 2 (ISBN 0-911060-05-7). Ohio Lib Foun.

--Eighteen Twenty Federal Population Census Index of Ohio. 1976. Repr. of 1964 ed. 29.75 (ISBN 0-685-70950-7). Ohio Lib Foun.

Ohio State University. Nursing Skills. 1077p. 1980. pap. text ed. 18.95 (ISBN 0-8359-5039-5). Reston.

Ohkawa, Kazushi & Key, Bernard. Asian Socioeconomical Development: A National Accounts Approach. 326p. 1980. text ed. 27.50. U Pr of Hawaii.

Ohkawa, Kazushi & Key, Bernard, eds. Asian Socioeconomic Development: A National Accounts Approach. 326p. 1980. text ed. 27.50x (ISBN 0-8248-0743-X). U Pr of Hawaii.

Ohle, W., ed. see Sladecek, Vladimir.

Ohlendorf, Sheila, tr. see Torres, Elias L.

Ohlendorf, Sheila M., ed. see Berlandier, Jean L., et al.

Ohles, John F., ed. Biographical Dictionary of American Educators, 3 vols. LC 77-84750. 1978. lib. bdg. 115.00 (ISBN 0-8371-9893-3, OHB/). Greenwood.

Ohlin, Lloyd E., jt. auth. see Cloward, Richard A.

Ohlsen, Woodrow & Hammond, Frank L., eds. From Paragraph to Essay: Readings for Progress in Writing. 3rd ed. LC 76-27897. 320p. (For accelerated classes). (gr. 9-12). 1976. pap. text ed. 7.95x (ISBN 0-684-14832-3, ScribC). Scribner.

Ohmer, M. M. Mathematics for a Liberal Education. LC 79-119669. (Mathematics Ser). (Illus.). 1971. text ed. 13.95x (ISBN 0-201-05435-3); instructor's manual 2.75 (ISBN 0-201-05436-1). A-W.

Ohmer, Merlin M., et al. Elementary Contemporary Mathematics. 2nd ed. LC 70-186167. 1972. pap. text ed. 19.50x o.p. (ISBN 0-471-00401-4). Wiley.

Ohnuki, Masako, tr. see Uyeda, Seiya.

Ohnuki-Tierney, Emiko. The Ainu of the Northwest Coast of Southern Sakhalin. Spindler, George & Spindler, Louise, eds. (Case Studies in Cultural Anthropology). (Illus.). 144p. pap. text ed. 4.95x (ISBN 0-8290-0276-6). Irvington.

--Illness & Healing Among the Sakhalin Ainu: A Symbolic Interpretation. LC 80-24268. (Illus.). 272p. Date not set. price not set (ISBN 0-521-23636-3). Cambridge U Pr.

Ohnysty, James. Aids to Ethics & Professional Conduct for Student Radiologic Technologists. 2nd ed. 176p. 1979. 11.75 (ISBN 0-398-01419-1). C C Thomas.

Oho, Kenkichi. Practical Fiberoptic Bronchoscopy. LC 79-92553. (Illus.). 1980. 36.00 (ISBN 0-89640-041-7). Igaku-Shoin.

Ohrn, Y., jt. auth. see Lowdin, P. O.

Ohrt, Wallace L. The Rogue I Remember. LC 79-17166. (Illus.). 128p. 1979. pap. 6.95 (ISBN 0-916890-94-5). Mountaineers.

Ohrwalder, Joseph. Ten Years' Captivity in the Mahdi's Camp, 1882-1892. 13th, rev. & abr. ed. LC 80-2199. (Illus.). 1981. Repr. of 1893 ed. 54.00 (ISBN 0-404-18981-4). AMS Pr.

Ohsawa, George. Atomic Age & the Philosophy of the Far East. (Illus.). 1977. 7.95 o.s.i. (ISBN 0-918860-28-8). G Ohsawa.

--Jack & Mitie. Rothman, Sandy, ed. Burns, Ken, tr. from Fr. Orig. Title: Jack et Madame Mitie En Occident. 224p. (Orig.). 1981. pap. 9.50 (ISBN 0-918860-36-9). G Ohsawa.

--Kiso Nihongo Jo Jikan: Four Hours to Basic Japanese. Alhara, Herman, ed. (Illus.). 1974. pap. 1.35 o.p. (ISBN 0-918860-06-7). G Ohsawa.

--Life & Death. 30p. 1971. pap. 1.00 o.p. (ISBN 0-918860-03-2). G Ohsawa.

--Macrobiotics: An Invitation to Health & Happiness. 77p. 1971. pap. 3.95 (ISBN 0-918860-02-4). G Ohsawa.

--Practical Guide to Far-Eastern Macrobiotic Medicine. Alhara, Herman, ed. (Illus.). 260p. 1973. pap. 7.50 o.p. (ISBN 0-918860-21-0). G Ohsawa.

Ohta, T. Evolution & Variation of Multigene Families. (Lecture Notes in Biomathematics: Vol. 37). 131p. 1980. pap. 9.80 (ISBN 0-387-09998-0). Springer-Verlag.

Ohta, T., ed. Solar-Hydrogen Energy System: An Authoritative Review of Water-Splitting Systems by Solar Beam & Solar Heat; Hydrogen Production, Storage & Utilisation. LC 79-40694. (Illus.). 1979. 48.00 (ISBN 0-08-022713-9). Pergamon.

Ohta, Tomoko, jt. auth. see Kimura, Motoo.

Oikawa, Kikuo. Trace Analysis of Atmospheric Samples. LC 77-3458. 1977. 29.95 (ISBN 0-470-99013-9). Halsted Pr.

Oil Shale Symposium, 11th. Proceedings. Gary, James H., ed. (Illus.). 389p. 1978. pap. 12.00 (ISBN 0-918062-03-9). Colo Sch Mines.

Oinas, Felix J., ed. Folklore Nationalism & Politics. 1977. pap. 9.95 (ISBN 0-89357-043-5). Slavica.

Oisteanu, Valery. Do Not Defuse. 1980. pap. 2.50 (ISBN 0-9601870-2-2). Pass.

Oisteanu, Valery. Underground Shadows. 1977. pap. 1.50 (ISBN 0-9601870-0-6). Pass.

Ojakangas, Beatrice A., jt. auth. see Consumer Guide Editors.

Ojeda, Enriave. Jorge Carrera Andrade: Introduccion A Su Vida. 1972. 16.95 (ISBN 0-88303-003-9); pap. 12.95 (ISBN 0-685-73209-6). E Torres & Sons.

Ojemann, George A., jt. auth. see Calvin, William H.

Ojha, B. S., jt. auth. see Gosal, Gurdev S.

Ojo, Oyedrian. The Climates of West Africa. 1977. text ed. 29.50 (ISBN 0-435-95700-7); pap. text ed. 14.50 (ISBN 0-435-95701-5). Heinemann Ed.

Oka, Hideyuki. How to Wrap Five More Eggs: Traditional Japanese Packaging. LC 74-23690. (Illus.). 216p. 1975. 18.75 (ISBN 0-8348-0108-6). Weatherhill.

Oka, S. Cardiovascular Hemorheology. (Illus.). 200p. Date not set. price not set (ISBN 0-521-23650-9). Cambridge U Pr.

Okabayashi, Atsushi & Kondo, Yoichiro. Masugi Nephritis & Its Immunopathologic Implications. LC 79-91335. (Illus.). 1980. 41.00 (ISBN 0-89640-039-5). Igaku-Shoin.

Okada, John. No-No Boy. LC 79-55834. 176p. 1978. pap. 5.95 (ISBN 0-295-95525-2). U of Wash Pr.

Okada, Kenzo, et al, illus. Okada, Shinoda, & Tsutaka. LC 79-84887. (Illus.). 50p. (Orig.). 1979. pap. 6.00 (ISBN 0-88397-034-1). Intl Exhibit Foun.

Okada, T. S., jt. auth. see Ebert, J. D.

Okafor, Festus C., ed. Philosophy of Education & Third World Perspective. LC 80-50732. 346p. (Orig.). 1981. 15.00x (ISBN 0-931494-06-0); pap. 10.00x (ISBN 0-931494-07-9). Brunswick Pub.

Okafor, Nduka. Development of Universities in Nigeria: A Study of the Influence of Political & Other Factors on University Development in Nigeria, 1868-1967. (Illus.). 1971. pap. text ed. 5.75x (ISBN 0-582-64060-1). Humanities.

Okagaki, Alan & Benson, Jim. County Energy Plan Guidebook. 2nd ed. (Illus.). 200p. (Orig.). 1979. pap. text ed. 10.00x (ISBN 0-937786-01-2). Inst Ecologica.

Okamoto, Shumpei. Japanese Oligarchy & the Russo-Japanese War. LC 74-114259. (Studies of the East Asian Institute of Col. Univ.). 1971. 20.00x (ISBN 0-231-03404-0). Columbia U Pr.

Okamoto, Shumpei, jt. ed. see Borg, Dorothy.

O'Kane, John, tr. from Persian. The Ship of Sulaiman. LC 70-186605. (Persian Heritage Ser). 250p. 1972. 17.50x (ISBN 0-231-03654-X). Columbia U Pr.

O'Kane, Richard H. Clear the Bridge. 496p. 1981. pap. 2.95 (ISBN 0-553-14516-9). Bantam.

Okara, Gabriel. The Voice. LC 76-90298. 1970. pap. text ed. 3.50x o.p. (ISBN 0-8419-0015-9, Africana). Holmes & Meier.

--The Voice. 96p. 1964. pap. 2.25 o.p. (ISBN 0-531-06048-9, Fontana Pap). Watts.

Okasha, Elizabeth. Hand-List of Anglo-Saxon Non-Runic Inscriptions. LC 75-129934. (Illus.). 1971. 58.00 (ISBN 0-521-07904-7). Cambridge U Pr.

Okazaki, Joji. Pure Land Buddhist Painting. Grotenhuis, Elizabeth T., tr. from Jap. LC 76-9354. (Japanese Arts Library: Vol. 4). 1977. 16.95 (ISBN 0-87011-287-2). Kodansha.

Oke, Janette. Love Comes Softly. 192p. (Orig.). 1979. pap. 3.50 (ISBN 0-87123-342-8, 210342). Bethany Fell.

--Love's Enduring Promise. 206p. (Orig.). 1980. pap. 3.50 (ISBN 0-87123-345-2, 210345). Bethany Fell.

Okebe, P. N. Preliminary Practical Physics. 1981. price not set (ISBN 0-471-27852-1, Pub. by Wiley-Interscience); pap. price not set (ISBN 0-471-27851-3). Wiley.

O'Keefe, Garrett J., jt. auth. see Mendelsohn, Harold.

O'Keefe, Rip. Sober Living Workbook. 1980. pap. 5.95. Hazelden.

O'Keeffe, Georgia. Georgia O'Keeffe: A Portrait by Alfred Stieglitz. LC 78-13467. (Illus., Co-pub. by Metropolitan Museum of Art). 1979. 45.00 (ISBN 0-670-51989-8, Studio). Viking Pr.

O'Keeffe, John. Wild Oats. 1977. pap. 3.25x (ISBN 0-87830-556-4). Theatre Arts.

O'Kelly De Galway, A. O. Tigran Petrosian - World Champion. 1967. text ed. 9.00 (ISBN 0-08-011013-4); pap. text ed. 5.50 (ISBN 0-08-011012-6). Pergamon.

O'Kelly de Galway, Alberic. Improve Your Chess Fast. 1978. pap. 9.95 (ISBN 0-7134-1054-X). David & Charles.

Oken, Alan. Alan Oken's Complete Astrology. 640p. 1980. pap. 9.95 (ISBN 0-553-01262-2). Bantam.

Oki, Masahiro. Healing Yourself Through Okida Yoga. LC 76-29339. 1977. pap. 7.95 (ISBN 0-87040-380-X). Japan Pubns.

--Meditation Yoga. Bradshaw, David N., tr. from Japanese. LC 77-93244. 1978. 12.00 (ISBN 0-87040-435-0). Japan Pubns.

--Practical Yoga: A Pictorial Approach. LC 76-115846. (Illus.). 1973. pap. 6.95 (ISBN 0-87040-224-2). Japan Pubns.

--Zen Yoga Therapy. LC 79-1060. (Illus.). 1979. pap. 12.50 (ISBN 0-87040-459-8). Japan Pubns.

O'Kieffe, Charley. Western Story: The Recollections of Charley O'Kieffe 1884-1898. LC 60-5381. (Pioneer Heritage Ser: Vol. 2). (Illus.). xvi, 223p. 1960. 11.95x (ISBN 0-8032-0134-6); pap. 2.95 (ISBN 0-8032-5796-1, BB 585, Bison). U of Nebr Pr.

Okigbo, P. N. Nigerian Public Finance. (African Studies Ser.: No. 15). 1965. 12.95x o.s.i. (ISBN 0-8101-0181-5). Northwestern U Pr.

--Nigeria's Financial System. (Illus.). 320p. 1981. text ed. 25.00x (ISBN 0-582-59733-1). Longman.

Okimoto, Jean D. It's Just Too Much. 128p. (YA) (gr. 5-12). 1980. 8.95 (ISBN 0-399-20737-6). Putnam.

--My Mother Is Not Married to My Father. 1981. pap. price not set (ISBN 0-671-56079-4). Archway.

Okin, Josee & Schmitt, Conrad J. Francais: Commencons. 1970. text ed. 11.60 (ISBN 0-07-047500-8, W); tchr's. ed. 10.96 (ISBN 0-07-047501-6); wkbk. 3.60 (ISBN 0-07-047502-4); tapes 360.00 (ISBN 0-07-047503-2); tests 72.00 (ISBN 0-686-66095-1); Webster master replacements 36.00 (ISBN 0-07-047506-7); filmstrips 80.00 (ISBN 0-07-047504-0). McGraw.

--Let's Speak French, Bks. 1-3. 1966. Bks. 1-2. text ed. 5.28x ea. (W). Bk. 1 (ISBN 0-07-047642-X). Bk. 2 (ISBN 0-07-047644-6). Bk. 3. text ed. 11.72x (ISBN 0-07-047638-1); tchrs. guide bks. 1 & 2 8.08x (ISBN 0-07-047645-4). Bk. 3. tchrs. guide 9.32x (ISBN 0-07-047639-X). McGraw.

Okinshevich, Leo. United States History & Historiography in Post-War Soviet Writings, 1945-1970: A Bibliography. new ed. LC 76-3756. 431p. 1976. text ed. 10.25 (ISBN 0-87436-208-3). ABC-Clio.

Okita, Saburo, jt. ed. see Crawford, John.

Okker, Tom. Tennis in Pictures. 160p. 1976. pap. 2.95 o.s.i. (ISBN 0-346-12308-9). Cornerstone.

Okner, Benjamin A., jt. auth. see Pechman, Joseph A. B.

Okochi, Kazuo & Karsh, Bernard, eds. Workers & Employers in Japan: The Japanese Employment Relations System. 548p. 1974. 25.00x o.p. (ISBN 0-691-03097-9). Princeton U Pr.

Okoli, Ekwueme F. Institutional Structure & Conflict in Nigeria. LC 79-3425. 1980. pap. text ed. 7.75 (ISBN 0-8191-0888-X). U Pr of Amer.

Okolicsanyi, L. Familial Hyperbilirubinemia: Proceedings of the Workshop on Familial Disorders of Hepatic Bilirubin Metabolism Held in Venice, Italy 23rd-24th May 1980. 250p. 1981. 42.00 (ISBN 0-686-69369-8, Pub. by Wiley-Interscience). Wiley.

Okon, Wincenty & Wilgocka-Okon, Barbara. The School Readiness Project. (Experiments & Innovations in Education Ser.). 53p. (Orig.). 1973. pap. 2.50 (ISBN 92-3-101065-4, U568, UNESCO). Unipub.

Okoye, Mokwugo. Points of Discord: Studies in Tension & Conflict. 225p. 1974. 13.50x o.p. (ISBN 0-584-10221-6). Intl Pubns Serv.

Okpaku, Joseph. Superfight No. II: The Story Behind the Fights Between Muhammad Ali & Joe Frazier. LC 74-74429. 1974. 6.95 (ISBN 0-89388-165-1). Okpaku Communications.

Okpaku, S. Family Planning & Preventive Psychiatry. 1981. 20.00 (ISBN 0-89388-003-5). Okpaku Communications.

Okpewho, Isidore. The Epic in Africa. 1979. 17.50 (ISBN 0-231-04400-3). Columbia U Pr.

--The Victims. 200p. (Orig.). 1979. 9.00 (ISBN 0-89410-115-3); pap. 5.00 (ISBN 0-89410-114-5). Three Continents.

Okri, Benjamin. Flowers & Shadows. (Drum Beat Ser.). 274p. 1980. pap. 5.00 (ISBN 0-582-64301-5). Three Continents.

Oksenberg, Michel & Oxnam, Robert B. China & America: Past & Future. (Headline Ser.: 235). 1977. pap. 2.00 (ISBN 0-87124-041-6, 77-77822). Foreign Policy.

Okuda, Kunio & Peters, Robert L., eds. Hepatocellular Carcinoma. LC 76-6500. (Wiley Series on Diseases of the Liver). 512p. 1976. 64.95 (ISBN 0-471-65316-0, Pub. by Wiley Medical). Wiley.

Okudjava, Boulat. Nocturne: From the Notes of Lt. Amiran Amilakhvari, Retired. Bouis, Antonina W., tr. from Russian. LC 77-11544. 1978. 10.00 o.p. (ISBN 0-06-013289-2, HarpT). Har-Row.

Okudzhava, Bulat. Sixty-Five Songs; Sixty-Five Pesen. Frumkin, V., ed. (Eng. & Rus.). 1980. 18.00 (ISBN 0-88233-637-1); pap. 11.00 (ISBN 0-88233-638-X). Ardis Pubs.

Okumu, John J., jt. auth. see Barkan, Joel D.

Okun, Arthur M. Equality & Efficiency: The Big Tradeoff. 124p. 1975. 10.95 (ISBN 0-8157-6476-6); pap. 4.95 (ISBN 0-8157-6475-8). Brookings.

--Prices & Quantities: A Macroeconomic Analysis. 400p. 1981. 19.95 (ISBN 0-8157-6480-4); pap. 7.95 (ISBN 0-8157-6479-0). Brookings.

Okun, Arthur M. & Perry, George L., eds. Curing Chronic Inflation. 1978. 14.95 (ISBN 0-8157-6474-X); pap. 5.95 (ISBN 0-8157-6473-1). Brookings.

Okun, Daniel A. Regionalization of Water Management: A Revolution in England & Wales. (Illus.). 1977. 62.10x (ISBN 0-85334-738-7, Pub. by Applied Science). Burgess-Intl Ideas.

Okun, L. B. Weak Interaction of Elementary Particles. 1965. text ed. 30.00 (ISBN 0-08-011122-X); pap. text ed. 19.50 (ISBN 0-08-013702-4). Pergamon.

Okun, Lawrence. On the Eighth Day. LC 81-80093. 208p. 1981. pap. 2.25 (ISBN 0-87216-852-2). Playboy Pbks.

Okun, Ronald, jt. ed. see George, Robert.

O'Kunewick, James P. & Meredith, Ruby F., eds. Graft vs. Leukemia in Man & Animal Models. 304p. 1981. 69.95 (ISBN 0-8493-5745-4). CRC Pr.

Okutani, T. & McGowan, J. A. Systematics, Distribution & Abundance of the Epiplanktonic Squid. (U. C. Publ. in Oceanography: Vol. 14). 1969. pap. 7.00x (ISBN 0-520-09319-4). U of Cal Pr.

Olabisi, Olagoka & Robeson, Lloyd. Polymer-Polymer Miscibility. 1979. 45.60 (ISBN 0-12-525050-9). Acad Pr.

Olafson, Fred, ed. Society, Law & Morality: Readings in Social Philosophy. 1961. text ed. 14.95 o.p. (ISBN 0-13-820142-0). P-H.

Olaitan, Samson O. & Agusiobo, Obiora N. Introduction to the Teaching of Home Economics. 320p. 1981. write for info. (ISBN 0-471-27807-6, Pub. by Wiley-Interscience); pap. write for info. (ISBN 0-471-27806-8). Wiley.

Olaitan, Samson O. & Augusiobo, Obiora N. Handbook of Practice Teaching. LC 80-40291. 192p. 1981. write for info. (ISBN 0-471-27805-X, Pub. by Wiley-Interscience); pap. write for info. (ISBN 0-471-27804-1). Wiley.

Olander, J. & Greenberg, M. Literature of Horror & the Supernatural. 1978. 8.95 (ISBN 0-13-537761-7); pap. 2.95 (ISBN 0-13-537753-6). P-H.

--Literature of the Fantastic. 1978. 8.95 (ISBN 0-13-537662-9); pap. 2.95 (ISBN 0-13-537654-8). P-H.

Olander, Joseph, jt. auth. see Greenberg, Martin.

Olaru, H., tr. see Anapol'Skaya, L. E. & Gandin, L. S.

Olauson, Judith. The American Woman Playwright: A View of Criticism & Characterization. LC 80-51605. 190p. 1981. 12.50x (ISBN 0-87875-198-X). Whitston Pub.

Olausson, Eric & Cato, Ingemar. Chemistry & Biochemistry of Estuaries. LC 79-41211. 432p. 1980. 80.00 (ISBN 0-471-27679-0, Pub. by Wiley-Interscience). Wiley.

Olbricht, Thomas. The Power to Be. LC 79-67136. (Journey Bks.). 1979. pap. 2.35 (ISBN 0-8344-0108-8). Sweet.

Olbricht, Thomas H. He Loves Forever. LC 80-52461. (Journey Bks). (Orig.). 1980. pap. 2.60 (ISBN 0-8344-0117-7). Sweet.

Olcott, Frances J. Good Stories for Anniversaries. LC 77-167093. (Tower Bks). (Illus.). 1971. Repr. of 1937 ed. 22.00 (ISBN 0-8103-3910-2). Gale.

Olcott, Henry S. Inside the Occult: The True Story of Madame H. P. Blavatsky. LC 75-17044. Orig. Title: Old Diary Leaves. 1975. lib. bdg. 12.90 o.p. (ISBN 0-914294-31-8); pap. 3.95 o.p. (ISBN 0-914294-30-X). Running Pr.

Old-House Journal Staff, ed. The Old-House Journal 1981 Catalog: A Buyer's Guide. (Illus.). 142p. (Orig.). 1981. pap. 9.95 (ISBN 0-87951-125-7). Overlook Pr.

Old, K. M. Phytophthora & Forest Management in Australia. 1980. 13.00x (ISBN 0-643-02523-5, Pub. by CSIRO Australia). State Mutual Bk.

Old, R. W. & Primrose, S. B. Principles of Gene Manipulation: An Introduction to Genetic Engineering. (Studies in Microbiology: Vol. 2). 1980. 32.75x (ISBN 0-520-04143-7); pap. 12.75 (ISBN 0-520-04151-8). U of Cal Pr.

Oldaker, Wilfred H., ed. see Aristophanes.

Oldale, Adrienne & Oldale, Peter. Growing Food Under Glass: One-Thousand & One Questions Answered. 1978. 11.95 (ISBN 0-7153-7334-X). David & Charles.

--Navigating Britain's Coastline: Land's End to Portland. LC 79-91496. (Illus.). 1980. 17.95 (ISBN 0-7153-7579-2). David & Charles.

--Navigating Britain's Coastline: Portland to Dover. LC 80-68901. (Illus.). 88p. 1981. 18.50 (ISBN 0-7153-7960-7). David & Charles.

--Plant Propagation in Pictures. LC 75-4062. (Illus.). 96p. 1975. 14.95 (ISBN 0-7153-6875-3). David & Charles.

Oldale, Peter, jt. auth. see Oldale, Adrienne.

Oldenberg, tr. see Mueller, F. Max.

Oldenbourg, Zoe. Heirs of the Kingdom. Carter, Anne, tr. from Fr. LC 70-147805. 1971. Repr. 8.95 o.s.i. (ISBN 0-394-46835-X). Pantheon.

Oldenburg, tr. see Mueller, F. Max.

Oldenburg, Claes. Notes in Hand: Miniatures of My Notebook Pages. 1971. pap. 2.95 o.p. (ISBN 0-525-47325-4). Dutton.

--Raw Notes: Documents & Scripts of the Performances: Stars, Moveyhouse, Massage, the Typewriter with annotations by the author. LC 73-83224. (The Nova Scotia Ser). (Illus.). 544p. 1973. pap. 12.95, c (ISBN 0-919616-01-1). NYU Pr.

Oldenburg, Veena T. Say It in Hindi. (Say It Ser.). 192p. (Orig.). Date not set. pap. 2.00 (ISBN 0-486-23959-4). Dover.

Oldendorf, William H. The Quest for an Image of the Brain. (Computerized Tomography in the Perspective of Past & Future Imaging Methods). 160p. 1980. text ed. 21.00 (ISBN 0-89004-429-5). Raven.

Oldenquist, Andrew. Moral Philosophy: Text & Readings. 2nd ed. LC 77-77978. (Illus.). 1978. pap. text ed. 11.50 (ISBN 0-395-25433-7). HM.

Older, Anne, jt. auth. see Dumbleton, Susanne.

Older, Julia & Sherman, Steve. Soup & Bread: One Hundred Recipes for Bowl & Board. 2nd ed. 128p. 1981. pap. 8.95 (ISBN 0-8289-0338-7). Greene.

Oldfather, W. A. A Bibliography of Epictetus. 177p. 1952. octavo 7.00. Holmes.

Oldfield, Pamela. Melanie Brown & the Jar of Sweets. (Illus.). (ps-5). 1974. 8.50 (ISBN 0-571-10619-6, Pub. by Faber & Faber). Merrimack Bk Serv.

--Melanie Brown Goes to School. (Illus.). (ps-5). 1970. 5.95 o.p. (ISBN 0-571-09421-X, Pub. by Faber & Faber). Merrimack Bk Serv.

Oldfield, Rosamund, tr. see Swedrup, Ivan.

Oldham, Dale. The Sudden Land. (Orig.). 1980. pap. 1.75 (ISBN 0-505-51480-X). Tower Bks.

Oldham, Greg R., jt. auth. see Hackman, J. Richard.

Oldham, John. Works of Mr. John Oldham. LC 79-26304. 1980. Repr. of 1686 ed. 72.00x (ISBN 0-8201-1337-9). Schol Facsimiles.

Oldham, Mary. The White Pony. (Books for Young Readers). 128p. (gr. 4-9). 1981. 7.95g (ISBN 0-8038-0800-3). Hastings.

Oldham, Neild. The Firebug. Mooney, Tom, ed. (Pal Paperbacks Ser., (Illus., Orig.). (gr. 7-12). 1976. pap. text ed. 1.25 (ISBN 0-8374-3488-2). Xerox Ed Pubns.

Oldmixon, John. Reflections on the Stage & Mr. Collyer's Defence of the Short View. LC 73-170447. (The English Stage Ser.: Vol. 33). lib. bdg. 50.00 (ISBN 0-8240-0616-X). Garland Pub.

Oldroyd, David R. Darwinian Impacts. 1980. pap. text ed. 13.50x (ISBN 0-391-02091-9). Humanities.

Oldroyd, Harold. Insects & Their World. LC 60-50390. (Orig.). 1962. pap. 2.75 o.s.i. (ISBN 0-226-62636-9, P516, Phoen). U of Chicago Pr.

Olds, Helen D. Detour for Meg. (gr. 6-9). 1967. pap. 1.25 o.p. (ISBN 0-671-29836-4). Archway.

--Detour for Meg. (gr. 6-9). 1967. pap. 1.25 (ISBN 0-671-29836-4). PB.

Olds, James. Drives & Reinforcements: Behavioral Studies of Hypothalamic Functions. LC 75-31480. 1977. pap. 10.50 (ISBN 0-89004-087-7). Raven.

Olds, Marshall. Analysis of the Interchurch World Movement Report on the Steel Strike. LC 73-139199. (Civil Liberties in American History Ser). 1971. Repr. of 1923 ed. lib. bdg. 47.50 (ISBN 0-306-70082-4). Da Capo.

Olds, Mason. Religious Humanism in America: Dietrich, Reese & Potter. 1977. 10.00 (ISBN 0-8191-0267-9). U Pr of Amer.

Olds, R. J. A Colour Atlas of the Rat: Dissection Guide. LC 78-24742. 1979. text ed. 10.95 (ISBN 0-470-26647-3). Halsted Pr.

Olds, Robert. Managing Your Schools: What's Ahead. 1979. pap. 11.95 (ISBN 0-87545-016-4). Natl Sch PR.

Olds, Robert, ed. School Board Meeting. 1970. pap. text ed. 4.75 o.p. (ISBN 0-685-04603-6, 411-3131). Natl Sch Pr.

Olds, Sally W., jt. auth. see Papalia, Diane E.

Olds, W. J. Lubricants,Cutting Fluids & Coolants. LC 72-83305. 1973. 17.95 (ISBN 0-8436-0812-9). CBI Pub.

O'Leary, Brian. The Fertile Stars. (Illus.). 1981. 12.95. Everest Hse.

O'Leary, Brian & Beatty, J. Kelly, eds. The New Solar System. (Illus.). 192p. 1981. 19.95 (ISBN 0-933346-26-3). Sky Pub.

O'Leary, Cornelius, jt. auth. see Budge, Ian.

O'Leary, De Lacy. Arabic Thought and Its Place in History. rev. ed. LC 80-1917. 1981. Repr. of 1939 ed. 35.00 (ISBN 0-404-18982-2). AMS Pr.

--Colloquial Arabic. 3rd ed. (Trubner's Colloquial Manuals). 1963. pap. 7.95 (ISBN 0-7100-7909-5). Routledge & Kegan.

--How Greek Science Passed to the Arabs. 1979. 17.50 (ISBN 0-7100-1903-3). Routledge & Kegan.

--Islam at the Cross Roads: A Brief Survey of the Present Position and Problems of the World of Islam. LC 80-1916. 1981. Repr. of 1923 ed. 26.50 (ISBN 0-404-18983-0). AMS Pr.

O'Leary, Greg. The Shaping of Chinese Foreign Policy. LC 80-10231. 320p. 1980. 25.00 (ISBN 0-312-71620-6). St Martin.

O'Leary, James L. & Goldring, Sidney, eds. Science & Epilepsy: Neuroscience Gains in Epilepsy Research. LC 75-21860. 303p. 1976. 26.00 (ISBN 0-89004-072-9). Raven.

O'Leary, James P. Systems Theory & Regional Integration: The "Market Model" of International Politics. LC 78-66420. 1978. pap. text ed. 10.25 (ISBN 0-8191-0500-7). U Pr of Amer.

O'Leary, John. Recollections of Fenians & Fenianism, 2 vols. in 1. 248p. 1968. Repr. of 1896 ed. 20.00x (ISBN 0-7165-0606-8, Pub. by Irish Academic Pr Ireland). Biblio Dist.

O'Leary, K. Daniel & Wilson, G. Terence. Behavior Therapy: Application & Outcome. (Social Learning Theory Ser.). (Illus.). 480p. 1975. ref. ed. 19.95 (ISBN 0-13-073890-5). P-H.

O'Leary, K. Daniel, jt. auth. see Wilson, G. Terence.

O'Leary, K. Daniel & O'Leary, Susan G., eds. Classroom Management: The Successful Use of Behavior Modification. 2nd ed. LC 76-41004. 1977. text ed. 32.00 (ISBN 0-08-021396-0); pap. text ed. 9.95 (ISBN 0-08-021395-2). Pergamon.

O'Leary, Lawrence R. Interviewing for the Decisionmaker. LC 75-44322. 144p. 1976. 12.95 (ISBN 0-88229-215-3); pap. 7.95 (ISBN 0-88229-512-8). Nelson-Hall.

O'Leary, Liam. Rex Ingram: Master of the Silent Cinema. (Illus.). 224p. 1980. 28.50. B&N.

O'Leary, Maggie, jt. auth. see Rhea, Kay.

O'Leary, Michael K., jt. auth. see Coplin, William D.

O'Leary, Susan G., jt. ed. see O'Leary, K. Daniel.

O'Leary, Timothy, jt. auth. see Murdock, George P.

Oleck, Howard L. Modern Corporation Law, 6 Vols. 1958-1960. with 1978 suppl 325.00 (ISBN 0-672-83063-9, Bobbs-Merrill Law); 1978 suppl. 115.00 (ISBN 0-672-81982-1). Michie.

Oleksy, Jerome E. Practical Solid-State Circuit Design. 2nd ed. LC 73-90284. 1980. pap. 8.95 (ISBN 0-672-21787-2). Sams.

Oleksy, Walter. It's Women's Work, Too! LC 80-10879. (Illus.). 192p. (gr. 7 up). 1980. PLB 8.29 (ISBN 0-671-33041-1). Messner.

--Laugh, Clown, Cry: The Story of Charlie Chaplin. LC 76-15001. (Focus Ser). (Illus.). (gr. 5 up). 1976. 6.60 o.p. (ISBN 0-8172-0427-X); PLB 6.60 o.p. (ISBN 0-8172-0426-1). Raintree Pubs.

--The Old Country Cookbook: Recipes from Thirty-One Countries. LC 73-81082. 1974. 16.95 (ISBN 0-88229-105-X). Nelson-Hall.

Olenick, Arnold. Managing the Company Tax Function. 1976. 29.95 o.p. (ISBN 0-13-550723-5). P-H.

Olenick, Arnold see Rousmaniere, Peter F., et al.

Olesen, Sigrid. Summer Is from Winter Until Winter. (Illus.). 80p. 1980. 4.95 (ISBN 0-936748-02-8); pap. 3.50 (ISBN 0-936748-03-6). Fade In.

Olesha, Yuri. Envy & Other Works. MacAndrew, Andrew R., tr. 320p. 1981. pap. 4.95 (ISBN 0-393-00042-7). Norton.

--Zavist. (Illus., Rus.). 1977. 15.00 o.p. (ISBN 0-88233-126-4); pap. 4.00 o.p. (ISBN 0-88233-127-2). Ardis Pubs.

Olesha, Yury. Envy. Berczynski, Thomas, tr. from Rus. (Orig.). 1979. pap. 4.50 (ISBN 0-88233-091-8). Ardis Pubs.

Olesker, J. Bradford. Beyond Forever. (Orig.). 1981. pap. 1.95 (ISBN 0-451-09565-0, J9565, Sig). NAL.

Olesky, J. & Rutkowski, G. Microprocessors & Digital Computer Technology. 1981. 22.95 (ISBN 0-13-581116-3). P-H.

Olesky, Jerome E., jt. auth. see Rutkowski, George B.

Oleson, Trygovi J. The Witenagemot in the Reign of Edward the Confessor: A Study in the Constitutional History of Eleventh-Century England. LC 80-2217. 1981. Repr. of 1955 ed. 29.50 (ISBN 0-404-18769-2). AMS Pr.

Oleszek, Walter J., jt. auth. see Davidson, Roger H.

Olford, Stephen. Lord, Open the Heavens! A Heartcry for Revival. LC 80-52053. 144p. 1980. pap. 3.95x (ISBN 0-87788-335-1). Shaw Pubs.

Olfson, Lewy. Thunder in the West. Mooney, Thomas J., ed. (Pal Paperbacks Kit A Ser.). (Illus., Orig.). (gr. 7-12). 1976. pap. text ed. 1.25 (ISBN 0-8374-3490-4). Xerox Ed Pubns.

--You Can Put on a Show. LC 74-31712. (Illus.). 144p. (gr. 3 up). 1975. 6.95 o.p. (ISBN 0-8069-7020-0); PLB 6.69 o.p. (ISBN 0-8069-7021-9). Sterling.

Olgaard, Anders. Growth, Productivity & Relative Prices. (Institute of Economics Univ. of Copenhagen). 1966. text ed. 23.00x (ISBN 0-7204-3028-3, Pub. by North Holland). Humanities.

Olgilvie, Eric & George, David. Living Things-Environmental Sciences: Curriculum Enrichment Units for the Gifted & Academically Talented. (Special Education Ser.). (Illus.). 1980. 59.00 (ISBN 0-89568-231-1). Spec Learn Corp.

Olgin, Howard A. The Doctor Game. 1979. pap. 2.50 o.s.i. (ISBN 0-440-12006-3). Dell.

--The Doctor Game. LC 77-20032. 1978. 8.95 o.p. (ISBN 0-397-01246-2). Lippincott.

Olgin, Joseph. Illustrated Football Dictionary for Young People. (Treehouse Illustrated Sports Dictionaries Ser.). (Illus.). 1978. pap. 2.50 (ISBN 0-13-450874-2). P-H.

Oliger, James, jt. ed. see Golub, Gene.

Oliger, Joseph, jt. ed. see Golub, Gene.

Olin, Harold, et al. Construction: Principles, Materials & Methods. 4th ed. 1980. text ed. 29.95 (ISBN 0-8134-2110-1). Interstate.

Olin, J. C. The Catholic Reformation. 1969. 8.50 o.p. (ISBN 0-87061-001-5). Chr Classics.

Olin, John C., et al, eds. Luther, Erasmus, & the Reformation: A Catholic-Protestant Reappraisal. LC 68-8749. x, 150p. 1969. 12.50 o.p. (ISBN 0-8232-0830-3). Fordham.

Olin, Spencer C., Jr. California's Prodigal Sons: Hiram Johnson & the Progressives. 1968. 14.75 (ISBN 0-520-00973-8). U of Cal Pr.

Olin, William. Escape from Utopia: My Ten Years in Synanon. 300p. 1981. 12.95 (ISBN 0-913300-53-5); pap. 6.95 (ISBN 0-913300-54-3). Unity Pr.

Olinick, Michael. Introduction to Mathematical Models in the Social & Life Sciences. LC 77-77758. (Illus.). 1978. text ed. 22.95 (ISBN 0-201-05448-5). A-W.

Oliphant, Margaret O. Miss Marjoribanks, 1866. Wolff, Robert L., ed. (Victorian Fiction Ser.). lib. bdg. 66.00 (ISBN 0-8240-1615-7). Garland Pub.

--The Perpetual Curate. Wolff, Robert L., ed. LC 75-1544. (Victorian Fiction Ser). 1975. Repr. of 1864 ed. lib. bdg. 66.00 (ISBN 0-8240-1614-9). Garland Pub.

--Phoebe, Junior: A Last Chronicle of Carlingford, 1876. Wolff, Robert L., ed. LC 75-1548. (Victorian Fiction Ser). 1975. lib. bdg. 66.00 (ISBN 0-8240-1616-5). Garland Pub.

--The Rector & the Doctor's Family, 1863. Wolff, Robert L., ed. LC 75-1543. (Victorian Fiction Ser). 1975. lib. bdg. 66.00 (ISBN 0-8240-1613-0). Garland Pub.

Oliphant, Margaret W. Salem Chapel. Wolff, Robert L., ed. LC 75-1508. (Victorian Fiction Ser.). 1975. Repr. of 1863 ed. lib. bdg. 66.00 (ISBN 0-8240-1582-7). Garland Pub.

Oliphant, Mrs. Miss Marjoribanks. LC 70-487530. (The Zodiac Press Ser.). 1979. 9.95 (ISBN 0-7011-1503-3, Pub. by Chatto Bodley Jonathan). Merrimack Bk Serv.

Oliphant, Winford. AFDC Foster Care: Problems & Recommendations. LC 74-75319. (Orig.). 1974. pap. 1.75 o.p. (ISBN 0-87868-121-3). Child Welfare.

Oliva, L. S. Catherine the Great. 1971. 8.95 o.p. (ISBN 0-13-121160-9, Spec). P-H.

Oliva, Leo E. Fort Hays, Frontier Army Post, 1865-1889. LC 80-82227. (Illus.). 66p. 1980. pap. write for info. (ISBN 0-87726-020-6). Kansas St Hist.

Oliva, Ralph A. & Dale, Charles W. Basic Electricity & DC Circuits. 2nd ed. LC 79-92192. (Basic Electricity Ser.). (Illus.). 924p. 1980. text ed. 19.95 (ISBN 0-89512-034-8). Tex Instr Inc.

Olive, Jane E., jt. auth. see Mori, Allen A.

Olivecrona, H. & Ladenheim, J. Congenital Arteriovenous Aneurysms of the Carotid & Vertebral Arterial Systems. (Illus.). 1957. 69.70 o.p. (ISBN 0-387-02204-X). Springer-Verlag.

Oliveira, Fernandes E. de see De Oliveira, Fernandes E., et al.

Oliveira, Nuno. Reflections on Equestrian Art. Fields, Phyllis, tr. from Portuguese. (Illus.). 12.25 (ISBN 0-85131-257-8, Dist. by Sporting Book Center). J A Allen.

Oliveira Marques, Antonio H. De see De Olivera Marques, Antonia H.

Oliver, jt. auth. see Nathan.

Oliver, A. P. The Larousse Guide to Shells of the World. LC 79-91944. (The Larousse Guide Books). (Illus.). 1980. 15.95 (ISBN 0-88332-107-6); pap. 8.95 (ISBN 0-88332-133-5). Larousse.

Oliver, Albert I. Maximizing Minicourses: A Practical Guide to a Curriculum Alternative. LC 77-13942. 1978. pap. text ed. 6.50x (ISBN 0-8077-2520-X). Tchrs Coll.

Oliver, Alfreda. Power Is You. 1976. pap. 1.75 o.p. (ISBN 0-449-13640-X, GM). Fawcett.

Oliver, Andrew. Portraits of John & Abigail Adams. (The Adams Papers, Ser. 4, Adams Family Portraits). (Illus.). 1967. 15.00x (ISBN 0-674-69150-4). Harvard U Pr.

--Portraits of John Quincy Adams & His Wife. LC 70-128349. (The Adams Papers, Ser. 4, Adams Family Portraits). (Illus.). 1970. 17.50x (ISBN 0-674-69152-0). Harvard U Pr.

Oliver, Andrew & Tolles, Bryant F., Jr. Windows on the Past: Portraits at the Essex Institute. (E. I. Museum Booklet Ser.). (Illus.). 60p. (Orig.). 1981. pap. 4.95 (ISBN 0-88389-080-1). Essex Inst.

Oliver, Anthony. The Pew Group. LC 80-2079. (Crime Club Ser.). 192p. 1981. 9.95 (ISBN 0-385-17412-8). Doubleday.

Oliver, Carl. Plane Talk: Aviators' & Astronauts' Own Stories. (gr. 7 up). 1980. 7.95 (ISBN 0-395-29743-5). HM.

Oliver, Chad. The Discovery of Humanity: An Introduction to Anthropology. (Illus.). 1980. text ed. 17.50 scp (ISBN 0-397-47407-5, HarpC); instrs'. manual free. Har-Row.

Oliver, Clinton S. & Sills, Stephanie, eds. Contemporary Black Drama: Raisin in the Sun, Purlie Victorious, Funnyhouse of a Negro, Dutchman, Blues for Mister Charlie, Day of Absence, Happy Ending, Gentleman Caller, No Place to Be Somebody. 1971. pap. text ed. 10.95x (ISBN 0-684-41432-5, ScribC). Scribner.

Oliver, Donald W. Education & Community: A Radical Critique of Innovative Schooling. LC 76-2114. 1977. 19.75 (ISBN 0-8211-1406-9); text ed. 17.75x in copies of ten (ISBN 0-685-80407-0). McCutchan.

Oliver, Douglas L. Solomon Island Society. (Illus.). pap. 3.45x o.p. (ISBN 0-8070-4689-2, BP270). Beacon Pr.

Oliver, E. J. Honore De Balzac. 1964. 3.95 o.s.i. (ISBN 0-02-592880-5). Macmillan.

Oliver, Eric & Wilson, John. Practical Security in Commerce & Industry. 1979. pap. text ed. 36.00x (ISBN 0-566-02033-5, Pub. by Gower Pub Co England). Renouf.

--Security Manual. 1979. text ed. 8.00x (ISBN 0-566-02116-1, Pub. by Gower Pub Co England). Renouf.

Oliver, Eric & Wilson, John, eds. Security Manual. 3rd ed. (Illus.). 1976. 7.50 o.s.i. (ISBN 0-8464-0831-7). Beekman Pubs.

Oliver, Frederick S. A Dweller on Two Planets: The Dividing of the Way-Phylos the Thibetan. LC 80-8896. (The Harper Library of Spiritual Wisdom Ser.). (Illus.). 432p. 1981. pap. 6.95 (ISBN 0-06-066565-3). Har-Row.

Oliver, George. Practical Anthropology. MacConaill, M. A., tr. 344p. 1969. pap. 16.00 spiral (ISBN 0-398-01424-8). C C Thomas.

Oliver, Hugh & MacMillan, Keith. The American Limerick Book. LC 80-21813. (Illus.). 96p. 1981. 9.95 (ISBN 0-8253-0001-0). Beaufort Bks NY.

Oliver, J. L. The Development & Structure of the Furniture Industry. 1965. 13.75 (ISBN 0-08-011460-1). Pergamon.

Oliver, J. M. Data Response Questions in A Level Economics. 1976. pap. text ed. 3.50x o.p. (ISBN 0-435-84529-2). Heinemann Ed.

Oliver, James & Scott, Christina, eds. Religion & World History: A Selection from the Works of Christopher Dawson. LC 74-33612. 480p. 1975. pap. 2.45 (ISBN 0-385-09551-1, Im). Doubleday.

Oliver, John E. Climate & Man's Environment: An Introduction to Applied Climatology. LC 73-5707. 517p. 1973. text ed. 24.95x (ISBN 0-471-65338-1). Wiley.

Oliver, John S., ed. Forensic Toxicology. 320p. 1980. 50.00x (Pub. by Croom Helm England). State Mutual Bk.

Oliver, Kenneth A. Words Every College Student Should Know. 465p. (Orig.). 1981. pap. 12.95 (ISBN 0-913244-50-3). Hapi Pr.

Oliver, Libbey H. Colonial Williamsburg Decorates for Christmas. (Illus.). 80p. 1981. pap. 4.95 (ISBN 0-87935-056-3). Williamsburg.

Oliver, Lin. Rock Music Scrapbook. LC 79-3336. (Illus.). (gr. 5 up). 1980. 8.95 o.p. (ISBN 0-397-31856-1); PLB 8.79 o.p. (ISBN 0-397-31905-3). Lippincott.

Oliver, Lucille. Cry for the World. 1981. pap. price not set (ISBN 0-8309-0307-0). Herald Hse.

Oliver, Martha H. Add a Few Sprouts. LC 75-10539. (Pivot Original Health Bk). 128p. (Orig.). 1975. pap. 1.95 (ISBN 0-87983-104-9). Keats.

Oliver, Paul, ed. Shelter & Society. 1978. pap. 7.95 o.p. (ISBN 0-214-20200-3, 8009, Dist. by Arco). Barrie & Jenkins.

--Shelter in Africa. 1978. 8.50 o.p. (ISBN 0-214-20205-4, 8010, Dist. by Arco). Barrie & Jenkins.

--Shelter, Sign & Symbol. LC 77-77089. (Illus.). 1980. pap. 9.95 (ISBN 0-87951-112-5). Overlook Pr.

Oliver, R. & Atmore, A. Africa Since Eighteen Hundred. 2nd ed. LC 70-189595. (Illus.). 340p. 1972. 29.95 (ISBN 0-521-08522-5); pap. 8.95x (ISBN 0-521-29240-9). Cambridge U Pr.
--Africa Since Eighteen Hundred. 3rd ed. (Illus.). 396p. Date not set. price not set (ISBN 0-521-23485-9); pap. price not set (ISBN 0-521-29975-6). Cambridge U Pr.
--African Middle Ages. (Illus.). 245p. Date not set. price not set (ISBN 0-521-23301-1); pap. price not set (ISBN 0-521-29894-6). Cambridge U Pr.
Oliver, R., jt. auth. see Sherrington, P. J.
Oliver, R. A. & Fagan, B. M. Africa in the Iron Age. LC 74-25639. (Illus.). 300p. 1975. 29.95 (ISBN 0-521-20598-0); pap. 7.95x (ISBN 0-521-09900-5). Cambridge U Pr.
Oliver, R. A. & Lewis, D. G. The Content of Sixth-Form General Studies. 144p. 1974. 12.00x (ISBN 0-7190-0586-8, Pub. by Manchester U Pr England). State Mutual Bk.
Oliver, R. T., et al, eds. Bladder Cancer: Principles of Combination Therapy. (Illus.). 272p. 1981. text ed. 69.00 (ISBN 0-407-00187-5). Butterworth.
Oliver, Ray. Principles of the Use of Radioisotope Tracers in Clinical & Research Investigations. 1971. pap. 10.75 (ISBN 0-08-015718-1). Pergamon.
Oliver, Raymond. Poems Without Names: The English Lyric, 1200-1500. LC 77-82617. 1970. 16.50x (ISBN 0-520-01403-0). U of Cal Pr.
Oliver, Robert. Culture & Communication: The Problem of Penetrating National & Cultural Boundaries. 184p. 1962. pap. 8.25 spiral (ISBN 0-398-01422-1). C C Thomas.
Oliver, Robert C., jt. auth. see Hamill, Charlotte.
Oliver, Robert W. International Economic Co-Operation & the World Bank. 421p. 1975. text ed. 35.00x (ISBN 0-8419-5013-X). Holmes & Meier.
Oliver, Roger W. Dreams of Passion: The Theater of Luigi Pirandello. LC 79-2179. 1979. 16.00x (ISBN 0-8147-6157-7); pap. 7.00x (ISBN 0-8147-6158-5). NYU Pr.
Oliver, Roland. Missionary Factor in East Africa. (Illus.). 1967. pap. text ed. 4.00x (ISBN 0-582-60847-3). Humanities.
Oliver, Roland & Fage, J. D. A Short History of Africa. rev. ed. LC 63-11304. 1962. 15.00x (ISBN 0-8147-0329-1). NYU Pr.
Oliver, Roland, ed. Dawn of African History. 2nd ed. (Illus., Orig.). (gr. 9-12). 1968. pap. 3.95x (ISBN 0-19-500355-1). Oxford U Pr.
--The Middle Age of African History. (Orig.). (gr. 9-12). 1967. pap. 3.95x (ISBN 0-19-500356-X). Oxford U Pr.
Oliver, Roland A., jt. auth. see Fage, J. D.
Oliver, Stanley. O & M for First Line Managers. 1975. pap. 14.95x (ISBN 0-7131-3350-3). Intl Ideas.
Oliver, Stanley, ed. Accountants Guide to Management Techniques. 500p. 1975. 25.00 o.s.i. (ISBN 0-7161-0231-5). Herman Pub.
Oliver, Tess. Red, Red Rose. 192p. (Orig.). 1980. pap. 1.50 (ISBN 0-671-57014-5). S&S.
Oliver, Virginia, jt. auth. see Jakle, John A.
Oliver, W. H. Prophets & Millennialists: The Uses of Biblical Prophecy in England from the 1790s to the 1840s. 1979. 17.95x (ISBN 0-19-647962-2). Oxford U Pr.
Oliver, William I., ed. & tr. Voices of Change in the Spanish American Theater: An Anthology. (Texas Pan American Ser). 294p. 1971. 15.00 (ISBN 0-292-70123-3). U of Tex Pr.
Olivier, Daniel. The Trial of Luther. 1979. pap. 8.50 (ISBN 0-570-03785-9, 12-2743). Concordia.
Olivier, Robert L. Tidoon. LC 70-18934. 96p. 1972. 5.95 (ISBN 0-911116-62-1). Pelican.
--Tironc: Son of the Cajun Teche. (Illus.). 1974. 5.95 (ISBN 0-88289-054-9). Pelican.
Olivieri, Evelyn R. De see Blazier, Kenneth D.
Olivieri, Matilde Vilarino De see Vilarino De Olivieri, Matilde.
Olivo & Marsh. Principles of Refrigeration. LC 76-14089. 1979. 14.32 (ISBN 0-8273-1014-5); pap. text ed. 12.20 (ISBN 0-686-60690-6); instructor's guide 1.50 (ISBN 0-8273-1004-8). Delmar.
Olivo, C. Thomas & Olivo, Thomas P. Fundamentals of Applied Physics. LC 77-79381. 1978. text ed. 15.00 (ISBN 0-8273-1300-4); tchr's guide 3.00 (ISBN 0-8273-1301-2). Delmar.
Olivo, Thomas C. Basic Machine Technology. 1980. 19.95 (ISBN 0-672-97171-2); pap. 4.95 student's manual o.p. (ISBN 0-672-97172-0); instructor's guide 6.67 (ISBN 0-672-97173-9). Bobbs.
Olivo, Thomas P., jt. auth. see Olivo, C. Thomas.
Olk-Apire, P. A. Idi Amin's Rise to Power: The Inside Story. 192p. (Orig.). 1981. 15.95 (ISBN 0-905762-68-1, Pub. by Zed Pr); pap. 6.95 (ISBN 0-905762-67-3). Lawrence Hill.
Olken, Charles, et al. The Connoisseurs' Handbook of California Wines. LC 79-3476. 192p. 1980. pap. 4.95 (ISBN 0-394-73973-6). Knopf.
Olken, Hyman. The Technical Communicator's Handbook of Technology Transfer. 144p. 1980. pap. 12.50 (ISBN 0-934818-01-0). Olken Pubns.
Olken, Ilene T., ed. see Pratolini, Vasco.
Olkowski, William, jt. auth. see Carr, Anna.
Olla, B. L., jt. auth. see Winn, H. E.
Olla, Bori L., jt. ed. see Burger, Joanna.
Ollard, Richard. The Image of the King: A Biography of Charles I & Charles II. LC 79-50965. (Illus.). 1979. 12.95 (ISBN 0-689-11006-5). Atheneum.
Olle, Fernando Gonzalez. Manual Bibliografico De Estudios Espanoles (Handbook of Hispanic Bibliography) (Sp.). 1978. 61.50 (ISBN 84-313-0464-2, Dist. by Ediciones Universidad de Navarra, S.A.). Bowker.
Olle, James G. Library History. (Outlines of Modern Librarianship Ser.). 114p. 1979. text ed. 12.00 (ISBN 0-89664-414-6, Pub. by K G Saur). Shoe String.
Olle, T. W. The CODASYL Approach to Data Base Management. 287p. 1978. 26.95 (ISBN 0-471-99579-7, 1-320). Wiley.
Oller, John W., Jr. Language Tests at School: A Pragmatic Approach. (Applied Linguistics & Language Study). (Illus.). 1979. text ed. 18.75x (ISBN 0-582-55365-2); pap. text ed. 12.25x (ISBN 0-582-55294-X). Longman.
Olleson, Edward, ed. Modern Musical Scholarship: Studies in Musical History. (Illus.). 1980. write for info. (ISBN 0-85362-180-2, Oriel). Routledge & Kegan.
Olley, John W. Righteousness in the Septuagint of Isaiah: A Contextual Study. LC 78-3425. (Society of Biblical Literature, Septuagint & Cognate Studies: No. 8). 1979. 12.00 (ISBN 0-89130-226-3); pap. 7.50 (ISBN 0-89130-365-0). Scholars Pr Ca.
Olley, Peter M., jt. ed. see Coceani, Flavio.
Ollier, C. D. Tectonics & Landforms. (Geomorphology Texts Ser.). (Illus.). 304p. 1981. text ed. 50.00 (ISBN 0-582-30032-0). Longman.
--Weathering. rev. ed. LC 75-320198. (Geomorphology Text). (Illus.). 304p. 1975. pap. text ed. 18.95x (ISBN 0-582-48180-5). Longman.
Olliver, Jane, ed. The Living World. (Visual World Ser.). (Illus.). 1977. PLB 7.90 (ISBN 0-531-09085-X). Watts.
Ollman, B. Alienation. 2nd ed. LC 76-4234. (Studies in the History & Theory of Politics). 1977. 29.95 (ISBN 0-521-21281-2); pap. 8.50x (ISBN 0-521-29083-X). Cambridge U Pr.
Olm, et al. Management Decisions & Organizational Policy. 3rd ed. 560p. 1981. text ed. 21.95 (ISBN 0-205-07215-1, 0872156); free tchr's ed. (ISBN 0-205-07216-X). Allyn.
Olmedo, Alfonso, tr. see Benko, Stephen.
Olmo, Harold P., jt. auth. see Brooks, Reid M.
Olmos, Ralph A. An Introduction to Police-Community Relations: A Guide for the Pre-Service Student & Practicing Police Officer. 128p. 1974. 10.50 (ISBN 0-398-02941-5). C C Thomas.
Olmstead, Alan H. In Praise of Seasons. LC 76-23515. (Illus.). 1977. 6.95 o.s.i. (ISBN 0-06-013284-1, HarpT). Har-Row.
--Threshold: The First Days of Retirement. LC 75-6351. 224p. 1975. 8.95 o.p. (ISBN 0-06-013271-X, HarpT). Har-Row.
Olmstead, Marty & Weimer, Jan. Exotic Food Guide. Leonard, Jan, ed. LC 80-66583. (Savvy San Francisco Ser.). (Illus.). 64p. (Orig.). 1980. pap. text ed. 2.50 (ISBN 0-89395-050-5). Cal Living Bks.
Olmsted, Elizabeth H., ed. Music Library Association Catalog of Cards for Printed Music, 1953-1972: A Supplement to the Library of Congress Catalogs, 2 vols. 1974. Set. 100.00 o.p. (ISBN 0-87471-474-5). Rowman.
Olmsted, Frederick L. A Journey Through Texas: Or, a Saddle Trip on the Southwestern Frontier. LC 78-7028. (Barker Texas History Center Ser: No. 2). (Illus.). 1978. pap. 6.95 (ISBN 0-292-74008-5). U of Tex Pr.
Olmsted, John C. Victorian Painting: Essays & Reviews, Eighteen Thirty-Two to Eighteen Forty-Eight. LC 80-65711. (Garland Reference Library of Humanities). 700p. 1980. 75.00 (ISBN 0-8240-2742-6). Garland Pub.
Olmsted, John M. Advanced Calculus. (Illus.). 1961. text ed. 23.95 (ISBN 0-13-010983-5). P-H.
--Calculus with Analytic Geometry, Vol. 1. LC 66-11169. (Century Mathematics Ser.). (Illus.). 1966. 26.50x (ISBN 0-89197-061-4). Irvington.
--Intermediate Analysis: An Introduction to Theory of Functions of One Real Variable. LC 56-5844. (Illus.). 1956. 32.50x (ISBN 0-89197-796-1); pap. text ed. 18.50x (ISBN 0-8290-0385-1). Irvington.
--Solid Analytic Geometry. (Century Mathematics Ser.). 1947. text ed. 28.50x (ISBN 0-89197-417-2); pap. text ed. 16.50x (ISBN 0-89197-942-5). Irvington.
Olmsted, Lorena A. Journey to Adventure. (YA) 1977. 5.95 (ISBN 0-685-74274-1, Avalon). Bouregy.
--Strange Inheritance. (YA) 1978. 5.95 (ISBN 0-685-86415-4, Avalon). Bouregy.
Olmsted, Lorena Ann. Dangerous Memory. 192p. (YA) 1974. 5.95 (ISBN 0-685-39471-9, Avalon). Bouregy.
Olmsted, Mary, ed. see Danchik, Kathleen M. & Schoenborn, Charlotte A.
Olmsted, Mary, ed. see Foley, Daniel J.
Olmsted, Mary, ed. see Strahan, Geneviene W.
Olmsted, Robert. The Diesel Years. LC 75-17721. (Illus.). 1975. 19.95 (ISBN 0-87095-054-1). Golden West.
Olmsted, Robert P. Milwaukee Rails. LC 80-81260. (Illus.). 200p. 1980. 26.95 (ISBN 0-934228-04-3). McMillan Pubns.
Olnek, Jay I. The Invisible Hand. 1980. 14.95 (ISBN 0-938538-00-4). N Stonington.
Olness, Karen. Parenting Happy Healthy Children. 1981. 9.95 (ISBN 0-9602790-4-0). The Garden.
--Practical Pediatrics in Less-Developed Countries. 1980. pap. 9.95 (ISBN 0-9602790-2-4). The Garden.
--Practical Pediatrics in Less-Developed Countries. 1980. pap. 7.95 (ISBN 0-9602790-2-4). The Garden.
--Raising Happy Healthy Children. 1981. pap. 3.95 (ISBN 0-9602790-5-9). The Garden.
Olney, James. The Rhizome & the Flower: The Perennial Philosophy--Yeats & Jung. 1980. 23.50x (ISBN 0-520-03748-0). U of Cal Pr.
Olney, Judith. Entertainments. (Illus.). 196p. 1981. 19.95 (ISBN 0-8120-5410-5). Barron.
Olney, Pat, jt. auth. see Olney, Ross.
Olney, Richard. The French Menu Cookbook. LC 80-24423. (Illus.). 446p. Date not set. pap. 8.95 (ISBN 0-689-70607-3, 268). Atheneum. Postponed.
--Simple French Food. LC 73-80755. (Illus.). pap. 7.95 (ISBN 0-689-70546-8, 229). Atheneum.
Olney, Rose R., ed. Tales of Time & Space. (gr. 3 up). 1978. pap. 1.25 (ISBN 0-307-21628-4, Golden Pr). Western Pub.
Olney, Ross & Olney, Pat. Keeping Insects As Pets. LC 78-2578. (First Bks). (Illus.). (gr. 4 up). 1978. PLB 6.45 s&l (ISBN 0-531-01490-8). Watts.
--Pocket Calculator Fun & Games. (Illus.). (gr. 4 up). 1977. PLB 6.45 s&l (ISBN 0-531-00387-6). Watts.
Olney, Ross R. Driving: How to Get a License (and Keep It!) LC 73-23003. (Career Concise Guides Ser.). (Illus.). 72p. (gr. 9 up). 1974. PLB 4.90 o.p. (ISBN 0-531-02718-X). Watts.
--Gymnastics. (First Bks.). (Illus.). 96p. (gr. 4-6). 1976. PLB 6.45 (ISBN 0-531-00849-5). Watts.
--Gymnastics. 1980. pap. 1.75 (ISBN 0-380-49213-X, 49213, Camelot). Avon.
--Light Motorcycle Repair. LC 75-8901. (Career Concise Guides Ser.). (Illus.). 72p. (gr. 5 up). 1975. PLB 4.90 o.p. (ISBN 0-531-02832-1). Watts.
--Modern Drag Racing Superstars. LC 80-25908. (High Interest-Low Vocabulary Ser.). (Illus.). 112p. (gr. 4). 1981. PLB 5.95 (ISBN 0-396-07925-3). Dodd.
--Motorcycling. LC 74-10720. (Illus.). 64p. (gr. 5 up). 1975. PLB 4.47 o.p. (ISBN 0-531-02788-0). Watts.
--Offshore! LC 80-10908. (Illus.). 96p. (gr. 5-9). 1981. PLB 10.95 (ISBN 0-525-36305-X). Dutton.
--Photographing Action Sports. LC 75-34250. (Illus.). 160p. (gr. 7 up). 1976. PLB 5.90 o.p. (ISBN 0-531-01139-9). Watts.
--Riding High: Bicycling for Young People. LC 80-28566. (Illus.). 192p. (gr. 5 up). 1981. 8.95 (ISBN 0-688-41979-8); PLB 8.59 (ISBN 0-688-51979-2). Morrow.
--Simple Gasoline Engine Repair. LC 72-160876. 1972. pap. 3.50 (ISBN 0-385-03778-3, Dolp). Doubleday.
--They Said It Couldn't Be Done. LC 78-12405. (gr. 4-7). 1979. PLB 10.95 (ISBN 0-525-41060-0). Dutton.
--This Game Called Hockey. LC 77-16872. (gr. 5 up). 1978. 5.95 (ISBN 0-396-07524-X). Dodd.
Olney, Ross R. & Duganne, Mary Ann. How to Make Your Car Run Better. LC 77-1566. (Career Concise Guides Ser.). 1977. 6.45 (ISBN 0-531-01296-4). Watts.
Olney, Ross R., ed. Shudders. (gr. 3 up). 1979. pap. 1.25 (ISBN 0-307-21617-9, Golden Pr). Western Pub.
Olorunsola, Victor A. Soldiers & Power: The Development Performance of the Nigerian Military Regime. LC 76-48485. (Publication Ser: No. 168). 1977. pap. 8.95 (ISBN 0-8179-6681-1). Hoover Inst Pr.
Oloruntimehin, B. O. Segu Tukulor Empire. (Ibadan History Ser.). (Illus.). 357p. 1972. text ed. 14.00x (ISBN 0-391-00206-6). Humanities.
O'Loughlin, C. National Economic Accounting. 1971. 23.00 (ISBN 0-08-016395-5). Pergamon.
Olphen, H. Van see Van Olphen, H.
Olphen, H. Van see Van Olphen, H. & Fripiat, J. J.
Olschak, B. & Wangyal, T. Guide to the Jewel Island. 10.00 o.p. (ISBN 0-685-57295-1). Weiser.
Olschki, Leonardo. Marco Polo's Asia: An Introduction to His "Description of the World" Called "Il Milione". Scott, John A., tr. 1960. 27.50x (ISBN 0-520-00975-4). U of Cal Pr.
--The Myth of Felt. 1949. 12.95x (ISBN 0-520-00974-6). U of Cal Pr.
Olsen, Aileen. Big Fish. LC 75-116335. (Illus.). (gr. k-3). 1970. 6.75 (ISBN 0-688-41271-8); PLB 6.48 o.p. (ISBN 0-688-51271-2). Lothrop.
Olsen, Arvis J. Sexuality: Guidelines for Teenagers. 80p. (Orig.). 1981. pap. 1.95 (ISBN 0-8010-6674-3). Baker Bk.
Olsen, Edward A. Japan: Economic Growth, Resource Scarcity, & Environmental Constraints. LC 77-28013. (A Westview Replica Edition Ser.). 1978. lib. bdg. 18.50x (ISBN 0-89158-064-6). Westview.
Olsen, Einar, jt. auth. see Bucher, Charles.
Olsen, Eve C., jt. auth. see Strang, Paul D.
Olsen, Frederick L. The Kiln Book. 2nd ed. LC 72-94254. 1978. pap. 9.50 o.p. (ISBN 0-935066-02-0). Keramos Bks.
Olsen, G. Elements of Mechanics of Materials. 4th ed. 1981. 23.95 (ISBN 0-13-267013-5). P-H.
Olsen, George H. The Beginner's Handbook of Electronics. 1980. text ed. 19.95 (ISBN 0-13-074211-2, Spec); pap. text ed. 7.95 (ISBN 0-13-074203-1). P-H.
Olsen, Gerner A. Elements of Mechanics of Materials. 3rd ed. (Illus.). 704p. 1974. ref. ed 23.95 (ISBN 0-13-266999-4). P-H.
Olsen, Helen C. To Catch the Wind. (YA) 1978. 5.95 (ISBN 0-685-86416-2, Avalon). Bouregy.
Olsen, Herb. Herb Olsen's Guide to Watercolor Landscapes. 128p. 1980. pap. 12.95 (ISBN 0-442-25784-8). Van Nos Reinhold.
Olsen, Ib S. The Boy in the Moon. Jensen, Virginia A., tr. LC 74-1418. (Illus.). 40p. (ps-3). 1977. 6.95 (ISBN 0-590-17713-3, Four Winds); lib. bdg. 6.95 (ISBN 0-590-07713-9). Schol Bk Serv.
Olsen, Jack. Missing Persons. LC 80-69375. 1981. 12.95 (ISBN 0-689-11133-9). Atheneum.
--Night of the Grizzlies. 1971. pap. 1.75 (ISBN 0-451-08806-9, E8806, Sig). NAL.
--Night Watch. 1980. pap. 2.75 (ISBN 0-445-04609-0). Popular Lib.
Olsen, James. Joe Namath. LC 76-16187. 1974. PLB 5.95 (ISBN 0-87191-265-1); pap. 2.95 (ISBN 0-89812-165-5). Creative Ed.
--Mark Spitz. LC 76-5815. (Creative Superstars Ser.). 1974. o. p. 5.95 (ISBN 0-87191-263-5); pap. 2.95 (ISBN 0-686-66998-3). Creative Ed.
Olsen, James T. Aretha Franklin. LC 74-14672. (Rock'n Pop Stars Ser.). (Illus.). 32p. (gr. 4-12). 1974. PLB 5.95 (ISBN 0-87191-390-9); pap. 2.75 o. p. (ISBN 0-89812-100-0). Creative Ed.
--Bill Cosby. LC 74-6454. (Personal Closeups Ser). 32p. 1974. 5.75 o.p. (ISBN 0-87191-356-9). Creative Ed.
--Billie Jean King. LC 76-12090. (Creative Superstars Ser.). 1974. PLB 5.95 (ISBN 0-87191-275-9); pap. 2.95 (ISBN 0-89812-177-9). Creative Ed.
--Ralph Nader. LC 74-6421. (Personal Closeups Ser). 32p. 1974. 5.75 o.p. (ISBN 0-87191-355-0). Creative Ed.
Olsen, Johan P., jt. auth. see March, James G.
Olsen, Larry D. Outdoor Survival Skills. 4th rev ed. LC 72-94938. (Illus.). 200p. 1973. 8.95 (ISBN 0-8425-0001-4); pap. 7.95 (ISBN 0-8425-0002-2). Brigham.
Olsen, Magnus, jt. ed. see Munch, Peter A.
Olsen, Mary P. For the Greater Glory: A Church Needlepoint Handbook. (Illus.). 192p. 1980. 15.95 (ISBN 0-8164-0476-3). Seabury.
Olsen, Paul. Comprehensive Psychotherapy. (Vol. 2). 1981. price not set. Gordon.
--Sons & Mothers: Why Men Behave As They Do. Graver, Fred, ed. 300p. 1981. 11.95 (ISBN 0-87131-338-3). M Evans.
Olsen, Paul, jt. auth. see Murrell, Sandra.
Olsen, Paul, ed. Comprehensive Psychotherapy, Vol. 2. 1981. price not set. Gordon.
Olsen, Paul T., ed. Emotional Flooding, Vol. I: An Official Publication of the National Institute for the Psychotherapies. LC 74-12620. (New Directions in Psychotherapy Ser.). 1976. 22.95 (ISBN 0-87705-239-5). Human Sci Pr.
Olsen, Richard. Karl Marx. (World Leaders Ser.: No. 70). 1978. lib. bdg. 11.95 (ISBN 0-8057-7678-8). Twayne.
Olsen, Richard G. & Krakowka, Steven. Immunology & Immunopathology of Domestic Animals. (Illus.). 320p. 1979. text ed. 29.75 (ISBN 0-398-03815-5). C C Thomas.
Olsen, Richard P. The Textile Industry. LC 77-9167. (Lexington Casebook Ser. in Industry Analysis). (Illus.). 1978. 21.95 (ISBN 0-669-01807-4). Lexington Bks.

Olsen, Robert D., Sr. Scott's Fingerprint Mechanics. (Illus.). 480p. 1978. 32.75 (ISBN 0-398-03730-2). C C Thomas.
Olsen, Rolf, jt. ed. see Wing, J. K.
Olsen, Stanley J. Fish, Amphibian & Reptile Remains from Archaeological Sites, Part I: Southeastern & Southwestern United States. LC 68-56643. (Peabody Museum Papers: Vol. 56, No. 2). 1968. pap. text ed. 15.00 (ISBN 0-87365-192-8). Peabody Harvard.
--Mammal Remains from Archaeological Sites, Part I: Southeastern & Southwestern United States. LC 65-689. (Peabody Museum Papers: Vol. 56, No. 1). 1964. pap. 15.00 (ISBN 0-87365-162-6). Peabody Harvard.
Olsen, Stein H. The Structure of Literary Understanding. LC 77-77719. 1978. 28.50 (ISBN 0-521-21731-8). Cambridge U Pr.
Olsen, Stephen B. & Stevenson, David K. Commercial Marine Fish & Fisheries of Rhode Island. (Marine Technical Report Ser.: No. 34). 1975. pap. 3.50 o.p. (ISBN 0-686-18101-8). URI MAS.
Olsen, Steve, et al. An Interpretive Atlas of Narragansett Bay. (Marine Bulletin Ser.: No. 40). 1980. 2.00 (ISBN 0-938412-16-7). URI MAS.
Olsen, T. V. Bonner's Stallion. 1978. pap. 1.95 (ISBN 0-449-13925-5, GM). Fawcett.
--Canyon of the Gun. 1978. pap. 1.75 (ISBN 0-449-13943-3, GM). Fawcett.
--Day of the Buzzard. 1979. pap. 1.50 o.p. (ISBN 0-449-14161-6, GM). Fawcett.
Olsen, V. Norskov. John Foxe & the Elizabethan Church. 1973. 22.75x (ISBN 0-520-02075-8). U of Cal Pr.
Olsen, Viggo. Daktar. 1976. pap. 1.75 (ISBN 0-89129-166-0). Jove Pubns.
Olsen, Viggo B. The Agnostic Who Dared to Search. 64p. 1975. pap. 0.95 (ISBN 0-8024-0139-2). Moody.
Olshaker, Mark. Einstein's Brain. 324p. 1981. 10.95 (ISBN 0-87131-342-1). M Evans.
--The Instant Image: Edwin Land & the Polaroid Experience. LC 77-15965. (Illus.). 292p. 1980. pap. 8.95 (ISBN 0-8128-6093-4). Stein & Day.
Olshan, Neil & Dreyer, Julie. Fears & Phobias. (gr. 7 up). 1980. PLB 7.90 (ISBN 0-531-02865-8, B08). Watts.
Olshavsky, Richard W. Attitude Research Enters the Eighties. LC 80-20621. (Proceedings Ser.). 196p. 1980. pap. 12.00 (ISBN 0-87757-145-7). Am Mktg.
Olshavsky, Richard W., ed. Attitude Research Enters the Eighties. LC 80-20621. (Proceedings Ser.). 196p. 1980. 12.00 (ISBN 0-87757-145-7). Am Mktg.
Olshen, Barry N. John Fowles. LC 78-3149. (Modern Literature Ser.). 1978. 10.95 (ISBN 0-8044-2665-1). Ungar.
Olson. Bruchko. LC 73-81494. 1977. pap. 2.45 (ISBN 0-88419-133-8). Creation Hse.
--Conditioning Fundamentals. 1968. pap. text ed. 4.95 (ISBN 0-675-09684-7). Merrill.
Olson, Alison G. & Brown, Richard M., eds. Anglo-American Political Relations, Sixteen Seventy-Five to Seventeen Seventy-Five. LC 73-108758. 1970. 20.00 (ISBN 0-8135-0624-7). Rutgers U Pr.
Olson, Arlene R. Art Critics & the Avant-Garde: New York, 1900-1913. Kuspit, Donald B., ed. (Studies in Fine Arts - Criticism: No. 18). 118p. 1980. 21.95 (ISBN 0-8357-1093-9, Pub. by UMI Res Pr). Univ Microfilms.
Olson, Arne L., jt. auth. see Burris, Barbara J.
Olson, Arnold T. The Significance of Silence. 200p. 1980. write for info. Free Church Pubns.
Olson, Arnold T., ed. The Search for Identity. LC 80-66030. 160p. 1980. 8.95 (ISBN 0-911802-46-0). Free Church Pubns.
Olson, Bruce, tr. Por Esta Cruz Te Matare. (Spanish Bks.). (Span.). 1979. 1.90 (ISBN 0-8297-0592-9). Life Pubs Intl.
--Por Esta Cruz Te Matarei. (Portuguese Bks.). 1979. 1.40 (ISBN 0-8297-0797-2). Life Pubs Intl.
Olson, Charles & Creeley, Robert. Charles Olson & Robert Creeley: The Complete Correspondence, Vol. 3. Butterick, George F., ed. (Illus.). 200p. (Orig.). 1981. 20.00 (ISBN 0-87685-483-8); deluxe ed. 30.00 (ISBN 0-87685-484-6); pap. 7.50 (ISBN 0-87685-482-X). Black Sparrow.
--Charles Olson & Robert Creeley: The Complete Correspondence, Vol. 3. Butterick, George F., ed. (Illus.). 200p. (Orig.). 1981. 20.00 o.p. (ISBN 0-87685-483-8); deluxe ed. 30.00 o.p. (ISBN 0-87685-484-6); pap. 7.50 o.p. (ISBN 0-87685-501-X). Black Sparrow.
Olson, Charles F. The Fiery Hunt & Other Plays. Butterick, George F., ed. LC 76-48311. (Writing Ser: No. 36). 150p. 1977. pap. 4.00 (ISBN 0-87704-033-8). Four Seasons Foun.
--Muthologos: Collected Lectures & Interviews, Vol. II. Butterick, George F., ed. LC 77-1955. (Writing Ser.: No. 35). 1979. 12.00 (ISBN 0-87704-039-7); pap. 6.00 (ISBN 0-87704-040-0). Four Seasons Foun.
--Muthologos: The Collected Lectures & Interviews, Vol. I. Butterick, George F., ed. LC 77-1955. (Writing Ser.: No. 35). 1979. 12.00 (ISBN 0-87704-032-X); pap. 5.00 (ISBN 0-87704-031-1). Four Seasons Foun.
Olson, Clarinda E. Basic Science for Dental Auxiliaries. (Illus.). 1980. pap. 12.95 ref. ed. (ISBN 0-13-069245-X). P-H.
Olson, Craig. Craig Olson's Decorating with Plants. Grooms, Kathe, ed. (Illus.). 110p. 1981. pap. 2.95 (ISBN 0-915658-31-3). Meadowbrook Pr.
Olson, D. E., jt. ed. see Cromwell, R.
Olson, David F. Stone Grinding & Polishing. LC 73-83453. (Little Craft Book Ser.). (Illus.). 48p. (gr. 7 up). 1973. 5.95 (ISBN 0-8069-5286-5); PLB 6.69 (ISBN 0-8069-5287-3). Sterling.
Olson, David H., ed. Inventory of Marriage & Family Literature, Vol. 5. LC 67-63014. 1979. 60.00x (ISBN 0-8039-1232-3); pap. 29.95x (ISBN 0-8039-1233-1). Sage.
--Inventory of Marriage & Family Literature, Vol. 6. LC 67-63014. (Illus.). 390p. 60.00 (ISBN 0-8039-1474-1); pap. 29.95 (ISBN 0-8039-1475-X). Sage.
Olson, David M. The Legislative Process: A Comparative Approach. (Illus.). 1980. text ed. 17.50 scp (ISBN 0-06-044919-5, HarpC). Har-Row.
Olson, David M., jt. auth. see Jewell, Malcolm E.
Olson, Dean F. Alaska Reindeer Herdsmen: A Study of Native Management in Transition. LC 71-631923. (Institute of Social, Economic & Government Research Ser.: No. 22). (Illus.). 172p. 1969. pap. 5.00 (ISBN 0-295-95119-2). U of Wash Pr.
Olson, Everett & Thomas, Roger D. A Cold Look at the Warm-Blooded Dinosaurs. (American Association for the Advancement of Science Ser.). 1979. lib. bdg. 28.50x (ISBN 0-89158-350-5). Westview.
Olson, Everett C., jt. ed. see Thomas, Roger D. K.
Olson, Gary D., jt. auth. see Krause, Herbert.
Olson, Gene, jt. auth. see Olson, Joan.
Olson, Gerald, ed. Advances in Consumer Research: Proceedings of 1979 Meeting, Vol. VII. softcover 21.00 (ISBN 0-915552-05-1). Assn Consumer Res.
Olson, H. F. Music, Physics & Engineering. 2nd ed. (Illus.). 10.00 (ISBN 0-8446-2680-5). Peter Smith.
Olson, Harry A. Early Recollections: Their Use in Diagnosis & Psychotherapy. (Illus.). 416p. 1979. text ed. 29.75 (ISBN 0-398-03826-0). C C Thomas.
Olson, Harry E., Jr. Physician Recruitment & the Hospital. (Illus.). 160p. (Orig.). 1980. 15.00 (ISBN 0-87258-301-5, 1035). Am Hospital.
Olson, Harry F. Modern Sound Reproduction. LC 77-28682. 352p. 1978. Repr. of 1972 ed. lib. bdg. 21.00 (ISBN 0-88275-648-6). Krieger.
Olson, Helen K. The Secret of Spirit Mountain. LC 80-1014. (Illus.). (gr. 5 up). 1980. 6.95g (ISBN 0-396-07856-7). Dodd.
Olson, Jack L., jt. auth. see Price, Wilson T.
Olson, James C. History of Nebraska. 2nd ed. LC 54-8444. (Illus.). xvi, 387p. 1966. 14.95 (ISBN 0-8032-0135-4); pap. 9.95 (ISBN 0-8032-5790-2, BB 579, Bison). U of Nebr Pr.
--Red Cloud & the Sioux Problem. LC 65-10048. (Illus.). xii, 375p. 1965. 15.00x (ISBN 0-8032-0136-2); pap. 5.50 (ISBN 0-8032-5817-8, BB 602, Bison). U of Nebr Pr.
Olson, Joan & Olson, Gene. Silver Dust & Spanish Wine: A History of Mexico. LC 80-51869. (Illus.). 336p. (Orig.). (gr. 9 up). 1980. pap. text ed. 6.97x (ISBN 0-913366-06-4). Windyridge.
Olson, Joan & Williams, Elaine. Antique Shopping in Southern California: Comprehensive Guide to Shops in Seven Counties. (Illus.). 300p. (Orig.). 1980. pap. 8.95 (ISBN 0-9602924-0-3). Willows Pr.
Olson, Karen, jt. ed. see Brown, Cheryl L.
Olson, Keith W. The G. I. Bill, the Veterans, & the Colleges. LC 72-91667. (Illus.). 152p. 1974. 10.00x (ISBN 0-8131-1288-5). U Pr of Ky.
Olson, Ken. The Art of Hanging Loose in an Uptight World. 208p. 1978. pap. 2.25 (ISBN 0-449-23613-7, Crest). Fawcett.
--Can You Wait till Friday? The Psychology of Hope. 288p. 1976. pap. 1.75 o.p. (ISBN 0-449-23022-8, Crest). Fawcett.
--Hey Man!, Open Up & Live! 1978. pap. 1.95 o.p. (ISBN 0-449-14038-5, GM). Fawcett.
Olson, Kenneth E. Music & Musket: Bands & Bandsmen of the American Civil War. LC 79-6195. (Contributions to the Study of Music & Dance: No. 1). (Illus.). 296p. 1981. lib. bdg. 27.50 (ISBN 0-313-22112-X). Greenwood.
Olson, Lynn. Sculpting with Cement: Direct Modeling in a Permanent Medium. (Illus.). 106p. (Orig.). (gr. 11-12). 1981. pap. price not set (ISBN 0-9605678-0-1). Steelstone.
Olson, Margot, jt. auth. see Forrest, Mary.
Olson, Margrethe H. Organization of Information Services: Alternative Approaches. Dufey, Gunter, ed. (Research for Business Decisions: Vol. 21). 290p. 1980. 27.95 (ISBN 0-8357-1105-6, Pub. by UMI Res Pr). Univ Microfilms.
Olson, Marjorie E. Finton the Fish: Visual Discriminations for Children. (Illus.). 29p. (gr. k-1). 1974. pap. text ed. 2.00x (ISBN 0-89039-100-9). Ann Arbor FL.
Olson, Marjorie T. The Sly Spy & Other Stories. (Educational Ser.). (Illus.). (gr. 2-3). 1979. pap. 5.00 (ISBN 0-89039-242-0). Ann Arbor FL.
Olson, May, jt. auth. see Arndt, Karl J.
Olson, Mildred. Diamondola. 1980. pap. 3.25 (ISBN 0-8280-0046-8, 04305-9). Review & Herald.
Olson, Milton C. & Haber, F. Barry. Business Mathematics. 1981. pap. 12.95 (ISBN 0-672-97327-8); answer key 6.67 (ISBN 0-672-97328-6). Bobbs.
Olson, Nancy B. Cataloging of Audiovisual Materials: A Manual Using AACR2, with an Appendix Containing OCLC Worksheets for All Examples Given in the Text. LC 79-73907. 1980. 17.50 (ISBN 0-933474-07-5). Minn Scholarly.
Olson, Nancy B., jt. auth. see Aichele, Jean.
Olson, Nat. How to Win Your Family to Christ. LC 77-81561. pap. 2.95 (ISBN 0-89107-149-0). Good News.
Olson, Nels. Time in Many Places. 218p. 1980. 9.00 (ISBN 0-87839-036-7). North Star.
Olson, Richard F. Managing the Interview. LC 80-17112. (Self-Teaching Guide Ser.). 183p. 1980. 7.95 (ISBN 0-471-04859-3, Pub. by Wiley-Interscience). Wiley.
--Performance Appraisal: A Guide to Greater Productivity. (Self-Teaching Guide Ser.). 200p. 1981. pap. text ed. 8.95 (ISBN 0-471-09134-0). Wiley.
Olson, Robert E., ed. Protein-Calorie Malnutrition. (Nutrition Foundation Monograph Ser). 1975. 48.00 (ISBN 0-12-526150-0). Acad Pr.
Olson, Robert G. Introduction to Existentialism. (Orig.). 1962. pap. text ed. 3.50 (ISBN 0-486-20055-8). Dover.
--Music Dictation: A Stereo Taped Series. (Orig.). 1970. pap. 9.95x (ISBN 0-534-00671-X); stereo taped s 195.00x (ISBN 0-534-00672-8). Wadsworth Pub.
Olson, Robert K. U. S. Foreign Policy & the New International Economic Order. (Special Studies in International Relations). 184p. 1981. lib. bdg. 20.00x (ISBN 0-86531-125-0). Westview.
Olson, Robert L., ed. see Weigand, Dennis A.
Olson, Roberta J. Italian Drawings 1780-1890. LC 79-9648. (Illus.). 248p. 1980. 29.95x (ISBN 0-253-11963-4). Ind U Pr.
Olson, Sheldon R. Ideas & Data: The Process & Practice of Social Research. 1976. text ed. 17.50x (ISBN 0-256-01809-X). Dorsey.
--Issues in the Sociology of Criminal Justice. LC 74-31261. (Studies in Sociology Ser.). 58p. 1975. pap. text ed. 2.50 (ISBN 0-672-61348-4). Bobbs.
Olson, Sherry H. Baltimore: The Building of an American City. LC 79-21950. 289p. 1980. text ed. 22.95x (ISBN 0-8018-2224-6). Johns Hopkins.
--Depletion Myth: A History of Railroad Use of Timber. LC 70-148940. 1971. 11.00x (ISBN 0-674-19820-4). Harvard U Pr.
Olson, Sue, ed. see Bumgarner, Marlene A.
Olson, Theodore. Millennialism, Utopianism, & Progress. 1981. 35.00 (ISBN 0-8020-5506-0). U of Toronto Pr.
Olson, Theodore V. Arrow in the Sun. 1980. pap. write for info. (ISBN 0-671-83541-6). PB.
--Bitter Grass. 1980. pap. write for info. (ISBN 0-671-83541-6). PB.
Olson, Virgil J. Capitol Reef: The Story Behind the Scenery. DenDooven, Gweneth R., ed. LC 75-184671. (Illus.). 1972. 7.95 (ISBN 0-916122-36-0); pap. 2.50 (ISBN 0-916122-11-5). K C Pubns.
Olson, W. G. Charismatic Church. LC 74-10600. 1974. pap. 3.50 (ISBN 0-87123-080-1, 210080). Bethany Fell.
Olson, W. Kent, jt. auth. see Atkinson, Brooks.
Olson, William H. Practical Neurology for the Primary Care Physician. (Illus.). 360p. 1981. lexotone spiral bdg. 21.75 (ISBN 0-398-04135-0). C C Thomas.
Olsson, Axel A. Neogene Mollusks from Northwestern Ecuador. (Illus.). 1964. 12.00 (ISBN 0-87710-367-4). Paleo Res.
Olsson, Bengt. Memphis Blues. (The Paul Oliver Blues Ser.). pap. 2.95 (ISBN 0-913714-48-8). Legacy Bks.
Olsson, David L., jt. auth. see Raphael, Harold J.
Olszowy, Damon R. Horticulture for the Disabled & Disadvantaged. 240p. 1978. 17.50 (ISBN 0-398-03691-8). C C Thomas.
Olthius, James H. Facts, Values & Ethics. 1968. pap. text ed. 18.00x (ISBN 9-0232-0487-5). Humanities.
Olthuis, J. H. & Vandezande, G. Bunglers & Visionaries: Christian Labour at the Crossroads. 1972. pap. 1.50 o.p. (ISBN 0-686-11984-3). Wedge Pub.
Olthuis, J. H., et al. Out of Concern for the Church. 1970. pap. 2.95 o.p. (ISBN 0-686-11985-1). Wedge Pub.
--Will All the King's Men. 1972. pap. 3.95 o.p. (ISBN 0-686-11987-8). Wedge Pub.
Olthuis, James. I Pledge You My Troth: Marriage, Family, Friendship. LC 74-25695. 160p. 1975. 4.95 (ISBN 0-06-066394-4, RD-155, HarpR). Har-Row.
Oltman, Debra. Study Guide for Weinberg, Schumaker & Oltman's Statistics: An Intuitive Approach. 4th ed. 250p. (Orig.). 1981. pap. text ed. 7.95 (ISBN 0-8185-0442-0). Brooks-Cole.
Oltmanns, Thomas F., jt. auth. see Neale, John M.
Olton, D. & Noonberg, A. Biofeedback: Clinical Applications in Behavioral Medicine. 1980. 21.00 (ISBN 0-13-076315-2). P-H.
Olton, Roy, jt. auth. see Plano, Jack.
Olweny, Ch. L., et al, eds. Kaposi's Sarcoma. (Antibodies & Chemotherapy: Vol. 29). (Illus.). 200p. 1981. 72.00 (ISBN 3-8055-2076-X). S Karger.
Olynyk, Stephen D., ed. see Rakhmanny, Roman.
Olyslager Organization. The Observer's Book of Automobiles. (The Observer Bks). (Illus.). 1980. 4.95 (ISBN 0-684-16516-3, ScribT). Scribner.
Omaggio, Alice C. Games & Simulations in the Foreign Language Classroom. (Language in Education Ser. No. 13). (Orig.). 1979. pap. text ed. 5.95x (ISBN 0-87281-099-2). Ctr Appl Ling.
O'Maille, T. Breacadh. 146p. 1973. 10.00x (ISBN 0-7165-2237-3, Pub. by Irish Academic Pr Ireland). Biblio Dist.
--Liosta Focal As Ros Muc. 270p. 1974. 20.00x (ISBN 0-7165-2238-1, Pub. by Irish Academic Pr Ireland). Biblio Dist.
O'Malley, B. W. & Birnbaumer, L., eds. Receptors & Hormone Action, Vol. 1. 1978. 49.00 (ISBN 0-12-526301-5); by subscription 42.25 (ISBN 0-685-79544-6). Acad Pr.
O'Malley, Bert W., ed. Hormone Action, Vol. 2. 1978. 52.50 (ISBN 0-12-526302-3); by subscription 45.00 (ISBN 0-686-67867-2). Acad Pr.
O'Malley, C. D., ed. The History of Medical Education. LC 72-85449. (UCLA Forum in Medical Sciences: No. 12). (Illus.). 1970. 50.00x (ISBN 0-520-01578-9). U of Cal Pr.
--Leonardo's Legacy: An International Symposium. LC 68-14976. (UCLA Center for Medieval & Renaissance Studies). (Illus.). 1968. 36.75x (ISBN 0-520-00956-8). U of Cal Pr.
O'Malley, C. D., et al, trs. see Harvey, William.
O'Malley, Charles D., ed. see Vesalius, Andreas.
O'Malley, Conor, jt. auth. see Irvine, Alexander R.
O'Malley, J., ed. see Marx, Karl.
O'Malley, J. Steven. Pilgrimage of Faith: The Legacy of the Otterbeins. LC 73-5684. (ATLA Monograph: No. 4). 1973. 10.00 (ISBN 0-8108-0626-6). Scarecrow.
O'Malley, Jerry, ed. Me Either, and Other One-Act Plays. 1976. pap. 0.60 (ISBN 0-8272-2311-0). Bethany Pr.
O'Malley, John. Schaum's Outline of Basic Circuit Analysis. (Schaum's Outline Ser.). 400p. 1981. pap. 6.95 (ISBN 0-07-047820-1). McGraw.
O'Malley, John E., jt. auth. see Koocher, Gerald P.
O'Malley, John R. Circuit Analysis. 1980. text ed. 20.95 (ISBN 0-13-133827-7). P-H.
O'Malley, Joseph, ed. see Rubel, Maximilien.
O'Malley, L. S., ed. Modern India & the West: A Study of the Interaction of Their Civilizations. (Royal Institute of International Affairs Ser). 1941. 17.00x o.p. (ISBN 0-19-821541-X). Oxford U Pr.
O'Malley, Sarah A., jt. auth. see Fournier, William.
O'Malley, Susan G., ed. see Goffe, Thomas.
O'Malley, William J. The Living Word: How the Gospels Work, Vol. 2. LC 80-80534. (Orig.). (gr. 9-12). 1980. pap. 4.95 (ISBN 0-8091-9559-3). Paulist Pr.
--The Living Word: Scripture & Myth, Vol. 1. LC 80-80534. (Orig.). (gr. 9-12). 1980. pap. text ed. 4.95 (ISBN 0-8091-9558-5). Paulist Pr.
Oman, Charles. Caroline Silver. 1970. 31.95 (ISBN 0-571-09442-2, Pub. by Faber & Faber). Merrimack Bk Serv.
--English Engraved Silver. (Illus.). 1979. 42.00 (ISBN 0-571-10498-3, Pub. by Faber & Faber). Merrimack Bk Serv.
Oman, Robert M. Graphing Algebraic Functions. 1979. pap. 1.95 (ISBN 0-931660-02-5). R Oman Pubns.

O'Manique, John. Energy in Evolution: Teilhard's Physics of the Future. (Teilhard Study Library). 1969. text ed. 4.00x (ISBN 0-900391-23-5). Humanities.

Omar, M. Ali. Elementary Solid State Physics: Principles & Applications. LC 73-10593. 1974. text ed. 25.95 (ISBN 0-201-05482-5). A-W.

Omar, Saleh Beshara. Ibn Al-Haytham's Optics: A Study of the Origins of Experimental Science. LC 76-42611. (Studies in Islamic Philosophy & Science). (Illus.). 1977. 25.00x (ISBN 0-88297-015-1). Bibliotheca.

O'Mara, W. P., et al. Residential Development Handbook. LC 77-930497. (Community Builders Handbook Ser.). (Illus.). 350p. 1978. 34.00 (ISBN 0-87420-580-8). Urban Land.

O'Mara, W. Paul, et al. Adaptive Use. LC 78-56054. (Illus.). 246p. 1978. 26.25 (ISBN 0-87420-582-4). Urban Land.

Omar Khayyam. The Rubaiyat. Fitzgerald, Edward, tr. LC 64-20696. 1964. 6.95 o.p. (ISBN 0-690-71388-6). T Y Crowell.

Omarr, Sydney. Sydney Omarr's Astrological Guide for You in 1980. (Orig.). 1979. pap. 2.25 o.p. (ISBN 0-451-08835-2, E8835, Sig). NAL.

--Sydney Omarr's Astrological Revelation About You. 1973. pap. 1.25 (ISBN 0-451-05674-4, Y5674, Sig). NAL.

Omaya, T., jt. auth. see Stoeckel, H.

O'Meally, Robert G. The Craft of Ralph Ellison. LC 80-12680. 1980. text ed. 14.00x (ISBN 0-674-17548-4). Harvard U Pr.

O'Meara, Carra F. The Iconography of the Facade of Saint-Gilles-Du-Gard. LC 76-23668. (Outstanding Dissertations in the Fine Arts - Medieval). (Illus.). 1977. Repr. of 1975 ed. lib. bdg. 52.00 (ISBN 0-8240-2717-5). Garland Pub.

O'Meara, John J. The Mind of Eriugena. Bieler, L., ed. 208p. 1973. 19.00x (ISBN 0-7165-2158-X, Pub. by Irish Academic Pr Ireland). Biblio Dist.

--The Voyage of Saint Brendan: Journey to the Promised Land. (Dolmen Texts: No. 1). (Illus.). 1978. text ed. 9.00x (ISBN 0-391-00710-6, Dolmen Pr). Humanities.

O'Meara, John J., tr. see Cambrensis, Giraldus.

O'Meara, O. T. Lectures on Symplectic Groups. LC 78-19101. (Mathematical Surveys: No. 16). 1978. 22.80 o.p. (ISBN 0-8218-1516-4, SURV 16). Am Math.

O'Meara, Walter. Sioux Are Coming. (Illus.). (gr. 3-7). 1971. 6.95 (ISBN 0-395-12759-9). HM.

Omel, Myles. The Diet Chef's Gourmet Cookbook. LC 80-70958. 288p. 1981. 14.95 (ISBN 0-8119-0328-1). Fell.

Omenetto, N. Analytical Laser Spectroscopy, Vol. 50. 550p. 1979. 47.50 (ISBN 0-471-65371-3, 1-075). Wiley.

Omer, Garth St. see St. Omer, Garth.

Ominde, S. H., ed. Studies in East African Geography & Development. (Illus.). 1971. 27.50x (ISBN 0-520-02073-1). U of Cal Pr.

Ommanney, F. The Fishes. (Young Readers Library). (Illus.). 1977. lib. bdg. 7.95 (ISBN 0-686-51090-9). Silver.

Ommanney, F. D. Fishes. LC 63-10758. (Life Nature Library). (Illus.). (gr. 5 up). 1970. PLB 8.97 o.p. (ISBN 0-8094-0622-5, Pub. by Time-Life). Silver.

Ommen, Thomas B. The Hermeneutic of Dogma. LC 75-29493. (American Academy of Religion. Dissertation Ser.). 1975. pap. 7.50 (ISBN 0-89130-039-2, 010111). Scholars Pr Ca.

O'Morrow, Gerald S. Administration of Activity Therapy Service. (Illus.). 440p. 1976. 22.50 (ISBN 0-398-01425-6). C C Thomas.

--Therapeutic Recreation: A Helping Profession. 2nd ed. (Illus.). 336p. 1980. text ed. 14.95 (ISBN 0-8359-7659-9). Reston.

Omrcanin, Margaret. Norway-Sweden-Croatia: A Comparative Study of State Secession & Formation. 1976. pap. 6.95 (ISBN 0-8059-2309-8). Dorrance.

Omu, Fred I. Press & Politics in Nigeria Eighteen Eighty-Nineteen Thirty Seven. (Ibadan History Ser.). 1978. text ed. 20.75x (ISBN 0-391-00561-8). Humanities.

Omura, James K., jt. auth. see Viterbi, Andrew J.

Omura, Yoshiaki. Acupuncture Medicine. LC 79-1944. 1981. 19.95 (ISBN 0-87040-491-1). Japan Pubns.

--A New Approach to Self-Diagnosis: Introducing Applied Kinesiology. LC 79-89345. (Illus.). Date not set. 9.95 (ISBN 0-87040-468-7). Japan Pubns. Postponed.

Omura, Yoshiaki, et al. The Tofu-Miso High Efficiency Diet. 208p. 1981. 10.95 (ISBN 0-668-05178-7); pap. 6.95 (ISBN 0-668-05180-9). Arco.

On, Danny, jt. auth. see Shaw, Richard J.

Onat, Etta S. & Orgel, Stephen, eds. The Witch of Edmonton by Thomas Dekker: A Critical Edition. LC 79-54355. (Renaissance Drama Second Ser.). 400p. 1980. lib. bdg. 44.00 (ISBN 0-8240-4472-X). Garland Pub.

Onate, Andres D. Chairman Mao & the Chinese Communist Party. LC 78-11049. (Illus.). 1979. 18.95 (ISBN 0-88229-250-1); pap. 9.95 (ISBN 0-88229-646-9). Nelson-Hall.

On Bober, Wolffgang. The Carver Effect: A Paranormal Experience. (Illus.). 224p. 1979. 11.95 (ISBN 0-8117-0329-0). Stackpole.

Ondetti, Miklos A., jt. auth. see Bodanszky, M.

Ondori Company Staff. Simple Cross Stitch. (Ondori Young Handicrafts Ser). (Illus.). 104p. 1977. pap. 3.50 o.p. (ISBN 0-87040-399-0). Japan Pubns.

--Simple Stuffed Toys. (Ondori Young Handicrafts Ser). (Illus.). 1977. pap. 3.50 o.p. (ISBN 0-87040-398-2). Japan Pubns.

--Small Flowers in Embroidery. (Ondori Young Handicrafts Ser). (Illus.). 1977. pap. 3.95 (ISBN 0-87040-396-6). Japan Pubns.

Ondori Publishing Co. Embroidery for Children's Clothing. (Ondori Needlecraft Ser.). (Illus., Orig.). 1977. pap. 6.50 (ISBN 0-87040-414-8). Japan Pubns.

Ondori Publishing Co. Staff. Cross Stitch Designs. (Ondori Handicraft Er). (Illus.). 96p. 1976. pap. 5.95 (ISBN 0-87040-366-4). Japan Pubns.

--Floral Embroidery. (Ondori Handicrafts Ser). (Illus.). 64p. 1976. pap. 5.50 (ISBN 0-87040-365-6). Japan Pubns.

--Lovely Paper Flowers. (Ondori Handicrafts Ser). (Illus., Orig.). 1977. pap. 6.50 (ISBN 0-87040-413-X). Japan Pubns.

--Simple Embroidery. (Ondori Handicrafts Ser.). (Illus.). 72p. 1976. pap. 5.50 (ISBN 0-87040-377-X). Japan Pubns.

--Smocking. (Ondori Handicraft Ser). (Illus.). 64p. 1976. pap. 5.50 (ISBN 0-87040-367-2). Japan Pubns.

--Stuffed Toys. (Ondori Handicraft Ser). (Illus.). 96p. 1976. pap. 5.50 (ISBN 0-87040-368-0). Japan Pubns.

Ondori Publishing Co. Staff & Murayama, Misako. Cross Stitch Patterns. (Ondori Handicraft Ser.). (Illus.). 64p. 1976. pap. 3.95 (ISBN 0-87040-374-5). Japan Pubns.

Ondori Publishing Company. Stitches & Samplers. (Ondori Embroidery Ser: Vol. 2). (Illus.). 104p. 1974. pap. 5.50 (ISBN 0-87040-357-5). Japan Pubns.

Ondori Publishing Company Staff. Easy Embroidery. (Ondori Embroidery Ser.: Vol. 1). (Illus.). 81p. 1974. pap. 3.95 (ISBN 0-87040-356-7). Japan Pubns.

--Embroidery Designs. (Ondori Embroidery Ser: Vol. 3). (Illus.). 65p. 1975. pap. 4.50 (ISBN 0-87040-358-3). Japan Pubns.

--Embroidery for Fun. (Ondori Embroidery Ser: Vol. 4). (Illus.). 137p. 1975. pap. 5.95 (ISBN 0-87040-359-1). Japan Pubns.

--Illustrated Basic Crochet & Knit. (Illus.). 48p. 1977. pap. 2.95 (ISBN 0-87040-389-3). Japan Pubns.

--One-Point Embroidery & Applique. new ed. (Ondori Young Handicraft Ser). (Illus.). 1977. pap. 3.95 (ISBN 0-87040-397-4). Japan Pubns.

Ondori Staff. Crochet Lace with Complete Diagrams. (Ondori Needlecraft Ser.). (Illus.). 1978. pap. 6.95 (ISBN 0-87040-415-6). Japan Pubns.

--Embroidery for Beginners. (Ondori Needlework Ser.). (Orig.). (gr. 6 up). 1978. pap. 5.50 (ISBN 0-87040-429-6). Japan Pubns.

--A Treasury of Embroidery Samples. LC 80-84416. (Illus.). 96p. 1981. pap. 5.95 (ISBN 0-87040-496-2). Japan Pubns.

Ondov, Geraldine, jt. auth. see Grubb, Reba D.

O'Neal, Bill. Henry Brown: The Outlaw-Marshall. (Illus.). 165p. 12.95; leatherbound collector's edition 75.00. Creative Pubns.

O'Neal, Charles. Three Wishes for Jamie. LC 79-66116. 248p. 1980. 15.95 (ISBN 0-933256-08-6); pap. text ed. 7.95 (ISBN 0-933256-09-4). Second Chance.

O'Neal, L. Thomas. Maya in Sankara: Measuring the Immeasurable. 1980. 16.00x (ISBN 0-8364-0611-7). South Asia Bks.

O'Neal, Robert & Love, Alan C. English for You. 1972. pap. text ed. 8.95x o.p. (ISBN 0-669-74369-0); instructor's manual free o.p. (ISBN 0-669-74385-2). Heath.

O'Neal, W. B. Jefferson's Fine Arts Library. 1976. 20.00 (ISBN 0-8139-0648-2). Brown Bk.

O'Neal, William. Henry Brown: Outlaw Marshal. LC 80-65457. 165p. 1981. 12.95 (ISBN 0-932702-09-0); collector's edtion 75.00 (ISBN 0-932702-10-4). Creative Texas.

O'Neal, William see O'Neal, William B.

O'Neal, William B. Jefferson's Buildings at the University of Virginia: The Rotunda. (Illus.). 1960. 10.00 o.p. (ISBN 0-8139-0189-8). U Pr of Va.

O'Neal, William B. see O'Neal, William B.

O'Neal, William B., ed. American Association of Architectural Bibliographers' Papers, Vol. 1. Incl. Henry-Russell Hitchcock. Grady, James H; Walter Gropius. Shillaber, Carol; Philip C. Johnson. O'Neal, William; Early Architecture of Virginia. Nichols, Frederick D. LC 65-14273. 128p. 1965. 10.00x (ISBN 0-8139-0003-4). U Pr of Va.

--American Association of Architectural Bibliographers' Papers, Vol. 2. Incl. Sibyl Moholy-Nagy. Johnson, Philip C. & O'Neal, William B.; Holabird & Roche. Rudd, William; Early Architecture of Virginia. Nichols, Frederick D. LC 65-14273. 113p. 1966. 10.00x (ISBN 0-8139-0004-2). U Pr of Va.

--American Association of Architectural Bibliographers' Papers, Vol. 3. Incl. Walter Gropius. LC 65-14273. 138p. 1966. 10.00x (ISBN 0-8139-0005-0). U Pr of Va.

--American Association of Architectural Bibliographers' Papers, Vol. 5. Incl. Henry-Russell Hitchcock. Grady, James H; Architectural Comment in American Magazines, 1783-1815. Neil, J. Meredith; The Adam Style in America, 1770-1820. Boyd, Sterling M; Calvert Vaux. Sigle, John D; Alvar Aalto. Beal, Peter W. LC 65-14273. 106p. 1968. 10.00x (ISBN 0-8139-0007-7). U Pr of Va.

--American Association of Architectural Bibliographers' Papers, Vol. 6. Incl. Jefferson As an Architect. O'Neal, William B. LC 65-14273. (Illus.). 150p. 1969. 10.00x (ISBN 0-8139-0281-9). U Pr of Va.

--American Association of Architectural Bibliographers' Papers, Vol. 7. Incl. Sir Nikolaus Pevsner. Barr, John R. LC 65-14273. 124p. 1970. 10.00x (ISBN 0-8139-0299-1). U Pr of Va.

--American Association of Architectural Bibliographers' Papers, Vol. 9. Incl. A Supplement to the Bibliography of Walter Gropius. Gropius, Ise, ed; A Bibliography of Works About Sir Christopher Wren. Stringer, Gail G., ed; Benjamin Henry Latrobe. Norton, Paul F., ed; Frank Lloyd Wright in Print 1959-1970. Muggenberg, James, compiled by. LC 65-14273. 1972. 10.00x (ISBN 0-8139-0391-2). U Pr of Va.

--American Association of Architectural Bibliographers Papers, Vol. 10. Incl. A Bibliography of Antonio Gaudi & the Catalan Movement, 1870-1930. Collins, George R. & Farinas, Maurice E., eds. LC 65-14273. 1973. 12.50x (ISBN 0-8139-0477-3). U Pr of Va.

--American Association of Architectural Bibliographers Papers, Vol. 11: Index to Papers 1-10. LC 65-14273. 1975. 12.50x (ISBN 0-8139-0608-3). U Pr of Va.

--Architecture in Virginia: An Official Guide to Four Centuries of Building in the Old Dominion. LC 67-13230. (Illus., Orig.). 1968. 4.95 o.s.i. (ISBN 0-8027-0020-9); pap. 2.95 o.s.i. (ISBN 0-8027-7006-1). Walker & Co.

Oneal, Zibby. The Language of Goldfish. 192p. 1981. pap. 1.95 (ISBN 0-449-70005-4, Juniper). Fawcett.

--Turtle & Snail. LC 78-14826. (Lippincott I-Like-to-Read Book). (Illus.). (gr. k-2). 1979. 6.95 (ISBN 0-397-31829-4). Lippincott.

O'Neil, Doris C., ed. Life: The First Decade Nineteen Thirty-Six to Nineteen Forty-Five. LC 79-88091. (Illus.). 1980. 22.50 (ISBN 0-8212-0682-6, 528854); pap. 9.95 (ISBN 0-8212-0760-1, 524298PB). NYGS.

O'Neil, Edward N., ed. Teles: The Cynic Teacher. LC 76-41800. (Society of Biblical Literature. Texts & Translantion - Graeco-Roman Religion Ser.). 1977. pap. 6.00 (ISBN 0-89130-092-9, 060211). Scholars Pr Ca.

O'Neil, Harold F., ed. Computer-Based Instruction: A State-of-the-Art Assessment. (Educational Technology Ser.). 1981. price not set (ISBN 0-12-526760-6). Acad Pr.

O'Neil, Harold F., Jr., ed. Issues in Instructional Systems Development. 224p. 1979. 17.50 (ISBN 0-12-526640-5). Acad Pr.

O'Neil, Kitty & Libby, Bill. Kitty: A Story of Triumph in a Soundless World. (Illus.). 224p. 1981. 9.95 (ISBN 0-688-00355-9). Morrow.

O'Neil, Paul. Barnstormers & Speed Kings. Time-Life Bks. Eds., ed. (The Epic of Flight Ser.). (Illus.). 176p. 1981. 12.95 (ISBN 0-8094-3275-7). Time-Life.

--The Frontiersmen. LC 76-47101. (Old West Ser.). (Illus.). (gr. 5 up). 1977. 12.96 (ISBN 0-8094-1547-X, Pub. by Time-Life). Silver.

--The Frontiersmen. (Old West Ser.). 1977. 12.95 (ISBN 0-8094-1545-3). Time-Life.

--The Rivermen. (The Old West Ser.). (Illus.). 240p. 1975. 12.95 (ISBN 0-8094-1496-1). Time-Life.

--The Rivermen. LC 75-7193. (The Old West). (Illus.). (gr. 5 up). 1975. kivar 12.96 (ISBN 0-8094-1498-8, Pub. by Time-Life). Silver.

O'Neil, Peter V. Introduction to Linear Algebra. 1979. text ed. 19.95x (ISBN 0-534-00606-X). Wadsworth Pub.

O'Neil, Robert M. Discriminating Against Discrimination: Preferential Admissions & the DeFunis Case. LC 75-3888. 288p. 1976. 10.95x (ISBN 0-253-31800-9). Ind U Pr.

--Free Speech: Responsible Communication Under Law. 2nd ed. LC 71-182877. (Orig.). 1972. pap. 3.95 (ISBN 0-672-61301-8, SC11). Bobbs.

O'Neil, Russell. Venom. 1979. pap. 1.95 o.p. (ISBN 0-345-25419-8). Ballantine.

O'Neil, Sally M., et al. Behavioral Approaches to Children with Developmental Delays. (Illus.). 1977. pap. 9.50 (ISBN 0-8016-3709-0). Mosby.

O'Neil, Terry, jt. auth. see Bleier, Rocky.

O'Neill, Ana M. Etica Para la Era Atomica. facsimile ed. 6.25 (ISBN 0-8477-2815-3); pap. 5.00 o.s.i. (ISBN 0-8477-2807-2). U of PR Pr.

O'Neill, Bard. Armed Struggle in Palestine: A Political - Military Analysis. LC 78-2285. (Westview Special Studies on the Middle East Ser.). 1978. lib. bdg. 26.50x (ISBN 0-89158-333-5). Westview.

O'Neill, Bard E., jt. ed. see Szyliowicz, Joseph S.

O'Neill, Barrett. Elementary Differential Geometry. 1966. text ed. 20.95 (ISBN 0-12-526750-9); answer bklt. 3.00 (ISBN 0-12-526756-8). Acad Pr.

O'Neill, Bill. A Mountain Never Too High: The Story of J. E. O'Neill. LC 77-82899. (Illus.). 1977. 7.95 (ISBN 0-913548-46-4, Valley Calif). Western Tanager.

O'Neill, Dan. The Mark of Cain. 1979. pap. 2.95 (ISBN 0-89728-016-4, 546726). Omega Pubns OR.

O'Neill, Eugene. Emperor Jones. 2nd ed. Herzberg, Max J., ed. (Orig.). 1960. pap. 6.50x (ISBN 0-13-274902-5). P-H.

--Iceman Cometh. 1957. pap. 1.95 (ISBN 0-394-70018-X, Vin). Random.

--Seven Plays of the Sea. 199p. Date not set. pap. 2.95 (ISBN 0-394-71856-9, Vin). Random.

O'Neill, Eugene see Caputi, Anthony.

O'Neill, Eugene see Watson, E. Bradlee & Pressey, Benfield.

O'Neill, Eugene, et al. American Playwrights on Drama. 2nd ed. Frenz, Horst, ed. 196p. Date not set. text ed. price not set (ISBN 0-89676-059-6); pap. text ed. price not set (ISBN 0-89676-060-X). Drama Bk. Postponed.

O'Neill, Frank & Libby, Bill. Sports Conditioning: Getting in Shape, Playing Your Best, & Preventing Injuries. LC 78-68373. (Illus.). 1979. 10.00 (ISBN 0-385-14108-4). Doubleday.

O'Neill, George, jt. auth. see O'Neill, Nena.

O'Neill, Jack. Up from the South: A Prospector in New Guinea, Nineteen Thirty-One to Nineteen Thirty-Seven. Sinclair, James, ed. (Illus.). 224p. 1979. text ed. 23.50x (ISBN 0-19-550567-0). Oxford U Pr.

O'Neill, James M. Early American Furniture. (gr. 7 up). 1963. text ed. 14.00 (ISBN 0-87345-045-0). McKnight.

O'Neill, James Milton. Religion & Education Under the Constitution. LC 72-171389. (Civil Liberties in American History Ser). 338p. 1972. Repr. of 1949 ed. lib. bdg. 35.00 (ISBN 0-306-70228-2). Da Capo.

O'Neill, John, tr. see Merleau-Ponty, Maurice.

O'Neill, John J. & Oyer, Herbert J. Visual Communication for the Hard of Hearing: History, Research & Methods. 2nd ed. (Illus.). 224p. 1981. text ed. 14.95 (ISBN 0-13-942466-0). P-H.

O'Neill, John P., ed. Clyfford Still. (Illus.). 222p. 1979. text ed. 22.50 (ISBN 0-87099-213-9, MPL D1965); pap. write for info. (ISBN 0-87099-214-7). Metro Mus Art.

O'Neill, John T., jt. ed. see Baldwin, Woodrow W.

O'Neill, Joseph. Land Under England. LC 80-14273. 228p. 1980. pap. 10.95 (ISBN 0-87951-117-6). Overlook Pr.

O'Neill, Judith. Martin Luther. LC 74-12959. (Introduction to the History of Mankind). (Illus.). 48p. (gr. 6-11). 1975. pap. text ed. 3.95 (ISBN 0-521-20403-8). Cambridge U Pr.

--Transported to Van Diemen's Land. (Introduction to the History of Mankind Ser.). (Illus.). 1977. 3.95 (ISBN 0-521-21231-6). Cambridge U Pr.

O'Neill, June, jt. ed. see Chiswick, Barry R.

O'Neill, Martha, ed. see Chamberlain, Valerie & Kelly, Joan.

O'Neill, Martha, ed. see Shank, et al.

O'Neill, Mary. Hailstones & Halibut Bones. LC 60-7138. (gr. k-12). 6.95a (ISBN 0-385-07911-7); pap. 1.95 (ISBN 0-385-07912-5); Softbound 1.95 (ISBN 0-385-05374-6). Doubleday.

--Saints: Adventures in Courage. LC 63-17278. (Illus.). (gr. 4-7). 1963. 7.95 o.p. (ISBN 0-385-04970-6). Doubleday.

O'Neill, Michael W. & Dobry, Ricardo, eds. Dynamic Response of Pile Foundations: Analytical Aspects. LC 80-69151. 112p. 1980. pap. text ed. 12.00 (ISBN 0-87262-257-6). Am Soc Civil Eng.

O'Neill, Nena & O'Neill, George. Open Marriage: A New Lifestyle for Couples. 1976. pap. 2.25 (ISBN 0-380-00271-X, 37465). Avon.

O'Neill, P. G. Japanese Kana Workbook. 1957. pap. 4.95 (ISBN 0-87011-039-X). Kodansha.

O'Neill, P. J. The Wiley Metric Guide. 1976. 7.95 o.p. (ISBN 0-471-02142-3). Wiley.

O'Neill, Paul. The End & the Myth. (The Old West Ser.). (Illus.). 1979. lib. bdg. 12.96 (ISBN 0-686-51083-6). Silver.

O'Neill, Paul D. Lutyens: Country Houses. 168p. 1981. 19.95 (ISBN 0-8230-7361-0, Whitney Lib). Watson-Guptill.

O'Neill, Reginald F. Theories of Knowledge: With a New Preface. 242p. 1980. Repr. of 1959 ed. text ed. 26.50x (ISBN 0-8290-0227-8); pap. text ed. 12.95x (ISBN 0-8290-0386-X). Irvington.

O'Neill, Robert, jt. auth. see Brunelle, Wallace.

O'Neill, Robert, et al. American Kernel Lessons: Intermediate Student's Book. (Illus.). 1978. pap. text ed. 4.50x (ISBN 0-582-79706-3); tchr's guide 4.50 (ISBN 0-582-79707-1); students tests 1.50x (ISBN 0-582-79708-X); Set 1. cassettes 11.95 (ISBN 0-582-79715-2); Set 2. cassette 19.95x (ISBN 0-582-79716-0); Set 3. cassettes 34.95x (ISBN 0-582-79710-1); tapescript 2.25x (ISBN 0-582-79709-8). Longman.

O'Neill, Tom. A Place Called Hope: Caring for Children in Distress. (Practice of Social Work Ser.: No. 7). 128p. 1981. 22.50x (ISBN 0-631-12963-4, Pub. by Basil Blackwell England); pap. 8.95x (ISBN 0-631-12654-6). Biblio Dist.

O'Neill, William. Educational Ideologies. (Orig.). 1981. pap. text ed. 17.95x (ISBN 0-8302-2305-3). Goodyear.

--The Progressive Years: America Comes of Age. LC 74-26163. 1975. 5.95 (ISBN 0-396-07197-X). Dodd.

O'Neill, William J., jt. auth. see Eby, Frank H.

O'Nell, Carl W. Dreams, Culture & the Individual. LC 76-513. (Cross-Cultural Themes Ser.). 96p. 1976. pap. text ed. 3.00 o.s.i. (ISBN 0-88316-523-6). Chandler & Sharp.

Ong, Walter J. Barbarian Within, & Other Fugitive Essays & Studies. 1962. 9.95 (ISBN 0-02-593260-8). Macmillan.

--Fighting for Life: Contest, Sexuality, & Consciousness. LC 80-66968. (Illus.). 240p. 1981. 14.95 (ISBN 0-8014-1342-7). Cornell U Pr.

--In the Human Grain. 1967. 9.95 (ISBN 0-02-593340-X). Macmillan.

--The Presence of the Word: Some Prolegomena for Cultural & Religious History. 1967. 22.50x o.p. (ISBN 0-300-00810-4). Yale U Pr.

--The Presence of the Word: Some Prolegomena for Cultural & Religious History. xvi, 360p. 1981. pap. 8.95x (ISBN 0-8166-1043-6). U of Minn Pr.

Onigman, Marc. This Date in Braves History. LC 80-6158. (This Date Ser.). 288p. 1981. pap. 9.95 (ISBN 0-8128-6106-X). Stein & Day.

Onions, C. T., et al. The Fate of French-E in English: The Plural of Nouns Ending in-th, Vol. 7. Commager, Steele, ed. Incl. Basic; Problems of Spelling Reform; Pure English of the Soil; Inflected English; The Critique of Pure English; Retrospect. (Society of Pure English Ser.). 1979. lib. bdg. 42.00 (ISBN 0-8240-3671-9). Garland Pub.

Onions, Charles T. Shakespeare Glossary. 2nd rev ed. 1919. pap. 10.95 (ISBN 0-19-871094-1). Oxford U Pr.

Onions, Oliver. A Case in Camera. 320p. 1980. Repr. of 1918 ed. lib. bdg. 15.50x (ISBN 0-89968-205-7). Lightyear.

Onis, Federico de, jt. auth. see Seminario De Estudios Hispanicos.

Onis, Harriet de see Alegria, Ciro.

Onis, Harriet de, tr. see Alegria, Ciro.

Onis, Harriet De see De Onis, Harriet.

Onis, Jose De see De Onis, Jose.

Online Conference, Ltd., ed. Word Processing: Selection, Implementation & Uses. 1979. text ed. 63.50x (ISBN 0-903796-32-5). Renouf.

Online Conferences Ltd., ed. Personal Computers in Business. 1978. pap. text ed. 42.00x (ISBN 0-903796-33-3, Pub. by Online Conferences England). Renouf.

--Pragmatic Programming & Sensible Software. 1978. text ed. 94.00x (ISBN 0-903796-20-1, Pub by Online Conferences England). Renouf.

Online Conferences Ltd., ed. see European Computing Congress.

Onoh, J. K., ed. The Foundations of Nigeria's Financial Infrastructure. 318p. 1980. 50.00x (ISBN 0-7099-0448-7, Pub. by Croom Helm Ltd England). Biblio Dist.

Onopa, Robert. The Pleasure Tube. 1979. pap. 1.75 o.p. (ISBN 0-425-03941-2). Berkley Pub.

Onstott, Kyle. The Falconhurst Fancy. 1978. lib. bdg. 14.30x (ISBN 0-89966-248-X). Buccaneer Bks.

Onstott, Kyle & Horner, Lance. Flight to Falconhurst. (Falconhurst Plantation Ser.). 1978. pap. 2.50 (ISBN 0-449-14257-4, GM). Fawcett.

Ontjes, David A. & Underwood, Louis E. Endocrinology. (Medical Examination Review Books: Vol. 33). 1975. spiral bdg. 16.50 (ISBN 0-87488-131-5). Med Exam.

Onuf, Nicholas G, ed. Law Making in the Global Community. 600p. 1980. lib. bdg. write for info. (ISBN 0-89089-169-9). Carolina Acad Pr.

Ooi Jin-Bee. Peninsular Malaysia. 2nd ed. LC 75-42166. (Geographies for Advanced Study). Orig. Title: Land, People & Economy in Malaysia. 1976. text ed. 23.00x (ISBN 0-582-48185-6). Longman.

Ooka, D., tr. see Kobayashi, Keizo.

Ooka, D. T., tr. see Tsunoyama, Yokihiro.

Ooka, Diane, tr. see Watanabe, Yuichi.

Ooka, Shohei. Fires on the Plain. Morris, Ivan, tr. from Japanese. 254p. 1957. pap. 5.95 (ISBN 0-8048-1379-5). C E Tuttle.

Ooms, Theodora. Teenage Pregnancy in a Family Context: Implications for Policy. (Family Impact Seminar Ser.). 350p. 1981. 19.50x (ISBN 0-87722-204-5). Temple U Pr.

Oonsted, Christopher, jt. auth. see Oonsted, Margaret.

Oonsted, Margaret & Oonsted, Christopher. On Fetal Growth Rate. (Clinics in Developmental Medicine Ser.: Vol. 46). 1972. 19.50 (ISBN 0-685-34617-X). Lippincott.

Oorthuys, Cas. Oxford in Focus. (Illus.). 144p. 1981. pap. 7.50 (ISBN 0-85181-100-0, Pub. by Faber & Faber). Merrimack Bk Serv.

Oostens-Wittamer, Yolande. La Belle Epoque: Masterworks by Combaz, Leo Jo & Livemont. LC 79-92749. (Illus.). 64p. (Orig.). 1980. pap. 8.95 (ISBN 0-88397-027-9). Intl Exhibit Foun.

Oosterbaan, John. Population Dispersal: A National Imperative. LC 79-9672. 1980. 18.95 (ISBN 0-669-03615-3). Lexington Bks.

Oosterhuis, Huub. Fifty Psalms: A New Translation. 1974. pap. 3.50 (ISBN 0-8164-2581-7). Crossroad NY.

--Open Your Hearts. LC 74-140237. 1971. 4.50 (ISBN 0-8164-1098-4). Crossroad NY.

--Times of Life. Smith, N. D., tr. from Dutch. LC 79-89653. (Orig.). 1980. pap. 3.95 (ISBN 0-8091-2245-6). Paulist Pr.

Oosterman, Gordon, jt. auth. see Zondag, Jack.

Oosterwal, Gottfried. Mission, Possible. LC 72-95276. (Anvil Ser.). 1972. pap. 4.95 (ISBN 0-8127-0066-X). Southern Pub.

Oosthuizein, G. C. Theological Battleground in Asia & Africa: The Issues Facing the Churches & the Efforts to Overcome Western Divisions. 1116p. 1972. text ed. 28.50x (ISBN 0-391-00230-9). Humanities.

Oosting, Henry J. The Study of Plant Communities: An Introduction to Plant Ecology. 2nd ed. LC 56-11029. (Illus.). 1956. 21.95x (ISBN 0-7167-0703-9). W H Freeman.

Oota, K. Histological Typing of Gastric Oesophageal Tumours. (World Health Organization: International Histological Classification of Tumours Ser.). (Illus.). 1977. text ed. 31.00 (ISBN 0-685-99115-6, 70-1-018-20); with slides 98.80 (ISBN 0-685-99116-4, 70-1-018-00). Am Soc Clinical.

Oparil, Suzanne. Renin, Vol. 1. 1977. 26.40 (ISBN 0-88831-000-5). Eden Med Res.

Oparil, Suzanne & Katholi, Richard. Renin, Vol. 2. Horrobin, D., ed. 1978. 28.80 (ISBN 0-88831-014-5). Eden Med Res.

Oparil, Suzanne, jt. auth. see Snider, Arthur J.

Oparil, Suzanne, et al. Renin. Horrobin, D. F., ed. (Annual Research Reviews Ser.: Vol. 5). 368p. 1980. 38.00 (ISBN 0-88831-092-7). Eden Med Res.

Oparin, A. I. Genesis & Evolutionary Development of Life. 1969. 22.75 (ISBN 0-12-527446-7). Acad Pr.

Oparin, A. I., jt. ed. see Rohlfing, Duane.

Opdycke, John B. Harper's English Grammar. 1977. pap. 1.95 (ISBN 0-445-08387-5). Popular Lib.

Opdycke, Leonard E., jt. auth. see Lynes, David.

Opdyke, D. L., ed. Monographs on Fragrance Raw Materials. (Illus.). 1979. 140.00 (ISBN 0-08-023775-4). Pergamon.

OPEC (Organization of Petroleum Exporting Companies) Annual Statistical Bulletin, 1978. LC 74-640556. (Illus.). 179p. 1979. pap. 22.50x (ISBN 0-8002-2211-3). Intl Pubns Serv.

Open University. The Good Health Guide. 1980. text ed. 22.95 (ISBN 0-06-318150-9, IntlDept). Har-Row.

Open University Staff. Understanding the Twentieth Century: A Course Guide. (New Viewpoints-Vision Bks.). 1980. pap. 8.95 (ISBN 0-531-06505-7, EE59). Watts.

Openheim, A. K., ed. Gasdynamics of Explosions & Reactive Systems: Proceedings of the Sixth International Colloquium Held in Stockholm, Sweden, 22-26 August 1977. (Illus.). 782p. 1980. 100.00 (ISBN 0-08-025442-X). Pergamon.

Openshaw, Harry T. Laboratory Manual of Qualitative Organic Analysis. 3rd ed. 1955. 14.95x (ISBN 0-521-05865-1); pap. 9.95x (ISBN 0-521-29112-7). Cambridge U Pr.

Openshaw, K. Cost & Financial Accounting in Forestry. 1977. text ed. 33.00 (ISBN 0-08-021456-8); pap. text ed. 15.00 (ISBN 0-08-021455-X). Pergamon.

Opfell, Olga S. The Lady Laureates: Women Who Have Won the Nobel Prize. LC 78-15995. 1978. 14.00 (ISBN 0-8108-1161-8). Scarecrow.

Opheim, Edward N. Old Mike of Monk's Lagoon. 1981. 6.95 (ISBN 0-533-04853-2). Vantage.

Ophiel. Art & Practice of Talismanic Magic. pap. 5.00 (ISBN 0-87728-445-8). Weiser.

--Oracle of Fortuna. pap. 6.95 (ISBN 0-685-47280-9). Weiser.

Ophuls, William. Ecology & the Politics of Scarcity: Prologue to a Political Theory of Steady State. LC 76-46436. (Illus.). 1977. pap. text ed. 9.95x (ISBN 0-7167-0481-1). W H Freeman.

Opie, Amelia. Adeline Mowbray; or, the Mother & Daughter: A Tale, 3 vols. Luria, Gina, ed. (The Feminist Controversy in England, 1788-1810). 1974. lib. bdg. 50.00 ea. (ISBN 0-8240-0874-X). Garland Pub.

--Elegy to the Memory of the Late Duke of Bedford; Written on the Evening of His Interment, Repr. Of 1820. Bd. with Mary Tighe (Nee Blackford) (1772-1810) Psyche: with Other Poems. 3rd ed. Repr. of 1811 ed. LC 75-31245. (Romantic Context Ser.: Poetry 1789-1830: Vol. 94). 1978. lib. bdg. 47.00 (ISBN 0-8240-2193-2). Garland Pub.

--Poems. Reiman, Donald H., ed. LC 75-31242. (Romantic Context Ser.: Poetry 1789-1830 Ser.). 1978. Repr. of 1802 ed. lib. bdg. 47.00 (ISBN 0-8240-2191-6). Garland Pub.

Opie, Iona & Opie, Peter. The Classic Fairy Tales. (Illus.). 1974. 22.50x (ISBN 0-19-211559-6). Oxford U Pr.

--The Classic Fairy Tales. (Illus.). 352p. 1980. pap. 7.95 (ISBN 0-19-520219-8). Oxford U Pr.

--A Nursery Companion. (Illus.). 128p. 1980. 19.95 (ISBN 0-19-212213-4). Oxford U Pr.

Opie, Peter, jt. auth. see Opie, Iona.

Opie, Redvers, tr. see Schumpeter, Joseph A.

Opik, H., jt. auth. see Street, H. E.

Opitz, Glenn, jt. auth. see Collins, J. L.

Opitz, H. A Classification System to Describe Workpieces, Classification System. Taylor, R. A., tr. LC 71-112891. 1970. Set. 64.00 (ISBN 0-08-015758-0). Pergamon.

Opler, Paul A. Biology, Ecology & Host Specificity of Microlepidoptera Associated with Quercus Agrifolia (Fagaceae) (U. C. Publications in Entomology Vol. 1). 1974. pap. 9.25x (ISBN 0-520-09500-6). U of Cal Pr.

Opoku, Khamal S. Fired. 64p. 1980. pap. 5.00 (ISBN 0-682-49636-7). Exposition.

Oppe, Thomas E., jt. auth. see Paine, Richmond S.

Oppelt, Norman T. Guide to Prehistoric Ruins of the Southwest. 200p. (Orig.). 1981. pap. 6.95 (ISBN 0-87108-587-9). Pruett.

Oppen, William A., ed. The Riel Rebellions: A Cartographic History. LC 79-94166. (Illus.). 1980. pap. 15.00x (ISBN 0-8020-6427-2). U of Toronto Pr.

Oppeneer, Joan, jt. auth. see Vervoren, Thora.

Oppenheim. Living Today. (gr. 9-12). 1981. text ed. price not set (ISBN 0-87002-343-8). Bennett Co.

Oppenheim, A. K. Impact of Aerospace Technology on Studies of the Earth's Atmosphere. LC 74-5410. 1974. text ed. 23.00 (ISBN 0-08-018131-7). Pergamon.

Oppenheim, A. Leo & Reiner, Erica, eds. Assyrian Dictionary of the Oriental Institute of the University of Chicago. Incl. Vol. 1, A, Pt. 2. 1976. Repr. of 1968 ed. 42.00x (ISBN 0-918986-07-9); Vol. 3, D. 1977. Repr. of 1959 ed. 17.00x (ISBN 0-918986-09-5); Vol. 4, E. 1974. Repr. of 1958 ed. 31.00x (ISBN 0-918986-10-9); Vol. 7, I-J. 1974. Repr. of 1960 ed. 25.00x (ISBN 0-918986-13-3); Vol. 9, L. 1978. Repr. of 1973 ed. 35.00x (ISBN 0-918986-15-X); Vol. 10, M, Pts 1 & 2. LC 56-58292. 1978. 110.00x (ISBN 0-918986-16-8); Vol. 16, S. 1977. Repr. of 1962 ed. 22.00x (ISBN 0-918986-18-4). LC 56-58292. Oriental Inst.

Oppenheim, A. N. & Torney, J. The Measurement of Children's Civic Attitudes in Different Nations. LC 74-10468. (I E A Studies in Evaluation: No. 2). 84p. (Orig.). 1974. pap. 10.95 (ISBN 0-470-65480-5). Halsted Pr.

Oppenheim, Alan V. & Schafer, Ronald W. Digital Signal Processing. LC 74-17280. (Illus.). 608p. 1975. text ed. 27.95 (ISBN 0-13-214635-5). P-H.

Oppenheim, Felix. Political Concepts: A Reconstruction. LC 80-23846. (Illus.). 1981. lib. bdg. price not set (ISBN 0-226-63184-2). U of Chicago Pr.

Oppenheim, Frank M. Royces Voyage Down Under: A Journey of the Mind. LC 79-4007. 136p. 1980. 11.50 (ISBN 0-8131-1394-6). U Pr of Ky.

Oppenheim, Irene. Consumer Skills. 1977. 10.60 (ISBN 0-87002-184-2); tchr's guide 5.00 (ISBN 0-87002-186-9); student guide 4.40 (ISBN 0-87002-267-9). Bennett IL.

Oppenheim, Irwin A. Textbook for Laboratory Assistants. 3rd ed. (Illus.). 190p. 1981. pap. text ed. 12.95 (ISBN 0-8016-3722-8). Mosby.

Oppenheim, Joanne. On the Other Side of the River. (Illus.). 32p. (gr. k-3). 1972. PLB 4.90 o.p. (ISBN 0-531-02562-4). Watts.

Oppenheim, N. Models in Urban & Regional Analysis. 1980. 24.95 (ISBN 0-13-041467-0). P-H.

Oppenheim, S. Chesterfield & Weston, Glen E., eds. The Lawyer's Robinson-Patman Act Sourcebook: Opinions of the FTC & the Courts, & Related Materials, 4 vols. 2723p. 1971. 160.00 set (ISBN 0-316-65089-7). Little.

Oppenheim, Shulamith. The Selchie's Seed. LC 74-22854. (Illus.). 96p. (gr. 4-6). 1975. 7.95 o.p. (ISBN 0-87888-076-3). Bradbury Pr.

Oppenheimer. The Lost Summer. (gr. 7-12). pap. 1.25 (ISBN 0-686-68468-0, Schol Pap). Schol Bk Serv.

Oppenheimer, Ernest J. Natural Gas: The New Energy Leader. 156p. (Orig.). 1981. pap. 7.50 (ISBN 0-9603982-2-8). Pen & Podium.

Oppenheimer, Evelyn. Oral Book Reviewing to Stimulate Reading: A Practical Guide in Technique for Lecture & Broadcast. LC 80-20006. 168p. 1980. 10.00 (ISBN 0-8108-1352-1). Scarecrow.

Oppenheimer, J., jt. auth. see Frolick, N. J.

Oppenheimer, Joel. Houses. 1981. 2.00 (ISBN 0-686-69560-7). White Pine.

--Just Friends: Friends and Lovers, Poems, 1959-1962. LC 70-83559. 1980. 15.00 (ISBN 0-912330-26-0); pap. 7.50 (ISBN 0-912330-27-9). Jargon Soc.

Oppenheimer, Lillian & Epstein, Natalie. Decorative Napkin Folding for Beginners. (Illus.). 1980. pap. 1.75 (ISBN 0-486-23797-4). Dover.

Oppenheimer, Oscar. God & Man. LC 79-64099. 1979. pap. text ed. 9.00 (ISBN 0-8191-0753-0). U Pr of Amer.

Oppenheimer, Paul, tr. from Ger. A Pleasant Vintage of Till Eulenspiegel. LC 73-184361. (Illus.). 336p. 1972. 20.00x (ISBN 0-8195-4043-9, Pub. by Wesleyan U Pr). Columbia U Pr.

Oppenheimer, Peter, ed. Issues in International Economics. (Oxford International Symposia). 300p. 1980. 40.00 (ISBN 0-85362-186-1, Oriel). Routledge & Kegan.

Oppenheimer, Samuel. Semiconductor Logic & Switching Circuits. 2nd ed. LC 72-92573. 1973. text ed. 19.95x (ISBN 0-675-09016-4); instructor's manual 3.95 (ISBN 0-686-66490-6). Merrill.

Oppenheimer, Samuel L., ed. see Tocci, Ronald J.

Opper, Sylvia, jt. auth. see Ginsburg, Herbert.

Opperman, Hal N. Jean-Baptiste Oudry (Sixteen Eighty-Six to Seventeen Fifty-Five) LC 76-23674. (Outstanding Dissertations in the Fine Arts Ser.). 1977. lib. bdg. 133.00 (ISBN 0-8240-2718-3). Garland Pub.

Oppermann, Alfred, ed. Dictionary of Electronics: English-German. 692p. 1980. 120.00 (ISBN 3-598-10312-3, Dist. by Gale Research Co.). K G Saur.

--Dictionary of Modern Engineering, 2 vols. 3rd ed. Incl. Vol. 1. English-German. 912p. 1972. 80.00 (ISBN 3-7940-6001-6); Vol. 2. German-English. 952p. 1974. 80.00 (ISBN 3-7940-6002-4). 160.00 set (ISBN 3-7940-6003-2). Gale.

Oppermann, Edward B., jt. auth. see Plane, Donald R.

Oppert, J. Moving to Metrics in Home Economics. LC 77-81325. 1977. 2.50 (ISBN 0-686-20043-8, 26108430). Home Econ Educ.

Oppler, Ellen C. Fauvism Reexamined. LC 75-23805. (Outstanding Dissertations in the Fine Arts - 20th Century). (Illus.). 1976. lib. bdg. 45.00 (ISBN 0-8240-1999-7). Garland Pub.

Opplt, J. J., jt. ed. see Lewis, L. A.

Optner, Stanford L. Systems Analysis for Business Management. 3rd ed. (Illus.). 400p. 1974. ref. ed. 17.95 (ISBN 0-13-881276-4). P-H.

Oquist, Paul. Violence, Conflict, & Politics in Colombia. LC 79-6778. (Studies in Social Discontinuity Ser.). 1980. 25.00 (ISBN 0-12-527750-4). Acad Pr.

O'Raifeartaigh, L., ed. General Relativity: Papers in Honour of J. L. Synge. (Illus.). 287p. 1972. 29.00x o.p. (ISBN 0-19-851126-4). Oxford U Pr.

Oraison, Marc. Morality for Our Time. LC 68-11922. 1969. pap. 1.25 (ISBN 0-385-01490-2, D266, Im). Doubleday.

Oram, R. B. Cargo Handling in a Modern Port. 1965. 27.00 (ISBN 0-08-011306-0); pap. 14.00 (ISBN 0-08-011305-2). Pergamon.

Oram, R. B. & Baker, C. C. The Efficient Port. 1971. 17.25 (ISBN 0-08-016396-3). Pergamon.

Oram, Samuel. Clinical Heart Disease. (Illus.). 1971. 65.00x (ISBN 0-685-83723-8). Intl Ideas.

Oran, Dan & Hoklin, Lonn. Z Warning. 1979. 8.95 o.p. (ISBN 0-345-28096-2). Ballantine.

O'Rand, Angela & Vasey, Wayne, eds. Assuring the Legal Rights of Older Citizens. (Center for Gerontological Studies & Programs Ser.: Vol.27). Date not set. price not set. U Presses Fla.

Orange County Assoc. Frases Fundamentales Para Comunicarse. (gr. k-12). 1975. 3.15 (ISBN 0-89075-200-1). Crane Pub Co.

Orange County Genealogical Society. Index to the Eighteen Eighty-One Ruttenber & Clark History of Orange County, New York. LC 79-84908. 1980. 20.00 (ISBN 0-9604116-1-5). Orange County Genealog.

Oravas, G. A., ed. see Duhem, Pierre M.

Oravetz, Jules. Questions & Answers for Plumbers Examinations. 2nd ed. LC 73-85726. (Illus.). 1977. pap. 8.95 (ISBN 0-672-23285-5). Audel.

Oravetz, Jules, Sr. Building Maintenance. LC 76-45885. 1977. 9.95 (ISBN 0-672-23278-2). Audel.

--Gardening & Landscaping: Lawns, Vegetables, Flowers, Trees, & Shrubs. LC 74-28650. 1975. 9.95 (ISBN 0-672-23229-4, 23229). Audel.

Orazem, Frank, jt. auth. see Doll, John P.

Orbach, Michael K. Hunters, Seamen & Entrepreneurs: The Tuna Seinermen of San Diego. (Illus.). 1978. 15.75x (ISBN 0-520-03348-5). U of Cal Pr.

Orbach, Susie. Fat Is a Feminist Issue: The Anti-Diet Guide to Permanent Weight Loss. 203p. 1979. pap. 2.50 (ISBN 0-425-04380-0). Berkley Pub.

Orbach, William W. To Keep the Peace: The United Nations Condemnatory Resolution. LC 75-41989. (Illus.). 168p. 1977. 14.50x (ISBN 0-8131-1341-5). U Pr of Ky.

Orbelo, Beverly. A Texas Quilting Primer. 48p. 1980. pap. 5.00 (ISBN 0-931722-07-1). Corona Pub.

Orben, Robert. Encyclopedia of One-Liner Comedy. LC 73-150910. 1971. 8.95 (ISBN 0-385-06698-8). Doubleday.

--Joke Teller's Handbook or, One Thousand Nine Hundred Ninety-Nine Belly Laughs. LC 66-12229. 1966. 5.95 o.p. (ISBN 0-385-04042-3). Doubleday.

Orbison, Tucker. The Tragic Vision of John Ford. (Salzburg Studies in English Literature, Jacobean Drama Studies: No. 21). 1974. pap. text ed. 25.00x (ISBN 0-391-01492-7). Humanities.

Orchard, D. B. & Longstaff, R. W., eds. J. J. Griesbach. LC 77-27405. (Society for New Testament Studies Monographs: No. 34). 1979. 27.50 (ISBN 0-521-21706-7). Cambridge U Pr.

Orchard, D. F. Concrete Technology, Vol. 2. rev. 3rd ed. LC 72-13145. 1973. 39.95 (ISBN 0-470-65539-9). Halsted Pr.

--Concrete Technology, Vol. 3. 3rd ed. LC 72-13145. 1976. 44.95 (ISBN 0-470-65540-2). Halsted Pr.

--Concrete Techology: Vol. 2, Practice. 4th ed. 1979. 67.40 (ISBN 0-85334-837-5, Pub. by Applied Science). Burgess-Intl Ideas.

Orchard, W. R. & Sherratt, A. F. Combined Heat & Power Whole City Heating Planning: Tomorrows Energy Economy. LC 80-41444. 234p. 1980. 59.95 (ISBN 0-470-27088-8). Halsted Pr.

Orchin, Milton & Jaffe, H. H. Symmetry, Orbitals, & Spectra. LC 76-136720. 1971. 36.50 (ISBN 0-471-65550-3, Pub. by Wiley-Interscience). Wiley.

Orchin, Milton, et al. The Vocabulary of Organic Chemistry. LC 79-25930. 1980. 35.00 (ISBN 0-471-04491-1, Pub. by Wiley-Interscience). Wiley.

Orcutt, Ben A. Poverty & Social Casework Services: Selected Papers. LC 74-14917. 1974. 8.00 o.p. (ISBN 0-8108-0751-3). Scarecrow.

Orcutt, Georgia. Soups, Chowders & Stews. Taylor, Sandra, ed. (Flair of New England Ser.). 1981. pap. 8.95 (ISBN 0-911658-17-3, 3078). Yankee Bks.

Orcutt, Georgia & Taylor, Sandra, eds. The Holiday Entertaining. LC 80-52141. (Flavor of New England). 1980. pap. 8.95 (ISBN 0-911658-13-0, 3074). Yankee Bks.

Orcutt, Georgia, ed. see Withee, John.

Orcutt, Guy H., et al. Policy Exploration Through Microanalytic Stimulation. 370p. 1976. 12.50 (ISBN 0-87766-170-7, 15100); pap. 5.95 (ISBN 0-87766-169-3, 15300). Urban Inst.

Orcutt, William D. The Stradivari Memorial. LC 76-58561. (Music Reprint Series). 1977. Repr. of 1978 ed. lib. bdg. 14.95 (ISBN 0-306-70865-5). Da Capo.

Orczy, Emmuska. Beau Brocade. 275p. 1980. Repr. of 1905 ed. lib. bdg. 13.95x (ISBN 0-89968-194-8). Lightyear.

--Blue Eyes & Gray. 1976. lib. bdg. 14.75x (ISBN 0-89968-014-3). Lightyear.

--The Elusive Pimpernel. 1976. lib. bdg. 15.75x (ISBN 0-89968-073-9). Lightyear.

--Emperor's Candlesticks. 1976. lib. bdg. 13.75x (ISBN 0-89968-075-5). Lightyear.

--The Laughing Cavalier. 1976. lib. bdg. 18.50x (ISBN 0-89968-076-3). Lightyear.

--The League of the Scarlet Pimpernel. 238p. 1981. Repr. lib. bdg. 12.95x (ISBN 0-89966-286-2). Buccaneer Bks.

--Old Man in the Corner. 340p. 1980. Repr. of 1908 ed. lib. bdg. 15.95x (ISBN 0-89968-196-4). Lightyear.

--The Old Man in the Corner: Twelve Mysteries by the Baroness Orczy. Bleiler, E. G., ed. (Orig.). 1980. pap. 3.50. Dover.

--Scarlet Pimpernel. (gr. 7 up). 1964. 3.95 o.s.i. (ISBN 0-02-768630-2). Macmillan.

--The Scarlet Pimpernel. 1976. lib. bdg. 15.75x (ISBN 0-89968-072-0). Lightyear.

Ord, John. The Bothy Songs & Ballads of Aberdeen. Banff & Moray, Angus & the Mearns. 493p. 1980. Repr. of 1930 ed. lib. bdg. 25.00 (ISBN 0-8492-7307-2). R West.

Orde, Lewis. The Lion's Way. LC 80-66493. 1981. 12.95 (ISBN 0-87795-268-X). Arbor Hse.

Orde Browne, G. St. The African Labourer. 240p. 1967. Repr. of 1933 ed. 24.00x (ISBN 0-686-26224-7, F Cass Co). Biblio Dist.

Orden, Phyllis Van see Van Orden, Phyllis & Phillips, Edith B.

Ordish, George. The Constant Pest: A Short History of Crop Pests & Their Control. LC 75-35297. (Illus.). 1976. 12.95 o.p. (ISBN 0-684-14553-7, ScribT). Scribner.

--The Living American House: The 350-Year Story of a Home - an Ecological History. (Illus.). 1981. 11.95 (ISBN 0-686-69231-4). Morrow.

--The Year of the Ant. LC 78-2260. (Illus.). 1978. 9.95 o.p. (ISBN 0-684-15523-0, ScribT). Scribner.

Ordish, Olive, tr. see Abel, Wilhelm.

Ordonez, Francisco. Del Odio Al Amor. 1980. pap. 1.20 (ISBN 0-311-08223-8). Casa Bautista.

Ord-Smith, R. J. & Stephenson, J. Computer Simulation of Continous Systems. LC 74-12957. (Computer Science Texts Ser.: No. 3). (Illus.). 300p. 1975. pap. text ed. 16.95x (ISBN 0-521-09872-6). Cambridge U Pr.

Ordway, jt. auth. see Tosh.

Ordway, Frederick I. & Sharpe, Mitchell R. The Rocket Team. LC 78-3313. (Illus.). 1979. 14.95 (ISBN 0-690-01656-5, TYC-T). T Y Crowell.

Ordway, Frederick I., 3rd, ed. Advances in Space Science & Technology, Vols. 1-11. Incl. Vols. 1-7. 1959-65. 49.00 ea. Vol. 1 (ISBN 0-12-037301-7). Vol. 2. o.p. (ISBN 0-12-037302-5). Vol. 3 (ISBN 0-12-037303-3). Vol. 4 (ISBN 0-12-037304-1). Vol. 5. o.p. (ISBN 0-12-037305-X). Vol. 6 (ISBN 0-12-037306-8). Vol. 7 (ISBN 0-12-037307-6); Vol. 8. 1966. 40.00 (ISBN 0-12-037308-4); Vol. 9. 1967. 40.00 (ISBN 0-12-037309-2); Vol. 10. 1970. 49.00 (ISBN 0-12-037310-6); Vol. 11. 1972. 57.00 (ISBN 0-12-037311-4); Suppl. 1. Space Carrier Vehicles: Design, Development & Testing of Launching Rockets. Lange, O. H. & Stein, R. J. 1963. 43.50 (ISBN 0-12-037361-0); Suppl. 2. Lunar & Planetary Surface Conditions. Weil, N. A. 1965. 43.50 (ISBN 0-12-037362-9). Acad Pr.

Ordway, Nicholas, jt. auth. see Friedman, Jack.

Ordy, J. Mark & Brizzee, Ken, eds. Sensory Systems & Communication in the Elderly. LC 79-65426. (Aging Ser.: Vol. 10). 1979. text ed. 32.00 (ISBN 0-89004-235-7). Raven.

Ordy, Mark & Harman, Denham, eds. Nutrition & Aging. 1980. write for info. (ISBN 0-89004-477-5, 531). Raven.

Ore, Oystein. Niels Hendrik Abel, Mathematician Extraordinary. LC 73-14693. (Illus.). viii, 277p. 1974. Repr. of 1957 ed. text ed. 10.95 (ISBN 0-8284-0274-4). Chelsea Pub.

O'Regan, Susan K. Neil Diamond. (Rock 'n Pop Stars Ser.). (Illus.). (gr. 3-6). 1975. PLB 5.95 (ISBN 0-87191-464-6); pap. 2.95 (ISBN 0-89812-115-9). Creative Ed.

Oregon State University Biology Colloquium, 40th. Forests: Fresh Perspectives from Ecosystems Analysis. Proceedings. Waring, Richard H., ed. LC 80-14883. (Illus.). 210p. 1980. pap. 12.00 (ISBN 0-87071-179-2). Oreg St U Pr.

O'Reilly, E. A Chronological Account of Nearly Four Hundred Irish Writers. 256p. 1969. Repr. of 1820 ed. 25.00x (ISBN 0-7165-0026-4, Pub. by Irish Academic Pr Ireland). Biblio Dist.

O'Reilly, Elizabeth, ed. Measure for Measure: Calorie & Carbohydrate Recipes. (Illus.). 1974. wire bound 11.95x (ISBN 0-433-24220-5). Intl Ideas.

O'Reilly, James T. Unions' Rights to Company Information. 1980. pap. 18.00 (ISBN 0-89546-023-8). Indus Res Unit-Wharton.

O'Reilly, Marjorie I., jt. auth. see O'Reilly, Robert C.

O'Reilly, P H & Shields. Nuclear Medicine in Urology & Nephrology. (Illus.). 1979. text ed. 44.95 (ISBN 0-407-00151-4). Butterworths.

O'Reilly, Richard, jt. ed. see Nahmias, Andre J.

O'Reilly, Robert C. Understanding Collective Bargaining in Education: Negotiations, Contracts & Disputes Between Teachers & Boards. LC 78-64495. 1978. 11.00 (ISBN 0-8108-1167-7). Scarecrow.

O'Reilly, Robert C. & O'Reilly, Marjorie I. Librarians & Labor Relations: Employment Under Union Contracts. LC 80-1049. (Contributions in Librarianship & Information Science Ser.: No. 35). 208p. 1981. lib. bdg. 25.00 (ISBN 0-313-22485-4, OLL/). Greenwood.

O'Reilly, Sean. Bioethics & the Limits of Science. 176p. (Orig.). 1980. pap. 5.95 (ISBN 0-931888-02-6, Chris. Coll. Pr.). Christendom Pubns.

--Meet the Centers. (Meet the Players: Basketball). (Illus.). (gr. 2-4). 1977. PLB 5.95 (ISBN 0-87191-601-0); pap. 2.95 (ISBN 0-89812-203-1). Creative Ed.

--Meet the Coaches. LC 76-54899. (Meet the Players: Basketball). (Illus.). (gr. 2-4). 1977. PLB 5.95 (ISBN 0-87191-600-2); pap. 2.95 (ISBN 0-89812-206-6). Creative Ed.

--Meet the Forwards. LC 76-52952. (Meet the Players: Basketball). (Illus.). (gr. 2-4). 1977. PLB 5.95 (ISBN 0-87191-603-7); pap. 2.95 (ISBN 0-89812-205-8). Creative Ed.

--Meet the Guards. LC 76-51833. (Meet the Players: Basketball). (Illus.). (gr. 2-4). 1977. PLB 5.95 (ISBN 0-87191-602-9); pap. 2.95 (ISBN 0-89812-204-X). Creative Ed.

Orel, Harold, ed. Thomas Hardy's Personal Writings. 295p. 1981. text ed. 10.00x (ISBN 0-333-05493-8, Pub. by Macmillan, England). Humanities.

--World of Victorian Humor. LC 61-8018. (Goldentree Books in English Literature). (Illus., Orig.). 1961. pap. text ed. 8.95x (ISBN 0-89197-474-1). Irvington.

Orel, Harold, jt. ed. see Wiley, Paul L.

Orellana, Eugenio, tr. see Owen, Robert & Howard, David M.

O'Relley, Z. Edward. Soviet-Type Economic Systems: A Guide to Information Sources. LC 73-17583. (Economics Information Guide Ser.: Vol. 12). 1978. 30.00 (ISBN 0-8103-1306-5). Gale.

Orelli, Hans C. von. The Prophecies of Jeremiah. 1977. 13.50 (ISBN 0-686-12974-1). Klock & Klock.

--The Twelve Minor Prophets. 1977. 13.50 (ISBN 0-686-12973-3). Klock & Klock.

Orem, Dorothea E. Nursing: Concepts of Practice. 1971. pap. 9.95 o.p. (ISBN 0-07-047691-8, HP). McGraw.

Orem, J. & Barnes, C. D., eds. Physiology in Sleep. (Research Topics in Physiology Ser.). 1981. write for info. (ISBN 0-12-527650-8). Acad Pr.

Oremland, Evelyn K. & Oremland, Jerome D., eds. The Effects of Hospitalization on Children: Models for Their Care. (Illus.). 360p. 1973. text ed. 18.50 (ISBN 0-398-02729-3). C C Thomas.

Oremland, Jerome D., jt. ed. see Oremland, Evelyn K.

Oren, O. H., ed. Aquaculture of Grey Mullets. LC 79-53405. (International Biological Programme: No. 26). (Illus.). 450p. Date not set. price not set (ISBN 0-521-22926-X). Cambridge U Pr.

Orenstein, Alan & Phillips, William R. Understanding Social Research: An Introduction. 1978. text ed. 16.95 (ISBN 0-205-05947-3, 8159475); instr's manual o.p. avail. (ISBN 0-205-05948-1). Allyn.

Orenstein, Alex. Willard V. O. Quine. (World Leaders Ser.: No. 15). 1977. lib. bdg. 12.50 (ISBN 0-8057-7716-4). Twayne.

Orenstein, Arbie. Ravel: Man & Musican. LC 74-34022. (Illus.). 320p. 1975. 17.50x (ISBN 0-231-03902-6). Columbia U Pr.

Orenstein, Jeffrey R., jt. auth. see Fowler, Robert B.

Orfield, Gary. Must We Bus? Segregated Schools & National Policy. 1978. 18.95 (ISBN 0-8157-6638-6); pap. 9.95 (ISBN 0-8157-6637-8). Brookings.

Orfield, Gary & Taylor, William. Racial Segregation: Two Policy Views. LC 79-3166. (Illus.). 68p. 1979. pap. text ed. 3.95 (ISBN 0-916584-13-5). Ford Found.

Orfield, Lester B. Amending of the Federal Constitution. LC 74-146151. (American Constitutional & Legal History Ser). (Illus.). 1971. Repr. of 1942 ed. lib. bdg. 25.00 (ISBN 0-306-70094-8). Da Capo.

--Criminal Procedure Under the Federal Rules, 7 vols. LC 66-17952. 1968. Set. 297.50 (ISBN 0-686-14508-9). Lawyers Co-Op.

Orfield, Lester B. & Re, E. D. Cases & Materials on International Law. 2nd ed. 1965. 20.00 (ISBN 0-672-80979-6, Bobbs-Merrill Law). Michie.

Orfila, Alejandro. The Americas in the Nineteen Eighties: An Agenda for the Decade Ahead. LC 80-5935. 166p. 1980. lib. bdg. 17.25 (ISBN 0-8191-1333-6); pap. text ed. 8.75 (ISBN 0-8191-1334-4). U Pr of Amer.

Orford, Jim & Harwin, Judith, eds. Alcohol & the Family. 200p. 1980. 25.00x (Pub. by Croom Helm England). State Mutual Bk.

Orford, Jim, jt. ed. see Feldman, Philip.

Orga, Ates. Beethoven: His Life & Times. LC 78-53221. (Life & Time of the Composer Ser.). (Illus.). 1978. 16.95 (ISBN 0-8467-0487-0, Pub. by Two Continents); pap. 5.95 (ISBN 0-8467-0460-9). Hippocrene Bks.

--Chopin: His Life & Times. (Illus.). 1978. 16.95 (ISBN 0-8467-0415-3, Pub. by Two Continents); pap. 5.95 (ISBN 0-8467-0416-1). Hippocrene Bks.

--The Proms. LC 74-81007. (Illus.). 160p. 1974. 12.95 o.p. (ISBN 0-685-49929-4). David & Charles.

Orga, Ates, ed. Records & Recording Classical Guide 1978. 1978. pap. 5.95 (ISBN 0-8467-0450-1, Pub. by Two Continents). Hippocrene Bks.

Organ, Dennis W., jt. auth. see Hamner, W. Clay.

Organ, Dennis W., ed. The Applied Psychology of Work Behavior: A Book of Readings. 1978. pap. 10.95x (ISBN 0-256-02080-9). Business Pubns.

Organ, James A. A Manual for the Biology of the Vertebrates. (Illus.). 1977. lab manual 7.95 (ISBN 0-89529-009-X). Avery Pub.

Organ, Troy W. The Hindu Quest for the Perfection of Man. LC 73-81450. 1970. 14.00 o.p. (ISBN 0-8214-0066-5). Ohio U Pr.

--Hindu Quest for the Perfection of Man. LC 73-81450. x, 439p. 1981. pap. 10.00x (ISBN 0-8214-0575-6). Ohio U Pr.

--Western Approaches to Eastern Philosophy. LC 75-14554. 282p. 1975. 13.95x (ISBN 0-8214-0194-7). Ohio U Pr.

Organic Gardening & Farming Editors. The Green Thumb Cookbook. Moyer, Anne, ed. LC 77-1745. 1977. 14.95 (ISBN 0-87857-168-X). Rodale Pr Inc.

--Terrific Tomatoes: All About How to Grow & Enjoy Them. LC 75-1314. (Illus.). 240p. 1975. 8.95 (ISBN 0-87857-094-2); pap. 3.95 (ISBN 0-87857-111-6). Rodale Pr Inc.

Organic Gardening & Farming Magazine, ed. Encyclopedia of Organic Gardening. LC 77-25915. 1978. 21.95 (ISBN 0-87857-225-2). Rodale Pr Inc.

Organic Gardening Editors. Getting the Most from Your Garden. (Illus.). 1980. 14.95 (ISBN 0-87857-291-0). Rodale Pr Inc.

Organick, Elliot I. & Meissner, Loren P. Fortran Four: Standard Fortran Watfor-Watfiv. 1975. text ed. 13.95 (ISBN 0-201-05503-1). A-W.

Organick, Elliot I., jt. auth. see Meissner, Loren P.

Organick, Elliot I., et al. Programming Language Structure. (Computer Science & Applied Mathematics Ser.). 1978. text ed. 21.95 (ISBN 0-12-528260-5). Acad Pr.

Organisation for Economic Co-Operation & Development. Reviews of National Science Policy: United States. Cohen, I. Bernard, ed. LC 79-7979. (Three Centuries of Science in America Ser.). 1980. Repr. of 1968 ed. lib. bdg. 44.00x (ISBN 0-405-12561-5). Arno.

Organization for Economic Cooperation & Development, jt. auth. see Nuclear Energy Agency.

Organization for Economic Cooperation & Development, Secretary General. Activities of OECD in 1975. 1976. 5.00 o.p. (ISBN 92-64-11522-6). OECD.

Organization for Economic Cooperation & Development. Annual Reports on Competition Policy in OECD Member Countries, 2 pts. Incl. No. 1. 94p. 6.25 o.p. (ISBN 0-686-14856-8); No. 2. 109p. 6.25 o.p. (ISBN 92-64-11575-7). 1976. OECD.

--Building for School & Community: Vol. V, Sweden. (Programme on Educational Building Ser.). (Illus.). 172p. 1980. pap. text ed. 10.50x (ISBN 92-64-12025-4, 95 80 02 1). OECD.

--Construction of Roads on Compressible Soils. (Road Research Ser.). (Illus.). 147p. (Orig.). 1980. pap. text ed. 13.50x (ISBN 92-64-12062-9, 7780021). OECD.

--East-West Trade in Chemicals. (Document Ser.). (Illus.). 78p. (Orig.). 1980. pap. text ed. 4.50x (ISBN 92-64-12034-3, 22 80 01 1). OECD.

--The Employment Problem in Less Developed Countries. (Employment Ser.: No. 1). 156p. 1971. 7.50 o.p. (ISBN 0-686-14735-9). OECD.

Organization for Economic Cooperation & Development & IEA. Energy Balances of OECD Countries, 1974 to 1978. 166p. (Orig., Eng. & Fr.). 1980. pap. 9.00x (ISBN 92-64-02056-X, 6180013). OECD.

Organization for Economic Cooperation & Development. Environment Policies for the 1980's. 110p. (Orig.). 1980. pap. text ed. 9.00x (ISBN 92-64-12049-1, 9780021). OECD.

Organization for Economic Cooperation & Development & Kennedy-Brenner, C. Foreign Workers & Immigration Policy: The Case of France. (Development Center Studies). (Illus.). 106p. (Orig.). 1980. pap. text ed. 6.00x (ISBN 92-64-11964-7, 41 79 04 1). OECD.

Organization for Economic Cooperation & Development. Interim Radiation Protection Standards for the Design, Construction, Testing & Control of Radioisotopic Cardiac Pacemakers. 54p. 1974. 2.50 o.p. (ISBN 92-64-11246-4). OECD.

--International Direct Investment: Policies, Procedures & Practices in OECD Member Countries, 1979. 72p. (Orig.). 1980. pap. text ed. 4.25x (ISBN 92-64-12026-2, 21 80 02 1). OECD.

--International Standardization of Fruit & Vegetables. Incl. Tomatoes, Cauliflowers, Lettuces, Curled-Leaved Endives & Broad-Leaved Endives. 200p. 1971; Onions, Apricots, Plums, Strawberries, Table Grapes. 150p. 1965. 3.25 o.p. (ISBN 0-686-14864-9); Artichokes, Cherries, Cabbages, Cucumbers, Asparagus. 148p. 1969. 6.50 o.p. (ISBN 0-686-14865-7); o.p. (ISBN 0-686-14866-5); Apples & Pears. 74p. 1971. 5.25 o.p. (ISBN 0-686-14867-3); Citrus Fruit. 72p. 1971. 5.25 o.p. (ISBN 0-686-14868-1). OECD.

--Meat Balances in OECD Member Countries: 1973 to 1978. (Illus.). 85p. (Orig.). 1980. pap. text ed. 7.50x (ISBN 92-64-02090-X, 5180053). OECD.

--Protection of Foreign Property: Draft Convention on the Protection of Foreign Property & Resolution of the Council of the OECD on the Draft Convention. 62p. 1967. 1.20 o.p. (ISBN 0-686-14795-2). OECD.

--Revenue Statistics of OECD Member Countries, 1965-1974. 1976. 10.00 o.p. (ISBN 92-64-01563-9). OECD.

--Review of Agricultural Policies in OECD Member Countries, 1979. (Agricultural Policy Reports Ser.). (Illus.). 116p. (Orig.). 1980. pap. text ed. 12.00x (ISBN 0-686-27336-2, 51 80 04 1). OECD.

--Spain. (OECD Economic Surveys, 1980). (Illus.). 62p. (Orig.). 1980. cancelled (ISBN 92-64-12047-5, 1080241). OECD.

--Supervision of Private Insurance in Europe. Incl. General Study. 226p; Country Reports. (18 bklets in cardboard box). 1963. 9.00 ea. o.p. OECD.

--Turkey. (OECD Economic Surveys, 1980). (Illus.). 61p. (Orig.). 1980. cancelled (ISBN 92-64-12066-1, 1080271). OECD.

Organization for Economic Cooperation & Development & ECMT. Urban Transport & the Environment: Seminar OECD-ECMT, July 10-12, 1979, 4 pts. (Orig.). 1980. pap. text ed. 12.00x set (ISBN 92-64-12001-7, 97 79 08 1). Pt. I, Background Reports (319 P.) Pt. II, Case Studies (283 P.) Pt. III, Overview (7 P.) Pt. IV, Conclusions (15 P.) OECD.

Organization Fro Economic Cooperation & Development. Educational Policy & Planning: Goals for Educational Policy in Sweden. 185p. (Orig.). 1980. pap. text ed. 8.50x (ISBN 92-64-01999-5, 91 80 02 3). OECD.

Organization of American States. Charter of the Organization of American States, Bogota, 1948. (Treaty Ser.: No. 1). (Eng., Span., Port. & Fr.). 1948. pap. 1.00 (ISBN 0-8270-0245-9). OAS.

--Copyright Protection in the Americas. 1979. looseleaf 150.00 (ISBN 0-379-20675-7). Oceana.

--Copyright Protection in the Americas, Release 1, Vol. 2. 1980. 75.00 (ISBN 0-379-20675-7). Oceana.

--Mining & Petroleum Legislation. LC 78-16150. (Binder 1 & supplement). 1978. per. binder 75.00 (ISBN 0-379-20381-2). Oceana.

--Mining & Petroleum Legislation, Release 1. 1980. 35.00 (ISBN 0-379-20381-2). Oceana.

--Sectoral Study of Transnational Enterprises in Latin America: The Banana Industry. 1978. pap. text ed. 5.00 (ISBN 0-8270-3305-2). Span. Ed (ISBN 0-8270-3310-9). OAS.

Orgel, Doris. Merry, Merry FIBruary. LC 77-650. (Illus.). 40p. (ps-4). 1977. 7.95 (ISBN 0-590-17708-7, Four Winds); 7.95 (ISBN 0-590-07708-2). Schol Bk Serv.

Orgel, Leslie E., jt. auth. see Miller, Stanley L.

Orgel, Shelly & Fine, Bernard D., eds. Clinical Psychoanalysis. (Downstate Psychoanalytic Institute Twenty-Fifth Anniversary Ser: Vol. III). 1979. 25.00x (ISBN 0-87668-368-5). Aronson.

Orgel, Stephen. The Illusion of Power. LC 73-80827. (Quantum Bks). (Illus.). 1975. 11.95x (ISBN 0-520-02505-9); pap. 4.95 (ISBN 0-520-02741-8). U of Cal Pr.

Orgel, Stephen, ed. see Armin, Robert.

Orgel, Stephen, ed. see Barnes, Barnabe.

Orgel, Stephen, ed. see Bocchi, Achille.

Orgel, Stephen, ed. see Brome, Richard.

Orgel, Stephen, jt. ed. see Brooks, John B.

Orgel, Stephen, jt. ed. see Clark, James D.

Orgel, Stephen, ed. see Clugston, George A.

Orgel, Stephen, ed. see Conti, Natale & Tritonio, Antonio M.

Orgel, Stephen, ed. see Cousteau, Pierre.

Orgel, Stephen, ed. see Davenport, Robert.

Orgel, Stephen, ed. see Day, John.

Orgel, Stephen, ed. see Dinet, Pierre.

Orgel, Stephen, ed. see Dolce, Ludovico.

Orgel, Stephen, ed. see Fletcher, John.

Orgel, Stephen, ed. see Fraunce, Abraham, et al.

Orgel, Stephen, ed. see Giarda, Christophoro.

Orgel, Stephen, ed. see Goffe, Thomas.

Orgel, Stephen, ed. see Gordon, P. J.

Orgel, Stephen, ed. see Heroldt, Johann.

Orgel, Stephen, ed. see Heywood, Thomas.

Orgel, Stephen, jt. ed. see Hirsch, Richard S.

Orgel, Stephen, ed. see Itzoe, Linda V.

Orgel, Stephen, ed. see Jones, Thomas.

Orgel, Stephen, ed. see Kemp, William.

Orgel, Stephen, ed. see Legge, Thomas.

Orgel, Stephen, ed. see Markham, Gervase & Sampson, Willliam.

Orgel, Stephen, ed. see Marmion, Shakerly.

Orgel, Stephen, ed. see May, Thomas.

Orgel, Stephen, ed. see Meagher, John A.

Orgel, Stephen, ed. see Menestrier, Claude.

Orgel, Stephen, ed. see Menestrier, Claude F.

Orgel, Stephen, ed. see Metz, J. C.

Orgel, Stephen, jt. ed. see Onat, Etta S.

Orgel, Stephen, jt. ed. see Owen, John I.

Orgel, Stephen, jt. ed. see Pignoria, Lorenzo.

Orgel, Stephen, ed. see Richardson, George.

Orgel, Stephen, ed. see Ross, Alexander.

Orgel, Stephen, ed. see Rudd, Anthony.

Orgel, Stephen, ed. see Shirley, James.

Orgel, Stephen, ed. see Shirley, James, et al.

Orgel, Stephen, ed. see Shirley, James.

Orgel, Stephen, jt. ed. see Sider, J. W.

Orgel, Stephen, jt. ed. see Turner, John P., Jr.

Orgel, Stephen, ed. see Tyson, Archie M.

Orgel, Stephen, ed. see Vaenius, Otho.

Orgel, Stephen, ed. see Vaenius, Otho V.

Orgel, Stephen, ed. see Waleys, Thomas.

Orgel, Stephen, ed. see Weiner, Arlene W.

Orgel, Stephen, jt. ed. see Young, Stephen B.

Orgill, Douglas & Gribben, John. The Sixth Winter. 288p. 1981. pap. 2.75 (ISBN 0-345-29242-1). Ballantine.

Orgill, Michael. Anchored in Love. 1976. pap. 1.50 (ISBN 0-89129-152-0). Jove Pubns.

Oriental Economist, ed. New Japanese-English Dictionary of Economic Terms. 580p. 1977. 20.00x (ISBN 0-8002-1609-1). Intl Pubns Serv.

Origen. On First Principles: Being Koetschau's Text of the De Principiis. Butterworth, G. W., tr. 7.50 (ISBN 0-8446-2685-6). Peter Smith.

--The Philocalia of Origen. Robinson, J. Armitage, rev. by. & intro. by. LC 80-2359. 1981. Repr. of 1893 ed. 39.50 (ISBN 0-404-18911-3). AMS Pr.

Orihel, Thomas C., jt. auth. see Ash, Lawrence R.

Orilia, Lawrence, et al. Business Data Processing Systems, 2 pts. 2nd ed. 1971. Set. text ed. 24.95 (ISBN 0-471-65700-X); tchrs. manual avail. (ISBN 0-471-02612-3). Wiley.

Oringer, Maurice J. Electrosurgery in Dentistry. 2nd ed. LC 70-186952. (Illus.). 1150p. 1975. text ed. 65.00 (ISBN 0-7216-7001-6). Saunders.

O'Riordan, Timothy & Hey, Richard D. Environmental Impact Assessment. (Illus.). 1977. 24.95 (ISBN 0-685-81671-0, 00706-4, Pub. by Saxon Hse). Lexington Bks.

O'Riordan, Timothy & Sewell, W. R. Project Appraisal & Policy Review. (Studies in Environmental Management & Resource Development). 320p. 1981. 35.75 (ISBN 0-471-27853-X, Pub. by Wiley-Interscience). Wiley.

O'Riordan, Timothy, et al. Progress in Resource Management & Environmental Planning. LC 79-41729. Vol. 1, 1979. 44.50 (ISBN 0-471-27747-9, Pub. by Wiley-Interscience); Vol. 2, 1980, 272p. 49.00 (ISBN 0-471-27747-9). Wiley.

Oriti, Ronald & Starbird, William. Introduction to Astronomy. 1977. text ed. 14.95x (ISBN 0-02-478560-1). Macmillan.

Orizet, Louis, jt. auth. see Gerard, Max.

Orland, Frank J. Microbiology in Clinical Dentistry. (Illus.). 250p. 1981. 23.50 (ISBN 0-88416-171-4). PSG Pub.

Orland, Leonard. Justice, Punishment, Treatment: The Correctional Process. LC 72-94014. 1973. text ed. 25.00 (ISBN 0-02-923440-9). Free Pr.

--Prisons: Houses of Darkness. LC 75-8428. 1975. 14.95 (ISBN 0-02-923430-1). Free Pr.

--Prisons: Houses of Darkness. LC 75-8428. (Illus.). 1978. pap. text ed. 6.95 (ISBN 0-02-923420-4). Free Pr.

Orlando, Joseph. The Waterfront Cookbook: Secrets of San Francisco Restaurant Chefs. rev. ed. Larrick, Gail, ed. LC 80-66582. (Illus.). 144p. 1980. pap. 5.95 (ISBN 0-89395-045-9); spiral binding 8.95 (ISBN 0-89395-063-7). Cal Living Bks.

Orlans, Harold, ed. Nonprofit Organizations: A Government Management Tool. 1980. 22.95 (ISBN 0-03-053966-8). Praeger.

Orlans, Harold, ed. see Carnegie Commission on Higher Education.

Orlansky, Michael D. & Heward, William L. Voices: Interviews with Handicapped People. (Special Education Ser.). (Illus.). 352p. (Orig.). Date not set. pap. text ed. price not set (ISBN 0-675-08024-X). Merrill.

Orlansky, Michael D., jt. auth. see Heward, William L.

Orleans, Ilo. Gingerbread Children. (Beginning-to-Read Bks). (Illus.). 32p. (gr. 1-3). 1973. PLB 3.39 o.p. (ISBN 0-695-40433-4); pap. 1.50 o.p. (ISBN 0-695-30433-X). Follett.

Orleans, Leo A., ed. Science in Contemporary China. LC 79-65178. 640p. 1980. 35.00x (ISBN 0-8047-1078-3). Stanford U Pr.

Orleans, Peter & Ellis, William R., Jr., eds. Race, Change, & Urban Society. LC 70-127992. (Urban Affairs Annual Reviews: Vol. 5). 1971. 25.00x (ISBN 0-8039-0009-0); pap. 9.95x (ISBN 0-8039-0354-5). Sage.

Orlebar, John. A Midshipman's Journal on Board H.M.S. Seringapatam During the Year, 1830. LC 76-11841. 1976. pap. 3.95 (ISBN 0-914488-10-4). Rand-Tofua.

Orlen, Steve. Permission to Speak. LC 77-89038. (Wesleyan Poetry Program: Vol. 90). 1978. 10.00x (ISBN 0-8195-2090-X, Pub. by Wesleyan U Pr); pap. 4.95 (ISBN 0-8195-1090-4). Columbia U Pr.

Orlich, Donald C. Designing Sensible Surveys. (Orig.). 1979. pap. 11.90 (ISBN 0-913178-50-0, Pub. by Two Continents). Hippocrene Bks.

Orlich, Donald C. & Orlich, Patricia R. The Art of Writing Successful R & D Proposals. 1977. 9.40 (ISBN 0-913178-51-9). Redgrave Pub Co.

--The Art of Writing Successful R & D Proposals. 1979. pap. 9.40 (ISBN 0-913178-51-9, Pub. by Two Continents). Hippocrene Bks.

Orlich, Donald C., et al. Teaching Strategies: A Guide to Better Instruction. (Orig.). 1979. pap. text ed. 12.95 (ISBN 0-669-02700-6). Heath.

Orlich, Patricia R., jt. auth. see Orlich, Donald C.

Orlich, Rose. Rose-Bloom at My Fingertips. 80p. 1981. 6.95. Adams Minn.

Orlick, Terry. The Cooperative Sports & Games Book: Challenge Without Competition. LC 77-88771. 1978. 10.00 (ISBN 0-394-42215-5); pap. 3.95 (ISBN 0-394-73494-7). Pantheon.

Orlick, Terry & Botterill, Cal. Every Kid Can Win. LC 74-19385. 190p. 1975. 13.95 (ISBN 0-88229-194-7); pap. 8.95 (ISBN 0-88229-471-7). Nelson-Hall.

Orlinsky, David O. & Howard, Kenneth I. Varieties of Psychotherapeutic Experience. LC 74-22011. 1975. text ed. 15.70x (ISBN 0-8077-2458-0); pap. text ed. 11.95x (ISBN 0-8077-2478-5). Tchrs Coll.

Orlinsky, Harry M. Ancient Israel. 2nd ed. (Development of Western Civilization Ser). (Illus., Orig.). (gr. 10 up). 1960. 9.50x o.p. (ISBN 0-8014-0324-3); pap. text ed. 2.95x o.p. (ISBN 0-8014-9849-X). Cornell U Pr.

--International Organization for Masoretic Studies, Proceedings & Papers. LC 74-16568. (Society of Biblical Literature, Masoretic Studies). 1974. 9.00 (ISBN 0-89130-308-1, 060501). Scholars Pr Ca.

Orlovsky, Peter, jt. auth. see Ginsberg, Allen.

Orlowski, S., jt. ed. see Simon, R.

Orman, H. A. Van see Van Orman, H. A.

Orman, Larry, jt. auth. see Hart, John.

Ormandy, P. G. An Introduction to Metallurgical Laboratory Techniques. LC 68-18530. 1968. 11.25 (ISBN 0-08-012560-3). Pergamon.

Orme, Michael. Micros--A Pervasive Force: A Study of the Impact of Microelectronics on Business & Society 1946-1990. LC 79-23839. 214p. 1978. 31.95x (ISBN 0-470-26891-3). Halsted Pr.

Orme, O. R. Ireland. (The World's Landscapes Ser.). (Illus.). 1970. pap. text ed. 8.50x o.p. (ISBN 0-582-31155-1). Longman.

Ormerod, A. Management of Textile Production. (Illus.). 1979. text ed. 44.95 (ISBN 0-408-00381-2). Butterworths.

Ormerod, M. B. & Duckworth, D. Pupils Attitudes to Science: A Review of Research. (General Ser.). 160p. 1975. pap. text ed. 14.50x (ISBN 0-85633-077-9, NFER). Humanities.

Ormerod, Oliver. The Picture of a Papist: Whereunto Is Annexed a Certain Treatise, Intituled Pagano-Papismus. LC 74-28878. (English Experience Ser.: No. 756). 1975. Repr. of 1606 ed. 18.50 (ISBN 90-221-0756-6). Walter J Johnson.

--The Picture of a Puritane: Or, a Relation of the Opinions - of the Anabaptists in Germanie, & of the Puritanes in England. LC 74-28879. (English Experience Ser.: No. 757). 1975. Repr. of 1605 ed. 9.50 (ISBN 90-221-0757-4). Walter J Johnson.

Ormes, Robert M. Guide to the Colorado Mountains. rev. ed. LC 72-115033. 1970. 7.95 o.s.i. (ISBN 0-8040-0139-1, SB). Swallow.

Ormond, Clyde. Complete Book of Outdoor Lore. LC 64-13133. (Illus.). 1965. 9.95 o.p. (ISBN 0-06-071440-9, HarpT). Har-Row.

--How to Track & Find Game. (Funk & W Bk.). (Illus.). 160p. 1975. 8.95 (ISBN 0-308-10210-X, TYC-T); pap. 4.50 (ISBN 0-308-10211-8, TYC-T). T Y Crowell.

--Small Game Hunting. rev. ed. LC 67-14557. (Funk & W Bk.). (Illus.). 1977. 8.95 (ISBN 0-308-10328-9, TYC-T); pap. 4.95 o.s.i. (ISBN 0-308-10329-7, TYC-T). T Y Crowell.

Ormond, Leonee & Ormond, Richard. Lord Leighton. LC 75-2773. (Studies in British Art Ser.). 192p. 1976. 60.00x (ISBN 0-300-01896-7). Yale U Pr.

Ormond, Richard. Early Victorian Portraits, 2 vol. (Illus.). 900p. 1980. Set. 160.00 (ISBN 0-312-22480-X). St Martin.

--J. S. Sargent: Paintings, Drawings, Watercolors. LC 76-114743. (Illus.). 1970. 30.00 o.s.i. (ISBN 0-06-013249-3, HarpT). Har-Row.

Ormond, Richard, jt. auth. see Ormond, Leonee.

Ormond, Suzanne, et al. Favorite New Orleans Recipes. LC 78-18841. 1979. English Ed. spiral bdg. 4.95 (ISBN 0-88289-198-7); French Ed. spiral bdg. 5.95 (ISBN 0-88289-199-5); Spanish Ed. spiral bdg. 5.95 (ISBN 0-88289-200-2); Combined Ed. spiral bdg. 10.95 (ISBN 0-88289-197-9). Pelican.

Ormont, Louis & Strean, Herbert S. The Practice of Conjoint Therapy: Combining Individual & Group Treatment. LC 77-17079. 1978. text ed. 19.95 (ISBN 0-87705-355-3). Human Sci Pr.

Ormrod, J. A., tr. see Evola, Julius.

Orna, Elizabeth, ed. Relevance of School Learning Experience to Performance in Industry. 1977. 22.95x (ISBN 0-85083-339-6). Intl Ideas.

Ornato, Joseph P. & Romankiewicz, John A. Handbook of the Pharmacology of Emergency Drugs for Paramedics. LC 77-89812. 1977. pap. 120.00 (ISBN 0-914768-36-0). Drug Intl Pubns.

Ornduff, Robert. A Biosystematic Survey of the Goldfield Genus Lasthenia (Compositae: Heleneiae) (U. C. Publ. in Botany: Vol. 40). 1966. pap. 6.50x (ISBN 0-520-09013-6). U of Cal Pr.

--Introduction to California Plant Life. (California Natural History Guides). (Illus.). 1974. 12.95x (ISBN 0-520-02583-0); pap. 4.95 (ISBN 0-520-02735-3). U of Cal Pr.

Orne, M. T., jt. ed. see Shor, R. E.

Ornstein, Allan C. Metropolitan Schools: Administrative Decentralization vs. Community Control. LC 73-20487. 1974. 10.00 (ISBN 0-8108-0653-3). Scarecrow.

Ornstein, Allan C., ed. Accountability for Teachers & School Administrators. LC 72-95012. 1973. pap. 4.95 (ISBN 0-8224-0055-3). Pitman Learning.

Ornstein, Robert & Spencer, Hazelton. Elizabethan & Jacobean Tragedy: An Anthology. 1964. pap. text ed. 7.95x o.p. (ISBN 0-669-21477-9). Heath.

Ornstein, Robert E. The Psychology of Consciousness. 1975. pap. 2.95 (ISBN 0-14-021679-0, Pelican). Penguin.

Ornstein, Robert E., ed. The Nature of Human Consciousness: A Book of Readings. LC 73-4431. (Psychology Ser.). (Illus.). 1973. pap. text ed. 10.95x (ISBN 0-7167-0790-X). W H Freeman.

Oroge, Adeniyij, ed. see Tarikh.

Orosz, Arpad. The Foreign Trade Turnover of Latin America Until 1970 & Its Prospective Development up to 1980. LC 77-369256. (Studies on Developing Countries). 130p. (Orig.). 1976. pap. 8.50x (ISBN 0-8002-0494-8). Intl Pubns Serv.

O'Rourke, A. Desmond. Changing Dimensions of U. S. Agricultural Policy. (Illus.). 1978. ref. ed. 14.95 (ISBN 0-13-127936-X). P-H.

O'Rourke, Brian. The Conscience of the Race: Sex & Religion in Irish & French Novels 1941-1973. 72p. 1981. 10.00x (ISBN 0-906127-22-X, Pub. by Irish Academic Pr Ireland). Biblio Dist.

O'Rourke, Frank. Ambuscade. Bd. with Thunder on the Buckhorn. 1980. pap. 1.95 (ISBN 0-451-09490-5, Sig). NAL.

--A Texan Came Riding. Bd. with Desperate Rider. pap. cancelled o.s.i. (ISBN 0-451-09490-5, Sig). NAL.

O'Rourke, G. G. F-Four Phantom. (Famous Aircraft Ser.). (Illus., Orig.). 1969. pap. 4.95 o.p. (ISBN 0-668-02221-3). Arco.

--F-Four Phantom Two. LC 78-79407. (Illus.). 1979. pap. 4.95 (ISBN 0-8168-5645-1). Aero.

O'Rourke, Karen & Barton, S. R. Nurse Power: Unions & the Law. (Illus.). 420p. 1980. pap. text ed. 14.95 (ISBN 0-87619-669-5). R J Brady.

O'Rourke, Robert. What God Did for ZEKE the Fuzzy Caterpillar. Sparks, Judith, ed. (A Happy Day Book). (Illus.). 24p. (gr. 1-3). 1980. 0.98 (ISBN 0-87239-406-9, 3638). Standard Pub.

O'Rourke, Robert, jt. auth. see Simon, Sidney B.

O'Rourke, Robert A. & Ross, John, Jr. Self-Assessment of Current Knowledge in Cardiovascular Disease. 1973. spiral bdg. 14.00 (ISBN 0-87488-275-3). Med Exam.

O'Rourke, William. Idle Hands. 1981. 12.95 (ISBN 0-440-04064-7). Delacorte.

Orozco, C. R. Spanish-English, English-Spanish Commercial Dictionary. 1969. 21.00 (ISBN 0-08-006381-0); pap. 11.25 (ISBN 0-08-006380-2). Pergamon.

Orozco, E. C. Republican Protestantism in Aztlan. 261p. 1980. 22.00 (ISBN 0-686-28883-1); pap. 11.00 (ISBN 0-686-28884-X). Petereins Pr.

Orozco, J. C. Eight Lithographs: Murals at Jiquilpan. Set. 12.50 (ISBN 0-911268-06-5). Rogers Bk.

Orozco, Julio, tr. see Kunz, Marilyn & Schell, Catherine.

Orozco, Julio, tr. see Lewis, C. S.

Orozco, Julio, tr. see Lindskoog, Kathryn.

Orozco, Julio, tr. see Reid, James.

Orozco, O., tr. see Cho, Paul Y.

Orr, Alan R., jt. auth. see Kelly, James L.

Orr, C. E. Food for Lambs. 168p. pap. 1.50. Faith Pub Hse.

--Heavenly Life for Earthly Living. 60p. 0.40; 3 copies. Faith Pub Hse.

--Helps to Holy Living. 64p. pap. 0.40; pap. 1.00 3 copies. Faith Pub Hse.

--The Hidden Life. 112p. pap. 0.75. Faith Pub Hse.

--How to Live a Holy Life. 112p. 0.75; pap. 2.00 3 copies. Faith Pub Hse.

--Odors from Golden Vials. 78p. pap. 0.60. Faith Pub Hse.

Orr, C. W. Cyprus Under British Rule. (Bibliotheca Historica Cyprica). (Illus.). 1972. text ed. 11.75x (ISBN 0-900834-19-6). Humanities.

Orr, David B., ed. New Directions in Employability: Reducing Barriers to Full Employment. LC 73-6094. (Special Studies in U.S. Economic, Social & Political Issues). 1973. 28.50x (ISBN 0-275-28838-2). Irvington.

Orr, Dorothy B., jt. auth. see Orr, Robert T.

Orr, Francis S., jt. auth. see Bartholomew, Roy A.

Orr, Frank. Great Goalies of Pro Hockey. (Pro Hockey Library: No. 5). (Illus.). (gr. 5 up). 1973. 2.50 o.p. (ISBN 0-394-82539-X); PLB 3.69 (ISBN 0-394-92539-4). Random.

--Great Moments in Auto Racing. LC 73-18087. (Illus.). 160p. 1974. 2.50 o.p. (ISBN 0-394-82763-5); PLB 3.69 (ISBN 0-394-92763-X). Random.

--Story of Hockey. (Pro Hockey Library: No. 1). (Illus.). (gr. 5-9). 1971. 2.50 o.p. (ISBN 0-394-82303-6, BYR); PLB 3.69 (ISBN 0-394-92303-0). Random.

Orr, J., jt. auth. see Lidden, H. P.

Orr, J., jt. auth. see Moule, H. C.

Orr, J. B., jt. auth. see Beck, R. N.

Orr, J. Edwin. Evangelical Awakenings in Africa. LC 74-32018. (Awakening Ser). 272p. 1975. pap. 4.95 (ISBN 0-87123-128-X, 210138). Bethany Fell.

--Evangelical Awakenings in Eastern Asia. LC 74-30353. (Awakening Ser). 192p. (Orig.). 1975. pap. 4.95 (ISBN 0-87123-126-3, 210126). Bethany Fell.

--Evangelical Awakenings in Latin America. LC 77-16148. (Awakening Ser). 1978. pap. 4.95 (ISBN 0-87123-130-1, 210130). Bethany Fell.

--Evangelical Awakenings in Southern Asia. LC 74-32019. (Awakening Ser). 256p. (Orig.). 1975. pap. 4.95 (ISBN 0-87123-127-1, 210127). Bethany Fell.

--Evangelical Awakenings in the South Seas. LC 76-26966. (Awakening Ser). 1977. pap. 4.95 (ISBN 0-87123-129-8, 210129). Bethany Fell.

--The Faith That Persuades. LC 76-62924. (Harper Jubilee Book). 1977. pap. 1.95 o.p. (ISBN 0-06-066939-X, HJ 30, HarpR). Har-Row.

Orr, J. M. Designing Library Buildings for Activity. (Grafton Books on Library Science). 1977. lib. bdg. 16.00x (ISBN 0-233-96230-1). Westview.

--Libraries As Communication Systems. LC 76-8739. (Contributions in Librarianship & Information Science: No. 17). 240p. 1977. lib. bdg. 16.95 (ISBN 0-8371-8936-5, ORL/). Greenwood.

Orr, Jack. Black Athlete: His Story in American History. (gr. 6 up). 1969. PLB 8.95 (ISBN 0-87460-104-5). Lion.

Orr, John. Tragic Drama & Modern Society: Studies in the Social & Literary Theroy of Drama from 1870 to the Present. LC 80-18156. Date not set. price not set (ISBN 0-312-81354-6). St Martin.

Orr, Lea. A Year Between School & University. (General Ser). 60p. 1974. pap. text ed. 7.00x (ISBN 0-85633-053-1, NFER). Humanities.

Orr, Lea, jt. auth. see Choppin, Bruce.

Orr, Leon. Unleashed. LC 79-13290. (Orion Ser.). 1979. pap. 2.95 (ISBN 0-8127-0230-1). Southern Pub.

Orr, Leonard. Babaji. 1980. pap. 10.00 (ISBN 0-686-27683-3). L Orr.

--How to Make Democracy Work. 1972. pap. 3.00 o.p. (ISBN 0-686-09763-7). L Orr.

Orr, Marsha E. Acute Pancreatic & Hepatic Dysfunction. Percy, R. Craig, ed. (The Fleschner Series in Critical Care Nursings). (Illus.). 175p. (Orig.). 1981. pap. text ed. 9.95 (ISBN 0-937878-04-9). Fleschner.

Orr, Mary. Women Still Weep: A Sequel to Women Must Weep. 1980. pap. 1.25 (ISBN 0-686-68851-1). Dramatists Play.

Orr, Monica, ed. Special Rooms: Louisville, Kentucky. LC 80-83167. 72p. (Orig.). 1980. pap. 9.95 (ISBN 0-937246-01-8). Hawley Cooke Orr.

Orr, Rebecca. Gunner's Run. LC 79-9613. 160p. (gr. 4-7). 1980. 8.95 (ISBN 0-06-024617-0, HarpJ); PLB 8.79 (ISBN 0-06-024618-9). Har-Row.

Orr, Robert P. The Meaning of Transcendence. Dietrich, Wendell, ed. LC 80-12872. (American Academy of Religion Dissertation Ser.). 1981. 13.50 (ISBN 0-89130-407-X); pap. 9.00. Scholars Pr CA.

Orr, Robert T. Marine Mammals of California. LC 78-165233. (California Natural History Guides Ser.: No. 29). 88p. 1972. pap. 5.95 (ISBN 0-520-02077-4). U of Cal Pr.

Orr, Robert T. & Orr, Dorothy B. Mushrooms of Western North America. (Illus.). 1980. 12.95 (ISBN 0-520-03656-5). U of Cal Pr.

Orr, William F. Corinthians I. (Anchor Bible Ser.: Vol. 32). 1976. 14.00 (ISBN 0-385-02853-9). Doubleday.

Orr, William I. & Cowan, S. D. Simple Low-Cost Wire Antennas for Radio Amateurs. LC 76-190590. (Illus.). 192p. 1972. 6.95 (ISBN 0-933616-02-3). Radio Pubns.

Orr, William I. & Cowan, Stuart D. All About Cubical Quad Antennas. 2nd ed. LC 59-13141. (Illus.). 112p. 1959. 4.75 (ISBN 0-933616-03-1). Radio Pubns.

--Beam Antenna Handbook. 5th ed. LC 55-11982. 200p. 1958. 5.95 (ISBN 0-933616-04-X). Radio Pubns.

--Better Shortwave Reception. 4th ed. LC 57-14916. (Illus.). 156p. 1957. 4.95 (ISBN 0-933616-05-8). Radio Pubns.

--The Radio Amateur Antenna Handbook. LC 78-53340. (Illus.). 190p. 1978. 6.95 (ISBN 0-933616-07-4). Radio Pubns.

--The Truth About CB Antennas. LC 70-164932. (Illus.). 240p. 1971. 6.95 (ISBN 0-933616-08-2). Radio Pubns.

Orr, William I., jt. auth. see Brier, Herbert S.

Orrall, Frank, ed. Solar Active Regions. LC 79-565371. (Skylab Solar Workshop Ser.). 1981. 17.50x (ISBN 0-87081-085-5). Colo Assoc.

Orrell, K., jt. auth. see Tolley, H.

Orrey, Lesley. Opera in the High Baroque. 1981. 27.50 (ISBN 0-7145-3658-X). Riverrun NY.

Orsagh, Thomas, et al. The Economic History of the United States Prior to 1860: An Annotated Bibliography. new ed. LC 75-1162. 100p. 1975. text ed. 4.50 (ISBN 0-87436-205-9). ABC-Clio.

Orsborn, Peggy A. Meeting: A One-Act Play. LC 67-31721. (Illus.). (gr. 6-12). 1968. tchr's ed & spirit master reader 7.95 (ISBN 0-910030-06-5). Afro Am.

Orser, Mary, et al. Astrorhythms. LC 78-22160. (Orig.). 1979. pap. 4.95 (ISBN 0-06-090632-4, CN 632, CN). Har-Row.

Orsini, Joseph. The Cost in Pentecost. 1977. pap. 3.95 o.p. (ISBN 0-88270-243-2). Logos.

Orso, Kathryn W. Parenthood: A Commitment in Faith. LC 75-5219. 64p. (Orig.). 1975. pap. text ed. 2.95 (ISBN 0-8192-1198-2); tchr's ed. 3.75 (ISBN 0-8192-1204-0); wkbk. 3.95 (ISBN 0-8192-1199-0). Morehouse.

Orszagh. Hungarian Deluxe Dictionary: English-Hungarian, 2 vols. 4th ed. 1974. 60.00x (ISBN 963-05-0554-1, H-331). Vanous.

Orszagh, Laszlo. Hungarian Concise Dictionary: English-Hungarian. 9th ed. 1979. 20.00x (ISBN 963-05-1883-X, H-269). Vanous.

--Hungarian Concise Dictionary: Hungarian-English, Vol. 2. 7th ed. 1976. 20.00x (ISBN 9-6305-0612-2, H268). Vanous.

--Hungarian-English - English-Hungarian Dictionary, 2 vols. 11th, rev. ed. 1977. Set. 15.00 (ISBN 0-686-68937-2). Vol. 1, Hung.-Eng., 464pp (ISBN 963-05-1255-6). Vol. 2, Eng.-Hung., 608pp (ISBN 963-05-1256-4). Heinman.

Ortega, James M. Numerical Analysis: Second Course. (Computer Science & Applied Mathematics Ser.). 201p. 1972. 19.95 o.p. (ISBN 0-12-528560-4). Acad Pr.

Ortega, Jose. Alienacion y Agnesion En Juan Goytisolo En Senas De Identidad y Reivindicacion Del Conde Don Julian. 1973. 10.50 (ISBN 0-88303-012-8); pap. 7.50 (ISBN 0-685-73216-9). E Torres & Sons.

Ortega, Jose L. Devocionario Biblico Guadalupano. 64p. 1980. pap. 1.50 (ISBN 0-89243-130-X). Liguori Pubns.

Ortega, Wenceslao & Sampere, Alberto. Mecanografia Cien, Libro 1. (Span.). 1971. pap. text ed. 6.80 (ISBN 0-06-316640-2, IntlDept). Har-Row.

--Mecanografia Cien: Practicas Secretariales. 180p. (Span.). 1972. pap. text ed. 4.00 (ISBN 0-06-316641-0, IntlDept). Har-Row.

Ortega y Gasset, Jose. Invertebrate Spain. LC 73-16212. iv, 212p. 1974. Repr. of 1937 ed. 12.00 (ISBN 0-86527-107-0). Fertig.

--Meditaciones Del Quijote. Revista De Occidente, ed. 1957. pap. 3.65 o.p. (ISBN 0-8477-0721-0). U of PR Pr.

Orten, James M. & Neuhaus, Otto W. Human Biochemistry. 9th ed. LC 74-19436. 1975. text ed. 26.95 (ISBN 0-8016-3729-5). Mosby.

Orth, Marjorie, jt. auth. see Voth, Harold.

Orth, Rene. New York: The Largest City in the United States. (Q Book: Famous Cities). (Illus.). (gr. 2-6). 1978. 3.95 (ISBN 0-8467-0447-1, Pub. by Two Continents). Hippocrene Bks.

--Paris: Capital City of France. (Q Book: Famous Cities). (Illus.). (gr. 2-6). 1978. 3.95 (ISBN 0-8467-0445-5, Pub. by Two Continents). Hippocrene Bks.

Orth, Samuel P see Johnson, Allen & Nevins, Allan.

Orthner, Dennis K. Intimate Relationships: An Introduction to Marriage & the Family. LC 80-21527. (Sociology Ser.). (Illus.). 496p. 1981. text ed. 16.95 (ISBN 0-201-05519-8). A-W.

Ortho Books Editorial Staff. Adventures in Mexican Cooking. LC 78-57893. (Illus.). 1979. pap. text ed. 4.95 (ISBN 0-917102-71-1). Ortho.

--All About Pruning. LC 78-57891. (Illus.). 1979. pap. 4.95 (ISBN 0-917102-73-8). Ortho.

--Elegant Meals with Inexpensive Meats. LC 78-57890. (Illus.). 1979. pap. 4.95 (ISBN 0-917102-75-4). Ortho.

--The World of Herbs & Spices. LC 78-57892. (Illus.). 1979. pap. 4.95 (ISBN 0-917102-72-X). Ortho.

Ortho Books Editorial Staff, ed. Adventures in Oriental Cooking. LC 76-29252. 1977. 4.95 (ISBN 0-917102-24-X). Ortho.

--All About Ground Covers. LC 77-89688. (Illus.). 1978. pap. 4.95 Midwest-Northeast ed. (ISBN 0-917102-55-X); pap. 4.95 South ed. (ISBN 0-917102-56-8); pap. 4.95 West ed. (ISBN 0-917102-57-6). Ortho.

--How to Build & Use Greenhouses. LC 78-57889. (Illus.). 1979. pap. 4.95 (ISBN 0-917102-74-6). Ortho.

Ortho Books Editorial Staff, ed. see Burke, Ken & Doty, Walter.

Ortho Books Editorial Staff, ed. see Cottin, Lin.

Ortho Books Editorial Staff, ed. see Henkin, William A.

Ortho Books Editorial Staff, ed. see Hildebrand, Ron.

Ortho Books Editorial Staff, ed. see Howland, Joseph E.

Ortho Books Editorial Staff, ed. see McNair, James K.

Ortho Books Staff, ed. see Howland, Joseph E.

Orthodox Christian Educational Society, ed. see Agapius, et al.

Orthodox Christian Educational Society, ed. see Livadeas, Themistocles & Charitos, Minas.

Orthodox Christian Educational Society, ed. see Makrakis, Apostolos.

Orthodox Christian Educational Society, ed. see Philaretos, S. D.

Orthodox Christian Educational Society, ed. see Philaretos, Sotirios D.

Orthodox Christian Educational Society, ed. see Vassilakos, Aristarchus.

Ortiz, Alfonso, ed. Southwest. LC 77-17162. (Handbook of North American Indians Ser.: Vol. 9). (Illus.). 700p. 1980. text ed. 17.00x (ISBN 0-87474-189-0). Smithsonian.

Ortiz, Elisabeth L. The Complete Book of Mexican Cooking. LC 67-18534. (Illus.). 352p. 1967. 8.95 (ISBN 0-87131-074-0); 5.95 (ISBN 0-87131-333-2). M Evans.

--The Complete Book of Mexican Cooking. (Illus.). 352p. 1980. pap. 5.95 o.p. (ISBN 0-87131-333-2). M Evans.

Ortiz, Juan Carlos. Cry of the Human Heart. LC 76-24099. 1977. pap. 3.95 (ISBN 0-88419-010-2). Creation Hse.

Ortiz, Roxanne D. Roots of Resistance: Land Tenure in New Mexico, Sixteen Eighty to Nineteen Eighty. LC 80-18935. 202p. (Orig.). 1980. 14.95 (ISBN 0-89551-050-2); pap. 9.95 (ISBN 0-89551-050-2). UCLA Chicano Stud.

Ortiz, Simon J. Fightback: For the Sake of the People, for the Sake of the Land. LC 80-51953. (Literature Ser.: No. 1). (Orig.). 1980. pap. 6.95 (ISBN 0-934090-03-3). U of NM Nat Am Stud.

--A Good Journey. LC 77-82789. (New World Writing Ser.). (Illus.). 1977. 15.00 o.p. (ISBN 0-913666-21-1); pap. 6.95 o.p. (ISBN 0-913666-20-3). Turtle Isl Foun.

Ortiz, Sutti R. De see De Ortiz, Sutti R.

Ortland, G. J. Handbook of Professional Telephone Selling. 1981. write for info. (ISBN 0-201-05490-6). A-W.

Ortloff, George C. & Ortloff, Stephen C. Lake Placid: The Olympic Years, 1932-1980. LC 76-45314. 1976. 19.95 (ISBN 0-9601170-1-6); pap. 9.95 o.p. (ISBN 0-9601170-2-4). Macromedia Inc.

Ortloff, H. Stuart & Raymore, Henry B. The Book of Landscape Design. LC 59-12871. (Illus.). 320p. 1975. pap. 3.25 o.p. (ISBN 0-685-52306-3). Morrow.

Ortloff, Stephen C., jt. auth. see Ortloff, George C.

Ortlund, Anne. Love Me with Tough Love. 1979. 7.95 (ISBN 0-8499-0145-6). Word Bks.

Ortlund, Raymond C. Lord, Make My Life a Miracle. LC 73-89714. (Orig.). 1974. pap. 2.50 (ISBN 0-8307-0284-9, 50-117-01); study guide 1.59 (ISBN 0-8307-0626-7, 6101305). Regal.

Ortmann, Otto. The Physiological Mechanics of Piano Technique. (Music Ser.). (Illus.). xvi, 396p. 1981. Repr. of 1929 ed. lib. bdg. 39.50 (ISBN 0-306-76058-4). Da Capo.

Orton, C., jt. auth. see Hodder, I.

Orton, Carles, jt. ed. see Carlson, Gene.

Orton, Charles, ed. see IFSTA Committee.

Orton, Charles, ed. see IFSTA Committee & Walker, Lorrin.

Orton, Colin G., et al, eds. Radiological Physics Examination Review Book, Vol. 1. 2nd ed. 1978. spiral bdg. 13.50 (ISBN 0-87488-486-1). Med Exam.

Orton, D. A. The Merlins of the Welsh Marches. LC 80-66090. 192p. 1980. 19.95 (ISBN 0-7153-7992-5). David & Charles.

Orton, D. H., et al. The Solid State Maser. LC 74-101374. 1970. 35.00 (ISBN 0-08-006819-7); pap. 14.50 (ISBN 0-08-006818-9). Pergamon.

Orton, Diana. Made of Gold: The Life of Angela Burdett Coutts. (Illus.). 1980. 45.00 (ISBN 0-241-89656-8, Pub. by Hamish Hamilton England). David & Charles.

Orton, Gavin. Eyvind Johnson. (World Authors Ser.: Sweden: No. 150). lib. bdg. 10.95 (ISBN 0-8057-2468-0). Twayne.

Orton, Graham see Ibsen, Henrik.

Orton, Helen F. Mystery in the Old Red Barn. LC 52-7461. (Illus.). (gr. 4-6). 1952. 5.95 o.p. (ISBN 0-397-30217-7). Lippincott.

--Mystery of the Hidden Book. (Illus.). (gr. 4-6). 1949. 8.95 o.p. (ISBN 0-397-30245-2). Lippincott.

--Secret of the Rosewood Box. LC 37-28568. (Illus.). (gr. 4-6). 1937. 8.95 (ISBN 0-397-31596-1). Lippincott.

Orton, Joe. Up Against It. LC 79-52099. 1979. pap. 4.95 (ISBN 0-394-17475-5, E736, Ever). Grove.

Orton, Lawrence D. Polish Detroit & the Kolasinski Affair. (Illus.). 268p. 1981. 17.95 (ISBN 0-8143-1671-9). Wayne St U Pr.

Orton, Mildred E. Cooking with Wholegrains. LC 77-148706. (Illus.). 72p. 1971. pap. 2.95 (ISBN 0-374-50936-0, N410). FS&G.

Orton, Richard, compiled by. Records of California Men in the War of the Rebellion: 1861-1867. LC 78-23517. 1979. Repr. of 1890 ed. 64.00 (ISBN 0-8103-3347-3). Gale.

Orton, Vrest. Vermont Afternoons with Robert Frost. (Illus.). 63p. 1979. pap. 4.50 o.s.i. (ISBN 0-911570-17-9). Vermont Bks.

Ortony, Andrew, ed. Metaphor & Thought. LC 78-32011. (Illus.). 1979. 45.00 (ISBN 0-521-22727-5); pap. 13.95x (ISBN 0-521-29626-9). Cambridge U Pr.

Orum, Anthony M. Introduction to Political Sociology: The Social Anatomy of Body Politics. (P-H Ser. in Sociology). (Illus.). 1978. ref. ed. 17.95 (ISBN 0-13-491381-7). P-H.

Orville-Thomas, W. J., jt. auth. see Ratajczak, H.

Orville-Thomas, W. J., jt. ed. see Ratajczak, H.

Orwell, George. Burmese Days. LC 73-12947. 287p. 1974. pap. 3.95 (ISBN 0-15-614850-1, HPL62, HPL). HarBraceJ.

--Clergyman's Daughter. LC 60-10943. 1969. pap. 3.95 (ISBN 0-15-618065-0, HPL37, HPL). HarBraceJ.

--Collected Essays, Journalism & Letters, Vol. 1: An Age Like This, 1920-1940. Orwell, Sonia & Angus, Ian, eds. LC 68-12591. 1971. pap. 6.95 (ISBN 0-15-618620-9, HB209, Harv). HarBraceJ.

--Collected Essays, Journalism & Letters, Vol. 4: In Front of Your Nose, 1945-1950. Orwell, Sonia & Angus, Ian, eds. LC 68-12591. 1971. pap. 6.95 (ISBN 0-15-618623-3, HB212, Harv). HarBraceJ.

--Collection of Essays. LC 54-7594. 1970. pap. 3.95 (ISBN 0-15-618600-4, HPL48, HPL). HarBraceJ.

--Coming up for Air. LC 50-5002. 1969. pap. 4.95 (ISBN 0-15-619625-5, HPL44, HPL). HarBraceJ.

--Keep the Aspidistra Flying. LC 56-5326. 1969. pap. 4.95 (ISBN 0-15-646899-9, HPL38, HPL). HarBraceJ.

--Nineteen Eighty-Four. LC 66-91393. (gr. 10 up). 8.95 (ISBN 0-15-166035-2). HarBraceJ.
--Orwell Reader: Fiction, Essays, & Reportage. LC 61-1439. 1961. pap. 5.95 (ISBN 0-15-670176-6, HB42, Harv). HarBraceJ.
Orwell, Sonia, ed. see Orwell, George.
Orwen, Gifford. Introduction to Italian. 1971. 7.75 (ISBN 0-913298-11-5). S F Vanni.
--Upgrade Your Italian: A Review Grammar. 1977. pap. 7.75 (ISBN 0-913298-12-3). S F Vanni.
Orwen, Gifford P. Cecco Angiolieri: A Study. (Studies in the Romance Languages & Literatures: No. 215). 104p. 1980. pap. 7.50 (ISBN 0-8078-9215-7). U of NC Pr.
Orynski, Wanda, ed. Henrik Bsen's Theatre Hengel Highlights. 1960. 4.75 (ISBN 0-8022-1245-X). Philos Lib.
Orzech. Plane Algerbraic Curves. 224p. 1981. 29.75 (ISBN 0-8247-1159-9). Dekker.
Orzel, Nick & Smith, Michael, eds. Eight Plays from Off-Off Broadway. 1966. pap. 4.95 o.p. (ISBN 0-672-50656-4). Bobbs.
Osa, Veronica De see De Osa, Veronica.
Osadchy, Mykhaylo. Cataract. Carynnyk, Marco, tr. from Ukrainian. LC 75-34371. (Helen & Kurt Wolff Bk.). 264p. 1976. 8.95 o.p. (ISBN 0-15-615550-8). HarBraceJ.
Osaki, S. & Nishio, T. Reliability Evaluation of Some Fault-Tolerant Computer Architectures. (Lecture Notes in Computer Science Ser.: Vol. 97). 129p. 1981. pap. 9.80 (ISBN 0-387-10274-4). Springer-Verlag.
Osbaldeston, Michael, jt. auth. see Hepworth, Andrew.
Osbeck, Kenneth W. My Choir Workbook. 1973. pap. 3.50 o.p. (ISBN 0-8254-3409-2). Kregel.
Osbon, D. Keith. Early Childhood Education in Historical Perspective. rev. ed. 1980. 11.95 (ISBN 0-918772-08-7); pap. 5.95 (ISBN 0-918772-07-9). Ed Assocs.
Osborn, Albert S. Problem of Proof: Especially As Exemplified in Disputed Documents Trials. LC 75-20212. 1975. Repr. of 1926 ed. 38.95 (ISBN 0-88229-300-1). Nelson-Hall.
Osborn, Alex F. Your Creative Power. (Lib. Rep. Ed.). 1972. 20.00x (ISBN 0-684-15314-9, ScribT). Scribner.
Osborn, Andrew D. Serial Publications. 3rd ed. LC 80-11686. 486p. 1980. 20.00 (ISBN 0-8389-0299-5). ALA.
Osborn, Anne G. An Introduction to Cerebral Angiography. (Illus.). 424p. 1980. text ed. 42.50 (ISBN 0-06-141829-3, Harper Medical). Har-Row.
Osborn, D. Keith. Early Childhood Education in Historical Perspective. LC 75-30492. 1977. pap. 4.95 o.p. (ISBN 0-918772-01-X). Ed Assocs.
Osborn, E. Ethical Patterns in Early Christian Thought. LC 75-10040. 288p. 1976. 34.00 (ISBN 0-521-20835-1). Cambridge U Pr.
Osborn, E. F. The Beginning of Christian Philosophy. LC 79-8911. 256p. Date not set. price not set; pap. price not set (ISBN 0-521-29855-5). Cambridge U Pr.
Osborn, George. The Role of the British Press in the 1976 Presidential Election. 64p. 1981. 10.00 (ISBN 0-682-49667-7). Exposition.
Osborn, Henry F., jt. auth. see Department of the Interior, U. S. Geological Survey, Monograph.
Osborn, Jack L. Personal Information: Privacy at the Workplace. LC 78-18223. 1978. pap. 7.50 o.p. (ISBN 0-8144-2223-3). Am Mgmt.
Osborn, John F. Statistical Exercises in Medical Research. LC 79-12451. 1979. 16.95x (ISBN 0-470-26744-5). Halsted Pr.
Osborn, John J., Jr. The Man Who Owned New York. 256p. 1981. 10.95 (ISBN 0-686-69052-4). HM.
Osborn, Leslie A. King of the Hill. Date not set. 7.95 (ISBN 0-533-04592-4). Vantage.
Osborn, Mary E. Who Tempers the Wind. LC 63-117821. 115p. 1963. pap. 2.75 (ISBN 0-8040-0320-3). Swallow.
Osborn, Richard N., et al. Organization Theory: An Integrated Contingency Approach. (Wiley Ser. in Management). 1980. text ed. 21.95 (ISBN 0-471-02173-3); tchrs' manual avail. (ISBN 0-471-02174-1). Wiley.
Osborn, Richards C. Business Finance: The Management Approach. LC 65-15300. (Illus.). 1965. text ed. 10.95x (ISBN 0-89197-053-3); instructor's manual free (ISBN 0-89197-054-1). Irvington.
Osborn, Robert, jt. auth. see Mannes, Marya.
Osborn, Roger. Mathematics of Investment. (Illus.). 9.50 (ISBN 0-8363-0066-1). Jenkins.
Osborn, Ronald E. Experiment in Liberty. 1978. 2.95 (ISBN 0-8272-0804-9). Bethany Pr.
--In Christ's Place: Christian Ministry in Today's World. Orig. Title: In Christ's Place. 256p. 1977. pap. 2.50 (ISBN 0-8272-1605-X). Bethany Pr.
Osborn, Royce R. A Professional Approach to Radiology Administration. (Illus.). 228p. 1980. 29.75 (ISBN 0-398-04097-4). C C Thomas.
Osborn, Scott C. & Phillips, Robert. Richard Harding Davis. (United States Authors Ser.: No. 289). 1978. lib. bdg. 12.50 (ISBN 0-8057-7192-1). Twayne.
Osborn, Tom, tr. see Wedekind, Frank.
Osborne, ed. Consolidated List of Approved Common Names of Insecticides & Certain Other Pesticides. LC 52-44516. 1979. 3.35 (ISBN 0-686-18865-9). Entomol Soc.
Osborne, A., et al. Micro Systems in Business. (Micro Monograph Ser.: No. 1). 122p. 1980. pap. text ed. 27.00x (ISBN 0-903796-63-5, Pub. by Online Conferences England). Renouf.
Osborne, Adam. A Business System Buyer's Guide. 600p. (Orig.). 1981. pap. 7.95 (ISBN 0-931988-47-0). Osborne-McGraw.
--An Introduction to Microcomputers: Vol. 1, Basic Concepts. rev. ed. 1980. pap. 12.99 (ISBN 0-931988-34-9). Osborne-McGraw.
--The Osborne Four & Eight Bit Microprocessor Handbook. 600p. 1981. pap. text ed. 19.95 (ISBN 0-931988-42-X). Osborne-McGraw.
--The Osborne Sixteen-Bit Microprocessor Handbook. 500p. 1981. pap. 19.95 (ISBN 0-931988-43-8). Osborne-McGraw.
--PET-CBM Personal Computer Guide. 2nd ed. 530p. 1980. pap. 15.00 (ISBN 0-931988-55-1). Osborne-McGraw.
--Running Wild the Next Industrial Revolution. (Orig.). 1979. pap. 3.95 (ISBN 0-931988-28-4). Osborne-McGraw.
--The Sixty-Eight Thousand Microprocessor Handbook. 200p. (Orig.). 1981. pap. 6.99 (ISBN 0-931988-41-1). Osborne-McGraw.
Osborne, Adam & Kane, Jerry. An Introduction to Microcomputers: Some Real Microprocessors. (Intro. to Microcomputers Ser.: Vol. 2). (Orig.). 1978. pap. text ed. 30.00 (ISBN 0-931988-15-2). Osborne-McGraw.
--An Introduction to Microcomputers: Some Real Support Devices. 1978. pap. text ed. 20.00 (ISBN 0-931988-18-7). Osborne-McGraw.
Osborne, Alford E., Jr., jt. auth. see Bobo, Benjamin F.
Osborne, Cecil. The Art of Learning to Love Yourself. 1976. 2.50 (ISBN 0-310-30572-1). Zondervan.
--Art of Understanding Yourself. LC 67-11612. (Orig.). 1968. pap. 3.50 (ISBN 0-310-30592-6); 1.50 (ISBN 0-310-30593-4). Zondervan.
Osborne, Cecil G. You're in Charge. 1976. pap. 1.25 (ISBN 0-89129-221-7). Jove Pubns.
Osborne, Charles. Richard Wagner & His World. LC 76-56892. (Encore Edition). (Illus.). 1977. 3.95 (ISBN 0-684-16915-0, ScribT). Scribner.
Osborne, Charles, tr. see Leider, Frida.
Osborne, Ernest L. & West, Victor. Men of Action: A History of the U. S. Life Saving Service on the Pacific Coast. LC 80-69563. (Illus.). 150p. (Orig.). 1981. pap. 10.00 (ISBN 0-932368-05-0). Bandon Hist.
Osborne, G. S. Changes in Scottish Education. 1968. text ed. 3.25x (ISBN 0-582-32415-7). Humanities.
Osborne, George E., et al. Handbook on Real Estate Finance Law. LC 79-284. (Hornbook Ser.). 885p. 1979. 18.95 (ISBN 0-8299-2034-X). West Pub.
Osborne, Harold. Abstraction & Artifice in Twentieth Century Art. (Illus.). 1979. 24.95x (ISBN 0-19-817359-8). Oxford U Pr.
--Aesthetics & Art Theory. (Illus.). 1970. pap. 4.95 o.p. (ISBN 0-525-47258-4). Dutton.
Osborne, Harrison. In Defense of Fascism: A New Critical Evaluation of the Fascist Experience in Modern History. (Science of Man Library Bk.). 1978. 51.75 (ISBN 0-89266-128-3). Am Classical Coll Pr.
Osborne, J. Grayson, jt. ed. see Martin, Gary L.
Osborne, J. W. John Cartwright. LC 74-190422. (Conference on British Studies, Biographical Ser). 168p. 1972. 36.00 (ISBN 0-521-08537-3). Cambridge U Pr.
--William Cobbett: His Thoughts & His Times. LC 66-18874. 10.00 (ISBN 0-910294-35-6). Brown Bk.
Osborne, John. End of Me Old Cigar & Jack & Jill. 1975. 8.95 o.p. (ISBN 0-571-10856-3, Pub. by Faber & Faber); pap. 3.95 (ISBN 0-571-10857-1). Merrimack Bk Serv.
--Hedda Gabler. 1972. 5.95 o.p. (ISBN 0-571-09887-8, Pub. by Faber & Faber); pap. 3.95 (ISBN 0-571-09888-6). Merrimack Bk Serv.
--Look Back in Anger. Taylor, John R., ed. LC 76-127573. (Casebook Ser). 1970. pap. text ed. 2.50 o.s.i. (ISBN 0-87695-044-6). Aurora Pubs.
--A Sense of Detachment. 1973. 5.95 o.p. (ISBN 0-571-10211-5, Pub. by Faber & Faber). Merrimack Bk Serv.
--Tom Jones: A Film Script. 1964. 4.95 (ISBN 0-571-05723-3, Pub. by Faber & Faber). Merrimack Bk Serv.
--Watch It Come Down. 1975. 8.50 (ISBN 0-571-10854-7, Pub. by Faber & Faber); pap. 3.95 o.p. (ISBN 0-571-10855-5). Merrimack Bk Serv.
Osborne, John J., Jr. The Only Thing I've Done Wrong. 1977. pap. 1.75 (ISBN 0-380-01870-5, 36970). Avon.
Osborne, Juanita T. The Ashes of Windrow. 192p. (YA) 1976. 5.95 (ISBN 0-685-59251-0, Avalon). Bouregy.
--Dark Season at Aerie. (YA) 1977. 5.95 (ISBN 0-685-81423-8, Avalon). Bouregy.
--Rendezvous at the Hallows. 192p. (YA) 1975. 5.95 (ISBN 0-685-50529-4, Avalon). Bouregy.
--Shadow Over Wyndham Hall. 192p. (YA) 1976. 5.95 (ISBN 0-685-66478-3, Avalon). Bouregy.
--The Shrinking Pond. 192p. (YA) 1974. 5.95 (ISBN 0-685-39179-5, Avalon). Bouregy.
Osborne, Juanita Tyree. The House on Hibiscus Hill. (YA) 1977. 4.95 o.p. (ISBN 0-685-74266-0, Avalon). Bouregy.
Osborne, Linda B. The Song of the Harp. LC 76-28047. 1977. 5.95 o.p. (ISBN 0-312-74480-3). St Martin.
Osborne, Louise. Keys of Hell. 256p. 1975. pap. 1.25 o.p. (ISBN 0-445-00284-0). Popular Lib.
Osborne, M. Region of Revolt: Focus on Southeast Asia. LC 75-133332. 1970. 11.50 (ISBN 0-08-017533-3). Pergamon.
Osborne, Maggie. Salem's Daughter. (Orig.). 1981. pap. 2.75 (ISBN 0-451-09602-9, E9602, Sig). NAL.
Osborne, Margaret. Collies. (Foyle's Handbks). 1973. 3.95 (ISBN 0-685-55800-2). Palmetto Pub.
Osborne, Mary C., et al, trs. see Price, Douglas B. & Twombly, Neil J.
Osborne, Mary C, et al, trs. see Price, Douglas B. & Twombly, Neil J.
Osborne, Michael, jt. auth. see De Meza, David.
Osborne, Neville N. Microchemical Analysis of Nervous Tissue. 1974. text ed. 37.00 (ISBN 0-08-018100-7). Pergamon.
Osborne, Neville N., ed. Biochemistry of Characterized Neurons. LC 76-55379. 1978. text ed. 50.00 (ISBN 0-08-021503-3). Pergamon.
Osborne, Richard H., ed. The Biological & Social Meaning of Race. LC 75-150652. (Psychology Ser). (Illus.). 1971. text ed. 16.95x (ISBN 0-7167-0935-X); pap. text ed. 8.95x (ISBN 0-7167-0934-1). W H Freeman.
Osborne, Robert. Academy Awards Best Actor Oscar Winners. 1977. pap. 4.95 (ISBN 0-912076-03-8). ESE Calif.
--Academy Awards Best Actress Oscar Winners. 1977. pap. 4.95 (ISBN 0-912076-02-X). ESE Calif.
--Academy Awards Best Picture Oscar Winners. 1977. pap. 4.95 (ISBN 0-912076-05-4). ESE Calif.
--Academy Awards, Nineteen Seventy-Four: Oscar Annual. (Illus.). 96p. 1974. 11.95 (ISBN 0-912076-14-3). ESE Calif.
--Academy Awards Nineteen Seventy-Six Oscar Annual. (Illus.). 1976. lib. bdg. 11.95 (ISBN 0-912076-23-2); pap. 4.95 (ISBN 0-912076-22-4). ESE Calif.
--Academy Awards Nineteen Seventy-Three Oscar Annual. annual (Illus.). 96p. 1973. 11.95 (ISBN 0-912076-11-9). ESE Calif.
--Fifty Golden Years of Oscar: The Official History of the Academy of Motion Picture Arts & Sciences. (Illus.). 1979. 24.95 (ISBN 0-912076-30-5); pap. 12.97 o.s.i. (ISBN 0-912076-29-1). ESE Calif.
Osborne, Roy. Lights & Pigments: Color Principles for Artists. LC 80-8790. (Icon Editions). (Illus.). 176p. (Orig.). 1981. pap. 5.95 (ISBN 0-06-430113-3, HarpT). Har-Row.
Osborne, Ruth F., jt. auth. see Kirkendall, Lester A.
Osborne, Valerie. One Big Yo to Go. (Illus.). 32p. (gr. 1 up). 1981. 9.95 (ISBN 0-19-554265-7). Oxford U Pr.
Osborne, W. C. Fans. 1977. text ed. 26.00 (ISBN 0-08-021725-7); pap. text ed. 14.00 (ISBN 0-08-021726-5). Pergamon.
Osborne, W. H., jt. auth. see Love, Harold D.
Osborne, William S. Caroline M. Kirkland. (U. S. Authors Ser.: No. 207). lib. bdg. 10.95 (ISBN 0-8057-0424-8). Twayne.
--Lydia Maria Child. (United States Authors Ser.: No. 380). 1980. lib. bdg. 12.95 (ISBN 0-8057-7315-0). Twayne.
Osbourn, William, Jr. A Hebrew & English Lexicon to the Old Testament. 287p. 1981. pap. 5.95 (ISBN 0-310-20361-9). Zondervan.
Osburn, Bernice B., jt. auth. see Osburn, Burl N.
Osburn, Burl N. & Osburn, Bernice B. Measured Drawings of Early American Furniture. LC 74-79936. (Illus.). 96p. 1975. pap. 3.50 (ISBN 0-486-23057-0). Dover.
Osburn, Charles B. Guide to French Studies: Supplement, with Cumulative Indexes. LC 68-12638. 1972. 13.50 (ISBN 0-8108-0493-X). Scarecrow.
--Present State of French Studies: A Collection of Research Reviews. LC 78-149990. 1971. 30.00 (ISBN 0-8108-0373-9). Scarecrow.
Osburn, Donald & Schneeberger, Kenneth. Modern Agricultural Management. 2nd ed. 370p. 1982. text ed. 16.95 (ISBN 0-8359-4550-2); instr's. manual free (ISBN 0-8359-4551-0). Reston.
Osburn, Donald O. & Schneeberger, Kenneth C. Modern Agriculture Management. 1978. 16.95 (ISBN 0-87909-495-8); instrs'. manual avail. Reston.
Osburn, Robert L. Essential Mathematics for General Chemistry. LC 74-32574. 128p. 1975. text ed. 5.95 o.p. (ISBN 0-471-65704-2). Wiley.
Oschry, Leonard, tr. see Katz, Jacob.
Osei-Kwame, Peter. A New Conceptual Model for the Study of Political Integration in Africa. LC 80-5708. 307p. 1980. lib. bdg. 20.00 (ISBN 0-8191-1316-6); pap. 11.50 (ISBN 0-8191-1317-4). U Pr of Amer.
Osek, Andrzej & Skrodzki, Woljciech. Contemporary Polish Sculpture. Keplicz, Krystyna, tr. from Pol. LC 79-304319. Orig. Title: Wspolczesna Rzezba Polska. (Illus.). 160p. 1977. 15.00x (ISBN 0-8002-2296-2). Intl Pubns Serv.
Oser, Jacob. Henry George. (World Leaders Ser.). 1974. lib. bdg. 9.95 (ISBN 0-8057-3682-4). Twayne.
Osers, Ewald, tr. see Strauss, Richard & Von Hofmannsthal, Hugo.
O'Seyenko-Antonov, A. V. The Time of Stalin: Portrait of a Tyranny. LC 80-8681. (Illus.). 384p. 1981. 15.00 (ISBN 0-06-010148-2, HarpT). Har-Row.
Osgood, Arthur F. The Art of Playing Safe in Wall Street: Wall Street Discoveries Capable of Maximizing Your Stock Market Profits & of Practically Eliminating Your Stock Market Potential Losses. (Illus.). 99p. 1981. 23.75 (ISBN 0-918968-88-7). Inst Econ Finan.
Osgood, C. E. Lectures on Language Performance. (Springer Ser. in Language & Communication: Vol. 7). (Illus.). 368p. 1980. 22.00 (ISBN 0-387-09901-8). Springer-Verlag.
Osgood, Carl C. Fatigue Design. 2nd ed. (International Series on the Strenth & Fracture of Materials & Structures). 500p. 1981. 65.00 (ISBN 0-08-026167-1); pap. 33.00 (ISBN 0-08-026166-3). Pergamon.
Osgood, Charles. Nothing Could Be Finer Than a Crisis That Is Minor in the Morning. LC 79-14377. 204p. 1979. 9.95 (ISBN 0-03-047646-1); pap. 3.95 (ISBN 0-03-057646-6). HR&W.
Osgood, Charles E. Method & Theory in Experimental Psychology. 1953. text ed. 17.95x (ISBN 0-19-501008-6). Oxford U Pr.
Osgood, Charles G. Concordance to the Poems of Edmund Spenser. 1963. 35.00 (ISBN 0-8446-1332-0). Peter Smith.
Osgood, Charles G., tr. see Boccaccio, Giovanni.
Osgood, Cornelius. Jug & Related Stoneware of Bennington. LC 73-152111. (Illus.). 1971. 16.50 o.p. (ISBN 0-8048-0888-0). C E Tuttle.
Osgood, DeWitt S. Preparing for the Latter Rain. LC 73-75219. 144p. 1973. pap. 4.50 (ISBN 0-8127-0070-8). Southern Pub.
Osgood, Don. Thirty Days to a Less Stressful You. LC 80-65434. 96p. (Orig.). 1980. pap. 4.50 (ISBN 0-915684-66-7). Christian Herald.
Osgood, Henry O. So This Is Jazz. LC 77-17859. (Roots of Jazz Ser.). (Illus.). 1978. Repr. of 1926 ed. lib. bdg. 22.50 (ISBN 0-306-77540-9). Da Capo.
Osgood, Lawrence see Corrigan, Robert W.
Osgood, Robert E. Limited War Revisited. (Westview Special Study). 1979. lib. bdg. 16.50x (ISBN 0-89158-465-X). Westview.
Osgood, Samuel. French Royalism Under the Third & Fourth Republics. LC 79-2289. 1981. Repr. of 1961 ed. 19.00 (ISBN 0-88355-965-X). Hyperion Conn.
Osgood, Samuel M. Napoleon Third & the Second Empire: Buffoon, Modern Dictator, or Sphinx. 2nd ed. (Problems in European Civilization Ser). Orig. Title: Napoleon Third: Buffoon, Modern Dictator, or Sphinx. 1973. pap. text ed. 4.95x o.p. (ISBN 0-669-81653-1). Heath.
Osgood, William F. Funktionentheorie, 2 Vols. LC 63-11319. (Ger). Vol. 1. 12.50 (ISBN 0-8284-0193-4); Vol. 2. 17.50 (ISBN 0-8284-0182-9). Chelsea Pub.
Osgood, William R. How to Plan & Finance Your Business. LC 79-28070. 224p. 1980. pap. 18.95 (ISBN 0-8436-0757-2). CBI Pub.
Osguthorpe, Russel T. Manager's Guide to the Tutor-Notetaker. 122p. 1980. pap. text ed. 6.00 (ISBN 0-88200-129-9, N6796). Alexander Graham.
--Tutor-Notetaker. 98p. (Orig.). 1980. pap. text ed. 6.00 (ISBN 0-88200-131-0, N6680). Alexander Graham.
O'Shaughnessy, Arthur. An Epic of Women. Fletcher, Ian & Stokes, John, eds. LC 76-20148. (Decadent Consciousness Ser.). 1978. lib. bdg. 38.00 (ISBN 0-8240-2780-9). Garland Pub.
--Music & Moonlight. Fletcher, Ian & Stokes, John, eds. LC 76-20153. (Decadent Consciousness Ser.: Vol. 31). 1977. Repr. of 1874 ed. lib. bdg. 38.00 (ISBN 0-8240-2781-7). Garland Pub.

--Songs of a Worker. Fletcher, Ian & Stokes, John, eds. LC 76-20159. (Decadent Consciousness Ser.). 1978. lib. bdg. 38.00 (ISBN 0-8240-2782-5). Garland Pub.

O'Shaughnessy, Brian. The Will, 2 vols. LC 79-13524. 1980. Vol. 1, 240 P. 57.50 (ISBN 0-521-22679-1); Vol. 2, 360 P. 62.50 (ISBN 0-521-22680-5). Cambridge U Pr.

O'Shaughnessy, J. Business Organization. (Studies in Management). 1966. pap. text ed. 10.95x (ISBN 0-04-658043-3). Allen Unwin.

--Patterns of Business Organization. LC 76-26116. 1976. 21.95 (ISBN 0-470-98927-0). Halsted Pr.

O'Shaughnessy, P. J. Trauma. 1978. pap. 1.95 o.p. (ISBN 0-523-40359-3, Dist. by Independent News Co.). Pinnacle Bks.

O'Shay, Don K. For Whom the Trumphets Sound. 1981. 13.95 (ISBN 0-533-04840-0). Vantage.

O'Shea, Donald C., et al. Introduction to Lasers & Their Applications. (Physics Ser.). 1977. text ed. 20.95 (ISBN 0-201-05509-0). A-W.

O'Shea, Edward. Yeats As Editor. (New Yeats Papers: Vol.12). (Illus.). 141p. 1975. pap. text ed. 6.50 (ISBN 0-85105-276-2, Dolmen Pr). Humanities.

O'Shea, J., ed. see Third IFAC Symposium, Montreal, Canada, 18-20 August 1980.

O'Shea, John P. Scientific Principles & Methods of Strength Fitness. 2nd ed. LC 75-18158. (Physical Education Ser.). (Illus.). 208p. 1976. pap. text ed. 9.50 (ISBN 0-201-05517-1). A-W.

O'Shea, Kevin. The Way of Tenderness. LC 78-61728. (Orig.). 1978. pap. 2.45 (ISBN 0-8091-2166-2). Paulist Pr.

O'Shea, Lester. Tampering with the Machinery: Roots of Economic & Political Malaise. 256p. 1980. 11.95 (ISBN 0-07-047749-3, GB). McGraw.

O'Shea, Mary J. Chicago. (Rock 'n Pop Stars Ser.). (Illus.). (gr. 4-12). 1975. PLB 5.95 (ISBN 0-87191-458-1); pap. 2.95 (ISBN 0-89812-114-0). Creative Ed.

O'Shea, Patrick, jt. auth. see Kingsbury, Roy.

Osheim, Duane J. An Italian Lordship: The Bishopric of Lucca in the Late Middle Ages. (UCLA Center for Medieval & Renaissance Studies: Vol. 11). 1977. 15.75x (ISBN 0-520-03005-2). U of Cal Pr.

O'Shell, Maggie. Prisoner--Cell Block H: The Karen Travers Story, No. 3. 224p. (Orig.). 1981. pap. 2.25 (ISBN 0-523-41176-6). Pinnacle Bks.

Osherson, Daniel N. Logical Abilities in Children, 4 vols. Incl. Vol. 1. Organization of Length & Class: Empirical Consequences of a Piagetion Formulism. 11.95 (ISBN 0-470-65723-5); Vol. 2. Logical Inference. 11.95 (ISBN 0-470-65724-3); Vol. 3. Reasoning in Adolesence-Deductive Inference. LC 75-25623. 1975. 14.95 (ISBN 0-470-65730-8); Vol. 4. Reasoning & Concepts. 14.95 (ISBN 0-470-99009-0). LC 74-2298. 1974-77. Halsted Pr.

Oshima, Keichi, jt. ed. see Harris, Stuart.

Oshima, Tsutomu, tr. see Funakoshi, Gichin.

Oshinsky, David M. Senator Joe McCarthy. LC 77-18474. 1981. 12.95 (ISBN 0-02-923490-5). Free Pr.

Oshiro, Hide. Don't Run: An Illustrated Poem of Juan Ramon Jimenez. (Illus.). 1981. 2.00 (ISBN 0-934834-21-0). White Pine.

Osiek, Betty T. Jose Asuncion Silva. (World Authors Ser.: No. 505 (Columbia)). 1978. 13.50 (ISBN 0-8057-6346-5). Twayne.

Osiek, Carolyn. Galatians. (New Testament Message Ser.). 9.95 (ISBN 0-89453-135-2); pap. 4.95 (ISBN 0-89453-200-6). M Glazier.

Osing, Gordon, ed. The Good People of Gomorrah. LC 78-31841. (Illus.). 1979. pap. 6.95x (ISBN 0-918518-13-X). St Luke TN.

O'Siochain, Conchur. The Man from Cape Clear. Breatnach, Riobard P., tr. 1975. pap. 6.25 (ISBN 0-686-28551-4). Irish Bk Ctr.

Osipova, Nonna. Bridges Between Clouds. (Illus.). 61p. (Rus.). 1980. pap. 3.00 (ISBN 0-935500-03-0, TXU 9-644). Am Samizdat.

--Bridges Between Clouds. (Illus.). 100p. (Orig.). 1981. pap. 4.00 (ISBN 0-935500-07-3). Am Samizdat.

--Life-Stories. (Illus.). 60p. (Orig.). 1980. pap. 4.00 o.s.i. (ISBN 0-935500-02-2, TX198-101). Am Samizdat.

--Stories Created by Life. (Illus.). 60p. (Rus.). pap. cancelled (ISBN 0-935500-26-X, TX 198-101). Am Samizdat.

Osipow, Samuel H., ed. Emerging Woman: Career Analysis & Outlooks. (Career Programs Ser). 176p. 1975. pap. text ed. 11.95x (ISBN 0-675-08733-3). Merrill.

Osipow, Samuel H., et al. Theories of Career Development. 2nd & rev. ed. LC 68-15785. (Illus.). 1973. pap. 17.95 (ISBN 0-13-913442-5). P-H.

--A Survey of Counseling Methods. 1980. pap. 10.50x (ISBN 0-256-02189-9). Dorsey.

Osis, Karlis. Deathbed Observations by Physicians & Nurses. 3rd ed. LC 61-18247. (Parapsychological Monograph No. 3). 1961. pap. 2.50 (ISBN 0-912328-06-1). Parapsych Foun.

Osis, Karlis & Haraldsson, Erlendur. At the Hour of Death. 1980. pap. 3.95 (ISBN 0-686-69250-0, 49486, Discus). Avon.

Oskamp, S. Attitudes & Opinions. LC 76-52999. 1977. 19.95 (ISBN 0-13-050393-2). P-H.

Oskarsson, Mats. Approaches to Self-Assessment in Foreign Language Learning. (PIE Council of Europe Language Learning Ser.). 1980. pap. 4.95 (ISBN 0-08-024594-3). Pergamon.

Osler, A. Complement: Mechanisms & Functions. 1976. 22.95 (ISBN 0-13-155226-0). P-H.

Osler, Dorothy. Machine Patchwork: Technique & Design. LC 79-57311. (Illus.). 120p. 1980. 19.95 (ISBN 0-7134-3295-0, Pub. by Batsford England). David & Charles.

Osler, Jack. Fifty Great Mini-Trips for Illinois. (Illus.). 1978. pap. 2.95 o.s.i. (ISBN 0-89645-006-6). Media Ventures.

Osler, Jack & Burgin, Tricia. Fifty Great Mini-Trips for Washington D. C. - Virginia. (Jack Osler's Mini-Trip Ser.). Date not set. pap. price not set (ISBN 0-89645-009-0). Media Ventures. Postponed.

Osler, Jack & Griffin, George. Fifty Great Mini-Trips in Florida. rev ed. (Jack Osler's Mini Trips Ser.). (Illus.). Date not set. pap. cancelled (ISBN 0-89645-012-0). Media Ventures.

Osler, Robert W. & Bickley, John S., eds. Glossary of Insurance Terms. 1972. 4.95 o.p. (ISBN 0-88245-004-2); pap. 3.00 o.p. (ISBN 0-88245-005-0). Merritt Co.

Osler, William. Way of Life: An Address Delivered to Yale Students Sunday Evening, April 20, 1913. (Illus.). 56p. 1969. 6.75 (ISBN 0-398-01433-7). C C Thomas.

Osley, A. S., ed. Calligraphy & Palaeography. 1965. 19.95 o.p. (ISBN 0-571-06499-X, Pub. by Faber & Faber). Merrimack Bk Serv.

Osman, Alice H. & McConochie, Jean. If You Feel Like Singing: American Folksongs & Activities for Students of English. (Illus.). 1979. pap. text ed. 3.95x (ISBN 0-582-79724-1); cassettes 11.50x (ISBN 0-582-79725-X); cassette & book 13.50x (ISBN 0-582-78310-0). Longman.

Osman, Colin & Turner, Peter, eds. Creative Camera Collection: No. 5. (Illus.). 1978. 27.50 (ISBN 0-685-67248-4, Pub. by Two Continents). Hippocrene Bks.

Osman, Jack & Van Dolson, Bobbie J. Thin from Within. 160p. 1981. pap. write for info. (ISBN 0-8280-0027-1). Review & Herald.

Osmond, C. B., et al. Physiological Processes in Plant Ecology: Towards a Synthesis with Atriplex. (Ecololgical Studies: Vol. 36). (Illus.). 500p. 1980. 49.80 (ISBN 0-387-10060-1). Springer-Verlag.

Osmond, Humphrey, jt. auth. see Siegler, Miriam.

Osmond, Humphry, jt. auth. see Siegler, Miriam.

Osmond, N., ed. see Rimbaud, Arthur.

Osmunson, Robert L. Hannah. LC 76-22295. (Destiny Ser). 1976. pap. 4.95 (ISBN 0-8163-0256-1, 08050-7). Pacific Pr Pub Assn.

Osofsky, Gilbert. Harlem: The Making of a Ghetto, 1890-1930. LC 66-10913. 1966. 9.95 o.s.i. (ISBN 0-06-054962-9, HarpT). Har-Row.

Osofsky, Howard J. The Pregnant Teen-Ager: A Medical, Educational, & Social Analysis. (Illus.). 136p. 1972. 9.75 (ISBN 0-398-01434-5). C C Thomas.

Osofsky, Howard J. & Osofsky, Joy. Answers for New Parents: Adjusting to Your New Role. 212p. 1980. 11.95 (ISBN 0-8027-0666-5); 6.95 (ISBN 0-8027-7169-6). Walker & Co.

Osofsky, Joy, jt. auth. see Osofsky, Howard J.

Osofsky, Joy D., ed. The Handbook of Infant Development. LC 78-17605. (Personality Processes Ser.). 1979. 46.50 (ISBN 0-471-65703-4, Pub. by Wiley-Interscience). Wiley.

Osofsky, Stephen. Peter Kropotkin. (World Leaders Ser.: No. 77). 1979. lib. bdg. 13.50 (ISBN 0-8057-7724-5). Twayne.

Osorgin, Mikhail. Selected Stories, Reminiscences, & Essays. Fiene, Donald, tr. from Rus. 300p. 1981. 15.00 (ISBN 0-88233-445-X). Ardis Pubs.

Osorio, Fernando C., jt. auth. see Glorioso, Robert M.

Oss, Melvin. Sixty-Five Plus. LC 72-88857. (Better Living Ser.). 64p. 1972. pap. 0.95 (ISBN 0-8127-0063-5). Southern Pub.

Osselton, J. W., jt. auth. see Cooper, R.

Ossenberg, R. Canadian Society: Pluralism, Change & Conflict. 1971. pap. 6.95 o.p. (ISBN 0-13-113282-2). P-H.

Ossman, David. Sullen Art: Interviews with Modern American Poets. (Orig.). 1963. pap. 1.45 o.s.i. (ISBN 0-87091-053-1). Corinth Bks.

Ossowski, Stanislaw. Class Structure in the Social Consciousness. LC 63-13183. 1963. 14.95 (ISBN 0-02-923500-6). Free Pr.

Ost, Hans. Leonardo-Studien. (Beitraege Zur Kunstgeschichte: Vol. 11). (Illus.). xii, 750p. (Ger.). 1975. 78.50x (ISBN 3-11-005727-1). De Gruyter.

Ost, John W., et al. A Laboratory Introduction to Psychology. 214p. 1969. 10.95 (ISBN 0-12-528856-5). Acad Pr.

Ostberg, Donald E., jt. auth. see Finney, Ross L.

Ostby, C. Kittelsen, Theodore: Drawings & Water Colors. 1976. 60.00x (ISBN 0-686-68011-1, N-534). Vanous.

Oster, Ernst, tr. see Schenker, Heinrich.

Oster, George F., ed. Some Mathematical Questions in Biology. (Lectures on Mathematics in the Life Sciences: Vol. 13). 1980. 11.20 (ISBN 0-8218-1163-0). Am Math.

Oster, Harry. Living Country Blues. (Funk & W Bk.). (Illus.). 464p. 1976. pap. 5.95 o.s.i. (ISBN 0-308-10236-3, TYC-T). T Y Crowell.

Oster, Jerry. Municipal Bonds. 288p. 1981. 10.95 (ISBN 0-395-30538-1). HM.

Oster, Ludwig. Modern Astronomy. LC 72-83247. 500p. 1973. text ed. 18.95x (ISBN 0-8162-6523-2). Holden-Day.

Oster, Merrill J., et al. Multiply Your Money Trading Soybeans: A Beginner's Guide to Speculating in Soybean Futures. 198p. 1981. 14.95 (ISBN 0-914230-10-7). Investor Pubns.

Oster, Rick. Acts of the Apostles, Pt. 2. LC 79-63268. (Living Word Commentary Ser.: Vol. 6). 1979. 7.95 (ISBN 0-8344-0099-5). Sweet.

Oster, S. M., et al. The Definition & Measurement of Poverty: A Review, Vol. 1. LC 77-5233. 1977. lib. bdg. 26.50x (ISBN 0-89158-245-2). Westview.

Oster, Sharon M., et al, eds. The Definition & Measurement of Poverty: Annotated Bibliography, Vol. 2. LC 77-5233. (Westview Special Studies in Applied Social Research Ser.). 1978. lib. bdg. 37.50x (ISBN 0-89158-246-0). Westview.

Osterbind, Carter C., ed. New Careers for Older People. LC 53-12339. (Center for Gerontological Studies & Programs Ser.: Vol. 20). 1971. pap. 4.25 (ISBN 0-8130-0332-6). U Presses Fla.

Osterbrock, Donald E. Astrophysics of Gaseous Nebulae. LC 74-11264. (Astronomy & Astrophysics Ser.). (Illus.). 1974. text ed. 29.95x (ISBN 0-7167-0348-3). W H Freeman.

Osterburg, James W., jt. auth. see O'Hara, Charles E.

Ostergaard, Donald. Gynecologic Urology & Urodynamics: Theory & Practice. (Illus.). 374p. 1980. lib. bdg. 40.00 (ISBN 0-683-06645-5). Williams & Wilkins.

Ostergard, Susan, et al. The Metric World: A Survival Guide. LC 75-6919. (Illus.). 176p. 1975. pap. text ed. 9.50 (ISBN 0-8299-0059-4); instrs.' manual avail. (ISBN 0-8299-0605-3). West Pub.

Osterhaven, M. Eugene, jt. tr. see Miller, Allen O.

Osterheld, William, jt. auth. see Slurzberg, Morris.

Osterholm, Jewell L. The Pathophysiology of Spinal Cord Trauma. (Illus.). 232p. 1978. 22.75 (ISBN 0-398-03705-1). C C Thomas.

Osterhoudt, Robert G., ed. The Philosophy of Sport: A Collection of Original Essays. 374p. 1973. 18.75 (ISBN 0-398-02871-0). C C Thomas.

Osterhout, Connie, ed. see IFSTA Committee.

Osterhout, Connie, jt. ed. see Laughlin, Jerry.

Osterhout, Connie, et al, eds. see IFSTA Committee.

Osterhout, Marilyn M., ed. Decontamination & Decommissioning of Nuclear Facilities. 820p. 1980. 75.00 (ISBN 0-306-40429-X, Plenum Pr). Plenum Pub.

Osterloh, William J. Police Supervisory Practice. LC 74-23482. 1975. text ed. 15.95x o.p. (ISBN 0-471-65712-3). Wiley.

Osterlund, Steven. Twenty Love Poems. 1977. pap. 2.95 (ISBN 0-931534-05-4). Windflower Pr.

Ostermann, Georg von see Von Ostermann, Georg F.

Ostermoeller, Wolfgang. Fish Breeding Recipes. (Illus.). 1973. pap. 5.95 (ISBN 0-87666-071-5, PS-693). TFH Pubns.

Osterrieth, P., et al. Improving Education for Disadvantaged Children: Some Belgian Studies. LC 79-4086. 1979. 28.00 (ISBN 0-08-024265-0). Pergamon.

Osterud, Oivind. Agrarian Structure & Peasant Politics in Scandinavia. 1978. pap. 19.00x (ISBN 82-00-01702-8, Dist. by Columbia U Pr.). Universitet.

Osteryoung, Jerome S. Capital Budgeting: Long-Term Asset Selection. 2nd ed. LC 77-85044. (Finance Ser.). 1979. text ed. 20.95 (ISBN 0-88244-139-6). Grid Pub.

--Financial Management: Self-Correcting Problems. (Finance & Real Estate Ser.). 1976. pap. text ed. 7.95 o.p. (ISBN 0-88244-105-1). Grid Pub.

Osteryoung, Jerome S. & McCarty, Daniel E. Analytical Techniques for Financial Management. LC 79-17196. (Finance Ser.). 1980. pap. text ed. 11.95 (ISBN 0-88244-196-5). Grid Pub.

Ostino, Guiseppe, ed. see Symposium Milan, Italy, November 1978.

Ostler, Carolyn H. Collecting People: Your Ancestors & Mine. (gr. 6 up). 1981. 10.00x (ISBN 0-686-08736-4). Genealog Inst.

Ostlere, Gordon & Bryce-Smith, Roger. Anaesthetics for Medical Students. 9th ed. 148p. 1981. text ed. 9.75 (ISBN 0-443-01863-4). Churchill.

Ostman, Ronald E., ed. Communication Research & Drug Education. LC 75-11132. (International Yearbooks of Drug Addiction & Society: Vol. 3). 1976. 20.00x (ISBN 0-8039-0420-7); pap. 9.95x (ISBN 0-8039-0511-4). Sage.

Ostor, Akos. The Play of the Gods: Locality, Ideology, Structure & Time in the Festivals of a Bengali Town. LC 79-25661. 264p. 1980. lib. bdg. 27.00x (ISBN 0-226-63954-1). U of Chicago Pr.

Ostova, Pat. Great Danes in Canada. 1980. 19.95 (ISBN 0-87714-080-4). Caroline Hse.

Ostovar, Terry. Fly Through the Baha'i Year. (Illus.). 48p. (Orig.). (gr. 2-6). 1980. pap. 4.95 (ISBN 0-933770-13-8). Kalimat.

Ostow, Miriam, jt. auth. see Ginzberg, Eli.

Ostrander, Lee E. Proceedings of the Seventh New England (Northeast) Bioengineering Conference: Held March 22-23, 1979, at Rensselaer Polytechnic Institute, Troy, New York. LC 79-83927. (New England Bio-Engineering Conference Ser.: Vol. 7). (Illus.). 1979. 62.00 (ISBN 0-08-024634-6). Pergamon.

Ostrander, Linda, jt. auth. see Owyang, Lily.

Ostrander, Sheila. Etiquette for Today. (Illus., Orig.). (gr. 9-12). 1967. pap. 3.50 (ISBN 0-06-463272-5, EH 272, EH). Har-Row.

Ostrander, Sheila & Schroeder, Lynn. Handbook of PSI Discoveries. (Illus.). 224p. 1974. 9.95 o.p. (ISBN 0-399-11288-X, Dist. by Putnam). Berkley Pub.

--Psychic Experience: ESP Investigated. LC 77-79512. (gr. 5 up). 1977. 7.95 o.p. (ISBN 0-8069-3092-6); PLB 7.49 o.p. (ISBN 0-8069-3093-4). Sterling.

Ostriker, Alicia. A Dream of Springtime. LC 78-59769. (Illus., Orig.). 1979. pap. 3.50 (ISBN 0-912292-52-0). The Smith.

Ostrogorskii, Moisei A. The Rights of Women: A Comparative Study in History & Legislation. Repr. of 1893 ed. lib. bdg. 16.00x (ISBN 0-87991-960-4). Porcupine Pr.

Ostrom, Elinor. Decision-Related Research on the Organization of Service Delivery Systems in Metropolitan Areas: Police Protection. LC 79-83821. 1979. codebook 26.00 (ISBN 0-89138-983-0). ICPSR.

Ostrosky, Anthony L., Jr. & Koch, James V. Introduction to Mathematical Economics. LC 78-69569. (Illus.). 1979. text ed. 18.95 (ISBN 0-395-27052-9); solutions manual 1.10 (ISBN 0-395-27053-7). HM.

Ostrovsky see Bentley, Eric.

Ostrovsky, Everett. Self Discovery & Social Awareness. LC 73-17333. 320p. 1974. pap. text ed. 12.95x o.p. (ISBN 0-471-65716-6). Wiley.

Ostrow, Eileen J., ed. Center Stage: An Anthology of 21 Contemporary Black American Plays. LC 80-53143. (Illus.). 352p. (Orig.). 1981. pap. price not set. Sea Urchin.

Ostrow, Marshall. Bettas. (Illus.). 96p. 1980. 2.95 (ISBN 0-87666-522-9, KW052). TFH Pubns.

Ostrowsky, O. Engineering Drawing for Technicians, Vol. 1. (Illus.). 94p. 1979. pap. 11.00x (ISBN 0-7131-3408-9). Intl Ideas.

Ostwald, Martin, ed. see Plato.

Ostwald, Martin, tr. see Aristotle.

Ostwald, Martin, tr. see Plato.

O'Suilleabhain, Sean. Handbook of Irish Folklore. LC 73-129100. 1970. Repr. of 1942 ed. 30.00 (ISBN 0-8103-3561-1). Gale.

O'Sullivan, Bernard J., compiled by. Bloodstock Sales Analysis, 1962. 1.75 (ISBN 0-85131-058-3, Dist. by Sporting Book Center). J A Allen.

O'Sullivan, Gahagan. Sure & There's More. (Contemporary Poets of Dorrance Ser.). 64p. 1981. 3.95 (ISBN 0-8059-2781-6). Dorrance.

O'Sullivan, Humphrey. The Diary of Humphrey O'Sullivan 1827-1835. De Bhaldraithe, Tomas, tr. from Irish. Orig. Title: Cin Lae Amhlaoibh. (Illus.). 139p. 1979. pap. 5.50 (ISBN 0-85342-588-4). Irish Bk Ctr.

O'Sullivan, James N., ed. Lexicon to Achilles Tatius. (Unter Suchungen Zur Antiken Literatur und Gesschichte: No. 18). 442p. 1980. text ed. 124.00x (ISBN 3-11-007844-9). De Gruyter.

O'Sullivan, Jeremiah F., tr. see Idung Of Prufening.

O'Sullivan, P., jt. auth. see Chisholm, M.

O'Sullivan, Patrick. Geographical Economics. 195p. 1981. 24.95 (ISBN 0-470-27122-1). Halsted Pr.

--The Sabbath of the New Testament. (Illus.). 52p. 1981. pap. 2.50 (ISBN 0-933464-12-6). D M Battle Pubns.
--Transport Policy: Geographic, Economic & Planning Aspects. 1981. 22.50x (ISBN 0-389-20143-X). B&N.
O'Sullivan, Sean. The Folklore of Ireland. 1974. 19.95 (ISBN 0-7134-2803-1, Pub. by Batsford England). David & Charles.
O'Sullivan, Susan B., et al. Physical Rehabilitation: Evaluation & Treatment Procedures. LC 80-10890. (Illus.). 521p. 1980. pap. text ed. 23.50 (ISBN 0-8036-6697-7). Davis Co.
O'Sullivan, Tim. Glitter Street. 1981. pap. 2.75 (ISBN 0-440-12902-8). Dell.
O'Sullivan, Timothy. Julian Hooge: A Biography. 1981. price not set (ISBN 0-7100-0592-X). Routledge & Kegan.
O'Sullivan, Vincent. The Houses of Sin, Repr. Of 1897 Ed. Fletcher, Ian & Stokes, John, eds. Bd. with Poems. Sullivan, Vincent. LC 76-25930. (Decadent Consciousness Ser.: Vol. 33). 1977. lib. bdg. 38.00 (ISBN 0-8240-2783-3). Garland Pub.
O'Sullivan, Vincent, ed. Anthology of Twentieth-Century New Zealand Poetry. (Oxford Paperbacks Ser). 1970. pap. 6.50x o.p. (ISBN 0-19-281092-8). Oxford U Pr.
Osuntokun, Akinjide. Nigeria in the First World War. (Ibadan History Ser.). 1979. text ed. 30.75x (ISBN 0-391-00916-8). Humanities.
Oswald, Helen. Precious Harvest. LC 79-88027. (Destiny Ser.). 1979. pap. 4.95 (ISBN 0-8163-0326-6, 16496-2). Pacific Pr Pub Assn.
Oswald, J. W., jt. auth. see Krar, S. F.
Oswald, John C. Benjamin Franklin, Printer. LC 74-3020. 1974. Repr. of 1917 ed. 24.00 (ISBN 0-8103-3642-1). Gale.
Oswald, Russell G. Attica: My Story. LC 72-77002. 1972. 7.95 o.p. (ISBN 0-385-08199-5). Doubleday.
Oswalk, Ellen K. That Book in the Attic. LC 63-22374. 1963. pap. 4.95 (ISBN 0-8163-0146-8, 20240-8). Pacific Pr Pub Assn.
Oswalt, Wendell H. Eskimos & Explorers. LC 78-10723. (Illus.). 368p. 1979. 15.00 (ISBN 0-88316-532-5). Chandler & Sharp.
--Kolmakovskiy Redoubt: The Ethnoarchaeology of a Russian Fort in Alaska. LC 80-53304. (Monumenta Archaeologica Ser.: No. 8). (Illus.). 212p. 1980. 10.50 (ISBN 0-917956-17-6). UCLA Arch.
--This Land Was Theirs: A Study of North American Indians. 3rd ed. LC 77-14986. 1978. text ed. 20.95 (ISBN 0-471-02342-6). Wiley.
Oswalt, Wendell H., et al. An Anthropological Analysis of Food-Getting Technology. LC 76-17640. 1976. 27.50 (ISBN 0-471-65729-8, Pub. by Wiley-Interscience). Wiley.
Oswin, jt. auth. see Cairns.
Oswin, Maureen. Holes in the Welfare Net. 168p. 1978. text ed. 13.75x (ISBN 0-7199-0939-2, Pub. by Bedford England). Renouf.
Otaki, Tadao, jt. auth. see Draeger, Donn F.
Otanes, Fe T., jt. auth. see Schachter, Paul.
Oteri, Laura, ed. see International Conference, Geneva, 1974.
Oteri, Laura, jt. ed. see Van Over, Raymond.
Otero, Lisandro. Cultural Policy in Cuba. (Studies & Documents on Cultural Policies). 55p. (Orig.). 1972. pap. 4.75 (ISBN 92-3-100967-2, U114, UNESCO). Unipub.
Otero, Ray, ed. see De Ford, Tamara.
Otero, Raymond B. Laboratory Exercises in Microbiology. 200p. 1973. 4.95 o.p. (ISBN 0-397-54147-3). Lippincott.
--Laboratory Exercises in Microbiology. 2nd ed. 1977. pap. text ed. 6.50 (ISBN 0-8403-1743-3). Kendall-Hunt.
Otfinoski, Steve. Death on Wheels. Verdick, Mary, ed. (Pal Paperbacks, Pal Skills Ser.). (Illus., Orig.). (gr. 7-12). 1978. pap. text ed. 1.25 (ISBN 0-8374-6708-X). Xerox Ed Pubns.
--The Monster That Wouldn't Die. Verdick, Mary, ed. (Pal Paperbacks Ser., Kit A). (Illus., Orig.). (gr. 7-12). 1976. pap. text ed. 1.25 (ISBN 0-8374-3497-1). Xerox Ed Pubns.
Otfinoski, Steven. High Flier. Verdick, Mary, ed. (Beginning Pal Paperbacks Ser.). (Illus., Orig.). (gr. 7-12). 1977. pap. text ed. 1.25 (ISBN 0-8374-3459-9). Xerox Ed Pubns.
--Monsters to Know & Love. Verdick, Mary, ed. (Beginning Pal Paperbacks Ser.). (Illus., Orig.). (gr. 7-12). 1977. pap. text ed. 1.25 (ISBN 0-8374-3455-6). Xerox Ed Pubns.
--The Red Ghost. Verdick, Mary, ed. (Beginning Pal Paperbacks Ser.). (Illus., Orig.). (gr. 7-12). 1977. pap. text ed. 1.25 (ISBN 0-8374-3466-1). Xerox Ed Pubns.
--Sky Ride. Mooney, Thomas J., ed. (Beginning Pal Paperbacks Ser.). (Illus., Orig.). (gr. 7-12). 1977. pap. text ed. 1.25 (ISBN 0-8374-3450-5). Xerox Ed Pubns.
--The Third Arm. Verdick, Mary, ed. (Beginning Pal Paperbacks Ser.). (Illus., Orig.). (gr. 7-12). pap. text ed. 1.25 (ISBN 0-8374-3464-5). Xerox Ed Pubns.
--The Verlaine Crossing. LC 78-15460. (Pacesetters Ser.). (Illus.). (gr. 4 up). 1978. PLB 7.95 (ISBN 0-516-02161-3). Childrens.
--The World's Darkest Days. Mooney, Thomas J., ed. (Beginning Pal Paperbacks Ser.). (Illus., Orig.). (gr. 7-12). 1977. pap. text ed. 1.25 (ISBN 0-8374-3462-9). Xerox Ed Pubns.
--The Zombie Maker. Uhlich, Richard, ed. (Bluejeans Paperback Ser.). (Illus., Orig.). (gr. 7-12). 1978. pap. text ed. 1.25 (ISBN 0-8374-5002-0). Xerox Ed Pubns.
Otfinoski, Steven, ed. Fun for All. (Beginning Pal Paperbacks Ser.). (Illus., Orig.). (gr. 7-12). 1977. pap. text ed. 1.25 (ISBN 0-8374-3467-X). Xerox Ed Pubns.
Othmer, jt. auth. see Kirk.
Othmer, D. F., jt. ed. see Kirk, R. E.
Otis, Brooks. Ovid As an Epic Poet. 2nd ed. LC 75-96098. 1971. 56.00 (ISBN 0-521-07615-3). Cambridge U Pr.
Otis, Calvin N. A Practical Guidebook in "Spontaneous" Art. (A Promotion of the Arts Library Book). (Illus.). 123p. 1981. 29.85 (ISBN 0-930582-99-3). Gloucester Art.
Otis, D. S. The Dawes Act & the Allotment of Indian Land. (Civilization of the American Indian Ser.: Vol. 123). 215p. 1973. 9.95x (ISBN 0-8061-1039-2). U of Okla Pr.
Otis, Denise & Maia, Ronaldo. Decorating with Flowers. (Illus.). 1978. 40.00 (ISBN 0-8109-0808-5). Abrams.
Otis, Don. Keeping Fit. 1979. pap. 2.25 (ISBN 0-89728-013-X). Omega Pubns OR.
Otis, George. The Blue Print. pap. 1.95 (ISBN 0-89728-021-0, 564816). Omega Pubns OR.
--Eldridge Cleaver: Ice & Fire. pap. 1.95 (ISBN 0-89728-026-1, 664956). Omega Pubns OR.
--The Ghost of Hagar. pap. 2.50 (ISBN 0-89728-033-4, 581116). Omega Pubns OR.
--God, Money & You. pap. 1.95 (ISBN 0-89728-034-2, 546638). Omega Pubns OR.
--God, Money & You. 1975. pap. 1.50 (ISBN 0-89129-004-4). Jove Pubns.
--The God They Never Knew. 1978. pap. 3.95 (ISBN 0-89728-011-3, 678276). Omega Pubns OR.
--High Adventure. pap. 1.95 (ISBN 0-89728-036-9, 533135). Omega Pubns OR.
--High Adventure. 1977. pap. 1.50 (ISBN 0-89129-014-1). Jove Pubns.
--Jesus: 220 Names. pap. 1.50 (ISBN 0-89728-041-5, 533144). Omega Pubns OR.
--Millennium Man. 8.95; pap. 4.95 (ISBN 0-89728-043-1, 615644). Omega Pubns OR.
--Peace, Power & Happiness. Orig. Title: Like a Roaring Lion. pap. 1.95 (ISBN 0-89728-051-2, 658302). Omega Pubns OR.
--Thunder of His Power. 1978. 5.95 (ISBN 0-89728-012-1). Omega Pubns OR.
--You Shall Receive. pap. 1.50 (ISBN 0-89728-064-4, 533250). Omega Pubns OR.
Otis, George & Walker, Mary. God, the Holy Spirit. pap. 1.25 (ISBN 0-685-60971-5, 532877). Omega Pubns OR.
Otis, George, Jr. The Polished Pilgrim. pap. 1.50 (ISBN 0-89728-053-9, 533180). Omega Pubns OR.
Otis, James. Toby Tyler: Or, Ten Weeks with a Circus. LC 75-32185. (Classics of Children's Literature, 1621-1932: Vol. 48). 1977. Repr. of 1881 ed. PLB 38.00 (ISBN 0-8240-2297-1). Garland Pub.
Otis, Jay L. & Leukart, R. H. Job Evaluation. 2nd ed. 1954. ref. ed. 19.95 (ISBN 0-13-509562-X). P-H.
Otis, Jorge, tr. Como Leon Rugiente. (Spanish Bks.). (Span.). 1978. 1.90 (ISBN 0-8297-0516-3). Life Pubs Intl.
Otis, Raymond. Little Valley. LC 79-56813. (Zia Bks.). 285p. 1980. pap. 5.95 (ISBN 0-8263-0534-2). U of NM Pr.
Otis, Todd. Hidden Power. 150p. (Orig.). 1980. text ed. cancelled (ISBN 0-936106-02-6); pap. cancelled (ISBN 0-686-65870-1). River Basin.
Otnes, Robert K. & Enochson, Loren. Digital Time Series Analysis. LC 72-637. (Wiley Series in Probability & Mathematical Statistics: Applied Probability & Statistics Section). 552p. 1972. 32.95 (ISBN 0-471-65719-0, Pub. by Wiley-Interscience). Wiley.
Oton, E. U., ed. Nigeria's Educator-Statesman: Selected Writings of Eyo Ita. 1980. 25.00x (ISBN 0-7146-2731-3, F Cass Co). Biblio Dist.
O'Toole, Edward J. Mystery of Commitment. LC 68-55034. 1969. 3.95 o.p. (ISBN 0-8189-0098-9). Alba.
O'Toole, Edward T. How to Gain Financial Independence. (Orig.). pap. 1.50 o.p. (ISBN 0-671-10344-X, Pub by S & S). Benjamin Co.
O'Toole, G. J. The Cosgrove Report. 1981. pap. 2.95 (ISBN 0-440-11594-9). Dell.
O'Toole, George. The Assassination Tapes. LC 74-21057. 1975. 8.95 o.p. (ISBN 0-89110-000-8). Penthouse Pr.
O'Toole, James. Making America Work: Productivity & Responsibility. 244p. 1981. 14.95 (ISBN 0-8264-0045-0). Continuum.
O'Toole, Roger S. Stag at Large. LC 68-19824. 1968. 5.95 o.s.i. (ISBN 0-02-594060-0). Macmillan.
O'Toole, Thomas, tr. see Kalck, Pierre.
O'Toole, Thomas E. Historical Dictionary of Guinea: Republic of Guinea-Conakry. LC 77-28145. (African Historical Dictionaries Ser.: No. 16). 1978. 9.50 (ISBN 0-8108-1112-X). Scarecrow.
Otsu, T. & Takayanagi, M., eds. Progress in Polymer Science, Japan, Vol. 7. (Ser. of Progress in Polymer Science in Japan). 1974. 39.95 (ISBN 0-470-65725-1). Halsted Pr.
Otsuka, Masanori & Hall, Z. W., eds. Neurobiology of Chemical Transmission. LC 78-24602. 1979. 31.50 (ISBN 0-471-03974-8, Pub. by Wiley-Medical). Wiley.
Otsuka, Sei, jt. ed. see Newton, William E.
Otsuka, Yuzo. Suho & the White Horse. Herring, Ann, tr. from Japanese. LC 80-26789. (Illus.). 48p. (gr. k-3). 1981. 10.95 (ISBN 0-670-68149-0). Viking Pr.
Ott, jt. auth. see Mendenhall.
Ott, Attiat F., jt. auth. see Ott, David J.
Ott, David J. & Ott, Attiat F. Federal Budget Policy. 3rd ed. (Studies of Government Finance). 1977. 12.95 (ISBN 0-8157-6710-2); pap. 4.95 (ISBN 0-8157-6709-9). Brookings.
Ott, Gil. Maize. (Illus.). 1980. ltd. signed ed. 20.00x (ISBN 0-915316-70-6); pap. 5.00x (ISBN 0-915316-69-2). Pentagram.
Ott, John N. The Dynamics of Color & Light: How They Affect Human Health & Behavior. (Illus.). 256p. 1981. 10.00 (ISBN 0-8159-5314-3). Devin.
Ott, Jonathan & Bigwood, Jeremy, eds. Teonanacatl: Hallucinogenic Mushrooms of North America. LC 78-14794. 1978. 14.50 (ISBN 0-914842-32-3); pap. 8.95 (ISBN 0-914842-29-3). Madrona Pubs.
Ott, Richard F., ed. see Vistnes, Lars M., et al.
Ott, Thomas O. The Haitian Revolution, 1789-1804. LC 72-85085. (Illus.). 1973. 12.50x (ISBN 0-87049-143-1). U of Tenn Pr.
Ott, William G., jt. auth. see Rosenberg, R. Robert.
Ottaway, David & Ottaway, Marina. Afrocommunism. LC 80-24289. (New Library of African Affairs Ser.). 320p. 1981. text ed. 25.00x (ISBN 0-8419-0664-5, Africana). Holmes & Meier.
--Algeria: The Politics of a Socialist Revolution. LC 70-83210. (Illus.). 1970. 20.00x (ISBN 0-520-01655-6). U of Cal Pr.
Ottaway, Hugh. Shostakovich Symphonies. LC 77-82651. (BBC Music Guides: No. 39). (Illus.). 64p. (Orig.). 1978. pap. 2.95 (ISBN 0-295-95573-2). U of Wash Pr.
Ottaway, Hugh & Hutchings, Arthur. Pelican History of Music, Vol. 3, Classical & Romantic. Stevens, Denis & Robertson, Alec, eds. (Orig.). 1968. pap. 2.50 o.p. (ISBN 0-14-020494-6, Pelican). Penguin.
Ottaway, J. M. & Ure, A. M. Practical Atomic Absorption Spectrometry. Date not set. 30.00 (ISBN 0-08-023800-9). Pergamon.
Ottaway, Marina, jt. auth. see Ottaway, David.
Otte, E., jt. auth. see Lockhart, J.
Otte, H. M. & Locke, S. R., eds. Materials Science Research Series, Vol. 2. LC 63-17645. 319p. 1965. 39.50 (ISBN 0-306-38502-3, Plenum Pr). Plenum Pub.
Otten, Anna, ed. Meistererzahlungen. (Orig., Ger.). 1969. pap. text ed. 8.50 (ISBN 0-13-574251-X). P-H.
--Mensch und Zeit: An Anthology of German Radio Plays. Incl. Knopfe. Aichinger, Ilse; Schildkrotenspiel. Von Der Vring, Georg; Verschlossene Tur. Von Hoerschelmann, Fred; Zinngeschrei. Eich, Gunter; Begegnung in Balkanexpress. Hildesheimer, Wolfgang; Nachtliches Gesprach Mit Einem Verachteten Menschen. Durrenmatt, Friedrich. LC 66-19203. (Illus., Orig., Ger.). 1966. pap. text ed. 5.95x (ISBN 0-89197-300-1); script 1.00x (ISBN 0-89197-301-X). Irvington.
--Voix et silences: Les Meilleures pieces radiophoniques francaises. Incl. Silences de Paris. Camus, Albert & Vives, V.; Une L'arme. Forest, Jean & Clair, Rene.; C'est vrai mais il ne faut pas le croire. Aveline, Claude; Frederic General. Constant, Jacques; Interview. Pinget, Robert. LC 68-11212. (Illus., Fr.). 1968. pap. text ed. 5.95x (ISBN 0-89197-466-0). Irvington.
Otten, C. Michael. Power, Values, & Society: An Introduction to Sociology. 1981. pap. text ed. 11.95x (ISBN 0-673-15260-X). Scott F.
--University Authority & the Student: The Berkeley Experience. LC 72-99485. (Illus.). 1970. 19.50x (ISBN 0-520-01607-6). U of Cal Pr.
Otten, Charlotte M., ed. Aggression & Evolution. LC 79-179422. 1973. text ed. 7.50 o.p. (ISBN 0-471-00407-3). Wiley.
--Anthropology & Art: Readings in Cross-Cultural Aesthetics. LC 75-43853. (Texas Press Source Books in Anthropology: No. 10). 1976. pap. 9.95 (ISBN 0-292-70313-9). U of Tex Pr.
Otten, Jane & Shelley, Florence D. When Your Parents Grow Old. LC 76-10697. (Funk & W Bk.). 1976. 9.95 o.s.i. (ISBN 0-308-10256-8, TYC-T). T Y Crowell.
Otten, Terry. The Deserted Stage: The Search for Dramatic Form in Nineteenth-Century England. LC 74-181685. 200p. 1972. 9.50x o.p. (ISBN 0-8214-0102-5). Ohio U Pr.
Ottersen, Signe R., ed. see International Institute for Environment & Development (I.I.E.D.).
Ottesen, Frances. Sun-Spaces. (Illus.). 76p. 1981. 7.95 (ISBN 0-9605220-0-X). Otafra.
Ottesen, Walter O., jt. auth. see Apfelbaum, H. Jack.
Ottewell, Guy. Astronomical Calendar: 1981. (Illus.). 1980. pap. 8.00 (ISBN 0-934546-04-5). Astron Cal.
--Astronomical Companion. (Illus.). 1979. pap. 12.00 (ISBN 0-934546-01-0). Astron Cal.
--The View from the Earth, 1981. (Illus.). 1980. pap. 4.00 (ISBN 0-934546-05-3). Astron Cal.
Ottis, Kenneth, et al. Experimental Animal Physiology: A Contemporary Systems Approach. 3rd ed. (Orig.). 1980. pap. text ed. 11.95 (ISBN 0-8403-2151-1). Kendall-Hunt.
Ottley, Reginald. Bates Family. LC 69-18627. (gr. 4-6). 1969. 4.50 o.p. (ISBN 0-15-205726-9, HJ). HarBraceJ.
Ottley, William Y. An Inquiry into the Origin & Early History of Engraving Upon Copper & Wood, 2 vols. Freedberg, Sydney J., ed. LC 77-25757. (Connoisseurship Criticism & Art History Ser.: Vol. 14). 835p. 1979. Set. lib. bdg. 80.00 (ISBN 0-8240-3272-1). Garland Pub.
--The Italian School of Design; Being a Series of Facsimiles of Original Drawings by the Most Eminent Painters & Sculptors of Italy, 3 vols. Freedberg, Sydney J., ed. LC 77-25758. (Connoisseurship Criticism & Art History Ser.: Vol. 15). (Illus.). 1980. Set. lib. bdg. 250.00 (ISBN 0-8240-3273-X). Garland Pub.
Ottman, R. More Music for Sight Singing. 1981. pap. 11.95 (ISBN 0-13-601211-6). P-H.
Ottman, Robert & Mainous, Frank. Programmed Rudiments of Music. 1979. pap. 14.95 (ISBN 0-13-729962-1). P-H.
Ottman, Robert W. Advanced Harmony: Theory & Practice. 2nd ed. LC 72-173655. (Illus.). 304p. 1972. text ed. 17.50 (ISBN 0-13-012955-0). P-H.
--Elementary Harmony: Theory & Practice. 2nd ed. LC 70-105451. 1970. text ed. 16.95 (ISBN 0-13-257451-9); wkbk 10.95 (ISBN 0-13-257469-1). P-H.
--Music for Sight Singing. 2nd ed. 1967. pap. text ed. 11.95 (ISBN 0-13-607440-5). P-H.
Ottman, Robert W. & Mainous, Frank D. Rudiments of Music. 1970. pap. text ed. 14.95 (ISBN 0-13-783662-7). P-H.
Otto, C. P. & Glaser, R. O. The Management of Training: A Handbook for Training Directors. 1970. 20.95 (ISBN 0-201-05510-4). A-W.
Otto, Frei, et al. Il Twenty Tasks. (Illus.). 334p. (Orig., Eng. & Ger.). 1979. lib. bdg. write for info. (ISBN 0-8150-0905-4). Wittenborn.
Otto, Henry J. & Sanders, David C. Elementary School Organization & Administration. 4th ed. LC 64-11518. (Illus.). 1960. text ed. 24.50x (ISBN 0-89197-529-2); pap. text ed. 12.95x (ISBN 0-89197-743-0). Irvington.
Otto, Herbert A., ed. Family in Search of a Future: Alternate Models for Moderns. LC 75-111879. 1970. pap. text ed. 9.95 (ISBN 0-13-302869-0). P-H.
--Marriage & Family Enrichment: New Perspectives & Programs. LC 75-30743. 1976. 14.95 (ISBN 0-687-23621-5); pap. 8.95 (ISBN 0-687-23620-7). Abingdon.
Otto, Herbert A. & Knight, James W., eds. Dimensions in Wholistic Healing: New Frontiers in the Treatment of the Whole Person. LC 78-27071. 1979. 23.95 (ISBN 0-88229-513-6); pap. text ed. 13.95 (ISBN 0-88229-697-3). Nelson-Hall.
Otto, Herbert R. The Linguistic Basis of Logic Translation. LC 78-63261. 1978. pap. text ed. 9.25 (ISBN 0-8191-0617-8). U Pr of Amer.
Otto, John A., tr. see Oury, Guy-Marie.
Otto, Lois, jt. auth. see Fields, Joanne.
Otto, Rudolf. Idea of the Holy: An Inquiry into the Non-Rational Factor in the Idea of the Divine & Its Relation to the Rational. 2nd ed. Harvey, John W., tr. 1950. 10.95 o.p. (ISBN 0-19-501331-X). Oxford U Pr.
Otto, Rudolph. Mysticism East & West. 1970. pap. 2.95 o.s.i. (ISBN 0-02-088230-0, Collier). Macmillan.
Otto, Svend. Taxi Dog. LC 77-24127. (Illus.). 40p. (ps-3). 1978. PLB 7.95 (ISBN 0-590-07722-8, Four Winds). Schol Bk Serv.
Otto, Svend S., illus. Tom Thumb. (Grimm's Fairy Tales). (Illus.). (gr. 2). 1976. PLB 4.95 (ISBN 0-88332-043-6, 8077). Larousse.
Otto, Walter F. Dionysus: Myth & Cult. Palmer, Robert B., tr. LC 65-11792. (Midland Bks.: No. 95). (Illus.). 1965. pap. 2.95x o.p. (ISBN 0-253-20095-4). Ind U Pr.

Otto, Wayne & Chester, Robert D. Objective Based Reading. LC 75-12100. (Illus.). 288p. 1976. text ed. 7.95 (ISBN 0-201-19311-6); tchr's guide 2.95 (ISBN 0-201-19321-3). A-W.

Otto, Wayne & Smith, Richard J. Corrective & Remedial Teaching. 3rd ed. LC 79-89740. (Illus.). 1980. text ed. 17.95 (ISBN 0-395-28355-8). HM.

Otto, Wayne, et al. Reading Problems: A Multidisciplinary Perspective. LC 76-23987. (Illus.). 1977. text ed. 17.95 (ISBN 0-201-05513-9). A-W.

--Corrective & Remedial Teaching. 2nd ed. LC 72-4799. 500p. 1973. text ed. 17.95 o.p. (ISBN 0-395-12662-2, 3-42395). HM.

Ottobre, Frances M., ed. see International Association for Educational Assessment, Third Annual Conference Narrobi, May 23, 1977.

Ottoson, Robert. A Reference Guie to the American Film Noir: 1940-1958. LC 80-23176. 290p. 1981. 15.00 (ISBN 0-8108-1363-7). Scarecrow.

Ottum, Bob. The Airplane Book. (ps-1). 1972. PLB 5.38 (ISBN 0-307-68936-0, Golden Pr). Western Pub.

--Big & Little Are Not the Same. (Tell-a-Tale Reader). 32p. (ps-3). 1980. PLB 4.77 (ISBN 0-307-68422-9, Golden Pr). Western Pub.

--Cars. (Illus.). (ps-1). 1973. PLB 5.00 (ISBN 0-307-60566-3, Golden Pr). Western Pub.

--See the Kid Run. 272p. 1981. pap. 2.75 (ISBN 0-446-95123-4). Warner Bks.

--The Tuesday Blade. 368p. 1978. pap. 2.75 (ISBN 0-446-95643-0). Warner Bks.

Ottum, Bob, ed. The Three Bears. (Illus.). (ps-1). 1973. PLB 5.38 (ISBN 0-307-68971-9, Golden Pr). Western Pub.

Ottun, Bob. Los Aviones. Sanchez, Rene, tr. (ps-3). 1977. PLB 5.92 o.p. (ISBN 0-307-68836-4, Golden Pr). Western Pub.

O'Tuama, Sean & Kinsella, Thomas. An Dunaire, Sixteen Hundred to Nineteen Hundred: Poems of the Dispossessed. (Illus.). 432p. 1980. text ed. 30.00x (ISBN 0-85105-363-7, Dolmen Pr); pap. text ed. 11.75x (ISBN 0-85105-364-5, Dolmen Pr). Humanities.

Otway, Thomas. Venice Preserved. Kelsall, Malcolm, ed. LC 69-12902. (Regents Restoration Drama Ser.). 1969. 7.95x (ISBN 0-8032-0366-7); pap. 2.65x (ISBN 0-8032-5366-4, BB 271, Bison). U of Nebr Pr.

Otwell, John, jt. auth. see Hordern, William.

Otypka, Oldrich. The Room of Delight. LC 73-22598. (Illus.). 288p. 1976. 15.00 o.p. (ISBN 0-498-01467-3). A S Barnes.

Ouchi, Hajime. Japanese Optical & Geometrical Art. LC 77-82360. (Orig.). 1977. pap. 5.00 (ISBN 0-486-23553-X). Dover.

Oudar, Jacques. Physics & Chemistry of Surfaces. (Illus.). 1975. 24.00x (ISBN 0-216-90020-4). Intl Ideas.

Ouden, Bernard D. The Fusion of Naturalism & Humanism. LC 79-5348. 1979. pap. text ed. 9.00 (ISBN 0-8191-0869-3). U Pr of Amer.

Oudenhoven, van Nico J. see Van Oudenhoven, Nico J.

Ouellette, Robert P., et al. Low-Temperature Plasma Technology Applications. LC 80-65514. (Electrotechnology Ser.: Vol. 5). (Illus.). 148p. 1980. 29.95 (ISBN 0-250-40375-7). Ann Arbor Science.

Ough, Anne R. New Directions in Crochet. LC 80-52646. (Illus.). 248p. 1981. 17.95 (ISBN 0-670-40008-4, Studio). Viking Pr.

Oughton, Frederick. The History & Practice of Woodcarving. (Illus.). 1976. Repr. 8.95 (ISBN 0-918036-03-8). Woodcraft Supply.

Oulanoff, Hongor. The Prose Fiction of Veniamin A. Kaverin. 1976. soft cover 9.95 (ISBN 0-89357-032-X). Slavica.

Oumet, Ronald P. Eighty Woodcraft Projects. 320p. 1980. 17.95 (ISBN 0-8246-0260-9). Jonathan David.

Ounsted, C., et al. Biological Factors in Temporal Lobe Epilepsy. (Clinics in Developmental Medicine Ser. No. 22). 135p. 1966. 9.00 (ISBN 0-685-24721-X). Lippincott.

Oursler, Fulton. Greatest Book Ever Written. 8.95 (ISBN 0-385-04175-6). Doubleday.

--Greatest Story Ever Told. 1949. pap. 2.45 (ISBN 0-385-08028-X, D121, Im). Doubleday.

Oursler, Will, jt. auth. see Klimo, Vernon.

Oury, Guy-Marie. St. Benedict: Blessed by God. Otto, John A., tr. from Fr. LC 80-13253. Orig. Title: Ce que croyait Benoit. (Orig.). 1980. pap. text ed. 4.50 (ISBN 0-8146-1181-8). Liturgical Pr.

Ouseg, H. L. Twenty-One Language Dictionary: International Dictionary. write for info. Philos Lib.

Ouspensky, P. D. Fourth Way. 1971. pap. 3.95 (ISBN 0-394-71672-8, Vin). Random.

--Letters from Russia, 1919. 1978. pap. 5.06 (ISBN 0-7100-0077-4). Routledge & Kegan.

--New Model of the Universe: Principles of the Psychological Method in Its Application to Problems of Science, Religion & Art. LC 35-8632. 1971. pap. 4.95 (ISBN 0-394-71524-1, Vin). Random.

Outcalt, David, jt. auth. see Wood, June.

Outcalt, David L., jt. auth. see Ceder, Jack G.

Outcast, Gabriel, pseud. Modern Times: Or, the Adventures of Gabriel Outcastt, 3 vols. in 1. LC 80-2493. 1981. Repr. of 1785 ed. 123.50 (ISBN 0-404-19127-4). AMS Pr.

Outerbridge, David & Thayer, Julie. The Last Shepherds. (Illus.). 1979. 15.95 o.p. (ISBN 0-670-41891-9, Studio). Viking Pr.

Outka, Darryl E., jt. auth. see Elliot, Alfred.

Outlaw, Alain C. Governor's Land Archaeological District Excavations: The Nineteen Seventy-Six Season. (Illus.). Date not set. write for info. (ISBN 0-8139-0875-2). U Pr of Va. Postponed.

Outler, Albert, ed. John Wesley. 516p. 1980. pap. 9.95 (ISBN 0-19-502810-4). Oxford U Pr.

Outterson, Leslie A. This I Believe-Thank You, Billy Sunday, for the Goodness & Mercy Which I Know. 1977. 7.00 o.p. (ISBN 0-682-48685-X). Exposition.

Ovchinnikov, V. V. Britain Observed: A Russian's View. LC 80-40657. 224p. 1981. 22.50 (ISBN 0-08-023603-0); pap. 8.50 (ISBN 0-08-023608-1). Pergamon.

Ovchinnikov, Yu. A., jt. ed. see Tosteson, D. C.

Ove Arup Partnership. Building Design for Energy Economics. 160p. 1981. 38.00 (ISBN 0-86095-850-7). Longman.

Ovenden, Graham. Alphonse Mucha Photographs. LC 73-89210. (Illus.). 1974. 15.95 o.p. (ISBN 0-685-48994-9). St Martin.

Ovennell, C. H., jt. auth. see Ovennell, Marjorie.

Ovennell, Marjorie & Ovennell, C. H. A History of Everyday Things in England, 5 vols. Incl. Volume I, 1066-1499. 1969 (ISBN 0-7134-1650-5); Volume II, 1500-1799. 1976 (ISBN 0-7134-1651-3); Volume III, 1733-1851. 1977 (ISBN 0-7134-1652-1); Volume IV, 1851-1914. 1976 (ISBN 0-7134-1653-X); Volume V, 1914-1968. Ellan, S. E. 1977 (ISBN 0-7134-1654-8). 17.95 ea. (Pub. by Batsford England). David & Charles.

Over, Ira Earl, jt. auth. see Chang, Huan-Yang.

Over, Raymond Van see Van Over, Raymond & Oteri, Laura.

Overall, John E. & Klett, C. James. Applied Multivariate Analysis. 522p. 1981. Repr. of 1972 ed. lib. bdg. price not set (ISBN 0-89874-325-7). Krieger.

Overbeck, Cynthia. Elephants. (Lerner Natural Science Bks.). (Illus.). (gr. 4-9). 1981. PLB 7.95 (ISBN 0-8225-1452-4). Lerner Pubns.

--Lions. (Lerner Natural Science Bks.). (Illus.). (gr. 4-10). 1981. PLB 7.95 (ISBN 0-8225-1463-X). Lerner Pubns.

--Monkeys. (Lerner Natural Science Bks.). (Illus.). (gr. 4-10). 1981. PLB 7.95 (ISBN 0-8225-1464-8). Lerner Pubns.

--Sunflowers. (Lerner Natural Science Bks.). (Illus.). (gr. 4-10). 1981. PLB 7.95 (ISBN 0-8225-1457-5). Lerner Pubns.

Overbeek, Johannes. The Population Challenge: A Handbook for Non-Specialists. LC 76-5328. (Contributions in Sociology: No. 19). (Illus.). 224p. 1976. lib. bdg. 16.95 (ISBN 0-8371-8896-2, OPC/). Greenwood.

Overbeek, Johannes, ed. The Evolution of Population Theory: A Documentary Sourcebook. LC 76-43138. (Contributions in Sociology: No. 23). 1977. lib. bdg. 16.95 (ISBN 0-8371-9313-3, OVP/). Greenwood.

Overberg, Kenneth R. An Inconsistent Ethic? Teachings of the American Catholic Bishops. LC 80-512. 220p. 1980. lib. bdg. 17.75 (ISBN 0-8191-1318-2); pap. text ed. 9.75 (ISBN 0-8191-1319-0). U Pr of Amer.

Overberger, C. & Mark, H. International Symposium on Macromolecules. (JPS Symposium: No. 62). 1978. 40.50 (ISBN 0-471-05602-2, Pub by Wiley-Interscience). Wiley.

Overbury, Thomas. Conceited News of Sir Thomas Overbury & His Friends: With Sir Thomas Overbury His Wife. Savage, James E., ed. LC 68-29084. 1968. 41.00x (ISBN 0-8201-1039-6). Schol Facsimiles.

Overcash, Michael R. & Davidson, James M., eds. Environmental Impact of Nonpoint Source Pollution. LC 79-56118. (Illus.). 1981. 29.95 (ISBN 0-250-40339-0). Ann Arbor Science.

Overgard, William. The Divide. pap. 2.50 (ISBN 0-515-05492-5). Jove Pubns.

Overholser, Stephen. Field of Death. LC 77-75875. 1977. 6.95 o.p. (ISBN 0-385-13204-2). Doubleday.

--A Hanging in Sweetwater. 224p. 1975. pap. 1.25 o.p. (ISBN 0-523-22655-1). Pinnacle Bks.

Overholser, Wayne. Sun on the Wall. 1981. pap. 1.75 (ISBN 0-345-29493-9). Ballantine.

Overholser, Wayne D. Cast a Long Shadow. Date not set. pap. 1.95 (ISBN 0-440-11423-3). Dell.

--Draw or Drag. 1981. pap. 1.95 (ISBN 0-440-13263-0). Dell.

--Gunlock. 1980. pap. 1.95 o.s.i. (ISBN 0-440-13322-X). Dell.

--Ride into Danger. 144p. (Orig.). 1980. pap. 1.75 (ISBN 0-553-13575-9). Bantam.

--Valley of the Guns. 1981. pap. 1.95 (ISBN 0-440-18825-3). Dell.

--West of the Rimrock. 1981. pap. 1.95 o.s.i. (ISBN 0-440-19586-1). Dell.

Overholt, W. H. Asia's Nuclear Future. LC 77-778. 1977. lib. bdg. 26.50x (ISBN 0-89158-217-7). Westview.

Overholt, William. The Future of Brazil. (Westview Special Studies on Latin America). 1978. lib. bdg. 27.50x (ISBN 0-89158-268-1). Westview.

Overington, Ian. Vision & Acquisition. LC 75-45872. 1976. 44.50x (ISBN 0-8448-0917-9). Crane-Russak Co.

Overland, Gordon W. Magic Tools for Stock Market Success. (Illus.). 149p. 1980. deluxe ed. 67.85 (ISBN 0-918968-77-1). Inst Econ Pol.

Overland, O., jt. auth. see Dietrichson, J.

Overland, Orm. The Making & Meaning of an American Classic: James Fenimore Cooper's 'the Prairie' 1973. text ed. 21.00x (ISBN 8-200-04613-3, Dist. by Columbia U Pr). Universitet.

Overman, Dean L. Effective Writing Techniques. LC 79-1212. (Orig.). 1980. pap. 4.95 (ISBN 0-671-09168-9). Monarch Pr.

Overman, Edward S. Taxation of Public Utilities in Tennessee. LC 61-13683. 1962. pap. 5.00x o.p. (ISBN 0-87049-038-9). U of Tenn Pr.

Overman, Michael, jt. auth. see Kind, Stuart.

Overmyer, Allen, jt. auth. see Brezina, Dennis W.

Overmyer, Wayne S., jt. auth. see Holmes, Arthur W.

Overs, Robert P., et al. Avocational Activities for the Handicapped: A Handbook for Avocational Counseling. (American Lectures in Social & Rehabilitation Psychology Ser.). 208p. 1974. 13.75 (ISBN 0-398-02975-X). C C Thomas.

Overseas Development Council, jt. auth. see McLaughlin, Martin M.

Overseas Development Council Staff, jt. auth. see Hansen, Roger D.

Overseas Development Council Staff, jt. auth. see Howe, James W.

Overseas Development Council Staff, jt. auth. see Hunter, Robert E.

Overseas Development Council Staff, jt. auth. see McLaughlin, Martin M.

Overseas Development Council Staff, jt. auth. see Sewell, John.

Overseas Development Council Staff, jt. auth. see Sewell, John W.

Overshiner, Elwyn E. Course Zero-Nine-Five to Eternity: The Saga of Destroyer Squadron Eleven. LC 80-82005. (Illus.). 224p. (Orig.). 1981. pap. 4.95 (ISBN 0-937480-00-2). Overshiner.

Overstreet, Bonaro, jt. auth. see Overstreet, H. A.

Overstreet, H. A. Mature Mind. (Keith Jennison Large Type Bks). (gr. 9 up). 1965. PLB 8.95 o.p. (ISBN 0-531-00234-9). Watts.

Overstreet, H. A. & Overstreet, Bonaro. Strange Tactics of Extremism. 1964. 5.95 (ISBN 0-393-05268-0); pap. 4.95x (ISBN 0-393-09749-8). Norton.

Overstreet, Helen-Mary F., jt. auth. see Kline, Draza.

Overstreet, Phoebe L., jt. auth. see Super, Donald E.

Overton, Jenny. Creed Country. (gr. 7 up). 1970. 4.95g o.s.i. (ISBN 0-02-769000-8). Macmillan.

--The Nightwatch Winter. 1973. 6.50 (ISBN 0-571-09969-6, Pub. by Faber & Faber). Merrimack Bk Serv.

Overton, John R., ed. see Ettinger, Karl E.

Overton, M. A. The Subject Departmentalized Public Library. 1969. 10.00x (ISBN 0-85365-051-9, Pub. by Lib Assn England). Oryx Pr.

Overton, Marie. Time Explorers & the Phoenix & the Carpet. pap. text ed. 2.50x o.p. (ISBN 0-435-21016-5). Heinemann Ed.

Overton, Richard C. Burlington Route: A History of the Burlington Lines. LC 76-17079. (Illus.). 1976. pap. 8.95 (ISBN 0-8032-5853-4, BB 632, Bison). U of Nebr Pr.

Overton, Robert. Palm Court. 1979. 17.95 (ISBN 0-241-10110-7, Pub. by Hamish Hamilton England). David & Charles.

Overy, Paul. Kandinsky: The Language of the Eye. 1969. pap. 17.50 (ISBN 0-236-17770-2, Pub. by Paul Elek). Merrimack Bk Serv.

Overy, R. J. The Air War, Nineteen Thirty-Nine to Nineteen Forty-Five. LC 80-6200. 288p. 1981. 16.95 (ISBN 0-8128-2792-9). Stein & Day.

Ovesy, Regina, ed. see Members & Friends of the Fashiion Group Inc.

Ovid. Amores. Kenney, E. J., ed. Incl. Medicamina Faciei Femineae; Ars Amatoria; Remedia Amoria. (Oxford Classical Texts Ser). 1961. 15.95x (ISBN 0-19-814642-6). Oxford U Pr.

--Metamorphoseon. Pontanus, Jacobus, ed. LC 75-27868. (Renaissance & the Gods Ser.: Vol. 24). (Illus.). 1977. Repr. of 1618 ed. lib. bdg. 73.00 (ISBN 0-8240-2073-1). Garland Pub.

--Metamorphoseos. LC 75-278944. (Renaissance & the Gods Ser.: Vol. 3). (Illus.). 1977. Repr. of 1518 ed. lib. bdg. 73.00 (ISBN 0-8240-2052-9). Garland Pub.

--Metamorphoses. Garth, et al, trs. LC 75-27884. (Renaissance & the Gods Ser.: Vol. 39). (Illus.). 1976. Repr. of 1732 ed. lib. bdg. 73.00 (ISBN 0-8240-2088-X). Garland Pub.

--Metamorphoses, Bk. 1. Lee, A. G., ed. 1953. pap. text ed. 7.50 (ISBN 0-521-05870-8). Cambridge U Pr.

--Metamorphoses, Bk. 8. Hollis, A. S., ed. (Illus.). 1970. 17.95x (ISBN 0-19-814440-7). Oxford U Pr.

--Metamorphosis. Watts, A. E., tr. from Latin. (Illus.). 440p. 1980. pap. 9.50 (ISBN 0-86547-019-7). N Point Pr.

--Tristia. Lind, L. R., tr. LC 73-88363. 177p. 1975. 10.00x (ISBN 0-8203-0330-5). U of Ga Pr.

Ovid & Sandys, George. Ovid's Metamorphoses English Ed. LC 75-27873. (Renaissance & the Gods Ser.: Vol. 27). (Illus.). 1976. Repr. of 1632 ed. lib. bdg. 73.00 (ISBN 0-8240-2076-6). Garland Pub.

Ovington, Ray. Freshwater Fishing. 1977. pap. 3.95 (ISBN 0-8015-2837-2, Hawthorn). Dutton.

--The Trout & the Fly. 1977. 9.95 o.p. (ISBN 0-8015-7982-1, Hawthorn); pap. 5.95 (ISBN 0-8015-7983-X, Hawthorn). Dutton.

Owen. Handbook of Statistical Tables. 1962. 26.95 (ISBN 0-201-05550-3). A-W.

--Star Streak: Stories of Space. (gr. 7-9). Date not set. pap. cancelled (ISBN 0-590-31264-2, Schol Pap). Schol Bk Serv.

--Working Hours: An Economic Analysis. LC 78-22287. (Illus.). 1979. 21.95 (ISBN 0-669-02740-5). Lexington Bks.

Owen, et al. Educational Psychology: An Introduction. 2nd ed. 1981. pap. text ed. 15.95 (ISBN 0-316-67729-9); tchrs'. manual free (ISBN 0-316-67730-2). Little.

Owen, A. L. Selig Perlman's Lectures on Capitalism & Socialism. LC 74-27312. 264p. 1976. 17.50 (ISBN 0-299-06780-7). U of Wis Pr.

Owen, A. R. Can We Explain the Poltergeist. LC 64-23925. 1964. 8.50 o.p. (ISBN 0-912326-10-7). Garrett-Helix.

--Hysteria, Hypnosis, & Healing: The Work of J. M. Charcot. LC 75-88055. (Illus.). 1970. 7.50 o.p. (ISBN 0-912326-25-5). Garrett-Helix.

Owen, Aloysius, tr. see Philipon, M. M.

Owen, Anita Y., jt. auth. see Frankle, Reva T.

Owen, Ann. The Sands of Time. 192p. (Orig.). 1980. pap. 1.50 (ISBN 0-671-57041-2). S&S.

Owen, Brian E. & Kops, W. J. The Impact of Policy Change on Decisions in the Mineral Industry. 116p. (Orig.). 1979. pap. text ed. 7.00x (ISBN 0-88757-015-1, Pub. by Ctr Resource Stud Canada). Renouf.

Owen, Brian E., et al. Introduction to Canadian Business. 1980. 21.95 (ISBN 0-205-06998-3, 0869988); tchrs. ed. free (ISBN 0-205-07007-8, 0870072). Allyn.

Owen, Bruce, et al. Television Economics. LC 74-926. (Illus.). 1974. 19.95 (ISBN 0-669-92999-9). Lexington Bks.

Owen, Carol. Social Stratification. (Students Library of Sociology). 1968. text ed. 4.25x (ISBN 0-7100-6086-6). Humanities.

Owen, D. B. History of Statistics & Probability. 1976. 37.55 (ISBN 0-8247-6390-4). Dekker.

Owen, D. F. Animal Ecology in Tropical Africa. new ed. LC 75-46586. (Tropical Ecology Ser). (Illus.). 1976. text ed. 18.95x (ISBN 0-582-44363-6); pap. text ed. 8.50x (ISBN 0-582-44362-8). Longman.

--Man in Tropical Africa: Human Ecology in Tropical Africa. 220p. 1973. 12.95x (ISBN 0-19-519746-1). Oxford U Pr.

--Tropical Butterflies: The Ecology & Behaviour of Butterflies in the Tropics with Special Reference to African Species. (Illus.). 1971. 34.95x (ISBN 0-19-857351-0). Oxford U Pr.

Owen, David. High School. 252p. 1981. 12.95 (ISBN 0-670-37149-1). Viking Pr.

Owen, David L. Providence Their Guide: The Story of the Long Range Desert Group 1940-1945. (Elite Unit Ser.: No. 3). (Illus.). 238p. 1981. 19.95 (ISBN 0-89839-040-0). Battery Pr.

Owen, Dean. Trackdown. (Latigo Ser.: Vol. I). 224p. 1981. pap. 1.95 (ISBN 0-445-04644-9). Popular Lib.

Owen, Dolores & Hanchey, Marguerite. Abstracts & Indexes in Science & Technology: A Descriptive Guide. LC 74-1345. 1974. 10.00 (ISBN 0-8108-0709-2). Scarecrow.

Owen, Dolores B., jt. auth. see Levine, Herbert M.

Owen, Dorothy L. Piers Plowman. 173p. 1980. Repr. of 1912 ed. lib. bdg. 30.00 (ISBN 0-8495-4226-X). Arden Lib.

Owen, Emily S. A Return to...The Joys of Parenthood: Tots to Teens Training for Family Unity. LC 77-89860. 1980. 12.95 (ISBN 0-86533-002-6, Pub. by New World Comm.). Amber Crest.

Owen, G. E., jt. ed. see Lloyd, G. E.

Owen, George & Sims, Victor. Science & the Spook. LC 71-88054. (Illus.). 1970. 4.50 o.p. (ISBN 0-912326-26-3). Garrett-Helix.

Owen, Gwyneth, jt. auth. see Heater, Derek.

Owen, H. P. Christian Knowledge of God. 1969. text ed. 34.00x (ISBN 0-485-11107-1, Athlone Pr). Humanities.

--W. R. Matthews: Philosopher & Theologian. 80p. 1976. pap. text ed. 7.00x (ISBN 0-485-12027-5, Athlone Pr). Humanities.

Owen, Harold, ed. see Owen, Wilfred.

Owen, Henry & Schultze, Charles L., eds. Setting National Priorities: A the Next Ten Years. 325p. 1976. 18.95 (ISBN 0-8157-6764-1); pap. 8.95 (ISBN 0-8157-6763-3). Brookings.

Owen, Henry, et al, eds. The Next Phase in Foreign Policy. 1973. 14.95 (ISBN 0-8157-6766-8); pap. 5.95 (ISBN 0-8157-6765-X). Brookings.

Owen, Hylda F. How to Raise & Train a Bloodhound. (Orig.). pap. 2.00 (ISBN 0-87666-248-3, DS1058). TFH Pubns.

Owen, J. I., ed. Brassey's Warsaw Pact Infantry & Its Weapons: Defense Publications. LC 76-6841. 1976. 17.00x (ISBN 0-89158-531-1). Westview.

Owen, John. The Glory of Christ. 288p. 1980. pap. 6.95 (ISBN 0-8024-2988-2). Moody.

--Grace & Duty of Being Spiritually Minded. (Summit Bks). 1977. pap. 3.45 (ISBN 0-8010-6663-8). Baker Bk.

--The Works of John Owen, 16 vols. 14.95 ea. Banner of Truth.

Owen, John B. Sheep Production. (Illus.). 436p. 1976. text ed. 18.50 (ISBN 0-8121-0748-9). Lea & Febiger.

Owen, John E. Sociology: Readings on Human Society. 1981. pap. text ed. 7.95x (ISBN 0-673-15265-0). Scott F.

Owen, John I. & Orgel, Stephen, eds. The Rare Triumphs of Love & Fortune. LC 78-66840. (Renaissance Drama Ser.). 1979. lib. bdg. 44.00 (ISBN 0-8240-9736-X). Garland Pub.

Owen, Lewis J. & Owen, Nancy H., eds. Middle English Poetry: An Anthology. LC 76-138662. (Library of Literature Ser). 1971. pap. 7.50 (ISBN 0-672-60984-3, LL-12). Bobbs.

Owen, M. E., jt. ed. see Jenkins, D.

Owen, Maribel V. Fun of Figure Skating. LC 60-10433. (Illus.). 1960. 11.95 o.s.i. (ISBN 0-06-071470-0, HarpT). Har-Row.

Owen, Maureen, ed. see Hartman, Yuki.

Owen, Myrfyn. Wild Geese of the World. (Illus.). 236p. 1981. 45.00 (ISBN 0-686-69428-7, Pub. by Batsford England). David & Charles.

Owen, Nancy H., jt. ed. see Owen, Lewis J.

Owen, Nancy L. The Illustrated Standard of the Dairy Goat. Date not set. 10.00 (ISBN 0-686-26679-X). Dairy Goat.

Owen, Norman G., ed. Compadre Colonialism: Studies on the Philippines Under American Rule. LC 75-175623. (Michigan Papers on South & Southeast Asia: No. 3). (Illus.). 252p. 1971. pap. 4.00x o.p. (ISBN 0-89148-003-X). Ctr S&SE Asian.

Owen, R. & Sutcliffe, R., eds. Studies in the Theory of Imperialism. (Illus.). 390p. 1972. pap. text ed. 14.95x (ISBN 0-582-48753-6). Longman.

Owen, R. J. Trial of Faith. 1.55 (ISBN 0-08-017609-7). Pergamon.

Owen, Ray, jt. auth. see Woods, Sylvia.

Owen, Richard. Nightmare. LC 79-16339. 1979. 10.95 (ISBN 0-312-57328-6). St Martin.

Owen, Robert & Howard, David M. Victor el Victorioso. Orellana, Eugenio, tr. from Eng. 152p. (Orig., Span.). 1981. pap. 2.95 (ISBN 0-89922-206-4). Edit Caribe.

Owen, Robert D. Hints on Public Architecture. LC 77-17509. (Illus.). 119p. 1978. Repr. of 1849 ed. 49.50x (ISBN 0-87474-736-8). Smithsonian.

--Hints on Public Architecture. (Architecture & Decorative Art Ser.). (Illus.). 1978. Repr. of 1849 ed. lib. bdg. 59.50 (ISBN 0-306-77545-X). Da Capo.

Owen, Roger, jt. ed. see Naff, Thomas.

Owen, Sri. The Home Book of Indonesian Cookery. 1976. 9.95 o.p. (ISBN 0-571-10850-4, Pub. by Faber & Faber). Merrimack Bk Serv.

--Indonesian Food & Cooking. rev. ed. (Illus.). 256p. 1980. pap. 10.95x (ISBN 0-907325-00-9, Pub. by Prospectengland). U Pr of Va.

Owen, T., jt. auth. see Goldsmith, D.

Owen, T. R. Geology Explained in South Wales. (Geology Explained Ser.). (Illus.). 1973. 14.95 (ISBN 0-7153-5860-X). David & Charles.

Owen, T. R., jt. auth. see Anderson, J. G.

Owen, T. R., jt. auth. see Anderson, J. G. C.

Owen, Thomas C. Capitalism & Politics in Russia: A Social History of the Moscow Merchants, 1855 to 1905. LC 80-11279. (Illus.). 352p. Date not set. 35.00 (ISBN 0-521-23173-6). Cambridge U Pr.

Owen, Trefor, jt. auth. see Fenton, Alexander.

Owen, Trevor. The Manager & Industrial Relations. 1979. 35.00 (ISBN 0-08-022471-7); pap. 12.75 (ISBN 0-08-022472-5). Pergamon.

Owen, W. J., ed. see Wordsworth, William.

Owen, Wanda. The Captain's Vixen. 400p. (Orig.). 1981. pap. 2.50 (ISBN 0-89083-709-0). Zebra.

Owen, Wilfred. The Accessible City. 150p. 1972. 10.95 (ISBN 0-8157-6770-6); pap. 4.95 (ISBN 0-8157-6769-2). Brookings.

--Collected Letters. Owen, Harold & Bell, John, eds. 1967. 29.50x (ISBN 0-19-211180-9). Oxford U Pr.

--Distance & Development: Transport & Communications in India. LC 67-30599. (Transport Research Program). 1968. 10.95 (ISBN 0-8157-6768-4). Brookings.

--Metropolitan Transportation Problem. rev. ed. 1966. 11.95 (ISBN 0-8157-6772-2). Brookings.

--Transportation for Cities: The Role of Federal Policy. 1976. pap. 3.95 (ISBN 0-8157-6773-0). Brookings.

Owen, William. The Cambrian Biography; or Historical Notices of Celebrated Men Among the Ancient Britons. Feldman, Burton & Richardson, Robert, eds. LC 78-60896. (Myth & Romanticism Ser.: Vol. 20). (Illus.). 1980. lib. bdg. 66.00 (ISBN 0-8240-3569-0). Garland Pub.

Owen, William, jt. auth. see Brown, Tom, Jr.

Owen, William B. & Goodspeed, Edgar J. Homeric Vocabularies: Greek & English Word-Lists for the Study of Homer. LC 68-31669. (Gr, & Eng). (YA) (gr. 9 up). 1969. pap. 2.95x (ISBN 0-8061-0828-2). U of Okla Pr.

Owen, Wyn F. & Antoine, George H. Guide to Graduate Study in Economics & Agricultural Economics. 5th ed. 1980. 11.50x (ISBN 0-256-02540-1). Irwin.

Owens, Alberta F. A Book for Ab. 1981. 4.75 (ISBN 0-8062-1677-8). Carlton.

Owens, Charles E. & Bell, Jimmy, eds. Blacks & Criminal Justice. LC 76-43639. 1977. 16.95 (ISBN 0-669-01101-0). Lexington Bks.

Owens, Claire M. Zen & the Lady. LC 79-50288. 311p. (Orig.). 1981. pap. 6.95 (ISBN 0-88238-996-3). Great Eastern.

Owens, Eleanor, et al. Tennis: Easy on-Easy off. 70p. 1975. 3.95 (ISBN 0-938822-10-1). USTA.

Owens, Elisabeth A. International Aspects of U. S. Income Taxation: Cases & Materials, Vol. III, Parts Four & Five. LC 80-18605. 512p. 1980. pap. text ed. 12.50x (ISBN 0-915506-24-6). Harvard Law Intl Tax.

Owens, Fred. Making It in Hollywood: An Actor's Guide. 96p. (Orig.). 1980. pap. 5.00 (ISBN 0-936182-01-6). Diamond Heights.

--Theatre Games. (Illus.). 220p. (Orig.). 1979. pap. 10.00 (ISBN 0-936182-00-8). Diamond Heights.

Owens, Gary, jt. auth. see Meagher, Sylvia.

Owens, Iris. After Claude. 224p. 1974. pap. 1.50 o.p. (ISBN 0-446-78427-3). Warner Bks.

Owens, J. Garfield. All God's Chillun. LC 79-134251. 1971. 3.75 o.p. (ISBN 0-687-01020-9). Abingdon.

Owens, J. J., jt. auth. see Yates, Kyle M.

Owens, J. J., ed. see Yates, Kyle M.

Owens, Jesse & Neimark, Paul. Jesse. 1978. 6.95 o.p. (ISBN 0-88270-314-5). Logos.

Owens, Joan L. The Graduate's Guide to the Business World. LC 73-77700. (Illus.). 96p. 4.95x o.p. (ISBN 0-686-09301-1, Dist. by Hippocrene Books Inc.); pap. 2.50x o.p. (ISBN 0-686-09302-X). Leviathan Hse.

Owens, Leslie H. This Species of Property: Slave Life & Culture in the Old South. LC 75-38110. 1977. pap. 4.95 (ISBN 0-19-502245-9, GB517, GB). Oxford U Pr.

Owens, Mary F. Salt from the Psalter. LC 80-67147. 1981. pap. 4.50 (ISBN 0-8054-1218-2). Broadman.

Owens, N. P., jt. auth. see Castle, E. F.

Owens, Norma F., jt. auth. see Bouchard, Rosemary.

Owens, Paul. Stereo Troubleshooting & Repair Manual. (Illus.). 1979. ref. 16.95 (ISBN 0-8359-7082-5). Reston.

Owens, Richard & Wolman, Baron. Levi's Denim Art Contest: Catalogue of Winners. (Illus.). 1974. pap. 3.00 o.p. (ISBN 0-916290-00-X). Squarebooks.

Owens, Robert G. Organizational Behavior in Education. 2nd ed. (Illus.). 368p. 1981. text ed. 17.95 (ISBN 0-13-641050-2). P-H.

--Organizational Behavior in Schools. LC 78-86521. (Education Ser). 1969. ref. ed. 14.95 (ISBN 0-13-641027-8). P-H.

Owens, Robert G. & Steinhoff, Carl R. Administering Change in Schools. (Illus.). 192p. 1976. Ref. Ed. 14.95 (ISBN 0-13-004929-8). P-H.

Owens, Rochelle. The Joe Chronicles Sacre Coeur. 1981. pap. 4.95 (ISBN 0-915298-16-3). Sagarin Pr.

Owens, W. R., ed. Seventeenth-Century England: A Changing Culture, Modern Studies, Vol. 2. 1981. 28.50x (ISBN 0-389-20169-3). B&N.

Owens, William A. This Stubborn Soil. LC 66-23604. 1966. 6.95 o.p. (ISBN 0-684-10444-X, ScribT). Scribner.

--Three Friends: Bedichek, Dobie, Webb - a Personal History. LC 70-82957. 335p. 1975. pap. 5.95 (ISBN 0-292-78012-5). U of Tex Pr.

Owensby, Clenton E. Kansas Prairie Wildflowers. (Illus.). 1980. text ed. 15.00 (ISBN 0-8138-0850-2); pap. text ed. 6.95 (ISBN 0-8138-1160-0). Iowa St U Pr.

Owenson, Lady Morgan S. Dramatic Scenes from Real Life, 2vols. Wolff, Robert L., ed. (Ireland-Nineteenth Century Fiction, Ser. Two: Vol. 10). 1979. lib. bdg. 92.00 (ISBN 0-8240-3459-7). Garland Pub.

--The O'Briens & The O'Flahertys. Wolff, Robert L., ed. (Ireland-Nineteenth Century Fiction, Ser. Two: Vol. 9). 1979. lib. bdg. 184.00 (ISBN 0-8240-3458-9); lib. bdg. 46.00 ea. Garland Pub.

--The Wild Irish Girl. Wolff, Robert L., ed. (Ireland-Nineteenth Century Fiction, Ser. Two: Vol. 6). 1979. lib. bdg. 126.00 (ISBN 0-8240-3455-4); lib. bdg. 46.00 ea. Garland Pub.

Owers, L. W. Electronics: An Elementary Introduction for Beginners. 2nd ed. (Illus.). (gr. 10-12). 1978. pap. text ed. 11.95x (ISBN 0-291-39659-3). Intl Ideas.

Owicki, Susan S. Axiomatic Proof Techniques for Parallel Programs. LC 79-50560. (Outstanding Dissertations in the Computer Sciences Ser.: Vol. 14). 203p. 1980. lib. bdg. 22.00 (ISBN 0-8240-4413-4). Garland Pub.

Owings, Loren C., ed. Environmental Values, 1860-1972: A Guide to Information Sources. LC 73-17539. (Man & the Environment Information Guide Ser.: Vol. 4). 593p. 1976. 30.00 (ISBN 0-8103-1343-X). Gale.

Owings, Mark, jt. ed. see Levack, Daniel J.

Owler, L. W. Intermediate Accounts. 3rd ed. 400p. 1975. pap. text ed. 12.95x (ISBN 0-7121-0936-6, Pub. by Macdonald & Evans England). Intl Ideas.

Owler, L. W. & Brown, J. L. Wheldon Costing Simplified. 5th ed. (Illus.). 336p. 1978. pap. text ed. 11.95x (ISBN 0-7121-2309-1, Pub. by Macdonald & Evans England). Intl Ideas.

--Wheldon's Cost Accounting & Costing Methods. 14th ed. (Illus.). 784p. 1978. text ed. 21.00x (ISBN 0-7121-2334-2, Pub. by Macdonald & Evans England). Intl Ideas.

Owman, Christer & Edvinsson, Lars, eds. Neurogenic Control of the Brain Circulation. LC 77-30303. 1977. text ed. 66.00 (ISBN 0-08-021553-X). Pergamon.

Owram, Doug. Promise of Eden: The Canadian Expansionist Movement & the Idea of the West, 1856-1900. 1980. 25.00x (ISBN 0-8020-5483-8); pap. 10.00 (ISBN 0-8020-6385-3). U of Toronto Pr.

Owre, J. Riis, ed. see Casona, Alejandro.

Owsley, Frank L., Jr. The Struggle for the Gulf Borderlands: The Creek War & the Battle of New Orleans, Eighteen Twelve to Eighteen Fifteen. LC 80-11109. 20.00 (ISBN 0-8130-0662-7). U Presses Fla.

Owsley, Harriet C., jt. ed. see Smith, Sam B.

Owsley, John Q., Jr. & Peterson, Rex A. Symposium on Aesthetic Surgery of the Breast. LC 78-17489. (Symposia of the Educational Foundation of the American Society of Plastic & Reconstructive Surgeons, Inc. Ser.). 1978. 67.50 (ISBN 0-8016-3793-7). Mosby.

Owyang, Lily & Ostrander, Linda. Creative Piano: A Modular Approach for Adult Beginners. LC 77-78909. (Illus.). 1978. pap. text ed. 14.50 (ISBN 0-395-25569-4). HM.

Oxaal, Ivar, et al, eds. Beyond the Sociology of Development. (International Library of Sociology). 1975. 25.00 (ISBN 0-7100-8049-2); pap. 12.00 (ISBN 0-7100-8050-6). Routledge & Kegan.

Oxborough, J., jt. auth. see Grear, A. C.

Oxborrow, John, jt. auth. see Glynn, Sean.

Oxbridge Communications, Inc. Legal Periodicals Directory. 150p. 1981. lib. bdg. 35.00 (ISBN 0-87196-335-3). Facts on File.

Oxenbury, Helen. Curious Creatures. LC 79-2980. (Heads, Bodies, Legs Ser.). (Illus.). 9p. (ps-3). 1980. 3.95 (ISBN 0-06-024597-2, HarpJ). Har-Row.

--Dressing. (Baby Board Bks.). (Illus.). 12p. (ps-k). Date not set. boards 3.50 (ISBN 0-671-42113-1, Little Simon). S&S.

--Family. (Baby Board Bks.). (Illus.). 12p. (ps-k). Date not set. boards 3.50 (ISBN 0-671-42110-7, Little Simon). S&S.

--Friends. (Baby Board Bks.). (Illus.). 12p. (ps). Date not set. boards 3.50 (ISBN 0-671-42111-5, Little Simon). S&S.

--Helen Oxenbury's ABC of Things. (Illus.). 64p. (ps-2). 1972. PLB 4.95 o.p. (ISBN 0-531-02020-7). Watts.

--Numbers of Things. LC 68-10048. (Illus.). (gr. k-3). 1968. PLB 4.90 o.p. (ISBN 0-531-01751-6). Watts.

--Pig Tale. LC 73-6357. (Illus.). 32p. (gr. k-3). 1973. PLB 7.92 (ISBN 0-688-30092-8). Morrow.

--Playing. (Baby Board Bks.). (Illus.). 12p. (ps-k). Date not set. boards 3.50 (ISBN 0-671-42109-3, Little Simon). S&S.

--The Queen & Rosie Randall. LC 78-10375. (Illus.). (gr. k-3). 1979. 7.95 (ISBN 0-688-22171-8); PLB 7.63 (ISBN 0-688-32171-2). Morrow.

--Working. (Baby Board Bks.). (Illus.). 12p. (ps-k). Date not set. boards 3.50 (ISBN 0-671-42112-3, Little Simon). S&S.

Oxender, Dale & Fox, C. Fred, eds. Molecular Aspects of Membrane Transport: Proceedings of the ICN-UCLA Symposium Held at Keystone, Col., Mar. 1977. LC 78-541. (Progress in Clinical & Biological Research: Vol. 22). 1978. 67.00 (ISBN 0-8451-0022-X). A R Liss.

Oxendine, J. Psychology of Motor Learning. 1968. text ed. 17.95 (ISBN 0-13-736595-0). P-H.

Oxenfeldt, Alfred R. Pricing Strategies. LC 74-78207. (Illus.). 272p. 1975. 18.95 (ISBN 0-8144-5368-6). Am Mgmt.

Oxenfeldt, Alfred R., ed. Models of Markets. LC 63-18435. (Illus.). 1963. 20.00x (ISBN 0-231-02643-9). Columbia U Pr.

Oxenfeldt, Alfred R., et al. A Basic Approach to Executive Decision Making. (Illus.). 1978. 14.95 (ISBN 0-8144-5467-4). Am Mgmt.

Oxenford, Lyn. Design for Movement. 1951. pap. 5.95 (ISBN 0-87830-561-0). Theatre Arts.

Oxenford, Vilma R. Challenge to Parents: Improve Your Child's Reading. LC 77-84744. (Illus.). 1977. pap. 8.95 (ISBN 0-9601474-1-1). Point Pr.

Oxenhandler, Neal. Change of Gods. LC 62-16727. 1962. 4.50 o.p. (ISBN 0-15-116640-4). HarBraceJ.

Oxenhandler, Neal, jt. ed. see Nelson, Robert J.

Oxern, jt. auth. see Fried.

Oxford Energy Seminar, First & Mabro, Robert. World Energy; Issues & Policies: Proceedings. 384p. 1980. 44.00x (ISBN 0-19-920119-6). Oxford U Pr.

Oxford English Dict., ed. see Brandreth, Cyles.

Oxford Scientific Films. Dragonflies. (Illus.). 32p. 1980. 7.95 (ISBN 0-399-20731-7). Putnam.

Oxley, R. & Poskitt, J. Management Techniques Applied to the Construction Industry. 2nd ed. 1971. pap. 14.95x (ISBN 0-8464-0593-8). Beekman Pubs.

Oxnam, Robert B., jt. auth. see Oksenberg, Michel.

Oxnam, Robert B. & Bush, Richardc., eds. China Briefing Nineteen Eighty. 120p. (Published in cooperation with the China Council of the Asia Society, Inc.). 1980. lib. bdg. 14.50x (ISBN 0-86531-028-9); pap. text ed. 6.50x (ISBN 0-86531-070-X). Westview.

Oxorn. Human Labor & Birth. 3rd ed. (Illus.). 1975. pap. text ed. 15.50 o.p. (ISBN 0-8385-3938-6). ACC.

Oxtoby, J. C. Measure & Category. 2nd ed. (Graduate Texts in Mathematics: Vol. 2). 106p. 1980. 19.80 (ISBN 0-387-90508-1). Springer-Verlag.

--Measure & Category: A Survey of the Analogies Between Topological & Measure Spaces. LC 73-149248. (Graduate Texts in Mathematics: Vol. 2). 1971. 14.50 o.p. (ISBN 0-387-90025-X); pap. text ed. 7.50 o.p. (ISBN 0-387-05349-2). Springer-Verlag.

Oxtoby, L., tr. see Denecke, H. J. & Meyer, R.

Oyama, Mas. Mas Oyama's Essential Karate. LC 77-79509. (Illus.). 1978. 14.95 (ISBN 0-8069-4120-0); lib. bdg. 14.99 (ISBN 0-8069-4121-9). Sterling.

Oyama, Masutatsu. The Kyokushin Way. LC 79-1961. 1979. 8.95 (ISBN 0-87040-460-1). Japan Pubns.

--This Is Karate. rev. ed. LC 65-17218. (Illus.). 368p. 1973. boxed 28.00 (ISBN 0-87040-254-4). Japan Pubns.

--Vital Karate. LC 67-19867. (Illus.). pap. 5.95 (ISBN 0-87040-143-2). Japan Pubns.

--What Is Karate? LC 66-21210. (Illus.). 176p. 1974. 22.00 (ISBN 0-87040-147-5). Japan Pubns.

Oye, Kenneth A., et al, eds. Eagle Entangled. (Illus.). 1978. 19.95 (ISBN 0-582-29003-1); pap. text ed. 10.95 (ISBN 0-582-29002-3). Longman.

Oyer, Herbert J., jt. auth. see O'Neill, John J.

Oyewole, Fola. Reluctant Rebel. 210p. 1975. 10.75x o.p. (ISBN 0-8476-1234-1). Rowman.

Oyle, Irving. Magic, Mysticism, & Modern Medicine. LC 75-28763. 1976. pap. 4.95 o.p. (ISBN 0-89087-121-3). Celestial Arts.

Oyono, Ferdinand. Old Man & the Medal. (African-American Library). 1971. pap. 1.50 o.s.i. (ISBN 0-02-053190-7, Collier). Macmillan.

Oystaeyen, F. Van see Van Oystaeyen, F.

Oyugi, Walter O. Rural Development Administration: A Kenyan Experience. 192p. 1981. text ed. 20.00x (ISBN 0-7069-1131-8, Pub. by Vikas India). Advent Bk.

Oz, Amos. Soumchi. LC 80-8457. (Illus.). 96p. (gr. 4-7). 1981. 8.95 (ISBN 0-06-024621-9, HarpJ); PLB 8.79g (ISBN 0-06-024622-7). Har-Row.

--Where the Jackals Howl & Other Stories. De Lange, Nicholas & Simpson, Philip, trs. (Helen & Kurt Wolff Bk.). 1981. 12.95 (ISBN 0-15-196038-0). HarBraceJ.

Ozaeta, Pablo. Canciones Dramatizadas. Frank, Marjorie & Lono, Luz P., eds. LC 75-16545. 20p. (gr. 4-8). 1975. pap. text ed. 2.95 songbook (ISBN 0-88499-240-3); cassette 7.95 (ISBN 0-88499-200-4); program package 79.95 (ISBN 0-88499-239-X). Inst Mod Lang.

--Mis Primeros Cuentos. Frank, Marjorie & Lono, Luz P., eds. LC 75-16546. (Illus.). (gr. 4-8). 1975. pap. 4.95 student ed. (ISBN 0-88499-241-1); teachers's ed. 7.95 (ISBN 0-88499-242-X); program package (1 teacher's ed. & 10 student wkbks.) 38.95 (ISBN 0-88499-243-8). Inst Mod Lang.

Ozanne, Charles G. The First Seven Thousand Years: A Study in Bible Chronology. LC 73-114063. (Illus.). 1970. 5.00 o.p. (ISBN 0-682-47084-8, Testament). Exposition.

Ozanne, Larry & Struyk, Raymond J. Housing from the Existing Stock: Comparative, Economic Analyses of Owner-Occupants & Landlords. (An Institute Paper). 196p. 1976. pap. 5.50 (ISBN 0-87766-168-5, 14900). Urban Inst.

Ozanne, Larry, jt. auth. see Vanski, Jean.

Ozell, John, ed. see Castillo Solorzano, Alonso De.

Ozenfant, Amedee. Foundations of Modern Art. Rodker, John, tr. (Illus.). 1952. pap. text ed. 5.00 (ISBN 0-486-20215-1). Dover.

Ozer, Jerome S., jt. auth. see Blumenthal, Shirley.

Ozer, Jerome S., ed. Film Review Annual, 1979. 1980. lib. bdg. 60.00x (ISBN 0-89198-124-1). Ozer.

Ozer, Mark N., ed. A Cybernetic Approach to the Assessment of Children: Toward a More Humane Use of Human Beings. (Westview Special Study). 1979. lib. bdg. 25.00x (ISBN 0-89158-466-8). Westview.

Ozias, Blake. All About Wine. (Apollo Eds.). (Illus.). 144p. 1972. pap. 4.95 o.s.i. (ISBN 0-8152-0332-2, A332, TYC-T). T Y Crowell.

Ozick, Cynthia. Levitation: Five Fictions. LC 80-7997. 256p. 1981. cancelled (ISBN 0-394-94563-8). Knopf.

Oziel, L. Jerome, jt. auth. see Munjack, Dennis J.

Ozima, Minoru. The Earth: Its Birth & Growth. Wakabayashi, J. F., tr. (Illus.). 180p. Date not set. price not set (ISBN 0-521-23500-6); pap. price not set (ISBN 0-521-28005-2). Cambridge U Pr.

Ozisik, M. Necati. Basic Heat Transfer. (Illus.). 1976. text ed. 23.95 (ISBN 0-07-047980-1, C); student manual 4.95 (ISBN 0-07-047981-X). McGraw.

--Heat Conduction. LC 79-990. 1980. 29.95 (ISBN 0-471-05481-X, Pub. by Wiley-Interscience). Wiley.

--Radiative Transfer & Interactions with Conduction & Convection. LC 72-12824. 608p. 1973. 37.50 (ISBN 0-471-65722-0, Pub. by Wiley-Interscience). Wiley.

Ozmon, Howard & Craver, Samuel. Philosophical Foundations of Education. new ed. (Coordinated Teacher Preparation Ser.). 240p. 1976. text ed. 14.95x (ISBN 0-675-08669-8). Merrill.

--Philosophical Foundations of Education. 2nd ed. (General Education Ser.). 320p. Date not set. text ed. 14.95 (ISBN 0-675-08049-5). Merrill.

Ozols, Violet, tr. see Lorber, Jakob.

Ozols, Violet, tr. see Lorber, Jokob.

Ozols, Violet, tr. see Martin, Bischof.

Ozols, Violet, tr. see Mohr, Victor.

P

P. A. R. Editorial Staff. Phonics Review. rev. ed. 59p. 1973. pap. text ed. 3.95 (ISBN 0-913310-12-3). PAR Inc.

P-H Staff. Prentice-Hall Federal Tax Course. students ed. Rubin, A., ed. 1981. 21.00 (ISBN 0-13-312488-6); pap. 7.95 study guide (ISBN 0-13-312496-7). P-H.

--Prentice-Hall Federal Tax Course: Nineteen Seventy-Nine Student's Edition. 1979. 17.95 o.p. (ISBN 0-13-312413-4). P-H.

P. S. Associates see Summerlin, Lee R.

Paalman, Anthony. Training Showjumpers. Holstein, G., tr. from Ger. (Illus.). 1978. 38.35 (ISBN 0-85131-260-8, Dist. by Sporting Book Center). J A Allen.

Paananen, Lauri A., jt. auth. see Engle, Eloise.

Paananen, Victor. William Blake. (English Authors Ser.: No. 202). 1977. lib. bdg. 10.95 (ISBN 0-8057-6672-3). Twayne.

Paarlberg, Don. Farm & Food Policy: Issues of the 1980s. LC 79-17496. x, 338p. 1980. 16.50x (ISBN 0-8032-3656-5). U of Nebr Pr.

--Great Myths of Economics. LC 68-16213. (Principles of Freedom Ser.). (Illus.). 206p. 1968. 9.95 (ISBN 0-89617-044-6). Inst Humane.

--Great Myths of Economics. LC 68-16213. (Principles of Freedom Ser.). 1976. Repr. of 1968 ed. 9.95x o.p. (ISBN 0-916054-20-9). Green Hill.

Paasivirt, Juhani. Finland & Europe: The Period of Autonomy & the International Crises, 1808-1914. Kirby, D. G., ed. Upton, Anthony F., tr. from Finnish. (The Nordic Ser.: Vol. 7). 300p. 1981. 29.50x (ISBN 0-8166-1046-0). U of Minn Pr.

Paaswell, Robert E. & Recker, Wilfred W. Problems of the Carless. LC 77-13730. (Praeger Special Studies). 1978. 23.95 (ISBN 0-03-040926-8). Praeger.

Paatz, Walter. The Arts of the Italian Renaissance: The Painting, Sculpture, Architecture. (Illus.). 264p. 1974. text ed. 14.95 (ISBN 0-13-047316-2). P-H.

Pabst, M. B. The Flora of the Chuckanut Formation of Northwestern Washington, the Equisetales, Filicales, & Coniferales. (U. C. Publ. in Geological Sciences: Vol. 76). 1968. pap. 7.00x (ISBN 0-520-09179-5). U of Cal Pr.

Paccagnini, Giovanni. Pisanello. Carroll, Jane, tr. LC 72-86573. (Illus.). 298p. (It.). 1973. 45.00x o.p. (ISBN 0-7148-1556-X, Pub. by Phaidon Pr England). Hennessey.

Paccard, Andre. Traditional Islamic Craft in Moroccan Architecture, 2 vols. 1980. 495.00x (Pub. by Editions Atelier England). State Mutual Bk.

Paccia-Cooper, Jeanne, jt. auth. see Cooper, William E.

Pace, C. Robert, ed. see Carnegie Commission on Higher Education.

Pace, David & Hunter, John. Direct Participation in Action: The New Bureaucracy. 1978. 17.95 (ISBN 0-566-00205-1, 02012-5, Pub. by Saxon Hse England). Lexington Bks.

Pace, Dean F. Negotiation & Management of Defense Contracts. LC 69-13681. 1970. 69.95 (ISBN 0-471-65741-7, Pub. by Wiley-Interscience). Wiley.

Pace, Frank J., jt. auth. see Mosier, Alice.

Pace, George B. & David, Alfred, eds. The Minor Poems, Pt. 1. LC 80-5943. (Works of Geoffrey Chaucer Ser., Variorum Ed.: Vol. V). 200p. 1981. 25.00 (ISBN 0-8061-1629-3). U of Okla Pr.

Pace, Graham, jt. auth. see Brandejs, Jan F.

Pace, J. Blair. Pain: A Personal Experience. LC 76-15951. (Illus.). 156p. 1976. 11.95 (ISBN 0-88229-238-2). Nelson-Hall.

Pace, Mildred M. The Pyramids: Tombs for Eternity. LC 79-11999. (Illus.). 192p. (gr. 7-9). 1980. 7.95 (ISBN 0-07-048054-0, GB). McGraw.

Pace, R. Wayne, et al. Techniques of Effective Communication. LC 78-18634. (Speech Ser.). (Illus.). 1979. pap. text ed. 11.50 (ISBN 0-201-05703-4). A-W.

Pace, Robert. Piano for Classroom Music. 2nd ed. LC 71-98966. (Music Ser). (Illus.). 1970. pap. text ed. 12.95 (ISBN 0-13-674994-1). P-H.

Pacejka, Hans B., ed. see IUTAM Symposium Held at the Delft University of Technology, Department of Mechanical Engineering, Delft, August 1975.

Pacey, May. West Highland White Terriers. (Foyle's Handbks). 1973. 3.95 (ISBN 0-685-55803-7). Palmetto Pub.

Pach, Walter. Renoir. (Library of Great Painters Ser). (Illus.). 1950. 35.00 (ISBN 0-8109-0446-2). Abrams.

Pachai, Bridglal, ed. South Africa's Indians: The Evolution of a Minority. LC 78-65358. 1978. pap. text ed. 17.50 (ISBN 0-8191-0656-9). U Pr of Amer.

Pachard, jt. auth. see Nichols.

Pachauri. International Energy Policy. 600p. 1980. 35.00 (ISBN 0-471-08984-2, Wiley-Interscience). Wiley.

Pachauri, R. K. The Dynamics of Electrical Energy Supply & Demand: An Economic Analysis. LC 75-19806. (Special Studies). (Illus.). 202p. 1975. text ed. 24.95 (ISBN 0-275-01530-0). Praeger.

--Energy & Economic Development in India. LC 77-12718. (Praeger Special Studies). 1977. 23.95 (ISBN 0-03-022371-7). Praeger.

Pachauri, Rajendra K., ed. Energy Policy for India. 1980. 22.50x (ISBN 0-8364-0620-6, Pub by Macmillan India). South Asia Bks.

Pache, Rene. The Future Life. 1979. pap. 6.95 (ISBN 0-8024-2900-9). Moody.

Pacheco, Blanca Silvestrini De see Silvestrini De Pacheco, Blanca.

Pacheco, Jose E. Don't Ask Me How the Time Goes by. Reid, Alastair, tr. from Span. 1978. 15.00x (ISBN 0-231-04284-1); pap. 5.95 (ISBN 0-231-04285-X). Columbia U Pr.

Pacheko, Jose, tr. from Eng. Electricidad Basica Para Apparatas Caseros. (Illus.). 140p. (Span.). 1975. 20.00 (ISBN 0-938336-10-X). Whirlpool.

Pa Chin. Family. 7.95 (ISBN 0-8351-0589-X). China Bks.

Pachman, Ludek. Checkmate in Prague: The Memoirs of a Grand Master. Sling, Marian, tr. (Illus.). 216p. 1975. 8.95 o.s.i. (ISBN 0-02-594300-6). Macmillan.

--Complete Chess Strategy: Play on the Wings, Vol. 3. 176p. 1981. 3.95 (ISBN 0-346-12517-0). Cornerstone.

Pachmuss, Tamira. A Russian Cultural Renaissance: A Critical Anthology of Russian Emigre Literature Before Nineteen Thirty Nine. LC 80-20670. 416p. 1981. 29.50x (ISBN 0-87049-296-9); pap. 9.95x (ISBN 0-87049-306-X). U of Tenn Pr. Postponed.

Pacholczyk, A. G. Radio Astrophysics: Nonthermal Processes in Galactic & Extragalactic Sources. LC 70-95657. (Astronomy & Astrophysics Ser.). (Illus.). 1970. text ed. 29.95x (ISBN 0-7167-0329-7). W H Freeman.

Pacholski, L., et al, eds. Model Theory of Algebra & Arithmetics: Procedings. (Lecture Notes in Mathematics Ser.: Vol. 834). 410p. 1981. pap. 24.50 (ISBN 0-686-69431-7). Springer-Verlag.

Pachow, W. Chinese Buddhism: Aspects of Interaction & Reinterpretation. LC 80-5432. 275p. 1980. lib. bdg. 19.00 (ISBN 0-8191-1090-6); pap. text ed. 10.50 (ISBN 0-8191-1091-4). U Pr of Amer.

Pachter, Henry M. Modern Germany: A Social, Cultural, & Political History. (Illus.). 1979. lib. bdg. 28.50x (ISBN 0-89158-166-9). Westview.

Pachter, Marc. A Gallery of Presidents. LC 78-22471. (Illus.). 95p. 1979. pap. 5.95 (ISBN 0-87474-743-0). Smithsonian.

Pachter, Marc, ed. see Edel, Leon, et al.

Pacific Northwest Laboratory. Export Potential for Photovoltaic Systems. 210p. 1980. pap. 19.95 (ISBN 0-89934-014-8). Solar Energy Info.

--Sitting Handbook for Small Wind Energy Conversion Systems. 85p. Date not set. 21.95 (ISBN 0-89934-121-7); pap. 10.95 (ISBN 0-89934-122-5). Solar Energy Info.

Pacific Search Press. The Northwest Adventure Guide. LC 80-24309. (Illus.). 1981. pap. 5.95 (ISBN 0-914718-54-1). Pacific Search.

Pacific War Research Society. The Day Man Lost: Hiroshima, 6 August 1945. LC 76-174219. (Illus.). 312p. 1972. 10.00x (ISBN 0-87011-174-4). Kodansha.

Pacific War Research Society, ed. Japan's Longest Day. LC 68-17573. (Illus.). 340p. 1980. pap. 4.95 (ISBN 0-87011-422-0). Kodansha.

Pacifici, Sergio. A Guide to Contemporary Italian Literature: From Futurism to Neorealism. LC 72-5472. (Arcturus Books Paperbacks). 352p. pap. 9.95 (ISBN 0-8093-0593-3). S Ill U Pr.

--The Modern Italian Novel: From Capuana to Tozzi. LC 75-156786. (Crosscurrents-Modern Critiques Ser.). 1973. 10.95 (ISBN 0-8093-0614-X). S Ill U Pr.

--The Modern Italian Novel: From Manzoni to Svevo. LC 67-13047. (Crosscurrents-Modern Critiques Ser.). 215p. 1967. 10.95 (ISBN 0-8093-0267-5). S Ill U Pr.

--The Modern Italian Novel: From Pea to Moravia. LC 67-13047. (Crosscurrents Modern Critiques Ser.). 288p. 1979. 16.95 (ISBN 0-8093-0873-8). S Ill U Pr.

Pacifico, Carl R. & Witwer, Daniel B. Practical Industrial Management: Insights for Managers. 550p. 1981. 19.95 (ISBN 0-471-08190-6, Pub. by Wiley-Interscience). Wiley.

Pacilio, John, Jr. & Stites, William H. Introduction to Debate. LC 67-25696. (gr. 10-12). 1967. pap. text ed. 7.95 o.p. (ISBN 0-87108-140-7). Pruett.

Pacini, Kathy, ed. see Albert, Burton, Jr.

Pacini, Kathy, ed. see Battles, Edith.

Pacini, Kathy, ed. see Brown, Fern G.

Pacini, Kathy, ed. see Delton, Judy.

Pacini, Kathy, ed. see Delton, Judy & Knox-Wagner, Elaine.

Pacini, Kathy, ed. see Gemme, Leila B.

Pacini, Kathy, ed. see Heide, Florence P. & Heide, Roxanne.

Pacini, Kathy, ed. see Hooker, Ruth & Smith, Carole.

Pacini, Kathy, ed. see Lapp, Eleanor J.

Pacini, Kathy, ed. see McGinnis, Lila S.

Pacini, Kathy, ed. see Nixon, Joan L.

Pacini, Kathy, ed. see Pfeffer, Susan B.

Pacini, Kathy, ed. see Quackenbush, Robert.

Pacini, Kathy, ed. see Robison, Nancy.

Pacini, Kathy, ed. see Stanek, Muriel.

Pacini, Kathy, ed. see Van Steenwyk, Elizabeth.

Pack, Alice & Henrichsen, Lynn. Sentence Combination: Writing & Combining Standard English Sentences, Bk. II. 1980. pap. 4.95 (ISBN 0-88377-174-8). Newbury Hse.

Pack, Alice C. Pronouns & Determiners. (Dyad Learning Program Ser.). 1977. pap. text ed. 6.50 bound with teacher's ed. (ISBN 0-88377-081-4); tchr's ed. avail. (ISBN 0-88377-082-2). Newbury Hse.

Pack, Alice C. & Henrichsen, Lynn. Sentence Combination: Writing & Combining Standard English Sentences, Bk. II. 128p. (Orig.). 1981. pap. text ed. 5.95 (ISBN 0-88377-174-8). Newbury Hse.

Pack, Alice C. & Joy, Robert O. Learning to Type in English As a Second Language. 1976. pap. text ed. 9.00x (ISBN 0-8191-0025-0). U Pr of Amer.

Pack, Frank. Gospel According to John, Pt. 1. Ferguson, Everett, ed. LC 74-7628. (Living Word Commentary Ser., Vol 5). 1975. 7.95 (ISBN 0-8344-0068-5). Sweet.

--The Gospel According to John, Pt. 2. LC 77-8725. (Living Word Commentary Ser.: Vol. 5). 1977. 7.95 (ISBN 0-8344-0088-X). Sweet.

Pack, Greta. Jewelry Making by the Lost Wax Process. rev. ed. 96p. 1979. pap. 4.95 (ISBN 0-442-25176-9). Van Nos Reinhold.

--Jewelry Making for the Beginning Craftsman. 78p. 1980. pap. 6.95 (ISBN 0-442-20173-7). Van Nos Reinhold.

Pack, Robert, jt. ed. see Hall, Donald.

Pack, Roger A. The Greek & Latin Literary Texts from Greco-Roman Egypt. LC 65-10786. 1967. 8.50 (ISBN 0-910294-22-4). Brown Bk.

Pack, S. W. Cunningham: The Commander. (Illus.). 1975. 21.00 o.s.i. (ISBN 0-7134-2788-4). Hippocrene Bks.

Pack, S. W. C. The Battle of Sirte. LC 74-31677. (Sea Battles in Close-up Ser.: No. 14). 1975. 7.50 (ISBN 0-87021-813-1). Naval Inst Pr.

Packard & Carter. Sugarcane Island. (Make up Your Own Mind Ser.: No. 1). 1976. 4.00 (ISBN 0-915248-12-3). Vermont Crossroads.

Packard, et al. Fashion Buying & Merchandising. LC 76-13571. (Illus.). 384p. 1976. 13.95 (ISBN 0-87005-142-3). Fairchild.

Packard, David W. Minoan Linear A. (Illus.). 1974. 20.00x (ISBN 0-520-02580-6). U of Cal Pr.

Packard, Edward. Deadwood City. (Choose Your Own Adventure Ser.: No. 8). 128p. 1980. pap. 1.50 (ISBN 0-553-13994-0). Bantam.

--Sugarcane Island. (Illus.). (gr. 3-6). 1978. pap. 1.50 (ISBN 0-686-68480-X). PB.

--Sugarcane Island. (gr. 3-6). 1978. pap. 1.25 (ISBN 0-671-56104-9). Archway.

--Who Killed Harlowe Thrombey, No. 9. (Choose Your Own Adventure Ser.). 128p. (Orig.). (gr. 3-8). 1981. pap. 1.50 (ISBN 0-553-14357-3). Bantam.

Packard, George R., jt. ed. see Johnson, U. Alexis.

Packard, Jerrold. Queen & Her Court. (Illus.). 256p. 1981. 12.50 (ISBN 0-684-16796-4, ScribT). Scribner.

Packard, Jerrold M. The Queen & Her Court: A Guide to the British Monarchy Today. 256p. 1981. 14.95 (ISBN 0-684-16796-4, ScribT). Scribner.

Packard, Joan. Natural Breast Enlargement: Through Effective Relaxation Techniques. (Illus.). 96p. (Orig.). 1981. pap. 6.95 (ISBN 0-915190-30-3). Jalmar Pr.

Packard, Olga, ed. see Stubbs, Bettie.

Packard, Pamela M. & Clement, Paul A. Corpus Vasorum Antiquorum. (The Los Angeles County Museum of Art. Ser: Fascicule 1, U.S.A., Fascicole 18). 1977. 49.50x (ISBN 0-520-02850-3). U of Cal Pr.

Packard, Robert G. Psychology of Learning & Instruction: A Performance Based Course. new ed. (Educational Psychology Ser.). 496p. 1975. pap. text ed. 14.95x (ISBN 0-675-08761-9); instructor's manual 3.95 (ISBN 0-686-67073-6). Merrill.

Packard, Sidney & Axelrod, Nathan. Concepts & Cases in Fashion Buying & Merchandising. LC 76-50439. 1977. text ed. 12.95 (ISBN 0-87005-182-2). Fairchild.

Packard, Sidney & Guerreiro, Miriam. The Buying Game: Fashion Buying & Merchandising. (Illus.). 1979. pap. text ed. 10.00 (ISBN 0-87005-315-9). Fairchild.

Packard, Vance. Hidden Persuaders. rev. ed. 1981. pap. write for info. (ISBN 0-671-83572-6). PB.

--Naked Society. (gr. 9 up). 1964. 9.95 o.p. (ISBN 0-679-50066-9). McKay.

Packard, William, ed. The Craft of Poetry. LC 74-2831. 240p. 1974. pap. 4.50 o.p. (ISBN 0-385-03468-7); pap. 4.50 Softbound o.p. (ISBN 0-385-03496-2). Doubleday.

--Desire. 176p. 1980. 12.95 (ISBN 0-312-19469-2). St Martin.

--Do Not Go Gentle. 128p. 1981. 9.95 (ISBN 0-312-21469-3). St Martin.

Packer, Boyd K. The Mediator. 1978. 3.95 (ISBN 0-87747-738-8); pap. text ed. 1.95 (ISBN 0-87747-736-1). Deseret Bk.

--Mothers. (Illus.). 1977. pap. 0.50 o.p. (ISBN 0-87747-650-0). Deseret Bk.

Packer, Diane, jt. auth. see Mason, Anita.

Packer, Herbert L., ed. see Carnegie Commission on Higher Education.

Packer, J. I. Beyond the Battle for the Bible. LC 80-68331. 160p. 1980. text ed. 7.95 (ISBN 0-89107-195-4, Cornerstone Bks). Good News.
--God Has Spoken. rev. ed. LC 80-7789. (Orig.). 1980. pap. 3.95 (ISBN 0-87784-656-1). Inter-Varsity.

Packer, J. I., tr. see Luther, Martin.

Packer, James I., pref. by. Knowing God: Study Guide. 1975. pap. 1.95 (ISBN 0-87784-413-5). Inter-Varsity.

Packer, James S. Saints, Sinners, & Christian History. (Orig.). 1980. pap. 6.25 (ISBN 0-9604090-0-9). Paladium Pr.

Packer, Lester. Experiments in Cell Physiology. 1967. text ed. 14.50 (ISBN 0-12-543450-2). Acad Pr.

Packer, Lona M. Christina Rossetti. (Illus.). 1963. 25.00x o.p. (ISBN 0-520-00980-0). U of Cal Pr.

Packer, Peter. Death of the Other Self. 1979. pap. 1.75 (ISBN 0-505-51356-0). Tower Bks.

Packer, William, tr. see Amendola, Giorgio.

Packer, William A., tr. see Medvedev, Roy.

Packman, Jean. Child Care: Needs & Numbers. (National Institute Social Services Library). 1969. text ed. 27.50x (ISBN 0-04-360016-6). Allen Unwin.
--The Child's Generation: Child Care Policy from Curtis to Houghton. (Aspects of Social Policy Ser.). 1975. 15.00x (ISBN 0-631-16590-8, Pub. by Basil Blackwell); pap. 11.95x (ISBN 0-631-16600-9). Biblio Dist.
--The Child's Generation: Child Care Policy in Britain. 2nd ed. (Aspects of Social Policy Ser.). 200p. 1981. pap. 12.50x (ISBN 0-631-12664-3, Pub. by Basil Blackwell England). Biblio Dist.

Pack-Miller, Lisa, et al. Easy Natural Breads Even a Kid Can Bake. Frompovich, Catherine J., ed. (Illus.). 14p. (gr. 3 up). 1980. pap. 1.50 (ISBN 0-935322-07-8). C J Frompovich.

Packo, John E. Find and Use Your Spiritual Gifts. 117p. (Orig.). 1980. pap. 2.95 (ISBN 0-87509-293-4); avail. leaders guide 1.25 (ISBN 0-87509-294-2). Chr Pubns.

Packull, Werner O., jt. auth. see Stayer, James M.

Pacyga, Dominic A., jt. auth. see Holt, Glen.

Pacyga, Dominic A., jt. auth. see Holt, Glen E.

Padamsee, Sultan. Poems. (Redbird Bk.). 1976. 9.00 (ISBN 0-89253-123-1); flexible bdg. 6.75 (ISBN 0-89253-138-X). Ind-US Inc.

Padden, R. C., ed. see Arzans de Orsua y Vela, Bartolome.

Paddington Press. Europe Business Travel Guide. 480p. 1981. 19.95 (ISBN 0-87196-338-8); pap. 11.95 (ISBN 0-87196-344-2). Facts on File.
--Latin America Business Travel Guide. 448p. 1981. 19.95 (ISBN 0-87196-339-6); pap. 11.95 (ISBN 0-87196-345-0). Facts on File.
--Middle East Business Travel Guide. 288p. 1981. 19.95 (ISBN 0-87196-343-4); pap. 11.95 (ISBN 0-87196-323-X). Facts on File.

Paddison, Ronan, jt. ed. see Muir, Richard.

Paddock, C. L. Bring a Bigger Basket. (Uplook Ser.). 32p. 1962. pap. 0.75 (ISBN 0-8163-0066-6, 02605-4). Pacific Pr Pub Assn.
--Life's Detours. (Uplook Ser.). 32p. 1952. pap. 0.75 (ISBN 0-8163-0074-7, 12225-9). Pacific Pr Pub Assn.
--When My Ship Comes in. (Uplook Ser.). 32p. 1962. pap. 0.75 (ISBN 0-8163-0080-1, 23345-2). Pacific Pr Pub Assn.

Paddock, Paul. China Diary: Crisis Diplomacy in Dairen. 1977. 3.75 (ISBN 0-8138-0240-7). Iowa St U Pr.

Paddon, M., jt. auth. see Busfield, Joan.

Paden, John N. Religion & Political Culture in Kano. LC 74-153548. 1973. 27.50x (ISBN 0-520-02020-0). U of Cal Pr.
--Values, Identities, & National Integration: Empirical Research in Africa. 1980. 37.95 (ISBN 0-8101-0467-9). Northwestern U Pr.

Paden, W. D., tr. see Gronbech, Vilhelm.

Paderewski, Ignacy J., ed. see Chopin, Frederic.

Padfield, Harland & Williams, Roy. Stay Where You Were: A Study of Unemployables in Industry. LC 72-11972. 250p. 1973. 7.50 o.p. (ISBN 0-397-47289-7); pap. text ed. 3.25 o.p. (ISBN 0-397-47280-3). Lippincott.

Padfield, Peter. History of Western Seapower: From the Campaign of Discovery to the Rise of England. (Illus.). Date not set. 14.95 o.p. (ISBN 0-679-51075-3). McKay.

Padgett, Ron. Toujours L'Amour: Poems. LC 76-7710. 1976. 10.00 (ISBN 0-915342-11-1); pap. 4.00 (ISBN 0-915342-10-3). SUN.

Padgett, Vincent L. The Mexican Political System. 2nd ed. LC 75-27497. (Illus.). 352p. 1976. pap. text ed. 9.75 (ISBN 0-395-20364-3). HM.

Padilla, Amado M., ed. Acculturation: Theory, Models & Some New Findings. LC 79-21617. (AAAS Selected Symposium Ser.: No. 39). (Illus.). 165p. 1980. lib. bdg. 17.00x (ISBN 0-89158-859-0). Westview.

Padilla, Elena. Up from Puerto Rico. LC 58-7171. 1958. 17.50x (ISBN 0-231-02213-1). Columbia U Pr.

Padilla, G. M., jt. ed. see Padilla Y Padilla, C. A.

Padilla, George M., jt. ed. see Cameron, Ivan L.

Padilla Y Padilla, C. A. & Padilla, G. M., eds. Amebiasis in Man. (Illus.). 198p. 1974. 19.75 (ISBN 0-398-03165-7). C C Thomas.

Padley, G. A. Grammatical Theory in Western Europe 1500-1700. LC 75-44573. 320p. 1976. 47.50 (ISBN 0-521-21079-8). Cambridge U Pr.

Padmanab, S. A. A Separate Life. 9.00 (ISBN 0-89253-712-4); flexible cloth 4.80 (ISBN 0-89253-713-2). Ind-US Inc.

Padmanabhan, Neela. The Generations. Subramanyam, Ka N., tr. from Tamil. (Orient Paperback Ser). 192p. 1972. pap. 2.50 (ISBN 0-88253-110-7). Ind-US Inc.

Padmananda, Swami, ed. see Swami Sivananda Radha.

Padolecchia, S. P. Marketing in the Developing World. 190p. 1979. 14.00x (ISBN 0-7069-0667-5, Pub. by Croom Helm Ltd England). Biblio Dist.

Padovani, G. & Silvestri, R. Dictionnaire bilingue Larousse, francais-italien et italien-francais. (Apollo). (Fr.). 10.50 (ISBN 0-685-13854-2, 3784). Larousse.

Padover, Saul, ed. Thomas K. Jefferson on Democracy. pap. 1.50 o.p. (ISBN 0-451-61509-3, MW1509, Ment). NAL.

Padover, Saul K. Karl Marx: An Intimate Biography. abr. ed. (Illus.). 1980. pap. 3.50 (ISBN 0-451-61897-1, ME1897, Ment). NAL.

Padulo, Louis & Arbib, Michael A. System Theory: A Unified State-Space Approach to Continuous & Discrete Systems. LC 73-77941. (Illus.). 1974. text ed. 24.95 (ISBN 0-7216-7035-0). Hemisphere Pub.

Padwa. Organic Photochemistry. 1981. 65.00. Dekker.

Padwal, S. M., jt. auth. see Bandyopadhyay, R.

Padwee, Howard. Live-Longer Diet for Dogs & Cats. (Illus.). 128p. 1980. 8.95 (ISBN 0-312-48885-8). St Martin.

Padzensky, Herbert R. & Gibson, Jane. Goalguide: A Minicourse in Writing Goals & Behavioral Objectives for Special Education. 1975. instructors manual, (free with participant's manual & wkbk.) 1.00 (ISBN 0-8224-3487-3); wkbk. 2.50 (ISBN 0-8224-3486-5); participant's manual 3.00 (ISBN 0-8224-3485-7). Pitman Learning.

Paelinck, J. H., et al. Spatial Econometrics. (Illus.). 1979. 25.95 (ISBN 0-566-00264-7, 02932-7, Pub. by Saxon Hse England). Lexington Bks.

Paelinck, Jean H. & Nijkamp, Peter. Operational Theory & Method in Regional Economics. LC 75-28609. (Regional Science Monograph Ser.). 488p. 1975. 32.95 (ISBN 0-347-01117-9, 00199-6, Pub. by Saxon Hse). Lexington Bks.

Paenson, Isaac. Systematic Glossary of the Terminology of Statistical Methods: English, French, Spanish, Russian. 1971. 120.00 (ISBN 0-08-012285-X). Pergamon.

Paepe, R. see Bowen, D. Q.

Paetow, Louis J. Guide to the Study of Medieval History. rev. ed. LC 80-81364. Repr. of 1931 ed. 55.00 (ISBN 0-527-69101-1). Kraus Repr.

Paetro, Maxine. How to Put Your Book Together & Get a Job in Advertising. LC 79-81012. (Illus.). 1979. write for info. o.p. (ISBN 0-685-97191-0). Executive Comm.

Pagan, Juan A. Lorca En la Lirica Puertorriquena. LC 80-17628. (Mente y Palabra Ser.). (Illus.). 486p. 1980. 6.25 (ISBN 0-8477-0574-9); pap. 5.00 (ISBN 0-8477-0575-7). U of PR Pr.

Pagano, Jules, jt. auth. see Hoffman, Hy.

Pagano, LeRoy E., jt. auth. see Ursic, Henry S.

Pagano, Robert R. Understanding Statistics in the Behavioral Sciences. (Illus.). 520p. 1981. text ed. write for info. (ISBN 0-8299-0316-X). West Pub.

Page, Athol. Playing String Quartets. 4.95 (ISBN 0-8283-1407-1). Branden.

Page, B. G. & Thomson, W. T. Insecticide, Herbicide, Fungicide Quick Guide, 1978. 1979. 10.00 o.p. (ISBN 0-686-19192-7). Thomson Pub CA.
--The Nineteen Eighty-One Insecticide, Herbicide, Fungicide Quick Guide. 140p. 1981. pap. 11.00 (ISBN 0-913702-11-0). Thomson Pub Ca.

Page, Benjamin B. The Czechoslovak Reform Movement, 1963-1968: A Study in the Theory of Socialism. (Philosophical Currents Ser: No. 4). 127p. 1973. pap. text ed. 15.00x (ISBN 90-6032-007-7). Humanities.

Page, Carole G. The Surgeon's Family. 1980. pap. 4.95 (ISBN 0-8423-6683-0). Tyndale.
--The Two Worlds of Tracy Corbett. LC 79-54117. 128p. 1980. pap. 2.75 (ISBN 0-8066-1767-5, 10-6727). Augsburg.

Page, Connie. From Bed to Verse. Date not set. 4.75 (ISBN 0-8062-1641-7). Carlton.

Page, D. L., jt. auth. see Gow, Andrew S.

Page, D. L., ed. Further Greek Epigrams. LC 79-42646. (Illus.). 700p. Date not set. price not set (ISBN 0-521-22903-0). Cambridge U Pr.

Page, Daniel & Braun, Hugo. Michigan Supplement for Modern Real Estate Practice. 2nd ed. 150p. (Orig.). 1980. pap. 7.95 (ISBN 0-88462-257-6). Real Estate Ed Co.

Page, Denys, ed. Epigrammata Graeca: From the Beginning to the Garland of Phillip. (Oxford Classical Texts Ser). 350p. 1975. 24.95x (ISBN 0-19-814581-0). Oxford U Pr.

Page, Denys, ed. see Euripides.

Page, Denys L. History & the Homeric Iliad. (Sather Classical Lectures: Vol. 31). (Illus.). 1959. 15.75x (ISBN 0-520-03246-2). U of Cal Pr.

Page, Don, jt. auth. see Whittinghill, Dick.

Page, E. S. & Wilson, L. B. Information, Representation & Manipulation in a Computer. 2nd ed. (Computer Science Texts Ser.). (Illus.). 1978. 40.75 (ISBN 0-521-22088-2); pap. 12.95x (ISBN 0-521-29357-X). Cambridge U Pr.
--An Introduction to Computational Combinatorics. LC 78-54722. (Computer Science Texts Ser.). (Illus.). 1979. 32.95 (ISBN 0-521-22427-6); pap. 10.95x (ISBN 0-521-29492-4). Cambridge U Pr.

Page, Elwin L. Judicial Beginnings in New Hampshire,1640-1700. LC 59-3040. (Illus.). 278p. 1959. text ed. 10.00x (ISBN 0-915916-02-9). U Pr of New Eng.

Page, Ernest W., et al. Human Reproduction: Essentials of Obstetrics, Gynecology, & Reproductive Medicine. 1981. text ed. price not set (ISBN 0-7216-7053-9). Saunders.

Page, Frank. Alone Against the Atlantic: The Observer Single-Handed Transatlantic Race, 1960-1980. LC 80-69349. (Illus.). 128p. 1981. 27.00x (ISBN 0-7153-8116-4). David & Charles.

Page, G. Terry, ed. see Association for Programmed Learning & Educational Technology Conference, 1979.

Page, G. Terry, et al, eds. International Dictionary of Education. (Illus.). 1977. 25.00 (ISBN 0-89397-003-4). Nichols Pub.

Page, Harry R. Public Purchasing & Materials Management. LC 79-2039. 528p. 1980. 32.95x (ISBN 0-669-03059-7). Lexington Bks.

Page, James. Forgotten Railways: South Wales. LC 79-51099. (Illus.). 1979. 19.95 (ISBN 0-7153-7734-5). David & Charles.

Page, James D. Psychopathology: The Science of Understanding Deviance. 2nd ed. (Illus.). 498p. 1975. 17.95x (ISBN 0-19-502293-9); instructor's manual avail., by Margaret & Herbert Rappaport (ISBN 0-19-502313-7). Oxford U Pr.

Page, James O. Hardwood County Rescue Squad. 132p. (Orig.). (gr. 8-12). 1980. pap. 5.75 (ISBN 0-936174-01-3). Backdraft.

Page, Jane. The Other Awkward Age. (Illus.). 1977. 8.95 o.p. (ISBN 0-913668-67-2); pap. 4.95 o.p. (ISBN 0-913668-65-6). Ten Speed Pr.

Page, L. W. Astronomy. new ed. (Orig.). (gr. 7-12). 1973. pap. text ed. 6.44 (ISBN 0-201-05651-8, Sch Div); tchr's manual 2.84 (ISBN 0-201-05652-6). A-W.
--Astronomy: How Man Learned About the Universe. (gr. 9-12). 1969. pap. 6.95 (ISBN 0-201-05650-X). A-W.

Page, Lou W. Geology. new ed. (Orig.). 1973. pap. text ed. 6.44 (ISBN 0-201-05653-4, Sch Div); tchr's manual 2.84 (ISBN 0-201-05654-2). A-W.
--Rocks & Minerals. (Illus.). (gr. 2-3). 1962. lib. ed. 2.97 o.p. (ISBN 0-695-47774-9). Follett.

Page, Monte M. & Arnold, William J., eds. Nebraska Symposium on Motivation, 1970. LC 53-11655. (Nebraska Symposia on Motivation Ser: Vol. 18). 1971. 13.50x (ISBN 0-8032-0612-7); pap. 5.50x (ISBN 0-8032-5618-3). U of Nebr Pr.

Page, Monte M., ed. see Nebraska Symposium on Motivation, 1979.

Page, Norman. Thomas Hardy. 212p. (Orig.). 1981. pap. price not set (ISBN 0-7100-8615-6). Routledge & Kegan.
--Thomas Hardy. 1977. 18.00 (ISBN 0-7100-8614-8). Routledge & Kegan.

Page, Norman, ed. D. H. Lawrence: Interviews & Recollections, 2 vols. 1981. Vol. 1, 160p. 26.50x (ISBN 0-389-20070-0); Vol. 2, 160p. 26.50x (ISBN 0-686-62941-8). B&N.
--Tennyson: Interviews & Recollections. 1981. 26.50x (ISBN 0-389-20066-2). B&N.
--Wilkie Collins: The Critical Heritage. (Critical Heritage Ser.). 1974. 27.00x (ISBN 0-7100-7843-9). Routledge & Kegan.

Page, Norman, ed. see Hardy, Thomas.

Page, Norvell W. Sons of the Bear God. 1979. pap. 1.75 o.p. (ISBN 0-425-03889-0). Berkley Pub.

Page, Phyllis. The Handbook for Flower Arrangers. (Color Ser.). (Illus.). 1965. 9.95 (ISBN 0-7137-0765-8, Pub by Blandford Pr England). Sterling.

Page, R. Man & Machines. pap. text ed. 3.35 (ISBN 0-08-016889-2). Pergamon.

Page, R. I. Life in Anglo-Saxon England. 1972. 19.95 (ISBN 0-7134-1461-8, Pub. by Batsford England). David & Charles.

Page, Rex & Didday, Richard. FORTRAN Seventy-Seven for Humans. (Illus.). 1980. pap. 10.95 (ISBN 0-8299-0271-6); instrs.' manual avail. (ISBN 0-8299-0615-0). West Pub.

Page, Rex, jt. auth. see Didday, Richard.

Page, Robert C. How to Lick Executive Stress. 1977. Repr. 4.95 (ISBN 0-346-12252-X). Cornerstone.

Page, Robert J. D., jt. auth. see Hodgins, Bruce W.

Page, Robert M. Plants As Organisms, Laboratory Studies of Plant Structure & Function. 1967. 7.95x (ISBN 0-7167-0710-1); individual studies 0.50 ea.; instr's manual avail. W H Freeman.

Page, S. F. Cassell Book of Austin Farina. 8.50x (ISBN 0-392-05820-0, SpS). Soccer.

Page, Stanley W. The Formation of the Baltic States: A Study of the Effects of Great Power Politics Upon the Emergence of Lithuania,Latvia, & Estonia. LC 74-80578. 1970. Repr. 14.00 (ISBN 0-86527-068-6). Fertig.

Page, Susie. Let's Talk Cats. LC 80-12852. (Illus.). 1980. 12.95 (ISBN 0-8289-0392-1). Greene.

Page, T. E., ed. see Virgil.

Page, Thomas. Sigmet Active. 288p. 1980. pap. 2.25 (ISBN 0-441-76330-8). Charter Bks.

Page, Thomas N. Two Little Confederates, Repr. Of 1888 Ed. Bd. with The Little Colonel. Johnston, Annie F. Repr. of 1896 ed. LC 75-32194. (Classics of Children's Literature, 1621-1932: Vol. 56). 1976. PLB 38.00 (ISBN 0-8240-2305-6). Garland Pub.

Page, Victor W. Ford Model A Service Manual & Handbook of Repair & Maintenance. Clymer Publications, ed. 1961. pap. 9.00 o.p. (ISBN 0-89287-265-9, H525). Clymer Pubns.
--Ford Owner's Handbook: Models T & a Nineteen Hundred & Eight to Nineteen Twenty-Eight. Clymer Publications, ed. (Illus.). 1958. pap. 9.00 o.p. (ISBN 0-89287-258-6, H509). Clymer Pubns.
--Model A Ford: Care & Maintenance of Automobiles & Trucks. (Illus.). 1948. pap. 4.00 o.p. (ISBN 0-89287-264-0, H524). Clymer Pubns.

Page, Warren. The Accurate Rifle. 11.95 (ISBN 0-87691-102-5). Winchester Pr.
--Topological Uniform Structures. LC 78-930. (Pure & Applied Mathematics. Wiley-Interscience Ser. of Texts, Monographs & Tracts: A Wiley Interscience Series of Texts, Monographs & Tracts). 1978. 41.95 (ISBN 0-471-02231-4, Pub. by Wiley-Interscience). Wiley.

Page-Jones, Meilir. The Practical Guide to Structured Systems Design. LC 79-67259. (Illus., Orig.). 1980. pap. 22.50 (ISBN 0-917072-17-0). Yourdon.

Pages, Irene, jt. ed. see Erickson, John.

Paget, Francis E. St. Antholin's; or, Old Churches & New: A Tale for the Times, 1841. Wolff, Robert L., ed. Bd. with Milford Malvoisin; or, Pews & Pew-Holders, 1842. LC 75-469. (Victorian Fiction Ser.). 1975. lib. bdg. 66.00 (ISBN 0-8240-1547-9). Garland Pub.

Paget, Julian. The Pageantry of Britain. (Illus.). 1980. 25.95 (ISBN 0-686-28008-3, Pub. by Michael Joseph). Merrimack Bk Serv.

Paget, Violet, jt. auth. see Lee, Vernon.

Paget-Tomlinson, E. Britain's Canal & River Craft. 144p. 1980. 37.50x (ISBN 0-903485-90-7, Pub. by Moorland England). State Mutual Bk.

Pagliaro, Louis A., et al, eds. Problems in Pediatric Drug Therapy. LC 78-50204. 313p. 1979. text ed. 19.50 (ISBN 0-914768-29-8, 16). Drug Intl Pubns.

Paglin, Morton. Poverty & Transfers In-Kind: A Re-Evaluation of Poverty in the United States. LC 79-88586. (Publication: No. 219). 108p. 1980. pap. 6.95 (ISBN 0-8179-7192-0). Hoover Inst Pr.

Pagliotti, Rick. How to Meet Girls: A Guide for Nice Guys. (Illus.). 1979. saddle stitched 2.95 (ISBN 0-9602694-0-1). R Pagliotti.

Pagnol. Le Chateau de ma Mere. (Easy Reader, C). pap. 3.75 (ISBN 0-88436-045-8, FRA201055). EMC.

Pagnol, Marcel. The Time of Love. 208p. 1980. 19.95 (ISBN 0-241-10009-7, Pub. by Hamish Hamilton England). David & Charles.

Paher, Stanley W. Colorado River Ghost Towns. (Illus.). 1976. 9.95 (ISBN 0-913814-08-3); pap. 5.95 (ISBN 0-913814-31-8). Nevada Pubns.
--Death Valley Teamsters. (Illus.). 1973. pap. 1.00 (ISBN 0-913814-07-5). Nevada Pubns.
--Nevada: An Annoted Bibliography. (Illus.). 1980. 95.00x (ISBN 0-913814-26-1). Nevada Pubns.
--Northwestern Arizona Ghost Towns. (Illus.). 1981. pap. 2.95 (ISBN 0-913814-30-X). Nevada Pubns.

--Southwestern Arizona Ghost Tours. (Illus.). 2.95 (ISBN 0-913814-32-6). Nevada Pubns.

Pahl, Aleta, jt. auth. see Harris, John.

Pahl, R. E. Patterns of Urban Life. (Aspects of Modern Sociology Ser). 1970. pap. text ed. 5.25x (ISBN 0-582-48803-6). Humanities.

Pahl, R. E., ed. Readings in Urban Sociology. 1968. text ed. 16.50 (ISBN 0-08-013303-7); pap. 7.75 (ISBN 0-08-013293-6). Pergamon.

Pai, Anna C. & Marcue-Roberts, Helen. Genetics: Its Concepts & Implications. (Illus.). 736p. 1981. text ed. 24.95 (ISBN 0-13-351007-7). P-H.

Pai, Young. Teaching, Learning, & the Mind. LC 72-3512. 250p. (Orig.). 1973. pap. text ed. 10.95 (ISBN 0-395-12663-0, 3-42835). HM.

Pai, Young, jt. auth. see Morris, Van C.

Paige, David. Bob Newhart. (Stars of Stage & Screen Ser.). (Illus.). (gr. 3-8). 1977. PLB 5.95 (ISBN 0-87191-561-8). Creative Ed.

--Carol Burnett. (Stars of Stage & Screen Ser.). (Illus.). (gr. 3-8). 1977. PLB 5.95 (ISBN 0-87191-555-3). Creative Ed.

--A Day in the Life of a Marine Biologist. LC 80-54097. (Illus.). 32p. (gr. 4 up). 1980. PLB 5.89 (ISBN 0-89375-446-3); pap. 2.50 (ISBN 0-89375-447-1). Troll Assocs.

--A Day in the Life of a Police Detective. LC 80-54102. (Illus.). 32p. (gr. 4 up). 1980. PLB 5.89 (ISBN 0-89375-442-0); pap. 2.50. Troll Assocs.

--A Day in the Life of a School Basketball Coach. LC 80-54101. (Illus.). 32p. (gr. 4 up). 1980. PLB 5.89 (ISBN 0-686-63461-6); pap. 2.50 (ISBN 0-89375-453-6). Troll Assocs.

--John Wayne. (Stars of Stage & Screen Ser.). (Illus.). (gr. 4-12). 1976. PLB 5.50 o.p. (ISBN 0-87191-551-0). Creative Ed.

--Johnny Carson. (Stars of Stage & Screen Ser.). (Illus.). (gr. 4-12). 1977. PLB 5.95 (ISBN 0-87191-560-X). Creative Ed.

--Liza Minnelli. (Stars of Stage & Screen Ser.). (Illus.). (gr. 4-12). 1977. PLB 5.95 (ISBN 0-87191-558-8). Creative Ed.

--Lucille Ball. (Stars of Stage & Screen Ser.). (Illus.). (gr. 4-12). 1977. PLB 5.95 (ISBN 0-87191-557-X). Creative Ed.

--Marlon Brando. (Stars of Stage & Screen Ser.). (Illus.). (gr. 4-12). 1977. PLB 5.95 (ISBN 0-87191-552-9). Creative Ed.

--Mary Tyler Moore. (Stars of Stage & Screen Ser.). (Illus.). (gr. 4-12). 1977. PLB 5.50 o.p. (ISBN 0-87191-559-6). Creative Ed.

--Moving a Rocket, a Sub, & the London Bridge. LC 80-22125. (On the Move Ser.). (Illus.). 48p. (gr. 3-6). 1980. PLB 9.25 (ISBN 0-516-03890-7). Childrens.

--Paul Newman. (Stars of Stage & Screen Ser.). (Illus.). (gr. 4-12). 1977. PLB 5.95 (ISBN 0-87191-553-7). Creative Ed.

--Pro Baseball: An Almanac of Facts & Records. (Sports Records Ser.). (Illus.). (gr. 3-12). 1977. lib. bdg. 6.75 (ISBN 0-87191-607-X). Creative Ed.

--Pro Basketball: An Almanac of Facts & Records. (Sports Records Ser.). (Illus.). 40p. (gr. 3-12). 1977. lib. bdg. 6.75 (ISBN 0-87191-605-3). Creative Ed.

--Pro Football: An Almanac of Facts & Records. LC 77-857. (Sports Records Ser.). (Illus.). (gr. 3-12). 1977. PLB 6.75 (ISBN 0-87191-604-5). Creative Ed.

--Robert Redford. (Stars of Stage & Screen Ser.). (Illus.). (gr. 4-12). 1977. PLB 5.50 o.p. (ISBN 0-87191-554-5). Creative Ed.

--Sidney Poitier. (Stars of Stage & Screen Ser.). (Illus.). (gr. 4-12). 1977. PLB 5.95 (ISBN 0-87191-556-1). Creative Ed.

--Track & Field: An Almanac of Facts & Records. (Sports Records Ser.). (Illus.). (gr. 3-12). 1977. PLB 6.75 (ISBN 0-87191-606-1). Creative Ed.

Paige, Donald D., et al. Elementary Mathematical Methods. LC 77-2683. 1978. 19.95 (ISBN 0-471-65756-5); tchrs. manual avail. (ISBN 0-471-04057-6). Wiley.

Paige, Glenn. Political Leadership. LC 76-169237. 1972. 15.95 (ISBN 0-02-923610-X). Free Pr.

Paige, Jeffery M. Agrarian Revolution: Social Movements & Export Agriculture in the Underdeveloped World. LC 74-25601. 1978. pap. text ed. 8.95 (ISBN 0-02-923550-2). Free Pr.

Paige, Jeffrey M., ed. see Paige, Karen E.

Paige, Karen E. The Politics of Reproductive Ritual. Paige, Jeffrey M., ed. 416p. 1981. 25.00 (ISBN 0-520-03071-0). U of Cal Pr.

Paige, Woodrow, Jr. Orange Madness: The Incredible Odyssey of the Denver Broncos. LC 78-4767. (Illus.). 1978. 8.95 o.p. (ISBN 0-690-01776-6, TYC-T). T Y Crowell.

Paik, Woon Ki & Sangduk Kim. Protein Methylation. LC 79-19557. (Biochemistry: a Series of Monographs). 1980. 31.50 (ISBN 0-471-04867-4, Pub. by Wiley-Interscience). Wiley.

Paillot, Jean Le see Le Paillot, Jean.

Paimblanc, Jean-Jacques R. Decorative Napkin Folding: A Lost Art Revived & Made Simple. (Foodservice Guides Ser.). (Illus.). 128p. 1981. 19.95 (ISBN 0-89046-072-8). Herman Pub.

Pain, F. Practical Wood Turner. rev. ed. LC 74-6436. (Illus.). 1979. pap. 5.95 (ISBN 0-8069-8580-1). Sterling.

Pain, H. J. The Physics of Vibrations & Waves. 2nd ed. 357p. 1976. 32.50 (ISBN 0-471-99407-3); pap. 16.50 (ISBN 0-471-99408-1). Wiley.

Paine. Organizational Strategy & Policy. 2nd ed. 1978. pap. 16.95. Dryden Pr.

Paine, Albert B. Girl in White Armor. new ed. (gr. 7 up). 1967. 4.50g o.s.i. (ISBN 0-02-769650-2). Macmillan.

--Mark Twain, 3 vols. LC 80-18842. (American Men & Women of Letters Ser.). 1730p. 1980. Set. pap. 19.95 (ISBN 0-87754-170-1). Chelsea Hse.

--Thomas Nast: His Period & His Pictures. LC 80-20105. (American Men & Women of Letters Ser.). (Illus.). 624p. 1981. pap. 8.95 (ISBN 0-87754-169-8). Chelsea Hse.

Paine, David, jt. auth. see Buzby, Walter J.

Paine, Donald F. Tennessee Law of Evidence. 1974. with 1976 suppl. 30.00 (ISBN 0-672-82543-0, Bobb-Merrill Law); 1976 suppl. 9.50 (ISBN 0-672-82452-3). Michie.

Paine, F. A. The Packaging Media. 444p. 1978. 43.95 (ISBN 0-470-99369-3). Wiley.

Paine, Harriett, jt. auth. see McWilliams, Margaret.

Paine, John K. History of Music to the Death of Schubert. LC 78-127280. (Music Ser). (Illus.). 1970. Repr. of 1907 ed. lib. bdg. 27.50 (ISBN 0-306-70038-7). Da Capo.

--Symphony No. One: Opus 23. LC 73-171077. (Earlier American Music Ser.: No. 1). 180p. 1972. Repr. of 1908 ed. lib. bdg. 25.00 (ISBN 0-306-77301-5). Da Capo.

Paine, Josephine Ruth, jt. auth. see Hodgson, Mary Anne.

Paine, Lauran. Dakota Death Trap. 1979. pap. 1.50 (ISBN 0-505-51421-4). Tower Bks.

Paine, Ralph D see Johnson, Allen & Nevins, Allan.

Paine, Richmond S. & Oppe, Thomas E. Neurological Examination of Children. (Clinics in Developmental Medicine Ser. Nos. 20 & 21). 280p. 1966. 19.50 (ISBN 0-685-24720-1). Lippincott.

Paine, Robert, ed. Politically Speaking: Cross-Cultural Studies of Rhetoric. LC 80-25411. 256p. 1981. text ed. 17.50x (ISBN 0-89727-017-7). Inst Study Human.

Paine, Sheperd. How to Build Dioramas. Hayden, Bob, ed. LC 80-82164. (Illus.). 104p. (Orig.). 1980. pap. 8.95 (ISBN 0-89024-551-7). Kalmbach.

Paine, Suzanne. Exporting Workers. LC 74-19528. (Department of Applied Economics, Occasional Papers Ser.: No. 41). 224p. 1974. 34.95 (ISBN 0-521-20631-6); pap. 15.95x (ISBN 0-521-09879-3). Cambridge U Pr.

Paine, Thomas. Age of Reason, Pt. 1. 2nd ed. Castell, Alburey, ed. 1957. pap. 2.50 (ISBN 0-672-60167-2, LLA5). Bobbs.

--Common Sense & Other Political Writings. Adkins, Nelson F., ed. LC 53-11326. 1953. pap. 5.50 (ISBN 0-672-60004-8, AHS5). Bobbs.

--Common Sense & the Crisis. 1970. pap. 2.95 (ISBN 0-385-09527-9, Anch). Doubleday.

--Selections from the Works of Thomas Paine. Peach, A. W., ed. 378p. 1980. Repr. lib. bdg. 30.00 (ISBN 0-8495-4385-1). Arden Lib.

Painter, A. A. Consumer Protection for Boat Users. 104p. 1980. 12.00x (ISBN 0-245-53450-4, Pub. by Nautical England). State Mutual Bk.

Painter, Charlotte. Seeing Things. 1976. 8.95 o.p. (ISBN 0-394-49739-2). Random.

--Seeing Things. 1981. pap. 6.95 (ISBN 0-932654-02-9). Context Pubns.

Painter, Desmond. Columbus. Yapp, Malcolm, et al, eds. (World History Ser.). (Illus.). 32p. (gr. 10). 1980. Repr. of 1977 ed. lib. bdg. 5.95 (ISBN 0-89908-042-1); pap. text ed. 1.95 (ISBN 0-89908-017-0). Greenhaven.

--Mao Tse-Tung. Yapp, Malcolm & Killingray, Margaret, eds. (World History Ser.). (Illus.). (gr. 10). 1980. lib. bdg. 5.95 (ISBN 0-89908-127-4); pap. write for info. (ISBN 0-89908-102-9). Greenhaven.

Painter, Desmond & Shepard, John. Religion. Yapp, Malcolm & Killinger, Margaret, eds. (World History Ser.). (Illus.). 32p. (gr. 10). 1980. lib. bdg. 5.95 (ISBN 0-89908-145-2); pap. text ed. 1.95 (ISBN 0-89908-120-7). Greenhaven.

Painter, John. Reading John's Gospel Today. LC 79-25332. (Biblical Foundations Ser.). Orig. Title: John: Witness & Theologian. 170p. 1980. pap. 5.95 (ISBN 0-8042-0522-1). John Knox.

Painter, K. S. The Severn Basin: Regional Archaeology. 1967. 3.95x o.p. (ISBN 0-435-32962-6). Heinemann Ed.

Painter, William. The Palace of Pleasure, 3 Vols. Jacobs, Joseph, ed. 1966. pap. text ed. 4.00 ea.; Vol. 1. pap. text ed. (ISBN 0-486-21691-8); Vol. 2. pap. text ed. (ISBN 0-486-21692-6); Vol. 3. pap. text ed. (ISBN 0-486-21693-4). Dover.

Painter, William E. Corporate & Tax Aspects of Closely Held Corporations. 670p. 1981. write for info (ISBN 0-316-68868-1). Little.

Painter, William H. Corporate & Tax Aspects of Closely Held Corporations. 1971. 40.00 (ISBN 0-316-68866-5); 1977 supplement 12.50 (ISBN 0-316-68864-9). Little.

Painting, Norman. Forever Ambridge. 1980. 9.95 o.p. (ISBN 0-7181-1422-1, Pub. by Michael Joseph). Merrimack Bk Serv.

Paisey, H. Alan. The Behavioural Strategy of Teachers. (General Ser). 192p. (Orig.). 1975. pap. text ed. 17.50x (ISBN 0-85633-054-X, NFER). Humanities.

Paish, F. W. How the Economy Works & Other Essays. 1970. text ed. 17.00x (ISBN 0-333-11067-6). Humanities.

Pai Shih-I. Radiation Gas Dynamics. (Illus.). 1966. 31.90 o.p. (ISBN 0-387-80776-4). Springer-Verlag.

Paisley, Rod. Tale Goes with the Hide. 1980. 4.75 o.p. (ISBN 0-8062-1223-3). Carlton.

Paisley, William, jt. auth. see Butler, Matilda.

Paitio, M. H. Finnish for Foreigners, Pt. 3. 1975. 13.50x (ISBN 9-5110-1919-8, F-566). Vanous.

Paivio, Allan. Imagery & Verbal Processes. LC 73-150787. 596p. 1979. text ed. 29.95 (ISBN 0-89859-069-8). L Erlbaum Assocs.

Pak, Ty. An Axiomatic Theory of Language with Applications to English. LC 80-12010. (Edward Sapir Monograph Ser. in Language, Culture & Cognition: No. 6). vi, 129p. (Orig.). 1979. pap. 6.00x (ISBN 0-933104-08-1). Jupiter Pr.

Pakenham, Thomas. The Boer War. LC 79-4779. 1979. 19.95 (ISBN 0-394-42742-4). Random.

Pakenham-Walsh, W. S. Tudor Story. 1963. 8.95 (ISBN 0-227-67678-5). Attic Pr.

Pakkala, Lorraine. Yea God! The True Story of a Spiritual Leader, Freedom, Who Led His Followers from Eastern Mysticism to Christianity. LC 80-11503. 250p. 1980. 11.95 (ISBN 0-89594-030-2); pap. 5.95 (ISBN 0-89594-029-9). Crossing Pr.

Pakvasa, S. & Peterson, V. S., eds. Proceedings of the Eighth Hawaii Topical Conference in Particle Physics, 1979. (Particle Physics Conference Proceedings). 1980. pap. text ed. 20.00x (ISBN 0-8248-0716-2). U Pr of Hawaii.

Pal, Anjali. Jataka Tales from the Ajanta Murals. (Illus.). 103p. (gr. 4-6). 1968. 1.00 (ISBN 0-88253-330-4). Ind-US Inc.

Pal, George & Mahain, Jo. The Time Machine. (Orig.). 1981. pap. 2.50 (ISBN 0-440-18632-3). Dell.

Pal, Yash, ed. Space & Development: Proceedings of Vikram Sarabhi Symposium of the Twenty-Second Plenary Meeting of the Committee on Space Research, Bangalore, India, 29 May--9 June 1979. LC 79-41358. (Illus.). 100p. 1980. 21.00 (ISBN 0-08-024441-6). Pergamon.

Pala, Dolores. Trumpet for a Walled City. 1979. pap. 1.75 o.p. (ISBN 0-449-23913-6, Crest). Fawcett.

Palacios, Agentina, tr. see Aruego, Jose & Aruego, Ariane.

Palacios, Argentina, jt. auth. see Rothman, Joel.

Palacios, Enrique, et al. Multiplanar Anatomy of the Head & Neck: For Computed Tomography. LC 80-11368. 208p. 1980. 148.00 (ISBN 0-471-05820-3, Pub. by WileyMed). Wiley.

Palacios, Marco. Coffee in Colombia, Eighteen Hundred to Nineteen Hundred Seventy: An Economic, Social & Political History. LC 78-73251. (Cambridge Latin American Studies: No. 36). (Illus.). 1980. 34.50 (ISBN 0-521-22204-4). Cambridge U Pr.

Palacios, Rafael, jt. ed. see Mora, Jaime.

Paladin Press, jt. ed. see Henderson, Martha.

Palairet, Michael, jt. ed. see Emmerich, Anne C.

Palaiseul, Jean. The Green Guide to Health from Plants. 1978. 10.95 o.p. (ISBN 0-214-66891-6, 4087, Dist. by Arco). Barrie & Jenkins.

Palandri, Angela C. Yuan Chen. (World Authors Ser.: No. 442). 1977. lib. bdg. 12.50 (ISBN 0-8057-6279-5). Twayne.

Palandri, Angela J., tr. Modern Verse from Taiwan. LC 79-161994. 1972. 18.50x (ISBN 0-520-02061-8). U of Cal Pr.

Palangyo, K. Dying in the Sun. (African Writers Ser.). 1968. pap. text ed. 3.95 (ISBN 0-435-90053-6). Heinemann Ed.

Palau, Luis. Con Quien Me Casare? LC 76-42154. 127p. (Orig., Span.). 1975. pap. 2.25 (ISBN 0-89922-050-9). Edit Caribe.

--Exito. Sipowicz, Edwin, tr. from Eng. LC 78-57804. 144p. (Orig., Span.). 1978. pap. 3.50 (ISBN 0-89922-115-7). Edit Caribe.

--The Luis Palau Story. (Illus.). 160p. 1980. 8.95 (ISBN 0-8007-1134-3). Revell.

--Sexo y Juventud. 83p. (Orig., Span.). (YA) 1974. pap. 1.95 (ISBN 0-89922-032-0). Edit Caribe.

Palay, Steven. I Love My Grandma. LC 76-46601. (Interaction 2 Ser.). (Illus.). (gr. k-3). 1977. PLB 7.95 o.p. (ISBN 0-8172-0067-3, Raintree Editions). Raintree Pubs.

Palazzo, Tony. The Biggest & the Littlest Animals. LC 77-112374. (Illus.). 40p. (gr. k-3). 1973. PLB 7.21 (ISBN 0-87460-225-4). Lion.

Palazzolo, Charles. Small Groups: An Introduction. 1980. text ed. 15.95 (ISBN 0-442-25868-2). D Van Nostrand.

Palecek, Joseph. The Surprise Kitten. LC 76-4806. (Illus.). 40p. (ps-2). 1976. 5.95 o.s.i. (ISBN 0-8193-0877-3, Four Winds); PLB 5.41 o.s.i. (ISBN 0-8193-0878-1). Schol Bk Serv.

Palekar, S. A. Problems of Wage Policy for Economic Development. 16.00x o.p. (ISBN 0-210-33924-1). Asia.

Palen. City Scenes: Problems & Prospects. 2nd ed. 1981. pap. text ed. 9.95 (ISBN 0-316-68871-1). Little.

Palen, J. John. The Urban World. 2nd ed. Munson, Eric M., ed. 480p. 1981. text ed. 17.95 (ISBN 0-07-048107-5, C). McGraw.

Palencia, Elaine F. Heart on Holiday. (Orig.). 1980. pap. 1.50 o.s.i. (ISBN 0-440-13476-5). Dell.

Palermo, David, jt. ed. see Weimer, Walter B.

Palermo, Patrick F. Lincoln Steffens. (United States Authors Ser.: No. 320). 1978. 12.50 (ISBN 0-8057-7253-7). Twayne.

Palese, Peter & Roizman, Bernard, eds. The Genetic Variation of Viruses, Vol. 354. LC 80-25770. 501p. 1980. write for info. (ISBN 0-89766-097-8); pap. write for info. (ISBN 0-89766-098-6). NY Acad Sci.

Pales Matos, Luis. Obras: Luis Pales Matos, Nineteen Fourteen to Nineteen Fifty-Nine, 2 vols. Arce de Vazquez, Margot, ed. LC 79-16469. 609p. (Sp.). 1980. Vol. I: Poetry. write for info. (ISBN 0-8477-3220-7); Vol. II: Prose. write for info (ISBN 0-8477-3221-5). Set (ISBN 0-8477-3219-3). U of PR Pr.

Paletta, Jeanne L., et al. Gynecologic Nursing. (Nursng Outline Ser.). pap. 9.50 (ISBN 0-87488-388-1). Med Exam.

Paletz, David L. & Entman, Robert M. Media Power Politics. LC 80-1642. 1981. 15.95 (ISBN 0-02-923650-9). Free Pr.

Paletz, David L., et al. Politics in Public Service Advertising on Television. LC 76-24363. (Special Studies). 1977. text ed. 23.95 (ISBN 0-275-23880-6). Praeger.

Paley, Frederick A. Greek Wit: A Collection of Smart Sayings & Anecdotes. 128p. 1980. Repr. of 1881 ed. lib. bdg. 20.00 (ISBN 0-8492-2190-0). R West.

Paley, Hiram & Weichsel, Paul M. Elements of Abstract Linear Algebra. LC 76-160668. 1972. text ed. 29.50x (ISBN 0-03-081311-5). Irvington.

Paley, James J., jt. ed. see Zavala, Albert.

Paley, Morton D. Energy & the Imagination: A Study of the Development of Blake's Thought. 1970. 27.00x (ISBN 0-19-811682-9). Oxford U Pr.

Paley, William. Natural Theology. Repr. of 1972 ed. 3.95 o.p. (ISBN 0-686-05047-9). St Thomas.

--The Principles of Moral & Political Philosophy. Wellek, Rene, ed. LC 75-11246. (British Philosophers & Theologians of the 17th & 18th Centuries: Vol. 45). 1977. Repr. of 1785 ed. lib. bdg. 42.00 (ISBN 0-8240-1797-8). Garland Pub.

Palgrave, Francis. The History of Normandy & England, 4 vols. LC 80-2218. 1981. Repr. of 1919 ed. 345.00 (ISBN 0-404-18770-6). AMS Pr.

Palgrave, Francis T. Golden Treasury of Songs & Lyrics. 8th ed. (gr. 9 up). 1944. 6.95 o.s.i. (ISBN 0-02-594410-X). Macmillan.

Palgrave, Francis T., ed. Golden Treasury of the Best Songs & Lyrical Poems in the English Language. 5th ed. (Oxford Standard Authors Ser.). (gr. 5-9). 1964. 27.00 (ISBN 0-19-254156-0). Oxford U Pr.

Palgrave, Robert H. Dictionary of Political Economy, 3 vols. LC 74-31358. 1976. Repr. of 1910 ed. Set. 130.00 (ISBN 0-8103-4210-3). Gale.

Pal'guev, S. F., ed. Thermodynamics of Salt & Oxide Systems. LC 61-15178. (Electrochemistry of Molten & Solid Electrolytes Ser.: Vol. 9, Trudy No. 12). (Illus.). 107p. 1972. 30.00 (ISBN 0-306-18009-X, Consultants). Plenum Pub.

Palic, Vladimir M. Government Publications. 1979. text ed. 37.00 (ISBN 0-08-021457-6). Pergamon.

Palin, G. R. Chemistry for Technologists. LC 70-142175. 355p. 1972. text ed. 25.00 (ISBN 0-08-016385-8); pap. text ed. 12.75 (ISBN 0-08-016386-6). Pergamon.

Palin, Michael & Jones, Terry. More Ripping Yarns. (Illus.). 1981. pap. 5.95 (ISBN 0-394-74810-7). Pantheon.

Palinski, Christine O., jt. auth. see Pizer, Hank.

Palisca, Claude. Baroque Music. 2nd ed. (P-H History of Music Ser.). (Illus.). 1980. text ed. 13.95 (ISBN 0-13-055954-7); pap. text ed. 8.45 (ISBN 0-13-055947-4). P-H.

Palisca, Claude V. Baroque Music. (Prentice-Hall History of Music Series). (Orig.). 1968. pap. 10.95 ref. ed. (ISBN 0-13-055962-8). P-H.

Palkes, Helen, jt. auth. see Prensky, Arthur L.

Palkovich, Ann M. & Schwartz, Douglas W. Pueblo Population & Society: The Arroyo Hondo Skeletal & Mortuary Remains. LC 80-5310. (Arroyo Hondo Archaeological Ser.: Vol. 3). (Illus.). 1981. pap. 6.25 (ISBN 0-933452-03-9). Schol Am Res.

Palkovitz, Harry P., jt. auth. see Lubic, Lowell G.

Palla, Patricia. A Bummer Is... 1977. pap. 1.50 o.p. (ISBN 0-8431-0415-5). Price Stern.

Palladio, Andrea. Four Books of Architecture. Ware, Isaac, ed. 1738. pap. text ed. 8.95 (ISBN 0-486-21308-0). Dover.

Pallain, G., ed. Ambassade De Talleyrand: A Londres. LC 72-12238. (Europe 1815-1945 Ser.). 464p. 1973. Repr. of 1891 ed. lib. bdg. 49.50 (ISBN 0-306-70575-3). Da Capo.

Pallas, Norvin. Calculator Puzzles, Tricks & Games. LC 76-1166. (Illus.). 96p. (YA) 1976. 5.95 (ISBN 0-8069-4534-6); PLB 6.69 (ISBN 0-8069-4535-4). Sterling.

--Short Short Stories. (Newbury Hse Readers Ser.: Stage 4 - Intermediate Level). (Illus.). (gr. 7-12). 1981. pap. text ed. 2.80 (ISBN 0-88377-198-5). Newbury Hse.

Pallas, Norvin, jt. auth. see McWhirter, Norris.

Pallasch, Thomas J. Pharmacology for Dental Students & Practioners. LC 79-16786. (Illus.). 458p. 1980. text ed. 27.00 (ISBN 0-8121-0689-X). Lea & Febiger.

Pallaschke, D., jt. ed. see Moeschlin, O.

Pallaschke, D., ed. see Symposium on Game Theory & Related Topics, Hagen & Bonn, Sept. 1978.

Pallavicino, Carlo. L' Amazzone Corsara, Overo L'avilda Regina De Goti. LC 76-21006. (Italian Opera 1640-1770 Ser.). 1978. lib. bdg. 70.00 (ISBN 0-8240-2612-8). Garland Pub.

Pallenberg, Corrado. Vatican Finances. 1971. text ed. 10.50x (ISBN 0-391-00194-9). Humanities.

Palley, Howard A., jt. auth. see Palley, Marian L.

Palley, Marian L. & Palley, Howard A. Urban America & Public Policies. 2nd ed. 336p. 1981. pap. text ed. 8.95 (ISBN 0-669-04004-5). Heath.

Palley, Marian L. & Preston, Michael B., eds. Race, Sex, & Policy Problems. (Policy Studies Organization Ser.). (Illus.). 1979. 22.95 (ISBN 0-669-01985-2). Lexington Bks.

Pallidini, Jody R. & Dubin, Beverly. Roll Your Own: The Complete Guide to Living in a Truck, Bus, Van, or Camper. (Illus.). 192p. 1974. pap. 3.95 o.s.i. (ISBN 0-02-081050-4, Collier). Macmillan.

Palling, S. J., ed. Developments in Food Packaging - One. (Illus.). xv, 192p. 1980. 45.00x (ISBN 0-85334-917-7). Burgess-Intl Ideas.

Palliser. Palliser's New Cottage Homes & Details. LC 75-4887. (Architecture & Decorative Arts Ser). (Illus.). 180p. 1975. Repr. of 1887 ed. lib. bdg. 45.00 (ISBN 0-306-70744-6). Da Capo.

Palliser, Fanny M. Historic Devices, Badges, & War-Cries. LC 68-18030. (Illus.). 1971. Repr. of 1870 ed. 26.00 (ISBN 0-8103-3381-3). Gale.

--History of Lace. LC 75-78219. (Illus.). x, 454p. 1972. Repr. of 1875 ed. 30.00 (ISBN 0-8103-3941-2). Gale.

Pallister, Anne. Magna Carta: The Heritage of Liberty. 144p. 1971. 22.50x (ISBN 0-19-827181-6). Oxford U Pr.

Pallot, Judith & Shaw, Denis. Planning in the Soviet Union. LC 80-24723. 320p. 1981. lib. bdg. 25.00x (ISBN 0-8203-0550-2). U of Ga Pr.

Pallottino, Massimo. Etruscans. rev. ed. Ridgway, David, ed. Cremona, J., tr. from It. LC 74-6082. (Illus.). 320p. 1975. 12.50x (ISBN 0-253-32080-1). Ind U Pr.

Palm, Charles G. & Reed, Dale, eds. Guide to the Hoover Institution Archives. (Bibliographical Ser.: No. 59). 430p. 1980. pap. 50.00 (ISBN 0-8179-2591-0). Hoover Inst Pr.

Palm, Franklin C. Calvinisim & the Religious Wars. LC 78-80579. 1971. Repr. 12.50 (ISBN 0-86527-020-1). Fertig.

Palm, Goran. The Flight from Work. Smith, P., tr. LC 77-76077. 1977. 16.95 (ISBN 0-521-21668-0). Cambridge U Pr.

Palm, Richard S. Physical Geography: A Multimedia Approach. (Geography Ser.). 1978. pap. text ed. 15.95 (ISBN 0-675-08403-2); media 595.00 (ISBN 0-675-08402-4); instructor's manual 3.95 (ISBN 0-686-66344-6); 2-4 sets 350.00 (ISBN 0-686-66345-4); 5-9 sets 250.00 (ISBN 0-686-66346-2); 10-14 sets 200.00 (ISBN 0-686-66347-0); 15 sets or more 165.00. Merrill.

Palm, Risa. The Geography of American Cities. (Illus.). 384p. 1981. text ed. 18.95x (ISBN 0-19-502785-X). Oxford U Pr.

Palm, Septima & Brewer, Ingrid. Cinderella Syndrome. (Illus.). 1980. pap. 3.50 (ISBN 0-686-28643-X). Septima.

Palma, Anthony D. Truth-Antidote for Error. LC 76-52177. (Radiant Life). 1977. pap. 1.95 (ISBN 0-88243-904-9, 02-0904); teacher's ed 2.50 (ISBN 0-88243-174-9, 32-017X). Gospel Pub.

Palma, Anthony F. De see Association of Bone & Joint Surgeons.

Palma, Gloria M. see Palma, Marigloria, pseud.

Palma, Gregory J. Chaff & the Wheat: Nineteen Twenty-Nine Seventy-Nine. LC 79-56716. (Orig.). 1979. 12.00 (ISBN 0-933402-08-2); pap. 6.95 (ISBN 0-933402-01-5). Charisma Pr.

Palma, Laurie D. The Good Morning Nutritional Breakfast Cookbook. LC 77-73996. 1978. 3.95 (ISBN 0-89430-005-9). Morgan-Pacific.

Palma, Marigloria, pseud. Versos De Cada Dia: Estampas Numeradas. LC 79-10463. (Coleccion UPREX, Ser. Poesia: No. 58). 100p. (Orig.). pap. 1.85 (ISBN 0-8477-0058-5). U of PR Pr.

Palma, Michael, ed. The Man I Pretend to Be: The Colloquies & Selected Poems of Guido Gozzano. LC 80-8551. (Lockert Library of Poetry in Translation). 264p. 1981. 16.00x (ISBN 0-691-06467-9); pap. 5.95x (ISBN 0-691-01378-0). Princeton U Pr.

Palmer. Sound Exploration & Discovery. write for info. (ISBN 0-87628-217-6). Ctr Appl Res.

Palmer & Weinert. Where Is Bone? 1980. pap. 1.50 (ISBN 0-380-75242-5, 75242, Camelot). Avon.

Palmer, tr. see Mueller, F. Max.

Palmer, A. Dean. Heinrich August Marschner, Seventeen Ninety-Five to Eighteen Sixty-One: His Life & Stage Works. Buelow, George, ed. (Studies in Musicology). 327p. 1981. 34.95 (ISBN 0-8357-1114-5, Pub. by UMI Res Pr). Univ Microfilms.

Palmer, A. J., ed. see Fuller, W. H.

Palmer, Abram S. Some Curios from a Word-Collector's Cabinet. LC 79-145517. Repr. of 1907 ed. 15.00 (ISBN 0-8103-3670-7). Gale.

Palmer, Adrienne. Dealer's Choice. 1978. pap. 1.75 (ISBN 0-505-51323-4). Tower Bks.

Palmer, Alan. The Russia of War & Peace. LC 72-89539. (Illus.). 1973. 10.00 o.s.i. (ISBN 0-02-594600-5). Macmillan.

Palmer, Andrew C. Structural Mechanics. (Oxford Engineering Science Texts). (Illus.). 1976. 36.00x (ISBN 0-19-856127-X); pap. 16.95x (ISBN 0-19-856128-8). Oxford U Pr.

Palmer, Arnold & Puckett, Earl. Four Hundred & Ninety-Five Golf Lessons by Arnold Palmer. 1973. pap. 4.95 o.p. (ISBN 0-695-80402-2). Follett.

Palmer, Arthur N. A Geological Guide to Mammoth Cave National Park. (Speleologia Ser.). (Illus.). 1981. write for info. (ISBN 0-914264-27-3, Dist. by Caroline Hse); pap. write for info. (ISBN 0-914264-28-1). Zephyrus Pr.

--Geology of Mammoth Cave National Park: A Geological Guide. 1980. 9.95 (ISBN 0-914264-27-3); pap. 5.95 (ISBN 0-914264-28-1). Caroline Hse.

Palmer, B. M. Life & Letters of J. H. Thornwell. 1974. 13.95 (ISBN 0-85151-195-3). Banner of Truth.

Palmer, Bernard. The Case of the Missing Dinosaur. LC 80-65059. (Powell Family Ser.). 160p. (Orig.). (gr. 7-10). 1981. pap. 2.25 (ISBN 0-89636-050-4). Accent Bks.

--Clue of the Old Sea Chest. LC 80-65060. (Powell Family Ser.). 160p. (Orig.). (gr. 7-10). 1981. pap. 2.25 (ISBN 0-89636-051-2). Accent Bks.

--The Mystery at Poor Boy's Folly. LC 80-65058. (The Powell Family Ser.). 160p. (Orig.). (gr. 7-10). 1981. pap. 2.25 (ISBN 0-89636-049-0). Accent Bks.

--Silent Thunder. LC 74-21363. 96p. (gr. 6-10). 1975. pap. 1.50 (ISBN 0-87123-531-5, 200531). Bethany Fell.

Palmer, Bernard & Palmer, Marjorie. Who Cares? (The Who Books Ser.). (Illus.). 1979. pap. 1.25 (ISBN 0-87123-713-X, 260713). Bethany Fell.

--Who Loves? (The Who Books Ser.). (Illus.). 1979. pap. 1.25 (ISBN 0-87123-711-3, 260711). Bethany Fell.

--Who Made. (The Who Books Ser.). (Illus.). 1979. pap. 1.25 (ISBN 0-87123-714-8, 260714). Bethany Fell.

--Who Tells? (The Who Books Ser.). (Illus.). 1979. pap. 1.25 (ISBN 0-87123-712-1, 260712). Bethany Fell.

Palmer, Bernard, jt. auth. see Eggerichs, Fred.

Palmer, Brooks. Book of American Clocks. (Illus.). 1950. 19.95 (ISBN 0-02-594590-4). Macmillan.

--Treasury of American Clocks. 2nd ed. 1967. 19.95 (ISBN 0-02-594580-7). Macmillan.

Palmer, Bruce. Body Weather. 1977. pap. 1.75 o.s.i. (ISBN 0-515-04386-9). Jove Pubns.

--Man Over Money: The Southern Populist Critique of American Capitalism. LC 79-24698. (Fred W. Morrison Ser. in Southern Studies). xviii, 311p. 1980. 19.50x (ISBN 0-8078-1427-X). U of NC Pr.

Palmer, C. Everard. Dog Called Houdini. (Illus.). (gr. 2-7). 1979. PLB 6.50 (ISBN 0-233-96985-3). Andre Deutsch.

Palmer, Charles A., jt. ed. see Cooper, Alice C.

Palmer, Charles E. Speech & Hearing Problems: A Guide for Teachers & Parents. 152p. 1961. pap. 7.25 spiral (ISBN 0-398-01441-8). C C Thomas.

Palmer, Charles E., jt. auth. see Brock, Horace R.

Palmer, Cherie. Perfect Fit: Charting & Finishing Knitted Garments. LC 74-8427. (Encore Edition). (Illus.). 1975. 4.95 o.p. (ISBN 0-684-15260-6, ScribT). Scribner.

Palmer, Colin. Quantitative Aids for Management Decision Making. 1979. text ed. 21.50x (ISBN 0-566-00284-1, Pub. by Gower Pub Co England). Renouf.

Palmer County Historical Society. Parmer County History. (Illus.). 414p. 1974. 17.95 (ISBN 0-89015-073-7). Nortex Pr.

Palmer, D., jt. ed. see Bradbury, M.

Palmer, D. J., ed. Shakespeare: The Tempest. (Casebook Ser.). 1970. 2.50 o.s.i. (ISBN 0-87695-053-5). Aurora Pubs.

Palmer, D. J., ed. see Shakespeare, William.

Palmer, David, jt. ed. see Bradbury, Malcolm.

Palmer, David S. In Search of Cumorah. LC 80-83866. (Illus.). 300p. 1981. 7.75 (ISBN 0-88290-169-9, 1063). Horizon Utah.

Palmer, Derecke. The Generalized Reciprocal Method of Seismic Refraction Prospecting. Burke, Kenneth B., ed. (Illus.). 112p. 1980. write for info. (ISBN 0-931830-14-1). Soc Exploration.

Palmer, Donald F., jt. auth. see Allison, Ira S.

Palmer, Eddy D. Practical Points in Gastroenterology. 3rd. ed. LC 80-17916. 1980. 14.50 (ISBN 0-87488-733-X). Med Exam.

Palmer, Edward L. Children & the Faces of Television: Teaching, Violence, Selling. 1980. 24.50 (ISBN 0-12-544480-X). Acad Pr.

--How to Prepare for the Graduate Record Examination (GRE) in Psychology. LC 77-12747. 1978. pap. 6.95 (ISBN 0-8120-0530-9). Barron.

Palmer, Edwin H. Doctrinas Claves. 2.50 (ISBN 0-686-12552-5). Banner of Truth.

--Five Points of Calvinism: A Study Guide. 1972. pap. 3.95 (ISBN 0-8010-6926-2). Baker Bk.

--El Spiritu Santo. 3.95 (ISBN 0-686-12551-7). Banner of Truth.

Palmer, Eogar Z. The Plummers of Harmony Grove. new ed. LC 74-8976. 1974. pap. 3.95 o.p. (ISBN 0-913408-12-3). Friends United.

Palmer, F. R. The English Verb. (Linguistics Library). (Illus.). 280p. 1974. text ed. 16.95x (ISBN 0-582-52454-7); pap. text ed. 10.95x (ISBN 0-582-52458-X). Longman.

--Semantics: A New Outline. LC 75-9089. (Illus.). 160p. 1976. 23.50 (ISBN 0-521-20927-7); pap. 7.95x (ISBN 0-521-09999-4). Cambridge U Pr.

Palmer, Florence K. The Confession Writer's Handbook. rev. ed. LC 80-12270. 216p. 1980. 10.95 (ISBN 0-89879-032-8). Writers Digest.

Palmer, Sir Francis B. Peerage Law in England: A Practical Treatise for Lawyers & Laymen. with an Appendix of Peerage Charters & Letters Patent (in English) Berkowitz, David & Thorne, Samuel, eds. LC 77-89217. (Classics of English Legal History in the Modern Era Ser.: Vol. 128). 1979. Repr. of 1907 ed. lib. bdg. 55.00 (ISBN 0-8240-3165-2). Garland Pub.

Palmer, Frank R., et al. Tool Steel Simplified. rev. ed. LC 78-7181. 1978. 14.50 (ISBN 0-8019-6747-3). Chilton.

Palmer, Frederick. Sequences. 1973. pap. text ed. 13.50x o.p. (ISBN 0-435-10685-6). Heinemann Ed.

Palmer, Friend. Early Days in Detroit: Papers Written by General Friend Palmer, of Detroit, Being His Personal Reminiscences of Important Events & Descriptions of the City for Over Eighty Years. LC 74-13871. (Illus.). 1032p. 1979. Repr. of 1906 ed. 29.00 (ISBN 0-8103-4068-2). Gale.

Palmer, G. E., tr. see Kadloubowsky, E.

Palmer, Gene C., ed. Neuropharmacology of Central Nervous System & Behavioral Disorders. LC 80-1107. 1981. 59.00 (ISBN 0-12-544760-4). Acad Pr.

Palmer, Geoffrey. Archaeology. LC 68-112513. (Pegasus Books: No. 12). (Illus.). (gr. 9 up). 1968. 10.50x (ISBN 0-234-77996-9). Intl Pubns Serv.

--Compensation for Incapacity: A Study of Law & Social Change in New Zealand & Australia. 448p. 1980. 49.50x (ISBN 0-19-558045-1). Oxford U Pr.

Palmer, George, jt. auth. see Dawson, John.

Palmer, George E. The Law of Restitution, 4 vols. 1978. Set. 200.00 (ISBN 0-316-69005-8); pap. 25.00 supp. 1980 (ISBN 0-316-69006-6). Little.

Palmer, Gladys L. & Wood, Katherine D. Urban Workers on Relief, 2 Vols. in 1. LC 75-165688. (FDR & the Era of the New Deal Ser.). 1971. Repr. of 1936 ed. Set. lib. bdg. 49.50 (ISBN 0-306-70336-X). Da Capo.

Palmer, Gordon. By Freedom's Holy Light. 1980. 3.75 (ISBN 0-8159-5110-8). Devin.

Palmer, Greg, ed. Bibliography of Loyalist Source Material in the United States, Canada & Great Britain. 700p. 1981. Set. lib. bdg. 85.00x (ISBN 0-930466-26-8). Meckler Bks.

Palmer, H. E. A Grammar of Spoken English. 3rd ed. Kingdon, R., ed. LC 75-26276. 341p. 1975. 36.00 (ISBN 0-521-21097-6); pap. 10.50x (ISBN 0-521-29040-6). Cambridge U Pr.

Palmer, H. R. The Seaplanes. LC 65-16861. 52p. 1980. 4.95 (ISBN 0-8168-5649-4). Aero.

Palmer, Helen, jt. tr. see Rivera, Carlos.

Palmer, Helen M., jt. ed. see Williams, E. T.

Palmer, Henry R., Jr. Seaplanes. LC 65-16861. (Famous Aircraft Ser). (Illus.). 1965. pap. 4.95 o.p. (ISBN 0-668-01293-5). Arco.

Palmer, Humphrey, tr. see Nelson, Leonard.

Palmer, J. W. Textile Processing & Finishing Aids: Recent Advances. LC 77-89629. (Chemical Technology Review Ser.: No. 96). (Illus.). 1978. 39.00 (ISBN 0-8155-0673-2). Noyes.

Palmer, James O. Psychological Assessment of Children. LC 70-101976. 1970. 28.95 (ISBN 0-471-65772-7). Wiley.

Palmer, Jan, illus. My First Book of Words. (Illus.). (ps). 1980. 1.50 (ISBN 0-307-11982-3, Golden Pr); PLB 6.08 (ISBN 0-307-61982-6). Western Pub.

--Who Lives in the Zoo? (Golden Storytime Bks.). (Illus.). 24p. (ps). 1981. 1.95 (ISBN 0-307-11958-0, Golden Pr); PLB 1.56 (ISBN 0-686-69208-X). Western Pub.

Palmer, Joe. Names in Pedgrees. 11.00 o.p. (ISBN 0-936032-05-7). Thoroughbred Own and Breed.

Palmer, Joe, jt. ed. see Mackay, Ronald.

Palmer, John L., ed. Creating Jobs: Public Employment Programs & Wage Subsidies. (Studies in Social Economics). 1978. 17.95 (ISBN 0-8157-6892-3); pap. 6.95 (ISBN 0-8157-6891-5). Brookings.

--Welfare in Rural Areas: The North Carolina-Iowa Income Maintenance Experiment. Pechman, Joseph A. L. (Studies in Social Experimentation). 1978. 14.95 (ISBN 0-8157-6896-6); pap. 5.95 (ISBN 0-8157-6895-8). Brookings.

Palmer, Julia R. Read for Your Life: Two Successful Efforts to Help People Read & an Annotated List of Books That Made Them Want to. LC 73-14695. 1974. 18.50 (ISBN 0-8108-0654-1). Scarecrow.

Palmer, King C. Orchestration. (Teach Yourself Ser.). 1975. pap. 2.95 o.p. (ISBN 0-679-10438-0). McKay.

Palmer, L. R. The Latin Language. (Great Languages Ser). 1961. text ed. 19.50x (ISBN 0-571-06813-8). Humanities.

Palmer, Lacie A. God Gave Me Miracle Hands. 1981. 5.95 (ISBN 0-533-04578-9). Vantage.

Palmer, Laura. Board Games to Color & Play. (Illus.). 32p. (gr. 1-12). 1979. pap. 3.50 (ISBN 0-89844-002-5). Troubador Pr.

Palmer, Leonard. Mt. Saint Helens, the Volcano Explodes. 15.00; pap. 7.95 (ISBN 0-86519-004-6). Green Hill.

Palmer, Lilli. Change Lobsters & Dance: The Autobiography of Lilli Palmer. LC 75-15924. (Illus.). 336p. 1975. 8.95 o.s.i. (ISBN 0-02-594610-2, 59461). Macmillan.

Palmer, Linda. Starstruck. 400p. 1981. 12.95 (ISBN 0-399-12512-4). Putnam.

Palmer, Lynne. Prosperity Signs. (Orig.). 1981. pap. 3.25 (ISBN 0-440-17144-X). Dell.

Palmer, Marjorie, jt. auth. see Palmer, Bernard.

Palmer, Melvyn D., jt. ed. see Zepp, Ira G., Jr.

Palmer, Michael. The European Paraliament: What It Is - What It Does - How It Works. 128p. 1981. 14.50 (ISBN 0-08-024536-6); pap. 7.20 (ISBN 0-08-024535-8). Pergamon.

Palmer, Monte. Dilemmas of Political Development. 2nd ed. LC 79-91100. 291p. 1980. pap. text ed. 7.95 (ISBN 0-87581-255-4). Peacock Pubs.

Palmer, Monte, jt. auth. see Fathaly, Omar I.

Palmer, Myles. Woody Allen. (Illus.). 128p. 1980. pap. 6.95 (ISBN 0-906071-39-9). Proteus Pub NY.

Palmer, Pamela, ed. The Robert R. Church Family of Memphis: Guide to the Papers with Selected Facsimiles of Documents & Photographs. LC 79-124374. (Mississippi Valley Collection Bulletin: No. 10). (Illus.). 87p. 1979. 12.95x (ISBN 0-87870-059-5); pap. 8.95x (ISBN 0-87870-060-9). Memphis St Univ.

Palmer, Peggy. Crafts for Bible Discovery. LC 79-55015. (Bible Discovery Books). 1979. pap. 4.25 (ISBN 0-8344-0111-8). Sweet.

Palmer, Peggy, ed. An American Original: The Story of Kwik-Kopy Printing. (Illus.). 139p. 1980. text ed. 8.95 (ISBN 0-918464-29-3); pap. text ed. 2.95 (ISBN 0-918464-30-7). D Armstrong.

Palmer, Pete, ed. see Treat, Roger.

Palmer, Philip E., jt. auth. see Reeder, Maurice M.

Palmer, R., jt. auth. see Weiner, S.

Palmer, R., jt. ed. see Leach, R.

Palmer, R. A., jt. ed. see Ladd, M. F.

Palmer, R. L. Anorexia Nervosa. 160p. 1981. pap. 3.95 (ISBN 0-14-022065-8, Pelican). Penguin.

Palmer, Ransford W. Caribbean Dependence on the United States Economy. LC 78-19770. (Praeger Special Studies). 1979. 22.95 (ISBN 0-03-041426-1). Praeger.

Palmer, Richard J., tr. see Goldin, Augusta.

Palmer, Richard J., tr. see Showers, Paul.

Palmer, Robert. Baby, That Was Rock & Roll: The Legendary Leiber & Stoller. 1978. pap. 8.95 (ISBN 0-89396-037-3). Urizen Bks.

--Deep Blues. LC 80-52000. (Illus.). 1981. 13.95 (ISBN 0-670-49511-5). Viking Pr.

Palmer, Robert B., tr. see Otto, Walter F.

Palmer, Robert L., ed. Electroconvulsive Therapy: An Appraisal. (Illus.). 320p. 1981. text ed. 59.50x (ISBN 0-19-261266-2). Oxford U Pr.

Palmer, Robin & Parsons, Neil, eds. Roots of Rural Poverty in Central & Southern Africa. (Campus Ser.: No. 199). 1978. 22.75x (ISBN 0-520-03318-3); pap. 7.95x (ISBN 0-520-03505-4). U of Cal Pr.

Palmer, Roger C., jt. ed. see Cassata, Mary B.

Palmer, Roy, ed. Everyman's Book of British Ballads. (Illus.). 256p. 1981. 22.50x (ISBN 0-460-04452-4, Pub. by J. M. Dent England). Biblio Dist.

Palmer, Samuel, jt. auth. see Palmer, Susann.

Palmer, Spencer J., ed. Studies in Asian Genealogy. LC 70-158453. (Illus.). 281p. 1972. 12.50 o.p. (ISBN 0-8425-0587-3). Brigham.

Palmer, Susann. Mesolithic Cultures of Britain. (Illus.). 1978. 9.95 o.p. (ISBN 0-85642-062-X, Pub. by Blandford Pr England). Sterling.

Palmer, Susann & Palmer, Samuel. The Hurdy-Gurdy. LC 79-56052. (Illus.). 192p. 1980. 45.00 (ISBN 0-7153-7888-0). David & Charles.

Palmer, Sushma & Ekvall, Shirley. Pediatric Nutrition in Developmental Disorders. (Illus.). 640p. 1978. 54.50 (ISBN 0-398-03652-7). C C Thomas.

Palmer, T. S. Place Names of the Death Valley Region in California & Nevada. LC 80-51783. (Illus.). 1980. wrappers 5.00 (ISBN 0-930704-04-5). Sagebrush Pr.

Palmer, Ted. Correctional Intervention & Research: Current Issues & Future Prospects. LC 77-25777. (Illus.). 1978. 21.00 (ISBN 0-669-02166-0). Lexington Bks.

Palmer, Tobias. An Angel in My House. 64p. 1981. pap. 1.95x (ISBN 0-912484-21-7). Joseph Nichols.

--Angel in My House. LC 75-22990. (Illus.). 64p. 1975. pap. 1.95 o.p. (ISBN 0-87793-103-8). Ave Maria.

Palmer, W. Robert. How to Understand the Bible. rev. ed. 112p. 1980. pap. 2.95 (ISBN 0-89900-140-8). College Pr Pub.

--What the Bible Says About Faith & Opinion. LC 79-57088. (What the Bible Says Ser.). 1980. 13.50 (ISBN 0-89900-076-2). College Pr Pub.

Palmer, William R. Freelance Business Writing Business. LC 78-78221. (Illus.). 1979. postpaid (14.95 price) 16.10 (ISBN 0-9602350-0-0); pap. 12.95 postpaid (11.95 price) (ISBN 0-9602350-1-9). Heathcote.

--Why the North Star Stands Still: And Other Indian Legends. (Illus.). 118p. 1978. 2.50. Zion.

Palmeri, Joseph. Conversational & Cultural French. (Fr.). 1966. text ed. 14.95 (ISBN 0-13-171900-9). P-H.

Palmes, J. C. Architectural Drawing in the R. I. B. A. pap. 2.50 (ISBN 0-685-20562-2). Transatlantic.

Palmguist, Roland E. House Wiring. 4th ed. LC 78-50216. (Illus.). 1978. 8.95 (ISBN 0-672-23315-0). Audel.

Palmier, L. H. Social Status & Power in Java. (Monographs on Social Anthropology: No. 20). 1969. pap. text ed. 9.00x (ISBN 0-485-19620-4, Athlone Pr). Humanities.

Palmier, Leslie H. Indonesia. (Nations & Peoples Library). (Illus.). 1966. 8.50x o.s.i. (ISBN 0-8027-2108-7). Walker & Co.

Palmieri, Anthony F. Elmer Rice: A Playwright's Vision of America. LC 78-75182. 248p. 1980. 19.50 (ISBN 0-8386-2333-6). Fairleigh Dickinson.

Palmisano, A. International Distributor Locator. LC 77-82718. 1977. pap. 35.00 o.p. (ISBN 0-917408-03-9). Intercontinental Pubns.

Palmore, Phyllis & Andre, Nevin. Small Appliance Repair. Schuler, Charles A., ed. LC 79-19186. (Basic Skills in Electricity & Electronics Ser.). (Illus.). 192p. (gr. 9-12). 1980. 11.60 (ISBN 0-07-048361-2, G); tchrs. manual 2.00 (ISBN 0-07-048363-9); activities manual 5.96 (ISBN 0-07-048362-0). McGraw.

Palmquist, Al. The Real Centurions. 1979. 2.25 (ISBN 0-89728-014-8). Omega Pubns OR.

Palmquist, Al & Stone, John. The Minnesota Connection. pap. cancelled o.s.i. (ISBN 0-681-12881-X, 698511). Omega Pubns OR.

Palmquist, Roland. Air Conditioning: Home & Commercial. LC 77-71586. 1977. 10.95 (ISBN 0-672-23288-X). Audel.

--Answers on Blueprint Reading. 3rd ed. LC 77-71585. 1977. 9.95 (ISBN 0-672-23283-9). Audel.

--Electrical Course for Apprentices & Journeymen. LC 73-85725. 1973. 10.95 (ISBN 0-672-23209-X). Audel.

--Questions & Answers for Electricians Examinations. 6th ed. 1978. 8.95 (ISBN 0-672-23307-X). Audel.

--Refrigeration: Home & Commercial. LC 77-71583. 1977. 12.95 (ISBN 0-672-23286-3). Audel.

Palmquist, Roland E. Guide to the Nineteen Seventy-Eight National Electrical Code. 1978. 12.95 (ISBN 0-672-23308-8). Audel.

Palms, Catherine. Realism, an Educational Philosophy of a Democratic Society. 1979. cancelled (ISBN 0-682-48937-9). Exposition.

Palms, Roger C., compiled by see Bunyan, John.

Palms, Roger C., tr. Dios Guia Tu Futuro. (Spanish Bks.). (Span.). 1977. 1.60 (ISBN 0-8297-0767-0). Life Pubs Intl.

Palomares, Uvaldo & Ball, Gerry. Yo Puedo: Bilingual Leadership Program for Junior & Senior High. 1980. 89.95 (ISBN 0-86584-036-9). Human Dev Train.

Palomares, Uvaldo & Logan, Ben. A Curriculum on Conflict Management. 1975. 5.95 (ISBN 0-86584-014-8). Human Dev Train.

Palomba, Neil A., jt. auth. see Jakubauskas, Edward B.

Palshof, T., jt. ed. see Mouridsen, H. T.

Palsson, Hermann & Edwards, Paul, trs. Egil's Saga. 1977. pap. 2.95 (ISBN 0-14-044321-5). Penguin.

Palsson, Hermann, jt. tr. see Magnusson, Magnus.

Palsson, Hermann & Edwards, Paul, illus. A Viking Romance: Gongu-Hrolf's Saga. 144p. 1981. 10.00x (ISBN 0-8020-2392-4). U of Toronto Pr.

Palsule, G. B., tr. see Deussen, Paul.

Palti, Josef. Toxigenic Fusaria, Their Distribution & Significance As Causes of Disease in Animal & Man. (Acta Phytomedica Ser.: Vol. 6). (Illus.). 112p. (Orig.). 1978. pap. text ed. 24.00 (ISBN 3-489-60326-5). Parey Sci Pubs.

Paltock, Robert. The Life & Adventures of Peter Wilkins, a Cornish Man, 1751, 2 vols. in 1. LC 74-16040. (Novel in England, 1700-1775 Ser). 1974. lib. bdg. 50.00 (ISBN 0-8240-1134-1). Garland Pub.

Paltsits, Victor H., ed. see Albany County Sessions.

Paludan, et al, eds. Issues Past & Present: An American History Sourcebook, 2 vols. 1978. Vol. 1. pap. text ed. 6.95x (ISBN 0-669-00784-6); Vol. 2. pap. text ed. 6.95x (ISBN 0-669-00954-7). Heath.

Palumbo, Dennis, ed. Evaluating & Optimizing Public Policy. 1980. pap. 5.00 (ISBN 0-686-62286-3). Policy Studies.

Palumbo, Dennis & Taylor, George A., eds. Urban Policy: A Guide to Information Sources. LC 78-25957. (Urban Studies Information Guide Ser.: Vol. 6). 1979. 30.00 (ISBN 0-8103-1428-2). Gale.

Palumbo, Dennis J. Statistics in Political & Behavioral Science. 2nd ed. LC 76-15572. 1977. 22.50x (ISBN 0-231-04010-5). Columbia U Pr.

Palumbo, Dennis J. & Harder, Marvin A. Implementing Public Policy. LC 80-8597. (Policy Studies Organization Bks.). 1981. price not set (ISBN 0-669-04305-2). Lexington Bks.

Palumbo, Dennis J., et al, eds. Evaluating & Optimizing Public Policy. LC 80-8598. (Policy). 1981. price not set (ISBN 0-669-04306-0). Lexington Bks.

Palumbo, Michael & Shanahan, William O., eds. Nationalism: Essays in Honor of Louis L. Snyder. 1981. 19.95 (ISBN 0-935764-02-X). Ark Hse NY.

Paluszek, John L. Will the Corporation Survive? LC 77-5730. (Illus.). 1977. 11.95 o.p. (ISBN 0-87909-894-5); pap. 7.95 (ISBN 0-87909-893-7). Reston.

Paluszny, Maria J. Autism: A Practical Guide for Parents & Professionals. 200p. 1980. pap. 9.95x (ISBN 0-8156-2225-2). Syracuse U Pr.

Palz, W. & Chartier, P., eds. Energy from Biomass in Europe. (Illus.). xii, 248p. 1981. 35.00x (ISBN 0-85334-934-7). Intl Ideas.

Palz, W & Steemers, Tc, eds. Solar Houses in Europe: How They Have Worked. LC 80-49715. (Illus.). 320p. 1981. 40.00 (ISBN 0-08-026743-2); pap. 20.00 (ISBN 0-08-026744-0). Pergamon.

Pam, Martin, jt. ed. see Meisel, Jurgen.

Pamart, J. Riverain, jt. auth. see Giraud, J.

Pampatti. Dance, Snake! Dance! Buck, David C., tr. (Translated from Tamil). 12.00 (ISBN 0-89253-797-3); flexible cloth 8.00 (ISBN 0-89253-798-1). Ind-US Inc.

Pampel, Fred C. Social Change & the Aged: Recent Trends in the United States. LC 79-4752. (Illus.). 240p. 1981. 22.95 (ISBN 0-669-02928-9). Lexington Bks.

Pamplin, Brian, jt. ed. see Elwell, Dennis.

Pamplin, Brian R. Crystal Growth. LC 73-21909. 1975. text ed. 82.00 (ISBN 0-08-017003-X); pap. text ed. 32.00 (ISBN 0-08-021310-3). Pergamon.

--Molecular Beam Epitaxy. (Illus.). 178p. 1980. 40.00 (ISBN 0-08-025050-5). Pergamon.

Pamplin, Brian R., ed. Progress in Crystal Growth & Characterization, Vol. 1. 1977. Pt. 1 1977. pap. text ed. 21.00 (ISBN 0-08-021663-3); Pt. 2 1978. pap. text ed. 23.00 (ISBN 0-08-023050-4); Pt. 3 1978. pap. text ed. 23.00 (ISBN 0-08-023051-2); Pt. 4. pap. text ed. 17.75 (ISBN 0-08-023083-0). Pergamon.

Pamplin, P., ed. Progress in Crystal Growth, Vol. 2, Complete. (Illus.). 404p. 1980. 112.50 (ISBN 0-08-026040-3). Pergamon.

Pan Am. Pan Am World Guide. LC 80-14222. (Illus.). 1072p. 1980. 8.95 (ISBN 0-07-048431-7, GB). McGraw.

Pan Am World Airways, ed. Pan Am's U. S. A. Guide. 3rd ed. (Illus.). 1980. 7.95 (ISBN 0-07-048422-8). McGraw.

Pan Am World Airways, Inc. Pan Am's World Guide. 24th ed. 1978. 7.95 o.p. (ISBN 0-07-048418-X, GB). McGraw.

Pan American Navigation Service Staff, ed. Airframe Mechanics Manual. rev. ed. LC 79-138652. (Zweng Manual Ser.). (Illus.). 1977. soft cover 15.95 (ISBN 0-87219-017-X). Pan Am Nav.

--Federal Aviation Regulations for Pilots: 1981 Edition. LC 73-644468. 1981. soft bdg. 3.50 (ISBN 0-87219-014-5). Pan Am Nav.

Pan, Elizabeth, et al. Annual Review of Rehabilitation, Vol. 1, 1980. 1980. text ed. 27.50 (ISBN 0-8261-3090-9). Springer Pub.

Pan, Stephen, ed. see Yeh Ch'ing.

Panandiker, V. A., et al. Family Planning Under the Emergency: Policy Implications of Incentives & Disincentives. (Illus.). 1979. text ed. 8.50x (ISBN 0-391-01011-5). Humanities.

Panassie, Hugues. Louis Armstrong. (Illus.). 148p. 1980. lib. bdg. 19.50 (ISBN 0-306-79611-2); pap. 5.95 (ISBN 0-306-80116-7). Da Capo.

Panati, Charles. Breakthroughs. 1981. pap. 3.25 (ISBN 0-425-04925-6). Berkley Pub.

--Links. 1979. pap. 2.25 o.p. (ISBN 0-425-04048-8). Berkley Pub.

Panati, Charles & Hudson, Michael. The Silent Intruder: Surviving the Radiation Age. 224p. 1981. 9.95 (ISBN 0-686-69062-1). HM.

Panayi, G. S. Rheumatoid Arthritis & Related Conditions, Vol. 1. (Annual Research Reviews Ser.). 1977. 14.40 (ISBN 0-88831-003-X). Eden Med Res.

--Rheumatoid Arthritis & Related Conditions, Vol. 2. LC 78-317911. (Annual Research Reviews Ser.). 1978. 19.20 (ISBN 0-88831-022-6). Eden Med Res.

Panayotova, Dora. Bulgarian Mural Paintings of the 14th Century. Alexieva, Marguerite & Athanassova, Theodora, trs. (Illus.). 28.50x (ISBN 0-8057-5003-7). Irvington.

Panc, V. Theories of Elastic Plates. (Mechanics of Surface Structures Ser.: No. 2). 736p. 1975. 80.00x (ISBN 90-286-0104-X). Sijthoff & Noordhoff.

Panchapakesan, S., jt. auth. see Gupta, Shanti C.

Pancheri, P., jt. ed. see Zichella, L.

Pancheri, Paolo, jt. auth. see Butcher, James N.

Panchev, S. Random Functions & Turbulence. LC 70-124852. 1971. 67.00 (ISBN 0-08-015826-9). Pergamon.

Panckhurst, J. Focus on Physical Handicap. 158p. 1981. pap. text ed. 16.00x (ISBN 0-85633-217-8, NFER). Humanities.

Panckhurst, John & McAllister, Arthur G. An Approach to the Further Education of the Physically Handicapped. (Illus.). 139p. 1980. pap. text ed. 13.75x (ISBN 0-85633-195-3, NFER). Humanities.

Pancoast, Harry M. & Junk, W. Ray. Handbook of Sugars. 2nd ed. (Illus.). 1980. text ed. 47.50 (ISBN 0-87055-348-8). AVI.

Pancoast, Harry M., jt. auth. see Junk, Ray.

Pancoast, Patricia, jt. auth. see Detmer, Josephine.

Pancoast, Patricia, et al. Portland. 2nd ed. LC 72-172820. (Illus.). 236p. 1973. 15.00 (ISBN 0-9600612-2-3); pap. 6.95 (ISBN 0-9600612-1-5). Greater Portland.

Panconcelli-Calzia, Giulio. Geschichtszahlen der Phonetik (1941) Together with Quellenatlas der Phonetik (1940) (Studies in the History of Linguistics: No. 16). 1980. text ed. 40.00x (ISBN 0-391-01649-0). Humanities.

Panda, N. Principles of Host-Plant Resistance to Insect Pests. LC 78-59169. (Illus.). 400p. 1980. text ed. 32.50 (ISBN 0-87663-836-1). Allanheld.

Pandell, Karen & Stall, Chris. Animal Tracks of the Pacific Northwest. (Illus.). 96p. (Orig.). 1981. pap. 3.95 (ISBN 0-89886-012-1). Mountaineers.

Pandey, I. M. Capital Structure & the Cost of Capital. 600p. 1980. text ed. 20.00x (ISBN 0-7069-0999-2, Pub. by Vikas India). Advent Bk.

Pandey, S. N. & Sinha, B. K. Plant Physiology. 1978. 17.50 (ISBN 0-7069-0720-5, Pub. by Vikas India). Advent Bk.

Pandey, S. N. & Trivedi, P. S. A Textbook of Botany, Vol. I: Algae, Fungi, Bacteria, Virus, Lichens, Mycoplasma & Elementary Plant Pathology. 1976. 18.95 (ISBN 0-7069-0516-4, Pub. by Vikas India). Advent Bk.

Pandey, S. N., et al. A Textbook of Botany, Vol. II: Bryophyta, Pteridophyta, Gymnosperms & Paleobotany. 1974. 17.50 (ISBN 0-7069-0213-0, Pub. by Vikas India). Advent Bk.

Pandit, D. P. Earning One's Livelihood in Mahuva. 5.25x o.p. (ISBN 0-210-22622-6). Asia.

Pandit, M. P. Aditi & Other Deities in the Veda. 1979. 3.95 (ISBN 0-89744-960-6). Auromere.

--Dynamics of Yoga, 3 vols. 1979. Vol. I. 8.00 (ISBN 0-89744-961-4); Vol. II. 8.00 (ISBN 0-89744-962-2); Vol. III. 9.00 (ISBN 0-89744-963-0). Auromere.

--Occult Lines Behind Life. LC 79-63488. 1979. pap. 3.95 (ISBN 0-89744-001-3). Auromere.

--Sadhana in Sri Aurobindo's Yoga. LC 78-59851. 1978. pap. 3.95 (ISBN 0-89744-000-5, Pub. by Atmaniketan Ashram). Auromere.

Pandit, M. P., tr. see Parasurama.

Pandit, M. P. Sri. Thoughts of a Shakta. 1979. pap. 1.75 (ISBN 0-89744-130-3, Pub. by Ganesh & Co India). Auromere.

Pandit, Sri M. Yoga of Works. 1979. 8.00 (ISBN 0-89744-943-6). Auromere.

Pandit, Sri M., ed. see Aurobindo, Sri.

Pandolfini, Bruce. Let's Play Chess: A Step-by-Step Guide for Beginners. LC 80-11410. (Illus.). 160p. (gr. 7-12). 1980. PLB 7.79 (ISBN 0-671-34054-9). Messner.

Panek, Dennis. Catastrophe Cat. LC 77-90951. (Illus.). (ps-1). 1978. 8.95 (ISBN 0-87888-130-1). Bradbury Pr.

--Catastrophe Cat at the Zoo. LC 78-26369. (Illus.). (ps-1). 1979. 8.95 (ISBN 0-87888-147-6). Bradbury Pr.

--Matilda Hippo Has a Big Mouth. LC 80-13260. (Illus.). (ps-2). 1980. 8.95 (ISBN 0-87888-161-1). Bradbury Pr.

Panel on Atmospheric Chemistry, Committee on Impacts of Stratospheric Change, National Research Council. Halocarbons: Effects on Stratospheric Ozone. 1976. pap. 10.25 (ISBN 0-309-02532-X). Natl Acad Pr.

Panel on the Public Policy Implications of Earthquake Prediction, Advisory Committee on Emergency Planning, Natl Research Council. Earthquake Prediction & Public Policy. LC 75-31953. ix, 142p. 1975. pap. 8.00 (ISBN 0-309-02404-8). Natl Acad Pr.

Panel, Vienna, March 18-22, 1974. Requirements for the Irradiaton of Food on a Commercial Scale: Proceedings. (Illus.). 216p. 1975. pap. 16.75 (ISBN 92-0-111275-0, IAEA). Unipub.

Panel, Washington D.C., Sept. 4-7, 1973. Radon in Uranium Mining: Proceedings. (Illus.). 173p. 1975. pap. 16.25 (ISBN 92-0-041075-8, ISP391, IAEA). Unipub.

Paneth, Donald. News Dictionary 1980. 400p. 1981. 14.95 (ISBN 0-87196-111-3). Facts on File.

Pang, P. K. & Epple, A. Evolution of Vertebrate Endocrine Systems. (Texas Tech Univ. Graduate Studies: No. 21). 404p. (Orig.). 1980. 35.00 (ISBN 0-89672-077-2); pap. 25.00 (ISBN 0-89672-076-4). Tex Tech Pr.

Pang, Rosemary, jt. auth. see Jacobson, Morris.

Pangborn, Edgar. Davy. 288p. 1976. pap. 1.50 o.p. (ISBN 0-345-24968-2). Ballantine.

--Good Neighbors & Other Strangers. LC 75-182023. 195p. 1973. pap. 1.50 o.s.i. (ISBN 0-02-023600-X, Collier). Macmillan.

Pangborn, Edward. Still I Persist in Wondering. 1978. pap. 1.75 o.s.i. (ISBN 0-440-18277-8). Dell.

Pangrazi & Dauer. Movement in Early Childhood & Primary Education. 1981. write for info. (ISBN 0-8087-1659-X); write for info. instr's guide (ISBN 0-8087-3314-1). Burgess.

Panigrahi, D. Charles Metcalfe in India-Ideas & Administration, 1806-35. 1968. 8.75x o.p. (ISBN 0-8426-1463-X). Verry.

Panikar, P. G., jt. auth. see Pillai, Velu R.

Paniker, C. K., jt. auth. see Ananthanarayan, R.

Panikkar, Kavalam M. Angola in Flames. 1962. 5.00x (ISBN 0-210-26856-5). Asia.

--In Defense of Liberalism. 1962. 6.50x (ISBN 0-210-34059-2). Asia.
--State & the Citizen. 3.50x o.p. (ISBN 0-210-33763-X). Asia.
Panikkar, Raimundo. Mantramanjari: The Vedic Experience. 1977. 33.75x (ISBN 0-520-02854-6). U of Cal Pr.
--Myth, Faith & Hermeneutics: Toward Cross-Cultural Religious Understanding. LC 77-99306. 1980. 19.95 (ISBN 0-8091-0232-3). Paulist Pr.
--Worship & Secular Man. LC 72-93339. 126p. 1973. pap. 4.95x o.p. (ISBN 0-88344-788-6). Orbis Bks.
Panitz, Esther L. The Alien in Their Midst: Images of the Jews in English Literature. LC 78-75183. 150p. 1981. 10.50 (ISBN 0-8386-2318-2). Fairleigh Dickinson.
Panjabi, Manohar, jt. auth. see White, Augustus A.
Pankell, Dora, jt. auth. see MacGregor, Ellen.
Pankhurst, Jerry & Sacks, Michael P., eds. Contemporary Soviet Society: Sociological Perspectives. 310p. 1980. 23.95 (ISBN 0-03-055916-2); pap. 9.95 (ISBN 0-03-055911-1). Praeger.
Pankhurst, Richard. Introduction to the Economic History of Ethiopia. 1961. text ed. 12.50x (ISBN 0-391-01992-9). Humanities.
--Saint Simonian's Mill & Carlyle: A Preface to Modern Thought. 1957. text ed. 4.75x (ISBN 0-391-02042-0). Humanities.
Pankove, J. I., ed. Display Devices. (Topics in Applied Physics Ser.: Vol. 40). (Illus.). 300p. 1980. 49.80 (ISBN 0-387-09868-2). Springer-Verlag.
Panksepp, jt. auth. see Morgane.
Panksepp, J., jt. auth. see Morgane, P.
Pan Ku. A History of the Former Han Dynasty, 3 vols. Dubs, H. H., tr. from Chinese. Incl. Vol. 1. 9.00x (ISBN 0-685-32338-2); Vol. 2. 10.00x (ISBN 0-87950-281-9); Vol. 3. 12.00x (ISBN 0-87950-282-7). LC 43-46839. 1980. Repr. of 1955 ed. Set. 25.00x (ISBN 0-87950-283-5). Spoken Lang Serv.
Pannall, P. R., jt. auth. see Zilva, Joan F.
Pannekoek, A., tr. A History of Astronomy. 521p. 1961. 19.50x (ISBN 0-87471-365-X). Rowman.
Pannell, Clifton W. & Salter, Christopher L., eds. China Geographer. (Illus.). 200p. 1981. lib. bdg. 24.50x (ISBN 0-89158-860-4). Westview.
Pannenberg, Wolfhart. What Is Man: Contemporary Anthropology in Theological Perepective. Priebe, Duane A., tr. from Ger. LC 74-101429. 168p. 1972. pap. 3.75 (ISBN 0-8006-1252-3, 1-1252). Fortress.
Pannenborg, Charles O. A New International Health Order. 476p. 1979. 32.50x (ISBN 90-286-0239-9). Sijthoff & Noordhoff.
Pannese, E. The Satellite Cells of the Sensory Canglia. (Advances in Antomy, Embryology & Cell Biology Ser.: Vol. 65). (Illus.). 98p. 1981. pap. 33.00 (ISBN 0-387-10219-1). Springer-Verlag.
Pannick, Gerald. Richard Palmer Blackmur. (United States Authors Ser.: No. 409). 1981. lib. bdg. 12.95 (ISBN 0-8057-7338-X). Twayne.
Panning, Armin J. The Life of Christ. 1971. pap. 2.50 (ISBN 0-8100-0018-0, 09-0932). Northwest Pub.
Pannwitt, Barbara, jt. auth. see Ogden, John B.
Panofsky, Erwin. Early Netherlandish Painting, 2 vols, Vols. 1 & 2. (Icon Edition). (Illus.). 1971. Vol. 1. pap. 11.95x (ISBN 0-06-430002-1, IN-2, HarpT); Vol. 2. pap. 8.95x (ISBN 0-06-430003-X, IN-3). Har-Row.
--Meaning in the Visual Arts. LC 55-9754. 1955. pap. 3.50 o.p. (ISBN 0-385-09248-2, A59, Anch). Doubleday.
--Renaissance & Renascences in Western Art. (Icon Edition). (Illus.). 380p. 1972. pap. 7.95 (ISBN 0-06-430026-9, IN-26, HarpT). Har-Row.
Panofsky, Hans E. A Bibliography of Africana. LC 72-823. (Contributions in Librarianship & Information Science Ser.: No. 11). 1975. lib. bdg. 18.95 (ISBN 0-8371-6391-9, PAA/). Greenwood.
Panofsky, W. K. Arms Control & Salt II. LC 79-5182. (Jessie & John Danz Lecture Ser.). 88p. 1979. pap. 2.95 (ISBN 0-295-95700-X). U of Wash Pr.
Panofsky, Wolfgang K. & Phillips, Melba. Classical Electricity & Magnetism. 2nd ed. 1962. 24.95 (ISBN 0-201-05702-6). A-W.
Panoletti, Rodolfo, jt. ed. see Gotto, Antonio.
Panov, V., jt. auth. see Estrin, Y.
Panshin, Alexei & Panshin, Cory. SF in Dimension. 2nd ed. LC 80-68572. 1980. pap. 6.00 (ISBN 0-911682-24-4). Advent.
Panshin, Cory, jt. auth. see Panshin, Alexei.
Pansini, Anthony J. Basic Electrical Power Distribution, 2 Vols. rev. 2nd ed. (Illus.). 1971. pap. 6.75 ea.; Vol. 1. pap. (ISBN 0-8104-0818-X); Vol. 2. pap. (ISBN 0-8104-0819-8); exam set vol. 1 0.30 (ISBN 0-8104-0821-X); exam set vol. 2 0.30 (ISBN 0-8104-0822-8). Hayden.
--Basic Electrical Power Transformers. 1976. pap. 6.75 (ISBN 0-8104-0020-0); final exam 0.30 (ISBN 0-8104-0600-4). Hayden.
--Basic Electrical Power Transmission. (Illus.). 128p. 1975. pap. 7.50 (ISBN 0-8104-5928-0); final exam 0.30 (ISBN 0-8104-0599-7). Hayden.
--Machiavelli & the United States, 6 vols. in 1. LC 70-108252. 1371p. (500th anniv. ed). 1969. 20.00 (ISBN 0-685-23384-7, 911876-02). Greenvale.
--Undergrounding Electric Lines. (gr. 10 up). 1978. pap. 7.15 (ISBN 0-8104-0827-9); final exam 0.30 (ISBN 0-686-67928-8). Hayden.
Pant, Gauri. Staircase Seventeen. (Writers Workshop Redbird Ser.). 1975. 8.00 (ISBN 0-88253-644-3); pap. text ed. 4.00 (ISBN 0-88253-643-5). Ind-US Inc.
--Voodoo. 1972. 8.00 (ISBN 0-88253-707-5); pap. text ed. 4.00 (ISBN 0-88253-845-4). Ind-US Inc.
--Weeping Season. (Redbird Book). 36p. 1975. 4.80 (ISBN 0-88253-717-2); pap. 4.00 (ISBN 0-88253-847-0). Ind-US Inc.
Pant, Niranjan. Politics of Panchaytirai Administration. 1979. text ed. 8.00x (ISBN 0-391-01850-7). Humanities.
Pantaleoni, C. A. & Bigler, James C. California Criminal Law: A Guide for Policemen. 1969. text ed. 16.95 (ISBN 0-13-112565-6). P-H.
Pantelides, Sokrates T., ed. Physics of Silicon Dioxide & Its Interfaces: An International Topical Conference. 1978. text ed. 43.00 (ISBN 0-08-023049-0). Pergamon.
Pantell, Dora, jt. auth. see Alesi, Gladys.
Pantell, Dora, jt. auth. see MacGregor, Ellen.
Pantell, R. H. Techniques of Environmental Systems Analysis. LC 76-98. 224p. 1976. 27.00 (ISBN 0-471-65791-3, Pub. by Wiley-Interscience). Wiley.
Pantelouris, E. M. Introduction to Animal Physiology & Physiological Genetics. 1966. text ed. 29.00 o.p. (ISBN 0-08-011722-8); pap. text ed. 15.50 o.p. (ISBN 0-08-018981-4). Pergamon.
Panter, Carol, jt. auth. see Liman, Ellen.
Panter-Brick, S. K., ed. Nigerian Politics & Military Rule: Prelude to the Civil War. (Athlone Commonwealth Papers: No. 13). 1970. text ed. 9.75x (ISBN 0-485-17613-0, Athlone Pr). Humanities.
Panter-Brick, Simone. Gandhi Against Machiavellism: Non-Violence in Politics. 1967. 7.50x (ISBN 0-210-34085-1). Asia.
Panther, Ida S. Doctor & Annie. 1981. 5.75 (ISBN 0-8062-1628-X). Carlton.
Pantin, Gerard. A Mole Cricket Called Servol: An Account of Experiences in Education & Community Development in Trinidad & Tobago, West Indies. (Illus.). 1979. text ed. 22.00 (ISBN 0-08-024278-2). Pergamon.
Pantin, W. A. The English Church in the Fourteenth Century. (Medieval Academy Reprints for Teaching Ser.). 1980. pap. 5.00x (ISBN 0-8020-6411-6). U of Toronto Pr.
Pantistico, E. B. Postharvest Physiology, Handling & Utilization of Tropical & Subtropical Fruits & Vegetables. (Illus.). 1975. lib. bdg. 45.00 (ISBN 0-87055-156-6). AVI.
Panum, Hortense. Stringed Instruments of the Middle Ages. LC 73-127279. (Music Ser). (Illus.). 1970. Repr. of 1939 ed. lib. bdg. 39.50 (ISBN 0-306-70039-5). Da Capo.
Panunzio, Constantine M. Deportation Cases of Nineteen-Nineteen to Nineteen-Twenty. LC 77-109547. (Civil Liberties in American History Ser). 1970. Repr. of 1921 ed. lib. bdg. 14.50 (ISBN 0-306-71901-0). Da Capo.
P'an Wei-Tung. The Chinese Constitution: A Study of Forty Years of Constitution-Making in China. LC 79-1639. 1981. Repr. of 1945 ed. 25.00 (ISBN 0-88355-942-0). Hyperion Conn.
Panyan, Marion V. How to Use Shaping. 1980. pap. 3.25 (ISBN 0-89079-050-7). H & H Ent.
Panzar, John C. Regulation, Service Quality, & Market Performance: A Model of Airline Rivalry. LC 78-75053. (Outstanding Dissertations in Economics Ser.). 1979. lib. bdg. 16.00 (ISBN 0-8240-4131-3). Garland Pub.
Panzarella, Andrew. Religion & Human Experience. LC 73-87024. 1974. pap. 3.30x (ISBN 0-88489-058-9); tchr's ed 2.60x (ISBN 0-88489-080-5). St Marys.
Panzarella, Joseph J., M.D. & Kittler, Glenn D. Spirit Makes a Man. LC 77-11766. 1978. 6.95 o.p. (ISBN 0-385-12117-2). Doubleday.
Panzion, Leo. The Pleasures of Being a Catholic, 2 vols. new ed. (Human Development Library Bk.). (Illus.). 1979. Set. 39.75 o.p. (ISBN 0-89266-155-0). Am Classical Coll Pr.
Paola, Tomie de. Four Stories for Four Seasons. LC 76-8837. (Illus.). (ps-2). 1977. PLB 7.95 (ISBN 0-13-330175-3); pap. 3.95 (ISBN 0-13-330100-1). P-H.
Paola, Tomie De see De Paola, Tomie.
Paola, Tomie de see De Paola, Tomie.
Paola, Tomie De see De Paola, Tomie.
Paola, Tomie de see De Paola, Tomie.
Paoletti, John T. The Siena Baptistry Font: A Study of an Early Renaissance Collaborative Program, 1416-1434. LC 78-74374. (Fine Arts Dissertations, Fourth Ser.). (Illus.). 1980. lib. bdg. 33.00 (ISBN 0-8240-3961-0). Garland Pub.
Paoletti, R. & Kritchevsky, D., eds. Advances in Lipid Research, Vols. 1-16. Incl. Vol. 1. 1964. 52.00 (ISBN 0-12-024901-4); Vol. 2. 1964. 52.00 (ISBN 0-12-024902-2); Vol. 3. 1965. 52.00 (ISBN 0-12-024903-0); Vol. 4. 1967. 52.00 (ISBN 0-12-024904-9); Vol. 5. 1967. 52.00 (ISBN 0-12-024905-7); Vol. 6. 1968. 52.00 (ISBN 0-12-024906-5); Vol. 7. 1969. 52.00 (ISBN 0-12-024907-3); Vol. 8. 1970. 52.00 (ISBN 0-12-024908-1); Vol. 9. 1971. 52.00 (ISBN 0-12-024909-X); Vol. 10. 1972. 52.00 (ISBN 0-12-024910-3); Vol. 11. 1973. 52.00 (ISBN 0-12-024911-1); Vol. 12. 1974. 52.00 (ISBN 0-12-024912-X); Vol. 13. 1975. 52.00 (ISBN 0-12-024913-8); Vol. 14. 1976. 52.00 (ISBN 0-12-024914-6); lib ed. 67.00 (ISBN 0-12-024974-X); microfiche 37.50 (ISBN 0-12-024975-8); Vol. 15. 1977. 45.50 (ISBN 0-12-024915-4); lib ed. 58.00 (ISBN 0-12-024976-6); microfiche 33.00 (ISBN 0-12-024977-4); Vol. 16. 1978. 42.50 (ISBN 0-12-024916-2); lib. ed. 54.00 (ISBN 0-12-024979-0); microfiche 31.00 (ISBN 0-12-024979-0). LC 63-22330. Acad Pr.
Paoletti, R., jt. ed. see Samuelsson, B.
Paoletti, R., et al, eds. Lipids: Proceedings, 2 vols. Incl. Vol. 1. Biochemistry. LC 75-21982. 298p. 37.50 (ISBN 0-89004-028-1); Vol. 2. Technology. LC 75-26387. 286p. 37.50 (ISBN 0-89004-029-X). 1975. Set. 68.00 (ISBN 0-685-61106-X). Raven.
Paoletti, Rodolfo, ed. Hearing on Hypolipidemic Drugs. 1981. text ed. price not set (ISBN 0-89004-649-2). Raven.
Paoletti, Rodolfo & Gotto, Antonio M., eds. Atherosclerosis Reviews, Vol. 2. LC 75-14582. 1977. 25.00 (ISBN 0-89004-061-3). Raven.
--Atherosclerosis Reviews, Vol. 4. LC 75-14582. 1978. 28.00 (ISBN 0-89004-218-7). Raven.
--Atherosclerosis Reviews, Vol. 5. LC 75-14582. 1979. text ed. 28.00 (ISBN 0-89004-275-6). Raven.
Paoletti, Rodolfo & Gotto, Antonio M., Jr., eds. Atherosclerosis Reviews, Vol. 1. LC 75-14582. 1976. 24.50 (ISBN 0-89004-038-9). Raven.
--Atherosclerosis Reviews, Vol. 3. LC 75-14582. 1978. 27.00 (ISBN 0-89004-217-9). Raven.
Paoletti, Rodolfo, jt. ed. see Kritchevsky, David.
Paoli, Arturo. Meditations on Saint Luke. McWilliams, Bernard, tr. from Spanish. LC 76-58539. 1977. 8.95x o.p. (ISBN 0-88344-314-7); pap. 4.95x o.p. (ISBN 0-88344-315-5). Orbis Bks.
Paolino, Thomas J., Jr. Psychoanalytic Psychotherapy: Theory, Technique, Therapeutic Relationship & Treatability. 350p. 1981. 20.00 (ISBN 0-87630-261-4). Brunner-Mazel.
Paolo, Tomie de see De Paola, Tomie.
Paolozzi & Sedwick. Conversation in Italian: Points of Departure. 2nd ed. (Illus., Orig.). 1981. pap. text ed. write for info. (ISBN 0-442-24474-6). D Van Nostrand.
Paolucci, Anne. From Tension to Tonic: The Plays of Edward Albee. LC 75-179594. (Crosscurrents-Modern Critiques Ser.). 158p. 1972. 9.95 (ISBN 0-8093-0551-8). S Ill U Pr.
Paolucci, Anne, ed. see Hegel, G. W.
Paolucci, Anne, tr. see Machiavelli, Niccolo.
Paolucci, Antonia. Ravenna. (Scala Art Book). (Illus., Orig.). 1978. pap. 7.95 (ISBN 0-8467-0470-6, Pub. by Two Continents). Hippocrene Bks.
Paolucci, Henry, ed. see Hegel, G. W.
Paolucci, Henry, tr. see Beccaria, Cesare.
Paolucci, Henry, tr. see Machiavelli, Niccolo.
Pap, A., jt. auth. see Edwards, Paul.
Pap, Leo. The Portuguese-Americans. (Immigrant Heritage of America Ser.). 1981. lib. bdg. 14.95 (ISBN 0-8057-8417-9). Twayne.
Papadatos, Constantine J., jt. ed. see Bartsocas, Christos S.
Papadimitriou, Christos H., jt. auth. see Lewis, Harry R.
Papadopoulos, C. True Visual Magnitude Photographic Star Atlas, 2 vols. LC 78-41254. 1979. Set. 550.00 (ISBN 0-08-021622-6); Vol. 1. 225.00 (ISBN 0-08-023435-6); Vol. 2. 325.00 (ISBN 0-08-021623-4). Pergamon.
Papadoupoulos, G. & Devreese, J. T., eds. Path Integrals & Their Applications in Quantum Statistical & Solid State Physics. (NATO Advanced Study Institutes Ser.: Series B, Physics, Vol. 34). 508p. 1978. 49.50 (ISBN 0-306-40017-0, Plenum Pr). Plenum Pub.
Papaefstratiou, Louka T. Transmission of External Price Disturbances in Small, Open Economies. LC 78-75064. (Outstanding Dissertations in Economics Ser.). 1979. lib. bdg. 20.00 (ISBN 0-8240-4141-0). Garland Pub.
Papageorge, Tod, ed. Walker Evans & Robert Frank: A Study of Experience. (Illus.). 72p. 1981. pap. write for info. (ISBN 0-89467-015-8). Yale Art Gallery.
Papageorgiou, George J. Mathematical Land Use Theory. LC 75-21303. (Illus.). 1976. 32.95 (ISBN 0-669-00164-3). Lexington Bks.
Papageorgiou, J. C. Management Science & Environmental Problems. (Illus.). 160p. 1980. 16.75 (ISBN 0-398-03995-X). C C Thomas.
Papageorgiou, Nikolaos. Population Energy Relationships of the Agrimi (Capra Aegagrus Cretica) on Theodorou Island, Greece. (Illus.). 56p. (Orig.). pap. text ed. 14.10 (ISBN 3-490-21518-4). Parey Sci Pubs.
Papagno, et al. Desairology: Hairdressing for Decedents. LC 80-82330. (The Family, the Funeral & the Hairdresser). (Illus.). 104p. (Orig.). 1980. 17.95x (ISBN 0-9604610-0-0); lib. bdg. 15.50 (ISBN 0-686-27695-7); pap. 12.95 (ISBN 0-9604610-1-9). JJ Pub Fl.
Papaioannou, A. N. The Prevention of Breast Cancer. 1981. write for info. (ISBN 0-87527-227-4). Green.
Papaioannou, G. From Mars Hill to Manhattan. 1976. pap. 5.95 (ISBN 0-937032-08-5). Light & Life Pub Co MN.
Papajohn, John C. Intensive Behavior Therapy. (General Psychology Ser.). Date not set. 15.00 (ISBN 0-08-025544-2). Pergamon. Postponed.
Papalia, Anthony & Mendoza, Jose A. Lecturas Para Hoy. (Orig.). (gr. 9-12). 1972. pap. text ed. 4.58 (ISBN 0-87720-512-4). AMSCO Sch.
--Por Fronteras Culturales. (Orig.). (gr. 11). 1976. pap. text ed. 6.25 (ISBN 0-87720-518-3). AMSCO Sch.
Papalia, Diane E. & Olds, Sally W. A Child's World: Infancy Through Adolescence. LC 74-31496. (Illus.). 672p. 1975. text ed. 15.95 (ISBN 0-07-048458-9, C); instructors' manual 2.95 (ISBN 0-685-50939-7); test file 5.95 (ISBN 0-07-048459-7). McGraw.
Papallo, George. What Makes It Work. LC 76-14838. 1976. 9.95 (ISBN 0-668-03962-0); pap. 4.95 (ISBN 0-668-03963-9). Arco.
Papanek, Gustav F., ed. The Indonesian Economy. LC 80-18752. 300p. 1981. 26.95 (ISBN 0-03-057429-3). Praeger.
Papanek, H., jt. ed. see Jahan, Rounaq.
Papanek, Hanna, jt. ed. see Jahan, Rounaq.
Papanikolas, Helen Z., ed. The Peoples of Utah. LC 76-12311. (Illus.). 498p. 7.50 o.p. (ISBN 0-913738-26-3). Utah St Hist Soc.
Paparella, ed. Biochemical Mechanisms in Hearing & Deafness. (Illus.). 416p. 1970. 27.50 (ISBN 0-398-01445-0). C C Thomas.
Paparella, Michael M., et al. Sensorineural Hearing Loss, Vertigo & Tinnitus: International Symposium. 232p. 1981. write for info. (6750-8). Williams & Wilkins.
Papas, William. People of Old Jerusalem. LC 80-197. (Illus.). 216p. 1980. 34.95 (ISBN 0-03-057483-8); prepub. 29.95 pre-Jan. HR&W.
Papashvily, George & Papashvily, Helen. Anything Can Happen. LC 44-41894. 1945. lib. bdg. 8.29 o.s.i. (ISBN 0-06-013256-6, HarpT). Har-Row.
Papashvily, George, jt. auth. see Papashvily, Helen.
Papashvily, Helen & Papashvily, George. Russian Cooking. (Foods of the World Ser). (Illus.). 1969. 14.95 (ISBN 0-8094-0043-X). Time-Life.
--Russian Cooking. LC 78-103302. (Foods of the World Ser). (Illus.). (gr. 6 up). 1969. PLB 14.94 (ISBN 0-8094-0070-7, Pub. by Time-Life). Silver.
Papashvily, Helen, jt. auth. see Papashvily, George.
Papavizas, George C., ed. Biological Control in Crop Production. (Beltsville Symposia in Agricultural Research Ser.: No. 5). 1981. text ed. 35.00 (ISBN 0-86598-037-3). Allanheld.
Papazian, Charlie. Joy of Brewing. rev. ed. (Illus.). 88p. 1980. pap. 4.50 (ISBN 0-9604130-0-6). Log Boom.
Pape, Ambrosius. Bettel und Garteteuffel. Graves, Oliver F., ed. LC 80-23210. liv, 440p. (Orig.). 1981. pap. 25.00 (ISBN 0-8173-0059-7). U of Ala Pr.
Pape, D. Gerbil for a Friend. (Illus.). 1979. pap. 1.50 (ISBN 0-13-353987-3). P-H.
Pape, Donna L. Big Words for Little People. 1973. pap. 1.49 o.p. (ISBN 0-87239-280-5, 2741). Standard Pub.
--Come Out, Come Out, Wherever You Are. LC 78-73528. (First Reader Ser.). (Illus.). (gr. k-3). Date not set. price not set (ISBN 0-89799-153-2); pap. price not set (ISBN 0-89799-071-4). Dandelion Pr. Postponed.
--The Little Bird. LC 78-73535. (First Reader Ser.). (Illus.). (gr. k-3). Date not set. price not set (ISBN 0-89799-157-5); pap. price not set (ISBN 0-89799-075-7). Dandelion Pr. Postponed.
--The Mouse at the Show. (Illus.). 32p. (ps-2). 1981. 5.95 (ISBN 0-525-66722-9). Elsevier-Nelson.
--Puzzle Panic. (gr. 4-6). 1977. pap. 1.25 (ISBN 0-590-10314-8, Schol Pap). Schol Bk Serv.

Pape, Donna L. & Grote, Jeanette. Pack of Puzzles. (gr. 4-6). 1976. pap. 1.25 (ISBN 0-590-10145-5, Schol Pap). Schol Bk Serv.

Pape, Donna L. & Mueller, Virginia. Bible Activities for Kids, No. 1. (Illus.). 64p. (Orig.). (gr. 3-7). 1980. pap. 1.95 (ISBN 0-87123-148-4, 21048). Bethany Fell.

Pape, Donna L., et al. Puzzles & Silly Riddles. (gr. 4-6). 1974. pap. 1.25 (ISBN 0-590-06120-8, Schol Pap). Schol Bk Serv.

Pape, Dorothy R. In Search of Gods Ideal Woman: A Personal Examination of the New Testament. LC 75-21453. 366p. (Orig.). 1976. pap. 5.95 (ISBN 0-87784-854-8). Inter-Varsity.

Pape, Gordon & Aspler, Tony. Chain Reaction. 1978. 9.95 o.p. (ISBN 0-670-21102-8). Viking Pr.

--The Scorpion Sanction. LC 79-56262. 372p. 1980. 13.95 (ISBN 0-670-19965-6). Viking Pr.

Pape, Richard. Boldness Be My Friend. 1955. 12.95 (ISBN 0-236-30836-X, Pub. by Paul Elek). Merrimack Bk Serv.

Papenfuse, Edward C. & Stiverson, Gregory A., Jr., eds. Maryland Manual: 1979-1980. (Illus.). 1979. 8.00 (ISBN 0-686-21209-6). MD Hall Records.

Papenfuse, Edward C., et al. A Guide to the Maryland Hall of Records: Local Judicial & Administrative Records on Microform, Vol. 1. 231p. 1978. 9.00 (ISBN 0-686-27482-2). MD Hall Records.

Paper, Lewis J. John F. Kennedy: The Promise & the Performance. xi, 408p. 1980. pap. 7.95 (ISBN 0-306-80114-0). Da Capo.

Paperno, V. A., jt. auth. see Nakhimovsky, A. D.

Papers from the First Annual Conference on Shock, Airlie, Va., June 1978. Advances in Shock Research: Proceedings, Vol. 1. Lefer, Allan M. & Mela, Leena M., eds. LC 79-63007. 288p. 1979. 30.00x (ISBN 0-8451-0600-7). A R Liss.

Papers from the First Annual Conference on Shock, Airlie, Va. June 1978. Advances in Shock Research: Proceedings, Vol. 2. Schumer, William, et al, eds. LC 79-63007. 308p. 1979. 30.00x (ISBN 0-8451-0601-5). A R Liss.

Papers from the Second Annual Conference on Shock, Williamsburg, Va. June 1979. Advances in Shock Research: Proceedings, Vol. 3. Lefer, Allan M. & Saba, Thomas M., eds. LC 79-63007. 316p. 1980. 34.00x (ISBN 0-8451-0602-3). A R Liss.

Papers from the Second Annual Conference on Shock, Williamsburg, Va., June 1979. Advances in Shock Research: Proceedings, Vol. 4. Spitzer, John J. & Marshall, Bryan E., eds. LC 79-63007. 232p. 1980. 26.00x (ISBN 0-8451-0603-1). A R Liss.

Papers Presented Before the College of Sports Medicine & Serfass, Robert. Exercise & Aging: The Scientific Basis. (Illus.). 224p. 1981. text ed. 12.95 (ISBN 0-89490-042-0). Enslow Pubs.

Papert, Seymour. Mindstorms: Children, Computers, & Powerful Ideas. LC 79-5200. 1980. 12.95 (ISBN 0-465-04627-4). Basic.

Papert, Seymour, jt. auth. see Minsky, Marvin L.

Papian, U. N., jt. auth. see Gates, D. M.

Papillon, Alfred L. Foundations of Educational Research. LC 78-69861. 1978. pap. text ed. 12.00 (ISBN 0-8191-0583-X). U Pr of Amer.

Papineau, David. Theory & Meaning. 218p. 1979. text ed. 19.95x (ISBN 0-19-824585-8). Oxford U Pr.

Papmehl, K. A., tr. see Soloviev, Sergei M.

Papola, T. S. Urban Informal Sector in an Urban Economy: A Study in Ahmedabad. 156p. 1981. text ed. 15.95x (ISBN 0-7069-1133-4, Pub by Vikas India). Advent Bk.

Papon, Donald. The Lure of the Heavens: A History of Astrology. (Illus.). 320p. 1980. pap. 7.95 (ISBN 0-87728-502-0). Weiser.

Papovych, Orest. Tetraphenylborates. (IUPAC Solubility Data Ser.: Vol. 18). 260p. 1981. 100.00 (ISBN 0-08-023928-5). Pergamon.

Papp, Charles S., jt. auth. see Swan, Lester A.

Papp, Daniel S. Vietnam: The View from Moscow, Peking, Washington. LC 80-20117. (Illus.). 263p. 1981. lib. bdg. 17.95x (ISBN 0-89950-010-2). McFarland & Co.

Papp, Peggy, ed. Family Therapy: Full Length Case Studies. LC 77-16641. 1977. 14.95 o.p. (ISBN 0-470-99355-3). Halsted Pr.

Pappas, James L. & Brigham, Eugene F. Fundamentals of Managerial Economics. LC 79-51063. 560p. 1981. text ed. 17.95 (ISBN 0-03-040841-5). Dryden Pr.

Pappas, Lou S. Cookies. Reynolds, Maureen, ed. LC 80-81247. (Illus.). 192p. 1980. pap. 4.95 (ISBN 0-911954-57-0). Nitty Gritty.

Pappas, S. Peter, ed. UV Curing: Science & Technology. LC 78-56293. (Illus.). 1978. perfect bdg. 95.00 (ISBN 0-686-23773-0). Tech Marketing.

Pappas, S. Peter & Winslow, F. H., eds. Photodegradation & Photostabilization of Coatings. (ACS Symposium Ser: No. 151). 1981. price not set (ISBN 0-8412-0611-2). Am Chemical.

Papper. Managerial Economics. 3rd ed. 1979. 21.95 (ISBN 0-03-045126-4). Dryden Pr.

Pappin, Charlene. Arithmetic, Complete Course. Maier, Eugene, ed. 1970. pap. text ed. 10.95x (ISBN 0-02-476650-X, 47665); progress tests 9.95x (ISBN 0-02-476640-2, 47664). Macmillan.

Pappworth. A Primer of Medicine. 4th ed. LC 77-30428. (Primer Ser.). 1978. 27.50 (ISBN 0-407-62603-4). Butterworths.

Pappworth, M. H. Passing Medical Exams. 1975. 9.95 (ISBN 0-407-00013-5). Butterworths.

Papworth, Joseph. New Politics. 336p. 1980. text ed. 37.50x (ISBN 0-7069-1273-X, Pub. by Vikas India). Advent Bk.

Papy, jt. auth. see Frederique.

Paque, Boris. Medical Astrology. Broglio, John, tr. from Fr. Date not set. 20.00 (ISBN 0-88231-051-8). ASI Pubs Inc. Postponed.

Paquette, F. Andre see Bird, Thomas E.

Paquette, Laurence, jt. auth. see Emerson, Lloyd.

Paquette, Lawrence, jt. auth. see Emerson, Lloyd.

Paquette, Radnor J., et al. Transportation Engineering: Planning & Design. 760p. 1972. 25.95 (ISBN 0-471-06670-2). Wiley.

Paquin, J. R. Die Design Fundamentals. (Illus.). (gr. 11-12). 1962. 19.00 (ISBN 0-8311-1010-4); wkbk. 7.00 (ISBN 0-8311-1011-2). Indus Pr.

Paquot, C., ed. Standard Methods for the Analysis of Oils, Fats & Derivatives. 6th ed. LC 78-40305. 1978. text ed. 25.00 (ISBN 0-08-022379-6). Pergamon.

Para Research, Inc. Astrological Books in Print, 1981-82. 144p. (Orig.). 1981. pap. 4.95 (ISBN 0-686-69331-0). Para Res.

Paracelsus. The Hermetic & Alchemical Writings of Paracelsus, Vol. 1: Hermetic Chemistry. Waite, Arthur E., ed. LC 75-40261. 394p. (Orig.). 1976. pap. 7.50 o.p. (ISBN 0-394-73184-0). Shambhala Pubns.

--The Hermetic & Alchemical Writings of Paracelsus, Vol. 2: Hermetic Medicine & Hermetic Philosophy. Waite, Arthur E., ed. & tr. from Ger. LC 75-40261. 396p. 1976. pap. 7.50 o.p. (ISBN 0-394-73185-9). Shambhala Pubns.

Paradis, James G. T. H. Huxley: Man's Place in Nature. LC 78-5492. 1978. 16.50x (ISBN 0-8032-0917-7). U of Nebr Pr.

Paradise, ed. see Ginsburg.

Paradise, Lee. Readings in English: The Arts, Bk 4. (Readings in English Ser.). 112p. (gr. 9-12). 1981. pap. text ed. price not set (ISBN 0-88345-426-2, 18885). Regents Pub.

Paradise, Paul. Gerbils. (Illus.). 96p. 1980. 2.95 (ISBN 0-87666-757-4, KW-037). TFH Pubns.

Paradise, Paul, jt. auth. see Evans, Irene.

Paradise, Paul R., ed. Goldfish. (Illus.). 1979. 2.95 (ISBN 0-87666-511-3, KW-014). TFH Pubns.

Parajon, Arturo, tr. see Robertson, A. T.

Paramanandhan, T. L., jt. auth. see Janovski, N. A.

Parameswaran, Uma. Cyclic Hope, Cyclic Pain. (Writers Workshop Redbird Ser.). 23p. 1975. 8.00 (ISBN 0-88253-520-X); pap. text ed. 4.00 (ISBN 0-88253-519-6). Ind-US Inc.

Paramount Pictures Corporation. The Mork & Mindy Super Activity Book. 128p. (gr. 2-6). 1980. pap. cancelled o.s.i. (ISBN 0-448-15497-8). G&D.

Paranavitana, Senarat. Sinhalayo. rev. 2nd ed. 67p. 1975. text ed. 6.00x o.p. (ISBN 0-8426-0794-3). Verry.

Paranavitana, Senarat. Ceylon & Malaysia. (Illus.). 234p. 1975. text ed. 10.00x o.p. (ISBN 0-8426-0791-9). Verry.

Paranjpe, A. C. In Search of Identity. LC 75-257. 1976. 17.95 (ISBN 0-470-65856-8). Halsted Pr.

Paranjpe, V. G., tr. see Bergaigne, Abel.

Parapsychological Association. Research in Parapsychology 1972: Abstracts & Papers from the 15th Annual Convention of the Parapsychological Association, 1972. Roll, W. G., et al, eds. LC 66-28580. 1973. 11.00 (ISBN 0-8108-0666-5). Scarecrow.

--Research in Parapsychology 1973: Abstracts & Papers from the 16th Annual Convention of the Parapsychological Association, 1973. Roll, W. G., et al, eds. LC 66-28580. 1974. 11.00 (ISBN 0-8108-0708-4). Scarecrow.

--Research in Parapsychology 1974: Abstracts & Papers from the 17th Annual Convention of the Parapsychological Association, 1974. Morris, J. D. & Roll, W. G., eds. LC 66-28580. 272p. 1975. 11.00 (ISBN 0-8108-0850-1). Scarecrow.

--Research in Parapsychology 1975: Abstracts & Papers from the 18th Annual Convention of the Parapsychological Association, 1975. Morris, J. D., et al, eds. LC 66-28580. 277p. 1976. 11.00 (ISBN 0-8108-0895-1). Scarecrow.

--Research in Parapsychology 1976: Abstracts & Papers from the 19th Annual Convention of the Parapsychological Association, 1976. Morris, J. D., et al, eds. LC 66-28580. 1977. 11.00 (ISBN 0-8108-1080-8). Scarecrow.

--Research in Parapsychology 1977: Abstracts & Papers from the 20th Annual Convention of the Parapsychological Association, 1977. Roll, William G., ed. LC 66-28580. 1978. lib. bdg. 11.00 (ISBN 0-8108-1131-6). Scarecrow.

--Research in Parapsychology 1978. Roll, William G., ed. LC 66-28580. 1979. 11.00 (ISBN 0-8108-1195-2). Scarecrow.

Parascandola, John, ed. The History of Antibiotics: A Symposium. (Illus.). 137p. (Orig.). 1980. pap. 5.40 (ISBN 0-931292-08-5). Am Inst Pharmacy.

Paraskevopoulos, George N. An Econometric Analysis of International Tourism. (Lecture Ser.: No. 31). (Illus.). 110p. (Orig.). 1977. pap. 8.50x (ISBN 0-8002-2743-3). Intl Pubns Serv.

Parasurama. Bases of Tantra Sadhana. Pandit, M. P., tr. 52p. (Sanskrit.). 1980. 2.00 (ISBN 0-89744-983-5, Pub. by Dipti Pubns India). Auromere.

Parcel, Guy S., et al. Teaching Myself About Asthma. 1st ed. LC 79-13166. (Illus.). 1979. pap. 10.00 (ISBN 0-8016-3755-4). Mosby.

Parcel, John I. & Moorman, R. B. Analysis of Statically Indeterminate Structures. 1955. 32.50 (ISBN 0-471-65868-5, Pub. by Wiley-Interscience). Wiley.

Parcher. Soil Mechanics & Foundations. 1968. text ed. 22.95x (ISBN 0-675-09746-0). Merrill.

Pardee, Dennis. Handbook of Ancient Hebrew Letters. LC 79-22372. (Society of Biblical Literature, Sources for Biblical Study: 15). Date not set. 15.00x (ISBN 0-89130-359-6, 060315); pap. 10.50x (ISBN 0-89130-360-X). Scholars Pr CA.

Pardee, Michael, jt. auth. see Waite, Mitchell.

Pardes, Herbert, jt. auth. see Simons, Richard C.

Pardey, Larry, jt. auth. see Pardey, Lin.

Pardey, Lin & Pardey, Larry. The Care & Feeding of the Offshore Crew. (Illus.). 1980. 17.95 (ISBN 0-393-03249-3). Norton.

Pardo Bazan, Emilia. The Son of the Bondwoman. Hearn, E. H., tr. 328p. 1976. Repr. of 1908 ed. 17.50 (ISBN 0-86527-307-3). Fertig.

Pardoe, E. F. Communication in Writing. 1965. 8.50 (ISBN 0-08-011136-X); pap. 4.20 (ISBN 0-08-011135-1). Pergamon.

Pardoen, Alan, ed. see Boyle, Patrick G.

Pardoen, Alan, ed. see Seaman, Donald.

Pardue, P. Buddhism: A Brief Account. 1971. pap. 1.95 o.s.i. (ISBN 0-02-088260-2, Collier). Macmillan.

Pare, Madeline F. & Fireman, Bert M. Arizona Pageant: A Short History of the 48th State. LC 65-65080. 1978. text ed. 7.00 (ISBN 0-685-67966-7). AZ Hist Foun.

Paredes, Americo, tr. see Cosio Villegas, Daniel.

Paredes, J. Anthony, ed. Anishinabe: Six Studies of Modern Chippewa. LC 79-20091. (Illus.). xi, 436p. 1980. 27.50 (ISBN 0-8130-0625-2). U Presses Fla.

Parelius, Ann P. & Parelius, Robert J. The Sociology of Education. LC 77-10948. (P-H Series in Sociology). (Illus.). 1978. 17.95 (ISBN 0-13-821173-6). P-H.

Parelius, Robert J., jt. auth. see Parelius, Ann P.

Parent, David J., ed. see Kalwies, Howard.

Parent, David J., ed. see Ley, Ralph.

Parent, David J., tr. see Landauer, Gustav.

Parent, Gail. The Best Laid Plans. 300p. 1981. 10.95 (ISBN 0-399-12510-8). Putnam.

--David Meyer Is a Mother. LC 74-15885. 256p. 1976. 7.95 o.s.i. (ISBN 0-06-013274-4, HarpT). Har-Row.

Parents Magazine Enterprises. Parents' Magazine's Mother's Encyclopedia & Everyday Guide to Family Health. Rossman, Isidore, ed. 1981. pap. 9.95 (Delta). Dell.

Parents Nursery School. Kids Are Natural Cooks. (Illus.). (ps-6). 1974. pap. 5.95 (ISBN 0-395-18521-1, Sandpiper). HM.

Paret, Peter. Clausewitz & the State. LC 75-16901. (Illus.). 560p. 1976. 25.95x (ISBN 0-19-501988-1). Oxford U Pr.

Paret, Peter, ed. Frederick the Great: A Profile. (World Profiles Ser). (Orig.). 1972. 7.95 o.p. (ISBN 0-8090-4678-4); pap. 3.95 o.p. (ISBN 0-8090-1402-5). Hill & Wang.

Paret, Peter, ed. see Von Clausewitz, Carl.

Paret, Peter, tr. see Meinecke, Friedrich.

Paret, Peter, tr. & intro. by see Ritter, Gerhard.

Pareto, Vilfredo. The Historical Theory of the Ruling Class. (The Most Meaningful Classics in World Culture Ser.). (Illus.). 1979. 49.75 (ISBN 0-89266-193-3). Am Classical Coll Pr.

--The Ruling Class in Italy Before 1900. LC 73-20130. 143p. 1975. Repr. of 1950 ed. 14.00 (ISBN 0-86527-176-3). Fertig.

Paretti, Sandra. Maria Canossa. 294p. 1981. 11.95 (ISBN 0-312-51449-2). St Martin.

--Wishing Tree. 1978. pap. 1.95 o.p. (ISBN 0-449-23604-8, Crest). Fawcett.

Parfit, Jessie. Helping the Handicapped Child: In Day & Residential Care, No. 3. (General Ser.). (Illus.). 48p. 1975. pap. text ed. 2.25x (ISBN 0-85633-060-4, NFER). Humanities.

Parfit, Jessie, ed. Community's Children. 1967. pap. text ed. 2.50x (ISBN 0-582-32417-3). Humanities.

Parfitt, G., ed. The Plays of Cyril Tourneur. LC 77-77014. (Plays by Renaissance & Restoration Dramatists Ser.). 1978. 29.95 (ISBN 0-521-21697-4); pap. 7.50x (ISBN 0-521-29235-2). Cambridge U Pr.

Parfitt, G. D., jt. auth. see Jaycock, M. J.

Parfitt, G. D., jt. auth. see Trotman-Dickenson, A. F.

Pargeter, Margaret. Autumn Song. (Harlequin Romances Ser.). 192p. 1980. pap. 1.25 o.p. (ISBN 0-373-02350-2, Pub. by Harlequin). PB.

--The Dark Oasis. (Harlequin Presents Ser.). 192p. 1981. pap. 1.50 (ISBN 0-373-10431-6, Pub. by Harlequin). PB.

--Kiss of a Tyrant. (Harlequin Romances Ser.). 192p. 1980. pap. 1.25 (ISBN 0-373-02375-8, Pub. by Harlequin). PB.

Pargment, Lila, tr. see Chaplina, Vera.

Parham, Sydney F. A Virginia Title Examiners' Manual. rev. ed. 517p. 1973. 35.00 (ISBN 0-87215-151-4); 1977 suppl 15.00 (ISBN 0-87215-290-1). Michie.

Parham, William. The Book of Melvin. LC 80-53663. (Illus.). 64p. (Orig.). 1981. pap. 3.95 (ISBN 0-938264-00-1). Veritas Pubns.

--Requiems & Other Celebrations. LC 80-53538. 80p. (Orig.). 1981. pap. 4.75 (ISBN 0-938264-01-X). Veritas.

Paribatra, Mom D., ed. Reluctant Princess: A Legend of Love in Siam. LC 63-8716. (Illus.). (gr. 9 up). 5.00 o.p. (ISBN 0-8048-0501-6). C E Tuttle.

Parikh, C. K. Parikh's Textbook of Medical Jurisprudence & Toxicology: For Classrooms & Courtrooms. (Illus.). 1108p. 1980. 91.00 (ISBN 0-08-025522-1). Pergamon.

Parikh, Girish. How to Measure Programmer Productivity. 86p. 1981. pap. 15.00 (ISBN 0-932888-02-X). Shetal Ent.

Parikh, V. M. Absorption Spectroscopy of Organic Molecules. LC 72-3460. 1974. pap. text ed. 16.95 (ISBN 0-201-05708-5). A-W.

Paringer, Lynn, et al. Health Status & Use of Medical Services: Evidence on the Poor, the Black, & the Rural Elderly. (An Institute Paper). 111p. 1979. pap. 7.50 (ISBN 0-87766-241-X, 24800). Urban Inst.

Parini, Jay. The Love Run. 1980. 10.95 (ISBN 0-316-69065-1, Pub. by Atlantic-Little Brown). Little.

Parins, James W., jt. auth. see Bender, Todd K.

Paris, Beltran. Beltran: Basque Sheepman of the American West. Douglass, William A., as told to. LC 79-20311. (Basque Book Ser.). (Illus.). 186p. 1979. 10.00 (ISBN 0-87417-054-0). U of Nev Pr.

Paris, Bernard J. Psychological Approach to Fiction: Studies in Thackeray, Stendhal, George Eliot, Dostoevsky, & Conrad. LC 73-15239. 320p. 1974. 12.50x (ISBN 0-253-34650-9). Ind U Pr.

Paris, Claudine & Casey, Bill. Project: You, a Manual of Rational Assertiveness Training. LC 78-66974. 1974. 5.95 (ISBN 0-686-23447-2). Bridges Pr.

Paris, Jeanne. Your Future As a Home Economist. LC 77-114119. (Career Guidance Ser). 1971. pap. 3.50 (ISBN 0-668-02247-7). Arco.

--Your Future As a Home Economist. LC 72-95601. (Careers in Depth Ser). (Illus.). (gr. 7 up). 1970. PLB 5.97 o.p. (ISBN 0-8239-0191-2). Rosen Pr.

Paris, Katherine W., ed. Gloria Dell' Arte: A Renaissance Perspective. LC 79-89876. (Illus.). 88p. (Orig.). 1979. pap. 6.00 (ISBN 0-686-28885-8). Philbrook.

Paris, Leslie, et al see Constable, John.

Paris, Mike & Comber, Chris. Jimmie the Kid: The Life of Jimmie Rodgers. (Da Capo Quality Paperbacks Ser.). (Illus.). 211p. 1981. pap. 6.95 (ISBN 0-306-80133-7). Da Capo.

Paris, Robert L., jt. auth. see Boucher, John.

Paris, Robert L., jt. auth. see Boucher, John G.

Parish. Teach Us, Amelia Bedelia. (ps-3). 1980. pap. 1.25 (ISBN 0-590-05797-9, Schol Pap). Schol Bk Serv.

Parish, Charles. Tristram Shandy Notes. (Orig.). 1968. pap. 2.25 (ISBN 0-8220-1311-8). Cliffs.

Parish, David W. State Government Reference Publications: An Annotated Bibliography. 2nd ed. 250p. 1981. lib. bdg. price not set (ISBN 0-87287-253-X). Libs Unl.

--State Government Reference Publications: An Annotated Bibliography. LC 74-81322. 1974. lib. bdg. 11.50 o.p. (ISBN 0-87287-100-2). Libs Unl.

Parish, Desmond & Parish, Marjorie. Wild Flowers: A Photographic Guide. (Illus.). 1979. 12.95 (ISBN 0-7137-0947-2, Pub by Blandford Pr England). Sterling.

Parish, Helen R. Estebanico. 128p. (gr. 7 up). 1974. 5.95 o.p. (ISBN 0-670-29814-X). Viking Pr.

Parish, J. H. Principles & Practice of Experiments with Nucleic Acids. LC 72-6424. 511p. 1972. 43.95 (ISBN 0-470-65922-X). Halsted Pr.

Parish, J. H., ed. Developmental Biology of Prokaryotes. (Studies in Microbiology: Vol. 1). 1980. 52.50x (ISBN 0-520-04016-3). U of Cal Pr.

Parish, James R. Actors' Television Credits Nineteen Fifty to Nineteen Seventy-Two. LC 73-9914. 1973. 25.00 (ISBN 0-8108-0673-8). Scarecrow.

--Actors' Television Credits: Supplement 1. LC 77-10741. 1978. 19.50 (ISBN 0-8108-1053-0). Scarecrow.

--Elvis Presley Scrapbook. 160p. (Orig.). 1975. pap. 7.95 o.p. (ISBN 0-345-27594-2). Ballantine.

--Film Actors Guide: Western Europe. LC 77-22485. 1977. 28.50 (ISBN 0-8108-1044-1). Scarecrow.

--Hollywood's Great Love Teams. (Illus.). 1974. 14.95 o.p. (ISBN 0-87000-245-7). Arlington Hse.

Parish, James R. & Pitts, Michael R. Film Directors: A Guide to Their American Films. LC 74-17398. (Illus.). 1974. 18.50 (ISBN 0-8108-0752-1). Scarecrow.

--Great Gangster Pictures. LC 75-32402. (Illus.). 1976. 18.00 (ISBN 0-8108-0881-1). Scarecrow.

--The Great Science Fiction Pictures. LC 77-5426. 1977. 18.00 (ISBN 0-8108-1029-8). Scarecrow.

--The Great Spy Pictures. LC 73-19509. (Illus.). 1974. 21.00 (ISBN 0-8108-0655-X). Scarecrow.

--The Great Western Pictures. LC 76-28224. (Illus.). 1976. 20.00 (ISBN 0-8108-0980-X). Scarecrow.

Parish, James R., ed. The Great Movie Series. LC 78-146771. (Illus.). 1971. 5.98 o.p. (ISBN 0-498-07847-7, Encore). A S Barnes.

Parish, James R., et al. Film Directors Guide: Western Europe. LC 76-1891. (Illus.). 1976. 13.50 (ISBN 0-8108-0908-7). Scarecrow.

Parish, Marjorie, jt. auth. see Parish, Desmond.

Parish, Peggy. Amelia Bedelia. (Illus.). (gr. 2-3). 1970. pap. 1.25 (ISBN 0-590-09069-0, Schol Pap); pap. 3.50 bk. & record (ISBN 0-590-20642-7). Schol Bk Serv.

--Amelia Bedelia & the Baby. LC 80-22263. (Read-Alone Bk.). (Illus.). 64p. (gr. 1-3). 1981. 5.95 (ISBN 0-688-00316-8); PLB 5.71 (ISBN 0-688-00321-4). Greenwillow.

--Amelia Bedelia Helps Out. 64p. (gr. 1-3). 1981. pap. 1.95 (ISBN 0-380-53405-3, Camelot). Avon.

--Be Ready at Eight. LC 78-11847. (Ready-to-Read Ser.). (Illus.). (gr. 1-4). 1979. 7.95 (ISBN 0-02-769830-0). Macmillan.

--Beginning Mobiles. LC 79-9950. (Ready-to-Read Handbook). (Illus.). (gr. 1-4). 1979. 7.95 (ISBN 0-02-770030-5). Macmillan.

--Clues in the Woods. LC 68-20607. (Illus.). (gr. 2-4). 1968. 8.95g (ISBN 0-02-769880-7); pap. 1.25 (ISBN 0-02-769880-7). Macmillan.

--Clues in the Woods. LC 68-20607. 128p. (gr. 2-4). 1972. pap. 1.25 o.s.i. (ISBN 0-02-044860-0, Collier). Macmillan.

--Costumes to Make. LC 75-102969. (Illus.). 1970. 7.95 (ISBN 0-02-769950-1). Macmillan.

--December Decorations. LC 75-14285. (Illus.). 64p. (gr. 1-4). 1975. 7.95 (ISBN 0-02-769920-X, 76992). Macmillan.

--Good Work, Amelia Bedelia. 1980. pap. 1.75 (49171, Camelot). Avon.

--Granny & the Desperadoes. (Illus.). 40p. (gr. 1-3). 1970. 7.95g (ISBN 0-02-769890-4). Macmillan.

--Granny & the Indians. LC 69-11304. (Illus.). (gr. 1-3). 1969. 7.95 (ISBN 0-02-769940-4). Macmillan.

--Granny, the Baby, & the Big Gray Thing. (Illus.). (gr. k-4). 1972. 6.95g (ISBN 0-02-769860-2). Macmillan.

--Haunted House. LC 71-119833. (Illus.). (gr. 2-4). 1971. 8.95 (ISBN 0-02-769960-9). Macmillan.

--Haunted House. (gr. k-6). 1981. pap. 1.50 (ISBN 0-440-43459-9, YB). Dell.

--Hermit Dan. (gr. k-6). 1981. pap. 1.50 (ISBN 0-440-43501-3, YB). Dell.

--Hermit Dan. LC 77-5748. (Illus.). (gr. 2-5). 1977. 8.95 (ISBN 0-02-769840-8, 76984). Macmillan.

--I Can--Can You, 4 bks. LC 79-26041. (Illus.). (ps). 1980. Set. 4.95 (ISBN 0-688-80279-6); write for info. pre-pack set. Greenwillow.

--Key to the Treasure. (gr. k-6). 1980. pap. 1.50 (ISBN 0-440-44438-1, YB). Dell.

--My Golden Book of Manners. (ps-3). 1962. PLB 7.62 (ISBN 0-307-60416-0, Golden Pr). Western Pub.

--Pirate Island Adventure. LC 75-12946. (Illus.). 176p. (gr. 2-5). 1975. 6.95 o.s.i. (ISBN 0-02-769900-5, 76990). Macmillan.

--Pirate Island Adventure. (gr. k-6). 1981. pap. 1.50 (ISBN 0-440-47394-2, YB). Dell.

--Sheet Magic: Games, Toys & Gifts from Old Sheets. (Illus.). (gr. 4-6). 1971. 6.95g (ISBN 0-02-769870-X). Macmillan.

--Too Many Rabbits. LC 73-11690. (Ready-to-Read Ser). (Illus.). 48p. (gr. 1-4). 1974. 7.95 (ISBN 0-02-769850-5). Macmillan.

Parish, Peter. The American Civil War. LC 74-84660. 750p. 1975. text ed. 29.50x (ISBN 0-8419-0176-7); pap. text ed. 17.50 o.p. (ISBN 0-8419-0197-X). Holmes & Meier.

--The Doctors & Patients Handbook of Medicines & Drugs. 1977. 12.95 o.p. (ISBN 0-394-49407-5); pap. 6.95 o.p. (ISBN 0-394-73337-1). Knopf.

Parish, R. V. The Metallic Elements. 1977. pap. text ed. 21.00x (ISBN 0-582-44278-8). Longman.

Parish, W., jt. auth. see Kingstather, W.

Parish, William L. & Whyte, Martin K. Village & Family in Contemporary China. LC 78-3411. xvi, 420p. 1980. pap. 8.95 (ISBN 0-226-64591-6, P899, Phoen). U of Chicago Pr.

Parisi, Gino. Intermediate Spanish Review Grammar. 336p. Date not set. pap. text ed. 8.95 (ISBN 0-669-02632-8); wkbk. 3.95 (ISBN 0-669-02633-6). Heath. Postponed.

Parisious, Roger N., et al, eds. see Ussher, Arland.

Parizeau, Alice & Szabo, Denis. The Canadian Criminal Justice System. LC 77-211. (Illus.). 1977. 19.95 (ISBN 0-669-01448-6). Lexington Bks.

Park, Brad & Fischler, Stan. Play the Man: Defenseman's Journal. LC 73-181824. (Illus.). 1971. 6.95 (ISBN 0-396-06433-7). Dodd.

Park, C. C. Ecology & Environmental Management: A Geographical Perspective. LC 79-5208. (Westview Studies in Physical Geography). 224p. 1980. lib. bdg. 24.50x (ISBN 0-89158-698-9). Westview.

Park, C. W. The Population Explosion. (Liberal Studies Ser.). 1965. pap. text ed. 3.00x o.p. (ISBN 0-435-46532-5). Heinemann Ed.

Park, Charles F., Jr. & MacDiarmid, Roy A. Ore Deposits. 3rd ed. LC 75-14157. (Geology Ser.). (Illus.). 1975. text ed. 28.95x (ISBN 0-7167-0272-X). W H Freeman.

Park, D. A. Classical Dynamics & Its Quantum Analogues. (Lecture Notes in Physics: Vol. 110). 339p. 1980. pap. 18.00 (ISBN 0-387-09565-9). Springer-Verlag.

Park, David. The Image of Eternity: Roots of Time in the Physical World. 1981. pap. 5.95 (ISBN 0-452-00551-5, F551, Mer). NAL.

Park-Davis & Company. Medical Word Building. 1970. pap. 7.95 (ISBN 0-87489-043-8). Med Economics.

Park, Dorothy M., jt. auth. see Smith, James A.

Park, Helen. A List of Architectural Books Available in America Before the Revolution. rev. ed. LC 76-189461. (Art & Architecture Bibliographies Ser: No. 1). (Illus.). 80p. 1973. 12.95x (ISBN 0-912158-21-2). Hennessey.

Park, J. D. Oil & Gas in Comecon. 1979. 39.50x (ISBN 0-89397-040-9). Nichols Pub.

Park, Jack. The Wind Power Book. (Illus.). 1981. 19.95 (ISBN 0-917352-05-X); pap. 11.95 (ISBN 0-917352-06-8). Cheshire.

Park, James. Absurdity, Insecurity & Despair. (Existential Freedom Ser.: No. 8). 1975. pap. 2.00x (ISBN 0-89231-008-1). Existential Bks.

--Authentic Love: An Existential Vision. 2nd ed. LC 76-5602. 232p. 1978. pap. 6.00x (ISBN 0-89231-510-5). Existential Bks.

--Depression, Fragmentation, & the Void. (Existential Freedom Ser.: No. 9). 1976. pap. 2.00x (ISBN 0-89231-009-X). Existential Bks.

--Existential Anxiety: Angst. (Existential Freedom Ser.: No. 5). 1974. pap. 2.00x (ISBN 0-89231-005-7). Existential Bks.

--Existential Freedom, No. 3. 1973. pap. 2.00x (ISBN 0-89231-003-0). Existential Bks.

--An Existential Understanding of Death: A Phenomenology of Ontological Anxiety. (Existential Freedom Ser.: No. 6). 72p. 1975. pap. 2.00x (ISBN 0-89231-006-5). Existential Bks.

--Loneliness & Existential Freedom. (Existential Freedom Ser.: No. 4). 1974. pap. 2.00x (ISBN 0-89231-004-9). Existential Bks.

--Obstacles to Existential Freedom. (Existential Freedom Ser.: No. 10). 1976. pap. 2.00x (ISBN 0-89231-010-3). Existential Bks.

Park, O'Hyun, ed. see Phillips, Bernard.

Park, R. & Gamble, W. L. Reinforced Concrete Slabs. LC 80-10229. 1980. 40.00 (ISBN 0-471-65915-0, Pub. by Wiley-Interscience). Wiley.

Park, R. D. & Eddowes, Maurice. Crop Husbandry. 2nd ed. (Illus.). 332p. 1975. 36.00x (ISBN 0-19-859443-7). Oxford U Pr.

Park, R. D., et al. Animal Husbandry. 2nd ed. (Illus.). 1970. pap. 16.95x (ISBN 0-19-859422-4). Oxford U Pr.

Park, Richard L., jt. auth. see Cohen, Stephen P.

Park, Robert, ed. Selected Letters of John Keats. pap. 1.95 (ISBN 0-451-50697-9, CJ697, Sig Classics). NAL.

Park, Robert E. Race & Culture. 1964. 8.95 o.s.i. (ISBN 0-02-923780-7); pap. text ed. 5.95 (ISBN 0-02-923790-4). Free Pr.

Park, Robert E. & Burgess, Ernest W. City. Janowitz, Morris, ed. LC 66-23694. (Heritage of Sociology Ser). 1967. 12.50x o.s.i. (ISBN 0-226-64607-6). U of Chicago Pr.

Park, Roy, ed. see Lamb, Charles.

Park, Ruth. The Gigantic Balloon. LC 76-3408. (Illus.). 40p. (gr. k-4). 1976. 5.95 o.s.i. (ISBN 0-685-66683-2, Four Winds); PLB 5.41 o.s.i. (ISBN 0-8193-0849-8); pap. 1.95 o.s.i. (ISBN 0-8193-0909-5, Pippin). Schol Bk Serv.

--When the Wind Changed. (Illus.). 32p. (Orig.). (ps-3). 1981. 8.95 (ISBN 0-698-20525-1, Peppercorn); pap. 4.95 (ISBN 0-698-20526-X). Coward.

Park, Sung H. Bridge Inspection & Structural Analysis: Handbook of Bridge Inspection. LC 80-81421. (Illus.). 312p. (Orig.). 1980. pap. text ed. 15.00 (ISBN 0-9604440-0-9). S H Park.

Park, W. M. & Reece, B. L. Fundamental Aspects of Medical Thermography. 1980. 18.00x (Pub. by Brit Inst Radiology England). State Mutual Bk.

Park, Willard Z. Shamanism in Western North America. LC 74-12553. 166p. 1975. Repr. of 1938 ed. lib. bdg. 16.50x (ISBN 0-8154-0497-2). Cooper Sq.

Park, William R. Cost Engineering Analysis: A Guide to the Economic Evaluation of Engineering Projects. LC 72-10237. (Illus.). 373p. 1973. 29.50 (ISBN 0-471-65914-2, Pub. by Wiley-Interscience). Wiley.

Park, William R. & Chapin-Park, Sue. How to Succeed in Your Own Business. LC 77-28955. 1978. 19.95 (ISBN 0-471-03189-5, Pub. by Wiley-Interscience). Wiley.

Park, Yoon S. Oil Money & the World Economy. LC 75-40467. (Special Studies in International Economics Ser). 1976. 35.00x (ISBN 0-89158-018-2). Westview.

Parkavich, Tamar J., jt. auth. see McCormick, Rose M.

Parke, jt. ed. see Parke, Dennis V.

Parke, D. V. The Biochemistry of Foreign Compounds. 1968. 27.00 (ISBN 0-08-012202-7). Pergamon.

Parke, D. V. & Smith, R. L. Drug Metabolism: From Microbe to Man. 1977. 57.50x o.p. (ISBN 0-8448-1127-0). Crane-Russak Co.

Parke, Dennis V. & Parke, eds. Mucus in Health & Disease. LC 77-22376. (Advances in Experimental Medicine & Biology: Vol. 89). 558p. 1977. 45.00 (ISBN 0-306-32689-2, Plenum Pr). Plenum Pub.

Parke, Herbert W. Greek Oracles. 1967. pap. text ed. 6.25x (ISBN 0-09-084111-5, Hutchinson U Lib). Humanities.

Parke, Ross D. see Hetherington, E. Mavis.

Parke, W. T. Musical Memoirs, Comprising an Account of the General State of Music in England. 2 Vols. in 1. LC 77-125058. (Music Ser). 1970. Repr. of 1830 ed. lib. bdg. 55.00 (ISBN 0-306-70023-9). Da Capo.

Parker & Silbey. BASIC for Business. (Illus.). 1980. 15.95 (ISBN 0-8359-0351-6); pap. text ed. 10.95 (ISBN 0-8359-0349-4); solutions manual free (ISBN 0-8359-0350-8). Reston.

Parker & Voyles. Official Guide to Pocket Knives. 2nd rev. ed. LC 78-72038. (Illus.). 1979. pap. 9.95 o.p. (ISBN 0-87637-101-2). Hse of Collectibles.

Parker, et al. Are Those Your Good Pants? 128p. (Orig.). 1981. pap. 1.75 (ISBN 0-449-14390-2, GM). Fawcett.

Parker, A. Cottage & Country Recipes. (Illus.). 1975. 7.95 (ISBN 0-571-10500-9, Pub. by Faber & Faber). Merrimack Bk Serv.

Parker, A. J. VS Basic for Business: For the IBM 360-370. 1982. pap. text ed. 12.95 (ISBN 0-8359-8439-7). Reston.

Parker, A. K. & Pye, D. The Fenland. LC 76-29114. (British Topographical Ser.). (Illus.). 1977. 14.95 (ISBN 0-7153-7296-3). David & Charles.

Parker, Alan & Stewart, John. Apple Basic for Business: For the Apple II. 1981. text ed. 16.95 (ISBN 0-8359-0228-5); pap. text ed. 11.95 (ISBN 0-8359-0226-9); instrs'. manual avail. (ISBN 0-8359-0229-3). Reston.

Parker, Alfred E. The Berkeley Police Story. (Illus.). 308p. 1972. 29.50 (ISBN 0-398-02373-5). C C Thomas.

Parker, Alice. Terrariums. (Easy-Read Fact Bks.). (Illus.). (gr. 2-4). 1977. PLB 6.45 s&l (ISBN 0-531-01315-4). Watts.

Parker & Son Staff. Parker Directory of Attorneys. LC 75-41995. 1981. 1980 suppl. incl. 11.50 (ISBN 0-911110-18-6). Parker & Son.

Parker, Angela & Parker, Geoffrey. European Solders Fifteen Fifty to Sixteen Fifty. (Cambridge Introduction to the History of Mankind Ser.). (gr. 4-5). 1977. pap. text ed. 3.95 (ISBN 0-521-21020-8). Cambridge U Pr.

Parker, Ann E. Astrology & Alcoholism: Genetic Key to the Horoscope. 1981. pap. 7.95 (ISBN 0-87728-519-5). Weiser.

Parker, Anne, tr. see Beckman, Gunnel.

Parker, Arthur C. Skunny Wundy Seneca Indian Tales. LC 73-115899. (Folklore Ser). (Illus.). (gr. 3 up). 1970. 5.95g o.p. (ISBN 0-8075-7405-8). A Whitman.

Parker, Bertha M. The Wonders of the Seasons. (gr. 3-6). 1974. PLB 7.15 o.p. (ISBN 0-307-60477-2, Golden Pr). Western Pub.

Parker, Betty & Martin, Edith. Embroidery Magic on Patterned Fabrics. LC 76-14976. (Encore Edition). (Illus.). 160p. 1976. 5.95 o.p. (ISBN 0-684-15704-7, ScribT). Scribner.

Parker, Betty J., jt. auth. see Parker, Francis.

Parker, Betty J., jt. ed. see Parker, Franklin.

Parker, Beulah. A Mingled Yarn: Chronicle of a Troubled Family. LC 72-75206. 320p. 1972. 15.00x (ISBN 0-300-01568-2); pap. 5.95x (ISBN 0-300-02292-1). Yale U Pr.

--My Language Is Me. 352p. 1975. pap. 1.95 o.p. (ISBN 0-345-24587-3). Ballantine.

Parker, Brant & Hart, Johnny. Every Man Is Innocent Until Proven Broke. (Wizard of Id Ser.). (Illus.). 1978. pap. 1.50 (ISBN 0-449-13650-7, GM). Fawcett.

Parker, Brant, jt. auth. see Hart, Johnny.

Parker, Brant, et al. I Hate Mondays! 1978. pap. 1.25 o.p. (ISBN 0-449-13978-6, GM). Fawcett.

Parker, Bruce C. see Holt, Perry C., et al.

Parker, Bruce R. & Castellino, Ronald A. Pediatric Oncologic Radiology. LC 77-23952. (Illus.). 1977. 47.50 o.p. (ISBN 0-8016-3756-2). Mosby.

Parker, Charles W. Radioimmunoassay of Biologically Active Compounds. (Illus.). 272p. 1976. pap. text ed. 22.95 (ISBN 0-13-750505-1). P-H.

Parker, Chauncey G., 3rd. The Visitor. 1981. pap. 2.50 (ISBN 0-451-09562-6, E9562, Sig). NAL.

Parker, Clifford S. & Maubrey, Pierre. Foundation Course in French Language & Culture. rev. ed. LC 68-12139. Orig. Title: Foundation Course in French. (Illus., Fr.). 1969. text ed. 15.95x (ISBN 0-669-44149-X); tapes avail. (ISBN 0-669-44156-2); tapes. 10 reels 50.00 (ISBN 0-669-44164-3); student test bk. 1.75x (ISBN 0-669-50468-8). Heath.

Parker, Constance-Anne. Mr. Stubbs: Horsepainter. (Illus.). 24.50 (ISBN 0-85131-123-7, Dist. by Sporting Book Center). J A Allen.

Parker, D. B. V. Polymer Chemistry. (Illus.). 1974. text ed. 22.30x (ISBN 0-85334-571-6). Intl Ideas.

Parker, D. Coffey. The Divinity of Marriage. 1980. 5.00. D C Parker.

Parker, David L. & Siegel, Esther. Guide to Dance in Films: A Guide to Information Sources. LC 76-20339. (Performing Arts Information Guide Series: Vol. 3). 1978. 30.00 (ISBN 0-8103-1377-4). Gale.

Parker, David M. Ocean Voyaging. LC 74-78837. 1975. 15.00 (ISBN 0-8286-0068-6). De Graff.

Parker, Dennis J. & Penning-Rowsell, Edmund C. Water Planning in Britain. (Resource Management Ser.: No. 1). (Illus.). 288p. (Orig.). 1980. text ed. 34.00x (ISBN 0-04-711006-6); pap. text ed. 17.95x (ISBN 0-04-711007-4). Allen Unwin.

Parker, Derek. Familiar to All. (Illus.). 1978. 8.95 o.p. (ISBN 0-224-01112-X, Pub. by Chatto Bodley Jonathan). Merrimack Bk Serv.

--Radio: The Great Years. LC 77-89378. 1977. 14.95 (ISBN 0-7153-7430-3). David & Charles.

Parker, Derek & Parker, Julia. The Story & the Song. 1979. 22.50 (ISBN 0-903443-25-2, Pub. by Hamish Hamilton England). David & Charles.

Parker, Don H., et al. The Metric System: Syllabus. 1974. pap. text ed. 16.50 units of 10 (ISBN 0-89420-052-6, 280222); cassette recordings 18.15 (ISBN 0-89420-163-8, 280000). Natl Book.

Parker, Donn. Computer Security Management. 304p. 1981. text ed. 21.95 (ISBN 0-8359-0905-0). Reston.

Parker, Donn B. Ethical Conflicts in Computer Science & Technology. vi, 201p. 1979. 20.00 (ISBN 0-88283-009-0); wkbk 15.00 (ISBN 0-88283-010-4). AFIPS Pr.

Parker, E. H. China: The History, Diplomacy & Commerce from the Earliest Times to the Present Day. LC 78-74314. (The Modern Chinese Economy Ser.: Vol. 6). 394p. 1980. lib. bdg. 44.00 (ISBN 0-8240-4255-7). Garland Pub.

Parker, Ed. Secrets of Chinese Karate. (Funk & W Bk.). (Illus.). 1968. pap. 2.95 (ISBN 0-308-90041-3, F23, TYC-T). T Y Crowell.

Parker, Ed, illus. Jack & the Beanstalk. LC 78-18072. (Illus.). (gr. 1-4). 1979. PLB 5.21 (ISBN 0-89375-125-1); pap. 1.50 (ISBN 0-89375-103-0). Troll Assocs.

Parker, Edmund K. Secrets of Chinese Karate. 1963. 8.95 (ISBN 0-13-797852-9); pap. 5.95 (ISBN 0-13-797845-6). P-H.

Parker, Elinor. Cooking for One. 5th, rev. ed. LC 76-15365. 1976. 10.95 (ISBN 0-690-01176-8, TYC-T). T Y Crowell.

Parker, Elizabeth C. The Descent from the Cross: Its Relation to the Extra-Liturgical Depositio Drama. LC 77-94713. (Outstanding Dissertations in the Fine Arts Ser.). 1978. lib. bdg. 34.00 (ISBN 0-8240-3245-4). Garland Pub.

Parker, Elliott S. & Parker, Emelia M. Asian Journalism: A Selected Bibliography of Sources on Journalism in China & Southeast Asia. LC 79-22785. 484p. 1979. 25.00 (ISBN 0-8108-1269-X). Scarecrow.

Parker, Else. Astrology & Its Practical Application. LC 80-20026. 202p. 1980. Repr. of 1977 ed. lib. bdg. 11.95x (ISBN 0-89370-639-6). Borgo Pr.

Parker, Emelia M., jt. auth. see Parker, Elliott S.

Parker, Emmett, tr. see Peyre, Henri.

Parker, F. M. Skinner. LC 80-1863. (Double D Western Ser.). 192p. 1981. 9.95 (ISBN 0-385-17382-2). Doubleday.

Parker, Fan & Parker, Stephen J. Russia on Canvas: Ilya Repin. LC 79-20577. (Illus.). 196p. 1980. 27.50x (ISBN 0-271-00252-2). Pa St U Pr.

Parker, Francis & Parker, Betty J. American Dissertations on Foreign Education: Israel, Vol. XIII. 464p. 1980. 32.00x (ISBN 0-87875-152-1). Whitston Pub.

--American Dissertations on Foreign Education: Iran & Iraq, Vol. XII. 425p. 1980. 28.50x (ISBN 0-87875-151-3). Whitston Pub.

Parker, Frank. The Law & the Poor. LC 72-97696. 256p. 1973. pap. 4.95x o.p. (ISBN 0-88344-276-0). Orbis Bks.

Parker, Frank A. Whither Civilization? 1981. 10.00 (ISBN 0-533-04882-6). Vantage.

Parker, Frank J. Caryl Chessman: The Red Light Bandit. LC 75-8760. (Illus.). 245p. 1975. 13.95 (ISBN 0-88229-188-2). Nelson-Hall.

Parker, Franklin & Parker, Betty J., eds. U. S. Higher Education: A Guide to Information Sources. (Education Information Guide Ser.: Vol. 9). 400p. 1980. 30.00 (ISBN 0-8103-1476-2). Gale.

Parker, Gail T. Mind Cure in New England: From the Civil War to World War I. LC 72-92704. 209p. 1973. text ed. 12.50x (ISBN 0-87451-073-2). U Pr of New Eng.

Parker, Gary E. & Mertens, Thomas R. Life's Basis: Biomolecules. LC 72-10744. (Self-Teaching Guides Ser.). 1973. pap. text ed. 2.95 o.p. (ISBN 0-471-65919-3). Wiley.

Parker, Geoffrey. Army of Flanders & the Spanish Road: 1567-1659. LC 76-180021. (Cambridge Studies in Early Modern History). (Illus.). 288p. 1972. 43.95 (ISBN 0-521-08462-8); pap. 11.95x (ISBN 0-521-09907-2). Cambridge U Pr.

--The Dutch Revolt. 320p. 1977. 20.00 (ISBN 0-8014-1136-X). Cornell U Pr.

--Europe in Crisis Fifteen Ninety-Eight to Sixteen Forty-Eight. LC 80-66912. (History of Europe Ser.; Cornell Paperbacks Ser.). 384p. 1980. pap. 5.95 (ISBN 0-8014-9209-2). Cornell U Pr.

--Logic of Unity. 3rd ed. (Illus.). 224p. 1981. pap. text ed. 14.95 (ISBN 0-582-30031-2). Longman.

Parker, Geoffrey, jt. auth. see Parker, Angela.

Parker, George. Lexico-Concordancia Del Nuevo Testamento En Griego y Espanol. Orig. Title: Lexicon-Concordance of the New Testament in Greek & Spanish. 1000p. (Span.). Date not set. pap. price not set (ISBN 0-311-42066-4). Casa Bautista.

Parker, George S. Five Historic Ships from Plan to Model. LC 81-22137. (Illus.). 1980. 17.50 (ISBN 0-87033-258-9). Cornell Maritime.

Parker, Gilbert. Battle of the Strong. 1976. lib. bdg. 18.50x (ISBN 0-89968-078-X). Lightyear.

--Born with a Golden Spoon. 1976. lib. bdg. 13.85x (ISBN 0-89968-081-X). Lightyear.

--The Hill of Pains. 1976. lib. bdg. 9.95x (ISBN 0-89968-082-8). Lightyear.

--The Judgement House. 1976. lib. bdg. 19.50x (ISBN 0-89968-080-1). Lightyear.

--The Right of Way. 1976. lib. bdg. 16.25x (ISBN 0-89968-079-8). Lightyear.

--Seats of the Mighty. 1976. lib. bdg. 16.75x (ISBN 0-89968-077-1). Lightyear.

--The Trespasser. 1976. lib. bdg. 13.85x (ISBN 0-89968-083-6). Lightyear.

Parker, Grant. Mayday: The History of a Village Holocaust. LC 80-83408. 260p. (Orig.). 1980. pap. 5.95 (ISBN 0-9604958-0-0). Libty Pr MI.

Parker, Harry & Hauf, H. D. Simplified Design of Structural Wood. 2nd ed. LC 78-9888. 1979. 19.95 (ISBN 0-471-66630-0, Pub. by Wiley-Interscience). Wiley.

Parker, Harry & Hauf, Harold D. Simplified Design of Reinforced Concrete. 4th ed. LC 75-38840. 1976. 21.95 (ISBN 0-471-66069-8, Pub. by Wiley-Interscience). Wiley.

--Simplified Design of Structural Steel. 4th ed. LC 73-13562. 326p. 1974. 22.00 (ISBN 0-471-66432-4, Pub. by Wiley-Interscience). Wiley.

--Simplified Engineering for Architects & Builders. 5th ed. LC 74-18068. 362p. 1975. 24.50 (ISBN 0-471-66201-1, Pub. by Wiley-Interscience). Wiley.

--Simplified Mechanics & Strength of Materials. 3rd ed. LC 76-56465. 304p. 1977. 22.95 (ISBN 0-471-66562-2, Pub. by Wiley-Interscience). Wiley.

Parker, Harry, jt. auth. see Kidder, Frank E.

Parker, Harry, et al. Materials & Methods of Architectural Construction. 3rd ed. LC 58-8213. 1958. 34.00 (ISBN 0-471-66297-6, Pub. by Wiley-Interscience). Wiley.

Parker, Harry L. Clinical Studies in Neurology. 384p. 1969. 12.75 (ISBN 0-398-01449-3). C C Thomas.

Parker, Henry. The Rich & the Pore. LC 77-7419. (English Experience Ser.: No. 882). 1977. Repr. of 1493 ed. lib. bdg. 69.00 (ISBN 90-221-0882-1). Walter J Johnson.

Parker, Hershel, jt. ed. see Hayford, Harrison.

Parker, Homer. Wastewater Systems Engineering. (Illus.). 464p. 1975. 27.95 (ISBN 0-13-945758-5). P-H.

Parker, Homer W. Air Pollution. (Illus.). 1977. 26.95x (ISBN 0-13-021006-4). P-H.

Parker, Horatio. Hora Novissima (Opus 30) LC 75-169652. (Earlier American Music Ser.: No. 2). 167p. 1972. Repr. of 1900 ed. lib. bdg. 25.00 (ISBN 0-306-77302-3). Da Capo.

Parker, Howard J. View from the Boys: A Sociology of Downtown Adolescents. LC 74-76184. (People, Plans & Problems Ser.). 1974. 17.95 (ISBN 0-7153-6456-1). David & Charles.

Parker, J. Carlyle, ed. City-County Index to Eighteen-Fifty Census Schedules. LC 79-11644. (Genealogy & Local History Ser.: Vol. 6). 1979. 30.00 (ISBN 0-8103-1385-5). Gale.

--An Index to the Biographees in Nineteenth Century California County Histories. LC 79-11900. (Genealogy & Local History Ser.: Vol. 7). 1979. 30.00 (ISBN 0-8103-1406-1). Gale.

--Library Service for Genealogists. LC 80-26032. (The Gale Genealogy & Local History Ser.: Vol. 15). 285p. 1981. 30.00 (ISBN 0-8103-1489-4). Gale.

Parker, J. Carlyle, compiled by. A Personal Name Index to Orton's Records of California Men in the War of the Rebellion, 1861 to 1867. LC 78-15674. (Gale's Genealogy & Local History Ser.: Vol. 5). 1978. 30.00 (ISBN 0-8103-1402-9). Gale.

Parker, J. D., et al. Introduction to Fluid Mechanics & Heat Transfer. (Engineering Ser). 1969. text ed. 25.95 (ISBN 0-201-05710-7). A-W.

Parker, J. H. Juan Perez De Montalvan. LC 74-23740. (World Authors Ser.: Spain: No. 352). 1975. lib. bdg. 12.50 (ISBN 0-8057-2625-X). Twayne.

Parker, James. Glossary of Terms Used in Heraldry. LC 77-94021. (Illus.). (gr. 9 up). 1970. 12.50 (ISBN 0-8048-0715-9). C E Tuttle.

Parker, James, jt. auth. see Gough, Henry.

Parker, James E. Programmed Guide to Tax Research. 272p. 1979. pap. text ed. 9.95x (ISBN 0-534-00796-1). Wadsworth Pub.

Parker, Jeri. Uneasy Survivors: Five Women Writers. LC 75-37705. 224p. 1975. pap. 5.95 o.s.i. (ISBN 0-87905-061-6). Peregrine Smith.

Parker, Joan H. & Parker, Robert B. Three Weeks in Spring. 1979. pap. 2.25 o.p. (ISBN 0-425-04018-6). Berkley Pub.

Parker, John. The World for a Marketplace: Episodes in the History of European Expansion. LC 78-71068. (Illus.). 1978. 15.00 (ISBN 0-9601798-0-1). Assocs James Bell.

Parker, John & Urness, Carol, eds. The American Revolution: A Heritage of Change. LC 75-24503. 1975. 10.00 (ISBN 0-9601798-0-1). Assocs James Bell.

Parker, John, tr. see Duffy, John.

Parker, John E. The Economics of Innovation. 2nd ed. (Illus.). 1978. text ed. 38.00x (ISBN 0-582-44612-0). Longman.

Parker, John L., jt. auth. see Liquori, Marty.

Parker, John R., ed. The Euterpeiad or Musical Intelligencer, 3 Vols. LC 65-23389. (Music Ser). 1977. Repr. of 1820 ed. Set. lib. bdg. 75.00 (ISBN 0-306-70920-1). Da Capo.

Parker, Julia. Aires. (Pocket Guides to Astrology Ser.). (Orig.). 1980. pap. write for info. (ISBN 0-671-25551-7, Fireside). S&S.

--Aquarius. (Pocket Guides to Astrology Ser.). (Orig.). 1980. pap. write for info. (ISBN 0-671-25555-X, Fireside). S&S.

--Cancer. (Pocket Guide to Astrology Ser.). (Orig.). 1980. pap. write for info. (ISBN 0-671-25557-6, Fireside). S&S.

--Capricorn. (Pocket Guide to Astrology Ser.). (Orig.). 1980. pap. (ISBN 0-671-25548-7, Fireside). S&S.

--Gemini. (Pocket Guide to Astrology Ser.). (Orig.). 1980. pap. write for info. (ISBN 0-671-25559-2, Fireside). S&S.

--Leo. (Pocket Guide to Astrology Ser.). (Orig.). 1980. pap. write for info. (ISBN 0-671-25553-3, Fireside). S&S.

--Libra. (Pocket Guide to Astrology Ser.). (Orig.). 1980. pap. write for info. (ISBN 0-671-25554-1, Fireside). S&S.

--Pisces. (Pocket Guide to Astrology Ser.). (Orig.). 1980. pap. write for info. (ISBN 0-671-25558-4, Fireside). S&S.

--Sagittarius. (Pocket Guide to Astrology Ser.). (Orig.). 1980. pap. write for info. (ISBN 0-671-25556-8, Fireside). S&S.

--Scorpio. (Pocket Guide to Astrology Ser.). (Orig.). 1980. pap. write for info. (ISBN 0-671-25550-9, Fireside). S&S.

--Taurus. (Pocket Guides to Astrology Ser.). (Orig.). 1980. pap. write for info. (ISBN 0-671-25560-6, Fireside). S&S.

--Virgo. (Pocket Guides to Astrology Ser.). (Orig.). 1980. pap. write for info. (ISBN 0-671-25549-5, Fireside). S&S.

Parker, Julia, jt. auth. see Parker, Derek.

Parker, K. J., jt. ed. see Birch, G. G.

Parker, Kay. Quilted Tessellations: Designs from M. C. Escher. (Illus.). 140p. 1981. 16.95 (ISBN 0-89594-045-0); pap. 9.95 (ISBN 0-89594-044-2). Crossing Pr.

Parker, Lois. Duncan, Son of Malcolm. LC 77-12724. (Crown Ser.). 1977. pap. 4.50 (ISBN 0-8127-0156-9). Southern Pub.

--They of Rome. 128p. 1980. pap. write for info. (ISBN 0-8127-0308-1). Southern Pub.

Parker, Lois & McConnell, David. A Little Peoples' Beginning on Michigan. (Illus.). 32p. (Orig.). (gr. 1-2). 1981. pap. 2.75 (ISBN 0-910726-06-X). Hillsdale Educ.

Parker, Lois M. Thee, Patience. Van Dolson, Bobbie J., ed. LC 74-78021. (Illus.). (gr. 4-7). 1974. pap. 4.50 (ISBN 0-8280-0061-1). Review & Herald.

Parker, Lucile. Mississippi Wildflowers. (Illus.). 144p. 1981. 29.95 (ISBN 0-88289-165-0). Pelican.

Parker, Lynn, et al. Frac's Guide to Quality School Lunch & Breakfast Programs. rev. ed. Perry, Cecilia, ed. Orig. Title: Frac's Guide to the School Lunch & Breakfast Programs. 52p. 1980. pap. text ed. 1.00 (ISBN 0-934220-04-2). Food Res Action.

Parker, M. M. A Garden of Stones. LC 80-13966. 224p. 1980. 8.95 (ISBN 0-396-07858-3). Dodd.

Parker, Margaret T. Lowell: A Study of Industrial Development. LC 73-118421. 1970. Repr. of 1940 ed. 15.00 o.p. (ISBN 0-8046-1373-7). Kennikat.

Parker, Mark. Horses, Airplanes, & Frogs. LC 76-54805. (Illus.). (ps-3). 1977. 5.50 (ISBN 0-913778-71-0). Childs World.

Parker, Mattie E. & Price, William S., Jr., eds. Colonial Records of North Carolina: Second Series, 5 vols. Incl. Vol. 1. North Carolina Charters & Constitutions, 1578-1698. 247p. 1963. 10.00 (ISBN 0-86526-022-2); Vol. 2. North Carolina Higher-Court Records, 1670-1696. 533p. 1968. 11.00 (ISBN 0-86526-023-0); Vol. 3. North Carolina Higher Court Records, 1697-1701. 622p. 1971. 12.00 (ISBN 0-86526-024-9); Vol. 4. North Carolina Higher-Court Records, 1702-1708. 533p. 1974. 16.00 (ISBN 0-86526-025-7); Vol. 5. North Carolina Higher Court Minutes, 1709-1723. 1977. 21.00 (ISBN 0-86526-026-5). Set (ISBN 0-86526-020-6). NC Archives.

Parker, Michael, jt. auth. see Walters, John.

Parker, Monique, jt. auth. see Cahen, Michel.

Parker, Nancy W. Cooper, the McNallys' Big Black Dog. LC 80-21905. (Illus.). 32p. (gr. k-3). 1981. PLB 7.95 (ISBN 0-396-07914-8). Dodd.

--The Crocodile Under Louis Finneberg's Bed. LC 77-16875. (ps-4). 1978. 5.50 (ISBN 0-396-07542-8). Dodd.

--Love from Uncle Clyde. LC 76-54957. (gr. k-3). 1977. 5.95 (ISBN 0-396-07426-X). Dodd.

--Mrs. Wilson Wanders Off. LC 76-6112. (gr. k-5). 1976. 5.95 (ISBN 0-396-07333-6). Dodd.

--The Ordeal of Byron B. Blackbear. LC 79-12140. (Illus.). (ps). 1979. 6.95 (ISBN 0-396-07642-4). Dodd.

--President's Cabinet: And How It Grew. LC 77-10090. (Illus.). 40p. (gr. 1 up). 1978. 7.95 (ISBN 0-590-17711-7, Four Winds); lib. bdg. 7.95 (ISBN 0-590-07711-2). Schol Bk Serv.

--The Spotted Dog: The Strange Tale of a Witch's Revenge. LC 80-13313. (Illus.). 48p. (gr. 6-9). 1980. PLB 6.95 (ISBN 0-396-07845-1). Dodd.

Parker, Nathan C., ed. Personal Name Index to the 1856 City Directories of California. LC 79-24246. (Gale Genealogy & Local History Ser.: Vol. 10). 250p. 30.00 (ISBN 0-8103-1414-2). Gale.

Parker, Netta. Best Dishes from Europe & the Orient: A New Collection of Recipes. 1970. 10.00 (ISBN 0-571-08442-7). Transatlantic.

Parker, Norton S. Audiovisual Script Writing. 1974. pap. 7.00 (ISBN 0-8135-0797-9). Rutgers U Pr.

Parker, Owen. Tack Now, Skipper. 1979. 18.95x (ISBN 0-8464-0065-0). Beekman Pubs.

Parker, Philip. Electricity & Atomic Physics. 1971. text ed. 6.95x o.p. (ISBN 0-435-68650-X). Heinemann Ed.

--Heat. 1971. text ed. 8.50x o.p. (ISBN 0-435-68644-5). Heinemann Ed.

Parker, R. A. Coke of Norfolk: A Financial & Agricultural Study, 1707-1842. (Illus.). 232p. 1975. 37.50x (ISBN 0-19-822403-6). Oxford U Pr.

--The Rents of Council Houses. 90p. 1967. pap. text ed. 5.00x (Pub. by Bedford England). Renouf.

Parker, R. H. An Introduction to Chemical Metallurgy: In SI-Metric Units. 2nd ed. 1978. text ed. 52.00 (ISBN 0-08-022125-4); pap. text ed. 14.00 (ISBN 0-08-022126-2). Pergamon.

Parker, R. H. & Harcourt, G. C., eds. Readings in the Concept & Measurement of Income. LC 75-87137. (Illus.). 1969. 47.50 (ISBN 0-521-07463-0); pap. 15.95x (ISBN 0-521-09591-3). Cambridge U Pr.

Parker, Ray, jt. auth. see Van Dyke, Dick.

Parker, Richard A. Demotic Mathematical Papyri. LC 77-177501. (Brown University Studies: No. 7). (Illus.). 86p. 1972. 25.00x (ISBN 0-87057-132-X, Pub. by Brown U Pr). Univ Pr of New England.

--Vienna Demotic Papyrus on Eclipse & Lunar-Omina. (Brown University Studies: No. 2). (Illus.). 59p. 1959. 25.00x (ISBN 0-87057-057-9, Pub. by Brown U Pr). Univ Pr of New England.

Parker, Richard A., et al. The Edifice of Taharqa by the Sacred Lake of Karnak. LC 77-76345. (Brown Egyptological Studies: No. 8). 154p. 1979. 60.00x (ISBN 0-87057-151-6, Pub. by Brown U Pr). Univ Pr of New England.

Parker, Robert A. Sweet Betsy from Pike: A Song from the Gold Rush Days. (Illus.). (gr. 1-4). 1978. 7.95 o.p. (ISBN 0-670-68632-8). Viking Pr.

Parker, Robert B. Early Autum. 1981. 10.95 (ISBN 0-440-02248-7, Sey Lawr). Delacorte.

--The Judas Goat. 1979. pap. 1.95 o.p. (ISBN 0-425-04204-9). Berkley Pub.

--Looking for Rachel Wallace. 1981. pap. 2.50 (ISBN 0-440-15316-6). Dell.

--Mature Advertising: A Handbook of Effective Advertising Copy. 176p. 1981. 19.95 (ISBN 0-201-05714-X). A-W.

Parker, Robert B., jt. auth. see Parker, Joan H.

Parker, Robert P., Jr. & Daly, Maxine E. Teaching English in the Secondary School. LC 72-88812. (Orig.). 1973. pap. text ed. 7.95 (ISBN 0-02-923870-6). Free Pr.

Parker, Roger, ed. see Mann, William.

Parker, Roger, tr. see Baldini, Gabriele.

Parker, Rolland S. Effective Decisions & Emotional Fulfillment. LC 76-54652. 1977. 13.95 (ISBN 0-88229-303-6). Nelson-Hall.

--Emotional Common Sense: How to Avoid Self-Destructiveness. LC 72-9758. 238p. 1973. 9.95 o.p. (ISBN 0-06-013278-7, HarpT). Har-Row.

--Psychology & Counseling Careers. (Career Concise Guides Ser.). (gr. 7 up). 1977. PLB 6.45 (ISBN 0-531-01309-X). Watts.

Parker, Rollin J. & Studders, R. J. Permanent Magnets & Their Applications. LC 62-10930. 1962. 43.50 (ISBN 0-471-66264-X, Pub. by Wiley-Interscience). Wiley.

Parker, Ronald K., jt. auth. see Day, Mary C.

Parker, Rowland. The Men of Denwich: The Story of a Vanished Town. LC 78-14167. (Illus.). 1979. 11.95 o.p. (ISBN 0-03-046801-9). HR&W.

Parker, Scott, jt. auth. see Terrace, Herbert S.

Parker, Sheila. Coloured Things: Stages 1 & 2. LC 77-83009. (Science 5-13 Ser.). (Illus.). 1977. pap. text ed. 9.30 (ISBN 0-356-04348-7). Raintree Child.

--Minibeasts: Stages 1 & 2. LC 77-82989. (Science 5-13 Ser.). (Illus.). 1977. pap. text ed. 9.30 (ISBN 0-356-04106-9). Raintree Child.

--Trees: Stages 1 & 2. LC 77-83008. (Science 5-13 Ser.). (Illus.). 1977. pap. text ed. 9.30 (ISBN 0-356-04347-9). Raintree Child.

--Working with Wood: Background Information. LC 77-82995. (Science 5-13 Ser.). (Illus.). 1977. pap. text ed. 8.25 (ISBN 0-356-04010-0). Raintree Child.

--Working with Wood: Stages 1 & 2. LC 77-82995. (Science 5-13 Ser.). (Illus.). 1977. pap. text ed. 8.25 (ISBN 0-356-04011-9). Raintree Child.

Parker, Stephen J., jt. auth. see Parker, Fan.

Parker, Sybil P., ed. see McGraw-Hill Book Co.

Parker, Sybil P., ed. see McGraw-Hill Encyclopedia of Science & Technology Staff.

Parker, T. H., tr. see Calvin, John.

Parker, T. H., et al, trs. see Barth, Karl.

Parker, Thomas D., jt. ed. see Evans, Robert A.

Parker, W., ed. Alicyclic Chemistry, Vols. 2-6. Incl. Vols. 2 & 3. 1972 Literature. LC 72-82047. Vol. 2, 1974. 49.50 (ISBN 0-85186-522-4); Vol. 3, 1973 Literature. 66.00 (ISBN 0-85186-552-6); Vol. 4. 1974 Literature. LC 72-82047. 1976. 75.50 (ISBN 0-85186-582-8); Vol. 5. 1975 Literature. 1977. 77.00 (ISBN 0-85186-612-3); Vol. 6. 1976 Literature. 1978. 79.75 (ISBN 0-85186-632-8). LC 72-82047. Am Chemical.

--Aliphatic, Alicyclic, & Saturated Heterocyclic Chemistry: 1970-1971 Literature, Vol. 1 In 3 Pts. LC 72-83454. 1973. pt. 1 30.25 (ISBN 0-85186-502-X); pt. 2 44.00 (ISBN 0-685-55721-9); pt. 3 44.00 (ISBN 0-685-55722-7). Am Chemical.

Parker, W. H. Health & Disease in Farm Animals: An Introduction to Farm Animal Medicine. 3rd ed. Date not set. 42.00 (ISBN 0-08-025900-6); pap. 13.25 (ISBN 0-08-025899-9). Pergamon. Postponed.
--The Russians: How They Live & Work. LC 72-93295. 179p. 1973. text ed. 8.95 (ISBN 0-03-029581-5, HoltC). HR&W.
Parker, Watson. Deadwood: The Golden Years. LC 80-24100. (Illus.). xiv, 293p. 1981. 17.50 (ISBN 0-8032-0973-8). U of Nebr Pr.
--Gold in the Black Hills. (Illus.). 1966. 12.95 o.p. (ISBN 0-8061-0723-5). U of Okla Pr.
Parker, Watson & Lambert, Hugh. Black Hills Ghost Towns. LC 73-1501. (Illus.). 215p. 1974. 21.95 (ISBN 0-8040-0637-7, SB); pap. 11.95 (ISBN 0-8040-0638-5). Swallow.
Parker, William. Homosexuality: A Selective Bibliography of Over Three Thousand Items. LC 71-163430. 1971. 11.00 o.p. (ISBN 0-8108-0425-5). Scarecrow.
--Homosexuality Bibliography: Supplement, 1970-1975. LC 77-1114. 1977. 15.00 (ISBN 0-8108-1050-6). Scarecrow.
Parker, William B. Life & Public Services of Justin Smith Morrill. LC 79-87371. (American Scene Ser). (Illus.). 1971. Repr. of 1924 ed. lib. bdg. 42.50 (ISBN 0-306-71595-3). Da Capo.
Parker, William R; see Bishop, G. Reginald, Jr.
Parker, Xenia L. A Beginner's Book of off-Loom Weaving. LC 77-16880. (gr. 5 up). 1978. 6.95 (ISBN 0-396-07558-4). Dodd.
--Mosaics in Needlepoint. LC 77-5045. (Encore Edition). (Illus.). 1977. encore ed. 5.95 (ISBN 0-684-16201-6, ScribT); pap. 3.95 encore ed. (ISBN 0-684-15036-0, SL713, ScribT). Scribner.
Parker, Xenia L., ed. Wooden Toys. LC 77-92312. (Illus.). 1978. 12.95 o.p. (ISBN 0-8015-4809-8, Hawthorn); pap. 7.95 (ISBN 0-8015-8817-0, Hawthorn). Dutton.
Parkes, Don & Thrift, Nigel. Times, Spaces & Places: A Chronogeographic Perspective. 1980. 64.75 (ISBN 0-471-27616-2, Pub. by Wiley-Interscience). Wiley.
Parkes, E. W. Braced Frameworks: An Introduction to the Theory of Structures. 2nd ed. LC 74-10556. 1974. text ed. 23.00 (ISBN 0-08-018078-7); pap. text ed. 11.25 (ISBN 0-08-018077-9). Pergamon.
Parkes, G. D., jt. auth. see Mellor, J. W.
Parkes, James W. The Jew in the Medieval Community. 456p. 1976. 14.95 o.p. (ISBN 0-87203-059-8); pap. 9.75 (ISBN 0-87203-060-1). Hermon.
Parkes, M. B. English Cursive Book Hands, Twelve Hundred to Fifteen Hundred. 1980. 27.50x (ISBN 0-520-04080-5). U of Cal Pr.
Parkes, M. B., compiled by. Medieval Manuscripts of Keble College, Oxford: A Descriptive Catalogue with Summary Descriptions of the Greek & Oriental Manuscripts. (Illus.). 365p. 1979. 175.00x (ISBN 0-85967-504-1, Pub. by Scolar Pr England). Biblio Dist.
Parkes, M. B. & Watson, Andrew G., eds. Medieval Scribes, Manuscripts & Libraries: Essays Presented to N. R. Ker. (Illus.). 408p. 1978. 80.00x (ISBN 0-85967-450-9, Pub. by Scolar Pr England). Biblio Dist.
Parkes, Patricia. Queen's Lady. 504p. 1981. 12.95 (ISBN 0-312-66008-1). St Martin.
Parkes, W. Raymond. Occupational Lung Disorders. 2nd ed. 1981. text ed. price not set (ISBN 0-407-33731-8). Butterworth.
Parkes, William. The Curtaine-Drawer of the World: Or, Chamberlaine of That Inne of Iniquity. LC 79-84130. (English Experience Ser.: No.934). 76p. 1979. Repr. of 1612 ed. lib. bdg. 9.00 (ISBN 90-221-0948-8). Walter J Johnson.
Parkey, Robert W., et al, eds. Clinical Nuclear Cardiology. LC 78-12673. 1978. 34.50 (ISBN 0-8385-1146-5). ACC.
Parkhill, Joe. Health, Beauty & Happiness. spiral 5.95 (ISBN 0-88427-014-9). Green Hill.
--Wonderful World of Honey. 6.95 (ISBN 0-936744-01-4). Green Hill.
Parkhill, Joe M. Here's to You Honey: The Book That Takes Where the World of Honey Leaves off, Vol. 2. 160p. 1980. spiral bdg 6.95. Country Bazaar.
--Honey-God's Gift-for Health & Beauty: Cooking & Canning with Honey, Food Value Versus Sugar. 158p. 1980. spiral bdg 6.95 (ISBN 0-936744-03-0). Country Bazaar.
--The NO DIET Way to Health, Beauty, Happiness, How to Have It, How to Keep It: Natures Way Cookbook & Canning with Honey. 157p. 1979. spiral bdg. 6.95 (ISBN 0-936744-00-6). Country Bazaar.
Parkhomenko, A. S., jt. auth. see Modenov, P. S.
Parkhouse, Bonnie L. & Lapin, Jackie. Women Who Win: Exercising Your Rights in Sports. (Illus.). 272p. 1980. 11.95 (ISBN 0-13-962365-5, Spec); pap. 5.95 (ISBN 0-13-962357-4). P-H.
Parkhurst, Genevieve. Healing & Wholeness. 5.95 (ISBN 0-910924-90-2). Macalester.
Parkhurst, Helen H. Cathedral: A Gothic Pilgrimage. 304p. 1980. Repr. of 1936 ed. lib. bdg. 40.00 (ISBN 0-8492-2174-9). R West.
Parkhurst, Jane. Isobel. 1977. pap. 1.95 o.s.i. (ISBN 0-515-04334-6). Jove Pubns.
Parkhurst, L. G., ed. see Finney, Charles G.
Parkin, Beverly. The Gift of Flowers. 64p. 1976. 4.95 o.p. (ISBN 0-8028-3479-5). Eerdmans.
Parkin, David, ed. Town & Country in Central & Eastern Africa: International African Seminar, 12th, Lusaka, Sept. 1972. (Illus.). 1976. 36.00x (ISBN 0-19-724199-9). Oxford U Pr.
Parkin, Frank. Marxism & Class Theory: A Bourgeois Critique. LC 79-14222. 1979. 17.50x (ISBN 0-231-04880-7). Columbia U Pr.
Parkin, J. M. & Nobay, A. R., eds. Current Economic Problems. 1975. 52.50 (ISBN 0-521-20818-1). Cambridge U Pr.
Parkin, Michael & Sumner, Michael T., eds. Inflation in the United Kingdom. 1978. 25.00x o.p. (ISBN 0-8020-2321-5). U of Toronto Pr.
Parkin, Michael, ed. see Myint, H.
Parkin, Molly. Molly's Manhattan. 200p. Date not set. cancelled (ISBN 0-686-68788-4). Riverrun NY.
--Switchback. 160p. Date not set. cancelled (ISBN 0-686-68789-2). Riverrun NY.
Parkin, N. & Flood, C. R. Welding Craft Practice, Pt. 1, Vols. 1-2. 1969. Pt. 1. pap. 4.40 (ISBN 0-08-012980-3); Pt. 2. pap. 5.25 (ISBN 0-08-013000-3). Pergamon.
Parkin, P. H., et al. Acoustics, Noise & Buildings. 4th ed. LC 79-670251. 1979. 24.00 (ISBN 0-571-04952-4, Pub. by Faber & Faber); pap. 15.95 (ISBN 0-571-04953-2, Pub. by Faber & Faber). Merrimack Bk Serv.
Parkin, Rex. Red Carpet. (Illus.). (gr. k-3). 1967. 8.95g (ISBN 0-02-770020-8). Macmillan.
Parkin, S. F., jt. auth. see Oakley, Janet.
Parkings, Mac. Owyhee Mountain Ballads & Other Poems. 1980. 4.50 o.p. (ISBN 0-8062-1086-9). Carlton.
Parkins, Almon E. Historical Geography of Detroit. LC 77-118422. 1970. Repr. of 1918 ed. 15.50 o.p. (ISBN 0-8046-1371-0). Kennikat.
Parkins, John W. Geology Explained in Dorset. LC 76-54070. (Geology Explained Ser.). (Illus.). 1977. 8.95 (ISBN 0-7153-7319-6). David & Charles.
Parkins, R. N., jt. auth. see Arup, H.
Parkinson, C. Northcote. Dead Reckoning. LC 80-81631. 272p. 1980. pap. 2.25 (ISBN 0-87216-728-3). Playboy Pbks.
Parkinson, C. Northcote & Armstrong, O. K. Great Issues: A Forum on Important Questions Facing the American Public. 1971. 5.95. TSU Pr.
Parkinson, C. Northcote & LeCompte, Herman. The Law of Longer Life. (Illus.). 1980. 10.95 (ISBN 0-916624-31-5). TSU Pr.
Parkinson, Cornelia M. Historical Tales of Old Reynoldsburg: Selections from the First Five Years of the Courier. (Illus.). 152p. (Orig.). 1980. pap. 7.50 (ISBN 0-938404-00-8). Hist Tales.
--History of Reynoldsburg & Truro Township, Ohio. (Illus.). 200p. 1981. 25.00 (ISBN 0-938404-02-4). Hist Tales.
--The Reynoldsburg Book of Lists. (Orig.). 1981. pap. text ed. 7.50 (ISBN 0-938404-03-2). Hist Tales.
Parkinson, D. A. Value Added Taxation in the ECC. 200p. 1980. 33.00x (ISBN 0-86010-190-8, Pub. by Graham & Trotman England). State Mutual Bk.
Parkinson, Dan & Hicks, David L. The Texians: Pre-Revolutionary Texas. LC 79-91599. 272p. 8.95 (ISBN 0-89896-000-2). Larksdale.
Parkinson, G. H., tr. see Leibniz, Gottfried.
Parkinson, George H. Georg Lukacs. 1977. 16.00x (ISBN 0-7100-8678-4). Routledge & Kegan.
Parkinson, James W. Focus on Your Language. LC 75-17952. 279p. 1976. pap. 7.95 (ISBN 0-672-61358-1); tchrs.' manual 5.00 (ISBN 0-685-50625-8). Bobbs.
Parkinson, John. Paradisi in Sole, Paradisus Terrestris, or a Garden of All Sorts of Pleasant Flowers Which Our English Ayre Will Permit. LC 74-28880. (English Experience Ser.: No. 758). 1975. Repr. of 1629 ed. 110.00 (ISBN 90-221-0758-2). Walter J Johnson.
Parkinson, John R., jt. auth. see Faaland, Just.
Parkinson, Michael, jt. auth. see Litt, Edgar.
Parkinson, Northcote. Jeeves. 192p. 1981. 8.95 (ISBN 0-312-44144-4). St Martin.
Parkinson, R. N. Edward Gibbon. (English Authors Ser.: No. 159). 1973. lib. bdg. 10.95 (ISBN 0-8057-1218-6). Twayne.
Parkinson, Roger. Zapata: A Biography. LC 74-28202. (Illus.). 256p. (Orig.). 1980. pap. cancelled (ISBN 0-8128-6072-1). Stein & Day.
Parkinson, Thomas. Hart Crane & Yvor Winters: Their Literary Correspondence. 1978. 12.95 (ISBN 0-520-03538-0). U of Cal Pr.
Parkinson, Virginia. Kindness to Pets. (Pointers for Little Persons Ser.). (Illus.). (gr. k-3). 1961. PLB 5.99 (ISBN 0-8178-5032-5). Harvey.
--Safety. (Pointers for Little Persons Ser.). (Illus.). (ps-2). 1963. PLB 5.99 (ISBN 0-8178-5062-7). Harvey.
Parkland Research. Guide to National Practices in Western Europe. 1973. 17.50 (ISBN 0-685-88894-0). CBI Pub.
Parkman, Frances. Oregon Trail. Feltskog, E. N., ed. (Illus.). 1969. 27.50 (ISBN 0-299-05070-X). U of Wis Pr.
Parkman, Francis. Montcalm & Wolfe. 1962. pap. 1.50 o.s.i. (ISBN 0-02-035920-9, Collier). Macmillan.
--Oregon Trail. (Keith Jennison Large Type Bks). (gr. 6 up). PLB 7.95 o.p. (ISBN 0-531-00257-8). Watts.
Parkman, N., jt. auth. see Tapley, J. G.
Parkman, R. The Cybernetic Society. 400p. 1972. text ed. 27.00 (ISBN 0-08-016949-X); pap. text ed. 12.75 (ISBN 0-08-017185-0). Pergamon.
Parks, Alex L. Law of Tug, Tow & Pilotage. 2nd, rev. ed. 1981. text ed. 40.00 (ISBN 0-87033-263-5). Cornell Maritime.
--The Law of Tug, Tow & Pilotage. 2nd ed. 1981. 60.00x (ISBN 0-87033-265-1). Cornell Maritime.
Parks, Alexis. People Heaters: A People's Guide to Keeping Warm in Winter. LC 80-21930. (Illus.). 128p. (Orig.). 1980. pap. 4.95 (ISBN 0-931790-16-6). Brick Hse Pub.
Parks, Annette W. Qhawala-li: Water Coming Down Place; "A History of Gualalal, Mendocino County, California. LC 80-82462. (Illus.). 150p. 1981. 24.95 (ISBN 0-9605550-0-5); pap. 12.95 (ISBN 0-9605550-1-3). FreshCut.
Parks, Arnold G. Urban Education: An Annotated Bibliography. LC 80-69234. 135p. 1981. perfect bdg 9.50 (ISBN 0-86548-053-2). Century Twenty One.
Parks, Betsy M. The Dictionary of Initials. 1981. 12.95 (ISBN 0-8065-0750-0). Lyle Stuart.
Parks, Douglas R. A Grammar of Pawnee. LC 75-25121. (American Indian Linguistics Ser.). 1976. lib. bdg. 42.00 (ISBN 0-8240-1971-7). Garland Pub.
Parks, Gerald. Real Estate Profit Power: Managing Your Own Real Estate Office. 1981. text ed. 16.95 (ISBN 0-8359-6595-3); instr's manual free (ISBN 0-8359-6596-1). Reston.
Parks, Gordon. Choice of Weapons. LC 64-25119. 1966. 9.95 o.s.i. (ISBN 0-06-013281-7, HarpT). Har-Row.
Parks, Janet B. Physical Education: The Profession. LC 79-24507. (Illus.). 1980. pap. text ed. 8.95 (ISBN 0-8016-3759-7). Mosby.
Parks, Lillian R. & Leighton, Frances S. The Roosevelts: A Family in Turmoil. (Illus.). 300p. 1981. 12.50 (ISBN 0-13-783043-2). P-H.
Parks, Lloyd C., tr. see Stendhal.
Parks, Lois F., ed. see Chivers, Thomas H.
Parks, M. G., ed. see Howe, Joseph.
Parks, Mercer H. The Task Worthy of Travail. LC 74-11835. 1975. 15.00 (ISBN 0-88415-784-9). Pacesetter Pr.
Parks, Michael. The Prince of the Golden Apple. 1975. 6.50 (ISBN 0-571-10702-8, Pub. by Faber & Faber). Merrimack Bk Serv.
Parks, Pat. Railroad That Died at Sea: FEC's Key West Ext. LC 68-54448. (Shortline Railroad Series). (Illus.). 1968. pap. 4.95 (ISBN 0-8289-0151-1). Greene.
Parks, Paul B. Evaluation of the CDS-CDTE Heterojuction Solar Cell. LC 78-74996. (Outstanding Dissertations on Energy Ser.). 1979. lib. bdg. 14.00 (ISBN 0-8240-3991-2). Garland Pub.
--Model of an Ablating Solid Hydrogen Pellet in a Plasma. LC 78-74999. (Outstanding Dissertations on Energy Ser.). 1979. lib. bdg. 14.00 (ISBN 0-8240-3989-0). Garland Pub.
Parks, Robert J. Democracy's Railroads: Public Enterprise in Jacksonian Michigan. LC 79-189557. (National University Publications). 1972. 17.50 (ISBN 0-8046-9027-8). Kennikat.
Parks, Roland D. Examination & Valuation of Mineral Property. 4th ed. (Illus.). 1957. 27.50 (ISBN 0-201-05730-1, Adv Bk Prog). A-W.
Parks, Stephen, ed. The English Book Trade, Sixteen Sixty to Eighteen Fifty-Three. Incl. Vol. 1 (ISBN 0-8240-0950-9); Vol. 2 (ISBN 0-8240-0951-7); Vol. 3 (ISBN 0-8240-0952-5); Vol. 4 (ISBN 0-8240-0953-3); Vol. 5 (ISBN 0-8240-0954-1); Vol. 6 (ISBN 0-8240-0955-X); Vol. 7 (ISBN 0-8240-0956-8); Vol. 8 (ISBN 0-8240-0957-6); Vol. 9 (ISBN 0-8240-0958-4); Vol. 10 (ISBN 0-8240-0959-2); Vol. 11 (ISBN 0-8240-0960-6); Vol. 12 (ISBN 0-8240-0961-4); Vol. 13 (ISBN 0-8240-0962-2); Vol. 14 (ISBN 0-8240-0963-0); Vol. 15 (ISBN 0-8240-0964-9); Vol. 16 (ISBN 0-8240-0965-7); Vol. 17 (ISBN 0-8240-0966-5); Vol. 18 (ISBN 0-8240-0967-3); Vol. 19 (ISBN 0-8240-0968-1); Vol. 20 (ISBN 0-8240-0969-X); Vol. 21 (ISBN 0-8240-0970-3); Vol. 22 (ISBN 0-8240-0971-1); Vol. 23 (ISBN 0-8240-0972-X); Vol. 24 (ISBN 0-8240-0973-8); Vol. 25 (ISBN 0-8240-0974-6); Vol. 26 (ISBN 0-8240-0975-4); Vol. 27 (ISBN 0-8240-0976-2); Vol. 28 (ISBN 0-8240-0977-0). 1974. lib. bdg. 50.00 per vol. (ISBN 0-686-57687-X). Garland Pub.
--English Book Trade, Sixteen Sixty to Eighteen Fifty-Three. Incl. Vol. 29 (ISBN 0-8240-0978-9); Vol. 30 (ISBN 0-8240-0979-7); Vol. 31 (ISBN 0-8240-0980-0); Vol. 32 (ISBN 0-8240-0981-9); Vol. 33, 2 vols (ISBN 0-8240-0982-7); Vol. 34 (ISBN 0-8240-0983-5); Vol. 35 (ISBN 0-8240-0984-3); Vol. 36 (ISBN 0-8240-0985-1); Vol. 37 (ISBN 0-8240-0986-X); Vol. 38 (ISBN 0-8240-0987-8). 1974. lib. bdg. 50.00 per vol. (ISBN 0-686-57688-8). Garland Pub.
Parks, W. Robert. Soil Conservation Districts in Action. (Illus.). 1952. 2.00x o.p. (ISBN 0-685-99406-6). Iowa St U Pr.
Parkus, H. Thermoelasticity. 2nd rev. & enl. ed. 1976. soft cover 24.80 (ISBN 0-387-81375-6). Springer-Verlag.
Parkus, H., ed. Electromagnetic Interactions in Elastic Solids. (CISM Courses & Lectures: Vol. 257). (Illus.). 425p. 1980. pap. 38.10 (ISBN 0-387-81509-0). Springer-Verlag.
Parlakian, Nishan, tr. see Shirvanzade, Alexandre.
Parlato, Salvatore J. Films Ex Libris: Literature in Sixteen mm & Video. LC 80-10181. (Illus.). 283p. 1980. lib. bdg. 15.95x (ISBN 0-89950-006-4). McFarland & Co.
Parlato, Salvatore J., Jr. Superfilms: An International Guide to Award Winning Educational Films. LC 76-10801. 1976. 16.50 (ISBN 0-8108-0953-2). Scarecrow.
Parlett, Beresford N. The Symmetric Eigenvalue Problem. (Illus.). 1980. text ed. 25.95 (ISBN 0-13-880047-2). P-H.
Parlett, David. All the Best Card Games. 1979. 19.95 (ISBN 0-7134-0387-X, Pub. by Batsford England). David & Charles.
Parlin, Bradley W. Immigrant Professionals in the United States: Discrimination in the Scientific Labor Market. LC 75-8409. (Special Studies). 96p. 1976. text ed. 22.95 (ISBN 0-275-01050-3). Praeger.
Parmaji, S. Education & Jobs. 1979. text ed. 9.25x (ISBN 0-391-01828-0). Humanities.
Parmalee, Paul W. & Loomis, Forrest D. Decoys & Decoy Carvers of Illinois. LC 69-19824. (Illus.). 408p. 1969. pap. 25.00 (ISBN 0-87580-524-8). N Ill U Pr.
Parmar, H. A., jt. auth. see Taylor, S. E.
Parmar, Shyam. Folk Music & Mass Media. 1978. 7.50x o.p. (ISBN 0-8364-0137-9). South Asia Bks.
Parmee, Douglas, tr. see Merimee, Prosper.
Parmelee, C. W. Ceramic Glazes. 3rd ed. Harman, Cameron G., ed. LC 70-183371. 1973. 21.50 (ISBN 0-8436-0609-6). CBI Pub.
Parmelee, Dean X., jt. ed. see Jacobson, Alan M.
Parmelin, Helene. Art Anti-Art: Anartism Explored. Underwood, J. A., tr. from Fr. 1980. pap. 5.95 (ISBN 0-7145-2571-5, Pub. by M Boyars). Merrimack Bk Serv.
--Art Anti-Art: Anartism Explored. 1977. text ed. 9.25x (ISBN 0-7145-2570-7). Humanities.
Parmet, Herbert S. The Democrats: The Years After FDR. LC 75-25990. (Illus.). 384p. 1976. 14.95 (ISBN 0-02-594770-2, 59477). Macmillan.
--Jack: The Struggles of John F. Kennedy. 1980. 14.95 (ISBN 0-8037-4452-8). Dial.
Parmeter, J. R., ed. Rhizoctonia Solani: Biology & Pathology. LC 69-16510. (Illus.). 1970. 30.00x (ISBN 0-520-01497-9). U of Cal Pr.
Parming, Tonu & Jarvesoo, Elmar, eds. A Case Study of a Soviet Republic: The Estonian SSR. LC 77-671. (Westview Special Studies on the Soviet Union & Eastern Europe). 1978. lib. bdg. 30.00x (ISBN 0-89158-247-9). Westview.
Parmley, Robert O. Field Engineer's Manual. 608p. 1981. 19.50 (ISBN 0-07-048513-5, P&RB). McGraw.
Parnell, Joy, ed. see Howard, Will.
Parnell, Wilma T. & Taber, Robert. The Killing of Corporal Kunze. (Illus.). 224p. 1981. 10.00 (ISBN 0-8184-0313-6). Lyle Stuart.

Parnes, Herbert S. From Mid-Career Through Retirement: Longitudinal Studies of the Male Work Force. (Illus.). 352p. 1981. text ed. 27.50x (ISBN 0-262-16079-X). MIT Pr.
Parnes, Robert. Canoeing the Jersey Pine Barrens. LC 77-70413. (Illus.). 288p. (Orig.). 1978. lib. bdg. 10.25 o.p. (ISBN 0-914788-03-5). East Woods.
Parnwell, E. C., jt. ed. see Hornby, A. S.
Parnwell, E. C., jt. ed. see Hornby, Albert S.
Parodi, Pierre. The Use of Poor Means in Helping the Third World. Gravalos, Elizabeth, tr. Orig. Title: Fr. 44p. 1970. pap. 1.25 (ISBN 0-934676-10-0). Greenlf Bks.
Parr, Carmen S., jt. auth. see De La Vega, Sara L.
Parr, John B., jt. auth. see Maclennan, Duncan.
Parr, Lucy C. Not of the World: A Living Account of the United Order. LC 75-5320. (Illus.). 232p. 1975. 6.95 (ISBN 0-88290-047-1). Horizon Utah.
Parrack, James D. The Naturalist in Majorca. (Regional Naturalist Ser). (Illus.). 208p. 1973. 5.95 (ISBN 0-7153-5948-7). David & Charles.
Parramon, J. M. Color. (Orig.). Date not set. pap. 4.95 (ISBN 0-89586-075-9). H P Bks. Postponed.
--Composition. (Orig.). 1981. pap. 4.95 (ISBN 0-89586-084-8). H P Bks.
--Drawing. (Orig.). 1980. pap. 4.95 (ISBN 0-89586-072-4). H P Bks.
--Oils. (Art Ser.). (Orig.). 1980. pap. 4.95 (ISBN 0-89586-073-2). H P Bks.
--Perspective. (Art Ser.). (Orig.). 1981. pap. 4.95 (ISBN 0-89586-082-1). H P Bks.
Parramon, J. M. & Fresquet, G. Watercolors. (Art Ser.). (Orig.). 1980. pap. 4.95 (ISBN 0-89586-074-0). H P Bks.
Parramon, J. M., ed. Painting the Nude. LC 77-361625. (Illus., Orig.). 1976. pap. 10.50x (ISBN 0-85242-449-3). Intl Pubns Serv.
Parravicini, Pastori, jt. auth. see Bassani, F.
Parret, H. H., ed. Meaning & Understanding International Conference, June 1979. (Foundation of Communication Ser.). 288p. 1980. text ed. 61.50x (ISBN 3-11-008116-4). De Gruyter.
Parret, Herman, ed. Le Language en Contexte: Etudes Philosophiques et Linguistiques de Pragmatique. (Linguisticae Investigationes Supplementa: No. 3). (Fr.). 1980. text ed. 85.50x (ISBN 90-272-3112-5). Humanities.
Parrette, James. Gallows Gold. (Orig.). 1980. pap. 1.95 (ISBN 0-89083-687-6, Kable News Co). Zebra.
Parrick, Jerry. A Twentieth Century Miracle. (Orig.). 1981. pap. 4.95 (ISBN 0-88270-488-5). Logos.
Parrillo, Vincent M. Strangers to These Shores: Race & Ethnic Relations in the United States. LC 79-87856. 1979. text ed. 16.25 (ISBN 0-395-28562-3); inst manual 0.65 (ISBN 0-395-28563-1). HM.
Parrinder, Geoffrey. African Traditional Religion. LC 75-39900. 160p. 1976. pap. 3.95x o.p. (ISBN 0-06-066472-X, RD150, HarpR). Har-Row.
--Jesus in the Qur'an. 1977. pap. 7.95 (ISBN 0-19-519963-4). Oxford U Pr.
--Mysticism in the World's Religions. 1977. pap. text ed. 4.95 (ISBN 0-19-502185-1, 497, GB). Oxford U Pr.
Parrinder, Patrick, ed. H. G. Wells: The Critical Heritage. (Critical Heritage Ser.). 1972. 29.00x (ISBN 0-7100-7387-9). Routledge & Kegan.
Parrinder, Patrick & Philmus, Robert, eds. H. G. Wells's Literary Criticism. 261p. 1980. 27.50x (ISBN 0-389-20035-2). B&N.
Parrington, Michael. The Excavation of an Iron Age Settlement, Bronze Age Ring-Ditches & Roman Features at Ashville Trading Estate, Abingdon (Oxfordshire) 166p. 1980. pap. 24.00x (ISBN 0-900312-50-5, Pub. by Coun Brit Arch England). Intl Schol Bk Serv.
Parriott, Sara. Calories Don't Count When... 1979. pap. 2.95 o.p. (ISBN 0-312-90453-3); prepack 29.50 o.p. (ISBN 0-312-90454-1). St Martin.
--Calories Don't Count When... LC 79-84900. (Illus.). 96p. 1979. pap. 2.95 (ISBN 0-87477-105-6). J P Tarcher.
--Sex Doesn't Count When... LC 79-66310. (Illus.). 96p. 1979. pap. 2.95 (ISBN 0-87477-113-7). J P Tarcher.
Parris, Henry. Staff Relations in the Civil Service: 50 Years of Whitleyism. (Royal Institute of Public Administration). 1973. text ed. 35.00x (ISBN 0-04-351046-9). Allen Unwin.
Parris, Judith H. The Convention Problem: Issues in Reform of Presidential Nominating Procedures. (Studies in Presidential Selection). 176p. 1972. 10.95 (ISBN 0-8157-6928-8); pap. 4.95 (ISBN 0-8157-6927-X). Brookings.
Parris, Judith H., jt. auth. see Bain, Richard C.
Parris, Judith H., jt. auth. see Sayre, Wallace S.
Parris, Leslie. The Pre-Raphaelites. (Tate Gallery: Little Art Book Ser.). (Illus.). 1977. pap. 1.95 (ISBN 0-8120-0856-1). Barron.
Parris, Leslie, jt. auth. see Shields, Conal.
Parris, Nina G., compiled by. Checklist of the Paintings, Prints, & Drawings in the Collection of the Robert Hull Fleming Museum. (Illus.). 166p. (Orig.). 1977. pap. 7.50 (ISBN 0-87451-989-6). U Pr of New Eng.
Parris, Wayne, jt. auth. see Holmes, Lowell E.
Parrish, Alvin E. Kidney Disease Case Studies. 2nd. ed. 1979. 14.75 (ISBN 0-87488-022-X). Med Exam.
Parrish, Anne. All Kneeling. 1976. lib. bdg. 13.95 (ISBN 0-89968-154-9). Lightyear.
--The Perennial Bachelor. 1976. lib. bdg. 13.95x (ISBN 0-89968-153-0). Lightyear.
Parrish, Frank. Fire in the Barley. LC 78-27819. (A Dan Mallet Novel of Suspense Ser.). 1979. 7.95 (ISBN 0-396-07684-X). Dodd.
--Sting of the Honeybee. LC 79-10518. 1979. 7.95 (ISBN 0-396-07702-1). Dodd.
Parrish, Henry M. Poisonous Snakebites in the United States. LC 78-18625. 1980. 15.00 (ISBN 0-533-03838-3). Vantage.
Parrish, John, et al. Uv-A: Biological Effects of Ultraviolet Radiation. LC 78-14968. (Illus.). 272p. 1978. 25.00 (ISBN 0-306-31121-6, Plenum Pr). Plenum Pub.
Parrish, Mary P. Book of Mormon Story. LC 66-10962. pap. 1.50 o.p. (ISBN 0-87747-024-3). Deseret Bk.
Parrish, Mary V. Then Comes the Joy. LC 76-44383. 1977. pap. 3.75 o.p. (ISBN 0-687-41439-3). Abingdon.
Parrish, Michael. The U S S R in World War II: An Annotated Bibliography of Books Published in the Soviet Union, 1945 to 1975. LC 80-8502. 925p. 1981. lib. bdg. 110.00 (ISBN 0-8240-9485-9). Garland Pub.
Parrish, Randall. Bob Hampton of Placer. 1976. lib. bdg. 16.70x (ISBN 0-89968-084-4). Lightyear.
--Contraband, A Romance of the North Atlantic. 1976. lib. bdg. 18.25x (ISBN 0-89968-085-2). Lightyear.
--My Lady of the North. 1976. lib. bdg. 16.30x (ISBN 0-89968-086-0). Lightyear.
--My Lady of the South. 1976. lib. bdg. 16.30x (ISBN 0-89968-087-9). Lightyear.
--When Wilderness Was King. 1976. lib. bdg. 17.25x (ISBN 0-89968-088-7). Lightyear.
Parrish, Roy J., Jr., jt. auth. see Beck, Henry J.
Parrish, Stephen, ed. see Austen, Jane.
Parrish, Wayland M. Reading Aloud. 4th ed. 1966. 13.95 o.p. (ISBN 0-8260-6995-9). Wiley.
Parrott, Bob W. Ontology of Humor. 1981. 10.95 (ISBN 0-8022-2387-7). Philos Lib.
Parrott, Cecil, tr. see Hasek, Jaroslav.
Parrott, Ian. Guide to Musical Thought. (Student's Music Library Ser). 1955. 6.95 (ISBN 0-234-77309-X). Dufour.
--Method in Orchestration. (Student's Music Library Ser). 1956. 6.95 (ISBN 0-234-77310-3). Dufour.
Parrott, Ray, tr. see Eikhenbaum, Boris.
Parry, Alan, jt. auth. see Robertson, Jenny.
Parry, Albert. Peter Kapitsa on Life & Science. 1968. 7.50 o.s.i. (ISBN 0-02-594810-5). Macmillan.
--The Russian Scientist. Koslow, Jules, ed. LC 72-92454. (Russia Old & New Series). (Illus.). 192p. 1973. 5.95 o.s.i. (ISBN 0-02-594820-2). Macmillan.
--Tattoo. 1971. pap. 1.95 o.s.i. (ISBN 0-02-081080-6, Collier). Macmillan.
Parry, Benita. Delusions & Discoveries: Studies on India in the British Imagination 1880-1930. 1972. 24.50x (ISBN 0-520-02215-7). U of Cal Pr.
Parry, C. English Through Drama. LC 72-184902. (Illus.). 250p. 1972. 24.95 (ISBN 0-521-08483-0); pap. 9.95x (ISBN 0-521-09741-X). Cambridge U Pr.
--Index Guide to Treaties, Vol. 1. 1979. 75.00 (ISBN 0-379-13002-5). Oceana.
Parry, C., ed. Lord McNair: Selected Papers & Bibliography. 1974. 32.00 (ISBN 0-379-00228-0). Oceana.
Parry, C. B. W. Rehabilitation of the Hand. 3rd ed. 1973. Repr. of 1977 ed. 49.95 (ISBN 0-407-38501-0). Butterworths.
Parry, David. Households of God. (Cistercian Studies Ser.: No. 39). (Orig.). 1980. pap. 7.95 (ISBN 0-87907-939-8). Cistercian Pubns.
--This Promise Is for You. LC 77-99305. 1978. pap. 2.95 (ISBN 0-8091-2098-4). Paulist Pr.
Parry, E. H. Principles of Medicine in Africa. (Illus.). 1976. text ed. 29.95x (ISBN 0-19-264223-5). Oxford U Pr.
Parry, Edward A. The Law & the Poor: London, Nineteen Fourteen. LC 79-56966. (The English Working Class Ser.). 1980. lib. bdg. 30.00 (ISBN 0-8240-0117-6). Garland Pub.
Parry, Geraint. John Locke. (Political Thinkers Ser.). 1978. text ed. 21.00x o.p. (ISBN 0-04-320130-X); pap. text ed. 8.95x (ISBN 0-04-320131-8). Allen Unwin.
Parry, H. B., ed. Population & Its Problems: A Plain Man's Guide. 432p. 1974. text ed. 34.95x (ISBN 0-19-857380-4). Oxford U Pr.
Parry, J. P. The Provision of Education in England & Wales. 1971. text ed. 27.50x (ISBN 0-04-371015-8). Allen Unwin.
Parry, James. The Discovery. LC 77-1904. 1978. 10.95 o.s.i. (ISBN 0-690-01166-0, TYC-T). T Y Crowell.
Parry, John H., ed. Establishment of the European Hegemony: 1415-1715: Trade & Exploration in the Age of the Renaissance. pap. 3.95x (ISBN 0-06-131045-X, TB1045, Torch). Har-Row.
Parry, John J., tr. see Capellanus, Andreas.
Parry, Keith. Trans-Pennine Heritage: People & Transport. LC 80-68691. (Illus.). 1981. 19.95 (ISBN 0-7153-8019-2). David & Charles.
Parry, Marian, illus. City Mouse - Country Mouse & Two More Mouse Tales from Aesop. (Illus.). (gr. 2-3). 1971. pap. 1.50 (ISBN 0-590-04438-9, Schol Pap); pap. 3.50 bk. & record (ISBN 0-590-04353-6). Schol Bk Serv.
Parry, Michel, ed. The Devil's Children. pap. 1.50 o.p. (ISBN 0-425-03202-7). Berkley Pub.
Parry, Noel, et al, eds. Social Work, Welfare & the State. LC 79-67578. 202p. 1980. pap. 9.95x (ISBN 0-8039-1415-6). Sage.
Parry, R. H., ed. The English Civil War & After, 1642-1658. LC 74-111423. 1970. pap. 4.95x (ISBN 0-520-01783-8, CAMPUS 30). U of Cal Pr.
--Stress-Strain Behaviour of Soils. (Illus.). 1973. text ed. 54.00x (ISBN 0-85429-121-0). Intl Ideas.
Parry, Robert W. & Kodama, Goji. Boron Chemistry Four: Fourth International Meeting on Boron Chemistry, Salt Lake City & Snowbird, Utah, USA, 8-13 July 1979. (IUPAC Symposium Ser.). 150p. 1980. 57.00 (ISBN 0-08-025256-7). Pergamon.
Parry, V. J. & Yapp, M. E. War, Technology, & Society in the Middle East. (Illus.). 464p. 1975. 33.00x (ISBN 0-19-713581-1). Oxford U Pr.
Parry, W. Topics in Ergodic Theory. LC 79-7815. (Tracts in Mathematics Ser.). Date not set. price not set (ISBN 0-521-22986-3). Cambridge U Pr.
Parsa, Mohamad H., et al. Safe Central Venous Nutrition: Guidelines for Prevention & Management of Complications. 280p. 1974. pap. 22.25 spiral (ISBN 0-398-02785-4). C C Thomas.
Parse. Man-Living-Health: A Theory of Nursing. 192p. 1981. pap. 11.95 (ISBN 0-471-04443-1, Pub. by Wiley Med). Wiley.
Parse, Rosemarie R., ed. Nursing Fundamentals. (Nursing Outline Ser.). 1974. 8.00 (ISBN 0-87488-378-4). Med Exam.
Parsegian, V. L. Introduction to Natural Science, Pt. 2, The Life Sciences. 1970. text ed. 21.50 (ISBN 0-12-545202-0); lab. suppl. 5.50 (ISBN 0-12-545256-X); tchrs' guide 5.00 (ISBN 0-12-545257-8). Acad Pr.
Parshall, G. W. Inorganic Syntheses, Vol. 15. (Inorganic Synthesis Ser.). 1974. 25.95 o.p. (ISBN 0-07-048521-6, P&RB). McGraw.
Parshall, Linda B. The Art of Narration in Wolfram's "Parzival" & Albrecht's "Jungerer Titurel". LC 79-21146. (Anglica Germanica Ser.: No. 2). 380p. Date not set. price not set (ISBN 0-521-22237-0). Cambridge U Pr.
Parshall, Phil. New Paths in Muslim Evangelism: Evangelical Approaches to Contextualization. 200p. (Orig.). 1980. pap. 6.95 (ISBN 0-8010-7056-2). Baker Bk.
Parsler, Ron & Shapiro, Dan. The Social Impact of Oil in Scotland. 192p. 1980. text ed. 27.75x (ISBN 0-566-00375-9, Pub. by Gower Pub Co England). Renouf.
Parsley, Mary, ed. My Book of Stories for All Seasons. LC 74-78600. (Illus.). 120p. (gr. 1-3). 1974. 4.95 o.p. (ISBN 0-88332-063-0, 8024). Larousse.
Parsloe, Phyllida. Juvenile Justice in Britain & the United States: The Balance of Needs & Rights. (Library of Social Work). 1978. 21.50x (ISBN 0-7100-8772-1). Routledge & Kegan.
Parson, Ruben A., et al. Conserving American Resources. 3rd ed. 640p. 1972. 20.95 (ISBN 0-13-167767-5). P-H.
Parson, Theodore. Achieving Classroom Communication Through Self Analysis. 1976. kit (instructor's manual, worktext, audiotape cassettes, instruction sheets) 21.50leader's (ISBN 0-574-23040-8, 13-6040); group leader's manual 4.95 (ISBN 0-574-23042-4, 13-6042); worktext 8.95 (ISBN 0-574-23041-6, 13-6041); studio kit (worktext, audiotape, instruction sheet) 17.50 (ISBN 0-574-23045-9, 3-6045); pre-recorded audiotape cassette 9.95 (13-6043). SRA.
Parson, Thomas E. How to Dance. 2nd ed. (Illus.). 1969. pap. 2.50 (ISBN 0-06-463202-4, EH 202, EH). Har-Row.
Parsonage, M. J. & Caldwell, A. D., eds. The Place of Sodium Valproate in the Treatment of Epilepsy. (Royal Society of Medicine International Congress & Symposium Ser.: No. 30). 1980. 29.00 (ISBN 0-8089-1293-3). Grune.
Parsonage, William H., ed. Perspectives on Victimology. LC 79-15524. (Sage Research Progress Series in Criminology: Vol. 11). 1979. 12.95x (ISBN 0-8039-1323-0); pap. 6.50x (ISBN 0-8039-1324-9). Sage.
Parsons. Russian-English Dictionary of...OCTB Words. 1978. 10.00 o.p. (ISBN 0-686-64130-2). Translation Research.
Parsons, C., jt. auth. see Wilson, John.
Parsons, C. G. Inside View of Slavery: Or a Tour Among the Planters. 1969. Repr. of 1855 ed. 15.00 (ISBN 0-87266-025-7). Argosy.
Parsons, C. J. Problems in Business Communications. 1977. pap. 11.00x (ISBN 0-7131-0107-5). Intl Ideas.
Parsons, Carole W., ed. see Scientific Personnel Office.
Parsons, Charles. Russian Dictionary of... (a, e, i, ya) Tel' Words. (Orig.). 1980. pap. 5.00x o.p. (ISBN 0-917564-08-1). Translation Research.
--Russian-English Dictionary of...(a,e,i,ya) tel' Words. (Orig.). 1980. pap. 5.00x (ISBN 0-917564-08-1). Translation Research.
Parsons, D. S. Roy Campbell: A Descriptive & Annotated Bibliography. LC 79-7930. (Illus.). 250p. 1980. 20.00cancelled o.p. (ISBN 0-8240-9526-X). Garland Pub.
Parsons, David, ed. Tenth-Century Studies: Essays in Commemoration of the Millennium of the Council of Winchester & Regulars Concordia. (Illus.). 270p. 1975. 35.00x (ISBN 0-87471-781-7). Rowman.
Parsons, Derrick. Do Your Own Horse. (Illus.). 12.25 (ISBN 0-85131-280-2). J A Allen.
Parsons, Donald. The Holy Eucharist: Rite Two a Devotional Commentary. 1976. pap. 3.95 (ISBN 0-8164-2129-3). Crossroad NY.
Parsons, Donald F., ed. Ultrasoft X-Ray Microscopy: Its Application to Biological & Physical Sciences. (N.Y. Academy of Sciences: Vol. 342). 402p. 1980. 70.00 (ISBN 0-89766-066-8); pap. write for info. (ISBN 0-89766-067-6). NY Acad Sci.
Parsons, Elia S., jt. auth. see Kelly, Marguerite.
Parsons, Elizabeth. The Upside-Down Cat. LC 80-13507. (Illus.). 48p. (gr. 3-6). 1981. 9.95 (ISBN 0-689-50187-0, McElderry Bk). Atheneum.
Parsons, Elsie C., ed. American Indian Life. LC 22-16158. (Illus.). 1967. 15.00x (ISBN 0-8032-3651-4); pap. 4.50 (ISBN 0-8032-5148-3, BB 364, Bison). U of Nebr Pr.
Parsons, Frank A. The Psychology of Dress. LC 74-19187. (Illus.). 1975. Repr. of 1920 ed. 24.00 (ISBN 0-8103-4087-9). Gale.
Parsons, Howard L. Ethics in the Soviet Union Today. 1967. pap. 1.00 (ISBN 0-89977-016-9). Am Inst Marxist.
--Humanistic Philosophy in Poland & Yugoslavia Today. (Occasional Papers Ser.: No. 4). 1968. pap. 1.00 (ISBN 0-89977-021-5). Am Inst Marxist.
--Man East & West: Essays in East-West Philosophy. (Philosophical Currents Ser: No. 8). 211p. 1975. pap. text ed. 20.50x (ISBN 90-6032-020-4). Humanities.
Parsons, Howard L., ed. Marx & Engels on Ecology. LC 77-71866. (Contributions in Philosophy: No.8). 1977. lib. bdg. 18.95 (ISBN 0-8371-9538-1, PME/). Greenwood.
Parsons, Ian, ed. see Rosenberg, Isaac.
Parsons, Jack. Population Fallacies. 1977. 14.95 o.p. (ISBN 0-301-74031-3, Pub. by Paul Elek); pap. 9.95 o.p. (ISBN 0-301-74032-1). Merrimack Bk Serv.
Parsons, James J. Antioqueno Colonization in Western Colombia. rev. ed. LC 68-58002. (Illus.). 1968. 20.00x (ISBN 0-520-01464-2). U of Cal Pr.
Parsons, Jeffrey R. Prehistoric Settlement Patterns in the Southern Valley of Mexico: The Chalco-Xochimilco Region. (Memoir Ser.: No. 14). (Orig.). 1981. pap. write for info. (ISBN 0-932206-88-3). U Mich Mus Anthro.
Parsons, John A., ed. Calcium Metabolism. (Comprehensive Endocrinology Ser.). 1981. 36.00 (ISBN 0-89004-344-2, 393). Raven.
--Endocrinology of Calcium Metabolism. (Comprehensive Endocrinology Ser.). 375p. 1981. 36.00 (ISBN 0-89004-344-2). Raven.
Parsons, Judith N. Math-a-Dot Series, Math Learning Games. Incl. Level I. Addition & Subtraction. (gr. 1-2). 1975 (ISBN 0-8224-4415-1); Level II. Addition & Subtraction. (gr. 1-3). 1975 (ISBN 0-8224-4416-X); Level III. Addition & Subtraction. (gr. 2-4). 1974 (ISBN 0-8224-4417-8); Level IV. Multiplication. (gr. 3-4). 1979 (ISBN 0-8224-4418-6); Level V. Division. (gr. 4-5). 1979 (ISBN 0-8224-4419-4). (Makemaster Bk.). pap. 5.50 ea. Pitman Learning.
--Math-a-Riddle Secret-Message Challenges to Build Basic Skills. Incl. Bk. I. Subtraction. (gr. 2-4) (ISBN 0-8224-4433-X); Bk. II. Multiplication. (gr. 3-5) (ISBN 0-8224-4434-8). (Makemaster Bk.). 1979. pap. 5.50 ea. Pitman Learning.
Parsons, Leonard J., jt. auth. see Dalrymple, Douglas J.

Parsons, Marilyn. Our Universe, Mine & Yours. 1980. 4.00 (ISBN 0-8062-1364-7). Carlton.
Parsons, Mothey. Almonds to Zoybeans: A Natural Foods Cookbook. (Illus.). 192p. 1973. pap. 1.50. Larchmont Bks.
Parsons, Neil, jt. ed. see Palmer, Robin.
Parsons, P. A. Behavioural & Ecological Genetics: A Study in Drosophila. (Illus.). 231p. 1973. 37.50x (ISBN 0-19-857354-5). Oxford U Pr.
Parsons, Peter, jt. auth. see Ehrman, Lee.
Parsons, Robert. A Conference About the Next Succession to the Crown of Ingland. LC 70-38217. (English Experience Ser.: No. 481). 1972. Repr. of 1594 ed. 32.50 (ISBN 90-221-0481-8). Walter J Johnson.
Parsons, Robert T., ed. Windows on Africa: A Symposium. 1972. text ed. 27.50x (ISBN 9-0040-1705-4). Humanities.
Parsons, S. A. How to Find Out About Engineering. 285p. 1972. text ed. 21.00 (ISBN 0-08-016919-8). Pergamon.
Parsons, Stanley, et al. United States Congressional Districts, 1788-1841. LC 77-83897. (Illus.). 1978. lib. bdg. 37.50x (ISBN 0-8371-9828-3, PUS/). Greenwood.
Parsons, Talcott. Essays in Sociological Theory. rev. ed. 1964. pap. text ed. 9.95 o.s.i. (ISBN 0-02-924030-1). Free Pr.
--Politics and Social Structure. LC 75-88631. 1969. 15.50 o.s.i. (ISBN 0-02-923960-5). Free Pr.
--Social Structure & Personality. LC 64-11218. 1964. 15.95 (ISBN 0-02-924850-7); pap. 3.45 (ISBN 0-02-924840-X). Free Pr.
--Social System. 1964. pap. text ed. 8.95 (ISBN 0-02-924190-1). Free Pr.
--Sociological Theory & Modern Society. LC 67-12517. 1967. 25.00 (ISBN 0-02-924200-2). Free Pr.
--Structure & Process in Modern Societies. 1960. 15.95 (ISBN 0-02-924340-8). Free Pr.
--Structure of Social Action. LC 49-49353. 1949. 15.95 (ISBN 0-02-924260-6); Vol. 1. pap. text ed. 7.95 (ISBN 0-02-924240-1); Vol. 2. pap. text ed. 6.95 (ISBN 0-02-924250-9). Free Pr.
Parsons, Talcott & Smelser, Neil J. Economy & Society: A Study in the Integration of Economic & Social Theory. 1965. pap. 2.95 o.s.i. (ISBN 0-02-923950-8). Free Pr.
Parsons, Talcott, tr. see Weber, Max.
Parsons, Talcott, et al. Working Papers in the Theory of Action. LC 80-24475. 269p. 1981. Repr. of 1953 ed. lib. bdg. 25.00x (ISBN 0-313-22468-4, PAWP). Greenwood.
Parsons, Theophilus. Memoir of Theophilus Parsons. LC 71-118032. (American Constitutional & Legal History Ser). 1970. Repr. of 1859 ed. lib. bdg. 45.00 (ISBN 0-306-71939-8). Da Capo.
Parsons, Thomas W. Incidents & Experiences in the Life of Thomas W. Parsons from 1826 to 1900. Mathias, Frank F., ed. LC 74-7878. (Illus.). 1975. 14.00x (ISBN 0-8131-1319-9). U Pr of Ky.
Parsons, Thornton H. John Crowe Ransom. (U. S. Authors Ser.: No. 150). 1969. lib. bdg. 10.95 (ISBN 0-8057-0604-6). Twayne.
Parsons, Timothy R. & Takahashi, M. Biological Oceanographic Processes. LC 73-7758. 196p. 1974. text ed. 19.80 o.p. (ISBN 0-08-017603-8); pap. text ed. 12.10 o.p. (ISBN 0-08-017604-6). Pergamon.
Parsons, Timothy R., et al. Biological Oceanographic Processes. 2nd ed. 1978. text ed. 38.00 (ISBN 0-08-021502-5); pap. text ed. 19.75 (ISBN 0-08-021501-7). Pergamon.
Parsons, Virgil & Sanford, Nancy. Interpersonal Interaction in Nursing. 1979. 7.95 (ISBN 0-201-05551-1, 05551, M&N Div). A-W.
Parsons, Virginia. Los Caballos. Sánchez, Rene, tr. from Eng. Orig. Title: The Horse Book. (Illus.). 24p. (Span.). (ps-3). 1977. PLB 5.92 o.p. (ISBN 0-307-68837-2, Golden Pr). Western Pub.
--The Horse Book. (Illus.). (ps-1). 1968. PLB 5.38 (ISBN 0-307-68937-9, Golden Pr). Western Pub.
Parsons, Virginia, illus. Things in My House. (Block Bk.). (ps). 1981. 2.50 (ISBN 0-686-69205-5, Golden Pr). Western Pub.
Parsons, William B. An American Engineer in China. LC 78-74326. (The Modern Chinese Economy Ser.). 315p. 1980. lib. bdg. 33.00 (ISBN 0-8240-4256-5). Garland Pub.
--Engineers & Engineering of the Renaissance. 1968. 18.50x o.p. (ISBN 0-262-16024-2); pap. 9.95x (ISBN 0-262-66026-1). MIT Pr.
Parsons, William E., Jr. Silly Putty & Other Children's Sermons. LC 73-3451. 112p. 1978. pap. 3.95 (ISBN 0-687-38464-8). Abingdon.
Parsons, William T. The Pennsylvania Dutch. LC 75-22044. (Immigrant Heritage of America Ser.). 1976. lib. bdg. 10.95 (ISBN 0-8057-8408-X). Twayne.
Parsonson, S. L. Pure Mathematics, 2 vols. LC 70-100026. (Illus.). 1971. Vol. 1. text ed. 14.50x (ISBN 0-521-07683-8); Vol. 2. text ed. 16.95x (ISBN 0-521-08032-0). Cambridge U Pr.
Parston, Gregory. Planners, Politics & Health Services. 196p. 1980. 25.50x (ISBN 0-85664-909-0, Pub. by Croom Helm Ltd England). Biblio Dist.
Partch, Harry. The Genesis of a Music. 2nd ed. LC 73-4333. (Music Reprint Ser.). 1974. lib. bdg. 29.50 (ISBN 0-306-71597-X); pap. 9.50 (ISBN 0-306-80106-X). Da Capo.
Partee, Barbara H. Subject & Object in Modern English. Hankamer, Jorge, ed. LC 78-66576. (Outstanding Dissertations in Linguistics Ser.). 1979. lib. bdg. 15.50 (ISBN 0-8240-9679-7). Garland Pub.
Parter, Seymour, jt. ed. see Meyer, Richard.
Parthasarathy, Indira. Tricky Ground. (Indian Novels Ser.). 191p. 1975. 9.50 (ISBN 0-89253-014-6). Ind-US Inc.
Parthasarathy, K. R. Multipliers on Locally Compact Groups. LC 71-84142. (Lecture Notes in Mathematics: Vol. 93). (Orig.). 1969. pap. 10.70 (ISBN 0-387-04612-7). Springer-Verlag.
Parthasarathy, R., ed. Ten Twentieth Century Indian Poets. (Three Crowns New Poetry from India Ser.). 1977. pap. 3.95x (ISBN 0-19-560665-5). Oxford U Pr.
Parthasarathy, S., jt. auth. see Srinivasan, B.
Partin, Harry, ed. see American Academy of Religion, 1974.
Partington, A. M. Bradley CPA Review Q & A Theory. LC 79-83865. 1979. pap. 12.00 (ISBN 0-932788-08-4). Bradley CPA.
--Q & A Theory. LC 79-83864. 12.00 (ISBN 0-932788-08-4). Bradley CPA.
Partington, A. M. & Nieminsky, Arthur C. Bradley CPA Review Practice & Theory. 10th, rev. ed. LC 79-89147. 1979. pap. 19.50 (ISBN 0-932788-11-4). Bradley CPA.
--Practice & Theory Manual. 10th ed. 19.50 (ISBN 0-932788-11-4). Bradley CPA.
Partington, A. M. & Weinberg, Frank. Q & A Practice. LC 79-83860. 16.00 (ISBN 0-932788-06-8). Bradley CPA.
Partington, Geoffrey. The Idea of an Historical Education. 257p. 1981. pap. text ed. 20.75x (ISBN 0-85633-202-X, NFER). Humanities.
--Women Teachers in the Twentieth Century in England & Wales. (General Ser.). (Orig.). 1976. pap. text ed. 10.75x (ISBN 0-85633-100-7, NFER). Humanities.
Partington, I., jt. auth. see Carter, H.
Partington, Martin. Landlord & Tenant: Text & Materials on Housing & Law. 2nd ed. (Law in Context Ser.). xxxviii, 554p. 1981. 54.00x (ISBN 0-297-77790-4, Pub. by Weidenfeld & Nicolson England). Rothman.
Partington, Martin & Jowell, J. L., eds. Welfare Law & Policy: Studies in Teaching, Practice & Research. 1979. 37.50x (ISBN 0-89397-051-4). Nichols Pub.
Partington, Paul G. W. E. B. Du Bois: A Bibliography of His Published Writings. rev. ed. LC 79-17920. 1979. lib. bdg. 15.00 (ISBN 0-9602538-1-5). P G Partington.
--Who's Who on the Postage Stamps of Eastern Europe. LC 79-22183. (Illus.). viii, 498p. 1979. lib. bdg. 31.50 (ISBN 0-8108-1266-5). Scarecrow.
Partisan Press Staff, ed. see Background GmBH.
Partlow, Robert B., ed. D. H. Lawrence, the Man Who Lived: Papers. LC 80-15262. 320p. 1980. 18.95 (ISBN 0-8093-0981-5). S Ill U Pr.
Partner, Peter. The Lands of St. Peter: The Papal State in the Middle Ages & the Early Renaissance. LC 73-182793. (Illus.). 494p. 1972. 32.50x (ISBN 0-520-02181-9). U of Cal Pr.
--Renaissance Rome: A Portrait of a Society, 1500-1559. 1977. 22.75x (ISBN 0-520-03026-5); pap. 6.95 (ISBN 0-520-03945-9). U of Cal Pr.
Partnow, Elaine. Breaking the Age Barrier. 288p. (Orig.). 1981. pap. 2.95 (ISBN 0-523-40845-5). Pinnacle Bks.
Parton, James. Life & Times of Benjamin Franklin, 2 vols. LC 72-126603. (American Scene Ser). (Illus.). 1971. Repr. of 1864 ed. Set. lib. bdg. 95.00 (ISBN 0-306-70048-4). Da Capo.
--Life of Thomas Jefferson. LC 76-126604. (American Scene Ser). (Illus.). 1971. Repr. of 1874 ed. lib. bdg. 59.50 (ISBN 0-306-70049-2). Da Capo.
Partridge. Concise Usage & Abusage. 4.95 o.p. (ISBN 0-8277-0094-6). British Bk Ctr.
Partridge, A. C. English Biblical Translation. (Andre Deutsch Language Library). 1973. lib. bdg. 20.00x (ISBN 0-233-96129-1). Westview.
--John Donne: Language & Style. (Andre Deutsch Language Library). 1979. lib. bdg. 26.50x (ISBN 0-233-97030-4). Westview.
--The Language of Modern Poetry: Yeats, Elliot, Auden. (Andre Deutsch Language Library). 1977. lib. bdg. 32.50x (ISBN 0-233-96642-0). Westview.
Partridge, Bellamy. Country Lawyer. (Illus.). 330p. 1979. pap. 6.95 (ISBN 0-89062-070-9, Pub. by Hughes Press). Pub Ctr Cult Res.
Partridge, Chuck. Mile High Surprise. (Pal Paperbacks, - Pal Skills II Ser.). (Illus.). (gr. 5-12). 1980. pap. text ed. 1.25 (ISBN 0-8374-6804-3). Xerox Ed Pubns.
Partridge, Colin, jt. ed. see Coustillas, Pierre.
Partridge, Edward, ed. see Jonson, Ben.
Partridge, Eric. Dictionary of Slang & Unconventional English. 7th ed. 1970. 39.95 (ISBN 0-02-594970-5). Macmillan.
--Macmillan Dictionary of Historical Slang. Simpson, Jacqueline, ed. 1072p. 1975. 29.95 (ISBN 0-02-594950-0). Macmillan.
--Origins: A Short Etymological Dictionary of Modern English. 1977. 45.00 (ISBN 0-02-594840-7). Macmillan.
--Slang Today & Yesterday: With a Short Historical Sketch & Vocabularies of English, American & Australian Slang. 4th ed. 1970. 30.00 (ISBN 0-7100-6922-7). Routledge & Kegan.
--Smaller Slang Dictionary. 1968. 16.95 (ISBN 0-7100-1938-6); pap. 7.95 (ISBN 0-7100-8331-9). Routledge & Kegan.
--You Have a Point There: A New & Complete Guide to Punctuation. (Orig.). 1978. pap. 7.95 (ISBN 0-7100-8753-5). Routledge & Kegan.
Partridge, Eric, ed. Smaller Slang Dictionary. 1961. 6.00 o.p. (ISBN 0-8022-1280-8). Philos Lib.
Partridge, Ernest, ed. Responsibilities to Future Generations: Environmental Ethics. 275p. (Orig.). 1981. 17.95 (ISBN 0-87975-153-3); pap. text ed. 8.95 (ISBN 0-87975-142-8). Prometheus Bks.
Partridge, Frances, tr. see Asturias, Miguel.
Partridge, Frances, tr. see Martineau, Gilbert.
Partridge, Loren & Starn, Randolph. A Renaissance Likeness: Art & Culture in Raphael's Julius II. (Quantum Ser.). (Illus.). 1980. 16.95x (ISBN 0-520-03901-7). U of Cal Pr.
Partridge, Michael. Motorcycle Pioneers: The Man, the Machines, the Events, 1860-1930. LC 76-12553. 1977. 8.95 (ISBN 0-668-04035-1). Arco.
Partridge, P. H. Society, Schools & Progress in Australia. LC 68-24067. 1968. 22.00 (ISBN 0-08-012919-6); pap. 11.25 (ISBN 0-08-012918-8). Pergamon.
Partridge, William L., jt. ed. see Eddy, Elizabeth M.
Partrow, Elaine. The Quotable Woman, 2 vols. Incl. Vol. 1. Eighteen Hundred to Eighteen Ninety-Nine (ISBN 0-523-40859-5); Nineteen Hundred to the Present (ISBN 0-523-40874-9). (Orig.). 1980. pap. 3.95 ea.; pap. 7.90 boxed set (ISBN 0-686-65984-8). Pinnacle Bks.
Parvate, T. V. Mahadev Govind Ranade. 1964. 10.75x o.p. (ISBN 0-210-26898-0). Asia.
Pasachoff, Jay M. & Kutner, Marc L. Invitation to Physics. 1980. text ed. 16.95x (ISBN 0-393-95164-2); tchr's manual & test bank free (ISBN 0-393-95167-7). Norton.
Pasachoff, Naomi. Playwrights, Preachers & Politicians: A Study of Four Tudor Old Testament Dramas. (Salzburg Studies in English Literature, Elizabethan & Renaissance Studies Ser.: No. 45). 162p. (Orig.). 1975. pap. text ed. 25.00x (ISBN 0-391-01493-5). Humanities.
Pasadena Art Alliance. All Things Wise & Wonderful. 1975. pap. 4.50 (ISBN 0-937042-00-5). Pasadena Art.
--Let's Celebrate. (Orig.). 1980. pap. 4.50. Pasadena Art.
--Wish You Were Here. 1979. pap. 4.50 (ISBN 0-937042-02-1). Pasadena Art.
Pasadena Junior League. The California Heritage Cookbook. LC 75-42495. 256p. 1976. 11.95 (ISBN 0-385-03995-6). Doubleday.
Pasamanick, Benjamin, et al. Schizophrenics in the Community: An Experimental Study in the Prevention of Hospitalization. LC 66-25455. (Illus.). 1967. 24.00x (ISBN 0-89197-390-7); pap. text ed. 6.95x (ISBN 0-89197-391-5). Irvington.
Pasamanik, Luisa. The Banished Angel. Aldridge, Carter, tr. LC 75-516551. 1978. 12.00 o.p. (ISBN 0-686-18968-X). Green River.
Pasanella, Anne L. & Volkmor, Cara B. Coming Back...or Never Leaving: Instructional Programming for Handicapped Students in the Mainstream. 1977. pap. text ed. 13.95 (ISBN 0-675-08460-1); filmstrip & cassette 135.00 (ISBN 0-675-08459-8); 2-5 sets 85.00, 6 or more sets 65.00 (ISBN 0-685-75490-1); instructor's manual 3.95 (ISBN 0-686-67642-4). Merrill.
--Teaching Handicapped Students in the Mainstream: Coming Back...or Never Leaving. 2nd ed. (Special Education Ser.). (Illus.). 384p. 1981. pap. text ed. 10.95 (ISBN 0-675-08026-6). Merrill.
Pasanen, Jack, jt. auth. see Easterling, Jack.
Pascal, A. Michael. Hospital Security & Safety. LC 77-14083. 1977. text ed. 28.00 (ISBN 0-89443-029-7). Aspen Systems.
Pascal, Blaise. The Nature of Man. (Illus.). 1980. 33.75 (ISBN 0-89901-007-5). Found Class Reprints.
--Pensees. Trotter, W. F., tr. 1958. pap. 3.25 (ISBN 0-525-47018-2, Evman). Dutton.
--Pensees. Krailsheimer, A. J., tr. (Classics Ser.). (Orig.). 1966. pap. 3.50 (ISBN 0-14-044171-9). Penguin.
Pascal, F. P. Save Johanna. 254p. 1981. 10.95 (ISBN 0-688-00448-2). Morrow.
Pascal, Francine. Hangin' Out with Cici. (YA) (gr. 7-9). 1978. pap. 1.75 (ISBN 0-671-41057-1). PB.
--My First Love & Other Disasters. (gr. 7-12). 1980. pap. 1.50 (ISBN 0-440-95447-9, LFL). Dell.
Pascale, Alfred C. The Secretarial Specialist. LC 73-34193. (Illus.). 216p. 1968. pap. text ed. 11.25 (ISBN 0-913310-02-6). PAR Inc.
Paschal, Andrew G., ed. W. E. B. DuBois Reader. LC 70-150672. 1971. 8.95 o.s.i. (ISBN 0-02-595100-9). Macmillan.
Paschal, Joel F. Mister Justice Sutherland, a Man Against the State. Repr. of 1951 ed. lib. bdg. 15.75x (ISBN 0-8371-2517-0, PAJS). Greenwood.
Paschal, Mary. The Structure of the Roman De Thebes. LC 80-66540. 96p. 1980. pap. 9.95 (ISBN 0-89729-261-8). Ediciones.
Paschall, Andrew G. W. E. B. DuBois Reader. 1971. pap. 2.45 o.s.i. (ISBN 0-02-035950-0, Collier). Macmillan.
Paschall, Eugene F., jt. ed. see Whistler, Roy L.
Paschke, V., tr. from Span. see Garcia, Manuel, II.
Pascoe, Elizabeth J., jt. auth. see Deaton, John G.
Pascoe, L. C. Teach Yourself New Mathematics. (Orig.). 1979. pap. 4.95 (ISBN 0-679-12326-1). McKay.
Pascual, J. F. & Calcagno, P. L., eds. Recent Advances in Pediatric Nephrology. (Contributions to Nephrology Ser.: Vol. 27). (Illus.). vi, 150p. 1981. pap. 54.00 (ISBN 3-8055-1851-X). S Karger.
Pasek, Jan C. Memoirs of the Polish Baroque: The Writings of Jan Chryzostom Pasek, a Squire of the Commonwealth of Poland & Lithuania. Leach, Catherine S., ed. LC 74-77731. 1977. 32.50 (ISBN 0-520-02752-3, CAL 447); pap. 5.95 (ISBN 0-520-04089-9). U of Cal Pr.
Pashdag, John & Woller, Jim. All Night L.A. Harper, Susan & Vandenburgh, Jane, eds. LC 78-3557. (Illus.). 1978. pap. 4.95 o.p. (ISBN 0-87701-112-5). Chronicle Bks.
Pasinetti, L. Structural Change & Economic Growth. (Illus.). 337p. Date not set. price not set (ISBN 0-521-23607-X). Cambridge U Pr.
Pasinetti, L. L. Growth & Income Distribution. LC 74-76579. (Illus.). 180p. 1974. 29.95 (ISBN 0-521-20474-7); pap. 13.95x (ISBN 0-521-29543-2). Cambridge U Pr.
Pasinetti, Luigi. Lectures in the Theory of Production. LC 77-1541. Orig. Title: Lezioni Di Teoria Della Produzione. 1977. 17.50x (ISBN 0-231-04100-4). Columbia U Pr.
Pask, Edward H. Enter the Colonies Dancing: A History of Dance in Australia Nineteen Thirty-Five to Nineteen Forty. 188p. 1980. 32.00x (ISBN 0-19-550589-1). Oxford U Pr.
Pask, Joseph A. see Fulrath, Richard M.
Paske-Smith, M., ed. see Raffles, Sir Stanford.
Paske-Smith, Montague, ed. Japanese Traditions of Christianity: Being Some Old Translations from the Japanese, with British Consular Reports of the Persecutions of 1868-1872. (Studies in Japanese History & Civilization). 1979. Repr. of 1930 ed. 17.50 (ISBN 0-89093-257-3). U Pubns Amer.
Paskevska, Anna. Both Sides of the Mirror: The Science & Art of Ballet. LC 79-51362. (Illus.). 200p. 1981. 22.50 (ISBN 0-87127-112-5). Dance Horiz.
Pasley, Fred D. Al Capone. (Illus., Orig.). 1968. pap. 3.95 o.p. (ISBN 0-571-06726-3, Pub. by Faber & Faber). Merrimack Bk Serv.
Pasley, Malcolm, ed. Nietzsche: Imagery & Thought. 1978. 23.75x (ISBN 0-520-03577-1). U of Cal Pr.
Pasmore, William A. & Sherwood, John J., eds. Sociotechnical Systems: A Sourcebook. LC 77-20543. 366p. 1978. pap. 14.95 (ISBN 0-88390-142-0). Univ Assocs.
Pasquali, Elaine A., et al. Mental Health Nursing: A Bio-Psycho-Cultural Approach. (Illus.). 635p. 1981. text ed. 19.95 (ISBN 0-8016-3758-9). Mosby.
Pasqualini, J. R., ed. Recent Advances in Steroid Biochemistry, Vols. 2-3. LC 75-4332. Vol. 2, 312p., 1975. pap. text ed. 55.00 (ISBN 0-08-019709-4); Vol. 3, 1977. pap. text ed. 50.00 (ISBN 0-08-021307-3). Pergamon.
Pasqualini, J. R., jt. ed. see James, V. H.
Pasquariello, Anthony, ed. see Buero Vallejo, A.
Pasquill, Frank. Atmospheric Diffusion. 2nd ed. LC 74-7054. 429p. 1974. 79.95 (ISBN 0-470-66892-X). Halsted Pr.

Pasquini, Bernardo. L'Idalma Overo Chi la Dura la Vince. Brown, Howard M., ed. LC 76-20996. (Italian Opera 1640-1770 Ser.). 1978. lib. bdg. 70.00 (ISBN 0-8240-2610-1). Garland Pub.
Pass, G. & Sutcliffe, H. Practical Inorganic Chemistry: Preparations, Reactions & Instrumental Methods. 2nd ed. 256p. 1979. pap. 9.95x (ISBN 0-412-16150-8, Pub. by Chapman & Hall). Methuen Inc.
Pass, Gail. Surviving Sisters. LC 80-69373. 1981. 10.95 (ISBN 0-689-11134-7). Atheneum.
Passage, Charles. Character Names in Dostoevsky's Fiction. 1981. 16.00 (ISBN 0-88233-616-9). Ardis Pubs.
Passage, Charles, tr. see Novalis.
Passage, Charles E. Dostoevski the Adapter. (Studies in Comp. Lit.: No. 10). lib. bdg. 12.50x (ISBN 0-8078-7010-2); pap. text ed. 6.50x (ISBN 0-8078-7010-2). U of NC Pr.
--Friedrich Schiller. LC 74-76129. (World Dramatists Ser). (Illus.). 180p. 1975. 10.95 (ISBN 0-8044-2734-8). Ungar.
Passage, Charles E. & Mantinbard, James H., trs. Amphitryon: Three Plays in New Verse Translation. (Studies in Comparative Literature: No. 57). 307p. 1974. 16.50x (ISBN 0-8078-7057-9); pap. 8.00 (ISBN 0-8078-7057-9). U of NC Pr.
Passage, Charles E., tr. see Von Goethe, Johann W.
Passalacqua, Carlos M. Noche, Fuente: Poesia. 2nd ed. LC 79-23317. (Illus.). 104p. 1980. pap. write for info. (ISBN 0-8477-3226-6). U of PR Pr.
Passamaneck, Stephen M., ed. see Bazak, Jacob.
Passamonti, Gino. Atlas of Complete Dentures. (Illus.). 140p. 1979. 48.00 (ISBN 0-931386-08-X). Quint Pub Co.
Passant, Ernest J. Short History of Germany: Eighteen Fifteen - Nineteen Forty-Five. 1962. 32.95 (ISBN 0-521-05915-1); pap. 8.95x (ISBN 0-521-09173-X). Cambridge U Pr.
Passantino, Robert, et al. Answer to the Cultist at Your Door. LC 80-83850. 1981. pap. 4.95 (ISBN 0-89081-275-6). Harvest Hse.
Passavant, Johann D. Raphael of Urbino & His Father Giovanni Santi. Freedberg, Sydney J., ed. LC 77-25762. (Connoisseurship Criticism & Art History Ser.: Vol. 17). (Illus.). 1979. lib. bdg. 33.00 (ISBN 0-8240-3275-6). Garland Pub.
--Tour of a German Artist in England, 2 vols. Freedberg, Sydney J., ed. LC 77-25761. (Connoisseurship Criticism & Art History Ser.: Vol. 16). (Illus.). 658p. 1979. Set. lib. bdg. 70.00 (ISBN 0-8240-3274-8). Garland Pub.
Passe, Crispin Van de see Van de Pusse, Crispin.
Passell, Peter. How to. 1977. pap. 1.75 o.p. (ISBN 0-345-25506-2). Ballantine.
Passell, Peter & Ross, Leonard. State Policies & Federal Programs: Priorities & Constraints. LC 77-27498. (Praeger Special Studies). 1978. 21.95 (ISBN 0-03-042591-3). Praeger.
Passen, Barry J. Programming Flowcharting for the Business Data Processing. LC 77-25509. 1978. pap. text ed. 16.95 (ISBN 0-471-01410-9). Wiley.
Passeron, Rene. Rene Magritte. (Filipacchi Art Bks). (Illus.). 96p. 1981. 25.00 (ISBN 2-8501-8098-X); pap. 9.95 (ISBN 2-8501-8099-8). Hippocrene Bks.
Passin, Herbert. Japanese Education. LC 74-93507. 1970. pap. 5.75x (ISBN 0-8077-1879-3). Tchrs Coll.
--Society & Education in Japan. LC 65-19168. (Orig.). 1965. pap. text ed. 7.00x (ISBN 0-8077-1875-0). Tchrs Coll.
Passin, Herbert, jt. auth. see Kahn, Herman.
Passin, Herbert & Iriye, Akira, eds. Encounter at Shimoda: Search for a New Pacific Partnership. (Special Studies on China & East Asia). 1979. lib. bdg. 24.50x (ISBN 0-89158-467-6). Westview.
Passler, David L. Time, Form & Style in Boswell's Life of Johnson. LC 70-151585. 1971. 12.50x o.p. (ISBN 0-300-01427-9). Yale U Pr.
Passm, Herbert, ed. Season of Voting: Japanese Elections of 1976 & 1977. 1979. pap. 6.25 (ISBN 0-8447-3343-1). Am Enterprise.
Passman, Donald S. The Algebraic Structure of Group Rings. LC 77-4898. (Pure & Applied Mathematics Ser.). 1977. 45.00 (ISBN 0-471-02272-1, Pub. by Wiley-Interscience). Wiley.
Passmore, John. Hume's Intentions. 3rd ed. 180p. 1980. 26.50x (ISBN 0-7156-0918-1, Pub. by Duckworth England). Biblio Dist.
--Perfectability of Man. LC 77-129625. 1970. 20.00x (ISBN 0-684-15521-4, ScribT). Scribner.
--Science & Its Critics. (Mason Welch Gross Lecture Ser). 1978. 9.00 (ISBN 0-8135-0852-5). Rutgers U Pr.
Passonneau, Janet V. & Hawkins, Richard A. Cerebral Metabolism & Neural Function. (Illus.). 370p. 1980. lib. bdg. 57.00 (ISBN 0-683-06788-5). Williams & Wilkins.
Passos, John Dos see Dos Passos, John.
Passow, A. H., et al. The National Case Study: An Empirical Comparative Study of 21 Educational Systems. LC 76-6078. (International Studies in Evaluation: Vol. 7). 379p. 1976. pap. 29.95 (ISBN 0-470-15119-6). Halsted Pr.
Passow, A. Harry, ed. Developing Programs for the Educationally Disadvantaged. LC 67-19026. 1968. text ed. 13.75 (ISBN 0-8077-1885-8); pap. text ed. 7.50x (ISBN 0-8077-1884-X). Tchrs Coll.
--Education in Depressed Areas. LC 63-15449. 1963. pap. 7.25x (ISBN 0-8077-1887-4). Tchrs Coll.
--Opening Opportunities for Disadvantaged Learners. LC 72-178197. 1972. text ed. 12.75x (ISBN 0-8077-1886-6); pap. 8.00x (ISBN 0-8077-1894-7). Tchrs Coll.
--Reaching the Disadvantaged Learner. LC 69-11364. 1970. text ed. 12.95x (ISBN 0-8077-1889-0); pap. text ed. 9.95x (ISBN 0-8077-1888-2). Tchrs Coll.
--Urban Education in the 1970's: Reflections & a Look Ahead. LC 73-154693. 1971. text ed. 10.95x (ISBN 0-8077-1883-1); pap. 7.25x (ISBN 0-8077-1882-3). Tchrs Coll.
Passwater, Richard. Supernutrition for Healthy Hearts. 1978. pap. 2.95 (ISBN 0-515-05725-8). Jove Pubns.
Passwater, Richard A. Selenium As Food & As Medicine. LC 80-82325. 200p. 1981. 10.95 (ISBN 0-87983-237-1); pap. 2.95 (ISBN 0-87983-229-0). Keats.
Pastan, Linda. Perfect Circle of the Sun. LC 76-171879. (New Poetry Ser.: No. 44). 1971. 5.00 o.p. (ISBN 0-8040-0553-2); pap. 2.75 o.p. (ISBN 0-8040-0621-0). Swallow.
Pasternak, Boris. Boris Pasternak: Stikhotvoreniia I Poemy. 731p. (Rus.). 1981. pap. write for info. (ISBN 0-89830-038-X). Russica Pubs.
--Dr. Zhivago. 576p. 1981. pap. 3.50 (ISBN 0-345-29310-X). Ballantine.
--Doktor Zhivago. LC 60-15772. 1959. 19.95 (ISBN 0-472-71796-0). U of Mich Pr.
--Fifty Poems. (Unwin Books). 1963. 6.50 o.p. (ISBN 0-04-891022-8); pap. 2.95 (ISBN 0-04-891023-6). Allen Unwin.
--I Remember: Sketch for an Autobiography. Magarshack, David, tr. (Illus., With an essay "Translating Shakespeare"). 8.00 (ISBN 0-8446-2710-0). Peter Smith.
--My Sister, Life. Carlisle, Olga A., tr. (Helen & Kurt Wolff Bk.). 1976. 14.95 o.p. (ISBN 0-15-163964-7). HarBraceJ.
--Sestra Moia Zhizn' 1976. 11.00 o.p. (ISBN 0-88233-231-7); pap. 3.50 o.p. (ISBN 0-88233-232-5). Ardis Pubs.
--Vozdushnye Puti 1976. 12.00 (ISBN 0-88233-229-5); pap. 4.50 (ISBN 0-88233-230-9). Ardis Pubs.
Pasternak, Burton. Introduction to Kinship & Social Organization. (Illus.). 208p. 1976. Ref. Ed. pap. 8.95 (ISBN 0-13-485466-7). P-H.
Pasternak, Velvel, ed. Songs of the Chassidim. 1968. Vol. 1. 1968. 12.50x (ISBN 0-8197-0170-X); Vol. 2. 1971. 15.00x (ISBN 0-8197-0276-5). Bloch.
Pasteur, D. The Management of Squatter Upgrading. 1979. text ed. 30.75x (ISBN 0-566-00266-3, Pub. by Gower Pub Co England). Renouf.
Pasto, Daniel & Johnson, Carl. Organic Structure Determination. 1969. ref. ed. 23.95 (ISBN 0-13-640854-0). P-H.
Pasto, Daniel G., jt. auth. see Gutsche, C. David.
Pasto, Daniel J. & Johnson, Carol R. Laboratory Text for Organic Chemistry: A Source Book of Chemical & Physical Techniques. 1979. pap. 17.95 (ISBN 0-13-521302-9). P-H.
Paston, Linda. Waiting for My Life, Poems. 1981. 14.95 (ISBN 0-393-01441-X); pap. 4.95 (ISBN 0-393-00049-4). Norton.
Pastor, Beatriz. Roberto Arlt y la Rebelion Alienada. LC 80-70560. 135p. (Span.). 1980. pap. write for info. (ISBN 0-935318-05-4). Edins Hispamerica.
Pastor, Robert A. Congress & the Politics of U. S. Foreign Economic Policy, 1929 to 1976. 416p. 1980. 24.50x (ISBN 0-520-03904-1). U of Cal Pr.
Pastoral Care Office. Empowered to Care. 1980. pap. 8.25 (ISBN 0-8309-0291-0). Herald Hse.
Pastorelli, Pietro, ed. see Sonnino, Sidney.
Pastrovicchi, Angelo. St Joseph of Copertino. LC 79-91298. 135p. 1979. Repr. of 1918 ed. pap. write for info. o.p. (ISBN 0-89555-135-7). Tan Bks Pubs.
Pasvolsky, Leo. Russia in the Far East. LC 79-2918. 181p. 1981. Repr. of 1922 ed. 17.50 (ISBN 0-8305-0087-1). Hyperion Conn.
Paszkiewicz, Magdalena M., tr. see Pokropek, Marian.
Pasztor, E. Concise Neurosurgery. (Illus.). 292p. 1980. 56.50 (ISBN 3-8055-1431-X). S Karger.
Pasztory, Esther. The Murals of Tepantitla, Teotihaucan. LC 75-23806. (Outstanding Dissertations in the Fine Arts - Native American Arts). (Illus.). 1976. lib. bdg. 45.00 (ISBN 0-8240-2000-6). Garland Pub.
Pasztory, Esther, ed. Middle Classic Mesoamerica: 400-700 A. D. (Illus.). 1978. 25.00x (ISBN 0-231-04270-1). Columbia U Pr.
Patai, Raphael. Golden River to Golden Road: Society, Culture & Change in the Middle East. 3rd rev. ed. LC 70-84742. 1969. 17.00x (ISBN 0-8122-7289-7). U of Pa Pr.
--The Messiah Texts. 1979. pap. 7.95 (ISBN 0-686-68433-8, 46482). Avon.
--Society, Culture & Change in the Middle East. LC 70-84742. Orig. Title: Golden River to Golden Road. (Illus.). 1971. pap. 7.95x (ISBN 0-8122-1009-3, Pa Paperbks). U of Pa Pr.
--The Vanished World of Jewry: Pictures by Eugene Rosow & Vivian Kleiman. (Illus.). 192p. 1981. 17.95 (ISBN 0-02-595120-3). Macmillan.
Patai, Raphael & Wing, Jennifer. Myth of the Jewish Race. (Encore Edition). 1975. 6.95 o.p. (ISBN 0-684-15435-8, ScribT). Scribner.
Patai, S. Supplement E Chemistry of Ethers Crown Ethers Hydroxyl Group & Their Sulphur Analogs. 1192p. 1980. Set. write for info. (ISBN 0-471-27618-9, Pub. by Wiley-Interscience). Pt. 1 (ISBN 0-471-27771-1). Pt. 2 (ISBN 0-471-27772-X). Wiley.
Pataki, L. & Zapp, E. Basic Analytical Chemistry. (Analytical Chemistry Ser.: Vol. 2). (Illus.). 1980. 38.00 (ISBN 0-08-023850-5). Pergamon.
Patanjali. Patanjali's Yoga Sutras. 2nd ed. Prasada, Rama, tr. from Sanskrit. 321p. 1981. Repr. of 1912 ed. 15.95 (ISBN 0-89744-996-7, Pub. by Orient Reprint India). Auromere.
Patanjali, Bhagwan S. Aphorisms of Yoga. (Illus., Orig.). 1973. pap. 5.50 (ISBN 0-571-10320-0, Pub. by Faber & Faber). Merrimack Bk Serv.
Patanjali, Swami S. The Ten Principal Upanishads. Yeats, W. B., tr. (Orig.). 1970. pap. 4.95 (ISBN 0-571-09363-9, Pub. by Faber & Faber). Merrimack Bk Serv.
Patanjali, V. & Muralidhar, A., eds. Modern Telugu Short Stories: An Anthology. Muralidhar, A., tr. 261p. 1968. pap. 2.45 (ISBN 0-88253-065-8). Ind-US Inc.
Patankar, Suhas V. Numerical Heat Transfer & Fluid Flow. LC 79-28286. (Hemisphere Series on Computational Methods in Mechanics & Thermal Sciences). (Illus.). 208p. 1980. text ed. 22.50 (ISBN 0-07-048740-5). McGraw.
Patashinskii, A. Z., et al. Fluctuation Theory of Phase Transitions. Shepherd, P. J., ed. (International Series in Natural Philosophy: Vol. 98). (Illus.). 1979. text ed. 60.00 (ISBN 0-08-021664-1). Pergamon.
Patchen, Kenneth. Still Another Pelican in the Breadbox. Morgan, Richard, ed. LC 80-82905. 96p. 1980. pap. 5.95 (ISBN 0-917530-14-4). Pig Iron Pr.
Pate, Don. Episodes at the Olive Press. LC 79-24125. (Horizon Ser.). 1980. pap. 4.50 (ISBN 0-8127-0269-7). Southern Pub.
--He Shall Be Like a Tree. (Horizon Ser.). 128p. 1981. pap. price not set (ISBN 0-8127-0315-4). Southern Pub.
Pate, Ellen & Spengler, Barbara. Handbook for Typists. 96p. 1980. 6.95 (ISBN 0-8403-2194-5). Kendall-Hunt.
--Handbook for Typists: Operation of the Selectric Typewriter, Technical Information, Format Illustrations & Procedures. 96p. (Orig.). 1980. pap. text ed. 6.95 o.p. (ISBN 0-8403-2194-5). Kendall-Hunt.
--Typewriting for the Modern Office: A Self-Paced Learning Activity Program. 288p. 1980. 10.95 (ISBN 0-8403-2196-1). Kendall-Hunt.
Patel, Dinker I. Exurbs: Urban Residential Developments in the Countryside. LC 79-48040. 151p. 1980. text ed. 15.50 (ISBN 0-8191-1001-9); pap. text ed. 8.00 (ISBN 0-8191-1002-7). U Pr of Amer.
Patel, Kant. Dimensions of States' Education & Public Health Policies. LC 78-64563. 1978. pap. text ed. 7.75 (ISBN 0-8191-0636-4). U Pr of Amer.
Patel, S. J. Essays in Economic Transition. 10.00x (ISBN 0-210-22659-5). Asia.
Patel, Satyavrata. Hinduism: Religion & Way of Life. 165p. 1980. text ed. 21.00x (ISBN 0-8426-1661-6). Verry.
Pateman, Carole. Participation & Democratic Theory. LC 71-120193. 1970. 17.50 (ISBN 0-521-07856-3); pap. 5.95x (ISBN 0-521-29004-X). Cambridge U Pr.
Patent, Dorothy H. Bacteria: How They Affect Other Living Things. LC 79-21567. (Illus.). 128p. (gr. 9 up). 1980. 8.95 (ISBN 0-8234-0401-3). Holiday.
--Fish & How They Reproduce. LC 76-10349. (Illus.). (gr. 3-7). 1976. 8.95 (ISBN 0-8234-0285-1). Holiday.
--Frogs, Toads, Salamanders & How They Reproduce. LC 74-26567. (Illus.). 144p. (gr. 4-7). 1975. 8.95 (ISBN 0-8234-0255-X). Holiday.
--Horses & Their Wild Relatives. LC 80-23559. (Illus.). 128p. (gr. 5 up). 1981. 8.95 (ISBN 0-8234-0383-1). Holiday.
--Hunters & the Hunted: Surviving in the Animal World. LC 80-23559. (Illus.). 64p. (gr. 4-8). 1981. PLB 7.95 (ISBN 0-8234-0386-6). Holiday.
--Reptiles & How They Reproduce. LC 77-3817. (Illus.). (gr. 5-7). 1977. 8.95 (ISBN 0-8234-0310-6). Holiday.
--The World of Worms. LC 77-17117. (Illus.). (gr. 5-9). 1978. 7.95 (ISBN 0-8234-0319-X). Holiday.
Patent, Greg. More Big Sky Cooking. (Big Sky Cooking Ser.: No. 2). (Illus.). 151p. (Orig.). 1980. pap. 9.50. Eagle Comm.
Pater, Alan F., ed. Nineteen Eighty One Anthology of Magazine Verse & Yearbook of American Poetry. 650p. lib. bdg. write for info. (ISBN 0-917734-05-X); lib. bdg. price not set (ISBN 0-917734-05-X). Monitor.
Pater, Walter. Cupid & Psyche. (Illus.). 1978. 9.95 (ISBN 0-571-11115-7, Pub. by Faber & Faber). Merrimack Bk Serv.
--Marius the Epicurean. Wolff, Robert L., ed. (Victorian Fiction Ser.). 1975. Repr. of 1885 ed. lib. bdg. 66.00 (ISBN 0-8240-1558-4). Garland Pub.
Patera, jt. auth. see McKay.
Paterno, Gianfranco, jt. auth. see Barone, Antonio.
Paternoster, Lewis M. & Frager, Ruth L. Three Dimensions of Vocabulary Growth. (Orig.). (gr. 10-12). 1971. pap. text ed. 5.25 (ISBN 0-87720-345-8). AMSCO Sch.
Paterson, A. B. Mulga Bill's Bicycle. LC 74-12286. (Illus.). 40p. (ps-3). 1975. 5.95 o.s.i. (ISBN 0-8193-0777-7, Four Winds); PLB 5.41 o.s.i. (ISBN 0-8193-0778-5). Schol Bk Serv.
Paterson, A. J. Golden Years of Clyde Steamers. LC 79-56430. (Illus.). 1979. 19.95 (ISBN 0-7153-4290-8). David & Charles.
Paterson, A. K., ed. see Tirso De Molina.
Paterson, A. R., jt. auth. see Henderson, J. Frank.
Paterson, Alexander. Across the Bridges or Life by the South London River-Side, London Nineteen Eleven. LC 79-56967. (The English Working Class Ser.). 1980. lib. bdg. 25.00 (ISBN 0-8240-0118-4). Garland Pub.
Paterson, Antoinette M. Francis Bacon & Socialized Science. (American Lectures in Philosophy). 208p. 1973. 16.75 (ISBN 0-398-02867-2). C C Thomas.
--Infinite Worlds of Giordano Bruno. (Amer. Lec. in Philosophy Ser.). (Illus.). 240p. 1970. 19.75 (ISBN 0-398-01452-3). C C Thomas.
Paterson, Betty J., jt. auth. see McCarty, Janet.
Paterson, J. G., jt. auth. see Lafkas, C.
Paterson, J. H. North America. 6th ed. (Illus.). 1979. text ed. 17.95 (ISBN 0-19-502484-2). Oxford U Pr.
Paterson, James. Commentaries on the Liberty of the Subject & the Laws of England Relating to the Security of the Person, 2 vols. 1010p. 1980. Repr. of 1877 ed. Set. lib. bdg. 75.00x (ISBN 0-8377-1005-7). Rothman.
Paterson, James & Macnaughton, Edwin. The Approach to Latin. (Illus.). Pt. 1 1938. text ed. 5.00x (ISBN 0-05-000292-9); Pt. 2 1969. text ed. 5.00x (ISBN 0-05-000293-7). Longman.
Paterson, Jane. Interpreting Handwriting. 1977. 7.95 o.p. (ISBN 0-679-50700-0); pap. 4.95 o.p. (ISBN 0-679-50701-9). McKay.
Paterson, Josephine G. & Zderad, Loretta T. Humanistic Nursing. LC 75-40431. 1976. 15.50 (ISBN 0-471-66946-6, Pub. by Wiley Medical). Wiley.
Paterson, Katherine. Angels & Other Strangers. (Illus.). 128p. (gr. 1-8). 1980. pap. 1.95 (ISBN 0-380-51144-4, 51144, Camelot). Avon.
--Angels & Other Strangers: Family Christmas Stories. LC 79-63797. (gr. 1 up). 1979. 8.95 (ISBN 0-690-03992-1, TYC-J). T Y Crowell.
--Bridge to Terabithia. (gr. 10 up). 1979. pap. 1.75 (ISBN 0-380-43281-1, 52365, Camelot). Avon.
--The Great Gilly Hopkins. LC 77-27075. (gr. 5 up). 1978. 7.95 (ISBN 0-690-03837-2, TYC-J); PLB 7.89 (ISBN 0-690-03838-0). T Y Crowell.
--The Master Puppeteer. (Illus.). 192p. (gr. 5 up). 1981. pap. 1.95 (ISBN 0-380-53322-7, 53322, Camelot). Avon.
--Of Nightingales That Weep. Wells, Haru, tr. (Illus.). (gr. 5 up). 1980. pap. 1.95 (ISBN 0-380-51110-X, 51110, Camelot). Avon.
--The Sign of the Chrysanthemum. (Illus.). (gr. 6 up). 1980. pap. 1.75 (ISBN 0-380-49288-1, 49288, Camelot). Avon.
Paterson, Linda M. Troubadours & Eloquence. 244p. 1975. 36.00x (ISBN 0-19-815711-8). Oxford U Pr.
Paterson, R. W. Nihilist Egoist: Max Stirner. 1971. 24.95x (ISBN 0-19-713413-0). Oxford U Pr.
--Values, Education & the Adult. (International Library of the Philosophy of Education). 1978. 20.00x (ISBN 0-7100-8968-6). Routledge & Kegan.

Paterson, Thomas G. Major Problems in American Foreign Policy. 1978. Vol. 1. pap. text ed. 8.95x (ISBN 0-669-00475-8); Vol. 2. pap. text ed. 9.95x (ISBN 0-669-00476-6). Heath.
--On Every Front: The Making of the Cold War. 1979. 14.95 (ISBN 0-393-01238-7); pap. 4.95x (ISBN 0-393-95014-X). Norton.
Paterson, Thomas G., et al. American Foreign Policy: A History. 1977. text ed. 16.95x (ISBN 0-669-94698-2). Heath.
Paterson, W., jt. auth. see Guile, A. E.
Paterson, W. E., jt. ed. see Wallace, William.
Paterson, W. S. The Physics of Glaciers. LC 71-82909. 1970. 37.00 (ISBN 0-08-013972-8); pap. 7.75 (ISBN 0-08-013971-X). Pergamon.
Paterson, William. Glimpses of Colonial Society & Life at Princeton College, 1766-1773, by One of the Class of 1763. Mills, W. Jay, ed. LC 72-179711. (Illus.). 182p. (Six songs). 1972. Repr. of 1903 ed. 18.00 (ISBN 0-8103-3810-6). Gale.
Paterson, William B. Marine Engine Room Blue Book. LC 65-25382. (Illus.). 1966. pap. 8.50x (ISBN 0-87033-044-6). Cornell Maritime.
--Red Book of Marine Engineering Questions & Answers, Vol. 1: Third & Second Assistant Engineers. 3rd ed. LC 76-153141. (Illus.). 1971. pap. 9.00x (ISBN 0-87033-088-8). Cornell Maritime.
--Red Book of Marine Engineering Questions & Answers, Vol. 2: First Assistant & Chief Engineer. 2nd ed. LC 65-13. (Illus.). 1973. pap. 9.00x (ISBN 0-87033-089-6). Cornell Maritime.
Paterson, Wilma. A Country Cup: Old & New Recipes for Drinks of All Kinds Made from Wild Plants & Herbs. (Illus.). 88p. (Orig.). 1981. 11.95 (ISBN 0-7207-1234-3). Merrimack Bk Serv.
Path, M. R., jt. auth. see Dumonde, D. C.
Pathak, N. N., jt. auth. see Ranjhan, S. K.
Pathak, R. C. English Hindi Dictionary. 1979. 11.00 (ISBN 0-89744-970-3). Auromere.
--Hindi English Dictionary. 1979. 11.00 (ISBN 0-89744-969-X). Auromere.
Pathak, R. C., ed. Hindi-English - English-Hindi Illustrated Dictionary, 2 vols. (Illus.). 1978. Set. 25.00 (ISBN 0-686-68936-4). Vol. 1, Hindi-Eng., 1512pp. Vol. 2. Eng.-Hindi, 1432pp. Heinman.
Pathak, Shankar. Social Welfare Manpower in North India. 180p. 1980. text ed. 15.95x (ISBN 0-7069-1075-3, Pub. by Vikas India). Advent Bk.
Pathria, R. K. Advanced Statistical Mechanics. 1972. text ed. 50.00 (ISBN 0-08-016747-0); pap. text ed. 24.00 (ISBN 0-08-018994-6). Pergamon.
--The Theory of Relativity. 2nd ed. 1974. text ed. 45.00 (ISBN 0-08-018032-9); pap. text ed. 24.00 (ISBN 0-08-018995-4). Pergamon.
Pathy, T. V. Elura: Art & Culture. (Illus.). 190p. 1980. text ed. 31.00x (ISBN 0-391-01758-6). Humanities.
Patillo, Manning M., Jr., et al. How to Get Your Fair Share of Foundation Grants. 12.00 o.p. (ISBN 0-686-24212-2). Public Serv Materials.
Patinkin, Don. Essays on & in the Chicago Tradition. LC 79-55770. (Illus.). xii, 315p. 1981. 29.75 (ISBN 0-8223-0439-2). Duke.
Patitucci, F., jt. auth. see Rapp, B.
Patka, Frederick. Existentialist Thinkers & Thoughts. LC 62-9770. 1962. 4.75 o.p. (ISBN 0-8022-1285-9). Philos Lib.
Patnaik, Deba, ed. Geography of Holiness: The Photography of Thomas Merton. LC 80-18604. 1980. 17.50 (ISBN 0-8298-0401-3). Pilgrim NY.
Patnode, Robert, jt. auth. see Hyde, R. M.
Paton, A. Instrument of Thy Peace: The Prayer of St. Francis. (Illus., Orig.). 1976. pap. 4.95 (ISBN 0-8164-2596-5). Crossroad NY.
Paton, Alan. Cry, the Beloved Country. (Lib. Rep. Ed.). (YA) 1961. 15.00x (ISBN 0-684-15559-1, ScribT); pap. 3.95 (ISBN 0-684-71863-4, SL7, ScribT); pap. text ed. 4.96 (ISBN 0-684-51544-X, SSP7, ScribC). Scribner.
--Instrument of Thy Peace. 1967. 5.95 (ISBN 0-8164-0152-7). Crossroad NY.
--The Land & People of South Africa. rev. ed. LC 79-3795. (Portraits of the Nations Ser.). (Illus.). (gr. 6 up). 1972. 8.79 (ISBN 0-397-31302-0). Lippincott.
--Tales from a Troubled Land. 1961. lib.rep. ed. 12.50x (ISBN 0-684-15135-9, ScribT). Scribner.
Paton, D. M., ed. The Transport of Neurotransmitters. (Journal: Pharmacology: Vol. 21, No. 2). (Illus.). 74p. 1980. pap. 14.50 (ISBN 3-8055-1316-X). S Karger.
Paton, David. Breaking Barriers: the Report of the Fifth Assembly of World Council of Churches, Nairobi, 1975. 384p. 1976. pap. 4.95 o.p. (ISBN 0-8028-1639-8). Eerdmans.
--The Relation of Angioid Streaks to Systemic Disease. (Amer. Lec. Living Chemistry Ser). (Illus.). 96p. 1972. 11.50 (ISBN 0-398-02375-1). C C Thomas.
Paton, David M., ed. The Mechanism of Neuronal & Extraneuronal Transport of Catecholamines. LC 74-14477. 405p. 1976. 37.50 (ISBN 0-89004-014-1). Raven.
--The Release of Catecholamines from Adrenergic Neurons. new ed. 1978. text ed. 60.00 (ISBN 0-08-021536-X); pap. text ed. 29.00 (ISBN 0-08-023755-X). Pergamon.
Paton, H. J. The Categorical Imperative: A Study in Kant's Moral Philosophy. 1971. pap. 4.95x (ISBN 0-8122-1023-9, Pa Paperbks). U of Pa Pr.
Paton, James. Jugs: A Collector's Guide. (Illus.). 1977. 9.95 o.p. (ISBN 0-684-14885-4, ScribT). Scribner.
Paton, L. B. Esther. LC 8-30156. (International Critical Commentary Ser.). 360p. Repr. of 1908 ed. text ed. 20.00x (ISBN 0-567-05009-2). Attic Pr.
Paton, Lewis B. The Early History of Syria & Palestine. LC 79-2878. (Illus.). 302p. 1981. Repr. of 1901 ed. 26.50 (ISBN 0-8305-0046-4). Hyperion Conn.
Paton, T. R. The Formation of Soil Material. (Illus.). 1978. text ed. 20.00x (ISBN 0-04-631009-6); pap. text ed. 9.95x (ISBN 0-04-641010-4). Allen Unwin.
Paton, Tam & Wale, Michael. The Bay City Rollers. pap. 0.95 o.p. (ISBN 0-425-03044-X). Berkley Pub.
Paton, William A. Accounting Theory. LC 73-84526. 1973. Repr. of 1962 ed. text ed. 15.00 (ISBN 0-914348-06-X). Scholars Bk.
Paton, William D., ed. see International Congress of Pharmacology, 7th, Reims, 1978. Satellite Symposium.
Patoski, Margaret, tr. see Denikin, Anton I.
Patoski, Margaret, tr. see Von Bock, Maria P.
Patourel, John Le see Le Patourel, John.
Patra, Atul C. Indian Contract Act: Vol. 1. 1967. Vol. 1. 20.00x (ISBN 0-210-27073-X). Asia.
Patricius, Bro. & Crifer, Sr. Carmel. Review Text in Health. (30 Line Drawings, Index, 336p). (gr. 7-12). 1962. pap. text ed. 5.58 (ISBN 0-87720-161-7). AMSCO Sch.
Patrick, Brennan. The Night Caller. (Orig.). 1981. pap. 2.25 (ISBN 0-440-16674-8). Dell.
Patrick, C. R., jt. auth. see Allen, P. E.
Patrick, Clarence H., ed. Police, Crime, & Society. 320p. 1972. 14.75 (ISBN 0-398-02376-X). C C Thomas.
Patrick, Dale. Arguing with God: The Angry Prayers of Job. 1977. pap. 2.95 (ISBN 0-8272-0013-7). Bethany Pr.
--The Rendering of God in the Old Testament, No. 10. Brueggemann, Walter & Donahue, John R., eds. LC 80-2389. (Overtures to Biblical Theology Ser.). 176p. (Orig.). 1981. pap. 8.95 (ISBN 0-8006-1533-6, 1-1533). Fortress.
Patrick, Dale & Dugger, William E., Jr. Electricity & Electronics Laboratory Manual. rev. ed. (Illus.). 372p. (gr. 7 up). 1980. 4.96. Goodheart.
Patrick, Dale R. Instrumentation Training Course: Electronic Instruments, 2 vols, Vol. 2. 2nd ed. LC 79-63866. 1979. pap. 11.95 (ISBN 0-672-21580-2, 21580); pap. 24.95 set (ISBN 0-672-21581-0). Sams.
Patrick, Dale R. & Fardo, Stephen W. Electrical Power Systems Technology. LC 79-63821. 1979. pap. 12.95 (ISBN 0-672-21607-8). Sams.
--Industrial Process Control Systems. LC 79-65744. 1979. pap. 13.95 (ISBN 0-672-21625-6). Sams.
Patrick, Dale R. & Patrick, Stephen. Instrumentation Training Course: Pneumatic Instruments, Vol. 1. 2nd ed. LC 79-63866. 1979. pap. 13.95 (ISBN 0-672-21579-9, 21579). Sams.
Patrick, Dale R., jt. auth. see Dugger, William.
Patrick, Derrick. Fetch Felix. (Illus.). 192p. 1981. 22.50 (ISBN 0-241-10371-1, Pub. by Hamish Hamilton England). David & Charles.
Patrick, Homer & Schaible, P. J. Poultry: Feeds & Nutrition. 2nd ed. (Illus.). 1980. 39.50 (ISBN 0-87055-353-4); pap. 25.00 (ISBN 0-87055-349-6). AVI.
Patrick, Hugh. Japanese Industrialization & Its Social Consequences. LC 75-7199. 1976. 27.50x o.p. (ISBN 0-520-03000-1); pap. 8.95x (ISBN 0-520-03285-3, CAMPUS 179). U of Cal Pr.
Patrick, Hugh & Rosovsky, Henry, eds. Asia's New Giant: How the Japanese Economy Works. 1976. 24.95 (ISBN 0-8157-6934-2); pap. 14.95 (ISBN 0-8157-6933-4). Brookings.
Patrick, James A. Architecture in Tennessee: Seventeen Sixty-Eight to Eighteen Ninety-Seven. (Illus.). 1981. 24.95 (ISBN 0-87049-223-3). U of Tenn Pr.
Patrick, Jane G. How to Get Your Child into Commercials & Modeling. LC 79-8031. (Illus.). 264p. 1981. 11.95 (ISBN 0-385-15317-1). Doubleday.
Patrick, Maxine. April of Enchantment. (Orig.). 1981. pap. 1.75 (ISBN 0-451-09579-0, Sig). NAL.
Patrick, Michael D, et al. Christabel: A Brief Critical History & Reconsideration. (Salzburg Studies in English Literature, Romantic Reassessment: No. 11). 118p. (Orig.). 1973. pap. text ed. 25.00x (ISBN 0-391-01494-3). Humanities.
Patrick, Robert. Mercy Drop & Other Plays. LC 79-53945. (Illus.). 1980. pap. 5.00 (ISBN 0-930762-03-7). Calamus Bks.
Patrick, Robert see Hoffmann, William M.
Patrick, Robert L. Application Design Handbook for Distributed Systems. LC 79-27205. (Illus.). 212p. 1980. text ed. 22.50 (ISBN 0-8436-1601-6). CBI Pub.
Patrick, Stephen, jt. auth. see Patrick, Dale R.
Patrick, Ted & Dulack, Tom. Let Our Children Go. 1977. pap. 2.25 (ISBN 0-345-25663-8). Ballantine.
Patrick, Walton R. Ring Lardner. (U. S. Authors Ser.: No. 32). lib. bdg. 10.95 (ISBN 0-8057-0440-X). Twayne.
Patrick, Walton R., jt. auth. see Current-Garcia, Eugene.
Patrides, C. A., ed. The Age of Milton: Backgrounds to Seventeenth-Century Literature. Waddington, Raymond B. (Illus.). 438p. 1980. 33.50x (ISBN 0-389-20051-4); pap. 14.00x (ISBN 0-389-20052-2). B&N.
--Approaches to Marvell: The York Tercentenary Lectures. (Illus.). 1978. 28.00x (ISBN 0-7100-8818-3). Routledge & Kegan.
--The Cambridge Platonists. LC 79-28412. 376p. 1980. 49.50 (ISBN 0-521-23417-4); pap. 12.95 (ISBN 0-521-29942-X). Cambridge U Pr.
Patrides, C. A., ed. see Herbert, George.
Patrie, James. The Genetic Relationship of the Ainu Language. (Oceanic Linguistics Special Publications Ser.: No. 17). 380p. (Orig.). 1981. pap. text ed. price not set (ISBN 0-8248-0724-3). U Pr of Hawaii.
Patrikas, Elaine O., et al. Medical Records Administration Continuing Education Review. 1975. spiral bdg. 14.00 (ISBN 0-87488-369-5). Med Exam.
Patsis, A. V. & Seanor, D. A. Photoconductivity in Polymers. LC 74-80461. (Illus.). 349p. (Orig.). 1976. 30.00x (ISBN 0-87762-136-5). Technomic.
Patsouras, Louis, jt. auth. see Thomas, Jack R.
Patt, Donald I. & Patt, Gail R. An Introduction to Modern Genetics. LC 74-12803. (Life Sciences Ser.). (Illus.). 384p. 1975. text ed. 19.95 (ISBN 0-201-05743-3); sol. manual 2.50 (ISBN 0-201-05742-5). A-W.
Patt, Gail R., jt. auth. see Patt, Donald I.
Patt, Jerry, jt. auth. see Ladley, Betty A.
Patt, Richard. Psallite. (Psallite Ser.: Series A). 1977. pap. 2.75 (ISBN 0-570-03764-6, 12-2698). Concordia.
--Psallite-Series B. 1978. pap. 2.75 (ISBN 0-570-03784-0, 12-2738). Concordia.
Patte, Daniel. Early Jewish Hermeneutic in Palestine. LC 75-22225. (Society of Biblical Literature. Dissertation Ser.). 350p. 1975. pap. 9.00 (ISBN 0-89130-015-5, 060122). Scholars Pr Ca.
Patte, Daniel, tr. see Calloud, Jean.
Pattee, Fred L. Development of the American Short Story. LC 66-13477. 1923. 15.00x (ISBN 0-8196-0175-6). Biblo.
Pattee, Fred L., ed. Century Readings in the American Short Story. 562p. 1980. Repr. of 1927 ed. lib. bdg. 40.00 (ISBN 0-89760-708-2). Telegraph Bks.
Pattee, Howard H., Jr., et al, eds. see Frinternational Symposium on X-Ray Optics & X-Ray Microanalysis - 3rd - Stanford - California - 1962.
Patten, Bernard C., ed. Systems Analysis & Simulation in Ecology, 3 vols. Vol. 1. 1971. 52.75 ea. (ISBN 0-12-547201-3). Vol. 1, 1971. Vol. 2, 1972 (ISBN 0-12-547202-1). Vol. 3, 1975. Acad Pr.
Patten, Brian. Little Johnny's Confession. 62p. (Orig.). 1968. 3.95 (ISBN 0-8090-6580-0); pap. 1.50 o.p. (ISBN 0-8090-1340-1). Hill & Wang.
Patten, Donald W. The Biblical Flood & the Ice Epoch. 1966. 9.00; pap. 7.50. Pacific Mer.
Patten, John, jt. ed. see Blake, Robert.
Patten, Lawton M. & Rogness, Milton. Architectural Drawing. 3rd ed. (Illus.). 1977. pap. text ed. 9.95 (ISBN 0-8403-1809-X). Kendall-Hunt.
Patten, Lewis B. Posse from Poison Creek. Bd. with Red Runs the River. 1980. pap. 1.95 (ISBN 0-451-09534-0, Sig). NAL.
--Ride a Tall Horse. 1981. pap. price not set (ISBN 0-451-09816-1, Signet Bks). NAL.
--Six Ways of Dying. 144p. 1976. pap. 1.95 (ISBN 0-441-76843-1). Ace Bks.
--Top Man with a Gun. 1979. pap. 1.75 (ISBN 0-449-14191-8, GM). Fawcett.
--The Trail of the Apache Kid. (Large Print Bks.). 1980. lib. bdg. 10.95 (ISBN 0-8161-3130-9). G K Hall.
Patten, Marion & Sherwin, Mary. Know Your America, Vols. 1 & 2. 1981. 16.95 (ISBN 0-385-18503-0). Doubleday.
Patten, Priscilla, jt. auth. see Patten, Rebecca.
Patten, Rebecca & Patten, Priscilla. Before the Times. LC 80-36848. (Illus.). 1980. pap. 6.95 (ISBN 0-89407-038-X); casebound 9.95 (ISBN 0-89407-047-9). Strawberry Hill.
Patten, Simon. The Development of English Thought: A Study in the Economic Interpretation of History. (The Neglected American Economists Ser.). 1974. lib. bdg. 50.00 (ISBN 0-8240-1026-4). Garland Pub.
--The Economic Basis of Protection. (The Neglected American Economists Ser.). 1974. lib. bdg. 50.00 (ISBN 0-8240-1025-6). Garland Pub.
--Essays in Economic Theory. Tugwell, Rexford G., ed. (The Neglected American Economists Ser.). 1974. lib. bdg. 50.00 (ISBN 0-8240-1029-9). Garland Pub.
--The Social Basis of Religion. (The Neglected American Economists Ser.). 1974. lib. bdg. 50.00 (ISBN 0-8240-1028-0). Garland Pub.
--The Theory of Prosperity. (The Neglected American Economists Ser.). 1974. lib. bdg. 50.00 (ISBN 0-8240-1027-2). Garland Pub.
Patten, Simon N. The Theory of Dynamic Economics. LC 79-1587. 1981. 16.00 (ISBN 0-88355-892-0). Hyperion Conn.
Patten, Thomas H., Jr. Manpower Planning & the Development of Human Resources. LC 76-137109. 1971. 45.95 (ISBN 0-471-66944-X, Pub. by Wiley-Interscience). Wiley.
--Organizational Development Through Teambuilding. LC 80-20726. 350p. 1981. 21.95 (ISBN 0-471-66945-8, Pub. by Wiley-Interscience). Wiley.
Patten, Tom C. & Carpenter, Robert. Rosita. (Illus.). 1975. 4.95 o.p. (ISBN 0-88415-795-4). Pacesetter Pr.
Patter, Douglas M. Van see Marion, Jerry B. & Van Patter, Douglas M.
Patterson, A. M. French-English Dictionary for Chemists. 2nd ed. 1954. 20.95 o.p. (ISBN 0-471-66957-1, Pub. by Wiley-Interscience). Wiley.
--German-English Dictionary for Chemists. 3rd ed. 1950. 21.95 (ISBN 0-471-66990-3, Pub. by Wiley-Interscience). Wiley.
Patterson, A. Temple. Hampshire & the Isle of Wight. 1976. 17.95 (ISBN 0-7134-3221-7, Pub. by Batsford England). David & Charles.
Patterson, Allen. The Gardens of Britain, Two: Dorset, Hampshire and the Isle of Wight. 1978. 24.00 (ISBN 0-7134-0992-4, Pub. by Batsford England). David & Charles.
Patterson, Angelo T., jt. auth. see Do Carmo, Pamela B.
Patterson, Archibald L. The Administration of Public Employee Retirement Systems: Georgia & the Nation. 100p. (Orig.). 1981. pap. price not set (ISBN 0-89854-073-9). U of GA Inst Govt.
Patterson, Bessie. The Wise Woman Builds Her House. 1979. pap. 3.75 (ISBN 0-89137-413-2). Quality Pubns.
Patterson, Buel R., jt. auth. see Carson, Ray F.
Patterson, C. H., jt. auth. see Kaczkowski, Henry.
Patterson, Charles H. Western Philosophy. Incl. Vol. 1. 600 B.C.-1600 A.D (ISBN 0-8220-1550-1); Vol. 2. Since 1600. pap. text ed. o.p. (ISBN 0-8220-1552-8). (Cliffs Course Outlines Ser.). 1971. pap. text ed. 2.95 o.p. (ISBN 0-685-41966-5). Cliffs.
Patterson, Clara E. How to Get Rid of Wrinkles. rev ed. LC 79-27184. (Illus.). 1980. 7.95 (ISBN 0-688-06546-5, Quill); pap. 2.95 (ISBN 0-688-03673-2, Quill). Morrow.
Patterson, David, ed. Pigments: An Introduction to Their Physical Chemistry. (Illus.). 1967. 33.60x (ISBN 0-444-20009-6). Intl Ideas.
Patterson, Doris T. Varieties of E. S. P. in the Edgar Cayce Readings. Orig. Title: Unfettered Mind. 77p. 1968. pap. 2.00 o.p. (ISBN 0-87604-036-9). ARE Pr.
Patterson, Dorothy, jt. auth. see Maca-Roueche, Suanne.
Patterson, E. Law in the Scientific Age. LC 63-9872. 1963. 12.50x (ISBN 0-231-02617-X). Columbia U Pr.
Patterson, Mrs. Elmer. Wisely Train the Younger Women. 1973. pap. 3.45 (ISBN 0-89137-406-X). Quality Pubns.
Patterson, F. W. Manual De Finanzas Para Iglesias. (Illus.). 118p. 1980. pap. 1.95 (ISBN 0-311-17005-6). Casa Bautista.
Patterson, F. W., tr. see Robertson, A. T.
Patterson, Frank A., ed. The Student's Milton. rev. ed. 1930. 44.50x (ISBN 0-89197-430-X). Irvington.
Patterson, G. A. Celestial Navigation with a Pocket Calculator. 1980. softbound 14.95 (ISBN 0-917410-03-3). Basic Sci Pr.
Patterson, G. R., et al. A Social Learning Approach to Family Intervention, Vol. 1: Families with Aggressive Children. LC 75-27000. 179p. 1975. pap. 10.95 (ISBN 0-916154-00-9). Castalia Pub.
Patterson, Gardner. Docker. LC 80-13514. 156p. (gr. 7 up). 1980. 8.95 (ISBN 0-689-50182-X, McElderry Bk). Atheneum.

Patterson, Geoffrey. Chestnut Farm Eighteen Sixty. (Illus.). (gr. k-3). 1980. 8.95 (ISBN 0-233-97208-0). Andre Deutsch.

Patterson, Gerald R. Living with Children: New Methods for Parents & Teachers. rev. ed. LC 76-23974. 1976. pap. text ed. 5.95 (ISBN 0-87822-130-1). Res Press.

--Professional Guide for Families & Living with Children. (Illus., Orig.). 1975. pap. text ed. 2.95 (ISBN 0-87822-160-3). Res Press.

--Social Learning Approach to Family Intervention: Coercive Family Process, Vol. 3. 1981. pap. write for info. Castalia Pub.

Patterson, H. W. Small Boat Building. (Illus.). 144p. pap. 7.50 (ISBN 0-8466-6052-0). Shorey.

Patterson, Harry. To Catch a King. 1980. pap. 2.95 (ISBN 0-449-24323-0, Crest). Fawcett.

Patterson, Ian, tr. see Guerin, Daniel.

Patterson, J. G. Zola Dictionary. LC 68-27179. 1969. Repr. of 1912 ed. 18.00 (ISBN 0-8103-3173-X). Gale.

Patterson, James. The Jericho Commandment. 1981. pap. 2.50 (ISBN 0-345-29241-3). Ballantine.

--The Thomas Berryman Number. 1977. pap. 1.75 o.p. (ISBN 0-685-75042-6, 345-255526-175). Ballantine.

Patterson, James H., jt. auth. see Pfaffenberger, Roger C.

Patterson, James T. Congressional Conservatism & the New Deal: The Growth of the Conservative Coalition in Congress, 1933-1939. LC 67-17845. (Illus.). 1967. pap. 6.50x (ISBN 0-8131-0123-9). U Pr of Ky.

Patterson, Janet & Patterson, Robert C. How to Live with a Pregnant Wife. LC 76-2014. 192p. 1976. pap. 3.95 o.p. (ISBN 0-8407-5603-8). Nelson.

Patterson, Jerry L. Blackjack's Winning Formula. 91p. 1980. write for info. (ISBN 0-9605112-0-2). Casino Gaming.

Patterson, John M., jt. auth. see Bliss, Edward, Jr.

Patterson, K. David. The Northern Gabon Coast to 1875. (Oxford Studies in African Affairs Ser). (Illus.). 176p. 1975. 29.95x (ISBN 0-19-821696-3). Oxford U Pr.

Patterson, Katherine. Partners in Pluralism: A Study Guide. (Orig.). 1981. pap. 2.95 (ISBN 0-377-00111-2). Friend Pr.

Patterson, LeRoy. Good Morning, Lord: Devotions for Athletes. (Good Morning, Lord Ser.). 1979. 2.45 (ISBN 0-8010-7044-9). Baker Bk.

Patterson, Lillie. Meet Miss Liberty. (gr. 4-6). 1962. 7.95g (ISBN 0-02-770570-6). Macmillan.

Patterson, Lindsay, compiled by. Black Films & Film-Makers: A Comprehensive Anthology from Stereotype to Superhero. LC 73-11545. 1975. 12.50 o.p. (ISBN 0-396-06843-X). Dodd.

Patterson, Margaret C., ed. Author Newsletters & Journals. LC 79-63742. (American Literature, English Literature, & World Literature in English Information Guide Ser.: Vol. 19). 1979. 30.00 (ISBN 0-8103-1432-0). Gale.

--Literary Research Guide. LC 75-13925. 1976. 28.00 (ISBN 0-8103-1102-X). Gale.

Patterson, Mary Ann, jt. auth. see Jackson, Sarah.

Patterson, Michael. The Revolution in German Theatre, Nineteen Hundred to Nineteen Thirty-Three. (Illus.). 226p. 1981. price not set (ISBN 0-7100-0659-4). Routledge & Kegan.

Patterson, Michael, jt. ed. see Thompson, Richard F.

Patterson, Michael M. & Kesner, Raymond P., eds. Electrical Stimulation Research Techniques. (Methods in Physiological Psychology Ser.). 1981. price not set (ISBN 0-12-547440-7). Acad Pr.

Patterson, P. R., et al. Psychological Aspects of Cystic Fibrosis. 1973. 17.50x (ISBN 0-88238-702-2). Columbia U Pr.

Patterson, Pam. Introduction to Enamelling. (Illus.). 1978. 14.50 (ISBN 0-589-50050-3, Pub by Reed Books Australia). C E Tuttle.

Patterson, Richard N. The Lasko Tangent. 208p. 1980. pap. 1.95 (ISBN 0-345-28705-3). Ballantine.

--The Outside Man. 252p. 1981. 11.95 (ISBN 0-316-69362-6). Little.

Patterson, Robert C., jt. auth. see Patterson, Janet.

Patterson, Roger L. Maintaining Effective Token Economies. (Illus.). 192p. 1976. 19.50 (ISBN 0-398-03435-4). C C Thomas.

Patterson, Roy. Allergic Diseases: Diagnosis & Management. 2nd ed. (Illus.). 624p. 1980. text ed. 42.50 (ISBN 0-397-50468-3). Lippincott.

Patterson, Samuel. Illinois Lobbyists Study, 1964. 2nd ed. LC 75-38490. 1975. Repr. of 1969 ed. codebk 8.00 (ISBN 0-89138-006-X). ICPSR.

Patterson, Samuel C., et al. A More Perfect Union: Introduction to American Government. 1979. 17.95x (ISBN 0-256-02095-7); study guide 5.50x (ISBN 0-256-02104-X). Dorsey.

Patterson, Stephen E. Political Parties in Revolutionary Massachusetts. LC 72-7991. 320p. 1973. 25.00 (ISBN 0-299-06260-0). U of Wis Pr.

Patterson, T. Archaeology: The Evaluation of Ancient Societies. 1981. pap. 11.95 (ISBN 0-13-044040-X). P-H.

Patterson, T. T. Job Evaluation: A Manual for the Patterson Method, Vol. II. 208p. 1978. text ed. 22.00x (ISBN 0-220-66844-2, Pub. by Busn Bks England). Renouf.

Patterson, Thomas C. America's Past: A New World Archaeology. 168p. 1973. pap. 5.95x (ISBN 0-673-05273-7). Scott F.

--Pattern & Process in the Early Intermediate Period Pottery of the Central Coast of Peru. (U. C. Publ. in Anthropology: Vol. 3). 1966. pap. 6.50x (ISBN 0-520-09002-0). U of Cal Pr.

Patterson, Thomas E. The Mass Media: How Americans Choose Their President. 220p. 1980. 21.95 (ISBN 0-03-057728-4); pap. 8.95 (ISBN 0-03-057729-2). Praeger.

Patterson, W. R. Colloquial Spanish. 4th ed. (Trubners Colloquial Manuals Ser.). 8.75 (ISBN 0-7100-4325-2); pap. 6.95 (ISBN 0-7100-6385-7). Routledge & Kegan.

Patterson, Yvonne. Doubting Thomas. (Arch Bk.: No. 18). 1981. pap. 0.79 (ISBN 0-570-06144-X, 59-1261). Concordia.

--The Wise King & the Baby. LC 59-1258. (Arch Bk.: No. 18). (Illus.). (gr. k-4). 1981. pap. 0.79 (ISBN 0-686-69321-3). Concordia.

Patti, Archimedes L. Why Vietnam: Prelude to America's Albatross. (Illus.). 700p. 1981. 19.50 (ISBN 0-520-04156-9). U of Cal Pr.

Pattie, Alice, jt. auth. see Kreis, Bernadine.

Pattis, Richard E. Karel the Robot: A Gentle Introduction to the Art of Programming. 128p. 1981. pap. text ed. 8.95 (ISBN 0-471-08928-1). Wiley.

Pattison, Anna, jt. auth. see Pattison, Gordon.

Pattison, Bruce. Music & Poetry of the English Renaissance. LC 70-127278. (Music Ser). (Illus.). 1970. Repr. of 1948 ed. lib. bdg. 22.50 (ISBN 0-306-71298-9). Da Capo.

Pattison, E. Mansell. The Experience of Dying. 1977. text ed. 13.95 (ISBN 0-13-294629-7, Spec); pap. text ed. 4.95 (ISBN 0-13-294611-4). P-H.

--Pastor & Parish: A Systems Approach. Clinebell, Howard J. & Stone, Howard W., eds. LC 76-62619. (Creative Pastoral Care & Counseling Ser.). 96p. 1977. pap. 3.25 (ISBN 0-8006-0559-4, 1-559). Fortress.

Pattison, E. Mansell, ed. Selection of Treatment for Alcoholics. LC 79-620007. (NIAAA-RUCAS Alcoholism Treatment Ser.: No. 1). 1981. pap. 10.00 (ISBN 0-911290-47-8). Rutgers Ctr Alcohol.

Pattison, Gordon & Pattison, Anna. Peridontal Instrumentation: A Clinical Manual. (Illus.). 1979. text ed. 21.95 (ISBN 0-87909-604-7). Reston.

Pattison, Patrick, jt. auth. see Reed, Donald A.

Pattison, Robert. The Child Figure in English Literature. LC 76-2893. 190p. 1978. 13.50x (ISBN 0-8203-0409-3). U of Ga Pr.

Pattison, W. T. Life & Works of the Troubadour Raimbaut D'Orange. LC 80-2182. 1981. Repr. of 1952 ed. 35.00 (ISBN 0-404-19015-4). AMS Pr.

Pattison, Walter T. Benito Perez Galdos. (World Authors Ser.: Spain: No. 341). 184p. 1975. lib. bdg. 12.50 (ISBN 0-8057-2689-6). Twayne.

Patton, Bobby R. & Giffin, Kim. Interpersonal Communication in Action: Basic Text & Readings. 3rd ed. (Illus.). 448p. 1980. pap. 12.95 scp (ISBN 0-06-045062-2, HarpC); avail. Har-Row.

--Interpersonal Communication in Action: Basic Text & Readings. 2nd ed. (Auer Ser.). 1977. pap. text ed. 14.50 scp o.p. (ISBN 0-06-042316-1, HarpC); instructor's manual free o.p. (ISBN 0-06-364974-8). Har-Row.

Patton, Bobby R. & Patton, Bonnie R. Female-Male: Living Together. (Interpersonal Communication Ser.). (Illus.). 1976. pap. text ed. 5.95 (ISBN 0-675-08643-4); instructor's manual 3.95 (ISBN 0-686-67248-8). Merrill.

Patton, Bonnie R., jt. auth. see Patton, Bobby R.

Patton, Carl S. Sources of the Synoptic Gospels. 263p. 1980. Repr. of 1915 ed. lib. bdg. 50.00 (ISBN 0-89984-385-9). Century Bookbindery.

Patton, Cliff. The Omni Strain. 432p. (Orig.). 1980. pap. 2.75 (ISBN 0-89083-689-2). Zebra.

Patton, Dennis D., jt. ed. see Nudelman, Sol.

Patton, George S., Jr. Patton on Armor. Province, Charles M., ed. (The Patton Ser.: Vol. 8). 60p. 1980. pap. 2.00 (ISBN 0-932348-12-2). Province Pub.

Patton, James R., jt. auth. see Payne, James S.

Patton, L. T. The Geology of Potter County. (Illus.). 180p. 1923. 0.50 (BULL 2330). Bur Econ Geology.

--The Geology of Stonewall County, Texas. (Illus.). 77p. 1930. 0.50 (BULL 3027). Bur Econ Geology.

Patton, Michael J., jt. auth. see Pepinsky, Harold B.

Patton, Oliver. My Heart Turns Back. 1981. pap. 2.75 (ISBN 0-445-04241-9). Popular Lib.

Patton, Oliver B. The Hollow Mountains. 384p. 1981. pap. 2.75 (ISBN 0-445-08462-6). Popular Lib.

--Western Wind. 384p. 1981. pap. 2.95 (ISBN 0-445-04634-1). Popular Lib.

Patton, Peter C., jt. auth. see Thurber, Kenneth J.

Patton, Peter C. & Holoien, Renee A., eds. Computing in the Humanities. LC 79-3185. 1981. price not set (ISBN 0-669-03397-9). Lexington Bks.

Patton, Robert D., jt. auth. see Moss, Arthur J.

Patton, Stuart & Jensen, Robert G. Biomedical Aspects of Lactation. 1976. pap. text ed. 13.25 (ISBN 0-08-020192-X). Pergamon.

Patton, Temple C. Paint Flow & Pigment Dispersion: A Rheological Approach to Coating & Ink Technology. 2nd ed. LC 78-10774. 1979. 52.50 (ISBN 0-471-03272-7, Pub. by Wiley-Interscience). Wiley.

Patton, W. Construction Materials. 1976. 19.95 (ISBN 0-13-168724-7). P-H.

Patton, W. J. Plastics Technology: Theory, Design & Manufacture. (Illus.). 1976. 17.95 o.p. (ISBN 0-87909-635-7). Reston.

Patton, William J. Kinematics. (Illus.). 1979. text ed. 18.95 (ISBN 0-8359-3693-7); students manual avail. (ISBN 0-8359-3694-5). Reston.

Pattou & Vaughn. Furniture Finishing. LC 73-24061. (Illus.). 1973. pap. 4.95 o.p. (ISBN 0-8473-1125-2). Sterling.

Patty, F. A. Industrial Hygiene & Toxicology, 2 vols. 2nd ed. LC 58-9220. 1958. Vol. 1, General Principles. o.p.; Vol. 2, Toxicology. 85.00 (ISBN 0-470-67188-2, Pub. by Wiley-Interscience). Wiley.

Patty, James S., ed. see Giraudoux, Jean.

Patz. Nobody Knows I Have Delicate Toes. (gr. k-3). 1980. 5.95 (ISBN 0-531-02392-3, C15); PLB 7.90 (ISBN 0-686-65252-5, B25). Watts.

Patz, Alan. Strategic Decision Analysis: A Managerial Approach to Policy. 1981. text ed. 18.95 (ISBN 0-316-69400-2); tchrs'. manual free (ISBN 0-316-69401-0). Little.

Patz, Alan L. & Rowe, A. J. Management Control & Decision Systems: Text, Cases, & Readings. (Ser. on Management, Accounting & Information Systems). 1977. 24.50 (ISBN 0-471-67195-9). Wiley.

Patz, Arnall & Hoover, Richard E. Protection of Vision in Children. (Illus.). 184p. 1969. text ed. 14.75 (ISBN 0-398-01456-6). C C Thomas.

Patz, Nancy. Pumpernickle Tickle & Mean Green Cheese. (Illus.). (gr. k-3). 1978. 6.95 (ISBN 0-531-02492-X); PLB 7.90 (ISBN 0-531-02221-8). Watts.

Pau. Failure Diagnoses & Performance Monitoring. Date not set. price not set (ISBN 0-8247-1018-5). Dekker.

Pauck, Wilhelm, ed. Melanchton & Bucer. (Library of Christian Classics Ichthus Edition). 1980. pap. 9.95 (ISBN 0-664-24164-6). Westminster.

Paudler, William W. Nuclear Magnetic Resonance. 1971. pap. text ed. 12.95 (ISBN 0-205-02888-8, 6828884). Allyn.

Pauerstein, Carl J., jt. ed. see Shain, Rochelle.

Pauk, W. & Millman, J. How to Take Tests. 1969. pap. 3.50 (ISBN 0-07-048915-7, SP). McGraw.

Pauk, Walter. Essential Skills Series, 20 bks. Incl. Bk. 1 (ISBN 0-89061-100-9, ESS1); Bk. 2 (ISBN 0-89061-101-7, ESS2); Bk. 3 (ISBN 0-89061-102-5, ESS3); Bk. 4 (ISBN 0-89061-103-3, ESS4); Bk. 5 (ISBN 0-89061-104-1, ESS5); Bk. 6 (ISBN 0-89061-105-X, ESS6); Bk. 7 (ISBN 0-89061-106-8, ESS7); Bk. 8 (ISBN 0-89061-107-6, ESS8); Bk. 9 (ISBN 0-89061-108-4, ESS9); Bk. 10 (ISBN 0-89061-109-2, ESS10); Bk. 11 (ISBN 0-89061-110-6, ESS11); Bk. 12 (ISBN 0-89061-111-4, ESS12); Bk. 13 (ISBN 0-89061-112-2, ESS13); Bk. 14 (ISBN 0-89061-113-0, ESS14); Bk. 15 (ISBN 0-89061-114-9, ESS15); Bk. 16 (ISBN 0-89061-115-7, ES516); Bk. 17 (ISBN 0-89061-116-5, ESS17); Bk. 18 (ISBN 0-89061-117-3, ESS18); Bk. 19 (ISBN 0-89061-118-1, ESS19); Bk. 20 (ISBN 0-89061-119-X, ESS20). (gr. 6-12). 1976. pap. 2.40x ea; 20 bk. set (ISBN 0-89061-098-3). Jamestown Pubs.

--Getting the Author's Tone: Is He Humorous, Serious, Satirical? (A Skill at a Time Ser). 64p. (gr. 9-12). 1975. pap. text ed. 2.40x (ISBN 0-89061-024-X). Jamestown Pubs.

--Getting the Main Point: Separating the Wheat from the Chaff. (A Skill at a Time Ser). 64p. (gr. 9-12). 1975. pap. text ed. 2.40x (ISBN 0-89061-026-6). Jamestown Pubs.

--How to Read Factual Literature. LC 70-113589. 1970. Bk. 1, Levels 7-8. pap. text ed. 5.95 (ISBN 0-574-17061-8, 13-0061); Bk. 2, Levels 9-10. instr's guide avail. (ISBN 0-574-17062-6, 13-0062); Bk. 3, Levels 11-12. pap. text ed. 5.95 (ISBN 0-574-17063-4, 13-0063); instr's guide 1.50 (ISBN 0-574-17065-0, 13-0065). SRA.

--How to Study in College. 2nd ed. LC 72-7923. 1974. pap. text ed. 7.50 (ISBN 0-395-17815-0). HM.

--Perceiving Structure: How Are the Ideas Organized? (A Skill at a Time Ser). 64p. (gr. 9-12). 1975. pap. text ed. 2.40x (ISBN 0-89061-030-4). Jamestown Pubs.

--Perceiving the Author's Intent: What Is the Author's Real Message? (A Skill at a Time Ser). 64p. (gr. 9-12). 1975. pap. text ed. 2.40x (ISBN 0-89061-029-0). Jamestown Pubs.

--Reading Between the Lines: Drawing Correct Inferences. (A Skill at a Time Ser). 64p. (gr. 9-12). 1975. pap. text ed. 2.40x (ISBN 0-89061-025-8). Jamestown Pubs.

--Recognizing Points of View: Whose Mind; Where's He Standing? (A Skill at a Time Ser). 64p. (gr. 9-12). 1975. pap. text ed. 2.40x (ISBN 0-89061-028-2). Jamestown Pubs.

--Recognizing Traits of Character: How Does the Author Build His Characters? (A Skill at a Time Ser). 64p. (gr. 9-12). 1975. pap. text ed. 2.40x (ISBN 0-89061-027-4). Jamestown Pubs.

--Six-Way Paragraphs. (Illus.). 224p. (gr. 9 up). 1974. pap. text ed. 4.00x (ISBN 0-89061-009-6). Jamestown Pubs.

--Understanding Figurative Language: What Effect Did the Author Intend? (A Skill at a Time Ser). 64p. (gr. 9 up). 1975. pap. text ed. 2.40x (ISBN 0-89061-023-1). Jamestown Pubs.

--Using the Signal Words: Making Transitional Words Work for You. (A Skill at a Time Ser). 64p. (gr. 9 up). 1975. pap. text ed. 2.40x (ISBN 0-89061-022-3). Jamestown Pubs.

--Vocabulary in Context: Getting the Precise Meaning. (A Skill at a Time Ser). 64p. (gr. 9 up). 1975. pap. text ed. 2.40x (ISBN 0-89061-021-5). Jamestown Pubs.

Pauk, Walter & Wilson, Josephine M. Reading for Facts. 1978. pap. 8.95x (ISBN 0-582-28028-1). Longman.

Pauk, Walter, ed. see Conan Doyle, Arthur.

Pauk, Walter, ed. see Harte, Bret.

Pauk, Walter, ed. see London, Jack.

Pauk, Walter, ed. see O'Henry.

Pauk, Walter, ed. see O. Henry.

Pauk, Walter, ed. see O'Henry.

Pauker, John. Angry Candy, the American As Consumer. LC 76-24127. (Illus.). 1976. pap. 2.50 (ISBN 0-917530-01-2). Pig Iron Pr.

Paukert, Felix, et al. Income Distribution, Structure of Economy & Employment: A Comparative Study for Four Asian Countries. 176p. 1981. 35.00x (ISBN 0-7099-2006-7, Pub. by Croom Helm LTD England). Biblio Dist.

Paul, Aileen. Kids' Fifty-State Cookbook. LC 76-2812. (gr. 3-7). 1976. PLB 6.95 (ISBN 0-385-11228-9). Doubleday.

--Kids Indoor Gardening. (gr. 4-7). 1975. pap. 0.75 o.s.i. (ISBN 0-671-29608-6). Archway.

--Kids' Indoor Gardening. (gr. 4-7). pap. 0.75 (ISBN 0-671-29608-6). PB.

Paul, Aileen & Hawkins, Arthur. Candies, Cookies, Cakes. LC 79-79701. 144p. (gr. 3-7). 1974. 4.95 o.p. (ISBN 0-385-03019-3). Doubleday.

Paul, Arnold M. Conservative Crisis & the Rule of Law: Attitudes of Bar & Bench 1887-1895. 7.50 (ISBN 0-8446-0839-4). Peter Smith.

Paul, Barbara. Devil Fire, Love's Revenge. 1977. pap. 1.95 o.p. (ISBN 0-345-25950-5). Ballantine.

--The Fourth Wall. 474p. 1980. Repr. of 1979 ed. large print ed. 12.95 (ISBN 0-89621-254-8). Thorndike Pr.

--The Seventeenth Stair. 1976. pap. 1.75 o.p. (ISBN 0-345-25200-4). Ballantine.

--To Love a Stranger. 1980. lib. bdg. 14.95 (ISBN 0-8161-3169-4, Large Print Bks). G K Hall.

--Your Eyelids Are Growing Heavy. LC 80-2462. 192p. 1981. 9.95 (ISBN 0-385-17466-7). Doubleday.

Paul, Bil. Bicycling California's Spine: Touring the Length of the Sierra Nevada. LC 80-70010. (Bikeroots Ser.). (Illus.). 64p. (Orig.). 1981. pap. 3.95 (ISBN 0-9600650-3-2). Alchemist-Light.

Paul, Burton. Kinematics & Dynamics of Planar Machinery. (Illus.). 1979. text ed. 32.95 (ISBN 0-13-516062-6). P-H.

Paul, C. Kegan, tr. see Huysmans, Joris K.

Paul, Cecil R. Passages of a Pastor. 128p. 1981. 6.95 (ISBN 0-310-43070-4, 11160). Zondervan.

Paul, Cedar, tr. see Marx, Karl.

Paul, Charles B. Science & Immortality: The Eloges of the Paris Academy of Sciences (1699-1791) 250p. 1980. 19.50x (ISBN 0-520-03986-6). U of Cal Pr.

Paul, Charlotte. A Child Is Missing. 1978. pap. 2.75 (ISBN 0-425-04354-1, Medallion). Berkley Pub.

--Gold Mountain. 1977. pap. 2.25 (ISBN 0-441-29749-8). Ace Bks.

--The Image. (Orig.). 1980. pap. 2.75 (ISBN 0-446-95145-5). Warner Bks.

--Phoenix Island. 1976. pap. 2.50 (ISBN 0-451-09413-1, E9413, Sig). NAI

Paul, D. R. & Newman, Seymour, eds. Polymer Blends, Vols. 1 & 2. 1978. Vol. 1. 50.50 (ISBN 0-12-546801-6); Vol. 2. 51.50 (ISBN 0-12-546802-4); 86.50 set (ISBN 0-685-80434-8). Acad Pr.
Paul, David W. Czechoslovakia: Profile of a Binational Socialist Country. (Nations of Contemporary Eastern Europe Ser.). 128p. 1981. lib. bdg. 16.50x (ISBN 0-89158-861-2). Westview.
Paul, Diana. The Buddhist Feminine Ideal: Queen Srimala & the Tathagatagarbha American Academy of Religion. LC 79-12031. (Dissertation Ser.: No. 30). 12.00x (ISBN 0-89130-284-0); pap. 7.50x (ISBN 0-89130-303-0). Scholars Pr CA.
--Women in Buddhism. 1980. 19.00 (ISBN 0-89581-456-0, Asian Humanities). Lancaster-Miller.
Paul, Doris A., jt. auth. see Issari, M. Ali.
Paul, Ellen F. & Russo, Philip A., Jr., eds. Public Policy: Issues, Analysis & Ideology. (Chatham House Ser. on Change in American Politics). 1981. pap. text ed. 8.95x (ISBN 0-934540-04-7). Chatham Hse Pubs.
Paul, Ellen F., jt. ed. see Jacobs, Dan N.
Paul, Hugo. Condominium Trap. LC 79-65558. 1981. 7.50 (ISBN 0-916620-36-0). Portals Pr.
Paul, J., jt. auth. see Mills, K.
Paul, J. Ellis. Manual of Four-Handed Dentistry. (Illus.). 155p. 1980. 42.00 (ISBN 0-931386-09-8). Quint Pub Co.
Paul, J. K. Fruit & Vegetable Juice Processing. LC 75-532. (Food Technology Review Ser: No. 21). (Illus.). 277p. 1975. 36.00 o.p. (ISBN 0-8155-0565-5). Noyes.
Paul, J. K., ed. Ethyl Alcohol Production & Use As a Motor Fuel. LC 79-22900. (Energy Tech Review, Chemical Tech Review No. 51: No. 144). (Illus.). 1980. 48.00 (ISBN 0-8155-0780-1). Noyes.
--Large & Small Scale Ethyl Alcohol Manufacturing Processes from Agricultural Raw Materials. LC 80-20219. (Chemical Tech. Rev. 169, Energy Tech. Rev. 58). (Illus.). 576p. 1981. 48.00 (ISBN 0-8155-0815-8). Noyes.
Paul, James L., jt. auth. see Rhodes, William.
Paul, Jean. Des Feldpredigers Schmelzle Reise Nach Flatz. Smeed, J. W., ed. (Clarendon German Ser). (Ger.). 1966. 3.25x o.p. (ISBN 0-19-832450-2). Oxford U Pr.
Paul, Jeffrey, ed. Reading Nozick. (Philosophy & Society Ser.). 1981. 25.00x (ISBN 0-8476-6279-9); pap. 10.95x (ISBN 0-8476-6280-2). Rowman.
Paul, Jennifer L. Nobody Home. 1978. pap. 1.95 o.s.i. (ISBN 0-446-89591-1). Warner Bks.
Paul, John, jt. auth. see Calman, Kenneth C.
Paul, Kathleen. Aries. (Sun Signs). (Illus.). (gr. 4-12). 1978. PLB 5.95 (ISBN 0-87191-641-X); pap. 2.95 (ISBN 0-89812-071-3). Creative Ed.
--Taurus. (Sun Signs Ser.). (Illus.). (gr. 4-12). 1978. PLB 5.95 (ISBN 0-87191-642-8); pap. 2.95 (ISBN 0-89812-072-1). Creative Ed.
Paul, Martin, tr. see Alberti, Rafael.
Paul, Mimi F., jt. auth. see Liebing, Ralph W.
Paul, Paula G. Inn of the Clowns. 192p. (YA) 1976. 5.95 (ISBN 0-685-67081-3, Avalon). Bouregy.
--You Can Hear a Magpie Smile. (gr. 5-8). 1980. 7.95 (ISBN 0-525-66709-1). Elsevier-Nelson.
Paul, Richard S. & Haeusler, Ernest F., Jr. Algebra & Trigonometry: For College Students. (Illus.). 1978. ref. 17.95 (ISBN 0-87909-031-6); instructor's manual free. Reston.
Paul, Richard S. & Shaevel, M. Leonard. Contemporary Technical Mathematics with Calculus. (Technical Mathematics Ser). 1970. text ed. 15.95 o.p. (ISBN 0-13-170654-3). P-H.
Paul, Rodman W. California Gold: The Beginning of Mining in the Far West. LC 47-54111. (Illus.). 1965. pap. 3.95 (ISBN 0-8032-5149-1, BB 313, Bison). U of Nebr Pr.
--The Frontier & the American West. Etulain, Richard W., ed. LC 76-11622. (Goldentree Bibliographies in American History). 1977. pap. text ed. 12.95x (ISBN 0-88295-542-X). AHM Pub.
--Mining Frontiers of the Far West,1848-1880. LC 63-8818. (Histories of the American Frontier Ser). (Illus.). 256p. 1980. pap. 6.50x (ISBN 0-8263-0315-3). U of NM Pr.
Paul, Roland A. American Military Commitments Abroad. 1973. 16.50 (ISBN 0-8135-0739-1). Rutgers U Pr.
Paul, Sherman. Emerson's Angle of Vision: Man & Nature in American Experience. LC 80-2542. 1981. Repr. of 1952 ed. 33.50 (ISBN 0-404-19267-X). AMS Pr.
--Hart's Bridge. LC 76-188133. 320p. 1972. 15.00 (ISBN 0-252-00257-1). U of Ill Pr.
Paul, Sherry. Ancient Skyscrapers: The Native American Pueblos. LC 78-23992. (Famous Firsts Ser.). (Illus.). 1978. lib. bdg. 7.35 (ISBN 0-686-51097-6). Silver.
Paul, William H. The Gray-Flannel Pigskin: Movers & Shakers of Pro Football. LC 74-10669. 1974. 7.95 o.p. (ISBN 0-397-01025-7). Lippincott.
Paula, F. Clive De see De Paula, F. Clive.
Paulaha, Richard, ed. see Engelmeier, Philip A.
Paulden, S. How to Deliver on Time. 128p. 1977. text ed. 19.25x (ISBN 0-566-02075-0, Pub. by Gower Pub Co England). Renouf.
Paulden, Sydney, jt. auth. see MacMillan, Colin.
Paulet, William. The Lord Marques Idlenes: Conteining Mainfold Matters of Acceptable Devise. LC 79-84131. (English Experience Ser.: No. 949). 112p. 1979. Repr. of 1586 ed. lib. bdg. 11.50 (ISBN 90-221-0949-6). Walter J Johnson.
Pauley, Bruce. Hitler & the Forgotten Nazis. LC 80-17006. 360p. 1981. 19.00x (ISBN 0-8078-1456-3). U of NC Pr.
Pauley, Steven. Technical Report Writing Today. 2nd ed. LC 78-69557. (Illus.). 1979. text ed. 14.50 (ISBN 0-395-27111-8); inst. manual 0.20 (ISBN 0-395-27110-X). HM.
Pauley, Steven E., jt. auth. see Ferre, John P.
Pauli, Max. Prayers for the Time Being. 1971. pap. 1.75 o.p. (ISBN 0-89243-017-6, 42500). Liguori Pubns.
Pauli, W. General Principles of Quantum Mechanics. 212p. 1980. pap. 17.20 (ISBN 0-387-09842-9). Springer-Verlag.
Pauli, Wolfgang. Pauli Lectures on Physics. Enz, C. P., ed. Marguilies, S. & Lewis, H. R., trs. Incl. Vol. 1. Electrodynamics. LC 76-155320 (ISBN 0-262-66033-4); Vol. 2. Optics & the Theory of Electronics. LC 72-7802 (ISBN 0-262-66034-2); Vol. 3. Thermodynamics & the Kinetic Theory of Gases. LC 72-7803 (ISBN 0-262-66035-0); Vol. 4. Statistical Mechanics. LC 72-7804 (ISBN 0-262-66036-9); Vol. 5. Wave Mechanics. LC 72-7805 (ISBN 0-262-66037-7); Vol. 6. Selected Topics in Field Quantization. LC 72-7807 (ISBN 0-262-66038-5). 1977. pap. text ed. 25.00x set (ISBN 0-262-66032-6); pap. text ed. 4.95x ea. MIT Pr.
Pauliat, P. Dictionnaire russe-francais. 11.95 (ISBN 0-685-13884-4, 3790). Larousse.
Paulin, Tom. The Strange Museum. 64p. (Orig.). 1980. pap. 9.95 (ISBN 0-571-11511-X, Pub. by Faber & Faber). Merrimack Bk Serv.
Pauling, Linus. Vitamin C, the Common Cold, & the Flu. LC 76-28516. (Illus.). 1976. pap. 6.95x (ISBN 0-7167-0361-0). W H Freeman.
Pauling, Linus & Pauling, Peter. Chemistry. LC 74-34071. (Chemistry Ser.). (Illus.). 770p. 1975. 23.95x (ISBN 0-7167-0176-6); ans. bk. avail. (ISBN 0-685-55250-0). W H Freeman.
Pauling, Linus, jt. auth. see Cameron, Ewan.
Pauling, Linus, jt. ed. see Hawkins, David.
Pauling, Linus C. The Chemical Bond: A Brief Introduction to Modern Structural Chemistry. abr. ed. (Illus.). 278p. (gr. 11-12). 1967. text ed. 20.00x (ISBN 0-8014-9829-5); pap. text ed. 7.95x (ISBN 0-8014-9829-5). Cornell U Pr.
Pauling, Peter, jt. auth. see Pauling, Linus.
Paulist Press Editorial & Catechetical Team. Spirit of the Lord, 12 units. (Come to the Father Program). (gr. 7-8). 1974. Student Booklets, Units 1-12. pap. text ed. 0.50 ea.; CCD tchr's. manual. gr. 7 6.95 (ISBN 0-8091-9116-4); parochial tchr's. manual gr. 7 7.95 (ISBN 0-8091-9115-6); CCD tchr's. manual gr. 8 6.95 (ISBN 0-8091-9125-3); parochial tchr's. manual gr. 8 7.95 (ISBN 0-8091-9124-5). Paulist Pr.
Paulist Press Team of Canadian & American Catechists. Gathered in Love. (Come to the Father Program Ser.). (Audio-vis. aids avail). (gr. 3). 1973. text ed. 2.75 child-parent bk. (ISBN 0-8091-9096-6); text ed. 2.75 spanish ed. (ISBN 0-8091-9105-9); cCD tchr. manual 7.95 (ISBN 0-8091-9098-2); parochial tchr. man. 7.95 (ISBN 0-8091-9097-4). Paulist Pr.
Paull, Rachel K. & Paull, Richard A. Geology of Wisconsin & Upper Michigan: Including Parts of Adjacent States. LC 76-27036. (Illus.). 1977. pap. text ed. 9.95 (ISBN 0-8403-1596-1). Kendall-Hunt.
Paull, Raymond. Old Walhalla: Portrait of a Gold Town. 148p. 1980. pap. 8.00x (ISBN 0-522-84212-7, Pub. by Melbourne U Pr Australia). Intl Schol Bk Serv.
Paull, Richard A., jt. auth. see Paull, Rachel K.
Paulos, John A. Mathematics & Humor. LC 80-12742. 1980. 12.95 (ISBN 0-226-65024-3). U of Chicago Pr.
Paulsen. Curse of the Cobra-CB Radio Caper. (gr. 3-5). pap. 1.25 (ISBN 0-590-12081-6, Schol Pap). Schol Bk Serv.
Paulsen, F. R. Plant Mutations & Radiations: Genetics for the Layman. 1960. 6.50 (ISBN 0-911268-25-1). Rogers Bk.
Paulsen, Gary. Careers in an Airport. LC 76-44241. (Whole Works Ser.). (Illus.). (gr. 3-7). 1977. PLB 9.65 (ISBN 0-8172-0707-4). Raintree Pubs.
--The CB Radio Caper. LC 76-47631. (Mallard Mystery Ser.). (Illus.). (gr. 3-6). 1977. PLB 7.75 (ISBN 0-8172-0926-3). Raintree Pubs.
--The Curse of the Cobra. LC 76-54275. (Mallard Mystery Ser.). (Illus.). (gr. 3-6). 1977. 7.75 (ISBN 0-8172-0928-X). Raintree Pubs.
--Downhill, Hotdogging, & Cross-Country--If the Snow Isn't Sticky. LC 78-26256. (Sports on the Light Side Ser.). (Illus.). (gr. 4-6). 1979. PLB 9.65 (ISBN 0-8172-0187-4). Raintree Pubs.
--Dribbling, Shooting, & Scoring Sometimes. LC 76-12614. (Sports on the Light Side Ser.). (Illus.). 32p. (gr. 3-6). 1976. PLB 9.65 (ISBN 0-8172-0179-3). Raintree Pubs.
--Facing off, Checking, & Goaltending--Perhaps. LC 78-21079. (Sports on the Light Side Ser.). (Illus.). (gr. 4-6). 1979. PLB 9.65 (ISBN 0-8172-0183-1). Raintree Pubs.
--Forehanding & Backhanding - If You're Lucky. LC 77-27046. (Sports on the Light Side Ser.). (Illus.). (gr. 3-6). 1978. PLB 9.65 (ISBN 0-8172-1158-6). Raintree Pubs.
--The Foxman. LC 76-57974. (gr. 6 up). 1977. 7.95 o.p. (ISBN 0-525-66543-9). Elsevier-Nelson.
--Going Very Fast in a Circle--If You Don't Run Out of Gas. LC 78-21109. (Sports on the Light Side Ser.). (Illus.). (gr. 4-6). 1979. PLB 9.65 (ISBN 0-8172-0185-8). Raintree Pubs.
--The Golden Stick. LC 76-47670. (Sports Fiction Ser.). (gr. 5-10). 1977. 7.75 (ISBN 0-8172-0800-3). Raintree Pubs.
--The Grass Eaters. LC 76-10313. (Real Animals Ser.). (Illus.). 64p. (gr. 5 up). 1976. PLB 8.65 (ISBN 0-8172-0602-7). Raintree Pubs.
--Hitting, Pitching & Running Maybe. LC 76-18092. (Sports on the Light Side Ser.). (Illus.). 32p. (gr. 3-6). 1976. PLB 9.65 (ISBN 0-8172-0177-7). Raintree Pubs.
--Launching, Floating High & Landing--If Your Pilot Light Doesn't Go Out. LC 78-26835. (Sports on the Light Side Ser.). (Illus.). (gr. 4-6). 1979. PLB 9.65 (ISBN 0-8172-0193-9). Raintree Pubs.
--Pummeling, Falling, & Getting up--Sometimes. LC 78-26997. (Sports on the Light Side Ser.). (Illus.). (gr. 4-6). 1979. PLB 9.65 (ISBN 0-8172-0195-5). Raintree Pubs.
--Running, Jumping, & Throwing - If You Can. LC 77-27479. (Sports on the Light Side Ser.). (Illus.). (gr. 3-6). 1978. PLB 9.65 (ISBN 0-8172-1160-8). Raintree Pubs.
--Slab Cowboy. LC 79-63130. Date not set. pap. 4.50 cancelled (ISBN 0-931328-04-7). Timely Bks.
--The Small Ones. LC 76-12635. (Real Animals Ser.). (Illus.). 64p. (gr. 4 up). 1976. PLB 8.65 (ISBN 0-8172-0600-0). Raintree Pubs.
--Successful Home Repair: When Not to Call the Contractor. LC 78-9107. (Illus.). 1978. 13.95 (ISBN 0-912336-69-2); pap. 6.95 (ISBN 0-912336-70-6). Structures Pub.
--Tackling, Running, & Kicking--Now & Again. LC 77-7786. (Sports on the Light Side Ser.). (Illus.). (gr. 3-6). 1977. PLB 9.65 (ISBN 0-8172-0966-2). Raintree Pubs.
--Track, Enduro, & Motocross--Unless You Fall Over. LC 78-21022. (Sports on the Light Side Ser.). (Illus.). (gr. 4-6). 1979. PLB 9.65 (ISBN 0-8172-0181-5). Raintree Pubs.
Paulsen, Gary & Browne, Art, Jr. TV & Movie Animals. LC 79-25861. (Illus.). 96p. (gr. 4-6). 1980. PLB 7.29 (ISBN 0-671-32989-8). Messner.
Paulsen, Gary & Theis, Dan. Martin Luther King: The Man Who Climbed the Mountain. LC 76-13483. (Illus.). 64p. (gr. 4-6). 1976. 6.60 o.p. (ISBN 0-8172-0415-6); PLB 6.60 o.p. (ISBN 0-8172-0414-8). Raintree Pubs.
Paulsen, Kathryn. Complete Book of Magic & Witchcraft. (Orig.). 1970. pap. 1.25 o.p. (ISBN 0-451-05589-6, Y5589, Sig). NAL.
Paulsen, Kathryn & Kuhn, Ryan A., eds. Woman's Almanac: Twelve How to Handbooks in One. LC 76-2055. (Illus.). 1976. 12.50 o.p. (ISBN 0-397-01113-X); pap. 8.95 (ISBN 0-397-01138-5). Lippincott.
Paulson, Arvid, tr. see Strindberg, August.
Paulson, David. Footprints of Faith. LC 78-69673. (Redwood Ser.). 1978. pap. 3.95 (ISBN 0-8163-0196-4, 06390-9). Pacific Pr Pub Assn.
Paulson, Michael G. The Fallen Crown: Three French Mary Stuart Plays of the Seventeenth Century. LC 79-6812. 207p. 1980. text ed. 17.00 (ISBN 0-8191-0959-2); pap. text ed. 9.25 (ISBN 0-8191-0960-6). U Pr of Amer.
Paulson, Ronald, jt. auth. see Bage, Robert.
Paulson, Ronald, ed. see Bage, Robert.
Paulson, Ronald, ed. see Brooke, Henry.
Paulson, Ronald, ed. see Collyer, Mary.
Paulson, Ronald, ed. see Fenelon & De Salignac De La Mothe, Francois.
Paulson, Ronald, ed. see Godwin, William.
Paulson, Ronald, ed. see Haywood, Eliza.
Paulson, Ronald, ed. see Holcroft, Thomas.
Paulson, Ronald, ed. see Johnstone, Charles.
Paulson, Ronald, ed. see MacKenzie, Henry.
Paulson, Ross E. Radicalism & Reform: The Vrooman Family & American Social Thought, 1837-1937. LC 68-12970. 324p. 1968. 12.00x (ISBN 0-8131-1156-0). U Pr of Ky.
Paulson, Walter G., et al. Planning a Corrugated Container Plant. (Tappi Press Reports). (Illus.). 125p. 1980. 93.95 (ISBN 0-89852-387-7, 01-01-R087). Tappi.
Paulston, Christina B. Bilingual Education: Theories & Issues. 90p. 1980. pap. 8.95 (ISBN 0-88377-146-2). Newbury Hse.
Paulston, Roland G. Society, Schools & Progress in Peru. 336p. 1972. text ed. 23.00 (ISBN 0-08-016428-5). Pergamon.
Paulston, Rolland G. Educational Change in Sweden. LC 68-29907. (Illus.). 1968. text ed. 9.25x (ISBN 0-8077-1892-0). Tchrs Coll.
Paulston, Rolland G., ed. Non-Formal Education: An Annotated International Bibliography. LC 72-186197. (Special Studies in International Economics & Development). 1972. 34.50x (ISBN 0-275-28623-1). Irvington.
Paul The Deacon. History of the Lombards. Foulke, William D., tr. LC 72-80382. (Middle Ages Ser). 1974. 15.00x (ISBN 0-8122-7671-X); pap. 4.95x (ISBN 0-8122-1079-4). U of Pa Pr.
Paulu, Burton. Television & Radio in the United Kingdom. 544p. 1981. 39.50x (ISBN 0-8166-0941-1). U of Minn Pr.
Pauly, Mark V. Doctors & Their Workshops: Economic Models of Physician Behavior. LC 80-16112. (National Bureau of Economic Research Ser.). (Illus.). 144p. 1980. lib. bdg. 17.00x (ISBN 0-226-65044-8). U of Chicago Pr.
Pauly, Mark V., ed. National Health Insurance: What Now, What Later, What Never? 1980. 16.95 (ISBN 0-8447-2184-0); pap. 8.25 (ISBN 0-8447-2185-9). Am Enterprise.
Pauly, Reinhard G. Music & the Theater: An Introduction to Opera. 1970. 18.50 (ISBN 0-13-607002-7). P-H.
--Music in the Classic Period. 2nd ed. (History of Music Ser). 224p. 1973. pap. text ed. 10.95 (ISBN 0-13-607630-0). P-H.
Pauncz, ed. Spin Eigenfunctions: Construction & Use. (Illus.). 1979. 35.00 (ISBN 0-306-40141-X, Plenum Pr). Plenum Pub.
Paunio, J. J. Theoretical Analysis of Growth & Cycles. (Illus.). 80p. 1974. 47.50 (ISBN 0-913314-38-2). Am Classical Coll Pr.
Pau On Lau, Estelle. Ellen C. Sabin: Proponent of Higher Education for Women. 1978. pap. text ed. 7.50x (ISBN 0-8191-0469-8). U Pr of Amer.
Pausanias. Description of Greece, 6 Vols. 2nd ed. Frazer, J. G., tr. LC 65-13634. (Illus.). 1897. Set. 95.00x (ISBN 0-8196-0144-6). Biblo.
Paushkin, Ya. M., et al. Organic Polymeric Semiconductors. Sultzkin, A. E., ed. Kondor, R., tr. Orig. Title: Rus. 242p. 1974. 32.95 (ISBN 0-470-67275-7). Halsted Pr.
Paust, Gil. The Complete Beginner's Guide to Horseback Riding. LC 76-42380. 1977. 6.95 o.p. (ISBN 0-385-01747-2); PLB write for info. o.p. (ISBN 0-385-03347-8). Doubleday.
--Model Railroading: How to Plan, Build, & Maintain Your Trains & Pikes. LC 80-1817. (Illus.). 160p. (gr. 4 up). 1981. 9.95a (ISBN 0-385-13033-3); PLB (ISBN 0-385-13034-1). Doubleday.
Pautler, Albert J., Jr. Job Seeking Guide. LC 78-57903. 1979. pap. text ed. 3.80 (ISBN 0-8273-1771-9). Delmar.
--Shop & Laboratory Instructor's Handbook: A Guide to Improving Education. new ed. 1978. text ed. 17.95 o.p. (ISBN 0-205-05841-8). Allyn.
Pauw, B. A. The Second Generation. (Xhosa in Town Ser.). 261p. 1973. pap. 15.95x (ISBN 0-19-570028-7). Oxford U Pr.
Pauw, John W. De see De Pauw, John W.
Pauwels, F. Biomechanics of the Locomotor Apparatus. (Illus.). 520p. 1980. 175.90 (ISBN 0-387-09131-9). Springer-Verlag.
Pauze, Denis, jt. auth. see Schieler, Leroy.
Pavan-Langston, D., et al, eds. Adenine Arabinoside: An Antiviral Agent. LC 75-4087. 425p. 1975. 34.50 (ISBN 0-89004-024-9). Raven.
Pavan-Langston, Deborah. Manual of Occular Diagnosis & Therapy. 1980. 12.95 (ISBN 0-316-69537-8). Little.
Pavarotti, Luciano & Wright, William. Pavarotti: My Own Story. LC 80-1990. (Illus.). 240p. 1981. 14.95 (ISBN 0-385-15340-6). Doubleday.
Pavelec, Barry J. & Kirschner, Stephen M. Take This Test. LC 80-972. 288p. Date not set. pap. 6.95 (ISBN 0-8019-6924-7). Chilton.
Pavelich, Michael J., jt. auth. see Abraham, Michael R.
Pavese, C. La Lune. Thompson, A. D., ed. 208p. 1980. 15.00x (ISBN 0-7190-0771-2, Pub. by Manchester U Pr England). State Mutual Bk.
Pavey, Peter. I'm Taggarty Toad. LC 80-16696. (Illus.). 32p. (ps-2). 9.95 (ISBN 0-87888-172-7). Bradbury Pr.
Pavey, Peter, illus. One Dragon's Dream. LC 79-12008. (Illus.). (ps-2). 1979. 8.95 (ISBN 0-87888-148-4). Bradbury Pr.

Pavithran, A. K. Bangladesh: Principles & Perspectives. LC 70-183008. viii, 109p. 1971. pap. text ed. 6.25x (ISBN 0-912004-02-9). W W Gaunt.
Pavitrananda, Swami. Modern Man in Search of Religion. pap. 1.00 o.s.i. (ISBN 0-87481-060-4). Vedanta Pr.
Pavitt & Worboye. Science Technology & the Modern Industrial State. (Sicon Bks.). 1977. pap. 3.95 (ISBN 0-408-71299-6). Butterworths.
Pavitt, Kate, jt. auth. see Pavitt, William T.
Pavitt, Keith. Technical Innovation & British Economic Performance. 353p. 1981. text ed. 50.00x (ISBN 0-333-26225-5, Pub. by Macmillan, England). Humanities.
Pavitt, William T. & Pavitt, Kate. Book of Talismans, Amulets & Zodiacal Gems. LC 72-157497. (Tower Bks). (Illus.). 1971. Repr. of 1914 ed. 26.00 (ISBN 0-8103-3901-3). Gale.
Pavlidis, George & Miles, Timothy R. Dyslexia Research & Its Applications to Education. 264p. 1981. 29.75 (ISBN 0-471-27841-6, Pub. by Wiley Interscience). Wiley.
Pavlidis, Theo. Computer Graphics & Pictorial Information Processing. (Illus.). 1981. text ed. price not set (ISBN 0-914894-65-X). Computer Sci.
Pavlik, Zdenek V. Lotto-Keno Supersystems: Winning Combinations & Systems for Lotto 6/40 & Keno Players. (Illus.). 80p. 1980. 6.00 (ISBN 0-682-49616-2). Exposition.
Pavlos, Andrew J. Social Psychology & the Study of Deviant Behavior. LC 78-65426. 1978. pap. text ed. 12.00 (ISBN 0-8191-0664-X). U Pr of Amer.
Pavlov, A. Pamiatniki Drevnerrusskago Kanonicheskago Prava. LC 80-2366. (Russkaya Istorischeskaya Biblioteka: Vol. 6). 76.00 (ISBN 0-404-18912-1). AMS Pr.
Pavlov, Ivan P. Conditioned Reflexes: An Investigation of the Physiological Activity of the Cerebral Cortex. Anrep, G. V., ed. 1927. pap. text ed. 4.50 (ISBN 0-486-60614-7). Dover.
Pavlova, Karolina. A Double Life. Monter, Barbara H., tr. from Russian. 1978. 12.00 (ISBN 0-88233-223-6); pap. 3.95 o.p. (ISBN 0-88233-224-4). Ardis Pubs.
Pavlovich, Natalie. Nursing Research: A Learning Guide. LC 77-22518. 1978. pap. text ed. 9.50 (ISBN 0-8016-3763-5). Mosby.
Pavlovich, Natalie, jt. auth. see Krampitz, Sydney D.
Pavlovsky, Michel N. Chinese-Russian Relations. Krader, Ruth, tr. from Fr. LC 79-5209. (Illus.). 194p. 1981. Repr. of 1949 ed. 19.00 (ISBN 0-8305-0088-X). Hyperion Conn.
Pavon, jt. auth. see Francisco, Garcia.
Pawelczynska, Anna. Values & Violence in Auschwitz: A Sociological Analysis. 1979. 12.95 (ISBN 0-520-03210-1); pap. 4.95 (ISBN 0-520-04242-5, CAL-479). U of Cal Pr.
Pawlak, Elizabeth A, & Hoag. Essentials of Periodontics. 2nd ed. LC 80-13361. (Illus.). 1980. pap. text ed. 13.95 (ISBN 0-8016-3764-3). Mosby.
Pawley, Bernard. Rome & Canterbury: From Henry VIII to the 1970's with an American Epilogue by Arthur A. Vogel. 1975. 13.50 (ISBN 0-8164-1178-6). Crossroad NY.
Pawlick, Thomas. Exploring Journalism Careers. (Career in Depth Ser.). (Illus.). 1981. lib. bdg. 5.97 (ISBN 0-8239-0515-2). Rosen Pr.
Pawlicki, T. How to Build a Flying Saucer: And Other Proposals in Specultive Engineering. 1980. pap. 6.95 (ISBN 0-13-402461-3). P-H.
Pawlik, Peter S., jt. auth. see Reismann, Herbert.
Pawlikowski, John T. What Are They Saying About Christian-Jewish Relations? LC 79-56135. 144p. (Orig.). 1980. pap. 2.95 (ISBN 0-8091-2239-1). Paulist Pr.
Pawlowski, J. Vehicle Body Engineering. Tidbury, Guy, tr. (Illus.). 1970. 28.00x o.p. (ISBN 0-8464-0952-6). Beekman Pubs.
Pawson, Eric. The Early Industrial Revolution. 1979. 29.95 o.p. (ISBN 0-7134-1625-4, Pub. by Batsford England); pap. 16.95 o.p. (ISBN 0-7134-1626-2). David & Charles.
Pawson, Ivan G. Physical Anthropology: Human Evolution. LC 77-2412. (Self-Teaching Guides). 1977. pap. text ed. 4.95 o.p. (ISBN 0-471-07280-7). Wiley.
Pawson, John R. Delaware Valley Rails. (Illus.). 1979. pap. 11.50 (ISBN 0-9602080-0-3). Pawson.
Pax, Noel. Simply Christmas. (Illus.). 72p. (Orig.). 1980. pap. 3.95 (ISBN 0-8027-7168-8); 5.95 (ISBN 0-8027-0672-X). Walker & Co.
Paxman, John M., ed. The World Population Crisis: Policy Implications & the Role of Law: Proceedings of the American Society of International Law Regional Meeting & the John Bassett Moore Society of International Law Symposium. LC 80-19753. vi, 179p. 1980. Repr. of 1971 ed. lib. bdg. 22.50x (ISBN 0-313-22619-9, PAWO). Greenwood.
Paxson, Ruth. Rios De Agua Viva. 1979. pap. 1.60 (ISBN 0-311-46065-8). Casa Bautista.
--Rivers of Living Water. pap. 1.50 (ISBN 0-8024-7367-9). Moody.
Paxson, William. The Business Writing Handbook. 288p. (Orig.). 1981. pap. 3.95 (ISBN 0-553-14344-1). Bantam.
Paxton, J. M., ed. Manual of Civil Engineering Plant & Equipment. 2nd ed. (Illus.). 1971. 123.00x (ISBN 0-85334-500-7). Intl Ideas.
Paxton, John & Fairfield, Sheila. Calendar of Creative Man. (Illus.). 544p. 1980. 27.50 (ISBN 0-87196-470-8). Facts on File.
Paxton, John, ed. Everyman's Dictionary of Abbreviations. rev. ed. 408p. 1981. 20.00x (ISBN 0-8476-6973-4). Rowman.
--Statesman's Year-Book World Gazetteer. 2nd ed. (Illus.). 800p. 1980. 25.00x (ISBN 0-312-76126-0). St. Martin.
--Statesman's Year Book, 1980-81. 117th ed. 1700p. 1980. 30.00x (ISBN 0-312-76093-0). St Martin.
Paxton, John G., ed. Civil War Letters of General Frank "Bull" Paxton: A Lieutenant of Lee & Jackson. LC 78-68427. 1978. 8.50 (ISBN 0-912172-23-1). Hill Jr Coll.
Pay, Don. Thunder from Heaven: The Story of the 17th Airborne Division in WW II. LC 80-69273. (Airborne Ser.: No. 4). (Illus.). 179p. 1980. Repr. 22.50 (ISBN 0-89839-037-0). Battery Pr.
Payack, Paul. Solstice III. (Illus.). 1977. pap. 1.00 o.p. (ISBN 0-686-20639-8). Samisdat.
Payack, Peter. Rainbow Bridges. 1978. pap. 1.00x (ISBN 0-686-07205-7). Samisdat.
Payan, Irene. Live: Poetry for Students, Awakening Students to Their Potential for Self-Expression. 1980. 2.95 (ISBN 0-932212-20-4). Avery Color.
Payer, Cheryl. The Debt Trap: The IMF & the Third World. LC 74-24794. 256p. 1975. 11.50 o.p. (ISBN 0-85345-375-6, CL3756); pap. 5.00 (ISBN 0-85345-376-4, PB3764). Monthly Rev.
Payer, Cheryl, ed. Commodity Trade of the Third World. LC 75-23282. 1976. 34.95 (ISBN 0-470-67282-X). Halsted Pr.
Payer, Sue. Second Body. 1979. pap. 1.95 (ISBN 0-505-51381-1). Tower Bks.
Payes, Rachel C. Love's Escapade. LC 80-85108. (Seven Sisters Regency Romance Ser.: No. 5). 192p. (Orig.). 1981. pap. 1.95 (ISBN 0-87216-834-4). Playboy Pbks.
--Love's Promenade. LC 80-83568. (Seven Sisters Regency Romance Ser.: No. 3). 192p. (Orig.). 1981. pap. 1.95 (ISBN 0-87216-805-0). Playboy Pbks.
--Love's Renegade. LC 80-83594. (Seven Sisters Regency Romance Ser.: No. 2). 192p. (Orig.). 1981. pap. text ed. 1.95 (ISBN 0-87216-809-3). Playboy Pbks.
--Love's Serenade. LC 80-84374. (A Seven Sisters Regency Romance Ser.). 192p. 1981. pap. 1.95 (ISBN 0-87216-817-4). Playboy Pbks.
--The Sapphire Legacy. large type ed. pap. 1.25 o.p. (ISBN 0-425-03185-3). Berkley Pub.
--Satan's Mistress. LC 80-81632. 352p. (Orig.). 1981. pap. 2.75 (ISBN 0-87216-726-7). Playboy Pbks.
Payler, Frederick. Law Courts, Lawyers & Litigants. xiv, 242p. 1980. Repr. of 1926 ed. lib. bdg. 24.00x (ISBN 0-8377-1006-5). Rothman.
Payne, Alma S., jt. auth. see Callahan, Dorothy.
Payne, Anthony. Schoenberg. (Oxford Studies of Composers). 1968. pap. 7.95x (ISBN 0-19-314116-7). Oxford U Pr.
--Social Behaviour in Vertebrates. (Scholarship Series in Biology). 1976. text ed. 12.95x (ISBN 0-435-61670-6). Heinemann Ed.
Payne, Barbara, jt. auth. see Peterson, James A.
Payne, Bruce L., jt. auth. see Fleishman, Joel L.
Payne, C. J. & White, K. J., eds. Caring for Deprived Children: International Case Studies of Residential Setting. 1979. 19.95 (ISBN 0-312-12166-0). St Martin.
Payne, Charles A. & Falls, William R. Modern Physical Science: A Student Study Guide. 1976. pap. text ed. 4.95 (ISBN 0-8403-1364-0). Kendall-Hunt.
Payne, Charlotte. The Glitterati. Date not set. pap. 2.75 (ISBN 0-440-13067-0). Dell.
Payne, Christina & Cutts, Paddy. Pedigree Cats & Kittens: How to Choose & Care for Them. (Illus.). 64p. 1981. pap. 5.95 (ISBN 0-7134-3915-7, Pub. by Batsford England). David & Charles.
Payne, Clive. Time to Be Myself. 4.50 o.p. (ISBN 0-8062-1203-9). Carlton.
Payne, Darwin R. A Christmas Carol. LC 80-18827. 128p. 1981. pap. price not set (ISBN 0-8093-0999-8). S Ill U Pr.
--The Scenographic Imagination. (Illus.). 1981. price not set (ISBN 0-8093-1009-0); pap. price not set (ISBN 0-8093-1010-4). S Ill U Pr.
Payne, David. The Kingdoms of the Lord. 304p. (Orig.). 1981. pap. 9.95 (ISBN 0-8028-1856-0). Eerdmans. Postponed.
Payne, David A., ed. Specification & Measurement of Learning Outcomes. (Education & Psychology Ser). (Orig.). 1960. pap. 10.50 (ISBN 0-471-00413-8). Wiley.
Payne, Dorris B. Psychiatric-Mental Health Nursing. 2nd. ed. Clunn, Patricia A., ed. LC 77-71852. (Nursing Outline Ser.). 1977. pap. 8.50 spiral bdg. (ISBN 0-87488-379-2). Med Exam.
Payne, E. F., tr. see Schopenhauer, Arthur.
Payne, E. M. F., jt. auth. see Godman, A.
Payne, Elizabeth. The Pharaohs of Ancient Egypt. LC 80-21392. (Landmark Bks.). (Illus.). 192p. (gr. 5-9). 1981. pap. 2.95 (ISBN 0-394-84699-0). Random.
Payne, Emmy. Katy No-Pocket. (gr. 1-3). 1969. reinforced bdg. 9.95 (ISBN 0-395-17104-0). HM.
Payne, Ernest A. The Saktas, an Introductory & Comparative Study: Calcutta & London, Nineteen Thirty-Three. LC 78-74270. (Oriental Religions Ser.: Vol. 8). (Illus.). 167p. 1980. lib. bdg. 22.00 (ISBN 0-8240-3905-X). Garland Pub.
Payne, F. Anne. Chaucer & Menippean Satire. LC 79-5412. 320p. 1981. 22.50 (ISBN 0-299-08170-2). U of Wis Pr.
Payne, Geoff, et al. Sociology & Social Research. (International Library of Sociology). 272p. 1981. price not set (ISBN 0-7100-0626-8). Routledge & Kegan.
Payne, George. Solar System Astronomy. 1980. text ed. 7.95 wire coil bdg. (ISBN 0-88252-103-9). Paladin Hse.
Payne, Gordon. Energy Managers' Handbook. 2nd ed. 1980. text ed. 25.00 (ISBN 0-86103-032-X); pap. text ed. 19.50 (ISBN 0-86103-033-8). Butterworths.
Payne, H. F. Organic Coating Technology, 2 Vols. LC 54-5971. 1954-61. Vol. 1. 45.00 (ISBN 0-471-67286-6); Vol. 2. 49.95 (ISBN 0-471-67353-6, Pub by Wiley-Interscience). Wiley.
Payne, Harry C., ed. Studies in Eighteenth Century Culture, Vol. 10. 384p. 1981. 25.00 (ISBN 0-299-08170-2). U of Wis Pr.
Payne, Howard & Payne, Rosemary. Athletics: Throwing. (Pelham Pictorial Sports Instruction Ser.). (Illus.). 1979. 9.95 (ISBN 0-7207-0925-3). Transatlantic.
Payne, J. Barton. New Perspectives on the Old Testament. Date not set. 14.95 (ISBN 0-88469-134-9). BMH Bks.
--Theology of the Older Testament. 1962. kivar 9.95 (ISBN 0-310-30721-X). Zondervan.
Payne, J. P. & Hill, D. W. Oxygen Measurement in Biology & Medicine. 1975. 64.95 (ISBN 0-407-00020-8). Butterworths.
Payne, J. S., et al. Head Start, a Tragicomedy with Epilogue. LC 72-10924. (Illus.). 1973. 22.95 (ISBN 0-87705-099-6); pap. 9.95 (ISBN 0-87705-098-8). Human Sci Pr.
Payne, J. W. Microorganisms & Nitrogen Sources Transport & Utilization of Amino Acids Peptides, Proteins & Related Subjects. LC 79-42900. 800p. 1980. 135.00 (ISBN 0-471-27697-9). Wiley.
Payne, Jack. The Complete New Encyclopedia of Little-Known, Highly Profitable Business Opportunities. rev. ed. LC 74-75380. 256p. 1980. Repr. of 1971 ed. 10.95 (ISBN 0-8119-0345-1). Fell.
--How to Make a Fortune in Finders' Fees. rev. ed. 1981. 10.95 (ISBN 0-8119-0346-X). Fell.
Payne, James F. & Kennedy, Michael L. Laboratory Studies in Zoology. (Illus.). 165p. 1980. lab. manual 8.95 (ISBN 0-89459-073-1). Hunter NC.
Payne, James S. & Patton, James R. Mental Retardation. (Special Education Ser.). (Illus.). 480p. 1981. text ed. 24.95 (ISBN 0-675-08027-4); write for info. Merrill.
Payne, James S., jt. auth. see Smith, James E., Jr.
Payne, James S., jt. ed. see Kauffman, James M.
Payne, James S., et al. Education & Rehabilitation Techniques. LC 74-6176. 322p. 1974. text ed. 24.95 (ISBN 0-87705-163-1); pap. text ed. 9.95 (ISBN 0-87705-225-5). Human Sci Pr.
--Strategies for Teaching the Mentally Retarded. 2nd ed. (Special Education Ser.). 368p. 1981. text ed. 17.95 (ISBN 0-675-08067-3). Merrill.
--Living in the Classroom: The Currency-Based Token Economy. LC 75-19004. 1976. text ed. 19.95 (ISBN 0-87705-276-X); pap. text ed. 8.95 (ISBN 0-87705-283-2). Human Sci Pr.
Payne, Joan B. Raven & Other Fairy Tales. LC 72-81379. (Illus.). (gr. k-3). 1969. PLB 3.72 o.s.i. (ISBN 0-8038-6310-1). Hastings.
Payne, John W., jt. ed. see Carroll, J. S.
Payne, Ladell. Black Novelists & the Southern Literary Tradition. LC 80-21747. 144p. 1981. 11.00x (ISBN 0-8203-0536-7). U of Ga Pr.
Payne, Leanne. The Healing Presence. 176p. 1981. pap. 4.95 (ISBN 0-89107-215-2). Good News.
Payne, Les, et al. The Life & Death of the SLA. 1976. pap. 1.95 o.p. (ISBN 0-345-25449-X). Ballantine.
Payne, Lucille V. Lively Art of Writing. pap. 1.95 (ISBN 0-451-61896-3, MJ1896, Ment). NAL.
Payne, Michael. Irony in Shakespeare's Roman Plays. (Salzburg Studies in English Literature, Elizabethan & Renaissance Studies: No. 19). 224p. 1976. pap. text ed. 25.00x (ISBN 0-391-01495-1). Humanities.
Payne, Peter L. The Early Scottish Limited Companies, Eighteen Fifty-Six to Eighteen Ninety-Five. 144p. 1981. 22.00x (Pub. by Scottish Academic Pr Scotland). Columbia U Pr.
Payne, R. The Apocalypse of Our Time & Other Writings by Vasily Razanov. 1977. text ed. 10.95 (ISBN 0-03-028911-4, HoltC). HR&W.
Payne, R., jt. auth. see Cooper, C. L.
Payne, R. L., jt. auth. see Pugh, Derek S.
Payne, Richard. How to Get a Better Job Quicker. 1975. pap. 1.75 o.p. (ISBN 0-451-07327-4, E7327, Sig). NAL.
--Study Guide to Accompany Unfinished Democracy. 1981. pap. 5.95x (ISBN 0-673-15487-4). Scott F.
Payne, Robert. The Holy Fire. LC 79-27594. 328p. 1980. pap. 8.95 (ISBN 0-913836-61-3). St Vladimirs.
--Massacre. (Illus.). 192p. 1973. 5.95 o.s.i. (ISBN 0-02-595240-4). Macmillan.
Payne, Rosemary, jt. auth. see Payne, Howard.
Payne, Roy, jt. auth. see Cooper, Cary L.
Payne, Samuel B., Jr. The Soviet Union & SALT. 224p. 1980. text ed. 19.95x (ISBN 0-262-16077-3). MIT Pr.
Payne, Selma & Payne, W. J. Cooking with Exotic Fruit. (Illus.). 144p. 1980. 19.95 (ISBN 0-7134-1192-9, Pub. by Batsford England). David & Charles.
Payne, Stanley G. A History of Spain & Portugal, 2 vols. LC 72-7992. (Illus.). 802p. 1973. text ed. 25.00 ea.; Vol. 1. (ISBN 0-299-06270-8); Vol. 2. (ISBN 0-299-06880-3); pap. text ed. 7.95 ea.; Vol. 1. (ISBN 0-299-06274-0); Vol. 2. (ISBN 0-299-06284-8). U of Wis Pr.
Payne, Stanley L. The Art of Asking Questions. 1980 ed. LC 80-7824. 264p. 1980. 22.50x (ISBN 0-691-08104-2); pap. 6.95 (ISBN 0-691-02367-0). Princeton U Pr.
Payne, Viola. Three Angels Over Rancho Grande. LC 75-32711. (Destiny Ser.). 1976. pap. 4.95 (ISBN 0-8163-0218-9, 20407-3). Pacific Pr Pub Assn.
Payne, W. J., jt. auth. see Payne, Selma.
Payne, W. J., jt. auth. see Williamson, G.
Payne, William H. Rousseau's Emile. 363p. 1980. Repr. of 1911 ed. lib. bdg. 35.00 (ISBN 0-89987-659-5). Darby Bks.
Payne-Gallwey, Ralph. The Projectile-Throwing Engines of the Ancients & Turkish & Other Oriental Bows of Mediaeval & Later Times. (Illus.). 70p. 1973. Repr. of 1907 ed. 12.50x o.p. (ISBN 0-87471-144-4). Rowman.
Paynell, Thomas, tr. see Erasmus, Desiderius.
Payne Smith, J., ed. see Smith, R. Payne.
Paynter, David H. Must Our Schools Die? A Plan to Meet the Current Crisis in Education. LC 80-23367. (Orig.). 1981. pap. 6.95 (ISBN 0-930014-41-3). Multnomah.
Payson, Harold H. Instant Boats. LC 78-64738. (Illus.). 1979. 15.00 (ISBN 0-87742-110-2). Intl Marine.
Payton, G., jt. ed. see Harber, K.
Payton, Geoffrey & Payton, Mary. Observer's Book of Pottery & Porcelain. (Observer Bks.). (Illus.). 1977. 2.95 (ISBN 0-684-15215-0, ScribT). Scribner.
Payton, Geoffrey, jt. auth. see Payton, Mary.
Payton, Joseph. Air Taxi Charter & Rental Directory of North America & Connection Points of Commuter Airlines with Other Scheduled Air Carriers. LC 75-648387. 100p. 1980. pap. 15.00 perfect bdg (ISBN 0-9603908-0-4). Aircraft Chart & Rent.
Payton, Mary & Payton, Geoffrey. The Observer's Book of Glass. (Illus.). 1977. 2.95 (ISBN 0-684-14940-0, ScribT). Scribner.
Payton, Mary, jt. auth. see Payton, Geoffrey.
Paz, D. G. The Politics of Working-Class Education in Britain, 1830-1850. 199p. 1981. lib. bdg. 30.00x (ISBN 0-87023-326-2). U of Mass Pr.
Paz, Octavio. Configurations. LC 78-145932. (Span. & Eng.). 1971. pap. 4.95 (ISBN 0-8112-0150-3, NDP303). New Directions.
--A Draft of Shadows & Other Poems. Weinberger, Eliot, tr. from Sp. LC 79-15588. 1979. 11.95 (ISBN 0-8112-0737-4); pap. 4.95 (ISBN 0-8112-0738-2, NDP489). New Directions.
--Early Poems 1935-1955. Rukeyser, Muriel, et al, trs. from Span. LC 72-93981. (Poetry Ser.). Orig. Title: Selected Poems. 160p. 1973. 7.95x (ISBN 0-253-31867-X). Ind U Pr.
Peabody, A. L., tr. see Karasik, V. M., et al.
Peabody, Albert, tr. see Pokrovskaya, Vera N.
Peabody, Albert, tr. see Traynis, V. V.
Peabody, Albert L., tr. see Turchaninov, S. P.
Peabody, James B., ed. see Adams, John.

Peabody Museum of Archaeology & Ethnology. Author & Subject Catalogues of the Library of the Peabody Museum of Archaeology & Ethnology: Fourth Supplement, 7 vols. (Library Catalogs Bib Guides). 1979. lib. bdg. 980.00 set (ISBN 0-8161-0253-8). G K Hall.

Peace, Adrian J. Choice, Class & Conflict: A Study of Southern Nigerian Factory Workers. LC 79-12658. (Harvester Studies in African Political Economy.). 1979. text ed. 38.75x (ISBN 0-391-01027-1). Humanities.

Peace Convention - Washington D.C. - Feb 1861. Report of the Debates: Proceedings. Chittenden, L. E., ed. (Law Politics & History Ser). 1971. Repr. of 1864 ed. lib. bdg. 59.50 (ISBN 0-306-70190-1). Da Capo.

Peace, Richard. Aprendamos a Amar a Dios. Roberts, Grace S., tr. from Eng. LC 75-29951. (Orig., Span.). 1975. pap. 1.50 (ISBN 0-89922-056-8). Edit Caribe.

--Aprendamos a Amar a Otros. Roberts, Grace S., tr. from Eng. LC 75-29980. 71p. (Orig., Span.). 1975. pap. 1.50 (ISBN 0-89922-057-6). Edit Caribe.

--Aprendamos a Amarnos a Nosotros Mismos. Roberts, Grace S., tr. from Eng. LC 75-29987. 69p. (Orig., Span.). 1975. pap. 1.50 (ISBN 0-89922-058-4). Edit Caribe.

--Learning to Love, 3 vols. Incl. Vol. 1. Learning to Love God. pap. 1.95 (ISBN 0-310-30751-1); Vol. 2. Learning to Love Ourselves. pap. 1.25 (ISBN 0-310-30761-9); Vol. 3. Learning to Love People. pap. 1.95 (ISBN 0-310-30771-6). Set. pap. 4.90 (ISBN 0-310-30788-0). Zondervan.

Peace, Richard A. Dostoyevsky. LC 77-116838. 1971. 48.00 (ISBN 0-521-07911-X); text ed. 10.95x (ISBN 0-521-09994-3). Cambridge U Pr.

Peacey, J. G. & Davenport, W. G. The Iron Blast Furnace: Theory & Practice. 1979. text ed. 41.00 (ISBN 0-08-023218-3); pap. text ed. 16.25 (ISBN 0-08-023258-2). Pergamon.

Peach. Pilgrim Fathers. (Ladybird Ser.). 1972. 1.49 (ISBN 0-87508-855-4). Chr Lit.

Peach, A. W., ed. see Paine, Thomas.

Peach, Bernard, ed. see Hutcheson, Francis.

Peach, David A. & Livernash, E. Robert. Grievance Initiation & Resolution: A Study in Steel. 1975. text ed. 8.50 (ISBN 0-87584-112-0). Harvard U Pr.

Peach, G. C. Urban Social Segregation. LC 74-80434. (Illus.). 450p. 1976. text ed. 23.00x (ISBN 0-582-48088-4). Longman.

Peach, James T., jt. auth. see Jannuzi, F. Tomasson.

Peacher, Georgiana. How to Improve Your Speaking Voice. LC 66-10277. 1966. 9.95 (ISBN 0-8119-0090-8). Fell.

Peachey, Mark. Facing Terminal-Illness. 72p. 1981. pap. 2.25 (ISBN 0-8361-1948-7). Herald Pr.

Peachment, Brian. An Aeroplane or a Grave. 1976. pap. 1.55 (ISBN 0-08-017841-3). Pergamon.

--Devil's Island. 1976. pap. 1.55 (ISBN 0-08-017613-5). Pergamon.

--Down Among the Dead Men. 1976. pap. 1.55 (ISBN 0-08-017615-1). Pergamon.

--Educational Drama. (Illus.). 232p. 1976. pap. 13.95x (ISBN 0-7121-0552-2, Pub. by Macdonald & Evans England). Intl Ideas.

--Three Fighters for Freedom. pap. 1.55 (ISBN 0-08-017617-8). Pergamon.

Peacock, A. D. & Uhlan, Edward. To Save a Boy: The Story of Boys Home, North Carolina. LC 75-171711. 1971. 6.00 o.p. (ISBN 0-682-47313-8). Exposition.

Peacock, A. T., jt. auth. see Rowley, C. K.

Peacock, Alan, jt. auth. see Edey, Harold C.

Peacock, Alan T. & Wiseman, Jack. The Growth of Public Expenditure in the United Kingdom. (University of York Studies in Economics). 1967. pap. text ed. 7.95x o.p. (ISBN 0-04-336011-4). Allen Unwin.

Peacock, Carol. Hand-Me-Down-Dreams. LC 80-26048. 192p. 1981. 12.95x (ISBN 0-8052-3761-5); pap. 8.95 (ISBN 0-8052-0678-7). Schocken.

Peacock, D., jt. auth. see Tribe, M. A.

Peacock, D. G., jt. ed. see Richardson, J. R.

Peacock, Donald. People, Peregrines, & Arctic Pipelines: The Critical Battle to Build Canada's Northern Gas Pipelines. LC 77-375197. (Illus.). 224p. 1977. pap. 5.95 (ISBN 0-295-95722-0). U of Wash Pr.

Peacock, Frederick & Gaston, Thomas. Automotive Engine Repair & Overhaul. (Illus.). 480p. 1980. text ed. 17.95 (ISBN 0-8359-0276-5). Reston.

Peacock, H. L. British History, Seventeen Fourteen - Present Day. 1968. pap. text ed. 10.50x o.p. (ISBN 0-435-31705-9). Heinemann Ed.

--A History of Modern Britain 1815-1975. 3rd ed. 1976. pap. text ed. 10.50x o.p. (ISBN 0-435-31710-5). Heinemann Ed.

Peacock, J. & Kirsch, A. Human Direction: An Evolutionary Approach to Social & Cultural Anthropology. 3rd ed. 1980. pap. 11.95 (ISBN 0-13-444851-0). P-H.

Peacock, J. B., jt. auth. see Hastings, N. A.

Peacock, James L. Consciousness & Change: Symbolic Anthropology in Evolutionary Perspective. LC 75-1349. 264p. 1975. 20.95 (ISBN 0-470-67452-0). Halsted Pr.

--Muslim Puritans: Reformist Psychology in Southeast Asian Islam. LC 76-55571. 1978. 20.00x (ISBN 0-520-03403-1). U of Cal Pr.

--Purifying the Faith: The Muhammadijah Movement in Indonesian Islam. LC 78-61992. 1978. 6.95 (ISBN 0-8053-7824-3). Benjamin-Cummings.

Peacock, Julia E. & Tomar, Russell H. Manual of Laboratory Immunology. LC 80-16716. (Illus.). 228p. 1980. pap. 17.00 (ISBN 0-8121-0719-5). Lea & Febiger.

Peacock, Kenneth. Twenty Ethnic Songs from Western Canada. (Illus.). 1966. pap. 5.00 (ISBN 0-660-02053-X, 56524-6, Pub. by Natl Mus Canada). U of Chicago Pr.

Peacock, R. see Kemmit, R.

Peacock, Ronald. The Art of Drama. LC 73-3026. 263p. 1974. Repr. of 1957 ed. lib. bdg. 18.75x (ISBN 0-8371-6825-2, PEAD). Greenwood.

Peacock, Thomas L. The Plays of Thomas Love Peacock. 157p. 1980. Repr. of 1910 ed. lib. bdg. 25.00 (ISBN 0-8495-4374-6). Arden Lib.

Peacock, William. English Verse, 5 vols. Incl. Vol. 1. Early Lyrics to Shakespeare. 6.95 (ISBN 0-19-250308-1); Vol. 2. Campion to the Ballads. 7.95 (ISBN 0-19-250309-X); Vol. 3. Dryden to Wordsworth. 7.95 (ISBN 0-19-250310-3); Vol. 4. Scott to E. B. Browning. 10.95 (ISBN 0-19-250311-1); Vol. 5. Longfellow to Rupert Brooke. 7.95 (ISBN 0-19-250312-X). (World's Classics Ser). Oxford U Pr.

Peacocke, A. R. Science & the Christian Experiment. 224p. 1971. 13.00x (ISBN 0-19-213953-3); pap. 6.95x (ISBN 0-19-213956-8). Oxford U Pr.

--The Sciences & Theology in the Twentiety Century. (Oxford International Symposia). 320p. 1981. price not set (ISBN 0-85362-188-8). Routledge & Kegan.

Peak, Carl E. The Decorative Touch: How to Decorate, Glaze, & Fire Your Pots. (Creative Handicrafts Ser.). (Illus.). 160p. 1981. 17.95 (ISBN 0-13-198085-8, Spec); pap. 8.95 (ISBN 0-13-198077-7). P-H.

Peak, Ellen, jt. auth. see Peak, Hugh S.

Peak, Hugh S. & Peak, Ellen. Supermarket Merchandising & Management. LC 76-17604. (Illus.). 1977. ref. ed. 15.95 (ISBN 0-13-876037-3). P-H.

Peake, Cyrus H. Nationalism & Education in Modern China. LC 72-80580. 1970. Repr. of 1932 ed. 14.50 (ISBN 0-86527-138-0). Fertig.

Peake, Katy. The Indian Heart of Carrie Hodges. (Illus.). 128p. (gr. 7 up). 1972. PLB 4.95 o.p. (ISBN 0-670-39788-1). Viking Pr.

Peake, Lilian. Gregg Barratt's Woman. (Harlequin Presents Ser.). 192p. 1981. pap. 1.50 (ISBN 0-373-10424-3, Pub. by Harlequin). PB.

--Promise at Midnight. (Harlequin Romances Ser.). 192p. 1981. pap. 1.25 (ISBN 0-373-02404-5, Pub. by Harlequin). PB.

--A Ring for a Fortune. (Harlequin Presents Ser.). 192p. 1980. pap. 1.50 (ISBN 0-373-10384-0, Pub. by Harlequin). PB.

--A Secret Affair. (Harlequin Presents Ser.). 192p. (Orig.). 1981. pap. 1.50 (ISBN 0-373-10407-3, Pub. by Harlequin). PB.

Peake, Mervin. A Book of Nonsense. LC 75-4108. 1975. 7.95 (ISBN 0-7206-0412-5). Dufour.

Peake, Mervyn. Gormenghast. 1976. pap. 2.50 (ISBN 0-345-27699-X). Ballantine.

--Peake's Progress: Selected Writings & Drawings of Mervyn Peake. Gilmore, Maeve, ed. LC 80-83054. (Illus.). 576p. 1981. 25.00 (ISBN 0-87951-121-4). Overlook Pr.

Peake, Mervyn, illus. Ride a Cock-Horse. LC 75-509235. (Illus.). (ps-2). 1979. 7.95 (ISBN 0-7011-5015-7, Pub. by Chatto Bodley Jonathan); pap. 2.95 (ISBN 0-7011-1945-4, Pub. by Chatto Bodley Jonathan). Merrimack Bk Serv.

Peake, Thomas, jt. auth. see Gilbert, Sir Gefrey.

Peaker, G. F. The Plowden Children Four Years Later. (General Ser.). 50p. 1971. pap. text ed. 7.00x (ISBN 0-901225-80-0, NFER). Humanities.

Peaker, Gilbert F. An Empirical Study of Education in Twenty-One Countries: A Technical Report. LC 75-30533. (International Studies in Evaluation Ser: No. 8). 232p. 1976. 12.95 o.p. (ISBN 0-470-67456-3). Halsted Pr.

Peaker, M. & Linzell, J. L. Salt Glands in Birds & Reptiles. LC 74-12966. (Physiological Society Monographs: No. 32). (Illus.). 296p. 1975. 53.50 (ISBN 0-521-20629-4). Cambridge U Pr.

Peale, Norman V. Bible Stories. pap. 2.25 (ISBN 0-89129-049-4). Jove Pubns.

--Enthusiasm Makes the Difference. LC 67-26078. 1967. 8.95 o.p. (ISBN 0-13-283200-3). P-H.

--The New Art of Living. 160p. 1977. pap. 2.25 (ISBN 0-449-23938-1, Crest). Fawcett.

--Norman Vincent Peale's Treasury of Joy & Enthusiasm. 1981. 9.95 (ISBN 0-8007-1180-7). Revell.

--The Positive Power of Jesus Christ. 8.95 (ISBN 0-8423-4874-3). Tyndale.

--Power of Positive Thinking. 1954. 7.95 (ISBN 0-13-686402-3). P-H.

--Sin, Sex & Self-Control. 1978. pap. 2.25 (ISBN 0-449-23921-7, Crest). Fawcett.

--The Tough-Minded Optimist. 1979. pap. 2.25 (ISBN 0-449-24247-1, Crest). Fawcett.

--You Can If You Think You Can. 1979. pap. 2.25 (ISBN 0-8007-8381-6). Revell.

Peale, Mrs. Norman V. Adventures of Being a Wife. 1977. pap. 1.95 o.p. (ISBN 0-449-23439-8, Crest). Fawcett.

Peano, Giuseppe. Selected Works of Giuseppe Peano. Kennedy, Hubert C., tr. LC 70-185719. 272p. 1973. 15.00x o.p. (ISBN 0-8020-5267-3). U of Toronto Pr.

Pear, Joseph & Martin, Gary. Behavior Modification: What Is It & How to Do It. LC 77-10849. (Illus.). 1978. pap. text ed. 14.95 (ISBN 0-13-066787-0). P-H.

Pearce, Brian, tr. see Bettelheim, Charles.

Pearce, Brian, tr. see Claudin-Urondo, Carmen.

Pearce, Brian, tr. see Emmanuel, Arghiri.

Pearce, Brian, tr. see Valentinov, Nikolay.

Pearce, Charles E. Sims Reeves, Fifty Years of Music in England. (Music Reprint Ser.). 1980. Repr. of 1924 ed. lib. bdg. 22.50 (ISBN 0-306-76007-X). Da Capo.

Pearce, Clifford. The Machinery of Change in Local Government: 1888-1974. (Institute of Local Government Studies). 240p. 1980. text ed. 37.50x (ISBN 0-04-352091-X, 2541). Allen Unwin.

Pearce, D. W., et al. Decision Making for Energy Futures: A Case Study on the Windscale Inquiry into the Reprocessing of Spent Oxide Fuels. 1979. text ed. 26.00x (ISBN 0-333-27438-5). Humanities.

Pearce, David & Nash, Christopher. Social Appraisal of Projects: A Text in Cost-Benefit Analysis. 400p. 1981. 22.95 (ISBN 0-470-27137-X). Halsted Pr.

Pearce, David W. Environmental Economics. LC 75-44207. (Modern Economics Ser.). 1976. text ed. 19.95x (ISBN 0-582-44622-8); pap. text ed. 10.95x (ISBN 0-582-44623-6). Longman.

Pearce, Donald, ed. see Pound, Ezra.

Pearce, Evelyn. Anatomy & Physiology for Nurses. new ed. 1975. pap. text ed. 4.95 (ISBN 0-571-04891-9, Pub. by Faber & Faber). Merrimack Bk Serv.

--A General Textbook of Nursing. 19th ed. 1975. text ed. 19.95 o.p. (ISBN 0-571-04855-2, Pub. by Faber & Faber). Merrimack Bk Serv.

Pearce, G. H. The Medical Report & Testimony. 104p. 1980. 35.00x (Pub. by Beaconsfield England). State Mutual Bk.

--The Medical Report & Testimony. (Illus.). 1979. text ed. 17.95x (ISBN 0-04-610012-1). Allen Unwin.

Pearce, George F. The U S Navy in Pensacola: From Sailing Ships to Naval Aviation, Eighteen Twenty-Five to Nineteen Thirty. LC 80-12167. (Illus.). vii, 207p. 1980. 17.00 (ISBN 0-8130-0665-1). U Presses Fla.

--The U. S. Navy in Pensacola: From Sailing Ships to Naval Aviation, Eighteen Twenty-Five to Nineteen Thirty. LC 80-12167. 1980. write for info. (ISBN 0-8130-0665-1). U Presses Fla.

Pearce, I. F., et al, eds. A Model of Output, Employment, Wages & Prices in the UK. LC 75-46134. (Illus.). 1976. 29.95 (ISBN 0-521-21210-3). Cambridge U Pr.

Pearce, J. H., jt. ed. see Smith, H.

Pearce, J. Kenneth & Stenzel, George. Logging & Pulpwood Production. 400p. 1972. 24.95 (ISBN 0-471-06839-X, Pub. by Wiley-Interscience). Wiley.

Pearce, Janice, jt. auth. see Pearce, Wayne.

Pearce, Joseph C. The Bond of Power. 1981. 10.95 (ISBN 0-525-06950-X). Dutton.

Pearce, Mary. Apple Tree, Lean Down. 1977. pap. 2.50 o.p. (ISBN 0-345-25655-7). Ballantine.

--The Land Endures. 252p. 1981. 10.95 (ISBN 0-312-46440-1). St Martin.

Pearce, Philippa. Battle of Bubble & Sqeak. (Illus.). (gr. 2-7). 1979. PLB 7.95 (ISBN 0-233-96986-1). Andre Deutsch.

Pearce, R. P., jt. ed. see Lighthill, J.

Pearce, T. M. New Mexico Place Names: A Geographical Dictionary. LC 64-17808. 1980. pap. 4.95 (ISBN 0-8263-0082-0). U of NM Pr.

Pearce, T. S. T. S. Eliot. LC 69-16155. (Literary Critiques Ser.). (Illus.). 1969. Repr. lib. bdg. 4.95 o.p. (ISBN 0-668-01883-6). Arco.

Pearce, Virginia, jt. auth. see Barnes, Kathleen.

Pearce, W. B., Jr., jt. auth. see Rossiter, Charles M.

Pearce, W. Barnett & Cronen, Vernon E. Communication, Action & Meaning: The Creation of Social Realities. 308p. 1980. 29.95 (ISBN 0-03-057611-3). Praeger.

Pearce, Wayne & Pearce, Janice. Tennis. (Sport Ser). (Illus.). 1971. pap. 4.25 ref. ed. (ISBN 0-13-903435-8). P-H.

Pearcy, Carl M. Some Recent Developments in Operator Theory. LC 78-8754. (Conference Board of the Mathematical Sciences Ser.: No. 36). 1980. Repr. of 1978 ed. 8.00 (ISBN 0-8218-1686-1, CBMS 36). Am Math.

Peardon, Thomas P., ed. see Locke, John.

Peare, Catherine O. John Woolman: Child of Light. LC 54-6990. (gr. 7-9). 6.95 (ISBN 0-8149-0376-2). Vanguard.

Pearl. Cleanness, Patience & Sir Gawain. (Early English Text Society Ser.). 1923. 69.00x (ISBN 0-19-722162-9). Oxford U Pr.

Pearl, Arthur & Riessman, F. New Careers for the Poor. LC 65-14910. 1965. 6.95 o.s.i. (ISBN 0-02-925200-8). Free Pr.

Pearl, David & Gray, Kevin. A Textbook of Social Welfare Law. 240p. 1981. 31.00x (ISBN 0-85664-644-X, Pub. by Croom Helm LTD England). Biblio Dist.

Pearl, Esther E. Deeper Than Shame. 384p. (Orig.). 1980. pap. 2.50 (ISBN 0-515-05533-6). Jove Pubns.

Pearl, Joseph, tr. see Caesar, Julius.

Pearl, Joseph, tr. see Cicero.

Pearl, Leon. Descartes. (World Leaders Ser.: No. 63). 1977. lib. bdg. 10.95 (ISBN 0-8057-7714-8). Twayne.

Pearl, Minnie. Minnie Pearl Cooks. LC 73-104838. (Illus.). 1977. 4.95 o.s.i. (ISBN 0-87695-137-X). Aurora Pubs.

Pearl, Richard M. Colorado Gem Trails & Mineral Guide. rev., 3rd ed. LC 75-132587. (Illus.). 223p. 1972. 12.95 (ISBN 0-8040-0052-2, SB). Swallow.

--Exploring Rocks, Minerals, Fossils in Colorado. LC 64-25339. (Illus.). 215p. 1969. 12.95 (ISBN 0-8040-0105-7, SB). Swallow.

--Gems, Minerals, Crystals & Ores. 1977. pap. 4.95 o.p. (ISBN 0-307-44385-X, Golden Pr). Western Pub.

--Geology. 4th rev. ed. 1975. pap. 4.95 (ISBN 0-06-460160-9, CO 160, Cos). Har-Row.

--Rocks & Minerals. (Orig.). 1969. pap. 2.75 (ISBN 0-06-463260-1, EH 260, EH). Har-Row.

Pearlman & Resnikoff. Leader's Guide to Back to School, Back to Work. 24p. 1973. pap. 3.75 (ISBN 0-686-11451-5). Am Personnel.

Pearlman, et al. Leader's Guide to Assertive Training Procedures for Women. 24p. 1973. pap. 3.75 (ISBN 0-686-11452-3). Am Personnel.

Pearlman, Barbara. Barbara Pearlman's Dance Exercises. LC 76-52009. 1978. 6.95 (ISBN 0-385-12665-4, Dolp). Doubleday.

Pearlman, Daniel & Pearlman, Paula R. Guide to Rapid Revision. 2nd ed. LC 73-20076. 1974. pap. text ed. 2.50 (ISBN 0-672-63300-0). Odyssey Pr.

Pearlman, Gilbert. Young Frankenstein. (Illus.). 160p. 1974. pap. 1.50 o.p. (ISBN 0-345-24268-8). Ballantine.

Pearlman, Jerome T., et al. Psychiatric Problems in Opthalmology. (Illus.). 180p. 1977. 16.75 (ISBN 0-398-03596-2). C C Thomas.

Pearlman, Moshe. In the Footsteps of the Prophets. LC 75-11965. (Illus.). 1975. 19.95 o.p. (ISBN 0-690-00962-3, TYC-T). T Y Crowell.

--The Maccabees. (Illus.). 272p. 1973. 12.95 o.s.i. (ISBN 0-02-595300-1). Macmillan.

Pearlman, Moshe, jt. auth. see Comay, Joan.

Pearlman, Myer. Through the Bible Book by Book, 4 vols. 1935. pap. 1.95 ea.; Vol. 1. (ISBN 0-88243-660-0, 02-0660); Vol. 2. (ISBN 0-88243-661-9, 02-0661); Vol. 3. (ISBN 0-88243-662-7, 02-0662); Vol. 4. (ISBN 0-88243-663-5, 02-0663). Gospel Pub.

Pearlman, Myer, tr. A Traves De la Biblia. (Spanish Bks.). 1977. 4.25 (ISBN 0-8297-0501-5); pap. 3.25 (ISBN 0-686-28805-X). Life Pubs Intl.

--Atraves Da Biblia. (Portugese Bks.). (Port.). 1979. 3.95 (ISBN 0-8297-0641-0). Life Pubs Intl.

--Conhecendo As Doutrinas Da Biblia. (Portugese Bks.). (Port.). 1979. 2.95 (ISBN 0-8297-0647-X). Life Pubs Intl.

--Ensenando Con Exito. (Spanish Bks.). 1978. 1.75 (ISBN 0-8297-0548-1). Vida Pubs.

--Evangelismo Personal. (Spanish Bks.). 1978. 1.25 (ISBN 0-8297-0552-X). Life Pubs Intl.

--Teologia Biblica y Sistematica. (Spanish Bks.). 1978. 4.25 (ISBN 0-8297-0603-8); pap. 3.25 (ISBN 0-8297-0602-X). Life Pubs Intl.

Pearlman, Paula R., jt. auth. see Pearlman, Daniel.

Pearlmutter, Simha. The Tents of Shem. LC 79-56104. 1980. 8.95 (ISBN 0-533-04505-3). Vantage.

Pearman, John W. & England, Ernest J. The Urological Management of the Patient Following Spinal Cord Injury. (Illus.). 304p. 1973. 21.75 (ISBN 0-398-02470-7). C C Thomas.

Pearman, Richard. Power Electronics: Solid Stare Motor Control. (Illus.). 1980. text ed. 19.95 (ISBN 0-8359-5585-0); instr's manual avail. Reston.

Pearman, William A. & Rotz, Robert A. The Province of Sociology: Selected Profiles. LC 79-17996. 212p. 1981. text ed. 15.95 (ISBN 0-88229-434-2); pap. text ed. 8.95 (ISBN 0-88229-735-X). Nelson-Hall.

Pears, D. F., tr. see Wittgenstein, Ludwig.

Pears, Nigel V. Basic Biogeography. LC 77-8108. (Illus.). 1977. pap. text ed. 12.95x (ISBN 0-582-48401-4). Longman.

Pearsall, D. A., ed. The Floure & the Leafe" & "the Assembly of Ladies". (Old & Middle English Texts). 191p. 1980. pap. 13.00x (ISBN 0-389-20026-3). B&N.

Pearsall, Derek. Old English & Middle English Poetry. (History of English Poetry Ser.). 1977. 28.00x (ISBN 0-7100-8396-3). Routledge & Kegan.

Pearsall, Derek, jt. ed. see Edwards, A. S.

Pearsall, Margaret E. Guide to Successful Dog Training. 2nd ed. LC 76-6806. 1976. 11.95 o.p. (ISBN 0-87605-758-X). Howell Bk.

Pearsall, Margaret E., jt. auth. see Pearsall, Milo D.

Pearsall, Milo & Leedham, Charles G. Dog Obedience Training. rev. ed. (Illus.). 1978. 12.95 o.p. (ISBN 0-684-16158-3, ScribT). Scribner.

Pearsall, Milo D. & Pearsall, Margaret E. Your Dog: Companion & Helper. LC 80-14115. (Illus.). 160p. 1980. 11.95 (ISBN 0-931866-07-3). Alpine Pubns.

Pearsall, R. Is That My Hook in Your Ear. 9.95x (ISBN 0-392-06563-0, SpS). Soccer.

Pearsall, R. B. Rupert Brooke: The Man & Poet. 174p. (Orig.). 1975. pap. text ed. 14.25x (ISBN 90-6203-437-3). Humanities.

Pearsall, Robert B. The Life & Writings of Ernest Hemingway. LC 72-93573. 282p. (Orig.). 1973. pap. text ed. 20.00x (ISBN 0-391-02005-6). Humanities.

--Robert Browning. (English Authors Ser.: No. 168). 1974. lib. bdg. 9.95 (ISBN 0-8057-1065-5). Twayne.

Pearsall, Robert B., ed. The Symbionese Liberation Army: Documents & Communications. (Melville Studies in American Culture: Vol.4). (Illus.). 158p. (Orig.). 1974. pap. text ed. 9.25x (ISBN 90-6203-128-5). Humanities.

Pearsall, Ronald. Victorian Sheet Music Covers. LC 72-6422. (Illus.). 116p. 1972. 16.00 (ISBN 0-8103-2001-0). Gale.

Pearsall, Thomas E. Audience Analysis for Technical Writing. (Illus., Orig.). 1969. pap. text ed. 5.95x (ISBN 0-02-476490-6, 47649). Macmillan.

Pearsall, Thomas E., jt. auth. see Houp, Kenneth W.

Pearse, A. Everson. Preparative & Optical Technology Ser. Theoretical & Applied, Vol. 1. 4th ed. (Preperative & Optical Technology Ser.). (Illus.). 480p. 1980. text ed. 62.50 (ISBN 0-443-01998-3). Churchill.

Pearse, Andrew. Seeds of Plenty, Seeds of Want: A Critical Analysis of the Green Revolution. 280p. 1980. 22.50 (ISBN 0-19-877150-9). Oxford U Pr.

Pearse, Maggie M. Traditional British Cookery. (International Wine & Food Society Ser.). (Illus.). 15.00 o.p. (ISBN 0-7153-5183-4). David & Charles.

Pearse, P. H. The Letters of P. H. Pearse. O'Buachalla, Seamas, ed. 528p. 1980. text ed. 31.25x (ISBN 0-391-01678-4). Humanities.

Pearse, Padraic. The Murder Machine & Other Essays. 1976. pap. 3.50 o.p. (ISBN 0-85342-471-3). Irish Bk Ctr.

Pearse, Patrick. Na Scribhinni Liteartha le Padraig Mac Pearais. O'Buachalla, Seamus, ed. 180p. (Irish.). 1979. pap. 4.95 (ISBN 0-85342-607-4). Irish Bk Ctr.

Pearse, R. W. & Gaydon, A. G. The Identification of Molecular Spectra. 4th ed. LC 76-18734. 407p. 1976. text ed. 53.95x o.p. (ISBN 0-412-14350-X, Pub. by Chapman & Hall). Methuen Inc.

--The Identification of Molecular Spectra. 4th ed. LC 76-18734. 1976. 53.95 o.p. (ISBN 0-470-15164-1). Halsted Pr.

Pearson, A. E., jt. ed. see Lane-Petter, W.

Pearson, Bill. Olive & Swee' Pea Wash up! Mann, Philip, ed. (Shape Board Play Book). (Illus.). 14p. (gr. k-3). 1980. bds. 2.95 comb bdg. (ISBN 0-89828-126-1, 6008). Tuffy Bks.

--Popeye & His Pals Stay in Shape. Mann, Philip, ed. (Shape Board Play Book). (Illus.). 14p. (gr. k-3). 1980. bds. 2.95 comb bdg. (ISBN 0-89828-125-3, 6007). Tuffy Bks.

--Wimpy in What's Good to Eat? Mann, Philip, ed. (Shape Board Play Book). (Illus.). 14p. (gr. k-3). 1980. bds. 2.95 comb bdg. (ISBN 0-89828-127-X, 6009). Tuffy Bks.

Pearson, Birger A. The Pneumatikos-Psychikos Terminology in First Corinthians. LC 73-92202. (Society of Biblical Literature. Dissertation Ser.). 1975. pap. 7.50 (ISBN 0-88414-034-2, 060112). Scholars Pr Ca.

Pearson, Birger A., ed. Religious Syncretism in Antiquity. LC 75-29421. (American Academy of Religion-University of California Institute of Religious Studies). 225p. 1975. pap. 7.50 (ISBN 0-89130-037-6, 010401). Scholars Pr Ca.

Pearson, Charles & Pryor, Anthony. Environment: North & South an Economic Interpretation. LC 77-11143. 37.95 (ISBN 0-471-02741-3, Pub. by Wiley-Interscience). Wiley.

Pearson, Charles H. Russia: By a Recent Traveler. (Russia Through European Eyes Ser). 1971. Repr. of 1859 ed. lib. bdg. 39.50 (ISBN 0-306-77030-X). Da Capo.

Pearson, Craig. Resolving Classroom Conflict. LC 74-16805. (Learning Handbooks Ser.). 1974. pap. 3.95 (ISBN 0-8224-1910-6). Pitman Learning.

Pearson, Craig M., et al. Independent Living: Being on Your Own. LC 79-16892. (Independent Living Ser.). (Illus.). 464p. (gr. 11-12). 1979. text ed. 13.32 (ISBN 0-07-049061-9); tchrs. manual & key 3.00 (ISBN 0-07-049063-5); student wkbk. 5.28 (ISBN 0-07-049062-7). McGraw.

Pearson, David. Laboratory Techniques in Food Analysis. LC 72-14169. 315p. 1973. 28.95 (ISBN 0-470-67539-X). Halsted Pr.

Pearson, Diane. Csardas. LC 75-5880. 1975. 10.00 o.p. (ISBN 0-397-01085-0). Lippincott.

Pearson, Donald E., jt. auth. see Buehler, Calvin A.

Pearson, Donald H., jt. auth. see Salmon, James H.

Pearson, Drew & Allen, Robert S. The Nine Old Men. LC 73-21727. (American Constitutional & Legal History Ser). 325p. 1974. Repr. of 1966 ed. lib. bdg. 39.50 (ISBN 0-306-70609-1). Da Capo.

Pearson, Durk. Life Extension: Adding Years to Your Life & Life to Your Years, a Practical Approach. (Orig.). 1981. 12.95 (ISBN 0-446-51229-X). Warner Bks.

Pearson, E. S., jt. auth. see Neyman, Jerzy.

Pearson, E. S. & Hartley, H. O., eds. Biometrika Tables for Statisticians, Vol. 1. 3rd ed. 270p. 1976. lib. bdg. 25.95x. Lubrecht & Cramer.

--Biometrika Tables for Statisticians, Vol. 1. 270p. 1976. 25.00x (ISBN 0-85264-700-X, Pub. by Griffin England). State Mutual Bk.

--Biometrika Tables for Statisticians, Vol. 2. 1976. 30.00x (ISBN 0-85264-701-8, Pub. by Griffin England). State Mutual Bk.

--Biometrika Tables for Statisticians: Reprint with Corrections, Vol. 2. 385p. 1976. Repr. lib. bdg. 30.50x. Lubrecht & Cramer.

Pearson, Edmund. More Studies in Murder. 317p. 1980. Repr. of 1936 ed. lib. bdg. 30.00 (ISBN 0-89760-715-5). Telegraph Bks.

Pearson, Edmund L. The Adventure of the Lost Manuscripts & One Other. (Illus.). 40p. (Orig.). 1974. pap. 4.00 o.p. (ISBN 0-915230-05-4). Rue Morgue.

--The Librarian at Play. 2nd ed. LC 79-53459. (Short Story Index in Reprint Ser.). Date not set. Repr. of 1912 ed. 22.50x (ISBN 0-8486-5010-7). Core Collection. Postponed.

Pearson, Eileen. Hitler's Reich. Yapp, Malcolm & Killingray, Margaret, eds. (World History Ser.). (Illus.). (gr. 10). 1980. Repr. of 1977 ed. lib. bdg. 5.95 (ISBN 0-89908-208-4); pap. text ed. 1.95 (ISBN 0-89908-233-5). Greenhaven.

Pearson, Esther. Early Churches of Washington State. LC 79-57216. (Illus.). 182p. 1980. 22.50 (ISBN 0-295-95713-1). U of Wash Pr.

Pearson, Geoff, jt. ed. see Mungham, Geoff.

Pearson, Geoffrey. The Deviant Imagination: Psychiatry, Social Work & Social Change. LC 75-9815. 252p. 1980. text ed. 27.50x (ISBN 0-8419-0209-7); pap. text ed. 11.50x (ISBN 0-8419-0616-5). Holmes & Meier.

Pearson, H. L. Projects for the School Foundry. (Illus.). 1970. 15.95x (ISBN 0-291-39673-9). Intl Ideas.

Pearson, Henry G. Your Hidden Skills: Clues to Careers & Future Pursuits. (Illus.). 150p. (Orig.). 1981. pap. price not set (ISBN 0-9605368-0-9). Mowry Pr.

Pearson, Hesketh. The Life of Oscar Wilde. 389p. 1980. Repr. of 1947 ed. lib. bdg. 35.00 (ISBN 0-89987-658-7). Century Bookbindery.

Pearson, Howard A., jt. auth. see Miller, Denis R.

Pearson, J. D., ed. see Matthews, Noel & Wainwright, M. Doreen.

Pearson, J. M. & Stolka, M. Poly (N-Vinylcarbazole) (Polymer Monographs Ser.). 1981. price not set. Gordon.

Pearson, Jack, ed. Employee Benefits Institutes & Seminars for Company Sponsored Plans, 1978: Proceedings. (Orig.). 1979. pap. 7.50 (ISBN 0-89154-095-4). Intl Found Employ.

Pearson, Jacqueline. Tragedy & Tragicomedy in the Plays of John Webster. 151p. 1980. 20.50x (ISBN 0-389-20030-1). B&N.

Pearson, James, et al. Cube-O-Gram Math Teacher Lesson Plan & Activity Book. (Cube-O-Math Ser.). (Illus.). 194p. (gr. k-3). 1979. pap. 9.95 (ISBN 0-933358-57-1). Enrich.

Pearson, Jeffrey & Pearson, Jessica. No Time but Place. (Illus.). 256p. 1980. 16.95 (ISBN 0-07-049030-9). McGraw.

Pearson, Jessica, jt. auth. see Pearson, Jeffrey.

Pearson, John. The Sitwells. LC 80-14371. 1980. pap. 7.95 (ISBN 0-15-682676-3, Harv). HarBraceJ.

--The Sitwells: A Family's Biography. 1979. 15.00 o.p. (ISBN 0-15-182703-6). HarBraceJ.

Pearson, John E, jt. auth. see Curry, O. J.

Pearson, John G., et al. Math Skills for the Sciences. LC 75-40065. (Wiley Self-Teaching Guides Ser). 1976. text ed. 5.95 (ISBN 0-471-67541-5). Wiley.

Pearson, Judy C., jt. auth. see Nelson, Paul E.

Pearson, K. Tables of the Incomplete Beta-Function. 505p. 1968. 60.00x (ISBN 0-85264-704-2, Pub. by England Griffin). State Mutual Bk.

--Tables of the Incomplete Gamma-Function. 164p. 1965. 30.00x (ISBN 0-85264-703-4, Pub. by Griffin England). State Mutual Bk.

Pearson, Karl G. & Litka, Michael P. Real Estate: Principles & Practices. 3rd ed. LC 79-20017. (Real Estate Ser.). 1980. text ed. 19.95 (ISBN 0-88244-202-3). Grid Pub.

Pearson, Larry, jt. ed. see Curry, Georgene.

Pearson, Lon. Nicomedes Guzman: Proletarian Author in Chile's Literary Generation of 1938. LC 75-19334. 320p. 1976. 15.00x (ISBN 0-8262-0178-4). U of Mo Pr.

Pearson, Lu E. Elizabethans at Home. (Illus.). 1957. 32.50x (ISBN 0-8047-0494-5); pap. 6.95 o.p. (ISBN 0-8047-0495-3, SP46). Stanford U Pr.

Pearson, M. N. Merchants & Rulers in Gujarat: The Response to the Portuguese in the Sixteenth Century. 1976. 18.50x (ISBN 0-520-02809-0). U of Cal Pr.

Pearson, Michael. The Store. 1981. 16.95 (ISBN 0-671-25114-7). S&S.

Pearson, Norman H., ed. see H. D.

Pearson, P. L. & Lewis, K. R., eds. Chromosomes Today, Vol. 5. LC 75-43619. 1976. 74.95 (ISBN 0-470-14997-3). Halsted Pr.

Pearson, Paul H. & Williams, Carol E., eds. Physical Therapy Services in the Developmental Disabilities. (Illus.). 448p. 1980. 25.50 (ISBN 0-398-02377-8). C C Thomas.

Pearson, R. G., jt. auth. see Frost, Arthur A.

Pearson, Ralph G. Symmetry Rules for Chemical Reactions: Orbital Topology & Elementary Processes. LC 76-10314. 600p. 1976. 37.50 (ISBN 0-471-01495-8, Pub. by Wiley-Interscience). Wiley.

Pearson, Richard, et al. Criminal Justice Education: The End of the Beginning. 220p. (Orig.). 1980. pap. 5.50x (ISBN 0-89444-030-6). John Jay Pr.

Pearson, Roger, ed. Korea in the World Today. 1976. pap. 10.00 (ISBN 0-685-79962-X). Coun Am Affairs.

--Sino-Soviet Intervention in Africa. 1977. pap. 10.00 (ISBN 0-685-79965-4). Coun Am Affairs.

Pearson, Roger W. & Lynch, Donald F. Alaska: A Geography. 300p. 1981. lib. bdg. 35.00x (ISBN 0-89158-903-1); text ed. 20.00x (ISBN 0-89158-903-1). Westview.

Pearson, Ronald & Ball, John N. Lecture Notes on Vertebrate Zoology. 225p. 1981. pap. 19.95 (ISBN 0-470-27143-4). Halsted Pr.

Pearson, Ross N. Physical Geography: A Survey of Man's Physical Environment. (Maps, Orig). 1971. pap. 4.25 (ISBN 0-06-460074-2, CO 74, COS). Har-Row.

Pearson, Scott R. & Stryker, J. Dirck. Rice in West Africa: Policy & Economics. LC 80-50906. (Illus.). 472p. 1981. 39.00x (ISBN 0-8047-1095-3). Stanford U Pr.

Pearson, Sidney A., Jr. Arthur Koestler. (English Authors Ser.: No. 228). 1978. lib. bdg. 12.50 (ISBN 0-8057-6699-5). Twayne.

Pearson, Susan. Monday I Was an Alligator. LC 78-23618. (Lippincott-I-Like-to-Read Books). (Illus.). (gr. k-2). 1979. 6.95 (ISBN 0-397-31830-8). Lippincott.

Pearson, T. Gilbert. Birds of America. 1936. 17.95 (ISBN 0-385-00024-3). Doubleday.

Pearson, W. N. see Sebrell, W. H., Jr. & Harris, Robert S.

Pearson, William B. Crystal Chemistry & Physics of Metals & Alloys. LC 70-176284. (Series on the Science & Technology of Materials). 1972. 58.00 o.p. (ISBN 0-471-67540-7, Pub. by Wiley-Interscience). Wiley.

Peart, E; see Cullen, William.

Peart, Jane. Portrait in Shadows. (Orig.). 1981. pap. 1.50 (ISBN 0-440-16693-4). Dell.

Peary, Dannis, jt. auth. see Peary, Gerald.

Peary, Gerald & Peary, Dannis. American Animated Cartoon. (Illus.). 1980. pap. 10.95 (ISBN 0-525-47639-3). Dutton.

Pease, Daniel C., ed. Cellular Aspects of Neural Growth & Differentiation. LC 73-126760. (UCLA Forum in Medical Sciences: No. 14). (Illus.). 1971. 50.00x (ISBN 0-520-01793-5). U of Cal Pr.

Pease, Edward M. & Wadsworth, George P. Calculus with Analytic Geometry. LC 68-56150. 1071p. 1969. 19.95x o.p. (ISBN 0-8260-7055-8). Wiley.

Pease, Esther E., jt. auth. see Lockhart, Aileene S.

Pease, Jack G. & Russell, Robert. Arithmetic Fundamentals. new ed. 240p. 1975. pap. text ed. 11.95x (ISBN 0-675-08767-8). Merrill.

Pease, Marguerite J., jt. auth. see Pease, Theodore C.

Pease, Norval F. Saint Under Stress. LC 70-88927. (Dimension Ser.). 1969. pap. 5.95 (ISBN 0-8163-0384-3, 19129-6). Pacific Pr Pub Assn.

Pease, Theodore C. & Pease, Marguerite J. George Rogers Clark & the Revolution in Illinois, Seventeen Sixty-Three to Seventeen Eighty-Seven. 1929. 3.00 (ISBN 0-912226-12-9). Ill St Hist So.

Pease, Victor P. Anxiety into Energy. 1981. 12.95 (ISBN 0-8015-0335-3, Hawthorn). Dutton.

Peasner, Tom. Emergency Powers: The Executive Order. pap. 1.75 (ISBN 0-918700-07-8). Duverus Pub.

Peat, Marwick, Mitchell & Co., ed. Taxation of Intercompany Transactions in Selected Countries in Europe & the USA. 119p. 1979. pap. 15.80 (ISBN 90-200-0589-8, Pub. by Kluwer Law & Taxation). Kluwer Boston.

Peat, R. C. Presenting Shakespeare. 1947. pap. 10.00x (ISBN 0-245-53047-9). Intl Ideas.

Peate, Iorwerth C. Tradition & Folk Life. (Illus.). 1972. 12.95 (ISBN 0-571-09804-5, Pub. by Faber & Faber). Merrimack Bk Serv.

Peatfield, A. E. Mechanical Engineering. Incl. Vol. 1. Hand Tools. 1973; Vol. 2. Engineering Components. 1974 (ISBN 0-679-10480-1); Vol. 3. Workshop Practice. 1973. o.p. (ISBN 0-679-10481-X). (Teach Yourself Ser.). pap. 2.95 ea. o.p. McKay.

Peatling, John H. Religious Education in a Psychological Key. 380p. (Orig.). 1981. pap. price not set (ISBN 0-89135-027-6). Religious Educ.

Peattie, Donald C. A Natural History of Western Trees. LC 80-12263. (Illus.). xvi, 751p. 1980. pap. 14.95 (ISBN 0-8032-8701-1, BB 741, Bison). U of Nebr Pr.

Peavy, Charles D. Larry McMurtry. (United States Authors Ser.: No. 291). 1977. lib. bdg. 12.50 (ISBN 0-8057-7194-8). Twayne.

Peavy, Charles D., ed. Afro-American Literature & Culture, Nineteen Forty-Five to Nineteen Seventy-Three: A Guide to Information Sources. LC 73-17561. (American Studies Information Guide Ser.: Vol. 6). 1979. 30.00 (ISBN 0-8103-1254-9). Gale.

Peavy, Linda. Have a Healthy Baby: Section on What to Eat After Your Baby Is Born. LC 76-46807. 1977. 9.95 (ISBN 0-8069-8376-0); PLB 8.29 (ISBN 0-8069-8377-9). Sterling.

Peavy, William. Southern Gardner's Soil Handbook. LC 78-58245. (Illus.). 1979. pap. 3.95 (ISBN 0-88415-817-9). Pacesetter Pr.

Peay, Marilyn, jt. auth. see Winefield, Helen.

Pebay-Peyroula, J. C., jt. auth. see Cagnac, B.

Peberdy, John F. Developmental Microbiology. LC 80-14825. (Tertiary Level Biology Ser.). 230p. 1980. pap. 29.95x (ISBN 0-470-26989-8). Halsted Pr.

Pebworth, Ted-Larry. Owen Felltham. LC 76-4863. (English Authors Ser.: No. 189). 1976. lib. bdg. 10.95 (ISBN 0-8057-6655-3). Twayne.

Pebworth, Ted-Larry, jt. auth. see Summers, Claude J.

Pebworth, Ted-Larry, jt. ed. see Summers, Claude J.

Peccei, A. Chasm Ahead. 1969. 7.50 o.s.i. (ISBN 0-02-595360-5). Macmillan.

Peccei, Aurelio. The Human Quality. 216p. 1977. text ed. 19.50 (ISBN 0-08-021479-7); pap. text ed. 9.25 (ISBN 0-08-021480-0). Pergamon.

Pecher, R. & Schmiermann, W. The Southern Cordillera Real. (Illus.). 57p. (Orig.). 1977. pap. 7.95 (ISBN 0-686-69199-7). Bradt Ent.

Pecherer & Vertuno. How to Calculate Drug Dosages. 1978. pap. text ed. 6.50 o.s.i. (ISBN 0-8273-1834-0). Delmar.

Pecherer, A. & Vertuno, S. How to Calculate Drug Dosages. 1978. pap. 7.50 (ISBN 0-87489-140-X). Med Economics.

Pechman, Joseph A. Federal Tax Policy. rev. ed. (Brookings Institute Studies of Government Finance). 1971. pap. text ed. 5.95x (ISBN 0-393-09987-3). Norton.

Pechman, Joseph A., ed. Setting National Priorities: K Agenda for the 1980s. 1980. 18.95 (ISBN 0-8157-6988-1); pap. 9.95 (ISBN 0-8157-6987-3). Brookings.

Pechman, Joseph A. A. Federal Tax Policy. 3rd ed. LC 76-54901. (Studies of Government Finance). 1977. 14.95 (ISBN 0-8157-6978-4); pap. 6.95 (ISBN 0-8157-6977-6). Brookings.

Pechman, Joseph A. B. & Okner, Benjamin A. Who Bears the Tax Burden? LC 74-280. (Studies of Government Finance). 120p. 1974. 9.95 (ISBN 0-8157-6968-7); pap. 3.95 (ISBN 0-8157-6967-9). Brookings.

Pechman, Joseph A. D. Comprehensive Income Taxation. LC 77-24246. (Studies of Government Finance). 1977. 14.95 (ISBN 0-8157-6982-2); pap. 5.95 (ISBN 0-8157-6981-4). Brookings.

Pechman, Joseph A. E. Setting National Priorities: H the 1978 Budget. 1977. 14.95 (ISBN 0-8157-6980-6); pap. 5.95 (ISBN 0-8157-6979-2). Brookings.

Pechman, Joseph A. K. Work Incentives & Income Guarantees: The New Jersey Negative Income Tax Experiment. Timpane, P. Michael, ed. (Studies in Social Experimentation). 232p. 1975. 11.95 (ISBN 0-8157-6976-8); pap. 4.95 (ISBN 0-8157-6975-X). Brookings.

Pechman, Joseph A. L. see Palmer, John L.

Pechman, Joseph A. M., et al. Social Security: Perspectives for Reform. LC 68-31836. (Studies in Social Economics). 352p. 1968. 14.95 (ISBN 0-8157-6974-1); pap. 5.95 (ISBN 0-8157-6973-3). Brookings.

Pechter, William S. Movies Plus One: Seven Years of Film Reviewing. 380p. 1981. 16.95 (ISBN 0-8180-0709-5). Horizon.

Pecile, A., jt. ed. see Martini, L.

Peck, Abraham J. Radicals & Reactionaries: The Crisis of Conservatism in Wilhelmine Germany. LC 78-62921. (Illus.). 1978. pap. text ed. 12.00 (ISBN 0-8191-0601-1). U Pr of Amer.

Peck, Bonita H. Personal Pronoun Photo Book. (Illus.). 64p. 1980. pap. 7.50x (ISBN 0-8134-2135-7). Interstate.

Peck, Charles, jt. auth. see Murphy, Herta.

Peck, David & Fine, David. L. A. Culture Quiz. (Illus.). 96p. (Orig.). 1981. 5.95 (ISBN 0-935232-07-9); pap. 3.95 (ISBN 0-935232-06-0). Deep River Pr.

Peck, David, jt. auth. see Bullock, Chris.

Peck, David R. American Marxist Literary Criticism: 1926-1941-a Bibliography. (Bibliographical Ser.: No. 10). 1975. 1.00 (ISBN 0-89977-012-6). Am Inst Marxist.

Peck, Ellen, jt. auth. see Lieberman, E. J.

Peck, Judith. Leap to the Sun: Learning Through Dynamic Play. (Illus.). 1979. 12.95 (ISBN 0-13-527275-0, Spec); pap. 5.95 (ISBN 0-13-527267-X). P-H.

Peck, Phyllis & Konkel, Gilbert. Your Future in Word Processing. (Careers in Depth Ser.). (Illus.). 140p. (gr. 7-12). 1981. lib. bdg. 5.97 (ISBN 0-8239-0532-2). Rosen Pr.

Peck, R. B. & Terzaghi, Karl. Theoretical Soil Mechanics. 1943. 35.00 (ISBN 0-471-85305-4, Pub. by Wiley-Interscience). Wiley.

Peck, R. B., jt. auth. see Terzaghi, Karl.

Peck, Ralph B., et al. Foundation Engineering. 2nd ed. LC 73-9877. 544p. 1974. 27.95 (ISBN 0-471-67585-7). Wiley.

Peck, Ralph H. Hotel & Motel Careers. (Career Concise Guides Ser.). (Illus.). (gr. 6 up). 1977. PLB 6.45 s&l (ISBN 0-531-00374-4). Watts.

--Travel Careers. (Career Concise Guides Ser.). (Illus.). 96p. (gr. 7 up). 1976. PLB 6.45 (ISBN 0-531-01154-2). Watts.

Peck, Richard. Amanda-Miranda. 544p. 1981. pap. 2.95 (ISBN 0-380-53850-4). Avon.

--New York Time. 1981. 9.95 (ISBN 0-440-06346-9). Delacorte.

--Representing Super Doll. 192p. (gr. 7 up). 1974. 6.95 o.p. (ISBN 0-670-59492-X). Viking Pr.

Peck, Richard, ed. Mindscapes: Poems for the Real World. LC 70-146821. (gr. 7 up). 1971. 5.95 o.s.i. (ISBN 0-440-05644-6). Delacorte.

Peck, Robert M., ed. & intro. by see Bartram, William.

Peck, Robert N. Bee Tree & Other Stuff. LC 75-10054. (Illus.). 128p. (gr. 3 up). 1975. 6.95 o.s.i. (ISBN 0-8027-6227-1); PLB 6.85 o.s.i. (ISBN 0-8027-6232-8). Walker & Co.

--Justice Lion. 264p. (gr. 7 up). 1981. 9.95 (ISBN 0-316-69658-7). Little.

--Mr. Little. LC 78-22347. (Illus.). 1979. 7.95a (ISBN 0-385-13657-9); PLB (ISBN 0-385-13658-7). Doubleday.

--Rabbits & Redcoats. (Illus.). 64p. (gr. 3-6). 1976. 6.95 o.s.i. (ISBN 0-8027-6241-7); PLB 6.85 o.s.i. (ISBN 0-8027-6242-5). Walker & Co.

--Rabbits & Redcoats. (N. H.-Vermont Historiettes). (Illus.). 64p. (gr. 3-4). 1976. pap. 0.95x (ISBN 0-915892-06-5). Regional Ctr Educ.

--Soup on Wheels. LC 80-17661. (Illus.). 128p. (gr. 3 up). 1981. 6.95 (ISBN 0-394-84581-1); PLB 6.99 (ISBN 0-394-94581-6). Knopf.

--Trig Goes Ape. (Illus.). 96p. (gr. 3-6). 1980. 7.95g (ISBN 0-316-69657-9). Little.

Peck, Robert Newton. Basket Case. LC 78-60298. (gr. 10 up). 1979. 5.95 (ISBN 0-385-14362-1). Doubleday.

Peck, Russell A. Kingship & Common Profit in Gower's "Confessio Amantis". LC 78-8984. (Literary Structures Ser.). 232p. 1978. 13.95x (ISBN 0-8093-0801-0). S Ill U Pr.

Peck, Russell A., ed. see Gower, John.

Peck, Ruth L. Best of Teacher's Arts & Crafts Workshop. 1974. 12.95 o.p. (ISBN 0-13-073668-6). P-H.

Peck, Theodore P., ed. Chemical Industries Information Sources. LC 76-6891. (Management Information Guide Ser.: No. 29). 1979. 30.00 (ISBN 0-8103-0829-0). Gale.

--Employee Counseling in Industry & Government: A Guide to Information Sources. LC 79-16028. (Management Information Guide Ser.: No. 37). 1979. 30.00 (ISBN 0-8103-0837-1). Gale.

--Occupational Safety & Health: A Guide to Information Sources. LC 74-7199. (Management Information Guide Ser.: No. 28). 262p. 1974. 30.00 (ISBN 0-8103-0828-2). Gale.

Peck, Wilbur. Volleyball. (Orig.). 1970. pap. 3.95 o.s.i. (ISBN 0-02-029570-7, Collier). Macmillan.

Peck, William. Anatomy of Local Radio-TV Copy. 4th ed. 1976. vinyl 5.95 o.p. (ISBN 0-8306-6890-X, 890). TAB Bks.

Peck, William & Ross, John. Egyptian Drawings. LC 78-52246. (Illus.). 1978. 24.95 o.p. (ISBN 0-525-09691-4). Dutton.

Pecker The Cat. A Rug Before My Time: Memoirs of Pecker the Cat. (Illus.). 32p. 1981. pap. 1.18 (ISBN 0-9604894-1-X). Borf Bks.

Peckham, Sir George. A True Reporte of the Late Discoueries of the Newfound Landes. LC 78-25630. (English Experience Ser.: No. 341). 1971. Repr. of 1583 ed. 11.50 (ISBN 90-221-0341-2). Walter J Johnson.

Peckham, Herbert C. BASIC: A Hands-on Method. 2nd ed. (Illus.). 320p. 1980. pap. text ed. 12.95 (ISBN 0-07-049160-7). McGraw.

Peckham, Howard H. Indiana, a History. (States & the Nation Ser.). (Illus.). 1978. 12.95 (ISBN 0-393-05670-8, Co-Pub by AASLH). Norton.

Peckham, Howard H., jt. ed. see Brown, Lloyd A.

Peckham, Morse. Humanistic Education for Business Executives. LC 60-9884. 1960. 10.00x (ISBN 0-8122-7177-7). U of Pa Pr.

--Victorian Revolutionaries: Speculations on Some Heroes of a Culture Crisis. LC 78-104701. 1970. 7.50 o.s.i. (ISBN 0-8076-0543-3). Braziller.

Peckham, Morse, ed. Romanticism: The Culture of the Nineteenth Century. LC 65-23181. (Cultures of Mankind Ser). (Illus.). 1965. 6.95 o.s.i. (ISBN 0-8076-0314-7). Braziller.

Peckham, Morse, ed. see Swinburne, Algernon C.

Pecora, Robert, jt. auth. see Berne, Bruce J.

Pecqueur, Constantin. Le Salut Du Peuple, Journal De la Science Sociale. 236p. (Fr.). 1977. lib. bdg. 32.50x o.p. (ISBN 0-8287-0673-5); pap. text ed. 22.50x o.p. (ISBN 0-685-75618-1). Clearwater Pub.

Pecsok, Robert L., jt. auth. see Laub, Richard J.

Pecsok, Robert L., et al. Modern Methods of Chemical Analysis. 2nd ed. LC 76-13894. 1976. 23.95x (ISBN 0-471-67662-4); solution manual avail. (ISBN 0-471-02878-9). Wiley.

Pecznick, Ira, jt. auth. see Hoffman, Paul.

Pedde, Lawrence D., et al. Metric Manual. rev. ed. (Illus.). 1979. 24.00 (ISBN 0-8103-1020-1). Gale.

Pedder, I. J. & Wynne, E. G. Genetics: A Basic Guide. 183p. 1974. pap. text ed. 5.95x (ISBN 0-393-09267-4). Norton.

Peddersen, Ray. Specs: The Comprehensive Foodservice Purchasing and Specification Manual. LC 76-56460. 1977. 85.00 (ISBN 0-8436-2084-6). CBI Pub.

Peddersen, Raymond B. Foodservice Purchasing. 460p. 1981. text ed. 19.95 (ISBN 0-8436-2192-3). CBI Pub.

Pedderson, Raymond B., et al, eds. Increasing Productivity in Foodservice. LC 73-84798. 1973. 14.95 (ISBN 0-8436-0560-X). CBI Pub.

Peddicord, Herschel, Jr., jt. auth. see Karnes, Frances A.

Peddie, Robert A. Place-Names in Imprints: An Index to the Latin & Other Forms Used on Title-Pages. LC 68-30594. 1968. Repr. of 1932 ed. 15.00 (ISBN 0-8103-3239-6). Gale.

Peddle, Frank. Thought & Being: Hegel's Criticism of Kant's System of Cosmological Ideas. LC 79-9695. 204p. 1980. text ed. 17.75 (ISBN 0-8191-0987-8); pap. text ed. 9.50 (ISBN 0-8191-0988-6). U Pr of Amer.

Peden, Creighton, jt. auth. see Hartshorne, Charles.

Peden, Margaret S., tr. see Fuentes, Carlos.

Peden, Margaret S., tr. see Neruda, Pablo.

Pedersen, Frank A., ed. The Father-Infant Relationship: Observational Studies in Family Settings. LC 79-20514. (Praeger Special Studies Ser.). 196p. 1980. 22.95 (ISBN 0-03-049506-7). Praeger.

Pedersen, Holger. A Glance at the History of Linguistics, with Particular Regard to the Historical Study of Phonology. Henriksen, C. & Henriksen, P., trs. (Studies in the History of Linguistics: No. 7). (Illus.). 1980. text ed. 18.75x (ISBN 0-391-01648-2). Humanities.

Pedersen, Knud, et al. Applied Nuclear Power for Practicing Engineers. LC 78-170128. 1972. 11.95 (ISBN 0-8436-0326-7). CBI Pub.

Pedersen, L. G., jt. auth. see Johnson, Charles S.

Pedersen, O. Almages, a Survey. (Illus.). 1974. 60.00x (ISBN 87-7492-087-1, D-751). Vanous.

Pedersen, Paul B., jt. auth. see Marsella, Anthony.

Pedersen, Paul B., et al, eds. Counseling Across Cultures. rev. & expanded ed. 368p. (Orig.). 1981. pap. 10.00x (ISBN 0-8248-0725-1). U Pr of Hawaii.

Pederson, Carl S. Microbiology of Food Fermentations. 2nd ed. (Illus.). 1979. text ed. 27.50 (ISBN 0-87055-277-5). AVI.

Pederson, Carlton A. & Wright, Milburn D. Selling: Principles & Methods. 6th ed. 1976. text ed. 17.95 (ISBN 0-256-01646-1). Irwin.

Pederson, Duane. How to Establish a Jail & Prison Ministry. 132p. 1981. pap. 3.95 (ISBN 0-8407-5675-5). Nelson.

Pederson, E. O. Transportation in Cities. 1980. 12.50 (ISBN 0-08-024666-4). Pergamon.

Pederson, Edith S. The Witchs Lamp. (Childrens Bk). Orig. Title: Teddy & the Witchs Lamp. (Illus.). 128p. (gr. 1-5). 1970. pap. 1.50 (ISBN 0-8024-1960-7). Moody.

Pederson, Ejner. Spasticity: Mechanism, Measurement, Management. 144p. 1969. pap. 10.00 spiral (ISBN 0-398-01462-0). C C Thomas.

Pederson, Johannes. Israel: Its Life & Culture, 4 bks. Incl. Bks. 1 & 2. 1973. Repr. of 1926 ed. 59.00x (ISBN 0-19-647899-5); Bks. 3 & 4. 2nd ed. 1973. Repr. of 1964 ed. o.p. (ISBN 0-19-647900-2). Oxford U Pr.

Pederson, Les. Missionary Go Home? 1980. pap. 3.50 (ISBN 0-8024-4881-X). Moody.

Pederzoli, G., jt. auth. see Mathai, A. M.

Pedicord, Harry W. & Bergmann, Frederick L., eds. The Plays of David Garrick, Vol. 1: Garrick's Own Plays, 1740-1766. LC 79-28443. (The Plays of David Garrick). (Illus.). 480p. 1980. 35.00x (ISBN 0-8093-0862-2). S Ill U Pr.

--The Plays of David Garrick, Vol. 2: Garrick's Own Play's 1767-1775. LC 79-28443. (Illus.). 444p. 1980. 35.00x (ISBN 0-8093-0863-0). S Ill U Pr.

Pedicord, Harry W. & Bergmann, Fredrick L., eds. The Plays of David Garrick: A Complete Collection of the Social Satires, French Adaptations, Pantomimes, Christmas & Musical Plays, Preludes, Interludes, & Burlesques, to Which Are Added the Alterations & Adaptations of the Plays of Shakespeare & Other Dramatists from the Sixteenth & Seventeenth Centuries: Vol. 3, Garrick's Adaptations of Shakespeare, 1744-1756. LC 79-28443. 496p. write for info. (ISBN 0-8093-0968-8). S Ill U Pr.

Pedicord, Harry W., ed. see Rowe, Nicholas.

Pedler, Margaret. The Hermit of Far End. 1976. lib. bdg. 15.75x (ISBN 0-89968-216-2). Lightyear.

--The Lamp of Fate. 1976. lib. bdg. 15.25x (ISBN 0-89968-217-0). Lightyear.

--The Splendid Folly. 1976. lib. bdg. 13.75x (ISBN 0-89968-218-9). Lightyear.

Pedley, A. J. The Manuscript Collections of the Maryland Historical Society. LC 68-23074. 1968. 15.00 (ISBN 0-938420-08-9). Md Hist.

Pedley, John, ed. New Light on Ancient Carthage. (Illus.). 160p. 1980. 20.00x (ISBN 0-472-10003-3). U of Mich Pr.

Pedley, John G. Sardis in the Age of Croesus. (Centers of Civilization Ser.: No. 24). (Illus.). 1968. 4.95x o.p. (ISBN 0-8061-0786-3). U of Okla Pr.

Pedley, T. J. The Fluid Mechanics of Large Blood Vessels. LC 78-73814. (Cambridge Monographs on Mechanics & Applied Mathematics). (Illus.). 1980. 89.50 (ISBN 0-521-22626-0). Cambridge U Pr.

Pedlow, J. C. Windows on the Holy Land. 150p. pap. text ed. 8.95 (ISBN 0-227-67839-7). Attic Pr.

Pedoe, Dan. Circles, a Mathematical View. LC 78-73522. (Illus.). 1979. pap. text ed. 2.75 (ISBN 0-486-63698-4). Dover.

Pedretti. Leonardo. 1980. pap. cancelled (ISBN 0-8120-2303-X). Barron.

Pedretti, Carlo. Leonardo Da Vinci Nature Studies from the Royal Library at Windsor Castle. (Illus.). 95p. (Orig.). 1980. pap. 10.00 (ISBN 0-384-32298-0). J P Getty Mus.

--Literary Works of Leonardo Da Vinci: A Commentary of Jean Paul Richter's Edition, 2 vols. 1977. Set. 88.50x (ISBN 0-520-03329-9). U of Cal Pr.

Pedretti, Lorraine W. Occupational Therapy: Practice Skills for Physical Dysfunction. (Illus.). 676p. 1981. pap. text ed. 23.95 (ISBN 0-8016-3772-4). Mosby.

Pedrick, Jean. Pride & Splendor. LC 75-23818. 72p. 1976. pap. 4.95 (ISBN 0-914086-10-3). Alicejamesbooks.

--Saints. (Chapbook Ser.: No. 1). 40p. (Orig.). 1980. pap. 4.95 (ISBN 0-937672-00-9). Rowan Tree.

--Wolf Moon. LC 73-94067. 72p. 1974. pap. 4.95 (ISBN 0-914086-03-0). Alicejamesbooks.

Pedrini, Duilio T. & Pedrini, Lura N. Pedrini Supplementary Aid to the Administration of the Stanford-Binet Intelligence Scale (Form L-M) A Handbook. LC 74-95256. (Professional Handbk Ser). 1970. pap. 8.75x (ISBN 0-87424-114-6). Western Psych.

Pedrini, Lura N., jt. auth. see Pedrini, Duilio T.

Pedro Calderon, De La Barca see Calderon De La Barca, Pedro.

Peebles, Leighton H. Molecular Weight Distribution in Polymers. LC 70-143175. (Polymer Reviews Ser: Vol. 18). 1971. 30.95 o.p. (ISBN 0-471-67710-8, Pub. by Wiley-Interscience). Wiley.

Peebles, Malcolm W. Evolution of the Gas Industry. 256p. 1981. 25.00x (ISBN 0-8147-6580-7). NYU Pr.

Peebles, Margaret & Howell, J. B., eds. History of Mississippi Libraries. 437p. 1975. 10.00 (ISBN 0-88289-190-1). Pelican.

Peebles, Marvin L. Directory of Management Resources for Community Based Organizations: Third Annual. 100p. 1981. spiral bdg. 12.00 (ISBN 0-939020-03-3). MLP Ent.

Peebles, Peyton Z. Communication System Principles. (Illus.). 1976. 27.50 (ISBN 0-201-05758-1, Adv Bk Prog); pap. 3.50 (ISBN 0-201-05759-X). A-W.

Peebles Press International. Cheap & Cheaper Restaurant Guide to Paris. 192p. 1980. 8.95 (ISBN 0-13-128488-6, Spec); pap. 3.95 (ISBN 0-13-128470-3). P-H.

Peebles Press International & Zabronski, Ann. The Cheap & Cheaper Restaurant Guide to Manhattan. 192p. 1980. 8.95 (ISBN 0-686-69278-0, Spec); pap. 3.95 (ISBN 0-686-69279-9). P-H.

--Cheap & Cheaper Restaurant Guide to Manhattan. 192p. 1980. 8.95 (ISBN 0-13-128421-5, Spec); pap. 3.95 (ISBN 0-13-128413-4). P-H.

Peebls, Melvin Van see Van Peebles, Melvin.

Peek, George A., ed. The Political Writings of John Adams: Representative Selections. LC 54-4998. 1954. 24.50x (ISBN 0-672-50965-2). Irvington.

Peek, Hedley & Aflalo, F. G., eds. Encyclopaedia of Sport, 2 vols. LC 75-23210. (Illus.). 1976. Repr. of 1897 ed. Set. 135.00 (ISBN 0-8103-4207-3). Gale.

Peek, Merle. Roll Over! A Counting Song Book. (Illus.). 32p. (ps-2). 1981. 8.95 (ISBN 0-395-29438-X, Clarion). HM.

Peek, Walter W., jt. auth. see Sanders, Thomas E.

Peeke, Harmon V. & Herz, Michael J., eds. Habituation, 2 vols. Incl. Vol. 1. Behavioral Studies. 1973. 40.50 (ISBN 0-12-549801-2); Vol. 2. Electrophysiological Substrates. 1973. 35.50 (ISBN 0-12-549802-0). Set. 61.00 (ISBN 0-685-40604-0). Acad Pr.

Peel, A. J. Transport of Nutrients in Plants. LC 73-17354. 1974. 19.95 (ISBN 0-470-67717-1). Halsted Pr.

Peel, Albert see Carlson, Leland H.

Peel, Colin. Flameout. LC 77-15918. 1978. 7.95 o.p. (ISBN 0-312-29546-4). St Martin.

Peel, Colin D. Flameout. LC 80-83595. 192p. 1981. pap. 2.25 (ISBN 0-87216-792-5). Playboy Pbks.

Peel, J. & Potts, D. M. Textbook of Contraceptive Practice. (Illus.). 1969. 47.50 (ISBN 0-521-07515-7); pap. 14.50x (ISBN 0-521-09598-0). Cambridge U Pr.

Peel, J. H. Along the Pennine Way. LC 79-52376. (Illus.). 1979. 19.95 (ISBN 0-7153-7833-3). David & Charles.

--England in Colour. 1969. 14.95 (ISBN 0-7134-0017-X, Pub. by Batsford England). David & Charles.

--An Englishman's Home. LC 78-52159. 1978. 14.95 (ISBN 0-7153-7637-3). David & Charles.

--Peel's England. LC 77-73586. 1977. 14.95 (ISBN 0-7153-7380-3). David & Charles.

--Portrait of Exmoor. LC 75-522868. (Portrait Bks.). (Illus.). 1970. 10.50x (ISBN 0-7091-1606-1). Intl Pubns Serv.

--Portrait of the Severn. LC 79-365046. (Portrait Bks.). (Illus.). 1968. 10.50x (ISBN 0-7091-0432-4). Intl Pubns Serv.

--Portrait of the Thames from Teddington to the Source. LC 67-84564. (Portrait Books Ser). (Illus.). 1967. 10.50x (ISBN 0-7091-0748-X). Intl Pubns Serv.

Peel, John D. Fundamentals of Training for Security Officers: A Comprehensive Guide to What You Should Be, Know & Do to Have a Successful Career As a Private Patrolman or Security Officer. (Illus.). 344p. 1980. 17.95 (ISBN 0-398-03966-6). C C Thomas.

--Story of Private Security. 168p. 1971. 12.75 (ISBN 0-398-01465-5). C C Thomas.

--The Training, Licensing & Guidance of Private Security Officers. 288p. 1973. 14.75 (ISBN 0-398-02813-3). C C Thomas.

Peel, Robert. Mary Baker Eddy, Vol. 1: The Years of Discovery, 1821-1875. 1972. 7.50 o.p. (ISBN 0-03-057555-9); pap. 3.95 (ISBN 0-03-086648-0). HR&W.

Peel, Roy V. & Donnelly, Thomas C. The Nineteen Thirty-Two Campaign. LC 73-454. (FDR & the Era of the New Deal Ser.). 252p. 1973. Repr. of 1935 ed. lib. bdg. 29.50 (ISBN 0-306-70567-2). Da Capo.

Peel, William J., jt. auth. see Dwight, John A.

Peele, David A., ed. Racket & Paddle Games: A Guide to Information Sources. LC 80-23977. (Sports, Games & Pastimes Information Guide Ser., Part of the Gale Information Guide Library: Vol. 9). 300p. 1980. 30.00 (ISBN 0-8103-1480-0). Gale.

Peele, Gillian, jt. auth. see Beloff, Max.

Peele, R. Mining Engineers' Handbook, 2 vols. 3rd ed. (Engineering Handbook Ser.). 1941. Set. 75.00 (ISBN 0-471-67716-7, Pub. by Wiley-Interscience). Wiley.

Peele, Stanton. The Addiction Experience. 1980. pap. 1.50. Hazelden.

Peelle, Howard. APL: An Introduction. (gr. 10 up). 1978. pap. text ed. 10.50 (ISBN 0-8104-5122-0). Hayden.

Peeples, Kenneth E., Jr., jt. auth. see Josey, E. J.

Peeples, W. D., jt. auth. see Wheeler, Ruric E.

Peeples, W. D., Jr., jt. auth. see Wheeler, Ruric E.

Peer Review Committee of the American Psychiatric Assn., et al, eds. Manual of Psychiatric Peer Review. 160p. 1981. spiral bdg. 11.00 (ISBN 0-685-76788-4, P168-0). Am Psychiatric.

Peerbolte, M. Lietaert. Psychic Energy. 1979. 12.95 (ISBN 0-685-95695-4, Pub. by Servire BV Netherlands). Hunter Hse.

Peerless, S. & McCormick, C. W., eds. Microsurgery for Cerebral Ischemia. (Illus.). 362p. 1981. 89.80 (ISBN 0-387-90495-6). Springer-Verlag.

Peerman, Dean G., jt. auth. see Marty, Martin E.

Peerman, Dean G., jt. ed. see Marty, Martin E.

Peers, E. Allison see John Of The Cross.

Peers, J. Allison, tr. see Lull, Ramon.

Peery, Rex & Umbach, Arnold. Wrestling. rev. ed. LC 61-12052. (Athletic Institute Ser). (Illus.). (gr. 6 up). 1967. 7.95 (ISBN 0-8069-4334-3); PLB 8.29 (ISBN 0-8069-4335-1). Sterling.

Peet, Bill. The Ant & the Elephant. LC 74-179918. (Illus.). 48p. (gr. k-3). 1972. reinforced bdg. 8.95 (ISBN 0-395-16963-1); pap. 2.95 (ISBN 0-395-29205-0). HM.

--Capyboppy. (Illus.). (gr. 2-4). 1966. reinforced bdg. 6.95 (ISBN 0-395-24378-5); pap. 3.00 o.p. (ISBN 0-395-07019-8). HM.

--Chester the Worldly Pig. (Illus.). (gr. k-3). 1965. reinforced bdg. 10.95 (ISBN 0-395-18470-3). HM.

--Eli. LC 77-17500. (gr. k-3). 1978. reinforced bdg. 8.95 (ISBN 0-395-26454-5). HM.

--Encore for Eleanor. (gr. k-3). 1981. 9.95 (ISBN 0-395-29860-1). HM.

--Farewell to Shady Glade. (gr. k-3). 1981. pap. 3.95x (ISBN 0-395-31128-4). HM.

--Jennifer & Josephine. (Illus.). (ps-3). 1980. pap. 3.45 (ISBN 0-395-29608-0, Sandpiper). HM.

--Kermit the Hermit. (Illus.). (gr. k-3). 1965. 8.95 (ISBN 0-395-15084-1). HM.

--Kermit the Hermit. (Illus.). (ps-3). 1980. pap. 3.45 (ISBN 0-395-29607-2, Sandpiper). HM.

--The Wump World. (gr. k-3). 1981. pap. 3.95x (ISBN 0-395-31129-2). HM.

Peet, Creighton. First Book of Skyscrapers. LC 64-17781. (First Bks). (Illus.). (gr. 4-6). 1964. PLB 4.90 o.p. (ISBN 0-531-00629-8). Watts.

Peet, Louis H. Handy Book of American Authors. LC 75-156928. 1971. Repr. of 1907 ed. 24.00 (ISBN 0-8103-3360-0). Gale.

Peet, Louise J., et al. Household Equipment. 8th ed. LC 78-11749. 1979. text ed. 20.95 (ISBN 0-471-02694-8); tchrs. manual avail. (ISBN 0-471-04876-3). Wiley.

Peeters, H., ed. Protides of the Biological Fluids: Prceedings, Colloquium on Protides of the Biological Fluids, 26th. LC 58-5908. (Illus.). 1978. text ed. 150.00 (ISBN 0-08-023182-9). Pergamon.

--Protides of the Biological Fluids: Proceedings, Colloquium on Protides of the Biological Fluids, 24th. 1977. 150.00 (ISBN 0-08-020359-0). Pergamon.

--Separation of Cells & Subcellular Elements. (Illus.). 1979. 22.00 (ISBN 0-08-024957-4). Pergamon.

Peeters, H., ed. see Colloquium on Protides of the Biological Fluids, 27th, Brussels, Apr. 30-May 3, 1979.

Peeters, Henk, jt. auth. see Ketting, Kees.

Peeters, Theo, jt. ed. see Fratianni, Michele.

Pefley, Richard K., ed. Proceedings of Third International Symposium on Alcohol Fuel Technology. 1000p. 1980. 79.95 (ISBN 0-686-65544-3); pap. 59.95 (ISBN 0-89934-020-2). Solar Energy Info.

Pegalis, Steven & Wachsman, Harvey. American Law of Medical Malpractice, 2 vols. LC 79-90712. 1980. 95.00. Lawyers Co-Op.

Pegals, C. Carl. Health Care & the Elderly. 300p. 1980. text ed. write for info. (ISBN 0-89443-333-4). Aspen Systems.

Pegden, Claude D., jt. auth. see Pritsker, A. Alan.

Pegels, C. Carl & Verkler, R. C. BASIC: A Computer Programming Language with Business & Management Applications. 3rd ed. 1978. pap. text ed. 12.95 (ISBN 0-8162-6684-0); instr'. manual 1.95 (ISBN 0-8162-6683-2). Holden-Day.

Pegels, C. Carl, jt. ed. see Mahajan, Vijay.

Pegis, Anton C., ed. see Thomas Aquinas, Saint.

Pegler, H. S. The Book of the Goat. Date not set. 6.00 (ISBN 0-686-26688-9). Dairy Goat.

Pegler, Martin, ed. Store Windows That Sell, 1980-81. (Illus.). 178p. 1980. 34.95 (ISBN 0-934590-04-4). Retail Report.

Pegler, Martin M. Tell & Sell. 1979. 7.95 (ISBN 0-911380-46-9). Signs of Times.

Pegram, Marjorie. Time & Chance. 1979. pap. 1.95 (ISBN 0-87508-594-6). Chr Lit.

Peheim, E., tr. see Eastham, R. C.

Pehrson, Robert N. The Bilateral Network of Social Relations in Konkama Lapp District. 3rd ed. 1971. pap. text ed. 10.00x (ISBN 8-200-04133-6, Dist. by Columbia U Pr). Universitet.

Pei, Mario. One Language for the World & How to Achieve It. LC 68-56449. 1958. 10.00x (ISBN 0-8196-0218-3). Biblo.

--The World's Chief Languages. 1960. 16.50 (ISBN 0-913298-07-7). S F Vanni.

Pei, Mario & Gaynor, Frank. Dictionary of Linguistics. (Quality Paperback: No. 177). 1980. pap. 4.95 (ISBN 0-8226-0177-X). Littlefield.

Pei, Mario A. Glossary of Linguistic Terminology. 1966. 20.00x (ISBN 0-231-03012-6). Columbia U Pr.

Peich, Michael, jt. auth. see McCurdy, Michael.

Peich, Michael, ed. see Steiner, Robert.

Peierls, Rudolf E. Quantum Theory of Solids. (International Series of Monographs on Physics). (Orig.). 1964. pap. 29.95x (ISBN 0-19-851240-6). Oxford U Pr.

Peige, John, et al, eds. Fire Service First Aid Practices, IFSTA Committee: 109. LC 77-75409. 1977. pap. text ed. 7.00 (ISBN 0-87939-009-3). Intl Fire Serv.

Peige, John, et al, eds. see IFSTA Committee.

Peige, John D. & Laughlin, Jerry, eds. Fire Service Reference Guide: 502. LC 77-80386. 1977. pap. text ed. 6.00 (ISBN 0-87939-031-X). Intl Fire Serv.

Peige, John D., et al, eds. see IFSTA Committee.

Peikari, Behrouz. Fundamentals of Network Analysis & Synthesis. (Illus.). 544p. 1974. ref. ed. 26.95 (ISBN 0-13-341321-7). P-H.

Peil, Margaret. Cities & Suburbs: Urban Life in West Africa. LC 80-26440. (New Library of African Affairs). 330p. 1981. text ed. 24.00x (ISBN 0-8419-0685-8). Holmes & Meier.

--Consensus & Conflict in African Societies. (African Studies Ser). (Illus.). 1977. text ed. 21.00x (ISBN 0-582-64173-X); pap. text ed. 9.95x (ISBN 0-582-64174-8). Longman.

Peil, William. The Big Story. (Illus.). 62p. (gr. 2-4). 1973. pap. 0.95 (ISBN 0-87793-124-0). Ave Maria.

Peirce, Charles S. Chance, Love & Logic. 317p. 1980. Repr. of 1923 ed. lib. bdg. 50.00 (ISBN 0-89984-386-7). Century Bookbindery.

--Charles S. Peirce: Selected Writings. Wiener, Philip P., ed. Orig. Title: Values in a Universe of Chance: Selected Writings of Charles S. (Peirce). pap. text ed. 6.00 (ISBN 0-486-21634-9). Dover.

Peirce, Neal R. & Longley, Lawrence D. The People's President: The Electoral College in American History & the Direct Vote Alternative. rev. ed. LC 80-24260. (Illus.). 416p. 1981. text ed. 40.00x (ISBN 0-300-02612-9); pap. 9.95 (ISBN 0-300-02704-4). Yale U Pr.

Peire Vidal. Poesie: Edizione Critica e Commento a Cura Di D'Arco Silvio Avalle, 2 vols. in 1. LC 80-2186. 1981. Repr. of 1960 ed. 72.50 (ISBN 0-404-19011-1). AMS Pr.

Peirol D'Auvergne & Aston, S. C. Peirol, Troubadour of Auvergne. LC 80-2185. 1981. Repr. of 1953 ed. 32.00 (ISBN 0-404-19012-X). AMS Pr.

Peirson, Gwynne. Police Operations. LC 75-44334. (Nelson-Hall Law Enforcement Ser.). 182p. 1976. 17.95 (ISBN 0-911012-86-9). Nelson-Hall.

Peisert, Hansgert. Systems of Higher Education: Federal Republic of Germany. (Design & Management of Systems of Higher Education Ser.). 240p. (Orig.). 1978. pap. text ed. 8.00 (ISBN 0-89192-206-7). Interbk Inc.

Peithmann, Irvin M. Broken Peace Pipes: A Four-Hundred Year History of the American Indian. 320p. 1964. 11.75 (ISBN 0-398-01468-X). C C Thomas.

Pejovich, Svetozar. The Codetermination Movement in the West. LC 77-18480. 1978. 21.00 (ISBN 0-669-02112-1). Lexington Bks.

Pejovich, Svetozar, jt. auth. see Furubotn, Eirik G.

Pejovich, Svetozar, ed. Governmental Controls & the Free Market: The U. S. Economy in the 1970's. LC 76-17976. 240p. 1976. 19.50x (ISBN 0-89096-020-8). Tex A&M Univ Pr.

Pekar, Peter P., jt. auth. see Ellis, Darryl J.

Pekarik, Andrew J. Japanese Lacquer, 1600-1900: Selections from the Charles A. Greenfield Collection. Wasserman, Rosanne, ed. (Illus.). 146p. 1980. 19.95 (ISBN 0-87099-247-3). Metro Mus Art.

Pekelis, Alexander H. Law & Social Action: Selected Essays of Alexander H. Pekelis. Konvitz, Milton, ed. LC 77-87376. (American Constitutional & Legal History Ser). (Illus.). 1970. Repr. of 1950 ed. lib. bdg. 29.50 (ISBN 0-306-71600-3). Da Capo.

Pekelis, V. Cybernetics A to Z. (Illus.). 310p. 1975. 10.00x o.p. (ISBN 0-8464-0310-2). Beekman Pubs.

Peking University Faculty. Modern Chinese: A Basic Course. LC 78-169835. Orig. Title: Modern Chinese Reader. 1971. pap. text ed. 3.50 (ISBN 0-486-22755-3); record & manual o.p. 12.95 (ISBN 0-686-66298-9). Dover.

--Modern Chinese: A Second Course. rev. ed. 500p. 1981. pap. price not set (ISBN 0-486-24155-6). Dover.

Pekkanen, John. Travel Ontario. 1971. 3.95 o.p. (ISBN 0-695-80233-X). Follett.

Peklenik, J. Advances in Manufacturing Systems - Research & Development. 196p. 1972. text ed. 50.00 (ISBN 0-08-016497-8). Pergamon.

Pel, Mario, tr. see Mazzolani, Lidia S.

Peladeau, Marius B. Stephen R. Deane: Early Maine Folk Calligrapher. (Illus.). 128p. 1981. 22.50 (ISBN 0-931474-15-9). TBW Bks.

Peladeau, Marius B., ed. see Tyler, Royall.

Pelczar, Michael, Jr & Chan, E. C. S. Elements of Microbiology. 1st ed. (Illus.). 704p. (Orig.). text ed. 19.95 (ISBN 0-07-049240-9, C); 10.95 (ISBN 0-07-049241-7); instrs'. 5.50 (ISBN 0-07-049230-1). McGraw.

Pelczynski, Aleksander. Banach Spaces of Analytic Functions & Absolutely Summing Operators. LC 77-9884. (Conference Board of the Mathematical Sciences Ser.: No. 30). 1980. Repr. of 1977 ed. 7.00 (ISBN 0-8218-1680-2, CBMS30). Am Math.

Peled, Abraham & Liu, Bede. Digital Signal Processing: Theory, Design & Implemetation. LC 76-17326. 1976. text ed. 24.95 (ISBN 0-471-01941-0); avail. solutions manual (ISBN 0-471-03634-X). Wiley.

Pelegrin, M. J., et al, eds. Comparison of Automatic & Oprations Research Techniques Applied to Large Systems Analysis. LC 80-40979. (Illus.). 240p. 40.00 (ISBN 0-08-024454-8). Pergamon.

Pelegrinis, Theodosius N. Kant's Conceptions of the Categorical Imperative & the Will. 236p. 1980. text ed. 12.50x (ISBN 0-391-01922-8). Humanities.

Pelenski, Jaroslaw, ed. The American & European Revolutions, 1776-1848: Sociopolitical & Ideological Aspects. LC 79-22599. (Illus.). 430p. 1980. text ed. 17.50x (ISBN 0-87745-097-8, 8294). U of Iowa Pr.

Pelgrom, Els. The Winter When Time Was Frozen. Rudnik, Maryka & Rudnik, Raphael, trs. from Dutch. LC 80-21224. Orig. Title: De Kinderen Van Het Achtste Woud. 224p. (gr. 4-6). 1980. 8.95 (ISBN 0-688-22247-1); PLB 8.59 (ISBN 0-688-32247-6). Morrow.

Pelham, Joseph, et al. To Hear & to Heed. 1978. 1.50 (ISBN 0-686-28797-5). Forward Movement.

Pelham, Thomas G. State Land-Use Planning & Regulation: Florida, the Model Code, & Beyond. LC 79-2390. (Lincoln Institute of Land Policy Books). 224p. 1979. 23.95 (ISBN 0-669-03062-7). Lexington Bks.

Pelikan, Jaroslav. The Christian Tradition, a History of the Development of Doctrine: The Spirit of Eastern Christendom (600-1700, Vol. 2. LC 79-142042. 1977. pap. 7.50 (ISBN 0-226-65373-0, P738, Phoen). U of Chicago Pr.

--The Christian Tradition: A History of the Development of Doctrine, Vol. 1: Emergence of the Catholic Tradition, 100-600. LC 79-142042. 1971. 20.00 (ISBN 0-226-65370-6). U of Chicago Pr.

Pelikan, Phyllis K. see Saxton, Dolores F., et al.

Pell, Arthur R. Police Leadership. (Illus.). 152p. 1967. 8.75 (ISBN 0-398-01471-X). C C Thomas.

Pell, Erik M., ed. Proceedings: International Conference on Photoconductivity - 3rd - Stanford University - Aug. 12 1969. 1972. 82.00 (ISBN 0-08-016137-5). Pergamon.

Pell, P. S., ed. Developments in Highway-Pavement Engineering, Vol. 1. (Illus.). 1978. 54.00x (ISBN 0-85334-781-6, Pub. by Applied Science). Burgess-Intl Ideas.

--Developments in Highway Pavement Engineering, Vol. 2. (Illus.). 1978. 36.80x (ISBN 0-85334-804-9, Pub. by Applied Science). Burgess-Intl Ideas.

Pell, Sylvia. The Shadow of the Sun. 384p. 1981. pap. 2.50 (ISBN 0-380-50658-0, 50658). Avon.

Pellaprat, H. P. Modern French Culinary Art. rev. ed. Fuller, John, ed. Orig. Title: L'art Culinaire Moderne. (Illus.). 1974. 89.95 (ISBN 0-00-435143-6, Virtue & Co.). CBI Pub.

Pellat, Charles. The Life & Works of Jahiz. Hawke, D. M, tr. (Islamic World Series). 1969. 18.50x (ISBN 0-520-01498-7). U of Cal Pr.

Pellegreno, Ann H. Iowa Takes to the Air: 1845-1918, Vol. 1. LC 79-55458. (Illus.). (YA) 1981. 14.95 (ISBN 0-935092-01-3). Aerodrome Pr.

Pellegrini, Angelo M. Food-Lover's Garden. LC 76-106621. (Illus.). 1970. pap. 4.95 (ISBN 0-914842-06-4). Madrona Pubs.

Pellegrino, Edmund D. & Thomasma, David C. A Philosophical Basis of Medical Practice: Toward a Philosophy & Ethic of the Healing Professions. (Illus.). 368p. 1981. 19.95x (ISBN 0-19-502790-6). Oxford U Pr.

--A Philosophical Basis of Medical Practice: Toward a Philosophy & Ethic of the Healing Professions. (Illus.). 368p. 1981. text ed. 11.95x (ISBN 0-19-502789-2). Oxford U Pr.

Pellegrino, Victoria Y., jt. auth. see DeRosis, Helen.

Pelleprat. Modern French Culinary Art. 1978. 92.50 (ISBN 0-685-47809-2). Radio City.

Pellet, P. L. & Shadarevian, Sossy. Food Composition: Tables for Use in the Middle East. 1970. pap. 10.00x (ISBN 0-8156-6032-4, Am U Beirut). Syracuse U Pr.

Pelletier, Kenneth R., ed. Holistic Medicine: From Pathology to Optimum Health. (A Merloyd Lawrence Bk.). 1979. 10.00 (ISBN 0-440-05288-2, Sey Lawr). Delacorte.

Pelletier, Paul. Prominent Scientists: An Index to Collected Bibliographies. 250p. 1980. 29.95 (ISBN 0-918212-41-3). Neal-Schuman.

Pellew, George. John Jay. LC 80-19992. (American Statesmen Ser.). 342p. 1980. pap. 5.95 (ISBN 0-87754-193-0). Chelsea Hse.

Pellicani, Luciano. Gramsci & the Communist Question. Watts, Mimi, tr. from Ital. (Publication Ser.: No. 243). 128p. (Orig.). 1981. pap. write for info. (ISBN 0-8179-7432-6). Hoover Inst Pr.

Pelling, H. Britain & the Second World War. 1970. pap. 1.95 o.p. (ISBN 0-531-06001-2, Fontana Pap). Watts.

Pelling, Margaret. Cholera, Fever & English Medicine, 1825 - 1865. (Historical Monographs). 1978. text ed. 29.95x (ISBN 0-19-821872-9). Oxford U Pr.

Pelling, Margaret, jt. ed. see Maddison, Francis.

Pelliot, Paul. Les Mongols et la Papaute, 3 pts. in 1 vol. LC 80-2365. 1981. Repr. of 1923 ed. 34.50 (ISBN 0-404-18913-X). AMS Pr.

Pellowski, Anne. Willow Wind Farm: Betsy's Story. (Illus.). 176p. (gr. 9-12). 1981. 8.95 (ISBN 0-399-20781-3). Philomel.

Pelly, Brian R. Thyristor Phase-Controlled Converters & Cycloconverters: Operation, Control, & Performance. LC 70-125276. 1971. 44.50 (ISBN 0-471-67790-6, Pub. by Wiley-Interscience). Wiley.

Pelnar, Premysl U. Health Effects of Asbestos & of Some Other Minerals & Fibres As Reflected in the World Literature: A Compendium of References, 1906-1979. 1981. 25.00 set (ISBN 0-930376-25-0). Pathotox Pubs.

Peloquin, Peter J. Laypersons Handbook of Radiation & How to Protect Yourself. (Orig.). 1980. pap. 1.95 (ISBN 0-936448-01-6). Peloquin Pubn.

--Reflections of a Nuclear War & the Energy Shortage. 64p. 1980. pap. 2.95 (ISBN 0-936448-00-8). Peloquin Pubns.

Peloro, Filomena C; see Eddy, Frederick D.

Pelosi, John W., jt. ed. see Wiegerink, Ronald.

Peloubet, F. N., ed. see Smith, William.

Peloubet, M. A., ed. see Smith, William.

Pels, Gertrude. Care of Water Pets. LC 54-9768. (Illus.). (gr. 2-5). 1955. 8.95 (ISBN 0-690-17070-X, TYC-J); PLB 8.79 (ISBN 0-690-17071-8). T Y Crowell.

Pelson, Wickes, jt. auth. see Liebert, Robert M.

Pelstring, Linda & Hauck, Jo A. Food to Improve Your Health. 256p. 1975. pap. 1.50 o.p. (ISBN 0-523-00637-3). Pinnacle Bks.

Pelstring, Linda & Mauck, JoAnn. Foods to Improve Your Health: A Complete Guide to Over Three Hundred Foods for One Hundred One Common Ailments. LC 73-83298. 224p. 1974. 3.95 (ISBN 0-8027-7147-5). Walker & Co.

Pelt, Ethel Van see Van Pelt, Ethel.

Pelt, Nancy Van see Van Pelt, Nancy.

Pelta, Kathy. What Does a Lifeguard Do? LC 76-53440. (What Do They Do Ser.). (gr. 4 up). 1977. 5.95 (ISBN 0-396-07406-5). Dodd.

--What Does an Airplane Pilot Do? LC 80-23530. (What Do They Do Ser.). (Illus.). 80p. (gr. 5 up). 1981. PLB 5.95 (ISBN 0-396-07910-5). Dodd.

Peltier, Leslie C. Guideposts to the Stars: Exploring the Skies Through the Year. LC 72-187797. (Illus.). (gr. 7 up). 1972. 9.95 (ISBN 0-02-770600-1). Macmillan.

Pelto. The Nature of Anthropology. 1966. pap. text ed. 4.95x (ISBN 0-675-09715-0). Merrill.

--The Study of Anthropology. 1965. pap. text ed. 4.95x (ISBN 0-675-09700-2). Merrill.

Pelto, Gretel H., jt. auth. see Glasser, Morton.

Pelto, Gretel H., jt. auth. see Pelto, Pertti J.

Pelto, Pertti J. The Snowmobile Revolution: Technology & Social Change in the Arctic. LC 72-89138. 210p. 1973. 6.95 (ISBN 0-8465-3755-9). Benjamin-Cummings.

Pelto, Pertti J. & Muessig, Raymond H. The Study & Teaching of Anthropology. 2nd ed. (Social Science Seminar, Secondary Education Ser.: No. C28). 136p. 1980. pap. text ed. 5.95 (ISBN 0-675-08192-0). Merrill.

Pelto, Pertti J & Pelto, Gretel H. Anthropological Research: The Structure of Inquiry. 2d ed. LC 76-62583. 1978. 29.95 (ISBN 0-521-21673-7); pap. 10.95x (ISBN 0-521-29228-X). Cambridge U Pr.

Pelton. Social Context of Child Abuse & Neglect. LC 80-13922. 1980. 24.95 (ISBN 0-87705-504-1). Human Sci Pr.

Pelton, Barry C. Badminton. (Prentice-Hall Sports Ser.). (Illus.). 1971. pap. text ed. 4.25x (ISBN 0-13-055327-1). P-H.

Pelton, Charles L. The Sex Book for Those Who Think They Know It All. Klinkel, Sheryl, ed. (Illus.). 227p. 1980. lib. bdg. 24.95 (ISBN 0-931470-03-X); pap. 14.95 (ISBN 0-931470-04-8). C L Pelton.

Pelton, Joseph N. Global Talk. LC 80-83261. 320p. 1980. write for info. (ISBN 90-286-0240-2). Sijthoff & Noordhoff.

Pelton, Joseph N. & Snow, Marcellus S., eds. Economic & Policy Problems in Satellite Communications. LC 75-44937. 1976. text ed. 25.95 (ISBN 0-275-23730-3). Praeger.

Pelton, Leroy H. The Psychology of Nonviolence. LC 74-2156. 310p. 1975. text ed. 23.00 (ISBN 0-08-018099-X). Pergamon.

Pelton, Robert D. The Trickster in West Africa: A Study of Mythic Irony & Sacred Delight. (Hermeneutics: Studies in the History of Religions). 1980. 27.50x (ISBN 0-520-03477-5). U of Cal Pr.

Pelton, Robert W. Loony Laws: You Never Knew You Were Breaking. LC 80-54814. (Illus.). 160p. 1981. 9.95 (ISBN 0-8027-0687-8); pap. 4.95 (ISBN 0-8027-7174-2). Walker & Co.

Pelton, Robert W., jt. auth. see Carden, Karen W.

Peltz, Leslie R. Fashion Accessories. 2nd ed. 1980. pap. 8.95 (ISBN 0-672-97275-1); tchrs. manual 3.33 (ISBN 0-672-97276-X). Bobbs.

--Fashion, Color, Line, & Design. 2nd ed. 1980. 9.90 (ISBN 0-672-97278-6); pap. 3.33 (ISBN 0-672-97277-8). Bobbs.

--Merchandising Mathematics. LC 79-494. 1979. pap. 9.50 (ISBN 0-672-97273-5); tchr's manual 3.33 (ISBN 0-672-97274-3). Bobbs.

Peluso, A. P., jt. auth. see Bauer, C. R.

Peluso, Ada. Background for Calculus. 1978. pap. text ed. 15.95 (ISBN 0-8403-2295-X, 40229501). Kendall-Hunt.

Peluso, Anthony P., et al. Basic BASIC Programming: Self-Instructional Manual & Text. (Computer Science Ser). 1971. pap. 13.95 (ISBN 0-201-05845-6). A-W.

Peluso, J. J., jt. ed. see Hafez, E. S.

Pelz, T., tr. see Ogibalov, P. M., et al.

Pelz, Werner. The Scope of Understanding in Sociology. 1974. 22.50x (ISBN 0-7100-7854-4); pap. 10.00 (ISBN 0-7100-8009-3). Routledge & Kegan.

Pelz, William. Basic Keyboard Skills: An Introduction to Accompaniment Improvisation, Transposition & Modulation, with an Appendix on Sight Reading. LC 80-22820. vii, 173p. 1981. Repr. of 1963 ed. PLB 23.50x (ISBN 0-313-22882-5, PEBK). Greenwood.

Pelzel, Thomas. Anton Raphael Mengs & Neoclassicism. LC 78-74375. (Fine Arts Dissertations, Fourth Ser.). (Illus.). 1980. lib. bdg. 27.50 (ISBN 0-8240-3962-9). Garland Pub.

Pember, Don. Mass Media in America. 3rd ed. 416p. 1981. pap. text ed. 11.95 (ISBN 0-574-22715-6, 13-5715); instr's. guide avail. (ISBN 0-574-22716-4, 13-5716). SRA.

--Mass Media in America. 2nd ed. LC 76-50018. (Illus.). 1977. pap. text ed. 11.95 (ISBN 0-574-22705-9, 13-5705); instr's guide avail. (ISBN 0-574-22706-7, 13-5706). SRA.

Pember, Don R. Mass Media Law. 2nd ed. 500p. 1981. text ed. write for info. (ISBN 0-697-04347-9). Wm C Brown.

--Privacy & the Press: The Law, the Mass Media, & the First Amendment. LC 79-152335. (Washington Paperback Ser.: No. 64). (Illus.). 312p. 1972. 11.50 (ISBN 0-295-95152-4); pap. 3.45 (ISBN 0-295-95265-2). U of Wash Pr.

Pember, G. H. Earth's Earliest Ages. LC 75-13928. 1975. 8.95 (ISBN 0-8254-3508-0). Kregel.

Pember-Reeves, M. S. Round About a Pound a Week: London, Ninetee Thirteen. LC 79-56968. (The English Working Class Ser.). 1980. lib. bdg. 25.00 (ISBN 0-8240-0119-2). Garland Pub.

Pemberton, J. E. British Official Publications. 2nd ed. LC 73-16231. 328p. 1974. text ed. 13.80 (ISBN 0-08-017797-2). Pergamon.

--How to Find Out in Mathematics. 2nd ed. 1970. 22.00 (ISBN 0-08-006824-3); pap. 10.75 (ISBN 0-08-006823-5). Pergamon.

--Politics & Public Libraries in England & Wales, 1850 - 1970. 1977. 13.25x (ISBN 0-85365-109-4, Pub. by Lib Assn England). Oryx Pr.

Pemberton, LeRoy A., jt. auth. see Archer, E. C.

Pemberton, Margaret. Shadows Over Silver Sands. large type ed. pap. 1.25 o.p. (ISBN 0-425-03049-0). Berkley Pub.

--Some Distant Shore. (Orig.). 1981. pap. 2.75 (ISBN 0-671-42772-5). Archway.

Pemberton, S. Macpherson. Disestablishment in Ireland: Implications for Catholic Objectives in Higher Education, 1869-1879. LC 79-64245. 1979. pap. text ed. 7.75 (ISBN 0-8191-0759-X). U Pr of Amer.

Pembrey, Sue. The Ward Sister. (RCN Research Monograph). 184p. 1981. pap. text ed. 10.00 (ISBN 0-443-02411-1). Churchill.

Pembrook, Linda. How to Beat Fatigue. 1975. pap. 1.75 (ISBN 0-380-00671-5, 29371). Avon.

Pempel, T. J. Patterns of Japanese Policy-Making: Experiences from Higher Education. 1978. lib. bdg. 21.50 o.p. (ISBN 0-89158-270-3). Westview.

Pemsteen, Hans. Clash of the Titans Storybook. (Illus.). 32p. (gr. 4-6). 1981. 4.95 (ISBN 0-307-16801-8, Golden Pr). Western Pub.

Pena, Alberto & De Bliek, Ruth. Cost Effectiveness in Training & Instruction. LC 80-82294. (Guideline Ser.). 60p. Date not set. pap. 6.95x (ISBN 0-931816-01-7). Kumarian Pr. Postponed.

Pena, Augustin De La see De La Pena, Augustin.

Pena, William, et al. Problem Seeking: An Architectural Programming Primer. LC 77-73637. 1977. 16.95 (ISBN 0-8436-2172-9). CBI Pub.

Penalosa, Fernando. Introduction to the Sociology of Language. 320p. (Orig.). 1981. pap. text ed. 13.95 (ISBN 0-88377-183-7). Newbury Hse.

Pencak, William. War, Politics, & Revolution in Provincial Massachusetts. (Illus.). 276p. 1980. write for info. (ISBN 0-930350-10-3). NE U Pr.

Pence, Danny B. Keys, Species & Host List, & Bibliography for Nasal Mites of North American Birds (Acarina: Rhinonyssinae, Turbinoptinae, Speleognathinae, & Cytoditidae) (Special Publications: No. 8). (Illus., Orig.). 1975. pap. 6.00 (ISBN 0-89672-033-0). Tex Tech Pr.

Penczek, S., ed. Polymerization of Heterocycles (Ring-Opening) LC 76-44623. 1977. text ed. 30.00 (ISBN 0-08-021367-7). Pergamon.

Penczek, S., et al. Cationic Ring-Opening Polymerization of Heterocyclic Monomers. (Advances in Polymer Science Ser.: Vol. 37). (Illus.). 156p. 1981. 46.00 (ISBN 0-387-10209-4). Springer-Verlag.

Pendar, Kenneth. Adventure in Diplomacy. LC 76-5479. (World War II Ser.). 1976. Repr. of 1945 ed. lib. bdg. 22.50 (ISBN 0-306-70774-8). Da Capo.

Pender, H. & Del Mar, W. Electrical Engineers Handbook: Electrical Power. 4th ed. (Wiley Engineers Handbook Ser.). 1949. 40.00 (ISBN 0-471-67881-3, Pub. by Wiley-Interscience). Wiley.

Pender, H. & McIlwain, K. Electrical Engineers Handbook: Electric Communication & Electronics. 4th ed. (Wiley Engineers Handbook Ser.). 1950. 39.95 (ISBN 0-471-67848-1, Pub. by Wiley-Interscience). Wiley.

Pender, Lydia. The Useless Donkeys. LC 79-25304. (Illus.). 40p. (gr. k-3). 1980. 9.95g (ISBN 0-7232-6194-6). Warne.

Pendered, Maureen, jt. auth. see Launay, Andre.

Pendered, Norman C., jt. auth. see Wilber, Gordon O.

Pendergrass, Virginia E., ed. Women Winning: A Handbook for Action Against Sex Discrimination. LC 78-27379. 1979. 16.95 (ISBN 0-88229-450-4); pap. 8.95 (ISBN 0-88229-699-X). Nelson-Hall.

Pendle, George. Land & People of Chile. (gr. 5-9). 1960. 3.95g o.s.i. (ISBN 0-02-770790-3). Macmillan.

--Land & People of Peru. (gr. 5-9). 1968. 3.95 o.s.i. (ISBN 0-02-770890-X). Macmillan.

Pendlebury, David, tr. The Walled Garden of Truth. 1976. pap. 2.95 o.p. (ISBN 0-525-47414-5). Dutton.

Pendlebury, John D. Archaeology of Crete. LC 63-18049. (Illus.). 12.00x (ISBN 0-8196-0121-7). Biblo.

Pendleton, Conrad. West: Manhattan to Oregon. LC 66-20103. 72p. 1966. 4.75 (ISBN 0-8040-0318-1). Swallow.

Pendleton, Don. Colorado Kill Zone. (Executioner Ser.: No. 25). 192p. (Orig.). 1976. pap. 1.95 (ISBN 0-523-40761-0). Pinnacle Bks.

--Executioner: Miami Massacre. (Executioner Ser, No. 4). 1970. pap. 1.95 (ISBN 0-523-41068-9). Pinnacle Bks.

--Executioner: Nightmare in New York. (Executioner Ser, No. 7). (Orig.). 1971. pap. 1.95 (ISBN 0-523-41071-9). Pinnacle Bks.

--Executioner: Vegas Vendetta. (Executioner Ser. No. 9). (Orig.). 1971. pap. 1.95 (ISBN 0-523-41073-5). Pinnacle Bks.

--Friday's Feast. (Executioner Ser.: No. 37). (Orig.). 1979. pap. 1.95 (ISBN 0-523-41101-4). Pinnacle Bks.

--Monday's Mob. (Executioner Ser.: No. 33). pap. 1.95 (ISBN 0-523-41097-2, Dist. by Independent News Co.). Pinnacle Bks.

--Sicilian Slaughter. (Executioner Ser. No. 16). pap. 1.95 (ISBN 0-523-40752-1). Pinnacle Bks.

--Tennessee Smash. (The Executioner Ser.: No. 32). 1978. pap. 1.95 (ISBN 0-523-41096-4). Pinnacle Bks.

--Wednesday's Wrath. (The Executioner Ser.: No. 35). 1979. pap. 1.95 (ISBN 0-523-41099-9). Pinnacle Bks.

Pendleton, Madge, et al. The Green Book: Guide for Living in Saudi Arabia. 3rd ed. LC 80-82276. (Illus.). 187p. 1980. pap. 12.00x (ISBN 0-918992-03-6). Middle East Edit.

Pendleton, Mary. Navajo & Hopi Weaving Techniques. (Illus.). 224p. 1974. 13.95 (ISBN 0-02-595500-4). Macmillan.

Pendleton, Niel. Fundraising: A Guide for Non-Profit Organizations. (Illus.). 192p. 1981. 13.95 (ISBN 0-13-332163-0, Spec); pap. 6.95 (ISBN 0-13-332155-X). P-H.

Pendleton, Winston K. Pursuit of Happiness. 1963. 3.95 o.p. (ISBN 0-8272-2922-4). Bethany Pr.

Pendry, E. D. Elizabethan Prisons & Prison Scenes, 2 vols. (Salzburg Studies in English Literature, Elizabethan & Renaissance Studies: No. 17). (Illus.). 385p. 1974. Set. pap. text ed. 50.25 (ISBN 0-391-01496-X). Humanities.

Pendry, Eric. The Way to Go Home. 1978. 8.95 (ISBN 0-393-08834-0). Norton.

Pene Du Bois, William. Bear Circus. (Viking Seafarer Ser). (Illus.). (gr. k-2). 1973. pap. 1.50 o.s.i. (ISBN 0-670-05085-7, Puffin). Penguin.

--Lion. (Viking Seafarer Ser). (Illus.). (gr. 1-3). 1974. pap. 1.50 o.p. (ISBN 0-670-05093-8, Puffin). Penguin.

--Squirrel Hotel. (Children's Literature Ser.). 1980. PLB 5.95 (ISBN 0-8398-2606-0). Gregg.

Penella, Robert J. The Letters of Apollonius of Tyana: A Critical Text with Prolegomena, Translation & Commentary. 146p. 1980. text ed. 25.25x (ISBN 90-04-05972-5). Humanities.

Penelope, Sr., tr. William of St. Thierry: On Contemplating God, Prayer, Meditations. (Cistercian Fathers Ser.: No. 3). 1970. pap. 4.00 (ISBN 0-87907-903-7). Cistercian Pubns.

Penfield, Marjorie, jt. auth. see Campbell, Ada M.

Penfield, Wilder & Roberts, Lamar. Speech & Brain Mechanisms. LC 59-5602. (Illus.). 304p. 1981. 25.00x; pap. 6.95. Princeton U Pr.

--Speech & Brain-Mechanisms. 1959. 25.00x (ISBN 0-691-08039-9). Princeton U Pr.

Penfold, Alastair, ed. Thomas Telford: Engineer. 192p. 1980. 40.00x (ISBN 0-7277-0084-7, Pub. by Telford England). State Mutual Bk.

Peng, Fred C., ed. Sign Language & Language Acquisition in Man & Ape. (AAAS Selected Symposium Ser.: No. 15). (Illus.). 1978. lib. bdg. 19.50x (ISBN 0-89158-445-5). Westview.

Peng, Syd S. Coal Mine Ground Control. LC 78-8965. 1978. 32.95 (ISBN 0-471-04121-1, Pub. by Wiley-Interscience). Wiley.

Peniakoff, Vladimir. Popski's Private Army. 368p. 1980. pap. 2.50 (ISBN 0-553-13048-X). Bantam.

Penick, Bettye, ed. see Committee on National Statistics, National Research Council.

Penick, Ib. The Lone Ranger: A Pop-up Book. LC 80-52868. (Pop-up Bks.: No. 43). (Illus.). 16p. (ps-3). 1981. pap. 4.95 boards o.p. (ISBN 0-394-84691-5). Random.

--Popeye: A Pop-up Book. LC 80-52840. (Pop-up Bks.: No. 42). (Illus.). 16p. (ps-3). 1981. pap. 4.95 boards (ISBN 0-394-84584-6). Random.

Peninou, Georges, et al. Multinational Corporations & European Public Opinion. LC 78-58894. (Praeger Special Studies). 1978. 23.95 (ISBN 0-03-046191-X). Praeger.

Penland & Williams. Community Psychology & Coordination. Date not set. price not set (ISBN 0-8247-6144-8). Dekker.

Penman, Kenneth A. Planning Physical Education & Athletic Facilities in Schools. LC 76-18134. 1977. text ed. 21.95 (ISBN 0-471-67915-1). Wiley.

--Using Statistics in Teaching Physical Education: A Linear Programmed Presentation. LC 76-3703. 1976. text ed. 12.95 (ISBN 0-471-67916-X). Wiley.

Penn, Elizabeth H. Individualized Arts & Crafts Lessons for the Elementary School. 1975. 13.95 o.p. (ISBN 0-685-73741-1). P-H.

Penn, Gerald M. & Batya, Judith. Interpretation of Immunoelectrophoretic Patterns. LC 77-93640. (Atlas Ser.). (Illus.). 1978. text ed. 30.00 (ISBN 0-89189-036-X, 16-A-001-00); incl. slides 140.00 (ISBN 0-89189-098-X, 15-A-001-00). Am Soc Clinical.

Penn, Jules. Jottings of a Stock Market Jackass. 3rd ed. 80p. (Orig.). 1973. pap. 5.00 o.p. (ISBN 0-912070-16-1). Bale Bks.

Penn, Margaret. The Foolish Virgin. 256p. Date not set. pap. 8.95 (ISBN 0-521-28297-7). Cambridge U Pr.

--Manchester Fourteen Miles. 244p. Date not set. pap. 8.95 (ISBN 0-521-28065-6). Cambridge U Pr.

--The Young Mrs. Burton. 256p. Date not set. pap. 8.95 (ISBN 0-521-28298-5). Cambridge U Pr.

Penn, William. Fruits of Solitude. pap. 3.95 (ISBN 0-913408-39-5). Friends United.

Penn, William & Myers, Albert C. William Penn's Own Account of the Lenni Lenape or Delaware Indians. rev. ed. (Illus.). 96p. 1981. pap. 4.95 (ISBN 0-912608-13-7). Mid Atlantic.

Pennak, Robert W. Collegiate Dictionary of Zoology. 1964. 21.50 (ISBN 0-8260-7100-7, Pub. by Wiley-Interscience). Wiley.

--Fresh-Water Invertebrates of the United States. 2nd ed. LC 78-8130. 1978. 32.50 (ISBN 0-471-04249-8, Pub. by Wiley-Interscience). Wiley.

Pennance, F. G., jt. auth. see Seldon, Arthur.

Pennar, Jaan, et al. Modernization & Diversity in Soviet Education: With Special Reference to Nationality Groups. LC 70-105285. (Special Studies in International Economics Development). 1971. 39.50x (ISBN 0-89197-854-2); pap. text ed. 16.50x (ISBN 0-89197-855-0). Irvington.

Pennell, Joseph. Illustration of Books: A Manual for the Use of Students. LC 78-146921. 1971. Repr. of 1896 ed. 18.00 (ISBN 0-8103-3641-3). Gale.

Pennell, Joseph & Bryant, Edward. Pennell's New York City Etchings: Ninety-One Prints. (Illus.). 112p. (Orig.). 1981. pap. write for info. (ISBN 0-486-23913-6). Dover.

Pennells, Ernest. Concrete Bridge Designer's Manual. (Viewpoint Publication Ser.). (Illus.). 1978. text ed. 40.00 (ISBN 0-7210-1083-0). Scholium Intl.

Penner, Allen R. Alan Sillitoe. LC 72-161822. (English Authors Ser.: No. 141). lib. bdg. 10.95 (ISBN 0-8057-1496-0). Twayne.

Penner, David A., jt. auth. see Bristol, James D.

Penner, Dick. Fiction of the Absurd: Pratfalls in the Void. (Orig.). 1980. pap. 3.50 (ISBN 0-451-61904-8, ME1904, Ment). NAL.

Penner, Jonathon. Going Blind. 1978. pap. 1.75 o.s.i. (ISBN 0-515-04541-1). Jove Pubns.

Penner, N. Canadian Left: A Critical Analysis. 1977. pap. 9.50 (ISBN 0-13-113126-5). P-H.

Penner, Rudolph G., jt. ed. see Moore, W. S.

Penney, Alexandra. How to Make Love to a Man. Southern, Carol, ed. 160p. 1981. 10.00 (ISBN 0-517-54145-9). Potter.

Penney, C., jt. auth. see Dugas, H.

Penney, James F. Perspective & Challenge in College Personnel Work. 108p. 1972. 9.75 (ISBN 0-398-02378-6). C C Thomas.

Penney, Sharon H. Patrician in Politics: Daniel Dewey Barnard of New York. new ed. LC 74-77652. 220p. 1974. 15.00 (ISBN 0-8046-9067-7, Natl U). Kennikat.

Penney, William M., ed. MOS Integrated Circuits: Theory, Fabrication, Design, & Systems Applications of MOS LSI. Lau, Lillian. LC 79-1039. 494p. 1979. Repr. of 1972 ed. lib. bdg. 24.50 o.p. (ISBN 0-88275-897-7). Krieger.

Penniman, Howard R., ed. Australian National Elections of 1977. 1980. pap. 8.25 (ISBN 0-8447-3357-1). Am Enterprise.

--New Zealand at the Polls: The General Election of 1978. 1980. pap. 7.95 (ISBN 0-8447-3376-8). Am Enterprise.

Penninger, F. Elaine, ed. English Drama to Sixteen Sixty (Excluding Shakespeare): A Guide to Information Sources. LC 73-16988. (American Literature, English Literature, & World Literatures in English Information Guide Ser.: Vol. 5). vi, 520p. 1976. 30.00 (ISBN 0-8103-1223-9). Gale.

Penninger, Frieda E. William Caxton. (English Authors Ser.: No. 263). 1979. lib. bdg. 12.95 (ISBN 0-8057-6759-2). Twayne.

Penning-Rowsell, Edmund C., jt. auth. see Parker, Dennis J.

Pennings, Johannes M. Interlocking Directorates: Origins & Consequences of Connections Among Organizations' Boards of Directors. LC 80-8001. (Social & Behavioral Science Ser.). 1980. text ed. 14.95x (ISBN 0-87589-469-0). Jossey-Bass.

Pennington, A. E., ed. see Kotosixin, Grigorij.

Pennington, Campbell W. The Pima Bajo of Central Sonora, Mexico: Vol. 1, The Material Culture. (Illus.). 372p. 1981. 25.00 (ISBN 0-87480-126-5). U of Utah Pr.

--The Tepehuan of Chihuahua: Their Material Culture. LC 73-99792. (Illus.). 1969. 10.00x (ISBN 0-87480-013-7); pap. 7.50x (ISBN 0-87480-147-8). U of Utah Pr.

Pennington, Campbell W., ed. The Pima Bajo (Nevome) of Central Sonora, Mexico: Vocabulario en la Lengua Nevome. 1979. 16.00x (ISBN 0-87480-125-7). U of Utah Pr.

Pennington, Chester, jt. auth. see Kingsbury, Jack D.

Pennington, D. H. Seventeenth Century Europe. (General History of Europe Ser.). (Illus.). 1972. pap. text ed. 10.95x (ISBN 0-582-48312-3). Longman.

Pennington, Donald & Thomas, Keith, eds. Puritans & Revolutionaries: Essays in Seventeenth-Century History Presented to Christopher Hill. 1978. 45.00x (ISBN 0-19-822439-7). Oxford U Pr.

Pennington, Earl, jt. auth. see Oestereich, James.

Pennington, G. W. & Naik, Sandra. Hormone Analysis, Vol. 1. 304p. 1981. 69.95 (ISBN 0-8493-5539-7). CRC Pr.

Pennington, Harvard C. TRS-Eighty Disk! And Other Mysteries. (TRS-80 Information Ser.: Vol. 1). (Illus.). 133p. (Orig.). 1979. pap. 22.50 (ISBN 0-936200-00-6). IJG Inc.

Pennington, Jean & Church, Helen N. Food Values of Portions Commonly Used. 13th ed. LC 80-7594. 200p. 1980. pap. 5.95 (ISBN 0-06-090819-X, CN819, CN). Har-Row.

Pennington, Jean A. Dietary Nutrient Guide. (Illus.). 1976. pap. text ed. 21.50 (ISBN 0-87055-196-5). AVI.

Pennington, Jean A. Thompson see Pennington, Jean A.

Pennington, Malcom W. & Allio, Robert J. Corporate Planning: Techniques & Applications. LC 78-25803. (Illus.). 1979. 21.95 (ISBN 0-8144-5497-6). Am Mgmt.

Pennington, R. Corbin & James, Elizabeth. For Parents of a Child Whose Speech Is Delayed. 2nd ed. 1980. pap. 0.50 (ISBN 0-8134-2137-3, 2137). Interstate.

--For the Parents of a Child Whose Speech Is Delayed. LC 64-25221. 1965. pap. 0.50 o.p. (ISBN 0-8134-0015-5, 15); pap. 0.40 ea. 2-24 copies o.p.; pap. 0.32 ea. 25 or more copies o.p. Interstate.

Penn-Lewis, Jessie. Magna Charta of Woman. LC 75-28655. 1975. pap. 2.50 (ISBN 0-87123-377-0, 200377). Bethany Fell.

--Thy Hidden Ones. 1962. pap. 3.50 (ISBN 0-87508-998-4). Chr Lit.

Pennock, J. Roland & Chapman, John W., eds. Property. LC 79-55007. (Nomos XXII). 1980. 24.90x (ISBN 0-8147-6576-9). NYU Pr.

Pennock, Michael. The Sacraments & You. (Illus.). 272p. (gr. 10-12). 1981. pap. 3.95 (ISBN 0-87793-221-2); teachers ed. 2.25 (ISBN 0-87793-222-0). Ave Maria.

Pennsylvania State Univ. Chemistry Dept., jt. auth. see Haas, Charles G.

Pennsylvania State University Nutrition Education Curriculum Study. Nutrition in a Changing World: Grade Four. LC 80-20736. (Illus.). 152p. (Orig.). (gr. 4). 1981. pap. text ed. 8.95x (ISBN 0-8425-1864-9). Brigham.

Pennsylvania University Bicentennial Conference. Conservation of Renewable Natural Resources. Zon, Raphael & Cooper, William, eds. LC 68-26200. Repr. of 1941 ed. 12.50 (ISBN 0-8046-0356-1). Kennikat.

Penny, Nicholas. Church Monuments in Romantic England. LC 76-58912. (Studies in British Art). (Illus.). 1977. 27.50x (ISBN 0-300-02075-9). Yale U Pr.

Penny, Nicholas, jt. auth. see Haskell, Francis.

Pennycock, Andrew. The Indoor Games Book. (Illus.). 1973. 10.95 (ISBN 0-571-09970-X, Pub. by Faber & Faber). Merrimack Bk Serv.

Pennycook, Andrew. Codes & Ciphers: Amazing Ways to Scramble & Unscramble Secret Messages. 1978. 12.50 (ISBN 0-679-50856-2); pap. 7.95 (ISBN 0-679-50966-6). McKay.

Pennycuick, C. J. Handy Matrices of Unit Conversion Factors for Biology & Mechanics. LC 74-26762. 47p. 1976. pap. 4.95 o.p. (ISBN 0-470-67948-4). Halsted Pr.

Pennypacker, Arabelle, ed. Reading for Young People: The Middle Atlantic. LC 80-16021. 162p. 1980. pap. 8.00 (ISBN 0-8389-0295-2). ALA.

Pennypacker, H. S., jt. auth. see Johnston, James M.

Penoyre, Jane, jt. auth. see Penoyre, John.

Penoyre, John & Penoyre, Jane. Houses in the Landscape: A Regional Study of Vernacular Building Styles in England & Wales. (Illus.). 1978. 18.95 (ISBN 0-571-11055-X, Pub. by Faber & Faber). Merrimack Bk Serv.

Penoyre, John & Ryan, Michael. Observer's Book of Architecture. (Observer Bks.). (Illus.). 1977. 4.95 (ISBN 0-684-15208-8, ScribT). Scribner.

Penrice, John. Dictionary & Glossary of the Koran. 17.00 (ISBN 0-686-63545-0). Intl Bk Ctr.

--Dictionary & Glossary of the Koran, with Copious Grammatical References & Explanations. LC 70-90039. 1969. Repr. of 1873 ed. 17.50x (ISBN 0-8196-0252-3). Biblo.

--A Dictionary & Glossary of the Koran: With Copious Grammatical References & Explanations of the Text. 176p. 1976. Repr. of 1971 ed. 12.50x o.p. (ISBN 0-87471-787-6). Rowman.

Penrock, J. Roland & Chapman, John W., eds. Human Rights. (Nomos Ser.: Vol. 22). 336p. 1980. 19.50x (ISBN 0-8147-6578-5). NYU Pr.

Penrod, D. A., jt. auth. see Hanson, D. P.

Penrod, James & Plastino, Janice. The Dancer Prepares: Modern Dance for Beginners. 2nd, rev. ed. LC 79-91836. (Illus.). 77p. 1980. pap. text ed. 3.95 (ISBN 0-87484-340-5). Mayfield Pub.

Penrose, Barry & Courtiour, Roger. The Pencourt File. LC 78-2152. (Illus.). 1978. 12.95 o.s.i. (ISBN 0-06-013343-0, HarpT). Har-Row.

Penrose, E. F., jt. auth. see Penrose, Edith.

Penrose, Edith & Penrose, E. F. Iraq: Economics, Oil & Politics. LC 77-16007. (Nations of the Modern World Ser.). 1978. lib. bdg. 38.50x (ISBN 0-89158-804-3). Westview.

Penrose, Edith Tilton, et al, eds. New Orientations: Essays in International Relations. 136p. 1970. 24.00x (ISBN 0-7146-2593-0, F Cass Co). Biblio Dist.

Penrose, Gordon. Dr. Zed's Brilliant Book of Science Experiments. LC 77-88864. (Illus.). (gr. 3-6). 1977. pap. 3.75 (ISBN 0-8120-0892-8). Barron.

Penrose, John M. Applications in Business Communication. 1981. pap. text ed. 7.95 (ISBN 0-03-058202-4). Dryden Pr.

Penrose, L. S. On the Objective Study of Crowd Behavior. 78p. 1981. Repr. of 1952 ed. text ed. price not set. Krieger.

--Outline of Human Genetics. 3rd ed. 1973. text ed. 6.50x o.p. (ISBN 0-435-60701-4). Heinemann Ed.

Penrose, O. Foundations of Statistical Mechanics: A Deductive Treatment. LC 70-89513. (International Series in Natural Philosophy: Vol. 22). (Illus.). 1970. 23.10 o.p. (ISBN 0-08-013314-2). Pergamon.

Penrose, Roland. Picasso: His Life & Work. rev ed. LC 72-180702. (Icon Editions). (Illus.). 544p. 1973. pap. 6.95 o.s.i. (ISBN 0-06-430016-1, IN-16, HarpT). Har-Row.

--Picasso: His Life & Work. 1980. pap. 8.95 (ISBN 0-520-04207-7, CAL 487). U of Cal Pr.

Penrose, Roland, ed. see Cirlot, Juan-Eduardo.

Penry, J. K. see Newmark, M. E.

Penry, J. K. & Daly, D. D., eds. Complex Partial Seizures & Their Treatment. LC 75-14584. (Advances in Neurology: Vol. 11). 480p. 1975. 32.00 (ISBN 0-89004-040-0). Raven.

Penry, J. K., jt. ed. see Newmark, M.

Penry, J. Kiffin see Glaser, G. H., et al.

Penry, J. Kiffin, jt. auth. see Lacy, Joseph R.

Penry, J. Kiffin, ed. Epilepsy: The Eighth International Symposium. LC 76-58059. 1977. 19.00 (ISBN 0-89004-190-3). Raven.

Penry, J. Kiffin & Dam, Mogens, eds. Advances in Epileptology Research. (Twelfth Epilepsy International Symposium, Copenhagen, Denmark). 1981. text ed. price not set (ISBN 0-89004-611-5). Raven.

Penry, J. Kiffin, ed. see Epilepsy International Symposium, 10th.

Penry, Jacques. Looking at Faces & Remembering Them. 1971. pap. 9.95 (ISBN 0-236-17664-1, Pub. by Paul Elek). Merrimack Bk Serv.

Pensee (Editors of) Velikovsky Reconsidered. LC 74-33637. 288p. 1976. 8.95 o.p. (ISBN 0-385-03118-1). Doubleday.

Penson, John B., Jr. & Lins, David A. Agricultural Finance: An Introduction to Micro & Macro Concepts. (Illus.). 1980. text ed. 20.95 (ISBN 0-13-018903-0). P-H.

Pentacost, Hugh. Random Killer. Date not set. pap. price not set (ISBN 0-440-17210-1). Dell.

Pentecost, D., tr. Dieu Repond-Problemes-Hommes. (French Bks.). (Fr.). 1979. write for info. Life Pubs Intl.

Pentecost, Dwight. Designed to Be Like Him. 1981. pap. 5.95 (ISBN 0-8024-2132-6). Moody.

Pentecost, Hugh. Death After Breakfast. 1980. pap. 2.25 (ISBN 0-440-11687-2). Dell.

--Death Mask. LC 80-15717. (A Julian Quist Mystery Novel Ser.). 224p. 1980. 8.95 (ISBN 0-396-07883-4). Dodd.

--Murder in Luxury. LC 80-22250. 196p. 1981. 8.95 (ISBN 0-396-07921-0). Dodd.

--Random Killer. LC 79-271. (Pierre Chambrun Mystery & Red Badge Novel of Suspense Ser.). 1979. 7.95 (ISBN 0-396-07654-8). Dodd.

Pentecost, J. Dwight. The Joy of Fellowship. 1977. pap. 4.95 (ISBN 0-310-30921-2). Zondervan.

--The Joy of Living. 160p. 1973. pap. text ed. 5.95 (ISBN 0-310-30871-2). Zondervan.

--Things to Come. 1958. 14.95 (ISBN 0-310-30890-9, Pub by Dunhan). Zondervan.

--The Words & Works of Jesus Christ. 576p. 1981. 16.95 (ISBN 0-310-30940-9, 17015). Zondervan.

--Your Adversary the Devil. 192p. 1976. pap. 4.95 (ISBN 0-310-30911-5). Zondervan.

Pentland, Charles. International Theory & European Integration. LC 73-10832. 1973. 17.95 (ISBN 0-02-925210-5). Free Pr.

Pentland, Charles, jt. ed. see Boyd, Gavin.

Pentony, De Vere, et al. Unfinished Rebellions. LC 72-148658. (Higher Education Ser.). 1971. 14.95x o.p. (ISBN 0-87589-095-4). Jossey-Bass.

Pentreath, R. J. Nuclear Power, Man & the Environment. LC 80-20173. (Wykeham Science Ser.: No. 51). 250p. 1981. pap. price not set (ISBN 0-8448-1381-8). Crane-Russak Co.

Pentz, Croft M. Expository Outlines from Romans. (Sermon Outline Ser.). 48p. (Orig.). 1980. pap. 1.95 (ISBN 0-8010-7045-7). Baker Bk.

--Outlines on Revelation. (Sermon Outline Ser.). 1978. pap. 1.95 (ISBN 0-8010-7030-9). Baker Bk.

--Outlines on the Holy Spirit. (Sermon Outline Ser). 1978. pap. 1.95 (ISBN 0-8010-7029-5). Baker Bk.

--Sermon Outlines from Acts. (Sermon Outline Ser.). 1978. pap. 1.95 (ISBN 0-8010-7039-2). Baker Bk.

Pentzer, Wilbur T., jt. auth. see Ryall, A. L.

Penzel, Frederick. Theatre Lighting Before Electricity. LC 77-14840. 1978. 20.00 (ISBN 0-8195-5021-3, Pub. by Wesleyan U Pr). Columbia U Pr.

Penzias, Walter & Goodman, M. W. Man Beneath the Sea: A Review of Underwater Ocean Engineering. LC 70-148506. 1973. 59.95 (ISBN 0-471-68018-4). Wiley.

Penzler, Otto, et al, eds. see Roseman, Mill.

Penzo, P. A., et al, eds. Astrodynamics, 1979, 2 pts. (Advances in the Astronautical Sciences Ser.: Vol. 40). 1980. lib. bdg. 45.00 ea. Pt. 1 (ISBN 0-87703-107-X). Pt. 2 (ISBN 0-87703-109-6). Pt. 1. pap. 35.00 ea. (ISBN 0-87703-108-8). Pt. 2 (ISBN 0-87703-110-X). fiche suppl. 20.00 (ISBN 0-87703-139-8). Univelt Inc.

Penzoldt, Peter. Supernatural in Fiction. 1952. text ed. 15.00x (ISBN 0-391-00461-1). Humanities.

People of 'Ksan. Gathering What the Great Nature Provided: Food Traditions of the Gitksan. LC 79-3871. (Illus.). 128p. 1980. 17.95 (ISBN 0-295-95710-7). U of Wash Pr.

People's Computer Company. Dr. Dobb's Journal of Computer Calesthenics & Orthodontia: Running Light Without Overbyte, 3 vols. 1980. pap. 18.95 ea.; Vol. 1. pap. (ISBN 0-8104-5475-0); Vol. 2. pap. (ISBN 0-8104-5484-X); Vol. 3. pap. (ISBN 0-8104-5490-4). Hayden.

Peoples Computer Company. What to Do After You Hit Return. 180p. 1980. 14.95 (ISBN 0-8104-5476-9). Hayden.

People's Court, Munich & Hitler, Adolph. Hitler Trial: Before the People's Court in Munich. Freniere, H. Francis, et al, trs. 1976. 130.00 (ISBN 0-89093-050-3). U Pubns Amer.

Peoria Tennis Association Facilities Committee. Let's Cure the Court Crunch. 1977. pap. text ed. 2.00 (ISBN 0-938822-05-5). USTA.

Pepe. No-Hitter. (gr. 7 up). 1977. pap. 1.25 o.p. (ISBN 0-590-02977-0). Schol Bk Serv.

Pepe, Frank, et al, eds. Motility in Cell Function: Proceedings of the First John M. Marshall Symposium on Cell Biology. LC 78-11880. 1979. 31.00 (ISBN 0-12-551750-5). Acad Pr.

Pepe, Thomas J. A Guide for Understanding School Law. LC 76-19897. 1976. pap. 6.95x o.p. (ISBN 0-8134-1835-6, 1835). Interstate.

Peper, Erik, et al, eds. Mind-Body Integration: Essential Readings in Biofeedback. LC 78-27224. (Illus.). 606p. 1978. 25.00 (ISBN 0-306-40102-9, Plenum Pr). Plenum Pub.

Pepeu, Giancarlo, et al, eds. Receptors for Neurotransmitters & Peptide Hormones. (Advances in Biological Psychopharmacology Ser.: Vol. 21). 1980. text ed. 56.00 (ISBN 0-89004-408-2). Raven.

Pepinsky, Harold B. People & Information. 1970. 28.00 (ISBN 0-08-015624-X). Pergamon.

Pepinsky, Harold B. & Patton, Michael J. The Psychological Experiment: A Practical Accomplishment. LC 75-134829. 208p. 1971. 16.00 (ISBN 0-08-016515-X). Pergamon.

Pepitone-Rockwell, Fran, ed. Dual Career Couples. LC 80-15747. (Sage Focus Editions Ser.: Vol. 24). (Illus.). 294p. 1980. 18.95 (ISBN 0-8039-1436-9); pap. 9.95x (ISBN 0-8039-1437-7). Sage.

Peppard, Alan P., jt. auth. see Riegler, Hubert F.

Peppard, Murray B. Friedrich Durrenmatt. (World Authors Ser.: Germany: No. 87). lib. bdg. 10.95 (ISBN 0-8057-2284-X). Twayne.

Peppe, G., tr. see Kaiser, Artur.

Peppe, Kathryn K., jt. ed. see Curry, Judith B.

Peppe, Rodney. Circus Numbers. LC 75-86381. (Illus.). (ps-3). 1969. 5.95 o.p. (ISBN 0-440-01288-0); PLB 5.47 o.p. (ISBN 0-440-01289-9). Delacorte.

--Rodney Peppe's Moving Toys. (Illus.). 128p. 1981. 14.95 (ISBN 0-8069-5422-1); lib. bdg. 13.29 (ISBN 0-8069-5423-X); pap. 6.95 (ISBN 0-8069-5424-8). Sterling.

Peppe, Rodney, illus. Rodney Peppe's Puzzle Book. 1977. 7.95 o.p. (ISBN 0-670-60261-2). Viking Pr.

Pepper. Affirmative Action Plan Workbook for Federal Contractors. 2nd ed. 1979. pap. 45.00 (ISBN 0-917386-31-0). Exec Ent.

Pepper, Art & Pepper, Laurie. Straight Life: The Story of Art Pepper. LC 79-7363. (Illus.). 1979. 12.95 (ISBN 0-02-871820-8). Schirmer Bks.

Pepper, Elizabeth & Wilcock, John. Magical & Mystical Sites: Europe & the British Isles. LC 76-5533. (Illus.). (YA) 1977. 10.95 o.s.i. (ISBN 0-06-014614-1, HarpT). Har-Row.

Pepper, Laurie, jt. auth. see Pepper, Art.

Pepper, Max, jt. auth. see Coe, Rodney M.

Pepper, Robert, jt. auth. see Avery, Robert K.

Pepper, Stephen C. Aesthetic Quality: A Contextualistic Theory of Beauty. LC 79-110052. 239p. Repr. of 1937 ed. lib. bdg. 19.75x (ISBN 0-8371-4437-X, PEAQ). Greenwood.

--The Sources of Value. 1958. 27.50x (ISBN 0-520-01798-6). U of Cal Pr.

--World Hypotheses: A Study in Evidence. 1970. pap. 6.95x (ISBN 0-520-00994-0, CAMPUS31). U of Cal Pr.

Pepper, Suzanne. Civil War in China: The Political Struggle, 1945-1949. 1978. 20.00x (ISBN 0-520-02440-0); pap. 6.95x (ISBN 0-520-04085-6). U of Cal Pr.

Pepper, Thomas, jt. auth. see Kahn, Herman.

Pepper, William. The Medical Side of Benjamin Franklin. (Illus.). 137p. 1970. Repr. of 1910 ed. 15.00 (ISBN 0-87266-039-7). Argosy.

Pepper, Wilma D. Fairy Tales for Me. 184p. (gr. 1). 1967. 2.50x o.p. (ISBN 0-89039-053-3). Ann Arbor Pubs.

--More Fairy Tales for Me. 180p. (gr. 1). 1967. 2.50x o.p. (ISBN 0-89039-054-1). Ann Arbor Pubs.

Pepperell, R. J., et al, eds. The Infertile Couple. (Illus.). 320p. 1980. text ed. 25.00x (ISBN 0-443-01727-1). Churchill.

Peppin, Brigid. Dictionary of Book Illustrators, 1800-1970. (Illus.). 544p. Date not set. 30.00 (ISBN 0-668-04366-0). Arco.

--Fantasy: The Golden Age of Fantastic Illustration. (Signet Art Books). (Illus.). 1976. pap. 6.95 o.p. (ISBN 0-451-79971-2, G9971, Sig). NAL.

Peppler, Henry J., jt. auth. see Reed, Gerald.

Pepys, Samuel. Diary, 3 Vols. 1953. Vol. 1. 8.50x (ISBN 0-460-00053-5, Evman); Vol. 2. 12.95x (ISBN 0-460-00054-3); Vol. 3. 12.95 (ISBN 0-460-00055-1). Dutton.

--Diary of Samuel Pepys. Morshead, O. F., ed. (Illus.). 1960. 8.50 (ISBN 0-8446-2727-5). Peter Smith.

--The Diary of Samuel Pepys, 3 vols. Latham, Robert & Matthews, William, eds. Incl. Vol. 1. 1660. 1970. 27.50 (ISBN 0-520-01575-4); Vol. 2. 1661. 22.75 (ISBN 0-520-01576-2); Vol. 3. 1662. 22.75 (ISBN 0-520-01577-0); Vol. 4. 1663. 22.75 (ISBN 0-520-01857-5); Vol. 5. 1664. 21.50 (ISBN 0-520-01858-3); Vol. 6. 1665. 21.50 (ISBN 0-520-01859-1); Vol. 7. 1666. 22.75 (ISBN 0-520-02094-4); Vol. 8. 1667. 24.50 (ISBN 0-520-02095-2); Vol. 9. 1668-1669. 24.50 (ISBN 0-520-02096-0). U of Cal Pr.

--A Pepysian Garland: Black-Letter Broadside Ballads of the Years 1595-1639, Chiefly from the Collection of Samuel Pepys. Rollins, Hyder E., ed. LC 74-176041. (Illus.). 491p. 1971. 22.50x (ISBN 0-674-66185-0). Harvard U Pr.

Perceval, A. History of Music. (Teach Yourself Ser.). 1974. pap. 3.95 o.p. (ISBN 0-679-10437-2). McKay.

Perceval, Edward, tr. see Huysmans, Joris K.

Percival, A. E., ed. The English Association Handbook of Societies & Collections. 1977. pap. 5.50x (ISBN 0-85365-449-2, Pub. by Lib Assn England). Oryx Pr.

Percival, Allen. English Love Songs. (Illus.). 256p. 1980. 27.50x (ISBN 0-389-20147-2). B&N.

Percival, James G. Uncollected Letters of James Gates Percival, Poet & Geologist, 1795-1856. Warfel, Harry R., ed. LC 59-62964. (U of Fla. Humanities Monographs: No. 1). 1959. pap. 3.00 (ISBN 0-8130-0186-2). U Presses Fla.

Percival, John. Roman Villa: A Historical Introduction. 1976. 28.50x (ISBN 0-520-03233-0). U of Cal Pr.

Percival, Julia. The Stewardess & Pixie Burger. 1975. pap. 1.75 o.p. (ISBN 0-380-01562-5, 24539). Avon.

Percival, M. Floral Biology. 1965. 10.50 (ISBN 0-08-010610-2); pap. 7.00 (ISBN 0-08-010609-9). Pergamon.

Percival, Rachel A. The Court of Elizabeth the First. (Illus.). 110p. 1976. 13.75x (ISBN 0-8476-6238-1). Rowman.

Percy, Ann, jt. ed. see Hiesinger, Ulrich W.

Percy, Bernard, jt. auth. see Hollander, Rene.

Percy, Bishop. Bishop Percy's Folio Manuscript Ballards & Romances, 3 vols. Hales, John W., et al, eds. LC 67-23962. 1866p. 1968. Repr. of 1868 ed. 110.00 (ISBN 0-8103-3409-7). Gale.

Percy, Charles, Senator. I Want to Know About the United States Senate. 96p. (gr. 3-7). 1976. 5.95 o.p. (ISBN 0-385-00192-4). Doubleday.

Percy, Cyril H. Us Four. (Illus.). 1963. 2.95 o.p. (ISBN 0-571-05636-9, Pub. by Faber & Faber). Merrimack Bk Serv.

Percy, Eustace. John Knox. LC 65-11937. 1965. 6.95 (ISBN 0-8042-0924-3). John Knox.

--John Knox. 1964. 8.95 (ISBN 0-227-67510-X). Attic Pr.

Percy, F. H. A History of Whitgift School. 1976. 16.95 (ISBN 0-7134-3158-X, Pub. by Batsford England). David & Charles.

Percy, George. Seven Card Stud: The Waiting Game. (Gambler's Book Shelf). 1979. pap. 2.95 (ISBN 0-89650-903-6). Gamblers.

Percy, H. M. New Materials in Sculpture. 2nd ed. 1966. 8.95 (ISBN 0-85458-998-8); pap. 6.50 (ISBN 0-85458-996-1). Transatlantic.

Percy, Larry & Rossiter, John R. Advertising Strategy: A Communication Theory Approach. LC 79-25228. 314p. 1980. 26.50 (ISBN 0-03-055906-5). Praeger.

Percy, R. Craig, ed. see Comer, Joyce B.

Percy, R. Craig, ed. see Emanuelsen, Kathy L. & Densmore, Mary J.

Percy, R. Craig, ed. see Orr, Marsha E.

Percy, Thomas. Reliques of Ancient English Poetry, 3 Vols. Wheatley, Henry B., ed. 1966. pap. text ed. 4.00 ea.; Vol. 1. pap. text ed. o.p. (ISBN 0-486-21611-X); Vol. 2. pap. text ed. (ISBN 0-486-21612-8); Vol. 3. pap. text ed. (ISBN 0-486-21613-6). Dover.

Percy, Walker. Love in the Ruins. LC 71-143301. 416p. 1971. 15.95 (ISBN 0-374-19302-9). FS&G.

--Love in the Ruins. 384p. 1981. pap. 2.95 (ISBN 0-380-38984-3, 53843). Avon.

--The Moviegoer. 242p. 1967. pap. 2.95 (ISBN 0-374-50596-9). FS&G.

--The Moviegoer. 1979. pap. 2.50 (ISBN 0-380-47076-4, 47076). Avon.

--The Second Coming. 368p. 1980. 12.95 (ISBN 0-374-25674-8); signed, limited ed. 60.00 (ISBN 0-374-25675-6). FS&G.

Perdue, K. S., ed. Pattern Recognition. (Communications & Cybernetics: Vol. 10). (Illus.). 270p. 1976. 37.70 o.p. (ISBN 0-387-07511-9). Springer-Verlag.

Perdue, Leo G. Wisdom & Cult: A Critical Analysis of the Views of Cult in the Wisdom Literatures of Israel & the Ancient Near East. LC 76-47453. (Society of Biblical Literature. Dissertation Ser.: No. 30). 1977. pap. 9.00 (ISBN 0-89130-094-5, 060130). Scholars Pr Ca.

Perdue, Theda. Nations Remembered: An Oral History of the Five Civilized Tribes, 1865-1907. LC 79-6828. (Contributions in Ethnic Studies: No. 1). xxiv, 221p. 1980. lib. bdg. 23.95 (ISBN 0-313-22097-2, PFN/). Greenwood.

Pereda, Jose M. Jose Maria Pereda: Selections from Sotileza & Penas Arriba. Talamantes, Florence W., ed. 1978. pap. text ed. 9.00x (ISBN 0-8191-0379-9). U Pr of Amer.

Pereira, Anthony. Naples, Pompeii & Southern Italy. 1977. 24.00 (ISBN 0-7134-0815-4, Pub. by Batsford England). David & Charles.

--Rome. (Illus.). 1975. 12.50 o.p. (ISBN 0-8038-6334-9). Hastings.

Pereira, Frederick A., jt. auth. see Selmanowitz, Victor J.

Pereira, H. C. Land Use & Water Resources. LC 72-85437. (Illus.). 180p. (Orig.). 1973. 39.00 (ISBN 0-521-08677-9); pap. 10.95x (ISBN 0-521-09750-9). Cambridge U Pr.

Pereira, Norman C., jt. ed. see Wang, Lawrence K.

Perel, Morton L. Dental Implantology & Prostheses. LC 76-2596. 226p. 1977. 44.75 o.p. (ISBN 0-397-50347-4). Lippincott.

Perella, Nicolas J. The Kiss Sacred & Profane: An Interpretative History of Kiss Symbolism & Related Religio-Erotic Themes. LC 75-83292. (Illus.). 1969. 28.50x (ISBN 0-520-01392-1). U of Cal Pr.

--Night & the Sublime in Giacomo Leopardi. (U. C. Publ. in Modern Philology: Vol. 99). 1971. pap. 9.00x (ISBN 0-520-09368-2). U of Cal Pr.

Perelman, Chaim. Idea of Justice & the Problems of Argument. (International Library of Philosophy & Scientific Method). 1963. text ed. 13.75x (ISBN 0-7100-3610-8). Humanities.

--Justice, Law & Argument: Essays on Moral & Legal Reasoning. (Synthese Library: No. 142). 175p. 1980. lib. bdg. 28.50 (ISBN 90-277-1089-9, Pub. by D. Reidel); pap. 10.50 (ISBN 90-277-1090-2). Kluwer Boston.

Perelman, Leslie, jt. auth. see Dimarco, Vincent.

Perelman, Lewis J., et al, eds. Energy Transitions: Long-Term Perspectives. (AAAS Selected Symposium: No. 48). 250p. 1980. lib. bdg. 18.50x (ISBN 0-89158-862-0). Westview.

Perelman, Michael. Farming for Profit in a Hungry World: Capital & the Crisis in Agriculture. LC 76-43229. 256p. 1978. text ed. 16.00 (ISBN 0-916672-88-3); pap. text ed. 7.50 (ISBN 0-916672-55-7). Allanheld.

Perenich, Reagan. The Textiles Laboratory Manual. 320p. (Orig.). 1980. pap. 10.95 (ISBN 0-933340-03-6). Prince Scientific.

Perepechko, I. I. Low-Temperature Properties of Polymers. 272p. 1981. 40.00 (ISBN 0-08-025301-6). Pergamon.

Perera, Gretchen, jt. auth. see Perera, Thomas.

Perera, Thomas & Perera, Gretchen. Louder & Louder: The Dangers of Noise Pollution. LC 72-10868. (Illus.). 64p. (gr. 4-6). 1973. PLB 4.90 o.p. (ISBN 0-531-02618-3). Watts.

Peretz, Don. The Government & Politics of Israel. 1979. lib. bdg. 23.50x (ISBN 0-89158-086-7); pap. text ed. 10.00x (ISBN 0-89158-087-5). Westview.

--Israel and the Palestine Arabs. LC 80-1915. 1981. Repr. of 1958 ed. 31.00 (ISBN 0-404-18984-9). AMS Pr.

Peretz, Don, et al. Islam: Legacy of the Past, Challenge of the Future. 1981. 9.95 (ISBN 0-88427-048-3). Green Hill.

--Islam: Legacy of the Past, Challenge of the Future. 160p. 1981. 9.95 (ISBN 0-88427-048-3, Dist. by Caroline Hse). North River.

Perez, A. & Coussement, R., eds. Site Characterization & Aggregation of Implanted Atoms in Materials. (NATO Advanced Study Institutes, Ser. B, Physics: Vol. 47). 530p. 1980. 55.00 (ISBN 0-306-40299-8, Plenum Pr). Plenum Pub.

Perez, Guillermo H. Lo Que los Jovenes Deben Saber Acerca De las Drogas. 1978. pap. 0.85 (ISBN 0-311-46070-4). Casa Bautista.

Perez, Louis A., Jr. Army Politics in Cuba, 1898-1958. LC 75-35440. (Pitt Latin American Ser.). 1976. 12.95x (ISBN 0-8229-3303-9). U of Pittsburgh Pr.

--The Cuban Revolutionary War, 1953-1958: A Bibliography. LC 76-18742. 1976. 11.00 (ISBN 0-8108-0954-0). Scarecrow.

Perez, Louis C., jt. auth. see Weiss, Beno.

Perez, Maria E. Lo Americano En el Teatro De Sor Juana Ines De la Cruz. 1975. 14.00 (ISBN 0-88303-020-9); pap. 11.00 (ISBN 0-685-73221-5). E Torres & Sons.

Perez, Ramon A. Liability Risk Management for Local Governments. 1981. spiral bdg. 25.00 (ISBN 0-88406-148-5). GA St U Busn Pub.

Perez, Roman & Ferrie, Carmen. Introduction to Business Translation: A Handbook in English - Spanish Contrastive Linguistics. LC 80-18052. 196p. 1980. pap. write for info. (ISBN 0-8477-3328-9). U of PR Pr.

Perez, Rosanne H. Protocols for Perinatal Practice. (Illus.). 450p. 1981. text ed. 19.95 (ISBN 0-8016-3805-4). Mosby.

Perez de Ayala, Ramon. Belarmino & Apolonio. Berns, Gabriel & Baumgarten, Murray, trs. 1971. 16.95x (ISBN 0-520-01786-2). U of Cal Pr.

--Honeymoon, Bittermoon. Eisenberg, Barry, tr. LC 79-116667. 1972. 16.95x (ISBN 0-520-01727-7). U of Cal Pr.

Perez-Diaz, Victor M. State, Bureaucracy & Civil Society: A Critical Discussion of the Political Theory of Karl Marx. (New Studies in Sociology Ser.). 1978. text ed. 15.25x (ISBN 0-333-23788-9); pap. text ed. 6.25x (ISBN 0-391-00555-3). Humanities.

Perez Galdos, Benita. La Sombra De Galdos: Libra De Lectura, Repaso y Conversacion. Cardona, Rudolph, ed. (Span). 1966. 6.95x (ISBN 0-393-09645-9); pap. 3.25x (ISBN 0-393-09632-7, NortonC); tapes 70.00 (ISBN 0-393-99114-8). Norton.

Perez Galdos, Benito. Gloria, 2 vols. in 1. Bell, C., tr. from Span. LC 73-21667. 692p. 1975. Repr. of 1882 ed. 27.50 (ISBN 0-86527-255-7). Fertig.

Perez-Mendez, Victor, jt. ed. see Thomas, Ralph H.

Perez-Ramon, Joacquin. Self & Non-Self in Early Buddhism. (Religon & Society Ser.: No. 17). 1980. 47.00x (ISBN 90-279-7987-1). Mouton.

Perez Y Sabido, J., jt. auth. see Howell, G.

Perfetti, Charles A., jt. ed. see Lesgold, Alan M.

Perham, ed. see Lord Lugard, et al.

Perham, Margery. Ten Africans. (Illus.). 1969. 7.95 (ISBN 0-571-05525-7, Pub. by Faber & Faber). Merrimack Bk Serv.

Perica, Esther. The American Woman: Her Role in the Revolutionary War. LC 80-28294. (Cameo Series of Notable Women). 1981. pap. price not set (ISBN 0-912526-28-9). Lib Res.

Perica, Lou & Boselovic, Len, eds. Guidelines for Writers of SI Metric Standards & Other Documents. 1975. pap. text ed. 8.00 (ISBN 0-916148-04-1). Am Natl.

Pericynthion. Man on the Spot. 1981. 12.95 (ISBN 0-936278-02-1). Green Hill.

Periers, Bonaventure Des see La Charite, Raymond C. & La Charite, Raymond.

Perigord, Emily M. Translation of French Foot-notes of The Dawn-Breakers. 1939. pap. 3.60 o.p. (ISBN 0-87743-075-6, 7-31-55). Baha'i.

Perillo, jt. auth. see Stevens.

Perillo, Joseph M., jt. auth. see Calamari, John D.

Perino, Joseph, jt. auth. see Perino, Sheila C.

Perino, Sheila C. & Perino, Joseph. Parenting Exceptional Children: A Manual. 208p. 1981. 19.95 (ISBN 0-8352-1354-4). Bowker.

Perisic, Zoran. Special Optical Effects. LC 80-41005. (Illus.). 1981. 29.95 (ISBN 0-240-51007-0). Focal Pr.

Perkin, Harold. Origins of Modern English Society: 1780-1880. LC 76-384509. 1969. pap. 10.95 (ISBN 0-8020-6141-9). U of Toronto Pr.

--The Structured Crowd: Essays in English Social History. 224p. 1981. 28.50x (ISBN 0-389-20116-2). B&N.

Perkin, Harold, ed. History: An Outline for the Intending Student. (Outline Ser). 1970. cased 14.95 (ISBN 0-7100-6814-X); pap. 7.95 (ISBN 0-7100-6815-8). Routledge & Kegan.

Perkins, Al. Hand, Hand, Fingers, Thumb. LC 76-77841. (Bright & Early Bk.). (Illus.). (ps-1). 1969. 3.95 (ISBN 0-394-81076-7, BYR); PLB 4.99 (ISBN 0-394-91076-1). Random.

Perkins, Ann. The Art of Dura-Europos. (Illus.). 140p. 1973. 45.00x (ISBN 0-19-813164-X). Oxford U Pr.

Perkins, Ann L. The Comparative Archeology of Early Mesopotamia. LC 49-10748. (Studies in Ancient Oriental Civilization: No. 25). (Illus.). xx, 201p. (Orig.). 1977. pap. text ed. 14.00x (ISBN 0-226-62396-3). Oriental Inst.

Perkins, Bradford. Castlereagh & Adams: England & the United States, 1812-1823. 1964. 20.00x (ISBN 0-520-00997-5). U of Cal Pr.

--The First Rapprochement: England & the United States, 1795-1805. 1967. Repr. 20.00x (ISBN 0-520-00998-3). U of Cal Pr.

--Prologue to War: England & the United States, 1805-1812. 1961. pap. 6.95x (ISBN 0-520-00996-7). U of Cal Pr.

Perkins, Carol. Renewal in Song: No. 2. pap. 3.95 (ISBN 0-88270-333-1). Logos.

Perkins, Courtland D. & Hage, R. E. Airplane Performance, Stability & Control. 1949. 29.95 (ISBN 0-471-68046-X). Wiley.

Perkins, Dan G., et al. Student's Resource Book & Study Guide to Accompany Psychology & You. 1978. pap. 5.95x (ISBN 0-673-15087-9). Scott F.

Perkins, David & Tanis, Norman. Native Americans of North America: A Bibliography Based on Collections in the Libraries of California State University, Northridge. (Illus.). 1975. 14.50 (ISBN 0-8108-0878-1). Scarecrow.

Perkins, Dexter. The Monroe Doctrine, 3 vols. Incl. 1823-1826. 8.00 (ISBN 0-685-22731-6); 1826-1867. 9.50 (ISBN 0-685-22732-4); 1867-1907. 9.50 (ISBN 0-685-22733-2). Set (ISBN 0-8446-1346-0). Peter Smith.

Perkins, Donald H. An Introduction to High Energy Physics. LC 74-137836. (Advanced Physics Ser). 1972. text ed. 20.95 (ISBN 0-201-05785-9). A-W.

Perkins, Dorothy. The Passionate Wisdom of Henry Miller: The Religious Dimension of His Life & Art. (Orig.). 1980. pap. 3.00 (ISBN 0-9604742-1-8). D J Perkins.

--Separation & Suffering: Hindu & Christian Views of Love. (Orig.). 1980. pap. 3.00 (ISBN 0-9604742-0-X). D J Perkins.

Perkins, Dwight, ed. Rural Small-Scale Industry in the People's Republic of China. LC 76-20015. 1977. 20.00x (ISBN 0-520-03284-5). U of Cal Pr.

--Rural Small-Scale Industry in the People's Republic of China. 1981. pap. 7.95 (ISBN 0-520-04401-0, CAL 499). U of Cal Pr.

Perkins, Edward A., jt. auth. see Reigel, Charles E.

Perkins, Elizabeth, jt. auth. see Sprague, Stuart.

Perkins, Elizabeth R. Education for Childbirth & Parenthood. 180p. 1980. bds. 27.50x (ISBN 0-7099-0273-5, Pub. by Croom Helm Ltd England). Biblio Dist.

Perkins, F. T., ed. see Permanent Section of Microbiological Standardization, 31st Symposium, Omstotite of Child Health, Ondon, 1969.

Perkins, G., jt. auth. see Drummond, David A.

Perkins, Hugh V. Human Development. 1975. text ed. 13.95x (ISBN 0-534-00383-4). Wadsworth Pub.

--Human Development & Learning. 2nd ed. 1974. 17.95x (ISBN 0-534-00345-1). Wadsworth Pub.

Perkins, J. M., jt. ed. see Butler, A. R.

Perkins, James A. Access to Higher Education: Two Perspectives. 84p. 1978. pap. 2.50 (ISBN 0-89192-219-9, Pub. by Intl Coun Ed Dev). Interbk Inc.

Perkins, James A., ed. see Carnegie Commission on Higher Education.

Perkins, John. A Profitable Book...Treating of the Lawes of England. And Now Translated Out of French into English, Vol. 63. Berkowitz, David S. & Thorne, Samuel E., eds. LC 77-86556. (Classics of English Legal History in the Modern Era Ser.). 1979. Repr. of 1827 ed. lib. bdg. 55.00 (ISBN 0-8240-3050-8). Garland Pub.

--With Justice for All. LC 80-50262. 192p. 1981. text ed. 7.95 (ISBN 0-8307-0754-9, 5108802). Regal. Postponed.

Perkins, John H., jt. ed. see Pimentel, David.

Perkins, John J. Principles & Methods of Sterilization in Health Sciences. 2nd ed. (Illus.). 584p. 1980. 23.75 (ISBN 0-398-01478-7). C C Thomas.

Perkins, John M. Let Justice Roll Down. LC 74-30172. 1976. pap. 4.95 (ISBN 0-8307-0345-4, 54-040-02). Regal.

Perkins, Lucy F. Scotch Twins. (Twin Ser). (Illus.). (gr. 3-5). 1969. Repr. PLB 4.85 o.s.i. (ISBN 0-8027-6062-7). Walker & Co.

--Spanish Twins. (Twins Ser). (Illus.). (gr. 4-6). 1969. PLB 4.85 o.s.i. (ISBN 0-8027-6070-8). Walker & Co.

Perkins, Maxwell, ed. see DeJong, Dola.

Perkins, Maxwell E. Editor to Author: The Letters of Maxwell E. Perkins. (Illus.). 1979. 12.50 o.p. (ISBN 0-684-16173-7, ScribT). Scribner.

Perkins, Michael. The Secret Record: Modern Erotic Literature. LC 76-18832. 1976. 7.95 o.p. (ISBN 0-688-03121-8); pap. 4.50 (ISBN 0-688-08121-5). Morrow.

Perkins, Molly. Bite of the Apple. 1981. 10.95. Riverrun NY.

Perkins, Percy H., Jr. Gemstones of the Bible. 2nd ed. (Illus.). 150p. 1980. pap. write for info. (ISBN 0-9603090-1-2). P H Perkins.

Perkins, Pheme. The Gnostic Dialogue. LC 80-81441. (Theological Inquiries Ser.). 256p. 1980. pap. 6.95 (ISBN 0-8091-2320-7). Paulist Pr.

--Hearing the Parables of Jesus. 216p. (Orig.). 1981. pap. 6.95 (ISBN 0-8091-2352-5). Paulist Pr.

Perkins, Philip H., jt. auth. see Green, J. Keith.

Perkins, Robert F., et al, eds. The Boston Athenaeum Art Exhibition Index: 1827-1874. (Illus.). 1980. 50.00x (ISBN 0-262-16075-7). MIT Pr.

Perkins, Robert L. Soren Kierkegaard. Nineham, Dennis E. & Robertson, E. H., eds. LC 69-14337. (Makers of Contemporary Theology Ser). (Orig.). 1969. pap. 3.45 (ISBN 0-8042-0710-0). John Knox.

Perkins, Rodney, jt. auth. see Barrager, Diane.

Perkins, Sheldon. Polaris. 1979. pap. 1.75 (ISBN 0-505-51386-2). Tower Bks.

Perkins, V. F. Film As Film: Understanding & Judging Movies. lib. bdg. 9.50x o.p. (ISBN 0-88307-423-0). Gannon.

Perkins, V. T. Film As Film. (Orig.). 1972. pap. 2.25 o.p. (ISBN 0-14-021477-1, Pelican). Penguin.

Perkins, William. Three Years in California: Journal of Life at Sonora, 1849-1852. 1964. 16.95 (ISBN 0-520-01000-0). U of Cal Pr.

Perkins, William C., jt. auth. see Martin, E. W., Jr.

Perkins, William H. Speech Pathology: An Applied Behavioral Science. 2nd ed. LC 76-25839. (Illus.). 1977. text ed. 23.95 (ISBN 0-8016-3785-6). Mosby.

Perkins, Wilma L. The Fanny Farmer Junior Cookbook. rev. ed. (Illus.). (gr. 5 up). 1957. 6.95 (ISBN 0-316-69932-2). Little.

Perkinson, Henry. Since Socrates. 1979. pap. text ed. 8.95x (ISBN 0-582-28098-2). Longman.

Perkinson, Henry J. Since Socrates: Studies in the History of Western Educational Thought. LC 79-9150. 222p. 1980. pap. 8.95 (ISBN 0-582-28098-2). Longman.

Perkinson, Henry J., ed. Two Hundred Years of American Educational Thought. LC 75-43907. (Educational Policy, Planning, & Theory Ser.). 1980. pap. 9.95x (ISBN 0-582-28198-9). Longman.

--Two Hundred Years of American Educational Thought. LC 75-43907. (Educational Policy, Planning, & Theory Ser.). 1976. pap. 8.95x o.p. (ISBN 0-679-30305-7, Pub. by MacKay). Longman.

Perkinson, Richard C. Handbook of Data Analysis & Data Base Design. 175p. 1981. pap. 29.50 (ISBN 0-89435-045-5). QED Info Sci.

Perkinson, Roy L., jt. auth. see Dolloff, Francis W.

Perkoff, Gerald T. Changing Health Care: Perspectives from a New Medical Care Setting. 1980. 18.50 (ISBN 0-914904-38-8). Health Admin Pr.

Perkoff, Stuart Z. Only Just Above the Ground: Special Issues 28. pap. 1.00 o.p. (ISBN 0-685-78406-1). The Smith.

Perkov, Yury, tr. see Afanasev, Aleksandr N.

Perkowski, Jan L., ed. Vampires of the Slavs. 1976. soft cover 9.95 (ISBN 0-89357-026-5). Slavica.

Perl, Lila. Don't Ask Miranda. LC 78-23835. (gr. 3-6). 1979. 7.50 (ISBN 0-395-28961-0, Clarion). HM.

--Dumb Like Me, Olivia Potts. LC 76-7986. (gr. 5 up). 1976. 7.95 (ISBN 0-395-28870-3, Clarion). HM.

--East Africa: Kenya, Tanzania, Uganda. 160p. (gr. 5-9). 1973. PLB 7.44 (ISBN 0-688-30088-X). Morrow.

--Eating the Vegetarian Way: Good Food from the Earth. LC 80-18416. (Illus.). 96p. (gr. 4-6). 1980. 7.95 (ISBN 0-688-22248-X); PLB 7.63 (ISBN 0-688-32248-4). Morrow.

--Egypt: Rebirth on the Nile. (gr. 5-9). 1977. 8.75 o.p. (ISBN 0-688-22106-8); lib. bdg. 8.88 (ISBN 0-688-32106-2). Morrow.

--Ghana & Ivory Coast, Spotlight on West Africa. LC 74-23106. (Illus.). 160p. (gr. 5-9). 1975. 7.92 (ISBN 0-688-31833-9). Morrow.

--The Global Food Shortage. LC 75-35860. 128p. (gr. 5-9). 1976. PLB 6.96 (ISBN 0-688-32068-6). Morrow.

--The Hamburger Book: All About Hamburgers & Hamburger Cookery. LC 73-7173. (Illus.). 128p. (gr. 5 up). 1974. 7.95 (ISBN 0-395-28921-1, Clarion). HM.

--Hunter's Stew & Hangtown Fry. LC 77-5366. (gr. 6 up). 1977. 8.95 (ISBN 0-395-28922-X, Clarion). HM.

--Junk Food, Fast Food, Health Food What America Eats & Why. 192p. (gr. 5 up). 1980. 9.95 (ISBN 0-395-29108-9, Clarion); pap. 4.95 (ISBN 0-395-30060-6). HM.

--Me & Fat Glenda. LC 71-179439. 192p. (gr. 3-6). 1972. 8.95 (ISBN 0-395-28871-1, Clarion). HM.

--Me & Fat Glenda. (gr. 4-6). 1973. pap. 1.75 (ISBN 0-671-42190-5). Archway.

--Mexico, Crucible of the Americas. LC 77-20203. (Illus.). (gr. 5-9). 1978. 8.95 (ISBN 0-688-22148-3); PLB 8.59 (ISBN 0-688-32148-8). Morrow.

--Puerto Rico, Island Between Two Worlds. LC 79-1130. (Illus.). (gr. 7-9). 1979. 9.50 (ISBN 0-688-22181-5); PLB 9.12 (ISBN 0-688-32181-X). Morrow.

--Slumps, Grunts, & Snickerdoodles: What Colonial America Ate & Why. LC 75-4894. (Illus.). 128p. (gr. 6 up). 1975. 7.95 (ISBN 0-395-28923-8, Clarion). HM.

--The Telltale Summer of Tina C. LC 75-9518. 192p. (gr. 4-8). 1975. 6.95 (ISBN 0-395-28872-X, Clarion). HM.

--That Crazy April. LC 73-14812. (gr. 4-8). 1974. 6.95 (ISBN 0-395-28869-X, Clarion). HM.

Perl, Martin L. High Energy Hadron Physics. LC 74-6348. 584p. 1974. 37.50 (ISBN 0-471-68049-4, Pub. by Wiley-Interscience). Wiley.

Perl, P. Ferns. (Encyclopedia of Gardening Ser.). (gr. 6 up). 1977. PLB 11.97 (ISBN 0-8094-2559-9). Silver.

Perl, Philip. Cacti & Succulents. Time-Life Books, ed. (Time-Life Encyclopedia of Gardening Ser.). 1978. 11.95 (ISBN 0-8094-2587-4). Time-Life.

--Ferns. (Encyclopedia of Gardening). 1977. 11.95 (ISBN 0-8094-2558-0). Time-Life.

Perl, Philip, jt. auth. see Crockett, James U.

Perl, Teri, jt. auth. see Freedman, Miriam.

Perl, William, jt. auth. see Lassen, Niels A.

Perle, George. The Operas of Alban Berg: Vol. I, Wozzeck. 325p. 1980. 20.00 (ISBN 0-520-03440-6). U of Cal Pr.

--Serial Compositon & Atonality: An Introduction to the Music of Schoenberg, Berg, & Webern. 5th ed. 1981. 16.50x (ISBN 0-520-04365-0). U of Cal Pr.

--Twelve-Tone Tonality. 1978. 18.50x (ISBN 0-520-03387-6). U of Cal Pr.

Perles, Anthony. The People's Railway. Walker, Jim, ed. (Interurbans Special Ser.: 69). (Illus.). 300p. 1980. write for info. (ISBN 0-916374-42-4). Interurban.

Perles, B. & Sullivan, C. Freund & Williams' Modern Business Statistics. rev. ed. 1969. text ed. 17.95 (ISBN 0-13-589580-4); lab. manual & wkbk. 6.95 (ISBN 0-13-589598-7). P-H.

Perlick. Plaid for Introduction to Business. 3rd ed. 1980. 5.50 (ISBN 0-256-02352-2, 08-0566-03). Learning Syst.

Perlick, Walter W. Plaid for Introduction to Business. 1976. pap. 5.50 (ISBN 0-256-01269-5, 08-056600). Learning Syst.

Perlick, Walter W. & Lesikar, Raymond V. Introduction to Business: A Societal Approach. 3rd ed. 1979. 16.95x (ISBN 0-256-02086-8). Business Pubns.

Perlick, Walter W., jt. auth. see Alexander, David P.

Perlin, John, jt. auth. see Butti, Ken.

Perlin, Martin S. Managing Institutional Planning: Health Facilities & PL93-641. LC 76-29788. 1976. 24.75 (ISBN 0-912862-31-9). Aspen Systems.

Perlin, Seymour, jt. auth. see Beauchamp, Thom.

Perlis, jt. auth. see Galler.

Perlis, Harlan J., jt. auth. see Cheremisinoff, Paul N.

Perlis, Harlan J., jt. ed. see Cheremisinoff, Paul N.

Perlman. Fermentation: 1977: Annual Reports. 1977. 29.50 (ISBN 0-12-040301-3). Acad Pr.

Perlman, D. & Laskin, A. I., eds. Advances in Applied Microbiology, Vol. 27. (Serial Publication). 1981. 26.00 (ISBN 0-12-002627-9). Acad Pr.

Perlman, D. & Tsao, G. T., eds. Annual Reports on Fermentation Processes. 1978. 25.00 (ISBN 0-12-040302-1). Acad Pr.

Perlman, D. see Umbreit, Wayne W.

Perlman, David see Umbreit, Wayne W.

Perlman, Dorothy. The Magic of Honey. 1978: pap. 1.95 (ISBN 0-380-00029-6, 39099). Avon.

Perlman, Helen H. So You Want to Be a Social Worker. rev. ed. LC 77-106939. (So You Want to Be Ser). 1970. 8.95 o.p. (ISBN 0-06-013318-X, HarpT); lib. bdg. 6.79 o.p. (ISBN 0-06-013319-8, HarpT). Har-Row.

Perlman, Janice E. The Myth of Marginality: Urban Poeverty & Politics in Rio De Janeiro. LC 73-87246. 250p. 1976. 22.75x (ISBN 0-520-02596-2); pap. 6.95x (ISBN 0-520-03952-1). U of Cal Pr.

Perlman, Jim, ed. see Bly, et al.

Perlman, Mark, ed. The Organization & Retrieval of Economic Knowledge. LC 76-30513. (International Economic Association Ser). 1977. lib. bdg. 46.65x (ISBN 0-89158-721-7). Westview.

Perlman, Mark, ed. see International Economic Association Conference, Tokyo.

Perlman, Mark, et al, eds. Index of Economic Articles, Vol. 15, 1978. LC 61-8020. 1978. 50.00x (ISBN 0-917290-04-6). Irwin.

--Index of Economic Articles, Vol. 14,1972. LC 61-8020. 1977. 50.00x (ISBN 0-917290-03-8). Irwin.

Perlman, Philip. Essentials of Modern Chemistry. rev. ed. 472p. (gr. 9-12). 1981. pap. text ed. 6.95 (ISBN 0-8120-2278-5). Barron. Postponed.

--Essentials of Modern Chemistry. LC 78-2344. (gr. 9-12). 1979. pap. 6.95 (ISBN 0-8120-0646-1). Barron.

Perlman, Philip B., ed. see U. S. Department of Justice.

Perlman, Richard. Labor Theory. LC 80-12286. 250p. 1981. Repr. of 1969 ed. lib. bdg. price not set (ISBN 0-89874-163-7). Krieger.

Perlman, Robert & Gurin, Arnold. Community Organization & Social Planning. LC 71-177887. 1972. 17.95 (ISBN 0-471-68050-8). Wiley.

Perlmann, Moshe. Sa'd B. Mansur Ibn Kammuna's Examination of the Inquiries into the Three Faiths. (U. C. Publ. in Near Eastern Studies: Vol. 6). 1967. pap. 8.00x (ISBN 0-520-09299-6). U of Cal Pr.

Perlmann, Moshe. ed. & tr. from Arabic. Ibn Kammuna's Examination of the Three Faiths: A Thirteenth-Century Essay in the Comparative Study of Religion. LC 73-102659. 1971. 20.00 (ISBN 0-520-01658-0). U of Cal Pr.

Perlmann, Moshe. ed. Shaykh Al-Damanhuri Against the Churches of Cairo (1739) (Publications in Near Eastern Studies: Vol. 19). 1975. pap. 11.50x (ISBN 0-520-09513-8). U of Cal Pr.

Perlmutter, Alfred. Guide to Marine Fishes. LC 60-14491. (Illus.). 431p. 1961. 15.00x (ISBN 0-8147-0336-4); pap. 5.95 (ISBN 0-8147-6561-0). NYU Pr.

Perlmutter, Amos. Military & Politics in Israel: Nation Building & Role Expansion. 2nd rev. ed. (Illus.). 161p. 1969. 23.50x (ISBN 0-7146-3100-0, F Cass Co). Biblio Dist.

--Military & Politics in Israel 1948-1967. rev ed. 1980. 23.50x (ISBN 0-7146-3100-0, F Cass Co). Biblio Dist.

--Political Roles & Military Rulers. 314p. 1980. 24.00x (ISBN 0-7146-3122-1, F Cass Co). Biblio Dist.

Perlmutter, Arnold, ed. see Center for Theoretical Studies.

Perlmutter, Arnold, jt. ed. see Kursunoglu, Behram.

Perlmutter, Arnold, et al, eds. High-Energy Physics in the Einstein Centennial Year. (Studies in the Natural Science: Vol. 16). 1979. 55.00 (ISBN 0-306-40297-1, Plenum Pr). Plenum Pub.

Perlmutter, David M. & Soames, Scott. Syntactic Argumentation & the Structure of English. 1979. 27.50x (ISBN 0-520-03828-2); pap. 10.50x (ISBN 0-520-03833-9, CAMPUS NO. 231). U of Cal Pr.

Perlmutter, Felice D., ed. A Design for Social Work Practice. LC 74-1200. 1974. 15.00x (ISBN 0-231-03808-9). Columbia U Pr.

Perlmutter, Howard V. & Sagafi-Nejad, Tagi. International Technology Transfer: Guidelines, Codes & a Muffled Quadrilogue. (Pergamon Policy Studies on International Developement). (Illus.). 250p. 1981. 27.50 (ISBN 0-08-027519-2). Pergamon.

Perlmutter, Howard V., jt. auth. see Heenan, David A.

Perlo, Ellen & Perlo, Victor. Dynamic Stability: The Soviet Economy Today. (Illus.). 365p. (Orig.). 1981. pap. 4.75 (ISBN 0-7178-0577-8). Intl Pub Co.

Perlo, Victor, jt. auth. see Perlo, Ellen.

Perloff, Harvey S. Planning the Post-Industrial City. LC 80-67753. (Illus.). 328p. 1980. 23.95 (ISBN 0-918286-21-2). Planners Pr.

Perloff, Harvey S., et al. Modernizing the Central City: New Towns Intown... & Beyond. LC 74-14687. 448p. 1975. text ed. 18.00 o.p. (ISBN 0-88410-414-1). Ballinger Pub.

Perloff, Marjorie. Frank O'Hara: Poet Among Painters. LC 76-16636. 1977. 12.50 o.s.i. (ISBN 0-8076-0835-1). Braziller.

--Poetry After Symbolism: Rimbaud to Cage. LC 80-8569. (Illus.). 360p. 1981. 20.00x (ISBN 0-691-06462-8). Princeton U Pr.

Perloff, Robert, jt. ed. see Datta, Lois-Ellin.

Perlongo, Robert. The Lamp Is Low. 8.00 (ISBN 0-89253-714-0); flexible cloth 4.80 (ISBN 0-89253-715-9). Ind-US Inc.

Perlow, Austin H. Communications for Trade Unions. (Continuing Education-Labor Studies Ser.). 350p. (Orig.). 1980. write for info. BNA.

Perls, Frederick S. Ego, Hunger & Aggression: The Beginning of Gestalt Therapy. LC 68-28547. 1969. pap. 2.95 (ISBN 0-394-70558-0, Vin). Random.

Perlstein, Israel. How to Relieve or Eliminate Chronic Pains - Discomforts Acquired During Sleep: A Doctor's Solution to Your Sleeping Problems. (Illus.). 64p. (Orig.). 1981. pap. 1.95 (ISBN 0-8326-2252-4, 7445). Delair.

Perman, David. Change & the Churches: An Anatomy of Religion in Britain. 1978. 18.00 (ISBN 0-370-10329-7). Transatlantic.

Perman, M. Reunion Without Compromise: The South & Reconstruction, 1865-1868. LC 72-86418. (Illus.). 384p. 1973. 37.95 (ISBN 0-521-20044-X); pap. 11.95x (ISBN 0-521-09779-7). Cambridge U Pr.

Permanent International Altaistic Conference, 18th Meeting, Bloomington, June 29-July 5, 1975. Aspects of Altaic Civilization II: Proceedings. Draghi, Paul A. & Clark, Larry V., eds. (Indiana University Uralic & Altaic Ser.: Vol. 134). 212p. 1978. 34.00 (ISBN 0-933070-02-0). Ind U Res Inst.

Permanent International Altaistic Conference, Indiana University, 1962. Aspects of Altaic Civilization: Proceedings. Francis, David & Sinor, Denis, eds. LC 80-28299. (Uralic & Altaic Ser.: Vol. 23). ix, 263p. 1981. Repr. of 1962 ed. lib. bdg. 25.00x (ISBN 0-313-22945-7, PIAA). Greenwood.

Permanent Section of Microbiological Standardization, 31st Symposium, Omstotite of Child Health, Ondon, 1969. Interferon & Interferon Inducers. Perkins, F. T. & Regamey, R. H., eds. (Immunobiological Standardization: Vol. 14). 1970. 36.00 (ISBN 3-8055-0637-6). S Karger.

Permin, Ib. Hokus Pokus: Coin Tricks. LC 77-79507. (The Little Magic Books). (Illus.). (gr. 2 up). 1977. 6.95 (ISBN 0-8069-4574-5); PLB 6.69 (ISBN 0-8069-4575-3). Sterling.

--Hokus Pokus: Rope & Scarf Tricks. LC 77-79506. (Illus.). (gr. 2 up). 1977. 6.95 (ISBN 0-8069-4576-1); PLB 6.69 (ISBN 0-8069-4577-X). Sterling.

--Hokus Pokus with Wands, Water & Glasses. LC 77-93314. (Illus.). (gr. 4 up). 1978. 6.95 (ISBN 0-8069-4578-8); PLB 6.69 (ISBN 0-8069-4579-6). Sterling.

Permut, S., ed. see Mokwa, Michael P. & Dawson, William M.

Pernia, Ernesto D. Urbanization, Population Growth & Economic Deveopment in the Philippines. (Studies in Population & Urban Demography: No. 3). 1977. lib. bdg. 19.95 (ISBN 0-8371-9721-X, PEU/). Greenwood.

Pernis, Benvenuto & Vogel, Henry J., eds. Regulatory T Lymphocytes. (P & S Biomedical Science Ser.). 1980. 47.50 (ISBN 0-12-551860-9). Acad Pr.

Pernkopf, Eduard. Atlas of Topograhical & Applied Human Anatomy Index, Vol. 3, Index. 2nd ed. Ferner, Helmut, ed. LC 79-25264. 100p. 1980. text ed. 12.00 (ISBN 0-8067-1572-3). Urban & S.

--Atlas of Topographical & Applied Human Anatomy: Head & Neck, Vol. 1. 2nd ed. Ferner, Helmut, ed. Monsen, Harry, tr. from Ger. LC 79-25264. (Illus.). 1980. text ed. 98.00 (ISBN 0-8067-1552-9). Urban & S.

--Atlas of Topographical & Applied Human Anatomy: Thorax, Abdomen & Extremities, Vol. 2. 2nd ed. Ferner, Helmut, ed. Monsen, Harry, tr. from Ger. LC 79-25264. (Illus.). 1980. text ed. 98.00 (ISBN 0-8067-1562-6). Urban & S.

Pernkoph, Eduard. Atlas of Topographical & Applied Human Anatomy: Head & Neck, Vol. 1. rev. 2nd ed. Ferner, Helmut, ed. Monsen, Harry, tr. from Ger. LC 79-25264. Orig. Title: Atlas der Topographischen und Angewamdten Anatomie Des Menschen. (Illus.). 308p. 1980. Repr. of 1963 ed. text ed. 98.00 (ISBN 0-7216-7198-5). Saunders.

Pernow, Bengt, jt. ed. see Carlson, Lars A.

Pernow, Bengt, jt. ed. see Von Euler, Ulf S.

Peron. A Dictionary of Business Terms. 29.95 (ISBN 2-03-020609-1). Larousse.

Peron, Michel, et al. Dictionnaire francais-anglais, anglais-francais des affaires: A French-English English-French Dictionary of Business Terms. rev. ed. 512p. 1974. 29.95 (ISBN 2-03-020609-1, 3764). Larousse.

Peroni, Peter A. The Burg: An Italian-American Community at Bay in Trenton. LC 79-63258. 1979. pap. text ed. 8.00 (ISBN 0-8191-0724-7). U Pr of Amer.

Perosa, Sergio. Henry James & the Experimental Novel. LC 77-16847. 1978. 12.95x (ISBN 0-8139-0727-6). U Pr of Va.

Perotti, James L. Heidegger on the Divine: The Thinker, the Poet & God. LC 73-92904. x, 134p. 1974. 9.50x (ISBN 0-8214-0144-0). Ohio U Pr.

Perotto, Aldo, jt. auth. see Delagi, Edward F.

Perouse, de La see De la Perouse.

Perovitch, Milosh. Radiological Evaluation of the Spinal Cord, 2 vols. 1981. Vol. 1, 240p. 64.95 (ISBN 0-8493-5041-7); Vol. 2, 192p. 52.95 (ISBN 0-8493-5043-3). CRC Pr.

Perowne, Barry. Raffles Revisited: New Adventures of a Famous Gentleman Crook. LC 73-14321. (Illus.). 332p. 1974. 9.95 o.s.i. (ISBN 0-06-013314-7, HarpT). Har-Row.

Perowne, J. J. Stewart. The Book of Psalms. 1976. 22.95 (ISBN 0-310-31040-7). Zondervan.

Perowne, Stewart. Holy Places of Christendom. LC 76-9272. (Illus.). 1976. 14.95 (ISBN 0-19-519878-6). Oxford U Pr.

Perper, Hazel. Citrus Seed Grower's Indoor How-to Book. LC 73-179694. (Illus.). 1971. 4.50 (ISBN 0-396-06434-5). Dodd.

Perper, Joshua A. & Wecht, Cyril H. Microscopic Diagnosis in Forensic Pathology. (Illus.). 472p. 1980. 54.75 (ISBN 0-398-03969-0). C C Thomas.

Perpillou, Aime V. Human Geography. 2d ed. LC 76-55302. (Geographies for Advanced Study Ser.). (Illus.). 1977. text ed. 21.00x (ISBN 0-582-48571-1); pap. text ed. 15.95x (ISBN 0-582-48572-X). Longman.

Perraton, J. & Baxter, R. Models, Evaluations & Information Systems for Planners, Vol. 1. (Land Use & Built Form Studies). 1978. text ed. 38.00x (ISBN 0-904406-50-4). Longman.

Perrault, Charles. Cinderella. new ed. LC 78-18067. (Illus.). (gr. 1-4). 1979. PLB 5.21 (ISBN 0-89375-120-0); pap. 1.50 (ISBN 0-89375-098-0). Troll Assocs.

--Histories, or Tales of Past Times. Lurie, Alison & Schiller, Justin G., eds. LC 75-32139. (Classics of Children's Literature Ser.: 1621-1932). PLB 38.00 (ISBN 0-8240-2255-6). Garland Pub.

--Perrault's Fairy Tales. LC 72-79522. (Illus.). (gr. 4-6). 1969. pap. 3.50 (ISBN 0-486-22311-6). Dover.

--The Sleeping Beauty. Walker, David, tr. & illus. LC 76-22697. (Illus.). (gr. k-5). 1977. 6.95 o.p. (ISBN 0-690-01278-0, TYC-J); PLB 7.89 (ISBN 0-690-01279-9). T Y Crowell.

--Thorn Rose. (Illus.). 1978. pap. 2.50 (ISBN 0-14-050222-X, Puffin). Penguin.

Perrault, Charles, jt. auth. see Brown, Marcia.

Perrell, O. C., jt. auth. see Pride, William M.

Perren, G. E. & Trim, J. L., eds. Applications of Linguistics: Selected Papers on the Second International Congress of Applied Linguistics, Cambridge. (Illus.). 1972. 69.50 (ISBN 0-521-08088-6). Cambridge U Pr.

Perret, Yvonne M., jt. auth. see Batshaw, Mark L.

Perriam, Wendy. Bourbon for Breakfast. LC 80-1865. 288p. 1981. 11.95 (ISBN 0-385-17374-1). Doubleday.

Perrich, Jerry R., ed. Congressional Staff Directory, Ltd. 272p. 1981. 69.95 (ISBN 0-8493-5693-8). CRC Pr.

Perrie, Maureen. The Agrarian Policy of the Russian Socialist-Revolutionary Party. LC 76-644. (Soviet & East European Studies Ser.). 1977. 27.50 (ISBN 0-521-21213-8). Cambridge U Pr.
Perrigo, Lynn I. The American Southwest: Its Peoples & Cultures. LC 76-146926. 1980. Repr. of 1971 ed. 14.95x (ISBN 0-8263-0403-6). U of NM Pr.
Perrin, Arnold. View from Hill Cabin. 1979. 10.95 (ISBN 0-89002-120-1); pap. 3.50 (ISBN 0-89002-119-8). Northwoods Pr.
Perrin, Blanche. Horses. (Illus.). 24p. (ps-4). 1962. PLB 5.00 (ISBN 0-307-60459-4, Golden Pr). Western Pub.
Perrin, Charles E. La Societe Feodale Allemande et Ses Institutions Du Xe Au XIIe Siecle. LC 80-2013. 1981. Repr. of 1956 ed. 34.50 (ISBN 0-404-18583-5). AMS Pr.
Perrin, D. D., ed. Stability Constants of Metal-Ion Complexes, Pt. B: Organic Ligands. (Chemical Data Ser.: No. 22). 1280p. 1979. 195.00 (ISBN 0-08-020958-0). Pergamon.
Perrin, D. D., et al. Purification of Laboratory Chemicals. 2nd ed. LC 79-41708. 580p. 1980. 72.00 (ISBN 0-08-022961-1). Pergamon.
Perrin, Linda. Coming to America: Immigrants from the Far East. LC 80-65840. 160p. (gr. 9-12). 1980. 9.95 (ISBN 0-440-01072-1). Delacorte.
Perrin, Noel. Giving up the Gun. LC 80-50744. 122p. 1980. pap. 4.95 (ISBN 0-394-73949-3). Random.
--Giving up the Gun: Japan's Reversion to the Sword Fifteen Forty-Three to Eighteen Seventy-Nine. LC 80-50744. (Illus.). 122p. 1980. pap. 4.95 (ISBN 0-394-73949-3). Shambhala Pubns.
Perrin, Norman. Jesus & the Language of the Kingdom: Symbol & Metaphor in New Testament Interpretation. LC 80-20822. 240p. 1980. pap. 8.95 (ISBN 0-8006-1432-1, 1-1432). Fortress.
--The Promise of Bultmann. LC 78-19639. 112p. 1979. pap. 3.95 (ISBN 0-8006-1357-0, 1-1357). Fortress.
--Resurrection According to Matthew, Mark, & Luke. LC 76-47913. 96p. (Orig.). 1977. pap. 3.50 (ISBN 0-8006-1248-5, 1-1248). Fortress.
--What Is Redaction Criticism? Via, Dan O., Jr., ed. LC 72-81529. (Guides to Biblical Scholarship). 96p. (Orig.). 1969. pap. 2.75 (ISBN 0-8006-0181-5, 1-181). Fortress.
Perrin, Norman, tr. see Jeremias, Joachim.
Perrin, Porter G. Reference Handbook of Grammar & Usage. (Derived from Writer's guide & Index to English). 1972. 7.95 (ISBN 0-688-00061-4). Morrow.
Perrin, Richard W. Historic Wisconsin Buildings: A Survey in Pioneer Architecture 1835-1870. 2nd ed. (Publication in History Ser.: No. 4). (Illus.). 150p. 1981. pap. 7.95. Milwaukee Pub.
Perrin, Ursula. Heart Failures. 1980. pap. 1.95 (ISBN 0-380-47589-8, 47589). Avon.
Perrin, William F. Variation of Spotted & Spinner Porpoise (Genus Stennella) in the Eastern Pacific & Hawaii. LC 74-22939. (Scripps Institution of Oceanography Bulletin: Vol. 21). 1975. pap. 12.50x (ISBN 0-520-09527-8). U of Cal Pr.
Perrins, Leslie. Showing Your Dog. (Foyle's Handbks). (Illus.). 1973. 3.95 (ISBN 0-685-55790-1). Palmetto Pub.
--Showing Your Dog. LC 76-11724. (Illus.). 1976. bds. 2.25 o.p. (ISBN 0-668-03977-9). Arco.
Perris, C. & Von Knorring, L., eds. Clinical Neurophysiological Aspects of Psychopathological Conditions. (Advances in Biological Psychiatry: Vol. 4). (Illus.). viii, 192p. 1980. pap. 36.75 (ISBN 3-8055-0604-X). S Karger.
Perritt, Richard A., jt. auth. see Berland, Theodore.
Perrolle, Pierre M., ed. see Xu Liangying & Fan Dianian.
Perrone, Fernando, ed. Portugal Political Struggle & the Mass Media. new ed. (Marxism & the Mass Media Ser.: No. 8). (Illus.). 1981. pap. 5.00 (ISBN 0-88477-012-5). Intl General.
Perrone, N., jt. ed. see Herrmann, G.
Perrone, Nicholas, jt. ed. see Pilkey, Walter D.
Perrone, Philip, jt. auth. see Male, Robert A.
Perrot, D. V. Swahili Dictionary. (Teach Yourself Ser.). 1974. pap. 2.95 o.p. (ISBN 0-679-10015-6). McKay.
Perrott, Eleanor S. It Happened in Pennsylvania. (gr. 4-5). 1952. pap. 3.50 (ISBN 0-931992-11-7). Penns Valley.
Perrott, R. H., jt. ed. see Hoare, C. A.
Perrow, Charles. Complex Organizations: A Critical Essay. 2nd ed. 1979. pap. text ed. 8.95x (ISBN 0-673-15205-7). Scott F.
Perroy, Edouard. La Feodalite En France Du X. Au XII. Siecle. LC 80-2012. 1981. Repr. of 1956 ed. 24.50 (ISBN 0-404-18584-3). AMS Pr.
Perry, A. H. & Walker, J. M. The Ocean-Atmosphere System. (Illus.). 1977. text ed. 22.00x (ISBN 0-582-48559-2); pap. text ed. 14.95x (ISBN 0-582-48560-6). Longman.
Perry, Allen H. Environmental Hazards in the British Isles. (Illus.). 192p. (Orig.). 1981. text ed. 27.50 (ISBN 0-04-910069-6, 2601); pap. text ed. 14.95 (ISBN 0-04-910070-X, 2602). Allen Unwin.
Perry, Anne. Callander Square. 256p. 1981. pap. 2.25 (ISBN 0-449-24365-6, Crest). Fawcett.
--Paragon Walk. 224p. 1981. 9.95 (ISBN 0-312-59598-0). St Martin.
Perry, B. E. Origin of the Book of Sindbad. 1960. 17.35x (ISBN 3-11-000538-7). De Gruyter.
Perry, Ben E. The Ancient Romances: A Literary-Historical Account of Their Origins. (Sather Classical Lectures: No. 37). 1967. 20.00x (ISBN 0-520-01003-5). U of Cal Pr.
Perry, Benjamin F. The Writings of Benjamin F. Perry. Meats, Stephen & Arnold, Edwin T., eds. Incl. Vol. I. Essays, Public Letters, & Speeches. 640p. 35.00 (ISBN 0-87152-340-X); Vols. II & III. Reminiscences of Public Men. Vol. II, 576p. 35.00 ea. (ISBN 0-87152-341-8); Vol. III, 572p. 35.00 (ISBN 0-87152-342-6). LC 80-19568. (The South Carolina Ser.: Bibliographical & Textual: No. 6). 1980. Repr. Set. 105.00 (ISBN 0-87152-339-6). Reprint.
Perry, Bliss. Walt Whitman. LC 80-25319. (American Men & Women of Letters Ser.). 346p. 1981. pap. 5.95 (ISBN 0-87754-151-5). Chelsea Hse.
Perry, Bliss see Johnson, Allen & Nevins, Allan.
Perry, Bliss, ed. The Heart of Emerson's Journals. 357p. 1980. Repr. of 1926 ed. lib. bdg. 30.00 (ISBN 0-89987-670-6). Darby Bks.
Perry, C. Seat Weaving. 1917. pap. 3.80 (ISBN 0-87002-015-3). Bennett IL.
Perry, Cecilia, ed. see Parker, Lynn, et al.
Perry, David W., ed. Homegrown Christian Education: Planning & Programming in the Local Congregation. (Orig.). 1979. pap. 4.95 (ISBN 0-8164-2212-5). Crossroad NY.
Perry, Donald & Merschel, Sylvia. Journey into a Hollow Tree. LC 80-14284. (Illus.). 64p. (gr. 4-12). 1980. PLB 7.95 (ISBN 0-89490-038-2). Enslow Pubs.
Perry, E. Caswell, ed. see Perry, Lilla S.
Perry, E. S., jt. auth. see Weissberger, A.
Perry, Edward D. Sanskrit Primer. LC 36-19814. 1959. 15.00x (ISBN 0-231-00858-9). Columbia U Pr.
--A Sanskrit Primer. 4th. ed. 1978. 6.95 (ISBN 0-89684-026-3, Pub. by Motilal Banarsidass India); pap. text ed. 4.95 (ISBN 0-89684-027-1). Orient Bk Dist.
Perry, Edward S., ed. Techniques of Chemistry Seperation & Purification. 3rd ed. Weissberger, A. LC 77-114920. (Techniques of Chemistry Ser.: Vol. 12). 1978. 42.50 (ISBN 0-471-02655-7, Pub. by Wiley-Interscience). Wiley.
Perry, Elizabeth J. Chinese Perspectives on the Nien Rebellion. 150p. 1981. 18.50 (ISBN 0-87332-191-X). M E Sharpe.
--Rebels & Revolutionaries in North China, 1845-1945. LC 79-65179. (Illus.). xvi, 324p. 1980. 25.00x (ISBN 0-8047-1055-4). Stanford U Pr.
Perry, Enos. Inspiring Boyhoods of Fifteen U. S. Presidents. 1979. 6.00 o.p. (ISBN 0-8062-1190-3). Carlton.
Perry, Enos C., jt. auth. see Haas, Kenneth B.
Perry, Enos J. Artificial Insemination of Farm Animals. 473p. 1968. 20.00 (ISBN 0-8135-0577-1). Rutgers U Pr.
Perry, F. E. A Dictionary of Banking. 304p. 1979. text ed. 19.95x (ISBN 0-7121-0428-3, Pub. by Macdonald & Evans England). Intl Ideas.
Perry, G. E., jt. auth. see Wilson, J. G.
Perry, Gaylord. Me & the Spitter. 1974. pap. 1.25 o.p. (ISBN 0-451-05927-1, Y5927, Sig). NAL.
Perry, George L., jt. ed. see Brainard, William C.
Perry, George L., jt. ed. see Okun, Arthur M.
Perry, Glenn & Fiorenza, Joseph. How to Start a Jukebox & Pinball Business with Little or No Money: Part-Time, Full-Time or Absentee: A Guide to the Electronic Amusement Game Business. LC 80-83931. (Illus., Orig.). 1981. 20.95 (ISBN 0-9602586-5-5); pap. 16.95 (ISBN 0-9602586-4-7). Perry Omega.
Perry, J. W. Lord of the Four Quarters: Myths of the Royal Father. (Patterns of Myth). (Illus.). 1970. pap. 1.50 o.s.i. (ISBN 0-02-066810-4, Collier). Macmillan.
Perry, James L. & Angle, Harold L. Labor-Management Relations & Public Agency Effectiveness: A Study of Urban Mass Transit. LC 80-10746. (Pergamon Policy Studies on Business). 208p. 1980. 24.00 (ISBN 0-08-025953-7). Pergamon.
Perry, James L. & Kraemer, Kenneth L., eds. Technological Innovation in American Local Governments: The Case of Computing. LC 78-26458. (Pergamon Policy Studies). (Illus.). 22.00 (ISBN 0-08-023707-X). Pergamon.
Perry, John. Zoos. LC 70-161071. (First Bks). (Illus.). (gr. 4 up). 1971. PLB 4.90 o.p. (ISBN 0-531-00754-5). Watts.
Perry, John, ed. Personal Identity. 246p. 1975. pap. 4.95x (ISBN 0-520-02960-7). U of Cal Pr.
Perry, John C. Beneath the Eagle's Wings: Americans in Occupied Japan. LC 80-15331. (Illus.). 256p. 1980. 12.95 (ISBN 0-396-07876-1). Dodd.
Perry, John J., tr. see Andreas Capellanus.
Perry, John W. Lord of the Four Quarters: Myths of the Royal Father. Watts, Alan W., ed. LC 65-19324. (Patterns of Myth Ser). 1965. 6.95 o.p. (ISBN 0-8076-0321-X). Braziller.
--Roots of Renewal in Myth & Madness: The Meaning of Psychotic Episodes. LC 76-19500. (Social & Behavioral Science Ser.). 1976. 14.95x (ISBN 0-87589-297-3). Jossey-Bass.
Perry, Josephine. Cookies from Many Lands. (Dover Cook Book Ser). 160p. (gr. 6-12). 1972. pap. 2.50 (ISBN 0-486-22832-0). Dover.
Perry, Judith J., et al, eds. see Texas Symposium on Relativistic Astrophysics, 9th.
Perry, K. R. The Bourgeois Century: A History of Europe 1780-1870. (Evolution of Western Society Ser.). 1972. text ed. 8.50x (ISBN 0-391-00225-2). Humanities.
Perry, Lilla S. Chinese Snuff Bottles. LC 60-12196. (Illus.). 1960. 35.00 (ISBN 0-8048-0106-1). C E Tuttle.
--My Friend Carl Sandburg: The Biography of a Friendship. Perry, E. Caswell, ed. LC 80-21908. 234p. 1981. 12.00 (ISBN 0-8108-1367-X). Scarecrow.
Perry, Lloyd M. Biblical Preaching for Today's World. 256p. 1973. 9.95 (ISBN 0-8024-0707-2). Moody.
Perry, Lloyd M., jt. auth. see Whitesell, Faris D.
Perry, Louis B. & Perry, Richard S. A History of the Los Angeles Labor Movement, 1911-1941. 1963. 22.75x (ISBN 0-520-01002-7). U of Cal Pr.
Perry, Louise M. & Schwengel, Jeanne S. Marine Shells of the Western Coast of Florida. rev. ed. 1955. 10.00 (ISBN 0-87710-370-4); pap. 8.00 (ISBN 0-87710-369-0). Paleo Res.
Perry, Mac. The Bible: Why Trust It? (Orig.). 1981. pap. 4.95 (ISBN 0-88270-493-1). Logos.
--Mac Perry's Florida Lawn & Garden Care. 1980. pap. 7.95 (ISBN 0-916224-57-0). Banyan Bks.
Perry, Marvin, et al. Man's Unfinished Journey: A World History. 1978. text ed. 19.04 (ISBN 0-395-25382-9); instructor's guide & key pap. 8.96 (ISBN 0-395-18017-1); workguide 5.48 (ISBN 0-395-18284-0). HM.
--Western Civilization: A Concise History. (Illus.). 704p. 1981. pap. text ed. 14.95 (ISBN 0-395-29313-8); write for info. instr's manual. HM.
Perry, Marvin, et al, eds. Western Civilization: A Concise History. Incl. Vol. 1. To 1789. pap. text ed. 9.95 (ISBN 0-395-29314-6); Vol. 2. From the 1600s. pap. text ed. 9.95 (ISBN 0-395-29315-4). (Illus.). 400p. 1981. price not set instrs. manual (ISBN 0-395-29316-2). HM.
Perry, Mary E. Crime & Society in Early Modern Seville. LC 79-66452. (Illus.). 310p. 1980. text ed. 14.00x (ISBN 0-87451-177-1). U Pr of New Eng.
Perry, Nance & Perry, Ron. Practical Gemcutting. (Illus.). 96p. (Orig.). 1980. pap. 13.50 (ISBN 0-589-50192-5, Pub. by Reed Bks Australia). C E Tuttle.
Perry, Natalie. Teaching the Mentally Retarded Child. 2nd ed. LC 73-20246. 800p. 1974. 20.00x (ISBN 0-231-03652-3). Columbia U Pr.
Perry, Olney R., jt. auth. see Freeman, Donald E.
Perry, Paul. Fasting Safely. LC 78-68564. 128p. (Orig.). 1981. pap. 4.95 (ISBN 0-89037-217-9). Anderson World.
--Rodeo. LC 78-68562. (Illus.). 144p. 1980. pap. cancelled (ISBN 0-89037-224-1). Anderson World.
Perry, Phillip M. China Business Directory. LC 80-52703. (Illus.). 352p. 1980. 55.00 (ISBN 0-87762-286-8). Technomic.
Perry, R., ed. see Institute of Criminology, University of Cambridge, England.
Perry, R. A., jt. ed. see Goodall, D. W.
Perry, R. B. Bibliography of William James. 1979. 28.50 o.p. (ISBN 0-685-94326-7). Porter.
--Bibliography of William James. 1977. 34.50 o.p. (ISBN 0-685-81151-4). Porter.
Perry, R. L., jt. auth. see Henderson, S. M.
Perry, Richard. Wildlife in Britain & Ireland. (Illus.). 253p. 1978. 16.00x (ISBN 0-85664-306-8, Pub. by Croom Helm Ltd England). Biblio Dist.
Perry, Richard S., jt. auth. see Perry, Louis B.
Perry, Ritchie. Bishop's Pawn, No. 4. 192p. 1981. pap. 2.25 (ISBN 0-345-28971-4). Ballantine.
--Brazil. LC 78-56598. (Countries Ser.). (Illus.). 1978. lib. bdg. 7.95 (ISBN 0-686-51149-2). Silver.
--Ritchie Perry Promotion, a Hard Man to Kill, No. 2. (Super Secret Agent Thrillers Ser.: No. 2), 1981. pap. 2.25 (ISBN 0-345-29056-9). Ballantine.
--Ritchie Perry Promotion, the Fall Guy, No. 1. (Super Secret Agent Thrillers Ser.: No. 2). 1981. pap. 2.25 (ISBN 0-345-29055-0). Ballantine.
--Ticket to Ride Number Three. 192p. 1981. pap. 2.25 (ISBN 0-345-29057-7). Ballantine.
Perry, Roger. Wonders of Llamas. LC 77-6492. (Wonders Ser.). (Illus.). (gr. 5 up). 1977. 5.95 (ISBN 0-396-07460-X). Dodd.
Perry, Ron, jt. auth. see Perry, Nance.
Perry, Ronald W. Racial Discrimination & Military Justice. LC 76-53541. (Special Studies). 1976. text ed. 20.95 (ISBN 0-275-24180-7). Praeger.
Perry, Stewart E. San Francisco Scavengers: Dirty Work & the Pride of Ownership. 1978. 12.95 (ISBN 0-520-03518-6). U of Cal Pr.
Perry, Susan. How Did We Get Clocks & Calendars? (Creative's Questions & Answers Library). (Illus.). 32p. (gr. 3-4). Date not set. PLB 5.75 (ISBN 0-87191-746-7); pap. 2.75 (ISBN 0-89812-215-5). Creative Ed. Postponed.
--How to Play Backgammon. (Creative Games, Activities, Projects Ser.). (Illus.). 40p. (gr. 4-8). 1980. PLB 5.95 (ISBN 0-87191-749-1); pap. 2.95 (ISBN 0-89812-218-X). Creative Ed.
--How to Play Rummy Card Games. (Creative Games, Activities, Projects Ser.). (Illus.). 32p. (gr. 4-8). 1980. PLB 5.95 (ISBN 0-87191-777-7); pap. 2.95 (ISBN 0-89812-245-7). Creative Ed.
Perry, T. W. Feed Formulations. 2nd ed. LC 74-83600. 1975. 12.35 o.p. (ISBN 0-8134-1670-1); text ed. 9.25x o.p. (ISBN 0-685-64706-4, 1670). Interstate.
Perry, T. W., ed. Feed Formulations. 3rd ed. 1981. 12.35 (ISBN 0-8134-2174-8); text ed. 9.25x. Interstate.
Perry, Thomas D. Moral Reasoning & Truth: An Essay in Philosophy & Jurisprudence. 1976. 27.00x (ISBN 0-19-824532-7). Oxford U Pr.
Perry, Vincent G. Skitch: The Message of the Roses. 6.95. Green Hill.
Perry, W. H. Fishermen's Handbook. 1980. 60.00x (ISBN 0-686-64736-X, Pub. by Fishing News England). State Mutual Bk.
Perry, W. H., ed. Fishermen's Handbook. 344p. 1980. cloth 29.95x (ISBN 0-85238-106-9, Pub. by Fishing News England). State Mutual Bk.
Perry, William E. Effective Methods of EDP Quality Assurance. (Illus.). 347p. (Orig.). 1978. pap. 28.50 (ISBN 0-89435-007-2). QED Info Sci.
--Management Guide to Computer Security & Control. (Business Data Processing: a Wiley Ser.). 275p. 1981. 20.95 (ISBN 0-471-05235-3, Pub. by Wiley-Interscience). Wiley.
--Orchestrating Your Career. 192p. 1981. pap. 13.95 (ISBN 0-8436-0799-8). CBI Pub.
Perry, William E. & Kuong, Javier F. Effective Computer Audit Practices Manual ECAP-Map-11: A Manual in Installments. 1980. 495.00 (ISBN 0-686-27136-X). Management Advisory Pubns.
Perryman, F. J. How to Resist the Devil. pap. 0.50. Faith Pub Hse.
Perryman, James H., ed. Oral Physiology & Occlusion: An International Symposium. LC 78-17812. 268p. 1979. 30.00 (ISBN 0-08-023183-7). Pergamon.
Perschia, Doris. The Fluger. (Science Fiction Ser.). 1980. pap. 1.95 (ISBN 0-87997-577-6, UJ1577). DAW Bks.
Perschke, Louis M. Helps & Hints at Bible Study. 176p. 1981. 8.50 (ISBN 0-682-49733-9). Exposition.
Perse, John. St.-John Perse: Letters. Knodel, Arthur J., ed. LC 79-9080. (Bollingen Ser.: LXXXVII: 2). (Illus.). 712p. 1981. 20.00x (ISBN 0-691-09868-9); pap. 8.50 (ISBN 0-691-01836-7). Princeton U Pr.
Perse, St. John. Collected Poems. Auden, W. H., tr. 1972. 27.50x o.p. (ISBN 0-691-09858-1). Princeton U Pr.
Perse, Saint-John. Exil. Little, Roger, ed. (Athlone French Poets Ser.). 1973. text ed. 19.50x (ISBN 0-685-45862-8, Athlone Pr); pap. text ed. 10.50x (ISBN 0-485-12706-7). Humanities.
Persell, Caroline H. Education & Inequality. LC 76-46707. 1977. 12.95 o.s.i. (ISBN 0-02-925140-0). Free Pr.
Pershad, Chitra. The Raging Moon. 6.75 (ISBN 0-89253-716-7); flexible cloth 4.80 (ISBN 0-89253-717-5). Ind-US Inc.
Persico, Enrico, ed. see Levi-Civita, Tullio.
Persico, Joseph. The Spiderweb. 224p. 1981. pap. 2.50 (ISBN 0-553-14334-4). Bantam.
Persing, Bobbye S. Business Communication Dynamics. (General Business Ser.). 475p. 1981. text ed. price not set (ISBN 0-675-08153-X). Merrill.
Persinger, Michael A. Weather Matrix & Human Behavior. LC 80-18422. 300p. 1980. 27.95 (ISBN 0-03-057731-4). Praeger.

Persinger, Michael A. & Lafreniere, Gyslaine F. Space-Time Transients & Unusual Events. LC 76-12634. 224p. 1977. 13.95 (ISBN 0-88229-334-6); pap. 7.95 (ISBN 0-88229-462-8). Nelson-Hall.

Persinger, Michael A., et al. TM & Cult Mania. 208p. 1980. 10.95 (ISBN 0-8158-0392-3). Chris Mass.

Persius & Juvenal. Saturae with Juvenal's Saturae. Clausen, W. V., ed. (Oxford Classical Texts Ser). 1959. 14.95x (ISBN 0-19-814640-X). Oxford U Pr.

Perske, Robert. New Life in the Neighborhood: How Persons with Retardation & Other Disabilities Can Help Make a Good Community Better. LC 80-15517. (Illus.). 80p. (Orig.). 1980. pap. 4.95 (ISBN 0-687-27800-7). Abingdon.

Person, Ethel S., jt. ed. see Stimpson, Catherine.

Person, Russell V. Essentials of Mathematics. 4th ed. LC 79-10708. 1980. text ed. 19.95 (ISBN 0-471-05184-5); study guide avail. (ISBN 0-471-06288-X); solutions manual avail. (ISBN 0-471-07752-6). Wiley.

Person, Russell V. & Person, Vernon J. Practical Mathematics. LC 76-21732. 400p. 1977. 19.95 (ISBN 0-471-68216-0). Wiley.

Person, Vernon J., jt. auth. see Person, Russell V.

Personick, Stewart D. Optical Fiber Transmission Systems. (Applications of Communications Theory Ser.). 210p. 1981. 25.00 (ISBN 0-306-40580-6, Plenum Pr). Plenum Pub.

Persons, Edgar. What You Need to Know to Own & Operate a Small Business: Youth Entrepreneurship. (Orig.). 1981. pap. write for info. (ISBN 0-89514-031-4). Am Voc Assn.

Persons, S., jt. auth. see Egbert, Donald D.

Persons, Stow. The Decline of American Gentility. LC 73-534. 352p. 1973. 20.00x (ISBN 0-231-03015-0); pap. 7.50x (ISBN 0-231-08347-5). Columbia U Pr.

--Free Religion: An American Faith. 5.00 o.p. (ISBN 0-8446-2736-4). Peter Smith.

Persse, Mary K., jt. auth. see Smith, Michael H.

Pertek, Jerzy. Poles on the High Seas. Jordan, Alexander, tr. (Library of Polish Studies: Vol. 9). text ed. 8.95 (ISBN 0-917004-13-2). Kosciuszko.

Perteron, Harold L. American Knives. 1980. 15.00 (ISBN 0-88227-016-8). Gun Room.

Pertwee, Bill. Pertwee's Promenades & Pierrots: One Hundred Years of Seaside Entertainment. LC 79-51084. (Illus.). 1979. 10.50 (ISBN 0-7153-7794-9). David & Charles.

Perusse, Roland I. Historical Dictionary of Haiti. LC 76-30264. (Latin American Historical Dictionaries Ser: No. 15). (Illus.). 1977. 10.00 (ISBN 0-8108-1006-9). Scarecrow.

Perutz, Kathrin. Reigning Passions. LC 77-20701. 1978. 10.00 o.p. (ISBN 0-397-01247-0). Lippincott.

Perutz, M. F., jt. auth. see Fermi, G.

Pervin, Lawrence A. Current Controversies & Issues in Personality. LC 78-15361. 1978. pap. text ed. 10.95 (ISBN 0-471-02035-4). Wiley.

Pervo, Richard I. & Carl, William J., III. Epiphany. Achtemeier, Elizabeth, et al, eds. LC 79-7377. (Proclamation 2: Aids for Interpreting the Lessons of the Church Year, Ser. C). 64p. 1979. pap. 2.50 (ISBN 0-8006-4085-3, 1-4085). Fortress.

Pesaran, M. H. & Slater, L. J. Dynamic Regression: Theory & Algorithms. LC 79-41652. (Computers & Their Applications Ser.). 363p. 1980. 74.95 (ISBN 0-470-26939-1). Halsted Pr.

Pesce, B., ed. Electrolytes. 1962. 37.00 (ISBN 0-08-009597-6); pap. 22.00 (ISBN 0-08-013778-4). Pergamon.

Pesce, Giovanni. And No Quarter: An Italian Partisan in World War II-Memoirs of Giovanni Pesce. Shaine, Frederick, tr. from It. LC 75-127826. 269p. 1972. 10.95x (ISBN 0-8214-0081-9). Ohio U Pr.

Pesch, Imelda M. Macrame. LC 76-126848. (Little Craft Book Ser.). (gr. 6 up). 1970. 5.95 (ISBN 0-8069-5158-3); PLB 6.69 (ISBN 0-8069-5159-1). Sterling.

Peschel, Enid R., ed. Medicine & Literature. 1980. 15.00 (ISBN 0-88202-127-3); text ed. 12.95. N Watson.

Peschel, Enid R., tr. see Rimbaud, Arthur.

Pesek, R., jt. ed. see Billingham, J.

Peseroff, Joyce. The Hardness Scale. LC 77-82224. 72p. 1977. pap. 4.95 (ISBN 0-914086-18-9). Alicejamesbooks.

Peskett, Peter. The Growplan Vegetable Book: A Monthly Guide Vegetable Book. (Illus.). 1978. 14.95 (ISBN 0-7153-7621-7). David & Charles.

Peski, Adrian M. Van see Van Peski, Adrian M.

Peskin, Dean B. Womaning: Overcoming Male Dominance of Executive Row. Ashton, Sylvia, ed. 1980. 15.95 (ISBN 0-87949-165-5). Ashley Bks.

Pesonen, M., jt. auth. see Hurme, R.

Pessemier, Edgar A. Product Management: Strategy & Organization. LC 77-2337. (Marketing Ser.). 1977. text ed. 24.95 (ISBN 0-471-68235-7). Wiley.

Pessen, Edward. Jacksonian America: Society, Personality, & Politics. rev. ed. (Orig.). 1978. pap. text ed. 10.25x (ISBN 0-256-01651-8). Dorsey.

--The Many-Faceted Jacksonian Era: New Interpretations. (Contributions in American History: No. 67). (Illus.). 1977. lib. bdg. 22.50 (ISBN 0-8371-9720-1, PJE/). Greenwood.

Pessen, Edward, ed. Jacksonian Panorama. LC 75-20140. (AHS Ser: No. 85). 1976. pap. 8.95 (ISBN 0-672-60142-7). Bobbs.

Pessin, Deborah. History of the Jews in America. (Illus.). 1957. pap. 4.95x (ISBN 0-8381-0189-5). United Syn Bk.

Pessino, Catherine, jt. auth. see Hussey, Lois J.

Pesso, Albert. Experience in Action: A Psychomotor Psychology. LC 72-96481. 263p. 1973. 13.00x (ISBN 0-8147-6559-9). NYU Pr.

--Movement in Psychotherapy: Psychomotor Techniques & Training. LC 69-19257. 1969. 12.00x (ISBN 0-8147-0340-2). NYU Pr.

Pestalozzi, Johann H. Pestalozzi's Educational Writings. Green, John A., tr. from Ger. Bd. with How Gertrude Teaches Her Children. (Contributions to the History of Psychology Ser., Vol. II, Pt. B: Psychometrics). 1978. Repr. of 1898 ed. 30.00 (ISBN 0-89093-163-1). U Pubns Amer.

Pestana, Carlos. Fluids & Electrolytes in the Surgical Patient. 2nd ed. (Illus.). 192p. 1981. softcover 14.95 (ISBN 0-683-06860-1). Williams & Wilkins.

--Fluids & Electrolytes in the Surgical Patient. 1977. pap. 10.95 o.p. (ISBN 0-683-06859-8). Williams & Wilkins.

Pestana, Ken, jt. auth. see McLean, Gordon.

Pestel, Eduard, jt. auth. see Mesarovic, Mihajlo.

Pestoff, Victor A. Voluntary Associations & Nordic Party Systems. 210p. 1982. 24.95 (ISBN 0-87855-354-1). Transaction Bks. Postponed.

Pestolesi, Robert A. & Sinclair, William A. Creative Administration in Physical Education & Athletics. LC 77-7075. (Illus.). 1978. 16.95 (ISBN 0-13-188987-7). P-H.

Pestolesi, Robert A., jt. auth. see Arnheim, Daniel B.

Peston, M. H. The British Economy. 224p. 1980. 30.00x (ISBN 0-86003-014-8, Pub. by Allan Pubs England); pap. 19.95x (ISBN 0-86003-115-2). State Mutual Bk.

--Theory of Macroeconomic Policy. 224p. 1974. pap. 19.50x (ISBN 0-86003-113-6, Pub. by Allan Pubs England). State Mutual Bk.

Pet Library Ltd. Know First Aid for Dogs. (Know Your Pet Ser.: No. 584). (Illus.). pap. 1.50 o.p. (ISBN 0-385-09301-2). Doubleday.

--Know How to Breed Egglayers. (Know Your Pet Ser.: No. 705). (Illus.). pap. 1.50 o.p. (ISBN 0-385-09343-8). Doubleday.

--Know How to Breed Livebearers. (Know Your Pet Ser.: No. 706). (Illus.). pap. 1.50 o.p. (ISBN 0-385-09345-4). Doubleday.

--Know How to Breed Tropical Fish. (Know Your Pet Ser.: No. 704). (Illus.). pap. 1.50 o.p. (ISBN 0-385-09340-3). Doubleday.

--Know How to Choose Your Dog. (Know Your Pet Ser.: No. 581). (Illus.). pap. 1.50 o.p. (ISBN 0-385-09294-6). Doubleday.

--Know How to Clip a Poodle. (Know Your Pet Ser.: No. 582). (Illus.). pap. 1.50 o.p. (ISBN 0-385-09295-4). Doubleday.

--Know How to Groom Your Dog. (Know Your Pet Ser.: No. 583). (Illus.). pap. 1.50 o.p. (ISBN 0-385-09298-9). Doubleday.

--Know How to Keep Salt Water Fishes. (Know Your Pet Ser.: No. 720). (Illus.). pap. 1.50 o.p. (ISBN 0-385-09363-2). Doubleday.

--Know How to Raise Your Puppy. (Know Your Pet Ser.: No. 586). (Illus.). pap. 1.50 o.p. (ISBN 0-385-09304-7). Doubleday.

--Know How to Train Your Dog. (Know Your Pet Ser.: No. 540). (Illus.). pap. 1.50 o.p. (ISBN 0-385-04480-1). Doubleday.

--Know Obedience & Show Training. (Know Your Pet Ser.: No. 539). (Illus.). pap. 1.50 o.p. (ISBN 0-385-09291-1). Doubleday.

--Know Your Airedale. (Know Your Pet Ser.: No. 530). (Illus.). pap. 1.50 o.p. (ISBN 0-385-09277-6). Doubleday.

--Know Your Aquarium. (Know Your Pet Ser.: No. 702). (Illus.). pap. 1.50 o.p. (ISBN 0-385-09338-1). Doubleday.

--Know Your Aquarium Plants. (Know Your Pet Ser.: No. 717). (Illus.). 1971. pap. 1.50 o.p. (ISBN 0-385-05849-7). Doubleday.

--Know Your Basset Hound. (Know Your Pet Ser.: No. 501). (Illus.). pap. 1.50 o.p. (ISBN 0-385-09195-8). Doubleday.

--Know Your Beagle. (Know Your Pet Ser.: No. 502). (Illus.). pap. 1.50 o.p. (ISBN 0-385-09196-6). Doubleday.

--Know Your Bettas. (Know Your Pet Ser.: No. 710). 64p. 1973. pap. 1.50 o.p. (ISBN 0-385-04533-6). Doubleday.

--Know Your Boston Terrier. (Know Your Pet Ser.: No. 503). (Illus.). pap. 1.50 o.p. (ISBN 0-385-09198-2). Doubleday.

--Know Your Boxer. (Know Your Pet Ser.: No. 504). (Illus.). pap. 1.50 o.p. (ISBN 0-385-09199-0). Doubleday.

--Know Your Bulldog. (Know Your Pet Ser.: No. 505). (Illus.). pap. 1.50 o.p. (ISBN 0-385-09201-6). Doubleday.

--Know Your Cairn Terrier. (Know Your Pet Ser.: No. 532). (Illus.). pap. 1.50 o.p. (ISBN 0-385-09279-2). Doubleday.

--Know Your Canary. (Know Your Pet Ser.: No. 652). (Illus.). pap. 1.50 o.p. (ISBN 0-385-09323-3). Doubleday.

--Know Your Chihuahua. (Know Your Pet Ser.: No. 506). (Illus.). pap. 1.50 o.p. (ISBN 0-385-09203-2). Doubleday.

--Know Your Cocker Spaniel. (Know Your Pet Ser.: No. 507). (Illus.). pap. 1.50 o.p. (ISBN 0-385-09211-3). Doubleday.

--Know Your Collie. (Know Your Pet Ser.: No. 508). (Illus.). pap. 1.50 o.p. (ISBN 0-385-09217-2). Doubleday.

--Know Your Dachshund. (Know Your Pet Ser.: No. 509). (Illus.). pap. 1.50 o.p. (ISBN 0-385-09218-0). Doubleday.

--Know Your Dalmatian. (Know Your Pet Ser.: No. 510). (Illus.). pap. 1.50 o.p. (ISBN 0-385-09221-0). Doubleday.

--Know Your Doberman Pinscher. (Know Your Pet Ser.: No. 511). (Illus.). pap. 1.50 o.p. (ISBN 0-385-09223-7). Doubleday.

--Know Your Domestic & Exotic Cats. (Know Your Pet Ser.: No. 602). (Illus.). pap. 1.50 o.p. (ISBN 0-385-09305-5). Doubleday.

--Know Your Fox Terrier. (Know Your Pet Ser.: No. 512). (Illus.). pap. 1.50 o.p. (ISBN 0-385-09226-1). Doubleday.

--Know Your Gerbils. (Know Your Pet Ser.: No. 757). 64p. 1973. pap. 1.50 o.p. (ISBN 0-385-04512-3). Doubleday.

--Know Your German Shepherd. (Know Your Pet Ser.: No. 513). (Illus.). pap. 1.50 o.p. (ISBN 0-385-09228-8). Doubleday.

--Know Your Goldfish. (Know Your Pet Ser.: No. 711). (Illus.). pap. 1.50 o.p. (ISBN 0-385-09346-2). Doubleday.

--Know Your Great Dane. (Know Your Pet Ser.: No. 514). (Illus.). pap. 1.50 o.p. (ISBN 0-385-01515-1). Doubleday.

--Know Your Guinea Pigs. (Know Your Pet Ser.: No. 753). 64p. 1973. pap. 1.50 o.p. (ISBN 0-385-04510-7). Doubleday.

--Know Your Guppies. (Know Your Pet Ser.: No. 714). (Illus.). pap. 1.50 o.p. (ISBN 0-385-09362-4). Doubleday.

--Know Your Hamster. (Know Your Pet Ser.: No. 754). (Illus.). pap. 1.50 o.p. (ISBN 0-385-09365-9). Doubleday.

--Know Your Irish Setter. (Know Your Pet Ser.: No. 515). (Illus.). pap. 1.50 o.p. (ISBN 0-385-01520-8). Doubleday.

--Know Your Kerry Blue. (Know Your Pet Ser.: No. 534). (Illus.). pap. 1.50 o.p. (ISBN 0-385-09283-0). Doubleday.

--Know Your Labrador Retriever. (Know Your Pet Ser.: No. 542). 64p. 1973. pap. 1.50 o.p. (ISBN 0-385-04507-7). Doubleday.

--Know Your Lhasa Apso. (Know Your Pet Ser.: No. 529). (Illus.). pap. 1.50 o.p. (ISBN 0-385-09276-8). Doubleday.

--Know Your Lovable Mutt. (Know Your Pet Ser.: No. 527). (Illus.). pap. 1.50 o.p. (ISBN 0-385-09268-7). Doubleday.

--Know Your Maltese. (Know Your Pet Ser.: No. 516). (Illus.). pap. 1.50 o.p. (ISBN 0-385-09231-8). Doubleday.

--Know Your Miniature Schnauzer. (Know Your Pet Ser.: No. 517). (Illus.). pap. 1.50 o.p. (ISBN 0-385-09232-6). Doubleday.

--Know Your Monkey. (Know Your Pet Ser.: No. 755). (Illus.). pap. 1.50 o.p. (ISBN 0-385-09368-3). Doubleday.

--Know Your Ocelots & Margays. (Know Your Pet Ser.: No. 756). (Illus.). pap. 1.50 o.p. (ISBN 0-385-09369-1). Doubleday.

--Know Your Old English Sheepdog. (Know Your Pet Ser.: No. 535). (Illus.). pap. 1.50 o.p. (ISBN 0-385-09284-9). Doubleday.

--Know Your Parakeet. (Know Your Pet Ser.: No. 656). (Illus.). pap. 1.50 o.p. (ISBN 0-385-09327-6). Doubleday.

--Know Your Parrot. (Know Your Pet Ser.: No. 657). (Illus.). pap. 1.50 o.p. (ISBN 0-385-09335-7). Doubleday.

--Know Your Pekingese. (Know Your Pet Ser.: No. 518). (Illus.). pap. 1.50 o.p. (ISBN 0-385-09241-5). Doubleday.

--Know Your Persian Cat. (Know Your Pet Ser.: No. 605). (Illus.). pap. 1.50 o.p. (ISBN 0-385-09310-1). Doubleday.

--Know Your Poodle. (Know Your Pet Ser.: No. 520). (Illus.). pap. 1.50 o.p. (ISBN 0-385-09243-1). Doubleday.

--Know Your Popular Cage Birds. (Know Your Pet Ser.: No. 651). (Illus.). pap. 1.50 o.p. (ISBN 0-385-09316-0). Doubleday.

--Know Your Pug. (Know Your Pet Ser.: No. 521). (Illus.). pap. 1.50 o.p. (ISBN 0-385-09244-X). Doubleday.

--Know Your Retriever. (Know Your Pet Ser.: No. 522). (Illus.). pap. 1.50 o.p. (ISBN 0-385-09250-4). Doubleday.

--Know Your Saint Bernard. (Know Your Pet Ser.: No. 533). (Illus.). pap. 1.50 o.p. (ISBN 0-385-09282-2). Doubleday.

--Know Your Scottish Terrier. (Know Your Pet Ser.: No. 423). (Illus.). pap. 1.50 o.p. (ISBN 0-385-09256-3). Doubleday.

--Know Your Setters & Pointer. (Know Your Pet Ser.: No. 538). (Illus.). pap. 1.50 o.p. (ISBN 0-385-09287-3). Doubleday.

--Know Your Shetland Sheepdog. (Know Your Pet Ser.: No. 524). (Illus.). pap. 1.50 o.p. (ISBN 0-385-09258-X). Doubleday.

--Know Your Shih Tzu. (Know Your Pet Ser.: No. 528). (Illus.). pap. 1.50 o.p. (ISBN 0-385-09274-1). Doubleday.

--Know Your Siamese Cat. (Know Your Pet Ser.: No. 605). (Illus.). pap. 1.50 o.p. (ISBN 0-385-09315-2). Doubleday.

--Know Your Toy Fox Terrier. (Know Your Pet Ser.: No. 536). (Illus.). pap. 1.50 o.p. (ISBN 0-385-09285-7). Doubleday.

--Know Your Weimaraner. (Know Your Pet Ser.: No. 525). (Illus.). pap. 1.50 o.p. (ISBN 0-385-09262-8). Doubleday.

--Know Your Welsh Corgi. (Know Your Pet Ser.: No. 541). (Illus.). pap. 1.50 o.p. (ISBN 0-385-05470-X). Doubleday.

--Know Your West Highland White Terrier. (Know Your Pet Ser.: No. 531). (Illus.). pap. 1.50 o.p. (ISBN 0-385-09278-4). Doubleday.

--Know Your Wild Birds. (Know Your Pet Ser.: No. 659). (Illus.). pap. 1.50 o.p. (ISBN 0-385-09337-3). Doubleday.

--Know Your Yorkshire Terrier. (Know Your Pet Ser.: No. 526). (Illus.). pap. 1.50 o.p. (ISBN 0-385-09266-0). Doubleday.

Petacchi, Donald. Work for Being in the Machine Age. LC 80-82646. 1980. 12.50 (ISBN 0-8022-2376-1). Philos Lib.

Petacco, Arrigo. Joe Petrosino. Markmann, Charles Lam, tr. (Illus.). 192p. 1974. 5.95 o.s.i. (ISBN 0-02-595160-2). Macmillan.

Peter, Ellis. Monk's-Hood. 224p. 1981. 9.95. Morrow.

Peter, Emmett B., Jr., ed. see Barbour, George M.

Peter, Gilbert M., jt. auth. see Peterson, Daniel R.

Peter, Laurence J. & Hull, Raymond. The Peter Principle: Why Things Always Go Wrong. (Illus.). 1969. 7.95 (ISBN 0-688-02289-8); pap. 3.95 (ISBN 0-688-27544-3). Morrow.

Peter, Roche De Coppens see Roche De Coppens, Peter.

Peter, Rozsa. Playing with Infinity: Mathematical Explorations & Excursions. LC 75-26467. 288p. 1976. pap. text ed. 3.50 (ISBN 0-486-23265-4). Dover.

Peterdi, Gabor. Printmaking. rev. & expanded ed. LC 80-12888. (Illus.). 336p. 1980. 24.95 (ISBN 0-02-596060-1). Macmillan.

Peterec, R. J. Dakar & West African Economic Development. LC 67-19651. 1967. 20.00x (ISBN 0-231-03016-9). Columbia U Pr.

Peterken, G. F. Guide to the Check Sheet of International Biological Programme Areas. (International Biological Program Handbook No. 4). (Illus.). 1967. pap. 3.50 (ISBN 0-632-04670-8, Blackwell). Mosby.

Peterkiewicz, J., ed. Polish Prose & Verse. 1956. text ed. 13.25x (ISBN 0-485-17502-9, Athlone Pr). Humanities.

Peterkiewicz, Jerzy. The Third Adam: The Mariavite Experiment in Mystical Marriage. (Illus.). 256p. 1975. 27.50x (ISBN 0-19-212198-7). Oxford U Pr.

Peterle, Tony J., ed. see International Congress of Game Biologists, Thirteenth, Atlanta, Ga., March 11-15, 1977.

Peters, A. J. British Further Education. 1967. 26.00 (ISBN 0-08-011893-3). Pergamon.

Peters, Amalia B. de see Lombardi, Ronald P. & De Peters, Amalia B.

Peters, Arthur K. Jean Cocteau & Andre Gide: An Abrasive Friendship. LC 73-185393. 1973. 30.00 (ISBN 0-8135-0709-X). Rutgers U Pr.

Peters, B. Guy. The Politics of Bureaucracy: A Comparative Perspective. LC 77-24584. (Comparative Studies of Political Life Ser.). (Illus.). 1978. text ed. 15.95x (ISBN 0-582-28001-X); pap. text ed. 9.95x (ISBN 0-582-28000-1). Longman.

Peters, Barbara H. & Hopkins, Phil. The Students' Survival Guide to San Diego. 3rd ed. (Illus.). 1980. cancelled (ISBN 0-931854-01-6). Humbird Hopkins.

Peters, C. F. Complete String Quartets Transcribed for Four-Hand Piano, 2 series. unabr. ed. Ser. 1, 320p. pap. 7.95 (ISBN 0-486-23974-8); Ser. 2, 256p. pap. 6.95 (ISBN 0-486-23975-6). Dover.

Peters, D. A. The Principles & Practice of Supervision. 1967. 15.00 (ISBN 0-08-012684-7); pap. 5.75 (ISBN 0-08-012683-9). Pergamon.

Peters, Donald A. Day Care: Problems, Process, Prospects. LC 75-34609. 1975. 11.95 (ISBN 0-87705-279-4); pap. 6.95 (ISBN 0-87705-290-5). Human Sci Pr.

Peters, Donald L. & Willis, Sherry L. Early Childhood. LC 77-12237. (Brooks-Cole Life-Span Developmental Psychology Ser.). (Illus.). 1978. pap. text ed. 6.95 (ISBN 0-8185-0248-7). Brooks-Cole.

Peters, Edward. The Magician, the Witch & the Law. LC 78-51341. (Middle Ages Ser.). 1978. 16.95x (ISBN 0-8122-7746-5). U of Pa Pr.

Peters, Edward, jt. auth. see Prasow, Paul.

Peters, Edward, ed. Christian Society & the Crusades, 1198-1229: Sources in Translation, Including the Capture of Damietta. LC 78-163385. (Middle Ages Ser). 1971. 7.50x (ISBN 0-8122-7644-2); pap. 4.95x (ISBN 0-8122-1024-7, Pa Paperbks). U of Pa Pr.

--First Crusade: The Chronicle of Fulcher of Chartres & Other Source Materials. LC 74-163384. (Middle Ages Ser). 1971. 9.50x (ISBN 0-8122-7643-4); pap. text ed. 5.95x (ISBN 0-8122-1017-4, Pa Paperbks). U of Pa Pr.

--Heresy & Authority in Medieval Europe. LC 79-5262. (Middle Ages Ser.). 384p. 1980. 25.00x (ISBN 0-8122-7779-1); pap. 11.95x (ISBN 0-8122-1103-0). U of Pa Pr.

--Monks, Bishops, & Pagans: Christian Culture in Gaul & Italy. Incl. Selections from the Minor Writings. Gregory Of Tours. McDermott, William C., ed. LC 74-33702. (Middle Ages Ser). 256p. 1975. pap. text ed. 5.95x (ISBN 0-8122-1069-7, Pa Paperbks). U of Pa Pr.

Peters, Edward, jt. ed. see Kors, Alan C.

Peters, Edward M. Europe: The World of the Middle Ages. (Illus.). 1977. text ed. 24.95 (ISBN 0-13-291898-6). P-H.

Peters, Elizabeth. Crocodile on the Sandbank. LC 74-31490. 1975. 7.95 (ISBN 0-396-07080-9). Dodd.

--Crocodile on the Sandbank. 1978. pap. 1.75 o.p. (ISBN 0-449-23713-3, Crest). Fawcett.

--The Curse of the Pharoahs. LC 80-27945. 320p. 1981. 9.95 (ISBN 0-396-07963-6). Dodd.

--Devil-May-Care. 1977. 7.95 o.p. (ISBN 0-396-07413-8). Dodd.

--Devil-May-Care. 1978. pap. 1.75 o.p. (ISBN 0-449-23581-5, Crest). Fawcett.

--Legend in Green Velvet. LC 76-3617. 1976. 7.95 (ISBN 0-396-07283-6). Dodd.

--The Love Talker. LC 79-22104. 256p. 1980. 8.95 (ISBN 0-396-07780-3). Dodd.

--The Love Talker. (Large Print Bks.). 1980. lib. bdg. 13.95 (ISBN 0-8161-3135-X). G K Hall.

--Street of the Five Moons. LC 74-4278. 1978. 7.95 (ISBN 0-396-07528-2). Dodd.

--Summer of the Dragon. LC 79-9782. 1979. 8.95 (ISBN 0-396-07689-0). Dodd.

Peters, Elizabeth & Keeler, Sr. Jerome. Pour Lire et Parler. (Illus.). (gr. 9-12). 1950. text ed. 2.00 o.p. (ISBN 0-8294-0132-6). Loyola.

Peters, Ellen A. Commercial Transactions: Text & Problems on Personalty, Realty & Services. 1971. text ed. 22.00 (ISBN 0-672-81703-9, Bobbs-Merrill Law). Michie.

Peters, Ellis. One Corpse Too Many. 192p. 1981. pap. 2.25 (ISBN 0-445-04653-8). Popular Lib.

Peters, F. E. Aristotle & the Arabs: The Aristotelian Tradition in Islam. LC 68-29431. (New York Studies in Near Eastern Civilization: No. 1). 1968. 15.00x (ISBN 0-8147-0342-9). NYU Pr.

--Greek Philosophical Terms: A Historical Lexicon. LC 67-25043. 234p. 1967. 10.95x o.p. (ISBN 0-8147-0343-7); pap. 5.95 (ISBN 0-8147-6552-1). NYU Pr.

--Ours: The Making & Unmaking of a Jesuit. 192p. 1981. 11.95 (ISBN 0-399-90113-2). Marek.

Peters, Frederick G. Robert Musil, Master of the Hoveny Life. LC 78-5158. 1978. 17.50x (ISBN 0-231-04476-3). Columbia U Pr.

Peters, Fritz. Boyhood with Gurdjieff. 192p. 1980. pap. 4.95 (ISBN 0-88496-146-X). Capra Pr.

Peters, George. A Theology of Church Growth. 368p. 1981. pap. 8.95 (ISBN 0-310-43101-8, 11285P). Zondervan.

Peters, H., ed. see Moreau, J. J., et al.

Peters, Hannah & McNatty, Kenneth P. The Ovary: A Correlation of Structure & Function in Mammals. 1980. 36.00 (ISBN 0-520-04124-0). U of Cal Pr.

Peters, Harry B. Literature of the Woodwind Quintet. LC 70-149999. 1971. 10.00 (ISBN 0-8108-0368-2). Scarecrow.

Peters, Harvey W. America's Coming Bankruptcy: How the Government Is Wrecking Your Dollar. LC 72-91216. 1973. 7.95 o.p. (ISBN 0-87000-200-7). Arlington Hse.

Peters, Helen, ed. see Donne, John.

Peters, Helen Hall. Physical Fitness & Mental Health Before & After Retirement. 1977. 6.50 o.p. (ISBN 0-682-48837-2, Banner). Exposition.

Peters, Herman J. & Shertzer, Bruce. Guidance: Program Development & Management. 3rd ed. (Education-Guidance & Counseling Ser.). 640p. 1974. text ed. 19.95x (ISBN 0-675-08825-9). Merrill.

Peters, Herman J., jt. auth. see Cunningham, Louis.

Peters, J. E. The Development of Farm Buildings. 298p. 1969. 35.00x (ISBN 0-7190-0386-5). State Mutual Bk.

Peters, Jackson. Bong! How to Make & Use Waterpipes. (Illus.). 96p. (Orig.). 1980. pap. 5.95 (ISBN 0-935232-00-1). Deep River Pr.

Peters, Jamie. Backpacking. LC 79-56581. (Illus.). 128p. 1980. 13.50 (ISBN 0-7153-7966-6). David & Charles.

Peters, Jean. Eight-Place Tables of Trigonometric Functions for Every Second of Arc. 1963. 35.00 (ISBN 0-8284-0174-8); thumb index ed. 39.00 (ISBN 0-8284-0185-3). Chelsea Pub.

Peters, John G., jt. ed. see Welch, Susan.

Peters, Joseph P. A Guide to Strategic Planning for Hospitals. LC 79-10063. 148p. (Orig.). 1979. 16.00 (ISBN 0-87258-259-0, 1200). Am Hospital.

Peters, Lawrence J. Software Design: Methods & Techniques. LC 80-50609. (Orig.). 1981. pap. 22.00 (ISBN 0-917072-19-7). Yourdon.

Peters, M. C., jt. auth. see Francis, W.

Peters, Margot, ed. see Shaw, George B.

Peters, Maureen. The Virgin Queen. 1979. pap. 1.95 o.p. (ISBN 0-523-40510-3). Pinnacle Bks.

Peters, Max, jt. auth. see Kaplan, Stanley H.

Peters, Melvin K. An Analysis of the Textual Character of the Bohairic Deuteronomy. LC 78-12958. (Society of Biblical Literature, Septuagint & Cognate Studies: No. 9). 1980. pap. 10.50 (ISBN 0-89130-264-6, 060409). Scholars Pr Ca.

Peters, Michael P. & Hisrich, Robert D. Marketing a New Product: Its Planning, Development & Control. LC 77-84070. 1978. 17.95 (ISBN 0-8053-4102-1). Benjamin-Cummings.

Peters, Mollie C., tr. see Von Staden, Wendelgard.

Peters, Nancy J., jt. auth. see Ferlinghetti, Lawrence.

Peters, Nancy J., et al, eds. Free Spirits. 1981. pap. price not set (ISBN 0-87286-128-7). City Lights.

Peters, Natasha. Savage Surrender. 1977. pap. 2.50 (ISBN 0-441-75156-3). Ace Bks.

Peters, R. S. Authority, Responsibility & Education. 3rd ed. 1973. pap. text ed. 7.95x (ISBN 0-04-170028-7). Allen Unwin.

--Concept of Motivation. 2nd ed. (Studies in Philosophical Psychology). 1969. pap. text ed. 6.50x (ISBN 0-391-00060-8). Humanities.

--Education & the Education of Teachers. (International Library of the Philosophy of Education). 1977. 18.00x (ISBN 0-7100-8469-2). Routledge & Kegan.

--Essays on Educators. (Unwin Education Bks). 160p. 1981. text ed. 19.95x (ISBN 0-04-370103-5, 2626-7); pap. text ed. 7.95x (ISBN 0-04-370104-3). Allen Unwin.

--Psychology & Ethical Development. 1974. text ed. 25.00x o.p. (ISBN 0-04-150049-0); pap. text ed. 15.95x (ISBN 0-04-150050-4). Allen Unwin.

Peters, R. S., jt. auth. see Benn, S. I.

Peters, R. S., ed. John Dewey Reconsidered. (International Library of the Philosophy of Education Ser.). 1977. 16.50x (ISBN 0-7100-8623-7). Routledge & Kegan.

Peters, Ralph. Bravo Romeo. 320p. 1981. 11.95 (ISBN 0-399-90097-7). Marek.

Peters, Richard, jt. auth. see Agazarian, Yvonne.

Peters, Richard S., ed. Perspectives on Plowden. (Students Library of Education). 1969. pap. text ed. 2.00x (ISBN 0-7100-6387-3). Humanities.

Peters, Robert. The Great American Poetry Bake-off. LC 79-16090. 290p. 1979. 14.50 (ISBN 0-8108-1231-2). Scarecrow.

--The Poet As Ice-Skater. pap. 10.00 signed ed. o.p. (ISBN 0-686-18852-7). Man-Root.

Peters, Robert A. ROI: Practical Theory & Innovative Application. rev. & enl. ed. 1979. 23.95 (ISBN 0-8144-5496-8). Am Mgmt.

Peters, Robert L., jt. ed. see Okuda, Kunio.

Peters, Roger. Mammalian Communication: A Behavioral Analysis of Meaning. LC 80-15229. (Orig.). 1980. pap. text ed. 9.95 (ISBN 0-8185-0388-2). Brooks-Cole.

Peters, Rudilph. Islam & Colonialism. (Religion & Society Ser.). 1980. text ed. 37.50x (ISBN 90-279-3347-2). Mouton.

Peters, Sharon. Fun at Camp. (Illus.). 32p. (gr. k-2). 1980. PLB 2.96 (ISBN 0-89375-378-5); pap. 0.95 (ISBN 0-89375-278-9). Troll Assocs.

--Happy Jack. (Illus.). 32p. (gr. k-2). 1980. PLB 2.96 (ISBN 0-89375-380-7); pap. 0.95 (ISBN 0-89375-280-0). Troll Assocs.

--Messy Mark. (Illus.). 32p. (gr. k-2). 1980. PLB 2.96 (ISBN 0-89375-381-5); pap. 0.95 (ISBN 0-89375-281-9). Troll Assocs.

--Puppet Show. (Illus.). 32p. (gr. k-2). 1980. PLB 2.96 (ISBN 0-89375-385-8); pap. 0.95 (ISBN 0-89375-286-X). Troll Assocs.

--Ready, Get Set, Go! (Illus.). 32p. (gr. k-2). 1980. PLB 2.96 (ISBN 0-89375-386-6); pap. 0.95 (ISBN 0-89375-285-1). Troll Assocs.

--Stop That Rabbit. (Illus.). 32p. (gr. k-2). 1980. PLB 2.96 (ISBN 0-89375-388-2); pap. 0.95 (ISBN 0-89375-288-6). Troll Assocs.

--Trick or Treat Halloween. (Illus.). 32p. (gr. k-2). 1980. PLB 2.96 (ISBN 0-89375-392-0); pap. 0.95 (ISBN 0-89375-292-4). Troll Assocs.

Peters, Sue. Shadow of an Eagle. (Harlequin Romances Ser.). 192p. 1980. pap. 1.25 (ISBN 0-373-02351-0, Pub. by Harlequin). PB.

Peters, Susan D., ed. see McCausland, Elizabeth.

Peters, Terry, jt. ed. see Callcott, M. V.

Peters, Will, jt. ed. see Currie, David.

Peters, William S., jt. auth. see Summers, George W.

Petersen. On the Track of the Dixie Limited. (Illus.). 64p. 8.50 (ISBN 0-936610-00-X). Colophon.

Petersen, Barbara. Building Blocks: For Developing Basic Language. 560p. 1977. 34.95 (ISBN 0-86575-036-X). Dormac.

Petersen, Carol. Albert Camus. Gode, Alexander, tr. LC 68-31455. (Modern Literature Ser.). 1969. 10.95 (ISBN 0-8044-2691-0); pap. 3.45 (ISBN 0-8044-6646-7). Ungar.

--Max Frisch. LaRue, Charlotte, tr. LC 72-153124. (Modern Literature Ser.). 10.95 (ISBN 0-8044-2692-9). Ungar.

Petersen, David L. Late Israelite Prophecy. LC 76-26014. (Society of Biblical Literature. Monograph: Vol. 23). 1977. 9.00 (ISBN 0-89130-076-7, 060023); pap. 7.50 (ISBN 0-89130-146-1). Scholars Pr Ca.

Petersen, David M. & Thomas, Charles W. Corrections: Problems & Prospects. (Law Enforcement Ser.). 288p. 1975. pap. text ed. 10.95 o.p. (ISBN 0-13-178293-2). P-H.

Petersen, David M., jt. auth. see Thomas, Charles W.

Petersen, David M., jt. ed. see Truzzi, Marcello.

Petersen, Donald. The Spectral Boy. LC 64-13611. (Wesleyan Poetry Program: Vol. 22). (Orig.). 1964. 10.00x (ISBN 0-8195-2022-5, Pub. by Wesleyan U Pr); pap. 4.95 (ISBN 0-8195-1022-X). Columbia U Pr.

Petersen, Dorothy G. Elementary School Teacher. LC 64-11899. (Illus.). 1964. 25.00x (ISBN 0-89197-139-4); pap. text ed. 14.95x (ISBN 0-89197-744-9). Irvington.

Petersen, Eggert. A Reassessment of the Concept of Criminality: An Analysis of Criminal Behavior in Terms of Individual & Current Environment: the Application of a Stochastic Model. LC 76-51327. 1977. 36.95 (ISBN 0-470-99034-1). Halsted Pr.

Petersen, Esther M. Foster Sons of the Desert. 6.95 o.p. (ISBN 0-685-58702-9). Vantage.

Petersen, Grete, jt. auth. see Bruun-Rasmussen, Ole.

Petersen, I., jt. ed. see Kellaway, P.

Petersen, Ingemar S., jt. ed. see Kellaway, Peter.

Petersen, J. Allan. Conquering Family Stress. 1978. pap. 3.95 (ISBN 0-88207-632-9). Victor Bks.

Petersen, J. L. Computer Programs for Spelling Correction. (Lecture Notes in Computer Science Ser.: Vol. 96). 213p. 1981. pap. 14.00 (ISBN 0-387-10259-0). Springer-Verlag.

Petersen, James C., jt. ed. see Markle, Gerald E.

Petersen, Jim. Evangelism As a Lifestyle. LC 80-83874. 1980. pap. 3.95 (ISBN 0-89109-475-X). NavPress.

Petersen, John. Silly Mysteries. (Illus.). (gr. k-3). 1976. pap. 1.25 o.p. (ISBN 0-590-10151-X, Schol Pap). Schol Bk Serv.

Petersen, Julius see Ball, W. Rouse, et al.

Petersen, K. E. Brownian Motion, Hardy Spaces & Bounded Mean Oscillation. LC 76-46860. (London Mathematical Society Lecture Notes: No. 28). (Illus.). 1977. limp bdg. 14.50x (ISBN 0-521-21512-9). Cambridge U Pr.

Petersen, Karen & Wilson, J. J. Women Artists: Recognition & Reappraisal from the Early Middle Ages to the Twentieth Century. (Illus., Orig.). 1976. pap. 6.95 (ISBN 0-06-090387-2, CN387, CN). Har-Row.

--Women Artists: Recognition & Reappraisal From the Early Middle Ages to the Twentieth Century. LC 76-23505. 212p. 1976. 15.00x (ISBN 0-8147-6567-X). NYU Pr.

Petersen, Kristelle L. The Single Person's Home-Buying Handbook. 320p. 1980. 14.95 (ISBN 0-8015-6840-4, Hawthorn); pap. 7.95 (ISBN 0-8015-6842-0). Dutton.

Petersen, Mark E. The Great Prologue. LC 75-14997. 136p. 1976. pap. 1.50. Deseret Bk.

--Three Kings of Israel. LC 80-36697. 179p. 1980. 6.95 (ISBN 0-87747-829-5). Deseret Bk.

Petersen, Morris S. & Rigby, J. Keith. Interpreting Earth History: A Manual in Historical Geology. 2nd ed. 202p. 1978. wire coil bdg. write for info. (ISBN 0-697-05080-7); instrs'. manual avail. Wm C Brown.

Petersen, P. J. Would You Settle for Improbable? LC 80-69465. 160p. (gr. 5 up). 1981. 8.95 (ISBN 0-440-09601-4); PLB 8.44 (ISBN 0-440-09672-3). Delacorte.

Petersen, Palle. Sally Can't See. LC 77-628. (Illus.). (gr. k-4). 1977. PLB 5.79 o.p. (ISBN 0-381-90058-4, JD-J). John Day.

Petersen, R. David, jt. auth. see Tobias, Marc W.

Petersen, R. H. A Monograph of Ramaria Subgenus Echinoramaria. (Bibliotheca Mycologica). (Illus.). 150p. 1980. lib. bdg. 30.00x (ISBN 0-686-28365-1). Lubrecht & Cramer.

Petersen, Robert, jt. ed. see Licata, Salvatore J.

Petersen, Ronald H. B & C: Mycological Association of M. J. Berkeley & M. A. Curtis. (Bibliotheca Mycologica: 72). (Illus.). 120p. 1980. pap. text ed. 15.00 (ISBN 3-7682-1258-0). Lubrecht & Cramer.

Petersen, T. M. Elementary FORTRAN. (Illus.). 176p. 1976. pap. text ed. 10.95x (ISBN 0-7121-0548-4, Pub. by Macdonald & Evans England). Intl Ideas.

Petersen, W. P. & Fehr, Terry. Meditation Made Easy. (Concise Guides Ser.). (Illus.). (gr. 6 up). 1979. s&l 6.45 (ISBN 0-531-02894-1). Watts.

Petersen, William A. Interrogating the Oracle: A History of the London Browning Society. 290p. 1979. 4.40x (ISBN 0-686-64109-4, Pub. by Browning Inst). Pub Ctr Cult Res.

Petersen, William J. Meet Me on the Mountain. 1979. pap. 2.95 (ISBN 0-88207-784-8). Victor Bks.

--Run Your Life by the Stars? 1977. pap. 1.50 o.p. (ISBN 0-88207-506-3). Victor Bks.

Petersen-Dyggve, Holger N. Chansons Francaises Du XIIIe Siecle. LC 80-2167. 1981. 29.50 (ISBN 0-404-19030-8). AMS Pr.

Petersen-Dyggve, Holgern. Trouveres et Protecteurs De Trouveres Dans les Cours Seigneuriales De France. LC 80-2168. 1981. Repr. of 1942 ed. 41.50 (ISBN 0-404-19032-4). AMS Pr.

Petersham, Maud & Petersham, Miska. Box with Red Wheels. (gr. k-3). 1949. 8.95 (ISBN 0-02-771340-7). Macmillan.

--Circus Baby. (Illus.). (gr. k-3). 1950. 9.95g (ISBN 0-02-771670-8). Macmillan.

--David. (Illus.). (gr. 4-6). 1967. 4.95g o.s.i. (ISBN 0-02-771900-6). Macmillan.

--Joseph & His Brothers. (Illus.). (gr. 3-4). 1958. 4.95g o.s.i. (ISBN 0-02-772240-6). Macmillan.

--Rooster Crows. (Illus.). (gr. k-1). 1945. 10.95g (ISBN 0-02-773100-6). Macmillan.

--Silver Mace. (gr. 4-6). 1964. 4.75g o.s.i. (ISBN 0-02-773660-1). Macmillan.

--Story of Jesus. rev. ed. (gr. 2-4). 1967. 6.95g (ISBN 0-02-773850-7). Macmillan.

--Story of the Presidents of the United States of America. rev. ed. (Illus.). (gr. 4-6). 1966. 6.95g (ISBN 0-02-773890-6). Macmillan.

Petersham, Miska, jt. auth. see Petersham, Maud.

Peterson & Hey. Parenthood. 1981. write for info. (ISBN 0-8087-1673-5). Burgess.

Peterson, jt. auth. see Kerin.

Peterson, Arthur, jt. ed. see Carlson, Norman.

Peterson, Arthur G. Viking & Cherokee. LC 79-89769. (Illus.). 170p. 1980. pap. 8.75. A G Peterson.

Peterson, Barbara H. & Kellogg, Carolyn J. Current Practice in Oncologic Nursing, Vol. 1. LC 75-31734. 232p. 1976. case bound 11.95 o.p. (ISBN 0-8016-3791-0); pap. 8.95 o.p. (ISBN 0-8016-3792-9). Mosby.

Peterson, Bob. Seattle Discovered. LC 76-41333. (Illus.). 1976. pap. 8.95 (ISBN 0-914842-13-7). Madrona Pubs.

Peterson, C. R., jt. auth. see Hill, Philip G.

Peterson, Candida C. A Child Grows Up: A New Approach to Child Development. LC 73-89779. 1974. pap. text ed. 7.95x (ISBN 0-88284-012-6). Alfred Pub.

Peterson, Carolyn S. Reference Books for Elementary & Junior High School Libraries. 2nd ed. LC 75-8537. 321p. 1975. 12.00 (ISBN 0-8108-0816-1). Scarecrow.

Peterson, Carolyn S. & Hall, Brenny. Story Programs: A Source Book of Materials. LC 80-15112. 300p. 1980. pap. 12.50 (ISBN 0-8108-1317-3). Scarecrow.

Peterson, Carroll V. John Davidson. (English Authors Ser.: No. 143). lib. bdg. 10.95 (ISBN 0-8057-1140-6). Twayne.

Peterson, Charles S. Utah: A History. (States & the Nation Ser.). (Illus.). 1977. 12.95 (ISBN 0-393-05629-5, Co-Pub. by AASLH). Norton.

Peterson, Clifford, ed. Saint Erkenwald. new ed. LC 76-53197. (Haney Foundation Ser). 1977. 10.00x (ISBN 0-8122-7723-6). U of Pa Pr.

Peterson, Craig. The Wacky World of Skiing. (Illus.). 128p. 1980. 9.95 (ISBN 0-913276-31-6). Stone Wall Pr.

Peterson, Dale E. The Clement Vision: Poetic Realism in Turgenev & James. (National University Publications Literary Criticism Ser.). 1975. 12.00 (ISBN 0-8046-9107-X, Natl U). Kennikat.

Peterson, Daniel. Functional Mathematics for the Mentally Retarded. LC 70-188780. text ed. 21.50x (ISBN 0-675-09097-0). Merrill.

Peterson, Daniel R. & Peter, Gilbert M. Introduction to Technical Mathematics. 416p. 1974. 12.95x (ISBN 0-673-07784-5). Scott F.

Peterson, David E. Hebrew Old Testament Slidaverb Tm Conjugation Chart. laminated plastic 3.95 o.p. (ISBN 0-310-31090-3). Zondervan.

Peterson, David M. & Thomas, Charles W. Corrections: Problems & Prospects. 2nd ed. (Criminal Justice Ser.). 1980. pap. text ed. 13.95 (ISBN 0-13-178350-5). P-H.

Peterson, Donovan & Ward, Annie, eds. Due Process in Teacher Evaluation. LC 80-5233. 223p. 1980. lib. bdg. 17.00 (ISBN 0-8191-1063-9); pap. text ed. 9.50 (ISBN 0-8191-1064-7). U Pr of Amer.

Peterson, Douglas L. Time, Tide & Tempest: A Study of Shakespeare's Romances. LC 72-94155. 1973. 10.00 (ISBN 0-87328-058-X). Huntington Lib.

Peterson, Edward C., jt. ed. see Bullock, Henry M.

Peterson, Elmer. Tristan Tzara: Dada & Surrational Theorist. 1971. 17.50 (ISBN 0-8135-0673-5). Rutgers U Pr.

Peterson, Eugene H. Five Smooth Stones for Pastoral Work. LC 79-87751. 1980. pap. 8.95 (ISBN 0-8042-1103-5). John Knox.

--Growing up in Christ: A Guide for Families with Adolescents. LC 76-12396. 1976. pap. 3.95 (ISBN 0-8042-2026-3). John Knox.

Peterson, F. Ross. Idaho: A Bicentennial History. (State & the Nation Ser.). 1976. 12.95 (ISBN 0-393-05600-7, Co-Pub by AASLH). Norton.

--Prophet Without Honor: Glenn H. Taylor & the Fight for American Liberalism. LC 72-91668. 1974. 13.50x (ISBN 0-8131-1286-9). U Pr of Ky.

Peterson, Florence. American Labor Unions. 2nd, rev. ed. LC 63-10629. 1963. 12.50x o.p. (ISBN 0-06-034830-5, HarpT). Har-Row.

Peterson, Franklyn, ed. Handbook of Landmower Repair. rev. ed. LC 77-92313. (Illus.). 1978. pap. 5.95 (ISBN 0-8015-3256-6, Hawthorn). Dutton.

Peterson, Franklynn, jt. auth. see Kesselman, Judi R.

Peterson, Franklynn, jt. auth. see Turkel, Judi K.

Peterson, George. The Most Ridiculous Book on Gardening Ever. 1981. 6.95 (ISBN 0-533-04590-8). Vantage.

Peterson, George E., jt. auth. see Hochman, Harold M.

Peterson, George E., ed. Property Tax Reform. 1973. pap. 4.95 (ISBN 0-87766-099-9, 49000). Urban Inst.

Peterson, Gerald R., jt. auth. see Hill, Frederick J.

Peterson, Gilbert A. How to Get Results with Adults. 1977. pap. 1.45 (ISBN 0-88207-178-5). Victor Bks.

Peterson, H. & Marquardt, J. Appraisal & Diagnosis of Speech & Language Disorders. 1981. 18.95 (ISBN 0-13-043505-8). P-H.

Peterson, H. C. & Fite, Gilbert C. Opponents of War, 1917-1918. LC 57-5239. (Illus.). 1968. Repr. of 1957 ed. pap. 2.95 o.p. (ISBN 0-295-78560-8, WP41). U of Wash Pr.

Peterson, Harold L. American Indian Tomahawks: Contributions, Vol. 19. 2nd ed. LC 67-30973. (Illus.). 1971. 10.00 o.p. (ISBN 0-934490-24-4). Mus Am Ind.

--American Knives. LC 58-7523. 1975. pap. 4.95 (ISBN 0-684-16943-6, SL611, ScribT). Scribner.

--The American Sword, Seventeen Seventy-Five to Nineteen Forty-Five. LC 65-25409. (Illus.). 1977. 22.50 (ISBN 0-686-15789-3). Ray Riling.

--How Do You Know It's Old? LC 74-13118. (Encore Edition). (Illus.). 1975. 6.95 o.p. (ISBN 0-684-15286-X, ScribT). Scribner.

--Picture Book of American Interiors: From Colonial Times to the Late Victorians. (Encore Edition). (Illus.). 1979. pap. 4.95 (ISBN 0-684-16918-5, SL861, ScribT). Scribner.

Peterson, Horace C. Propaganda for War. LC 68-15832. 1968. Repr. of 1939 ed. 16.00 (ISBN 0-8046-0365-0). Kennikat.

Peterson, Howard, jt. ed. see Lier, Hal.

Peterson, Jack E. Industrial Health. (Illus.). 1977. ref. ed. 26.95 (ISBN 0-13-459552-1). P-H.

Peterson, James, ed. Computer Organization & Assembly Language Programming. (Computer Science & Applied Mathematics Ser.). 1978. 20.95 (ISBN 0-12-552250-9). Acad Pr.

Peterson, James A. Counseling & Values: A Philosophical Examination. LC 74-117427. 1976. pap. text ed. 9.95 (ISBN 0-910328-24-2). Carroll Pr.

--Finding & Preparing Precious & Semiprecious Stones. (Illus.). 96p. 1974. pap. 6.95 o.p. (ISBN 0-8096-1826-5, Assn Pr). Follett.

--Intramural Administration: Theory & Practice. 384p. 1976. 15.95 (ISBN 0-13-477232-6). P-H.

Peterson, James A. & Payne, Barbara. Love in the Later Years: The Emotional, Physical, Sexual & Social Potential of the Elderly. 192p. 1975. 7.95 o.p. (ISBN 0-8096-1898-2, Assn Pr). Follett.

Peterson, James C., jt. ed. see Markle, Gerald E.

Peterson, John E., et al. Enhancing Hospital Efficiency: A Guide to Expanding Beds Without Bricks. (Illus.). 1980. text ed. 15.00 (ISBN 0-914904-45-0). Health Admin Pr.

Peterson, John M., jt. auth. see Gray, Ralph.

Peterson, K., ed. Health Services Administration Education, 2 vols. Incl. Vol. I. 46.00 (ISBN 0-914904-55-8); pap. text ed. price not set; Vol. II. text ed. price not set (ISBN 0-914904-56-6); pap. text ed. price not set. (Illus.). 350p. 1981. Health Admin Pr.

Peterson, Kenneth G. The University of California Library at Berkeley, 1900-1945. (U. C. Publ. in Librarianship: Vol. 8). 1970. pap. 10.00x (ISBN 0-520-09211-2). U of Cal Pr.

Peterson, Knut. The Lost Frontier. 1981. 10.95 (ISBN 0-87949-172-8). Ashley Bks.

Peterson, L. E., ed. see Committee on Space Research.

Peterson, Lorraine. If God Loves Me, Why Can't I Get My Locker Open? 192p. (Orig.). (gr. 6-12). 1980. pap. 3.95 (ISBN 0-87123-251-0, 210251). Bethany Fell.

Peterson, Louis J., jt. auth. see Schifferes, Justus J.

Peterson, M. Jeanne. The Medical Profession in Mid-Victorian London. 1978. 22.75x (ISBN 0-520-03343-4). U of Cal Pr.

Peterson, Martin, jt. ed. see Johnson, Arnold.

Peterson, Martin L. The Complete Montana Travel Guide. LC 79-88126. (Illus.). 224p. 1980. pap. 5.95 (ISBN 0-686-28763-0). Lake County.

Peterson, Martin S. & Johnson, Arnold H. Encyclopedia of Food Science. (Illus.). 1978. lib. bdg. 79.50 (ISBN 0-87055-227-9). AVI.

Peterson, Melvin N. Flight Deck Uses for HP-25: Vol. 1, Professional Assortment. 66p. 1979. spiral bdg. 10.00x (ISBN 0-938880-00-4). MNP Star.

--Flight Deck Uses for the HP-41c: Vol. 1, Manual Run Mode Edition. 59p. 1981. spiral bdg. 12.00x (ISBN 0-938880-01-2). MNP Star.

Peterson, Merrill D. Thomas Jefferson & the New Nation: A Biography. LC 70-110394. (Illus.). 1090p. 1975. pap. 9.95 (ISBN 0-19-501909-1, GB436, GB). Oxford U Pr.

Peterson, Mike & Gadbois, Robert. The Biggest Giraffe. LC 77-1981. (Books by Children for Children). (Illus.). (gr. 2-6). 1977. PLB 6.45 (ISBN 0-87191-609-6). Creative Ed.

Peterson, N. L. & Harkness, S. D., eds. Radiation Damage in Metals. (TA 460.r23). 1976. 38.00 (ISBN 0-87170-055-7). ASM.

Peterson, Nancy L. Our Lives for Ourselves: Women Who Have Never Married. 320p. 1981. 13.95 (ISBN 0-399-12476-4). Putnam.

Peterson, P., jt. auth. see Sims, J.

Peterson, Paul. Final Take. 1980. pap. write for info. (ISBN 0-671-81678-0). PB.

Peterson, Paul E. City Limits. 288p. 1981. lib. bdg. price not set (ISBN 0-226-66292-6); pap. price not set (ISBN 0-226-66293-4). U of Chicago Pr.

Peterson, Penelope L. & Walberg, Herbert J., eds. Research on Teaching: Concepts, Findings & Implications. LC 78-62102. (Education Ser.). 1979. 15.50 (ISBN 0-8211-1518-9); text ed. 14.00 in ten or more copies (ISBN 0-685-63681-X). McCutchan.

Peterson, R. Industrial Order & Social Policy. 1973. pap. 8.95 ref. ed. (ISBN 0-13-464297-X). P-H.

Peterson, R. A., jt. auth. see Demerath, N. S.

Peterson, R. V., jt. ed. see Richardson, J. H.

Peterson, Raymond M. & Cleveland, James O. Medical Problems in the Classroom: An Educator's Guide. (Illus.). 328p. 1976. 24.75 (ISBN 0-398-03287-4). C C Thomas.

Peterson, Rein & Silver, Edward A. Decision Systems for Inventory Management & Production Planning. LC 78-4980. (Ser. in Management Administration). 1979. text ed. 27.95 (ISBN 0-471-68327-2). Wiley.

Peterson, Reona. Tomorrow You Die. pap. 2.95 (ISBN 0-89728-060-1, 659262). Omega Pubns OR.

Peterson, Rex A., jt. auth. see Owsley, John Q., Jr.

Peterson, Richard. Mary Lavin. (English Author Ser.: No. 239). 1978. 12.50 (ISBN 0-8057-6707-X). Twayne.

Peterson, Richard B. & Tracy, Lane. Systematic Management of Human Resources. LC 78-55826. 1979. text ed. 17.95 (ISBN 0-201-05814-6); readings book avail. 10.95 (ISBN 0-201-05815-4). A-W.

Peterson, Richard L., jt. auth. see Kidwell, David S.

Peterson, Richard S. Imitation & Praise in the Poems of Ben Jonson. LC 80-26261. (Illus.). 280p. 1981. 18.50x (ISBN 0-300-02586-6). Yale U Pr.

Peterson, Robert. Leaving Taos. LC 80-8693. (The National Poetry Ser.). 96p. 1981. pap. 5.95 (ISBN 0-06-090875-0, CN 875, CN). Har-Row.

--Leaving Taos. LC 80-8693. (National Poetry Ser.). 1981. 9.95 (ISBN 0-06-014839-X, CN875, HarpT); pap. 5.95 (ISBN 0-06-090875-0). Har-Row.

--Leaving Taos. LC 80-8693. (The National Poetry Ser.). 96p. 1981. 9.95 (ISBN 0-06-014839-X, HarpT). Har-Row.

Peterson, Robert A., jt. auth. see Kerin, Roger A.

Peterson, Robin. Marketing: A Contemporary Introduction. LC 76-25215. (Marketing Ser.). 1977. pap. text ed. 21.95 (ISBN 0-471-68331-0); instructor's manual avail. (ISBN 0-471-01859-7); study guide avail. (ISBN 0-471-01551-2). Wiley.

Peterson, Robin, et al. Marketing in Action: An Experiential Approach. (Illus.). 1978. pap. text ed. 9.95 (ISBN 0-8299-0204-X); instrs.' manual avail. (ISBN 0-8299-0565-0). West Pub.

Peterson, Robin T. Personal Selling: An Introduction. LC 77-10979. (Marketing Ser.). 1978. text ed. 20.95 (ISBN 0-471-01743-4); tchrs. manual avail. (ISBN 0-471-01744-2). Wiley.

Peterson, Robin T., jt. auth. see Gross, Charles W.

Peterson, Roger T. Audubon Birds. LC 79-57407. (Abbeville Library of Art: No. 4). (Illus.). 112p. 1980. pap. 4.95 (ISBN 0-89659-091-7). Abbeville Pr.

--Birds. LC 63-16281. (Life Nature Library). (Illus.). (gr. 5 up). 1968. PLB 8.97 o.p. (ISBN 0-8094-0624-1, Pub. by Time-Life). Silver.

--The Birds. (Young Readers Library). (Illus.). 1977. lib. bdg. 7.95 (ISBN 0-686-51085-2). Silver.

--A Field Guide to the Birds. 4th ed. 1980. 15.00 (ISBN 0-395-26621-1); limited ed. 75.00 (ISBN 0-395-29930-6); pap. 9.95 (ISBN 0-395-26619-X). HM.

--A Field Guide to the Birds: A Completely New Guide to All the Birds of Eastern and Central North America. 4th ed. 1980. 15.00 (ISBN 0-395-26621-1); ltd. ed. 50.00 (ISBN 0-686-65213-4); pap. 9.95 (ISBN 0-395-26619-X). HM.

Peterson, Roland. The Good Humor Book. (Orig.). 1977. pap. 1.75 o.s.i. (ISBN 0-88449-060-2). Vision Hse.

Peterson, Roy R. A Cross-Sectional Approach to Anatomy. (Illus.). 1980. 49.95 (ISBN 0-8151-6668-0). Year Bk Med.

Peterson, Rudolph E. Stress Concentration Factors. LC 53-11283. 336p. 1974. 32.50 (ISBN 0-471-68329-9, Pub. by Wiley-Interscience). Wiley.

Peterson, Samiha S., et al. The Two-Career Family: Issues & Alternatives. LC 78-66418. 1978. pap. text ed. 10.25 (ISBN 0-8191-0020-X). U Pr of Amer.

Peterson, Shailer. Comprehensive Review for Dental Hygienists. 4th ed. LC 79-28109. (Illus.). 1980. pap. text ed. 18.95 (ISBN 0-8016-3802-X). Mosby.

Peterson, Shailer, ed. Clinical Dental Hygiene. 4th ed. LC 72-77196. (Illus.). 448p. 1972. text ed. 15.95 o.p. (ISBN 0-8016-3810-0). Mosby.

Peterson, Sidney. The Dark of the Screen. (Anthology Film Archives Ser.: No. 4). (Illus.). 220p. 1980. 22.50x (ISBN 0-8147-6581-5); pap. 9.00x (ISBN 0-8147-6582-3). NYU Pr.

Peterson, Susan. Shoji Hamada: A Potter's Way & Work. LC 74-77957. (Illus.). 240p. 1974. 22.50 (ISBN 0-87011-228-7). Kodansha.

Peterson, Thomas D. Wittgenstein for Preaching: A Model for Communication. LC 80-5802. 192p. 1980. lib. bdg. 17.00 (ISBN 0-8191-1342-5); pap. text ed. 8.75 (ISBN 0-8191-1343-3). U Pr of Amer.

Peterson, Thomas V. Ham & Japheth: The Mythic World of Whites in the Antebellum South. LC 78-15716. (ATLA Monograph: No. 12). 1978. lib. bdg. 11.00 (ISBN 0-8108-1162-6). Scarecrow.

Peterson, Thurman S. & Hobby, Charles R. Intermediate Algebra for College Students. 5th ed. 1980. text ed. 16.50 scp (ISBN 0-06-045184-X, HarpC); answer key avail. (ISBN 0-06-365152-1). Har-Row.

Peterson, Trudy H. Agricultural Exports, Farm Income, & the Eisenhower Administration. LC 79-15825. 1979. 15.95x (ISBN 0-8032-3659-X). U of Nebr Pr.

Peterson, Trudy H., ed. Farmers, Bureaucrats, & Middlemen: Historical Perspectives on American Agriculture. LC 80-14609. (Illus.). 514p. 1981. 19.95 (ISBN 0-88258-083-3). Howard U Pr.

Peterson, V. S., jt. ed. see Pakvasa, S.

Peterson, Virgilia, tr. see Romanowicz, Zofia.

Peterson, W. S. Victorian Heretic: Mrs. Humphry Ward's Robert Elsmere. 288p. 1976. text ed. 9.25x (ISBN 0-7185-1147-6, Leicester). Humanities.

Peterson, W. Wesley. Introduction to Programming Languages. 1974. 21.95 (ISBN 0-13-493486-5). P-H.

Peterson, Wallace C. Elements of Economics. 500p. 1973. text ed. 15.95x (ISBN 0-393-09417-0). Norton.

--Income, Employment & Economic Growth. 4th ed. Incl. Macroeconomics: Problems, Concepts & Self Tests. Williams, Harold R. 1978. pap. text ed. 9.95x wkbk. (ISBN 0-393-09058-2). 1978. text ed. 15.95x (ISBN 0-393-09069-8). Norton.

Peterson, William. Anita Bryant, Dale Evans Rogers: Two Stars for God. 1974. pap. 1.25 o.s.i. (ISBN 0-446-76508-2). Warner Bks.

Peterson, William S. Browning Institute Studies. Incl. Vol. 1. 1973; Vol. 2. 1974; Vol. 3. 1975; Vol. 4. 1976; Vol. 5. 1977; Vol. 6. 1978; Vol. 7. 1979. 21.50x (ISBN 0-686-67542-8); Vol. 8. 1980. 23.50x (ISBN 0-686-67543-6). LC 73-80684. (Illus.). 23.00x (ISBN 0-685-92147-6, Pub. by Browning Inst). Pub. Ctr Cult Res.

--Interrogating the Oracle: A History of the London Browning Society. LC 69-15916. (Illus.). xii, 276p. 1970. 14.00x (ISBN 0-8214-0056-8). Ohio U Pr.

--Robert & Elizabeth Barrett Browning: An Annotated Bibliography, 1951-1970. LC 74-24915. (Illus.). 1974. 26.50x (ISBN 0-685-27180-3, Pub. by Browning Inst). Pub Ctr Cult Res.

Peterson, Willis. Glory of Nature's Form. Shangle, Robert D., ed. LC 79-12418. (Illus.). 160p. 1979. 27.50 (ISBN 0-89802-001-8). Beautiful Am.

Peterson, Willis L. Principles of Economics, 2 vols. 3rd. ed. 1977. pap. text ed. 9.50x macro o.p. (ISBN 0-256-01912-6); pap. text ed. 9.50x micro o.p. (ISBN 0-256-01914-2). study guide macro 2.95x o.p. (ISBN 0-256-01913-4); study guide micro 2.95x o.p. (ISBN 0-256-01915-0). Irwin.

--Principles of Economics, 2 vols. 4th ed. Incl. Vol. 1. Macro. pap. 10.50x (ISBN 0-256-02335-2); study guide 4.50x (ISBN 0-256-02336-0); Vol. 2. Micro. pap. 10.50x (ISBN 0-256-02337-9); study guide 4.50x (ISBN 0-256-02338-7). 1980. Irwin.

Peterson's Guides Editors, ed. Who Offers Part-Time Degree Programs? A National Survey of Postsecondary Institutions Offering Daytime, Evening, Weekend, Summer & External Degree Programs-1981 Edition. 250p. 1981. pap. 6.00 (ISBN 0-87866-121-2). Petersons Guid.

Peterson's Guides Editors, compiled by. The Competitive Colleges: Who Are They? 250p. 1981. pap. 6.95 (ISBN 0-87866-127-1). Petersons Guid.

--After Scholarships, What: Sixteen Ways to Reduce Your College Costs. 400p. 1981. pap. 8.00 (ISBN 0-87866-129-8). Petersons Guid.

Petersson, Torsten. Cicero: A Biography. LC 63-10768. 1920. 15.00x (ISBN 0-8196-0119-5). Biblo.

Pethes, G. & Frenyo, V. L. Advances in Animal & Comparative Physiology: Proceedings of the 28th International Congress of Physiological Sciences, Budapest, 1980. LC 80-41894. (Advances in Physiological Sciences: Vol. 20). (Illus.). 400p. 1981. 50.00 (ISBN 0-08-027341-6). Pergamon.

Pethes, G., et al, eds. Recent Advances of Avian Endocrinology: Proceedings of a Satellite Symposium of the 28th International Congress of Physiological Sciences, Budapest, Hungary, 1980. LC 80-42007. (Advances in Physiological Sciences: Vol. 33). (Illus.). 450p. 1981. 50.00 (ISBN 0-08-027355-6). Pergamon.

Pethybridge. History of Postwar Russia. pap. 2.45 (ISBN 0-452-25011-0, Z5011, Plume). NAL.

Pethybridge, Roger, ed. Development of the Communist Bloc. (History & Politics Ser.). 1965. pap. text ed. 2.95x o.p. (ISBN 0-669-23267-X). Heath.

Petie, Haris. Billions of Bugs. (Illus.). (ps-2). 1975. 5.95 (ISBN 0-13-076240-7); pap. 2.50 (ISBN 0-13-076174-5). P-H.

Petis De La Croix, Francois. The Persian & the Turkish Tales, Pt. 1. LC 77-170535. (Novel in England, 1700-1775 Ser). lib. bdg. 50.00 (ISBN 0-8240-0535-X). Garland Pub.

--The Persian & the Turkish Tales, Pt. 2. LC 77-170535. (Novel in England, 1700-1775 Ser). lib. bdg. 50.00 (ISBN 0-8240-0536-8). Garland Pub.

Petit, Gaston & Arboleda, Amadio. Evolving Techniques in Japanese Woodblock Prints. LC 77-75974. (Illus.). 1978. 18.50 (ISBN 0-87011-309-7). Kodansha.

Petit, Jean Francois Le see Le Petit, Jean Francois.

Petit, Paul. Pax Romana. Willis, James, tr. 1976. 27.50x (ISBN 0-520-02171-1). U of Cal Pr.

Petit, R. Electromagnetic Theory of Gratings. (Topics in Current Physics Ser.: Vol. 22). (Illus.). 284p. 1981. 38.35 (ISBN 0-387-10193-4). Springer-Verlag.

Petit Bois, G. Tables of Indefinite Integrals. 1906. pap. text ed. 5.00 (ISBN 0-486-60225-7). Dover.

Petit-Dutaillis, Charles E. The Feudal Monarchy in France & England from the Tenth to the Thirteenth Century. LC 80-2011. 1981. Repr. of 1936 ed. 44.50 (ISBN 0-404-18585-1). AMS Pr.

Petitjean, Pierre. Backstage: With the Ballet. Seaver, Richard & Seaver, Jeannette, trs. (Large Format Ser.). 1979. pap. 9.95 o.p. (ISBN 0-14-005185-6). Penguin.

Petitt, William, jt. auth. see Manocchio, Tony.

Petrak, F. & Sydow, H. Die Gattungen der Pyrenomyceten, Sphaeropsideen und Melanconieen, Pt. 1. (Feddes Repertorium: Beiheft 27). 551p. (Ger.). 1979. Repr. of 1926 ed. lib. bdg. 97.20x (ISBN 3-87429-071-9). Lubrecht & Cramer.

Petrak, Margaret L., ed. Diseases of Cage & Aviary Birds. 2nd ed. (Illus.). 540p. 1981. text ed. price not set (ISBN 0-8121-0692-X). Lea & Febiger.

Petrarca, Francesco. Physicke Against Fortune. Twyne, Thomas, tr. LC 80-22768. 1980. Repr. of 1579 ed. 75.00x (ISBN 0-8201-1359-X). Schol Facsimiles.

Petras, Herman, jt. auth. see Logan, William.

Petras, James. Class, State & Power in the Third World: With Case Studies on Class Conflict in Latin America. 300p. 1981. text ed. 19.95 (ISBN 0-86598-018-7). Allanheld.

--Politics & Social Forces in Chilean Development. 1969. 19.50x (ISBN 0-520-01463-4). U of Cal Pr.

Petras, James & Zemelman Merino, Hugo. Peasants in Revolt: A Chilean Case Study, 1965-1971. Flory, Thomas, tr. LC 72-1578. (Latin American Monographs: No. 28). 164p. 1973. 8.50 (ISBN 0-292-76404-9). U of Tex Pr.

Petras, James F., et al. The Nationalization of Venezuelan Oil. LC 77-7822. (Praeger Special Studies). 1977. text ed. 24.95 (ISBN 0-03-022656-2). Praeger.

Petras, John. The Social Meaning of Human Sexuality. 2nd ed. 1978. pap. text ed. 8.35 (ISBN 0-205-06013-7, 8160139). Allyn.

Petras, John W. Sex: Male-Gender: Masculine. LC 74-32335. 265p. 1975. pap. text ed. 7.95x (ISBN 0-88284-019-3). Alfred Pub.

Petras, John W., ed. George Herbert Mead: Essays on His Social Philosophy. LC 59-11329. 1968. 9.25x (ISBN 0-8077-1902-1). Tchrs Coll.

Petre, F. Loraine. Napoleon's Conquest of Prussia, 1806. LC 77-72679. 1977. 14.95 (ISBN 0-88254-435-7). Hippocrene Bks.

Petrello, George J., jt. auth. see Brown, Richard D.

Petre-Quadens, Olga & Schlag, John D., eds. Basic Sleep Mechanisms. (NATO Advanced Study Institute Ser.). 1974. 43.50 (ISBN 0-12-552950-3). Acad Pr.

Petri, R. Construction Estimating. 1978. ref. ed. 20.95 (ISBN 0-87909-152-5); text ed. 18.95 (ISBN 0-87909-152-5). Reston.

Petric, Vlada, ed. Film & Dreams. 1981. pap. 8.50 (ISBN 0-913178-61-6). Redgrave Pub Co.

Petrick, Paul J. Fiberglass Repairs. LC 76-17811. (Illus.). 1976. 6.00 (ISBN 0-87033-222-8). Cornell Maritime.

Petrie, Cairine. The Nowhere Boys: A Comparative Study of Open & Closed Residential Placement. 184p. 1980. 18.50x (ISBN 0-566-00302-3, 02835-5, Pub. by Saxon Hse England). Lexington Bks.

Petrie, George. Church & State in Early Maryland. 1973. Repr. of 1892 ed. pap. 7.00 (ISBN 0-384-45970-6). Johnson Repr.

Petrie, Glen. Mariamme. 1978. pap. 1.95 o.s.i. (ISBN 0-515-04561-6). Jove Pubns.

Petrie, Graham. The Cinema of Francois Truffaut. LC 72-106791. (Film Guide Ser). (Illus.). 1970. pap. 3.50 o.p. (ISBN 0-498-07649-0). A S Barnes.

--Hungarian Cinema Today: History Must Answer to Man. (Illus.). 284p. (Orig.). 1980. pap. 8.95 (ISBN 9-6313-0485-X). NY Zoetrope.

Petrie, John, tr. see Weil, Simone.

Petrie, Sidney & Stone, Robert B. Martinis & Whipped Cream. 272p. 1968. pap. 2.25 o.s.i. (ISBN 0-446-82506-9). Warner Bks.

Petrie, W. & Campbell, M. Guide to Orchids of Canada & the United States: Excluding the Tropicals of Florida & Hawaii & the Asiatics of Alaska. (Illus.). 1981. pap. price not set (ISBN 0-88839-089-0). Hancock Hse.

Petrie, W. M. Religious Life in Ancient Egypt. LC 72-78238. (Illus.). 1972. Repr. of 1924 ed. lib. bdg. 22.50x (ISBN 0-8154-0422-0). Cooper Sq.

Petrillo, H. V. & Bullock, C. L. Processing Securities Transactions: Administrative Procedures of Brokerage Firms. LC 73-89818. 260p. 1969. 23.95 (ISBN 0-8260-7145-7, 75801). Ronald Pr.

Petrillo, Madeline & Sanger, Sirgay. Emotional Care of Hospitalized Children: An Environmental Approach. 2nd ed. LC 79-27462. 450p. 1980. pap. text ed. 10.95 (ISBN 0-397-54343-3). Lippincott.

Petrocelli, Orlando R. Olympia's Inheritance. 1977. pap. 1.75 o.p. (ISBN 0-523-40006-3). Pinnacle Bks.

Petrocik, John R. Party Coalitions: Realignments & the Decline of the New Deal Party System. LC 80-22212. (Illus.). 1981. lib. bdg. price not set (ISBN 0-226-66378-7). U of Chicago Pr.

Petrone, Fred R. The Developmental Kindergarten: Individualized Instruction Through Diagnostic Grouping. (Illus.). 240p. 1976. 18.75 (ISBN 0-398-03506-7). C C Thomas.

Petronius. The Satyricon. Arrowsmith, William, tr. from Lat. LC 59-6026. 1959. 24.00x (ISBN 0-472-72935-7). Irvington.

Petrosy'Ants, A. M. Problems of Nuclear Science & Technology: The Soviet Union As a World Nuclear Power. 4th rev. & enl. ed. LC 80-40818. (Illus.). 400p. 1981. 56.00 (ISBN 0-08-025462-4). Pergamon.

Petrov, George, tr. see Rudnitsky, Konstantin.

Petrov, M. P. Deserts of the World. LC 75-12921. 1977. 87.95 (ISBN 0-470-68447-X). Halsted Pr.

Petrov, M. P., jt. auth. see Turov, E. A.

Petrova, Luba, jt. auth. see Lesnin, I. M.

Petrovich, S. B., jt. ed. see Hess, Eckhard H.

Petrovsky, Boris V., ed. Atlas of Thoracic Surgery, 2 vols. LC 78-23699. (Illus.). 1979. Set. 150.00 (ISBN 0-8016-3832-1). Mosby.

Petruck, Marvin, tr. see Kushyar Ibn Labban.

Petrunkevitch, Alexander, et al. Studies of Fossiliferous Amber Arthropods of Chiapas, Mexico, Pt. II. (U. C. Publ. in Entomology: Vol. 63). 1971. pap. 8.50x (ISBN 0-520-09375-5). U of Cal Pr.

Petry, Ann. Harriet Tubman: Conductor on the Underground Railroad. (gr. 6-9). 1971. pap. 1.95 (ISBN 0-671-42167-0). Archway.

--Street. (gr. 9-12). 1969. pap. 1.25 (ISBN 0-515-01997-6). Jove Pubns.

Petry, Glenn H., jt. auth. see Karvel, George.

Petry, Loren C. A Beachcomber's Botany. LC 68-26716. (Illus.). 160p. 1975. 5.95 (ISBN 0-85699-119-8). Chatham Pr.

Petry, Ray C., ed. Late Medieval Mysticism. (Library of Christian Classics Ichthus Edition). 1980. pap. 9.95 (ISBN 0-664-24163-8). Westminster.

Petsche, Hellmuth, jt. ed. see Brazier, Mary A.

Petschek, Joyce S. The Silver Bird: A Tale for Those Who Dream. LC 80-70049. (Illus.). 192p. 1981. pap. 8.95 (ISBN 0-89087-318-6). Celestial Arts.

Petschek, Rodolfo, jt. auth. see Bohn, Dave.

Petschull, Jurgen. The Great Balloon Escape. Searls, Courtney, tr. 1981. 10.95 (ISBN 0-686-62158-1). Times Bks.

Pettee, George S. Process of Revolution. LC 76-80581. 1971. Repr. 12.75 (ISBN 0-86527-159-3). Fertig.

Pettegrove, James P. Sailing with Dr. Summers. Date not set. 6.95 (ISBN 0-533-04668-8). Vantage.

Pettengill, Robert B. & Uppal, J. S. Can Cities Survive: A Study of Some Urban Fiscal Problems. 128p. 1974. text ed. 14.95 (ISBN 0-312-11515-6); pap. text ed. 6.95 (ISBN 0-312-11480-X). St Martin.

Pettengill, Samuel B. The Yankee Pioneers: A Saga of Courage. Bohannon, Laura, ed. (Bicentennial Historiettes). (Illus.). 86p. (gr. 7-9). 1977. pap. text ed. 0.95x (ISBN 0-915892-11-1). Regional Ctr Educ.

Petter, Hugo M. Concordancia Greco-Espanola. Carroll, Betty De, ed. Date not set. Repr. of 1976 ed. 12.95 (ISBN 0-311-42047-8). Casa Bautista.

Petteruto, Ray. How to Open & Operate a Restaurant. LC 80-67823. (Food Service Ser.). 269p. 1981. pap. 8.60 (ISBN 0-8273-1966-5); instr's. guide 1.90 (ISBN 0-8273-1967-3). Delmar.

Pettes, Dorothy E. Staff & Student Supervision: A Task Centered Approach. (National Institute Social Services Library). 1979. text ed. 16.95x (ISBN 0-04-361033-1); pap. text ed. 7.95x (ISBN 0-04-361034-X). Allen Unwin.

Pettibone, Marian H. Some Scale-bearing Polychaetes of Puget Sound & Adjacent Waters. LC 53-6933. (Illus.). 136p. 1953. pap. 7.50 (ISBN 0-295-73936-3). U of Wash Pr.

Pettigrew, Helen. Bible Word Quest. new ed. 96p. 1975. pap. 1.95 (ISBN 0-8010-6965-3). Baker Bk.

Pettigrew, John, ed. Robert Browning, the Poems, Vol. I. LC 80-53976. 1218p. 1981. text ed. 35.00x (ISBN 0-300-02675-7); pap. 12.95 (ISBN 0-300-02683-8). Yale U Pr.

--Robert Browning, the Poems, Vol. II. LC 80-53976. 1156p. 1981. text ed. 35.00x (ISBN 0-300-02676-5); pap. 12.95 (ISBN 0-300-02684-6). Yale U Pr.

Pettigrew, Joyce. Robber Noblemen. 1975. 24.00 (ISBN 0-7100-7999-0). Routledge & Kegan.

Pettigrew, Thomas F. The Sociology of Race Relations: Reflection & Reform. LC 79-54666. (Illus.). 1980. pap. text ed. 10.95 (ISBN 0-02-925110-9). Free Pr.

Pettijohn, F. J., et al. Sand & Sandstone. LC 79-168605. 1972. 31.10 o.p. (ISBN 0-387-05528-2); pap. 19.80 (ISBN 0-387-90071-3). Springer-Verlag.

Pettinato, Giovanni. The Archives of Ebla: An Empire Inscribed in Clay. LC 77-16939. (Illus.). 384p. 1981. 15.95 (ISBN 0-385-13152-6). Doubleday.

Pettit, Arthur G. Mark Twain & the South. LC 73-86405. 240p. 1974. 13.00x (ISBN 0-8131-1310-5). U Pr of Ky.

Pettit, Ed, jt. auth. see Schul, Bill.

Pettit, George R. Synthetic Peptides, Vol. 3. 1975. 55.25 (ISBN 0-12-552403-X). Acad Pr.

Pettit, Michael. The Axmann Agenda. (Orig.). 1980. pap. 2.50 o.s.i. (ISBN 0-440-10152-2). Dell.

Pettit, Neila T. Real Readers & Human Teachers. 1974. 4.50x (ISBN 0-87543-119-4). Lucas.

Pettit, Neila T. & Cockriel, Irwin W. Petriel Reading Comprehension Test. 1973. 1.00 (ISBN 0-87543-097-X); 0.75 (ISBN 0-87543-091-0). Lucas.

Pettit, P., jt. ed. see Hookway, C.

Pettit, Philip. The Concept of Structuralism: A Critical Analysis. LC 74-22971. 198p. 1975. 12.95x (ISBN 0-520-02882-1); pap. 2.95 (ISBN 0-520-03416-3). U of Cal Pr.

--Judging Justice: An Introduction to Contemporary Political Philosophy. 192p. 1980. 25.00x (ISBN 0-7100-0563-6); pap. 11.95 (ISBN 0-7100-0571-7). Routledge & Kegan.

Pettitt, George A. Clayton: Not Quite Shangri-la. LC 79-76597. (Illus.). 1969. 5.00 o.p. (ISBN 0-685-72718-1). Brooks-Sterling.

--Prisoners of Culture. LC 68-57070. 1970. 8.50 o.p. (ISBN 0-684-31100-3, ScribT). Scribner.

Pettman, Barrie O., ed. Labour Turnover & Retention. LC 75-18452. 204p. 1976. 21.95 (ISBN 0-470-68448-8). Halsted Pr.

Pettman, Charles. Africanderisms. LC 68-18007. 1968. Repr. of 1913 ed. 28.00 (ISBN 0-8103-3289-2). Gale.

Pettman, Ralph. The Biopolitics of International Relations. LC 80-22926. (Pergamon Policy Studies on Biopolitics). 200p. 1981. 20.00 (ISBN 0-08-026329-1); pap. 9.95 (ISBN 0-08-026328-3). Pergamon.

Pettofrezzo, Anthony J. Matrices & Transformations. 1978. pap. text ed. 3.00 (ISBN 0-486-63634-8). Dover.

Pettofrezzo, Anthony J. & Armstrong, Lee H. Elementary Algebra: A Programmed Approach. 1980. pap. text ed. 14.95x (ISBN 0-673-15293-6). Scott F.

--Intermediate Algebra: A Programmed Approach. 1981. pap. text ed. 13.95 (ISBN 0-673-15315-0). Scott F.

Pettus, Beryl E. & Bland, Randall W. Texas Government Today: Structures, Functions, Political Processes. rev. ed. 1979. pap. text ed. 10.95x (ISBN 0-256-02199-6). Dorsey.

Pettus, Sir John. The Constitution of Parliaments in England. Berkowitz, David S. & Thorne, Samuel E., eds. LC 77-89214. (Classics of English Legal History in the Modern Era Ser.: Vol. 63). 446p. 1979. lib. bdg. 40.00 (ISBN 0-8240-3162-8). Garland Pub.

Petty, Barbara. Bad Blood. 1980. pap. 2.25 o.s.i. (ISBN 0-440-10438-6). Dell.

Petty, Francey, jt. auth. see Baker, Oleda.

Petty, J. William, II, jt. auth. see Walker, Ernest W.

Petty, Jo. Golden Praises. LC 80-944. 192p. 1981. 7.95 (ISBN 0-385-15892-0, Galilee). Doubleday.

Petty, Richard. King of the Road. (Illus.). 1977. 9.95 o.s.i. (ISBN 0-02-596030-X, 59603). Macmillan.

Petty, Richard E., et al, eds. Cognitive Responses in Persuasion. LC 80-26388. 512p. 1981. text ed. 29.95 (ISBN 0-89859-025-6). L Erlbaum Assocs.

Petty, Roy. Contemporary Tennis. LC 77-91165. 1978. 6.95 o.p. (ISBN 0-8092-7548-1); pap. 3.95 (ISBN 0-8092-7574-0). Contemp Bks.

Petty, Ryan. How to Make More Money with Your Garage Sale. 96p. 1981. pap. 3.95 (ISBN 0-312-39602-3). St Martin.

Petty, Thomas L. & Nett, Louise M. For Those Who Live & Breathe: A Manual for Patients with Emphysema & Chronic Bronchitis. 2nd ed. (Illus.). 128p. 1975. 9.75 (ISBN 0-398-02380-8). C C Thomas.

Petty, Thurman, Jr. Siege. (Orion Ser.). 144p. (gr. 7-10). 1980. pap. write for info. (ISBN 0-8127-0302-2). Southern Pub.

Petty, W. The Political Anatomy of Ireland. 260p. 1970. Repr. of 1691 ed. 30.00x (ISBN 0-7165-0093-0, Pub. by Irish Academic Pr Ireland). Biblio Dist.

Petty, Walter T. & Bowen, Mary. Slithery Snakes & Other Aids to Children's Writing. (Orig.). 1967. text ed. 7.95 (ISBN 0-13-813097-3). P-H.

Petty, Walter T., jt. auth. see Greene, Harry A.

Petty, Walter T., et al. Experiences in Language: Tools & Techniques for Language Arts Methods. 2nd ed. 544p. 1976. text ed. 14.95x o.p. (ISBN 0-205-05474-9). Allyn.

Petuchowski, Jakob J. Ever Since Sinai. 3rd ed. LC 79-64324. 1979. pap. text ed. 4.95 (ISBN 0-930038-11-8). Arbit.

--Prayerbook Reform in Europe: The Liturgy of European Liberal & Reform Judaism. LC 68-8262. 1969. 13.50 (ISBN 0-8074-0091-2, 387580, Pub. by World Union). UAHC.

Petuchowski, Jakob L. & Brocke, Michael. The Lord's Prayer & Jewish Liturgy. 1978. 14.50 (ISBN 0-8164-0381-3). Crossroad NY.

Petulengro, Gipsy. Romany Remedies & Recipes. LC 80-20035. 126p. 1980. Repr. of 1972 ed. lib. bdg. 9.95x (ISBN 0-89370-616-7). Borgo Pr.

Petulla, Joseph M. American Environmental History: The Exploitation & Conservation of Natural Resources. LC 75-4870. (Illus.). 1977. 18.00x (ISBN 0-87835-058-6); pap. text ed. 10.95x (ISBN 0-87835-055-1). Boyd & Fraser.

Petyt, George. Lex Parliamentaria; or, a Treatise of Law & Custom of the Parliaments of England. Berkowitz, David & Thorne, Samuel, eds. LC 77-89215. (Classics of English Legal History in the Modern Era Ser.: Vol. 126). 1979. Repr. of 1690 ed. lib. bdg. 55.00 (ISBN 0-8240-3163-6). Garland Pub.

Petyt, K. M. The Study of Dialect: An Introduction to Dialectology. (Andre Deutsch Language Library). 240p. 1980. lib. bdg. 26.50x (ISBN 0-86531-060-2). Westview.

Petz & Swisher. Clinical Practice of Blood Transfusion. Date not set. text ed. price not set (ISBN 0-443-08067-4). Churchill.

Petz, Lawrence D. & Swisher, Scott N., eds. Clinical Practice of Blood Transfusion. (Illus.). 640p. 1981. lib. bdg. 55.00 (ISBN 0-443-08067-4). Churchill.

Petzal, David. Twenty-Two Caliber Rifle. (Illus.). 1973. 9.95 (ISBN 0-87691-077-0). Winchester Pr.

Petzold, jt. auth. see Gaunt.

Petzold, A. & Rohrs, M. Concrete for High Temperatures. 2nd ed. Phillips, A. R. & Turner, F. H., trs. from Ger. (Illus.). 1970. text ed. 37.30x (ISBN 0-85334-033-1, Pub. by Applied Science). Burgess-Intl Ideas.

Petzold, Paul, jt. auth. see Englander, A. Arthur.

Petzold, Paul, jt. auth. see Young, Freddie.

Petzoldt, Rudiger. Speaking of: Diabetes. Heyden, Fransois, tr. from Ger. LC 80-68763. (The Medical Adviser Ser.). (Illus.). 1980. pap. 3.95 (ISBN 0-8326-2243-5, 7457). Delair.

Petzow, Gunter. Metallographic Etching. 1978. 24.00 (ISBN 0-87170-002-6). ASM.

Peucker, T. J. Computer Cartography. LC 72-75261. (CCG Resource Papers Ser.: No. 17). 1972. pap. text ed. 4.00 (ISBN 0-89291-064-X). Assn Am Geographers.

Peusner, Leonardo. Concepts in Bioenergetics. (Concepts of Modern Biology Ser). (Illus.). 272p. 1974. pap. 11.95 reference ed. (ISBN 0-13-166264-3). P-H.

Pevsner, Nicholas. Some Architectural Writers of the Nineteenth Century. (Illus.). 340p. 1972. 37.50x (ISBN 0-19-817315-6). Oxford U Pr.

Pevsner, Nikolaus. Academies of Art, Past & Present. LC 78-87379. (Illus.). 332p. 1973. Repr. of 1940 ed. lib. bdg. 30.00 (ISBN 0-306-71603-8). Da Capo.

--Pioneers of Modern Design. 1961. pap. 4.95 (ISBN 0-14-020497-0, Pelican). Penguin.

--The Sources of Modern Architecture & Design. (World of Art Ser.). (Illus.). 1977. pap. 9.95 (ISBN 0-19-519939-1). Oxford U Pr.

--Studies in Art, Architecture, & Design, 2 vols. 15.00 ea o.s.i. Vol. 1 (ISBN 0-8027-0276-7). Vol. 2 (ISBN 0-8027-0277-5). Walker & Co.

Pevsner, Nikolaus, jt. auth. see Fleming, John.

Pevsner, Nikolaus & Richards, J. M., eds. The Anti-Rationalists: Art Nouveau Architecture & Design. LC 76-12192. (Icon Editions). (Illus.). 210p. 1976. pap. 7.95 o.s.i. (ISBN 0-06-430076-5, IN-76, HarpT). Har-Row.

Pevsner, Nikolaus, et al. A Dictionary of Architecture. LC 75-27325. (Illus.). 554p. 1976. 22.50 (ISBN 0-87951-040-4). Overlook Pr.

Pevsner, Stella. And You Give Me a Pain, Elaine. LC 78-5857. (gr. 6 up). 1978. 7.50 (ISBN 0-395-28877-0, Clarion). HM.

--And You Give Me a Pain, Elaine. (gr. 7-9). 1981. pap. 1.95 (ISBN 0-671-56020-4). Archway.

--Call Me Heller, That's My Name. LC 72-90084. (Illus.). 192p. (gr. 3-6). 1973. 7.95 (ISBN 0-395-28874-6, Clarion). HM.

--Keep Stompin' till the Music Stops. LC 76-27845. (gr. 4-7). 1977. 6.95 (ISBN 0-395-28875-4, Clarion). HM.

--A Smart Kid Like You. LC 74-19320. 192p. (gr. 4-8). 1974. 7.50 (ISBN 0-395-28876-2, Clarion). HM.
Pexieder, Tomas, ed. Mechanisms of Cardiac Morphogenesis & Teratogenesis. (Perspectives in Cardiovascular Research Ser.: Vol. 5). (Illus.). 525p. 1980. text ed. 48.00 (ISBN 0-89004-460-0). Raven.
Peyman, Gholam A., et al, eds. Principles & Practice of Ophthalmology, 3 vols. (Illus.). 2000p. Date not set. Set. text ed. 250.00 (ISBN 0-7216-7228-0); Vol. 1. text ed. 82.50 (ISBN 0-7216-7211-6); Vol. 2. text ed. 82.50 (ISBN 0-7216-7212-4); Vol. 3. text ed. 85.00 (ISBN 0-7216-7213-2). Saunders.
Peyrazat, Jean E. Histoires Droles. (Illus.). 1972. pap. text ed. 2.75 (ISBN 0-88345-063-1, 18069); 2 tapes o.p. 15.00 (ISBN 0-685-59048-8, 58265); 2 cassettes 25.00 (ISBN 0-685-59049-6, 58422). Regents Pub.
Peyre, Henri. The Failures of Criticism. rev. ed. Orig. Title: Writers & Their Critics. 363p. (Orig.). 1944. 15.00x (ISBN 0-8014-0335-9); pap. 4.95 (ISBN 0-8014-9055-3, CP55). Cornell U Pr.
--Observations on Life, Literature & Learning in America. LC 61-8218. 1961. 7.95x o.p. (ISBN 0-8093-0043-5). S Ill U Pr.
--What Is Symbolism? Parker, Emmett, tr. from Fr. LC 79-4686. 176p. 1980. 15.75 (ISBN 0-8173-7004-8). U of Ala Pr.
Peyre, Henri & Seronde, Joseph, eds. Nine Classic French Plays. rev. ed. 1974. pap. text ed. 12.95x (ISBN 0-669-90241-1). Heath.
Peyrefitte, Roger. Knights of Malta. LC 59-12194. 1959. 12.95 (ISBN 0-87599-087-8). S G Phillips.
Peyser, Joan. Twentieth-Century Music: The Sense Behind the Sound. LC 79-57286. (Illus.). 1980. pap. 5.95 (ISBN 0-02-871880-1). Schirmer Bks.
Peyton, K. M. The Beethoven Medal. LC 71-175109. (Illus.). (gr. 6-9). 1972. 8.95 (ISBN 0-690-12846-0, TYC-J). T Y Crowell.
--Flambards. pap. 3.95 (ISBN 0-14-005461-8). Penguin.
--A Pattern of Roses. LC 73-3387. (Illus.). 132p. (gr. 6 up). 1973. 8.95 (ISBN 0-690-61199-4, TYC-J). T Y Crowell.
--Pennington's Last Term. LC 75-13099. (Illus.). (gr. 7-9). 1971. 8.95 (ISBN 0-690-61271-0, TYC-J). T Y Crowell.
--Sea Fever. 1980. pap. 1.50 (ISBN 0-448-17129-5, Tempo). G&D.
--The Team. LC 75-34092. (Illus.). (gr. 6 up). 1976. 8.95 (ISBN 0-690-01083-4, TYC-J). T Y Crowell.
Peyton, Mike. Finish with Engines. 96p. 1980. 9.00x (ISBN 0-245-53409-1, Pub. by Nautical England). State Mutual Bk.
--Hurrican Zoe & Other Sailing. 96p. 1980. 9.00x (ISBN 0-245-53132-7, Pub. by Nautical England). State Mutual Bk.
Peyton, Patricia, ed. Reel Change: A Guide to Social Issue Films. LC 79-54657. (Film Fund Ser.). (Illus., Orig.). 1980. pap. 6.95. NY Zoetrope.
Pezet, A. W., jt. auth. see Abrahamson, E. M.
Pezzano, Chuck, jt. auth. see Sperber, Paula.
Pezzano, Chuck, jt. auth. see Weiskopf, Herm.
Pezzullo, Thomas R. & Brittingham, Barbara E. Salary Equity: Detecting Sex Bias in Salaries Among College & University Professors. LC 78-24634. 1979. 17.95 (ISBN 0-669-02770-7). Lexington Bks.
Pfadt, Robert. Animals Without Backbones. (Beginning-to-Read Bks). (Illus.). (gr. 2-4). 1967. pap. 1.50 o.p. (ISBN 0-695-30428-3); PLB 3.39 o.p. (ISBN 0-695-80428-6). Follett.
Pfaff, D. W. Estrogens & Brain Function: Neural Analysis of a Hormone-Controlled Mammalian Reproductive Behavior. (Illus.). 272p. 1980. 24.90 (ISBN 0-387-90487-5). Springer-Verlag.
Pfaff, Richard W. Montague Rhodes James. (Illus.). 461p. 1980. 40.00x (ISBN 0-85967-554-8, Pub. by Scolar Pr England). Biblio Dist.
Pfaffenberger, jt. ed. see Johnsonbaugh.
Pfaffenberger, Roger C. & Patterson, James H. Statistical Methods: For Business & Economics. 1977. 20.95x (ISBN 0-256-01797-2). Irwin.
Pfafflin, James & Ziegler, Edward, eds. Advances in Environmental Science & Engineering, Vol. 4. 240p. 1981. write for info. (ISBN 0-677-16250-2). Gordon.
Pfahl, Peter B. Retail Florist Business. 3rd ed. LC 76-50302. (Illus.). 1977. 16.65 (ISBN 0-8134-1898-4); text ed. 12.50x (ISBN 0-685-85669-0). Interstate.
Pfaltz, Marilyn, jt. auth. see Reed, Ann.
Pfaltzgraff, Diane K., jt. auth. see Dougherty, James E.
Pfaltzgraff, Robert, Jr., ed. Study of International Relations: A Guide to Information Sources. LC 73-17511. (International Relations Information Guide Ser.: Vol. 5). 220p. 1977. 30.00 (ISBN 0-8103-1331-6). Gale.
Pfaltzgraff, Robert L., ed. Politics & the International System. 2nd ed. LC 70-161414. 612p. 1972. pap. text ed. 7.50 o.p. (ISBN 0-397-47218-8). Lippincott.
Pfaltzgraff, Robert L., Jr. Britain Faces Europe: 1957 to 1967. LC 69-17748. 1969. 7.50 o.p. (ISBN 0-8122-7590-X). U of Pa Pr.
--Energy Issues & Alliance Relationships: The United States, Western Europe and Japan. LC 80-81711. (Special Reports). 72p. 1980. 6.50 (ISBN 0-89549-019-6). Inst Foreign Policy Anal.
Pfaltzgraff, Robert L., Jr. & Davis, Jacquelyn K. The Cruise Missile: Bargaining Chip or Defense Bargain? LC 76-51854. (Special Reports Ser.). 1977. 3.00 (ISBN 0-89549-002-1). Inst Foreign Policy Anal.
Pfatteicher, Philip. The Lesser Festivals, Vols. 1 & 2. LC 74-24917. (Proclamation 1: Aids for Interpretig the Lessons of the Church Year Ser.). 64p. 1975. pap. 1.95 ea. (1-1309); Vol. 1. pap. (ISBN 0-8006-1309-0, 1-1310); Vol. 2. pap. (ISBN 0-8006-1310-4). Fortress.
Pfeffer, Alan J. German Review Grammar. 2nd ed. 1970. text ed. 13.95x o.p. (ISBN 0-669-52241-4); tapes. 6 reels 30.00 o.p. (ISBN 0-669-90407-4); lab drill manual o.p 1.50x o.p. (ISBN 0-669-52266-X). Heath.
Pfeffer, Irving & Klock, David R. Perspectives on Insurance. (Illus.). 448p. 1974. ref. ed. 18.95 (ISBN 0-13-661066-8). P-H.
Pfeffer, Irwin, jt. auth. see Abraham, Henry.
Pfeffer, J., et al. Basic Spoken German Grammar. LC 73-8875. (Illus.). 384p. 1974. text ed. 13.95 (ISBN 0-13-061994-9); tapes o.p. 150.00 (ISBN 0-13-062182-X); wkbk. & guide to tapes 6.95 (ISBN 0-13-062000-9). P-H.
Pfeffer, J. Alan. Kontexte. 1976. pap. 7.95x (ISBN 0-669-73940-5). Heath.
Pfeffer, Jeffrey. Organizational Design. Mackenzie, Kenneth D., ed. LC 77-86024. (Organizational Behavior Ser.). (Illus.). 1978. pap. text ed. 9.95x (ISBN 0-88295-453-9). AHM Pub.
Pfeffer, Leo. Liberties of an American: The Supreme Court Speaks. 2nd ed. 5.25 o.p. (ISBN 0-8446-2739-9). Peter Smith.
Pfeffer, Pierre. Asia: A Natural History. LC 68-28330. (The Continents We Live On, Ser, Vol. 6). (Illus.). 1968. 20.00 o.p. (ISBN 0-394-41570-1). Random.
Pfeffer, Richard. Working for Capitalism. 1979. 22.50 (ISBN 0-231-04426-7); pap. 8.00 (ISBN 0-231-04427-5). Columbia U Pr.
Pfeffer, Richard M., ed. No More Vietnams: The War & the Future of American Foreign Policy. LC 68-58302. 1968. 8.95 o.s.i. (ISBN 0-06-013324-4, HarpT). Har-Row.
Pfeffer, Susan. Starring Peter & Leigh. (gr. 7-12). 1980. pap. 1.75 (ISBN 0-440-98200-6, LFL). Dell.
Pfeffer, Susan B. About David. LC 80-65837. 176p. (gr. 8-12). 1980. 8.95 (ISBN 0-440-00093-9). Delacorte.
--Awful Evelina. Pacini, Kathy, ed. LC 79-108. (Concept Bk.: Level I). (Illus.). (gr. k-3). 1979. 6.95g (ISBN 0-8075-0494-7). A Whitman.
--Just Between Us. LC 79-53606. (gr. 4-7). 1980. 7.95 (ISBN 0-440-07823-7); PLB 7.45 (ISBN 0-440-05046-4). Delacorte.
--Kid Power. LC 77-1975. (gr. 4-6). 1977. PLB 6.90 s&l (ISBN 0-531-00123-7). Watts.
--What Do You Do When Your Mouth Won't Open? LC 80-68731. (Illus.). 128p. (gr. 4-7). 1981. 7.95 (ISBN 0-440-09471-2); PLB 7.44 (ISBN 0-440-09475-5). Delacorte.
Pfeifer, Luanne. Ski California: A Guide to Downhill & Cross-Country Skiing. LC 80-13731. (Illus.). 1980. pap. 7.95 (ISBN 0-89141-091-0). Presidio Pr.
Pfeiffer, C. Boyd. Field Guide to Outdoor Photography. LC 76-55380. (Illus.). 224p. 1977. pap. 3.95 (ISBN 0-8117-2261-9). Stackpole.
Pfeiffer, Carl C., et al. Schizophrenias: Yours & Mine. 1970. pap. 2.50 (ISBN 0-515-05835-1). Jove Pubns.
Pfeiffer, Carl J., et al. Gastro-Intestinal Ultrastructure: An Atlas of Scanning & Transmission Electron Micrographs. 1974. 55.25 (ISBN 0-12-553750-6). Acad Pr.
Pfeiffer, Charles F. Baker's Bible Atlas. rev. ed. (Illus.). 1961. Repr. 14.95 (ISBN 0-8010-6930-0). Baker Bk.
--The Bible Atlas. LC 60-15536. 1975. 14.95 (ISBN 0-8054-1129-1). Broadman.
--Book of Leviticus: A Study Manual. (Shield Bible Study Ser). (Orig.). pap. 2.95 (ISBN 0-8010-6889-4). Baker Bk.
--Dead Sea Scrolls & the Bible. rev. & enl. ed. Pfeiffer, Charles F., ed. (Baker Studies in Biblical Archaeology). (Illus.). 1969. pap. 3.95 (ISBN 0-8010-6898-3). Baker Bk.
--Tell el Amarna & the Bible. (Baker Studies in Biblical Archaeology). 1976. pap. 2.95 (ISBN 0-8010-7002-3). Baker Bk.
Pfeiffer, Charles F. & Vos, Howard F. Wycliffe Historical Geography of Bible Lands. 1967. 14.95 (ISBN 0-8024-9699-7). Moody.
Pfeiffer, Charles F., jt. ed. see Harrison, Everett.
Pfeiffer, Charles F., et al, eds. Wycliffe Bible Encyclopedia, 2 vols. (Illus.). 1875p. 1975. 40.00 (ISBN 0-8024-9697-0). Moody.
Pfeiffer, Charles M. The Art of Making Wax Flowers & Fruit As an Interesting & Profitable Career. (Illus.). 117p. 1981. 39.85 (ISBN 0-930582-87-X). Gloucester Art.
Pfeiffer, Douglas, ed. see Krantz, Les.
Pfeiffer, Douglas, ed. see Smith, Clyde.
Pfeiffer, Douglas A., ed. see Foster, Lee.
Pfeiffer, Douglas A., ed. see Gibbs, James A.
Pfeiffer, Eric, jt. auth. see Busse, Ewald W.
Pfeiffer, Guy O. & Nikel, Casimir M. The Household Environment & Chronic Illness: Guidelines for Constructing & Maintaining a Less Polluted Residence. (Illus.). 208p. 1980. text ed. 14.75 (ISBN 0-398-03961-5). C C Thomas.
Pfeiffer, J. William & Jones, John E. Reference Guide to Handbooks & Annuals. rev. ed. LC 75-14661. 150p. 1981. pap. 9.50 (ISBN 0-88390-069-6). Univ Assocs.
Pfeiffer, J. William, jt. auth. see Jones, John E.
Pfeiffer, J. William & Jones, John E., eds. Annual Handbook for Group Facilitators, 1974. LC 73-92841. (Series in Human Relations Training). 290p. 1974. pap. 20.00 (ISBN 0-88390-082-3); looseleaf 44.50 (ISBN 0-88390-074-2). Univ Assocs.
--Annual Handbook for Group Facilitators, 1972. LC 73-92841. (Series in Human Relations Training). 272p. 1972. pap. 20.00 (ISBN 0-88390-085-8); pap. 14.50 (ISBN 0-88390-072-6). Univ Assocs.
--Annual Handbook for Group Facilitators, 1976. LC 73-92841. (Series in Human Relations Training). 292p. 1976. pap. 20.00 (ISBN 0-88390-088-2); looseleaf notebk. 44.50 (ISBN 0-88390-087-4). Univ Assocs.
--The Annual Handbook for Group Facilitators, 1980. LC 73-92841. (Series in Human Relations Training). 296p. 1980. pap. 20.00 (ISBN 0-88390-097-1); looseleaf notebook 44.50 (ISBN 0-88390-096-3). Univ Assocs.
--Annual Handbook for Group Facilitators, 1978. LC 73-92841. (Series in Human Relations Training). 296p. 1978. pap. 20.00 (ISBN 0-88390-099-8); looseleaf notebook 44.50 (ISBN 0-88390-098-X). Univ Assocs.
--A Handbook of Structured Experiences for Human Relations Training, 7 vols. LC 73-92840. (Series in Human Relations Training). 1973-81. pap. 9.50 ea.; Vol. 1. Rev. Ed. (ISBN 0-88390-041-6); Vol. 2. Rev. Ed. (ISBN 0-88390-042-4); Vol. 3. Rev. Ed. (ISBN 0-88390-043-2); Vol. 4. (ISBN 0-88390-044-0). Vol. 5 (ISBN 0-88390-045-9). Vol. 6 (ISBN 0-88390-046-7). Vol. 7 (ISBN 0-88390-047-5). Vol.8 (ISBN 0-88390-048-3). Univ Assocs.
--A Handbook of Structured Experiences for Human Relations Training, Vol. VIII. LC 73-92840. (Ser. in Human Relations Training). 154p. (Orig.). 1981. pap. 9.50 (ISBN 0-88390-048-3). Univ Assocs.
Pfeiffer, J. William, jt. ed. see Jones, John E.
Pfeiffer, J. William, et al. Instrumentation in Human Relations Training, 2nd Ed. A Guide to 92 Instruments with Wide Application to the Behavioral Sciences. LC 76-6621. 328p. 1976. pap. 17.50 (ISBN 0-88390-116-1). Univ Assocs.
Pfeiffer, John. Cell. rev. ed. LC 64-15570. (Life Science Library). (Illus.). (gr. 5 up). 1969. PLB 8.97 o.p. (ISBN 0-8094-0462-1, Pub. by Time-Life). Silver.
Pfeiffer, John E. The Emergence of Man. enl. & rev. ed. LC 72-79686. (Illus.). 576p. (YA) 1972. 17.95 o.p. (ISBN 0-06-013329-5, HarpT). Har-Row.
Pfeiffer, Kenneth, jt. auth. see Rubinstein, Moshe.
Pfeiffer, Paul E. & Schum, David A., eds. Introduction to Applied Probability. 1973. text ed. 20.95 (ISBN 0-12-553150-8); instrs' manual 3.00 (ISBN 0-12-553156-7). Acad Pr.
Pfeiffer, Rudolf. History of Classical Scholarship from 1300 to 1850. 1976. 32.50x (ISBN 0-19-814364-8). Oxford U Pr.
Pfeiffer, Rudolph. History of Classical Scholarship: From the Beginning to the End of the Hellenistic Age. 1968. 37.50x (ISBN 0-19-814342-7). Oxford U Pr.
Pfeiffer, William B. & Voegele, Walter O. Correct Maid for Hotels & Motels. rev. 2nd ed. (Illus., Orig.). 1965. pap. 2.99 (ISBN 0-8104-9456-6). Hayden.
Pfeiffer-Dennis, Nancy A. Easy-to-Make Patchwork Skirts. (Illus., Orig.). 1980. pap. 3.50 (ISBN 0-486-23888-1). Dover.
Pfeil, Donald J. Through the Reality Warp. 1976. pap. 1.50 o.p. (ISBN 0-345-25377-9). Ballantine.
Pfeil, E., jt. ed. see Hofmann, E.
Pfhal, John, photos by. Altered Landscapes. (Untitled 26 Ser.). (Illus.). 56p. (Orig.). 1981. pap. 10.95 (ISBN 0-933286-23-6). Friends Photography.
Pfiffner, James P. The President, the Budget, & Congress: Impoundment & the 1974 Budget Act. (Special Studies in Public Policy & Public Systems Management). 1979. lib. bdg. 19.50x (ISBN 0-89158-468-4); pap. text ed. 8.00x (ISBN 0-89158-495-1). Westview.
Pfiffner, John M. & Sherwood, F. Administrative Organization. 1960. 19.95x (ISBN 0-13-008615-0). P-H.
Pfister, Adrienne, jt. auth. see Schick, Allen.
Pflatzgraff, Robert L., Jr., jt. ed. see Hahn, Walter F.
Pflaum, R. T., jt. auth. see Popov, Alexander I.
Pflaum-Connor, Susanna. The Development of Language & Reading in the Young Child. 2nd ed. Heilman, Arthur W., ed. (Early Childhood Education Ser.). 1978. text ed. 9.95 (ISBN 0-675-08392-3). Merrill.
Pflaum-Connor, Susanna, ed. Aspects of Reading Education. LC 77-95250. (National Society for the Study of Educ., Series on Contemp Educ. Issues). 1978. 16.00 (ISBN 0-8211-1517-0); text ed. 14.50 (ISBN 0-685-04964-7). McCutchan.
Pfleiderer, A., ed. Probleme der Krebsnachsorge. (Beitraege zur Onkologie: Band 4). (Illus.). 112p. 1980. pap. 24.00 (ISBN 3-8055-1378-X). S Karger.
Pfloog, Jan. Animal Friends & Neighbors. (ps-2). 1973. PLB 10.69 o.p. (ISBN 0-307-65773-6, Golden Pr). Western Pub.
--Animals on the Farm. (Illus.). 24p. (ps-4). 1968. PLB 5.00 (ISBN 0-307-60573-6, Golden Pr). Western Pub.
--The Bear Book. (Illus.). 24p. (gr. k-1). 1976. PLB 5.38 (ISBN 0-307-68977-8, Golden Pr). Western Pub.
--The Cat Book. (Illus.). (ps-1). 1964. PLB 5.38 (ISBN 0-307-68901-8, Golden Pr). Western Pub.
--The Dog Book. (ps-2). 1964. PLB 5.38 (ISBN 0-307-68900-X, Golden Pr). Western Pub.
--The Farm Book. (ps-1). 1964. PLB 5.38 (ISBN 0-307-68905-0, Golden Pr). Western Pub.
--The Fox Book. (Illus.). 24p. (gr. k-1). 1976. PLB 5.38 (ISBN 0-307-68978-6, Golden Pr). Western Pub.
--The Kitten Book. (Illus.). (gr. k-1). 1976. PLB 5.38 (ISBN 0-307-68947-6, Golden Pr). Western Pub.
--The Monkey Book. (Illus.). 24p. (ps-4). 1977. Repr. of 1969 ed. PLB 5.38 (ISBN 0-307-68953-0, Golden Pr). Western Pub.
--The Puppy Book. (Illus.). (ps-1). 1968. PLB 5.38 (ISBN 0-307-68946-8, Golden Pr). Western Pub.
--The Squirrel Book. (Illus.). 24p. (ps-4). 1977. Repr. of 1965 ed. PLB 5.38 (ISBN 0-307-68918-2, Golden Pr). Western Pub.
--The Tiger Book. (Illus.). 24p. (gr. k-1). 1976. PLB 5.38 (ISBN 0-307-68983-2, Golden Pr). Western Pub.
--The Zoo Book. (ps-1). 1967. PLB 5.38 (ISBN 0-307-68939-5, Golden Pr). Western Pub.
Pfloong, Jan. Los Gatitos. Sanchez, Rene, tr. (Illus.). 24p. (Span.). (ps-3). 1977. PLB 5.92 o.p. (ISBN 0-307-68847-X, Golden Pr). Western Pub.
Pfluger, A. Karate: Basic Principles. 1970. pap. 2.95 (ISBN 0-06-463307-1, EH 307, EH). Har-Row.
--Karate Kiai! Perfecting Your Power. Banister, Manly, tr. from Ger. LC 76-58748. (Illus.). 1977. 7.95 (ISBN 0-8069-4448-X); lib. bdg. 7.49 (ISBN 0-8069-4449-8). Sterling.
Pfnister, Allan O. Planning for Higher Education: Background & Application. LC 76-5906. (Special Studies in Higher Education Ser). 1976. 23.75x (ISBN 0-89158-035-2). Westview.
Pfohl, Stephen J. Predicting Dangerousness. LC 77-25742. (Illus.). 1978. 21.50 (ISBN 0-669-01509-1). Lexington Bks.
Pfordresher, John. A Variorum Edition of Idylls of the King. 1088p. 1973. 30.00x (ISBN 0-231-03691-4). Columbia U Pr.
Pfordresher, John, jt. ed. see Dawson, Carl.
Pfrommer, Marian. On the Range: Cooking Western Style. LC 80-18380. (Illus.). 104p. 1981. 8.95 (ISBN 0-689-30826-4). Atheneum.
Pfuhl, John J. Oil & Its' Impact: A Case Study of Community Change. LC 80-5090. 164p. 1980. text ed. 17.25 (ISBN 0-8191-1043-4); pap. text ed. 9.00 (ISBN 0-8191-1044-2). U Pr of Amer.
PGA Tour. Official PGA Tour Media Guide Nineteen Eighty-One. 240p. 1981. pap. 5.95 (ISBN 0-89480-142-2). Workman Pub.
Phadnis, U. Towards the Integration of Indian States, 1919-1947. 8.50x (ISBN 0-210-31180-0). Asia.
Phadnis, Urmila. Studies on Sri Lanka & India Relations. 1981. 15.00x (ISBN 0-88386-893-8). South Asia Bks.
Phalon, Richard. Your Money. (Illus.). 320p. 1981. 5.95 (ISBN 0-312-89823-1). St Martin.
Phaneuf. The Nursing Audit: Self-Regulation in Nursing Practice. 2nd ed. (Illus.). 1976. pap. 13.50 (ISBN 0-8385-7005-4). ACC.

Phares, E. Jerry. Clinical Psychology: Concepts, Methods, & Profession. 1979. 18.95x (ISBN 0-256-02190-2). Dorsey.
Phares, Ross. Bible in Pocket, Gun in Hand: The Story of Frontier Religion. LC 64-11375. 1971. pap. 3.95 (ISBN 0-8032-5725-2, BB 524, Bison). U of Nebr Pr.
Pharis, Mary, jt. auth. see Gottesfeld, Mary.
Pharmaceutical Society of Great Britain, ed. British Pharmacopoeia, 2 vols. 2nd ed. 1980. 150.00 (ISBN 0-11-320688-7, Pub. by Pharmaceutical). Vol. 1, 552 Pg. Vol. 2, 688 Pg. Rittenhouse.
Pharmaceutical Society of Great Britain. European Pharmacopoeia, Vol. 1. 1st ed. 400p. 1969. 45.00 o.p. (ISBN 0-85369-066-9, Pub. by Pharmaceutical). Rittenhouse.
--European Pharmacopoeia, Vol. 2. 1st ed. 568p. 1971. 45.00 o.p. (ISBN 0-85369-079-0, Pub. by Pharmaceutical). Rittenhouse.
Pharmaceutical Society of Great Britain, ed. The Pharmaceutical Codex. 11th ed. 1125p. 1979. 68.00 (ISBN 0-85369-129-0, Pub. by Pharmaceutical). Rittenhouse.
--Pharmaceutical Handbook. 19th ed. 800p. 1980. 35.00 (ISBN 0-85369-130-4, Pub. by Pharmaceutical). Rittenhouse.
Pharoah, Timothy M., jt. auth. see Collins, Michael F.
Pharr, Clyde. Homeric Greek: A Book for Beginners. (Illus.). (YA) (gr. 9 up). 1980. Repr. of 1959 ed. 7.95x (ISBN 0-8061-1275-1). U of Okla Pr.
Pharr, Robert D. The Soul Murder Case: A Confession of the Victim. 1975. pap. 2.95 (ISBN 0-380-00404-6, 26070). Avon.
Pharr, Susan J. Political Women in Japan: The Search for a Place in Political Life. 275p. 1981. 17.50x (ISBN 0-520-04071-6). U of Cal Pr.
Phatak, Arvind V. Managing Multinational Corporations. LC 73-18134. (Special Studies). 364p. 1974. text ed. 19.95 o.p. (ISBN 0-275-08600-3); pap. text ed. 10.95 o.p. (ISBN 0-275-88940-8). Praeger.
Phaustos Of Byzantium. Patmowtiwn Hayots. Date not set. Repr. of 1883 ed. cancelled (ISBN 0-88206-033-3). Caravan Bks.
--Patmowtiwn Hayots: History of the Armenians. Garsoian, Nina G., ed. 1981. write for info. (ISBN 0-88206-033-3). Caravan Bks.
Phayre, Thomas. A Newe Boke of Presidentes in Maner of a Register. LC 73-6100. (English Experience Ser.: No. 569). 1973. Repr. of 1543 ed. 21.00 (ISBN 90-221-0569-5). Walter J Johnson.
Pheby, John. The Oxford-Duden Pictorial German-English Dictionary. The Dudenredaktion & German Section of Oxford Pr Dictionary Department, eds. (Illus.). 776p. 1980. text ed. 24.95x (ISBN 0-19-864135-4). Oxford U Pr.
Pheifer, J. D., ed. Old English Glosses in the Ephinal-Erfurt Glossary. 259p. 1974. 24.95x (ISBN 0-19-811164-9). Oxford U Pr.
Pheiffer, Susan G., ed. see Lappin, Kendall E.
Phelan, James. Worlds from Words: A Theory of Language in Fiction. LC 80-25844. (Chicago Originals Ser.). 256p. lib. bdg. 19.00x (ISBN 0-226-66690-5). U of Chicago Pr.
Phelan, John L. Hispanization of the Philippines: Spanish Aims & Filipino Responses, 1565-1700. (Illus.). 1959. 21.50x (ISBN 0-299-01810-5). U of Wis Pr.
--The Millennial Kingdom of the Franciscans in the New World. 2nd rev ed. 1970. 17.50x (ISBN 0-520-01404-9). U of Cal Pr.
--The People & the King: The Comunero Revolution in Colombia, 1781. LC 76-53654. 1978. 27.50 (ISBN 0-299-07290-8). U of Wis Pr.
Phelan, Mary K. The Burning of Washington: August 1814. LC 74-30025. (Illus.). (gr. 5-10). 1975. 8.95 (ISBN 0-690-00486-9, TYC-J). T Y Crowell.
--Circus: A Book to Begin On. LC 63-9083. (Book to Begin on Ser.). 48p. (gr. k-4). 1963. pap. 0.95 o.p. (ISBN 0-03-080113-3). HR&W.
--Election Day. LC 67-15402. (Holiday Ser.). (Illus.). (gr. k-3). 1967. 8.95 (ISBN 0-690-25661-2, TYC-J); PLB 6.89 (ISBN 0-690-25662-0). T Y Crowell.
--Four Days in Philadelphia- 1776. LC 67-18521. (gr. 5 up). 1967. 8.95 (ISBN 0-690-31485-X, TYC-J). T Y Crowell.
--Fourth of July. LC 65-25909. (Holiday Ser.). (Illus.). (gr. k-3). 1966. PLB 7.89 (ISBN 0-690-31415-9, TYC-J). T Y Crowell.
--Martha Berry. LC 77-158699. (Biography Ser.). (Illus.). (gr. 2-5). 1972. PLB 7.89 (ISBN 0-690-52113-8, TYC-J). T Y Crowell.
--Midnight Alarm: The Story of Paul Revere's Ride. LC 68-17080. (Illus.). (gr. 4-7). 1968. 8.95 (ISBN 0-690-53638-0, TYC-J). T Y Crowell.
--Mr. Lincoln's Inaugural Journey. LC 76-175110. (Illus.). (gr. 5-8). 1972. 8.95 (ISBN 0-685-24997-2, TYC-J). T Y Crowell.
--Mother's Day. LC 65-11646. (Holiday Ser.). (Illus.). (gr. 1-3). 1965. PLB 7.89 (ISBN 0-690-56195-4, TYC-J). T Y Crowell.
--The Story of the Boston Massacre. LC 75-25961. (Illus.). 160p. (gr. 5-9). 1976. 8.95 (ISBN 0-690-00716-7, TYC-J). T Y Crowell.
--The Story of the Boston Tea Party. LC 72-7554. (Illus.). (gr. 5-9). 1973. 8.95 (ISBN 0-690-77653-5, TYC-J). T Y Crowell.
--Story of the Great Chicago Fire, 1871. LC 72-109910. (Illus.). (gr. 5-8). 1971. 8.95 (ISBN 0-690-77671-3, TYC-J). T Y Crowell.
--Waterway West: The Story of the Erie Canal. LC 77-1787. (Illus.). (gr. 5-9). 1977. 8.95 (ISBN 0-690-01333-7, TYC-J). T Y Crowell.
Phelan, Terry W. The Week Mom Unplugged the TVs. LC 78-12180. (Illus.). 48p. (gr. 2-6). 1979. 5.95 (ISBN 0-590-07561-6, Four Winds). Schol Bk Serv.
Phelan, Thomas P. Catholics in Colonial Days. LC 74-145706. Repr. of 1935 ed. 18.00 (ISBN 0-8103-3685-5). Gale.
Phelon, Sheldon & Marsar Inc., ed. Phelon's Discount Jobbing 1981-1982. 9th ed. 1980. 70.00 (ISBN 0-686-27107-6). P S & M Inc.
Phelon, Sheldon, & Masar, Inc., ed. Sheldon's Retail & Phelon's Resident Byers Book. 97th ed. 1981. pap. 70.00 (ISBN 0-686-28951-X). P S & M Inc.
Phelps, Austin. The Still Hour. 1979. pap. 2.45 (ISBN 0-85151-202-X). Banner of Truth.
Phelps, Bailey. They Loved the Land: History of Foard County. 25.00 (ISBN 0-685-48796-2). Nortex Pr.
Phelps, Dennis & Phelps, Patricia. A Critical Analysis of Radical Economics, the New Left, in Relationship to Karl Marx's Economic Theories: Radical Effects Upon Orthodox & Marxian Economic Doctrines. 1976. pap. text ed. 10.25x (ISBN 0-8191-0036-6). U Pr of Amer.
Phelps, Dryden L., tr. see Huang Shou-Fu & T'An Chung-Yo.
Phelps, E. R., jt. auth. see Wolfe, John H.
Phelps, Edmund S. Inflation, Policy & Unemployment Theory. (Illus.). 1972. 15.95x (ISBN 0-393-09395-6). Norton.
Phelps, Ethel J. The Maid of the North & Other Folk Tales Heroines. LC 80-21500. (Illus.). 192p. (gr. 2-6). 1981. 10.95 (ISBN 0-03-056893-5). HR&W.
Phelps, Gilbert, ed. see Herriot, James, et al.
Phelps, Gilbert, intro. by see Waterton, Charles.
Phelps, John, ed. Complete Building Construction. LC 78-65477. 1978. 19.95 (ISBN 0-672-23323-1). Audel.
Phelps, John, ed. see Herriot, James, et al.
Phelps, Lynn & Dewine, Sue. Interpersonal Communication Journal. LC 76-3576. (Illus.). 200p. 1976. pap. text ed. 9.50 (ISBN 0-8299-0102-7); instrs.' manual avail. (ISBN 0-8299-0566-9). West Pub.
Phelps, Lynn A., jt. auth. see Morse, Ben W.
Phelps, Michael E., jt. auth. see Sorenson, James A.
Phelps, Noah A. see Hutchinson, K. M.
Phelps, Patricia, jt. auth. see Phelps, Dennis.
Phelps, Robert, ed. see Colette.
Phelps, Tony. Poisonous Snakes. (Illus.). 320p. 1981. 27.50 (ISBN 0-7137-0877-8, Pub. by Blanford Pr England). Sterling.
Phelps, Tricia, jt. auth. see Phelps-Tersaki, Diana.
Phelps, Trisha, jt. auth. see Phelps-Terasaki, Diana.
Phelps Brown, E. H. The Inequality of Pay. LC 76-7768. 23.75x (ISBN 0-520-03380-9). U of Cal Pr.
Phelps-Terasaki, Diana & Phelps, Trisha. Disorders of Written Language: Methods & Programming for Redemiation. 350p. 1981. text ed. price not set (ISBN 0-89443-360-1). Aspen Systems.
Phelps-Tersaki, Diana & Phelps, Tricia. Teaching Written Expression: The Phelps Sentence Guide Program. 112p. 1980. pap. text ed. 7.00 (ISBN 0-87879-248-1). Acad Therapy.
Pheng, Lee T. Prospect of a Drowning. (Writing in Asia Ser.). 1980. text ed. 3.50 (00245). Heinemann Ed.
Phenice, Lillian A. Children's Perceptions of Elderly Persons. LC 80-65604. 145p. 1981. perfect bdg. 10.50 (ISBN 0-86548-054-0). Century Twenty One.
Phenice, Terrell W., jt. auth. see Sauer, Norman J.
Phenix, Philip H. Religious Concerns in Contemporary Education. LC 59-11329. 1959. 5.75x (ISBN 0-8077-1905-6). Tchrs Coll.
Phenix, Philip H., tr. see Manach, Jorge.
Phi Delta Kappa Symposium on Educational Research, 12th. Leadership: The Science & Art Today, Proceedings. Gephart, William J. & Cunningham, Lavern, eds. LC 60-2874. 320p. 1973. 8.50 (ISBN 0-87581-155-8). Phi Delta Kappa.
Phibbs, Brendan. The Cardiac Arrhythmias. 3rd ed. LC 78-7265. 1978. pap. text ed. 17.50 (ISBN 0-8016-3911-5). Mosby.
--The Human Heart: A Guide to Heart Disease. 4th ed. LC 79-17665. 1979. pap. text ed. 14.95 (ISBN 0-8016-3917-4). Mosby.
Philadelphia Maritime Museum. George Robert Bonfield: Philadelphia Marine Painter, 1805 to 1898. LC 78-71198. (Illus.). 78p. (Orig.). 1978. pap. text ed. 8.00 (ISBN 0-913346-04-7). Phila Maritime Mus.
--Thomas Birch Seventeen Seventy-Nine to Eighteen Fifty-One: Paintings & Drawings. (Illus.). 64p. 1966. pap. 2.00 (ISBN 0-913346-06-3). Phila Maritime Mus.
Philadelphia Museum of Art & Detroit Institute of Arts, Grand Palais, Paris. The Second Empire, Eighteen Fifty-Two to Eighteen Seventy: Art in France Under Napoleon III. LC 78-60516. (Illus.). 1978. 18.95x (ISBN 0-8143-1630-1, Pub. by Phila Mus Art). Wayne St U Pr.
Philadelphia Suburban School Study Council Group B. Southeast Asia & the Soviet Union. LC 66-28972. 1966. pap. text ed. 1.50x o.p. (ISBN 0-8134-0895-4, 895). Interstate.
Philadelphia Working Party. Guide to Global Giving. 59p. 1976. pap. 1.50 (ISBN 0-86571-006-6). Movement New Soc.
Philaretos, S. D. The Idea of Being. Orthodox Christian Educational Society, ed. Cummings, D., tr. from Hellenic. 287p. 1963. 3.00x (ISBN 0-938366-09-2). Orthodox Chr.
Philaretos, Sotirios D. The Decalogue & the Gospel. Orthodox Christian Educational Society, ed. Cummings, D., tr. from Hellenic. 62p. (Orig.). Date not set. pap. 1.50x (ISBN 0-938366-43-2). Orthodox Chr.
Philbin, Janis, jt. auth. see Schmidt, Werner J.
Philbin, Tom. Basic Plumbing. (Illus.). 1977. 14.50 (ISBN 0-87909-065-0). Reston.
--Cabinets & Bookcases. Horowitz, Shirley M., ed. LC 80-67152. (Illus.). 144p. (Orig.). 1980. 12.95 (ISBN 0-932944-21-3); pap. 5.95 (ISBN 0-932944-22-1). Creative Homeowner.
--The Encyclopedia of Hardware. LC 78-52965. 1978. 12.00 o.p. (ISBN 0-8015-2335-4, Hawthorn); pap. 6.95 (ISBN 0-8015-2336-2, Hawthorn). Dutton.
--Home Fix-It Secrets of the Pros. (Illus.). 1980. cancelled (ISBN 0-525-93118-X); pap. 6.95 (ISBN 0-525-93104-X). Dutton.
--The Yearbook Killer. (Orig.). 1981. pap. 1.95 (ISBN 0-449-14400-3, GM). Fawcett.
Philbin, Tom & Koelbel, Fritz. How to Add a Room to Your House. (Illus.). 192p. 1980. 14.95 (ISBN 0-684-16494-9, ScribT). Scribner.
Philbin, William J. To You Simonides: Versions from Greek Anthology. (Dolmen Editions: No. 19). 120p. 1973. bds. 12.00x (ISBN 0-85105-231-2, Dolmen Pr). Humanities.
Philbrick, Francis S. Rise of the West, 1754-1830. LC 65-21377. (New American Nation Ser.). 1965. 15.00x o.s.i. (ISBN 0-06-013330-9, HarpT). Har-Row.
Philbrick, Helen, jt. auth. see Philbrick, John.
Philbrick, John & Philbrick, Helen. Gardening for Health & Nutrition. LC 79-3595. 96p. 1980. pap. 3.95 (ISBN 0-06-066535-1, RD 402). Har-Row.
Philbrick, Ralph N., ed. Symposium on the Biology of the California Islands: Proceedings. (Illus.). 1967. 12.50 (ISBN 0-916436-01-2). Santa Barb Botanic.
Philbrook Art Center. Native American Art at Philbrook. LC 80-82374. (Orig.). 1980. pap. 8.00 (ISBN 0-86659-001-3). Philbrook.
Philbrook, Clem. Ollie's Team & the Baseball Computer. Date not set. 3.99 (ISBN 0-8038-5348-3). Hastings.
Philbrook, Marilyn M., compiled by. Medical Books for the Layperson: An Annotated Bibliography, Supplement. 1978. pap. 2.00 (ISBN 0-89073-060-1). Boston Public Lib.
Philby, H. Saudi Arabia. (Arab Background Ser.). 18.00x (ISBN 0-685-72057-8). Intl Bk Ctr.
Philby, H. St. John. The Heart of Arabia, 2 vols. 1980. Repr. Set. 55.00x (ISBN 0-7146-3072-1, F Cass Co). Biblio Dist.
Philby, J. B. Arabian Highlands. LC 76-10643. (Middle East in the 20th Century). 1976. Repr. of 1952 ed. lib. bdg. 55.00 (ISBN 0-306-70765-9). Da Capo.
Philby, Kim. My Silent War. 4.95 (ISBN 0-686-28852-1). Academy Chi Ltd.
Philip, A. Butt, jt. auth. see Bayliss, B. T.
Philip, A. E., jt. auth. see McCulloch, J. W.
Philip, Alistair G. Neonatology - A Practical Guide. 2nd ed. LC 80-21108. 1980. pap. 18.50 (ISBN 0-87488-671-6). Med Exam.
Philip, D. Frank. Manual of Elocution for the Ministry. 122p. Repr. of 1948 ed. text ed. 3.50 (ISBN 0-567-02207-2). Attic Pr.
Philip, G. D. The Rise & Fall of the Peruvian Military Radicals 1968-1976. (Univ. of London Institute of Latin American Studies Monographs: No. 9). 1978. text ed. 31.25x (ISBN 0-485-17709-9, Athlone Pr). Humanities.
Philip, Hugh, jt. auth. see Goyen, Judith.
Philip, Lotte B. The Ghent Altarpiece & the Art of Jan Van Eyck. LC 73-113007. (Illus.). 380p. 1980. 50.00x (ISBN 0-691-03870-8); pap. 15.00 (ISBN 0-691-00316-5). Princeton U Pr.
Philip, Mary. Who Wants to Cook? 1977. pap. text ed. 4.95x o.p. (ISBN 0-435-42650-8). Heinemann Ed.
Philip, P. & Atterbury, P. World Furniture. (Illus.). Date not set. 30.00 (ISBN 0-686-68700-0). Mayflower Bks.
Philip, T. & Distler, A., eds. Hypertension: Mechanisms & Management. 279p. 1981. pap. 42.00 (ISBN 0-387-10171-3). Springer-Verlag.
Philipon, M. M. Conchita: A Mother's Diary. Owen, Aloysius, tr. LC 78-1929. 1978. pap. 6.95 (ISBN 0-8189-0368-6). Alba.
Philippakis, Andreas S. & Kazmier, Leonard. Structured COBAL. 2nd ed. Stewart, Charles E., ed. (Illus.). 448p. 1980. pap. text ed. 13.95 (ISBN 0-07-049801-6); instructor's manual 7.95 (ISBN 0-07-049802-4). McGraw.
Philippakis, Andreas S. & Kazmier, Leonard J. Structured COBOL. 2nd ed. Stewart, Charles E., ed. (Illus.). 448p. 1981. pap. text ed. 13.95 (ISBN 0-07-049801-6); instrs'. manual 5.95 (ISBN 0-07-049802-4). McGraw.
Philippatos, George C. Essentials of Financial Management: Text & Cases. LC 73-86413. 1974. text ed. 17.95x (ISBN 0-8162-6716-2); wkbk. 4.95 (ISBN 0-8162-6696-4). Holden-Day.
Philippe, Joseph. Coffee. (Q Books: Where Do Things Come from?). (Illus.). 1978. 3.95 (ISBN 0-8467-0443-9, Pub. by Two Continents). Hippocrene Bks.
--Cotton. (Q Books: Where Do Things Come from?). (Illus.). 1978. 3.95 (ISBN 0-8467-0444-7, Pub. by Two Continents). Hippocrene Bks.
--Glass. (Q Books: Where Do Things Come from?). (Illus.). 28p. 1978. 3.95 (ISBN 0-8467-0442-0, Pub. by Two Continents). Hippocrene Bks.
Philippe, Louis. Diary of My Travels in America. Becker, Stephen, tr. (Illus.). 1977. 14.95 o.p. (ISBN 0-440-01844-7). Delacorte.
Philippi, Herbert. Stagecraft & Scene Design. LC 53-6010. 1953. text ed. 18.95 (ISBN 0-395-05053-7). HM.
Philippon, Catherine, tr. see Vossler, Otto.
Philippou, A. J. Orthodoxy Life & Freedom. LC 80-20616. 160p. 1980. lib. bdg. 17.95x (ISBN 0-89370-088-6); pap. 11.95x (ISBN 0-89370-089-4). Borgo Pr.
Philips, A., jt. auth. see Stone, J.
Philips, Barbara. Don't Call Me Fatso. LC 79-23888. (Life & Living from a Child's Point of View Ser.). (Illus.). (gr. k-5). 1980. PLB 9.65 (ISBN 0-8172-1350-3). Raintree Child.
Philips, C. H. The Young Wellington in India. (The Creighton Lecture in History Ser). (Illus., Orig.). 1974. pap. text ed. 2.50x (ISBN 0-485-14120-5, Athlone Pr). Humanities.
Philips, C. H., et al, eds. Indian Studies Abroad. 1964. 6.50x o.p. (ISBN 0-210-33635-8). Asia.
Philips, Clare, jt. auth. see Rachman, S. J.
Philips, Cyril H., ed. see Bentinck, William A.
Philips, Frederik. Forty-Five Years with Philips. (Illus.). 1978. 17.95 (ISBN 0-7137-0931-6, Pub. by Blandford Pr England). Sterling.
Philips, Janet & Phillips, Peter. Victorians at Home & Away. (Illus.). 220p. 1978. 16.00x (ISBN 0-85664-688-1, Pub. by Croom Helm Ltd England). Biblio Dist.
Philips, Judson. Death Is a Dirty Trick. LC 79-27738. (A Peter Styles Mystery Novel Ser.). 192p. 1980. 7.95 (ISBN 0-396-07820-6). Dodd.
Philips, Ronald J., jt. ed. see Mercer, James L.
Philipson, Morris. The Wallpaper Fox. 1978. pap. 1.95 (ISBN 0-515-04436-9). Jove Pubns.
Philliber, Susan G., et al. Social Research. LC 79-91097. 189p. 1980. pap. text ed. 6.50 (ISBN 0-87581-252-X). Peacock Pubs.
Philliber, William W. & McCoy, Clyde B., eds. The Invisible Minority: Urban Appalachians. LC 79-4008. (Illus.). 192p. 1981. 15.50x (ISBN 0-8131-1395-4). U Pr of Ky.
Phillimore, Robert. The Principal Ecclesiastical Judgments Delivered in the Court of Arches 1867 to 1875. xiii, 420p. 1981. Repr. of 1876 ed. lib. bdg. 35.00x (ISBN 0-8377-2504-6). Rothman.
Phillimore, W. P. How to Write the History of a Family: A Guide for the Genealogist. LC 70-179653. (Illus.). viii, 206p. 1972. Repr. of 1876 ed. 22.00 (ISBN 0-8103-3117-9). Gale.
Phillimore, W. P. & Fry, E. A. Index to Changes of Name. LC 68-27180. 1969. Repr. of 1905 ed. 18.00 (ISBN 0-8103-3132-2). Gale.
Phillimore, Walter G. Three Centuries of Peace Treaties & Their Teachings, 1582-1913. LC 73-147602. (Library of War & Peace; International Law). lib. bdg. 38.00 (ISBN 0-8240-0363-2). Garland Pub.
Phillip, Alban M. Prison-Breakers: A Book of Escapes from Captivity. LC 76-174093. (Illus.). 1971. Repr. of 1927 ed. 18.00 (ISBN 0-8103-3803-3). Gale.

Phillip, P. Joseph & Dombrosk, Stephen J. Seasonal Patterns of Hospital Activity. LC 79-1752. 160p. 1979. 15.95 (ISBN 0-669-02926-2). Lexington Bks.
Phillipov, Vladimir, tr. see Levchev, Lyumbomir.
Phillippo, Gene. The Professional Guide to Real Estate Development. LC 75-26106. (Illus.). 306p. 1976. 19.95 (ISBN 0-87094-111-9). Dow Jones-Irwin.
Phillipps, S. M., intro. by. Famous Cases of Circumstantial Evidence, 2 vols. in 1. 1980. Repr. of 1878 ed. lib. bdg. 42.50x (ISBN 0-8377-1002-2). Rothman.
Phillipps. Basic Life Support: Skills Manual. LC 77-8351. 1977. pap. 11.95 (ISBN 0-87618-883-8). R J Brady.
Phillips, A. B., tr. see Seiffert, Karl.
Phillips, A. D. & Turton, B. J., eds. Environment, Man & Economic Change: Essays Presented to S.H. Beaver. (Illus.). 500p. 1975. text ed. 42.00x (ISBN 0-582-50114-8). Longman.
Phillips, A. R., tr. see Petzold, A. & Rohrs, M.
Phillips, Almarin, ed. Promoting Competition in Regulated Markets. (Studies in the Regulation of Economic Activity). 397p. 1975. 15.95 (ISBN 0-8157-7052-9); pap. 6.95 (ISBN 0-8157-7051-0). Brookings.
Phillips, Amelia, ed. see Houston, Ralph.
Phillips, Archie & Phillips, Bubba. How to Mount Fish. (Illus.). 144p. 1981. 19.95 (ISBN 0-8117-0787-3). Stackpole.
Phillips, Arthur M., 3rd. Grand Canyon Wildflowers. Priehs, T. J., ed. LC 79-54236. (Illus.). 145p. 1979. pap. 6.50 (ISBN 0-938216-01-5). GCNHA.
Phillips, Audrey E., ed. see University of California, Berkeley, Library.
Phillips, B. J., et al. Public Libraries: Legislation, Administration, & Finance. 1977. pap. text ed. 6.75x (ISBN 0-85365-750-5, Pub. by Lib Assn England). Oryx Pr.
Phillips, Beeman N. School Stress & Anxiety. LC 77-21658. 1978. 16.95 (ISBN 0-87705-324-3). Human Sci Pr.
Phillips, Beeman N., jt. ed. see Oakland, Thomas.
Phillips, Bernard. Religion & the Life of Man. Park, O'Hyun, ed. LC 77-74731. 1977. pap. 3.75 o.p. (ISBN 0-87707-181-0). CSA Pr.
Phillips, Betty L. Go! Fight! Win! LC 79-53607. (Illus.). (YA) (gr. 8 up). 1981. PLB 8.89 (ISBN 0-440-02957-0); pap. 7.95 (ISBN 0-440-02956-2). Delacorte.
--The Picture Story of Nancy Lopez. LC 79-25344. (Illus.). 64p. (gr. 4-6). 1980. PLB 6.97 (ISBN 0-671-33050-0). Messner.
Phillips, Betty W., ed. Management of Behavior in the Classroom: A Handbook of Psychological Strategies. LC 79-66965. 232p. 1980. pap. text ed. 9.80x (ISBN 0-87424-162-6). Western Psych.
Phillips, Billie M. & Brown, Virginia S. New Discovery Technique for Art Instruction: An Innovative Handbook for the Elementary Teacher. 1976. 13.95 o.p. (ISBN 0-13-612507-7). P-H.
Phillips, Bob. The Fun Joke Book. pap. 1.95 (ISBN 0-89081-235-7). Harvest Hse.
--A Humorous Look at Love & Marriage. LC 80-83841. 128p. 1981. pap. 2.25 (ISBN 0-89081-268-3). Harvest Hse.
--The World's Greatest Collection of Clean Jokes. (Orig.). 1974. pap. 1.75 o.s.i. (ISBN 0-87801-018-1). Vision Hse.
Phillips, Bruce F., jt. ed. see Cobb, J. Stanley.
Phillips, Bubba, jt. auth. see Phillips, Archie.
Phillips, C., jt. auth. see Baxter, R. E.
Phillips, C. G., ed. see Holmes, Gordon.
Phillips, C. S. & Williams, R. J. Inorganic Chemistry, 2 vols. Incl. Vol. 1. Principles & Non-Metals. 1965 (ISBN 0-19-501021-3, OxfordC); Vol. 2. Metals. 1966 (ISBN 0-19-501022-1). 12.95x ea. Oxford U Pr.
Phillips, Carolyn E. Michelle. LC 80-52202. (Illus.). 176p. 1980. text ed. 7.95 (ISBN 0-8307-0757-3, 5109000). Regal.
Phillips, Celeste R. & Anzalone, Joseph T. Fathering: Participation in Labor & Birth. LC 77-13224. (Illus.). 1978. pap. 9.50 (ISBN 0-8016-3919-0). Mosby.
Phillips, Charles. Paderewski: The Story of a Modern Immortal. LC 77-17399. (Music Reprint Ser.: 1978). (Illus.). 1978. Repr. of 1934 ed. lib. bdg. 35.00 (ISBN 0-306-77534-4). Da Capo.
--Paramedic Skills Manual. 288p. 1980. pap. text ed. 14.95 (ISBN 0-87619-436-6). R J Brady.
Phillips, Charles D. Sentencing Councils in the Federal Courts: An Evaluation. LC 79-3784. 128p. 1980. 19.95x (ISBN 0-669-03514-9). Lexington Bks.
Phillips, Clyde B. The Driver. 1978. pap. 1.95 (ISBN 0-345-27295-1). Ballantine.
Phillips, Cobell. The Forties. 1974. 12.95 o.s.i. (ISBN 0-686-66970-3). Macmillan.
Phillips, D. Z. Religion Without Explanation. 1976. 18.50x (ISBN 0-631-17100-2, Pub. by Basil Blackwell). Biblio Dist.
Phillips, D. Z., ed. see Anderson, John.
Phillips, David J. Quantitative Aquatic Biological Indicators: Their Use to Monitor Trace Metal & Organochlorine Pollution. (Illus.). xii, 460p. 1980. 65.00x (ISBN 0-85334-884-7). Burgess-Intl Ideas.
Phillips, David S. Basic Statistics for Health Science Students. LC 77-13865. (Psychology Ser.). (Illus.). 1978. text ed. 14.95x (ISBN 0-7167-0051-4); pap. text ed. 7.95x (ISBN 0-7167-0050-6). W H Freeman.
Phillips, Don T. & Garcia-Diaz, Alberto. Fundamentals of Network Analysis. (Illus.). 496p. 1981. text ed. 26.95 (ISBN 0-13-341552-X). P-H.
Phillips, Don T., et al. Operations Research: Principles & Practices. LC 75-44395. 585p. 1976. text ed. 23.95 (ISBN 0-471-68707-3). Wiley.
Phillips, Donald E. Student Protest Nineteen Sixty-Nineteen Sixty-Nine: An Analysis of the Issues & Speeches. LC 79-3716. 1980. text ed. 14.75 (ISBN 0-8191-0911-8); pap. text ed. 9.00 (ISBN 0-8191-0912-6). U Pr of Amer.
Phillips, Donald T., jt. auth. see Beightler, Charles S.
Phillips, E. Barbara & LeGates, Richard T. City Lights: An Introduction to Urban Studies. (Illus.). 608p. 1981. pap. text ed. 14.95x (ISBN 0-19-502797-3). Oxford U Pr.
Phillips, E. J. Corpus Signorium Imperii Romani: Hadrian's Wall, East of North Tyne, Vol. I, Fsc. I. (British Academy Ser.). (Illus.). 1977. 69.00x (ISBN 0-19-725954-5). Oxford U Pr.
Phillips, E. L., jt. auth. see Haring, Norris G.
Phillips, E. Lakin. Counseling & Psychotherapy: A Behavioral Approach. LC 77-1771. (Personality Processes Ser.). 1977. 25.95 (ISBN 0-471-01881-3, Pub. by Wiley-Interscience). Wiley.
Phillips, Edith B., jt. ed. see Van Orden, Phyllis.
Phillips, Elisabeth C., jt. auth. see Leone, Nicholas C.
Phillips, Elizabeth C. Monarch Notes on Faulkner's Absalom, Absalom. (Orig.). pap. 1.95 (ISBN 0-671-00664-9). Monarch Pr.
Phillips, Ellis L., Jr., jt. auth. see Lon Hefferlin, JB.
Phillips, Evelyn M. The Illustrated Guidebook to the Frescoes in the Sistine Chapel. (Illus.). 124p. 1981. Repr. of 1901 ed. 49.85 (ISBN 0-89901-029-6). Found Class Reprints.
Phillips, F. C. An Introduction to Crystallography. 4th ed. 1979. pap. text ed. 25.95 (ISBN 0-470-26347-4). Halsted Pr.
Phillips, Frances. For a Living. 1981. pap. 4.00 (ISBN 0-914610-26-0). Hanging Loose.
Phillips, G., jt. auth. see Milner, G. W.
Phillips, G. Frank, jt. auth. see Woodroof, J. G.
Phillips, Gene D. Evelyn Waugh's Officers, Gentlemen & Rogues: The Fact Behind His Fiction. LC 75-26546. 195p. 1975. 11.95 (ISBN 0-88229-172-6); pap. 7.95 (ISBN 0-88229-495-4). Nelson Hall.
--The Films of Tennessee Williams. LC 76-50204. (Illus.). 256p. 1980. 20.00 o.p. (ISBN 0-87982-025-X). Art Alliance.
--Graham Greene: The Films of His Fiction. LC 73-85252. 1974. pap. 7.950 (ISBN 0-8077-2376-2). Tchrs Coll.
--Hemingway & Film. LC 80-7563. (Ungar Film Library). (Illus.). 250p. 1980. 10.95 (ISBN 0-8044-2695-3); pap. 5.95 (ISBN 0-8044-6644-0). Ungar.
--Ken Russell. (Theatrical Arts Ser.). 1979. lib. bdg. 10.95 (ISBN 0-8057-9266-X). Twayne.
--The Movie Makers: Artists in an Industry. LC 73-75524. 1973. 19.95 (ISBN 0-911012-43-5). Nelson-Hall.
Phillips, George H. Chiefs & Challengers. 1975. 15.95 (ISBN 0-520-02719-1). U of Cal Pr.
Phillips, Gerald M. Communication & the Small Group. 2nd ed. LC 74-179366. (Speech Communication Ser.: No. 12). 180p. 1973. pap. text ed. 4.50 (ISBN 0-672-61302-6, SC12R). Bobbs.
Phillips, Gerald M. & Metzger, Nancy J. The Study of Intimate Communication. 464p. 1976. text ed. 12.95x o.p. (ISBN 0-205-04876-5); instr's manual free o.p. (ISBN 0-205-04877-3). Allyn.
Phillips, Gerald M. & Zolten, J. Jerome. Structuring Speech: A How-to-Do-It-Book About Public Speaking. (Speech Communication Ser.). 1976. pap. 6.50 (ISBN 0-672-61366-2, SC-22). Bobbs.
Phillips, Gerald M., et al. Group Discussion: A Practical Guide to Participation & Leadership. LC 78-56441. (Illus.). 1978. text ed. 13.95 (ISBN 0-395-25415-9); inst. manual 0.65 (ISBN 0-395-25416-7). HM.
Phillips, H. L., jt. auth. see Kurtz, M. A.
Phillips, H. M. Educational Cooperation Between Developed & Developing Countries. LC 75-19807. (Praeger Special Studies). (Illus.). 352p. 1976. text ed. 32.00 (ISBN 0-275-55900-9). Praeger.
Phillips, Helen, tr. see Galilea, Segundo.
Phillips, Henry. The Theatre & Its Critics in Seventeenth-Century France. (Modern Language & Literature Monographs). 272p. 1980. 36.00 (ISBN 0-19-815535-2). Oxford U Pr.
Phillips, Herbert E. Innovative Idea Bank. LC 80-65052. 192p. 1980. pap. 15.00 (ISBN 0-8408-0501-2). Carrollton Pr.
Phillips, Herbert P. Thai Peasant Personality: The Patterning of Interpersonal Behavior in the Village of Bang Chan. 1965. 17.50x (ISBN 0-520-01008-6). U of Cal Pr.
Phillips, Howard M. All You Need to Know About Defined Benefit Keogh Plans. 120p. 1980. text ed. 20.00 looseleaf (ISBN 0-89529-130-4). Avery Pub.
Phillips, I. & Collier, J., eds. Metronidazole. (Royal Society of Medicine International Congress & Symposium Ser.: No. 18). 1980. 29.50 (ISBN 0-8089-1236-4). Grune.
Phillips, I. D., jt. auth. see Wareing, P. F.
Phillips, J. & Knights, B. Estuarine & Coastal Land Reclamation & Water Storage. (Illus.). 256p. 1979. 28.95 (ISBN 0-566-00252-3, Pub. by Teakfield Ltd England). Lexington Bks.
Phillips, J. B. New Testament in Modern English. rev ed. student ed. 9.95 (ISBN 0-02-596970-6). student ed 3.95 (ISBN 0-686-67531-2, 59697). Macmillan.
--The Newborn Christian. 1978. 9.95 (ISBN 0-02-596120-9). Macmillan.
--Peter's Portrait of Jesus. 1976. 7.95 (ISBN 0-00-215628-8, A1154, Pub. by Collins Pubs). Abingdon.
Phillips, J. G., ed. Environmental Physiology. LC 74-22107. 198p. 1975. 12.95x (ISBN 0-470-68490-9). Halsted Pr.
Phillips, J. P., et al. Organic Electronic Spectral Data. LC 60-16428. Vol. 13, 1971. 66.00 (ISBN 0-471-03563-7, Pub. by Wiley-Interscience); Vol. 14, 1978. 85.00 (ISBN 0-471-05076-8); Vol. 15, 1979. 80.00 (ISBN 0-471-05572-7). Wiley.
Phillips, James E. Images of a Queen: Mary Stuart in Sixteenth-Century Literature. 1964. 20.00x (ISBN 0-520-01007-8). U of Cal Pr.
Phillips, James E., ed. Twentieth Century Interpretations of Coriolanus. (Twentieth Century Interpretations Ser). 1970. 8.95 (ISBN 0-13-172676-5, Spec); pap. 1.25 (ISBN 0-13-172668-4, Spec). P-H.
Phillips, James M. From the Rising of the Sun: Christians & Society in Contemporary Japan. LC 80-24609. (Illus.). 352p. (Orig.). 1981. pap. 14.95 (ISBN 0-88344-145-4). Orbis Bks.
Phillips, James W. Washington State Place Names. rev. ed. LC 73-159435. (Illus.). 186p. 1971. 11.50 (ISBN 0-295-95158-3); pap. 6.95 (ISBN 0-295-95498-1). U of Wash Pr.
Phillips, Jerry J., jt. auth. see Noel, Dix.
Phillips, Jill. Annus Mirabilis: A Bibliography of Medieval Times. (Bibliographies for Librarians Ser.). 1980. lib. bdg. 75.00 (ISBN 0-8490-1398-4). Gordon Pr.
Phillips, Jill M. The Darkling Plain: A Bibliography of Books About World War I. (Bibliographies for Librarians Ser.). 1980. lib. bdg. 69.95 (ISBN 0-8490-3207-5). Gordon Pr.
Phillips, Jo. Exploring Triangles: Paper-Folding Geometry. LC 74-14862. (Young Math Ser.). (Illus.). 40p. (gr. k-3). 1975. 6.95 o.p. (ISBN 0-690-00644-6, TYC-J); PLB 7.89 (ISBN 0-690-00645-4). T Y Crowell.
--Right Angles: Paper-Folding Geometry. LC 72-171007. (Young Math Ser.). (Illus.). (gr. 1-4). 1972. 6.95 o.p. (ISBN 0-690-60916-7, TYC-J); PLB 7.89 (ISBN 0-690-60917-5). T Y Crowell.
Phillips, Joel & Wynne, Ronald D. Cocaine: The Mystique & the Reality. 1980. pap. 3.50 (ISBN 0-380-48678-4, 48678, Discus). Avon.
Phillips, John. Dear Parrot. (Illus.). 1979. 5.95 (ISBN 0-517-53868-7). Potter.
--Exploring Genesis. 582p. 1980. 10.95 (ISBN 0-8024-2408-2). Moody.
--Exploring Hebrews. 1977. 10.95 (ISBN 0-8024-2406-6). Moody.
--Exploring Revelation. 288p. 1974. 10.95 (ISBN 0-8024-2407-4). Moody.
--Exploring Romans. 250p. 1971. 10.95 (ISBN 0-8024-2405-8). Moody.
--Exploring the Scriptures. 1965. Repr. 10.95 (ISBN 0-8024-2410-4). Moody.
--How to Live Forever. (Teach Yourself the Bible Ser). 1964. pap. 1.75 (ISBN 0-8024-3700-1). Moody.
Phillips, John B. Your God Is Too Small. 8.95 (ISBN 0-02-597410-6). Macmillan.
Phillips, John L., Jr. The Origins of Intellect: Piaget's Theory. 2nd ed. LC 75-5703. (Illus.). 1975. text ed. 14.95x (ISBN 0-7167-0579-6); pap. text ed. 7.95x (ISBN 0-7167-0580-X). W H Freeman.
--Piaget's Theory: A Primer. LC 80-20800. (Psychology Ser.). (Illus.). 1981. text ed. 12.95x (ISBN 0-7167-1235-0); pap. text ed. 5.95x (ISBN 0-7167-1236-9). W H Freeman.
--Statistical Thinking: A Structural Approach. LC 73-3035. (Psychology Ser). (Illus.). 1973. text ed. 11.95x (ISBN 0-7167-0832-9); pap. text ed. 5.95x (ISBN 0-7167-0831-0). W H Freeman.
Phillips, John P., et al. Organic Electronic Spectral Data, Vol. 16. LC 60-16428. (Data Vol. Xvi, 1974). 1126p. 1980. 90.00 (ISBN 0-471-06058-5, Pub. by Wiley-Interscience). Wiley.
Phillips, John R. The Reformation of Images: Destruction of Art in England, 1530-1665. 1974. 20.00x (ISBN 0-520-02424-9). U of Cal Pr.
Phillips, Joy B. Development of Vertebrate Anatomy. LC 74-14876. 1975. text ed. 17.95 (ISBN 0-8016-3927-1). Mosby.
Phillips, K. A., jt. auth. see Stove, J. D.
Phillips, Kathleen C. Katie McCrary & the Wiggins Crusade. (gr. 4-7). 1980. 9.95 (ISBN 0-525-66717-2). Elsevier-Nelson.
Phillips, Keith. The Making of a Disciple. 1981. 7.95 (ISBN 0-8007-1181-5). Revell.
Phillips, L. F., jt. auth. see McEwan, M. J.
Phillips, Lawrence C. & Hoffman, William H. West's Federal Taxation: 1979 Annual: Individual Incomes Taxes. new rev. ed. 1978. text ed. 17.95 (ISBN 0-8299-0178-7); solutions manual avail. (ISBN 0-8299-0567-7). West Pub.
Phillips, Leslie. Human Adaptation & Its Failures. LC 68-14646. (Personality & Psychopathology Ser.: Vol. 3). 1968. 32.50 o.p. (ISBN 0-12-553850-2). Acad Pr.
Phillips, Linda R., jt. auth. see Wolanin, Mary O.
Phillips, Lionel. All That Glittered: Selected Correspondence of Lionel Phillips, 1890-1924. Fraser, Maryna & Jeeves, Alan, eds. (Illus.). 444p. 1977. text ed. 31.00x (ISBN 0-19-570100-3). Oxford U Pr.
Phillips, Louis. The Animated Thumbtack Railroad, Dollhouse & All-Around Surprise Book: (Evening Edition) LC 75-12637. (Illus.). 96p. (gr. 3 up). 1975. 6.95 (ISBN 0-397-31646-1); pap. 2.95 o.p. (ISBN 0-397-31647-X, LSC-37). Lippincott.
--Freaky Facts. Schneider, Meg, ed. (Funnybones Ser.). 64p. 1981. pap. 1.50 (ISBN 0-671-42247-2). S&S.
--The Man Who Stole the Atlantic Ocean. 1979. pap. 1.25 (ISBN 0-380-48173-1, 48173, Camelot). Avon.
Phillips, Louis & Markoe, Karen. Nuttier Nock Nocks. Schneider, Meg, ed. (Funnybones Ser.). (Illus.). 64p. (gr. 3-7). 1981. pap. 1.50 (ISBN 0-671-42248-0, Wanderer). S&S.
--The Super Duper American History Fun Book. (Illus.). (gr. 4-6). 1978. PLB 7.90 s&l (ISBN 0-531-01468-1). Watts.
Phillips, Louis, jt. auth. see Markoe, Karen.
Phillips, M., ed. Interpreting Blake. LC 78-8322. (Illus.). 1979. 42.00 (ISBN 0-521-22176-5). Cambridge U Pr.
Phillips, M. Ian. Brain Unit Activity During Behavior. (Illus.). 376p. 1973. text ed. 22.50 (ISBN 0-398-02769-2). C C Thomas.
Phillips, McCandlish. The Bible, the Supernatural & the Jews. LC 77-92532. 1970. pap. 6.95 (ISBN 0-87123-036-4, 210036). Bethany Fell.
--Spirit World of the Bible, the Supernatural, & the Jews. abr. ed. LC 72-77015. 192p. 1972. pap. 1.75 o.p. (ISBN 0-88207-048-7). Victor Bks.
Phillips, Margaret. Songs of the Good Earth. LC 79-10731. 62p. 1980. pap. 4.95 (ISBN 0-88289-221-5). Pelican.
Phillips, Margaret M; see Erasmus, Desiderius.
Phillips, Margaret M., tr. see Erasmus.
Phillips, Margot & Culinary Arts Institute Staff. The Greek Cookbook. Finnegan, Edward G., ed. LC 79-51590. (Adventures in Cooking Ser.). (Illus.). 1980. cancelled (ISBN 0-8326-0612-X, 1520); pap. 3.95 (ISBN 0-8326-0611-1, 2520). Delair.
Phillips, Mary W. Knitting. (Illus.). (gr. 5 up). 1977. PLB 5.20 s&l o.p. (ISBN 0-531-00837-1). Watts.
--Macrame, Step by Step. (Step by Step Craft Ser). 1974. pap. 2.95 (ISBN 0-307-42005-1, Golden Pr). Western Pub.
Phillips, Maurice. Lightning on Ice. LC 63-8733. (gr. 6-9). 1963. 5.95 o.p. (ISBN 0-385-05139-5). Doubleday.
Phillips, Melba, jt. auth. see Panofsky, Wolfgang K.
Phillips, Michael J. Edwin Muir: A Master of Modern Poetry. LC 78-67103. 1978. 19.50 (ISBN 0-915144-54-9). Hackett Pub.
--Selected Love Poems. 120p. 1980. 18.50 (ISBN 0-915144-87-5); pap. 6.95 (ISBN 0-915144-88-3). Hackett Pub.
Phillips, Mike. Blueprint for Raising a Child. 1978. pap. 3.95 (ISBN 0-88270-280-7). Logos.
--A Christian Family in Action. LC 77-1887. 1977. pap. 2.95 (ISBN 0-87123-085-2, 210085). Bethany Fell.
--Does Christianity Make Sense? 1978. pap. 1.95 (ISBN 0-88207-513-6). Victor Bks.

--A Survival Guide for Tough Times. LC 79-4261. 1979. pap. 3.50 (ISBN 0-87123-498-X, 210498). Bethany Fell.

Phillips, Mike, et al. Forbidden Fantasies. (Illus.). 128p. 1980. pap. 14.95 (ISBN 0-02-006300-8, Collier). Macmillan.

Phillips, Nina. Conversational English for the Non-English-Speaking Child. LC 68-23006. 1968. pap. text ed. 5.50x (ISBN 0-8077-1907-2). Tchrs Coll.

Phillips, O. A. & Buck, Ray. He Ain't No Bum. 1980. pap. 1.95 (ISBN 0-451-09540-5, J9450, Sig). NAL.

Phillips, O. M. The Dynamics of the Upper Ocean. 2nd ed. LC 76-26371. (Monographs on Mechanics & Applied Mathematics). (Illus.). 1977. 59.95 (ISBN 0-521-21421-1). Cambridge U Pr.

--The Dynamics of the Upper Ocean. LC 76-26371. (Cambridge Monographs on Mechanics & Applied Mathematics). 344p. 1980. pap. 21.50x (ISBN 0-521-29801-6). Cambridge U Pr.

Phillips, Pat. Invitation to Danger. 192p. (YA) 1976. 4.95 o.p. (ISBN 0-685-64246-1, Avalon). Bouregy.

--Love Waits at Penrhyn. 192p. (YA) 1975. 5.95 (ISBN 0-685-53495-2, Avalon). Bouregy.

Phillips, Patricia. Anise. (Orig.). 1978. pap. 1.95 o.s.i. (ISBN 0-515-04515-2). Jove Pubns.

--Captive Flame. 384p. (Orig.). 1980. pap. 2.50 (ISBN 0-515-05190-X). Jove Pubns.

--Jenny. (Histoical Romance Ser.). 432p. (Orig.). 1981. pap. 2.75 (ISBN 0-515-05538-7). Jove Pubns.

--Love's Defiant Prisoner. 1978. pap. 1.95 o.s.i. (ISBN 0-515-04375-3). Jove Pubns.

--Prehistory of Europe. LC 79-3787. 352p. 1980. 17.50x (ISBN 0-253-11956-1). Ind U Pr.

Phillips, Paul. Marx & Engels on Law & Laws. 238p. 1981. 27.50x (ISBN 0-389-20120-0). B&N.

Phillips, Paul, jt. auth. see Lazenby, David.

Phillips, Paul C., ed. see Stuart, Granville.

Phillips, Peter, jt. auth. see Philips, Janet.

Phillips, Philip. Archaeological Survey in the Lower Yazoo Basin, Mississippi: 1949-1955. LC 77-80028. (Peabody Museum Papers: Vol. 60). 1970. pap. text ed. 50.00 (ISBN 0-87365-173-1). Peabody Harvard.

Phillips, Philip & Brown, James A. Pre-Columbian Shell Engravings from the Craig Mound at Spiro, Oklahoma, 4 vols. Flnt, Emily & Condon, Lorna, eds. LC 74-77557. (Illus.). 1978. Limited Ed. lib. bdg. 240.00 (ISBN 0-87365-777-2). Peabody Harvard.

--Pre-Columbian Shell Engravings from the Craig Mound at Spiro, Oklahoma, Pt. 1. (Illus.). 1978. pap. 35.00 (ISBN 0-87365-795-0). Peabody Harvard.

Phillips, Philip A. Paul De Lamerie, Citizen & Goldsmith of London 1688-1751. 75.00x (ISBN 0-87556-510-7). Saifer.

Phillips, R., jt. auth. see Nussbaum, A.

Phillips, Ralph W., jt. auth. see Hine, Maynard K.

Phillips, Raymond E. & Feeney, Mary K. The Cardiac Rhythms: A Systematic Approach to Interpretation. LC 72-86451. (Illus.). 320p. 1973. text ed. 15.50 o.p. (ISBN 0-7216-7220-5). Saunders.

Phillips, Rob. Making Tracks. 1981. pap. 2.25 (ISBN 0-8439-0888-2, Leisure Bks). Nordon Pubns.

Phillips, Robert. Denton Welch. (English Authors Ser.: No. 163). 1974. lib. bdg. 12.50 (ISBN 0-8057-1567-3). Twayne.

--Land of Lost Content. LC 70-134667. 1970. 7.95 (ISBN 0-8149-0674-5). Vanguard.

--Last & Lost Poems of Delmore Schwartz. LC 78-63244. 1979. 8.95 (ISBN 0-8149-0808-X). Vanguard.

--Running on Empty: New Poems. LC 80-2429. 72p. 1981. 8.95 (ISBN 0-385-17304-0); pap. 4.95 (ISBN 0-385-17305-9). Doubleday.

--William Goyen. (United States Authors Ser.: No. 329). 1979. lib. bdg. 12.50 (ISBN 0-8057-7269-3). Twayne.

Phillips, Robert & Marquez, Olga. Visiones De Latinoamerica: A Cultural Reader. 2nd ed. (Illus.). 224p. 1980. pap. text ed. 10.50 scp (ISBN 0-06-045223-4, HarpC). Har-Row.

Phillips, Robert, jt. auth. see Osborn, Scott C.

Phillips, Robert, ed. Aspects of Alice: Lewis Carroll's Dreamchild As Seen Through the Critics' Looking Glasses. LC 70-178822. (Illus.). 15.00 (ISBN 0-8149-0700-8). Vanguard.

--Moonstruck: An Anthology of Lunar Poetry. LC 73-83042. (Illus.). 224p. 1974. 8.95 (ISBN 0-8149-0734-2). Vanguard.

Phillips, Roderick. Family Breakdown in Late Eighteenth Century France: Divorces in Rouen 1792-1803. (Illus.). 288p. 1980. 55.00 (ISBN 0-19-822572-5). Oxford U Pr.

Phillips, Roger. Concise Russian Review Grammar with Exercises. 1974. pap. 3.95x (ISBN 0-299-06544-8). U of Wis Pr.

--Wild Flowers of Britain. LC 78-303430. (Illus.). 1977. Repr. of 1977 ed. 27.50x (ISBN 0-7063-5580-6). Intl Pubns Serv.

Phillips, Stanton. Phillips Conveyances. 136p. (Orig.). 1980. pap. 4.66 (ISBN 0-9605268-0-3). A J Phillips.

Phillips, Steven R., jt. auth. see Bergquist, William H.

Phillips, Susan & Zecher, Richard. The SEC & the Public Interest. (Illus.). 184p. 1981. text ed. 19.95x (ISBN 0-262-16080-3). MIT Pr.

Phillips, U. B. Correspondence of Robert Toombs, Alexander H. Stephens, & Howell Cobb. LC 68-54846. (American Scene Ser). 1970. Repr. of 1911 ed. lib. bdg. 79.50 (ISBN 0-306-71191-5). Da Capo.

Phillips, U. Utah. Starlight on the Rails & Other Songs. (Illus.). 1973. pap. 3.95 o.s.i. (ISBN 0-8256-9905-3). Wooden Shoe.

Phillips, Ulrich B. American Negro Slavery. 12.50 (ISBN 0-8446-1348-7). Peter Smith.

Phillips, W. A., jt. auth. see Sproull, R. L.

Phillips, W. A., ed. Amorphous Solids. (Topics in Current Physics Ser.: Vol. 24). (Illus.). 190p. 1981. 32.00 (ISBN 0-387-10330-9). Springer-Verlag.

Phillips, W. R., jt. auth. see Grant, I. S.

Phillips, W. W. A Nineteen Seventy-Five Annotated Checklist of the Birds of Ceylon (Sri Lanka) rev. ed. (Illus.). 92p. 1975. pap. text ed. 7.95x (ISBN 0-87474-761-9). Smithsonian.

Phillips, Wendell. Oman a History. 14.00x (ISBN 0-685-72053-5). Intl Bk Ctr.

--Unknown Oman. (Arab Background Ser.). 1972. 14.00x (ISBN 0-685-77102-4). Intl Bk Ctr.

Phillips, William R. Mineral Optics: Principles & Techniques. LC 78-134208. (Geology Ser.). (Illus.). 1971. text ed. 28.95x (ISBN 0-7167-0251-7). W H Freeman.

Phillips, William R., jt. auth. see Orenstein, Alan.

Phillips, Wm. Revell & Griffen, Dana T. Optical Mineralogy: The Nonopaque Minerals. LC 80-12435. (Illus.). 1981. text ed. 39.95x (ISBN 0-7167-1129-X). W H Freeman.

Phillips-Birt, Douglas. Sailing Yacht Design. (Illus.). 1979. 32.50 (ISBN 0-229-11563-2, ScribT). Scribner.

Phillis, J. W. The Pharmacology of Synapses. 376p. 1970. 55.00 (ISBN 0-08-015558-8). Pergamon.

Phillis, J. W., jt. ed. see Kerkut, G. A.

Phillpotts, Beatrice. The Book of Fairies. (Illus.). 1979. 15.00 (ISBN 0-345-28091-1). Ballantine.

Phillpotts, Eden. My Adventure in the Flying Scotsman. Schantz, Tom, ed. (Illus.). 40p. 1975. pap. 4.00 (ISBN 0-915230-09-7). Rue Morgue.

Philmus, Robert, jt. ed. see Parrinder, Patrick.

Philmus, Robert M., ed. see Wells, H. G.

Philo, Harry, et al. Lawyers Desk Reference, 2 vols. 6th ed. Date not set. 85.00 (ISBN 0-686-27087-8). Lawyers Co-Op.

Philomusus, S. Mr. Law's Unlawfulness of the Stage Entertainment Examin'd. Bd. with The Entertainment of the Stage; Some Few Hints in Defence of Dramatical Entertainments. Ramsay, Allan. (The English Stage Ser.: Vol. 50). lib. bdg. 50.00 (ISBN 0-8240-0633-X). Garland Pub.

Philon, Helen. Early Islamic Ceramics. (Catalogue of Islamic Art in the Benaki Museum: Vol. 1). (Illus.). 376p. 1981. 147.50x (ISBN 0-85667-098-7, Pub. by Sotheby Parke Bernet England). Biblio Dist.

Philosophy of Science Association, Biennial Meeting, 1978. PSA 1978: Symposia, Special Sessions & Invited Lectures, Vol. 2. Asqwith, Peter D. & Hacking, Ian, eds. 1981. write for info. (ISBN 0-917586-10-7); pap. write for info. (ISBN 0-917586-09-3). Philos Sci Assn.

Philosophy of Science Biennial Meeting, 1976. S a, Nineteen Seventy-Six: Symposia, Vol. 2. Asquith, Peter D. & Suppe, Frederick, eds. LC 76-27152. 1977. 9.75 (ISBN 0-917586-04-2); pap. 6.25 (ISBN 0-917586-03-4). Philos Sci Assn.

Philostratus. Les Images. De Vigenere, Blaise, tr. LC 75-27866. (Renaissance & the Gods Ser.: Vol. 22). (Illus., Fr.). 1977. Repr. of 1614 ed. lib. bdg. 73.00 (ISBN 0-8240-2071-5). Garland Pub.

Philp, Kenneth R. & West, Elliott, eds. Essays on Walter Prescott Webb. (Walter Prescott Webb Memorial Lectures: No. 10). 160p. 1976. 8.95 (ISBN 0-292-72016-5). U of Tex Pr.

Philp, Kenneth R., jt. ed. see Lackner, Bede K.

Philpot, Frank A. Three Months to Earn. Sandman, Peter M., ed. (Career Ser). (Orig.). 1970. pap. 1.25 o.s.i. (ISBN 0-02-081110-1, Collier). Macmillan.

Philpot, Gordon A. The National Economy: An Introduction to Macroeconomics. LC 80-20615. (Introduction to Economics Ser.). 256p. 1981. pap. text ed. 7.95 (ISBN 0-471-05591-3). Wiley.

Philpot, J. H. The Seceders. pap. 2.25 (ISBN 0-686-12539-8). Banner of Truth.

Philpot, Joseph C. Letters & Memoir of Joseph Charles Philpot. (Giant Summit Ser.). 568p. 1981. pap. 9.95 (ISBN 0-8010-7060-0). Baker Bk.

Philpott, A. R. Let's Look at Puppets. LC 67-26517. (Let's Look Ser). (Illus.). (gr. 4-8). 1966. 4.95g o.p. (ISBN 0-8075-4494-9). A Whitman.

Philpott, Bryan. Fighters Defending the Reich. (World War Two Photo Album: No. 4). (Illus.). 96p. 1981. pap. 5.95 (ISBN 0-89404-044-8). Aztex.

--Fighters Over the Mediterranean. (World War Two Photo Album: No. 6). (Illus.). 96p. 1981. pap. 6.95 (ISBN 0-89404-048-0). Aztex.

--German Bombers Over England. (World War Two Photo Album: No. 2). (Illus.). 96p. 1981. pap. 5.95 (ISBN 0-89404-042-1). Aztex.

--German Bombers Over Russia: World War Two Photo Album. (Illus.). 96p. 1981. pap. 5.95 (ISBN 0-89404-050-2). Aztex.

--German Bombers Over the Med. (World War Two Photo Album Ser.: No. 13). (Illus.). 1980. 17.95 o.p. (ISBN 0-85059-393-X); pap. 11.95 o.p. (ISBN 0-85059-394-8). Aztex.

--German Bombers Over the Med: World War Two Photo Album. (Illus.). 96p. 1981. pap. 5.95 (ISBN 0-89404-037-5). Aztex.

--German Fighters Over England. Reach, D., ed. (World War 2 Photo Album: 10). (Illus.). 1979. 17.95 o.p. (ISBN 0-85059-355-7); pap. 11.75 o.p. (ISBN 0-85059-356-5). Aztex.

--German Fighters Over England: World War Two Photo Album. (Illus.). 96p. 1981. softcover 5.95 (ISBN 0-89404-056-1). Aztex.

--German Fighters Over Russia. (World War Two Photo Album: No. 16). (Illus.). 96p. 1980. pap. 5.95 (ISBN 0-89404-040-5). Aztex.

--German Maritime Aircraft. (World War Two Photo Album: No. 18). (Illus.). 96p. 1981. pap. 5.95 (ISBN 0-89404-046-4). Aztex.

--Luftwaffe Camouflage of World War Two. (Illus.). 64p. 1975. 4.95 o.p. (ISBN 0-85059-213-5). Aztex.

--Modelling Jet Fighters. (Illus.). 1976. 5.75 o.p. (ISBN 0-85059-231-3). Aztex.

--Modelling World War 2 Fighters. (Illus.). 1977. 5.65 o.p. (ISBN 0-85059-262-3). Aztex.

--World War 2 Photo Album 13: German Bombers Over the Med. 96p. 1980. 17.95 o.p. (ISBN 0-85059-393-X); pap. 11.95 o.p. (ISBN 0-85059-394-8). Aztex.

Philpott, Bryan, jt. auth. see Bowyer, Michael J.

Philpott, Kent. The Gay Theology. 1977. pap. 2.50 o.p. (ISBN 0-88270-241-6). Logos.

--If the Devil Wrote a Bible. 1975. pap. 1.95 o.p. (ISBN 0-88270-105-3). Logos.

--The Third Sex? LC 75-13177. 1975. 5.95 o.p. (ISBN 0-88270-131-2); pap. 2.50 o.p. (ISBN 0-88270-259-9). Logos.

Philpott, Kent & Hymers, R. L. The Deliverance Book. pap. cancelled o.s.i. (ISBN 0-89728-024-5, 677389). Omega Pubns OR.

Philpott, R. H. & Sapire, K. E. Obstetrics, Family Planning & Paediatrics: A Manual of Practical Management for Doctors & Nurses. 1977. pap. text ed. 7.50 o.p. (ISBN 0-86980-109-0). Verry.

Philpott, Stuart. West Indian Migration: The Montserrat Case. (Monographs on Social Anthropology). (Illus.). 228p. 1973. text ed. 19.50x (ISBN 0-391-00287-2, Athlone Pr). Humanities.

Philpott, William H. & Kalita, Dwight K. Brain Allergies: The Psycho-Nutrient Connection. LC 79-93429. (Illus.). 260p. 1980. 15.00 (ISBN 0-87983-224-X). Keats.

Phipps, Charles T. Browning's Clerical Characters. (Salzburg Studies in English Literature: Romantic Reassessment: No. 62). 336p. 1976. pap. text ed. 25.00x (ISBN 0-391-01497-8). Humanities.

Phipps, D. A. Metals & Metabolism, No. 26. (Oxford Chemistry Ser). (Illus.). 1976. pap. 12.50x (ISBN 0-19-855413-3). Oxford U Pr.

Phipps, Frances. Collector's Complete Dictionary of American Antiques. LC 72-97256. 656p. 1974. 15.95 (ISBN 0-385-03337-0). Doubleday.

--Colonial Kitchens, Their Furnishings & Their Gardens: The First Definitive Account Based on Settlers' Journals & Travelers' Diaries. LC 80-65251. (Illus.). 376p. 1980. pap. 8.95 (ISBN 0-8015-1435-5, Hawthorn). Dutton.

Phipps, Graeme, jt. auth. see Stanbury, Peter.

Phipps, Lloyd J. Mechanics in Agriculture. 2nd ed. LC 76-24049. 1977. 19.65 (ISBN 0-685-80737-1); text ed. 14.75x (ISBN 0-8134-1841-0). Interstate.

Phipps, Lloyd J., jt. auth. see Cook, G. C.

Phipps, Nancy, tr. see Sheldon, William D.

Phipps, Rita. For Students About Studying: A Study Skills Handbook. 1981. write for info. U of Wash Pr.

--The Successful Student's Handbook: A Step-by-Step Guide to Study Skills. LC 80-54427. (Illus.). 160p. (Orig.). 1981. pap. price not set (ISBN 0-295-95813-8). U of Wash Pr.

Phipps, William E. Influential Theologians on Wo-Man. LC 79-5431. 1980. pap. text ed. 7.50 (ISBN 0-8191-0880-4). U Pr of Amer.

--The Sexuality of Jesus. LC 74-126282. 1979. pap. 3.95 o.p. (ISBN 0-06-066562-9, RD141, HarpR). Har-Row.

Phipps, Wilma H. & Rich, Rosemary. Patient Care Studies in Medical-Surgical Nursing. 1972. pap. 7.50 o.p. (ISBN 0-8016-3930-1). Mosby.

Phipps, Wilma J., et al. Medical-Surgical Nursing: Concepts & Clinical Practice. LC 78-27863. (Illus.). 1979. text ed. 30.95 (ISBN 0-8016-3932-8). Mosby.

--Shafer's Medical-Surgical Nursing. 7th ed. LC 79-27334. (Illus.). 1014p. 1980. text ed. 25.95 (ISBN 0-8016-3934-4). Mosby.

Phipson, Joan. Family Conspiracy. LC 64-11494. (Illus.). (gr. 4-6). 1964. 5.95 o.p. (ISBN 0-15-227110-4, HJ). HarBraceJ.

--Threat to the Barkers. LC 65-10962. (Illus.). (gr. 4-6). 1965. 4.95 o.p. (ISBN 0-15-286310-9, HJ). HarBraceJ.

--A Tide Flowing. LC 80-24375. 168p. (gr. 7 up). 1981. 8.95 (ISBN 0-689-50196-X, McElderry Bk). Atheneum.

Phister, Montgomery, Jr. Data Processing Technology & Economics. LC 76-24121. (Illus.). 1977. text ed. 29.95 o.p. (ISBN 0-917640-01-2); pap. text ed. 19.95x o.p. (ISBN 0-917640-02-0). Santa Monica Pub.

--Data Processing Technology & Economics. 2nd ed. (Illus.). 1979. 45.00 (ISBN 0-932376-03-7, Co-Pub. by Santa Monica Pub); pap. 30.00 (ISBN 0-932376-04-5). Digital Pr.

--Data Processing Technology & Economics: 1975-1978 Supplement. (Illus.). 1979. pap. 10.00x (ISBN 0-917640-03-9). Santa Monica Pub.

Phistiklakis, Nicholas G., ed. see Eliopoulos, Nicholas C.

Phizacklea, Annie & Miles, Bob. Labour & Racism. 256p. 1980. 30.00 (ISBN 0-7100-0678-0); pap. 18.50 (ISBN 0-7100-0679-9). Routledge & Kegan.

Phizacklea, Annie, jt. ed. see Miles, Robert.

Pholeric, Janet J. Folk Dances Around the World, Vol. 1. LC 79-63544. 188p. 1980. 12.00 (ISBN 0-498-02259-5). A S Barnes.

Photiadis, John D. & Schwarzweller, Harry K., eds. Change in Rural Appalachia: Implications for Action Programs. LC 75-122381. (Illus.). 1971. 17.00x (ISBN 0-8122-7618-3). U of Pa Pr.

PhotoGraphic Magazine Editors, jt. auth. see Helprin, Ben.

Phylos The Tibetan. A Dweller on Two Planets. (Illus.). 450p. 1974. pap. 3.95 (ISBN 0-8334-1753-3). Steinerbks.

Phypers, David, jt. auth. see Bridge, Donald.

Physics Survey Committee. Physics in Perspective: The Nature of Physics and the Subfields of Physics (Student Edition) (Illus.). 368p. 1973. pap. 7.00x (ISBN 0-309-02118-9). Natl Acad Pr.

--Physics in Perspective Vol. 2 Pt. a: The Core Subfields of Physics. (Illus.). 768p. 1972. pap. 18.75 (ISBN 0-309-02100-6). Natl Acad Pr.

--Physics in Perspective, Volume 2, Part B: The Interfaces. (Illus.). 728p. 1973. pap. 18.75 (ISBN 0-309-02101-4). Natl Acad Pr.

Phythian, B. A., ed. A Concise Dictionary of Correct English. (Littlefield, Adams Quality Paperback Ser.: No. 349). 1979. pap. 5.50 (ISBN 0-8226-0349-7). Littlefield.

Phytochemical Society. Perspectives in Phytochemistry: Proceedings. Harborne, J. B. & Swain, T., eds. 1969. 29.00 (ISBN 0-12-324660-1). Acad Pr.

--Phytochemical Phylogeny: Proceedings. Harborne, J. B., ed. 1970. 47.50 (ISBN 0-12-324666-0). Acad Pr.

Phytochemical Society of North American Symposium. Recent Advances in Phytochemistry: Structure, Biogenesis, Distribution. Runeckles, V. C. & Mabry, T. J., eds. 1974. Vol. 7. 37.00 (ISBN 0-12-612407-8); Vol. 8. 37.00 (ISBN 0-12-612408-6). Acad Pr.

Phytochemical Society of North America. Symposia, Vols. 5 & 6. Runeckles, V. C. & Tso, T. C., eds. Incl. Vol. 5. Structural & Functional Aspects of Phytochemistry. 1972. 48.50 (ISBN 0-12-612405-1); Vol. 6. Terpenoids: Structure, Biogenesis, Distribution. 1973. 37.00 (ISBN 0-12-612406-X). Acad Pr.

Pi Sigma Alpha Committee on Publications. Major Problems in State Constitutional Revision. Graves, W. Brooke, ed. LC 78-779. xiv, 306p. 1978. Repr. of 1960 ed. lib. bdg. 24.50x (ISBN 0-313-20266-4, PSAM). Greenwood.

Pia, H. W., et al, eds. Spontaneous Intracerebral Haematomas: Advances in Diagnosis & Therapy. (Illus.). 500p. 1981. 116.90 (ISBN 0-387-10146-2). Springer Verlag.

Piaget, Jean. Adaptation & Intelligence: Organic Selection & Phenocopy. Eames, Steward, tr. LC 79-25592. 130p. 11.00 (ISBN 0-226-66777-4). U of Chicago Pr.

--Child's Conception of Physical Causality. 1966. Repr. of 1930 ed. text ed. 17.75x (ISBN 0-7100-3068-1). Humanities.

--The Grasp of Consciousness: Action & Concept in the Young Child. LC 75-43687. 352p. 1976. 16.50x (ISBN 0-674-36033-8); pap. 5.95 (ISBN 0-674-36034-6). Harvard U Pr.

--John Amos Comenius on Education. LC 67-21499. 1968. text ed. 9.75 (ISBN 0-8077-1911-0); pap. text ed. 5.25x (ISBN 0-8077-1908-0). Tchrs Coll.

--Language & Thought of the Child. 3rd ed. 1962. text ed. 15.50x (ISBN 0-7100-3041-X). Humanities.

--Main Trends in Interdisciplinary Research. 1973. pap. 1.95x o.p. (ISBN 0-06-131755-1, TB1755, Torch). Har-Row.

--The Psychology of Intelligence. 1971. Repr. of 1950 ed. 16.95 (ISBN 0-7100-3136-X). Routledge & Kegan.

Piaget, Jean, jt. auth. see Inhelder, Barbel.

Piaget, Jean, et al. The Child's Conception of Geometry. Lunzer, E. A., tr. 432p. 1981. pap. 8.95 (ISBN 0-393-00057-5). Norton.

Pianka, Phyllis T. Nurse of the Island. 192p. (YA) 1976. 5.95 (ISBN 0-685-66476-7, Avalon). Bouregy.

--The Paisley Butterfly. (Orig.). 1980. pap. 1.50 o.s.i. (ISBN 0-440-17105-9). Dell.

Piarron De Chamousset, C. - H. Vues D'un Citoyen. 535p. (Fr.). 1977. Repr. of 1757 ed. lib. bdg. 47.50x o.p. (ISBN 0-8287-0690-5). Clearwater Pub.

Piatagorsky, Gregor. Cellist Music. 1979. Repr. of 1965 ed. 27.50 (ISBN 0-306-70822-1). Da Capo.

Piattelli-Palmarini, Massimo, ed. Language & Learning: The Debate Between Jean Piaget & Noam Chomsky. LC 80-10588. 1980. text ed. 20.00x (ISBN 0-674-50940-4). Harvard U Pr.

Piatti, G., ed. Advances in Composite Materials. (Illus.). 1978. text ed. 91.10x (ISBN 0-85334-770-0, Pub. by Applied Science). Burgess-Intl Ideas.

Piave, F. M. Rigoletto. Dent, E. J., ed. 1939. 2.50 o.p. (ISBN 0-19-313314-8). Oxford U Pr.

Piazza, Paul. Christopher Isherwood: Myth & Anti-Myth. LC 77-14271. 1978. 15.00x (ISBN 0-231-04118-7). Columbia U Pr.

Piazza, Robert, ed. Learning Disabilities: Revision. (Special Education Ser.). (Illus., Orig.). 1980. pap. text ed. 9.95 (ISBN 0-89568-119-6). Spec Learn Corp.

Pica, George, ed. see Doran, Jeffry W.

Picano, Felice. An Asian Minor: The True Story of Ganymede. (Illus.). 80p. 1981. 19.95 (ISBN 0-933322-07-0); pap. 5.95 (ISBN 0-933322-06-2). Sea Horse.

--Eyes. 1977. pap. 1.95 o.s.i. (ISBN 0-440-12427-1). Dell.

Picano, Felice, ed. A True Likeness: An Anthology of Lesbian and Gay Writing Today. 320p. 1980. pap. 9.95 (ISBN 0-933322-04-6). Sea Horse.

Picard, Barbara L. Tales of the Norse Gods & Heroes. (Illus.). 312p. (gr. 6 up). 1980. Repr. of 1953 ed. 14.95 (ISBN 0-19-274513-1). Oxford U Pr.

Picard, Emile & Simart, G. Theorie Des Fonctions Algebriques De Deux Variables Independantes 2 Vols. in 1. LC 67-31156. (Fr). 1971. 29.00 (ISBN 0-8284-0248-5). Chelsea Pub.

Picard, Raymond C., jt. ed. see Bryan, John L.

Picasso, Juan R. Senderos De Navidad. 1980. pap. 0.65 (ISBN 0-311-08218-1). Casa Bautista.

Picasso, Pablo. Hunk of Skin. LC 68-8390. (Pocket Poet Ser.: No. 25). (Orig., Span. & Eng.). 1969. pap. 1.00 o.p. (ISBN 0-87286-040-X). City Lights.

--Picasso. Jaffe, Hans L., ed. (Library of Great Painters Ser). 1964. 35.00 (ISBN 0-8109-0368-7). Abrams.

Piccard, Betty. An Introduction to Social Work: A Primer. rev. ed. 1979. pap. text ed. 7.95x (ISBN 0-256-02109-0). Dorsey.

Picchio, Riccardo. Etudes Litteraires Slavo-Romanes. (Studia Historica et Philologica Ser.: Vol. VI). (Fr.). 1978. write for info. o.p. (ISBN 8-7774-0005-4, Pub. by Licosa Editrice Italy). Schoenhof.

Picchiuti, Paul. Up in the Air. (Hello World Ser.). 1967. pap. 1.65 (ISBN 0-8163-0305-3, 21620-0). Pacific Pr Pub Assn.

Piccini, A. A Fishy Story. (Illus.). (ps-3). 0.75 o.s.i. (ISBN 0-8198-0197-6). Dghtrs St Paul.

Piccirillo, Martin L., jt. auth. see Prostano, Emanuel T.

Piccolpasso, Cipriano. Three Books of the Potter's Art, 2 vols. Lightbown, Ronald & Caiger-Smith, Alan, trs. (Illus.). 358p. 1980. Repr. 210.00x set (ISBN 0-85967-452-5, Pub. by Scolar Pr England). Biblio Dist.

Piccone, Paul, jt. ed. see Cavalcanti, Pedro.

Piccone, Paul, ed. see International Telos Conference, 1st, Waterloo, Ont., Oct. 8-11, 1970.

Pice, Margaret La see La Pice, Margaret.

Pichanick, Valerie. Harriet Martineau: The Woman & Her Work, Eighteen Hundred & Two to Eighteen Seventy-Six. (Women & Culture Ser.). 336p. 1980. 15.00x (ISBN 0-472-10002-5). U of Mich Pr.

Pichaske, David. A Generation in Motion: Popular Music & Culture in the 1960's. LC 78-63033. (Illus.). 1979. 15.00 (ISBN 0-02-871860-7); pap. 5.95 (ISBN 0-02-871850-X). Schirmer Bks.

Pichaske, David R. The Poetry of Rock: The Golden Years. 192p. (Orig.). 1981. pap. 5.95 (ISBN 0-933180-17-9). Ellis Pr.

--Writing Sense: A Handbook of Composition. LC 74-15134. 1975. pap. text ed. 5.95 (ISBN 0-02-925170-2). Free Pr.

Pichierei, L. Music in New Hampshire, 1623-1800. LC 60-13940. 1960. 20.00x (ISBN 0-231-02377-4). Columbia U Pr.

Pichler, F. & Hanika, F. de P. Progress in Cybernetics & Systems Research, Vol. 7. LC 75-6641. (Progress in Cybernetics & Systems Research Ser.). (Illus.). 393p. 1980. text ed. 50.00 (ISBN 0-89116-195-3). Hemisphere Pub.

Pichler, F. & Trappl, R., eds. Progress in Cybernetics & Systems Research, Vol. 6. LC 75-6641. (Progress in Cybernetics & Systems Research Ser.). (Illus.). 500p. Date not set. text ed. 50.00 (ISBN 0-89116-194-5). Hemisphere Pub. Postponed.

Picinelli, Filippo. Mundus Symbolicus, 2 vols. LC 75-27878. (Renaissance & the Gods Ser.: Vol. 33). (Illus.). 1977. Repr. of 1694 ed. Set. lib. bdg. 146.00 (ISBN 0-8240-2082-0); lib. bdg. 73.00 ea. Garland Pub.

Pick, A., ed. see Kozhevnikov, A. V.

Pick, Anne D., et al see Hetherington, E. Mavis.

Pick, Arnold. Aphasia. (Illus.). 168p. 1973. text ed. 14.75 (ISBN 0-398-02658-0). C C Thomas.

Pick, Bernard. The Cabala. LC 13-26188. 160p. 1974. pap. 2.95 o.p. (ISBN 0-87548-199-X). Open Court.

Pick, Christopher. The Young Scientist Book of the Undersea. LC 78-17796. (Young Scientist Ser.). (Illus.). (gr. 4-5). 1978. text ed. 6.95 (ISBN 0-88436-529-8). EMC.

Pick, Christopher C. Oil Machines. LC 78-26333. (Machine World Ser.). (Illus.). (gr. 2-4). 1979. PLB 9.95 (ISBN 0-8172-1327-9). Raintree Pubs.

--Undersea Machines. LC 78-27420. (Machine World Ser.). (Illus.). (gr. 2-4). 1979. PLB 9.95 (ISBN 0-8172-1326-0). Raintree Pubs.

Pick, Franz. Pick's Currency Yearbook 1977-1979. 22nd ed. 1981. 180.00 (ISBN 0-87551-277-1). Pick Pub.

Pick, Fred L. & Knight, Norman. Pocket History of Freemasonry. 5th ed. 1969. 13.50x (ISBN 0-584-10256-9). Intl Pubns Serv.

Pick, Herbert L., Jr. & Saltzman, Elliot, eds. Modes of Perceiving & Processing Information. LC 77-21025. 1977. 14.95 (ISBN 0-470-99342-1). Halsted Pr.

Pick, Joseph. Autonomic Nervous System: Morphological, Comparative, Clinical & Surgical Aspects. LC 68-20600. (Illus.). 1970. 69.00 o.p. (ISBN 0-397-50257-5). Lippincott.

Pick, Philip L., ed. Tree of Life: An Anthology of Articles Appearing in the Jewish Vegetarian, 1966-1974. LC 76-18476. 1977. 6.95 o.p. (ISBN 0-498-01945-4). A S Barnes.

Pick, R. M., jt. ed. see Bratos, S.

Pickard, David. Dawn Wind. 1980. pap. 2.50 (ISBN 0-85363-133-6). OMF Bks.

Pickard, Eileen. The Development of Creative Ability. (Orig.). 1979. pap. text ed. 20.75x (ISBN 0-85633-178-3, NEFR). Humanities.

Pickard, G. L. Descriptive Physical Oceanography. 2nd ed. 220p. 1976. text ed. 12.10 o.p. (ISBN 0-08-018159-7); pap. text ed. 7.00 o.p. (ISBN 0-08-018158-9). Pergamon.

--Descriptive Physical Oceanography. 3rd ed. (International Series in Geophysics). (Illus.). 1979. text ed. 35.00 (ISBN 0-08-023824-6); pap. text ed. 11.50 (ISBN 0-08-023825-4). Pergamon.

Pickard, G. L. & Pond, S. Introductory Dynamic Oceanography. LC 77-4427. 1978. text ed. 45.00 (ISBN 0-08-021614-5); pap. text ed. 12.50 (ISBN 0-08-021615-3). Pergamon.

Pickard, H. M. Manual of Operative Dentistry. 4th ed. (Illus.). 1976. pap. 15.50x (ISBN 0-19-267004-2). Oxford U Pr.

Pickard, Mary A. Feasting Naturally: From Your Own Recipes. LC 80-68229. 1980. spiral bdg. 7.95 (ISBN 0-934474-18-4). Cookbook Pubs.

--Feasting...Naturally. LC 79-64450. 1979. softbound with spiral plastic bdg. 6.95 (ISBN 0-934474-05-2). Cookbook Pubs.

Pickard, P. M. The Activity of Children. 1965. text ed. 4.75x (ISBN 0-582-32420-3). Humanities.

--If You Think Your Child Is Gifted. (Illus.). 160p. (Orig.). 1976. pap. 6.75 o.p. (ISBN 0-04-370072-1). Allen Unwin.

Pickard, Roy. The Award Movies: A Complete Guide from A to Z. LC 80-54142. (Illus.). 354p. 1981. 14.95 (ISBN 0-8052-3767-4); pap. 6.95 (ISBN 0-8052-0677-9). Schocken.

--Who Played Who in the Movies. LC 80-26546. 304p. 1981. 14.95 (ISBN 0-8052-3766-6); pap. 5.95 (ISBN 0-8052-0676-0). Schocken.

Pickard, Tom. The Jarrow March. (Illus.). 96p. 1981. 11.95 (ISBN 0-8052-8079-0, Pub. by Allison & Busby England); pap. 5.95. Schocken.

Picken, Laurence, ed. Musica Asiatica Two. (Illus.). 195p. 1980. pap. 32.00x (ISBN 0-19-323235-9). Oxford U Pr.

Picken, Mary B. & White, Doris. Needlepoint for Everyone. LC 67-22543. (Illus.). 1970. 13.95 o.s.i. (ISBN 0-06-005761-0, HarpT). Har-Row.

Picken, Mary B., ed. The Fashion Dictionary: Fabric, Sewing, & Apparel As Expressed in the Language of Fashion. enl. ed. LC 72-83771. (Funk & W Bk.). (Illus.). 448p. 1972. 12.95 o.s.i. (ISBN 0-308-10052-2, F64, TYC-T). T Y Crowell.

Picken, Stuart D. & Reischauer, Edwin O. Shinto: Japan's Spiritual Roots. LC 79-91520. (Illus.). 80p. 1980. 17.50 (ISBN 0-87011-410-7). Kodansha.

Picker, Martin. The Chanson Albums of Marguerite of Austria. 1965. 55.00x (ISBN 0-520-01009-4). U of Cal Pr.

Pickerell, Albert G. & Dornin, May. The University of California: A Pictorial History. (Illus.). 1968. 19.95 (ISBN 0-520-01010-8). U of Cal Pr.

Pickering, F. B. Physical Metallurgy & Design of Steels. (Illus.). 1978. text ed. 62.60x (ISBN 0-85334-752-2). Intl Ideas.

Pickering, F. B., ed. The Metallurgical Evolution of Stainless Steels. 1979. 38.00 (ISBN 0-87170-077-8). ASM.

Pickering, George. Creative Malady. 1974. 13.95 (ISBN 0-19-519800-X). Oxford U Pr.

Pickering, I. S. Exercises for the Autonomic Nervous System: You Need Them! (Illus.). 112p. 1981. price not set (ISBN 0-398-04454-6); pap. price not set (ISBN 0-398-04466-X). C C Thomas.

Pickering, J. F. Industrial Structure & Market Conduct. 335p. 1974. bds. 36.00x (ISBN 0-85520-040-5, Pub by Martin Robertson England); pap. 14.95x (ISBN 0-85520-039-1). Biblio Dist.

Pickering, James H., ed. The World Turned Upside Down: The Prose and Poetry of the American Revolution. 1975. 17.50 (ISBN 0-8046-9082-0, Natl U). Kennikat.

Pickering, Jerry. Theatre: A Contemporary Introduction. 3rd ed. (Illus.). 380p. 1981. pap. text ed. 10.36 (ISBN 0-8299-0403-4). West Pub.

Pickering, Larry K., jt. auth. see Dupont, Herbert L.

Pickering, Samuel F. Be Merry & Wise: John Locke & Eighteenth-Century English Children's Books. Date not set. 16.50 (ISBN 0-87049-290-X). U of Tenn Pr. Postponed.

Pickering, W. J., jt. auth. see Mallows, D. F.

Pickering, W. S., ed. Durkheim on Religion. 1975. 28.00x (ISBN 0-7100-8108-1). Routledge & Kegan.

Pickering, W. S. F. A Social History of the Diocese of Newcastle. (Illus.). 1981. 35.00 (ISBN 0-85362-189-6, Oriel). Routledge & Kegan.

Pickering, Wilbur. The Identity of the New Testament, Text. LC 77-1559. 1977. 7.95 o.p. (ISBN 0-8407-5113-3). Nelson.

Pickersgill, Gary M. & Pickersgill, Joyce E. Contemporary Economic Systems: A Comparative View. (Illus.). 352p. 1974. ref. ed. 18.95x (ISBN 0-13-169342-5). P-H.

Pickersgill, Joyce E., jt. auth. see Pickersgill, Gary M.

Pickett, George E., jt. auth. see Hanlon, John J.

Pickett, Hazel. God's Perfect Way for You. 1.95 o.p. (ISBN 0-910924-32-5). Macalester.

Pickett, L. M. Derld. (Chess Player Ser.). 1977. pap. 5.95 o.p. (ISBN 0-900928-52-2, H-1160). Hippocrene Bks.

--Sicilian Defence Series 8: Lines with B-QN5. (Chess Player Ser.). 1977. pap. 5.95 o.p. (ISBN 0-900928-85-9, H-1193). Hippocrene Bks.

Pickett, Nell A. & Laster, Ann A. Technical English: Writing, Reading, & Speaking. 3rd ed. (Illus.). 1980. pap. 14.50 scp (ISBN 0-06-045221-8, HarpC); instr's manual avail. Har-Row.

Pickett, Ronald, jt. auth. see Triggs, Thomas.

Pickhardt, Robert C., jt. auth. see McLaughlin, Frank S.

Pickle, H. B. & Abrahson, R. L. Small Business Management. 2nd ed. (Wiley Series in Management). 500p. 1981. text ed. 20.95 (ISBN 0-471-06218-9). Wiley.

Pickle, Hal B. & Abrahamson, Royce L. Small Business Management. LC 75-29035. 512p. 1976. text ed. 20.95 (ISBN 0-471-68806-1); instr's. guide avail. (ISBN 0-471-68927-0); study guide 7.95 (ISBN 0-471-68811-8). Wiley.

Pickles, Wilfred. Wilfred Pickles Invites You to Have Another Go. LC 77-85030. 1978. 14.95 (ISBN 0-7153-7393-5). David & Charles.

Pickrell, Annie D. Pioneer Women in Texas. 1970. 15.00 (ISBN 0-8363-0126-9). Jenkins.

Pickrell, John A., ed. Lung Connective Tissue. 240p. 1981. 59.95 (ISBN 0-8493-5749-7). CRC Pr.

Pickthall, M. M., ed. Holy Quran with English Translation. 1976. Repr. 14.50x (ISBN 0-8364-0415-7). South Asia Bks.

Pickthall, Marmaduke, ed. The Glorious Koran. bilingual ed. 1696p. 1976. text ed. 50.00x (ISBN 0-04-297036-9). Allen Unwin.

Pickthall, Muhammed M., tr. from Arabic. The Glorious Koran. 1979. deluxe ed. 50.00 (ISBN 0-87773-713-4). Great Eastern.

Pickup, Madelaine. German Shepherd Guide. 6.98 o.p. (ISBN 0-385-01575-5). Doubleday.

Pickup, Madeleine. All About the German Shepherd Dog. (All About Ser.). (Illus.). 170p. 1980. 16.95 (ISBN 0-7207-1219-X, Pub. by Michael Joseph). Merrimack Bk Serv.

--The Alsatian Owner's Encyclopaedia. 1964. 8.95 (ISBN 0-7207-0001-9, Pub. by Michael Joseph). Merrimack Bk Serv.

Pico Della Mirandola, Giovanni. On the Dignity of Man. Wallis, Charles G., et al, trs. Bd. with On Being & Unity; Heptaplus. LC 65-26540. 1965. pap. 5.50 (ISBN 0-672-60483-3, LLA227). Bobbs.

Picon-Salas, Mariano. A Cultural History of Spanish America: From Conquest to Independence. Leonard, Irving A., tr. 1962. pap. 4.95x (ISBN 0-520-01012-4, CAMPUS15). U of Cal Pr.

Pictorius, Georg see Albricus.

Pidal, M. Manual De Gramatica Historica. 12.50x (ISBN 0-686-00874-X). Colton Bk.

Piddock, Charles A. The Monster Fly. McCarthy, Patricia, ed. (Pal Paperbacks Kit Ser.). (Illus., Orig.). (gr. 7-12). pap. text ed. 1.25 (ISBN 0-8374-3475-0). Xerox Ed Pubns.

Pidmohylny, Valerian. A Little Touch of Drama. Luckyj, George S., tr. from Ukrainian. LC 72-86407. (Ukrainian Classics in Translation Ser: No. 1). 1972. lib. bdg. 11.50x (ISBN 0-87287-051-0). Ukrainian Acad.

Pidoll, Carl. Eroica: A Novel About Beethoven. LC 57-7677. 7.95 (ISBN 0-8149-0184-0). Vanguard.

PIE Seminar,Papers, Oxford, April 1979. Foreign Language Teaching: Meeting Individual Needs. Altman, Howard B., ed. 128p. pap. 7.95 (ISBN 0-08-024604-4). Pergamon.

Piechowiak, Ann & Cook, Myra. Complete Guide to the Elementary Learning Center. 252p. pap. 8.95 (ISBN 0-13-160309-4, Reward). P-H.

Piediscalzi, N., et al. Distinguishing Moral Education, Values Clarification & Religion-Studies: Proceedings. Swyhart, B., ed. LC 76-26670. (American Academy of Religion. Section Papers). 1976. pap. 4.50 (ISBN 0-89130-082-1, 010918). Scholars Pr Ca.

Piekalkiewicz, Janusz. Arnheim 1944. Barker, H. A. & Barker, A. J., trs. from Ger. (Illus.). 1977. 17.50x (ISBN 0-7110-0826-4). Intl Pubns Serv.

--Arnhem Nineteen Hundred & Forty-Four: Germany's Last Victory. (Encore Edition). (Illus.). 1978. 4.95 (ISBN 0-684-16551-1, ScribT). Scribner.

--The Cavalry of World War II. LC 80-5800. (Illus.). 256p. 1980. 25.00 (ISBN 0-8128-2749-X). Stein & Day.

Piekalkiewicz, Jaroslaw. Communist Local Government: A Study of Poland. LC 72-85539. xiv, 282p. 1975. 16.00x (ISBN 0-8214-0140-8). Ohio U Pr.

Piele, Linda J., jt. auth. see Tyson, John C.

Pielou, E. C. Biogeography. LC 79-13306. 1979. 23.50 (ISBN 0-471-05845-9, Pub. by Wiley-Interscience). Wiley.

Pielou, Evelyn C. Ecological Diversity. LC 75-9663. 165p. 1975. 21.95 (ISBN 0-471-68925-4, Pub. by Wiley-Interscience). Wiley.

Piene, Otto, et al. Centerbeam. (Illus.). 1980. pap. 15.00 (ISBN 0-262-66047-4). MIT Pr.

Pienkowski, Jan. The Haunted House. (Illus.). (ps-3). 1979. 8.95 (ISBN 0-525-31520-9). Dutton.

--Numbers. LC 74-83405. (Concept Bks). (Illus.). 32p. (ps-2). 1975. PLB 5.29 (ISBN 0-8178-5242-5). Harvey.

--Sizes. LC 74-8308. (Concept Bks). (Illus.). 32p. (ps-2). 1975. PLB 5.29 (ISBN 0-8178-5262-X). Harvey.

Pienkowski, Jan, jt. auth. see Nicoll, Helen.

Piepe, Anthony, et al. Mass Media & Cultural Relationships. 184p. 1977. text ed. 23.00x (ISBN 0-566-00161-6, Pub. by Gower Pub Co England). Renouf.

Piepenburg, Robert. Raku Pottery. (Illus.). 160p. 1976. pap. 9.95 (ISBN 0-02-011860-0, Collier). Macmillan.

Pieper, August. Isaiah II. 1980. pap. 24.50 (ISBN 0-8100-0109-8). Northwest Pub.

Pieper, Elizabeth. Sticks & Stones Book. 1976. 4.00 (ISBN 0-937540-06-4, HPP-8). Human Policy Pr.

Pierard, Richard V., jt. auth. see Linder, Robert D.

Pieraut-Le Bonniec, Gilbert. The Development of Modal Reasoning: Genesis of Necessity & Probability Notions. LC 79-24969. (Developmental Psychology Ser.). 1980. 16.50 (ISBN 0-12-554650-5). Acad Pr.

Pierce, A. J. & Pierce, D. K. Victorian & Edwardian Children from Old Photographs. LC 79-56442. (Illus.). 120p. 1980. 17.95 (ISBN 0-7134-2327-7, Pub. by Batsford England). David & Charles.

Pierce, Allan D. Acoustics: An Introducton to Its Physical Principles & Applications. (Illus.). 656p. 1981. text ed. 28.95x (ISBN 0-07-049961-6, C); write for info solutions manual (ISBN 0-07-049962-4). McGraw.

Pierce, Anthony. Canal People. (Junior Reference Ser.). (Illus.). 64p. (gr. 7 up). 7.95 (ISBN 0-7136-1811-6). Dufour.

Pierce, Bess. Moline: A Pictorial History. Friedman, Donna R., ed. (Illus.). 208p. 1981. pap. write for info. (ISBN 0-89865-095-X). Donning Co.

Pierce, Bessie L. A History of Chicago, 3 vols. Incl. Vol. 1. The Beginning of a City. xxii, 488p. Repr. of 1937 ed (ISBN 0-226-66817-7); Vol. 2. From Town to City, 1848-1871. xviii, 582p. Repr. of 1940 ed (ISBN 0-226-66818-5); Vol. 3. The Rise of a Modern City, 1871-1893. xvi, 612p. Repr. of 1957 ed (ISBN 0-226-66819-3). LC 75-24667. 1976. lib. bdg. 20.00x ea. U of Chicago Pr.

--Public Opinion & the Teaching of History in the United States. LC 71-107416. (Civil Liberties in American History Ser.). 1970. Repr. of 1926 ed. lib. bdg. 37.50 (ISBN 0-306-71883-9). Da Capo.

Pierce, C. C. Secret & Secure: Privacy, Cryptography & Secure Communication. LC 77-73804. (Illus.). 1977. pap. 3.25 o.s.i. (ISBN 0-9601564-1-0). C C Pierce.

Pierce, Carole & Pierce, Robert. Buck Rogers. (Golden Storybook). (Illus.). (gr. 4-6). 1979. PLB 9.15 o.p. (ISBN 0-307-62083-2, Golden Pr); pap. 1.25 o.p. (ISBN 0-307-12083-X, Golden Pr). Western Pub.

Pierce, Clayton C. Secret & Secure: Privacy, Cryptography & Secure Communication. rev. ed. LC 77-73804. (Illus.). 1979. cancelled (ISBN 0-9601564-2-9); pap. 5.95 (ISBN 0-9601564-3-7). C C Pierce.

Pierce, Conway, jt. auth. see Smith, R. Nelson.

Pierce, D. K., jt. auth. see Pierce, A. J.

Pierce, David G. & Shaw, David M. Monetary Economics: Theories, Evidence & Policy. LC 73-91530. 1974. 27.00x (ISBN 0-8448-0267-0); pap. 14.50x (ISBN 0-8448-0268-9). Crane-Russak Co.

Pierce, Douglas J. All You Must Know About Psychology in Order to Know Yourself. (Illus.). 1980. 27.45 (ISBN 0-89920-008-7). Am Inst Psych.

Pierce, F. F., ed. see Cervantes-Saavedra, Miguel De.

Pierce, Frank. Amadis De Gaula. LC 75-25907. (World Authors Ser.: Spain: No. 372). 1976. lib. bdg. 12.50 (ISBN 0-8057-6220-5). Twayne.

Pierce, Franklin. Federal Usurpation. xx, 437p. 1980. Repr. of 1908 ed. lib. bdg. 35.00x (ISBN 0-8377-1007-3). Rothman.

Pierce, G. Barry, et al. Cancer: A Problem of Developmental Biology. (Foundations of Developmental Biology Ser.). 1978. 18.95 (ISBN 0-13-113373-X). P-H.

Pierce, Glenn. The Condor. (Orig.). 1980. pap. 1.95 (ISBN 0-505-51520-2). Tower Bks.

Pierce, Guy, compiled by. Cuttings: The Pick of "Country Life" from Punch. (Illus.). 64p. 1981. pap. 4.50 (ISBN 0-241-10496-3, Pub. by Hamish Hamilton England). David & Charles.

Pierce, J. From Abacus to Zeus: A Handbook of Art History. 1977. pap. text ed. 8.95 (ISBN 0-13-331686-6). P-H.

Pierce, J. R. An Introduction to Information Theory: Symbols, Signals & Noise. 2nd, rev. ed. 320p. pap. write for info. (ISBN 0-486-24061-4). Dover.

Pierce, James S. Paul Klee & Primitive Art. LC 75-23807. (Outstanding Dissertations in the Fine Arts - 20th Century). 1976. lib. bdg. 31.00 (ISBN 0-8240-2001-4). Garland Pub.

Pierce, Joe E. Development of Linguistic System in English Speaking American Children, Vol. 2. 185p. (Orig.). 1981. pap. 8.95 (ISBN 0-913244-51-1). Hapi Pr.

--How English Really Works. LC 79-202. (Illus.). 1979. pap. 11.95 (ISBN 0-913244-18-X). Hapi Pr.

--How English Really Works. 235p. pap. 12.95 (ISBN 0-913244-18-X). Hapi Pr.

--Languages & Linguistics. 2nd ed. 188p. 1980. pap. 11.95 (ISBN 0-913244-23-6). Hapi Pr.

--Languages & Linguistics: An Introduction. 2nd ed. (Illus.). 190p. 1980. pap. 10.95 (ISBN 0-913244-23-6). Hapi Pr.

--A Linguistic Method of Teaching Second Languages. 145p. 1973. pap. 6.95 (ISBN 0-913244-05-8). Hapi Pr.

--A Theory of Language, Culture & Human Behavior. 161p. 1972. pap. 7.95. Hapi Pr.

Pierce, Jotham D., Jr. Construction Contracts in the Eighties. LC 80-80760. (Real Estate Law & Practice Course Handbook Ser.). 896p. 1980. pap. text ed. 25.00 (ISBN 0-686-68821-X, N4-4348). PLI.

Pierce, Judith, jt. auth. see Saurman, Judith.

Pierce, Leona, jt. auth. see De Regniers, Beatrice S.

Pierce, Lucia & Pierce, Lucia. International Training. 1981. pap. 7.95x (ISBN 0-915432-81-1). NE Conf Teach Foreign.

Pierce, Margaret, jt. auth. see Pierce, Robert.

Pierce, Marjorie. East of the Gabilans. LC 76-56566. 190p. 1981. 17.95 (ISBN 0-934136-14-9); pap. 9.95 (ISBN 0-934136-11-4). Western Tanager.

Pierce, Milton. How to Collect Your Overdue Bills: A Guide to Collection Techniques & Customer Relations. LC 80-66023. 1980. 19.95 (ISBN 0-87094-198-4). Dow Jones-Irwin.

Pierce, Milton, jt. auth. see Lee, John W.

Pierce, R. C. & Tebeaux, W. Gene. Operational Mathematics for Business. 512p. 1980. text ed. 16.95x (ISBN 0-534-00789-9). Wadsworth Pub.

Pierce, R. C., Jr., jt. auth. see Anderson, Chaney.

Pierce, Richard A. Russia's Hawaiian Adventure, 1815-1817. (Materials for the Study of Alaska History Ser.: No. 8). (Illus.). 1976. 10.00x (ISBN 0-919642-68-3); pap. 5.50x (ISBN 0-919642-69-1). Limestone Pr.

Pierce, Richard A., ed. Documents for the History of the Russian-American Company. Ramsay, Marina, tr. (Materials for the Study of Alaska History Ser.: No. 7). (Illus.). 1976. 10.00x (ISBN 0-919642-56-X). Limestone Pr.

Pierce, Richard A., ed. see Huggins, Eli L.

Pierce, Richard A., ed. see Shelikhov, Grigorii I.

Pierce, Richard A., ed. see Wrangell, Ferdinand P.

Pierce, Richard J., Jr. Natural Gas Regulation Handbook. 1980. pap. 25.00 (ISBN 0-917386-29-9). Exec Ent.

Pierce, Robert & Pierce, Margaret. High Sierra Hiking Guide to Merced Peak. Winnett, Thomas, ed. LC 72-89915. (High Sierra Hiking Guide Ser: Vol. 11). (Illus., Orig.). 1973. pap. 3.95 (ISBN 0-911824-23-5). Wilderness.

Pierce, Robert, jt. auth. see Pierce, Carole.

Pierce, Ruth, jt. auth. see Baldwin, Linda.

Pierce, W. C., et al. Quantitative Analysis. 4th ed. LC 58-7905. 1958. 23.95 (ISBN 0-471-68904-1). Wiley.

Pierce, Walter D. & Gray, Charles E. Deciphering the Learning Domains: A Second Generation Classification Model for Educational Objectives. LC 79-66225. 1979. pap. text ed. 10.50 (ISBN 0-8191-0816-2). U Pr of Amer.

Pierce, Walter M. Oregon Cattleman, Governor, Congressman: Memoirs & Times of Walter M. Pierce. Bone, Arthur H., ed. LC 80-81718. (Illus.). 528p. 1981. pap. 14.95 (ISBN 0-87595-071-X). Oreg Hist Soc.

Piercey, Dorothy. Reading Activities in Content Areas: An Ideabook for Middle & Secondary Schools. abr. ed. 1976. pap. text ed. 19.95x o.p. (ISBN 0-205-05510-9). Allyn.

Piercy, Marge. Breaking Camp. LC 68-16007. (Wesleyan Poetry Program: Vol. 39). 1968. 10.00x (ISBN 0-8195-2039-X, Pub. by Wesleyan U Pr); pap. 4.95 (ISBN 0-8195-1039-4). Columbia U Pr.

--Hard Loving. LC 70-82544. (Wesleyan Poetry Program: Vol. 46). 1969. 10.00x (ISBN 0-8195-2046-2, Pub. by Wesleyan U Pr); pap. 4.95 (ISBN 0-8195-1046-7). Columbia U Pr.

--The High Cost of Living. LC 77-6149. 1978. 10.00 o.s.i. (ISBN 0-06-013339-2, HarpT). Har-Row.

--Small Changes. 544p. 1978. pap. 2.75 (ISBN 0-449-23671-4, Crest). Fawcett.

Piercy, Marge & Wood, Ira. The Last White Class: A Play About Neighborhood Terror. LC 79-18884. 160p. 1979. 10.95 (ISBN 0-89594-028-0); pap. 4.95 (ISBN 0-89594-027-2). Crossing Pr.

Piermattei, D. L. & Greeley, R. G. An Atlas of Surgical Approaches to the Bones of the Dog & Cat. 2nd ed. LC 77-27755. (Illus.). 1979. text ed. 25.00 (ISBN 0-7216-7241-8). Saunders.

Piero & Chiara. I Giovedi Della Signora Giulia. (Easy Readers, B). 1979. pap. 3.75 (ISBN 0-88436-292-2). EMC.

Pierog, Sophie H., jt. ed. see Dube, Shiv K.

Pieroni, David. Physician Compensation. new ed. LC 78-59104. 1978. text ed. 26.00 (ISBN 0-89443-049-1). Aspen Systems.

Pieroni, Goffredo G., jt. ed. see Freeman, Herbert.

Pieroni, Robert E. Family Practice Review, Vol. 2. LC 79-91973. 1980. pap. 14.50 (ISBN 0-87488-181-1). Med Exam.

--Internal Medicine Review. LC 75-21781. (Arco Medical Review Ser.). pap. text ed. 11.00 (ISBN 0-668-03881-0, 3881). Arco.

--Self-Assessment of Current Knowledge in Rheumatology. 2nd ed. 1976. spiral bdg. 13.00 o.s.i. (ISBN 0-87488-258-3). Med Exam.

Pieroni, Robert E. & Beetham, William P., Jr. Rheumatology. (Medical Examination Review Book: Vol. 31). 1974. spiral bdg. 16.50 (ISBN 0-87488-144-7). Med Exam.

Pieroni, Robert E. & Scutchfield, F. Family Practice Review. 1978. spiral bdg. 16.50 (ISBN 0-87488-134-X). Med Exam.

Pierot, Suzanne. The Ivy Book: The Growing & Care of Ivy & Ivy Topiary. LC 73-1855. (Illus.). 160p. 1974. 8.95 (ISBN 0-02-597500-5). Macmillan.

Pierot, Suzanne W. Suzanne's Cooking Secrets. (Illus.). 1981. 12.95 (ISBN 0-393-01458-4); pap. 5.95 (ISBN 0-393-00055-9). Norton.

Pierpoint, Robert C. At the White House: Assignments to Six Presidents. (Illus.). 192p. 1981. 10.95 (ISBN 0-399-12281-8). Putnam.

Pierpont Morgan Library. British Watercolors, Seventeen Fifty to Eighteen Fifty. (Illus.). 1966. 5.00 (ISBN 0-685-19430-2). Pierpont Morgan.

Pierre, Andrew J. & Moyne, Claudia W. Nuclear Proliferation: A Strategy for Control. LC 76-29317. (Headline Ser.: 232). (Illus., Orig.). 1976. pap. 2.00 (ISBN 0-87124-037-8). Foreign Policy.

Pierre, Jose. An Illustrated Dictionary of Surrealism. (Illus.). (gr. 10-12). 1978. pap. 3.95 (ISBN 0-8120-0987-8). Barron.

--Surrealism. (Masters of Art Ser.). (Illus.). 1979. pap. 3.95 (ISBN 0-8120-2156-8). Barron.

--Symbolism. (Masters of Art Ser.). (Illus.). 1979. pap. 3.95 (ISBN 0-8120-2155-X). Barron.

--Wolfgang Paalen. (Filipacchi Art Ser.). (Illus.). 76p. 1980. 25.00 (ISBN 2-8501-8106-4); pap. cancelled (ISBN 2-85018-095-5). Hippocrene Bks.

Pierre, Joseph H. When Timber Stood Tall. LC 79-21006. (Illus.). 192p. 1980. 19.95 (ISBN 0-87564-909-2). Superior Pub.

Pierrot-Bults, A. C., jt. ed. see Van der Spoel, S.

Piers, Anthony. Split Infinity. 368p. 1981. pap. 2.50 (ISBN 0-345-28213-2, Del Rey). Ballantine.

Piers, Helen. Kitten Book & Other Stories. (Illus.). (gr. k-3). 1970. PLB 4.90 o.p. (ISBN 0-531-01934-9). Watts.

Piers, Maria W. & Landau, Genevieve M. The Gift of Play. 123p. 1980. 9.95 (ISBN 0-8027-0657-6). Walker & Co.

Piersol, Allan G., jt. auth. see Bendat, Julius S.

Pierson, Arthur T. George Muller of Bristol. 1971. 9.95 (ISBN 0-8007-0106-2). Revell.

Pierson, Daniel J. Man & Woman Teacher Manual. rev. ed. (To Live in Christ Ser.). 264p. 1980. pap. 4.75 (ISBN 0-697-01751-6). Wm C Brown.

Pierson, Frank C. The Minimum Level of Unemployment & Public Policy. 194p. 1980. text ed. 8.50 (ISBN 0-911558-76-4); pap. text ed. 5.50 (ISBN 0-911558-75-6). Upjohn Inst.

Pierson, Jack D. What a Teenager Ought to Know About Sex & God. (Teenager's Essential Education Library). (Illus.). 147p. 1981. 21.75 (ISBN 0-89266-288-3). Am Classical Coll Pr.

Pierson, John H. Full Employment Without Inflation. LC 79-5446. 254p. 1980. text ed. 18.50 (ISBN 0-916672-39-5). Allanheld.

Pierson, Lance, jt. auth. see Mandeville, Sylvia.

Pierson, R. H. So You Want to Be a Leader. LC 66-20341. (Dimension Ser.). pap. 5.95 (ISBN 0-8163-0156-5, 19410-0). Pacific Pr Pub Assn.

Pierson, R. H. & Stevenson, G. S. Final Countdown. LC 66-23433. (Stories That Win Ser.). 1966. pap. 0.95 o.p. (ISBN 0-8163-0118-2, 06100-2). Pacific Pr Pub Assn.

Pierson, Richard N., Jr., et al, eds. Quantitative Nuclear Cardiography. LC 74-201990. 304p. 1975. text ed. 37.50 o.p. (ISBN 0-471-68950-5, Pub. by Wiley Medical). Wiley.

Pierson, Robert. What's Just Ahead. LC 78-14219. (Flame Ser.). 1978. pap. 0.95 (ISBN 0-8127-0203-4). Southern Pub.

Pierson, Vernon C. The New Attempts at the Monetization of Gold & Their Meaning for the Future of the World. (Illus.). 127p. 1980. 49.75 (ISBN 0-918968-72-0). Inst Econ Finan.

Pierson, W. J., jt. auth. see Neumann, Gerhard.

Pierson, Welcome D. Defense Attorney & Basic Defense Tactics. 1956. incl. 1966 suppl. 15.00 (ISBN 0-672-80022-5, Bobbs-Merrill Law); 1966 suppl. 6.00 (ISBN 0-672-80024-1). Michie.

Piesinger, Gregory H. Nuclear Radiation: What It Is, How to Detect It, How to Protect Yourself from It. (Illus.). 150p. (Orig.). 1980. pap. 9.95 (ISBN 0-937224-00-6). Dyco Inc.

Piest, Oskar, ed. see Mill, John S.

Piest, Oskar, ed. see Plato.

Piet, John H. A Path Through the Bible. 1981. pap. 8.95 (ISBN 0-664-24369-X). Westminster.

Pieters, Eli E. The Statue of Pedro Vito. 1981. 4.95 (ISBN 0-8062-1671-9). Carlton.

Pieters, Richard S., jt. auth. see Lux, J. Richard.

Pietersma, Albert, et al. The Apocalypse of Elijah. LC 79-24788. 1981. price not set (ISBN 0-89130-371-5, 060219); pap. 7.50 (ISBN 0-89130-372-3). Scholars Pr CA.

Pietrasinski, Z. The Art of Learning. 1969. 21.00 (ISBN 0-08-012019-9). Pergamon.

--The Psychology of Efficient Thinking. 1969. 27.00 (ISBN 0-08-012544-1). Pergamon.

Pietri, Paul H., Jr., jt. auth. see Mosley, Donald C.

Pietri, Pedro. Puerto Rican Obituary. LC 73-8058. 144p. 1974. 7.50 o.p. (ISBN 0-85345-300-4, CL-3004). Monthly Rev.

Pietropinto, Anthony & Congress, Elaine. The Clinic. 1981. 11.95 (ISBN 0-8129-0887-2). Times Bks.

Pietrzyk, Donald J. & Frank, Clyde. Analytical Chemistry. 2nd ed. 700p. 1979. 18.95 (ISBN 0-12-555160-6); pap. text ed. 3.00 instr's manual (ISBN 0-12-555162-2). Acad Pr.

Pietsch, Paul. Shufflebrain. (Illus.). 288p. 1981. 10.95 (ISBN 0-395-29480-0). HM.

Pietsch, William V. Human Be-Ing: How to Have a Creative Relationship Instead of a Power Struggle. 1975. pap. 1.95 (ISBN 0-451-08784-4, J8784, Sig). NAL.

--Human Be-Ing: How to Have a Creative Relationship Instead of a Power Struggle. LC 73-20379. 256p. 1974. 7.95 o.p. (ISBN 0-88208-042-3). Lawrence Hill.

Pietschmann, D., jt. ed. see Boeninger, Hildegard R.

Pigeaud, Theodore G. Literature of Java: Supplement Catalogue Raisonne of Javanese Manuscripts in the Library of the University of Leiden & Other Public Collections in the Netherlands. (Codices Manuscript Ser.: No. XX). (Illus.). 390p. 1980. pap. 64.10 (ISBN 90-6021-453-6, Pub. by Leiden University Press). Kluwer Boston.

Pigg, R. Morgan, jt. auth. see Rash, J. Keogh.

Piggott, Derek. Beginning Gliding: The Fundamentals of Soaring Flight. (Illus.). 1977. 20.00x (ISBN 0-06-495569-9). B&N.

--Gliding: A Handbook on Soaring Flight. 4th ed. (Illus.). 270p. 1976. 18.50x (ISBN 0-06-495570-2). B&N.

--Going Solo: A Simple Guide to Soaring. (Illus.). 112p. 1978. pap. 8.95x. B&N.

Piggott, F. T. The Music & Musical Instruments of Japan. LC 70-155234. (Music Ser). 1971. Repr. of 1909 ed. lib. bdg. 22.50 (ISBN 0-306-70160-X). Da Capo.

Piggott, Michael R. Load-Bearing Composite Materials. 1980. 39.00 (ISBN 0-08-024230-8); pap. 15.00 (ISBN 0-08-024231-6). Pergamon.

Piggott, Patrick. The Life & Music of John Field, 1782-1837: Creator of the Nocturne. (Illus.). 1974. 37.50x (ISBN 0-520-02412-5). U of Cal Pr.

Piggott, S., ed. The Agrarian History of England & Wales, Vol. 1, Pt. 1: Prehistory. LC 66-19763. (Agrarian History of England & Wales Ser.). Date not set. 64.50 (ISBN 0-521-08741-4). Cambridge U Pr.

Piggott, Stuart. Ancient Europe: From the Beginnings of Agriculture to Classical Antiquity. LC 64-21369. (Illus.). 1966. 22.95x (ISBN 0-202-33002-8). Aldine Pub.

--Ruins in a Landscape. 1976. 12.00x (ISBN 0-85224-303-0, Pub. by Edinburgh U Pr Scotland); pap. 6.95 (ISBN 0-85224-311-1). Columbia U Pr.

Piggott, Stuart, ed. The Prehistoric Peoples of Scotland. LC 80-27371. (Studies in Ancient History & Archaeology). (Illus.). ix, 165p. 1981. Repr. of 1962 ed. lib. bdg. 25.00x (ISBN 0-313-22916-3, PIPR). Greenwood.

Pigman, W. Carbohydrates: Chemistry & Biochemistry, Vol. 1b. 2nd ed. LC 68-26647. 1981. 69.50 (ISBN 0-12-556351-5). Acad Pr.

Pigman, W. & Horton, D. The Carbohydrates. 2nd ed. Incl. Vol. 1A. 1972. 68.50 (ISBN 0-12-556301-9); subscription 58.75 (ISBN 0-686-66782-4); Vol. 2A. 1970. 56.00, subscription 48.00 (ISBN 0-12-556302-7); Vol. 2B. 1970. 72.50, subscription 62.00 (ISBN 0-12-556352-3). Acad Pr.

Pigman, Ward & Wolfrom, Melville L., eds. Advances in Carbohydrate Chemistry. Incl. Vol. 1. 1945 (ISBN 0-12-007201-7); Vol. 2. 1946 (ISBN 0-12-007202-5); Vol. 3. 1948 (ISBN 0-12-007203-3); Vol. 4. 1949 (ISBN 0-12-007204-1); Vol. 5. Hudson, C. S. & Cantor, S. M., eds. 1950 (ISBN 0-12-007205-X); Vol. 6. 1951 (ISBN 0-12-007206-8); Vol. 7. Hudson, C. S., et al, eds. 1952 (ISBN 0-12-007207-6); Vol. 8. Hudson, C. S. & Wolfrom, Melville, eds. 1953 (ISBN 0-12-007208-4); Vol. 9. Wolfrom, Melville L. & Tipson, R. Stuart, eds. 1954 (ISBN 0-12-007209-2); Vol. 10. 1955 (ISBN 0-12-007210-6); Vol. 11. 1956 (ISBN 0-12-007211-4); Vol. 12. 1957 (ISBN 0-12-007212-2); Vol. 13. 1958 (ISBN 0-12-007213-0); Vol. 14. 1959 (ISBN 0-12-007214-9); Vol. 15. 1960 (ISBN 0-12-007215-7); Vol. 16. 1962 (ISBN 0-12-007216-5); Vol. 17. 1963 (ISBN 0-12-007217-3); Vol. 18. 1963 (ISBN 0-12-007218-1); Vol. 19. 1964 (ISBN 0-12-007219-X); Vol. 20. 1965 (ISBN 0-12-007220-3); Vol. 21. 1967 (ISBN 0-12-007221-1); Vol. 22. 1967 (ISBN 0-12-007222-X); Vol. 23. **1968 (ISBN 0-12-007223-8); Vol. 24. 1970 (ISBN 0-12-007224-6); Vol. 25. 1971. 49.50 (ISBN 0-12-007225-4); Vol. 26. Tipson, Stuart R. & Horton, Derek, eds. 1971. 49.50 (ISBN 0-12-007226-2); Vol. 27. 1972. 49.50 (ISBN 0-12-007227-0); Vol. 28. 1973. 58.00 (ISBN 0-12-007228-9); Vol. 29. 1974. 58.00 (ISBN 0-12-007229-7). Vols. 1-19. 49.50 ea.; Vols. 20-24. 49.50 ea. Acad Pr.**

Pignani, Tullio J. & Haggard, Paul W. Modern Analytic Geometry. 1970. text ed. 14.95x o.p. (ISBN 0-669-49536-0); instructor's guide gratis o.p. (ISBN 0-669-49544-1). Heath.

Pignataro, Louis J. Traffic Engineering: Theory & Practice. (Illus.). 512p. 1973. 28.95 (ISBN 0-13-926220-2). P-H.

Pignoria, Lorenzo & Orgel, Stephen, eds. Vere e Nove Imagini de gli Dei delli Antichi. LC 78-68193. (The Renaissance & the Gods: the Philosophy of Images Ser.). (Illus.). 1980. lib. bdg. 66.00 (ISBN 0-8240-3686-7). Garland Pub.

Pigors, Faith, jt. auth. see Pigors, Paul.

Pigors, Paul & Myers, Charles A. Personnel Administration: A Point of View & a Method. 9th ed. (Illus.). 560p. 1981. text ed. 18.95x (ISBN 0-07-049971-3, C); instructor's manual 7.95 (ISBN 0-07-049972-1). McGraw.

Pigors, Paul & Pigors, Faith. The Pigors Incident Process of Case Study. LC 79-23530. 1980. 13.95 (ISBN 0-87778-149-4). Educ Tech Pubns.

Pigou, A. C., jt. auth. see Rountree, B. Seebohm.

Pigou, Arthur C. Essays in Applied Economics. Repr. of 1930 ed. 21.00x (ISBN 0-678-05077-5). Kelley.

Pijlman, F. The Grebe. (Animal Environment Ser.). (Illus.). 30p. 1980. 4.95 (ISBN 0-8120-5377-X). Barron.

Pijpers, F. W., jt. auth. see Kateman, G.

Pikarsky, Milton & Christensen, Daphne. Urban Transportation Policy & Management. (Illus.). 1976. 22.95 (ISBN 0-669-00955-5). Lexington Bks.

Pike, Arnold. Viewpoint on Nutrition. LC 80-24024. 221p. 1980. Repr. of 1973 ed. lib. bdg. 9.95x (ISBN 0-89370-621-3). Borgo Pr.

Pike, Arthur, jt. auth. see Popkin, Gary.

Pike, Arthur L., jt. auth. see Timbie, William H.

Pike, Arthur M., jt. auth. see Popkin, Gary S.

Pike, Charles R. Ashes & Blood. LC 80-70093. (Jubal Cade Westerns Ser.). 160p. 1981. pap. 2.95 (ISBN 0-87754-242-2). Chelsea Hse.

--Bounty Road. LC 80-70092. (Jubal Cade Westerns Ser.). 142p. 1981. pap. 2.95 (ISBN 0-87754-241-4). Chelsea Hse.

--Brand of Vengeance. LC 80-70091. (Jubal Cade Westerns Ser.). 142p. 1981. pap. 2.95 (ISBN 0-87754-240-6). Chelsea Hse.

--The Burning Man. LC 80-69220. (Jubal Cade Westerns Ser.). 128p. 1980. pap. 2.95 (ISBN 0-87754-235-X). Chelsea Hse.

--Days of Blood. LC 80-69749. (Jubal Cade Westerns Ser.). 125p. 1981. pap. 2.95 (ISBN 0-87754-238-4). Chelsea Hse.

--Death Wears Grey. LC 80-69221. (Jubal Cade Westerns Ser.). 144p. 1981. pap. 2.95 (ISBN 0-87754-237-6). Chelsea Hse.

--Double Cross. LC 80-68160. (Jubal Cade Westerns Ser.). 128p. 1980. pap. 2.95 (ISBN 0-87754-231-7). Chelsea Hse.

--The Golden Dead. LC 80-69219. (Jubal Cade Westerns Ser.). 128p. 1981. pap. 2.95 (ISBN 0-87754-236-8). Chelsea Hse.

--The Hungry Gun. LC 80-68158. (Jubal Cade Westerns Ser.). 112p. 1980. pap. 2.95 (ISBN 0-87754-232-5). Chelsea Hse.

--Killer Silver. LC 80-68163. (Jubal Cade Westerns Ser.). 144p. 1980. pap. 2.95 (ISBN 0-87754-233-3). Chelsea Hse.

--The Killing Ground. LC 80-70090. (Jubal Cade Westerns Ser.). 144p. 1981. pap. 2.95 (ISBN 0-87754-239-2). Chelsea Hse.

--The Killing Trail. LC 80-68159. (Jubal Cade Westerns Ser.). 128p. 1980. pap. 2.95 (ISBN 0-87754-230-9). Chelsea Hse.

--Vengeance Hunt. LC 80-69218. (Jubal Cade Westerns Ser.). 128p. 1980. pap. 2.95 (ISBN 0-87754-234-1). Chelsea Hse.

Pike, D. Australia: The Quiet Continent. 2nd ed. (Illus.). 1970. 29.95 (ISBN 0-521-07745-1); pap. 9.95x (ISBN 0-521-09604-9, 365). Cambridge U Pr.

Pike, Diane K. A Roadmap for Seekers of the Journey into Self. (Illus., Orig.). 1981. pap. price not set (ISBN 0-916192-17-2). L P Pubns.

Pike, Diane K., jt. auth. see Lorrance, Arleen.

Pike, Donald & Muench, David. Big Sur. DenDooven, Gweneth R., ed. LC 78-51408. (Illus.). 1979. 8.95 (ISBN 0-916122-68-9); pap. 3.75 (ISBN 0-916122-67-0). K C Pubns.

Pike, Earl A. Protection Against Bombs & Incendiaries: For Business, Industrial & Educational Institutions. (Illus.). 92p. 1973. 9.50 (ISBN 0-398-02517-7). C C Thomas.

Pike, James. Scout & Ranger. LC 74-39282. (The American Scene Ser). (Illus.). 164p. 1972. Repr. of 1932 ed. lib. bdg. 19.50 (ISBN 0-306-70458-7). Da Capo.

Pike, James A. Beyond the Law. LC 73-10754. 102p. 1974. Repr. of 1963 ed. lib. bdg. 11.75x (ISBN 0-8371-7021-4, PIBL). Greenwood.

Pike, James A. & Pittenger, W. Norman. Faith of the Church. (Orig.). 1951. pap. 3.95 (ISBN 0-8164-2019-X, SP3). Crossroad NY.

Pike, Kenneth L. Phonemics: A Technique for Reducing Language to Writing. 1947. pap. 6.50x (ISBN 0-472-08732-0). U of Mich Pr.

--Phonetics: A Critical Analysis of Phonetic Theory & a Technic for the Practical Description of Sounds. 1943. pap. 6.50x (ISBN 0-472-08733-9). U of Mich Pr.

--Tone Languages: A Technique for Determining the Number & Type of Pitch Contrasts in a Language, with Studies in Tonemic Substitution & Fusion. 1948. pap. 6.95x (ISBN 0-472-08734-7). U of Mich Pr.

Pike, Kenneth L., jt. ed. see Brend, Ruthm M.

Pike, Lionel. Beethoven, Sibelius & "the Profound Logic". (Studies in Symphonic Analysis). (Illus.). 1978. text ed. 44.25x (ISBN 0-485-11178-0, Athlone Pr). Humanities.

Pike, Nelson. God & Evil: Reading on the Theological Problem of Evil. 1964. pap. 7.95 ref. ed (ISBN 0-13-357665-5). P-H.

Pike, Nelson, ed. see Hume, David.

Pike, Robert M., et al, eds. Innovation in Access to Higher Education: Ontario, Canada,England, Wales, & Sweden. (Access to Higher Education Ser.: No. 5). 336p. 1978. pap. 10.00 (ISBN 0-89192-217-2, Pub. by Intl Coun Ed Dev). Interbk Inc.

Pike, Royston E. Britain's Prime Ministers from Walpole to Wilson. (Illus.). 1970. 8.95 (ISBN 0-600-72032-2). Transatlantic.

--Human Documents of the Lloyd George Era. (Illus.). 272p. 1972. text ed. 9.95x (ISBN 0-04-942098-4, 9095). Allen Unwin.

Pike, Royston E, ed. Human Documents of Adam Smith's Time. 1973. pap. text ed. 9.95x (ISBN 0-04-942119-0). Allen Unwin.

Pike, Royston E., ed. Human Documents of the Industrial Revolution in Britain. 1966. text ed. 13.50x o.p. (ISBN 0-04-942059-3); pap. text ed. 12.50x (ISBN 0-04-942060-7). Allen Unwin.

--Human Documents of the Victorian Golden Age. 1967. text ed. 12.50x o.p. (ISBN 0-04-942068-2); pap. text ed. 9.50x (ISBN 0-04-942136-0). Allen Unwin.

Pike, Ruth. Aristocrats & Traders: Sevillian Society in the Sixteenth Century. LC 76-37756. 256p. 1972. 17.50 (ISBN 0-8014-0699-4). Cornell U Pr.

Pike, S. W., jt. auth. see Agnew, Neil M.

Pikelner, S. B., jt. auth. see Kaplan, S. A.

Pikelny, Philip S., jt. auth. see Evans, Donald P.

Pikl, Barbara H., ed. see Massachusetts General Hospital Pediatric Nursing Service.

Piland, Sherry, jt. auth. see Bachmann, Donna G.

Pilapil, F. & Studva, K., eds. Programmed Instruction: Radiation Therapy. 55p. 1979. pap. 6.50 (ISBN 0-89352-099-3). Masson Pub.

--Programmed Instruction: Understanding Cancer & Chemotherapy. 80p. 1979. pap. 6.50 (ISBN 0-89352-081-0). Masson Pub.

Pilat, J. F. Ecological Politics: The Rise of the Green Movement. LC 80-52547. (The Washington Papers: No. 77). 96p. 1980. pap. 3.50 (ISBN 0-8039-1535-7). Sage.

Pilch, John J. Wellness: Your Invitation to Full Life. Frost, Miriam, ed. Orig. Title: Wellness. 128p. (Orig.). 1981. pap. text ed. 5.95 (ISBN 0-03-059062-0). Winston Pr.

--What Are They Saying About the Book of Revelation? LC 78-51594. 1978. pap. 2.45 (ISBN 0-8091-2126-3). Paulist Pr.

Pilch, Judith, jt. auth. see Neff, Herbert.

Pilch, Michael & Wood, V. Pension Schemes. 1979. text ed. 34.25x (ISBN 0-566-02117-X, Pub. by Gower Pub Co England). Renouf.

Pilcher, G., jt. auth. see Cox, J. D.

Pilcher, George W. Samuel Davies: Apostle of Dissent in Colonial Virginia. LC 77-134737. 1971. 13.50x (ISBN 0-87049-121-0). U of Tenn Pr.

Pilcher, Mary A. Macrame. 1972. 5.50 o.p. (ISBN 0-8231-5038-0). Branford.

Pilcher, Rosamunde. The Day of the Storm. LC 75-26190. 1976. 7.95 o.p. (ISBN 0-312-18445-X). St Martin.

--The End of the Summer. 160p. 1976. pap. 1.25 o.p. (ISBN 0-345-24858-9). Ballantine.

--Under Gemini. LC 75-26192. 1976. 8.95 o.p. (ISBN 0-312-82915-9). St Martin.

Pildas, Ave, photos by. Art Deco Los Angeles. LC 77-4581. (Illus.). 1977. pap. 4.95 o.s.i. (ISBN 0-06-013338-4, TD-295, HarpT). Har-Row.

Pilecki, Francis J., jt. auth. see Immegart, Glenn L.

Pileggi, Stephen. If You Love Your Kids, Don't Let Them Grow up to Be Jerks. LC 80-16882. (Open Mind Bk.). 64p. (Orig.). 1980. pap. 4.95 (ISBN 0-916392-58-9). Oak Tree Pubns.

--Why Not Be for Real? LC 80-17814. (Open Mind Bk.). 64p. (Orig.). 1980. pap. 4.95 (ISBN 0-916392-57-0). Oak Tree Pubns.

Pilgrim, C. E. New Siwalik Primates: Their Bearing on the Question of Evolution of Man & the Anthropoidea. Bd. with A Sivapithecus Palate. LC 77-86436. (India Geological Survey. Records of the Geological Survey of India: Vol. 45). 1977. Repr. of 1915 ed. 15.00 (ISBN 0-404-16675-X). AMS Pr.

Pilhes, Rene-Victor. The Provocateur. Lindley, Denver & Lindley, Helen, trs. from Fr. LC 76-5555. 1977. 10.00 o.s.i. (ISBN 0-06-013337-6, HarpT). Har-Row.

Piliavin, Jane A., et al, eds. Emergency Intervention. 1981. price not set (ISBN 0-12-556450-3). Acad Pr.

Piliawsky, Monte. Exit Thirteen. LC 78-59599. 1979. 10.00 o.p. (ISBN 0-89430-026-1). Morgan-Pacific.

Pilinszky, Janos. Selected Poems. Hughes, Ted & Csokits, Janos, trs. LC 76-52273. 1977. 8.95 (ISBN 0-89255-017-1); pap. 4.95 (ISBN 0-89255-018-X). Persea Bks.

Pilkey, Walter D. & Perrone, Nicholas, eds. Structural Mechanics Software Series, Vol. III. (Illus.). 450p. 1980. 25.00x (ISBN 0-8139-0857-4). U Pr of Va.

Pilkey, Walter D., jt. ed. see Moyar, Gerald J.

Pilkington, A. E. Bergson and His Influence. LC 75-22555. 300p. 1976. 45.00 (ISBN 0-521-20971-4). Cambridge U Pr.

Pilkington, A. E., ed. Appollinaire Guillaume: Alcools. (French Texts Ser.). 1970. pap. text ed. 10.00x (ISBN 0-631-00710-5, Pub. by Basil Blackwell). Biblio Dist.

Pilkington, James P. Methodist Publishing House: A History, Vol. 1. (Illus.). 1968. 7.50 (ISBN 0-687-26700-5). Abingdon.

Pilkington, John, jt. auth. see Bradt, Hilary.

Pilkington, William T. Critical Essays on the Western American Novel. (Reference Bks). 1980. lib. bdg. 25.00 (ISBN 0-8161-8351-1). G K Hall.

--Harvey Fergusson. (U. S. Authors Ser.: No. 257). 1975. lib. bdg. 10.95 (ISBN 0-8057-7157-3). Twayne.

Pilkington, William T & Graham, Don, eds. Western Movies. LC 78-21427. (Illus.). 184p. 1979. 13.95 o.p. (ISBN 0-8263-0496-6); pap. 6.95 (ISBN 0-8263-0497-4). U of NM Pr.

Pillai, S. Devadas, ed. Winners & Losers: Styles of Development & Change in an Indian Region. Baks, C. 407p. 1979. text ed. 36.00 (ISBN 0-8426-1679-9). Verry.

Pillai, Thakazhi S. Chemmeen. Menon, Narayana, tr. 221p. 1964. pap. 3.00 (ISBN 0-88253-066-6). Ind-US Inc.

--Scavenger's Son. Asher, R. E., tr. from Malayalam. 143p. 1975. pap. 2.50 (ISBN 0-89253-025-1). Ind-US Inc.

--The Unchaste. Bhaskaran, M. K., tr. 112p. 1971. pap. 2.10 (ISBN 0-88253-067-4). Ind-US Inc.

Pillai, Velu R. & Panikar, P. G. Land Reclamation in Kerala. 1965. 10.50x o.p. (ISBN 0-210-31242-4). Asia.

Pillay, Bala. British Indians in the Transvaal: Trade, Politics & Imperial Relations, 1885-1906. 1977. text ed. 11.00x (ISBN 0-582-64201-9). Longman.

Pillin, William. The Abandoned Music Room. (Illus.). 60p. 1975. pap. 2.00 o.p. (ISBN 0-87711-059-X). Kayak.

--Pavanne for a Fading Memory. LC 63-16650. 82p. 1963. 5.00 (ISBN 0-8040-0240-1). Swallow.

Pilling, Doria. The Child with a Chronic Medical Problem: Cardiac Disorders, Diabetes, Haemophilia, Social, Emotional, & Educational Adjustment. (General Ser.). 60p. 1973. pap. text ed. 6.25x (ISBN 0-85633-027-2, NFER). Humanities.

--The Child with Asthma: Social, Emotional & Educational Adjustment - an Annotated Bibliography. (General Ser.). 84p. 1975. pap. text ed. 7.00x (ISBN 0-85633-071-X, NFER). Humanities.

--The Child with Cerebral Palsy: Social, Emotional & Educational Adjustment: an Annotated Bibliography. (General Ser.). 61p. (Orig.). 1973. pap. text ed. 7.00x (ISBN 0-85633-016-7, NFER). Humanities.

--The Child with Spinal Bifida: Social, Emotional, & Educational Adjustment, an Annotated Bibliography. (General Ser.). 1973. pap. text ed. 6.25x (ISBN 0-85633-021-3, NFER). Humanities.

--Orthopaedically Handicapped Child: Social, Emotional & Educational Adjustment, an Annotated Bibliography to the End of 1964. (General Ser). 60p. (Orig.). 1973. pap. text ed. 6.25x (ISBN 0-85633-004-3, NFER). Humanities.

Pilling, John. Autobiography & Imagination: Studies in Self-Scrutiny. 200p. 1981. price not set (ISBN 0-7100-0730-2). Routledge & Kegan.

--Samuel Beckett. 1976. 18.00 (ISBN 0-7100-8323-8). Routledge & Kegan.

Pilling, John, jt. auth. see Knowlson, James.

Pilling, M. J. Reaction Kinetics. (Oxford Chemistry Ser). (Illus.). 144p. 1975. 24.95x (ISBN 0-19-855481-8). Oxford U Pr.

Pillitteri, Adele. Child Health Nursing: Care of the Growing Family. 2nd ed. 1981. text ed. write for info (ISBN 0-316-70793-7). Little.

--Maternal-Newborn Nursing: Care of the Growing Family. 2nd ed. 1981. text ed. write for info. (ISBN 0-316-70792-9). Little.

Pillsbury, Barbara L. Mosque & Pagoda: The Muslim Chinese. 344p. Date not set. text ed. cancelled (ISBN 0-292-75056-0). U of Tex Pr.

Pillsbury, Donald M. & Heaton, Charles L. A Manual of Dermatology. 2nd ed. LC 79-3927. (Illus.). 360p. 1980. text ed. 25.00 (ISBN 0-7216-7242-6). Saunders.

Pillsbury, Dorothy L. Star Over Adobe. LC 63-21376. (Illus.). 1977. pap. 3.95 (ISBN 0-8263-0179-7). U of NM Pr.

Pillsbury, Kent L., et al. Social Issues & Education in the America Urban & Suburban Society: A Textbook for Teacher Education. LC 76-6887. 260p. 1977. 16.95 (ISBN 0-88229-154-8). Nelson-Hall.

Pil'Niak, Boris. Golyi God. 79p. (Orig., Rus.). 1980. 12.00 o.p. (ISBN 0-88233-452-2); pap. 5.00 (ISBN 0-88233-453-0). Ardis Pubs.

Pilon, A. Barbara. Teaching Language Arts Creatively in the Elementary Grades. LC 77-23508. 1978. 13.50 (ISBN 0-471-68980-7). Wiley.

Pilot Books Staff, jt. auth. see Small, Samuel.

Piltch, Benjamin. Popular Stars. 64p. (gr. 3-7). 1980. 3.50 (ISBN 0-934618-02-X). Skyview Pub.

Piltch, Benjamin, ed. see Funes, Marilyn & Lazarus, Alan.

Piltz, Albert & Sund, Robert. Creative Teaching of Science in the Elementary School. 2nd ed. 320p. 1974. pap. text ed. 11.95x (ISBN 0-205-04278-3). Allyn.

Piltz, Anders. The World of Medieval Learning. Jones, Davis, tr. (Illus.). 1981. 30.00x (ISBN 0-389-20206-1). B&N.

Pim, Alan. Financial & Economic History of the African Tropical Territories. 1970. Repr. of 1940 ed. 15.00 (ISBN 0-87266-046-X). Argosy.

Pim, Linda. The Invisible Additives: Environmental Contamination of Food. 195p. 1981. 9.95 (ISBN 0-385-17001-7); pap. 6.95 (ISBN 0-385-17002-5). Doubleday.

Pimentel, David. Food, Energy & Future of Society. 1980. pap. 3.00x (ISBN 0-87081-089-8). Colo Assoc.

Pimentel, David & Pimentel, Marcia. Food, Energy & Society. LC 79-9484. 1979. pap. 14.95x (ISBN 0-470-26840-9). Halsted Pr.

Pimentel, David, ed. Handbook of Pest Management in Agriculture. 1981. Vol. 1. 69.95 (ISBN 0-8493-3841-7); Vol. 2. 67.95 (ISBN 0-8493-3842-5); Vol. 3. 69.95 (ISBN 0-8493-3843-3). CRC Pr.

--World Food, Pest Losses & the Environment. LC 77-90418. (AAAS Selected Symposium Ser.: No. 13). (Illus.). 1978. lib. bdg. 22.00x (ISBN 0-89158-441-2). Westview.

Pimentel, David & Perkins, John H., eds. Pest Control: Cultural & Environmental Aspects. LC 79-18516. (AAAS Selected Symposium: No. 43). (Illus.). 243p. 1980. lib. bdg. 22.00x (ISBN 0-89158-753-5). Westview.

Pimentel, George C. & Spratley, Richard D. Understanding Chemistry. LC 70-142944. 1971. 26.50x (ISBN 0-8162-6761-8); solution manual o.p. 6.95 (ISBN 0-8162-6741-3). Holden-Day.

Pimentel, George C., ed. Chemistry: An Experimental Science. LC 63-18323. (Chemical Education Material Study). (Illus.). 1963. text ed. 11.95x (ISBN 0-7167-0001-8); tchrs guide o.p. 14.95x (ISBN 0-7167-0003-4); lab manual ed. by Lloyd E Malm 2.00x (ISBN 0-7167-0002-6). W H Freeman.

Pimentel, Marcia, jt. auth. see Pimentel, David.

Pimlott, Douglas H., jt. auth. see Rutter, Russell J.

Pimlott, John, jt. auth. see Willmott, Ned.

Pimsleur. Opinions, Committees on Professional Ethics, Release 1. 1980. 150.00 (ISBN 0-379-20670-6). Oceana.

Pimsleur, M. G., ed. Checklists of Basic American Legal Publications, 5 pts. Incl. Pt. 1. Statutes; Pt. 2. Session Laws; Pt. 3. Attorneys General Opinions & Reports; Pt. 4. Judicial Councils; Pt. 5. Restatements. (AALL Publications Ser: No. 4). (5 sections with 1978 supplement). looseleaf bdg., 1978 supplement incl. 140.00x (ISBN 0-8377-0104-X). Rothman.

Pimsleur, Meira G. Opinions: Committees on Professional Ethics: the Association of the Bar of the City of New York, the New York County Lawyer's Association, New York State Bar Association. LC 80-14204. 1000p. 1980. Set. looseleaf bdg. 150.00 (ISBN 0-379-20670-6). Oceana.

Pimsleur, Meura G. Law Book Published, 1975-1977. 50.00 (ISBN 0-686-60607-8, 1971-1977); 85.00. ea. (1980-1981); 70.00 (ISBN 0-686-60608-6, 1980). Glanville.

Pimsleur, Paul & Quinn, Terence, eds. Psychology of Second Language Learning. (Illus.). 1971. 27.50 (ISBN 0-521-08236-6). Cambridge U Pr.

Pinar, William. Heightened Consciousness, Cultural Revolution, & Curriculum Theory. LC 73-17615. 1974. 15.25 (ISBN 0-8211-1511-1); text ed. 13.75 (ISBN 0-685-42641-6). McCutchan.

Pinar, William, ed. Curriculum Theorizing: The Reconceptualists. LC 74-12821. 472p. 1974. 15.75 o.p. (ISBN 0-8211-1513-8); text ed. 14.15 o.p. (ISBN 0-685-52300-4). McCutchan.

Pinard, Adrien. The Conservation of Conservation: The Child's Acquisition of a Fundamental Concept. Feider, Helga, tr. LC 80-26339. (Chicago Originals Ser.). 200p. 1981. lib. bdg. 14.00x (ISBN 0-226-66834-7). U of Chicago Pr.

Pinaud, Yves-Louis. Sailing from Start to Finish. 1979. 19.95 (ISBN 0-229-11548-9, Scribner-T). Scribner.

Pinay, Maurice. The Plot Against the Church. 1978. 15.00x (ISBN 0-911038-39-6). Noontide.

Pinchbeck, Ivy. Women Workers & the Industrial Revolution, 1750-1850. LC 75-96378. Repr. of 1930 ed. 25.00x (ISBN 0-678-05106-2). Kelley.

Pincherle, L. Worked Problems in Heat, Thermodynamics & Kinetic Theory. 1966. 22.00 (ISBN 0-08-012016-4); pap. 10.75 (ISBN 0-08-012015-6). Pergamon.

Pincherle, Marc. Corelli. (Music Reprint Ser.). 1979. Repr. of 1956 ed. lib. bdg. 22.50 (ISBN 0-306-79576-0). Da Capo.

Pinchot, Ann. Certain Rich Girls. 288p. 1980. pap. 2.50 (ISBN 0-553-13195-8). Bantam.

--Doctors & Wives. 352p. 1981. pap. 2.75 (ISBN 0-553-14804-4). Bantam.

Pinchot, Gifford. The Fight for Conservation. LC 10-19948. (Americana Library Ser.: No. 5). 180p. 1967. Repr. of 1910 ed. 10.50 (ISBN 0-295-97861-9, AL5). U of Wash Pr.

--To the South Seas; the Cruise of the Schooner Mary Pinchot to the Galapogos, the Marquesas, & the Tuamotu Islands, & Tahiti. LC 70-174094. (Illus.). xiv, 500p. 1972. Repr. of 1930 ed. 24.00 (ISBN 0-8103-3933-1). Gale.

Pinchot, Jane. Mexicans in America. rev. ed. (In America Bks.). (Illus.). 104p. (gr. 5-11). PLB 5.95. Lerner Pubns.

--Mexicans in America. LC 72-3587. (In America Bks.). (Illus.). 104p. (gr. 5-11). 1973. PLB 5.95 o.p. (ISBN 0-8225-0222-4). Lerner Pubns.

Pinchuck, Isadore. Scientific & Technical Translation. LC 77-4933. 1977. lib. bdg. 23.50 o.p. (ISBN 0-89158-737-3). Westview.

Pinckney, Richard P., jt. auth. see Evett, Jack.

Pincus, Allen & Minahan, Anne. Social Work Practice: Model & Method. LC 73-82647. 355p. 1973. text ed. 12.95 (ISBN 0-87581-132-9). Peacock Pubs.

Pincus, Cynthia, et al. The Roots of Success. LC 80-18462. 1980. 8.95 (ISBN 0-13-783258-3). P-H.

Pincus, Debra. The Arco Foscari: the Building of a Triumphal Gateway in Fifteenth Century Venice. LC 75-23808. (Outstanding Dissertations in the Fine Arts - Fifteenth Century). (Illus.). 1976. lib. bdg. 53.00 (ISBN 0-8240-2002-2). Garland Pub.

Pincus, Gregory, ed. Hormones & Atherosclerosis: Proceedings. 1959. 38.50 (ISBN 0-12-557050-3). Acad Pr.

Pincus, Gregory & Thimann, Kenneth V., eds. The Hormones: Physiology, Chemistry & Applications, 5 vols. Incl. Vol. 1. 1948. 72.50 (ISBN 0-12-557001-5); Vol. 2. 1950. 72.50 (ISBN 0-12-557002-3); Vol. 3. 1955. 72.50 (ISBN 0-12-557003-1); Vol. 4. Pincus, Gregory, et al, eds. 1964. 72.50 (ISBN 0-12-557004-X); Vol. 5. Pincus, Gregory, et al, eds. 1964. 72.50 (ISBN 0-12-557005-8). Set. 292.50 (ISBN 0-685-23215-8). Acad Pr.

Pincus, Gregory, ed. see Laurentian Hormone Conferences.

Pincus, Harriet. Little Red Riding Hood. LC 68-11505. (Illus.). 32p. (ps-3). 1973. pap. 1.25 (ISBN 0-15-652850-9, AVB75, VoyB). HarBraceJ.

Pincus, Harriet, ed. & illus. Little Red Riding Hood. LC 68-11505. (Illus.). (gr. k-3). 1968. 6.95 (ISBN 0-15-247132-4, HJ). HarBraceJ.

Pincus, J. J. Pressure Groups & Politics in Antebellum Tariffs. LC 76-51733. 1977. 17.50x (ISBN 0-231-03963-8). Columbia U Pr.

Pincus, Leo I. Practical Boiler Water Treatment: Including Air-Conditioning Systems. 284p. 1981. Repr. lib. bdg. price not set (ISBN 0-89874-255-2). Krieger.

Pincus, Lily. Death & the Family. 1976. pap. 2.95 (ISBN 0-394-71900-X, Vin). Random.

Pincus, Stanley. Respiratory Therapist Manual. LC 74-79838. (Allied Health Ser). 1975. pap. 7.05 (ISBN 0-672-61389-1). Bobbs.

Pincus-Witten, Robert. Occult Symbolism in France: Josephin Peladan & the Salons De la Rose-Croix. LC 75-23809. (Outstanding Dissertations in the Fine Arts - 20th Century). (Illus.). 1976. lib. bdg. 41.00 (ISBN 0-8240-2003-0). Garland Pub.

--Postminimalism: American Art of the Decade. LC 77-77010. (Illus.). 1981. pap. text ed. 11.95 (ISBN 0-915570-07-6). Oolp Pr.

Pincus-Witten, Robert, jt. auth. see Delehanty, Suzanne.

Pindar. Carmina Cum Fragmentis. Bowra, C. M., ed. (Oxford Classical Texts Ser). 1935. 18.95x (ISBN 0-19-814539-X). Oxford U Pr.

Pindar, Norris T., 3rd. Engineering Wall & Partition Components for Prefabrication. (Illus.). 128p. 1981. 13.50 (ISBN 0-89047-008-1). Herman Pub. Postponed.

Pindborg. Atlas of Diseases of the Oral Mucosa. 3rd ed. LC 78-54520. 1980. 75.00 (ISBN 0-7216-7277-9). Saunders.

Pindborg, J. J. & Kramer, I. R. Histological Typing of Odontogenic Tumours, Jaw Cysts & Allied Lesions. (World Health Organization: International Histological Classification of Tumours Ser.). 1971. incl. slides 112.50 (ISBN 0-685-77234-9, 70-1-005-00). Am Soc Clinical.

Pinder, David. The Netherlands. new ed. Thompson, Ian, ed. LC 76-18924. (Westview Special Studies in Industrial Geography). (Illus.). 1976. lib. bdg. 26.00 o.p. (ISBN 0-89158-626-1). Westview.

Pinder, David, jt. ed. see Hoyle, Brian.

Pinder, Glenn D., jt. auth. see Harris, Dale B.

Pinder, J., jt. ed. see Henig, S.

Pinder, John, ed. The International Implications of National Industrial Strategies. 320p. 1981. text ed. 32.50 (ISBN 0-86598-040-3). Allanheld.

Pine, A. DuGuay. The Magic Picture Book. 125p. 1980. 6.95 (ISBN 0-8059-2738-7). Dorrance.

Pine, Eli S. How to Enjoy Calculus. LC 80-10974. 128p. 1980. lib. bdg. 7.95 (ISBN 0-668-04949-9); pap. 4.95 (ISBN 0-668-04951-0). Arco.

Pine, R. Dean. Beginning the Third Century: The Liberal-Led March to Communism. 1977. 4.95 o.p. (ISBN 0-533-02844-2). Vantage.

Pine, Tillie S. & Levine, Joseph. The Polynesians Knew. new ed. (Illus.). (ps-4). 1974. PLB 7.95 o.p. (ISBN 0-07-050090-8, GB). McGraw.

Pine, Vanderlyn R. Introduction to Social Statistics. (Methods of Social Science Ser.). (Illus.). 1977. text ed. 18.95 (ISBN 0-13-496844-1). P-H.

Pine, Vanderlyn R., et al, eds. Acute Grief & the Funeral. (Illus.). 328p. 1976. 21.75 (ISBN 0-398-03434-6). C C Thomas.

Pinel, Philippe. The Clinical Training of Doctors: An Essay of 1793. Weiner, Dora B., ed. & tr. from Fr. LC 80-14500. (The Henry E. Sigerist Supplements to the Bulletin of the History of Medicine, New Ser.: No. 3). 108p. 1981. pap. text ed. 7.50x (ISBN 0-8018-2448-6). Johns Hopkins.

--Treatise on Insanity. Davis, D. D., tr. from Fr. Bd. with Responsibility in Mental Disease. (Contributions to the History of Psychology Ser., Vol. III, Pt. C: Medical Psychology). 1978. Repr. of 1806 ed. 30.00 (ISBN 0-89093-167-4). U Pubns Amer.

Pinera-Llera, Humberto. Introduccion E Historica De la Filosofia. 3rd ed. LC 89-65885. (Coleccion Textos). (Illus.). 348p. (Span.). 1980. pap. 12.95 (ISBN 0-89729-254-5). Ediciones.

Pinero, Arthur W; see Salerno, Henry F.

Pines, Ayala, et al. Burnout: From Tedium to Personal Growth. LC 80-755. (Illus.). 224p. 1981. 17.95 (ISBN 0-02-925350-0). Free Pr.

Pines, Ayala M. & Maslach, Christina. Experiencing Social Psychology. 1978. pap. text ed. 8.95x (ISBN 0-394-31281-3). Random.

Pines, Herman. The Chemistry of Catalytic Hydrocarbon Conversions. 1981. price not set (ISBN 0-12-557160-7). Acad Pr.

Pines, Maya. The Brain Changers: Scientists & the New Mind Control. LC 73-8721. (Illus.). 1973. 10.00 o.p. (ISBN 0-15-113700-5). HarBraceJ.

--Revolution in Learning: The Years from Birth to Six. LC 66-10657. 1967. 10.00 o.s.i. (ISBN 0-06-034866-6, HarpT). Har-Row.

Pinfield, Edward R., jt. auth. see Aikawa, Jerry K.

Pinfold, Geoffrey M. Reinforced Concrete Chimneys & Towers. (C & CA Viewpoint Publication Ser.). (Illus.). 1976. text ed. 21.50 (ISBN 0-7210-0993-X). Scholium Intl.

Pinfold, Tom see Norcliffe, Glen.

Ping, Lee Poh. Chinese Society in Nineteenth Century Singapore. (East Asian Historical Monographs). (Illus.). 1978. 19.95x (ISBN 0-19-580384-1). Oxford U Pr.

Pinget, Robert. Plays, Vol. I. 1980. pap. 4.95 (ISBN 0-7145-0474-2). Riverrun NY.

--Plays, Vol. II. 1980. pap. 4.95 (ISBN 0-7145-0036-4). Riverrun NY.

--Robert Pinget: Plays, 2 vols. Bray, Barbara & Beckett, Samuel, trs. pap. 4.95 ea.; Vol. I. (ISBN 0-7145-0474-2); Vol. II. (ISBN 0-7145-0036-4). Riverrun NY.

--Robert Pinget: Three Plays, Vol. 2. 192p. 1968. 5.00 (ISBN 0-8090-7631-4). Hill & Wang.

Pinget, Robert see Otten, Anna.

Pingree, David, ed. see Hashimi, Ali Ibn Sulayman al.

Pinhey, E. C. A Survey of the Dragonflies (Order Odonata) of Eastern Africa. (Illus.). vii, 214p. 1961. 18.50x (ISBN 0-565-00216-3, Pub. by Brit Mus Nat Hist England). Sabbot-Natural Hist Bks.

Pinion, F. B. A Jane Austen Companion. rev. ed. (A Critical Survey & Reference Book). 1980. text ed. 31.25x (ISBN 0-333-12489-8). Humanities.

Pink, A. W. The Application of the Scriptures: A Refutation of Dispensationalism. pap. 1.25 (ISBN 0-685-88366-3). Reiner.

--Los Attributos De Dios. 2.50 (ISBN 0-686-12561-4). Banner of Truth.

--Effectual Fervent Prayer. White, Donald R., ed. 176p. 1981. 8.95 (ISBN 0-8010-7059-7). Baker Bk.

--Letters of A. W. Pink. 1978. pap. 2.50 (ISBN 0-85151-262-3). Banner of Truth.

--The Life of Elijah. 1976. pap. 4.95 (ISBN 0-85151-041-8). Banner of Truth.

--Profiting from the Word. 1977. pap. 2.45 (ISBN 0-85151-032-9). Banner of Truth.

--La Soberania De Dios. 2.95 (ISBN 0-686-12562-2). Banner of Truth.

--The Sovereignty of God. 1976. pap. 3.45 (ISBN 0-85151-133-3). Banner of Truth.

Pink, Arthur W. Attributes of God. 1961. pap. 2.95 (ISBN 0-685-19823-5). Reiner.

--Exposition of the Gospel of John, 4 Vols. in 1. 1945. 22.95 (ISBN 0-310-31180-2). Zondervan.

--Gleanings from Elisha. LC 79-181591. 288p. 1972. 10.95 (ISBN 0-8024-2962-9). Moody.

--Gleanings from Paul. 1967. write for info. (ISBN 0-8024-2965-3). Moody.

--Gleanings from the Scriptures: Man's Total Depravity. LC 73-80942. 1970. 10.95 (ISBN 0-8024-2966-1). Moody.

--Gleanings in Exodus. 1964. 10.95 (ISBN 0-8024-2975-0). Moody.

--Gleanings in Genesis. 1922. 10.95 (ISBN 0-8024-2968-8). Moody.

--Gleanings in Joshua. 1964. 10.95 (ISBN 0-8024-2982-3). Moody.

--Gleanings in the Godhead. 256p. 10.95 (ISBN 0-8024-2977-7). Moody.

--Holy Spirit. 1970. pap. 4.95 (ISBN 0-8010-7041-4). Baker Bk.

--Interpretation of the Scriptures. 1972. pap. 3.95 (ISBN 0-8010-7025-2). Baker Bk.

--The Life of David, 2 vols. in one. (Giant Summit Ser.). 768p. 1981. pap. 10.95 (ISBN 0-8010-7061-9). Baker Bk.

--Seven Sayings of Our Saviour on the Cross. (Summit Bks). 1977. pap. 2.45 (ISBN 0-8010-7015-5). Baker Bk.

Pink, Heinz-Guenther. Mathpower U. S. A. Thirty Subject Volume. 1980. write for info. (ISBN 0-915946-08-4). Pink Hse Pub.

Pink, Marilyn. How to Catalogue Works of Art: A Guide for the Private Collector. LC 72-86380. (Illus.). 54p. (Orig.). 1972. pap. 3.50x (ISBN 0-686-02501-6). Mus Sys.

Pinkas, Danny, jt. auth. see Golan, Aviezier.

Pinkele, Carl F., jt. auth. see Ginsburgs, George.

Pinkepank, Jerry A. Second Diesel Spotter's Guide. LC 66-22894. (Illus.). 459p. 1973. 12.75 (ISBN 0-89024-025-6); pap. 10.95 (ISBN 0-89024-026-4). Kalmbach.

Pinker, Robert. English Hospital Statistics: Eighteen Sixty Seven to Nineteen Thirty Eight. 1966. text ed. 6.95x o.p. (ISBN 0-435-32700-3). Heinemann Ed.

--Social Theory & Social Policy. 240p. 1971. 14.50x (ISBN 0-8448-0185-2). Crane-Russak Co.

Pinkerton, Betsy, jt. auth. see Pinkerton, Steve.

Pinkerton, Edward C. Word for Word. LC 77-20391. Date not set. price not set (ISBN 0-930454-06-5, Dist. by Stein & Day). Verbatim. Postponed.

Pinkerton, Kathrene. Hidden Harbor. LC 51-13350. (Illus.). (gr. 9 up). 1951. 3.95 o.p. (ISBN 0-15-233973-6, HJ). HarBraceJ.

Pinkerton, Kathrene S. Steer North. LC 62-8346. (gr. 7 up). 1962. 4.95 o.p. (ISBN 0-15-280210-X, HJ). HarBraceJ.

Pinkerton, Philip. Childhood Disorder: A Psychosomatic Approach. (Illus.). 200p. 1975. 15.00x (ISBN 0-231-03955-7). Columbia U Pr.

Pinkerton, Steve & Pinkerton, Betsy. The Great Book of Catalogs. 8.95 (ISBN 0-9602882-0-1). Green Hill.

Pinkerton, Todd. Breaking Communication Barriers with Roleplay. LC 75-32944. 1976. pap. 4.95 (ISBN 0-8042-1097-7). John Knox.

Pinkham, Joan, tr. see Cesaire, Aime.

Pinkham, Mary E. Mary Ellen's Best of Helpful Kitchen Hints. (Illus., Orig.). 1980. pap. 4.50 (ISBN 0-446-97212-6). Warner Bks.

Pinkham, Mary E. & Higgenbotham, Pearl. Mary Ellen's Best of Helpful Hints. (Illus.). 144p. 1979. deluxe ed. 7.95 (ISBN 0-446-51211-7); pap. 4.50 (ISBN 0-446-97752-7). Warner Bks.

Pinkley, Virgil & Scheer, James F. Eisenhower Declassified. 1979. 12.95 o.p. (ISBN 0-8007-1063-0). Revell.

Pinkney, A. Red, Black & Green. LC 75-22550. 256p. 1976. 29.95 (ISBN 0-521-20887-4); pap. 6.95 (ISBN 0-521-29459-2). Cambridge U Pr.

Pinkney, Alphonse. Black Americans. 2nd ed. (Ethnic Groups in American Life Ser.). (Illus.). 272p. 1975. text ed. 8.95 o.p. (ISBN 0-13-077537-1); pap. text ed. 7.95x (ISBN 0-13-077529-0). P-H.

Pinkney, William, Jr. Life of William Pinkney. LC 75-75276. (American History, Politics & Law Ser). 1969. Repr. of 1853 ed. lib. bdg. 39.50 (ISBN 0-306-71307-1). Da Capo.

Pinkstaff, Dick & Pinkstaff, Marlene A. Personal Skill Building for the Emerging Manager. LC 79-16920. 1979. pap. 8.95 (ISBN 0-8436-0785-8). CBI Pub.

Pinkstaff, Marlene A., jt. auth. see Pinkstaff, Dick.

Pinkus, Herman. A Guide to Dermatohistopathology. 3rd ed. 672p. 1981. 40.00 (ISBN 0-8385-3151-2). ACC.

Pinkus, Susan. Going into Hospital. new ed. LC 73-595891. (New Citizen Book). (Illus.). 80p. 1973. 10.50x (ISBN 0-85340-230-2). Intl Pubns Serv.

Pinkus, Theo, ed. Conversations with Lukacs. LC 74-34021. 1975. 9.95x (ISBN 0-262-16062-5); pap. 4.95 (ISBN 0-262-66044-X). MIT Pr.

Pinkwater, D. Manus. Fat Men from Space. (Illus.). (gr. 4-6). 1980. pap. 0.95 (ISBN 0-440-44542-6, YB). Dell.

--The Hoboken Chicken Emergency. LC 76-41910. (Illus.). (gr. 3-7). 1977. 7.95 (ISBN 0-13-392514-5). P-H.

Pinkwater, D. Manus, jt. auth. see Pinkwater, Jill.

Pinkwater, Daniel. The Magic Moscow. LC 80-12785. (Illus.). 64p. (gr. 5 up). 1980. 7.95 (ISBN 0-590-07583-7, Four Winds). Schol Bk Serv.

--Tooth-Gnasher Superflash. LC 80-69996. (Illus.). 32p. (gr. k-3). 1981. 9.95 (ISBN 0-590-07624-8, Four Winds). Schol Bk Serv.

--The Words of Kukumlima. LC 80-24713. (gr. 4-7). 1981. 9.95 (ISBN 0-525-43380-5). Dutton.

Pinkwater, Daniel, jt. auth. see Keele, Luqman.

Pinkwater, Daniel M. Alan Mendelsohn, the Boy from Mars. LC 78-12052. (gr. 4-7). 1979. PLB 9.95 (ISBN 0-525-25360-2). Dutton.

--Alan Mendelsohn: The Boy from Mars. 224p. (gr. 5-8). 1981. pap. 1.95 (ISBN 0-553-14522-3). Bantam.

--Fat Men from Space. LC 77-6091. (gr. 4up). 1977. 5.50 (ISBN 0-396-07461-8). Dodd.

--The Last Guru. LC 78-14260. (gr. 5 up). 1978. 6.95 (ISBN 0-396-07636-X). Dodd.

--Return of the Moose. LC 78-22434. (Illus.). (gr. 5 up). 1979. 6.95 (ISBN 0-396-07674-2). Dodd.

--The Wuggie Norple Story. LC 79-19014. (Illus.). 40p. (gr. k-3). 1980. 9.95 (ISBN 0-590-07569-1, Four Winds). Schol Bk Serv.

--Yobgorgle: Mystery Monster of Lake Ontario rev. ed. 160p. (gr. 3-6). 1981. pap. 1.75 (ISB 0-553-15109-6). Bantam.

Pinkwater, Jill. The Natural Snack Cookbook. LC 75-11717. (Illus.). 272p. (gr. 7 up). 1975. 14.95 (ISBN 0-590-07374-5, Four Winds). Schol Bk Serv.

Pinkwater, Jill & Pinkwater, D. Manus. Superpuppy: How to Choose, Raise & Train the Best Possible Dog for You. LC 76-8825. (Illus.). (gr. 3 up). 1977. 9.95 (ISBN 0-395-28878-9, Clarion). HM.

Pinkwater, Manus. Three Big Hogs. LC 75-4780. (Illus.). 40p. (ps-3). 1975. 6.95 (ISBN 0-395-28819-3, Clarion). HM.

Pinkwater, Manus M. Pickle Creature. LC 78-11157. (Illus.). 32p. (gr. k-3). 1979. 8.95 (ISBN 0-590-07579-9, Four Winds). Schol Bk Serv.

Pinloche, A. & Jolivet, A. Dictionnaire bilingue Larousse, francais-alemand et allemand-francais. (Apollo). (Fr. & Ger.). 10.50 (ISBN 0-685-13853-4, 3779). Larousse.

Pinnell, Gay S., ed. Discovering Language with Children. LC 80-24795. 132p. (Orig.). 1980. pap. 5.50 (ISBN 0-8141-1210-2, 12102). NCTE.

Pinnell, Richard T. Francesco Corbetta & the Baroque Guitar: With a Transcription of His Works, 2 vols. Buelow, George, ed. (Studies in Musicology). 714p. 1980. Set. 49.95 (ISBN 0-8357-1140-4, Pub. by UMI Res Pr); Vol. 1. (ISBN 0-8357-1141-2); Vol. 2. (ISBN 0-8357-1142-0). Univ Microfilms.

Pinneo. Congestive Heart Failure. 1978. pap. 6.95 (ISBN 0-8385-1169-4). ACC.

Pinney, Edward L., Jr. A First Group Therapy Book. 224p. 1970. text ed. 11.50 (ISBN 0-398-01490-6). C C Thomas.

Pinney, Roy. The Snake Book. LC 78-68336. (Illus.). 256p. 1981. 12.95 (ISBN 0-385-13547-5). Doubleday.

Pinney, T., ed. The Letters of Thomas Babington Macaulay, Vol. 5. LC 73-75860. (Illus.). 425p. Date not set. 85.00 (ISBN 0-521-22749-6). Cambridge U Pr.

--The Letters of Thomas Babington Macaulay, Vol. 6. LC 73-75860. (Illus.). 350p. Date not set. price not set (ISBN 0-521-22750-X). Cambridge U Pr.

Pinney, Thomas, ed. Essays of George Eliot. LC 74-18488. 1963. 20.00x (ISBN 0-231-02619-6). Columbia U Pr.

Pinnock, Clark. Reason Enough. LC 79-3632. (Orig.). 1980. pap. 3.50 (ISBN 0-87784-623-5). Inter-Varsity.

Pinnock, Clark H. Are There Any Answers? 48p. 1976. pap. 1.75 (ISBN 0-87123-009-7). Bethany Fell.

--Grace Unlimited. LC 75-22161. 272p. 1975. pap. 5.95 (ISBN 0-87123-185-9, 210185). Bethany Fell.

Pino, David. The Clarinet & Clarinet Playing. (Illus.). 288p. 1980. 15.95 (ISBN 0-684-16624-0, ScribT). Scribner.

Pinowski, J. & Kendeigh, S. C., eds. Granivorous Birds in Ecosystems. LC 76-47189. (International Biological Programme Ser.: No. 12). (Illus.). 1978. 79.50 (ISBN 0-521-21504-8). Cambridge U Pr.

Pinsker, Harold & Willis, William D., Jr., eds. Information Processing in the Nervous System. 378p. 1980. text ed. 38.00 (ISBN 0-89004-422-8). Raven.

Pinsker, Sanford. Between Two Worlds: The American Novel in the Nineteen Sixties. LC 79-64168. 139p. 1980. 7.50 (ISBN 0-87875-169-6). Whitston Pub.

Pinson, Elliot N., jt. auth. see Denes, Peter B.

Pinson, William M. Practiquemos el Evangelio. Orig. Title: Applying the Gospel. 1976. pap. 1.85 (ISBN 0-311-46071-2). Casa Bautista.

Pinson, William M., Jr., jt. auth. see Maston, T. B.

Pintauro, Joseph. Cold Hands. 1980. pap. 2.50 (ISBN 0-451-09482-4, E9482, Sig). NAL.

Pintauro, Joseph & Kent, Sr. Corita. To Believe in God. LC 68-11741. 1968. 4.95 o.p. (ISBN 0-06-066640-4, HarpR). Har-Row.

Pintel, G., jt. auth. see Diamond, J.

Pintel, Gerald, jt. auth. see Diamond, Jay.

Pinter, Charles C. Set Theory. LC 77-131203. (Mathematics Ser). 1971. text ed. 15.95 (ISBN 0-201-05827-8). A-W.

Pinter, Harold. Poems & Prose: 1949-1977. LC 78-56046. 1978. pap. 5.95 (ISBN 0-394-17070-9, E722, Ever). Grove.

--The Proust Screenplay. LC 77-78081. 1977. pap. 3.95 (ISBN 0-394-17018-0, E690, Ever). Grove.

Pintner, Rudolf, et al. Educational Psychology. 6th ed. (Orig.). 1970. pap. 4.95 (ISBN 0-06-460023-8, CO 23, COS). Har-Row.

Pinto, Cesar M. Acupuncture: Science or Charlatanism? (Illus.). 440p. 1978. 14.95 (ISBN 0-8059-2433-7). Dorrance.

Pinto, Diana, ed. Contemporary Italian Sociology: A Reader. (Illus.). 224p. Date not set. price not set (ISBN 0-521-23738-6); pap. price not set (ISBN 0-521-28191-1). Cambridge U Pr.

Pinto, Edward H. Treen & Other Wooden Bygones. (Illus.). 1978. 50.00 o.p. (ISBN 0-684-15906-6, ScribT). Scribner.

Pinto, J. D. Behavior & Taxonomy of the Epicauta Maculata Group (Coleoptera: Meloidae) (U. C. Publications in Entomology Ser.: Vol. 89). 1980. pap. 12.00 (ISBN 0-520-09616-9). U of Cal Pr.

Pinto, Vivian De Sola. Crisis in English Poetry, Eighteen Eighty to Nineteen Forty. (Repr. of 1951 ed). 1967. text ed. 6.25x (ISBN 0-09-024411-7, Hutchinson U Lib); pap. text ed. 3.00x (ISBN 0-09-024412-5, Hutchinson U Lib). Humanities.

Pintus, P., jt. auth. see Gibbs, G. W.

Pinzon, Alvaro. Calculo, Bk. I. 2nd ed. (Span.). 1978. pap. text ed. 6.00 (ISBN 0-06-316986-X, Pub. by HarLA Mexico). Har-Row.

--Calculo, Bk. II. 2nd ed. (Span.). 1978. pap. text ed. 6.00 (ISBN 0-06-316987-8, Pub. by HarLA Mexico). Har-Row.

--Fisica, Vol. I. 2nd ed. (Span.). 1978. pap. text ed. 6.00 (ISBN 0-06-316668-2, Pub. by HarLA Mexico). Har-Row.

--Fisica, Vol. II. 2nd ed. (Span.). 1978. pap. text ed. 6.00 (ISBN 0-06-316669-0, Pub. by HarLA Mexico). Har-Row.

Piomelli, Sergio & Yachnin, Stanley. Current Topics in Hematology, Vol. 1. LC 78-19681. 247p. 1978. 28.00x (ISBN 0-8451-0350-4). A R Liss.

Piomelli, Sergio & Yachnin, Stanley, eds. Current Topics in Hematology, Vol. 3. LC 78-19681. 280p. 1980. 30.00x (ISBN 0-8451-0352-0). A R Liss.

Piore, M. J. Birds of Passage. LC 78-12067. 1979. 21.50 (ISBN 0-521-22452-7). Cambridge U Pr.

Piore, Michael, jt. auth. see Berger, Suzanne.

Piore, Michael J. Birds of Passage: Migrant Labor & Industrial Societies. LC 78-12067. (Illus.). 192p. 1980. pap. 6.95 (ISBN 0-521-28058-3). Cambridge U Pr.

Piore, Michael J., jt. auth. see Doeringer, Peter B.

Piore, Michael J., ed. Unemployment & Inflation: Institutional & Structuralist Views. LC 79-55274. 1980. 20.00 (ISBN 0-87332-143-X); pap. 7.95 (ISBN 0-87332-165-0). M E Sharpe.

Piore, Nancy K. Lightning: The Poetry of Rene Char. LC 80-22001. (Illus.). 150p. 1981. 17.95x (ISBN 0-930350-08-1). NE U Pr.

Piotrow, Phyllis T. World Population: The Present & Futue Crisis, No. 251. 1st ed. LC 80-69582. (Headline Ser.: No. 251). (Illus.). 80p. (Orig.). 1980. pap. 2.00 (ISBN 0-87124-064-5). Foreign Policy.

--World Population: The Present & Future Crisis. LC 80-69582. (Headline Ser.: No. 251). (Illus.). 80p. (Orig.). 1980. pap. 2.00 (ISBN 0-87124-064-5). Foreign Policy.

Pious, Richard M. Civil Rights & Liberties in the 1970's. 1973. pap. text ed. 3.95 (ISBN 0-394-31707-6). Random.

Pipard, Maurice. Travel Games. (Panda Paperbacks). (Illus.). 96p. (gr. 3-7). 1975. pap. 1.95 (ISBN 0-531-02734-1). Watts.

Pipe, Ann K. Bonsai: The Art of Dwarfing Trees. (Illus.). 1964. pap. 3.95 (ISBN 0-8015-0796-0, Hawthorn). Dutton.

--Reproducing Furniture in Miniature. LC 75-32981. (Illus.). 224p. 1976. 15.00 o.p. (ISBN 0-8092-8294-1); pap. 5.95 o.p. (ISBN 0-8092-8072-8). Contemp Bks.

Pipe, Peter. Objectives-Tool for Change. LC 74-83218. 1975. pap. 4.20 (ISBN 0-8224-4900-5). Pitman Learning.

Pipe, Peter, jt. auth. see Mager, Robert F.

Pipe, Ted. Gas Engine Manual. 2nd ed. LC 76-45883. 1977. 9.95 (ISBN 0-672-23245-6). Audel.

Piper. Stories from Ugidali: Cherokee Story Teller. 1981. pap. 1.95 (ISBN 0-89992-078-0). MT Coun Indian.

Piper, Charles V. & Morse, W. J. The Soybean. (Illus.). 8.00 (ISBN 0-8446-1350-9). Peter Smith.

Piper, D. W., jt. ed. see Powell, L. W.

Piper, David. The Companion Guide to London. LC 77-72102. 1977. pap. 6.95 o.p. (ISBN 0-684-14954-0, ScribT). Scribner.

--The Genius of British Painting. (Illus.). 352p. 1975. 27.50 o.p. (ISBN 0-688-00313-3). Morrow.

--Kings & Queens of England & Scotland. (Illus.). 1980. 17.95 (ISBN 0-571-11560-8, Pub. by Faber & Faber). Merrimack Bk Serv.

Piper, David, jt. auth. see Wise, Susan.

Piper, David W. & Glatter, Ron. The Changing University: A Report on the Staff Development in Universities Programme 72-74. (General Ser.). (Illus., Orig.). 1977. pap. text ed. 38.50x (ISBN 0-85633-121-X, NFER). Humanities.

Piper, Doris D. A Home for Jamie. (N. H.-Vermont Historiettes). (Illus.). 58p. (Orig.). (gr. 3-4). 1976. 4.95x (ISBN 0-915892-08-1); pap. 1.45 (ISBN 0-915892-13-8). Regional Ctr Educ.

Piper, H. Beam. Little Fuzzy. 160p. (Orig.). 1976. pap. 1.95 (ISBN 0-441-48492-1). Ace Bks.

Piper, Helen. Charley O'Toole the Leprechaun. 1980. pap. 2.00 (ISBN 0-89502-041-6). FEB.

Piper, Henry D., ed. Fitzgerald's the Great Gatsby: The Novel, the Critics, the Background. (Research Anthologies Ser). (Illus., Orig.). 1970. pap. text ed. 7.95x (ISBN 0-684-41402-3, ScribC). Scribner.

Piper, Henry D., ed. see Cowley, Malcolm.

Piper, James. Personal Filmmaking. (Illus.). 368p. 1975. 9.95 (ISBN 0-87909-612-8); instrs' manual avail. Reston.

Piper, Joanne. Filing: Syllabus. 2nd ed. 1979. pap. text ed. 6.95 (ISBN 0-89420-037-2, 327007); cassette recordings 104.25 (ISBN 0-89420-146-8, 106000). Natl Book.

--Personal Shorthand Master Dictionary. 1978. pap. 10.75 (ISBN 0-89420-043-7, 212000). Natl Book.

--Vowel Sounds & Silent Letters: Syllabus. 1975. pap. text ed. 4.85 (ISBN 0-89420-023-2, 240008); cassette recordings 22.05 (ISBN 0-89420-196-4, 240000). Natl Book.

Piper, Joanne & Yerian, Theo. Personal Shorthand: Syllabus. 1975. pap. text ed. 8.95 (ISBN 0-89420-083-6, 217000); cassette recordings 246.90 (ISBN 0-89420-172-7, 178000). Natl Book.

--Personal Shorthand: Teacher's Manual & Key to Syllabus. 1975. tchr's ed. 4.95 (ISBN 0-89420-094-1, 217007). Natl Book.

Piper, John, jt. auth. see Cheetham, J. H.

Piper, Patricia L., et al. Manual on K F: The Library of Congress Classification Schedule for Law of the United States. LC 72-86471. (AALL Publications Ser.: No. 11). 135p. 1972. text ed. 22.50x (ISBN 0-8377-0109-0). Rothman.

Piper, Priscilla J., jt. auth. see Annual Symposium of Basic Medical Sciences, 10th.

Piper, Roger. Story of Computers. LC 64-20226. (Illus.). (gr. 7 up). 1964. 4.95 o.p. (ISBN 0-15-280847-7, HJ). HarBraceJ.

--The Story of Oil. (Junior Reference Ser.). (Illus.). 64p. (gr. 7 up). 7.95 (ISBN 0-7136-1911-2). Dufour.

Piper, Steven. The North Ships: The Life of a Trawlerman. LC 74-76187. 1974. 5.50 o.p. (ISBN 0-7153-6483-9). David & Charles.

Piper, Sue, ed. see Jones, Terri & Jones, Evelyn J.

Piper, Terrence. Classroom Management & Behavioral Objectives. LC 73-91797. 1974. pap. 4.95 (ISBN 0-8224-1412-0); duplicatable materials 4.95. Pitman Learning.

--Materials for Classroom Management. LC 73-91796. 1974. duplicatable materials 4.95 (ISBN 0-8224-4412-7). Pitman Learning.

Piper, Terrence J. & Elgart, Denise B. Teacher Supervision Through Behavioral Objectives: An Operationally Described System. LC 79-15648. (Illus., Orig.). 1979. pap. text ed. 6.50 (ISBN 0-933716-03-6). P H Brookes.

Piper, W. Stephen, jt. auth. see Schilling, Otto F.

Pipes, Daniel. Slave Soldiers & Islam: The Genesis of a Military System. LC 80-23969. 272p. 1981. text ed. 25.00x (ISBN 0-300-02447-9). Yale U Pr.

Pipes, Peggy. Nutrition in Infancy & Childhood. LC 76-39865. (Illus.). 1977. pap. 9.95 (ISBN 0-8016-3940-9). Mosby.

Pipes, Peggy L. Nutrition in Infancy & Childhood. 2nd ed. (Illus.). 288p. 1981. pap. text ed. 11.95 (ISBN 0-8016-3941-7). Mosby.

Pipes, Richard. Karamzin's Memoir on Ancient & Modern Russia. LC 59-6484. 1966. pap. text ed. 4.95x (ISBN 0-689-70157-8, 83). Atheneum.

--Struve: Liberal on the Left, 1870-1905. (Russian Research Center Studies: No. 64). 1970. 20.00x (ISBN 0-674-84595-1). Harvard U Pr.

--U. S. Soviet Relations in the Era of Detente: A Tragedy of Errors. 230p. (Orig.). 1981. lib. bdg. 22.00x (ISBN 0-86531-154-4); pap. text ed. 10.00x (ISBN 0-86531-155-2). Westview.

Pipes, Richard, ed. Soviet Strategy in Europe. LC 76-1555. 1976. 19.50x (ISBN 0-8448-0854-7). Crane-Russak Co.

Pipkin, Bernard W., et al. Laboratory Exercises in Oceanography. (Illus.). 1977. lab. manual 9.95x (ISBN 0-7167-0181-2); tchrs. manual avail. W H Freeman.

Pippard, A. B. Elements of Classical Thermodynamics. 1966. pap. text ed. 9.95x (ISBN 0-521-09101-2). Cambridge U Pr.

Pippard, Brian. The Physics of Vibration, Vol. 1. LC 77-85685. (Illus.). 1978. 78.00 (ISBN 0-521-21899-3). Cambridge U Pr.

Pippenger, C. E., et al, eds. Anti-Epileptic Drugs: Quantitative Analysis & Interpretation. LC 76-58055. 1978. 36.50 (ISBN 0-89004-197-0). Raven.

Pippert, Wesley. Faith at the Top. LC 73-88676. 192p. 1973. pap. 1.50 o.p. (ISBN 0-912692-28-6). Cook.

Pippin, Horace. The Phillips Collection. LC 76-52613. (Illus.). 64p. (Orig.). 1981. pap. 10.00 (ISBN 0-295-95818-9, Pub. by Phillips). U of Wash Pr.

Pippin, James A. Developing Casework Skills. LC 80-18799. (Sage Human Services Guides: No. 15). 160p. 1980. pap. 8.00 (ISBN 0-8039-1503-9). Sage.

Pirages, Dennis C. & Ehrlich, Paul R. Ark II: Social Response to Environmental Imperatives. (Illus.). 1974. pap. text ed. 9.95x (ISBN 0-7167-0847-7). W H Freeman.

Pirandello, Luigi. Naked Masks: Five Plays. Bentley, Eric, ed. Incl. It Is So If You Think So; Henry Fourth; Six Characters in Search of an Author; Each in His Own Way; Liola. 1957. pap. 4.50 (ISBN 0-525-47006-9). Dutton.

--One, None and a Hundred-Thousand. Putnam, S., tr. from Ital. LC 76-50039. 268p. 1981. Repr. of 1933 ed. 19.00 (ISBN 0-686-69134-2). Fertig.

--Shoot! (Si Gira) The Notebooks of Serafino Gubbio, Cinematograph Operator. Moncrieff, C. K., tr. from It. LC 74-12380. 334p. 1975. Repr. of 1926 ed. 17.50 (ISBN 0-86527-302-2). Fertig.

Pirandello, Luigi see Caputi, Anthony.

Pirandello, Luigi see Watson, E. Bradlee & Pressey, Benfield.

Pirani, Conrad L., jt. auth. see McCluskey, Robert T.

Pirenne, Henri. Mohammed & Charlemagne. Miall, Bernard, tr. 293p. 1974. pap. text ed. 9.50x (ISBN 0-04-940025-8). Allen Unwin.

Pirenne, Jacqueline. A la Decouverte De L'arabie. (Arabia Past & Present Ser.: Vol. 14). (Fr.). 32.50 (ISBN 0-902675-53-2). Oleander Pr.

Pirenne, M. H. Optics, Painting & Photography. LC 71-108109. (Illus.). 1970. 58.00x (ISBN 0-521-07686-2). Cambridge U Pr.

Pires, Deborah S., jt. auth. see Malkemes, Fred.

Pires, Deborah S., jt. auth. see Malkenes, Fred.

Pirie, David. A Heritage of Horror: The English Gothic Cinema, 1946-1972. 1975. pap. 2.95 (ISBN 0-380-00069-5, 20099). Avon.

Pirie, N. W., ed. Food Protein Sources. LC 74-12962. (International Biological Programme Ser.: No. 4). (Illus.). 288p. 1975. 47.50 (ISBN 0-521-20588-3). Cambridge U Pr.

Pirie, R. Gordon, ed. Oceanography: Contemporary Readings in Ocean Sciences. 2nd ed. (Illus.). 1977. pap. text ed. 8.95x (ISBN 0-19-502119-3). Oxford U Pr.

Piriou, Jean-Pierre J., ed. see Green, Julien.

Pirmanten, Patricia. Beatles. LC 74-14656. (Rock'n Pop Stars Ser.). (Illus.). 32p. (gr. 4-12). 1974. PLB 5.95 (ISBN 0-87191-398-4); pap. 2.95 (ISBN 0-89812-106-X). Creative Ed.

Pirnicory, Vincent see Rousmaniere, Peter F., et al.

Pirnot, Thomas L., jt. auth. see Hunkins, Dalton R.

Pirofsky, Bernard, et al. Blood Banking Principles Review Book: Essay Questions & Answers. 1973. spiral bdg. 12.00 (ISBN 0-87488-339-3). Med Exam.

Pirone, P. P. Tree Maintenance. 5th ed. (Illus.). 1978. 29.95 (ISBN 0-19-502321-8). Oxford U Pr.

Pirozzolo, Francis J. The Neuropsychology of Developmental Reading Disorders. LC 78-19752. 1979. 18.95 (ISBN 0-03-046121-9). Praeger.

Pirozzolo, Francis J. & Wittrock, Merlin C. Neuropsychological & Cognitive Processes in Reading. (Perspectives in Neurolinguistics & Psycholinguistics Ser.). 1981. price not set (ISBN 0-12-557360-X). Acad Pr.

Pirozzolo, Francis J., jt. ed. see Maletta, Gabe J.

Pirruccello, Frank W. Plastic & Reconstructive Surgery of the Face: Cosmetic Surgery. (Illus.). 200p. 1981. write for info. (6891-1). Williams & Wilkins.

Pirserchia, Doris. Doomtime. (Science Fiction Ser.). 1981. pap. 2.25 (ISBN 0-87997-619-5, UE1619). DAW Bks.

Pirson, Sylvain J. Handbook of Well Log Analysis: For Oil & Gas Formation Evaluation. 1963. ref. ed. 31.95 (ISBN 0-13-382804-2). P-H.

--Oil Reservoir Engineering. LC 76-56806. (Illus.). 746p. 1977. Repr. of 1958 ed. lib. bdg. 34.50 o.p. (ISBN 0-88275-500-5). Krieger.

Pirt, S. John. Principles of Microbe & Cell Cultivation. LC 74-28380. 1975. 46.95 (ISBN 0-470-69038-0). Halsted Pr.

Pirtle, Caleb. Fort Worth: The Civilized West. Blakey, Ellen S. & Silvey, Larry P., eds. LC 80-66338. (The American Portrait Ser.). (Illus.). 240p. 1980. 24.95 (ISBN 0-932986-11-0). Continent Herit.

Pirtle, Wayne, jt. auth. see Grant, John J.

Pisan, Christine De see De Pisan, Christine.

Pisano, Beverly. Afghan Hounds. (Illus.). 125p. 1980. 2.95 (ISBN 0-87666-682-9, KW-077). TFH Pubns.

--Chow Chows. (Illus.). 125p. 2.95 (ISBN 0-87666-702-7, KW-089). TFH Pubns.

--Old English Sheepdogs. (Illus.). 128p. 1980. 2.95 (ISBN 0-87666-723-X, KW-093). TFH Pubns.

--Siberian Huskies. (Illus.). 128p. 1979. 2.95 (ISBN 0-87666-677-2, KW-068). TFH Pubns.

Pisano, Beverly & Holcombe, A. D. Beagles. (Illus.). 125p. 1979. 2.95 (ISBN 0-87666-686-1, KW-080). TFH Pubns.

Pisano, Beverly & Taynton, Mark. Shetland Sheepdogs. 125p. 1979. 2.95 (ISBN 0-87666-685-3, KW-079). TFH Pubns.

Pisano, Beverly & Thurmer, Tressa E. Chihuahuas. (Illus.). 128p. 1980. 2.95 (ISBN 0-87666-701-9, KW-087). TFH Pubns.

Pisano, Beverly, ed. English Setters. (Illus.). 128p. 1980. 2.95 (ISBN 0-87666-716-7, KW102). TFH Pubns.

Pisano, Beverly & Monte, Evelyn, eds. Brittany Spaniels. (Illus.). 128p. 1980. lib. bdg. 2.95 (ISBN 0-87666-708-6, KW092). TFH Pubns.

Pisarev, Dimitri I. Selected Philosophical, Social, & Political Essays. Dixon, R. & Katzer, J., trs. LC 79-2919. (Illus.). 711p. 1981. Repr. of 1958 ed. 45.00 (ISBN 0-8305-0089-8). Hyperion Conn.

Piscano, John & Lichter, Henry. A Matter of Taste-Doctors Discovery for Permanent Weight Loss. LC 78-26573. 1979. 9.95 (ISBN 0-8119-0318-4). Fell.

Pisciotte, Joe, jt. auth. see Gertz, Elmer.

Piscope, John. Kinesiology: The Science of Movement. LC 80-21545. 650p. 1981. text ed. 18.95 (ISBN 0-471-03483-5). Wiley.

Pisk, Litz. The Actor & His Body. LC 76-8369. (Illus.). 1976. 8.65 (ISBN 0-87830-008-2); pap. 4.75 (ISBN 0-87830-553-X). Theatre Arts.

Pissarides, C. A. Labour Market Adjustment. LC 75-21035. 1976. 44.50 (ISBN 0-521-21064-X). Cambridge U Pr.

Pister, K., ed. Structural Engineering & Structural Mechanics: A Volume Honoring Egor P. Popov. 1980. 29.95 (ISBN 0-13-853671-6). P-H.

Pistoleta. Der Trobador Pistolta. Bd. with Der Trobador Guillem Margret. Magret, Guillem. LC 80-2184. 1981. 27.00 (ISBN 0-404-19013-8). AMS Pr.

Piston, Walter. Orchestration. (Illus.). 1955. 15.95x (ISBN 0-393-09740-4, NortonC). Norton.

Pi-Sunyer, Oriol & Salzmann, Zdenek. Humanity & Culture: An Intro to Anthropology. LC 77-76336. (Illus.). 1978. text ed. 19.95 (ISBN 0-395-25051-X); inst. manual 0.65 (ISBN 0-395-26239-9). HM.

Pita, Edward G. Air Conditioning Principles & Systems: An Energy Approach. LC 80-18958. 608p. 1981. text ed. 19.95 (ISBN 0-471-04214-5). Wiley.

Pitblado, J. Roger. The North Mkata Plain, Tanzania: A Study of Land Capability & Land Tenure. (Department of Geography Research Publications Ser.). 200p. 1981. pap. 8.50x (ISBN 0-8020-3378-4). U of Toronto Pr.

Pitcairn, Leonora. Young Students' Book of Child Care. 4th ed. LC 76-58076. 1978. 6.50x (ISBN 0-521-21671-0). Cambridge U Pr.

Pitch, Anthony S. Peace. (Illus.). 200p. 1979. 18.95 (ISBN 0-89961-001-3). SBS Pub.

Pitcher, Diana. Tokoloshi. 64p. 1980. 14.75x (ISBN 0-7050-0081-8, Pub. by Skilton & Shaw England). State Mutual Bk.

--Tokoloshi: African Folk Tales Retold. LC 80-69843. (Illus.). 64p. (gr. 3 up). 1981. Repr. 9.95 (ISBN 0-89742-049-7). Dawne-Leigh.

Pitcher, Donald E. An Historical Geography of the Ottoman Empire: From Earliest Times to the End of the Sixteenth Century. (Illus.). 171p. 1972. Repr. of 1968 ed. text ed. 156.75x (ISBN 9-0040-3945-7). Humanities.

Pitcher, George. Berkeley. (The Arguments of the Philosophers Ser.). 1977. 22.50 (ISBN 0-7100-8685-7). Routledge & Kegan.

Pitcher, Tony, jt. auth. see Hart, Paul.

Pitcher, W. & Berger, A. The Geology of Donegal. 435p. 1972. 55.00 o.p. (ISBN 0-471-69055-4, Pub. by Wiley). Krieger.

Pitcher, Wayne H., Jr. Immobilized Enzymes for Food Processing. 256p. 1980. 63.95 (ISBN 0-8493-5345-9). CRC Pr.

Pitches, Douglas O. Man in Orbit: And Down to Earth. LC 80-50670. 81p. 1981. 5.95 (ISBN 0-533-04649-1). Vantage.

Pitcoff, Ramsey K. & Powell, Herb. Neuroradiology with Computed Tomography. 575p. 1981. text ed. price not set (ISBN 0-7216-7444-5). Saunders.

Pitkin, Anne. Notes for Continuing the Performance. 1977. 2.50 (ISBN 0-918116-04-X). Jawbone Pr.

Pitkin, Dorothy. Sea Change. (gr. 7-11). 1964. PLB 5.69 o.p. (ISBN 0-394-91592-5). Pantheon.

--Wiser Than Winter. (gr. 7-9). 1960. PLB 5.69 o.p. (ISBN 0-394-91828-2). Pantheon.

Pitkin, Gary M. Serials Automation in the United States: A Bibliographic History. LC 76-18116. 1976. 10.00 (ISBN 0-8108-0955-9). Scarecrow.

Pitkin, Hanna F. The Concept of Representation. (Campus Ser.: No. 75). 1978. pap. 6.95x (ISBN 0-520-02156-8). U of Cal Pr.

--Wittgenstein & Justice: On the Significance of Ludwig Wittgenstein for Social & Political Thought. LC 76-138508. 1972. 20.00x (ISBN 0-520-01841-9); pap. 7.95x (ISBN 0-520-02329-3). U of Cal Pr.

Pitkin, Thomas M. The Captain Departs: Ulysses S. Grant's Last Campaign. LC 73-4321. 185p. 1973. 10.95x (ISBN 0-8093-0637-9). S Ill U Pr.

Pitkin, Thomas M., jt. auth. see Cordasco, Francesco.

Pitkin, Timothy. Political & Civil History of the United States of America from the Year 1763 to the Close of the Administration of President Washington in March, 1797, 2 Vols. LC 79-109613. (Ear of the American Revolution Ser). 1970. Repr. of 1823 ed. lib. bdg. 95.00 (ISBN 0-306-71908-8). Da Capo.

Pitler, Robert M. New York Criminal Practice Under the CPL. LC 74-181692. 1972. with 1979 suppl. 50.00 (ISBN 0-87632-087-6). Boardman.

Pitman, John C., jt. auth. see Roueche, John E.

Pitrone, Jean M. Myra: The Life & Times of Myra Wolfgang, Trade-Union Leader. LC 80-68386. (Illus.). 226p. 1980. 10.00 (ISBN 0-686-28855-6). Calibre Bks.

Pitseolak, Peter. Peter Pitseolak's Escape from Death. Eber, Dorothy, ed. LC 77-83236. 1978. 7.95 o.s.i. (ISBN 0-440-06894-0, Sey Lawr); PLB 7.45 (ISBN 0-440-06896-7). Delacorte.

Pitt, Angela. Shakespeare's Women. (Illus.). 224p. 1981. 16.50x (ISBN 0-389-20122-7). B&N.

Pitt, Barrie. Battle of the Atlantic. LC 79-74822. (World War II Ser.). (Illus.). (gr. 6 up). 1977. PLB 14.94 (ISBN 0-8094-2467-3, Pub. by Time-Life). Silver.

--Battle of the Atlantic. Time-Life Books, ed. (World War II). 1977. 12.95 (ISBN 0-8094-2466-5). Time-Life.

--Churchill & His Generals. 224p. 1981. pap. 2.50 (ISBN 0-553-14610-6). Bantam.

Pitt, Bertram, jt. auth. see Strauss, H. William.

Pitt, D. C. & Smith, B. C. Government Department: An Organizational Perspective. 166p. (Orig.). 1981. pap. 20.00 (ISBN 0-7100-0742-6). Routledge & Kegan.

Pitt, Dennis. Lysosomes & Cell Function. LC 75-308385. (Integrated Themes in Biology Ser). (Illus.). 160p. 1975. pap. text ed. 11.50x (ISBN 0-582-44344-X). Longman.

Pitt, Douglas C. Telecommunications Function of the British Post Office. 1979. text ed. 20.50x (ISBN 0-566-00273-6, Pub. by Gower Pub Co England). Renouf.

Pitt, Leonard. The Decline of the Californios: A Social History of the Spanish-Speaking Californians, 1846-1890. 1966. 11.95 (ISBN 0-520-01019-1); pap. 5.95 (ISBN 0-520-01637-8, CAL186). U of Cal Pr.

--We Americans: A Topical History of the United States. (Single volume edition). 1976. 16.95x o.p. (ISBN 0-673-05974-X). Scott F.

Pitt, V., jt. auth. see Hoke, H.

Pitt, Valerie. Bats. LC 76-12535. (First Bks.). (Illus.). 72p. (gr. 5-8). 1976. PLB 4.90 o.p. (ISBN 0-531-00335-3). Watts.

--Let's Find Out About Communications. LC 72-7084. (Let's Find Out Bks). (Illus.). 48p. (gr. 3-4). 1973. PLB 4.47 o.p. (ISBN 0-531-00083-4). Watts.

--Let's Find Out About Manners. LC 70-183898. (Let's Find Out Bks). (Illus.). 48p. (gr. 3-4). 1972. PLB 4.47 o.p. (ISBN 0-531-00082-6). Watts.

--Let's Find Out About Names. LC 76-131156. (Let's Find Out Bks). (Illus.). (gr. k-3). 1971. PLB 4.47 o.p. (ISBN 0-531-00069-9). Watts.

--Let's Find Out About Neighbors. LC 78-101750. (Let's Find Out Bks). (Illus.). (gr. k-3). 1970. PLB 4.47 o.p. (ISBN 0-531-00058-3). Watts.

--Let's Find Out About Streets. LC 72-87932. (Let's Find Out Bks). (Illus.). (gr. k-3). 1969. PLB 4.47 o.p. (ISBN 0-531-00063-X). Watts.

--Let's Find Out About the City. LC 68-10507. (Let's Find Out Bks). (Illus.). (gr. k-3). 1968. PLB 4.47 o.p. (ISBN 0-531-00012-5). Watts.

--Let's Find Out About the Community. LC 79-185688. (Let's Find Out Bks). (Illus.). 48p. (gr. 3-4). 1972. PLB 4.47 o.p. (ISBN 0-531-00080-X). Watts.

--Let's Find Out About the Family. LC 78-117180. (Let's Find Out Bks). (gr. k-3). 1970. PLB 4.90 o.p. (ISBN 0-531-00065-6). Watts.

--Tennyson Laureate. LC 63-6002. 1962. 15.00x o.p. (ISBN 0-8020-1228-0); pap. 4.50 o.p. (ISBN 0-8020-6098-6). U of Toronto Pr.

Pitt, Valerie & Cook, David. A Closer Look at Ants. LC 75-4358. (A Closer Look at Ser). (Illus.). 32p. (gr. 4 up). 1975. 2.95 (ISBN 0-531-02423-7); PLB 6.90 (ISBN 0-531-01098-8). Watts.

Pitt, Valerie, jt. auth. see Hoke, Helen.

Pittard, Kay & Mitchell, Robert W. Comparative Morphology of the Life Stages of Cryptocellus pelaezi (Arachnida, Ricinulei) (Graduate Studies: No. 1). (Illus., Orig.). 1972. pap. 4.00 (ISBN 0-89672-008-X). Tex Tech Pr.

Pittaro, John M. Cuentos Faciles De Hoy y Ayer. (Illus.). 128p. (gr. 8). 1973. pap. text ed. 2.75x (ISBN 0-88334-059-3). Ind Sch Pr.

Pittaro, Johnm. Cuentecitos. 128p. (gr. 8-10). 1968. pap. text ed. 2.75 (ISBN 0-88345-034-8, 17444); cassettes 25.00 (ISBN 0-686-67013-2). Regents Pub.

Pittaway, Margaret. The Rainforest Children. (Illus.). 32p. (ps-3). 1980. 7.95 (ISBN 0-19-554238-X). Oxford U Pr.

Pittenger, Donald B. Projecting State & Local Populations. LC 75-38694. 144p. 1975. 17.50 o.p. (ISBN 0-88410-356-0). Ballinger Pub.

Pittenger, Norman. After Death-Life in God. 96p. 1980. 4.95 (ISBN 0-8164-0108-X). Crossroad NY.

--Unbounded Love: God & Man in Process. (Orig.). 1976. pap. 3.95 (ISBN 0-8164-2119-6). Crossroad NY.

Pittenger, Norman W. Early Britain: The Celts, Romans, & Anglo-Saxons. LC 72-256. (First Bks). (Illus.). 96p. (gr. 5-8). 1972. PLB 4.90 o.p. (ISBN 0-531-00742-1). Watts.

Pittenger, W. Norman. Plato: His Life & Teaching. LC 76-150375. (Biography Ser). (gr. 7 up). 1971. PLB 5.90 o.p. (ISBN 0-531-00964-5). Watts.

Pittenger, W. Norman, jt. auth. see Pike, James A.

Pitti, Buonaccorso & Dati, Gregorio. Two Memoirs of Renaissance Florence: The Diaries of Buonaccorso Pitti & Gregorio Dati. pap. 2.95x (ISBN 0-06-131333-5, TB1333, Torch). Har-Row.

Pittillo, Elen S., jt. auth. see Heyden, Siegfried.

Pittillo, Elen S., jt. auth. see Sizemore, Chris C.

Pittman, Brenda S. The Feelings Are There. 1981. 4.50 (ISBN 0-8062-1553-4). Carlton.

Pittman, David J. & Snyder, Charles R. Society, Culture & Drinking Patterns. LC 62-15188. 1962. 28.95 (ISBN 0-471-69102-X, Pub. by Wiley-Interscience). Wiley.

Pittman, David J. & Snyder, Charles R., eds. Society, Culture & Drinking Patterns. LC 65-15188. (Arcturus Books Paperbacks). 633p. 1968. pap. 12.95 (ISBN 0-8093-0326-4). S Ill U Pr.

Pittman, Philip. The Present State of the European Settlements on the Mississippi. facsimile, new ed. McDermott, John Francis, ed. LC 76-44247. (Illus.). 221p. 1977. 24.95x (ISBN 0-87870-011-0). Memphis St Univ.

Pittock, A. B., et al, eds. Climatic Change & Variability: A Southern Perspective. LC 76-53521. (Illus.). 1978. 65.50 (ISBN 0-521-21562-5). Cambridge U Pr.

Pitt-Rivers, Julian. People of the Sierra. 2nd ed. LC 70-153710. 1972. pap. 5.50 (ISBN 0-226-67010-4, P55, Phoen). U of Chicago Pr.

Pitt-Rivers, Michael. Dorset: A Shell Guide. (Shell Guide Ser.). (Illus.). 1969. 7.95 (ISBN 0-686-24603-9, Pub. by Faber & Faber). Merrimack Bk Serv.

Pitts, Denis. This City Is Ours. 1977. pap. 1.95 o.p. (ISBN 0-380-01851-9, 36483). Avon.

Pitts, Forrest R. Japan. rev. ed. LC 77-87223. (World Cultures Ser.). (Illus.). 192p. (gr. 6 up). 1979. text ed. 9.95, 5 or more copies 7.96 ea. o.p. (ISBN 0-88296-119-5); tchrs'. guide 8.94 o.p. (ISBN 0-686-67105-8). Fideler.

Pitts, Forrest R., jt. auth. see Dicken, Samuel N.

Pitts, J. R. The Life & Confession of the Noted Outlaw James Copeland. facsimile ed. LC 80-20865. (Illus.). 256p. 1980. Repr. of 1909 ed. 12.50 (ISBN 0-87805-125-2). U Pr of Miss.

Pitts, James N., et al. Advances in Photochemistry. LC 66-13592. Vol. 10, 1977. 38.50 (ISBN 0-471-02145-8, Pub. by Wiley-Interscience); Vol. 11, 1979. 43.95 (ISBN 0-471-04797-X); Vol. 12, 1980. 42.50 (ISBN 0-471-06286-3). Wiley.

Pitts, James N., Jr. & Metcalf, Robert L., eds. Advances in Environmental Science & Technology. LC 69-18013. 1977. Vol. 4. 30.95 o.p. (ISBN 0-471-69087-2); Vol. 7. 43.50 (ISBN 0-471-01365-X, Pub. by Wiley-Interscience). Wiley.

Pitts, Michael R. Famous Movie Detectives. LC 79-17474. 367p. 1979. 18.50 (ISBN 0-8108-1236-3). Scarecrow.

--Horror Film Stars. LC 80-11241. (Illus.). 333p. 1981. lib. bdg. 16.95x (ISBN 0-89950-003-X); pap. 12.95x (ISBN 0-89950-004-8). McFarland & Co.

--Radio Soundtracks: A Reference Guide. LC 76-18888. 1976. 10.00 (ISBN 0-8108-0956-7). Scarecrow.

Pitts, Michael R. & Harrison, Louis H. Hollywood on Record: The Film Stars' Discography. LC 77-17144. (Illus.). 1978. 19.50 (ISBN 0-8108-1093-X). Scarecrow.

Pitts, Michael R., jt. auth. see Parish, James R.

Pitts, V. Peter, ed. Children's Pictures of God. (Illus.). (gr. 1-4). 1979. pap. 3.95 (ISBN 0-915744-20-1). Character Res.

Pitz, jt. auth. see Wallace.

Pitz, Henry C. Charcoal Drawing. LC 73-133980. (Illus.). 1971. 13.95 o.p. (ISBN 0-8230-0615-8); pap. 9.95 o.p. (ISBN 0-8230-0616-6). Watson-Guptill.

Pivar, William H. The Real Estate Career Guide. LC 80-11544. 240p. 1980. lib. bdg. 11.95 (ISBN 0-668-04789-5); pap. 7.95 (ISBN 0-668-04970-7). Arco.

Pivcevic, E., ed. Phenomenology & Philisophical Understanding. LC 74-19533. 304p. 1975. 38.50 (ISBN 0-521-20637-5); pap. 11.50x (ISBN 0-521-09914-5). Cambridge U Pr.

Pivovarov, A. A. Thermal Conditions in Freezing Lakes & Rivers. Vilim, E., tr. from Rus. LC 73-12269. 136p. 1973. 32.95 (ISBN 0-470-69103-4). Halsted Pr.

Piwonka, Mario P. Lucilius und Kallimachos. Commager, Steele, ed. LC 77-70830. (Latin Poetry Ser.). 1978. lib. bdg. 41.00 (ISBN 0-8240-2976-3). Garland Pub.

Piwonka, Ruth & Blackburn, Roderic H. A Visible Heritage, Columbia County, New York: A History in Art & Architecture. LC 77-9093. 160p. 1977. 14.95 (ISBN 0-89062-053-9, Pub. by Columbia County); pap. 10.95 (ISBN 0-89062-028-8). Pub Ctr Cult Res.

Pixler, Paul. Hiking Trails of the San Juans. (Illus.). 120p. (Orig.). 1981. pap. 5.95 (ISBN 0-87108-579-8). Pruett.

Pixley, Alden F. Applied Linear Algebra. LC 80-8241. 264p. 1980. lib. bdg. 18.50 (ISBN 0-8191-1169-4); pap. text ed. 10.50 (ISBN 0-8191-1170-8). U Pr of Amer.

Pizarro, Agueda. Shadowinnower. Miller, Barbara S., tr. from Sp. LC 79-12561. 1979. 12.50x (ISBN 0-231-04828-9); pap. 4.95 (ISBN 0-231-04829-7). Columbia U Pr.

Pizer, Donald. Critical Essays on Theodore Dreiser. (Critical Essays on American Literature). 1981. lib. bdg. 25.00 (ISBN 0-8161-8257-4). Twayne.

Pizer, Donald, ed. see Garland, Hamlin.

Pizer, Donald, ed. see Norris, Frank.

Pizer, Hank & Garfink, Christine. The Post Partum Book: How to Cope with & Enjoy the First Year of Parenting. LC 78-19710. 1979. 9.95 (ISBN 0-394-50524-7, GP821). Grove.

Pizer, Hank & Palinski, Christine O. Coping with a Miscarriage. (Illus.). 1980. 10.95 (ISBN 0-8037-1380-0). Dial.

Pizey, J. S. Synthetic Reagents, Vols. 1-2. LC 73-14417. 411p. 1974. Vol. 1. 74.95 (ISBN 0-470-69104-2); Vol. 2. 54.95 (ISBN 0-470-69107-7). Halsted Pr.

--Synthetic Reagents Vol. 4: Mercuric Acetate Periodic Acid & Periodates Sulfuryl Chloride. 200p. 1981. 110.00 (ISBN 0-470-27133-7). Halsted Pr.

Pizey, J. S., ed. Synthetic Reagents, Vol. 3. LC 73-14417. 1977. 59.95 (ISBN 0-470-99118-6). Halsted Pr.

Pizzarello, Donald J., jt. auth. see Cooper, Jay S.

Pizzat, Frank. Behavior Modification in Residential Treatment for Children: Model of a Program. LC 72-11554. 98p. 1973. text ed. 12.95 (ISBN 0-87705-097-X). Human Sci Pr.

Pizzetti, Ippolito & Cocker, Henry. Flowers: A Guide for Your Garden, 2 vols. LC 73-7526. (Illus.). 1300p. 1975. 60.00 o.p. (ISBN 0-8109-0127-7). Abrams.

Pizzi, Bobby. Remnants of Every Day Life. 1979. 6.95 (ISBN 0-533-04529-0). Vantage.

Pizzo, Joan. Little Crumb. (Illus.). 29p. (Orig.). (gr. k-6). 1980. PLB 10.95; pap. 7.95. Back Bay.

Pizzorno, Alessandro, jt. ed. see Crouch, Colin.

Pizzuto, Joseph. Fabric Science. 4th ed. Price, Arthur & Cohen, Alan, eds. (Illus.). 1980. ring-binder, wkbk. 14.50 (ISBN 0-87005-265-9). Fairchild.

Plaat, Otto. Ordinary Differential Equations. LC 70-156869. 350p. 1971. 18.50x (ISBN 0-8162-6844-4). Holden-Day.

Plaatje, Sol T., illus. Mhudi. new ed. 1978. pap. 5.00 (ISBN 0-89410-031-9, Co-Pub by Heinemann Educ. Bks). Three Continents.

Plaatje, Solomon T. Mhudi. Couzens, Tim, ed. (Illus.). 165p. 1975. Repr. 22.00x (ISBN 0-909078-01-7, Pub. by Quagga Press). Three Continents.

Plaats G. J. Van, Der see Van Der Plaats, G. J.

Place. The Vikings. (gr. 5 up). 1980. pap. 6.90 (ISBN 0-531-09170-8, G32). Watts.

Place, Carol, jt. ed. see Weiss, Iris R.

Place, Charles A. Charles Bulfinch: Architect & Citizen. LC 68-27717. (Architecture & Decorative Art Ser). (Illus.). 1968. Repr. of 1925 ed. lib. bdg. 29.50 (ISBN 0-306-71150-8). Da Capo.

Place, Irene & Byers, Edward E. Executive Secretarial Procedures. 5th ed. LC 79-9097. (Illus.). 1980. text ed. 15.80 (ISBN 0-07-050255-2); instrs'. manual & key 5.50 (ISBN 0-07-050257-9). McGraw.

Place, Irene, et al. Fundamental Filing Practice. (Office Occupations Ser). (Illus.). 256p. 1973. pap. text ed. 9.95x (ISBN 0-13-332742-6). P-H.

Place, Irene M. & Popham, E. L. Filing & Records Management. 1966. text ed. 12.95x (ISBN 0-13-314625-1). P-H.

Place, Linna F., et al. Aging & the Aged: An Annotated Bibliography & Research Guide. (Westview Guides to Library Research). 175p. 1980. lib. bdg. 17.50x (ISBN 0-89158-934-1). Westview.

Place, Lucille. Fell's Beginner's Guide to Bridge for All Ages. LC 75-13971. 1975. pap. 4.95 (ISBN 0-8119-0362-1). Fell.

--Parliamentary Procedures Simplified. LC 76-16466. 160p. 1976. 9.95 (ISBN 0-8119-0269-2); pap. 4.95 (ISBN 0-88391-049-7). Fell.

Place, Marian T. Bigfoot All Over the Country. LC 78-7728. (Illus.). 1978. 6.50 (ISBN 0-396-07610-6). Dodd.

--The Boy Who Saw Bigfoot. LC 78-23199. (gr. 4-6). 1979. 5.95 (ISBN 0-396-07644-0). Dodd.

--Comanches & Other Indians of Texas. LC 79-103829. (Curriculum Related Bks). (gr. 7 up). 1970. 5.50 o.p. (ISBN 0-15-219451-7, HJ). HarBraceJ.

--Gold Down Under: Story of the Australian Gold Rush. (Illus.). (gr. 7 up). 1969. 4.50g o.s.i. (ISBN 0-02-774440-X, CCPr). Macmillan.

--Nobody Meets Bigfoot. LC 75-40030. (gr. 4-7). 1976. 4.95 (ISBN 0-396-07290-9). Dodd.

--The Resident Witch. (Illus.). (gr. 2-5). 1974. pap. 1.75 (ISBN 0-380-00852-1, 51425, Camelot). Avon.

Place, Marion T. On the Track of Bigfoot. (Illus.). (gr. 5 up). 1979. pap. 1.75 (ISBN 0-671-29944-1). PB.

Place, Robin & Ross, Anne. The Celts. LC 77-86183. (Peoples of the Past Ser.). (Illus.). 1977. lib. bdg. 7.95 (ISBN 0-686-51155-7). Silver.

Place, Stan & Budd, Elaine. Stan Place's Guide to Make-Up: How to Look Like Yourself Only Better. (Illus.). 192p. 1981. 17.95 (ISBN 0-385-15537-9). Doubleday.

Placek, Paul J., ed. see Hendershot, Gerry E.

Placzek, Beverley, ed. Record of a Friendship: The Correspondence of Wilhelm Reich and A.S. Neill. 1981. 15.95 (ISBN 0-374-24807-9). FS&G.

Plahter, Leif E., et al. Gothic Painted Altar Frontals from the Church of Tingelstad. (Medieval Art in Norway Ser). 107p. 1974. 32.00x (ISBN 8-200-08953-3, Dist. by Columbia U Pr). Universitet.

Plaice, Neville, tr. see Bernhard, Thomas.

Plaice, Stephen, tr. see Bernhard, Thomas.

Plaidy, Jean. The Battle of the Queens. 320p. 1981. 10.95 (ISBN 0-399-12604-X). Putnam.

--Beyond the Blue Mountains. 480p. 1976. pap. 1.95 o.p. (ISBN 0-449-22773-1, Crest). Fawcett.

--The Captive Queen of Scots. 448p. 1977. pap. 1.75 o.p. (ISBN 0-449-23287-5, Crest). Fawcett.

--A Health Unto His Majesty. 288p. 1973. pap. 1.75 o.p. (ISBN 0-449-22019-2, P2019, Crest). Fawcett.

--Here Lies Our Sovereign Lord. 288p. 1977. pap. 1.75 o.p. (ISBN 0-449-23256-5, Crest). Fawcett.

--Light on Lucrezia. 240p. 1977. pap. 1.75 o.p. (ISBN 0-449-23108-9, Crest). Fawcett.

--Madonna of the Seven Hills. 288p. 1976. pap. 1.75 o.p. (ISBN 0-449-23026-0, Crest). Fawcett.

--The Passionate Enemies. 320p. 1981. pap. 2.50 (ISBN 0-449-24390-7, Crest). Fawcett.

--The Prince of Darkness. 320p. 1981. 10.95 (ISBN 0-686-69594-1). Putnam.

--Queen & Lord M. 1978. pap. 1.75 o.p. (ISBN 0-449-23605-6, Crest). Fawcett.

--The Sixth Wife. 1975. pap. 1.25 o.p. (ISBN 0-449-22343-4, P2343, Crest). Fawcett.

Plain, Belva. Random Winds. 1981. pap. 3.50 (ISBN 0-440-17158-X). Dell.

Plaister, T. Developing Listening Comprehension for ESL Students: The Kingdom of Kochen. 1976. pap. 8.50 (ISBN 0-13-204479-X); tapes 125.00 (ISBN 0-13-204495-1). P-H.

Plaister, Ted. English Monosyllables: A Minimal Pair Locator List for English As a Second Language. 1965. pap. 2.00x o.p. (ISBN 0-8248-0022-2, Eastwest Ctr). U Pr of Hawaii.

Plakogiannis, Fotios M. & Cutie, Anthony J. Self-Assessment of Current Knowledge in Pharmacy. 1976. spiral bdg. 9.50 (ISBN 0-87488-272-9). Med Exam.

Plamenatz, John. Democracy & Illusion: An Examination of Certain Aspects of Modern Democratic Theory. 1977. pap. text ed. 10.50x (ISBN 0-582-48575-4). Longman.

--English Utilitarians. 2nd ed. 1958. text ed. 18.50x (ISBN 0-631-05420-0). Humanities.

--Karl Marx's Philosophy of Man. 292p. 1975. 37.50x (ISBN 0-19-824551-3); pap. 13.95 (ISBN 0-19-824649-8). Oxford U Pr.

--Man & Society: A Critical Examination of Some Important Social & Political Theories from Machiavelli to Marx, Vol. 2. 1975. pap. text ed. 14.95 (ISBN 0-582-48046-9). Longman.

Plamenatz, John P. German Marxism & Russian Communism. LC 75-1135. 356p. 1975. Repr. of 1954 ed. lib. bdg. 25.25x (ISBN 0-8371-7986-6, PLGM). Greenwood.

Planche, James R. The Pursuivant of Arms; or, Heraldry Founded Upon Facts. LC 72-10610. (Illus.). 299p. 1973. Repr. of 1874 ed. 15.00 (ISBN 0-8103-3171-3). Gale.

--Recollections & Reflections. (Music Reprint, 1978 Ser.). (Illus.). 1978. Repr. of 1901 ed. lib. bdg. 42.50 (ISBN 0-306-79501-9). Da Capo.

Planck, Dennistown W. Ver see Ver Planck, Dennistown W. & Teare, B. R.

Plane, Donald R. & Kochenberger, Gary A. Operations Research for Managerial Decisions. 1972. text ed. 13.90 (ISBN 0-256-00451-X). Irwin.

Plane, Donald R. & Oppermann, Edward B. Statistics for Management Decisions. 1977. 18.50x (ISBN 0-256-01814-6). Business Pubns.

Plane, Donald R., et al. Simulation of the Denver Fire Department for Development Policy Analysis. 1975. 2.50 (ISBN 0-686-64196-5). U CO Busn Res Div.

Plane, Robert A., jt. auth. see Sienko, Michell J.

Planelli, Antonio. Dell'Opera in Musica. LC 80-2292. 1981. Repr. of 1772 ed. 31.50 (ISBN 0-404-18861-3). AMS Pr.

Plank, J. E. Van Der see Van Der Plank, J. E.

Plank, John N., et al, eds. Cuba & the United States: Long Range Perspectives. 1967. 11.95 (ISBN 0-8157-7100-2). Brookings.

Planned Parenthood Federation of America, Inc. Echoes from the Past. (Illus.). 128p. 1979. 25.00 (ISBN 0-934586-03-9). Plan Parent.

Planning & Conservation Foundation, ed. see Sedway-Cooke.

Plano, Jack & Olton, Roy. International Relations Dictionary. 2nd ed. 1978. 6.50 o.p. (ISBN 0-932826-00-8). New Issues MI.

Plano, Jack C., jt. auth. see Kamara, Marjon V.

Plano, Jack C., jt. auth. see Rossi, Ernest E.

Plant, Sir Arnold. Selected Economic Essays & Addresses. Seldon, Arthur, ed. 260p. 1974. 26.00 (ISBN 0-7100-7935-4). Routledge & Kegan.

Plant, Majorie. The English Book Trade. 1974. text ed. 27.50x o.p. (ISBN 0-04-655012-7). Allen Unwin.

Plant, Michael, jt. ed. see Hore, Brian.

Plant, Raymond. Social & Moral Theory in Casework. (Library of Social Work). 1970. 10.00x (ISBN 0-7100-6808-5); pap. 3.50 (ISBN 0-7100-6809-3). Routledge & Kegan.

Plant, Raymond, et al. Political Philosophy & Social Welfare: Essays on the Normative Basis of Welfare Provision. (International Library of Welfare & Philosophy). 280p. 1981. 27.50 (ISBN 0-7100-0611-X); pap. 15.00 (ISBN 0-7100-0631-4). Routledge & Kegan.

Plant, Richard, ed. see Boll, Heinrich.

Plant, Richard M. Formulae for the Mariner. LC 78-21543. (Illus.). 1978. spiral bdg. 7.00x (ISBN 0-87033-251-1). Cornell Maritime.

Plant, Richard M., jt. auth. see James, Richard.

Plante, David. Ghost of Henry James. LC 71-118217. Date not set. cancelled (ISBN 0-87645-025-7). Gambit.

Plante, Edmund. The New Neighbors. (Orig.). 1979. pap. 1.95 (ISBN 0-686-68909-7). Manor Bks.

Plante, Jacques. Goaltending. (Illus.). 128p. 1973. pap. 2.95 o.s.i. (ISBN 0-02-081120-9, Collier). Macmillan.

Plante, Patricia. Monarch Notes on Stendhal's the Red & the Black & Charterhouse of Parma. (Orig.). pap. 1.95 (ISBN 0-671-00570-7). Monarch Pr.

Plantinga, Alvin. The Nature of Necessity. 1979. pap. 9.95x (ISBN 0-19-824414-2). Oxford U Pr.

Plantinga, Cornelius, Jr. Beyond Doubt: A Devotional Response to Questions of Faith. LC 80-10647. (Illus.). 256p. (Orig.). 1980. pap. text ed. 4.95 (ISBN 0-933140-12-6). Bd of Pubns CRC.

Plantinga, Leon B. Schumann As Critic. LC 76-7599. (Music Reprint Ser.). 1976. Repr. of 1967 ed. pap. 27.50 (ISBN 0-306-70785-3). Da Capo.

Plantley. The International Civil Service: Law & Management. 1981. write for info. (ISBN 0-89352-103-5). Masson Pub.

Plants, Helen & Venable, Wallace. Introduction to Statics. LC 74-32425. (Illus.). 1045p. 1975. text ed. 19.50 (ISBN 0-8299-0023-3); tchrs' ed. avail. (ISBN 0-8299-0568-5); notebook avail. (ISBN 0-8299-0047-0). West Pub.

Plascov, A. O. The Palestinian Refugees in Jordan 1948-57. 256p. 1980. 32.50x (ISBN 0-7146-3120-5, F Cass Co). Biblio Dist.

Plasitics Education Foundation. Curriculum Guide for Plastics Education. LC 77-4080. 1977. pap. 12.95 (ISBN 0-672-97113-5). Bobbs.

Plaskow, Judith, jt. auth. see Christ, Carol P.

Plass, H. J., Jr., jt. auth. see Hagerty, W. W.

Plasschaert, Sylvain R. Transfer Pricing & Multinational Corporation: An Overview of Concepts, Mechanisms & Regulations. LC 79-84708. (Praeger Special Studies Ser.). 126p. 1979. 21.95 (ISBN 0-03-052396-6). Praeger.

Plaster, C., et al, eds. Milling, Vol. 1. 2nd ed. (Engineering Craftsmen: No. H4). (Illus.). 1977. spiral bdg. 16.50x (ISBN 0-85083-404-X). Intl Ideas.

Plaster, H. J. Blast Cleaning & Allied Processes. LC 73-155194. (Illus.). 374p. 1972. 57.50x (ISBN 0-901994-03-0). Intl Pubns Serv.

Plastics Technology Editors, ed. Plastics Manufacturing Handbook & Buyers Guide. 250p. (Annual). Date not set. pap. 22.95x (ISBN 0-89047-049-9). Herman Pub.

Plastino, Janice, jt. auth. see Penrod, James.

Plater, William M. Grim Phoenix: Reconstructing Thomas Pynchon. LC 77-12833. 288p. 1978. 12.50x (ISBN 0-253-32670-2). Ind U Pr.

Plateris, Alexander A. & Shipp, Audrey. Duration of Marriage to Divorce United States. (Ser. 21: No. 38). 50p. 1981. pap. text ed. 1.75 (ISBN 0-8406-0217-0). Natl Ctr Health Stats.

Plath, David W., jt. auth. see Sugihara, Yoshie.

Plath, Sylvia. Crossing the Water. LC 71-138756. 1971. 8.95 (ISBN 0-06-013366-X, HarpT); pap. 3.95 (ISBN 0-06-013374-0, TD230, HarpT). Har-Row.

Platner, W. S. & Meyer, D. K. Laboratory Guide for Elements of Physiology. 5th ed. text ed. 3.95x spiral bdg. (ISBN 0-87543-039-2). Lucas.

Platnick, Norman I., jt. auth. see Nelson, Gareth.

Plato. Apology. Adam, A. M., ed. (Gr). text ed. 5.50x (ISBN 0-521-05958-5). Cambridge U Pr.

--Crito. Adam, James, ed. (Gr). text ed. 6.50x with vocab. (ISBN 0-521-05959-3). Cambridge U Pr.

--The Dialogues of Plato. Greene, William C., ed. Jowett, B., tr. 1954. 7.95x o.p. (ISBN 0-87140-858-9). Liveright.

--Dialogues of Plato. Kaplan, Justin E., ed. Jowett, Benjamin E., tr. pap. 2.95 (ISBN 0-671-42137-9). WSP.

--Euthyphro. Burnet, John, ed. Bd. with Apology of Socrates; Crito. 1924. 11.95x (ISBN 0-19-814015-0). Oxford U Pr.

--Euthyphro, Apology Crito: With the Death Scene from Phaedo. Church, F. J. & Cummings, R. D., trs. Bd. with Apology; Crito. (gr. 9up). 1956. pap. 2.50 (ISBN 0-672-60166-4, LLA4). Bobbs.

--Gorgias. Helmbold, W. C., tr. LC 52-9226. 1952. pap. 3.50 (ISBN 0-672-60181-8, LLA20). Bobbs.

--Gorgias. Dodds, E. R., ed. 1959. 34.50x (ISBN 0-19-814153-X). Oxford U Pr.

--Gorgias. Irwin, Terence, tr. from Greek. (Clarendon Plato Ser.). 278p. 1979. text ed. 29.00x (ISBN 0-19-872087-4); pap. text ed. 14.95x (ISBN 0-19-872091-2). Oxford U Pr.

--Laches & Charmides. Sprague, Rosamond K., ed. LC 72-86556. (Liberal Arts Library Ser.). 112p. 1973. pap. text ed. 3.95 (ISBN 0-672-60379-9). Bobbs.

--The Last Days of Socrates. Tredennick, Hugh, tr. Incl. Euthyphro; Apology; Crito; Phaedo. (Classics Ser.). 1954. pap. 2.25 (ISBN 0-14-044037-2). Penguin.

--Meno. Jowett, Benjamin, tr. LC 51-7881. 1949. pap. 2.50 (ISBN 0-672-60173-7, LLA12). Bobbs.

--Meno. Bluck, R. S., ed. (Gr). 1961. text ed. 63.00 (ISBN 0-521-05961-5). Cambridge U Pr.

--Opera, 5 vols. Burnet, John, ed. Incl. Vol. 1. Euthyphro, Apologia Socratis, Crito, Phaedo, Cratylus, Theaetetus, Sophista, Politicus. 2nd ed. 1905. 17.50x (ISBN 0-19-814540-3); Vol. 2. Parmenides, Philebus, Symposium, Phaedrus, Alcibiades 1 & 2, Hipparchus, Amatores. 2nd ed. 1910. 17.50x (ISBN 0-19-814541-1); Vol. 3. Theages, Charmides, Laches, Lysis, Euthydemus, Protagoras, Gorgias, Meno, Hippias Maior, Hippas Minor, Io, Menexenus. 1903. 18.95x (ISBN 0-19-814542-X); Vol. 4. Clitopho, Respublica, Timaeus, Critias. 1905. 18.95x (ISBN 0-19-814544-6); Vol. 5. Minos, Leges, Epinomis, Epistulae, Definitiones. 1907. 22.50x (ISBN 0-19-814546-2). Oxford U Pr.

--Phaedo. Church, F. J., tr. LC 51-10496. 1951. pap. 2.95 (ISBN 0-672-60192-3, LLA30). Bobbs.

--Phaedo. Hackforth, R., ed. 200p. 1972. 23.95 (ISBN 0-521-08458-X); pap. 6.50x (ISBN 0-521-09702-9). Cambridge U Pr.

--Phaedo. Gallop, David, tr. & notes by. (Clarendon Plato Ser). 224p. 1975. pap. 17.95x (ISBN 0-19-872049-1). Oxford U Pr.

--Phaedo. Burnet, John, ed. 1979. pap. 11.95x (ISBN 0-19-814014-2). Oxford U Pr.

--Phaedrus. Helmbold, W. C. & Rabinowitz, W. G., trs. 1956. pap. 2.50 (ISBN 0-672-60207-5, LLA40). Bobbs.

--Phaedrus. Hackforth, R., ed. 200p. 1972. 23.95 (ISBN 0-521-08459-8); pap. 6.50x (ISBN 0-521-09703-7). Cambridge U Pr.

--Philebus. Hackforth, R., ed. 200p. 1972. 23.95 (ISBN 0-521-08460-1); pap. 6.50x (ISBN 0-521-09704-5). Cambridge U Pr.

--Philebus. Gosling, J. C., tr. & notes by. (Clarendon Plato Ser). 256p. 1975. 15.50x (ISBN 0-19-872044-0); pap. 17.95x (ISBN 0-19-872054-8). Oxford U Pr.

--Plato & Parmenides: Way of Truth & Plato's Parmenides. Cornford, Francis M., tr. 1957. pap. 5.95 (ISBN 0-672-60297-0, LLA102). Bobbs.

--Plato: Protagoras. Taylor, C. C., tr. (Clarendon Plato Ser.). 1976. 22.00x (ISBN 0-19-872045-9); pap. 11.50 o.p. (ISBN 0-19-872088-2). Oxford U Pr.

--Plato's Cosmology: The Timaeus of Plato. Cornford, Francis M., tr. LC 57-4253. 1957. pap. 7.95 (ISBN 0-672-60296-2, LLA101). Bobbs.

--Plato's Phaedo. Bluck, R. S., tr. 1959. pap. 5.50 (ISBN 0-672-60308-X, LLA110). Bobbs.

--Plato's Republic. Jowett, Benjamin, tr. (Classics Ser). (gr. 11 up). 1968. pap. 1.95 (ISBN 0-8049-0172-4, CL-172). Airmont.

--Plato's Theory of Knowledge: The Theaetetus & the Sophist of Plato. Cornford, Francis M., tr. LC 57-4254. 1957. pap. 6.95 (ISBN 0-672-60294-6, LLA100). Bobbs.

--Protagoras. Vlastos, Gregory, ed. Jowett, Benjamin & Ostwald, Martin, trs. LC 56-14580. 1956. pap. 3.50 (ISBN 0-672-60232-6, LLA59). Bobbs.

--Protagoras. Adam, James & Adam, A. M., eds. (Gr). text ed. 8.95x (ISBN 0-521-05962-3). Cambridge U Pr.

--Protagoras & Meno. Guthrie, W. K., tr. Bd. with Meno. (Classics Ser.). 1957. pap. 2.50 (ISBN 0-14-044068-2). Penguin.

--Republic, 2 Vols. rev. ed. Adam, James, ed. (Gr.). Vol. 1, Bks. 1-5. text ed. 56.00x (ISBN 0-521-05963-1); Vol. 2, Bks. 6-10. text ed. 66.00x (ISBN 0-521-05964-X). Cambridge U Pr.

--Republic. Lindsay, A. D., tr. 1957. pap. 5.95 (ISBN 0-525-47004-2). Dutton.

--The Republic & Other Works. Jowett, Benjamin, tr. Incl. Symposium; Parmenides; Euthyphro; Apology; Crito; Phaedo. pap. 4.95 (ISBN 0-385-09497-3, C12, Anch). Doubleday.

--Statesman. Ostwald, Martin, ed. Skemp, B. J., tr. LC 57-14633. 1957. pap. 3.95 (ISBN 0-672-60230-X, LLA57). Bobbs.

--Symposium. Jowett, Benjamin, tr. 1956. pap. 1.95 (ISBN 0-672-60169-9, LLA7). Bobbs.

--Symposium & Other Dialogues. Joyce, Michael, et al, eds. 1964. 12.95x (ISBN 0-460-00418-2, Evman). Dutton.

--Theaetetus. Jowett, Benjamin, tr. 1949. pap. 2.50 (ISBN 0-672-60174-5, LLA13). Bobbs.

--Theaetetus (Including Part I of Theory of Knowledge) Cornford, Francis M., tr. pap. 3.95 (ISBN 0-672-60299-7, LLA105). Bobbs.

--The Theaetetus of Plato. Levett, M. J., tr. 1981. lib. bdg. 12.50 (ISBN 0-915144-82-4); pap. text ed. 4.95 (ISBN 0-915144-81-6). Hackett Pub. Postponed.

--Timaeus. Jowett, Benjamin, tr. 1949. pap. 2.95 (ISBN 0-672-60175-3, LLA14). Bobbs.

--Timaeus (from Plato's Cosmology) Piest, Oskar, ed. Cornford, Francis M., tr. pap. 3.95 (ISBN 0-672-60301-2, LLA106). Bobbs.

Plato, Chris C., jt. ed. see Wertelecki, Wladimir.

Platt, Alan & Weiler, Lawrence D., eds. Congress & Arms Control. LC 77-28307. (Westview Special Studies in International Relations & Foreign Policy Ser.). 1978. lib. bdg. 24.50 o.p. (ISBN 0-89158-157-X). Westview.

Platt, Alan A. The U.S. Senate & Strategic Arms Policy: 1969-1977. LC 78-7151. (A Westview Replica Edition). 1978. lib. bdg. 17.50x (ISBN 0-89158-199-5). Westview.

Platt, Anthony M., ed. Politics of Riot Commissions. 1971. pap. 3.95 o.s.i. (ISBN 0-02-074590-7, Collier). Macmillan.

Platt, Charles. Garbage World. 1977. pap. 1.25 (ISBN 0-505-51164-9). Tower Bks.

--Outdoor Survival. LC 75-35883. (Career Concise Guides Ser.). (Illus.). 72p. (gr. 6 up). 1976. PLB 6.45 (ISBN 0-531-01128-3). Watts.

--Popular Superstitions. LC 70-167114. 244p. 1973. Repr. of 1925 ed. 24.00 (ISBN 0-8103-3170-5). Gale.

--Sweet Evil. 1977. pap. 1.25 o.p. (ISBN 0-425-03298-1). Berkley Pub.

--Twilight of the City. LC 76-40913. 1977. 8.95 o.s.i. (ISBN 0-02-597620-6, 59762). Macmillan.

Platt, Colin. Medieval Southampton: The Port & Trading Community A. D. 1000-1600. (Illus.). 300p. 1973. 27.50x (ISBN 0-7100-7653-3). Routledge & Kegan.

Platt, Colin, et al. Excavations in Medievel Southampton 1953-1969. Incl. Vol. 1. The Excavation; Vol. 2. The Finds. (Illus.). 1975. Set. text ed. 75.00x (ISBN 0-7185-1123-9, Leicester). Humanities.

Platt, D. C. Latin America & British Trade: 1806-1914. (Merchant Adventurers). (Illus.). 1972. text ed. 11.25x (ISBN 0-7136-1309-2). Humanities.
Platt, Deborah, ed. see Bolton, David.
Platt, Deborah, ed. see Lakey, H. L.
Platt, Deborah, ed. see Lakey, Harold.
Platt, Deborah L. & Wiesley, Keith. Forgotten Airplanes: Interesting History of Aviation Firsts. 176p. 1981. 10.50 (ISBN 0-934506-04-3). Westminster Comm Pubns.
Platt, Eugene. South Carolina State Line. LC 80-83405. 144p. 1980. 7.95 (ISBN 0-9605064-0-3); pap. 5.00 (ISBN 0-9605064-1-1). Huguley Co.
Platt, G. N. Van Der see Boogman, J. C. & Van Der Plaat, G. N.
Platt, Gerald M., jt. auth. see Weinstein, Fred.
Platt, Jennifer. Realities of Social Research. LC 75-30275. 224p. 1976. 24.95 (ISBN 0-470-69119-0). Halsted Pr.
Platt, Jerome & Labate, Christina. Heroin Addiction: Theory, Research, & Treatment. LC 76-5794. (Personality Processes Ser.). 417p. 1976. 29.95 (ISBN 0-471-69114-3, Pub. by Wiley-Interscience). Wiley.
Platt, Jerome & Wicks, Robert. Drug Abuse: A Criminal Justice Primer. 1977. pap. text ed. 6.95x (ISBN 0-02-477200-3). Macmillan.
Platt, John. The Petrology, Structure, & Geologic History of the Catalina Schist Terrain, Southern California. LC 74-22941. (Publications in Geological Sciences: Vol. 112). 1976. pap. 11.00x (ISBN 0-520-09525-1). U of Cal Pr.
--Selected Exercises Upon Geological Maps. 1974. pap. text ed. 3.25x (ISBN 0-04-550021-5). Allen Unwin.
--A Series of Elementary Exercises Upon Geological Maps. 1974. pap. text ed. 3.25x (ISBN 0-04-550019-3). Allen Unwin.
Platt, John & Challinor, John. Simple Geological Structures. 1974. pap. text ed. 4.95x (ISBN 0-04-550020-7). Allen Unwin.
Platt, Kin. The Doomsday Gang. LC 77-18864. (gr. 7-9). 1978. 7.95 (ISBN 0-688-80143-9); PLB 7.63 (ISBN 0-688-84143-0). Greenwillow.
--Dracula, Go Home. (gr. 7-12). 1981. pap. 1.25 (ISBN 0-440-92022-1, LE). Dell.
--Headman. LC 75-11808. 192p. (gr. 7 up). 1975. PLB 7.92 (ISBN 0-688-84011-6). Greenwillow.
--Run for Your Life. LC 77-3172. (Triumph Bks.). (Illus.). (gr. 4up). 1977. PLB 6.90 (ISBN 0-531-01327-8). Watts.
Platt, Michael. Rome & Romans According to Shakespeare. (Salzburg Studies in English Literature, Jacobean Drama Studies: No. 51). 295p. (Orig.). 1976. pap. text ed. 25.00x (ISBN 0-391-01498-6). Humanities.
Platt, Nancy Van Dyke see Van Dyke Platt, Nancy.
Platt, P. Libraries in Colleges of Education. 2nd ed. 1972. 19.50x (ISBN 0-85365-335-6, Pub. by Lib Assn England). Oryx Pr.
Platt, R. I-Opener. 1976. pap. 11.95 (ISBN 0-13-448779-6). P-H.
Platt, Robert T., jt. auth. see Brodsky, Carroll M.
Platt, Rutherford. One Thousand & One Questions Answered About Trees. LC 59-6900. 6.50 o.p. (ISBN 0-396-04233-3). Dodd.
Platt, Rutherford H. Land Use Control: Interface of Law & Geography. Natoli, Salvatore J., ed. LC 76-18389. (Resource Papers for College Geography Ser.). (Illus.). 1976. pap. text ed. 4.00 (ISBN 0-89291-109-3). Assn Am Geographers.
Platt, Tony & Takagi, Paul, eds. Punishment & Penal Discipline: Essays on the Prison & the Prisoner's Movement. LC 79-90275. (Vol. I). (Illus., Orig.). 1980. pap. 8.50 (ISBN 0-935206-00-0). Crime & Soc Justice.
Platt, Tony, et al. The Iron Fist & the Velvet Glove: An Analysis of the U. S. Police. 2nd ed. (Illus.). 1977. pap. text ed. 3.50 (ISBN 0-917404-02-5). Ctr Res Criminal.
Platt, Washington. National Character in Action: Intelligence Factors in Foreign Relations. 1961. 17.50x (ISBN 0-8135-0382-5). Rutgers U Pr.
Platt, William R. Color Atlas & Textbook of Hematology: A Slide Presentation. LC 75-733020. (Illus.). 48p. 1975. 185.00 o.p. (ISBN 0-397-50345-8). Lippincott.
Platten, David. Making Camping & Outdoor Gear. LC 80-68902. (Illus.). 160p. 1981. 16.95 (ISBN 0-7153-8023-0). David & Charles.
--The Outdoor Survival Handbook. 13.50 (ISBN 0-7153-7793-0, Pub. by Batsford England). David & Charles.
Platts, John T. Dictionary of Urdu, Classical Hindi, & English. 1930. 74.00x (ISBN 0-19-864309-8). Oxford U Pr.
Platts, Mark. Ways of Meaning: An Introduction to a Philosophy of Language. 1978. 22.00x (ISBN 0-7100-0000-6); pap. 11.00 (ISBN 0-7100-0001-4). Routledge & Kegan.
Platzer, M. F., ed. see Project SQUID Workshop on Transonic Flow Problems in Turbomachinery, Feb. 1976.
Platzer, Michael, jt. auth. see Cohn, Michael.
Platzman, P. M. & Wolff, P. A. Waves & Interactions in Solid State Plasmas. (Solid State Physics: Suppl. 13). 1973. 26.50 (ISBN 0-12-607773-8). Acad Pr.
Platzner, Robert L. The Metaphysical Novel in England: The Romantic Phase. Varma, Devendra P., ed. LC 79-8468. (Gothic Studies & Dissertations Ser.). 1980. lib. bdg. 29.00x (ISBN 0-405-12656-5). Arno.
Plauger, P. J., jt. auth. see Kernighan, Brian W.
Plaut, Thomas R. & Anderson, Mildred C. The Gross Regional Product of Texas & Its Regions: Growth Trends & the Structure of Output. (Illus.). 100p. (Orig.). 1981. pap. text ed. 6.00 (ISBN 0-87755-244-4). U of Tex Busn Res.
Plaut, W. Gunther. Commentary on Genesis. (Pardes Torah; Jewish Commentary on the Torah Ser.). 1974. 10.00 (ISBN 0-8074-0001-7, 381611); pap. 8.00 (ISBN 0-685-48959-0, 381601). UAHC.
--The Rise of Reform Judaism: A Sourcebook of Its European Origins. Incl. Growth of Reform Judaism: American & European Sources to 1948. 1965. 1963. 10.00 (ISBN 0-8074-0089-0, 382770, Pub. by World Union). UAHC.
--The Torah: A Modern Commentary: Exodus. (The Torah Commentary Ser.). 476p. 1981. 17.50 (ISBN 0-8074-0040-8, 381606). UAHC.
Plaut, W. Gunther, ed. Growth of Reform Judaism: American & European Sources Until 1948. 1965. 10.00 (ISBN 0-8074-0086-6, 382780). UAHC.
Plaut, W. Gunther, ed. see Bamberger, Bernard J.
Plautus. Amphitryon & Two Other Plays. Casson, Lionel, ed. 1971. pap. 4.95 (ISBN 0-393-00601-8, Norton Lib.). Norton.
--Comoediae, 2 Vols. Lindsay, W. M., ed. 1905. Vol. 1. 24.00x (ISBN 0-19-814628-0); Vol. 2. 22.50x (ISBN 0-19-814629-9). Oxford U Pr.
--Menaechmi. Copley, Frank O., tr. LC 50-5706. 1956. pap. 3.75 (ISBN 0-672-60178-8, LLA17). Bobbs.
--Rudens. abr. ed. Sonnenschein, W. A., ed. 1901. 12.95x (ISBN 0-19-872093-9). Oxford U Pr.
--Selections. Westaway, K. M., ed. text ed. 4.25x (ISBN 0-521-07197-6). Cambridge U Pr.
Plautus see Aristophanes.
Playbody Editors. Playboy's Party Jokes, No. 2. (Illus.). 192p. 1980. pap. 1.95 (ISBN 0-87216-715-1). Playboy Pbks.
Playboy Editors. Playboy's Party Jokes. 192p. (Orig.). 1980. pap. 1.95 (ISBN 0-87216-710-0). Playboy Pbks.
--Playboy's Party Jokes No. 3. 192p. 1980. pap. 1.95 (ISBN 0-87216-720-8). Playboy Pbks.
Playboy Magazine Editors. Playboy's Party Jokes, No. 6. (Party Joke Ser.). 160p. 1980. pap. 1.95 (ISBN 0-87216-735-6). Playboy Pbks.
--Playboy's Party Jokes, No. 5. (Party Joke Ser.: No. 5). (Illus.). 160p. 1980. pap. 1.95 (ISBN 0-87216-730-5). Playboy Pbks.
Player, Gary. Gary Player's Golf Clinic. LC 81-65104. (Illus.). 160p. 1981. pap. 6.95 (ISBN 0-910676-23-2, 6036). DBI.
Player, Gary & Sullivan, George. Gary Player's Golf Book for Young People. LC 79-55882. (Illus.). 112p. (gr. 7-12). 1980. 8.95 (ISBN 0-914178-35-0, 25483-9). Golf Digest.
Player, Mack A. Cases & Materials on Employment Discrimination Law. LC 79-28069. (American Casebook Ser.). 915p. 1980. text ed. 18.95 (ISBN 0-8299-2075-7). West Pub.
--Federal Law of Employment Discrimination in a Nutshell. rev. ed. LC 80-22475. (Nutshell Ser.). 357p. 1980. pap. text ed. 6.95 (ISBN 0-8299-2111-7). West Pub.
Playfair, Guy L. This House Is Haunted: The True Story of a Poltergeist. LC 80-5387. (Illus.). 288p. 1980. 11.95 (ISBN 0-8128-2732-5). Stein & Day.
Playfair, Guy L. & Hill, Scott. The Cycles of Heaven. 1979. pap. 2.75 (ISBN 0-380-45419-X, 45419). Avon.
Playford, John & Purcell, Henry. An Introduction to the Skill of Musick. LC 67-27551. (Music Reprint Ser.). 282p. 1972. Repr. of 1694 ed. lib. bdg. 29.50 (ISBN 0-306-70937-6). Da Capo.
Playne, C. E. The Neuroses of the Nations. 468p. 1980. Repr. of 1925 ed. lib. bdg. 35.00 (ISBN 0-8495-4373-8). Arden Lib.
Pleasance, Peggy, jt. auth. see Cameron, W. M.
Pleasants, Jeanne V; see Bottiglia, William F.
Pleasants, Jeanne V; see Bree, Germaine.
Pledger, D. M. Complete Guide to Demolition. (Illus.). 1978. text ed. 18.00x (ISBN 0-904406-22-9). Longman.
Pleh, Csaba, jt. ed. see Kardos, Lajos.
Plehn, Heinz, jt. auth. see Kling, Bernard.
Pleket, H. W., jt. auth. see Finley, M. I.
Plekhanov, G. V. Essays in the History of Materialism. 1968. 16.50 (ISBN 0-86527-061-9). Fertig.
Plekhanov, George V. Development of the Monist View of History. 1982. 19.95 (ISBN 0-87855-322-3); pap. 4.95 (ISBN 0-87855-704-0). Transaction Bks.
--Fundamental Problems of Marxism. rev. ed. LC 69-20358. 1969. 5.95 o.p. (ISBN 0-7178-0074-1); pap. 2.25 (ISBN 0-7178-0073-3). Intl Pub Co.
Plekhanov, Georgii V. Anarchism & Socialism. Aveling, Eleanor M., tr. LC 79-2921. 148p. 1981. Repr. of 1912 ed. 15.00 (ISBN 0-8305-0090-1). Hyperion Conn.
Plenderleith, H. J. & Werner, A. E. Conservation of Antiquities & Works of Art: Treatment, Repair, & Restoration. 2nd ed. 1971. 42.00x (ISBN 0-19-212960-0). Oxford U Pr.
Plenn. El Arbol De la Violeta. 1964. 6.95 (ISBN 0-87751-015-6, Pub by Troutman Press). E Torres & Sons.
--La Cancion Verde. 1956. 6.95 (ISBN 0-87751-014-8, Pub by Troutman Press). E Torres & Sons.
Plentl, Albert A. & Friedman, Emanuel A. Lymphatic System of the Female Genitalia. LC 70-158402. (Major Problems in Obstetrics & Gynecology Ser.: Vol. 2). (Illus.). 1971. 17.50 (ISBN 0-7216-7266-3). Saunders.
Plenzdorf, Ulrich. Die Neuen Lieden Des Jungen W. 1978. pap. text ed. 9.95 (ISBN 0-471-02855-X). Wiley.
Plescia, O. J., ed. see Symposium of the Institute of Microbiology, Rutgers University, 1967.
Pleslova-Stikova, Emilie, jt. auth. see Ehrich, Robert W.
Plesner, A. I. Spectral Theory of Linear Operators, 2 Vols. Nestell, Merlynd & Gibbs, Alan G., trs. LC 68-20524. 1969. Vol. 1. 15.00 (ISBN 0-8044-4767-5); Vol. 2. 15.00 (ISBN 0-8044-4768-3); Set. 25.00 (ISBN 0-8044-4766-7). Ungar.
Plessis, N. Du see Du Plessis, N.
Pletcher, Barbara A. Readings in Business Today. 1980. 6.95x (ISBN 0-256-02376-X). Irwin.
Pletcher, Barbara A., jt. auth. see Buffa, Elwood S.
Pletsch, Bill. Integrated Circuits: Making the Miracle Chip. 80p. 1978. pap. 6.00 (ISBN 0-686-27006-1). Palmer-Pletsch.
Pletta, D. H. & Frederick, D. Engineering Mechanics: Statics & Dynamics. (Illus.). 1969. 25.95 (ISBN 0-8260-7190-2). Wiley.
Plews, R. W., ed. Analytical Methods Used in Sugar Refining. (Illus.). 1969. 37.30x (ISBN 0-444-20046-0, Pub. by Applied Science). Burgess-Intl Ideas.
Plimmer, Jack R., ed. Pesticide Chemistry in the Twentieth Century. LC 76-51748. (ACS Symposium Ser: No. 37). 1977. 23.00 (ISBN 0-8412-0364-4). Am Chemical.
Plimpton, Florus B. see Diffenderffer, Henry.
Plimpton, George. Bogey Man. LC 68-28213. (Illus.). 1968. 10.95 o.p. (ISBN 0-06-013362-7, HarpT). Har-Row.
--One for the Record: The Inside Story of Hank Aaron's Chase for the Home-Run Record. LC 74-7026. (Illus.). 160p. (YA) 1974. 8.95 o.p. (ISBN 0-06-013373-2, HarpT). Har-Row.
--Open Net. 300p. 1981. 11.95 (ISBN 0-399-12558-2). Putnam.
--Shadow Box. LC 77-4275. (Illus.). (YA) 1977. 9.95 o.p. (ISBN 0-399-11995-7, Dist. by Putnam). Berkley Pub.
Plimpton, George, ed. Writers at Work. LC 80-18030. (The Paris Review Interviews Ser.: No. 5). (Illus.). 416p. 1981. 17.95 (ISBN 0-670-79098-2). Viking Pr.
--Writers at Work, Vol. 5. (Writers at Work Ser.). 416p. 1981. pap. 8.95 (ISBN 0-14-005818-4). Penguin.
Pliner, Robert. The Lazy Indoor Gardener. 1976. pap. 3.95 (ISBN 0-394-73160-3). Random.
Pliner, Roberta L., jt. auth. see Evans, Charles M.
Plint, M. A. & Boswirth, L. Fluid Mechanics: A Laboratory Course. 186p. 1978. 30.00x (ISBN 0-85264-245-8, Pub. by Griffin England). State Mutual Bk.
Pliny. The Elizabethan Zoo. Byrne, M. St. Clare, ed. Holland, Philemon & Topsell, Edward, trs. LC 79-88477. (Illus.). 192p. 1979. 15.00 (ISBN 0-87923-300-1, Nonpareil Bks.); pap. 7.95 (ISBN 0-87923-299-4). Godine.
--Epistularum Libri Decem. Mynors, Roger A., ed. (Oxford Classical Texts). 1963. 18.95x (ISBN 0-19-814643-4). Oxford U Pr.
Pliny, jt. auth. see Martial.
Plischke, Elmer, ed. Modern Diplomacy: The Art &The Artisans. 1979. pap. 9.25 (ISBN 0-8447-3350-4). Am Enterprise.
Plochmann, George K. Ordeal of Southern Illinois University. LC 59-7379. (Illus.). 1959. 693pp. 10.00x (ISBN 0-8093-0020-6); 2 vols. set boxed 704pp. 15.00x (ISBN 0-8093-0021-4). S Ill U Pr.
Plog, Fred, jt. auth. see Bates, Daniel.
Plog, Fred, jt. auth. see Dittert, Alfred E., Jr.
Plog, Stanley C., ed. The Year Two Thousand & Mental Retardation. (Current Topics in Mental Health Ser.). (Illus.). 240p. 1980. 19.95 (ISBN 0-306-40252-1, Plenum Pr). Plenum Pub.
Plog, Stephen. Stylistic Variation in Prehistoric Ceramics. (New Studies in Archaeology). (Illus.). 130p. 1980. 19.95 (ISBN 0-521-22581-7). Cambridge U Pr.
Ploghoft, Milton E. & Shuster, Albert H. Social Science Education in the Elementary School. 2nd ed. (Elementary Education Ser.). 400p. 1976. text ed. 17.95 (ISBN 0-675-08692-2). Merrill.
Ploman, Edward W. Broadcasting in Sweden. (Case Studies on Broadcasting Systems). (Orig.). 1976. pap. 14.00 (ISBN 0-685-76681-0). Routledge & Kegan.
Plomer, Henry R. English Printing Fourteen Seventy-Six to Nineteen Hundred. 360p. 1980. Repr. of 1916 ed. lib. bdg. 35.00 (ISBN 0-8482-5576-3). Norwood Edns.
Plommer, W. H., ed. Vitruvius & Later Roman Building Manuals. LC 72-90487. (Classical Studies). (Illus.). 128p. 1973. 16.95 (ISBN 0-521-20141-1). Cambridge U Pr.
Plossi, George. Manufacturing Control: The Last Frontier for Profits. LC 73-8965. 1973. 16.95 (ISBN 0-87909-483-4). Reston.
Plossl, G. & Wright, O. Production & Inventory Control: Principles & Techniques. 1967. ref. ed. 21.95 (ISBN 0-13-725127-0). P-H.
Plossl, George W. & Welch, W. Evert. The Role of Top Management in the Control of Inventory. (Illus.). 1978. 16.95 (ISBN 0-8359-6697-6). Reston.
Plotch, Walter, jt. ed. see Tumin, Melvin M.
Plotinus. Opera. Vol. 1, Porphyrii Vita Plotini: Enneades 1-3. Henry, P. & Schwyzer, H. R., eds. (Oxford Classical Texts Ser.). 1964. 31.00x (ISBN 0-19-814561-6). Oxford U Pr.
Plotkin, Irving H., jt. auth. see Shick, Blair C.
Plotnicov, Leonard, jt. auth. see Tuden, Arthur.
Plotnik, Arthur. Library Life - American Style: A Journalist's Field Report. LC 75-16280. (Illus.). 226p. 1975. 10.00 (ISBN 0-8108-0852-8). Scarecrow.
Plott, John C. Global History of Philosophy: The Patristic-Sutra Period, Vol. 3. 1980. 27.00 (ISBN 0-8426-1680-2). Verry.
Plotz, Helen. As I Walked Out One Evening: A Book of Ballads. LC 76-10306. 288p. (gr. 5-9). 1976. 9.25 (ISBN 0-688-80054-8); PLB 8.88 (ISBN 0-688-84054-X). Greenwillow.
--This Powerful Rhyme: A Book of Sonnets. LC 79-14037. (gr. 6 up). 1979. 7.95 (ISBN 0-688-80226-5); PLB 7.63 (ISBN 0-688-84226-7). Greenwillow.
Plotz, Helen, ed. The Gift Outright: America to Her Poets. LC 77-8555. (gr. 7 up). 1977. 9.25 (ISBN 0-688-80109-9); PLB 8.88 (ISBN 0-688-84109-0). Greenwillow.
--Life Hungers to Abound: Poems of the Family. LC 78-5829. (gr. 5-9). 1978. 8.95 (ISBN 0-688-80176-5); PLB 8.59 (ISBN 0-688-84176-7). Greenwillow.
Plotz, Helen, ed. see Hardy, Thomas.
Plotz, Helen, ed. see Stevenson, Robert L.
Plou, Dafne C. De see Drakeford, John W.
Ploutz, Paul F. The Metric System: Content & Methods. 2nd ed. (Elementary Education Ser.). 1977. pap. text ed. 8.95 (ISBN 0-675-08538-1). Merrill.
Plow, Sabanes De see Simmons, Paul D. & Crawford, Kenneth.
Plowden, Alison. The House of Tudor. LC 76-6936. 272p. 1981. pap. 8.95 (ISBN 0-8128-6123-X). Stein & Day.
--The Young Victoria. LC 80-5908. (Illus.). 208p. 1981. 12.95 (ISBN 0-8128-2766-X). Stein & Day.
Plowden, David. Tugboat. LC 76-13464. (Illus.). (gr. 3 up). 1976. 8.95 (ISBN 0-02-774550-3, 77455). Macmillan.
Plowman, E. Grosvenor, ed. Coordinated Transportation: Problems & Requirements. LC 76-78376. 1968. pap. 7.50x (ISBN 0-87033-151-5). Cornell Maritime.
Plowman, Max, ed. see Blake, William.
Plowright, Piers. Read English. 1973. pap. text ed. 2.95x (ISBN 0-435-28705-2); tape 26.00x (ISBN 0-435-28706-0); cassette 22.00x (ISBN 0-435-28707-9). Heinemann Ed.
Plowright, Piers see Milne, John.
Pluchart-Simon, Bernard. Proust: L'amour comme verite humaine et romanesque. new ed. (Collection themes et textes). 191p. (Orig., Fr.). 1975. pap. 6.75 (ISBN 2-03-035029-X, 2683). Larousse.
Plucker, Lina S. & Roerick, Kaye L., eds. Brevet's Illinois Historical Markers & Sites. LC 75-253. (Historical Markers-Sites Ser.). (Illus.). 300p. (Orig.). 1976. 10.95 o.p. (ISBN 0-88498-028-6); text ed. 6.95 o.p. (ISBN 0-685-52607-0); pap. 6.95 (ISBN 0-88498-029-4); pap. text ed. 4.95 o.p. (ISBN 0-685-52608-9). Brevet Pr.
Plucknett, Donald A. Managing Pastures & Cattle Under Coconuts. (Tropical Agriculture Ser.). 1979. lib. bdg. 27.50x (ISBN 0-89158-299-1). Westview.

Plucknett, Donald L. Small-Scale Processing & Storage of Tropical Root Crops. (Tropical Agriculture Ser.). 1979. lib. bdg. 30.00x (ISBN 0-89158-471-4). Westview.

Plucknett, Donald L., jt. auth. see Lumpkin, Thomas A.

Plucknett, Donald L. & Beemer, Halsey, eds. Vegetable Farming Systems in the People's Republic of China. (Westview Special Studies in Agricultural Science). 350p. 1980. lib. bdg. 28.50x (ISBN 0-89158-999-6). Westview.

Plucknett, Theodore F. A Concise History of the Common Law. 5th ed. 802p. 1956. 21.50 (ISBN 0-316-71083-0). Little.

Pluckrose, Henry. Creative Themes. (Illus.). 1969. 5.25x o.p. (ISBN 0-237-28647-5). Intl Pubns Serv.

Pluckrose, Henry, ed. Small World of Apes. (Small World Ser.). (Illus.). 1979. (gr. 5-8) 2.95 (ISBN 0-531-03443-7); PLB 5.90 s&l (gr. k-3) (ISBN 0-531-03407-0). Watts.

--Small World of Bears. (Small Worlds Ser.). (Illus.). (gr. k-3). 1979. PLB 5.90 s&l (ISBN 0-531-03403-8). Watts.

--Small World of Birds. (Small World Ser.). (Illus.). 1979. 9 (gr. 5-8) 5.90 (ISBN 0-531-03444-5); PLB 4.90 s&l (gr. k-3) (ISBN 0-531-03408-9). Watts.

--Small World of Elephants. (Small Worlds Ser.). (Illus.). (gr. k-3). 1979. PLB 5.90 s&l (ISBN 0-531-03404-6). Watts.

--Small World of Horses. (Small Worlds Ser.). (Illus.). (gr. k-3). 1979. PLB 5.90 s&l (ISBN 0-531-03405-4). Watts.

--Small World of Whales. (Small Worlds Ser.). (Illus.). (gr. k-3). 1979. PLB 5.90 s&l (ISBN 0-531-03406-2). Watts.

Plueger, Aaron L. Things to Come for Planet Earth. 1977. pap. 3.50 (ISBN 0-570-03762-X, 12-2691). Concordia.

Plum, jt. auth. see Wayman.

Plum, Fred, ed. see Association for Research in Nervous & Mental Disease.

Plum, Judy, ed. see Oblander, Ruth, et al.

Plumb, David. The Music Stopped & Your Monkey's on Fire. 7.50 (ISBN 0-930324-10-2). Green Hill.

Plumb, J. H. Death of the Past. 152p. 1978. text ed. 12.50x (ISBN 0-333-06050-4). Humanities.

--The Horizon Book of the Renaissance. Ketchum, Richard M., ed. LC 61-11489. (Illus.). 432p. 1961. deluxe ed. 19.95 o.p. (ISBN 0-8281-0285-6, BO97D1-16). Am Heritage.

Plumb, J. H., ed. see McKendrick, Melveena.

Plumb, J. H., et al. The English Heritage. LC 77-92987. (Illus., Orig.). 1978. pap. text ed. 11.95x (ISBN 0-88273-350-8). Forum Pr MO.

Plumb, R. T., jt. auth. see Jenkyn, J. F.

Plumb, S. C. Introduction to Fortran: A Program for Self-Instruction. 1964. pap. text ed. 13.50 o.p. (ISBN 0-07-050350-8, C). McGraw.

Plume, Ilse. The Bremen Town Musicians. LC 79-6622. (Illus.). 32p. (ps-3). 1980. 8.95a (ISBN 0-385-15161-6); PLB (ISBN 0-385-15162-4). Doubleday.

Plumer, W. S. Psalms. (Geneva Commentaries Ser.). 1978. 26.95 (ISBN 0-85151-209-7). Banner of Truth.

Plumer, William, Jr. Life of William Plumer. LC 77-87384. (American History, Politics & Law Ser). 1969. Repr. of 1857 ed. lib. bdg. 55.00 (ISBN 0-306-71608-9). Da Capo.

Plumer, William S. Commentary on the Epistle of Paul to the Hebrews. (Giant Summit Ser.). 560p. 1980. Repr. of 1872 ed. pap. 9.95 (ISBN 0-8010-7054-6). Baker Bk.

Plummer, A., jt. auth. see Robertson, A.

Plummer, Alfred. Corinthians II. LC 16-915. (International Critical Commentary Ser.). 462p. Repr. of 1916 ed. text ed. 23.00x (ISBN 0-567-05028-9). Attic Pr.

--St. Luke. 5th ed. (International Critical Commentary Ser.). 688p. Repr. of 1901 ed. text ed. 23.00x (ISBN 0-567-05023-8). Attic Pr.

Plummer, C. J. Ship Handling in Narrow Channels. 3rd ed. LC 78-15384. (Illus.). 1966. pap. 7.00x (ISBN 0-87033-247-3). Cornell Maritime.

Plummer, Charles. Vitae Sanctorum Hiberniae, 2 Vols. 1910. 48.00x set (ISBN 0-19-821390-5). Oxford U Pr.

Plummer, Charles, ed. Lives of Irish Saints, 2 Vols. 1922. 44.00x set (ISBN 0-19-821389-1). Oxford U Pr.

Plummer, F. B. The Carboniferous Rocks of the Llano Region of Central Texas. (Illus.). 170p. 1943. 2.00 (PUB 4329). Bur Econ Geology.

Plummer, F. B. & Sargent, E. C. Underground Waters & Subsurface Temperatures of the Woodbine Sand in Northeast Texas. (Illus.). 178p. 1931. 1.00 (BULL 3138). Bur Econ Geology.

Plummer, Kenneth, ed. The Making of the Modern Homosexual. 1980. 22.50x (ISBN 0-389-20159-6). B&N.

Plummer, William. The Holy Goof: A Biography of Neal Cassady. (Illus.). 150p. Date not set. 10.00 (ISBN 0-13-392605-2). P-H. Postponed.

Plummer, William J. A Quail in the Family. 128p. 1975. pap. 1.50 o.p. (ISBN 0-449-22568-2, Q2568, Crest). Fawcett.

Plumpe, J., ed. see Augustine, St.

Plumpe, J., jt. ed. see Wuasten, J.

Plumpton, C. & Macilwaine, P. S. New Tertiary Mathematics: Applied Mathematics, Vol. 1, Pt. 2: Basic Applied Mathematics. (Illus.). 42.00 (ISBN 0-08-025035-1); pap. 14.00 (ISBN 0-08-021645-5). Pergamon.

--New Tertiary Mathematics: Further Applied Mathematics, Vol. 2, Pt. 2. (Illus.). Date not set. 42.00 (ISBN 0-08-025037-8); pap. 16.75 (ISBN 0-08-025026-2); F/non-net 14.00 (ISBN 0-08-025036-X). Pergamon.

--New Tertiary Mathematics: Further Pure Mathematics, Vol. 2, Pt. 1. LC 79-41454. (Illus.). 408p. 1981. 42.00 (ISBN 0-08-025033-5); pap. 16.75 (ISBN 0-08-021644-7). Pergamon.

--New Tertiary Mathematics: The Core. (Pure Mathematics: Vol. 1). (Illus.). 1980. 42.00 (ISBN 0-08-025031-9); pap. 14.00 (ISBN 0-08-021643-9). Pergamon.

Plumpton, C. & Tomkys, W. H. Sixth Form Pure Mathematics, Vols. 1-2. 1968. Vol. 1. pap. 9.50 (ISBN 0-686-57456-7); Vol. 2. pap. 11.00 (ISBN 0-08-009383-3). Pergamon.

--Theoretical Mechanics in SI Units: In SI Units, Vols. 1-2. 2nd ed. 1972. Vol. 1. pap. 8.55 (ISBN 0-08-016268-1); Vol. 2. pap. 9.25 (ISBN 0-08-016591-5). Pergamon.

Plumpton, C. A., jt. auth. see Chirgwin, B.

Plunkett, Barbara. Sam Diego, a Coloring Adventure in San Diego, California. (Illus.). (ps). 1977. pap. 1.25 (ISBN 0-914488-14-7). Rand-Tofua.

Plunkett, H. Dudley & Bowman, Mary J. Elites & Change in the Kentucky Mountains. LC 76-160049. (Illus.). 216p. 1973. 13.50x (ISBN 0-8131-1275-3). U Pr of Ky.

Plunkett, H. Dudley, jt. auth. see Lynch, James.

Plunkett, Orda A., jt. auth. see Wilson, J. Walter.

Plunz, Richard, ed. Housing Form & Public Policy in the United States. LC 77-22686. 264p. 1980. 29.95 (ISBN 0-03-056839-0). Praeger.

Pluta, Joseph, ed. Economic & Business Issues of the Nineteen Eighties. LC 80-68658. 235p. (Orig.). 1980. pap. 7.00 (ISBN 0-87755-242-8). U of Tex Busn Res.

Pluta, Joseph E., ed. Economic & Business: Issues of the 1980's. 1980. 7.00. U of Tex Busn Res.

--The Energy Picture: Problems & Prospects. LC 80-68659. 185p. 1980. pap. 6.00. U of Tex Busn Res.

Pluta, Joseph E., et al. Texas Fact Book 1981. rev. ed. 200p. (Orig.). 1981. pap. 6.00 (ISBN 0-87755-246-0). U of Tex Busn Res.

Plutarch. The Age of Alexander. Scott-Kilvert, Ian, tr. (Classics Ser). 1973. pap. 3.95 (ISBN 0-14-044286-3). Penguin.

--Makers of Rome. Scott-Kilvert, Ian, tr. (Classics Ser.). 368p. 1965. pap. 3.25 (ISBN 0-14-044158-1). Penguin.

--Plutarch's Lives. White, John S., ed. LC 66-28487. (Illus.). 468p. (gr. 7 up). 1900. 9.50x (ISBN 0-8196-0174-8). Biblo.

Plutarchus. The Roman Questions of Plutarchus. Rose, H. J., tr. 1924. 15.00x (ISBN 0-8196-0284-1). Biblo.

Plutchik, Robert. Fundamentos De Investigacion Experimental. rev. ed. 1975. pap. text ed. 7.00 (ISBN 0-06-316991-6, IntlDept). Har-Row.

Pluto Press. State of the World Atlas. 1981. 14.95 (ISBN 0-671-42438-6, Touchstone); pap. 9.95 (ISBN 0-671-42439-4). S&S.

Plutzik, Hyam. Apples from Shinar. LC 59-12479. (Wesleyan Poetry Program: Vol. 2). (Orig.). 1959. 10.00x (ISBN 0-8195-2002-0, Pub. by Wesleyan U Pr); pap. 4.95x (ISBN 0-8195-1002-5). Columbia U Pr.

Plympton, Bill. Medium Rare. 1978. 2.95 o.p. (ISBN 0-03-021466-1). HR&W.

Plywood Clinic, 3rd, Portland, Mar.1975. Modern Plywood Techniques Vol. 3: Proceedings. Lambert, Herbert G., ed. LC 74-20159. (Plywood Clinic Library: A Forest Industries Book). (Illus.). 240p. 1976. pap. 29.50 o.p. (ISBN 0-87930-048-5). Miller Freeman.

Poag, James F. Wolfram Von Eschenbach. (World Authors Ser.: Germany: No. 233). lib. bdg. 10.95 (ISBN 0-8057-2304-8). Twayne.

Poage, Michael. Born. 1975. pap. 15.00 (ISBN 0-685-82994-4). Black Stone.

--Handbook of Ornament. 1979. pap. 7.50 (ISBN 0-686-25597-6); 30.00 o.p. (ISBN 0-686-25596-8). Black Stone.

Poage, Scott. Quantitative Management Methods for Practicing Engineers. LC 77-133267. 1970. 11.95 (ISBN 0-389-00531-2); pap. 9.95 (ISBN 0-8436-0334-8). CBI Pub.

Poala, Tomie De see De Paola, Tomie.

Poate, J. M., et al, eds. Thin Films: Interdiffusion & Reactions. LC 77-25348. (Electrochemical Society Ser.). 1978. 43.50 (ISBN 0-471-02238-1, Pub. by Wiley-Interscience). Wiley.

Poats, Rutherford M. Technology for Developing Nations: New Directions for U. S. Technical Assistance. 225p. 1972. 11.95 (ISBN 0-8157-7118-5). Brookings.

Pochan, Andre. The Mysteries of the Great Pyramids. 1977. pap. 2.25 o.p. (ISBN 0-380-00881-5, 31492). Avon.

Poche, Emanuel. Porcelain Marks of the World. LC 73-92270. (Illus.). 256p. 1975. 6.95 o.p. (ISBN 0-668-03403-3). Arco.

Pochedly, Carl. Leukemia & Lymphoma in the Nervous System. (Illus.). 248p. 1977. 30.00 (ISBN 0-685-73596-6). C C Thomas.

Pochin-Mould, Daphne. The Aran Islands. (Island Set). (Illus.). 171p. 1973. 16.95 (ISBN 0-7153-5782-4). David & Charles.

Pocklington, John. Sunday No Sabbath: A Sermon. LC 74-28881. (English Experience Ser.: No. 759). 1975. Repr. of 1636 ed. 6.00 (ISBN 90-221-0759-0). Walter J Johnson.

Pocock, D. F., tr. see Durkheim, Emile.

Pocock, David. Understanding Social Anthropology. (Teach Yourself Ser). (gr. 7 up). 1976. pap. 4.95 o.p. (ISBN 0-679-10496-8). McKay.

Pocock, Douglas & Hudson, Ray. Images of the Urban Environment. LC 77-14371. (Illus.). 1978. 15.00 (ISBN 0-231-04502-6). Columbia U Pr.

Pocock, Douglas, ed. Humanistic Geography & Literature: Essays on the Experience of Place. 224p. 1981. 27.00x (ISBN 0-389-20158-8). B&N.

Pocock, Gordon. Boileau & the Nature of Neo-Classism. LC 79-50885. (Major European Authors Ser.). 1980. 34.00 (ISBN 0-521-22772-0). Cambridge U Pr.

Pocock, J. G., ed. The Political Works of James Harrington. LC 75-41712. (Studies in the History and Theory of Politics: No. 27). 1977. 72.50 (ISBN 0-521-21161-1). Cambridge U Pr.

--Three British Revolutions: 1641, 1688, 1776. LC 79-27572. (Folger Institute Essays, Published for the Folger Shakespeare Library). 456p. 1980. 32.50 (ISBN 0-691-05293-X); pap. 12.50 (ISBN 0-691-10087-X). Princeton U Pr.

Pocock, Philip. The Obvious Illusion. LC 80-69634. (Illus.). 96p. 1980. 25.00 (ISBN 0-8076-0987-0); pap. 14.95 (ISBN 0-8076-0994-3). Braziller.

Pocock, Robine, et al. The Burmese Cat. (Illus.). 182p. 1980. 22.50 (ISBN 0-7134-2937-2, Pub. by Batsford England). David & Charles.

Poctarnees, Welleran. All Mirrors Are Magic Mirrors. (Illus.). 1981. 16.95 (ISBN 0-914676-30-X, Star & Elephant Bk); pap. 9.95 (ISBN 0-914676-33-4). Green Tiger.

Pocztar, Jerry. The Theory & Practice of Programmed Instruction: A Guide for Teachers. (Monographs on Education, No. 7). (Illus.). 179p. (Orig.). 1972. pap. 7.00 (ISBN 92-3-100936-2, U679, UNESCO). Unipub.

Podair, Simon, jt. auth. see Spiegel, Allen D.

Podeschi, John B. Dickens & Dickensiana: A Catalogue of the Richard Gimbel Collection in the Yale University Library. LC 79-66938. 594p. 1981. text ed. 65.00x (ISBN 0-300-03506-3). Yale U Pr.

Podgorecki, Adam. Law & Society. 1974. 23.50x (ISBN 0-7100-7983-4); pap. 10.00 (ISBN 0-7100-8035-2). Routledge & Kegan.

--Practical Social Sciences. (International Library of Sociology). 200p. 1975. 16.00x (ISBN 0-7100-8175-8). Routledge & Kegan.

Podhajsky, Alois. The Riding Teacher: A Basic Guide to Correct Methods of Classical Instruction. LC 72-84937. 240p. 1973. 7.95 o.p. (ISBN 0-385-02540-8). Doubleday.

Podol, Peter L. Fernando Arrabal. (World Authors Ser.: No. 499 (Spain)). 1978. 13.50 (ISBN 0-8057-6340-6). Twayne.

Podolny, Walter, Jr. & Scalzi, John B. Construction & Design of Cable-Stayed Bridges. LC 75-46578. (Practical Construction Guides Ser.). 506p. 1976. 47.50 (ISBN 0-471-75625-3, Pub. by Wiley-Interscience). Wiley.

Podolsky, Stephen, ed. Clinical Diabetes: Modern Management. 608p. 1980. 30.00x (ISBN 0-8385-1123-6). ACC.

Podolsky, Stephen & Viswanathan, M., eds. Secondary Diabetes: The Spectrum of the Diabetics Syndromes. 1980. 52.00 (ISBN 0-89004-372-8). Raven.

Podos, Batya. Ariadne. LC 80-70233. 52p. (Orig.). 1980. pap. 3.00 (ISBN 0-9603628-2-7). Frog in Well.

Podracky, John. Photographic Retouching & Airbrush Techniques. (Illus.). 1980. text ed. 13.95 (ISBN 0-13-665257-3). P-H.

Podsakoff, Philip M., jt. auth. see Simpson, Douglas B.

Poduska, Bernard. You Can Cope: Be the Person You Want to Be Through Self Help. 1975. 12.95 (ISBN 0-13-972562-8, Spec); pap. 3.95 (ISBN 0-13-972570-9). P-H.

Poe, Edgar A. The Cask of Amontillado. (Creative's Classics Ser.). (Illus.). 32p. (gr. 5-9). 1980. lib. bdg. 6.95 (ISBN 0-87191-773-4). Creative Ed.

--Complete Poetry & Selected Criticism of Edgar Allan Poe. Tate, Allen, ed. 1981. pap. 5.95 (ISBN 0-452-00548-5, F548, Mer). NAL.

--The Complete Works of Edgar Allen Poe, 10 vols. 1981. Repr. of 1908 ed. Set. lib. bdg. 400.00 (ISBN 0-89987-660-9). Darby Bks.

--Edgar Allan Poe, Stories & Poems. (Classics Ser). (gr. 9 up). pap. 1.50 (ISBN 0-8049-0008-6, CL-8). Airmont.

--The Gold Bug. LC 76-94830. 1969. 3.00 (ISBN 0-937684-01-5). Tradd St Pr.

--Key Writings: Representative Selections. rev. ed. Craig, Hardin & Alterton, Margaret, eds. 7.50 o.p. (ISBN 0-8446-0225-6). Peter Smith.

--Marginalia. LC 80-22585. 1980. write for info. (ISBN 0-8139-0812-4). U Pr of Va.

--Murders in the Rue Morgue. rev. ed. Dixson, Robert J., ed. Bd. with The Gold Bug. (American Classics Ser.: Bk. 3). (gr. 9 up). 1973. pap. text ed. 2.75 (ISBN 0-88345-199-9, 18122); cassettes 40.00 (ISBN 0-685-38998-7); tapes 40.00 (ISBN 0-685-38999-5). Regents Pub.

--The Pit & the Pendulum. (Creative's Classics Ser.). (Illus.). 48p. (gr. 4-9). 1980. PLB 6.95 (ISBN 0-87191-771-8). Creative Ed.

--Poems. 225p. 1980. Repr. of 1900 ed. text ed. 14.00x (ISBN 0-8419-7300-8). Holmes & Meier.

--Poems & Essays. 1955. 11.50x (ISBN 0-460-00791-2, Evman); pap. 7.95 (ISBN 0-460-01791-8). Dutton.

--Poems of Edgar Allan Poe. Macdonald, Dwight, ed. LC 65-21417. (Apollo Eds.). (Illus.). 1971. pap. 1.95 o.p. (ISBN 0-8152-0311-X, A311, TYC-T). T Y Crowell.

--Poems of Edgar Allan Poe. Stovall, Floyd, ed. LC 65-23455. 1977. Repr. 12.95x (ISBN 0-8139-0194-4). U Pr of Va.

--Short Fiction of Edgar Allan Poe: An Annotated Edition. Levine, Stuart & Levine, Susan, eds. LC 74-12377. (LL Ser: No. 40). (Illus.). 672p. 1975. 14.95 o.p. (ISBN 0-672-51462-1); pap. text ed. 14.95 (ISBN 0-672-61032-9). Bobbs.

--Tales of Edgar Allan Poe. LC 80-14064. (Raintree Short Classics). (Illus.). 48p. (gr. 4 up). 1981. PLB 9.95 (ISBN 0-8172-1662-6). Raintree Pubs.

--The Tell-Tale Heart. (Creative's Classics Ser.). (Illus.). 32p. (gr. 4-9). 1980. PLB 6.95 (ISBN 0-87191-772-6). Creative Ed.

Poe, Edgar A. & Foye, Raymond. The Unknown Poe. LC 80-2431. 1980. 10.95x (ISBN 0-87286-119-8); pap. 5.95x (ISBN 0-87286-110-4). City Lights.

Poe, Edgar A., jt. auth. see Gardette, Charles D.

Poe, Edgar Allan. Complete Stories & Poems of Edgar Allan Poe. LC 66-24310. 9.95 (ISBN 0-385-07407-7). Doubleday.

--Letters & Documents in the Enoch Pratt Free Library. Bd. with Merun & Recollections of Edgar A. Poe. Wilmer, Lambert A. LC 41-10640. 30.00x (ISBN 0-8201-1199-6). Schol Facsimiles.

Poe, Jerry B. An Introduction to American Business Enterprise: Introductory Text & Cases. 3rd ed. 1976. text ed. 16.95 o.p. (ISBN 0-256-01822-7); pap. 6.50x wkbk o.p. (ISBN 0-256-01823-5). Irwin.

--An Introduction to American Business Enterprises. 4th ed. 1980. 16.95x (ISBN 0-256-02280-1). Irwin.

Poe, Roy, et al. Getting Involved with Business. (Illus.). 576p. (gr. 9-10). 1980. text ed. 12.16 (ISBN 0-07-050335-4, G); learning activity kit 4.60 (ISBN 0-07-050336-2). McGraw.

Poe, Sophie A. Buckboard Days. Cunningham, Eugene, ed. (Illus.). 304p. 1981. pap. write for info. (ISBN 0-8263-0572-5); pap. price not set (ISBN 0-8263-0573-3). U of NM Pr.

Poe, Susan. Americana Mazes. 32p. (Orig.). (gr. 3 up). 1980. pap. 1.50 (ISBN 0-937518-07-7). Hartley Hse.

--Best Ever Fantasy Mazes. (Illus.). 32p. (Orig.). (gr. 3 up). 1980. pap. 1.50 (ISBN 0-937518-04-2). Hartley Hse.

Poebel, Arno. Grammatical Texts. (Publications of the Babylonian Section: Vol. 6). 122p. 1914. soft bound 3.00 o.p. (ISBN 0-686-11920-7). Univ Mus of U PA.

Poehlman, J. M. Breeding Field Crops. (Illus.). 1977. text ed. 19.50 o.p. (ISBN 0-87055-251-1). AVI.

Poehlman, John M. Breeding Field Crops. 2nd ed. (Illus.). 1979. text ed. 26.50 (ISBN 0-87055-328-3). AVI.

Poehlman, William R., tr. see Lohse, Eduard.

Poellot, Luther. Revelation: The Last Book in the Bible. LC 61-18228. 1976. lib. bdg. 8.25 (ISBN 0-8100-0048-2, 15N0355); pap. 5.25 (ISBN 0-8100-0049-0, 15N0356). Northwest Pub.

Poesse, Walter. Juan Ruiz de Alarcon. (World Authors Ser.: Spain: No. 231). lib. bdg. 10.95 (ISBN 0-8057-2012-X). Twayne.

Poets & Writers, Inc. A Writer's Guide to Copyright. Herron, Caroline R., ed. LC 79-25019. (Illus.). 49p. (Orig.). 1979. pap. 4.95 (ISBN 0-913734-10-1). Poets & Writers.

--A Directory of American Fiction Writers, 1976 Edition. LC 75-25710. 104p. 1976. 10.00 o.p. (ISBN 0-913734-04-7); pap. 5.00 o.p. (ISBN 0-913734-05-5). Poets & Writers.

Poff, Mike. Coaches' Guide to Offensive Line Fundamentals & Techniques. LC 80-83977. (Illus.). 160p. (Orig.). 1981. pap. text ed. 5.95 (ISBN 0-918438-62-4). Leisure Pr.

Poffenberger, Mark. Patterns of Change in the Nepal Himalaya. 111p. 1981. lib. bdg. 15.50x (ISBN 0-86531-184-6). Westview.

Poffenberger, Thomas. Fertility & Family Life in an Indian Village. LC 75-9025. (Michigan Papers on South & Southeast Asia: No. 10). (Illus.). 114p. 1975. pap. 4.50x (ISBN 0-89148-010-2). Ctr S&SE Asian.

Poffenberger, Thomas & Sebaly, Kim. The Socialization of Family Size Values: Youth & Family Planning in an Indian Village. LC 76-53996. (Michigan Papers on South and Southeast Asia: No. 12). (Illus.). 150p. 1976. pap. 5.00x (ISBN 0-89148-012-9). Ctr S&SE Asian.

Pogany-Balas, Edit. The Influence of Rome's Antique Monumental Sculptures on the Great Master's of the Renaissance. Debreczeni, Arpad, tr. (Illus.). 115p. 1980. 25.00x (ISBN 963-05-1682-9). Intl Pubns Serv.

Pogash, Jeffrey. How to Read a Wine Label. (Illus., Orig.). 1978. pap. 5.95 o.p. (ISBN 0-8015-3742-8). Dutton.

Poggie, John J. & Gersuny, Carl. Fishermen of Galilee: The Human Ecology of a New England Coastal Community. LC 73-93703. (Marine Bulletin: No. 17). 1974. pap. 3.00 (ISBN 0-938412-09-4). URI MAS.

Poggie, John J., Jr. & Lynch, Robert N., eds. Rethinking Modernization. LC 72-826. 352p. 1974. lib. bdg. 17.95x (ISBN 0-8371-6394-3, POM/). Greenwood.

Poggio, Tomaso, jt. ed. see Reichardt, Werner E.

Pogony, G. E. Wing Beat: A Collection of Eagle Woodcuts. Graham, Douglas J., tr. from Hungarian. LC 76-22176. (Illus.). 1976. 20.00x (ISBN 0-933652-10-0). Domjan Studio.

Pogrebin, Lottie C. Growing up Free: Raising Your Kids in the 80's. LC 80-13054. 528p. 1980. 15.95 (ISBN 0-07-050370-2, GB). McGraw.

Pogrund, Phyllis, jt. auth. see Grebel, Rosemary.

Pogue, Forrest C. George C. Marshall: Ordeal & Hope, 1939-1943. 1966. 12.50 o.s.i. (ISBN 0-670-33686-6). Viking Pr.

Pogue, Jim C., ed. see Barnes, Barnabe.

Pogue, Kate. Fritzie Goes Home. (A Young Reader Ser.). (Illus.). (gr. k-3). 1979. PLB 5.00 (ISBN 0-307-60301-6, Golden Pr). Western Pub.

Pogue, Thomas F. & Sgontz, Larry G. Government & Economic Choice: An Introduction to Public Finance. LC 77-75157. (Illus.). 1978. text ed. 18.95 (ISBN 0-395-25112-5). HM.

Pohier, Jacques & Mieth, Dietmar, eds. The Dignity of the Despised on Earth. (The New Concilium: Vol. 130). 120p. (Orig.). 1980. pap. 4.95 (ISBN 0-8164-2038-6). Crossroad NY.

Pohier, Jacques, jt. ed. see Bockle, Franz.

Pohier, Jacques, jt. ed. see Mieth, Dietmar.

Pohier, Jacques-Marie, jt. auth. see Bockle, Franz.

Pohier, Jacques-Marie, jt. ed. see Bockle, Franz.

Pohier, Jean-Marie, jt. ed. see Bockle, Franz.

Pohl, C. F. Mozart & Haydn in London, 2 vols. in 1. LC 70-125059. (Music Ser). 1970. Repr. of 1867 ed. lib. bdg. 35.00 (ISBN 0-306-70024-7). Da Capo.

Pohl, Frederick. Frederick Pohl's Favorite Stories: Forty Years As a Science Fiction Editor. 448p. 1981. 14.95 (ISBN 0-399-12592-2). Putnam.

--Gold at the Starbow's End. pap. 1.25 o.p. (ISBN 0-345-22775-1). Ballantine.

Pohl, Frederick & Williamson, Jack. Undersea Fleet. 1977. pap. 1.50 o.p. (ISBN 0-345-25618-2). Ballantine.

Pohl, Frederick, ed. Nebula Winners Fourteen. LC 66-20974. (Harper Science Fiction Ser.). 240p. 1980. 11.95 (ISBN 0-06-013382-1, HarpT). Har-Row.

Pohl, Frederick, et al, eds. The Great Science Fiction Series: Stories from the Best of the Science Fiction Series from 1944 to 1980 by 20 All-Time Favorite Writers. LC 79-1705. 416p. 1980. 16.95 (HarpT). Har-Row.

Pohl, Frederik. Beyond the Blue Event Horizon. 1980. pap. 2.50 (ISBN 0-345-27535-7). Ballantine.

--Gateway. (A Del Rey Bk). 1978. pap. 2.50 (ISBN 0-345-29300-2). Ballantine.

--The Space Merchants. 2nd ed. 224p. 1981. pap. 1.50 (ISBN 0-345-29697-4). Ballantine.

Pohl, Frederik & Kornbluth, C. M. Before the Universe. 224p. (Orig.). 1980. pap. 1.95 (ISBN 0-553-11042-X). Bantam.

Pohl, Frederik & Williamson, Jack. Reefs of Space. 1973. pap. 1.25 o.p. (ISBN 0-345-23448-0). Ballantine.

--Rogue Star. 1973. pap. 1.25 o.p. (ISBN 0-345-23450-2). Ballantine.

--Starchild. 1973. pap. 1.25 o.p. (ISBN 0-345-23449-9). Ballantine.

Pohl, H. A. Dielectrophoresis. LC 77-71421. (Cambridge Monographs on Physics). (Illus.). 1978. 99.50 (ISBN 0-521-21657-5). Cambridge U Pr.

Pohl, Ira & Shaw, Alan. The Nature of Computation: An Introduction to Computer Science. (Illus.). 1981. text ed. 16.95 (ISBN 0-914894-12-9). Computer Sci.

Pohl, William. The Voice of Maine. (Illus.). 176p. Date not set. 18.95 (ISBN 0-8159-7104-4). Devin. Postponed.

Pohl, William, tr. see Husserl, Edmund.

Poignant, Raymond. Education & Development in Western Europe, the United States, & the U.S.S.R. A Comparative Study. LC 72-77012. (Illus.). 1969. text ed. 12.75x (ISBN 0-8077-2009-7). Tchrs Coll.

Poignant, Roselyn. Discovery Under the Southern Cross. (International Library). (Illus.). 128p. (gr. 7 up). 1976. PLB 6.90 o.p. (ISBN 0-531-02121-1). Watts.

Poincelot, R. Horticulture: Principles & Practical Applications. 1980. 19.95 (ISBN 0-13-394809-9). P-H.

Poindexter. Macroeconomics. 1976. 18.95 (ISBN 0-03-089419-0). Dryden Pr.

Poindexter, J. Carl, Jr. Macroeconomics. 2nd ed. LC 79-51107. 560p. 1981. text ed. 17.95 (ISBN 0-03-050271-3). Dryden Pr.

Poinsett, Brenda. When Jesus Prayed. LC 80-67896. 1981. pap. 3.25 (ISBN 0-8054-5179-X). Broadman.

Pointen, A. J., jt. auth. see Elwell, D.

Pointer, Horst, jt. auth. see Komoda, Shusul.

Pointillart, Marie-Blanche. Costumes from Crepe Paper. (Little Craft Book Ser). (Illus.). 48p. (gr. 5 up). 1974. 4.95 o.p. (ISBN 0-8069-5302-0); PLB 5.89 o.p. (ISBN 0-8069-5303-9). Sterling.

Pointon, A. J., jt. auth. see Elwell, D.

Pointon, Marcia. History of Art: A Student's Handbook. (Illus.). 104p. 1980. text ed. 14.95x (ISBN 0-04-701010-X, 2573); pap. text ed. 7.50x (ISBN 0-04-701011-8, 2574). Allen Unwin.

Poirer, Richard. Comic Sense of Henry James: A Study of the Early Novels. 1967. pap. 4.95 (ISBN 0-19-500438-8, GB). Oxford U Pr.

Poirier, D. R., jt. auth. see Geiger, G. H.

Poirier, Frank E. Fossil Evidence: The Human Evolutionary Journey. 3rd ed. (Illus.). 360p. 1981. pap. text ed. 12.95 (ISBN 0-8016-3952-2). Mosby.

--In Search of Ourselves: An Introduction to Physical Anthropology. 3rd rev. ed. 1981. pap. text ed. price not set (ISBN 0-8087-1666-2). Burgess.

Poirier, Jacques & Dumas, Jean-Louis R. Review of Medical Histology. Taube, Ursula, tr. LC 76-28944. (Illus.). 1977. pap. text ed. 10.95 (ISBN 0-7216-7273-6). Saunders.

Poirier, Jacques, jt. auth. see Escourolle, Raymond.

Poirier, Louis J., et al, eds. see International Conference on Parkinson's Disease, No. 6.

Poirier, Richard. Performing Self: Compositions & Decompositions in the Languages of Contemporary Life. 1971. 11.95 (ISBN 0-19-501368-9). Oxford U Pr.

--World Elsewhere: The Place of Style in American Literature. 1966. 12.95 (ISBN 0-19-500061-7). Oxford U Pr.

--A World Elsewhere: The Place of Style in American Literature. 270p. 1966. pap. 4.95 (ISBN 0-19-500778-6, 264, GB). Oxford U Pr.

Poirier, Richard, jt. ed. see Kermode, Frank.

Poirot, James, jt. auth. see Horn, Carin.

Poirot, James, et al. Practice in Computers & Mathematics. 227p. (Orig.). (gr. 11-12). 1980. pap. text ed. 5.95 (ISBN 0-88408-126-5). Sterling Swift.

Poirot, James L. Computers & Education. (Illus.). 96p. (Orig.). 1980. pap. 6.95 (ISBN 0-88408-137-0). Sterling Swift.

--Microcomputer Systems & Applied BASIC. (Illus.). 150p. (Orig.). (gr. 6-12). 1980. pap. 8.95 (ISBN 0-88408-136-2). Sterling Swift.

Poirot, James L. & Retzlaff, Danold A. Microcomputer Workbook: TRS-80ed. 128p. 1979. pap. 4.95 wkbk. (ISBN 0-88408-121-4). Sterling Swift.

Poirot, James L. & Retzlaff, Don A. Microcomputer Workbook: Apple II Ed. 2nd ed. 137p. (gr. 11-12). 1981. pap. text ed. 5.95 (ISBN 0-88408-139-7). Sterling Swift.

Poirot, James L. & Retzlaff, Donald A. Microcomputer Workbook: Apple II Edition. 144p. (Orig.). (gr. 11-12). 1979. wkbk 4.95 (ISBN 0-88408-120-6). Sterling Swift.

Poirot, James L., jt. auth. see Groves, David N.

Pois, Joseph. Watchdog on the Potomac: A Study of the Comptroller General of the United States. LC 78-66276. 1979. pap. text ed. 12.00 (ISBN 0-8191-0691-7). U Pr of Amer.

Pois, Robert A. Friedrich Meinecke & German Politics in the Twentieth Century. LC 70-157818. 192p. 1972. 20.00x (ISBN 0-520-02045-6). U of Cal Pr.

Poisson De Gomez, Madeleine Angelique. The Memoirs of the Baron Du Tan, to Which Is Added the Calabrian; or, the History of Charles Brachy, & the Hermit, 1744. LC 74-16060. (Novel in England, 1700-1775 Ser). 1974. lib. bdg. 50.00 (ISBN 0-8240-1111-2). Garland Pub.

Poister, Theodore H., et al. Applied Program Evaluation in Local Government. LC 78-20374. 240p. 1979. 23.95 (ISBN 0-669-02731-6). Lexington Bks.

Poitier, Sidney. This Life. 416p. 1981. pap. 2.95 (ISBN 0-345-29407-6). Ballantine.

Poitras, G., jt. auth. see Adie, R.

Poix, Carol de see De Poix, Carol.

Pokotilov, Dmitri & Loewenthal, Rudolf. History of the Eastern Mongols During the Ming Dynasty from 1368 to 1631. (Studies in Chinese History & Civilization). 148p. 1977. Repr. of 1947 ed. 17.00 (ISBN 0-89093-087-2). U Pubns Amer.

Pokras, Fran. Leaving. 1978. pap. 1.75 o.s.i. (ISBN 0-515-04526-8). Jove Pubns.

Pokras, Robert, jt. auth. see Gardocki, Gloria J.

Pokropek, Marian. Guide to Folk Art & Folklore in Poland. Paszkiewicz, Magdalena M., tr. from Polish. (Illus.). 307p. 1980. 20.00x (ISBN 83-213-3014-2). Intl Pubns Serv.

Pokrovskaya, Vera N. Means for Increasing the Effectiveness of Hydrotransport. Cooley, W. C. & Faddick, R. R., eds. Peabody, Albert, tr. from Rus. LC 77-77841. (Illus., Eng.). 1977. 40.00x o.p. (ISBN 0-918990-02-5). Terraspace.

Polack, W. G. The Handbook to the Lutheran Hymnal. 3rd rev. ed. 1975. Repr. of 1942 ed. lib. bdg. 13.95 (ISBN 0-8100-0003-2, 03-0700). Northwest Pub.

Polak, A. Norwegian Silver. (Illus.). 158p. 1972. 30.00x (ISBN 8-2090-1050-6, N520). Vanous.

Polak, A. Laurence. Legal Fictions. 127p. 1980. Repr. of 1945 ed. lib. bdg. 25.00 (ISBN 0-89987-699-4). Century Bookbindery.

Polak, H. S., et al. Mahatma Gandhi. 1966. pap. 3.00 (ISBN 0-88253-170-0). Ind-US Inc.

Polak, J. J., tr. see Tinbergen, Jan.

Polak, Jacques J., jt. ed. see Mundell, Robert A.

Polakoff, Keith I. Political Parties in American History. LC 80-21505. 550p. 1981. pap. text ed. 14.95 (ISBN 0-471-07747-X). Wiley.

Polakoff, Murray E., et al. Financial Institutions & Markets. 1970. text ed. 21.95 (ISBN 0-395-05062-6). HM.

Polakoski, Kenneth, jt. ed. see Boyarsky, Saul.

Polakowski, N. H. & Ripling, E. Strength & Structure of Engineering Materials. 1965. text ed. 26.95 (ISBN 0-13-851790-8). P-H.

Poland, James L. Medical Physiology Textbook Study Guide. 2nd ed. LC 79-51989. 1979. pap. 8.50 (ISBN 0-87488-155-2). Med Exam.

Poland, James L., et al. Musculoskeletal System. 1981. pap. write for info. (ISBN 0-87488-667-8). Med Exam.

Poland, Jefferson, ed. Sex Marchers. 1968. 5.95 (ISBN 0-910550-13-1). Elysium.

Polansky, Joseph & Nielsen, Greg. Pendulum Power. (Warner Destiny Bk.). (Orig.). 1977. pap. 1.95 o.s.i. (ISBN 0-446-89348-X). Warner Bks.

Polansky, Norman A. Ego Psychology & Communication: Theory for the Interview. LC 74-116533. 1971. 17.95x (ISBN 0-202-26052-6). Aldine Pub.

Polansky, Norman A., et al. Damaged Parents: An Anatomy of Child Neglect. LC 80-22793. (Illus.). 288p. 1981. 15.00 (ISBN 0-226-67221-2). U of Chicago Pr.

Polanyi, John C., jt. ed. see Griffiths, Franklyn.

Polanyi, Karl. Great Transformation: The Political & Economic Origins of Our Time. 1957. pap. 6.95 (ISBN 0-8070-5679-0, BP45). Beacon Pr.

Polanyi, Michael. The Logic of Liberty: Reflections & Rejoinders. LC 51-8809. (Midway Reprint Ser.). 1981. 9.00x (ISBN 0-226-67296-4). U of Chicago Pr.

--Tacit Dimension. LC 66-21015. 1967. pap. 2.50 (ISBN 0-385-06988-X, A540, Anch). Doubleday.

Polcyn, Kenneth A. An Educator's Guide to Communication. LC 78-89216. 116p. 1973. pap. text ed. 2.50 (ISBN 0-89192-017-X, Pub. by Acad Ed Dev). Interbk Inc.

Poldauf, J. Czech-English-Czech Dictionary. new ed. 1980. text ed. 13.50x (ISBN 0-89918-253-4, C253). Vanous.

Polden, Margaret, jt. auth. see McKenna, Julie.

Pole, J. R. American Individualism & the Promise of Progress: Inaugural Lecture. (Inaugural Lecture Ser.). 30p. pap. 5.95 (ISBN 0-19-951526-3). Oxford U Pr.

--Paths to the American Past. LC 79-830. 1979. 19.95 (ISBN 0-19-502579-2). Oxford U Pr.

--Political Representation in England & the Origins of the American Republic. 1971. pap. 5.95x (ISBN 0-520-01903-2, CAMPUS50). U of Cal Pr.

--The Pursuit of Equality in American History. LC 76-20020. (Jefferson Memorial Lecture Ser.). 1978. 18.50x (ISBN 0-520-03286-1); pap. 5.95 (ISBN 0-520-03947-5). U of Cal Pr.

Pole, Thomas. Pole's History of Adult Schools. Verner, Coolie, ed. 1967. 11.50 (ISBN 0-88379-005-X). Adult Ed.

Polednak, Anthony P. The Longevity of Athletes. (Illus.). 284p. 1979. text ed. 13.75 (ISBN 0-398-03867-8). C C Thomas.

Poleman, Thomas T., jt. auth. see Ewell, Peter T.

Polemis, D. I. Doukai: A Contribution to Byzantine Prosopography. (Univ. of London Historical Studies: No. 22). 1968. text ed. 30.00x (ISBN 0-485-13122-6, Athlone Pr). Humanities.

Polemological Centre of the Free University of Brussels. Possibilities of Civilian Defence in Western Europe: Proceedings. Geeraerts, Gustaff, ed. (Vol. 6). 180p. 1977. pap. text ed. 19.25 (ISBN 90-265-0252-4, Pub. by Swets Pub Serv Holland). Swets North Am.

Polen, O. W. Editorially Speaking. 1975. pap. 1.25 (ISBN 0-87148-300-9). Pathway Pr.

--Living by the Word. LC 77-79942. 1977. pap. 1.25 (ISBN 0-87148-509-5). Pathway Pr.

Polenberg, Richard. One Nation Divisible: Class, Race & Ethnicity in the U.S. Since 1938. (Pelican History of the United States Ser.). 1980. pap. 4.95 (ISBN 0-14-021246-9). Penguin.

Polenske, Karen R. State Estimates of Technology, 1963. LC 73-1641. (Multiregional Input-Output Study: Vol. 4). (Illus.). 1974. 25.95 (ISBN 0-669-87007-2). Lexington Bks.

--State Estimates of the Gross National Product 1947, 1958, 1963. LC 79-145900. (Multiregional Input Output Study: Vol. 1). 320p. 1972. 29.95 (ISBN 0-669-62539-6). Lexington Bks.

--The United States Multiregional Input-Output Accounts & Model. LC 78-332. (Illus.). 1980. 36.00x (ISBN 0-669-02173-3). Lexington Bks.

Polenz, G. Donald. Helping As a Humanistic Process: Perspectives & Viewpoints. 1976. pap. text ed. 8.95x o.p. (ISBN 0-8191-0079-X). U Pr of Amer.

Polette, Nancy. Developing Methods of Inquiry: A Source Book for Elementary Media Personnel. LC 72-11992. 1973. 10.00 (ISBN 0-8108-0575-8). Scarecrow.

--E Is for Everybody: A Manual for Bringing Fine Picture Books into the Hands & Hearts of Children. LC 76-16199. (Illus.). 165p. 1976. 10.00 (ISBN 0-8108-0966-4). Scarecrow.

--In-Service: School Library - Media Workshops & Conferences. LC 73-12095. 1973. 11.50 (ISBN 0-8108-0658-4). Scarecrow.

Polette, Nancy & Hamlin, Marjorie. Celebrating with Books. LC 77-3862. (Illus.). 1977. 10.00 (ISBN 0-8108-1032-8). Scarecrow.

--Exploring Books with Gifted Children. LC 80-23721. 1980. lib. bdg. 17.50x (ISBN 0-87287-216-5). Libs Unl.

--Reading Guidance in a Media Age. LC 75-26833. (Illus.). 1975. 12.00 (ISBN 0-8108-0873-0). Scarecrow.

Polezhaev, L. V. Organ Regeneration in Animals: Recovery of Organ Regeneration Ability in Animals. (Amer. Lec. in Living Chemistry Ser.). (Illus.). 200p. 1972. 19.75 (ISBN 0-398-02381-6). C C Thomas.

Polgar, Steven, ed. Culture & Population: A Collection of Current Studies. LC 80-20070. (Carolina Population Center, Monograph: 9). vi, 195p. 1980. Repr. of 1971 ed. lib. bdg. 19.75x (ISBN 0-313-22620-2, POCP). Greenwood.

Polgreen, Cathleen, jt. auth. see Polgreen, John.

Polgreen, John & Polgreen, Cathleen. Earth in Space. 1963. 2.95 o.p. (ISBN 0-394-80127-X, BYR). Random.

Polhamus, J. & Funai, M. Dinosaur Funny Bones. 1974. 4.95 (ISBN 0-13-214536-7); pap. 1.95 (ISBN 0-13-214585-5). P-H.

Polhemus, Robert M. The Changing World of Anthony Trollope. 1968. 16.75x (ISBN 0-520-01021-3). U of Cal Pr.

--Comic Faith: The Great Tradition from Austen to Joyce. LC 79-24856. 1980. 25.00 (ISBN 0-226-67320-0). U of Chicago Pr.

Poli, jt. auth. see Boothroyd.

Poliakov, Leon. The History of Anti-Semitism: From Voltaire to Wagner, Vol. 3. LC 75-2826. 1975. 15.00 (ISBN 0-8149-0762-8). Vanguard.

Police Foundation. Progress in Policing: Essays on Change. Staufenberger, Richard A., ed. 1980. prof. reference 19.50 (ISBN 0-88410-843-0). Ballinger Pub.

Polich, J. Michael & Armor, David J. The Course of Alcoholism: Four Years After Treatment. Braiker, Harriet B., ed. (Personality Processes Ser.). 312p. 1981. 25.00 (ISBN 0-471-08682-7, Pub. by Wiley-Interscience). Wiley.

Polichak, C. W., jt. auth. see Merenda, Merilyn.

Polimeni, Ralph S., jt. auth. see Cashin, James.

Polimeros, George. Energy Cogeneration Handbook: Criteria for Central Plant Design. 264p. 1981. 39.50 (ISBN 0-8311-1130-5). Indus Pr.

Polis, M., ed. see Third IFAC Symposium, Montreal, Canada, 18-20 August 1980.

Polisar, Ira A., jt. auth. see Miller, Maurice H.

Polisensky, J. V. The Thirty Years War. Evans, Robert, tr. 1971. 22.75x (ISBN 0-520-01868-0). U of Cal Pr.
--War & Society in Europe, 1618-1648. LC 77-71423. (Illus.). 1978. 35.50 (ISBN 0-521-21659-1). Cambridge U Pr.
Polish Academy of Science. Poetic Potentials in Information of Astronomy. 1976. pap. 1.95. Primary Pr.
Polish, Virginia. Alphabet. (Starting off with Phonics Ser.: Bk. 2). (Illus.). (gr. k). 1980. pap. text ed. 2.21 (ISBN 0-87895-052-4); tchrs. manual 2.00 (ISBN 0-87895-062-1). Modern Curr.
--Auditory & Motor Skills. (Starting off with Phonics Ser.: Bk. 1). (gr. k). 1980. pap. text ed. 2.21 (ISBN 0-87895-051-6); tchr's manual 2.00 (ISBN 0-87895-061-3). Modern Curr.
--Consonant Sounds. (Starting off with Phonics Ser.: Bk. 3). (gr. k). 1980. pap. text ed. 2.21 (ISBN 0-87895-053-2); tchrs. ed. 2.00 (ISBN 0-87895-063-X). Modern Curr.
--Long Vowels. (Starting off with Phonics Ser.: Bk. 6). (gr. k). 1980. pap. text ed. 2.21 (ISBN 0-87895-056-7); tchrs. manual 2.00 (ISBN 0-87895-066-4). Modern Curr.
--More Consonant Sounds. (Starting off with Phonics Ser.: Bk. 4). (Illus.). (gr. k). 1980. pap. text ed. 2.21 (ISBN 0-87895-054-0); tchrs. ed. 2.00 (ISBN 0-87895-064-8). Modern Curr.
--Short Vowels. (Starting off with Phonics Ser.: Bk. 5). (Illus.). (gr. k). 1980. pap. text ed. 2.12 (ISBN 0-87895-055-9); tchrs. ed. 2.00 (ISBN 0-87895-065-6). Modern Curr.
Polishook, Irwin H. Rhode Island & the Union, 1774-1795. (Studies in History Ser.: No. 5). 1969. 12.95x o.s.i. (ISBN 0-8101-0003-7). Northwestern U Pr.
Politaske, Daniel. Music. 2nd ed. 1979. 17.95 (ISBN 0-13-607556-8); study guide & workbook 5.95 (ISBN 0-13-607564-9); records set 16.95 (ISBN 0-13-607580-0). P-H.
Politi, Leo. Boat for Peppe. (Encore Ed.). (Illus.). 1950. pap. 1.49 o.p. (ISBN 0-684-15845-0, ScribJ). Scribner.
--Song of the Swallows. (Illus.). (gr. k-3). 1949. reinforced bdg. 8.95 (ISBN 0-684-92309-2, ScribJ); pap. 0.95 o.p. (ISBN 0-684-12780-6, SBF19, ScribJ). Scribner.
--Song of the Swallows. (Illus.). 32p. (gr. k-3). pap. 2.95 (ISBN 0-689-70494-1, A-121, Aladdin). Atheneum.
Politis, Linos. A History of Modern Greek Literature. 341p. 1973. 31.00x (ISBN 0-19-815721-5). Oxford U Pr.
Polito, Nat A., jt. auth. see Joerg, Ernest A.
Politz, Murray J. Clinical Podiatric Laboratory Diagnosis. Fielding, Morton D., ed. LC 77-80657. (Podiatric Medicine & Surgery Ser.: Vol. 9). 1977. 27.50 (ISBN 0-87993-096-9). Futura Pub.
Politzer, Frieda N., jt. auth. see Politzer, Robert L.
Politzer, R. L. & Urrutibeheity, H. N. Peldanos. 2nd ed. LC 72-75117. 1972. pap. text ed. 17.95x (ISBN 0-471-00848-6); wkbk. 6.50x (ISBN 0-471-00854-0). Wiley.
Politzer, R. L., et al. L' Echelle: Structures Essentielles du Francais. 1966. 18.95 (ISBN 0-471-00432-4); wkbk. 7.95x (ISBN 0-471-00433-2). Wiley.
Politzer, Robert L. Linguistics & Applied Linguistics: Aims & Methods. 1972. 5.95. Heinle & Heinle.
--Speaking German. LC 69-10287. 1969. text ed. 10.50 (ISBN 0-13-825794-9). P-H.
--Teaching French: An Introduction to Applied Linguistics. 2nd ed. LC 65-14561. 1965. text ed. 14.95 (ISBN 0-471-00430-8). Wiley.
Politzer, Robert L. & Hagiwara, Michio P. Active Review of French: Selected Patterns, Vocabulary & Pronunciation Problems for Speakers of English. LC 63-155633. 1963. pap. 14.95x (ISBN 0-471-00438-3); tapes avail. (ISBN 0-471-00439-1). Wiley.
Politzer, Robert L. & Politzer, Frieda N. Teaching English As a Second Language. 264p. 1981. Repr. of 1972 ed. lib. bdg. write for info. (ISBN 0-89874-068-1). Krieger.
Polk, Donice, ed. see Cook, et al.
Polk, Dora. Vernon Watkins & the Spring of Vision. 1977. text ed. 14.50x (ISBN 0-7154-0349-4). Humanities.
Polk, Edwin, jt. auth. see Polk, Ralph W.
Polk, Frank. F-F-Frank Polk: An Uncommonly Frank Autobiography. LC 78-51848. 136p. pap. 9.50 (ISBN 0-87358-276-4). Northland.
Polk, James. The Passion of Loreen Bright Weasel. 192p. 1981. 8.95 (ISBN 0-686-69056-7). HM.
Polk, Lee & LeShan, Eda. The Incredible Television Machine. LC 77-6247. (Illus.). (gr. 5 up). 1977. 8.95 (ISBN 0-02-774700-X, 77470). Macmillan.
Polk, Noel & Privratsky, Kenneth L. The Sound & the Fury: A Concordance to the Novel. LC 80-12310. (The Faulkner Concordances Ser.: No. 5). 412p. 1980. Set. 62.00 (ISBN 0-8357-0513-7, IS-00108, Pub. by Faulkner Concordance). A-L (ISBN 0-8357-0558-7). M-Z (ISBN 0-8357-0559-5). Univ Microfilms.
Polk, Ralph W. Elementary Platen Presswork. rev. ed. (gr. 11-12). 1971. 7.96 (ISBN 0-87002-109-5). Bennett IL.
Polk, Ralph W. & Polk, Edwin. Practice of Printing. rev. ed. (Illus.). (gr. 9-12). 1971. text ed. 11.80 (ISBN 0-87002-101-X); elem. ptg. job sheets. 2.60 (ISBN 0-87002-029-3). Bennett IL.
Polk, Stella G. Glory Girl. (gr. 5-8). 1970. 6.95 o.p. (ISBN 0-8363-0036-X). Jenkins.
Polk, T. C., Jr. Hospital Acquired Infections. (Illus.). 1977. 19.50 (ISBN 0-8391-1102-9). Univ Park.
Polk, William R. The Arab World: Fourth Edition of the United States & the Arab World. LC 80-16995. (American Foreign Policy Library). 1981. text ed. 22.50x (ISBN 0-674-04316-2); pap. text ed. 8.95x (ISBN 0-674-04317-0). Harvard U Pr.
Polking, Kirk. The Private Pilot's Dictionary & Handbook. LC 72-95274. (Illus.). 280p. 1974. lib. bdg. 5.95 o. p. o.p. (ISBN 0-668-02932-3); lib. bdg. 5.95 o.p. (ISBN 0-668-02931-5). Arco.
Polking, Kirk, ed. Internships Nineteen Hundred Eighty-One. (Orig.). 1981. pap. 6.95 (ISBN 0-89879-036-0). Writers Digest.
--Jobs for Writers. LC 80-16070. 256p. 1980. 10.95 (ISBN 0-89879-019-0). Writers Digest.
Polkinghorn, R. Stephen. Micro-Theory & Economic Choices. 1979. 17.95x (ISBN 0-256-02143-0). Irwin.
Polkinghorne, J. C. Models of High Energy Processes. LC 79-296. (Monographs on Mathematical Physics). (Illus.). 1980. 29.95 (ISBN 0-521-22369-5). Cambridge U Pr.
--The Particle Play: An Account of the Ultimate Constituents of Matter. LC 79-17846. (Illus.). 1979. text ed. 13.95x (ISBN 0-7167-1177-X). W H Freeman.
Polkinghorne, Ruby K. Weaving & Other Pleasant Occupations. LC 71-143640. 1971. Repr. of 1940 ed. 18.00 (ISBN 0-8103-3659-6). Gale.
Poll, Richard D. Howard J. Stoddard: Founder of the Michigan National Bank. (Illus.). x, 260p. 1980. 17.50x (ISBN 0-87013-220-2). Mich St U Pr.
Pollack. The Disco Handbook. (gr. 7-12). 1980. pap. 1.50 (ISBN 0-590-30003-2, Schol Pap). Schol Bk Serv.
--Material Science & Metallurgy. 3rd ed. (Illus.). 416p. 1980. text ed. 21.95 (ISBN 0-8359-4280-5). Reston.
Pollack, Alan, jt. auth. see Guillemin, Victor.
Pollack, Doreen. Educational Audiology for the Limited Hearing Infant. (Illus.). 256p. 1979. text ed. 14.75 (ISBN 0-398-01501-5). C C Thomas.
Pollack, Ervin H. Human Rights: Amintaphil, IVR-Northam, Vol. 1. LC 70-173834. 1971. lib. bdg. 32.50 (ISBN 0-930342-65-8). W S Hein.
Pollack, H. E. The Puuc: An Architectural Survey of the Hill Country of Yucatan & North Casmpeche, Mexico, Memoirs, Vol. 19. (Illus.). 612p. 1980. pap. 50.00 cancelled (ISBN 0-87365-693-8). Peabody Harvard.
Pollack, Herman. Tool Design. (Illus.). 528p. 1976. 19.95 (ISBN 0-87909-840-6); students manual avail. Reston.
Pollack, Jonathan D., jt. ed. see Marwah, Onkar.
Pollack, Margaret. Adaptive Development. (Studies in Developmental Pediatrics Ser: Vol. 3). 240p. 1981. text ed. 17.50 (ISBN 0-88416-380-6). PSG Pub.
Pollack, Michael, jt. auth. see Nelkin, Dorothy.
Pollack, Neuman. Fundamentals of American Government: A Programmed Approach. 1978. pap. text ed. 13.60 (ISBN 0-205-06008-0). Allyn.
Pollack, Norman, ed. Populist Mind. (Orig.). 1967. pap. 8.50 (ISBN 0-672-60076-5, AHS50). Bobbs.
--The Populist Mind. LC 66-16752. 539p. 1967. text ed. 28.50x (ISBN 0-8290-0197-2). Irvington.
Pollack, Randy B. Study Guide to Accompany in Search of Ourselves. 3rd ed. 1981. pap. text ed. price not set o.p. (ISBN 0-8087-3326-5). Burgess.
Pollack, Richard & Sloane, Irving. Guitar Repair: A Manual of Repair for Guitars & Fretted Instruments. 1973. 14.95 (ISBN 0-525-12002-5). Dutton.
Pollack, Robert, ed. Readings in Mammalian Cell Culture. rev. ed. LC 75-15101. (Illus.). 884p. 1975. pap. text ed. 24.00 (ISBN 0-87969-116-6). Cold Spring Harbor.
--Readings in Mammalian Cell Culture. 2nd ed. 1981. pap. text ed. 26.00 (ISBN 0-686-69552-6). Cold Spring Harbor.
Pollack, Seymour V. Guide to Fortran Four. LC 65-8201. 1966. 17.50x (ISBN 0-231-02904-7). Columbia U Pr.
Pollack, Seymour V., jt. auth. see Sterling, Theodor D.
Pollak, F. Pump Users' Handbook. 2nd ed. (Illus.). 208p. 1980. 19.95 (ISBN 0-87201-770-2). Gulf Pub.
Pollak, Karen, jt. auth. see Pollak, Oliver.
Pollak, O. J. & Kritchevsky, D. Sitosterol. (Monographs on Atherosclerosis: Vol. 10). (Illus.). 1980. pap. 75.00 (ISBN 3-8055-0568-X). S Karger.
Pollak, Oliver & Pollak, Karen. Rhodesia-Zimbabwe. (World Bibliographical Ser.: No. 4). 197p. 1979. 25.25 (ISBN 0-903450-14-3). ABC-Clio.
Pollak, Otto & Kelley, Nancy L. The Challenges of Aging. 224p. 1981. 9.95 (ISBN 0-88427-045-9, Dist. by Caroline Hse). North River.
Pollak, Richard. Up Against Apartheid: The Role & the Plight of the Press in South Africa. LC 80-22363. (Science & International Affairs Ser.). 160p. 1981. price not set (ISBN 0-8093-1013-9). S Ill U Pr.
Polland, Madeleine. Sabrina. 1978. 9.95 (ISBN 0-440-07893-8). Delacorte.
Polland, Madeleine A. All Their Kingdoms. 1981. 11.95 (ISBN 0-440-00019-X). Delacorte.
Pollard. Official Guide to Collector Prints. rev. ed. LC 78-72033. (Illus.). 1979. pap. 9.95 o.p. (ISBN 0-87637-108-X). Hse of Collectibles.
--Official Price Guide to Collector Prints. 3rd ed. (House of Collectibles Ser.). Date not set. 9.95 (ISBN 0-87637-147-0, 5003). Arco.
Pollard, A. B. & Schofield, C. W. Basic Physical Science for Technicians. (Illus.). 1977. pap. 11.00x (ISBN 0-7131-3384-8). Intl Ideas.
Pollard, A. H. An Introduction to the Mathematics of Finance. rev. ed. 1978. pap. 7.00 (ISBN 0-08-021796-6). Pergamon.
--Introductory Statistics: A Service Course. 1973. pap. 12.00 (ISBN 0-08-017352-7). Pergamon.
Pollard, A. H., et al. Demographic Techniques. 161p. 1974. 17.75 (ISBN 0-08-017378-0). Pergamon.
Pollard, A. W., ed. English Miracle Plays, Moralities & Interludes: Specimens of the Pre-Elizabethan Drama. 8th ed. 1979. pap. 16.95x (ISBN 0-19-871098-4). Oxford U Pr.
Pollard, Al, jt. auth. see Sherman, Harold.
Pollard, Albert J. The Salad Bar Syndrome. 1981. 6.95 (ISBN 0-533-04573-8). Vantage.
Pollard, Arthur. Anthony Trollope. 1978. 15.00x (ISBN 0-7100-8811-6). Routledge & Kegan.
--Crabbe: The Critical Heritage. (The Critical Heritage Ser.). 510p. 1972. 38.50 (ISBN 0-7100-7258-9). Routledge & Kegan.
Pollard, B. R., jt. auth. see Gibson, W. M.
Pollard, David E. A Chinese Look at Literature: The Literary Values of Chou Tso-Jen in Relation to the Tradition. 1974. 20.00x (ISBN 0-520-02409-5). U of Cal Pr.
Pollard, Harold R. Developments in Management Thought. LC 72-84394. 288p. 1975. pap. 14.50x (ISBN 0-8448-0772-9). Crane-Russak Co.
Pollard, Hazel B., jt. auth. see Pollard, Richard.
Pollard, Hazel M. From Heroics to Sentimentalism: A Study of Thomas Otway's Tragedies. (Salzburg Studies in English Literature, Poetic Drama & Poetic Theory: No. 10). 301p. 1974. pap. text ed. 25.00x (ISBN 0-391-01500-1). Humanities.
Pollard, J. H. Mathematical Models for the Growth of Human Populations. LC 72-91957. 204p. 1973. 29.50 (ISBN 0-521-20111-X); pap. 9.95x (ISBN 0-521-29442-8). Cambridge U Pr.
Pollard, J. M. A Handbook of Numerical & Statistical Techniques. LC 76-27908. (Illus.). 1977. 48.00 (ISBN 0-521-21440-8); pap. 14.95 (ISBN 0-521-29750-8). Cambridge U Pr.
Pollard, Jack, ed. Australian & New Zealand Fishing. LC 73-473961. (Illus.). 960p. 1977. 15.00x (ISBN 0-7271-0168-4). Intl Pubns Serv.
Pollard, Joseph P. Mister Justice Cardozo, a Liberal Mind in Action. Repr. of 1935 ed. lib. bdg. 18.75x (ISBN 0-8371-2815-3, POJD). Greenwood.
Pollard, Michael. How Things Work. LC 78-54638. (Illus.). (gr. 5-7). 1979. 8.95 (ISBN 0-88332-097-5, 8129). Larousse.
--The Victorians. 1978. pap. text ed. 4.95x o.p. (ISBN 0-435-31724-5). Heinemann Ed.
Pollard, Morris, ed. Perspectives in Virology: The Gustav Stern Symposium, Vol. 10. LC 77-84126. (The Gustav Stern Symposium Ser.). 1978. 31.50 (ISBN 0-89004-214-4). Raven.
--Virus-Induced Immunopathology. (Perspectives in Virology: Vol. 6). 1969. 37.50 (ISBN 0-12-560556-0). Acad Pr.
Pollard, Morris, ed. see Eleventh Gustave Stern Symposium on Perspectives in Virology, New York, February 1980.
Pollard, Richard & Pollard, Hazel B. From Human Sentience to Drama: Principles of Critical Analysis, Tragic & Comedic. LC 73-85447. ix, 310p. 1974. 14.00x (ISBN 0-8214-0135-1). Ohio U Pr.
Pollard, Sidney. Integration of the European Economy Since 1815. (Studies on Contemporary Europe: No. 4). 96p. 1981. text ed. 15.95x (ISBN 0-04-336069-6, 2615-6); pap. text ed. 6.95x (ISBN 0-04-336070-X). Allen Unwin.
Pollen, Gerry, jt. auth. see Goodwin, Mary T.
Poller, Nidra. Eggs As Usual Breakfast Etc. 26p. (gr. 2 up). 1980. PLB 10.00 stiched binding (ISBN 0-686-68704-3). Lawrence Hill.
Polley, Joseph. Applied Real Estate Math. 2nd ed. (Illus.). 256p. 1980. pap. text ed. 10.95 (ISBN 0-8359-0252-8). Reston.
Polley, Judith. Val Verde. 1974. 6.95 o.p. (ISBN 0-440-06092-3). Delacorte.
Polley, Maxine. Dance Aerobics. LC 80-23906. (Illus.). 160p. (Orig.). 1981. pap. 5.95 (ISBN 0-89037-186-5). Anderson World.
Polley, Roger. Making Wooden Toys. 1978. 17.95 (ISBN 0-7134-0823-5, Pub. by Batsford England). David & Charles.
Pollin, Burton. Music for Shelley's Poetry. LC 74-4446. (Music Reprint Ser.). 174p. 1974. lib. bdg. 19.50 (ISBN 0-306-70640-7). Da Capo.
Pollin, Burton R. Dictionary of Names & Titles in Poe's Collected Works. LC 68-28982. (Paperback Ser.). 1968. lib. bdg. 19.50 (ISBN 0-306-71154-0). Da Capo.
Pollio, Howard. Behavior & Existence: An Introduction to Empirical Humanistic Psychology. 512p. 1981. text ed. 18.95 (ISBN 0-8185-0425-0). Brooks-Cole.
Pollio, Howard R. The Psychology of Symbolic Activity. LC 72-1943. 1974. text ed. 20.95 (ISBN 0-201-05851-0). A-W.
Pollis, Adamantia & Schwab, Peter, eds. Human Rights: Cultural & Ideological Perspectives. LC 78-19771. (Praeger Special Studies). 1979. 22.95 (ISBN 0-03-046631-8); pap. 9.95 (ISBN 0-03-046631-8). Praeger.
Pollit, Kimball, jt. auth. see Abbott, Derek.
Pollitt, Ernesto. Poverty & Malnutrition in Latin America: Early Childhood Intervention Programs. LC 80-18811. 150p. 1980. 21.95 (ISBN 0-03-058031-5). Praeger.
Pollitt, J. J. Art & Experience in Classical Greece. LC 74-160094. (Illus.). 1972. 32.50 (ISBN 0-521-08065-7); pap. 8.95x (ISBN 0-521-09662-6). Cambridge U Pr.
Pollitt, Jerry J. The Art of Greece - 1400-31 B.C. Sources & Documents. 1965. pap. text ed. 10.95 (ISBN 0-13-047183-6). P-H.
Pollitt, Ronald & Curry, Herbert F., eds. Portraits in British History. 1975. pap. text ed. 9.95x (ISBN 0-256-01679-8). Dorsey.
Pollitz, Edward A. The Forty-First Thief. 1975. 8.95 o.p. (ISBN 0-440-04837-0). Delacorte.
Pollnitz, Karl L. Les Amusemens De Spa; or, the Gallantries of the Spaw in Germany, Pt. 1. LC 78-170597. (Foundations of the Novel Ser.: Vol. 67). lib. bdg. 50.00 (ISBN 0-8240-0579-1). Garland Pub.
--Les Amusemens De Spa; or, the Gallantries of the Spaw in Germany, Pt. 2. LC 78-170597. (Foundations of the Novel Ser.: Vol. 68). lib. bdg. 50.00 (ISBN 0-8240-0580-5). Garland Pub.
--La Saxe Gallante; or, the Amorous Adventures & Intrigues of Frederick-Augustus 2. LC 78-170589. (Foundations of the Novel Ser.: Vol. 59). lib. bdg. 50.00 (ISBN 0-8240-0571-6). Garland Pub.
Pollo, Stefanaq & Puto, Arben. History of Albania: From Its Origins to the Present Day. (Illus.). 1980. 50.00x (ISBN 0-7100-0365-X). Routledge & Kegan.
Pollock, Bruce. In Their Own Words: Lyrics & Lyricists, 1955-74. 224p. 1975. pap. 4.95 o.s.i. (ISBN 0-02-061420-9, Collier). Macmillan.
--In Their Own Words: Lyrics & Lyricists, 1955-74. 224p. 1975. 10.95 (ISBN 0-02-597950-7). Macmillan.
--It's Only Rock & Roll. (gr. 12 up). 1980. 7.95 (ISBN 0-395-29182-8). HM.
--Playing for Change. (YA) (gr. 7-9). 1978. pap. 1.50 (ISBN 0-671-29877-1). PB.
--Playing for Change. (gr. 7-9). 1978. pap. 1.50 o.s.i. (ISBN 0-671-29877-1). Archway.
--When Rock Was Young: A Nostalgic Review of the Top Forty Era. LC 80-23460. (Illus.). 224p. 1981. 13.95 (ISBN 0-03-049836-8, Owl Books); pap. 6.95 (ISBN 0-03-049841-4). HR&W.
Pollock, Bruce & Wagman, John. The Face of Rock & Roll. LC 78-2402. (Illus.). 1978. pap. 12.95 o.p. (ISBN 0-03-042871-8). HR&W.
Pollock, David A. Methods of Electronic Audio Surveillance. 2nd pt. ed. (Illus.). 418p. 1979. pap. text ed. 16.50 (ISBN 0-398-02382-4). C C Thomas.
Pollock, Edward & Maitland, Frederic W. History of English Law Before the Time of Edward First, 2 vols. Vol. 2. 59.00 (ISBN 0-521-07062-7); Vol. 1. pap. 24.95x (ISBN 0-521-09515-8); Vol. 2. pap. 24.95x (ISBN 0-521-09516-6). Cambridge U Pr.
Pollock, Frederick. Introduction to the History of the Science of Politics. 6.00 o.p. (ISBN 0-8446-2750-X). Peter Smith.

Pollock, Griselda. Millet. 1977. 15.95 (ISBN 0-8467-0252-5, Pub. by Two Continents); pap. 9.95 (ISBN 0-8467-0251-7). Hippocrene Bks.

Pollock, Ian. Beware of the Cat. LC 77-82688. (Illus.). 1977. pap. 2.95 (ISBN 0-8467-0385-8, Pub. by Two Continents). Hippocrene Bks.

--Unmarried Couples. (Illus., Orig.). 1978. pap. 3.95 (ISBN 0-8467-0521-4, Pub. by Two Continents). Hippocrene Bks.

Pollock, John. Amazing Grace: John Newton's Story. LC 78-3142. 192p. 1980. 9.95 (ISBN 0-06-066653-6). Har-Row.

--Apostle. Orig. Title: Man Who Shook the World. 244p. 1972. pap. 3.95 (ISBN 0-88207-233-1). Victor Bks.

Pollock, Michael L. & Schmidt, Donald H. Heart Disease & Rehabilitation. 1979. 45.00x (ISBN 0-89289-407-5). HM Prof Med Div.

Pollock, Penny. Garlanda: The Ups & Downs of an Uppity Teapot. (Illus.). 80p. (gr. 2-6). 1980. 7.95 (ISBN 0-399-20713-9). Putnam.

Pollock, Sheldon. Aspects of Verification in Sanskrit Lyric Poetry. (American Oriental Ser.: Vol. 61). 1977. 11.00. Am Orient Soc.

Pollock, Shirley. Adventures in Being a Parent: Family Enrichment Ideas for Busy Parents. (Orig.). 1981. pap. 3.50 (ISBN 0-87239-458-1, 2971). Standard Pub.

Pollock, Steven H. Magic Mushroom Cultivation. (Illus.). 1981. pap. 6.00 (ISBN 0-930074-01-7). Herbal Med.

--Building Playground Sculpture & Homes. LC 74-20319. (Illus.). pap. 7.95 (ISBN 0-9600818-1-X). Master Pr.

Pollock, T. C. & Spaulding, J. G. General Semantics: A Theory of Meaning Analyzed. (Monographs: No. 3). 3.00x (ISBN 0-910780-03-X). Inst Gen Semantics.

Pollock, Ted. Managing Creatively: A Very Practical Guide, 2 vols. Incl. Vol. 1. Managing Yourself Creatively. LC 75-145863. 9.95 (ISBN 0-8436-0714-9); Vol. 2. Managing Others Creatively. LC 70-161280. 9.95 (ISBN 0-8436-0715-7). 1971. 16.95 set (ISBN 0-8436-0717-3). CBI Pub.

--Managing Others Creatively. 1974. pap. 4.50 (ISBN 0-8015-4854-3, Hawthorn). Dutton.

--Managing Yourself Creatively. 1974. pap. 3.95 (ISBN 0-8015-4860-8, Hawthorn). Dutton.

Pollock, Vera & Weiner, Jack. Corrosion of Pulp & Paper Mill Equipment. LC 76-21187. (Bibliographic Ser.: No. 269). 1976. pap. 40.00 (ISBN 0-87010-054-8). Inst Paper Chem.

Polmar, Norman. The Ships & Aircraft of the U. S. Fleet. 12th ed. 416p. 1981. 24.95 (ISBN 0-87021-643-0). Naval Inst Pr.

Polnaszek, Frank. Five Hundred Five Hockey Questions Your Friends Can't Answer. 192p. 1980. 9.95 (ISBN 0-8027-0669-X); pap. 5.95 (ISBN 0-8027-7167-X). Walker & Co.

Polner, Murray. Rabbi: The American Experience. LC 77-23123. 1977. 8.95 o.p. (ISBN 0-03-017716-2). HR&W.

Polome, Edgar C., ed. see Conference on Indo-European Studies, U. of Texas, Austin, Feb. 4-5, 1980.

Polonsky, A. & Drukier, Boleslaw. The Beginnings of Communist Rule in Poland, December 1943-June 1945. 400p. 1980. 37.50x (ISBN 0-7100-0540-7). Routledge & Kegan.

Polonsky, Abraham. Zenia's Way. 1980. 9.95 (ISBN 0-690-01896-7). Lippincott & Crowell.

Polonsky, Antony. Little Dictators. 1975. 22.00 (ISBN 0-7100-8095-6). Routledge & Kegan.

Polos, Nicholas C. John Swett: California's Frontier Schoolmaster. LC 78-69836. (Illus.). 1978. pap. text ed. 10.25 (ISBN 0-8191-0580-5). U Pr of Amer.

Polow, Nancy. An Articulation Curriculum for the S Sound. (Illus.). 108p. 1975. pap. 9.75 spiral bdg. (ISBN 0-685-57027-4). C C Thomas.

Polow, Nancy G. A Stuttering Manual for the Speech Therapist. 84p. 1975. pap. 9.75 (ISBN 0-398-03492-3). C C Thomas.

Polsby, N. W., jt. auth. see Greenstein, F. I.

Polsby, Nelson & Wildavsky, Aaron. Presidential Elections: Strategies of American Electoral Politics. 5th ed. LC 70-162761. 1976. 12.50 (ISBN 0-684-16415-9). Scribner.

Polsby, Nelson W. & Smith, Geoffrey. British Government & Its Discontents. LC 79-56372. 208p. 1981. 12.95 (ISBN 0-465-00765-1). Basic.

Polsby, Nelson W., ed. Reapportionment in the 1970s. LC 73-142046. (Institute of Governmental Studies, UC Berkely). 1971. 21.50x (ISBN 0-520-01885-0). U of Cal Pr.

Polsby, Nelson W., ed. see National Journal.

Polsky, Howard W., jt. auth. see Bakal, Yitzhak.

Polsky, Ned. Hustlers, Beats & Others. 1969. pap. 2.50 o.p. (ISBN 0-385-03400-8, A656, Anch). Doubleday.

Polsky, Nelson. Congress & the Presidency. 3rd ed. 192p. 1976. pap. text ed. 7.95 (ISBN 0-13-167692-X). P-H.

Polson, C. J. & Gee, D. J. Essentials of Forensic Medicine. 3rd rev. ed. LC 72-87949. 732p. 1973. 75.00 (ISBN 0-08-017023-4). Pergamon.

Polster, Diane, ed. see Edney, Margon & Grimm, Ede.

Polster, Edythe & Marks, Alfred H. Surimono: Prints by Elbow. (Illus.). 494p. 1980. 1500.00 (ISBN 0-8188-0120-4, Lovejoy). Paragon.

Poltarnees, Welleran. Further Up & Further in. 1981. pap. cancelled (ISBN 0-914676-03-2). Green Tiger.

Poltarnees, Welleran, intro. by. A Book of Unicorns. (Illus.). 1978. 18.95 (ISBN 0-914676-08-3, Star & Elephant); pap. 10.95 (ISBN 0-914676-16-4). Green Tiger.

Poltoratzky, Marianna, jt. auth. see Wolkonsky, Catherine.

Poltroon, Milford. How to Fish Good. pap. 3.95 (ISBN 0-87691-051-7). Winchester Pr.

Poltroon, Milford S. The Happy Fish Hooker: A Piscatorial Perpetration. LC 77-5000. 1977. pap. 3.95 (ISBN 0-87691-242-0). Winchester Pr.

--The Phony Phone Book. 1979. pap. 4.95 (ISBN 0-87691-280-3). Winchester Pr.

Poluga, Charles, jt. auth. see Auvil, Daniel L.

Polugayevsky, Lyev. Grandmaster Preparation. Neat, K. P., tr. (Pergamon Russian Chess Ser.). (Illus.). 200p. 1981. 22.00 (ISBN 0-08-024099-2); pap. 12.00 (ISBN 0-08-024098-4). Pergamon.

Polunin, Nicholas, ed. see International Conference on Environment Future, 2nd.

Polunin, Oleg. Flowers of Greece & the Balkans: A Field Guide. 474p. 1980. 125.00x (ISBN 0-19-217626-9). Oxford U Pr.

Polunin, Oleg & Huxley, Anthony. Flowers of the Mediterranean. LC 79-670242. (Illus.). 1979. 15.95 (ISBN 0-7011-1029-5, Pub. by Chatto Bodley Jonathan); pap. 9.95 (ISBN 0-7011-2284-6). Merrimack Bk Serv.

Polunin, Oleg & Smythies, B. E. Flowers of South-West Europe. (Illus.). 1973. 45.00x (ISBN 0-19-217625-0). Oxford U Pr.

Polushkin, Maria. Mother, Mother, I Want Another. (Illus.). 1980. Repr. 1.50 (ISBN 0-590-30375-9). Schol Bk Serv.

Polvay, Marina. Cucina Magra, Cucina Sana: Slim & Healthy Italian Cooking. (Illus.). 192p. 1981. 13.95 (ISBN 0-13-195081-9, Spec); pap. 6.95 (ISBN 0-13-195073-8). P-H.

--The Energy Saver's Cookbook. (Creative Cooking Ser.). (Illus.). 320p. 1980. 19.95 (ISBN 0-13-277616-2, Spec); pap. 9.95 (ISBN 0-13-277608-1). P-H.

Polwhele, Richard. The Unsex'd Females: A Poem. Luria, Gina, ed. Bd. with The Female Advocate; or, an Attempt to Recover the Rights of Women from Male Usurpation. Radcliffe, Mary Ann. (The Feminist Controversy in England, 1788-1810 Ser.). 1974. lib. bdg. 50.00 (ISBN 0-8240-0875-8). Garland Pub.

Polya, George & Kilpatrick, Jeremy. The Stanford Mathematics Problem Book: With Hints & Solutions. LC 73-86270. 1974. pap. text ed. 4.50x (ISBN 0-8077-2416-5). Tchrs Coll.

Polya, George & Latta, Gordon. Complex Variables. LC 73-14882. 352p. 1974. text ed. 24.95 (ISBN 0-471-69330-8). Wiley.

Polya, Gyorgy. Mathematical Discovery on Understanding, Learning & Teaching Problem Solving, 2 Vols. LC 62-8784. 1962. Vol. 1. 18.95 (ISBN 0-471-69333-2); Vol. 2. 16.95 o.p. (ISBN 0-471-69335-9). Wiley.

Polybius. The Histories. Badian, E., ed. 1966. text ed. 20.00x (ISBN 0-8290-0196-4). Irvington.

Polyviou, Polyvios G. Cyprus: Conflict & Negotiation 1960-1980. 246p. 1981. text ed. 40.00x (ISBN 0-8419-0683-1). Holmes & Meier.

Polzin, Robert. Late Biblical Hebrew: Toward an Historical Typology of Biblical Hebrew Prose. LC 76-3559. (Harvard Semitic Monographs). (Illus.). 1976. 7.50 (ISBN 0-89130-101-1, 040012). Scholars Pr Ca.

Polzin, Robert M. Moses & the Deuteronomist: A Literary Study of the Deuteronomic History. 224p. Date not set. 14.95 (ISBN 0-8245-4740-3); pap. 7.95 (ISBN 0-8245-4739-X). Crossroad NY.

Poma, Huaman. Letter to a King: A Picture History of the Inca Civilization. Dilke, Christopher, tr. 1978. 10.00 o.p. (ISBN 0-525-14480-3). Dutton.

Pomer, Marshall. Intergenerational Occupational Mobility in the United States. LC 80-20626. (University of Florida Social Science Monograph: No. 66). write for info. (ISBN 0-8130-0674-0). U Presses Fla.

Pomerance, Arnold, tr. see Maser, Werner.

Pomerance, Bernard. The Elephant Man. LC 79-7792. 1979. 8.95 (ISBN 0-394-50642-1). Grove.

Pomerans, A. J., tr. see De Wit, H. C.

Pomerans, Arnold, tr. see Romein, Jan.

Pomerantz, Charlotte. The Ballad of the Long-Tailed Rat. LC 74-13611. (Illus.). 32p. (ps-2). 1975. 6.95g (ISBN 0-02-774890-1, 77489). Macmillan.

--The Mango Tooth. LC 76-22664. (Illus.). (gr. k-3). 1977. PLB 7.92 (ISBN 0-688-84070-1). Greenwillow.

--The Piggy in the Puddle. LC 73-6047. (Illus.). 32p. (ps-2). 1974. 7.95 (ISBN 0-02-774900-2). Macmillan.

Pomerantz, Edward. Brisburial. 1981. 14.95x (ISBN 0-913660-13-2); pap. 7.95x (ISBN 0-913660-14-0). Magic Circle Pr.

Pomerantz, James, jt. ed. see Kubovy, Michael.

Pomeranz, Felix, et al. Pensions: An Accounting & Management Guide. LC 75-35288. 1976. 31.95 (ISBN 0-8260-7199-6). Ronald Pr.

Pomeranz, Ruth. The Lady Apprentices. 144p. 1973. pap. text ed. 5.00x (ISBN 0-7135-1868-5, Pub. by Bedford England). Renouf.

Pomeranz, Y. & Meloan, Clifton E. Food Analysis: Theory & Practice. rev. ed. 1978. 23.50 (ISBN 0-87055-238-4). AVI.

Pomeranz, Y. & Shellenberger, J. A. Bread Science & Technology. (Illus.). 1971. 29.50 (ISBN 0-87055-104-3). AVI.

Pomeranz, Y., jt. auth. see Meloan, Clifton.

Pomeranz, Y., jt. auth. see Meloan, Clifton E.

Pomerol, C. Cenozoic Era. 280p. 1981. 74.95 (ISBN 0-470-27140-X). Halsted Pr.

Pomeroy, Earl S. The Pacific Slope: A History of California, Oregon, Washington, Idaho, Utah, & Nevada. LC 65-11128. (Washington Paperback Ser: No. 69). (Illus.). 436p. 1973. Repr. of 1965 ed. 15.00 (ISBN 0-295-95303-9). U of Wash Pr.

--The Territories & the United States, 1861-1890: Studies in Colonial Administration. LC 70-8872. (Americana Library Ser.: No. 15). 1969. 10.50 (ISBN 0-295-95030-7, AL15); pap. 2.95 (ISBN 0-295-95101-X, ALP15). U of Wash Pr.

Pomeroy, Graham, jt. auth. see Fagan, Brian M.

Pomeroy, John N., ed. see Sedgwick, Theodore.

Pomeroy, Pete. Wipeout! (gr. 7-12). 1972. pap. 0.95 o.p. (ISBN 0-590-08769-X, Schol Pap). Schol Bk Serv.

Pomeroy, Ruth. Redbook's Guide to Buying Your First Home. 1980. 11.95 (ISBN 0-686-60933-6, 24716); pap. 4.95 (ISBN 0-686-60934-4, 25385). S&S.

Pomeroy, Ruth, ed. see Redbook Magazine.

Pomeroy, William J. American Neo-Colonialism: Its Emergence in the Philippines & Asia. LC 71-10385. 1970. 7.50 o.p. (ISBN 0-7178-0251-5); pap. 2.85 (ISBN 0-7178-0252-3). Intl Pub Co.

Pomery, Claire. Fight It Out, Work It Out, Love It Out. LC 76-56499. 1977. 8.95 o.p. (ISBN 0-385-00468-0). Doubleday.

Pomey, Antoine. The Pantheon. LC 75-27879. (Renaissance & the Gods Ser.: Vol. 34). (Illus.). 1976. Repr. of 1694 ed. lib. bdg. 73.00 (ISBN 0-8240-2083-9). Garland Pub.

Pomiane, Edouard de see De Pomiane, Edouard.

Pommery, Jean. How Human the Animals. LC 78-24613. 224p. 1981. pap. 6.95 (ISBN 0-8128-6086-1). Stein & Day.

Pomonis, Carolyn. Lord How Different. Hausman, Gerald, ed. LC 80-299. 128p. (Orig.). 1980. pap. 6.95 (ISBN 0-913270-85-7, Sundial Bks). Sunstone Pr.

Pompa, L. Vico: A Study of the New Science. LC 74-79140. 216p. 1975. 26.95 (ISBN 0-521-20584-0). Cambridge U Pr.

Pompeiano, O. & Ajmone-Marsan, C., eds. Brain Mechanisms & Perceptual Awareness. (IBRO Ser.: No. 8). 1981. text ed. price not set (ISBN 0-89004-603-4). Raven.

Pompeiano, O., ed. see IBRO Symposium, Italy, September 1978.

Pomper, Gerald M. The Election of 1980: Reports & Interpretations. 224p. (Orig.). 1980. 12.95 (ISBN 0-934540-10-1); pap. text ed. 7.95 (ISBN 0-934540-09-8). Chatham Hse Pubs.

--Performance of American Government. LC 71-163607. 416p. 1972. text ed. 9.95 o.s.i. (ISBN 0-02-925270-9). Free Pr.

Pomper, Philip. Russian Revolutionary Intelligentsia. LC 75-107303. (AHM Europe Since 1500 Ser.). 1970. pap. 5.95x (ISBN 0-88295-749-X). AHM Pub.

--Sergei Nechaev. (Illus.). 1979. 19.50 (ISBN 0-8135-0867-3). Rutgers U Pr.

Pomraning, G. C. Radiation Hydrodynamics. 304p. 1973. text ed. 50.00 (ISBN 0-08-016893-0). Pergamon.

Pomraning, Gerald C., jt. ed. see Goodjohn, Albert J.

Pomroy, Martha. What Every Woman Needs to Know About the Law. LC 80-85109. 432p. 1981. pap. 3.95 (ISBN 0-87216-835-2). Playboy Pbks.

Ponce, Juan G. Alejandro Obregon. (Illus.). 1970. pap. 2.00 (ISBN 0-913456-09-8). Interbk Inc.

Ponce De Leon, Jose L. El Arte de la Conversacion, el Arte de la Composicion. 2nd ed. 264p. (Span.). 1975. pap. text ed. 12.95x scp (ISBN 0-06-045249-8, HarpC); tapes 195.00 (ISBN 0-685-54221-1). Har-Row.

Poncela, Enrique J. Noche de Primavera sin Sueno: Comedia Humoristica en Tres Actos. Lacosta, Francisco C., ed. LC 67-25113. (Span.). (YA) (gr. 9 up). 1967. pap. text ed. 3.95x (ISBN 0-89197-320-6). Irvington.

Pond, Grace. Cats & Kittens. 1976. pap. 5.95 (ISBN 0-7134-3247-0, Pub. by Batsford England). David & Charles.

--Complete Cat Guide. 6.98 o.p. (ISBN 0-385-01607-7). Doubleday.

--The Observer's Book of Cats. rev. ed. (Illus.). 1979. 3.95 (ISBN 0-684-16589-9, ScribT). Scribner.

--Persian Cats. Foyle, Christina, ed. (Foyle's Handbks). 1973. 3.95 (ISBN 0-685-55820-7). Palmetto Pub.

Pond, Grace, jt. auth. see Ing, Catherine.

Pond, S., jt. auth. see Pickard, G. L.

Pond, Samuel A., jt. auth. see Bricker, George W.

Pond, Samuel A. & Bricker, George W., eds. Bricker's International Directory of University Executive Development Programs: 1981. 12th ed. LC 73-110249. 1980. 85.00 (ISBN 0-9604804-0-4). Bricker's Intl.

--Bricker's International Directory: University Executive Development Programs. 12th ed. LC 73-110249. 600p. 1980. 85.00x (ISBN 0-9604804-0-4). S A Pond.

Pond, Wilson G. & Houpt, Katherine A. The Biology of the Pig. LC 77-90909. (Illus.). 352p. 1978. 25.00x (ISBN 0-8014-1137-8). Comstock.

Pond, Wilson G. & Maner, Jerome H. Swine Production in Temperate & Tropical Environments. LC 73-16068. (Illus.). 1974. text ed. 30.95x (ISBN 0-7167-0840-X). W H Freeman.

Pond, Wilson G., et al, eds. Animal Agriculture: Human Needs in the 21st Century. 600p. 1980. lib. bdg. 20.00x (ISBN 0-86531-032-7). Westview.

Ponder, E. P. Red Cell Structure & Its Breakdown. (Protoplasmatologia: Vol. 10, Pt. 2). (Illus.). 1955. pap. 34.90 o.p. (ISBN 0-387-80388-2). Springer-Verlag.

Ponder, L. United States Tax Court Practice & Procedure. 1976. 29.95 o.p. (ISBN 0-13-938688-2). P-H.

Ponder, Winifred. Clara Butt: Her Life Story. LC 77-16530. (Music Reprint Ser.: 1978). (Illus.). 1978. Repr. of 1928 ed. lib. bdg. 27.50 (ISBN 0-306-77529-8). Da Capo.

Pondrom, Cyrena N., jt. ed. see Dembo, L. S.

Pondy, Louis R., jt. auth. see Leavitt, Harold J.

Pondy, Louis R., jt. ed. see Leavitt, Harold J.

Pong, K. Lee & Chi, Sik R. Let's Talk in Korean. LC 78-72953. 1978. 3.50 (ISBN 0-930878-10-8). Hollym Intl.

Pong, Ted. Quilt. (Illus.). 87p. (Orig.). 1981. pap. 3.95. Pong.

Ponge, Francis. Le Parti Pris Des Choses. Higgins, Ian, ed. (Athlone French Poets Ser.). 1979. text ed. 27.50x (ISBN 0-485-14714-9, Athlone Pr); pap. text ed. 13.00x (ISBN 0-485-12212-X, Athlone Pr). Humanities.

--Sun Placed in the Abyss & Other Texts. Gavronsky, Serge, tr. from Fr. LC 77-3631. 1977. pap. 4.00 (ISBN 0-915342-22-7). SUN.

Poniachek, Harvey A. Monetary Independence Under Flexible Exchange Rates. (Illus.). 1979. 18.95 (ISBN 0-669-02728-6). Lexington Bks.

Ponicsan, Darryl. Goldengrove. LC 78-163586. 1971. 5.95 o.p. (ISBN 0-440-01971-0). D Ponicsan.

--The Ringmaster. 1978. 8.95 o.p. (ISBN 0-440-07579-3). Delacorte.

--Tom Mix Died for Your Sins. 1975. 8.95 o.p. (ISBN 0-440-05969-0). Delacorte.

Ponnambalam, Satchi. Dependent Capitalism in Crisis: Sri Lanka 1948-1978. 256p. 1981. 16.95 (ISBN 0-905762-85-1, Pub. by Zed Pr). Lawrence Hill.

Ponnamperuma, Cyril & Cameron, A. G. W., eds. Interstellar Communication: Scientific Perspectives. (Illus.). 272p. 1974. pap. text ed. 11.50 (ISBN 0-395-17809-6). HM.

Ponnamperuma, Cyril & Margulis, Lynn, eds. Limits of Life. 200p. 1980. PLB 26.50 (ISBN 90-277-1155-0, Pub. by D. Reidel). Kluwer Boston.

Ponomareff, Constantin V. Sergey Esenin. (World Authors Ser.: No. 478). 1978. lib. bdg. 12.50 (ISBN 0-8057-6319-8). Twayne.

Ponomarev, Boris N. Selected Speeches & Writings. LC 80-40182. 384p. Date not set. 47.50 (ISBN 0-08-023606-5). Pergamon.

Pons, Maurice. The Seasons of the Ram. Frenaye, Frances, tr. LC 76-28052. 1977. 7.95 o.p. (ISBN 0-312-70822-X). St Martin.

Ponse, Barbara. Identities in the Lesbian World: The Social Construction of Self. LC 77-84763. (Contributions in Sociology: No. 28). 1978. lib. bdg. 18.95x (ISBN 0-8371-9889-5, PLW/). Greenwood.

Ponsonby, Arthur. English Diaries: A Review of English Diaries from the Sixteenth to the Twentieth Century with an Introduction on Diary Writing. LC 75-152247. 1971. Repr. of 1923 ed. 21.00 (ISBN 0-8103-3711-8). Gale.

--Samuel Pepys. 160p. 1980. Repr. of 1928 ed. lib. bdg. 20.00 (ISBN 0-89760-706-6). Telegraph Bks.
Ponsonby-Fane, Richard A. Fortunes of the Emperors: Studies in Revolution, Exile, Abdication, Usurpation, & Deposition in Ancient Japan. (Studies in Japanese History & Civilization). 1979. 28.00 (ISBN 0-89093-250-6). U Pubns Amer.
--Imperial Cities: The Capitals of Japan from the Oldest Times Until 1229. (Studies in Japanese History & Civilization). 1979. 21.50 (ISBN 0-89093-251-4). U Pubns Amer.
Ponsot, Marie. Admit Impediment. LC 80-2727. (Knopf Poetry Ser.: No. 5). 1981. 10.95 (ISBN 0-394-51450-5); pap. 5.95 (ISBN 0-394-74845-X). Knopf.
Ponsot, Marie, tr. from Chinese. Chinese Fairy Tales. (Illus.). (gr. 4-6). 1974. PLB 10.69 o.p. (ISBN 0-307-66820-7, Golden Pr). Western Pub.
Ponstein, J. Approaches to the Theory of Optimization. LC 79-41419. (Cambridge Tracts in Mathematics: No. 77). (Illus.). 140p. 1980. 36.50 (ISBN 0-521-23155-8). Cambridge U Pr.
Pontalis, J. B. Frontiers in Psychoanalysis: Between the Dream & the Pain. 1981. write for info. (ISBN 0-8236-2090-5). Intl Univs Pr.
Pontanus, Jacobus. Symbolarum Libri XVII Virgilii, 3 vols. LC 75-27860. (Renaissance & the Gods Ser.: Vol. 18). (Illus.). 1976. Repr. of 1599 ed. Set. lib. bdg. 73.00 (ISBN 0-8240-2066-9); lib. bdg. 30.00 (ISBN 0-685-76406-0). Garland Pub.
Pontanus, Jacobus, ed. see Ovid.
Ponte, Lowell. The Cooling. LC 76-7963. 288p. 1976. 8.95 o.p. (ISBN 0-13-172312-X). P-H.
Pontecorvo, G. Trends in Genetic Analysis. LC 58-8805. (Columbia Biological Ser.: No. 18). 1958. 19.00x (ISBN 0-231-02268-9). Columbia U Pr.
Pontecorvo, Giulio, ed. Fisheries Conflict in the North Atlantic: Problems of Management & Jurisdiction. LC 74-9665. (Law of the Sea Institute Ser). 1974. text ed. 17.50 o.p. (ISBN 0-88410-020-0). Ballinger Pub.
Pontefract, Roger. Feel Fit-Come Alive. (Illus.). 144p. 1979. text ed. 19.50x (ISBN 0-19-217583-1). Oxford U Pr.
Ponterotto, Italo L., jt. auth. see Mondelli, R. J.
Pontet, R. L. Du see Caesar.
Pontiero, G. An Anthology of Brazilian Modernist Poetry. 1969. text ed. 18.75 (ISBN 0-08-013327-4); pap. text ed. 9.25 (ISBN 0-08-013326-6). Pergamon.
Pontifical Institute of Mediaeval Studies, Toronto. Dictionary Catalog of the Library of the Pontifical Institute of Mediaeval Studies: First Supplement. (Library Catalogs-Bib. Guides). 1979. lib. bdg. 125.00 (ISBN 0-8161-1061-1). G K Hall.
Pontifical Institute of Mediaeval Studies, Ontario. Dictionary Catalogue of the Library of the Pontifical Institute of Mediaeval Studies: First Supplement, 5 vols. 1979. Set. lib. bdg. 125.00 (ISBN 0-8161-1061-1). G K Hall.
Ponting, Herbert & Hurley, Frank. Nineteen Ten to Nineteen Sixteen Antarctic Photographs: The Scott, Mawson, & Schackleton Expeditions. (Illus.). 1980. 12.50 o.p. (ISBN 0-312-57443-6). Berkley Pub.
Ponting, Kenneth. Sheep of the World in Color. (Illus.). 132p. 1980. 14.95 (ISBN 0-7137-0941-3, Pub. by Blandford Pr England). Sterling.
Ponting, Kenneth G. & Litt, M. Leonardo da Vinci: Drawings of Textile Machines. (Illus.). 1979. text ed. 26.00x (ISBN 0-239-00193-1). Humanities.
Pooch, U. & Chattergy, R. Designing Microcomputer Systems. (Microcomputer Ser.). 224p. 1979. pap. 9.95 (ISBN 0-8104-5679-6). Hayden.
Pooch, Udo, jt. auth. see Chattergy, Rahul.
Poochoo. Methuselah's Gang. Segal, Nelly, tr. from Hebrew. LC 80-1010. (Illus.). 192p. (gr. 3-6). 1980. 7.95g (ISBN 0-396-07886-9). Dodd.
Pool, Ethel, jt. auth. see Bailey, Henry T.
Pool, J. Lawrence, et al. Acoustic Nerve Tumors: Early Diagnosis & Treatment. 2nd ed. (Illus.). 252p. 1970. 18.75 (ISBN 0-398-01507-4). C C Thomas.
Pool, Phoebe. Impressionism. (World of Art Ser.). (Illus.). 1967. pap. 9.95 (ISBN 0-19-519930-8). Oxford U Pr.
Pool, Thomas B., jt. ed. see Cameron, Ivan L.
Pool, William C. Eugene C. Barker: Historian. LC 76-627820. (Illus.). 1971. 10.50 (ISBN 0-87611-025-1). Tex St Hist Assn.
Poole, A. Joe Foreword by see Machen, Elizabeth M.
Poole, Austin L. From Domesday Book to Magna Carta, 1087-1216. 2nd ed. (Oxford History of England Ser). 1955. 33.00x (ISBN 0-19-821707-2). Oxford U Pr.
--Obligations of Society in the Turlfth & Thirteenth Centuries: The Ford Lectures Delivered in the University of Oxford in Michaelmas Term. LC 80-2007. 1981. Repr. of 1946 ed. 18.50 (ISBN 0-404-18587-8). AMS Pr.
Poole, C. P. Electron Spin Resonance: A Comprehensive Treatise on Experimental Technique. 922p. 1967. 50.00 (ISBN 0-470-69386-X). Wiley.
Poole, C. P., Jr. & Farach, H. A. The Theory of Magnetic Resonance. 452p. 1972. 31.95 (ISBN 0-471-69383-9). Wiley.
Poole, Catherine A., jt. auth. see Wexler, Howard A.
Poole, Ernest. The Harbor. 1976. lib. bdg. 17.25x (ISBN 0-89968-099-2). Lightyear.
--His Family. 1976. lib. bdg. 14.75x (ISBN 0-89968-100-X). Lightyear.
--His Second Wife. 1976. lib. bdg. 14.25x (ISBN 0-89968-101-8). Lightyear.
Poole, F., jt. ed. see Draffan, I. W.
Poole, Frederick K. First Book of Indonesia. LC 70-134368. (First Bks). (Illus.). (gr. 4-6). 1971. PLB 4.90 o.p. (ISBN 0-531-00735-9). Watts.
--Jordan. LC 73-14618. (First Bks). (Illus.). 72p. (gr. 5-8). 1974. PLB 6.45 (ISBN 0-531-00818-5). Watts.
--Jordan. rev. ed. O'Brien, Linda, ed. (First Bks). (Illus.). (gr. 4-6). 1978. PLB 6.45 s&l (ISBN 0-531-02241-2). Watts.
--Malaysia & Singapore. LC 74-13439. (Illus.). 92p. (gr. 5-8). 1975. PLB 3.90 o.p. (ISBN 0-531-02778-3). Watts.
--Southeast Asia. rev ed. LC 72-5404. (First Bks.). (Illus.). 96p. (gr. 7-9). 1973. 5.90 (ISBN 0-531-00801-0); text ed. 3.90 (ISBN 0-531-00637-9). Watts.
--Thailand. LC 72-10392. (First Bks). (Illus.). 72p. (gr. 5-7). 1973. PLB 4.90 o.p. (ISBN 0-531-00791-X). Watts.
Poole, Gary. Gag Galaxy Outer Space Jokes & Riddles. (Illus.). 128p. (Orig.). 1981. pap. 1.25 (ISBN 0-448-17165-1, Tempo). G&D.
--Tales of the Spooky Natural & Vampire Jokes. (Illus.). 128p. 1980. lib. bdg. write for info. (ISBN 0-448-13446-2, Tempo); pap. 1.25 (ISBN 0-448-14516-2). G&D.
--Who's Zoo: Animal Jokes & Riddles. (Orig.). (gr. 3 up). pap. 1.25 (ISBN 0-448-17279-8, Tempo). G&D.
Poole, K. P. The Local Government Service: In England & Wales. (New Local Government Ser.). (Illus.). 1978. text ed. 25.00x (ISBN 0-04-352073-1); pap. text ed. 10.95x (ISBN 0-04-352074-X). Allen Unwin.
Poole, Lon. Accounts Payable: CBM-PET Edition. 200p. (Orig.). 1980. pap. cancelled (ISBN 0-931988-42-X). Osborne-McGraw.
--The Apple II User's Guide. 500p. 1981. pap. 15.00 (ISBN 0-931988-46-2). Osborne-McGraw.
Poole, Lon & Borchers, Mary. Some Common BASIC Programs. 3rd ed. 195p. (Orig.). 1979. pap. 14.99 (ISBN 0-931988-06-3). Osborne-McGraw.
Poole, Lon, ed. Accounts Receivable: CBM-PET Edition. 200p. (Orig.). 1980. pap. cancelled (ISBN 0-931988-43-8). Osborne-McGraw.
--General Ledger: COM-PET Edition. 200p. 1980. pap. cancelled (ISBN 0-931988-44-6). Osborne-McGraw.
--Payroll: COM-PET Edition. 180p. (Orig.). 1980. pap. cancelled (ISBN 0-931988-41-1). Osborne-McGraw.
--Practical BASIC Programs. 250p. (Orig.). 1980. pap. 15.99 (ISBN 0-931988-38-1). Osborne-McGraw.
--Some Common BASIC Programs for Commodore Business Machines. 200p. 1980. pap. 14.99 (ISBN 0-931988-40-3). Osborne-McGraw.
Poole, Lon, et al. General Ledger-WANG. 144p. (Orig.). 1979. pap. 20.00 (ISBN 0-931988-20-9). Osborne-McGraw.
--Payroll with Cost Accounting-CBASIC. 364p. (Orig.). 1979. pap. 20.00 (ISBN 0-931988-22-5). Osborne-McGraw.
Poole, M. J., jt. auth. see Egelstaff, P. A.
Poole, Matthew. A Commentary on the Holy Bible, 3 vols. 1979. Set. 79.95 (ISBN 0-85151-211-9); Vol. 1 Genesis-Job. 28.95 (ISBN 0-85151-054-X); Vol. 2 Psalms-Malachi. 28.95 (ISBN 0-85151-134-1); Vol. 3 Matthew-Revelation. 28.95 (ISBN 0-85151-135-X). Banner of Truth.
Poole, Michael. Theories of Trade Unionism. 280p. 1981. 35.00 (ISBN 0-7100-0695-0). Routledge & Kegan.
Poole, Michael & Mansfield, Roger. Managerial Roles in Industrial Relations: Towards a Definitive Survey of Research & Formulation of Models. 1980. text ed. 27.75x (ISBN 0-566-00377-5, Pub. by Gower Pub Co England). Renouf.
Poole, N. J., jt. auth. see Lynch, J. M.
Poole, Peter A. China Enters the United Nations: A New Era for the World Organization. LC 74-584. (World Focus Bks.). (Illus.). 96p. (gr. 7 up). 1974. PLB 6.45 (ISBN 0-531-02713-9). Watts.
--Profiles in American Foreign Policy: Stimson, Kennan, Acheson, Dulles, Rusk, Kissinger, & Vance. LC 80-5624. (Illus.). 54p. (Orig.). 1981. lib. bdg. 17.00 (ISBN 0-8191-1422-7); pap. text ed. 7.75 (ISBN 0-8191-1423-5). U Pr of Amer.
Poole, Phillip. Dien Bien Phu, 1954: The Battle That Ended the First Indochina War. LC 79-185286. (World Focus Bks). (Illus.). 96p. (gr. 7 up). 1972. PLB 4.90 o.p. (ISBN 0-531-02156-4). Watts.
Poole, R. H. & Shepherd, P. J. Junior Impact. Incl. One. It's a Fact (ISBN 0-435-01736-5); Two. The Senses (ISBN 0-435-01737-3); Three. Creatures (ISBN 0-435-01738-1); Four. Myth & Legend. 1976 (ISBN 0-435-01739-X). (gr. 6-9). 1976. pap. text ed. 3.95x ea. o.p.; pap. text ed. 8.50 tchrs' bk o.p. (ISBN 0-435-01740-3). Heinemann Ed.
Poole, Richard. Gun Vote at Valdoro. 1979. pap. 1.50 (ISBN 0-505-51440-0). Tower Bks.
Poole, Robert, Jr. Cutting Back City Hall. LC 79-6411. 224p. 1981. pap. 5.95 (ISBN 0-87663-557-5). Universe.
--Cutting Back City Hall. LC 79-6411. (A Free Life Editions Bk.). 224p. 1980. 12.50x (ISBN 0-87663-266-5). Universe.
Poole, Rogers. The Unknown Virginia Woolf. LC 78-3458. 1978. 17.95 (ISBN 0-521-21987-6). Cambridge U Pr.
Poole, Shona C. The Christmas Cookbook. LC 79-63631. 259p. 1981. pap. 5.95 (ISBN 0-689-70606-5, 267). Atheneum.
Poole, Susan. Booker T. Washington. LC 78-64423. (Illus.). (gr. 1-4). Date not set. price not set (ISBN 0-89799-091-9); pap. price not set (ISBN 0-89799-060-9). Dandelion Pr. Postponed.
--John Paul Jones. LC 78-74129. (Illus.). (gr. 2-5). Date not set. price not set (ISBN 0-89799-180-X); pap. price not set (ISBN 0-89799-179-6). Dandelion Pr. Postponed.
Poole, Victoria. Thursday's Child. 1980. 10.95 (ISBN 0-316-71334-1). Little.
Pooler, William S. Data Management & Analysis Using SPSS. (Learning Packages in the Policy Sciences: No. 16). 68p. (Orig.). 1978. pap. text ed. 3.50 (ISBN 0-936826-05-3). Pol Stud Assocs.
Pooley, Robert C. Teaching English Grammar. LC 57-11455. 1957. 24.00x (ISBN 0-89197-440-7); pap. text ed. 12.95x (ISBN 0-89197-441-5). Irvington.
Poon, Leonard, ed. Aging in the Nineteen-Eighties: Psychological Issues. LC 80-18515. 1980. 19.50. Am Psychol
Poon, Leonard W., et al, eds. see George A. Talland Memorial Conference.
Poor, Walter A. Differential Geometric Structures. (Illus.). 320p. 1981. text ed. 44.95 (ISBN 0-07-050435-0, C). McGraw.
Poore, Benjamin. Half-Breed in Johsonville. 1981. 5.75 (ISBN 0-8062-1579-3). Carlton.
Poortinga, Ype H., ed. Basic Problems in Cross-Cultural Psychology: Selected Papers from the 3rd International Conference of the International Association for Cross-Cultural Psychology, Tilburg, July 12-16, 1976. 380p. 1977. pap. text ed. 27.75 (ISBN 90-265-0247-8, Pub. by Swets Pub Serv Holland). Swets North Am.
Poortsmans, J., jt. ed. see Di Prampero, P. E.
Popa, Vasko. The Little Box. Simic, Charles, tr. LC 78-134539. 1973. 7.50 (ISBN 0-685-31528-2). Charioteer.
Pope, Alan & Harper, J. J. Low-Speed Wind Tunnel Testing. LC 66-17619. 1966. 37.50 (ISBN 0-471-69392-8, Pub. by Wiley-Interscience). Wiley.
Pope, Alexander. A Choice of Pope's Verse. Porter, Peter, ed. 1971. 7.50 (ISBN 0-571-09291-8, Pub. by Faber & Faber); pap. 3.95 (ISBN 0-571-09292-6). Merrimack Bk Serv.
--Collected Poems. Dobree, Bonamy, ed. 1976. 7.50x (ISBN 0-460-00760-2, Evman); pap. 3.75 (ISBN 0-460-01760-8, Evman). Dutton.
--Essay on Man. Brady, Frank, ed. 1965. pap. 2.50 (ISBN 0-672-61159-7, LLA103). Bobbs.
--Literary Criticism of Alexander Pope. Goldgar, Bertrand A., ed. LC 64-17231. (Landmark Edns.). 1979. 15.00x (ISBN 0-8032-0459-0). U of Nebr Pr.
--Rape of the Lock. Hunt, John D., ed. LC 70-127574. (Casebook Ser). 1970. pap. text ed. 2.50 o.s.i. (ISBN 0-87695-045-4). Aurora Pubs.
Pope, Antoinette. Antoinette Pope's New School Cookbook. 1088p. 1973. 14.95 (ISBN 0-02-598060-2). Macmillan.
Pope, Benjamin, jt. auth. see Siegman, Aron Wolfe.
Pope, Dudley. The Buccaneer King: The Biography of the Notorious Sir Henry Morgan, 1635-1688. LC 76-12156. (Illus.). 1978. 11.95 (ISBN 0-396-07566-5). Dodd.
Pope, Harrison, Jr. The Road East: America's New Discovery of Eastern Wisdom. LC 73-16887. 256p. 1974. pap. 3.45 o.p. (ISBN 0-8070-1127-4, BP476). Beacon Pr.
Pope, Jean A. Comprehension & Experimental Analysis in "A" Level Physics. 1973. pap. text ed. 4.25x o.p. (ISBN 0-435-68725-5). Heinemann Ed.
Pope, John A. Chinese Porcelains from the Ardebil Shrine. 2nd ed. (Illus.). 496p. 1981. 100.00x (ISBN 0-85667-097-9, Pub. by Sotheby Parke Bernet England). Biblio Dist.
Pope, John A., et al. The Freer Gallery of Art, Washington D. C. LC 80-82645. (Oriental Ceramics Ser.: Vol. 9). (Illus.). 180p. 1981. 65.00 (ISBN 0-87011-448-4). Kodansha.
Pope John XXIII. Journal of a Soul. White, Dorothy, tr. LC 79-7786. (Illus.). 504p. 1980. pap. 5.95 (ISBN 0-385-14842-9, Im). Doubleday.
Pope, Joyce. A Closer Look at Jungles. LC 78-4834. (Closer Look at Ser.). (Illus.). (gr. 5 up). 1978. PLB 6.90 s&l (ISBN 0-531-01485-1). Watts.
Pope, Kenneth S., et al. On Love & Loving: Psychological Perspectives on the Nature & Experience of Romantic Love. LC 80-8012. (Social & Behavioral Science Ser.). 1980. text ed. 16.95x (ISBN 0-87589-479-8). Jossey-Bass.
Pope, M., jt. ed. see Kogan, M.
Pope, Maurice. The Ancient Greeks: How They Lived & Worked. LC 75-41966. 192p. 1976. 11.95 (ISBN 0-8023-1264-0). Dufour.
Pope, Michael. Introducing Oil Painting. 1977. pap. 16.95 (ISBN 0-7134-0238-5, Pub. by Batsford England). David & Charles.
--Introducing Watercolour Painting. 1973. 19.95 (ISBN 0-7134-2434-6, Pub. by Batsford England). David & Charles.
Pope, Norris, Jr. Dickens & Charity. 1978. 18.00x (ISBN 0-231-04478-X). Columbia U Pr.
Pope, Robert G. Half-Way Covenant: Church Membership in Puritan New England. LC 69-18067. 1969. 18.50 o.p. (ISBN 0-691-07156-X). Princeton U Pr.
Pope, S. Elspeth. The Time-Lag in Cataloging. (Illus.). 1973. 10.00 (ISBN 0-8108-0551-0). Scarecrow.
Pope, Saxton T. Bows & Arrows. (California Library Reprint Ser.). 1974. Repr. 13.75x (ISBN 0-520-02641-1). U of Cal Pr.
Pope-Hennessy, James. The Houses of Parliament. (Folio Miniature Ser.). 1975. 4.95 (ISBN 0-7181-1302-0, Pub. by Michael Joseph). Merrimack Bk Serv.
Pope-Hennessy, John. Luca della Robbia. LC 79-13566. (Illus.). 1980. 95.00x (ISBN 0-8014-1256-0). Cornell U Pr.
--Raphael. LC 70-88138. (Wrightsman Lectures: Vol. 4). (Illus.). 1970. 20.00, uk (ISBN 0-8147-0476-X). NYU Pr.
Pope John Paul. Brazil - Journey in the Light of the Eucharist. 1980. write for info. (ISBN 0-8198-1102-5); pap. write for info. (ISBN 0-8198-1103-3). Dghtrs St Paul.
Pope John Paul, II. You Are the Future You Are My Hope. 1979. 4.95 o.s.i. (ISBN 0-8198-0632-3); pap. 3.95 (ISBN 0-8198-0633-1). Dghtrs St Paul.
Pope John Paul II. Africa: Apostolic Pilgrimage. 1980. 8.00 (ISBN 0-8198-0708-7); pap. 7.00 (ISBN 0-8198-0709-5). Dghtrs St Paul.
--Love & Responsibility. Willetts, H. T., tr. 1981. 11.95 (ISBN 0-374-19247-2). FS&G.
--Words of Certitude: Excerpts from His Talks & Writings As Bishop & Pope. Buono, Anthon, tr. from It. LC 80-81440. 136p. 1980. pap. 2.95 (ISBN 0-8091-2302-9). Paulist Pr.
Popence, W. P., jt. auth. see Dailey, D. H.
Popenfus, John R. Classroom Application Theory & Practice in Secondary School Social Studies. LC 78-60694. 1978. pap. text ed. 9.00 o.p. (ISBN 0-8191-0563-5). U Pr of Amer.
Popenoe, David. Sociology. 3rd ed. (Illus.). 1977. text ed. 17.95 (ISBN 0-13-821694-0); wkbk & study guide 4.95x (ISBN 0-13-821660-6). P-H.
--Sociology. 4th ed. 1980. text ed. 17.95 (ISBN 0-13-820944-8); wkbk. 5.95 (ISBN 0-13-820977-4). P-H.
Popescu, I. M., jt. auth. see Agarbiceanu, I. I.
Popescu, J. Italian for Commerce. 1968. 18.75 (ISBN 0-08-012454-2). Pergamon.
Pope-Selman, Linda, jt. auth. see Selman, Lawrence H.
Popham, A. E. The Drawings of Leonardo da Vinci. (Illus.). 320p. 1981. 15.95 (ISBN 0-224-00909-5, Pub. by Chatto-Bodley-Jonathan). Merrimack Bk Serv.
Popham, E. L., jt. auth. see Place, Irene M.
Popham, Hugh. Fabulous Voyage of the Pegasus. LC 59-6591. (Illus.). (gr. 4-8). 1959. 7.95 (ISBN 0-87599-092-4). S G Phillips.
Popham, J. K. Spiritual Counsel to the Young. (Summit Bks). Orig. Title: Letters to the Young. 1977. pap. 1.95 (ISBN 0-8010-7020-1). Baker Bk.
Popham, James & Baker, Eva. Establishing Instructional Goals. 1970. pap. text ed. 8.95 (ISBN 0-13-289256-1). P-H.

--Planning an Instructional Sequence. (Illus.). 1970. pap. text ed. 8.95 (ISBN 0-13-679704-0). P-H.

Popham, W. Educational Evaluation. 1975. 18.95 (ISBN 0-13-240515-6). P-H.

Popham, W. & Baker, Eva. Systematic Instruction. 1970. pap. text ed. 8.95 (ISBN 0-13-880690-X). P-H.

Popham, W. James. Advising Schools: A Handbook for Concerned Citizens. 1977. pap. 7.95 (ISBN 0-932166-00-8). Instruct Object.

--Criterion-Referenced Measurement. (Illus.). 1978. pap. 12.95 (ISBN 0-13-193607-7). P-H.

--Evaluation in Education. new ed. LC 74-12822. 601p. 1974. 21.00 (ISBN 0-8211-1512-X); text ed. 19.00 (ISBN 0-685-57220-X). McCutchan.

--An Evalution Guidebook-a Set of Practical Guidelines for the Educational Evaluator. 1972. pap. 5.95 o.p. (ISBN 0-932166-01-6). Instruct Object.

--Uses of Instructional Objectives: A Personal Perspective. LC 72-95013. 1973. pap. text ed. 4.95 (ISBN 0-8224-7182-5). Pitman Learning.

Popiel, Elda S. Nursing & the Process of Continuing Education, Nineteen Seventy-Seven. 2nd ed. LC 76-57997. (Illus.). 1977. pap. text ed. 10.95 (ISBN 0-8016-3969-7). Mosby.

Popkin, Arlene. My April Fool Book. (Illus.). (ps-3). 1974. PLB 5.65 (ISBN 0-914844-04-0). J Alden.

Popkin, Gary. Introductory Structured Cobol Programming. (Orig.). 1980. pap. text ed. 16.95 (ISBN 0-442-23166-0); instr's. manual 4.95 (ISBN 0-442-26773-8). D Van Nostrand.

Popkin, Gary & Pike, Arthur. Introduction to Data Processing. LC 76-10893. (Illus.). 1977. pap. text ed. 17.95 (ISBN 0-395-20628-6); inst. manual 1.25 (ISBN 0-395-20629-4). HM.

Popkin, Gary S. Introductory Structured COBOL Programming. 496p. 1981. text ed. 18.95 (ISBN 0-442-26771-1). Van Nos Reinhold.

Popkin, Gary S. & Pike, Arthur M. Introduction to Data Processing with BASIC. 2nd ed. (Illus.). 592p. 1981. text ed. 17.50 (ISBN 0-395-29483-5); wkbk 6.95 (ISBN 0-395-29485-1); write for info. instr's manual (ISBN 0-395-29484-3). HM.

Popkin, P. R., jt. auth. see Hill, Leslie.

Popkin, Richard H. History of Scepticism from Erasmus to Descartes. rev. ed. (Philosophical Texts & Studies). 1964. text ed. 28.50x (ISBN 9-0232-0438-7). Humanities.

--The History of Scepticism from Erasmus to Spinoza. 1979. 20.00x (ISBN 0-520-03827-4); pap. 6.95x (ISBN 0-520-03876-2, CAMPUS NO. 226). U of Cal Pr.

--Philosophy of the Sixteenth & Seventeenth Centuries. LC 66-10365. (Orig.). 1966. pap. text ed. 6.95 (ISBN 0-02-925490-6). Free Pr.

Popkin, Richard H. & Stroll, Avrum. Philosophy Made Simple. 1956. pap. 3.50 (ISBN 0-385-01217-9, Made). Doubleday.

Popkin, Richard H., tr. see Bayle, Pierre.

Popkin, Samuel. The Rational Peasant: The Political Economy of Rural Society in Vietnam. 1979. 16.50x (ISBN 0-520-03561-5); pap. 5.95x (ISBN 0-520-03954-8, CAMPUS NO. 236). U of Cal Pr.

Popkin, Zelda. Dear Once. LC 75-11870. 384p. 1975. 8.95 o.s.i. (ISBN 0-397-01053-2). Lippincott.

Popko, Rhonda. The Book of Basic Sewing. (Illus.). 104p. (Orig.). 1981. pap. 4.95 (ISBN 0-8326-2248-6, 7445). Delair.

POPLAB Staff. Un Cuestionario Demografico Basico: Recoleccion de Patos y Analysis en Encuestas por Muestro. (Manual Ser.: No. 7). (Span.). 1980. pap. 3.50 (ISBN 0-89383-068-2). Intl Program Labs.

Poplasen, Ilija. The Struggle for the Good, 2 pts. (Illus.). 1981. Repr. of 1978 ed. Pt. I, 61 Pgs. 10.00 (ISBN 0-935352-03-1); Pt. II, 128 Pgs. 20.00 (ISBN 0-935352-04-X). MIR PA.

Poplavskii, Boris I. Snezhnyi Chas: Stikhi, 1931-35. 2nd ed. Karlinsky, Simon, ed. (Modern Russian Literature & Culture, Studies & Texts: Vol. 8). 110p. (Rus.). 1980. pap. 7.00 (ISBN 0-933884-13-3). Berkeley Slavic.

Popley, H. A., ed. & tr. The Sacred Kural. 2nd. ed. Orig. Title: The Tamil Veda of Tiruvalluvar. 159p. pap. 2.80 (ISBN 0-88253-386-X). Ind-US Inc.

Poplin, Dennis E. Social Problems. 1978. 14.95x (ISBN 0-673-07973-2). Scott F.

Popoff, Peter. Calamities, Catastrophies, & Chaos. Tanner, Don, ed. LC 80-69974. (Illus.). 108p. 1980. pap. 2.50 (ISBN 0-938544-01-2). Faith Messenger.

--A New Fire Is Blazing. Tanner, Don, ed. LC 80-67993. (Illus.). 194p. (Orig.). 1980. pap. 4.95 (ISBN 0-938544-02-0). Faith Messenger.

Popoff, Peter & Tanner, Don. Forecasts for Nineteen-Eighty Two. LC 80-69975. (Illus.). 50p. 1980. pap. 1.00 (ISBN 0-938544-00-4). Faith Messenger.

Popolato, Alphonse, jt. ed. see Gibbs, Terry R.

Popov, Alexander I. & Pflaum, R. T. Introductory Analytical Chemistry. 1966. text ed. 12.95x o.p. (ISBN 0-669-25239-5). Heath.

Popov, Dusko. Spy-Counter Spy. 4.95 (ISBN 0-686-28850-5). Academy Chi Ltd.

Popov, Egor O. Mechanics of Materials: SI Version. 2nd ed. (Illus.). 1978. 24.95 (ISBN 0-13-571299-8). P-H.

Popov, Egor P. Introduction to Mechanics of Solids. 1968. ref. ed. 24.95 (ISBN 0-13-487769-1). P-H.

Popov, Howard P. Mechanics of Materials. 2nd ed. 1976. 24.95 (ISBN 0-13-571356-0). P-H.

Popov, V. N., jt. auth. see Konoplyova, N. P.

Popova, Ludmila G., tr. see Bogolubov, Nikolai N., et al.

Popovic, ed. Nikola Tesla (1856-1943) Lectures, Patents, Articles. 1977. 60.00 o.p. (ISBN 0-89918-639-4, Y-639). Vanous.

Popovic, Branko D. Introductory Engineering Electromagnetics. (Engineering Ser). 1971. text ed. 25.95 (ISBN 0-201-05871-5). A-W.

Popovich, Dorothy. Effective Educational & Behavioral Programming for Severely & Profoundly Handicapped Students. (Illus.). 300p. (Orig.). 1981. pap. text ed. 14.95 (ISBN 0-933716-14-1). P H Brookes.

Popovich, Dorothy & Laham, Sandra L. The Adaptive Behavior Curriculum (ABC) Prescriptive Behavior Analyses for Moderately, Severely, & Profoundly Handicapped Persons, Vol. 1. 336p. (Orig.). 1980. pap. text ed. 13.95 (ISBN 0-933716-13-3). P H Brookes.

--The Adaptive Behavior Curriculum: Thirty-Five Hundred Prescriptive Behavior Analyses for Moderately, Severely, & Profoundly Handicapped Students. 230p. 1980. pap. 13.95 (ISBN 0-933716-13-3). P H Brookes.

Popovich, Dorothy & Loham, Sandra L. The Adaptive Behavior Curriculum: Prescriptive Behavioral Analyses for Moderately, Severely, & Profoundly Handicapped Students, Vol. 1. 336p. 1981. pap. text ed. 13.95 (ISBN 0-933716-13-3). P H Brookes.

Popoviciu, L., et al, eds. see European Congress on Sleep Research, 4th, Tirgu-Mures, September 1978.

Popovych, Orest & Tomkins, Reginald. Nonaqueous Solution Chemistry. LC 80-21693. 450p. 1981. 32.00 (ISBN 0-471-02673-5, Pub. by Wiley-Interscience). Wiley.

Popp, A. John, et al, eds. Neural Trauma. LC 78-24627. (Seminars in Neurological Surgery). 1979. text ed. 38.00 (ISBN 0-89004-257-8). Raven.

Popp, Adelheid D. The Autobiography of a Working Woman. Harvey, E. C., tr. LC 79-2950. (Illus.). 135p. 1981. Repr. of 1912 ed. 14.50 (ISBN 0-8305-0113-4). Hyperion Conn.

Poppe, Nicholas. Diamond Sutra: Three Mongolian Versions of the Vajracchedika Prajnaparamita. 1971. 52.50x (ISBN 3-447-00594-7). Intl Pubns Serv.

--Mongolian Language Handbook. LC 72-125673. (Language Handbook Ser.). 1970. pap. text ed. 5.00 (ISBN 0-87281-003-8). Ctr Appl Ling.

Poppeliers, John, et al. What Style Is It? (Illus.). 1977. text ed. 4.95 (ISBN 0-89133-065-8). Preservation Pr.

Popper, Frank. The Politics of Land-Use Reform. 312p. 1981. 20.00 (ISBN 0-299-08530-9); pap. text ed. 7.50 (ISBN 0-299-08534-1). U of Wis Pr.

Popper, Karl R. Conjectures & Refutations: The Growth of Scientific Knowledge. 1968. pap. 7.50x (ISBN 0-06-131376-9, TB1376, Torch). Har-Row.

--Logic of Scientific Discovery. rev. ed. pap. 6.95x (ISBN 0-06-130576-6, TB576, Torch). Har-Row.

--Objective Knowledge: An Evolutionary Approach. 360p. 1972. text ed. 14.95x o.p. (ISBN 0-19-824370-7); pap. text ed. 6.95x (ISBN 0-19-875024-2). Oxford U Pr.

--The Poverty of Historicism. 1977. pap. text ed. 5.95x (ISBN 0-06-131126-X, TB1126, Torch). Har-Row.

Popson, Martha. That We Might Have Life. LC 80-2080. 128p. (gr. 6 up). 1981. pap. 2.75 (ISBN 0-385-17438-1, Im). Doubleday.

Popular Science Authors. Woodworking Projects for the Home. LC 73-86629. (Popular Science Ser). (Illus.). 312p. 1974. 12.95 o.s.i. (ISBN 0-06-013394-5, HarpT). Har-Row.

Population Council. Catalogue of the Population Council Library. 1979. lib. bdg. 280.00 (ISBN 0-8161-0278-3). G K Hall.

Population Institute. Population Activist's Handbook. (Illus.). 192p. 1974. pap. 4.95 o.s.i. (ISBN 0-02-053270-9, Collier). Macmillan.

--The Population Activist's Handbook. LC 73-21298. (Illus.). 192p. 1974. 8.95 o.s.i. (ISBN 0-02-598350-4). Macmillan.

Population Reference Bureau. People! rev ed. Cook, Robert C. & Lecht, Jane, eds. LC 68-20456. (Illus.). 63p. (gr. 7-9). 1973. pap. text ed. 2.50 o.p. (ISBN 0-910416-21-4). Columbia Bks.

Poqueras-Mayo, A., jt. auth. see Laurenti, Joseph L.

Poquette, Radnor J., jt. auth. see Wright, P. H.

Porambo, Ron. No Cause for Indictment: An Autopsy of Newark. 408p. 1972. pap. 3.95 o.p. (ISBN 0-03-003301-2). HR&W.

Porat, Dan I. & Barna, Arpad. Introduction to Digital Techniques. LC 78-17696. (Electronic Technology Ser.). 1979. text ed. 23.95x (ISBN 0-471-02924-6); solutions manual (ISBN 0-471-04351-6). Wiley.

Porat, Dan I., jt. auth. see Barna, Arpad.

Porat, Frieda. Creative Procrastination. LC 80-7750. 192p. (Orig.). 1980. pap. text ed. 4.95 (ISBN 0-06-250690-0, BN3003, HarpR). Har-Row.

Porcellati, Giuseppe, et al, eds. Function & Metabolism of Phospholipids in the Central & Peripheral Nervous Systems. LC 76-15617. (Advances in Experimental Medicine & Biology Ser.: Vol. 72). 412p. 1976. 45.00 (ISBN 0-306-39072-8, Plenum Pr). Plenum Pub.

--Ganglioside Function: Biochemical & Pharmacological Implications. LC 76-7403. (Advances in Experimental Medicine & Biology Ser.: Vol. 71). 306p. 1976. 35.00 (ISBN 0-306-39071-X, Plenum Pr). Plenum Pub.

Porch, Douglas. The Portuguese Armed Forces & the Revolution. (Publications Ser.: No. 188). (Illus.). 11.00 (ISBN 0-85664-391-2). Hoover Inst Pr.

Porche, Verandah. The Body's Symmetry: Poems. pap. 2.95 o.p. (ISBN 0-06-090370-8, CN370, CN). Har-Row.

Porchey. Ermine Tales: More Memoirs of the Earl of Carnarvon. (Illus.). 158p. 1980. 14.50x (ISBN 0-297-77763-7, Pub. by Weidenfeld & Nicolson England). Biblio Dist.

--No Regrets: Memoirs of the Earl of Carnarvon. (Illus.). 227p. 1980. Repr. 17.00x (ISBN 0-297-77246-5, Pub. by Weidenfeld & Nicolson England). Biblio Dist.

Porends, Norman J., jt. auth. see Benes, Vaclav.

Poresky, Louise A. The Elusive Self: Psyche & Spirit in Virginia Woolf's Novels. LC 79-64503. 288p. 1981. 22.50 (ISBN 0-87413-170-7, 170). U Delaware Pr.

Porges, F., ed. see Porges, J.

Porges, G. Applied Acoustics. 1979. pap. 18.95 (ISBN 0-470-26748-8). Halsted Pr.

Porges, Irwin. Edgar Rice Burroughs: The Man Who Created Tarzan, 2 vols. 640p. 1976. Set. pap. 10.00 o.p. (ISBN 0-345-25131-8); Vol. 1. (ISBN 0-345-25947-5); Vol. 2. (ISBN 0-685-66521-6). Ballantine.

Porges, J. Handbook of Heating, Ventilating & Air Conditioning. 7th ed. Porges, F., ed. (Illus.). 1977. 40.00x (ISBN 0-408-00233-6). Transatlantic.

Porges, Peter P. How-Not-to-Do-It Book. (Mad Ser.). (Illus., Orig.). 1981. pap. 1.75 (ISBN 0-446-94190-5). Warner Bks.

Porges, Peter P., jt. auth. see Frank.

Poriss, M. How to Live Cheap but Good: A Primer for People with High Tastes & Low Income. 1971. 6.95 o.p. (ISBN 0-07-050522-5, GB). McGraw.

Porizek, Radoslav, jt. auth. see Puzman, Josef.

Porn, Ingmar. The Logic of Power. 1970. pap. 6.50x o.p. (ISBN 0-631-12510-8, Pub. by Basil Blackwell). Biblio Dist.

Porsild, A. E. Rocky Mountain Wild Flowers. (Illus.). 1974. pap. 7.95 (ISBN 0-660-00073-3, 56495-9, Pub. by Natl Gallery Canada). U of Chicago Pr.

Porsild, A. Erling, jt. auth. see Cody, William J.

Port, Michael, ed. The Houses of Parliament. LC 76-3374. (Studies in British Art Ser.). 1976. 50.00x (ISBN 0-300-02022-8). Yale U Pr.

Porta, G. Della see International Pigment Cell Conference - 6th.

Porta, Giambattista Della. Gli Duoi Fratelli Rivali: The Two Rival Brothers. Clubb, Louise G., tr. from Italian. 350p. 1980. 22.50x (ISBN 0-520-03786-3). U of Cal Pr.

Porte, J. F. Sir Charles V Stanford. LC 76-12570. (Music Reprint Ser.). 1976. Repr. of 1921 ed. lib. bdg. 18.50 (ISBN 0-306-70790-X). Da Capo.

Porte, Joel. Emerson & Thoreau: Transcendentalists in Conflict. LC 80-2512. 1981. Repr. of 1966 ed. 29.50 (ISBN 0-404-19060-X). AMS Pr.

--Representative Man: Ralph Waldo Emerson in His Time. (Illus.). 1979. 17.50x (ISBN 0-19-502436-2). Oxford U Pr.

--The Romance in America. LC 69-17795. 1972. 9.00x (ISBN 0-8195-6024-3, Pub. by Wesleyan U Pr England). Columbia U Pr.

Porten, Bezalel. Archives from Elephantine: The Life of an Ancient Jewish Military Colony. (Illus.). 1968. 27.50x (ISBN 0-520-01028-0). U of Cal Pr.

Porten, Ronald P. Von Der see Von Der Porten, Ronald P.

Porteous, Alexander. Forest Folklore, Mythology & Romance. LC 68-26597. 1968. Repr. of 1928 ed. 18.00 (ISBN 0-8103-3456-9). Gale.

Porteous, I. R. Topological Geometry. 2nd ed. LC 79-41611. Date not set. 59.50 (ISBN 0-521-23160-4); pap. 22.50 (ISBN 0-521-29839-3). Cambridge U Pr.

Porteous, J. Douglas. Environment & Behavior: Planning & Everyday Urban Life. LC 76-1752. 1977. text ed. 16.95 (ISBN 0-201-05867-7). A-W.

Porter. Poems of the Ancients. 3.50 o.s.i. (ISBN 0-8027-6054-6). Walker & Co.

Porter, jt. auth. see Wortabet.

Porter, A. Kingsley. Lombard Architecture, 4 Vols. LC 67-8936. (Illus.). 1967. 150.00 o.p. (ISBN 0-87817-018-9). Hacker.

Porter, Andrew, tr. see Wagner, Richard.

Porter, Anna Maria. Walsh Colville; or, a Young Man's First Entrance into Life: A Novel. Luria, Gina, ed. (The Feminist Controversy in England, 1788-1810 Ser.). 1974. lib. bdg. 50.00 (ISBN 0-8240-0876-6). Garland Pub.

Porter, Bern. Vestigia: Notes on the Life & Work of Janelle Viglini. 1975. pap. 7.50 o.p. (ISBN 0-685-53396-4, 0-911156-15-3). Porter.

--The Viglini Letters: February 1973 - June 1974, Vol. 1. 1975. pap. 7.50 o.p. (ISBN 0-685-53395-6, 0-911156-15-2). Porter.

Porter, Bernard. The Lion's Share: A Short History of British Imperialism, 1850-1970. LC 75-16224. 400p. 1976. text ed. 22.00x (ISBN 0-582-48103-1); pap. text ed. 11.95x (ISBN 0-582-48104-X). Longman.

--The Refugee Question in Mid-Victorian Politics. LC 78-73947. (Illus.). 1980. 41.50 (ISBN 0-521-22638-4). Cambridge U Pr.

Porter, Bernard H. H. L. Mencken Bibliography. Porter, Bernard H., ed. (Illus.). 28p. 1972. 8.50 o.p. (ISBN 0-911156-01-1). Porter.

--I Ricordi Di Firenze. 60p. 1981. lib. bdg. 28.50 (ISBN 0-686-68872-4). Porter.

--Knox County, Maine. (Illus.). 1969. 15.00 o.p. (ISBN 0-685-19456-6). Porter.

--What Henry Miller Said & Why It Is Important. 2nd ed. (Illus.). 1972. 8.50 o.p. (ISBN 0-685-19458-2). Porter.

Porter, C. Burnham, jt. auth. see Moffat, Alex W.

Porter, Carolyn. Seeing & Being: The Plight of the Participant-Observer in Emerson, Jones, Adams, Faulkner. 400p. 1981. 22.50x (ISBN 0-8195-5054-X). Wesleyan U Pr.

Porter, Cathy. Alexandra Kollontai: The Lonely Struggle of the Woman Who Defied Lenin. (Illus.). 553p. 1980. 14.95 (ISBN 0-8037-0129-2). Dial.

Porter, Cedric L. Taxonomy of Flowering Plants. 2nd ed. LC 66-19914. (Illus.). 1967. 24.95x (ISBN 0-7167-0709-8). W H Freeman.

Porter, Charles E., ed. Statistical Theories of Spectra: Fluctuations. (Perspectives in Physics Ser.). (Illus., Orig.). 1965. pap. 24.00 (ISBN 0-12-562356-9). Acad Pr.

Porter, Cliff. Basic Appliance Repair, Vol. 1: Dishwashers, Garbage Disposers, Electric Ranges & Ovens. (Illus.). 1971. 5.95 o.p. (ISBN 0-8104-0785-X); Set. transparencies 151.15s.p. o.p. (ISBN 0-685-03715-0, C001); transparencies 2.15 ea. o.p. Hayden.

--Basic Appliance Repair, Vol. 2: Laundry Equipment - Washers & Dryers. (Illus.). 1975. pap. 5.98 o.p. (ISBN 0-8104-5846-2). Hayden.

Porter, Curt C. Chemical Mechanisms of Drug Action. (American Lectures in Living Chemistry Ser). (Illus.). 184p. 1970. 15.50 (ISBN 0-398-01509-0). C C Thomas.

Porter, Darwin. Marika. 1979. pap. 2.50 o.p. (ISBN 0-425-04262-6). Berkley Pub.

Porter, David. Dickinson: The Modern Idiom. LC 80-24322. 336p. 1981. text ed. 20.00 (ISBN 0-674-20444-1). Harvard U Pr.

--Managing Hospital Architecture, Health Facilities Programming & Design. (Illus.). 450p. text ed. write for info. (ISBN 0-914904-53-1); pap. text ed. write for info. Health Admin Pr.

Porter, Donald. Making Loose Covers. 1975. 17.95 (ISBN 0-7134-2911-9, Pub. by Batsford England). David & Charles.

Porter, Donald C. The Sachem. 352p. 1981. pap. 2.95 (ISBN 0-553-13681-X). Bantam.

--War Chief. (Colonization of America Ser.). 384p. (Orig.). 1980. pap. 2.75 (ISBN 0-553-13803-0). Bantam.

Porter, Dorothy. This Is for You. (Illus.). 57p. 1974. 6.95 o.p. (ISBN 0-89015-064-8). Nortex Pr.

Porter, Earl W. Trinity & Duke, 1892-1924: Foundations of Duke University. LC 64-15199. (Illus.). 1964. 9.75 o.p. (ISBN 0-8223-0137-7); pap. 5.75 (ISBN 0-8223-0350-7). Duke.

Porter, Edward A., jt. auth. see Fitch, Richard D.

Porter, Edwin & Libris, Edouard, eds. The Fall River Tragedy: With an Essay on the True Borden Murderer by Edouard Libris. rev. ed. 350p. 1981. lib. bdg. 15.00; pap. 10.00. Forty Whacks.

Porter, Eleanor. Pollyanna Grows up. 308p. 1980. Repr. of 1915 ed. lib. bdg. 14.50x (ISBN 0-89968-193-X). Lightyear.

Porter, Eleanor H. Just David. 1976. lib. bdg. 15.25x (ISBN 0-89968-107-7). Lightyear.
--Mary-Marie. 1976. lib. bdg. 14.25x (ISBN 0-89968-102-6). Lightyear.
--Miss Billy - Married. 1976. lib. bdg. 16.75x (ISBN 0-89968-104-2). Lightyear.
--Miss Billy's Decision. 1976. lib. bdg. 16.25x (ISBN 0-89968-105-0). Lightyear.
--Pollyanna. 1976. lib. bdg. 14.75x (ISBN 0-89968-106-9). Lightyear.
--Road to Understanding. 1976. lib. bdg. 16.75x (ISBN 0-89968-108-5). Lightyear.
Porter, Eleanor P. Miss Billy. 1976. lib. bdg. 16.25x (ISBN 0-89968-103-4). Lightyear.
Porter, Eliot. Baja California. 1969. pap. 3.95 o.p. (ISBN 0-345-21640-7). Ballantine.
--Birds of North America: A Personal Selection. 1972. 19.95 o.p. (ISBN 0-525-06698-5). Dutton.
--Eliot Porter Calendar 1981. 1981. 6.95 (ISBN 0-525-03004-2). Dutton.
--The Greek World. Levi, Peter, ed. (Illus.). 1980. 45.00 (ISBN 0-525-11812-8). Dutton.
Porter, Eliot & Abbey, Edward. Appalachian Wilderness: The Great Smoky Mountains. rev. ed. (Illus.). 1973. 12.95 o.p. (ISBN 0-525-05686-6). Dutton.
Porter, Elizabeth. Water Management in England & Wales. LC 77-83998. (Cambridge Geographical Studies: No. 10). (Illus.). 1979. 40.50 (ISBN 0-521-21865-9). Cambridge U Pr.
Porter, Ernest G. Schubert's Song Technique. (Student's Music Library Ser). (Illus.). 1959. bds. 10.95 (ISBN 0-234-77457-6). Dufour.
Porter, Ethel & Porter, Hugh. Pilgrim Hymnal. organist's ed. 596p. 8.00. Pilgrim Pr.
Porter, Ethel & Porter, Hugh, eds. Pilgrim Hymnal. 596p. 1931. 6.50 (ISBN 0-8298-0107-3). Pilgrim Pr.
Porter, Ethel K., jt. auth. see Ronander, Albert C.
Porter, Eugene. San Elizario. (Illus.). 14.95 (ISBN 0-8363-0117-X); special ed 125.00 (ISBN 0-685-83963-X). Jenkins.
Porter, Frank W. Indians in Maryland & Delaware: A Critical Bibliography. LC 79-2460. (Newberry Library Center for the History of the American Indian Bibliographical Ser.). 128p. 1980. pap. 4.95x (ISBN 0-253-30954-9). Ind U Pr.
Porter, Gareth. Peace Denied: The United States, Vietnam, & the Paris Agreement. LC 75-3890. (Illus.). 384p. 1976. 15.00x (ISBN 0-253-16160-6). Ind U Pr.
--Vietnam: a History in Documents. pap. write for info. (F553, Meridian Bks). NAL.
Porter, Gene S. Freckles. 1977. 9.95x (ISBN 0-89967-003-2). Harmony & Co.
--Freckles. 254p. 1980. Repr. PLB 14.95x (ISBN 0-89966-224-2). Buccaneer Bks.
--The Harvester. 1977. 9.95x (ISBN 0-89967-004-0). Harmony & Co.
--The Harvester. 560p. 1977. PLB 22.50x (ISBN 0-89966-225-0). Buccaneer Bks.
Porter, George & Lane-Petter, William, eds. Notes for Breeders of Common Laboratory Animals. 1964. 28.50 (ISBN 0-12-562750-5). Acad Pr.
Porter, George, jt. ed. see Bragg, William L.
Porter, H. Boone. Keeping the Church Year. 1978. pap. 3.95 (ISBN 0-8164-2161-7). Crossroad NY.
Porter, Henry. The Two Angry Women of Abington: A Critical Edition. Evett, Marianne B., ed. LC 79-54336. (Renaissance Drama Ser.). 304p. 1980. lib. bdg. 33.00 (ISBN 0-8240-4454-1). Garland Pub.
Porter, Hugh, jt. auth. see Porter, Ethel.
Porter, Hugh, jt. ed. see Porter, Ethel.
Porter, Ian H. & Hook, Ernest B., eds. Human Embryonic & Fetal Death. LC 80-19011. (Birth Defects Institute Symposium X Ser.). 1980. 27.00 (ISBN 0-12-562860-9). Acad Pr.
Porter, J. The Making of the Central Pennines. 160p. 1980. 20.85x (ISBN 0-903485-80-X, Pub. by Allan Pubs England). State Mutual Bk.
Porter, J. A. The Drama of Speech Acts: Shakespeare's Lancastrian Tetralogy. 1979. 14.50x (ISBN 0-520-03702-2). U of Cal Pr.
Porter, J. F., jt. ed. see Manniche, P.
Porter, J. R. & Russell, W. M., eds. Animals in Folklore. (Folklore Society Mistletoe Ser.). (Illus.). 1978. 22.50x o.p. (ISBN 0-8476-6065-6). Rowman.
Porter, Jean. Psychic Development. (Illus.). 1974. pap. 2.75 o.p. (ISBN 0-394-70939-X). Random.
Porter, Jean & Cahn, Leonard. San Francisco: Cool, Gray City of Love. 1981. 19.95 (ISBN 0-525-93180-5, Hawthorn); pap. 10.95 (ISBN 0-525-47663-6). Dutton.
Porter, Jimathan & Chapple, Jonathan. Integrating the Computer with Your Business: Accounting for Computer Charges. LC 80-13930. 308p. 1980. pap. 29.95x (ISBN 0-470-26984-7). Halsted Pr.
Porter, John H., et al. Workbook to Accompany Weimer Introduction to Business. 5th ed. 1974. pap. text ed. 6.50x o.p. (ISBN 0-256-01618-6). Irwin.
Porter, John W. & Spurgeon, Sandra L. Biosynthesis of Isoprenoid Compounds. 350p. 1981. 35.00 (ISBN 0-471-04807-0, Pub. by Wiley-Interscience). Wiley.
Porter, K., jt. auth. see Ellinwood, L.
Porter, Katherine A., tr. & intro. by see Fernandez De Lizardi, Jose J.
Porter, Kingsley A. Construction of Lombard & Gothic Vaults. 1911. 49.50x (ISBN 0-685-69851-3). Elliots Bks.
Porter, Lyman W., jt. ed. see Rosenzweig, Mark R.
Porter, M. Cambodia: Starvation & Revolution. 1979. 24.50 o.p. (ISBN 0-685-67801-6). Porter.
Porter, Mae R. & Davenport, Odessa. Scotsman in Buckskin: Sir William Drummond Stewart & the Rocky Mountain Fur Trade. Date not set. 9.50 (ISBN 0-8038-6648-8). Hastings.
Porter, Marilyn M., jt. auth. see Wallower, Lucille.
Porter, Michael E. Competitive Strategy: Techniques for Analyzing Industries & Competitors. (Illus.). 1980. 15.95 (ISBN 0-02-925360-8). Macmillan.
--Competitive Strategy: Techniques for Analyzing Industries & Competitors. LC 80-65200. (Illus.). 400p. 1980. 14.95 (ISBN 0-02-925360-8). Free Pr.
Porter, Mike. Funny Mouth: Comedy Material for All Occasions. 1981. spiral bdg. 12.95 (ISBN 0-914598-70-8); pap. 9.95 (ISBN 0-914598-71-6). Padre Prods.
Porter, P. W., jt. auth. see DeSouza, A. R.
Porter, Paul R. The Recovery of American Cities. LC 75-39090. (Illus.). 192p. 1976. 8.95 (ISBN 0-8467-0152-9, Pub. by Two Continents). Hippocrene Bks.
Porter, Peter. English Subtitles. 64p. 1981. pap. 11.95 (ISBN 0-19-211942-7). Oxford U Pr.
--Sydney. new ed. Time-Life Books Editors, ed. (The Great Cities Ser.). (Illus.). 200p. 1980. 14.95 (ISBN 0-8094-3108-4, Silver Burdett). Time-Life.
Porter, Peter, ed. see Pope, Alexander.
Porter, Philip W. Food & Development in the Semi-Arid Zone of East Africa. LC 79-20312. (Foreign & Comparative Studies-African Ser.: No. XXXII). 110p. 1979. pap. text ed. 7.00x (ISBN 0-915984-54-7). Syracuse U Foreign Comp.
Porter Productions. Rodney Rabbit Builds a House. (Rodney Rabbit Build-up Board Ser.). (Illus.). 18p. (ps-1). 1980. bds. 2.95 (ISBN 0-675-01021-7). Merrill.
Porter, R., ed. Studies in Neurophysiology. LC 87-51674. (Illus.). 1978. 110.00 (ISBN 0-521-22019-X). Cambridge U Pr.
Porter, R., jt. ed. see Rousseau, G. S.
Porter, R. F., et al. Flight Identification of European Raptors. 2nd ed. (Illus.). 1976. 26.00 (ISBN 0-85661-012-7, Pub by T & A D Poyser). Buteo.
Porter, Raymond J. P. H. Pearse. (English Authors Ser.: No. 154). 1973. lib. bdg. 10.95 (ISBN 0-8057-1434-0). Twayne.
Porter, Robert, ed. The Arts & City Planning. LC 80-14076. 1980. pap. text ed. 9.95 (ISBN 0-915400-20-0). Am Council Arts.
--A Guide to Corporate Giving in the Arts. 1981. 29.95 (ISBN 0-915400-23-5). Am Council Arts.
--United Arts Fundraising Manual. 77p. (Orig.). 1980. pap. text ed. 7.95 (ISBN 0-915400-19-7). Am Council Arts.
--United Arts Fundraising: Nineteen Eighty Campaign Analysis. (Illus., Orig.). 1980. pap. 9.95 (ISBN 0-915400-29-4). Am Council Arts.
Porter, Robert T., jt. auth. see Josephson, Martin M.
Porter, Rosalee G. The Rhyming Reporter. LC 80-68921. 178p. (Orig.). 1981. pap. 5.95x (ISBN 0-935774-00-9). Elgen Pub Co.
Porter, Roy. The Making of Geology: Earth Science in Britain, 1660-1815. LC 76-56220. 1977. 35.50 (ISBN 0-521-21521-8). Cambridge U Pr.
Porter, Roy, et al. Writer's Manual. rev. ed. 1979. 27.95 (ISBN 0-88280-087-6); pap. 17.95 (ISBN 0-88280-088-4). ETC Pubns.
Porter, Roy E., et al. The Writer's Manual. LC 75-43588. 1979. pap. 16.95 (ISBN 0-88280-088-4); pap. 14.95 (ISBN 0-88280-063-9). Chicago Review.
Porter, Roze M. Thistle Hill, the Cattle Baron's Legacy. LC 80-67827. 456p. 1980. 19.95x (ISBN 0-87706-113-0). Branch-Smith.
Porter, Russell W. The Arctic Diary of Russell Williams Porter. Friis, Herman R., ed. LC 75-45375. (Illus.). 160p. 1976. 12.95x (ISBN 0-8139-0649-0). U Pr of Va.
Porter Sargent Staff, ed. The Directory for Exceptional Children. 9th ed. LC 54-4975. (Special Education Ser.). (Illus.). 1384p. 1981. 30.00 (ISBN 0-87558-097-1). Porter Sargent.
Porter, Standish, jt. auth. see Ingamells, Lynn.
Porter, Stuart R., jt. auth. see Angel, Allen R.
Porter, Susan W., jt. auth. see Tinker, Jack.
Porter, Sylvia. Sylvia Porter's Money Book. 1976. pap. 6.95 o.s.i. (ISBN 0-380-00638-3, 40089). Avon.
Porter, Tom & Greenstreet, Robert. Manual of Graphic Techniques. (Illus.). 1980. pap. 9.95 (ISBN 0-684-16504-X, ScribT). Scribner.
Porter, W. Curtis & Waters, J. Erwin. Porter-Waters Debate. pap. 4.50 (ISBN 0-89315-205-6). Lambert Bk.
Porter, Wesley. Kate Shelley & the Midnight Express. (Illus.). 1979. (gr. 5-8) 2.95 (ISBN 0-531-02504-7); PLB 5.90 s&l (gr. k-3) (ISBN 0-531-04083-6). Watts.
Porter, William, jt. auth. see Heffer, Marjorie.
Porter, William N., tr. see Tsurayuki, Kino.
Porterfield, Ernest. Black & White Mixed Marriages. LC 77-87996. 1978. 15.95 (ISBN 0-88229-131-9); pap. 7.95 (ISBN 0-88229-484-9). Nelson-Hall.
Porterfield, James T. Investment Decisions & Capital Costs. (Illus.). 1965. pap. 10.95 ref. ed. (ISBN 0-13-502617-2). P-H.
Porterfield, William M. Concepts of Chemistry. (Illus.). 1972. text ed. 18.95x (ISBN 0-393-09385-9). Norton.
Portes, Alejandro & Walton, John. Labor, Class, & the International System. 1981. price not set (ISBN 0-12-562020-9). Acad Pr.
Portes, Alejandro & Browning, Harley L., eds. Current Perspectives in Latin American Urban Research. LC 75-620107. (Institute of Latin American Studies Special Pubn. Ser.). 176p. 1976. 9.95x (ISBN 0-292-71036-4); pap. 4.95 (ISBN 0-292-71037-2). U of Tex Pr.
Porteus, A., ed. Developments in Environmental Control & Public Health, Vol. 1. (Illus.). 1979. 51.80x (ISBN 0-85334-834-0, Pub. by Applied Science). Burgess-Intl Ideas.
Portis, Alan M. Electromagnetic Fields: Sources & Media. LC 78-7585. 1978. text ed. 29.95 (ISBN 0-471-01906-2); solutions manual o.p. (ISBN 0-471-03717-6). Wiley.
Portis, Charles. True Grit. (RL 8). pap. 1.25 (ISBN 0-451-05419-9, Y5419, Sig). NAL.
Portis, Rowe, tr. see Champigny, Robert.
Portisch, Lajos & Sarkozy, Balazs. Six Hundred Endings. Eszenyi, Sandor, et al, trs. (Pergamon Chess Ser.). (Illus.). 328p. 1981. text ed. 16.75 (ISBN 0-08-024137-9). Pergamon.
Portland Cement Association. Administrative Practices in Concrete Construction. LC 74-28259. (National Concrete Technology Curriculum Project Ser). 230p. 1975. text ed. 25.95 (ISBN 0-471-67433-8). Wiley.
--Basic Concrete Construction Practices. LC 74-28253. (National Concrete Technology Curriculum Project Ser). 480p. 1975. text ed. 29.95 (ISBN 0-471-67430-3); instructor's guide avail. (ISBN 0-471-67436-2). Wiley.
--Concrete Construction & Estimating. Avery, Craig, ed. LC 80-12349. (Illus.). 576p. 1980. pap. 14.00 (ISBN 0-910460-75-2). Craftsman.
--Concrete Inspection Procedures. LC 74-28254. (National Concrete Technology Curriculum Project Ser). 146p. 1975. text ed. 17.95 (ISBN 0-471-67431-1). Wiley.
Portlock, Carol S. & Goffinet, Donald R. Manual of Clinical Problems in Oncology. (Little, Brown Spiral Manual Series). 1980. pap. 12.95 (ISBN 0-316-71424-0). Little.
Portman, David N. The Universities & the Public: A History of Adult Higher Education in the United States. LC 78-9333. 1979. text ed. 16.95 (ISBN 0-88229-116-5). Nelson-Hall.
Portman, David N., ed. Early Reform in American Higher Education. LC 72-186982. 1972. 16.95x (ISBN 0-911012-41-9). Nelson-Hall.
Portmann, Michel, et al. The Ear & Temporal Bone. LC 78-61476. (Illus.). 464p. 1979. 71.50 (ISBN 0-89352-034-9). Masson Pub.
Portnoy, Julius. The Philosopher & Music. (Music Reprint Ser.: 1980). 1980. Repr. of 1954 ed. lib. bdg. 25.00 (ISBN 0-306-76006-1). Da Capo.
Portnoy, William M., et al, eds. Emergency Medical Care. LC 77-70083. (Illus.). 1977. 19.95 (ISBN 0-669-01364-1). Lexington Bks.
Portugal, Franklin H. & Cohen, Jack S. A Century of DNA. (Illus.). 400p. 1980. 20.00 (ISBN 0-262-16067-6); pap. 6.95 (ISBN 0-262-16067-6). MIT Pr.
Portugal, Nancy, jt. auth. see Main, Jody.
Portugali, Juval. Distribution, Allocation, Social Structure & Spatial Form: Elements of Planning Theory. (Progress in Planning: Vol. 14, Part 3). (Illus.). 83p. 1980. pap. 13.50 (ISBN 0-08-026808-0). Pergamon.
Portuondo, Augusto A. Diez Comedias Atribuidas a Lope De Vega: Estudio Do Su Autenticidad. 1980. pap. 17.00 (ISBN 84-499-3788-4). Biblio Siglo.
Porush, David. Rope Dances. LC 78-68135. 8.95 o.p. (ISBN 0-914590-50-2); pap. 3.95 o.p. (ISBN 0-914590-51-0). Braziller.
Porzecanski, Arturo C. Uruguay's Tupamaros: The Urban Guerilla. LC 73-13340. (Special Studies in International Politics & Government). 1973. 18.95x (ISBN 0-275-28802-1). Irvington.
Posa, John G., ed. see Electronics Magazine.
Posada, Jose G. Posada's Popular Mexican Prints. Berdecio, Robert & Appelbaum, Stanley, eds. LC 77-178994. (Illus.). 192p. (Orig.). 1972. pap. 6.00 (ISBN 0-486-22854-1). Dover.
Posamentier, Alfred. Teaching Mathematics in the Secondary School. 1981. pap. text ed. 15.95 (ISBN 0-675-08033-9). Merrill.
Posavac, Emile J. & Carey, Raymond G. Program Evaluation: Methods & Case Studies. (Illus.). 1980. text ed. 18.95 (ISBN 0-13-729665-7). P-H.
Poschel, Reinhard, jt. auth. see Kaluznin, Lev.
Poser, Ernest G., jt. ed. see Ashem, Beatrice A.
Poser, Hans. Philosophie und Mythos. 1979. text ed. 52.00x (ISBN 3-11-007601-2). De Gruyter.
Posey, Jeanne K. The Horsekeeper's Handbook. 1974. 9.95 (ISBN 0-87691-134-3). Winchester Pr.
Posey, Walter B. Frontier Mission: A History of Religion West of the Southern Appalachians to 1861. LC 66-16229. (Illus.). 448p. 1966. 14.00x (ISBN 0-8131-1119-6). U Pr of Ky.
Positron Annihilation Conference - Wayne State University - 1965. Positron Annihilation: Proceedings. Stewart, Alec & Roellig, Leonard, eds. 1967. 52.50 o.p. (ISBN 0-12-669350-1). Acad Pr.
Poskitt, J., jt. auth. see Oxley, R.
Poslusney, Venard. Prayer of Love: The Art of Aspiration. 128p. (Orig.). 1975. pap. 1.95 (ISBN 0-914544-07-1). Living Flame Pr.
Posner, Barbara M. Nutrition & the Elderly. LC 77-17683. 1979. 19.95 (ISBN 0-669-02085-0). Lexington Bks.
Posner, Charles. Reflections on the Revolution in France: 1968. 6.75 (ISBN 0-8446-0852-1). Peter Smith.
Posner, Donald, jt. auth. see Held, Julius.
Posner, Gary H. Introduction to Synthesis Using Organocopper Reagents. LC 80-13538. 140p. 1980. 23.50 (ISBN 0-471-69538-6, Pub. by Wiley-Interscience). Wiley.
Posner, George J. & Rudnitsky, Alan N. Course Design: A Guide to Curriculum Development for Teachers. LC 77-17712. 1978. pap. text ed. 9.95x (ISBN 0-582-28038-9). Longman.
Posner, Grace. In My Sister's Eyes. LC 80-20781. 160p. (gr. 7 up). 1980. 7.95 (ISBN 0-8253-0013-4). Beaufort Bks NY.
Posner, M. Practice in English: Test Papers for Foreign Students. 1971. pap. 11.00x (ISBN 0-17-555059-X). Intl Ideas.
Posner, Marcy, ed. see Cole, John.
Posner, R. The Romance Languages: A Linguistic Introduction. 7.75 (ISBN 0-8446-0853-X). Peter Smith.
Posner, Richard. The Impassioned. 352p. (Orig.). 1980. pap. 2.75 (ISBN 0-515-04624-8). Jove Pubns.
--The Lovers. 1978. pap. 1.95 o.p. (ISBN 0-449-13989-1, GM). Fawcett.
Posner, Richard A. The Economics of Justice. LC 80-25075. (Illus.). 448p. 1981. text ed. 25.00 (ISBN 0-674-23525-8). Harvard U Pr.
Posner, Richard A. & Easterbrook, Frank H. Antitrust - Cases, Economic Notes, & Other Materials. 2nd ed. LC 80-25590. (American Casebook Ser.). (Illus.). 1980. text ed. 22.95 (ISBN 0-8299-2115-X). West Pub.
Posner, Richard A. & Scott, Kenneth E. Economics of Corporation & Securities Regulation. (Orig.). 1981. text ed. write for info (ISBN 0-316-71435-6). Little.
Posner, Richard A., jt. auth. see Kronman, Anthony T.
Posner, Roland. Poetic Communications & Rational Discourse: Methods of Linguistics, Literary & Philosophical Analysis. (Janua Linguarum, Series Minor). 1979. pap. text ed. 17.50x (ISBN 90-279-3138-0). Mouton.
Posner, Steve, jt. auth. see Sandler, Bernard.
Posner, Zalman I. Think Jewish: A Contemporary View of Judaism, a Jewish View of Today's World. LC 78-71323. 1979. 8.95 (ISBN 0-9602394-0-5); pap. 4.95 (ISBN 0-9602394-1-3). Kesher.
Posnick, Paul, jt. auth. see Leokum, Leonard.
Posovac, Emil J. Impacts of Program Evaluation on Mental Health Care. (Westview Special Studies in Health Care). 1979. lib. bdg. 22.50x (ISBN 0-89158-271-1). Westview.
Pospesel, Howard. Introduction to Logic: Predicate Logic. (Illus.). 224p. 1976. text ed. 9.95 (ISBN 0-13-486225-2). P-H.
--Introduction to Logic: Propositional Logic. (Illus.). 224p. 1974. pap. text ed. 8.95 (ISBN 0-13-486217-1). P-H.
Pospisil, Leopold J. The Ethnology of Law. 2nd ed. LC 77-75811. 1978. pap. text ed. 6.95 (ISBN 0-8465-5825-4). Benjamin-Cummings.
Possehl, Gregory L. Trade & Culture Change in Asia. (Illus.). 165p. 1980. lib. bdg. write for info. (ISBN 0-89089-173-7). Carolina Acad Pr.

Posses, F. The Art of International Negotiation. 195p. 1978. text ed. 23.50x (ISBN 0-220-66315-7, Pub. by Busn Bks England). Renouf.

Possien, Wilma M. They All Need to Talk: Oral Communication in the Language Arts Program. (Orig.). 1969. pap. 8.95 (ISBN 0-13-917088-X). P-H.

Possony, Stefan T., jt. auth. see Glaser, Kurt.

Post, Argie W. How to Get in Shape. (Illus.). 1977. 4.50 o.p. (ISBN 0-682-48548-9). Exposition.

--Rape of Detroit. 50p. 1975. 4.00 o.p. (ISBN 0-682-48133-5). Exposition.

Post, C. Gordon. Supreme Court & Political Questions. LC 74-87386. (American History, Politics & Law Ser). 1969. Repr. of 1936 ed. lib. bdg. 19.50 (ISBN 0-306-71610-0). Da Capo.

Post, C. Gordon, ed. see Calhoun, John C. A.

Post, Elizabeth. The New Emily Post's Etiquette. LC 74-14667. (Funk & W Bk.). (Illus.). 880p. 1975. 13.95 (ISBN 0-308-10167-7, TYC-T); thumb-indexed 12.95 (ISBN 0-308-10168-5). T Y Crowell.

Post, Elizabeth & Staffieri, Anthony. The Complete Book of Entertaining. LC 80-7879. (Illus.). 384p. 1981. 14.95 (ISBN 0-690-01970-X, HarpT). Har-Row.

Post, Elizabeth L., ed. Emily Post Book of Etiquette for Young People. LC 67-25416. (Funk & W Bk.). (gr. 7 up). 1967. 9.95 o.s.i. (ISBN 0-308-50002-4, TYC-T). T Y Crowell.

--Emily Post's Wedding Etiquette: Wonderful World of Weddings. (Funk & W Bk.). (Illus.). 1970. 14.95 (ISBN 0-308-50005-9, TYC-T). T Y Crowell.

Post, Emily. The Emily Post Institute Book of Home Entertaining. 1981. 12.95 (ISBN 0-690-01970-X). Lippincott & Crowell.

Post, Emily & Staffieri, Anthony. The Complete Book of Entertaining from the Emily Post Institute. LC 80-7879. 320p. 1981. 14.95. Lippincott & Crowell.

Post, James E. Risk & Response. (Illus.). 1976. 21.50 (ISBN 0-669-00645-9). Lexington Bks.

Post, James E., jt. auth. see Preston, Lee E.

Post, Jeremiah, jt. ed. see Post, Joyce.

Post, Joyce & Post, Jeremiah, eds. Travel in the United States: A Guide to Information Sources. (Geography & Travel Information Guide Ser.: Vol. 3). 600p. 1981. 30.00 (ISBN 0-8103-1423-1). Gale.

Post, Kalmon D., et al, eds. The Pituitary Adenoma. 530p. 1980. 59.50 (ISBN 0-306-40382-X, Plenum Pr). Plenum Pub.

Post, Kenneth & Vickers, Michael. Structure & Conflict in Nigeria. 1974. 22.50 (ISBN 0-299-06470-0). U of Wis Pr.

Post, Laurens Van Der see Van Der Post, Laurens.

Post, Louis F. Deportations Delirium of Nineteen-Twenty. LC 73-114343. (Civil Liberties in American History Ser). 1970. Repr. of 1923 ed. lib. bdg. 32.50 (ISBN 0-306-71882-0). Da Capo.

Post, Melville D. The Bradmoor Murder. 297p. 1980. Repr. of 1929 ed. lib. bdg. 14.25x (ISBN 0-89968-197-2). Lightyear.

--The Man of Last Resort. 284p. 1980. Repr. of 1897 ed. lib. bdg. 14.25x (ISBN 0-89968-198-0). Lightyear.

--The Methods of Uncle Abner. Schantz, Tom & Schantz, Enid, eds. (Illus.). 96p. 1974. 6.95 (ISBN 0-915230-03-8). Rue Morgue.

--The Mountain School Teacher. 196p. 1980. Repr. of 1922 ed. lib. bdg. 12.75x (ISBN 0-89968-199-9). Lightyear.

--The Strange Schemes of Randolph Mason. 280p. 1980. Repr. of 1901 ed. lib. bdg. 14.25x (ISBN 0-89968-200-6). Lightyear.

Post, Richard S., ed. Combating Crime Against Small Business. 160p. 1972. 9.75 (ISBN 0-398-02383-2). C C Thomas.

Post, Robert C., ed. Every Four Years: The American Presidency. 1980. 21.95 (ISBN 0-89599-005-9). Smithsonian Expo Bks.

Postal, Bernard & Koppman, Lionel. American Jewish Landmarks: A Travel Guide and History, Vol. 1. LC 76-27401. (Orig.). 1977. 18.50 (ISBN 0-8303-0151-8); pap. 10.50 (ISBN 0-8303-0152-6). Fleet.

Postal, Paul M., jt. auth. see Johnson, David E.

Postan, Cynthia, tr. see Bairoch, Paul.

Postan, Cynthia, tr. see Duby, Georges.

Postan, E., jt. auth. see Holbrook, D.

Postan, M. M. Essays on Medieval Agriculture & General Problems of the Medieval Economy. (Illus.). 300p. 1973. 38.50 (ISBN 0-521-08744-9). Cambridge U Pr.

--Fact & Relevance: Essays on Historical Method. 1971. 26.95 (ISBN 0-521-07841-5). Cambridge U Pr.

--The Medieval Economy & Society: An Economic History of Britain, 1100-1500. LC 72-87202. 1973. 18.50x (ISBN 0-520-02325-0). U of Cal Pr.

--Medieval Trade & Finance. (Illus.). 350p. 1973. 41.95 (ISBN 0-521-08745-7). Cambridge U Pr.

Poster, M. Existential Marxism in Postwar France: From Sartre to Althusser. 1975. 23.50x (ISBN 0-691-07212-4); pap. 5.95 (ISBN 0-691-01994-0). Princeton U Pr.

Poster, Mark, tr. see Baudrillard, Jean.

Postgate & Firmin. Mr. Rumbletum's Gumboot. 1975. 3.95 (ISBN 0-7207-0781-1, Pub. by Michael Joseph). Merrimack Bk Serv.

--Silly Old Uncle Feedle. 1975. 3.95 (ISBN 0-7207-0783-8, Pub. by Michael Joseph). Merrimack Bk Serv.

--The Song of the Pongo. 1975. 3.95 (ISBN 0-7207-0782-X, Pub. by Michael Joseph). Merrimack Bk Serv.

Postgate, J. R. The Sulphate Reducing Bacteria. LC 78-73600. (Illus.). 1979. 35.50 (ISBN 0-521-22188-9). Cambridge U Pr.

Postgate, J. R., jt. ed. see Gray, T. G.

Postill, Frederick J., jt. auth. see Kalinich, David P.

Postill, Ronald, jt. auth. see Bryant, Victor.

Postle, Denis. Fabric of the Universe. (Illus.). 208p. 1976. 5.95 (ISBN 0-517-52623-9). Crown.

Postlethwait, S. N., et al. The Audio-Tutorial Approach to Learning: Through Independent Study & Integrated Experiences. 3rd ed. LC 70-187724. 1972. pap. text ed. 8.95 o.p. (ISBN 0-8087-6002-5). Burgess.

Postlethwaite, N., jt. ed. see Choppin, B.

Postlethwaite, T. N., jt. ed. see Choppin, B. H.

Postman, Neil. Crazy Talk, Stupid Talk. 1976. 8.95 o.s.i. (ISBN 0-440-01554-5). Delacorte.

--Television & the Teaching of English. LC 61-13519. (Orig.). 1961. pap. text ed. 10.95x (ISBN 0-89197-445-8). Irvington.

Postman, Neil, et al, eds. Language in America: A Report on Our Deteriorating Semantic Environment. LC 73-77137. 1969. pap. 5.50 (ISBN 0-672-63552-6). Pegasus.

--Language in America: A Report on Our Deteriorating Semantic Environment. LC 73-77137. 1969. text ed. 22.50x (ISBN 0-672-53552-1). Irvington.

Postnikov, A. G. Tauberian Theory & Its Applications. (Trudy Steklov: No. 144). 1980. 26.00 (ISBN 0-8218-3048-1). Am Math.

Poston, Carol H., ed. see Wollstonecraft, Mary.

Poston, Dudley L., Jr. & Weller, Robert H., eds. Population of the South: Structure & Change in Social Demographic Context. 288p. 1981. text ed. 25.00x (ISBN 0-292-76467-7). U of Tex Pr.

Poston, M., jt. auth. see Power, Eileen.

Poston, Richard W. Action Now! A Citizen's Guide to Better Communities. LC 76-949. 270p. 1976. 11.85x (ISBN 0-8093-0760-X); pap. 7.95 (ISBN 0-8093-0763-4). S Ill U Pr.

Potash, Robert A. The Army & Politics in Argentina, 1945-1962: Peron to Frondizi. LC 79-64220. (Illus.). xiv, 418p. 1980. 25.00x (ISBN 0-8047-1056-2). Stanford U Pr.

Poteet, David. How to Trace Your Family Tree. LC 79-84344. 1979. pap. 3.50 (ISBN 0-87123-209-X, 210209). Bethany Fell.

Poten, U., ed. see International Symposium on Intracranial Pressure, 2nd.

Poter, Wesley. Dragons of Peking. (Illus.). (gr. k-3). 1979. 2.95 (ISBN 0-531-02500-4); PLB 6.90 s&l o.p. (ISBN 0-531-04079-8). Watts.

Pothier, Patricia C. Psychiatric Nursing: A Basic Text. 1980. pap. text ed. 12.95 (ISBN 0-316-71484-4). Little.

Potholm, C. P. & Morgan, R. E., eds. Focus on Police: The Police in American Society. 1976. pap. text ed. 6.95 o.p. (ISBN 0-470-15075-0); pap. text ed. 6.95 (ISBN 0-470-15077-7). Halsted Pr.

Potholm, Christian & Dale, Richard, eds. Southern Africa in Perspective: Essays in Regional Politics. LC 79-143520. 1972. 19.95 (ISBN 0-02-925290-3); pap. text ed. 9.95 (ISBN 0-02-925320-9). Free Pr.

Potholm, Christian P. Liberation & Exploitation: The Struggle for Ethiopia. 1977. pap. text ed. 7.00x (ISBN 0-8191-0040-4). U Pr of Amer.

--Strategy & Conflict: The Search for Historical Malleability. LC 78-71368. (Illus.). 1979. pap. 7.50 (ISBN 0-8191-0668-2). U Pr of Amer.

Potholm, Christian P. & Fredland, Richard A., eds. Integration & Disintegration in East Africa. LC 80-5914. 229p. 1980. lib. bdg. 17.75 (ISBN 0-8191-1298-4); pap. text ed. 9.75 (ISBN 0-8191-1299-2). U Pr of Amer.

Poti, S. J. Quantitive Studies in Life Science. 250p. 1980. text ed. 25.00x (ISBN 0-7069-1247-0, Pub by Vikas India). Advent Bk.

Potichnyj, Peter J. & Shapiro, Jane P., eds. From the Cold War to Detente. LC 75-19808. (Praeger Special Studies Ser.). 238p. 1976. text ed. 31.95 (ISBN 0-275-56200-X). Praeger.

Potichnyj, Peter J., jt. ed. see Shapiro, Jane P.

Potok, Andrew. Ordinary Daylight. 256p. 1981. pap. 2.95 (ISBN 0-553-14432-4). Bantam.

Potok, Chaim. The Chosen. 1978. pap. 2.50 (ISBN 0-449-24200-5, Crest). Fawcett.

--Wanderings: Chaim Potok's History of the Jews. LC 78-54915. 1978. 20.00 (ISBN 0-394-50110-1). Knopf.

Potoker, Edward M. Ronald Firbank. LC 76-92032. (Columbia Essays on Modern Writers Ser.: No. 43). 1970. pap. 2.00 (ISBN 0-231-03168-8, MW43). Columbia U Pr.

Potomac Corral of the Westerners. Great Western Indian Fights. LC 60-15191. (Illus.). 1966. pap. 3.50 (ISBN 0-8032-5186-6, BB 339, Bison). U of Nebr Pr.

Pott, August F. Einleitung in die Allegemeine Sprachwissenschaft. Bd. with Zur Literature der Sprachenkunde. (Amsterdam Classics in Linguistics, 1800-1925: No. 10). (Orig.). 1979. pap. text ed. 62.75x (ISBN 90-272-0871-9). Humanities.

Pott, Eckart. Rivers & Lakes. (Illus.). 144p. 1981. pap. 5.95 (ISBN 0-7011-2544-6, Pub. by Chatto-Bodley-Jonathan). Merrimack Bk Serv.

Pott, J. A. & Wright, F. A., trs. Martial, the Twelve Books Epigrams. 402p. 1981. Repr. lib. bdg. 65.00 (ISBN 0-89987-566-1). Darby Bks.

Pott, William S. Chinese Political Philosophy. LC 79-2290. 1981. Repr. of 1925 ed. 13.50 (ISBN 0-88355-966-8). Hyperion Conn.

Pottebaum, G. A. The Christmas Story. (Little People's Paperbacks Ser.). 1979. pap. 0.99 (ISBN 0-8164-2241-9). Crossroad NY.

--The Cloud. (Little People's Paperbacks Ser.). 1979. pap. 0.99 (ISBN 0-8164-2245-1). Crossroad NY.

--The Easter Lamb. (Little People's Paperbacks Ser.). 1979. pap. 0.99 (ISBN 0-8164-2247-8). Crossroad NY.

--The Generous Vine Grower. (Little People's Paperbacks Ser.). 1979. pap. 0.99 (ISBN 0-8164-2252-4). Crossroad NY.

--God Made the World. (Little People's Paperbacks Ser.). 1979. pap. 0.99 (ISBN 0-8164-2239-7). Crossroad NY.

--God So Loves the World. (Little People's Paperbacks Ser.). 1979. pap. 0.99 (ISBN 0-8164-2244-3). Crossroad NY.

--The Good Samaritan. (Little People's Paperbacks Ser.). 1979. pap. 0.99 (ISBN 0-8164-2249-4). Crossroad NY.

--The Great Harvest. (Little People's Paperbacks Ser.). 1979. pap. 0.99 (ISBN 0-8164-2253-2). Crossroad NY.

--How the Animals Got Their Names. (Little People's Paperbacks Ser.). pap. 0.99 (ISBN 0-8164-2240-0). Crossroad NY.

--The King & the Servant. (Little People's Paperbacks Ser.). pap. 0.99 (ISBN 0-8164-2251-6). Crossroad NY.

--The Little Grain of Wheat. (Little People's Paperbacks Ser.). 1979. pap. 0.99 (ISBN 0-8164-2243-5). Crossroad NY.

--The Loving Father. (Little People's Paperbacks Ser.). 1979. pap. 0.99 (ISBN 0-8164-2250-8). Crossroad NY.

--Psalm Eight from Voices of Children. (Little People's Paperbacks Ser.). 1979. pap. 0.99 (ISBN 0-8164-2254-0). Crossroad NY.

--Psalm Eighty-Four the Sparrow Finds a Home. (Little People's Paperbacks Ser.). 1979. pap. 0.99 (ISBN 0-8164-2256-7). Crossroad NY.

--Psalm Ninety-Eight Sing a New Song. (Little People's Paperbacks Ser.). 1979. pap. 0.99 (ISBN 0-8164-2257-5). Crossroad NY.

--Psalm One Hundred Fifty the Praise Parade. (Little People's Paperback Ser.). 1979. pap. 0.99 (ISBN 0-8164-2258-3). Crossroad NY.

--Psalm Twenty-Three My Shepherd Is the Lord. (Little People's Paperbacks Ser.). 1979. pap. 0.99 (ISBN 0-8164-2255-9). Crossroad NY.

--The Story of Emmaus. (Little People's Paperbacks Ser.). 1979. pap. 0.99 (ISBN 0-8164-2248-6). Crossroad NY.

--The Three Wise Men. (Little People's Paperbacks Ser.). 1979. pap. 0.99 (ISBN 0-8164-2242-7). Crossroad NY.

Potten, C. S., jt. ed. see Lord, B. I.

Potter. Tale of Peter Rabbit. (ps-3). pap. 1.25 (ISBN 0-590-09141-7, Schol Pap). Schol Bk Serv.

Potter, B. The Story of Miss Moppett. (Peter Possum Paperbacks Ser). 1967. pap. 0.95 o.p. (ISBN 0-531-05118-8). Watts.

--The Tailor of Gloucester. (Peter Possum Paperbacks Ser). 1967. pap. 0.95 o.p. (ISBN 0-531-05103-X). Watts.

--The Tale of Benjamin Bunny. (Peter Possum Paperbacks Ser). 1967. pap. 0.95 o.p. (ISBN 0-531-05126-9). Watts.

--The Tale of Squirrel Nutkin. (Peter Possum Paperbacks Ser). 1967. pap. 0.95 o.p. (ISBN 0-531-05116-1). Watts.

Potter, Beatrix. Beatrix Potter's Birthday Book. Linder, Enid, ed. LC 73-89833. (Illus.). 160p. (gr. 3 up). 1974. 6.95 (ISBN 0-7232-1758-0); leather bdg. 11.95 (ISBN 0-7232-1815-3). Warne.

--Pie & the Patty Pan. (Peter Possum Paperbacks). (gr. k-3). 1975. pap. 0.95 o.p. (ISBN 0-531-05115-3). Watts.

--Songs of Peter Rabbit: Music by Dudley Glass. (Illus.). 1952. 3.95 (ISBN 0-7232-1035-7). Warne.

--Tale of Peter Rabbit. (Illus.). (gr. k-2). 1970. 1.95 (ISBN 0-307-10486-9, Golden Pr); PLB 7.62 (ISBN 0-307-60486-1). Western Pub.

--Tale of Peter Rabbit. pap. 3.50 incl. record (ISBN 0-590-04358-7, Schol Pap). Schol Bk Serv.

Potter, C. F. The Lost Years of Jesus Revealed. 1979. pap. 1.75 o.p. (ISBN 0-449-14194-2, GM). Fawcett.

Potter, C. W., et al. Introduction to Medical Microbiology. 1968. 8.95 (ISBN 0-407-56500-0). Butterworths.

Potter, Charles H. Greenhouse: Place of Magic. (Illus.). 1966. 7.95 o.p. (ISBN 0-525-11818-7); Rev. Ed. 1976. pap. 4.95 o.p. (ISBN 0-87690-199-2). Dutton.

--Perennials in the Garden. LC 59-6124. (Illus.). 1959. 10.95 (ISBN 0-87599-094-0). S G Phillips.

Potter, Chas. Is That in the Bible? 1978. pap. 2.25 (ISBN 0-449-23540-8, Crest). Fawcett.

Potter, David. History & American Society: The Essays of David Potter. Fehrenbacher, Don E., ed. 448p. 1973. 15.95 (ISBN 0-19-501628-9). Oxford U Pr.

--Understanding Government. 1975. 17.95 (ISBN 0-7134-2910-0, Pub. by Batsford England). David & Charles.

--Understanding Money. 1972. 17.95 (ISBN 0-7134-2163-0, Pub. by Batsford England). David & Charles.

Potter, David & Anderson, Martin P. Discussion in Small Groups. 3rd ed. 1976. pap. text ed. 9.95x (ISBN 0-534-00426-1). Wadsworth Pub.

Potter, David C., jt. ed. see Lewis, Paul G.

Potter, David M. Division & the Stresses of Reunion: 1845-1876. 240p. 1973. pap. 7.95x (ISBN 0-673-05786-0). Scott F.

Potter, Edgar. Cowboy Slang. LC 70-170899. (Illus.). 1971. 6.95 o.p. (ISBN 0-87564-105-9). Superior Pub.

Potter, Eloise F., et al. Birds of the Carolinas. LC 79-14201. (Illus.). viii, 408p. 1980. 14.95 (ISBN 0-8078-1399-0). U of NC Pr.

Potter, G. R. Zwingli. LC 75-46136. (Illus.). 1977. 59.50 (ISBN 0-521-20939-0). Cambridge U Pr.

Potter, Helen R. Social & Economic Dimensions of Health & Illness Behavior in New Mexico: An Annotated Bibliography. LC 75-99570. 1969. pap. 5.00x o.p. (ISBN 0-8263-0163-0). U of NM Pr.

Potter, Israel R. Life & Remarkable Adventures of Israel R. Potter. 4.50 o.p. (ISBN 0-8446-2752-6). Peter Smith.

Potter, J. M. Capitalism & the Chinese Peasant: Social & Economic Change in a Hong Kong Village. (Center for Chinese Studies, UC Berkeley). 1968. 18.50x (ISBN 0-520-01024-8). U of Cal Pr.

Potter, J. Reid. North Carolina Appellate Handbook. 1978. 28.50 (ISBN 0-87215-211-1, Bobbs-Merrill Law). Michie.

Potter, Jack & Lowell, Mark. Assessing the Effectiveness of Advertising. 281p. 1975. text ed. 24.50x (ISBN 0-220-69730-2, Pub. by Busn Bks England). Renouf.

Potter, James L. & Fich, S. Theory of Networks & Lines. (Illus.). 1963. ref. ed. 24.95 (ISBN 0-13-913228-7). P-H.

Potter, Jerry. Silence in Eden. LC 77-18639. 1978. 9.95 o.s.i. (ISBN 0-690-01742-1, TYC-T). T Y Crowell.

Potter, John. Archaeologica Graeca: Or, the Antiquities of Greece, 2 vols. Feldman, Burton & Richardson, Robert, eds. LC 78-60893. (Myth & Romanticism Ser.: Vol. 19). (Illus.). 1980. Set. lib. bdg. 120.00 (ISBN 0-8240-3568-2); lib. bdg. 66.00 ea. Garland Pub.

Potter, Joy H. Elio Vittorini. (World Authors Ser.: No. 518). 1979. lib. bdg. 14.95 (ISBN 0-8057-6359-7). Twayne.

Potter, Karl H., ed. The Encyclopedia of Indian Philosophies: Bibliography of Indian Philosophies. 844p. 1970. Vol. 1, 1973. 25.00x (ISBN 0-7189-2126-7); Vol. 2, 1977. 32.50x (ISBN 0-691-07183-7). Intl Pubns Serv.

Potter, Lance D. & Mazzocco, Alexis. Guide to Government Agency Programs. LC 80-116020. 145p. (Orig.). 1979. pap. 3.50 (ISBN 0-89763-019-X). Natl Clearinghse Bilingual Ed.

Potter, Leo G. My Bible Is Jesus. 1976. pap. 1.25 (ISBN 0-8272-2310-2). Bethany Pr.

Potter, M. C. & Foss, J. F. Fluid Mechanics. 1975. 26.95 (ISBN 0-8260-7207-0); tchrs. manual avail. (ISBN 0-471-07509-4). Wiley.

Potter, Marian. Blatherskite. LC 80-18450. 192p. (gr. 4-6). 1980. 6.95 (ISBN 0-688-22249-8); PLB 6.67 (ISBN 0-688-32249-2). Morrow.

Potter, Merle C. Mathematical Methods in the Physical Sciences. (Illus.). 1978. ref. ed. 24.95 (ISBN 0-13-561134-2). P-H.

Potter, Neil. Oil Rig. LC 78-61231. (Careers Ser.). (Illus.). 1978. lib. bdg. 7.95 (ISBN 0-686-51122-0). Silver.

Potter, Norman N. Food Science. 3rd ed. 1978. text ed. 22.00 (ISBN 0-87055-275-9). AVI.

Potter, Philip J. Power Plant Theory & Design. 2nd ed. (Illus.). 1959. 25.95 (ISBN 0-8260-7205-4). Wiley.

Potter, S. Changing English. (Andre Deutsch Language Library). 1977. lib. bdg. 12.50x (ISBN 0-233-96648-X). Westview.
--Modern Linguistics. (Andre Deutsch Language Library). 1977. lib. bdg. 12.50x (ISBN 0-233-95546-1). Westview.
Potter, Sulamith H. Family Life in a Northern Thai Village: A Study of the Structural Significance of Women. 1978. 12.00x (ISBN 0-520-03430-9); pap. 4.95x (ISBN 0-520-04044-9). U of Cal Pr.
Potter, T., jt. auth. see Rae, G.
Potter, T. W. The Changing Landscape of South Etruria. (Illus.). 1979. 27.50 (ISBN 0-312-12953-X). St Martin.
Potter, Thomas C. & Rae, Gwenneth R. Informal Reading Diagnosis: A Practical Guide for the Classroom Teacher. LC 72-4727. (Illus.). 336p. 1973. pap. 11.95 ref. ed. (ISBN 0-13-464453-0). P-H.
Potter, Van R. Bioethics: Bridge to the Future. (Illus.). 1971. pap. 10.95 ref. ed. (ISBN 0-13-076505-8). P-H.
Potter, William C., ed. Verification & SALT. (Westview Special Studies in National Security & Defense Policy). 200p. 1980. lib. bdg. 25.00x (ISBN 0-89158-886-8). Westview.
Potterbaum, Charlene. Thanks Lord, I Needed That. 1979. Repr. of 1977 ed. pocket size 2.95 (ISBN 0-88270-411-7). Logos.
Potthoff, Harvey H. Loneliness: Understanding & Dealing with It. LC 76-13900. 128p. 1976. 5.95 o.p. (ISBN 0-687-22579-5). Abingdon.
Pottieger, Anne E., jt. ed. see Inciardi, James A.
Pottinger, Don, jt. auth. see Norman, A. V.
Pottinger, George. The Bubble Reputation. 256p. 1981. 15.00x (ISBN 0-7073-0286-2, Pub. by Scottish Academic Pr Scotland). Columbia U Pr.
--Muirfield & the Honorable Company. 1972. 10.00x (ISBN 0-7073-0154-8, Pub. by Scottish Academic Pr Scotland). Columbia U Pr.
Pottker, Janice, jt. auth. see Fishel, Andrew.
Pottle, Frederick A. Stretchers: The Story of a Hospital Unit on the Western Front. 1929. 34.50x (ISBN 0-685-89785-0). Elliots Bks.
Pottle, Ralph R. Tuning the School Band & Orchestra. 3rd ed. Orig. Title: Tuning the School Band. (Illus.). (gr. 7-12). 1980. lib. bdg. 9.00 (ISBN 0-911162-01-1). Pottle.
Potts, Albert M. The World's Eye. LC 79-4009. (Illus.). 1981. price not set (ISBN 0-8131-1387-3). U Pr of Ky.
Potts, D. Gordon, jt. auth. see Newton, Thomas H.
Potts, D. Gordon, jt. ed. see Newton, Thomas H.
Potts, D. M., jt. auth. see Peel, J.
Potts, F. A., jt. auth. see Borradaile, L. A.
Potts, Gordon, jt. auth. see Newton, Thomas H.
Potts, James L., et al. Prisoner's Self Help Litigation Manual. LC 77-6191. 1977. 15.95 (ISBN 0-669-01640-3). Lexington Bks.
Potts, Louis W. Arthur Lee: A Virtuous Revolutionary. LC 80-21831. (Southern Biography Ser.). 320p. 1981. 25.00x (ISBN 0-8071-0785-9). La State U Pr.
Potts, Malcolm & Selman, Peter. Society & Fertility. (Illus.). 384p. 1979. 27.50x (ISBN 0-7121-1960-4, Pub. by Macdonald & Evans England). Intl Ideas.
Potts, Malcolm, et al. Abortion. LC 76-27907. (Illus.). 1977. 66.00 (ISBN 0-521-21442-4); pap. 17.95x (ISBN 0-521-29150-X). Cambridge U Pr.
Potts, Marion, et al. Structure & Development in Child Language: The Preschool Years. LC 78-10968. 1979. 17.50x (ISBN 0-8014-1184-X). Cornell U Pr.
Potts, Nancy. Loneliness: Living Between the Times. 1978. pap. 3.95 (ISBN 0-88207-630-2). Victor Bks.
Potts, Phil. Survival Is the Bottom Line. 58p. (Orig.). 1980. pap. 2.95 (ISBN 0-89260-182-5). Hwong Pub.
Potts, T. C. Conscience in Medieval Philosophy. 180p. 1980. 47.50 (ISBN 0-521-23287-2). Cambridge U Pr.
Potvin, Claude, tr. see Wade, Harlan.
Potvin, Douglas, ed. see Long, Michael, et al.
Potvin, Rose-Ella, tr. see Wade, Harlan.
Potz, Veronica. Umericks for Children. (See-Hear-Color Me Bk). 1981. 8.95 (ISBN 0-912492-15-5). Pyquag.
Potz, Veronica & Babin, Lawrence J. Limericks for Children. (See-Hear-Color Me Book Ser.). 1981. 6.95 (ISBN 0-912492-15-5). Pyquag.
Pough, Frederick H. All About Volcanoes & Earthquakes. (Allabout Ser: No. 4). (Illus.). (gr. 4-6). 1953. PLB 4.39 o.p. (ISBN 0-394-90204-1, BYR). Random.
Pougin, Arthur. Les Vrais Createurs De l'Opera Francais: Perrin et Cambert. LC 80-2296. 1981. Repr. of 1881 ed. 33.50 (ISBN 0-404-18862-1). AMS Pr.
Poulet, Virginia. Blue Bug's Book of Colors. LC 80-23229. (Blue Bug Bks). (Illus.). 32p. (ps-3). 1981. PLB 7.95 (ISBN 0-516-03442-1). Childrens.
Poulik, M. D., ed. Beta Two-Microglobulin: Its Significance in Clinical Medicine. (Journal: Vox Sanguinis: Vol. 38, No. 6). (Illus.). 1980. soft cover 19.75 (ISBN 3-8055-1560-X). S Karger.
Poulin, A., Jr. Contemporary American Poetry. 2nd ed. 1975. pap. text ed. 9.95 o.p. (ISBN 0-395-18618-8). HM.
Poulin, Clarence. Tailoring Suits the Professional Way. rev. ed. (Illus.). (gr. 9-12). 1973. text ed. 9.20 (ISBN 0-87002-128-1). Bennett IL.
Poulin, Jacques. The Jimmy Trilogy. Fischman, Sheila, tr. from Fr. (Anansi Fiction Ser.: No. 39). 250p. (Orig.). 1979. pap. 8.95 (ISBN 0-88784-074-4, Pub. by Hse Anansi Pr Canada). U of Toronto Pr.
Poulos, George. Orthodox Saints: Spiritual Profiles for Modern Man, Vol. 3. Vaporis, Nomikos M., ed. (Illus.). 211p. 1980. text ed. 9.50 (ISBN 0-916586-40-5); pap. text ed. 5.50 (ISBN 0-916586-41-3). Holy Cross Orthodox.
Poulos, H. G. & Davis, E. H. Elastic Solutions for Soil & Rock Mechanics. LC 73-17171. (Soil Engineering Ser.). 424p. 1974. text ed. 39.95 (ISBN 0-471-69565-3). Wiley.
Poulos, Kathleen, jt. ed. see Boydston, Jo Ann.
Poulos, Nellie. Life's Story & Healings. 160p. pap. 1.50. Faith Pub Hse.
Poulson, Barry W., et al, eds. U. S.-Mexico Economic Relations. (Special Studies in International Economics & Business). 1979. lib. bdg. 35.00x (ISBN 0-89158-469-2). Westview.
Poulson, Joan. Yorkshire Cookery. 1979. 24.00 (ISBN 0-7134-0142-7, Pub. by Batsford England). David & Charles.
Poulson, Mary H., jt. auth. see Garret, Maxwell R.
Poulsson, Emilie. Finger Plays for Nursery & Kindergarten. LC 74-165397. (Illus.). (ps-k). 1971. pap. 2.00 (ISBN 0-486-22588-7). Dover.
Poulton, Diana. John Dowland. 1972. 38.50x o.p. (ISBN 0-520-02109-6). U of Cal Pr.
Poulton, E. C. Environment & Human Efficiency. (American Lectures in Living Chemistry Ser.). (Illus.). 336p. 1972. 26.75 (ISBN 0-398-01515-5). C C Thomas.
Poulton, G. A. & James, Terry. Pre-Schooling in the Community. 160p. 1975. 12.95x (ISBN 0-7100-8245-2); pap. 6.95 (ISBN 0-7100-8246-0). Routledge & Kegan.
Poulton, Helen J. & Howland, Marguerite S. The Historian's Handbook. LC 71-165774. 300p. 1972. 15.95x o.p. (ISBN 0-8061-0985-8); pap. 7.95x (ISBN 0-8061-1009-0). U of Okla Pr.
Pouncey, Peter. The Necessities of War: A Study of Thucydides' Pessimism. LC 80-16887. 232p. 1981. 19.50x (ISBN 0-231-04994-3). Columbia U Pr.
Pound, Ezra. Antheil & the Treatise on Harmony. 2nd ed. LC 68-27463. (Music Ser.). (gr. 9 up). 1968. Repr. of 1927 ed. lib. bdg. 17.50 (ISBN 0-306-70981-3). Da Capo.
--Confucian Analects. 1970. Repr. of 1956 ed. text ed. 18.25x (ISBN 0-7206-1850-9). Humanities.
--Confucius: The Great Digest, the Unwobbling Pivot, the Analects. 288p. 1951. 5.95 (ISBN 0-8112-0154-6, NDP-285). New Directions.
--Ezra Pound & the Visual Arts. Zinnes, Harriet, ed. LC 80-36720. 352p. 1980. 25.95 (ISBN 0-8112-0772-2). New Directions.
--Letters to John Theobald. Pearce, Donald & Schneidau, Herbert, eds. (Illus.). 196p. 1981. 20.00 (ISBN 0-933806-02-7). Black Swan CT.
--Selected Poems. LC 57-8603. 1957. pap. 2.95 (ISBN 0-8112-0162-7, NDP66). New Directions.
Pound, Ezra, tr. see De Gourmont, Remy.
Pound, Gomer. A Handbook for Writing Graduate Theses. LC 77-80739. 1977. pap. text ed. 5.5000 (ISBN 0-8403-1767-0). Kendall-Hunt.
Pound, Merritt B. & Saye, Albert B. Handbook on the Constitutions of the United States & Georgia. rev. ed. LC 46-27121. 184p. 1975. pap. 2.00x (ISBN 0-8203-0216-3). U of Ga Pr.
Pound, Roscoe. Criminal Justice in America. LC 79-37841. (American Constitutional & Legal History Ser). 224p. 1972. Repr. of 1930 ed. lib. bdg. 22.50 (ISBN 0-306-70435-8). Da Capo.
--The Development of Constitutional Guarantees of Liberty. LC 75-14600. 207p. 1975. Repr. of 1957 ed. lib. bdg. 18.50x (ISBN 0-8371-8225-5, PODC). Greenwood.
--Introduction to the Philosophy of Law. rev. ed. (Storrs Lectures Ser.). 1954. 14.50x (ISBN 0-300-00839-2); pap. 4.95 1959 (ISBN 0-300-00188-6, Y10). Yale U Pr.
Pounds, N. J. An Economic History of Medieval Europe. LC 73-93716. (Illus.). 544p. 1974. text ed. 21.00x (ISBN 0-582-48266-6); pap. 10.95x, 1977 (ISBN 0-582-48680-7). Longman.
--An Historical Geography of Europe, 450 Bc-1330 AD. 1973. 59.50 (ISBN 0-521-08563-2); pap. 22.95x (ISBN 0-521-29126-7). Cambridge U Pr.
Pounds, Norman J. Geography of Iron & Steel. 4th rev. ed. (Orig.). 1968. pap. text ed. 6.00x (ISBN 0-09-106261-6, Hutchinson U Lib). Humanities.
Pountney, Harold. Police Photography. (Illus.). 1971. 26.00x (ISBN 0-85334-621-6). Intl Ideas.
Pountney, Kate. Make a Mobile. LC 74-9824. (Illus.). 64p. (gr. 3 up). 1974. 9.95 (ISBN 0-87599-206-4). S G Phillips.
Pountney, Michael. The First Four Years Are the Hardest: A Handbook for Campus Christians. LC 80-19792. (Illus.). 110p. (Orig.). 1980. pap. 3.95 (ISBN 0-87784-451-3). Inter-Varsity.
Pourade, Richard F. The Rising Tide. LC 67-11865. (Historic Birthplace of California Ser.: Vol. 6). (Illus.). 267p. 1967. 14.50 (ISBN 0-913938-06-8). Copley Bks.
Pourade, Richard F., ed. see Minshall, Herbert L.
Pourjavady, N., jt. auth. see Wilson, P. L.
Pournelle, Jerry. King David's Spaceship. 1981. 11.95 (ISBN 0-671-25328-X). S&S.
--Red Heroin. Date not set. pap. 1.95 o.p. (ISBN 0-425-04195-6). Berkley Pub.
Poussard, Wendy, jt. auth. see Eastman, Moira.
Poussin, Charles D., jt. auth. see Bernstein, Serge.
Povah, Nigel. Chess Training. 176p. 1981. 19.95 (ISBN 0-571-11604-3, Pub. by Faber & Faber); pap. 8.95 (ISBN 0-571-11608-6). Merrimack Bk Serv.
Poverman, C. E. Solomon's Daughter. 1981. 12.95 (ISBN 0-670-36144-5). Viking Pr.
Povey, John. Roy Campbell. (World Authors Ser.: No. 439). 1977. lib. bdg. 12.50 (ISBN 0-8057-6277-9). Twayne.
Powdermaker, Hortense. Stranger & Friend: The Way of an Anthropologist. 1966. 7.50x (ISBN 0-393-07442-0, Norton Lib); pap. 3.95 1967 (ISBN 0-393-00410-4). Norton.
Powell. Brain & Personality. LC 79-87638. (Illus.). 122p. 1979. 21.95 (ISBN 0-03-052701-5). Praeger.
--Renaissance Italy. (Warwick Press Ser.). (gr. 5 up). 1980. PLB 6.90 (ISBN 0-531-09164-3, B34). Watts.
Powell & Van Dyke. Minnesota & Manitoba One Hundred Years Ago. (Illus.). pap. 3.50 (ISBN 0-89540-056-1). Sun Pub.
Powell, Anthony. At Lady Molly's. (A Dance to the Music of Time: Vol. 2). 1976. pap. 2.50 (ISBN 0-445-08446-4). Popular Lib.
--Faces in My Time. LC 80-14843. (No. 3). (Illus.). 256p. 1981. 14.95 (ISBN 0-03-021001-1). HR&W.
--From a View to a Death. 1978. pap. 2.25 o.p. (ISBN 0-445-04295-8). Popular Lib.
--The Kindly Ones. (A Dance to the Music of Time: No. 2). 1976. pap. 2.50 (ISBN 0-445-08446-4). Popular Lib.
--The Military Philosophers. (Dance to the Music of Time: No.3). pap. 2.50 (ISBN 0-445-08447-2). Popular Lib.
Powell, Anton & Vanags, Patricia. Ancient Greeks. LC 78-2646. (Civilization Library). (Illus.). (gr. 5 up). 1978. PLB 6.90 s&l (ISBN 0-531-01446-0). Watts.
Powell, Barbara. How to Raise a Successful Daughter. LC 78-16975. 1979. 12.95 (ISBN 0-88229-457-1); pap. 6.95 (ISBN 0-88229-679-5). Nelson-Hall.
Powell, Betty. Knowledge of Actions. 1967. text ed. 5.00x (ISBN 0-04-121004-2). Humanities.
Powell, C Randall & Kirts, Donald K. Career Sevices Today: A Dynamic College Profession. LC 79-54801. 1980. pap. 11.95 (ISBN 0-913936-13-8). Coll Placement.
Powell, Charles. The Poets in the Nursery. 79p. Repr. of 1920 ed. lib. bdg. 25.00 (ISBN 0-8492-4221-5). R West.
Powell, Christopher & Butler, Arthur, eds. The Parliamentary & Scientific Committee: The First Forty Years 1939-1979. (Illus.). 102p. 1980. 17.50x (ISBN 0-7099-0347-2, Pub. by Croom Helm Ltd England). Biblio Dist.
Powell, D., jt. auth. see Skrabanek, P.
Powell, David, jt. auth. see Skrabanek, Petr.
Powell, David, ed. see Rossetti, Christina.
Powell, David, tr. see Mears, Henrietta C.
Powell, David J. Clinical Supervision. LC 79-20586. 1979. manual 19.95x (ISBN 0-87705-406-1); trainee wkbk. 7.95x (ISBN 0-87705-407-X). Human Sci Pr.
Powell, Enoch. No Easy Answers. LC 73-17906. 1974. 6.95 (ISBN 0-8164-0251-5). Crossroad NY.
Powell, Enoch & Ritchie, Richard. A Nation or No Nation? Six Years in British Politics. 1978. 24.00 (ISBN 0-7134-1542-3, Pub. by Batsford England). David & Charles.
Powell, Eric. Kelp, the Health Giver. 1980. pap. 1.95 (ISBN 0-87904-041-6). Lust.
Powell, Eric F. Biochemistry up to Date. 1980. 25.00 (ISBN 0-85032-175-1, Pub. by Daniel Co England). State Mutual Bk.
--Biochemistry Up to Date. 66p. 1963. pap. 5.00x (ISBN 0-8464-0995-X). Beekman Pubs.
--Building a Healthy Heart. 64p. 1961. pap. 3.00x o.p. (ISBN 0-8464-0997-6). Beekman Pubs.
--The Group Remedy Prescriber. 1980. 7.95 o.p. (ISBN 0-8464-1015-X). Beekman Pubs.
--Health from the Kitchen. 64p. 1969. pap. 2.50x (ISBN 0-8464-1018-4). Beekman Pubs.
--A Home Course in Nutrition. 104p. 1978. pap. 7.50x (ISBN 0-8464-1019-2). Beekman Pubs.
--Kelp the Health Giver. 1980. 2.25 (ISBN 0-8464-1028-1). Beekman Pubs.
--The Natural Home Physician. LC 79-50415. Date not set. 8.95 (ISBN 0-448-16558-9); pap. 5.95. G&D. Postponed.
--Tranquilization with Harmless Herbs. 1980. 3.00x (ISBN 0-8464-1054-0). Beekman Pubs.
Powell, Evan. Complete Guide to Home Appliance Repair. rev. ed. LC 80-5262. (A Popular Science Bk.). (Illus.). 464p. 1981. 15.95 (ISBN 0-06-013384-8, HarpT). Har-Row. Postponed.
Powell, Fred W., ed. Hall J. Kelley on Oregon. LC 79-87635. (The American Scene Ser). (Illus.). 412p. 1972. Repr. of 1932 ed. lib. bdg. 39.50 (ISBN 0-306-71796-4). Da Capo.
Powell, Geoffery & Fullick, Roy. Suez: The Double War. (Illus.). 240p. 1979. 24.00 (ISBN 0-241-10182-4, Pub. by Hamish Hamilton England). David & Charles.
Powell, Herb, jt. auth. see Pitcoff, Ramsey K.
Powell, Hugh, ed. see Gryphius, Andreas.
Powell, J. A. Biological & Taxonomic Studies on Tortricine Moths, with Reference to the Species in California. (U. C. Publ. in Entomology: Vol. 32). 1964. pap. 10.00x (ISBN 0-520-09100-0). U of Cal Pr.
Powell, J. L., jt. auth. see Faure, G.
Powell, J. U. & Barber, E. A., eds. New Chapters in the History of Greek Literature. 1921. 15.00x (ISBN 0-8196-0286-8). Biblo.
--New Chapters in the History of Greek Literature. (Second Ser). 1929. 15.00x (ISBN 0-8196-0287-6). Biblo.
Powell, James D. Building Plastic Ship Models. (Illus.). 350p. 1981. cancelled (ISBN 0-498-02286-2). A S Barnes.
Powell, James D. & Kelley, C. Aron. Students Resource Manual: Hicks-Gullett Management of Organization. th ed. 368p. Date not set. text ed. price not set (ISBN 0-07-028777-5). McGraw.
Powell, James M. & Powers, Mary Nelle H. Biography of N. B. Hardeman. 9.00 o.p. (ISBN 0-89225-045-3). Gospel Advocate.
Powell, James N. Global Employment Guide: Worldwide Opportunities for Profitable & Exciting Year-Round or Seasonal Jobs in Every Corner of the Globe. LC 79-83725. 1979. 7.95 (ISBN 0-87863-171-2). Farnswth Pub.
--Mandalas: The Dynamics of Vedic Symbolism. Ghai, S. K., ed. 127p. 1980. 9.95 (ISBN 0-914794-36-1). Wisdom Garden.
Powell, Jerry A. & Hogue, Charles L. California Insects. (Illus.). 1980. 15.95 (ISBN 0-520-03806-1); pap. 7.95 (ISBN 0-520-03782-0). U of Cal Pr.
Powell, John. My Pilgrimage of Prayer. (Prayer in My Life Ser.: Ser. II). 1974. pap. 1.00x (ISBN 0-8358-0313-9). Upper Room.
Powell, John B. My Twenty-Five Years in China. LC 76-27721. (China in the 20th Century Ser.). 1976. Repr. of 1945 ed. lib. bdg. 35.00 (ISBN 0-306-70761-6). Da Capo.
Powell, John D. Political Mobilization of the Venezuelan Peasant. LC 70-134947. (Center for International Affairs Ser). (Illus.). 1971. 12.50x (ISBN 0-674-68626-8). Harvard U Pr.
Powell, John J. Essays Upon the Law of Contracts & Agreements, 2 vols. in 1. Berkowitz, David & Thorne, Samuel, eds. LC 77-86628. (Classics of English Legal History in the Modern Era Ser.: Vol. 86). 1979. Repr. of 1970 ed. lib. bdg. 55.00 (ISBN 0-8240-3073-7). Garland Pub.
Powell, John L. & Crasemann, B. Quantum Mechanics. (Illus.). 1961. 24.95 (ISBN 0-201-05920-7). A-W.
Powell, John W. Campus Security & Law Enforcement. 250p. 1981. text ed. 19.95 (ISBN 0-409-95028-9). Butterworth.
--Exploration of the Colorado River & Its Canyons. Orig. Title: Canyons of the Colorado. (Illus.). 1895. pap. 5.00 (ISBN 0-486-20094-9). Dover.
Powell, Jouett L. Three Uses of Christian Discourse in John Henry Newman. LC 75-29423. (American Academy of Religion. Dissertation Ser.). 1975. pap. 7.50 (ISBN 0-89130-042-2, 010110). Scholars Pr Ca.
Powell, L. W. & Piper, D. W., eds. Fundamentals of Gastroenterology: With Self-Assessment Workbook. 3rd ed. (Illus.). 222p. 1980. pap. text ed. 17.50 incl. wkbk. (ISBN 0-909337-26-8); wkbk. avail. ADIS Pr.
Powell, Lawrence C. Arizona. (States & the Nation Ser.). (Illus.). 1976. 12.95 (ISBN 0-393-05575-2, Co-Pub by AASLH). Norton.

--Where Water Flows: The Rivers of Arizona. (Illus.). 120p. 1980. 25.00 (ISBN 0-87358-222-5). Northland.
Powell, Lawrence C., ed. & compiled by see Whitman, Walt.
Powell, Linton E. History of Spanish Piano Music. LC 79-3761. 256p. 1980. 17.50x (ISBN 0-253-18114-3). Ind U Pr.
Powell, M. J. Approximation Theory & Methods. (Illus.). 300p. Date not set. price not set (ISBN 0-521-22472-1); pap. price not set (ISBN 0-521-29514-9). Cambridge U Pr.
Powell, M. J. V., ed. House Builders Reference Book. (Illus.). 1979. text ed. 84.95 (ISBN 0-408-00337-5). Butterworths.
Powell, Marcene L. Assessment & Management of Developmental Changes & Problems in Children. (Illus.). 350p. 1981. pap. 12.95 (ISBN 0-8016-1520-8). Mosby.
Powell, Marcia & Graeme, Lynn. The Honeymoon Handbook: A Guide to Life's Most Romantic Adventure. (Illus.). 256p. 1980. 12.95 (ISBN 0-02-598520-5). Macmillan.
Powell, Marian, tr. see Born, Wina.
Powell, N. W. Handbook for Radiologic Technologists & Special Procedures Nurses in Radiology. (Illus.). 104p. 1974. 11.75 (ISBN 0-398-03066-9). C C Thomas.
Powell, P. C. The Selection & Use of Thermoplastics. (Engineering Design Guides Ser.). (Illus.). 1977. pap. 4.50x o.p. (ISBN 0-19-859156-X). Oxford U Pr.
Powell, Paul W. Why Me, Lord? 120p. 1981. pap. 3.95 (ISBN 0-89693-007-6). Victor Bks.
Powell, Peter J. Cheyennes, Ma Heo O's People: A Critical Bibliography. LC 80-8033. (The Newberry Library Center for the History of the American Indian Bibliographical Ser.). 128p. 1980. pap. 4.95x (ISBN 0-253-30416-4). Ind U Pr.
Powell, R. Ventures in Education with Black Baptists in Tennessee. 5.95 o.p. (ISBN 0-8062-1142-3). Carlton.
Powell, R. E., jt. auth. see Daugherty, J. S.
Powell, Ralph, tr. see Den Tex, Jan.
Powell, Ray M. Budgetary Control Procedures for Institutions. LC 78-51520. (Studies in the Managment of Not-for-Profit Institutions: No. 3). (Illus.). 1980. text ed. 12.95x (ISBN 0-268-00658-X). U of Notre Dame Pr.
--Management Procedures for Institutions. LC 78-51525. (Studies in the Management of Not-for-Profit Institutions: No. 2). (Illus.). 1980. text ed. 12.95x (ISBN 0-268-01344-6). U of Notre Dame Pr.
Powell, Raymond. Shakespeare & the Critics' Debate. 167p. 1980. 19.50x (ISBN 0-8476-6227-6). Rowman.
Powell, Rex R. The Functional Morphology of the Fore-Guts of the Thalassind Crustaceans, "Callianassa californiensis" & "Upogebia pugettensis". (U. C. Publications in Zoology: Vol. 102). 1974. pap. 6.00x (ISBN 0-520-09504-9). U of Cal Pr.
Powell, Robert. Crisis in Consciousness. 11.50 (ISBN 0-227-67426-X). Attic Pr.
--Return to Meaningfulness. LC 80-54613. 180p. 1981. pap. text ed. 7.95 (ISBN 0-932238-07-6). Word Shop.
Powell, Roger. Equilibrium Thermodynamics in Petrology: An Introduction. 1978. text ed. 21.60 (ISBN 0-06-318061-8, IntlDept); pap. text ed. 15.70 (ISBN 0-06-318073-1, IntlDept). Har-Row.
Powell, Russell H. Television Repair & Servicing: A Bibliography & Index for 1960-1976. LC 77-4058. 1977. 16.95x (ISBN 0-918596-00-9). Commonweal Bks.
Powell, Sumner C. Puritan Village: The Formation of a New England Town. LC 63-8862. (Illus.). 1963. 27.50x (ISBN 0-8195-3034-4, Pub. by Wesleyan U Pr); pap. 6.95 (ISBN 0-8195-6014-6). Columbia U Pr.
Powell, T. G. Mexico & the Spanish Civil War. 240p. 1981. 17.50x (ISBN 0-8263-0546-6). U of NM Pr.
--Prehistoric Art. (World of Art Ser.). (Illus.). 1966. pap. 9.95 (ISBN 0-19-519920-0). Oxford U Pr.
Powell, Terry. Nobody's Perfect. 1979. pap. 1.95 (ISBN 0-88207-577-2). Victor Bks.
Powell, Thomas F. Josiah Royce. (World Leaders Ser). lib. bdg. 10.95 (ISBN 0-8057-3713-8). Twayne.
Powell, Victor G. Warehousing: Analysis for Effective Operations. 240p. 1976. text ed. 29.50x (ISBN 0-220-66301-7, Pub. by Busn Bks England). Renouf.
Powell, W. J., jt. auth. see Fynn, G. W.
Powell, W. R., jt. auth. see Berl, W. G.
Powell, William S. Annals of Progress: The Story of Lenoir County & Kinston, North Carolina. 1963. pap. 2.00 (ISBN 0-86526-124-5). NC Archives.
--North Carolina Colony. LC 69-11795. (Forge of Freedom Ser). (Illus.). (gr. 4-7). 1969. 5.95g o.s.i. (ISBN 0-02-775100-7, CCPr). Macmillan.
--Proprietors of North Carolina. (Illus.). 1968. pap. 1.00 (ISBN 0-86526-101-6). NC Archives.
Powell-Smith, V. A Modern View of the Law for Builders & Surveyors. 1967. 25.00 (ISBN 0-08-012297-3). Pergamon.
Powell-Smith, Vincent, jt. auth. see Whyte, W. S.
Powelson, J., jt. auth. see Loehr, Wm.
Powelson, John P. A Select Bibliography on Economic Development: With Annotations. (Special Studies in Social, Political & Economic Development). 1979. lib. bdg. 29.50x (ISBN 0-89158-497-8). Westview.
Power Computation Conference, 7th, Lausanne, Switzerland, July 12-17, 1980. Procedings. 1981. text ed. price not set (ISBN 0-86103-025-7). Butterworth.
Power, David, jt. auth. see Schmidt, Herman.
Power, David, jt. ed. see Maldonado, Luis.
Power, David, jt. ed. see Schmidt, Herman.
Power, Dennis M., ed. The California Islands: Proceedings of a Multidisciplinary Symposium. LC 80-463. 787p. (Orig.). 1980. pap. text ed. 20.00 (ISBN 0-936494-01-8). Santa Barbara Mus Nat Hist.
Power, Effie. Bag O' Tales. LC 68-26598. 1968. Repr. of 1934 ed. 19.00 (ISBN 0-8103-3486-0). Gale.
Power, Eileen. Medieval People. 10th rev. & enl. ed. 1963. pap. 3.95 (ISBN 0-06-463253-9, EH 253, EH). Har-Row.
--Medieval People. 10th rev. & enl. ed. 210p. 1963. 13.50x (ISBN 0-686-63945-6). B&N.
Power, Eileen & Poston, M. Medieval Women. LC 75-7212. (Illus.). 144p. 1976. pap. 21.50 (ISBN 0-521-20769-X); pap. 5.50x (ISBN 0-521-09946-3). Cambridge U Pr.
Power, Frank, Jr., jt. auth. see Cousy, Robert J.
Power, John & Brown, Jeremy. Fisherman's Handbook. LC 70-38529. 1972. pap. 2.95 o.p. (ISBN 0-684-13752-6, SL512, ScribT). Scribner.
Power, John H. & Sicat, Gerardo P. Philippines. (Organization for Economic Cooperation & Development Industry & Trade in Some Developing Countries Ser). 1971. pap. 9.00x (ISBN 0-19-215337-4). Oxford U Pr.
Power, Jonathan. Western Europe's Migrant Workers. (Minority Rights Group: No. 28). 1976. pap. 2.50 (ISBN 0-89192-085-4). Interbk Inc.
Power, Jonothan, et al. Migrant Workers in Western Europe & the United States. LC 78-41199. 1979. 28.00 (ISBN 0-08-023385-6); pap. 12.75 (ISBN 0-08-023384-8). Pergamon.
Power, Lawrence, et al. Diabetes Outpatient Care Through Physician Assistants: A Model for Health Maintenance Organizations. (Illus.). 116p. 1973. text ed. 9.75 (ISBN 0-398-02676-9). C C Thomas.
Power, Marjory W., jt. auth. see Haviland, William.
Power, P. The Role of the Family in the Rehabilitation of the Physically Disabled. 1980. 19.95 (ISBN 0-8391-1549-0). Univ Park.
Power, P. B. A Book of Comfort. 1974. pap. 2.25 (ISBN 0-85151-203-8). Banner of Truth.
Power, Patrick, tr. see O'Brien, Flann.
Power, Patrick C. The Book of Irish Curses. 1975. pap. 4.95 (ISBN 0-87243-060-X). Templegate.
Power, Richard. Don Juan in Tulsa. 1981. 12.50 (ISBN 0-916620-54-9). Portals Pr.
Powers, Anne. Blacks in American Movies: A Selected Bibliography. LC 74-1925. 1974. 10.00 (ISBN 0-8108-0753-X). Scarecrow.
--Ride East, Ride West. 1978. pap. 1.95 (ISBN 0-505-51300-5). Tower Bks.
Powers, Bill. Break Him Down! (Target Books). (Illus.). (gr. 3 up). 1977. PLB 6.45 s&l (ISBN 0-531-01273-5). Watts.
--Flying High. (Target Bks.). (Illus.). (gr. 3 up). 1978. PLB 6.45 s&l (ISBN 0-531-01461-4). Watts.
--The Weekend. (Triumph Books). (Illus.). (gr. 6 up). 1978. PLB 6.90 s&l (ISBN 0-531-01467-3). Watts.
Powers, Bob & Barasch, Marc. Crafting Turquoise Jewelry. LC 78-12277. (Illus.). 192p. 1978. 16.95 (ISBN 0-8117-1803-4). Stackpole.
Powers, Bonnie. Dancing All the Way: (How to Dance Your Way to Success) (Illus.). 1980. pap. 12.95 o.p. (ISBN 0-930490-24-X). Future Shop.
Powers, Brian, jt. auth. see Wachtel, Betsy.
Powers, Bruce P., ed. Christian Education Handbook. 1981. pap. 7.95 (ISBN 0-8054-3229-9). Broadman.
Powers, Charles W. & Vogel, David. Ethics in the Education of Business Managers. LC 80-10147. (The Teaching of Ethics Ser.). 81p. 1980. pap. 5.00 (ISBN 0-916558-10-X). Hastings Ctr Inst Soc.
Powers, David G. First Book of How to Make a Speech. (First Bks). (Illus.). (gr. 4-6). 1963. PLB 4.90 o.p. (ISBN 0-531-00552-6); pap. 1.25 o.p. (ISBN 0-531-02301-X). Watts.
--First Book of How to Run a Meeting. LC 67-17556. (First Bks). (Illus.). (gr. 4-6). 1967. PLB 4.90 o.p. (ISBN 0-531-00553-4); pap. 1.25 o.p. (ISBN 0-531-02302-8). Watts.
Powers, David L. Boundary Value Problems. 2nd ed. 351p. 1979. 19.95 (ISBN 0-12-563760-8); instr'. manual 3.00 (ISBN 0-12-563762-4). Acad Pr.
Powers, Elizabeth. The Journal of Madame Royale. LC 75-43990. (Illus.). 192p. (gr. 5 up). 1976. 7.50 o.s.i. (ISBN 0-8027-6251-4); PLB 7.39 (ISBN 0-8027-6252-2). Walker & Co.
Powers, Gene R. Cleft Palate. LC 72-86554. (Studies in Communicative Disorders Ser.). 37p. 1973. pap. text ed. 3.50 (ISBN 0-672-61288-7). Bobbs.
Powers, Harold, ed. Studies in Music History: Essays for Oliver Strunk. LC 80-14086. (Illus.). x, 527p. 1980. Repr. of 1968 ed. lib. bdg. 39.75x (ISBN 0-313-22501-X, POSM). Greenwood.
Powers, J. F. Look How the Fish Live. 1976. pap. 1.95 o.p. (ISBN 0-345-25225-X). Ballantine.
Powers, J. Patrick. Construction Dewatering: A Guide to Theory & Practice. LC 80-18851. (Wiley Ser. of Practical Construction Guides). 300p. 1981. 29.95 (ISBN 0-471-69591-2, Pub. by Wiley-Interscience). Wiley.
Powers, John R. The Last Catholic in America. LC 79-24431. 1981. Repr. of 1973 ed. lib. bdg. 10.00x (ISBN 0-8376-0439-7). Bentley.
Powers, Joseph M. Eucharistic Theology. 1972. pap. 3.95 (ISBN 0-8164-2545-0). Crossroad NY.
Powers, Katherine R. The Influence of William Godwin on the Novels of Mary Shelley. Varma, Devendra P., ed. LC 79-7469. (Gothic Studies & Dissertations Ser.). 1980. lib. bdg. 17.00x (ISBN 0-405-12657-3). Arno.
Powers, Lyall H. Faulkner's Yoknapatawpha Comedy. 296p. 1980. 18.50x (ISBN 0-472-08727-4). U of Mich Pr.
Powers, Marcella. Soft Hands That Kill. LC 77-74001. 1979. 8.00 o.p. (ISBN 0-89430-010-5). Morgan-Pacific.
Powers, Mark J. & Vogel, David J. Inside the Financial Futures Markets. 260p. 1980. 23.95 (ISBN 0-471-08136-1). Ronald Pr.
Powers, Mary Nelle H., jt. auth. see Powell, James M.
Powers, Melvin. How to Get Rich in Mail Order. 1980. pap. 10.00 (ISBN 0-87980-373-8). Wilshire.
--Mental Power Thru Sleep Suggestion. pap. 3.00 (ISBN 0-87980-097-6). Wilshire.
--Self-Hypnosis: Its Theory, Technique & Application. pap. 3.00 (ISBN 0-87980-138-7). Wilshire.
Powers, Nora. Affairs of the Heart. 192p. (Orig.). 1980. pap. 1.50 (ISBN 0-671-57003-X). S&S.
--Design for Love. 192p. (Orig.). 1980. pap. 1.50 (ISBN 0-671-57042-0). S&S.
Powers, P. W. How to Dispose of Toxic Substances & Industrial Wastes. LC 76-2317. (Environmental Technology Handbook Ser.: No. 4). (Illus.). 1976. 48.00 o.p. (ISBN 0-8155-0615-5). Noyes.
Powers, Richard, jt. auth. see Madden, David.
Powers, Robert M. Planetary Encounters. 1980. pap. 2.95 (ISBN 0-446-93330-9). Warner Bks.
--Shuttle. LC 79-652. (Illus.). 256p. 1979. 16.95 o.p. (ISBN 0-8117-1686-4); pap. 12.95 (ISBN 0-8117-2112-4). Stackpole.
--Shuttle: The World's First Spaceship. 1980. pap. 2.75 (ISBN 0-446-95331-8). Warner Bks.
Powers, Ron. The Newscasters: The News Business As Show Business. LC 76-62789. 256p. 1977. 8.95 o.p. (ISBN 0-312-57207-7). St Martin.
--The Newscasters: The News Business As Show Business. LC 76-62789. 1978. pap. 4.95 o.p. (ISBN 0-312-57208-5). St Martin.
--Toot-Toot-Tootsie, Good-Bye. 1981. 10.95 (ISBN 0-440-08190-4). Delacorte.
Powers, Stanley P., et al, eds. Developing the Municipal Organization. LC 74-79125. (Municipal Management Ser.). 1974. text ed. 22.00 (ISBN 0-87326-001-5). Intl City Mgt.
Powers, Stephen. Tribes of California. LC 75-13150. 1977. 27.50x (ISBN 0-520-03023-0); pap. 5.95 (ISBN 0-520-03172-5, CAL 327). U of Cal Pr.
Powers, Susan. The Inspirational Series, 12 bks. (Illus.). 1980. 2.95 ea. Mayflower Bks.
Powers, Thomas. The Man Who Kept the Secrets: Richard Helms & the CIA. 1981. pap. 3.50 (ISBN 0-671-83654-4). PB.
Powers, Thomas F. Introduction to Management in the Hospitality Industry. LC 78-23205. (Service Management Ser.). 1979. text ed. 17.95c (ISBN 0-471-03128-3); tchrs. manual (ISBN 0-471-05355-4). Wiley.
Powers, W. L., jt. auth. see Kirkham, Don.
Powers, William F. & Rauch, Herbert E., eds. Astrodynamics, 1975. new ed. LC 57-43769. (Advances in the Astronautical Science Ser: Vol. 33). (Illus.). 1976. lib. bdg. 35.00x (ISBN 0-87703-079-0); microfiche supplement 35.00 (ISBN 0-87703-142-8). Am Astronaut.
Powers, William G., jt. auth. see Scott, Michael D.
Powers, William T. Behavior: The Control of Perception. LC 73-75697. 320p. 1973. text ed. 16.95x (ISBN 0-202-25113-6). Aldine Pub.
Powers, William T., jt. auth. see Glasser, William.
Power-Waters, Brian. Power-Waters, Brian, Margin for Error, None. LC 80-22289. (Illus.). 250p. 1980. 12.95 (ISBN 0-9603980-0-7). Pierce Pubs.
Powicke, Frederick M. Reformation in England. (Oxford Paperbacks Ser). 1961. pap. 3.95x (ISBN 0-19-285001-6). Oxford U Pr.
--Thirteenth Century, 1216-1307. 2nd ed. (Illus.). 1962. 33.00x (ISBN 0-19-821708-0). Oxford U Pr.
--Ways of Medieval Life & Thought. LC 64-13394. (Illus.). 1949. 9.50x (ISBN 0-8196-0137-3). Biblo.
Powledge, Fred. Engineering of Restraint. 1.00 (ISBN 0-686-68336-6). Pub Aff Pr.
--Journeys Through the South. LC 77-93299. 1979. 10.00 (ISBN 0-8149-0796-2). Vanguard.
Pownall, David. The Bunch from Bananas. LC 80-27422. (Illus.). 96p. (gr. 3-6). 1981. 7.95 (ISBN 0-02-775090-6). Macmillan.
--The Dream of Chief Crazy Horse. (gr. 5 up). 1975. 6.95 (ISBN 0-571-10672-2, Pub. by Faber & Faber); pap. 2.95 (ISBN 0-571-10673-0). Merrimack Bk Serv.
Pownall, Glen. Basketry. (New Craft Bk.). 80p. 1980. 7.50 (ISBN 0-85467-023-8, Pub. by Viking Sevenseas New Zealand). Intl Schol Bk Serv.
--Jewellery & Gemcraft. (New Crafts Books Ser.). 1980. 7.50 (ISBN 0-85467-018-1, Pub. by Viking Sevenseas New Zealand). Intl Schol Bk Serv.
--Knotting Crafts. (New Crafts Books Ser.). 76p. 1980. 8.25 (ISBN 0-85467-020-3, Pub. by Viking Sevenseas New Zealand). Intl Schol Bk Serv.
--Leathercraft. (Creative Leisure Ser.). (Illus.). 76p. 1974. 7.50x (ISBN 0-85467-019-X). Intl Pubns Serv.
--Leathercraft. (New Crafts Books Ser.). 76p. 1980. 7.50 (ISBN 0-85467-019-X, Pub. by Viking Sevenseas New Zealand). Intl Schol Bk Serv.
--Lighting Craft. (New Crafts Ser.). 84p. 1980. 8.25 (ISBN 0-85467-022-X, Pub. by Viking Sevenseas New Zealand). Intl Schol Bk Serv.
--Lighting Crafts. (Creative Leisure Ser.). (Illus.). 84p. 1974. 7.50x (ISBN 0-85467-022-X). Intl Pubns Serv.
--New Zealand Flora & Fauna. 60p. 1980. pap. 1.95 (ISBN 0-85467-032-7, Pub. by Viking Sevenseas New Zealand). Intl Schol Bk Serv.
--New Zealand Shells and Shellfish. 88p. 1980. pap. 7.50 (ISBN 0-85467-033-5, Pub. by Viking Sevenseas New Zealand). Intl Schol Bk Serv.
--Perfumery. (New Crafts Books Ser.). 72p. 1980. 7.50 (ISBN 0-85467-026-2, Pub. by Viking Sevenseas New Zealand). Intl Schol Bk Serv.
--Shell Craft. (New Crafts Books Ser.). 72p. 1980. 7.50 (ISBN 0-85467-021-1, Pub. by Viking Sevenseas New Zealand). Intl Schol Bk Serv.
--Soft Toys. 80p. 1980. 7.50 (ISBN 0-85467-008-4, Pub. by Viking Sevenseas New Zealnd). Intl Schol Bk Serv.
Pownall, Peter. Fisheries of Australia. (Illus.). 160p. 1979. 20.50 (ISBN 0-85238-101-8, FN). Unipub.
Pownall, T. Administration of the Colonies. LC 79-146155. (Era of the American Revolution Ser). 1971. Repr. of 1768 ed. lib. bdg. 39.50 (ISBN 0-306-70123-5). Da Capo.
Powney, Derek J., jt. auth. see Collieu, A.
Poyer, D. C. White Continent. (Orig.). pap. 2.50 (ISBN 0-515-05479-8). Jove Pubns.
Poynter, Dan. Business Letters for Publishers: Creative Correspondence Outlines. 82p. 1981. 14.95 (ISBN 0-915516-28-4); magnetic recorded disc 29.95 (ISBN 0-915516-29-2). Para Pub.
--Hang Gliding Manual with Log. 6th ed. LC 76-14105. (Illus.). 1980. pap. 1.50 (ISBN 0-915516-12-8). Para Pub.
--Hang Gliding: The Basic Handbook of Skysurfing. 9th ed. LC 75-46185. (Illus.). 1979. 11.95 (ISBN 0-915516-08-X); pap. 6.95 (ISBN 0-915516-07-1). Para Pub.
--Manned Kiting: The Basic Handbook of Tow Launched Hang Gliding. 2nd ed. LC 74-20186. (Illus.). 1975. pap. 3.95 (ISBN 0-915516-04-7). Para Pub.
--The Parachute Manual: A Technical Treatise on the Parachute. 2nd ed. LC 77-71447. (Illus.). 1977. lab. manual 29.95 (ISBN 0-915516-06-3). Para Pub.
--Parachute Rigging Course: A Course of Study for the FAA Rigger Certificate. 2nd ed. LC 77-71448. (Illus.). 1981. pap. 11.95 (ISBN 0-915516-14-4). Para Pub.

--Parachuting I-E Course. 3rd ed. LC 78-50571. (Illus.). 1978. pap. 9.95 (ISBN 0-915516-18-7). Para Pub.
--Parachuting Manual with Log. 5th ed. LC 76-14106. (Illus.). 1980. pap. 1.50 (ISBN 0-915516-11-X). Para Pub.
--Parachuting: The Skydivers' Handbook. 3rd ed. LC 77-83469. (Illus.). 1980. 11.95 (ISBN 0-915516-17-9); pap. 6.95 (ISBN 0-915516-16-0). Para Pub.
--Publishing Short-Run Books: How to Pasteup & Reproduce Books Instantly Using Your Copy Shop. new ed. LC 80-13614. (Illus.). 104p. (Orig.). 1980. pap. 6.95 (ISBN 0-915516-23-3). Para Pub.
--The Self-Publishing Manual: How to Write, Print & Sell Your Own Book. 2nd ed. LC 79-712. (Illus.). 1980. 14.95 (ISBN 0-915516-22-5); pap. 9.95 (ISBN 0-915516-21-7). Para Pub.
--Toobee Players' Handook: The Amazing Flying Can. new ed. LC 80-20529. (Illus.). 52p. (Orig.). 1981. pap. 4.95 (ISBN 0-915516-25-X). Para Pub.
Poynter, Dan & Danna, Mark. Frisbee Players' Handbook. 3rd ed. LC 77-79101. (Illus.). 1980. pap. text ed. 6.95 (ISBN 0-915516-20-9); pap. 9.95 with disc (ISBN 0-915516-15-2); pap. 6.95 without disc (ISBN 0-915516-19-5). Para Pub.
Poynter, Margaret. Frisbee Fun. (Illus.). (gr. 3-6). 1978. pap. 1.25 (ISBN 0-671-29885-2). PB.
Poynter, Margaret & Lane, Arthur. Voyager: The Story of a Space Mission. LC 80-18723. (Illus.). 160p. 1981. 9.95 (ISBN 0-689-30827-2). Atheneum.
Pozgar, George D. Legal Aspects of Health Care Administration. LC 78-17276. 1979. text ed. 21.95 (ISBN 0-89443-044-0). Aspen Systems.
Pozhela, J. Plasma & Current Instabilities in Semiconductors. Germogenova, O. A., tr. (International Series in the Science of the Solid State: Vol. 18). (Illus.). 314p. 1981. 54.00 (ISBN 0-08-025048-3). Pergamon.
PPP Inc. Simple Spanish Cookery. 1977. 2.95 (ISBN 0-442-82575-7). Peter Pauper.
Praag, Van see Van Praag.
Prabha, Krishna. Towns: A Structural Analysis. 1979. text ed. 13.50x (ISBN 0-391-01860-4). Humanities.
Prabhavananda, Swami & Isherwood, Christopher, trs. Bhagavad-Gita: Song of God. 3rd ed. LC 46-1825. 1972. 6.95 (ISBN 0-87481-008-6). Vedanta Pr.
Prabhavananda, Swami & Manchester, Frederick, trs. Upanishads: Breath of the Eternal. LC 48-5935. 6.95 (ISBN 0-87481-007-8). Vedanta Pr.
Prabhu, N. U. Stochastic Storage Processes: Queues, Insurance Risk & Dams. (Applications of Mathematics Ser.: Vol. 15). 140p. 1981. 19.80 (ISBN 0-387-90522-7). Springer Verlag.
Pracy, R., et al. A Short Textbook Ear Nose & Throat. 2nd ed. (Illus.). 1975. pap. 7.00 o.p. (ISBN 0-397-58151-3). Lippincott.
--Ear, Nose, Throat: Surgery & Nursing. LC 77-84317. 1977. 14.50 (ISBN 0-471-03918-7). Wiley.
Prada, Beatriz-Maria. Great Quick & Easy Cooking. 192p. (Orig.). 1975. pap. 1.50 o.p. (ISBN 0-345-24282-3). Ballantine.
Prade, Ernstfried. Windsurfing. (EP Sport Ser.). (Illus.). 1979. 12.95 (ISBN 0-8069-9166-6, Pub. by EP Publishing England). Sterling.
Prade, Henri, jt. auth. see Dubois, Didier.
Pradi, Julie, tr. see Lettau, Reinhard.
Prado, Carlos Del see Calvo, Juan A. & Del Prado, Carlos.
Praeger, Donald L., jt. auth. see Kwitko, Marvin L.
Praetorius, Michael. Syntagma Musicum, 2 vols. Blumenfeld, Harold, tr. from Ger. (Music Reprint Ser.: 1979). Orig. Title: De Organographia, First & Second Parts. (Illus.). 1979. Repr. of 1962 ed. lib. bdg. 19.50 (ISBN 0-306-70563-X). Da Capo.
Prag, A., jt. auth. see Lockwood, Edward H.
Prager, Annabelle. The Surprise Party: An I Am Reading Book. LC 76-40309. (Illus.). (ps-4). 1977. 4.95 (ISBN 0-394-83235-3); PLB 3.99 (ISBN 0-394-93235-8). Pantheon.
Prager, Arthur. The Mahogany Tree: A Very Informal History of "Punch". LC 77-81360. 1979. 15.00 (ISBN 0-8015-4780-6, Hawthorn). Dutton.
--Underhanded Backgammon. 1977. pap. 4.95 (ISBN 0-8015-8125-7, Hawthorn). Dutton.
Prager, Audrey & Gettleman, Barry. Job Creation in the Community: An Evaluation of Locally Initiated Employment Projects in Massachusetts. 1977. 17.50 (ISBN 0-89011-506-0, EMT 114). Abt Assoc.
Prager, William. Introduction to Mechanics of Continua. 6.75 o.p. (ISBN 0-8446-4797-7). Peter Smith.
Prago, Albert. The Revolutions in Spanish America: The Independence Movements of 1808-1825. (gr. 8 up). 1970. 5.95g o.s.i. (ISBN 0-02-775110-4). Macmillan.
Prahalad, C. K., jt. auth. see Silvers, John B.
Prain, D. see Jackson, B. D., et al.

Prais, S. J. The Evolution of Giant Firms in Britain. LC 76-18410. (NIEST Economic & Social Studies Ser.: No. 30). (Illus.). 1977. 41.50 (ISBN 0-521-21356-8). Cambridge U Pr.
Prajnanananda, Swami. Christ the Savior. 1.25 o.p. (ISBN 0-87481-627-0). Vedanta Pr.
Prakash, B. Aspects of Indian History & Civilization. 1965. 8.50 (ISBN 0-8426-1681-0). Verry.
Prakash, Louise, et al, eds. Molecular & Environmental Aspects of Mutagenesis. (Illus.). 296p. 1975. 31.75 (ISBN 0-398-03137-1). C C Thomas.
Prakash, Om & Fyle, Clifford M. Books for the Developing Countries: Asia, Africa. 1965. pap. 2.50 (ISBN 92-3-100605-3, U58, UNESCO). Unipub.
Prakash, S. Financing of Planned Development in India. 1968. 7.50 (ISBN 0-8426-1682-9). Verry.
Prakash, Shamsher. Soil Dynamics. (Illus.). 432p. 1981. text ed. 26.95 (ISBN 0-07-050658-2, C); student's manual 4.95 (ISBN 0-07-050659-0). McGraw.
Prakash, Shamsher & Ranjan, Gopal. Problems in Soil Mechanics. 150p. 1972. 8.00x (ISBN 0-210-27101-9). Asia.
Prakash, Shri. Educational System of India. 1980. 9.50 (ISBN 0-391-02182-6). Humanities.
Prampero, P. E. Di see Di Prampero, P. E. & Poortsmans, J.
Prance, Anne E., jt. auth. see Prance, Ghillean T.
Prance, Ghillean T. Biological Diversification in the Tropics. 752p. 1981. 40.00x (ISBN 0-231-04876-9). Columbia U Pr.
Prance, Ghillean T. & Mori, Scott A. Lecythidaceae - Part One the Actinomonophic-Flowered New World Lecythidaceae: Asteranthos, Gustavia, Grias, Allantoma & Cariniana. LC 79-4659. (Flora Neotropica Ser.: Vol. 21). 1979. pap. 28.00 (ISBN 0-89327-193-4). NY Botanical.
Prance, Ghillean T. & Prance, Anne E. The Amazon Forest & River. (Illus.). 1981. 14.95 (ISBN 0-8120-5330-3). Barron.
Prandtl, Ludwig & Tietjens, O. G. Applied Hydro & Aeromechanics. Den Hartog, Jacob P., ed. (Illus.). 1934. pap. text ed. 5.00 (ISBN 0-486-60375-X). Dover.
--Fundamentals of Hydro & Aeromechanics. Rosenhead, L., tr. (Illus.). pap. text ed. 4.00 (ISBN 0-486-60374-1). Dover.
Prandy, Ken, ed. see Stewart, Alexander, et al.
Prange, Arthur J., Jr. The Thyroid Axis, Drugs & Behavior. LC 73-90468. 213p. 1974. 24.50 (ISBN 0-911216-34-0). Raven.
Praninskas, Jean. Rapid Review of English Grammar. 2nd ed. (Illus.). 352p. 1975. pap. 10.95 (ISBN 0-13-753145-1). P-H.
Prasad, Amba & Kashyap, G. P. Elementary Chemical Calculations. 3rd rev. ed. 1967. pap. 2.50x o.p. (ISBN 0-210-27017-9). Asia.
Prasad, Bhrigunath. Structure of the Epididymis of Birds & the Seasonal Changes in the Epididymis of the Parrot. 1965. pap. 5.00x (ISBN 0-210-98100-8). Asia.
Prasad, Birjadish. The Poetry of Thomas Hårdy, 2 vols. (Salzburg Studies in English Literature, Romantic Reassessment Ser: 57). 1977. Set. pap. text ed. 50.25x (ISBN 0-391-01501-X). Humanities.
Prasad, C. V., jt. auth. see Khan, M. E.
Prasad, Kedar N. & Vernadakis, Antonia, eds. Mechanisms of Neurotoxic Substances. 1981. text ed. price not set (ISBN 0-89004-638-7). Raven.
Prasad, Manchar, jt. auth. see Kadambi, V.
Prasad, Narmadeshwar. Iconography of Time. (Redbird Bk.). 1976. flexible bdg. 4.80 (ISBN 0-89253-093-6). Ind-US Inc.
Prasad, Prakash C. Foreign Trade & Commerce in Ancient India. 1977. 20.00x o.p. (ISBN 0-88386-981-0). South Asia Bks.
Prasad, R. C. Early English Travellers in India. 2nd rev. ed. 391p. 1980. text ed. 27.00 (ISBN 0-8426-1649-7). Verry.
Prasad, S. Benjamin & Shetty, Y. Krishna. An Introduction to Multinational Management. (Illus.). 256p. 1976. 11.95 (ISBN 0-13-489203-8). P-H.
Prasad, S. Benjamin, ed. Management in International Perspective. LC 67-10930. (Orig.). 1967. pap. text ed. 6.95x (ISBN 0-89197-289-7). Irvington.
Prasad, S. N. Life of Invertebrates. 800p. 1980. text ed. 50.00 (ISBN 0-7069-1042-7, Pub. by Vikas India). Advent Bk.
Prasad, Vikram & Cook, David. Taxonomy of Water Mite Larvae. (Memoirs Ser: No. 18). (Illus.). 326p. 1972. 22.00 (ISBN 0-686-08727-5). Am Entom Inst.
Prasada, Rama, tr. see Patanjali.
Prasanna, A. R., et al, eds. Gravitation Quanta & the Universe. LC 80-17051. 326p. 1981. 34.95 (ISBN 0-470-27007-1). Halsted Pr.

Prasanna, A. R., et al, eds. Gravitation, Quanta & the Universe: Proceedings of the Einstein Centenary Symposium Held at Ahmedabad, India 29 January to 3 February, 1979. LC 80-17051. 326p. 1981. 34.95 (ISBN 0-470-27007-1). Halsted Pr.
Prasow, Paul & Peters, Edward. Arbitration & Collective Bargaining. 2nd ed. 480p. 22.00x (ISBN 0-07-050674-4, C). McGraw.
Prasse, Leona E. Lyonel Feininger: A Definitive Catalogue of His Graphic Work: Etchings, Lithographs, Woodcuts. LC 74-108899. (Illus.). 304p. 1972. 35.00x (ISBN 0-910386-18-8, Pub. by Cleveland Mus Art). Ind U Pr.
Prassel, Frank R. The Western Peace Officer: A Legacy of Law & Order. 330p. 1980. pap. 7.95 (ISBN 0-8061-1694-3). U of Okla Pr.
Prast, William G. Securing U. S. Energy Supplies: The Private Sector As an Instrument of Public Policy. LC 79-2978. 1981. 15.95x (ISBN 0-669-03305-7). Lexington Bks.
Prasuhn, Alan L. Fundamentals of Fluid Mechanics. (Illus.). 1980. text ed. 24.95 (ISBN 0-13-339507-3). P-H.
Pratap, Dharma. The Advisory Jurisdiction of the International Court. 310p. 1972. text ed. 39.50x (ISBN 0-19-825302-8). Oxford U Pr.
Pratapaditya Pal. Nepal: Where the Gods Are Young. LC 75-769. (Illus.). 136p. 1975. 19.95 (ISBN 0-87848-045-5). Asia Soc.
Pratchett, Terry. The Dark Side of the Sun. LC 75-29644. 1976. 7.95 o.p. (ISBN 0-312-18270-8). St Martin.
Prater, Arnold. Miracle Living. (Orig.). pap. 2.95 (ISBN 0-89081-125-3). Harvest Hse.
Prater, Yvonne. Snoqualmie Pass: From Indian Trail to Interstate. Earnest, Rebecca, ed. (Illus.). 120p. (Orig.). 1981. pap. 6.95 (ISBN 0-89886-015-6). Mountaineers.
Pratesi, R. & Sacchi, C. A., eds. Lasers in Photomedicine & Photobiology: Proceedings. (Springer Series in Optical Sciences: Vol. 22). (Illus.). 235p. 1980. 29.50 (ISBN 0-387-10178-0). Springer-Verlag.
Prather, Hugh. A Book of Games: A Course in Spiritual Play. LC 80-2840. (Illus.). 176p. 1981. pap. 5.95 (ISBN 0-385-14779-1, Dolp). Doubleday.
--I Touch the Earth, the Earth Touches Me. LC 72-79420. 160p. 1972. pap. 3.95 (ISBN 0-385-05063-1). Doubleday.
--Notes on Love & Courage. LC 77-75873. 1977. pap. 4.95 (ISBN 0-385-12772-3). Doubleday.
--There Is a Place Where You Are Not Alone. LC 80-912. 224p. 1980. pap. 5.95 (ISBN 0-385-14778-3, Dolp). Doubleday.
Prather, Ray. Anthony & Sabrina. LC 73-3888. (Illus.). 32p. (gr. k-3). 1973. 4.95g o.s.i. (ISBN 0-02-775030-2). Macmillan.
--Double-Dog-Dare. LC 74-13316. (Ready-to-Read Ser.). (Illus.). 40p. (gr. 1-3). 1975. 4.95g o.s.i. (ISBN 0-02-775040-X). Macmillan.
--No Trespassing. LC 73-19056. (Illus.). 32p. (gr. k-3). 1974. 4.95g o.s.i. (ISBN 0-02-775020-5). Macmillan.
Prather, Ronald E. Discrete Mathematical Structures for Computer Science. LC 75-25014. (Illus.). 680p. 1976. text ed. 20.95 (ISBN 0-395-20622-7); solutions manual 1.50 (ISBN 0-395-20623-5). HM.
Pratney, Winkie. Doorways to Discipleship. LC 77-80008. 1977. pap. 3.95 (ISBN 0-87123-106-9, 210106). Bethany Fell.
--A Handbook for Followers of Jesus. LC 76-44385. 1976. pap. 4.95 (ISBN 0-87123-378-9, 210378). Bethany Fell.
--Star Wars, Star Trek. 1978. pap. 1.75 (ISBN 0-89728-057-1, 693400). Omega Pubns OR.
Pratolini, Vasco. Cronaca Familiare. Olken, Ilene T., ed. LC 73-130788. (Orig., Ital.). 1971. pap. text ed. 8.95x (ISBN 0-89197-117-3). Irvington.
Prats, A. J. The Autonomous Image: Cinematic Narration & Humanism. xvi, 171p. 1981. price not set (ISBN 0-8131-1406-3). U Pr of Ky.
Pratt, Charles. Here on the Island: Being an Account of a Way of Life Several Miles off the Maine Coast. LC 73-14282. (Illus.). 192p. 1974. 17.50 o.s.i. (ISBN 0-06-013409-7, HarpT). Har-Row.
Pratt, Charles & Maxwell, William. The Garden & the Wilderness. (Illus.). 159p. 1980. 50.00 (ISBN 0-8180-1420-2). Horizon.
Pratt, Cranford, jt. ed. see Mwansasu, Bismarck.
Pratt, Derek & Burton, Anthony. Canal. (Illus.). 96p. 1976. 11.95 (ISBN 0-7153-6932-6). David & Charles.
Pratt, Douglas R. Basics of Model Rocketry. Angle, Burr, ed. LC 80-84580. (Illus., Orig.). 1981. pap. 2.50 (ISBN 0-89024-557-6). Kalmbach.
Pratt, Ellen. Amy & the Cloudbasket. LC 75-25035. (Illus.). 38p. (Orig.). (ps-3). 1975. pap. 3.00 (ISBN 0-914996-08-8). Lollipop Power.
Pratt, Fletcher, jt. auth. see De Camp, L. Sprague.
Pratt, Fletcher see Johnson, Allen & Nevins, Allan.

Pratt, Francis. The United States in World Affairs: What Is Its Role? Fraenkel, Jack R., ed. (Crucial Issues in American Government Ser.). (gr. 9-12). 1976. pap. text ed. 4.96 (ISBN 0-205-04906-0, 7649061). Allyn.
Pratt, George J., et al. A Clinical Hypnosis Primer. LC 79-92665. 1980. 12.95 (ISBN 0-930626-07-9). Psych & Consul Assocs.
Pratt, Helen G. China & Her Unfinished Revolution. (Studies in Chinese History & Civilization). 173p. 1977. Repr. of 1937 ed. 16.00 (ISBN 0-89093-091-0). U Pubns Amer.
Pratt, J. G. On the Evaluation of Verbal Material in Parapsychology. LC 70-94866. (Parapsychological Monograph No. 10). 1969. pap. 2.50 (ISBN 0-912328-14-2). Parapsych Foun.
Pratt, J. G., jt. auth. see Rhine, J. B.
Pratt, J. Gaither. ESP Research Today: A Study of Developments in Parapsychology Since 1960. LC 73-3098. 1973. 10.00 (ISBN 0-8108-0609-6). Scarecrow.
--Parapsychology: An Insider's View of ESP. LC 76-45437. 1977. Repr. of 1966 ed. 12.00 (ISBN 0-8108-0991-5). Scarecrow.
Pratt, James N. The Wine Bibber's Bible. rev. ed. (Illus.). 192p. 1981. pap. 6.95 (ISBN 0-89286-182-7). One Hurd One Prods.
Pratt, John, et al. Costs & Control in Further Education. (General Ser.). 1978. text ed. 36.75x (ISBN 0-85633-159-7, NFER). Humanities.
Pratt, John C., ed. George Eliot's Middlemarch Notebooks: A Transcription. Neufeldt, Victor A. LC 74-16715. 1979. 30.00x (ISBN 0-520-02867-8). U of Cal Pr.
Pratt, John T. The Law Relating to Friendly Societies. Berkowitz, David S. & Thorne, Samuel E., eds. LC 77-86656. (Classics of English Legal History in the Modern Era Ser.: Vol. 40). 160p. 1979. lib. bdg. 40.00 (ISBN 0-8240-3089-3). Garland Pub.
Pratt, Josiah, ed. Thought of the Evangelical Leaders: John Newton, Thomas Scott, Charles Simeon, Etc. 1978. 15.95 (ISBN 0-85151-270-4). Banner of Truth.
Pratt, Julius W. America's Colonial Experiment. 1964. 7.50 o.p. (ISBN 0-8446-1362-2). Peter Smith.
--History of U. S. Foreign Policy. 3rd ed. LC 72-149978. (Illus.). 1972. ref. ed. 18.95 o.p. (ISBN 0-13-392316-9). P-H.
Pratt, Julius W., et al. A History of United States Foreign Policy. 4th ed. 1980. text ed. 19.95 (ISBN 0-13-392282-0). P-H.
Pratt, Kevin. Thirty Bike Rides in the Austin Area. 76p. 1973. 3.50 o.p. (ISBN 0-8363-0127-7). Jenkins.
Pratt, L. R. East of Malta West of Suez. LC 75-23534. (Illus.). 224p. 1975. 31.95 (ISBN 0-521-20869-6). Cambridge U Pr.
Pratt, Lois. Family Structure & Effective Health Behavior: The Energized Family. LC 75-29817. (Illus.). 256p. 1976. pap. text ed. 10.50 (ISBN 0-395-18702-8). HM.
Pratt, Louis H. James Baldwin. (United States Authors Ser.: No. 290). 1978. lib. bdg. 9.95 (ISBN 0-8057-7193-X). Twayne.
Pratt, M. J., jt. auth. see Faux, I. D.
Pratt, Mary M. Better Angling with Simple Science. (Illus.). 144p. 9.50 (ISBN 0-85238-069-0, FN). Unipub.
Pratt, Michael. Mugging As a Social Problem. 256p. 1980. 32.50 (ISBN 0-7100-0564-4). Routledge & Kegan.
Pratt, Noel. Homoeopathic Prescribing. 96p. 1980. 25.00x (Pub. by Beaconsfield England). State Mutual Bk.
Pratt, Peter, ed. History of Japan: Compiled from the Records of the English East India Company at the Instance of the Court of Directors, 2 vols. (Studies in Japanese History & Civilization). 1979. Repr. of 1931 ed. Set. 62.00 (ISBN 0-89093-261-1). U Pubns Amer.
Pratt, Robert A., ed. see Chaucer, Geoffrey.
Pratt, S. D., jt. auth. see Seavey, George R.
Pratt, Shannon. Valuing a Business: The Analysis & Appraisal of Closely Held Companies. 500p. 1981. 42.50 (ISBN 0-87094-205-0). Dow Jones-Irwin.
Pratt, Stanley E. Guide to Venture Capital Sources. 5th ed. 1981. 49.50 (ISBN 0-914470-12-4). Capital Pub Corp.
Pratt, Terence. Programming Languages: Design & Implementation. (Illus.). 496p. 1975. 24.95 (ISBN 0-13-730432-3). P-H.
Pratt, Vaughan R. Shellsort & Sorting Networks. LC 79-50559. (Outstanding Dissertations in the Computer Sciences). 1980. lib. bdg. 11.00 (ISBN 0-8240-4406-1). Garland Pub.
Pratt, W. V. Journals of Two Cruises Aboard the Privateer Yankee. 1967. 4.95 o.s.i. (ISBN 0-02-598580-9). Macmillan.
Pratt, William K. Digital Image Processing. LC 77-20888. 1978. 42.50 (ISBN 0-471-01888-0, Pub. by Wiley-Interscience). Wiley.
Pratte, Richard. Pluralism in Education: Conflict, Clarity, & Commitment. (Illus.). 232p. 1979. text ed. 16.50 (ISBN 0-398-03911-9); pap. text ed. 10.50 (ISBN 0-398-03912-7). C C Thomas.

Pratten, C. F. Comparisons of the Performance of Swedish & U.K. Companies. LC 76-19625. (Applied Economics Ser.: Occasional Papers, No. 47). (Illus.). 1976. pap. 16.95x (ISBN 0-521-29134-8). Cambridge U Pr.

--Labour Productivity Differentials Within International Companies. LC 76-8294. (Department of Applied Economics. Occasional Papers: No. 50). (Illus.). 1976. pap. 15.95x (ISBN 0-521-29102-X). Cambridge U Pr.

Prausnitz, J. Computer Calculations for Multicomponent Vapor-Liquid & Liquid-Liquid Equilibrium. 1980. 24.95 (ISBN 0-13-164962-0). P-H.

Prausnitz, J. M. Molecular Thermodynamics of Fluid-Phase Equilibria. LC 69-16866. 1969. ref. ed. 28.95 (ISBN 0-13-599639-2). P-H.

Prawer, Joshua. Crusader Institutions. (Illus.). 536p. 1980. 89.00x (ISBN 0-19-822536-9). Oxford U Pr.

Prawer, S. S. Karl Marx & World Literature. 1976. 39.95x (ISBN 0-19-815745-2). Oxford U Pr.

Pray, Thomas & Strong, Daniel. Decide: A Managerial Decision Game to Accompany Principles of Management by Kurtz & Boone. 120p. 1981. pap. text ed. 6.95 (ISBN 0-394-32698-9). Random.

Praz, Manrio. Studies in Seventeenth Century Imagery, 2 vols. in 1. LC 40-3654. Repr. 40.00 (ISBN 0-403-07208-5). Somerset Pub.

Praz, Mario. On Neoclassicism. Davidson, Angus, tr. 1969. 19.95x o.s.i. (ISBN 0-8101-0009-6). Northwestern U Pr.

PRC Energy Analysis Co. Design, Installation & Operation of Small, Stand-Alone Photovoltaic Powersystems. 300p. 1981. pap. 34.50 (ISBN 0-89934-092-X). Solar Energy Info.

Prc Energy Analysis Company & Weinstein, Stephen. Architectural & Engineering Concerns in Solar System Design, Installation & Operation. 51p. 1980. pap. 10.95 (ISBN 0-89934-052-0, H044-PP). Solar Energy Info.

Pre, Donn R. Grand. Confessions of an Arms Peddler. 1979. 9.95 (ISBN 0-912376-39-2). Chosen Bks Pub.

Preas, Jerry L. Champions & the All Americans. (Illus.). 1979. pap. 4.95 (ISBN 0-686-26660-9). Texan-Am Pub.

Preble, Amanda. Half-Heart. (Orig.). 1981. pap. 1.50 (ISBN 0-440-13442-0). Dell.

Preble, George H. The Symbols, Standards, Flags & Banners of Ancient & Modern Nations. 1980. lib. bdg. 12.00 (ISBN 0-8161-8476-3). G K Hall.

Prechtl, Heinz & Beintema, David. The Neurological Examination of the Full Term Newborn Infant. 2nd ed. (Clinics in Developmental Medicine Ser.: No. 63). 68p. 1977. Repr. of 1965 ed. 21.00 (ISBN 0-685-24716-3). Lippincott.

Pred, A. R. Major Job-Providing Organizations & Systems of Cities. LC 74-79830. (CCG Resource Papers Ser.: No. 27). (Illus.). 1974. pap. text ed. 4.00 (ISBN 0-89291-074-7). Assn Am Geographers.

Pred, Allan. Urban Growth & City-Systems in the United States, 1840-1860. LC 80-12098. (Studies in Urban History). 1980. text ed. 28.00x (ISBN 0-674-93091-6). Harvard U Pr.

Predmore, Richard L. World of Don Quixote. LC 67-20879. 1967. 7.50x (ISBN 0-674-96090-4). Harvard U Pr.

Pree, Gladis de see De Pree, Gordon & De Pree, Gladis.

Pree, Gordon De see De Pree, Gordon & De Pree, Gladis.

Pree, Mildred De see DePree, Mildred.

Preece, A. W. & Sabolovic, D., eds. Cell Electrophoresis: Clinical Application & Methodology. 496p. 1979. 56.00 (ISBN 0-7204-0674-9). Elsevier.

Preece, Harold. Lone Star Man: The Life of Ira Aten. 1960. 6.95 (ISBN 0-8038-4255-4). Hastings.

Preece, Warren E., ed. Encyclopaedia Britannica, 30 vols. 1980. write for info. (ISBN 0-85229-387-9). Ency Brit Ed.

Preeg, Ernest H. Traders & Diplomats: An Analysis of the Kennedy Round of Negotiations Under the General Agreement on Tariffs & Trade. LC 69-19693. 1970. 12.95 (ISBN 0-8157-7176-2). Brookings.

Preger, Elfriede. Ancient Egypt: A Survey. LC 78-54099. (Illus.). 1978. pap. 6.95 (ISBN 0-89708-001-7). And Bks.

Pregnall, William S. Laity & Liturgy: A Handbook for the Parish Worship Committee. 128p. (Orig.). 1975. pap. 3.95 (ISBN 0-8164-2593-0). Crossroad NY.

Preis, S. & Cocks, G. Arithmetic. 2nd ed. 1980. pap. 14.95 o.p. (ISBN 0-13-046201-2). P-H.

Preiskel, H. W. Precision Attachment in Dentistry. 3rd ed. (Illus.). 1979. text ed. 45.00 (ISBN 0-8016-8424-2). Mosby.

Preiss, Byron. The Electric Company Joke Book. (gr. 1-5). 1973. PLB 5.38 (ISBN 0-307-64824-9, Golden Pr). Western Pub.

--The Silent "E's" from Outer Space. (Electric Company Ser.). (Illus.). (gr. 1-5). 1973. PLB 5.38 (ISBN 0-307-64821-4, Golden Pr). Western Pub.

--Weird Heroes. 1975. pap. 1.50 o.p. (ISBN 0-515-03746-X). Jove Pubns.

Preiss, Byron & Goulart, Ron. Weird Heroes, Vol. 7, Bk. 2: Eye of the Vulture. (Orig.). 1977. pap. 1.50 o.p. (ISBN 0-515-04293-5). Jove Pubns.

Preiss, Byron, ed. Weird Heroes, Vol. 8. (Orig.). 1977. pap. 1.75 o.p. (ISBN 0-515-04257-9). Jove Pubns.

Prekopa, A., ed. see Conference on Mathematical Programming, 3rd, Matrafured, Hungary, 1975.

Prekopa, A., jt. ed. see Kall, P.

Preksto, Peter W., Jr. Library Skills. (Basic Skills Library). (Illus.). (gr. 4 up). 1979. PLB 5.95 (ISBN 0-87191-714-9). Creative Ed.

--Map Reading Skills. (Basic Skills Library). (Illus.). (gr. 4 up). 1979. PLB 5.95 (ISBN 0-87191-715-7). Creative Ed.

Preksto, Peter W., Jr. & Schaefer, Patricia S. Spelling Skills. (Basic Skills Library). (Illus.). (gr. 4 up). 1979. PLB 5.95 (ISBN 0-87191-713-0). Creative Ed.

--Writing Skills. (Basic Skills Library). (Illus.). (gr. 4 up). 1979. PLB 5.95 (ISBN 0-87191-716-5). Creative Ed.

Prelutsky, Jack. Circus. LC 73-6055. (Illus.). 32p. (gr. k-3). 1974. 7.95g (ISBN 0-02-775060-4). Macmillan.

--It's Halloween. (Illus.). 48p. 1980. Repr. pap. 1.50 (ISBN 0-590-03275-5, Schol Pap). Schol Bk Serv.

--The Mean Old Mean Hyena. LC 78-2300. (Illus.). (gr. k-3). 1978. 7.95 (ISBN 0-688-80163-3); PLB 7.63 (ISBN 0-688-84163-5). Greenwillow.

--Nightmares: Poems to Trouble Your Sleep. LC 76-4820. (Illus.). 40p. (gr. 3 up). 1976. 8.25 (ISBN 0-688-80053-X); PLB 7.92 (ISBN 0-688-84053-1). Greenwillow.

--Pack Rat's Day & Other Poems. LC 73-81061. (Illus.). 32p. (gr. k-4). 1974. 5.95g o.s.i. (ISBN 0-02-775050-7). Macmillan.

--The Queen of Eene. LC 77-17311. (Illus.). (gr. k-3). 1978. 7.95 (ISBN 0-688-80144-7); PLB 7.63 (ISBN 0-688-84144-9). Greenwillow.

--The Snopp on the Sidewalk & Other Poems. LC 76-46323. (Illus.). (gr. 3 up). 1977. PLB 6.96 (ISBN 0-688-84084-1). Greenwillow.

--Terrible Tiger. LC 75-89592. (Illus.). (gr. k-3). 1970. 4.95g o.s.i. (ISBN 0-02-775130-9). Macmillan.

--Toucans Two & Other Poems. LC 70-102970. (Illus.). (gr. k-3). 1970. 6.95g (ISBN 0-02-775070-1). Macmillan.

Prelutsky, Jack, tr. see Neumann, Rudolf.

Premchand. Godan. Lal, P., tr. 1972. pap. 3.50 (ISBN 0-88253-069-0). Ind-US Inc.

Premiere et Deuxieme Commissions Du Bureau De Paris. Proces De l'Association Internationale Des Travailleurs. (Fr.). 1977. lib. bdg. 18.75x o.p. (ISBN 0-8287-0705-7); pap. text ed. 8.75x o.p. (ISBN 0-685-74934-7). Clearwater Pub.

Premm, Mattias. Dogmatic Theology for the Laity. LC 67-21425. 1977. pap. 10.00 (ISBN 0-89555-022-9, 183). TAN Bks Pubs.

Premoe, David, ed. Zion, the Growing Symbol. 1980. pap. 5.75 (ISBN 0-8309-0301-1). Herald Hse.

Prempree, Thongbliew, et al. Radiobiology Examination Review Book. 1975. spiral bdg. 10.00 (ISBN 0-87488-487-X). Med Exam.

Prendergast, Alice. Medical Terminology: A Text-Workbook. LC 76-62907. 1977. pap. text ed. 10.95 (ISBN 0-201-05966-5, M&N Div); instr's man. 9.95 (ISBN 0-201-05967-3). A-W.

Prendergast, C., jt. auth. see Crockett, James U.

Prendergast, Curt. The First Aviators. (The Epic of Flight). (Illus.). 176p. (Orig.). 1981. 12.95 (ISBN 0-8094-3262-5). Time-Life.

Prendergast, Curtis. Easy Gardens. Time-Life Books, ed. (Encyclopedia of Gardening Ser.). (Illus.). 1979. 11.95 (ISBN 0-8094-2637-4). Time-Life.

Prendergast, Terrence, tr. see Leon-Dufour, Xavier.

Prenis, John, ed. Energybook, No. 1: Natural Sources & Backyard Applications. LC 74-84854. (Illus.). 117p. (Orig.). 1975. lib. bdg. 12.90 (ISBN 0-914294-22-9); pap. 5.95 (ISBN 0-914294-21-0). Running Pr.

Prenowitz, Walter & Jordan, M. Basic Concepts of Geometry. (Illus.). 1965. text ed. 24.95x (ISBN 0-471-00451-0). Wiley.

Prenshaw, Peggy W., jt. ed. see Fazio, Michael W.

Prensky, Arthur L. & Palkes, Helen. Care of the Neurologically Handicapped Child. (Illus.). 350p. 1981. text ed. 18.95x (ISBN 0-19-502917-8). Oxford U Pr.

Prensky, Sol & Seidman, Arthur. Manual of Linear Integrated Circuits. 2nd ed. (Illus.). 1981. text ed. 19.95 (ISBN 0-8359-4241-4). Reston.

Prensky, Sol D. Electronic Instrumentation. 2nd ed. 1971. ref. ed. 21.95 (ISBN 0-13-251645-4). P-H.

Prentice, Ann E. The Public Library Trustee: Image & Performance on Funding. LC 73-1648. 1973. 10.00 (ISBN 0-8108-0597-9). Scarecrow.

--Suicide: A Selective Bibliography of Over 2,200 Items. LC 74-19231. 1974. 10.00 (ISBN 0-8108-0773-4). Scarecrow.

Prentice, Archibald. History of the Anti-Corn-Law League, 2 Vols. LC 68-21442. Repr. of 1853 ed. 32.50x (ISBN 0-678-05191-7). Kelley.

Prentice, D. M. Your Book of Parliament. (Your Book Ser.). (Illus.). (gr. 5 up). 1967. 7.95 (ISBN 0-571-08129-0, Pub. by Faber & Faber). Merrimack Bk Serv.

Prentice, Diana, jt. auth. see Hensley, Dana.

Prentice-Hall Tax Editorial Staff. Ten-Forty Handbook. 1979. 18.50 (ISBN 0-13-903393-9). P-H.

Prentice, J. M. Dynamics of Mechanical Systems. 2nd ed. LC 79-41460. 486p. 1980. 59.95x (ISBN 0-470-26938-3). Halsted Pr.

Prentice, Lloyd. Words, Pictures, Media: Communication in Educational Politics. 91p. 1976. pap. text ed. 4.00 (ISBN 0-917754-01-8). Inst Responsive.

Prentice, Roger & Kirk, John M., trs. A Fist & the Letter: Revolutionary Poems of Latin America. (Illus.). 1978. pap. 3.50 o.p. (ISBN 0-8467-0558-3, Pub. by Two Continents). Hippocrene Bks.

Prentice, Sartell. The Heritage of the Cathedral. 328p. 1980. Repr. of 1936 ed. lib. bdg. 40.00 (ISBN 0-8495-4399-1). Arden Lib.

Prentice, T. Merrill & Sargent, Elizabeth O. Weeds & Wildflowers of Eastern North America. 1973. 25.00 (ISBN 0-87577-063-0). Peabody Mus Salem.

Prentis, Edmund A., jt. ed. see White, Lazarus.

Prentiss. Oscilloscopes. (Illus.). 1980. text ed. 16.95 (ISBN 0-8359-5354-8); pap. text ed. 9.95 (ISBN 0-8359-5353-X). Reston.

Prentiss, Charlotte. Love's Savage Embrace. 304p. (Orig.). 1981. pap. 2.75 (ISBN 0-515-05272-8). Jove Pubns.

Prentiss, Hervey Putnam. Timothy Pickering As the Leader of New England Federalism, 1800-1815. LC 71-124882. (American Scene Ser). (Illus.). 118p. 1972. Repr. of 1934 ed. lib. bdg. 17.50 (ISBN 0-306-71052-8). Da Capo.

Prentiss, Stan. Magnavox Color TV Service Manual, Vol. 2. LC 70-117189. (Schematic Servicing Manual Ser). (Illus.). 1972. pap. 7.95 (ISBN 0-8306-1589-X, 589). TAB Bks.

--Servicing Sony TV for 1974-1975, Vol. 1. LC 75-17001. (Illus.). 1975. pap. 12.95 (ISBN 0-672-21223-4, 21223). Sams.

--Servicing the New Modular Color TV Receivers, Vol. 1. LC 73-78195. (Schematic Servicing Manual Ser). (Illus.). 178p. 1973. leatherette o.p. 9.95 (ISBN 0-8306-3662-5); pap. 6.95 (ISBN 0-8306-2662-X, 662). TAB Bks.

Prentky, Robert A. Creativity & Psychopathology: A Neurocognitive Perspective. 282p. 1980. 27.95 (ISBN 0-03-053376-7). Praeger.

Prentout, Henri. Essai Sur les Origines et la Fondation Du Duche De Normandie. LC 80-2214. 1981. Repr. of 1911 ed. 39.00 (ISBN 0-404-18776-5). AMS Pr.

Prentup, Frank. Skipping the Rope. 2nd, rev. ed. 36p. 1980. pap. 3.95 (ISBN 0-87108-572-0). Pruett.

Prentup, Frank B. Skipping the Rope for Fun & Fitness. (Illus.). pap. 2.25 o.p. (ISBN 0-87108-021-4). Pruett.

Preobrazhensky, Alexander G. Etymological Dictionary of the Russian Language. LC 52-3699. (Columbia Slavic Studies). 50.00 (ISBN 0-231-01889-4). Columbia U Pr.

Preparata, G. & Aubert, J. J., eds. Probing Hadrons with Leptons. (Ettore Majorana International Science Ser., Physical Sciences: Vol. 5). 502p. 1980. 59.50 (ISBN 0-306-40438-9, Plenum Pr). Plenum Pub.

Prescot, Dray. Rebel of Antares. (Science Fiction Ser.). 1980. pap. 1.95 (ISBN 0-87997-582-2, UJ1582). DAW Bks.

Prescott, Daniel A. Emotion & the Educative Process: A Report of the Committee on the Relation of Emotion to the Educative Process. 323p. 1980. Repr. of 1938 ed. lib. bdg. 25.00 (ISBN 0-89760-707-4). Telegraph Bks.

Prescott, David & Turner, James, eds. Methods in Cell Biology: Three-Dimensioal Ultrastructure in Biology, Vol. 22. 1981. write for info. (ISBN 0-12-564122-2). Acad Pr.

Prescott, David, jt. ed. see Goldstein, L.

Prescott, David M., ed. Methods in Cell Physiology. Incl. Vol. 1. 1964. 47.50 (ISBN 0-12-564101-X); Vol. 2. 1966. 47.50 (ISBN 0-12-564102-8); Vol. 3. 1969. 47.50 (ISBN 0-12-564103-6); Vol. 4. 1970. 47.50 (ISBN 0-12-564104-4); Vol. 5. 1972. 47.50 (ISBN 0-12-564105-2); Vol. 6. 1973. 47.50 (ISBN 0-12-564106-0); Vol. 7. 1974. 47.50 (ISBN 0-12-564107-9); Vol. 8. 1974. 49.00 (ISBN 0-12-564108-7); Vol. 9. 1975. 47.50 (ISBN 0-12-564109-5); Vol. 10. 1975. 47.50 (ISBN 0-12-564110-9); Vol. 11. Yeast Cells. 1975. 47.50 (ISBN 0-12-564111-7); Vol. 12. 1975. 47.50 (ISBN 0-12-564112-5); Vol. 13. 1976. 47.50 (ISBN 0-12-564113-3); Vol. 14. 1976. 48.00 (ISBN 0-12-564114-1); Vol. 15. 1977. 47.00 (ISBN 0-12-564115-X); Vol. 16. Chromatin & Chromosomal Protein Research I. Stein, Gary & Stein, Janet, eds. 1977. 48.50 (ISBN 0-12-564116-8). Acad Pr.

Prescott, David M. & Harris, Curtis, eds. Methods in Cell Biology: Vol. 21, Methods to Culture Normal Human Tissues & Cells, Pt. A: Respiratory, Cardiovascular, & Intgumentary Systems. (Serial Publication Ser.). 1980. 39.50 (ISBN 0-12-564121-4). Acad Pr.

--Methods in Cell Biology: Vol. 21, Methods to Culture Normal Human Tissues & Cells, Pt. B: Endocrine, Urogenital, & Gastro-Intestinal Systems. (Serial Publication Ser.). 1980. 49.50 (ISBN 0-12-564140-0). Acad Pr.

Prescott, Ernest. Creatures That Help Each Other. (Easy-Read Wildlife Bk.). (Illus.). 31p. (gr. 2-4). 1976. PLB 4.90 o.p. (ISBN 0-531-00354-X). Watts.

--Flying Creatures. (Easy-Read Wildlife Bk.). (Illus.). 48p. (gr. 2-4). 1976. PLB 4.90 o.p. (ISBN 0-531-00355-8). Watts.

--Slow Creatures. (Easy-Read Wildlife Bk.). (Illus.). 31p. (gr. 2-4). 1976. PLB 4.90 o.p. (ISBN 0-531-01219-0). Watts.

--What Comes Out of an Egg. (Easy-Read Wildlife Ser.). (Illus.). 32p. (gr. 2-4). 1976. PLB 4.90 o.p. (ISBN 0-531-00362-0). Watts.

Prescott, Evarts, Jr. How to Prepare for the College Level Examination Program (CLEP) 1980. pap. 6.95 (ISBN 0-07-019764-4, SP). McGraw.

Prescott, Frank W. & Zimmerman, Joseph F. The Politics of the Vets Legislation in New York State, 2 vols. LC 79-9696. 649p. 1980. Vol. 1. pap. 17.50 (ISBN 0-8191-0985-1); softcover set 33.50 (ISBN 0-8191-0986-X); Vol. 2. 26.75 (ISBN 0-8191-0983-5); text ed. 51.50 hardback set (ISBN 0-8191-0984-3). U Pr of Amer.

Prescott, Frederick C., ed. Selections from the Critical Writings of Edgar Allan Poe. 425p. 1981. Repr. of 1909 ed. 15.00 (ISBN 0-87752-182-4). Gordian.

Prescott, G. W. Algae of the Western Great Lakes Area. 1962. text ed. 24.95x o.p. (ISBN 0-697-04552-8). Wm C Brown.

Prescott, G. W., et al. Desmidiales, Sarccodermae, Mesotaeniaceae. LC 70-183418. (North American Flora, Ser. II: Part 6). 1972. pap. 5.75 (ISBN 0-89327-018-0). NY Botanical.

--A Synopsis of North American Desmids Part II: Desmidiaceae: Placodermae Section 3. LC 70-183418. (Illus.). x, 720p. Date not set. 58.50x (ISBN 0-8032-3660-3). U of Nebr Pr.

Prescott, H. F. The Man on a Donkey. 640p. 1981. pap. 8.95 (ISBN 0-02-023830-4). Macmillan.

Prescott, J. R. The Geography of State Policies. 1968. text ed. 6.00x (ISBN 0-09-088860-X, Hutchinson U Lib). Humanities.

--Political Geography of the Oceans. LC 74-31813. 247p. 1975. 19.95 (ISBN 0-470-69672-9). Halsted Pr.

Prescott, L. F., ed. see International Conference on Drug Absorption, Edinburgh, 1979.

Prescott, Mary A. How to Raise & Train a Bullmastiff. (Orig.). pap. 2.00 (ISBN 0-87666-260-2, DS1065). TFH Pubns.

Prescott, Peter S. The Child Savers. LC 80-2705. 320p. 1981. 12.95 (ISBN 0-394-50235-3). Knopf.

Prescott, W. H. Correspondence of William Hickling Prescott, 1833-1847. Wolcott, Roger, ed. LC 76-112312. (American Public Figures Ser). 1970. Repr. of 1925 ed. lib. bdg. 42.50 (ISBN 0-306-71912-6). Da Capo.

Prescott, William H. Conquest of Mexico & Peru. Howell, Roger, ed. text ed. 20.00x (ISBN 0-8290-0220-0). Irvington.

--History of the Conquest of Mexico, 2 Vols. 1957. 6.00x ea. o.p. (Evman). Vol. 1 (ISBN 0-460-00397-6). Vol. 2 (ISBN 0-460-00398-4). Dutton.

--Literary Memoranda of William Hickling Prescott, 2 vols. Gardiner, C. Harvey, ed. LC 61-9004. (Illus.). 1961. boxed 22.50x (ISBN 0-8061-0495-3); pap. 8.95x (ISBN 0-8061-1161-5). U of Okla Pr.

President's Commission for a National Agenda for the Eighties. A National Agenda for the Eighties. 1981. pap. 2.95 (ISBN 0-451-62011-9, ME2011, Ment). NAL.

President's Commission On Immigration & Naturalization. Whom We Shall Welcome. LC 73-146270. (Civil Liberties in American History Ser). 1971. Repr. of 1953 ed. lib. bdg. 35.00 (ISBN 0-306-70145-6). Da Capo.
President's Commission on Law Enforcement & Administration of Justice. Task Force Report: The Police. LC 73-154585. (Police in America Ser). 1971. Repr. of 1967 ed. 17.00 (ISBN 0-405-03383-4). Arno.
Preslan, Kristina. Group Crafts for Teachers & Librarians on Limited Budgets. LC 80-13145. (Illus.). 1980. pap. 9.00x (ISBN 0-87287-218-1). Libs Unl.
Presley, Dee, et al. Elvis, We Love You Tender. 1981. pap. 3.50 o.s.i. (ISBN 0-440-12323-2). Dell.
Presley, Delma E., jt. auth. see Harper, Francis.
Presley, James, jt. auth. see McCamy, John C.
Presley, John R., jt. ed. see O'Brien, D. P.
Presno, C., jt. auth. see Presno, V.
Presno, V. & Presno, C. The Value Realms: Activities for Helping Students Develop Values. 1980. pap. text ed. 8.50x (ISBN 0-8077-2584-6). Tchrs Coll.
Presper, Mary. Joys of Woodstoves & Fireplaces. LC 78-73323. pap. 6.95 (ISBN 0-448-14847-1). G&D.
Press. The Adventures of the Black Hand Gang. (gr. 3-5). 1980. pap. 1.25 (ISBN 0-590-30000-8, Schol Pap). Schol Bk Serv.
Press, Chaim. What Is the Reason? Repr. of 1975 ed. Vols 1,2,3, except where noted 5.95x ea.; Vol. 6. 5.95 o.p. (ISBN 0-8197-0377-X). Bloch.
Press, Charles. American Policy Studies. 200p. 1981. pap. text ed. 7.95 (ISBN 0-471-07866-2). Wiley.
--Political Cartoons. LC 76-2309. (Illus.). 360p. 1981. 18.00 (ISBN 0-8386-1901-0). Fairleigh Dickinson.
Press, Charles & VerBerg, Kenneth. State & Community Governments in the Federal System. LC 78-22064. 1979. text ed. 16.95x (ISBN 0-471-02725-1); tchrs. manual avail. (ISBN 0-471-04909-3). Wiley.
Press, Frank & Siever, Raymond. Earth. 2nd ed. LC 77-25209. (Illus.). 1978. text ed. 21.95x (ISBN 0-7167-0289-4); instr' guide avail. W H Freeman.
Press, Frank & Siever, Raymondintro. by. Planet Earth: Readings from Scientific American. LC 74-14919. (Illus.). 1974. text ed. 19.95x (ISBN 0-7167-0507-9); pap. text ed. 9.95x (ISBN 0-7167-0506-0). W H Freeman.
Press, Hans J. The Adventures of the Black Hand Gang. Littlewood, Barbara, tr. from Ger. LC 77-5950. (Illus.). (gr. 2-5). 1977. PLB 6.95 (ISBN 0-13-013938-6). P-H.
--Simple Science Experiments. 1974. 14.95 (ISBN 0-7134-2894-5, Pub. by Batsford England). David & Charles.
Press, Larry & Whittaker, Lou, eds. Personal Computing Digest. (Illus.). vi, 211p. 1980. pap. 12.00 (ISBN 0-88283-012-0). AFIPS Pr.
Press, Margaret L. Chemehuevi: A Grammar & Lexicon. (U. C. Publications in Linguistics Ser.: Vol. 92). 1980. pap. 12.00 (ISBN 0-520-09600-2). U of Cal Pr.
Press, Max, jt. auth. see Wilson, Chris.
Pressat, Roland. Demographic Analysis: Methods, Results & Applications. LC 69-11228. 1972. 26.95x (ISBN 0-202-30093-5). Aldine Pub.
Presseau, Jack R. I'm Saved, You're Saved--Maybe. LC 76-12401. 1977. 6.95 (ISBN 0-8042-0832-8). John Knox.
Presseisen, Ernst L. Germany & Japan: A Study in Totalitarian Diplomacy, 1933-1941. LC 68-57832. 1970. Repr. of 1958 ed. 18.50 (ISBN 0-86527-082-1). Fertig.
Presser, Stephen B. & Zainaldin, Jamil S. Law & American History: Cases & Materials. LC 80-15905. (American Casebook Ser.). 897p. 1980. text ed. 19.95 (ISBN 0-8299-2094-3). West Pub.
Pressey, Benfield, jt. ed. see Watson, E. Bradlee.
Pressly, Thomas J. Americans Interpret Their Civil War. LC 62-17572. 1965. pap. text ed. 6.95 (ISBN 0-02-925450-7). Free Pr.
Pressman, Abraham I. Switching & Linear Power Supply, Power Converter Design. (Illus.). 1977. text ed. 23.95 (ISBN 0-8104-5847-0); net solutions manual 1.95 (ISBN 0-8104-5827-6). Hayden.
Pressman, Israel, jt. auth. see Gordon, Gilbert.
Pressman, Jeffrey L. Federal Programs & City Politics: The Dynamics of the Aid Process in Oakland. (Oakland Project Ser). 1975. 18.50x (ISBN 0-520-02749-3); pap. 4.95x (ISBN 0-520-03508-9). U of Cal Pr.
Pressman, Jeffrey L. & Wildavsky, Aaron. Implementation; How Great Expectations in Washington Are Dashed in Oakland: Or Why It's Amazing That Federal Programs Work at All, This Being the Saga of the Economic Development Administration As Told to by Two Sympathetic Observers Who Seek to Build Morals on Ruined Hopes. 2nd, exp. ed. (The Oakland Project). 1979. 15.75x (ISBN 0-520-03959-9); pap. 3.95x (ISBN 0-520-03946-7, CAMPUS NO. 247). U of Cal Pr.
Pressman, R. S. & Williams, J. E. Numerical Control & Computer-Aided Manufacturing. 310p. 1977. text ed. 24.95 (ISBN 0-471-01555-5). Wiley.
--Numerical Control & Computer-Aided Manufacturing. 310p. 1977. 24.95 (ISBN 0-471-01555-5). Wiley.
Presson, Hazel. Student Journalist & Keys to Successful Reporting. LC 65-22256. (Student Journalist Ser). (gr. 7 up). Date not set. PLB 7.97 (ISBN 0-8239-0124-6). Rosen Pr. Postponed.
Presson, Kay P. Irish Legacy. 1978. 4.50 (ISBN 0-533-03573-2). Vantage.
Prest, A. R. Financing University Education. (Institute of Economic Affairs, Occasional Papers Ser.: No. 12). pap. 2.50 (ISBN 0-255-69603-5). Transatlantic.
--Value-Added Taxation: The Experience of the United Kingdom. 1980. pap. 4.25 (ISBN 0-8447-3404-7). Am Enterprise.
Prest, Wilfrid, ed. Lawyers in Early Modern Europe & America. LC 80-22574. 224p. 1981. text ed. 27.50x (ISBN 0-8419-0679-3). Holmes & Meier.
Prestage, Jewel L., jt. ed. see Githens, Marianne.
Prestayko, A. W., jt. ed. see Crooke, S. T.
Prestayko, Archie W., jt. auth. see Crooke, Stanley T.
Presthus, R. Public Administration. 6th ed. 1975. text ed. 16.95x (ISBN 0-8260-7225-9). Wiley.
Presthus, Robert, ed. Cross-National Perspectives, United States & Canada. (International Studies in Sociology & Social Anthropology: No.XXIV). 1977. text ed. 32.00x (ISBN 90-04-05238-0). Humanities.
Presto, Linda. The Bath Book. (Illus.). (gr. k-2). 1978. PLB 5.38 (ISBN 0-307-68935-2, Golden Pr). Western Pub.
--Pink Panther Book. (A Golden Book for Early Childhood Ser.). (Illus.). (gr. k-3). 1979. PLB 5.38 (ISBN 0-307-68944-1, Golden Pr). Western Pub.
Prestol, Sack & Schneider, Herman, eds. Tax Planning for Investors. rev. ed. LC 79-10505. 1979. pap. 6.95 (ISBN 0-87128-574-6, Pub. by Dow Jones). Dow Jones-Irwin.
Preston, A. Cruisers. LC 79-89592. 192p. 1980. 16.95 (ISBN 0-13-194902-0). P-H.
Preston, A., jt. auth. see Mahan, A.
Preston, Antony. Super Destroyers. 72p. 1980. 11.50x (ISBN 0-85177-131-9, Pub. by Cornell England). State Mutual Bk.
--Warships of the World. (Illus.). 1979. 19.95 o.s.i. (ISBN 0-8464-0962-3). Beekman Pubs.
Preston, C. Random Fields. (Lecture Notes in Mathematics: Vol. 534). 1976. soft cover 12.10 (ISBN 0-387-07852-5). Springer-Verlag.
Preston, Charles. Dow Jones Crosswords for the Serious, Bk. 3. 60p. 1981. pap. 3.50 (ISBN 0-87094-238-7). Dow Jones-Irwin.
--Dow Jones Crosswords for the Serious, Bk. 4. 60p. 1981. pap. 3.50 (ISBN 0-87094-239-5). Dow Jones-Irwin.
Preston, Charles, ed. The Wall Street Journal Book of Wit. 160p. (Orig.). 1981. pap. 7.95 (ISBN 0-87094-227-1). Dow Jones-Irwin.
--The Wall Street Journal Cartoon Portfolio. LC 79-20777. (Illus.). 1979. 12.95 o.p. (ISBN 0-87128-584-3, Pub. by Dow Jones); pap. 7.95 (ISBN 0-87128-581-9). Dow Jones-Irwin.
Preston, David A. Environment, Society & Rural Change in Latin America: The Past, Present & Future in the Country. LC 79-41481. 1980. write for info. (ISBN 0-471-27713-4, Pub. by Wiley-Interscience). Wiley.
--Farmers & Towns, Rural-Urban Relations in Highland Bolivia. 197p. 1980. 14.95x (ISBN 0-86094-009-8, Pub. by GEO Abstracts England); pap. 11.40x (ISBN 0-86094-008-X, Pub. by GEO Abstracts England). State Mutual Bk.
Preston, Don & Preston, Sue. Crazy Fox Remembers. 224p. 11.95 (ISBN 0-13-188896-X). P-H.
Preston, Don, jt. auth. see Warrick, Ruth.
Preston, Edna M. The Sad Story of the Little Bluebird & the Hungry Cat. (gr. k-3). 1977. pap. 0.95 o.p. (ISBN 0-590-10276-1, Schol Pap). Schol Bk Serv.
--Where Did My Mother Go? LC 77-15064. (Illus.). 32p. (gr. k-3). 1978. 7.95 (ISBN 0-590-07347-8, Four Winds). Schol Bk Serv.
Preston, Edna M. & Cooney, Barbara. Squawk to the Moon, Little Goose. (Illus.). 32p. (gr. k-3). 1976. pap. 1.50 o.s.i. (ISBN 0-670-05103-9, Puffin). Penguin.
Preston, Effa E. The Popular Commencement Book. LC 70-175776. 434p. 1975. Repr. of 1931 ed. 20.00 (ISBN 0-8103-4034-8). Gale.
Preston, G. B., jt. auth. see Clifford, A. H.
Preston, Harriet W., tr. see Sainte-Beuve, Charles A.
Preston, Hayter, jt. auth. see Brangwyn, Frank.
Preston, Ivan L. The Great American Blow-up: Puffery in Advertising & Selling. LC 74-27313. 1975. 27.50 (ISBN 0-299-06730-0); pap. 7.95 (ISBN 0-299-06734-3). U of Wis Pr.
Preston, J. B., ed. see Lombardi, Thomas P.
Preston, Jack D. & Bergen, Stephen F. Color Science & Dental Art. LC 80-17295. (Illus.). 88p. 1980. pap. 49.50 (ISBN 0-8016-4038-5). Mosby.
Preston, Lee E. & Post, James E. Private Management & Public Policy: The Principle of Public Responsibility. (Illus.). 192p. 1975. pap. text ed. 10.95 (ISBN 0-13-710970-9). P-H.
Preston, M. A. & Bhaduri, R. K. Structure of the Nucleus. 475p. 1975. 37.50 (ISBN 0-201-05976-2, Adv Bk Prog); pap. text ed. 25.50 (ISBN 0-201-05977-0, Adv Bk Prog). A-W.
Preston, Michael B., jt. ed. see Palley, Marian L.
Preston, Michael J., ed. see Lyons, Anne K. & Lyons, Thomas R.
Preston, P. Communication for Managers. 1979. 17.95 (ISBN 0-13-153957-4). P-H.
Preston, P. N. Benzimidazoles & Congeneric Tricyclic Compounds, Pt. 1, Vol. 40. (Chemistry of Heterocyclic Compounds Ser.). 848p. 1981. write for info. (ISBN 0-471-03792-3, Pub. by Wiley-Interscience). Wiley.
--Benzimidazoles & Congeneric Tricyclic Compounds, Vol. 40, Pt. 2. LC 80-17383. (Chemistry of Heterocyclic Compounds Ser.). 1200p. 1980. 120.00 (ISBN 0-471-03792-3, Pub. by Wiley-Interscience). Wiley.
Preston, Paul & Nelson, Ralph. Salesmanship: A Contemporary Approach. 1981. 15.95 (ISBN 0-8359-6933-9); instr's manual free. Reston.
Preston, Paul & Zimmerer, Thomas W. Business: An Introduction to American Enterprise. 1976. 18.95 (ISBN 0-13-091272-7); student guide 7.95 (ISBN 0-13-091280-8). P-H.
Preston, Paul, jt. auth. see Thornton, Billy M.
Preston, Philip. White Mountains - East. (Illus.). 270p. (Orig.). 1981. pap. 8.50 (ISBN 0-9603106-1-4). Waumbek.
Preston, Ralph C. & Botel, Morton. How to Study. 4th ed. 176p. 1981. pap. 6.95 (ISBN 0-574-19625-0, 13-3625); instr's. guide avail. (ISBN 0-574-19626-9, 13-3626). SRA.
--How to Study. 1974. pap. text ed. 6.00 (ISBN 0-574-51295-0, 5-1295); instr's guide avail. (ISBN 0-574-51296-9, 5-1296); specimen set 7.47 (ISBN 0-574-51299-3, 5-1299). SRA.
Preston, Ralph N. Early Washington Atlas. LC 78-57006. (Illus.). 1980. pap. 6.50 (ISBN 0-8323-0311-9). Binford.
Preston, Richard A. & Wise, Sidney. Men in Arms: A History of Warfare & Its Interrelationships with Western Society. rev. ed. 2nd ed. LC 76-101676. (Illus.). 440p. (Orig.). 1970. pap. text ed. 11.95 (ISBN 0-03-045681-9). Praeger.
Preston, Stuart. Vuillard. LC 74-142739. (Library of Great Painters). (Illus.). 1971. 35.00 (ISBN 0-8109-0538-8). Abrams.
Preston, Sue, jt. auth. see Preston, Don.
Preston, T. R. & Willis, M. B. Intensive Beef Production. 2nd ed. 1974. 24.00 (ISBN 0-08-018980-6); text ed. 40.00 (ISBN 0-08-017788-3). Pergamon.
Preston, Thomas. Cambises: A Critical Edition. Johnson, Robert C., ed. (Salzburg Studies in English Literature, Elizabethan & Renaissance Studies Ser.: No. 23). 193p. (Orig.). 1975. pap. text ed. 25.00x (ISBN 0-391-01502-8). Humanities.
Preston, Thomas A. Coronary Artery Surgery: A Critical Review. LC 76-51977. 1977. 15.50 (ISBN 0-89004-165-2). Raven.
Preston, Valerie. Handbook for Modern Educational Dance. rev. ed. (Movement & Creative Drama Ser.). 1980. pap. 10.95 (ISBN 0-8238-0247-7). Plays.
Preston, Wheeler. American Biographies. LC 73-10407. x, 1147p. 1975. Repr. of 1940 ed. 48.00 (ISBN 0-8103-4054-2). Gale.
Preston, William L. Vanishing Landscapes: Land & Life in the Tulare Lake Basin. (Illus.). 290p. 1981. 15.95 (ISBN 0-520-04053-8). U of Cal Pr.
Preston-Mafham, Ken. Practical Wildlife Photography. LC 80-40792. (Practical Photography Ser.). (Illus.). 144p. 1981. 19.95 (ISBN 0-240-51081-X). Focal Pr.
Prestwich, Michael, ed. Documents Illustrating the Crisis of 1297-98 in England. (Royal Historical Society: Camden Society Fourth Ser.: Vol. 24). 216p. 1980. 20.00x (ISBN 0-8476-3307-1). Rowman.
Prete, Barbara, jt. ed. see Bradford, Peter.
Prete, John Di see Di Prete, John.
Pretest Series. PreTest for Students Preparing for the National Board Examination, Pt. 1. 4th ed. LC 77-78442. (Illus.). 1977. pap. 17.50 (ISBN 0-07-079138-4). McGraw-Pretest.
Pretest Series, ed. PreTest for Students Preparing for the National Board Examination, Pt. II. 4th ed. LC 77-78442. 1978. pap. 17.50 (ISBN 0-07-079139-2). McGraw-Pretest.
--PreTest for Students Preparing for the State Board Examinations for Practical Nurse Licensure. 2nd ed. LC 78-56568. 1979. pap. 13.95 (ISBN 0-07-079132-5). McGraw-Pretest.
--PreTest for Students Preparing for the State Board Examinations for Registered Nurse Licensure. 4th ed. LC 78-51705. 1979. pap. 13.95 (ISBN 0-07-079130-9). McGraw-Pretest.
PreTest Service, Inc. Internal Medicine: PreTest Self-Assessment & Review. (Illus.). 1977. pap. text ed. 25.00 o.p. (ISBN 0-07-050798-8, HP). McGraw.
Pretner, Lee. Pro Sports Trivia. LC 74-34548. (Illus.). 160p. (gr. 4 up). 1975. 5.88 o.p. (ISBN 0-531-01091-0). Watts.
Preto-Rodas, Richard A., jt. ed. see Hower, Alfred.
Pretty. Weapon Systems Nineteen Eighty to Nineteen Eighty-One. 1980. 135.00 (ISBN 0-531-03935-8). Watts.
--Weapon Systems Nineteen Seventy-Nine to Nineteen Eighty. 1980. 84.50 (ISBN 0-531-03299-X). Watts.
Pretty, Ronald T., ed. Jane's Weapon Systems. 1976. 72.50 o.p. (ISBN 0-531-03267-1). Watts.
Preu, James. Florida Educators. LC 56-63392. (Florida State Univ. Studies). 1959. 4.50 (ISBN 0-8130-0494-2). U Presses Fla.
Preus, Herman A. A Theology to Live By. 1977. pap. 7.95 (ISBN 0-570-03739-5, 12-2643). Concordia.
Preus, James S. Carlstadts Ordinaciones & Luther's Liberty. (Harvard Theological Review & Studies). 1974. pap. 6.00 (ISBN 0-89130-223-9, 020027). Scholars Pr Ca.
Preus, Robert D. Theology of Post-Reformation Lutheranism: A Study of Theological Prolegomena. LC 70-121877. 1970. 15.50 (ISBN 0-570-03211-3, 15-2110). Concordia.
--Theology of Post-Reformation Lutheranism, Vol. 2. 350p. 1972. 15.50 (ISBN 0-570-03226-1, 15-2123). Concordia.
Preuss, Angela & Stevens, Sherrill. Angela Preuss: Ten Million Dollar Lady. 125p. 1980. 10.95 (ISBN 0-931804-07-8). Skipworth Pr.
Preuss, Arthur, ed. Dictionary of Secret & Other Societies. LC 66-21186. 1966. Repr. of 1924 ed. 26.00 (ISBN 0-8103-3083-0). Gale.
Preuss, Paul. Re-Entry. (Orig.). 1981. pap. 2.25 (ISBN 0-553-14834-6). Bantam.
Preuss, Peter, tr. see Nietzsche, Friedrich.
Preussler, Otfried. The Satanic Mill. Bell, Anthea, tr. from Ger. 240p. (gr. 7 up). 1973. 7.95g (ISBN 0-02-775170-8). Macmillan.
Prevention Magazine. The Complete Book of Vitamins. 1977. 16.95 (ISBN 0-87857-176-0). Rodale Pr Inc.
Prevert, Jacques. Paroles. Ferlinghetti, Lawrence, tr. LC 56-8586. (Pocket Poet Ser.: No. 9). 1958. pap. 2.50 (ISBN 0-87286-042-6, PP9). City Lights.
Previn, Dory. Midnight Baby: An Autobiography. 1976. 8.95 o.s.i. (ISBN 0-02-599000-4). Macmillan.
Previte-Orton, C. W. Outlines of Medieval History. 2nd ed. LC 64-25837. 1916. 14.00x (ISBN 0-8196-0147-0). Biblo.
--The Shorter Cambridge Medieval History, 2 vols. Incl. Vol. 1. The Later Roman Empire to the Twelfth Century. (Illus.). 644p (ISBN 0-521-20962-5). pap. (ISBN 0-521-09976-5); Vol. 2. The Twelfth Century to the Renaissance. (Illus.). 558p. pap. (ISBN 0-521-09977-3). (Medieval History Ser). 1975. 53.95 ea.; pap. 15.95 ea. Cambridge U Pr.
Previte-Orton, C. W., ed. The Shorter Cambridge Medieval History, 2 vols. Set. 89.50 (ISBN 0-521-05993-3); Set. pap. 27.95 (ISBN 0-521-08758-9). Cambridge U Pr.
Previts, Gary J. & Merino, Barabara D. A History of Accounting in America: An Historical Interpretation of the Cultural Significance of Accounting. LC 79-616. 1979. 24.50 (ISBN 0-471-05172-1, Pub by Ronald Pr). Wiley.
Previts, Gary J., ed. see Edwards, James D.
Prewett, Omer, jt. ed. see Huff, Douglas.
Prewitt, Cheryl & Slattery, Kathryn S. The Cheryl Prewitt Story. LC 80-2896. (Illus.). 216p. 1981. 11.95 (ISBN 0-385-17021-1, Galilee). Doubleday.
Prewitt, Kenneth, jt. ed. see Knowles, Louis.
Prez, Caroline S. De see De Prez, Caroline S. & De Prez, Richard J.
Prez, Richard J. De see De Prez, Caroline S. & De Prez, Richard J.
Prezbindowski, Kathleen. A Guide to Learning Anatomy & Physiology. (Illus.). 1980. pap. text ed. 9.95 (ISBN 0-8016-4040-7). Mosby.

Preziosi, Donald. Semiotics of the Built Environment: An Introduction to Architectonic Analysis. LC 78-20404. (Advances in Semiotics Ser.). (Illus.). 128p. 1979. 15.00x (ISBN 0-253-17638-7). Ind U Pr.

Pribram, Karl H., jt. ed. see Isaacson, Robert L.

Price, Alfred. Aircraft Versus Submarine. LC 74-75792. 1973. 15.50 (ISBN 0-87021-802-6). Naval Inst Pr.

--Focke-Wulf 190 at War. encore ed. LC 77-78704. (Illus.). 1978. 4.95 o.p. (ISBN 0-684-16364-0, ScribT). Scribner.

--Luftwaffe Handbook. (Encore Edition). (Illus.). 1977. 3.95 (ISBN 0-684-16691-7, ScribT). Scribner.

Price, Anthony. The Forty-Four Vintage. LC 77-92229. 1978. 7.95 o.p. (ISBN 0-385-14028-2). Doubleday.

Price, Archibald G. The Western Invasions of the Pacific & Its Continents: A Study of Moving Frontiers & Changing Landscapes, 1513-1958. LC 80-14037. (Illus.). xi, 236p. 1980. Repr. of 1963 ed. lib. bdg. 20.75x (ISBN 0-313-22433-1, PRWE). Greenwood.

Price, Arthur, ed. see Pizzuto, Joseph.

Price, Barbara A. & Price, Theodore. Federico Fellini: An Annotated International Bibliography. LC 77-26310. 1978. 13.50 (ISBN 0-8108-1104-9). Scarecrow.

Price, Barbara R. Police Professionalism. LC 76-58246. 1977. 14.95 (ISBN 0-669-01341-2). Lexington Bks.

Price, Barbara R. & Baunach, Phyllis J., eds. Criminal Justice Research: New Models & Findings. LC 80-20145. (Illus.). 143p. 1980. 12.95 (ISBN 0-8039-1509-8); pap. 6.50 (ISBN 0-8039-1510-1). Sage.

Price, Bertram, jt. auth. see Chatterjee, Samprit.

Price, Bill, jt. auth. see Lemons, Wayne.

Price, Billy, jt. auth. see Lemons, Wayne.

Price, Billy L. & Price, James. Homeowner's Guide to Saving Energy. LC 76-24785. (Illus.). 1976. pap. 5.95 (ISBN 0-8306-5904-8, 904). TAB Bks.

Price, Blanche A; see Bottiglia, William F.

Price, Brian. Pictorial World Atlas. LC 79-50872. (Illus.). 224p. 1980. 29.95 (ISBN 0-528-83105-4). Rand.

Price, Brian, et al. Rounding Third: Professional Baseball in Washington. (Commentaries on the National Pastime Ser.). (Illus., Orig.). 1979. pap. 1.25 o.s.i. (ISBN 0-89133-083-6). Preservation Pr.

Price, Brick. Audi Service-Repair Handbook: 100 LS Series, 1970-1977. 2nd ed. Robinson, Jeff, ed. (Illus.). 1976. pap. 10.95 (ISBN 0-89287-096-6, A131). Clymer Pubns.

--BSA Service-Repair Handbook: All 500 & 650cc Unit Construction Twins. Jorgensen, Eric, ed. (Illus.). 1977. pap. 9.95 (ISBN 0-89287-182-2, M302). Clymer Pubns.

--Hodaka Service - Repair Handbook: 90-125cc Singles, 1964-1975. Robinson, Jeff, ed. (Illus.). 168p. 1975. pap. text ed. 9.95 (ISBN 0-89287-005-2, M307). Clymer Pubns.

--Husqvarna Service - Repair Handbook: 125-450cc Singles, 1966-1975. Robinson, Jeff, ed. (Illus.). 168p. 1976. pap. text ed. 9.95 (ISBN 0-89287-014-1, M423). Clymer Pubns.

--Mustang Service - Repair Handbook: All Models, 1964-1973. Robinson, Jeff, ed. (Illus.). 232p. 1976. pap. text ed. 10.95 (ISBN 0-89287-088-5, A167). Clymer Pubns.

--Ossa Service - Repair Handbook: 125-250cc Singles, 1971-1978. 2nd ed. Robinson, Jeff, ed. (Illus.). 160p. 1976. pap. text ed. 9.95 (ISBN 0-89287-092-3, M362). Clymer Pubns.

--Sailboat Auxiliary Engine Maintenance: Atomic, Chrysler, Ford, Perkins, Pisces, Volvo-Penta, Westerbeke, Yanmar. Robinson, Jeff, ed. (Illus.). 144p. 1975. pap. text ed. 9.00 o.p. (ISBN 0-89287-079-6). Clymer Pubns.

--Triumph Service-Repair Handbook: TR2-TR6 & GT6, 1954-1976. Robinson, Jeff, ed. (Illus.). 1976. pap. text ed. 10.95 (ISBN 0-89287-103-2, A210). Clymer Pubns.

Price, Brynmor F. & Nida, Eugene A. A Translators Handbook on the Book of Jonah. (Helps for Translators Ser.). 1978. soft cover 2.80 (ISBN 0-8267-0199-X, 08552). United Bible.

Price, Carl E. Worship Without Walls. LC 80-51409. (Orig.). 1980. pap. 1.00x (ISBN 0-8358-0404-6). Upper Room.

Price, Cecil, ed. see Sheridan, Richard B.

Price, Charles M., jt. auth. see Bell, Charles G.

Price, Charles P. Introducing the Book of Common Prayer. LC 77-6125. 1977. pap. 1.75 (ISBN 0-8164-2171-4). Crossroad NY.

Price, Christine. Happy Days. LC 77-95577. (Illus.). (gr. 3-6). 2.00 (ISBN 0-935738-02-9, 5004). US Comm UNICEF.

--Made in West Africa. LC 74-4202. 160p. (gr. 5 up). 1975. PLB 9.95 o.p. (ISBN 0-525-34400-4). Dutton.

Price, Christine, jt. auth. see Keely, H. H.

Price, Christopher P. & Spencer, Kevin, eds. Centrifugal Analysers in Clinical Chemistry. 520p. 1980. 59.95 (ISBN 0-03-058854-5). Praeger.

Price, D. C. Patrons & Musicians of the English Renaissance. LC 80-40054. (Cambridge Studies in Music). (Illus.). 250p. Date not set. 55.00 (ISBN 0-521-22806-9). Cambridge U Pr.

Price, David. Magic: A Pictorial History of Conjuring in the Theater. LC 78-75326. (Illus.). Date not set. cancelled (ISBN 0-498-02359-1). A S Barnes. Postponed.

Price, Derek J. Little Science, Big Science. LC 63-10524. (George B. Pegram Lecture Ser). (Illus.). 1963. pap. 5.00x (ISBN 0-231-08562-1). Columbia U Pr.

Price, Derek J. De Solla see Price, Derek J.

Price, Douglas B. & Twombly, Neil J. Georgetown University Papers on Languages & Linguistics, No. 10. Osborne, Mary C., et al, trs. (Illus.). 1978. pap. 5.95 o.p. (ISBN 0-87840-065-6). Georgetown U Pr.

--Phantom Limb Phenomenon - A Medical, Folkloric, & Historical Study: Texts & Translations of 10th to 20th Century Miracle Accounts. Osborne, Mary C, et al, trs. 526p. 1979. pap. text ed. 6.95 (ISBN 0-87840-168-7). Georgetown U Pr.

Price, E. M., tr. see Bordewijk, Ferdinand.

Price, Edward O. & Stokes, Allen W. Animal Behavior in Laboratory & Field. 2nd ed. (Illus.). 1975. pap. text ed. 9.95x (ISBN 0-7167-0762-4); tchr's manual avail. W H Freeman.

Price, Elizabeth C. & Cheremisinoff, Paul N. Biogas Production & Utilization. LC 79-56113. (Illus.). 1981. 29.95 (ISBN 0-250-40334-X). Ann Arbor Science.

Price, Eugenia. Beloved Invader. LC 65-20589. 1965. 10.95 (ISBN 0-397-10013-2). Lippincott.

--Burden Is Light. rev. ed. 1975. pap. 1.50 (ISBN 0-89129-005-2). Jove Pubns.

--Diary of a Novel: The Story of Writing Margaret's Story. LC 80-7869. 160p. 1980. 9.95 (ISBN 0-690-01937-8). Lippincott & Crowell.

--Don Juan McQueen. LC 74-8941. 1974. 8.95 o.s.i. (ISBN 0-397-01057-5). Lippincott.

--God Speaks to Women Today. pap. 2.95 (ISBN 0-310-31302-3). Zondervan.

--Just As I Am. 1968. 4.95 o.p. (ISBN 0-397-10060-4, Holman). Lippincott.

--Just As I Am. (Orig.). 1976. pap. 1.75 (ISBN 0-89129-187-3). Jove Pubns.

--Learning to Live. (Orig.). pap. 1.95 (ISBN 0-89129-193-8). Jove Pubns.

--Lighthouse. LC 79-163223. 1971. 8.95 o.s.i. (ISBN 0-685-00291-8). Lippincott.

--Make Love Your Aim. 192p. 1972. pap. 2.95 (ISBN 0-310-31312-0). Zondervan.

--Maria. LC 77-1707. 1977. 10.00 o.s.i. (ISBN 0-397-01058-3). Lippincott.

--New Moon Rising. LC 69-14496. 1969. 10.00 o.s.i. (ISBN 0-397-10079-5). Lippincott.

--No Pat Answers. pap. 2.95 (ISBN 0-310-31332-5); study guide 0.75 (ISBN 0-310-31333-3). Zondervan.

--Woman to Woman. pap. 2.95 (ISBN 0-310-31392-9). Zondervan.

--Woman's Choice. pap. 2.95 (ISBN 0-310-31382-1). Zondervan.

Price, F. W. Basic Molecular Biology. 497p. 1979. 25.95 (ISBN 0-471-69729-X). Wiley.

Price, Flo. Quick & Easy Casseroles. 1976. pap. 1.50 (ISBN 0-89129-158-X). Jove Pubns.

Price, Frank W., tr. see Sun Yat-sen.

Price, Glanville & Wells, David A., eds. The Year's Work in Modern Language Studies: 1978, Vol. 40. LC 31-32540. 1198p. 1979. 80.00x (ISBN 0-900547-70-7); Vols. 1-39. write for info. Intl Pubns Serv.

Price, Glenn W. Origins of the War with Mexico: The Polk-Stockton Intrigue. 1967. pap. 5.95x (ISBN 0-292-76003-5). U of Tex Pr.

Price, H., tr. see Weil, Simone.

Price, H. H. Essays in the Philosophy of Religion: Based on the Sarum Lectures, 1971. 130p. 1972. 11.95x (ISBN 0-19-824376-6). Oxford U Pr.

Price, J., jt. auth. see Flanders, H.

Price, J. H. The Political Institutions of West Africa. 2nd ed. (Illus.). 288p. 1975. pap. text ed. 5.75x (ISBN 0-09-123111-6, Hutchinson U Lib). Humanities.

Price, J. R. & Putney, Valerie F. In This Corner. (Orig.). 1981. pap. 2.95 o.s.i. (ISBN 0-440-13970-8). Dell.

Price, Jacob M. Capital & Credit in British Overseas Trade: The View from the Chesapeake 1770-1776. LC 80-13815. 1980. text ed. 18.50x (ISBN 0-674-09480-8). Harvard U Pr.

Price, James, jt. auth. see Price, Billy L.

Price, James H., jt. auth. see Steen, Edwin B.

Price, James L. & Mueller, Charles W. Professional Turnover: The Case of Nurses. (Health Systems Management Ser.). 218p. 1980. write for info. (ISBN 0-89335-124-5). Spectrum Pub.

Price, James L., jt. auth. see Hall, Thor.

Price, Jane. How to Have a Child & Keep Your Job. LC 79-16316. 1979. 10.95 (ISBN 0-312-39592-2). St Martin.

--You're Not Too Old to Have a Baby. 147p. 1977. 7.95 (ISBN 0-374-29606-5). FS&G.

Price, Joe X. Redd Foxx, B. S. (Before Sanford) LC 77-75839. (Illus.). 1979. 8.95 o.p. (ISBN 0-8092-7856-1). Contemp Bks.

Price, John F. Lie Groups & Compact Groups. LC 76-14034. (London Mathematical Society Lecture Notes Ser.: No. 25). 1977. pap. 16.95x (ISBN 0-521-21340-1). Cambridge U Pr.

Price, John H., jt. auth. see Lovins, Amory B.

Price, John V. David Hume. LC 68-24287. (English Authors Ser.: No. 77). 1969. lib. bdg. 10.95 (ISBN 0-8057-1280-1). Twayne.

Price, Jonathan. Thirty Days to More Powerful Writing. 192p. (Orig.). 1981. pap. 5.95 (ISBN 0-449-90047-9, Columbine). Fawcett.

Price, Jones D., jt. auth. see Cavalla, J. F.

Price, Justin, jt. auth. see Flanders, Harley.

Price, Justin J., jt. auth. see Flanders, H.

Price, Justin J., jt. auth. see Flanders, Harley.

Price, Karl F. & Walker, James W. Issues in Business: An Introduction to American Enterprise. 3rd ed. LC 76-30750. 1977. text ed. 20.95x (ISBN 0-471-69734-6); instructors manual avail. (ISBN 0-471-02613-1). Wiley.

Price, Kenneth P., jt. ed. see Gatchel, Robert J.

Price, L. W. Periglacial Environment, Permafrost & Man. LC 79-188229. (CCG Resource Papers Ser.: No. 14). (Illus.). 1972. pap. text ed. 4.00 (ISBN 0-89291-061-5). Assn Am Geographers.

Price, Larry W. Mountains & the Man: A Study of Process & Environment. (Illus.). 496p. 1981. 22.50 (ISBN 0-520-03263-2). U of Cal Pr.

Price, Lew P. Aquarian Anastasis. LC 65-9503. 1975. pap. 5.95 (ISBN 0-917578-01-5). Eternal Ent.

--Astrology-the Cosmic Stradivarius. LC 51-6501. 1974. pap. 12.00 (ISBN 0-685-46895-X). Eternal Ent.

Price, Marion T. Witch Who Saved Halloween. 1980. pap. 1.75 (ISBN 0-380-00097-0, 51417, Camelot). Avon.

Price, Martin. Swift's Rhetorical Art: A Study in Structure & Meaning. LC 73-7764. (Arcturus Books Paperbacks). 125p. 1973. pap. 3.95 (ISBN 0-8093-0646-8). S Ill U Pr.

--To the Palace of Wisdom: Studies in Order & Energy from Dryden to Blake. LC 63-10846. 1970. Repr. of 1964 ed. 7.00x o.p. (ISBN 0-8093-0474-0). S Ill U Pr.

Price, Martin, ed. see Swift, Jonathan.

Price, Martin J., ed. Coins: An Illustrated Survey, 650 B.C. to the Present Day. (Illus.). 320p. 1980. slipcased 50.00 (ISBN 0-416-00691-4). Methuen Inc.

Price, Mary R., jt. auth. see Lindsay, Donald.

Price, Michael H. & Turner, George E. Human Monsters in the Cinema. LC 78-75327. (Illus.). Date not set. cancelled 17.50 (ISBN 0-498-02360-5). A S Barnes. Postponed.

Price, Monroe E. Law & the American Indian: Readings, Notes & Cases. (Contemporary Legal Education Ser.). 1973. 22.00 (ISBN 0-672-81770-5, Bobbs-Merrill Law). Michie.

Price, Morgan P. My Reminiscences of the Russian Revolution. LC 79-2922. (Illus.). 402p. 1981. Repr. of 1921 ed. 27.50 (ISBN 0-8305-0091-X). Hyperion Conn.

Price, N. J. Fault & Joint Development in Brittle & Semi-Brittle Rock. 1966. 23.00 (ISBN 0-08-011275-7); pap. 10.75 (ISBN 0-08-011274-9). Pergamon.

Price, Nancy W., jt. auth. see Van der Meulen, Jan.

Price, Nelson L. Only the Beginning. LC 79-55662. (gr. 10 up). 1980. 4.95 (ISBN 0-8054-5331-8). Broadman.

Price, Nicholas & Dwek, Raymond. Principles & Problems in Physical Chemistry for Biochemists. 2nd ed. (Illus.). 1980. 23.00x (ISBN 0-19-855511-3); pap. 9.95x (ISBN 0-19-855512-1). Oxford U Pr.

Price, Pamela V. Entertaining with Wine. 1976. 15.95x (ISBN 0-7198-2613-6). Intl Ideas.

Price, Peter W. Insect Ecology. LC 75-12720. 514p. 1975. 23.50 (ISBN 0-471-69721-4, Pub. by Wiley-Interscience). Wiley.

Price, R. Masters, Unions & Men. LC 79-21229. (Illus.). 1980. 39.95 (ISBN 0-521-22882-4). Cambridge U Pr.

Price, R. F. Reference Book of English Words & Phrases for Foreign Science Students. 1976. text ed. 18.75 (ISBN 0-08-011750-3); pap. text ed. 6.50 (ISBN 0-08-020381-7). Pergamon.

Price, R. J. Glacial & Fluvioglacial Landforms. (Geomorphology Texts: Vol. 5). (Illus.). 242p. 1973. pap. text ed. 16.95 (ISBN 0-582-48435-9). Longman.

Price, R. J. see Bowen, D. Q.

Price, Reynolds. Permanent Errors. LC 70-124974. 1970. 6.50 o.p. (ISBN 0-689-10357-3). Atheneum.

--Permanent Errors. LC 70-124974. 1980. pap. 4.95 (ISBN 0-689-70599-9, 258). Atheneum.

--The Source of Light. LC 80-69650. 1981. 12.95 (ISBN 0-689-11136-3). Atheneum.

Price, Richard. A Free Discussion of the Doctrine of Materialism and Philosophical Necessity, 1778. Wellek, Rene, ed. LC 75-11247. (British Philosophers & Theologians of the 17th & 18th Centuries Ser.). 1978. lib. bdg. 42.00 (ISBN 0-8240-1798-6). Garland Pub.

--The Spirit of the Alberta Indian Treaties. 202p. 1979. pap. text ed. 8.95x (ISBN 0-920380-23-9, Pub. by Inst Res Pub Canada). Renouf.

--Two Tracts on Civil Liberties. LC 74-169641. (Era of the American Revolution Ser.). 1972. Repr. lib. bdg. 35.00 (ISBN 0-306-70233-9). Da Capo.

Price, Richard, jt. auth. see Price, Sally.

Price, Richard H., et al, eds. Prevention in Mental Health: Research, Policy, & Practice. LC 80-14676. (Sage Annual Reviews of Community Mental Health: Vol. 1). (Illus.). 320p. 1980. 20.00x (ISBN 0-8039-1468-7); pap. 9.95x (ISBN 0-8039-1469-5). Sage.

Price, Robert M. Society & Bureaucracy in Contemporary Ghana. LC 74-81439. 275p. 1975. 21.50x (ISBN 0-520-02811-2). U of Cal Pr.

Price, Roger. The Economic Modernization of France, 1730-1880. LC 75-14447. 1975. 24.95 (ISBN 0-470-69722-9). Halsted Pr.

--The French Second Republic: A Social History. 1972. 32.00 (ISBN 0-7134-1117-1, Pub. by Batsford England). David & Charles.

Price, Roger & Sloan, Larry. World's Worst California Jokes. 1980. 1.50 o.p. (ISBN 0-8431-0691-3). Price Stern.

Price, Roger & Stern, Leonard. Mad Libs, No. 11. 48p. 1980. pap. 1.75 (ISBN 0-8431-0248-9). Price Stern.

--Mad Libs, No. 12. 48p. 1980. pap. 1.75 (ISBN 0-8431-0249-7). Price Stern.

--Mad Libs No. 2. 1959. pap. 1.75 (ISBN 0-8431-0056-7). Price Stern.

Price, Ronald R., et al, eds. Single Photon Emission Computed Tomography & Other Selected Computer Topics. LC 80-52817. (Illus.). 244p. 1980. pap. 29.50 (ISBN 0-932004-06-7). Soc Nuclear Med.

Price, S. G. Introducing the Electronic Office. (Illus.). 161p. 1979. pap. 22.50x (ISBN 0-85012-204-X). Intl Pubns Serv.

Price, Sally & Price, Richard. Afro-American Arts of the Suriname Rain Forest. (Illus.). 240p. 1981. 37.50 (ISBN 0-520-04345-6, CAL 516); pap. 14.95 (ISBN 0-520-04412-6). U of Cal Pr.

Price, Seymour G. Air Conditioning for Building Engineers & Managers. 1970. 25.00 (ISBN 0-8311-3001-6). Indus Pr.

Price, Steve. Wild Places of the South. LC 79-26290. (Illus.). 200p. 1980. lib. bdg. 11.25 o.p. (ISBN 0-914788-22-1). East Woods.

Price, Susan. Christopher Uptake. 208p. (gr. 5-12). 1981. 14.95 (ISBN 0-571-11660-4, Pub. by Faber & Faber). Merrimack Bk Serv.

--Home from Home. (gr. 6-8). 1978. 8.95 (ISBN 0-571-11022-3, Pub. by Faber & Faber). Merrimack Bk Serv.

Price, Theodora H. Kourotrophos: Cults & Representations of the Greek Nursing Dieties. 1978. text ed. 54.00x (ISBN 90-04052-51-8). Humanities.

Price, Theodore, jt. auth. see Price, Barbara A.

Price, Thomas R., ed. see Princeton Conference on Cerebrovascular Disease, 11th., Mar. 1978.

Price, Vladimir, ed. see Hume, David.

Price, W. C., ed. see International Organization of Citrus Virologists, 5th Conference.

Price, W. G., jt. auth. see Bishop, R. E.

Price, W. R., ed. see Maupassant, Guy De.

Price, W. V., jt. auth. see Van Slyke, L. L.

Price Waterhouse & Co., compiled by. Abingdon Clergy Income Tax Guide, 1979. 7th ed. 1978. pap. 2.95 o.p. (ISBN 0-687-00390-3). Abingdon.

Price Waterhouse & Co., ed. Abingdon Clergy Income Tax Guide, 1981 Edition for 1980 Returns. (Orig.). 1980. pap. 2.95 (ISBN 0-687-00394-6). Abingdon.

Price Waterhouse & Co., rev. by. Abingdon Clergy Income Tax Guide, 1980. (Orig.). 1979. pap. 2.95 o.p. (ISBN 0-687-00392-X). Abingdon.

Price, Wendel S., jt. ed. see David, Georges.

Price, Willard. Amazon Adventure. (gr. 6-9). 1949. 7.95 o.p. (ISBN 0-381-99732-4, A02200, JD-J). John Day.

--Gorilla Adventure. (Illus.). 222p. (gr. 3-6). 1980. 8.95 (ISBN 0-224-61636-6, Pub. by Chatto Bodley Jonathan). Merrimack Bk Serv.

Price, William S., Jr., jt. ed. see Parker, Mattie E.

Price, Wilson T. & Olson, Jack L. Elements of Cobol Programming. LC 77-187112. 1977. pap. text ed. 14.50 (ISBN 0-03-018371-5). Dryden Pr.

Price-Jones, D. & Solomon, M. E., eds. Biology in Pest & Disease Control: Symposium of the British Ecological Society, 13th Oxford, 4-7 Jan. 72. LC 73-12466. (British Ecological Society Symposia Ser.). 1974. 34.95 (ISBN 0-470-69727-X). Halsted Pr.

Price-Williams, Douglass R. Explorations in Cross-Cultural Psychology. LC 74-28740. (Publications in Anthropology Ser.). 144p. 1975. 7.50x (ISBN 0-88316-515-5). Chandler & Sharp.

Prichard, Allyn & Taylor, Jean. Accelerating Learning: The Use of Suggestion in the Classroom. 176p. 1980. pap. text ed. 7.00 (ISBN 0-87879-249-X). Acad Therapy.

Prichard, Elizabeth & Collard, Jean, eds. Social Work with the Dying Patient & the Family. LC 77-8679. 1977. 22.50x (ISBN 0-231-04021-0). Columbia U Pr.

Prichard, Elizabeth, et al, eds. Social Work with the Dying Patient & the Family. Lefkowitz, Irene, et al, trs. (Foundation of Thanatology Ser.). (Illus.). 1980. pap. 12.50x (ISBN 0-231-08371-8). Columbia U Pr.

Prichard, Elizabeth R., et al, eds. Home Health Care & the Quality of Life. (Foundation of Thanatology Ser.). 1979. 20.00x (ISBN 0-231-04258-2). Columbia U Pr.

Prichard, H. A. Kant's Theory of Knowledge. Beck, Lewis W., ed. LC 75-32042. (The Philosophy of Immanuel Kant Ser.: Vol. 5). 1977. Repr. of 1909 ed. lib. bdg. 26.00 (ISBN 0-8240-2329-3). Garland Pub.

Prichard, Hesketh. Where Black Rules White: A Journey Across & About Hayti. 298p. 1971. Repr. of 1900 ed. 24.00x (ISBN 0-7165-1819-8, Pub. by Irish Academic Pr Ireland). Biblio Dist.

Prichard, James. On the Different Forms of Insanity in Relation to Jurisprudence. Bd. with Suggestions for the Future Provision of Criminal Lunatics. Hood, W. C; Statistics of Insanity. Hood, W. C. (Contributions to the History of Psychology Ser., Vol. III, Pt. E: Insanity & Jurisprudence). 1980. Repr. of 1842 ed. 30.00 (ISBN 0-89093-328-6). U Pubns Amer.

Prichard, Katharine S. The Wild Oats of Han. (Illus.). 160p. (gr. 4-7). 1973. 4.95g o.s.i. (ISBN 0-02-775200-3). Macmillan.

Prick, J. J. Infantile Autistic Behaviour & Experience: A New Clinical Picture. (Modern Approaches to the Diagnosis & Instruction of Multi-Handicapped Children: Vol. 1). 102p. 1971. text ed. 21.50 (ISBN 90-237-4101-3, Pub. by Swets Pub Serv Holland). Swets North Am.

Prickett, Stephen. Romanticism and Religion. LC 75-2254. 320p. 1976. 44.50 (ISBN 0-521-21072-0). Cambridge U Pr.

Priddin, Deirdre. Art of the Dance in French Literature from Theophile Gautier to Paul Valery. 1952. text ed. 4.00x (ISBN 0-391-01947-3). Humanities.

Priddy, Frances. Ghosts of Lee House. LC 68-27813. (gr. 7-8). 1968. 5.95 o.p. (ISBN 0-385-08952-X). Doubleday.

Pride, William M. & Ferrell, O. C. Marketing: Basic Concepts & Decisions. LC 76-10892. (Illus.). 1976. text ed. 17.50 o.p. (ISBN 0-395-24529-X); inst. manual 4.00 o.p. (ISBN 0-395-24530-3); study guide 6.95 o.p. (ISBN 0-395-24756-X). HM.

Pride, William M. & Perrell, O. C. Marketing: Basic Concepts & Decisions. 2nd ed. LC 79-88040. 1980. text ed. 18.50 (ISBN 0-395-28059-1); study guide pap. 7.25 (ISBN 0-395-28163-6); instr's manual 3.25 (ISBN 0-395-28161-X). HM.

Pride, William M., jt. auth. see Robicheaux, Robert A.

Prideaux, G. Experimental Linguistics: Integration of Theories & Applications. (Story-Scientia Linguistics Ser.: No. 3). 1980. text ed. 57.75x (ISBN 90-6439-164-5). Humanities.

Prideaux, J. D. Lynton & Barnstable Railway Album. 1974. 17.95 (ISBN 0-7153-6809-5). David & Charles.

--The Welsh Narrow Gauge Railway. (Illus.). 1976. 11.95 (ISBN 0-7153-7184-3). David & Charles.

Prideaux, James. The Orphans: A Play in Two Acts. 1980. pap. 2.50 (ISBN 0-686-68850-3). Dramatists Play.

Prideaux, Tom. Cro-Magnon Man. LC 73-79435. (Emergence of Man Ser). (Illus.). (gr. 6 up). 1973. lib. bdg. 11.56 o.p. (ISBN 0-8094-1272-1, Pub. by Time-Life). Silver.

--Cro-Magnon Man. (Emergence of Man Ser.). (Illus.). 1973. 9.95 (ISBN 0-8094-1271-3); lib. bdg. avail. (ISBN 0-685-41617-8). Time-Life.

--World of Delacroix. (Library of Art). (Illus.). 1966. 15.95 (ISBN 0-8094-0233-5). Time-Life.

--World of Delacroix. LC 66-21130. (Library of Art Ser.). (Illus.). (gr. 6 up). 1966. 12.96 (ISBN 0-8094-0262-9, Pub. by Time-Life). Silver.

--World of Whistler. (Time-Life Library of Art). (Illus.). (gr. 5 up). 1970. 15.95 (ISBN 0-8094-0256-4). Time-Life.

--World of Whistler. LC 70-116437. (Library of Art Ser.). (Illus.). (gr. 6 up). 1970. 12.96 (ISBN 0-8094-0285-8, Pub. by Time-Life). Silver.

Prider, Rex T. Mining in Western Australia. 328p. 1980. 22.50x (ISBN 0-85564-153-3, Pub. by U of West Australia Pr Australia). Intl Schol Bk Serv.

Pridham, G. J. Electronic Devices & Circuits, Vols. 1-3. LC 67-26692. Vol. 1. 1968. 22.00 (ISBN 0-08-012549-2); Vol. 2. 1969. o.p. (ISBN 0-08-013461-0); Vol. 3. 1972. 21.00 (ISBN 0-08-016626-1); Vol. 1. pap. 9.25 (ISBN 0-08-012548-4); Vol. 3. pap. 7.75 (ISBN 0-08-016755-1). Pergamon.

--Solid State Circuits. 196p. 1973. text ed. 25.00 (ISBN 0-08-016932-5); pap. text ed. 12.75 (ISBN 0-08-016933-3). Pergamon.

Pridham, Geoffrey & Pridham, Pippa. Transnational Party Co-Operation & European Integration. 304p. 1981. text ed. 34.00x (ISBN 0-04-329032-9, 2591). Allen Unwin.

Pridham, Pippa, jt. auth. see Pridham, Geoffrey.

Priebe, Duane A., tr. see Pannenberg, Wolfhart.

Priehs, T. J., ed. see Phillips, Arthur M., 3rd.

Priehs, Timothy J. Thomas Moran: The Grand Canyon Sketches. 1978. 2.95 (ISBN 0-938216-07-4). GCNHA.

Prien, Erich P., et al. Mental Health in Organizations: Personal Adjustment & Constructive Intervention. LC 78-16757. 1978. 15.95 (ISBN 0-88229-175-0). Nelson-Hall.

Prier. Basic Medical Virology. LC 66-22708. 724p. 1966. 18.50 o.p. (ISBN 0-685-54436-2, Pub. by Williams & Wilkins). Krieger.

Prier, James E., jt. ed. see Friedman, Herman.

Priest, Christopher. The Affirmation. 240p. 1981. 10.95 (ISBN 0-684-16957-6, ScribT). Scribner.

--An Infinite Summer. 1981. pap. 2.75 (ISBN 0-440-14067-6). Dell.

--Inverted World. 256p. 1975. pap. 1.25 o.p. (ISBN 0-445-00309-X). Popular Lib.

Priest, Joseph. Problems of Our Physical Environment: Energy - Transportation - Pollution. LC 72-9317. 1973. text ed. 16.95 (ISBN 0-201-05972-X). A-W.

Priest, Loring B. Uncle Sam's Stepchildren: The Reformation of United States Indian Policy, 1865-1887. LC 75-5983. x, 310p. 1975. pap. 3.95 (ISBN 0-8032-5818-6, BB 601, Bison). U of Nebr Pr.

Priest, R., ed. see Annual Conference for Psychosomatic Research, 20th, London, Nov. 15-16, 1976.

Priestley, Barbara, ed. British Qualifications. 10th ed. 1979. 40.00x (ISBN 0-85038-222-X, Pub by Kogan Pg). Nichols Pub.

Priestley, G., jt. ed. see Stephens, H. S.

Priestley, Harold E. Truly Bizarre. LC 78-68689. (Illus.). 1979. 9.95 (ISBN 0-8069-0134-9); lib. bdg. 9.29 (ISBN 0-8069-0135-7). Sterling.

Priestley, Heather. All About the Beagle. 1973. 9.95 (ISBN 0-7207-0613-0, Pub. by Michael Joseph). Merrimack Bk Serv.

Priestley, Herbert I. Tristan De Luna, Conquistador of the Old South: A Study of Spanish Imperial Strategy. (Perspectives in American History Ser.: No. 49). (Illus.). Repr. lib. bdg. 16.00x (ISBN 0-87991-375-4). Porcupine Pr.

Priestley, Joseph. Disquisitions Relating Matter & Spirit, 2 vols. in 1. Wellek, Rene, ed. Bd. with The Doctrine of Philosophical Necessity Illustrated: Being an Appendix to the Disquestions Relating to Matter & Spirit. LC 75-11248. (British Philosophers & Theologians of the 17th & 18th Centuries: Vol. 47). 1977. Repr. of 1777 ed. lib. bdg. 42.00 (ISBN 0-8240-1799-4). Garland Pub.

--An Examination of Dr. Reid's Inquiry into the Human Mind. Wellek, Rene, ed. LC 75-11249. (British Philosophers & Theologians of the 17th & 18th Centuries Ser.). 1978. Repr. of 1774 ed. lib. bdg. 42.00 (ISBN 0-8240-1800-1). Garland Pub.

--Historical Account of the Navigable Rivers, Canals, & Railways Throughout Great Britain. LC 67-19729. (Illus.). Repr. of 1831 ed. 32.50x (ISBN 0-678-05081-3). Kelley.

Priestley, Margaret. West African Trade & Coast Society: A Family Study. (West African History Ser.). 1969. 9.50x o.p. (ISBN 0-19-215638-1). Oxford U Pr.

Priestley, Philip. Community of Scapegoats: The Segregation of Sex Offenders & Informers in Prisons. 150p. 1980. 24.00 (ISBN 0-08-025231-1). Pergamon.

Priestley, Philip, et al. Justice for Juveniles: The Nineteen Hundred Sixty-Nine Children & Young Persons Act-A Case for Reform? (Library of Social Work). 1978. 13.00 (ISBN 0-7100-8703-9). Routledge & Kegan.

Priestly, Lee. Giant Who Wanted Company. (A Young Reader Ser.). (Illus.). (gr. k-3). 1979. PLB 5.00 (ISBN 0-307-60207-9, Golden Pr). Western Pub.

Priestly, R. J., ed. Effects of Heating on Foodstuffs. (Illus.). 1979. 62.10x (ISBN 0-85334-797-2, Pub. by Applied Science). Burgess-Intl Ideas.

Priestman, Kathleen, ed. see Borland, D. M.

Prieto, Mariana B. Tomato Boy. LC 67-10158. (Illus.). (gr. 2-4). 1967. PLB 7.89 (ISBN 0-381-99725-1, A80800, JD-J). John Day.

Prigg, Edward. Report of the Case of Edward Prigg Against the Commonwealth of Pennsylvania. LC 70-111587. Repr. of 1842 ed. 11.75x (ISBN 0-8371-4613-5). Negro U Pr.

Prigogine, I. & Rice, Stuart A. Advances in Chemical Physics, Vol. 48. (Advances in Chemical Physics Ser.). 530p. 1981. 53.00 (ISBN 0-471-08294-5, Pub. by Wiley-Interscience). Wiley.

Prigogine, I., jt. auth. see Glansdorff, P.

Prigogine, I., ed. Advances in Chemical Physics, Vol. 26. 317p. 1974. 32.50 (ISBN 0-471-69931-4). Krieger.

--Stochastic Processes in Chemical Physics, Vol. 18. 321p. 1970. 31.50 (ISBN 0-471-69923-3). Krieger.

Prigogine, I. & Rice, Stuart A., eds. Advances in Chemical Physics, Vols. 27, 31-37, 43-44 & 46. Incl. Vol. 27. 50.50 (ISBN 0-471-69932-2); Vol. 31. 45.50 (ISBN 0-471-69933-0); Vol. 32. 35.95 (ISBN 0-471-69934-9); Vol. 33. 41.95 (ISBN 0-471-69935-7); Vol. 34. 41.50 (ISBN 0-471-69936-5); Vol. 35. 42.50 (ISBN 0-471-69937-3); Vol. 36. 52.50 (ISBN 0-471-02274-8); Vol. 37. 40.50 (ISBN 0-471-03459-2); Vol. 43. 1980. 36.50 (ISBN 0-471-05741-X); Vol. 44. 1980. 65.00 (ISBN 0-471-06025-9); Vol. 46. 432p. 1980. 42.50 (ISBN 0-471-08295-3). LC 58-9935 (Pub. by Wiley-Interscience). Wiley.

Prigogine, Ilya. From Being to Becoming: Time & Complexity in the Physical Sciences. LC 79-26774. (Illus.). 1980. text ed. 24.95x (ISBN 0-7167-1107-9); pap. text ed. 12.95x (ISBN 0-7167-1108-7). W H Freeman.

Primack, M. L. & Willis, J. F. An Economic History of the United States. 1980. 16.95. A-W.

Primack, Martin L. & Willis, James F. An Economic History of the United States. 1979. 18.95 (ISBN 0-8053-8010-8). Benjamin-Cummings.

Primack, Martin L., jt. auth. see Willis, James F.

Prime, Alfred C., ed. Arts & Crafts in Philadelphia, Maryland, & South Carolina, 1721-1785, 2 Vols. LC 79-75356. (Architecture & Decorative Art Ser). 1969. Repr. of 1929 ed. Set. lib. bdg. 45.00 (ISBN 0-306-71320-9). Da Capo.

Prime, Derek. Created to Praise. 128p. (Orig.). 1981. pap. 2.95 (ISBN 0-87784-825-4). Inter-Varsity.

Prime, Honor. Mathew's Ear. (Illus.). (ps-5). 1964. 5.95 (ISBN 0-571-06063-3, Pub. by Faber & Faber). Merrimack Bk Serv.

Prime, Joan C. Love's Way. (YA) 1978. 5.95 (ISBN 0-685-85779-4, Avalon). Bouregy.

Primeau, Ronald. Beyond "Spoon River". The Legacy of Edgar Lee Masters. 208p. 1981. text ed. 22.50x (ISBN 0-292-70731-2). U of Tex Pr.

--The Rhetoric of Television. LC 78-2492. (English & Humanities Ser.). 1978. pap. text ed. 9.95x (ISBN 0-582-28058-3). Longman.

Primeau, Ronald, ed. Influx: Essays on Literary Influence. (Literary Criticism Ser). 1977. 14.50 (ISBN 0-8046-9151-7, Natl U). Kennikat.

Primeaux, Patrick. Richard R. Niebuhr on Christ & Religion: The Four-Stage Development of His Thought. (Toronto Studies in Theology: Vol. 4). 1981. soft cover 19.95x (ISBN 0-88946-973-3). E Mellen.

Primlani, Kala. Indian Cooking, with Useful Hints on Good Housekeeping. Ramchandani, R. V., tr. from Sindhi. 166p. 1975. pap. 2.40 (ISBN 0-88253-748-2). Ind-US Inc.

Primm. St. Louis-A History. (Western Urban History Ser.). (Illus.). 1981. 16.95 (ISBN 0-87108-546-1). Pruett.

Primmer, Brian. The Berlioz Style. 1973. 16.50x (ISBN 0-19-713136-0). Oxford U Pr.

Primmer, Phyllis. Til Night Is Gone. 1980. pap. 1.95 mass mkt. (ISBN 0-310-26342-5). Zondervan.

Primrose, D. A., jt. auth. see Kekstadt, H.

Primrose, S. B. Introduction to Modern Virology. LC 74-23739. (Basic Microbiology Ser.: No. 2). 1975. pap. text ed. 10.95 o.p. (ISBN 0-470-70038-6). Halsted Pr.

Primrose, S. B. & Dimmock, N. J. Introduction to Modern Virology. 2nd ed. (Basic Microbiology Ser.: Vol. 2). 251p. 1980. pap. text ed. 19.95x (ISBN 0-470-26941-3). Halsted Pr.

Primrose, S. B., jt. auth. see Old, R. W.

Primrose, William, ed. see Menuhin, Yehudi.

Prince, Alison. The Doubting Kind. (gr. 7 up). 1977. 8.25 (ISBN 0-688-22126-2); PLB 7.92 (ISBN 0-688-32126-7). Morrow.

--The Doubting Kind. 228p. 1981. pap. 1.95 (ISBN 0-448-16499-X, Tempo). G&D.

--Willow Farm. 224p. (gr. 7 up). 1981. pap. 1.95 (ISBN 0-448-17270-4, Tempo). G&D.

Prince, Derek. The Baptism in the Holy Spirit. 1966. pap. 1.25 (ISBN 0-934920-07-9, B-19). Derek Prince.

--Burial by Baptism. 1970. pap. 0.75 o.p. (ISBN 0-934920-15-X, B-22). Derek Prince.

--Discipleship, Shepherding, Commitment. 1.50 (ISBN 0-934920-15-X, B-27). Derek Prince.

--Eternal Judgment. (Foundation Ser.: Bk. VII). 1965-66. pap. 1.50 (ISBN 0-934920-06-0, B-16). Derek Prince.

--Faith to Live by. 1977. pap. 3.50 (ISBN 0-686-12768-4, B-29). Derek Prince.

--Faith to Live By. 1977. pap. 3.50 (ISBN 0-89283-042-5). Servant.

--Foundation for Faith. (Foundation Ser.: Bk. I). 1965-66. pap. 1.75 (ISBN 0-934920-00-1, B-10). Derek Prince.

--From Jordan to Pentecost. (Foundation Ser.). pap. 1.75 (ISBN 0-934920-02-8, B-12). Derek Prince.

--The Grace of Yielding. 1977. pap. 1.50 (ISBN 0-934920-20-6, B-30). Derek Prince.

--How to Fast Successfully. 1976. pap. 1.50 (ISBN 0-934920-19-2, B-28). Derek Prince.

--Laying on of Hands. (Foundation Ser.: Bk. V). 1965-66. pap. 1.50 (ISBN 0-934920-04-4, B-14). Derek Prince.

--Praying for the Government. 1970. pap. 0.75 o.p. (ISBN 0-934920-11-7, B-20). Derek Prince.

--Purposes of Pentecost. (Foundation Ser.: Bk. IV). 1965-66. pap. 2.50 (ISBN 0-934920-03-6). Derek Prince.

--Repent & Believe. (Foundation Ser.: Bk. II). 1965-66. pap. 1.75 (ISBN 0-934920-01-X, B-11). Derek Prince.

--Resurrection of the Dead. (Foundation Ser.: Bk. VI). 1965-66. pap. 1.75 (ISBN 0-934920-05-2, B-15). Derek Prince.

--Self Study Bible Course. 1969. pap. 3.95 (ISBN 0-934920-08-7, B-90). Derek Prince.

--Three Messages for Israel. 1969. pap. 1.50 jewish ed. (ISBN 0-934920-21-4, BJ-18). Derek Prince.

--Three Messages for Israel: Jewish Edition. 64p. (Orig.). 1977. pap. 1.50 (ISBN 0-934920-21-4). Derek Prince.

Prince, Derek, jt. auth. see Prince, Lydia.

Prince, Eleanor F., illus. Basic Horsemanship-English & Western: A Complete Guide for Riders & Instructors. LC 71-144289. 384p. 1974. 12.95 (ISBN 0-385-06587-6). Doubleday.

--Basic Training for Horses--English & Western. LC 76-42383. (Illus.). 1979. 12.95 (ISBN 0-385-03244-7). Doubleday.

Prince, F. T. The Italian Element in Milton's Verse. 183p. 1980. Repr. of 1954 ed. lib. bdg. 30.00 (ISBN 0-8492-2191-9). R West.

Prince, F. T., ed. see Milton, John.

Prince, Francine. Diet for Life. 1981. pap. 4.95 (ISBN 0-346-12496-4). Cornerstone.

Prince, Hugh, jt. auth. see Kain, Roger.

Prince, J. H. How Animals Hunt. (Illus.). 1980. 8.95 (ISBN 0-525-66688-5). Elsevier-Nelson.

--How Animals Move. (Illus.). 160p. (YA) 1981. 10.95 (ISBN 0-525-66712-1). Elsevier-Nelson.

--Neville Cayley. (Illus.). 80p. 1981. 40.00x (ISBN 0-87663-355-6). Universe.

--Weather & the Animal World. 1975. 6.95 (ISBN 0-525-66416-5). Elsevier-Nelson.

Prince, John R. & Schmidt, Lewis D. Statistics & Mathematics in the Nuclear Medicine Laboratory. LC 75-39797. (Illus.). 89p. 1976. pap. text ed. 18.00 perfect bdg. (ISBN 0-89189-020-3, 45-8-007-00). Am Soc Clinical.

Prince, Judith S., jt. auth. see Miller, Theodore K.

Prince, Lydia & Prince, Derek. Appointment in Jerusalem. 1978. pap. 2.50 o.p. (ISBN 0-8499-4109-1, 4109-1, Dist. by Word Bks.). Chosen Bks Pub.

Prince, Marjorie M. The Cheese Stands Alone. LC 73-6737. (Illus.). 176p. (gr. 5 up). 1973. 7.95 (ISBN 0-395-17511-9). HM.

--The Cheese Stands Alone. (gr. 7-9). 1975. pap. 1.95 (ISBN 0-671-42449-1). Archway.

--The Cheese Stands Alone. (Illus.). (YA) (gr. 7-9). 1979. pap. 1.75 (ISBN 0-671-56042-5). PB.

Prince, Michael J. Provincial Mineral Policies: Newfoundland 1945-75. 60p. (Orig.). 1977. pap. text ed. 3.50x (ISBN 0-686-63140-4, Pub. by Ctr Resource Stud Canada). Renouf.

Prince, Thomas R. Information Systems for Management Planning & Control. 3rd ed. 1975. text ed. 20.50 (ISBN 0-256-01647-X). Irwin.

Prince Of Wales. The Old Man of Lochnagar. (gr. k up). 1980. 10.95 (ISBN 0-374-35613-0). FS&G.

Princeton Center for Infancy. The Parenting Advisor. 1977. pap. 6.95 (ISBN 0-385-14330-3, Anch). Doubleday.

--Parents' Yellow Pages. Caplan, Frank, ed. LC 76-52002. 1978. pap. 7.95 (ISBN 0-385-12410-4, Anch). Doubleday.

Princeton Conference on Cerebrovascular Disease, 11th., Mar. 1978. Proceedings. Price, Thomas R. & Nelson, Erland, eds. LC 77-84127. 1979. text ed. 30.00 (ISBN 0-89004-292-6). Raven.

Princeton Conferences on Cerebrovascular Diseases, 10th. Cerebrovascular Diseases. Scheinberg, Peritz, ed. LC 75-25125. 1976. 27.00 (ISBN 0-89004-095-8). Raven.

Prindiville, Kathleen. First Ladies. (gr. 4-6). 1964. 4.95 o.s.i. (ISBN 0-02-775150-3). Macmillan.

Pring, Julian T., ed. Oxford Dictionary of Modern Greek. Greek-English. 1965. 13.50x (ISBN 0-19-864207-5). Oxford U Pr.

Pring, Martin J. How to Forecast Interest Rates: A Guide to Profits for Consumers, Managers & Investors. 192p. 1981. 14.95 (ISBN 0-07-050865-8, P&RB). McGraw.

--International Investing Made Easy. new ed. 224p. 1980. 15.95 (ISBN 0-07-050872-0, P&RB). McGraw.

Pringle, A., jt. auth. see Burtt, E. T.

Pringle, Charles D., jt. auth. see Longenecker, Justin G.

Pringle, J. W., ed. Biology & the Human Sciences. 1972. pap. 3.50x (ISBN 0-19-857122-4). Oxford U Pr.

Pringle, Laurence. Animals & Their Niches: How Species Share Resources. (Illus.). (gr. 3-7). 1977. 6.25 (ISBN 0-688-22127-0); PLB 6.00 (ISBN 0-688-32127-5). Morrow.

--City & Suburb: Exploring an Ecosystem. LC 75-16161. (Illus.). 69p. (gr. 3-6). 1975. 9.95 (ISBN 0-02-775350-6, 77535). Macmillan.

--Cockroaches: Here, There & Everywhere. LC 79-132301. (A Let's-Read & Find-Out Science Bk). (Illus.). (gr. k-3). 1971. PLB 7.89 (ISBN 0-690-19680-6, TYC-J). T Y Crowell.

--Death Is Natural. LC 76-48923. (Illus.). 64p. (gr. 1-5). 1977. 6.95 (ISBN 0-590-07440-7, Four Winds). Schol Bk Serv.

--Ecology: Science of Survival. (Illus.). (gr. 7 up). 1971. 8.95 (ISBN 0-02-775230-5). Macmillan.

--Energy: Power for People. (Science for Survival Ser.). (Illus.). 128p. (gr. 7 up). 1975. 9.95 (ISBN 0-02-775330-1). Macmillan.

--Follow a Fisher. LC 72-83784. (Illus.). (gr. 2-5). 1973. 7.89 o.p. (ISBN 0-690-31237-7, TYC-J). T Y Crowell.

--From Pond to Prairie: The Changing World of a Pond & Its Life. LC 70-175599. (Illus.). 40p. (gr. 4-6). 1972. 4.95g o.s.i. (ISBN 0-02-775220-8). Macmillan.

--The Gentle Desert: Exploring an Ecosystem. LC 77-5875. (Illus.). (gr. 3-7). 1977. 7.95 (ISBN 0-02-775380-8, 77538). Macmillan.

--The Hidden World: Life Under a Rock. LC 76-47641. (Exploring an Ecosystem Ser.). (Illus.). (gr. 3-7). 1977. 8.95 (ISBN 0-02-775340-9, 77534). Macmillan.

--Into the Woods: Exploring the Forest Ecosystem. LC 72-92448. (Illus.). 64p. (gr. 3-6). 1973. 7.95 (ISBN 0-02-775320-4). Macmillan.

--Lives at Stake: The Science & Politics of Environmental Health. LC 80-14272. (Illus.). 144p. (gr. 6 up). 1980. PLB 8.95 (ISBN 0-02-775410-3). Macmillan.

--The Minnow Family. LC 75-28335. (Illus.). 64p. (gr. 3-7). 1976. 6.25 (ISBN 0-688-22060-6); PLB 6.00 (ISBN 0-688-32060-0). Morrow.

--Natural Fire, Its Ecology in Forests. LC 79-13606. (Illus.). 64p. (gr. 4-6). 1979. 5.95 (ISBN 0-688-22210-2); PLB 5.71 (ISBN 0-688-32210-7). Morrow.

--Nuclear Power: From Physics to Politics. LC 78-27180. (Science for Survival Ser.). 144p. (gr. 6 up). 1979. PLB 8.95 (ISBN 0-02-775390-5, 77539). Macmillan.

--One Earth, Many People: The Challenge of Human Population Growth. LC 71-133559. (Illus.). (gr. 5 up). 1971. 4.95g o.s.i. (ISBN 0-02-775260-7); text ed. 1.96 o.s.i. (ISBN 0-02-775280-1). Macmillan.

--Only Earth We Have. LC 71-78076. (Illus.). (gr. 5-8). 1971. pap. 0.95 o.s.i. (ISBN 0-02-044880-5, Collier). Macmillan.

--Only Earth We Have. LC 71-78076. (Illus.). (gr. 4-8). 1969. 5.95g o.s.i. (ISBN 0-02-775210-0); text ed. 1.96 o.s.i. (ISBN 0-02-775250-X). Macmillan.

--Our Hungry Earth: The World Food Crisis. LC 76-10828. (Science for Survival Ser.). 128p. (gr. 7 up). 1976. 7.95 (ISBN 0-02-775290-9, 77529). Macmillan.

--Pests & People: The Search for Sensible Pest Control. LC 71-165104. (Illus.). (gr. 7up). 1972. 7.95 (ISBN 0-02-775270-4). Macmillan.

--Recycling Resources. LC 72-81062. (Illus.). 128p. (gr. 7 up). 1974. 5.95g o.s.i. (ISBN 0-02-775310-7). Macmillan.

--This Is a River: Exploring an Ecosystem. LC 70-160074. (Illus.). (gr. 4 up). 1972. 4.95g o.s.i. (ISBN 0-02-775240-2). Macmillan.

--Twist, Wiggle, & Squirm: A Book About Earthworms. LC 74-184983. (A Let's-Read-&-Find-Out Science Bk). (Illus.). 33p. (gr. k-3). 1973. 7.95 (ISBN 0-690-84154-X, TYC-J); PLB 7.89 (ISBN 0-690-84155-8). T Y Crowell.

--Water Plants. LC 74-23942. (A Let's-Read & Find-Out Science Bk). (Illus.). 40p. (gr. k-3). 1975. 6.95 o.p. (ISBN 0-690-00737-X, TYC-J); PLB 7.89 (ISBN 0-690-00738-8). T Y Crowell.

--Wild Foods: A Beginner's Guide to Identifying, Harvesting & Preparing Safe & Tasty Plants from the Outdoors. LC 78-1910. (Illus.). 192p. (gr. 7 up). 1978. 10.95 (ISBN 0-590-07511-X, Four Winds). Schol Bk Serv.

Pringle, M. L., jt. auth. see Gooch, Stan.

Pringle, M. L., ed. Caring for Children: A Symposium on Co-Operation in Child Care. (Studies in Child Development). (Orig.). 1969. pap. text ed. 4.50x (ISBN 0-582-32439-4). Humanities.

Pringle, Mary Beth & Stericker, Anne. Sex Roles in Literature. (English & Humanities Ser.). 1980. pap. text ed. 9.95 (ISBN 0-582-28103-2). Longman.

Pringle, P., ed. see Bussell, Jan.

Pringle, P., ed. see Mitchell, Peggy.

Pringle, Patrick. Smugglers. LC 68-1842. (Pegasus Books: No. 6). (Illus.). 1965. 7.50x (ISBN 0-234-77877-6). Intl Pubns Serv.

Pringle, Robert. Indonesia & the Philippines: American Interests in Island Southeast Asia. LC 80-13474. (Illus.). 296p. 1980. 30.00x (ISBN 0-231-05008-9); pap. 8.00x (ISBN 0-231-05009-7). Columbia U Pr.

Pringle, Roger, ed. A Portrait of Elizabeth I: In the Words of the Queen & Her Contemporaries. (Illus.). 128p. 1980. 10.75x (ISBN 0-389-20088-3). B&N.

Pringles, Laurence. The Economic Growth Debate: Are There Limits to Growth? (Impact Ser). (gr. 9 up). 1978. lib. bdg. 6.90 s&l (ISBN 0-531-01322-7). Watts.

Pringsheim, E. G. Pure Cultures of Algae: Their Preparation & Maintenance. 1967. Repr. of 1946 ed. 5.95 o.s.i. (ISBN 0-02-850370-8). Hafner.

Prins, Gwyn. The Hidden Hippopotamus: Reappraisal in African History, the Early Colonial Experience. LC 79-41658. (African Studies: No. 28). (Illus.). 320p. 1980. 45.00 (ISBN 0-521-22915-4). Cambridge U Pr.

Prins, H. A. & Whyte, M. B. Social Work & Medical Practice. LC 71-184453. 94p. 1972. text ed. 15.00 (ISBN 0-08-016847-7). Pergamon.

Prins, Herschel. Criminal Behaviour: An Introduction to Its Causes & Treatment. 240p. 1974. pap. 6.95x o.p. (ISBN 0-8464-0299-8). Beekman Pubs.

Prins, R., jt. ed. see Schuit, G. G.

Prins, Warner, illus. The Haggadah. (Illus.). 10.00 o.p. (ISBN 0-498-06401-8, Yoseloff). A S Barnes.

Prinsep, H. T. History of the Political & Military Transactions in India During the Administration of the Marquis of Hastings, 1813-1823, 2 vols. (Illus.). 988p. 1972. Repr. of 1825 ed. 84.00x (ISBN 0-7165-2134-2, Pub. by Irish Academic Pr Ireland). Biblio Dist.

Print Project. The Unusual-by-Mail Catalog. (Illus.). 192p. 1980. 14.95 (ISBN 0-312-83374-1); pap. 7.95 (ISBN 0-312-83375-X). St Martin.

Printz, Peggy & Steinle, Paul. Commune: Life in Rural China. LC 76-58427. (Illus.). 1977. 6.95 (ISBN 0-396-07420-0). Dodd.

Printz-Pahlson, Goran, jt. tr. see Matthias, John.

Prinz, Karl E., ed. see Abraham, Nicholas A.

Priolo, Joan. Decoupage: Simple & Sophisticated. LC 73-93597. (Little Craft Book Ser). (Illus.). 48p. (gr. 4 up). 1974. 5.95 (ISBN 0-8069-5300-4); PLB 6.69 (ISBN 0-8069-5301-2). Sterling.

Priolo, Louis A. As for Me & My House. (Orig.). 1976. pap. 1.75 o.p. (ISBN 0-88368-077-7). Whitaker Hse.

Prior, Arthur. Past, Present & Future. 1967. 27.50x (ISBN 0-19-824311-1). Oxford U Pr.

Prior, Arthur N. Formal Logic. 2nd ed. 1962. 35.00x (ISBN 0-19-824156-9). Oxford U Pr.

Prior, Brenda G. La Pequena Bella Durmiente. Ross, Ronald, tr. from Eng. (Libros Arco). (Illus.). 32p. (Orig., Span.). (gr. 1-3). 1972. pap. 0.95 o.s.i. (ISBN 0-89922-045-2). Edit Caribe.

Prior, Mike, ed. The Popular & the Political: Essays on Socialism in the 1980's. 220p. 1981. pap. price not set (ISBN 0-7100-0627-6). Routledge & Kegan.

Prior, Mike, et al. Politics & Power I. Purdy, David, et al, eds. 240p. (Orig.). 1980. pap. 12.50 (ISBN 0-7100-0593-8). Routledge & Kegan.

Prior, Moody E. The Drama of Power: Studies in Shakespeare's History Plays. 1973. 16.75x o.s.i. (ISBN 0-8101-0421-0). Northwestern U Pr.

--Language of Tragedy. LC 66-12753. (Midland Bks.: No. 86). 1966. pap. 2.95x o.p. (ISBN 0-253-20086-5). Ind U Pr.

Prior, Pamela. Monitoring Cerebral Function: Long-Term Recordings of Cerebral Electrical Activity. LC 78-14390. (Illus.). 1979. text ed. 30.00x (ISBN 0-397-58251-X). Lippincott.

Priovolos, Theophilos. Coffee & the Ivory Coast: An Econometric Study. LC 80-8630. (The Wharton Econometric Studies). (Illus.). 240p. 1981. 24.95 (ISBN 0-669-04331-1). Lexington Bks.

Prip-Moller, Johannes. Chinese Buddhist Monasteries. (Illus.). 410p. 1981. 65.00 (ISBN 0-85656-034-0). Great Eastern.

Prisco, Salvatore, III. An Introduction to Psychohistory: Theories & Case Studies. LC 80-8245. 190p. 1980. lib. bdg. 17.50 (ISBN 0-8191-1335-2); pap. text ed. 9.00 (ISBN 0-8191-1336-0). U Pr of Amer.

Priselkov, Mikhail D. Khanskie Iarlyki Russkim Metropolitam. LC 80-2364. 1981. Repr. of 1916 ed. 25.50 (ISBN 0-686-69404-X). AMS Pr.

Prisma-Lagersson, R. Swedish-English Modern Dictionary. 4th ed. 1979. 20.00x (ISBN 9-1518-0942-7, SW204). Vanous.

Prisma-Lagersson, Rolf. Svensk-Engelsk Modern Ordbok. 4th ed. 1979. 20.00x (ISBN 9-1518-0942-7, SW-204). Vanous.

Prista, Alexander da R. Essential Portuguese Grammar. LC 66-20416. 1966. lib. bdg. 9.50x (ISBN 0-88307-579-2). Gannon.

Pritam, Amrita. A Line in the Water. Gorowara, Krishna, tr. from Punjabi. (Mayfair Paperbacks). 141p. 1975. 5.95 (ISBN 0-89253-012-X); pap. 2.50 (ISBN 0-89253-023-5). Ind-US Inc.

Pritchard. Building Science & Materials Two: Checkbook. 1981. text ed. price not set. Butterworth.

Pritchard, A. E., jt. auth. see Cole, F. R.

Pritchard, Alan. Alchemy: A Bibliography of English Language Writings. 400p. 1980. 75.00x (ISBN 0-7100-0472-9). Routledge & Kegan.

Pritchard, Anthony. The World Champions. LC 73-15147. (Illus.). 1974. 7.95 o.s.i. (ISBN 0-02-599210-4). Macmillan.

Pritchard, C. West Midlands. (Geography of the British Isles Ser). (Illus.). 116p. 1975. 6.95x (ISBN 0-521-20029-6). Cambridge U Pr.

Pritchard, Colin & Taylor, Richard. Social Work: Reform or Revolution? (Library of Social Work). 1978. 16.00x (ISBN 0-7100-8882-5); pap. 8.00 (ISBN 0-7100-8884-1). Routledge & Kegan.

Pritchard, Colin, jt. auth. see Jones, Ray.

Pritchard, Colin, jt. auth. see Taylor, Richard.

Pritchard, D. C. Lighting. 2nd ed. (Environmental Physics Ser.). (Illus.). 1978. pap. text ed. 11.95x (ISBN 0-582-41083-5). Longman.

Pritchard, David A. Mental Health Law in Mississippi. LC 78-62247. 1978. pap. text ed. 11.25 (ISBN 0-8191-0568-6). U Pr of Amer.

Pritchard, Elaine. Chess for Pleasure. (Illus.). 1971. 7.95 (ISBN 0-571-09201-2, Pub. by Faber & Faber). Merrimack Bk Serv.

Pritchard, F. H. Essays of To-Day. 258p. 1980. Repr. lib. bdg. 20.00 (ISBN 0-89984-378-6). Century Bookbindery.

Pritchard, G., ed. Developments in Reinforced Plastics, No. 1. (Illus.). xii, 283p. 1981. 62.00x (ISBN 0-85334-919-3). Intl Ideas.

Pritchard, H. O., jt. auth. see Allen, G.

Pritchard, James B., ed. Ancient Near East in Pictures with Supplement. 2nd ed. Incl. Ancient Near Eastern Texts Relating to the Old Testament with Supplement. 3rd ed (ISBN 0-691-03502-4). 1969. deluxe ed. 46.50x ea. (ISBN 0-691-03502-4); Set. 82.50x (ISBN 0-686-66606-2). Princeton U Pr.

Pritchard, John P. A Literary Approach to the New Testament. LC 72-1793. (Illus.). 355p. 1981. pap. 7.95 (ISBN 0-8061-1710-9). U of Okla Pr.

Pritchard, Peter. Turtles of the World. 1966. 20.00 o.p. (ISBN 0-87666-228-9, H922). TFH Pubns.

Pritchard, Peter C., jt. ed. see Ward, Daniel B.

Pritchard, R. John & Zaide, Sonia M., eds. Tokyo War Crimes Trial, 22 vols. Incl. Vol. 1. 1981 (ISBN 0-8240-4750-8); Vol. 2. 1981 (ISBN 0-8240-4751-6); Vol. 3. 1981 (ISBN 0-8240-4752-4); Vol. 4. 1981 (ISBN 0-8240-4753-2); Vol. 5. 1981 (ISBN 0-8240-4754-0); Vol. 6. 1981 (ISBN 0-8240-4755-9); Vol. 7. 1981 (ISBN 0-8240-4756-7); Vol. 8. 1981 (ISBN 0-8240-4757-5); Vol. 9. 1981 (ISBN 0-8240-4758-3); Vol. 10. 1981 (ISBN 0-8240-4759-1); Vol. 11. 1981 (ISBN 0-8240-4760-5); Vol. 12. 1981 (ISBN 0-8240-4761-3); Vol. 13. 1981 (ISBN 0-8240-4762-1); Vol. 14. 1981 (ISBN 0-8240-4763-X); Vol. 15. 1981 (ISBN 0-8240-4764-8); Vol. 16. 1981 (ISBN 0-8240-4765-6); Vol. 17. 1981 (ISBN 0-8240-4766-4); Vol. 18. 1981 (ISBN 0-8240-4767-2); Vol. 19, 1981 (ISBN 0-8240-4768-0); Vol. 20. 1981 (ISBN 0-8240-4769-9); Vol. 21. 1981 (ISBN 0-8240-4770-2); Vol. 22. 1981 (ISBN 0-8240-4771-0). lib. bdg. 77.00 ea. Garland Pub.

Pritchard, R. M. Housing & the Spatial Structure of the City. LC 75-3859. (Cambridge Geographical Studies). (Illus.). 403p. 1976. 41.50 (ISBN 0-521-20882-3). Cambridge U Pr.

Pritchard, Robert. Operational Financial Management. LC 76-25062. (Illus.). 1977. text ed. 18.95 (ISBN 0-13-637827-7). P-H.

Pritchard, Violet. English Medieval Graffiti. 1967. 47.50 (ISBN 0-521-05998-4). Cambridge U Pr.

Pritchett, C. H. The American Constitutional System. 5th ed. Munson, Eric M., ed. (American Government Ser.). 160p. 1981. pap. text ed. 6.95 (ISBN 0-07-050893-3). McGraw.

Pritchett, C. W. Sicilian Scheveningen. 1977. 21.50 (ISBN 0-7134-0087-0, Pub. by Batsford England). David & Charles.

Pritchett, G. Herman. The Federal System in Constitutional Law. (Illus.). 1978. pap. 11.95 ref. ed. (ISBN 0-13-308460-4). P-H.

Pritchett, Herman C., jt. ed. see Murphy, Walter F.

Pritchett, V. S. Blind Love & Other Stories. Epstein, Jason, ed. LC 70-85570. 1969. 7.95 o.p. (ISBN 0-394-41714-3). Random.

--On the Edge of the Cliff & Other Stories. LC 79-4805. 1979. 10.00 (ISBN 0-394-50485-2). Random.

Pritchett, V. S., ed. The Oxford Book of Short Stories. 750p. 1981. 19.95 (ISBN 0-19-214116-3). Oxford U Pr.

Pritchett, Victor S. London Perceived. LC 62-14471. 1966. pap. 2.25 o.p. (ISBN 0-15-652970-X, HB103, Harv). HarBraceJ.

Pritchett, W. Kendrick. The Choiseul Marble. (U. C. Publ. in Classical Studies: Vol. 5). 1970. pap. 7.50x (ISBN 0-520-09051-9). U of Cal Pr.

--Dionysius of Halicarnassus: On Thucydides. 1975. 14.50x (ISBN 0-520-02922-4); pap. 7.95x (ISBN 0-520-02959-3). U of Cal Pr.

--The Greek State at War, Pt. 1. LC 71-633960. 1975. 18.50x (ISBN 0-520-02758-2). U of Cal Pr.

--The Greek State at War, Pt. 2. LC 74-77991. 1975. 20.00x (ISBN 0-520-02565-2). U of Cal Pr.

--The Greek State at War, Pt. 3. 1980. 24.50 (ISBN 0-520-03781-2). U of Cal Pr.

--Studies in Ancient Greek Topography, Pt. 2: Battlefields. (U. C. Publ. in Classical Studies: Vol. 4). 1969. pap. 11.50x (ISBN 0-520-09050-0). U of Cal Pr.

Pritchett, William L. Properties & Management of Forest Soils. LC 78-23196. 1979. text ed. 26.95 (ISBN 0-471-03718-4). Wiley.

Pritkin, Nathan & McGrady, Patrick, Jr. The Pritkin Program for Diet & Exercise. 1979. 14.95 (ISBN 0-448-14302-X). G&D.

Pritsker, A. Alan. Modeling & Analysis Using Q-Gert Networks. 2nd ed. LC 78-71976. 1979. 19.50x o.p. (ISBN 0-470-26648-1). Halsted Pr.

Pritsker, A. Alan & Pegden, Claude D. Introduction to Simulation & Slam. LC 78-23385. 1978. 28.95 (ISBN 0-470-26588-4). Halsted Pr.

Prittie, Terence. The Velvet Chancellors: A History of Post-War Germany. (Illus.). 286p. 1981. text ed. 26.00x (ISBN 0-8419-6750-4). Holmes & Meier.

Prittie, Terence, jt. auth. see Loeb, O. W.

Pritts, Joseph. Incidents of Border Life Illustrative of the Times & Condition of the First Settlements in Parts of the Middle & Western States... Compiled from Authentic Sources. LC 75-7080. (Indian Captivities Ser.: Vol. 57). 1977. Repr. of 1839 ed. lib. bdg. 44.00 (ISBN 0-8240-1681-5). Garland Pub.

Pritzker, Alan B. & Young, Robert E. Simulation with Gasp PL I: A PL I Based Continuous Discrete Simulation Language. LC 75-23182. 335p. 1975. 24.00 (ISBN 0-471-70046-0, Pub. by Wiley-Interscience). Wiley.

Privratsky, Kenneth L., jt. auth. see Polk, Noel.

Prizzi, Elaine & Hoffman, Jeanne. Teaching off the Wall. 1980. pap. 6.95 (ISBN 0-8224-6830-1). Pitman Learning.

Probert, S. D. & Hub, D. R., eds. Thermal Insulation. (Illus.). 1968. text ed. 26.00x (ISBN 0-444-20025-8, Pub. by Applied Science). Burgess-Intl Ideas.

Probert, Walter. Law, Language & Communication. (Amer. Lec. Behavioral Science & Law Ser.). 408p. 1972. 19.50 (ISBN 0-398-02477-4). C C Thomas.

Probst, Calvin, ed. Hospital Purchasing Guide: Nineteen Eighty-One. 5th ed. (Annual Ser.). 1981. pap. text ed. 85.00 (ISBN 0-933916-05-1). Medical Busn.

Probst, Raymond E., ed. Obstetrics & Gynecology Specialty Board Review. 5th ed. 1977. spiral bdg. 16.50 (ISBN 0-87488-304-0). Med Exam.

Probstein, Ronald F., jt. ed. see Hayes, Wallace D.

Proby, Kathryn H. Audubon in Florida: With Selections from the Writings of John James Audubon. LC 72-85114. (Illus.). 384p. 1974. pap. 14.95 (ISBN 0-87024-301-2). U of Miami Pr.

Proceedings of a Workshop, Palo Alto, California, July 1979, et al. Conduction Velocity Distributions: A Population Approach to Electrophysiology of Nerve. Dorfman, Leslie J. & Cummins, Kenneth L., eds. (Progress in Clinical & Biological Research Ser.: No. 52). 338p. 1981. 30.00x (ISBN 0-8451-0052-1). A R Liss.

Proceedings of an International Conference, France, 1969. PSI Factors in Creativity. Angoff, Allan & Shapin, Betty, eds. LC 71-140141. 1970. 7.00 (ISBN 0-912328-18-5). Parapsych Foun.

Proceedings of the Colloquium on Numerical Analysis, Lausanne, Oct. 11-13, 1976. Numerical Analysis. Descloux, J. & Marti, J. T., eds. (International Series of Numerical Mathematics: No. 37). 248p. 1977. pap. 30.00 (ISBN 3-7643-0939-3). Birkhauser.

Proceedings of the International Conference, Paris, France, 1977. PSI & States of Awareness. Shapin, Betty & Coly, Lisette, eds. LC 78-50167. 1978. 14.00 (ISBN 0-912328-30-4). Parapsych Foun.

Proceedings, Schlitz, September 1975. First International Symposium on Groundwater Ecology. Husmann, Siegfried, ed. 232p. 1976. pap. text ed. 29.95 (ISBN 90-265-0240-0, Pub. by Swets Pub Serv Holland). Swets North Am.

Prochaska, F. K. Women & Philanthropy in Nineteenth-Century England. (Illus.). 312p. 1980. 36.00 (ISBN 0-19-822627-6); pap. 21.00 (ISBN 0-19-822628-4). Oxford U Pr.

Prochaska, Georg. Dissertation on the Functions of the Nervous System. Laycock, T., tr. Bd. with On the Study of Character. (Contributions to the History of Psychology Ser., Vol. XIV, Pt. A: Orientations). 1980. Repr. of 1851 ed. 30.00 (ISBN 0-89093-316-2). U Pubns Amer.

Prochaska, James O. Systems of Psychotherapy: A Transtheoretical Analysis. 1979. 17.95x (ISBN 0-256-02064-7). Dorsey.

Prochnow, Herbert V. Public Speaker's Treasure Chest. new, rev. ed. LC 75-25058. 1977. 15.95 (ISBN 0-06-013404-6, HarpT). Har-Row.

Prochoroff, Marina see Bottiglia, William F.

Procler, Jesse H., ed. Islam & International Relations. LC 80-1914. 1981. Repr. of 1965 ed. 27.50 (ISBN 0-404-18969-5). AMS Pr.

Proclus. Elements of Theology. 2nd ed. Dodds, E. R., tr. 1963. 23.50x o.p. (ISBN 0-19-814160-2). Oxford U Pr.

Procopius. The Secret History. (Penguin Classics). 1980. pap. 3.95 (ISBN 0-14-044182-4). Penguin.

Procopuis. Procopius. LC 67-28144. 351p. 1967. text ed. 20.00x (ISBN 0-8290-0199-9). Irvington.

Procter, Ben, jt. auth. see McDonald, Archie.

Procter, Evelyn S. Alfonso X of Castile, Patron of Literature & Learning. LC 80-10508. (Norman Macoll Lectures: 1949). vi, 149p. 1980. Repr. of 1951 ed. lib. bdg. 19.50x (ISBN 0-313-22347-5, PRAL). Greenwood.

--Curia & Cortes in Leon & Castille, Ten Seventy-Two to Twelve Ninety-Five. LC 79-51750. (Cambridge Iberian & Latin American Studies). (Illus.). 350p. 1980. 42.50 (ISBN 0-521-22639-2). Cambridge U Pr.

Proctor, Andrew, jt. ed. see Ward, R. Gerard.

Proctor, C. R., jt. ed. see Loeffler, F. J.

Proctor, D. F. Breathing, Speech, & Song. (Illus.). 180p. 1980. 19.80 (ISBN 0-387-81580-5). Springer-Verlag.

Proctor, Dennis, ed. The Autobiography of G. Lowes Dickinson. (Illus.). 287p. 1973. 12.50x (ISBN 0-7156-0647-6, Pub. by Duckworth England). Biblio Dist.

Proctor, Ellen A. A Brief Memoir of Christina G. Rossetti. 84p. 1980. Repr. of 1895 ed. lib. bdg. 10.00 (ISBN 0-8495-4391-6). Arden Lib.

Proctor, George A. Canadian Music of the Twentieth Century. 1980. 27.50 (ISBN 0-8020-5419-6). U of Toronto Pr.

Proctor, J. O. Techniques, Notes, Tips for Teachers. 1968. pap. text ed. 4.40 (ISBN 0-8273-0361-0). Delmar.

Proctor, Marion B. Figure Skating. (Physical Education Activities Ser). 1969. pap. text ed. 3.25x (ISBN 0-697-07011-5); teacher's manual avail. Wm C Brown.

Proctor, Paul, ed. Longman Dictionary of Contemporary English. (Illus.). 1979. text ed. 12.95x (ISBN 0-582-52571-3). Longman.

Proctor, Richard W. The Barber's Shop. rev. & enl. ed. LC 74-79753. (Illus.). 1971. Repr. of 1883 ed. 15.00 (ISBN 0-8103-3036-9). Gale.

Proctor, Samuel, ed. Eighteenth-Century Florida: Life on the Frontier. LC 76-5852. (Papers on the Annual Bicentennial Symposia: No. 3). 1976. 7.00 (ISBN 0-8130-0523-X). U Presses Fla.

--Eighteenth-Century Florida: The Impact of the American Revolution. LC 78-1870. (Papers of the Annual Bicentennail Symposia: No. 5). 1978. 9.00 (ISBN 0-8130-0589-2). U Presses Fla.

Proctor, Tony & Stone, Marilyn A. Marketing Research. (Illus.). 192p. 1978. pap. text ed. 9.95x (ISBN 0-7121-1291-X, Pub. by Macdonald & Evans England). Intl Ideas.

Proctor, William, jt. auth. see Boa, Kenneth.

Prodan, M. Forest Biometrics. 1968. 55.00 o.p. (ISBN 0-08-012441-0). Pergamon.

Prodano, Sylvio, jt. auth. see Denman, D. R.

Proddow, Penelope. Spirit of Spring. LC 76-104339. (Illus.). (gr. 5-8). 1970. 4.95 o.p. (ISBN 0-87888-020-8). Bradbury Pr.

Prodham, B. The Board & Financial Management. 175p. 1979. text ed. 24.50 (ISBN 0-220-66354-8, Pub. by Business Books England). Renouf.

Prod'Homme, J. G. Les Symphonies De Beethoven. 13th ed. LC 76-52485. (Music Reprint Ser.). (Illus., Fr.). 1978. Repr. of 1906 ed. lib. bdg. 39.50 (ISBN 0-306-70859-0). Da Capo.

Product Safety Letter Staff. Index of "Substantial Hazard". Reports to the Consumer Product Safety Commission. 1979. 45.00 (ISBN 0-914176-14-5). Wash Busn Info.

Professional Publications. Directory of Construction Associations. 2nd ed. MacDonald, Joseph A., ed. (Orig.). 1980. pap. 19.95 (ISBN 0-932836-01-1). Prof Pubns NY.

--Handbook of Construction Resources & Support Services. MacDonald, Joseph A., ed. (Orig.). 1980. pap. 49.50 (ISBN 0-932836-02-X). Prof Pubns NY.

Professional Report Editors & Kirk, John. Incorporating Your Business. (Illus.). 1981. 15.00 (ISBN 0-8092-5903-6). Contemp Bks.

Professional Staff of Hewlett-Woodmere Public Library, compiled by. Index to Art Reproductions in Books. Thomson, Elizabeth, ed. LC 74-1286. 1974. 15.00 (ISBN 0-8108-0711-4). Scarecrow.

Proffer, Carl, ed. Modern Russian Poets on Poetry. 1976. 15.00 (ISBN 0-88233-185-X). Ardis Pubs.

Proffer, Carl & Proffer, Ellendea, eds. The Ardis Anthology of Russian Futurism. (Illus.). 413p. 1980. 22.50 (ISBN 0-88233-469-7); pap. 7.50. Ardis Pubs.

Proffer, Carl R. & Proffer, Ellendea, eds. Ardis Anthology of Recent Russian Literature. 1976. pap. 6.95 o.p. (ISBN 0-394-73291-X). Random.

--Glagol III: Al'manakh "Ardisa". (Rus.). 1981. 15.00 (ISBN 0-88233-477-8); pap. 5.00 (ISBN 0-88233-478-6). Ardis Pubs.

Proffer, Ellendea. Mikhail Bulgakov. 1981. 22.00 (ISBN 0-88233-198-1). Ardis Pubs.

Proffer, Ellendea, ed. Tsvetaeva: A Pictorial Biography. 1980. 20.00 (ISBN 0-88233-358-5); pap. 11.00 (ISBN 0-88233-359-3). Ardis Pubs.

Proffer, Ellendea, jt. ed. see Proffer, Carl.

Proffer, Ellendea, jt. ed. see Proffer, Carl R.

Proffer, Ellendea, jt. ed. see Trifonov, Yury V.

Proffer, Ellendea C., ed. Marina Tsvetaeva: A Pictorial Biography, Eighteen Ninety-Two to Nineteen Forty-One. (Illus.). 1980. 20.00 (ISBN 0-88233-358-5); pap. 11.00 (ISBN 0-88233-359-3). Ardis Pubs.

Proffitt, Edward. Poetry: An Introduction & Anthology. LC 80-80842. 384p. 1981. pap. text ed. 8.95 (ISBN 0-395-29486-X); instr's. manual 0.40 (ISBN 0-395-29487-8). HM.

Profio, A. Edward. Experimental Reactor Physics. LC 75-35735. 832p. 1976. 42.50 (ISBN 0-471-70095-9, Pub. by Wiley-Interscience). Wiley.

--Radiation Shielding & Dosimetry. LC 78-15649. 1979. 36.50 (ISBN 0-471-04329-X, Pub. by Wiley-Interscience). Wiley.

Profumo, Tony. The Mime. 1978. pap. 1.95 o.s.i. (ISBN 0-515-04255-2). Jove Pubns.

Progoff, Ira. At a Journal Workshop: The Basic Text & Guide for Using the Intensive Journal. LC 75-13932. 1975. 12.50 (ISBN 0-87941-003-5); pap. 6.95, 1977 (ISBN 0-87941-006-X). Dialogue Hse.

--Image of an Oracle: A Report on Research into the Mediumship of Eileen J. Garrett. LC 64-24081. 1964. 7.50 o.p. (ISBN 0-912326-11-5). Garrett-Helix.

--Jung's Psychology & Its Social Meaning. LC 72-97273. 320p. 1973. pap. 3.50 (ISBN 0-385-03273-0, Anch). Doubleday.

--The Practice of Process Meditation: The Intensive Journal Way to Spiritual Experience. 1980. 12.95 (ISBN 0-87941-008-6). Dialogue Hse.

--The Star Cross. LC 70-176111. (Entrance Meditation Ser.). 1971. pap. 2.95 (ISBN 0-87941-001-9). Dialogue Hse.

--The Well & the Cathedral: With an Introduction on Its Use in the Practice of Meditation. 2nd ed. LC 76-20823. (Entrance Meditation Ser.). 1977. 8.95 (ISBN 0-87941-004-3); pap. 3.95 1980 (ISBN 0-87941-005-1). Dialogue Hse.

Progress Publishers, Moscow. Lenin: Collected Works, 45 vols. 1975. 299.00x set (ISBN 0-8464-0557-1). Beekman Pubs.

Progressive Farmer Food Staff & Harvey, Ann, eds. Progressive Farmer Country Living Recipes: 1980. (Illus.). 128p. 1981. 9.95 (ISBN 0-8487-0514-9). Oxmoor Hse.

Progressive Grocer Magazine Staff. Grocery Retailing in the Eighties. (Illus.). 1980. 12.95 (ISBN 0-911790-75-6). Prog Grocer.

Progressive Grocer's Marketing Guidebook Staff. Display & Merchandising Idea Book. 2nd ed. (Illus.). 1981. 19.95 (ISBN 0-911790-55-1). Prog Grocer.

--New Idea Book. 2nd ed. (Illus.). 1980. 18.95 (ISBN 0-911790-59-4). Prog Grocer.

Prohaska, Dorothy. Raimund & Vienna. LC 70-116749. (Anglica Germanica Ser.: No. 2). (Illus.). 1971. 44.50 (ISBN 0-521-07789-3). Cambridge U Pr.

Prohias, Antonio. The All New Mad Secret File on Spy Vs. Spy. (Mad Ser). (Illus.). 192p. 1973. pap. 1.75 (ISBN 0-446-94421-1). Warner Bks.

--Fifth Mad Report on Spy Vs. Spy. (Mad Ser.). (Illus., Orig.). 1978. pap. 1.75 (ISBN 0-446-94422-X). Warner Bks.

--The Fourth Mad Declassified Papers on Spy Vs. Spy. (Mad Ser.). (Illus.). 192p. 1974. pap. 1.75 (ISBN 0-446-94423-8). Warner Bks.

--Spy Vs. Spy Follow-up File. (Mad Ser.). (Illus.). 1975. pap. 1.75 (ISBN 0-446-94424-6). Warner Bks.

--The Third Mad Dossier of Spy vs. Spy. (Mad Ser.). (Illus.). 192p. 1972. pap. 1.75 (ISBN 0-446-94425-4). Warner Bks.

Proia, Nicholas C. Barron's Handbook of College Transfer Information. (Barron's Educational Ser.). 304p. 1980. pap. 5.95 (ISBN 0-8120-2166-5). Barron.

Project SQUID Workshop on Transonic Flow Problems in Turbomachinery, Feb. 1976. Transonic Flow Problems in Turbomachinery: Proceedings. new ed. Adamson, T. C. & Platzer, M. F., eds. LC 77-22185. (Illus.). 1977. text ed. 57.50 (ISBN 0-89116-069-8). Hemisphere Pub.

Project Squid Workshop on Turbulence in Internal Flows: Turbomachinery & Other Applications, Airlie House, Warrenton, Va., June 14-15, 1976. Turbulence in Internal Flows: Turbomachinery & Other Engineering Applications, Proceedings. new ed. Murthy, S. N., ed. LC 77-15615. (Illus.). 1977. text ed. 57.50 (ISBN 0-89116-073-6). Hemisphere Pub.

Prokasy, William F., ed. Classical Conditioning. LC 65-16466. (Century Psychology Ser.). (Illus.). 1965. 24.50x (ISBN 0-89197-082-7); pap. text ed. 8.95x (ISBN 0-89197-083-5). Irvington.

Prokofiev, Sergei. Peter & the Wolf. LC 79-92902. (Illus.). 32p. (ps-5). 1980. 10.00g (ISBN 0-87923-331-1). Godine.

Prokop, Charles & Bradley, L. A., eds. Medical Psychology: Contributions to Behavioral Medicine. LC 80-1676. 1981. price not set (ISBN 0-12-565960-1). Acad Pr.

Prokop, F. W. The Future Economic Significance of Large Lowgrade Copper & Nickel Deposits. Borchert, H., ed. (Illus.). 67p. (Orig.). 1975. pap. 32.50x (ISBN 3-443-12013-X). Intl Pubns Serv.

Prokopoff, Stephen, jt. auth. see Ferrer, Rafael.

Prokopoff, Stephen S. & Siegfried, Joan C. The Nineteenth-Century Architecture of Saratoga Springs. (Architecture Worth Saving in New York State Ser.). (Illus.). 104p. 1980. pap. write for info. (ISBN 0-89062-001-6). NYSCA.

Prokopoff-Giannini, Paula, ed. see Moon, Warren G.

Prokosch, Frederic. America, My Wilderness. 256p. 1972. 6.95 o.p. (ISBN 0-374-10388-7). FS&G.

--The Missolonghi Manuscript. 1968. 5.95 o.p. (ISBN 0-374-21064-0). FS&G.

--The Wreck of the Cassandra. 1966. 4.95 o.p. (ISBN 0-374-29324-4). FS&G.

Proktor, Noel J. Simple Propagation: Propagation by Seed, Division, Layering, Cuttings, Budding & Grafting. (Illus.). 246p. 1981. pap. 8.95 (ISBN 0-571-11707-4, Pub. by Faber & Faber). Merrimack Bk Serv.

Pronay, Nicholas, jt. auth. see Thorpe, Frances.

Pronin, Monica, ed. Energy Index Nineteen Eighty. LC 73-89098. 600p. 1981. 135.00 (ISBN 0-89947-010-6). Environ Info.

--Environment Index Nineteen Eighty. LC 73-189498. 800p. 1981. 135.00 (ISBN 0-89947-011-4). Environ Info.

Pronk, Cornelis, tr. see Bakker, F.

Pronk, Fredericka, tr. see Bakker, F.

Pronko, Leonard C. Eugene Ionesco. LC 65-16380. (Columbia Essays on Modern Writers Ser.: No. 7). (Orig.). 1965. pap. 2.00 (ISBN 0-231-02681-1, MW7). Columbia U Pr.

--Theater East & West: Perspectives Toward a Total Theater. 1967. 11.50x o.p. (ISBN 0-520-01041-8); pap. 3.85 (ISBN 0-520-02622-5). U of Cal Pr.

Pronko, N. H. Psychology from the Standpoint of an Interbehaviorist. LC 80-10247. 600p. 1980. text ed. 19.95 (ISBN 0-8185-0397-1). Brooks-Cole.

Pronzini, Bill. Creature! A Chrestomathy of "Monstery". LC 80-70221. 304p. 1981. 12.95 (ISBN 0-87795-310-4); pap. 5.95 (ISBN 0-87795-321-X). Arbor Hse.

--Games. 1978. pap. 1.75 o.p. (ISBN 0-449-23484-3, Crest). Fawcett.

--Masques. LC 80-70219. 288p. 1981. 11.95 (ISBN 0-87795-308-2). Arbor Hse.

Pronzini, Bill & Malzberg, Barry N. Night Screams. LC 80-83596. 304p. 1981. pap. 2.75 (ISBN 0-87216-788-7). Playboy Pbks.

Pronzini, Bill, jt. auth. see Anderson, Jack.

Pronzini, Bill, jt. auth. see Malzberg, Barry N.

Pronzini, Bill, jt. ed. see Malzberg, Barry N.

Pronzini, Bill, et al, eds. The Arbor House Treasury of Horror & the Supernatural. LC 80-70220. 512p. (Orig.). 1981. 19.95 (ISBN 0-87795-309-0); pap. 8.95 (ISBN 0-87795-319-8). Arbor Hse.

Proper, Churchill. Footwear: Leathercraft. LC 78-185669. (Handicraft Ser.: No. 1). (Illus.). 32p. (Orig.). (gr. 7-12). 1971. lib. bdg. 2.45 incl. catalog cards (ISBN 0-87157-901-4); pap. 1.45 vinyl laminated covers (ISBN 0-87157-401-2). SamHar Pr.

Propertius. Elegies, 3 bks. Camps, W. A., ed. 1961-67. Bk. 1. text ed. 22.50 (ISBN 0-521-06000-1); pap. 8.50x (ISBN 0-521-29210-7); Bk. 2. text ed. 22.50 (ISBN 0-521-06001-X); Bk. 3. text ed. 16.95 (ISBN 0-521-06002-8). Cambridge U Pr.

Propertius, Sextus. The Poems of Sextus Propertius. McCulloch, J. P., tr. LC 78-115490. (Bilingual ed.). 1975. 22.75x (ISBN 0-520-01714-5); pap. 2.95 (ISBN 0-520-02774-4). U of Cal Pr.

Property Managers. The Condominium Community: A Guide for Owners, Boards, & Managers. 1978. 18.95 (ISBN 0-912104-22-8). Inst Real Estate.

Propes, S. Those Oldies but Goodies. 1973. pap. 1.95 o.s.i. (ISBN 0-02-061430-6, Collier). Macmillan.

Propes, Stephen. Those Oldies but Goodies: A Guide to 50's Record Collecting. 160p. 1973. 5.95 o.p. (ISBN 0-02-599270-8); pap. 1.95 (ISBN 0-02-061430-6). Macmillan.

Prophet, Elizabeth, jt. auth. see Prophet, Mark.

Prophet, Elizabeth C., ed. Pearls of Wisdom 1968, Vol. 11. LC 78-64502. 9.95 (ISBN 0-916766-33-0). Summit Univ.

Prophet, Mark & Prophet, Elizabeth. Climb the Highest Mountain. LC 72-175101. (Illus.). 1978. pap. 9.95 (ISBN 0-916766-26-8). Summit Univ.

Prophit, jt. auth. see Long.

Propper, Dan. The Tale of the Amazing Tramp. LC 76-58849. 1977. pap. 2.50x o.p. (ISBN 0-916156-20-6). Cherry Valley.

Propper, Robert A., illus. High Diddle Diddle. LC 75-15062. (Illus.). (ps-3). 1975. 5.95 (ISBN 0-87070-377-3). Museum Mod Art.

Prose, Francine. Animal Magnetism. 1979. pap. 1.95 o.p. (ISBN 0-425-04099-2). Berkley Pub.

--Household Saints. 224p. 1981. 10.95 (ISBN 0-312-39341-5). St Martin.

--Marie Laveau. 1977. 8.95 o.p. (ISBN 0-399-11873-X). Berkley Pub.

--Marie Laveau. 1977. pap. 2.25 o.p. (ISBN 0-425-03727-4). Berkley Pub.

Prose, Mary R. Spiritual Journeying: Directions on the Path for Prayer. LC 79-67513. 94p. 1980. 6.95 (ISBN 0-533-04472-3). Vantage.

Proskauer, Julien J. Spook Crooks: Exposing the Secrets of the Propheteers Who Conduct Our Wickedest Industry. LC 70-162517. (Illus.). 1971. Repr. of 1932 ed. 18.00 (ISBN 0-8103-3760-6). Gale.

Proskine, Alec. No Two Rivers Alike: Fifty Canoeable Rivers of New York & Pennsylvania. LC 80-11648. (Illus.). 1980. 9.95 (ISBN 0-89594-020-5). Crossing Pr.

Proskouriakoff, Tatiana. Jades from the Cenote of Sacrifice, Chichen Itza, Yucatan. LC 74-77555. (Peabody Museum Memoirs: Vol. 10, No. 1). 1974. pap. text ed. 40.00 (ISBN 0-87365-682-2). Peabody Harvard.

Prosser. Bibliography with Abstracts on Pump Sumps & Intakes. 1978. pap. 21.00 (ISBN 0-900983-70-1, Dist. by Air Science Co). BHRA Fluid.

Prosser, Eleanor. Shakespeare's Anonymous Editors: Scribe & Compositor in the Folio Text of "2 Henry IV". LC 79-66179. (Illus.). xiv, 219p. 1981. 18.50x (ISBN 0-8047-1033-3). Stanford U Pr.

Prosser, Franklin P., jt. auth. see Winkel, David E.

Prosser, Hilary. Perspectives on Foster Care. (General Ser.). 1978. pap. text ed. 20.75x (ISBN 0-85633-147-3, NFER). Humanities.

--Perspectives on Residential Child Care: An Annotated Bibliography. (National Children's Bureau Report). 1976. pap. text ed. 8.75x (ISBN 0-85633-113-9, NFER). Humanities.

Prosser, M. J. The Hydraulic Design of Pump Sumps & Intakes. (Illus.). 1977. pap. 34.00 (ISBN 0-86017-027-6, Dist. by Air Science Co.). BHRA Fluid.

Prosser, Michael H. The Cultural Dialogue: An Introduction to Intercultural Communication. LC 77-89049. (Illus.). 1978. text ed. 13.95 (ISBN 0-395-24448-X). HM.

Prosser, Reese T. New Formulation of Particle Mechanics. LC 52-42839. (Memoirs: No. 61). 1980. pap. 6.00 (ISBN 0-8218-1261-0, MEMO-61). Am Math.

Prosser, Robert. Geology Explained in the Lake District. (Geology Explained Ser.). 1977. 14.95 (ISBN 0-7153-7397-8). David & Charles.
Prostano, Emanuel T. Audiovisual Media & Libraries: Selected Readings. LC 72-89111. 276p. 1972. lib. bdg. 18.50x (ISBN 0-87287-053-7). Libs Unl.
Prostano, Emanuel T. & Piccirillo, Martin L. Law Enforcement: A Selective Bibliography. LC 73-86399. 1974. lib. bdg. 13.50 o.p. (ISBN 0-87287-077-4). Libs Unl.
Prostano, Emanuel T. & Prostano, Joyce S. The School Library Media Center. 2nd ed. LC 76-30402. (Library Science Text Ser). (Illus.). 1977. lib. bdg. 15.00x (ISBN 0-87287-137-1). Libs Unl.
Prostano, Joyce S., jt. auth. see Prostano, Emanuel T.
Protein-Calorie Advisory Group. The P A G Compendium, 9 vols. LC 74-19367. 7000p. 1975. Set. 699.95 (ISBN 0-470-70107-2). Halsted Pr.
Prothero, George W., ed. Peace Handbooks, 25 vols. LC 73-82619. 1973. Repr. of 1920 ed. Set. 875.00 (ISBN 0-8420-1704-6). Scholarly Res Inc.
Prothero, R. E., ed. see Byron, George G.
Prothero, R. Mansell, ed. People & Land in Africa South of the Sahara: Readings in Social Geography. (Illus.). 1972. pap. text ed. 9.95x (ISBN 0-19-501287-9). Oxford U Pr.
Protheroe, David R. Imports & Politics. 170p. 1980. pap. text ed. 8.95x (ISBN 0-920380-45-X, Pub. by Inst Res Pub Canada). Renouf.
Protheroe, W., et al. Exploring the Universe. (Science Ser.). 1979. text ed. 19.95 (ISBN 0-675-08313-3); instructor's manual 3.95 (ISBN 0-686-67277-1). Merrill.
Protheroe, William M., et al. Exploring the Universe. 2nd ed. (Illus.). 480p. 1981. text ed. 19.95 (ISBN 0-675-08154-8); instr's. manual 3.95 (ISBN 0-686-69491-0). Merrill.
Protherough, Robert, jt. auth. see Torbe, Mike.
Prottas, Jeffrey M. People-Processing. LC 78-19567. 1979. 18.95 (ISBN 0-669-02628-X). Lexington Bks.
Protter, Eric, ed. A Harvest of Horrors: Classic Tales of the Macabre. LC 79-56028. (Illus.). 286p. 1980. 12.50 (ISBN 0-8149-0755-5). Vanguard.
--Monster Festival: Classic Tales of the Macabre. LC 79-56028. (Illus.). (gr. 7 up). 10.00 (ISBN 0-8149-0377-0). Vanguard.
Protter, Murray H. & Morrey, Charles B., Jr. Calculus with Analytic Geometry: A First Course. 3rd ed. LC 76-12801. (Mathematics Ser.). 1977. text ed. 20.95 (ISBN 0-201-06037-X). A-W.
--Calculus with Analytic Geometry: A Second Course. LC 70-153066. (Mathematics Ser). 1971. text ed. 21.95 (ISBN 0-201-06021-3). A-W.
--College Calculus with Analytic Geometry. 3rd ed. LC 76-12800. (Mathematics Ser.). 1977. text ed. 25.95 (ISBN 0-201-06030-2). A-W.
Proudfoot, Christopher. Collecting Phonographs & Gramophones. (The Christies International Collectors Ser.). (Illus.). 128p. 1980. 14.95 (ISBN 0-8317-3952-5). Mayflower Bks.
Proudfoot, G. R., ed. see Fletcher, John & Shakespeare, William.
Proudfoot, Mary. The Republic of Austria, Nineteen Eighteen to Nineteen Thirty-Four: A Study in the Failure of Democratic Government. LC 79-2291. 1981. Repr. of 1946 ed. 16.50 (ISBN 0-88355-967-6). Hyperion Conn.
Proudley, Brian & Proudley, Valerie. Fuchsias in Color. (Illus.). 206p. 1981. 12.95 (ISBN 0-7137-0754-2, Pub. by Blandford Pr England). Sterling.
--Garden Conifers in Color. (Color Ser.). (Illus.). 1976. 9.95 (ISBN 0-7137-0807-7, Pub by Blandford Pr England). Sterling.
--Garden Flowers in Color. (Illus.). 1979. 12.95 (ISBN 0-7137-0911-1, Pub. by Blandford Pr England). Sterling.
--Heathers in Color. (Color Ser.). (Illus.). 1974. 9.95 (ISBN 0-7137-0635-X, Pub by Blandford Pr England). Sterling.
Proudley, Valerie, jt. auth. see Proudley, Brian.
Proudman, Robert. AMC Field Guide to Trail Building & Maintenance. (Illus.). 1977. pap. 5.95 o.p. (ISBN 0-910146-13-6). Appalach Mtn.
Proudman, Robert & Rajala, Reuben. AMC Field Guide to Trail Building & Maintenance. 2nd ed. (Illus.). 210p. 1981. pap. 5.95 (ISBN 0-910146-30-6). Appalach Mtn.
Proulx, Annie & Nichols, Lew. Cider. (Illus.). 272p. 1980. pap. 9.95 (ISBN 0-88266-242-2). Garden Way Pub.
Proulx, Donald A. Local Differences & Time Differences in Nasca Pottery. (U. C. Publ. in Anthropology: Vol. 5). 1968. pap. 8.00x (ISBN 0-520-09004-7). U of Cal Pr.
Prouse, Howard L., jt. auth. see Turner, V. Dean.
Proust, Marcel. A L Ombre Des Jeunes Filles En Fleurs. (Coll. Folio). 1965. pap. 4.50 (ISBN 0-685-23900-4, 1428). French & Eur.
--On Reading. Autret, Jean & Burford, William, eds. Autret, Jean & Burford, William, trs. 1971. 7.95 o.s.i. (ISBN 0-02-599240-6). Macmillan.
--Pleasures & Days: & Other Writings. Varese, L., et al, trs. from Fr. LC 78-2432. 1978. Repr. of 1957 ed. 18.50 (ISBN 0-86527-293-X). Fertig.
Proutfoot, L. Dryden's Aeneid & Its Seventeenth Century Predecessors. 278p. 1980. Repr. of 1960 ed. text ed. 30.00 (ISBN 0-8495-2173-4). R West.
Prouty, Charles T. Contention & Shakespeare's 2 Henry V. 1954. 32.50x (ISBN 0-685-69852-1). Elliots Bks.
Prouty, Olive H. Conflict. 224p. 1975. pap. 1.50 o.p. (ISBN 0-445-03069-0). Popular Lib.
Provder, Theodore, ed. Size Exclusion Chromatography (GPC) LC 80-22015. (ACS Symposium Ser.: No. 138). 1980. 30.75 (ISBN 0-8412-0586-8). Am Chemical.
Provence, Sally, et al. The Challenge of Daycare. LC 75-43331. 1977. 20.00x (ISBN 0-300-01964-5); pap. 7.95x (ISBN 0-300-02354-5). Yale U Pr.
Provensen, Alice & Provensen, Martin. My Little Hen. (Illus.). (ps-1). 1973. PLB 4.99 (ISBN 0-394-92684-6, BYR). Random.
--Our Animal Friends at Maple Hill Farm. LC 74-828. (Illus.). 64p. (gr. k-3). 1974. 3.95 o.p. (ISBN 0-394-82123-8, BYR); PLB 6.99 (ISBN 0-394-92123-2). Random.
--Play on Words. (ps-2). 1972. 2.95 (ISBN 0-394-82124-6, BYR); PLB 4.69 (ISBN 0-394-92124-0). Random.
Provensen, Alice & Provensen, Martin, illus. The Golden Mother Goose. (Illus.). 1976. 2.95 o.p. (ISBN 0-307-13766-X, Golden Pr); PLB 7.62 o.p. (ISBN 0-307-63766-2). Western Pub.
--A Peaceable Kingdom: The Shaker Abecedarius. (Picture Puffins Ser.). (Illus.). (gr. k-3). pap. 2.95 (ISBN 0-14-050370-6, Puffin). Penguin.
Provensen, Martin, jt. auth. see Provensen, Alice.
Provenzano, Natalie. First Things. (Illus.). (ps-1). 1980. 2.95 (ISBN 0-525-69408-0, Gingerbread). Dutton.
Provenzo, Asterie B. & Provenzo, Eugene F. Play It Again: Historic Board Games You Can Make & Play. (Illus.). 288p. 1981. 17.95 (ISBN 0-13-683367-5, Spec); pap. 8.95 (ISBN 0-13-683359-4, Spec). P-H.
Provenzo, Asterie B., jt. auth. see Provenzo, Eugene F.
Provenzo, Asterie B., jt. auth. see Provenzo, Eugene F., Jr.
Provenzo, Eugene F. & Provenzo, Asterie B. Rediscovering Photography. LC 80-17769. (Young Inventor's Ser.). 128p. 1980. 8.95 (ISBN 0-916392-55-4). Oak Tree Pubns.
Provenzo, Eugene F., jt. auth. see Provenzo, Asterie B.
Provenzo, Eugene F., Jr. & Provenzo, Asterie B. Rediscovering Astronomy. LC 80-17210. (Young Inventor's Ser.). (Illus.). 128p. 1980. 8.95 (ISBN 0-916392-61-9). Oak Tree Pubns.
Provenzo, Eugene F., Jr., jt. auth. see Young, Andrew D.
Province, Charles M., ed. see Patton, George S., Jr.
Provost, Gary. Make Every Word Count. LC 80-23699. 256p. 1980. 10.95 (ISBN 0-89879-020-4). Writers Digest.
Provus, Malcolm D. The Grand Experiment: The Life and Death of the TTT Program As Seen Through the Eyes of Its Evaluators. LC 74-30961. 277p. 1975. 16.00 (ISBN 0-8211-1514-6); text ed. 14.50 (ISBN 0-685-52140-0). McCutchan.
Provus, Malcolm M. Discrepancy Evaluation: For Educational Program Improvement & Assessment. LC 75-146312. 1971. 19.00 (ISBN 0-8211-1509-X); text ed. 17.00 (ISBN 0-685-04199-9). McCutchan.
Prowant, Forest S. Today, Tomorrow, Yesterday. 1981. 5.95 (ISBN 0-533-04777-3). Vantage.
Prowse, D. W. History of Newfoundland from the English, Colonial & Foreign Records. 1971. Repr. of 1895 ed. pap. text ed. 51.50x (ISBN 90-6041-084-X). Humanities.
Prowse, Philip. This Is London. (Illus.). 1977. pap. 1.25x (ISBN 0-435-27045-1). Heinemann Ed.
Prowse, Philip see Milne, John.
Prpic, George J. South Slavic Immigration in America. (The Immigrant Heritage of America Ser.). 1978. lib. bdg. 13.50 (ISBN 0-8057-8413-6). Twayne.
Prtho Books Editorial Staff, ed. All About Growing Fruits & Berries. LC 76-29250. (Illus.). 1977. pap. 4.95; pap. midwest-northeast ed. (ISBN 0-917102-29-0); pap. west ed. (ISBN 0-917102-28-2); pap. south ed. (ISBN 0-917102-30-4). Ortho.
Prucha, Francis P. American Indian Policy in the Formative Years: The Indian Trade & Intercourse Acts, 1790-1834. LC 62-9428. 1970. pap. 3.25 (ISBN 0-8032-5706-6, BB 510, Bison). U of Nebr Pr.
--A Bibliographical Guide to the History of Indian-White Relations in the United States. LC 76-16045. 1977. lib. bdg. 25.00x (ISBN 0-226-68476-8); pap. 11.00x (ISBN 0-226-68477-6). U of Chicago Pr.
--Broadax & Bayonet: The Role of the United States Army in the Development of the Northwest, Seventeen Ninety to Eighteen Thirty-Four. LC 53-6511. 279p. 1967. pap. 1.95 o.p. (ISBN 0-8032-5151-3, BB 360, Bison). U of Nebr Pr.
--The Churches & the Indian Schools, 1888-1912. LC 79-12220. (Illus.). 1979. 16.50x (ISBN 0-8032-3657-3). U of Nebr Pr.
--Sword of the Republic: The U. S. Army on the Frontier, 1783-1846. LC 77-74431. (Wars of the United States Ser.). (Illus.). 458p. 1977. pap. 6.95x (ISBN 0-253-28800-2). Ind U Pr.
Prucha, Francis P., ed. Americanizing the American Indians: Writings by the "Friends of the Indian," 1880-1900. LC 77-14102. 1978. pap. 4.95 (ISBN 0-8032-5881-X, BB 643, Bison). U of Nebr Pr.
--Documents of United States Indian Policy. LC 74-14081. x, 278p. 1975. 14.95x (ISBN 0-8032-0852-9); pap. 4.95x (ISBN 0-8032-5814-3, BB 599, Bison). U of Nebr Pr.
Prudden, Bonnie. Bonnie Prudden's Fitness Book: A Picture Guide with Exercises & Reducing Plans. 1959. 14.95 (ISBN 0-8260-7235-6). Ronald Pr.
--Exer-Sex. (Illus.). 1980. pap. 3.95 (ISBN 0-553-10698-8). Aquarian Pr.
--Fitness from Six to Twelve. LC 67-13726. (Illus.). 1972. 9.95 o.s.i. (ISBN 0-06-013436-4, HarpT). Har-Row.
--Pain Erasure: The Bonnie Prudden Way. (Illus.). 288p. 1980. 14.95 (ISBN 0-87131-328-6). M Evans.
Prudhoe, John, tr. see Von Goethe, Johann W.
Prue, J. E. Ionic Equilibria. 1966. 15.00 (ISBN 0-08-011344-3). Pergamon.
Pruet, Janet E. When the Roses Fade. 1981. 4.95 (ISBN 0-8062-1644-1). Carlton.
Pruett, James & Rigsby, Lee. Selective Music Bibliography from the Period 1663-1763. (Illus.). 1962. pap. 1.00 (ISBN 0-86526-109-1). NC Archives.
Prufer, Olaf. Raven Rocks: A Woodland Rockshelter in Belmont County, Ohio. Seeman, Mark F., ed. LC 80-84664. (Kent State Research Papers in Archaeology: No. 1). (Illus.). 104p. (Orig.). 1981. pap. 6.00x (ISBN 0-87338-254-4). Kent St U Pr.
Pruginin, Yoel, jt. auth. see Hepher, Dalfour.
Prugovecki, Eduard. Quantum Mechanics in Hilbert Space. 2nd ed. LC 80-534. (Pure & Applied Mathematics Ser.). 1981. write for info. (ISBN 0-12-566060-X). Acad Pr.
Pruitt, Basil A., jt. auth. see Salisbury, Roger E.
Pruitt, Cay. Rays from Sunshine. 56p. 1980. 3.50 (ISBN 0-8059-2766-2). Dorrance.
Pruitt, Fred. The New Testament Church & Its Symbols. 131p. 1.00. Faith Pub Hse.
--Past, Present & Future of the Church. 72p. 0.60. Faith Pub Hse.
Pruitt, Fred & Pruitt, Lawrence. God's Gracious Dealings. (Illus.). 496p. 5.00. Faith Pub Hse.
Pruitt, Ida. Old Madam Yin: A Memoir of Peking Life. LC 78-68782. 1979. 8.95x (ISBN 0-8047-1038-4); pap. 2.95 (ISBN 0-8047-1099-6, SP24). Stanford U Pr.
Pruitt, Lawrence, jt. auth. see Pruitt, Fred.
Pruner, Leonora. Love's Secret Storm. (Orig.). 1981. pap. 3.95 (ISBN 0-87123-347-9, 210347). Bethany Fell.
Prunieras, M., ed. Epidermal Keratinocyte Differentiation & Fibrillogenesis. (Frontiers of Matrix Biology Ser.: Vol. 9). (Illus.). 240p. 1980. 72.00 (ISBN 3-8055-0893-X). S Karger.
Prusek, Jaroslav. Lyrical & the Epic: Studies of Modern Chinese Literature. Lee, Leo Ou-fan, ed. LC 80-7491. (Studies in Chinese Literature & Society). 320p. 1980. 22.50x (ISBN 0-253-10283-9). Ind U Pr.
Prussin, Jeffrey A. Employee Health Benefits: HMOs & Mandatory Dual Choice. LC 76-24131. 1976. 49.50 (ISBN 0-912862-27-0). Aspen Systems.
Prussin, Labelle. Architecture in Northern Ghana: A Study of Forms & Functions. LC 75-84789. (Illus.). 1969. 18.50x (ISBN 0-520-01613-0). U of Cal Pr.
Pruter, A. T. & Alverson, Dayton L., eds. The Columbia River Estuary & Adjacent Ocean Waters: Bioenvironmental Studies. LC 79-178705. (Illus.). 882p. 1972. 25.00 (ISBN 0-295-95177-X). U of Wash Pr.
Prutskov, Nikita I. Gleb Uspensky. (World Authors Ser.: Russia: No. 190). lib. bdg. 10.95 (ISBN 0-8057-2914-3). Twayne.
Prybyla, Jan S. Issues in Socialist Economic Modernization. 140p. 1980. 19.95 (ISBN 0-03-057962-7). Praeger.
Pryce, Betty H. Mastering English. LC 75-2090. (High School Equivalency Prog. Ser.). 161p. (Orig.). (gr. 9-12). 1975. pap. text ed. 5.00 (ISBN 0-913310-39-5). Par Inc.
Pryce, J. D. Basic Methods of Linear Functional Analysis. 1973. text ed. 12.00x (ISBN 0-09-113411-0, Hutchinson). Humanities.
Pryce, Larry. The Bee Gees. LC 80-68161. (Illus.). 144p. 1981. pap. 2.95 (ISBN 0-87754-251-1). Chelsea Hse.
Pryce-Jones, David. Vienna. Time-Life Books, ed. (Great Cities Ser.). (Illus.). 1978. 14.95 (ISBN 0-8094-2327-8). Time-Life.
Pryke, E. J. Redactional Style in the Marcan Gospel. LC 76-52184. (Society for New Testament Studies Monographs). 1978. 37.00 (ISBN 0-521-21430-0). Cambridge U Pr.
Pryke, Richard. The Nationalised Industries: Policies & Performance. 282p. 1981. 32.50x (ISBN 0-85520-241-6, Pub. by Martin Robertson England); pap. 12.95x (ISBN 0-85520-242-4). Biblio Dist.
Pryke, Richard & Dodgson, John. The British Rail Problem: A Case Study in Economic Disaster. LC 75-30589. 288p. 1975. 28.75x (ISBN 0-89158-521-4). Westview.
Prynne, William, et al. William Prynne. Berkowitz, David S. & Thorne, Samuel E., eds. (English Legal History Ser.: Vol. 124). 589p. 1979. lib. bdg. 55.00 (ISBN 0-8240-3161-X). Garland Pub.
Prynne, William. Histriomastix. LC 75-170418. (The English Stage Ser: Vol. 13). lib. bdg. 50.00 (ISBN 0-8240-0596-1). Garland Pub.
Pryor, A. W., jt. auth. see Willis, B. T.
Pryor, Anthony, jt. auth. see Pearson, Charles.
Pryor, Judith, jt. auth. see Gruber, James.
Pryor, Karen. Lads Before the Wind: Adventures in Porpoise Training. LC 74-15846. (Illus.). 288p. (YA) 1975. 9.95 o.p. (ISBN 0-06-013442-9, HarpT). Har-Row.
Pryor, Nancy. The Amazing Diet Secret of a Desperate Housewife. (Illus.). 180p. 1981. 9.95 (ISBN 0-8119-0420-2, Pegasus Rex). Fell.
Pryor, Pauline. The Faint-Hearted Felon. (Candlelight Romance Ser.). (Orig.). Date not set. pap. 1.50 (ISBN 0-440-12506-5). Dell.
Pryor, R., ed. see Watkins, Vernon.
Pryor, Sam & Burnett, John. All God's Creatures: The Autobiography of Sam Pryor. 1981. 10.00 (ISBN 0-533-04946-6). Vantage.
Pryor, William A. Frontiers of Free Radical Chemistry. LC 80-19007. 1980. 27.00 (ISBN 0-12-566550-4). Acad Pr.
--Introduction to Free Radical Chemistry. (Illus.). 1966. pap. 9.95 ref. ed. (ISBN 0-13-484154-9). P-H.
Pryor, William A. see Calvin, Melvin.
Pryos, John. William Wantling: A Biography & Selected Writings. 80p. (Orig.). 1981. pap. 4.50 (ISBN 0-933180-09-8). Spoon Riv Poetry.
Pryse, B. Elizabeth. Successful Communication in Business. 272p. 1981. pap. 10.95x (ISBN 0-631-11601-X, Pub. by Basil Blackwell). Biblio Dist.
Pryse-Phillips, William & Murray, T. J. Essential Neurology. LC 77-91653. 1978. 25.00 (ISBN 0-87488-740-2). Med Exam.
Prytherch, Reginald. Modern Waterskiing: A Guide for Skiers & Boat Divers. (Illus.). 1979. 9.95 (ISBN 0-7137-0927-8, Pub by Blandford Pr England). Sterling.
Prytz, Ulla, jt. auth. see Von Bornstedt, Marianne.
Prywes, M., jt. ed. see Sela, M.
Przebienda, Edward, jt. auth. see Wall, C. Edward.
Przebienda, Edward, ed. Cumulative Personal Author Indexes for the Monthly Catalog of U.S. Government Publications, 1941-1975, 5 vols. Incl. Decennial Cumulative Personal Author Index, 1941-50. 1971. 35.00 (ISBN 0-87650-007-6); Decennial Cumulative Personal Author Index, 1951-60. 1971. 35.00 (ISBN 0-87650-008-4); Quinquennial Cumulative Personal Author Index, 1961-65. 1971. 35.00 (ISBN 0-87650-009-2); Quinquennial Cumulative Personal Author Index, 1966-70. 1971. 35.00 (ISBN 0-87650-016-5); Quinquennial Cumulative Personal Author Index, 1971-75. 1979. 35.00 (ISBN 0-87650-097-1). LC 4-18088. (Cumulative Author Index Ser.: No. 2). Set. 150.00. Pierian.
Przeworski, Adam & Teune, Henry. Logic of Comparative Social Inquiry. (Comparative Studies in Behavioral Science Ser). 1970. 20.50 (ISBN 0-471-70142-4, Pub. by Wiley-Interscience). Wiley.
Przybylski, Benno. Righteousness in Matthew & His World of Thought. LC 79-41371. (Society for New Testament Studies Monographs: No. 41). 240p. 1981. 24.50 (ISBN 0-521-22566-3). Cambridge U Pr.
Psaltis, Cynthia D. & Spallato, Sonja L. Programmed Articulation Therapy: Time to Modify. 248p. 1973. pap. 12.50 (ISBN 0-398-02745-5). C C Thomas.
Psathas, George, ed. Phenomenological Sociology: Issues & Applications. LC 73-2805. 384p. 1973. 20.95 (ISBN 0-471-70152-1, Pub. by Wiley-Interscience). Wiley.

Pshezhetsky, S. Ya., et al. E P R of Free Radicals in Radiation Chemistry. Slutzkin, D., ed. Shelnitz, P., tr. LC 74-8760. 446p. 1974. 54.95 (ISBN 0-470-70154-4). Halsted Pr.

Psychoudakis, George. Cretan Runner. Fermor, Patrick L., tr. (Illus.). 1978. pap. 8.50 (ISBN 0-7195-3475-5). Transatlantic.

Ptacek, Paul H., et al. Index to Speech, Language & Hearing Journal Titles, 1954-78. LC 79-20058. 328p. 1979. text ed. 25.00 (ISBN 0-933014-54-6). College-Hill.

Public Archives of Canada. Catalogue of the Public Archives of Canada: Collection of Published Material with a Chronological List of Pamphlets. 1979. lib. bdg. 1200.00 (ISBN 0-8161-0316-X). G K Hall.

Public Interest Economics Foundation. Benefits of Health & Safety Regulation. Ferguson, Allen R. & Behn, Judith, eds. 1981. write for info. (ISBN 0-88410-721-3). Ballinger Pub.

Public Securities Assoc. Fundamentals of Municipal Bonds. (Illus.). 1980. cancelled (ISBN 0-89490-048-X). Enslow Pubs.

Public Servie Co. of New Mexico. Technical & Economic Assessment of Solar Hybrid Repowering. 450p. 1981. pap. 39.50 (ISBN 0-89934-083-0). Solar Energy Info.

Publication Associates, ed. see May, Julian.

Publisher's Editorial Staff. Indiana Banking & Related Laws. 3rd ed. LC 78-15745. 1977. 50.00, with 1978 suppl (ISBN 0-672-83720-X, Bobbs-Merrill Law); 1978 suppl. 10.00 (ISBN 0-672-83721-8). Michie.

Pubreuil, Linda. Private Practice. 1976. pap. 1.50 o.p. (ISBN 0-685-69158-6, LB366DK, Leisure Bks). Nordon Pubns.

Pucciani, Oreste F., ed. French Theater Since 1930: Six Contemporary Full Length Plays. 1954. 15.95x o.p. (ISBN 0-471-00449-9). Wiley.

Puchala, Donald J., jt. ed. see Eckhard, Frederic.

Puchala, Donald J., jt. ed. see Eckhard, Frederick.

Pucini, Kathy, ed. see Heide, Florence P. & Heide, Roxanne.

Puckett, Earl, jt. auth. see Palmer, Arnold.

Puckett, R. E., jt. auth. see Romanowitz, H. A.

Puckett, Richard H. Introduction to Mathematical Economics: Matrix Algebra & Linear Economic Models. LC 70-142830. (Illus.). 276p. text ed. 8.95x o.p. (ISBN 0-669-49783-5). Heath.

Pucknat, A. W., ed. Health Impacts of Polynuclear Aromatic Hydrocarbons. LC 80-28039. (Environmental Health Review Ser.: No. 5). (Illus.). 271p. 1981. 39.00 (ISBN 0-8155-0840-9). Noyes.

Puddephatt, Noel. Signposts to Homoeopathic Remedies. 1980. text ed. 4.50 o.p. (ISBN 0-8464-1049-4). Beekman Pubs.

Puddephatt, R. J. The Periodic Table of the Elements. (Oxford Chemistry Ser.). (Illus.). 108p. 1972. pap. text ed. 8.50x (ISBN 0-19-855407-9). Oxford U Pr.

Puddicombe, Ann, jt. auth. see Maughan, Jackie J.

Pudney, John. Brunel & His World. (Illus.). 128p. 1974. 8.75 o.p. (ISBN 0-500-13047-7). Transatlantic.

Puel, Gaston. The Song Between Two Stars. (Translated from French). 6.75 (ISBN 0-89253-770-1); flexible cloth 4.80 (ISBN 0-89253-771-X). Ind-US Inc.

Pueschal, Siegfried M., jt. ed. see Sadick, Tamah L.

Pueschel, Siegfried M., et al. Down's Syndrome: Growing & Learning. 1978. 8.95 (ISBN 0-8362-2804-9); pap. 5.95 (ISBN 0-8362-2805-7). Andrews & McMeel.

Puffer, S. Adams. The Boy & His Gang. 188p. 1980. Repr. of 1912 ed. lib. bdg. 25.00 (ISBN 0-89987-657-9). Darby Bks.

Pugachev, V. S. Theory of Random Functions. 1965. text ed. 51.00 (ISBN 0-08-010421-5). Pergamon.

Pugel, Jane W. Your Pre-Teens Can Be Fun. (Uplook Ser.). 30p. 1972. pap. 0.75 (ISBN 0-8163-0084-4, 24515-9). Pacific Pr Pub Assn.

Pugh, Anthony. Introduction to Tensegrity. LC 75-5951. 150p. 1976. 14.50x (ISBN 0-520-02996-8); pap. 4.95 (ISBN 0-520-03055-9, CAL 325). U of Cal Pr.

--Polyhedra: A Visual Approach. LC 74-27297. 150p. 1976. 14.50x (ISBN 0-520-02926-7); pap. 4.95 (ISBN 0-520-03056-7, CAL 324). U of Cal Pr.

Pugh, B. Friction & Wear: A Trilogy Text for Students. 19.95 (ISBN 0-408-00097-X); pap. 6.95 (ISBN 0-408-00098-8). Butterworths.

Pugh, Cedric. Housing in Capitalist Societies. 320p. 1980. lib. bdg. 44.00 (ISBN 0-566-00336-8, Pub. by Gower Pub Co England). Renouf.

Pugh, D. S. & Hickson, D. J. Organizational Structure in Its Context: The Aston Programme One. LC 75-26469. 248p. 1976. 21.95 (ISBN 0-347-01114-4, 00206-2, Pub. by Saxon Hse). Lexington Bks.

Pugh, Derek S. & Payne, R. L. Organizational Behavior in Its Context: The Aston Programme 3. 1977. 19.95 o.p. (ISBN 0-566-00159-4, 01086-3, Pub. by Saxon Hse England). Lexington Bks.

Pugh, Emerson M. & Pugh, Emerson W. Principles of Electricity & Magnetism. 2nd ed. LC 70-87043. (Physics Ser). 1970. text ed. 22.95 (ISBN 0-201-06014-0). A-W.

Pugh, Emerson W., jt. auth. see Pugh, Emerson M.

Pugh, Francis, jt. auth. see Baynes, Ken.

Pugh, H. L., ed. Mechanical Behaviour of Materials Under Pressure. (Illus.). 1970. 104.40x (ISBN 0-444-20043-6). Intl Ideas.

Pugh, James M., jt. auth. see Schwartz, Bernard.

Pugh, Martin. Electoral Reform in War & Peace, 1906-1918. 1978. 20.00 (ISBN 0-7100-8792-6). Routledge & Kegan.

Pugh, Ralph B. Imprisonment in Medieval England. LC 68-12061. (Illus.). 54.50 (ISBN 0-521-06005-2). Cambridge U Pr.

Pugh, W., jt. ed. see Huth, H.

Pu Gill Gwon. Dynamic Breaking Techniques. LC 77-89191. (Ser. 128). 1977. pap. 6.95 (ISBN 0-89750-023-7). Ohara Pubns.

--Skills in Counterattacks, No. 135. 1980. pap. 6.95 (ISBN 0-89750-067-9). Ohara Pubns.

Pugliese, Anthony, ed. Ability Grouping: Homogenous Vs. Hetergoneous. 39p. 1977. pap. 9.00 o.p. (ISBN 0-686-00900-2, D-107). Essence Pubns.

--Alternative Education: Programs & Research. 1978. pap. 10.00 o.p. (ISBN 0-686-00901-0, D-117). Essence Pubns.

--Education of the Gifted Child. 39p. 1977. pap. 9.00 o.p. (ISBN 0-686-00905-3, D-108). Essence Pubns.

--The Effects of Drugs on Learning & Memory. 1977. pap. 9.50 o.p. (ISBN 0-686-00906-1, D-109). Essence Pubns.

--Sex Education: Attitudes & Research. 1978. pap. 9.50 o.p. (ISBN 0-686-00912-6, D-114). Essence Pubns.

Pugliese, Joseph M. To Reach the Green Valley. 1977. 4.50 o.p. (ISBN 0-533-02782-9). Vantage.

Puglise, Francis. Too Smart? (Illus.). 23p. (Orig.). 1980. 1.00 (ISBN 0-936920-01-7). Ridgeview Jr High Pr.

Pugmire, M. C. Experiences in Music for Young Children. LC 76-4304. (gr. 10-12). 1977. pap. text ed. 10.00 (ISBN 0-8273-0567-2); instructor's guide 2.00 (ISBN 0-8273-0568-0); tape cassette 5.75 (ISBN 0-8273-0566-4). Delmar.

Pugsley, Alfred, ed. The Works of Isambard Kingdom Brunel - an Engineering Appreciation. 232p. 1980. 40.00x (ISBN 0-7277-0030-8, Pub. by Telford England). State Mutual Bk.

--The Works of Isambard Kingdom Brunel: An Engineering Appreciation. LC 79-41470. (Illus.). 232p. 1980. 29.95 (ISBN 0-521-23239-2). Cambridge U Pr.

Puhalo, L. Innokenty of Alaska. 1977. pap. 5.00 (ISBN 0-913026-86-7). St Nectarios.

--Lives of the Saints, Vols. 2 & 3. 1977. pap. 2.50 ea.; Vol. 2. (ISBN 0-913026-75-1); Vol. 3. (ISBN 0-913026-77-8). St Nectarios.

Puhalo, Lev. God's Fools: Lives of Fools for Christ's Sake. 1976. pap. 6.00 (ISBN 0-913026-79-4). St Nectarios.

--Kiev Caves Paterikon: A Hagiography of the Kiev Caves Monastery. 1980. pap. 7.50 (ISBN 0-913026-80-8). St Nectarios.

--Lives of Saints for Young People, Vol. 1. 1975. pap. 2.50 (ISBN 0-913026-11-5). St Nectarios.

--Lives of Saints for Young People, Vol. 4. 1977. pap. 2.50 (ISBN 0-913026-91-3). St Nectarios.

Puhl, Frederick, ed. Science Fiction of the Forties. 1978. pap. 4.95 (ISBN 0-380-40097-9, 40097). Avon.

Puhvel, Jaan, jt. ed. see Anderson, William S.

Pukui, Mary K., jt. auth. see Handy, E. S.

Pula, Robert, ed. see Korzybski, Alfred.

Pulaski, Mary Ann. Understanding Piaget. rev. ed. LC 80-7595. 256p. 1980. 11.95 (ISBN 0-06-013454-2, HarpT). Har-Row.

Puliafito, Carmen A., jt. ed. see Albert, Daniel M.

Pulido, Mei Mei A., ed. see Statt, David A.

Puligandla, R. Fact & Fiction in B. F. Skinner's & Utopia. LC 73-21001. 114p. 1974. 10.00 (ISBN 0-87527-130-8). Green.

Pullan, Brian. Sources for the History of Medieval Europe from the Mid-Eighth to the Mid-Thirteenth Century. 228p. 1980. pap. 7.95x (ISBN 0-631-12371-7, Pub. by Basil Blackwell). Biblio Dist.

Pullan, Brian, tr. see Tenenti, Alberto.

Pullan, Janet, tr. see Tenenti, Alberto.

Pullar, Philippa. Gilded Butterflies: The Rise & Fall of the London Season. 1979. 22.50 (ISBN 0-241-89965-6, Pub. by Hamish Hamilton England). David & Charles.

Pullein-Thompson, Diana. Boy & the Donkey. LC 58-11463. (Illus.). (gr. 2-6). 1958. 7.95 (ISBN 0-87599-089-4). S G Phillips.

Pullein-Thompson, Josephine, et al. Black Beauty's Clan. (Illus.). 288p. (gr. 7-9). 1980. 7.95 (ISBN 0-07-050913-1). McGraw.

--Black Beauty's Family. (Illus.). 288p. (gr. 7-9). 1980. 7.95 (ISBN 0-07-050914-X). McGraw.

Pullen, John. The Twentieth Maine. 1980. 17.50 (ISBN 0-686-68805-8). Pr of Morningside.

Pullen, Mary-Helen, jt. auth. see Swank, Roy L., M.D., Ph.D.

Pulliam, John D. History of Education in America. 2nd ed. (Educational Foundations Ser.). 196p. 1976. pap. text ed. 9.50 (ISBN 0-675-08660-4). Merrill.

Pulliam, John P. & Bowman, Jim R. Educational Futurism: In Pursuance of Survival. 164p. 1975. pap. 3.95x (ISBN 0-8061-1299-9). U of Okla Pr.

Pullman, Bernard, et al, eds. Carcinogenesis: Fundamental Mechanisms & Environmental Effects. (Jerusalem Symposium: No. 13). 560p. PLB 63.00 (ISBN 90-277-1171-2, Pub. by D. Reidel). Kluwer Boston.

Pullum, Geoffrey, jt. ed. see Goyvaerts, Didier.

Pulman, Jack. Collision. 256p. 1981. pap. 2.25 (ISBN 0-449-24362-1, Crest). Fawcett.

Pulman, Michael B. The Elizabethan Privy Council in the Fifteen Seventies. LC 73-115497. 1971. 22.75x (ISBN 0-520-01716-1). U of Cal Pr.

Pulsipher, Gerreld L., jt. auth. see Rosenow, John E.

Pulton, Ferdinand. De Pace Regis et Regni. Berkowitz, David S. & Thorne, Samuel E., eds. LC 77-86638. (Classics of English Legal History in the Modern Era Ser.: Vol.29). 574p. 1979. lib. bdg. 40.00 (ISBN 0-8240-3078-8). Garland Pub.

Pulver, Ann E., jt. ed. see Bergsma, Daniel.

Pulver, Jeffery. A Biographical Dictionary of English Music. LC 69-16666. (Music Ser). 538p. 1972. Repr. of 1927 ed. lib. bdg. 42.50 (ISBN 0-306-71103-6). Da Capo.

Pulver, Jeffrey. Paganini: The Romantic Virtuoso. LC 69-11669. (Music Ser). 1970. Repr. of 1936 ed. lib. bdg. 25.00 (ISBN 0-306-71199-0). Da Capo.

Pulvertaft, R. G. Hand. 3rd ed. (Operative Surgery Ser.). 1977. 94.95 (ISBN 0-407-00618-4). Butterworths.

Pulvino, Charles J., jt. auth. see Lee, James L.

Pumphrey, Jean. Sheltered at the Edge. 1981. 4.95. Solo Pr.

Pumphrey, Muriel W., jt. ed. see Pumphrey, Ralph E.

Pumphrey, Ralph E. & Pumphrey, Muriel W., eds. Heritage of American Social Work: Readings in Its Philosophical & Institutional Development. LC 61-8989. 1961. 22.50x (ISBN 0-231-02486-X); pap. 9.00x (ISBN 0-231-08619-9). Columbia U Pr.

Pumroy, Donald K. & Pumroy, Shirley S. Modern Childrearing: A Behavioral Approach. LC 77-26964. (Illus.). 1978. text ed. 14.95 (ISBN 0-88229-185-8). Nelson-Hall.

Pumroy, Shirley S., jt. auth. see Pumroy, Donald K.

Pun, Lucas. Introduction to Optimization Practice. 1969. 29.50 o.p. (ISBN 0-471-70233-1, Pub. by Wiley-Interscience). Wiley.

Puner, Morton. To the Good Long Life: What We Know About Growing Old. LC 73-80054. 320p. 1974. 10.00x o.p. (ISBN 0-87663-191-X). Universe.

--Vital Maturity: Living Longer & Better. 1979. 12.50x (ISBN 0-87663-232-0); pap. 6.95 (ISBN 0-87663-994-5). Universe.

Pungor. Ion-Selective Electrodes. 1977. 18.50 (ISBN 0-9960003-5-6, Pub. by Kaido Hungary). Heyden.

Pungor, E. & Buzas, L., eds. Coulometric Analysis. (Illus.). 301p. 1979. 32.50x (ISBN 963-05-2021-4). Intl Pubns Serv.

Punithalingham, E. Plant Diseases Attributed to Botryodiplodia Theobromae Pat. (Bibliotheca Mycologica: No. 71). (Illus.). 200p. 1980. lib. bdg. 20.00 (ISBN 3-7682-1256-4). Lubrecht & Cramer.

Punke, Harold H. Mythology in American Education. 384p. 1981. pap. write for info. (ISBN 0-8134-2136-5). Interstate.

--Vocation As the Core of American Social Philosophy. LC 75-3521. 1975. text ed. 9.50x (ISBN 0-8134-1718-X, 1718). Interstate.

Punt, Norman A. The Singer's & Actor's Throat. 3rd ed. (Illus.). 112p. 1979. pap. text ed. 7.95x (ISBN 0-433-26451-9). Drama Bk.

--The Singer's & Actor's Throat: The Vocal Mechanism of the Professional Voice User & Its Care in Health & Disease. 4th, rev. ed. (Illus.). 100p. 1979. pap. write for info. o.p. Heinman.

Punter, David. The Literature of Terror: A History of Gothic Fiction from 1765 to the Present Day. (Illus.). 256p. 1980. lib. bdg. 30.00 (ISBN 0-582-48920-2); pap. text ed. 14.95 (ISBN 0-582-48921-0). Longman.

Punter, Ian. Woodwork Projects & Design. (Illus.). 96p. 1981. 14.95 (ISBN 0-7134-3549-6, Pub. by Batsford England). David & Charles.

Puntila, L. A. The Political History of Finland: 1809-1966. 248p. 1976. 22.50x (ISBN 0-8448-0913-6). Crane-Russak Co.

Puotinen, C. J. Career Astrology: Vocational Counseling for the Nineteen Eighties. 240p. 1980. pap. 8.95 (ISBN 0-930840-10-0). Ninth Sign.

Puotinen, C. J., ed. Astrological Self-Publishing. 1977. pap. 5.95 o.p. (ISBN 0-930840-04-6). Ninth Sign.

Puppenthal, G. C., ed. Nursery Care of Nonhuman Primates. LC 78-322018. (Advances in Primatology Ser.). 349p. 1979. 32.50 (ISBN 0-306-40150-9, Plenum Pr). Plenum Pub.

Puppi, Lionello. Andrea Palladio. LC 74-21496. (Illus.). 456p. 1975. 60.00 (ISBN 0-8212-0645-1, 039705). NYGS.

Puppo, Giancarlo. Argentine Art before the Hispanic Domination. (Illus.). 276p. 1980. 50.00 (ISBN 0-295-95772-7, Pub. by Edicolor Argentina). U of Wash Pr.

Purce, Jill. The Mystic Spiral: Journey of the Soul. (Art & Imagination Ser.). (Illus.). 128p. 1980. pap. 8.95 (ISBN 0-500-81005-2). Thames Hudson.

Purcell, Arthur H. The Waste Watchers: A Citizen's Handbook for Conserving Energy & Resources. LC 79-8438. (Illus.). 1980. pap. 4.50 (ISBN 0-385-14220-X, Anch). Doubleday.

Purcell, Carl. Carl Purcell's Complete Guide to Travel Photography. (Illus.). 1980. 14.95 (ISBN 0-87165-053-3); pap. 7.95 (ISBN 0-87165-054-1). Ziff-Davis Pub.

Purcell, Edmund S. Life of Cardinal Mannings, Archbishop of Westminster, 2 vols. LC 70-126605. (Europe 1815-1945 Ser.). 1534p. 1974. Repr. of 1896 ed. Set. lib. bdg. 85.00 (ISBN 0-306-70050-6). Da Capo.

Purcell, Edward A., Jr. The Crisis of Democratic Theory: Scientific Naturalism & the Problem of Value. LC 72-91669. 344p. 1979. pap. 7.50x (ISBN 0-8131-0141-7). U Pr of Ky.

Purcell, Edwin J. Calculus with Analytic Geometry. 3rd ed. LC 77-7977. (Illus.). 1978. 25.95 (ISBN 0-13-112052-2); Solutions Manual by Patterson 4.95 (ISBN 0-13-112037-9); pap. text ed. 1.00 linear algebra suppl. (ISBN 0-13-112029-8). P-H.

Purcell, Henry, jt. auth. see Playford, John.

Purcell, John. Best-Kept Secret: The Story of the Atomic Bomb. LC 63-13795. (Illus.). (gr. 7 up). 1963. 6.95 (ISBN 0-8149-0378-9). Vanguard.

Purcell, Mary & Wylder, Robert C., eds. Narrative Impulse: Short Stories for Analysis. LC 63-14021. (Orig.). 1963. pap. 6.50 (ISBN 0-672-63067-2). Odyssey Pr.

Purcell, Patrick. Computing in Design. 1981. text ed. price not set (ISBN 0-86103-045-1, Westbury Hse). Butterworth.

Purcell, Phillip. Malaysia. (Nations & Peoples Library). (Illus.). 1965. 8.50x o.s.i. (ISBN 0-8027-2112-5); pap. 3.50 o.s.i. (ISBN 0-8027-7059-2). Walker & Co.

Purcell, Sally, ed. Charles of Orleans: Selected Poems. (Fyfield). 112p. 1979. 6.95 (ISBN 0-902145-68-1, Pub. by Carcanet New Pr England); pap. 3.95 o.s.i. (ISBN 0-902145-69-X). Persea Bks.

Purcell, Susan K. The Mexican Profit-Sharing Decision. LC 74-84148. 224p. 1976. 24.50x (ISBN 0-520-02843-0). U of Cal Pr.

Purcell, Theodore & Cavanagh, Gerald. Blacks in the Industrial World: Issues for the Manager. LC 74-184530. 1972. 15.95 (ISBN 0-02-925520-1); pap. text ed. 5.95 (ISBN 0-02-925480-9). Free Pr.

Purcell, Victor. The Chinese in Southeast Asia. 2nd ed. (Royal Institute of International Affairs Ser.). (Illus.). 640p. 1980. pap. 22.00x (ISBN 0-19-580463-5). Oxford U Pr.

Purcell, W. R., Jr. Visualizing Business Finance. Date not set. 25.00 (ISBN 0-8436-0760-2). CBI Pub. Postponed.

Purchase, I. F., ed. Mycotoxins in Human Health: Symposium. LC 72-3778. 306p. 1971. 39.95 (ISBN 0-470-70232-X). Halsted Pr.

Purdie, Edna, ed. see Hebbel, Friedrich.

Purdom, Charles, jt. auth. see Schloss, Malcolm.

Purdon, Noel. The Words of Mercury: Shakespeare & English Mythography of the Renaissance. (Salzburg Studies in English Literature, Elizabethan & Renaissance Studies: No. 39). (Illus.). 246p. 1974. pap. text ed. 25.00x (ISBN 0-391-01503-6). Humanities.

Purdue, jt. auth. see Reasons.

Purdue University Industrial Waste Conference, 35th. Proceedings. Bell, John M., ed. 1981. text ed. 59.95 (ISBN 0-250-40363-3). Ann Arbor Science.

Purdy, A. T. Needle-Punching. 69.00x (ISBN 0-686-63775-5). State Mutual Bk.

Purdy, Al. Poems for All the Annettes. LC 72-357343. (House of Anansi Poetry Ser.: No. 7). 108p. 1973. 10.95 (ISBN 0-88784-107-4, Pub. by Hse Anansi Pr Canada); pap. 4.95 (ISBN 0-88784-007-8). U of Toronto Pr.

Purdy, David, et al, eds. see Prior, Mike, et al.

Purdy, Dorothy, jt. auth. see Spiegelberg, Nancy.
Purdy, James. Malcolm. 1980. pap. 3.95 (ISBN 0-14-005595-9). Penguin.
--Mourners Below. 1981. 13.95 (ISBN 0-670-49142-X). Viking Pr.
--The Nephew. 152p. 1980. pap. 3.95 (ISBN 0-14-005670-X). Penguin.
--Proud Flesh. 58p. 1981. limited signed ed. 40.00 (ISBN 0-935716-07-6). Lord John.
--Sixty-Three: Dream Palace & Other Stories. 176p. 1981. pap. 3.95 (ISBN 0-14-005732-3). Penguin.
Purdy, Linda, jt. auth. see Woodard, James.
Purdy, Richard Little & Millgate, Michael, eds. The Collected Letters of Thomas Hardy: Vol. 2 1893-1901. (Illus.). 320p. 1980. 49.95 (ISBN 0-19-812619-0). Oxford U Pr.
Purdy, Susan. Books for You to Make. LC 73-4568. (gr. 6 up). 1973. 8.79 (ISBN 0-397-31318-7). Lippincott.
--Christmas Decorations for You to Make. LC 65-21673. (Illus.). (gr. 1-9). 1965. 9.79 (ISBN 0-397-31486-8). Lippincott.
--Christmas Gifts for You to Make. LC 76-10160. (Illus.). (gr. 5-12). 1976. 8.79 (ISBN 0-397-31695-X); pap. 4.95 (ISBN 0-397-31696-8). Lippincott.
--Holiday Cards for You to Make. LC 67-10375. (Illus.). (gr. 4-9). 1967. 7.89 (ISBN 0-397-31574-0). Lippincott.
Purdy, Susan G. Jewish Holiday Cookbook. (Holiday Cookbook Ser.). (Illus.). (gr. 4 up). 1979. s&l 7.90 (ISBN 0-531-02281-1); pap. 2.95 (ISBN 0-531-03430-5). Watts.
Purgraski. Sorting Life Out. LC 66-7533. 1978. 24.00x (ISBN 0-930004-00-0). C E M Comp.
Purgraski, Carolyn B., et al. Sorting Out Money Values & Student Packet of Ready-to-Be-Duplicated Worksheets. rev. ed. (Sorting Life Out Ser.). 292p. 1981. tchr's. ed. 25.00 (ISBN 0-930004-02-7); student packet, 68p. free. C E M Comp.
Purgraski, I. Sorting Out Money Values. LC 76-3347. 1979. 6.95x o.p. (ISBN 0-930004-01-9). C E M Comp.
Purhoit, Swami S., tr. The Bhagavad Gita. (Illus.). 1977. 10.00 o.p. (ISBN 0-394-40671-0); pap. 5.95 (ISBN 0-394-72394-5). Knopf.
Puri, G. S., et al. Research Methods in Plant Ecology. 1968. 12.50x (ISBN 0-210-26925-1). Asia.
Puri, M. L. & Sen, P. K. Nonparametric Methods in Multivariate Analysis. LC 79-129052. (Ser. in Probability & Mathematical Statistics). 1971. 40.95 (ISBN 0-471-70240-4, Pub. by Wiley-Interscience). Wiley.
Puri, M. L., ed. Nonparametric Techniques in Statistical Inference. LC 74-116750. (Illus.). 1970. 86.50 (ISBN 0-521-07817-2). Cambridge U Pr.
Puri, Rakshat. Nineteen Poems. (Writers Workshop Redbird Ser.). 1975. 8.00 (ISBN 0-89253-521-0); pap. text ed. 4.80 (ISBN 0-88253-724-5). Ind-US Inc.
--Poems. 8.00 (ISBN 0-89253-718-3); flexible cloth 4.80 (ISBN 0-89253-719-1). Ind-US Inc.
Puri, S. P. Special Theory of Relativity. 1973. text ed. 15.00x (ISBN 0-210-22586-6). Asia.
Puri, Vishnu. Bhakti Ratnavali: An Anthology from the Bhagavata. Tapasyananda, Swami, tr. from Sanskrit. 256p. 1980. pap. 5.95 (ISBN 0-87481-499-5). Vedanta Pr.
Purin, C. M. Standard German Vocabulary. 1937. text ed. 3.95x o.p. (ISBN 0-669-29678-3). Heath.
Purintun, Ann-Elizabeth, jt. auth. see Kraft, Robert A.
Purkart, Josef, ed. see Boncompagno da Signa.
Purkayastha, Pratyush. The Romantics Third Voice: A Study of the Dramatic Works of the English Romantic Poets. (Salzburg Studies in English Literature, Poetic Drama & Poetic Theory: No. 41). 1978. pap. text ed. 25.00x (ISBN 0-391-01505-2). Humanities.
Purkey, William W., Sr. Self-Concept & School Achievement. 1970. pap. text ed. 7.95 (ISBN 0-13-803163-0). P-H.
Purkis, H. J. Building Physics: Acoustics. 1966. 23.00 (ISBN 0-08-011443-1); pap. 11.25 (ISBN 0-08-011442-3). Pergamon.
Purkis, Helen M. French Course for West Africa, 4 bks. 1962-65. Bk. 1. text ed. 5.95x (ISBN 0-521-06009-5); Bk. 2. text ed. 5.95x (ISBN 0-521-06010-9); Bk. 3. text ed. 5.95x (ISBN 0-521-06011-7); Bk. 4. text ed. 5.95x (ISBN 0-521-06012-5). Cambridge U Pr.
Purkis, John. A Preface to Wordsworth. (Preface Bks). (Illus.). 1970. pap. text ed. 5.95x (ISBN 0-582-31503-4). Longman.
Purohit, R. K., jt. auth. see Sharma, B. L.
Purpel, David & Belanger, Maurice. Curriculum & the Cultural Revolutions: A Book of Essays & Readings. LC 76-183259. 300p. 1972. 20.00x (ISBN 0-685-23647-1); text ed. 18.00x (ISBN 0-8211-1509-X). McCutchan.
Purpel, David & Ryan, Kevin, eds. Moral Education...It Comes with the Territory. LC 76-18041. xix, 424p. 1976. 15.75x (ISBN 0-8211-1516-2, Co-Pub. & Co-Distrib. by McCutchan). Phi Delta Kappa.
Purpel, David E. & Ryan, Kevin, eds. Moral Education. LC 76-18041. 1976. 20.00 (ISBN 0-8211-1516-2); text ed. 18.00x (ISBN 0-685-71410-1). McCutchan.
Purpel, David E., jt. ed. see Gress, James R.
Purpura, D. P., et al, eds. Experimental Models of Epilepsy: A Manual for the Laboratory Worker. LC 72-181308. (Illus.). 615p. 1972. 39.00 (ISBN 0-911216-26-X). Raven.
--Neurosurgical Management of the Epilepsies. LC 74-80533. (Advances in Neurology Ser: Vol. 8). 1975. 32.00 (ISBN 0-911216-88-X). Raven.
Purpura, Dominick P., jt. ed. see Yahr, Melvin D.
Pursall, B. R. & King, A. L., eds. Aerodynamics & Ventilation of Vehicle Tunnels Review & Bibliography. (BHRA Fluid Engineering Ser.: Vol. 2). 1977. pap. 52.00 (ISBN 0-900983-62-0, Dist. by Air Science Co.). BHRA Fluid.
Purseglove, J. W. Tropical Crops: Monocotyledons, Vol. 3. 1972-73. Pt. 2. 18.95 (ISBN 0-471-70242-0). Halsted Pr.
--Tropical Crops: Monocotyledons, Vol 3, Pts. 1 & 2. LC 68-16628. 607p. 1972. pap. 38.95 (ISBN 0-470-70228-1). Halsted Pr.
Purser, L. C., ed. see Cicero.
Pursey, Helen L. Wild Flowers. (Hamlyn Nature Guide Ser.). (Illus.). 1978. 8.95 (ISBN 0-600-39381-X). Transatlantic.
Pursley & Snortland. Managing Government Organizations: An Intro to Public Administration. (Illus.). 1980. text ed. 16.95 (ISBN 0-87872-245-9). Duxbury Pr.
Pursley, Robert. Introduction to Criminal Justice. 1977. text ed. 14.95x (ISBN 0-02-477540-1). Macmillan.
Pursuit, Dan G., et al, eds. Police Programs for Preventing Crime & Delinquency. (Illus.). 512p. 1972. 24.75 (ISBN 0-398-02456-1); pap. 14.75 (ISBN 0-398-02488-X). C C Thomas.
Purtill, Richard. The Stolen Goddess. (Science Fiction Ser.). 1980. pap. 1.75 (ISBN 0-87997-584-9, UE1584). DAW Bks.
Purtilo, David T. A Survey of Human Diseases. LC 77-81550. 1978. 21.95 (ISBN 0-201-05782-4, M&N Div). A-W.
Purtilo, Ruth B. & Cassel, Christine K. Ethical Dimensions in the Health Professions. 200p. 1981. text ed. price not set (ISBN 0-7216-7411-9). Saunders.
Purtle, Dale, jt. auth. see Noss, Richard B.
Purucker, G. De see De Purucker, G.
Purucker, G De see De Purucker, G.
Purucker, G. De see De Purucker, G.
Purver, Jonathan & Taylor, Lawrence. Handlin Criminal Appeals, Vol. 1. LC 80-81271. 1980. 47.50. Lawyers Co-Op.
Purves, A. C., ed. Theodore Spencer: Selected Essays. 1967. 22.00 (ISBN 0-8135-0539-9). Rutgers U Pr.
Purves, A. C., et al, eds. Literature Education in Ten Countries. LC 73-8044. (International Studies in Evaluation Ser.: Vol. 2). 428p. 1973. pap. 14.95 (ISBN 0-470-70229-X). Halsted Pr.
Purves, Alan C., et al, eds. Educational Policy & International Assessment: Implications of the IEA Surveys of Achievement. LC 74-30962. (National Society for the Study of Education, Contemporary Educational Issues Ser). 250p. 1975. 15.25 (ISBN 0-8211-1515-4); pap. text ed. 13.75 (ISBN 0-685-52137-0). McCutchan.
Purves, Jock. The Unlisted Legion. 1978. pap. 3.45 (ISBN 0-85151-245-3). Banner of Truth.
Purves, John. Italian Dictionary. (Routledge Pocket Dictionaries Ser.). 862p. 1980. pap. 8.95 (ISBN 0-7100-0602-0). Routledge & Kegan.
Purves, John, ed. A Dictionary of Modern Italian. 1953. 12.00 (ISBN 0-7100-1977-7). Routledge & Kegan.
Purves, M. J. The Physiology of the Cerebral Circulation. LC 70-169577. (Physiological Society Monographs: No. 28). (Illus.). 40p. 1972. 72.00 (ISBN 0-521-08300-1). Cambridge U Pr.
Purves, M. J., ed. The Peripheral Arterial Chemoreceptors. LC 74-16996. (Illus.). 500p. 1975. 77.00 (ISBN 0-521-20522-0). Cambridge U Pr.
Puryear, Edgar F., Jr. Stars in Flight: Studies in Air Force Leadership. 310p. 1981. 14.95 (ISBN 0-89141-127-5); pap. 8.95 (ISBN 0-89141-128-3). Presidio Pr.
Puryear, Herbert B. Reflections on the Path. (Illus.). 183p. (Orig.). 1979. pap. 3.95 (ISBN 0-87604-113-6). ARE Pr.
--Sex & the Spiritual Path. 225p. (Orig.). 1980. pap. 5.95 (ISBN 0-87604-129-2). ARE Pr.
Puryear, Herbert B. & Thurston, Mark. Meditation & the Mind of Man. rev. ed. 1975. pap. 4.95 (ISBN 0-87604-105-5). ARE Pr.
Pusateri, C. Joseph. Enterprise in Radio: WWL & the Business of Broadcasting in America. LC 79-9598. 378p. 1980. text ed. 20.25 (ISBN 0-8191-0954-1); pap. text ed. 12.00 (ISBN 0-8191-0955-X). U Pr of Amer.
Pusch, Hans. Working Together on Rudolf Stein's Mystery Dramas: Steiner's Mystery Dramas. LC 80-67024. (Illus.). 144p. (Orig.). 1980. pap. text ed. 9.95 (ISBN 0-910142-91-2). Anthroposophic.
Pusch, Margaret D., ed. see Lanier, Alison R.
Pusey, Edward B. Daniel the Prophet. 1978. 19.50 (ISBN 0-686-12942-3). Klock & Klock.
Pusey, Merlo J. The Supreme Court Crisis. LC 74-171699. (FDR & the Era of the New Deal Ser). 108p. 1972. Repr. of 1937 ed. lib. bdg. 15.00 (ISBN 0-306-70389-0). Da Capo.
Pushkarev, Boris, jt. auth. see Tunnard, Christopher.
Pushkin, Aleksandr. Eugene Onegin: A Novel in Verse, 2 vols. Nabokov, Vladimir, tr. from Russ. LC 80-8730. (Bollingen Ser.: Vol. LXXII). 1460p. 1981. 80.00x (ISBN 0-691-09744-5); pap. 18.00 (ISBN 0-691-01837-5). Princeton U Pr.
Pushkin, Alexander. Eugene Onegin: Revised & Enlarged Edition. rev. enlarged ed. Arndt, Walter, tr. 304p. 1981. pap. 5.95 (ISBN 0-525-47591-5). Dutton.
--Tale of Csar Saltan: Or the Prince & the Swan Princess. Lowe, Patricia T., tr. LC 75-5655. 1975. 5.95 (ISBN 0-690-00792-2, TYC-J). T Y Crowell.
Pustay, John S. Counterinsurgency Warfare. LC 65-11319. 1965. 9.95 o.s.i. (ISBN 0-02-925530-9). Free Pr.
Pusterla, E., ed. see Gautherie, M., et al.
Put, Van Der M. see Gerritzen, L. & Van Der Put, M.
Puter, S. A. Looters of the Public Domain. LC 70-38833. (Illus.). 495p. 1972. Repr. of 1908 ed. lib. bdg. 55.00 (ISBN 0-306-70449-8). Da Capo.
Puterbaugh, Donald L., jt. auth. see Fling, Paul N.
Puth, Robert C., ed. Current Issues in American Economy, 1980-1981. (Orig.). 1980. pap. text ed. 7.95 (ISBN 0-669-02479-1). Heath.
Puthoff, Harold, jt. auth. see Targ, Russell.
Puthucheary, Mavis. The Politics of Administration: The Malaysian Experience. 1978. 29.00x (ISBN 0-19-580386-8). Oxford U Pr.
Putigny, Bob. Easter Island. LC 75-39804. (Island Ser.). (Illus.). 128p. 1976. pap. 7.95 (ISBN 0-8467-0164-2, Pub. by Two Continents). Hippocrene Bks.
Putman, Charles E. Diagnostic Imaging in Pulmonary Disease. 1981. 32.50 (ISBN 0-8385-1682-3). ACC.
Putman, Charles E., jt. auth. see Goodman, Lawrence R.
Putman, Marc, jt. auth. see Engstrom, Robert E.
Putnam, Arnold O., et al. Unified Operations Management: A Practical Approach to a Management Information System. rev. ed. LC 63-1546. (Illus.). 1969. 10.95 (ISBN 0-89047-024-3). Herman Pub.
Putnam, Bluford H. & Wilford, D. Sykes, eds. The Monetary Approach to International Adjustment. LC 78-19753. 1979. 24.50 (ISBN 0-03-046711-X); pap. 9.95 (ISBN 0-03-056211-2). Praeger.
Putnam, C., jt. auth. see Goodman, Lawrence R.
Putnam, D. F., jt. auth. see Chapman, L. J.
Putnam, Frank B., jt. auth. see Cleland, Robert G.
Putnam, George H. Books & Their Makers During the Middle Ages, 2 Vols. 1962. Set. text ed. 42.50x (ISBN 0-391-01060-3). Humanities.
Putnam, H. Philosophical Papers, 2 vols. Incl. Vol. 1. Mathematics, Matter & Method. (Illus.). 32.95 (ISBN 0-521-20665-0); Vol. 2. Mind, Language & Reality. 38.50 (ISBN 0-521-20668-5); pap. 12.95x (ISBN 0-521-29551-3). 1975. Cambridge U Pr.
--Philosophical Papers: Mathematics, Matter & Methods, Vol. 1. 2nd ed. LC 75-8315. 1979. 38.50 (ISBN 0-521-22553-1); pap. 11.95 (ISBN 0-521-29550-5). Cambridge U Pr.
Putnam, H. Phelps. Collected Poems of H. Phelps Putnam. Walker, Charles R., ed. 232p. (Index of first lines). 1971. 10.00 o.p. (ISBN 0-374-12627-5). FS&G.
Putnam, Hilary. Meaning & the Moral Sciences. (International Library of Philosophy). 1979. pap. 6.95 (ISBN 0-7100-0437-0). Routledge & Kegan.
--Meaning & the Moral Sciences. (International Library of Philosophy & Scientific Method). 1978. 16.00 (ISBN 0-7100-8754-3). Routledge & Kegan.
Putnam, Peter. Keep Your Head Up, Mr. Putnam. LC 52-5468. 1952. lib. bdg. 9.87 o.s.i. (ISBN 0-06-013441-0, HarpT). Har-Row.
Putnam, Robert D. Comparative Study of Political Elites. (Illus.). 256p. 1976. pap. 10.95x (ISBN 0-13-154195-1). P-H.
Putnam, Roy C. Getting It All Together: A Study in Ephesians. LC 76-28456. 1977. pap. 3.95 o.p. (ISBN 0-687-14114-1). Abingdon.
Putnam, S., tr. see Pirandello, Luigi.
Putney, Valerie F., jt. auth. see Price, J. R.
Puto, Arben, jt. auth. see Pollo, Stefanaq.
Putt, A. Putt's Law & the Successful Technocrat. (Illus.). 124p. 1981. 8.00 (ISBN 0-682-49702-9). Exposition.
Putt, Arlene M. General Systems Theory Applied to Nursing. 1978. text ed. 10.95 (ISBN 0-316-72300-2). Little.
Putt, Samuel G. Henry James: A Reader's Guide. LC 66-17350. (YA) (gr. 9-12). 1967. pap. 4.95 (ISBN 0-8014-9027-8). Cornell U Pr.
Puttcamp, Rita. Operation Bro-Kee. (Bro-Kee Ser.). (gr. 5-9). 1978. pap. 3.50 (ISBN 0-570-07761-3, 39-1107). Concordia.
Puttenham, G. Arte of English Poesie. Willcock, G. D. & Walker, A., eds. 1970. 65.00 (ISBN 0-521-07782-6). Cambridge U Pr.
Putterill, Martin & Bloch, Cheree. Providing for Leisure for the City Dweller: A Review of Needs & Processes with Guidelines for Charge. (Illus.). 141p. 1978. pap. 16.00x (ISBN 0-8476-3113-3). Rowman.
Putterman, Barry. Merrie Melodies & Looney Tunes. LC 78-69637. (Illus.). 1979. 17.50 o.p. (ISBN 0-498-02211-0). A S Barnes.
Putz, Geo & Spectre, Peter, eds. Mariner's Catalog, Vol. 7. LC 73-88647. (Illus.). 1979. pap. 8.95 (ISBN 0-87742-115-3). Intl Marine.
Putz, George, jt. auth. see Spectre, Peter H.
Puurade, Richard F., ed. see Lindsay, Diana E.
Puxon, Grattan. Rom: Europe's Gypsies. (Minority Rights Group: No. 14). 1973. pap. 2.50 (ISBN 0-89192-113-3). Interbk Inc.
Pu Yi, Aisin-Gioro. From Emperor to Citizen, Vol. I. 2nd ed. 1980. 5.95 o.p. (ISBN 0-8351-0619-5); pap. 6.95 o.p. (ISBN 0-8351-0621-7). China Bks.
--From Emperor to Citizen, Vol. II. 2nd ed. 1980. 5.95 o.p. (ISBN 0-8351-0620-9); pap. 6.95 o.p. (ISBN 0-8351-0622-5). China Bks.
Puysegur, A. M. J. Chastenet de see Chastenet de Puysegur, A. M.
Puzman, Josef & Porizek, Radoslav. Communication Control in Computer Networks. (Wiley Series in Computing). 300p. 1981. 36.00 (ISBN 0-471-27894-7, Pub. by Wiley Interscience). Wiley.
Puzo, Mario. The Fortunate Pilgrim. 1978. pap. 2.25 (ISBN 0-449-23456-8, Crest). Fawcett.
--The Godfather. (RL 10). 1979. pap. 2.95 (ISBN 0-451-09438-7, E9438, Sig). NAL.
Pyatt, Edward. Mountains & Mountaineering Facts & Feats. (Guinness Superlatives Ser.). (Illus.). 256p. 1980. 19.95 (ISBN 0-8069-9246-8, Pub. by Guinness Superlatives England). Sterling.
Pyatt, G., et al. Social Accounting for Development Planning with Special Reference to Sri Lanka. LC 76-53523. 1978. 34.50 (ISBN 0-521-21578-1). Cambridge U Pr.
Pycock, C. J., jt. auth. see Kruk, Z. L.
Pycock, C. J. & Taberner, P. V., eds. Central Neurotransmitter Turnover. 200p. 1980. 30.00x (Pub. by Croom Helm England). State Mutual Bk.
Pycraft, David. Observer's Book of Garden Flowers. (Observer Bks.). (Illus.). 1977. 2.95 (ISBN 0-684-15219-3, ScribT). Scribner.
Pye, D., jt. auth. see Parker, A. K.
Pye, David. Nature & Art of Workmanship. LC 68-12062. (Illus.). 1968. 24.50 (ISBN 0-521-06016-8); pap. 8.95 (ISBN 0-521-29356-1). Cambridge U Pr.
Pye, J. K. A Grand National Commentary. (Illus.). 11.35 (ISBN 0-85131-121-0, Dist. by Sporting Book Center). J A Allen.
Pye, Lloyd. That Prosser Kid. 1978. pap. 1.95 o.p. (ISBN 0-449-23659-5, Crest). Fawcett.
Pye, Lucian W. Southeast Asia's Political Systems. 2nd ed. (Comparative Asian Government Ser). (Illus.). 128p. 1974. 7.95 (ISBN 0-13-823690-9); pap. text ed. 6.95 (ISBN 0-13-823682-8). P-H.
Pye, Michael. The King Over the Water. (Illus.). 288p. 1981. 12.95 (ISBN 0-03-057551-6). HR&W.
--Zen & Modern Japanese Religions. LC 74-155691. (Living Religions Series). (Illus.). 1973. pap. 3.50x (ISBN 0-7062-3148-1). Intl Pubns Serv.
Pyeatt, Nancy. The Consultant's Legal Guide. (The Consultant's Library). 1980. text ed. 30.00 (ISBN 0-930686-09-8). Bermont Bks.
Pyenson, Louis L. Fundamentals of Entomology & Plant Pathology. 2nd ed. (Illus.). 1980. text ed. 22.00 (ISBN 0-87055-334-8). AVI.
--Fundamentals of Entomology & Plant Pathology. 2nd ed. (Illus.). 1977. 20.50 o.p. (ISBN 0-87055-237-6). AVI.
--Healthy Plant Handbook. (Illus.). 1981. lib. bdg. 15.00 (ISBN 0-87055-377-1). AVI.
Pyenson, Louis L. & Barke, Harvey E. Laboratory Manual for Entomology & Plant Pathology. (Illus.). 1976. pap. text ed. 12.00 (ISBN 0-87055-200-7). AVI.
Pyhrr, Peter A. Zero-Base Budgeting: A Practical Management Tool for Evaluating Expenses. LC 72-8358. (Systems & Controls for Financial Management Ser). 240p. 1973. 26.50 (ISBN 0-471-70234-X); pap. 12.95 (ISBN 0-471-03721-4, Pub. by Wiley-Interscience). Wiley.

Pykare, Nina. The Innocent Heart. (Orig.). 1981. pap. 1.50 (ISBN 0-440-14475-2). Dell.
Pyke, Gertrude V. & Pyke, Helen G. Student Nurse. LC 77-70846. (Nova Ser.). 1977. pap. 4.95 (ISBN 0-8127-0134-8). Southern Pub.
Pyke, Helen G., jt. auth. see Pyke, Gertrude V.
Pyke, M. Nutrition. (Teach Yourself Ser.). 1974. pap. 2.95 o.p. (ISBN 0-679-10371-6). McKay.
Pyke, Magnus. Butter Side up! The Delights of Science. (Illus.). 1977. 8.95 o.p. (ISBN 0-8069-0106-3); lib. bdg. 8.29 o.p. (ISBN 0-8069-0107-1). Sterling.
--Technological Eating. (Illus.). 114p. 1972. 10.50 o.p. (ISBN 0-7195-2576-4). Transatlantic.
Pylant, Agnes D., ed. Fun Plans for Church Recreation. LC 58-8924. 1958. 4.95 (ISBN 0-8054-7501-X). Broadman.
--Valentine Banquets. LC 63-21601. (Illus., Orig.). 1963. pap. 0.95 (ISBN 0-8054-9913-X). Broadman.
Pyle & Larson. Plaid for Elementary Accounting, 2 vols. rev ed. 1979. Vol. 1. 5.50 (ISBN 0-256-02130-9, 01-0589-02); Vol. 2. 5.50 (ISBN 0-256-02131-7, 01-0590-02). Learning Syst.
Pyle, David W. Intelligence: An Introduction. (Illus.). 1979. 16.00x (ISBN 0-7100-0306-4); pap. 7.95 (ISBN 0-7100-0307-2). Routledge & Kegan.
Pyle, Ernie. Brave Men. LC 74-70. 474p. 1974. Repr. of 1944 ed. lib. bdg. 35.00x (ISBN 0-8371-7368-X, PYBM). Greenwood.
Pyle, Gerald F., ed. New Directions in Medical Geography: Medical Geography Papers from the 75th Anniversary Meeting of the Association of American Geographers, Philadelphia Pa., April 1979. (Illus.). 86p. 1980. 14.95 (ISBN 0-08-025817-4). Pergamon.
Pyle, H. Pepper. (Peter Possum Paperbacks). (gr. k-3). 1975. pap. 0.95 o.p. (ISBN 0-531-05123-4). Watts.
Pyle, Howard. Some Merry Adventures of Robin Hood. (Keith Jennison Large Type Bks). (gr. 5 up). 1967. PLB 7.95 o.p. (ISBN 0-531-00283-7). Watts.
--Some Merry Adventures of Robin Hood. rev. ed. (Illus.). 1954. 4.95 o.p. (ISBN 0-684-13066-1, ScribJ). Scribner.
--The Story of the Champions of the Round Table. (Illus.). (ps-4). 1968. pap. 5.00 (ISBN 0-486-21883-X). Dover.
Pyle, Howard, ed. see Exquemelin, Alexandre O.
Pyle, Kenneth B. The Making of Modern Japan: An Introduction. (Civilization & Society Ser.). 1978. pap. text ed. 6.95x (ISBN 0-669-84657-0). Heath.
Pyle, Robert. The Audubon Society Field Guide to North American Butterflies. LC 80-84240. (Illus.). 864p. 1981. 11.95 (ISBN 0-394-51914-0). Knopf.
Pyle, William, et al. Fundamental Accounting Principles. 3rd canadian ed. 1980. text ed. 21.95x (ISBN 0-256-02293-3); workbook of study guides 7.95x (ISBN 0-256-02295-X); working papers 7.95x ea. Nos. 1-14 (ISBN 0-256-02295-X). Nos. 15-28 (ISBN 0-256-02296-8). practice sets 7.95x ea. No. 1 (ISBN 0-256-02297-6). No. 2 (ISBN 0-256-02298-4). Irwin.
Pyle, William W. & Larson, Kermit D. Financial Accounting. 1980. 19.50x (ISBN 0-256-02259-3). Irwin.
Pyle, William W., et al. Fundamental Accounting Principles. 8th ed. (Willard J. Graham Ser. in Accounting). 900p. 1978. text ed. 19.95x (ISBN 0-256-01994-0); practice sets nos. 1 & 2, wkbk. of study guides 5.95 work papers 1-14 & 15-29 5.95 ea. 5.95 ea. Irwin.
--Initiation a la Compatibilite Financiere et Administrative. 2nd canadienne francaise ed. 1980. text ed. 26.85x (ISBN 0-256-02517-7); practice set 8.30x (ISBN 0-256-02541-X). Irwin.
Pylee, M. V. India's Constitution. 3rd rev. ed. (Illus.). ix, 471p. (Orig.). 1980. pap. text ed. 11.95x (ISBN 0-210-33709-5). Asia.
Pylyshyn, Z., ed. Perspectives on the Computer Revolution. ref. ed. 13.95x o.p. (ISBN 0-13-660761-6). P-H.
Pym, David. The Religious Thought of Samuel Taylor Coleridge. 1979. text ed. 12.50x (ISBN 0-901072-65-6). Humanities.
Pym, J. S., ed. see Flett, T. M.
Pym, Mrs. Michael, jt. auth. see Nelms, Mrs. Henning.
Pyman, Avril. Aleksandr Blok: a Biography, Vol. I: The Distant Thunder, 1880-1908. (Illus.). 1979. 29.50x (ISBN 0-19-211714-9). Oxford U Pr.
Pyman, Avril, ed. Alexander Blok: Selected Poems. LC 67-31506. 388p. 1972. text ed. 30.00 (ISBN 0-08-012185-3). Pergamon.
--Mikhail Bulgakov: Selected Works. 259p. 1972. pap. text ed. 17.00 (ISBN 0-08-015506-5). Pergamon.
--Yevgeniy Shvarts: Three Plays. 288p. 1972. text ed. 14.00 (ISBN 0-08-016294-0). Pergamon.
Pynchon, Thomas. Crying of Lot Forty-Nine. LC 66-12340. 1966. 5.95 o.p. (ISBN 0-397-00418-4). Lippincott.
Pyner, David. Simplefied Painless Endodontics for the General Dentist: An Alternative to N 2. (Illus.). 171p. 1980. 48.00 (ISBN 0-931386-12-8). Quint Pub Co.
Pynn, Ronald. American Politics: Changing Expectations. 1981. text ed. write for info. (ISBN 0-442-25865-8). D Van Nostrand.
Pynoos, Jon, et al, eds. Housing Urban America. 2nd ed. LC 80-12108. 1980. text ed. 37.95 (ISBN 0-202-32010-3); pap. text ed. 15.95 (ISBN 0-202-32011-1). Aldine Pub.
Pynsent, R., ed. Czech Prose & Verse: A Selection with an Introductory Essay. (London East European). 1979. pap. text ed. 26.25x (ISBN 0-485-17519-3, Athlone Pr). Humanities.
Pyrnelle, Louise-Clarke. Diddie, Dumps & Tot. 1963. 8.95 (ISBN 0-911116-17-6). Pelican.
Pytkowicz, Ricardo M. Activity Coefficients in Electrolyte Solutions, 2 vols. 1979. Vol. 2, 336p. 69.95 (ISBN 0-8493-5411-0); Vol. 2. 74.95 (ISBN 0-8493-5412-9). CRC Pr.
Pyun, Hae Soo. Nature, Intelligibility & Metaphysics: Studies in the Philosophy of F.J.E. Woodbridge. (Philosophical Currents Ser.: No. 2). 108p. 1972. pap. text ed. 15.00x (ISBN 90-6032-004-2). Humanities.

Q

Qafisheh, Hamdi. Basic Course in Gulf Arabic. 16.00x (ISBN 0-686-63543-4). Intl Bk Ctr.
Qafisheh, Hamdi see McCarus, Ernest, et al.
Qamber, Akhtar. Sabbatical in Japan. 1976. 8.00 (ISBN 0-89253-819-8); flexible cloth 4.00 (ISBN 0-89253-820-1). Ind-US Inc.
Qayum, Abdul. Social Cost-Benefit Analysis. 250p. 1979. pap. 9.95 (ISBN 0-913244-16-3). Hapi Pr.
Quackenbush, Robert. Along Came the Model T! How Henry Ford Put the World on Wheels. LC 77-10057. (Illus.). 40p. (gr. k-5). 1978. 6.50 (ISBN 0-590-07714-7, Four Winds); PLB 6.19 o.p. (ISBN 0-8193-0953-2). Schol Bk Serv.
--Animal Cracks. LC 75-1199. (A Fun-To-Read Bk.). (Illus.). 64p. (gr. 1-4). 1975. 6.95 o.p. (ISBN 0-688-41702-7); PLB 6.67 (ISBN 0-688-51702-1). Lothrop.
--The Boy Who Dreamed of Rockets. LC 78-21882. (Illus.). 32p. (gr. k-5). 1978. lib. bdg. 6.95 (ISBN 0-590-07724-4, Four Winds); lib. bdg. 5.41 o.p. (ISBN 0-8193-0996-6). Schol Bk Serv.
--City Trucks. Tucker, Kathleen, ed. (Illus.). 40p. (ps-4). 1981. 6.95 (ISBN 0-8075-1163-3). A Whitman.
--Clementine. LC 73-13990. (Illus.). 40p. (gr. k-3). 1974. 8.79 (ISBN 0-397-31506-6). Lippincott.
--Detective Mole & the Halloween Mystery. LC 80-20784. (Illus.). 32p. (gr. 1-3). 1981. 7.95 (ISBN 0-688-41988-7); PLB 7.63 (ISBN 0-688-51988-1). Morrow.
--Henry's Awful Mistake. (Illus.). 48p. (ps-3). 1981. 4.95 (ISBN 0-8193-1039-5); PLB 5.95 (ISBN 0-8193-1040-9). Parents.
--Movie Monsters & Their Masters: The Birth of the Horror Film. Tucker, Kathleen, ed. LC 79-27291. (Illus.). (gr. 3 up). 1980. 6.50g (ISBN 0-8075-5299-2). A Whitman.
--She'll Be Comin' 'round the Mountain. LC 73-2943. (Illus.). 40p. (gr. k-2). 1973. 8.95 (ISBN 0-397-31480-9). Lippincott.
--Take Me Out to the Airfield: How the Wright Brothers Invented the Airplane. LC 76-2558. (Illus.). 40p. (gr. 1-6). 1976. 5.95 o.s.i. (ISBN 0-8193-0879-X, Four Winds); PLB 5.41 o.s.i. (ISBN 0-8193-0880-3). Schol Bk Serv.
--Too Many Lollipops. LC 75-12546. (Illus.). 40p. (gr. k-3). 1975. 5.95 o.s.i. (ISBN 0-8193-0825-0, Four Winds); PLB 5.41 o.s.i. (ISBN 0-8193-0826-9). Schol Bk Serv.
--Who Threw That Pie? The Birth of Movie Comedy. Pacini, Kathy, ed. LC 78-27047. (Illus.). (gr. 3 up). 1979. 6.50g (ISBN 0-8075-9058-4). A Whitman.
Quade, Edward S., jt. auth. see Majone, Giandomenico.
Quadling, D., jt. auth. see Shuard, H.
Quadrupani, R. P. Light & Peace. LC 79-67860. 193p. 1980. pap. 3.00 (ISBN 0-89555-133-0). Tan Bks Pubs.
Quagliano, James & Vallarino, L. Chemistry. 3rd ed. 1969. ref. ed. 21.95x (ISBN 0-13-128926-8); answers to selected problems 0.25 (ISBN 0-13-128934-9). P-H.
Quagliariello, E., et al. Horizons in Biochemistry & Biophysics, Vol. 4. (Illus.). text ed. write for info. o.s.i. (ISBN 0-201-02714-3, Adv Bk Prog). A-W.
--Horizons in Biochemistry & Biophysics, Vol. 5. (Illus.). text ed. cancelled o.s.i. (ISBN 0-201-02715-1, Adv Bk Prog). A-W.
Quagliariello, E., et al, eds. Horizons in Biochemistry & Biophysics, 3 vols. Incl. Vol. 1. cancelled o.s.i. (ISBN 0-201-02711-9); pap. cancelled o.s.i. (ISBN 0-201-02721-6); Vol. 2. cancelled o.s.i. (ISBN 0-201-02712-7); pap. cancelled o.s.i. (ISBN 0-201-02722-4); Vol. 3. cancelled o.s.i. (ISBN 0-201-02713-5); pap. cancelled o.s.i. (ISBN 0-201-02723-2). (Illus., Adv Bk Prog). A-W.
Quagliariello, E., et al, eds. see International Symposium on Function & Molecular Aspects of Biomembrane Transport, Italy, April 1979.
Quaife, M. M., ed. see Davis, Britton.
Quaife, M. M., ed. see Kelly, Luther S.
Quaife, Milo M., ed. see Boller, Henry A.
Quaife, Milo M., ed. see Carson, Kit.
Quaife, Milo M., ed. see Conard, Howard L.
Quaife, Milo M., ed. see Custer, George A.
Quaife, Milo M., ed. see Finerty, John F.
Quaife, Milo M., ed. see Gillett, James B.
Quaife, Milo M., ed. see Gregg, Josiah.
Quainton, Malcolm. Ronsard's Ordered Chaos: Visions of Flux & Stability in the Poetry of Pierre de Ronsard. 252p. 1980. 25.00x (ISBN 0-389-20023-9). B&N.
Quale, G. Robina. Eastern Civilizations. 2nd ed. (Illus., Orig.). 1975. 19.95 (ISBN 0-13-222976-5); pap. text ed. 15.95 (ISBN 0-13-222992-7). P-H.
Qualey, Carlton C., ed. Thorstein Veblen: The Carleton College Veblen Seminar Essays. LC 68-28400. 1968. 15.00x (ISBN 0-231-03111-4). Columbia U Pr.
Quanbeck, Alton H. & Blechman, Barry M. D. Strategic Forces: Issues for the Mid-Seventies. (Studies in Defense Policy). 110p. 1973. pap. 3.95 (ISBN 0-8157-7283-1). Brookings.
Quanbeck, B. Alton H. & Woods, Archie L. Modernizing the Strategic Bomber Force. (Studies in Defense Policy). 1976. 3.95 (ISBN 0-8157-7281-5). Brookings.
Quandt, Jean B. From the Small Town to the Great Community: The Social Thought of Progressive Intellectuals. 1970. 16.00 (ISBN 0-8135-0679-4). Rutgers U Pr.
Quandt, William B. Decade of Decisions: American Policy Toward the Arab-Israeli Conflict, 1967-1976. 1977. 14.95 o.p. (ISBN 0-520-03469-4); pap. 5.95x (ISBN 0-520-03536-4). U of Cal Pr.
Quandt, William B., et al. The Politics of Palestinian Nationalism. 1973. 15.95x (ISBN 0-520-02336-6); pap. 3.95 (ISBN 0-520-02372-2, CAMPUS 93). U of Cal Pr.
Quante, Wolfgang. The Exodus of Corporate Headquarters from New York City. LC 75-19809. (Special Studies). (Illus.). 234p. 1976. text ed. 27.95 (ISBN 0-275-55770-7). Praeger.
Quanty, Carol & Davis, Anthony. Observing Children: A Child Development Manual. LC 74-79515. 1974. pap. text ed. 5.95x o.p. (ISBN 0-88284-016-9). Alfred Pub.
Quantz, Johann J. On Playing the Flute. Reilly, Edward R., tr. LC 75-10986. (Illus.). 1975. 19.95 (ISBN 0-02-871940-9); pap. 8.95 (ISBN 0-02-871930-1). Schirmer Bks.
Quaranta Di San Severino, B., ed. see Mussolini, Benito.
Quarantelli, E. L., ed. Disasters: Theory & Research. LC 76-52786. (Sage Studies in International Sociology: Vol. 13). 1978. 18.00x (ISBN 0-8039-9851-1); pap. 9.95x (ISBN 0-8039-9852-X). Sage.
Quarles, Benjamin. The Negro in the American Revolution. 256p. 1973. pap. 4.95 (ISBN 0-393-00674-3, Norton Lib.). Norton.
--Negro in the Making of America. (Orig.). (gr. 9 up). 1964. pap. 2.95 (ISBN 0-02-036130-0, Collier). Macmillan.
Quarles, Jaime C., tr. see Brown, Jamieson-Fausett.
Quarles, Jaime C., tr. see Latourette, Kenneth S.
Quarles, Lemuel C., tr. see Brown, Jamieson-Fausett.
Quarles, Lemuel C., tr. see Latourette, Kenneth S.
Quarrie, Bruce. German Mountain Troops. (World War Two Photo Album: No. 15). (Illus.). 96p. 1980. pap. 5.95 (ISBN 0-89404-039-1). Aztex.
--German Paratroops in the Mediterranean: World War Two Photo Album. (Illus.). 96p. 1981. pap. 5.95 (ISBN 0-89404-049-9). Aztex.
--Modelling Miniature Figures. (Illus.). 1978. pap. 11.75 (ISBN 0-85059-331-X). Aztex.
--Panzers in North West Europe. (World War Two Photo Album: No. 5). (Illus.). 96p. 1981. pap. 5.95 (ISBN 0-89404-047-2). Aztex.
--Panzers in Russia, 1941-1943: World War II Photo Album. (Illus.). 96p. 1981. pap. 5.95 (ISBN 0-89404-055-3). Aztex.
--Panzers in the Desert. (World War Two Photo Album: No. 1). (Illus.). 96p. 1981. pap. 5.95 (ISBN 0-89404-041-3). Aztex.
--Waffen-SS in Russia. (World War Two Photo Album: No. 3). (Illus.). 96p. 1981. pap. 5.95 (ISBN 0-89404-043-X). Aztex.
--World War Two Photo Album: Panzers in the Balkans & Italy. (Illus.). 96p. 1981. pap. 5.95 (ISBN 0-89404-059-6). Aztex.
Quarrie, P. R., tr. see Alfonsi, Petrus.
Quartermain, L. B. New Zealand & the Antarctic. (Illus.). 1971. 11.50x o.p. (ISBN 0-8426-1477-X). Verry.
Quarternary Stratigraphy Symposium, 1975. Quarternary Stratigraphy of North America: Proceedings. Mahaney, W. C., ed. 1976. 47.00 (ISBN 0-12-787045-8). Acad Pr.
Quasem, M. A. Al-Ghazali on Islamic Guidance. 124p. 1980. 9.95x (ISBN 0-89955-208-0, Pub. by M A Quasem Malaysia); pap. 6.95x (ISBN 0-89955-209-9). Intl Schol Bk Serv.
--The Jewels of the Qur'an: Al-Ghazali's Theory. 244p. 1980. 13.95x (ISBN 0-89955-204-8, Pub. by M A Quasem Malaysia); pap. 7.95x (ISBN 0-89955-205-6). Intl Schol Bk Serv.
--The Recitation & Interpretation of the Qur'an. 121p. 1980. 9.95x (ISBN 0-89955-206-4, Pub. by M A Quasem Malaysia); pap. 6.95x (ISBN 0-89955-207-2). Intl Schol Bk Serv.
Quasten, J., ed. see Augustine, St.
Quastler, I. E. Pioneer of the Third Level: A History of Air Midwest. (Illus.). 174p. 1980. pap. 7.50 (ISBN 0-9602554-1-9). Commuter Airlines.
--Swift Aire Lines: History of an American Commuter Airline. (Illus.). 126p. 1979. pap. 5.50 (ISBN 0-9602554-0-0). Commuter Airlines.
--Swift Aire Lines, 1969-79: Commuter Air Lines. (Illus.). 1979. pap. 6.00 (ISBN 0-9602554-0-0, Pub by Commuter). Aviation.
Quat, Helen. Wonderful World of Freezer Cooking. (Illus.). 1969. pap. 1.50 o.p. (ISBN 0-451-06788-6, W6788, Sig). NAL.
Quatremere. Prolegomenes D'ebn-Khaldoun, 3 vols. Arabic 40.00x (ISBN 0-685-77123-7). Intl Bk Ctr.
Quatremere de Quincy, A. C. An Essay on the Nature, the End, and the Means of Imitation in the Fine Arts. Freedberg, Sydney J., ed. LC 77-25763. (Connoisseurship, Criticism, & Art History: Vol. 18). 468p. 1979. lib. bdg. 48.00 (ISBN 0-8240-3276-4). Garland Pub.
Quay, Herbert C. & Werry, John S. Psychopathological Disorders of Childhood. 2nd ed. LC 78-24238. 1979. text ed. 22.95 (ISBN 0-471-04268-4). Wiley.
Quay, Richard H. In Pursuit of Equality of Educational Opportunity: A Selective Bibliography & Guide to the Research Literature. LC 76-52691. 200p. 1978. lib. bdg. 23.00 (ISBN 0-8240-9872-2). Garland Pub.
Quay, W. B. Pineal Chemistry: In Cellular & Physiological Mechanisms. (American Lectures in Living Chemistry). (Illus.). 448p. 1974. 33.50 (ISBN 0-398-02802-8). C C Thomas.
Quayle, Eric. Old Cook Books: An Illustrated History. 1978. 14.95 o.p. (ISBN 0-87690-283-2). Dutton.
Quayle, H. I. & Jenkins, S. C. Branch Lines into the Eighties. LC 79-56065. (Illus.). 96p. 1980. 16.95 (ISBN 0-7153-7980-1). David & Charles.
Quayle, Jacqueline, tr. see Fals-Borda, Orlando.
Quebedeaux, Richard. The Worldly Evangelicals: Who They Are--& Where They're Headed. LC 77-20446. 204p. 1980. pap. 5.95 (ISBN 0-06-066728-1, RD 338, HarpR). Har-Row.
Quebedeaux, Richard & Sawatsky, Rodney, eds. Evangelical-Unification Dialogue. LC 79-89421. (Conference Ser.: No. 3). (Orig.). 1979. pap. text ed. 7.95 (ISBN 0-932894-02-X). Unif Theol Seminary.
Queen, Ellery. And on the Eighth Day. 1976. pap. 1.75 (ISBN 0-345-28291-4). Ballantine.
--Chinese Orange Mystery. 1979. 1.75 o.p. (ISBN 0-686-63173-0, Sig). NAL.
--Detective Short Story: A Bibliography. LC 73-79517. 1969. 17.00x (ISBN 0-8196-0237-X); signed 30.00x (ISBN 0-685-06922-2). Biblo.
--Double, Double. 1976. pap. 1.75 (ISBN 0-345-28289-2). Ballantine.
--Double Ellery Queen. 1978. pap. 1.75 (ISBN 0-451-08025-4, E8025, Sig). NAL.
--The Fourth Side of the Triangle. 192p. 1975. pap. 1.75 (ISBN 0-345-28288-4). Ballantine.
--In the Queens' Parlor & Other Leaves from the Editors' Notebook. LC 70-79516. 1969. Repr. of 1957 ed. 12.00x (ISBN 0-8196-0238-8). Biblo.
--Murderer Is a Fox. 1976. pap. 1.50 o.p. (ISBN 0-345-25289-6). Ballantine.
--The Scarlet Letters. Bd. with The Glass Village. 1981. pap. 2.25 (ISBN 0-451-09675-4, E9675, Sig). NAL.
--Ten Days' Wonder. Bd. with The King Is Dead. 1980. pap. 2.25 (ISBN 0-451-09488-3, E9488, Sig). NAL.
--There Was an Old Woman. Bd. with The Origin of Evil. 1980. pap. 1.95 (ISBN 0-451-09306-2, J9306, Sig). NAL.
--Wife or Death & the Golden Goose. 1978. pap. 1.75 (ISBN 0-451-08087-4, E8087, Sig). NAL.
Queen, Ellery, ed. Ellery Queen Presents: Erle Stanley Gardner's The Amazing Adventures of Lester Leith. 192p. 1981. 9.95 (ISBN 0-8037-1653-2). Davis Pubns.

--Ellery Queen's Circumstantial Evidence. 287p. 1980. 9.95 (ISBN 0-8037-2213-3). Davis Pubns.
--Ellery Queen's Cops & Capers. LC 77-81935. 1977. pap. 1.50 o.p. (ISBN 0-89559-001-8). Davis Pubns.
--Ellery Queen's Crime Cruise Round the World. 288p. 1981. 9.95 (ISBN 0-8037-2189-7). Davis Pubns.
--Ellery Queen's Crimes & Consequences. LC 77-82626. 1977. pap. 1.50 o.p. (ISBN 0-89559-002-6). Davis Pubns.
--Ellery Queen's Doors to Mystery. 288p. 1981. 9.95 (ISBN 0-8037-2194-3). Davis Pubns.
--Ellery Queen's X Marks the Plot. LC 77-81937. pap. 1.95 o.p. (ISBN 0-89559-004-2). Davis Pubns.
Queen, Ellery, ed. see Ellin, Stanley.
Queen, Ellery, intro. by see Gardner, Erle S.
Queeney, K. M. Direct Broadcast Satellites & the United Nations. 344p. 1978. 41.00x (ISBN 90-286-0069-8). Sijthoff & Noordhoff.
Que Hee, Shane S. & Sutherland, Ronald G. The Phenoxyalkanoic Herbicides: Volume 1 Chemistry, Analysis & Environmental Pollution. 272p. 1981. 62.95 (ISBN 0-8493-5851-5). CRC Pr.
Quehen, Hugh De see Butler, Samuel.
Quehl, Gary H., ed. see Bergquist, William H. & Phillips, Steven R.
Queisser, H. J., jt. ed. see Madelung, O.
Quelet, Lucien. Les Champignons du Jura et des Vosges, 22 pts. in 1 vol. (Illus.). 1964. 76.80 o.p. (ISBN 0-686-21595-8). Lubrecht & Cramer.
Quemere, Erwan, jt. ed. see Asaria, Gerald.
Queneau, Raymond. Exercises in Style. 2nd ed. Wright, Barbara, tr. from Fr. LC 80-26102. Orig. Title: Exercises De Style. (Illus.). 208p. 1981. 12.95 (ISBN 0-8112-0803-6); pap. 4.95 (ISBN 0-8112-0789-7, ND513). New Directions.
--The Flight of Icarus. Wright, Barbara, tr. from Fr. LC 73-76900. Orig. Title: Le Vol D'Icare. 192p. 1973. pap. 4.95 (ISBN 0-8112-0483-9, NDP358). New Directions.
--Selected Poems. Savory, Teo, tr. LC 69-13017. (French Ser). (Eng. & Fr., Fr). 1970. 10.00 (ISBN 0-87775-084-X); pap. 4.00 (ISBN 0-87775-084-X). Unicorn Pr.
--The Skin of Dreams. Kaplan, H. J., tr. from Fr. LC 77-11668. 1979. Repr. of 1948 ed. 13.50 (ISBN 0-86527-305-7). Fertig.
Quennell, C. H. Everyday Life in Roman & Anglo-Saxon Times. 1969. 19.95 (ISBN 0-7134-1675-0, Pub. by Batsford England). David & Charles.
Quennell, C. H., jt. auth. see Quennell, Marjorie.
Quennell, Marjorie & Quennell, C. H. Everyday Life in Prehistoric Times. 1959. 19.95 (ISBN 0-7134-1673-4, Pub. by Batsford England). David & Charles.
Quennell, Peter. Affairs of the Mind: The Salon in Europe & America from the 18th to the 20th Century. (Illus.). 1980. 14.95 o.p. (ISBN 0-915220-57-1). New Republic.
--Romantic England. LC 78-119142. (Illus.). 1970. 11.95 o.s.i. (ISBN 0-02-600100-4). Macmillan.
--The Sign of the Fish. (Illus.). 255p. 1980. Repr. of 1960 ed. lib. bdg. 30.00 (ISBN 0-8492-2209-5). R West.
--Singular Preference: Portraits & Essays. LC 70-132091. (Essay & General Literature Index Reprint Ser). 1971. Repr. of 1953 ed. 12.25 (ISBN 0-8046-1419-9). Kennikat.
Quennell, Peter, ed. Memoirs of William Hickey. (Illus.). 470p. 1975. 25.00 (ISBN 0-7100-8129-4). Routledge & Kegan.
--Vladimir Nabokov: A Tribute. (Illus.). 150p. 1981. pap. 5.95. Morrow.
Quennell, Peter, ed. see Byron, George G.
Quenouille, M. H. Introductory Statistics. 2nd ed. 1968. pap. text ed. 11.25 (ISBN 0-08-013783-0). Pergamon.
Quentin, Patrick. Puzzle for Puppets. 1979. pap. 2.25 (ISBN 0-380-48579-6, 48579). Avon.
--Puzzle Forwantons. 208p. 1980. pap. 2.25 (ISBN 0-380-49643-7, 49643). Avon.
Quera, Leon. Advertising Campaigns: Formulation & Tactics. 2nd ed. LC 76-42684. (Advertising & Journalism Ser.). 1977. text ed. 20.95 (ISBN 0-88244-130-2). Grid Pub.
Quereshi, M. Y. Statistics & Behavior: An Introduction. LC 79-5514. 1980. pap. text ed. 11.50 (ISBN 0-8191-0901-0). U Pr of Amer.
Quericize, F. De see Chaffurin, L. & De Quericize, F.
Querido, Arie. Development of Socio-Medical Care in the Netherlands. (Library of Social Policy & Administration). 1968. text ed. 4.75x (ISBN 0-7100-4032-6). Humanities.
Queriere, Yves de La see La Queriere, Yves de.
Quertermous, Russel & Quertermous, Steve. Modern Guns, Identification & Values. 2nd, rev. ed. (Illus.). 416p. 1980. pap. 11.95 o.p. (ISBN 0-89145-118-8). Collector Bks.
Quertermous, Steve, jt. auth. see Quertermous, Russel.
Quest, Erica. The Silver Castle. LC 77-26527. 1978. 7.95 o.p. (ISBN 0-385-14172-6). Doubleday.
Quester, George, ed. Sea Power in the 1970's. LC 73-88666. 1975. 15.00 (ISBN 0-8046-7088-9). Kennikat.
Quetelet, Lambert A. Treatise on Man & the Development of His Faculties, 1842. LC 77-81364. (Hist. of Psych. Ser.). (Illus., Fr.). 1969. 22.00x (ISBN 0-8201-1061-2). Schol Facsimiles.
Quevedo, Francisco De & Ife, Barry. Francisco De Quevedo: La Vida del Buscon Llamado Don Pablos. 1977. 27.00 (ISBN 0-08-021855-5). Pergamon.
Quevedo y Villegas, Francisco G. de. The Comical Works of Don Francisco de Quevedo. 2nd ed. Stevens, John, tr. LC 80-2494. 1981. Repr. of 1709 ed. 69.50 (ISBN 0-404-19128-2). AMS Pr.
Quible, Zane K., et al. Introduction to Business Communication. (Illus.). 496p. 1981. text ed. 16.95 (ISBN 0-13-479055-3). P-H.
Quick, Anne, jt. ed. see Leyerle, John.
Quick, Armand J. The Hemorrhagic Diseases & the Pathology of Hemostasis. (Illus.). 404p. 1974. text ed. 33.50 (ISBN 0-398-02998-9). C C Thomas.
Quick, Horace F. Population Ecology. LC 73-19664. (Biological Sciences Curriculum Ser). 1974. pap. 4.95 (ISBN 0-672-63678-6). Pegasus.
Quick, James. Fishing the Nymph. (Illus.). 1960. 12.95 (ISBN 0-8260-7265-8). Ronald Pr.
Quick, John & LaBau, Tom. Dictionary of Motion Picture & Video Terms. (Illus.). 1981. 14.95 (ISBN 0-89046-067-1). Herman Pub.
Quick, Joseph H., et al. Work-Factor Time Standards: Measurement of Manual & Mental Work. (Illus.). 1962. 24.50 o.p. (ISBN 0-07-051061-X). McGraw.
Quick, Robert H. Essays on Educational Reformers. 568p. 1980. Repr. of 1902 ed. lib. bdg. 35.00 (ISBN 0-8495-4428-9). Arden Lib.
Quie, Paul G., jt. ed. see Gallin, John I.
Quigley, Althea E., jt. ed. see Salmon, Margaret B.
Quigley, Hugh & Clark, R. T. Republican Germany. LC 67-24592. (Illus.). 1968. Repr. of 1928 ed. 16.50 (ISBN 0-86527-166-6). Fertig.
Quigley, Isabel, tr. see Ceccherini, Silvano.
Quigley, Isabel, tr. see Marcorelles, Louis.
Quigley, Isabel, tr. see Veraldi, Attilio.
Quigley, John. Queen's Royal. 1978. pap. 2.25 o.p. (ISBN 0-449-23574-2, Crest). Fawcett.
Quigley, Lillian. The Blind Man & the Elephant. LC 59-7209. (Illus.). (gr. k-4). 1959. reinforced bdg. 6.95 o.p. (ISBN 0-684-13276-1, ScribJ); pap. 0.95 o.p. (ISBN 0-684-12780-6, SBF19, ScribJ). Scribner.
Quigley, Lillian F. Ireland. (Illus.). (gr. 7 up). 1964. 2.95 o.s.i. (ISBN 0-02-775690-4). Macmillan.
Quigley, Martin. Mr. Blood's Last Night. 167p. 1980. pap. 5.95 (ISBN 0-86629-023-0). Sunrise MO.
Quigley, Pax & Hodgetts, Victoria. The Story of Pregnancy: In Cartoons. (Illus.). 1979. pap. 2.50 (ISBN 0-685-46344-3). Budlong.
Quigley, Robert, jt. auth. see Sears, William.
Quigley, Stacy. Do I Have to? LC 79-23890. (Life & Living from a Child's Point of View Ser.). (Illus.). (gr. k-5). 1980. PLB 9.65 (ISBN 0-8172-1352-X). Raintree Child.
Quill, J. Michael. Prelude to the Radicals: The North & Reconstruction During 1865. LC 79-9674. 179p. 1980. text ed. 17.75 (ISBN 0-8191-0978-9); pap. text ed. 9.00 (ISBN 0-8191-0979-7). U Pr of Amer.
Quill, Monica. Not a Blessed Thing! (A Sister Mary Teresa Mystery Ser.). 224p. 1981. 9.95 (ISBN 0-8149-0849-7). Vanguard.
Quiller, Andrew. Blood on the Sand. (Gladiator Ser.: No. 4). 1978. pap. 1.25 o.p. (ISBN 0-523-40094-2). Pinnacle Bks.
--The Gladiator: The Hill of the Dead. 176p. (Orig.). 1975. pap. 1.25 o.p. (ISBN 0-523-22765-5). Pinnacle Bks.
--Hill of the Dead. LC 80-71033. (The Gladiators Ser.). Orig. Title: Eagles: the Hill of the Dead. 128p. 1981. pap. 2.95 (ISBN 0-87754-226-0). Chelsea Hse.
--Land of Mist. (The Gladiators Ser.). 144p. 1981. pap. 2.95 (ISBN 0-87754-225-2). Chelsea Hse.
--The Land of Mist. (Gladiator Ser.: No. 2). 1976. pap. 1.25 o.p. (ISBN 0-523-22896-1). Pinnacle Bks.
Quiller-Couch, Arthur & Dumaurier, Daphne. Castle D'or. 274p. 1976. Repr. of 1962 ed. lib. bdg. 9.50x (ISBN 0-89244-091-0). Queens Hse.
Quiller-Couch, Arthur, ed. The Oxford Book of Ballads, 2 vols in one. Repr. of 1955 ed. 75.00 (ISBN 0-403-08625-6). Somerset Pub.
Quiller-Couch, Arthur, et al, eds. see Shakespeare, William.
Quilligan, E. J. & Kretchmer, Norman, eds. Fetal & Maternal Medicine. LC 79-4345. 1979. 44.50 (ISBN 0-471-50737-7, Pub. by Wiley Medical). Wiley.
Quilligan, E. J., ed. see Battagila, Frederick C. & Hageman, Dwain D.
Quilligan, Edward J. Current Therapy in Obstetrics & Gynecology. LC 79-65461. (Illus.). 224p. 1980. text ed. 22.50 (ISBN 0-7216-7414-3). Saunders.
Quillinan, Edward. Consolation; a Poem Addressed to Lady Brydges, Repr. Of 1815 Ed. Bd. with Monthermer; a Poem. Repr. of 1815 ed; The Sacrifice of Isabel. A Poem. Repr. of 1816 ed; Elegiac Verses, Addressed to a Lady. Repr. of 1817 ed; Woodcuts & Verses. Repr. of 1820 ed; Carmina Brugensiana. Domestic Poems. Repr. of 1822 ed. LC 75-31249. (Romantic Context Ser.: Poetry 1789-1830: Vol. 98). 1978. lib. bdg. 47.00 (ISBN 0-8240-2197-5). Garland Pub.
Quillinan, Edward, jt. auth. see Brydges, Samuel E.
Quilter, E. S. Searoom Handbook with Radar Anti-Collision Tables. LC 76-240. 1976. 15.00x (ISBN 0-87033-221-X). Cornell Maritime.
Quimby, Charles W., Jr. Law for the Medical Practitioner. 1979. text ed. 17.50 (ISBN 0-914904-39-6). Health Admin Pr.
Quimby, Ian M. Material Culture & the Study of American Life. (A Winterthur Bk.). (Illus.). 1978. 12.95x (ISBN 0-393-05661-9); pap. 5.95x (ISBN 0-393-09037-X). Norton.
Quimby, Ian M., ed. Ceramics in America: Winterthur Conference Report 1972. LC 72-96715. (Winterthur Conference Report). 350p. 1980. 12.50x (ISBN 0-8139-0870-1); pap. 6.95x (ISBN 0-8139-0476-5). U Pr of Va.
--A Winterthur Bk, No. 7. (Winterthur Bk.). (Illus.). 1972. 15.00 (ISBN 0-8139-0370-X). U of Chicago Pr.
Quimby, Ian M. & Swank, Scott T., eds. Perspectives on American Folk Art. (A Winterthur Bk.). (Illus.). 1980. 21.95 (ISBN 0-393-01273-5); pap. 9.95x (ISBN 0-393-95088-3). Norton.
Quimby, Paul & Youngsberg, Norma. Yankee on the Yangtze. LC 76-49387. (Nova Ser.). 1977. pap. 4.95 (ISBN 0-8127-0131-3). Southern Pub.
Quimme, Peter. The Signet Book of Coffee & Tea. 1976. pap. 1.75 o.p. (ISBN 0-451-07149-2, E7149, Sig). NAL.
Quin, Louis D. The Heterocyclic Chemistry of Phosphorus: Systems Based on the Phosphorus Carbon Bond. LC 80-19721. 420p. 1981. 35.00 (ISBN 0-471-06461-0, Pub. by Wiley-Interscience). Wiley.
Quince, Peter. Country Life. (Illus.). 1975. 10.95 o.p. (ISBN 0-04-630007-4). Allen Unwin.
Quincer, Sheldon B. Whitefield's Sermon Outlines. pap. 3.95 (ISBN 0-8028-1157-4). Eerdmans.
Quincer, Sheldon B., ed. Matthew Henry's Sermon Outlines. 1955. pap. 3.95 (ISBN 0-8028-1155-8). Eerdmans.
Quincey, Thomas De see De Quincey, Thomas.
Quincy, A. C. De see De Quincy, A. C.
Quincy, A. C. Quatremere de see Quatremere de Quincy, A. C.
Quincy, H. Keith. The Seamy Side of Government: Essays on Punishment & Coercion. LC 78-78400. 1979. pap. text ed. 7.50 (ISBN 0-8191-0707-7). U Pr of Amer.
Quincy, Josiah. Memoir of the Life of Josiah Quincy. LC 78-146274. (Era of American Revolution Ser.). 1971. Repr. of 1825 ed. lib. bdg. 49.50 (ISBN 0-306-70098-0). Da Capo.
Quindry, Kenneth E. & Schoening, Niles. State & Local Tax Performance Nineteen Seventy-Eight. rev. ed. 1980. pap. 3.00. S Regional Ed.
Quine, W. V. Philosophy of Logic. 1970. pap. 7.95x ref. ed. (ISBN 0-13-663625-X). P-H.
--Ways of Paradox & Other Essays. (Orig.). 1966. pap. text ed. 4.95 o.p. (ISBN 0-394-30449-7). Random.
Quine, Willard. From a Logical Point of View: Logico-Philosophical Essays. pap. 3.95x (ISBN 0-06-130566-9, TB566, Torch). Har-Row.
Quine, Willard V. From a Logical Point of View: Nine Logico-Philosophical Essays. 2nd rev. ed. LC 61-15277. 1961. 9.00x (ISBN 0-674-32350-5); pap. 3.95x (ISBN 0-674-32351-3). Harvard U Pr.
--Ontological Relativity & Other Essays. LC 72-91121. (John Dewey Lectures Ser.: No. 1). 1969. 15.00x (ISBN 0-231-03307-9); pap. 5.00x (ISBN 0-231-08357-2). Columbia U Pr.
Quin-Harkin, Janet. Magic Growing Powder. LC 80-18019. (Illus.). 48p. (ps-3). 1981. 4.95 (ISBN 0-8193-1037-9); PLB 5.95 (ISBN 0-8193-1038-7). Parents.
Quinlan, Charles, Jr. Orthographic Projection Simplified. rev. ed. (gr. 9-10). 1969. pap. text ed. 4.48 (ISBN 0-87345-056-6). McKnight.
Quinlan, Maurice J. Samuel Johnson: A Layman's Religion. (Illus.). 1964. 20.00x (ISBN 0-299-03030-X). U of Wis Pr.
Quinlan, P. M. & Compton, W. V. Espanol Rapido. Hargreaves, P. H., ed. 1971. 6.50 (ISBN 0-249-44089-X). Transatlantic.
Quinn, Arthur. Broken Shore: The Marin Peninsula, a Perspective on California History. (Illus.). 288p. 1981. 14.95 (ISBN 0-87905-085-3). Peregrine Smith.
--The Confidence of British Philosophers: An Essay in Historical Narrative. (Studies in the History of Christian Thought: No. XVII). 1977. text ed. 45.75x (ISBN 9-0040-5397-2). Humanities.
Quinn, Arthur H. American Fiction: An Historical & Critical Survey. (gr. 11 up). 1981. Repr. of 1947 ed. text ed. 23.50x (ISBN 0-8290-0032-1). Irvington.
--A History of the American Drama: From the Beginning to the Civil War. 2nd ed. 1943. 29.50x (ISBN 0-89197-218-8). Irvington.
--A History of the American Drama: From the Civil War to the Present Day. rev ed. 1946. 29.50x (ISBN 0-89197-219-6). Irvington.
Quinn, Arthur H., ed. Literature of the American People. 1172p. 1951. 59.50x (ISBN 0-89197-279-X). Irvington.
Quinn, Bernetta. Ezra Pound: An Introduction to the Poetry. LC 72-6830. (Introductions to Modern American Poetry Ser.). 225p. 1973. 15.00x (ISBN 0-231-03282-X). Columbia U Pr.
Quinn, Sr. Bernetta. Randall Jarrell. (United States Authors Ser.: No. 398). 1981. lib. bdg. 10.95 (ISBN 0-8057-7266-9). Twayne.
Quinn, Brennan, jt. auth. see Ballard, Jim.
Quinn, Brian S. The New Euromarkets: A Theoretical & Practical Study of International Financing in the Eurobond & Eurocurrency Markets. LC 75-4755. 1975. 24.95 (ISBN 0-470-70266-4). Halsted Pr.
Quinn, Bridie & Cashman, Seamus. Irish Poems for Young People; Wolfhound Book of. (Illus.). (gr. 6-12). 1976. 9.95 (ISBN 0-9503454-3-1). Irish Bk Ctr.
Quinn, Carin. Your Career As a Physician. LC 79-802. 1979. lib. bdg. 5.95 (ISBN 0-668-04742-9, 4742); pap. 3.50 (ISBN 0-668-04753-4, 4753). Arco.
Quinn, Daniel & Cook, Emilie C. Beginning Metric Measurement Learning Module. 1974. pap. text ed. 124.00 (ISBN 0-89290-132-2, CM-53). Soc for Visual.
Quinn, Daniel & Mills, Richard G. Multiplication Learning Module. 1975. pap. text ed. 225.00 (ISBN 0-89290-133-0). Soc for Visual.
Quinn, Daniel & Weatherall, Donald M. Addition & Subtraction Learning Module. (ps). 1974. pap. text ed. 330.25 (ISBN 0-89290-131-4, CM-52). Soc for Visual.
Quinn, Edward, tr. see Kung, Hans.
Quinn, Edward, tr. see Rahner, Karl.
Quinn, Edward, tr. see Vorgrimler, Herbert.
Quinn, Edward, et al. The Major Shakespearean Tragedies: A Critical Bibliography. LC 72-77284. 1973. 12.95 (ISBN 0-02-925590-2). Free Pr.
Quinn, Edward G. & Dolan, Paul J. Sense of the Sixties. LC 68-12834. (Orig.). 1968. pap. text ed. 7.95 (ISBN 0-02-925560-0). Free Pr.
Quinn, Edward G., jt. ed. see Campbell, Oscar J.
Quinn, J. H. Miocene Equidae of the Texas Gulf Coastal Plain. (Illus.). 102p. 1955. 1.75 (PUB 5516). Bur Econ Geology.
Quinn, Jake. The Mindbenders. (Shannon Ser: No. 3). 1975. pap. 1.25 o.p. (ISBN 0-685-51412-9, LB226ZK, Leisure Bks). Nordon Pubns.
Quinn, James B. Strategies for Change: Logical Incrementalism. LC 80-82098. 230p. 1980. 15.95 (ISBN 0-87094-220-4). Dow Jones-Irwin.
Quinn, Jane B. Everyone's Money Book. 1980. pap. 9.95 (ISBN 0-440-55725-9, Dell Trade Pbks). Dell.
Quinn, Jim. American Tongue & Cheek: A Populist Guide to Our Language. 1981. 11.95 (ISBN 0-394-50905-6). Pantheon.
--Never Eat Out on a Saturday Night. 224p. 1981. pap. 6.95 (ISBN 0-525-47657-1). Dutton.
Quinn, Kenneth. Catullan Revolution. 1971. pap. 1.95 o.p. (ISBN 0-472-06175-5, 175, AA). U of Mich Pr.
--Virgil's Aeneid: A Critical Description. LC 68-12248. 1968. 9.75x o.p. (ISBN 0-472-08739-8). U of Mich Pr.
Quinn, Michael A., jt. ed. see Mendelson, Robert E.
Quinn, Mildred D., jt. auth. see Reinhardt, Adina M.
Quinn, Mildred D., jt. ed. see Reinhardt, Adina M.
Quinn, Seabury. The Hellfire Files of Jules De Grandin. (Jules De Grandin Ser.: No. 5). pap. 1.25 o.p. (ISBN 0-445-00428-2). Popular Lib.
--The Horror Chambers of Jules De Grandin. (Jules De Grandin Ser.: No. 6). 1977. pap. 1.50 o.p. (ISBN 0-445-03183-2). Popular Lib.

Quinn, Sheila, ed. Nursing in the European Community. 192p. 1980. 25.00x (ISBN 0-7099-0080-5, Pub. by Croom Helm Ltd England). Biblio Dist.

Quinn, Terence, jt. ed. see Pimsleur, Paul.

Quinn, Thomas. Dairy Farm Management. LC 77-90330. 1980. pap. text ed. 13.80 (ISBN 0-8273-1679-8); instructor's guide 1.75 (ISBN 0-8273-1679-8). Delmar.

Quinn, Vincent. Hart Crane. (U. S. Authors Ser.: No. 35). 1963. lib. bdg. 10.95 (ISBN 0-8057-0164-8). Twayne.

Quinney, Richard. Capitalist Society: Readings for a Critical Sociology. 1979. pap. text ed. 11.50x (ISBN 0-256-02233-X). Dorsey.

Quinones, Nathan, ed. see Curriculum Adaptation Network for Bilingual Bicultural Education.

Quinones, Nathan, ed. see Silverstein, et al.

Quinones, Ricardo. Dante Alighieri. (World Authors Ser.: No. 563). 1979. lib. bdg. 13.50 (ISBN 0-8057-6405-4). Twayne.

Quint, B. G. Clear & Simple Guide to Bookkeeping. (Clear & Simple Guides Ser.). (Illus.). 96p. (Orig.). 1981. pap. 4.95 (ISBN 0-671-42108-5). Monarch Pr.

Quint, Emanuel B. & Hecht, Neil S. Jewish Jurisprudence: Its Sources & Modern Applications, Vol. II. (Jewish Jurisprudence Ser.). 1981. price not set (ISBN 3-7186-0064-1). Harwood Academic.

--Jewish Jurisprudence Its Sources & Modern Applications, Vol. 1. 268p. 1980. 28.00 (ISBN 3-7186-0055-2); pap. 10.00 (ISBN 3-7186-0054-4). Harwood Academic.

Quint, Howard H. & Cantor, Milton, eds. Men, Women & Issues in American History, 2 vols. rev. ed. 1980. pap. text ed. 9.50x ea. Vol. 1 (ISBN 0-256-02311-5). Vol. 2 (ISBN 0-256-02312-3). Dorsey.

Quint, Howard H., et al, eds. Main Problems in American History, 2 Vols. 4th ed. 1978. text ed. 11.25x ea. (ISBN 0-686-66399-3); Vol. 1. (ISBN 0-256-02051-5); Vol. 2. (ISBN 0-256-02052-3). Dorsey.

Quintana, Richardo. The Mind & Art of Jonathan Swift. 8.50 (ISBN 0-8446-1370-3). Peter Smith.

Quintanilha, A. La Probleme De la Sexualite Chez les Champignons: Recherches Sur le Genre Coprinus. (Illus.). 1968. pap. 20.00 (ISBN 3-7682-0556-8). Lubrecht & Cramer.

Quintanilla, Efren. Aventuras De Bartolillo. (Span.). 7.95 (ISBN 84-241-5634-X). E Torres & Sons.

Quintanilla, Guadalupe C. & Silman, James B. El Espiritu Siempre Eterno Del Mexico Americano. 1977. pap. text ed. 8.25 (ISBN 0-8191-0121-4). U Pr of Amer.

Quintero, Jorge A. Laws, Theories & Values. 2nd ed. (Illus.). 144p. 1980. 10.50 (ISBN 0-87527-147-2). Green.

Quintilian. On the Early Education of the Citizen-Orator. rev. ed. Watson, John S., tr. 1965. 5.50 (ISBN 0-672-60474-4). Bobbs.

Quinton, A., tr. see Ajdukiewicz, K.

Quinton, Anthony. Bacon. (Past Masters Ser.). 1981. 7.95 (ISBN 0-8090-2790-9); pap. 2.95 (ISBN 0-8090-1414-9). Hill & Wang.

--The Nature of Things. 400p. 1973. 25.00x (ISBN 0-7100-7453-0). Routledge & Kegan.

--The Nature of Things. 1978. pap. 8.95 (ISBN 0-7100-8903-1). Routledge & Kegan.

Qui-Phiet, Tran. Faulkner & the French New Novelist. LC 80-66067. (Scholarly Monographs). 85p. 1980. pap. 7.50 (ISBN 0-8408-0503-9). Carrollton Pr.

Quirin, Jim & Cohen, Barry. Rock One Hundred. 2nd ed. LC 76-12441. (Illus.). 1976. Set. pap. text ed. 5.00 (ISBN 0-917190-01-7); pap. 0.75 ea. Suppl., 1976 (ISBN 0-917190-03-3). Suppl., 1977 (ISBN 0-917190-03-3). Suppl., 1978 (ISBN 0-917190-05-X). Suppl., 1979 (ISBN 0-917190-06-8). Chartmasters.

Quirk, Cathleen. Rue & Grace: Poems. 64p. 1981. 7.95 (ISBN 0-89594-054-X); pap. 3.95 (ISBN 0-89594-055-8). Crossing Pr.

Quirk, James, jt. auth. see McDougal, Duncan.

Quirk, James P. Intermediate Microeconomics. LC 75-34009. (Illus.). 448p. 1976. text ed. 18.50 (ISBN 0-574-19265-4, 13-2265); instr's guide avail. (ISBN 0-574-19266-2, 13-2266); mathematical notes 3.95 (ISBN 0-574-19267-0, 13-2267). SRA.

Quirk, James P. & McDougall, Duncan. Microeconomics. 1981. pap. text ed. 11.95 (ISBN 0-574-19410-X, 13-2410); instr's guide avail. (ISBN 0-574-19411-8, 13-2411). SRA.

Quirk, James P., jt. auth. see McDougall, Duncan.

Quirk, Lawrence J. The Films of Ingrid Bergman. (Illus.). 226p. 1975. pap. 6.95 (ISBN 0-8065-0480-3). Citadel Pr.

--The Films of Myrna Loy. 1980. 16.95 (ISBN 0-8065-0735-7). Lyle Stuart.

--The Films of Robert Taylor. (Illus.). 1979. pap. 6.95 (ISBN 0-8065-0667-9). Citadel Pr.

--The Films of Ronald Colman. (Illus.). 1979. pap. 6.95 (ISBN 0-8065-0668-7). Citadel Pr.

--The Films of William Holden. 256p. 1973. 12.00 (ISBN 0-8065-0375-0); pap. 6.95 (ISBN 0-8065-0517-6). Citadel Pr.

Quirk, Paul J. Industry Influence in Federal Regulatory Agencies. LC 80-8571. 264p. 1981. 18.50x (ISBN 0-691-09388-1); pap. 4.95x (ISBN 0-691-02823-0). Princeton U Pr.

Quirk, R., et al. Grammar of Contemporary English. 1976. text ed. 42.00x (ISBN 0-582-52444-X). Longman.

Quirk, Robert E. Mexican Revolution & the Catholic Church, 1910-1929. LC 73-75399. 288p. 1973. 10.00x (ISBN 0-253-33800-X). Ind U Pr.

--The Mexican Revolution, Nineteen Fourteen to Nineteen Fifteen: The Convention of Aquascalientes. LC 80-28130. 325p. 1981. Repr. of 1960 ed. lib. bdg. 27.50x (ISBN 0-313-22894-9, QUMR). Greenwood.

Quirke, Lillian M. The Rug Book: How to Make All Kinds of Rugs. (Creative Handcrafts Ser.). (Illus.). 1980. 16.95 (ISBN 0-13-783704-6, Spec); pap. 8.95 (ISBN 0-13-783712-7). P-H.

Quiroga, Horacio. Horacio Quiroga: Cuentos escogidos. Franco, Jean, ed. 1968. 10.00 (ISBN 0-08-012792-4); pap. 6.25 (ISBN 0-08-012791-6). Pergamon.

Quiros, J. De see De Quiros, J. & Schrager, O.

Quiros, T. E. Por Sendas Biblicas. 162p. (Span.). Date not set. pap. price not set (ISBN 0-311-08753-1). Casa Bautista.

Quiroz, Adrian Gonzalez. Llegando Al Alcoholico. 1979. pap. 0.85 (ISBN 0-311-46077-1). Casa Bautista.

Quisling, Ronald G. Correlative Neuroradiology. LC 79-26947. 1980. 45.00 (ISBN 0-471-05737-1, Pub. by Wiley Medical). Wiley.

Quist, Allen. The Abortion Revolution. 1980. 4.95 (ISBN 0-8100-0115-2). Northwest Pub.

Quitoriano, James H. The Psychology of the Soul. (Illus.). 1979. 37.50 (ISBN 0-89266-204-2). Am Classical Coll Pr.

Quitt, Martin & Fox, Vivian. Loving, Parenting, & Dying: The Family Cycle in England & America, Past & Present. 200p. 1980. 27.00 (ISBN 0-914434-14-4); pap. 10.95 (ISBN 0-914434-15-2). Psychohistory Pr.

Quoist, Michel. Christ Is Alive. LC 71-131101. 1972. pap. 1.95 (ISBN 0-385-09484-1, Im). Doubleday.

--I've Met Jesus Christ. LC 73-79643. 160p. 1975. pap. 1.95 (ISBN 0-385-02802-4, Im). Doubleday.

Qureishi, S. Aleem. Pakistan. (World Bibliographical Ser.: No. 10). 1981. write for info. (ISBN 0-903450-13-5). ABC-Clio.

Qureshi, A. H. Edinburgh Review & Poetic Truth. (Costerus New Ser.: No. 16). 1978. pap. text ed. 8.75x (ISBN 90-6203-752-6). Humanities.

R

R. B. Uleck Associates. Federal Career Guide. (Illus., Orig.). 1979. pap. 5.95 (ISBN 0-937562-03-3). Uleck Assoc.

R. B Uleck Associates. Life Sciences Jobs Handbook. (Illus., Orig.). 1979. pap. 9.95 (ISBN 0-937562-01-7). Uleck Assoc.

R. B. Uleck Associates. Social & Behavioral Sciences Jobs Handbook. (Illus.). 48p. (Orig.). 1979. pap. 9.95 (ISBN 0-937562-02-5). Uleck Assoc.

R. D. Cortina Company. Conversational Brazilian-Portuguese in 20 Lessons. 192p. 1980. pap. 3.95 (ISBN 0-06-463607-0, EH 607, EH). Har-Row.

--Conversational Japanese in Twenty Lessons. 256p. 1980. pap. 4.95 (ISBN 0-06-463606-2, EH 606, EH). Har-Row.

--Conversational Modern Greek in Twenty Lessons. 288p. 1980. pap. 4.95 (ISBN 0-06-463604-6, EH 604, EH). Har-Row.

--Ingles EN Twenty Lecciones. 384p. 1980. pap. 4.95 (ISBN 0-06-463608-9, EH 608, EH). Har-Row.

R. G. On the Way: Thoughts for Pilgrims. 1975. 3.95 o.s.i. (ISBN 0-8198-0447-9). Dghtrs St Paul.

R. Hoe & Co. Catalogue of Printing Presses & Printers' Materials, Lithographic Presses, Stereotyping & Electrotyping Machinery, Binders' Presses & Materials. Bidwell, John, ed. LC 78-74397. (Nineteenth-Century Book Arts & Printing History Ser.: Vol. 11). (Illus.). 1980. lib. bdg. 22.00 (ISBN 0-8240-3885-1). Garland Pub.

Raab, Carl & Raab, Joan. The Student Biologist Explores Genetics. (gr. 7-12). 1977. PLB 7.97 o.p. (ISBN 0-8239-0378-8). Rosen Pr.

Raab, Felix. English Face of Machiavelli. LC 65-1256. 1964. 15.00x o.p. (ISBN 0-8020-1300-7). U of Toronto Pr.

Raab, Joan, jt. auth. see Raab, Carl.

Raabe, Janis. Primary Readers. 1978. Set 3 Blends 10 Bks. pap. text ed. 7.68 (ISBN 0-87895-039-7). Modern Curr.

Raabe, Janis A. Primary Readers, Set 1: Short Vowels. (Illus.). (gr. k-1). 1974. pap. text ed. 7.68 incl. tchrs' guide (ISBN 0-87895-011-7). Modern Curr.

--Primary Readers, Set 2: Long Vowels. (Illus.). (gr. k-1). 1975. pap. text ed. 7.68 (ISBN 0-87895-026-5); tchrs. guide avail. Modern Curr.

Raabe, Paul. Era of German Expressionism. 1980. 25.00 (ISBN 0-7145-0698-2); pap. 8.95 (ISBN 0-7145-0699-0). Riverrun NY.

Raaen, V. F., et al. Carbon Fourteen. (Advanced Chemistry Ser.). 1968. text ed. 27.00 o.p. (ISBN 0-07-051085-7, C). McGraw.

Ra'Anan, Gavriel D. Yugoslavia After Tito: Scenarios & Implications. LC 77-4164. (Special Studies on the Soviet Union & Eastern Europe Ser.). 1978. lib. bdg. 22.00x (ISBN 0-89158-335-1). Westview.

Ra'Anan, Uri, ed. Ethnic Resurgence in Modern Democratic States: A Multidisciplinary Approach to Human Resources & Conflict. (Pergamon Policy Studies). 1980. 32.50 (ISBN 0-08-024647-8). Pergamon.

Ra'Anan, Uri, et al. Arms Transfer to the Third World: Problems & Policies. LC 77-17949. (Westview Special Studies in International Relations & U.S. Foreign Policy). 1978. lib. bdg. 37.50x (ISBN 0-89158-092-1). Westview.

Rabalais, J. Wayne. Principles of Ultraviolet Photoelectron Spectroscopy. LC 76-28413. (Wiley-Interscience Monographs in Chemical Physics). 1977. 42.50 (ISBN 0-471-70285-4, Pub by Wiley-Interscience). Wiley.

Rabalais, Maria & Hall, Howard. Children, Celebrate! LC 73-94242. (Orig.). 1974. pap. 5.95 (ISBN 0-8091-1820-3). Paulist Pr.

Rabalais, Nancy N., jt. ed. see Flint, R. Warren.

Rabalivas, Andreas D., jt. ed. see Boulougouris, John C.

Raban, Jonathan, ed. Robert Lowell's Poems: A Selection. Lowell, Robert. 1974. 9.95 (ISBN 0-571-10594-7, Pub. by Faber & Faber); pap. 5.95 (ISBN 0-571-10182-8). Merrimack Bk Serv.

Rabassa, Gregory, tr. see Cortazar, Julio.

Rabassa, Gregory, tr. see Coutinho, Alfranio.

Rabassa, Gregory, tr. see Garcia-Marquez, Gabriel.

Rabassa, Gregory, tr. see Sanchez, Luis R.

Rabasse, Maurice. Du Regime Des Fiefs En Normandie Au Moyen Age. LC 80-2006. 1981. Repr. of 1905 ed. 29.50 (ISBN 0-404-18588-6). AMS Pr.

Rabb, Maurice F., jt. auth. see Apple, David J.

Rabb, Theodore K., ed. Thirty Years' War: Problems of Motive, Extent, & Effect. 2nd ed. (Problems in European Civilization Ser.). 1972. pap. text ed. 4.95x o.p. (ISBN 0-669-82503-4). Heath.

Rabbani, Ruhiyyih. Prescription for Living. 2nd rev. ed. 1978. 7.95 (ISBN 0-85398-002-0, 7-31-23, Pub. by G Ronald England); pap. 2.50 (ISBN 0-85398-003-9, 7-31-24, Pub. by G. Ronald England). Baha'i.

--The Priceless Pearl. (Illus.). 1969. pap. 8.00 (ISBN 0-900125-03-9, 7-31-48). Baha'i.

Rabbeno, Ugo. American Commercial Policy: Three Historical Essays. (The Neglected American Economists Ser.). 1974. lib. bdg. 50.00 (ISBN 0-8240-1031-0). Garland Pub.

Rabbitt, Thomas. The Booth Interstate. LC 80-7975. 96p. 1981. 9.95 (ISBN 0-394-51382-7); pap. 4.95 (ISBN 0-394-73962-0). Knopf.

Rabby, Rami. Locating, Recruiting, & Hiring the Disabled. 1981. pap. 3.95 (ISBN 0-87576-095-3). Pilot Bks.

Rabe, Bernice. Who's Afraid? LC 79-23289. (Illus.). (gr. 7 up). 1980. PLB 7.95 (ISBN 0-525-42708-2, Skinny Book); pap. 2.50 (ISBN 0-525-45051-3, Skinny Book). Dutton.

Rabe, Berniece. The Orphans. (gr. 4-7). 1978. PLB 7.95 (ISBN 0-525-36450-1). Dutton.

Rabe, Claire. Sicily Enough. LC 76-28246. 73p. 1980. pap. 3.75 (ISBN 0-88496-070-6). Ross-Erikson.

Rabe, Olive, jt. auth. see Fisher, Aileen.

Rabelais, Francois. Heroic Deeds of Gargantua & Pantagruel, 2 Vols. 1954. 5.00x (ISBN 0-460-00826-9, Evman); Vol 1 O.p. o.p. Vol. 2 (ISBN 0-460-00827-7). Dutton.

Rabelsky, Freda, ed. see Forman, George E. & Sigel, Irving E.

Raben, Joseph. Computer Assisted Research in the Humanities: A Directory of Scholars Active, 1966-1972. LC 75-16447. 1977. text ed. 69.50 (ISBN 0-08-019870-8). Pergamon.

Raben, Marguerite. Textile Mill. LC 78-1614. (Industry at Work Ser.). (Illus.). (gr. 4-6). 1978. PLB 4.90 s&l o.p. (ISBN 0-531-02209-9). Watts.

Rabenstein, Albert. Introduction to Ordinary Differential Equations. 2nd ed. 538p. 1972. 20.95 (ISBN 0-12-573957-5). Acad Pr.

Rabianski, Joseph, jt. auth. see Epley, Donald R.

Rabier, Jacques-Rene & Inglehart, Ronald. Eurobarometer Three: European Men & Women, May 1975. LC 79-83750. 1979. codebook 8.00 (ISBN 0-89138-989-X). ICPSR.

Rabin, Albert. Assessment with Projective Techniques: A Concise Introduction. 1981. text ed. 22.95 (ISBN 0-8261-3550-1); pap. text ed. cancelled (ISBN 0-8261-3551-X). Springer Pub.

Rabin, Albert I. Further Explorations in Personality. LC 80-19407. (Personality Processes Ser.). 240p. 1980. 19.95 (ISBN 0-471-07721-6, Pub. by Wiley-Interscience). Wiley.

Rabin, Carol. A Guide to Music Festivals in America. LC 78-74201. 1979. pap. 5.95 o.p. (ISBN 0-912944-51-X). Berkshire Traveller.

--Guide to Music Festivals in North America. rev., enl. ed. LC 78-74201. 260p. 1981. 6.95 (ISBN 0-912944-67-6). Berkshire Traveller.

Rabin, Lucy F. Ford Madox Brown & the Pre-Raphaelite History-Picture. LC 77-94725. (Outstanding Dissertations in the Fine Arts Ser.). 1979. lib. bdg. 31.00 (ISBN 0-8240-3246-2). Garland Pub.

Rabineau, Phyllis. Feather Arts: Beauty, Wealth, & Spirit from Five Continents. Williams, Patricia, ed. LC 78-774595. (Illus.). 88p. (Orig.). 1979. pap. 7.95 (ISBN 0-914868-08-X). Field Mus.

Rabiner, L. R., jt. ed. see Flanagan, J. L.

Rabiner, Lawrence R. & Schafer, Ronald W. Digital Processing of Speech Signals. (P-H Signal Processing Ser.). 1978. ref. ed. 29.95 (ISBN 0-13-213603-1). P-H.

Rabinovitch, B. S., et al, eds. Annual Review of Physical Chemistry, Vol. 31. LC 51-1658. (Illus.). 1980. text ed. 20.00 (ISBN 0-8243-1031-4). Annual Reviews.

Rabinovitch, Sacha, tr. see Robert, Marthe.

Rabinovitz, Francine F. City Politics & Planning. LC 69-19454. 1970. 15.95x (ISBN 0-202-24091-6). Aldine Pub.

Rabinovitz, Francine J. & Trueblood, Felicity M., eds. Latin American Urban Research, Vol. 1. LC 78-103483. 1971. 20.00x (ISBN 0-8039-0062-7); pap. 9.95x (ISBN 0-8039-0619-6). Sage.

Rabinovitz, Rubin. Iris Murdoch. LC 68-19756. (Columbia Essays on Modern Writers Ser.: No. 34). (Orig.). (gr. 9 up). 1968. pap. 2.00 (ISBN 0-231-03000-2, MW34). Columbia U Pr.

Rabinow, Paul. Reflections on Fieldwork in Morocco. (Quantum Ser.). 1977. 14.50x (ISBN 0-520-03450-3); pap. 4.95x (ISBN 0-520-03529-1). U of Cal Pr.

Rabinow, Paul & Sullivan, William M., eds. Interpretive Social Science: A Reader. LC 77-85743. (Campus Ser.: No. 218). 1979. 24.50x (ISBN 0-520-03588-7); pap. 6.95x (ISBN 0-520-03834-7). U of Cal Pr.

Rabinowich, Ellen. Horses & Foals. (Easy-Read Fact Bk.). (Illus.). (gr. 2-4). 1979. PLB 6.45 s&l (ISBN 0-531-02272-2). Watts.

--Kangaroos, Koalas, & Other Marsupials. LC 78-5805. (First Bks). (Illus.). (gr. 4-6). 1978. PLB 6.45 s&l (ISBN 0-531-01489-4). Watts.

--The Loch Ness Monster. (Easy-Read Fact Bks.). (Illus.). (gr. 2-4). 1979. PLB 6.45 s&l (ISBN 0-531-02274-9). Watts.

--Rock Fever, No. 4. (Hi Lo Ser.). 96p. (gr. 6 up). 1981. pap. 1.50 (ISBN 0-553-14621-1). Bantam.

--Seals, Sea Lions, & Walruses. (gr. 4 up). 1980. PLB 6.90 (ISBN 0-531-04106-9). Watts.

--Toni's Crowd. LC 78-1549. (Triumph Bks). (Illus.). (gr. 7-10). 1978. PLB 6.90 s&l (ISBN 0-531-02210-2). Watts.

Rabinowicz, Ernest. Introduction to Experimentation. LC 72-93989. 1970. pap. 7.95 (ISBN 0-201-06481-2). A-W.

Rabinowitch, E., jt. ed. see Rabinowitch, V.

Rabinowitch, V. & Rabinowitch, E., eds. Views on Science, Technology & Development. LC 74-32201. 300p. 1975. text ed. 37.00 (ISBN 0-08-018241-0). Pergamon.

Rabinowitz, D. & Nielsen, Y. Home Life. Orig. Title: Would You Like to Come & Live Here. 1971. 5.95 o.s.i. (ISBN 0-02-600300-7). Macmillan.

Rabinowitz, Harvey Z. Building in Use Study: Research Report, 2 pts. Incl. Pt. 1. Technical Factors; Pt. 2. Functional Factors. (Publications in Architecture & Urban Planning Ser.). (Illus.). 258p. 1975. 10.00 set (ISBN 0-686-28214-0, R75-1). U of Wis Ctr Arch-Urban.

Rabinowitz, Howard N. Race Relations in the Urban South 1865-1890. (Urban Life in America Ser.). (Illus.). 1978. 19.95x (ISBN 0-19-502283-1). Oxford U Pr.

Rabinowitz, Peter M., ed. Talking Medicine: America's Doctors Tell Their Stories. 1981. 14.95 (ISBN 0-393-01397-9). Norton.

Rabinowitz, Sacha, tr. see Moscovici, Serge.

Rabinowitz, Sandy. How I Trained My Colt. LC 79-3162. (Reading-on-My-Own Bk.). (Illus.). 64p. (gr. 2). 1981. 4.95a (ISBN 0-385-15423-2); PLB (ISBN 0-385-15424-0). Doubleday.

Rabinowitz, Stanley J. Sologub's Literary Children: Keys to a Symbolist's Prose. (Illus.). 176p. 1980. pap. 9.95 (ISBN 0-89357-069-9). Slavica.

Rabinowitz, Victor. In Re Alger Hiss, Vol. 2. Tiger, Edith, ed. 1981. pap. 9.95 (ISBN 0-8090-0150-0). Hill & Wang.

Rabinowitz, W. G., tr. see Plato.

Rabjohn, N. Organic Syntheses Collective Volumes, Vol. 4. 1036p. 1963. 39.00 (ISBN 0-471-70470-9, 2-203). Wiley.

Rabkin, Eric, jt. auth. see Scholes, Robert.

Rabkin, Eric S. Arthur C. Clarke. LC 80-25922. (Starmont Reader's Guide: No. 1). 80p. 1980. Repr. of 1979 ed. lib. bdg. 9.95x (ISBN 0-89370-032-0). Borgo Pr.

Rabkin, Eric S., ed. Fantastic Worlds: Myths, Tales, & Stories. 1979. 17.95 (ISBN 0-19-502542-3, GB 572); pap. 6.95 (ISBN 0-19-502541-5). Oxford U Pr.

Rabkin, Judith G., jt. ed. see Klein, Donald F.

Rabkin, Norman. Shakespeare & the Common Understanding. LC 67-19237. (Orig.). 1967. 8.95 o.s.i. (ISBN 0-02-925660-7); pap. 2.95 (ISBN 0-02-925650-X). Free Pr.

--Shakespeare & the Problem of Meaning. LC 80-18538. 1981. lib. bdg. 16.00x (ISBN 0-226-70177-8). U of Chicago Pr.

Rabkin, Peggy A. Fathers to Daughters: The Legal Foundations of Female Emancipation. LC 79-6830. (Contributions in Legal Studies: No. 11). ix, 214p. 1980. lib. bdg. 25.00 (ISBN 0-313-20670-8, RFD/). Greenwood.

Rabkin, Richard, jt. auth. see Skjei, Eric.

Rabl, S. S. Boatbuilding in Your Own Backyard. 2nd ed. LC 57-11361. (Illus.). 1958. 12.75 (ISBN 0-87033-009-8). Cornell Maritime.

--Ship & Aircraft Fairing & Development: For Draftsman & Loftsmen & Sheet Metal Workers. (Illus.). 1941. pap. 6.00x spiral bdg. (ISBN 0-87033-096-9). Cornell Maritime.

Raboff, Ernest. Da Vinci. LC 78-139054. (gr. 3-7). PLB 6.95 (ISBN 0-385-07738-6). Doubleday.

--Frederic Remington. LC 73-75361. 36p. (gr. 3-7). 1976. 6.95 (ISBN 0-385-05033-X). Doubleday.

--Michelangelo. LC 71-139055. (gr. 3-7). 6.95 (ISBN 0-385-07517-0). Doubleday.

--Pierre-Auguste Renoir. LC 72-93205. (gr. 3-7). 1970. PLB 6.95 (ISBN 0-385-03775-9). Doubleday.

--Vincent Van Gogh. LC 73-75362. 36p. (gr. 3-7). 1975. 6.95a o.p. (ISBN 0-385-05009-7); PLB (ISBN 0-385-06999-5). Doubleday.

Raboteau, Albert J. Slave Religion: The Invisible Institution in the Antebellum South. (Illus.). 1980. pap. 6.95 (ISBN 0-19-502705-1, GB 594, GB). Oxford U Pr.

Rabushka, Alvin, jt. ed. see Duignan, Peter.

Raby, William L. Income Tax & Business Decisions: An Introductory Tax Text. 4th ed. LC 77-25840. (Illus.). 1978. ref. ed. 21.00 (ISBN 0-13-454363-7). P-H.

Raby, William L., jt. auth. see Tidwell, Victor H.

Rac, G. & Potter, T. Informal Reading Diagnosis: A Practical Guide for the Classroom Teacher. 2nd ed. 1981. 14.95 (ISBN 0-13-464628-2); pap. 10.95 (ISBN 0-13-464610-X). P-H.

Raccagni, Michelle. The Modern Arab Woman: A Bibliography. LC 78-15528. 1978. lib. bdg. 14.50 (ISBN 0-8108-1165-0). Scarecrow.

Race, George J., ed. see Loose Leaf References Services.

Race, Jeffrey. War Comes to Long An: Revolutionary Conflict in a Vietnamese Province. LC 79-145793. 1971. 22.75x (ISBN 0-520-01914-8); pap. 5.95x (ISBN 0-520-02361-7, CAL254). U of Cal Pr.

Rachels, James. Understanding Moral Philosophy. 1976. text ed. 17.95x (ISBN 0-8221-0172-6). Dickenson.

Rachet, G. & Rachet, M. F. Dictionnaire civilisation grecque. (Illus., Fr.). pap. 8.50 (ISBN 0-685-13861-5, 3715). Larousse.

Rachet, M. F., jt. auth. see Rachet, G.

Rachewiltz, Mary de see De Rachewiltz, Mary.

Rachie, Kenneth O. The Millets & Minor Cereals. LC 73-22142. 1974. 10.00 (ISBN 0-8108-0700-9). Scarecrow.

Rachie, Kenneth O. & Majmudar, J. V. Pearl Millet. LC 79-5144. (Illus.). 320p. 1980. lib. bdg. 29.75x (ISBN 0-271-00234-4). Pa St U Pr.

Rachleff, Owen. Exploring the Bible. LC 78-15262. (Illus.). 360p. 1981. 39.95 (ISBN 0-89659-008-9). Abbeville Pr.

Rachleff, Owen S. Young Israel: A History of the Modern Nation the First 20 Years. (Illus.). (gr. 7 up). 1981. PLB 7.95 (ISBN 0-87460-115-0). Lion.

Rachlin, Carol K., jt. auth. see Marriott, Alice.

Rachlin, Harvey. The Songwriter's Handbook. LC 77-2946. (Funk & W Bk.). (Illus.). 1977. 10.95 (ISBN 0-308-10321-1, TYC-T). T Y Crowell.

Rachlin, Howard. Behavior & Learning. LC 76-2068. (Psychology Ser.). (Illus.). 1976. text ed. 21.95x (ISBN 0-7167-0568-0). W H Freeman.

--Introduction to Modern Behaviorism. 2nd ed. LC 76-1151. (Illus.). 1976. text ed. 17.95x (ISBN 0-7167-0493-5); pap. text ed. 9.95x (ISBN 0-7167-0492-7). W H Freeman.

Rachlin, Robert. Profit Strategies for Business. 144p. 1981. 12.95 (ISBN 0-13-726216-7, Spec); pap. 4.95 (ISBN 0-13-726208-6). P-H.

--Profit Strategies for Business. LC 79-88674. 1980. 14.95 (ISBN 0-938712-01-2). Marr Pubns.

--Return on Investment: Strategies for Profit. LC 75-44668. 1976. 14.95 (ISBN 0-938712-00-4). Marr Pubns.

--Successful Techniques for Higher Profits. 260p. 1981. 16.95 (ISBN 0-938712-02-0). Marr Pubns.

Rachlin, Robert, jt. auth. see Sweeny, H. W.

Rachlis, Eugene & Ewers, John C. Indians of the Plains. LC 60-6402. (American Heritage Junior Library). (Illus.). 153p. (gr. 5 up). 1960. 9.95 (ISBN 0-8281-0385-2, J001-0). Am Heritage.

Rachman, Arnold W. Identity Group Psychotherapy with Adolescents. 336p. 1975. 23.50 (ISBN 0-398-03255-6). C C Thomas.

Rachman, David. Marketing Strategy & Structure. LC 73-17352. (Illus.). 448p. 1974. text ed. 17.95 (ISBN 0-13-558338-1). P-H.

Rachman, David J. Retail Strategy & Structure. 2nd ed. (Illus.). 496p. 1975. 18.95 (ISBN 0-13-780478-4). P-H.

Rachman, David J., jt. auth. see Mescon, Michael M.

Rachman, S. Critical Essays on Psychoanalysis. 1963. 19.25 o.p. (ISBN 0-08-010181-X). Pergamon.

--The Effects of Psychotherapy. 196p. 1971. 25.00 (ISBN 0-08-016805-1); pap. 12.75 (ISBN 0-08-016807-8). Pergamon.

Rachman, S., ed. Advances in Behaviour Research & Therapy, Vol. 2. (Illus.). 186p. 1980. 84.00 (ISBN 0-08-027110-3). Pergamon.

--Contributions to Medical Psychology, Vol. 2. (Illus.). 352p. 1980. 36.00 (ISBN 0-08-024684-2). Pergamon.

Rachman, S. J. & Philips, Clare. Psychology & Behavioral Medicine. LC 79-8589. (Illus.). 1980. 22.95 (ISBN 0-521-23178-7); pap. 6.95 (ISBN 0-521-29850-4). Cambridge U Pr.

Rachman, S. J. & Wilson, G. T. The Effects of Psychological Therapy. 2nd, enl. ed. (FEBS Ser.: Vol. 24). 400p. 1980. 53.00 (ISBN 0-08-024675-3); pap. 16.00 (ISBN 0-08-024674-5). Pergamon.

Rachman, Stanley J. Fear & Courage. LC 78-464. (Psychology Ser.). (Illus.). 1978. text ed. 17.95x (ISBN 0-7167-0089-1); pap. text ed. 8.95x (ISBN 0-7167-0087-5). W H Freeman.

Rachow, Louis A., ed. Theatre & Performing Arts Collections. (Special Collections Ser.: Vol. 1, No. 1). 128p. 1981. text ed. 19.95 (ISBN 0-917724-47-X). Haworth Pr.

Rachwiltz, I. de see De Rachwiltz, I. & Wang, M.

Racin, John. Sir Walter Raleigh As Historian: An Analysis of 'the History of the World' (Salzburg Studies in English Literature, Elizabethan & Renaissance Studies: No. 2). 216p. 1976. pap. text ed. 25.00x (ISBN 0-391-01506-0). Humanities.

Racina, Thom. Nine to Five. 160p. (Orig.). 1980. pap. 2.25 (ISBN 0-553-14496-0). Bantam.

Racina, Thom & Johnson, Joe. The Gannon Girls. (Orig.). 1979. pap. 2.25 (ISBN 0-515-05384-8). Jove Pubns.

Racina, Thom, jt. auth. see Shaw, Robert J.

Racina, Tom. The Great Los Angeles Blizzard. 1978. pap. 2.25 o.s.i. (ISBN 0-515-04718-X). Jove Pubns.

Racine, Daniel L. Leon-Gontran, Damas, 1912-1978. Founder of Negritude: A Memorial Casebook. LC 79-64101. 1979. pap. text ed. 11.25 (ISBN 0-8191-0727-1). U Pr of Amer.

Racine, Jean. Bajazet. Girdlestone, Cuthbert, ed. (French Texts Ser.). 1964. pap. text ed. 4.50x o.p. (ISBN 0-631-00560-9, Pub. by Basil Blackwell). Biblio Dist.

--Mithridate. Rudler, Gustave, ed. (French Texts Ser.). 1965. pap. text ed. 4.50x o.p. (ISBN 0-631-00440-8, Pub. by Basil Blackwell). Biblio Dist.

--Plaideurs. (Documentation thematique). (Illus., Fr). pap. 2.95 (ISBN 0-685-14041-5, 269). Larousse.

--Racine: Five Plays. Muir, Kenneth, tr. & intro. by. Incl. Andromache; Britannicus; Berenice; Phaedra; Athaliah. 288p. (Orig.). 1969. pap. 7.95 (ISBN 0-8090-0717-7, Mermaid). Hill & Wang.

Racine, Jean B. Andromache. Briffault, Herma, tr. from Fr. 1957. 4.75 (ISBN 0-8120-5006-1); pap. text ed. 1.95 (ISBN 0-8120-0028-5). Barron.

--Britannicus. Butler, Philip F., ed. LC 68-10026. (Illus.). 1967. text ed. 9.95x (ISBN 0-521-29197-6). Cambridge U Pr.

Racioppo, Larry. Halloween. LC 80-19119. (Illus.). 32p. (gr. 1 up). 1980. 8.95 (ISBN 0-684-16708-5). Scribner.

Rack, Lillian, jt. auth. see Rack, Norman.

Rack, Norman & Rack, Lillian. Macrame: Advanced Technique & Design. LC 72-175416. 144p. 1972. pap. 3.95 o.p. (ISBN 0-385-08749-7). Doubleday.

Racker, Efraim. A New Look at Mechanisms in Bioenergetics. 1976. 18.00 (ISBN 0-12-574670-9); pap. text ed. 10.00 (ISBN 0-12-574672-5). Acad Pr.

Racker, Efraim, ed. Membranes of Mitochondria & Chloroplasts. LC 72-97168. (ACS Monograph: No. 165). 1970. 28.50 (ISBN 0-8412-0287-7). Am Chemical.

Rackham, Arthur, illus. Fairy Tales from Many Lands. (Large Format Ser.). (Illus.). 1978. pap. 5.95 o.p. (ISBN 0-14-004914-2). Penguin.

Rackham, George. Diving Complete. (Illus.). 232p. 1976. 18.00 (ISBN 0-571-10342-1). Transatlantic.

Rackley, Charles E. Critical Care Cardiology. Brest, Albert N., ed. (Cardiovascular Clinics Ser.: Vol. 11, No. 3). (Illus.). 245p. 1981. text ed. 40.00 (ISBN 0-8036-7242-X). Davis Co.

Rackman, Emanuel. One Man's Judaism. LC 73-100583. 1970. 8.95 o.p. (ISBN 0-8022-2323-0). Philos Lib.

Rackmill, Ruth. Let's Have Fun with English. LC 80-68407. 120p. 1981. perfect bdg. 6.95 (ISBN 0-86548-061-3). Century Twenty One.

Racowsky, Dave & Hay, Thomas. Physical Anthropology - Laboratory Approach. rev. ed. LC 79-65361. (Illus.). 256p. 1979. pap. text ed. 13.50x (ISBN 0-686-63523-X). U MO-St Louis.

Racz, Attila. Courts & Tribunals: A Comparative Study. Zehery, Miklos, tr. 246p. 1980. 25.00x (ISBN 963-05-1799-X). Intl Pubns Serv.

Racz, Eva, tr. see Babits, Mihaly.

Racz, Evz, tr. see Mojzer, Miklos.

Rad, Gerhard Von see Von Rad, Gerhard.

Rad, P. F. I A H S International Symposium on Housing Problems, 1976: Proceedings, 2 vols. Rad, P. F., et al, eds. 1977. pap. 76.00 (ISBN 0-08-022121-1). Pergamon.

Radanovic, L., ed. Sensitivity Methods in Control Theory. 1966. 28.00 (ISBN 0-08-011827-5); pap. 14.50 (ISBN 0-08-013784-9). Pergamon.

Radband, D., jt. auth. see Stephens, H. S.

Radcliff, Ruth K. & Ogden, Sheila J. Calculation of Drug Dosages: A Workbook. 2nd ed. 290p. 1980. pap. text ed. 9.95 (ISBN 0-8016-4067-9). Mosby.

Radcliff, Ruth K. & Ogden, Shelia J. Nursing & Medical Terminology: A Workbook. LC 76-17597. (Illus.). 1977. pap. text ed. 12.50 (ISBN 0-8016-3714-7). Mosby.

Radcliff-Brown, Alfred R., ed. African Systems of Kinship & Marriage. 1950. pap. 14.95x (ISBN 0-19-724147-6). Oxford U Pr.

Radcliffe, Ann. Italian, Or, the Confessional of the Black Penitents. Garber, Frederick, ed. (Oxford English Novels Ser.). 1968. 17.95x (ISBN 0-19-255315-1). Oxford U Pr.

--The Mysteries of Udolpho. rev. ed. Dobree, Bonamy, ed. (World Classics Paper Ser.). 1980. pap. 5.95x. Oxford U Pr.

Radcliffe, C. W., jt. auth. see Suh, C. H.

Radcliffe, Elsa J. Gothic Novels of the Twentieth Century: An Annotated Bibliography. LC 78-24357. 291p. 1979. lib. bdg. 13.00 (ISBN 0-8108-1190-1). Scarecrow.

Radcliffe, Mary Ann see Polwhele, Richard.

Radcliffe, P. Beethoven's String Quartets. LC 77-26271. (Illus.). 1978. 22.50 (ISBN 0-521-21963-9); pap. 5.95 (ISBN 0-521-29326-X). Cambridge U Pr.

Radcliffe, Philip. Mozart Piano Concertos. LC 75-27958. (BBC Music Guides: No. 34). (Illus.). 64p. (Orig.). 1978. pap. 2.95 (ISBN 0-295-95477-9). U of Wash Pr.

Radcliffe, Virginia. Carribean Heritage. LC 75-12189. (Illus.). 288p. 1976. 17.50 (ISBN 0-8027-0518-9). Walker & Co.

Radcliffe-Brown, Alfred R. Andaman Islanders. 1964. pap. text ed. 5.95 (ISBN 0-02-925580-5). Free Pr.

--Structure & Function in Primitive Society. 1952. 12.95 (ISBN 0-02-925630-5); pap. text ed. 6.95 (ISBN 0-02-925620-8). Free Pr.

Radde, Paul O. The Supervision Decision! Employee Guide. (Illus.). 150p. 1981. price not set vinyl binder (ISBN 0-89384-060-2); price not set wkbk. (ISBN 0-89384-061-0). Learning Concepts.

Radding, Charles. The Modern Presidency. (American Government Ser.). (gr. 7 up). 1979. PLB 6.90 s&l (ISBN 0-531-02266-8). Watts.

Radding, Shirley B., jt. ed. see Jones, Jerry L.

Rade, Lennart. Take a Chance with Your Calculator: Probability Problems for Programmable Calculators. LC 77-88868. 1977. pap. 9.95 (ISBN 0-918398-07-X). Dilithium Pr.

Radel, J. Lucien. Roots of Totalitarianism: Fascism, National Socialism, and Communism. 1975. text ed. 19.50x (ISBN 0-8448-0374-X); pap. text ed. 9.50x (ISBN 0-8448-0600-5). Crane-Russak Co.

Radeleff, R. D. Veterinary Toxicology. 2nd ed. LC 74-85846. (Illus.). 1970. text ed. 9.50 o.s.i. (ISBN 0-8121-0200-2). Lea & Febiger.

Radelet, Louis. The Police and the Community. 1977. text ed. 14.95x (ISBN 0-02-477510-X). Macmillan.

Radelet, Louis A. The Police & the Community: Studies. LC 72-11489. (Criminal Justice Ser.). 240p. 1973. text ed. 8.95x o.p. (ISBN 0-02-476710-7). Glencoe.

Radeloff, D. J., jt. auth. see Charlesworth, R.

Radeloff, Deanna J. & Zechman, Roberta. Children in Your Life: A Guide to Child Care & Parenting. LC 80-67826. (Home Economics Ser.). 384p. 1981. pap. 12.40 (ISBN 0-8273-1748-4); instr's. guide 1.10 (ISBN 0-8273-1749-2). Delmar.

Rademaker, C. S. Life & Work of Gerardus Joannes Vossius (1577-1659) (Respublica Literaria Neerlandica). 472p. 1980. text ed. 48.50x (ISBN 90-232-1785-3). Humanities.

Rader, Charles M., jt. auth. see McClellen, Joseph H.

Rader, H., ed. Faculty Involvement in Library Instruction. LC 76-21914. (Library Orientation Ser.: No. 6). 1976. 10.00 (ISBN 0-87650-070-X). Pierian.

Rader, Melvin. Marx's Interpretation of History. 1979. 14.95x (ISBN 0-19-502474-5); pap. text ed. 5.95x (ISBN 0-19-502475-3). Oxford U Pr.

Rader, Ralph W. Tennyson's Maud: The Biographical Genesis. (Library Reprint Ser.: Vol. 90). 1978. 15.75x (ISBN 0-520-03617-4). U of Cal Pr.

Rader, Robert J. Advanced Software Design Techniques. (Illus.). 172p. text ed. 16.50 (ISBN 0-89433-046-2). Petrocelli.

Rader, Trout. Theory of Microeconomics. 1972. text ed. 22.50 (ISBN 0-12-575050-1). Acad Pr.

Rader, Wendelin, jt. ed. see Eschlach, Achim.

Rader, William. Dr. Rader's "No-Diet Program for Permanent Weight Control". LC 79-66688. 239p. 1981. 9.95 (ISBN 0-87477-139-0). J P Tarcher.

Radetzki, Marian. Uranium: Economic & Political Instability in a Strategic Commodity Market. 1981. 30.00 (ISBN 0-312-83424-1). St Martin.

Radetzki, Marian & Zorn, Stephen. Financing Mining Projects in Developing Countries. 1980. 35.00x (Pub. by Mining Journal England). State Mutual Bk.

Radford, A., ed. Italian Syntax. LC 77-71424. (Cambridge Studies in Linguistics: No. 21). 1977. 42.50 (ISBN 0-521-21643-5). Cambridge U Pr.

Radford, Charles D. What No One, but Absolutely No One Knows About Money. (Illus.). 127p. 1981. 31.25 (ISBN 0-89266-284-0). Am Classical Coll Pr.

Radford, Don. Changes: Stage 3. LC 77-83001. (Science 5-13 Ser.). (Illus.). 1977. pap. text ed. 9.30 (ISBN 0-356-04346-0). Raintree Child.

--Changes: Stages 1 & 2 & Background. LC 77-83001. (Science 5-13 Ser.). (Illus.). 1977. pap. text ed. 9.30 (ISBN 0-356-04105-0). Raintree Child.

--Metals: Background Information. LC 77-83004. (Science 5-13 Ser.). (Illus.). 1977. pap. text ed. 8.25 (ISBN 0-356-04104-2). Raintree Child.

--Metals: Stages 1 & 2. LC 77-83004. (Science 5-13). (Illus.). 1977. pap. text ed. 8.25 (ISBN 0-356-04103-4). Raintree Child.

--Science from Toys: Stages 1 & 2 & Background. LC 77-83000. (Science 5-13 Ser.). (Illus.). 1977. pap. text ed. 9.30 (ISBN 0-356-04006-2). Raintree Child.

--Science, Models & Toys: Stage 3. LC 77-82998. (Science 5-13 Ser.). (Illus.). 1977. pap. text ed. 9.30 (ISBN 0-356-04351-7). Raintree Child.

Radford, Evelyn, jt. auth. see Radford, Maisie.

Radford, John & Rose, David. The Teaching of Psychology: Method, Content, & Context. LC 79-40824. 1980. 40.00 (ISBN 0-471-27665-0, Pub. by Wiley-Interscience). Wiley.

Radford, K. J. Complex Decision Problems: An Integrated Strategy for Resolution. (Illus.). 224p. 1977. text ed. 13.95 (ISBN 0-87909-171-1). Reston.

--Information Systems for Strategic Decisions. (Illus.). 1978. ref. ed. 14.95 (ISBN 0-87909-389-7). Reston.

--Information Systems in Management. LC 73-80911. 1973. 15.95 (ISBN 0-87909-352-8). Reston.

--Managerial Decision Making. (Illus.). 256p. 1975. 14.95 (ISBN 0-87909-473-7). Reston.

--Modern Managerial Decision Making. 1981. text ed. 17.95 (ISBN 0-8359-4571-5); instr's. manual avail. (ISBN 0-8359-4229-5). Reston.

--Strategic Planning: An Analytical Approach. (Illus.). 1980. text ed. 14.95 (ISBN 0-8359-7068-X). Reston.

Radford, K. W., jt. auth. see Ball, Robert W.

Radford, Ken. Tales of South Wales. 192p. 1980. 12.00x (ISBN 0-7050-0080-X, Pub. by Skilton & Shaw England). State Mutual Bk.

Radford, Maisie & Radford, Evelyn. Musical Adventures in Cornwall. 1965. 6.95 o.p. (ISBN 0-685-56922-5). David & Charles.

Radhakrishna, S., ed. Science Technology & Global Problems--Views from the Developing World. (Illus.). 1980. 45.00 (ISBN 0-08-024489-0). Pergamon.

Radhakrishnan. Hindu Moral Life & Action. 1980. text ed. write for info. (ISBN 0-391-02011-0). Humanities.

Radhakrishnan, C. Zero. (Indian Writers Ser.). 110p. 1974. 6.50 (ISBN 0-88253-462-9). Ind-US Inc.

Radhakrishnan, S. The Bhagavadgita. 2nd ed. 388p. 1949. 12.50 (ISBN 0-04-891029-5). Allen Unwin.

--The Bhagavadgita. 2nd ed. 1949. 12.50 (ISBN 0-04-891028-7); pap. 10.95 (ISBN 0-04-891029-5). Allen Unwin.

--The Brahma Sutra: The Philosophy of Spiritual Life. 1959. 16.95 (ISBN 0-04-294043-5). Allen Unwin.

--Eastern Religions & Western Thought. 2nd ed. 396p. 1975. pap. text ed. 6.95x (ISBN 0-19-560604-3). Oxford U Pr.

--Hindu View of Life. (Unwin Paperbacks Ser.). 92p. 1980. pap. 4.95 (ISBN 0-04-294045-1, 9048). Allen Unwin.

--An Idealist View of Life. (Paperbacks Ser.). 288p. 1980. pap. 6.75 (ISBN 0-04-141009-2, 1614). Allen Unwin.

--An Idealist View of Life. (Unwin Bks.). 1961. pap. 2.95 o.p. (ISBN 0-04-141005-X). Allen Unwin.

Radhakrishnan, Sarvepalli. The Creative Life. 146p. 1976. pap. 2.40 (ISBN 0-89253-049-9). Ind-US Inc.

--Our Heritage. (Orient Paperback Ser.). 156p. (Orig.). 1973. pap. 2.35 (ISBN 0-88253-249-9). Ind-US Inc.

--Religion & Culture. 176p. 1971. pap. 2.40 (ISBN 0-88253-074-7). Ind-US Inc.

Radhakrishnan, Sarvepelli. Indian Philosophy, 2 Vols. (Muirhead Library of Philosophy). 1962. Set. text ed. 36.00x (ISBN 0-04-181009-0). Humanities.

Radhakrishnan, Sarvepelli & Muirhead, J. H., eds. Contemporary Indian Philosophy. 2nd ed. (Muirhead Library of Philosophy). 1963. Repr. of 1958 ed. text ed. 31.25x (ISBN 0-04-199004-8). Humanities.

Radharkrishnan, R., jt. auth. see Asher, R. E.

Radhuber, Stanley. Beautiful Michigan. Shangle, Robert D., ed. LC 78-52648. (Illus.). 72p. 1978. 14.95 (ISBN 0-915796-10-4); pap. 7.95 (ISBN 0-915796-09-0). Beautiful Am.

Radi, Heather, et al. Biographical Register of the New South Wales Parliament 1901-70. (Australian Parliaments, Biographical Notes: No. 6). 302p. 1979. text ed. 37.95 (ISBN 0-7081-1756-2, 0575, Pub. by ANUP Australia); pap. text ed. 18.95 (ISBN 0-7081-1757-0, 0574). Bks Australia.

Radice, Lisanne. Prelude to Appeasement: East European Central Diplomacy in the Early 1930's. (East European Quarterly Ser.: No. 80). 256p. 1981. text ed. 17.50x (ISBN 0-914710-74-5). East Eur Quarterly.

Radice, William, tr. see Raychaudhuri, Upendrakishore.

Radics, Stephen P., Jr. & Geisman, Miriam S. Tax Breaks for Homeowners: Tax Breaks for Homeowners. (Illus.). 96p. 1981. pap. 5.95 (ISBN 0-87863-024-4). Farnswth Pub.

Radigan, John D. The Silver Revolution & the New Monetary Order of the World. (Illus.). 129p. 1981. 49.85 (ISBN 0-89266-283-2). Am Classical Coll Pr.

Radiguet. Le Diable au Corps. (Easy Reader, B). pap. 3.75 (ISBN 0-88436-059-8, FRA201057). EMC.

Radin, Beryl. Implementation, Change, in the Federal Bureaucracy: School Desegregation Policy in HEW, 1964-1968. LC 76-58320. 1977. pap. text ed. 10.95x (ISBN 0-8077-2522-6). Tchrs Coll.

Radin, P., tr. see Adler, Alfred.

Radin, Paul. African Folktales. (Bollingen Ser., Vol. 32). 1970. pap. 6.95 o.p. (ISBN 0-691-01762-X). Princeton U Pr.

--Primitive Religion: Its Nature & Origin. 1937. pap. text ed. 3.50 (ISBN 0-486-20393-X). Dover.

--Winnebago Tribe. LC 64-63594. (Illus.). 1970. pap. 8.50 (ISBN 0-8032-5710-4, BB 512, Bison). U of Nebr Pr.

--World of Primitive Man. 1971. pap. 2.45 o.p. (ISBN 0-525-47298-3). Dutton.

Radine, Lawrence B. The Taming of the Troops: Social Control in the United States Army. LC 76-5262. (Contributions in Sociology Ser.: No. 22). (Orig.). 1976. lib. bdg. 16.95x (ISBN 0-8371-8911-X, RTT/). Greenwood.

Radiopress-Tokyo, ed. China Directory-1971. 9th ed. 657p. 1980. 85.00x (ISBN 0-8002-2752-2). Intl Pubns Serv.

Radiquet, Raymond. Cheeks on Fire. Stone, Alan, tr. 1980. pap. 4.95 (ISBN 0-686-68795-7). Riverrun NY.

Radke, Don. Cheese Making at Home: The Complete Illustrated Guide. LC 74-1505. 168p. 1974. 5.95 o.p. (ISBN 0-385-01887-8). Doubleday.

Radl, Shirley L. Mother's Day Is Over. 1974. pap. 1.95 o.s.i. (ISBN 0-446-89673-X). Warner Bks.

Radlauer, Dan, jt. auth. see Radlauer, Ed.

Radlauer, E. & Radlauer, R. S. Bonneville Cars. LC 73-3076. (Sports Action Bks). (gr. 3 up). 1973. PLB 5.90 o.p. (ISBN 0-531-02092-4). Watts.

--Buggy-Go-Round. LC 76-15188. (Sports Action Bks). (Illus.). (gr. 3 up). 1971. PLB 5.90 o.p. (ISBN 0-531-01991-8). Watts.

--Chopper Cycle. LC 79-180239. (Sports Action Bks). (Illus.). 48p. (gr. 3 up). 1972. PLB 5.90 o.p. (ISBN 0-531-02033-9). Watts.

--Foolish Filly. LC 73-17048. (gr. 3 up). 1974. PLB 5.90 o.p. (ISBN 0-531-02680-9). Watts.

--Horsing Around. LC 77-180241. (Sports Action Bks). (Illus.). 48p. (gr. 3 up). 1972. PLB 6.45 (ISBN 0-531-02034-7). Watts.

--Motorcycle Mutt. LC 73-942. (Sports Action Bks). (gr. 3 up). 1973. PLB 6.90 o.p. (ISBN 0-531-02091-6). Watts.

--On the Drag Strip. LC 70-151889. (Sports Action Ser). (Illus.). (gr. 3 up). 1971. 5.20 o.p. (ISBN 0-531-01995-0). Watts.

--On the Sand. LC 73-180240. (Sports Action Bks). (Illus.). 48p. (gr. 3 up). 1972. PLB 5.20 o.p. (ISBN 0-531-02035-5). Watts.

--On the Water. LC 72-7085. (Sports Action Bks.). (Illus.). 48p. (gr. 3 up). 1973. PLB 5.20 o.p. (ISBN 0-531-02586-1). Watts.

--Racing on the Wind. LC 73-17055. (Sports Action Books). (Illus.). 48p. (gr. 3 up). 1974. PLB 5.90 o.p. (ISBN 0-531-02681-7). Watts.

--Salt Cycle. LC 72-7113. (Sports Action Bks.). (Illus.). 48p. (gr. 3 up). 1973. PLB 5.20 o.p. (ISBN 0-531-02585-3). Watts.

--Scramble Cycle. LC 72-151887. (Sports Action Bks). (Illus.). (gr. 3 up). 1971. 5.90 o.p. (ISBN 0-531-01999-3). Watts.

Radlauer, Ed. Reading Incentive Program Series: Spanish Edition. Covarrubias, Ana, tr. from Eng. Incl. Carros Chistosos de Carreras de Arrastre. Orig. Title: Drag Racing - Funny Cars (ISBN 0-8372-0990-0); Carros Hechos a la Orden. Orig. Title: Custom Cars (ISBN 0-8372-0991-9); Los VW - Bugs. Orig. Title: VW - Bugs (ISBN 0-8372-0989-7). Orig. Title: Title Minibikes. (Illus., Span.). (gr. 3-12). 1973. pap. 2.85 ea.; multimedia kits with cassettes & filmstrips avail. Bowmar-Noble.

--Some Basics About Radio-Control Cars. LC 80-22039. (Gemini Bks). 32p. (gr. 4 up). 1981. PLB 8.65g (ISBN 0-516-07691-4, Elk Grove Bks). Childrens.

--Some Basics About Rock Climbing. LC 80-22053. (Gemini Bks). 32p. (gr. 4 up). 1981. PLB 8.65g (ISBN 0-516-07692-2, Elk Grove Bks). Childrens.

Radlauer, Ed & Radlauer, Dan. Race Car Drivers School. LC 74-34061. (Schools for Action Ser). (Illus.). 48p. (gr. 3 up). 1975. PLB 6.90 o.p. (ISBN 0-531-02099-1). Watts.

Radlauer, Ed & Radlauer, Ruth. Clown Mania. LC 80-21826. (Mania Bks). (Illus.). 32p. (gr. k-4). 1981. PLB 7.95g (ISBN 0-516-07783-X, Elk Grove Bks). Childrens.

--Horse Mania. LC 80-21550. (Mania Bks). (Illus.). 32p. (gr. k-5). 1981. PLB 7.95g (ISBN 0-516-07784-8, Elk Grove Bks). Childrens.

--Reptile Mania. LC 80-21575. (Mania Bks). (Illus.). 32p. (gr. k-5). 1981. PLB 7.95g (ISBN 0-516-07785-6, Elk Grove Bks). Childrens.

--Some Basics About Women's Gymnastics. LC 79-21826. (Gemini Bks.). (Illus.). 32p. (gr. 3 up). 1980. PLB 8.65 (ISBN 0-516-07687-6, Elk Grove Bks.); pap. 2.50 (ISBN 0-516-47687-4). Childrens.

Radlauer, Ed, jt. auth. see Radlauer, Ruth.

Radlauer, R. S., jt. auth. see Radlauer, E.

Radlauer, Ruth. Bryce Canyon National Park. LC 79-22722. (Parks for People Ser.). (Illus.). 48p. (gr. 3 up). 1980. PLB 9.25 (ISBN 0-516-07484-9, Elk Grove Bks.). Childrens.

--Virgin Islands National Park. LC 80-22457. (Parks for People Ser.). (Illus.). 48p. (gr. 3 up). 1981. PLB 9.25 (ISBN 0-516-07741-4). Childrens.

--Volcanoes. LC 80-25464. (Illus.). 48p. (gr. 3 up). 1981. PLB 9.25g (ISBN 0-516-07835-6, Elk Grove Bks). Childrens.

Radlauer, Ruth & Radlauer, Ed. Bird Mania. LC 80-21833. (Mania Bks). (Illus.). 32p. (gr. k-4). 1981. PLB 7.95g (ISBN 0-516-07782-1, Elk Grove Bks). Childrens.

Radlauer, Ruth, jt. auth. see Radlauer, Ed.

Radler, Albert J., jt. tr. see Ault, Hugh J.

Radler, K-H., jt. auth. see Krause, F.

Radley, G. W. Managing the Computer. 1975. text ed. 21.00x (ISBN 0-7002-0256-0). Intl Ideas.

Radley, J. A. Starch Production Technology. (Illus.). 1976. 145.40x (ISBN 0-85334-662-3, Pub. by Applied Science). Burgess-Intl Ideas.

Radley, J. A., ed. Examination & Analysis of Starch & Starch Products. (Illus.). 1976. 63.30x (ISBN 0-85334-692-5, Pub. by Applied Science). Burgess-Intl Ideas.

--Industrial Uses of Starch & Its Derivatives. 1976. 63.30x (ISBN 0-85334-691-7). Intl Ideas.

Radley, Roger J., jt. auth. see Cargas, Harry J.

Radley, Sheila. The Chief Inspector's Daughter. 256p. 1981. 9.95 (ISBN 0-684-16730-1, ScribT). Scribner.

--Death in the Morning. 1981. lib. bdg. 13.95 (ISBN 0-8161-3199-6, Large Print Bks). G K Hall.

Radley, Virginia L. Elizabeth Barrett Browning. (English Authors Ser.: No. 136). lib. bdg. 9.95 (ISBN 0-8057-1064-7). Twayne.

--Samuel Taylor Coleridge. (English Authors Ser.: No. 36). 1966. lib. bdg. 9.95 (ISBN 0-8057-1100-7). Twayne.

Radlowski, Roger J. & Kirvan, John. The Spirit of Poland: A Photographic Meditation. (Illus.). 60p. (Orig.). 1980. pap. 6.95 (ISBN 0-03-056666-5). Winston Pr.

Radner, K., ed. see Carnegie Commission on Higher Educaion.

Rado, George T. & Suhl, H., eds. Magnetism: A Treatise on Modern Theory & Materials, 5 vols. 1963-1973. Vol. 1. 55.25 (ISBN 0-12-575301-2); Vol. 2A. 48.50 (ISBN 0-12-575302-0); Vol. 2B. 48.50 (ISBN 0-12-575342-X); Vol. 3. 48.75 (ISBN 0-12-575303-9); Vol. 4. 45.50 (ISBN 0-12-575304-7); Vol. 5. 52.50 (ISBN 0-12-575305-5). Acad Pr.

Rado, P. An Introduction to the Technology of Pottery. LC 79-90454. 1969. 22.00 (ISBN 0-08-006458-2); pap. 9.25 (ISBN 0-08-006457-4). Pergamon.

Rado, Sandor. Adaptational Psychodynamics Motivation & Control. Jameson, Jean & Klein, Henriette, eds. LC 70-82528. 1969. 25.00 (ISBN 0-87668-018-X). Aronson.

Rado, T. On the Problem of Plateau - Subharmonic Functions. LC 71-160175. (Illus.). 1971. pap. 19.90 (ISBN 0-387-05479-0). Springer-Verlag.

Radocy, Rudolf E. & Boyle, J. David. Psychological Foundations of Musical Behavior. (Illus.). 360p. 1979. text ed. 25.75 (ISBN 0-398-03841-4). C C Thomas.

Radojcic, Svetozar. Geschichte der Serbischen Kunst von den Anfaengen bis zum Ende des Mittelalters. (Illus., Ger.). 1969. 29.40x (ISBN 3-11-000267-1). De Gruyter.

Radola, B. J., ed. Electrophoresis Nineteen Seventy-Nine: Methods & Theories, Biochemical & Clinical Applications. 700p. 1980. 116.00x (ISBN 3-11-008154-7). De Gruyter.

Radom, Matthew. The Social Scientist in American Industry: Self-Perception of Role, Motivation, & Career. LC 76-125193. 1970. 15.00 (ISBN 0-8135-0665-4). Rutgers U Pr.

Rados, David L. Marketing for Non-Profit Organizations. LC 80-25948. (Illus.). 512p. 1981. 24.95 (ISBN 0-86569-055-3). Auburn Hse.

Radosh, Ronald, ed. Debs. (Great Lives Observed Ser). 1971. pap. 2.45 o.p. (ISBN 0-13-197673-7, S728, Spec). P-H.

Radovsky, F. J. The Macronyssidae & Laelepidae (Acarina: Mesostigmata) Parasitic on Bats. (U. C. Publ. in Entomology: Vol. 46). 1967. pap. 10.00x (ISBN 0-520-09118-3). U of Cal Pr.

Radtke, George A. Budgerigars. Orig. Title: Wellensittiche-Mein Hobby. (Illus.). 1979. 2.95 (ISBN 0-87666-984-4, KW-011). TFH Pubns.

Radycki, J. Diane, tr. The Letters & Journals of Paula Modersohn-Becker. LC 80-18993. 370p. 1980. 17.50 (ISBN 0-8108-1344-0). Scarecrow.

Radzialowski. Hypertention Research: Methods & Models. Date not set. price not set (ISBN 0-8247-1344-3). Dekker.

Radzinowics, Mary Ann, ed. see Milton, J.

Radzinowicz, Leon. Ideology & Crime. LC 66-15724. (James S. Carpentier Fund Lecture Ser). 1966. 15.00x (ISBN 0-231-02926-8). Columbia U Pr.

Radzivilover, Cantor M. Now or Never: A Time for Survival. LC 78-26200. 1979. 9.95 (ISBN 0-8119-0314-1). Fell.

Rae, B. Bennet. The Lemon Sole. (Illus.). 108p. 7.00 (ISBN 0-85238-013-5). Unipub.

Rae, Donna. The Donna Rae Easy Exercise Program. 160p. (Orig.). 1980. pap. cancelled (ISBN 0-346-12459-X). Cornerstone.

Rae, G., ed. Seminar on AACR2. 1980. pap. 17.50 (ISBN 0-85365-563-4, Pub. by Lib Assn England). Oryx Pr.

Rae, Gwenneth R., jt. auth. see Potter, Thomas C.

Rae, Gwynedd. Mary Plain Goes to America. 1957. 6.25 (ISBN 0-7100-1997-1). Routledge & Kegan.

--Mary Plain's 'whodunit' 1965. 7.25 (ISBN 0-7100-1999-8). Routledge & Kegan.

Rae, Hugh C. The Travelling Soul. 1977. pap. 1.50 o.p. (ISBN 0-380-01854-3, 36517). Avon.

Rae, John. Conscience & Politics: British Government & the Conscientious Objector to Military Service, 1916-1919. (Illus.). 1970. text ed. 11.25x o.p. (ISBN 0-19-215176-2). Oxford U Pr.

--The Third Twin. LC 80-16001. 128p. (gr. 5-9). 1981. 8.95 (ISBN 0-7232-6192-X). Warne.

Rae, Patricia. Charge Nurse. 368p. (Orig.). 1980. pap. 2.50 (ISBN 0-89083-663-9). Zebra.

Raeburn, Ben, ed. see Wright, Frank L.

Raeder, Erich. My Life. Drexel, Henry W., tr. LC 79-6121. (Navies & Men Ser.). (Illus.). 1980. Repr. of 1960 ed. lib. bdg. 35.00x (ISBN 0-405-13075-9). Arno.

Raef, Laura C. Waikiki Nurse. 192p. (YA) 1976. 4.95 o.p. (ISBN 0-685-62027-1, Avalon). Bouregy.

Raeff, Marc. Michael Speransky: Statesman of Imperial Russia, 1772 to 1839. LC 78-59037. 1980. Repr. of 1957 ed. 27.50 (ISBN 0-88355-709-6). Hyperion Conn.

Raeff, Marc, ed. Catherine the Great: A Profile. LC 77-163575. (World Profiles Ser.). 1972. 7.95 o.p. (ISBN 0-8090-3367-4); pap. 5.95 o.p. (ISBN 0-8090-1400-9). Hill & Wang.

Rael, Leyla & Rudhyar, Dane. Astrological Aspects. 1980. pap. 9.95 (ISBN 0-88231-112-3). ASI Pubs Inc.

Raelin, Joseph A. Building a Career: The Effect of Initial Job Experiences & Related Work Attitudes on Later Employment. LC 80-24848. 178p. 1980. text ed. 7.00 (ISBN 0-911558-74-8); pap. text ed. 4.50 (ISBN 0-911558-73-X). Upjohn Inst.

Raemsch, Dorothy C. October Dawn. 26p. 1980. 3.75 (ISBN 0-9605398-0-8). D C Raemsch.

Raese, Jon W., jt. auth. see Willard, Beatrice L.

Raf, Zee. A Message for the Youth of America. LC 79-64406. 1980. 7.95 (ISBN 0-533-04302-6). Vantage.

Rafael, Gideon. Destination Peace: Three Decades of Israeli Foreign Policy. LC 80-9060. 400p. 1981. 16.95 (ISBN 0-8128-2812-7). Stein & Day.

Rafalski, Piotr, jt. auth. see Jankowski, Stanislaw.

Raff, Beverly, jt. ed. see Anderson, Gene C.

Raff, Beverly, ed. see Friesner, Arlyne.

Raff, Martin J. Infectious Diseases. (Medical Examination Review Bks.: Vol. 30). 1974. spiral bdg. 16.50 (ISBN 0-87488-147-1). Med Exam.

Raff, Rudolf A. see Bourne, G. H. & Danielli, J. F.

Raffael, Michael. Bistro Style Cookery. 1978. 14.95 (ISBN 0-7198-2634-9, Northwood Pub.). CBI Pub.

Raffaele, Joseph A. Labor Leadership in Italy & Denmark. 1962. 35.00 (ISBN 0-299-02660-4). U of Wis Pr.

--The Management of Technology: Change in a Society of Organized Advocacies. rev. ed. LC 79-63752. 1979. pap. text ed. 11.75 (ISBN 0-8191-0739-5). U Pr of Amer.

Raffauf, Robert F. Handbook of Alkaloids & Alkaloid-Containing Plants. LC 73-113713. 1970. 105.00 (ISBN 0-471-70478-4, Pub. by Wiley-Interscience). Wiley.

Raffel, B., intro. by. Sir Gawain & the Green Knight. (Orig.). 1970. pap. 1.75 (ISBN 0-451-61848-3, ME1848, Ment). NAL.

Raffel, Burton, tr. Poems from the Old English. 2nd, rev & enl. ed. LC 60-14776. 1964. 7.95x (ISBN 0-8032-0150-8); pap. 1.95x (ISBN 0-8032-5154-8, BB 106, Bison). U of Nebr Pr.

Raffel, Marshall. The U. S. Health System: Origins & Functions. LC 80-86. 1980. 17.95 (ISBN 0-471-04512-8, Pub. by Wiley Med). Wiley.

Raffel, Stanley. Matters of Fact: A Sociological Inquiry. 1979. 18.00 (ISBN 0-7100-0034-0). Routledge & Kegan.

Raffensperger, John G., ed. Swenson's Pediatric Surgery. 4th ed. 960p. 1980. 78.50x (ISBN 0-8385-8756-9). ACC.

Raffensperger, John G., et al. Acute Abdomen in Infancy & Childhood. LC 71-130975. (Illus., Span. ed. avail). 1970. 13.00 o.p. (ISBN 0-397-50259-1). Lippincott.

Rafferty, Kathleen. Dell Crossword Dictionary. 1981. pap. 2.95 (ISBN 0-440-16314-5). Dell.

--Dell Word Search, No. 20. 1981. pap. 1.95 (ISBN 0-440-12071-3). Dell.

Rafferty, Kathleen, ed. The Big Dell Book of Crosswords & Pencil Puzzles. (Orig.). 1981. pap. 6.95 (ISBN 0-440-50970-X, Dell Trade Pbks). Dell.

Rafferty, Milton D. & Harris, Scott. Basic World Place Location. (Illus.). 1977. pap. text ed. 2.95 (ISBN 0-8403-1791-3). Kendall-Hunt.

Rafferty, S. S. Fatal Flourishes. (gr. 7 up). 1978. pap. 1.95 (ISBN 0-380-41772-3, 41772). Avon.

Rafferty, Sadie, jt. auth. see Rossi, Nick.

Raffini, James P. Discipline: Negotiating Conflict with Today's Kids. 160p. 1980. 10.95 (ISBN 0-13-215731-4, Spec); pap. 3.95 (ISBN 0-13-215723-3). P-H.

--Discipline: Negotiating Conflicts with Today's Kids. 192p. 1980. 10.95 (Spec); pap. 3.95. P-H.

Raffler-Engel, Walburga Von see Von Raffler-Engel, Walburga & Hutcheson, Robert H.

Raffler-Engel, Walburga von see Von Raffler-Engel, Walburga & Lebrun, Yvan.

Raffles, Stamford. Statement of the Services of Sir Stamford Raffles. (Oxford in Asia Historical Reprints Ser.). 1979. 24.95x (ISBN 0-19-580318-3). Oxford U Pr.

Raffles, Sir Stanford. Report on Japan to the Secret Committee of the English East India Company. Paske-Smith, M., ed. (Records of Asian History). (Illus.). 1971. text ed. 13.00x (ISBN 0-7007-0003-X). Humanities.

Raffucci de Garcia, Carmen I. El Gobierno civil y la Ley Foraker (Antecedentes historicos) LC 79-16454. Orig. Title: Las Instituciones de Gobierno Civil en la Elaboracion de la Ley Foraker y Sus Antecedentes Historicos. xi, 213p. (Sp.). 1980. pap. write for info. (ISBN 0-8477-0864-0). U of PR Pr.

Rafroidi, Patrick. Irish Literature in English: The Romantic Period (1789-1850, Vol. II, Pts. IV, Bibliography. 1980. text ed. write for info. (ISBN 0-391-01033-6). Humanities.

--Irish Literature in English: The Romantic Period (1789-1850, Vol. I, Pts. 1, 2 & 3. (Illus.). 1980. text ed. write for info. (ISBN 0-391-01032-8). Humanities.

Rafroidi, Patrick & Brown, Terence. The Irish Short Story. 1979. text ed. 29.25x (ISBN 0-391-01703-9). Humanities.

Rafter, Rosalie & Alaia, Cheri. RCT Writing: A Workbook. 225p. (gr. 9-12). 1981. pap. 5.75 (ISBN 0-937820-10-5). Westsea Pub.

Ragaller, Klaus, ed. Current Interruption in High-Voltage Networks. LC 78-6057. (Brown Boveri Symposia Ser.). 380p. 1978. 37.50 (ISBN 0-306-40007-3, Plenum Pr). Plenum Pub.

Ragan, Lise B., ed. see Garcia, Mary H. & Gonzalez-Mena, Janet.

Ragan, Pauline K., ed. Aging Parents. LC 78-66073. 1979. pap. 6.00 (ISBN 0-88474-087-0). USC Andrus Geron.

--Work & Retirement: Policy Issues. LC 79-91688. 178p. 1980. pap. 6.00 (ISBN 0-88474-094-3). USC Andrus Geron.

Ragan Report Editors. Organizational Communication: Questions & Answers. 124p. (Orig.). 1980. pap. 10.00 (ISBN 0-931368-04-9). Ragan Comm.

Ragan, W. Gordon. Georgia Cookbook. 2nd ed. LC 78-70630. (Illus.). 1980. 9.95 (ISBN 0-916620-50-6). Portals Pr.

Ragatz, L. J. Guide for the Study of British Caribbean History, 1763-1834, Including the Abolitions & Emancipation Movements. LC 71-75275. (Law, Politics, & History Ser). 1970. Repr. of 1932 ed. lib. bdg. 65.00 (ISBN 0-306-71308-X). Da Capo.

Ragaway, Martin. Funny, Funny World Almanac. (Laughter Library). (Illus., Orig.). 1979. pap. 1.95 o.p. (ISBN 0-8431-0526-7). Price Stern.

Ragazzini, Giuseppe & Gagliardelli, Giancarlo. Italian-English, English-Italian Commercial Dictionary (1977) 1978. 50.00 (ISBN 0-685-25202-7). Heinman.

Ragazzini, Giuseppe & Biagi, Adele, eds. Concise English-Italian Italian-English Dictionary. LC 73-17088. 1214p. 1973. pap. 11.50 (ISBN 0-582-55505-1). Longman.

Rager, G. The Development of Retinotectal Projection in the Chicken. (Advances in Anatomy, Embryology & Cell Biology: Vol. 63). (Illus.). 92p. 1980. pap. 30.70 (ISBN 0-387-10121-7). Springer-Verlag.

Ragette, Friedrich. Baalbek. LC 80-19626. (Illus.). 128p. 1981. 18.00 (ISBN 0-8155-5059-6). Noyes.

Ragg, N. M. People Not Cases. (International Library of Welfare & Philosophy). 1977. 15.00x (ISBN 0-7100-8482-X). Routledge & Kegan.

Raggatt, Peter C., ed. Education in the Cities of England. LC 73-94130. (Sage Contemporary Social Science Issues: No. 11). 1974. pap. 4.95x (ISBN 0-8039-0395-2). Sage.

Raggett. Military Communications Nineteen Seventy-Nine to Nineteen Eighty. 1980. 99.50 (ISBN 0-531-03914-5). Watts.

Raghavacharyulu, D. V. The Critical Response: Selected Essays on the American, Commonwealth,Indian & British Traditions in Literature. 1980. 13.50x (ISBN 0-8364-0632-X, Pub. by Macmillan India). South Asia Bks.

Raghavan, M. D. India in Ceylonese History, Society & Culture. 2nd ed. 1970. 10.00x (ISBN 0-210-31211-4). Asia.

Raghunath, H. M. Dimensional Analysis & Hydraulic Model Testing. 1968. 5.50x o.p. (ISBN 0-210-22655-2). Asia.

Ragland, Margaret. Full of Joy. 1980. pap. 3.95 (ISBN 0-89137-415-9). Quality Pubns.

--What's It Worth? Probing Our Values with Questions Jesus Asked. 1977. pap. 3.75 (ISBN 0-89137-409-4). Quality Pubns.

Ragland, Mary E. Rabelais & Panurge: A Psychological Approach to Literary Character. 1976. pap. text ed. 20.00x (ISBN 90-6203-339-3). Humanities.

Ragland, Phillda, jt. auth. see Scovel, Myra.

Ragont, Joe. Failure: The Back Door to Success-Leader's Guide. pap. 3.95 (ISBN 0-8024-2517-8). Moody.

--How to Witness Successfully - Leader's Guide. 1979. pap. 3.25 (ISBN 0-8024-3793-1). Moody.

Ragosta, Millie J. Gerait's Daughter. LC 80-2759. 192p. 1981. 9.95 (ISBN 0-385-17274-5). Doubleday.

Ragsdale, John G. Dutch Oven Cooking. LC 73-75475. (Illus.). 61p. (Orig.). 1973. pap. 2.50 (ISBN 0-88415-200-6). Pacesetter Pr.

Ragsdale, Ronald O., jt. auth. see Latimer, George W.

Ragusa & Cherubini. One Thousand One Pitfalls in Italian. 1980. pap. 6.95 (ISBN 0-8120-0589-9). Barron.

Ragusa, Olga. Luigi Pirandello. LC 68-54457. (Columbia Essays on Modern Writers Ser.: No. 37). (Orig.). 1968. pap. 2.00 (ISBN 0-231-02952-7, MW37). Columbia U Pr.

--Verga's Milanese Tales. 1964. 6.00 (ISBN 0-913298-33-6). S F Vanni.

Rahani, Ameen. Book of Khalid. (Arab Background Ser.). 12.00x (ISBN 0-685-77103-2). Intl Bk Ctr.

Rahe, Richard H., jt. ed. see Gunderson, E. K.

Raheja, P. C. Soil Productivity & Crop Growth. 1967. 15.00x (ISBN 0-210-27008-X). Asia.

Rahim, Abdur. The Principles of Muhammadan Jurisprudence According to the Hanali, Maliki, Shafi'i & Hanbali Schools. LC 79-2879. 443p. 1981. Repr. of 1911 ed. 33.50 (ISBN 0-8305-0047-2). Hyperion Conn.

Rahlfs, A., ed. Septuaginta, 2 vols. 1965. Repr. of 1935 ed. 30.35 (ISBN 3-438-05120-6, 56400). United Bible.

Rahm, David A. Reading the Rocks: A Layman's Guide to the Geologic Secrets of Canyons, Mesas & Buttes in the American Southwest. LC 74-78915. (Totebook). (Illus.). 192p. 1974. pap. 7.95 o.p. (ISBN 0-87156-103-4). Sierra.

Rahman, F., ed. see Avicenna.

Rahman, Fazlur. Islam. 2nd ed. LC 78-68547. 1979. pap. 6.50 (ISBN 0-226-70280-4); pap. 6.50 (ISBN 0-226-70281-2, P806, Phoen). U of Chicago Pr.

Rahman, Hossainur. Hindu-Muslim Relations in Bengal, 1905-1947. 1977. text ed. 12.50 (ISBN 0-210-40605-4). Asia.

Rahman, Mushtaqur & Iowa State University Research Foundation. Agrarian Egalitarianism, Land Tenures & Land Reforms in South Asia. 224p. 1980. pap. text ed. 9.95 (ISBN 0-8403-2343-3). Kendall-Hunt.

Rahman, N. A. Course in the Theoretical Statistics. 1968. 14.25 o.s.i. (ISBN 0-02-850780-0). Hafner.

--Exercises in Probability & Statistics for Mathematics Undergraduates. 1967. 10.95 o.s.i. (ISBN 0-02-850770-3). Hafner.

--Exercises in Probability & Statistics. 2nd ed. 1981. 35.00 (ISBN 0-02-850760-6). Macmillan Info.

Rahmas, D. Steve, ed. see Fleissner, Else M.

Rahmas, D. Steve, ed. see Foy, Elizabeth & Schurer, John.

Rahmas, D. Steve, ed. see Kurland, Gerald.

Rahmas, D. Steve, ed. see Mallin, Jay.

Rahmel, A., jt. ed. see Holmes, D. R.

Rahn, Arthur O., jt. auth. see Heartwell, Charles M., Jr.

Rahn, Hermann, ed. see American Physiological Society.

Rahn, Joan E. Eyes & Seeing. LC 80-23988. (Illus.). 128p. (gr. 5-9). 1981. PLB 8.95 (ISBN 0-689-30828-0). Atheneum.

--Nature in the City: Plants. LC 76-44324. (Science Information Ser.). (Illus.). (gr. k-5). 1977. PLB 8.65 (ISBN 0-8172-0661-2). Raintree Pubs.

--Seven Ways to Collect Plants. LC 77-21181. (gr. 4-6). 1978. 6.95 (ISBN 0-689-30640-7). Atheneum.

Rahner, Hugo. Greek Myths & Christian Mystery. LC 79-156736. (Illus.). 1971. Repr. of 1963 ed. 17.50x (ISBN 0-8196-0270-1). Biblo.

--Man at Play. 1972. pap. 1.95 (ISBN 0-8164-2556-6). Crossroad NY.

Rahner, Karl. Christian at the Crossroads. Moiser, Jeremy, tr. from Ger. 250p. 1976. 5.95 (ISBN 0-8164-4712-8). Crossroad NY.

--Concern for the Church: Theological Investigations Vol. XX. (Theological Investigations Ser.). 272p. (Ger.). 1981. 12.95 (ISBN 0-8245-0027-X). Crossroad NY.

--Foundations of Christian Faith. 1978. 19.50 (ISBN 0-8164-0354-6). Crossroad NY.

--Free Speech in the Church. LC 79-8717. Orig. Title: Das Freie Wort in der Kirche. 112p. 1981. Repr. of 1959 ed. lib. bdg. 17.50x (ISBN 0-313-20849-2, RAFS). Greenwood.

--Hearers of the Word. 1969. 9.50 (ISBN 0-8164-1041-0). Crossroad NY.

--Meditations on Freedom & the Spirit. 1978. pap. 3.95 (ISBN 0-8164-2162-5). Crossroad NY.

--Meditations on Hope & Love. LC 77-76614. 1977. pap. 3.95 (ISBN 0-8164-2155-2). Crossroad NY.

--Meditations on the Sacraments. 1977. 5.95 (ISBN 0-8164-0344-9). Crossroad NY.

--Opportunities for Faith: Elements of a Modern Spirituality. 1975. 8.95 (ISBN 0-8164-1180-8). Crossroad NY.

--Prayers & Meditations: An Anthology of the Spiritual Writings of Karl Rahner. Griffiths, John, ed. 128p. 1980. pap. 3.95 (ISBN 0-8245-2619-8). Crossroad NY.

--The Priesthood. Quinn, Edward, tr. from German. LC 72-94304. 288p. 1973. Repr. of 1970 ed. 8.95 (ISBN 0-8164-1106-9). Crossroad NY.

--The Religious Life Today. 1976. 5.95 (ISBN 0-8164-0323-6). Crossroad NY.

--Shape of the Church to Come. 1974. 6.95 (ISBN 0-8164-1181-6). Crossroad NY.

--The Spirit in the Church. 1979. pap. 3.95 (ISBN 0-8164-2189-7). Crossroad NY.

--Spirit in the World. Lynch, William, tr. LC 67-29676. 1968. 13.50 (ISBN 0-8164-1122-0). Crossroad NY.

--Theological Investigations, Vols. 1-13. Incl. Vol. 1. 12.95 (ISBN 0-8164-1154-9); Vol. 2. 12.95 (ISBN 0-8164-1190-5); Vol. 3. 12.95 (ISBN 0-8164-1155-7); Vol. 4. 12.95 (ISBN 0-8164-1156-5); Vol. 5. 14.95 (ISBN 0-8164-1191-3); Vol. 6. 12.95 (ISBN 0-8164-1157-3); Vol. 7. 13.95 (ISBN 0-8164-1126-3); Vol. 8. 12.95 (ISBN 0-8164-1127-1); Vol. 9. 10.95 (ISBN 0-8164-1128-X); Vol. 10. 14.95 (ISBN 0-8164-1129-8); Vol. 11. 12.95 (ISBN 0-8164-1143-3); Vol. 12. 10.95 (ISBN 0-8164-1179-4); Vol. 13. 12.95 (ISBN 0-8164-1193-X). Crossroad NY.

--Theological Investigations, Vol. 14. 12.95 (ISBN 0-8164-1203-0). Crossroad NY.

--Theological Investigations XVI: Experience of the Spirit: Source of Theology. 1979. 14.95 (ISBN 0-8164-0417-8). Crossroad NY.

--Trinity. LC 72-87766. 128p. 1970. 5.95 (ISBN 0-8164-1133-6). Crossroad NY.

--Watch & Pray with Me: The Seven Last Words. 1977. pap. 4.95 (ISBN 0-8164-2126-9). Crossroad NY.

Rahner, Karl & Metz, Johann B. The Courage to Pray. 112p. (Orig.). 1980. pap. 3.95 (ISBN 0-8245-2024-6). Crossroad NY.

Rahner, Karl & Thusing, Wilhelm. A New Christology. 256p. 1980. 12.95 (ISBN 0-8164-0211-6). Crossroad NY.

Rahner, Karl & Vorgrimler, Herbert. Dictionary of Theology. 2nd ed. 500p. (Ger.). 1981. 24.50 (ISBN 0-8245-0040-7). Crossroad NY.

Rahner, Karl & Weger, Karl-Heinz. Our Christian Faith: Answers for the Future. 208p. (Orig.). 1980. 10.95 (ISBN 0-8245-0145-4); pap. 4.95 (ISBN 0-8245-2032-7). Crossroad NY.

Rahner, Karl, ed. Encyclopedia of Theology: The Concise Sacramentum Mundi. rev., abr. ed. 1536p. 1975. 39.50 (ISBN 0-8164-1182-4). Crossroad NY.

Raht, John, jt. auth. see Elwood, Ann.

Rahtz, P. A. Excavations at Little Waltham. 74p. 1980. pap. 48.00 (ISBN 0-900312-64-5, Pub. by Coun Brit Arch England). Intl Schol Bk Serv.

--Excavations at St. Mary's Church, Deerhurst. 74p. 1980. pap. 11.95x (ISBN 0-900312-35-1, Pub. by Coun Brit Arch England). Intl Schol Bk Serv.

Rahula, Walpola. What the Buddha Taught. (Illus.). 1967. pap. 6.95 (ISBN 0-900406-02-X). Dufour.

--What the Buddha Taught. rev. ed. (Illus.). 168p. 1974. pap. 4.95 (ISBN 0-394-17827-0, E641, Ever). Grove.

--Zen & the Taming of the Bull: Towards the Definition of Buddhist Thought. 1978. text ed. 17.25x (ISBN 0-900406-69-0). Humanities.

Rahv, Betty T. From Sartre to the New Novel. LC 74-77655. 176p. 1974. 12.50 (ISBN 0-8046-9076-6, Natl U). Kennikat.

Rahv, Philip, ed. Modern Occasions Two: New Fiction, Criticism, Poetry. LC 66-18863. (National Univ. Pubns.). 320p. 1974. 15.00 (ISBN 0-8046-9068-5). Kennikat.

Rai, Rajkumar. The Geomorphology of Sonar Basin. 1980. text ed. write for info. (ISBN 0-391-01835-3). Humanities.

Raiborn, Mitchell H., jt. auth. see Anderson, Henry R.

Raichle, Donald R. From a Normal Beginning: The Origins of Kean College of New Jersey. (Illus.). 432p. 1980. 20.00 (ISBN 0-8386-4500-3). Fairleigh Dickinson.

Raichur, S. & Liske, C. T., eds. The Politics of Aid, Trade & Investment. LC 75-31886. (Comparative Political Economics & Public Policy Ser.). 218p. 1976. 25.95 (ISBN 0-470-54117-2). Halsted Pr.

Raico, Ralph, tr. see Von Mises, Ludwig.

Raiffa, H., jt. auth. see Luce, Robert D.

Raigan, E. F. The Saturday Evening Post Dried Foods Cookbook. LC 80-67060. (Illus.). 1980. pap. 5.95 (ISBN 0-89387-041-2). Sat Eve Post.

Railey, Jay M., jt. auth. see Gallant, Robert W.

Railsearch Publishing, Inc., ed. Modern Railroad Roadway Maintenance & Management. (Railsearch Railroad Management Ser.: No. 4). (Illus.). 600p. 1980. 147.50 (ISBN 0-937060-03-8); lib. bdg. 48.00 (ISBN 0-937060-07-0). Railsearch.

--The New Dictionary of Railroad Working Terminology. (Railsearch Railroad Management Ser.). (Illus.). 400p. 1980. 28.00 (ISBN 0-686-27634-5); lib. bdg. 29.25 (ISBN 0-686-27635-3). Railsearch.

Raimes, Ann. Focus on Composition. (Illus.). 1978. pap. 6.95x (ISBN 0-19-502238-6). Oxford U Pr.

--Problems & Teaching Strategies in ESL Composition. (Language in Education Ser.: No. 14). (Orig.). 1979. pap. text ed. 2.95x (ISBN 0-87281-100-X). Ctr Appl Ling.

Raimon, Peire. Le Poesie Di Peire Raimon De Tolosa. Cavaliere, Alfredo, ed. LC 80-2181. 1981. Repr. of 1935 ed. 29.50 (ISBN 0-404-19010-3). AMS Pr.

Raimondi, Anthony J., et al. The Dandy-Walker Syndrome. (Illus.). vi, 80p. 1981. 34.75 (ISBN 3-8055-1722-X). S Karger.

Raimondi, Emily. Secret of the Sea Legacy. LC 73-83033. 192p. (gr. 5-8). 1974. 6.95 (ISBN 0-8149-0725-3). Vanguard.

Raimy, Eric. Shared Houses, Shared Lives: The New Extended Families. LC 78-65366. 1979. 10.00 o.p. (ISBN 0-312-90859-8); pap. 4.95 o.p. (ISBN 0-312-90860-1). St Martin.

Raina, Asoka. Inside R.A.W. The Story of India's Secret Service. 175p. 1981. 12.50x (ISBN 0-7069-1299-3, Pub. by Vikas India). Advent Bk.

Raina, Trilokinath, ed. An Anthology of Modern Kashmiri Verse 1930-1960. Raina, Trithokinath, tr. from Kashmiri. 280p. 1974. lib. bdg. 12.50 (ISBN 0-88253-469-6). Ind-US Inc.

Raina, Trithokinath, tr. see Raina, Trilokinath.

Rainbolt, John C. From Prescription to Persuasion: Manipulation of Seventeenth Century Virginia Economy. LC 73-83268. 1974. 13.95 (ISBN 0-8046-9057-X). Kennikat.

Raine, Harmony & Heyer, Georgette. The Georgette Heyer Compendium. 1979. 4.95x (ISBN 0-89967-000-8). Harmony & Co.

Raine, James W. Land of Saddle-Bags: A Study of the Mountain People of Appalachia. LC 70-78223. (Illus.). 1969. Repr. of 1924 ed. 15.00 (ISBN 0-8103-0160-1). Gale.

Raine, K. Blake & Antiquity. (A. W. Mellon Lecture: No. 11). 1978. 16.50x (ISBN 0-691-09943-X, 330); pap. 5.95 (ISBN 0-691-01802-2). Princeton U Pr.

Raine, Katharine. All About the Dachshund. (All About Ser.). (Illus.). 1980. 16.95 (ISBN 0-7207-1178-9, Pub. by Michael Joseph). Merrimack Bk Serv.

Raine, Kathleen. Collected Poems. 1966. 10.95 o.p. (ISBN 0-241-90115-4). Dufour.

--Death in Life & Life in Death: Cuchulain Comforted & News for the Delphic Oracle. (New Yeats Papers Ser: No. 8). 62p. 1974. pap. text ed. 7.50x (ISBN 0-85105-245-2, Dolmen Pr). Humanities.

--From Blake to a Vision. (New Yeats Papers Ser.: No. 17). 1979. pap. text ed. 11.75x (ISBN 0-85105-339-4, Dolmen Pr). Humanities.

--The Lost Country. 1971. text ed. 5.00x (ISBN 0-85105-194-4, Dolmen Pr). Humanities.

--On a Deserted Shore. 1973. text ed. 6.00x (ISBN 0-85105-248-7, Dolmen Pr). Humanities.

--The Oracle in the Heart. 87p. (Orig.). 1980. pap. 8.50 (ISBN 0-04-821045-5, 2487). Allen Unwin.

--William Blake. (World of Art Ser). (Illus.). 1970. pap. 9.95 (ISBN 0-19-519931-6). Oxford U Pr.

--Yeats, the Tarot & the Golden Dawn. 2nd rev. ed. (New Yeats Papers Ser: Vol. 2). (Illus.). 1976. pap. text ed. 7.50x (ISBN 0-85105-195-2, Dolmen Pr). Humanities.

Raine, Kathleen, tr. see Calderon De La Barca, Pedro.

Raine, W. R. The Last Shot. 1976. Repr. of 1926 ed. lib. bdg. 9.60 (ISBN 0-88411-553-4). Amereon Ltd.

Rainer, Lick F. Atlas a Color De Oirugia. 600p. 1981. pap. text ed. write for info. (ISBN 0-06-315030-1, Pub. by HarlA Mexico). Har-Row.

Rainer, Tristine. The New Diary: How to Use a Journal for Self-Guidance & Expanded Creativity. LC 76-62677. 1978. 9.95 o.p. (ISBN 0-87477-061-0). J P Tarcher.

--The New Diary: How to Use a Journal for Self-Guidance & Expanded Creativity. LC 76-62677. 1979. pap. 5.95 (ISBN 0-87477-150-1). J P Tarcher.

--The New Diary: Recreating Oneself Through Journal Writing. LC 76-6277. Date not set. cancelled (ISBN 0-312-90736-2). St Martin.

Raineri, A., et al, eds. Selected Topics in Exercise Cardiology & Rehabilitation. (Ettore Majorana International Science Ser.--Life Sciences: Vol. 4). 285p. 1981. pap. 35.00 (ISBN 0-306-40566-0, Plenum Pr). Plenum Pub.

Raines, Charles A. Monarch Notes on Rawlings' the Yearling. (Orig.). pap. 1.95 (ISBN 0-671-00859-5). Monarch Pr.

Raines, Howell. Whiskey Man. 1980. pap. 2.50 (ISBN 0-449-24335-4, Crest). Fawcett.

Raines, John C. Attack on Privacy. LC 73-16691. 160p. 1974. 4.95 o.p. (ISBN 0-8170-0621-4). Judson.

Raines, Kathleen, ed. see Blake, Robert.

Raines, Margaret. Consumers' Management. rev. ed. Orig. Title: Managing Livingtime. (Illus.). (gr. 9-12). 1973. text ed. 14.32 (ISBN 0-87002-123-0); tchr's guide avail. (ISBN 0-685-06849-8). Bennett IL.

Rainey, Anne. Mosaics in Roman Britain. (Illus.). 205p. 1973. 12.00x o.p. (ISBN 0-87471-158-4). Rowman.

Rainey, Homer P. Tower & the Dome: A Free University Vs Political Control. LC 76-161831. 1971. 5.95 o.p. (ISBN 0-87108-047-8). Pruett.

Rainey, R. C. Insect Flight. LC 75-22091. (Royal Entomological Society of London Symposium Ser.). 287p. 1976. 60.95 (ISBN 0-470-70550-7). Halsted Pr.

Rainey, Reuben M. Freud As Student of Religion: Perspectives on the Background & Development of His Thought. LC 75-17536. (American Academy of Religion. Dissertation Ser.: No. 7). 1975. pap. 7.50 (ISBN 0-89130-012-0, 010107). Scholars Pr Ca.

Rainich, Gabrielle & Kuipers, A. H., eds. Russian-English Vocabulary with Grammatical Sketch. 66p. 1980. Repr. of 1972 ed. with corrections 5.20 (ISBN 0-8218-0037-X, REV). Am Math.

Rainolde, Richard. A Booke Called the Foundacion of Rhetorike. LC 78-6210. (English Experience Ser.: No. 91). 1969. Repr. of 1563 ed. 16.00 (ISBN 90-221-0091-X). Walter J Johnson.

Rainoldes, John, et al. Th'overthrow of Stage-Players. LC 70-170414. (The English Stage Ser.: Vol. 11). lib. bdg. 50.00 (ISBN 0-8240-0594-5). Garland Pub.

Rains, A. J. Harding & Ritchie, H. David, eds. Bailey & Love's Short Practice of Surgery. 17th ed. Orig. Title: Short Practice of Surgery. (Illus.). 1977. text ed. 64.00 (ISBN 0-87488-900-6). Med Exam.

Rains, Donald W., et al, eds. Genetic Engineering of Osmoregulation: Impact of Plant Productivity for Food, Chemicals & Energy. (Basic Life Sciences Ser.: Vol. 14). 395p. 1980. 39.50 (ISBN 0-306-40454-0, Plenum Pr). Plenum Pub.

Rainsberger, Todd. Eloquent Light: The Cinematography of James Wong Howe. LC 80-26542. (Illus.). 218p. 1981. 17.50 (ISBN 0-498-02405-9). A S Barnes.

Rainsbury, Robert. Written English: An Introduction for Beginning Students of English As a Second Language. 1977. pap. 7.95 (ISBN 0-13-970673-9). P-H.

Rainsford, Christina. Spring Laughter. 1980. 5.50 (ISBN 0-8233-0316-0). Golden Quill.

Rainsford, George N. Congress & Higher Education in the Nineteenth Century. LC 72-83343. 1972. 10.50x (ISBN 0-87049-140-7). U of Tenn Pr.

Raintree, Diane, ed. The Household Book of Hints & Tips. 272p. 1980. pap. 2.25 (ISBN 0-345-28927-7). Ballantine.

Raintree, Lee. Dallas. 1980. pap. 2.50 (ISBN 0-440-11752-6). Dell.

Rainwater, Frank. Lord Byron: A Study of the Development of His Philosophy, with Special Emphasis Upon the Dramas. 50p. 1980. Repr. of 1949 ed. lib. bdg. 8.50 (ISBN 0-8492-7731-0). R West.

Rainwater, Janette. You're in Charge. LC 79-65000. 1979. pap. 8.50 (ISBN 0-89615-021-6). Guild of Tutors Pr.

Rainwater, Lee. Behind Ghetto Walls: Black Family Life in a Federal Slum. LC 77-113083. 1970. text ed. 20.95x (ISBN 0-202-30113-3); pap. text ed. 9.95x (ISBN 0-202-30114-1). Aldine Pub.

Rainwater, Percy L. Mississippi: Storm Center of Secession, 1856-1861. LC 72-84188. (American Scene, Comments & Commentators Ser). 1969. Repr. of 1938 ed. lib. bdg. 27.50 (ISBN 0-306-71614-3). Da Capo.

Raison, Timothy. Power & Parliament. 1979. 20.00x (ISBN 0-631-11301-0, Pub. by Basil Blackwell England); pap. 8.50x (ISBN 0-631-12892-1). Biblio Dist.

Raison, Timothy, ed. The Founding Fathers of Social Science. rev. ed. 319p. 1979. 15.95 o.p. (ISBN 0-85967-458-4, Pub. by Scolar Pr England); pap. 7.95 (ISBN 0-85967-459-2). Biblio Dist.

Raitt, Jill. The Eucharistic Theology of Theodore Beza: Development of the Reformed Doctrine. LC 74-188907. (American Academy of Religion. Studies in Religion). 1972. pap. 7.50 (ISBN 0-89130-156-9, 010004). Scholars Pr Ca.

Raitt, Thomas M. A Theology of Exile: Judgment-Deliverance in Jeremiah & Ezekiel. LC 76-62610. 288p. 1977. 15.95 (ISBN 0-8006-0497-0, 1-497). Fortress.

Raizis, M. Byron. Dionysios Solomos. (World Authors Ser.: Greece: No. 193). lib. bdg. 10.95 (ISBN 0-8057-2846-5). Twayne.

Raj, Jagdish. Mutiny & British Land Policy in North India, 1856-1868. 1967. 6.25x o.p. (ISBN 0-210-22660-9). Asia.

Raj, Praskah A. Kathmandu & the Kingdom of Nepal. 2nd ed. (Illus.). 1978. pap. 3.95 o.p. (ISBN 0-908086-01-6, Pub. by Two Continents). Hippocrene Bks.

Raja, C. Kunhan. Poet Philosophers of the Rig Veda. (Sanskrit & eng.). 8.95 (ISBN 0-89744-121-4, Pub. by Ganesh & Co. India). Auromere.

Raja, C. Kunhan, tr. from Sanskrit. Asya Vamasya Hymn (The Riddle of the Universe) 6.50 (ISBN 0-89744-120-6, Pub. by Ganesh & Co. India). Auromere.

Rajagopal, R., ed. Environmental Mediation & Conflict Management: A Selection of Papers Presented at the 5th Annual Conference of the NAEP, Washington Dc, April 21-23 1980. 120p. 1981. pap. 10.00 (ISBN 0-08-026261-9). Pergamon.

Rajagopalachari, C. Mahabharata. 1979. pap. 3.50 (ISBN 0-89744-929-0). Auromere.

--Ramayana. 1979. pap. 3.95 (ISBN 0-89744-930-4). Auromere.

Rajala, Reuben, jt. auth. see Proudman, Robert.

Rajan, B. & George, A. G., eds. Makers of Literary Criticism, Vol. 1. 10.00x (ISBN 0-210-26992-8). Asia.

--Makers of Literary Criticism, Vol. 2. 10.00x (ISBN 0-210-26991-X). Asia.

Rajan, B., ed. see Hawthorne, Nathaniel.

Rajan, Bhalchandra. Too Long in the West. 1961. pap. 2.00 (ISBN 0-88253-175-1). Ind-US Inc.

Rajan, K. T., jt. ed. see Richards, R. J.

Rajan, M. S. United Nations & Domestic Jurisdiction. 1958. 25.00x (ISBN 0-210-33974-8). Asia.

Rajan, M. S. & Ganguly, Shivaji, eds. India & the International System: A Selection from the Major Writings of Sisir Gupta. 400p. 1981. text ed. 40.00x (ISBN 0-7069-1072-9, Pub. by Vikas India). Advent Bk.

Rajan, Mohini, jt. auth. see Lynton, Harriet R.

Rajan, S. V. & Rao, H. G. Soil & Crop Productivity. 1973. 10.00x (ISBN 0-210-27100-0). Asia.

Rajan, Tilottama. Myth in a Metal Mirror. (Writers Workshop Redbird Ser.). 1975. 8.00 (ISBN 0-88253-580-3); pap. text ed. 4.80 (ISBN 0-88253-579-X). Ind-US Inc.

Rajana, Cecil. The Chemical & Petro-Chemical Industries of Russia & Eastern Europe, 1960-1980. 1975. 62.50 (ISBN 0-85621-040-4, Pub. by Scottish Academic Pr Scotland). Columbia U Pr.

Rajanen, Aini. The Legend of St. Urho. LC 81-295. (Illus.). 48p. (ps up). 1981. 8.95 (ISBN 0-87518-215-1). Dillon.

--Of Finnish Ways. LC 80-28932. (Heritage Books). (Illus.). 232p. 1981. 8.95 (ISBN 0-87518-214-3). Dillon.

Rajec, E. M. The Study of Names in Literature: A Bibliography. 261p. 1978. 38.00 (ISBN 0-89664-000-0, Pub. by K G Saur). Gale.

Rajendra, Ram. History of Buddhism in Nepal: AD 704-1396. 1979. 17.50x o.p. (ISBN 0-89684-035-2). South Asia Bks.

Raj Gupta, Giri, ed. Religions in Modern India, Vol. 5. 368p. 1981. text ed. 27.50x (ISBN 0-7069-0793-0, Pub. by Vikas India). Advent Bk.

Rajhan, S. K., jt. auth. see Krishna, G.

Rajhans, Gyan S. & Sullivan, John. Asbestos Sampling & Analysis. 1981. text ed. 37.50 (ISBN 0-686-69577-1). Ann Arbor Science.

Rajiva, Stanley E. The Permanent Element. 8.00 (ISBN 0-89253-720-5); flexible cloth 4.80 (ISBN 0-89253-721-3). Ind-US Inc.

Rajka, George. Atopic Dermatitis. LC 74-14868. (Major Problems in Dermatology Ser: No. 3). (Illus.). 165p. 1975. 25.00 (ISBN 0-7216-7448-8). Saunders.

Rajki, Bela. Teaching to Swim, Learning to Swim. Hepp, Ferenc, tr. from Hung. Orig. Title: Uszastanitas--Uszastanulas. (Illus.). 83p. 1980. 12.50x (ISBN 963-13-0957-6). Intl Pubns Serv.

Rajki, Sandor, ed. Proceedings of a Workshop on Agricultural Potentiality Directed by Nutritional Needs. (Illus.). 238p. 1979. 25.00x (ISBN 963-05-1991-7). Intl Pubns Serv.

Rajnath. T. S. Eliot's Theory of Poetry. 1980. text ed. 12.50x (ISBN 0-391-01755-1). Humanities.

Rajneesh, Bhagwan S. I Am the Gate: Initiation & Discipleship. (Orig.). 1977. pap. 4.95 (ISBN 0-06-090573-5, CN-573, CN). Har-Row.

--Meditation: The Art of Ecstasy. (Orig.). 1976. pap. 5.95 (ISBN 0-06-090529-8, CN529, CN). Har-Row.

--Meditation: The Art of Ecstasy. Bharti, Ma S., ed. 1978. pap. 2.95 (ISBN 0-06-080394-0, P394, PL). Har-Row.

--The Mustard Seed: Discourses on the Sayings of Jesus from the Gospel According to Thomas. LC 77-20461. 1978. pap. 6.95 (ISBN 0-06-066785-0, RD-255, HarpR). Har-Row.

--The Supreme Doctrine: Discourses on the Kenopanishad. 356p. (Orig.). 1980. pap. 14.95 (ISBN 0-7100-0572-5). Routledge & Kegan.

--The Way of Tao, Pt. I. Didi, Dolli, tr. 1978. 24.00 (ISBN 0-89684-025-5, Pub. by Motilal Barnarsidass India). Orient Bk Dist.

--Words Like Fire: Discourses on Jesus. LC 80-8343. 288p. (Orig.). 1981. pap. 5.95 (ISBN 0-06-066787-7, RD 347, HarpR). Har-Row.

Rajneesh, Bhagwan Sri. Dimensions Beyond the Known. (Orig.). 1979. pap. 6.95 (ISBN 0-914794-35-3). Wisdom Garden.

--Nirvana: The Last Nightmare. Rajneesh Foundation, ed. (Illus.). 278p. (Orig.). 1981. pap. 7.95 (ISBN 0-914794-37-X). Wisdom Garden Bks.

Rajneesh Foundation, ed. see Rajneesh, Bhagwan Sri.

Raju, C. No Exit. (Writers Workshop Redbird Ser.). 1975. 6.75 (ISBN 0-88253-586-2); pap. text ed. 4.00 (ISBN 0-88253-585-4). Ind-US Inc.

Raju, K. Ranga, jt. auth. see Garde, R. J.

Raju, P. T. Introduction to Comparative Philosophy. LC 62-7870. (Arcturus Books Paperbacks). 376p. 1970. pap. 9.95 (ISBN 0-8093-0419-8). S Ill U Pr.

Rakech. Managing Health Care Org. 1977. 18.95 (ISBN 0-7216-7451-8). Dryden Pr.

Rakel, Robert E. Principles of Family Medicine. LC 76-41541. (Illus.). 1977. text ed. 19.95 (ISBN 0-7216-7449-6). Saunders.

Rakesh, Mohan. Lingering Shadows. Ratan, Jai, tr. 214p. 1970. pap. 2.50 (ISBN 0-88253-075-5). Ind-US Inc.

Rakestraw, jt. ed. see Kieffer, W. F.

Rakhmanny, Roman. In Defense of the Ukrainian Cause. Olynyk, Stephen D., ed. 256p. 1979. 12.95 (ISBN 0-8158-0385-0). Chris Mass.

Raknem, Ingvald. Joan of Arc in History, Legend & Literature. (Scandinavian University Books). 284p. 1972. 22.00x (ISBN 8-200-02247-1, Dist. by Columbia U Pr). Universitet.

Rakoczi, Basil I. Foreseeing the Future. 128p. 1973. pap. 1.25 o.p. (ISBN 0-06-087039-7, HW). Har-Row.

Rakoff, Stuart H., jt. auth. see Friedman, Kenneth M.

Rakosi, Carl. Droles De Journal. LC 80-28307. 1981. 25.00 (ISBN 0-915124-43-2, Bookslinger); pap. 5.00 (ISBN 0-915124-44-0). Toothpaste.

Rakosnik, J., jt. auth. see Tichy, M.

Rakov, Lois E. My First Haggadah. new ed. (gr. k-3). 1978. 3.95 (ISBN 0-87243-075-8). Templegate.

Rakow, Edwin, ed. Lyric Verse. LC 63-12620. 1962. pap. 3.95 (ISBN 0-672-73225-4). Odyssey Pr.

Rakowska-Harmstone, Teresa, ed. Perspectives for Change in Communist Societies. (Special Studies on the Soviet Union & Eastern Europe). 1979. lib. bdg. 22.50x (ISBN 0-89158-336-X). Westview.

Rakowski, Cathy A., jt. auth. see Saulniers, Suzanne S.

Rakowski, James P., ed. Transportation Economics: A Guide to Information Sources. LC 73-17584. (Economics Information Guide Series: Vol. 5). 200p. 1976. 30.00 (ISBN 0-8103-1307-3). Gale.

Raktoe, B. L., et al. Factorial Design. (Wiley Series in Probability & Mathematical Statistics). 250p. 1981. 23.95 (ISBN 0-471-09040-9, Pub. by Wiley-Interscience). Wiley.

Raleigh, Alexander. The Book of Esther. Date not set. 9.00 (ISBN 0-86524-037-X). Klock & Klock.

Raleigh, John H. The Chronicle of Leopold & Molly Bloom: "Ulysses" As Narrative. 1978. 17.50x (ISBN 0-520-03301-9). U of Cal Pr.

Raleigh, Walter. A Choice of Sir Walter Raleigh's Verse. Nye, Robert, ed. 1972. 7.95 (ISBN 0-571-08253-X, Pub. by Faber & Faber); pap. 3.95 (ISBN 0-571-08753-1). Merrimack Bk Serv.

--Selected Prose & Poetry. Latham, Agnes M., ed. 1965. text ed. 3.00x (ISBN 0-485-61005-1, Athlone Pr). Humanities.

Raleigh, Walter, et al, eds. Shakespeare's England: An Account of the Life & Manners of His Age, 2 Vols. (Illus.). 1916. 59.00x (ISBN 0-19-821252-6). Oxford U Pr.

Raleigh, Sir Walter, et al. The Prerogative of Parliaments in England, Proved in a Dialogue, 4 vols. in 1. Berkowitz, David S. & Thorne, Samuel E., eds. LC 77-89209. (Classics of English Legal History in the Modern Era Ser.: Vol. 123). 1979. lib. bdg. 55.00 (ISBN 0-8240-3160-1). Garland Pub.

Ralescu, D. A., jt. auth. see Negoita, C. V.

Rall, Karen. Beautifood: Looking Better Through Nutrition. LC 80-83615. (Illus.). 160p. (Orig.). 1981. pap. 6.95 (ISBN 0-89087-307-0). Celestial Arts.

Ralley, Thomas G., jt. auth. see Dudewicz, Edward J.

Rallis, Stephen & Schiffmann, Gerard. Weil Representation I: Intertwining Distributions & Discrete Spectrum. LC 80-12191. (Memoirs of the American Mathematical Society Ser.). 1980. 6.40 (ISBN 0-8218-2231-4, MEMO-231). Am Math.

Rallis, T. Intercity Transportation: Engineering & Planning. 1978. 39.95 (ISBN 0-470-01394-X). Halsted Pr.

Ralls, Kenneth, et al. Introduction to Materials Science & Engineering. LC 76-10813. 608p. 1976. text ed. 26.95 (ISBN 0-471-70665-5); solution manual avail. (ISBN 0-471-02397-3). Wiley.

Ralph, James. Case of Authors by Profession or Trade, 1758, Champion 1739. LC 66-10008. 1966. 26.00x (ISBN 0-8201-1037-X). Schol Facsimiles.

--The Touchstone: Historical Essays on the Reigning Diversions of the Town. LC 78-170491. (The English Stage Ser.: Vol. 47). lib. bdg. 50.00 (ISBN 0-8240-0630-5). Garland Pub.

Ralph, Margaret. Historias Que Jesus Conto. (Serie Jirafa). Orig. Title: Stories Jesus Told. 1979. 2.95 (ISBN 0-311-38537-0, Edit Mundo). Casa Bautista.

--Jesus: Historias de su Vida. LaValle, Teresa, tr. (Serie Jirafa). Orig. Title: The Life of Jesus. 1979. 2.95 (ISBN 0-311-38536-2, Edit Mundo). Casa Bautista.

--Personas Escogidas De Dios. (Serie Jirafa). Orig. Title: God's Special People. 1979. 2.95 (ISBN 0-311-38535-4, Edit Mundo). Casa Bautista.

Ralph, Philip L., jt. auth. see Burns, Edward M.

Ralston, Anthony & Wilf, H. S., eds. Mathematical Methods for Digital Computers, 2 Vols. LC 60-6509. 1960. Vol. 1. 29.95 (ISBN 0-471-70686-8); Vol. 2. 31.95 (ISBN 0-471-70689-2, Pub by Wiley-Interscience). Wiley.

Ralston, Jackson H. International Arbitration from Athens to Locarno. LC 75-147737. (Library of War & Peace; Int'l. Organization, Arbitration & Law). 38.00 (ISBN 0-8240-0472-8). Garland Pub.

--Law & Procedure of International Tribunals. LC 75-147738. (Library of War & Peace; International Law). lib. bdg. 38.00 (ISBN 0-8240-0496-5). Garland Pub.

Ralston, Mark A. Pierce Arrow. LC 80-15214. (Illus.). 366p. 1980. 25.00 (ISBN 0-498-02451-2). A S Barnes.

Ralston, Melvin B. & Cox, Don R. Emblems of Reality: Discovering Experience in Language. LC 72-81654. 256p. 1973. pap. text ed. 5.95x (ISBN 0-02-476750-6). Macmillan.

Ralston, Penny, jt. auth. see Schultz, Jerelyn.

Ram, K. S. Basic Nuclear Engineering. LC 77-795. 1977. 12.95 (ISBN 0-470-99105-4). Halsted Pr.

Ram, Lily P. Manual of Nursing Arts & Procedures. 1978. 10.00 (ISBN 0-7069-0686-1, Pub. by Vikas India). Advent Bk.

Ram, M. D. Surgery. 6th ed. (Medical Examination Review Book: Vol. 5). 1977. spiral bdg. 8.50 (ISBN 0-87488-105-6). Med Exam.

Ram, M. D., ed. Self-Assessment of Current Knowledge in Surgery. LC 80-18730. 1980. pap. 16.50 (ISBN 0-87488-223-0). Med Exam.

Ramabhadran, N., jt. auth. see Balakrishnan, B.

Ramachandra, Rgo S. A Game of Words. 1976. 8.00 (ISBN 0-89253-809-0); flexible cloth 4.80 (ISBN 0-89253-810-4). Ind-US Inc.

Ramachandran. Sri Sankara Vijayam. 1977. pap. 2.25 (ISBN 0-89744-123-0, Pub. by Ganesh & Co. India). Auromere.

Ramachandran, B., tr. see Kagan, A. M., et al.

Ramachandran, G. N. & Srinivasan, R. Fourier Methods in Crystallography. 259p. 1970. 23.95 (ISBN 0-471-70705-8). Krieger.

Ramachandran, H. Village Clusters & Rural Development. 140p. 1980. text ed. 12.50 (ISBN 0-391-02138-9). Humanities.

Ramachandran, K. S. Archaeology of South India: Tamilnadu. 1980. 40.00x (ISBN 0-8364-0669-9, Pub. by Sundeep). South Asia Bks.

Ramachandran, V. S. Calcium Chloride in Concrete: Science & Technology. (Illus.). 1976. text ed. 63.30x (ISBN 0-85334-682-8, Pub. by Applied Science). Burgess-Intl Ideas.

Ramachandran, V. S., jt. auth. see Josephson, B. D.

Ramaer, R. Steam Locomotives of the East African Railways. 1974. 14.95 (ISBN 0-7153-6437-5). David & Charles.

Ramage, Craufurd T. Familiar Quotations from French & Italian Authors. LC 68-22042. Orig. Title: Beautiful Thoughts from French & Italian Authors Ser. 1968. Repr. of 1904 ed. 18.00 (ISBN 0-8103-3191-8). Gale.

--Familiar Quotations from German & Spanish Authors. LC 68-2043. (With English translations). Repr. of 1904 ed. 18.00 (ISBN 0-8103-3192-6). Gale.

--Familiar Quotations from Greek Authors. LC 68-22044. Orig. Title: Beautiful Thoughts from Greek Authors. 1968. Repr. of 1895 ed. 18.00 (ISBN 0-8103-3193-4). Gale.

Ramakrishna, D., ed. Indian-English Prose: An Anthology. 1981. text ed. write for info. (ISBN 0-391-02190-7). Humanities.

Ramakrishna, Rao V. Emerson, His Muse & Message. 312p. 1980. lib. bdg. 35.00 (ISBN 0-8482-5869-X). Norwood Edns.
Ramaley, Judith A., jt. auth. see Bevelander, Gerrit.
Ramalingam, P. Operations Research & Management Science: An Applications Approach. Date not set. text ed. 19.95 (ISBN 0-8162-6996-3). Holden-Day.
--Systems Analysis for Managerial Decisions: A Computer Approach. LC 76-10534. 1976. 29.95 (ISBN 0-471-70710-4). Wiley.
Raman, A. S. Tales from Indian Mythology. (Illus.). 123p. (gr. 7-12). 74. 3.60 (ISBN 0-88253-473-4). Ind-US Inc.
Raman, T. A. India. rev. ed. LC 78-54252. (World Cultures Ser). (Illus.). (gr. 6 up). 1980. 1-4 copies 9.95 (ISBN 0-88296-127-6); 5 or more 7.96 (ISBN 0-685-14487-9); tchrs'. guide 8.94 (ISBN 0-88296-369-4). Fideler.
Raman, T. A., et al. India & Southeast Asia. LC 78-54253. (World Cultures Ser.). (Illus.). (gr. 6 up). 1979. text ed. 12.43 1-4 copies o.p. (ISBN 0-88296-160-8); text ed. 9.94 5 or more o.p. (ISBN 0-685-14493-3); tchr's guide skills manual incl. 8.94 o.p. (ISBN 0-88296-369-4). Fideler.
Ramanadham, V. V. Public Enterprise in Britain. 176p. 1950. 22.50x (ISBN 0-7146-1245-6, F Cass Co). Biblio Dist.
Ramanathan, G. Quest for General Education: Reflections on the Harvard Report. 10.50x o.p. (ISBN 0-210-22539-4). Asia.
Ramanuja Research Society. Vishishadvaita: Philosophy & Religion. 273p. 1975. 10.75 (ISBN 0-88253-683-4). Ind-US Inc.
Ramanujan, A. K. & Krishnamurthi, M. G., eds. Some Kannada Poems. 1975. 8.00 (ISBN 0-88253-636-2); pap. text ed. 4.00 (ISBN 0-88253-635-4). Ind-US Inc.
Ramanujan, A. K., tr. Fifteen Poems from a Classical Tamil Anthology. (Translated from Tamil). 8.00 (ISBN 0-89253-774-4); flexible cloth 4.00 (ISBN 0-89253-775-2). Ind-US Inc.
Ramanujan, A. K., tr. see Adiga, M. G.
Ramanujan, S. Collected Papers. LC 62-8326. 1962. 13.95 (ISBN 0-8284-0159-4). Chelsea Pub.
Rama Rao, R. V. Of Men, Matter & Me. 4.50x o.p. (ISBN 0-210-34006-1). Asia.
Rama Rau, Santha. Cooking of India. (Foods of the World Ser). (Illus.). 1969. 14.95 (ISBN 0-8094-0042-1). Time-Life.
Ramati, Alexander. Barbed Wire on the Isle of Man. LC 79-3361. 252p. 1980. 10.95 (ISBN 0-15-256039-4). HarBraceJ.
Ramati, Racquel & Urban Design Group of the Department of City Planning, New York. How to Save Your Own Street. LC 78-14709. (Illus.). 176p. 1981. pap. 19.95 (ISBN 0-385-14814-3, Dolp). Doubleday.
Ramazani, P. K. The Persian Gulf & the Strait of Hormuz. (International Straits of the World Ser.: No. 3). 200p. 1979. 35.00x (ISBN 90-286-0069-8). Sijthoff & Noordhoff.
Ramazani, R. K. Beyond the Arab-Israeli Settlement: New Directions for U. S. Policy in the Middle East. LC 77-87564. (Foreign Policy Reports Ser.). 69p. 1977. 5.00 (ISBN 0-89549-006-4). Inst Foreign Policy Anal.
Ramazani, Rouhollah K. Foreign Policy of Iran, 1500-1941: A Developing Nation in World Affairs. LC 66-12469. 1966. 12.95x (ISBN 0-8139-0200-2). U Pr of Va.
--Middle East & the European Common Market. LC 64-13718. 1964. 7.50x o.p. (ISBN 0-8139-0201-0). U Pr of Va.
Rambeau, John. Guidebook to Better Reading: Levels 6-Adult. (Guidebook to Better Reading Ser.). 1976. text ed. 2.67 (ISBN 0-87892-560-0); tchr's manual 2.67 (ISBN 0-87892-561-9). Economy Co.
Rambisoon, Amar B. The Essentials of Successful Preaching. 1981. 6.50 (ISBN 0-8062-1706-5). Carlton.
Rambo, Dottie. Down by the Creek Bank. (Creek Bank Kids Ser.: Vol. 1). (ps-8). 1979. 3.95 (ISBN 0-914850-50-4). Impact Tenn.
--Love Is. (Creek Bank Kids Ser.: Vol. 9). (ps-8). 1980. 3.95 (ISBN 0-914850-92-X). Impact Tenn.
Rambo, Dottie & Huntsinger, Dave. Is There Anything I Can Do for You? (Creek Bank Kids Ser.: Vol. 5). (ps-8). 1979. 3.95 (ISBN 0-914850-74-1). Impact Tenn.
--Multiply. (Creek Bank Kids Ser.: Vol. 8). (ps-8). 1980. 3.95 (ISBN 0-914850-91-1). Impact Tenn.
--Puzzles. (Creek Bank Kids Ser.: Vol. 6). (ps-8). 1979. 3.95 (ISBN 0-914850-76-8). Impact Tenn.
Ramchand, Kenneth. West Indian Narrative: An Introductory Anthology. 1966. pap. text ed. 3.75x (ISBN 0-17-566009-3). Humanities.
Ramchandani, R. H. India & Africa. 314p. 1980. text ed. 16.50x (ISBN 0-391-01796-9). Humanities.
Ramchandani, R. V., tr. see Primlani, Kala.
Ramee, Pierre De La see La Ramee, Pierre De.
Rameh, Clea, jt. auth. see Abreu, Maria I.
Ramesh, Jairam & Weiss, Charles, Jr., eds. Mobilizing Technology for World Development. LC 79-5349. 240p. 1979. pap. 6.95 (ISBN 0-03-055451-9). Overseas Dev Council.
Rameshwar Rao, S., tr. The Mahabharata. 2nd ed. Orig. Title: The Children's Mahabharata. 219p. 1976. pap. text ed. 2.85 (ISBN 0-89253-041-3). Ind-US Inc.
Ramette, Richard W. Chemical Equilibrium & Analysis. (Chemistry Ser). (Illus.). 672p. 1981. text ed. 23.95 (ISBN 0-201-06107-4). A-W.
Ramey, Emmett & Wong, Alex. The Loan Package. 180p. 1981. 3 ring binder 29.95 (ISBN 0-916378-12-8). Oasis Pr.
Ramey, J. Intimate Friendships. 1976. 9.95 o.p. (ISBN 0-13-476903-1); pap. 3.95 o.p. (ISBN 0-13-476895-7). P-H.
Ramfjord, Sigurd & Ash, McKinley, Jr. Occlusion. 2nd ed. LC 78-151682. (Illus.). 1971. 22.00 (ISBN 0-7216-7441-0). Saunders.
Ramig, Christopher J., jt. auth. see Hall, Mary A.
Raming, Ida. The Exclusion of Women from the Priesthood: Divine Law or Sex Discrimination? Adams, Norman R., tr. LC 76-23322. 280p. 1976. 13.50 (ISBN 0-8108-0957-5). Scarecrow.
Ramirez, Bruno. When Workers Fight: The Politics of Industrial Relations in the Progressive Era, 1898-1916. LC 77-83895. (Contributions in Labor History: No. 2). 1978. lib. bdg. 18.95 (ISBN 0-8371-9826-7, RAW/). Greenwood.
Ramirez, Miguel, jt. ed. see Scheer, Linda.
Ramke, Bin. White Monkeys. LC 80-24582. (Contemporary Poetry Ser.). 85p. 1981. 8.50 (ISBN 0-8203-0544-8); pap. 4.50 (ISBN 0-8203-0551-0). U of Ga Pr.
Ramm, A. Theory & Applications of Some New Classes of Integral Equations. 344p. 1981. pap. 18.80 (ISBN 0-387-90540-5). Springer-Verlag.
Ramm, Bernard. Handbook of Contemporary Theology. (Orig.). 1966. pap. 2.65 o.p. (ISBN 0-8028-1159-0). Eerdmans.
Ramm, Bernard L. His Way Out. LC 73-87284. (Orig.). 1974. pap. 2.95 (ISBN 0-8307-0277-6, S282-1-27). Regal.
Rammuny, Raji see McCarus, Ernest, et al.
Ramo, Simon. America's Technology Slip. LC 80-21525. 350p. 1980. 14.95 (ISBN 0-471-05976-5, Pub. by Wiley-Interscience). Wiley.
Ramon Y Cajal, Santiago. Structure of Ammon's Horn. Kraft, Lisbeth M., tr. (Illus.). 100p. 1968. pap. 11.50 photocopy ed. spiral (ISBN 0-398-01543-0). C C Thomas.
--Structure of the Retina. Thorpe, Sylvia A., tr. (Illus.). 224p. 1972. text ed. 17.75 (ISBN 0-398-02385-9). C C Thomas.
Ramos, Adam & Ramos, Joseph. California Brandy: The Wine Drinker's Spirit. (Illus.). 1981. 12.95 (ISBN 0-914598-66-X). Padre Prods.
Ramos, Alberto G. The New Science of Organizations: A Reconceptualization of the Wealth of Nations. 224p. 1981. 25.00 (ISBN 0-8020-5527-3). U of Toronto Pr.
Ramos, David. Prune Orchard Management. (Illus.). 144p. (Orig.). Date not set. pap. text ed. price not set (ISBN 0-931876-45-1). AG Sci Pubns.
Ramos, Joseph, jt. auth. see Ramos, Adam.
Ramos, Joseph R. Labor & Development in Latin America. LC 74-108095. (Institute of Latin American Studies). (Illus.). 1970. 20.00x (ISBN 0-231-03250-1). Columbia U Pr.
Ramos, Mel. Mel Ramos: Watercolors. (Lancaster-Miller Art Ser.). (Illus.). 1980. 8.95 (ISBN 0-89581-009-3). Lancaster-Miller.
Ramos, Myra B., tr. see Freire, Paulo.
Ramos-Diaz, Emma, tr. see Jackins, Harvey.
Ramos-Garcia, Luis A., ed. Tales from Austin. 1980. 5.95 (ISBN 0-934840-02-4). U Tex Studia.
Ramos-Garcia, Luis A. & Lugones, Nestor, eds. Studia Hispanica I in Honor of Rodolfo Cardona. 1980. 12.95 (ISBN 0-934840-01-6). U Tex Studia.
Ramos-Garcia, Luis A. & O'Hara, Edgar, eds. The Newest Peruvian Poetry in Translation. 1979. 4.95 (ISBN 0-934840-00-8). U Tex Studia.
Ramp, Eugene & Semb, George. Behavior Analysis: Areas of Research & Application. LC 74-340095. (Illus.). 432p. 1975. ref. ed. 19.95 (ISBN 0-13-074195-7). P-H.
Rampa, Mama S. Pussywillow. 1976. pap. 2.50 (ISBN 0-685-72712-2). Weiser.
--Tigerlily. 1978. pap. 2.50 (ISBN 0-685-90229-3). Weiser.
Rampa, T. Cave of the Ancients. pap. 2.50 (ISBN 0-685-88123-7). Weiser.
--Doctor from Lhasa. pap. 2.50 (ISBN 0-685-88124-5). Weiser.
--I Believe. pap. 2.50 (ISBN 0-685-88125-3). Weiser.
--The Third Eye. pap. 2.50 (ISBN 0-685-88126-1). Weiser.
Rampa, T. Lobsang. Beyond the Tenth. pap. 2.50 (ISBN 0-685-22168-7). Weiser.
--Candlelight. 174p. (Orig.). 1974. pap. 2.50 (ISBN 0-685-50987-7). Weiser.
--Chapters of Life. pap. 2.50 (ISBN 0-685-22170-9). Weiser.
--Feeding the Flame. pap. 2.50 (ISBN 0-685-01079-1). Weiser.
--The Hermit. pap. 2.50 (ISBN 0-685-27226-5). Weiser.
--Living with the Lama. pap. 2.50 (ISBN 0-685-01080-5). Weiser.
--The Rampa Story. pap. 2.50 (ISBN 0-685-91301-5). Weiser.
--The Saffron Robe. 1974. pap. 2.50 (ISBN 0-685-70567-6). Weiser.
--The Thirteenth Candle. pap. 2.50 (ISBN 0-685-27227-3). Weiser.
--Three Lives. pap. 2.50 (ISBN 0-685-91302-3). Weiser.
--Twilight, 1977. pap. 2.50 (ISBN 0-685-91303-1). Weiser.
--Wisdom of the Ancients. 1975. pap. 2.50 (ISBN 0-685-70568-4). Weiser.
--You. Forever. pap. 2.50 (ISBN 0-685-22178-4). Weiser.
Rampaul, Hoobasar. Pipe Welding Procedures. (Illus.). 208p. 1973. 18.50 (ISBN 0-8311-1100-3). Indus Pr.
Rampersad, Arnold. The Art & Imagination of W. E. B. Dubois. 1976. 15.00x (ISBN 0-674-04711-7). Harvard U Pr.
--Melville's Israel Potter: A Pilgrimage & Progress. 133p. 1969. 4.95 (ISBN 0-87972-000-X); pap. 1.95x (ISBN 0-87972-001-8). Bowling Green Univ.
Rampp, Donald L. Classroom Activities for Auditory Perceptual Disorders. 1976. pap. text ed. 2.95x (ISBN 0-8134-1794-5, 1794). Interstate.
Ramquist, Grace. Complete Christmas Programs, No. 6. 64p. 1980. pap. 1.95 (ISBN 0-310-31571-9, 10638P). Zondervan.
--Complete Christmas Programs, No. 7. 80p. 1980. pap. 1.95 (ISBN 0-310-31581-6, 10639P). Zondervan.
Ramroop, Govinda V. The Voices of India. 1980. 4.95 (ISBN 0-533-03273-3). Vantage.
Rams, Edwin. Analysis & Valuation of Retail Locations. 1976. 29.95 (ISBN 0-87909-033-2). Reston.
Ramsay, A. T. Oceanic Micropalaeontology, Vol. 1. 1977. 120.00 (ISBN 0-12-577301-3). Acad Pr.
Ramsay, Allan see Philomusus, S.
Ramsay, Graham & Harris, Paul. The Joy of Coaching Youth Soccer. LC 79-54131. (Illus., Orig.). 1979. pap. 4.95 (ISBN 0-916802-15-9). Soccer for Am.
Ramsay, I. Synopsis of Endrocrinology & Metabolism. 2nd ed. (Illus.). 1980. pap. 18.95 (ISBN 0-8151-7033-5). Year Bk Med.
Ramsay, James A. Experimental Basis of Modern Biology. LC 64-21564. (Illus.). 1969. text ed. 49.50x (ISBN 0-521-06027-3); pap. 12.50x (ISBN 0-521-09575-1). Cambridge U Pr.
--Physiological Approach to the Lower Animals. 2nd ed. LC 68-21398. (Illus.). 1968. text ed. 29.50 (ISBN 0-521-07185-2); pap. 8.50x (ISBN 0-521-09537-9). Cambridge U Pr.
Ramsay, James H. The Foundations of England: Or, Twelve Centuries of British History, 2 vols. LC 80-2215. 1981. Repr. of 1898 ed. Set. 125.00 (ISBN 0-404-18780-3). Vol. 1 (ISBN 0-404-18781-1). Vol. 2 (ISBN 0-404-18782-X). AMS Pr.
Ramsay, James O. Multiscale: Four Programs for Multidimensional Scaling by the Method of Maximum Likelihood. pap. 9.00 (ISBN 0-89498-002-5). Natl Ed Res.
Ramsay, Marina, tr. see Pierce, Richard A.
Ramsay, Marion L. Pyramids of Power: The Story of Roosevelt, Insull & the Utility Wars. (FDR & the Era of the New Deal Ser.). (Illus.). 342p. 1975. Repr. of 1937 ed. lib. bdg. 32.50 (ISBN 0-306-70707-1). Da Capo.
Ramsay, Natalie R. Norwegian Society. 1974. text ed. 15.00x (ISBN 82-00-04834-9, Dist. by Columbia U Pr); pap. text ed. 11.00x (ISBN 82-00-04610-9). Universitet.
Ramsay, Robert. Hawaiian Tramways. (Illus.). 36p. 1976. pap. 4.00 o.p. (ISBN 0-87095-062-2). Golden West.
Ramsay, Roland T. Management's Guide to Effective Employment Interviewing. 1980. 59.50 (ISBN 0-85013-089-1). Dartnell Corp.
Ramsay, Verna, ed. see Academy of Motion Picture Arts & Sciences.
Ramsay, W. M. & Bell, Gertrude L. Two Thousand & One Churches. (Illus.). xiv, 580p. Repr. of 1905 ed. lib. bdg. 80.00x (ISBN 0-89241-121-X). Caratzas Bros.
Ramsay, William H. Historical Commentary on the Epistle to the Galatians. 1978. 15.75 (ISBN 0-686-12953-9). Klock & Klock.
Ramsay, William M. The Layman's Guide to the New Testament. LC 79-87742. (Layman's Bible Commentary Ser.). 273p. (Orig.). 1980. pap. 10.00 (ISBN 0-8042-0322-9). John Knox.
--Meaning of Jesus Christ. (Orig.). (gr. 9-10). 1964. pap. 3.45 (ISBN 0-8042-9220-5); tchrs' guide pap. 2.60. John Knox.
Ramsburg, Janelle S., jt. auth. see Forman, Louis H.
Ramsdale, Jeanne. Persian Cats. (Orig.). 1962. pap. 2.00 (ISBN 0-87666-178-9, M507). TFH Pubns.
Ramsdell, Charles, tr. see Sierra, Justo.
Ramsden, Caroline. Farewell Manchester. (Illus.). 6.50 o.p. (ISBN 0-85131-066-4, Dist. by Sporting Book Center). J A Allen.
--Racing Without Tears. (Illus.). pap. 4.35 (ISBN 0-85131-004-4, Dist. by Sporting Book Center). J A Allen.
Ramsden, David. Peripheral Metabolism & Action of Thyroid Hormones, Vol. 1. 1977. 19.20 (ISBN 0-904406-54-7). Eden Med Res.
Ramsden, David B. Peripheral Metabolism & Action of Thyroid Hormones, Vol. 2, 1977. (Annual Research Reviews). 1978. 28.80 (ISBN 0-88831-029-3). Eden Med Res.
Ramsden, John. The Age of Balfour & Baldwin: 1902-1940. (A History of the Conservative Party). (Illus.). 1978. text ed. 40.00x (ISBN 0-582-50714-6). Longman.
Ramsden, William E. Ministries Through Non-Parish Institutions. LC 80-22294. (Into Our Third Century Ser.). 96p. (Orig.). 1981. pap. 3.95 (ISBN 0-687-27037-5). Abingdon.
Ramsen, John, ed. The Country Gentleman in Politics: The Political Diaries of Sir Robert Sanders, First Lord of Bayford 1910-1935. 280p. 1980. text ed. 62.50x (ISBN 0-391-01778-0). Humanities.
Ramsey, A. H. The Nameless War. 1978. pap. 4.00x (ISBN 0-911038-38-8). Noontide.
Ramsey, Bette. My Mother's Welcome Home. (Illus.). 1977. pap. 0.95 o.p. (ISBN 0-917726-10-3). Hunter Bks.
Ramsey, Charles E., jt. auth. see McCarty, Donald J.
Ramsey, Dan. Budget Flying. (McGraw-Hill Series in Aviation). (Illus.). 176p. 1980. 16.95 (ISBN 0-07-051202-7). McGraw.
--How to Make One Hundred Thousand Dollars a Year Selling Residential Real Estate. 297p. 1980. 14.95 (ISBN 0-13-423582-7, Busn). P-H.
--One Hundred & One Successful Ways to Turn Weekends into Wealth. 216p. 1980. 10.95 (ISBN 0-13-634808-4, Parker). P-H.
Ramsey, Elizabeth M. & Donner, Martin W. Placental Vasculature & Circulation. LC 79-65527. (Illus.). 101p. 1980. text ed. 65.00 (ISBN 0-7216-7446-1). Saunders.
Ramsey, F. P., intro. by. Foundations: Essays in Philosophy, Logic, Mathematics & Economics. (International Library of Psychology, Philosophy & Scientific Method). 1978. text ed. 24.75x (ISBN 0-391-00814-5). Humanities.
Ramsey, Frederick, Jr. A Guide to Longplay Jazz Records. LC 77-9065. (Roots of Jazz Ser.). (Illus.). 1977. Repr. of 1954 ed. lib. bdg. 25.00 (ISBN 0-306-70891-4). Da Capo.
Ramsey, George W. Quest for the Historical Israel. LC 80-82188. 208p. (Orig.). 1981. pap. 12.50 (ISBN 0-8042-0187-0). John Knox.
Ramsey, Gerald. Morning, Noon & Night Cookbook. 2nd ed. LC 63-16652. 272p. 8.95 (ISBN 0-87074-178-0). SMU Press.
Ramsey, Gloria. Couching: Decorative Laid Thread Embroidery. 1976. 19.94 o.p. (ISBN 0-7134-3130-X, Pub. by Batsford England). David & Charles.
Ramsey, Gregory, ed. see Historic Restoration Project.
Ramsey, Ian T. On Being Sure in Religion. 1963. text ed. 11.25x (ISBN 0-485-11063-6, Athlone Pr). Humanities.
Ramsey, James. The Education of Jesus Christ. LC 80-84438. (Shepherd Classics Ser.). 130p. 1979. pap. 5.95 (ISBN 0-87983-236-3). Keats.
Ramsey, James B. Economic Forecasting-Models or Markets? LC 80-21911: (Cato Papers Ser.: No. 15). 112p. 1980. pap. 5.00 (ISBN 0-932790-28-3). Cato Inst.
--Revelation: An Exposition of the First Eleven Chapters. (Geneva Commentary Ser.). 1977. 14.95 (ISBN 0-85151-256-9). Banner of Truth.
Ramsey, James B. & Musgrave, Gerald L. APL-STAT: A Do-It-Yourself Guide to Computational Statistics Using APL. LC 80-15016. 340p. 1981. pap. 14.95 solutions manual (ISBN 0-534-97985-8). Lifetime Learn.
Ramsey, James B., jt. ed. see Kmenta, Jan.
Ramsey, Jarold, ed. Coyote Was Going There: Indian Literature of the Oregon Country. LC 76-49158. (Illus.). 336p. 1977. 14.95 (ISBN 0-295-95441-8); pap. 7.95 (ISBN 0-295-95731-X). U of Wash Pr.
Ramsey, Marina, tr. see Shelikhov, Grigorii I.
Ramsey, Marjorie E. & Bayless, Kathleen. Kindergarten: Program & Practices. LC 80-11478. (Illus.). 1980. pap. text ed. 12.95 (ISBN 0-8016-4076-8). Mosby.
Ramsey, Paul. The Art of John Dryden. LC 70-80088. 224p. 1969. 10.00x (ISBN 0-8131-1184-6). U Pr of Ky.
--Basic Christian Ethics. LC 78-56925. 424p. 1980. pap. text ed. 9.50x (ISBN 0-226-70383-5). U of Chicago Pr.

--The Ethics of Fetal Research. LC 74-27633. 96p. 1975. 8.95x (ISBN 0-300-01879-7); pap. 2.95x (ISBN 0-300-01880-0). Yale U Pr.
--Fabricated Man: The Ethics of Genetic Control. LC 78-123395. 1970. 12.00x (ISBN 0-300-01373-6); pap. 3.45x (ISBN 0-300-01374-4, YF6). Yale U Pr.
--No Running on the Boardwalk. LC 74-75941. (Contemporary Poetry Ser.). 59p. 1975. pap. 4.50 (ISBN 0-8203-0356-9). U of Ga Pr.
--The Patient As Person: Exploration in Medical Ethics. LC 77-118737. 1970. 20.00x (ISBN 0-300-01357-4); pap. 4.95x (ISBN 0-300-01741-3, Y263). Yale U Pr.
Ramsey, Stanley C. & Harvey, J. D. Small Georgian Houses & Their Details. Date not set. 17.95 o.p. (ISBN 0-8038-0235-8). Hastings.
Ramsey, Verna, ed. see Academy of Motion Picture Arts & Sciences.
Ramsgard, William C. Making Systems Work: The Psychology of Business Systems. LC 77-5933. (Business Data Processing Ser.). 1977. 29.50 (ISBN 0-471-01522-9, Pub. by Wiley-Interscience). Wiley.
Ramsland, Clement, jt. ed. see Bowditch, John.
Ramstetter, Victoria. The Marquise & the Novice. LC 80-83118. (Illus.). 100p. (Orig.). 1981. pap. 4.95 (ISBN 0-930044-16-9). Naiad Pr.
Ramu, S. Anantha, jt. auth. see Iyengar, K. T.
Ramus, J. Developmental Sequence of the Marine Red Alga Pseudogloiophloea in Culture. (U. C. Publ. in Botany: Vol. 52). 1969. pap. 6.50x (ISBN 0-520-09026-8). U of Cal Pr.
Ramwell, Peter, ed. Prostaglandin Synthetase Inhibitors: New Clinical Applications Proceedings. LC 80-7797. (Prostaglandins & Related Lipids Ser.: Vol. 1). 410p. 1980. 34.00x (ISBN 0-8451-2100-6). A R Liss.
Ranald, Margaret L. Monarch Notes on Shakespeare's Winter's Tale. (Orig.). pap. 1.75 o.p. (ISBN 0-671-00656-8). Monarch Pr.
Ranald, Ralph. Monarch Notes on Browning's Poetry. (Orig.). pap. 1.75 (ISBN 0-671-00776-9). Monarch Pr.
Ranald, Ralph A. Monarch Notes on Shakespeare's the Tempest. (Orig.). pap. 1.75 (ISBN 0-671-00644-4). Monarch Pr.
Rance, Nicholas. The Historical Novel & Popular Politics in Nineteenth-Century England. (Critical Studies Ser.). 176p. 1975. 13.50x (ISBN 0-06-495805-1). B&N.
Rancourt, Karen L. Yeah, but Children Need.... 1978. 8.95 (ISBN 0-8467-0451-X, Pub. by Two Continents). Hippocrene Bks.
Rancurello, Antos C., et al, trs. see Brentano, Franz.
Rand, Ann & Eksell, Olle. Edward & the Horse. LC 61-6121. (Illus.). (gr. k-2). 1961. 3.25 o.p. (ISBN 0-15-225202-9, HJ). HarBraceJ.
Rand, Ayn. Atlas Shrugged. 1957. 15.00 (ISBN 0-394-41576-0). Random.
Rand, Christopher C., tr. see Ts'ao Yu.
Rand, E. M. Founders of the Middle Ages. Date not set. 7.50 (ISBN 0-8446-2779-8). Peter Smith.
Rand, Elias, ed. Recent Advances in Diagnostic Ultrasound. (Illus.). 160p. 1971. 15.50 (ISBN 0-398-02386-7). C C Thomas.
Rand, Elizabeth, ed. see Edney, Margon & Grimm, Ede.
Rand, Elizabeth, ed. see Wheeler, Grace.
Rand, Elizabeth H., ed. see Boyko, Walter N.
Rand, Ellen, jt. auth. see Derven, Ronald.
Rand, Harry. Arshile Gorky: The Implication of Symbols. LC 77-25046. (Illus.). 256p. 1981. text ed. 40.00 (ISBN 0-8390-0209-2). Allanheld & Schram.
--Arshile Gorky: The Implication of Symbols. LC 77-25046. (Illus.). 256p. 1981. 40.00 (ISBN 0-8390-0209-2). Allanheld.
Rand McNally. Guide to Florida. 5th ed. LC 79-656302. (Illus.). 1979. pap. 4.95 (ISBN 0-528-84109-2). Rand.
--The New International Atlas. LC 80-51969. (Illus.). 568p. 1980. 60.00 (ISBN 0-528-83111-9); deluxe ed. 100.00 (ISBN 0-528-83112-7). Rand.
--Pocket Atlas. LC 80-83201. (Illus.). 160p. 1980. pap. 4.95 (ISBN 0-528-83097-X). Rand.
--Pocket Vacation Guide. 1981. pap. 3.95 (ISBN 0-528-84547-0). Rand.
Rand McNally & Company & Southern Living Travel Editors. Southern Living Travel South - 1981. (Illus.). 192p. 1981. pap. 9.95 (ISBN 0-686-69039-7). Oxmoor Hse.
Rand, Peter. The Time of the Emergency. LC 77-75388. 1977. 6.95 o.p. (ISBN 0-385-07033-0). Doubleday.
Rand, Robert W. Microneurosurgery. 2nd ed. LC 78-7230. 1978. text ed. 74.50 (ISBN 0-8016-4077-6). Mosby.
Rand School of Social Science. Trial of Scott Nearing & the the American Socialist Party. LC 73-147523. (Library of War & Peace; Labor, Socialism & War). lib. bdg. 38.00 (ISBN 0-8240-0311-X). Garland Pub.
Rand, W. W. Diccionario De la Santa Biblia. Orig. Title: Dictionary of the Holy Bible. (Illus.). 768p. (Span.). 1969. pap. 10.95 (ISBN 0-89922-003-7). Edit Caribe.
Randa, James, jt. ed. see Mahanthappa, K. T.
Randall, Arne, jt. auth. see Conant, Howard.
Randall, Bob. The Fan. 288p. 1978. pap. 2.50 (ISBN 0-446-91887-3). Warner Bks.
--The Next. 352p. (Orig.). 1981. pap. 2.75 (ISBN 0-446-95740-2). Warner Bks.
Randall, Bruce. Barbell Way to Physical Fitness. (Illus.). 1970. 9.95 (ISBN 0-385-09053-6). Doubleday.
Randall, C., jt. auth. see Youngman, W.
Randall, Cher. Total Preparation for Childbirth. 1979. pap. 4.95 (ISBN 0-88270-331-5). Logos.
Randall, Clifford W. & Benefield, Larry D. Biological Processes Design for Wastewater Treatment. (Environmental Sciences Ser.). (Illus.). 1980. text ed. 27.95 (ISBN 0-13-076406-X). P-H.
Randall, D. J., et al. The Evolution of Air Breathing in Vertebrates. LC 80-462. (Illus.). 176p. Date not set. 27.50 (ISBN 0-521-22259-1). Cambridge U Pr.
Randall, Derek. Young Player's Guide to Cricket. LC 80-66427. (Illus.). 96p. 1980. 13.50 (ISBN 0-7153-7991-7). David & Charles.
Randall, F. British Government & Politics. (Illus.). 288p. (Orig.). 1979. pap. text ed. 12.95x (ISBN 0-7121-0247-7, Pub. by Macdonald & Evans England). Intl Ideas.
--Stalin's Russia. LC 65-18559. 1965. 12.95 (ISBN 0-02-925810-3). Free Pr.
Randall, J. G. Mr. Lincoln. Current, Richard N., ed. Date not set. 5.00 (ISBN 0-8446-0865-3). Peter Smith.
Randall, J. K. Something Medieval. LC 80-80808. 41p. 1981. 14.25. Lingua Pr.
Randall, James G. Lincoln & the South. LC 80-22084. (The Walter Lynwood Fleming Lectures in Southern History, L. S. U.). (Illus.). viii, 161p. 1980. Repr. of 1946 ed. lib. bdg. 18.75x (ISBN 0-313-22843-4, RALS). Greenwood.
Randall, John H. Aristotle. LC 60-6030. 1960. 20.00x (ISBN 0-231-02359-6); pap. 6.00x (ISBN 0-231-08529-X). Columbia U Pr.
--The Career of Philosophy Vol. 1: From the Middle Ages to the Enlightenment. LC 62-10454. 1970. 27.50x (ISBN 0-231-08677-6); pap. 12.50x (ISBN 0-231-08637-7). Columbia U Pr.
--Career of Philosophy Vol. 2. From the German Enlightenment to the Age of Darwin. LC 62-10454. 1970. 20.00x (ISBN 0-231-08678-4); pap. 12.50x (ISBN 0-231-08639-3). Columbia U Pr.
--Hellenistic Ways of Deliverance & the Making of the Christian Synthesis. LC 74-137339. 1970. 17.50x (ISBN 0-231-03327-3). Columbia U Pr.
--How Philosophy Uses Its Past. LC 63-20464. (Matchette Foundation Lecture Ser.: No. 14). 1963. 15.00 o.p. (ISBN 0-231-02663-3). Columbia U Pr.
Randall, John H., Jr. Philosophy After Darwin: Chapters for the Career of Philosophy & Other Essays, Vol. 3. Singer, Beth J., ed. LC 62-10454. 1977. 20.00x (ISBN 0-231-04114-4). Columbia U Pr.
Randall, John H., Jr. & Buchler, Justus. Philosophy: An Introduction. rev. ed. 1971. pap. 3.95 (ISBN 0-06-460041-6, CO 41, COS). Har-Row.
Randall, John H., Jr., et al. Readings in Philosophy. 3rd ed. 1972. pap. 5.95 (ISBN 0-06-460059-9, CO 59, COS). Har-Row.
Randall, Laura. A Comparative Economic History of Latin America, 1500-1914. Incl. Vol. 2. Argentina. 18.75 (ISBN 0-8357-0272-3, SS-00043); Vol. 3. Brazil. 18.75 (ISBN 0-8357-0273-1, SS-00044); Vol. 4. Peru. 16.75 (ISBN 0-8357-0274-X, SS-00045). LC 77-81283. 1977. Univ Microfilms.
--An Economic History of Argentina. LC 77-24388. 1977. 20.00x (ISBN 0-231-03358-3). Columbia U Pr.
Randall, Lilian M. Images in the Margins of Gothic Manuscripts. (California Studies in the History of Art: No. IV). 1966. 60.00x (ISBN 0-520-01047-7). U of Cal Pr.
Randall, Margaret. Women in Cuba--Twenty Years Later. (Illus.). 182p. 1981. 15.95 (ISBN 0-918266-15-7); pap. 6.95 (ISBN 0-918266-14-9). Smyrna.
Randall, Marta. Dangerous Games. (Orig.). 1980. pap. write for info. (ISBN 0-671-82417-1). PB.
Randall, Paula. After the Big Bang. 105p. (Orig.). 1980. pap. 3.95 (ISBN 0-89260-186-8). Hwong Pub.
Randall, Peter, jt. ed. see Whitaker, Linton A.
Randall, Richard S. Censorship of the Movies: The Social & Political Control of a Mass Medium. LC 68-14035. 1968. 22.50 (ISBN 0-299-04731-8); pap. 6.95x (ISBN 0-299-04734-2). U of Wis Pr.
Randall, Rona. Dragonmede. 320p. 1975. pap. 1.75 o.p. (ISBN 0-345-24351-X). Ballantine.
--The Eagle at the Gate. 1978. pap. 2.25 (ISBN 0-380-42846-6, 42846). Avon.
--Gods of Mars. 1977. pap. 1.95 (ISBN 0-345-27835-6). Ballantine.
--The Mating Dance. 1980. pap. 2.75 (ISBN 0-686-69245-4, 50591). Avon.
--Watchman's Stone. 240p. 1976. pap. 1.75 o.p. (ISBN 0-345-25107-5). Ballantine.
--The Willow Herb. 160p. (Orig.). Date not set. pap. 1.75 (ISBN 0-345-28586-7). Ballantine.
Randall-Stevens, H. C. Atlantis to the Latter Days. 3rd ed. (Illus.). 1966. 12.50 (ISBN 0-685-22167-9). Weiser.
--Teachings of Osiris. new ed. 1970. Repr. of 1927 ed. 9.50 (ISBN 0-685-22177-6). Weiser.
--Wisdom of the Soul. 3rd ed. (Illus.). 1974. 10.00 (ISBN 0-685-27228-1). Weiser.
Randegart, Lyle J. Mary's Baby. 1981. 6.75 (ISBN 0-8062-1656-5). Carlton.
Randel, Fred V. The World of Elia: Charles Lamb's Essayistic Romanticism. (National University Publications Literary Criticism Ser.). 1975. 12.95 (ISBN 0-8046-9118-5, Natl U). Kennikat.
Randel, William, et al, eds. Contributions to Science. (Florida State U. Ser). (Illus.). 173p. 1950. pap. 2.50 o.p. (ISBN 0-8130-0451-9). U Presses Fla.
Randell, B., jt. ed. see Anderson, T.
Randeraat, J. Van & Setterington, R. E., eds. Piezoelectric Ceramics. 2nd ed. (Mullard Publications Ser.). (Illus.). 211p. 1974. text ed. 24.50x (ISBN 0-901232-75-0). Scholium Intl.
Randhawa, M. S. The Green Revolution: A Case Study of Punjab. LC 73-5851. 207p. 1974. 15.95 (ISBN 0-470-70795-X). Halsted Pr.
Randi, James. Flim-Flam. (Illus.). 1980. 12.95 (ISBN 0-690-01877-0). Lippincott.
Randier, Jean. Marine Navigation Instruments. (Illus.). 219p. 1980. text ed. 47.50x (ISBN 0-7195-3733-9). Humanities.
Randle, Gretchen R., ed. Electronic Industries Information Sources. LC 67-31262. (Management Information Guide Ser.: No. 13). 1968. 30.00 (ISBN 0-8103-0813-4). Gale.
Randle, John. Understanding Britain: A History of the British People & Their Culture. (Illus.). 288p. 1981. 25.00x (ISBN 0-631-12471-3, Pub. by Basil Blackwell England); pap. 8.95x (ISBN 0-631-12883-2). Biblio Dist.
Randle, Paul A. & Swensen, Philip R. Financial Planning for the Executive. (Finance Ser.). (Illus.). 300p. 1981. text ed. 15.95. Lifetime Learn.
Randle, Robert F. Origins of Peace: A Study of Peacemaking & the Structure of Peace Settlements. LC 72-80078. (Illus.). 1973. 19.95 (ISBN 0-02-925800-6). Free Pr.
Randles, Slim. Dogsled. 1978. pap. 3.95 (ISBN 0-87691-261-7). Winchester Pr.
Randlett, Samuel. The Best of Origami. (Illus.). 185p. 1981. 12.95 (ISBN 0-571-10275-1, Pub. by Faber & Faber). Merrimack Bk Serv.
Rando, Guy L., jt. auth. see Jones, Rees L.
Randolph, Boris. Bible Verses in Verse. LC 80-67992. 144p. 1980. pap. 3.95 (ISBN 0-87516-424-2). De Vorss.
Randolph, David & Kingsbury, Jack D. Pentecost 1. LC 75-24959. (Proclamation 1: Aids for Interpreting the Lessons of the Church Year, Ser. B). 64p. 1975. pap. 1.95 (ISBN 0-8006-4076-4, 1-4076). Fortress.
Randolph, David J., ed. Ventures in Worship 3. 224p. (Orig.). 1973. pap. 3.95 o.p. (ISBN 0-687-43689-3). Abingdon.
Randolph, David J. & Garrett, Bill, eds. Ventures in Song. (Orig.). 1972. pap. 2.95 o.p. (ISBN 0-687-43682-6). Abingdon.
Randolph, Edmund. Beef, Leather & Grass. LC 80-18818. (Illus.). 304p. 1981. 14.95 (ISBN 0-8061-1517-3). U of Okla Pr.
--Mostly Fools: A Romance of Civilization, 1886. (Victorian Fiction Ser.). 1975. lib. bdg. 66.00 (ISBN 0-8240-1539-8). Garland Pub.
Randolph, Elizabeth. How to Be Your Cat's Best Friend. (Illus.). 224p. 1981. 11.95 (ISBN 0-316-73376-8). Little.
Randolph, Erwin P. William Law. (English Author Ser.: No. 282). 1980. lib. bdg. 10.95 (ISBN 0-8057-6765-7). Twayne.
Randolph, Francis L. Studies for a Byron Bibliography. LC 79-13752. 1979. 25.00 (ISBN 0-915010-26-7). Sutter House.
Randolph, Henry F., ed. Fifty Years of English Song, 2 vols. (Illus.). 290p. 1981. Repr. of 1888 ed. lib. bdg. 150.00 (ISBN 0-8495-4574-9). Arden Lib.
Randolph, J. Ralph, ed. Forts of Tennessee. (The Tennessee Ser.: Vol. 4). (Illus.). 1981. 12.95 (ISBN 0-87870-109-5). Memphis St Univ.
Randolph, Jerry, jt. auth. see Taylor, James B.
Randolph, Patricia M. Diet, Nutrition & Dentistry. (Illus.). 358p. 1980. pap. text ed. 14.95 (ISBN 0-8016-4088-1). Mosby.
Randolph, Paul H. & Meeks, Howard D. Applied Linear Optimization. LC 78-50044. (Industrial Engineering Ser.). 1978. pap. text ed. 8.95 o.p. (ISBN 0-88244-144-2). Grid Pub.
Randolph, Robert M. Planagement: Moving Concept into Reality. LC 79-17075. 1979. Repr. of 1975 ed. 17.95 (ISBN 0-89384-056-4). Learning Concepts.
Randolph, Theron G. Human Ecology & Susceptibility to the Chemical Environment. (Illus.). 160p. 1978. 12.50 (ISBN 0-398-01548-1). C C Thomas.
Randolph, Theron G. & Moss, Ralph W. An Alternative Approach to Allergies: The New Field of Clinical Ecology Unravels the Environmental Causes of Mental & Physical Ills. LC 80-7866. 264p. 1980. 11.95 (ISBN 0-690-01998-X). Lippincott & Crowell.
Randsborg, Klavs. From Period Three to Period Four: Chronological Studies of the Bronze Age in Southern Scandinavia & Northern Germany. (Archaeological Historical Ser.: No. 15). (Illus.). 1972. pap. text ed. 27.75x (ISBN 87-480-7622-8). Humanities.
Ranelagh, E. L. The Past We Share: The Near Eastern Ancestry of Western Folk Literature. (Illus.). 288p. 1980. 21.95 (ISBN 0-7043-2234-X, Pub. by Quartet England). Horizon.
Ranere, Anthony J., jt. auth. see Linares, Olga F.
Raney, Ken, tr. see Gresham, Stephen, et al.
Raney, R. Beverly, jt. auth. see Brashear, H. Robert.
Ranganadha, S. Industrial Management & Market Research-Conceptual Framework. 1969. 5.50x o.p. (ISBN 0-8426-0061-2). Verry.
Rangel-Ribeiro, Victor. Baroque Music: A Practical Guide for the Performer. LC 80-5222. (Illus.). 260p. 1981. 15.00 (ISBN 0-02-871980-8). Schirmer Bks.
Ranger, Dan. Pacific Coast Shay. LC 64-8046. 14.95 (ISBN 0-87095-022-3). Golden West.
Ranger, Mary. Benjamin of Nazareth. (Starlight Ser.). (Illus.). (gr. 5-8). 1981. pap. 1.95 (ISBN 0-570-03615-1, 39-1103). Concordia.
--Rebellious Rebecca. (Starlight Ser.). (Illus.). (gr. 5-8). 1977. pap. 2.25 (ISBN 0-570-03612-7, 39-1100). Concordia.
--Simon the Small. (Starlight Ser.). (Illus.). (gr. 5-8). 1977. pap. 2.25 (ISBN 0-570-03613-5, 39-1101). Concordia.
Ranger, T. O. Dance & Society in Eastern Africa 1890-1970: The Beni Ngoma. LC 74-76389. 1974. 20.00x (ISBN 0-520-02729-9). U of Cal Pr.
Ranger, T. O. & Kimambo, Isaria, eds. The Historical Study of African Religion. (Library Reprint Ser.). 1976. 24.75x (ISBN 0-520-03179-2). U of Cal Pr.
Ranger, T. O. & Weller, John, eds. Themes in the Christian History of Central Africa. 1975. 27.50x (ISBN 0-520-02536-9). U of Cal Pr.
Rani, Nisha, jt. auth. see Gupta, S. L.
Ranis, Gustav. The United States & the Developing Economies. rev. ed. 1973. 8.95x (ISBN 0-393-05461-6, NortonC); pap. 5.95x (ISBN 0-393-09999-7). Norton.
Ranis, Gustav, jt. ed. see Beranek, William.
Ranjan, Gopal, jt. auth. see Prakash, Shamsher.
Ranjhan, S. K. Animal Nutrition & Feeding Practices in India. 2nd ed. 350p. 1980. 13.50x (ISBN 0-7069-0509-1). Intl Pubns Serv.
Ranjhan, S. K. & Pathak, N. N. Management & Feeding of Buffaloes. Date not set. text ed. 15.00x (ISBN 0-7069-0778-7, Pub. by Vikas India). Advent Bk.
Ranjhan, S. K., jt. auth. see Krishna, G.
Rank, Hugh. Edwin O'Connor. (U. S. Authors Ser.: No. 242). 1974. lib. bdg. 9.95 (ISBN 0-8057-0555-4). Twayne.
Rank, Otto. Beyond Psychology. pap. text ed. 4.00 (ISBN 0-486-20485-5). Dover.
Ranke, Leopold Von see Von Ranke, Leopold.
Ranke, von L. see Von Ranke, Leopold.
Ranki, Gyorgy, jt. tr. see Berend, Ivan T.
Rankilor, P. R. Membranes in Ground Engineering. LC 80-40504. 432p. 1981. 49.50 (ISBN 0-471-27808-4, Pub. by Wiley-Interscience). Wiley.
Rankin, Carroll W. Dandelion Cottage. 4th ed. 1977. Repr. of 1904 ed. 4.95 (ISBN 0-938746-00-6). Marquette Cnty Hist.
Rankin, Ernest H., jt. ed. see Carter, James L.
Rankin, Hugh F. Pirates of Colonial North Carolina. (Illus.). 1979. pap. 1.00 (ISBN 0-86526-100-8). NC Archives.
Rankin, Jake & Rankin, Marni. Getaway Guide II: More Short Vacations in the Pacific Northwest. 192p. 1981. pap. 8.95 (ISBN 0-914718-56-8). Pacific Search.
Rankin, Judy & Aronstein, Michael. A Natural Way to Golf Power. LC 74-20407. (Illus.). 224p. (YA) 1976. 8.95 o.s.i. (ISBN 0-06-013517-4, HarpT). Har-Row.
Rankin, Lois, jt. tr. see Abrahams, Roger D.
Rankin, Marni, jt. auth. see Rankin, Jake.
Rankin, Molly K. I Heard Singing. LC 74-27533. (Destiny Ser.). 1976. pap. 4.95 (ISBN 0-8163-0227-8, 09035-7). Pacific Pr Pub Assn.
--No Chance to Panic. LC 79-87734. (Destiny Ser.). 1980. pap. 4.95 (ISBN 0-8163-0383-5, 14484-0). Pacific Pr Pub Assn.

Rankin, O. S. Israel's Wisdom Literature: Its Bearing on Theology & the History of Religions. LC 36-33127. 288p. Repr. of 1936 ed. text ed. 7.50 (ISBN 0-567-02214-5). Attic Pr.

Rankin, Paula. Augers. LC 80-70565. (Poetry Ser.). 1980. 9.95 (ISBN 0-915604-45-0); pap. 4.95 (ISBN 0-915604-46-9). Carnegie-Mellon.

Rankin, R. A. Modular Forms & Functions. LC 76-11089. (Illus.). 1977. 68.50 (ISBN 0-521-21212-X). Cambridge U Pr.

Rankin, Robert, ed. see Bloy, Myron B., Jr., et al.

Rankin, Robert P., jt. auth. see Lowry, Ritchie P.

Rankin, Robert S. & Dallmayr, Winfried R. Freedom & Emergency Powers in the Cold War. LC 63-21213. 1964. pap. text ed. 10.95x (ISBN 0-89197-531-4). Irvington.

Rankin, Sloan. Dink. LC 80-81545. (Illus.). 96p. 1980. 6.95 (ISBN 0-396-07837-0). Dodd.

Rankins, William. A Mirrour of Monsters. Bd. with Menaphon. Nashe, Thomas; Kind Harts Dream. Chettle, Henry. (The English Stage Ser.: Vol. 9). lib. bdg. 50.00 (ISBN 0-8240-0592-9). Garland Pub.

Ranlett, John G. Money & Banking: An Introduction to Analysis & Policy. 3rd ed. LC 77-23251. 1977. text ed. 23.50 (ISBN 0-471-70815-1). Wiley.

Ranlett, William. The Architect, 2 vols. LC 76-21851. (Architecture & Decorative Art Ser.). (Illus.). 1976. Repr. of 1857 ed. lib. bdg. 85.00 (ISBN 0-306-70799-3). Da Capo.

Ranney, Austin. Curing the Mischiefs of Faction: Party Reform in America. (Jefferson Memorial Lectures). 1975. 16.95x (ISBN 0-520-02650-0); pap. 3.25 (ISBN 0-520-03215-2, CAL 335). U of Cal Pr.

--Federalization of Presidential Primaries. 1978. pap. 3.25 (ISBN 0-8447-3297-4). Am Enterprise.

--Pathways to Parliament: Candidate Selection in Britain. 1965. 25.00 (ISBN 0-299-03560-3). U of Wis Pr.

Ranney, Austin, jt. auth. see Bone, Hugh A.

Ranney, Austin, ed. Past & Future of Presidential Debates. 1979. pap. 7.25 (ISBN 0-8447-3330-X). Am Enterprise.

--Presidential Nominating Process: Can It Be Improved? 1980. pap. 3.25 (ISBN 0-8447-3397-0). Am Enterprise.

Ranney, M. W. Heat Exchange Fluids & Techniques. LC 79-20336. (Energy Tech Review, No. 50, Chemical Review Ser.: No. 143). (Illus.). 1980. 42.00 (ISBN 0-8155-0778-X). Noyes.

--Oil Shale & Tar Sands Technology. LC 79-16122. (Energy Technology Review No. 49; Chemical Technology Review No. 137). (Illus.). 1980. 48.00 (ISBN 0-8155-0769-0). Noyes.

--Silicones, 2 vols. Incl. Vol. 1. Rubber, Electrical Molding Resins & Functional Fluids (ISBN 0-8155-0665-1); Vol. 2. Coatings, Printing Inks, Cellular Plastics, Textiles & Consumer Products (ISBN 0-8155-0669-4). LC 77-77019. (Chemical Technology Review Ser.: Vols. 91-92). (Illus.). 1977. 39.00 ea. Noyes.

Ranney, M. W., ed. Flotation Agents & Processes: Technology & Applications. LC 80-19191. (Chemical Tech. Rev. 172). (Illus.). 372p. 1981. 48.00 (ISBN 0-8155-0821-2). Noyes.

Ranney, M. William. Lubricant Additives-Recent Developments. LC 77-94235. (Chemical Technology Review Ser.: No. 104). (Illus.). 1978. 39.00 o.p. (ISBN 0-8155-0693-7). Noyes.

Ranney, M. William, ed. Synthetic Oils & Additives for Lubricants: Advances Since 1977. LC 79-24355. (Chemical Technology Review Ser.: No. 145). (Illus.). 1980. 48.00 (ISBN 0-8155-0781-X). Noyes.

Ranniaia, Tom I., tr. see Bulgakov, Mikhail.

Ranofsky, Abraham L. Surgical Operations in Short-Stay Hospitals, U.S. 1973. Shipp, Audrey M., ed. (Ser. 13: No. 24). 61p. 1976. pap. text ed. 1.25 (ISBN 0-8406-0069-0). Natl Ctr Health Stats.

Rans, L., jt. auth. see Sturgeon, S.

Ransford, jt. auth. see Jeffries.

Ransley, P. G. & Ridson, R. A. Reflux & Renal Scarring. 1980. 15.00x (Pub. by Brit Inst Radiology). State Mutual Bk.

Ransom, Bill, jt. auth. see Herbert, Frank.

Ransom, C. J. The Age of Velikovsky. LC 76-22381. (Illus.). 1977. 12.95 (ISBN 0-917994-01-9). Kronos Pr.

Ransom, Grayce A. & Stowe, Elaine. Crackerjacks. rev. ed. (Cornerstone Ser.). (gr. 4-5). 1978. pap. text ed. 4.52 (ISBN 0-201-41026-5, Sch Div); tchr's ed. 5.56 (ISBN 0-201-41027-3). A-W.

--Drumbeats. rev. ed. (Cornerstone Ser.). (gr. 4-5). 1978. pap. text ed. 4.52 (ISBN 0-201-41028-1, Sch Div); tchr's ed. 5.56 (ISBN 0-201-41029-X). A-W.

Ransom, Jay E. Gems & Minerals of America: A Guide to Rock Collecting. LC 72-9147. (Illus.). 730p. (YA) 1975. 22.50 o.p. (ISBN 0-06-013512-3, HarpT); lib. bdg. 21.79 o.p. (ISBN 0-06-013513-1); (ISBN 0-685-50280-5). Har-Row.

--The Gold Hunter's Field Book: How & Where to Find Gold in the United States & Canada. LC 74-20409. 1980. pap. 5.95 (ISBN 0-06-090775-4, CN 775, CN). Har-Row.

--The Gold Hunter's Field Book: How & Where to Prospect for Colors, Nuggets, & Mineral Ores of Gold by Amateur Serious Followers of Jason & the Golden Fleece. LC 74-20409. (Illus.). 382p. (YA) 1975. 10.95 o.p. (ISBN 0-06-013511-5, HarpT). Har-Row.

Ransom, Jay E., ed. Harper & Row's Complete Field Guide to North American Wildlife: Western Edition. LC 79-2635. (Illus.). 910p. 1981. 17.50 o.p. (ISBN 0-690-01979-3, HarpT); flexible vinyl cover 12.95 o.p. (ISBN 0-690-01971-8). Har-Row.

Ransom, M. A. & Engle, Eloise K. Sea of the Bear. LC 79-6122. (Navies & Men Ser.). (Illus.). 1980. Repr. of 1964 ed. lib. bdg. 19.00x (ISBN 0-405-13076-7). Arno.

Ransom, P. J. Railways Revived. (Illus.). 1973. 7.95 (ISBN 0-571-09972-6, Pub. by Faber & Faber). Merrimack Bk Serv.

--Your Book of Canals. (Your Book Ser.). (Illus.). 1977. 6.95 (ISBN 0-571-10971-3, Pub. by Faber & Faber). Merrimack Bk Serv.

Ransom, R. & Sutch, R. One Kind of Freedom. LC 76-27909. 1978. 35.50 (ISBN 0-521-21450-5); pap. 11.95x (ISBN 0-521-29203-4). Cambridge U Pr.

Ransom, Stewart, et al. Clergy, Ministers & Priests. (International Library of Sociology Ser.). 1977. 20.00 (ISBN 0-7100-8713-6). Routledge & Kegan.

Ransom, Timothy W. The Beach Troop of the Gombe. LC 77-92573. 1979. 18.00 (ISBN 0-8387-1704-7). Bucknell U Pr.

Ransom, W. M. Last Rites. 1978. 2.50 (ISBN 0-918116-13-9). Jawbone Pr.

Ransom, William L. Majority Rule & the Judiciary. LC 78-166099. (American Constitutional & Legal History Ser). 1971. Repr. of 1912 ed. pap. 19.50 (ISBN 0-306-70205-3). Da Capo.

Ransome, Arthur. Coot Club. (Illus.). 352p. (gr. 4-7). 1980. 9.95 (ISBN 0-224-60635-2, Pub. by Chatto Bodley Jonathan). Merrimack Bk Serv.

--Swallows & Amazons. 352p. (gr. 3-7). 1981. 9.95 (ISBN 0-224-60631-X, Pub. by Chatto-Bodley-Jonathan). Merrimack Bk Serv.

--We Didn't Mean to Go to Sea. (Children's Literature Ser.). 1981. PLB 11.98 (ISBN 0-8398-2698-2). Gregg.

Ransome, Eleanor. The Terrific Kemble: A Victorian Self-Portrait from the Writings of Fanny Kemble. 1979. 22.50 (ISBN 0-241-89884-6, Pub. by Hamish Hamilton England). David & Charles.

Ransome, Roger. The Greater Horseshoe Bat. (Mammal Society Ser.). (Illus.). 50p. 1980. 6.95 (ISBN 0-7137-0986-3, Pub. by Blandford Pr England). Sterling.

Ranson, Stephen W. Anatomy of the Nervous System. 10th rev. ed. Clark, Sam L., ed. LC 59-5080. (Illus.). 1959. 18.00 (ISBN 0-7216-7455-0). Saunders.

Rantz, Marilyn & Courtial, Donald C. Lifting, Moving & Transferring Patients: A Manual. (Illus.). 219p. 1981. pap. text ed. 9.95 (ISBN 0-8016-4087-3). Mosby.

Rantzen, M. J. Little Ship Astro-Navigation. 1978. 10.95 o.p. (ISBN 0-214-20373-5, 8039, Dist. by Arco). Barrie & Jenkins.

--Little Ship Handling. 1978. 8.50 o.p. (ISBN 0-214-20040-X, 8041, Dist. by Arco). Barrie & Jenkins.

--Little Ship Meteorology. 1978. 9.95 o.p. (ISBN 0-214-20006-X, 8042, Dist. by Arco). Barrie & Jenkins.

--Little Ship Navigation. 1978. 11.95 o.p. (ISBN 0-214-20374-3, 8043, Dist. by Arco). Barrie & Jenkins.

Ranwez, Alain D. Jean-Paul Satre's "Les Temps Modernes". LC 80-50077. 163p. 1980. 15.00x (ISBN 0-87875-191-2). Whitston Pub.

Rao, Adapa R. Emerson & Social Reform. 132p. 1981. text ed. 10.25 (ISBN 0-391-02199-0). Humanities.

Rao, Anthony. The Dinosaur Coloring Book. (Illus.). 48p. (Orig.). (gr. 1-4). 1980. pap. 2.00 (ISBN 0-486-24022-3). Dover.

Rao, C. N. & Ferraro, J. R. Spectroscopy in Inorganic Chemistry. 1970-1971. Vol. 1. 48.50 (ISBN 0-12-580201-3); Vol. 2. 48.50 (ISBN 0-12-580202-1). Acad Pr.

Rao, C. R. Essays on Econometrics & Planning. 1965. 37.00 (ISBN 0-08-011025-8). Pergamon.

Rao, C. R. & Mitra, Sujit K. Generalized Inverse of Matrices & Its Applications. LC 74-158528. (Ser. in Probability & Statistics Section). 1971. 29.95 (ISBN 0-471-70821-6, Pub. by Wiley-Interscience). Wiley.

Rao, C. Radhakrishna. Linear Statistical Inference & Its Applications. 2nd ed. LC 72-13093. (Ser. in Probability & Mathematical Statistics). 608p. 1973. 36.95 (ISBN 0-471-70823-2). Wiley.

Rao, G. Gopal, jt. auth. see Skelton, Mary L.

Rao, G. Lakshmana. Brain Drain & Foreign Students. LC 78-10903. (Illus.). 1979. 25.00x (ISBN 0-312-09437-X). St Martin.

Rao, H. G., jt. auth. see Rajan, S. V.

Rao, H. K. Reinforced Cement Concrete: A Textbook for Polytechnic Students. pap. 5.00x (ISBN 0-210-34062-2). Asia.

Rao, J. S., ed. see Indian Society of Theoretical & Applied Mechanics, 20th Congress, India, 1975.

Rao, K. Bhaskara. Rudyard Kipling's India. 1975. pap. 4.95x (ISBN 0-8061-1243-3). U of Okla Pr.

Rao, K. K., ed. Food Consumption & Planning. 1976. 94.00 (ISBN 0-08-016459-5). Pergamon.

Rao, K. L. Mahatma Gandhi & Comparative Religion. 1979. 15.00x (ISBN 0-89684-034-4). South Asia Bks.

Rao, K. P., jt. ed. see Chennakesavan, S.

Rao, K. R., jt. auth. see Sailaja, P.

Rao, K. Ramamohan, jt. auth. see Elliott, Douglas F.

Rao, M. M. Foundations of Stochastic Analysis. (Probability & Mathematical Statistics Ser.). 1981. price not set (ISBN 0-12-580850-X). Acad Pr.

Rao, Malithi. Khajuraho & Other Poems. 1976. 8.00 (ISBN 0-89253-821-X); flexible cloth 4.80 (ISBN 0-89253-822-8). Ind-US Inc.

Rao, N. Narayana. Elements of Engineering Electromagnetics. (Illus.). 1977. 25.95 (ISBN 0-13-264150-X). P-H.

Rao, P. Parameswara, jt. auth. see Chatterjee, Nirmal C.

Rao, P. Syamasundar & Miller, Max D. Pediatric Cardiology. LC 61-66847. (Medical Examination Review Ser.: Vol. 37). 1980. pap. 19.50 (ISBN 0-87488-140-4). Med Exam.

Rao, Potluri M. & Miller, Roger L. Applied Econometrics. 1971. 18.95x (ISBN 0-534-00031-2). Wadsworth Pub.

Rao, R. V. Small Industries & a Developing Economy. 1979. text ed. 11.50x (ISBN 0-391-01829-9). Humanities.

Rao, Raghavendra. Poems. 8.00 (ISBN 0-89253-722-1); flexible cloth 4.00 (ISBN 0-89253-723-X). Ind-US Inc.

Rao, Raja. The Cat & Shakespeare: A Tale of Modern India. (Orient Paperback Ser.). 119p. 1975. pap. 2.00 o.p. (ISBN 0-88253-775-X). Ind-US Inc.

--Kanthapura. LC 63-18637. 1967. Repr. 4.95 (ISBN 0-8112-0168-6). New Directions.

Rao, S. R., jt ed. see Sundaralingham, M.

Rao, S. S. Optimization: Theory & Applications. LC 77-28171. 1980. 19.95 (ISBN 0-470-26784-4). Halsted Pr.

Rao, S. S., ed. The Finite Element Method in Engineering. LC 80-40817. 400p. 1981. 51.00 (ISBN 0-08-025467-5); pap. 18.00 (ISBN 0-08-025466-7). Pergamon.

Rao, T. V. & Bhatt, Anil. Adult Education for Social Change. 1980. 15.00x (ISBN 0-8364-0648-6, Pub. by Manohar India). South Asia Bks.

Rao, V. G. The Corporation Income Tax in India. 240p. 1980. text ed. 13.50x (ISBN 0-391-02133-8). Humanities.

Rao, V. K. Essays in Economic Development. 1966. pap. 5.50x o.p. (ISBN 0-210-98182-2). Asia.

Rao, V. V. Decibel Notation. 7.50x (ISBN 0-210-33831-8). Asia.

Rao, Vimala. Banaras, 1974 Poems. 1976. 8.00 (ISBN 0-89253-827-9); flexible cloth 4.80 (ISBN 0-89253-828-7). Ind-US Inc.

Rapaccini, L. Parlo Italiano. (It). 12.10 (ISBN 0-685-20245-3). Schoenhof.

Rapado, A., et al, eds. Purine Metabolism in Man III: Biochemical, Immunological, & Cancer Research, Pt. B. (Advances in Experimental Medicine & Biology Ser.: Vol. 122B). 482p. 1980. 45.00 (ISBN 0-306-40311-0, Plenum Pr). Plenum Pub.

--Purine Metabolism in Man III: Clinical & Therapeutic Aspects, Pt. A. (Advances in Experimental Medicine & Biology Ser.: Vol. 122A). 466p. 1980. 45.00 (ISBN 0-306-40310-2, Plenum Pr). Plenum Pub.

Rapalje, Stewart. A Treatise on Contempt Including Civil & Criminal Contempts of Judicial Tribunals, Justices of the Peace, Legislative Bodies, Municipal Boards, Committees, Notaries, Commissioners, Referees & Other Officers Exercising Judicial & Quasi-judicial Functions: With Practice & Forms. xliv, 273p. 1981. Repr. of 1890 ed. lib. bdg. 32.50x (ISBN 0-8377-1030-8). Rothman.

Raper, C. David & Kramer, Paul J. Crop Reactions to Water & Temperature Stresses in Humid, Temperate Climates. (Special Studies in Agricultural Science & Policy). 425p. 1981. lib. bdg. 30.00x (ISBN 0-686-69585-2). Westview.

Raper, J. R., ed. see International Congress of Botany, Edinburgh, 1964.

Raph, Jane B., et al. Bright Underachievers. LC 66-25459. 1966. text ed. 11.50x (ISBN 0-8077-2021-6). Tchrs Coll.

Raphael, Alice. Goethe & the Philosophers' Stone: Symbolical Patterns in the Parable & the Second Part of Faust. LC 64-7535. 8.50 o.p. (ISBN 0-912326-13-1). Garrett-Helix.

Raphael, Bertram. The Thinking Computer: Mind Inside Matter. LC 75-30839. (Psychology Ser.). (Illus.). 1976. pap. text ed. 10.95x (ISBN 0-7167-0723-3). W H Freeman.

Raphael, D. D., ed. British Moralists, Sixteen Fifty to Eighteen Hundred, 2 Vols. 1969. Set. pap. 14.95x (ISBN 0-19-875010-2). Oxford U Pr.

Raphael, D. D., ed. see Smith, Adam.

Raphael, David. Justice & Liberty. 1980. text ed. 40.00x (ISBN 0-485-11195-0, Athlone Pr). Humanities.

Raphael, Elaine & Bolognese, Don. Turnabout. LC 80-11866. (Illus.). 32p. (gr. 1-3). 1980. 8.95 (ISBN 0-670-73281-8). Viking Pr.

Raphael, F. & McLeish, K., trs. Aeschylus: The Oresteia. LC 78-6013. (Greek & Roman Authors Ser.). 1979. 14.95 (ISBN 0-521-22060-2); pap. 4.50 (ISBN 0-521-29344-8). Cambridge U Pr.

Raphael, Frederic, ed. Bookmarks. 1978. 7.95 (ISBN 0-224-01074-3, Pub. by Chatto Bodley Jonathan). Merrimack Bk Serv.

Raphael, Frederic, et al. List of Books. 1981. 10.95 (ISBN 0-517-54017-7, Harmony). Crown.

Raphael, Frederick. W. Somerset Maugham & His World. LC 76-19742. (Encore Edition). (Illus.). 1977. 3.95 (ISBN 0-684-16552-X, ScribT). Scribner.

Raphael, Harold J. & Olsson, David L. Package Production Management. 2nd ed. (Illus.). 1976. lib. bdg. 26.50 (ISBN 0-87055-217-1); pap. text ed. 18.00 (ISBN 0-87055-307-0). AVI.

Raphael, Jesse S. Governmental Regulation of Business. LC 66-12081. 1966. 7.95 o.s.i. (ISBN 0-02-925820-0). Free Pr.

Raphael Katzen Associates. Grain Motor Fuel Alcohol Technical & Economic Assessment Study. 344p. 1981. pap. 39.50 (ISBN 0-89934-063-6). Solar Energy Info.

Raphael Katzen Associates International, Inc. Farm & Cooperative Alcohol Plant Study: Technical & Economic Assessment As a Commercial Venture. 230p. 1981. pap. 20.00 (ISBN 0-89934-117-9). Solar Energy Info.

Raphael, Max. Demands of Art. Guterman, Norbert, tr. LC 65-10431. (Bollingen Ser.: Vol. 78). (Illus.). 1968. 30.00 o.p. (ISBN 0-691-09722-4). Princeton U Pr.

Raphael, Ray. An Everyday History of Somewhere. (Illus.). 192p. pap. 10.00 (ISBN 0-933280-11-4). Island Pr.

Raphael, Rick. The President Must Die. 1981. 12.95 (ISBN 0-393-01445-2). Norton.

Raphael, Robert. Richard Wagner. (World Authors Ser.: Germany: No. 77). lib. bdg. 10.95 (ISBN 0-8057-2976-3). Twayne.

Raphaelson, Joel, jt. auth. see Roman, Kenneth.

Rapid Excavation & Tunneling Conference, 1979. R E T C Proceedings, 2 vols. Hustrulid, William A. & Maevis, Alfred C., eds. LC 79-52280. (Illus.). 1819p. 1979. 55.00x (ISBN 0-89520-266-2). Soc Mining Eng.

Rapier, Regina. Saga of Felix Senac: Being the Legend & Biography of a Confederate Agent in Europe. (Illus.). 216p. 1972. 10.00x (ISBN 0-9600584-2-7). R C Rapier.

--Tales Out of Time, Vol. 1: The Mad Compactor & Other Science Fiction Short Stories. 1980. 7.50 (ISBN 0-686-69469-4). R C Rapier.

Rapin, P., jt. ed. see Sachs, H. K.

Rapin, Rene. Willa Cather. 115p. 1980. Repr. of 1930 ed. lib. bdg. 12.50 (ISBN 0-8492-7730-2). R West.

Rapkin, Richard H., ed. Practical Pediatrics: Selected Abstracts. 234p. 1981. 22.50 (ISBN 0-88416-342-3, 342). PSG Pub.

Rapoport, Amnon, jt. auth. see Fillenbaum, Samuel.

Rapoport, Amos. House Form & Culture. LC 69-14550. (Geography Ser). 1969. pap. 6.95 ref. ed. (ISBN 0-13-395673-3). P-H.

--Human Aspects of Urban Form: Towards a Man-Environment Approach to Urban Form & Design. 1977. text ed. 36.00 (ISBN 0-08-017974-6). Pergamon.

Rapoport, Anatol. The Big Two: Soviet-American Perceptions of Foreign Policy. LC 72-124676. 1972. 28.50x (ISBN 0-672-53507-6). Irvington.

--Two-Person Game Theory: The Essential Ideas. LC 66-11082. (Ann Arbor Science Library Ser). 1966. 5.95 o.p. (ISBN 0-472-00115-9). U of Mich Pr.

--Two-Person Game Theory: The Essential Ideas. (Ann Arbor Science Library Ser). (Orig.). 1966. pap. 4.95 (ISBN 0-472-05015-X, 515, AA). U of Mich Pr.

Rapoport, Anatol, ed. see Von Clausewitz, Karl.

Rapoport, Henry, jt. auth. see Cason, James.

Rapoport, Louis. The Lost Jews: Last of the Ethiopian Falashas. LC 79-92340. (Illus.). 264p. 1980. 13.95 (ISBN 0-8128-2720-1). Stein & Day.

Rapoport, Nathan. Monuments & Sculptures. LC 80-52914. (Illus.). 96p. 1981. 20.00 (ISBN 0-88400-073-7). Shengold.

Rapoport, Nessa. Preparing for Sabbath. LC 80-21539. 304p. 1981. 10.95 (ISBN 0-688-00294-3). Morrow.

Rapoport, Rhona & Rapoport, Robert N. Dual-Career Families Re-Examined: New Integrations of Work & Family. 2nd ed. 382p. 1976. 25.50x (ISBN 0-85520-125-8, Pub. by Martin Robertson England); pap. 10.95x (ISBN 0-85520-124-X). Biblio Dist.

--Leisure & the Family Life Cycle. 1975. 32.00x (ISBN 0-7100-8134-0). Routledge & Kegan.

--Leisure & the Family Life Cycle. 1978. pap. 12.50 (ISBN 0-7100-8825-6). Routledge & Kegan.

Rapoport, Robert N., jt. auth. see Rapoport, Rhona.

Rapoport, Roger & Lind, Margot. The California Catalogue: Everything You Need to Know About Living, Working, Playing, Shopping & Traveling in the Golden State. LC 76-12524. (Illus.). 1977. pap. 7.95 o.p. (ISBN 0-525-03153-7). Dutton.

Rapoport, Roger, jt. auth. see Uston, Ken.

Rapoport, Ron, jt. auth. see McGregor, Jim.

Rapoport, Stanley I. Blood-Brain Barrier in Physiology & Medicine. LC 75-26280. 1976. 33.50 (ISBN 0-89004-079-6). Raven.

Rapp, B. & Patitucci, F. Managing Local Government for Improved Performance: A Practical Approach. LC 76-25240. 1977. lib. bdg. 35.00x (ISBN 0-89158-121-9); pap. 14.50x (ISBN 0-89158-412-9). Westview.

Rapp, Birger. Models for Optimal Investment & Maintenance Decisions. LC 74-25084. 461p. 1975. 41.95 (ISBN 0-470-70911-1). Halsted Pr.

Rapp, Clifford. Stranger Within Me. 176p. 1981. 7.95 (ISBN 0-8059-2780-8). Dorrance.

Rapp, Doris J. Allergies & Your Child. LC 71-155528. 1972. 6.95 o.p. (ISBN 0-03-086578-6). HR&W.

--Allergies & Your Family. LC 79-93250. (Illus.). 352p. 1980. 12.95 (ISBN 0-8069-5558-9); lib. bdg. 11.69 (ISBN 0-8069-5559-7); pap. 6.95 (ISBN 0-8069-8878-9). Sterling.

Rapp, Fred, ed. Oncogenic Herpes Viruses, Vols. 1 & 2. 1980. Vol. 1, 240p. 59.95 (ISBN 0-8493-5619-9); Vol. 2, 160p. 49.95 (ISBN 0-8493-5620-2). CRC Pr.

Rapp, G. Color of Minerals. (Earth Science Curriculum Project Pamphlet Ser). 1971. pap. 3.20 (ISBN 0-395-02620-2). HM.

Rapp, Georg, tr. see Fried, Erich.

Rapp, Herbert J. & Borsos, Tibor. Molecular Basis of Complement Action. LC 75-110165. 164p. 1970. 19.50 (ISBN 0-306-50065-5, Plenum Pr). Plenum Pub.

Rapp, Joel, jt. auth. see Rapp, Lynn.

Rapp, Lea B. Put Your Kid in Show Biz. LC 80-54346. (Illus.). 160p. 1981. 12.95 (ISBN 0-8069-7040-5); lib. bdg. 11.69 (ISBN 0-8069-7041-3); pap. 6.95 (ISBN 0-8069-7508-3). Sterling.

Rapp, Lynn & Rapp, Joel. Mother Earth's Houseplant Coloring Album. (Illus., Orig.). 1976. pap. 2.95 o.p. (ISBN 0-912300-72-8, 72-8). Troubador Pr.

Rapp, Marvin A. New York. LC 68-9256. 1968. pap. 2.95 (ISBN 0-8077-2022-4). Tchrs Coll.

Rappaport, A., jt. auth. see Mathe, G.

Rappaport, Alfred. Information for Decision-Making: Quantitative & Behavioral Dimensions. 2nd ed. (Illus.). 384p. 1975. ref. ed. 19.95 (ISBN 0-13-464388-7). P-H.

Rappaport, Louis H. SEC Accounting Practice & Procedure. 3rd ed. 1260p. 1972. 42.50 (ISBN 0-8260-7325-5, 77831). Ronald Pr.

Rappaport, Suzanne, tr. see Kundera, Milan.

Rappaport, Victor. Making It in Music. 1979. 12.95 (ISBN 0-13-547612-7, Spec); pap. 5.95 (ISBN 0-13-547604-6, Spec). P-H.

Rappolt, Hedwig, tr. see Wolf, Christa.

Rappoport, Angelo S. Folklore of the Jews. LC 71-167125. Repr. of 1937 ed. 18.00 (ISBN 0-8103-3864-5). Gale.

--Superstitions of Sailors. LC 71-158207. 1971. Repr. of 1928 ed. 20.00 (ISBN 0-8103-3739-8). Gale.

Rappoport, Leon & Summers, David, eds. Human Judgement & Social Interaction. LC 72-84872. 1973. 28.50x (ISBN 0-03-085870-4). Irvington.

Rapport, Leonard & Northwood, Arthur, Jr. Rendezvous with Destiny. (Illus.). 1977. 14.00 (ISBN 0-686-26296-4). One Hund First Air.

Rapson, Richard L. Denials of Doubt: An Interpretation of American History. LC 78-58595. 1978. pap. text ed. 13.50 (ISBN 0-8191-0541-4). U Pr of Amer.

Rapson, Richard L. & Rapson, Susan B. The Pursuit of Meaning: America - 1600-2000. 1977. pap. text ed. 11.25x (ISBN 0-8191-0175-3). U Pr of Amer.

Rapson, Richard L., ed. Cult of Youth in Middle-Class America. LC 74-146876. (Problems in American Civilization Ser.). 118p. pap. text ed. 4.95x o.p. (ISBN 0-669-73387-3). Heath.

--Major Interpretations of the American Past. LC 72-149210. (Literature of History Ser). (Orig.). 1971. 18.95x (ISBN 0-89197-284-6); pap. text ed. 7.95x (ISBN 0-89197-285-4). Irvington.

Rapson, Susan B., jt. auth. see Rapson, Richard L.

Raraty, M., ed. see Hoffman, E. T.

Rardon, James. Understanding the Federal Air Regulations. (Aviation Technician Training Course Ser.). 96p. (Orig.). 1980. pap. text ed. 4.95 (ISBN 0-89100-123-9). Aviation Maintenance.

Rasberry, Leslie. Computer Age Copyfitting. (An Art Direction Book). Date not set. pap. 8.95 o.p. (ISBN 0-8038-1250-7). Hastings.

Rasberry, Robert W. The Technique of Political Lying. LC 80-5976. 301p. 1981. lib. bdg. 19.75 (ISBN 0-8191-1482-0); pap. text ed. 11.25 (ISBN 0-8191-1483-9). U Pr of Amer.

Rasch, G. Probabalistic Models for Some Intelligence & Attainment Tests. LC 80-16546. 208p. 1980. lib. bdg. 9.00x (ISBN 0-226-70554-4). U of Chicago Pr.

--Probalistic Models for Some Intelligence & Attainment Tests. LC 80-16546. 208p. 1980. lib. bdg. 21.00x (ISBN 0-226-70553-6). U of Chicago Pr.

Rasch, Gerald. Hands Are Handy. 20p. (Orig.). 1981. pap. 3.50 (ISBN 0-86629-011-7). Sunrise MO.

Rasch, Joseph, jt. auth. see Harris, Homer I.

Raschke, Carl A. Moral Action, God, & History in the Thought of Immanuel Kant. LC 75-11787. (American Academy of Religion. Dissertation Ser.). xiv, 236p. 1975. pap. 7.50 (ISBN 0-89130-003-1, 010105). Scholars Pr Ca.

Rase, H. F. & Barrow, M. H. Piping Design for Process Plants. LC 63-17483. 1963. 36.95 (ISBN 0-471-70920-4, Pub. by Wiley-Interscience). Wiley.

--Project Engineering of Process Plants. 1957. 39.00 (ISBN 0-471-70917-4, Pub. by Wiley-Interscience). Wiley.

Rase, Howard F. Chemical Reactor Design for Process Plants, 2 vols. Incl. Vol. 1. Principles & Techniques. 50.00 (ISBN 0-471-01891-0); Vol. 2. Case Studies & Design Data. 27.95 (ISBN 0-471-01890-2). LC 77-1285. 1977 (Pub. by Wiley-Interscience). Wiley.

Rash, J. E. & Hudson, C. S. Freeze-Fracture: Methods, Artifacts, & Interpretations. LC 79-109. 1979. text ed. 21.00 (ISBN 0-89004-386-8). Raven.

Rash, J. Keogh & Pigg, R. Morgan. Health Education Curriculum: A Guide for Curriculum Development in Health Education. LC 78-24493. 1979. text ed. 17.95 (ISBN 0-471-03765-6). Wiley.

Rashid, A. An Introduction to Pteridophyta. 1976. 12.50 (ISBN 0-7069-0447-8, Pub. by Vikas India). Advent Bk.

Rashid, Haroun Er. Geography of Bangladesh. (Illus.). 1978. lib. bdg. 30.00x (ISBN 0-89158-356-4). Westview.

Rashid, S. Anwar & Archer, Maurice. Organizational Behavior. 336p. 1980. pap. text ed. 17.95 (ISBN 0-8403-2221-6). Kendall-Hunt.

Rashke, Richard. The Killing of Karen Silkwood. 1981. 12.95 (ISBN 0-395-30233-1). HM.

Rashkis, Zora, jt. ed. see Carter, Candy.

Rask, Rasmus K. A Grammar of the Icelandic or Old Norse Tonque. Dasent, George W., tr. from Danish. (Amsterdam Classics in Linguistics 1800-1925: No. 2). Orig. Title: Vejledning til det Islandskeeller gamle Nordisk Sprog. 1979. text ed. 40.00x (ISBN 90-272-0871-9). Humanities.

Raskhodoff, Nicholas M. The Complete Mobile Home Book: The Guide to Manufactured Homes. LC 80-5798. 240p. 1981. 19.95 (ISBN 0-8128-2781-3). Stein & Day.

--Electronic Drafting & Design. 3rd ed. (Illus.). 1977. text ed. 19.95 (ISBN 0-13-250613-0). P-H.

Raskin, A., jt. ed. see Gershon, S.

Raskin, Allen, jt. ed. see Schulterbrandt, Joy G.

Raskin, Edith, jt. auth. see Raskin, H. Joseph.

Raskin, Ellen. Moe Q McGlutch, He Smoked Too Much. LC 73-4383. (Illus.). 48p. (gr. k-3). 1973. 5.95 o.s.i. (ISBN 0-8193-0686-X, Four Winds); PLB 5.41 o.s.i. (ISBN 0-8193-0687-8). Schol Bk Serv.

--Moose, Goose & Little Nobody. LC 80-15287. (Illus.). 32p. (ps-3). 1980. Repr. of 1974 ed. 8.95 (ISBN 0-590-07775-9, Four Winds). Schol Bk Serv.

--The Mysterious Disappearance of Leon (I Mean Noel) (Illus.). 160p. (gr. 4-7). 1980. pap. 1.95 (ISBN 0-380-51177-0, 51177, Camelot). Avon.

--The Westing Game. 1980. pap. 1.75 (ISBN 0-380-49346-2, 49346, Camelot). Avon.

Raskin, Eugene. Architecturally Speaking. 1970. pap. 3.95x (ISBN 0-8197-0003-7). Bloch.

--Architecture & People. 192p. 1974. ref. ed. 16.95 (ISBN 0-13-044594-0). P-H.

Raskin, H. Joseph & Raskin, Edith. The Witch House & Other Tales Our Settlers Told. (gr. 4-6). 1978. pap. 1.25 (ISBN 0-590-11916-8, Schol Pap). Schol Bk Serv.

Raskin, Herbert A., jt. auth. see Krystal, Henry.

Raskin, Neil H. & Appenzeller, Otto. Headache. LC 79-66042. (Monograph in Major Problems in Internal Medicine: No. 19). (Illus.). 244p. 1980. 19.50 (ISBN 0-7216-7467-4). Saunders.

Raskin, Philip, jt. ed. see Rifkin, Harold.

Raskin, Saul. Our Father Our King. (Illus., Heb. & eng). 1966. 15.00 (ISBN 0-8197-0288-9); deluxe ed. 25.00. Bloch.

Raskova, H., ed. Pharmacology & Toxicology of Naturally Occurring Toxins, 2 vols. LC 77-130797. 1972. Vol. 1. 60.00 (ISBN 0-08-016319-X); Vol. 2. 52.00 (ISBN 0-08-016798-5); Set. 81.00 (ISBN 0-08-016797-7). Pergamon.

Rasmussen, B. H., tr. see Keller, Werner.

Rasmussen, Carl, tr. see Nygren, Anders.

Rasmussen, Chrys, jt. ed. see O'Brien, Aline.

Rasmussen, Claire, jt. auth. see Jackle, Mary.

Rasmussen, Grant L. & Windle, William F. Neural Mechanisms of the Auditory & Vestibular Systems. 436p. 1965. pap. 20.25 spiral (ISBN 0-398-01554-6). C C Thomas.

Rasmussen, Henry. Ferraris for the Road. (Illus.). 1980. 39.95 (ISBN 0-87938-117-5). Motorbooks Intl.

Rasmussen, Jorgen S., jt. auth. see Dragnich, Alex N.

Rasmussen, Knud. The People of the Polar North. LC 75-167126. 1975. Repr. of 1908 ed. 18.00 (ISBN 0-685-52348-9). Gale.

Rasmussen, Linda, et al, eds. A Harvest Yet to Reap: A History of Prairie Women. (Illus.). 240p. 1976. pap. 12.50 (ISBN 0-88961-050-9). U of Nebr Pr.

Rasmussen, Peter, ed. see Hawley, Newton & Suppes, Patrick.

Rasmussen, R. Kent. Historical Dictionary of Rhodesia-Zimbabwe. Wilgus, A. Curtis, ed. LC 78-23671. (African Historical Dictionaries Ser.: No. 18). 1979. lib. bdg. 22.50 (ISBN 0-8108-1187-1). Scarecrow.

Rasmussen, Steen E. London: The Unique City. 2nd ed. (Illus.). Date not set. pap. 9.95 (ISBN 0-262-68027-0). MIT Pr.

Rasmussen, T. B. Bucchero Pottery from Southern Etruria. LC 78-13464. (Cambridge Classical Studies). (Illus.). 1979. 42.50 (ISBN 0-521-22316-4). Cambridge U Pr.

Rasmussen, Theodore & Marino, Raul, eds. Functional Neurosurgery. LC 77-85871. 1979. text ed. 34.50 (ISBN 0-89004-228-4). Raven.

Rasmussen, Wayne. Agriculture in the United States: A Documentary History, 3 vols. 1975. Set. 135.00 o.p. (ISBN 0-394-47320-5). Random.

Rasp, R., et al. New Writers Nine. (New Writing & Writers Ser.). 1971. text ed. 13.00x (ISBN 0-7145-0016-X). Humanities.

Rasp, Renate, et al. New Writers Nine. 1980. pap. 6.00 (ISBN 0-7145-0017-8). Riverrun NY.

Raspa, Anthony, ed. John Donne: Devotions Upon Emergent Occasions. 248p. 1976. 18.00x o.s.i. (ISBN 0-7735-0194-0). McGill-Queens U Pr.

Raspe, G., ed. Life Science Monograph, No. 2. Long, J., et al, trs. 221p. 1972. text ed. 36.00 (ISBN 0-08-017596-1). Pergamon.

Rasp-Nuri, Grace. Yusuf, Boy of Cyprus. LC 58-5901. (Illus.). (gr. 5-9). 1958. 8.95 (ISBN 0-87599-095-9). S G Phillips.

Rasputin, Maria & Barham, Patte. Rasputin: The Man Behind the Myth. (Illus.). 1978. pap. 2.95 (ISBN 0-446-93878-5). Warner Bks.

Rasputin, Maria & Barrham, Patte. Rasputin: The Man Behind the Myth. 328p. 1981. pap. 2.95. Warner Bks.

Rasputin, Valentin. Live & Remember. Bouis, Antonina W., tr. from Rus. 1978. 11.95 (ISBN 0-02-601130-1). Macmillan.

Rassias, John A. & De Lachapelle-Skubly, Jacqueline. Le Francais: Depart-Arrivee. 577p. 1980. text ed. 18.95 scp (ISBN 0-06-045316-8, HarpC); instrs'. manual avail.; scp student wkbk. 6.50 (ISBN 0-06-045317-6); scp tapes 295.00 (ISBN 0-06-047493-9). Har-Row.

Rassmussen, David & Haworth, Charles. Economics: Principles & Applications. LC 78-2245. 672p. 1979. text ed. 17.95 (ISBN 0-574-19280-8, 13-2280); instr's guide avail. (ISBN 0-574-19281-6, 13-2281); study guide 6.50 (ISBN 0-574-19282-4, 13-2282); lecture resource supplement 3.75 (ISBN 0-574-19284-0, 13-2284). SRA.

Rassner, Gernot. Atlas of Dermatology. Kahn, Guinter, ed. LC 78-5704. (Illus.). 1978. text ed. 27.50 (ISBN 0-8067-1601-0). Urban & S.

Rast, Harold W., ed. see Jeske, Richard L.

Rastetter, J., jt. auth. see Begemann, H.

Rastogi, R. P. & Misra, R. R. An Introduction to Chemical Thermodynamics. 1978. 22.50 (ISBN 0-7069-0638-1, Pub. by Vikas India). Advent Bk.

Rat, M. Dictionnaire des locutions françaises. (Fr). 23.50 (ISBN 0-685-13866-6, 3613). Larousse.

Ratajczak, H. & Orville-Thomas, W. J. Molecular Interactions. Vol. 1, 448 Pp. 78.00 (ISBN 0-471-27664-2, 1-500); Vol. 2. write for info. (ISBN 0-471-27681-2). Wiley.

Ratajczak, H. & Orville-Thomas, W. J., eds. Molecular Interactions, Vol. 2. LC 79-40825. 1981. write for info. (ISBN 0-471-27681-2, Pub. by Wiley-Interscience). Wiley.

Ratan, Jai. The Angry Goddess. 8.00 (ISBN 0-89253-634-9). Ind-US Inc.

Ratan, Jai, tr. Contemporary Hindi Short Stories. (Writers Workshop Saffronbird Ser.). 180p. 1975. 12.00 (ISBN 0-88253-518-8); pap. text ed. 4.80 (ISBN 0-88253-517-X). Ind-US Inc.

Ratan, Jai, tr. see Askh, Upendranath.

Ratan, Jai, tr. see Chander, Krishan.

Ratan, Jai, tr. see Rakesh, Mohan.

Ratan, Jai, tr. see Varma, Shrikant.

Ratan, Jai, tr. see Yadav, Rajendra.

Ratan, Jai, et al, trs. see Sahni, Bhisham.

Ratchford, Fannie E., ed. see Bronte, Emily J.

Ratcliff, Carter. Fernando Botero. LC 80-66283. (Illus.). 272p. 1980. 75.00 (ISBN 0-89659-146-8). Abbeville Pr.

Ratcliff, J. D. Your Body & How It Works. 1975. 8.95 o.s.i. (ISBN 0-440-09896-3). Delacorte.

Ratcliff, Rosemary. Dear Worried Brown Eyes. 1969. 10.00 (ISBN 0-08-007041-8). Pergamon.

Ratcliff, Ruth. Scottish Folk Tales. (Illus.). 1977. 10.00 (ISBN 0-584-62393-3). Transatlantic.

Ratcliffe, D. A., ed. A Nature Conservation, 2 vols. Incl. Vol. 1. 115.00 (ISBN 0-521-21159-X); Vol. 2. 90.00 (ISBN 0-521-21403-3). LC 76-11065. (Illus.). 1977. Cambridge U Pr.

Ratcliffe, F. N., jt. auth. see Fenner, Frank.

Ratcliffe, J. A. An Introduction to the Ionosphere & Magnetosphere. LC 74-171680. (Illus.). 200p. 1972. 35.50 (ISBN 0-521-08341-9); pap. 11.50x (ISBN 0-521-09970-6). Cambridge U Pr.

Ratcliffe, Jane. Fly High, Run Free. (Illus.). 168p. 1981. 10.95 (ISBN 0-7011-2365-6, Pub. by Chatto-Bodley-Jonathan). Merrimack Bk Serv.

Ratcliffe, Jeanira, jt. auth. see Dallas, Rita.

Ratcliffe, Peter. Racism & Reaction: A Profile of Handsworth. (International Library of Sociology). 280p. 1981. price not set (ISBN 0-7100-0696-9). Routledge & Kegan.

Ratcliffe, T. A. The Development of Personality. 1967. text ed. 5.50x (ISBN 0-04-150013-X). Humanities.

Rateaver, Bargyla & Rateaver, Gylver. The Organic Method Primer: A Practical Explanation, the Why & How for the Beginner & the Experienced. LC 73-85165. (Conservation Gardening & Farming Ser). 1975. pap. 10.00 (ISBN 0-9600698-1-X). Rateavers.

Rateaver, Bargyla, ed. see Cotten, Emmi.

Rateaver, Bargyla, ed. see Hills, Lawrence D.

Rateaver, Gylver, jt. auth. see Rateaver, Bargyla.

Rateaver, Gylver, ed. see Corley, Hugh.

Rateaver, Gylver, ed. see Cotten, Emmi.

Rateaver, Gylver, ed. see Hainsworth, P. H.

Rateaver, Gylver, ed. see Hills, Lawrence D.

Rateaver, Gylver, ed. see Leatherbarrow, Margaret.

Rateaver, Gylver, ed. see Stephenson, W. A.

Rath, Eric. Container Systems. LC 72-13139. (Materials Handling & Packaging Ser.). 608p. 1973. 49.50 (ISBN 0-471-70921-2, Pub. by Wiley-Interscience). Wiley.

Rath, Frederick L. & O'Connell, Merrilyn R. Administration: A Bibliography on Historical Organization Practices, Vol. 5. 250p. 1980. text ed. 14.95x (ISBN 0-910050-44-9). AASLH.

Rath, Frederick L., Jr. & O'Connell, Merrilyn, eds. Care & Conservation of Collections: A Bibliography on Historical Organization Practices, Vol. 2. LC 75-26770. 1977. 10.00x (ISBN 0-910050-28-7). AASLH.

Rath, Frederick L., Jr., jt. ed. see Reese, Rosemary S.

Rath, P. M., jt. auth. see Mason, R. E.

Rath, Patricia M., et al. Case Studies in Marketing & Distribution. (Illus.). (gr. 9-12). 1965. pap. text ed. 2.95x (ISBN 0-8134-0835-0, 835). Interstate.

Rathbone, David. How to Keep the Money You Owe: One Hundred One (Legal(Ways to Confound Your Creditors. (Illus.). 70p. (Orig.). 1981. pap. 10.00. Phoenix Laguna.

Rathbone, Josephine & Lucas, Carol. Recreation in Total Rehabilitation. 424p. 1970. lexofone 13.50 (ISBN 0-398-01555-4). C C Thomas.

Rathbone, Julian. Base Case. 1981. 9.95 (ISBN 0-394-50911-0). Pantheon.

--Carnival. LC 76-27622. 1976. 7.95 o.p. (ISBN 0-312-12250-0). St Martin.

Rathbone, Percy C. The Forsyth Wickes Collection. LC 68-27635. (Illus.). 1968. pap. 2.50 (ISBN 0-87846-036-5, Pub. by Mus Fine Arts Boston). C E Tuttle.

Rathbone, Perry T. Forsyth Wickes Collection. (Illus.). 1968. 8.50 (ISBN 0-87846-164-7). Mus Fine Arts Boston.

Rathbone, Perry T., intro. by. One Hundred Paintings from the Boston Museum. (Illus.). 1970. pap. 4.95 o.p. (ISBN 0-87846-176-0). Mus Fine Arts Boston.

Rathbone, R. J., ed. see African Studies Association of the United Kingdom, 1972.

Rathbone, Robert R. Communicating Technical Information. LC 66-25632. (Engineering Ser). (Illus., Orig.). 1966. pap. 8.95 (ISBN 0-201-06305-0). A-W.

Rathbun, G. B. The Social Structure & Ecology of Elephant-Shrews. (Advances in Ethology Ser.: Vol. 20). (Illus.). 84p. (Orig.). 1979. pap. text ed. 29.50 (ISBN 3-489-60836-4). Parey Sci Pubs.

Rathbun, John. American Literary Criticism: Vol. I, 1800-1860. (United States Authors Ser.: No. 339). 1979. lib. bdg. 12.50 (ISBN 0-8057-7263-4). Twayne.

Rathbun, John, jt. auth. see Clark, Harry.

Rathburn, Seward H. Background for Architecture. 1926. 42.50x (ISBN 0-685-69854-8). Elliots Bks.

Rathe, John C. Radiographic Tumor Localizer. 196p. 1981. 15.00 (ISBN 0-87527-249-5). Green.

Rather, Dan & Herskowitz, Mickey. The Camera Never Blinks: Adventures of a TV Journalist. 1978. pap. 2.50 (ISBN 0-345-29025-9). Ballantine.

Rather, L. J. Addison & the White Corpuscles: An Aspect of Nineteenth-Century Biology. LC 71-149940. (Wellcome Institute of the History of Medicine). 1972. 17.50x (ISBN 0-520-01972-5). U of Cal Pr.

--Mind & Body in Eighteenth Century Medicine: A Study Based on Jerome Gaub's De Regimine Mentis. (Wellcome Institute of the History of Medicine). 1965. 20.00x (ISBN 0-520-01049-3). U of Cal Pr.

Rather, Lois. Jessie Fremont at Black Point. (Illus.). 1974. ltd. ed. 15.00 o.p. (ISBN 0-686-20622-3). Rather Pr.

Rathgeb, Marlene M. Success Signs. (Illus.). 224p. 1981. 10.95 (ISBN 0-312-77485-0); pap. 5.95 (ISBN 0-312-77486-9). St Martin.

Rathgeber, Eva-Maria, jt. auth. see Altbach, Philip G.

Rathi, M., jt. ed. see Kumar, S.

Rathi, Manohar & Kumar, Sudhir, eds. Perinatal Medicine, Vol. 2. 224p. 1981. text ed. 35.00 (ISBN 0-89116-181-3). Hemisphere Pub.

Rathje, William L., jt. ed. see Sabloff, Jeremy A.

Rathjen, Diana P. & Foreyt, John P., eds. Social Competence: Interventions for Children & Adults. LC 80-118. (Pergamon General Psychology Ser.: No. 91). (Illus.). 300p. 1980. 26.50 (ISBN 0-08-025965-0). Pergamon.

Rathjen, Gregory, jt. auth. see Stephens, Otis H.

Rathjens, George W. The Future of the Strategic Arms Race: Options for the 1970's. 1969. pap. 0.90 (ISBN 0-87003-028-0). Carnegie Endow.

Rathjens, George W., jt. ed. see Long, Franklin A.

Rathkopf, Arden H., jt. auth. see Rathkopf, Charles A.

Rathkopf, Charles A. & Rathkopf, Arden H. The Law of Zoning & Planning, with Forms, 4 vols. LC 56-2013. 1977. Set. looseleaf with 1979 suppl. 175.00 (ISBN 0-87632-020-5). Boardman.

Rathman, R. Annabel, ed. see Travis, John W.

Rathmore, Fateh S., et al. With Tigers in the Wild: An Experience in an Indian Forest. (Illus.). 196p. 1981. text ed. 75.00 (ISBN 0-7069-1023-0, Pub. by Vikas India). Advent Bk.

Raths, James, et al. Studying Teaching. 2nd ed. LC 70-123086. 1971. pap. text ed. 13.95 (ISBN 0-13-858878-3). P-H.

Raths, Louis, et al. Values & Teaching. 2nd ed. (Educational Foundations Ser.). 1978. pap. text ed. 9.95x (ISBN 0-675-08514-4). Merrill.

Rational Dress Association. Exhibition Catalogue, 1883 & Gazette, 1888-1889. Stansky, Peter & Shewan, Rodney, eds. LC 76-18323. (Aesthetic Movement & the Arts & Crafts Movement Ser.). 1978. lib. bdg. 44.00x (ISBN 0-8240-2456-7). Garland Pub.

Ratkevich, Ronald P. Dinosaurs of the Southwest. LC 75-40837. (Illus.). 115p. 1977. pap. 4.95 (ISBN 0-8263-0406-0). U of NM Pr.

Ratkevich, Ronald P., jt. auth. see Casanova, Richard L.

Ratkevich, Ronald P., ed. see Murphy, Lawrence & Murphy, Bernadette.

Ratledge, Marcus W. Don't Become the Victim. 120p. 1981. pap. 6.00 (ISBN 0-87364-211-2). Paladin Ent.

Ratliff, A. H., jt. auth. see Lloyd-Roberts, G. C.

Ratliff, Bascom W. Leaving the Hospital: Discharge Planning for Total Patient Care. 176p. 1981. 19.75 (ISBN 0-398-04146-6). C C Thomas.

Ratliff, Dale H. Minor Sexual Deviance: Diagnosis & Pastoral Treatment. LC 76-29284. 1976. pap. text ed. 3.95 o.p. (ISBN 0-8403-1605-4). Kendall-Hunt.

Ratliff, Gerald L. The Theatre Student: Learning Scenes. (Theatre Student Ser.). (Illus.). 140p. 1981. lib. bdg. 12.50 (ISBN 0-8239-0531-4). Rosen Pr.

Ratliff, Richard C. Constitutional Rights of College Students: A Study in Case Law. LC 72-5729. 1972. 10.00 (ISBN 0-8108-0532-4). Scarecrow.

Ratliff, William F. Creaciones y Creadores: A Basic Literary Reader. 128p. 1981. pap. text ed. 7.95 (ISBN 0-394-32654-7). Random.

Ratnagar, Shereen. Encounters: India's Westerly Trade in the Bronze Age. 240p. 1981. 17.95 (ISBN 0-19-561253-1). Oxford U Pr.

Ratner, Elaine & Ware, Tim. The Golden Gate Bridge! LC 80-52139. (Illus.). 1981. 18.50 (ISBN 0-916290-12-3); pap. 10.95. Squarebooks.

Ratner, Elaine, ed. see Milne, Terry.

Ratner, Leonard. Classic Music: A Handbook for Analysis. LC 76-57808. (Illus.). 1980. 35.00 (ISBN 0-02-872020-2). Schirmer Bks.

Ratner, Marc L. William Styron. (U. S. Authors Ser.: No. 196). lib. bdg. 10.95 (ISBN 0-8057-0708-5). Twayne.

Ratner, Marilyn, jt. auth. see Cooper, Terry.

Ratner, Marilyn, jt. auth. see Cooper, Terry Touff.

Ratner, V. A. Molecular Genetic Regulatory Systems. 1981. write for info. (ISBN 0-201-06190-2). A-W.

Ratsma, P. Rotterdam in Drawings: Rotterdam Getekend. (Illus.). 1979. 35.00x (ISBN 90-247-2261-6). Heinman.

Rattazzi, Mario C., et al, eds. Isozymes: Current Topics in Biological & Medical Research, Vol. 3. LC 77-12288. 1979. 22.00x (ISBN 0-8451-0252-4). A R Liss.

--Isozymes: Current Topics in Biological & Medical Research, Vol. 4. LC 77-12288. 218p. 1980. 26.00 (ISBN 0-8451-0253-2). A R Liss.

Rattenbury, J. M. Amino Acid Analysis. 320p. 1981. 89.95 (ISBN 0-470-27141-8). Halsted Pr.

Rattey, B. K. A Short History of the Hebrews: From the Patriarchs to Herod the Great. (Illus.). 1976. pap. 6.95x (ISBN 0-19-832121-X). Oxford U Pr.

Ratti, Jogindar & Manougian, Manoug. Introductory Calculus with Applications. 2nd ed. LC 76-13096. (Illus.). 1977. pap. text ed. 17.50 (ISBN 0-395-24545-1); inst. manual 1.75 (ISBN 0-395-24544-3). HM.

Ratti, O. & Westbrook, A. Secrets of the Samurai: A Survey of the Martial Arts of Feudal Japan. LC 72-91551. 1973. 35.00 (ISBN 0-8048-0917-8). C E Tuttle.

Rattner, Abraham. Abraham Rattner. Leepa, Allen, ed. LC 79-133447. (Contemporary Artists Ser.). (Illus.). 196p. 1974. 65.00 o.p. (ISBN 0-8109-0429-2). Abrams.

Rattray, Everett T. The South Fork: The Land & the People of Eastern Long Island. LC 78-23692. (Illus.). 1979. 10.00 (ISBN 0-394-41860-3). Random.

Rattray, R. S. Ashanti. (Illus.). 1981. Repr. of 1923 ed. 27.00 (ISBN 0-19-823149-0). Oxford U Pr.

--Ashanti Proverbs: The Primitive Ethics of a Savage People. 1981. 14.95x (ISBN 0-19-823147-4). Oxford U Pr.

Ratyck, Joanna see Crean, John E., et al.

Ratzer, Erick R., jt. auth. see Morift, H. Mason.

Ratzinger, Joseph. Introduction to Christianity. 1970. 8.95 (ISBN 0-8164-2262-1). Crossroad NY.

Ratzlaff, Ruben M. & Butler, Paul T. Ezra-Nehemiah-Esther. (Bible Study Textbook Ser.). 1979. 13.00 (ISBN 0-89900-014-2). College Pr Pub.

Ratzlaff, Ruby. A Good Fight. LC 78-57356. (Redwood Ser.). pap. 3.95 (ISBN 0-8163-0232-4). Pacific Pr Pub Assn.

Rau, Nicholas. Matrices & Mathematical Prgramming: An Introduction for Economists. 1980. 18.50 (ISBN 0-312-52299-1). St Martin.

Rau, Santha R. Cooking of India. LC 79-98164. (Foods of the World Ser). (Illus.). (gr. 6 up). 1969. PLB 14.94 (ISBN 0-8094-0069-3, Pub. by Time-Life). Silver.

Rau, Santha Rama, jt. auth. see Devi, Gayatri.

Rau, Santha Rama see Rama Rau, Santha.

Raubinger, Frederick M., et al. Leadership in the Secondary School. new ed. (Education-Administration Ser.). 464p. 1974. text ed. 20.95x (ISBN 0-675-08796-1). Merrill.

Rauch, B., jt. auth. see Malone, D.

Rauch, Basil. Roosevelt: From Munich to Pearl Harbor. LC 74-34446. (FDR & the Era of the New Deal Ser). 527p. 1975. Repr. of 1967 ed. lib. bdg. 39.50 (ISBN 0-306-70739-X). Da Capo.

Rauch, Constance. The Landlady. 256p. 1976. pap. 1.75 o.p. (ISBN 0-445-08468-5). Popular Lib.

Rauch, David. Priorities in Adult Education. 1972. 10.00 o.p. (ISBN 0-88379-006-8). Adult Ed.

Rauch, Georg von. A History of Soviet Russia. 6th ed. Jacobsohn, Peter & Jacobsohn, Annette, trs. from German. LC 76-185777. 541p. 1972. pap. text ed. 7.95x. Praeger.

Rauch, George Von see Von Rauch, George.

Rauch, H. E., ed. Control Programs of Nonlinear Programming: Proceedings of the IFAC Workshop, Denver, Colorado, USA, June 1979. (IFAC Proceedings). 130p. 1980. 35.00 (ISBN 0-08-024491-2). Pergamon.

Rauch, Hans-Georg. Battle Lines. (Illus.). 1977. 6.95 o.p. (ISBN 0-684-15139-1, ScribT). Scribner.

--The Lines Are Coming: A Book About Drawing. LC 78-12861. (Illus.). (gr. 2 up). 1978. reinforced bdg 8.95 (ISBN 0-684-15989-9, ScribJ). Scribner.

Rauch, Herbert E., jt. ed. see Powers, William F.

Rauch, Irmengard & Carr, Gerald F., eds. Signifying Animal. LC 79-3624. (Advances in Semiotics). 384p. 1980. 24.95x (ISBN 0-253-18496-7). Ind U Pr.

Rauch, Irmengard & Scott, Charles T., eds. Approaches in Linguistic Methodology. 1967. 17.50x (ISBN 0-299-04240-5). U of Wis Pr.

Rauch, Leo. Monarch Notes on Plato's the Republic & Selected Dialogues. pap. 1.95 (ISBN 0-671-00505-7). Monarch Pr.

Raucher, Herman. There Should Have Been Castles. 1978. 9.95 o.s.i. (ISBN 0-440-09038-5). Delacorte.

Raudkivi, A. J. Hydrology. 1979. 68.00 (ISBN 0-08-024261-8). Pergamon.

--Loose Boundary Hydraulics. 2nd ed. Francis, J. D., ed. 326p. 1976. text ed. 37.00 (ISBN 0-08-018772-2); pap. text ed. 23.00 (ISBN 0-08-018771-4). Pergamon.

Raudkivi, A. J. & Callander, R. A. Analysis of Groundwater Flow. LC 76-10776. 1976. 28.50 o.p. (ISBN 0-470-15117-X). Halsted Pr.

Raudsepp, Eugene. Essential Self. (Best Thoughts Ser.). (Illus.). 80p. (Orig.). 1981. pap. 2.50 (ISBN 0-8431-0388-4). Price Stern.

--How Creative Are You? 196p. 1981. pap. 4.95 (ISBN 0-686-69593-3, Perigee). Putnam.

--Love & Loving. (Best Thoughts Ser.). (Illus.). 80p. 1981. pap. 2.50 (ISBN 0-8431-0389-2). Price Stern.

--Love & Sexuality. (Best Thoughts Ser.). (Illus.). 80p. 1981. pap. 2.50 (ISBN 0-8431-0387-6). Price Stern.

--Success & Failure. (Best Thoughts Ser.). (Illus.). 80p. (Orig.). 1981. pap. 2.50 (ISBN 0-8431-0390-6). Price Stern.

Raudsepp, Eugene & Hough, George P. Creative Growth Games. LC 77-2522. (Illus.). 1977. pap. 3.95 o.p. (ISBN 0-15-622735-5, Harv). HarBraceJ.

Raudsepp, Eugene & Yeager, Joseph C. How to Sell New Ideas: Your Company's & Your Own. (Illus.). 224p. 1981. 15.95 (ISBN 0-13-432427-7, Spec); pap. 6.95. P-H.

Rauff, Edward A. Why People Join the Church. LC 79-90741. (Orig.). 1980. pap. 5.95 (ISBN 0-8298-0387-4). Pilgrim NY.

Raumer, Frederick Von see Von Raumer, Frederick.

Raun, Donald L., jt. auth. see Anderson, Donald L.

Rauner, Judy A. Helping People Volunteer. LC 80-82556. (Illus.). 96p. (Orig.). 1980. pap. 10.50 (ISBN 0-9604594-0-5). Marlborough Pubns.

Raup, David M. & Stanley, Steven M. Principles of Paleontology. 2nd ed. LC 77-17443. (Illus.). 1978. text ed. 24.95x (ISBN 0-7167-0022-0). W H Freeman.

Raupach, Manfred, jt. ed. see Dechert, Hans.

Rausa, Rosario. The Blue Angels: An Illustrated History. (Illus.). 1979. 14.50 (ISBN 0-911721-82-7, Pub. by Moran). Aviation.

--Gold Wings, Blue Sea: A Naval Aviator's Story. 216p. 1981. 15.95 (ISBN 0-87021-219-2). Naval Inst Pr.

Rausa, Rosario, jt. auth. see Heinemann, Edward H.

Rausch, Edwin, ed. Management in Institutions of Higher Learning. LC 79-650. 1980. 26.95 (ISBN 0-669-02856-8). Lexington Bks.

Rausch, Gerald, jt. auth. see Tonnis, John.

Rausch, Tondra S., jt. auth. see Rund, Douglas A.

Rauschenbusch, Walter. Theology for the Social Gospel. (Series E). 1978. pap. 6.95 (ISBN 0-687-41580-2). Abingdon.

Rausen, Ruth G., ed. see Tennyson, Alfred.

Rauter, Rosemarie, compiled by. Printed for Children. 448p. 1978. pap. 28.00 (ISBN 0-89664-111-2, Pub. by K G Saur). Gale.

Ravage, John A. The Television: The Director's Viewpoint. (Westview Special Studies in Communications). 1978. lib. bdg. 20.00x (ISBN 0-89158-337-8); text ed. 9.50 (ISBN 0-89158-337-8). Westview.

Ravel, O. E. Numismatique Grecque Falsifications Moyens Pour les Reconnaitre. 105p. (Fr.). 1980. Repr. of 1946 ed. 20.00 (ISBN 0-916710-71-8). Obol Intl.

--Les "Poulains" De Corinthe. (Illus.). 1979. text ed. 80.00 (ISBN 0-916710-47-5). Obol Intl.

Raven, A. J. & Kuan, L. K. Modern Mathematics Check-up. 1977. pap. text ed. 6.50x o.p. (ISBN 0-435-50812-1). Heinemann Ed.

Raven, Bertram H., ed. Policy Studies Review Annual, Vol. 4. LC 77-72938. (Illus.). 768p. 1980. 35.00 (ISBN 0-8039-1119-X). Sage.

Raven, Bertran & Rubin, Jeffrey. Social Psychology: People in Groups. LC 75-32693. 592p. 1976. 21.95 (ISBN 0-471-70970-0); instructor's resource book 2.50 (ISBN 0-471-01498-2). Wiley.

Raven, C. P. Outline of Developmental Physiology. 3rd ed. 1966. 15.00 (ISBN 0-08-011343-5). Pergamon.

Raven, Charles E. War & the Christian. LC 75-147675. (Library of War & Peace; Relig. & Ethical Positions on War). lib. bdg. 38.00 (ISBN 0-8240-0432-9). Garland Pub.

Raven, Francis H. Mathematics of Engineering Systems. 1966. text ed. 29.95x (ISBN 0-07-051230-2, C). McGraw.

Raven, John E., jt. auth. see Kirk, Geoffrey S.

Raven, Peter & Evert, Ray. Biology of Plants. 2nd ed. LC 75-42980. (Illus.). 1976. 18.95x o.p. (ISBN 0-87901-054-1). Worth.

Raven, Peter H. & Axelrod, Daniel I. Origin & Relationships of the California Flora. (Publications in Botany: No. 72). 1978. pap. 7.50x (ISBN 0-520-09573-1). U of Cal Pr.

Raven, Peter H., et al. Biology of Plants. 3rd ed. 1981. text ed. write for info. (ISBN 0-87901-132-7); write for info. lab manual (ISBN 0-87901-142-4); prep guide avail. (ISBN 0-87901-143-2). Worth.

Raven, Simon. Bring Forth the Body. LC 75-31244. 1974. 12.50x (ISBN 0-85634-017-0). Intl Pubns Serv.

--Places Where They Sing. LC 73-508962. (Alms for Oblivion Ser.: No. 6). 1970. 8.50x (ISBN 0-85634-997-6). Intl Pubns Serv.

Raven, Susan & Weir, Alison. Women in History. (Illus.). 288p. 1981. 19.95 (ISBN 0-517-53982-9, Harmony). Crown.

Ravenal, Earl C. Strategic Disengagement & World Peace: Toward a Noninterventionist American Foreign Policy. (The Cato Papers Ser.: No. 7). 64p. 1979. pap. 2.00 (ISBN 0-932790-07-0). Cato Inst.

Ravenel, Shannon, jt. ed. see Elkin, Stanley.

Ravenette, A. T. Dimensions of Reading Difficulties. 1968. 11.25 (ISBN 0-08-012956-0); pap. 5.75 (ISBN 0-08-012955-2). Pergamon.

Ravenhill, Leonard. Meat for Men. LC 51-418. 1979. pap. 3.50 (ISBN 0-87123-362-2, 210362). Bethany Fell.

--Revival Praying. 1962. pap. 3.50 (ISBN 0-87123-482-3, 210482). Bethany Fell.

--Sodom Had No Bible. 1979. pap. 2.95 (ISBN 0-87123-496-3, 210496). Bethany Fell.

Ravenhill, Philip L. Baule Statuary Art: Meaning & Modernization. Bd. with Beauty in the Eyes of the Baule: Aesthetics & Cultural Values. Vogel, Susan M. LC 79-24004. (Working Papers in the Traditional Arts: Nos. 5 & 6). (Illus.). 1980. pap. text ed. 4.95x (ISBN 0-89727-006-1). Inst Study Human.

Ravensdale, J. R. Liable to Floods: Village Landscape on the Edge of Fens. LC 73-80473. (Illus.). 254p. 1974. 31.95 (ISBN 0-521-20285-X). Cambridge U Pr.

Ravensdale, T. Coral Fishes. (Encore Editions). (Illus.). 1973. 3.50 o.p. (ISBN 0-684-14995-8, ScribT). Scribner.

Ravera, O., ed. Biological Aspects of Freshwater Pollution: Proceedings of the Course Held at the Joint Research Centre, Ispra, Italy, 5-9 June 1978. (Illus.). 1979. 36.00 (ISBN 0-08-023442-9). Pergamon.

Ravetz, Alison. Remaking Cities. 375p. 1980. 37.50x (ISBN 0-85664-293-2, Pub. by Croom Helm Ltd England). Biblio Dist.

Ravetz, J. R. Scientific Knowledge & Its Social Problems. 1971. 42.00x (ISBN 0-19-827213-8). Oxford U Pr.

Ravi, K. V. Imperfections & Impurities in Semiconductor Silicon. LC 80-21978. 425p. 1981. 32.50 (ISBN 0-471-07817-4, Pub. by Wiley-Interscience). Wiley.

Ravich, M. G. & Kamenev, E. N. Crystalline Basement of the Antarctic Platform. Bogosh, R., ed. Kaner, N., tr. from Rus. LC 74-13646. 582p. 1975. 79.95 (ISBN 0-470-70990-1). Halsted Pr.

Ravielli, Anthony. What Are Street Games? LC 80-22657. 1981. 10.95 (ISBN 0-689-30838-8). Atheneum.

Ravin, A. W., jt. ed. see Caspari, E. W.

Ravindra, H, jt. ed. see Cropley, A. J.

Ravindranath, B. & Chander, M. Power System Protection & Switchgear. 1978. 16.95 (ISBN 0-470-99311-1). Halsted Pr.

Ravitch, Diane & Goodenow, Ronald, eds. Educating an Urban People: The New York Experience. 1981. text ed. 22.50 (ISBN 0-8077-2600-1). Tchrs Coll.

Ravitch, Mark M. A Century of Surgery: History of the American Surgical Association, 2 vols. (Illus.). 1600p. 1981. Set. 195.00. Lippincott.

--Intussusception in Infants & Children. 156p. 1981. 28.50 (ISBN 0-87527-169-3). Green. Postponed.

Raw, Barbara C. The Art & Background of Old English Poetry. LC 78-390. 1978. 19.95x (ISBN 0-312-04984-6). St Martin.

Raw, Charles. A Financial Phenomenon: An Investigation of the Rise & Fall of the Slater Walker Empire. LC 77-17675. 1978. 12.95 o.p. (ISBN 0-06-013506-9, HarpT). Har-Row.

Rawcliffe, C. T. & Rawson, D. H., eds. Principles of Inorganic & Theoretical Chemistry. 1974. pap. text ed. 15.95x (ISBN 0-435-66747-5). Heinemann Ed.

Rawcliffe, Carole. The Staffords, Earls of Stafford & Dukes of Buckingham 1394-1521. LC 77-71425. (Studies in Medieval Life & Thought: No. 11). (Illus.). 1978. 39.95 (ISBN 0-521-21663-X). Cambridge U Pr.

Rawcliffe, Michael. The Roosevelt File. (Illus.). 96p. (gr. 9-12). 1980. 14.95 (ISBN 0-7134-1921-0, Pub. by Batsford England). David & Charles.

Rawding, F. W. The Buddha. LC 74-14436. (Introduction to the History of Mankind Ser). (Illus.). 48p. (YA) 1975. pap. 3.95 (ISBN 0-521-20368-6). Cambridge U Pr.

--Gandhi. LC 79-11008. (Cambridge Introduction to the History of Mankind Topic Book). (Illus.). (gr. 6). 1980. pap. 3.95 (ISBN 0-521-20715-0). Cambridge U Pr.

--The Rebellion in India, 1857. (Cambridge Introduction to the History of Mankind Ser.). (Illus.). (gr. 4-5). 1977. pap. 3.95 (ISBN 0-521-20683-9). Cambridge U Pr.

Rawle, William. View of the Constitution of the United States of America. LC 70-109548. (American Constitutional & Legal History Ser). 1970. Repr. of 1829 ed. lib. bdg. 35.00 (ISBN 0-306-71902-9). Da Capo.

Rawley, James A. The Politics of Union: Northern Politics During the Civil War. LC 80-17173. vi, 202p. 1980. 15.50x (ISBN 0-8032-3856-8); pap. 3.95x (ISBN 0-8032-8902-2, BB 743, Bison). U of Nebr Pr.

--Turning Points of the Civil War. LC 66-19266. (Illus.). 1974. pap. 5.50x (ISBN 0-8032-5155-6, BB 382, Bison). U of Nebr Pr.

Rawley, James A., ed. see Wolseley, Garnet.

Rawley, Michael. Book. (Illus.). 128p. 1981. 19.95 (ISBN 0-938580-00-0). Please Pr.

Rawlings, Gertrude B. The Story of Books. 160p. 1980. Repr. of 1901 ed. lib. bdg. 25.00 (ISBN 0-89984-431-6). Century Bookbindery.

Rawlings, Hunter R. Structure of Thucydides' History. LC 80-8572. 312p. 1981. 21.00x (ISBN 0-691-03555-5). Princeton U Pr.

Rawlings, Marjorie K. Cross Creek Cookery. LC 42-25465. (Illus.). 1942. 12.95 (ISBN 0-684-10487-3, ScribT). Scribner.

--Secret River. (Illus.). (gr. 1-4). 1955. pap. 0.95 o.p. (ISBN 0-684-12636-2, SBF8, ScribT). Scribner.

--When the Whippoorwill. pap. 1.75 o.p. (ISBN 0-89176-522-0, 6522). Mockingbird Bks.

--When the Whippoorwill. 1980. pap. 2.25 (ISBN 0-89176-035-0). Mockingbird Bks.

--The Yearling. (Illus.). 1962. 20.00 (ISBN 0-684-20922-5, ScribJ); text ed. 5.56 (ISBN 0-684-51547-4, ScribC); pap. o.p. (ISBN 0-684-71878-2, SL40, ScribJ); pap. text ed. 2.84 o.p. (ISBN 0-684-51548-2, ScribC). Scribner.

Rawlings, Maurice. Before Death Comes. 224p. 1980. 7.95 (ISBN 0-8407-5191-5). Nelson.

Rawlings, Ronald. Antique-Hunter's Handbook. LC 77-91720. (Leisure & Travel Ser.). (Illus.). 1978. 7.50 (ISBN 0-7153-7578-4). David & Charles.

--Making & Managing an Antique Shop. LC 79-51100. (Making & Managing Ser.). (Illus.). 1980. 17.95 (ISBN 0-7153-7800-7). David & Charles.

Rawlins, Jack P. Thackeray's Novels: A Fiction That Is True. 1975. 18.50x (ISBN 0-520-02562-8). U of Cal Pr.

Rawlins, M. D., jt. auth. see Smith, S. E.

Rawlins, N. Omri. Introduction to Agribusiness. (Illus.). 1980. text ed. 11.95 (ISBN 0-13-477703-4). P-H.

Rawlinson, D. H. Practice of Criticism. 1968. 34.00 (ISBN 0-521-06045-1); pap. 8.95x (ISBN 0-521-09540-9). Cambridge U Pr.

Rawlinson, J. Geoffrey. Creative Thinking & Brainstorming. LC 80-22724. 144p. 1981. 14.95 (ISBN 0-470-27091-8). Halsted Pr.

Rawls, Eugene. A Handbook of Yoga for Modern Living. (Orig.). pap. 1.50 (ISBN 0-515-00958-X). Jove Pubns.

Rawls, Eugene S. & Diskin, Eve. Joy of Life Through Yoga. 1976. pap. 1.25 o.s.i. (ISBN 0-446-76736-0). Warner Bks.

Rawls, Walton. The Great Book of Currier & Ives' America. LC 79-89549. (Illus.). 488p. 1979. 85.00 (ISBN 0-89659-070-4). Abbeville Pr.

Rawls, Wilson. Where the Red Fern Grows. LC 61-9201. 7.95a (ISBN 0-385-02059-7); PLB (ISBN 0-385-05619-2). Doubleday.

Rawnsley, Howard M., jt. auth. see Mitruka, Brij M.

Rawski, Thomas G. China's Transition to Industrialism: Producer Goods & Economic Development in the Twentieth Century. (Michigan Studies on China). (Illus.). 226p. 1980. 16.50x (ISBN 0-472-08755-X). U of Mich Pr.

Rawson, C. J. Gulliver & the Gentle Reader: Studies in Swift & Our Time. 200p. 1973. 18.50x (ISBN 0-7100-7602-9). Routledge & Kegan.

Rawson, D. H., jt. ed. see Rawcliffe, C. T.

Rawson, Geoffrey. Pandora's Last Voyage. LC 64-18291. (Illus.). 1964. 3.95 o.p. (ISBN 0-15-170826-6). HarBraceJ.

Rawson, Jessica. Animals in Art. (Illus.). 1978. 14.95 (ISBN 0-684-15650-4, ScribT); pap. 9.95 (ISBN 0-684-16920-7, SL791, ScribT). Scribner.

Rawson, K. J. & Tupper, E. C. Basic Ship Theory, Vols. 1 & 2. 2nd ed. (Illus.). 352p. 1976. Vol. 1. pap. text ed. 19.95x (ISBN 0-582-44523-X); Vol. 2. pap. text ed. 21.00x (ISBN 0-582-44524-8). Longman.

Rawson, M., jt. auth. see Blegen, C. W.

Rawson, Natasha. Search for Truth. 100p. 1981. write for info. (Pub. by the Linolean Press). Larksdale.

Rawson, P. F., jt. auth. see Casey, R.

Rawson, Philip. The Art of Tantra. LC 77-18400. (World of Art Ser.). (Illus.). 1978. pap. 9.95 (ISBN 0-19-520055-1). Oxford U Pr.

--Tantra: The Indian Cult of Ecstasy. (Illus.). 1977. pap. 8.95 (ISBN 0-500-81001-X). Thames Hudson.

Rawson, Phillip. The Art of Southeast Asia: Cambodia, Vietnam, Thailand, Loas, Burma, Java & Bali. (World of Art Ser.). (Illus.). 1967. pap. 9.95 (ISBN 0-19-520005-5). Oxford U Pr.

Rawstron, E. M., jt. auth. see Wise, M. J.

Ray & Lewis. Exploring Professional Cooking. rev. ed. (gr. 9-12). 1980. text ed. 14.60 (ISBN 0-87002-315-2); student guide 6.08 (ISBN 0-87002-163-X); tchr's guide 10.00 (ISBN 0-87002-302-0); visual masters 10.60 (ISBN 0-87002-172-9). Bennett IL.

Ray, ed. Immunobiology & Transplantation, Cancer & Pregnancy. 500p. Date not set. text ed. price not set (ISBN 0-08-025994-4). Pergamon.

Ray, Amal. Inter-Governmental Relations in India: A Study in Indian Federalism. 1967. 4.75x o.p. (ISBN 0-210-22719-2). Asia.

Ray, Ami. Apocalypso. 10.00 (ISBN 0-89253-637-3); flexible cloth 5.00 (ISBN 0-89253-638-1). Ind-US Inc.

Ray, Ann, ed. see Hills, Christopher.

Ray, Arthur J. Indians in the Fur Trade: Their Role As Trappers, Hunters, & Middle Man in the Lands Southwest of Hudson Bay, 1660-1860. LC 73-89848. (Illus.). 1974. pap. 7.50 (ISBN 0-8020-6226-1). U of Toronto Pr.

Ray, B. Two-Six Compounds. LC 72-93126. 1970. 37.00 (ISBN 0-08-006624-0). Pergamon.

Ray, C. A. La Vida Responsable: Orientacion Biblica Sobre Nuestro Estilo De Vivir. Lopez, Albert C., tr. Orig. Title: Living the Responsible Life. 1980. 3.00 (ISBN 0-311-46079-8). Casa Bautista.

Ray, C. T., ed. see Walker, W. C., et al.

Ray, Colin, ed. Library Service to Children: An International Survey, Vol. 12. (IFLA Publications Ser.). 1978. 24.50 (ISBN 0-89664-004-3, Pub. by K G Saur). Shoe String.

Ray, Cyril. Cyril Ray's Book of Wine. (Illus.). 1978. 12.95 o.p. (ISBN 0-688-03333-4). Morrow.

Ray, David. The Farm in Calabria & Other Poems. Sklar, Morty, ed. LC 80-123410. (Outstanding Author Ser.: No. 3). (Illus.). 32p. (Orig.). 1980. pap. 2.00 (ISBN 0-930370-08-2). Spirit That Moves.

--Gathering Firewood: New Poems & Selected. LC 74-5968. (Wesleyan Poetry Program: Vol. 75). 88p. 1974. pap. 4.95 (ISBN 0-8195-1075-0, Pub. by Wesleyan U Pr). Columbia U Pr.

Ray, David, jt. auth. see Frank, Ted.

Ray, David, ed. From A to Z: 200 Contemporary American Poets. LC 80-27328. xi, 243p. 1981. 16.95 (ISBN 0-8040-0369-6); pap. 8.95 (ISBN 0-8040-0370-X). Swallow.

Ray, David, ed. see Mayo, E. L.

Ray, Deborah. Sunday Morning We Went to the Zoo. LC 80-7915. (Illus.). (ps-2). 1981. 8.95 (ISBN 0-06-024841-6, HarpJ); PLB 8.79 (ISBN 0-06-024842-4). Har-Row.

Ray, Dorothy J. Aleut & Eskimo Art: Tradition & Innovation in South Alaska. LC 79-56591. (Illus.). 224p. 1981. 29.95 (ISBN 0-295-95709-3). U of Wash Pr.

Ray, Edgar. Grand Huckster: Houston's Judge Roy Hofheintz, Genius of the Astrodome. (Illus.). 1980. 19.95 (ISBN 0-87870-069-2); deluxe ed. 29.95 (ISBN 0-87870-195-8). Memphis St Univ.

Ray, G. F. & Uhlmann, L. The Innovation Process in the Energy Industry. LC 78-17064. (National Institute of Economic & Social Research, Occasional Papers Ser.: No. 30). 1979. 21.95 (ISBN 0-521-22371-7). Cambridge U Pr.

Ray, G. F., jt. auth. see Nabseth, L.

Ray, George & Robinson, Colin. European Energy Outlook to Nineteen Eighty-Five. LC 80-455974. 123p. 1978. pap. text ed. 135.00x (ISBN 0-8002-1405-6). Intl Pubns Serv.

Ray, J. Edgar. Art of Bricklaying. Johnson, Harold V., ed. (Illus.). (gr. 9-12). 1971. pap. text ed. 11.00 (ISBN 0-87002-271-7). Bennett IL.

Ray, J. P., ed. The Diary of a Dead Man, Eighteen Sixty-Two to Eighteen Sixty-Four. (Illus.). 430p. (Orig.). 1979. pap. 4.00 (ISBN 0-686-27871-2, Pub. by Eastern Natl Park). Eastern Acorn.

Ray, James L. Global Politics. LC 78-69552. (Illus.). 1978. text ed. 15.95 (ISBN 0-395-26542-8); inst. manual 0.65 (ISBN 0-395-26540-1). HM.

Ray, Jayanta K. Public Policy & Global Reality: Some Aspects of American Alliance Policy. 1977. text ed. 15.00x (ISBN 0-391-01002-6). Humanities.

Ray, John. Britain & the Modern World. 1974. pap. text ed. 7.95x o.p. (ISBN 0-435-31751-2). Heinemann Ed.

--Cars. (Junior Reference Ser.). (Illus.). 96p. (gr. 7 up). 7.96 (ISBN 0-7136-1322-X). Dufour.

--A History of British Transport 1700 to the Present. 1969. pap. text ed. 4.95x o.p. (ISBN 0-435-31753-9). Heinemann Ed.

--The History of Flight. 1968. pap. text ed. 4.95x o.p. (ISBN 0-435-31750-4). Heinemann Ed.

--A History of the Railways. 1969. pap. text ed. 4.95x o.p. (ISBN 0-435-31754-7). Heinemann Ed.

--Hitler & Mussolini. 1970. pap. text ed. 2.95x (ISBN 0-435-31755-5). Heinemann Ed.

Ray, Karl, ed. see Tsunoyama, Yokihiro.

Ray, Keith, ed. see Architectural Record Magazine.

Ray, Kenneth C., jt. auth. see Drury, Robert L.

Ray, Lila. Entrance. (Redbird Bk.). 1976. 6.75 (ISBN 0-89253-512-1); flexible bdg. 4.00 (ISBN 0-89253-124-X). Ind-US Inc.

Ray, Marie B. The Importance of Feeling Inferior. LC 80-19319. 266p. 1980. Repr. of 1971 ed. lib. bdg. 9.95x (ISBN 0-89370-606-X). Borgo Pr.

Ray, Mary. Shout Against the Wind. (Faber Fanfares Ser.). (Illus.). 176p. (Orig.). (gr. 4-9). 1980. pap. 3.25 (ISBN 0-571-11489-X, Pub. by Faber & Faber). Merrimack Bk Serv.

--A Tent for the Sun. 1971. 6.95 (ISBN 0-571-09770-7, Pub. by Faber & Faber). Merrimack Bk Serv.

Ray, Mary & Lewis, Evelyn. Exploring Professional Cooking. (gr. 10-12). 1976. text ed. 12.80 o.p. (ISBN 0-87002-161-3); tchr guide 10.00 o.p. (ISBN 0-87002-167-2); wkbk 6.08 o.p. (ISBN 0-87002-163-X). Bennett IL.

Ray, Mary F. & Dondi, Beda. Professional Cooking & Baking. (Illus.). 450p. 1981. text ed. 13.20 (ISBN 0-87002-328-4); write for info. tchr's guide (ISBN 0-87002-329-2); write for info. student guide (ISBN 0-87002-330-6). Bennett IL.

Ray, Michael L. & Ward, Scott, eds. Communicating with Consumers: The Information Processing Approach. LC 75-32370. (Sage Contemporary Social Science Issues Ser.: Vol. 21). 1976. 4.95x (ISBN 0-8039-0579-3). Sage.

Ray, N. L. There Was This Man Running. LC 80-27225. 156p. (gr. 5-9). 1981. PLB 8.95 (ISBN 0-02-775760-9). Macmillan.

Ray, Oakley S. Drugs, Society & Human Behavior. 2nd ed. LC 77-20660. (Illus.). 1978. pap. text ed. 14.50 (ISBN 0-8016-4094-6). Mosby.

Ray, P. K. Agricultural Insurance: Theory & Practice & Application to Developing Countries. 2nd ed. (Illus.). 360p. Date not set. 86.01 (ISBN 0-08-025787-9). Pergamon.

Ray, P. Orman, jt. auth. see Ogg, Frederic A.

Ray, Ratnalakha. Change in Bengal Agrarian Society, Seventeen Sixty to Eighteen Fifty. 1980. 20.00x (ISBN 0-8364-0646-X, Pub. by Manohar India). South Asia Bks.

Ray, Richard & MacCaskey, Michael. Roses. (Gardening Ser.). (Orig.). 1981. pap. 7.95 (ISBN 0-89586-079-1). H P Bks.

Ray, Richard & Walheim, Lance. Citrus. (Gardening Ser.). (Orig.). 1980. pap. 7.95 (ISBN 0-89586-076-7). H P Bks.

Ray, Robert J. Cage of Mirrors. LC 80-7867. 320p. 1980. 11.95 (ISBN 0-690-01938-6). Lippincott & Crowell.

Ray, Robin. Robin Ray's Music Quiz. 1978. 13.50 (ISBN 0-7134-1492-8, Pub. by Batsford England). David & Charles.

Ray, S. H. see Haddon, A. C.

Ray, S. K. Economics of the Black Market. (Replica Edition Ser.). 250p. 1981. lib. bdg. 20.00x (ISBN 0-86531-149-8). Westview.

Ray, Satyajit, jt. auth. see Ray, Sukumar.

Ray, Satyajit, tr. see Ray, Sukumar & Ray, Satyajit.

Ray, Sibnarayan. Autumnal Equinox. (Redbird Ser). 1975. 10.00 (ISBN 0-89253-601-2); pap. text ed. 4.80 (ISBN 0-88253-711-3). Ind-US Inc.

Ray, Sibnarayan, ed. Vak: An Anthology of Australian, European & Indian Verse. 14.00 (ISBN 0-89253-623-3). Ind-US Inc.

Ray, Sidney F. The Lens & All Its Jobs. (Media Manuals Ser.). Date not set. pap. 8.95 (ISBN 0-8038-4299-6). Hastings.

Ray, Sukumar & Ray, Satyajit. Nonsense Rhymes. Ray, Satyajit, tr. from Bengali. (Writers Workshop Saffronbird Ser.). 1975. 8.00 (ISBN 0-88253-588-9); pap. text ed. 4.00 (ISBN 0-88253-587-0). Ind-US Inc.

Ray, Susan, tr. see Zauner, Renate.

Ray, Talton F. The Politics of the Barrios of Venezuela. rev. ed. (Illus.). 1969. 19.50x (ISBN 0-520-01461-8). U of Cal Pr.

Ray, Verne F., et al. Apache Indians X. Horr, David A., ed. (American Indian Ethnohistory Ser.). 1978. lib. bdg. 42.00 (ISBN 0-8240-0718-2). Garland Pub.

Ray, W. Harmon. Advanced Process Control. (Chemical Engineering Ser.). (Illus.). 1980. text ed. 29.50 (ISBN 0-07-051250-7, C). McGraw.

Ray, Walheim L. The Best Book on CB Radio. LC 76-41094. (Illus.). 1976. pap. cancelled o.p. (ISBN 0-685-71227-3). H P Bks.

Ray, William, ed. Conversations: Reynolds Price & William Ray. (Mississippi Collection Bulletin, No. 9). (Illus.). 82p. 1976. pap. 5.95x (ISBN 0-87870-086-2). Memphis St Univ.

Ray, William J., jt. auth. see Stern, Robert M.

Ray, Willis. Introduction to Manufacturing Careers. (gr. 7-10). 1975. pap. text ed. 5.00 activity ed. (ISBN 0-87345-177-5). McKnight.

Ray, Willis H. & Szekely, Julian. Process Optimization with Applications in Metallurgy & Chemical Engineering. LC 73-936. 400p. 1973. 39.00 (ISBN 0-471-71070-9, Pub. by Wiley-Interscience). Wiley.

Ray, Winifred, tr. see Bonn, M. J.

Ray, Worth S. Austin Colony Pioneers. LC 77-144991. (Illus.). 17.50 (ISBN 0-8363-0007-6). Jenkins.

Raya, Joseph & De Vinck, Jose. Byzantine Daily Worship. (Illus.). 1969. plastic bdg. o.s.i. 15.75x o.p. (ISBN 0-911726-07-1); deluxe ed. morocco o.s.i. 35.00x o.p. (ISBN 0-911726-09-8); pap. 15.75x o.p. (ISBN 0-911726-00-4). Alleluia Pr.

Rayan, Krishna. Suggestions & Statement in Poetry. 1972. text ed. 19.50x (ISBN 0-485-11134-9, Athlone Pr). Humanities.

Rayaprol, Srinivas. Bones & Distances. 2nd ed. (Redbird Bk.). 1976. 8.00 (ISBN 0-89253-117-7); flexible bdg. 4.00 (ISBN 0-89253-135-5). Ind-US Inc.

--Married Love & Other Poems. (Writers Workshop Redbird Ser.). 1976. 8.00 (ISBN 0-89253-724-8); pap. text ed. 4.00 (ISBN 0-89253-725-6). Ind-US Inc.

Rayback, J. G. History of American Labor. 1959. 6.95 o.s.i. (ISBN 0-02-601140-9). Macmillan.

Rayback, Joseph G. History of American Labor. LC 59-5344. 1966. pap. text ed. 7.95 (ISBN 0-02-925850-2). Free Pr.

Raybould, E. C., jt. auth. see Leach, D. J.

Rayburn, John. Gregorian Chant: A History of Controversy Concerning Its Rhythm. LC 80-27616. xiv, 90p. 1981. Repr. of 1964 ed. lib. bdg. 19.75x (ISBN 0-313-22811-6, RAGR). Greenwood.

Rayburn, L. Gayle. Principles of Cost Accounting with Managerial Implications. 1979. 19.95 (ISBN 0-256-02144-9). Irwin.

Rayburn, Wallace. The Men in White. 1975. 8.95 o.p. (ISBN 0-7207-0831-1, Pub. by Michael Joseph). Merrimack Bk Serv.

Raychard, Al. Al Raychard's Fly Fishing in Maine. LC 80-12126. (Illus.). 176p. (Orig.). 1980. pap. 6.95 (ISBN 0-89621-055-3). Thorndike Pr.

Ray-Chaudhuri, D. K., ed. Relations Between Combinatorics & Other Parts of Mathematics. LC 78-25979. (Proceedings of Symposia in Pure Mathematics: Vol. 34). 1980. Repr. of 1979 ed. 16.00 (ISBN 0-8218-1434-6). Am Math.

--Relations Between Combinatorics, & Other Parts of Mathematics: Proceedings of Symposia in Pure Mathematics, Vol. 34. 1979. write for info. o.p. (ISBN 0-8218-1434-6). Am Math.

Raychaudhuri, Upendrakishore. The Stupid Tiger & Other Tales. Radice, William, tr. LC 80-2691. (Illus.). 96p. (gr. 1-5). 1981. 8.95 (ISBN 0-233-97256-0). Andre Deutsch.

Raycraft, Carol, jt. auth. see Raycraft, Don.
Raycraft, Don. Collector's Guide to Kitchen Antiques. (Illus.). 1980. 17.95 (ISBN 0-89145-140-4). Collector Bks.
Raycraft, Don & Raycraft, Carol. American Country Pottery. 1975. 6.95 o.p. (ISBN 0-87069-120-1). Wallace-Homestead.
--Early American Furniture. 6.95 o.p. (ISBN 0-87069-026-4). Wallace-Homestead.
--Price Guide to American Country Pottery. 1976. 1.50 o.p. (ISBN 0-87069-150-3). Wallace-Homestead.
--Wallace-Homestead Price Guide to American Country Antiques. (Illus.). 1978. sofbound 8.95 o.p. (ISBN 0-87069-230-5). Wallace-Homestead.
Rayer, F. G. Electronic Experiments. (Pegasus Books). 1971. 10.50x (ISBN 0-234-77485-1). Intl Pubns Serv.
--Electronic Projects in Hobbies. 1979. pap. 7.95 o.p. (ISBN 0-686-60308-7, NB 98). Hayden.
Rayer, Francis G. Electrical Experiments. LC 75-368193. (Pegasus Books: No. 13). (Illus.). (gr. 9 up). 1968. 7.50x (ISBN 0-234-77997-7). Intl Pubns Serv.
--Radio Experiments. LC 78-431666. (Pegasus Books: No. 20). (Illus.). 1968. 7.50x (ISBN 0-234-77182-8). Intl Pubns Serv.
Rayess, George. Art of Lebanese Cooking. 14.00 (ISBN 0-685-77131-8). Intl Bk Ctr.
Rayfield, Joan, tr. see Maquet, Jacques.
Raygor, A. & Scnmelzer, R. Word Attack & Spelling: An Audio Tutorial. 1981. 250.00 (ISBN 0-13-963215-8); student wkbk. 7.95 (ISBN 0-13-963223-9). P-H.
Raygor, Alton, ed. see Lewick-Wallace, Mary.
Raygor, Alton, ed. see Wallace, Mary L.
Raygor, Alton L. & Schick, George B. Reading at Efficient Rates. 2nd ed. (McGraw-Hill Basic Skills). (Illus.). 192p. 1980. pap. text ed. 9.95 (ISBN 0-07-044418-8, C). McGraw.
Raygor, Alton L., ed. see Learning Technology Incorporated.
Raygor, Larry. Catherine's Twins. (Orig.). 1979. pap. 1.95 (ISBN 0-532-23107-4). Manor Bks.
Rayleigh, Baron, jt. auth. see Strutt, John W.
Raylor, A. J. Revolutions & Revolutionaries. LC 80-66006. 1980. 12.95 (ISBN 0-689-11069-3). Atheneum.
Rayman, Paula, jt. ed. see Bruyn, Severyn T.
Raymond, Alex & Hammett, Dashiell. Secret Agent Nine. Gelman, Woody, ed. LC 76-19616. (Illus.). 176p. 1976. pap. 8.95 (ISBN 0-686-65518-4). Nostalgia Pr.
Raymond, Boris. Krupskaia & Soviet Russian Librarianship: 1917-1939. LC 79-1041. 1979. 13.00 (ISBN 0-8108-1209-6). Scarecrow.
Raymond, Charlotte C., ed. see Weston, George F., Jr.
Raymond, Corey E., et al. Problems in Marketing. 6th ed. (Illus.). 832p. 20.95 (ISBN 0-07-013141-4); instrs'. 4.95 (ISBN 0-07-013142-2). McGraw.
Raymond, Ellsworth. The Soviet State. 2nd ed. LC 76-46138. 462p. 1978. 18.00x (ISBN 0-8147-7370-2). NYU Pr.
Raymond, Gregory A. Conflict Resolution & the Structure of the State System. LC 79-53702. (Illus.). 122p. 1980. text ed. 22.50 (ISBN 0-916672-12-3). Allanheld.
Raymond, Gregory A., jt. auth. see Fry, Earl H.
Raymond, Jacque, jt. auth. see Banerji, Dilip.
Raymond, Jim, jt. auth. see Young, Dean.
Raymond, John. Twenty-Six Lessons on Matthew, Vol. II. (Bible Student Study Guide Ser.). 180p. 1981. pap. 2.95 (ISBN 0-89900-171-8). College Pr Pub.
--Twenty-Six Lessons on Matthew, Vol. 1. LC 80-67734. (Bible Student Study Guides). 150p. (Orig.). 1980. pap. 2.95 (ISBN 0-89900-167-X). College Pr Pub.
Raymond, Ronald R., Jr., et al. Grow Your Roots Anywhere, Anytime. Date not set. 12.95. Wyden.
Raymond, Stephen, jt. auth. see Gruberg, Edward.
Raymond, Walter J. Dictionary of Politics. LC 78-50189. (Illus.). deluxe ed. 24.95x (ISBN 0-931494-00-1). Brunswick Pub.
Raymont, J. E. Plankton & Productivity in the Oceans. 1963. 36.00 (ISBN 0-08-010185-2); pap. 15.00 (ISBN 0-08-019009-X). Pergamon.
Raymont, John E., et al. Plankton & Productivity in the Oceans: Vol. 1, Phytoplankton. 2nd ed. (Illus.). 1980. text ed. 75.00 (ISBN 0-08-021552-1); pap. text ed. 19.95 (ISBN 0-08-021551-3). Pergamon.
Raymore, Henry B., jt. auth. see Ortloff, H. Stuart.
Rayner, Claire. The Body Book. LC 79-23363. (Illus.). (gr. k-7). 1980. 6.95 (ISBN 0-8120-5325-7). Barron.
--Paddington Green. 1977. pap. 1.95 o.p. (ISBN 0-449-23265-4, Crest). Fawcett.
Rayner, D. Stratigraphy of the British Isles. 2nd ed. LC 79-8523. (Illus.). 400p. Date not set. price not set (ISBN 0-521-23452-2); pap. price not set (ISBN 0-521-29961-6). Cambridge U Pr.
Rayner, D. H. Stratigraphy of the British Isles. (Illus.). 1967. 44.50 (ISBN 0-521-06047-8). Cambridge U Pr.
Rayner, Dorothy H. Stratigraphy of the British Isles. (Illus.). 1980. pap. 15.50 (ISBN 0-521-29820-2). Cambridge U Pr.
Rayner, E. G., jt. auth. see Dexter, N. C.
Rayner, Eric. Human Development. 2nd ed. 1977. text ed. 25.00x (ISBN 0-04-155009-9); pap. text ed. 9.95x (ISBN 0-04-155008-0). Allen Unwin.
Rayner, J. N. Conservation, Equilibrium & Feedback Applied to Atmospheric & Fluvial Processes. LC 77-189377. (CCG Resource Papers Ser.: No. 15). (Illus.). 1972. pap. text ed. 4.00 (ISBN 0-89291-062-3). Assn Am Geographers.
Rayner, Mary. Garth Pig & the Ice-Cream Lady. (ps-3). pap. 2.95 (ISBN 0-689-70495-X, A-122, Aladdin). Atheneum.
--The Rain Cloud. LC 79-3069. (Illus.). 32p. (ps-2). 1980. 8.95 (ISBN 0-689-30763-2). Atheneum.
--The Witchfinder. LC 76-22600. (Illus.). (gr. 5-9). 1976. 7.25 (ISBN 0-688-22082-7); PLB 6.96 (ISBN 0-688-32082-1). Morrow.
Rayner, Ronald. Mushrooms & Toadstools. (Illus.). 128p. 1980. 8.95 (ISBN 0-600-36283-3). Transatlantic.
Rayner, William. Stag Boy. LC 72-91232. (gr. 7 up). 1973. 4.25 o.p. (ISBN 0-15-278400-4, HJ). HarBraceJ.
--The Trail to Bear Pawn Mountain. 1976. pap. 1.50 o.p. (ISBN 0-345-25391-4). Ballantine.
Raynes, John. Painting Seascapes. LC 79-56607. (Start to Paint Ser.). (Illus.). 104p. 1980. pap. 3.95 (ISBN 0-8008-6205-8, Pentalic). Taplinger.
--Starting to Paint in Oils. LC 79-56681. (Start to Paint Ser.). (Illus.). 104p. 1980. pap. 3.95 (ISBN 0-8008-7386-6, Pentalic). Taplinger.
--Starting to Paint with Acrylics. LC 79-56682. (Start to Paint Ser.). (Illus.). 104p. 1980. pap. 3.95 (ISBN 0-8008-7385-8, Pentalic). Taplinger.
Raynes, Norma V., et al. Organisational Structure & the Care of the Mentally Retarded. LC 79-83740. (Praeger Special Studies Ser.). 240p. 1979. 24.95 (ISBN 0-03-051516-5). Praeger.
--Organisational Structure & the Care of the Mentally Retarded. 192p. 1980. 25.00x (ISBN 0-85664-532-X, Pub. by Croom Helm England). State Mutual Bk.
Raynor, Dorka. Grandparents Around the World. Rubin, Caroline, ed. LC 76-57661. (Concept Books Ser.). (Illus.). (gr. k). 1977. 6.95g (ISBN 0-8075-3037-9). A Whitman.
--My Friends Live in Many Places. Tucker, Kathleen, ed. LC 79-27655. (Concept Bk.: Level 1). (Illus.). (ps up). 1980. 6.95g (ISBN 0-8075-5353-0). A Whitman.
--This Is My Father & Me. LC 73-7320. (Concept Bks.). (Illus.). 40p. (ps up). 1973. 6.95g (ISBN 0-8075-7883-5). A Whitman.
Raynor, Henry & Landon, H. Robbins. Hayden. (Great Composers Ser.). (Illus.). 1972. 8.95 (ISBN 0-571-08361-7, Pub. by Faber & Faber). Merrimack Bk Serv.
Raynor, Joel O. & Entin, Elliot E. Motivation, Career Striving, & Aging. LC 80-27082. (Illus.). 496p. Date not set. text ed. 24.95 (ISBN 0-89116-189-9). Hemisphere Pub. Postponed.
Raynor, Joel O., jt. auth. see Atkinson, John W.
Raynor, John. Anatomy & Physiology. 1977. text ed. 19.50 scp (ISBN 0-06-045339-7, HarpC); instructor's manual free (ISBN 0-06-365350-8); scp study guide 6.50 (ISBN 0-06-045338-9). Har-Row.
Raytheon Service Co. Wind Energy Systems Program Summary Nineteen Eighty. 230p. 1981. pap. 19.50 (ISBN 0-89934-108-X). Solar Energy Info.
Rayward, W. Boyd. The Public Library: Circumstances & Prospects: (Papers Presented at the 39th Annual Conference) LC 78-19604. (The University of Chicago Studies in Library Science). 1979. lib. bdg. 10.00x (ISBN 0-226-70585-4). U of Chicago Pr.
Raz, J., jt. ed. see Hacker, P. M.
Raz, Joseph. Concept of a Legal System: An Introduction to the Theory of Legal System. 1970. 14.95x o.p. (ISBN 0-19-825189-0). Oxford U Pr.
--The Concept of a Legal System: An Introduction to the Theory of a Legal System. 2nd ed. 244p. 1980. 24.95x (ISBN 0-19-825362-1); pap. 11.95x (ISBN 0-19-825363-X). Oxford U Pr.
Razi, Zvi. Life, Marriage & Death in a Medieval Parish. LC 79-8491. (Past & Present Publications). (Illus.). 1980. 27.50 (ISBN 0-521-23252-X). Cambridge U Pr.
Razin, Andrew M, jt. auth. see Gurman, Alan S.
Razin, Assaf, jt. ed. see Flanders, M. June.
Razzi, James. Bag of Tricks: Fun Things to Make & Do with the Groceries. LC 75-136996. (Illus.). (gr. k-3). 1971. 5.95 o.s.i. (ISBN 0-8193-0449-2, Four Winds); PLB 5.41 o.s.i. (ISBN 0-8193-0450-6). Schol Bk Serv.
--Don't Open This Box. LC 72-10219. (Illus.). 48p. (ps-2). 1973. 5.95 o.s.i. (ISBN 0-8193-0669-X, Four Winds); PLB 5.41 o.s.i. (ISBN 0-8193-0670-3). Schol Bk Serv.
--Just for Kids: Things to Make, Do & See, Easy As 1-2-3. LC 73-13521. 64p. (ps-3). 1974. 5.95 o.s.i. (ISBN 0-8193-0723-8, Four Winds); PLB 5.41 o.s.i. (ISBN 0-8193-0724-6). Schol Bk Serv.
--Star-Spangled Fun! Things to Make, Do & See from American History. LC 74-30397. (Illus.). 64p. (ps-4). 1976. 5.95 o.s.i. (ISBN 0-8193-0817-X, Four Winds); PLB 5.41 o.s.i. (ISBN 0-8193-0818-8). Schol Bk Serv.
--The Star Trek Action Toy Book. (Illus.). (ps-5). 1976. pap. 3.95 (ISBN 0-394-83277-9, BYR). Random.
--The Toy Book. (Illus.). (ps-4). 1976. pap. 3.95 (ISBN 0-394-83146-2, BYR). Random.
Razzi, Jim. Encyclopedia Brown Activity Book. (gr. 2-5). 1980. pap. 1.25 (ISBN 0-686-57990-9). Bantam.
--Encyclopedia Brown Puzzle & Game Books. (gr. 4-8). 1980. pap. 1.25 (ISBN 0-686-57991-7). Bantam.
--Encyclopedia Brown's Fourth Book of Games & Puzzles. 64p. (gr. 4-6). 1981. pap. 1.50 (ISBN 0-553-15110-X). Bantam.
--Encyclopedia Brown's Third Book of Games & Puzzles. 64p. (Orig.). (gr. 4-6). 1981. pap. 1.50 (ISBN 0-553-15077-4). Bantam.
Re, E. D., jt. auth. see Orfield, Lester B.
Re, Edward D. Brief Writing & Oral Argument. 4th rev. ed. LC 73-11059. 1977. 15.00 (ISBN 0-913338-22-2). Trans-Media Pub.
Rea, Kenneth. Canton in Revolution: The Collected Papers of Earl Swisher, 1925-1928. 1977. lib. bdg. 23.50x (ISBN 0-89158-304-1). Westview.
Rea, Kenneth, ed. Early Sino-American Relations (1841-1912) The Collected Articles of Earl Swisher. LC 77-13252. 1977. lib. bdg. 21.00 o.p. (ISBN 0-89158-305-X). Westview.
Rea, Kenneth W. & Brewer, John C., eds. The Forgotten Ambassador: The Reports of John Leighton Stuart, 1946-1949. (Replica Edition Ser.). 350p. 1981. lib. bdg. 25.00x (ISBN 0-86531-157-9). Westview.
REA Staff. Computer Science. 960p. 1980. 22.85 (ISBN 0-87891-525-7). Res & Educ.
--Handbook for Applied Mathematics. 800p. 1980. 16.85 (ISBN 0-87891-521-4). Res & Educ.
--Optics. 960p. 1980. 22.85 (ISBN 0-87891-526-5). Res & Educ.
--Strength of Materials - Mechanics of Solids. 896p. 1980. 22.85 (ISBN 0-87891-522-2). Res & Educ.
Reach, D., ed. see Featherstone, Donald F.
Reach, D., ed. see Philpott, Bryan.
Read. Beginner's Guide to Gemmology. 9.95 (ISBN 0-686-27953-0). Butterworths.
Read, A. J. Physics: A Descriptive Analysis. 1970. 14.95 (ISBN 0-201-06304-2). A-W.
Read, Ann K., jt. auth. see Garrison, Linda.
Read, B. E. & Dean, G. D. Determination of Dynamic Properties of Polymers & Composites. LC 78-12690. 1979. 60.95 (ISBN 0-470-26543-4). Halsted Pr.
Read, Brenda. Better Hockey for Girls. (Better Ser.). (Illus.). text ed. 14.50x (ISBN 0-7182-1445-5, SpS). Soccer.
Read, C. P., jt. auth. see Chandler, Asa C.
Read, Carol I., jt. auth. see Gammon, Margaret.
Read, Clark P. Parasitism & Symbiology: An Introductory Text. LC 75-110390. 320p. 1970. 17.95 o.p. (ISBN 0-8260-7355-7). Wiley.
Read, Conyers. Tudors: Personalities & Practical Politics in Sixteenth-Century England. (Illus.). 1969. pap. 6.95 (ISBN 0-393-00129-6, Norton Lib). Norton.
Read, D., et al. Health Education: The Search for Values. 1977. 12.95 (ISBN 0-13-384511-7). P-H.
Read, D. H. I Am Persuaded. (Scholar As Preacher Ser.). 190p. Repr. of 1961 ed. text ed. 7.75 (ISBN 0-567-04430-0). Attic Pr.
Read, David H. The Faith Is Still There. LC 80-21395. (Orig.). 1981. pap. 4.95 (ISBN 0-687-12650-9). Abingdon.
Read, Donald. The Concept of Health. 3rd ed. 1978. 11.95 (ISBN 0-205-05686-5, 715686-3); instructor's manual free (ISBN 0-205-05687-3, 715687-1). Allyn.
Read, Donald A. Drugs & People. (gr. 6-12). 1972. pap. text ed. 3.80 (ISBN 0-205-03381-4, 7133812); tchr's guide 2.40 (ISBN 0-205-02613-3, 7126131). Allyn.
--Looking in: Exploring One's Personal Health Values. (Health Education Ser.). (Illus.). 1977. pap. text ed. 8.95 (ISBN 0-13-540484-3). P-H.
Read, Donald C. & Simon, Sidney B. Humanistic Education Sourcebook. (Illus.). 480p. 1975. ref. ed. 16.95 (ISBN 0-13-447714-6); pap. 12.50 (ISBN 0-13-447706-5). P-H.
Read, Edwin A., et al. Continuous Progress in Spelling (CPS) 1. rev. ed. (gr. 1-3). 1977. 2.97 (ISBN 0-87892-286-5); 2.97 (ISBN 0-87892-287-3); kit 124.50 (ISBN 0-87892-285-7). Economy Co.
--Continuous Progress in Spelling (CPS) 2. rev. ed. (gr. 4-6). 1977. 2.16 (ISBN 0-87892-289-X); tchrs' manual 2.16 (ISBN 0-87892-290-3); 124.50 (ISBN 0-87892-288-1). Economy Co.
Read, Ethel M. Lo, the Poor Indian: A Saga of the Suisun Indians of California. LC 80-82306. 580p. (Orig.). 1980. 18.00 (ISBN 0-914330-34-9); pap. 10.00 (ISBN 0-914330-37-3). Panorama West.
Read, F. H. Electromagnetic Radiation. LC 79-41484. (Manchester Physics Ser.). 352p. 1980. 58.50 (ISBN 0-471-27718-5); pap. 23.00 (ISBN 0-471-27714-2). Wiley.
Read, Forrest. Seventy-Six: One World & the Cantos of Ezra Pound. LC 80-15892. (Illus.). 475p. 1981. 25.00x (ISBN 0-8078-1455-5); pap. 14.00x (ISBN 0-8078-4076-9). U of NC Pr.
Read, Frank T. & McGough, Lucy S. Let Them Be Judged: The Judicial Integration of the Deep South. LC 78-876. 1978. 27.50 (ISBN 0-8108-1118-9). Scarecrow.
Read, H. H. & Watson, Janet. Introduction & Geology, 2 vols. Incl. Vol. 1. Principles. 2nd ed. LC 76-50637. 1977. 27.95 (ISBN 0-470-99031-7); Vol. 2, 2 pts. LC 75-501. 1975; Pt. 1. Early Stages of Earth History. 221p. 19.95 (ISBN 0-470-71165-5); Pt. 2. Later Stages of Earth History. 371p. 24.95 (ISBN 0-470-71166-3). Halsted Pr.
Read, Herbert. A Concise History of Modern Painting. (World of Art Ser.). (Illus.). 1974. pap. 9.95 (ISBN 0-19-519940-5). Oxford U Pr.
--A Concise History of Modern Sculpture. (World of Art Ser.). (Illus.). 1964. pap. 9.95 (ISBN 0-19-519941-3). Oxford U Pr.
--The Philosophy of Modern Art. 1964. pap. 7.50 (ISBN 0-571-06506-6, Pub. by Faber & Faber). Merrimack Bk Serv.
Read, Herbert E., ed. The Knapsack: A Pocket-Book of Prose & Verse. 7th ed. LC 79-51960. (Granger Poetry Library). 1981. Repr. of 1947 ed. 43.75x (ISBN 0-89609-193-7). Granger Bk.
Read, James & Yapp, Malcolm. Law. Killingray, Margaret & O'Connor, Edmund, eds. (World History Ser.). (Illus.). (gr. 10). 1980. Repr. of 1977 ed. lib. bdg. 5.95 (ISBN 0-89908-144-4); pap. text ed. 1.95 (ISBN 0-89908-119-3). Greenhaven.
Read, Jan. The Catalans. 1979. 21.95 (ISBN 0-571-10969-1, Pub. by Faber & Faber). Merrimack Bk Serv.
--Wines of Spain & Portugal. (Illus.). 1980. 13.95 (ISBN 0-571-10266-2, Pub. by Faber & Faber). Merrimack Bk Serv.
Read, John. Humour & Humanism in Chemistry. LC 79-8621. Repr. of 1947 ed. 38.00 (ISBN 0-404-18487-1). AMS Pr.
--Prelude to Chemistry: An Outline of Alchemy, Its Literature & Relationships. LC 79-8622. (Illus.). Repr. of 1937 ed. 39.50 (ISBN 0-404-18488-X). AMS Pr.
Read, Kenneth E. High Valley. LC 65-20581. (Illus.). lib. rep. ed. 17.50x (ISBN 0-684-15134-0, ScribT). Scribner.
--Other Voices. LC 79-26194. (Anthropology Ser.). 1980. pap. 6.95 (ISBN 0-88316-534-1). Chandler & Sharp.
Read, Leonard E. Freedom Freeway. 128p. 1979. 3.00 (ISBN 0-910614-61-X). Foun Econ Ed.
--Seeds of Progess. 128p. 1980. 3.00 (ISBN 0-910614-65-2); pap. 1.00 (ISBN 0-910614-66-0). Foun Econ Ed.
--Thoughts Rule the World. 128p. 1981. 6.00 (ISBN 0-910614-67-9). Foun Econ Ed.
Read, M. K. Juan Huarte de San Juan. (World Authors Ser.: No. 619). 1981. lib. bdg. 14.95 (ISBN 0-8057-6461-5). Twayne.
Read, Malcolm, jt. auth. see Murdoch, Brian.
Read, Miss The White Robin. 1980. 8.95 (ISBN 0-395-29452-5); pap. write for info. HM.
Read, P. G. Gemmological Instruments. 1978. 29.95 (ISBN 0-408-00316-2). Butterworths.
Read, Piers P. Alive: The Story of the Andes Survivors. 1975. pap. 2.50 (ISBN 0-380-00321-X, 51714). Avon.
--Polonaise. LC 76-15306. 1976. 10.00 o.p. (ISBN 0-397-01150-4). Lippincott.
--The Professor's Daughter. 1980. pap. 2.25 (ISBN 0-380-49981-9, 49981). Avon.
Read, Piers Paul. The Train Robbers. LC 78-4890. (Illus.). 1978. 10.95 o.s.i. (ISBN 0-397-01283-7). Lippincott.
--The Upstart. 352p. 1979. pap. 2.25 (ISBN 0-380-49023-4, 49023). Avon.
Read, R. B. San Francisco Affordable Feasts, Vol. 1. LC 77-74627. (A California Living Book). (Illus.). 1977. pap. 3.95 (ISBN 0-89395-001-7). Cal Living Bks.
Read, Ralph. When the Cook Can't Look: A Cooking Handbook for the Blind & Visually Impaired. 144p. 1981. 9.95 (ISBN 0-8264-0034-5). Continuum.
Read, Randy, jt. auth. see Rusk, Tom.
Read, Ronald C. Tangrams: Three Hundred & Thirty Puzzles. 1978. pap. 2.50 (ISBN 0-486-21483-4). Dover.

Read, Stanley E. & Zabriskie, John B., eds. Streptococcal Diseases & the Immune Response. LC 79-26638. 1980. 45.00 (ISBN 0-12-583880-8). Acad Pr.

Read, Thomas. The Female Poets of America: With Portraits, Biographical Notices, & Specimens of Their Writings. LC 76-9777. (Illus.). 1978. Repr. of 1857 ed. 50.00 (ISBN 0-8103-4290-1). Gale.

Read, W. L., jt. auth. see Chappell, R. T.

Read, William M. Michigan Manuscript 18 of the Gospels. LC 44-13750. (Publications in Language & Literature: No. 11). (Illus.). 75p. 1942. pap. 5.00 (ISBN 0-295-95219-9). U of Wash Pr.

Read, William R. & Ineson, Frank A. Brazil 1980: The Protestant Handbook. 1973. pap. 4.95 (ISBN 0-912552-04-2). MARC.

Reade, Charles. Cloister & the Hearth. 1955. 7.50x o.p. (ISBN 0-460-00029-2, Evman). Dutton.

--Cream... Contains Jack of All Trades, a Matter-of-Fact Romance, & the Autobiography of a Thief. LC 80-2495. 1981. Repr. of 1858 ed. 35.00 (ISBN 0-404-19129-0). AMS Pr.

--It Is Never Too Late to Mend: A Matter-of-Fact Romance, 3 vols. in 2. LC 80-2496. 1981. Repr. of 1857 ed. Set. 104.00 (ISBN 0-404-19130-4). Vol. 1 (ISBN 0-404-19131-2). Vol. 2 (ISBN 0-404-19132-0). AMS Pr.

Reade, Eric. History & Heartburn: The Saga of Australian Film, 1896-1978. 353p. 1980. 40.00 (ISBN 0-8386-3082-0). Fairleigh Dickinson.

Reade, Isabel, tr. see Anderson Imbert, Enrique.

Reade, Quinn. Quest of the Dark Lady. 1976. pap. 1.25 (ISBN 0-505-51101-0). Tower Bks.

Reade, William W. The Outcast. Wolff, Robert L., ed. LC 75-1525. (Victorian Fiction Ser.). 1975. Repr. of 1875 ed. lib. bdg. 66.00 (ISBN 0-8240-1597-5). Garland Pub.

Reade, Winwood & Hosking, Eric. Nesting Birds, Eggs & Fledglings in Color. rev. ed. (Color Ser.). (Illus.). 1974. 9.95 (ISBN 0-7137-0710-0, Pub by Blandford Pr England). Sterling.

Reader, D. H. Zulu Tribe in Transition. 1966. text ed. 8.75x (ISBN 0-7190-0258-3). Humanities.

Reader, Dennis J. Coming Back Alive. LC 79-5147. (Illus.). 256p. (gr. 7 up). 1981. 8.95 (ISBN 0-686-68070-7); PLB 8.99 (ISBN 0-686-68071-5). Random.

Reader, John. Missing Links & the Men Who Found Them. (Illus.). 181p. 1981. 19.95 (ISBN 0-316-73590-6). Little.

Reader, John & Croze, Harvey. Pyramids of Life: Illuminations of Nature's Fearful Symmetry. LC 76-50638. 1977. 12.95 o.p. (ISBN 0-397-01151-2). Lippincott.

Reader, Mark, et al, eds. Atom's Eve: Ending the Nuclear Age, an Anthology. (McGraw-Hill Paperbacks Ser.). 288p. (Orig.). 1980. pap. 5.95 (ISBN 0-07-051287-6, SB). McGraw.

Reader, W. J. A House in the City. 1979. 30.00 (ISBN 0-7134-1647-5, Pub. by Batsford England). David & Charles.

Reader's Digest. Almanac & Yearbook 1981. (Illus.). 1981. 6.95 (ISBN 0-89577-090-3, Pub. by Reader's Digest). Norton.

Readers Digest. Animals Can Be Almost Human. 1980. 16.95 (ISBN 0-89577-069-5, Pub. by Readers Digest Assoc). Norton.

Reader's Digest. Back to Basics. (Illus.). 1981. 19.95 (ISBN 0-89577-086-5, Pub. by Reader's Digest). Norton.

--Crafts & Hobbies: A Step-by-Step Guide to Creative Skills. Date not set. 19.95 (ISBN 0-686-69221-7). Readers Digest Pr.

--Drive America. (Illus.). 1981. 22.95 (ISBN 0-89577-085-7, Pub. by Reader's Digest). Norton.

--Joy of Nature. (Illus.). 1977. 16.95 (ISBN 0-89577-036-9, Pub. by Reader's Digest). Norton.

--Reader's Digest Crafts & Hobbies. (Illus.). 1980. 19.95 (ISBN 0-89577-063-6, Pub. by Readers Digest Assoc). Norton.

--Reader's Digest Stories Behind Everyday Things. (Illus.). 1980. 19.95 (ISBN 0-89577-068-7, Pub. by Readers Digest Assoc). Norton.

--Stories Behind Everyday Things. 19.95 (ISBN 0-89577-068-7). Readers Digest Pr.

Readers Digest. Treasury for Young Readers. 1979. 14.95 (ISBN 0-89577-064-4, Pub. by Readers Digest Assoc). Norton.

Reader's Digest, ed. Natural Wonders of the World. (Illus.). 464p. 1980. 19.95 (ISBN 0-89577-087-3, Pub by Reader's Digest Assoc). Norton.

--Reader's Digest Nineteen-Eighty One Almanac & Yearbook. 16th ed. (Illus.). 1981. 6.95 (ISBN 0-89577-090-3, Pub. by Reader's Digest Assoc). Norton.

--The World's Best Fairy Tales. (Illus.). 1980. 16.95 (ISBN 0-89577-078-4, Pub. by Reader's Digest). Norton.

Reader's Digest Association, Canada. Outdoors Canada. (Illus.). 1980. 24.95 (ISBN 0-393-01366-9). Norton.

Readers Digest Editorial Staff. Animals You Will Never Forget. (Illus.). 1969. 16.95 (ISBN 0-393-21422-2). Norton.

Reader's Digest Editors. Book of Christmas. (Illus.). 304p. 1973. 15.95 o.p. (ISBN 0-393-21418-4). Norton.

Readers Digest Editors. Family Word Finder. 832p. 1975. 16.95 (ISBN 0-89577-023-7, Pub by Reader's Digest). Norton.

--The Story of America. (Illus.). 527p. 1975. 17.95 (ISBN 0-89577-024-5, Pub by Reader's Digest). Norton.

Reader's Digest Editors, ed. The Art of Living. (Orig.). 1980. pap. 2.50 (ISBN 0-425-04549-8). Berkley Pub.

--Secrets of the Past. (Orig.). 1980. pap. 2.50 (ISBN 0-425-04551-X). Berkley Pub.

--Tests & Teasers. (Orig.). 1980. pap. 2.50 (ISBN 0-425-04552-8). Berkley Pub.

Readey, Helen & Readey, William. Mathematical Concepts for Nursing: A Workbook. LC 79-20751. 1980. 7.95 (ISBN 0-201-06166-X). A-W.

Readey, Helen, jt. auth. see Berni, Rosemarian.

Readey, Helen, et al. Introduction to Nursing Essentials: A Handbook. LC 76-41198. (Illus.). 1977. pap. text ed. 9.50 (ISBN 0-8016-4099-7). Mosby.

Readey, William, jt. auth. see Readey, Helen.

Reading, H. G., jt. ed. see Ballance, P. F.

Reading, Hugo F. A Dictionary of the Social Sciences. 1977. 14.00 (ISBN 0-7100-8642-3); pap. 6.95 (ISBN 0-7100-8650-4). Routledge & Kegan.

Ready, John, ed. Lasers in Modern Industry. LC 79-66705. (Manufacturing Update Ser.). (Illus.). 1979. 29.00 (ISBN 0-87263-052-8). SME.

Ready, Robert. Hazlitt at Table. LC 79-22811. 128p. 1981. 13.50 (ISBN 0-8386-2414-6). Fairleigh Dickinson.

Reagan, Charles E. Ethics for Scientific Researchers. 2nd ed. 184p. 1971. 11.75 (ISBN 0-398-01558-9). C C Thomas.

Reagan, Cora L. Handbook of Auditory Perceptual Training. 168p. 1973. 11.75 (ISBN 0-398-02885-0). C C Thomas.

Reagan, Cora L., jt. auth. see Cunningham, Susanne A.

Reagan, J., et al, eds. Electrical Maintenance & Installation: Supplementary Training Material. (Engineering Craftsmen: No. J22S). (Illus.). 1976. pap. text ed. 19.95x (ISBN 0-85083-329-9). Intl Ideas.

Reagan, James W., jt. ed. see Keebler, Catherine M.

Reagan, John H. Memoirs of John H. Reagan, Postmaster General of the Confederacy & Early Texas Statesman. 12.50 o.p. (ISBN 0-8363-0068-8). Jenkins.

Reagan, Michael D. The New Federalism. 192p. 1972. 3.95 (ISBN 0-19-501585-1). Oxford U Pr.

--The New Federalism. 175p. 1972. pap. text ed. 2.95x o.p. (ISBN 0-19-501584-3). Oxford U Pr.

Reagan, Michael D. & Sanzone, John G. The New Federalism. 2nd ed. 208p. 1981. pap. text ed. 3.95x (ISBN 0-19-502772-8). Oxford U Pr.

Reagan, Reginald. One Man's Research: The Autobiography of Reginald L. Reagan. LC 80-66703. 1980. 10.95 (ISBN 0-89754-011-5); pap. 3.50 (ISBN 0-89754-010-7). Dan River Pr.

Reagan, Ronald & Hobbs, Charles. Ronald Reagan's Call to Action. (Illus.). 176p. 1976. pap. 1.75 o.s.i. (ISBN 0-446-84233-8). Warner Bks.

Reage, Pauline. Story of O: Part Two, Return to the Chateau. D'Estree, Sabine, tr. from Fr. LC 77-155130. Orig. Title: Retour a Roissy. 158p. 1980. pap. 2.25 (ISBN 0-394-17658-8, B364, BC). Grove.

Reagen, Michael V. & Stoughton, Donald M., eds. School Behind Bars: A Descriptive Overview of Correctional Education in the American. LC 75-40001. 1976. 15.00 (ISBN 0-8108-0891-9). Scarecrow.

Reagen, Michael V., ed. see American Foundation for Continuing Education at Syracuse University.

Real Estate Education Co. & Grubb & Ellis Commercial Brokerage Co. Successful Leasing & Selling of Office Property. 1980. 3-ring binder 49.95 (ISBN 0-88462-312-2). Real Estate Ed Co.

Real Estate Education Company & Grub & Ellis Commercial Brokerage Co. Successful Industrial Real Estate Brokerage. 2nd ed. 327p. 1980. 3-ring binder 49.95 o.p. (ISBN 0-695-81501-6). Real Estate Ed Co.

Real Estate Education Company Staff & Grubb & Ellis Company. Successful Leasing & Selling of Retail Property. 250p. 1980. 49.95 (ISBN 0-88462-315-7). Real Estate Ed Co.

Real Estate Research Corporation. Air Rights & Highways. rev. ed. LC 77-97085. (Technical Bulletin Ser.: No. 64). (Illus.). 1969. pap. 4.75 (ISBN 0-87420-064-4). Urban Land.

Real, H. G., jt. auth. see Fox, R. M.

Real, Linton M. First Steps in Horsemastership. LC 72-92314. (Illus.). 7.50 o.p. (ISBN 0-668-02761-4). Arco.

Reams, Bernard D., Jr. & Dunn, Donald J. Immigration & Nationality Law Review: 1976-77, 3 vols. 1977. Vol. 1. lib. bdg. 32.50 (ISBN 0-930342-08-9); Vol. 2, 1978-79. lib. bdg. 32.50 (ISBN 0-930342-67-4); Vol. 3. lib. bdg. 32.50 (ISBN 0-89941-061-8). W S Hein.

Reamy, Lois. TravelAbility: A Guide for Physically Disabled Travelers in the United States. 1978. 11.95 (ISBN 0-02-601170-0). Macmillan.

Reaney, P. H. A Dictionary of British Surnames. 2nd ed. 1976. 42.00 (ISBN 0-7100-8106-5). Routledge & Kegan.

--The Origin of English Surnames. 1980. pap. 8.95 (ISBN 0-7100-0353-6). Routledge & Kegan.

Reap, James. Athens: A Pictorial History. Friedman, Donna R., ed. (Illus.). 208p. 1981. pap. price not set (ISBN 0-89865-110-7). Donning Co.

Reapsome, James, et al, eds. Evangelical Missions Quarterly, Vols. 10-12. LC 71-186301. (Illus.). 1978. Set. 16.95x (ISBN 0-87808-708-7). William Carey Lib.

--Evangelical Missions Quarterly, Vols. 13-15. LC 71-186301. 803p. 1980. Repr. 19.95 (ISBN 0-87808-709-5). William Carey Lib.

Reapsome, James W., et al, eds. Evangelical Missions Quarterly, Vols. 7-9. LC 71-186301. 1973. Set. 13.95x (ISBN 0-87808-707-9). William Carey Lib.

Reardon. A Guide to Plastic Surgery for Men. 1981. write for info. Everest Hse.

Reardon, B. Liberalism & Tradition. LC 75-7214. 320p. 1975. 42.00 (ISBN 0-521-20776-2). Cambridge U Pr.

Reardon, B. M. From Coleridge to Gore: A Century of Religious Thought in Britain. 1971. 15.00x o.p. (ISBN 0-582-48510-X). Longman.

Reardon, Bernard M. Religious Thought in the Nineteenth Century. (Orig.). 1966. 49.50 (ISBN 0-521-06049-4); pap. 12.50x (ISBN 0-521-09386-4). Cambridge U Pr.

Reardon, James. The Sweet Life of Jimmy Riley. 1981. 13.95 (ISBN 0-686-68760-4, Wyndham Bks). S&S.

Reardon, Joan & Thorsen, Kristine A. Poetry by American Women, 1900-1975: A Bibliography. LC 78-11944. 1979. 27.50 (ISBN 0-8108-1173-1). Scarecrow.

Reardon, Maureen & Sanders, Peter. Match Point. LC 75-22012. (The Venture Ser, a Reading Incentive Program). (Illus.). 76p. (gr. 7-12,RL 4.5-6.5). 1975. text ed. 23.25 ea. pack of 5 (ISBN 0-8172-0235-8). Follett.

Reardon, Maureen, jt. auth. see Conta, Marcia.

Reardon, Patrick, jt. auth. see Stanat, Kirby W.

Reardon, Ray. Classic Snooker. LC 76-20094. 1976. 10.50 (ISBN 0-7153-7244-0). David & Charles.

--Ray Reardon's Fifty Best Trick Shots. LC 80-69348. (Illus.). 128p. 1980. 11.95 (ISBN 0-7153-7993-3). David & Charles.

Reaske, Herbert. Monarch Notes on Tolstoy's Anna Karenina. (Orig.). pap. 1.95 (ISBN 0-671-00571-5). Monarch Pr.

Reason, Joyce. To Be a Pilgrim (John Bunyan) 1961. pap. 1.95 (ISBN 0-87508-625-X). Chr Lit.

Reason, Peter & Rowan, John. Human Inquiry: A Sourcebook of New Paradigm Research. 1981. price not set (ISBN 0-471-27936-6, Pub. by Wiley Interscience). Wiley.

Reasoner, Charles F., intro. by. For Kids Only. LC 76-28183. (Illus.). (gr. 1 up). 1977. 8.95 o.s.i. (ISBN 0-440-02738-1); pap. 4.95 (ISBN 0-440-02690-3). Delacorte.

Reasoner, James M. Texas Wind. (Orig.). 1980. pap. 1.95 (ISBN 0-532-23201-1). Manor Bks.

Reasons & Purdue. Ideology of Social Problems. 15.95 (ISBN 0-88284-110-6). Alfred Pub.

Reasons, C., jt. auth. see Goff, C.

Reaves, Paul M., jt. auth. see Etgen, William M.

Reavey, George, ed. & tr. The New Russian Poets. bilingual ed. 320p. 1981. pap. 9.95 (ISBN 0-7145-2715-7, Pub. by M. Boyars). Merrimack Bk Serv.

Reavey, George, tr. see Mayakovsky, Vladimir.

Reavin, Sam. Hurray for Captain Jane. LC 79-153793. (Illus.). (gr. k-3). 1971. 5.95 o.s.i. (ISBN 0-8193-0511-1, Four Winds); PLB 5.41 o.s.i. (ISBN 0-8193-0512-X). Schol Bk Serv.

Reavin, Sara. Elise. (Orig.). 1980. pap. 2.95 (ISBN 0-451-09483-2, Sig). NAL.

Reay, D. A. Industrial Energy Conservation: A Handbook for Engineers & Managers. 2nd ed. (Illus.). 1979. 60.00 (ISBN 0-08-023273-6). Pergamon.

Reay, D. A., jt. auth. see Dunn, P. D.

Reay, David A. History of Man-Powered Flight. 1977. text ed. 23.00 (ISBN 0-08-021738-9). Pergamon.

Reay, Lee. Incredible Journey: Through the Hole-in-the-Rock. Hechtle, Ranier, ed. (Illus.). 128p. (Orig.). 1981. 5.95 (ISBN 0-934826-05-6); pap. 3.95 (ISBN 0-934826-06-4). Meadow Lane.

--Lambs in the Meadow. LC 79-66222. (Illus.). 1979. 8.95 (ISBN 0-934826-00-5); pap. 5.95 (ISBN 0-934826-01-3). Meadow Lane.

Reay-Smith, John. Discovering Spanish Wine. (Illus.). 1977. 14.00 (ISBN 0-7091-5464-X). Transatlantic.

Rebarchek, Ray. Memoirs of an Alaskan Farmer. LC 79-56330. 1981. 8.95 (ISBN 0-533-04526-6). Vantage.

Rebay, Luciano. Alberto Moravia. LC 77-126544. (Columbia Essays on Modern Writers Ser.: No. 52). (Orig.). 1970. pap. 2.00 (ISBN 0-231-02762-1, MW52). Columbia U Pr.

Reber, Jan & Shaw, Paul. Executive Protection Manual. 1976. 39.95 (ISBN 0-916070-02-6); soft cover 29.95. MTI Tele.

Reber, Ralph W. & Terry, Gloria B. Behavioral Insights for Supervision. new ed. (Illus.). 320p. 1975. pap. 11.95 ref. ed. (ISBN 0-13-073163-3). P-H.

Rebert, Jo & O'Hara, Jean. Copper Enameling. 2.95 (ISBN 0-934706-00-X). Prof Pubns Ohio.

Rebeta-Burditt, Joyce. The Cracker Factory. 1977. 8.95 o.s.i. (ISBN 0-02-601250-2, 60125). Macmillan.

Rebholz, R. A., ed. Sir Thomas Wyatt: The Complete Poems. LC 80-53980. 558p. 1981. text ed. 25.00x (ISBN 0-300-02681-1); pap. 5.95x (ISBN 0-300-02688-9). Yale U Pr.

Rebhorn, Eldon. Woodturning. (gr. 9-12). 1970. text ed. 13.28 (ISBN 0-87345-047-7). McKnight.

Rebisz, J., ed. see Woodford, Protase E. & Kernan, Doris.

Reblitz, Arthur A. & Bowers, Q. David. Treasures of Mechanical Music. (Illus.). 634p. 1981. 25.00 (ISBN 0-911572-20-1). Vestal.

Reboul, P., jt. auth. see Wordingham, J. A.

Reboullet, et al. Methode Orange, Bk 1. (Methode Orange Ser.). (Illus., Fr.). (gr. 7-12). 1979. pap. text ed. 4.25 (ISBN 0-88345-406-8). Regents Pub.

--Methode Orange - Workbook 1. (Methode Orange Ser.). (Illus., Fr.). (gr. 7-12). 1979. pap. text ed. 4.25 (ISBN 0-686-67708-0); tchrs' manual 5.95 (ISBN 0-88345-411-4); cassettes 70.00 (ISBN 0-686-60844-5); slides 120.00 (ISBN 0-686-60845-3). Regents Pub.

Rebreau, Liviu. Ion. Aderman, Ralph M., ed. LC 67-25190. 1967. 16.95x (ISBN 0-8057-5695-7). Irvington.

Rebuck, John, et al. The Reticuloendothelial System. LC 79-23857. (International Academy of Pathology Monograph). 342p. 1980. Repr. 21.50 (ISBN 0-89874-101-7). Krieger.

Reburn, Rockne. How to Pass the California Bar Exam. (Illus.). 141p. (Orig.). 1980. 14.00 (ISBN 0-9605672-0-8). Bar-None.

Rech, R. & Moore, K. E., eds. Introduction to Psychopharmacology. LC 78-116995. 1971. 15.50 (ISBN 0-911216-12-X). Raven.

Rechcigl, M., Jr., ed. Nitrogen, Electrolytes Water & Metabolism. (Comparative Animal Nutrition: Vol. 3). (Illus.). 1979. 78.00 (ISBN 3-8055-2829-9). S Karger.

Rechcigl, Miloslav, ed. Handbook of Nutritional Requirements in a Functional Context. 1981. Vol. 1. 72.95 (ISBN 0-686-69343-4); Vol. 2. 77.95 (ISBN 0-8493-3958-8). CRC Pr.

Rechcigl, Miroslav, ed. Handbook in Nutrition & Food, CRC: Section E-Nutritional Disorders, Vols. 2-3. 1978. Vol. II, 548p. 69.95 (ISBN 0-8493-2797-0); Vol. III, 388p. 59.95 (ISBN 0-8493-2798-9). CRC Pr.

Rechowicz, Michael. Electric Power at Low Temperatures. (Monographs in Electrical & Electronic Engineering). (Illus.). 150p. 1975. 36.00x (ISBN 0-19-859312-0). Oxford U Pr.

Rechs, James R., jt. auth. see Regestein, Quentin R.

Rechs, Robert J. Helicopter External Loads, Vol. 1. (Planning & Operation Ser.). (Illus.). 100p. (Orig.). 1981. pap. text ed. 5.00 (ISBN 0-937568-19-8). Rechs Pubns.

--Helicopter External Loads, Vol. 2. (Certification & Training Ser.). 100p. 1980. pap. text ed. 5.00 (ISBN 0-937568-21-X). Rechs Pubns.

Rechtschaffen, Bernard & Marck, Louis. Two Thousand & One German & English Idioms: 2001 Deutsche und Englische Idiome. Date not set. pap. 9.95 (ISBN 0-8120-0474-4). Barron. Postponed.

Rechy, John. Rushes. LC 79-2302. 288p. 1981. pap. 3.50 (ISBN 0-394-17883-1, BC). Grove.

Recinos, Adrian & Goetz, Delia, trs. Popol Vuh: The Sacred Book of the Ancient Quiche: Spanish Version of the Original Maya. (Civilization of the American Indian Ser.: No. 29). (Eng). 1978. Repr. of 1950 ed. 9.95 (ISBN 0-8061-0205-5). U of Okla Pr.

Reck, Andrew J., ed. Selected Writings: George Herbert Mead. LC 80-27248. lxxii, 416p. 1981. 24.00x (ISBN 0-226-51672-5); pap. 10.95 (ISBN 0-226-51671-7). U of Chicago Pr.

Reck, David. Music of the Whole Earth. LC 76-12493. 1977. 19.95 (ISBN 0-684-14631-2, ScribT); pap. 15.95 (ISBN 0-684-14633-9, SL648, ScribT). Scribner.

Reck, Franklin M. Romance of American Transportation. rev. ed. LC 62-18235. (Illus.). (gr. 5 up). 1962. 7.95 o.p. (ISBN 0-690-71033-X, TYC-J). T Y Crowell.

Recker, Wilfred W., jt. auth. see Paaswell, Robert E.

Reck-Malleczewen, Friedrich P. Diary of a Man in Despair. Rubens, Paul, tr. LC 74-85783. 1970. 6.95 o.s.i. (ISBN 0-02-601400-9). Macmillan.

Record, Jane C. Staffing Primary Care in Nineteen Ninety: Physician Replacement & Cost Savings. (Health Care & Society Ser.: No. 6). 1981. text ed. 23.50 (ISBN 0-8261-3370-3); pap. text ed. cancelled (ISBN 0-8261-3371-1). Springer Pub.

Record, Jeffrey. Force Reductions in Europe: Starting Over. LC 80-83753. (Special Report Ser.). 92p. 1980. 6.50 (ISBN 0-89549-027-7). Inst Foreign Policy Anal.

--Sizing up the Soviet Army. (Studies in Defense Policy). 51p. 1975. pap. 3.95 (ISBN 0-8157-7367-6). Brookings.

--U. S. Nuclear Weapons in Europe: Issues & Alternatives. (Studies in Defense Policy). 70p. 1974. pap. 3.95 (ISBN 0-8157-7365-X). Brookings.

Record, Jeffrey, jt. auth. see Binkin, Martin.

Record, K. Jeffrey, jt. auth. see Lawrence, Richard D.

Record, Robert. The Castle of Knowledge. LC 74-28882. (English Experience Ser.: No. 760). 1975. Repr. of 1556 ed. 44.00 (ISBN 90-221-0760-4). Walter J Johnson.

--The Path-Way to Knowledg, Containing the First Principles of Geometrie. LC 74-80206. (English Experience Ser.: No. 687). 1974. Repr. of 1551 ed. 18.50 (ISBN 90-221-0687-X). Walter J Johnson.

Record, Wilson. Race & Radicalism: The NAACP & the Communist Party in Conflict. 237p. 1966. pap. 3.95 (ISBN 0-8014-9035-9, CP35). Cornell U Pr.

Rector, Barry M. & Rector, Floyd C., eds. The Kidney, 2 vols. 2nd ed. 1981. Vol. 1. text ed. write for info. (ISBN 0-7216-1967-3); Vol. 2. text ed. write for info. (ISBN 0-7216-1968-1); Set. text ed. write for info. (ISBN 0-7216-1969-X). Saunders.

Rector, Floyd C., jt. ed. see Rector, Barry M.

Rector, Justine J., jt. auth. see Tinney, James S.

Rector, Robert E. & Zwick, Earl J. Finite Mathematics & Its Applications. LC 78-69547. (Illus.). 1979. text ed. 17.50 (ISBN 0-395-27206-8); inst. manual 0.75 (ISBN 0-395-27207-6). HM.

Rector, Russell & Alexy, George. The Eight Thousand & Eighty Six Book. 1980. pap. 16.99 (ISBN 0-931988-29-2). Osborne-McGraw.

Redbook Editors. The Expectant Mother. pap. 2.50 (ISBN 0-671-42413-0). PB.

Redbook Magazine. Redbook Wise Woman's Diet: All-Time Favorite Recipes. Pomeroy, Ruth, ed. (Illus.). 176p. 1980. 14.95 (ISBN 0-88421-161-4). Butterick Pub.

Redcliff, M. R. Agrarian Reform & Peasant Organization on the Ecuadorian Coast. (Univ. of London Institute of Latin American Studies Monographs: No. 8). (Illus.). 1978. text ed. 25.75x (ISBN 0-485-17708-0, Athlone Pr). Humanities.

Redd, Kathleen M. & Harkins, Arthur M., eds. Educational Futures Sourcebook II: Selections from the Second Conference of the World Future Society's Education Section. 1980. write for info. World Future.

Reddall, Henry. Fact, Fancy & Fable. LC 68-25519. 1968. Repr. of 1889 ed. 18.00 (ISBN 0-8103-3093-8). Gale.

Reddan, Harold J. Sociology: Advanced Test for the G. R. E. 2nd ed. LC 66-16410. (Orig.). 1972. pap. 4.95 o.p. (ISBN 0-668-01444-X). Arco.

Reddding, S. G. The Working Class Manager. 1979. text ed. 23.00x (ISBN 0-566-00291-4, Pub. by Gower Pub Co England). Renouf.

Reddell, James R. A Preliminary Bibliography of Mexican Cave Biology with a Checklist of Published Records. (Association for Mexican Cave Studies: Bulletin 3). 184p. 1971. 10.00. Speleo Pr.

Reddell, James R., ed. Studies on the Caves & Cave Fauna of the Yucatan Peninsula. (Association for Mexican Cave Studies: Bulletin 6). 296p. 1977. 13.00. Speleo Pr.

Reddell, James R. & Mitchell, Robert W., eds. Studies on the Cavernicole Fauna of Mexico. (Association for Mexican Cave Studies: Bulletin 4). 239p. 1971. 13.00. Speleo Pr.

Reddell, James R., jt. ed. see Mitchell, Robert W.

Redden, Kenneth R. & Veron, Enid L. Modern Legal Glossary. 576p. 1980. 19.00 (ISBN 0-87215-237-5). Michie.

Redden, Kenneth R., jt. auth. see Saltzburg, Stephen A.

Redder, Ronald. Perforated Mood-Swing Book. LC 76-186644. (Illus.). 100p. (Orig.). (YA) 1972. pap. 2.50 (ISBN 0-570-03134-6, 12-2381). Concordia.

Reddick, De Witt C. The Mass Media & the School Newspaper. 1976. text ed. 13.95x (ISBN 0-534-00436-9). Wadsworth Pub.

Reddick, John. Danzig Trilogy of Gunter Grass: A Study of The Tin Drum, Cat & Mouse, & Dog Years. 1974. 13.50 o.p. (ISBN 0-15-123815-4). HarBraceJ.

Reddick, Marshall E., jt. auth. see Cohen, William A.

Reddin, Chitra P. Forms of Evil in the Gothic Novel. Varma, Devendra P., ed. LC 79-8472. (Gothic Studies & Dissertations Ser.). 1980. lib. bdg. 28.00x (ISBN 0-405-12669-7). Arno.

Reddin, Opal. Have It His Way. LC 78-73143. 1980. pap. 1.95 (ISBN 0-88243-717-8, 02-0717). Gospel Pub.

Redding, David A. Lives He Touched: The Relationships of Jesus. LC 77-20443. 1978. 5.95 o.p. (ISBN 0-06-066815-6, HarpR). Har-Row.

--The Parables He Told. LC 76-9972. (Harper Jubilee Book). 192p. 1976. pap. 1.95 o.p. (ISBN 0-06-066813-X, HJ-29, HarpR). Har-Row.

Redding, J. Saunders. They Came in Chains. rev. ed. LC 73-401. 1973. 6.25 o.s.i. (ISBN 0-397-00812-0). Lippincott.

Redding, Robert H. The Partners. LC 80-1660. (Double D Western Ser.). 192p. 1981. 9.95 (ISBN 0-385-17007-6). Doubleday.

Redding, Saunders, jt. ed. see Davis, Arthur P.

Reddish, V. C. The Physics of Stellar Interiors. 1975. 19.50x (ISBN 0-8448-0610-2). Crane-Russak Co.

--Stellar Formation. 225p. 1976. text ed. 45.00 (ISBN 0-08-018062-0); pap. text ed. 19.50 (ISBN 0-08-023053-9). Pergamon.

Reddoch, Mildred L. So White, the Lilies. 1981. 5.95 (ISBN 0-8062-1629-8). Carlton.

Reddy, A. K. Technology, Development & the Environment: A Re-Appraisal. (Illus.). 60p. 1980. 5.75 (ISBN 0-08-025693-7). Pergamon.

Reddy, J. N., jt. auth. see Oden, J. T.

Reddy, K. N., jt. auth. see Kline, Daniel L.

Reddy, M. N., jt. auth. see Tuma, Jan J.

Reddy, P. S., et al, eds. Pericardial Disease. 1981. text ed. price not set (ISBN 0-89004-586-0). Raven.

Reddy, T. J. Less Than a Score, but a Point: Poems. LC 74-7173. 1974. pap. 2.95 o.p. (ISBN 0-394-71080-0, V-80, Vin). Random.

Reddy, T. Ramakrishna. India's Policy in the United Nations. LC 67-26816. 1968. 12.50 (ISBN 0-8386-6755-4). Fairleigh Dickinson.

Redei, L. Algebra, Vol. 1. 1966. 72.00 (ISBN 0-08-010954-3). Pergamon.

--Foundation of Euclidean & Non-Euclidean Geometries According to F. Klein. (International Series in Pure & Applied Mathematics: Vol. 97). 1968. 52.00 o.p. (ISBN 0-08-011965-4). Pergamon.

--The Theory of Finitely Generated Commutative Semigroups. (International Series in Pure & Applied Mathematics: Vol. 82). (Illus.). 1966. 42.00 (ISBN 0-08-010520-3). Pergamon.

Redekop, Calvin. Strangers Become Neighbors. (Studies in Anabaptist & Mennonite History Ser.: No. 22). (Illus.). 312p. 1980. 19.95x (ISBN 0-8361-1228-8). Herald Pr.

Redekop, J. Approaches to Canadian Politics. 1978. pap. 11.25 (ISBN 0-13-043729-8). P-H.

Redemptorist Pastoral Publication. The Illustrated Catechism. 112p. (Orig.). 1981. pap. 3.95 (ISBN 0-89243-135-0). Liguori Pubns.

Redenbaugh, Al. Trailer Tramp-Gone Fishing. Martin, Paul & Whattam, Al, eds. (Illus.). 101p. 1979. pap. 3.95 (ISBN 0-918146-15-1). Peninsula WA.

Redenius, Charles. The American Ideal of Equality & Constitutional Change: From Jefferson's Declaration to the Burger Court. (National University Publications, Political Science Ser.). 1981. 17.50 (ISBN 0-8046-9282-3). Kennikat.

Reder, Jack & Reeder, Carolyn. Shenandoah Vestiges: What the Mountain People Left Behind. LC 80-81761. 72p. 1980. pap. 3.75 (ISBN 0-915746-14-X). Potomac Appalach.

Redfern, George B. Evaluating Teachers & Administrators: A Performance Objective Approach. (Westview Special Studies in Education). 186p. 1980. lib. bdg. 18.50x (ISBN 0-89158-760-8); pap. text ed. 9.50x (ISBN 0-89158-890-6). Westview.

Redfern, M., ed. see Totterdell, B. & Bird, J.

Redfern, Roger A. Portrait of the Pennines. LC 75-434154. (Portrait Bks.). (Illus.). 192p. 1969. 10.50x (ISBN 0-7091-0872-9). Intl Pubns Serv.

Redfern, Ron. Corridors of Time: 1,700,000,000 Years of Earth. 200p. 1980. 50.00 (ISBN 0-8129-0922-4). Times Bks.

Redfield, Margaret, jt. ed. see Fei, Hsiao-Tung.

Redfield, Marion H., tr. see Bright, Robert.

Redford, Ken & Tremayne, Nick. Success in Golf. (Success Sportbooks Ser.). (Illus.). 1977. 9.95 (ISBN 0-7195-2862-3). Transatlantic.

Redford, Lawrence H., ed. The Occupation of Japan & Its Legacy to the Postwar World. 158p. pap. 4.00. MacArthur Memorial.

--The Occupation of Japan: Impact of Legal Refor, 212p. pap. 5.00. MacArthur Memorial.

Redgate, John. The Last Decathlon. 1980. pap. 2.50 o.s.i. (ISBN 0-440-14643-7). Dell.

Redgrave, Michael. Actor's Ways & Means. 1979. pap. 4.85 (ISBN 0-87830-516-5). Theatre Arts.

Redgrove, H. Stanley. Alchemy, Ancient & Modern. (Illus.). 141p. 1980. 20.00 (ISBN 0-89005-344-8). Ares.

Redgrove, Herbert S. Alchemy: Ancient & Modern. LC 79-8624. Repr. of 1922 ed. 23.50 (ISBN 0-404-18490-1). AMS Pr.

Redgrove, Hugh. Growing Trees & Shrubs. (Practical Gardening Ser.). (Illus.). 96p. (Orig.). 1979. pap. 10.50 (ISBN 0-589-01247-9, Pub. by Reed Bks Australia). C E Tuttle.

Redgrove, Peter. In the Country of the Skin. 1973. 12.00 (ISBN 0-7100-7514-6). Routledge & Kegan.

--Miss Carstairs Dress for Bloodings. 108p. 1981. pap. 5.95 (ISBN 0-7145-2557-X, Pub. by M Boyars). Merrimack Bk Serv.

--Weddings at Nether Powers & Other New Poems. 1979. pap. 7.95 (ISBN 0-7100-0255-6). Routledge & Kegan.

Redheffer, Raymond, jt. auth. see Levinson, Norman.

Redhouse, James. A Turkish & English Lexicon. 80.00x (ISBN 0-685-72063-2). Intl Bk Ctr.

Redinger, Reul O. Silver: An Instructional Guide to the Silversmith's Art. (Illus.). 144p. 1980. 14.95 (ISBN 0-13-810218-X, Spec); pap. 6.95 (ISBN 0-13-810200-7). P-H.

Redish, Martin H. Federal Jurisdiction: Tensions in the Allocation of Judicial Power. 370p. 1980. 25.00 (ISBN 0-672-84196-7). Michie.

Redknap, Christopher. Focus on Teachers' Centers. (General Ser.). 1977. pap. text ed. 13.25x (ISBN 0-85633-126-0, NFER). Humanities.

Redl, Fritz. Pre-Adolescents: What Makes Them Tick? 17p. 1974. pap. 1.00 (ISBN 0-686-12276-3). Jewish Bd Family.

Redl, Fritz & Wineman, David. Aggressive Child. 1957. 16.95 (ISBN 0-02-925870-7). Free Pr.

Redlich, F. C., jt. auth. see Hollingshead, A. B.

Redlich, F. C., ed. Social Psychiatry. LC 68-27002. (ARNMD Research Publications Ser: Vol.47). 1969. 25.00 (ISBN 0-89004-159-8). Raven.

Redlich, Josef. Austrian War Government. (Economic & Social History of the World War Ser.). 1929. 47.50x (ISBN 0-685-69855-6). Elliots Bks.

Redman, Alvin, ed. see Wilde, Oscar.

Redman, Barbara J. Consumer Behavior: Theory & Applications. (Illus.). 1979. pap. text ed. 12.50 (ISBN 0-87055-324-0). AVI.

Redman, Barbara J., jt. auth. see Redman, John C.

Redman, Barbara K. Issues and Concepts in Patient Education. (The Patient Education Series). 160p. 1981. pap. 11.50 (ISBN 0-8385-4405-3). ACC.

--The Process of Patient Teaching in Nursing. 4th ed. LC 80-15310. (Illus.). 294p. 1980. pap. text ed. 11.95 (ISBN 0-8016-4100-4). Mosby.

Redman, Barbara K., ed. Patterns for Distribution of Patient Education. (The Patient Education Series). 176p. 1981. pap. 11.50 (ISBN 0-8385-7776-8). ACC.

Redman, Ben R., tr. see Giraudoux, Jean.

Redman, Charles L. Research & Theory in Current Archeology. LC 73-6717. 384p. 1973. pap. text ed. 17.50 (ISBN 0-471-71291-4, Pub. by Wiley-Interscience). Wiley.

--The Rise of Civilization: From Early Farmers to Urban Society in the Ancient Near East. LC 78-1493. (Illus.). 1978. text ed. 24.95x (ISBN 0-7167-0056-5); pap. text ed. 14.95x (ISBN 0-7167-0055-7). W H Freeman.

Redman, Charles L., ed. Research & Theory in Current Archeology. 400p. 1980. Repr. of 1973 ed. lib. bdg. write for info. (ISBN 0-89874-226-9). Krieger.

Redman, Edith. Recipes for Healthier Childern. rev. ed. 1977. pap. 4.95 o.s.i. (ISBN 0-7715-9329-5). Vanguard.

Redman, John C. & Redman, Barbara J. Microeconomics: Resource Allocation & Price Theory. (Illus.). 1981. text ed. 17.50 (ISBN 0-87055-367-4). AVI.

Redman, William, jt. ed. see Borchardt, Jack.

Redmen, Edith. Recipes for Healthier Families. 208p. 1976. 9.95 o.s.i. (ISBN 0-7715-9940-4). Vanguard.

Redmile, Brenda. Make Your Own Dress Patterns. 1978. 17.95 (ISBN 0-7134-0389-6, Pub. by Batsford England). David & Charles.

--Making Patterns for Children's Clothes. (Illus.). 120p. 1980. 17.95 (ISBN 0-7134-2141-X, Pub. by Batsford England). David & Charles.

Redmond, C. F., jt. ed. see Lodge, H. C.

Redmond, Eugene, ed. see Dumas, Henry.

Redmond, J. Drama, Dance & Music. (Themes in Drama Ser.: No. 3). (Illus.). 260p. Date not set. 36.00 (ISBN 0-521-22180-3). Cambridge U Pr.

Redmond, J., et al, eds. Year's Work in English Studies, Vol. 58, 1977. 639p. 1980. text ed. 39.00x (ISBN 0-391-01320-3). Humanities.

Redmond, James, ed. see Morris, William.

Redmond, Kent C. & Smith, Thomas M. Project Whirlwind: The History of a Pioneer Computer. (History of Computing Ser.). (Illus.). 1980. 21.00 (ISBN 0-932376-09-6). Digital Pr.

Redmore, Fred H. Fundamentals of Chemistry. (Illus.). 1979. ref. ed. 20.95 (ISBN 0-13-335158-0); lab. manual 8.95 (ISBN 0-13-335174-2); 7.95 (ISBN 0-13-335182-3); sol. manual 6.95 (ISBN 0-13-335166-1). P-H.

Redmount, R. S., et al. Grievance-Response Mechanisms in the Ghetto. LC 74-151046. (Symposia on Law & Society Ser). 1971. Repr. of 1968 ed. lib. bdg. 17.50 (ISBN 0-306-70117-0). Da Capo.

Redpath, A. A. Why Do We Laugh? (Creative's Questions & Answers Ser.). (Illus.). 32p. (gr. 3-4). Date not set. PLB 5.65 (ISBN 0-87191-751-3); pap. 2.75 (ISBN 0-89812-220-1). Creative Ed. Postponed.

Redpath, Alan. Faith for the Times, Pt. 3: The Fruit of Deliverance. 1976. 3.95 o.p. (ISBN 0-8007-0779-6). Revell.

Redpath, Ann. Jim Boen--a Man of Opposites. 48p. (gr. 4-8). 1980. PLB 5.95 (ISBN 0-87191-744-0). Creative Ed.

Redpath, Ann, ed. see Frevert, Patricia D.

Redpath, Ann, ed. see Larson, Norita D.

Redpath, Peter A. A Simplified Introduction to the Wisdom of St. Thomas. LC 80-5230. 180p. 1980. lib. bdg. 17.50 (ISBN 0-8191-1058-2); pap. text ed. 8.50 (ISBN 0-8191-1059-0). U Pr of Amer.

Redshaw, L. C., ed. see Ilyushin, A. A. & Lenskii, V. S.

Redshaw, Thomas D. Heimaey. 40p. (Orig.). 1974. pap. text ed. 3.75x (ISBN 0-85105-258-4, Dolmen Pr). Humanities.

Redwood, Christopher, ed. A Delius Companion: A 70th Birthday Tribute to Eric Fenby. LC 76-57756. (Music Reprint Ser.). (Illus.). 1977. Repr. of 1976 ed. lib. bdg. 25.00 (ISBN 0-306-77532-8). Da Capo.

Redwood, John. Public Enterprise in Crisis: The Future of the Nationalised Industries. 211p. 1981. 19.50x (ISBN 0-631-12582-5, Pub. by Basil Blackwell England). Biblio Dist.

Ree, Gerry De La see De La Ree, Gerry.

Ree, J. Philosophy & Its Past. (Philosophy Now Ser.). 1978. text ed. 20.00x (ISBN 0-391-00544-8); pap. text ed. 9.25x (ISBN 0-391-00556-1). Humanities.

Reebie Associates, et al. Transguide: A Guide to Sources of Freight Transportation Information. LC 80-53144. 392p. 1980. 40.00 (ISBN 0-9604776-0-8). Reebie Assoc.

Reeby, Ellis A., et al. Continuous Advancement Program 2: Individualized Mathematics Objectives & Self-Tests. (Illus.). 207p. (Orig., Prog. Bk.). (gr. 8). 1973. pap. text ed. 3.50x o.p. (ISBN 0-686-66760-3). Ind Sch Pr.

--Continuous Advancement Program 2: Individualized Mathematics Self-Learning Packet. (Illus.). 315p. (Orig., Prog. Bk.). (gr. 8). 1973. pap. text ed. 4.50x o.p. (ISBN 0-686-66759-X). Ind Sch Pr.

--Continuous Advancement Program 2: Individualized Mathematics Tests & Answers. 345p. (Orig., Prog. Bk.). (gr. 8). 1973. pap. text ed. 15.00x o.p. (ISBN 0-88334-082-8). Ind Sch Pr.

Reece, B. L., jt. auth. see Park, W. M.

Reece, Colleen L. Heritage of Nurse O'Hara. (YA) 1977. 4.95 o.p. (ISBN 0-685-74272-5, Avalon). Bouregy.

--In Search of Twilight. (YA) 1978. 5.95 (ISBN 0-685-84748-9, Avalon). Bouregy.

--Nurse Autumn's Secret Love. 1979. 5.95 (ISBN 0-686-52547-7, Avalon). Bouregy.

--The Other Nine. (Orig.). 1981. pap. 6.50 (ISBN 0-8309-0288-0). Herald Hse.

Reece, Daphne E., jt. auth. see Storey, Joan.

Reece, Eileen. The Dieting Gourmet. 1976. 10.50 o.p. (ISBN 0-04-641028-7). Allen Unwin.

--Soups for All Seasons & a Collation of Sandwiches. 1976. 9.50 o.p. (ISBN 0-04-641032-5). Allen Unwin.

Reece, James S. & Anthony, Robert N. Accounting Principles Workbook. 5th ed. 1979. pap. text ed. 6.95 (ISBN 0-256-02171-6). Irwin.

Reece, James S., jt. auth. see Anthony, Robert N.

Reed. Electron Microprobe Analysis. LC 74-94356. (Monographs on Physics). (Illus.). 350p. 1975. 59.95 (ISBN 0-521-20466-6). Cambridge U Pr.

Reed, Ann & Pfaltz, Marilyn. Ladies Who Lunch. LC 72-1212. 1972. pap. 2.95 o.p. (ISBN 0-684-15059-X, SL723, ScribT). Scribner.

Reed, Arthur. Airport. LC 78-61230. (Careers Ser.). (Illus.). 1978. lib. bdg. 7.95 (ISBN 0-686-51119-0). Silver.
--F-Fourteen Tomcat. (Illus.). 1978. 12.50 (ISBN 0-684-15881-7, ScribT). Scribner.
Reed, Barry. The Verdict. 1980. lib. bdg. 14.95 (ISBN 0-8161-3175-9, Large Print Bks). G K Hall.
Reed, Bika. The Fields of Transformation. (Illus.). 1981. 8.95 (ISBN 0-89281-016-5). Inner Tradit.
Reed, Bill. Mr. Siggie Morrison with His Comb & Paper. (Australian Theatre Workshop Ser.). 1972. pap. text ed. 4.25x (ISBN 0-686-65323-8, 00525). Heinemann Ed.
--Truganinni. (Austalian Theatre Workshop Ser.). 1977. pap. text ed. 4.50x (ISBN 0-686-65425-0, 00529). Heinemann Ed.
Reed, Bobbie. Single on Sunday: A Manual for Successful Single Adult Ministries. 1979. pap. 5.50 (ISBN 0-570-03781-6, 12-2735). Concordia.
Reed, Bobbie & Johnson, Rex E. Bible Learning Activities: Youth - Grades Seven to Twelve. LC 73-87520. (Illus.). 155p. (Orig.). (gr. 7-12). 1974. pap. 2.95 o.p. (ISBN 0-8307-0239-3, 97-013-03). Regal.
Reed, Brenda & Walker, Freda. Advanced Hockey for Women. (Illus.). 182p. 1976. 18.50 (ISBN 0-571-09881-9). Transatlantic.
Reed, Brian. Diesel Hydraulic Locomotives of the Western Region: England. LC 74-81059. (Locomotive Studies). (Illus.). 112p. 1981. 16.95 (ISBN 0-7153-6769-2). David & Charles.
--One-Hundred Fifty Years of British Steam Locomotives. LC 75-10514. (Illus.). 128p. 1975. 19.95 (ISBN 0-7153-7051-0). David & Charles.
Reed, Brian & Rowledge, J. W. Stanier 4-6-0's of the LMS. 1977. 14.95 (ISBN 0-7153-7385-4). David & Charles.
Reed, Charles E., jt. ed. see Dempsey, Jerry A.
Reed, Chester A. Bird Guide: Land Birds East of the Rockies. 5.95 (ISBN 0-385-04809-2). Doubleday.
Reed, Dale, jt. ed. see Palm, Charles G.
Reed, Don C. Notes from an Underwater Zoo. (Illus.). 1981. 11.95. Dial.
Reed, Donald A. & Pattison, Patrick. Science Fiction Film Awards. 1981. lib. bdg. 14.95 (ISBN 0-912076-39-9); pap. 9.95 (ISBN 0-686-65799-3). Ese Calif.
Reed, Douglas. Behind the Scene. (Pt. 2 of Far & Wide). 1976. pap. 3.50x (ISBN 0-911038-41-8). Noontide.
--The Grand Design. 1977. pap. 2.00x (ISBN 0-911038-49-3). Noontide.
Reed, E., et al. Commercial Banking. 2nd ed. 1980. 18.95 (ISBN 0-13-152785-1). P-H.
Reed, Edward A., jt. auth. see Eary, Donald F.
Reed, Edward W., et al. Casebook in Commercial Banking. (Illus.). 1977. ref. ed. 9.95 (ISBN 0-13-117473-8). P-H.
Reed, G. A., jt. auth. see Sander, K. F.
Reed, G. H. Refrigeration. LC 74-15129. (Illus.). 1969. 8.95 (ISBN 0-8306-0295-X); pap. 4.95 (ISBN 0-8306-9295-9, 295). TAB Bks.
--Refrigeration: A Practical Manual for Apprentices. 3rd ed. (Illus.). 1974. pap. text ed. 12.40x (ISBN 0-85334-605-4). Intl Ideas.
--Refrigeration: A Practical Manual for Mechanics. (Illus.). 1972. 26.00x (ISBN 0-85334-531-7, Pub. by Applied Science). Burgess-Intl Ideas.
Reed, Gary. All About Swimming Pools. LC 76-20375. (Illus.). 1976. 6.95 o.p. (ISBN 0-8306-6844-6); pap. 4.95 (ISBN 0-8306-5844-0, 844). TAB Bks.
Reed, Gerald. Prescott & Dunn's Industrial Microbiology. 4th ed. (Illus.). 1981. lib. bdg. 59.00 (ISBN 0-87055-374-7). AVI.
Reed, Gerald & Peppler, Henry J. Yeast Technology. (Illus.). 1973. 35.00 (ISBN 0-87055-136-1). AVI.
Reed, Gervais, jt. auth. see Moseley, Spencer.
Reed, Glenn, jt. auth. see McCarter, Albert D.
Reed, Graham. Magic for Every Occasion. (Illus.). 128p. (gr. 5 up). 1981. 9.95 (ISBN 0-525-66733-4). Elsevier-Nelson.
--The Psychology of Anomalous Experience: A Cognitive Approach. 1972. text ed. 8.25x (ISBN 0-09-113240-1, Hutchinson U Lib). Humanities.
Reed, H. Clay. Delaware Colony. LC 77-95297. (Forge of Freedom Ser). (Illus.). (gr. 5-8). 1970. 8.95 (ISBN 0-02-775730-7, CCPr). Macmillan.
Reed, H. O. & Sidnell, R. G. The Materials of Music Composition Through Jazz, Rock, Pop, Folk, & Art Music, Book II: Exploring The Parameters. 1980. 14.95 (ISBN 0-201-06126-0); write for info. (ISBN 0-201-06122-8). A-W.
Reed, H. Owen & Sidnell, Robert G. Materials of Music Composition Book 1: Fundamentals. LC 76-55643. 1978. pap. text ed. 14.95 (ISBN 0-201-06125-2). A-W.
Reed, Henry. Lectures on English Literature from Chaucer to Tennyson. 411p. 1980. Repr. of 1876 ed. lib. bdg. 40.00 (ISBN 0-89984-430-8). Century Bookbindery.
Reed, Ione. Twenty-Five Oregon Weekend Adventures, Vol. II. LC 75-27462. (Illus.). 1979. pap. 4.95 (ISBN 0-89802-064-6). Beautiful Am.
Reed, Ishmael. Mumbo Jumbo. 1978. pap. 2.25 (ISBN 0-380-01860-8, 36566). Avon.
Reed, Ishmael, ed. Calafia: The California Poetry. LC 78-51132. 1979. 15.00 (ISBN 0-931676-04-5); pap. 8.95 (ISBN 0-931676-03-7). Y'bird.
Reed, J. D. Pursuit. 1981. pap. 2.75 (ISBN 0-440-17167-9). Dell.
Reed, Jackson. The Raptures of Love. (Orig.). 1976. pap. 1.95 o.s.i. (ISBN 0-515-04082-7). Jove Pubns.
Reed, James. The Border Ballads. (Illus.). 232p. 1973. text ed. 18.75x (ISBN 0-485-11144-6, Athlone Pr). Humanities.
--Sir Walter Scott: Locality & Landscape. 1980. text ed. 40.00x (ISBN 0-485-11197-7, Athlone Pr). Humanities.
Reed, James H., jt. auth. see Williams, Walter E.
Reed, John. Schubert. (The Great Composer Ser). (Illus.). 1978. 9.50 o.p. (ISBN 0-571-10327-8, Pub. by Faber & Faber). Merrimack Bk Serv.
Reed, John, tr. see Sassine, Williams.
Reed, John Q. Benjamin Penhallow Shillaber. (U. S. Authors Ser.: No. 209). lib. bdg. 10.95 (ISBN 0-8057-0664-X). Twayne.
Reed, John R. A Gallery of Spiders: Poems. LC 80-81894. (Ontario Review Press Poetry Ser.). 80p. 1980. 9.95 (ISBN 0-86538-005-8); pap. 4.95 (ISBN 0-86538-006-6). Ontario Rev NJ.
--Old School Ties, the Public Schools in British Literature. LC 64-23341. 1964. 7.95x (ISBN 0-8156-2070-5). Syracuse U Pr.
--Perception & Design in Tennyson's "Idylls of the King". LC 77-122100. 270p. 1969. 12.00x (ISBN 0-8214-0078-9). Ohio U Pr.
--Victorian Conventions. LC 73-92908. xiii, 561p. 1975. 20.00x (ISBN 0-8214-0147-5). Ohio U Pr.
Reed, John S., ed. see Black, Merle.
Reed, Jon-Michael, ed. see Miller, Ron.
Reed, Jon-Michael, ed. see Naha, Ed.
Reed, Kathlyn L. & Sanderson, Sharon T. Concepts of Occupational Therapy. (Illus.). 29p. 1980. pap. 19.95 (ISBN 0-683-07200-5). Williams & Wilkins.
Reed, Ken. The Silent Sage. LC 74-27531. (Illus.). 1974. 6.95 (ISBN 0-914794-00-0); pap. 3.95 (ISBN 0-685-53189-9). Wisdom Garden.
Reed, Ken, ed. see Avital, Samuel.
Reed, Kenneth. Truman Capote. (United States Authors Ser.: No. 388). 1981. lib. bdg. 9.95 (ISBN 0-8057-7321-5). Twayne.
Reed, Kenneth T. S. N. Behrman. LC 75-2085. (U. S. Authors Ser.: No. 256). 152p. 1975. lib. bdg. 10.95 (ISBN 0-8057-7154-9). Twayne.
Reed, Kit. The Ballad of T. Rantula. 224p. 1981. pap. 1.95 (ISBN 0-449-70003-8, Juniper). Fawcett.
--Captain Grownup. 1978. pap. 1.95 o.p. (ISBN 0-449-23692-7, Crest). Fawcett.
--Magic Time. 240p. 1981. pap. 2.25 (ISBN 0-425-04745-8). Berkley Pub.
Reed, L. C. & Longnecker, O. M., Jr. The Geology of Hemphill County, Texas. (Illus.). 98p. 1932. price not set (BULL 3231). Bur Econ Geology.
Reed, Langford. The Complete Limerick Book: The Origin, History & Achievements of the Limerick. LC 78-175778. (Illus.) 147p. 1974. Repr. of 1925 ed. 15.00 (ISBN 0-8103-3974-9). Gale.
--Writer's Rhyming Dictionary. 7.95 (ISBN 0-87116-044-7). Writer.
Reed, Leon. Two Faces of Life. 60p. (Orig.). 1980. pap. 3.95 (ISBN 0-89260-197-3). Hwong Pub.
Reed, Louis S., et al. Health Insurance & Psychiatric Care: Utilization & Cost. 412p. 1972. 8.00 (ISBN 0-685-31187-2, 217). Am Psychiatric.
Reed, M. C. Investment Railways in Britain, 1820-1844: A Study in the Development of the Capital Market. (Illus.). 240p. 1975. write for info. (ISBN 0-19-821852-4). Oxford U Pr.
Reed, Mabel, jt. auth. see Arnold, Mary E.
Reed, Maxine K. The Video Programs Update. (Illus.). 64p. (Orig.). 1981. (ISBN 0-935478-09-4). Natl Video.
Reed, Maxine K., ed. The Video Source Book. 2nd ed. (Illus.). 1260p. (Orig.). 1980. 64.95x (ISBN 0-935478-05-1); pap. 59.95. Natl Video.
--Le Video Source Book: France. (Illus.). 250p. (Orig.). 1981. pap. 30.00 (ISBN 0-935478-08-6). Natl Video. Postponed.
--The Video Source Book: UK. (Illus.). 280p. (Orig.). 1981. pap. 24.00 (ISBN 0-935478-07-8). Natl Video.
--The Video Tape - Disc Guide: Religion. (Illus.). 200p. (Orig.). 1981. pap. 19.95 (ISBN 0-935478-06-X). Natl Video.
Reed, Michael & Simon, Barry. Methods of Modern Mathematical Physics, 4 vols. Incl. Vol. 1. Functional Analysis. 1972. 24.95 (ISBN 0-12-585001-8); Vol. 2. Fourier Analysis Self-Adjointness. 1975. 34.50 (ISBN 0-12-585002-6); Vol. 3. Scattering Theory. 1979. 42.00 (ISBN 0-12-585003-4); Vol. 4. 1978. 34.00 (ISBN 0-12-585004-2). Acad Pr.
Reed, Michael & Simon, Barry, eds. Methods of Modern Mathematical Physics: Functional Analysis, Vol. 1. rev. & enl. ed. 1980. 24.00 (ISBN 0-12-585050-6). Acad Pr.
Reed, Millard. Solar Energy in Tomorrow's World. LC 79-25256. (Illus.). 192p. (gr. 7-12). 1980. PLB 8.79 (ISBN 0-671-33043-8). Messner.
Reed, Muriel. Visites Chez les Francais. Carre, Jeffrey J. & Carre, Marie-Rose, eds. (Illus., Orig., Fr.). 1966. pap. text ed. 8.50 (ISBN 0-13-942250-1). P-H.
Reed, Myril B., jt. auth. see Maxwell, Lee M.
Reed, Myrtle. Flower of the Dusk. 1976. lib. bdg. 15.75x (ISBN 0-89968-109-3). Lightyear.
--Lavender & Old Lace. 1976. lib. bdg. 13.50x (ISBN 0-89968-110-7). Lightyear.
--A Spinner in the Sun. 1976. lib. bdg. 17.25x (ISBN 0-89968-111-5). Lightyear.
Reed, Pat B. Nutrition: An Applied Science. (Illus.). 650p. 1980. text ed. 19.95 (ISBN 0-8299-0311-9); instrs.' manual avail. (ISBN 0-8299-0570-7). West Pub.
Reed, Peter J. Kurt Vonnegut, Jr. (Writers for the Seventies Ser.). 214p. 1976. 9.95 (ISBN 0-690-01048-6, TYC-T); pap. 2.95 (ISBN 0-690-01049-4, TYC-T). T Y Crowell.
Reed, R. P., jt. ed. see Clark, A. F.
Reed, Rex. People Are Crazy Here. (Illus.). 352p. 1974. 7.95 o.p. (ISBN 0-440-07365-0). Delacorte.
--Valentines & Vitrol. 1977. 8.95 o.s.i. (ISBN 0-440-09336-8). Delacorte.
Reed, Richard J. Cutaneous Vasculitides: Immunologic & Histologic Correlations. LC 77-22502. (Illus.). 1978. text ed. 16.00 (ISBN 0-89189-033-5, 16-1-028-00); slides 58.00 (ISBN 0-89189-097-1, 15-1-028-00). Am Soc Clinical.
--Melanocytic Nevi & Related Tumors of the Skin. (Atlas Ser.). 1975. 58.00 (ISBN 0-89189-100-5, 15-1-013-00). Am Soc Clinical.
Reed, Robert, ed. Thirty-Two Picture Postcards of Old Washington D.C. 1977. pap. 2.75 (ISBN 0-486-23418-5). Dover.
Reed, Robert D. Furnace Operations. 3rd ed. 230p. 1981. 18.95 (ISBN 0-87201-301-4). Gulf Pub.
Reed, Robert R. Colonial Manila: The Context of Hispanic Urbanism & Process of Morphogenesis. (Publications in Geography Ser.: Vol. 22). 1978. pap. 12.00x (ISBN 0-520-09579-0). U of Cal Pr.
Reed, Rowena, ed. see Albion, Robert G.
Reed, Rufus M. Conquerors of the Dark Hills. 1978. 6.95 (ISBN 0-533-03701-8). Vantage.
Reed, Sheldon, ed. Counseling in Medical Genetics. 246p. 1980. 26.00 (ISBN 0-8451-0208-7). A R Liss.
Reed, Sue W., jt. auth. see Worthen, Amy N.
Reed, T. J. Thomas Mann: The Uses of Tradition. 442p. 1974. 36.00x (ISBN 0-19-815742-8); pap. 8.25x (ISBN 0-19-815747-9). Oxford U Pr.
Reed, Walter L. An Exemplary History of the Novel: The Quixotic Versus the Picaresque. LC 80-17908. 1981. lib. bdg. 22.00x (ISBN 0-226-70683-4). U of Chicago Pr.
Reed, William. Olaf Wieghorst. LC 76-101419. (Illus.). 1976. 30.00 o.p. (ISBN 0-87358-045-1). Northland.
Reed, William, jt. auth. see Holden, Michael.
Reed, William G. & Maunder, Elwood R. Four Generations of Management: The Simpson-Reed Story. (Illus.). 1977. 16.50 o.p. (ISBN 0-89030-033-X). Forest Hist Soc.
Reeder. Educating Our Masters. 1980. text ed. 30.00x (ISBN 0-7185-5036-6, Leicester). Humanities.
Reeder, Carolyn, jt. auth. see Reder, Jack.
Reeder, Carolyn, jt. auth. see Reeder, Jack.
Reeder, Jack & Reeder, Carolyn. Hikes to Abandoned Homesites in Shenandoah National Park. LC 80-81761. 72p. (Orig.). 1980. pap. write for info. o.p. (ISBN 0-915746-13-1). Potomac Appalach.
--Shenandoah Vestiges: What the Mountain People Left Behind. LC 80-81761. 72p. (Orig.). 1980. pap. 3.75 (ISBN 0-915746-14-X). Potomac Appalach.
Reeder, Maurice M. & Palmer, Philip E. The Radiology of Tropical Disease with Epidemiological, Pathological & Clinical Correlation. (Illus.). 1080p. 1981. lib. bdg. 110.00 (ISBN 0-683-07199-8). Williams & Wilkins.
Reeder, R. T., ed. Fifth Institute on Coal Mine Health & Safety: Proceedings. (Fifth Proceedings Ser.). (Illus.). 380p. (Orig.). 1980. pap. text ed. 12.00 (ISBN 0-918062-41-1). Colo Sch Mines.
--Fourth Institute on Coal Mine Health & Safety: Proceedings. 1979. 10.50 o.p. (ISBN 0-918062-07-1). Colo Sch Mines.
Reeder, Red. The French & Indian War. LC 76-181680. (gr. 5-9). 1972. 7.95 (ISBN 0-525-66208-1). Elsevier-Nelson.
--Medal of Honor Heroes. (gr. 4-8). 1965. 2.95 o.p. (ISBN 0-394-80411-2). Random.
Reeder, Red, jt. auth. see Campion, Nardi R.
Reeder, Robert C. The Sourcebook of Medical Communications. (Illus.). 325p. 1981. text ed. 29.00 (ISBN 0-8016-4177-2). Mosby.
Reeder, Sharon, et al. Maternity Nursing. LC 79-22993. 775p. 1980. text ed. 22.95x (ISBN 0-397-54253-4). Lippincott.
Reeder, W. Donald. Letters of John & Jude. (Teach Yourself the Bible Ser). 1965. pap. 1.75 (ISBN 0-8024-4674-4). Moody.
Reedman, J. H. Techniques in Mineral Exploration: Popular Edition. (Illus.). 1979. 50.00x (ISBN 0-85334-851-0, Pub. by Applied Science). Burgess-Intl Ideas.
Reedy, George. The Presidency in Flux. 200p. 1973. 12.50x (ISBN 0-231-03736-8). Columbia U Pr.
Reefe, Thomas O. The Rainbow & the Kings: A History of the Luba Empire to 1891. 1981. 21.00x (ISBN 0-520-04140-2). U of Cal Pr.
Reejhsinghani, Aroona. Tasty Snacks. 158p. 1975. pap. 2.00 (ISBN 0-88253-773-3). Ind-US Inc.
Reekie, Fraser. Draughtsmanship: Architectural & Building Graphics. 3rd ed. (Illus.). 248p. 1976. pap. 12.95x (ISBN 0-7131-3368-6). Intl Ideas.
Reekie, W. Duncan. The Economics of the Pharmaceutical Industry. 145p. 1975. text ed. 26.00x (ISBN 0-8419-5009-1). Holmes & Meier.
--Industry, Prices & Markets. LC 79-14543. 166p. 1979. 18.95x (ISBN 0-470-26709-7). Halsted Pr.
--Macroeconomics for Managers. 160p. 1980. 18.00x (ISBN 0-86003-510-7, Pub. by Allan Pubs England); pap. 9.00x (ISBN 0-86003-610-3). State Mutual Bk.
--Managerial Economics. 440p. 1975. 45.00x (ISBN 0-86003-007-5, Pub. by Allan Pubs England); pap. 22.50x (ISBN 0-86003-108-X). State Mutual Bk.
Reel, J. R., jt. ed. see Hafez, E. S.
Reel, Jerry R., jt. ed. see Menon, K. M.
Reel, Joseph P. Use Both Brains. LC 80-82602. (Illus.). 104p. (Orig.). 1980. pap. 14.95 (ISBN 0-938024-00-0). Human Dev Pr.
Reeman, Douglas. Dive in the Sun. 240p. 1981. pap. 2.50 (ISBN 0-515-05876-9). Jove Pubns.
--The Greatest Enemy. pap. 2.25 (ISBN 0-515-05448-8). Jove Pubns.
--The Last Raider. pap. 2.25 (ISBN 0-515-05730-4). Jove Pubns.
--Path of the Storm. pap. 1.95 (ISBN 0-515-05373-2). Jove Pubns.
--A Prayer for the Ship. 256p. 1981. pap. 2.50 (ISBN 0-515-05783-5). Jove Pubns.
--The Pride & the Anguish. pap. 1.95 (ISBN 0-515-05357-0). Jove Pubns.
--Rendezvous - South Atlantic. pap. 2.25 (ISBN 0-515-05717-7). Jove Pubns.
--A Ship Must Die. 256p. 1981. pap. 2.50 (ISBN 0-515-05954-4). Jove Pubns.
--To Risks Unknown. pap. 1.95 (ISBN 0-515-05411-9). Jove Pubns.
Rees, jt. auth. see Gray.
Rees, ed. see Greville, Fulke.
Rees, Alan M. & Young, Blanche A. Consumer Health Information Source Book. (Consumer Health Information Publications Program Ser.). 480p. 1981. 32.50 (ISBN 0-8352-1336-6). Bowker.
Rees, Alan M. & Crawford, Susan, eds. Directory of Health Sciences Libraries in the United States. LC 80-65893. 356p. 1980. 25.00. Med Lib Assn.
Rees, Albert. The Economics of Work & Pay. 2nd ed. (Illus.). 1979. text ed. 14.95 scp (ISBN 0-06-045354-0, HarpC). Har-Row.
Rees, Albert & Shultz, George P. Workers & Wages in an Urban Labor Market. LC 75-110114. (Studies in Business & Society Ser). 1970. 12.50x (ISBN 0-226-70705-9). U of Chicago Pr.
Rees, Alwyn & Rees, Brinley. Celtic Heritage: Ancient Tradition in Ireland & Wales. (Illus.). 1977. pap. 8.95 (ISBN 0-500-27039-2). Thames Hudson.
Rees, B. R. & Jervis, Margaret E. Lampas: A New Approach to Greek. 1972. pap. 4.95x o.p. (ISBN 0-631-12270-2, Pub. by Basil Blackwell). Biblio Dist.
Rees, B. R., ed. Classics: An Outline for the Intending Student. (Outlines Ser). 1970. 8.25 (ISBN 0-7100-6914-6); pap. 7.50 (ISBN 0-7100-6915-4). Routledge & Kegan.
Rees, Barbara. Harriet Dark: Branwell Bronte's Lost Novel. 1980. pap. 1.95 (ISBN 0-446-90356-6). Warner Bks.
Rees, Brinley, jt. auth. see Rees, Alwyn.
Rees, C., et al, eds. Theory & Applications of Fourier Analysis. (Pure & Applied Mathematics Ser.). 1980. 37.50 (ISBN 0-8247-6903-1). Dekker.

Rees, Charles, jt. auth. see Rees, Paul.
Rees, Charles, et al. Plane Trigonometry with Tables. 7th ed. (Illus.). 1977. text ed. 16.95 (ISBN 0-13-679209-X). P-H.
Rees, Clair & Wixom, Hartt. The Penny-Pinching Guide to Bigger Fish & Better Hunting. (Illus.). 256p. 1980. 9.95 (ISBN 0-87691-319-2). Winchester Pr.
Rees, Clair F. Profitable Part-Time - Full-Time Freelancing. LC 79-22724. 214p. 1980. 11.95 (ISBN 0-89879-012-3). Writers Digest.
Rees, D. A., ed. & pref. by see Farquharson, Arthur.
Rees, D. Morgan. Industrial Archaeology of Wales. LC 74-82832. (Industrial Archaeology of the British Isles Ser.). (Illus.). 288p. 1975. 22.50 (ISBN 0-7153-6819-2). David & Charles.
Rees, Daniel, jt. auth. see English Benedictine Congregation Members.
Rees, David. The Exeter Blitz. (gr. 6 up). 1980. 7.95 (ISBN 0-525-66683-4). Elsevier-Nelson.
Rees, Eloise R. Once in Six Thousand Years. (Orig.). 1980. pap. 1.95 (ISBN 0-532-23185-6). Manor Bks.
Rees, Ennis, tr. see Homer.
Rees, G. Brychan, ed. see Hebbel, Friedrich.
Rees, Gareth & Rees, Teresa L., eds. Poverty & Social Inequality in Wales. 279p. 1980. 30.00x (ISBN 0-7099-2200-0, Pub. by Croom Helm Ltd England). Biblio Dist.
Rees, Garnet. Baudelaire, Sartre & Camus: Lectures & Commentaries. 86p. 1976. pap. text ed. 10.00x (ISBN 0-7083-0601-2). Verry.
Rees, Garnet, ed. see Apollinaire, Guillaume.
Rees, Henry. British Isles: A Regional Geography. 2nd ed. (Illus.). 1972. text ed. 19.95x (ISBN 0-245-50745-0). Intl Ideas.
Rees, J. Larcombe. The Fire Brand. (The Pathfinder Ser.). 128p. (gr. 2-6). 1980. pap. 2.50 (ISBN 0-310-37911-3, 0017P). Zondervan.
Rees, Joan. Fulke Greville, Lord Brooke, 1554-1628: A Critical Biography. LC 79-132064. (Illus.). 1971. 17.50x (ISBN 0-520-01824-9). U of Cal Pr.
--The Poetry of Dante Gabriel Rossetti. 150p. Date not set. 39.95 (ISBN 0-521-23537-5). Cambridge U Pr.
--Shakespeare & the Story: Aspects of the Creation. 1978. text ed. 31.25x (ISBN 0-485-11179-9, Athlone Pr). Humanities.
Rees, John, et al, eds. Industrial Location & Regional Systems: Spatial Organization in the Economic Sector. (Illus.). 320p. 1981. text ed. 24.95x (ISBN 0-89789-008-6). J F Bergin.
Rees, Joseph D. Poems to Shape Lives: Inspirational Verse on the Gospel, Life Love & Family. LC 76-3993. (Illus.). 112p. 1976. pap. 3.95 o.p. (ISBN 0-88290-059-5). Horizon Utah.
Rees, L. H., jt. ed. see Van Wimersma Greidanus, T. B.
Rees, Margaret, ed. see De Musset, Alfred.
Rees, Michael K. The Complete Family Guide to Living with High Blood Pressure. LC 80-18767. 1980. 9.95 (ISBN 0-13-160432-5). P-H.
Rees, Nigel. Love, Death & the Universe. (Illus.). 128p. 1981. pap. 6.95 (ISBN 0-02-029340-2). Macmillan.
Rees, Paul & Rees, Charles. Principles of Mathematics. 3rd ed. (Illus.). 1977. 17.95 (ISBN 0-13-709683-6). P-H.
Rees, Paul K., et al. College Algebra. 8th, rev. ed. (Illus.). 560p. 1981. text ed. 17.95 (ISBN 0-07-051733-9); write for info instr.' manual (ISBN 0-07-051734-7). McGraw.
Rees, Philip. Fascism in Britain: An Annotated Bibliography. 1978. text ed. 27.50x (ISBN 0-391-00908-7). Humanities.
Rees, Philip, ed. Hong Kong 1978: A Review of 1977. LC 78-640270. (Illus.). 1978. 10.00x o.p. (ISBN 0-8002-1514-1). Intl Pubns Serv.
Rees, Philip, jt. ed. see Hobcraft, John.
Rees, R. & Gravelle, H. F. E. Microeconomics. 2nd ed. (Modern Economics Ser.). (Illus.). 620p. 1981. pap. text ed. 8.50 (ISBN 0-582-44075-0). Longman.
Rees, R., jt. auth. see Gravelle, H.
Rees, R. A., jt. ed. see Bryer, J. R.
Rees, Richard. Simone Weil: A Sketch for a Portrait. LC 66-11154. (Crosscurrents-Modern Critiques Ser.). 215p. 1966. 10.95 (ISBN 0-8093-0191-1). S Ill U Pr.
--Simone Weil: A Sketch for a Protrait. LC 77-24990. (Arcturus Books Paperbacks). 215p. 1978. pap. 6.95 (ISBN 0-8093-0852-5). S Ill U Pr.
Rees, Robert A. & Harbert, Earl N., eds. Fifteen American Authors Before 1900: Bibliographic Essays on Research & Criticism. LC 77-157395. 1971. 30.00x (ISBN 0-299-05910-3); pap. 8.95x (ISBN 0-299-05913-8). U of Wis Pr.
Rees, Samuel. David Jones. (English Authors Ser.: No. 246). 1978. 12.50 (ISBN 0-8057-6726-6). Twayne.
Rees, Stuart. Social Work Face to Face. 1979. 15.50x (ISBN 0-231-04764-9). Columbia U Pr.
Rees, Teresa L., jt. ed. see Rees, Gareth.
Rees, Thomas. Reminiscences of Literary London from 1779 - 1853. LC 68-24476. 1969. Repr. of 1896 ed. 15.00 (ISBN 0-8103-3888-2). Gale.
Rees, Thomas D. Aesthetic Plastic Surgery, 2 vols. (Illus.). 1168p. 1980. Vol. 1. text ed. 75.00 (ISBN 0-7216-7519-0); Vol. 2. text ed. 85.00 (ISBN 0-7216-7521-2); Set. text ed. 160.00 (ISBN 0-7216-7522-0). Saunders.
Rees, Vyvyan. South-West Wales: Pembrokeshire & Camarthenshire: Pembrokeshire & Camarthenshire, a Shell Guide. 2nd ed. (Shell Guide Ser.). (Illus.). 1976. 13.95 (ISBN 0-571-04810-2, Pub. by Faber & Faber). Merrimack Bk Serv.
Reese, Bob. Arbor Day. Jordan, Alton, ed. (Holidays Ser.). (Illus.). (gr. k-3). 1977. PLB 3.50 (ISBN 0-89868-031-X, Read Res); pap. text ed. 1.75 (ISBN 0-89868-064-6). ARO Pub.
--Crab Apple. Wasserman, Dan, ed. (Ten Word Bks.). (Illus.). (gr. k-1). 1979. PLB 4.50 (ISBN 0-89868-072-7); pap. 1.95 (ISBN 0-89868-083-2). ARO Pub.
--Easter. Jordan, Alton, ed. (Holidays Ser.). (Illus.). (gr. k-3). 1977. PLB 3.50 (ISBN 0-89868-032-8, Read Res); pap. text ed. 1.75 (ISBN 0-89868-065-4). ARO Pub.
--Little Dinosaur. Wasserman, Dan, ed. (Ten Word Bks.). (Illus.). (gr. k-1). 1979. PLB 4.50 (ISBN 0-89868-070-0); pap. 1.95 (ISBN 0-89868-081-6). ARO Pub.
--Saint Patrick's Day. Jordan, Alton, ed. (Holidays Ser.). (Illus.). (gr. k-3). 1977. PLB 3.50 (ISBN 0-89868-030-1, Read Res); pap. text ed. 1.75 (ISBN 0-89868-063-8). ARO Pub.
--Sunshine. Wasserman, Dan, ed. (Ten Word Bks.). (Illus.). (gr. k-1). 1979. PLB 4.50 (ISBN 0-89868-073-5); pap. 1.95 (ISBN 0-89868-084-0). ARO Pub.
--Who's a Silly Egg? Jordan, Alton, ed. (Buppet Series). (Illus.). (gr. k-3). 1981. PLB 4.50 (ISBN 0-89868-092-1, Read Res); pap. text ed. 1.95 (ISBN 0-89868-103-0). ARO Pub.
--Who's New at the Zoo. Wasserman, Dan, ed. (Ten Word Bks.). (Illus.). (gr. k-1). 1979. PLB 4.50 (ISBN 0-89868-074-3); pap. 1.95 (ISBN 0-89868-085-9). Aro Pub.
Reese, Bob, et al. Buppet Character Book Set, 10 bks. Jordan, Alton, ed. (Illus.). (gr. k-3). 1981. Set. PLB 45.00 (ISBN 0-89868-088-3, Read Res); pap. 19.50 set (ISBN 0-89868-099-9). ARO Pub.
--Elephant Set, 10 bks. Jordon, Alton, ed. (Illus.). (gr. k-6). 1977. Set. PLB 35.00 (ISBN 0-89868-011-5); Set. pap. 17.50 (ISBN 0-89868-044-1). ARO Pub.
--Holiday Series, 10 bks. Jordan, Alton, ed. (Illus.). (gr. k-6). 1977. Set. PLB 35.00 (ISBN 0-89868-022-0); Set. pap. 17.50 (ISBN 0-89868-055-7). ARO Pub.
--I Can Read Underwater Series, 10 bks. Jordan, Alton, ed. (Illus.). (gr. k-6). 1974. Set. PLB 35.00 (ISBN 0-89868-000-X); Set. pap. 17.50 (ISBN 0-89868-033-6). ARO Pub.
--Ten Word Books, 10 bks. Wasserman, Dan, ed. (Illus.). (gr. k-6). Set. PLB 45.00 (ISBN 0-89868-066-2); Set. pap. 19.50 (ISBN 0-89868-077-8). ARO Pub.
--Fire Drill. Wasserman, Dan, ed. (Ten Word Bks.). (Illus.). (gr. k-1). 1979. PLB 4.50 (ISBN 0-89868-071-9); pap. 1.95 (ISBN 0-89868-082-4). ARO Pub.
--Flowers. Wasserman, Dan, ed. (Ten Word Bks.). (Illus.). (gr. k-1). 1979. PLB 4.50 (ISBN 0-89868-076-X); pap. 1.95 (ISBN 0-89868-087-5). ARO Pub.
Reese, Edward, compiled by. The Reese Chronological Bible. 1649p. 1980. Repr. of 1977 ed. 24.95 (ISBN 0-87123-115-8, 230115). Bethany Fell.
Reese, Ellen P. Experiments in Operant Behavior. LC 64-18142. (Century Psychology Ser.). (Illus.). 1981. pap. text ed. 12.95x (ISBN 0-89197-159-9). Irvington.
Reese, George, ed. The Official Papers of Francis Fauquier, Lieutenant Governor of Virginia, 1758-1768: Vol. II, 1761-1763. LC 80-19866. (Virginia Historical Society Documents Ser.: Vol. 15). 1981. price not set (ISBN 0-8139-0895-7). U Pr of Va.
--The Official Papers of Francis Fauquier, Lieutenant Governor of Virginia, Seventeen Fifty-Eight to Seventeen Sixty-Eight, Vol. 1. LC 80-19866. (Virginia Historical Society Documents Ser.: Vol. 14). 1981. 37.50x (ISBN 0-8139-0856-6). U Pr of Va.
Reese, Gustave. Fourscore Classics of Music Literature. LC 78-87616. (Music Reprint Ser). 1969. Repr. of 1957 ed. lib. bdg. 17.50 (ISBN 0-306-71620-8). Da Capo.
--Music in the Middle Ages. (Illus.). 1940. 24.95x (ISBN 0-393-09750-1, NortonC). Norton.
--Music in the Renaissance. rev. ed. (Illus.). 1959. 29.95x (ISBN 0-393-09530-4, NortonC). Norton.
Reese, Gustave & Brandel, R. Commonwealth of Music. 1965. 7.50 o.s.i. (ISBN 0-02-926080-9). Free Pr.
Reese, Gustave & Snow, Robert J., eds. Essays in Musicology: In Honor of Dragan Plamenac on His 70th Birthday. LC 77-8220. (Music Reprint, 1978 Ser.). (Illus.). 1977. Repr. of 1969 ed. lib. bdg. 32.50 (ISBN 0-306-77408-9). Da Capo.
Reese, H. W. & Lipsitt, L. P., eds. Advances in Child Development & Behavior, Vol. 15. 1980. 28.00 (ISBN 0-12-009715-X); lib. bdg. 36.50 (ISBN 0-12-009784-2); microfiche ed. 19.50 (ISBN 0-12-009785-0). Acad Pr.
Reese, Hayne, ed. Advances in Child Development & Behavior. Incl. Vol. 1. 1964. 36.00 (ISBN 0-12-009701-X); Vol. 2. Lipsitt, Lewis P. & Spiker, Charles G, eds. 1965. 36.00 (ISBN 0-12-009702-8); Vol. 3. 1967. 36.00 (ISBN 0-12-009703-6); Vol. 4. Lipsitt, Lewis P & Reese, Hayne W., eds. 1969. 36.00 (ISBN 0-12-009704-4); Vol. 5. 1970. 36.00 (ISBN 0-12-009705-2); Vol. 6. 1971. 36.00 (ISBN 0-12-009706-0); Vol. 7. 1973. 32.50 (ISBN 0-12-009707-9); Vol. 8. 1974. 32.50 (ISBN 0-12-009708-7); Vol. 9. 1974. 32.50 (ISBN 0-12-009709-5); Vol. 10. 1975. 32.50 (ISBN 0-12-009710-9); lib. ed. 43.00 (ISBN 0-12-009774-5); microfiche 23.50 (ISBN 0-12-009775-3); Vol. 11. 1976. 32.50 (ISBN 0-12-009711-7); lib ed. 43.00 (ISBN 0-12-009776-1); microfiche 23.50 (ISBN 0-12-009777-X); Vol. 12. 1978. 28.00 (ISBN 0-12-009712-5); lib ed. 36.00 (ISBN 0-12-009778-8); microfiche 19.50 (ISBN 0-12-009779-6); Vol. 13. 1979. 26.00 (ISBN 0-12-009713-3); lib ed. 33.50 (ISBN 0-12-009780-X); microfiche 18.50 (ISBN 0-12-009781-8). LC **63-23237. Acad Pr.**
Reese, Hayne W. see Reese, Hayne.
Reese, James M. First & Second Thessalonians. Harrington, Wilfrid & Senior, Donald, eds. (New Testament Message Ser.: Vol. 16). 130p. 1980. 9.95 (ISBN 0-89453-139-5); pap. 4.95 (ISBN 0-89453-204-9). M Glazier.
Reese, John. Angel Range. 1976. pap. 0.95 o.p. (ISBN 0-685-72360-7, LB386NK, Leisure Bks). Nordon Pubns.
--Big Mutt. (Illus.). (gr. 5-7). 1969. pap. 1.75 (ISBN 0-671-29987-5). PB.
--Halter-Broke. 1978. pap. 1.50 o.s.i. (ISBN 0-515-04580-2). Jove Pubns.
--The Wild One. 1978. pap. 1.25 o.p. (ISBN 0-449-13953-0, GM). Fawcett.
Reese, Lee F. Men of the Blue Ghost (USS Lexington CV-16) Historic Events of World War II in the Pacific As Told by the Men Who Lived Them, 1943-6. (Illus.). 980p. 1980. 50.00 (ISBN 0-686-64547-2). Lex Bk Co CA.
Reese, Loretta. Fifty Craft Ideas with Patterns. LC 80-53363. (Illus.). 64p. (Orig.). pap. 3.50 (ISBN 0-87239-427-1, 2144). Standard Pub.
Reese, M. M., ed. Elizabethan Verse Romances. (Routledge English Texts). 1971. 7.95 (ISBN 0-7100-4517-4); pap. 2.95 (ISBN 0-7100-4518-2). Routledge & Kegan.
Reese, M. M., ed. see Gibbon, Edward.
Reese, Nancy. The Bee. Jordan, Alton, ed. (I Can Read Underwater Books). (Illus.). (gr. k-3). 1974. PLB 3.50 (ISBN 0-89868-005-0, Read Res); pap. text ed. 1.75 (ISBN 0-89868-038-7). ARO Pub.
--I Can Eat an Elephant. Jordan, Alton, ed. (Elephant Ser.). (Illus.). (gr. k-3). 1975. PLB 3.50 (ISBN 0-89868-012-3, Read Res); text ed. 1.75 softbd. (ISBN 0-89868-045-X). ARO Pub.
--Purple Bear. Jordan, Alton, ed. (Elephant Ser.). (Illus.). (gr. k-3). 1975. PLB 3.50 (ISBN 0-89868-013-1, Read Res); pap. text ed. 1.75 (ISBN 0-89868-046-8). ARO Pub.
--Silly Egg. Jordan, Alton, ed. (Illus.). (gr. k-3). 1974. PLB 3.50 (ISBN 0-89868-004-2, Read Res); pap. text ed. 1.75 (ISBN 0-89868-037-9). ARO Pub.
--Smiley Snake. Jordan, Alton, ed. (I Can Read Underwater Bks). (Illus.). (gr. k-3). 1974. PLB 3.50 (ISBN 0-89868-010-7, Read Res); pap. text ed. 1.75 (ISBN 0-89868-043-3). ARO Pub.
--Valentine's Day. Jordan, Alton, ed. (Holidays Ser.). (Illus.). (gr. k-3). 1977. PLB 3.50 (ISBN 0-89868-029-8, Read Res); pap. text ed. 1.75 (ISBN 0-89868-062-X). ARO Pub.
Reese, Reuben A. The True Doctrine of Ultra Vires in the Law of Corporations, Being a Concise Presentation of the Doctrine in Its Application to the Powers & Liabilities of Private & Municipal Corporations. lxxi, 338p. 1981. Repr. of 1897 ed. lib. bdg. 30.00x (ISBN 0-8377-1031-6). Rothman.
Reese, Ron. Crazy Cat. Jordan, Alton, ed. (I Can Read Underwater Bks). (Illus.). (gr. k-3). 1974. PLB 3.50 (ISBN 0-89868-002-6, Read Res); pap. text ed. 1.75 (ISBN 0-89868-065-4). ARO Pub.
--Crazy Cat's Bad Day. Jordan, Alton, ed. (Buppet Series). (Illus.). (gr. k-3). 1981. PLB 4.50 (ISBN 0-89868-090-5, Read Res); pap. text ed. 1.95 (ISBN 0-89868-101-4). ARO Pub.
--Halloween. Jordan, Alton, ed. (Holidays Ser.). (Illus.). (gr. k-3). 1977. PLB 3.50 (ISBN 0-89868-023-9, Read Res); pap. text ed. 1.75 (ISBN 0-89868-056-5). ARO Pub.
--Mosquito. Jordan, Alton, ed. (Elephant Ser:). (Illus.). (gr. k-3). 1975. PLB 3.50 (ISBN 0-89868-014-X, Read Res); text ed. 1.75 soft bd. (ISBN 0-89868-047-6). ARO Pub.
--Sammy Skunk. Jordan, Alton, ed. (I Can Read Underwater Bks). (Illus.). (gr. k-3). 1974. PLB 3.50 (ISBN 0-89868-009-3, Read Res); pap. text ed. 1.75 (ISBN 0-89868-042-5). ARO Pub.
--Toy Bear. Jordan, Alton, ed. (Elephant Ser.). (Illus.). (gr. k-3). 1975. PLB 3.50 (ISBN 0-89868-016-6, Read Res); pap. text ed. 1.75 (ISBN 0-89868-049-2). ARO Pub.
Reese, Rosemary S. & Rath, Frederick L., Jr., eds. Documentation of Collections. (A Bibliography on Historical Organization Practices: Vol. 4). 1979. text ed. 12.50x (ISBN 0-910050-38-4). AASLH.
Reese, Terence. Begin Bridge with Reese. LC 77-79501. (Illus.). (gr. 6 up). 1977. 6.95 o.p. (ISBN 0-8069-4932-5); PLB 6.69 o.p. (ISBN 0-8069-4933-3). Sterling.
--Bidding a Bridge Hand. Orig. Title: Develop Your Bidding Judgment. 254p. 1972. pap. 3.50 (ISBN 0-486-22830-4). Dover.
--Bridge at the Top. 1977. 14.95 (ISBN 0-571-11123-8, Pub. by Faber & Faber). Merrimack Bk Serv.
--The Most Puzzling Situations in Bridge Play. LC 78-57884. (Illus.). 1978. 6.95 o.p. (ISBN 0-8069-4936-8); lib. bdg. 6.69 o.p. (ISBN 0-8069-4937-6). Sterling.
--The Most Puzzling Situations in Bridge Play. 1980. pap. 1.95 (ISBN 0-451-09538-3, J9538, Sig). NAL.
--Winning at Casino Gambling. 1979. pap. 1.75 (ISBN 0-451-08617-1, E8617, Sig). NAL.
--Winning at Casino Gambling: An International Guide. LC 78-62195. 1978. 9.95 (ISBN 0-8069-0138-1); lib. bdg. 9.29 (ISBN 0-8069-0139-X). Sterling.
--Your Book of Contract Bridge. (gr. 7 up). 1971. 5.50 (ISBN 0-571-06387-X). Transatlantic.
Reese, Terence & Brinig, Robert. Backgammon: The Modern Game. LC 76-19770. (Illus.). 1976. 9.95 (ISBN 0-8069-4930-9); PLB 9.29 (ISBN 0-8069-4931-7). Sterling.
Reese, Terence & Dormer, Albert. The Bridge Player's Alphabetical Handbook. 224p. 1981. 19.95 (ISBN 0-571-11599-3, Pub. by Faber & Faber). Merrimack Bk Serv.
Reese, Terence & Trezel, Roger. Blocking & Unblocking Plays in Bridge. LC 76-13614. 64p. 1976. pap. 3.95 (ISBN 0-8119-0359-1). Fell.
--Elimination Play in Bridge. LC 76-55902. 1977. pap. 3.95 (ISBN 0-8119-0361-3). Fell.
--Safety Plays in Bridge. LC 76-13613. 64p. 1976. pap. 3.95 (ISBN 0-8119-0395-8). Fell.
--Snares & Swindles in Bridge. LC 76-55903. 1977. pap. 3.95 (ISBN 0-8119-0397-4). Fell.
--Those Extra Chances in Bridge. LC 77-23675. 1978. pap. 3.95 (ISBN 0-8119-0398-2). Fell.
--When to Duck--When to Win in Bridge. LC 77-23677. 1978. pap. 3.95 (ISBN 0-8119-0401-6). Fell.
Reese, Terence & Watkins, A. T. How to Win at Poker. pap. 3.00 (ISBN 0-87980-070-4). Wilshire.
Reese, Terence, ed. see Vinje, Helge.
Reese, Thomas. The Architecture of Ventura Rodriguez, 2 vols. LC 75-23810. (Outstanding Dissertations in the Fine Arts - 18th Century). (Illus.). 1976. Set. lib. bdg. 121.00 (ISBN 0-8240-2004-9). Garland Pub.
Reese, Thomas J. The Politics of Taxation. LC 79-8413. (Illus.). xxv, 237p. 1980. lib. bdg. 25.00 (ISBN 0-89930-003-0, RPT/, Quorum Bks). Greenwood.
Reese, W. S. Six Score: The 120. LC 76-8956. (Illus.). 100p. 1976. 30.00 (ISBN 0-8363-0144-7). Jenkins.
Reese, William L. & Freeman, Eugene, eds. Process & Divinity: The Hartshorne Festschrift. LC 64-13547. 633p. 1964. 25.00 (ISBN 0-87548-054-3); pap. 8.95 o.p. (ISBN 0-87548-055-1). Open Court.
Reesman, Richard T. Contributions of the Major Philosophers into the Problem of Body Resurrection & Personal Immortality. (Illus.). 117p. 1981. 41.85 (ISBN 0-89920-021-4). Am Inst Psych.
Reesor, James B. Gospel Sermons for Saint & Sinner. 107p. 1968. 2.95 (ISBN 0-87148-356-4); pap. 2.25 (ISBN 0-87148-357-2). Pathway Pr.
Reeve, Clara. Plans of Education, with Remarks on the Systems of Other Writers: In a Series of Letters Between Mrs. Darnford & Her Friends. (The Feminist Controversy in England, 1788-1810 Ser.). 1974. lib. bdg. 50.00 (ISBN 0-8240-0877-4). Garland Pub.
Reeve, F. A. Victorian & Edwardian Cambridge. 1971. pap. 11.95 (ISBN 0-7134-0093-5, Pub. by Batsford England). David & Charles.

--Victorian & Edwardian Cambridgeshire. 1976. 16.95 o.p. (ISBN 0-7134-3079-6, Pub. by Batsford England). David & Charles.

Reeve, F. D. The Blue Cat. 1973. 6.95 o.p. (ISBN 0-374-11474-9); pap. 2.95 o.p. (ISBN 0-374-51048-2). FS&G.

--The Brother. 1971. 6.95 o.p. (ISBN 0-374-11697-0). FS&G.

--White Colors. 1973. 7.95 o.p. (ISBN 0-374-28927-1). FS&G.

Reeve, Frank A. Spaziergange Durch Cambridge. (Illus., Ger.). 1978. pap. 4.00 (ISBN 0-900891-44-0). Oleander Pr.

Reeve, Joel. Goal Ahead. LC 67-22811. (gr. 7-10). 1967. 8.95 (ISBN 0-87599-137-8). S G Phillips.

Reeves, Andrew L. Toxicology: Principles & Practice, Vol. 1. LC 80-19259. 240p. 1981. 24.50 (ISBN 0-471-71340-6, Pub. by Wiley-Interscience). Wiley.

Reeves, Bruce. Street Smarts. LC 80-28256. 192p. (gr. 6 up). 1981. 8.95 (ISBN 0-8253-0047-9). Beaufort Bks NY.

Reeves, C. C., Jr. Caliche-Origin Classification, Morphology & Uses. LC 76-2234. 1976. text ed. 39.95x (ISBN 0-686-16733-3). Estacado Bks.

Reeves, C. M. An Introduction to Logical Design of Digital Circuits. LC 77-182029. (Computer Science Texts Ser: No. 1). (Illus.). 200p. 1972. text ed. 11.95x (ISBN 0-521-09705-3). Cambridge U Pr.

Reeves, Earl, jt. ed. see Filipovitch, Anthony.

Reeves, James. The King Who Took Sunshine. pap. text ed. 2.50x o.p. (ISBN 0-435-21000-9). Heinemann Ed.

--Mulcaster Market. 1951. pap. text ed. 2.95 o.p. (ISBN 0-435-21003-3). Heinemann Ed.

--Understanding Poetry. 1965. text ed. 9.95x (ISBN 0-435-18768-6). Heinemann Ed.

Reeves, James, ed. Cassell Book of English Poetry. LC 65-20998. (YA) 1965. 15.00x o.s.i. (ISBN 0-06-005910-9, HarpT). Har-Row.

--Five Late Romantic Poets. (The Poetry Bookshelf). 1974. pap. text ed. 3.95 (ISBN 0-435-15074-X). Heinemann Ed.

Reeves, James, retold by. Giants & Warriors. (Illus., Orig.). 1978. pap. 2.95 (ISBN 0-8467-0540-0, Pub. by Two Continents). Hippocrene Bks.

Reeves, James, ed. Golden Land. (gr. 4 up). 1963. 10.95 o.p. (ISBN 0-582-15284-4). Dufour.

Reeves, James, retold by. Heroes & Monsters. (Illus., Orig.). 1978. pap. 2.95 (ISBN 0-8467-0539-7, Pub. by Two Continents). Hippocrene Bks.

Reeves, James, ed. Selected Poems of S. T. Coleridge. (The Poetry Bookshelf). 1959. pap. text ed. 6.50x (ISBN 0-435-15021-9). Heinemann Ed.

Reeves, James & Gittings, Robert, eds. Selected Poems of Thomas Hardy. (The Poetry Bookself Ser.). 1981. 11.50x (ISBN 0-389-20080-8). B&N.

Reeves, James & Seymour-Smith, Martin, eds. The Poems of Andrew Marvell. (The Poetry Bookshelf). 1969. pap. text ed. 4.95 (ISBN 0-435-15064-2). Heinemann Ed.

Reeves, James, ed. see De France, Marie.

Reeves, James, jt. ed. see Flower, Desmond.

Reeves, John. Murder by Microphone. 224p. 1980. pap. 2.25 (ISBN 0-380-43729-5, 43729). Avon.

Reeves, John A. & Simon, J. Malcolm. Coaches' Collection of Soccer Drills. LC 80-84212. (Illus.). 96p. (Orig.). 1981. pap. text ed. 4.95 (ISBN 0-918438-63-2). Leisure Pr.

Reeves, John R. Questions & Answers About Acne. LC 76-28514. (Illus.). (gr. 7 up). 1977. 6.95 (ISBN 0-13-748434-8). P-H.

Reeves, Joyce A. Motherless Victim. 1981. 5.95 (ISBN 0-8062-1576-3). Carlton.

Reeves, M. E. The Medieval Village. (Then & There Ser.). (Illus.). 1972. pap. text ed. 2.65x (ISBN 0-582-20375-9). Longman.

Reeves, Marjorie & Hirsch-Reich, Beatrice. The Figurae of Joachim of Fiore. (Oxford-Warburg Studies). (Illus.). 380p. 1972. text ed. 36.00x (ISBN 0-19-920038-6). Oxford U Pr.

Reeves, Mavis M., jt. auth. see Glendening, Parris N.

Reeves, Michael. Travolta: A Photo Bio. (Illus.). 1978. pap. 1.95 (ISBN 0-515-04850-X). Jove Pubns.

Reeves, Nigel. Heirich Heine: Poetry & Politics. (Oxford Modern Languages & Literature Monographs). 215p. 1974. 29.95x (ISBN 0-19-815524-7). Oxford U Pr.

Reeves, Nigel, jt. auth. see Dewhurst, Kenneth.

Reeves, R. D. & Brooks, R. R. Trace Element Analysis of Geological Materials. LC 78-8064. (Chemical Analysis: Monographs on Analytical Chemistry & Its Applications). 1978. 35.00 (ISBN 0-471-71338-4, Pub. by Wiley-Interscience). Wiley.

Reeves, Richard S. & Robinson, Patrick. Decade of Champions: The Greatest Years in the History of Thoroughbred Racing, 1970-1980. LC 79-92604. (Illus.). 192p. 1980. 75.00 (ISBN 0-8487-0508-4). Oxmoor Hse.

Reeves, Richard W., jt. auth. see Cooke, Ronald U.

Reeves, Robert G. Flora of Central Texas. Orig. Title: Flora of South Central Texas. 1977. pap. text ed. 8.00x (ISBN 0-934786-00-3). G Davis.

Reeves, Rosser. Popo. LC 79-56380. (Illus.). 196p. 1980. 10.00 (ISBN 0-8149-0838-1). Vanguard.

Reeves, Troy D. An Annoted Index to the Sermons of John Donne, 2 vols. Incl. Vol. 1 (ISBN 0-391-02146-X); Vol. 2 (ISBN 0-391-02147-8). (Elizabethan Studies: No. 95). 1980. pap. text ed. 25.00 ea. Humanities.

Reeves, W. G., jt. ed. see Holborow, E. J.

Reference International. Encyclopedia of Aviation. LC 77-72699. (Encore Edition). (Illus.). 1977. 5.95 (ISBN 0-684-16921-5, ScribT). Scribner.

Reff, Theodore. The Notebooks of Edgar Degas: A Catalogue of the Thirty-Eight Notebooks in the Bibliotheque Nationale & Other Collections, 2 vols. 1977. Set. 159.00x (ISBN 0-19-817333-4). Oxford U Pr.

Reff, Theodore, ed. Exhibition of Character & Genre Pictures. (Modern Art in Paris 1855 to 1900 Ser.). 112p. 1981. lib. bdg. 44.00 (ISBN 0-8240-4727-3). Garland Pub.

--Exhibitions of Art Nouveau. (Modern Art in Paris Ser.). 486p. 1981. lib. bdg. 44.00 (ISBN 0-8240-4732-X). Garland Pub.

--Exhibitions of Barbizon & Landscape Art. (Modern Art in Paris 1855 to 1900 Ser.). 449p. 1981. lib. bdg. 44.00 (ISBN 0-8240-4737-0). Garland Pub.

--Exhibitions of Classicizing Art. (Modern Art in Paris 1855 to 1900 Ser.). 395p. 1981. lib. bdg. 44.00 (ISBN 0-8240-4735-4). Garland Pub.

--Exhibitions of Draftsmen & Illustrations. (Modern Art in Paris, 1855 to 1900, Ser.). 241p. 1981. lib. bdg. 44.00 (ISBN 0-8240-4744-3). Garland Pub.

--Exhibitions of Impressionist Art, Bk. I. (Modern Art in Paris 1855 to 1900 Ser.). 356p. 1981. lib. bdg. 44.00 (ISBN 0-8240-4741-9). Garland Pub.

--Exhibitions of Impressionist Art, Bk. II. (Modern Art in Paris 1855 to 1900 Ser.). 259p. 1981. lib. bdg. 44.00 (ISBN 0-8240-4742-7). Garland Pub.

--Exhibitions of Later Realist Art. (Modern Art in Paris 1855 to 1900 Ser.). 320p. 1981. lib. bdg. 44.00 (ISBN 0-8240-4740-0). Garland Pub.

--Exhibitions of Modern Drawings. (Modern Art in Paris 1855 to 1900 Ser.). 251p. 1981. lib. bdg. 44.00 (ISBN 0-8240-4724-9). Garland Pub.

--Exhibitions of Modern European Art. (Modern Art in Paris 1855 to 1900 Ser.). 500p. 1981. lib. bdg. 44.00 (ISBN 0-8240-4725-7). Garland Pub.

--Exhibitions of Modern Prints. (Modern Art in Paris 1855 to 1900 Ser.). 339p. 1981. lib. bdg. 44.00 (ISBN 0-8240-4726-5). Garland Pub.

--Exhibitions of Realist Art, Bk. I. (Modern Art in Paris 1855 to 1900 Ser.). 518p. 1981. lib. bdg. 44.00 (ISBN 0-8240-4738-9). Garland Pub.

--Exhibitions of Realist Art, Bk. II. (Modern Art in Paris 1855 to 1900 Ser.). 345p. 1981. lib. bdg. 44.00 (ISBN 0-8240-4739-7). Garland Pub.

--Exhibitions of Romantic Art. (Modern Art in Paris 1855 to 1900 Ser.). 340p. 1981. lib. bdg. 44.00 (ISBN 0-8240-4736-2). Garland Pub.

--Exhibitions of Sculpture. (Modern Art in Paris 1855 to 1900 Ser.). 394p. 1981. lib. bdg. 44.00 (ISBN 0-8240-4745-1). Garland Pub.

--Exhibitions of Symbolists & Nabi. (Modern Art in Paris 1855 to 1900 Ser.). 254p. 1981. lib. bdg. 44.00 (ISBN 0-8240-4743-5). Garland Pub.

--Exhibitions of the Rosicrucian Salon. (Modern Art in Paris 1855 to 1900 Ser.). 354p. 1981. lib. bdg. 44.00 (ISBN 0-8240-4730-3). Garland Pub.

--Exhibitions of the Salon Des Cent, 1894 to 1895. (Modern Art in Paris 1855 to 1900 Ser.). 175p. 1981. lib. bdg. 44.00 (ISBN 0-8240-4731-1). Garland Pub.

--Exhibitions of the Society of Printmakers. (Modern Art in Paris 1855 to 1900 Ser.). 262p. 1981. lib. bdg. 44.00 (ISBN 0-8240-4729-X). Garland Pub.

--Impressionist Group Exhibitions. (Modern Art in Paris 1855 to 1900 Ser.). 157p. 1981. lib. bdg. 44.00 (ISBN 0-8240-4723-0). Garland Pub.

--Miscellaneous Group Exhibitions. (Modern Art in Paris 1855 to 1900 Ser.). 219p. 1981. lib. bdg. 44.00 (ISBN 0-8240-4734-6). Garland Pub.

--National Fine Arts Exhibitions. (Modern Art in Paris 1855 to 1900 Ser.). 396p. 1981. lib. bdg. 44.00 (ISBN 0-8240-4733-8). Garland Pub.

--Post-Impressionist Group Exhibitions. (Modern Art in Paris Ser.). 302p. 1981. lib. bdg. 44.00 (ISBN 0-8240-4728-1). Garland Pub.

--Retrospective Exhibition of Gustave Dore. (Modern Art in Paris 1855 to 1900 Ser.). 221p. 1981. lib. bdg. 44.00 (ISBN 0-8240-4746-X). Garland Pub.

--Retrospective Exhibitions of Ernest Meissonier. (Modern Art in Paris 1855 to 1900 Ser.). 353p. 1981. lib. bdg. 44.00 (ISBN 0-8240-4747-8). Garland Pub.

--Salons of the "Independants", 1884 to 1891. (Modern Art in Paris 1855 to 1900 Ser.). 253p. 1981. lib. bdg. 44.00 (ISBN 0-8240-4709-5). Garland Pub.

--Salons of the "Independants", 1892 to 1895. (Modern Art in Paris 1855 to 1900 Ser.). 320p. 1981. lib. bdg. 44.00 (ISBN 0-8240-4710-9). Garland Pub.

--Salons of the "Independants", 1896 to 1900. (Modern Art in Paris 1855 to 1900 Ser.). 280p. 1981. lib. bdg. 44.00 (ISBN 0-8240-4711-7). Garland Pub.

--Salons of the "Nationale", 1890. (Modern Art in Paris 1855 to 1900 Ser.). (Illus.). 256p. 1981. lib. bdg. 44.00 (ISBN 0-8240-4712-5). Garland Pub.

--Salons of the "Nationale", 1891. (Modern Art in Paris 1855 to 1900 Ser.). (Illus.). 302p. 1981. lib. bdg. 44.00 (ISBN 0-8240-4713-3). Garland Pub.

--Salons of the "Nationale", 1892. (Modern Art in Paris 1855 to 1900 Ser.). (Illus.). 294p. 1981. lib. bdg. 44.00 (ISBN 0-8240-4714-1). Garland Pub.

--Salons of the "Nationale", 1893. (Modern Art in Paris 1855 to 1900 Ser.). (Illus.). 275p. 1981. lib. bdg. 44.00 (ISBN 0-8240-4715-X). Garland Pub.

--Salons of the "Nationale", 1894. (Modern Art in Paris 1855 to 1900 Ser.). (Illus.). 254p. 1981. lib. bdg. 44.00 (ISBN 0-8240-4716-8). Garland Pub.

--Salons of the "Nationale", 1895. (Modern Art in Paris 1855 to 1900 Ser.). (Illus.). 288p. 1981. lib. bdg. 44.00 (ISBN 0-8240-4717-6). Garland Pub.

--Salons of the "Nationale", 1896. (Modern Art in Paris 1855 to 1900 Ser.). (Illus.). 263p. 1981. lib. bdg. 44.00 (ISBN 0-8240-4718-4). Garland Pub.

--Salons of the "Nationale", 1897. (Modern Art in Paris 1855 to 1900 Ser.). (Illus.). 291p. 1981. lib. bdg. 44.00 (ISBN 0-8240-4719-2). Garland Pub.

--Salons of the "Nationale", 1898. (Modern Art in Paris 1855 to 1900 Ser.). (Illus.). 259p. 1981. lib. bdg. 44.00 (ISBN 0-8240-4720-6). Garland Pub.

--Salons of the "Nationale", 1899. (Modern Art in Paris 1855 to 1900 Ser.). (Illus.). 256p. 1981. lib. bdg. 44.00 (ISBN 0-8240-4721-4). Garland Pub.

--Salons of the "Refuses". (Modern Art in Paris 1855 to 1900 Ser.). 133p. 1981. lib. bdg. 44.00 (ISBN 0-8240-4722-2). Garland Pub.

--World's Fair of Eighteen Eighty-Nine. (Modern Art in Paris 1855 to 1900). 330p. 1981. lib. bdg. 44.00 (ISBN 0-8240-4704-4). Garland Pub.

--World's Fair of Eighteen Eighty-Nine: Retrospective Exhibition of Fine Arts, 1789 to 1889. (Modern Art in Paris 1855 to 1900). (Illus.). 250p. 1981. lib. bdg. 44.00 (ISBN 0-8240-4705-2). Garland Pub.

--World's Fair of Eighteen Fifty-Five: Modern Art in Paris 1855-1900. 694p. 1981. lib. bdg. 44.00 (ISBN 0-8240-4701-X). Garland Pub.

--World's Fair of Eighteen Seventy-Eight. (Modern Art in Paris 1855 to 1900). 388p. 1981. lib. bdg. 44.00 (ISBN 0-8240-4703-6). Garland Pub.

--World's Fair of Eighteen Sixty-Seven. (Modern Art in Paris 1855 to 1900). 224p. 1981. lib. bdg. 44.00 (ISBN 0-8240-4702-8). Garland Pub.

--World's Fair of Nineteen Hundred: General Catalogue. (Modern Art in Part in Paris 1855 to 1900). 582p. 1981. lib. bdg. 44.00 (ISBN 0-8240-4706-0). Garland Pub.

--World's Fair of Nineteen Hundred: Retrospective Exhibition of French Art, 1800 to 1889. (Modern Art in Paris 1855 to 1900). (Illus.). 442p. 1981. lib. bdg. 44.00 (ISBN 0-8240-4707-9). Garland Pub.

--World's Fair of Nineteen Hundred: Retrospective Exhibition of Fine Art,1889 to 1900. (Modern Art in Paris 1855 to 1900). 581p. 1981. lib. bdg. 44.00 (ISBN 0-8240-4708-7). Garland Pub.

Regamey, R. H., ed. see Permanent Section of Microbiological Standardization, 31st Symposium, Omstotite of Child Health, Ondon, 1969.

Regan, D. E. Local Government & Education. 2nd ed. (New Local Government Ser.). 1979. pap. text ed. 11.95x (ISBN 0-04-352065-0). Allen Unwin.

Regan, David J. Mourning Glory: The Making of a Marine. 1980. 8.95 (ISBN 0-8159-6218-5). Devin.

Regan, Donald. Utilitarianism & Cooperation. 296p. 1980. text ed. 37.50x (ISBN 0-19-824609-9); pap. 15.95x. Oxford U Pr.

Regan, Tom & Singer, P. Animal Rights & Human Obligation. 256p. 1976. pap. 8.50 (ISBN 0-13-037523-3). P-H.

Regardie, Israel. Art & Meaning of Magic. 3.00 o.p. (ISBN 0-685-22166-0). Weiser.

Regato, Juan A. del see Del Regato, Juan A. & Spjut, Harlan J.

Regazzi, John J. & Hines, Theodore C. A Guide to Indexed Periodicals in Religion. LC 75-22277. 328p. 1975. 12.00 (ISBN 0-8108-0868-4). Scarecrow.

Regel, C. Von see Von Wiesner, J. & Von Regel, C.

Regelski, Thomas A. General Music Methods. LC 80-5561. (Illus.). 448p. 1981. text ed. 12.95 (ISBN 0-02-872070-9). Schirmer Bks.

--Principles & Problems of Music Education. (Illus.). 328p. 1975. ref. ed. 16.95 (ISBN 0-13-709840-5); pap. 13.95 ref. ed. (ISBN 0-13-709832-4). P-H.

--Teaching General Music: Action Learning for Middle & Secondary Schools. LC 80-5561. (Illus.). 448p. 1981. text ed. 12.95 (ISBN 0-02-872070-9). Schirmer Bks.

Regen, Frank. Apuleius philosophus Platonicus: Untersuchungen zur Apologie (De magia) und zu De Mundo. (Untersuchungen zur antiken Literatur und Geschichte, 10). 123p. 1971. 26.00x (ISBN 3-11-003678-9). De Gruyter.

Regener, Eric. Pitch Notation & Equal Temperament: A Formal Study. (U. C. Publ: Occasional Papers: No. 6). pap. 14.50x (ISBN 0-520-09453-0). U of Cal Pr.

Regensburg, Jeannette. Toward Education for Health Professions. 1978. text ed. 14.95 scp (ISBN 0-06-045357-5, HarpC). Har-Row.

Regenstein, Lewis. The Politics of Extinction: The Shocking Story of the World's Endangered Wildlife. (Illus.). 400p. 1975. 9.95 o.s.i. (ISBN 0-02-601910-8). Macmillan.

Regensteiner, Henry, ed. see Durrenmatt, Friedrich.

Reger, Roger. Preschool Programming of Children with Disabilities. (Illus.). 136p. 1974. 13.75 (ISBN 0-398-01564-3). C C Thomas.

Regestein, Quentin R. & Rechs, James R. Sound Sleep. 1980. 10.95 (ISBN 0-671-24960-6, 24960). S&S.

Reggio Emilia see Higgins, Dick.

Regier, Henry A. A Balanced Science of Renewable Resources with Particular Reference to Fisheries. LC 78-4979. (Washington Sea Grant Ser.). 110p. 1978. pap. 10.50 (ISBN 0-295-95602-X). U of Wash Pr.

Regier, Marilyn C. Social Policy in Action: Perspectives on the Implementation of Alcoholism Reforms. LC 78-20274. 1979. 19.95 (ISBN 0-669-02716-2). Lexington Bks.

Regin, Deric. Traders, Artists, Burghers: A Cultural History of Amsterdam in the 17th Century. (Illus.). 1976. pap. text ed. 18.00x (ISBN 9-0232-1427-7). Humanities.

Reginald, R. By Any Other Name: A Comprehensive Checklist of Science Fiction & Fantasy Pseudonyms. LC 80-10924. (Borgo Reference Library: Vol. 9). 64p. 1981. lib. bdg. 8.95 (ISBN 0-89370-805-4); pap. 2.95x (ISBN 0-89370-905-0). Borgo Pr.

--A Guide to Science Fiction & Fantasy in the Library of Congress Classification Scheme. LC 80-11418. (Borgo Reference Library: Vol. 8). 64p. 1981. lib. bdg. 8.95x (ISBN 0-89370-807-0); pap. 2.95x (ISBN 0-89370-907-7). Borgo Pr.

--To Be Continued... An Annotated Bibliography of Science Fiction & Fantasy Series & Sequels. LC 80-11206. (Borgo Reference Library: Vol. 11). 64p. 1981. lib. bdg. 8.95x (ISBN 0-89370-808-9); pap. 2.95x (ISBN 0-89370-908-5). Borgo Pr.

--X, Y & Z: A List of Those Books Examined in the Course of Compiling Science Fiction & Fantasy Literature, a Checklist, 1700 to 1974, with Contemporary Science Fiction Authors II, Which Were Judged to Fall Outside the Genre of Fantastic Literature; an Anti-Bibliography. LC 80-11697. (Borgo Reference Library: Vol. 10). 160p. 1981. lib. bdg. 19.95x (ISBN 0-89370-809-7); pap. 9.95x (ISBN 0-89370-909-3). Borgo Pr.

Reginald, R. & Burgess, Mary A. The Milford Series: Popular Writers of Today; an Index to Volumes 1 to 30. LC 80-15340. (Borgo Reference Library: Vol. 5). 64p. 1981. lib. bdg. 8.95x (ISBN 0-89370-803-8); pap. 2.95x (ISBN 0-89370-903-4). Borgo Pr.

Reginald, R. & Currey, L. W. Science-Fiction Price Guide. (Borgo Reference Library: Vol. 7). 256p. (Orig.). 1981. lib. bdg. 29.95x (ISBN 0-89370-150-5); pap. text ed. 19.95 (ISBN 0-89370-250-1). Borgo Pr.

Reginald, R. & Lewis, Dan. In His Native Habitat: Characteristics of the Science-Fiction Writer. LC 80-11207. (Borgo Reference Library: Vol. 1). 64p. 1981. lib. bdg. 8.95x (ISBN 0-89370-810-0); pap. text ed. 2.95x (ISBN 0-89370-910-7). Borgo Pr.

--Science Fiction & Fantasy Statistics. LC 80-10690. (Borgo Reference Library: Vol. 3). 64p. 1981. lib. bdg. 8.95x (ISBN 0-89370-804-6); pap. 2.95x (ISBN 0-89370-904-2). Borgo Pr.
Reginald, R., jt. auth. see Barron, Neil.
Reginald, R., jt. auth. see Currey, L. W.
Reginald, R., jt. auth. see Elliot, Jeffrey M.
Reginald, R. & Menville, Douglas, eds. Jaufry the Knight & the Fair Brunissende: A Tale of the Times of King Arthur. LC 80-19436. (Newcastle Forgotten Fantasy Library: Vol. 21). 156p. 1980. Repr. of 1979 ed. lib. bdg. 10.95x (ISBN 0-89370-520-9). Borgo Pr.
Reginald, R., ed. see Arnold, Edwin L.
Reginald, R., ed. see Barringer, Leslie.
Reginald, R., ed. see Coblentz, Stanton A.
Reginald, R., ed. see Dunsany, Lord Edward.
Reginald, R., ed. see Haggard, H. Rider.
Reginald, R., ed. see Lindsay, David.
Reginald, R., ed. see Morris, Kenneth.
Reginald, R., ed. see Morris, William.
Reginald, R., ed. see Newbolt, Henry.
Reginald, R., ed. see Stoker, Bram.
Reginald, Robert, ed. Science Fiction & Fantasy Literature: A Checklist from 1700 to 1974...with Contemporary Science Fiction Authors II, 2 vols. LC 76-46130. 1979. 85.00 set (ISBN 0-8103-1051-1). Gale.
Regional Employment Programme for Latin America & the Caribbean. Employment in Latin America. (Praeger Special Studies). 1978. 22.95 (ISBN 0-03-042131-4). Praeger.
Regmi, Mahesh C. Landownership in Nepal. LC 74-77734. 1976. 22.75x (ISBN 0-520-02750-7). U of Cal Pr.
--Thatched Huts & Stucco Places: Peasants & Landlords in Nineteenth Century Nepal. 173p. 1978. 14.00x (ISBN 0-7069-0672-1, Pub. by Croom Helm Ltd. England). Biblio Dist.
Regnier, Beatrice S. De see De Regnier, Beatrice S.
Regnier, Victor. Planning for the Elderly: Alternative Community Analysis Techniques. LC 79-90975. 152p. 1980. pap. 6.00 (ISBN 0-88474-093-5). USC Andrus Geron.
Regniers, Beatrice De see De Regniers, Beatrice & Gilman, Esther.
Regniers, Beatrice S. De see De Regniers, Beatrice S.
Regniers, Beatrice S. De see De Regniers, Beatrice S. & Gordon, Isabel.
Regniers, Beatrice S. De see De Regniers, Beatrice S. & Pierce, Leona.
Regnon, Theodore De. Etudes De Theologie Positive Sur la Sainte Trinite: Theories Grecques Des Processions Divines. LC 80-2363. (Troisieme Ser., II). 1981. Repr. of 1893 ed. 67.00 (ISBN 0-404-18915-6). AMS Pr.
Regosin, Richard. The Matter of My Book: Montaigne's "Essais" As the Book of the Self. 1977. 14.95x (ISBN 0-520-03476-7). U of Cal Pr.
Rehder, A. The Bradley Bibliography: A Guide to the Literature of the Woody Plants of the World, Published Before the Beginning of the 20th Century, 5 vols. Sargent, C. S., ed. 3895p. 1976. Repr. Set. lib. bdg. 745.20x (ISBN 0-686-27682-5). Vol. I. Vol. II (ISBN 3-87429-107-3). Vol. III (ISBN 3-87429-108-1). Vol. IV (ISBN 3-87429-109-X). Vol. V (ISBN 3-87429-110-3). Lubrecht & Cramer.
--Manual of Cultivated Trees & Shrubs. 2nd ed. 1940. 14.95 o.s.i. (ISBN 0-02-601920-5). Macmillan.
Rehder, Herald A. The Audubon Society Field Guide to North American Seashells. LC 80-84239. 864p. 1981. 9.95 (ISBN 0-394-51913-2). Knopf.
Rehder, Jessie, ed. Young Writer at Work. LC 62-11938. 1962. 8.95 (ISBN 0-672-63148-2). Odyssey Pr.
Rehder, Jessie & Kaufman, Wallace, eds. Act of Writing. LC 68-21800. 1969. pap. 6.95 (ISBN 0-672-63002-8). Odyssey Pr.
Rehfeldt, Phillip. New Directions for Clarinet. (The New Instrumentation Ser.: Vol. 4). 1978. 17.95x (ISBN 0-520-03379-5). U of Cal Pr.
Rehfuss, John, jt. auth. see Murphy, Thomas P.
Rehg, Kenneth L. & Sohl, Damian G. Ponapean Reference Grammar. LC 80-13276. (Pali Language Texts: Micronesia). 1980. pap. text ed. 16.00x (ISBN 0-8248-0718-9). U Pr of Hawaii.
Rehkopf, Donald C., ed. Portraits in Words: An Introduction to the Study of Biography. LC 62-13410. 1962. 4.95 (ISBN 0-672-73251-3); pap. 3.50 o.p. (ISBN 0-672-73229-7). Odyssey Pr.
Rehm, J., jt. auth. see Winold, A.
Rehm, Lynn P., ed. Behavior Therapy for Depression: Present Status & Future Directions. 1980. 29.50 (ISBN 0-12-585880-9). Acad Pr.
Rehork, Joachim, ed. see Keller, Werner.
Rehr, Paula B. Why Is Everyone Growing up & I'm Still in the 8th Grade? Poems About School Life Today. (Illus.). 48p. pap. 3.50 (ISBN 0-686-63982-0). Garrett Pk.
Rehrauer, George. Cinema Booklist: Supplement One. LC 70-188378. 1974. 11.00 o.p. (ISBN 0-8108-0696-7). Scarecrow.
--Cinema Booklist: Supplement Two. LC 70-188378. 1977. 16.50 o.p. (ISBN 0-8108-0997-4). Scarecrow.
Rehwinkel, Alfred M. Wonders of Creation. LC 74-8416. 288p. 1973. pap. 6.95 (ISBN 0-87123-649-4, 210649). Bethany Fell.
Reich, Bernard, jt. ed. see Long, David E.
Reich, Hanns, ed. Baby Animals & Their Mothers. (Illus.). (gr. 3 up). 1965. 7.95 o.p. (ISBN 0-8090-2010-6, Terra Magica). Hill & Wang.
Reich, J. R. & Reich, Michael S. United States Government. (Illus.). 207p. (Orig.). (gr. 7-12). 1979. pap. text ed. 4.50 (ISBN 0-8372-3552-9); tchrs' guide 1.26 (ISBN 0-8372-3553-7). Bowmar-Noble.
Reich, L. & Stivala, S. S. Autoxidation of Hydrocarbons & Polyolefins: Kinetics & Mechanisms. 1969. 59.50 o.p. (ISBN 0-8247-1580-2). Dekker.
Reich, Michael. Racial Inequality: A Political-Economic Analysis. LC 80-8573. 320p. 1981. 20.00x (ISBN 0-691-04227-6); pap. 6.95 (ISBN 0-691-00365-3). Princeton U Pr.
Reich, Michael S., jt. auth. see Reich, J. R.
Reich, Norbert E., jt. auth. see Haaga, John.
Reich, Paul R. Hematology: Physiopathologic Basis for Clinical Practice. 1978. text ed. 22.95 (ISBN 0-316-73860-3); pap. text ed. 17.95 (ISBN 0-316-73861-1). Little.
Reich, Peter A., ed. see Linguistic Association of Canada & the U.S.
Reich, Sheldon. Francisco Zuniga: Sculptor. LC 80-18986. 1980. 35.00 (ISBN 0-8165-0665-5). U of Ariz Pr.
Reich, Steve. Writings About Music. LC 73-87481. (The Nova Scotia Ser). (Illus.). 82p. 1974. 10.00x, c o.p. (ISBN 0-8147-7358-3); pap. 4.00, C (ISBN 0-8147-7357-5). NYU Pr.
--Writings About Music. 1974. pap. 7.00 (ISBN 0-686-67541-X, 50-26921). Eur-Am Music.
Reich, Steven D., jt. ed. see Crooke, Stanley T.
Reich, Warren T., ed. Encyclopedia of Bioethics, 4 vols. LC 78-8821. 1978. Set. 230.00 (ISBN 0-02-926060-4). Free Pr.
Reich, Wilhelm. The Bion Experiments: On the Origin of Life. Jordan, Derek & Jordan, Inge, trs. (Octagon edition). 1979. 22.50 (ISBN 0-374-96768-7); pap. 8.95 (ISBN 0-374-51446-1). FS&G.
--Character Analysis. Carfagno, Vincent R., tr. 1980. pap. 7.95 (ISBN 0-374-50980-8). FS&G.
--Die Entdeckung des Orgons Erster Teil die Funktion des Orgasmus. 390p. 1968. 35.00 (ISBN 0-374-13976-8). FS&G.
--The Function of the Orgasm. Carfagno, V., tr. 416p. 1973. 10.95 (ISBN 0-374-15965-3). FS&G.
--Function of the Orgasm: The Discovery of the Orgone. Reich, Wilhelm, tr. (Illus.). pap. 3.95 o.p. (ISBN 0-452-00337-7, FM337, Mer). NAL.
--Ibsen's Peer Gynt. 74p. 1975. 10.00 (ISBN 0-374-17416-4). FS&G.
--Der Krebs. 461p. 1971. 40.00 (ISBN 0-374-13813-3). FS&G.
--The Mass Psychology of Fascism. Carfagno, Vincent R., tr. 1980. pap. write for info. (ISBN 0-374-50884-4). FS&G.
--The Murder of Christ: The Emotional Plague of Mankind. 228p. 1953. 5.95 (ISBN 0-374-21625-8); pap. 3.95 (ISBN 0-374-50476-8, N290). FS&G.
--Orgonomischer Funktionalismus. 110p. 1973. 35.00 (ISBN 0-374-22724-1). FS&G.
--Sex-Pol: Essays 1929-1934. Baxandall, Lee, ed. LC 72-2735. 1972. pap. 2.45 (ISBN 0-394-71791-0, V-791, Vin). Random.
--What Is Sexuality? 1981. 10.95 (ISBN 0-374-28843-7). FS&G.
Reichard, Gary W. The Reaffirmation of Republicanism: Eisenhower & the Eighty-Third Congress. LC 75-1017. (Twentieth Century America Ser.). 320p. 1975. 18.50x (ISBN 0-87049-167-9). U of Tenn Pr.
Reichard, Joseph R., jt. auth. see Roseler, Robert O.
Reichardt, Charles S., jt. ed. see Cook, Thomas D.
Reichardt, Werner E. & Poggio, Tomaso, eds. Theoretical Approaches in Neurobiology. (Illus.). 208p. 1980. text ed. 20.00x (ISBN 0-262-18100-2). MIT Pr.
Reichart, Walter A. & Schlissel, Lillian, eds. Washington Irving Journals & Notebooks, 1807-1822, Vol. 2. (Critical Editions Program Ser.). 1981. lib. bdg. 32.00 (ISBN 0-8057-8501-9). Twayne.
Reichenbach, Bruce R. Cosmological Argument: A Reassessment. (Illus.). 160p. 1972. 14.50 (ISBN 0-398-02387-5). C C Thomas.
Reichenbach, Hans. Axiomatization of the Theory of Relativity. Reichenbach, Maria, ed. & tr. LC 68-21540. 1968. 18.50x (ISBN 0-520-01525-8). U of Cal Pr.
--Elements of Symbolic Logic. 444p. 1980. pap. 7.00 (ISBN 0-486-24004-5). Dover.
--Laws, Modalities, & Counterfactuals. LC 74-29798. Orig. Title: Nomological Statements & Admissible Operations. 1977. 16.50x (ISBN 0-520-02966-6). U of Cal Pr.
--Philosophy of Space & Time. Reichenbach, Maria, tr. 1957. pap. text ed. 3.50 (ISBN 0-486-60443-8). Dover.
--The Rise of Scientific Philosophy. 1951. 17.95x (ISBN 0-520-01053-1); pap. 4.95 (ISBN 0-520-01055-8, CAL3). U of Cal Pr.
--The Theory of Probability: An Inquiry into the Logical & Mathematical Foundations of the Calculus of Probability. (California Library Reprint Series: No. 23). 1971. 23.75x (ISBN 0-520-01929-6). U of Cal Pr.
--The Theory of Relativity & A Priori Knowledge. 1965. 18.50x (ISBN 0-520-01059-0). U of Cal Pr.
Reichenbach, Heinrich G. Die Vollstandigste Naturgeschicte der affen. LC 78-72725. Repr. of 1863 ed. 72.50 (ISBN 0-404-18298-4). AMS Pr.
Reichenbach, Maria, ed. & tr. see Reichenbach, Hans.
Reichenbach, Maria, tr. see Reichenbach, Hans.
Reichenbach-Klinke, H., jt. auth. see Elkan, E.
Reichenberger, Arnold G., ed. see Vega Capiro, Lope F.
Reichert, John J. Color the Creatures. (Illus.). (gr. 4-12). 1979. pap. 2.50 (ISBN 0-930504-03-8). Polaris Pr.
Reichert, Katharine E. Primary Care of Young Adults: A Practitioner's Manual. 1976. pap. 13.00 (ISBN 0-87488-986-3). Med Exam.
Reichert, Richard. Born in the Spirit of Jesus. 84p. (Orig.). 1980. pap. text ed. 2.75 (ISBN 0-697-01725-7); tchr's manual 3.50 (ISBN 0-697-01726-5); spirit masters 10.95 (ISBN 0-697-01727-3). Wm C Brown.
--Making Moral Decisions. LC 79-63483. (Illus.). (gr. 11-12). 1979. pap. text ed. 3.30x (ISBN 0-88489-109-7); tchrs. guide 1.40x (ISBN 0-88489-118-6). St Marys.
Reichle, D. E., ed. Dynamic Properties of Forest Ecosystems. LC 78-72093. (International Biological Programme Ser.: No. 23). (Illus.). 850p. Date not set. 95.00 (ISBN 0-521-22508-6). Cambridge U Pr.
Reichler. The Macmillan Baseball Calendar, 1981. 108p. Date not set. 7.95 (ISBN 0-02-926130-9). Macmillan.
Reichler, Joseph L. The Great All-Time Baseball Record Book: A Unique Sourcebook of Facts, Feats & Figures. (Illus.). 608p. 1981. 19.95 (ISBN 0-02-603100-0). Macmillan.
Reichley, A. James. Conservatives in an Age of Change: The Nixon & Ford Administrations. 500p. 1981. 26.95 (ISBN 0-8157-7380-3); pap. 11.95 (ISBN 0-8157-7379-X). Brookings.
Reichlin, Seymour, et al, eds. The Hypothalamus, Vol. 56. LC 77-83691. (Association for Research in Nervous & Mental Disease Research Publications). 1978. 43.50 (ISBN 0-89004-167-9). Raven.
Reichman, L. & Wishart, B. J. Issues Four: Critical Questions for the '70s. 1972. pap. 7.95x (ISBN 0-02-476850-2, 47685). Macmillan.
Reichman, O. H., jt. ed. see Fein, J. M.
Reichmann, Felix. The Sources of Western Literacy: The Middle Eastern Civilizations. LC 79-8292. (Contributions in Librarianship & Information Science: No. 29). 274p. 1980. lib. bdg. 25.00 (ISBN 0-313-20948-0, RWL/). Greenwood.
Reid, A. S., jt. auth. see Hazel, A. C.
Reid, Adrian. The Goddaughter. 1980. pap. 2.25 (ISBN 0-380-47571-5, 47571, 47571). Avon.
Reid, Agnes J. Letters of Long Ago. (Utah, the Mormons & the West Ser.: No. 2). 93p. 1973. 9.50 (ISBN 0-87480-158-3, Tanner). U of Utah Pr.
Reid, Alan. Concise Encyclopedia of the Second World War. (Illus.). 232p. 1974. 14.95x o.p. (ISBN 0-8464-0273-4). Beekman Pubs.
Reid, Alastair, tr. see Borges, Jorge L.
Reid, Alastair, tr. see Neruda, Pablo.
Reid, Alastair, tr. see Pacheco, Jose E.
Reid, Alec, jt. ed. see Brown, Terence.
Reid, Alistair, jt. auth. see Monegal, Emir.
Reid, Anthony. The Blood of the People: Revolution & the End of Traditional Rule in Northern Sumatra. (Illus.). 308p. 1979. text ed. 34.50x (ISBN 0-19-580399-X). Oxford U Pr.
Reid, B., jt. auth. see Coppleson, M.
Reid, B. L. Tragic Occasions: Essays on Several Forms. LC 72-154032. 1971. 12.95 (ISBN 0-8046-9016-2, Natl U). Kennikat.
Reid, Barbara & Reid, Ewa. The Cobbler's Reward. LC 78-4638. (Illus.). (gr. k-3). 1978. 8.95 (ISBN 0-02-775800-1, 77580). Macmillan.
Reid, Barbara, jt. auth. see Markus, Julia.
Reid, C. Lestock. Commerce & Conquest. LC 78-115328. 1971. Repr. of 1947 ed. 12.95 (ISBN 0-8046-1119-X). Kennikat.
Reid, C. N. Deformation Geometry for Material Scientists. LC 73-4716. 220p. 1973. text ed. 25.00 (ISBN 0-08-017237-7); pap. text ed. 13.25 (ISBN 0-08-017745-X). Pergamon.
Reid, D. A. Construction Principles. 1973. text ed. 17.50x (ISBN 0-7114-3305-4). Intl Ideas.
Reid, D. Kim, jt. auth. see Gallagher, Jeanette.
Reid, David P. What Are They Saying About the Prophets? LC 80-80869. (Orig.). 1980. pap. 2.95 (ISBN 0-8091-2304-5). Paulist Pr.
Reid, Donald & Booth, Philip. Biology for the Individual. Incl. Introduction to the Series. 1971. pap. text ed. o.p. (ISBN 0-435-59766-3); Bk. 1. Sorting Animals & Plants into Groups. 1971. pap. text ed. 4.50x o.p. (ISBN 0-435-59750-7); tchrs guide 5.95 o.p. (ISBN 0-435-59751-5); Bk 2. How Life Begins (Human Reproduction) 1971. pap. text ed. 4.50x o.p. (ISBN 0-435-59752-3); tchrs guide 8.25x o.p. (ISBN 0-435-59753-1); Bk 3. Movement in Animals. 1971. pap. text ed. 2.95x o.p. (ISBN 0-435-59754-X); tchrs guide 5.95 o.p. (ISBN 0-435-59755-8); Bk 4. Support in Animals & Plants. 1972. pap. text ed. 2.95x o.p. (ISBN 0-435-59756-6); Bk 5. Problems of Life in Hot, Cold, & Dry Climates. 1972. pap. text ed. 4.50x o.p. (ISBN 0-435-59758-2); tchrs guide 5.00x o.p. (ISBN 0-435-59759-0); Bk 6. Working with Very Small Things. 1974. pap. text ed. 4.50x o.p. (ISBN 0-435-59760-4); Bk 7. The War Against Diseases. 1974. pap. text ed. 2.95x o.p. (ISBN 0-435-59762-0); Bks. 6 & 7. tchrs guide 5.50x o.p. (ISBN 0-435-59761-2); **Bk 8. Plant Reproduction. 1973. pap. text ed. 4.50x o.p. (ISBN 0-435-59764-7); Bk. 9. Skeletons & Muscles. 1973. pap. text ed. 4.50x o.p. (ISBN 0-435-59764-7). Heinemann Ed.**
--Skeletons & Muscles. (Biology for the Individual Ser.). pap. text ed. 4.50x o.p. (ISBN 0-435-59768-X). Heinemann Ed.
Reid, Donald M. Lawyers & Politics in the Arab World, 1880-1960. LC 80-71053. (Studies in Middle Eastern History: No. 5). 600p. 1981. 30.00 (ISBN 0-88297-028-3). Bibliotheca.
--The Odyssey of Farah Antun: A Syrian Christian's Quest for Secularism. LC 74-80598. (Studies in Middle Eastern History: No. 2). 1975. 23.50x (ISBN 0-88297-009-7). Bibliotheca.
Reid, Duncan E. & Christian, C. Donald, eds. Controversy in Obstetrics & Gynecology Two. 2nd ed. LC 73-93432. (Illus.). 365p. 1974. text ed. 38.00 (ISBN 0-7216-7528-X). Saunders.
Reid, E. Cell Populations. LC 79-40729. (Methodological Surveys in Biochemistry Ser.: Vol. 8). 1979. 59.95x (ISBN 0-470-26809-3). Halsted Pr.
--Trace-Organic Sample Handling. (Methodological Surveys Analysis). 400p. 1981. 110.00 (ISBN 0-470-27071-3). Halsted Pr.
Reid, E., ed. Blood Drugs & Other Analytical Challenges. LC 78-40411. (Methodological Surveys in Biology Ser.). 1978. 54.95 (ISBN 0-470-26445-4). Halsted Pr.
--Plant Organelles. LC 79-40730. (Methodological Surveys in Biochemistry Ser.: Vol. 9). 1979. 59.95 (ISBN 0-470-26810-7). Halsted Pr.
Reid, Eric, ed. Membranous Elements & Movement of Molecules. LC 77-77378. (Methodological Surveys Ser: Vol. 6). 1977. 53.95 (ISBN 0-470-99186-0). Halsted Pr.
Reid, Ewa, jt. auth. see Reid, Barbara.
Reid, Francis. Stage Lighting Handbook. LC 76-8319. (Illus.). 1976. 10.45 (ISBN 0-87830-156-9). Theatre Arts.
Reid, G. A. & Thompson, Evelina. Pitman Shorterhand. Angus, M., ed. LC 72-88594. 1972. text ed. 7.96 (ISBN 0-8224-1007-9); Drillbook One, spiral bdg. 4.60 (ISBN 0-8224-1735-9); 15 cassettes, tape program one 220.00 (ISBN 0-8224-1026-5). Pitman Learning.
--Shorterhand Dictionary of Common Words. Angus, M., ed. 1974. pap. 5.10 (ISBN 0-8224-4154-3). Pitman Learning.
Reid, George. Sound of the Trumpet. (Horizon Ser.). 224p. 1981. price not set (ISBN 0-8127-0328-6); pap. price not set (ISBN 0-8127-0321-9). Southern Pub.
Reid, Gordon. Politics of Financial Control: The Role of the House of Commons. (Orig.). 1966. text ed. 5.00x (ISBN 0-09-079260-2, Hutchinson U Lib); pap. text ed. 2.50x (ISBN 0-09-079261-0, Hutchinson U Lib). Humanities.
Reid, Ivan. Social Class Differences in Britain: A Sourcebook. (Illus.). 1977. text ed. 15.00x (ISBN 0-7291-0165-7); pap. text ed. 7.75x (ISBN 0-7291-0160-6). Humanities.
Reid, J. Calvin, ed. Psalms to Live by. Taylor, Kenneth N., tr. LC 72-86211. (Orig.). 1972. pap. 1.75 o.p. (ISBN 0-8307-0189-3, 50-071-00). Regal.
Reid, J. K., ed. see Calvin, John.
Reid, J. S., ed. see Cicero.
Reid, Jacinta. The Ditch Diggers. 1979. 6.95 o.p. (ISBN 0-533-03777-8). Vantage.

Reid, James. Dios, el Atomo, y el Universo. Orozco, Julio, tr. from Eng. LC 76-55491. 240p. (Orig., Span.). 1977. pap. 3.50 (ISBN 0-89922-083-5). Edit Caribe.
--The Offering. 1978. pap. 1.75 o.s.i. (ISBN 0-685-54631-4, 04768-6). Jove Pubns.
Reid, James M. & Silleck, Anne. Better Business Letters: A Programmed Book to Develop Skill in Writing. 2nd ed. LC 77-88056. 1978. pap. text ed. 8.95 (ISBN 0-201-06327-1). A-W.
Reid, James M., Jr., jt. auth. see Bossone, Richard M.
Reid, Jane. Metrics for Everyday Use. new ed. LC 74-24660. 24p. (gr. 7-12). 1975. pap. text ed. 2.60 (ISBN 0-87002-216-4). Bennett IL.
Reid, John. The Best Little Boy in the World. 1977. pap. 2.25 (ISBN 0-345-28872-6). Ballantine.
Reid, John C. Marriage Covenant. LC 67-11305. (Orig.). 1967. pap. 1.00 (ISBN 0-8042-1710-6). John Knox.
Reid, John G. Acadia, Maine, & New Scotland: Marginal Colonies in the Seventeenth Century. 320p. 1981. 27.50x (ISBN 0-8020-5508-7). U of Toronto Pr.
Reid, John K. The Authority of Scripture: A Study of the Reformation & Post-Reformation Understanding of the Bible. LC 79-8716. 286p. 1981. Repr. of 1962 ed. lib. bdg. 25.00x (ISBN 0-313-22191-X, REAS). Greenwood.
Reid, John P. In Defiance of the Law: The Standing-Army Controversy, the Two Constitutions, & the Coming of the American Revolution. LC 80-14002. (Studies in Legal History). 295p. 1981. 20.00x (ISBN 0-8078-1449-0). U of NC Pr.
--Law for the Elephant: Property & Social Behavior on the Overland Trail. LC 79-26989. (Illus.). 1980. 18.50 (ISBN 0-87328-104-7). Huntington Lib.
Reid, John P., ed. The Briefs of the American Revolution. (NYU School of Law Ser. in Anglo-American Legal History). 176p. 1981. text ed. 22.50x (ISBN 0-8147-7384-2). NYU Pr.
Reid, Kenneth E. From Character Building to Social Treatment: The History of the Use of Groups in Social Work. LC 79-6567. xviii, 249p. 1981. lib. bdg. 29.95 (ISBN 0-313-22016-6, RCB/). Greenwood.
Reid, Kim & Hresko, Wayne. Introduction to Learning Disabilities. (Illus.). 448p. Date not set. text ed. 16.95x (ISBN 0-07-051768-1, C). McGraw.
Reid, Lee. From a Coastal Kitchen: Food & Flavor from Lull Bay. (Illus.). 144p. 1981. pap. 7.95 (ISBN 0-87663-608-3). Universe.
Reid, Loren. Finally It's Friday: School & Work in Mid-America, 1921-1933. 288p. 1981. 19.95 (ISBN 0-8262-0330-2). U of Mo Pr.
Reid, Louis A. Meaning in the Arts. (Muirhead Library of Philosophy). 1969. text ed. 11.50x o.p. (ISBN 0-04-701004-5). Humanities.
--A Study in Aesthetics. 415p. 1980. Repr. of 1931 ed. lib. bdg. 45.00 (ISBN 0-8495-4635-4). Arden Lib.
Reid, Mado, jt. auth. see Cundiff, W. E.
Reid, Malcolm. The Shouting Signpainters: A Literary & Political Account of Quebec Revolutionary Nationalism. LC 75-158922. 320p. 1972. 8.95 o.p. (ISBN 0-85345-154-0, CL-1540); pap. 3.95 (ISBN 0-85345-283-0, PB-2830). Monthly Rev.
Reid, Margaret I. & McDowell, Robert J. Guidance in the Secondary School: An Annotated Bibliography of Literature, Materials & Tests. (Occasional Reports Ser.: No. 2). 1976. pap. text ed. 7.75x (ISBN 0-85633-102-3, NFER). Humanities.
Reid, Margaret I., et al. A Matter of Choice: A Study of Guidance & Subject Options. (Research Reports Ser.). (Illus.). 260p. (Orig.). 1974. pap. text ed. 18.25x (ISBN 0-85633-046-9, NFER). Humanities.
Reid, Meta M. The Two Rebels. 1969. 6.50 (ISBN 0-571-08967-4, Pub. by Faber & Faber). Merrimack Bk Serv.
Reid, Mildred I. Writers: Help Yourselves! 5.00 (ISBN 0-914062-02-6). Burkehaven Pr.
--Writers: Here's How! rev ed. 1978. 4.00 (ISBN 0-914062-01-8). Burkehaven Pr.
--Writers: Let's Plot! rev. ed. 1979. 5.50 (ISBN 0-914062-03-4). Burkehaven Pr.
--Writers: Make It Sell! rev. ed. 1976. 5.50 (ISBN 0-914062-04-2). Burkehaven Pr.
--Writers: Why Stop Now? rev ed. 1981. 6.00 (ISBN 0-914062-05-0). Burkehaven Pr.
Reid, Paul E. A Model of Interpersonal Speech Communication. LC 79-64197. 1979. pap. text ed. 6.25 (ISBN 0-8191-0755-7). U Pr of Amer.
Reid, Peter. Affirmative Action Compliance Kit: Eed Dictionary. 1980. pap. 10.00 (ISBN 0-917386-35-3). Exec Ent.
--Affirmative Action Compliance Kit: Reference Guide. 1980. pap. 15.00 (ISBN 0-917386-34-5). Exec Ent.
--Affirmative Action Compliance Kit: Working Manual. 1980. pap. 75.00 (ISBN 0-917386-33-7). Exec Ent.
Reid, R. J. Law of Moses & Its Lesson. pap. 0.30 (ISBN 0-87213-693-0). Loizeaux.
Reid, Richard & Crum, Milton, Jr. Lesser Festivals 3: Saints' Days & Special Occasions. Achtemeier, Elizabeth, et al, eds. LC 79-7377. (Proclamation 2: Aids for Interpreting the Lessons of the Church Year). 64p. (Orig.). 1981. pap. 2.50 (ISBN 0-8006-1395-3, 1-1395). Fortress.
Reid, Robert. Microbes & Men. 1975. 8.95 o.p. (ISBN 0-8415-0348-6). Dutton.
Reid, Robert A. & Leech, Rachel M. Biochemistry & Structure of Cell Organelles. (Tertiary Level Biology Series). 176p. 1980. 34.95x (ISBN 0-470-26980-4); pap. text ed. 18.95x (ISBN 0-470-26981-2). Halsted Pr.
Reid, Robert C., jt. auth. see Modell, Michael.
Reid, Ruby D. My Life. 1981. 4.95 (ISBN 0-8062-1694-8). Carlton.
Reid, S. W., ed. see Brown, Charles B.
Reid, Susan, ed. The Black Experience: A Manual for Students in the Helping Professions. 1976. pap. text ed. 6.75x (ISBN 0-8191-0001-3). U Pr of Amer.
Reid, T. R. Congressional Odyssey: The Saga of a Senate Bill. LC 80-10108. (Illus.). 1980. text ed. 10.95x (ISBN 0-7167-1171-0); pap. text ed. 5.95x (ISBN 0-7167-1172-9). W H Freeman.
Reid, Thomas. Essays on the Active Powers of Man. Wellek, Rene, ed. LC 75-11251. (British Philosophers & Theologians of the 17th & 18th Centuries: Vol. 50). 1977. Repr. of 1788 ed. lib. bdg. 42.00 (ISBN 0-8240-1802-8). Garland Pub.
--Thomas Reid's Inquiry & Essays. Lehrer, Keith & Beanblossom, Ronald E., eds. LC 75-1197. (LLA Ser: No. 156). 431p. 1975. pap. 8.50 (ISBN 0-672-61173-2). Bobbs.
--Thomas Reid's Lectures on Natural Theology (1780) Duncan, Elmer H., ed. LC 80-5964. 177p. 1981. lib. bdg. 19.00 (ISBN 0-8191-1354-9); pap. text ed. 9.00 (ISBN 0-8191-1355-7). U Pr of Amer.
Reid, Tim. As I Feel It. Maxwell, Daphne, ed. LC 80-54670. (Illus.). 62p. 1981. 8.95 (ISBN 0-931748-19-4). Lincoln Pub.
Reid, W., jt. auth. see Drazin, P.
Reid, W. A., jt. auth. see Taylor, Philip H.
Reid, W. A., jt. ed. see Taylor, P. H.
Reid, William A. Thinking About the Curriculum: The Nature & Treatment of Curriculum Problems. 1978. 16.00 (ISBN 0-7100-8979-1); pap. 7.95 (ISBN 0-7100-8980-5). Routledge & Kegan.
Reid, William A. & Walker, Decker F., eds. Case Studies in Curriculum Change. 1975. 24.00x (ISBN 0-7100-8037-9); pap. 10.00 (ISBN 0-7100-8038-7). Routledge & Kegan.
Reid, William D. Death Notices of Ontario. 417p. 1980. PLB 20.00 (ISBN 0-912606-06-1). Hunterdon Hse.
Reid, William J. Task-Centered System. 1978. 15.00x (ISBN 0-231-03797-X). Columbia U Pr.
Reid, William J. & Epstein, Laura. Task-Centered Casework. LC 72-4931. 350p. 1972. 13.00x (ISBN 0-231-03466-0). Columbia U Pr.
--Task-Centered Practice. LC 76-28177. 1977. 13.00x (ISBN 0-231-04072-5). Columbia U Pr.
Reid, William J. & Shyne, Ann W. Brief & Extended Casework. LC 70-79192. 1969. 13.00x (ISBN 0-231-03219-6). Columbia U Pr.
Reid, William T. Sturmian Theory for Ordinary Differential Equations. (Applied Mathematical Sciences: Vol. 31). 559p. 1981. pap. 26.80 (ISBN 0-387-90542-1). Springer-Verlag.
Reidei, Marc, jt ed. see Macnamara, Donal E.
Reidel, Arthur, ed. Fundamental Rock Climbing. 1973. pap. 1.75 (ISBN 0-9601698-0-6). MIT Outing.
Reider, Federic. Hitler's S. S. (Illus.). 256p. 1981. 24.95 (ISBN 0-89404-061-8). Aztex.
Reider, Frederic. Hitler's S.S. (Illus.). 256p. 1981. 24.95 (ISBN 0-89404-061-8). Aztex.
Reidman, Sarah R. Odd Habitats of Land Animals. (gr. 3-6). 1980. 6.95 o.p. (ISBN 0-679-20779-1). McKay.
Reied, Morton H., ed. Systems of Equality & Inequality in Human Society. 240p. 1981. 20.95 (ISBN 0-89789-012-4). J F Bergin.
Reierson, Gary B., jt. auth. see Campbell, Thomas C.
Reif, Dan. Solar Retrofit: How to Evaluate & Install Solar Heating in Existing Homes. (Illus.). 160p. (Orig.). 1980. 16.95 (ISBN 0-931790-50-6); pap. 8.95 (ISBN 0-931790-15-8). Brick Hse Pub.
Reif, Daniel K. Solar Retrofit: Adding Solar to Your Home. (Illus.). 200p. 1981. 17.95 (ISBN 0-931790-50-6); pap. 8.95 (ISBN 0-931790-15-8). Brick Hse Pub.
Reif, Joseph A. & Levinson, Hanna. Spoken Modern Hebrew. (Spoken Language Ser.). 590p. 1980. pap. 15.00x (ISBN 0-87950-683-0); text & cassette 175.00 (ISBN 0-87950-685-7); cassettes, 34 dual track 165.00x (ISBN 0-87950-684-9) (ISBN 0-87950-685-7). Spoken Lang Serv.
Reif, Joseph A., jt. auth. see Stern, A Z.
Reif, Joseph A., jt. ed. see Stern, A. Z.
Reiff, D. D., ed. Component Support Snubbers: Design, Application & Testing. (PVP: No. 42). 130p. 1980. 10.00 (H00169). ASME.
Reiff, Florence M. Steps in Home Living. rev. ed. (Illus.). (YA) (gr. 7-9). 1971. text ed. 15.96 (ISBN 0-87002-099-4); tchr's guide avail. (ISBN 0-685-06851-X). Bennett IL.
Reiff, Robert F. A Stylistic Analysis of Arshile Gorky's Art from 1943-1948. LC 76-23679. (Outstanding Dissertations in the Fine Arts - American). (Illus.). 1977. Repr. of 1961 ed. lib. bdg. 52.00 (ISBN 0-8240-2719-1). Garland Pub.
Reiff, Stephanie A. Secrets of Tut's Tomb & the Pyramids. LC 77-22770. (Great Unsolved Mysteries Ser.). (Illus.). (gr. 4-5). 1977. PLB 9.65 (ISBN 0-8172-1051-2). Raintree Pubs.
--Visions of the Future: Magic Numbers & Cards. LC 77-22801. (Myth, Magic & Superstition Ser.). (Illus.). (gr. 4-5). 1977. PLB 9.65 (ISBN 0-8172-1027-X). Raintree Pubs.
Reiffel, James, et al, eds. Psychosocial Aspects of Cardiovascular Disease: The Life-Threatened Patient, the Family & the Staff. Kutscher, Austin H. LC 79-27765. (Foundation of Thanatology Ser.). (Illus.). 1980. 25.00x (ISBN 0-231-04354-6). Columbia U Pr.
Reiffel, Leonard. The Contaminant. 1980. pap. 2.50 o.s.i. (ISBN 0-440-11473-X). Dell.
Reifsnyder, David N. Parasitic Diseases Case Studies. LC 80-81733. 1980. pap. 18.50 (ISBN 0-87488-049-1). Med Exam.
Reifsnyder, William E. Footloose in the Swiss Alps. LC 74-76313. (Totebook). (Illus.). 444p. 1974. pap. 7.95 (ISBN 0-87156-102-6). Sierra.
--Hut Hopping in the Austrian Alps. LC 73-77290. (Totebook Ser). (Illus.). 224p. 1973. pap. 5.95 (ISBN 0-87156-081-X). Sierra.
--Weathering the Wilderness: The Sierra Club Guide to Practical Meteorology. LC 79-20859. (Outdoor Guides Ser.). (Illus.). 272p. 1980. pap. 8.95 (ISBN 0-87156-266-9). Sierra.
Reigel, Charles E. & Perkins, Edward A. Executive Typewriting. 2nd ed. (Illus.). 256p. (gr. 12 up). 1980. practice set in envelope container 13.75 (ISBN 0-07-051826-2); instrs'. guide & visual key 4.95 (ISBN 0-07-051827-0). McGraw.
Reiger, John F. American Sportsmen & the Origins of Conservation. (Illus.). 352p. 1975. 11.95 (ISBN 0-87691-173-4). Winchester Pr.
Reiget. Wake up It's Night. (ps-3). pap. 1.25 (ISBN 0-590-05404-X, Schol Pap). Schol Bk Serv.
Reighley, Joan, jt. auth. see Creighton, Margo N.
Reihlen, H., intro. by. Export Directory of German Industries, 1980. 27th ed. LC 57-16210. 1332p. (Orig.). 1980. pap. 55.00x (ISBN 0-8002-2695-X). Intl Pubns Serv.
Reik, Theodor. The Creation of Woman: A Psychoanalytic Inquiry into the Myth of Eve. LC 60-5613. 160p. 1973. Repr. of 1960 ed. pap. 1.95 o.p. (ISBN 0-07-051813-0, SP). McGraw.
--Listening with the Third Ear. 1977. pap. 2.25 o.p. (ISBN 0-685-86426-X). Jove Pubns.
--Psychology of Sex Relations. LC 74-28525. 243p. 1975. Repr. of 1945 ed. lib. bdg. 21.00x (ISBN 0-8371-7916-5, RESR). Greenwood.
--Ritual: Psychoanalytic Studies. LC 73-2645. (Illus.). 367p. 1975. Repr. of 1946 ed. lib. bdg. 25.25x (ISBN 0-8371-6814-7, RERI). Greenwood.
Reik, Theodore. Of Love & Lust. 1976. pap. 2.25 o.s.i. (ISBN 0-515-03971-3). Jove Pubns.
Reiley, H. Edward & Shry, Carroll L., Jr. Introductory Horticulture. LC 77-81006. 1979. pap. text ed. 22.00 (ISBN 0-8273-1893-6); instructor's guide 1.60 (ISBN 0-8273-1645-3). Delmar.
Reiling, J. & Swellengrebel, J. L. Translators Handbook on the Gospel of Luke. (Helps for Translators Ser.). 1971. 11.75 (ISBN 0-8267-0136-1, 08512). United Bible.
Reill, Peter H. The German Enlightenment & the Rise of Historicism. LC 73-87244. 318p. 1975. 27.50x (ISBN 0-520-02594-6). U of Cal Pr.
Reilly, Adam. Harold Lloyd: The King of Daredevil Comedy. (Illus.). 1977. 14.95 o.s.i. (ISBN 0-02-601940-X). Macmillan.
Reilly, Conor. Metal Contamination of Food. xvi, 231p. 1980. 42.50x (ISBN 0-85334-905-3). Burgess-Intl Ideas.
Reilly, Cyril & Reilly, Renee. I Am of Ireland. (Illus.). 60p. (Orig.). 1981. pap. 6.95 (ISBN 0-03-059058-2). Winston Pr.
Reilly, Dorothy. Behavioral Objectives-Evaluation in Nursing. 2nd ed. 200p. 1980. pap. text ed. 11.95 (ISBN 0-8385-0634-8). ACC.
Reilly, Edgar M., Jr. The Audubon Illustrated Handbook of American Birds. (Illus.). 544p. 1968. 20.00 o.p. (ISBN 0-685-48741-5, Pub by National Audubon Society). Interbk Inc.
Reilly, Edward D., jt. auth. see Federighi, Francis.
Reilly, Edward R., tr. see Quantz, Johann J.
Reilly, Elizabeth C. Dictionary of Colonial American Printer's Ornaments & Illustrations. (Illus.). xxxvi, 514p. 1975. 45.00x (ISBN 0-912296-06-2, Dist. by U Pr of Va). Am Antiquarian.
Reilly, Harold J. & Brod, Ruth H. The Edgar Cayce Handbook for Health Through Drugless Therapy. (Illus.). 356p. 1975. 10.95 o.s.i. (ISBN 0-02-601960-4). Macmillan.
--Edgar Cayce Handbook for Health Through Drugless Therapy. 1977. pap. 3.50 (ISBN 0-515-05825-4). Jove Pubns.
Reilly, Harry, ed. see Guder, Robert F.
Reilly, Helen. McKee of Centre Street. 299p. 1980. Repr. of 1933 ed. lib. bdg. 14.25x (ISBN 0-89968-214-6). Lightyear.
Reilly, John & Vitousek, Paige. Questions & Answers to Help You Pass the Real Estate Exam. 200p. (Orig.). 1981. pap. 13.95 (ISBN 0-88462-395-5). Real Estate Ed Co.
--Questions & Answers to Help You Pass the Real Estate License Examination. 200p. 1980. pap. cancelled (ISBN 0-695-81506-7). Real Estate Ed Co.
Reilly, John C. & Scheina, Robert L. American Battleships, Eighteen Eighty-Six to Nineteen Twenty-Three: Predreadnought Design & Construction. LC 79-91326. 236p. 1980. 29.95 (ISBN 0-87021-524-8). Naval Inst Pr.
Reilly, John H. Arthur Adamov. LC 74-2162. (World Authors Ser.: France: No. 318). 1974. lib. bdg. 10.95 (ISBN 0-8057-2005-7). Twayne.
--Jean Giraudoux. (World Authors Ser.: No. 513 (France)). 1978. 12.50 (ISBN 0-8057-6354-6). Twayne.
Reilly, John H., ed. see Giraudoux, Jean.
Reilly, John M., ed. Twentieth Century Crime & Mystery Writers. (Twentieth Century Writers Ser.). 1600p. 1980. 50.00x (ISBN 0-312-82417-3). St Martin.
Reilly, John W. Language of Real Estate. 1977. 35.95 o.p. (ISBN 0-88462-362-9). Real Estate Ed Co.
--The Language of Real Estate. 585p. (Orig.). 1977. pap. 19.95 (ISBN 0-88462-354-8). Real Estate Ed Co.
Reilly, Marta T., et al. Guide to Resource Organizations. (Resources in Bilingual Education Ser.). (Orig.). 1981. pap. write for info. (ISBN 0-89763-053-X). Natl Clearinghse Bilingual Ed.
Reilly, Mary, ed. Play As Exploratory Learning. LC 72-98044. 1974. 20.00x (ISBN 0-8039-0159-3); pap. 8.95x (ISBN 0-8039-0845-8). Sage.
Reilly, Renee, jt. auth. see Reilly, Cyril.
Reilly, Robert T. Travel & Tourism Marketing Techniques. LC 79-92385. 1980. 14.95 (ISBN 0-916032-08-6). Merton Hse.
Reilly, Sidney. Britain's Master Spy: The Adventures of Sidney Reilly. 296p. 1980. Repr. of 1933 ed. lib. bdg. 35.00 (ISBN 0-89984-449-9). Century Bookbindery.
Reilly, Thomas, ed. Sports Fitness & Sports Injuries. (Illus.). 304p. 1981. 45.00 (ISBN 0-571-11628-0, Pub. by Faber & Faber); pap. 28.00 (ISBN 0-571-11629-9). Merrimack Bk Serv.
Reilly, Thomas A. & Sigall, Michael W. Political Bargaining: An Introduction to Modern Politics. LC 75-38837. (Illus.). 1976. text ed. 16.95x (ISBN 0-7167-0538-9); pap. text ed. 8.95x (ISBN 0-7167-0537-0). W H Freeman.
Reily, F. Investment Analysis & Portfolio Management. LC 78-56196. 1979. 20.95 (ISBN 0-03-013576-1). Dryden Pr.
Reim, G. Studien zum Altestamentlichen Hintergrund Des Johannesevangeliums. LC 72-76086. (New Testament Studies Monograph, No. 22). 280p. (Ger.). 1973. 51.00 (ISBN 0-521-08630-2). Cambridge U Pr.
Reiman, Doanld H., ed. John Thelwall. Incl. Ode to Science. Repr. of 1791 ed; John Gildin's Ghost. Repr. of 1795 ed; Poems. Repr. of 1801 ed. LC 75-31261. (Romantic Context Ser.: Poetry 1789-1830). 1978. lib. bdg. 47.00 (ISBN 0-8240-2207-6). Garland Pub.
Reiman, Donald, ed. English Romantic Poetry, Eighteen Hundred-Eighteen Thirty-Five: A Guide to Information Sources. LC 74-11527. (American Literature, English Literature, & World Literatures in English Information Guide Ser.: Vol. 27). 1979. 30.00 (ISBN 0-8103-1231-X). Gale.
Reiman, Donald, ed. see Dacre, Charlotte.
Reiman, Donald H. Percy Bysshe Shelley. (English Authors Ser.: No. 81). lib. bdg. 9.95 (ISBN 0-8057-1488-X). Twayne.
Reiman, Donald H., ed. Dramatic Scenes & Other Poems 1819; Marcian Colonna, 1820: Proctor Bryan Waller ("Barry Cornwall") (1787-1874) LC 75-31246. (Romantic Context Ser.: Poetry 1789-1830). 1978. lib. bdg. 47.00 (ISBN 0-8240-2194-0). Garland Pub.

--Edward Thurlow. Incl. Hermilda in Palestine...with Other Poems. Repr. of 1812 ed; The Sonnets of Edward, Lord Thurlow: Select Poems, 1821. Repr. of 1819 ed. LC 75-31267. (Romantic Context Ser.: Poetry 1789-1830). 1978. lib. bdg. 43.00 (ISBN 0-8240-2213-0). Garland Pub.

--Edward Thurlow, Second Baron Thurlow (1781-1829) LC 75-31265. (Romantic Context Ser.: Poetry 1789-1830). 1978. lib. bdg. 47.00 (ISBN 0-8240-2211-4). Garland Pub.

--The Flood of Thessaly: Proctor Bryan Waller. LC 75-31248. (Romantic Context Ser.: Poetry 1789-1830). 1978. Repr. of 1823 ed. lib. bdg. 47.00 (ISBN 0-8240-2196-7). Garland Pub.

--George Canning (Seventeen Seventy to Eighteen Twenty-Seven) & William Gifford (Seventeen Fifty-Six to Eighteen Twenty-Six. LC 75-31176. (Romantic Context: Poetry 1789-1830 Ser.). 1978. lib. bdg. 47.00 (ISBN 0-8240-2128-2). Garland Pub.

--George Crolx (Seventeen Eighty to Eighteen Sixty) LC 75-31189. (Romantic Context Ser.: Poetry 1789-1830 Ser.). 1978. lib. bdg. 47.00 (ISBN 0-8240-2140-1). Garland Pub.

--James Montgomery. LC 75-31239. (Romantic Context Ser.: Poetry 1789-1830). 1978. lib. bdg. 47.00 (ISBN 0-8240-2188-6). Garland Pub.

--James Montgomery (1771-1854) Incl. Prison Amusements. Repr. of 1797 ed; The Wanderer of Switzerland. Repr. of 1806 ed. LC 75-31235. (Romantic Context Ser.: Poetry 1789-1830). 1978. lib. bdg. 47.00 (ISBN 0-8240-2185-1). Garland Pub.

--John Chalk Claris. LC 75-31179. (Romantic Context Ser.: Poetry 1789-1830). 1977. lib. bdg. 47.00 (ISBN 0-8240-2131-2). Garland Pub.

--John Chalk Claris ("Arthur Brooke") (1797-1866) LC 75-31178. (Romantic Context Ser.: Poetry 1789-1830). 1978. lib. bdg. 47.00 (ISBN 0-8240-2130-4). Garland Pub.

--John Hamilton Reynolds. LC 75-31251. (Romantic Context Ser.: Poetry 1789-1830). 1977. lib. bdg. 47.00 (ISBN 0-8240-2199-1). Garland Pub.

--John Hamilton Reynolds. Incl. The Garden of Florence. Repr. of 1821 ed; The Press, or Literary Chit-Chat. Repr. of 1822 ed; Odes & Addresses to Great People. Repr. of 1825 ed. LC 75-31252. (Romantic Context Ser.: Poetry 1789-1830). 1978. lib. bdg. 47.00 (ISBN 0-8240-2200-9). Garland Pub.

--Josiah Conder. LC 75-31183. (Romantic Context Ser.: Poetry 1789-1830). 1977. lib. bdg. 47.00 (ISBN 0-8240-2134-7). Garland Pub.

--Miscellaneous Verse, Originally Published in Quarto, by Burges, Carv, Dyer, Lloyd, Merivale, Thelwall & Wilson. Bd. with James Bland Burges: The Birth & Triumph of Love, A Poem. Burges, James B. Repr. of 1796 ed; Henry Francis Cary (1755-1844) Sonnets & Odes. Repr. of 1788 ed; Ode to General Kosciusko. Repr. of 1797 ed; George Dyer: Poems. Repr. of 1792 ed; Charles Lloyd: Poems on the Death of Priscilla Farmer (Including Poems by Coleridge & Lamb) Repr. of 1796 ed; Lines Suggested by the Fast, Appointed on Wednesday, February 27, 1799. Repr. of 1799 ed; John Herman Merivale: The Minstrel: Book the Third (Continuation of a Poem by James Beattie) Repr. of 1808 ed; John Thelwall: Poems Written in Close Confinement in the Tower & Newgate, Under a Charge of High Treason. Repr. of 1795 ed; John Wilson: The Magic Mirror. Addressed to Walter Scott, Esq. Repr. of 1812 ed. LC 75-31175. (Romantic Context Ser.: Poetry 1789-1830: No. 28). 1978. lib. bdg. 47.00 (ISBN 0-8240-2127-4). Garland Pub.

Reiman, Donald H., ed. & intro. by. The Romantics Reviewed: A Collection in Depth of Periodical Reviews (1793-1830, 11 vols. Incl. Vols. I & II. Pt. A. lib. bdg. 93.00 each (ISBN 0-8240-0509-0); Vols. I To V. Pt. B. lib. bdg. 375.00 5 vol. set (ISBN 0-8240-0510-4); Vols. I & II. Pt. C. lib. bdg. 93.00 each 2 vol. set (ISBN 0-8240-0511-2); Vols. I & II. Bibliography of Literary Reviews in British Periodicals 1798-1820. Ward, William S., ed. lib. bdg. 60.00 ea.. Set. lib. bdg. 740.00 (ISBN 0-8240-0512-0); lib. bdg. 93.00 ea. vols. comprising pts. a,b, & c. Garland Pub.

Reiman, Donald H. & Reiman, Donald H., eds. A Sicilian Story, 1820; Mirandola 1821: Proctor Bryan Waller. LC 75-31247. (Romantic Context: Poetry 1789-1830 Ser.). 1977. lib. bdg. 47.00 (ISBN 0-8240-2195-9). Garland Pub.

Reiman, Donald H., ed. see Barrett, Eaton S.

Reiman, Donald H., ed. see Bland, Robert.

Reiman, Donald H., ed. see Bloomfield, Robert.

Reiman, Donald H., ed. see Bowles, William L.

Reiman, Donald H., ed. see Burges, James B.

Reiman, Donald H., ed. see Carr, Sir John.

Reiman, Donald H., ed. see Dallas, Robert C.

Reiman, Donald H., ed. see Darley, George.

Reiman, Donald H., ed. see Darwin, Erasmus.

Reiman, Donald H., ed. see Dermody, Thomas.

Reiman, Donald H., ed. see Dyer, George.

Reiman, Donald H., ed. see Elliott, Ebenezer.

Reiman, Donald H., ed. see Frere, John H.

Reiman, Donald H., ed. see Gent, Thomas.

Reiman, Donald H., ed. see Hayley, William.

Reiman, Donald H., ed. see Heber, Reginald.

Reiman, Donald H., ed. see Hemans, Felicia D.

Reiman, Donald H., ed. see Hobhouse, John C.

Reiman, Donald H., ed. see Hodgson, Francis.

Reiman, Donald H., ed. see Lloyd, Charles.

Reiman, Donald H., ed. see Mant, Richard.

Reiman, Donald H., ed. see Medwin, Thomas.

Reiman, Donald H., ed. see Merivale, John H.

Reiman, Donald H., ed. see Montgomery, James.

Reiman, Donald H., ed. see Opie, Amelia.

Reiman, Donald H., ed. see Reynolds, John H.

Reiman, Donald H., ed. see Shelley, Percy.

Reiman, Donald H., ed. see Smith, Horatio.

Reiman, Donald H., ed. see Smith, James & Smith, Horatio.

Reiman, Donald H., ed. see Sotheby, William.

Reiman, Donald H., ed. see Southey, Robert.

Reiman, Donald H., ed. see Thelwall, John.

Reiman, Donald H., ed. see Thurlow, Edward.

Reiman, Donald H., ed. see Tighe, Mary.

Reiman, Donald H., ed. see Walker, William S.

Reiman, Donald H., ed. see Wiffen, Jeremiah H.

Reiman, Donald H., ed. see Wilson, John.

Reiman, Donald H., et al, eds. The Evidence of the Imagination: Studies of Interactions Between Life & Art in English Romantic Literature. LC 77-14673. 1978. 17.50x (ISBN 0-8147-7372-9); pap. 5.00x (ISBN 0-8147-7373-7). NYU Pr.

Reiman, Hobart A. Acute Respiratory Tract Diseases: Prevention & Treatment. LC 74-8610. 154p. 1975. 15.00 (ISBN 0-8463-0152-0). Krieger.

Reimann see Weyl, Hermann, et al.

Reimann, et al. Uniform National Examination in Landscape Architecture: Candidate Review Manual. LC 78-55457. 1978. pap. 25.00 (ISBN 0-918436-04-4). Environ Des VA.

Reimann, Hobart A. & Juniper, Kerrison, Jr. Infectious & Parasitic Diseases of the Intestine - Discussions in Patient Management. 1977. spiral bdg. 8.50 (ISBN 0-87488-880-8). Med Exam.

Reimer, Bennett. Philosophy of Music Education. (Contemporary Perspectives in Music Education Ser). 1970. pap. text ed. 10.50 (ISBN 0-13-663872-4). P-H.

Reimer, Bennett & Evans, Edward. The Experience of Music. (Illus.). 384p. 1973. text ed. 18.95 (ISBN 0-13-294553-3); wkbk. 9.95 (ISBN 0-13-294876-1); records 18.95 (ISBN 0-13-294900-8); library of records 110.50 (ISBN 0-13-294892-3); demonstration record 129.95. P-H.

Rein, Irving J. The Great American Communication Catalogue. (Speech Communications Ser.). (Illus.). 160p. 1975. pap. 10.95 (ISBN 0-13-363580-5). P-H.

--Relevant Rhetoric. 1969. pap. text ed. 7.95 (ISBN 0-02-926140-6). Free Pr.

Rein, Lynn. Ladies & Gentlemen: A History of the School of Speech of North Western University. 1980. 15.95 (ISBN 0-8101-0538-1). Northwestern U Pr.

Rein, M. L., jt. auth. see Bass, Howard L.

Rein, Natalie. Daughters of Rachel: Women in Israel. 1980. pap. 4.95 (ISBN 0-14-005731-5). Penguin.

Reina, Reuben E., jt. auth. see Cochran, Thomas C.

Reinberg, A., jt. ed. see Smolensky, M. H.

Reinberg, A., et al, eds. Night & Shift Work-Biological & Social Aspects: Proceedings of the Vth International Symposium on Night and Shift Work-Scientific Committee on Shift Work of the Permanent Commission & International Association on Occupational Health (PCIAIH, Rouen, 12-16 May 1980. (Illus.). 516p. 1981. 80.00 (ISBN 0-08-025516-7). Pergamon.

Reinberg, Gerald, et al, eds. A Festschrift for Maurice Goldhaber. new ed. LC 80-20599. (Transaction Ser.: Vol. 40). 293p. 1980. 25.00 (ISBN 0-89766-086-2). NY Acad Sci.

Reincke, Mary & Stokes, Sylvia, eds. The American Bar - the Canadian Bar - the International Bar, 1979. 61st ed. LC 18-21110. 1979. 110.00 o.p. (ISBN 0-931398-04-5). R B Forster.

Reineck, H. E. & Singh, I. B. Depositional Sedimentary Environments-with Reference to Terrigenous Classics. (Illus.). 439p. 1974. 50.00 o.p. (ISBN 0-387-06115-0). Springer-Verlag.

--Depositional Sedimentary Environments with Reference to Terrigenous Clastics. 2nd rev. ed. (Illus.). 549p. 1980. pap. 29.80 (ISBN 0-387-10189-6). Springer-Verlag.

Reinecke. Introduction to Business: A Contemporary View. 3rd ed. 704p. 1980. text ed. 17.95 (ISBN 0-205-06879-0, 0868795). Allyn.

Reinecke, Esther E. Punkin's First Halloween. (Second Grade Bk.). (Illus.). (gr. 2-3). PLB 5.95 o.p. (ISBN 0-513-00395-9). Denison.

Reinecker, Herbert. Der Kommissar Lasst Bitten. (Easy Readers, B). 1978. pap. text ed. 3.75 (ISBN 0-88436-291-4). EMC.

Reinehr, Robert C. The Machine That Oils Itself: A Critical Look at the Mental Health Establishment. LC 75-23326. 264p. 1975. 14.95 (ISBN 0-88229-248-X). Nelson Hall.

Reiner, Erica, jt. ed. see Oppenheim, A. Leo.

Reiner, Erica, et al, eds. The Assyrian Dictionary of the Oriental Institute of the University of Chicago, 2 pts, Vol. 11, N. LC 56-58292. 1981. Pt. 1 & 2. lib. bdg. 110.00x (ISBN 0-918986-17-6). Oriental Inst.

Reiner, Irving & Curtis, Charles W. Representation Theory of Finite Groups & Orders. (Pure & Applied Mathematics: Texts, Monographs & Tracts). 900p. 1981. 60.00 (ISBN 0-471-18994-4, Pub. by Wiley-Interscience). Wiley.

Reiner, Irving, jt. auth. see Curtis, Charles W.

Reiner, J. Organism As an Adaptive Control System. 1968. 18.95 (ISBN 0-13-640920-2). P-H.

Reiner, Laurence E. Methods & Materials of Residential Construction. (Illus.). 336p. 1981. text ed. 24.95 (ISBN 0-13-578864-1). P-H.

Reiner, Miriam, et al, eds. Standard Methods of Clinical Chemistry. Incl. Vol. 1. Reiner, Miriam, ed. 1953. 26.00 (ISBN 0-12-609101-3); Vol. 2. Seligson, David, ed. 1958. 26.00 (ISBN 0-12-609102-1); Vol. 3. 1961. 26.00 (ISBN 0-12-609103-X); Vol. 4. 1964. 26.00 (ISBN 0-12-609104-8); Vol. 5. Meites, S., ed. 1965. 26.00 (ISBN 0-12-609105-6); Vol. 6. MacDonald, R. P., ed. 1970. 36.50 (ISBN 0-12-609106-4); Vol. 7. 1972. 42.50 (ISBN 0-12-609107-2). Acad Pr.

Reiner, R. The Blue-Coated Worker. LC 77-85695. (Cambridge Studies in Sociology: No. 10). (Illus.). 1978. 38.50 (ISBN 0-521-21889-6); pap. 11.95 (ISBN 0-521-29482-7). Cambridge U Pr.

Reiners, Ed, jt. auth. see Shear, Lee.

Reiners, Ludwig. Frederick the Great. 1960. 13.95 (ISBN 0-85496-251-4). Dufour.

Reinert, Harry. German First Year. (gr. 7-12). 1971. wkbk. 6.42 (ISBN 0-87720-583-3). AMSCO Sch.

--Review Text in German, First Year. (Orig.). (gr. 10-12). 1971. pap. text ed. 5.33 (ISBN 0-87720-581-7). AMSCO Sch.

Reinert, Henry R., jt. auth. see Swanson, H. Lee.

Reinertsen, Lauren. Clipart Book of Promotional & Program Artwork. LC 74-84398. (Illus.). 64p. 1974. pap. 9.95 (ISBN 0-87874-013-9). Galloway.

Reinfeld, Fred. Attack & Counterattack in Chess. 1970. pap. 1.95 (ISBN 0-06-463204-0, EH 204, EH). Har-Row.

--Chess for Children. rev. ed. LC 58-7612. (Illus.). 72p. (gr. 3-12). 1980. 6.95 (ISBN 0-8069-4904-X); PLB 6.69 (ISBN 0-8069-4905-8). Sterling.

--Chess in a Nutshell. LC 58-11323. 1958. 5.95 o.p. (ISBN 0-385-01754-5). Doubleday.

--Chess Is an Easy Game. LC 61-18952. (gr. 5 up). 1962. 6.95 (ISBN 0-8069-4906-6); PLB 6.69 (ISBN 0-8069-4907-4). Sterling.

--Complete Book of Chess Openings. 1963. pap. 2.95 (ISBN 0-06-463274-1, EH 274, EH). Har-Row.

--Complete Chess Course. LC 59-13043. 1959. 12.95 (ISBN 0-385-00464-8). Doubleday.

--Complete Chess Player. 1953. 6.95 o.p. (ISBN 0-13-159111-8). P-H.

--The Complete Chessplayer. 1978. pap. 2.25 (ISBN 0-449-14101-2, GM). Fawcett.

--Great Games by Chess Prodigies. (Illus.). 256p. 1972. pap. 2.95 o.s.i. (ISBN 0-02-029710-6, Collier). Macmillan.

--How to Build a Coin Collection. (Illus.). 160p. 1973. pap. 4.95 (ISBN 0-02-081230-2, Collier). Macmillan.

--How to Play Chess Like a Champion. 1977. pap. 1.75 o.p. (ISBN 0-449-23289-1, Crest). Fawcett.

--How to Win at Checkers. pap. 3.00 (ISBN 0-87980-068-2). Wilshire.

--How to Win Chess Games Quickly. 1963. pap. 2.95 (ISBN 0-06-463269-5, EH 269, EH). Har-Row.

--Improving Your Chess. 1963. pap. 3.50 (ISBN 0-06-463267-9, EH 267, EH). Har-Row.

--Improving Your Chess. (Illus., Orig.). 1970. pap. 2.95 o.p. (ISBN 0-571-09393-0, Pub. by Faber & Faber). Merrimack Bk Serv.

--The Joys of Chess. (Illus.). 288p. 1974. pap. 2.95 o.s.i. (ISBN 0-02-029730-0, Collier). Macmillan.

--Pony Express. LC 64-21330. (Illus.). 127p. 1973. pap. 2.95 (ISBN 0-8032-5786-4, BB 572, Bison). U of Nebr Pr.

--Win at Chess. Orig. Title: Chess Quiz. 1945. pap. 2.50 (ISBN 0-486-20438-3). Dover.

Reinfeld, Fred & Hobson, Burton. Catalogue of the World's Most Popular Coins. 10th ed. LC 78-66299. (Illus.). 1979. 19.95 (ISBN 0-8069-6070-1); lib. bdg. 17.59 (ISBN 0-8069-6071-X). Sterling.

Reinfeld, Fred & Hobson, Burton H. How to Build a Coin Collection. LC 58-12544. (Illus.). (gr. 3 up). 1977. 7.95 (ISBN 0-8069-6068-X); PLB 7.49 (ISBN 0-8069-6069-8). Sterling.

Reinfeld, Fred & Soltis, Andy. Morphy Chess Masterpieces. 176p. 1974. 6.95 o.s.i. (ISBN 0-02-601980-9). Macmillan.

Reinfeld, Fred, jt. auth. see Hobson, Burton.

Reinfeld, Fred, jt. auth. see Horowitz, I. A.

Reinfeld, Fred, ed. see Tarrasch, Siegbert.

Reinfeld, Nyles. Survival Management for Industry. 1981. text ed. 17.95 (ISBN 0-8359-7410-3); instr's. manual free (ISBN 0-8359-7411-1). Reston.

Reingold, et al. Combinatorial Algorithms: Theory & Practice. 1977. text ed. 23.95 (ISBN 0-13-152447-X). P-H.

Reingold, Carmel B. Convection Oven Cookbook. LC 80-7859. 170p. 1980. 13.95; pap. 7.95. Lippincott & Crowell.

--Convection Oven Cookbook. 1980. 13.95 (ISBN 0-690-01980-7, HarpT); pap. 7.95 (ISBN 0-690-01982-3, HarpT). Har-Row.

--The Crockery Pot Cookbook. (Orig.). 1975. pap. 1.50 (ISBN 0-515-03950-0). Jove Pubns.

--Cuisinart Food Processor Cookbook. 1981. pap. price not set (Delta). Dell.

--How to Be Happy If You Marry Again. 1977. pap. 2.50 (ISBN 0-06-080412-2, P412, PL). Har-Row.

--Johann Sebastian Bach: Revolutionary of Music. LC 72-114927. (Biography Ser). (Illus.). (gr. 7 up). 1970. PLB 5.90 o.p. (ISBN 0-531-00956-4). Watts.

Reingold, Carmel B. & Kaufman, William I. Fabulous Fondue Cookbook. (Orig.). 1970. pap. 1.50 o.s.i. (ISBN 0-515-02311-6, V2311). Jove Pubns.

Reingold, Nathan, ed. The Papers of Joseph Henry: The Princeton Years, January 1838-1840, Vol. 4. LC 72-2005. (The Papers of Joseph Henry Ser.). (Illus.). 432p. 1981. text ed. 30.00x (ISBN 0-87474-792-9). Smithsonian.

Reinhard, John. Clinical Pharmacology. 3rd ed. (Illus.). 1977. pap. text ed. 20.50 (ISBN 0-89147-039-5). CAS.

Reinhardt, Adina M. & Quinn, Mildred D. Current Practice in Family-Centered Community Nursing: A Sociocultural Framework, Vol. II. LC 73-8681. (Current Practice Ser.). (Illus.). 1980. pap. text ed. 12.95 (ISBN 0-8016-4121-7). Mosby.

--Current Practice in Gerontological Nursing. LC 78-31424. (Current Practice Ser.). 1979. text ed. 12.50 (ISBN 0-8016-4122-5); pap. text ed. 10.95 (ISBN 0-8016-4113-6). Mosby.

Reinhardt, Adina M. & Quinn, Mildred D., eds. Current Practice in Family-Centered Community Nursing. LC 76-26006. (Illus.). 1977. 11.95 o.p. (ISBN 0-8016-4114-4); pap. 8.95 o.p. (ISBN 0-8016-4107-1). Mosby.

--Family Centered Community Nursing: A Sociocultural Framework. LC 73-8681. 1973. pap. text ed. 12.50 (ISBN 0-8016-4102-0). Mosby.

Reinhardt, Howard E. & Loftsgaarden, Don O. Elementary Probability & Statistical Reasoning. 1976. text ed. 16.95x (ISBN 0-669-08300-3); instructor's manual free (ISBN 0-669-00241-0). Heath.

Reinhardt, Jon M. Foreign Policy & National Intergration: The Case of Indonesia. (Monograph: No. 17). (Illus.). vi, 230p. 1971. 6.50 o.p. (ISBN 0-686-63725-9). Yale U Pr.

Reinhardt, Kurt F. Germany: Two Thousand Years, 2 Vols. rev. ed. LC 60-53139. Vol.1. 12.00 (ISBN 0-8044-1783-0); Vol.2. 12.00 (ISBN 0-8044-1784-9); Vol.1. pap. 5.50 (ISBN 0-8044-6692-0); Vol.2. pap. 5.95 (ISBN 0-8044-6693-9). Set. pap. 10.95 (ISBN 0-8044-6691-2). Ungar.

Reinhart, Charles. You Can't Do That: Beatles Bootlegs & Novelty Records, 1963-1980. 1981. 11.95 (ISBN 0-87650-128-5). Pierian.

Reinharth, Leon, et al. The Practice of Planning: Strategic, Administrative, Operational. 352p. 1980. text ed. 19.95. Van Nos Reinhold.

Reinharz, Jehuda, jt. auth. see Mendes-Flohr, Paul R.

Reinhold, E., ed. Jahrestagung der Oesterreichischen Gesellschaft fur Gynaekologie und Geburtshilfe, Juni 1980, Krems. (Gynaekologische Rundschau: Vol. 20, Suppl. 2, 1981). (Illus.). vi, 294p. 1981. pap. 39.75 (ISBN 3-8055-2191-X). S Karger.

Reinhold, H. A., ed. The Soul Afire: Revelations of the Mystics. 440p. 1973. pap. 2.95 (ISBN 0-385-01489-9, Im). Doubleday.

Reinhold, L., et al. Progress in Phytochemistry, Vol. 7. LC 68-24347. (Illus.). 410p. 1981. 87.50 (ISBN 0-08-026362-3). Pergamon.

Reinhold, L., et al, eds. Progress in Phytochemistry, Vol. 6. LC 68-24347. (Illus.). 1980. 87.50 (ISBN 0-08-024946-9). Pergamon.

Reinhold, Robert see Smith Experimental Fiction Project.
Reining, Conrad C. Zande Scheme: An Anthropological Case Study of Economic Development in Africa. (African Studies Ser.: No. 17). 1966. 11.95x o.s.i. (ISBN 0-8101-0205-6). Northwestern U Pr.
Reining, Priscilla & Lenkerd, Barbara, eds. Village Viability in Contemporary Society. (AAAS Selected Symposium: No. 34). 1979. lib. bdg. 23.50x (ISBN 0-89158-472-2). Westview.
Reinis, Z., ed. Adaptibility of the Vascular Wall: Proceedings. (Illus.). 650p. 1980. 87.40 (ISBN 0-387-09907-7). Springer-Verlag.
Reinisch, Edith H. & Minear, Ralph E. Health of the Preschool Child. LC 78-8743. 1978. text ed. 17.95 (ISBN 0-471-60800-9). Wiley.
Reinitz, Richard. Irony & Consciousness: American Historiography & Reinhold Niebuhr's Vision. LC 77-92574. 232p. Date not set. 18.00 (ISBN 0-8387-2062-5). Bucknell U Pr.
Reino, Joseph. Karl Shapiro. (United States Authors Ser.: No. 404). 1981. lib. bdg. 12.95 (ISBN 0-8057-7333-9). Twayne.
Reinold, E., ed. Jahrestagung der Oesterreichischen Gesellschaft Fur Gynaekologie und Geburtshilfe, Juni 1980, Krems. (Journal: Gynaekologische Rundschau: Vol. 20, Suppl. 2). 300p. 1980. pap. write for info. (ISBN 3-8055-2191-X). S Karger.
Reinsch, Paul S. English Common Law in the Early American Colonies. LC 75-110969. (American Constitutional & Legal History Ser). 1970. Repr. of 1899 ed. lib. bdg. 14.95 (ISBN 0-306-71910-X). Da Capo.
Reinsmith, Richard. Bury the Past. (Orig.). 1980. pap. 1.75 (ISBN 0-505-51558-X). Tower Bks.
Reinstedt, Randall A. Ghostly Tales & Mysterious Happenings of Old Monterey. LC 79-110356. (Illus.). 1977. pap. 3.95 (ISBN 0-933818-04-1). Ghost Town.
--Ghosts, Bandits & Legends of Old Monterey. LC 74-189524. (Illus.). 1974. pap. 3.50 (ISBN 0-933818-00-9). Ghost Town.
--Incredible Ghosts of Old Monterey's Hotel Del Monte. (Illus.). 48p. pap. 2.95 (ISBN 0-933818-07-6). Ghost Town.
--Monterey's Mother Lode. LC 79-110351. (Illus.). 1977. pap. 5.50 (ISBN 0-933818-01-7). Ghost Town.
--Shipwrecks & Sea Monsters of California's Central Coast. LC 76-350548. (Illus.). 1975. pap. 5.95 (ISBN 0-933818-02-5). Ghost Town.
--Tales, Treasures, & Pirates of Old Monterey. LC 79-110354. (Illus.). 1976. pap. 4.95 (ISBN 0-933818-03-3). Ghost Town.
--Where Have All the Sardines Gone? LC 79-101716. (Illus.). 1978. pap. 5.95 (ISBN 0-933818-05-X). Ghost Town.
Reis, Claire R. Composers in America. LC 77-4158. (Music Reprint Ser., 1977). 1977. Repr. of 1947 ed. lib. bdg. 29.50 (ISBN 0-306-70893-0). Da Capo.
Reis, L. Van der see Van der Reis, L.
Reis, Marion J., jt. tr. see Lemon, Lee T.
Reis, Victor H. Gardener's Trouble Shooter. (Illus.). 1958. 8.95 o.p. (ISBN 0-911378-09-X). Sheridan.
Reisberg, Barry. Brain Failure: An Introduction to Current Concepts of Senility. LC 80-69717. (Illus.). 1981. 19.95 (ISBN 0-02-926260-7). Free Pr.
Reisberg, Ken. Card Games. LC 78-11646. (First Bks.). (Illus.). (gr. 4 up). 1979. PLB 6.45 s&l (ISBN 0-531-02253-6). Watts.
--Card Tricks. (gr. 1-3). 1980. PLB 7.90 (ISBN 0-531-04137-9). Watts.
--Martial Arts. (First Bks.). (Illus.). (gr. 4 up). 1979. s&l 6.45 (ISBN 0-531-04077-1). Watts.
Reisbick, M. H., ed. Dental Materials in Clinical Dentistry, Vol. 11. LC 79-21849. (Post Graduate Dental Handbook Ser.). (Illus.). 350p. 1981. text ed. 29.50 (ISBN 0-88416-166-8). PSG Pub.
Reischauer, Edwin O. Japan: The Story of a Nation. rev. ed. (Illus.). 428p. 1974. 11.95 (ISBN 0-394-49510-1); pap. text ed. 10.95. Knopf.
Reischauer, Edwin O. & Craig, Albert M. Japan: Tradition & Transformation. LC 77-77979. (Illus.). 1978. text ed. 14.25 (ISBN 0-395-25814-6). HM.
Reischauer, Edwin O., jt. auth. see Fairbank, John K.
Reischauer, Edwin O., jt. auth. see Picken, Stuart D.
Reischauer, Jean, jt. auth. see Reischauer, Robert K.
Reischauer, Robert D., et al. Reforming School Finance. (Studies in Social Economics). 1973. 11.95 (ISBN 0-8157-7396-X); pap. 4.95 (ISBN 0-8157-7395-1). Brookings.
Reischauer, Robert K. & Reischauer, Jean. Early Japanese History (40 B. C.-A. D. 1167, 2 vols. 19.00 (ISBN 0-8446-1381-9). Peter Smith.
Reische, Diana, ed. Energy Demand Vs. Supply. (Reference Shelf Ser: Vol. 47, No. 5). 1975. 6.25 (ISBN 0-8242-0573-1). Wilson.
--Performing Arts in America. (Reference Shelf Ser.). 1973. 6.25 (ISBN 0-8242-0505-7). Wilson.
--Problems of Mass Transportation. (Reference Shelf Ser: Vol. 42, No. 5). 1970. 6.25 (ISBN 0-8242-0413-1). Wilson.
Reiser, A., ed. Photochemistry Seven: Seventh IUPAC Symposium on Photochemistry, Leuven, Belgium, 24-28 July, 1978. (IUPAC Symposia Ser.). 1979. 37.00 (ISBN 0-08-022358-3). Pergamon.
Reiser, Catherine L. Pittsburgh's Commercial Development: 1800-1850. LC 51-9480. 247p. 1951. 6.00 (ISBN 0-911124-36-5). Pa Hist & Mus.
Reiser, David E., et al. Patient Interviewing: The Human Dimension. (Illus.). 264p. 1980. softcover 14.95 (ISBN 0-683-07226-9). Williams & Wilkins.
Reiser, Howard. Skateboarding. (First Bks.). (Illus.). (gr. 4 up). 1978. PLB 6.45 s&l (ISBN 0-531-01412-6). Watts.
Reiser, Judy. And I Thought I Was Crazy! Quirks, Idiosyncrasies & Meshugass That People Are into. LC 80-15360. (Illus.). 138p. (Orig.). 1980. pap. 4.95 (ISBN 0-671-25399-9, 91707-2, Fireside). S&S.
Reiser, M. & Rostoker, N., eds. Collective Methods of Acceleration. (Accelerators & Storage Rings: Vol. 2). 752p. 1979. lib. bdg. 43.00 (ISBN 3-7186-0005-6). Harwood Academic.
Reiser, Martin. The Police Department Psychologist. 136p. 1972. 10.75 (ISBN 0-398-02483-5). C C Thomas.
--Practical Psychology for Police Officers. 196p. 1973. 13.50 (ISBN 0-398-02846-X). C C Thomas.
Reiser, Morton F., jt. auth. see Leigh, Hoyle.
Reiser, Oliver L. This Holyest Erthe. (Illus., Orig.). 1981. pap. 5.95 (ISBN 0-89407-022-3). Strawberry Hill.
Reiser, S. J. Medicine & the Reign of Technology. LC 77-87389. (Illus.). 1978. 21.50 (ISBN 0-521-21907-8). Cambridge U Pr.
Reiser, Stanley J. Medicine & the Reign of Technology. LC 77-87389. (Illus.). 317p. (Orig.). 1981. pap. 8.95 (ISBN 0-521-28223-3). Cambridge U Pr.
Reiser, Virginia S. Favorite Poems in Large Print. 1981. lib. bdg. 17.95 (ISBN 0-8161-3160-0, Large Print Bks). G K Hall.
Reiser, William E. What Are They Saying About Dogma? LC 78-58955. 1978. pap. 2.45 (ISBN 0-8091-2127-1). Paulist Pr.
Reisfeld, Ralph A. & Ferrone, Soldano, eds. Current Trends in Histocompatability, 2 vols. Incl. Vol. 1. Immunogenetic & Molecular Profiles. 565p. 49.50 (ISBN 0-306-40480-X); Vol. 2. Biological & Clinical Concepts. 310p. 2.50 (ISBN 0-306-40481-8). 1981 (Plenum Pr). Plenum Pub.
Reisinger, Ernest C. The Carnal Christian: What Should We Think of the Carnal Christian? 75p. Date not set. 0.75. Banner of Truth.
Reisman, Albert F., jt. ed. see Fritch, Bruce E.
Reisman, Arnold. Materials Management for Health Services. LC 79-3524. 1981. 35.95 (ISBN 0-669-03458-4). Lexington Bks.
--Systems Analysis in Health-Care Delivery. LC 79-3907. 336p. 1979. 24.95 (ISBN 0-669-02855-X). Lexington Bks.
Reisman, Arnold, jt. auth. see Clark, Jon D.
Reisman, Bernard. The Chavurah: A Contemporary Jewish Experience. 1977. pap. 5.50 (ISBN 0-8074-0048-3, 140050). UAHC.
Reisman, Daniel & Durst, Sanford J. Buying & Selling Country Land. (Illus.). 1980. lib. bdg. 30.00 (ISBN 0-915262-40-1). S J Durst.
Reisman, David. Galbraith & Market Capitalism. LC 79-9688. 1980. 25.00x (ISBN 0-8147-7380-X); pap. 11.00x (ISBN 0-8147-7381-8). NYU Pr.
Reisman, Fredericka K. & Kauffman, Samuel H. Teaching Mathematics to Children with Special Needs. (Special Education Ser.). 336p. 1980. text ed. 16.95x (ISBN 0-675-08175-0). Merrill.
Reisman, Fredricka K. A Guide to the Diagnostic Teaching of Arithmetic. (Elementary Education Ser.). 1978. pap. text ed. 7.95x (ISBN 0-675-08397-4). Merrill.
Reisman, J. M. Principles of Psychotherapy with Children. (Ser. on Personality Processes). 1973. 25.50 o.p. (ISBN 0-471-71568-9). Wiley.
Reisman, John M. Anatomy of a Friendship. 260p. 1981. pap. 6.95 (ISBN 0-86616-004-3). Lewis Pub Co.
--Principles of Psychotherapy with Children. LC 80-29581. 354p. 1981. Repr. of 1973 ed. lib. bdg. price not set (ISBN 0-89874-317-6). Krieger.
Reisman, L., et al. The New Orleans Voter: A Handbook of Political Description, Vol. 2. Bd. with Republicanism in New Orleans. Vines, K. N. 1955. 4.00 (ISBN 0-930598-01-6). Tulane Stud Pol.
Reisman, W. Michael & Weston, Burns H., eds. Toward World Order & Human Dignity: Essays in Honor of Myres S. McDougal. LC 75-36109. (Illus.). 1976. 25.00 (ISBN 0-02-926290-9). Free Pr.
Reismann, Herbert & Pawlik, Peter S. Elasticity, Theory & Applications. LC 80-10145. 1980. 36.00 (ISBN 0-471-03165-8, Pub. by Wiley Interscience). Wiley.
Reisner, George A. A Provincial Cemetary of the Pyramid Age Naga-Ed-der, Pt. 3. (U. C. Publ. in Egyptain Archaeology: Vol. 6). 1932. 68.50x (ISBN 0-520-01060-4). U of Cal Pr.
Reisner, Robert G., ed. Bird: The Legend of Charlie Parker. LC 74-30084. (Roots of Jazz Ser). (Illus.). 256p. 1975. lib. bdg. 22.50 (ISBN 0-306-70677-6); pap. 6.95 (ISBN 0-306-80069-1). Da Capo.
Reisner, Robert George. The Jazz Titans. LC 76-58559. (Roots of Jazz Ser.). 1977. Repr. of 1960 ed. lib. bdg. 19.50 (ISBN 0-306-70866-3). Da Capo.
Reiss, David. MASH: The Exclusive Inside Story of TV's Most Popular Show. LC 80-685. (Illus.). 160p. pap. 8.95 (ISBN 0-672-52656-5). Bobbs.
Reiss, David & Hoffman, Howard, eds. The American Family: Dying or Developing? LC 78-24447. 264p. 1979. 21.95 (ISBN 0-306-40117-7, Plenum Pr). Plenum Pub.
Reiss, Edmund. William Dunbar. (English Authors Ser.: No. 257). 1979. lib. bdg. 12.95 (ISBN 0-8057-6750-9). Twayne.
Reiss, H., et al, eds. Progress in Solid State Chemistry, Vols. 1, 3 & 5-7. Vol. 1, 1964. text ed. 81.00 (ISBN 0-08-010246-8). Vol. 3. 1967. text ed. 81.00 (ISBN 0-08-011886-0). Vol. 5. 1971. text ed. 81.00 (ISBN 0-08-015846-3); Vol. 6. 1971. text ed. 81.00 (ISBN 0-08-016723-3); Vol. 7. 1972. text ed. 81.00 (ISBN 0-08-016916-3). Pergamon.
Reiss, Hans, ed. see Nisbet, H. B.
Reiss, Ira L. Premarital Sexual Standards in America. LC 60-7095. 1960. 12.95 (ISBN 0-02-926190-2); pap. text ed. 5.95 (ISBN 0-02-926200-3). Free Pr.
--The Social Context of Premarital Sexual Permissiveness. LC 67-22609. 1967. 22.50x (ISBN 0-03-064880-7). Irvington.
Reiss, John J. Colors. LC 69-13653. (Illus.). (ps-1). 1969. 8.95 (ISBN 0-87888-008-9). Bradbury Pr.
--Numbers. LC 76-151313. (Illus.). (ps-1). 1971. 8.95 (ISBN 0-87888-029-1). Bradbury Pr.
--Shapes. LC 73-76545. (Illus.). 32p. (ps-2). 1974. 8.95 (ISBN 0-87888-053-4). Bradbury Pr.
Reiss, L. H. Reservoir Engineering Aspects of Fractured Formations. 200p. (Orig.). 1981. pap. text ed. 14.95 (ISBN 0-87201-303-0). Gulf Pub.
Reiss, Malcolm, jt. auth. see Campbell, Stuart D.
Reiss, Marguerite. Holy Nudges: Listening to God's Voice. 1976. 5.95 o.p. (ISBN 0-88270-185-1); pap. 2.95 o.p. (ISBN 0-88270-186-X). Logos.
Reiss, Robert. Summer Fires. 1980. pap. write for info. (ISBN 0-671-83414-2). PB.
Reiss, Timothy J. Tragedy & Truth: Studies in the Development of a Neoclassical Discourse. LC 80-10413. 320p. 1980. 24.50x (ISBN 0-300-02461-4). Yale U Pr.
Reiss, Walter. Thank God for My Breakdown. 1980. 4.95 (ISBN 0-8100-0114-4). Northwest Pub.
Reissman, Leonard. Class in American Society. 1960. text ed. 12.95 (ISBN 0-02-926270-4). Free Pr.
--Urban Process. LC 64-20301. 1964. text ed. 7.50 (ISBN 0-02-926310-7); pap. text ed. 5.95 (ISBN 0-02-926300-X). Free Pr.
Reister, Floyd N., ed. Private Aviation: A Guide to Information Sources. LC 79-84660. (Sports, Games, & Pastimes Information Guide Ser.: Vol. 3). 1979. 30.00 (ISBN 0-8103-1440-1). Gale.
Reit, Ann, ed. The World Outside: Collected Short Fiction About Women at Work. LC 77-7986. (gr. 7 up). 1977. 6.95g o.s.i. (ISBN 0-590-07484-9, Four Winds); pap. 3.95 o.s.i. (ISBN 0-685-79849-6, Four Winds). Schol Bk Serv.
Reit, Ann, ed. see Hays, H. R.
Reit, Seymour. All Kinds of Planes. (Golden Look-Look Bks.). (ps-3). 1978. PLB 5.38 (ISBN 0-307-61853-6, Golden Pr); pap. 0.95 (ISBN 0-307-11853-3). Western Pub.
--All Kinds of Ships. (Golden Look-Look Bks.). (ps-3). 1978. PLB 5.38 (ISBN 0-307-61854-4, Golden Pr); pap. 0.95 (ISBN 0-307-11854-1). Western Pub.
--All Kinds of Trains. (Golden Look-Look Bks.). (ps-3). 1978. PLB 5.38 (ISBN 0-307-61852-8, Golden Pr); pap. 0.95 (ISBN 0-307-11852-5). Western Pub.
--Bugs Bunny Goes to the Dentist. (Look-Look Bks.). (Illus.). 1978. PLB 5.38 (ISBN 0-307-61843-9, Golden Pr); pap. 0.95 (ISBN 0-307-11843-6). Western Pub.
--Bugs Bunny's Space Carrot. (Look-Look Ser.). (Illus.). 1977. PLB 5.38 (ISBN 0-307-61831-5, Golden Pr); pap. 0.95 (ISBN 0-307-11831-2). Western Pub.
--Ironclad. LC 76-50649. (gr. 4-6). 1977. 5.95 (ISBN 0-396-07403-0). Dodd.
--Masquerade: Amazing Deception & Camouflage Strategies of World War II. LC 77-70122. (Illus.). 1978. 11.95 o.p. (ISBN 0-8015-4931-0). Dutton.
--Tweety & Sylvester: Birds of a Feather. (Look-Look Ser.). (Illus.). 1977. PLB 5.38 (ISBN 0-307-61833-1, Golden Pr); pap. 0.95 (ISBN 0-307-11833-9). Western Pub.
Reit, Seymour, jt. auth. see Andujar, Claudia.
Reit, Seymour, jt. auth. see Bailey, Anne.
Reit, Seymour V. The Day They Stole the Mona Lisa. 1981. 11.95 (ISBN 0-671-25056-6). Summit Bks.
Reit, Sy. The Ginghams. (A Golden Book of Picture Postcards Ser.). (Illus.). (ps-4). 1977. pap. 0.95 o.p. (ISBN 0-307-11101-6, Golden Pr). Western Pub.
--Tiny & Tony. (Golden Book of Picture Postcards Ser.). (Illus.). (ps-4). 1977. pap. 0.95 o.p. (ISBN 0-307-11103-2, Golden Pr). Western Pub.
Reiter, B. P. The Saturday Night Knife & Gun Club. LC 76-51437. 1977. 8.95 o.p. (ISBN 0-397-01141-5). Lippincott.
Reiter, J. The Women. LC 78-1346. (The Old West Ser.). (Illus.). 1978. lib. bdg. 12.96 (ISBN 0-686-51082-8). Silver.
Reiter, Joan & Time-Life Books Editors. The Women. (Old West Ser.). (Illus.). 1978. 12.95 (ISBN 0-8094-1512-7). Time-Life.
Reiter, Paul, jt. auth. see Vivian, Gordon.
Reiter, R. J. & Follett, B. K., eds. Seasonal Reproduction in Higher Vertebrates. (Progress in Reproductive Biology Ser.: Vol. 5). (Illus.). 1980. 93.00 (ISBN 3-8055-0246-X). S Karger.
Reiter, Russel. The Pineal, Vol. 2. 1977. 21.60 (ISBN 0-88831-006-4). Eden Med Res.
Reiter, Russel J. The Pineal, Vol. 3. Horrobin, D. F., ed. 1979. 28.80 (ISBN 0-88831-039-0). Eden Med Res.
Reiter, Russel J., ed. The Pineal Gland: Volume 1, Anatomy & Biochemistry. 288p. 1981. 72.95 (ISBN 0-8493-5714-4). CRC Pr.
Reiter, Toni & Maier, Siegfried. Cross Country Skiing. (Illus.). 1980. pap. 4.95 (ISBN 0-8120-2040-5). Barron.
Reith, Edward J. & Ross, Michael H. Atlas of Descriptive Histology. 3rd ed. 1977. text ed. 17.95 scp (ISBN 0-06-045368-0, HarpC). Harrow.
Reith, G. St. John: Chapters 1-8, Vol. I. (Handbooks for Bible Classes Ser.). 197p. Repr. of 1889 ed. text ed. 7.50 (ISBN 0-567-08114-1). Attic Pr.
--St. John: Chapters 8-21, Vol. II. (Handbooks for Bible Classes). 178p. Repr. of 1889 ed. text ed. 7.50 (ISBN 0-567-08115-X). Attic Pr.
Reither, Joseph. World History: A Brief Introduction. new rev. ed. LC 65-17275. Orig. Title: World History at a Glance. (Illus.). 512p. 1973. pap. 5.95 (ISBN 0-07-051875-0, SP). McGraw.
Reithmaier, L. W., jt. auth. see Gentle, E. J.
Reithmaier, Larry. Computer Guide for Pilots. LC 78-94966. (Pilot Guides). pap. 1.00 (ISBN 0-8168-7200-7). Aero.
Reithmaior, Larry, ed. Aviation Mechanics Certification Guide. LC 80-11630. (Illus.). 1980. 6.95 (ISBN 0-932882-01-3). Palomar Bks.
Reitlinger, Gerald. The Final Solution. rev. ed. 1961. pap. 4.95 o.p. (ISBN 0-498-04021-6, Prpta). A S Barnes.
Reitman. Education, Society & Change. 496p. 1981. pap. text ed. 13.50 (ISBN 0-205-07254-2, 2373541); free tchr's ed. (ISBN 0-205-07255-0, 237255X). Allyn.
Reitman, A. The Election Process. 2nd ed. 1980. 5.95. Oceana.
Reitman, Alan. The Pulse of Freedom: American Liberties-1920-1970. 1976. pap. 1.95 o.p. (ISBN 0-451-61484-4, MJ1484, Ment). NAL.
Reitman, Alan, ed. Price of Liberty: Perspectives on Civil Liberties by Member of the A.C.L.U. 1968. 6.95x (ISBN 0-393-05284-2, Norton Lib); pap. 1.95 1969 (ISBN 0-393-00505-4). Norton.
Reitman, Anita, jt. auth. see Solomon, Lois.
Reitman, Julian. Computer Simulation Applications. 438p. 1981. Repr. lib. bdg. price not set (ISBN 0-89874-310-9). Krieger.
--Computer Simulation Applications Discrete Event Simulation for Synthesis & Analysis of Complex Systems. LC 74-161138. (Systems Engineering & Analysis Ser.). 1971. 36.50 o.p. (ISBN 0-471-71625-1, Pub. by Wiley-Interscience). Wiley.
Reitman, Sandford W. Foundations of Education for Prospective Teachers. 1977. text ed. 16.95x (ISBN 0-205-05677-6). Allyn.
Reitsch, Arthur, jt. auth. see Hanke, John E.

Reitz, Deneys. Commando: A Boer Journal Ofthe Boer War. (Orig.). 1929. pap. 5.95 (ISBN 0-571-08778-7, Pub. by Faber & Faber). Merrimack Bk Serv.

Reitz, H. Joseph. Behavior in Organizations. rev. ed. 1980. 19.95x (ISBN 0-256-01792-1). Irwin.

Reitz, John R., et al. Foundations of Electromagnetic Theory. 3rd ed. LC 78-18649. (Physics Ser.). (Illus.). 1979. text ed. 23.95 (ISBN 0-201-06332-8). A-W.

Reitz, Rosetta. Menopause: A Positive Approach. 1979. pap. 3.50 (ISBN 0-14-005120-1). Penguin.

Reitzel, J. David, jt. auth. see Dunfee, Thomas W.

Reitzel, William. Mediterranean: Its Role in American Foreign Policy. LC 71-79310. 1969. Repr. of 1948 ed. 12.50 (ISBN 0-8046-0531-9). Kennikat.

Reitzenstein, Richard. The Hellenistic Mystery-Religions. Steely, John E., tr. from Ger. LC 77-12980. (Pittsburgh Theological Monographs: No. 15). Orig. Title: Die Hellenistischen Mysterienreligionen Nach Ihren Arundgedanken und Wirkungen. 1978. pap. text ed. 12.95 (ISBN 0-915138-20-4). Pickwick.

Reizes, Haim. The Mechanics of Vehicle Collisions. (Illus.). 152p. 1973. 16.75 (ISBN 0-398-02639-4). C C Thomas.

Rejnis, Ruth. How to Buy Real Estate Without Getting Burned. LC 81-80094. 288p. (Orig.). 1981. pap. 3.50 (ISBN 0-87216-851-4). Playboy Pbks.

Rekoff. Analog Computer Programming. 1967. text ed. 17.95 (ISBN 0-675-09735-5). Merrill.

Relf, Pat. Muppet Manners (or the Night Gonzo Gave a Party) LC 80-24087. (Muppet Show Bks.). (Illus.). 32p. (gr. 1-5). 1981. pap. 1.95 (ISBN 0-394-84713-X). Random.

Relf, Patricia. Elizabeth's First Day at School. (Golden Storytime Bk.). (Illus.). 24p. 1981. 1.95 (ISBN 0-307-11957-2, Golden Pr). Western Pub.

--Show & Tell. (Sesame Street Early Bird Bks). (Illus.). 32p. (ps). 1981. 3.50 (ISBN 0-307-11606-9, Golden Pr). Western Pub.

--That New Baby! 24p. (ps). 1980. 1.50 (ISBN 0-307-11989-0); PLB 6.08 (ISBN 0-307-61989-3). Western Pub.

Religious Education Staff. Insights: Spirit Masters for Reading the New Testament. (To Live Is Christ Ser.). 1978. 12.95 (ISBN 0-697-01674-9). Wm C Brown.

--Lord & Savior: Friend & Brother, Spirit Masters for The Jesus Book. (To Live Is Christ Ser.). 1979. 10.95 (ISBN 0-697-01692-7). Wm C Brown.

--Man & Woman Spirit Masters. (To Live Is Christ Ser.). 1980. 10.95 (ISBN 0-697-01752-4). Wm C Brown.

--Mystery, Value, & Awareness: Spirit Masters for Religions of the World. (To Live Is Christ Ser.). 1979. 10.95 (ISBN 0-697-01730-3). Wm C Brown.

--Pluralism, Similarities, & Contrast: Spirit Masters for Religion in North America. (To Live Is Christ Ser.). 1979. 10.95 (ISBN 0-697-01735-4). Wm C Brown.

--The Spirit Alive in Prayer: Spirit Masters. (To Live Is Christ Ser.). 1979. 9.95 (ISBN 0-697-01699-4). Wm C Brown.

--The Spirit Alive in Service: Spirit Masters. (To Live Is Christ Ser.). 1979. 9.95 (ISBN 0-697-01712-5). Wm C Brown.

--The Spirit Alive in Vocations: Spirit Masters. (To Live Is Christ Ser.). 1980. 9.95 (ISBN 0-697-01755-9). Wm C Brown.

Relis, Nurie & Strauss, Gail. Sewing for Fashion Design. (Illus.). 1978. ref. 13.95 (ISBN 0-87909-755-8). Reston.

Relkin, Donald B., jt. auth. see Miller, Donald E.

Relkin, Richard. The Pineal, Vol. 1. 1976. 21.60 (ISBN 0-904406-26-1). Eden Med Res.

Reller, Theodore L., jt. ed. see Erickson, Donald A.

Relles, Daniel A., jt. auth. see Brelsford, William M.

Rels, Herbert. Rules of Printed English. 1980. 25.00x (ISBN 0-232-51038-5, Pub. by Darton-Longman-Todd England). State Mutual Bk.

Remak, Joachim. Origins of World War One: 1871-1914. 12.50 (ISBN 0-8446-0873-4). Peter Smith.

Remarque, Erich M. Full Circle. LC 74-1190. 1974. 6.95 o.p. (ISBN 0-15-134100-1). HarBraceJ.

Rembold, U., ed. Information-Control Problems in Manufacturing Technology: Proceedings of the Second IFAC/IFIP Symposium, Stuttgart, Federal Republic of Germany, 22-24 October, 1979. LC 80-49945. (IFAC Proceedings Ser.). (Illus.). 330p. 1980. 75.00 (ISBN 0-08-024452-1). Pergamon.

Remen, Naomi. The Human Patient. LC 77-16941. 264p. 1980. 10.95 (ISBN 0-385-13251-4, Anchor Pr). Doubleday.

Remenyi, Karoly. Combustion Stability. Darabant, E., tr. (Illus.). 175p. 1980. 20.00x (ISBN 963-05-2023-0). Intl Pubns Serv.

Remer, C. F. Readings in Economics for China. LC 78-74358. (The Modern Chinese Economy Ser.). 685p. 1980. lib. bdg. 77.00 (ISBN 0-8240-4278-6). Garland Pub.

Remick, Dorothy C. Stephen S. Townsend. (Illus.). 160p. 1981. 12.50 (ISBN 0-89962-050-7). Todd & Honeywell.

Remick, Jack. The Stolen House. LC 79-91912. (Fiction Ser.). 168p. (Orig.). 1980. pap. 4.95 (ISBN 0-917530-13-6). Pig Iron Pr.

Remington, et al. Criminal Justice Administration. (Contemporary Legal Education Ser.). 1969. 20.00 (ISBN 0-672-80989-3, Bobbs-Merrill Law). Michie.

Remington, Alexander M. Anatomy of the Economic Forces Which Decide the Life & Death of Our Modern Societies. (Illus.). 148p. 1981. 49.75 (ISBN 0-918968-91-7). Inst Econ Finan.

Remington, Frederick. Pony Tracks. (Western Frontier Library: No. 19). (Illus.). 1977. 6.95 (ISBN 0-8061-0499-6); pap. 3.95 (ISBN 0-8061-1248-4). U of Okla Pr.

Remington, Jack S. & Swartz, Morton N. Current Clinical Topics in Infectious Diseases, No. 1. (Illus.). 1980. text ed. 30.00 (ISBN 0-07-051850-5). McGraw.

--Current Clinical Topics in Infectious Diseases, No. 2. (Illus.). 304p. 1981. text ed. 30.00 (ISBN 0-07-051851-3, HP). McGraw.

Remington, Robin A., ed. The International Relations of Eastern Europe: A Guide to Information Sources. LC 73-17512. (International Relations Information Guide Ser.: Vol. 8). 1978. 30.00 (ISBN 0-8103-1320-0). Gale.

Remini, Robert, jt. auth. see Clark, James I.

Remini, Robert O., jt. auth. see Clark, James I.

Remini, Robert V. Andrew Jackson. (World Leaders Ser). 1966. lib. bdg. 8.95 o.p. (ISBN 0-8057-3048-6). Twayne.

--The Revolutionary Age of Andrew Jackson. 1977. pap. 1.50 (ISBN 0-380-01753-9, 34652). Avon.

Remini, Robert V. & Miles, Edwin A., eds. The Era of Good Feelings & the Age of Jackson, 1816-1841. LC 79-84211. (Goldentree Bibliographies in American History). 1979. text ed. 18.95x (ISBN 0-88295-578-0); pap. text ed. 13.95x (ISBN 0-88295-579-9). AHM Pub.

Remley, David A. Crooked Road: A History of the Alaska Highway. LC 75-23239. (Illus.). 1976. 10.95 o.p. (ISBN 0-07-051872-6, GB). McGraw.

Remley, Mary L., ed. Women in Sport: A Guide to Information Sources. LC 80-14773. (Sports, Games, & Pastimes Information Guide Ser.: Vol. 10). 140p. 1980. 30.00 (ISBN 0-8103-1461-4). Gale.

Remling, John. Brakes. LC 77-7262. (Automotive Mechanics Ser.). 1978. text ed. 14.95 (ISBN 0-471-71645-6). Wiley.

--Steering & Suspension. LC 77-10529. (Automotive Ser.). 1978. 15.95 (ISBN 0-471-71646-4); tchr'. manual avail. (ISBN 0-471-03763-X). Wiley.

Remmers, H. Lee, jt. auth. see Brooke, Michael Z.

Remmers, Hermann H. Introduction to Opinion & Attitude Measurement. LC 74-138127. 437p. 1972. Repr. of 1954 ed. lib. bdg. 29.75x (ISBN 0-8371-4166-4, REOA). Greenwood.

Remmers, Mary. Ducks on the Pond: A Little League Lexicon. (Illus.). (gr. 1-6). 1981. pap. price not set (ISBN 0-88319-056-7). Shoal Creek Pub.

Remmert, H. Arctic Animal Ecology. (Illus.). 250p. 1981. pap. 24.80 (ISBN 0-387-10169-1). Springer-Verlag.

--Ecology: A Textbook. (Illus.). 300p. 1980. pap. 21.30 (ISBN 0-387-10059-8). Springer-Verlag.

Remmling, Gunter W. The Sociology of Karl Mannheim: Chaos or Planning? With a Bibliographical Guide to the Sociology of Knowledge, Ideological Analysis, & Social Planning. (International Library of Sociology). 1974. text ed. 15.75x (ISBN 0-391-00376-3). Humanities.

Remmling, Gunter W., ed. Towards the Sociology of Knowledge: Origin & Development of a Sociological Thought Style. (International Library of Sociology). (Illus.). 463p. 1974. text ed. 32.50x (ISBN 0-391-00291-0). Humanities.

Remnant, Peter, ed. see Leibniz, G. W.

Remneck, Richard B., ed. Social Scientists & Policy Making in the USSR. LC 76-27587. (Praeger Special Studies). 1977. text ed. 22.95 (ISBN 0-275-56890-3). Praeger.

Remond De Saint-Mard, Toussaint. Reflexions Sur l'Opera. LC 80-2294. 1981. Repr. of 1741 ed. 18.50 (ISBN 0-404-18863-X). AMS Pr.

Rempel, John I. Building with Wood & Other Aspects of Nineteenth Century Building in Central Canada. rev. ed. LC 68-71816. (Illus.). 1980. 35.00 (ISBN 0-8020-2280-4); pap. 19.95 (ISBN 0-8020-6428-0). U of Toronto Pr.

Remsberg, Charles, jt. auth. see Gallagher, Richard.

Remuzzi, Giuseppe, et al, eds. Hemostasis, Prostaglandins & Renal Disease. (Monographs of the Mario Negri Institute for Pharmacological Research). 475p. 1980. text ed. 39.00 (ISBN 0-89004-484-8). Raven.

Remy, Bob. Louisiana Sports Encyclopedia. 1977. pap. 8.95 (ISBN 0-88289-120-0). Pelican.

Remy, Bob, jt. auth. see Mule, Marty.

Remy, Jules & Brenchley, Julius. A Journey to Great Salt-Lake City, 2 vols. LC 75-134399. (Illus.). 1124p. 1972. Repr. of 1861 ed. Set. write for info. (ISBN 0-404-08441-9). Vol. 1 (ISBN 0-404-08442-7). Vol. 2 (ISBN 0-404-08443-5). AMS Pr.

Remy, Pierre-Jean. Compartment East: Love & Adventure on the Orient Express. 1980. 13.95 (ISBN 0-688-03739-9). Morrow.

Remy, Richard C. Citizenship & Consumer Education: Key Assumptions & Basic Competencies. LC 79-93121. (Fastback Ser.: No. 144). (Orig.). 1980. pap. 0.75 (ISBN 0-87367-144-9). Phi Delta Kappa.

--Handbook of Basic Citizenship Competencies: Guidelines for Comparing Materials, Assessing Instruction & Setting Goals. Brandt, Ronald S., ed. LC 79-56888. 109p. (Orig.). 1980. pap. 4.75 (ISBN 0-87120-098-8, 611-80196). Assn Supervision.

Renaissance English Text Society & Cavendish, George. Metrical Visions. Edwards, A. S., ed. LC 80-12390. 260p. 1980. text ed. 19.50 (ISBN 0-87249-391-1). U of SC Pr.

Renard. Poil de Carotte. (Easy Reader, A). pap. 2.90 (ISBN 0-88436-046-6, FRA110051). EMC.

Renard, Jules. The Journal of Jules Renard. Bogan, Louise, ed. Roget, Elizabeth, tr. LC 64-21767. 1964. 6.00 o.s.i. (ISBN 0-8076-0276-0). Braziller.

Renauld, Ron. Times Change. 288p. (Orig.). 1981. pap. 2.50 (ISBN 0-523-41107-3). Pinnacle Bks.

Renault, Mary. Kind Are Her Answers. 287p. 1976. Repr. of 1940 ed. lib. bdg. 13.95x (ISBN 0-89244-078-3). Queens Hse.

--The Middle Mist. 288p. 1976. Repr. of 1945 ed. lib. bdg. 13.95x (ISBN 0-89244-080-5). Queens Hse.

--The Nature of Alexander. LC 74-15152. 1976. pap. 7.95 (ISBN 0-394-73254-5). Pantheon.

--North Face. 286p. 1976. Repr. of 1948 ed. lib. bdg. 13.95x (ISBN 0-89244-081-3). Queens Hse.

--Promise of Love. 1974. pap. 2.25 (ISBN 0-515-05147-0, A3422). Jove Pubns.

--Promise of Love. 382p. 1976. Repr. of 1939 ed. lib. bdg. 15.50x (ISBN 0-89244-079-1). Queens Hse.

--Return to Night. 1974. pap. 1.50 o.s.i. (ISBN 0-515-03337-5, A3337). Jove Pubns.

--Return to Night. 303p. 1976. Repr. of 1947 ed. lib. bdg. 13.95x (ISBN 0-89244-082-1). Queens Hse.

Renchlin, Johannes. Mysterium Cosmographicum. Goodman, Martin, tr. LC 77-86245. (Bilingual Editions of Classics in Philosophy & Science: Ser. 3). Date not set. 20.00 (ISBN 0-913870-56-0). Abaris Bks.

Rendel, Margherita. Administrative Functions of the French Conseil D' Etat. (LSE Research Monograph: No. 6). 1970. bds. 17.00x (ISBN 0-297-00042-X). Humanities.

Rendell. Flower Arrangement with a Marine Theme. 1972. 3.95 o.p. (ISBN 0-7153-4109-X). David & Charles.

Rendell, Joan. Your Book of Corn Dollies. (Illus.). 1976. 6.95 (ISBN 0-571-10841-5, Pub. by Faber & Faber). Merrimack Bk Serv.

--Your Book of Pressed & Dried Flowers. (gr. 4 up). 1979. 6.95 (ISBN 0-571-11249-8, Pub. by Faber Faber). Merrimack Bk Serv.

Rendell, Routh. The Best Man to Die. 1981. pap. 1.95 (ISBN 0-345-29693-1). Ballantine.

Rendell, Ruth. From Doon with Death. 160p. 1976. pap. 1.95 (ISBN 0-345-29287-1). Ballantine.

--Means of Evil. 160p. 1981. pap. 2.25 (ISBN 0-553-14153-8). Bantam.

--One Across, Two Down. 224p. 1981. pap. 2.25 (ISBN 0-553-14729-3). Bantam.

--Vanity Dies Hard. 160p. Date not set. pap. 1.25 (ISBN 0-345-29286-3). Ballantine.

--Wolf to the Slaughter. 192p. Date not set. pap. 1.95 (ISBN 0-345-29284-7). Ballantine.

Render, Barry & Stair, Ralph M., Jr. Management Science: A Self-Correcting Approach. 1978. pap. text ed. 12.95 (ISBN 0-205-06079-X, 1060791). Allyn.

Render, Barry, jt. auth. see Stair, Ralph M., Jr.

Rendle, Alfred B. Classification of Flowering Plants, 2 bks. Incl. Bk. 1. Gymnosperms & Monocotyledons. 72.50 (ISBN 0-521-06056-7); Bk. 2. Dicotyledons. 85.00 (ISBN 0-521-06057-5). Cambridge U Pr.

Rendle, B. J., compiled by. World Timbers, 3 vols. Incl. Vol. 1. Europe & Africa. 192p. 1969. o.p. (ISBN 0-8020-1570-0); Vol. 2. North & South America, Including Central America & the West Indies. 1969 (ISBN 0-8020-1667-7); Vol. 3. Asia, Australia & New Zealand. 1970 (ISBN 0-8020-1718-5). LC 74-398920. (Illus.). 35.00x ea. o.p. U of Toronto Pr.

Rendon, A. Chicano Manifesto. 1972. pap. 2.95 o.s.i. (ISBN 0-02-096330-0, Collier). Macmillan.

Rene de, Marie Alphonse, jt. auth. see Claviere, Maude la.

Renford, Beverly & Hendrickson, Linnea. Bibliographic Instruction: A Handbook. LC 80-12300. 1980. pap. 14.95x (ISBN 0-918212-24-3). Neal-Schuman.

Renfrew, C. E. Speech Disorders in Children. 78p. 1972. text ed. 8.25 (ISBN 0-08-016828-0). Pergamon.

Renfrew, Colin. Before Civilization. 1979. pap. 5.95 (ISBN 0-521-29643-9). Cambridge U Pr.

Renfrew, Colin see Cotterell, Arthur.

Renfrew, Jane. Paleoethnobotany: The Prehistoric Food Plants of the Near East & Europe. 300p. 1973. 22.50x (ISBN 0-231-03745-7). Columbia U Pr.

Renfro, Nancy. Puppet Corner in Every Library. (Illus.). 110p. 1977. pap. 8.95 (ISBN 0-931044-01-4). Renfro Studios.

--Puppetry & the Art of Story Creation. (Puppetry in Education Ser.). (Illus.). 164p. (Orig.). 1979. pap. 10.95 (ISBN 0-931044-02-2). Renfro Studios.

Renfro, Nancy, jt. auth. see Hunt, Tamara.

Renfroe, Cornelia M. Kitchen Communion. LC 59-11220. (Illus.). 1959. 2.50 (ISBN 0-8042-2400-5). John Knox.

Renich, Jill. To Have & to Hold. 145p. 1975. pap. 2.50 (ISBN 0-310-31812-2); study guide 0.95 (ISBN 0-310-31813-0). Zondervan.

Renick, Marion. Take a Long Jump. LC 71-158885. (Encore Ser.). (Illus.). 160p. (gr. 3-6). 1971. 5.95 (ISBN 0-684-12496-3, ScribJ). Scribner.

--A Touchdown for Doc. (Encore Ser.). (Illus.). (gr. 2-6). 1948. 5.95 (ISBN 0-684-13048-3, ScribJ). Scribner.

--Watch Those Red Wheels Roll. LC 65-14766. (Illus.). 128p. (gr. 2-6). 1965. 5.95 (ISBN 0-684-13172-2, ScribJ). Scribner.

Renier, Elizabeth. The Moving Dream. (Victorian Romance Ser.). 1978. pap. 1.50 o.p. (ISBN 0-449-23460-6, Crest). Fawcett.

Renier, F. G. Learn Dutch! A Dutch Grammar. 1960. pap. 3.95 o.p. (ISBN 0-7100-6818-2). Routledge & Kegan.

Renier, F. G., ed. Dutch-English & English-Dutch Dictionary. 1949. 12.00 (ISBN 0-7100-2023-6). Routledge & Kegan.

Renken, Aleda. Adventure on Padre Island. LC 75-5945. (Haley Adventure Bks.). 96p. (gr. 3-7). 1975. pap. 2.50 (ISBN 0-570-07231-X, 39-1029). Concordia.

--Donnie's Dangers. (Haley Adventures Ser.). 1981. pap. 2.50 (ISBN 0-570-07235-2, 39-1070). Concordia.

--Grandma Haley. (Haley Adventures Ser.). 1981. pap. 2.50 (ISBN 0-570-07234-4, 39-1069). Concordia.

--Pat's Problems. (Haley Adventures Ser.). 1981. pap. 2.50 (ISBN 0-570-07236-0, 39-1071). Concordia.

--Picked on Pat. LC 73-75864. (gr. 3-7). 1973. pap. 0.95 (ISBN 0-570-03601-1, 39-1024). Concordia.

--Rough Rapids Ahead. LC 74-38. (Haley Adventure Bks.). (Illus.). 96p. (gr. 3-7). 1974. pap. 2.50 (ISBN 0-570-03605-4, 39-1027). Concordia.

--The Two Christmases. LC 74-37. (Haley Adventure Bks.). (Illus.). 96p. (gr. 3-7). 1974. pap. 2.50 (ISBN 0-570-03604-6, 39-1026). Concordia.

Renmore, C. D. Silicon Chips: The Magical Mineral in Your Telephone, Calculator, Toys, Automobile, Hospital, Air Conditioning, Factory, Furnace, Sewing Machine, & Countless Other Future Inventions. LC 80-24153. (Illus.). 160p. 1980. 8.95 (ISBN 0-8253-0022-3). Beaufort Bks NY.

Renn, Derek F. Norman Castles of Britain. 1968. text ed. 21.00x (ISBN 0-391-00276-7). Humanities.

Renner. Complete Dentures: A Guide for Patient Treatment. (Monographs in Dentristry: Vol. 3). 1981. 32.50 (ISBN 0-89352-123-X). Masson Pub.

Renner, Adrienne G., jt. auth. see Layman, N. Kathryn.

Renner, Al G. Experimental Fun with the Yo-Yo. LC 78-23569. (Illus.). (gr. 5 up). 1979. 5.95 (ISBN 0-396-07657-2). Dodd.

--How to Build a Better Mousetrap Car -- & Other Experimental Science Fun. LC 76-48912. 1977. 5.95 (ISBN 0-396-07419-7). Dodd.

Renner, B. Current Algebras & Their Applications. 1968. 34.00 (ISBN 0-08-012504-2). Pergamon.
Renner, Frederic G. Charles M. Russell. concise ed. (Illus.). 1977. 17.50 o.p. (ISBN 0-8109-1590-1). Abrams.
Renner, John, jt. auth. see Stafford, Donald.
Renner, K. Edward. What's Wrong with the Mental Health Movement. LC 74-26831. 272p. 1975. 15.95 (ISBN 0-88229-180-7). Nelson-Hall.
Renner, Peter F. Basic Hotel Front Office Procedures: A Basic Guide. LC 80-17905. 295p. 1980. pap. text ed. 12.95 (ISBN 0-8436-2190-7). CBI Pub.
Renner, Thomas C., jt. auth. see Teresa, Vincent.
Rennert, Hugo A. Spanish Pastoral Romances. LC 67-29552. 1968. Repr. of 1912 ed. 11.00x (ISBN 0-8196-0214-0). Biblo.
Rennert, Jonathan. George Thalben-Ball. (Illus.). 1979. 17.95 (ISBN 0-7153-7863-5). David & Charles.
Rennert, Vincent P. Western Outlaws. LC 68-11268. (America in the Making Ser). (Illus.). (gr. 7 up). 1968. 4.95g o.s.i. (ISBN 0-02-775740-4, CCPr). Macmillan.
Renner-Tana, Patti. How Odd This Ritual of Harmony. (Poetry Discovery Ser.). 50p. (Orig.). 1981. pap. 4.75 (ISBN 0-933906-19-6). Gusto Pr.
Rennie, Susan, jt. auth. see Gearhart, Sally.
Rennie, Ysabel. The Search for Criminal Man. LC 77-3109. (Dangerous Offenders Project Ser.). 1978. 21.95 (ISBN 0-669-01480-X). Lexington Bks.
Renninger, John P. Multinational Cooperation for Development in West Africa. LC 78-15217. 176p. 1979. 22.00 (ISBN 0-08-022490-3). Pergamon.
Reno, Cora. Evolution & the Bible. 1979. pap. 1.25 (ISBN 0-8024-0131-7). Moody.
Reno, Edward A., Jr., ed. The New York Times Cumulative Subject & Personal Name Index: Environment Nineteen Sixty-Five to Nineteen Seventy-Five. 778p. 1978. 75.00 (ISBN 0-667-00606-0). Microfilming Corp.
Reno, Marie. Final Proof. 1977. pap. 1.25 o.p. (ISBN 0-445-04059-9). Popular Lib.
Reno, Marie R. When the Music Changed. 1980. pap. 12.95 (ISBN 0-453-00384-2, H384). NAL.
Reno, Ottie W. Pitching Championship Horseshoes. rev. ed. 1975. 8.95 o.p. (ISBN 0-498-01408-8); pap. 4.95 o.p. (ISBN 0-498-01410-X). A S Barnes.
Reno, Philip. Mother Earth, Father Sky, & Economic Development: Navajo Resources & Their Use. (Illus.). 200p. 1981. 12.95x (ISBN 0-8263-0550-4). U of NM Pr.
Reno, Phillip. Taos Pueblo. 2nd rev ed. LC 72-78538. 1972. pap. 2.50 (ISBN 0-8040-0329-7, SB). Swallow.
Renold, Albert E., ed. see American Physiological Society.
Renou, Louis, ed. Hinduism. LC 61-15496. (Great Religions of Modern Man Ser). 1961. 8.95 o.s.i. (ISBN 0-8076-0164-0). Braziller.
Renouf, Jane & Hulse, Stewart. First Aid for Hill Walkers & Climbers. (Illus.). 169p. 1978. pap. 5.95 (ISBN 0-14-046293-7). Bradt Ent.
Renouvin, Pierre. Forms of War Government in France. (Economic & Social History of the World War Ser.). 1927. 47.50x (ISBN 0-685-69856-4). Elliots Bks.
--The Immediate Origins of the War. LC 68-9591. 1969. 19.50 (ISBN 0-86527-101-1). Fertig.
Rensberger, Boyce. The Cult of the Wild. LC 76-53415. 1977. 7.95 o.p. (ISBN 0-385-09962-2); pap. 2.95 o.p. (ISBN 0-385-09963-0). Doubleday.
Rensberger, John M. Entoptychine Pocket Gophers (Mammalia, Geomyoidea) of the Early Miocene John Day Formation, Oregon. (U. C. Publ. in Geological Sciences: Vol. 90). 1973. pap. 11.50x (ISBN 0-520-09392-5). U of Cal Pr.
--New Iniid Cetacean from the Miocene of California. (Publcations in Geological Sciences Ser.: Vol. 82). 1969. pap. 5.75x (ISBN 0-520-09186-8). U of Cal Pr.
Rensberger, John M., jt. auth. see Fisher, Richard V.
Rensch, Bernard. Evolution Above the Species Level. Altevogt, tr. LC 58-13505. (Columbia Biological Ser.: No. 19). 1960. 30.00x (ISBN 0-231-02296-4). Columbia U Pr.
Rensch, Bernhard. Biophilosophy. Sym, Cecilia, tr. from Ger. LC 72-132692. 1971. 20.00x (ISBN 0-231-03299-4). Columbia U Pr.
--Homo Sapiens: From Man to DemiGod. LC 72-80482. 1972. 17.50x (ISBN 0-231-03683-3). Columbia U Pr.
Rensch, Roslyn. The Harp: Its History, Technique & Repertoire. (Illus.). 246p. 1971. 40.00x (ISBN 0-7156-0467-8, Pub. by Duckworth England). Biblio Dist.
Rense, Paige, ed. Architectural Digest American Interiors. LC 77-23652. (Illus.). 1978. 35.00x o.s.i. (ISBN 0-89535-002-5). Knapp Pr.
Renshaw, Domeena C. The Hyperactive Child. LC 73-86936. 1974. 13.95 (ISBN 0-911012-76-1). Nelson-Hall.
Renshon, Stanley A. Psychological Needs & Political Behavior: A Theory of Personality & Political Efficacy. LC 73-11735. 1974. 15.95 (ISBN 0-02-926320-4). Free Pr.
Renshon, Stanley A., ed. Handbook of Political Socialization: Theory and Research. LC 76-55102. 1977. 25.00 (ISBN 0-02-926340-9). Free Pr.
Renson, C. E. Oral Disease. (Illus.). 1978. text ed. 14.50x (ISBN 0-906141-04-4, Pub. by Update Pubns England). Kluwer Boston.
Rensselaer, John K. Van see Van Rensselaer, Mrs. John K.
Rensselaer, Phillip Van see Van Rensselaer, Phillip.
Renstrom, Richard. Motorcycle Milestones, Vol. 1. LC 80-66669. (Illus.). 112p. 1980. 19.00 (ISBN 0-936660-00-7); pap. 14.00 (ISBN 0-936660-01-5). Classics Unltd.
Renton, Bruce A. Drafting Projects for Today. 1975. pap. 8.80 (ISBN 0-8273-1926-6). Delmar.
Renton, Michael. Getting Better Results from the Meetings You Run. LC 80-51792. (Illus.). 95p. 1980. pap. text ed. 5.95 (ISBN 0-87822-214-6, 2146). Res Press.
Renty, Ivan De see De Renty, Ivan.
Renvoize, Jean. Children in Danger. 1975. 13.00x (ISBN 0-7100-7892-7). Routledge & Kegan.
--Coming Apart. LC 80-6202. 288p. 1981. 12.95 (ISBN 0-8128-2780-5). Stein & Day.
Renvoizie, Jean. Web of Violence: A Study of Violence in the Family. 1978. 16.00 (ISBN 0-7100-8804-3). Routledge & Kegan.
Renwick, A. M. Story of the Church. pap. 3.45 o.p. (ISBN 0-8028-1163-9). Eerdmans.
Renwick, Ethel. The Real Food Cookbook. 1978. spiral-bound kivar 8.95 (ISBN 0-310-31871-8). Zondervan.
Renwick, George W. Evaluation: Practical Guidelines. LC 79-92378. (Intercultural Handbks.). (Illus.). 1980. pap. text ed. 4.50 (ISBN 0-933662-08-4). Intercult Pr.
--InterAct: Australia-U.S. LC 80-83910. (Country Orientation Ser.). 80p. 1980. pap. text ed. 10.00 (ISBN 0-933662-16-5). Intercult Pr.
Renwick, George W., ed. see Condon, John C.
Renwick, George W., ed. see Fieg, John.
Renwick, Roger Dev. English Folk Poetry: Structure & Meaning. LC 79-5260. (American Folklore Society Ser.). 256p. 1980. 17.00x (ISBN 0-8122-7777-5). U of Pa Pr.
Renwick, Roger DeV see Renwick, Roger Dev.
Renyi, Alfred. Foundations of Probability. LC 72-105221. 1970. 18.95x (ISBN 0-8162-7114-3). Holden-Day.
Renyi, Alfred, tr. see Vekerdi, Laszlo.
Renz, G. W. The Distribution & Ecology of Radiolaria in the Central Pacific-Plankton & Surface Sediments. (Bulletin of the Scripps Institution of Oceanography: Vol. 22). 1976. pap. 14.00x (ISBN 0-520-09533-2). U of Cal Pr.
Renzo, D. J. De see De Renzo, D. J.
Renzulli, J. S., jt. ed. see Barbe, W. B.
Renzulli, Joseph S. Mark One-New Directions in Creativity. 23.84 (ISBN 0-06-539000-8, SchDept). Har-Row.
--Mark Three-New Directions in Creativity. 23.84 (ISBN 0-06-539002-4, SchDept). Har-Row.
--Mark Two-New Directions in Creativity. 23.84 (ISBN 0-06-539001-6, SchDept). Har-Row.
--New Directions in Creativity. 1976. 23.84 ea. (SchDept). Mark A (ISBN 0-06-538998-0). Mark B (ISBN 0-06-538999-9). Har-Row.
Renzulli, Joseph S. & Stoddard, Elizabeth P., eds. Under One Cover: Gifted & Talented Education in Perspective. LC 80-68284. 248p. 1980. pap. 11.25 (ISBN 0-86586-108-0). Coun Exc Child.
Renzulli, Joseph S., jt. ed. see Barbe, Walter B.
Renzulli, Joseph S., et al. Scales for Rating Behavioral Characteristics of Superior Students. 1977. pap. 5.95 (ISBN 0-936386-00-2). Creative Learning.
Repacholi, M. H. & Bewell, D. A., eds. Essentials of Medical Ultrasound. (Medical Methods Ser.). (Illus.). 1981. 24.50 (ISBN 0-89603-028-8). Humana.
Replogle, Justin. Auden's Poetry. LC 68-8508. (Washington Paperback Ser.: No. 60). 271p. 1971. 9.95 (ISBN 0-295-78563-2); pap. 2.95 (ISBN 0-295-95141-9, WP-60). U of Wash Pr.
Report of a Conference Held in January 1979. The Chronic Mental Patient: Problems, Solutions, & Recommendations for a Public Policy. Talbott, John A., ed. LC 78-73984. 1979. pap. 11.00x (ISBN 0-685-95862-0, P242-0). Am Psychiatric.
Report of Round Table, European Conference of Ministers of Transport on Transport Economics, 34th, Paris, May 6-7, 1976. Psychological Determinants of User Behavior: Proceedings. 1977. 3.75 o.p. (ISBN 92-82-11041-9). OECD.
Report of the AFIPS Panel on Transborder Data Flow. Proceedings. Turn, Rein, ed. LC 79-93002. (Transborder Data Flow: Concerns in Privacy Protection & Free Flow of Information: Vol. 1). (Illus.). xviii, 186p. 1979. pap. 15.00 (ISBN 0-88283-004-X). AFIPS Pr.
Report of the Goodman Committee. Charity Law & Voluntary Organisations. 150p. 1976. pap. text ed. 5.00x (ISBN 0-7199-0910-4, Pub. by Bedford England). Renouf.
Reports from the United Nations Conference in Rome. New Sources of Energy: Solar Two. (Illus.). 1978. lib. bdg. 16.00 (ISBN 0-88930-032-1, Pub. by Cloudburst Canada); pap. 8.50 (ISBN 0-88930-031-3). Madrona Pubs.
Repp, Victor, jt. auth. see McCarthy, Willard J.
Reppert, Charlotte P., ed. see Bishop, Morris.
Reppy, Judith, jt. ed. see Long, Franklin A.
Reppy, William A. & De Funiack, William Q. Community Property in the U. S. A Comparative Study by Cases, Materials & Problems. (Contemporary Legal Education Ser). 1975. 22.00 (ISBN 0-672-82067-6, Bobbs-Merrill Law); 1979 suppl. 4.00 (ISBN 0-672-83855-9). Michie.
Reps, John W. Town Planning in Frontier America. 320p. 1980. pap. 9.95 (ISBN 0-8262-0316-7). U of Mo Pr.
Reps, Paul. Juicing. LC 77-82770. 1978. pap. 3.50 o.p. (ISBN 0-385-13250-6, Anch). Doubleday.
--Paul Reps: Letters to a Friend (Writings & Drawings), 1939 to 1980. (Illus.). 186p. 1981. 60.00 (ISBN 0-938286-01-3); ltd. ed. 175.00 (ISBN 0-938286-00-5). Stillgate.
--Zen Flesh, Zen Bones. LC 57-10199. (Illus.). 1957. 10.50 (ISBN 0-8048-0644-6). C E Tuttle.
Reps, Paul, ed. Zen Flesh, Zen Bones: A Collection of Zen & Pre-Zen Writings. pap. 2.95 (ISBN 0-385-08130-8, A233, Anch). Doubleday.
Republic of China. Laws, Ordinances, Regulations, & Rules Relating to the Judicial Administration of the Republic of China. (Studies in Chinese Government & Law). 364p. 1977. Repr. of 1923 ed. 24.00 (ISBN 0-89093-062-7). U Pubns Amer.
ReQua, Eloise & Statham, Jane, eds. Developing Nations: A Guide to Information Sources. LC 65-17576. (Management Information Guide Ser.: No. 5). 1965. 30.00 (ISBN 0-8103-0805-3). Gale.
Requa-Clark, Barbara & Holroyd, Sam V. Applied Pharmacology for the Dental Hygienists. 427p. 1981. pap. 11.95 (ISBN 0-8016-2239-5). Mosby.
Requin, Jean, ed. Attention & Performance, Vol. 7. LC 78-13662. (International Symposium on Attention & Performance). 1978. 29.95 (ISBN 0-470-26521-3). Halsted Pr.
Reres, Mary, jt. auth. see Robinson, Alice.
Reschenthaler, G. B. Occupational Health & Safety in Canada. 152p. 1979. pap. text ed. 5.00x (ISBN 0-920380-35-2, Pub. by Inst Res Pub Canada). Renouf.
Reschenthaler, G. B. & Roberts, B. Perspectives on Canadian Airline Regulation. 266p. 1979. pap. text ed. 13.50x (ISBN 0-409-88604-1, Pub. by Inst Res Pub Canada). Renouf.
Rescher, Nicholas. Conceptual Idealism. 1973. 25.00x (ISBN 0-631-14950-3, Pub. by Basil Blackwell). Biblio Dist.
--Distributive Justice: A Constructive Critique of the Utilitarian Theory of Distribution. LC 66-29532. 1966. 18.50x (ISBN 0-672-60711-5); pap. text ed. 8.95x (ISBN 0-89197-733-3). Irvington.
--Induction. LC 80-52598. xii, 225p. 1981. 34.95 (ISBN 0-8229-3431-0). U of Pittsburgh Pr.
--The Primacy of Practice: Essays Towards a Pragmatically Kantian Theory of Empirical Knowledge. 1973. 25.00x (ISBN 0-631-15020-X, Pub. by Basil Blackwell). Biblio Dist.
--Scepticism: A Critical Reappraisal. 265p. 1980. 30.00x (ISBN 0-8476-6240-3). Rowman.
--Scientific Explanation. LC 71-80675. 1970. 12.95 (ISBN 0-02-926330-1). Free Pr.
--Studies in Moral Philosophy. (Monograph Ser.: No. 1). 1968. pap. 10.00x o.p. (ISBN 0-631-11450-5, Pub. by Basil Blackwell). Biblio Dist.
Rescher, Nicholas & Brandom, Robert. The Logic of Inconsistency: A Study in Nonstandard Possible-World Semantics & Ontology. (American Philosophical Quarterly Library of Philosophy). 174p. 1979. 22.50x (ISBN 0-8476-6248-9). Rowman.
Rescher, Nicholas, jt. auth. see Baier, Kurt.
Rescher, Nicholas, ed. Studies in Epistemology. (Monograph Ser.: Vol. 9). 1975. pap. 15.00x (ISBN 0-631-11530-7, Pub. by Basil Blackwell). Biblio Dist.
--Studies in Ethics. (Monograph Ser.: No. 7). 1973. pap. 19.00x (ISBN 0-631-11510-2, Pub. by Basil Blackwell). Biblio Dist.
--Studies in Modality. Manor, Ruth. (Monograph Ser.: No. 8). 1973. pap. 10.00x o.p. (ISBN 0-631-11520-X, Pub. by Basil Blackwell). Biblio Dist.
--Studies in Ontology. (American Philosophical Quarterly Monograph: No. 12). 1978. pap. 19.00x (ISBN 0-631-11560-9, Pub. by Basil Blackwell England). Biblio Dist.
--Studies in the Philosophy of Mind. (Monograph Ser.: No. 6). 1972. pap. 19.00x (ISBN 0-631-11500-5, Pub. by Basil Blackwell). Biblio Dist.
--Studies in the Philosophy of Science. (Monograph Ser.: No. 3). 1969. pap. 19.00x (ISBN 0-631-11470-X, Pub. by Basil Blackwell). Biblio Dist.
--Studies in the Theory of Knowledge. (Monograph Ser.: No. 4). 1970. pap. 19.00x (ISBN 0-631-11480-7, Pub. by Basil Blackwell). Biblio Dist.
Rescher, Nicholas, ed. see Almeder, Robert.
Rescher, Nicolas, ed. Negation & Non-Being. (Monograph Ser.: No. 10). 1976. pap. 10.00x o.p. (ISBN 0-631-11540-4, Pub. by Basil Blackwell). Biblio Dist.
Reschke, Robert C. Component & Modular Techniques: A Builder's Handbook. Case, Virginia, ed. (Illus.). 300p. 1981. 39.95 (ISBN 0-89999-016-9). Structures Pub.
--Successful How to Build Your Own Home. 2nd ed. LC 79-91999. (Successful Ser.). (Illus.). 1979. 15.95 (ISBN 0-912336-93-5); pap. 9.95 (ISBN 0-912336-94-3). Structures Pub.
--Successful Roofing & Siding. LC 76-54145. (Illus.). 160p. 1977. 14.95 (ISBN 0-912336-26-9); pap. 7.95 (ISBN 0-912336-27-7). Structures Pub.
Research & Education Association Staff. The Economics Problem Solver. LC 80-53175. (Illus.). 1088p. (Orig.). pap. text ed. 16.85x (ISBN 0-87891-524-9). Res & Educ.
--The Electric Circuits Problem Solver: A Supplement to Any Class Text. LC 79-92401. (Illus.). 1056p. 1980. pap. text ed. 22.85 (ISBN 0-87891-517-6). Res & Educ.
--Handbook of Mathematical Formulas, Tables, Functions, Graphs, Transforms. LC 80-52490. (Illus.). 800p. (Orig.). pap. text ed. 16.85x (ISBN 0-87891-521-4). Res & Educ.
--The Linear Algebra Problem Solver: A Supplement to Any Class Text. LC 79-92402. (Illus.). 1024p. 1980. pap. text ed. 22.85x (ISBN 0-87891-518-4). Res & Educ.
--The Mechanics Problem Solver: A Supplement to Any Class Text. LC 79-92403. (Illus.). 1088p. 1980. pap. text ed. 22.85x (ISBN 0-87891-519-2). Res & Educ.
--The Organic Chemistry Problem Solver: A Supplement to Any Class Text. LC 78-51952. 1978. pap. text ed. 22.85 (ISBN 0-87891-512-5). Res & Educ.
--Problem Solver in Strength of Materials & Mechanics of Solids. LC 80-83305. (Illus.). 896p. (Orig.). pap. text ed. 22.85x (ISBN 0-87891-522-2). Res & Educ.
--The Psychology Problem Solver. LC 80-53174. (Illus.). 1056p. (Orig.). pap. text ed. 16.85x (ISBN 0-87891-523-0). Res & Educ.
Research Co-Ordination Meeting & Panel. Tracer Studies on Non-Protein Nitrogen for Ruminants II: Proceedings. (Illus.). 208p. 1975. pap. 15.50 (ISBN 92-0-111175-4, IAEA). Unipub.
Research Department of the Universal House of Justice. Baha'i Education: A Compilation. Extracts from the Writings of Baha'u'llah, 'Abdu'l-Baha, & Shoghi Effendi. 1977. pap. 3.00 (ISBN 0-87743-117-5, 7-15-59). Baha'i.
Research for Better Schools, Inc. Educational Reform for a Changing Society. new ed. Rubin, Louis, ed. 1978. text ed. 19.95 (ISBN 0-205-05827-2). Allyn.
Research Group & Gingerich, Duane, eds. Medical Products Liability: A Comprehensive Guide & Sourcebook. (Health Care Economics & Technology Ser.). 500p. 1981. 59.50x (ISBN 0-86621-001-6). F&S Pr.
Research Institute of Geography, Hungarian Academy of Sciences, Budapest, ed. Man & Environment: Symposium containing contribution of 30 international scientists. 1974. 18.75 o.p. (ISBN 0-685-42226-6). Adler.
Research Libraries Fo the New York Public Library & the Library of Congress. Bibliographic Guide to Psychology: 1980. (Library Catalogs-Guides Ser.). 1981. lib. bdg. 70.00 (ISBN -08161-6893-8). G K Hall.
Research Libraries of the New York Public Library, the Schomburg Collection & the Library of Congress. Bibliographic Guide to Black Studies: 1980. (Library Catalogs-Bib. Guides Ser.). 1981. lib. bdg. 70.00 (ISBN 0-8161-6882-2). G K Hall.
Research Libraries of the New York Public Library & the Library of Congress. Bibliographic Guide to Business & Economics: 1980. (Library Catalogs-Bib. Guides). 1981. lib. bdg. 225.00 (ISBN 0-8161-6883-0). G K Hall.
--Bibliographic Guide to Conference Publication: 1980. (Library Catalogs-Bib. Guides Ser.). 1981. lib. bdg. 130.00 (ISBN 0-8161-6884-9). G K Hall.

Research Libraries of the New York Public Library. Bibliographic Guide to Dance: Nineteen Seventy-Nine. (Library Catalogs-Bib. Guides). 1980. lib. bdg. 170.00 (ISBN 0-8161-6867-9). G K Hall.

Research Libraries of the New York Public Library, ed. Bibliographic Guide to Dance: 1978. (Library Catalogs Bib.Guides). 1979. lib. bdg. 100.00 (ISBN 0-8161-6851-2). G K Hall.

Research Libraries of the New York Public Library & the Library of Congress. Bibliographic Guide to Government Publications - Foreign: 1980. (Library Catalogs-Bib. Guides Ser.). 1981. lib. bdg. 195.00 (ISBN 0-8161-6886-5). G K Hall.

--Bibliographic Guide to Government Publications - U. S. 1980. (Library Catalogs-Bib. Guides Ser.). 1981. lib. bdg. 195.00 (ISBN 0-8161-6887-3). G K Hall.

--Bibliographic Guide to Maps & Atlases: 1980. (Library Catalogs-Bib. Guides Ser.). 1981. lib. bdg. 95.00 (ISBN 0-8161-6890-3). G K Hall.

--Bibliographic Guide to Music: 1980. (Libraries Catalogs-Bib. Guides Sew.). 1981. lib. bdg. 90.00 (ISBN 0-8161-6891-1). G K Hall.

--Bibliographic Guide to Technology: 1979. (Library Catalogs-Bib. Guides). 1980. lib. bdg. 145.00 (ISBN 0-8161-6878-4). G K Hall.

--Bibliographic Guide to Theatre Arts: Nineteen Seventy-Nine. (Library Catalogs-Bib. Guides). 1980. lib. bdg. 70.00 (ISBN 0-8161-6862-8). G K Hall.

Research Libraries of the New York Public Library. The Imprint Catalog in the Rare Book Division: The Research Libraries of the New York Public Library. (Library Catalogs-Bib. Guides). 1979. lib. bdg. 1848.00 (ISBN 0-8161-0092-6). G K Hall.

Research Libraris of the New York Public Library & the Library of Congress. Bibliographic Guide to Business & Economics: Nineteen Seventy-Eight. (Library Catalogs-Bib. Guides). 1979. lib. bdg. 195.00 (ISBN 0-8161-6849-0). G K Hall.

Research Staff of Inst. of Texan Cultures. The Melting Pot: Ethnic Cuisine in Texas. (Illus.). 230p. 1977. 10.95 (ISBN 0-933164-18-1). U of Tex Inst Tex Culture.

Reseck, J., Jr. Scuba Safe & Simple. 1975. 8.95 o.p. (ISBN 0-13-796714-4); pap. 4.95 (ISBN 0-13-796680-6). P-H.

Reseck, John, Jr. Marine Biology. (Illus.). 1979. text ed. 16.95 (ISBN 0-8359-4276-7); instrs'. manual avail. Reston.

Resek, Carl, ed. The Progressives. (Orig.). 1967. pap. 7.50 (ISBN 0-672-60084-6, AHSJ4). Bobbs.

Resford, Eliza. Yet Softly Tread the Leaves. 1981. 10.95 (ISBN 0-533-04949-0). Vantage.

Resh, Howard M. Hydroponic Food Production: A Definitive Guide to Soilless Culture. LC 78-23468. (Illus.). 1978. text ed. 14.95 (ISBN 0-912800-54-2). Woodbridge Pr.

Reshevsky. Art of Positional Play. 1976. 14.95 o.p. (ISBN 0-679-13051-9). McKay.

Reshevsky, Samuel. Great Chess Upsets. LC 74-77098. 1975. 9.95 o.p. (ISBN 0-668-03492-0); pap. 3.95 o.p. (ISBN 0-668-03493-9). Arco.

Resibois, P. & De Leener, M. F. Classical Kinetic Theory of Fluids. LC 76-58852. 1977. 39.95 (ISBN 0-471-71694-4, Pub. by Wiley-Interscience). Wiley.

Resick, Matthew C., et al. Modern Administrative Practices in Physical Education & Athletics. 3rd ed. LC 78-67946. (Physical Education Ser.). (Illus.). 1979. text ed. 16.95 (ISBN 0-201-06249-6). A-W.

Resing, Henry A., jt. ed. see Fraissard, Jacques P.

Resnekov, Leon & Julian, Desmond, eds. Friedberg's: Diseases of the Heart. 4th ed. (Illus.). 1981. write for info. (ISBN 0-443-08003-8). Churchill.

Resnick. Official Guide to Comic & Science Fiction Books. 3rd rev. ed. LC 78-61693. (Illus.). 1979. pap. 7.95 o.p. (ISBN 0-87637-102-0). Hse of Collectibles.

Resnick, Charlotte A. & Resnick, Gloria R. To Your Good Health! (gr. 7-12). 1979. text ed. 14.50 (ISBN 0-87720-164-1); pap. text ed. 8.92 (ISBN 0-87720-163-3). AMSCO Sch.

Resnick, David, jt. auth. see Halliday, Robert.

Resnick, Donald & Niwayama, Gen. Diagnosis of Bone & Joint Disorders with Emphasis on Articlar Abnormalities. (Illus.). 2200p. Date not set. price not set (ISBN 0-7216-7561-1). Saunders. Postponed.

Resnick, Gloria R., jt. auth. see Resnick, Charlotte A.

Resnick, Lauren B. & Ford, Wendy W. The Psychology of Mathematics for Instruction. 368p. 1981. text ed. 24.95 (ISBN 0-89859-029-9). L Erlbaum Assocs.

Resnick, M., jt. auth. see Fong, B.

Resnick, Marcia. Landscape-Loftscape. new ed. pap. cancelled o.p. (ISBN 0-89439-006-6). Printed Matter.

Resnick, Martin I. Current Studies in Urology. (Illus.). 190p. 1981. write for info. (7216-1). Williams & Wilkins.

Resnick, Matthew C., jt. auth. see Seidel, Beverly L.

Resnick, Michael. Gymnastics & You: The Whole Story of the Sport. LC 77-8345. (Illus.). (gr. 5-9). 1977. pap. 3.95 (ISBN 0-528-87052-1). Rand.

Resnick, Miriam, jt. auth. see Fong, Bernadine.

Resnick, R. Basic Concepts in Relativity & Early Quantum Theory. 1972. pap. 11.95 (ISBN 0-471-71703-7). Wiley.

--Introduction to Special Relativity. 1972. pap. 10.95x (ISBN 0-471-71725-8). Wiley.

Resnick, Robert, jt. auth. see Eisberg, Robert.

Resnick, Robert, jt. auth. see Halliday, David.

Resnick, Seymour. Essential Spanish Grammar. (Orig.). 1963. pap. 2.00 (ISBN 0-486-20780-3). Dover.

--Essential Spanish Grammar. LC 63-4093. 1959. lib. bdg. 9.50x (ISBN 0-88307-577-6). Gannon.

Resnik, H. & Ruben, H. Emergency Psychiatric Care. LC 74-11791. (Illus.). 1975. pap. 12.95 (ISBN 0-913486-15-9). Charles.

Resnik, H. L., jt. auth. see Mitchell, Jeffrey.

Resnikoff, jt. auth. see Pearlman.

Resnikoff, H. L. & Wells, R. O. Mathematics in Civilization. LC 72-83805. (Illus.). 24.50x (ISBN 0-03-085035-5); pap. text ed. 8.95x (ISBN 0-89197-843-7). Irvington.

Resolutions of the Council of Ministers of Transport & Reports Approved in 1978. ECMT: 25th Annual Report, Vol. II. (4#149). 1979. 12.50 (ISBN 92-821-1054-0). OECD.

Resource Publications, Inc. Staff. MusiCatalog. Cunningham, W. P., ed. 1978. pap. 49.95 (ISBN 0-89390-013-3). Resource Pubns.

Ress, Etta S. Field & Meadow. LC 60-6114. (Community of Living Things Ser). (Illus.). (gr. 4-8). 1967. PLB 7.45 (ISBN 0-87191-016-0). Creative Ed.

--Transportation. LC 64-8099. (Illus.). (gr. 4-8). 1967. PLB 7.95 (ISBN 0-87191-003-9). Creative Ed.

Ress, Etta S. & Liebow, Gina. Man Builds Tomorrow. LC 66-25120. (Illus.). (gr. 4-8). 1966. PLB 7.95 (ISBN 0-87191-000-4). Creative Ed.

Ress, Etta S., ed. see Arbital, Samuel L.

Ressler, Ralp. A World of Choice: Careers and You- Student Workbook. LC 77-4182. (Illus.). 1978. pap. 7.95 (ISBN 0-88280-050-7); tchr's guide 9.95 (ISBN 0-88280-051-5). ETC Pubns.

Restak, Richard M. The Brain: The Last Frontier. 1980. pap. 3.50 (ISBN 0-446-96975-3). Warner Bks.

Restak, Richard M., M.D. The Brain: The Last Frontier. LC 78-68353. 1979. 12.95 (ISBN 0-385-13405-3). Doubleday.

Restall, Robin L. Finches & Other Seed-Eating Birds. (Illus.). 1975. 19.95 (ISBN 0-571-10353-7, Pub. by Faber & Faber). Merrimack Bk Serv.

Restany, Pierre. Chryssa. LC 77-1916. (Contemporary Artist Ser.). (Illus.). 1978. 55.00 o.p. (ISBN 0-8109-0366-0). Abrams.

Restarick, Henry B. Sun Yat Sen, Liberator of China. LC 79-2837. (Illus.). 167p. 1981. Repr. of 1931 ed. 16.50 (ISBN 0-8305-0014-6). Hyperion Conn.

Restaurant Business Inc. Menu Planning & Foods Merchandising. 1st ed. LC 73-163322. 1971. 14.50 (ISBN 0-672-96092-3); tchrs' manual 5.90 (ISBN 0-672-96094-X); wkbk. 6.50 (ISBN 0-672-96093-1). Bobbs.

Restif De la Bretonne, Nicolas - Edme. Le Plus Fort Des Pamphlets: L'ordre Des Paysans Aux Etats - Generaux. 80p. (Fr.). 1977. lib. bdg. 20.00x o.p. (ISBN 0-8287-0720-0); pap. text ed. 10.00x o.p. (ISBN 0-685-75616-5). Clearwater Pub.

Restino, Susan. Mrs. Restino's Country Kitchen. LC 74-28704. (Illus.). 304p. (Orig.). 1976. pap. 7.95 o.p. (ISBN 0-8256-3060-6, Quick Fox). Music Sales.

Reston, James. Artillery of the Press. LC 67-11330. 1967. 10.00 o.p. (ISBN 0-06-013542-5, HarpT). Har-Row.

Restrepo, Carlos S., tr. see Gitman, Lawrence J.

Resume Service Staff. Resumes That Get Jobs. LC 75-24504. (Orig.). 1976. lib. bdg. 7.00 (ISBN 0-668-03935-3); pap. 3.95 (ISBN 0-668-03909-4). Arco.

Reswick, James & Taft, Charles. Introduction to Dynamic Systems. 1967. ref. ed. 23.95 (ISBN 0-13-479907-0). P-H.

Reti, Richard. Modern Ideas in Chess. pap. 3.00 (ISBN 0-486-20638-6). Dover.

Retif, Andre. Pierre Larousse et son oeuvre. new ed. 335p. 1975. pap. 19.50x (ISBN 2-03-079950-5). Larousse.

Rettich, Margaret. The Silver Touch & Other Family Christmas Stories. Crawford, Elizabeth D., tr. (Illus.). (gr. 4-6). 1978. 7.50 o.p. (ISBN 0-688-22164-5); PLB 7.63 (ISBN 0-688-32164-X). Morrow.

Rettig, R. Bruce & Ginter, Jay J., eds. Limited Entry as a Fishery Management Tool. (Washington Sea Grant Ser.). 584p. 1980. pap. 15.00 (ISBN 0-295-95741-7). U of Wash Pr.

Rettinger, M. Studio Acoustics. 1981. 35.00 (ISBN 0-8206-0283-3). Chem Pub.

Rettke, Marian P. Georgiana. 224p. (Orig.). 1981. pap. 2.25 (ISBN 0-515-05656-1). Jove Pubns.

Rettke, Marion P. Highland Rapture. (Orig.). 1979. pap. 1.75 (ISBN 0-515-05318-X). Jove Pubns.

Retzlaff, Danold A., jt. auth. see Poirot, James L.

Retzlaff, Don A., jt. auth. see Poirot, James L.

Retzlaff, Donald A., jt. auth. see Poirot, James L.

Reuben, B. G. & Burstall, M. L. The Chemical Economy. LC 73-85210. (Illus.). 400p. 1974. text ed. 30.00x (ISBN 0-582-46307-6). Longman.

Reuben, Bryan G., jt. auth. see Wittcoff, Harold.

Reuben, Gabriel. Electricity Experiments for Children. (gr. 5-9). pap. 2.25 (ISBN 0-486-22030-3). Dover.

Reuben, John P., et al, eds. Electrobiology of Nerve, Synapse & Muscle. LC 75-14587. 1976. 34.50 (ISBN 0-89004-030-3). Raven.

Reuben, Paula, jt. auth. see Dodson, Fitzhugh.

Reuben, Ruth, tr. see Sheldon, Charles M.

Reuben, S., jt. auth. see Hartston, W. R.

Reubens, Beatrice G. Bridges to Work: International Comparisons of Transitional Services. LC 76-28562. (Conservation of Human Resources Ser.: No. 3). 288p. 1977. text ed. 18.00 (ISBN 0-916672-05-0). Allanheld.

--Hard-To-Employ: European Programs. (Illus.). 1970. 20.00x (ISBN 0-231-03388-5). Columbia U Pr.

--Preparation for Work: A Cross-Country Analysis. LC 77-84454. (Conservation of Human Resources Ser.: No. 4). 1981. text ed. 25.00x (ISBN 0-86598-028-4). Allanheld.

--The Youth Labor Force. LC 80-67390. (Conservation of Human Resources Ser.: No. 13). 1981. text ed. 32.50 (ISBN 0-86598-027-6). Allanheld.

Reubens, Edwin P., ed. The Challenge of the New International Economic Order. (Westview Special Studies in International Economics & Business). 220p. 1981. lib. bdg. 25.00x (ISBN 0-89158-762-4); pap. text ed. 11.50x (ISBN 0-86531-078-5). Westview.

Reuber, Grant, jt. ed. see Guinsburg, T. N.

Reuchlin, Abelard. The True Authorship of the New Testament. 1979. pap. 2.00. Vector Assocs.

Reucroft, P. J., et al. Surface Structure & Mechanisms of Gasification Catalyst Deactivation. De Vore, R. William, ed. (Illus.). 86p. (Orig.). 1980. pap. 4.50 (ISBN 0-89779-028-6, IMMR46-PD22-80); 1.50 (ISBN 0-89779-029-4). OES Pubns.

Reul, I. H., et al, eds. see International Conference on Mechanics in Medicine & Biology, 1st, Aachen, Germany, 1978.

Reuleaux, Franz. Kinematics of Machinery: Outlines of a Theory of Machines. Kennedy, Alexander B., tr. (Illus.). 1876. pap. text ed. 6.00 (ISBN 0-486-61124-8). Dover.

Reum, Earl & Cummings, Oveta. The Effective Student Council in the Mid-Seventies. rev ed. 48p. 1973. pap. text ed. 3.00 o.p. (ISBN 0-88210-047-5). Natl Assn Principals.

Reumann, John. Jesus in the Church's Gospels: Modern Scholarship & the Earliest Sources. LC 68-10933. 564p. 1973. pap. 6.95 (ISBN 0-8006-1091-1, 1-1091). Fortress.

Reumann, John, ed. The Church Emerging: A U. S. Lutheran Case Study. LC 76-62618. 288p. 1977. pap. 9.95 (ISBN 0-8006-1259-0, 1-1259). Fortress.

Reumann, John, ed. see Hahn, Ferdinand.

Reumann, John, ed. see Harner, Philip B.

Reumann, John, ed. see Jeremias, Joachim.

Reumann, John, ed. see Lewis, C S.

Reumann, John, ed. see Manson, T. W.

Reumann, John, ed. see Moule, C. F.

Reumert, Elith. Hans Andersen the Man. Brochner, Jessie, tr. from Danish. LC 71-110811. (Tower Bks). (Illus.). 1971. Repr. of 1927 ed. 20.00 (ISBN 0-8103-3902-1). Gale.

Reus, Violet, jt. auth. see Gorzelany, James A.

Reusch, William. An Introduction to Organic Chemistry. LC 76-50855. 1977. text ed. 27.50 (ISBN 0-8162-7161-5); study guide 9.95 (ISBN 0-686-28568-9). Holden Day.

Reuscher, John A. Essays on the Metaphysical Foundation of Personal Identity. LC 80-6067. 111p. 1981. lib. bdg. 16.50 (ISBN 0-8191-1471-5); pap. text ed. 7.25 (ISBN 0-8191-1472-3). U Pr of Amer.

Reuschlein, Harold G. Jurisprudence: Its American Prophets; a Survey of Taught Jurisprudence. LC 70-158741. 1971. Repr. of 1951 ed. lib. bdg. 29.75x (ISBN 0-8371-6180-0). Greenwood.

Reuschlein, Harold G. & Gregory, William A. Handbook on the Law of Agency & Partnership. LC 78-12853. (Hornbook Ser.). 625p. 1978. text ed. 17.95 (ISBN 0-8299-2016-1). West Pub.

Reusswig, William. A Picture Report of the Custer Fight. (Illus.). 192p. (gr. 6-9). 1967. 12.50 (ISBN 0-8038-5737-3). Hastings.

Reute, H., jt. auth. see Baker, P. F.

Reuter, Edward B. Handbook of Sociology. 233p. 1980. Repr. of 1941 ed. lib. bdg. 30.00 (ISBN 0-89987-156-9). Darby Bks.

Reuter, Fritz. Seed-Time & Harvest; or, During My Apprenticeship. 292p. 1976. Repr. of 1871 ed. 15.00 (ISBN 0-86527-301-4). Fertig.

Reuter, Margaret. Careers in a Fire Department. LC 77-8151. (Whole Works Ser.). (Illus.). (gr. 3-7). 1977. PLB 9.65 (ISBN 0-8172-0954-9). Raintree Pubs.

--Careers in a Police Department. LC 77-8113. (Whole Works Ser.). (Illus.). (gr. 3-7). 1977. PLB 9.65 (ISBN 0-8172-0956-5). Raintree Pubs.

--Earthquakes: Our Restless Planet. LC 76-45653. (Science Information Ser.). (Illus.). (gr. 4-6). 1977. PLB 8.65 (ISBN 0-8172-0352-4). Raintree Pubs.

--Two Thousand Plus Index & Glossary. (gr. k-3). 1977. PLB 7.30 (ISBN 0-8172-1025-3). Raintree Pubs.

Reutov, O. A., et al. CH-Acids. LC 77-30618. (Illus.). 1979. 41.00 (ISBN 0-08-021610-2). Pergamon.

Revard, Stella P. The War in Heaven. LC 79-23297. (Illus.). 1980. 18.50x (ISBN 0-8014-1138-6). Cornell U Pr.

Revelis, B. G. Greek-English Letterwriting. 5.00 (ISBN 0-685-09036-1). Divry.

Revell, Dorothy T. Gourmet Recipes for Diabetics: The International Diabetic Diet Book. 196p. 1971. 13.75 (ISBN 0-398-02153-8). C C Thomas.

Revell, E. J. Biblical Texts with Palestinian Pointing. LC 77-8893. (Society of Biblical Literature. Masoretic Studies). 1977. pap. 9.00 (ISBN 0-89130-141-0, 060504). Scholars Pr Ca.

Revell, Peter. James Whitcomb Riley. (U. S. Authors Ser.: No. 159). lib. bdg. 9.95 (ISBN 0-8057-0624-0). Twayne.

--Paul Laurence Dunbar. (United States Authors Ser.: No. 298). 1979. lib. bdg. 12.50 (ISBN 0-8057-7213-8). Twayne.

ReVelle. Environmental Studies: Issues & Choices for Society. 1980. text ed. 18.95 (ISBN 0-442-22069-3); instr's. manual 3.95 (ISBN 0-442-25753-8). D Van Nostrand.

ReVelle, Charles S. & ReVelle, Penelope L. Sourcebook on the Environment: The Scientific Perspective. 1974. pap. text ed. 9.95 (ISBN 0-395-17018-4). HM.

ReVelle, Jack B. Safety Training Methods. LC 80-16601. 300p. 1980. 24.95 (ISBN 0-471-07761-5, Pub. by Wiley-Interscience). Wiley.

ReVelle, Jack B., jt. auth. see Brown, Kenneth S.

ReVelle, Penelope L., jt. auth. see ReVelle, Charles S.

Revere, John, tr. see Magendie, Francois.

Revere, Lawrence. Playing Blackjack As a Business: 1977 Edition. (Illus.). 1977. 12.50 (ISBN 0-686-67857-5); pap. 8.95 (ISBN 0-8184-0064-1). Lyle Stuart.

Revesz, G. The Psychology of a Musical Prodigy. 180p. 1980. Repr. of 1925 ed. lib. bdg. 45.00 (ISBN 0-89987-715-X). Darby Bks.

Revesz, Therese R. Witches. LC 77-10626. (Myth, Magic & Superstition Ser.). (Illus.). (gr. 4-5). 1977. PLB 9.65 (ISBN 0-8172-1034-2). Raintree Pubs.

Revi, Albert C. American Art Nouveau Glass. LC 68-18778. (Illus.). 476p. 1981. Repr. 40.00 (ISBN 0-916838-40-4). Schiffer.

--The Spinning Wheel's Complete Book of Antiques. (Illus.). 9.95 o.p. (ISBN 0-686-51535-8). Wallace-Homestead.

Revien, Leon & Gabor, Mark. Dr. Revien's Eye Exercise Program for Athletes: How to Direct Your Eyes to Win in 15 Minutes a Day. LC 80-54623. (Illus.). 192p. 1981. pap. 4.95 (ISBN 0-89480-152-X). Workman Pub.

Revista De Occidente, ed. see Ortega Y Gasset, Jose.

Revold, Reidar, jt. auth. see Langaard, Johan H.

Revolutionary Health Committee of Hunan Province. A Barefoot Doctor's Manual. rev. ed. (Illus.). 1977. lib. bdg. 17.50 (ISBN 0-88930-037-2, Pub. by Cloudburst Canada); pap. 8.95 (ISBN 0-88930-012-7). Madrona Pubs.

Revsine, Lawrence. Replacement Cost Accounting. (Contemporary Topics in Accounting Ser). (Illus.). 224p. (Ref. ed). 1973. pap. 9.95 (ISBN 0-13-773630-4). P-H.

Rewald, John. The History of Impressionism. LC 68-17468. (Illus.). 672p. 1980. 40.00 (ISBN 0-87070-369-2, 365149, Pub. by Museum Mod Art); pap. 19.95 (ISBN 0-87070-369-2). NYGS.

Rewoldt, Stewart H., et al. Introduction to Marketing Management. 3rd. ed. 1977. text ed. 19.95 (ISBN 0-256-01928-2). Irwin.

Rex, Chris. Comfort Clothes. LC 80-69534. (Illus.). 80p. (Orig.). pap. 7.95 (ISBN 0-89087-312-7). Celestial Arts.

--Comfort Clothes: How to Make & Wear West African Style Garments. LC 80-69534. (Illus.). 80p. 1981. 7.95 (ISBN 0-89087-312-7). Celestial Arts.

Rex, John. Discovering Sociology: Studies in Sociological Theory & Method. 288p. 1973. 24.00 (ISBN 0-7100-7411-5). Routledge & Kegan.

--Key Problems of Sociological Theory. (International Library of Sociology & Social Reconstruction). 1970. text ed. 11.25x o.p. (ISBN 0-7100-3409-1); pap. text ed. 4.50x o.p. (ISBN 0-391-00091-8). Humanities.

--Race, Colonialism & the City. 324p. 1973. 25.00x (ISBN 0-7100-7412-3). Routledge & Kegan.

--Sociology & the Demystification of the Modern World. (International Library of Sociology Ser.). 1974. 22.00x (ISBN 0-7100-7858-7). Routledge & Kegan.

Rex, John, ed. Approaches to Sociology: An Introduction to the Major Trends in British Sociology. (International Library of Sociology Ser.). 1974. 23.50x (ISBN 0-7100-7824-2); pap. 10.00 (ISBN 0-7100-7825-0). Routledge & Kegan.

Rex, Percy F. The Prolific Pencil. Burrows, Fredrika A. & Sullwold, Stephen W., eds. LC 80-51482. (Illus.). 312p. 1980. 15.00 (ISBN 0-88492-037-2). W S Sullwold.

Rex, Walter, tr. see D'Alembert, Jean L.

Rexford, Kenneth. Electrical Control for Machines. LC 80-70918. (Electrical Maintenance Ser.). (Illus.). 332p. 1981. pap. text ed. 9.80 (ISBN 0-8273-1983-5); write for info. instr's guide (ISBN 0-8273-1984-3). Delmar.

Rexroad, Robert A. Technical Marketing to the Government. 325p. 1981. 69.50 (ISBN 0-85013-122-7). Dartnell Corp.

Rexroth, Kenneth. American Poetry in the Twentieth Century. LC 73-17882. 400p. 1973. pap. 2.95 o.p. (ISBN 0-8164-9167-4). Continuum.

--An Autobiographical Novel. LC 78-8823. 382p. 1978. pap. 6.95 (ISBN 0-915520-15-X). Ross-Erikson.

--The Elastic Retort: Essays in Literature & Ideas. LC 73-6425. 228p. 1973. 7.95 o.p. (ISBN 0-8164-9168-2). Continuum.

Rexroth, Kenneth, ed. The Buddhist Writings of Lafcadio Hearn. LC 77-2496. 312p. 1977. lib. bdg. 12.95 (ISBN 0-915520-05-2). Ross-Erikson.

Rey, H. A. Curious George. (Illus.). 48p. (gr. k-3). 1973. pap. 2.50 (ISBN 0-395-15023-X, Sandpiper). HM.

--Curious George Gets a Medal. (Illus.). (gr. k-3). 1957. reinforced bdg. 8.95 (ISBN 0-395-16973-9). HM.

--Curious George Learns the Alphabet. LC 62-12261. (Illus.). 72p. (gr. k-3). 1973. pap. 2.95 (ISBN 0-395-13718-7, Sandpiper). HM.

--The Stars: A New Way to See Them. 3rd ed. (gr. 8 up). 1967. 11.95 (ISBN 0-395-08121-1). HM.

--The Stars: A New Way to See Them. 1976. pap. 6.95 (ISBN 0-395-24830-2). HM.

Rey, J. Del see Del Rey, Judy Lynn.

Rey, Judy-Lynn Del see Del Rey, Judy-Lynn.

Rey, Lester Del see Del Rey, Lester.

Rey, Marilyn B. & Maloof, Katherine. Deutsch Macht Spass. (gr. 8-11). 1979. wkbk. 4.50 (ISBN 0-87720-582-5). AMSCO Sch.

Rey, Pierre. The Widow. 1978. pap. 2.50 o.p. (ISBN 0-425-04010-0, Dist. by Putnam). Berkley Pub.

Reyburn, Noel J. Thoughts from My Quiet Corner. 52p. 1978. 3.50 (ISBN 0-8059-2591-0). Dorrance.

Reyburn, Wallace. Twickenham: The Story of a Rugby Ground. 1976. 14.95 o.p. (ISBN 0-04-796044-2). Allen Unwin.

Reychler, Luc. Patterns of Diplomatic Thinking: A Cross National Study of Structural & Social-Psychological Determinants. LC 78-19774. (Praeger Special Studies). 1979. 24.95 (ISBN 0-03-046636-9). Praeger.

Reyer, Eduard. Questions on Geologic Principles. Keller, Allen, et al, trs. LC 79-89374. (Microform Publication: No. 9). (Illus.). 1979. 4.00x (ISBN 0-8137-6009-7). Geol Soc.

Reyer, Wilhelm. Einfuhrung in Die Phanomenologie. LC 78-66737. (Phenomenology Ser.: Vol. 11). 475p. 1980. lib. bdg. 44.00 (ISBN 0-8240-9559-6). Garland Pub.

Reyes-Guerra, David R. & Fischer, Alan M. Peterson's Guide to Undergraduate Engineering Study. (Orig.). 1981. pap. 14.00 (ISBN 0-87866-163-8). Petersons Guides.

Reymes, William, tr. see Secchi, Nicolo.

Reymond, Arnold. History of the Sciences in Greco-Roman Antiquity. Bray, Ruth G. De, tr. LC 63-18046. 1963. 10.50x (ISBN 0-8196-0128-4). Biblo.

Reymond, E. A. & Barns, J. W., eds. Four Martyrdoms from the Pierpont Morgan Coptic Codices. 278p. 1974. 24.95x (ISBN 0-19-815448-8). Oxford U Pr.

Reyna, Rudy De see De Reyna, Rudy.

Reynaud, C. B. Critical Path: Network Analysis & Resource Scheduling. 2nd ed. 1970. text ed. 17.50x (ISBN 0-7121-3301-1). Intl Ideas.

Reynaud, Joyce. Samoyeds. (Illus.). 128p. 1980. 2.95 (ISBN 0-87666-680-2, KW-072). TFH Pubns.

Reynaud-Dulaurier, Georges, ed. see Fullard, Harold & Darby, H. C.

Reynell, A. C., et al, eds. Ovid's Metamorphoses: Selections. 1972. pap. 4.50 (ISBN 0-571-10254-9, Pub. by Faber & Faber). Merrimack Bk Serv.

Reynell, Joan. Language Developement & Assessment. (Studies in Developmental Pediatrics Ser.: Vol. 1). 178p. 1980. text ed. 16.50 (ISBN 0-88416-377-6). PSG Pub.

Reynoldds, James J., jt. auth. see Harshbarger, Ronald J.

Reynolds. Social Work & Social Living. 2.50 (ISBN 0-8065-0332-7). Citadel Pr.

Reynolds & Michas. Plaid for Principles of Economics: Macro. 3rd ed. 1979. 5.50 (ISBN 0-256-02132-5, 05-0865-03). Learning Syst.

--Plaid for Principles of Economics: Micro. 3rd ed. 1979. 5.50 (ISBN 0-256-02133-3, 05-0866-03). Learning Syst.

Reynolds, jt. auth. see Waltar.

Reynolds, et al. Elementary Accounting. 1978. 18.95 (ISBN 0-03-018021-X). Dryden Pr.

Reynolds, Amy, ed. see Eads, Buryl.

Reynolds, Barbara. Cambridge Italian Dictionary. LC 74-77384. 1962. Vol. 1. Italian-English 1962. 115.00 (ISBN 0-521-06059-1). Cambridge U Pr.

--Concise Cambridge Italian Dictionary. 1974. 42.00 (ISBN 0-521-07273-5). Cambridge U Pr.

Reynolds, Barbara A. Jesse Jackson: The Man, the Movement, the Myth. LC 74-17813. 416p. 1975. 14.95 (ISBN 0-911012-80-X). Nelson-Hall.

Reynolds, Barrie. Magic, Divination & Witchcraft Among the Barotse of Northern Rhodesia. (Illus.). 1963. 17.95x (ISBN 0-520-01063-9). U of Cal Pr.

Reynolds, Beatrice, tr. see Bodin, Jean.

Reynolds, Ben, tr. see Ladurie, Emmanuel L.

Reynolds, Bonnie J. The Confetti Man. 448p. 1976. pap. 1.95 o.p. (ISBN 0-345-25251-9). Ballantine.

Reynolds, Bruford S. Money Saving Recipes Through Sprouting & Gardening. pap. 4.95 (ISBN 0-89036-134-7). Hawkes Pub Inc.

Reynolds, C. Sinhalese: An Introductory Course. 1980. 38.00x (ISBN 0-8364-0661-3, Pub. by London U England). South Asia Bks.

Reynolds, C. H. Sinhalese: An Introductory Course. 1980. 38.00x (ISBN 0-8364-0661-3). South Asia Bks.

Reynolds, Clark G. The Saga of Smokey Stover. LC 78-64485. 1978. 6.00 (ISBN 0-937684-06-6). Tradd St Pr.

Reynolds, Clyde. Minolta XD & XG Book. (Camera Book Series). (Illus.). 128p. 1980. pap. 9.95 (ISBN 0-240-51035-6). Focal Pr.

Reynolds, Cynthia. Teaching Child Development. 1975. pap. 14.95 (ISBN 0-7134-2990-9, Pub. by Batsford England). David & Charles.

Reynolds, David K. Morita Psychotherapy. LC 74-30530. 200p. 1976. 15.95 (ISBN 0-520-02937-2). U of Cal Pr.

--The Quiet Therapies: Japanese Pathways to Personal Growth. LC 80-17611. 144p. 1980. 8.95 (ISBN 0-8248-0690-5). U Pr of Hawaii.

Reynolds, David K. & Farberow, Norman L. Endangered Hope: Experiences in Psychiatric Aftercare Facilities. 1978. 12.95 (ISBN 0-520-03457-0). U of Cal Pr.

--The Family Shadow: Sources of Suicide & Schizophrenia. 188p. 1981. 14.95 (ISBN 0-520-04213-1). U of Cal Pr.

Reynolds, Donald C. & Collins, Thomas C. Excitons: Their Properties & Uses. 1981. 36.00 (ISBN 0-12-586580-5). Acad Pr.

Reynolds, Donald M. Hiram Powers & His Ideal Sculpture. LC 76-23685. (Outstanding Dissertations in the Fine Arts - American). (Illus.). 1977. Repr. of 1975 ed. lib. bdg. 63.00 (ISBN 0-8240-2720-5). Garland Pub.

Reynolds, E. E., ed. see Roper, William & Harpsfield, Nicholas.

Reynolds, E. G. & Fulton, Robin. Target Rifle Shooting. 1978. 11.95 o.p. (ISBN 0-686-01039-6, 8032, Dist. by Arco). Barrie & Jenkins.

Reynolds, E. H., jt. ed. see Botez, M. I.

Reynolds, Erma. Bible Places Quiz Book. (Quiz & Puzzle Books Ser.). 112p. (Orig.). 1981. pap. 2.45 (ISBN 0-8010-7703-6). Baker Bk.

Reynolds, G. F., tr. see Galus, Z.

Reynolds, G. W. Aloes of South Africa. 1975. Repr. 51.00 (ISBN 0-86961-064-3). Horticultural.

--Aloes of Tropical Africa & Madagascar. (Illus.). 1966. 51.00 (ISBN 0-685-12174-7). Horticultural.

Reynolds, George S., jt. auth. see Fantino, Edmund J.

Reynolds, Gerald, jt. auth. see Enterkin, Hugh.

Reynolds, Grace D., ed. Swimming Program for the Handicapped. 1973. pap. 4.95 o.p. (ISBN 0-8096-0471-X, Assn Pr). Follett.

Reynolds, Graham. A Concise History of Watercolors. (World of Art Ser.). (Illus.). 1978. pap. 9.95 (ISBN 0-19-520051-9). Oxford U Pr.

--Turner. (World of Art Ser.). (Illus.). 1969. pap. 9.95 (ISBN 0-19-519932-4). Oxford U Pr.

Reynolds, H. T. Analysis of Nominal Data. LC 77-72851. (University Papers: Quantitative Applications in the Social Sciences, No. 7). 1977. 3.50x (ISBN 0-8039-0653-6). Sage.

Reynolds, Helen. Cops & Dollars: The Economics of Criminal Law & Justice. (Illus.). 256p. 1981. pap. 15.75 (ISBN 0-398-04115-6). C C Thomas.

Reynolds, Helen, jt. auth. see Tramel, Mary E.

Reynolds, Hezekiah. Directions for House & Ship Painting. (AAS Facsimiles: No. 1). (Illus., Orig.). 1978. pap. 2.95 (ISBN 0-912296-16-X, Dist. by U Pr of Va). Am Antiquarian.

Reynolds, Isaac, jt. auth. see Slavin, Albert.

Reynolds, Issac N., et al. Elementary Accounting. 2nd ed. LC 80-65808. 1040p. 1981. pap. text ed. 19.95 (ISBN 0-03-058144-3). Dryden Pr.

Reynolds, J. Craft of Programming. 1981. 22.95 (ISBN 0-13-188862-5). P-H.

Reynolds, J., jt. auth. see Badcock, W.

Reynolds, J. F., jt. auth. see Jamieson, B. G.

Reynolds, Jan. William Callow. LC 79-56444. (Illus.). 272p. 1980. 150.00 (ISBN 0-7134-1438-3, Pub. by Batsford England). David & Charles.

Reynolds, Jane L. Music Lessons That Are Easy to Teach. 1976. 11.95 (ISBN 0-13-608059-6). P-H.

Reynolds, Jean K., compiled by. How to Choose & Use Child Care. LC 79-54920. (Orig.). 1980. pap. 2.50 (ISBN 0-8054-5275-3). Broadman.

Reynolds, Jesse A. & Hormachea, Marion. Public Recreation Administration. (Illus.). 480p. 1976. 16.95x (ISBN 0-87909-662-4). Reston.

Reynolds, John H. John Hamilton Reynolds. Reiman, Donald H., ed. LC 75-31250. (Romantic Context Ser.: Poetry 1789-1830). 1978. lib. bdg. 47.00 (ISBN 0-8240-2198-3). Garland Pub.

Reynolds, John I. Indian-American Joint Ventures: Business Policy Relationships. LC 77-18587. 1978. pap. text ed. 10.50x (ISBN 0-8191-0403-5). U Pr of Amer.

Reynolds, John J. Juan Timoneda. LC 75-9837. (World Author Ser.: Spain: No. 367). 1975. lib. bdg. 10.95 (ISBN 0-8057-6205-1). Twayne.

Reynolds, Kay, jt. auth. see Shell, Adeline G.

Reynolds, L. D. & Wilson, N. G. Scribes & Scholars: A Guide to the Transmission of Greek & Latin Literature. 2nd ed. (Illus.). 266p. 1974. pap. text ed. 11.50x (ISBN 0-19-814372-9). Oxford U Pr.

Reynolds, Larry T., jt. auth. see Henslin, James M.

Reynolds, Lloyd G. The American Economy in Perspective. Brooks, Barbara & Lieberman, Bonnie, eds. (Illus.). 480p. 1981. pap. text ed. 14.95x (ISBN 0-07-052028-3, C); write for info instrs.' manual (ISBN 0-07-052030-5). McGraw.

--Economics: A General Introduction. 4th ed. 1973. text ed. 18.95 (ISBN 0-256-01400-0). Irwin.

--Macroeconomics: Analysis & Policy. 3rd. ed. 1979. pap. text ed. 11.50 (ISBN 0-256-02173-2); review guide & wkbk. 5.95 (ISBN 0-256-02170-8). Irwin.

--Microeconomics: Analysis & Policy. 3rd. ed. 1979. pap. text ed. 11.50 (ISBN 0-256-02172-4); review guide & wkbk 5.95 (ISBN 0-256-02169-4). Irwin.

--Three Worlds of Economics. (Studies in Comparative Economics: No. 12). (Illus.). 1971. 27.50x (ISBN 0-300-01481-3); pap. 5.45x o.p. (ISBN 0-300-01491-0, Y245). Yale U Pr.

Reynolds, Lloyd G., ed. Agriculture in Development Theory. LC 74-20085. 528p. 1975. 30.00x (ISBN 0-300-01805-3); pap. 6.95x (ISBN 0-300-02188-7). Yale U Pr.

Reynolds, Lloyd G., et al. Current Issues of Economic Policy. 1973. pap. text ed. 9.95 (ISBN 0-256-01441-8). Irwin.

--Readings in Labor Economics & Labor Relations. 2nd ed. (Illus.). 1978. pap. text ed. 11.95 (ISBN 0-13-761569-8). P-H.

Reynolds, Lorna, jt. ed. see O'Driscoll, Robert.

Reynolds, Marjorie. Dark Horse Barnaby. (Illus.). (gr. 4-6). 1967. 3.95g o.s.i. (ISBN 0-02-776060-X). Macmillan.

--Ride the Wild Storm. LC 69-11305. (Illus.). (gr. 4-6). 1969. 4.95g o.s.i. (ISBN 0-02-776040-5). Macmillan.

--Sire Unknown. LC 68-20608. (Illus.). (gr. 4-6). 1968. 4.50g o.s.i. (ISBN 0-02-776110-X). Macmillan.

Reynolds, Mary T. Joyce & Dante: The Shaping Imagination. LC 80-7550. (Illus.). 400p. 1981. 22.50x (ISBN 0-691-06446-6). Princeton U Pr.

Reynolds, Maureen, ed. see Pappas, Lou S.

Reynolds, Maynard & Hively, Wells. Domain Referenced Testing in Special Education. 1975. pap. text ed. 4.00x o.p. (ISBN 0-86586-022-X). Coun Exc Child.

Reynolds, Maynard C. The Social Environment of the Schools. LC 80-65498. 104p. (Orig.). 1980. pap. 6.75 (ISBN 0-86586-103-X). Coun Exc Child.

Reynolds, Maynard C., jt. auth. see Hebeler, Jean R.

Reynolds, Maynard C., jt. ed. see Birch, Jack W.

Reynolds, Michael M., ed. Guide to Theses & Dissertations: An Annotated, International Bibliography of Bibliographies. LC 74-11184. 600p. 1975. 42.00 (ISBN 0-8103-0976-9). Gale.

Reynolds, Michael S. Hemingway's Reading, Nineteen Ten to Nineteen Forty: Commentary & Inventory. LC 80-7549. 200p. 1980. 17.50 (ISBN 0-691-06447-4). Princeton U Pr.

Reynolds, Moira D. The Outstretched Hand-Advances in Modern Medicine. (Illus.). 140p. 1980. lib. bdg. 7.97 (ISBN 0-8239-0502-0). Rosen Pr.

Reynolds, Nancy J, jt. auth. see Boundy, Suzanne S.

Reynolds, P. Iron Age Farming. (Cambridge Introduction to the History of Mankind Ser.). 48p. 1976. pap. 3.95 (ISBN 0-521-21084-4). Cambridge U Pr.

Reynolds, P. A. An Introduction to International Relations. 2nd ed. 352p. 1980. pap. text ed. 12.95 (ISBN 0-582-29502-5). Longman.

Reynolds, P. A. & Hughes, E. J. The Historian As Diplomat: Charles Kingsley Webster & the United Nations 1939-1946. 198p. 1976. 36.00x (ISBN 0-85520-131-2, Pub. by Martin Robertson England). Biblio Dist.

Reynolds, Pamela. Will the Real Monday Please Stand up. (gr. 7-9). 1976. pap. 1.75 (ISBN 0-671-42067-4). Archway.

--Will the Real Monday Please Stand up? (YA) (gr. 7-9). 1976. pap. 1.25 (ISBN 0-671-29789-9). PB.

Reynolds, Paul. International Commodity Agreements & the Common Fund: A Legal & Financial Analysis. LC 78-16265. (Praeger Special Studies). 1978. 26.95 (ISBN 0-03-044266-4). Praeger.

Reynolds, Paul D. Primer in Theory Construction. 194p. (Orig.). 1971. pap. 4.95 (ISBN 0-672-61196-1). Bobbs.

Reynolds, Paul R. Guy Carleton: A Biography. LC 80-81587. 192p. 1980. 10.95 (ISBN 0-688-03770-4). Morrow.

Reynolds, Quentin. Wright Brothers. (Landmark Ser). (Illus.). (gr. 4-6). 1950. PLB 5.99 (ISBN 0-394-90310-2, BYR). Random.

--Wright Brothers. (gr. 4-6). 1950. 2.95 o.p. (ISBN 0-394-80310-8, BYR). Random.

--The Wright Brothers. LC 50-11766. (Landmark Bks.). (Illus.). 160p. (gr. 5-9). 1981. pap. 2.95 (ISBN 0-394-84700-8). Random.

Reynolds, R. A. Computer Methods for Architects. (Illus.). 160p. 1980. text ed. 39.95 (ISBN 0-408-00476-2). Butterworths.

Reynolds, R. D. Ascomycete Systematics: The Luttrellian Concept. (Springer Series in Microbiology). (Illus.). 272p. 1981. 42.80 (ISBN 0-387-90488-3). Springer-Verlag.

Reynolds, R. J., jt. auth. see Thompson, K. C.

Reynolds, Ray P., ed. Bookhunter's Guide to the Northeast: 1979-80 Edition. 1979. pap. 6.60 (ISBN 0-934792-00-3). Ephemera.

--Bookhunter's Guide to the West & Southwest, 1980-1982. (Bookhunter's Guides Ser.). 130p. (Orig.). 1980. pap. 6.60 (ISBN 0-934792-01-1). Ephemera.

Reynolds, Reginald. The Wisdom of John Woolman: With a Selection from His Writings As a Guide to the Seekers of Today. LC 79-8724. xii, 178p. 1981. Repr. of 1948 ed. lib. bdg. 22.50x (ISBN 0-313-22190-1, REJW). Greenwood.

Reynolds, Robert L. Europe Emerges: Transition Toward an Industrial World-Wide Society, 600-1750. (Illus.). 1961. pap. 8.95x (ISBN 0-299-02294-3). U of Wis Pr.

Reynolds, Robert L. & MacArthur, Douglas, 2nd. Commodore Perry in Japan. LC 63-20168. (American Heritage Junior Library). (Illus.). 153p. (gr. 5 up). 1963. 9.95 (ISBN 0-8281-0396-8, J012-0); PLB 12.89 (ISBN 0-06-024951-X, Dist. by Har-Row). Am Heritage.

Reynolds, Sian, tr. see Braudel, Fernand.

Reynolds, Sian, tr. see Ladurie, Emmanuel L.

Reynolds, Susan. An Introduction to the History of English Medieval Towns. (Illus.). 1977. text ed. 27.00x (ISBN 0-19-822455-9). Oxford U Pr.

Reynolds, V., jt. ed. see Blurton-Jones, N.

Reynolds, Vernon. The Biology of Human Action. 2nd ed. LC 80-11856. (Illus.). 1981. text ed. 19.95x (ISBN 0-7167-1239-3); pap. text ed. 10.95x (ISBN 0-7167-1240-7). W H Freeman.

Reynolds, W. N. Physical Properties of Graphite. (Illus.). 1968. text ed. 29.90x (ISBN 0-444-20012-6). Intl Ideas.

Reynolds, Walter F. Commerically Available Chemical Agents for Paper & Board Manufacture. 3rd ed. (TAPPI PRESS Reports). 74p. 1980. pap. 54.95 (ISBN 0-89852-383-4, 01-01-R083). TAPPI.
--Dry Strength Additives. LC 79-67261. (TAPPI PRESS Bks.). 1980. 34.95 (ISBN 0-89855-204-4, 01-02-B044). TAPPI.
Reynolds, William H., jt. auth. see Myers, James H.
Reynolds, William L. Judicial Process in a Nutshell. LC 80-12730. (Nutshell Ser.). 322p. 1980. pap. text ed. 6.95 (ISBN 0-8299-2089-7). West Pub.
Reynoldson, George. Let's Reach for the Sun. (Illus.). 144p. 1978. pap. 9.95 o.p. (ISBN 0-9603570-0-9). Space-Time.
--Let's Reach for the Sun: 30 Original Solar & Earth Sheltered Home Designs. rev. ed. Erdahl, Jeanne, ed. (Illus.). 144p. 1981. pap. 9.95 (ISBN 0-9603570-1-7). Space-Time.
Rezatto, Helen. Mount Moriah: Kill a Man, Start a Cemetery. LC 80-81127. (Illus.). 256p. 1980. 7.95 (ISBN 0-87970-150-1). North Plains.
Rezits, Joseph. Guitar Music in Print. LC 80-84548. 1000p. (Orig.). 1981. pap. 50.00 (ISBN 0-8497-7802-6, Pub. by Kjos West). Kjos.
Rezk, A. M., ed. Heat & Fluid Flow in Power System Components. (Heat & Mass Transfer: Vol. 3). (Illus.). 300p. 1980. 55.00 (ISBN 0-08-024235-9). Pergamon.
Rezneck, Samuel. The Saga of an American Jewish Family Since the Revolution: A History of the Family of Jonas Phillips. LC 79-6725. 1980. text ed. 17.75 (ISBN 0-8191-0939-8); pap. text ed. 9.50 (ISBN 0-8191-0940-1). U Pr of Amer.
Reznik, John W. Racquetball. LC 78-66320. 1979. 9.95 (ISBN 0-8069-4138-3); lib. bdg. 9.29 (ISBN 0-8069-4139-1). Sterling.
Reznik, John W., jt. auth. see Mueller, Pat.
Reznikoff, Charles. Poems, Nineteen Eighteen to Nineteen Thirty-Six: The Complete Poems of Charles Reznikoff, Vol. 1. Cooney, Seamus, ed. 222p. (Orig.). 1978. 14.00 (ISBN 0-87685-262-2); pap. 5.00 (ISBN 0-87685-261-4). Black Sparrow.
--Poems, Nineteen Thirty-Seven to Nineteen Seventy-Five: The Complete Poems of Charles Reznikoff, Vol. 2. Cooney, Seamus, ed. 1978. 14.00 (ISBN 0-87685-301-7); pap. 6.00 (ISBN 0-87685-300-9). Black Sparrow.
Reznikoff, W. S., jt. ed. see Miller, J. H.
Rezzori, Gregor Von see Von Rezzori, Gregor.
Rezzuto, Thomas, jt. auth. see Selden, Samuel, Jr.
Rhea, Carolyn. Healing in His Wings. LC 68-31348. 1977. pap. 4.50 (ISBN 0-8054-5150-1). Broadman.
Rhea, Kay & O'Leary, Maggie. The Psychic Is You. LC 79-53023. 168p. 1981. pap. 5.95 (ISBN 0-89087-311-9). Celestial Arts.
Rhee, Jhoon. Chon-Ji of Tae Kwon Do Hyung. Alvarez, Roberto, tr. LC 74-120124. (Series 102). (Illus., Sp. & Eng.). 1970. pap. text ed. 5.95 (ISBN 0-89750-000-8). Ohara Pubns.
--Hwa-Rang & Chung-Mu of Tae Kwon Do Hyung. LC 77-163382. (Ser. 109). (Illus.). 1971. pap. text ed. 5.95 (ISBN 0-89750-004-0). Ohara Pubns.
Rhees, Rush, ed. Ludwig Wittgenstein: Personal Recollections. 256p. 1981. 22.50x (ISBN 0-8476-6253-5). Rowman.
Rhees, Rush, ed. see Wittgenstein, Ludwig.
Rhees, Rush, et al, eds. see Wittgenstein, Ludwig.
Rhein, Francis B. Understanding the New Testament. LC 65-23532. Orig. Title: An Analytical Approach to the New Testament. 1974. pap. text ed. 5.25 (ISBN 0-8120-0027-7). Barron.
Rhein, Phillip H. Albert Camus. (World Authors Ser.: France: No. 69). 1969. lib. bdg. 9.95 (ISBN 0-8057-2196-7). Twayne.
Rheinboldt, Cornelie J., tr. see Burger, Dionys.
Rheinboldt, W. C., tr. see Stiefel, E. L.
Rheinheimer, G. Aquatic Microbiology. 2nd ed. LC 79-40645. 240p. 1980. 28.00 (ISBN 0-471-27643-X, Pub. by Wiley-Interscience). Wiley.
Rheinheimer, Gerhard. Aquatic Microbiology. LC 72-8615. 220p. 1974. 21.00 o.p. (ISBN 0-471-71803-3, Pub. by Wiley-Interscience). Wiley.
Rhie, Marylin M. Fo-Kuang Ssu: Literary Evidences & Buddhist Images. LC 76-23690. (Outstanding Dissertations in the Fine Arts - Far Eastern). (Illus.). 1977. Repr. of 1970 ed. lib. bdg. 45.00 (ISBN 0-8240-2721-3). Garland Pub.
Rhie, Schi-Zhin. Soon-Hee in America. LC 77-81780. (Illus.). (gr. k-3). 1977. PLB 6.50 (ISBN 0-930878-00-0). Hollym Intl.
Rhine, J. B. & Pratt, J. G. Parapsychology: Frontier Science of the Mind. (Illus.). 236p. 1974. 9.75 (ISBN 0-398-01580-5). C C Thomas.
Rhine, Louisa E. The Invisible Picture: A Study of Psychic Experiences. LC 80-10545. (Illus.). 275p. 1981. lib. bdg. 15.95x (ISBN 0-89950-015-3). McFarland & Co.
--Mind Over Matter: The Story of PK. LC 70-90224. (Illus.). 1970. 11.95 (ISBN 0-02-602420-9). Macmillan.
Rhine, Shirley H. America's Aging Population: Issues Facing Business & Society, Report No. 785. (Illus.). viii, 60p. 1980. pap. 15.00 (ISBN 0-8237-0221-9). Conference Bd.
Rhine, W. Ray, ed. Making Schools More Effective: New Directions from Follow Through. (Educational Psychology Ser.). 1981. price not set (ISBN 0-12-587060-4). Acad Pr.
Rhinelander, John B., jt. auth. see Willrich, Mason.
Rhinelander, Philip H. Is Man Incomprehensible to Man? (Illus.). 1974. text ed. 10.95x (ISBN 0-7167-0765-9); pap. text ed. 5.95x (ISBN 0-7167-0764-0). W H Freeman.
Rhoades, Everett R. Federal Policy & American Indian Health Needs. LC 74-10495. 32p. 1974. pap. 1.00 o.p. (ISBN 0-913456-38-1). Interbk Inc.
Rhoades, George, jt. auth. see Rhoades, Lynn.
Rhoades, John. Linguistic Diversity & Language Belief in Kenya: The Special Position of Swahili. LC 77-20016. (Foreign & Comparative Studies-African Ser.: No. 26). 1977. pap. text ed. 6.00x (ISBN 0-915984-23-7). Syracuse U Foreign Comp.
Rhoades, Lynn & Rhoades, George. Teaching with Newspapers: The Living Curriculum. LC 80-82682. (Fastback Ser.: No. 149). (Orig.). 1980. pap. 0.75 (ISBN 0-87367-149-X). Phi Delta Kappa.
Rhoades, Robert B. Medical Aspects of the Imported Fire Ant. LC 77-1736. (Illus.). 1977. 4.75 o.p. (ISBN 0-8130-0559-0). U Presses Fla.
Rhoads, Bert. Bickie's Cow College. 1980. pap. 2.95 (ISBN 0-8280-0042-5). Review & Herald.
--Bickie's Thunder Egg. 1980. pap. 2.95 (ISBN 0-8280-0043-3, 02362-2). Review & Herald.
Rhoads, David M. Israel in Revolution, 6-74 C.E. A Political History Based on the Writings of Josephus. LC 75-36452. 208p. 1976. 9.95 (ISBN 0-8006-0442-3, 1-442); pap. 5.95 (ISBN 0-8006-1442-9, 1-1442). Fortress.
Rhoads, Donald C. & Lutz, Richard A., eds. Skeletal Growth of Acquatic Organisms: Biological Records of Environmental Change. (Topics in Geobiology Ser.: Vol. I). (Illus.). 720p. 1980. 47.50 (ISBN 0-306-40259-9, Plenum Pr). Plenum Pub.
Rhoads, Fred. Rhoads' West. LC 72-86327. (Illus.). 124p. 1972. 6.95 o.p. (ISBN 0-87358-102-4). Northland.
Rhoads, Jerry L. Basic Accounting & Budgeting for Nursing Homes. 460p. 1981. 24.95 (ISBN 0-8436-0795-5). CBI Pub.
Rhoads, William B. The Colonial Revival. LC 76-23695. (Outstanding Dissertations in the Fine Arts Ser.). 1977. lib. bdg. 133.00x (ISBN 0-8240-2722-1). Garland Pub.
Rhodabarger, T. D. Personal Money Management for Physicians. 1973. 16.50 (ISBN 0-87489-027-6). Med Economics.
Rhoden, Chris C. Economics: Facts, Theory & Policy. LC 75-35954. 1976. text ed. 16.95 (ISBN 0-471-71802-5); instructor's manual avail. (ISBN 0-471-71801-7). Wiley.
Rhoderick, E. H., jt. auth. see Rose-Innes, A. C.
Rhodes & Stone. The Language of the Earth. 350p. Date not set. text ed. 35.01 (ISBN 0-08-025981-2); pap. text ed. 17.51 (ISBN 0-08-025980-4). Pergamon.
Rhodes, A. & Fletcher, D. L. Principles of Industrial Microbiology. 1966. 19.50 (ISBN 0-08-011906-9); pap. 15.00 (ISBN 0-08-011905-0). Pergamon.
Rhodes, Anthony. Propaganda: The Art of Persuasion, World War II. Margolin, Victor, ed. LC 75-17545. (Illus.). 300p. 1981. pap. 15.95 (ISBN 0-87754-078-0). Chelsea Hse.
Rhodes, Arnold. The Republic F-84: From "Lead Sled" to "Super Hawg". (Illus.). 128p. 1981. pap. 9.95 (ISBN 0-89404-054-5). Aztex.
Rhodes, Buck A. & Croft, Barbara Y. Basics of Radiopharmacy. LC 77-26557. 1978. pap. text ed. 17.95 (ISBN 0-8016-4127-6). Mosby.
Rhodes, Buck A., ed. Quality Control in Nuclear Medicine: Radiopharmaceuticals, Instrumentation & in-Vitro Assays. (Illus.). 1977. 44.50 o.p. (ISBN 0-8016-4115-2). Mosby.
Rhodes, C. O. Let's Look at Musical Instruments & the Orchestra. LC 71-85229. (Let's Look Ser). (Illus.). (gr. 4-8). 1969. 4.95g o.p. (ISBN 0-8075-4483-3). A Whitman.
Rhodes, Carolyn H., ed. American Notes & Queries Supplement, First Person Female American: A Selected & Annotated Bibliography of the Autobiographies of American Women Living After 1950, Vol. II. LC 77-93778. 453p. 1980. 28.50 (ISBN 0-87875-140-8). Whitston Pub.
Rhodes, Charles M. Mastering the Decisive Power of Logical Thinking. (Illus.). 1980. deluxe ed. 39.75 (ISBN 0-89266-223-9). Am Classical Coll Pr.
Rhodes, Daniel. Tamba Pottery: The Timeless Art of a Japanese Village. LC 74-113180. (Illus.). 1970. 19.95 (ISBN 0-87011-118-3). Kodansha.
Rhodes, Donald R. Synthesis of Planar Antenna Sources. (Oxford Engineering Science Ser.). (Illus.). 230p. 1975. 45.00x (ISBN 0-19-856123-7). Oxford U Pr.
Rhodes, Frank H. Evolution. (Golden Guide Ser). (Illus.). 1974. PLB 9.15 (ISBN 0-307-64360-3, Golden Pr); pap. 1.95 o.p. (ISBN 0-307-24360-5). Western Pub.
Rhodes, G., jt. auth. see Brignell, J.
Rhodes, Gerald. Inspectorates in British Government. (Royal Institute of Public Administration Ser.). (Illus.). 276p. 1981. text ed. 34.00x (ISBN 0-04-351056-6, 2596). Allen Unwin.
Rhodes, Gerald & Ruck, S. K. The Government of Greater London. (New Local Government Ser.). 1970. pap. text ed. 9.50x o.p. (ISBN 0-04-352027-8); pap. text ed. 9.50x o. p. (ISBN 0-04-352028-6). Allen Unwin.
Rhodes, Helen. Doctor, What Can I Do? (Horizon Ser.). 128p. 1981. pap. price not set (ISBN 0-8127-0327-8). Southern Pub.
Rhodes, J. & Walker, A. C., eds. Thin-Walled Structures. 1980. 54.95x (ISBN 0-470-26906-5). Halsted Pr.
Rhodes, James. The Agricultural Marketing System. LC 77-95339. (Agricultural Economics Ser.). 1978. text ed. 20.95 (ISBN 0-88244-170-1). Grid Pub.
Rhodes, James M. The Hitler Movement: A Modern Millenarian Revolution. LC 78-70391. (Publications Ser.: 213). 263p. 1980. 14.95 (ISBN 0-8179-7131-9). Hoover Inst Pr.
Rhodes, John S., et al, eds. Advances in X-Ray Analysis, Vol. 23. 400p. 1980. 45.00 (ISBN 0-306-40435-4). Plenum Pub.
Rhodes, Lucien, jt. auth. see Little, Jeffrey B.
Rhodes, Lynette I. American Folk Art: From the Traditional to the Naive. LC 77-9240. (Themes in Art Ser.). (Illus.). 120p. 1978. pap. 7.95x (ISBN 0-910386-42-0, Pub. by Cleveland Mus Art). Ind U Pr.
--Science Within Art. LC 79-93193. (Illus.). 72p. 1980. pap. 7.95x (ISBN 0-910386-57-9, Pub. by Cleveland Mus Art). Ind U Pr.
Rhodes, Marie J. & Gruendemann, Barbara J. Alexander's Care of the Patient in Surgery. 6th ed. LC 77-26054. (Illus.). 1978. text ed. 29.95 (ISBN 0-8016-0431-1). Mosby.
Rhodes, Mary. Ideas for Canvas Work. (Illus.). 1969. 13.50 (ISBN 0-8231-4014-8). Branford.
Rhodes, Mitchell L., jt. auth. see Brashear, Richard E.
Rhodes, Neil. Elizabeth Grotesque. 208p. 1980. 35.00 (ISBN 0-7100-0599-7). Routledge & Kegan.
Rhodes, Neil S., jt. auth. see Lieberman, Jethro K.
Rhodes, Philip. The Value of Medicine. 1977. text ed. 15.95x (ISBN 0-04-610004-0). Allen Unwin.
Rhodes, R. A. Public Administration & Policy Analysis. 1979. text ed. 23.00x (ISBN 0-566-00239-6, Pub. by Gower Pub Co England). Renouf.
Rhodes, R. A. & Hull, C. Intergovernmental Relations in the European Community. 96p. 1977. text ed. 23.00x (ISBN 0-566-00191-8, Pub. by Gower Pub Co England). Renouf.
Rhodes, Richard. The Ozarks. (The American Wilderness Ser.). (Illus.). 240p. 1974. 12.95 (ISBN 0-8094-1196-2). Time-Life.
--The Ozarks. LC 73-90480. (American Wilderness Ser). (Illus.). (gr. 6 up). 1974. lib. bdg. 11.97 (ISBN 0-8094-1197-0, Pub. by Time-Life). Silver.
Rhodes, Robert E., jt. ed. see Casey, Daniel J.
Rhodes, Robert P. The Insoluble Problems of Crime. LC 76-46275. 1977. text ed. 11.95 (ISBN 0-471-71799-1). Wiley.
Rhodes, Russell. The Herod Conspiracy. LC 80-15323. 350p. 1980. 11.95 (ISBN 0-396-07865-6). Dodd.
--The Styx Complex. LC 77-654. 1977. 8.95 (ISBN 0-396-07435-9). Dodd.
Rhodes, William & Paul, James L. Emotionally Disturbed & Deviant Children: New Views & Approaches. LC 77-17630. 1978. ref. ed. 16.95 (ISBN 0-13-274662-X). P-H.
Rhodes, Winnie B. Cooking for Diabetics at Home & Away. 240p. 1976. pap. 16.75 (ISBN 0-398-03417-6). C C Thomas.
Rhodes-James, R. Memoirs of a Conservative. 1970. 9.95 o.s.i. (ISBN 0-02-602490-X). Macmillan.
Rhoer, Edward Van Der. Many a Secret Place: The Story Ofthe Master Spy Sidney George Reilly. 288p. 1981. 12.50 (ISBN 0-684-16870-7, ScribT). Scribner.
Rhoer, Edward Van Der see Van Der Rhoer, Edward.
Rhomiopoulou, Katerina, jt. ed. see Yalouris, Nicholas M.
Rhone, L. C. Total Auto Body Repair. LC 75-2551. (Illus.). 1975. pap. 19.95 (ISBN 0-685-93194-3). Bobbs.
--Total Auto Body Repair. LC 75-2551. 1978. tchr's guide 3.33 (ISBN 0-672-97137-2); student guide 7.95 (ISBN 0-672-97200-X). Bobbs.
Rhoton, Dale & Rhoton, Elaine. Can We Know? 1972. pap. 0.95 o.p. (ISBN 0-87508-465-6). Chr Lit.
Rhoton, Elaine, jt. auth. see Rhoton, Dale.
Rhymer, Joseph & Bullen, Anthony. Companion to the Good News: New Testament. (Fount Religious Paperbacks Ser). 1976. pap. 1.95 (ISBN 0-00-624742-3, FA4742, Pub. by Collins Pubs). World Bible.
--Companion to the Good News, Old Testament. (Fount Religious Paperbacks Ser.). 1976. pap. 1.95 (ISBN 0-00-623354-6, FA3354, Pub. by Collins Pubs). World Bible.
Rhymer, Joseph, ed. The Bible in Order. LC 75-11363. 1950p. 1976. 35.00 o.p. (ISBN 0-385-11062-6). Doubleday.
Rhymes, I. L., jt. auth. see Austen, D. E.
Rhyne, Jane M. Curriculum for Teaching the Visually Impaired. 320p. 1981. text ed. 27.50 (ISBN 0-398-04161-X); pap. text ed. 27.50 spiral bdg. (ISBN 0-398-04161-X). C C Thomas.
Rhyne, Janie. The Gestalt Art Experience. LC 73-84603. 1974. text ed. 16.95 (ISBN 0-8185-0102-2). Brooks-Cole.
Rhyne, Nancy. The Grand Stand: An Uncommon Guide to Myrtle Beach & Its Surroundings. (Illus.). 160p. (Orig.). 1981. pap. 4.95 (ISBN 0-914788-36-1). East Woods.
Rhyne, V. Thomas. Fundamentals of Digital Systems Design. LC 72-6903. (Illus.). 560p. 1973. 27.95 (ISBN 0-13-336156-X). P-H.
Rhys, Ernest, ed. see Manning, Anne, et al.
Rhys, Jean. Quartet. LC 77-138795. 1971. 8.95 o.s.i. (ISBN 0-06-013537-9, HarpT). Har-Row.
--Tigers Are Better Looking. LC 72-9175. 1974. 8.95 o.p. (ISBN 0-06-013561-1, HarpT). Har-Row.
Riachardson, Ron. Dinghy Racing. 11.95 (ISBN 0-7134-0319-5, SpS). Soccer.
Riano, J. F. Critical & Biographical Notes on Early Spanish Music. LC 79-158958. (Music Ser). 1971. Repr. of 1887 ed. lib. bdg. 19.50 (ISBN 0-306-70193-6). Da Capo.
Riasanovsky, A. V., ed. Generalizations in Historical Writing. LC 63-7860. 1964. 9.00x o.p. (ISBN 0-8122-7386-9). U of Pa Pr.
Riasanovsky, Nicholas V. A History of Russia. 3rd ed. LC 76-42634. (Illus.). 1977. 27.50 (ISBN 0-19-502129-0); text ed. 17.95x (ISBN 0-19-502128-2). Oxford U Pr.
--Nicholas I & Official Nationality in Russia, 1825-1855. (Russian & East European Studies). 1959. 18.50x (ISBN 0-520-01064-7); pap. 5.95x (ISBN 0-520-01065-5, CAMPUS 120). U of Cal Pr.
--A Parting of the Ways: Government & the Educated Public in Russia, 1801-1855. 1977. 45.00x (ISBN 0-19-822533-4). Oxford U Pr.
--The Teaching of Charles Fourier. LC 77-84043. 1969. 20.00x (ISBN 0-520-01405-7). U of Cal Pr.
Riasanovsky, Nicholas V. & Struve, Gleb, eds. California Slavic Studies, 7 vols. Incl. Vol. I. 1960 (ISBN 0-520-09037-3); Vol. II. 1963 (ISBN 0-520-09038-1); Vol. V. 1970 (ISBN 0-520-09043-8); Vol. VII. 1974 (ISBN 0-520-09485-9); Vol. VIII. 1975 (ISBN 0-520-09519-7); Vol. IX. 1976 (ISBN 0-520-09541-3); Vol. X. 1977 (ISBN 0-520-09564-2). (Vols. I, II pap. only). Set. 15.75 (ISBN 0-686-63969-3). U of Cal Pr.
Riasanovsky, V. A. Chinese Civil Law. (Studies in Chinese Government & Law). 1977. Repr. of 1938 ed. 22.50 (ISBN 0-89093-061-9). U Pubns Amer.
Ribalow, Harold U. The Jew in American Sports. rev. ed. 1980. 14.95 (ISBN 0-8197-0175-0). Bloch.
--The Tie That Binds: Conversations with Jewish Writers. LC 80-19433. 272p. 12.95 (ISBN 0-498-01963-2). A S Barnes.
Riban, David M. Introduction to Physical Science. (Illus.). 656p. 1981. text ed. 21.95 (ISBN 0-07-052140-9, C); instr's manual 4.95 (ISBN 0-07-052141-7). McGraw.
Ribbinck, Tony, jt. auth. see Jackson, P. B.
Ribble, Margaret A. The Rights of Infants. 128p. 1973. pap. 1.25 (ISBN 0-451-07735-0, Y7735, Sig). NAL.
Ribble, Margaretha A. Rights of Infants: Early Psychological Needs & Their Satisfaction. 2nd ed. LC 65-24832. 1965. 15.00x (ISBN 0-231-02849-0). Columbia U Pr.
Ribbon Publications. Soap Opera Word-Find Puzzles. 1977. pap. 1.50 o.p. (ISBN 0-685-75035-3, 345-25566-6-150). Ballantine.
Ribeiro, Lucia, jt. auth. see De Souza, Luis A.
Ribeiro, Manoel A., tr. Conversas Intimas. (Portugese Bks.). (Port.). 1979. 1.00 (ISBN 0-8297-0651-8). Life Pubs Intl.
Ribeiro, Victor R. see Rangel-Ribeiro, Victor.
Ribelin, William E. & McCoy, John R. Pathology of Laboratory Animals. (Illus.). 448p. 1971. 22.50 (ISBN 0-398-02203-8). C C Thomas.

Ribelin, William E. & Migaki, George, eds. Pathology of Fishes. LC 73-15261. 1975. pap. 70.00 (ISBN 0-299-06520-0, 652). U of Wis Pr.

Ribenboim, P. Algebraic Numbers. LC 74-37174. (Pure & Applied Mathematics Ser.). 360p. 1972. 35.50 (ISBN 0-471-71804-1, Pub. by Wiley-Interscience). Wiley.

Ribera, Gilbert J. Machine Calculation for Business & Personal Use. 2nd ed. LC 79-83523. 1979. pap. text ed. 13.95x (ISBN 0-8162-7180-1); solutions manual 2.50x (ISBN 0-686-67449-9). Holden-Day.

Ribera, Julian. Music in Ancient Arabia & Spain: Being La Musica De las Cantigas. LC 70-87614. (Music Ser). 1970. Repr. of 1929 ed. lib. bdg. 25.00 (ISBN 0-306-71622-4). Da Capo.

Riberholt, K. & Drastrup, A. Bookbinding at Home: The Basics of Bookbinding Simply Explained in Words & Diagrams. (Illus.). 96p. (Orig.). 1981. pap. 5.95 (ISBN 0-8069-9270-0). Sterling.

Ribich, Thomas I. Education & Poverty. LC 67-30600. (Studies in Social Economics). 1968. 10.95 (ISBN 0-8157-7430-3). Brookings.

Ribicoff, Abraham & Newman, Jon O. Politics: The American Way. rev. ed. (Illus.). (gr. 7-9). 1974. pap. text ed. 4.80 o.p. (ISBN 0-205-03973-1, 7639732). Allyn.

Ribner, Irving, ed. see Marlowe, Christopher.

Ribner, Irving, ed. see Shakespeare, William.

Ribot, Theodule A. Diseases of Memory. Smith, W. H. & Snell, M. M., trs. Bd. with Diseases of Personality. Repr. of 1891 ed; Diseases of the Will. Repr. of 1894 ed. (Contributions to the History of Psychology, Vol. I, Pt. C: Medical Psychology). 1978. Repr. of 1882 ed. 30.00 (ISBN 0-89093-165-8). U Pubns Amer.

Riboud, Marc. Visions of China: Photographs by Marc Riboud, 1957-1980. (Illus.). 1981. 30.00 (ISBN 0-394-51535-8); pap. 14.95 (ISBN 0-394-74840-9). Pantheon.

Rica, I., jt. auth. see Liteanu, C.

Ricard, Robert. The Spiritual Conquest of Mexico. Simpson, Lesley B., tr. (California Library Reprint Ser: No. 57). 1974. 21.75x (ISBN 0-520-02760-4). U of Cal Pr.

Ricardo, David. Principles of Political Economy & Taxation. 1972. 5.00x (ISBN 0-460-00590-1, Evman); pap. 5.95 (ISBN 0-460-01590-7). Dutton.

--Works & Correspondence, 11 vols. Sraffa, P., ed. 1951. Vols. 1-2, 4, 6 & 8-11. 49.50 ea.; Vols. 3, 5 & 7. 50.50 ea. Cambridge U Pr.

Ricca, F., ed. Absorption-Desorption Phenomena. 1972. 31.50 (ISBN 0-12-587750-1). Acad Pr.

Riccardi, Theodore, Jr., jt. auth. see Bender, Ernest.

Riccardi, Vincent M., jt. ed. see Mulvihill, John J.

Ricchiuti, P. B. Jeff. 1973. pap. 0.65 o.p. (ISBN 0-8163-0105-0, 10130-3). Pacific Pr Pub Assn.

Ricchiuti, Paul. Amy. (Uplook Ser.). 1976. pap. 0.75 (ISBN 0-8163-0252-9, 01550-3). Pacific Pr Pub Assn.

--Elijah Jeremiah Phillips' Great Journey. (Hello World Ser.). 1975. pap. 1.65 (ISBN 0-8163-0185-9, 05303-3). Pacific Pr Pub Assn.

--Ellen. LC 76-44051. (Destiny Ser). 1976. pap. 4.50 o.p. (ISBN 0-8163-0255-3, 05312-4). Pacific Pr Pub Assn.

--Five Little Gifts. (Hello World Ser.). 1975. pap. 1.65 (ISBN 0-8163-0186-7, 06265-3). Pacific Pr Pub Assn.

--I Found a Feather. LC 67-24371. (Hello World Ser.). 1967. pap. 1.65 (ISBN 0-8163-0309-6, 09020-9). Pacific Pr Pub Assn.

--Let's Play Make Believe. 1975. pap. 1.65 (ISBN 0-8163-0187-5, 12150-9). Pacific Pr Pub Assn.

--My Very Best Friend. (Hello World Ser.). 1975. pap. 1.65 (ISBN 0-8163-0188-3, 13950-1). Pacific Pr Pub Assn.

--When You Open Your Bible. LC 67-18008. (Hello World Ser.). 1967. pap. 1.65 (ISBN 0-8163-0307-X, 23380-9). Pacific Pr Pub Assn.

--Whose House Is It? (Hello World Ser.). 1967. pap. 1.40 o.p. (ISBN 0-8163-0308-8, 23610-9). Pacific Pr Pub Assn.

Ricchiuti, Paul B. General Lee. (Uplook Ser.). 1978. pap. 0.75 (ISBN 0-8163-0198-0, 07038-3). Pacific Pr Pub Assn.

--Mandy. (Uplook Ser.). 1978. pap. 0.75 (ISBN 0-8163-0206-5, 13105-2). Pacific Pr Pub Assn.

--Mike. (Uplook Ser.). 1978. pap. 0.75 (ISBN 0-8163-0207-3, 13496-5). Pacific Pr Pub Assn.

Ricci, A. James. Understanding & Training Horses. LC 64-14466. (Illus.). (gr. 10 up). 1964. 10.95 (ISBN 0-397-00356-0). Lippincott.

Ricci, Isolina. Mom's House, Dad's House: Making Shared Custody Work. 224p. 1980. 12.95 (ISBN 0-02-602550-7). Macmillan.

Ricci, Robert, jt. auth. see Fink, Robert R.

Riccio, Dolores & Bingham, Joan. The Complete All-in-the-Oven Cookbook: The Cookbook for Saving Time & Energy. LC 80-5712. 300p. 1981. 12.95 (ISBN 0-8128-2699-X). Stein & Day.

Riccio, Ottone M. The Intimate Art of Writing Poetry. 240p. 1980. 14.95 (ISBN 0-13-476846-9, Spec); pap. 5.95 (ISBN 0-686-65793-4). P-H.

Riccio, Richard V. The Belief Factor. 1980. 8.95 (ISBN 0-89962-009-4). Todd & Honeywell.

Ricciuti, Edward. Older Than the Dinosaurs: The Origin & Rise of the Mammals. LC 77-26606. (Illus.). 96p. (gr. 5-12). 1980. 7.95 (ISBN 0-690-01328-0, TYC-J); PLB 7.89 (ISBN 0-690-03879-8). T Y Crowell.

Ricciuti, Edward R. The Devil's Garden: Facts & Folklore of Perilous Plants. LC 77-79624. (Illus.). 1978. 10.95 o.s.i. (ISBN 0-8027-0581-2). Walker & Co.

--Killers of the Seas. (Illus.). 208p. 1973. 10.00 o.s.i. (ISBN 0-8027-0415-8). Walker & Co.

Ricciuti, Henry N., jt. auth. see Caldwell, Betty E.

Rice, Allan L., tr. see Mellerowicz, Harald.

Rice, Anne. The Feast of All Saints. 640p. 1981. pap. 2.95 (ISBN 0-449-24378-8, Crest). Fawcett.

Rice, Bernard J., jt. auth. see Strange, Jerry D.

Rice Blast Workshop. Proceedings. 222p. 1979. pap. 18.50 (R008, IRRI). Unipub.

Rice Center. The Cost of Delay Due to Government Regulation in the Houston Housing Market. LC 79-65687. (ULI Research Report Ser.: No. 28). (Illus.). 92p. 1979. pap. text ed. 9.75 (ISBN 0-87420-328-7). Urban Land.

Rice, Charles & Martyn, J. Louis. Easter. LC 74-24958. (Proclamation 1: Aids for Interpreting the Lessons of the Church Year, Ser. B). 64p. 1975. pap. 1.95 (ISBN 0-8006-4075-6, 1-4075). Fortress.

Rice, David & Rice, Tamara T. Icons & Their History. LC 74-78136. (Illus.). 192p. 1974. 45.00 (ISBN 0-87951-021-8). Overlook Pr.

Rice, David, jt. ed. see Botein, Michael.

Rice, David G. & Stambaugh, John E. Sources for the Study of Greek Religion. LC 79-18389. (Society of Biblical Literature. Sources for Biblical Study Ser.: No. 14). 1979. 12.00 (ISBN 0-89130-346-4, 060314); pap. 7.50 (ISBN 0-89130-347-2). Scholars Pr Ca.

Rice, David G., jt. ed. see Gurman, Alan S.

Rice, David H. Protective Philosophy: A Discussion of the Principles of the American Protective System, As Embodied in the McKinley Bill. (The Neglected American Economists Ser.). 1974. lib. bdg. 50.00 (ISBN 0-8240-1024-8). Garland Pub.

Rice, David T. Art of the Byzantine Era. (World of Art Ser.). (Illus.). 1963. pap. 9.95x (ISBN 0-19-519925-1). Oxford U Pr.

--English Art, 871-1100. (Oxford History of English Art Ser). (Illus.). 1952. 24.95x o.p. (ISBN 0-19-817201-X). Oxford U Pr.

--Islamic Art. (World of Art Ser.). (Illus.). 1975. pap. 9.95 (ISBN 0-19-519926-X). Oxford U Pr.

Rice, Don. Birds: A Picture Source Book. 160p. 1980. pap. 8.95 (ISBN 0-442-20395-0). Van Nos Reinhold.

Rice, Earle, Jr. Fear on Ice. (Storytellers Ser.). (Illus.). 64p. (gr. 5 up). 1981. PLB 7.95 (ISBN 0-516-02262-8). Childrens.

--Tiger, Lion, Hawk. (Pacesetters Ser.). (Illus.). 64p. (gr. 4 up). 1978. PLB 7.95 (ISBN 0-516-02174-5). Childrens.

Rice, Eddy. How to Grow, Preserve & Store All the Food You Need. (Illus.). 1977. 10.95 (ISBN 0-87909-350-1). Reston.

Rice, Edward. The Age of Charlemagne. 112p. 1963. 2.95 (ISBN 0-374-29492-5). FS&G.

--Eastern Definitions: A Short Encyclopedia of Religions of the Orient. LC 77-19359. 1978. 10.00 (ISBN 0-385-08563-X). Doubleday.

--The Five Great Religions. LC 72-87074. (Illus.). 192p. (gr. 7 up). 1973. 9.95 (ISBN 0-590-07175-0, Four Winds). Schol Bk Serv.

--The High Middle Ages. 128p. 1963. 2.95 (ISBN 0-374-29520-4). FS&G.

--Man in the Sycamore Tree: The Good Times & Hard Life of Thomas Merton. LC 76-121809. 1972. pap. 2.45 (ISBN 0-385-02730-3, Im). Doubleday.

--Marx, Engels & the Workers of the World. LC 76-56183. (Illus.). 192p. (gr. 7 up). 1977. 8.95 (ISBN 0-590-07407-5, Four Winds). Schol Bk Serv.

--Ten Religions of the East. LC 78-6186. (Illus.). 160p. (gr. 7 up). 1978. 8.95 (ISBN 0-590-07473-3, Four Winds). Schol Bk Serv.

Rice, Edward E. Mao's Way. LC 70-186116. (Center for Chinese Studies, Uc Berkeley). 600p. 1972. 25.00x (ISBN 0-520-02199-1); pap. 4.95 (ISBN 0-520-02623-3). U of Cal Pr.

Rice, Elmer. Elmer Rice: Three Plays. Incl. The Adding Machine; Street Scene; Dream Girl. 239p. 1965. 4.25 (ISBN 0-8090-0735-5, Mermaid). Hill & Wang.

Rice, Emmett A., et al. A Brief History of Physical Education. 5th ed. (Illus.). 1969. 17.95 (ISBN 0-8260-7430-8). Wiley.

Rice, Eve. Ebbie. LC 75-11688. (Illus.). 32p. (ps-3). 1975. 7.25 (ISBN 0-688-80017-3); PLB 6.96 (ISBN 0-688-84017-5). Greenwillow.

--Goodnight, Goodnight. LC 79-17253. (Illus.). (gr. k-1). 1980. 6.95 (ISBN 0-688-80254-0); PLB 6.67 (ISBN 0-688-84254-2). Greenwillow.

--Mr. Brimble's Hobby & Other Stories. LC 75-8872. (Greenwillow Read-Alone Bks.). (Illus.). 64p. (gr. 1-4). 1975. 5.95 o.p. (ISBN 0-688-80006-8); PLB 5.71 (ISBN 0-688-84006-X). Greenwillow.

--New Blue Shoes. LC 74-13259. (Illus.). 32p. (ps-1). 1975. 8.95 (ISBN 0-02-775960-1). Macmillan.

--Oh, Lewis! LC 73-19057. (Illus.). 32p. (ps-2). 1974. 7.95g (ISBN 0-02-775950-4). Macmillan.

--The Remarkable Return of Winston Potter Crisply. LC 77-28101. (gr. 5-9). 1978. 7.95 (ISBN 0-688-80145-5); PLB 7.63 (ISBN 0-688-84145-7). Greenwillow.

--Sam Who Never Forgets. LC 76-30370. (ps-3). 1977. 7.95 (ISBN 0-688-80088-2); PLB 7.63 (ISBN 0-688-84088-4). Greenwillow.

Rice, F. Philip. Marriage & Parenthood. 1979. text ed. 18.95 (ISBN 0-205-06517-1, 8165173); instr's man. avail. (ISBN 0-205-06539-2, 8165394). Allyn.

--Outdoor Life Gun Data Book. LC 74-83594. (An Outdoor Life Bk.). (Illus.). 576p. 1975. 12.95 o.p. (ISBN 0-06-013529-8, HarpT). Har-Row.

Rice, F. Philip & Dahl, John I. Hunting Dogs: An Outdoor Life Book. rev. ed. LC 67-14555. (Funk & W Bk.). (Illus.). 1978. 7.95 o.s.i. (ISBN 0-308-10324-6, TYC-T); pap. 4.50 o.s.i. (ISBN 0-308-10325-4, TYC-T). T Y Crowell.

Rice, F. Phillip. The Adolescent: Development, Relationships, & Culture. 3rd ed. 700p. 1981. text ed. 17.95 (ISBN 0-205-07303-4, 2473038); free tchr's ed. (ISBN 0-205-07304-2). Allyn.

Rice, F. Phillip & Dahl, John I. Game Bird Hunting. rev. ed. LC 65-14985. (Funk & W Bk.). (Illus.). 1977. 7.95 o.s.i. (ISBN 0-308-10322-X, TYC-T); pap. 4.50 (ISBN 0-308-10323-8, TYC-T). T Y Crowell.

Rice, Frank A. Eastern Arabic: An Introduction to the Spoken Arabic of Palestine, Syria & Lebanon. 1977. pap. 7.95x (ISBN 0-686-63542-6). Intl Bk Ctr.

Rice, Freddie & Rice, Freddie. Fly Tying Illustrated: For Nymphs & Lures. LC 76-2150. (Illus.). 112p. 1976. 11.95 (ISBN 0-7153-6952-0). David & Charles.

Rice, Hazel V. Gastrointestinal Nursing. (Nursing Outline Ser.). 1978. pap. 9.50 (ISBN 0-87488-392-X). Med Exam.

Rice, Helen S. Someone Cares: The Collected Poems of Helen Steiner Rice. (Illus.). 128p. 1972. 8.95 (ISBN 0-8007-0524-6); keepsake ed. 9.95 (ISBN 0-8007-0528-9). Revell.

Rice, Helen Steiner. Just for You: A Special Collection of Inspirational Verses. LC 67-10385. 1967. 4.50 (ISBN 0-385-07721-1). Doubleday.

Rice, Hugh A. L. Thomas Ken: Bishop & Non-Juror. 1958. pap. 7.50x (ISBN 0-8401-2008-7). Allenson.

Rice, James. A Cajun Alphabet. LC 76-28490. (Illus.). 1976. 9.95 (ISBN 0-88289-136-7). Pelican.

--Cajun Night Before Christmas Coloring Book. 1976. 1.25 (ISBN 0-88289-138-3). Pelican.

--Gaston Goes to Mardi Gras. LC 77-13302. (Illus.). 1977. 7.95 (ISBN 0-88289-158-8). Pelican.

--Gaston Goes to Texas. LC 78-12490. (Illus.). (ps-6). 1978. 7.95 (ISBN 0-88289-204-5). Pelican.

--Gaston Lays an Offshore Pipeline. (Illus.). 1979. 7.95 (ISBN 0-88289-177-4). Pelican.

Rice, James, illus. Gaston the Green-Nosed Alligator. 1974. 7.95 (ISBN 0-88289-049-2). Pelican.

Rice, Jean M. My Friend the Computer. (Illus.). 1976. tchrs'. guide 15.00 (ISBN 0-513-01496-9); wkbk. 3.95 (ISBN 0-513-01495-0). Denison.

Rice, John G. Build Program Technique: A Practical Approach for the Development of Automatic Software Generation Systems. LC 80-20742. (Business Data Processing Ser.). 375p. 1981. 29.95 (ISBN 0-471-05278-7, Pub. by Wiley-Interscience). Wiley.

Rice, John R. Matrix Computation & Mathematical Software. Stewart, Charles E., ed. (Computer Science Ser.). (Illus.). 288p. Date not set. text ed. 23.95 (ISBN 0-07-052145-X); solutions manual 5.95 (ISBN 0-07-052146-8). McGraw.

--Sign Language for Everyone: A Basic Course in Communication with the Deaf. LC 77-14592. 1978. 9.95 (ISBN 0-8407-9002-3). Nelson.

--When a Christian Sins. 1954. pap. 1.50 (ISBN 0-8024-9434-X). Moody.

Rice, Joseph B. A Positive Plan for a Revolutionary Change in the Political Structure of the United States. (American Culture Library Bk). (Illus.). 128p. 1981. 28.15 (ISBN 0-89266-290-5). Am Classical Coll Pr.

Rice, Joyce G. Love Never Ends. pap. 3.95 (ISBN 0-89036-147-9). Hawkes Pub Inc.

Rice, Laura N., jt. auth. see Wexler, David A.

Rice, Laura W. Cacti & Succulents for Modern Living. (Modern Living Ser.). (Illus.). 80p. (Orig.). 1976. pap. 2.95 (ISBN 0-89484-003-7, 10104). Merchants Pub Co.

Rice, Lee M., jt. auth. see Vernam, Glen R.

Rice, Lee W., jt. auth. see Grant, Bruce.

Rice, Leland, jt. auth. see Glenn, Constance W.

Rice, Max M. You Can Take It with You. LC 80-68885. 160p. 1981. pap. 3.95 (ISBN 0-89636-063-6). Accent Bks.

Rice, Michael S., ed. Pilot's Manual for the Grumman F6F Hellcat. (Illus.). 60p. 1975. pap. 4.95 (ISBN 0-87994-033-6, Pub. by AvPubns). Aviation.

Rice, Miriam C. How to Use Mushrooms for Color. rev. ed. (Illus.). 145p. 1980. pap. 7.95 (ISBN 0-916422-19-4). Mad River.

Rice, Myron A., jt. auth. see Muenscher, Walter C.

Rice, Ora E., jt. auth. see Lockhart, Noble L.

Rice, Oscar K. Statistical Mechanics, Thermodynamics, & Kinetics. LC 66-16379. (Chemistry Ser.). (Illus.). 1967. 28.95x (ISBN 0-7167-0133-2). W H Freeman.

Rice, Patty C. Amber: The Golden Gem of the Ages. 1980. 26.95 (ISBN 0-442-26138-1). Van Nos Reinhold.

Rice, R. J. Fundamentals of Geomorphology. (Illus.). 1977. text ed. 32.00 (ISBN 0-582-48429-4); pap. text ed. 17.95x (ISBN 0-582-48430-8). Longman.

Rice, Richard. Openness of God. (Horizon Ser.). 96p. 1981. pap. write for info. (ISBN 0-8127-0303-0). Southern Pub.

Rice, Rip G. Biological Activated Carbon for Drinking Water. 1981. text ed. 69.90 2 vol. set (ISBN 0-250-40429-X); text ed. 39.95 vol. 1 (ISBN 0-250-40427-3); text ed. 39.95 vol. 2 (ISBN 0-250-40428-1). Ann Arbor Science.

Rice, Stanley. CRT Typesetting Handbook. 415p. 1981. 35.00 (ISBN 0-442-23889-4). Van Nos Reinhold.

--Tell Time. LC 63-15403. (Illus.). (gr. 2-5). 1963. pap. 3.50 o.p. (ISBN 0-15-284380-9, HJ). HarBraceJ.

Rice, Stuart A., jt. auth. see Prigogine, I.

Rice, Stuart A., jt. ed. see Prigogine, I.

Rice, Tamara T. Ancient Arts of Central Asia. (World of Art Ser). (Illus.). 1965. pap. 9.95 (ISBN 0-19-520001-2). Oxford U Pr.

--A Concise History of Russian Art. (World of Art). (Illus.). 1963. pap. text ed. 9.95 (ISBN 0-19-520002-0). Oxford U Pr.

Rice, Tamara T., jt. auth. see Rice, David.

Rice, Thomas J., ed. English Fiction, Nineteen Hundred to Nineteen Fifty: A Guide to Information Sources. LC 73-16989. (American Literature, English Literature, and World Literatures in English Information Guide Ser.: Vol. 20). 680p. 1979. 30.00 (ISBN 0-8103-1217-4). Gale.

Rice, Tim, jt. auth. see Weber, Andrew.

Rice, Wayne, et al. Fun-N-Games. 1977. pap. 5.95 (ISBN 0-310-35001-8). Zondervan.

Rice, William & Wolf, Burton. Where to Eat in America. 1977. pap. 5.95 o.p. (ISBN 0-394-73438-6). Random.

Rice, William G. Tale of Two Courts: Judicial Settlement of Controversies Between the States of the Swiss & American Federations. 1967. 15.00x (ISBN 0-299-04390-8). U of Wis Pr.

Rice, William H. Hawaiian Legends. LC 77-83648. (Bernice P. Bishop Museum Publications: No. 63). (Illus.). 164p. 1977. pap. 23.50 (ISBN 0-295-95729-8). U of Wash Pr.

Rich, Alexander & Davidson, Norman, eds. Structural Chemistry & Molecular Biology: A Volume Dedicated to Linus Pauling by His Students, Colleagues, & Friends. LC 67-21127. (Illus.). 1968. 36.95x (ISBN 0-7167-0135-9). W H Freeman.

Rich, Barnett. Level One Mathematics: For the College Boards. (gr. 11-12). 1970. pap. text ed. 7.75 (ISBN 0-87720-231-1). AMSCO Sch.

--Mathematics for the College Boards: PSAT, SAT. (Illus., Orig.). (gr. 10-12). 1967. wkbk. 7.75 (ISBN 0-87720-201-X). AMSCO Sch.

Rich, Barnett, jt. auth. see Dressler, Isidore.

Rich, Beatrice. ABCDEFGHIJKLMNOPQRSTUVWXYZ in Eng & French. (Illus.). 64p. (gr. k-2). 1981. PLB 7.95 (ISBN 0-87460-353-6). Lion.

Rich, Craig. West Country Weather Guide. 1980. pap. 4.50 (ISBN 0-7153-8052-4). David & Charles.

Rich, Dale. How You Can Get Straight A's in College by Beating the System. 123p. (Orig.). 1981. 9.95 (ISBN 0-89896-099-1). Larksdale.

Rich, Daniel. The Flow of Art. LC 75-13774. 1975. 12.50 (ISBN 0-689-10692-0). Atheneum.

Rich, Daniel C. Degas. (Library Great Painters Ser). (Illus., Orig.). 1951. 35.00 (ISBN 0-8109-0067-X). Abrams.

Rich, Elizabeth. What It's Like to Be a Flight Attendant. LC 80-6152. 192p. 1981. 12.95 (ISBN 0-8128-2785-6). Stein & Day.

Rich, Guy J., jt. auth. see Smith, Tom W.
Rich, Harry, ed. see Verdick, Mary.
Rich, Harvey E. & Jolicoeur, Pamela M. Student Attitudes & Academic Environments: A Study of California Higher Education. LC 78-2953. (Praeger Special Studies). 1978. 19.95 (ISBN 0-03-041431-8). Praeger.
Rich, John M. Challenge & Response: Education in American Culture. LC 73-22100. 300p. 1974. text ed. 17.95 o.p. (ISBN 0-471-71900-5). Wiley.
--Innovations in Education: Reformers & Their Critics. 3rd ed. 350p. 1980. pap. text ed. 10.50 (ISBN 0-205-07141-4, 237141-3). Allyn.
--Innovations in Education: Reformers & Their Critics. 2nd ed. 1978. pap. text ed. 8.95x o.p. (ISBN 0-205-06059-5). Allyn.
Rich, Kathleen. The Lucifer Mask. 1977. pap. 1.50 (ISBN 0-505-51186-X). Tower Bks.
Rich, Lloyd. Understanding Microprocessors. (Illus.). 336p. 1980. text ed. 17.95 (ISBN 0-8359-8057-X). Reston.
Rich, Louise D. The Coast of Maine. rev ed. LC 75-6662. (Illus.). 385p. 1975. 9.95 o.s.i. (ISBN 0-690-00698-5, TYC-T); pap. 6.95 o.s.i. (ISBN 0-690-00957-7, TYC-T). T Y Crowell.
--First Book of New World Explorers. (First Bks). (Illus.). (gr. 4-6). 1960. PLB 4.90 o.p. (ISBN 0-531-00595-X); pap. 1.25 o.p. (ISBN 0-531-02315-X). Watts.
--First Book of the Early Settlers. (First Bks). (Illus.). (gr. 4-6). 1960. PLB 4.90 o.p. (ISBN 0-531-00518-6); pap. 1.25 o.p. (ISBN 0-531-02312-5). Watts.
--First Book of the Fur Trade. LC 65-10451. (First Bks). (Illus.). (gr. 4-6). 1965. PLB 4.90 o.p. (ISBN 0-531-00539-9). Watts.
--First Book of the Vikings. (First Bks). (Illus.). (gr. 4-6). 1962. PLB 4.90 o.p. (ISBN 0-531-00660-3). Watts.
--King Philip's War, 1675-76: The New England Indians Fight the Colonists. LC 78-183577. (Focus Bks). (Illus.). 96p. (gr. 7 up). 1972. PLB 4.47 o.p. (ISBN 0-531-02453-9). Watts.
--Three of a Kind. LC 76-101747. (gr. 4-6). 1970. PLB 4.90 o.p. (ISBN 0-531-01837-7). Watts.
Rich, Mark. Custom Cars & Trucks. (On the Move Ser.). (Illus.). 48p. (gr. 3-6). 1981. PLB 9.25 (ISBN 0-516-03886-9). Childrens.
--Custom Cycles. LC 80-26659. (On the Move Ser.). (Illus.). 48p. (gr. 3-6). 1981. PLB 9.25 (ISBN 0-516-03887-7). Childrens.
--Custom Vans. LC 80-25792. (On the Move Ser.). (Illus.). 48p. (gr. 3-6). 1981. PLB 9.25 (ISBN 0-516-03885-0). Childrens.
Rich, Meredith. Bare Essence. 320p. (Orig.). 1981. pap. 2.95 (ISBN 0-449-14386-4, GM). Fawcett.
Rich, Mildred K. Handcrafts for the Homebound Handicapped. (Illus.). 116p. 1960. photocopy ed. spiral 11.75 (ISBN 0-398-01585-6). C C Thomas.
Rich, Norman. The Age of Nationalism and Reform, 1850-1890. (Illus.). 1977 10.95x (ISBN 0-393-05607-4); pap. 4.95 1976 (ISBN 0-393-09183-X). Norton.
--Friedrich Von Holstein: Politics & Diplomacy in the Era of Bismarck & Wilhelm. 1965. 130.00 (ISBN 0-521-06077-X). Cambridge U Pr.
Rich, Robert F., jt. auth. see Morss, Elliott R.
Rich, Robert F., ed. Translating Evaluation into Policy. LC 79-21453. (Sage Research Progress Ser. in Evaluation: Vol. 3). (Illus.). 1979. 12.95x (ISBN 0-8039-1283-8); pap. 6.50x (ISBN 0-8039-1284-6). Sage.
Rich, Robert M. Crimes Without Victims: Deviance & the Criminal Law. LC 78-63258. 1978. pap. text ed. 10.25 (ISBN 0-8191-0618-6). U Pr of Amer.
--Juvenile Delinquency: A Paradigmatic Perspective. LC 78-53025. 1978. pap. text ed. 10.75x o.p. (ISBN 0-8191-0493-0). U Pr of Amer.
Rich, Rosemary, jt. auth. see Phipps, Wilma H.
Rich, Susan, ed. Kline Guide to the Packaging Industry. (Illus.). 324p. 1980. pap. 100.00. Kline.
Rich, Thomas A., jt. auth. see Gilmore, Alden S.
Rich, William. Smaller Families Through Social & Economic Progress. LC 72-97989. (Monographs: No. 7). 74p. 1973. 2.00 (ISBN 0-686-28688-X). Overseas Dev Council.
Richan, Willard C. & Mendelsohn, Allan R. Social Work: The Unloved Profession. 226p. 1973. 8.95 (ISBN 0-531-05350-4); pap. 4.95 (ISBN 0-531-05550-7). Watts.
Richan, Willard C., ed. Human Services & Social Work Responsibility. LC 72-108195. 382p. 1969. pap. 10.00 (ISBN 0-87101-053-4, CBO-058-C). Natl Assn Soc Wkrs.
Richard, jt. auth. see Frankel.
Richard, E. & Churchill, Linda R. The Bionic Banana. (YA) (gr. 7-12). pap. 1.50 (ISBN 0-440-90852-3, LE). Dell.
Richard, E., jt. auth. see Churchill, Linda R.
Richard, Earl. Acts Six: One to Eight: Four. LC 78-12926. (Society of Biblical Literature. Dissertation Ser.: No. 41). (Orig.). 1978. pap. 9.00 (ISBN 0-89130-261-1, 060141). Scholars Pr Ca.
Richard, Frederic M., jt. ed. see Tometsko, Andrew M.
Richard, Glasstone. Dancing As a Career for Men. LC 80-54339. (Illus.). 120p. (gr. 10 up). 1981. 8.95 (ISBN 0-8069-4640-7); lib. bdg. 9.29 (ISBN 0-8069-4641-5). Sterling.
Richard, Michel P. & Mann, John. Exploring Social Space: Participant's Manual. LC 72-88813. 1973. pap. text ed. 7.95 (ISBN 0-02-926410-3). Free Pr.
Richard, Patrick, jt. ed. see Marton, L.
Richard, Stanley. The Best Plays of the Seventies. LC 79-6634. 816p. 1980. 17.95 (ISBN 0-385-14739-2). Doubleday.
Richard, Van Den Tak see Van Den Tak, Richard.
Richards. A Horse Grows up. (ps-3). pap. 1.25 (ISBN 0-590-12090-5, Schol Pap). Schol Bk Serv.
--Quantum Pharmacology. 1977. text ed. 39.95 (ISBN 0-408-70919-7). Butterworths.
Richards, Adrian, ed. Marine Geotechnology: Marine Slope Stability Conference, Vol. 2. 1978. 45.00x (ISBN 0-8448-1352-4). Crane-Russak Co.
Richards, Alan J. British Birds: A Field Guide. LC 79-52375. (Illus.). 1979. 14.95 (ISBN 0-7153-7834-1). David & Charles.
Richards, Alison. Handmade Jewelry: Techniques & Design. LC 76-4644. (Funk & W Bk.). (Illus.). 1976. 12.95 o.s.i. (ISBN 0-308-10263-0, TYC-T). T Y Crowell.
Richards, Arlene K. & Willis, Irene. Leaving Home. LC 80-12721. 192p. (gr. 7 up). 1980. 8.95 (ISBN 0-689-30757-8). Atheneum.
Richards, Aurelia. The Mormon Trail: In Story Form. pap. 5.95 (ISBN 0-89036-137-1). Hawkes Pub Inc.
Richards, B., ed. Measurement of Unsteady Fluid Dynamic Phenomena. LC 76-11843. (Thermal & Fluids Engineering Series). (Illus.). 450p. 1977. text ed. 44.50 (ISBN 0-89116-012-4, Co-Pub. by McGraw Intl). Hemisphere Pub.
Richards, B. A., jt. auth. see Crowson, P. C.
Richards, B. N. Introduction to the Soil Ecosystem. LC 73-85688. (Illus.). 160p. (Orig.). 1974. pap. text ed. 16.95x (ISBN 0-582-44130-7). Longman.
Richards, Barry. The Barry Richards Story. (Illus.). 1978. 10.95 o.p. (ISBN 0-571-11187-4, Pub. by Faber & Faber). Merrimack Bk Serv.
Richards, Bernard, ed. English Verse Eighteen Thirty to Eighteen Ninety. (Longman Annotated Anthologies of English Verse: Vol. 6). 543p. 1980. text ed. 33.00 (ISBN 0-582-48387-5); pap. text ed. 19.95 (ISBN 0-582-48388-3). Longman.
Richards, Blair & Sigmund, Janice. Come, Let Us Celebrate. 160p. 1976. pap. 5.95 o.p. (ISBN 0-8015-1457-6). Dutton.
Richards, C. M., jt. auth. see Taylor, P. H.
Richards, Carl, et al. Stoneflies. (Illus.). 192p. 1980. 19.95 (ISBN 0-87691-327-3). Winchester Pr.
Richards, Carolyn, ed. see Coleman, Richard.
Richards, Clay. Marble Jungle. 1961. 7.95 (ISBN 0-8392-1064-7). Astor-Honor.
Richards, D. J., tr. see Suetin, A. S.
Richards, D. L. Telecommunication by Speech: A Transmission Performance-of-Telephone Networks. 1973. 52.95 (ISBN 0-470-71949-4). Halsted Pr.
Richards, David, ed. The Penguin Book of Russian Short Stories. 1981. pap. 4.50 (ISBN 0-14-004816-2). Penguin.
Richards, David A. The Moral Criticism of Law. 1977. pap. text ed. 11.95x (ISBN 0-8221-0198-X). Dickenson.
Richards, Dennis L., ed. Montana's Genealogical Records. (The Gale Genealogy & Local History Ser.: Vol. 11). 330p. 1981. 30.00 (ISBN 0-8103-1487-8). Gale.
Richards, Dorothy S. A Handbook of Pedigree Cat Breeding. (Illus.). 143p. 1980. pap. 14.95 (ISBN 0-7134-0422-1, Pub. by Batsford England). David & Charles.
Richards, E. G. & Dover, S. D. An Introduction to the Physical Properties of Large Molecules in Solution. LC 79-41583. (IUPAB Biophysics Ser.: No. 3). (Illus.). 200p. 1980. 29.50 (ISBN 0-521-23110-8); pap. 9.95 (ISBN 0-521-29817-2). Cambridge U Pr.
Richards, Elizabeth. Jilla. 1978. pap. 1.50 o.s.i. (ISBN 0-685-86425-1). Jove Pubns.
Richards, Frank. Old-Soldier Sahib. (Orig.). 1966. pap. 4.95 (ISBN 0-571-06574-0, Pub. by Faber & Faber). Merrimack Bk Serv.
Richards, Frank F., jt. auth. see Baumgarten, Alexander.
Richards, G. C., tr. see Wilcken, Ulrich.
Richards, Guy. The Salekov Kill. 256p. (Orig.). 1981. pap. 2.50 (ISBN 0-449-14405-4, GM). Fawcett.
Richards, H. M., Jr. Angels: Secret Agents of God & Satan. LC 80-22223. (Flame Ser.). 64p. 1980. pap. 0.95 (ISBN 0-8127-0313-8). Southern Pub.
--Faith & Prayer. (Uplook Ser.). 32p. 1971. pap. 0.75 (ISBN 0-8163-0071-2, 06010-3). Pacific Pr Pub Assn.
Richards, Harold. Earthquake. LC 79-13559. (Flame Ser.). 1979. pap. 0.95 (ISBN 0-8127-0240-9). Southern Pub.
Richards, Hubert. Reading Paul Today: A New Introduction to the Man & His Letters. LC 79-26287. (Biblical Foundations Ser.). (Illus.). 152p. 1980. pap. 4.95 (ISBN 0-8042-0374-1). John Knox.
Richards, I. A. Interpretation in Teaching. 2nd ed. 435p. 1973. text ed. 18.00x (ISBN 0-391-00282-1). Humanities.
--Tomorrow Morning, Faustus. LC 62-14468. 1962. 4.50 o.p. (ISBN 0-15-190490-1). HarBraceJ.
Richards, Ivor A. Mencius on the Mind: Experiments in Multiple Definition. LC 79-2838. (Illus.). 1981. Repr. of 1932 ed. 16.50 (ISBN 0-8305-0015-4). Hyperion Conn.
--Philosophy of Rhetoric. (YA) (gr. 9 up). 1965. pap. 3.95 (ISBN 0-19-500715-8, GB). Oxford U Pr.
--Plato's Republic. (Orig.). 23.95 (ISBN 0-521-05965-8); pap. 6.50x (ISBN 0-521-09359-7). Cambridge U Pr.
--Practical Criticism, a Study of Literary Judgment. LC 56-13740. 1956. pap. 4.95 (ISBN 0-15-673626-8, HB16, Harv). HarBraceJ.
Richards, Ivor A., et al. First Workbook of Spanish. pap. 0.75 o.s.i. (ISBN 0-671-46896-0). WSP.
--Second Workbook in Spanish. pap. 0.75 o.s.i. (ISBN 0-671-46897-9). WSP.
Richards, J. Swordsmen of the Screen. (Cinema & Society Ser.). (Illus.). 1977. 23.50 (ISBN 0-7100-8478-1). Routledge & Kegan.
Richards, J. F. Mughal Administration in Golconda. (Illus.). 360p. 1975. 45.00x (ISBN 0-19-821561-4). Oxford U Pr.
Richards, J. M. Eight-Hundred Years of Finnish Architecture. (Illus.). 1978. 32.00 (ISBN 0-7153-7512-1). David & Charles.
Richards, J. M., jt. ed. see Pevsner, Nikolaus.
Richards, J. Morris, jt. auth. see Tanner, George S.
Richards, J. T. A Generation Apart. (The Whitmarsh Chronicles Ser.: Vol. 1). 416p. (Orig.). 1981. pap. 2.75 (ISBN 0-515-05242-6). Jove Pubns.
Richards, J. W. Technical Development in the Small Plant. 1970. 16.50x (ISBN 0-249-44024-5). Intl Ideas.
Richards, Jack. Error Analysis: Perspectives on Second Language Acquisition. (Applied Linguistics & Language Study Ser.). 1974. pap. text ed. 9.00x (ISBN 0-582-55044-0). Longman.
Richards, Jack, jt. auth. see Tutko, Thomas.
Richards, Janet R. The Sceptical Feminist: A Philosophical Enquiry. 320p. 1980. 32.00 (ISBN 0-7100-0673-X). Routledge & Kegan.
Richards, Jeffrey. The Popes & the Papacy in the Early Middle Ages, 476-752. 1979. 40.00 (ISBN 0-7100-0098-7). Routledge & Kegan.
--Visions of Yesterday. (Illus.). 1974. 23.50 (ISBN 0-7100-7576-6). Routledge & Kegan.
Richards, Jeffrey, jt. auth. see Evans, Eric J.
Richards, Jessica. Mistress of the Western Wind. 208p. (Orig.). 1980. pap. 2.50 (ISBN 0-515-04755-4). Jove Pubns.
--Tularosa. 336p. (Orig.). pap. 2.25 (ISBN 0-515-04761-9). Jove Pubns.
Richards, John. Hidden Country: Nature on Your Doorstep. LC 72-12745. (Illus.). 144p. (gr. 5-8). 1973. PLB 9.95 (ISBN 0-87599-195-5). S G Phillips.
Richards, John T. Luminous Sanity: Literary Criticism of John G. Neihardt. 1973. pap. 4.20 (ISBN 0-686-27393-1). Neihardt Found.
Richards, Judith. How Does It Feel to Be Deaf? (Illus.). (gr. 4-7). Date not set. PLB price not set (ISBN 0-671-34030-1). Messner. Postponed.
--Sounds of Silence. 1981. pap. 2.75 (ISBN 0-671-43117-X). PB.
--Summer Lightning. LC 77-16761. 1978. 8.95 o.p. (ISBN 0-312-77544-X). St Martin.
Richards, Katharine L. How Christmas Came to the Sunday-Schools: The Observance of Christmas in the Protestant Church Schools of the United States. LC 70-159860. 1971. Repr. of 1934 ed. 18.00 (ISBN 0-8103-3793-2). Gale.
Richards, L. Israel! - Do You Know. 5.95 o.p. (ISBN 0-87747-124-X). Deseret Bk.
Richards, Larry. Born to Grow. LC 74-92603. 1974. pap. 2.50 (ISBN 0-88207-708-2). Victor Bks.
--The Complete Christian. 144p. 1975. pap. 2.50 (ISBN 0-88207-714-7). Victor Bks.
--Science & the Bible...Can We Believe Both? 32p. 1973. pap. 0.69 o.p. (ISBN 0-88207-372-9). Victor Bks.
Richards, Larry & Johnson, Paul. Death & the Caring Community. LC 80-19752. (Critical Concern Bks.). 1981. 8.95 (ISBN 0-930014-45-6). Multnomah.
Richards, Larry E., et al. Business Statistics: Why & When. (Illus.). 1978. text ed. 17.95 (ISBN 0-07-052273-1, C); wkbk. 6.95 (ISBN 0-07-052275-8); instructor's manual 4.95 (ISBN 0-07-052274-X). McGraw.
Richards, Laura E. Abigail Adams & Her Times. LC 78-143631. 1971. Repr. of 1917 ed. 18.00 (ISBN 0-8103-3640-5). Gale.
Richards, Lawrence O. Creative Bible Study. 1979. pap. 5.95 (ISBN 0-310-31911-0). Zondervan.
--Creative Bible Teaching. 1970. 8.95 (ISBN 0-8024-1640-3). Moody.
--How Far I Can Go. (Answers for Youth Ser.). 1980. pap. 3.95 (ISBN 0-310-38951-8). Zondervan.
--How I Can Be Real. (Answers for Youth Ser.). 1980. pap. 3.95 (ISBN 0-310-38971-2). Zondervan.
--How I Can Experience God. (Answers for Youth Ser.). 1980. pap. 3.95 (ISBN 0-310-38991-7). Zondervan.
--How I Can Fit in. (Answers for Youth Ser.). 1980. pap. 3.95 (ISBN 0-310-38961-5). Zondervan.
--A New Face for the Church. 288p. (Orig.). 1981. pap. 6.95 (ISBN 0-310-31901-3). Zondervan.
--A Theology of Christian Education. 320p. 1975. 12.95 (ISBN 0-310-31940-4). Zondervan.
Richards, Lawrence O. & Hoeldtke, Clyde. A Theology of Church Leadership. (Illus.). 352p. 1980. 12.95 (ISBN 0-310-31960-9). Zondervan.
Richards, Leigh. Spring Fires. (Silhouette Ser.: No. 21). pap. 1.50 (ISBN 0-686-68329-3). PB.
--Spring Fires. 192p. (Orig.). 1980. pap. 1.50 (ISBN 0-671-57021-8). S&S.
Richards, Leonard L. The Advent of American Democracy. 1977. pap. 7.95x (ISBN 0-673-07904-X). Scott F.
--Gentlemen of Property and Standing: Anti-Abolition Mobs in Jacksonian America. 1971. pap. 4.95 (ISBN 0-19-501351-4, 347, GB). Oxford U Pr.
--Gentlemen of Property & Standing: Anti-Abolition Mobs in Jacksonian America. LC 74-93862. 1970. 12.95 (ISBN 0-19-500082-X). Oxford U Pr.
Richards, Lockie. Dressage: Begin the Right Way. LC 75-6. (Illus.). 96p. 1975. 12.95 (ISBN 0-7153-6926-1). David & Charles.
Richards, M. & Whitby-Strevens, C. BCPL-The Language & Its Compiler. LC 77-71098. (Illus.). 1980. 26.50 (ISBN 0-521-21965-5). Cambridge U Pr.
Richards, M. P., ed. The Integration of the Child into a Social World. LC 73-82464. 320p. 1974. 35.00 (ISBN 0-521-20306-6); pap. 12.95x (ISBN 0-521-09830-0). Cambridge U Pr.
Richards, M. Ross & Richards, Marie C. Old Testament Charts. pap. 1.95 o.p. (ISBN 0-87747-447-8). Deseret Bk.
Richards, M. Ross & Richards, Marie C., eds. Book of Mormon Charts. pap. 1.95 o.p. (ISBN 0-87747-444-3). Deseret Bk.
Richards, Marie C., jt. auth. see Richards, M. Ross.
Richards, Marie C., jt. ed. see Richards, M. Ross.
Richards, Mary C. Centering in Pottery, Poetry, & the Person. LC 64-22372. 1969. pap. 6.95 (ISBN 0-8195-6011-1, Pub. by Wesleyan U Pr). Columbia U Pr.
--The Crossing Point: Selected Talks & Writings. LC 73-6010. (Illus.). 1973. 15.00x (ISBN 0-8195-4060-9, Pub. by Wesleyan U Pr); pap. 6.95 (ISBN 0-8195-6029-4). Columbia U Pr.
Richards, Mary H. Musical Sketchbook One. (Illus., Orig.). (gr. 1-3). 1967. pap. 1.40 (ISBN 0-8224-9011-0); tchrs' manual free (ISBN 0-8224-9015-3). Pitman Learning.
--Pentatonic Songs for Young Children. LC 67-29156. (Orig.). (gr. 1-3). 1967. pap. 0.96x (ISBN 0-8224-9013-7). Pitman Learning.
Richards, Max D. & Greenlaw, Paul S. Management: Decisions & Behavior. rev. ed. 1972. text ed. 18.95 (ISBN 0-256-00474-9). Irwin.
Richards, Michael E. Meat for Your Freezer. 1974. 6.95 (ISBN 0-571-10223-9, Pub. by Faber & Faber). Merrimack Bk Serv.
Richards, Norman. Tractors, Plows & Harvesters: A Book About Farm Machines. LC 77-83821. (gr. 1-3). 1978. 7.95 (ISBN 0-385-12347-7); PLB (ISBN 0-385-12348-5). Doubleday.
Richards, O. W. A Revisional Study of the Masarid Wasps (Hymenoptera, Vespoidea) (Illus.). 294p. 1962. 24.00x (ISBN 0-565-00697-5, Pub. by Brit Mus Nat Hist England). Sabbot-Natural Hist Bks.
Richards, P. & Leonor, M. Education & Income Distribution in Asia. 208p. 1981. 35.50x (ISBN 0-7099-2201-9, Pub. by Croom Helm Ltd England). Biblio Dist.

Richards, Paul G., jt. auth. see Aki, Keiiti.

Richards, Paul W. Tropical Rain Forest. LC 79-50507. (Illus.). 1952. 65.50 (ISBN 0-521-06079-6); pap. 22.50 (ISBN 0-521-29658-7). Cambridge U Pr.

Richards, Peter G. Reformed Local Government System. 4th ed. (New Local Government Ser.). 192p. 1980. pap. text ed. 8.95 (ISBN 0-04-352090-1, 2491). Allen Unwin.

Richards, Peter G., jt. auth. see Lucas, Bryan K.

Richards, Peter S., jt. auth. see O'Dell, Andrew C.

Richards, Philip, jt. auth. see Esbensen, Thorwald.

Richards, R. J. An Introduction to Dynamics & Control. 1979. text ed. 45.00 (ISBN 0-582-44182-X); pap. text ed. 24.00 (ISBN 0-582-44183-8). Longman.

Richards, R. J. & Rajan, K. T., eds. Tissue Culture in Medical Research (II) Second International Symposium on Tissue Culture in Medical Research, 1-3 April 1980, Cardiff, Wales. (Illus.). 281p. 1980. 48.00 (ISBN 0-08-025924-3). Pergamon.

Richards, Richard D. Ophthalmologic Disorders: A Practitioner's Guide. 1973. spiral bdg. 12.00 (ISBN 0-87488-703-8). Med Exam.

Richards, Roy. Early Experiences. LC 77-82994. (Science 5-13 Ser.). (Illus.). 1977. pap. text ed. 9.30 (ISBN 0-356-04005-4). Raintree Child.

--Holes, Gaps & Cavities: Stages 1 & 2. LC 77-82990. (Science 5-13 Ser.). (Illus.). 1977. pap. text ed. 9.30 (ISBN 0-356-04108-5). Raintree Child.

--Ourselves: Stages 1 & 2. LC 77-83006. (Science 5-13 Ser.). (Illus.). 1977. pap. text ed. 9.30 (ISBN 0-356-04349-5). Raintree Child.

--Time: Stages 1 & 2 & Background. LC 77-82997. (Science 5-13 Ser.). (Illus.). 1977. pap. text ed. 8.25 (ISBN 0-356-04008-9). Raintree Child.

Richards, Ruth & Abrams, Joy. Let's Do Yoga. LC 74-22199. (Illus.). 48p. (gr. 2-5). 1975. reinforced bdg. 5.95 o.p. (ISBN 0-03-014006-4). HR&W.

Richards, S. A. & Fielden, P. S. Temperature Regulation. LC 73-77794. (Wykeham Science Ser.: No. 27). 1973. pap. 8.75x (ISBN 0-8448-1335-4). Crane-Russak Co.

Richards, Stanley, ed. America on Stage: Ten Great Plays of American History. LC 75-7255. 960p. 1976. 12.50 o.p. (ISBN 0-385-03005-3). Doubleday.

--Best Mystery & Suspense Plays of the Modern Theatre. 1979. pap. 7.95 (ISBN 0-380-46466-7). Avon.

--The Best Short Plays, 1971. LC 38-8006. (Best Short Plays Ser). 1971. 12.95 (ISBN 0-8019-5587-4). Chilton.

--The Best Short Plays 1972. LC 38-8006. (Best Short Plays Ser). 479p. 1972. 12.95 (ISBN 0-8019-5588-2). Chilton.

--The Best Short Plays, 1973. (Best Short Plays Ser.). 400p. 1973. 12.95 (ISBN 0-8019-5589-0). Chilton.

--Best Short Plays, 1975. 352p. 1975. 12.95 (ISBN 0-8019-6082-7). Chilton.

--The Best Short Plays 1977. LC 38-8006. (Best Short Plays Ser.). (Illus.). 1977. 12.95 (ISBN 0-8019-6515-2, 6515). Chilton.

--The Best Short Plays, 1978. LC 38-8006. (Best Short Plays Ser.). 1978. 12.95 (ISBN 0-8019-6642-6). Chilton.

Richards, T. G., jt. auth. see Neame, K. D.

Richards, T. H. Energy Methods in Stress Analysis. LC 79-29647. (Engineering Science Ser.). 410p. 1980. pap. 26.95 (ISBN 0-470-27068-3). Halsted Pr.

--Energy Methods in Stress Analysis: With an Introduction to Finite Element Techniques. (Ellis Horwood Series in Engineering Science). 1977. 58.95 (ISBN 0-470-98960-2). Halsted Pr.

Richards, T. H. & Stanley., P., eds. Stability Problems in Engineering Structures & Components. (Illus.). 1979. 82.80x (ISBN 0-85334-836-7, Pub. by Applied Science). Burgess-Intl Ideas.

Richards, T. H., jt. ed. see Gibbs, H. G.

Richards, Tad, jt. auth. see Levy, Elizabeth.

Richards, Thomas C. Cobol: An Introduction. (Data Processing Ser.). 350p. 1981. pap. text ed. 12.95 (ISBN 0-675-08041-X). Merrill.

Richards, Thomas J., jt. auth. see Kempf, Albert F.

Richards, W. G., jt. auth. see Gasser, R. P.

Richards, W. G., et al. Bibliography of ab initio Molecular Wave Functions: Supplement for 1970-1973. 376p. 1974. pap. 33.50x (ISBN 0-19-855356-0). Oxford U Pr.

Richards, Whitman see Held, Richard.

Richards, William L. The Classification of the Greek Manuscripts of the Johannine Epistles. LC 77-23469. (Society of Biblical Literature. Dissertation Ser.). 1977. pap. 7.50 (ISBN 0-89130-140-2, 060135). Scholars Pr Ca.

Richardson. Laboratory Operations for Rotating Electric Machinery & Transformer Technology. 256p. 1980. pap. text ed. 7.95 (ISBN 0-8359-3925-1). Reston.

--Urban Economics. 1978. 20.95 (ISBN 0-275-24430-X). Dryden Pr.

Richardson & Baldwin. Public Administration: Government in Action. (Political Science Ser.). 1976. text ed. 15.50 o.p. (ISBN 0-675-08605-1); instructor's manual 3.95 o.p. (ISBN 0-686-67373-5). Merrill.

Richardson, jt. auth. see Baldwin.

Richardson, jt. auth. see Brady.

Richardson, A., jt. auth. see Carter, G. W.

Richardson, Agnes. Jesus Calls Us His Sheep. (Illus.). 1981. 4.95 (ISBN 0-8062-1636-0). Carlton.

Richardson, Albert E. Monumental Classic Architecture in Great Britain & Ireland. (Illus.). 1981. 25.00 (ISBN 0-393-01451-7); pap. 10.95 (ISBN 0-393-00053-2). Norton.

Richardson, Arleta. In Grandma's Attic. LC 74-75541. 112p. (Orig.). (gr. 4-8). 1974. pap. 1.95 (ISBN 0-912692-32-4). Cook.

--Stories from Grandma's Attic. (gr. 6-12). 1980. 5.95 (ISBN 0-89191-310-6). Cook.

Richardson, B. A. Wood Construction. 1978. text ed. 30.00x (ISBN 0-904406-14-8, Construction Pr). Longman.

Richardson, Barry. Remedial Treatment of Buildings. (The Construction Press Ser.). (Illus.). 236p. 1981. 42.00 (ISBN 0-904406-74-1). Longman.

Richardson, Ben & Fahey, William A. Great Black Americans. 2nd. rev. ed. LC 75-12841. Orig. Title: Great American Negroes. (Illus.). 352p. (gr. 5 up). 1976. 10.95 (ISBN 0-690-00994-1, TYC-J). T Y Crowell.

Richardson, Bradley. The Political Culture of Japan. 1974. pap. 7.95x (ISBN 0-520-03049-4); pap. 6.95x (ISBN 0-520-03049-4). U of Cal Pr.

Richardson, Brian, ed. & intro. by see Machiavelli, Niccolo.

Richardson, Christine A., jt. ed. see Thornton, Wendy A.

Richardson, Dana R., jt. auth. see Haidinger, Timothy P.

Richardson, Daniel. Basic Circulatory Physiology. 1976. text ed. 13.95 (ISBN 0-316-74422-0, Little Med Div). Little.

Richardson, David, jt. auth. see Emmons, Michael.

Richardson, David W., et al, eds. Frozen Human Semen: A Royal College of Obstetricians & Gynaecologists Workshop in the Cryobiology of Human Semen & Its Role on Artificial Insemination by Donor, March 22 & 23, 1979. (Developments in Obstetrics & Gynecology Ser.: No. 4). 280p. 1980. lib. bdg. 49.95 (ISBN 90-247-2370-1, Martinus Nijhoff Pubs). Kluwer Boston.

Richardson, Don. Eternity in Their Hearts. LC 80-50542. 1981. text ed. 8.95 (ISBN 0-8307-0739-5, 5108608). Regal. Postponed.

--Lords of the Earth. LC 77-74534. 1977. pap. 5.95 (ISBN 0-8307-0529-5, 54-057-18). Regal.

Richardson, Don, tr. Hijo De Paz. (Spanish Bks.). (Span.). 1977. 2.45 (ISBN 0-8297-0572-4). Life Pubs Intl.

Richardson, Donald V., ed. Handbook of Rotating Electric Machinery. (Illus.). 652p. 1980. text ed. 24.95 (ISBN 0-8359-2759-8). Reston.

Richardson, Douglas. Gothic Revival Architecture in Ireland. LC 76-23700. (Outstanding Dissertations in the Fine Arts Ser.). 1978. lib. bdg. 133.00x (ISBN 0-8240-2723-X). Garland Pub.

Richardson, E. Allen. Muslims in America. 96p. (Orig.). 1981. pap. 4.95 (ISBN 0-8298-0449-8). Pilgrim NY.

Richardson, Edgar P. Short History of Painting in America. (Orig.). 1963. pap. 10.95 scp (ISBN 0-690-73377-1, HarpC); pap. text ed. 6.50 o.p. (ISBN 0-686-68500-8). Har-Row.

Richardson, Elmo. Dams, Parks & Politics: Resource Development & Preservation in the Truman-Eisenhower Era. LC 72-91670. (Illus.). 256p. 1973. 14.00x (ISBN 0-8131-1284-2). U Pr of Ky.

Richardson, Emeline. The Etruscans: Their Art & Civilization. LC 64-15817. (Illus.). 1976. pap. 9.50 (ISBN 0-226-71235-4, P670, Phoen). U of Chicago Pr.

Richardson, F. C. Morphological Studies of the Nymphaeaceae, Vol. 4. Structure & Development of the Flower of Brasenia schreberi Geml. (U. C. Publ. in Botany: Vol. 47). 1969. pap. 7.00x (ISBN 0-520-09020-9). U of Cal Pr.

Richardson, Frank H. Solo Para Muchachos. 1980. pap. 1.60 (ISBN 0-311-46929-9). Casa Bautista.

Richardson, Gary. Where's It At? 1978. pap. 3.50 (ISBN 0-88207-182-3). Victor Bks.

Richardson, Gary L. & Birkin, Stanley J. Problem Solving Using Pl-C: An Introduction for Business & the Social Sciences. LC 75-4724. 480p. 1975. 17.95 (ISBN 0-471-72048-8); instructor's manual avail. (ISBN 0-471-72049-6). Wiley.

Richardson, Gary L., et al. A Primer of Structured Program Design. 1980. 17.50 (ISBN 0-89433-110-8); pap. 14.00 (ISBN 0-89433-085-3). Petrocelli.

Richardson, George. Iconology, 2 vols. Orgel, Stephen, ed. LC 78-68201. (Philosophy of Images Ser.: Vol. 20). (Illus.). 1980. Set. lib. bdg. 132.00 (ISBN 0-8240-3694-8). Garland Pub.

Richardson, George B. Economic Theory. (Orig.). 1964. pap. text ed. 2.50x (ISBN 0-09-072653-7, Hutchinson U Lib). Humanities.

Richardson, H. Edward. Cassius Marcellus Clay: Firebrand of Freedom. LC 74-7882. (The Kentucky Bicentennial Bookshelf Ser.). (Illus.). 168p. 1980. Repr. of 1976 ed. 5.95 (ISBN 0-8131-0205-7). U Pr of Ky.

--How to Think & Write. 1970. pap. 7.95x (ISBN 0-673-05289-3). Scott F.

Richardson, H. W. Regional Growth Theory. LC 73-5749. 264p. 1973. 27.95 (ISBN 0-470-71952-4). Halsted Pr.

Richardson, Harry W. Economic Aspects of the Energy Crisis. LC 75-8360. 256p. 1975. 19.95 (ISBN 0-669-03327-8). Lexington Bks.

--Regional Development Policy & Planning in Spain. (Illus.). 264p. 1975. 24.95 (ISBN 0-347-01091-1, 99440-5, Pub. by Saxon Hse). Lexington Bks.

Richardson, Henry B. Outline of French Grammar with Vocabularies. rev. ed. 1950. text ed. 12.50x (ISBN 0-89197-327-3); pap. text ed. 4.55x (ISBN 0-89197-328-1). Irvington.

Richardson, Herbert, ed. see Anselm Of Canterbury.

Richardson, Herbert W., ed. New Religions & Mental Health: A Guide to the Issues. (Symposium Ser.: Vol. 6). (Orig.). 1980. soft cover 11.95x (ISBN 0-88946-910-5). E Mellen.

Richardson, Herbert W., jt. ed. see Clark, Elizabeth.

Richardson, Howard & Berney, William. Dark of the Moon. LC 56-9611. (Orig.). 1966. pap. 2.65x (ISBN 0-87830-517-3). Theatre Arts.

Richardson, Hugh E., jt. auth. see Snellgrove, David L.

Richardson, J. Art: The Way It Is. 1974. pap. 10.95 (ISBN 0-13-049221-3). P-H.

Richardson, J., jt. auth. see Faires, V.

Richardson, J. A., et al. Books for the Retarded Reader. 6th ed. 1977. pap. text ed. 12.00x (ISBN 0-85563-152-X). Verry.

Richardson, J. H. & Peterson, R. V., eds. Systematic Materials Analysis. (Materials Science Ser.: Vol. 1). 1974. 48.50, by subscription 42.00 (ISBN 0-12-587801-X). Acad Pr.

Richardson, J. J. Policy-Making Process. (Library of Political Studies). 1969. text ed. 5.25x (ISBN 0-7100-6523-X). Humanities.

Richardson, J. J. & Jordan, A. G. Governing Under Pressure: The Policy Process in a Post Parliamentary Democracy. 212p. 1979. 33.50x (ISBN 0-85520-237-8, Pub by Martin Robertson England); pap. 12.50x (ISBN 0-85520-314-5). Biblio Dist.

Richardson, J. R. A Selection of Folk Dances, Vol. 1-5. Repr. Vol. 1. 1965. pap. 3.00 (ISBN 0-685-77384-1); Vol. 2. 1966. pap. 3.80 (ISBN 0-08-010842-3); Vol. 3. 1966. pap. 3.80 (ISBN 0-08-011926-3); Vol. 4. 1971. pap. 3.80 (ISBN 0-08-016190-1); Vol. 5. 1978. pap. 3.80 (ISBN 0-08-021589-0). Pergamon.

Richardson, J. R. & Peacock, D. G., eds. Chemical Engineering. (Chemical Engineering Ser.: Vol. 3). (Illus.). 1979. text ed. 75.00 (ISBN 0-08-023818-1); pap. text ed. 24.00 (ISBN 0-08-023819-X). Pergamon.

Richardson, James D., compiled by. The Messages & Papers of Jefferson Davis & the Confederacy, 1861-65, 2 vols. LC 66-29296. 1400p. 1981. Set. pap. 29.95 (ISBN 0-87754-206-6). Chelsea Hse.

Richardson, James M. History of Greenville County, South Carolina: Narrative & Biographical. LC 80-23330. 342p. 1980. Repr. of 1930 ed. 22.50 (ISBN 0-87152-343-4). Reprint.

Richardson, James T., jt. auth. see Brady, Allen H.

Richardson, Jeanne M., jt. auth. see Malinowsky, H. Robert.

Richardson, Joan. Wild Edible Plants of New England: A Field Guide, Including Poisonous Plants Often Encountered. (Illus.). 256p. (Orig.). 1981. pap. 9.95 (ISBN 0-89933-009-6). DeLorme Pub. Postponed.

Richardson, Joanna. Enid Starkie. LC 73-10563. (Illus.). 320p. 1974. 7.95 o.s.i. (ISBN 0-02-602910-3). Macmillan.

Richardson, Joanna, tr. from Fr. & see Gautier, Theophile.

Richardson, Joanna, tr. see Verlaine, Paul.

Richardson, Joe M. The Negro in the Reconstruction of Florida, 1865-1877. LC 73-84442. 272p. 1973. Repr. of 1965 ed. 10.00 o.p. (ISBN 0-88251-038-X). Trend House.

Richardson, John. The Canadian Brothers: Or the Prophecy Fulfilled: a Tale of the Late American War. Klinck, Carl F., ed. 1976. pap. 6.95 (ISBN 0-8020-6264-4). U of Toronto Pr.

Richardson, Judith K., jt. auth. see Richardson, Lloyd I.

Richardson, Kay. Briarwood Summer. 192p. (YA) 1976. 4.95 o.p. (ISBN 0-685-67080-5, Avalon). Bouregy.

--Come to Greenleaves. (YA) 1977. 4.95 o.p. (ISBN 0-685-75639-4, Avalon). Bouregy.

Richardson, Kenneth, ed. Twentieth Century Writing: A Reader's Guide to Contemporary Literature. 1970. 20.00 (ISBN 0-693-01700-7). Transatlantic.

Richardson, Larry N. The Philosophy of Nietzsche in Dramatic Representational Expressions. (Essence of the Great Philosophers Ser.). (Illus.). 97p. 1981. 19.75 (ISBN 0-89266-277-8). Am Classical Coll Pr.

Richardson, Laurel W. Readings in Sex & Gender. 416p. 1982. pap. text ed. 12.95 (ISBN 0-669-03370-7). Heath. Postponed.

Richardson, Lawrence. Poetical Theory in Republican Rome. Commager, Steele, ed. LC 77-70825. (Latin Poetry Ser.). 1978. lib. bdg. 22.00 (ISBN 0-8240-2977-1). Garland Pub.

Richardson, Linda. Banking & Sales: A Consultative Guide to Cross Selling Financial Products & Services. 165p. 1981. 19.95 (ISBN 0-471-09010-7, Pub. by Wiley-Interscience). Wiley.

Richardson, Lloyd I. & Richardson, Judith K. The Mathematics of Drugs & Solutions with Clinical Applications. 1976. 7.95 o.p. (ISBN 0-07-052309-6, HP); instructor's manual 2.95 o.p. (ISBN 0-07-052310-X). McGraw.

Richardson, M. O., ed. Polymer Engineering Composites. (Illus.). 1977. 102.60x (ISBN 0-85334-722-0). Intl Ideas.

Richardson, Michael L. After Amin: The Bloody Pearl. LC 80-23249. (Illus.). 224p. (Orig.). 1980. pap. 4.95 (ISBN 0-9604968-0-7, 737). Majestic Bks.

Richardson, Mozelle. Daughter of the Sacred Mountain. LC 76-46415. 1977. 7.95 o.p. (ISBN 0-688-03145-5). Morrow.

Richardson, Nancy. How to Stencil & Decorate Furniture & Tinware. 1956. 12.95 o.p. (ISBN 0-8260-7445-6). Ronald Pr.

Richardson, Norman & Stubbs, Thomas. Plants, Agriculture, & Human Society. LC 77-72644. 1978. pap. text ed. 9.95 (ISBN 0-8053-8215-1). Benjamin-Cummings.

Richardson, Otis Dunbar. Says Who?--Authority & Old Adam. 1978. 7.00 o.p. (ISBN 0-682-49010-5). Exposition.

--Start Point: Six Studies in Violence. 1973. 8.00 o.p. (ISBN 0-682-47672-2). Exposition.

Richardson, Peter N. German-Romance Contact: Name-Giving in Walser Settlements. LC 74-79043. (Amsterdamer Publikationen Zur Sprache und Literatur: No. 15). 372p. (Orig.). 1974. pap. text ed. 34.25x (ISBN 90-6203-221-4). Humanities.

Richardson, Peter R., jt. auth. see Cousoneau, Eric.

Richardson, R. C. Puritanism in North-West England: A Regional Study of the Diocese of Chester to 1642. 214p. 1972. 15.00x (ISBN 0-87471-093-6). Rowman.

Richardson, Richard C., Jr. & Leslie, Larry L. The Impossible Dream? Financing Community College's Evolving Mission. (Horizon Issues Monograph Ser.). 52p. (Orig.). 1980. pap. 5.00 (ISBN 0-87117-105-8). Am Assn Comm Jr Coll.

Richardson, Robert, ed. see Bryant, Jacob.

Richardson, Robert, ed. see De Camoens, Luis.

Richardson, Robert, ed. see Mallet, Paul H.

Richardson, Robert, ed. see Owen, William.

Richardson, Robert, ed. see Potter, John.

Richardson, Robert A., jt. auth. see Davis, Ann N.

Richardson, Robert D., jt. auth. see Feldman, Burton.

Richardson, Robert D., ed. see Bell, John.

Richardson, Robert D., ed. see Clavigero, Francesco S.

Richardson, Robert D., ed. see Davies, Edward.

Richardson, Robert D., ed. see Rowlands, Henry.

Richardson, Robert D., ed. see Volney, C. F.

Richardson, Robert G. Surgeon's Heart: History of Cardiac Surgery. (Illus.). 1969. 21.00x (ISBN 0-433-27590-1). Intl Ideas.

Richardson, Robert O. How to Get Your Own Patent. LC 80-54340. (Illus.). 128p. 1981. 16.95 (ISBN 0-8069-5564-3); lib. bdg. 14.99 (ISBN 0-8069-5565-1); pap. 8.95 (ISBN 0-8069-8990-4). Sterling.

Richardson, Robert S. Star Lovers. 1967. 7.50 o.s.i. (ISBN 0-02-602900-6). Macmillan.

Richardson, Rupert N., et al. Texas: The Lone Star State. 4th ed. (Illus.). 464p. 1981. text ed. 17.95 (ISBN 0-13-912444-6). P-H.

Richardson, S. A. Protecting Buildings. 1977. 14.95 (ISBN 0-7153-7321-8). David & Charles.

Richardson, S. Lee, ed. Dimensions of Communication. (Illus., Orig.). 1969. pap. text ed. 14.95 (ISBN 0-13-214494-8). P-H.

Richardson, Samuel. A Collection of the Moral & Instructive Sentiments, Maxims, Cautions, & Reflexions, Contained in the Histories of Pamela, Clarissa, & Sir Charles Grandison. LC 80-22492. 1980. Repr. of 1755 ed. 45.00x (ISBN 0-8201-1357-3). Schol Facsimilies.
--The History of Sir Charles Grandison, 3 vols. Harris, Jocelyn, ed. (Oxford English Novels Ser). (Illus.). 1720p. 1972. Set. boxed 47.00x o.p. (ISBN 0-19-255358-5). Oxford U Pr.
--Pamela, 2 Vols. 1955. Vol. 1. 10.50x (ISBN 0-460-00683-5, Evman); Vol. 2. 6.00x (ISBN 0-460-00684-3); Vol. 1. pap. 3.25x (ISBN 0-460-01683-0); pap. o.p. (ISBN 0-460-01684-9). Dutton.
--Pamela: Or Virtue Rewarded. Sabor, Peter, ed. (Penguin English Library). 480p. 1981. pap. 4.95 (ISBN 0-14-043140-3). Penguin.
--Pamela; or, Virtue Rewarded, 1801, 4 vols. Shugrue, Michael F., ed. (The Flowering of the Novel, 1740-1775 Ser: Vol. 1). 1974. lib. bdg. 50.00 ea. (ISBN 0-8240-1100-7). Garland Pub.
Richardson, Samuel & Fielding, Henry. Pamela, Shamela. 1980. pap. 3.50 (ISBN 0-451-51366-5, CE1366, Sig Classics). NAL.
Richardson, Selma K., ed. Research About Nineteenth-Century Children & Books: Portrait Studies. (Monograph: No. 17). (Illus.). 1980. pap. 8.00 (ISBN 0-87845-055-6). U of Ill Lib Sci.
Richardson, Susan M., jt. auth. see Merrill, Virginia.
Richardson, Terry. Modern Industrial Plastics. LC 72-92621. 17.95 (ISBN 0-672-20948-9). Bobbs.
Richardson, Treva M. Sanitation for Food Service Workers. 2nd ed. LC 74-23606. 1974. pap. 10.95 (ISBN 0-8436-0582-0). tchr's guide 1.95 (ISBN 0-8436-2049-8). CBI Pub.
Richardson, Vokes. Not All Our Pride. LC 65-14600. 1965. 4.50 o.p. (ISBN 0-8076-0296-5). Braziller.
Richardson, W. J. Cost Improvement, Work Sampling & Short Interval Scheduling. 1976. 18.95 (ISBN 0-87909-139-8). Reston.
Richardson, Walter & Kerr, Roberta. Lost Nickel. 1981. 4.50 (ISBN 0-533-03282-2). Vantage.
Richardson, Walter C. Mary Tudor, the White Queen. LC 68-11050. (Illus.). 1969. 10.00 o.p. (ISBN 0-295-95006-4). U of Wash Pr.
Richardson, William C., jt. auth. see Shortell, Stephen M.
Richardson, Wyman. House on Nauset Marsh. (Illus.). 1980. pap. 5.95 (ISBN 0-85699-046-9). Chatham Pr.
Richart, F. E., Jr., et al. Vibrations of Soils & Foundations. (Civil Engineering Ser). 1970. ref. ed. 25.95 (ISBN 0-13-941716-8). P-H.
Richart, Ralph M., jt. auth. see Ferenczy, Alex.
Richelle, M. & Lejeune, H. Time in Animal Behaviour. (Illus.). 1980. 51.00 (ISBN 0-08-023754-1); pap. 23.00 (ISBN 0-08-025489-6). Pergamon.
Richels, Richard G. R & D Under Uncertainty. LC 78-74997. (Outstanding Dissertations on Energy Ser.). 1979. lib. bdg. 18.00 (ISBN 0-8240-3978-5). Garland Pub.
Richelson, Geraldine, jt. auth. see Freudenberger, Herbert.
Richert, Barbara. Getting Your Kids to Eat Right. 192p. (Orig.). 1981. pap. 5.95 (ISBN 0-346-12519-7). Cornerstone.
Richert, Donald, jt. auth. see Kelley, John L.
Richert, G. H., et al. Retailing Principles & Practices. 5th ed. 1968. text ed. 13.96x (ISBN 0-07-052321-5, G); tchrs. manual & key 4.50x (ISBN 0-07-052323-1); Set. problems 4.96x (ISBN 0-07-052320-7); Set. projects 4.96x (ISBN 0-07-052322-3); tests 2.96x (ISBN 0-07-052324-X). McGraw.
Richert, H. E., jt. auth. see Halberstam, H.
Richey, David. The Brown Trout Fisherman's Guide. LC 78-53428. 1978. 10.95 o.p. (ISBN 0-8015-0952-1). Dutton.
--The Small-Boat Handbook. LC 78-3315. 224p. pap. 3.95 (ISBN 0-06-463535-X, EH 535, EH). Har-Row.
Richey, E. T. & Namon, Richard. EEG Instrumentation and Technology. (Illus.). 218p. 1976. 29.75 (ISBN 0-398-03426-5). C C Thomas.
Richey, Jim. Banking Language. (Spiritual Vocabulary Ser.). (Illus.). 48p. (gr. 7-12). 1980. pap. text ed. 2.45 (ISBN 0-915510-37-5). Janus Bks.
--Clothing Language. (Survival Vocabulary Ser.). (Illus.). 48p. (gr. 7-12). 1979. pap. text ed. 2.45 (ISBN 0-915510-33-2). Janus Bks.
--Credit Language. (Survival Vocabulary Ser.). (Illus.). 48p. (gr. 7-12). 1980. pap. text ed. 2.45 (ISBN 0-915510-36-7). Janus Bks.
--Drivers License Language. (Survival Vocabulary Ser.). (Illus.). 48p. (Orig.). (gr. 7 up). 1980. pap. 2.45 (ISBN 0-915510-49-9). Janus Bks.
--Entertainment Language. (Survival Vocabulary Ser.). (Illus.). 48p. (gr. 7-12). 1979. pap. text ed. 2.45 (ISBN 0-915510-34-0). Janus Bks.
--Medical Language. (Survival Vocabulary Ser.). (Illus.). 48p. (gr. 7 up). 1980. pap. text ed. 2.45 (ISBN 0-915510-48-0). Janus Bks.
Richey, Margaret F. & Sacker, Hugh, eds. Selected Poems of Walther Von der Vogelweide. 4th, new & rev. ed. (Blackwell's German Text Ser.). 1967. pap. 4.50x o.p. (ISBN 0-631-01820-4, Pub. by Basil Blackwell). Biblio Dist.
Richey, Russell E., ed. Denominationalism. LC 74-49103. 1977. 15.95 o.p. (ISBN 0-687-10469-6); pap. 6.95 o.p. (ISBN 0-687-10470-X). Abingdon.
Richie, Donald. Introducing Japan. LC 77-75966. (Illus.). 1978. 14.95 (ISBN 0-87011-308-9). Kodansha.
--Ozu: His Life & Films. (Illus.). 1974. 18.50 (ISBN 0-520-02445-1); pap. 5.95 (ISBN 0-520-03277-2). U of Cal Pr.
Richie, Donald & Burma, Ian. The Japanese Tattoo. LC 79-26738. (Illus.). 120p. 1980. 23.50 (ISBN 0-8348-0149-3, Pub. by John Weatherhill Inc Japan). C E Tuttle.
Richler, Mordecai. Apprenticeship of Duddy Kravitz. Young, George, ed. (Illus.). 288p. (Orig.). 1974. pap. 1.50 o.p. (ISBN 0-345-24154-1). Ballantine.
--The Apprenticeship of Duddy Kravitz. 304p. 1981. pap. 2.95 (ISBN 0-553-14584-3). Bantam.
--Jacob Two Two Meets the Hooded Fang. 1981. pap. 2.50 (ISBN 0-686-68904-6). Bantam.
--Joshua Then & Now. 384p. 1981. pap. 3.25 (ISBN 0-553-14583-5). Bantam.
Rich-McCoy, Lois. Late Bloomer: Profiles of Women Who Found Their True Callings. LC 79-1679. (Illus.). 224p. 1980. 10.95 (ISBN 0-06-013593-X, HarpT). Har-Row.
Richman, Barry M. & Farmer, Richard N. Leadership, Goals & Power in Higher Education: A Contingency & Open-Systems Approach to Effective Management. LC 74-9112. (Higher Education Ser.). 320p. 1974. 15.95x (ISBN 0-87589-235-3). Jossey-Bass.
Richman, Carol. Lekachmacher Family. LC 76-23409. (Illus.). 1976. 7.95 (ISBN 0-914842-14-5). Madrona Pubs.
Richman, Frances B. Windfalls. 1980. 5.50 (ISBN 0-8233-0313-6). Golden Quill.
Richman, Irwin. Historical Manuscript Depositories in Pennsylvania. LC 65-65225. 1965. 2.50 (ISBN 0-911124-08-X). Pa Hist & Mus.
Richman, Jeanne, ed. see League of Women Voters of New York State.
Richman, John. The United States & the Soviet Union: The Decision to Recognize. LC 79-92564. 287p. 1980. 11.95 (ISBN 0-935880-00-3). Camberleigh & Hall.
Richman, Phyllis, jt. auth. see Stapleton, Constance.
Richman, Sidney. Bernard Malamud. (U. S. Authors Ser.: No. 109). 1966. lib. bdg. 9.95 (ISBN 0-8057-0472-8). Twayne.
Richmind, Robert W., jt. ed. see Ripley, John W.
Richmond, Anthony & Kubat, Daniel, eds. Internal Migration: The New World & the Third World. LC 75-42537. (Sage Studies in International Sociology: Vol. 4). 1976. 18.00x (ISBN 0-8039-9960-7); pap. 9.95x (ISBN 0-8039-9974-7). Sage.
Richmond, Anthony H. Post-War Immigrants in Canada. LC 67-100218. 352p. 1967. 17.50x o.p. (ISBN 0-8020-1673-1). U of Toronto Pr.
--Readings in Race & Ethnic Relations. 350p. 1972. 27.00 (ISBN 0-08-016213-4); pap. 14.00 (ISBN 0-08-016212-6). Pergamon.
Richmond, Bruce L. The Pattern of Freedom. 266p. 1980. Repr. of 1911 ed. lib. bdg. 25.00 (ISBN 0-8492-7732-9). R West.
Richmond, C. John Hopton. (Illus.). 280p. Date not set. price not set (ISBN 0-521-23434-4). Cambridge U Pr.
Richmond, Donald. The Dunkirk Directive. LC 79-65119. 1980. 12.95 (ISBN 0-8128-2687-6). Stein & Day.
Richmond, Farley, tr. see Thakur, Asaita.
Richmond, H. M. Shakespeare's Political Plays. 7.50 (ISBN 0-8446-2804-2). Peter Smith.
Richmond, Hugh M. The Christian Revolutionary: John Milton. 1975. 16.50x (ISBN 0-520-02443-5). U of Cal Pr.
Richmond, John. Egypt in Modern Times. LC 77-1969. 1977. 17.50x (ISBN 0-231-04296-5). Columbia U Pr.
Richmond, Legh see Trimmer, Sarah.
Richmond, M. S. Prison Profiles. 1965. 9.00 (ISBN 0-379-00238-6). Oceana.
Richmond, P. E., ed. New Trends in Integrated Science Teaching: Education of Teachers, Vol. 3. (Illus.). 227p. (Orig.). 1974. pap. 18.00 (ISBN 92-3-101190-1, U419, UNESCO). Unipub.
Richmond, Phyllis A. Introduction to PRECIS for North American Usage. 340p. 1981. lib. bdg. 25.00x (ISBN 0-87287-240-8). Libs Unl.
Richmond, Robert. Kansas a Land of Contrast. rev ed. LC 74-77390. 1979. pap. text ed. 10.95x. Forum Pr MO.
Richmond, Robert P. Legacy of the Bloody Bride. (Orig.). 1979. pap. 1.95 (ISBN 0-532-23125-2). Manor Bks.
Richmond, Robert W. Kansas, a Land of Contrasts. rev. ed. (Illus., Orig.). 1977. text ed. 10.95x o.p. (ISBN 0-88273-010-X); pap. text ed. 7.95x o.p. (ISBN 0-88273-025-8). Forum Pr MO.
Richmond, Robert W. & Mardock, Robert W., eds. Nation Moving West: Readings in the History of the American Frontier. LC 66-10446. 1966. 15.95x (ISBN 0-8032-0152-4); pap. 3.50x (ISBN 0-8032-5157-2, BB 336, Bison). U of Nebr Pr.
Richmond, Roe. Lifeline of Texas. (Lashtrow Ser.: No. 6). 1981. pap. 1.95 (ISBN 0-8439-0892-0, Leisure Bks). Nordon Pubns.
Richmond, Samuel B. Operations Research for Management Decisions. LC 68-20552. (Illus.). 600p. 1968. 24.95 (ISBN 0-8260-7460-X); manual o.p. (ISBN 0-471-07476-4). Wiley.
--Statistical Analysis. 2nd ed. (Illus.). 1964. 22.50 (ISBN 0-8260-7475-8); manual o.p. (ISBN 0-471-07477-2). Wiley.
Richmond, Sonya. How to Be Healthy with Yoga. LC 62-20294. (Illus., Orig.). 1966. pap. 1.50 o.p. (ISBN 0-668-01004-5). Arc Bks.
--International Vegetarian Cookery. LC 66-21124. 1965. 3.75 o.p. (ISBN 0-668-01510-1). Arco.
Richmond, Stanley. Clarinet & Saxophone Experience. LC 70-183051. (Illus.). 1972. 8.95 o.p. (ISBN 0-312-14245-5, C30000). St Martin.
--Clarinet & Sax0 Phone Experience. 1980. 25.00x (Pub.by Darton-Longman-Todd England). State Mutual Bk.
Richmond, Steven, jt. auth. see Greenblatt, Michael.
Richmond, W., jt. auth. see Oakley, K.
Richter, Alice N., jt. auth. see Numeroff, Laura J.
Richter, Charles F. Elementary Seismology. LC 58-5970. (Geology Ser.). (Illus.). 1958. 31.95x (ISBN 0-7167-0211-8). W H Freeman.
Richter, Conrad. Light in the Forest. (Literature Ser.). (gr. 9-12). 1970. pap. text ed. 3.58 (ISBN 0-87720-755-0). AMSCO Sch.
--Trees. (Keith Jennison Large Type Bks). (gr. 7 up). PLB 8.95 o.p. (ISBN 0-531-00297-7). Watts.
Richter, Cynthia A. Pandora in Pinkralia. LC 79-66393. 61p. 1980. 4.95 (ISBN 0-533-04382-4). Vantage.
Richter, D., ed. Biochemical Factors Concerned in the Functional Activity of the Nervous System. 1969. pap. 27.00 (ISBN 0-08-013311-8). Pergamon.
Richter, Daniel K., jt. auth. see Vaughan, Alden T.
Richter, David. Forms of the Novella: 10 Short Novels. 833p. 1981. pap. text ed. 9.95 (ISBN 0-394-32030-1). Knopf.
Richter, Derek. The Challenge of Violence. 1973. text ed. 12.25 (ISBN 0-08-017809-X). Pergamon.
Richter, Derek, ed. Addiction & Brain Damage. 320p. 1980. 45.00x (Pub. by Croom Helm England). State Mutual Bk.
Richter, Dietmar, jt. auth. see Koch, Gebhard.
Richter, Dolores. Art, Economics & Change: The Kulebele of Northern Ivory Coast. (Illus.). 165p. (Orig.). 1980. pap. 8.95 (ISBN 0-932382-01-0). Psych Graphic.
Richter, Dorothy. Make Your Own Soap Plain & Fancy. LC 73-83663. 160p. 1974. pap. 1.95 (ISBN 0-385-01776-6, Dolp). Doubleday.
Richter, G. W. & Epstein, M. A., eds. International Review of Experimental Pathology. Incl. Vol. 1. 1962. 52.00 (ISBN 0-12-364901-3); Vol. 2. 1963. 52.00 (ISBN 0-12-364902-1); Vol. 3. 1965. 52.00 (ISBN 0-12-364903-X); Vol. 4. 1965. 52.00 (ISBN 0-12-364904-8); Vol. 5. 1967. 52.00 (ISBN 0-12-364905-6); Vol. 6. 1968. 52.00 (ISBN 0-12-364906-4); Vol. 7. 1969. 52.00 (ISBN 0-12-364907-2); Vol. 8. 1969. 52.00 (ISBN 0-12-364908-0); Vol. 9. 1971. 52.00 (ISBN 0-12-364909-9); Vol. 10. 1972. 52.00 (ISBN 0-12-364910-2); Vol. 11. 1972. 52.00 (ISBN 0-12-364911-0); Vol. 12. 1973. 52.00 (ISBN 0-12-364912-9); Vol. 17. 1977. 43.50 (ISBN 0-12-364917-X); Vol. 18. 1978. 52.50 (ISBN 0-12-364918-8); Vol. 19. 1979. 29.50 (ISBN 0-12-364919-6). Acad Pr.
--International Review of Experimental Pathology, Vol. 22. 1980. write for info. (ISBN 0-12-364922-6). Acad Pr.
Richter, Gerhard. Plant Metabolism. 450p. 1980. 60.95x (ISBN 0-85664-955-4, Pub. by Croom Helm England). State Mutual Bk.
Richter, Gisela. A Handbook of Greek Art: A Survey of the Visual Arts of Ancient Greece. (Illus.). 432p. 1980. pap. 10.95 (ISBN 0-525-47651-2). Dutton.
Richter, H. P. & Schwan, W. C., eds. Wiring Simplified. 33rd ed. LC 33-7980. 160p. 1981. 3.50 (ISBN 0-9603294-1-2). Park Pub.
Richter, H. V., jt. ed. see Shepherd, K. R.
Richter, Hans. Dada: Art & Anti-Art. (World of Art Ser.). (Illus.). 1978. pap. 9.95 (ISBN 0-19-520071-3). Oxford U Pr.
Richter, Hans P. Friedrich. Kroll, Edite, tr. LC 78-119098. (gr. 5-8). 1970. reinforced bdg. 5.95 o.p. (ISBN 0-03-012721-1). HR&W.
Richter, Liselotte. Jean-Paul Sartre. Wieck, Fred, tr. from Ger. LC 68-31456. (Modern Literature Ser.). 135p. 1970. 10.95 (ISBN 0-8044-2732-1); pap. 3.45 (ISBN 0-8044-6728-5). Ungar.
Richter, M., ed. Political Theory of Montesquieu. LC 76-4753. 400p. 1977. 29.95 (ISBN 0-521-21156-5); pap. 9.95x (ISBN 0-521-29061-9). Cambridge U Pr.
Richter, N., jt. auth. see Hoegner, W.
Richter, P., jt. auth. see La Fauci, H. M.
Richter, Peyton E., jt. auth. see Fogg, Walter L.
Richter, Peyton E., ed. Perspectives in Aesthetics: Plato to Camus. LC 66-19066. (Orig.). 1967. pap. 8.50 (ISBN 0-672-63082-6). Odyssey Pr.
Richter, S., jt. auth. see Forcese, D.
Richter, Steffen, jt. ed. see Mehrtens, Herbert.
Richterich, R. Clinical Chemistry: Theory, Practice & Interpretation. Colombo, J. P., ed. 672p. 1981. price not set (ISBN 0-471-27809-2, Pub. by Wiley-Interscience). Wiley.
Richthofen, Manfred Von see Von Richthofen, Manfred.
Richtmyer, Robert D. & Morton, K. W. Difference Methods for Initial-Value Problems. 2nd ed. LC 67-13959. (Pure & Applied Mathematics Ser.). (Illus.). 1967. 37.95 (ISBN 0-470-72040-9, Pub. by Wiley-Interscience). Wiley.
Rickard, Henry C., ed. Behavioral Intervention in Human Problems. LC 76-112398. 434p. 1971. 31.00 (ISBN 0-08-016327-0); pap. 11.55 (ISBN 0-08-017737-9). Pergamon.
Rickard, Jack, jt. auth. see Silverstone, Lou.
Rickard, Jack, jt. auth. see Siverstone, Lou.
Rickard, P., jt. auth. see Combe, T. G.
Rickard, P., ed. Chrestomathie de la Langue Francaise au Quinzieme Siecle. LC 74-12976. 464p. 1976. 115.00 (ISBN 0-521-20685-5). Cambridge U Pr.
Rickard, P., ed. see Harmer, Lewis.
Rickard, Peter. A History of the French Language. (Modern Languages Ser). 174p. 1974. text ed. 10.75x (ISBN 0-09-118740-0, Hutchinson U Lib); pap. text ed. 9.25x (ISBN 0-09-118741-9). Humanities.
--Langue Francaise au Seizieme Siecle. (Illus., Fr.). 1968. 74.00 (ISBN 0-521-06921-1). Cambridge U Pr.
Rickards, Colin, ed. The Caribbean Year Book 1979-1980. 50th ed. (Illus.). 1980. pap. 45.00x (ISBN 0-8002-2717-4). Intl Pubns Serv.
Rickards, Ralph. Understanding Medical Terms: A Self-Instructional Course. (Illus.). 112p. 1980. pap. text ed. 7.95 (ISBN 0-443-02029-9). Churchill.
Rickards, T., jt. auth. see Carson, J. W.
Rickels, Milton & Rickels, Patricia. Seba Smith. (U.S. Authors Ser.: No. 283). 1977. lib. bdg. 10.95 (ISBN 0-8057-7185-9). Twayne.
Rickels, Patricia, jt. auth. see Rickels, Milton.
Ricker, Kenneth S., jt. ed. see Hofman, Helenmarie.
Rickerson, Wayne. Family Fun & Togetherness. 1979. pap. 3.95 (ISBN 0-88207-641-8). Victor Bks.
Rickerson, Wayne E. Good Times for Your Family. LC 76-3934. (Orig.). 1976. pap. 3.25 o.p. (ISBN 0-8307-0427-2, 54-036-18). Regal.
--How to Help the Christian Home. LC 77-94923. 1978. pap. 3.25 (ISBN 0-8307-0588-0, 54-083-18). Regal.
Rickert, Edith, et al, eds. Chaucer's World. LC 48-6059. 1948. 25.00x (ISBN 0-231-01568-2); pap. 12.50x (ISBN 0-231-08530-3, 30). Columbia U Pr.
Rickert, R. T., ed. see Henslowe, Philip.
Rickert, Russell K. Astronomy & Space Exploration. 1974. text ed. 9.50 (ISBN 0-201-06431-6). A-W.
Ricketson, Anna & Ricketson, Walton, eds. Daniel Ricketson & His Friends: Letter, Poems, Sketches, Etc. LC 80-2513. 1981. Repr. of 1902 ed. 60.00 (ISBN 0-404-19061-8). AMS Pr.
Ricketson, Walton, jt. ed. see Ricketson, Anna.
Ricketson, William F., jt. auth. see Wilson, Jerome D.
Rickett, Adele A., tr. see Wang, Kuo-Wei.
Rickett, C. C. Drill for Skill. (Illus., Orig.). (gr. 9-10). 1946. pap. text ed. 3.92 (ISBN 0-87720-327-X). AMSCO Sch.
Ricketts, Carl E. El Lobo & Spanish Gold: A Texas Maverick in Mexico. LC 74-77508. (Illus.). 210p. 1974. 8.50 (ISBN 0-89052-006-2). Madrona Pr.
Ricketts, Edward F., jt. auth. see Steinbeck, John.
Ricketts, L. W., et al. EMP Radiation & Protective Techniques. LC 76-19091. 1976. 37.95 o.p. (ISBN 0-471-01403-6, Pub. by Wiley-Interscience). Wiley.
Ricketts, Martin J., jt. auth. see Webb, M. G.

Ricketts, S. W., jt. auth. see Rossdale, P. D.

Rickey, George. Constructivism. LC 67-27525. (Illus.). 1967. 25.00 o.s.i. (ISBN 0-8076-0426-7). Braziller.

Rickey, Michael & Street, Donald M., eds. The Sailing Encyclopedia. (Illus.). 1980. 29.95 (ISBN 0-690-01922-X). Lippincott.

Rickham, P. P. & Hecker, W. C. Management of the Burned Child. (Progress in Pediatric Surgery Ser.: Vol. 14). 1981. write for info. (ISBN 0-8067-1514-6). Urban & S.

Rickham, P. P. & Irving, Irene M. Neonatal Surgery. 2nd ed. 1978. 149.00x (ISBN 0-407-00069-0). Butterworths.

Ricklefs, M. C. Jogjakarta Under Sultan Mangkubumi 1749-1792: A History of the Division of Java. (London Oriental Ser: No. 30). 496p. 1974. text ed. 33.00x (ISBN 0-19-713578-1). Oxford U Pr.

Ricklefs, M. C. & Voorhoeve, P. Indonesian Manuscripts in Great Britain: A Catalogue of Manuscripts in Indonesian Languages in British Public Collections. (London Oriental Bibliographies 5). 1977. 55.00x (ISBN 0-19-713592-7). Oxford U Pr.

Rickles, Robert, jt. ed. see N. Y. Board of Trade.

Rickman, H. P. Wilhelm Dilthey: Pioneer of the Human Sciences. 1980. 16.50x (ISBN 0-520-03879-7). U of Cal Pr.

Rickman, John, ed. see Ferenczi, Sandor.

Ricks, Beatrice. Henry James: A Bibliography of Secondary Works. LC 75-22128. (Author Bibliographies Ser.: No. 24). 1975. 21.00 (ISBN 0-8108-0853-6). Scarecrow.

Ricks, Christopher, ed. A. E. Housman: A Collection of Critical Essays. (Twentieth Century Views Ser). 1968. 10.05 (ISBN 0-13-395913-9, Spec); pap. 1.95 (ISBN 0-13-395905-8, STC83, Spec). P-H.

--Poems & Critics. 1966. pap. 1.95 o.p. (ISBN 0-531-06037-3, Fontana Pap). Watts.

Ricks, David A. International Dimensions of Corporate Finance. LC 77-22693. (Foundations of Finance Ser.). (Illus.). 1978. pap. text ed. 10.95 (ISBN 0-13-471706-6). P-H.

Ricks, Eldin. Combination Reference. 3.95 o.p. (ISBN 0-87747-037-5); pocket ed. 2.50 (ISBN 0-87747-038-3). Deseret Bk.

Ricks, Truett A., et al. Principles of Security: An Introduction. (Illus.). 400p. 1981. text ed. price not set (ISBN 0-87084-744-9). Anderson Pub Co.

Rickwood, D., jt. auth. see Birnie, G. D.

Ricoeur, Paul. The Contribution of French Historiography to French History. (Zaharoff Lectures Ser.). 56p. 1980. pap. 8.95x (ISBN 0-19-952249-9). Oxford U Pr.

--Essays on Biblical Interpretation. Mudge, Lewis S., ed. LC 80-8052. 192p. (Orig.). 1980. pap. 7.95 (ISBN 0-8006-1407-0, 1-1407). Fortress.

--Freedom & Nature: The Voluntary & the Involuntary. Kohak, E. V., tr. (Studies in Phenomenology & Existential Philosophy Ser). 1966. 22.95x (ISBN 0-8101-0208-0); pap. 9.95x (ISBN 0-8101-0534-9). Northwestern U Pr.

--Freud & Philosophy: An Essay on Interpretation. Savage, Denis, tr. LC 70-89907. (Terry Lectures Ser). 1970. 30.00x (ISBN 0-300-01165-2); pap. 9.95 (ISBN 0-300-02189-5). Yale U Pr.

--Political & Social Essays. Stewart, David & Bien, Joseph, eds. LC 74-82500. ix, 293p. 1974. 15.00x (ISBN 0-8214-0169-6). Ohio U Pr.

Ricoeur, Paul, jt. auth. see MacIntyre, Alasdair.

Riddel, Alan. Eclipse. 1980. pap. 3.95 (ISBN 0-7145-0908-6). Riverrun NY.

Riddel, Joseph N. C. Day Lewis. (English Authors Ser.: No. 124). 1971. lib. bdg. 10.95 (ISBN 0-8057-1336-0). Twayne.

Riddell, Bob. Life on Ye Ol' Homestead: Tucson Mountains. (Illus.). 100p. (Orig.). 1980. pap. 3.95 (ISBN 0-9604184-0-7). Roberts Ent.

Riddell, C., jt. auth. see Coulson, Margaret A.

Riddell, Charlotte. Maxwell Drewitt. (Nineteenth Century Fiction Ser.: Ireland: Vol. 62). 888p. 1979. lib. bdg. 46.00 (ISBN 0-8240-3511-9). Garland Pub.

--The Nun's Curse. (Nineteenth Century Fiction Ser.: Ireland: Vol. 63). 932p. 1979. lib. bdg. 46.00 (ISBN 0-8240-3512-7). Garland Pub.

Riddell, James. Up & Down on the Farm. (Illus.). 32p. (ps-4). 1981. 7.95 (ISBN 0-224-01709-8, Pub. by Chatto-Bodley-Jonathan). Merrimack Bk Serv.

Riddell, Robert. Ecodevelopment. 1980. 27.50 (ISBN 0-312-22585-7). St Martin.

Riddell, Thomas A., et al. Economics: A Tool for Understanding Society. LC 78-62552. (Economics Ser.). (Illus.). 1979. text ed. 12.95 (ISBN 0-201-06352-2); instr's manual avail. (ISBN 0-201-06353-0). A-W.

Riddick, John A. see Weissberger, A.

Riddle, Douglas F. Analytic Geometry with Vectors. 2nd ed. 1978. 18.95x (ISBN 0-534-00485-7). Wadsworth Pub.

--Calculus & Analytic Geometry. 3rd ed. 1979. text ed. 29.95x (ISBN 0-534-00626-4). Wadsworth Pub.

Riddle, Janet T. & Dinner, Joan. Objective Tests for Nurses, Book 2. (Objective Tests for Nurses Ser.). (Illus.). 112p. 1981. pap. text ed. 6.95 (ISBN 0-443-01740-9). Churchill.

Riddle, Katharine P., jt. ed. see Taylor, Clara M.

Riddle, Marilyn R. Poems from the Oregon Sea Coast. (Illus.). 24p. (Orig.). 1979. pap. 3.00 large type ed. (ISBN 0-9603748-0-9). Sandpiper OR.

--Unicorns for Everyone: Large Type. (Illus.). 24p. (Orig.). (gr. k-12). 1980. pap. 3.00 (ISBN 0-9603748-1-7, 200). Sandpiper OR.

Riddle, Maxwell. Your Family Dog: The Complete Guide to Choosing, Caring for, Training & Showing. LC 78-60299. (Illus.). 528p. 1981. 16.95 (ISBN 0-385-12707-3). Doubleday.

Riddle, R. M. Pathology of Drug Induced & Tonic Diseases. 1981. text ed. write for info. (ISBN 0-443-08083-6). Churchill.

Riddle, W. E. & Fairley, R. E. Software Development Tools. (Illus.). 280p. 1980. pap. 19.80 (ISBN 0-387-10326-0). Springer-Verlag.

Ride, W. D. Guide to the Native Mammals of Australia. (Illus.). 1970. 32.00x (ISBN 0-19-550252-3). Oxford U Pr.

Ridenhour, Thomas E., jt. auth. see Micks, Marianne H.

Ridenour, Crea. Ocupate En Ensenar. 1979. pap. 0.95 (ISBN 0-311-11031-2). Casa Bautista.

Ridenour, Fritz. Faith It or Fake It? LC 73-120783. 1978. pap. 1.95 (ISBN 0-8307-0441-8, S114-1-86). Regal.

--How Do You Handle Life? 1976. pap. 1.95 (ISBN 0-8307-0430-2, S104156). Regal.

--How to Be a Christian in an Unchristian World. rev. ed. LC 72-169603. (Orig.). 1972. pap. 1.95 (ISBN 0-8307-0611-9, S123150). Regal.

--How to Be a Christian Without Being Religious. (Illus.). (gr. 9-12). 1967. pap. 1.95 (ISBN 0-8307-0435-3, S121158). Regal.

--I'm a Good Man, But. LC 75-96702. 1969. pap. 1.95 (ISBN 0-8307-0429-9, S102153). Regal.

--The Other Side of Morality. LC 68-8388. (Orig.). 1969. pap. 1.85 o.p. (ISBN 0-8307-0040-4, S112-1-59). Regal.

Ridenour, Fritz, tr. Di las Cosas Como Son. (Spanish Bks.). (Span.). 1978. 1.90 (ISBN 0-8297-0862-6). Life Pubs Intl.

--Le Dire Tel Quel. (French Bks.). (Fr.). 1979. 2.05 (ISBN 0-686-28822-X). Life Pubs Intl.

--Quien Dice? (Spanish Bks.). (Span.). 1978. 1.90 (ISBN 0-8297-0440-X). Life Pubs Intl.

Ridenour, Fritz, et al, eds. Who Says? LC 68-16268. (Illus., Orig.). (YA) 1968. pap. 1.85 o.p. (ISBN 0-8307-0002-1, S123118). Regal.

Ridenour, Nina & Johnson, Isabel. Some Special Problems of Children Aged 2-5. 1976. pap. 1.50 (ISBN 0-686-12268-2). Jewish Bd Family.

Rider, Alice D. A Story of Books & Libraries. LC 76-7596. 183p. 1976. 10.00 (ISBN 0-8108-0930-3). Scarecrow.

Rider, Don K. Energy: Hydrocarbon Fuels & Chemical Resources. 600p. 1981. 40.00 (ISBN 0-471-05915-3, Pub. by Wiley-Interscience). Wiley.

Rider, John R. Your Future in Broadcasting. LC 70-146047. (Career Guidance Ser). 125p. 1974. pap. 3.50 (ISBN 0-668-03427-0). Arco.

Rider, K. J. History of Science & Technology: A Select Bibliography. 1970. 13.75x (ISBN 0-85365-144-2, Pub. by Lib Assn England). Oryx Pr.

Rider, R. H. Teachers Skills. 1979. text ed. cancelled (ISBN 0-06-318115-0, Pub. by Har-Row Ltd England). Har-Row.

Rider, Warrick W. Dyed for Death. (Orig.). 1980. pap. 1.95 (ISBN 0-505-51497-4). Tower Bks.

Ridge, Antonia. For Love of a Rose. 1965. 8.95 (ISBN 0-571-06469-8, Pub. by Faber & Faber); pap. 4.95 (ISBN 0-571-10118-6). Merrimack Bk Serv.

--The Thirteenth Child. 1962. 3.95 o.p. (ISBN 0-571-07068-X, Pub. by Faber & Faber). Merrimack Bk Serv.

Ridge, Antonia & Bouhuys, Mies. Melodia: The Dutch Street-Organ. (Illus.). (ps-5). 1969. 6.95 (ISBN 0-571-08721-3, Pub. by Faber & Faber). Merrimack Bk Serv.

Ridge, Antonia, et al. Hurray for a Dutch Birthday. (Illus.). (ps-5). 1964. 6.95 (ISBN 0-571-06025-0, Pub. by Faber & Faber). Merrimack Bk Serv.

Ridge, G. R. The Hero in French Decadent Literature. LC 61-17538. 5.00 (ISBN 0-910294-23-2). Brown Bk.

--The Hero in French Romantic Literature. LC 59-14610. 5.00 (ISBN 0-910294-24-0). Brown Bk.

Ridgely-Nevitt, Cedric. American Steamships on the Atlantic, 3 vols. LC 78-66835. 550p. 1980. 75.00 (ISBN 0-87413-140-5). U Delaware Pr.

Ridgeway, James. Politics of Ecology. 1971. 6.95 o.p. (ISBN 0-525-18108-3); pap. 2.25 (ISBN 0-525-47304-1). Dutton.

Ridgeway, Rick. The Boldest Dream: The Story of Twelve Who Climbed Mount Everest. LC 78-14080. (Illus.). 1979. 10.95 (ISBN 0-15-113432-4). HarBraceJ.

--The Last Step: The American Ascent of K2. LC 80-19395. (Illus.). 400p. 1980. 25.00 (ISBN 0-89886-007-5). Mountaineers.

Ridgman, W. J. Experimentation in Biology: An Introduction to Design & Analysis. (Tertiary Level Biology Ser). 234p. 1976. pap. text ed. 14.95 (ISBN 0-470-15216-8). Halsted Pr.

Ridgway, A. & Thumm, W. Physics of Medical Radiography. 1968. 21.95 (ISBN 0-201-06460-X). A-W.

Ridgway, David, ed. see Pallottino, Massimo.

Ridiman, Bob. Simple Science Fun: Experiments with Light, Sound, Air & Water. LC 72-664. (A Humpty Dumpty Bk). (Illus.). 56p. (gr. k-3). 1972. 5.95 o.s.i. (ISBN 0-8193-0606-1, Four Winds); PLB 5.41 o.s.i. (ISBN 0-8193-0607-X). Schol Bk Serv.

--What Is a Shadow? Experiences with Gravity, Shadows, Mirrors & Electricity. LC 73-4368. (A Humpty Dumpty Bk.). (Illus.). 52p. (gr. k-3). 1973. 5.95 o.s.i. (ISBN 0-8193-0688-6, Four Winds); PLB 5.41 o.s.i. (ISBN 0-8193-0689-4). Schol Bk Serv.

Ridker, Ronald. Employment in South Asia: Problems, Prospects & Prescriptions. (Occasional Papers: No. 1). 74p. 1971. 1.00 (ISBN 0-686-28697-9). Overseas Dev Council.

Ridker, Ronald G. & Watson, William D., Jr. To Choose a Future. LC 79-3643. (Resources for the Future Ser.). 1980. 33.50x (ISBN 0-8018-2354-4). Johns Hopkins.

Ridler, Anne B., ed. Shakespeare Criticism, 1935-1960. (Oxford Paperbacks Ser). 1970. pap. 4.95x o.p. (ISBN 0-19-281082-0). Oxford U Pr.

Ridley, F. & Blondel, J. Public Administration in France. new ed. 1969. 25.00x (ISBN 0-7100-2037-6). Routledge & Kegan.

Ridley, F. F. Revolutionary Syndicalism in France. LC 73-123663. 1971. 38.50 (ISBN 0-521-07907-1). Cambridge U Pr.

--The Study of Government: Political Science & Public Administration. 1975. text ed. 25.00x (ISBN 0-04-320106-7); pap. text ed. 8.95x (ISBN 0-04-320107-5). Allen Unwin.

Ridley, Gordon, jt. auth. see Emmett, John.

Ridley, Hugh, tr. see Bley, Helmut.

Ridley, James. The History of James Lovegrove, Esq., 1761, 2 vols. in 1. (The Flowering of the Novel, 1740-1775 Ser: Vol. 58). 1974. lib. bdg. 50.00 (ISBN 0-8240-1157-0). Garland Pub.

Ridley, John H. Gynecologic Surgery: Errors, Safeguards, & Salvage. 430p. 1974. 27.00 o.p. (ISBN 0-683-07276-5). Williams & Wilkins.

Ridley, Michael. Buddhism. (Illus.). 1979. 14.95 (ISBN 0-7137-0886-7, Pub. by Blandford Pr England). Sterling.

--Megalithic Art of the Maltese Islands. (Illus.). 1978. 9.95 o.p. (ISBN 0-85642-056-5, Pub. by Blanford Pr England); pap. 3.50 o.p. (ISBN 0-85642-057-3). Sterling.

Ridley, Nancy. Portrait of Northumberland. LC 66-5457. (Portrait Bks.). (Illus.). 1966. 10.50x (ISBN 0-7091-6070-4). Intl Pubns Serv.

Ridlon, Marci. Kittens & More Kittens. (Beginning-to-Read Ser.). (Illus.). (gr. 2-4). 1967. pap. 1.50 o.p. (ISBN 0-695-34868-X). Follett.

Ridout, Ronald & Serraillier, Ian. The Wide Horizon Reading Scheme. Incl. Introductory Stage. Look Alive (ISBN 0-435-11771-8); Introductory Stage. Making Good (ISBN 0-435-11772-6); Introductory Stage. The Cave of Death (ISBN 0-435-11773-4); Stage One. I Dare You (ISBN 0-435-11774-2); Stage One. Jungle Adventure (ISBN 0-435-11775-0); Stage One. Katy at Home (ISBN 0-435-11770-X); Stage Two. Read to Enjoy (ISBN 0-435-11776-9); Stage Two. The Adventure of Dick Varley (ISBN 0-435-11777-7); Stage Two. Guns in the Wild (ISBN 0-435-11778-5); Stage Two. Katy at School (ISBN 0-435-11779-3); Stage Three. To Please You (ISBN 0-435-11780-7); Stage Three. Treasure Ahead (ISBN 0-435-11781-5); Stage Four. Whatever the Odds (ISBN 0-435-11782-3); Stage Four. Mountain Rescue (ISBN 0-435-11783-1); Stage Four. Fight for Freedom (ISBN 0-435-11784-X). (gr. 6-9). pap. text ed. 3.25x ea. o.p. Heinemann Ed.

Ridout, Samuel. The Church & Its Order According to Scripture. Date not set. pap. 1.95 (ISBN 0-87213-711-2). Loizeaux.

Ridpath, George. The Stage Condemn'd. LC 79-170443. (The English Stage Ser.: Vol. 29). lib. bdg. 50.00 (ISBN 0-8240-0612-7). Garland Pub.

Ridpath, Ian, ed. The Illustrated Encyclopedia of Astronomy & Space. LC 76-3577. (Illus.). 1976. 17.95 (ISBN 0-690-01132-6, TYC-T). T Y Crowell.

Ridson, R. A., jt. auth. see Ransley, P. G.

Rie, Ellen D., jt. ed. see Rie, Herbert E.

Rie, Herbert E. & Rie, Ellen D., eds. Handbook of Minimal Brain Dysfunctions: A Critical View. LC 78-25656. (Personality Processes Ser.). 1980. 44.50 (ISBN 0-471-02959-9, Pub. by Wiley-Interscience). Wiley.

Rieber, Robert W., ed. Psychology of Language & Thought: Essays on the Theory & History of Psycholinguistics. (Applied Psycholinguistics & Communication Disorders Ser.). (Illus.). 280p. 1980. 27.50 (ISBN 0-306-40361-7, Plenum Pr). Plenum Pub.

--Wilhelm Wundt & the Making of a Scientific Psychology. 260p. 1980. 24.50 (ISBN 0-306-40483-4, Plenum Pr). Plenum Pub.

Rieber, Robert W. & Salzinger, Kurt, eds. Psychology: Theoretical-Historical Perspectives. LC 79-6790. 1980. 21.00 (ISBN 0-12-588265-3). Acad Pr.

Rieber, Robert W., jt. ed. see Vetter, Harold J.

Rieche, Alfred. Outline of Industrial Organic Chemistry. 1968. 50.00 o.p. (ISBN 0-8206-0233-7). Chem Pub.

Riechel, Klaus-Walter. Economic Effects of Exchange-Rate Changes. new ed. LC 78-58926. 1978. 17.95 (ISBN 0-669-02376-0). Lexington Bks.

Riechert, T. Stereotactic Brain Operations: Methods, Clinical Aspects, Indications. (Illus.). 387p. 1980. 120.00 (ISBN 3-456-80457-1, Pub. by Hans Huber). J K Burgess.

Riecken, Henry W., ed. see Social Science Research Council Conference on Social Experiments.

Riede, David C. & Baker, J. Wayne. The Western Intellectual Tradition: Greece Through the Middle Ages, Vol. 1. 208p. 1980. pap. text ed. 8.50 (ISBN 0-8403-2259-3). Kendall-Hunt.

Riede, David G. Swinburne: A Study of Romantic Mythmaking. LC 78-4940. 1978. 12.95x (ISBN 0-8139-0745-4). U Pr of Va.

Riedel, Eunice, et al. The Book of the Bible. 560p. 1981. pap. 3.95 (ISBN 0-553-14649-1). Bantam.

Riedel, Manfred. Odds & Chances for Kids: A Look at Probability. (Illus.). (gr. 5-9). 1979. PLB 8.95 (ISBN 0-13-630442-7). P-H.

Riedel, Marc & Vales, Pedro A., eds. Treating the Offender: Problems & Issues. LC 76-12870. 1977. text ed. 24.50 (ISBN 0-275-56350-2). Praeger.

Riedel, W. R., jt. auth. see Funnell, B. M.

Riedesel, C. Alan. Guiding Discovery to Elementary School Math. 2nd ed. 1973. text ed. 19.95 (ISBN 0-13-371583-3). P-H.

--Teaching Elementary School Mathematics. (Illus.). 1980. text ed. 18.95 (ISBN 0-13-892549-6). P-H.

Riedl, Frederick. History of Hungarian Literature. Ginever, C. A., tr. LC 68-26602. 1968. Repr. of 1906 ed. 18.00 (ISBN 0-8103-3221-3). Gale.

Riedler, W., ed. Scientific Ballooning: Proceedings of a Symposium of the 21st Plenary Meeting of the Committee on Space Research, Innsbruck, Austria, May 29-June 10 1978. LC 78-41182. (Illus.). 226p. 63.00 (ISBN 0-08-023420-8). Pergamon.

Riedlsperger, Max E. Lingering Shadow of Nazism. (Eastern European Monographs: No. 42). 1978. 14.00x (ISBN 0-914710-35-4, Dist. by Columbia U Pr). East Eur Quarterly.

Riedman, Sarah. Allergies. (First Books Ser.). (Illus.). (gr. 4-6). 1978. PLB 6.45 s&l (ISBN 0-531-01352-9). Watts.

Riedman, Sarah R. Diabetes. (gr. 4 up). 1980. PLB 6.45 (ISBN 0-531-04107-7). Watts.

--Gardening Without Soil. LC 78-13088. (First Bks.). (Illus.). (gr. 4-6). 1979. PLB 6.45 s&l (ISBN 0-531-02256-0). Watts.

--Sharks. (Easy-Read Fact Bks.). (Illus.). (gr. 2-4). 1977. PLB 6.45 (ISBN 0-531-01314-6). Watts.

--Spiders. (Easy-Read Fact Bks.). (Illus.). (gr. 2-4). 1979. PLB 6.45 s&l (ISBN 0-531-02853-4). Watts.

Riedmann. The Story of Adamsville. 128p. 1980. pap. text ed. 3.95x (ISBN 0-534-00823-2). Wadsworth Pub.

Riefe, Alan. The Conspirators. (Cage Ser.: No. 2). 176p. 1975. pap. 0.95 o.p. (ISBN 0-445-00650-1). Popular Lib.

--Fire in the Wind. 1976. pap. 1.25 o.p. (ISBN 0-445-00423-1). Popular Lib.

--Killer with the Golden Touch. (Cage Ser.: No. 6). 176p. (Orig.). 1975. pap. 0.95 o.p. (ISBN 0-445-00672-2). Popular Lib.

--The Lady Killers. (Cage Ser.: No. 1). 176p. 1975. pap. 0.95 o.p. (ISBN 0-445-00649-8). Popular Lib.

Riefe, Barbara. Wild Fire. LC 80-83569. 384p. (Orig.). 1981. pap. 2.95 (ISBN 0-87216-798-4). Playboy Pbks.

Riegel, K. F. & Rosenwald, G. C. Structure & Transformation: Development & Historical Aspects. (Origins of Behavior Ser.: Vol. 3). 1975. 27.95 (ISBN 0-471-72140-9). Wiley.

Riegel, Klaus F. Psychology, Mon Amour: A Countertext. LC 77-89422. (Illus.). 1978. pap. text ed. 9.50 (ISBN 0-395-25748-4). HM.

Riegel, O. U. Crown of Glory: Life of J. J. Strang, Moses, of the Mormons. 1935. 45.00x (ISBN 0-685-69857-2). Elliots Bks.

Riegel, R. & Miller, J. Insurance Principles & Practices: Property & Liability. 6th ed. 1976. text ed. 20.95 (ISBN 0-13-468868-6). P-H.

Riegel, Robert E. The Story of the Western Railroads: From 1852 Through the Reign of the Giants. LC 26-9772. 1964. 14.95x (ISBN 0-8032-0903-7); pap. 7.25 (ISBN 0-8032-5159-9, BB 183, Bison). U of Nebr Pr.

Riegel, Rodney P. & Lovell, Ned B. Minimum Competency Testing. LC 79-93113. (Fastback Ser.: No. 137). (Orig.). 1980. pap. 0.75 (ISBN 0-87367-137-6). Phi Delta Kappa.

Rieger, James. Mutiny Within. LC 67-12475. (Orig.). 6.50 (ISBN 0-8076-0400-3); pap. 2.50 (ISBN 0-8076-0409-7). Braziller.

Rieger, James H., ed. see Shelley, Mary W.

Riegert, Eduard & Hiers, Richard H. Pentecost 2. LC 75-24960. (Proclamation 1: Aids for Interpreting the Lessons of the Church Year, Ser. B). 64p. 1965. pap. 1.95 (ISBN 0-8006-4077-2, 1-4077). Fortress.

Riegert, Paul W. From Arsenic to DDT: A History of Entomology in Western Canada. 400p. 1980. 30.00x (ISBN 0-8020-5499-4). U of Toronto Pr.

Riegler, Hubert F. & Peppard, Alan P. Surface Anatomy for Coaches & Athletic Trainers. (Illus.). 80p. 1979. pap. 10.75 spiral (ISBN 0-398-03856-2). C C Thomas.

Riehl, C. Luise. Emergency Nursing. (YA) (gr. 9 up). 1970. 10.64 (ISBN 0-87002-009-9). Bennett IL.

--Family Nursing. (Illus.). 384p. 1974. text ed. 15.00 (ISBN 0-87002-154-0). Bennett IL.

Riehl, Herbert, jt. auth. see Simpson, Robert H.

Riehl, Jospeh E. Charles Lamb's Children's Literature. (Romantic Reassessment Ser.: No. 94). 1980. pap. text ed. 25.00x (ISBN 0-391-02189-3). Humanities.

Riehle, Wolfgang. The Middle English Mystics. 256p. 1981. 32.50 (ISBN 0-7100-0612-8). Routledge & Kegan.

Riehn, Rainer, ed. Musik Wozu. (Edition Suhrkamp: Vol. 684). (Orig.). 1980. pap. text ed. 7.80 (ISBN 3-518-10684-8, Pub. by Insel Verlag Germany). Suhrkamp.

Riehn, Richard K., tr. see Udet, Ernst.

Rieke, Richard D. & Sillars, Malcolm O. Argumentation & the Decision Making Process. LC 74-20900. 288p. 1975. 13.95 (ISBN 0-471-72165-4). Wiley.

Riekes, Linda & Ackerly, Salley M. Lawmaking. 2nd ed. (Law in Action Ser.). (Illus.). (gr. 5-9). 1980. pap. 4.00 (ISBN 0-8299-1023-9); tchrs.' ed. 4.00 (ISBN 0-8299-1024-7). West Pub.

Riely, John C. The Age of Horace Walpole in Caricature: An Exhibition of Satirical Prints & Drawings from the Collection of W. S. Lewis. 48p. 1981. pap. text ed. 5.00x (ISBN 0-300-03509-8, 73-88450). Yale U Pr.

Riemann, H. Food-Borne Infections & Intoxications. (Food Science & Technology Ser. of Monographs). 1969. 67.50 o.p. (ISBN 0-12-588350-1). Acad Pr.

Riemann, Hugo. Dictionary of Music. LC 75-125060. (Music Ser). 1970. Repr. of 1908 ed. lib. bdg. 65.00 (ISBN 0-306-70025-5). Da Capo.

--History of Music Theory. rev. ed. Haggh, Raymond, tr. LC 75-125060. (Music Ser.). 435p. 1974. Repr. of 1966 ed. lib. bdg. 35.00 (ISBN 0-306-70637-7). Da Capo.

--Opern-Handbuch. LC 80-2295. 1981. 75.00 (ISBN 0-404-18864-8). AMS Pr.

Riemer, A. P. Antic Fables: Patterns of Evasion in Shakespeare's Comedies. LC 80-13330. 1980. 18.95 (ISBN 0-312-04369-4). St Martin.

Riemer, A. P., ed. Macbeth. 1980. pap. 3.50x (ISBN 0-424-00081-4, Pub. by Sydney U Pr Australia). Intl Schol Bk Serv.

Riemer, Edwin & Leibling, Louis. Barron's How to Prepare for Civil Service Examinations: Clerks, Stenographers, Typists. 4th ed. (Barron's Educational Ser.). 405p. 1981. pap. text ed. 5.95 (ISBN 0-8120-2033-2). Barron.

Riemer, Ruth, jt. auth. see Broom, Leonard.

Riemsdijk, H. C. A Case Study in Syntactic Markedness: The Binding Nature of Prepositional Phrases. 1978. pap. text ed. 23.00x o.p. (ISBN 90-316-0160-8). Humanities.

Riencourt, Amaury de see De Riencourt, Amaury.

Riepe, D. Indian Philosophy Since Independence. (Philosophical Currents Ser.: No. 25). 403p. 1980. text ed. 34.25x (ISBN 90-6032-113-8). Humanities.

Riepe; Dan, ed. Asian Philosophy Today. 300p. 1980. write for info. (ISBN 0-677-05530-7). Gordon.

Riera, Russell S. & Smith, Chris. Two Hundred Good Restaurants: A Guide to Eating in San Francisco & the Bay Area. 2nd ed. LC 80-81377. 1980. pap. 3.25 (ISBN 0-930870-02-6). Moss Pubns.

Ries, Al & Trout, Jack. Positioning: The Battle for Your Mind. 224p. 1980. 10.95 (ISBN 0-07-065263-5, P&RB). McGraw.

Ries, Lawrence R. Wolf Masks: Violence in Contemporary Poetry. LC 76-30540. (National University Pubns. Literary Criticism Ser.). 1977. 12.95 (ISBN 0-8046-9168-1). Kennikat.

Ries, Peter W., jt. auth. see Jack, Susan S.

Riesbeck, Christopher K., jt. auth. see Schank, Roger C.

Riese, Alan W. & LaSalle, Herbert J. All About the Dictionary. (Orig.). (gr. 8-11). 1976. pap. text ed. 5.25 (ISBN 0-87720-330-X). AMSCO Sch.

Riese, Walther. History of Neurology. LC 58-10645. (Illus.). 1959. 4.00 o.p. (ISBN 0-910922-09-8). MD Pubns.

Rieselbach, Leroy N. Legislative Reform. LC 77-223. (Policy Studies Organization Ser.). (Illus.). 1978. 18.95 (ISBN 0-669-01436-2). Lexington Bks.

--Roots of Isolationism: Congressional Voting & Presidential Leadership in Foreign Policy. (Orig.). 1966. 9.50 (ISBN 0-672-51169-X); pap. 4.35 o.p. (ISBN 0-672-60770-0). Bobbs.

Riesen, A. H. & Thompson, R. F. Advances in Psychobiology, Vol. 3. LC 70-178148. 1976. 37.50 (ISBN 0-471-72173-5). Wiley.

Riesen, Austin H. & Kinder, E. F. Postural Development of Infant Chimpanzees. 1952. 42.50x (ISBN 0-685-69858-0). Elliots Bks.

Riesenberg, Felix. Story of the Naval Academy. (Landmark Ser, No. 84). (Illus.). (gr. 4-6). 1958. PLB 4.39 o.p. (ISBN 0-394-90384-6). Random.

Riesenfeld, Stefan A. Cases & Materials on Creditors' Remedies & Debtors' Protection. 3rd ed. LC 79-9357. (American Casebook Ser.). 810p. 1979. text ed. 20.95 (ISBN 0-8299-2060-9). West Pub.

Rieser, Max. The True Founder of Christianity & the Hellenistic Philosophy. 1980. text ed. 14.25x (ISBN 90-6296-081-2). Humanities.

Riesman, D., ed. see Carnegie Commission on Higher Education.

Riesman, David. On Higher Education: Origins & Consequences of the Academic Counterrevolution in America. LC 80-8007. (Carnegie Council Ser.). 1981. text ed. 15.95 (ISBN 0-87589-484-4). Jossey-Bass.

Riesman, David, ed. see Carnegie Commission on Higher Education.

Riesner, Dieter, jt. auth. see Schweik, Robert C.

Riess, Fred, jt. auth. see Lucas, Ted.

Riess, R. Dean, jt. auth. see Johnson, Lee W.

Riess, Steven A. Touching Base: Professional Baseball & American Culture in the Progressive Era. LC 79-6570. (Contributions in American Studies: No. 48). (Illus.). xv, 268p. 1980. lib. bdg. 22.95 (ISBN 0-313-20671-6, RTB/). Greenwood.

Riessman, F., jt. auth. see Pearl, Arthur.

Riestra, Miguel A. Fundamentos Filosoficos De la Educacion. 3rd ed. 5.00 o.s.i. (ISBN 0-8477-2716-5); pap. 4.35 o.s.i. (ISBN 0-8477-2717-3). U of PR Pr.

Riethmuller, Gert, et al, eds. Natural & Induced Cell-Mediated Cytotoxicity: Effector & Regulatory Mechanisms. LC 79-14162. (Perspectives in Immunology Ser.). 1979. 19.00 (ISBN 0-12-584650-9). Acad Pr.

Riethmuller, John. Ports of the World, Nineteen Eighty. 33rd ed. LC 48-3083. (Illus.). 1076p. 1980. 100.00x (ISBN 0-510-49156-1). Intl Pubns Serv.

Rietti, Mario. Money & Banking in Latin America. LC 79-4157. 1979. 24.95 (ISBN 0-03-049156-8). Praeger.

Rietz, Carl A. Guide to the Selection, Combination & Cooking of Foods, 2 vols. Incl. Vol. 1. Selection & Combination. 1961. 28.00 o.p. (ISBN 0-87055-032-2); Vol. 2. Formulation & Cookery. 1965. 30.00 o.p. (ISBN 0-87055-033-0). (Illus.). AVI.

Rieux, Jacques, ed. see Arnauld, Antoine & Lancelot, Claude.

Rife, Carl B. Celebrating the Church Year: A Children's Worship Service. 1980. pap. text ed. 0.95 (ISBN 0-89536-443-3). CSS Pub.

Rife, John M. & Rife, W. R. John & Mary J. Rife of Greene County Ohio: Their Ancestors & Descendants. LC 80-83318. 1980. 5.00. Reiff Pr.

Rife, W. R., jt. auth. see Rife, John M.

Rifelj, Carol D., jt. auth. see Knox, Edward C.

Riffle, Kathryn L., ed. Rehabilitative Nursing Case Studies. 1979. pap. 9.50 (ISBN 0-87488-035-1). Med Exam.

Rifkin, Harold & Raskin, Philip, eds. Diabetes Mellitus, Vol. 5. new ed. (Illus.). 391p. 1980. text ed. 22.95 (ISBN 0-87619-747-0). R J Brady.

Rifkin, Jeremy & Howard, Ted. Entropy: A New World View. 324p. 1980. 11.95 (ISBN 0-670-29717-8). Viking Pr.

--Who Should Play God ? 1977. pap. 2.25 o.s.i. (ISBN 0-440-19504-7). Dell.

--Who Should Play God? 1977. 8.95 o.p. (ISBN 0-440-09552-2). Delacorte.

Rifkin, Natalie, ed. see Johnson, Fred.

Rifkin, Natalie, ed. see LaBastille, Anne.

Riforgiato, Leonard R. Missionary of Moderation: Henry Melchior Muhlenberg & the Lutheran Church in English America. LC 78-75203. 256p. Date not set. 19.50 (ISBN 0-8387-2379-9). Bucknell U Pr.

Riga, Peter J. The Death of the American Republic. LC 80-67050. (Scholarly Monographs). 250p. 1980. pap. 20.00 (ISBN 0-8408-0511-X). Carrollton Pr.

Rigaudy, J. & Klesney, S. P., eds. Nomenclature of Organic Chemistry: The Blue Book: 1978 Ed. Sections A-F & H. 1978. text ed. 82.00 (ISBN 0-08-022369-9). Pergamon.

Rigauer, Bero. Sport & Work. Guttmann, Allen, ed. 110p. (Eng.). 1981. 12.50x (ISBN 0-231-05200-6). Columbia U Pr.

Rigby, Andrew. Alternative Realities: A Study of Communes & Their Members. (International Library of Sociology). 1974. 25.00 (ISBN 0-7100-7715-7). Routledge & Kegan.

--Communes in Britain. 1974. 13.50 (ISBN 0-7100-7906-0). Routledge & Kegan.

Rigby, D. Sue, jt. auth. see Hanson, Robert N.

Rigby, Ida K. Karl Hofer. LC 75-23811. (Outstanding Dissertations in the Fine Arts - 20th Century). (Illus.). 1976. lib. bdg. 45.00 (ISBN 0-8240-2005-7). Garland Pub.

Rigby, J. Keith, jt. auth. see Petersen, Morris S.

Rigby, Keith, Jr., jt. ed. see Lucas, Spencer.

Rigby, T. H. Lenin's Government. LC 78-18754. (Soviet & East European Studies). 1979. 44.50 (ISBN 0-521-22281-8). Cambridge U Pr.

Rigdon, Charles. The Hamptons. 1979. pap. 2.50 o.p. (ISBN 0-523-40232-5). Pinnacle Bks.

Rigdon, R. H. Trauma & Cancer: Pathology for the Lawyer. 232p. 1975. 21.75 (ISBN 0-398-03441-9). C C Thomas.

Rigdon, Raymond, jt. auth. see Colson, Howard.

Rigdon, Raymond M., jt. auth. see Colson, Howard P.

Riger, Robert. The Athlete: Writings, Drawings, Photographs & Television Sports; an Original Collection of 25 Years of Work. 1980. 24.95 (ISBN 0-671-24940-1). S&S.

Rigg, A. G. Glastonbury Miscellany of the 15th Century: A Descriptive Index of Trinity College. (Oxford English Monographs). 1968. 5.00x o.p. (ISBN 0-19-811713-2). Oxford U Pr.

Rigg, Donald C. & Kramer, Melinda G. Prentice-Hall Workbook for Writers. 2nd ed. LC 77-26898. 1978. pap. text ed. 7.95 (ISBN 0-13-696039-1). P-H.

Rigg, George, ed. Editing Medieval Texts. LC 76-52722. (Conference on Editorial Problems Ser.: Vol. 12). 1977. lib. bdg. 16.50 (ISBN 0-8240-2426-5). Garland Pub.

Riggar, S. W., jt. auth. see Riggar, T. F.

Riggar, T. F. & Riggar, S. W. Career Education & Rehabilitation for the Mentally Handicapped. (Illus.). 272p. 1980. text ed. 24.75 (ISBN 0-398-04137-7). C C Thomas.

Rigge, Simon. War in the Outposts. Editors of Time-Life Books, ed. (World War II Ser.). (Illus.). 208p. 1981. 13.95 (ISBN 0-8094-3379-6). Time-Life.

Riggle, H. M. Beyond the Tomb. 288p. 4.00. Faith Pub Hse.

--Christian Baptism, Feet Washing & the Lord's Supper. 264p. 3.50. Faith Pub Hse.

--The Christian Church: Its Rise & Progress. 488p. 5.00. Faith Pub Hse.

--Jesus Is Coming Again. 111p. pap. 1.00. Faith Pub Hse.

--The Kingdom of God & the One Thousand Years Reign. 160p. pap. 1.50. Faith Pub Hse.

--The Sabbath & the Lord's Day. 160p. pap. 1.50. Faith Pub Hse.

--The Two Works of Grace. 56p. pap. 0.40; pap. 1.00 3 copies. Faith Pub Hse.

Riggle, H. M., jt. auth. see Warner, D. S.

Riggle, H. M., jt. ed. see Speck, S. L.

Riggs, Donald E., ed. Leadership in Librarianship: A Futuristic View. 1981. lib. bdg. 17.50x (ISBN 0-912700-64-5). Oryx Pr.

Riggs, Gene B., jt. auth. see Marks, H. S.

Riggs, Henry E. Accounting: A Survey. 1981. text ed. 18.95 (ISBN 0-07-052851-9, C); write for info instrs.' manual (ISBN 0-07-052852-7). McGraw.

Riggs, J. L. Productions Systems: Planning, Analysis, & Control. 2nd ed. (Ser. in Management & Administration). 1976. 25.95 (ISBN 0-471-72186-7); tchrs. manual avail. (ISBN 0-471-01698-5). Wiley.

Riggs, Maida L. Jump to Joy: Helping Children Grow Through Active Play. (Illus.). 176p. 1980. 12.95 (Spec); pap. 6.95. P-H.

Riggs, Ralph M. We Believe. 1954. 2.95 (ISBN 0-88243-780-1, 02-0780). Gospel Pub.

Riggs, Ralph M., tr. O Guia Do Pastor. (Portugese Bks.). (Port.). 1979. 3.25 (ISBN 0-8297-0665-8); pap. 2.25 (ISBN 0-686-28815-7). Life Pubs Intl.

Riggs, Robert F. The Apocalypse Unsealed. LC 80-81698. 1981. 18.95 (ISBN 0-8022-2367-2). Philos Lib.

Riggs, Timothy A. Hieronymus Cock: Printmaker & Publisher. LC 76-23706. (Outstanding Dissertations in the Fine Arts Ser.). 1977. lib. bdg. 73.00 (ISBN 0-8240-2724-8). Garland Pub.

Riggs, William G. The Christian Poet in Paradise Lost. 1972. 16.50x (ISBN 0-520-02081-2). U of Cal Pr.

Righetti, A., jt. ed. see Donath, A.

Righetti, Raymond R. Stock Market Strategy for Consistent Profits. LC 79-23006. 176p. 1981. 14.95 (ISBN 0-88229-574-8). Nelson-Hall.

Righter, William. Myth & Literature. (Concepts of Literature Ser.). 1975. 12.50x (ISBN 0-7100-8137-5). Routledge & Kegan.

Rightridge, Allan. Plato & the Metaphysics of the State. (The Most Meaningful Classics in World Culture). (Illus.). 108p. 1981. 43.75 (ISBN 0-89266-297-2). Am Classical Coll Pr.

Rights, Douglas L. American Indian in North Carolina. 2nd ed. LC 57-9277. (Illus.). 1981. Repr. of 1972 ed. 10.00 (ISBN 0-910244-09-X). Blair.

Rights, Mollie & Solga, Tim. Beastly Neighbors: Or Why Earwigs Make Good Mothers. (Brown Paper School Ser.). (Illus.). 128p. (Orig.). (gr. 3 up). 1981. 9.95 (ISBN 0-316-74576-6); pap. 5.95 (ISBN 0-316-74577-4). Little.

Rigney, Barbara H. Madness & Sexual Politics in the Feminist Novel: Studies in Bronte, Woolf, Lessing & Atwood. LC 78-53291. 1978. 15.00 (ISBN 0-299-07710-1); pap. 5.95 (ISBN 0-299-07714-4). U of Wis Pr.

Rigney, D. A. & Glaeser, W. A., eds. Source Book on Wear Control Technology. 1978. 38.00 (ISBN 0-87170-028-X). ASM.

Rigney, Francis J., jt. auth. see Murray, William D.

Rigsby, Howard. The Lone Gun. 144p. 1978. pap. 1.25 o.p. (ISBN 0-449-14005-9, GM). Fawcett.

Rigsby, Lee, jt. auth. see Pruett, James.

Rigterink, James M., jt. auth. see Ficker, Victor B.

Riha, I., jt. ed. see Sterzl, J.

Riha, Karl, intro. by. Figurinen der Comedia Dell'arte. (Insel Buecherei: 1007). 100p. pap. 9.10 (ISBN 3-458-19007-4, Pub. by Insel Verlag Germany). Suhrkamp.

Riha, Thomas, ed. Readings in Russian Civilization, 3 vols. rev. ed. Incl. Vol. 1. Russia Before Peter the Great, 900-1700. 8.75x (ISBN 0-226-71852-2); pap. 5.50 (ISBN 0-226-71853-0); Vol. 2. Imperial Russia, 1700-1917. o.s.i. (ISBN 0-226-71854-9); pap. 6.50 (ISBN 0-226-71855-7); Vol. 3. Soviet Russia, 1917-Present. 9.50x (ISBN 0-226-71856-5); pap. 8.00 (ISBN 0-226-71857-3). LC 69-14825. 1969. U of Chicago Pr.

Rihani, May. Development As If Women Mattered: An Annotated Bibliography with a Third World Focus. LC 78-57205. (Occasional Papers: No. 10). 144p. 1978. pap. 3.00 (ISBN 0-686-28694-4). Overseas Dev Council.

Riikon, E. & Tuomikowski, A. Finnish Dictionary. 10th ed. 1979. text ed. 45.00x (ISBN 9-5110-0343-7, F560). Vanous.

Rijk, Lambertus M. De see De Rijk, Lambertus M.

Rijn, Rembrandt Van see Van Rijn, Rembrandt.

Rijnberg, Elbert. A Trio of Tales. 64p. 1981. 5.00 (ISBN 0-682-49735-5). Exposition.

Riker. Finding My Way. (gr. 9-12). 1979. pap. 7.52 (ISBN 0-87002-304-7); student guide 2.52 (ISBN 0-87002-309-8); tchr's guide 2.64 (ISBN 0-87002-311-X). Bennett IL.

Riker, Audrey. Me: Understanding Myself & Others. 1977. 9.68 (ISBN 0-87002-182-6); student guide 2.92 (ISBN 0-87002-190-7); tchr's guide 3.40 (ISBN 0-87002-188-5). Bennett IL.

Riker, Audrey, et al. Married Life. rev. ed. (gr. 10-12). 1976. text ed. 14.20 (ISBN 0-87002-071-4); student guide 2.60 (ISBN 0-87002-208-3). tchr's guide avail. Bennett IL.

Riker, Dorothy L., jt. auth. see Barnhart, John D.

Riker, James. Harlem: Its Origins & Early Annals. LC 78-104551. Repr. of 1881 ed. lib. bdg. 38.50x (ISBN 0-8398-1759-2). Irvington.

Riker, Tom. City & Suburban Gardens: Frontyards, Backyards, Terraces, Rooftops & Window Boxes. LC 76-58532. (Illus.). 1977. 12.95 (ISBN 0-13-134544-3); pap. 8.95 o.p. (ISBN 0-13-134536-2). P-H.

--Sex in the Garden. LC 76-4135. (Illus.). 192p. 1976. 9.95 o.p. (ISBN 0-688-03063-7). Morrow.

Rikhoff, Jean. One of the Raymonds. 1977. pap. 1.95 o.p. (ISBN 0-449-23090-2, Crest). Fawcett.

Rikhye, I. J. The Sinai Blunder: Withdrawal of the United Nations Emergency Force Leading to the Six-Day War of June 1967. 240p. 1980. 24.00x (ISBN 0-7146-3136-1, F Cass Co). Biblio Dist.

Rikitake, Tsuneji, ed. Current Research in Earthquake Prediction, Vol. 1. (Developments in Earth & Planetary Sciences Ser.: No. 2). 400p. 1981. PLB 37.00 (ISBN 0-686-28846-7, Pub. by D. Reidel). Kluwer Boston.

Riland, George. New Steinerbooks Dictionary of the Paranormal. (Spiritual Science Library). 370p. 1980. 20.00x (ISBN 0-8334-0719-8). Multimedia.

Riley, Beauton. Washing on the Line. 4.95 o.p. (ISBN 0-685-48820-9). Nortex Pr.

Riley, Bill & Leake, Laura. History & Events of the Early Nineteen Twenties. LC 79-56202. 1981. 8.95 (ISBN 0-533-04515-0). Vantage.

Riley, Carroll L. & Hedrick, Basil C., eds. Across the Chichimec Sea: Papers in Honor of J. Charles Kelley. LC 78-802. (Illus.). 336p. 1978. 19.95x (ISBN 0-8093-0829-0). S Ill U Pr.

Riley, Carroll L., et al, eds. Man Across the Sea: Problems of Pre-Columbian Contacts. 1971. 25.00x (ISBN 0-292-70117-9). U of Tex Pr.

Riley, Clayton, jt. auth. see King, Martin L., Sr.

Riley, Coye F. Show Me the Way. 1981. 4.74 (ISBN 0-8062-1588-7). Carlton.

Riley, D. & Spolton, L. World Weather & Climate. LC 73-75858. (Illus.). 128p. 1974. 19.50 (ISBN 0-521-20176-4); pap. 7.95x (ISBN 0-521-20175-6). Cambridge U Pr.

Riley, Denis R. & Young, Anthony. World Vegetation. 1967. 6.95x (ISBN 0-521-06083-4). Cambridge U Pr.

Riley, Dick, ed. Critical Encounters: Writers & Themes in Science Fiction. LC 78-4300. (Recognitions Ser.). 1978. 10.95 (ISBN 0-8044-2713-5); pap. 3.95 (ISBN 0-8044-6732-3). Ungar.

Riley, Edward. Riley's Flute Melodies, 2vols. in 1. Hitchcock, H. Wiley, ed. & intro. by. LC 72-14213. (Earlier American Music Ser.: Vol. 18). 200p. 1973. Repr. of 1816 ed. lib. bdg. 17.50 (ISBN 0-306-70565-6). Da Capo.

Riley, Gary L. & Baldridge, Victor J., eds. Governing Academic Organizations: New Problems, New Perspectives. LC 76-56995. 1977. 20.00x (ISBN 0-8211-1715-7); text ed. 18.00x (ISBN 0-685-75001-9). McCutchan.

Riley, Glenda. Frontierswomen, the Iowa Experience. (Illus.). 1981. write for info. (ISBN 0-8138-1470-7). Iowa St U Pr.

Riley, Herbert P. Introduction to Genetics & Cytogenetics. (Illus.). 1967. Repr. of 1948 ed. 19.50 o.s.i. (ISBN 0-02-850960-9). Hafner.

Riley, Herbert P. & Majumdar, Shyamal K. The Aloineae: A Biosystematic Survey. LC 77-92927. (Illus.). 192p. 1980. 28.75x (ISBN 0-8131-1376-8). U Pr of Ky.

Riley, James C. International Government Finance & the Amsterdam Capital Market: 1740-1815. LC 79-152. (Illus.). 1980. 37.50 (ISBN 0-521-22677-5). Cambridge U Pr.

Riley, James W. The Eternal Poetry of Romantic Love. (Illus.). 1979. deluxe ed. 31.45 (ISBN 0-930582-47-0). Gloucester Art.

--The Gobble-Uns'll Git You Ef You Don't Watch Out! LC 74-23110. (gr. 3-5). 1975. 8.95 (ISBN 0-397-31621-6). Lippincott.

--Joyful Poems for Children. LC 60-14663. (gr. 2-6). 1960. 5.95 o.p. (ISBN 0-672-50342-5). Bobbs.

Riley, Jean, jt. auth. see Hall, Nancy.

Riley, Jeannie C. & Buckingham, Jamie. From Harper Valley to the Mountain Top. Orig. Title: Jeannie C. 180p. 1980. 8.95 (ISBN 0-912376-63-5). Chosen Bks Pub.

Riley, K. F. Mathematical Methods for the Physical Sciences. LC 73-89765. 512p. (Orig.). 1974. 57.50 (ISBN 0-521-20390-2); pap. 22.95x (ISBN 0-521-09839-4). Cambridge U Pr.

Riley, Laura & Riley, William. Guide to the National Wildlife Refuges. (Illus.). 672p. 1981. pap. 9.95 (ISBN 0-385-14015-0, Anch). Doubleday.

Riley, M. J., ed. Management Information Systems: Selected Readings. 2nd ed. 400p. 1981. pap. text ed. 14.50 (ISBN 0-8162-7190-9). Holden-Day.

Riley, Matilda W., ed. Aging from Birth to Death: Interdisciplinary Perspectives. (AAAS Selected Symposium: No. 30). (Illus.). 1979. lib. bdg. 20.00x (ISBN 0-89158-363-7). Westview.

Riley, Matilda W., jt. ed. see Merton, Robert K.

Riley, Maurice W. The History of the Viola. LC 79-66348. 1979. 27.50 (ISBN 0-9603150-0-4); pap. 22.50 (ISBN 0-9603150-1-2). M W Riley.

Riley, Michael J., jt. auth. see Crane, Dwight D.

Riley, N. D. Insects in Color. (European Ecology Ser.). (Illus.). 1963. 9.95 (ISBN 0-7137-0144-7, Pub by Blandford Pr England). Sterling.

Riley, Nevita, jt. auth. see McEoin, Gary.

Riley, P. A. & Cunningham, P. J. The Faber Pocket Medical Dictionary. rev. ed. (Illus.). 1974. 4.95 o.p. (ISBN 0-571-04844-7, Pub. by Faber & Faber). Merrimack Bk Serv.

Riley, P. W. King William & the Scottish Politicans. 1979. text ed. 32.50x (ISBN 0-85976-040-5). Humanities.

Riley, Patricia. Needlecraft Projects. 1978. 14.95 (ISBN 0-7134-0745-X). David & Charles.

--The Skirtmaking Book. 1979. 17.95 (ISBN 0-7134-1641-6, Pub. by Batsford England). David & Charles.

Riley, R. C. Great Western Album. 14.50x (ISBN 0-392-07860-0, SpS). Soccer.

Riley, Raymond C. Belgium. new ed. LC 76-18938. (Westview Special Studies in Industrial Geography). (Illus.). 1976. lib. bdg. 26.00x (ISBN 0-89158-625-3). Westview.

Riley, Ridge. Road to Number One: A Personal Chronicle of Penn State Football with a Foreword by Head Coach Joseph V. Paterno. LC 75-40740. 1977. 5.95 o.p. (ISBN 0-385-11397-8). Doubleday.

Riley, Terry & Day, Rosemary. The Witch & the Owl. (Illus.). 1981. 10.95x (ISBN 0-460-06886-5, Pub. by J. M. Dent England). Biblio Dist.

Riley, W. B. Electronic Computer Memory Technology. 1971. 27.50 o.p. (ISBN 0-07-052915-9, P&RB). McGraw.

Riley, William, jt. auth. see Riley, Laura.

Riley, William F., jt. auth. see Dally, James W.

Riley-Smith, Jonathan. What Were the Crusades? 1977. 12.50 o.p. (ISBN 0-87471-944-5). Rowman.

Rilke, Rainer M. For the Sake of a Single Verse. (Illus.). 40p. 1974. pap. 12.95 (ISBN 0-517-51205-X); pap. 6.95 (ISBN 0-517-51206-8). Potter.

--Poems. McKay, G. W., ed. (Clarendon German Ser). (gr. 9 up). 1965. pap. 2.95x (ISBN 0-19-500366-7). Oxford U Pr.

--Rodin. Firmage, Robert, tr. from Ger. (Illus.). 1979. pap. 9.95 (ISBN 0-87905-044-6). Peregrine Smith.

--Selected Poems of Rainer Maria Rilke: A Translation from the German & Commentary. Bly, Robert, tr. from Ger. LC 78-2114. 192p. 1981. 13.95 (ISBN 0-06-010432-5, CN727, HarpT); pap. 5.95. Har-Row.

--Selected Poems of Rainer Maria Rilke: A Translation from the German & Commentary. Bly, Robert, tr. LC 78-2114. (Ger.). 1981. pap. 5.95 (ISBN 0-06-090727-4, CN). Har-Row.

--Selected Works, Vol. II: Poetry. Leishman, J. B., tr. from Ger. LC 60-8714. 17.95 (ISBN 0-8112-0379-4). New Directions.

Rilke, Ravier M. Rilke on Love & Other Difficulties: Translations & Considerations of Rainer Maria Rilke. Mood, John, ed. 121p. 1975. 7.50 (ISBN 0-393-04390-8); pap. 5.95 (ISBN 0-393-04404-1). Norton.

Rilla, Wolf. The Illusionists. 1978. pap. 1.95 o.s.i. (ISBN 0-515-04560-8). Jove Pubns.

--The Writer & the Screen: On Writing for Film & Television. 1974. pap. 4.95 (ISBN 0-688-05234-7). Morrow.

Rima, I. H. Development of Economic Analysis. 3rd ed. 1978. text ed. 18.95 (ISBN 0-256-02030-2). Irwin.

Rimbaud, Arthur. Arthur Rimbaud: A Season in Hell & Illuminations. Peschel, Enid R., tr. (Illus.). 200p. 1973. 13.95 (ISBN 0-19-501727-7). Oxford U Pr.

--Complete Works with Selected Letters. Fowlie, Wallace, tr. LC 66-13885. (Fr & Eng). 1967. pap. 6.95 (ISBN 0-226-71973-1, P288, Phoen). U of Chicago Pr.

--Illuminations. Osmond, N., ed. (French Poets Ser.). (Illus.). 192p. 1976. text ed. 27.50x (ISBN 0-485-14710-6, Athlone Pr); pap. text ed. 13.00x (ISBN 0-485-12710-5, Athlone). Humanities.

--Season in Hell. Varese, Louise, tr. Bd. with Drunken Boat. LC 61-14900. (Eng. & Fr.). pap. 2.95 (ISBN 0-8112-0185-6, NDP97). New Directions.

--A Season in Hell. Peschel, Enid R., tr. Bd. with Illuminations. (Illus., Engl. & Fre.). 1974. pap. 4.95 (ISBN 0-19-501760-9, 403, GB). Oxford U Pr.

Rimbaud, Robert C. What Nobody, but Absolutely Nobody Knows About Sex, or New Discoveries into the Metaphysics of Sex. (Illus.). 113p. 1981. 18.25 (ISBN 0-89266-286-7). Am Classical Coll Pr.

Rimbault, Edward F., ed. The Old Cheque-Book, or Book of Rememberance of the Chapel Royal from 1561. LC 65-23407. (Music Ser.). 1966. Repr. of 1872 ed. lib. bdg. 25.00 (ISBN 0-306-70911-2). Da Capo.

Rimbeaux, B. C., jt. auth. see Cassidy, John.

Rimer, J. Thomas. Mori Ogai. LC 74-28163. (World Authors Ser.: No. 355). 1975. lib. bdg. 10.95 (ISBN 0-8057-2636-5). Twayne.

Rimland, Bernard. Infantile Autism: The Syndrome & Its Implications for a Neural Theory of Behavior. (Century Psychology Ser.). 1981. Repr. of 1964 ed. text ed. 18.50x (ISBN 0-8290-0061-5). Irvington.

Rimm, Alfred A., et al. Basic Biostatistics in Medicine & Epidemiology. 352p. 1980. pap. text ed. 16.50x (ISBN 0-8385-0528-7). ACC.

Rimm, David C. & Masters, John C. Behavior Theraphy: Techniques & Empirical Findings. 2nd ed. 538p. 1979. 18.95 (ISBN 0-12-588860-0). Acad Pr.

Rimm, David C. & Somervill, John W. Abnormal Psychology. 696p. 1977. 18.95 (ISBN 0-12-588840-6). Acad Pr.

Rimmer, C. Brandon. The Dirks Escape. LC 79-88496. (Orig.). 1979. pap. 2.50 (ISBN 0-87123-108-5, 200108). Bethany Fell.

Rimmer, Joan. The Irish Harp. 2nd ed. (Irish Life & Culture Series). (Illus.). 1977. pap. 3.95 (ISBN 0-85342-151-X). Irish Bk Ctr.

Rimmer, M. Race & Industrial Conflict. Clegg, Hugh & Bain, George, eds. 1972. text ed. 4.95x o.p. (ISBN 0-435-85765-7). Heinemann Ed.

Rimmer, Robert H. Gold Lovers. Orig. Title: Zolotov Affair. 227p. 1980. Repr. of 1967 ed. 12.50 (ISBN 0-8290-0224-3). Irvington.

--The Love Explosion. 1980. pap. 2.75 (ISBN 0-451-09519-7, E9519, Sig). NAL.

--That Girl from Boston. 224p. 1980. Repr. of 1962 ed. 12.50 (ISBN 0-8290-0226-X). Irvington.

Rimmer, William. Art Anatomy. pap. 5.00 (ISBN 0-486-20908-3). Dover.

Rimoin, David L., ed. International Nomenclature of Constitutional Diseases of Bone Wih Bibliography. LC 79-54820. (March of Dimes Birth Defects Foundation Ser.: Vol. 15, No. 10). 1979. write for info. March of Dimes.

Rimpoche, Lati, tr. see Nagarjuna.

Rimsky-Korsakov, Nikolay. Principles of Orchestration. 1922. pap. text ed. 6.00 (ISBN 0-486-21266-1). Dover.

Rinaldi, Ann. Term Paper. LC 80-7686. 202p. (gr. 5 up). 1980. 8.95 (ISBN 0-8027-6395-2). Walker & Co.

Rinaldi, John F. The Art & Science of Wall Street Scalping for the Gaining of Superlative Profits. 1980. 37.55 (ISBN 0-918968-50-X). Inst Econ Finan.

Rinaldi, Robert R., ed. see American Academy of Podiatric Sports Medicine.

Rinaldi, Robert R., ed. see Members of the American Academy of Podiatric Sports Medicine.

Rinalducci, Ralph J. The Japanese Police Establishment. 388p. 1974. 26.75 (ISBN 0-398-03577-6). C C Thomas.

Rinder, Robert M. A Practical Guide to Small Computers for Business & Professional Use. 288p. 1981. pap. 6.95 (ISBN 0-671-09259-6). Monarch Pr.

Rinder, Walter. Love Is an Attitude. LC 74-147246. (Illus., Orig.). 1970. 5.95 o.p. (ISBN 0-912310-04-9); pap. 4.95 (ISBN 0-912310-03-0). Celestial Arts.

Rindler, Lester, jt. auth. see Mirengoff, William.

Rindler, W. Essential Relativity. rev. ed. (Texts & Monographs in Physics). (Illus.). 284p. 1980. pap. 19.80 (ISBN 0-387-10090-3). Springer-Verlag.

Rinehart, J. S. Geysers & Geothermal Energy. (Illus.). 223p. 1980. 19.80 (ISBN 0-387-90489-1). Springer-Verlag.

Rinehart, Kenneth L., jt. auth. see DePuy, Charles H.

Rinehart, Kenneth L & Suami, Tetsuo, eds. Aminocyclitol Antibiotics. LC 80-10502. (ACS Symposium Ser.: No. 125). 1980. 39.50 (ISBN 0-8412-0554-X). Am Chemical.

Rinehart, Mary R. Case of Jenny Brice. 1976. lib. bdg. 12.95x (ISBN 0-89968-182-4). Lightyear.

--Circular Staircase. 1976. lib. bdg. 12.95x (ISBN 0-89968-181-6). Lightyear.

--The Man in Lower Ten. 1976. lib. bdg. 12.95x (ISBN 0-89968-180-8). Lightyear.

Rinehart, Russell. The Ugly Unicorn. LC 79-84875. 1979. pap. 2.00 (ISBN 0-934020-01-9). Illusive Unicorn.

Rinella, Richard J. & Robbins, Claire C. Career Power. 281p. 1981. 14.95 (ISBN 0-8144-5630-8); comb-bound 16.95 (ISBN 0-8144-7009-2). Am Mgmt.

Riner, John, et al. Mathematics of Finance. 4th ed. 1969. ref. ed. 19.95 (ISBN 0-13-565036-4). P-H.

Rines, Alice R. Evaluating Student Progress in Learning the Practice of Nursing. LC 63-19048. (Orig.). 1963. pap. 4.75x (ISBN 0-8077-2036-4). Tchrs Coll.

Rines, Alice R. & Montag, Mildred L. Nursing Concepts & Nursing Care. LC 75-40028. 505p. 1976. 15.95 o.p. (ISBN 0-471-72245-6, Pub. by Wiley Medical). Wiley.

Rines, Alice R., jt. auth. see Montag, Mildred L.

Rinet, Jacqueline & Hillard, Denise, eds. Catalogue Des Ouvrages Imprimes Au XVIe Siecle: Science, Techniques, Medicine. 450p. 1980. text ed. 45.00 (ISBN 3-598-10119-8). K G Saur.

Ring, Alfred A. Valuation of Real Estate. 2nd ed. 1970. ref. ed. 19.95 (ISBN 0-13-939892-9). P-H.

Ring, Alfred A. & Dasso, Jerome. Real Estate Principles & Practices. 9th ed. (Illus.). 752p. 1981. text ed. 21.00 (ISBN 0-13-765958-X). P-H.

Ring, Daniel F., ed. Studies in Creative Partnership: Federal Aid to Public Libraries During the New Deal. LC 80-15762. 154p. 1980. 10.00 (ISBN 0-8108-1319-X). Scarecrow.

Ring, Elizabeth. Up the Cockneys! 1974. 9.95 (ISBN 0-236-31081-X, Pub. by Paul Elek). Merrimack Bk Serv.

Ring, Jeanne, ed. Who's Who in Electronics. rev. ed. (Annual). 1981. 62.95 (ISBN 0-916512-66-5). Harris Pub.

Ringe, Donald A. James Fenimore Cooper. (U. S. Authors Ser.: No. 11). 9.95 (ISBN 0-8057-0156-7). Twayne.

--The Pictorial Mode: Space & Time in the Art of Bryant, Irving, & Cooper. LC 71-147859. (Illus.). 256p. 1971. 14.50x (ISBN 0-8131-1250-8). U Pr of Ky.

Ringel, Martin, ed. see Lanzano, Susan & Abreu, Rosendo.

Ringel, William E. Searches & Seizures, Arrests & Confessions. 2nd ed. LC 70-186243. 550p. 1979. 50.00 (ISBN 0-87632-079-5). Boardman.

Ringelblum, Emmanuel. Polish-Jewish Relations During the Second World War. Allon, Dafna, et al, trs. LC 76-1394. 330p. 1976. 24.00 (ISBN 0-86527-155-0). Fertig.

Ringer. Restoring the American Dream. 1981. pap. 2.95 (ISBN 0-449-24314-1). Fawcett.

Ringgold, Gene. The Films of Rita Hayworth. 1977. pap. 6.95 (ISBN 0-8065-0574-5). Citadel Pr.

Ringgren, Helmer, jt. ed. see Botterweck, G. Johannes.

Ringi, Kjell. Stranger. LC 68-23661. (Illus.). (ps-2). 1968. 3.95 (ISBN 0-394-81571-8); PLB 5.39 (ISBN 0-394-91571-2). Random.

Ringler, William A., Jr., ed. see Sidney, Philip.

Ringo, Miriam. Nobody Said It Better! Two Thousand Seven Hunred Wise & Witty Quotations About Famous People. LC 80-20404. 352p. 1980. 12.95 (ISBN 0-528-81104-5). Rand.

Ringold, Clay. The Night Hell's Corners Died. 1978. Repr. of 1972 ed. 1.25 (ISBN 0-505-51328-5). Tower Bks.

Ringold, Paul L. & Clark, John. The Coastal Almanac: For 1980--the Year of the Coast. LC 80-22501. (Geology Ser.). (Illus.). 1980. 19.95x (ISBN 0-7167-1285-7); pap. 9.95x (ISBN 0-7167-1286-5). W H Freeman.

Ringsdorf, W. M., Jr., jt. auth. see Cheraskin, E.

Ringstad, M. Adventures on Library Shelves. LC 68-16398. (Illus.). (gr. 2 up). 1967. PLB 7.99 prebound (ISBN 0-87783-156-4); pap. 2.75 (ISBN 0-686-66511-2). Oddo.

Ringwalt, J. Luther & Bidwell, John, eds. American Encyclopaedia of Printing. LC 78-74411. (Nineteenth-Century Book Arts & Printing History Ser.: Vol. 21). (Illus.). 1980. lib. bdg. 66.00 (ISBN 0-8240-3895-9). Garland Pub.

Rini, Lisa, jt. auth. see Werner, Peter H.

Rinkel, L. I. Money: A Labor Theory of Value. 202p. 1980. pap. text ed. 15.75x (ISBN 90-232-1744-6). Humanities.

Rinker, Richard N. The East Burlap Parables. LC 69-11775. (Illus.). xiv, 169p. 1969. 9.95x (ISBN 0-8032-0154-0); pap. 1.95 (ISBN 0-8032-5161-0, BB 394, Bison). U of Nebr Pr.

Rinker, Rosalind. Communicating Love Through Prayer. 1966. pap. 1.75 (ISBN 0-310-32072-0). Zondervan.

--Conversational Prayer. (Orig.). pap. 1.50 (ISBN 0-89129-210-1). Jove Pubns.

--Conversational Prayer. 1976. pap. 1.75 (ISBN 0-89129-210-1). Jove Pubns.

--Dentro del Circulo. Cochrane, James R., tr. from Eng. 110p. (Orig., Span.). 1976. pap. 2.25 (ISBN 0-89922-075-4). Edit Caribe.

--Prayer: Conversing with God. pap. 2.75 (ISBN 0-310-32092-5); pap. youth edition o.p. (ISBN 0-310-32101-8). Zondervan.

--Praying Together. rev. ed. 96p. 1980. pap. 2.95 (ISBN 0-310-32111-5). Zondervan.

Rinkoff, Barbara. Guess What Grasses Do. LC 76-177316. (gr. k-3). 1972. 7.25 o.p. (ISBN 0-688-41592-X); PLB 6.96 o.p. (ISBN 0-688-51592-4). Lothrop.

--Map Is a Picture. LC 65-11648. (A Let's-Read-&-Find-Out Science Bk). (Illus.). (gr. k-3). 1965. bds. 7.89 (ISBN 0-690-51793-9, TYC-J). T Y Crowell.

Rinn, Roger C. & Markle, Allan. Positive Parenting. (Illus.). 1977. pap. text ed. 4.95 (ISBN 0-89147-052-2). CAS.

Rinpoche, Namgyal. The Path of Victory: Discourses on the Paramita. Gelong, Karma S., ed. LC 80-84669. (Illus.). 75p. (Orig.). 1980. pap. 5.00 (ISBN 0-9602722-1-6). Open Path.

Rinsler, Norma. Gerard de Nerval. 1973. text ed. 17.50x (ISBN 0-485-14601-0, Athlone Pr); pap. text ed. 8.75x (ISBN 0-485-12706-7, Athlone Pr). Humanities.

Rinsler, Norma, ed. see De Nerval, Gerard.

Rinsley, Donald. Treatment of the Severly Disturbed Adolescent. 1979. 30.00 (ISBN 0-87668-320-0). Aronson.

Rintoul, William. Drilling Ahead. (Illus.). 300p. 1981. 16.95 (ISBN 0-934136-09-2, Valley Pub). Western Tanager.
--Oildorado: Boom Times on the West Side. LC 78-50141. (Illus.). 240p. 1980. pap. 7.95 (ISBN 0-934136-07-6, Valley Calif). Western Tanager.
--Spudding in: Recollections of Pioneer Days in the California Oil Fields. 240p. 1978. Repr. of 1976 ed. 12.95 (ISBN 0-910312-37-0). Calif Hist.
Rinzler, Alan, ed. Manifesto Addressed to the President of the United States from the Youth of America. 1970. pap. 1.50 o.s.i. (ISBN 0-02-074640-7, Collier). Macmillan.
Rinzler, Carol. Cosmetics: What the Ads Don't Tell You. 256p. 1979. pap. 1.95 o.p. (ISBN 0-441-11750-3). Charter Bks.
Rinzler, Carol A. Cosmetics: What the Ads Don't Tell You. LC 77-4675. 1977. 9.95 o.s.i. (ISBN 0-690-01459-7, TYC-T). T Y Crowell.
Rinzler, Carol E., ed. see McCarthy, Eugene.
Riofrancos, Maro, tr. see Vazquez, Adolfo S.
Rio Ianacio, Del see Del Rio, Ignacio.
Riordan, J. An Introduction to Combinatorial Analysis. LC 80-337. 1980. 18.00 (ISBN 0-691-08262-6); pap. 6.95 (ISBN 0-691-02365-4). Princeton U Pr.
--Sport in Soviet Society. LC 76-9729. (Soviet & East European Studies Ser.). (Illus.). 1977. 44.50 (ISBN 0-521-21284-7); pap. 14.95 (ISBN 0-521-28023-0). Cambridge U Pr.
Riordan, James, tr. The Three Magic Gifts. (Illus.). 28p. (gr. k-4). 1980. 9.95 (ISBN 0-19-520194-9). Oxford U Pr.
Riordan, Mary M. Lillian Hellman: A Bibliography, 1926-1978. LC 80-16147. (Author Bibliographies Ser.: No. 50). 244p. 1980. 13.50 (ISBN 0-8108-1320-3). Scarecrow.
Riordan, Michael, jt. auth. see Anderson, Bruce.
Riordan, William. On the Take. (Orig.). 1976. pap. 1.25 o.p. (ISBN 0-685-64015-9, LB342ZK, Leisure Bks). Nordon Pubns.
--Plunkitt of Tammany Hall. 98p. 1976. Repr. of 1905 ed. lib. bdg. 12.95x (ISBN 0-89244-088-0). Queens Hse.
Rios, Louis J., ed. see Munoz Martin, Luis.
Riotton, C. & Christopherson, William. Cytology of the Female Genital Tract. (World Health Organization: International Histological Classification of Tumours Ser.). 1977. 66.00 (ISBN 0-685-77240-3, 70-0-008-20); incl. slides 160.50 (ISBN 0-685-77241-1, 70-0-008-00). Am Soc Clinical.
Riotton, G. & Christopherson, W. M. Cytology of Non-Gynaecological Sites. (World Health Organization: International Histological Classification of Tumours Ser.). (Illus.). 1977. text ed. 66.00 (ISBN 92-4-176017-6, 70-1-017-20); with slides 195.00 (ISBN 92-4-176017-6, 70-1-017-00). Am Soc Clinical.
Rioux, William. You Can Improve Your Child's School. 1980. 12.95 (ISBN 0-686-68754-X, 25116). S&S.
Ripa, Cesare. Iconologie. Baudouin, Jean, tr. LC 75-27874. (Renaissance & the Gods Ser.: Vol. 29). (Illus., Fr.). 1976. Repr. of 1644 ed. lib. bdg. 73.00 (ISBN 0-8240-2078-2). Garland Pub.
Ripa, Cesare see Marolles, Michel de.
Ripalda, Jose-Maria. The Divided Nation: The Roots of a Bourgeois Thinker, G. W. F. Hegel. (Dialectic & Society: No. 3). 1977. text ed. 31.25x (ISBN 90-232-1514-1). Humanities.
Riper, Walker V., et al. Nature Photography with High Speed Flash. (Museum Pictorial: No. 5). 1952. pap. 1.10 o.p. (ISBN 0-916278-34-4). Denver Mus Natl Hist.
Ripert, Pierre, jt. auth. see Alauzen, Andre.
Ripka, Herbert. Munich, Before & After. LC 68-9630. 1969. Repr. of 1939 ed. 20.00 (ISBN 0-86527-133-X). Fertig.
Ripley, Alexandra, ed. Charleston. LC 79-8568. 504p. 1981. 14.95 (ISBN 0-385-14572-1). Doubleday.
Ripley, Brian D. Spatial Statistics. (Probability & Mathematical Statistics Ser.: Applied Probability & Statistics). 352p. 1981. 27.00 (ISBN 0-471-08367-4, Pub. by Wiley-Interscience). Wiley.
Ripley, Dillon, jt. auth. see Ali, Salim.
Ripley, Francis J. Last Gospel. 1962. 3.50 o.p. (ISBN 0-8362-0203-1, Pub. by Sheed). Guild Bks.
Ripley, John W. & Richmind, Robert W., eds. A Century of Healing Arts-Eighteen Fifty to Nineteen Fifty. (Illus.). 176p. 1980. pap. 5.95. Shawnee County Hist.
Ripley, Randall. Public Policies & Their Politics. 1967. 4.50x (ISBN 0-393-05337-7); pap. 3.95x (ISBN 0-393-09689-0, NortonC). Norton.
Ripley, Randall B. American National Government & Public Policy. LC 73-10574. (Illus., Orig.). 1974. pap. text ed. 7.95 (ISBN 0-02-926540-1). Free Pr.
--The Politics of Economic & Human Resource Development. LC 79-173977. (Policy Analysis Ser). 1972. 8.95 (ISBN 0-672-51479-6); pap. 4.35 o.p. (ISBN 0-672-61070-1). Bobbs.
Ripley, Randall B. & Franklin, Grace A. Congress, the Bureaucracy & Public Policy. 1980. pap. text ed. 8.50x o.p. (ISBN 0-256-02256-9). Dorsey.
--Congress, the Bureaucracy, & the Public Policy. rev. ed. 1980. pap. 9.50x (ISBN 0-256-02256-9). Dorsey.
Ripley, Randall B. & Franklin, Grace A., eds. Policy-Making in the Federal Executive Branch. LC 74-33093. (Illus.). 1975. 17.95 (ISBN 0-02-926490-1). Free Pr.
Ripley, Robert L. Ripley's Giant Book of "Believe It or Not". (Illus.). 256p. (Orig.). 1976. pap. 8.95 (ISBN 0-446-97686-5). Warner Bks.
Ripley, S. D., jt. auth. see Ali, Salim.
Ripley, S. Dillon. Land & Wildlife of Tropical Asia. LC 64-25408. (Life Nature Library). (Illus.). (gr. 5 up). 1964. PLB 8.97 o.p. (ISBN 0-8094-0632-2, Pub. by Time-Life). Silver.
--A Naturalist's Adventure in Nepal: Search for the Spiny Babbler. (Illus.). 301p. 1981. Repr. of 1953 ed. 12.50 (ISBN 0-87474-810-0). Smithsonian.
Ripley, S. Dillon, jt. auth. see Ali, Salim.
Ripley, Theresa M., jt. auth. see Loughary, John W.
Ripley, William. Main Street & Wall Street. LC 72-93640. 1973. Repr. of 1927 ed. text ed. 13.00 (ISBN 0-914348-07-8). Scholars Bk.
Ripling, E., jt. auth. see Polakowski, N. H.
Ripoll, Carlos. Archivo Jose Marti: Repertorio Critico, Medio Siglo De Estudios Martianos. 1971. 14.50 (ISBN 0-88303-010-1); pap. 11.50 (ISBN 0-685-73214-2). E Torres & Sons.
--Conciencia Intelectual De America: Antologia Del Ensayo Hispanoamericano. rev. 3rd ed. 1974. 9.50 (ISBN 0-88303-150-7). E Torres & Sons.
--Escritos Desconocidos De Jose Marti. 1971. 10.50 (ISBN 0-88303-001-2). E Torres & Sons.
--Indice Universal De la Obra De Jose Marti. 1971. 15.00 (ISBN 0-88303-009-8); pap. 10.95 (ISBN 0-685-73213-4). E Torres & Sons.
--Jose Marti, Letras y Huellas Desconocidas. 1976. 10.95 (ISBN 0-88303-024-1); pap. 6.50 (ISBN 0-685-73013-1). E Torres & Sons.
--Patria: El Periodico De Jose Marti, Registro General, 1892-1895. 1971. 9.95 (ISBN 0-88303-011-X); pap. 6.95 (ISBN 0-685-73215-0). E Torres & Sons.
Rippe, James M., jt. auth. see Alpert, Joseph S.
Ripper, Charles L. Moles & Shrews. (Illus.). (gr. 5-9). 1957. PLB 6.48 o.p. (ISBN 0-688-31513-5). Morrow.
Rippey, Robert M. The Evaluation of Teaching in Medical Schools. LC 80-19891. (Medical Education Ser.). 1980. text ed. 19.95 (ISBN 0-8261-3440-8). Springer Pub.
Ripple, Paula. Called to Be Friends. LC 80-67402. 160p. (Orig.). 1980. pap. 3.95 (ISBN 0-87793-212-3). Ave Maria.
Rippley, La Vern. The German-Americans. LC 75-26917. (Immigrant Heritage of America Ser.). 1976. lib. bdg. 9.95 (ISBN 0-8057-8405-5). Twayne.
Rips, Geoffrey. The Campaign Against the Underground Press in the United States: 1960-1979. 80p. 1981. pap. 2.50 (ISBN 0-87286-127-9). City Lights.
Rischbrith, Bessie S. March of Australian Women. 15.00x (ISBN 0-392-08104-0, SpS). Soccer.
Rischin, Moses. Immigration & the American Tradition. (AHS Ser: No. 79). 512p. 1976. pap. 9.95 (ISBN 0-672-60130-3). Bobbs.
Rischin, Moses, ed. see Dillon, Merton L.
Risdon, Donald H. Your Book of Pet Keeping. (Illus.). (gr. 3-7). 1964. 6.75 (ISBN 0-571-05771-3). Transatlantic.
Riseborough, Donald, ed. Canada & the French. LC 74-75155. 220p. 1975. lib. bdg. 17.50x (ISBN 0-87196-224-1). Facts on File.
Risedorf, Gwen. Born Today, Born Yesterday: Reincarnation. LC 77-21406. (Myth, Magic & Superstition Ser.). (Illus.). (gr. 4-5). 1977. PLB 9.65 (ISBN 0-8172-1045-8). Raintree Pubs.
--Ghosts & Ghouls. LC 77-14333. (Myth, Magic & Superstition Ser.). (Illus.). (gr. 4-5). 1977. PLB 9.65 (ISBN 0-8172-1038-5). Raintree Pubs.
Riser, Wayne. Your Future in Veterinary Medicine. LC 75-29656. 160p. (YA) 1976. pap. 3.50 (ISBN 0-668-03916-7). Arco.
Rising, Edward. Ambulatory Care Systems, Vol. 1: Design of Ambulatory Care Systems for Improved Patient Flow. LC 76-55865. 1977. 16.95 (ISBN 0-669-01323-4). Lexington Bks.
Rising, Gerald R. & Harkin, Joseph B. The Third "R". Mathematics Teaching for Grades K-8. 1978. text ed. 16.95x (ISBN 0-534-00567-5). Wadsworth Pub.
Rising, Gerald R., jt. auth. see Johnson, Donovan A.
Risinger, Hettie. Innovative Machine Quilting. LC 79-91393. (Illus.). 164p. 1980. 14.95 (ISBN 0-8069-5398-5); lib. bdg. 13.29 (ISBN 0-8069-5399-3). Sterling.
Risjord, Norman K. Chesapeake Politics, Seventeen Eighty One-Eighteen Hundred. LC 78-7996. 1978. 30.00x (ISBN 0-231-04328-7). Columbia U Pr.
--Forging the American Republic, 1760-1815. LC 72-4239. 1973. pap. text ed. 8.50 (ISBN 0-201-06301-8). A-W.
--Representative Americans: The Colonists, Vol. I. (Representative Americans Ser.). 272p. 1980. pap. text ed. 6.95 (ISBN 0-669-02831-2). Heath.
Risk, Clifford, tr. see Todorov, I. T.
Risk, L. M. De see De Rijk, L. M.
Riskind, Mary. Apple Is My Sign. (gr. 5-8). 1981. 7.95 (ISBN 0-395-30852-6). HM.
Risko, Victoria, jt. auth. see Mohan, Maden.
Riss, Richard. The Evidence for the Resurrection of Jesus Christ. LC 76-50978. 1977. pap. 1.95 (ISBN 0-87123-134-4, 200134). Bethany Fell.
Risse, G. B. Modern China & Traditional Chinese Medicine. 176p. 1973. 12.75 (ISBN 0-398-02816-8). C C Thomas.
Risser, Joy. OJT Traffic Clerk Resource Materials. 2nd ed. (Gregg Office Job Training Program). (Illus.). 112p. (gr. 11-12). 1980. soft cover 4.80 (ISBN 0-07-052960-4); training manual avail. (ISBN 0-07-052961-2). McGraw.
Risser, Paul G. & Cornelison, Kathy D. Man & the Biosphere. LC 79-4953. (Illus.). 109p. 1979. pap. 6.95 (ISBN 0-8061-1610-2). U of Okla Pr.
Rissover, F. & Birch, D. Mass Media & the Popular Arts. 12.95x (ISBN 0-07-052950-7, C); pap. 8.95 (ISBN 0-07-052944-2); instructor's manual 5.50 (ISBN 0-07-052944-2). McGraw.
Rist, J. M. Epicurus: An Introduction. LC 70-177939. 200p. 1972. 34.00 (ISBN 0-521-08426-1); pap. 7.95 (ISBN 0-521-29200-X). Cambridge U Pr.
--On the Independence of Matthew & Mark. LC 76-40840. (Society for New Testament Studies Monographs: No. 22). 1978. 19.95 (ISBN 0-521-21476-9). Cambridge U Pr.
--Plotinus: The Road to Reality. 1977. 38.00 (ISBN 0-521-06085-0); pap. 9.95 (ISBN 0-521-29202-6). Cambridge U Pr.
--Stoic Philosophy. LC 79-85736. 1969. 38.00 (ISBN 0-521-07620-X); pap. 9.95 (ISBN 0-521-29201-8). Cambridge U Pr.
Rist, John M., ed. The Stoics. (Major Thinkers Ser.: Vol. 1). 1978. 20.00x o.p. (ISBN 0-520-03135-0); pap. 5.95x (ISBN 0-520-03675-1). U of Cal Pr.
Rist, Ray C. Guestworkers in Germany: Prospects for Pluralism. LC 78-6282. (Praeger Special Studies). 1978. 27.95 (ISBN 0-03-040766-4). Praeger.
Rist, Ray C. & Anson, Ronald J. Education, Social Science, & the Judicial Process. LC 77-962. 1977. pap. text ed. 7.50x (ISBN 0-8077-2532-3). Tchrs Coll.
Rist, Ray C., ed. Confronting Youth Unemployment in the Nineteen Eighties: Rhetoric Versus Reality. LC 80-19730. (Pergamon Policy Studies on Social Issues). 236p. 1980. 20.00 (ISBN 0-08-026077-2). Pergamon.
Riste, Olav & Nokleby, Berit. Norway 1940-45: The Resistance Movement. (Illus.). 93p. (Orig.). 1970. pap. 6.50x (ISBN 82-518-0164-8). Intl Pubns Serv.
Riste, T., ed. Ordering in Strongly Fluctuating Condensed Matter Systems. (NATO Advanced Study Institute Ser.: Series B: Physics, Volume 50). 490p. 1980. 55.00 (ISBN 0-306-40341-2, Plenum Pr). Plenum Pub.
Ristelhueber, Rene. History of the Balkan Peoples. Spector, Sherman D., ed. & tr. from Fr. LC 78-147184. (Illus.). 470p. 1978. 28.50x (ISBN 0-8290-0176-X); pap. text ed. 12.50x (ISBN 0-8290-0177-8). Irvington.
Ritcher, Ann R. The Foxes of Kincarra. 128p. 1981. 7.95 (ISBN 0-89962-209-7). Todd & Honeywell.
Ritcheson, Charles R. Edmund Burke & the American Revolution. (Sir George Watson Lectures). 1976. pap. text ed. 1.25x (ISBN 0-7185-1154-9, Leicester). Humanities.
Ritchey, John A. & Hulley, O. S. Manufacturing Organization & Management. 3rd ed. (Int'l. Series in Industrial & Systems Engineering). (Illus.). 608p. 1975. 19.95 (ISBN 0-13-555854-9). P-H.
Ritchey, W., jt. ed. see Grasselli, J.
Ritchie, Alice. Treasure of Li-Po. LC 49-10204. (Illus.). (gr. 4-6). 1949. 4.50 o.p. (ISBN 0-15-290158-2, HJ). HarBraceJ.
Ritchie, Andrew C., intro. by. Selected Paintings & Sculptures from the Yale University Art Gallery. LC 76-179475. (University Ser.: No. 2). (Illus.). 380p. 1972. 25.00x o.p. (ISBN 0-300-01562-3). Yale U Pr.
Ritchie, Anna & Ritchie, Graham. Scotland; Archaeology & Early History. (Ancient People & Places Ser.). (Illus.). 192p. 1981. 19.95 (ISBN 0-500-02100-7). Thames Hudson.
Ritchie, Anne, jt. auth. see Ritchie, Graham.
Ritchie, Arthur W. Heros of Seventy-Six! They Aren't What They Used to Be, but Then They Never Were. LC 80-50612. (Illus.). 255p. 1981. 9.95 (ISBN 0-9604516-0-9). Sigma Pr.
Ritchie, Barbara, ed. see Douglass, Frederick.
Ritchie, Carson I. The Decorated Gun. LC 78-75331. (Illus.). Date not set. 15.00 o.p. (ISBN 0-498-02203-X). A S Barnes. Postponed.
--Food in Civilization: How History Has Been Affected by Human Tastes. 192p. 1981. 8.95 (ISBN 0-8253-0037-1). Beaufort Bks NY.
Ritchie, David. The Ring of Fire. LC 80-69391. (Illus.). 296p. 1981. 12.95 (ISBN 0-689-11150-9). Atheneum.
--The Ring of Fire. LC 80-69391. 1981. 12.95 (ISBN 0-689-11150-9). Atheneum.
Ritchie, Donald & Carola, Robert. Biology. LC 78-67450. (Life Sciences Ser.). 1979. text ed. 20.95 (ISBN 0-201-06335-2); inst. manual avail. (ISBN 0-201-06336-0); study guide avail. (ISBN 0-201-06337-9). A-W.
Ritchie, Donald A. James M. Landis: Dean of the Regulators. LC 80-12828. 1980. text ed. 17.50x (ISBN 0-674-47171-7). Harvard U Pr.
Ritchie, Donald D., jt. auth. see Fuller, Harry J.
Ritchie, Everett J., jt. auth. see Hehner, Nels E.
Ritchie, Gary A., ed. New Agricultural Crops. (AAAS Selected Symposium: No. 38). 1979. lib. bdg. 23.00x (ISBN 0-89158-473-0). Westview.
Ritchie, George. Electronics Construction & Assembly. (Illus.). 1980. lib. bdg. 16.95 (ISBN 0-13-250472-3). P-H.
Ritchie, George G., Jr. Return from Tomorrow. 1978. 6.95 (ISBN 0-912376-23-6). Chosen Bks Pub.
Ritchie, Graeme D. Computational Grammar: An Artificial Intelligence Approach to Linguistic Description. (Harvester Studies in Cognitive Science: No. 15). 1980. 26.50x (ISBN 0-389-20048-4). B&N.
Ritchie, Graham & Ritchie, Anne. Edinburgh & South-East Scotland: Regional Archaeology. 1972. 5.50x o.p. (ISBN 0-435-32971-5). Heinemann Ed.
Ritchie, Graham, jt. auth. see Ritchie, Anna.
Ritchie, H. David, jt. ed. see Rains, A. J. Harding.
Ritchie, J. H., jt. auth. see Crawshaw, B. H.
Ritchie, J. M. German Expressionist Drama. Weisstein, Ulrich J., ed. (World Author Ser.: No. 421). 1977. lib. bdg. 9.95 (ISBN 0-8057-6261-2). Twayne.
Ritchie, James. Successful Homeowner's Tools. (Successful Ser.). 192p. 1980. 14.95 (ISBN 0-912336-85-4); pap. 7.95 (ISBN 0-912336-86-2). Structures Pub.
Ritchie, James, jt. auth. see Ritchie, Jane.
Ritchie, James D. Energy Use on the Farm. Case, Virginia, ed. (Illus.). 400p. 1981. 32.50 (ISBN 0-89999-029-0). Structures Pub.
--Successful Alternate Energy Methods. Frohn, Peggy, ed. LC 80-13103. (Successful Ser.). (Illus.). 1980. 14.95 (ISBN 0-89999-000-2); pap. 8.95 (ISBN 0-89999-001-0). Structures Pub.
--Successful Log Homes. LC 78-15308. 1978. 13.95 (ISBN 0-912336-71-4); pap. 6.95 (ISBN 0-912336-72-2). Structures Pub.
Ritchie, James L., et al. Thallium--201 Myocardial Imaging. LC 78-3004. 1978. 18.50 (ISBN 0-89004-274-8). Raven.
Ritchie, James M., ed. Periods in German Literature, Vol. 1. 1967. 15.95 (ISBN 0-85496-031-7); pap. 12.95 (ISBN 0-85496-032-5). Dufour.
Ritchie, Jane & Ritchie, James. Growing up in New Zealand. LC 78-52238. 1978. text ed. 13.50x (ISBN 0-86861-104-2); pap. text ed. 7.50x o.p. (ISBN 0-86861-112-3). Allen Unwin.
--Growing up in Polynesia. 1979. text ed. 13.50x (ISBN 0-86861-201-4); pap. text ed. 9.50x (ISBN 0-86861-209-X). Allen Unwin.
Ritchie, Jo-An. Jonie Goes to Academy. LC 78-21271. (Orion Ser.). (gr. 6-12). 1979. pap. 1.95 (ISBN 0-8127-0193-3). Southern Pub.
--Jonie Graduates. LC 78-27431. (Orion Ser.). (gr. 6-12). 1979. pap. 1.95 (ISBN 0-8127-0201-8). Southern Pub.
--Jonie's Direct Line. LC 75-44644. (Crown Ser.). 1976. pap. 4.50 (ISBN 0-8127-0110-0). Southern Pub.
Ritchie, Juanita. Polynesian Twilight. (Illus.). 170p. (Orig.). 1980. pap. 3.95 (ISBN 0-89260-179-5). Hwong Pub.
Ritchie, Oscar W., jt. auth. see Koller, Marvin R.
Ritchie, Paul. Australia. (Illus.). 1968. 3.95g o.s.i. (ISBN 0-02-776140-1). Macmillan.
Ritchie, Richard, jt. auth. see Powell, Enoch.
Ritchie, Robert L. The Normans in Scotland. LC 80-2216. 1980. Repr. of 1954 ed. 57.50 (ISBN 0-404-18783-8). AMS Pr.
Ritchie, Robert L. & Simons, C. J. Essays in Translation from French. text ed. 27.50x (ISBN 0-521-06092-3); pap. 10.95x (ISBN 0-521-09205-1). Cambridge U Pr.

Ritchie, Ward. A Bowl of Quince. (Santa Susana Press Ser.). 1977. 30.00 (ISBN 0-937048-15-1). CSUN.

Ritenour, Jacob V., jt. auth. see Gutsch, Kenneth U.

Ritger, Dick & Allen, George. The Complete Guide to Bowling Spares: The Encyclopedia of Spares. LC 78-68659. (Illus.). 240p. 1979. 14.95 (ISBN 0-933554-04-4); pap. 9.95 (ISBN 0-933554-05-2). Ritger Sports.

Ritger, Dick, jt. auth. see Allen, George.

Ritner, Peter. Red Carpet for the Shah. LC 75-15806. 224p. 1975. 6.95 o.p. (ISBN 0-688-02957-4). Morrow.

Ritschel, W. A. Handbook of Basic Pharmacokinetics. 2nd ed. LC 79-90428. 1980. 19.50 (ISBN 0-914768-34-4). Drug Intl Pubns.

Ritsko, Alan J. Lighting for Location Motion Pictures. 224p. 1980. pap. 8.95 (ISBN 0-442-23136-9). Van Nos Reinhold.

Ritson, Joseph. Ancient Songs & Ballads, from the Reign of King Henry 2nd to the Revolution. LC 67-23930. 1968. Repr. of 1877 ed. 20.00 (ISBN 0-8103-3417-8). Gale.

Ritsos, Yannis. Subterranean Horses. Savvas, Minas, tr. from Greek. LC 80-83220. (International Poetry: Vol. 3). (Illus.). xii, 63p. 1980. 10.95 (ISBN 0-8214-0579-9); pap. 6.95 (ISBN 0-8214-0580-2). Ohio U Pr.

Ritt, Lawrence, jt. ed. see Bauer, Carol.

Rittberger, Volker, jt. ed. see Krippendorff, Ekkehart.

Rittel, Horst, jt. auth. see Kunz, Werner.

Rittenhouse, George A., ed. see Hegel, Georg W.

Ritter, A. Anarchism. LC 80-40589. 196p. 1981. 27.50 (ISBN 0-521-23324-0). Cambridge U Pr.

Ritter, Alan. The Political Thought of Pierre-Joseph Proudhon. LC 80-19558. (Illus.). xii, 222p. 1980. Repr. of 1969 ed. lib. bdg. 23.50x (ISBN 0-313-22719-5, RIPT). Greenwood.

Ritter, Archibald R. The Economic Development of Revolutionary Cuba: Strategy & Performance. LC 73-3670. (Special Studies). (Illus.). 350p. 1974. text ed. 34.95 (ISBN 0-275-28727-0). Praeger.

Ritter, E. A. Shaka Zulu. 408p. (RL 10). 1973. pap. 1.95 o.p. (ISBN 0-451-61231-0, MJ1231, Ment). NAL.

Ritter, Frank N. The Paranasal Sinuses: Anatomy & Surgical Techniques. 2nd ed. LC 73-7519. (Illus.). 1978. text ed. 31.50 (ISBN 0-8016-4129-2). Mosby.

Ritter, Gerhard. Frederick the Great: A Historical Profile. Paret, Peter, tr. & intro. by. 1968. 15.75x (ISBN 0-520-01074-4); pap. 4.95x (ISBN 0-520-02775-2). U of Cal Pr.

Ritter, Lawrence S. & Silber, William L. Money. 4th, rev. ed. 336p. 1981. 12.95x (ISBN 0-465-04718-1); pap. 6.95x (ISBN 0-465-04720-3). Basic.

Ritter, Lawrence S., jt. auth. see Honig, Donald.

Ritter, Margaret. The Burning Woman. 1980. pap. 2.75 (ISBN 0-425-04463-7). Berkley Pub.

Ritter, Paul. Educreation: Education for Creation, Growth & Change. 2nd ed. 1978. text ed. 51.00 (ISBN 0-08-021475-4); pap. text ed. 26.00 (ISBN 0-08-021476-2). Pergamon.

--Planning for Man & Motor. 1964. 37.00 (ISBN 0-08-010417-7). Pergamon.

Ritter, Paul M. The Business Manager in the Independent School. 1980. pap. 6.50 (ISBN 0-934338-41-8). NAIS.

Ritter, Rhoda. Rocks & Fossils. (Easy-Read Fact Book Ser.). (Illus.). 48p. (gr. 2-4). 1977. PLB 4.47 o.p. (ISBN 0-531-00358-2). Watts.

Ritterband, P. Education, Employment & Migration. LC 76-62584. (ASA Rose Monographs). (Illus.). 1978. 19.95 (ISBN 0-521-21586-2); pap. 6.95x (ISBN 0-521-29192-5). Cambridge U Pr.

Ritterberger, Volker, ed. Science & Technology in a Changing International Order: The United Nations Conference on Science & Technology for Development. (Special Studies in Social, Political, & Economic Development). 200p. 1981. lib. bdg. 25.00x (ISBN 0-86531-146-3). Westview.

Ritterbush, Philip. Overtures to Biology: Speculations of Eighteenth Century Naturalists. 1964. 42.50x (ISBN 0-685-69859-9). Elliots Bks.

Ritterbush, Philip C., jt. ed. see Starr, Chauncey.

Ritter-Sanders, M. Handbook of Advanced Solid-State Troubleshooting. 1977. 18.95 (ISBN 0-87909-321-8). Reston.

Rittershausen, Brian & Rittershausen, Wilma. Orchids As Indoor Plants. (Illus.). 90p. 1980. 12.50 (ISBN 0-7137-0998-7, Pub. by Blandford Pr England). Sterling.

Rittershausen, Wilma, jt. auth. see Rittershausen, Brian.

Ritti, R. Richard. Engineer & the Industrial Corporation. LC 73-133913. 1971. 17.50x (ISBN 0-231-03373-7). Columbia U Pr.

Ritti, Richard R., jt. auth. see Klein, Stuart M.

Ritums, John, ed. see Martin, Philip R.

Ritvo, Edward R., jt. auth. see Conroy, Mary.

Ritz, David. The Man Who Brought the Dodgers Back to Brooklyn. 1981. price not set (ISBN 0-671-25356-5). S&S.

Ritz, Jean-Georges. Le Poete Gerard Manley Hopkins, S. J. (1844-1889) 726p. 1980. Repr. of 1963 ed. lib. bdg. 100.00 (ISBN 0-8492-7748-5). R West.

Ritzen, Martin, et al, eds. Biology of Normal Human Growth. Date not set. price not set. Raven.

Ritzer. Issues Debates & Controversies: An Introduction to Sociology. 1972. 7.95x o.s.i. (ISBN 0-205-03499-3, 8134995); instr's manual free o.s.i. (ISBN 0-205-04467-0). Allyn.

--Sociology: A Multiple Paradigm Science. rev ed. 300p. 1980. pap. text ed. 9.40 (ISBN 0-205-07073-6, 8170738). Allyn.

Ritzer, George. Issues, Debates & Controversies: An Introduction to Sociology. 2nd ed. LC 81-67214. 1980. pap. text ed. 10.45 (ISBN 0-205-06721-2, 8167214). Allyn.

--Sociology: A Multiple Paradigm Science. 240p. 1975. text ed. 10.95x o.p. (ISBN 0-205-04428-X, 8144281). Allyn.

--Towards an Integrated Social Paradigm: The Search for an Exemplar & an Image of the Subject Matter. 300p. 1981. pap. text ed. 13.95 (ISBN 0-205-06721-2). Allyn.

Ritzer, George, jt. auth. see Antonio, Robert J.

Ritzmann, Stephan E. & Daniels, Jerry C., eds. Serum Protein Abnormalities: Diagnostic & Clinical Aspects. (Series in Laboratory Medicine). (Illus.). 440p. 1975. 32.50 (ISBN 0-316-74754-8). Little.

Rivas, Gilberto L. The Chicanos: Life & Struggles of the Mexican Minority in the United States, with Readings. Martinez, Elizabeth, ed. LC 73-8056. 224p. (Bilingual). 1974. 7.95 o.p. (ISBN 0-85345-298-9, CL2989); pap. 4.95 (ISBN 0-85345-329-2, PB3292). Monthly Rev.

Rivas, Jose G., tr. see Torrey, R. A.

Rivas, Rafael Alberto. Survival: My Life in Love & War. 1977. 8.50 o.p. (ISBN 0-682-48942-5). Exposition.

Rivenburgh, Viola K. Tales of the Menehune, the Little Pixie Folk of Hawaii. (Illus.). 48p. 1980. pap. 3.95 (ISBN 0-918146-19-4). Peninsula WA.

Rivenes, Richard, et al. Foundations of Physical Education. LC 77-75155. (Illus.). 1978. text ed. 14.75 (ISBN 0-395-25389-6). HM.

River Oaks Garden Club, ed. Garden Book for Houston & the Gulf Coast. LC 75-5316. (Illus.). 191p. (Includes planting calendar). 1975. 8.95 (ISBN 0-88415-350-9). Pacesetter Pr.

Rivera, A. Ramon & Gruenbaum, Thelma. To Music & Children with Love! Reflections for Parents & Teachers. 133p. 1979. pap. 6.95 (ISBN 0-936190-03-5). ExPressAll.

Rivera, Carlos & Eastman, P. D., trs. Are You My Mother? In English & Spanish. (Spanish Beginner Bks: No. 4). (gr. 2-4). 1967. 3.95 (ISBN 0-394-81596-3); PLB 5.99 (ISBN 0-394-91596-8). Random.

Rivera, Carlos & Palmer, Helen, trs. A Fish Out of Water in English & Spanish. (Spanish Beginner Bks: No. 2). (gr. 2-4). 1967. 2.95 (ISBN 0-394-81598-X); PLB 5.99 (ISBN 0-394-91598-4). Random.

Rivera, Francisco P. & Hurtado, Mario. Introduccion a la Literatura Espanola. (gr. 11-12). 1976. pap. text ed. 7.95 (ISBN 0-88345-275-8). Regents Pub.

Rivera, Geronimo A. The Life & Adventures of Alonso, the Chattering Lay Brother & Servant of Many Masters. LC 80-2468. 1981. Repr. of 1845 ed. 57.50 (ISBN 0-404-19100-2). AMS Pr.

Rivera, Julius. Latin America: A Sociocultural Interpretation. rev. ed. LC 77-27271. 268p. 1980. text ed. 18.95x (ISBN 0-8290-0129-8); pap. text ed. 8.95x (ISBN 0-8290-0444-0). Irvington.

Rivera, Louis R., ed. see Ismaili, Rashidah, et al.

Rivera, Louis R., ed. see Killens, John O.

Rivera Cianchini, Osvaldo & Mojica Sandoz, Luis. Pajaros Notables De Puerto Rico: Guia Para Observadores De Aves. (Illus.). v, 101p. 1980. write for info. (ISBN 0-8477-2324-0); pap. write for info. (ISBN 0-8477-2325-9). U of PR Pr.

Rivera-Martinez, Carmen, jt. auth. see San Juan Cafferty, Pastora.

Rivero, Juan A. Los Anfibios y Reptils de Puerto Rico. LC 76-11798. (Illus.). 448p. (Orig.). 1976. pap. write for info. (ISBN 0-8477-2317-8). U of PR Pr.

Rivero, Oswald De see De Rivero, Oswaldo.

Rivers, Caryl & Lupo, Alan. For Better! for Worse! 256p. 1981. 12.95 (ISBN 0-671-25446-4). Summit Bks.

Rivers, Charles L. Robert Browning's Theory of the Poet, 1833-1841. (Salzburg Studies in English Literature, Romantic Reassessment Ser.: No. 58). (Orig.). 1976. pap. text ed. 25.00x (ISBN 0-391-01507-9). Humanities.

Rivers, E. L. Thirty-Six Spanish Poems. LC 57-13596. 1957. pap. text ed. 5.00 (ISBN 0-395-05099-5). HM.

Rivers, Earl, jt. tr. see Wydeville, A.

Rivers, Elias L., tr. see Zaldivar, Gladys.

Rivers, Francine. Kathleen. 1979. pap. 2.25 (ISBN 0-515-04726-0). Jove Pubns.

--Sycamore Hill. 288p. (Orig.). 1981. pap. 2.50 (ISBN 0-523-41324-6). Pinnacle Bks.

Rivers, Gayle & Hudson, James. The Contract Rescue. LC 80-1850. (Illus.). 240p. 1981. 11.95 (ISBN 0-385-17200-1). Doubleday.

Rivers, Isabel. Classical & Christian Ideas in English Renaissance Poetry. 1979. text ed. 24.95x (ISBN 0-04-807002-5); pap. text ed. 8.95x (ISBN 0-04-807003-3). Allen Unwin.

Rivers, Kay M. Jill Wins a Friend. LC 76-16021. (Kids in Sports Ser.). (Illus.). (gr. 1-3). 1976. PLB 4.95 (ISBN 0-913778-59-1); pap. 2.75 (ISBN 0-89565-123-8). Childs World.

Rivers, Paul. Cuaderno de Espanol Practico Comercial. 231p. 1980. pap. text ed. 7.95 (ISBN 0-686-64979-6, HC). HarBraceJ.

Rivers, R. W. On-Scene Traffic Accident Investigator's Manual. (Illus.). 192p. 1981. 32.75 (ISBN 0-398-04121-0). C C Thomas.

Rivers, Tresa. The Biography of Alfonzo Love. 1981. 6.95 (ISBN 0-533-03330-6). Vantage.

Rivers, W. Finding Facts: Interviewing, Observing, Using Reference Sources. 1975. pap. 8.95 (ISBN 0-13-316364-4). P-H.

Rivers, Wilga M. Teaching Foreign Language Skills. 2nd, rev. ed. LC 80-24993. 1981. lib. bdg. 22.00x (ISBN 0-226-72098-5); pap. 12.50x (ISBN 0-226-72097-7). U of Chicago Pr.

Rivers, Wilga M. & Temperley, Mary S. A Practical Guide to the Teaching of English: As a Second or Foreign Language. 1977. pap. 8.95x (ISBN 0-19-502210-6). Oxford U Pr.

Rivers, William E. Business Reports: Samples from the "Real World". (Illus.). 272p. 1981. pap. 9.95 (ISBN 0-13-107656-6). P-H.

Rivers, William H. Kinship & Social Organization: Together with the Genealogical Method of Anthropological Enquiry. LC 67-17557. (Monographs on Social Anthropology). (Illus.). 1968. text ed. 10.75x (ISBN 0-485-19534-8, Athlone Pr). Humanities.

Rivers, William L. Free - Lancer & the Staff Writer. 2nd ed. 1976. text ed. 14.95x (ISBN 0-534-00453-9). Wadsworth Pub.

--Writing: Craft & Art. 256p. 1975. pap. text ed. 7.50 (ISBN 0-13-970202-4). P-H.

Rivers, William L. & Smolkin, Shelley. Free-Lancer & Staff Writer: Newspaper Features & Magazine Articles. 3rd ed. 352p. 1980. text ed. 14.95x (ISBN 0-534-00873-9). Wadsworth Pub.

Rivers, William L., jt. ed. see Nimmo, Dan.

Rivers, William L., et al. Responsibility in Mass Communication. 3rd ed. LC 79-3400. 320p. 1980. 14.95 (ISBN 0-06-013594-8, HarpT). Har-Row.

Rivers, William L., et al, eds. Aspen Handbook on the Media: 1977-1979 Edition, a Selective Guide to Research, Organizations, & Publications in Communications. LC 77-14556. (Praeger Special Studies). 1977. 32.50 (ISBN 0-03-023141-8). Praeger.

Rivers, William R., jt. auth. see Sellers, Leonard.

Rivers-Coffey, Rachel. The City Man. LC 77-97. 1978. 7.95 o.s.i. (ISBN 0-06-013576-X, HarpT). Har-Row.

Rivett, Patrick, jt. auth. see Ackoff, R. L.

Riviere, Bill, jt. auth. see Lyman, Tom.

Riviere, J. Industrial Applications of Microbiology. Smith, J. & Moss, M., eds. Smith, J. & Moss, M., trs. LC 77-22815. 1978. 27.95 (ISBN 0-470-99265-4). Halsted Pr.

Riviere, Marie-Claude. Pin Pictures with Wire & Thread. Egan, E. W., tr. from Fr. LC 75-14521. (Little Craft Book Ser.). (Illus.). 48p. 1975. 5.95 (ISBN 0-8069-5340-3); PLB 6.69 (ISBN 0-8069-5341-1). Sterling.

Rivin, Zelma, jt. auth. see Clark, Anne.

Rivinus, M. W., jt. auth. see Bidde, K. H.

Rivkin, Arnold. Nation-Building in Africa: Problems & Prospects. Morrow, John, ed. 1970. 22.00 (ISBN 0-8135-0618-2). Rutgers U Pr.

Rivkin, S. Technology Unbound. 1969. 11.50 (ISBN 0-08-006424-8); pap. 6.25 (ISBN 0-08-006391-8). Pergamon.

Rivkin, Steven R. Cable Television: A Guide to Federal Regulations. LC 73-90819. (Rand Cable Television Ser.). 1974. 19.50x (ISBN 0-8448-0259-X). Crane-Russak Co.

Rivlin, Alice M. Systematic Thinking for Social Action. LC 74-161600. 1971. 11.95 (ISBN 0-8157-7478-8); pap. 4.95 (ISBN 0-8157-7477-X). Brookings.

Rivlin, Alice M. & Timpane, P. Michael, eds. Ethical & Legal Issues of Social Experimentation. (Studies in Social Experimentation). 180p. 1975. 10.95 (ISBN 0-8157-7482-6); pap. 4.95 (ISBN 0-8157-7481-8). Brookings.

--Planned Variation in Education: Should We Give up or Try Harder? (Studies in Social Experimentation). 184p. 1975. 11.95 (ISBN 0-8157-7480-X); pap. 4.95 (ISBN 0-8157-7479-6). Brookings.

Rivlin, Harry N., ed. see Stent, Madelon D.

Rivlin, Theodore J. The Chebyshev Polynomials. LC 74-10876. (Pure & Applied Mathematics Ser). 192p. 1974. 27.95 (ISBN 0-471-72470-X, Pub. by Wiley-Interscience). Wiley.

--An Introduction to the Approximation of Functions. 160p. 1981. pap. price not set (ISBN 0-486-64069-8). Dover.

Riwkin-Brick, Anna. My Swedish Cousins. (gr. 2-4). 1967. 4.95 o.s.i. (ISBN 0-02-776970-4). Macmillan.

Rix, Alan G. Japan's Economic Aid: Policy-Making & Politics. 1980. write for info. (ISBN 0-312-44063-4). St Martin.

Rix, Herbert D. Rhetoric in Spenser's Poetry. 88p. 1980. Repr. of 1940 ed. lib. bdg. 15.00 (ISBN 0-89987-712-5). Darby Bks.

Rix, Keith B. Alcohol & Alcoholism, Vol. I. Horrobin, D. F., ed. (Alcohol Research Review Ser.). 250p. 1980. Repr. of 1977 ed. 24.95x (ISBN 0-87705-960-8). Human Sci Pr.

Rix, Sara E., jt. auth. see Sheppard, Harold L.

Rixon, A. E. Fossil Animal Remains: Their Preparation and Conservation. (Illus.). 296p. 1976. pap. text ed. 18.25x (ISBN 0-485-12028-3, Athlone Pr). Humanities.

Rixon, Shelagh, jt. auth. see Byrne, Don.

Rizza, Paul F., et al. Pennsylvania Atlas: A Thematic Atlas of the Keystone State. 1976. pap. 6.95x o.p. (ISBN 0-686-23264-X). Ptolemy Pr.

Rizzi, Ennio A. Design & Estimating for Heating, Ventilating, & Air Conditioning. 480p. 1980. text ed. 27.95 (ISBN 0-442-26952-8). Van Nos Reinhold.

Rizzo, John R. Management for Librarians: Fundamentals & Issues. LC 79-8950. (Contributions in Librarianship & Information Science: No. 33). (Illus.). xvii, 339p. 1980. lib. bdg. 35.00 (ISBN 0-313-21990-7, RML/). Greenwood.

Rizzo, Joseph V., jt. auth. see Suran, Bernard G.

Rizzo, Mario J., ed. Time, Uncertainty & Disequilibrium: Exploration of Austrian Themes. LC 78-13872. 1979. 21.00 (ISBN 0-669-02698-0). Lexington Bks.

Rizzo, Raymond. The Total Actor. LC 74-28493. 264p. 1975. pap. 8.50 (ISBN 0-672-63276-4). Odyssey Pr.

--The Voice As an Instrument. 2nd ed. LC 77-9433. 1977. pap. text ed. 8.50 (ISBN 0-672-61407-3). Bobbs.

Rizzuto, Ana-Maria. The Birth of the Living God: A Psychoanalytic Study. LC 78-10475. (Illus.). 1979. 15.00x (ISBN 0-226-72100-0); pap. 6.50 (ISBN 0-226-72102-7). U of Chicago Pr.

--The Birth of the Living God: A Psychoanalytic Study. LC 78-10475. x, 246p. 1981. pap. 6.50 (ISBN 0-226-72102-7). U of Chicago Pr.

Rizzuto, Anthony. Camus' Imperial Vision. 1981. price not set (ISBN 0-8093-1002-3). S Ill U Pr.

Rizzuto, Charlz, tr. see Balbin, Julius.

Rjndt, Phillipe Van see Van Rjndt, Phillipe.

Rmiker-Sebeok, Jean, jt. ed. see Winner, Irene P.

Roa, K. L. India's Water Wealth. rev. ed. 1980. 11.00x (ISBN 0-8364-0580-3, Pub. by Orient Longman). South Asia Bks.

Roach, Dale E., jt. auth. see Roth, David A.

Roach, Eugene & Kephart, Newell. Purdue Perceptual-Motor Survey. LC 66-14493. (To be used with The Slow Learner in the Classroom). 1966. pap. text ed. 13.95x spiral bdg. (ISBN 0-675-09797-5). Merrill.

Roach, John. Public Examinations in England, 1850-1900. LC 71-123668. (Cambridge Texts & Studies in the History of Education). 1971. 37.50 (ISBN 0-521-07931-4). Cambridge U Pr.

Roach, Marilynne. Down to Earth at Walden. (gr. 5 up). 1980. 7.95 (ISBN 0-395-29647-1). HM.

Roach, Marilynne K. Encounters with the Invisible World: Being Ten Tales of Ghosts, Witches, & the Devil Himself in New England. LC 76-22186. (Illus.). (gr. 5-9). 1977. 7.95 (ISBN 0-690-01277-2, TYC-J). T Y Crowell.

--The Mouse & the Song. LC 73-13877. (Illus.). 48p. (ps-3). 1974. 5.95 o.s.i. (ISBN 0-8193-0721-1, Four Winds); PLB 5.41 o.s.i. (ISBN 0-8193-0722-X). Schol Bk Serv.

Roach, Mary Ellen & Eicher, Joanne B., eds. Dress, Adornment, & the Social Order. LC 65-19482. 1965. pap. text ed. 14.95x (ISBN 0-471-72476-9). Wiley.

Roach, Penelope. Political Socialization in the New Nations of Africa. LC 66-24873. (Orig.). pap. text ed. 3.50x (ISBN 0-8077-2042-9). Tchrs Coll.

Road, Sinclair, tr. see Cocteau, Jean.

Roadarmel, Gordon, ed. & tr. Death in Delhi: Modern Hindi Short Stories. LC 74-187871. 1973. 12.95x (ISBN 0-520-02220-3). U of Cal Pr.

Roads, C., ed. see International Computer Music Conference, 1978.

Roaf, R. & Hodkinson, L. J. Basic Surgical Care. 2nd ed. (Illus.). 280p. 1977. 20.95x (ISBN 0-8464-0183-5); pap. text ed. 14.00x (ISBN 0-686-60819-4). Beekman Pubs.

Roalman, A. R. Investor Relations That Work. 148p. 1981. 34.95 (ISBN 0-8144-5620-0). Am Mgmt.

Roalman, Arthur R., ed. Investor Relations Handbook. LC 73-85192. 240p. 1974. 17.95 (ISBN 0-8144-5349-X). Am Mgmt.

Roane, Martha K. see Holt, Perry C., et al.

Roark, Albert E., jt. auth. see Stanford, Gene.

Roate, Mettja C. How to Make Wine in Your Own Kitchen. 12th ed. (Orig.). 1979. pap. 1.75 (ISBN 0-532-17241-8). Manor Bks.

--The New Hamburger & Hot Dog Cookbook. LC 74-20888. 1975. Repr. 8.95 o.p. (ISBN 0-87000-299-6). Arlington Hse.

Rob, ed. see Ballantyne, J.

Rob, ed. see Nixon, H. H.

Rob, C., ed. Vascular Surgery. 3rd ed. (Operative Surgery Ser.). 1976. 84.95 (ISBN 0-407-00644-3). Butterworths.

Rob, C., ed. see Logue, Valentine.

Rob, C., et al. General Principles & Breast & Hernia. (Operative Surgery Ser.). 1977. 67.95 (ISBN 0-407-00610-9). Butterworths.

Rob, Charles & Smith, Rodney, eds. Atlas of General Surgery. LC 80-41016. (Operative Surgery Ser.). (Illus.). 786p. 1980. text ed. 59.95 (ISBN 0-407-00206-5). Butterworths.

Rob, Charles, ed. see Roberts, David W.

Rob, Charles, ed. see Symon, Lindsay.

Robards, Karen. Island Flame. 1981. pap. 2.50 (ISBN 0-8439-0868-8, Leisure Bks). Nordon Pubns.

Robat, N. J., ed. see Erades, P. A.

Robaut, Alfred. L' Oeuvre Complet de Eugene Delacroix: Peintures, Dessins, Gravures Lithographies. LC 78-75310. (History & Literature of Art Ser). 1969. lib. bdg. 55.00 (ISBN 0-306-71628-3). Da Capo.

Robb. Lifestyle: The Autobiography of Robb. (Illus.). 1979. 19.95 (ISBN 0-241-10169-7, Pub. by Hamish Hamilton England). David & Charles.

Robb, Brian. Last of the Centaurs. (Illus.). (gr. k-4). 1979. PLB 6.95 (ISBN 0-233-97000-2). Andre Deutsch.

--My Grandmother's Djinn. LC 77-22646. (Illus.). 40p. (gr. k-4). 1978. lib. bdg. 6.95 (ISBN 0-590-07717-1, Four Winds); PLB 5.41 o.p. (ISBN 0-8193-0918-4). Schol Bk Serv.

--Twelve Adventures of the Celebrated Baron Munchausen. (Illus.). (gr. 2 up). 1979. PLB 7.95 (ISBN 0-233-97019-3). Andre Deutsch.

Robb, David M. The Art of the Illuminated Manuscript. LC 78-37830. (Illus.). 356p. 1973. 50.00 o.p. (ISBN 0-498-01118-6). A S Barnes.

Robb, George P. & Williamson, Ann P. An Introduction to Individual Appraisal. (Illus.). 360p. write for info. (ISBN 0-398-04473-2); pap. write for info. (ISBN 0-398-04474-0). C C Thomas.

Robb, John D. Hispanic Folk Music of New Mexico & the Southwest: A Self-Portrait of the People. LC 78-21392. (Illus.). 1980. 35.00 (ISBN 0-8061-1492-4). U of Okla Pr.

Robb, Louis. Dictionary of Modern Business. (Span. -Eng. & Eng. -Span.). 1960. 25.00 (ISBN 0-685-06098-5). Anderson Kramer.

Robb, Margaret D. Dynamics of Motor-Skill Acquisition. (Illus.). 192p. 1972. pap. text ed. 8.95 (ISBN 0-13-222059-8). P-H.

Robb, Peter. The Government of India & Reform: Polices Towards Politics & the Constitution 1916-1921, Vol. 32. (London Oriental Ser). 1977. 37.50x (ISBN 0-19-713590-0). Oxford U Pr.

Robb, Peter & Taylor, David, eds. Rule, Protest, Identity: Aspects of Modern South Asia. (Collected Papers on South Asia: No. 1). 1978. text ed. 11.75x (ISBN 0-391-00866-8). Humanities.

Robb, Sandra. Surrender in Paradise. 192p. (Orig.). 1980. pap. 1.50. S&S.

Robb, Thomas B. The Bonus Years. LC 68-28076. 1968. 5.95 o.p. (ISBN 0-8170-0410-6). Judson.

Robb, William, jt. auth. see Hamilton, Douglas M.

Robbe-Grillet, Alain, jt. auth. see Hamilton, David.

Robben, John. Coming to My Senses. 1977. pap. 1.75 o.p. (ISBN 0-345-24815-5). Ballantine.

Robbin, Ed. Woody Guthrie & Me: An Intimate Reminiscence. (Illus.). 1980. pap. 6.95 (ISBN 0-89581-015-8). Lancaster-Miller.

Robbin, Edward. Thursday's Child No. 2. LC 80-83893. (Anthology of Short Stories Ser.). (Illus.). 200p. (Orig.). 1980. pap. 5.00 (ISBN 0-9603518-2-5). Glen Pr.

Robbins. Political Economy: Past & Present. 1976. 15.00x (ISBN 0-231-04128-4). Columbia U Pr.

Robbins, Arthur. Expressive Therapy: A Creative Arts Approach to Depth-Oriented Therapy. LC 80-13005. 300p. 1980. text ed. 19.95x (ISBN 0-87705-101-1). Human Sci Pr.

Robbins, Carol & Robbins, Clive. Music for the Hearing Impaired. 1980. pap. 29.50 (ISBN 0-918812-11-9). Magnamusic.

Robbins, Charles. Harry Truman: Last of His Kind, an Informal Portrait. (Illus.). 1979. 10.95 (ISBN 0-688-03447-0). Morrow.

Robbins, Claire C., jt. auth. see Rinella, Richard J.

Robbins, Clive, jt. auth. see Robbins, Carol.

Robbins, David, jt. auth. see Brown, Richard.

Robbins, Franklyn A., jt. auth. see Mancini, Janet K.

Robbins, Harold. The Dream Merchants. 1980. pap. 3.50 (ISBN 0-671-83455-X). PB.

--Memories of Another Day. 1980. pap. 3.50. PB.

--Where Love Has Gone. 1977. pap. 3.50 (ISBN 0-671-82676-X). PB.

Robbins, Harry W., tr. see De Lorris, Guillaume & De Meun, Jean.

Robbins, Herbert, jt. auth. see Courant, Richard.

Robbins, Jack. Pharmacy: A Profession in Search of a Role. LC 79-90142. (Illus.). 164p. 1980. 14.95 (ISBN 0-686-65738-1). Technomic.

Robbins, Jack A., ed. James T. Farrell - Literary Essays, 1954-1974. (Literary Criticism Ser.). 1976. 11.50 (ISBN 0-8046-9125-8, Natl U). Kennikat.

Robbins, Jack A., ed. see Hicks, Granville.

Robbins, Jacob J. Asthma Is Curable. 1965. 6.00 o.p. (ISBN 0-682-43045-5, University). Exposition.

Robbins, Jane. Citizen Participation & Public Library Policy. LC 74-34248. 191p. 1975. 10.00 (ISBN 0-8108-0796-3). Scarecrow.

Robbins, Jhan. Bess & Harry. large print ed. LC 80-27985. 1981. Repr. of 1980 ed. 9.95 (ISBN 0-89621-263-7). Thorndike Pr.

--Your Pet's Secret Language. 176p. 1976. pap. 2.95 (ISBN 0-446-93912-9). Warner Bks.

Robbins, Keith. John Bright. (Illus.). 1979. 25.00x (ISBN 0-7100-8992-9). Routledge & Kegan.

Robbins, Lord. Higher Education Revisited. 230p. 1980. text ed. 34.00x (ISBN 0-8419-5082-2). Holmes & Meier.

Robbins, Martin D., et al. Who Runs the Computer? Strategies for the Management of Computers in Higher Education. LC 75-19416. 102p. 1975. 19.75x (ISBN 0-89158-000-X). Westview.

Robbins, Maurice & Irving, Mary B. The Amateur Archaeologist's Handbook. rev. ed. (Illus.). 304p. 1973. 11.95 (ISBN 0-690-05569-2, TYC-T). T Y Crowell.

--The Amateur Archaeologist's Handbook. 3rd ed. LC 80-7901. (Illus.). 304p. 11.95 (ISBN 0-690-01976-9, HarpT). Har-Row.

Robbins, Naomi, jt. auth. see Herstein, Sheila.

Robbins, Peter, jt. ed. see Edwards, John.

Robbins, R. H., ed. Sir Thomas Browne's Pseudodoxia Epidemica. (Oxford English Texts Ser.). (Illus.). 1000p. 1980. 129.00 (ISBN 0-19-812706-5). Oxford U Pr.

Robbins, Richard G., Jr. Famine in Russia, 1891-1892. LC 74-8528. (Studies of the Russian Institute of Columbia University). 1975. 17.50x (ISBN 0-231-03836-4). Columbia U Pr.

Robbins, Rossell H. see Rowland, Beryl.

Robbins, Roy M. Our Landed Heritage: The Public Domain, 1776-1970. 2nd rev. ed. LC 75-3569. (Illus.). xii, 503p. (A Bicentennial Edition). 1976. pap. 5.95x (ISBN 0-8032-5803-8, BB 588, Bison). U of Nebr Pr.

Robbins, Royal. Advanced Rockcraft. (Illus.). 1973. wrappers 3.95 (ISBN 0-910856-56-7). La Siesta.

--Basic Rockcraft. (Illus.). 1970. wrappers 2.95 (ISBN 0-910856-34-6). La Siesta.

Robbins, Shawn, as told to. Ahead of Myself: Confessions of a Professional Psychic, Shawn Robbins As Told to Milton Pierce. LC 80-20486. 80. 9.95 (ISBN 0-13-004002-9). P-H.

Robbins, Stephen P. The Administrative Process. 2nd ed. (Illus.). 1980. text ed. 21.95 (ISBN 0-13-007385-7); study guide 7.95 (ISBN 0-13-007369-5). P-H.

--The Administrative Process: Integrating Theory & Practice. 512p. 1976. 18.95 o.p. (ISBN 0-13-007419-5); 6.50 o.p. study guide (ISBN 0-13-007393-8). P-H.

--Organizational Behavior: Concepts & Controversies. (Illus.). 1979. ref. 19.95 (ISBN 0-13-641464-8). P-H.

--Personnel: The Management of Human Resources. LC 77-23046. (Illus.). 1978. text ed. 19.95 (ISBN 0-13-657833-0). P-H.

Robbins, Sterling. Auyana. Date not set. price not set o.p. (ISBN 0-295-95788-3). U of Wash Pr. Postponed.

Robbins, Tom. Another Roadside Attraction. 352p. 1981. pap. 6.95 (ISBN 0-345-29469-6). Ballantine.

--Another Roadside Attraction. 1975. pap. 2.95 (ISBN 0-345-29245-6). Ballantine.

--Still Life with Woodpecker. 288p. (Orig.). 1980. 12.95 (ISBN 0-553-05000-1); pap. 6.95 (ISBN 0-553-01260-6). Bantam.

Robbins, William J., et al. Growth. 1928. 29.50x (ISBN 0-685-89755-9). Elliots Bks.

Robe, Lucy B. Haunted Inheritance. LC 79-56903. (Illus., Orig.). 1980. pap. 5.95 (ISBN 0-89638-042-4). Compcare.

Robe, Stanley. Hispanic Folktales from New Mexico: Narratives from the R.D. Jameson Collection. (Publications in Folklore & Mythology: No. 30). 1977. pap. 10.50x o.p. (ISBN 0-520-09570-7). U of Cal Pr.

Robe, Stanley L. Amapa Storytellers. (U. C. Publ. in Folklore Studies: Vol. 24). 1972. pap. 10.00x (ISBN 0-520-09391-7). U of Cal Pr.

--Azuela & the Mexican Underdogs. LC 76-20031. 1979. 20.00x (ISBN 0-520-03293-4). U of Cal Pr.

Robeck, Bruce W. Legislators & Party Loyalty: The Impact of Reapportionment in California. LC 77-18634. 1978. pap. text ed. 7.50 (ISBN 0-8191-0424-8). U Pr of Amer.

Robeck, Mildred C. & Wilson, John A. Psychology of Reading: Foundations of Instruction. LC 73-13797. 600p. 1974. text ed. 23.95 (ISBN 0-471-72580-3). Wiley.

Roben, Paul, jt. ed. see Chapman, Caroline.

Roberg, Roy R. Police Management & Organizational Behavior: A Contingency Approach. (Criminal Justice Ser.). (Illus.). 1979. text ed. 18.50 (ISBN 0-8299-0275-9); instrs.' manual avail. (ISBN 0-8299-0599-5). West Pub.

Roberg, Roy R. & Webb, Vincent J. Critical Issues in Corrections: Problems, Trends, & Prospects. 300p. 1981. pap. text ed. 10.95 (ISBN 0-8299-0405-0). West Pub.

Roberge, James K., jt. auth. see Wedlock, Bruce D.

Roberge, Paul T., ed. see Hesseling, Dirk C.

Roberge, Paul T., ed. see Melcuk, Igor A.

Roberson, John & Roberson, Marie. Complete Barbecue Cookbook. 1967. pap. 1.95 o.s.i. (ISBN 0-02-081240-X, Collier). Macmillan.

Roberson, John A. & Crowe, Clayton T. Engineering Fluid Mechanics. 1975. text ed. 20.95 o.p. (ISBN 0-395-18607-2); sol. manual 5.35 o.p. (ISBN 0-395-18782-6). HM.

--Engineering Fluid Mechanics. 2nd ed. LC 79-87855. (Illus.). 1980. text ed. 24.50 (ISBN 0-395-28357-4); solutions manual 2.50 (ISBN 0-395-28358-2). HM.

Roberson, John R. China from Manchu to Mao. LC 79-22269. (Illus.). 208p. (gr. 5 up). 1980. 10.95 (ISBN 0-689-30758-6). Atheneum.

Roberson, Marie, jt. auth. see Roberson, John.

Roberson, Rick, jt. auth. see Engdahl, Sylvia L.

Robert, A. M. & Robert, L., eds. Biology & Pathology of Elastic Tissues. (Frontiers of Matrix Biology Ser.: Vol. 8). (Illus.). viii, 232p. 1980. 74.25 (ISBN 3-8055-3078-1). S Karger.

Robert Bentley, Inc. Audi Fox Service Manual, 1973, 1974, 1975, 1976, 1977, 1978, 1979. LC 79-53187. (Illus.). 1979. pap. 24.95 (ISBN 0-8376-0097-9). Bentley.

--Toyota Corolla Tercel Service Manual 1980-1981. pap. 18.50 (ISBN 0-8376-0250-5). Bentley.

--Toyota Corolla 1.8 Service Manual 1980-1981. pap. 18.50 (ISBN 0-8376-0245-9). Bentley.

--Volkswagen Dasher Service Manual Model Years 1974-1981. (Illus.). 1980. pap. 19.95 (ISBN 0-8376-0083-9). Bentley.

--Volkswagen Rabbit Diesel Service Manual, 1977-1981. (Illus.). 432p. (Orig.). 1980. pap. 18.50 (ISBN 0-8376-0104-5). Bentley.

--Volkswagen Rabbit Diesel Service Manual 1977-1981, Including Pickup Truck. rev. ed. (Illus.). 480p. (Orig.). 1981. pap. 18.50 (ISBN 0-8376-0104-5). Bentley.

--Volkswagen Rabbit-Scirocco Service Manual, Gasoline Models, 1975, 1976, 1977, 1978, 1979. rev. ed. LC 79-57170. (Illus.). 628p. (Orig.). 1980. pap. 18.50 (ISBN 0-8376-0098-7). Bentley.

--Volkswagen Rabbit-Scirocco Service Manual 1980-1981, Gasoline Models, Including Pickup Truck. rev. ed. (Illus.). 600p. (Orig.). 1981. pap. 18.50 (ISBN 0-8376-0099-5). Bentley.

Robert, Bruce & Stick, David. Cape Hatteras Seashore. LC 64-23727. (Illus.). 3.95 (ISBN 0-87461-950-5). McNally.

Robert, H. M. Robert's Rules of Order. (Spire Bk). 1967. pap. 1.95 (ISBN 0-8007-8038-8). Revell.

Robert, Henry M. Parliamentary Law. 588p. 1981. pap. 19.95 (ISBN 0-686-28898-X). Lewis Pub Co.

--Parliamentary Practice: An Introduction to Parliamentary Law. 203p. 1981. pap. 4.95 (ISBN 0-86616-008-6). Lewis Pub Co.

--Robert's Rules of Order. Vixman, Rachel, ed. (YA) (gr. 9-12). 1967. pap. 1.95 (ISBN 0-515-05366-X). Jove Pubns.

--Robert's Rules of Order Revised. 1971. pap. 3.95 (ISBN 0-688-05306-8). Morrow.

Robert, Henry M., et al. Robert's Rules of Order Newly Revised. 1970. 10.95x (ISBN 0-673-05714-3); lea. 24.95x (ISBN 0-673-07675-X). Scott F.

Robert, L., jt. ed. see Robert, A. M.

Robert Lang Adams & Associates, ed. The Chicago Job Bank: A Comprehensive Guide to Major Employers Throughout Greater Chicago. (Job Bank Ser.). 300p. (Orig.). 1981. pap. 9.95 (ISBN 0-937860-05-0). Adams Inc MA.

--The Los Angeles Job Bank: A Comprehensive Guide to Major Employers Throughout Greater Los Angeles. (Job Bank Ser.). 300p. (Orig.). 1981. pap. 9.95 (ISBN 0-937860-04-2). Adams Inc MA.

Robert Lang Adams Associates, ed. The New York Job Bank: Conprehensive Guide to Major Employers Throughout Greater New York City Including Northern New Jersey, Southwestern Connecticut, Long Island, Southeastern New York State, & All Five Boroughs of New York City. 450p. (Orig.). 1981. pap. 9.95 (ISBN 0-937860-03-4). Adams Inc MA.

Robert, Marthe. The Old & the New: From Don Quixote to Kafka. Cosman, Carol, tr. 1977. 19.50x (ISBN 0-520-02509-1). U of Cal Pr.

--Origins of the Novel. Rabinovitch, Sacha, tr. from Fr. LC 80-7970. 256p. 1980. 19.95x (ISBN 0-253-18824-5). Ind U Pr.

Robert, William J., jt. auth. see Corley, Robert N.

Robert Clark, Gillean. Resource Recovery Planning & Management. 1981. text ed. 24.00 (ISBN 0-250-40298-X). Ann Arbor Science.

Robertis, Eduardo De see DeRobertis, Eduardo & Schacht, Jochen.

Roberts. The Cardiac Conducting System & the HIS Bundle Electrogram. 1975. 18.50 o.p. (ISBN 0-8385-1040-X). ACC.

--A Century of Friedel-NCrafts Alkylations & Re-Arrangements. Date not set. price not set (ISBN 0-8247-6433-1). Dekker.

--Seven Bears. (gr. 3-5). pap. 1.25 (ISBN 0-590-05413-9, Schol Pap). Schol Bk Serv.

Roberts, A. Applied Geotechnology: A Text for Students & Engineers on Rock Excavation & Related Topics. (Illus.). 416p. 1981. 50.00 (ISBN 0-08-024015-1); pap. 25.00 (ISBN 0-08-024014-3). Pergamon.

Roberts, A. & Bush, B. M., eds. Neurones Without Impulses. LC 79-42572. (Society for Experimental Biology Seminar Ser.). (Illus.). 250p. Date not set. 59.50 (ISBN 0-521-23364-X); pap. 19.95 (ISBN 0-521-29935-7). Cambridge U Pr.

Roberts, A. Wayne. Introductory Calculus: Second Edition with Analytic Geometry & Linear Algebra. 1972. text ed. 20.95 (ISBN 0-12-589756-1); answer bk 3.00 (ISBN 0-12-589758-8). Acad Pr.

Roberts, Ada L. Love So Freely Given. 1981. 8.95 (ISBN 0-533-04814-1). Vantage.

--The New Book of Favorite Breads from Rose Lane Farm. 2nd, rev. ed. (Illus.). 192p. 1981. pap. 3.00 (ISBN 0-486-24091-6). Dover.

Roberts, Adam. Nations in Arms: The Theory & Practice of Territorial Defense. LC 76-10671. (Special Studies). (Illus.). 280p. 1976. text ed. 24.95 (ISBN 0-275-23170-4). Praeger.

Roberts, Adam, jt. auth. see Windsor, Philip.

Roberts, Alan W. Einstein As I Knew Him. 7.95 (ISBN 0-89523-001-1). Green Hill.

Roberts, Albert. Sourcebook on Prison Education: Past, Present, & Future. 224p. 1971. pap. 13.50 spiral (ISBN 0-398-02190-2). C C Thomas.

Roberts, Albert F. Geotechnology: An Introductory Text for Students & Engineers. LC 76-45440. 1977. text ed. 59.00 (ISBN 0-08-019602-0); pap. text ed. 24.75 (ISBN 0-08-021594-7). Pergamon.

Roberts, Albert O. The Nucleon Simplified. 1980. 4.95 (ISBN 0-533-04319-0). Vantage.

Roberts, Albert R. Self-Destructive Behavior. (Illus.). 232p. 1975. 22.75 (ISBN 0-398-03290-4). C C Thomas.

--Sheltering Battered Women: A National Study & Service Guide. LC 80-19827. (Focus on Women Ser.: No. 3). 228p. 1980. text ed. 22.95 (ISBN 0-8261-2690-1); pap. text ed. 15.95 (ISBN 0-8261-2691-X). Springer Pub.

Roberts, Albert R., ed. Childhood Deprivation. 232p. 1974. 14.75 (ISBN 0-398-03149-5). C C Thomas.

Roberts, Alice C. Aphasic Child: A Neurological Basis for His Education & Rehabilitation. 96p. 1970. 7.50 (ISBN 0-398-01595-3). C C Thomas.

Roberts, Alvin. Psychosocial Rehabilitation of the Blind. 100p. 1973. 11.75 (ISBN 0-398-02834-6). C C Thomas.

Roberts, Andrew O. A History of the Bemba: Political Growth & Change in North-Eastern Zambia Before 1900. LC 73-5813. 408p. 1974. 30.00 (ISBN 0-299-06450-6). U of Wis Pr.

Roberts, Ann. Growing Vegetables in Alaska: & Other Far North Climates. (Illus.). 200p. 1981. 10.95 (ISBN 0-918270-08-1). That New Pub.

Roberts, B., jt. auth. see Reschenthaler, G. B.

Roberts, B. C., et al. Reluctant Militants. 1972. text ed. 15.75x o.p. (ISBN 0-435-85780-0). Heinemann Ed.

Roberts, B. H. Comprehensive History of the Church of Jesus Christ of Latter-Day-Saints, 6 vols. 1978. pap. 9.95 set (ISBN 0-8425-1275-6). Brigham.

Roberts, B. H., intro. by. History of the Church, 7 vols. Incl. Vol. 1 (1820-1834) 511p. 1974 (ISBN 0-87747-074-X); Vol. 2 (1834-1837) 543p. 1974 (ISBN 0-87747-075-8); Vol. 3 (1834-1839) 478p (ISBN 0-87747-076-6); Vol. 4 (1839-1842) 620p (ISBN 0-87747-077-4); Vol. 5 (1842-1843) 563p (ISBN 0-87747-078-2); Vol. 6 (1843-1844) 641p (ISBN 0-87747-079-0); Vol. 7 (period 2, The Apostolic Interregnum) 640p (ISBN 0-87747-080-4). 9.95 ea.; index 9.95 (ISBN 0-87747-291-2). Deseret Bk.
Roberts, B. M., jt. auth. see Billington, N. S.
Roberts, B. M., jt. auth. see Croome, D. J.
Roberts, B. T. Holiness Teachings. pap. 2.95 o.p. (ISBN 0-686-12880-X). Schmul Pub Co.
--Pungent Truths. pap. 3.50 o.p. (ISBN 0-686-12903-2). Schmul Pub Co.
Roberts, Bernice R., jt. auth. see Gilchrist, Robert S.
Roberts, Bette B. The Gothic Romance: Its Appeal to Women Writers & Readers in Late Eighteenth-Century England. Varma, Devendra P., ed. LC 79-8474. (Gothic Studies & Dissertations Ser.). 1980. lib. bdg. 25.00x (ISBN 0-405-12658-1). Arno.
Roberts, Blaine & Schulze, David L. Modern Mathematics & Economic Analysis. 1973. 16.95x (ISBN 0-393-09392-1); study guide 4.95x (ISBN 0-393-09374-3). Norton.
Roberts, Bobby, II, ed. see Williams, Hobie L.
Roberts, Brian. Diamond Magnates. (Illus.). 1973. 8.95 o.p. (ISBN 0-684-14661-4, ScribT). Scribner.
Roberts, Brian & Furneaux, Barbara, eds. Autistic Children. (Special Needs in Education Ser.). 1979. pap. 7.95 (ISBN 0-7100-0348-X). Routledge & Kegan.
--Autistic Children: Teaching, Community & Research Approaches. (Special Needs in Education Ser.). 1977. 17.00x (ISBN 0-7100-8704-7). Routledge & Kegan.
Roberts, Brian R., jt. auth. see Buckley, Peter J.
Roberts, Bruce. Carolina Goldrush: America's First. LC 70-165464. 4.50 (ISBN 0-87461-958-0). McNally.
--Old Salem in Pictures. (Illus., Orig.). 1968. 3.95 (ISBN 0-87461-951-3). McNally.
--This Haunted Land. 5.95 (ISBN 0-87461-956-4). McNally.
Roberts, Bruce & Roberts, Nancy. Ghosts & Specters: Ten Supernatural Stories from the Deep South. LC 73-20909. 96p. (gr. 5-7). 1974. 4.95 o.p. (ISBN 0-385-00698-5). Doubleday.
--Ghosts of the Carolinas. LC 62-21045. (Orig.). 5.95 (ISBN 0-87461-952-1); pap. 4.50 (ISBN 0-87461-953-X). McNally.
--Ghosts of the Wild West. LC 76-2813. (YA) (gr. 6-7). 1976. 5.95 o.p. (ISBN 0-385-11299-8). Doubleday.
--The Goodliest Land: North Carolina. LC 72-89345. (Illus.). 160p. 1973. 11.95 (ISBN 0-385-04302-3). Doubleday.
--Illustrated Guide to Ghosts & Mysterious Occurrences in the Old North State. LC 59-14157. (Orig.). 5.95 (ISBN 0-87461-954-8); pap. 4.50 (ISBN 0-87461-955-6). McNally.
--Where Time Stood Still: A Portrait of Appalachia. (gr. 5-9). 1970. 6.95 o.s.i. (ISBN 0-02-777440-6, CCPr). Macmillan.
Roberts, Bruce, jt. auth. see West, John F.
Roberts, Bryan R., jt. ed. see Long, Norman.
Roberts, Carey & Seely, Rebecca. Tidewater Dynasty: The Lees of Stratford Hall. 1981. 12.95 (ISBN 0-15-190294-1). HarBraceJ.
Roberts, Carol, jt. auth. see Feuerstein, Phillis.
Roberts, Catherine. The Scientific Conscience: Reflections on the Modern Biologist & Humanism. LC 67-11553. (Orig.). 1967. pap. 1.95 o.s.i. (ISBN 0-8076-0410-0). Braziller.
Roberts, Cecil E. A Soldier from Texas. Snyder, Carey H., ed. LC 78-67480. (Illus.). 1978. 12.50 (ISBN 0-87706-104-1); pap. 6.95. Branch-Smith.
Roberts, Cecilia M. Doctor & Patient in the Teaching Hospital: A Tale of Two Life-Worlds. LC 75-40629. 1977. 16.95 (ISBN 0-669-00453-7). Lexington Bks.
Roberts, Charles, jt. auth. see Kidwell, Clara S.
Roberts, Charles C. Tangled Justice: Some Reasons for a Change of Policy in Africa. LC 72-89011. Repr. of 1937 ed. 11.75x (ISBN 0-8371-1724-0). Negro U Pr.
Roberts, Charles E., Jr. Ordinary Differential Equations: A Computational Approach. LC 78-13023. 1979. 19.95 (ISBN 0-13-639757-3). P-H.
Roberts, Charles G. Selected Poetry & Critical Prose. Keith, W. J., ed. LC 73-91558. (Literature of Canada Ser.). 1974. pap. 5.95 (ISBN 0-8020-6206-7). U of Toronto Pr.
Roberts, Clarence, et al. Sharing of Scripture. LC 78-61724. 1978. pap. 2.95 (ISBN 0-8091-2141-7). Paulist Pr.
Roberts, Colin H. Manuscript, Society & Belief in Early Christian Egypt. (Schweich Lectures Ser.). 1979. 23.50x (ISBN 0-19-725982-0). Oxford U Pr.
Roberts, D. F. Climate & Human Variability. 2nd ed. LC 76-2227. 1978. pap. text ed. 5.95 o.p. (ISBN 0-8465-6625-7). Benjamin-Cummings.
Roberts, D. V., ed. Enzyme Kinetics. LC 76-11091. (Cambridge Chemistry Texts Ser.). (Illus.). 1977. 57.50 (ISBN 0-521-21274-X); pap. 16.95x (ISBN 0-521-29080-5). Cambridge U Pr.
Roberts, D. W. Gynecology & Obstetrics. (Operative Surgery Ser.). 1977. 49.95 (ISBN 0-407-00615-X). Butterworths.
Roberts, Dana. Understanding Watchman Nee. (Orig.). 1981. pap. 4.95 (ISBN 0-88270-489-3). Logos.
Roberts, Daniel A. & Boothroyd, Carl W. Fundamentals of Plant Pathology. LC 77-169737. (Illus.). 1972. text ed. 24.95x (ISBN 0-7167-0822-1). W H Freeman.
Roberts, David. Deborah: A Wilderness Narrative. LC 76-134663. (Illus.). (gr. 7-12). 8.95 (ISBN 0-8149-0677-X). Vanguard.
--Great Exploration Hoaxes. Michaelman, Herbert, ed. 1981. 12.95 (ISBN 0-517-54075-4, Michaelman Books). Crown.
--Mountain of My Fear. LC 68-20393. (Illus.). (gr. 7-12). 1968. 8.95 (ISBN 0-8149-0192-1). Vanguard.
--Paternalism in Early Victorian England. 1979. 24.00 (ISBN 0-8135-0868-1). Rutgers U Pr.
Roberts, David & Gadbois, Robert. Adventure at Murray's: A Strange Shopping Trip. LC 77-1646. (Books by Children for Children). 1977. PLB 6.45 (ISBN 0-87191-611-8). Creative Ed.
Roberts, David R. Executive Compensation. LC 58-12851. 1959. 8.50 o.s.i. (ISBN 0-02-926590-8). Free Pr.
Roberts, David W. Clinical Surgery: Gynaecology & Obstetrics, Vol. 15. Rob, Charles & Smith, Rodney, eds. (Illus.). 1968. 12.00 o.p. (ISBN 0-397-58017-7). Lippincott.
Roberts, Del, ed. see Bodie, Idella F.
Roberts, Del, ed. see Wongrey, Jan.
Roberts, Dennis. Well... Excuse Me. LC 80-84233. 64p. (Orig.). 1981. pap. 1.25 (ISBN 0-89081-265-9). Harvest Hse.
Roberts, Diana, jt. auth. see Roberts, Don.
Roberts, Don. Prayers for the Young Child. 1981. pap. 5.95 (ISBN 0-570-04051-5, 56-1717). Concordia.
Roberts, Don & Roberts, Diana. Mount St. Helens the Volcano of Our Time. (Illus.). 48p. (Orig.). pap. 5.95 (ISBN 0-936608-10-2). F Amato Pubns.
Roberts, Doreen. Teaching Art. 1978. 19.95 (ISBN 0-7134-0634-8, Pub. by Batsford England); pap. 14.95 (ISBN 0-7134-2314-5). David & Charles.
Roberts, Doug. To Adam with Love. pap. 1.95 (ISBN 0-89728-059-8, 533232). Omega Pubns OR.
Roberts, Douglas. To Adam with Love. Orig. Title: Para Adan Con Amor. 1977. 1.50 (ISBN 0-8297-0745-X). Life Pubs Intl.
--To Adam with Love. 1975. pap. 1.50 (ISBN 0-89129-009-5). Jove Pubns.
Roberts, Douglas, tr. Ao Adao, Com Amor. (Portugese Bks.). (Port.). 1979. 1.55 (ISBN 0-8297-0857-X). Life Pubs Intl.
Roberts, Douglas L., et al. The Dynamics of Dental Practice Administration: A Guide for Efficient Dental Health Care Delivery. LC 77-84139. 1977. spiral bdg. 18.00 (ISBN 0-87488-974-X). Med Exam.
Roberts, E., et al, eds. GABA in Nervous System Function. LC 74-21983. 576p. 1976. 36.50 (ISBN 0-89004-043-5). Raven.
Roberts, Ed, jt. auth. see Winnett, Thomas.
Roberts, Edgar V. Writing Themes About Literature. 4th ed. 1977. pap. text ed. 7.95 (ISBN 0-13-970582-1). P-H.
Roberts, Edgar V., ed. see Fielding, Henry.
Roberts, Edgar V., ed. see Gay, John.
Roberts, Edmund. Fundamentals of Men's Fashion Design: A Guide to Casual Clothes. new ed. LC 75-13691. (Illus.). 224p. 1975. 14.50x (ISBN 0-87005-104-0). Fairchild.
Roberts, Elizabeth. Childhood Sexual Learning: The Unwritten Curriculum. 1980. 22.50 (ISBN 0-88410-374-9). Ballinger Pub.
Roberts, Elizabeth H. On Your Feet. 1977. pap. 1.75 o.s.i. (ISBN 0-515-04385-0). Jove Pubns.
Roberts, Elizabeth M. The Great Meadow. 224p. 1975. pap. 1.50 o.p. (ISBN 0-89176-446-1, 6446). Mockingbird Bks.
Roberts, Ellis W. Along the Susquehanna. 128p. 1980. 7.95 (ISBN 0-686-28856-4). Colwyn-Tangno.
Roberts, Eric. More Flower Arrangement. (Teach Yourself Ser.). 1975. pap. 2.95 o.p. (ISBN 0-679-10429-1). McKay.
Roberts, Eric B. From Football to Finance: The Story of Brady Keys Jr. LC 70-151026. (Illus.). (gr. 7 up). 1971. 4.75 o.p. (ISBN 0-15-230265-4, HJ). HarBraceJ.
Roberts, Ernie. Worker's Control. (Ruskin House Ser. in Trade Union Studies). 1973. text ed. 12.50x o.p. (ISBN 0-04-321013-9); pap. text ed. 6.95x (ISBN 0-04-321014-7). Allen Unwin.
Roberts, Estelle, et al, eds. The Horse World Catalog. LC 76-21819. 1977. pap. 7.95 o.p. (ISBN 0-397-01026-5). Lippincott.
Roberts, Florence B. Review of Pediatric Nursing. 2nd ed. LC 77-14579. 1978. pap. text ed. 9.50 (ISBN 0-8016-4133-0). Mosby.
Roberts, Frances. Angel in the Fire. 1979. pap. 2.50 (ISBN 0-932814-31-X). Kings Farspan.
Roberts, Frank. To All Generations, a Study of Church History. 276p. (Orig.). 1981. pap. text ed. price not set (ISBN 0-933140-17-7); price not set tchr's manual (ISBN 0-933140-18-5). Bd of Pubns CRC.
Roberts, Fred M. Nikonos Photography: The Camera & the System. 3rd ed. LC 77-80027. 1977. pap. 6.00 (ISBN 0-912746-00-9, Dist. by Aqua-Craft, Inc.). F M Roberts.
Roberts, Fred S. Discrete Mathematical Models with Applications to Social Biological & Environmental Problems. (Illus.). 560p. 1976. Ref. Ed. 22.95 (ISBN 0-13-214171-X). P-H.
Roberts, Geoffrey. Reading in the Primary School. (Students Library of Education). 1969. pap. text ed. 2.75x (ISBN 0-7100-6519-1). Humanities.
Roberts, Geoffrey R. English in Primary Schools. 1972. 12.00x (ISBN 0-7100-7308-9); pap. 5.00 (ISBN 0-7100-7309-7). Routledge & Kegan.
Roberts, Gerald, ed. see Hopkins, Gerard M.
Roberts, Glyn, jt. ed. see Landers, Daniel.
Roberts, Grace S., tr. see Hunt, Gladys.
Roberts, Grace S., tr. see Kunz, Marilyn & Schell, Catherine.
Roberts, Grace S., tr. see Peace, Richard.
Roberts, H. J. Causes, Ecology & Prevention of Traffic Accidents: With Emphasis Upon Traffic Medicine, Epidemiology Sociology & Logistics. (Illus.). 1200p. 1971. 54.75 (ISBN 0-398-02169-4). C C Thomas.
Roberts, Harry V. Conversational Statistics. (Data Analysis Series). 256p. 1974. pap. text ed. 15.95 (ISBN 0-07-053135-8, C). McGraw.
Roberts, Harry V., jt. auth. see Ling, Robert F.
Roberts, Harry V., jt. auth. see Wallis, W. Allen.
Roberts, Hayden. Community Development: Learning & Action. LC 78-12986. 1979. 15.00x (ISBN 0-8020-5437-4); pap. 6.50 (ISBN 0-8020-6351-9). U of Toronto Pr.
Roberts, Helen. Women, Health & Reproduction. 208p. (Orig.). 1981. pap. 11.95 (ISBN 0-7100-0703-5). Routledge & Kegan.
Roberts, Helen, ed. Doing Feminist Research. 224p. (Orig.). 1981. pap. price not set (ISBN 0-7100-0772-8). Routledge & Kegam.
Roberts, Helen H. Basketry of the San Carlos Apache Indians: Anthropological Papers of the Am. Museum of Natural History, Vol. 31, Pt. 2. LC 72-10331. (Beautiful Rio Grande Classics Ser). lib. bdg. 10.00 o.s.i. (ISBN 0-87380-096-6); pap. 8.00 o.p. (ISBN 0-87380-134-2). Rio Grande.
Roberts, Henry H. Occupational Hazards. 1981. pap. 2.50 (ISBN 0-8439-0904-8, Leisure Bks). Nordon Pubns.
Roberts, Herbert A. The Principles & Art of Cure by Homoeopathy. 286p. 1942. 14.95x (ISBN 0-8464-1042-7). Beekman Pubs.
Roberts, Howard R. Food Safety. 448p. 1981. 39.50 (ISBN 0-471-06458-0, Pub. by Wiley-Interscience). Wiley.
Roberts, I. F., jt. auth. see Cantor, Leonard M.
Roberts, J. & Whitehouse, D. G. Practical Plant Physiology. LC 75-46566. 1977. pap. text ed. 13.95x (ISBN 0-582-44127-7). Longman.
Roberts, J. Deotis, jt. ed. see Gardiner, James J.
Roberts, J. M. Europe, Eighteen Eighty to Nineteen Forty-Five. (General History of Europe Ser.). 1972. pap. text ed. 11.95x (ISBN 0-582-48310-7). Longman.
Roberts, J. W. Letters of John. Ferguson, Everett, ed. (Living Word New Testament Commentary Ser.: Vol. 18). 1968. 7.95 (ISBN 0-8344-0033-2). Sweet.
--Revelation to John. Ferguson, Everett, ed. LC 73-20857. (Living Word New Testament Commentary Ser.: Vol. 19). 1974. 7.95 (ISBN 0-8344-0074-X). Sweet.
Roberts, Jack. The Amazing Adventures of Lord Gore: A True Saga of the Old West. Collman, Russ, ed. (Illus.). 1977. 27.00 (ISBN 0-913582-07-7). Sundance.
--Lord Gore. (Illus.). 220p. 27.00 (ISBN 0-913582-07-7). Sundance.
--So You're Going to Take Tennis Seriously? (Illus.). 144p. 1974. pap. 3.50 (ISBN 0-911104-34-8). Workman Pub.
Roberts, James R., jt. auth. see Greenberg, Michael I.
Roberts, Jane. How to Develop Your ESP Power. new ed. LC 66-17331. 1980. pap. 5.95 (ISBN 0-8119-0354-0). Fell.
--Seth Speaks. LC 78-38925. (Illus.). 552p. 1972. 9.95 (ISBN 0-13-807206-X); pap. 5.95 (ISBN 0-13-807222-1). P-H.
--The Unknown Reality: Vol. One of a Seth Book. LC 77-1092. 308p. 1980. pap. 4.95 (ISBN 0-13-938779-X). P-H.
Roberts, Jane & Butts, Robert F. The Individual & the Nature of Mass Events: A Seth Book. LC 80-22600. 336p. 1981. 11.95 (ISBN 0-13-457259-9). P-H.
Roberts, Jane & Knower, Barry. Per-Se Award Plays, 1971: Special Issue 24. pap. 1.00 o.p. (ISBN 0-685-78409-6). The Smith.
Roberts, Janet L. Golden Lotus. (Orig.). 1981. pap. 2.50 (ISBN 0-446-81997-2). Warner Bks.
--Silver Jasmine. (Orig.). 1980. pap. 2.50 (ISBN 0-446-81998-0). Warner Bks.
Roberts, Jean & Ahuja, Elizabeth. Hearing Levels of U. S. Youths 12-17 Years. LC 74-11318. (Data from Health Examination Survey Ser. 11: No. 145). 65p. 1975. pap. 0.75 (ISBN 0-8406-0024-0). Natl Ctr Health Stats.
Roberts, Jean L., jt. auth. see Kimsey, Larry R.
Roberts, Jennifer. Tender Fugitive. (Orig.). 1980. pap. 2.50 (ISBN 0-505-51504-0). Tower Bks.
Roberts, Jim. The Original Floating Zoo. (Action Bks). (Illus.). 12p. (ps-3). 1975. pap. 3.50 (ISBN 0-570-07107-0, 56-1284). Concordia.
--Someone Who Cared. (Action Bks.). (Illus.). 12p. (ps-3). 1975. pap. 3.50 (ISBN 0-570-07104-6, 56-1281). Concordia.
--Star Force One Take Along Game. (gr. 3 up). 1980. pap. 3.95 (ISBN 0-671-95649-3). Wanderer Bks.
Roberts, John. Industrialization of Japan. LC 75-158425. (First Bks). (Illus.). (gr. 5-7). 1971. PLB 4.90 o.p. (ISBN 0-531-00747-2). Watts.
--Revolution & Improvement, 1775-1848. LC 75-17288. 1976. 28.50x (ISBN 0-520-03076-1). U of Cal Pr.
Roberts, John G. The Colonial Conquest of Asia. LC 75-38165. (Impact Bks Ser). (Illus.). 96p. (gr. 7 up). 1976. PLB 6.90 (ISBN 0-531-01126-7). Watts.
Roberts, John S. Black Music of Two Worlds. 1974. pap. 3.95 (ISBN 0-688-24344-4). Morrow.
--The Latin Tinge: The Impact of Latin American Music on the United States. LC 78-26534. (Illus.). 1979. 14.95 (ISBN 0-19-502564-4). Oxford U Pr.
--Oxytocin: Vol. 1. 1977. 14.40 (ISBN 0-88831-010-2). Eden Med Res.
Roberts, Joseph & Hawk, Bonnie. Legal Rights Primer: In & Out of the Classroom. 96p. (Orig.). 1980. pap. 5.00 (ISBN 0-87879-241-4). Acad Therapy.
Roberts, Joseph, jt. auth. see Holcenberg, John C.
Roberts, Joseph B., Jr. Of Love & Time. LC 80-50319. 1980. 7.95 (ISBN 0-916624-30-7). TSU Pr.
Roberts, Joseph M. O.S.H.A. Compliance Manual. (Illus.). 272p. 1976. 16.95 (ISBN 0-87909-599-7). Reston.
Roberts, Joseph M., Sr. Construction Management: An Effective Approach. (Illus.). 368p. 1980. 21.95; text ed. 15.95 (ISBN 0-8359-0927-1). Reston.
Roberts, Josephine A. Architectonic Knowledge in the New Arcadia (1590) Sidney's Use of Heroic Journey. (Salzburg Studies in English Literature: Elizabethan & Renaissance Ser.: No. 69). 1978. pap. text ed. 25.00x (ISBN 0-391-01510-9). Humanities.
Roberts, Julian L., jt. auth. see Ifft, James B.
Roberts, Julian L., Jr. & Ifft, James B. Frantz-Malm's Chemical Principles in the Laboratory. 2nd ed. (Illus.). 1977. lab. manual 10.95x (ISBN 0-7167-0184-7); tchr's manual avail.; individual experiments 0.50 ea. (ISBN 0-685-99797-9). W H Freeman.
Roberts, Julian L., Jr., jt. auth. see Ifft, James B.
Roberts, K., et al. Fragmentary Class Structure. 1977. pap. text ed. 17.95 (ISBN 0-435-82765-0); pap. text ed. 11.50 (ISBN 0-435-82766-9). Heinemann Ed.
Roberts, Kate L., ed. Hoyt's New Cyclopedia of Practical Quotations. rev. ed. LC 40-13383. (Funk & W Bk.). (YA) (gr. 9 up). 1940. thumb-indexed 10.95 o.p. (ISBN 0-308-40054-2, 429090, TYC-T). T Y Crowell.
Roberts, Keith. The Chalk Giants. LC 75-10687. (YA) 1975. 6.95 o.p. (ISBN 0-399-11559-5, Dist. by Putnam). Berkley Pub.
--Pavane. pap. 1.50 o.p. (ISBN 0-425-03142-X). Berkley Pub.
Roberts, Keith D. & Edwards, Jennifer M. Paediatric Intensive Care. 2nd ed. (Illus.). 1976. 28.25 (ISBN 0-632-08020-5, Blackwell). Mosby.
Roberts, Kenneth. Arundel. LC 33-19961. 1944. 12.95 (ISBN 0-385-04024-5). Doubleday.
--Arundel. 1976. pap. 1.95 o.p. (ISBN 0-449-30690-9, C690, Prem). Fawcett.
--Boon Island. 192p. 1981. pap. 2.50 (ISBN 0-449-24408-3, Crest). Fawcett.
--Captain Caution. 1977. pap. 1.50 o.p. (ISBN 0-449-30739-5, Q739, Prem). Fawcett.
--Captain Caution. 11.95 (ISBN 0-385-04794-0). Doubleday.
--Leisure. (Aspects of Modern Sociology, the Social Structure of Modern Britain Ser). 1970. pap. text ed. 9.75x (ISBN 0-582-48807-9). Humanities.

--Lively Lady. 1976. pap. 1.95 o.p. (ISBN 0-449-30784-0, Prem). Fawcett.
--The Lively Lady. 12.95 (ISBN 0-385-04261-2). Doubleday.
--Lydia Bailey. 1976. pap. 1.75 o.p. (ISBN 0-449-30693-3, X693, Prem). Fawcett.
--Lydia Bailey. 12.95 (ISBN 0-385-04271-X). Doubleday.
--Northwest Passage. 1981. pap. 2.95 (ISBN 0-449-24095-9, Crest). Fawcett.
--Oliver Wiswell. 1977. pap. 1.95 o.p. (ISBN 0-449-30696-8, C696, Prem). Fawcett.
--Rabble in Arms. 1977. pap. 1.95 o.p. (ISBN 0-449-30748-4, C748, Prem). Fawcett.

Roberts, Kenneth D. Contributions of Joseph Ives to Connecticut Clock Technology, 1810-1862. LC 77-118414. 1970. 24.00 (ISBN 0-913602-00-0). K Roberts.
--Eli Terry & the Connecticut Shelf Clock. LC 72-97556. 1973. 27.00 (ISBN 0-913602-06-X). K Roberts.
--Some Nineteenth Century English Woodworking Tools. (Illus.). 496p. 1980. text ed. 40.00x (ISBN 0-913602-40-X). K Roberts.

Roberts, Kenneth D., ed. Stanley Rule & Level Co. 1879 Price List of Tools & Hardware. 1973. 4.50 (ISBN 0-913602-05-1). K Roberts.
--Stanley Rule & Level Co. 1888 Price List of Tools. 1975. 4.50 (ISBN 0-913602-14-0). K Roberts.

Roberts, Kenneth H. & Sharples, Win, Jr. Primer for Film-Making: A Complete Guide to 16mm & 35mm Film Production. LC 70-91620. (Illus.). 1971. 16.50 o.p. (ISBN 0-672-53582-3); pap. 11.95 (ISBN 0-672-63582-8). Pegasus.

Roberts, Kenneth J. The Rest of the Week. LC 73-87984. 1975. pap. 2.95 (ISBN 0-87973-549-X). Our Sunday Visitor.

Roberts, L. W. Cytodifferentiation in Plants. LC 75-10041. (Developmental & Cell Biology Ser.: No. 2). (Illus.). 250p. 1976. 32.50 (ISBN 0-521-20804-1). Cambridge U Pr.

Roberts, Lamar, jt. auth. see Penfield, Wilder.

Roberts, Larry S., jt. auth. see Schmidt, Gerald D.

Roberts, Laura, jt. auth. see Kirby, Colleen.

Roberts, Leigh M., et al, eds. Comprehensive Mental Health: The Challenge of Evaluation. (Illus.). 1968. 27.50x (ISBN 0-299-05000-9). U of Wis Pr.

Roberts, Leonard. I Bought Me a Dog. (Illus.). 1976. pap. 1.25. Pikeville Coll.
--Old Greasybeard: Tales from the Cumberland Gap. LC 69-20398. (Illus.). 1980. pap. text ed. 7.95 (ISBN 0-933302-04-5). Pikeville Coll.
--Sang Branch Settlers: Folksongs & Tales of a Kentucky Mountain Family. LC 74-3357. (American Folklore Society Memoir Ser.: No. 61). (Illus.). 534p. 1974. 17.50x o.p. (ISBN 0-292-77510-5). U of Tex Pr.
--Sang Branch Settlers: Tales & Songs of an Eastern Kentucky Family. text ed. 12.00 (ISBN 0-933302-05-3); pap. text ed. 7.95 (ISBN 0-933302-06-1). Pikeville Coll.
--South from Hell-Fer Sartin. 287p. 1964. pap. 2.95. Pikeville Coll.

Roberts, Leonard W. & Agey, C. Buell. In the Pine: Selected Kentucky Folksongs. 2nd ed. LC 78-56599. 1979. 12.50 (ISBN 0-933302-25-8); pap. 7.95 (ISBN 0-933302-26-6). Pikeville Coll.

Roberts, Linda. Pepi. (Illus.). 32p. (gr. 4-6). 1977. 2.95 (ISBN 0-8059-2459-0). Dorrance.

Roberts, Margaret. California Pioneers: Tales of Explorers, Indians, & Settlers. (Illus.). 1981. 7.95 (ISBN 0-914598-42-2). Padre Prods.

Roberts, Martha D., jt. auth. see Roberts, Mervin F.

Roberts, Martin. Machines & Liberty 1789-1914. (A Portrait of Europe Ser.). (Illus.). 360p. 1973. pap. write for info. Oxford U Pr.

Roberts, Mary-Carter. Little Brother Fate. 1957. 3.75 o.p. (ISBN 0-374-18848-3). FS&G.

Roberts, Mervin F. All About Boas & Other Snakes. (Illus.). 96p. (Orig.). 1975. pap. 2.95 (ISBN 0-87666-904-6, PS-313). TFH Pubns.
--All About Chameleons & Anoles. (Illus.). 1977. pap. 2.50 (ISBN 0-87666-902-X, PS-310). TFH Pubns.
--All About Land Hermit Crabs. new ed. (Illus.). 1978. pap. text ed. 2.00 (ISBN 0-87666-920-8, PS-767). TFH Pubns.
--All About Salamanders. 96p. (Orig.). 1976. pap. 2.50 (ISBN 0-87666-901-1, PS-312). TFH Pubns.
--Breeding Zebra Finches. (Illus.). 96p. 1980. 2.95 (ISBN 0-87666-883-X, KW-056). TFH Pubns.
--Guinea Pigs for Beginners. (Illus.). 1972. pap. 2.00 (ISBN 0-87666-198-3, M-541). TFH Pubns.
--How to Raise Hamsters. pap. 2.00 (ISBN 0-87666-205-X, M508). TFH Pubns.
--Pigeons. (Orig.). pap. 2.00 (ISBN 0-87666-432-X, M512). TFH Pubns.
--Society Finches. (Illus.). 1979. 2.95 (ISBN 0-87666-990-9, KW-029). TFH Pubns.
--Society Finches, Breeding. (Illus.). 1979. 2.95 (ISBN 0-87666-991-7, KW-030). TFH Pubns.
--Teddy Bear Hamsters. (Illus.). 96p. (Orig.). 1974. pap. 2.50 (ISBN 0-87666-206-8, PS710). TFH Pubns.
--Turtles. (Illus.). 96p. 1980. 2.95 (ISBN 0-87666-928-3, KWO51). TFH Pubns.

Roberts, Mervin F. & Roberts, Martha D. All About Iguanas. (Orig.). 1976. pap. 2.50 (ISBN 0-87666-903-8, PS311). TFH Pubns.

Roberts, Mervin F., Jr. Your Terrarium. (Orig.). pap. 3.50 (ISBN 0-87666-225-4, M511). TFH Pubns.

Roberts, Michael. British Diplomacy & Swedish Politics, 1758-1773. LC 80-11499. 1980. 29.50x (ISBN 0-8166-0910-1). U of Minn Pr.
--Early Vasas. (Illus.). 1968. 59.95 (ISBN 0-521-06930-0). Cambridge U Pr.
--Fans: How We Go Crazy Over Sports. LC 76-26880. 1978. 8.95 o.s.i. (ISBN 0-915220-20-2); pap. 3.95 o.p. (ISBN 0-915220-46-6). New Republic.
--The Swedish Imperial Experience: Fifteen Sixty to Seventeen Eighteen. LC 78-58799. (Illus.). 1979. 23.50 (ISBN 0-521-22502-7). Cambridge U Pr.

Roberts, Michael, ed. The Faber Book of Comic Verse. 1978. 15.00 (ISBN 0-571-04833-1, Pub. by Faber & Faber); pap. 8.95 (ISBN 0-571-11263-3). Merrimack Bk Serv.

Roberts, Moss, tr. see Tse Tung, Mao.

Roberts, N. Use of Social Science Literature. (Information Sources in Sciences & Technology Ser.). 1976. 34.95 (ISBN 0-408-10602-6). Butterworths.

Roberts, Nancy. Week in Robert's World: The South. LC 69-16211. (Face to Face Books Ser). (Illus.). (gr. k-3). 1969. 4.50g o.s.i. (ISBN 0-685-16359-8, CCPr); text ed. 1.36 o.s.i. (ISBN 0-685-16360-1, CCPr). Macmillan.
--The Yoga Thing. 1973. 8.95 (ISBN 0-8015-9024-8, Hawthorn); pap. 5.95 (ISBN 0-8015-9025-6, Hawthorn). Dutton.

Roberts, Nancy, jt. auth. see Roberts, Bruce.

Roberts, Neal, ed. The Government As Land Developer. LC 75-41924. 1977. 21.95 (ISBN 0-669-00485-5). Lexington Bks.

Roberts, Neal A., ed. Property Tax Preferences for Agricultural Land. LC 79-52473. (Illus.). 140p. 1980. text ed. 18.00 (ISBN 0-916672-32-8). Allanheld.

Roberts, Nesta. Mental Health & Mental Illness. (Library of Social Policy & Administration). (Orig.). 1967. text ed. 4.50x (ISBN 0-7100-4022-9); pap. text ed. 3.25x (ISBN 0-7100-4025-3). Humanities.

Roberts, Newton. The Cyclical Theories of Stock Market Action. (Illus.). 1978. deluxe binder 49.75 (ISBN 0-918968-02-X). Inst Econ Finan.

Roberts, P. A. Regional Blocks for Nurse Anesthetists. (Illus.). 128p. 1978. 11.75 (ISBN 0-398-03808-2). C C Thomas.

Roberts, Pamela. Teaching the Child Rider. (Illus.). pap. 4.55 (ISBN 0-85131-195-4, Dist. by Sporting Book Center). J A Allen.

Roberts, Patricia. Patricia Roberts Knitting Patterns. (Illus.). 18.95x o.p. (ISBN 0-8464-0705-1). Beekman Pubs.

Roberts, Patrick. Psychology of Tragic Drama. 1975. 25.00x (ISBN 0-7100-8034-4). Routledge & Kegan.

Roberts, Paul, ed. see Biology Colloquium, 35th,Oregon State University,1974.

Roberts, Paul M. Review Text in United States History. rev. ed. (Illus., Orig.). (gr. 7-9). 1967. pap. text ed. 6.75 (ISBN 0-87720-601-5). AMSCO Sch.
--Understanding Grammar. 1954. text ed. 15.95x scp (ISBN 0-06-045480-6, HarpC). Har-Row.

Roberts, Paula. Run Away Home. (Orig.). 1980. pap. 1.75 (ISBN 0-505-51484-2). Tower Bks.

Roberts, Peter. Any Color So Long As It's Black: The First Fifty Years of Automobile Advertising. LC 76-6044. (Illus.). 1976. 14.95 o.p. (ISBN 0-688-03102-1). Morrow.
--Theater in Britain: A Playgoer's Guide. 2nd ed. 192p. 1975. pap. 8.95x o.p. (ISBN 0-8464-0915-1). Beekman Pubs.

Roberts, Peter C. Modelling Large Systems: Limits to Growth Revisited. LC 78-13339. (Orasa Text). 1978. pap. 19.95 (ISBN 0-470-26528-0). Halsted Pr.

Roberts, Peter J., et al, eds. Dopamine. LC 78-4355. (Advances in Biochemical Psychopharmacology Ser.: Vol. 19). 1978. 31.50 (ISBN 0-89004-239-X). Raven.

Roberts, Philip, ed. see Hamilton, David.

Roberts, R. B., jt. ed. see Stark, David C.

Roberts, R. S. Dictionary of Radio, TV & Audio. 1981. text ed. price not set (ISBN 0-408-00339-1, Newnes-Butterworth). Butterworth.

Roberts, Randy. Jack Dempsey: The Manassa Mauler. LC 80-992. (Illus.). 320p. 1980. pap. 6.95 (ISBN 0-394-17660-X, E759, Ever). Grove.

Roberts, Ray, ed. see Bergonzi, Bernard.

Roberts, Ray, ed. see Williams, Neville.

Roberts, Richard. Chess. (Quick & Easy Ser). (Orig.). 1965. pap. 1.95 o.s.i. (ISBN 0-02-081260-4, Collier). Macmillan.

Roberts, Richard, jt. auth. see Campbell, Joseph.

Roberts, Richard A. Custer's Last Battle. (Custer Monograph: No. 4). 60p. 1978. pap. 8.00x (ISBN 0-686-26878-4). Monroe County Lib.

Roberts, Richard A., jt. auth. see Gabel, Robert A.

Roberts, Richard B., et al. Studies of Biosynthesis in Escherichiacoli, 2 vols. (Illus.). 521p. 1958. pap. 21.50 ea. (607). Carnegie Inst.

Roberts, Rinalda. Four Marys. 256p. (Orig.). 1976. pap. 1.25 o.p. (ISBN 0-445-00366-9). Popular Lib.

Roberts, Robert W. & Northen, Helen. Theories for Social Work with Groups. LC 76-4967. 400p. 1976. 17.50x (ISBN 0-231-03885-2). Columbia U Pr.

Roberts, Robert W., ed. The Unwed Mother. LC 80-20554. (Readers in Social Problems). viii, 270p. 1980. Repr. of 1966 ed. lib. bdg. 25.00x (ISBN 0-313-22677-6, ROUM). Greenwood.

Roberts, Robert W. & Nee, Robert H., eds. Theories of Social Casework. LC 70-123358. 1971. text ed. 15.00x (ISBN 0-226-72105-1). U of Chicago Pr.

Roberts, Ron E. Social Problems: Human Possibilities. LC 78-163. (Illus.). 1978. pap. text ed. 12.95 (ISBN 0-8016-4143-8). Mosby.

Roberts, Ron E. & Kloss, Robert M. Social Movements: Between the Balcony & the Barricade. 2nd ed. LC 73-12577. (Illus.). 1979. pap. 13.95 (ISBN 0-8016-4135-7). Mosby.

Roberts, Ronald J. & Shepherd, C. Jonathan. Handbook of Trout & Salmon Diseases. (Illus.). 172p. 21.25 (ISBN 0-85238-066-6, FN). Unipub.

Roberts, Ronald J., jt. ed. see Muir, James F.

Roberts, S. Behavioral Concepts & the Critically Ill Patient. 1976. 15.95 (ISBN 0-13-074476-X). P-H.

Roberts, S. & Fischer, I. Handbook for Modal Counterpoint. LC 67-19238. 1967. pap. text ed. 12.95 (ISBN 0-02-926560-6). Free Pr.

Roberts, S. M. & Scheinmann, F., eds. Chemistry, Biochemistry & Pharmacology of Prostanoids. 1978. text ed. 90.00 (ISBN 0-08-023799-1). Pergamon.

Roberts, Sharon, jt. auth. see Roy, Callista.

Roberts, Sharon L. Behavioral Concepts & Nursing Throughout the Lifespan. 1978. ref. 14.95x (ISBN 0-13-074559-6); pap. text ed. 11.95x (ISBN 0-13-074567-7). P-H.

Roberts, Spencer E., tr. see Shestov, Lev.

Roberts, Susan A., et al. Civics for New Mexicans. LC 80-52284. 375p. 1980. 25.00 (ISBN 0-8263-0547-4). U of NM Pr.

Roberts, Suzanne. Danger in Paradise. (YA) 5.95 (ISBN 0-685-07427-7, Avalon). Bouregy.
--Gracie. LC 65-19890. (gr. 5-9). 1965. 5.95 o.p. (ISBN 0-385-05866-7). Doubleday.

Roberts, T., jt. auth. see Hendricks, G.

Roberts, T. R., jt. auth. see Hutson, D. H.

Roberts, Tanya, jt. auth. see O'Donoghue, Patrick.

Roberts, Thom. Summerdog. 1978. pap. 1.50 (ISBN 0-380-01950-7, 75788, Camelot). Avon.

Roberts, Thomas B., ed. Four Psychologies Applied to Education: Freudian, Behavioral, Humanistic, Transpersonal. LC 74-9729. 1975. text ed. 19.50 o.p. (ISBN 0-470-72586-9); pap. text ed. 12.95x (ISBN 0-470-72588-5). Halsted Pr.

Roberts, Tom. Developing Effective Managers. LC 75-318208. (Management in Perspective Ser.). 168p. 1974. pap. 7.50x (ISBN 0-85292-100-4). Intl Pubns Serv.

Roberts, Toni M., et al. Healthwise Handbook: A Guide to Responsible Health Care. LC 78-55852. 1979. 6.95 o.p. (ISBN 0-385-14339-7, Dolp). Doubleday.

Roberts, Verne L. Machine Guarding: A Historical Perspective. LC 80-84798. (Illus.). 282p. 1980. text ed. 59.95 (ISBN 0-938830-00-7). Inst Product.

Roberts, W. The Reproductive System: Disease, Diagnosis, Treatment. (Clinical Monographs Ser.). (Illus.). 1974. pap. 7.95 (ISBN 0-87618-062-4). R J Brady.

Roberts, W. G. The Quest for Oil. LC 76-54736. (Illus.). (gr. 9-12). 1977. 10.95 (ISBN 0-87599-225-0). S G Phillips.

Roberts, Walter O. & Lansford, Henry. The Climate Mandate. LC 78-25677. (Illus.). 1979. text ed. 16.95x (ISBN 0-7167-1054-4); pap. text ed. 8.95x (ISBN 0-7167-1055-2). W H Freeman.

Roberts, William. Earlier History of English Bookselling. LC 66-28043. 1967. Repr. of 1889 ed. 15.00 (ISBN 0-8103-3314-7). Gale.

Roberts, William C., et al. Cardiology: 81. (Illus.). 400p. 1981. text ed. 35.00 (ISBN 0-914316-22-2). Yorke Med.

Roberts, Willis J. & Bristow, Allen P. Introduction to Modern Police Firearms. Gourley, Douglas, ed. (Criminal Justice Ser). (Illus.). 1969. text ed. 10.95x (ISBN 0-02-477000-0, 47700). Macmillan.

Roberts, Willo D. Don't Hurt Laurie! LC 76-46569. (Illus.). (gr. 4-6). 1977. 8.95 (ISBN 0-689-30571-0). Atheneum.
--Don't Hurt Laurie! (gr. 3-7). pap. 2.95 (ISBN 0-689-70496-8, A-123, Aladdin). Atheneum.
--The Girl with the Silver Eyes. LC 80-12391. 192p. (gr. 4-6). 1980. 8.95 (ISBN 0-689-30786-1). Atheneum.
--House of Imposters. (Orig.). 1977. pap. 1.50 o.p. (ISBN 0-445-04039-4). Popular Lib.
--The Jaubert Ring. 1978. pap. 1.50 o.p. (ISBN 0-445-04169-2). Popular Lib.

Roberts-Baytop, Adrianne. Dido, Queen of Infinite Literary Variety: The English Renaissance Borrowings & Influences. (Salzburg Studies in English Literature, Elizabethan & Renaissance Studies: No. 25). 154p. 1974. pap. text ed. 25.00x (ISBN 0-391-01511-7). Humanities.

Robertshaw, Joseph E. & Mecca, Stephen J. Problem Solving: A Systems Approach. (Illus.). 1979. text ed. 19.25 (ISBN 0-89433-075-6). Petrocelli.

Robertshaw, Joseph E., jt. auth. see Dickerson, Steven L.

Robertshaw, Joseph E., jt. auth. see Mecca, Stephen J.

Robertson & Cassidy. Development of Modern English. 2nd ed. 1953. 16.95 (ISBN 0-13-208330-2). P-H.

Robertson, jt. auth. see Stevens, D.

Robertson, A. & Plummer, A. Corinthians I. (International Critical Commentary Ser.). 496p. Repr. of 1978 ed. write for info. (ISBN 0-567-05027-0). Attic Pr.

Robertson, A. F., jt. auth. see Dunn, J.

Robertson, A. H., ed. European Yearbook-Annuaire Europeen, Vol. XXVI. 696p. (Fr., Eng.). 1980. lib. bdg. 110.00 (ISBN 90-247-2298-5, Pub. by Marinus Nijhoff). Kluwer Boston.

Robertson, A. J., ed. The Laws of the Kings of England from Edmund to Henry I. LC 80-2210. 1981. Repr. of 1925 ed. 52.50 (ISBN 0-404-18784-6). AMS Pr.

Robertson, A. M., jt. auth. see Hobson, P. N.

Robertson, A. P. & Robertson, Wendy. Topologial Vector Spaces. 2nd ed. LC 72-89805. (Cambridge Tracts in Mathematics Ser: No. 53). 1980. 21.50 (ISBN 0-521-20124-1); pap. 10.95 (ISBN 0-521-29882-2). Cambridge U Pr.

Robertson, A. T. Una Armonia De los Cuatro Evangelios. Patterson, F. W. & Parajon, Arturo, trs. 1979. pap. 4.55 (ISBN 0-311-04302-X). Casa Bautista.
--Epochs in the Life of Jesus. (A. T. Robertson Library Ser). 1974. pap. 2.95 o.p. (ISBN 0-8010-7624-2). Baker Bk.
--Epochs in the Life of Simon Peter. (A. T. Robertson Library Ser). 1974. pap. 3.95 o.p. (ISBN 0-8010-7626-9). Baker Bk.
--Estudios En el Nuevo Testamento. Hale, Sara A., tr. from Eng. Orig. Title: Studies in the New Testament. 224p. (Span.). Date not set. pap. price not set (ISBN 0-311-03629-5). Casa Bautista.
--Estudios Sobre el Nuevo Testamento. 1978. Repr. of 1973 ed. 2.85 o.p. (ISBN 0-311-03629-5). Casa Bautista.
--Luke the Historian in the Light of Research. (A. T. Robertson Library). 1977. pap. 3.95 o.p. (ISBN 0-8010-7646-3). Baker Bk.
--Paul & the Intellectuals. LC 59-5859. pap. 2.50 (ISBN 0-8054-1344-8). Broadman.
--Some Minor Characters in the New Testament. (A.T. Robertson Library). 194p. 1976. pap. 2.95 o.p. (ISBN 0-8010-7637-4). Baker Bk.

Robertson, Alden. The No Baloney Sandwich Book. LC 77-80145. 1978. pap. 4.95 o.p. (ISBN 0-385-12429-5). Doubleday.
--The Wild Horse Gatherers. (Illus.). (gr. 7 up). 1978. pap. 10.95 (ISBN 0-684-15591-5, ScribJ, ScribJ). Scribner.
--The Wild Horse Gatherers. LC 77-17512. (Sierra Club-Scribner Juvenile Ser.). (Illus.). (gr. 7 up). 1978. 10.95 o.p. (ISBN 0-684-15589-3); pap. 6.95 (ISBN 0-684-15591-5). Sierra.

Robertson, Alec, ed. see Ottaway, Hugh & Hutchings, Arthur.

Robertson, Andrew. Strategic Marketing: A Business Response to Consumerism. LC 78-3. 27.95 (ISBN 0-470-26313-X). Halsted Pr.

Robertson, Andrew, jt. auth. see Neal, L. F.

Robertson, Angus, ed. From Television to Home Computer: The Future of Consumer Electronics. (Illus.). 336p. 1980. 27.50 (ISBN 0-7137-0973-1, Pub. by Blandford Pr England). Sterling.

Robertson, Anne S. Roman Imperial Coins in the Hunter Coin Cabinet, University of Glasgow: Pertinax to Aemilian, Vol. 3. (Illus.). 1977. 98.00x (ISBN 0-19-713306-1). Oxford U Pr.

Robertson, B. & Scarborough, G. Hawker Hurricane. (Illus.). 104p. 21.95 (ISBN 0-85059-124-4). Aztex.

Robertson, B. & Scarborough, G. JU 87 Stuka. (Illus.). 1976. 15.75 o.p. (ISBN 0-85059-193-7). Aztex.

Robertson, Barry C. Modern Physics for Applied Science. 368p. 1981. text ed. 20.95 (ISBN 0-471-05343-0). Wiley.

Robertson, Bruce. Air Aces of the Nineteen Fourteen to Nineteen Eighteen War. LC 59-13378. (Harleyford Ser). (Illus.). 1959. 18.95 (ISBN 0-8168-6350-4). Aero.

--Battle of Britain. (Caler Illustrated Ser.). (Illus.). 60p. 1970. pap. text ed. 4.95 o.p. (ISBN 0-87059-000-6, Pub. by Caler). Aviation.

--Lancaster - the Story of a Famous Bomber. 18.95 o.p. (ISBN 0-900435-10-0). Aero.

Robertson, C. Grant. Bismarck. LC 68-9604. 1969. Repr. of 1918 ed. 21.00 (ISBN 0-86527-008-2). Fertig.

Robertson, C. M. History of Greek Art, 2 vols. LC 73-79317. 1976. Set. 115.00 (ISBN 0-521-20277-9). Cambridge U Pr.

Robertson, C. M., jt. auth. see Boardman, J.

Robertson, Carolyn, jt. auth. see Robertson, James.

Robertson, Charles. Bath: An Architectural Guide. 1975. 33.00 (ISBN 0-571-10750-8, Pub. by Faber & Faber); pap. 9.95 (ISBN 0-571-10805-9). Merrimack Bk Serv.

Robertson, Charles L. International Politics Since World War II: A Short History. 2nd ed. LC 74-23998. 448p. 1975. pap. text ed. 15.95x (ISBN 0-471-72744-X). Wiley.

Robertson, Constance. Oneida Community: An Autobiography. (Illus.). 1981. pap. 9.95 (ISBN 0-8156-0166-2). Syracuse U Pr.

Robertson, D., jt. auth. see Corbet, H.

Robertson, D. B., ed. Power & Empowerment in Higher Education: Studies in Honor of Louis Smith. LC 77-76333. 168p. 1978. 13.00x (ISBN 0-8131-1373-3). U Pr of Ky.

Robertson, D. W., tr. see Augustine, Saint.

Robertson, David A. Linguistic Evidence in Dating Early Hebrew Poetry. LC 72-87886. (Society of Biblical Literature. Dissertation Ser.: No. 3). 1973. pap. 7.50 (ISBN 0-89130-159-3, 060103). Scholars Pr Ca.

Robertson, David H. & Smith, Craig R. Manual of Clinical Pharmacology. (Illus.). 290p. 1981. price not set softcover (ISBN 0-683-07300-1). Williams & Wilkins.

Robertson, Dennis & Dennison, S. Control of Industry. (Cambridge Economic Handbook Ser). 1960. 10.95x (ISBN 0-521-08766-X). Cambridge U Pr.

Robertson, Sir Dennis H. Economic Commentaries. LC 79-1589. 1981. Repr. of 1956 ed. 17.00 (ISBN 0-88355-894-7). Hyperion Conn.

Robertson, Don. The Greatest Thing That Almost Happened. 1977. pap. 1.95 o.s.i. (ISBN 0-446-89660-8). Warner Bks.

--Miss Margaret Ridpath & the Dismantling of the Universe. 1978. pap. 2.25 o.s.i. (ISBN 0-515-04569-1). Jove Pubns.

Robertson, Donald. Pre-Columbian Architecture. LC 63-7513. (Great Ages of World Architecture Ser). (Illus.). 1963. 7.95 o.p. (ISBN 0-8076-0213-2); pap. 3.95 o.p. (ISBN 0-8076-0342-2). Braziller.

Robertson, Donald S. Greek & Roman Architecture. 2nd ed. (Illus.). 1969. 52.00 (ISBN 0-521-06104-0); pap. 12.95x (ISBN 0-521-09452-6). Cambridge U Pr.

Robertson, Donald W. Mind's Eye of Richard Buckminster Fuller. 1976. 7.00 (ISBN 0-533-23314-3). Robertson.

Robertson, Dougal. Sea Survival. 9.95 (ISBN 0-236-31089-5, Pub. by Paul Elek). Merrimack Bk Serv.

Robertson, Durant W., Jr. Chaucer's London. LC 68-30920. (New-Dimensions Historical Cities Ser). (Illus.). 1968. pap. text ed. 9.50x o.p. (ISBN 0-471-72731-8). Wiley.

Robertson, E. Graeme. Pneumoencephalography. 2nd ed. (Illus.). 832p. 1967. 42.75 (ISBN 0-398-01596-1). C C Thomas.

Robertson, E. H., ed. see Henderson, Ian.

Robertson, E. H., ed. see Perkins, Robert L.

Robertson, E. H., ed. see Thomas, J. Heywood.

Robertson, E. H., ed. see Towers, Bernard.

Robertson, E. R., ed. The Engineering Uses of Coherent Optics. LC 75-22978. 560p. 1976. 145.00 (ISBN 0-521-20879-3). Cambridge U Pr.

Robertson, Edwin H. Dietrich Bonhoeffer. LC 66-15514. (Makers of Contemporary Theology Ser). (Orig.). 1966. pap. 3.45 (ISBN 0-8042-0535-3). John Knox.

Robertson, Elizabeth C. & Wood, Margaret I. Today's Child: A Modern Guide to Baby Care & Child Training. LC 71-37204. 288p. 1972. 7.95 o.p. (ISBN 0-684-12727-X, ScribT). Scribner.

Robertson, Frank. Triangle of Death: The Inside Story of the Triads--the Chinese Mafia. (Illus.). 1978. 14.95 (ISBN 0-7100-8732-2). Routledge & Kegan.

Robertson, Frank C. & Harris, Beth K. Soapy Smith. 1961. 7.95 (ISBN 0-8038-6661-5). Hastings.

Robertson, Giles. Giovanni Bellini. LC 79-93169. (Illus.). 171p. 1980. Repr. of 1968 ed. lib. bdg. 60.00 (ISBN 0-87817-273-4). Hacker.

Robertson, Ian. Sociology. 2nd ed. 1981. text ed. write for info. (ISBN 0-87901-134-3); write for info. study guide (ISBN 0-87901-144-0); write for info. reader (ISBN 0-87901-168-8). Worth.

--Sociology. LC 76-52248. (Illus.). 1977. 15.95x o.p. (ISBN 0-87901-116-5); study guide by Harris & Cole 5.95, o.p. (ISBN 0-87901-071-1). Worth.

Robertson, Ian W., tr. see Barth, Karl.

Robertson, J. M., jt. ed. see Dummer, Geoffrey W.

Robertson, J. T., jt. auth. see Smith, R. R.

Robertson, Jack C. Auditing. rev. ed. 1979. text ed. 19.95x (ISBN 0-256-02212-7). Business Pubns.

Robertson, Jack R. Genitourinary Problems in Women. (Amer. Lec. in Gynecology & Obstetrics Ser.). (Illus.). 168p. 1978. 21.75 (ISBN 0-398-03668-3). C C Thomas.

Robertson, James. Great American Beer Book. 1980. pap. 2.95 (ISBN 0-446-93073-3). Warner Bks.

--Power, Money & Sex: Towards a New Social Balance. (Ideas in Progress Ser.). 1978. 11.95 (ISBN 0-7145-2554-5, Pub. by M Boyars); pap. 7.95 (ISBN 0-7145-2555-3). Merrimack Bk Serv.

--Profit or People? The New Social Role of Money. (Ideas in Progress Ser.). 1978. 9.95 (ISBN 0-7145-0848-9, Pub. by M Boyars); pap. 4.95 (ISBN 0-7145-0773-3). Merrimack Bk Serv.

Robertson, James & Robertson, Carolyn. The Small Towns Book. LC 76-23813. 1978. pap. 5.95 (ISBN 0-385-11012-X, Anch). Doubleday.

Robertson, James C. Introduction to Fire Prevention. (Fire Science Ser.). 1975. text ed. 14.95x (ISBN 0-02-477080-9). Macmillan.

Robertson, James I., Jr., ed. see McAllister, Robert.

Robertson, James O. American Myth, American Reality. 1980. text ed. 16.95 (ISBN 0-8090-2504-3). Hill & Wang.

Robertson, James W., jt. auth. see Al Hashim, Dhia.

Robertson, James W., jt. auth. see Alhashim, Dhia D.

Robertson, Jenny & Parry, Alan. Jesus in Danger. (Ladybird Bible Ser.). (Illus.). 32p. (ps-4). 1980. Repr. 1.95 (ISBN 0-310-42870-X). Zondervan.

Robertson, Jenny. The Easter Story. (Ladybird Bible Ser.). (Illus.). 32p. (ps-4). 1980. Repr. 1.95 (ISBN 0-310-42860-2). Zondervan.

--Jesus, the Child. (Ladybird Bible Ser.). (Illus.). 32p. (ps-4). 1980. Repr. 1.95 (ISBN 0-310-42820-3). Zondervan.

--Jesus, the Leader. (Ladybird Bible Ser.). (Illus.). 32p. (ps-4). 1980. Repr. 1.95 (ISBN 0-310-42830-0). Zondervan.

--Paul Meets Jesus. (Ladybird Bible Ser.). (Illus.). 32p. (ps-4). 1980. Repr. 1.95 (ISBN 0-310-42880-7). Zondervan.

--Paul the Traveler. (Ladybird Bible Ser.). (Illus.). 32p. (ps-4). 1980. Repr. 1.95 (ISBN 0-310-42890-4). Zondervan.

Robertson, John J. A. G. Daniels. LC 77-80687. (Dimension Ser.). 1977. pap. 5.95 (ISBN 0-8163-0276-6). Pacific Pr Pub Assn.

Robertson, John K. Atomic Artillery & the Atomic Bomb. 1979. Repr. of 1945 ed. lib. bdg. 10.00 (ISBN 0-8492-7712-4). R West.

Robertson, Josephine. Meditations for the Later Years. LC 73-19935. 80p. 1974. 5.95 o.p. (ISBN 0-687-24099-9). Abingdon.

Robertson, Keith. Henry Reed Inc. (gr. 2-5). 1974. pap. 1.75 (ISBN 0-440-43552-8, YB). Dell.

--Henry Reeds Baby Sitting Service. (gr. 2-5). 1974. pap. 1.75 (ISBN 0-440-43565-X, YB). Dell.

--Henry Reed's Big Show. (Illus.). (gr. 4-6). 1970. PLB 9.95 (ISBN 0-670-36839-3). Viking Pr.

--Wreck of the Saginaw. (Illus.). (gr. 7 up). 1954. PLB 3.95 o.p. (ISBN 0-670-79060-5). Viking Pr.

Robertson, Kirk. Drinking Beer at Twenty-Two Below. 1980. 2.00 (ISBN 0-917554-04-3). Maelstrom.

--Origins, Initiations. 1980. 25.00 (ISBN 0-918824-19-2); pap. 4.00 (ISBN 0-918824-18-4). Turkey Pr.

Robertson, Kirk, ed. see Haslam, Gerald.

Robertson, Kirk, ed. see Masarik, Al.

Robertson, Kirk, ed. see Matte, Robert, Jr.

Robertson, Leon & Heagerty, Margaret. Medical Sociology: A General Systems Approach. LC 75-9779. 220p. 1975. 17.95 (ISBN 0-88229-127-0); pap. 9.95x (ISBN 0-88229-578-0). Nelson-Hall.

Robertson, Leon S., jt. auth. see Mazur, Allan.

Robertson, Leonard F., jt. auth. see Schantz, William T.

Robertson, Mary E. Tarantula & the Red Chigger. 192p. (gr. 5 up). 1980. PLB 7.95 (ISBN 0-316-75115-4). Little.

Robertson, Max. Wimbledon 1877-1977. LC 77-365693. (Illus.). 1979. 12.50x (ISBN 0-905418-50-6). Intl Pubns Serv.

Robertson, Merle G., ed. Third Palenque Round Table, Nineteen Seventy-Eight: Part Two, Vol. V. (Illus.). 200p. (Orig.). Date not set. pap. text ed. 35.00x (ISBN 0-292-78037-0). U of Tex Pr.

Robertson, O. Palmer. The Christ of the Covenants. 385p. (Orig.). 1981. pap. 7.50 (ISBN 0-8010-7699-4). Baker Bk.

Robertson, Pat & Buckingham, Jamie. Shout It from the Housetops: The Story of the Founder of the Christian Broadcasting Network. LC 72-76591. 248p. 1972. pap. 2.95 (ISBN 0-88270-097-9). Logos.

Robertson, Pat, tr. Milagro Del Amor Agape. (Spanish Bks.). (Span.). 1978. 1.90 (ISBN 0-8297-0914-2). Life Pubs Intl.

Robertson, R. Macdonald. Selected Highland Folktales. 1977. 11.95 (ISBN 0-7153-7436-2). David & Charles.

Robertson, Seonaid M. Creative Crafts in Education. (Illus.). 1967. Repr. of 1952 ed. 20.00 (ISBN 0-7100-2045-7). Routledge & Kegan.

--Rosegarden & Labyrinth: A Study in Art Education. (Illus.). 1963. 16.95x (ISBN 0-7100-2046-5). Routledge & Kegan.

Robertson, T. S., jt. auth. see Sumner, R.

Robertson, Thomas, jt. auth. see Kassarjian, Harold.

Robertson, Thomas, jt. ed. see Ward, Scott.

Robertson, Thomas S., et al. Televised Medicine Advertising & Children. 21.95 (ISBN 0-03-049161-4). Praeger.

Robertson, W. B. The Endometrium. (Postgraduate Pathology Ser.). 1981. text ed. 52.95 (ISBN 0-407-00171-9). Butterworth.

Robertson, Walter J. Gold Panning for Profit. Jones, William R., ed. (Illus.). 32p. 1978. pap. 2.50 (ISBN 0-89646-035-5). Outbooks.

Robertson, Wendy, jt. auth. see Robertson, A. P.

Robertson, Wilmot, ed. Best of Instauration 1976. 117p. 1980. pap. 10.00 (ISBN 0-914576-11-9). Howard Allen.

Robeson, James F., et al. Selling. 1978. text ed. 16.50 (ISBN 0-256-01967-3). Irwin.

Robeson, Kenneth. Satan Black & Cargo Unknown. (Doc Savage Ser.: Nos. 97 & 98). 224p. 1980. pap. 1.95 (ISBN 0-553-13421-3). Bantam.

--The Whisker of Hercules No. 103: The Man Who Was Scared No. 104. 208p. 1981. pap. 1.95 (ISBN 0-553-14616-5). Bantam.

Robeson, Lloyd, jt. auth. see Olabisi, Olagoka.

Robeson, Paul. Here I Stand. LC 70-159847. 1971. pap. 4.95 (ISBN 0-8070-6407-6, BP410). Beacon Pr.

Robeson, Susan. The Whole World in His Hands: A Pictoral Biography of Paul Robeson. (Illus.). 256p. 1981. 17.95 (ISBN 0-8065-0754-3). Citadel Pr.

Robey, David, ed. Structuralism: An Introduction-Wolfson College Lectures 1972. 1973. pap. text ed. 9.95x (ISBN 0-19-874017-4). Oxford U Pr.

Robey, Sidney J., jt. auth. see Bruyere, Toni M.

Robicheaux, Robert A. & Pride, William M. Marketing: Contemporary Dimensions. 2nd ed. LC 79-89125. 1980. pap. text ed. 9.50 (ISBN 0-395-28500-3). HM.

Robichek, Alexander A. & Myers, Stewart C. Optimal Financing Decisions. (Illus.). 1966. pap. 10.95x ref. ed. (ISBN 0-13-638114-6). P-H.

Robie, Joan H. What Your Handwriting Tells About You. LC 77-91726. 1978. 5.95 (ISBN 0-8054-6922-2). Broadman.

Robiette, A. G. Electric Melting Practice. 412p. 1972. 52.95 (ISBN 0-470-72787-X). Halsted Pr.

--Electric Smelting Processes. LC 73-2039. (Illus.). 276p. 1973. 42.95 (ISBN 0-470-72786-1). Halsted Pr.

Robigne, Bennel De see De Robigne, Bennel.

Robillard, Raymond A. Interdependence of Free Enterprise & Governments in the Global Marketplace. LC 79-66832. 1979. pap. text ed. 9.00 (ISBN 0-8191-0852-9). U Pr of Amer.

Robilliard, Eileen D. The Persistent Pianist: A Book for the Late Beginner & Adult Re-Starter. 1967. pap. 8.95x (ISBN 0-19-318416-8). Oxford U Pr.

Robin. Dog Horoscope Book: Your Dog Needs a Birthday. (Illus.). 1972. pap. 2.00 o.p. (ISBN 0-87666-317-X, PS-684). TFH Pubns.

--Higher Excited States of Polyatomic Molecules. Vol. 1. 1974. 48.50 (ISBN 0-12-589901-7); Vol. 2. 1975. 50.25 (ISBN 0-12-589902-5). Acad Pr.

--How to Get the Most Out of Your Audio Recording & Playback. (Illus.). 128p. 1980. pap. 5.95 (ISBN 0-8359-2957-4). Reston.

Robin, Christopher. How to Build Your Own Stereo Speakers: Construction, Applications, Circuits & Characteristics. (Illus.). 1978. ref. ed. 16.95 (ISBN 0-87909-374-9); pap. 6.95 (ISBN 0-8359-2936-1). Reston.

--Twenty-One Stereo Hi-Fi Stereo Speaker Cabinets You Can Build. (Illus.). 80p. 1980. pap. 4.95 (ISBN 0-8359-7896-6). Reston.

Robin, E. D. Claude Bernarde & the Internal Environment. 1979. 34.50 (ISBN 0-8247-6894-9). Dekker.

Robin, Gordon, ed. Scoliosis. 1973. 21.50 (ISBN 0-12-589850-9). Acad Pr.

Robin, Gordon C. Scoliosis & Neurological Disease. LC 75-19283. 1975. 36.95 (ISBN 0-470-72795-0). Halsted Pr.

Robin, J. P., ed. Colloquium Spectroscopium, Internationale, 2. 1977. text ed. 13.25 (ISBN 0-08-021569-6). Pergamon.

Robin, Jean. Elmdon, Continuity & Change in a Northwest Essex Village. LC 79-12964. (Illus.). 1980. 41.50 (ISBN 0-521-22820-4). Cambridge U Pr.

Robin, Leon. Pyrrhon et le Scepticisme Grec. LC 78-66561. (Ancient Philosophy Ser.). 264p. 1980. lib. bdg. 26.00 (ISBN 0-8240-9589-8). Garland Pub.

Robin, M. Canadian Provincial Politics. 2nd ed. 1978. pap. 11.25 (ISBN 0-13-113233-4). P-H.

Robinet, B., ed. International Symposium on Programming. (Lecture Notes in Computer Science: Vol. 83). 341p. 1980. pap. 19.50 (ISBN 0-387-09981-6). Springer-Verlag.

Robinette, Gary O. Plant Form Studies: Design Characteristics of Plant Materials. LC 80-68358. (Illus.). 244p. pap. text ed. 19.50 (ISBN 0-918436-12-5). Environ Des VA.

--Planting Details. 200p. 1980. pap. text ed. 20.00 (ISBN 0-918436-14-1). Environ Design.

Robins, Adrienne. The Writers Practical Handbook. LC 79-19667. 1980. text ed. 12.95 (ISBN 0-471-03033-3); tchrs. manual avail. (ISBN 0-471-07833-6). Wiley.

Robins, Alan & Himber, Jane A. The TM Program & Enlightenment: Dawn of a New Age. pap. 1.95 o.p. (ISBN 0-425-03250-7). Berkley Pub.

Robins, Denise. Desert Rapture. 1978. pap. 1.75 (ISBN 0-380-42416-9, 42416). Avon.

--The Long Shadow. 1979. pap. 1.75 (ISBN 0-380-47167-1, 47167). Avon.

--Love, Vol. VI. 592p. 1980. pap. 2.75 (ISBN 0-345-28520-4). Ballantine.

--Love, Vol. VII. 720p. 1980. pap. 2.75 (ISBN 0-345-28521-2). Ballantine.

--Love Like Ours. 1976. pap. 1.25 o.p. (ISBN 0-345-25494-5). Ballantine.

--Set the Stars Alight. 1978. pap. 1.75 (ISBN 0-380-42424-X, 42424). Avon.

Robins, Elizabeth. The Convert. 304p. 1980. pap. 5.95 (ISBN 0-912670-83-5). Feminist Pr.

Robins, Eric. Secret Eden: Africa's Enchanted Wilderness. (Illus.). 128p. 1981. 27.00 (ISBN 0-241-10423-8, Pub. by Hamish Hamilton England). David & Charles.

Robins, Madeleine. Althea. (Orig.). 1977. pap. 1.50 o.p. (ISBN 0-449-23268-9, Crest). Fawcett.

Robins, Natalie. Eclipse. 64p. 1981. 8.95 (ISBN 0-8040-0367-X); pap. 4.95 (ISBN 0-8040-0368-8). Swallow.

Robins, Philip K. & Weiner, Samuel, eds. Child Care & Public Policy. LC 77-17724. (Illus.). 1978. 21.00 (ISBN 0-669-02088-5). Lexington Bks.

Robins, R. H. General Linguistics: An Introductory Survey. 3rd ed. (Longman Linguistics Library). (Illus.). 1980. text ed. 30.00 (ISBN 0-582-55363-6); pap. text ed. 14.95 (ISBN 0-582-55364-4). Longman.

Robins, R. S., et al. Psychopathology & Political Leadership, Vol. 16. LC 77-85747. 1977. lib. bdg. 17.50 o.p. (ISBN 0-930598-17-2); pap. text ed. 6.00 (ISBN 0-930598-16-4). Tulane Stud Pol.

Robins, Sheila M., tr. see Ruwet, Nicolas.

Robinson. American Education: Its Organization & Control. 1968. pap. text ed. 10.95 (ISBN 0-675-09823-8). Merrill.

Robinson, jt. auth. see Manley.

Robinson, A., jt. auth. see Millward, R.

Robinson, A. T. & Marks, R. Woven Cloth Construction. 188p. 1967. 15.00 (ISBN 0-306-30662-X, Plenum Pr). Plenum Pub.

Robinson, Abraham. Numbers & Ideals. LC 65-16747. (Illus.). 1965. 10.95x (ISBN 0-8162-7234-4). Holden-Day.

Robinson, Adele J., ed. Portland Symphony Cookbook. LC 74-84052. 1974. 8.95 (ISBN 0-9601266-1-9). Portland Symphony.

Robinson, Adjai. Principles & Practice of Teaching. (Illus.). 176p. (Orig.). 1980. pap. text ed. 10.50x (ISBN 0-04-370098-5, AU449). Allen Unwin.

Robinson, Adrian, jt. auth. see Millward, Roy.

Robinson, Alan H. Virgin Islands National Park: The Story Behind the Scenery. DenDooven, Gweneth R., ed. LC 74-81560. (Illus.). 1974. 7.95 (ISBN 0-916122-39-5); pap. 3.50 (ISBN 0-916122-14-X). K C Pubns.

Robinson, Aletha. The Lao Handbook of Maternal & Child Health. 1980. pap. 0.50 (ISBN 0-9602790-1-6). The Garden.

Robinson, Alfred. Life in California Before the Conquest. LC 68-30553. (American Scene Ser). (Illus.). 1968. Repr. of 1846 ed. lib. bdg. 35.00 (ISBN 0-306-71142-7). Da Capo.

Robinson, Alice & Reres, Mary. Your Future in Nursing Careers. LC 72-75218. (Illus.). 128p. 1975. pap. 3.50 (ISBN 0-668-03429-7). Arco.

Robinson, Alice M. & Notter, Lucille. Clinical Writing for Health Professionals. (Illus.). 128p. (Orig.). 1981. pap. price not set (ISBN 0-87619-893-0). R J Brady.

Robinson, Anthony, ed. In the Cockpit. (Illus.). 316p. 1979. 29.95 (ISBN 0-87165-051-7, ZD Bks). Ziff-Davis Pub.

Robinson, Arthur, et al. Elements of Cartography. 4th ed. LC 78-1670. 1978. 24.95 (ISBN 0-471-01781-7). Wiley.

Robinson, Arthur, et al, eds. Sex Chromosome Aneuploidy: Prospective Studies on Children. LC 78-13921. (Alan R. Liss Ser.: Vol. 15, No. 1). 1979. 32.00 (ISBN 0-8451-1024-1). March of Dimes.

Robinson, Arthur H., et al. Atlas of Wisconsin. LC 73-15262. 124p. 1974. 22.50 (ISBN 0-299-06530-8); pap. 8.95 (ISBN 0-299-06534-0). U of Wis Pr.

Robinson, B. W. The Arts of the Japanese Sword. (Illus.). 1979. 38.00 (ISBN 0-571-04723-8, Pub. by Faber & Faber). Merrimack Bk Serv.

--Persian Paintings in the John Rylands Library: A Descriptive Catalog. (Illus.). 365p. 1980. 87.50x (ISBN 0-85667-072-3, Pub. by Sotheby Parke Bernet). Biblio Dist.

Robinson, B. W., et al. Islamic Painting & the Arts of the Book. LC 76-15727. 1976. 95.00 o.p. (ISBN 0-684-14789-0, ScribT). Scribner.

Robinson, Barbara. The Best Christmas Pageant Ever. (Illus.). (gr. 3-5). 1973. pap. 1.75 (ISBN 0-380-00769-X, 51441, Camelot). Avon.

--The Best Christmas Pageant Ever. 96p. 1979. pap. 1.75 (ISBN 0-380-48066-2, 48066). Avon.

Robinson, Barbara, jt. auth. see Blotnick, Elihu.

Robinson, Bill. Cruising: The Boats & the Places. (Illus.). 1981. 17.95 (ISBN 0-393-03258-2). Norton.

--Legendary Yachts. (Nautical Ser.). (Illus.). 1978. 7.98 o.p. (ISBN 0-679-51175-X). McKay.

Robinson, C., jt. ed. see Nitecki, Z.

Robinson, Cedric. Sand Pilot of Morecambe Bay. LC 79-56054. (Illus.). 168p. 1980. 14.95 (ISBN 0-7153-7915-1). David & Charles.

Robinson, Chandler A. J. Evetts Haley: Passing of the Old West. Date not set. 12.50 (ISBN 0-8363-0160-9). Jenkins.

Robinson, Charles A., Jr. Athens in the Age of Pericles. (Centers of Civilization Ser.: No. 1). (Illus.). 1959. pap. 3.95x (ISBN 0-8061-0935-1). U of Okla Pr.

--First Book of Ancient Egypt. (First Bks). (Illus.). (gr. 4-6). 1960. PLB 6.45 (ISBN 0-531-00462-7). Watts.

--First Book of Ancient Greece. (First Bks). (Illus.). (gr. 4-6). 1960. PLB 6.90 (ISBN 0-531-00463-5). Watts.

--First Book of Ancient Rome. rev. ed. (First Bks). (Illus.). (gr. 4-6). 1964. PLB 6.90 (ISBN 0-531-00466-X). Watts.

Robinson, Charles N. British Tar in Fact & Fiction. LC 68-26601. (Illus.). 1968. Repr. of 1909 ed. 20.00 (ISBN 0-8103-3514-X). Gale.

Robinson, Christopher. French Literature in the Twentieth Century. (Comparative Literature Ser.). 288p. 1981. 15.00x (ISBN 0-389-20121-9). B&N.

Robinson, Clayton, jt. ed. see Kalin, Berkeley.

Robinson, Colin, jt. auth. see Ray, George.

Robinson, Cyril E. Romani. 1941. text ed. 5.25x (ISBN 0-521-06108-3). Cambridge U Pr.

Robinson, D. M., jt. ed. see Jamieson, G. A.

Robinson, D. W., jt. ed. see Bratteli, O.

Robinson, Daniel N. Mind Unfolded: Essays on Psychology's Historic Texts. 1978. 24.00 (ISBN 0-89093-207-7); pap. 8.00 (ISBN 0-89093-209-3). U Pubns Amer.

Robinson, Daniel N., ed. Seminal Cases & Contemporary Commentaries: England. (Contributions to the History of Psychology Ser.: Insanity & Jurisprudence). 1980. 30.00 (ISBN 0-89093-331-6). U Pubns Amer.

--Seminal Cases & Contemporary Commentaries: The United States. (Insanity & Jurisprudence). 1980. 30.00 (ISBN 0-89093-330-8). U Pubns Amer.

Robinson, David. Chiefs & Clerics: Abdul Bokar Kan & the History of Futa Toro 1853-1891. (Studies in African Affairs). (Illus.). 306p. 1975. 19.50x o.p. (ISBN 0-19-822701-9). Oxford U Pr.

--Encyclopedia of Gerbils. 224p. 1980. 9.95 (ISBN 0-87666-915-1, H-974). TFH Pubns.

--Gerbils. LC 76-9037. (Illus.). (YA) 1976. bds. 2.25 o.p. (ISBN 0-668-03987-6). Arco.

--The History of World Cinema. rev. ed. LC 80-51767. (Illus.). 512p. 1981. 14.95 (ISBN 0-8128-2747-3). Stein & Day.

--The Process of Becoming Ill. (Medicine, Illness & Society Ser). 1971. 18.00x (ISBN 0-7100-7096-9). Routledge & Kegan.

--Research Inventory of the Mexican Collection of Colonial Parish Registers. (Finding Aids to the Microfilmed Manuscript Collection of the Genealogical Society of Utah). 350p. (Orig.). 1981. pap. 15.00 (ISBN 0-87480-181-8). U of Utah Pr.

--Talking Out of Alcoholism. 160p. 1980. 25.00x (ISBN 0-85664-755-1, Pub. by Croom Helm England). State Mutual Bk.

Robinson, David & Henry, Stuart. Self-Help & Health: Mutual Aid for Modern Problems. 164p. 1977. 21.95x (ISBN 0-85520-167-3, Pub. by Martin Robertson England). Biblio Dist.

--Self-Help & Health: Mutual Aid for Modern Problems. 1977. pap. 12.50x (ISBN 0-85520-317-X, Pub by Martin Robertson England). Biblio Dist.

Robinson, David & Robinson, Yvonne. From Self-Help to Health: A Guide to Self-Help Groups. 1979. 14.95 (ISBN 0-686-63745-3, Pub. by Batsford England). David & Charles.

Robinson, David, ed. see Aranda, Francisco.

Robinson, David, jt. ed. see Wadsworth, Michael.

Robinson, David A. Accounts Receivable & Inventory Lending: How to Establish & Operate a Department. 2nd ed. LC 80-21097. (Illus.). 1981. text ed. 43.00 (ISBN 0-87267-036-8). Bankers.

--Accounts Receivable & Inventory Lending: How to Establish & Operate a Department. LC 77-5322. (Illus.). 1977. 36.00 o.p. (ISBN 0-87267-029-5). Bankers.

Robinson, David E., jt. auth. see Garrett, William J.

Robinson, David F. Living Wild: The Secrets of Animal Survival. MacConomy, Alma D., ed. LC 80-80702. (Illus.). 208p. 1980. 14.95 (ISBN 0-912186-37-2). Natl Wildlife.

Robinson, David J. Studying Latin America: Essays in Honor of Preston E. James. LC 80-12413. (Dellplain Latin American Studies: No. 4). 290p. (Orig.). 1980. pap. 19.25 (ISBN 0-8357-0515-3, SS-00135, Pub. by Syracuse U Dept Geog). Univ Microfilms.

Robinson, David J., ed. see Carl, George E.

Robinson, Delmer. Appalachian Hill Country Cook Book. LC 80-83183. (Illus.). 156p. 1980. 9.95 (ISBN 0-934750-04-1). Jalamap.

Robinson, Dennis M., jt. auth. see Robinson, Jacqueline.

Robinson, Diana. The Monarch & the Princess. 1981. 5.95 (ISBN 0-533-04745-5). Vantage.

--To Stretch a Plank: A Survey of Psychokinesis. LC 80-12335. 282p. 1981. 15.95 (ISBN 0-88229-404-0). Nelson-Hall.

Robinson, Don. Backpacking. (Illus.). 112p. 1981. 12.95 (ISBN 0-8069-9180-1, Pub. by EP Publishing England); pap. 6.95 (ISBN 0-8069-9182-8). Sterling.

Robinson, Doris, ed. see Grimes, Janet & Daims, Diva.

Robinson, Douglas, ed. see Starr, Walter A., Jr.

Robinson, Douglas H. The Zeppelin in Combat: A History of the German Naval Airship Division, 1912-1918. LC 80-13791. (Illus.). 432p. 1980. Repr. of 1971 ed. 25.00 (ISBN 0-295-95752-2). U of Wash Pr.

Robinson, E. A. & Griffin, Keith, eds. The Economic Development of Bangladesh Within a Socialist Framework: Proceedings of a Conference Held by the International Economic Association at Daca. LC 74-8438. (International Economic Assoc. Ser.). 1974. 44.95 (ISBN 0-470-72803-5). Halsted Pr.

Robinson, E. E. The Roosevelt Leadership Nineteen Thirty Three to Nineteen Fourty Five. LC 75-146154. (American Scene Ser.). 1972. Repr. of 1955 ed. lib. bdg. 42.50 (ISBN 0-306-70202-9). Da Capo.

Robinson, E. R. Time Dependent Chemical Processes. LC 75-1124. 370p. 1975. 44.95 (ISBN 0-470-72802-7). Halsted Pr.

Robinson, E. S. Association Theory Today: An Essay in Systematic Psychology. 1964. pap. 7.95 o.s.i. (ISBN 0-02-851010-0). Hafner.

Robinson, Edward G. & Spigelgass, Leonard. All My Yesterdays. 1975. pap. 1.95 o.p. (ISBN 0-451-06428-3, J6428, Sig). NAL.

Robinson, Edward J. Public Relations & Survey Research: Achieving Organizational Goals in a Communication Context. LC 77-79167. (Illus., Orig.). 1969. 28.50x (ISBN 0-89197-365-6); pap. text ed. 12.95x (ISBN 0-89197-366-4). Irvington.

Robinson, Edward L. Sloth & Heathen Folly. LC 76-167930. 384p. 1972. 8.95 o.s.i. (ISBN 0-02-604090-5). Macmillan.

Robinson, Edwin A. Collected Poems. 1937. 19.95 o.s.i. (ISBN 0-02-604080-8). Macmillan.

Robinson, Ellis. A Commentary on Catulus, Oxford, Eighteen Eighty-Nine. 2nd ed. Commager, Steele, ed. LC 77-70812. (Latin Poetry-Editions, Commentations Critical Works). 1979. lib. bdg. 55.00 (ISBN 0-8240-2953-4). Garland Pub.

Robinson, Enders A. Multichannel Time Series Analysis with Digital Computer Programs. LC 67-28043. 1978. pap. text ed. 17.95x (ISBN 0-8162-7254-9). Holden-Day.

Robinson, Eric, ed. see Clare, John.

Robinson, F. A. The Vitamin Co-Factors of Enzyme Systems. 1966. 54.45 o.p. (ISBN 0-08-011319-2). Pergamon.

Robinson, F. M. Macroscopic Electromagnetism. LC 73-4280. 256p. 1973. 37.00 (ISBN 0-08-017647-X). Pergamon.

Robinson, F. N. Noise & Fluctuations in Electronic Devices & Circuits. (Monographs in Electrical & Electronic Engineering). (Illus.). 254p. 1975. 37.50x (ISBN 0-19-859319-8). Oxford U Pr.

Robinson, F. N., ed. see Chaucer, Geoffrey.

Robinson, Forrest, ed. see Sidney, Philip.

Robinson, Forrest G. & Robinson, Margaret G. Wallace Stegner. (U.S. Authors Ser.: No. 282). 1977. lib. bdg. 10.95 (ISBN 0-8057-7182-4). Twayne.

Robinson, Frank E., jt. auth. see Gerbracht, Carl.

Robinson, Frank K., ed. The Harmony of Deeper Music: Posthumous Poems of Edgar Lee Masters. LC 79-108963. (Tower Poetry Ser.: No. 10). 1976. commemorative ed. 15.00 (ISBN 0-87959-021-1); 7.50 (ISBN 0-87959-091-2); pap. 5.00 (ISBN 0-87959-096-3). U of Tex Hum Res.

Robinson, Frank M., jt. auth. see Scortia, Thomas N.

Robinson, Frank M., Jr., ed. Therapeutic Re-Creation: Ideas & Experiences. (Illus.). 200p. 1974. 15.50 (ISBN 0-398-03160-6); pap. 9.50 (ISBN 0-398-03161-4). C C Thomas.

Robinson, Frank S. Children of the Dragon. 1977. pap. 1.95 (ISBN 0-380-01819-5, 35774). Avon.

Robinson, Frank T. Living New England Artists: Biographical Sketches. Weinberg, H. Barbara, ed. LC 75-28880. (Art Experience in Late 19th Century America Ser.: Vol. 14). (Illus.). 1976. Repr. of 1888 ed. lib. bdg. 44.00 (ISBN 0-8240-2238-6). Garland Pub.

Robinson, Franklin W. & Wilson, William H. Flemish & Dutch Paintings Fourteen Hundred to Nineteen Hundred: From the John & Mable Ringling Museum of Art. LC 80-50842. (Illus.). 310p. (Orig.). 1980. pap. 25.00 (ISBN 0-916758-02-8). Ringling Mus Art.

Robinson, Fred C., jt. auth. see Greenfield, Stanley B.

Robinson, Fred M. The Comedy of Language: Studies in Modern Comic Literature. LC 80-125. 200p. 1980. lib. bdg. 15.00x (ISBN 0-87023-297-5). U of Mass Pr.

Robinson, Frederick W. Beyond the Church. Wolff, Robert L., ed. LC 75-1501. (Victorian Fiction Ser.). 1975. Repr. of 1866 ed. lib. bdg. 66.00 (ISBN 0-8240-1576-2). Garland Pub.

--Church & Chapel, 1863, 3 vols. in 1. Wolff, Robert L., ed. LC 75-1500. (Victorian Fiction Ser.). 1975. lib. bdg. 66.00 (ISBN 0-8240-1575-4). Garland Pub.

--High Church. Wolff, Robert L., ed. LC 75-498. (Victorian Fiction Ser.). 1975. Repr. of 1860 ed. lib. bdg. 66.00 (ISBN 0-8240-1573-8). Garland Pub.

--No Church. Wolff, Robert L., ed. LC 75-499. (Victorian Fiction Ser.). 1975. Repr. of 1861 ed. lib. bdg. 66.00 (ISBN 0-8240-1574-6). Garland Pub.

Robinson, G. E. & Newport, M. G. Dental Organization Management. (Illus.). 196p. 1974. 14.75 (ISBN 0-398-03045-6). C C Thomas.

Robinson, G. W. Guernsey. LC 76-58788. 1977. 14.95 (ISBN 0-7153-7341-2). David & Charles.

Robinson, Geoffrey C. & Clarke, Heather F. The Hospital Care of Children: A Review of Contemporary Issues. 288p. 1980. 18.95x (ISBN 0-19-502673-X). Oxford U Pr.

Robinson, George M., jt. auth. see Moulton, Janice.

Robinson, George W., ed. see Combs, Bert T.

Robinson, Gerald J. & Eppler, Klaus. Going Public - Securities Underwriting. LC 61-18675. (Illus.). 1971. looseleaf with 1978 rev. pages 60.00 (ISBN 0-87632-010-8). Boardman.

Robinson, Glen O., ed. Communications for Tomorrow: Policy Perspectives for the 1980's. 1978. 37.50 (ISBN 0-03-046546-X); pap. 12.95 student ed (ISBN 0-03-046541-9). Praeger.

Robinson, Glen O., et al. The Administrative Process. 2nd ed. LC 80-114. (American Casebook Ser.). 997p. 1980. text ed. 21.95 (ISBN 0-8299-2085-4). West Pub.

Robinson, Guernsey. Clinical Transplantation in Dental Specialties. 1979. 45.00 (ISBN 0-8016-4142-X). Mosby.

Robinson, H. A Geography of Tourism. (Illus.). 512p. 1976. pap. 17.50x (ISBN 0-7121-0721-5, Pub. by Macdonald & Evans England). Intl Ideas.

--Latin America. 4th ed. (Illus.). 544p. 1977. pap. text ed. 17.95x (Pub. by Macdonald & Evans England). Intl Ideas.

Robinson, H. & Smith, N. Reading Instruction for Today's Children. 1980. 17.95 (ISBN 0-13-755157-6). P-H.

Robinson, H. Alan. Teaching Reading & Study Strategies: The Content Areas. 2nd ed. 1978. text ed. 17.95 (ISBN 0-205-06084-6, 2360845). Allyn.

Robinson, H. Alan, jt. auth. see Thomas, Ellen L.

Robinson, H. Alan, et al. Strategies for Reading: Paragraphs. (gr. 7-12). 1978. pap. text ed. 4.96 (ISBN 0-205-05852-3, 5258529); tchr's ed. 4.96 (ISBN 0-205-05853-1, 5258537). Allyn.

--Strategies for Reading: Sentences. (gr. 7-12). 1978. pap. text ed. 4.96 (ISBN 0-205-05848-5, 5258480); tchr's ed. 4.96 (ISBN 0-205-05849-3, 5258499). Allyn.

--Strategies for Reading: Words in Context. (gr. 7-12). 1978. pap. text ed. 4.96 (ISBN 0-205-05850-7, 5258502); tchr's ed. 4.96 (ISBN 0-205-05128-6, 5258510). Allyn.

Robinson, H. J. & Vane, J. R., eds. Prostaglandin Synthetase Inhibitors. LC 74-83454. 1974. 37.50 (ISBN 0-89004-011-7). Raven.

Robinson, H. Russell. The Armour of Imperial Rome. LC 74-11777. (Illus.). 112p. 1974. 17.50 o.p. (ISBN 0-684-13956-1, ScribT). Scribner.

Robinson, H. Wheeler. The Christian Doctrine of Man. 392p. Repr. of 1926 ed. 10.00x (ISBN 0-567-22219-5). Attic Pr.

--History of Israel. 2nd rev. ed. (Studies in Theology). 1967. pap. 13.50x (ISBN 0-7156-0163-6, Pub. by Duckworth England). Biblio Dist.

Robinson, Haddon W. Psalm Twenty-Three. (Illus., Orig.). 1968. pap. 1.95 (ISBN 0-8024-6935-3); pap. 2.95 large print (ISBN 0-8024-6934-5). Moody.

Robinson, Harry M., Jr. The Diagnosis & Treatment of Fungal Infections: A Symposium. (Illus.). 580p. 1974. 41.75 (ISBN 0-398-02789-7). C C Thomas.

Robinson, Helene. Intermediate Piano for Adults, Vol. 1. 1970. pap. 10.95x (ISBN 0-534-00210-2). Wadsworth Pub.

Robinson, Henry, et al. Certain Considerations in Order to a More Speedy, Cheap, and Equal Distribution of Justice Throughout the Nation. Berkowitz, David S. & Thorne, Samuel E., eds. LC 77-86668. (Classics of English Legal History in the Modern Era Ser.: Vol. 49). 317p. 1979. lib. bdg. 40.00 (ISBN 0-8240-3098-2). Garland Pub.

Robinson, Henry H. Negotiability in the Federal Sector. 1981. 18.00 (ISBN 0-87546-080-1); pap. 12.95 (ISBN 0-87546-081-X). NY Sch Indus Rel.

Robinson, Henry M., jt. auth. see Campbell, Joseph.

Robinson, Hilary, jt. auth. see Ferri, Elsa.

Robinson, I. The New Grammarian's Funeral. LC 75-6009. (Illus.). 225p. 1975. 27.95 (ISBN 0-521-20856-4); pap. 9.95 (ISBN 0-521-29316-2). Cambridge U Pr.

Robinson, Ian. Chaucer & the English Tradition. LC 79-163179. 1972. 44.00 (ISBN 0-521-08231-5); pap. 9.95x (ISBN 0-521-09899-8). Cambridge U Pr.

--Chaucer's Prosody. LC 79-116841. 1971. 42.50 (ISBN 0-521-07920-9). Cambridge U Pr.

--The Survival of English Essays in the Criticism of Language. 300p. 1973. 34.00 (ISBN 0-521-20191-8); pap. 9.95x (ISBN 0-521-09898-X). Cambridge U Pr.

Robinson, J. Armitage, rev. by. & intro. see Origen.

Robinson, J. F. & Lowe, Stephen. Videotape Recording. 3rd ed. LC 80-41244. 1981. 27.95 (ISBN 0-240-51083-6). Focal Pr.

Robinson, J. Hedley & Muirden, James. Astronomy Data Book. 2nd ed. LC 78-21698. 1979. 14.95 (ISBN 0-470-26594-9). Halsted Pr.

--Astronomy Data Book. new ed. (Illus.). 1979. 21.50 (ISBN 0-7153-7743-4). David & Charles.

Robinson, J. Lewis, ed. British Columbia. (Studies in Canadian Geography). 1972. 10.00 o.p. (ISBN 0-8020-1922-6); pap. 5.50x o.p. (ISBN 0-8020-6162-1). U of Toronto Pr.

Robinson, J. O. The Psychology of Visual Illusion. (Illus.). 288p. 1974. text ed. 10.75x (ISBN 0-09-112280-5, Hutchinson U Lib); pap. text ed. 5.50x (ISBN 0-09-112281-3). Humanities.

Robinson, J. P. The Effects of Weapons on Ecosystems. LC 79-41226. (Illus.). 76p. 1979. 11.50 (ISBN 0-08-025656-2). Pergamon.

Robinson, J. S., ed. Fuels from Biomass: Technology & Feasibility. LC 80-23488. (Energy Tech. Re. 61; Chem. Tech. Rev. 176). (Illus.). 377p. 1981. 48.00 (ISBN 0-8155-0824-7). Noyes.

Robinson, J. W. Handbook of Spectroscopy, Vol. 3. 432p. 1981. 64.95 (ISBN 0-8493-0333-8). CRC Pr.

Robinson, J. W., jt. auth. see Arnott, James F.

Robinson, J. W., ed. Handbook of Spectroscopy, CRC, 2 vols. LC 73-77524. (Handbook Ser). 1974. Set. (ISBN 0-685-48941-8); Vol. 1, 913p. 69.95 (ISBN 0-87819-331-6); Vol. 2, 578p. 59.95 (ISBN 0-8493-0332-X). CRC Pr.

Robinson, Jacob S. A Journal of the Santa Fe Expedition Under Colonel Doniphan. LC 75-87634. (American Scene Ser.). (Illus.). 96p. 1972. Repr. of 1932 ed. lib. bdg. 12.50 (ISBN 0-306-71798-0). Da Capo.

Robinson, Jacqueline & Robinson, Dennis M. High School Entrance Examinations. LC 80-22278. 512p. 1981. lib. bdg. 9.00 (ISBN 0-668-05149-3); pap. 6.50 (ISBN 0-668-05155-8). Arco.

Robinson, James & Cox, Jimmie. In Search of a Father. 1979. pap. write for info. (ISBN 0-8423-1634-5). Tyndale.

Robinson, James, tr. see Abhayadatta.

Robinson, James A. Congress & Foreign Policy-Making: A Study in Legislative Influence & Initiative. LC 80-20372. x, 262p. 1980. Repr. of 1962 ed. lib. bdg. 27.50x (ISBN 0-313-22706-3, ROCF). Greenwood.

Robinson, James E. The Scope of Rhetoric: A Handbook for Composition & Literature. 1970. pap. 5.95x (ISBN 0-673-05246-X). Scott F.

Robinson, James H. & Darline, R. One Hundred Bible Quiz Activities for Church School Classes. 1981. pap. 3.95 (ISBN 0-570-03829-4, 12-2794). Concordia.

Robinson, James H. & Robinson, Rowena D. Bulletin Board Ideas. LC 72-94108. 80p. 1981. pap. 2.95 (ISBN 0-570-03141-9, 12-2525). Concordia.

Robinson, James K., ed. see Hardy, Thomas.

Robinson, James M. A New Quest of the Historical Jesus. LC 59-1300. (Scholars Press Reprint Ser.: No. 2). 1979. pap. 7.50 (ISBN 0-89130-328-6, 000702). Scholars Pr Ca.

--The Problem of History in Mark. LC 57-857. (Scholars Press Reprint Ser.). pap. 6.00 (ISBN 0-89130-334-0, 000703). Scholars Pr CA.

Robinson, James M. & Koester, Helmut. Trajectories through Early Christianity. LC 79-141254. 312p. 1971. pap. 7.95 (ISBN 0-8006-1362-7, 1-1362). Fortress.

Robinson, James W. & Dernoncourt, Wayne L. The Grievance Procedure & Arbitration: Text & Cases. LC 77-18573. 1978. pap. text ed. 11.00x (ISBN 0-8191-0411-6). U Pr of Amer.

Robinson, James W., et al, eds. Introduction to Labor. 1975. pap. 9.95 (ISBN 0-13-485490-X). P-H.

Robinson, Jean. Strange but Wonderful Cosmic Awareness of Duffy Moon. LC 73-15526. (Illus.). (gr. 3-6). 1974. 6.50 (ISBN 0-395-28880-0, Clarion). HM.

Robinson, Jeff, jt. auth. see Combs, Jim.

Robinson, Jeff, ed. Kawasaki Service--Repair Handbook: 80-450cc Singles, 1966-1977. (Illus.). 1977. pap. 9.95 (ISBN 0-89287-152-0, M350). Clymer Pubns.

--Kawasaki Service & Repair Handbook: Kz400 Twins, 1974-1979. (Illus.). 1979. pap. 9.95 (ISBN 0-89287-138-5, M355). Clymer Pubns.

Robinson, Jeff, ed. see Ahlstrand, Alan.

Robinson, Jeff, ed. see Bishop, Mike.

Robinson, Jeff, ed. see Clymer Publications.

Robinson, Jeff, ed. see Combs, Jim.

Robinson, Jeff, ed. see Davis, Pedr & McCarthy, Mike.

Robinson, Jeff, ed. see Hoy, Ray.

Robinson, Jeff, ed. see Jorgensen, Eric.

Robinson, Jeff, ed. see Lockwood, Tim.

Robinson, Jeff, ed. see Price, Brick.

Robinson, Jeff, ed. see Sales, David.

Robinson, Jerome B. Hunt Close! (Illus.). 1978. 12.95 (ISBN 0-87691-259-5). Winchester Pr.

Robinson, Jerry. The Nineteen Seventies: Best Editorial Cartoons of the Decade. (McGraw-Hill Paperbacks Ser.). (Illus.). 192p. (Orig.). 1980. pap. 7.95 (ISBN 0-07-053281-8). McGraw.

--Skippy & Percy Crosby. LC 78-53777. (Illus.). 1978. 16.95 o.p. (ISBN 0-03-018491-6). HR&W.

--World's Greatest Comics Quiz. 192p. (Orig.). 1981. pap. 1.50 (ISBN 0-448-14292-9, Tempo). G&D.

Robinson, Jerry W., Jr., jt. auth. see Christenson, James A.

Robinson, Jessie, jt. auth. see Abramson, Lillian.

Robinson, Jill. Bed-Time-Story. LC 74-8578. 1974. 7.95 o.p. (ISBN 0-394-48803-2, BYR). Random.

Robinson, Joan. Aspects of Development & Underdevelopment. LC 78-25610. (Modern Economics Ser.). 1979. 22.95 (ISBN 0-521-22637-6); pap. 5.95 (ISBN 0-521-29589-0). Cambridge U Pr.

--Essays in the Theory of Employment. LC 78-14138. (Illus.). 1981. Repr. of 1950 ed. 18.50 (ISBN 0-88355-812-2). Hyperion Conn.

--The Rate of Interest & Other Essays. LC 79-51867. 1981. Repr. of 1952 ed. 17.00 (ISBN 0-88355-959-5). Hyperion Conn.

--What Are the Questions? & Other Essays: Further Contributions to Economics. 214p. 1981. 17.50x (ISBN 0-87332-199-5); pap. 8.95x (ISBN 0-87332-200-2). M E Sharpe.

Robinson, Joe. Claret & Cross-Buttock: Rafferty's Prize-Fighters. 1976. 13.50 o.p. (ISBN 0-04-920048-8). Allen Unwin.

--The Life & Times of Francie Nichol of South Shields. 1975. 8.95 o.p. (ISBN 0-04-920042-9). Allen Unwin.

Robinson, John. How Americans Use Time: A Social-Psychological Analysis of Everyday Behavior. LC 76-58838. (Special Studies). 1977. text ed. 24.95 (ISBN 0-275-24200-5). Praeger.

--In Extremity. LC 77-77725. 176p. 1980. 23.95 (ISBN 0-521-21690-7); pap. 7.95 (ISBN 0-521-29730-3). Cambridge U Pr.

Robinson, John A. The Roots of a Radical. 176p. 1981. 9.95 (ISBN 0-8245-0028-8). Crossroad NY.

Robinson, John L. Living Hard: Southern Americans in the Great Depression. LC 80-5817. 272p. 1981. lib. bdg. 19.75 (ISBN 0-8191-1379-4); pap. text ed. 10.75 (ISBN 0-8191-1380-8). U Pr of Amer.

Robinson, John M. Introduction to Early Greek Philosophy. LC 68-1065. 1968. pap. text ed. 10.95 (ISBN 0-395-05316-1). HM.

Robinson, John W. High Sierra Hiking Guide to Mt. Goddard. 2nd ed. Winnett, Thomas, ed. (High Sierra Hiking Guide Ser.: Vol. 10). (Illus., Orig.). 1980. pap. 3.95 (ISBN 0-89997-002-8). Wilderness.

Robinson, Joseph A. Gilbert Crispin, Abbot of Westminster: A Study of the Abby Under Norman Rule. LC 80-2211. 1981. Repr. of 1911 ed. 32.50 (ISBN 0-404-18785-4). AMS Pr.

Robinson, Joseph R., ed. Ophthalmic Drug Delivery Systems. LC 80-66335. 144p. 1980. 18.00 (ISBN 0-917330-32-3). Am Pharm Assn.

Robinson, Julian. Fashion in the Thirties. (Oresko Art Bks). (Illus.). 1978. 15.95 (ISBN 0-8467-0426-9, Pub. by Two Continents); pap. 9.95 (ISBN 0-8467-0427-7). Hippocrene Bks.

Robinson, Keith, jt. auth. see Featherstone, Donald.

Robinson, Keith & Wilson, Robert, eds. Extending Economics Within the Curriculum. (Direct Editions Ser). (Orig.). 1978. pap. 16.00 (ISBN 0-7100-8629-6). Routledge & Kegan.

Robinson, Kenneth A. Thoreau & the Wild Appetite. LC 90-2682. 1981. Repr. of 1957 ed. 12.50 (ISBN 0-404-19079-0). AMS Pr.

Robinson, Kenneth L., jt. auth. see Tomek, William G.

Robinson, Kitty K. & Greene, Ethel J. Putting It All Together: Skills & Activities for the Elementary Child. 1978. pap. text ed. 10.00x (ISBN 0-8191-0362-4). U Pr of Amer.

Robinson, L. C. see Marton, L.

Robinson, Lafayette. The Second Coming of Christ Is Now. LC 80-83601. (Illus.). 160p. Date not set. pap. price not set (ISBN 0-8187-0041-6). Harlo Pr.

Robinson, Larry M. & Adler, Roy D. Selected Contributions to Marketing Thought: An Annotated Bibliography. (Research Monographs: No. 91). 150p. 1981. pap. 9.95 (ISBN 0-88406-142-6). Ga St U Busn Pub.

Robinson, Larry M., jt. auth. see Sturdivant, Frederick.

Robinson, Leigh. Landlording: A Handy Manual for Scrupulous Landlords & Landladies How Do It Themselves. 3rd ed. 272p. 1980. pap. text ed. 15.00 (ISBN 0-932956-01-7); pap. text ed. 17.50 canadian edition. Express.

Robinson, Lennox, jt. ed. see Macdonagh, Donagh.

Robinson, M. S. Catalogue of Drawings of Willem Van de Velde Senior & Junior, 2 vols. (Illus.). 240p. 1958. Vol. 1. 110.00 (ISBN 0-521-06114-8); Vol. 2, 1974. 110.00 (ISBN 0-521-06115-6). Cambridge U Pr.

Robinson, Mabel L. Runner of the Mountain Tops: The Life of Louis Agassiz. LC 73-167139. 1971. Repr. of 1939 ed. 18.00 (ISBN 0-8103-3806-8). Gale.

Robinson, Margaret. Schools & Social Work. 1978. 21.00x (ISBN 0-7100-0004-9); pap. 12.50 (ISBN 0-7100-0005-7). Routledge & Kegan.

Robinson, Margaret G., jt. auth. see Robinson, Forrest G.

Robinson, Marileta. Mr. Goat's Bad Good Idea: Three Stories. LC 77-26601. (gr. 1-4). 1979. 6.95 (ISBN 0-690-03862-3, TYC-J); PLB 7.89 (ISBN 0-690-03864-X). T Y Crowell.

Robinson, Marilynne. Housekeeping. 1981. 10.95 (ISBN 0-374-17313-3). FS&G.

Robinson, Mark, jt. auth. see Lambrick, George.

Robinson, Marsh. Osteotomy of Mandibular Ramus: Prognathism & Allied Problems. (Illus.). 168p. 1977. 19.50 (ISBN 0-398-03610-1). C C Thomas.

Robinson, Martha. Arthritis & You. 88p. 1980. 15.00x (ISBN 0-86025-847-5, Pub. by Ian Henry Pubns England). State Mutual Bk.

Robinson, Mary. Walsingham; or, the Pupil of Nature: A Domestic Story, 4 vols. Luria, Gina, ed. (The Feminist Controversy in England, 1788-1810 Ser.). 1974. Set. lib. bdg. 152.00 (ISBN 0-8240-0878-2); lib. bdg. 50.00 ea. Garland Pub.

Robinson, Matt. Gordon of Sesame Street Storybook. (Illus.). (gr. 7-9). 1951. 4.95 (ISBN 0-394-82406-7, BYR); PLB 5.99 (ISBN 0-394-92406-1). Random.

Robinson, Max, ed. see Rukert, Norman G.

Robinson, Michael C. Water for the West: The Bureau of Reclamation, 1902-1977. (Illus.). 1979. pap. text ed. 6.00 o.p. (ISBN 0-917084-30-6). Am Public Works.

Robinson, Michael F. Naples & Neapolitan Opera. (Oxford Monographs on Music). 200p. 1972. 36.00x (ISBN 0-19-816124-7). Oxford U Pr.

Robinson, Morton J. Self-Assessment of Current Knowledge in Pathology. 3rd ed. 1977. spiral bdg. 14.00 (ISBN 0-87488-253-2). Med Exam.

Robinson, Neville K. Villagers at War: Some Papua New Guinea Experience in World War II. Fisk, E. K., ed. (Pacific Research Series Monograph: No. 2). 223p. 1980. pap. text ed. 12.95 (0475). Bks Australia.

Robinson, P., ed. Fundamentals of Experimental Psychology: A Comparative Approach. 2nd ed. 19.95 (ISBN 0-13-339135-3); pap. 5.95 wkbk (ISBN 0-13-339127-2). P-H.

Robinson, Patricia, jt. auth. see Robinson, Stuart.

Robinson, Patrick, jt. auth. see Reeves, Richard S.

Robinson, Paul W. Fundamentals of Experimental Psychology: A Comparative Approach. 400p. 1976. 19.95x (ISBN 0-13-339168-X); student guide 6.95 (ISBN 0-13-339143-4). P-H.

Robinson, Pauline C. ESP (English for Specific Purposes) The Present Position. (Pergamon Institute of English). 1980. pap. 8.95 (ISBN 0-08-024585-4). Pergamon.

Robinson, Peggy. The Portland Walkbook. (Illus., Maps by Judith Farmer). 1978. pap. 5.95 o.p. (ISBN 0-918480-09-4). Victoria Hse.

--Profiles of Northwest Plants: Food Uses, Medicinal Uses, & Legends. 2nd ed. (Illus.). 168p. 1979. pap. 5.95 (ISBN 0-686-27923-9). P Robinson.

Robinson, Percy. Handel & His Orbit. (Music Reprint Ser.). 1979. Repr. of 1908 ed. lib. bdg. 27.50 (ISBN 0-306-79522-1). Da Capo.

Robinson, Peter. How to Appraise Commercial Properties. 1971. 24.95 o.p. (ISBN 0-13-401828-1). P-H.

Robinson, Peter, ed. see Stokes, Adrian.

Robinson, Peter G. Marine Engineer's Guide to Fluid Flow. LC 75-25933. (Illus.). 1975. 5.00x (ISBN 0-87033-215-5). Cornell Maritime.

Robinson, Peter S., ed. Foundation Guide for Religious Grant Seekers. LC 79-19006. (Scholars Press Handbooks in Humanities Ser.: No. 1). 1979. 10.50 (ISBN 0-89130-339-1, 001501); pap. 6.00 (ISBN 0-89130-340-5). Scholars Pr Ca.

Robinson, Phyllis. Great Ideas for Banquets: Possibilities, Plans, & Patterns. (Paperback Program Ser.). (Orig.). 1981. pap. 7.95 (ISBN 0-8010-7706-0). Baker Bk.

Robinson, R. Clinical Chemistry & Automation: A Study in Laboratory Proficiency. 188p. 1971. 21.95x (ISBN 0-85264-204-0, Pub. by Griffin England). State Mutual Bk.

--Ways to Move. (Topics in Geography Ser.). (Illus.). 1977. 16.95 (ISBN 0-521-21271-5); pap. 8.95 (ISBN 0-521-29081-3). Cambridge U Pr.

Robinson, R., et al. Africa & the Victorians: The Official Mind of Imperialism. 1967. pap. text ed. 13.50x (ISBN 0-333-05552-7). Humanities.

Robinson, R. W., et al. Combinatorial Mathematics VII: Proceedings. (Lecture Notes in Mathematics Ser.: Vol. 829). (Illus.). 256p. 1981. pap. 16.80 (ISBN 0-387-10254-X). Springer-Verlag.

Robinson, Ras, jt. auth. see Beasley, Manley.

Robinson, Ras, ed. The Finest of Fulness. 192p. 1979. pap. 3.95 (ISBN 0-937778-00-1). Fulness Hse.

Robinson, Ray & Winold, Allen. The Choral Experience: Literature, Materials, & Methods. 1976. text ed. 14.95x scp (ISBN 0-06-161419-X, HarpC). Har-Row.

Robinson, Raymond. The Growing of America: Seventeen Eighty-Nine to Eighteen Forty-Eight. LC 78-67275. 1979. pap. text ed. 6.95x (ISBN 0-88273-112-2). Forum Pr MO.

Robinson, Rich. How to Save Tax Dollars When You Sell Your House. 4th ed. 1980. pap. 1.95 (ISBN 0-88462-372-6). Real Estate Ed Co.

Robinson, Richard. An Atheist's Values. 1975. pap. 12.75x (ISBN 0-631-15970-3, Pub. by Basil Blackwell). Biblio Dist.

--The Video Primer: Equipment, Production & Concepts. LC 73-89670. 1974. pap. 8.95 (ISBN 0-8256-3139-4, 030033, Quick Fox). Music Sales.

Robinson, Richard, ed. Professor Hoffmann's Modern Magic. LC 77-78530. 1977. text ed. 11.95 o.p. (ISBN 0-8256-3073-8); pap. 6.95 o.p. (ISBN 0-8256-3084-3, 030073, Quick Fox). Music Sales.

Robinson, Richard D. National Control of Foreign Business: A Survey of Fifteen Countries. LC 75-44938. (Special Studies). (Illus.). 1976. text ed. 45.00 (ISBN 0-275-56500-9). Praeger.

Robinson, Richard D., et al. Foreign Investment in the Third World: A Comparative Study of Selected Developing Country Investment Promotion Programs. 1980. 10.00 (6005). Chamber Comm US.

Robinson, Richard H. Early Madhyamika in India & China. 1977. text ed. 13.50x o.p. (ISBN 0-8426-0904-0). Verry.

Robinson, Robert H. Lynchtree County. (Orig.). 1980. pap. 2.50 (ISBN 0-505-51553-9). Tower Bks.

Robinson, Robert L. Complete Course in Professional Locksmithing. LC 73-174584. (Illus.). 300p. 1973. 42.95 (ISBN 0-911012-15-X). Nelson-Hall.

--How to Burglar-Proof Your Home. LC 76-54352. 1978. 14.95 (ISBN 0-88229-245-5); pap. 7.95 (ISBN 0-88229-505-5). Nelson-Hall.

Robinson, Roger H. The Police Shotgun Manual. (Illus.). 168p. 1973. 14.75 (ISBN 0-398-02630-0). C C Thomas.

Robinson, Roland I. & Johnson, Robert W. Self-Correcting Problems in Finance. 3rd ed. 272p. 1976. pap. text ed. 12.95 (ISBN 0-205-05444-7, 0854441). Allyn.

Robinson, Roland I. & Wrightsman, Dwayne. Financial Markets: The Accumulation & Allocation of Wealth. Orig. Title: Money & Capital Markets. (Illus.). 512p. 1974. text ed. 18.95 o.p. (ISBN 0-07-053273-7, C). McGraw.

Robinson, Romney. Edward H. Chamberlin. LC 74-147309. 1971. pap. 2.00 (ISBN 0-231-03005-3). Columbia U Pr.

Robinson, Ronald. Tumors That Secrete Catecholamines: A Study Their Natural History & Their Diagnosis. LC 79-41731. 132p. 1980. 40.00 (ISBN 0-471-27748-7). Wiley.

Robinson, Rowena D., jt. auth. see Robinson, James H.

Robinson, Roy. Lepidoptera Genetics. 1971. 64.00 (ISBN 0-08-006659-3). Pergamon.

Robinson, Shari. A First Number Book. LC 80-83587. (Illus.). 96p. (gr. k-4). 1981. PLB 11.85 (ISBN 0-448-13922-7); pap. 3.95 (ISBN 0-448-47335-6). Platt.

Robinson, Sol. Radio Advertising: How to Sell It & Write It. LC 76-162410. 1974. 12.95 o.p. (ISBN 0-8306-4565-9, 565). TAB Bks.

Robinson, Sonda T. The Darkness of Love. 1977. pap. 1.25 o.s.i. (ISBN 0-515-04195-5). Jove Pubns.

Robinson, Spider. Telempath. (YA) 1976. 7.95 o.p. (ISBN 0-399-11796-2, Dist. by Putnam). Berkley Pub.

Robinson, Stearn. Dreamer's Dictionary. 1975. pap. 2.95 (ISBN 0-446-93917-X). Warner Bks.

Robinson, Stephen E. The Testament of Adam: An Examination of the Syriac & Greek Traditions. LC 80-12209. (Society of Biblical Literature Dissertation Ser.: No. 52). write for info. (ISBN 0-89130-398-7, 06-01-52); pap. write for info. (ISBN 0-89130-399-5). Scholars Pr CA.

Robinson, Stuart & Robinson, Patricia. Exploring Fabric Printing. (Illus.). (gr. 7 up). 1972. 12.00 (ISBN 0-8231-7021-7). Branford.

Robinson, T., jt. auth. see Beaton, W. R.

Robinson, Terry, jt. auth. see Strait, Raymond.

Robinson, Theodore H. Paradigms & Exercises in Syriac Grammar. 4th ed. Brockington, L. H., ed. 1962. 14.95x (ISBN 0-19-815416-X). Oxford U Pr.

--The Poetry of the Old Testament. LC 48-10111. (Studies in Theology: No. 49). 1947. pap. 8.50x (ISBN 0-8401-6049-6). Allenson.

Robinson, Thomas. The Schoole of Musicke, Wherein Is Taught the Perfect Method of True Fingering of the Lute, Pandora, Orpharion & Viol da Gamba. LC 73-6122. (English Experience Ser.: No. 589). 1973. Repr. of 1603 ed. 16.00 (ISBN 90-221-0589-X). Walter J Johnson.

Robinson, Thomas W., ed. The Cultural Revolution in China. LC 77-129609. 1971. 25.00x (ISBN 0-520-01811-7). U of Cal Pr.

Robinson, Thomas W., jt. ed. see Choucri, Nazli.

Robinson, Tim. In Worlds Apart-Professionals & Their Clients in the Welfare State. 87p. 1978. pap. text ed. 4.90x (ISBN 0-7199-0942-2, Pub. by Bedford England). Renouf.

Robinson, Tom. An Eskimo Birthday. LC 74-23750. (Illus.). (gr. 2-5). 1975. 5.25 (ISBN 0-396-07065-5). Dodd.

Robinson, Trevor. The Amateur Wind Instrument Maker, Revised Edition. LC 80-5381. (Illus.). 136p. 1981. pap. 8.95 (ISBN 0-87023-312-2). U of Mass Pr.

Robinson, Veronica. Delos. LC 80-65667. (Illus.). 128p. (gr. 6 up). 1980. 8.95 (ISBN 0-233-97259-5). Andre Deutsch.

Robinson, Vester. Basic Principles of Electricity. LC 72-91115. 464p. 1973. ref. ed. 14.95 (ISBN 0-87909-062-6). Reston.

Robinson, Virgil. James White. LC 75-16921. (Illus.). 1976. 7.50 (ISBN 0-8280-0049-2). Review & Herald.
--William Booth & His Army. LC 75-25226. (Panda Ser). 1976. pap. 4.95 (ISBN 0-8163-0272-3, 23685-1). Pacific Pr Pub Assn.
--Yankee Dan. (Uplook Ser.). 1976. pap. 0.75 (ISBN 0-8163-0273-1, 24000-2). Pacific Pr Pub Assn.
Robinson, W. Heath. How to Be a Motorist. (Illus.). 130p. 1975. 10.95 (ISBN 0-7156-1180-1, Pub. by Duckworth England). Biblio Dist.
--Humours of Golf. (Illus.). 96p. 13.50 (ISBN 0-7156-0915-7, Pub. by Duckworth England). Biblio Dist.
Robinson, W. Peter, jt. auth. see Giles, Howard.
Robinson, W. Stitt. The Southern Colonial Frontier: Sixteen Hundred Seven to Seventeen Sixty-Three. LC 78-21432. (Histories of the American Frontier Ser). 1979. 12.50x o.p. (ISBN 0-8263-0502-4); pap. 6.50x (ISBN 0-8263-0503-2). U of NM Pr.
Robinson, Wayne. I Once Spoke in Tongues. pap. 1.50 (ISBN 0-89129-013-3). Jove Pubns.
--Questions Are the Answer. LC 80-36780. 110p. 1980. pap. 5.95 (ISBN 0-8298-0409-9). Pilgrim NY.
Robinson, William A. Best Sales Promotions, Vol. 4. LC 80-66061. 1980. 24.95 (ISBN 0-87251-047-6). Crain Bks.
Robinson, William A., jt. ed. see Rossof, Arthur H.
Robinson, William C. Law of Patents, 3 vols. 1971. Repr. of 1890 ed. Set. 125.00 (ISBN 0-87632-039-6). Boardman.
Robinson, William H. Phillis Wheatley: A Bio-Bibliography. (Reference Books Ser.). 1981. 18.00 (ISBN 0-8161-8318-X). G K Hall.
Robinson, William J., jt. ed. see Szycher, Michael.
Robinson, William R., ed. Man & the Movies. LC 67-24549. (Illus.). 1967. 22.50 (ISBN 0-8071-0718-2). La State U Pr.
Robinson, Yvonne, jt. auth. see Robinson, David.
Robischon, Paulette, jt. auth. see Sobol, Evelyn G.
Robison, Bonnie & Sports Illustrated Editors. Sports Illustrated Volleyball. LC 72-3880. (Sports Illustrated Library Ser). 1970. 5.95 (ISBN 0-397-00842-2); pap. 2.95 (ISBN 0-397-00905-4). Lippincott.
Robison, Deborah. No Elephants Allowed. (Illus.). 32p. (ps-2). 1981. 8.95 (ISBN 0-395-30078-9, Clarion). HM.
Robison, G. A., jt. ed. see Greengard, P.
Robison, G. Alan & Greengard, Paul, eds. Advances in Cyclic Nucleotide Research, Vol. 13. 352p. 1980. text ed. 38.00 (ISBN 0-89004-471-6). Raven.
Robison, G. Alan, jt. ed. see Greengard, Paul.
Robison, Helen F. Exploring Teaching in Early Childhood Education. 1977. text ed. 16.95 (ISBN 0-205-05550-8). Allyn.
--New Directions in the Kindergarten. LC 65-22438. (Orig.). 1966. pap. 7.00x (ISBN 0-8077-2045-3). Tchrs Coll.
Robison, Jim, illus. The Elves & the Shoemaker. (Tell-a-Tale Readers). (Illus.). (gr. k-3). 1975. PLB 4.77 (ISBN 0-307-68496-2, Whitman). Western Pub.
Robison, John. Proofs of a Conspiracy. 1967. pap. 3.95 (ISBN 0-88279-121-4). Western Islands.
Robison, Joleen & Sellers, Kay. Advertising Dolls. (Illus.). 1980. pap. 9.95 (ISBN 0-89145-134-X). Collector Bks.
Robison, Mary. Oh! LC 80-2723. 1981. 10.95 (ISBN 0-394-50947-1). Knopf.
Robison, Nancy. Cheerleading. LC 80-80607. (Free Time Fun Ser.). (Illus.). 48p. (gr. 5 up). 1981. 6.79 (ISBN 0-8178-0005-0). Harvey.
--Kurt Thomas: International Winner. LC 79-25572. (Sports Stars Ser.). (Illus.). 48p. (gr. 2-8). 1980. PLB 7.35 (ISBN 0-516-04307-2); pap. 1.95 (ISBN 0-516-44307-0). Childrens.
--On the Balance Beam. Pacini, Kathy, ed. LC 78-15228. (Springboard Bks). (Illus.). (gr. 3-6). 1978. 5.75g (ISBN 0-8075-6067-7). A Whitman.
Robison, Nancy L. Baton Twirling. LC 78-73746. (Free Time Fun Ser.). (Illus.). 56p. (gr. 3 up). 1980. PLB 6.79 (ISBN 0-8178-5999-3). Harvey.
--Tracy Austin: Teen Tennis Champ. rev. ed. LC 79-56009. (Star People Ser.). (Illus.). 80p. (gr. 4 up). 1980. PLB 5.79 (ISBN 0-8178-5920-9). Harvey.
Robison, Richard A. & Tiechert, Curt, eds. Treatise on Invertebrate Paleontology: Introduction (Fossilization, Biogeography & Biostratigraphy, Pt. A. LC 53-12913. 1979. 25.00x (ISBN 0-8137-3001-5). Geol Soc.
Robison, Tom. Alas, Alas, That Great City & Other Essays. (Illus.). 65p. 1980. pap. 2.50 (ISBN 0-918700-05-1). Duverus Pub.
Roblee, C. & McKechnie, A. Investigation of Fires. 1981. 14.95 (ISBN 0-13-503169-9). P-H.
Robleto, Adolfo. Amor, Fe y Esperanza. (No. 2). 1980. 1.80 (ISBN 0-311-08757-4). Casa Bautista.
--Dramas y Poemas Para Dias Especiales, No. 1. 94p. (Span.). 1980. pap. 1.95 (ISBN 0-311-07004-3, Edit Mundo). Casa Bautista.
--Dramas y Poemas Para Dias Especiales, No. 2. 1979. Repr. of 1977 ed. 1.95 (ISBN 0-311-07008-6, Edit Mundo). Casa Bautista.
--Sermones Para Dias Especiales. (Tomo II). 1979. 2.25 (ISBN 0-311-07011-6). Casa Bautista.
--Sermones Para Dias Especiales. 1980. Repr. of 1978 ed. 1.95 (ISBN 0-311-07009-4). Casa Bautista.
--Todo Es Bello Alrededor. 80p. Date not set. pap. price not set (ISBN 0-311-08758-2, Edit Mundo). Casa Bautista.
Robleto, Adolfo, tr. see Conner, T.
Robleto, Adolfo, tr. see Dana, H. E. & Mantey, J. R.
Robley, Grace, jt. auth. see Robley, Wendel.
Robley, Grace, jt. auth. see Robley, Wendell.
Robley, Wendel & Robley, Grace. Spank Me If You Love Me. LC 76-1067. 128p. 1976. pap. 2.95 o.p. (ISBN 0-89221-019-2). New Leaf.
Robley, Wendell & Robley, Grace. The Spirit-Led Family. 1974. pap. 1.25 o.p. (ISBN 0-88368-033-5). Whitaker Hse.
Robock, Stefan H., et al. International Business & Multinational Enterprises. rev ed. 1977. text ed. 20.95 (ISBN 0-256-01974-6). Irwin.
Robotham, John & Shields, Gerald. Freedom of Access to Library Materials. 250p. Date not set. 16.95 (ISBN 0-918212-31-6). Neal-Schuman.
Robotham, John S. & LaFleur, Lydia. Library Programs: How to Select, Plan & Produce Them. LC 76-2033. 307p. 1976. 14.50 (ISBN 0-8108-0911-7). Scarecrow.
Robottom, John, jt. auth. see Claypole, William.
Robson, B. T. Urban Analysis. LC 68-25086. (Geographical Studies: No. 1). (Illus.). 1969. 47.50 (ISBN 0-521-07272-7); pap. 11.50 (ISBN 0-521-09989-7). Cambridge U Pr.
Robson, Barbara & Sutherland, Kentoncompiled by. A Selected Annotated Bibliography for Teaching English to Speakers of Vietnamese. LC 75-24859. (Vietnamese Refugee Education Ser.: No. 4). 1975. pap. text ed. 2.50x (ISBN 0-87281-046-1). Ctr Appl Ling.
Robson, D. & Fox, J. D., eds. Nuclear Analogue States. LC 76-17849. (Benchmark Papers in Nuclear Physics Ser.: Vol. 1). 1976. 48.50 (ISBN 0-12-787356-2). Acad Pr.
Robson, E. & Wimp, J., eds. Against Infinity. 1979. 17.00; pap. 8.95. Primary Pr.
Robson, E. R. School Architecture. Seaborne, Malcolm, ed. & intro. by. (Victorian Library). (Illus.). 440p. 1972. Repr. of 1874 ed. text ed. 15.50x (ISBN 0-391-00251-1, Leicester). Humanities.
Robson, Eric. The American Revolution. LC 74-171392. (Era of the American Revolution Ser.). 254p. 1972. Repr. of 1955 ed. lib. bdg. 25.00 (ISBN 0-306-70417-X). Da Capo.
Robson, Ernest. Phonetic Music. 1981. 19.00. Primary Pr.
--Tomas Onetwo. (Illus.). 1971. 6.95. Primary Pr.
--Transcualisticas. bilingual ed. Lopez de Thorogood, Lucy, tr. (Eng. & Span.). 1978. signed limited ed. 25.00; pap. 8.95. Primary Pr.
--Transwhichics. 1970. 15.00; pap. 7.95. Primary Pr.
Robson, Ernest M. Orchestra of the Language. 6.50 o.p. (ISBN 0-498-07111-1, Yoseloff). A S Barnes.
Robson, Graham. Motoring in the Thirties. 1980. 35.95 (ISBN 0-85059-365-4). Aztex.
Robson, J. R. Famine: Its Causes Effects & Management. (Food & Nutrition in History & Anthropology Ser.). 109p. 1980. write for info. (ISBN 0-677-16180-8). Gordon.
Robson, John M., ed. Editing Nineteenth Century Texts. (Conference on Editorial Problems Ser.). 1976. lib. bdg. 16.50 (ISBN 0-8240-2401-X). Garland Pub.
Robson, John M., ed. see Mill, John S.
Robson, Malcolm. Channel Island Pilot. 176p. 1980. 27.00 (ISBN 0-245-53413-X, Pub. by Nautical England). State Mutual Bk.
Robson, Malcom. French Pilot, Vol. 2. 256p. 1980. 33.00x (ISBN 0-245-53382-6, Pub. by Nautical England). State Mutual Bk.
Robson, N., jt. auth. see Cyrus, D.
Robson, P. D., jt. auth. see Harris, D. J.
Robson, P. M., jt. auth. see Wells, G. L.
Robson, Peter. Economic Integration in Africa. LC 68-25582. 1969. 14.95x o.s.i. (ISBN 0-8101-0033-9). Northwestern U Pr.
Robson, R. Thayne, jt. auth. see Nordlund, Willis J.
Robson, Thomas D. High-Alumina Cements & Concretes. 1963. 12.95 (ISBN 0-471-72846-2). Halsted Pr.
Robson, Vivian E. Astrology Guide to Your Sex Life. LC 67-16883. (Illus., Orig.). 1963. pap. 0.95 (ISBN 0-668-01628-0). Arc Bks.
--Fixed Stars & Constellations in Astrology. LC 73-16447. (Illus.). 1980. pap. 5.95 (ISBN 0-87728-033-9). Weiser.
Robson-Scott, W. D. The Younger Goethe & the Visual Arts. (Angelica Germanica Ser.). 200p. 49.50 (ISBN 0-521-23321-6). Cambridge U Pr.
Roby, Mary L. Christobel. large type ed. pap. 1.50 o.p. (ISBN 0-425-03141-1). Berkley Pub.
Roby, Pamela. Where Do We Go from Here: Conditions of Women in Blue-Collar Jobs. 258p. 1981. text ed. 15.50x (ISBN 0-87073-172-6); pap. text ed. 8.95x (ISBN 0-87073-173-4). Schenkman.
Roby, Pamela, ed. The Poverty Establishment. (Illus.). 224p. 1974. 7.95 o.p. (ISBN 0-13-693705-5, Spec); pap. 2.95 o.p. (ISBN 0-13-693697-0, S334, Spec). P-H.
Robyns, Gwen. The Mystery of Agatha Christie. LC 77-76259. 1978. 8.95 o.p. (ISBN 0-385-12623-9). Doubleday.
--The Potato Cookbook: From Thinning to Sinning Deliciously from Soups to Desserts. LC 76-43322. (Illus.). 136p. 1976. 9.95 (ISBN 0-916144-11-9). Stemmer Hse.
Robyns, Gwen, jt. auth. see Grace, Princess.
Roch, John, jt. tr. see Yannela, Donald.
Roch, Robert, tr. from Eng. La Recherche de Dieu, Livre Premier. (Fr.). 1978. pap. 10.00 (ISBN 0-87604-111-X). ARE Pr.
Roch, Sara E. Midwifery Revision. (Illus.). 352p. 1980. text ed. 10.00 (ISBN 0-443-01964-9). Churchill.
Rocha E Silva, M. & Leme, J. Garcia. Chemical Mediators in the Acute Inflammatory Reaction. 374p. 1973. text ed. 42.00 (ISBN 0-08-017040-4). Pergamon.
Rocha e Silva, M. & Suarez-Kurtz, G., eds. Concepts of Membranes in Regulation & Excitation. LC 74-21984. 1975. 22.50 (ISBN 0-89004-031-1). Raven.
Rochais, G. Les Recits de Resurrection des Morts dans le Nouveau Testament. LC 79-41615. (Society for New Testament Studies Monographs). 240p. (Fr.). Date not set. price not set (ISBN 0-521-22381-4). Cambridge U Pr.
Rochard, Henri. I Was a Male War Bride. (Illus.). 1977. Repr. lib. bdg. 5.00 (ISBN 0-686-21179-0). Maple Mont.
Roche, Alphonse. Alphonse Daudet. LC 75-25549. (World Authors Ser.: France: No. 380). 1976. lib. bdg. 12.50 (ISBN 0-8057-6223-X). Twayne.
Roche, John P. Sentenced to Life: Reflections on Politics, Education, & Law. LC 73-13361. 450p. 1974. 12.95 o.s.i. (ISBN 0-02-604350-5). Macmillan.
--Shadow & Substance. 1969. pap. 2.95 o.s.i. (ISBN 0-02-074650-4, Collier). Macmillan.
Roche, Judy, jt. auth. see Schuman, Donna.
Roche, Mazo De La see De La Roche, Mazo.
Roche, P. K. Goodbye, Arnold. LC 79-50750. (Illus.). 32p. (ps-2). 1981. pap. 2.75 (ISBN 0-8037-3033-0, Pied Piper Bk). Dial.
Roche, Thomas P., Jr. & O'Donnell, C. P., eds. Edmund Spenser: The Faerie Queene. 1247p. 1981. text ed. 40.00x (ISBN 0-300-02705-2); pap. 12.95x (ISBN 0-300-02706-0). Yale U Pr.
Roche, Thomas P., Jr., jt. ed. see Kullen, Patrick.
Roche De Coppens, Peter. The Spiritual Perspective: Key Issues & Themes Interpreted from the Standpoint of Spiritual Consciousness. LC 80-487. 163p. 1980. text ed. 17.75 (ISBN 0-8191-1017-5); pap. text ed. 8.00 (ISBN 0-8191-1018-3). U Pr of Amer.
Rochefoucauld, Francois De La see De La Rochefoucauld, Francois.
Rochefoucauld, Francois La see La Rochefoucauld, Francois.
Rochell, Carlton, ed. Wheeler & Goldhor's Practical Administration of Public Libraries. rev. ed. LC 79-3401. (Illus.). 480p. 1981. 27.50 (ISBN 0-06-013601-4, HarpT). Har-Row.
Rochelle, Pierre Drieu La see Drieu La Rochelle, Pierre.
Rocher, F. De see Hagiwara, M. P. & De Rocher, F.
Rocher, Francoise De see Hagiwara, Michio P. & De Rocher, Francoise.
Rocher, L., ed. see Bartholomaeo, Paulinus S.
Rocher, Rosane, ed. see Brown, W. Norman.
Rochester, Devereaux. Full Moon to France. LC 76-26250. 1977. 8.95 o.p. (ISBN 0-06-013586-7, HarpT). Har-Row.
Rochester, J. Martin & Stern, Jean. Controlling International Violence Through International Institutions: Empirical Policy Analysis Materials. rev. ed. Coplin, William D., ed. (Learning Packages in International Relations Ser.: No. 3). 88p. (Orig.). 1971. pap. text ed. 4.00x (ISBN 0-915984-73-3). Maxwell Schl Citizen.
Rochford, Thomas, jt. auth. see Gorer, Richard.
Rochlin, Gene I. Plutonium, Power, & Politics: International Arrangements for the Disposition of Spent Nuclear Fuel. 1979. 24.95x (ISBN 0-520-03887-8). U of Cal Pr.
Rochlin, Gene I., intro. by. Scientific Technology & Social Change: Readings from Scientific American. LC 74-3282. (Illus.). 1974. text ed. 19.95x (ISBN 0-7167-0501-X); pap. text ed. 9.95x (ISBN 0-7167-0500-1). W H Freeman.
Rochow, E. G. The Chemistry of Silicon. (Pergamon Texts in Inorganic Chemistry: Vol. 9). 146p. 1975. text ed. 27.00 (ISBN 0-08-018792-7); pap. text ed. 14.00 (ISBN 0-08-018791-9). Pergamon.
Rochow, E. G. & Abel, E. W. The Chemistry of Germanium, Tin & Lead. (Pergamon Texts in Inorganic Chemistry: Vol. 14). 146p. 1975. text ed. 27.00 (ISBN 0-08-018854-0); pap. text ed. 14.00 (ISBN 0-08-018853-2). Pergamon.
Rochstrasser, R. M., et al, eds. Picosecond Phenomena II: Proceedings. (Springer Series in Chemical Physics: Vol. 14). (Illus.). 382p. 1981. 38.00 (ISBN 0-387-10403-8). Springer-Verlag.
Rock, Gail. The House Without a Christmas Tree. 96p. (gr. 4-6). 1980. pap. 1.75 (Skylark). Bantam.
Rock, James M., ed. Money, Banking & Macroeconomics: A Guide to Information Sources. LC 73-17585. (Economics Information Guide Ser.: Vol. 11). 1977. 30.00 (ISBN 0-8103-1300-6). Gale.
Rock Mechanics International Society & the U. S. National Committee, 16th. Design Methods in Rock Mechanics: Proceedings. American Society of Civil Engineers, et al, eds. 432p. 1977. text ed. 31.00 (ISBN 0-87262-080-8). Am Soc Civil Eng.
Rock, Paul. Deviant Behavior. 1976. text ed. 9.50x (ISBN 0-09-115440-5, Hutchinson U Lib); pap. text ed. 4.75x (ISBN 0-09-115441-3). Humanities.
--Making People Pay. (International Library of Sociology). 1973. 25.00x (ISBN 0-7100-7684-3). Routledge & Kegan.
Rock, Philip. The Passing Bells. 1980. pap. 2.75 o.s.i. (ISBN 0-440-16837-6). Dell.
Rock, Robert C., jt. auth. see Burke, M. Desmond.
Rock, Robert H. The Chief Executive Officer. LC 77-6505. (Illus.). 1977. 15.95 (ISBN 0-669-01599-7). Lexington Bks.
Rock, Sidney & Miller, Samuel I. Career Mathematics: Practical Applications for Nonmechanical & Business Occupations. (gr. 10 up). 1978. text ed. 13.95x (ISBN 0-8104-5536-6); pap. text ed. 10.95x (ISBN 0-8104-5535-8); tchrs'. guide 1.95 (ISBN 0-8104-5625-7). Hayden.
Rock, V. P., jt. ed. see Hawley, Amos H.
Rockcastle, Verne, et al. Addison-Wesley Science Experience Records Books, Gr. 3-6. (Addison-Wesley Science Program Ser.). (gr. 1-6). 1980. 3.12 (Sch Div). Gr. 3 (ISBN 0-201-05383-7). Gr. 4. l.p. 3.92 (ISBN 0-201-05384-5); Gr. 5. l.p. 4.72 (ISBN 0-201-05385-3); Gr. 6. l.p. 4.72 (ISBN 0-201-05386-1). A-W.
Rockcastle, Verne N., et al. Space, Time, Energy, Matter: STEM - Student & Teacher's Editions. Incl. Bks. 1-6. Teacher's Guides, 6 bks. 2nd rev. ed. 1975. pap. o.p. Bk. 1. tchr's ed. gr. 1 o.p. (ISBN 0-201-05344-6); Bk. 2. tchr's ed. gr. 2 o.p. (ISBN 0-201-05345-4); Bk. 3. tchr's ed. gr. 3 o.p. (ISBN 0-201-05346-2); Bk. 4. tchr's ed. gr. 4 o.p. (ISBN 0-201-05347-0); Bk. 5. tchr's ed. gr. 5 o.p. (ISBN 0-201-05348-9); Bk. 6. tchr's ed. gr. 6 o.p. (ISBN 0-201-05349-7); Laboratory Record Books. 1976. Bk. 3. pap. text ed. 3.12 gr. 3 o.p. (ISBN 0-201-07591-1); Bk. 3. tchr's ed. 3.56 o.p. (ISBN 0-201-07595-4); Bk. 4. pap. text ed. 3.92 gr. 4 o.p. (ISBN 0-201-07592-X); Bk. 4. tchr's ed. 4.80 o.p. (ISBN 0-201-07596-2); Bk. 5. pap. text ed. 4.72 gr. 5 o.p. (ISBN 0-201-07593-8); Bk. 5. tchr's ed. 5.36 o.p. (ISBN 0-201-07597-0); Bk. 6. pap. text ed. 4.72 gr. 6 o.p. (ISBN 0-201-07594-6); Bk. 6. tchr's ed. 5.36 o.p. (ISBN 0-201-07598-9); Texts. (gr. k-6). 1975. Primer. pap. text ed. 3.60 gr. k o.p. (ISBN 0-201-05280-6); **Primer. tchr's ed. 6.92 o.p. (ISBN 0-201-05343-8); text ed. 7.36 gr. 1 o.p. (ISBN 0-201-05281-4); text ed. 7.68 gr. 2 o.p. (ISBN 0-201-05282-2); text ed. 8.20 gr. 3 o.p. (ISBN 0-201-05283-0); text ed. 8.80 gr. 4 o.p. (ISBN 0-201-05284-9); text ed. 10.00 gr. 5 o.p. (ISBN 0-201-05285-7); text ed. 10.00 gr. 6 o.p. (ISBN 0-201-05286-5). (Elementary School Science Ser.). (gr. 1-6, Sch Div). A-W.**
Rockefeller Brothers Foundation. The Use of Land. LC 73-8215. (Illus.). 318p. 1973. 10.00 o.s.i. (ISBN 0-690-00267-X, TYC-T); pap. 5.95 o.s.i. (ISBN 0-690-00275-0, TYC-T). T Y Crowell.
Rockey, C. J. Structured PL-1 Programming with Business Applications. 1981. pap. text ed. 13.95x (ISBN 0-697-08141-9); solutions manual avail. (ISBN 0-697-08145-1). Wm C Brown.
Rockey, Denyse. Speech Disorder in Nineteenth Century Britain: The History of Stuttering. 280p. 1980. 50.00x (ISBN 0-85664-809-4, Pub. by Croom Helm Ltd England). Biblio Dist.

Rockey, K. C., et al. The Finite Element Method: A Basic Introduction for Engineers. LC 74-6671. 239p. 1975. 25.95 o.p. (ISBN 0-470-72927-9). Halsted Pr.
--The Finite Element Method: A Basic Introduction. 239p. 1980. pap. text ed. 19.95x (ISBN 0-470-26979-0). Halsted Pr.
Rockland, Louis B. & Stewart, George F., eds. Water Activity: Influences on Food Quality: Proceedings of Second International Symposium on Properties of Water Affecting Food Quality. LC 79-26632. 1980. 60.00 (ISBN 0-12-591350-8). Acad Pr.
Rockland, Mae S. The New Jewish Yellow Pages. (Illus.). 288p. (Orig.). 1981. pap. 9.95 (ISBN 0-89961-016-1). SBS Pub.
Rockland, Michael A. Homes on Wheels. 192p. 1980. 12.95 (ISBN 0-8135-0892-4). Rutgers U Pr.
Rockley, Alicia A. History of Gardening in England. LC 68-21522. 1969. Repr. of 1896 ed. 18.00 (ISBN 0-8103-3845-9). Gale.
Rockley, L. E. Finance for the Non-Accountant. 3rd ed. 337p. 1979. pap. 12.25x (ISBN 0-220-67022-6, Pub. by Busn Bks England). Renouf.
--Finance for the Purchasing Executive. 191p. 1978. text ed. 24.50x (ISBN 0-220-66362-9, Pub. by Busn Bks England). Renouf.
Rockmaker, Gordon. One Hundred One Short Cuts in Math Anyone Can Do. LC 65-15500. (gr. 9 up). 1965. 8.95 (ISBN 0-8119-0136-X). Fell.
Rockman, Robert. Monarch Notes on Shaw's Plays. pap. 2.25 (ISBN 0-671-00646-0). Monarch Pr.
Rockmore, Renee & Rockmore, Steve. The Carpet Garden. LC 77-27434. (Illus.). 1978. 7.95 o.p. (ISBN 0-690-01679-4, TYC-T); pap. 4.95 o.p. (ISBN 0-690-01747-2, TYC-T). T Y Crowell.
Rockmore, Steve, jt. auth. see Rockmore, Renee.
Rockmore, Tom. Fichte, Marx, & the German Philosophical Tradition. LC 80-13194. 232p. 1980. 16.50x (ISBN 0-8093-0955-6). S Ill U Pr.
Rockowitz. Back to Basics, 3 bks. Incl. Bk. 1. English (ISBN 0-8120-2086-3); Bk. 2. Grammar (ISBN 0-8120-2087-1); Bk. 3. Reading (ISBN 0-8120-2103-7). 1981. pap. 3.95 ea. Barron.
Rockowitz, et al. Barron's How to Prepare for the High School Equivalency Exam (GED) rev. ed. (gr. 10-12). 1978. pap. text ed. 6.95 (ISBN 0-8120-0645-3). Barron.
Rockowitz, Murray. Arrow Word Puzzles. 64p. (gr. 3-7). 1980. pap. 1.25 (ISBN 0-590-30914-5, Schol Pap). Schol Bk Serv.
--Developing Skills for the High School Equivalency Examination in Grammar, Usage, Spelling & Vocabulary. 1972. pap. text ed. 5.50 (ISBN 0-8120-0485-X). Barron.
Rocksborough Smith, Simon, jt. auth. see Thomas, David S.
Rockstein, Morris & Sussman, Marvin. Biology of Aging. 1979. pap. text ed. 8.95x (ISBN 0-534-00687-6). Wadsworth Pub.
Rockville, Alphonse De see De Rockville, Alphonse.
Rockwell. A Bump in the Night. (ps-3). 1980. pap. 1.50 (ISBN 0-590-30071-7, Schol Pap). Schol Bk Serv.
Rockwell, Anne. The Awful Mess. LC 80-16779. (Illus.). 40p. (ps-2). 1980. Repr. of 1973 ed. 7.95 (ISBN 0-590-07784-8, Four Winds). Schol Bk Serv.
--A Bear, a Bobcat & Three Ghosts. LC 77-5084. (Ready-to-Read Ser.). (Illus.). (gr. 1-4). 1977. 7.95 (ISBN 0-02-777460-0, 77746). Macmillan.
--Big Boss. LC 74-13660. (Ready-to-Read Ser.). (Illus.). 64p. (gr. 1-3). 1975. 7.95g (ISBN 0-02-777570-4). Macmillan.
--Gift for a Gift. LC 73-12855. (Illus.). 48p. (gr. k-3). 1974. 5.95 o.s.i. (ISBN 0-8193-0711-4, Four Winds); PLB 5.41 o.s.i. (ISBN 0-8193-0712-2). Schol Bk Serv.
--Gogo's Car Breaks Down. LC 74-2523. (ps-k). 1978. 5.95a o.p. (ISBN 0-385-00555-5); PLB (ISBN 0-385-02365-0). Doubleday.
--Gollywhopper Egg. LC 73-6042. (Ready-to-Read Ser). (Illus.). 64p. (gr. 1-4). 1974. 8.95 (ISBN 0-02-777470-8). Macmillan.
--Gray Goose & Gander & Other Mother Goose Rhymes. LC 79-6839. (Illus.). 64p. (ps-1). 1980. 8.95 (ISBN 0-690-04048-2, TYC-J); PLB 8.79 (ISBN 0-690-04049-0). T Y Crowell.
--Machines. (Illus.). (ps-2). 1972. 7.95 (ISBN 0-02-777520-8). Macmillan.
--Paul & Arthur & the Little Explorer. LC 72-463. (Illus.). 64p. (gr. k-3). 1972. 5.95 o.s.i. (ISBN 0-8193-0592-8, Four Winds); PLB 5.41 o.s.i. (ISBN 0-8193-0593-6). Schol Bk Serv.
--The Story Snail. LC 73-19058. (Ready-to-Read Ser.). (Illus.). 64p. (gr. 1-4). 1974. 7.95g (ISBN 0-02-777560-7). Macmillan.
--Thump Thump Thump! LC 80-22142. (Illus.). (ps-1). 1981. 7.95 (ISBN 0-525-41300-6). Dutton.
--Timothy Todd's Good Things Are Gone. LC 78-6299. (Ready-to-Read Ser.). (Illus.). (gr. 1-4). 1978. 7.95 (ISBN 0-02-777600-X, 77760). Macmillan.
--Toolbox. LC 72-119836. (Illus.). (gr. k-1). 1971. 7.95 (ISBN 0-02-777540-2). Macmillan.
--Tuhurahura & the Whale. LC 71-153791. (Illus.). (gr. k-3). 1971. 5.95 o.s.i. (ISBN 0-8193-0509-X, Four Winds); PLB 5.41 o.s.i. (ISBN 0-8193-0510-3). Schol Bk Serv.
--Up a Tall Tree. LC 79-7695. (Reading-on-My-Own Bks.). (Illus.). 64p. (gr. 2). 1981. 4.95a (ISBN 0-385-15556-5); PLB (ISBN 0-385-15557-3). Doubleday.
--Walking Shoes. LC 79-7696. (Reading on My Own Ser.). (Illus.). (ps-3). 1980. 4.95a (ISBN 0-385-14730-9); PLB (ISBN 0-385-14731-7). Doubleday.
--When We Grow Up. LC 80-21768. (Illus.). (ps-1). 1981. PLB 10.95 (ISBN 0-525-42575-6). Dutton.
Rockwell, Anne & Rockwell, Harlow. Blackout. LC 78-12185. (Ready-to-Read Ser.). (Illus.). (gr. 1-4). 1979. 7.95 (ISBN 0-02-777610-7). Macmillan.
--My Barber. LC 80-29467. (Ready-to-Read Ser.). (Illus.). 24p. (ps-2). 1981. PLB 7.95 (ISBN 0-02-777630-1). Macmillan.
--The Supermarket. LC 79-11411. (Illus.). (ps-1). 1979. 7.95 (ISBN 0-02-777580-1). Macmillan.
--Thruway. LC 70-156842. (Illus.). (ps-1). 1972. 7.95 (ISBN 0-02-777510-0). Macmillan.
Rockwell, Coralie. Kagok: A Traditional Korean Vocal Form. LC 72-87568. (D (Monographs), No. 3). (Illus.). 312p. (Orig.). 1972. pap. text ed. 7.50x (ISBN 0-913360-05-8). Asian Music Pub.
Rockwell, D., jt. ed. see Naudascher, E.
Rockwell, D. M., jt. ed. see Sleeman, Phillip.
Rockwell, F. F. & Grayson, Esther C. The Complete Book of Bulbs. rev. ed. LC 77-4437. (Illus.). 1977. 10.00 o.p. (ISBN 0-397-01194-6). Lippincott.
Rockwell, Harlow. I Did It. LC 73-19059. (Ready-to-Read Ser.). (Illus.). 64p. (gr. 1-4). 1974. 6.95 (ISBN 0-02-777550-X). Macmillan.
--Look at This. LC 77-12716. (Ready-to-Read Ser.). (Illus.). (gr. 1-4). 1978. 7.95 (ISBN 0-02-777590-9, 77759). Macmillan.
--My Dentist. LC 75-6974. (Illus.). 32p. (ps-3). 1975. 7.95 (ISBN 0-688-80011-4); PLB 7.63 (ISBN 0-688-84011-6). Greenwillow.
--My Doctor. LC 72-92442. (Illus.). 24p. (ps-2). 1973. 8.95 (ISBN 0-02-777480-5). Macmillan.
--My Nursery School. LC 75-25871. (Illus.). 24p. (gr. k-3). 1976. 7.95 (ISBN 0-688-80025-4); PLB 7.63 (ISBN 0-688-84025-6). Greenwillow.
--Printmaking. LC 73-78479. 64p. (gr. 3-7). 1974. 4.95 o.p. (ISBN 0-385-01816-9). Doubleday.
Rockwell, Harlow, jt. auth. see Rockwell, Anne.
Rockwell International, et al. Wind Machines: Guide to Manufacturers, Products & Research Activities. Bereny, J. A., ed. LC 78-68748. cancelled (ISBN 0-930978-63-3); pap. 15.95 (ISBN 0-930978-28-5). Solar Energy Info.
Rockwell, Jane. Cats & Kittens. LC 73-14560. (First Bks). (Illus.). 72p. (gr. 4-7). 1974. PLB 6.45 (ISBN 0-531-00812-6). Watts.
--Dogs & Puppies. LC 75-25750. (First Bks. Ser). (Illus.). 96p. (gr. 5 up). 1976. PLB 6.45 (ISBN 0-531-00840-1). Watts.
--Dogs & Puppies. (Illus.). (gr. 4-6). 1979. pap. 1.50 (ISBN 0-671-56038-7). PB.
--Wolves. LC 77-1551. (First Bks.). (Illus.). (gr. 4-6). 1977. PLB 6.45 s&l (ISBN 0-531-02910-7). Watts.
Rockwell, Jeanne & Noonan, Thomas E., eds. Good Company: Poets at Michigan. LC 77-91403. 1978. 6.00 (ISBN 0-9602934-0-X). Noon Rock.
Rockwell, Kenneth G. Megalomania & Mediocrity in the Leadership of Nations: The Meaning for the World. (The Major Currents in Contemporary World History Library). (Illus.). 117p. 1981. 39.95 (ISBN 0-89266-292-1). Am Classical Coll Pr.
Rockwell, Norman. Norman Rockwell: My Adventures As an Illustrator. LC 79-55715. (Illus.). 1979. 13.95 (ISBN 0-89387-034-X). Sat Eve Post.
Rockwell, Robert B., jt. auth. see Niedrach, Robert J.
Rockwell, Robert E., jt. auth. see Endres, Jeannette.
Rockwell, Robert R., jt. auth. see Morneau, Robert H., Jr.
Rockwell, Thomas. Hey, Lover Boy. LC 80-68739. 160p. (YA) (gr. 8-12). 1981. 8.95 (ISBN 0-440-03583-X). Delacorte.
--How to Eat Fried Worms. LC 73-4262. (gr. 4-6). 1973. PLB 7.90 (ISBN 0-531-02631-0). Watts.
--How to Eat Fried Worms. 128p. 1975. pap. 1.50 (ISBN 0-440-44545-0, YB). Dell.
--How to Eat Fried Worms: And Other Plays. LC 78-72854. (gr. 4-7). 1980. 7.95 (ISBN 0-440-03498-1); PLB 7.45 (ISBN 0-440-03499-X). Delacorte.
--The Neon Motorcycle. LC 72-10350. (Illus.). 40p. (gr. k-3). 1973. PLB 4.90 o.p. (ISBN 0-531-02561-6). Watts.
Rockwell, Wilson, ed. Memoirs of a Lawman. LC 62-19354. 378p. 1962. 12.95 (ISBN 0-8040-0200-2, SB). Swallow.
Rockwood, D. Stephen, jt. ed. see Miller, William.
Rockwood, Frank E., ed. & intro. by. Cicero's Tusculan Disputations, Bk. 1. Bd. with Scipio's Dream. xiv, 22p. xiv, 109p. 1966. 5.95x (ISBN 0-8061-0718-9). U of Okla Pr.
Roda, Janet. No-Sew Decorating. (Orig.). 1981. pap. 9.95 (ISBN 0-440-56207-4, Delta). Dell.
Rodabaugh, John. Frenchtown. 200p. 1981. 19.95 (ISBN 0-86629-021-4). Sunrise MO.
Rodack, Madeleine T., tr. see Bandelier, Adolph F.
Rodale, Jerome I. Natural Way to Better Eyesight. (Orig.). 1968. pap. 1.50 (ISBN 0-515-01827-9, V1827). Jove Pubns.
Rodale, Robert. Sane Living in a Mad World. pap. 1.25 (ISBN 0-451-05385-0, Y5385, Sig). NAL.
Rodd, Laurel R. Nichiren: Selected Readings. LC 79-17054. (Asian Studies in Hawaii: No. 26). 224p. 1980. pap. text ed. 9.75x (ISBN 0-8248-0682-4). U Pr of Hawaii.
Rodda, Charles. The Placable Colonel Corby. 1981. 4.95 (ISBN 0-8062-1639-5). Carlton.
Rodda, J. C., et al. Systematic Hydrology. 1976. 49.95 (ISBN 0-408-00234-4). Butterworths.
Rodda, P. U., jt. auth. see Fisher, W. L.
Rodda, P. U., et al. Limestone & Dolomite Resources: Lower Cretaceous Rocks, Texas. (Illus.). 286p. 1966. 4.50 (RI 56). Bur Econ Geology.
Roddale, Jerome I. Natural Health, Sugar & the Criminal Mind. (Orig.). 1968. pap. 1.50 o.s.i. (ISBN 0-515-01828-7, N1828). Jove Pubns.
Roddick, D. Frisbee Disc Basics. 1980. 8.95 (ISBN 0-13-331322-0). P-H.
Roddick, Ellen. Holding Patterns. 224p. 1981. 10.95 (ISBN 0-312-38833-0). St Martin.
Roddon, G. Pastel Painting Techniques. 1979. 24.00 (ISBN 0-7134-1022-1, Pub. by Batsford England). David & Charles.
Roddy & Coolen. Electronic Communications. 2nd ed. (Illus.). 640p. 1980. text ed. 19.95 (ISBN 0-8359-1631-6); instr's. manual free. Reston.
Roddy, D. Introduction to Microelectronics. 2nd ed. 1978. text ed. 30.00 (ISBN 0-08-022687-6); pap. text ed. 14.00 (ISBN 0-08-022688-4). Pergamon.
--Radio & Line Transmission, Vol. 2. 1972. 30.00 (ISBN 0-08-016289-4); pap. 12.75 (ISBN 0-08-016288-6). Pergamon.
Roddy, D. J., et al, eds. see Symposium on Planetary Cratering Mechanics, Flagstaff, Ariz., 1976.
Roddy, Florence H. Faces of Nature: Fashioned by God. 96p. 1980. 3.95 (ISBN 0-8059-2759-X). Dorrance.
Roddy, Lee. Intimate Portraits of Women in the Bible. LC 80-65432. 256p. 1980. 9.95 (ISBN 0-915684-64-0). Christian Herald.
--The Mystery of Aloha House. (Chime Gothic 202 Ser.). 1981. pap. 2.50 (ISBN 0-89191-293-2). Cook.
--On Wings of Love. 128p. 1981. pap. 3.95 (ISBN 0-8407-5758-1). Nelson.
Rode, Pierre. Twenty-Four Caprices in Form Etudes for Violin. Saenger, Gustave, ed. (Carl Fischer Music Library: No.583). 52p. (gr. 6-12). 1910. pap. 4.00 (ISBN 0-686-64060-8, L583). Fischer Inc NY.
Rodee, Marian E. Old Navajo Rugs: Their Development from 1900 to 1940. (Illus.). 96p. 1981. price not set (ISBN 0-8263-0566-0); pap. price not set (ISBN 0-8263-0567-9). U of NM Pr.
Rodefeld, Richard D., et al. Change in Rural America: Causes, Consequences & Alternatives. LC 78-4644. (Illus.). 1978. pap. text ed. 17.95 (ISBN 0-8016-4145-4). Mosby.
Rodehaver, Gladys K., compiled by see Lord Easu.
Rodehaver, Myles W., et al. The Sociology of the School. LC 80-26021. x, 262p. 1981. Repr. of 1957 ed. lib. bdg. 27.50x (ISBN 0-313-22897-3, ROSSC). Greenwood.
Rodemacher, P. G., jt. auth. see Klem, Joan R.
Roden, Claudia. Book of Middle Eastern Food. 1974. pap. 4.95 (ISBN 0-394-71948-4, Vin). Random.
Roden, Donald T. Schooldays in Imperial Japan: A Study in the Culture of a Student Elite. (Illus.). 300p. 1980. 24.50x (ISBN 0-520-03910-6). U of Cal Pr.
Roden, Martin. Analog & Digital Communication Systems. 1979. 25.95 (ISBN 0-13-032722-0). P-H.
Roderick, G. W. & Stephens, M. D. Education & Industry in the Nineteenth Century: The English Disease? (Illus.). 196p. 1978. pap. text ed. 10.95 (ISBN 0-582-48719-6). Longman.
Roderick, G. W., jt. ed. see Stephens, M. D.
Roderick, Gordon W., jt. ed. see Stephens, Michael D.
Roderick, Jessie A., jt. auth. see Berman, Louise M.
Roderick, Robert. The Greek Position. Date not set. 14.95 (ISBN 0-671-61015-5, Wyndham). S&S.
Roderman, Winifred H. Getting Around Cities & Towns. (Survival Guide Ser.). (Illus.). 64p. (gr. 7-12). 1979. pap. text ed. 2.85 (ISBN 0-915510-30-8). Janus Bks.
Roderman, Winifred H., ed. see Jameson, Mack & Nist, Al.
Roderus, Frank. Cowboy. LC 80-1866. (Double D Western Ser.). 192p. 1981. 9.95 (ISBN 0-385-17120-X). Doubleday.
--Easy Money. LC 78-52121. 1978. 7.95 o.p. (ISBN 0-385-14423-7). Doubleday.
--Old Kyle's Boy. LC 80-1661. (Double D Western Ser.). 192p. 1981. 9.95 (ISBN 0-385-15937-4). Doubleday.
Rodes, David S., ed. see Shadwell, Thomas.
Rodes, John E. Germany: A History. 719p. 1964. 19.50 o.p. (ISBN 0-03-042600-6, Pub. by HR&W). Krieger.
Rodes, Richard. Running Free. LC 74-7514. (Illus.). 64p. (Orig.). 1974. pap. 3.00 o.p. (ISBN 0-8170-0637-0). Judson.
Rodger, L. W. Marketing Concepts & Strategies in the Next Decade. LC 73-1797. 248p. 1973. 18.95 (ISBN 0-470-72932-5). Halsted Pr.
--Marketing in a Competitive Economy. 3rd ed. LC 73-3342. 253p. 1965. pap. 18.95 (ISBN 0-470-72928-7). Halsted Pr.
Rodgers. Official Guide to Old Books. 2nd rev. ed. LC 78-72024. (Illus.). 1979. pap. 8.95 o.p. (ISBN 0-87637-113-6). Hse of Collectibles.
Rodgers, Andrew D., 3rd. Bernhard Eduard Fernow: A Story of North American Forestry. 1969. Repr. of 1951 ed. 13.95 o.s.i. (ISBN 0-02-851090-9). Hafner.
Rodgers, Barbara N. The Careers of Social Studies Students. 75p. 1964. pap. text ed. 3.75x (Pub. by Bedford England). Renouf.
Rodgers, Bernard F., Jr. Philip Roth. (United States Authors Ser.: No. 318). 1978. 9.95 (ISBN 0-8057-7249-9). Twayne.
--Philip Roth: A Bibliography. LC 74-16224. (Author Bibliographies Ser.: No. 19). 1974. 10.00 (ISBN 0-8108-0754-8). Scarecrow.
Rodgers, C. Leland. Essentials of Biology: A Basic Text of Current Biological Thought. LC 74-8166. (gr. 10-12). 1974. pap. 5.95 (ISBN 0-8120-0236-9). Barron.
Rodgers, Carolyn M. How I Got Ovah: New & Selected Poems. LC 74-12707. 81p. 1976. pap. 3.95 (ISBN 0-385-04673-1, Anch). Doubleday.
Rodgers, Charles A., jt. auth. see Juszli, Frank L.
Rodgers, Charles A., Jr., jt. auth. see Juszli, Frank L.
Rodgers, Diane, jt. auth. see Miller, Lani.
Rodgers, Eamon J., ed. Benito Perez Galdos: Tormento. 1976. text ed. 27.00 (ISBN 0-08-018089-2); pap. text ed. 14.00 (ISBN 0-08-018088-4). Pergamon.
Rodgers, Frank. A Guide to British Government Publications. 1980. 35.00 (ISBN 0-8242-0617-7). Wilson.
Rodgers, Gerry, et al. Population, Employment, & Inequality: The Bachue Model Applied to the Philippines. LC 78-60535. (Praeger Special Studies). 1978. 28.95 (ISBN 0-03-047216-4). Praeger.
Rodgers, Harrell R. & Harrington, Michael. Unfinished Democracy: The American Political Systems. 1981. text ed. 17.95x (ISBN 0-673-15458-0); pap. text ed. 14.95x (ISBN 0-673-15415-7). Scott F.
Rodgers, Harrell R., Jr. Crisis in Democracy: A Policy Analysis of American Government. LC 77-79458. (Political Science Ser.). 1978. pap. text ed. 8.95 (ISBN 0-201-06468-5). A-W.
--Poverty Amid Plenty: A Political & Economic Analysis. LC 78-18642. (Political Science Ser.). (Illus.). 1979. pap. text ed. 7.50 (ISBN 0-201-06471-5). A-W.
Rodgers, Harrell R., Jr. & Bullock, Charles S., 3rd. Coercion to Compliance. (Politics of Education Ser.). (Illus.). 1976. 17.95 (ISBN 0-669-00691-2); pap. 11.95 (ISBN 0-669-00965-2). Lexington Bks.
Rodgers, Harrell R., Jr., ed. Racism & Inequality: The Policy Alternatives. LC 75-15640. (Illus.). 1975. text ed. 12.00x (ISBN 0-7167-0796-9); pap. text ed. 4.50x (ISBN 0-7167-0795-0). W H Freeman.
Rodgers, John. Shorebirds & Predators: Birds of the Pacific Northwest, Part 1. (Illus.). 1974. 10.00 (ISBN 0-88894-067-X, Pub. by Douglas & McIntyre). Madrona Pubs.
Rodgers, John, jt. auth. see Dunbar, Carl O.
Rodgers, John F., jt. auth. see Crawford, H. Warren.
Rodgers, John M. State Estimates of Commodity Trade Flows, 1963. LC 73-8811. (Multiregional Input-Output Study: Vol. 5). (Illus.). 272p. 1973. 25.50 (ISBN 0-669-89227-0). Lexington Bks.

--State Estimates of Outputs, Employment & Payrolls 1947, 1958, 1963. LC 72-5759. (Multiregional Input-Output Study: Vol. 2). (Illus.). 1972. 25.95 (ISBN 0-669-73494-2). Lexington Bks.

Rodgers, Martin J. The Four States of America. 1980. 7.95 (ISBN 0-533-04562-2). Vantage.

Rodgers, Mary. Freaky Friday. (gr. 7 up). 1977. pap. 1.95 (ISBN 0-06-080392-4, P392, PL). Har-Row.

Rodgers, R. H., ed. Petri Diaconi: Ortus et Vita Iustorum Casinensis. (Publications in Classical Studies Ser.: Vol. 10). 1973. pap. 13.50x (ISBN 0-520-09393-3). U of Cal Pr.

Rodgers, Richard. Songs of Richard Rodgers: A Definitive Collection. LC 74-8879. 1974. pap. 8.95 (ISBN 0-394-70966-7). Random.

Rodgers, Richard C. Quality Control & Data Analysis of Binder-Ligand Assays: Radiommunoassay, Enzymeimmmunoassay, Flouroimmunoassay, a Programmed Text. (Illus.). 1981. 36.00 (ISBN 0-930914-07-4). Sci Newsletters.

Rodgers, Susan S., jt. auth. see Good, Shirley R.

Rodgers, William H., Jr. Cases & Materials on Energy & Natural Resources Law. LC 78-31515. (American Casebook Ser.). 995p. 1979. text ed. 23.95 (ISBN 0-8299-2029-3). West Pub.

Rodgers-Rose, La Frances, ed. The Black Woman. LC 79-28712. (Sage Focus Editions: Vol. 21). (Illus.). 316p. 1980. 18.95 (ISBN 0-8039-1311-7); pap. 9.95x (ISBN 0-8039-1312-5). Sage.

Rodgon, M. Single-Word Usage, Cognitive Development & the Beginnings of Combinatorial Speech. LC 75-7211. (Illus.). 192p. 1976. 27.50 (ISBN 0-521-20884-X). Cambridge U Pr.

Rodich, G., jt. auth. see Chao, Lincoln.

Rodieck, R. W. The Vertebrate Retina: Principles of Structure & Function. LC 79-190434. (Biology Ser.). (Illus.). 1973. text ed. 65.00x (ISBN 0-7167-0696-2). W H Freeman.

Rodin. Rodin on Art. 2nd ed. LC 70-132323. (Illus.). 304p. 1981. pap. 7.95 (ISBN 0-8180-0114-3). Horizon.

Rodin, Alvin E. The Influence of Matthew Baillie's Morbid Anatomy: Biography, Evaluation & Reprint. (American Lectures in History of Medicine & Science Ser.). (Illus.). 304p. 1973. 13.50 (ISBN 0-398-02781-1). C C Thomas.

Rodin, Auguste. Cathedrals of France. rev. ed. Geissbuhler, Elisabeth C., tr. from Fr. (Illus.). 278p. 20.00x (ISBN 0-933806-07-8). Black Swan CT.

Rodin, Burt. Calculus with Analytic Geometry. 1969. ref. ed. 25.95 (ISBN 0-13-112060-3). P-H.

Rodin, S., jt. auth. see Thompson, G. McKecknie.

Rodini, Robert J. Antonfrancesco Grazzini: Poet, Dramatist, & Novelliere 1503-1584. 1970. 25.00 (ISBN 0-299-05590-6). U of Wis Pr.

--Le Opere Di Dio. LC 75-39907. (It.). 1976. pap. text ed. 7.20 (ISBN 0-395-13399-8). HM.

Rodinson, Maxime. The Arabs. Goldhammer, Arthur, tr. LC 80-25916. (Illus.). 140p. 1981. lib. bdg. price not set (ISBN 0-226-72355-0); pap. price not set (ISBN 0-226-72356-9). U of Chicago Pr.

--Islam & Capitalism. LC 73-17297. 1974. 10.00 (ISBN 0-394-46719-1). Pantheon.

--Marxism & the Muslim World. 1979. text ed. 24.50 o.p. (ISBN 0-685-63693-3, 0-911156-33-2). Porter.

--Muhammad. Carter, Anne, tr. LC 69-20189. 1980. 15.95 (ISBN 0-394-50908-0); pap. 5.95 (ISBN 0-394-73822-5). Pantheon.

Roditi, Edouard. Dialogues on Art. LC 79-91612. 250p. 1980. pap. 6.95 (ISBN 0-915520-21-4). Ross-Erikson.

--Thrice Chosen. 135p. (Orig.). 1981. signed edition 17.50 (ISBN 0-87685-351-3); pap. 5.00 (ISBN 0-87685-350-5). Black Sparrow.

Rodker, John, tr. see Ozenfant, Amedee.

Rodman, Alexius. An Introduction to Logic: Mastering the Powers of Logical Thinking. (Illus.). 1980. deluxe ed. 37.75 (ISBN 0-89266-228-X). Am Classical Coll Pr.

Rodman, George. Mass Media Issues: Analysis & Debate. 320p. 1981. pap. text ed. 10.95 (ISBN 0-574-22570-6, 13-5570). SRA.

Rodman, Hyman, jt. auth. see Sarvis, Betty.

Rodman, M., jt. auth. see DiPalma, J.

Rodman, Richard B., tr. see Shklovskii, Iosif S.

Rodman, Selden. The Miracle of Haitian Art. LC 73-81447. 96p. (gr. 9 up). 1974. 6.95 o.p. (ISBN 0-385-07800-5). Doubleday.

--A Short History of Mexico. rev. ed. LC 80-6151. 264p. 1981. 14.95 (ISBN 0-8128-2808-9). Stein & Day.

Rodman, Selden, ed. One Hundred American Poems. (Orig.). pap. 1.50 (ISBN 0-451-61666-9, MW1666, Ment). NAL.

Rodmell, Ken. How to Use Type. 120p. 1981. pap. 7.95 (ISBN 0-442-29801-3). Van Nos Reinhold.

Rodney, Lynn S. & Joalson, Robert F. The Administration of Recreation, Parks, & Leisure Services. 2nd ed. 496p. 1981. text ed. 17.95 (ISBN 0-471-05806-8). Wiley.

Rodnick, David. Essays on an America in Transition. LC 75-126861. (Orig.). 1972. 10.00x (ISBN 0-912570-03-2). Caprock Pr.

--Postwar Germans. 1948. 37.50x (ISBN 0-685-89773-7). Elliots Bks.

--Strangled Democracy: Czechoslovakia 1948-1969. LC 70-125284. (Orig.). 1970. pap. 8.00x (ISBN 0-912570-01-6). Caprock Pr.

Rodnitzky, Jerome L. Minstrels of the Dawn: The Folk-Protest Singer As a Cultural Hero. LC 76-4520. 186p. 1976. 13.95 (ISBN 0-88229-284-6); pap. 7.95 (ISBN 0-88229-427-X). Nelson-Hall.

Rodolakis, A. & Tetrick, N. Buying Options: Wall Street on a Shoestring. 1976. 12.95 o.p. (ISBN 0-87909-109-6). Reston.

Rodoreda, Merce. Time of the Doves. Rosenthall, David, tr. LC 79-9652. 1980. 8.95 (ISBN 0-8008-7731-4). Taplinger.

Rodowski, Colby F. What About Me. 160p. (gr. 6 up). 1976. PLB 7.90 (ISBN 0-531-01209-3). Watts.

Rodowsky, Colby. P.S. Write Soon. (YA) (gr. 7-12). 1980. pap. 1.50 (ISBN 0-440-97119-5, LFL). Dell.

--P.S. Write Soon. (gr. 5 up). 1978. PLB 7.90 s&l (ISBN 0-531-01474-6). Watts.

Rodrick, Bruce. Teaching with Puppets. (Illus.). 48p. 1976. pap. 1.75 (ISBN 0-87239-075-6, 3281). Standard Pub.

Rodrigues, Jose H. Brazil & Africa. Mazzara, Richard A. & Hileman, Sam, trs. 1965. 23.75x (ISBN 0-520-01076-0). U of Cal Pr.

Rodrigues, Raymond J. & Badaczewski, Dennis. A Guidebook for Teaching Literature. new ed. 1978. pap. text ed. 17.95 (ISBN 0-205-06068-4). Allyn.

Rodrigues, Raymond J. & White, Robert H. Mainstreaming the Non-English Speaking Student. (Theory & Research into Practice Ser.). (Orig.). 1981. write for info. (ISBN 0-8141-3036-4, 30364). NCTE.

Rodriguez, Alejandro. Handbook of Child Abuse & Neglect. 1977. spiral bdg. 13.00 (ISBN 0-87488-648-1). Med Exam.

Rodriguez, Armando R. The Gypsy Wagon. (Creative Ser: No. 2). 1974. pap. 3.50 (ISBN 0-89551-005-7). UCLA Chicano Stud.

Rodriguez, Cookie, tr. Senhor, Faze-Me Chorar. (Portugese Bks.). (Port.). 1979. 1.50 (ISBN 0-8297-0690-9). Life Pubs Intl.

--Senor, Hazme Llorar. (Spanish Bks.). (Span.). 1978. 1.95 (ISBN 0-8297-0597-X). Life Pubs Intl.

Rodriguez, Eliseo, tr. see Kramer, Janice.

Rodriguez, Fred. The Treatment of Different Languages in the United States: A Brief Historical Survey. 1979. text ed. 2.50x saddle stitched o.p. (ISBN 0-87543-153-4). Lucas.

Rodriguez, Jaime E., jt. auth. see MacLachlan, Colin M.

Rodriguez, Jorge A., tr. see Westberg, Granger.

Rodriguez, Jose C. Eyes of the Mind. 1981. 12.50 (ISBN 0-533-04591-6). Vantage.

Rodriguez, Jose M., tr. see Campbell, Doak S.

Rodriguez, Judith. Mudcrab at Gambaro's. (Illus.). 91p. 1981. text ed. 13.25 (ISBN 0-7022-1574-0); pap. 7.25. U of Queensland Pr.

Rodriguez, M., ed. see Traven, B.

Rodriguez, Mario. The Cadiz Experiment in Central America, 1808-1826. 1978. 23.75x (ISBN 0-520-03394-9). U of Cal Pr.

Rodriguez, Mario B. Cuentistas de Hoy. LC 52-14409. (Span). 1952. pap. text ed. 7.50 (ISBN 0-395-05317-X). HM.

Rodriguez, O. Jaime. The Emergence of Spanish America: Vincente Rocafuerte & Spanish Americanism, 1808-1832. LC 74-22972. 392p. 1976. 26.50x (ISBN 0-520-02875-9). U of Cal Pr.

Rodriguez, Oscar E., tr. see Rusbuldt, Richard E., et al.

Rodriguez, Otilio, jt. tr. see Kavanaugh, Kieran.

Rodriguez, Rita M., jt. auth. see Carter, E. Eugene.

Rodriguez-Castellano, Juan, ed. see Mallo, Jeronimo.

Rodriguez-Monino, Antonio. Los Pliegos Poeticos de la Biblioteca Colombiana. (Publications in Modern Philology: Vol. 110). 1976. pap. 12.00x (ISBN 0-520-09521-9). U of Cal Pr.

Rodriguez-Seda de Laguna, Asela. Shaw en el mundo Hispanico. LC 79-22415. (Coleccion Mente y Palabra). 142p. (Sp.). 1980. 6.25 (ISBN 0-8477-0564-1); pap. 5.00 (ISBN 0-8477-0565-X). U of PR Pr.

Rodriques, A. & Tondeur, D., eds. Percolation Processes: Theory & Applications. (NATO Advanced Study Institute Ser.: Applied Science, No. 33). 594p. 1980. 65.00x (ISBN 90-286-0579-7). Sijthoff & Noordhoff.

Rodriquez, Judy Z. De see De Rodriquez, Judy Z. & Ziek, Nona M.

Rodriquez-Baez, Felix, jt. auth. see Feliciano-Mendoza, Ester.

Rodway, Allan. English Comedy. LC 74-25377. 1975. 20.00x (ISBN 0-520-02935-6). U of Cal Pr.

Rodway, Avril. Fairies. (The Leprechaun Library). (Illus.). 64p. 1981. 3.95 (ISBN 0-399-12610-4). Putnam.

--A Literary Herbal. (The Leprechaun Library). (Illus.). 64p. 1980. 3.95 (ISBN 0-399-12545-0). Putnam.

Rodwell, J. M., ed. & tr. Koran. 1953. 10.50x (ISBN 0-460-00380-1, Evman); pap. 4.95 (ISBN 0-460-01380-7). Dutton.

Rodzinski, Witold. History of China, Vol. 1. 1978. text ed. 52.00 (ISBN 0-08-021806-7). Pergamon.

Rodziszewski, Audrey Korwin see Konwicki, Tadeusz.

Rodziszewski, George Korwin see Konwicki, Tadeusz.

Roe, A. C., jt. auth. see Braymer, Daniel H.

Roe, A. K. & Sherwood, M. C. Learning Experience Guides for Nursing Students, 4 vols. 3rd ed. LC 78-8301. 1978. pap. 14.95 ea. Vol. 1 (ISBN 0-471-04186-6). Vol. 2 (ISBN 0-471-04614-0). Vol. 3 (ISBN 0-471-04187-4). Vol. 4 (ISBN 0-471-04613-2). Wiley.

Roe, Anne K. & Sherwood, Mary C. Nursing in the Seventies. LC 73-2874. 272p. 1973. pap. text ed. 12.50 (ISBN 0-471-72962-0). Wiley.

Roe, Clifford & Winick, Charles. The Great War on White Slavery or Fighting for the Protection of Our Girls. LC 78-66466. (Prostitution Ser.: Vol. 16). 448p. 1979. lib. bdg. 40.00 (ISBN 0-8240-9712-2). Garland Pub.

Roe, Daphne A. Alcohol & the Diet. (Illus.). 1979. lib. bdg. 17.50 (ISBN 0-87055-316-X). AVI.

--Drug Induced Nutritional Deficiencies. (Illus.). 1976. lib. bdg. 22.50 (ISBN 0-87055-205-8). AVI.

Roe, Derek. Prehistory: An Introduction. LC 70-81799. 1970. 17.50x (ISBN 0-520-01406-5); pap. 3.25 (ISBN 0-520-02252-1). U of Cal Pr.

Roe, Derek A. The Lower & Middle Paleolithic Periods in Britain. (Archaeology in Britain Ser.). (Illus.). 384p. 1981. 95.00 (ISBN 0-7100-0600-4). Routledge & Kegan.

Roe, F. Gordon. Home Furnishing with Antiques. (Illus.). 1965. 6.95 o.p. (ISBN 0-8038-2993-0). Hastings.

Roe, F. J., jt. ed. see Ambrose, E. J.

Roe, Frederick W., intro. by. Essays & Poems of Arnold. 497p. 1980. Repr. of 1928 ed. lib. bdg. 30.00 (ISBN 0-8492-7717-5). R West.

Roe, Frederick W., ed. Victorian Prose. 1947. 16.95 o.p. (ISBN 0-8260-7565-7). Wiley.

Roe, Halper. Tears of the Prophets. LC 75-33530. (Illus.). 1975. 15.00 (ISBN 0-916326-01-2). Bloch.

Roe, JoAnn. The North Cascadians. LC 80-21620. 200p. 1980. 14.95 (ISBN 0-914842-49-8). Madrona Pubs.

Roe, Keith E. & Frederick, Richard G. Dictionary of Theoretical Concepts in Biology. LC 80-19889. 312p. 1981. 17.50 (ISBN 0-8108-1353-X). Scarecrow.

Roe, P. H., jt. ed. see Savage, G. J.

Roe, Paul F. Choral Music Education. LC 77-100403. (Music Ser). 1970. ref. ed. 18.50 (ISBN 0-13-133348-8). P-H.

Roe, Shirley A. Matter, Life & Generation: Eighteenth Century Embryology & the Haller-Wolff Debate. LC 80-19611. (Illus.). 216p. Date not set. price not set (ISBN 0-521-23540-5). Cambridge U Pr.

Roebbelen, Gerhard & Sharp, Eugene L. Mode of Inheritance, Interaction & Application of Genes Conditioning Resistance to Yellow Rust. (Advances in Plant Breeding Ser.: Vol. 9). (Illus.). 88p. (Orig.). 1978. pap. text ed. 25.00 (ISBN 3-489-71110-6). Parey Sci Pubs.

Roeber, jt. auth. see Malone.

Roeber, A. G. Faithful Magistrates & Republican Lawyers: Creators of Virginia Legal Culture, 1680-1810. LC 80-19524. (Studies in Legal History). 352p. 1981. 24.00x (ISBN 0-8078-1461-X). U of NC Pr.

Roeber, Joe. Social Change at Work: The ICI Weekly Staff Agreement. LC 75-11849. 1975. 34.95 (ISBN 0-470-73000-5). Halsted Pr.

--Social Change at Work: The Imperial Chemical Industries Weekly Staff Agreement. 1975. 22.50x (ISBN 0-7156-0867-3). Intl Ideas.

Roeber, Richard J. The Organization in a Changing Environment. LC 72-11603. 1973. pap. text ed. 6.50 (ISBN 0-201-06501-0). A-W.

Roebling, Karl. Pentecostals Around the World. (Illus.). 1978. cancelled (ISBN 0-682-49109-8). Exposition.

Roebuck, Carl. World of Ancient Times. (Illus.). 1966. pap. text ed. 13.95x (ISBN 0-684-13726-7, ScribC). Scribner.

Roebuck, J. A., Jr., et al. Engineering Anthropometry Methods. LC 74-34272. (Human Factors Ser). 459p. 1975. 45.95 (ISBN 0-471-72975-2, Pub. by Wiley-Interscience). Wiley.

Roebuck, Janet. The Shaping of Urban Society: A History of City Forms & Functions. 2nd ed. LC 73-18205. (Illus.). 288p. 1974. 8.95 o.p. (ISBN 0-684-13644-9, ScribC); pap. text ed. 4.95x o.p. (ISBN 0-684-13700-3, ScribC). Scribner.

--Urban Development in Nineteenth Century London: Lambeth, Battersea & Wandsworth 1838-1888. (Illus.). 211p. 1979. 17.50x (ISBN 0-8476-3038-2). Rowman.

Roebuck, Julian & Weeber, Stanley C. Political Crime in the United States: Analyzing Crimes by & Against Government. LC 78-19463. (Praeger Special Studies). 1978. 25.95 (ISBN 0-03-044241-9). Praeger.

Roebuck, Julian B., jt. auth. see Cowie, James B.

Roeck, Alan L. Twenty-Four Hours a Day. large print ed. 1980. pap. 4.95 (ISBN 0-89486-108-5). Hazelden.

Roeda, Jack. Decisions: A Study of Christian Ethics. LC 80-189628. (Orig.). 1980. pap. text ed. 2.45 (ISBN 0-933140-14-2); tchr's manual 3.85 (ISBN 0-933140-15-0). Bd of Pubns CRC.

Roedder, Edwin & Kozlowski, Andrezj, eds. Fluid Inclusion Research: Proceedings of COFFI, Vol. 10, 1977. 270p. 1980. pap. 10.00x (ISBN 0-472-02010-2). U of Mich Pr.

Roedell, Wendy C., et al. Gifted Young Children. Tannenbaum, Abraham J., ed. LC 80-10707. (Perspectives on Gifted & Talented Education Ser.). (Orig.). 1980. pap. text ed. 6.50x (ISBN 0-8077-2587-0). Tchrs Coll.

Roeder, Ralph, tr. see Goncourt, Edmond L.

Roederer, J. G. Introduction to the Physics & Psychophysics of Music. LC 72-97698. (Heidelberg Science Library: Vol. 16). (Illus.). xii, 164p. 1973. pap. 7.10 o.p. (ISBN 0-387-90063-2). Springer-Verlag.

Roeh, Itzhak, et al. Almost Midnight: Reforming the Late Night News. LC 80-16991. (People & Communication: Vol. 11). (Illus.). 200p. 1980. 18.50 (ISBN 0-8039-1504-7). Sage.

--Almost Midnight: Reforming the Late Night News. LC 80-16991. (People & Communication: Vol. 11). (Illus.). 200p. 1980. pap. 8.95 (ISBN 0-8039-1505-5). Sage.

Roehl, Harvey N. Player Piano Treasury. 2nd ed. LC 73-77327. (Illus.). 1972. 15.00 (ISBN 0-911572-00-7). Vestal.

Roehl, Thomas, jt. ed. see Hanson, Kermit.

Roehm, Marjorie C., ed. The Letters of George Catlin & His Family: A Chronicle of the American West. 1966. 27.50x (ISBN 0-520-01078-7). U of Cal Pr.

Roehrick, Kaye L., ed. Brevet's North Dakota Historical Markers & Sites. LC 74-79978. (Historical Markers-Sites Ser). (Illus.). 176p. 1975. 10.95 (ISBN 0-88498-024-3); text ed. 6.95 o.p. (ISBN 0-685-52609-7); pap. 6.95 (ISBN 0-88498-025-1); pap. text ed. 4.46 o.p. (ISBN 0-685-52610-0). Brevet Pr.

Roellig, Leonard, ed. see Positron Annihilation Conference - Wayne State University - 1965.

Roeloffs, Karl. James Shirleys Beitrag Zur Entwicklung der Comedy of Manners. (Salzburg Studies in English Literature, Poetic Drama & Poetic Theory Ser.: No. 37). 1978. pap. text ed. 25.00x (ISBN 0-391-01508-7). Humanities.

Roelofs, Robert, et al. Environment & Society: A Book of Readings on Environmental Policy, Attitudes & Values. 448p. 1974. pap. text ed. 12.95 (ISBN 0-13-283374-3). P-H.

Roemer. Roemer Healthcare Systems & Comparative Manpower Policies. Date not set. price not set (ISBN 0-8247-1389-3). Dekker.

Roemer, John. Analytical Foundations of Marxian Economic Theory. LC 80-22646. (Illus.). 224p. Date not set. price not set (ISBN 0-521-23047-0). Cambridge U Pr.

Roemer, Michael & Stern, Joseph J. The Appraisal of Development Projects: A Practical Guide to Project Analysis with Case Studies & Solutions. LC 74-30710. (Special Studies). (Illus.). 252p. 1975. text ed. 24.95 (ISBN 0-275-05960-X). Praeger.

Roemer, Milton I., ed. see Sigerist, Henry E.

Roemer, Ruth & McKray, George, eds. Legal Aspects of Health Policy: Issues & Trends. LC 79-8583. (Illus.). x, 473p. 1980. lib. bdg. 45.00 (ISBN 0-313-21430-1, RIH/). Greenwood.

Roemer, Stern. Cases in Economic Development Projects: Policies & Statistics. 1981. text ed. price not set (ISBN 0-408-10730-8); pap. text ed. price not set (ISBN 0-408-10729-4). Butterworth.

Roen, Richard L., et al. The Helix Herbal Album. 1978. 8.95 (ISBN 0-394-50309-0). Random.

Roenfeld, Sybil. Georgian Scene Painters & Scene Painting. Date not set. price not set (ISBN 0-521-23339-9). Cambridge U Pr.

Roenigk, Henry H., Jr. Office Dermatology. (Illus.). 340p. 1981. write for info. (7316-8). Williams & Wilkins.

Roepke, Howard G. Movememts of the British Iron & Steel Industry, 1720 to 1951, Vol. 36. LC 80-23128. (Illinois Studies in the Social Sciences). (Illus.). vii, 198p. 1981. Repr. of 1956 ed. lib. bdg. 25.00x (ISBN 0-8371-9096-7, ROMB). Greenwood.

--Readings in Economic Geography. LC 67-19451. 1967. 15.95 o.p. (ISBN 0-471-72971-X). Wiley.

Roer, Kathleen. Minnesota Legal Forms-Real Estate. Mason Publishing Company Staff, ed. (Minnesota Legal Forms 1981 Ser.). 150p. 1981. ring binder 15.00 (ISBN 0-917126-86-6). Mason Pub.

Roerich, A. N. The Blue Annals. 2nd ed. 1976. 37.50 (ISBN 0-89684-179-0). Orient Bk Dist.

Roerick, Kaye L., jt. ed. see Plucker, Lina S.

Roering, jt. auth. see Block.

Roes, Carol. Mahalo Nui Translations. 1980. pap. 3.00 (ISBN 0-930932-20-X). M. Loke.

Roesch, Joseph E., tr. see Chapuis, Alfred.

Roesch, Roberta & De La Roche, Harry. Anyone's Son: A True Story. (Illus.). 1979. 9.95 o.p. (ISBN 0-8362-6608-0). Andrews & McMeel.

Roesch, Ronald & Golding, Stephen L. Competency to Stand Trial. LC 80-12456. 251p. 1981. 19.95 (ISBN 0-252-00825-1). U of Ill Pr.

Roeschl, Maria & Lehrs, Ernst. Second Man in U. S. 1978. pap. 7.95 (ISBN 0-904822-07-9, Pub by Henry Goulden, Ltd.). St George Bk Serv.

Roesler. Gansebraten. (Easy Reader, A). pap. 2.90 (ISBN 0-88436-109-8, GEA110054). EMC.

Roesser, Robert P., jt. auth. see Givone, Donald D.

Roessler, Edward B., jt. auth. see Alder, Henry L.

Roessler, Edward B., jt. auth. see Amerine, Maynard A.

Roethel, Louis & Weinstein, Abraham. Logic, Sets, & Numbers: A Positive Approach to Math. 2nd ed. 1976. 19.95x (ISBN 0-534-00491-1). Wadsworth Pub.

Roethenmund, Robert. Swiss Banking Handbook. LC 79-55800. (Illus.). 1980. 19.95 (ISBN 0-916728-33-1); pap. 8.95 o.s.i. (ISBN 0-916728-34-X). Bks in Focus.

Roethke, Theodore. Collected Poems. LC 65-23785. 288p. 1975. pap. 5.95 (ISBN 0-385-08601-6, Anch). Doubleday.

--Far Field. LC 64-12105. 1971. pap. 2.95 (ISBN 0-385-04692-8, Anch). Doubleday.

Roethlisberger, Marcel. Claude Lorrain: The Drawings, 2 vols., boxed. Incl. Vol. 1. Catalogue (ISBN 0-520-01458-8); Vol. 2. Plates (ISBN 0-520-01805-2). LC 66-24050. (Studies in the History of Art: No. 8). (Illus.). 1969. 70.00x ea. U of Cal Pr.

Roett, Riordan. Brazil: Politics in a Patrimonial Society. rev ed. LC 77-7825. (Praeger Special Studies). 1978. 23.95 (ISBN 0-03-022861-1); pap. 8.95 student ed (ISBN 0-03-022866-2). Praeger.

Roetzer, Elisabeth, jt. auth. see Trobisch, Ingrid.

Roetzer, Josef. Family Planning the Natural Way. Date not set. pap. 6.95 (ISBN 0-8007-1185-8). Revell. Postponed.

Rofes, Eric, ed. see Fayerweather Street School.

Roff, Charles L. A Boomtown Lawyer in the Osage. (Illus.). 180p. 1975. 6.00 o.p. (ISBN 0-89015-101-6). Nortex Pr.

Roff, Renee, compiled by. Directory of American Book Workers. 1981. 19.95 (ISBN 0-935164-05-7). N T Smith.

Roff, William R. Bibliography of Malay & Arabic Periodicals Eighteen Seventy-Six to Nineteen Forty-One. (London Oriental Bibliographies Ser: No. 3). 80p. 1972. 9.75x o.p. (ISBN 0-19-713572-2). Oxford U Pr.

Roffey, Maureen. Indoors. (Illus.). (ps). 1979. 1.25 (ISBN 0-370-02006-5, Pub. by Chatto Bodley Jonathan). Merrimack Bk Serv.

--Let's Have a Party. (Illus.). 1978. 6.95 (ISBN 0-370-01278-X, Pub. by Chatto Bodley Jonathan). Merrimack Bk Serv.

--Out of Doors. (Illus.). (ps). 1979. 1.25 (ISBN 0-370-02007-3, Pub. by Chatto Bodley Jonathan). Merrimack Bk Serv.

Roffey, Maureen & Lodge, Bernard. Door to Door. LC 80-50229. (Illus.). 32p. (gr. k-1). 1980. 7.95 (ISBN 0-688-41966-6). Lothrop.

--The Grand Old Duke of York. (Illus.). 1978. 6.95 (ISBN 0-370-10761-6, Pub. by Chatto Bodley Jonathan). Merrimack Bk Serv.

--Tinker Tailor Soldier Sailor. (Illus.). 1978. 6.95 (ISBN 0-370-01805-2, Pub. by Chatto Bodley Jonathan). Merrimack Bk Serv.

Roffman, Etomar Ben. The Great Christ Debate: A Quest for the Theological Reconciliation of Judaism, Christianity, & Islam. 1978. 8.50 o.p. (ISBN 0-682-49123-3). Exposition.

Rogal, Samuel J. Sisters of Sacred Song: Selected Listing of Women Hymnodists in Great Britain & America. LC 80-8482. 180p. 1981. lib. bdg. 22.00 (ISBN 0-8240-9482-4). Garland Pub.

--Teaching Composition in Senior High School. (Quality Paperback: No. 99). (Orig.). 1969. pap. 2.95 (ISBN 0-8226-0099-4). Littlefield.

Rogan, Barbara. Changing States. 192p. 1981. 10.95 (ISBN 0-385-17373-3). Doubleday.

Roger-Marx, Claude & Cotte, Sabine. Delacroix. LC 70-132366. (Great Draughtsmen Ser). (Illus.). 1971. 7.95 o.s.i. (ISBN 0-8076-0586-7). Braziller.

Rogers. Issues in Adolescent Psychology. 3rd ed. 1977. pap. 12.95 (ISBN 0-13-506428-7). P-H.

--Matrix Derivatives. 224p. 1980. 27.50 (ISBN 0-8247-1176-9). Dekker.

Rogers, jt. auth. see Turner.

Rogers, A. L., jt. auth. see Beneke, E. S.

Rogers, A. Robert. The Humanities: A Selective Guide to Information Sources. 2nd ed. LC 79-25335. (Library Science Text Ser.). 1980. lib. bdg. 25.00 (ISBN 0-87287-206-8); pap. text ed. 14.50 (ISBN 0-87287-222-X). Libs Unl.

Rogers, A. W. Techniques of Autoradiography. 3rd, rev. & enl. ed. LC 78-16861. 1979. 65.00 (ISBN 0-444-80063-8, North Holland). Elsevier.

Rogers, Alan. Empire & Liberty: American Resistance to British Authority, 1755-1763. 1975. 17.50x (ISBN 0-520-02275-0). U of Cal Pr.

--Landscapes & Documents. 85p. 1974. pap. text ed. 3.75x (ISBN 0-7199-0883-3, Pub. by Bedford England). Renouf.

Rogers, Andrei. Matrix Analysis of Interregional Population Growth & Distribution. 1968. 18.50x (ISBN 0-520-01083-3). U of Cal Pr.

Rogers, Andy, et al, eds. Proceedings of the Texas Conference on Performatives, Presuppositions, & Implicatures. LC 77-79322. 1977. pap. text ed. 9.95x o.p. (ISBN 0-87281-063-1). Ctr Appl Ling.

Rogers, Ann. The New Cookbook for Poor Poets & Others. rev ed. (Illus.). 1979. 8.95 o.p. (ISBN 0-684-16046-3, ScribT); pap. 3.95 (ISBN 0-684-16948-7, SL837, ScribT). Scribner.

Rogers, Anne. Cinderella. LC 78-50997. (Grimm Ser.). (Illus.). 24p. (gr. 2). 1978. lib. bdg. 6.95 o.p. (ISBN 0-88332-093-2, 8130). Larousse.

Rogers, Anne, tr. from Danish. Grimm's The Musicians of Bremen. LC 74-78599. (Illus.). 24p. (gr. 1-3). 1974. 6.95 (ISBN 0-88332-060-6, 8027). Larousse.

Rogers, Augustus J., 3rd. Choice: An Introduction to Economics. 2nd ed. (Illus.). 258p. 1974. pap. text ed. 11.95 (ISBN 0-13-133223-6). P-H.

Rogers, Barbara. The Doomsday Scroll. LC 79-7101. 1979. 8.95 (ISBN 0-396-07655-6). Dodd.

--Project Web. LC 79-25673. 256p. 1980. 8.95 (ISBN 0-396-07795-1). Dodd.

--White Wealth & Black Poverty: American Investments in Southern Africa. LC 75-35353. (Studies in Human Rights: No. 2). 288p. 1976. lib. bdg. 17.50 (ISBN 0-8371-8277-8, RWW/). Greenwood.

Rogers, Betty. Will Rogers. LC 79-4743. (Illus.). 1979. pap. 5.95 (ISBN 0-8061-1600-5). U of Okla Pr.

Rogers, Billi M., jt. ed. see Sewell, Ernestine.

Rogers, Bruce, jt. auth. see Watanabe, Masahiro.

Rogers, Carl. Freedom to Learn: A View of What Education Might Become. LC 72-75629. 1969. text ed. 11.95 (ISBN 0-675-09519-0); pap. text ed. 8.95x (ISBN 0-675-09579-4). Merrill.

Rogers, Carl R. Client Centered Therapy. LC 51-9139. 1951. pap. text ed. 13.50 (ISBN 0-395-05322-6). HM.

--Counseling & Psychotherapy. LC 42-24693. 1942. text ed. 18.95 (ISBN 0-395-05321-8). HM.

--A Way of Being. 288p. 1980. 14.95 (ISBN 0-395-29915-2). HM.

--A Way of Being. LC 80-82291. 288p. 1981. pap. text ed. 6.95 (ISBN 0-395-29735-4). HM.

Rogers, Carl R. & Dymond, Rosalind F., eds. Psychotherapy & Personality Change. LC 54-11211. (Midway Reprint Ser.). 1978. pap. text ed. 20.00x (ISBN 0-226-72375-5). U of Chicago Pr.

Rogers, Carole. How to Collect: A Complete Guide. 1981. 12.95 (ISBN 0-525-93190-2); pap. 6.95 (ISBN 0-525-47671-7). Dutton.

Rogers, Charles B. Art Observations. (Illus.). 64p. 1980. pap. 5.95 (ISBN 0-686-64396-8). Rogers Hse Mus.

Rogers, Claude A. Hausdorff Measures. (Illus.). 1970. 28.95 (ISBN 0-521-07970-5). Cambridge U Pr.

Rogers, Cyril H. Budgerigars. Foyle, Christina, ed. (Foyle's Handbooks). 1973. 3.95 (ISBN 0-685-55808-8). Palmetto Pub.

--Cage & Aviary Birds. Clear, Val, ed. LC 75-845. (Illus.). 224p. 1975. 6.98 o.s.i. (ISBN 0-02-604360-2). Macmillan.

--Canaries. Foyle, Christina, ed. (Foyle's Handbks). (Illus.). 1973. 3.95 (ISBN 0-685-55797-9). Palmetto Pub.

--Cockatiels. (Illus.). 80p. 1981. 3.95 (ISBN 0-903264-26-9, 5212-0, Pub. by K & R Bks England). Arco.

--The Encyclopedia of Cage & Aviary Birds. 15.95 (ISBN 0-7207-0802-8, Pub. by Michael Joseph). Merrimack Bk Serv.

--Foreign Birds. Foyle, Christina, ed. (Foyle's Handbks). 1973. 3.95 (ISBN 0-685-55809-6). Palmetto Pub.

--Parakeet Guide. 1971. 6.98 o.p. (ISBN 0-385-01652-2). Doubleday.

--Zebra Finches. (Illus.). 128p. 1980. 7.95 (ISBN 0-903264-19-6, 4904-9, Pub. by K & R Bks England). Arco.

Rogers, D. & Ruchlin, H. Economics & Education: Principles & Applications. LC 74-143519. 1971. text ed. 14.95 (ISBN 0-02-926690-4). Free Pr.

Rogers, D., ed. Gabriel Tellez: El Condenado por desconfiado. LC 73-7964. 172p. 1974. text ed. 22.00 (ISBN 0-08-017247-4); pap. text ed. 14.00 (ISBN 0-08-017248-2). Pergamon.

Rogers, Dale E. Angel Unaware. (Orig.). pap. 1.50 (ISBN 0-515-05325-2). Jove Pubns.

--Angel Unaware. 1975. pap. 1.25 (ISBN 0-685-84180-4, PV091). Jove Pubns.

--Dearest Debbie. 1966. pap. 1.25 o.s.i. (ISBN 0-89129-073-7). Jove Pubns.

--Finding the Way. Orig. Title: God Has the Answers. 64p. 1973. 3.95 o.p. (ISBN 0-8007-0604-8). Revell.

--Time Out, Ladies! (Spire Bk). 1969. 3.95 o.p. (ISBN 0-8007-0317-0). Revell.

--Trials, Tears & Triumph. 1977. 4.95 o.p. (ISBN 0-8007-0847-4). Revell.

--Where He Leads. (Illus.). 1974. deluxe ed. 5.95 (ISBN 0-8007-0723-0); pap. 1.50 o.p. (ISBN 0-8007-8194-5, Spire Bks). Revell.

--Where He Leads. 1975. pap. 1.50 (ISBN 0-89129-002-8). Jove Pubns.

--Woman at the Well. 1970. 6.95 (ISBN 0-8007-0385-5); pap. 1.95 (ISBN 0-8007-8090-6, Spire Bks). Revell.

Rogers, David. The Bedroom Set. 1979. pap. 1.75 o.p. (ISBN 0-449-14188-8, GM). Fawcett.

--The Great American Alimony Escape. 1979. pap. 1.95 o.p. (ISBN 0-449-14132-2, GM). Fawcett.

--Inventory of Educational Improvement Efforts in the New York City Public Schools. LC 77-10481. 1977. pap. text ed. 12.75x (ISBN 0-8077-2531-5). Tchrs Coll.

--Management of Big Cities: Interest Groups & Social Change Strategies. LC 77-151671. 1971. 12.50 (ISBN 0-8039-0092-9); pap. 8.95x. Sage.

--Monarch Notes on Tennyson's Idylls of the King & Other Poems. (Orig.). pap. 2.25 (ISBN 0-671-00734-3). Monarch Pr.

Rogers, David, jt. ed. see Hawley, Willis.

Rogers, David, ed. see Hawley, Willis.

Rogers, David, jt. ed. see Whiting, Larry.

Rogers, David C. Business Policy & Planning: Text & Cases. (Illus.). 1977. 21.95 (ISBN 0-13-107409-1). P-H.

Rogers, David E., et al. Year Book of Medicine, 1980. (Illus.). 640p. 1980. 29.95 (ISBN 0-8151-7441-1). Year Bk Med.

Rogers, David H. Consumer Banking in New York. 138p. 1975. 15.00x (ISBN 0-231-03935-2). Columbia U Pr.

Rogers, Dexter, jt. auth. see Touchstone, Joseph C.

Rogers, Diane P., et al. Inside World Politics 1974. (gr. 9-12). 1974. text ed. 7.60 (ISBN 0-205-03480-2, 7634803); tchrs'. guide 3.12 (ISBN 0-205-03481-0, 7634811). Allyn.

Rogers, Dilwyn J., ed. A Bibliography of African Ecology: A Geographically & Topically Classified List of Books & Articles. LC 78-19935. (Special Bibliographic Ser: No. 6). 1979. lib. bdg. 37.50 (ISBN 0-313-20552-3, RAE/). Greenwood.

Rogers, Donald I. Save It, Invest It & Retire: The Updated Guide to Carefree Retirement. (Illus.). 224p. 1973. 7.95 o.p. (ISBN 0-87000-202-3). Arlington Hse.

--Since You Went Away. LC 72-91642. 320p. 1973. 8.95 o.p. (ISBN 0-87000-195-7). Arlington Hse.

Rogers, Dorothy. Adolescence: A Psychological Perspective. 2nd ed. LC 77-16639. (Illus.). 1978. pap. text ed. 8.95 (ISBN 0-8185-0249-5); test items upon adoption of text free (ISBN 0-685-85040-4). Brooks-Cole.

--Adolescents & Youth. 4th ed. (Illus.). 544p. 1981. text ed. 18.95 (ISBN 0-13-008748-3). P-H.

--The Adult Years: An Introduction to Aging. (Illus.). 1979. text ed. 18.95 (ISBN 0-13-008987-7). P-H.

--Issues in Adult Development. LC 79-26993. 1980. pap. text ed. 9.95 (ISBN 0-8185-0385-8). Brooks-Cole.

--Issues in Child Psychology. 2nd ed. LC 76-28503. 1977. pap. text ed. 11.95 (ISBN 0-8185-0193-6); test items avail. (ISBN 0-685-74949-5). Brooks-Cole.

--Issues in Life-Span Human Development. LC 79-27550. 1980. pap. text ed. 9.95 (ISBN 0-8185-0390-4). Brooks-Cole.

--Life-Span Human Development. LC 80-25158. 512p. 1981. text ed. 17.95 (ISBN 0-8185-0389-0). Brooks-Cole.

--Psychology of Adolescence. 3rd ed. 1977. 18.95 (ISBN 0-13-734897-5). P-H.

Rogers, Douglas. Sherwood Anderson: A Selective, Annotated Bibliography. LC 75-45225. (Author Bibliographies Ser.: No. 26). 163p. 1976. 10.00 (ISBN 0-8108-0900-1). Scarecrow.

Rogers, Douglas G., ed. Many Marriages by Sherwood Anderson. LC 78-2353. 1978. 12.00 (ISBN 0-8108-1122-7). Scarecrow.

Rogers, E. & Shoemaker, F. Communication of Innovations. 2nd ed. LC 78-122276. 1971. text ed. 14.95 (ISBN 0-02-926680-7). Free Pr.

Rogers, Edmund. Elephants. LC 77-13964. (Animals of the World Ser.). (Illus.). (gr. 4-8). 1977. PLB 10.65 (ISBN 0-8172-1076-8). Raintree Pubs.

Rogers, Everett M. Communication Strategies for Family Planning. LC 73-1049. 1973. 17.95 (ISBN 0-02-926700-5). Free Pr.

Rogers, Everett M. & Agarwala-Rogers, Rekha. Communication in Organizations. LC 75-32368. (Illus.). 1976. pap. text ed. 7.95 (ISBN 0-02-926710-2). Free Pr.

Rogers, Everett M. & Burdge, Rabel J. Social Change in Rural Society. 2nd ed. (Illus.). 1972. text ed. 17.95 (ISBN 0-13-815464-3). P-H.

Rogers, Everett M. & Kincaid, D. Lawrence. Communication Networks: Towards a New Paradigm for Research. LC 80-65202. (Illus.). 1981. 19.95 (ISBN 0-02-926740-4). Free Pr.

Rogers, F. E. Illustrations in Applied Network Theory. LC 72-75949. 1973. 17.50x (ISBN 0-8448-0165-8). Crane-Russak Co.

Rogers, Felicity M. All About the Shetland Sheepdog. (All About Ser.). (Illus.). 140p. 1980. 16.95 (ISBN 0-7207-1222-X, Pub. by Michael Joseph). Merrimack Bk Serv.

--All About the Shetland Sheepdog. rev. ed. 1980. 14.95 o.p. (ISBN 0-7207-0618-1, Pub. by Michael Joseph). Merrimack Bk Serv.

Rogers, Ferial & Minter, Phyllis V. Goats: Their Care & Breeding. (Illus.). 100p. 1980. 3.95 (ISBN 0-686-63088-2, 4948-0, Pub. by K & R Bks England). Arco.

Rogers, Fred. Mr. Rogers' Neighborhood: The Costume Party. (ps-1). 1976. PLB 5.38 (ISBN 0-307-68958-1, Golden Pr). Western Pub.

--Mister Roger's Songbook. (Illus.). (gr. k-2). 1970. 4.95 o.p. (ISBN 0-394-80481-3). Random.

Rogers, G. F. & Mayhew, Y. R. Thermodynamic & Transport Properties of Fluids SI Units. 2nd ed. 20p. 1976. Repr. of 1964 ed. pap. text ed. 3.25x (ISBN 0-631-96400-2, Pub. by Basil Blackwell). Biblio Dist.

Rogers, H. J., jt. ed. see Stanier, R. Y.

Rogers, Harry E. How to Do a Bankruptcy. 2nd ed. 7.95. Green Hill.

--How to Do a Bankruptcy. 2nd ed. 1980. pap. 7.95. Caroline Hse.

Rogers, J. A. From "Superman to Man". rev. ed. 132p. 1941. 5.95 (ISBN 0-9602294-4-2). H M Rogers.

--World's Great Men of Color, Vols. 1 & 2. LC 73-186437. (Illus.). 972p. 1972. Vol. 1. 9.95 o.p. (ISBN 0-686-66675-5, 60437); Vol. 2. 9.95 o.s.i. (ISBN 0-02-604380-7, 60437). Macmillan.

Rogers, J. W. & Millan, W. H. Coil Slitting. LC 73-7903. 127p. 1973. pap. text ed. 9.25 (ISBN 0-08-017696-8). Pergamon.

Rogers, Jack B. & Baird, Forrest. Introduction to Philosophy: A Case Study Approach. LC 80-8344. (Case Study Ser.). 240p. (Orig.). 1981. pap. text ed. 8.95x (ISBN 0-06-066997-7, RD 346, HarpR). Har-Row.

Rogers, James H., et al. First Aid & Emergency Medical Care. 128p. 1980. pap. text ed. 6.95 (ISBN 0-8403-2242-9). Kendall-Hunt.

Rogers, Jean L. & Fortson, Walter L. Fair Employment Interviewing. LC 76-1747. 128p. 1976. text ed. 8.95 (ISBN 0-201-06469-3). A-W.

Rogers, Jim. Silver Streak. 1976. pap. 1.75 o.p. (ISBN 0-345-25458-9). Ballantine.

Rogers, JoAnn V. Libraries & Young Adults: Media, Services, & Librarianship. LC 79-15. 1979. 17.50x (ISBN 0-87287-195-9). Libs Unl.

Rogers, Joseph W. Why Are You Not a Criminal. LC 77-2005. 192p. 1977. 10.95 (ISBN 0-13-957811-0, Spec); pap. 3.95 (ISBN 0-13-957803-X). P-H.

Rogers, Joyce. The Wise Woman. LC 80-68538. 1981. 6.95 (ISBN 0-8054-5289-3). Broadman.

Rogers, Julia. Understanding People or, How to Be Your Very Own Shrink. LC 78-31175. 1979. 12.95 (ISBN 0-88229-273-0); pap. 7.95 (ISBN 0-88229-678-7). Nelson-Hall.

Rogers, L. A. Business Analysis for Marketing Managers. 1978. pap. 14.95x (ISBN 0-434-91738-9). Intl Ideas.

Rogers, Lee. The Radiology of Trauma. (Illus.). Date not set. text ed. price not set (ISBN 0-443-08038-0). Churchill. Postponed.

Rogers, Lou. First Thanksgiving. (Beginning-to-Read Ser.). (Illus.). (gr. 2-4). 1962. 2.50 o.p. (ISBN 0-695-82884-3); lib. ed. 2.97 o.p. (ISBN 0-695-42884-5). Follett.

Rogers, Mark E. The Bridge of Catzad-Dum & Other Stories. (Illus.). 62p. (Orig.). 1980. pap. 6.00 ltd. digest-sized (ISBN 0-937528-00-5). Burning Bush.

Rogers, Mary & Joyce, Nancy. Women & Money. 1979. pap. 2.25 (ISBN 0-686-68425-7, 46003). Avon.

Rogers, May. Waverly Dictionary. 2nd ed. LC 66-27850. 1967. Repr. of 1885 ed. 20.00 (ISBN 0-8103-3222-1). Gale.

Rogers, Michael, jt. auth. see Brookshire, Michael L.

Rogers, Michael A. Paraplegia. (Illus.). 1978. 11.95 o.p. (ISBN 0-571-11209-9, Pub. by Faber & Faber); pap. 7.95 (ISBN 0-571-11208-0). Merrimack Bk Serv.

Rogers, Millard F., Jr. Favorite Paintings from the Cincinnati Art Museum. LC 80-66965. (Illus.). 104p. (Orig.). 1980. pap. 14.95 (ISBN 0-89659-159-X). Abbeville Pr.

Rogers, Natalie. Farewell Fatigue. LC 78-17132. (Illus.). 1978. pap. 2.95 o.p. (ISBN 0-668-04664-3, 4664). Arco.

Rogers, Norman. Wessex Dialect. 1979. text ed. 9.25x (ISBN 0-239-00182-6). Humanities.

Rogers, Pat. Eighteenth-Century Encounters: Essays on Literature & Society in the Age of Walpole. 220p. 1980. 21.00x (ISBN 0-389-20090-5). B&N.

Rogers, Pat, ed. Defoe: The Critical Heritage. (The Critical Heritage Ser). 1972. 25.00 (ISBN 0-7100-7259-7). Routledge & Kegan.

--The Eighteenth Century. LC 78-15568. (The Context of English Literature). 1978. text ed. 28.50x (ISBN 0-8419-0421-9); pap. text ed. 14.50x (ISBN 0-8419-0422-7). Holmes & Meier.

Rogers, Patrick V. Colossians. (New Testament Message Ser.). 9.95 (ISBN 0-89453-138-7); pap. 4.95 (ISBN 0-89453-203-0). M Glazier.

Rogers, Paul, jt. auth. see Skellern, Claire.

Rogers, Peter V. Tragedy Is My Parish: Working for God in the Streets of New Orleans. 1979. 9.95 (ISBN 0-02-604390-4). Macmillan.

Rogers, Philip W., jt. auth. see Kurtzman, Neil A.

Rogers, R. M. & Watkins, Arthur R. German Through Conversational Patterns. 3rd ed. (Illus.). 544p. 1981. text ed. 17.50 scp (ISBN 0-06-045551-9, HarpC); avail. instrs' manual; wkbk. scp 7.50 (ISBN 0-06-045554-3); tapes 229.00. Har-Row.

Rogers, R. R. A Short Course in Cloud Physics. 2nd ed. 1979. 37.00 (ISBN 0-08-023040-7); pap. text ed. 17.50 (ISBN 0-08-023041-5). Pergamon.

Rogers, R. R., et al. A Short Course in Cloud Physics. Ter Haar, D. & Blaker, J. W., eds. 224p. 1975. text ed. 19.80 o.p. (ISBN 0-08-019694-2). Pergamon.

Rogers, R. Vashon, Jr. The Law & Medical Men. xiii, 214p. 1981. Repr. of 1884 ed. lib. bdg. 22.00x (ISBN 0-8377-1032-4). Rothman.

Rogers, Robert. Metaphor: A Psychoanalytic View. LC 77-80477. 1978. 11.95x (ISBN 0-520-03548-8). U of Cal Pr.

Rogers, Robert S. & Chamberlain, V. B., 3rd, eds. National Account Marketing Handbook. 426p. 1981. 24.95 (ISBN 0-8144-5618-9). Am Mgmt.

Rogers, Rolf E. Max Weber's Ideal Type Theory. LC 68-54974. 1969. 4.50 o.p. (ISBN 0-8022-2260-9). Philos Lib.

--The Political Process in Modern Organization. LC 79-171712. (Illus.). 158p. 1971. 6.50 o.p. (ISBN 0-682-47350-2, University). Exposition.

Rogers, Rosemary. The Crowd Pleasers. rev. ed. 528p. 1980. pap. 2.75 (ISBN 0-380-75622-6, 75622). Avon.

--The Crowd Pleasers. 1978. pap. 3.95 (ISBN 0-380-38927-4, 38927). Avon.

--Dark Fires. 1975. pap. write for info. (ISBN 0-380-00425-9, 76570). Avon.

--The Insiders. 1978. pap. 2.50 (ISBN 0-380-40576-8, 40576). Avon.

--Lost Love, Last Love. 1980. pap. 2.95 (ISBN 0-380-75515-7, 75515). Avon.

--Sweet Savage Love. 640p. 1980. pap. 2.95 (ISBN 0-380-00815-7, 76588). Avon.

Rogers, Roy & Evans, Dale. Happy Trails. 224p. 1981. 2.50 (ISBN 0-553-14253-4). Bantam.

Rogers, Ruth H. Fluid Mechanics. 1978. 28.00 (ISBN 0-7100-8681-4). Routledge & Kegan.

Rogers, Rutherford D. & Weber, David C. University Library Administration. (Illus.). 1971. 20.00 (ISBN 0-8242-0417-4). Wilson.

Rogers, Senta S. & Mohler, Irvin C., eds. Cardiovascular Disease - Epidemiology, Prevention & Rehabilitation: A Guide to the Literature, Vol. 1, 1960-1973. 606p. 1974. 65.00 (ISBN 0-306-67191-3). IFI Plenum.

Rogers, Stanley F., jt. auth. see Schulz, David A.

Rogers, T. Georgian Poetry, Nineteen Eleven to Nineteen Twenty-Two: The Critical Heritage. (The Critical Heritage Ser.). 1977. 29.00x (ISBN 0-7100-8278-9). Routledge & Kegan.

Rogers, T. Howard. Marine Corrosion. 1968. text ed. 34.95 (ISBN 0-600-41190-7). Butterworths.

Rogers, Terence A. Elementary Human Physiology. (Illus.). 1961. text ed. 18.95x (ISBN 0-471-73062-9). Wiley.

Rogers, W. R. You Can Give a Chalk Talk. LC 80-65775. 1981. saddlewire 4.95 (ISBN 0-8054-6931-1). Broadman.

Rogers, Wallace, jt. auth. see Wiebers, Jacob.

Rogers, Walter T. Dictionary of Abbreviations. LC 68-30662. 1969. Repr. of 1913 ed. 20.00 (ISBN 0-8103-3338-4). Gale.

Rogers, Wesley W. General Administration in the Nursing Home. 2nd, rev. ed. LC 75-22325. 1976. 16.95 o.p. (ISBN 0-8436-0573-1); text ed. 11.95 o.p. (ISBN 0-685-50116-7). CBI Pub.

--General Administration in the Nursing Home. 3rd ed. LC 80-19106. 456p. 1980. text ed. 17.95 (ISBN 0-8436-0788-2). CBI Pub.

Rogers, Will. The Illiterate Digest. LC 77-145720. (Illus.). 351p. 1975. Repr. of 1924 ed. 24.00 (ISBN 0-8103-3975-7). Gale.

Rogers, William I., jt. auth. see Wilder, Claudyne.

Roget, Elizabeth, tr. see Renard, Jules.

Roget, Peter M. Roget's International Thesaurus. 4th ed. LC 62-12806. 1977. 11.50 (ISBN 0-690-00010-3, TYC-T); thumb indexed 12.95 (ISBN 0-690-00011-1). T Y Crowell.

--Roget's University Thesaurus. Mawson, C. O., ed. (Apollo Eds.). (YA) (gr. 9-12). pap. 6.95 (ISBN 0-8152-0062-5, A62, TYC-T). T Y Crowell.

Rogge, O. John. First & the Fifth. LC 71-140377. (Civil Liberties in American History Ser). 1971. Repr. of 1960 ed. lib. bdg. 35.00 (ISBN 0-306-70087-5). Da Capo.

--Why Men Confess. LC 78-140376. (Civil Liberties in American History Ser). 1971. Repr. of 1959 ed. lib. bdg. 27.50 (ISBN 0-306-70088-3). Da Capo.

Rogger, Hans & Weber, Eugen, eds. The European Right: A Historical Profile. 1965. pap. 7.95x (ISBN 0-520-01080-9, CAL124). U of Cal Pr.

Rogin, Neal, ed. see Emery, Stewart.

Rogliatti, G. Leica & Leicaflex Lenses. 1978. 25.95 (ISBN 0-906447-00-3, Pub. by Fountain). Morgan.

--Leica: The First Fifty Years. 25.95 (ISBN 0-85242-594-5, Pub. by Fountain). Morgan.

Rogness, Milton, jt. auth. see Patten, Lawton M.

Rognoni, Luigi. Second Vienna School. Mann, Robert, tr. (Illus.). 420p. 1980. lib. bdg. 27.50 (ISBN 0-7145-3528-1). Riverrun NY.

Rogo, D. Scott. The Haunted Universe. 1977. pap. 1.50 o.p. (ISBN 0-451-07508-0, W7508, Sig). NAL.

--Man Does Survive Death. 1977. pap. 3.95 (ISBN 0-8065-0582-6). Citadel Pr.

--Methods & Models for Education in Parapsychology. LC 73-75209. (Parapsychological Monograph No. 14). 1973. pap. 2.50 (ISBN 0-912328-22-3). Parapsych Foun.

Rogo, D. Scott, jt. auth. see Druffel, Ann.

Rogoff, Joseph K. Manipulation, Traction & Massage. 2nd ed. (Rehabilitation Medicine Library Ser.). (Illus.). 250p. 1980. lib. bdg. 25.50 (ISBN 0-683-07324-9). Williams & Wilkins.

Rogoff, Maurice G. Laboratory Assistant's Manual: A Guide for Medical Laboratory Assistants. (McGraw-Hill International Health Services Ser.). (Illus.). 1977. pap. text ed. 6.95 o.p. (ISBN 0-07-099552-4, C). McGraw.

Rogosin, Elinor. The Dance Makers: Conversations with American Choreographers. (Illus.). 192p. 1980. 14.95 (ISBN 0-8027-0648-7). Walker & Co.

Rogosinski, W. W. Volume & Integral. (University Mathematical Texts Ser.). 1952. 7.95 (ISBN 0-471-73128-5). Halsted Pr.

Rogosinski, Werner. Fourier Series. 2nd ed. LC 50-6214. 6.95 (ISBN 0-8284-0067-9). Chelsea Pub.

Rogovin, Charles, jt. ed. see Edelhertz, Herbert.

Rogovin, Z. A., ed. Advances in Polymer Science. Kaner, N., tr. from Rus. LC 74-13580. 331p. 1974. 48.95 (ISBN 0-470-73132-X). Halsted Pr.

Rogowski, Piotr & Wala, Mario. Luge. (Illus.). 1979. pap. 15.00 (ISBN 0-8467-0586-9, Pub. by Two Continents). Hippocrene Bks.

Rogowski, Stephen J. Computer Clippings. 1976. 7.75 (ISBN 0-88488-083-4). Creative Pubns.

Rohatgi, V. K., jt. ed. see Gani, J.

Rohatgi-Mukherjee, K. K. Fundamentals of Photochemistry. LC 78-12088. 1979. 12.95 (ISBN 0-470-26547-7). Halsted Pr.

Rohde, David W. & Spaeth, Harold J. Supreme Court Decision Making. LC 75-25645. (Illus.). 1976. text ed. 18.95x (ISBN 0-7167-0717-9); pap. text ed. 9.95x (ISBN 0-7167-0716-0). W H Freeman.

Rohde, Eleanour S. Herbs & Herb Gardening. LC 70-180975. (Illus.). 1976. Repr. of 1936 ed. 24.00 (ISBN 0-8103-4303-7). Gale.

--Rose Recipes from Olden Times. (Illus.). 95p. 1973. pap. 2.00 (ISBN 0-486-22957-2). Dover.

--The Scented Garden. LC 70-175781. 1974. Repr. of 1931 ed. 22.00 (ISBN 0-8103-3874-2). Gale.

Rohde, Jill & Rohde, Ron. The New Good (but Cheap) Chicago Restaurant Book: Where to Find Great Meals at Little Neighborhood Restaurants from 1.50 to 4.95. rev & enl ed. LC 76-3133. 250p. 1977. pap. 3.95 (ISBN 0-8040-0698-9). Swallow.

Rohde, Ron, jt. auth. see Rohde, Jill.

Rohde, S. M. & Cheng, H. S., eds. Surface Roughness Effects in Hydrodymanic & Mixed Lubrication. 211p. 1980. 30.00 (G00193). ASME.

Rohe, Fred. The Zen of Running. 1975. pap. 3.95 o.p. (ISBN 0-394-73038-0). Random.

Rohl, J. S. & Barrett, H. J. Programming Via Pascal. LC 79-17433. (Cambridge Computer Science Texts Ser.: No. 12). 300p. 1980. 38.50 (ISBN 0-521-22628-7); pap. 15.95 (ISBN 0-521-29583-1). Cambridge U Pr.

Rohl, John. Germany Without Bismarck. LC 67-26960. 1967. 22.75x (ISBN 0-520-01086-8). U of Cal Pr.

Rohlen, Thomas P. For Harmony & Strength: Japanese White-Collar Organization in Anthropological Perspective. LC 73-91668. 1974. 21.50x (ISBN 0-520-02674-8); pap. 6.95x (ISBN 0-520-03849-5). U of Cal Pr.

Rohlf, F. James & Sokal, Robert R. Statistical Tables. 2nd ed. 1981. text ed. price not set (ISBN 0-7167-1257-1); pap. text ed. price not set (ISBN 0-7167-1258-X). W H Freeman.

--Statistical Tables. LC 68-54121. (Biology Ser.). (Illus.). 1969. text ed. 19.95x (ISBN 0-7167-0673-3); pap. text ed. 9.95x (ISBN 0-7167-0664-4). W H Freeman.

Rohlf, F. James, jt. auth. see Sokal, Robert R.

Rohlfing, Duane & Oparin, A. I., eds. Molecular Evolution: Prebiological & Biological. 481p. 1972. 39.50 (ISBN 0-306-30719-7, Plenum Pr). Plenum Pub.

Rohm, Robert. Guinness World Records Math Learning Module. LC 79-730909. (Illus.). (gr. 6-7). 1979. pap. text ed. 175.00 (ISBN 0-89290-091-1, CM-73). Soc for Visual.

Rohm, Robert & Shaw, John W. Real World Measurement. LC 79-730249. (Illus.). 1979. pap. text ed. 99.00 (ISBN 0-89290-097-0, A513-SATC). Soc for Visual.

Rohmer, Richard. Balls! 352p. 1980. 12.95 (ISBN 0-8253-0003-7). Beaufort Bks NY.

--Periscope Red. 352p. 1980. 12.95 (ISBN 0-8253-0020-7). Beaufort Bks NY.

Rohmer, Sax. The Bride of Fu Manchu. 1976. Repr. of 1933 ed. lib. bdg. 9.70 (ISBN 0-89190-801-3). Am Repr-Rivercity Pr.

--The Day the World Ended. 1976. Repr. of 1930 ed. lib. bdg. 13.10 (ISBN 0-89190-804-8). Am Repr-Rivercity Pr.

--The Insidious Dr. Fu Manchu. 1976. lib. bdg. 13.95x (ISBN 0-89968-143-3). Lightyear.

--Return of Dr. Fu Manchu. 1976. lib. bdg. 13.95x (ISBN 0-89968-141-7). Lightyear.

--The Romance of Sorcery. 1973. Repr. of 1914 ed. 18.00 (ISBN 0-685-70657-5). Gale.

--Wulfheim. 1972. 5.00 (ISBN 0-685-33438-4). Bookfinger.

--The Yellow Claw. 1976. lib. bdg. 13.95x (ISBN 0-89968-142-5). Lightyear.

Rohn, Peter H. Treaty Profiles. new ed. LC 73-83352. 300p. 1974. text ed. 35.00 (ISBN 0-87436-131-1). ABC-Clio.

--World Treaty Index & Treaty Profiles, 6 vols. new ed. LC 73-83352. 3300p. 1974. text ed. 510.00 (ISBN 0-87436-132-X). ABC-Clio.

Rohner, Peter. Fluid Power Logic Circuit Design: Analysis, Design Methods & Worked Examples. LC 79-14178. 226p. 1979. 32.95x (ISBN 0-470-26779-8). Halsted Pr.

Rohner, Ralph J., jt. auth. see Spanogle, John A., Jr.

Rohner, Traugott, jt. auth. see Mayer, Robert.

Rohr, Donald G., jt. auth. see Ergang, Robert.

Rohrbaugh, Richard L. The Biblical Interpreter: An Agrarian Bible in an Industrial Age. LC 78-54560. 132p. 1978. pap. 4.95 (ISBN 0-8006-1346-5, 1-1346). Fortress.

Rohrberger, Mary. Story to Anti-Story. LC 78-69581. 1978. pap. text ed. 8.50 (ISBN 0-395-26387-5); inst. manual 0.45 (ISBN 0-395-26388-3). HM.

Rohrbough, Malcolm J. The Trans-Appalachian Frontier. (Illus.). 1978. 22.50x (ISBN 0-19-502209-2). Oxford U Pr.

Rohrlich, F. Classical Charged Particles. 1965. text ed. 24.50 (ISBN 0-201-06492-8, Adv Bk Prog). A-W.

Rohrlich, F., jt. auth. see Jauch, J. M.

Rohrlich, Jay B. Work & Love: The Crucial Balance. LC 80-14727. 254p. 1980. 10.95 (ISBN 0-671-40087-8). Summit Bks.

Rohrs, M., jt. auth. see Petzold, A.

Rohsenow, Warren M. & Choi, H. Heat, Mass & Momentum Transfer. (Illus.). 1961. text ed. 27.95 (ISBN 0-13-385187-7). P-H.

Roid, Gale & Haladyna, Tom. A Technology for Test-Item Writing. 1981. price not set. Acad Pr.

Roiphe, Anne. Newcomer. 1981. price not set (ISBN 0-671-41455-0, Linden). S&S.

--Torch Song. 1978. pap. 1.95 o.p. (ISBN 0-451-07901-9, J7901, Sig). NAL.

Roizin, L. & Shiraki, H., eds. Neurotoxicology, Vol. 1. LC 77-4632. 1977. 68.50 (ISBN 0-89004-148-2). Raven.

Roizman, Bernard, jt. ed. see Palese, Peter.

Rojankovsky, Feodor. Great Big Wild Animal Book. (Illus.). (ps-2). 1962. PLB 7.62 (ISBN 0-307-60452-7, Golden Pr). Western Pub.

Rojankovsky, Feodor, illus. The Great Big Animal Book. (Illus.). 1976. PLB 7.62 (ISBN 0-307-60468-3, Golden Pr). Western Pub.

Rojansky, Vladimir. Electromagnetic Fields & Waves. LC 79-52648. 1980. pap. text ed. 7.95 (ISBN 0-486-63834-0). Dover.

Rojas, Guillermo. Manual De Ejercicios Espanol e Ingles. LC 77-84424. 1977. pap. 3.00 (ISBN 0-915808-25-0). Editorial Justa.

Rojas, Juan, tr. see Graham, Billy.

Rojas, Juan, tr. see Mayhall, Carole.

Rojas-Lombardi, Felipe. The A to Z No-Cook Cookbook. (Illus.). 64p. (gr. k-6). 1974. 3.95 o.p. (ISBN 0-307-15784-9, Golden Pr); PLB 9.15 o.p. (ISBN 0-307-65784-1). Western Pub.

Rojek, Dean G., jt. auth. see Jensen, Gary F.

Rokeach, Milton. Beliefs, Attitudes & Values: A Theory of Organization & Change. LC 68-21322. (Social & Behavioral Science Ser.). 1968. 14.95x (ISBN 0-87589-013-X). Jossey-Bass.

--The Nature of Human Values. LC 72-92870. 1973. 17.95 (ISBN 0-02-926750-1). Free Pr.

--The Three Christs of Ypsilanti: A Psychological Study. (Morningside Book Ser.). 360p. 1981. pap. 8.00x (ISBN 0-231-05271-5). Columbia U Pr.

Rokeah, David. Eyes in the Rock: Selected Poems. (Poetry in Europe Ser.). 78p. 1968. 5.95 (ISBN 0-8040-0106-5). Swallow.

Rokes, Willis P. Human Relations in Handling Insurance Claims. 1967. text ed. 12.00x (ISBN 0-256-00467-6). Irwin.

--No-Fault Insurance. LC 72-173308. 416p. 1972. 12.50 o.p. (ISBN 0-88245-006-9). Merritt Co.

Rokkan, S., jt. auth. see Lipset, Seymour M.

Rokkan, Stein, ed. A Quarter Century of International Social Science: Internal Social Science Council. 1979. text ed. 56.25x (ISBN 0-391-01930-9). Humanities.

Rokkan, Stein, jt. ed. see Crawford, Elisabeth.

Roland. The Song of Roland. Moncrieff, C. Scott, tr. 150p. 1959. pap. 2.95 (ISBN 0-472-06032-5, 32, AA). U of Mich Pr.

Roland, Alan & Harris, Barbara. Career & Motherhood: Struggles for a New Identity. LC 78-8026. 1978. 16.95 (ISBN 0-87705-372-3). Human Sci Pr.

Roland, Alan, ed. Psychoanalysis: Creativity & Literature. LC 77-26613. 1978. 22.50x (ISBN 0-231-04324-4). Columbia U Pr.

Roland, Albert. Great Indian Chiefs. (Illus.). (gr. 6 up). 1968. 5.95g o.s.i. (ISBN 0-02-777650-6, CCPr). Macmillan.

--Philippines. (Illus.). (gr. 7 up). 1967. 7.95 (ISBN 0-02-777850-9). Macmillan.

Roland, Charles P. Confederacy. LC 60-12573. (History of American Civilization Ser.). (Illus.). 1960. 8.50x (ISBN 0-226-72450-6); pap. 5.95 (ISBN 0-226-72451-4, CHAC18). U of Chicago Pr.

Roland, Hall C. The Armchair Engineer. 120p. (Orig.). 1981. pap. 4.95 (ISBN 0-918398-51-7). Dilithium Pr.

Roland, Howell, Jr. The Living Stone. (Orig.). 1979. pap. 1.95 (ISBN 0-532-23138-4). Manor Bks.

Roland, Maxwell. Management of the Infertile Couple. (Illus.). 256p. 1968. 14.75 (ISBN 0-398-01603-8). C C Thomas.

Rolander-Chilo, Brita, ed. Nutritional Research: An International Approach. (Illus.). 1979. text ed. 28.00 (ISBN 0-08-024399-1). Pergamon.

Rolerson, Darrell A. Boy & a Deer. LC 79-81623. (Illus.). (gr. 3 up). 1970. 4.50 o.p. (ISBN 0-396-07172-4). Dodd.

--A Boy Called Plum. LC 73-11987. (gr. 4 up). 1974. 5.95 (ISBN 0-396-06871-5). Dodd.

Roley, V. Vance. A Structural Model of the U. S. Government Securities Market. LC 78-75048. (Outstanding Dissertations in Economics Ser.). 1979. lib. bdg. 30.00 (ISBN 0-8240-4127-5). Garland Pub.

Rolf, Robert. Masamune Hakucho. (World Authors Ser.: No. 533). 1979. lib. bdg. 14.95 (ISBN 0-8057-6375-9). Twayne.

Rolfe, E. J., jt. ed. see Hawthorne, J.

Rolfe, Eugene, tr. see Neumann, Erich.

Rolfe, Lionel. Literary L. A. (Illus.). 96p. (Orig.). 1981. pap. 5.95 (ISBN 0-87701-177-X). Chronicle Bks.

Rolfe, Sidney E. & Burtle, James L. The Great Wheel: The World, Monetary System; a Reinterpretation. LC 73-79929. (McGraw-Hill Paperbacks). 304p. 1975. pap. 4.95 (ISBN 0-07-053562-0, SP). McGraw.

Rolfe, Stan & Barson, John. Fracture & Fatigue Control in Structures: Applications of Fracture Mechanics. (Illus.). 1977. text ed. 34.95 (ISBN 0-13-329953-8). P-H.

Rolichek. Management Fin. Inst. 2nd ed. 1976. 22.95 (ISBN 0-03-089912-5). Dryden Pr.

Roll, Charles R., Jr. The Distribution of Rural Incomes in China: A Comparison of the 1930's & 1950's. LC 78-74301. (The Modern Chinese Economy Ser.: Vol. 13). 223p. 1980. lib. bdg. 22.00 (ISBN 0-8240-4288-3). Garland Pub.

Roll, Charles W., Jr. & Cantril, Albert H. Polls: Their Use & Misuse in Politics. rev. ed. LC 80-50359. (Illus.). 224p. 1980. pap. 5.95 (ISBN 0-932020-01-1). Seven Locks Pr.

Roll, Eric. A History of Economic Thought. 1974. text ed. 15.95x o.p. (ISBN 0-256-01609-7). Irwin.

Roll, Richard J., jt. auth. see Downs, Hugh.

Roll, W. G., ed. see Parapsychological Association.

Roll, W. G., et al, eds. see Parapsychological Association.

Roll, William G. The Poltergeist. LC 76-25880. (Illus.). 224p. 1976. 10.00 (ISBN 0-8108-0984-2). Scarecrow.

Roll, William G., ed. Research in Parapsychology 1979: Abstracts & Papers from the Twenty-Second Annual Convention of the Parapsychological Association. LC 66-2858. 238p. 1980. 12.00 (ISBN 0-8108-1327-0). Scarecrow.

Roll, William G., ed. see Parapsychological Association.

Roll, Winifred. Mary I: The History of an Unhappy Tudor Queen. (Illus.). 1979. 9.95g (ISBN 0-13-559096-5). P-H.

Rollain, jt. auth. see Kraus.

Rolland, Romain. Life of Ramakrishna. 3.95 (ISBN 0-87481-080-9). Vedanta Pr.

--Life of Vivekananda. 7.95 (ISBN 0-87481-090-6). Vedanta Pr.

--Tolstoy. LC 71-147457. (Library of War & Peace; Peace Leaders: Biographies & Memoirs). lib. bdg. 38.00 (ISBN 0-8240-0316-0). Garland Pub.

Rollason, E. C. Metallurgy for Engineers. 4th ed. (Illus.). 1973. pap. 18.95x (ISBN 0-7131-3282-5). Intl Ideas.

Rolle, ed. see Jackson, Helen H.

Rolle, Andrew F. California: A History. 3rd ed. LC 77-90674. (Illus.). 1978. text ed. 16.50x (ISBN 0-88295-776-7). AHM Pub.

--Immigrant Upraised: Italian Adventurers & Colonists in an Expanding America. LC 68-10302. (Illus.). 1968. 17.95x (ISBN 0-8061-0810-X); pap. 6.95x o.p. (ISBN 0-8061-1204-2). U of Okla Pr.

Rolle, Andrew F. & Gaines, John S. The Golden State: A History of California. 2nd ed. LC 79-84210. (Illus.). 1979. text ed. 12.95x (ISBN 0-88295-796-1); pap. text ed. 7.95x (ISBN 0-88295-797-X). AHM Pub.

Rolle, Kurt A. Introduction to Thermodynamics. 2nd ed. 1980. text ed. 22.95 (ISBN 0-675-08268-4); instructor's manual 3.95 (ISBN 0-686-63342-3). Merrill.

Rolle, Kurt C. Introduction to Thermodynamics. LC 72-95278. 1973. text ed. 18.95x o.p. (ISBN 0-675-08994-8); instructor's manual 3.95 o.p. (ISBN 0-686-66872-3). Merrill.

Roller, Duane & Blum, Ronald. Fundamental Physics, 2 vols. Incl. Vol. 1. Mechanics, Waves & Thermodynamics; Vol. 2. Electricity, Magnetism, Light & Modern Physics. (Illus.). 1981. text ed. 22.95 ea.; text ed. 28.95 (ISBN 0-8162-7282-4); wkbk. & sol. manual avail. Holden-Day.

Roller, Duane, Sr. & Blum, Ronald. An Introduction to Fundamental & Applied Physics. 1200p. 1980. Vols. I & II. 28.95 (ISBN 0-8162-7282-4). Holden-Day.

Roller, Gil. Katie King: A Voice from Beyond. 1976. pap. 1.50 o.p. (ISBN 0-445-03100-X). Popular Lib.

Rollett, R., et al. Fertilizers & Soil Amendments. 1981. 24.00 (ISBN 0-13-314336-8). P-H.

Rollin, Bernard E., ed. see Arnauld, Antoine & Lancelot, Claude.

Rollin, Betty. First, You Cry. LC 76-16047. 1976. 7.95 o.p. (ISBN 0-397-01167-9). Lippincott.

Rollin, H. The Mentally Abnormal Offender & the Law. 1969. 15.00 (ISBN 0-08-013385-1); pap. 7.00 (ISBN 0-08-013384-3). Pergamon.

Rolling Stone Editors. Rolling Stone Interviews, No. 1. 464p. 1973. pap. 1.75 o.s.i. (ISBN 0-446-59866-6). Warner Bks.

Rolling Stone Press. Rolling Stone Illustrated History of Rock & Roll. 1976. pap. 10.95 o.p. (ISBN 0-394-73238-3). Random.

--The Rolling Stone Illustrated History of Rock & Roll, 1950-1980. rev. & updated ed. Miller, Jim, ed. (Illus.). 1980. 20.00 (ISBN 0-394-51322-3); pap. 10.95 (ISBN 0-394-73938-8). Random.

--The Rolling Stone Visits Saturday Night Live. LC 79-5123. (Illus.). 1979. pap. 8.95 o.p. (ISBN 0-385-15674-X, Dolp). Doubleday.

Rollins, Bryant. Danger Song. (African American Library). 1971. pap. 1.95 o.s.i. (ISBN 0-02-053500-7, Collier). Macmillan.

Rollins, Charlemae H. They Showed the Way: Forty American Negro Leaders. LC 64-20692. (gr. 4 up). 1964. 8.95 (ISBN 0-690-81612-X, TYC-J). T Y Crowell.

Rollins, Hyder E., ed. see Pepys, Samuel.

Rollins, Leighton. Disasters of War. LC 80-69430. 1981. signed limited ed. 20.00 (ISBN 0-932274-16-1); pap. 4.00 (ISBN 0-932274-15-3). Cadmus Eds.

Rollins, Yvonne B. Baudelaire et le Grotesque. LC 78-54094. (Fr.). 1978. pap. text ed. 9.75 (ISBN 0-8191-0498-1). U Pr of Amer.

Rollinson, C. L. The Chemistry of Chromium, Molybdenum & Tungsten. (Pergamon Texts in Inorganic Chemistry: Vol. 21). 148p. 1975. text ed. 28.00 (ISBN 0-08-018868-0); pap. text ed. 14.50 (ISBN 0-08-018867-2). Pergamon.

Rollo, V. Foster. The Black Experience in Maryland. LC 79-64802. 92p. 1980. perfect bound 7.00 (ISBN 0-917882-09-1). Maryland Hist.

Rollock, Barbara. Black Experience in Children's Books. 1974. pap. 2.50 o.p. (ISBN 0-87104-614-8, Branch Lib). NY Pub Lib.

Rolls, E. T. The Brain & Reward. LC 74-32290. 124p. 1975. pap. text ed. 12.75 (ISBN 0-08-018225-9). Pergamon.

Rolnick, Norma, jt. ed. see Hyatt, Ralph.

Roloff, Joan G. Encounter: Readings for Thinking, Talking, Writing. 2nd ed. LC 73-7356. (Illus.). 416p. 1974. pap. text ed. 6.95x (ISBN 0-02-477150-3). Macmillan.

Roloff, Joan G. & Wylder, Robert C. There Is No Away: Readings & Language Activities in Ecology. 1971. pap. text ed. 7.95x (ISBN 0-02-477170-8, 47717). Macmillan.

--The Writing Book. 1978. 7.95x (ISBN 0-02-477120-1). Macmillan.

Roloff, Michael, tr. see Handke, Peter.

Roloff, Michael, tr. see Hesse, Hermann.

Roloff, Michael E. & Miller, Gerald R., eds. Persuasion: New Directions in Theory & Research. LC 79-21202. (Sage Annual Reviews of Communication Research: Vol. 8). 311p. 1980. 20.00x (ISBN 0-8039-1213-7); pap. 9.95x (ISBN 0-8039-1214-5). Sage.

Rolph, C. H. London Particulars. 192p. 1980. 19.50x (ISBN 0-19-211755-6). Oxford U Pr.

Rolph, Earl R. The Theory of Fiscal Economics. (California Library Reprint Series: No. 21). 1971. 20.00x (ISBN 0-520-01926-1). U of Cal Pr.

Rolph, John, jt. auth. see Morris, Carl.

Rolt, L. T. Railway Adventure. 1977. 10.50 (ISBN 0-7153-7389-7). David & Charles.

--Red for Danger. new ed. LC 76-28618. (Illus.). 16.95 (ISBN 0-7153-4009-3). David & Charles.

Rolt, L. T. & Allen, J. S. The Steam Engine of Thomas Newcomen. (Illus.). 1977. 15.00 o.p. (ISBN 0-88202-171-0, Sci Hist). N Watson.

Rolte, J., tr. Palatinate - a Full Declaration of the Faith & Ceremonies Professed in the Dominions of Prince Fredericke, 5. Prince Elector Palatine. LC 79-84129. (English Experience Ser.: No. 947). 208p. 1979. Repr. of 1614 ed. lib. bdg. 20.00 (ISBN 90-221-0947-X). Walter J Johnson.

Rom, William N. & Archer, Victor E., eds. Health Implications of New Energy Technologies. (Illus.). 700p. 1980. 40.00 (ISBN 0-250-40361-7). Ann Arbor Science.

Romagnesi, H. Petit Atlas Des Champignons, 3 vols. (Illus.). 1964. Vols. 1 & 2. 25.00 (ISBN 0-934454-91-4). Lubrecht & Cramer.

Romagnoli, Franco G., jt. auth. see Romagnoli, Margaret.

Romagnoli, Margaret & Romagnoli, Franco G. The New Italian Cooking. 384p. 1980. 15.00 (ISBN 0-316-75565-6). Little.

Romaine, William. The Life of Faith. (Summit Bks.). 178p. 1981. pap. 1.95 (ISBN 0-8010-7704-4). Baker Bk.

Romains, Jules. The Death of Nobody. Maccarthy, D. & Waterlow, S., trs. from Fr. LC 74-23525. 1977. Repr. of 1944 ed. 13.75 (ISBN 0-86527-233-6). Fertig.

--Hommes de bonne volonte, 2 Vols. (Documentation thematique). (Illus., Fr.). pap. 2.95 ea. Larousse.

--Knock. Gidney, James B., tr. from Fr. LC 61-18360. 1962. text ed. o.p. (ISBN 0-8120-5052-5); pap. text ed. 1.95 (ISBN 0-8120-0084-6). Barron.

Roman, A. The World in Crisis. 1981. 11.95 (ISBN 0-533-04903-2). Vantage.

Roman, Herschel L., et al, eds. Annual Review of Genetics, Vol. 14. LC 67-29891. (Illus.). 1980. text ed. 20.00 (ISBN 0-8243-1214-7). Annual Reviews.

Roman, Kenneth & Raphaelson, Joel. Writing That Works. LC 80-8695. 160p. 1981. 9.95 (ISBN 0-06-014843-8, HarpT). Har-Row.

Roman, Klara G. Handwriting: A Key to Personality. 1977. pap. 5.95 (ISBN 0-394-73091-7). Pantheon.

Roman, Lulu. Lulu. (Illus.). 1978. 7.95 (ISBN 0-8007-0956-X). Revell.

Roman, Paul. Some Modern Mathematics for Physicists & Other Outsiders, 2 vols. LC 74-1385. 1975. Vol. 1. text ed. 40.00 (ISBN 0-08-018097-3); Vol. 2. text ed. 34.10 o.p. (ISBN 0-08-018134-1); Vol. 1. pap. text ed. 28.00 (ISBN 0-08-018096-5); Vol. 2. pap. text ed. 28.00 (ISBN 0-08-018133-3). Pergamon.

Roman, Stephen B. & Loebl, Eugen. The Responsible Society. LC 77-9155. 1978. 6.95 (ISBN 0-8467-0360-2, Pub. by Two Continents). Hippocrene Bks.

Roman, Zoltan, ed. see Internaional Conference on Industrial Economics, 2nd.

Romand, J., jt. auth. see Vodar, Boris.

Romanek, Richard J. Introduction to Electronic Technology. (Illus.). 480p. 1975. ref. ed. 19.95 (ISBN 0-13-468801-5). P-H.

Romanes, G. J. Cunningham's Manual of Practical Anatomy: Thorax and Abdomen, Vol. 2. 14th ed. (Illus.). 1977. pap. text ed. 10.95x (ISBN 0-19-263135-7). Oxford U Pr.

Romanes, G. J., ed. Cunningham's Manual of Practical Anatomy: Head & Neck & Brain, Vol. 3. 14th ed. (Illus.). 1979. pap. text ed. 10.95x (ISBN 0-19-263205-1). Oxford U Pr.

--Cunningham's Textbook of Anatomy. 12th ed. (Illus.). 1080p. 1981. text ed. 39.50x (ISBN 0-19-263134-9). Oxford U Pr.

Romanes, G. J., ed. see Cunningham.

Romanes, George J. Animal Intelligence. (Contributions to the History of Psychology Ser.: No. 7, Pt. a: Orientations). 1978. 30.00 (ISBN 0-89093-156-9). U Pubns Amer.

Romankiewicz, John A., jt. auth. see Ornato, Joseph P.

Romankiewicz, John A., et al. Handbook of Essential Drug Therapy for Critical Care Nurses. LC 79-90429. 211p. 1980. pap. text ed. 12.50 spiral bound (ISBN 0-914768-35-2). Drug Intl Pubns.

Romanne-James, Constance. Herb-Lore for Housewives. LC 71-180978. (Illus.). 264p. 1974. Repr. of 1938 ed. 18.00 (ISBN 0-8103-3976-5). Gale.

Romano, Albert. Applied Statistics for Science & Industry. 1977. text ed. 20.95x o.p. (ISBN 0-205-05575-3, 5655757); instr's manual avail. o.p. (ISBN 0-205-05576-1, 5655765). Allyn.

Romano, Anne T. Transactional Analysis for Police Personnel. write for info. (ISBN 0-398-04175-X). C C Thomas.

Romano, Clare & Ross, John. The Complete Collagraph: The Art & Technique of Printmaking from Collage Plates. LC 80-20685. (Illus.). 1980. 29.95 (ISBN 0-02-926770-6). Free Pr.

--The Complete Collagraph: The Art & Technique of Printmaking from Collage Plates. (Illus.). 1980. 29.95 (ISBN 0-02-926770-6). Macmillan.

Romano, Clare, jt. auth. see Ross, John.

Romano, Frank J. How to Build a Profitable Newspaper. LC 72-14136. 1973. 19.50 o.p. (ISBN 0-912920-15-7). North Am Pub Co.

Romano, John. Dickens & Reality. LC 77-10745. 1978. 15.00x (ISBN 0-231-04246-9). Columbia U Pr.

Romano, Joseph A. & Wiener, Matthew B. Mill's Pharmacy State Board Review. 29th ed. LC 76-14721. 1977. pap. 13.00 (ISBN 0-87488-430-6). Med Exam.

Romano, Louis G., et al, eds. The Middle School: Selected Readings on an Emerging School Program. LC 72-97847. 1973. 20.95 (ISBN 0-911012-82-6); pap. 11.95 (ISBN 0-88229-572-1). Nelson-Hall.

Romano, Richard & Leiman, Melvin. Views on Capitalism. 2nd ed. 1975. pap. text ed. 6.95x (ISBN 0-02-477220-8, 47722). Macmillan.

Romanofsky, Peter, ed. Social Service Organizations, 2 vols. LC 77-84754. (Greenwood Encyclopedia of American Institutions: No. 2). 1978. lib. bdg. 65.00 (ISBN 0-8371-9829-1, RSS/). Greenwood.

Romanos, Michael C., ed. Western European Cities in Crisis. LC 78-21445. (Illus.). 1979. 24.95 (ISBN 0-669-02800-2). Lexington Bks.

Romanov, V. G. Integral Geometry & Inverse Problems for Hyperbolic Equations. (Springer Tracts in Natural Philosophy: Vol. 26). (Illus.). 152p. 1974. 32.60 (ISBN 0-387-06429-X). Springer-Verlag.

Romanowicz, Zofia. Passage Through the Red Sea. Peterson, Virginia, tr. LC 62-19588. (Helen & Kurt Wolff Bk). 1962. 3.75 o.p. (ISBN 0-15-170995-5). HarBraceJ.

Romanowitz, H. A. & Puckett, R. E. Introduction to Electronics. 2nd ed. LC 75-23060. 531p. 1976. text ed. 24.95x (ISBN 0-471-73264-8); instructor's manual avail. (ISBN 0-471-01509-1). Wiley.

Romans, J. Thomas. Capital Exports & Growth Among U.S. Regions. LC 65-21131. (New England Research Ser: No. 1). 1965. 17.50x (ISBN 0-8195-8009-0, Pub. by Wesleyan U Pr). Columbia U Pr.

Romans, John R. & Ziegler, P. Thomas. The Meat We Eat. 11th ed. LC 77-70869. 1977. 23.35 (ISBN 0-8134-1945-X); pap. text ed. 17.50x (ISBN 0-685-86006-X). Interstate.

Romantik Hotels. Romantik Hotels & Restaurants. 160p. 1981. 4.98 (ISBN 0-912944-66-8). Berkshire Traveller.

Romanyshyn, John. Social Welfare: Charity to Justice. 1971. 15.95 (ISBN 0-394-31026-8). Random.

Rombauer, Irma, jt. auth. see Becker, Marion R.

Rombauer, Irma S. & Becker, Marion R. The Joy of Cooking. pap. 5.95 (ISBN 0-451-07166-2, E8978, Sig). NAL.

--Joy of Cooking. rev. ed. LC 75-10772. (Illus.). 930p. 1975. 14.95 (ISBN 0-672-51831-7); deluxe ed. 20.00 (ISBN 0-672-52385-X). Bobbs.

Rombauer, Marjorie D. Legal Problem Solving: Analysis Research & Writing. 3rd ed. LC 78-3468. (American Casebook Ser). 352p. 1978. text ed. 13.95 (ISBN 0-8299-2002-1). West Pub.

Romberg, Bertil. Carl Jonas Love Almqvist. LC 76-16859. (World Authors Ser: No. 401). 1977. lib. bdg. 12.50 (ISBN 0-8057-6241-8). Twayne.

Romberg, Thomas A. Individually Guided Mathematics. LC 75-40905. (Leadership Ser in Indiv. Guided Ed.). 160p. 1976. pap. text ed. 7.95 (ISBN 0-201-19411-2); instr's guide 2.95 (ISBN 0-201-19421-X). A-W.

Romberger, J. A. Meristems, Growth & Development in Woody Plants. (Landmark Reprints in Plant Science Ser.). 1963. text ed. 15.00 (ISBN 0-86598-005-5). Allanheld.

Romberger, J. A., jt. ed. see Diener, T. O.

Romberger, John A. Virology in Agriculture. LC 76-42139. (Beltsville Symposia in Agricultural Reasearch Ser.: No. 1). 320p. 1977. text ed. 23.50 (ISBN 0-916672-14-X). Allanheld.

Romberger, John A., ed. Biosystematics in Agriculture. LC 77-84408. (Beltsville Symposia in Agricultural Research Ser.: No. 2). 352p. 1978. text ed. 24.00. Allanheld.

Romberger, John A., ed. see Beltsville Symposia in Agricultural Research.

Romberger, Judy. Lolly. LC 80-2062. 256p. 1981. 12.95 (ISBN 0-385-15860-2). Doubleday.

Rome, John, ed. The Blandford Book of Traditional Handicrafts. (Illus.). 240p. 1981. 22.50 (ISBN 0-7137-0951-0, Pub. by Blandford Pr England). Sterling.

Rome, Margaret. Champagne Spring. (Harlequin Romances Ser.). (Orig.). 1980. pap. 1.25 o.p. (ISBN 0-373-02332-4, Pub. by Harlequin). PB.

Romein, Jan. The Watershed of Two Eras: Europe in 1900. Pomerans, Arnold, tr. from Dutch. LC 77-14841. 1978. 30.00x (ISBN 0-8195-5026-4, Pub. by Wesleyan U Pr). Columbia U Pr.

Romen, A. S. Self-Suggestion & Its Influence on the Human Organism. Lewis, A. S. & Forsky, V., eds. (Illus.). 220p. 1980. 20.00 (ISBN 0-87332-195-2). M E Sharpe.

Romeo. Ars Semiotica, Vol. 2, No. 3. 1979. pap. text ed. 20.50x. Humanities.

Romeo, Luigi. Ecce Homo: A Lexicon of Man. 1980. text ed. 20.00x (ISBN 90-272-2006-9). Humanities.

Romer, Alfred, ed. Radiochemistry & the Discovery of Isotopes. LC 74-91273. (Classics of Science Ser). (Orig., Fr. & Ger.). 1970. pap. text ed. 3.50 (ISBN 0-486-62507-9). Dover.

Romer, Nancy. The Sex-Role Cycle: Socialization from Infancy to Old Age. (Women's Lives - Women's Work Ser.). (Illus.). 190p. (Orig.). (gr. 11-12). 1981. pap. 5.95 (ISBN 0-912670-69-X). Feminist Pr.

Romer, Robert H. Energy: An Introduction to Physics. LC 75-35591. (Illus.). 1976. 21.95x (ISBN 0-7167-0357-2); tchr's guide avail. W H Freeman.

Romero, Donald G. A Handbook on Professional Magazine Article Writing. 1975. 3.95 (ISBN 0-87543-127-5). Lucas.

Romero, Francisco. Theory of Man. Cooper, William F., tr. 1965. 22.75x (ISBN 0-520-01087-6). U of Cal Pr.

Romero, Joan A., ed. see American Academy of Religion, 1972 & 1973.

Romero, Jose G., tr. see Statt, David A.

Romero, Jose R. La Vida Inutil De Pito Perez. Cord, W., ed. 1972. 8.95 o.p. (ISBN 0-13-517045-1); pap. 7.95 o.p. (ISBN 0-13-517037-0). P-H.

Romero, Juan, tr. Los Himnos De Juan Romero. (Spanish Bks.). (Span.). 1978. 1.60 (ISBN 0-8297-0878-2). Life Pubs Intl.

Romero, Oscar. A Martyr's Message of Hope: Six Homilies of Oscar Romero. 125p. (Orig.). 1981. pap. 4.95 (ISBN 0-934134-09-X). Natl Cath Reporter.

Romey, W. D. Field Guide to Plutonic & Metamorphic Rocks. (Earth Science Curriculum Project Pamphlet Ser). 1971. pap. 3.20 (ISBN 0-395-02619-9). HM.

Romfh, Richard F. Patients' Guide to Doctors: How to Hire & Fire Your Doctor to Save Your Life. Date not set. 15.95 (ISBN 0-87949-199-X). Ashley Bks.

Romfh, Richard F., jt. auth. see Anderson, Robert M.

Romig, Dennis A. Justice for Our Children. LC 77-9154. 1978. 21.00 (ISBN 0-669-01787-6) Lexington Bks.

Romig, Harry G., jt. auth. see Dodge, Harold F.

Romilly, Samuel, jt. auth. see Staunford, William.

Romine, Jack S. Sentence Mastery. 2nd ed. 1966. text ed. 8.95 (ISBN 0-13-806695-7). P-H.

Romine, Jack S., et al. College Business English. 2nd ed. (Illus.). 1972. pap. text ed. 13.95 (ISBN 0-13-141994-3). P-H.

Rommel, Kurt. Our Father Who Art in Heaven. Cooperrider, Edward A., tr. from Ger. LC 80-2373. 64p. 1981. pap. price not set (ISBN 0-8006-1448-8, 1-1448). Fortress.

Romney, Seymour, et al, eds. Gynecology & Obstetrics: The Health Care of Women. 2nd ed. (Illus.). 1980. text ed. 48.50 (ISBN 0-07-053582-5, HP). McGraw.

Rompelman, O., jt. auth. see Kitney, R. I.

Romtvedt, David. Moon. 80p. 1981. write for info. (ISBN 0-931460-14-X); pap. write for info. (ISBN 0-931460-16-6). Bieler.

Ron, Van Der Meer see Van Der Meer, Ron & Van Der Meer, Atie.

Rona, Peter A. The Central North Atlantic Ocean Basin & Continental Margins: Geology, Geophysics, Geochemistry, & Resources, Including the Trans-Atlantic Geotraverse (TAG) (Illus.). 99p. 1980. pap. 45.00 (ISBN 0-08-026259-7). Pergamon.

Ronai, Lili. Corals. LC 75-6865. (A Let's Read & Find Out Science Bk). (Illus.). 40p. (gr. k-3). 1976. 7.89 (ISBN 0-690-00921-6, TYC-J). T Y Crowell.

Ronald, Ann. Functions of Setting in the Novel: From Mrs. Radcliffe to Charles Dickens. Varma, Devendra P., ed. LC 79-8475. (Gothic Studies & Dissertations Ser.). 1980. lib. bdg. 25.00x (ISBN 0-405-12659-X). Arno.

Ronald, Charles P., ed. see Malone, Bill C.

Ronald, D. W. & Carter, R. J. The Longmoor Military Railway. 1974. 17.95 (ISBN 0-7153-6357-3). David & Charles.

Ronald, K., ed. see International Conference on the Mediterranean Monk Seal, 1st, Rhodes, Greece, 1978.

Ronalds, Francis S. The Attempted Whig Revolution of Sixteen Seventy-Eight to Sixteen Eighty-One. 202p. 1974. Repr. of 1937 ed. 12.50x o.p. (ISBN 0-87471-467-2). Rowman.

Ronalds, Francis S., jt. auth. see Fleming, Thomas J.

Ronan. Curse of the Vampires. (gr. 7-12). 1980. pap. 1.25 (ISBN 0-590-30062-8, Schol Pap). Schol Bk Serv.

--Master of the Dead, & Other Strange Unsolved Mysteries. (gr. 7-12). 1980. pap. 1.25 (ISBN 0-590-30005-9, Schol Pap). Schol Bk Serv.

Ronan & Hanisch. Epistolario De Juan Ignacio Molina. (Sp.). 1980. 11.60 (ISBN 0-8294-0360-4). Loyola.

Ronan, C. A. Isaac Newton. (Clarendon Biography Ser.). (Illus.). 1976. pap. 3.50 (ISBN 0-912728-05-1). Newbury Bks Inc.

--The Shorter Science & Civilisation in China, Vol. 1. LC 77-82513. (Illus.). 1978. 29.95 (ISBN 0-521-21821-7). Cambridge U Pr.

Ronan, Charles E. Francisco Javier Clavigero, S. J., Figure of the Mexican Enlightment: His Life & Work. 1977. pap. 20.00x (ISBN 0-8294-0347-7). Jesuit Hist.

Ronan, Colin A. & Needham, J. Shorter Science & Civilization in China, Vol. 1. LC 77-82513. (Illus.). 337p. 1980. pap. 12.95 (ISBN 0-521-29286-7). Cambridge U Pr.

Ronan, Frank. Planes & Copter. (gr. 4-6). 1977. pap. 0.59 o.p. (ISBN 0-590-05420-1, Schol Pap). Schol Bk Serv.

Ronan, Margaret. All About Our Fifty States. rev. ed. LC 78-16658. (gr. 5-9). 1978. 3.95 (ISBN 0-394-80244-6); PLB 4.99 (ISBN 0-394-90244-0). Random.

Ronan, Richard. Buddha's Kisses. 96p. 1980. pap. 4.95 (ISBN 0-917342-73-9, Pub. by Gay Sunshine). Bookpeople.

Ronander, Albert C. & Porter, Ethel K. Guide to the Pilgrim Hymnal. LC 65-26448. 456p. 1966. 10.95 (ISBN 0-8298-0055-7). Pilgrim Fr.

Ronay, Egon. Egon Ronay's Lucasa Guide 1981 To Hotels, Resturants, Inns in Great Britain & Ireland & Guide to 740 Furnished Apartments in London. rev. ed. LC 74-644899. (Illus.). 830p. 1981. pap. 12.95 (ISBN 0-03-058958-4). HR&W.

--Egon Ronay's Nineteen Eighty-One Pub Guide. rev. ed. (Illus.). 1981. pap. price not set (ISBN 0-14-005813-3, Pub. by Auto Assn-British Tourist Authority England). Merrimack Bk Serv.

--Just a Bite: Egon Ronay's Lucas Guide 1979 for Gourmets on a Family Budget. 1979. pap. 3.95 o.p. (ISBN 0-14-005143-0). Penguin.

Ronchi, C., et al, eds. see Joint Research Centre, Workshop, Karlslruhe Establishment (European Inst. for Transuranium Elements), Germany, October 1978.

Ronda, James P., jt. auth. see Bowden, Henry W.

Rondinelli, Dennis A. & Ruddle, Kenneth. Urbanization & Rural Development: A Spatial Policy for Equitable Growth. LC 78-17790. (Praeger Special Studies). 1978. 24.95 (ISBN 0-03-043111-5). Praeger.

Ronen, Joshua & Sadan, Simcha. Smoothing Income Numbers: Objectives, Means & Implications. LC 80-21350. (Paperback Series of Accounting). 1981. pap. text ed. 5.95 (ISBN 0-201-06347-6). A-W.

Ronen, Simcha. The Flexible Work Schedule: An Innovation in the Quality of Work Life. (Illus.). 352p. 1980. 18.95 (ISBN 0-07-053607-4). McGraw.

Ronertson, Jenny. Jesus, the Storyteller. (Ladybird Bible Ser.). (Illus.). 32p. (ps-4). 1980. Repr. 1.95 (ISBN 0-310-42840-8). Zondervan.

Roney, Raymond G., jt. auth. see Casciero, Albert J.

Rongier, Louis. The Genius of the West. LC 76-93466. (Principles of Freedom Ser.). 222p. 1971. 10.00 o.p. (ISBN 0-8402-5001-0). Nash Pub.

Ronning, Olaf & Bjaerevoll, Olav. Flowers of Svalbard. (Illus.). 56p. 1981. pap. 14.00x (ISBN 82-00-05398-9). Universitet.

Ronowicz, Doris, tr. see Krzyzanowski, Julian.

Ronsard, Pierre de see De Ronsard, Pierre.

Ronsheim, Milton. The Life of General Custer. (Custer Monograph: No. 1). (Illus.). 67p. 1978. pap. 8.00x limited ed. (ISBN 0-686-28492-5). Monroe County Lib.

Ronsivall, Louis J., jt. auth. see Nickerson, John T.

Ronstadt, Robert. Research & Development Abroad by U. S. Multinationals. LC 77-10672. (Praeger Special Studies). 1977. 21.95 (ISBN 0-03-022661-9). Praeger.

Rontgen, Robert E. Marks on German Bohemian & Austrian Porcelain, Seventeen Ten to the Present. Rontgen, Robert E., tr. (Illus.). 704p. 1981. 75.00 (ISBN 0-916838-38-2). Schiffer.

Rony, Peter R. Logic & Memory Experiments: Using TTL Integrated Circuits. Incl. Bk. 1. pap. 10.95 (ISBN 0-672-21542-X); Bk. 2. pap. 10.95 (ISBN 0-672-21543-8). LC 78-57209. 1978. Bks 1 & 2. pap. 19.95 (ISBN 0-672-21544-6). Sams.

Rony, Peter R., et al. Eighty-Eighty A Bugbook: Microcomputer Interfacing & Programming. LC 77-77399. 1977. pap. 11.95 (ISBN 0-672-21447-4). Sams.

--Introductory Experiments in Digital Electronics & 8080a Microcomputer Programming & Interfacing. Incl. Vol. 1. pap. 14.95 (ISBN 0-672-21550-0); Vol. 2. pap. 13.50 (ISBN 0-672-21551-9). 1978. 2 vol. set 25.50 (ISBN 0-672-21552-7). Sams.

Roo, Ann De see De Roo, Ann.

Rood, David S. Wichita Grammar. LC 75-25122. (American Indian Linguistics Ser.). 1976. lib. bdg. 42.00 (ISBN 0-8240-1972-5). Garland Pub.

Rood, Karen L., ed. American Writers in Paris, Nineteen Twenty to Nineteen Thirty-Nine. LC 79-26101. (Dictionary of Literary Biography Ser.: Vol. 4). (Illus.). 1980. 54.00 (ISBN 0-8103-0916-5, Bruccoli Clark Book). Gale.

Rood, Robert, jt. auth. see Trefil, James.

Rood, Ronald. The Loon in My Bathtub. LC 64-23363. (Illus.). 192p. 1974. 7.95 o.p. (ISBN 0-8289-0228-3); pap. 3.95 (ISBN 0-8289-0229-1). Greene.

Rood, Wayne R. Art of Teaching Christianity. (Illus., Orig.). 1968. pap. 5.95 (ISBN 0-687-01924-9). Abingdon.

Rook, A., et al. Textbook of Dermatology, 2 vols. 3rd ed. (Illus.). 1979. Set. 236.00 (ISBN 0-632-00465-7). Mosby.

Rook, Arthur & Savin, J. A., eds. Recent Advances in Dermatology, No. 5. (Recent Advances Ser.). (Illus.). 325p. 1980. text ed. 45.00x (ISBN 0-443-01958-4). Churchill.

Rooke, F. E., et al. Ophthalmic Nursing: Its Practice & Management. (Illus.). 256p. 1980. pap. text ed. 13.50x (ISBN 0-443-01494-9). Churchill.

Rooke, Leon. Fat Woman. LC 80-21893. 192p. 1981. 9.95 (ISBN 0-394-51642-7). Knopf.

Rooke, M. Leigh & Wingrove, C. Ray. Benefaction or Bondage? Social Policy & the Aged. LC 79-5437. 1980. pap. text ed. 7.50 (ISBN 0-8191-0885-5); text ed. 15.25 (ISBN 0-8191-1037-X). U Pr of Amer.

Rooke, Patrick, et al. The Normans. LC 78-56586. (Peoples of the Past Ser.). (Illus.). 1978. lib. bdg. 7.95 (ISBN 0-686-51159-X). Silver.

Rooks, George. Non-Stop Discussion Workbook! Problems for Intermediate & Advanced Students of English. (Orig.). 1980. pap. text ed. 2.95 (ISBN 0-88377-171-3). Newbury Hse.

Room, Adrian. Naming Names: A Consideration of Pseudonyms & Name Changes. LC 80-27801. 260p. 1981. lib. bdg. write for info. (ISBN 0-89950-025-0). McFarland & Co.

--Room's Dictionary of Confusibles. 1979. 16.00 (ISBN 0-7100-0120-7). Routledge & Kegan.

Room, Adrian, compiled by. Place-Name Changes Since Nineteen Hundred: A World Gazetteer. LC 79-4300. 1979. 11.00 (ISBN 0-8108-1210-X). Scarecrow.

Room, Thomas G. & Kirkpatrick, P. B. Miniquaternion Geometry. LC 79-123347. (Tracts in Mathematics: No. 60). 1971. 28.95 (ISBN 0-521-07926-8). Cambridge U Pr.

Roomet, Louise, jt. auth. see Hewitt, Karen.

Roomkin, Myron, jt. ed. see Juris, Hervey A.

Rooney, James. Bossmen: Bill Monroe & Muddy Waters. (Illus.). 160p. 1972. Repr. of 1971 ed. pap. 0.99 o.p. (ISBN 0-8104-6106-4). Hayden.

Rooney, James R. Mechanics of the Horse. 1980. lib. bdg. 12.50 (ISBN 0-88275-693-1). Krieger.

Rooney, John F., Jr. A Geography of American Sport: From Cabin Creek to Anaheim. 1974. text ed. 11.50 (ISBN 0-201-06491-X). A-W.

Rooney, Patrick, jt. ed. see Lee, James M.

Rooney, Victor M. Analysis of Linear Circuits: Passive & Active Components. 608p. 1975. text ed. 19.95 (ISBN 0-675-08886-0); instructor's manual 3.95 (ISBN 0-675-08886-0). Merrill.

Roos, Anne D., et al. Using Our Language: Level 1 of 6. LC 76-12418. (Illus.). (gr. 1). 1977. pap. text ed. 3.18 (ISBN 0-8372-9301-4); 3.90 (ISBN 0-8372-9302-2, C406-1). Bowmar-Noble.

--Using Our Language. Incl. Level 2 of 6. LC 72-12418. (Illus.). (gr. 2). text ed. 4.98 (ISBN 0-8372-9303-0); tchr's ed. bk. 2 6.51 (ISBN 0-8372-9304-9, C407-1); Level 3 of 6. LC 72-12418. (Illus.). (gr. 3). text ed. 6.96 (ISBN 0-8372-9307-3); tchr's ed. bk. 3 7.86 (ISBN 0-8372-9308-1, C408-1); Level 4 of 6. LC 72-12418. (Illus.). (gr. 4). text ed. 6.06 (ISBN 0-8372-9311-1); Level 5 of 6. LC 76-12418. (Illus.). (gr. 5). text ed. 6.51 (ISBN 0-8372-9315-4); tchr' ed. bk. 5 7.95 (ISBN 0-8372-9316-2); Level 6 of 6. LC 76-12418. (Illus.). (gr. 6). text ed. 6.51 (ISBN 0-8372-9319-7); tchr's ed. bk. 6 7.95 (ISBN 0-8372-9320-0). 1977. Bowmar-Noble.

Roos, C. F. NRA Economic Planning. LC 72-171693. (Fdr & the Era of the New Deal Ser.). 596p. 1972. Repr. of 1937 ed. lib. bdg. 55.00 (ISBN 0-306-70396-3). Da Capo.

Roos, Kelley. The Kidnapper. 1981. 9.95 (ISBN 0-8027-5436-8). Walker & Co.

Roosevelt, Anna C. Parmana: Prehistoric Maize & Manioc Subsistence Along the Orinoco & Amazon. (Studies in Archaeology). 1980. 29.50 (ISBN 0-12-595350-X). Acad Pr.

Roosevelt, Anna C. & Smith, James, eds. The Ancestors: Native Artisans of the Americas. LC 79-89536. (Illus.). 230p. (Orig.). 1980. pap. 17.50 (ISBN 0-295-95780-8, Pub. by Mus Am Ind). U of Wash Pr.

Roosevelt, Eleanor. You Learn by Living. LC 60-10416. 1960. 15.00 o.s.i. (ISBN 0-06-013645-6, HarpT). Har-Row.

Roosevelt, F. D. On Our Way. LC 72-2383. (FDR & the Era of the New Deal Ser.). 216p. 1973. Repr. of 1934 ed. lib. bdg. 29.50 (ISBN 0-306-70476-5). Da Capo.

Roosevelt, Franklin D. Franklin D. Roosevelt & Foreign Affairs: Second Series, Vols. 4-16. Schewe, Donald B., ed. LC 68-25617. 2327p. 1979. 27.00 ea.; Set, Jan. 1937-Aug. 1939. 375.00 (ISBN 0-88354-201-3). Vol. 4, Jan.-Mar. 1973 (ISBN 0-88354-202-1). Vol. 5, Apr.-June 1937 (ISBN 0-88354-203-X). Vol. 6, July-Sept. 1937 (ISBN 0-88354-204-8). Vol. 7, Oct.-Dec. 1937 (ISBN 0-88354-205-6). Vol. 8, Jan.-Feb. 1938 (ISBN 0-88354-206-4). Clearwater Pub.

--Looking Forward. LC 72-2382. (FDR & the Era of the New Deal Ser). 284p. 1973. Repr. of 1933 ed. lib. bdg. 27.50 (ISBN 0-306-70477-3). Da Capo.

Roosevelt, Kermit. Memories of My Father. (Illus.). 98p. Date not set. Repr. of 1920 ed. 44.85 (ISBN 0-89901-026-1). Found Class Reprints.

Roosevelt, Ruth. Living in Step. (Paperbacks Ser.). 1977. Repr. of 1976 ed. pap. 4.95 (ISBN 0-07-053596-5, SP). McGraw.

Roosevelt, Theodore. Gouverneur Morris. LC 80-24746. (American Statesmen Ser.). 340p. 1981. pap. 5.95 (ISBN 0-87754-188-4). Chelsea Hse.

--New Nationalism. 7.50 (ISBN 0-8446-0237-X). Peter Smith.

Root, George F. The Story of a Musical Life: An Autobiography. LC 70-126072. (Music Ser). 1970. Repr. of 1891 ed. lib. bdg. 29.50 (ISBN 0-306-70031-X). Da Capo.

Root, Leon & Kiernan, Thomas. Doctor's Guide to Tennis Elbow. 1980. 8.95 (ISBN 0-679-50460-5); pap. 4.95 (ISBN 0-679-50977-1). McKay.

--Oh, My Aching Back: A Doctor's Guide to Your Back Pain & How to Control It. LC 72-92649. 1980. 3.98 o.p. (ISBN 0-679-50384-6). McKay.

Root, Martha L. Tahirih the Pure. 1980. Repr. of 1938 ed. casebound 6.95 (ISBN 0-933770-14-6). Kalimat.

Root, Orrin. Training for Service: a Survey of the Bible: Instructor's Edition. (Illus., Orig.). 1964. pap. 2.50 (ISBN 0-87239-325-9, 3219). Standard Pub.

--Training for Service: a Survey of the Bible: Pupil's Edition. (Illus., Orig.). 1964. pap. 1.95 (ISBN 0-87239-326-7, 3220). Standard Pub.

Root, Orrin, ed. see Thomas, Roger W.

Root, Robert, jt. auth. see Gilmore, Gene.

Root, W. S. & Hoffman, F. G., eds. Physiological Pharmacology: A Comprehensive Treatise, 4 vols. Incl. Vol. 1. The Nervous System, Part A. 1963. 62.50 (ISBN 0-12-595701-7); Vol. 2. The Nervous System, Part B. 1965. 49.25 (ISBN 0-12-595702-5); Vol. 3. The Nervous System, Part C. 1967. 51.00 (ISBN 0-12-595703-3); Vol. 4. The Nervous System, Part D. 1967. 51.00 (ISBN 0-12-595704-1); Vol. 5. The Nervous System, Part E. 1974. 62.50 (ISBN 0-12-595705-X). Acad Pr.

Root, Waverley. Cooking of Italy. LC 68-19230. (Foods of the World Ser). (Illus.). (gr. 6 up). 1968. PLB 14.94 (ISBN 0-8094-0057-X, Pub. by Time-Life). Silver.

--Cooking of Italy. (Foods of the World Ser). (Illus.). 1968. 14.95 (ISBN 0-8094-0030-8). Time-Life.

--Food: An Informal Dictionary. (Illus.). 1980. 29.95 (ISBN 0-671-22589-8). S&S.

Root, Waverley & De Rochement, Richard. Eating in America: A History. LC 76-16145. 1976. 16.95 o.p. (ISBN 0-688-03096-3). Morrow.

Root, William P. Reasons for Going It on Foot. LC 80-69369. Orig. Title: Wheel Turning on the Hub of the Sun. 80p. 1981. 10.00 (ISBN 0-689-11138-X); pap. 5.95 (ISBN 0-689-11164-9). Atheneum.

Rooten, Luis Van see Van Rooten, Luis.

Rootes, Nina, tr. see Cendrars, Blaise.

Roots, B., jt. auth. see Johnston, P.

Roots, Ivan. The Great Rebellion, Sixteen Forty-Two to Sixteen Sixty. pap. 17.95 (ISBN 0-7134-1399-9, Pub. by Batsford England). David & Charles.

Roots, John McCook. Chou. LC 74-27588. 1978. 8.95 o.p. (ISBN 0-385-03804-6). Doubleday.

Roover, Raymond De see De Roover, Raymond.

Roozen, David A. Churched & Unchurched in America: A Comparative Profile. LC 77-94682. 1978. pap. 2.00 (ISBN 0-914422-07-3). Glenmary Res Ctr.

Roozen, David A., jt. ed. see Hoge, Dean R.

Roper, Alan see Dryden, John.

Roper, Burns W., et al. Polling on the Issues. LC 80-23439. 224p. 1980. 11.95 (ISBN 0-932020-02-X); pap. 7.95 (ISBN 0-932020-03-8). Seven Locks Pr.

Roper, C. A. Complete Handbook of Locks & Locksmithing. LC 76-43134. (Illus.). 1976. 12.95 (ISBN 0-8306-6920-5); pap. 7.95 (ISBN 0-8306-5920-X, 920). TAB Bks.

Roper, Derek. Wordsworth & Coleridge - Lyrical Ballads 1805. 2nd ed. 432p. 1976. pap. 12.95 (ISBN 0-7121-0140-3, Pub. by Macdonald & Evans England). Intl Ideas.

Roper, Fred & Boorkman, JoAnne. Introduction to Reference Sources in the Health Sciences. 256p. 1980. text ed. 18.00 (ISBN 0-912176-08-3). Med Lib Assn.

Roper, Fred W., compiled by. Alfred William Pollard: A Selection of His Essays. LC 76-25547. (Great Bibliographers Ser.: No. 2). 252p. 1976. 12.00 (ISBN 0-8108-0958-3). Scarecrow.

Roper, Gayle, jt. auth. see Fisher, Marianne.

Roper, L. V. Death As in Matador. 176p. (Orig.). 1975. pap. 0.95 o.p. (ISBN 0-445-00644-7). Popular Lib.

--The Emerald Chicks. (Renegade Roe Ser.: No. 2). 176p. 1976. pap. 1.25 o.p. (ISBN 0-445-00332-4). Popular Lib.

Roper, Les V., Jr. The Overlord. 1978. pap. 1.95 o.s.i. (ISBN 0-515-04754-6). Jove Pubns.

Roper, Nancy. Livingstone's Pocket Medical Dictionary. 1976. pap. 4.95 o.p. (ISBN 0-443-01603-8, SL674, ScribT). Scribner.

Roper, Nancy, et al. The Elements of Nursing. (Illus.). 1980. text ed. 44.00 (ISBN 0-443-02198-8); pap. text ed. 27.50x (ISBN 0-443-01577-5). Churchill.

Roper, R. G., jt. auth. see Kato, S.

Roper, Robert. On Spider Creek. 1979. pap. 2.25 o.p. (ISBN 0-449-23903-9, Crest). Fawcett.

--Royo County. 1979. pap. 1.95 o.p. (ISBN 0-449-23971-3, Crest). Fawcett.

Roper, Steve, jt. ed. see Steck, Allen.

Roper, William & Harpsfield, Nicholas. Lives of St. Thomas More. Reynolds, E. E., ed. 1963. 12.95x (ISBN 0-460-00019-5, Evman); pap. 1.95 o.p. (ISBN 0-460-01019-0). Dutton.

Ropes, J. H. Saint James. LC 16-6543. (International Critical Commentary Ser.). 336p. Repr. of 1916 ed. 17.50x (ISBN 0-567-05035-1). Attic Pr.

Ropes, John C. The Story of the Civil War, Vol. 4. 749p. 1980. Repr. of 1894 ed. lib. bdg. 375.00 (ISBN 0-8495-4634-6). Arden Lib.

Ropke, John C. Concrete: Problems, Causes, & Cures. (Illus.). 192p. 1981. 21.50 (ISBN 0-07-053609-0). McGraw.
Ropp, Robert S. De see De Ropp, Robert S.
Ropp, Theodore. War in the Modern World. rev. ed. 1962. pap. 3.95 (ISBN 0-02-036400-8, Collier). Macmillan.
Roquette, Peter, ed. see Hasse, Helmut.
Rorabacher, Louise E. A Concise Guide to Composition. 3rd ed. 304p. 1976. text ed. 8.95 scp (ISBN 0-06-045569-1, HarpC); scp practice pages 6.50 (ISBN 0-06-045568-3); answer manual avail. (ISBN 0-685-57572-1). Har-Row.
--Frank Dalby Davison. (World Authors Ser.: No. 514). 1979. lib. bdg. 12.50 (ISBN 0-8057-6355-4). Twayne.
Rorem, Ned. Critical Affairs: A Composer's Journal. LC 70-128574. 1970. 5.95 o.s.i. (ISBN 0-8076-0569-7). Braziller.
--Music from Inside Out. LC 67-12477. 1967. 4.00 o.s.i. (ISBN 0-8076-0402-X). Braziller.
--New York Diary. LC 67-27523. (Illus.). 1967. 5.95 o.p. (ISBN 0-685-07515-X). Braziller.
Rorig, Fritz. The Medieval Town. Matthew, D. J., tr. 1967. 20.00x (ISBN 0-520-01088-4); pap. 5.75x (ISBN 0-520-01579-7, CAMPUS23). U of Cal Pr.
Rorres, Chris, jt. auth. see Anton, Howard.
Rorty, Amelie O., ed. Essays on Aristotle's Ethics. (Major Thinkers Ser.). 1981. 20.00x (ISBN 0-520-03773-1, CAMPUS 245); pap. 4.95x (ISBN 0-520-04041-4). U of Cal Pr.
--Explaining Emotions. 1980. 30.00x (ISBN 0-520-03775-8); pap. 7.95x (ISBN 0-520-03921-1, CAMPUS NO. 232). U of Cal Pr.
--The Identities of Persons. LC 75-13156. (Topics in Philosophy: Vol. 3). 1976. 15.75 o.p. (ISBN 0-520-03030-3); pap. 5.95x (ISBN 0-520-03309-4, CAMPUS 180). U of Cal Pr.
Rorvik, David M. In His Image: The Cloning of a Man. LC 78-5226. 1978. 8.95 o.p. (ISBN 0-397-01255-1). Lippincott.
Rosa, Alfred F. & Eschholz, Paul A., eds. Contemporary Fiction in America & England, 1950-1970: A Guide to Information Sources. LC 73-16990. (American Literature, English Literature, & World Literatures in English Information Guide Series: Vol. 10). 220p. 1976. 30.00 (ISBN 0-8103-1219-0). Gale.
Rosa, Denise M. De la see Kolin, Michael J. & De la Rosa, Denise M.
Rosa, Joseph G. Gunfighter: Man or Myth? LC 68-31378. (Illus.). 1979. Repr. of 1969 ed. 9.95 (ISBN 0-8061-0825-8). U of Okla Pr.
--Gunfighter: Man or Myth? (Illus.). 229p. 1980. pap. 5.95 (ISBN 0-8061-1561-0). U of Okla Pr.
Rosa, Nicolas & Rosa, Sharon. Small Computers for the Small Businessman. LC 80-68531. 350p. 1980. pap. 12.95 (ISBN 0-918398-31-2). Dilithium Pr.
Rosa, Sharon, jt. auth. see Rosa, Nicolas.
Rosa, Veronica di see Feuer, Janice.
Rosai, Juan. Ackerman's Surgical Pathology. 6th ed. (Illus.). 1450p. 1981. text ed. 97.50 (ISBN 0-8016-0045-6). Mosby.
--Manual of Surgical Pathology Gross Room Procedures. (Illus.). 128p. 1981. 17.95x (ISBN 0-8166-1027-4). U of Minn Pr.
Rosaldo, Michael Z. Knowledge & Passion. LC 79-12632. (Cambridge Studies in Cultural Systems). (Illus.). 1980. 24.95 (ISBN 0-521-22582-5); pap. 6.95 (ISBN 0-521-29562-9). Cambridge U Pr.
Rosallo, Renato. Ilongot Headhunting, 1883-1974: A Study in Society & History. LC 79-64218. (Illus.). 1980. 18.50x (ISBN 0-8047-1046-5). Stanford U Pr.
Rosamond, Peggy J. Antique French Doll Coloring Books. 8p. (gr. 8-12). pap. 3.50 (ISBN 0-914510-06-1). Evergreen.
--Antique French Doll Paper Dolls. 8p. (gr. 8-12). 1976. pap. 3.50. Evergreen.
Rosand, David. Titian. (Library of Great Painters). (Illus.). 1978. 35.00 (ISBN 0-8109-1654-1). Abrams.
Rosand, David & Muraro, Michelangelo. Titian & the Venetian Woodcut. LC 75-25621. (Illus.). 1976. pap. 14.95 (ISBN 0-88397-067-8). Intl Exhibit Foun.
Rosanes-Berrett, Marilyn. Do You Really Need Eyeglasses? 1978. pap. 1.95 (ISBN 0-445-04154-4). Popular Lib.
Rosa-Nieves. Voz Folklorica De Puerto Rico. 1967. 16.95 (ISBN 0-87751-009-1, Pub by Troutman Press). E Torres & Sons.
Rosa-Nieves & Melon. Biografias Puertorriquenas. 1970. 18.95 (ISBN 0-685-73206-1, Pub by Troutman Press). E Torres & Sons.
Rosario. El Espanol De America. 1970. 12.95 (ISBN 0-685-73205-3, Pub by Troutman Press). E Torres & Sons.
Rosario, Idalia. Idalia's Project ABC-Proyecto ABC. LC 80-21013. (Illus.). 32p. (ps-2). 1981. 6.95 (ISBN 0-03-044141-2). HR&W.
Rosato, D. V., ed. see Society of the Plastics Industry.
Rosberg, Carl G. & Callaghy, Thomas M., eds. Socialism in Sub-Saharan Africa: A New Assessment. LC 79-84635. (Research Ser.: No. 38). (Illus.). 1979. pap. 9.50x (ISBN 0-87725-138-X). U of Cal Intl St.
Rosberg, Carl G., Jr., jt. ed. see Coleman, James S.
Rosberg, Robert, ed. see Mosler Anti-Crime Bureau.
Rosborough, E. H. Tying & Fishing the Fuzzy Nymphs. LC 78-13949. (Illus.). 192p. 1979. 14.95 (ISBN 0-8117-1811-5). Stackpole.
Rosbottom, Ronald C. Choderlos De Laclos. (World Authors Ser.: No. 502 (France)). 1978. 13.95 (ISBN 0-8057-6343-0). Twayne.
Rosburg, Bob. The Putter. 160p. 1975. pap. 2.95 (ISBN 0-346-12356-9). Cornerstone.
Roscher, Wilhelm & Hillman, James, eds. Pan & the Nightmare: Two Studies. (Dunquin Ser.). 1972. pap. text ed. 7.50 (ISBN 0-88214-204-6). Spring Pubns.
Rosci, Marco. The Hidden Leonardo. LC 77-70250. (Illus.). 1977. 19.95 o.p. (ISBN 0-528-81042-1). Rand.
Roscoe, A. A. Uhuru's Fires: African Literature East to South. LC 76-3038. 280p. 1977. 42.50 (ISBN 0-521-21295-2); pap. 11.95x (ISBN 0-521-29089-9). Cambridge U Pr.
Roscoe, Adrian A. Mother Is Gold: A Study in West African Literature. 1971. 21.50 (ISBN 0-521-08092-4); pap. 11.95x (ISBN 0-521-09644-8). Cambridge U Pr.
Roscoe, D. T. Mountaineering: A Manual for Teachers & Instructors. (Illus.). 1976. 18.00 (ISBN 0-571-09456-2). Transatlantic.
Roscoe, Edward S. The Growth of English Law. Being Studies in the Evolution of Law & Procedure in England. viii, 260p. 1980. Repr. of 1911 ed. lib. bdg. 26.00x (ISBN 0-8377-1029-4). Rothman.
Roscoe, Edwin S., et al. Organization for Production. 5th ed. 1971. text ed. 18.95 (ISBN 0-256-00470-6). Irwin.
Roscoe, Stanley N., et al. Aviation Psychology. 1980. text ed. 16.50 (ISBN 0-8138-1925-3). Iowa St U Pr.
Roscoe, Theodore. Lincoln's Assassination, April 14, 1865: Investigation of a President's Murder Uncovers a Web of Conspiracy. LC 73-152852. (Focus Bks). (Illus.). (gr. 7 up). 1971. PLB 4.47 o.p. (ISBN 0-531-00993-9). Watts.
--Tin Cans. (War Books). 1979. pap. 2.50 o.p. (ISBN 0-685-92502-1, 13037-4). Bantam.
--The Trent Affair, November, 1861: U.S. Detainment of a British Ship Nearly Brings War with England. LC 76-186758. (Focus Books). (Illus.). 72p. (gr. 7 up). 1972. PLB 6.45 (ISBN 0-531-02455-5). Watts.
Rosdahl, Caroline B., jt. auth. see Thompson, Ella M.
Rose. The Study of Sociology. 1966. pap. text ed. 4.95x (ISBN 0-675-09717-7). Merrill.
Rose, jt. ed. see Hughes, D. E.
Rose, A. H., et al, eds. Advances in Microbial Physiology. Incl. Vol. 1. 1967. o.p. (ISBN 0-12-027701-8); Vol. 2. 1968. 29.50 (ISBN 0-12-027702-6); Vol. 3. 1969. 34.50 (ISBN 0-12-027703-4); Vol. 4. 1970. 49.00 (ISBN 0-12-027704-2); Vol. 5. 1970. o.s.i (ISBN 0-12-027705-0); Vol. 6. 1971. 51.00 (ISBN 0-12-027706-9); Vol. 7. Rose, A. H. & Tempest, D. W., eds. 1972. 43.00 (ISBN 0-12-027707-7); Vol. 8. 1972. 37.50 (ISBN 0-12-027708-5); Vol. 9. 1973. 35.00 (ISBN 0-12-027709-3); Vol. 10. 1973. 41.50 (ISBN 0-12-027710-7); Vol. 14. 1977. 57.50 (ISBN 0-12-027714-X); Vol. 15. 1977. 61.50 (ISBN 0-12-027715-8); Vol. 16. 1978. 52.00 (ISBN 0-12-027716-6); Vol. 17. 1978. 55.50 (ISBN 0-12-027717-4). Acad Pr.
Rose, Adam, jt. auth. see Edmunds, Stahrl.
Rose, Adam Z., jt. ed. see Edmunds, Stahrl W.
Rose, Albert. Governing Metropolitan Toronto: A Social & Political Analysis 1953-1971. LC 72-157821. (Institute of Governmental Studies, U. C. Berkeley & Lane Studies in Regional Government). 1973. 20.00x (ISBN 0-520-02041-3). U of Cal Pr.
Rose, Allen J. & Schick, Barbara A. APL in Practice. LC 80-5351. 374p. 1980. 25.00 (ISBN 0-471-08275-9, Pub. by Wiley-Interscience). Wiley.
Rose, Allison. Wildflowers in Britain. 7.50x (ISBN 0-392-07390-0, LTB). Soccer.
Rose, Anne. How Does a Czar Eat Potatoes? LC 72-5140. (Illus.). 32p. (ps-3). 1973. PLB 6.96 o.p. (ISBN 0-688-51531-2). Lothrop.
Rose, Arden. Interacting Through Creative Arts Activities. LC 76-29237. (Learning Handbooks Ser.). 1976. pap. 3.95 (ISBN 0-8224-1905-X). Pitman Learning.
Rose, Arnold. The Singer & the Voice: Vocal Physiology & Technique for Singers. 2nd ed. (Illus.). 267p. 1978. 15.95 (ISBN 0-85967-446-0, Pub. by Scolar Pr England); pap. 7.95 (ISBN 0-85967-447-9). Biblio Dist.
Rose, Barbara. American Art Since Nineteen Hundred. LC 72-83563. (Illus.). 320p. 1975. text ed. 13.95x. Praeger.
Rose, Barbara, ed. see Namuth, Hans.
Rose, C. W. Agricultural Physics. 1966. 16.50 (ISBN 0-08-011885-2); pap. 12.00 (ISBN 0-08-011884-4). Pergamon.
Rose, Cissy. Willie & Billie & Other Tales for Children. 1980. 4.50 (ISBN 0-8062-1343-4). Carlton.
Rose, Clifford F. & Gawel, M. Migraine: The Facts. (Illus.). 150p. 1980. text ed. 11.95x (ISBN 0-19-261161-5). Oxford U Pr.
Rose, Darrell E. Audiological Assessment. 2nd ed. 1978. 20.95 (ISBN 0-13-050815-2). P-H.
Rose, David, jt. auth. see Radford, John.
Rose, David P. Endocrinology of Cancer, 2 vols. 1979. Vol. 1, 160p. 49.95 (ISBN 0-8493-5337-8); Vol. 2, 160p. 49.95 (ISBN 0-8493-5338-6). CRC Pr.
Rose, E. Cases of Conscience. LC 74-76947. 272p. 1975. 35.50 (ISBN 0-521-20462-3). Cambridge U Pr.
Rose, Edgar. Housing for the Aged. 1978. 24.95 (ISBN 0-566-00217-5, 02175-X, Pub. by Saxon Hse England). Lexington Bks.
Rose, Elizabeth, jt. auth. see Rose, Gerald.
Rose, Ellen C. The Novels of Margaret Drabble: Equivocal Figures. (Illus.). 141p. 1980. 26.50x (ISBN 0-389-20006-9). B&N.
Rose, Emily M., jt. ed. see Rose, Milton R.
Rose, Ernst. A History of German Literature. LC 60-9405. (Gotham Library). (Orig.). 1960. 12.00x (ISBN 0-8147-0362-3); pap. 6.00x (ISBN 0-8147-0363-1). NYU Pr.
Rose, George. All That Glitters. 1980. pap. 5.95 (ISBN 0-9602462-6-6). Working Pr CA.
Rose, George G., ed. Atlas of Vertebrate Cells in Tissue Culture. 1971. 53.50 (ISBN 0-12-596856-6). Acad Pr.
Rose, Gerald. Ahhh! said Stork. (Illus.). 1977. 7.95 (ISBN 0-571-11097-5, Pub. by Faber & Faber). Merrimack Bk Serv.
--Ironhead. (Illus.). (ps-5). 1973. 6.95 (ISBN 0-571-10301-4, Pub. by Faber & Faber). Merrimack Bk Serv.
--Nineteen Seventy-Nine Patent Law Handbook. LC 78-17713. 1979. 13.50 (ISBN 0-87632-251-8). Boardman.
--Rabbit Pie. (Illus.). 32p. (gr. 5-8). 1980. 9.95 (ISBN 0-571-11480-6, Pub. by Faber & Faber). Merrimack Bk Serv.
Rose, Gerald & Rose, Elizabeth. Albert & the Green Bottle. (Illus.). (ps-5). 1972. 6.95 (ISBN 0-571-09873-8, Pub. by Faber & Faber). Merrimack Bk Serv.
--Androcles & the Lion. (Illus.). (ps-5). 1971. 6.50 (ISBN 0-571-09774-X, Pub. by Faber & Faber). Merrimack Bk Serv.
--The Great Oak. (Illus.). (ps-5). 1970. 4.95 o.p. (ISBN 0-571-09251-9, Pub. by Faber & Faber). Merrimack Bk Serv.
--Lucky Hans. (Illus.). (ps-5). 1976. 8.95 (ISBN 0-571-10905-5, Pub. by Faber & Faber). Merrimack Bk Serv.
--Punch & Judy Carry on. (Illus.). (ps-5). 1962. 6.95 (ISBN 0-571-05161-8, Pub. by Faber & Faber). Merrimack Bk Serv.
--Wolf! Wolf! (Illus.). (ps-5). 1974. 6.95 (ISBN 0-571-10405-3, Pub. by Faber & Faber). Merrimack Bk Serv.
Rose, Gerald, ed. Intellectual Property Law Review: Annual. Incl. 1976 (ISBN 0-87632-142-2); 1977 (ISBN 0-87632-143-0); 1978 (ISBN 0-87632-144-9); 1979 (ISBN 0-87632-145-7). LC 79-88703. 42.50 ea. Boardman.
Rose, Gordon & Marshall, Tony M. Counselling & School Social Work: An Experimental Study. LC 74-1752. 345p. 1975. 27.95 (ISBN 0-471-73549-3, Pub. by Wiley-Interscience). Wiley.
Rose, Graham. Landscape with Weeds. (Illus.). 160p. 1980. 14.95 (ISBN 0-241-10353-3, Pub. by Hamish Hamilton England). David & Charles.
Rose, H. J., tr. see Plutarchus.
Rose, Harold M. Lethal Aspects of Urban Violence. LC 77-18680. (Illus.). 1979. 14.95 (ISBN 0-669-02117-2). Lexington Bks.
Rose, Harold M., jt. ed. see Gappert, Gary.
Rose, Herbert H. Life & Thought of A. D. Gordon. 1964. 3.50x (ISBN 0-8197-0176-9). Bloch.
Rose, Herbert J., ed. Gods & Heroes of the Greeks: An Introduction to Greek Mythology. 8.50 (ISBN 0-8446-5113-3). Peter Smith.
Rose, Hilarly. Doctors, Patients & Pathology. 79p. 1972. pap. text ed. 5.00x (ISBN 0-7135-1741-7, Pub. by Bedford England). Renouf.
Rose, Hilary & Rose, Steven. Ideology of-in the Natural Sciences. 363p. 1980. pap. text ed. 11.25x (ISBN 0-87073-881-X). Schenkman.
Rose, Howard. Twelve Ravens. Marek, R., ed. 1970. 6.95 o.s.i. (ISBN 0-02-604880-9). Macmillan.
Rose, Howard N. A Thesaurus of Slang. LC 72-167144. xii, 120p. Repr. of 1934 ed. 18.00 (ISBN 0-8103-3115-2). Gale.
Rose, J. & Bilciu, C., eds. Modern Trends in Cybernetics & Systems I-III: Proceedings of the Third International Congress of Cybernetics & Systems, Bucharest, Romania, August 25-29, 1975, 3 vols. Incl. Vol. 1 (ISBN 0-387-08196-8); Vol. 2 (ISBN 0-387-08197-6); Vol. 3 (ISBN 0-387-08198-4). 1977. Set. 173.20 (ISBN 3-540-08199-2); 69.30 ea. Springer-Verlag.
Rose, J. & Weidener, E. W., eds. Westview Environmental Studies, 3 vols. Incl. Vol. 1. Pesticides: Boon or Bane? Green, M. B. LC 76-5881. 18.00x (ISBN 0-89158-610-5); Vol. 2. Climate & the Environment: The Atmospheric Impact on Man. Griffiths, John F. LC 76-5801. pap. text ed. 11.00x (ISBN 0-236-40022-3); Vol. 3. Electromagnetism, Man & the Environment. Battocletti, Joseph H. LC 76-7905. 17.50x (ISBN 0-89158-612-1). 1976. Westview.
Rose, J., ed. see Hutchins, John G. B.
Rose, J. G. & De Vore, R. W., eds. Kentucky Coal Refuse Disposal & Utilization Seminar, Fourth: Proceedings. (Illus.). 1978. pap. text ed. 7.00 (ISBN 0-89779-010-3); microfiche 1.50 (ISBN 0-89779-011-1). OES Pubns.
Rose, J. H. The Revolutionary & Napoleonic Era. 387p. 1980. Repr. of 1894 ed. lib. bdg. 40.00 (ISBN 0-89760-737-6). Telegraph Bks.
Rose, J. W. & Cooper, J., eds. Technical Data on Fuel: S. I. Units. 7th rev. ed. LC 77-24872. 1978. 88.95 (ISBN 0-470-99239-5). Halsted Pr.
Rose, James M. & Brown, Barbara, eds. Black Roots in Southeastern Connecticut 1650-1900: A Guide to Information Sources. (Gale Genealogy & Local History Ser.: Vol. 8). 1980. 30.00 (ISBN 0-8103-1411-8). Gale.
Rose, James M. & Eichholz, Alice, eds. Black Genesis: An Annotated Bibliography for Black Genealogical Research. LC 77-74819. (Genealogy & Local History Ser.: Vol. 1). (Illus.). 1978. 30.00 (ISBN 0-8103-1400-2). Gale.
Rose, Jennifer. Out of a Dream. (Second Chance at Love, Contemporary Ser.: No. 4). (Orig.). 1981. pap. 1.75 (ISBN 0-515-05777-0). Jove Pubns.
Rose, John S. A Course on Group Theory. LC 76-22984. (Illus.). 1978. 57.50 (ISBN 0-521-21409-2); pap. 18.50x (ISBN 0-521-29142-9). Cambridge U Pr.
Rose, Joseph L., et al. Basic Physics in Diagnostic Ultrasound. LC 79-14932. 1979. 29.95 (ISBN 0-471-05735-5, Pub. by Wiley Medical). Wiley.
Rose, Joy, jt. ed. see Rose, Leon.
Rose, Karen. There Is a Season. 1969. pap. 1.25 (ISBN 0-380-39537-1, 39537). Avon.
Rose, L. M. The Application of Mathematical Modelling to Process Development & Design. LC 74-14543. 364p. 1974. 49.95 (ISBN 0-470-73351-9). Halsted Pr.
Rose, Leo E. Nepal: Strategy for Survival. LC 75-100022. (Center of South & Southeast Asia Studies, UC Berkeley). 1971. 22.75x (ISBN 0-520-01643-2). U of Cal Pr.
Rose, Leon & Rose, Joy, eds. Commodity Money Management Yearbook, 1980. (Illus.). 1981. 39.50 (ISBN 0-936624-01-9). LJR Inc.
Rose, Leslie I. & Lavine, Robert L., eds. New Concepts in Endocrinology & Metabolism. LC 77-9314. (The 39th Hahnemann Symposium on Endocrinology). 1977. 28.50 (ISBN 0-8089-1028-0). Grune.
Rose, Leu. Movie Kings. (Pal Paperbacks, - Pal Skills II Ser.). (Illus.). (gr. 5-12). 1980. pap. text ed. 1.25 (ISBN 0-8374-6807-8). Xerox Ed Pubns.
Rose, Linda. Hands. 1980. 14.95 (ISBN 0-671-24944-4). S&S.
Rose, Lisle A. Assault on Eternity: Richard E. Byrd & the Exploration of Antarctica, 1946-47. LC 79-93232. (Illus.). 352p. 1980. 19.95 (ISBN 0-87021-085-8). Naval Inst Pr.
--The Roots of Tragedy: The United States & the Struggle for Asia, 1945-1953. LC 75-35354. (Contributions in American History: No. 48). 352p. 1976. lib. bdg. 18.50 (ISBN 0-8371-8592-0, RRT/). Greenwood.
Rose, Louisa, et al, eds. The Menopause Book. Cornell, Elizabeth & Kemeny, Nancy. 272p. 1980. pap. 5.95 (ISBN 0-686-62823-3, Hawthorn). Dutton.
Rose, Mark, ed. Twentieth Century Interpretations of Anthony & Cleopatra. 1977. 8.95 (ISBN 0-13-038612-X, Spec); pap. 2.45 (ISBN 0-13-038604-9). P-H.
Rose, Martin R., et al. The Past Climate of Arroyo Hondo, New Mexico, Reconstructed from Tree Rings. (Arroyo Hondo Archaeological Ser.: Vol. 4). (Illus., Orig.). 1981. pap. 6.25 (ISBN 0-933452-05-5). Schol Am Res.
Rose, Michael. French Industrial Studies. 148p. 1977. text ed. 20.50x (ISBN 0-566-00207-8, Pub. by Gower Pub Co England). Renouf.

Rose, Milton R. & Rose, Emily M., eds. A Shaker Reader. LC 77-70773. (Antiques Magazine Library). (Illus.). 1977. 12.95x (ISBN 0-87663-297-5, Main Street); pap. 7.95 (ISBN 0-87663-969-4). Universe.

Rose, N. R. & Friedman, H., eds. Manual of Clinical Immunology. 2nd ed. (Illus.). 1980. 25.00 (ISBN 0-914826-25-5); flexible binding 21.00 (ISBN 0-914826-27-1). Am Soc Microbio.

Rose, Noel & Bigazzi, Pierluigi E. Methods in Immunodiagnosis. 2nd ed. LC 80-15273. 256p. 1980. 18.50 (ISBN 0-471-02208-X, Pub. by Wiley Med). Wiley.

Rose, Noel R., et al. Fundamentals of Immunology. Zulch, Joan C., ed. (Illus.). 448p. 1973. text ed. 15.25x o.p. (ISBN 0-02-403590-4); pap. text ed. 11.50x o.p. (ISBN 0-685-30318-7). Macmillan.

Rose, Norman. Lewis Namier & Zionism. 192p. 1980. 29.50x (ISBN 0-19-822621-7). Oxford U Pr.

Rose, Pat R. The Solar Boat Book. LC 80-69217. (Illus.). 266p. (Orig.). 1979. pap. 9.95 (ISBN 0-9604874-0-9). Aqua-Sol Ent.

Rose, Patricia. Wolf Huber Studies: Aspects of Renaissance Thought & Practice in Danube School Painting. LC 76-23711. (Outstanding Dissertations in the Fine Arts - 16th Century). (Illus.). 1977. Repr. of 1973 ed. lib. bdg. 63.00 (ISBN 0-8240-2725-6). Garland Pub.

Rose, Peter I. They & We: Racial & Ethnic Relations in the United States. 252p. 1981. pap. text ed. 7.95 (ISBN 0-394-32402-1). Random.

Rose, Peter L. De see De Rose, Peter L.

Rose, Peter Q. Ivies. (Illus.). 180p. 1980. 17.50 (ISBN 0-7137-0969-3, Pub. by Blandford Pr England). Sterling.

Rose, Peter S. & Fraser, Donald R. Financial Institutions. 1980. 18.95x (ISBN 0-256-02205-4). Business Pubns.

Rose, Peter S., jt. ed. see Fraser, Donald R.

Rose, R. M., et al see Wulff, J.

Rose, Reginald. Twelve Angry Men: A Screen Adaptation, Directed by Sidney Lumet. Garrett, George P., et al, eds. LC 71-135273. (Film Scripts Ser.). 1971. pap. text ed. 6.95x (ISBN 0-89197-970-0). Irvington.

Rose, Richard. Do Parties Make a Difference? pap. 8.95 (ISBN 0-934540-08-X). Chatham Hse Pubs.

--Electoral Behavior: A Comparative Handbook. LC 72-11285. (Illus.). 1974. 35.00 (ISBN 0-02-926810-9). Free Pr.

--Lessons from America: An Exploration. LC 74-925. 308p. 1974. 19.95 (ISBN 0-470-73350-0). Halsted Pr.

--Managing Presidential Objectives. LC 76-4424. 1976. 17.95 (ISBN 0-02-926840-0). Free Pr.

--Politics in England. 1974. 17.00 (ISBN 0-571-10297-2, Pub. by Faber & Faber); pap. 10.95 (ISBN 0-571-10534-3). Merrimack Bk Serv.

--The Problem of Party Government. LC 74-30329. (Illus.). 1975. 17.95 (ISBN 0-02-926780-3). Free Pr.

--What Is Governing? Purpose & Policy in Washington. LC 77-13476. (Illus.). 1978. pap. 9.95x ref. ed. (ISBN 0-13-952127-5). P-H.

--The Wolf. 288p. (Orig.). 1980. pap. 2.50 (ISBN 0-89083-657-4). Zebra.

Rose, Richard & McAllister, Ian. United Kingdom Facts. 240p. 1981. text ed. 48.50x (ISBN 0-8419-5578-6). Holmes & Meier.

Rose, Richard, jt. auth. see Mackie, Thomas T.

Rose, Richard, ed. Challenge to Governance: Studies in Overloaded Polities. LC 80-40148. 238p. 1980. 20.00 (ISBN 0-8039-9816-3); pap. 9.95 (ISBN 0-8039-1508-X). Sage.

--The Dynamics of Public Policy: A Comparative Analysis. LC 75-31293. 1976. 18.50x (ISBN 0-8039-9965-8); pap. 8.95x (ISBN 0-8039-9966-6). Sage.

--Electoral Participation: A Comparative Analysis. LC 80-41015. (Sage Studies in Contemporary Political Sociology). 358p. 1980. 25.00 (ISBN 0-8039-9811-2). Sage.

Rose, Richard & Suleiman, Ezra N., eds. Presidents & Prime Ministers. 1980. pap. 8.25 (ISBN 0-8447-3386-5). Am Enterprise.

Rose, Richard, ed. see Butler, David E.

Rose, Robert C. The Lonely Eagles. (Illus.). 1976. pap. 6.00 (ISBN 0-911720-68-5, Pub. by Tuskegee). Aviation.

Rose, Roger G. A Museum to Instruct & Delight. LC 80-69203. (Special Publication Ser.: No. 68). (Illus.). 96p. Date not set. pap. 6.50 (ISBN 0-910240-28-0). Bishop Mus.

Rose, Sheldon D. A Casebook in Group Therapy: A Behavioral-Cognitive Approach. (Social Work Practice Ser.). (Illus.). 1979. text ed. 14.95 (ISBN 0-13-117408-8). P-H.

--Group Therapy: A Behavioral Approach. (Illus.). 1977. 17.95 (ISBN 0-13-365239-4). P-H.

Rose, Steven, jt. auth. see Rose, Hilary.

Rose, Tom. Economics: Principles & Policy from a Christian Perspective. LC 76-41727. 1977. 12.95 (ISBN 0-915134-22-5); pap. instr's man. 3.95 (ISBN 0-915134-23-3). American Ent Texas.

--How to Succeed in Business: A Resource Unit on Understanding Business & Getting Ahead in the Business World. LC 74-33827. 1975. 4.95 (ISBN 0-686-10503-6); pap. 1.95 (ISBN 0-686-10504-4). American Ent Texas.

--When the Union Organizer Knocks. new ed. (Illus.). 150p. 1972. pap. 7.95 (ISBN 0-686-05611-6). American Ent Texas.

Rose, Tom & Metcalf, Robert. The Coming Victory. (The Coronation Ser.: No. 5). 206p. (Orig.). 1980. pap. 6.95x (ISBN 0-686-28757-6). Chr Stud Ctr.

--The Coming Victory: Proposals on How to Overcome the Troubles That Plague Us. LC 80-68679. 192p. 1980. pap. 6.95. American Ent Texas.

Rose, Tony. The Complete Book of Movie Making. Date not set. 8.50 o.p. (ISBN 0-8038-1260-4). Hastings.

--The Complete Book of Movie Making. 1972. 8.50 o.p. (ISBN 0-85242-083-8, Pub. by Fountain). Morgan.

Rose, Wendy. Lost Copper. 1980. 8.95 (ISBN 0-686-27943-3). Malki Mus Pr.

Rose, William J. Polish Memoirs of William John Rose. Stone, Daniel, ed. LC 74-79986. 1975. 17.50x o.p. (ISBN 0-8020-5306-8). U of Toronto Pr.

Rose, William K. Astrophysics. LC 72-89470. 1973. 24.50x (ISBN 0-03-079155-3); pap. text ed. 12.50x (ISBN 0-89197-667-1). Irvington.

Rose, Willie L. A Documentary History of Slavery in North America. LC 75-16906. 544p. 1976. 29.95x (ISBN 0-19-501976-8); pap. text ed. 8.95x (ISBN 0-19-501978-4). Oxford U Pr.

Rosebaum, Robert A., ed. see Neumann, Inge S.

Roseberry, Viola. Illustrated History of Indian Baskets & Plates. (Illus.). 1974. pap. 2.50 o.s.i. (ISBN 0-913668-73-7). Ten Speed Pr.

Roseboom, Eugene H. & Eckes, Alfred E., Jr. A History of Presidential Elections: From George Washington to Jimmy Carter. 1979. 15.95 (ISBN 0-02-604890-6); pap. 9.95 (ISBN 0-02-036420-2, Collier). Macmillan.

Roseborough, Margaret M. Outline of Middle English Grammar. Repr. of 1938 ed. lib. bdg. 15.00x (ISBN 0-8371-4324-1, ROMI). Greenwood.

Rosebury, Theodor. Microbes & Morals. 352p. 1976. pap. 1.95 o.p. (ISBN 0-345-24893-7). Ballantine.

Rosecrance, Richard N. Defense of the Realm: British Strategy in the Nuclear Epoch. LC 67-26368. 1968. 20.00x (ISBN 0-231-03065-7). Columbia U Pr.

Rosecrance, Richard N., ed. Dispersion of Nuclear Weapons: Strategy & Politics. LC 64-17019. 1964. 20.00x (ISBN 0-231-02709-5). Columbia U Pr.

Rosecrans, Thomas R. Adirondack Rock & Ice Climbs. (Illus.). 124p. 1978. lib. bdg. 9.25 o.p. (ISBN 0-914788-17-5). East Woods.

Rosefsky, Robert S. Personal Finance & Money Management. LC 77-20283. 1978. text ed. 15.95 (ISBN 0-471-01740-X); tchr.'s manual avail. (ISBN 0-471-03762-1); study guide by M. H. Ivener avail. Wiley.

Rosefsky, Robert S., jt. auth. see Ivener, Martin H.

Rosegger, Gerhard. The Economics of Production & Innovation: An Industrial Perspective. (Illus.). 1980. 41.00 (ISBN 0-08-024047-X); pap. 17.50 (ISBN 0-08-024046-1). Pergamon.

Rose-Innes, A. C. Introduction to Superconductivity. 244p. 1975. text ed. 26.40 o.p. (ISBN 0-08-013469-6); pap. 16.50 o.p. (ISBN 0-08-019011-1). Pergamon.

Rose-Innes, A. C. & Rhoderick, E. H. Introduction to Superconductivity. 2nd ed. 1977. text ed. 45.00 (ISBN 0-08-021651-X); pap. 24.00 (ISBN 0-08-021652-8). Pergamon.

Roseler, Robert & Duckert, Audrey, eds. Moderne Deutsche Erzaehler. 3rd ed. 1960. 7.95x (ISBN 0-393-09536-3, NortonC). Norton.

Roseler, Robert O. & Reichard, Joseph R. German Grammar Workbook. 1956. pap. text ed. 2.95x (ISBN 0-89197-533-0). Irvington.

Roseliep, Raymond. Listen to Light: Haiku. (Illus.). 128p. 1980. 10.00 (ISBN 0-934184-05-4); pap. 5.00 (ISBN 0-934184-06-2). Alembic Pr.

Rosell, Rosendo. Mas Cuentos Picantes de Rosendo Rosell. LC 79-5001. (Coleccion Caniqui). (Illus.). 138p. 1980. pap. 5.95 (ISBN 0-89729-219-7). Ediciones.

Rosellemar, Kenneth. How to Master the Art of Spiritual Intercourse. (The Society of Psychic Research Library). (Illus.). 1981. 45.75 (ISBN 0-89920-025-7). Am Inst Psych.

Roseman, Curtis C. Changing Migration Patterns Within the United States. Natoli, Salvatore J., ed. LC 76-57033. (Resource Papers for College Geography Ser.). (Illus.). 1977. pap. text ed. 4.00 (ISBN 0-89291-123-9). Assn Am Geographers.

Roseman, Ed. Career Planning for Salesmen. 2nd ed. 56p. 1981. spiral bdg 7.95 (ISBN 0-89047-041-3). Herman Pub.

Roseman, Edward. Confronting Nonpromotability: How to Manage a Stalled Career. LC 77-8013. (Illus.). 1977. 14.95 (ISBN 0-8144-5441-0). Am Mgmt.

--Managing Employee Turnover: A Postive Approach. 241p. 1981. 17.95 (ISBN 0-8144-5585-9). Am Mgmt.

Roseman, Mill. Detectionary. Penzler, Otto, et al, eds. LC 75-27326. (Illus.). 320p. 1980. pap. 5.95 (ISBN 0-87951-114-1). Overlook Pr.

Rosemergy, John C. Celestial Horizons: A Concise View of the Universe. 1977. pap. text ed. 12.95x (ISBN 0-205-05571-0); instr's manual avail. (ISBN 0-205-05572-9). Allyn.

Rosemont, Franklin, ed. Surrealism & Its Popular Accomplices. (Illus.). 112p. 1980. pap. 5.00 (ISBN 0-87286-121-X). City Lights.

Rosen. Mummy Jokes & Puzzles. (gr. 3-5). 1980. pap. 1.25 (ISBN 0-590-30052-0, Schol Pap). Schol Bk Serv.

--Philosophic Systems & Education. 1968. pap. text ed. 7.95x (ISBN 0-675-09592-1). Merrill.

Rosen, A. & Freiden, R. Word Processing. 2nd ed. 1981. 15.95 (ISBN 0-13-963488-6). P-H.

Rosen, A. & Frelden, R. Word Processing. 1977. text ed. 16.95 (ISBN 0-13-963504-1). P-H.

Rosen, Anne, et al. Family Passover. LC 79-89298. 64p. (gr. 2 up). 1980. 6.95 (ISBN 0-8276-0169-7, 452). Jewish Pubn.

Rosen, Bernard. Strategies of Ethics. LC 77-77431. (Illus.). 1978. text ed. 13.50 (ISBN 0-395-25077-3); inst. manual 0.60 (ISBN 0-395-25078-1). HM.

Rosen, Bernard & Caplan, Arthur L. Ethics in the Undergraduate Curriculum. LC 80-12351. (The Teaching of Ethics Ser.). 67p. 1980. pap. 4.00 (ISBN 0-916558-13-4). Hastings Ctr Inst Soc.

Rosen, Charles. Arnold Shoenberg. LC 80-8773. 113p. (Orig.). 1981. pap. 4.95 (ISBN 0-691-02706-4). Princeton U Pr.

--A Mile Above the Rim. 1978. pap. 1.95 o.p. (ISBN 0-345-25955-6). Ballantine.

--Scandal of '51: How the Gamblers Almost Killed College Basketball. LC 77-215355. (Illus.). 1978. 10.00 o.p. (ISBN 0-03-040701-X). HR&W.

Rosen, Charles, ed. see Auber, Daniel F.

Rosen, Charles, ed. see Bellini, Vincenzio.

Rosen, Charles, ed. see Bellini, Vincenzo.

Rosen, Charles, ed. see Cherubini, Maria L.

Rosen, Charles, ed. see Donizetti, Gaetano.

Rosen, Charles, ed. see Halevy, Jacques-Francois.

Rosen, Charles, ed. see Le Seur, Jean F.

Rosen, Charles, ed. see Mehul, Etienne.

Rosen, Charles, ed. see Mehul, Etienne N.

Rosen, Charles, ed. see Meyerbeer, Giacomo.

Rosen, Charles, ed. see Rossini, Gioachino.

Rosen, Charles, ed. see Scribe, Eugene & Delestre-Poirson, Charles-Gaspard.

Rosen, Charles, ed. see Spontini, Gasparo.

Rosen, Connie & Rosen, Harold. The Language of Primary School Children. (Education Ser.). (Orig.). 1973. pap. 3.95 o.p. (ISBN 0-14-080340-8). Penguin.

Rosen, David H. Lesbianism: A Study of Female Homosexuality. (Illus.). 140p. 1974. 11.75 (ISBN 0-398-02924-5); pap. 7.50 (ISBN 0-398-03116-9). C C Thomas.

Rosen, Donn E., jt. ed. see Nelson, Gareth.

Rosen, Doris B. Employment Testing & Minority Groups. (Key Issues Ser.: No. 6). 1970. pap. 2.00 (ISBN 0-87546-239-1). NY Sch Indus Rel.

Rosen, Elliot A. Hoover, Roosevelt, and the Brains Trust: From Depression to New Deal. LC 76-49976. 1977. 22.50x (ISBN 0-231-04172-1). Columbia U Pr.

Rosen, George. Decision Making Chicago-Style: The Genesis of a University of Illinois Campus. LC 79-25643. (Illus.). 224p. 1980. 15.00 (ISBN 0-252-00803-0). U of Ill Pr.

--Democracy & Economic Change in India. rev. ed. 1966. 20.00x (ISBN 0-520-01089-2). U of Cal Pr.

--History of Public Health. LC 58-8307. 1958. 9.95 (ISBN 0-910922-06-3). MD Pubns.

--Madness in Society: Chapters in the Historical Sociology of Mental Illness. LC 68-13112. 352p. 1980. pap. 7.50 (ISBN 0-226-72642-8, P913). U of Chicago Pr.

Rosen, Gerald. The Carmen Miranda Memorial Flagpole. LC 77-73554. 1977. 8.95 o.s.i. (ISBN 0-89141-032-5); pap. 3.95 o.s.i. (ISBN 0-89141-033-3). Presidio Pr.

--Don't Be Afraid: A Program for Overcoming Your Fears & Phobias. 1976. text ed. 8.95 o.p. (ISBN 0-13-218412-5, Spec); pap. text ed. 2.95 o.p. (ISBN 0-13-218404-4). P-H.

--The Relaxation Book: An Illustrated Self-Help Program. (Psychology Today Book Club). (Illus.). 1978. 10.95 (ISBN 0-13-772210-9, Spec); pap. 4.95 (ISBN 0-13-772202-8, Spec). P-H.

Rosen, Gerald M., et al, eds. Behavioral Science in Family Practice. 300p. 1980. 19.50x (ISBN 0-8385-0638-0). ACC.

Rosen, Harold, jt. auth. see Rosen, Connie.

Rosen, Harold J. Construction Specifications Writing Principles & Procedures. 2nd ed. 240p. 1981. 24.95 (ISBN 0-471-08328-3, Pub. by Wiley-Interscience). Wiley.

Rosen, Harold J. & Bennett, Philip M. Construction Materials Evaluation & Selection: A Systematic Approach. LC 79-15885. (Wiley Series of Practical Construction Guides). 1979. 21.95 (ISBN 0-471-73565-5, Pub. by Wiley-Interscience). Wiley.

Rosen, Hjalmar, jt. auth. see Stagner, Ross.

Rosen, Keith S., jt. auth. see Karst, Kenneth L.

Rosen, Kenneth. A Regional Model of Residential Construction. 220p. Date not set. 18.00 (ISBN 0-88410-618-7). Ballinger Pub.

--Voices of the Rainbow. LC 80-52071. 232p. 1980. pap. 4.95 (ISBN 0-394-17747-9). Seaver Bks.

Rosen, Kenneth, ed. Voices of the Rainbow. (Seaver-Grove Bk.). 1980. pap. 4.95 o.p. (ISBN 0-394-17747-9). Grove.

Rosen, Kenneth M., ed. Current Cardiology, Vol. 2. (Current Ser). (Illus.). 500p. 1980. 35.00x (ISBN 0-89289-109-2). HM Prof Med Div.

Rosen, Kenneth T., jt. ed. see Kaufman, George.

Rosen, Lawrence R. Dow Jones-Irwin Guide to Interest. LC 73-89120. (Illus.). 180p. 1974. 9.95 o.p. (ISBN 0-87094-067-8). Dow Jones-Irwin.

Rosen, Linda R., jt. auth. see Rosen, Raymond.

Rosen, Marvin. Notes & Blots from a Psychologist's Desk. LC 77-16183. 1978. 13.95 (ISBN 0-88229-199-8). Nelson-Hall.

Rosen, Marvin & Clark, Gerald R., eds. The History of Mental Retardation: Collected Papers, 2 vols. (Illus.). 700p. 1975. 24.50 ea. (ISBN 0-8391-0827-3). Vol. 2 (ISBN 0-685-56047-3). Univ Park.

Rosen, Marvin J. Introduction to Photography: A Self Directing Approach. LC 75-31013. (Illus.). 384p. 1976. pap. text ed. 14.25 (ISBN 0-395-20471-2); inst. manual 3.25 (ISBN 0-395-20472-0). HM.

Rosen, Michael. Mind Your Own Business. LC 74-9969. (Illus.). 96p. (gr. 3 up). 1974. 8.95 (ISBN 0-87599-209-9). S G Phillips.

Rosen, Paul P., jt. ed. see Sommers, Sheldon C.

Rosen, Philip T. The Modern Stentors: Radio Broadcasters & the Federal Government,1920-1934. LC 79-8952. (Contributions in Economics & Economic History: No. 31). (Illus.). 267p. 1980. lib. bdg. 25.00x (ISBN 0-313-21231-7, RMS/). Greenwood.

Rosen, Raymond & Rosen, Linda R. Human Sexuality. 576p. 1981. text ed. 17.95 (ISBN 0-394-32028-X). Random.

Rosen, Renee. It Happened in Three Counties. 1981. 10.95 (ISBN 0-8062-1586-0). Carlton.

Rosen, Robert. Dynamical Systems Theory in Biology: Stability Theory & Its Applications, Vol. 1. LC 74-126231. (Biomedical Engineering Ser.). 1970. 40.95 (ISBN 0-471-73550-7, Pub. by Wiley-Interscience). Wiley.

Rosen, S. Introduction to the Primates: Living & Fossil. 1974. pap. 9.95 (ISBN 0-13-493478-4). P-H.

Rosen, Sherman J. Manual for Environmental Impact Evaluation. (Illus.). 1976. 18.95x (ISBN 0-13-553453-4). P-H.

Rosen, Shirley. Truman of St. Helens: The Man & His Mountain. (Illus.). 200p. 1981. 9.95 (ISBN 0-914842-57-9). Madrona Pubs.

Rosen, Steven. Samuel Beckett & the Pessimistic Tradition. LC 76-2506. 1976. 17.00 (ISBN 0-8135-0809-6). Rutgers U Pr.

Rosen, Theodore & Martin, Sandy. Atlas of Black Dermatology. 1981. text ed. price not set (ISBN 0-316-75709-8). Little.

Rosen, Winifred. Henrietta & the Day of the Iguana. LC 77-19047. (Illus.). 32p. (gr. k-3). 1978. 6.95 (ISBN 0-590-07471-7, Four Winds). Schol Bk Serv.

--Henrietta & the Gong from Hong Kong. LC 80-19526. (Illus.). 32p. (gr. k-3). 1981. 7.95 (ISBN 0-590-07657-4, Four Winds). Schol Bk Serv.

--Henrietta, the Wild Woman of Borneo. LC 74-31017. (Illus.). 48p. (gr. k-3). 1975. 5.95 (ISBN 0-590-07390-7, Four Winds). Schol Bk Serv.

Rosenau, James, et al. The Analysis of International Politics. LC 70-184005. 1972. 17.95 (ISBN 0-02-927030-8). Free Pr.

Rosenau, James N. Citizenship Between Elections. LC 73-16907. (Illus.). 1974. 19.95 (ISBN 0-02-926970-9). Free Pr.

--Domestic Sources of Foreign Policy. LC 67-10347. 1967. 17.95 (ISBN 0-02-927000-6). Free Pr.

--The Dramas of Political Life. LC 79-17804. (Illus.). 1980. pap. text ed. 7.95 (ISBN 0-87872-246-7). Duxbury Pr.

--In Search of Global Patterns. LC 75-20950. (Illus.). 1976. 19.95 (ISBN 0-02-927050-2). Free Pr.

Rosenau, James N., et al. World Politics. LC 75-22766. (Illus.). 1976. text ed. 17.95 (ISBN 0-02-927040-5). Free Pr.

Rosenau, Milton D., Jr. Successful Project Management: A Step-by-Step Approach with Practical Examples. LC 80-24720. 350p. 1981. text ed. 24.95 (ISBN 0-534-97977-7). Lifetime Learn.

Rosenau, William. Jewish Ceremonial Institutions & Customs. rev. ed. 3rd. ed. LC 70-78222. (Illus.). 1971. Repr. of 1925 ed. 15.00 (ISBN 0-8103-3402-X). Gale.

Rosenauer, N. & Willis, A. H. Kinematics of Mechanisms. pap. text ed. 4.00 (ISBN 0-486-61796-3). Dover.

Rosenbach, A. S. American Jewish Bibliography. 1926. 10.00 o.p. (ISBN 0-685-05623-6). Am Jewish Hist Soc.

Rosenbach, Joseph B., et al. College Algebra. 5th ed. LC 79-135634. 1971. text ed. 18.95x (ISBN 0-471-00473-1); solutions manual avail. (ISBN 0-471-00474-X). Wiley.

--College Algebra with Trigonometry. LC 73-79572. (Illus.). 1963. text ed. 18.95x o.p. (ISBN 0-471-00476-6). Wiley.

--Essentials of Trigonometry. 2nd rev. ed. 1974. text ed. 18.95x (ISBN 0-471-01104-5). Wiley.

Rosenbaum, Alan S., ed. The Philosophy of Human Rights: International Perspectives. LC 79-6191. (Contributions in Philosophy: No. 15). xv, 272p. 1980. lib. bdg. 27.50 (ISBN 0-313-20985-5, RHR/). Greenwood.

Rosenbaum, Bernard L., ed. How to Motivate Today's Workers: Motivational Models for Managers & Supervisors. (Illus.). 192p. 1981. 14.95 (ISBN 0-07-053711-9, P&RB). McGraw.

Rosenbaum, E. & Sherman, A. J. M. M. Warburg & Co., 1798-1938 Merchant Bankers of Hamburg. LC 79-511. (Illus.). 1979. text ed. 24.50x o.p. (ISBN 0-8419-0477-4). Holmes & Meier.

Rosenbaum, Edward E. Rheumatology. (New Directions in Therapy Ser.). 1980. pap. 15.50 (ISBN 0-87488-683-X). Med Exam.

Rosenbaum, Ernest H., et al. Going Home: A Home Care Training Program. (Illus.). 160p. 1980. 12.00 (ISBN 0-915950-49-9); three ring binder 12.00 (ISBN 0-915950-48-0). Bull Pub.

Rosenbaum, H. Jon & Sederberg, Peter C., eds. Vigilante Politics. LC 75-11168. 1976. 15.00x (ISBN 0-8122-7702-3). U of Pa Pr.

Rosenbaum, H. Jon & Tyler, William G., eds. Contemporary Brazil: Issues in Economic & Political Development. LC 73-180851. (Special Studies in International Economics & Development). 1972. 28.00x (ISBN 0-275-28289-9). Irvington.

Rosenbaum, Harold D. Pearls in Diagnostic Radiology, Vol. 1. (Illus.). 240p. 1980. pap. 32.50x (ISBN 0-443-08097-6). Churchill.

Rosenbaum, James E. Making Inequality: The Hidden Curriculum of High School Tracking. LC 76-2008. 225p. 1976. 17.95 o.p. (ISBN 0-471-73605-8, Pub. by Wiley-Interscience). Wiley.

Rosenbaum, Jean, jt. auth. see Rosenbaum, Veryl.

Rosenbaum, Jonathan. Moving Places: A Life at the Movies. LC 80-7596. (Illus.). 288p. 1980. 11.95 (ISBN 0-06-013657-X, HarpT); pap. 5.95 (ISBN 0-06-090823-8, CN823). Har-Row.

Rosenbaum, Jonathan, tr. see Bazin, Andre.

Rosenbaum, Nelson M. Citizen Involvement in Land Use Governance: Issues & Methods. 82p. 1976. pap. 3.50 (ISBN 0-87766-140-5, 11500). Urban Inst.

--Land Use & the Legislatures: The Politics of State Innovation. 93p. 1976. pap. 3.50 (ISBN 0-87766-174-X, 15400). Urban Inst.

Rosenbaum, Peter. Peer-Mediated Instruction. LC 72-92363. 272p. 1973. text ed. 10.25x (ISBN 0-8077-2368-1). Tchrs Coll.

Rosenbaum, Peter S. Grammar of English Predicate Complement Constructions. (Press Research Monographs: No. 47). 1967. 12.50x o.p. (ISBN 0-262-18023-5). MIT Pr.

Rosenbaum, Peters S., jt. ed. see Jacobs, Roderick A.

Rosenbaum, Robert J. Mexicano Resistance in the Southwest: The Sacred Right of Self-Preservation. (Illus.). 245p. 1981. text ed. 14.95x (ISBN 0-292-77562-8). U of Tex Pr.

Rosenbaum, Samuel. A Yiddish Word Book for English Speaking People. 199p. 1980. pap. text ed. 6.95 (ISBN 0-442-21932-6). Van Nos Reinhold.

Rosenbaum, Veryl. Mother, Daughter, Self. 1979. pap. 1.95 (ISBN 0-505-51406-0). Tower Bks.

Rosenbaum, Veryl & Rosenbaum, Jean. Stepparenting. LC 77-22070. 160p. 1977. 7.95 (ISBN 0-88316-530-9). Chandler & Sharp.

Rosenbaum, Walter A. Coal & Crisis: The Political Dilemma of Energy Management. LC 78-8606. (Praeger Special Studies). 1978. 20.95 (ISBN 0-03-042596-4). Praeger.

--The Politics of Environmental Concern. 2nd ed. LC 76-41964. 1977. pap. 8.95 (ISBN 0-275-64820-6). Praeger.

Rosenberg, Alan S. Evaluating Tax Shelter Offerings: 1980 Course Handbook. LC 80-80759. 512p. 1980. pap. text ed. 25.00 (ISBN 0-686-68823-6, J4-3477). PLI.

Rosenberg, Alexander, jt. auth. see Beauchamp, Tom L.

Rosenberg, Ann E. Freudian Theory & American Religious Journals: Nineteen Hundred to Nineteen Sixty-Five. Berkhofer, Robert, ed. (Studies in American History & Culture, III). 255p. 1980. 26.95 (ISBN 0-8357-1099-8, Pub. by UMI Res Pr). Univ Microfilms.

Rosenberg, B. G., jt. auth. see Hyde, Janet.

Rosenberg, Bernard & Rosenberg, Deena. The Music Makers. 1979. 17.50 (ISBN 0-231-03953-0). Columbia U Pr.

Rosenberg, Bernard & Silverstein, Harry. The Real Tinsel. LC 73-112854. (Illus.). 436p. 1974. pap. 3.95 o.s.i. (ISBN 0-02-012550-X, Collier). Macmillan.

Rosenberg, Bruce A. Art of the American Folk Preacher. LC 77-111649. 1970. 15.95 (ISBN 0-19-500092-7). Oxford U Pr.

--Folksongs of Virginia: A Checklist of the WPA Holdings at Alderman Library, University of Virginia. LC 75-88185. 145p. 1969. 5.95 (ISBN 0-8139-0279-7). U Pr of Va.

Rosenberg, Bruce A., jt. ed. see Mandel, Jerome.

Rosenberg, Charles E., ed. The Family in History. LC 75-14962. (Haney Foundation Ser.). 1975. 12.95 (ISBN 0-8122-7702-3); pap. 5.95 (ISBN 0-8122-1100-6). U of Pa Pr.

Rosenberg, D. N. Oaten Reeds & Trumpets: Pastoral & Epic in Virgil, Spenser, & Milton. LC 80-17974. 288p. 1981. 22.50 (ISBN 0-8387-5002-8). Bucknell U Pr.

Rosenberg, Daniel. Mary Brown: From Harper's Ferry to California. (Occasional Papers: No. 17). 1976. pap. 1.50 (ISBN 0-89977-024-X). Am Inst Marxist.

Rosenberg, David. Chosen Days: Celebrating Jewish Festivals in Poetry & Art. LC 79-7906. (Illus.). 224p. 1980. 14.95 (ISBN 0-385-14365-6). Doubleday.

--Job Speaks. 101p. 1980. Repr. of 1977 ed. 3.95 (ISBN 0-934450-09-9). Unmuzzled Ox.

Rosenberg, Deena, jt. auth. see Rosenberg, Bernard.

Rosenberg, Dorothy, jt. auth. see Camurati, Mireya.

Rosenberg, E. & Rosenberg, N. Postwar America: Readings & Reminiscences. 336p. 1976. pap. 10.95 (ISBN 0-13-685495-8). P-H.

Rosenberg, Emily. Spreading the American Dream. 1981. 12.95 (ISBN 0-8090-8798-7); pap. 4.95 (ISBN 0-8090-0146-2). FS&G.

Rosenberg, H. M. The Solid State: An Introduction to the Physics of Crystals. 2nd ed. (Physics Ser.). (Illus.). 1979. 15.95x (ISBN 0-19-851844-7); pap. 11.50x (ISBN 0-19-851845-5). Oxford U Pr.

Rosenberg, Harold. Art on the Edge. (Illus.). 288p. 1975. 14.95 (ISBN 0-02-604900-7). Macmillan.

--Discovering the Present. 1973. pap. 3.95 o.s.i. (ISBN 0-226-72681-9, P691, Phoen). U of Chicago Pr.

--Discovering the Present: Three Decades in Art, Culture, & Politics. 1973. 7.00x (ISBN 0-226-72680-0). U of Chicago Pr.

Rosenberg, Harvey S. & Bolande, Robert P., eds. Perspectives in Pediatric Pathology, Vol. 5. (Illus.). 309p. 1979. 43.50 (ISBN 0-89352-061-6). Masson Pub.

Rosenberg, Isaac. The Collected Works of Isaac Rosenberg. Parsons, Ian, ed. (Illus.). 1979. 29.95 (ISBN 0-19-520143-4). Oxford U Pr.

Rosenberg, Israel. Shay Agnon's World of Mystery & Allegory: An Analysis of Iddo & 'Aynam. 145p. 1978. 5.95 (ISBN 0-8059-2538-4). Dorrance.

Rosenberg, J. Prescriber's Guide to Drug Interactions. 1978. pap. 12.95 (ISBN 0-87489-143-4). Med Economics.

Rosenberg, James L; see Corrigan, Robert W.

Rosenberg, Jay F. & Travis, Charles. Readings in the Philosophy of Language. LC 70-132170. 1971. text ed. 19.95 (ISBN 0-13-759332-5). P-H.

Rosenberg, Jerry M. Dictionary of Business & Management. LC 78-7796. 1978. 27.95 (ISBN 0-471-01681-0, Pub. by Wiley-Interscience). Wiley.

Rosenberg, John. Dorothy Richardson: The Genius They Forgot. 1979. pap. 10.95x o.p. (ISBN 0-7156-0655-7, Pub. by Duckworth England). Biblio Dist.

Rosenberg, John D., ed. The Genius of John Ruskin: Selections from His Writings. 1979. Repr. of 1963 ed. 27.50 (ISBN 0-7100-0354-4). Routledge & Kegan.

Rosenberg, Judith K. Young People's Literature in Series: Fiction, Non-Fiction, & Publishers' Series, 1973-1975. LC 77-57963. 1977. lib. bdg. 17.50x (ISBN 0-87287-140-1). Libs Unl.

Rosenberg, Judith K., jt. auth. see Rosenberg, Kenyon C.

Rosenberg, Kenyon C. & Doskey, John S. Media Equipment: A Guide & Dictionary. LC 76-25554. (Illus.). 150p. 1976. lib. bdg. 17.50x (ISBN 0-87287-155-X). Libs Unl.

Rosenberg, Kenyon C. & Rosenberg, Judith K. Watergate: An Annotated Bibliography. LC 75-6880. 141p. 1975. lib. bdg. 11.50x o.p. (ISBN 0-87287-116-9). Libs Unl.

Rosenberg, L. Marketing. (Illus.). 1977. 19.95 (ISBN 0-13-556100-0); wkbk. & study guide 4.95 (ISBN 0-13-556118-3). P-H.

Rosenberg, L., jt. auth. see Mandell, M.

Rosenberg, Larry J., jt. auth. see Mandell, Maurice.

Rosenberg, Leon E., jt. auth. see Scriver, Charles R.

Rosenberg, Leon J. Sangers' Pioneer Texas Merchants. LC 78-62426. (Illus.). 1978. 12.95 (ISBN 0-87611-037-5). Tex St Hist Assn.

Rosenberg, Marie E., ed. Women & Society: A Critical Review of the Literature with a Selected Annotated Bibliography. Bergstrom, Len V. LC 73-77874. 1975. 20.00x (ISBN 0-8039-0248-4). Sage.

Rosenberg, Mark L. Patients: The Experience of Illness. LC 79-67115. (Illus.). 208p. (Orig.). 1980. 14.95 o.p. (ISBN 0-03-056743-2); pap. 8.95 o.p. (ISBN 0-03-056742-4). HR&W.

Rosenberg, Marvin. The Masks of King Lear. LC 74-115492. 448p. 1972. 22.75x (ISBN 0-520-01718-8). U of Cal Pr.

--The Masks of Macbeth. 1978. 35.00x (ISBN 0-520-03262-4). U of Cal Pr.

Rosenberg, Maurice. Pretrial Conference & Effective Justice: A Controlled Test in Personal Injury Litigation. LC 64-8492. (Illus.). 1964. 20.00x (ISBN 0-231-02780-X). Columbia U Pr.

Rosenberg, Milton J., et al. Attitude Organization & Change: An Analysis of Consistency Among Attitude Components. LC 80-14704. (Yale Studies in Attitude & Communication: Vol. 3). (Illus.). x, 239p. 1980. Repr. of 1960 ed. lib. bdg. 22.25x (ISBN 0-313-22435-8, ROAT). Greenwood.

Rosenberg, N. Perspectives on Technology. LC 75-14623. 336p. 1976. 42.95 (ISBN 0-521-20957-9); pap. 12.50x (ISBN 0-521-29011-2). Cambridge U Pr.

Rosenberg, N., jt. auth. see Rosenberg, E.

Rosenberg, Neil V. Bill Monroe & His Blue Grass Boys: An Illustrated Discography. (Illus.). 122p. 1974. pap. 4.50 (ISBN 0-915608-02-2). Country Music Found.

Rosenberg, Norman D., jt. auth. see Ruggieri, George D.

Rosenberg, Norman J., ed. Drought in the Great Plains: Research on Impacts & Strategies. 1980. 16.50 (ISBN 0-918334-34-9). WRP.

--North American Droughts. LC 78-52024. (AAAS Selected Symposium Ser.). (Illus.). 1978. lib. bdg. 20.00x (ISBN 0-89158-443-9). Westview.

Rosenberg, Paul, ed. The Urban Information Thesaurus: A Vocabulary for Social Documentation. LC 76-52604. 1977. lib. bdg. 27.50 (ISBN 0-8371-9483-0, UTH/). Greenwood.

Rosenberg, Peter D. Patent Law Fundamentals. 2nd ed. LC 74-15799. 1980. 37.50 (ISBN 0-87632-098-1). Boardman.

Rosenberg, Philip, ed. Toxins: Animal, Plant & Microbial. 1978. text ed. 145.00 (ISBN 0-08-022640-X). Pergamon.

Rosenberg, Pierre. Chardin. LC 78-74107. (Illus.). 428p. 1979. 47.50x (ISBN 0-910386-48-X, Pub. by Cleveland Mus Art); pap. 32.50x (ISBN 0-910386-49-8, Pub. by Cleveland Mus Art). Ind U Pr.

Rosenberg, R. M., jt. auth. see Klotz, Irving M.

Rosenberg, R. Robert & Ott, William G. Business & the Law. (Illus.). 280p. 1975. pap. text ed. 12.25 o.p. (ISBN 0-07-053675-9, G); instructor's manual & key 6.00 o.p. (ISBN 0-07-053676-7). McGraw.

Rosenberg, Ronald C., jt. auth. see Karnopp, Dean C.

Rosenberg, Sharon & Bordow, Joan W. The Denim Book. LC 78-1984. (Creative Handcraft Ser.). (Illus.). 1978. 15.95 o.p.- (ISBN 0-13-198424-1, Spec); pap. 8.95 (ISBN 0-13-198416-0). P-H.

Rosenberg, Stephen, jt. auth. see Allan, Peter.

Rosenberg-Dishman, Marie B., jt. ed. see Een, Jo Ann D.

Rosenberger, Francis C., ed. Records of the Columbia Historical Society of Washington D.C. Incl. 1957-1959. (Illus.). 1961. 15.00x (ISBN 0-8139-0493-5); 1960-1962. (Illus.). 1963. 15.00x (ISBN 0-8139-0494-3); 1963-1965. (Illus.). 1966. 15.00x (ISBN 0-8139-0495-1); 1966-1968. (Illus.). 1969. 15.00x (ISBN 0-8139-0496-X); 1969-1970. LC 1-17677. (Illus.). 1971. 20.00x (ISBN 0-8139-0497-8); 1971-1972. 1973. 20.00x (ISBN 0-8139-0501-X); 1973-74. 1976. 20.00x (ISBN 0-685-38490-X). LC 73-84160. U Pr of Va.

--Records of the Columbia Historical Society of Washington D. C, Vol. 50. (Illus.). 550p. 1980. 20.00x (ISBN 0-8139-0866-3). U Pr of Va.

Rosenberger, Gustav. Clinical Examination of Cattle. (Illus.). 469p. 1980. 95.00 (ISBN 0-7216-7705-3). Saunders.

Rosenberger, Homer T. Adventures & Philosophy of a Pennsylvania Dutchman: An Autobiography in a Broad Setting. LC 79-165295. (Illus.). 665p. 1971. lib. bdg. 15.00 (ISBN 0-917264-03-7). Rose Hill.

--Grassroots Philosophy for the Modern Mind. LC 75-32703. (Horizons of the Humanities: Vol. 2). 255p. 1976. lib. bdg. 9.00 (ISBN 0-917264-00-2). Rose Hill.

--Man & Modern Society: Philosophical Essays. LC 72-85861. (Horizons of the Humanities Ser.: Vol. 1). 272p. 1972. lib. bdg. 8.00 (ISBN 0-917264-05-3). Rose Hill.

--The Philadelphia & Erie Railroad: Its Place in American Economic History. LC 74-75110. (Illus.). 748p. 1975. lib. bdg. 22.50 (ISBN 0-914932-02-0). Rose Hill.

--Vignettes of Philosophy: Thirty-Five Vital Subjects. LC 77-71070. (Horizons of the Humanities Ser.: Vol. 3). 258p. 1977. lib. bdg. 9.00 (ISBN 0-917264-01-0). Rose Hill.

Rosenberger, Joseph. The Burning Blue Death. (Death Merchant Ser.: No. 38). 192p. (Orig.). 1980. pap. 1.95 (ISBN 0-523-41382-3). Pinnacle Bks.

--The Cosmic Reality Kill. (Death Merchant Ser.: No. 36). (Orig.). 1979. pap. 1.95 (ISBN 0-523-41380-7). Pinnacle Bks.

--Death Merchant, No. 44. 192p. (Orig.). 1981. pap. 1.95 (ISBN 0-523-41325-4). Pinnacle Bks.

--Death Merchant No. 34: Operation Mind-Murder. 1979. pap. 1.95 (ISBN 0-523-41378-5). Pinnacle Bks.

--Death Merchant: The Devil's Trashcan, No. 45, 192p. (Orig.). 1981. pap. 1.95 (ISBN 0-523-41021-2). Pinnacle Bks.

--The Fourth Reich. (Death Merchant Ser.: No. 39). 192p. (Orig.). 1980. pap. 1.95 (ISBN 0-523-41383-1). Pinnacle Bks.

Rosenberger, Joseph N. The Death Merchant: No. 1. 1972. pap. 1.95 (ISBN 0-523-41345-9). Pinnacle Bks.

Rosenberry, Edward H. Melville. (Illus.). 1979. 17.00x (ISBN 0-7100-8989-9). Routledge & Kegan.

Rosenblatt, Bernard A. Two Generations of Zionism. LC 67-18134. 1967. 6.95 (ISBN 0-88400-017-6). Shengold.

Rosenblatt, G. M., ed. Progress in Solid State Chemistry, Vol. 12. (Illus.). 332p. 1980. 81.00 (ISBN 0-08-022846-1). Pergamon.

Rosenblatt, Jay S., et al, eds. Advances in the Study of Behavior, Vol. 11. 1980. 35.00 (ISBN 0-12-004511-7). Acad Pr.

Rosenblatt, Judah, jt. auth. see Rosenblatt, Lisa.

Rosenblatt, Jules. Key Punch. 1969. wkbk. 10.50 (ISBN 0-672-96027-3); wkbk. & kit 29.95 (ISBN 0-672-96029-X). Bobbs.

Rosenblatt, Lisa & Rosenblatt, Judah. Simplified BASIC Programming: With Companion Problems. 1973. pap. text ed. 8.95 (ISBN 0-201-06512-6). A-W.

--Simplified Fortran Programming: With Companion Problems. 1973. pap. text ed. 8.95 (ISBN 0-201-06511-8). A-W.

Rosenblatt, Louise M. The Reader, the Text, the Poem: The Transactional Theory of the Literary Work. LC 78-16335. 214p. 1978. 11.95x (ISBN 0-8093-0883-5). S Ill U Pr.

Rosenblatt, Ruth Y., jt. auth. see Beebe, Brooke M.

Rosenblatt, S. Bernard, et al. Communication in Business. 1977. 16.95 (ISBN 0-13-153262-6). P-H.

Rosenblatt, Samuel M., ed. Technology & Economic Development: A Realistic Perspective. (Special Studies in Social, Political & Economic Development). 1979. lib. bdg. 22.50x (ISBN 0-89158-474-9). Westview.

Rosenblatt, Seymour & Dodson, Reynolds. Beyond Valium: The Brave New World of Psychochemistry. 316p. 1981. 13.95 (ISBN 0-399-12577-9). Putnam.

Rosenblatt, Suzanne. Everyone Is Going Somewhere. LC 75-35920. (Illus.). 32p. (gr. k-2). 1976. 4.95 o.s.i. (ISBN 0-02-777700-6, 77770). Macmillan.

Rosenbloom. Marketing Channels. 1978. 20.95 (ISBN 0-03-017831-2). Dryden Pr.

Rosenbloom, Bert. Retail Marketing. 470p. 1981. text ed. 20.95 (ISBN 0-394-32191-X). Random.

Rosenbloom, David H. Federal Equal Employment Opportunity: Politics & Public Personnel Administration. LC 77-954. (Special Studies). 1976. text ed. 24.95 (ISBN 0-275-24420-2). Praeger.
Rosenbloom, David H., jt. auth. see Nachmias, David.
Rosenbloom, Donald T. Self-Assessment of Current Knowledge in Orthodontics. 1976. spiral bdg. 13.50 o.p. (ISBN 0-87488-244-3). Med Exam.
Rosenbloom, Jerry. A Case Study in Risk Management. 160p. 1972. pap. 11.95 (ISBN 0-13-116061-3). P-H.
Rosenbloom, Joseph. Bananas Don't Grow on Trees: A Guide to Popular Misconceptions. LC 78-57783. (Illus.). (gr. 6 up). 1978. 6.95 (ISBN 0-8069-3100-0); PLB 7.49 (ISBN 0-8069-3101-9). Sterling.
--Biggest Riddle Book in the World. LC 76-1165. (Illus.). 320p. (gr. 2 up). 1976. 7.95 (ISBN 0-8069-4532-X); PLB 8.29 (ISBN 0-8069-4533-8). Sterling.
--Consumer Complaint Guide. 8th ed. LC 73-182375. 1981. 12.50 (ISBN 0-02-469590-4). Macmillan.
--Consumer Protection Guide, 1978. LC 77-84961. 1978. pap. 4.95 (ISBN 0-02-695740-X). Macmillan Info.
--Daffy Dictionary: Funabridged Definitions from Aardvark to Zuider Zee. LC 76-51173. (Illus.). (gr. 3 up). 1977. 7.95 (ISBN 0-8069-4542-7); PLB 8.29 (ISBN 0-8069-4543-5). Sterling.
--A Dictionary of Dinosaurs. LC 80-18525. (Illus.). 96p. (gr. 4 up). 1980. PLB 8.29 (ISBN 0-671-34038-7). Messner.
--Gigantic Joke Book. LC 77-93310. (Illus.). (gr. 2 up). 1978. 7.95 (ISBN 0-8069-4590-7); PLB 8.29 (ISBN 0-8069-4591-5). Sterling.
--Maximillian, You're the Greatest. (gr. 4 up). 1980. 8.95 (ISBN 0-525-66705-9). Elsevier-Nelson.
--Monster Madness: Riddles, Jokes, & Fun. LC 80-52339. (Illus.). 128p. (gr. 2 up). 1980. 5.95 (ISBN 0-8069-4634-2); PLB 6.69 (ISBN 0-8069-4635-0). Sterling.
--Polar Bears Like It Hot. LC 79-91397. (Illus.). 160p. (gr. 8 up). 1980. 6.95 (ISBN 0-8069-4612-1); PLB 8.29 (ISBN 0-8069-4613-X). Sterling.
--Snappy Put-Downs & Funny Insults. LC 80-54348. (Illus.). 128p. (gr. 3-6). 1981. 5.95 (ISBN 0-8069-4646-6); lib. bdg. 6.69 (ISBN 0-8069-4647-4). Sterling.
Rosenbloom, P., jt. auth. see Evyatar, A.
Rosenbloom, Richard S. & Russell, John R. New Tools for Urban Management. 1971. text ed. 15.00 (ISBN 0-87584-093-0). Harvard U Pr.
Rosenbloom, Richard S., jt. auth. see McKenney, James L.
Rosenblueth, E., jt. auth. see Newmark, N. M.
Rosenblueth, Emilio, ed. Design of Earthquake Resistant Structures. LC 79-9499. 295p. 1980. 47.95x (ISBN 0-470-26839-5). Halsted Pr.
Rosenblum, Edwin E. How to Raise & Train a Brittany Spaniel. (Orig.). pap. 2.00 (ISBN 0-87666-257-2, DS1063). TFH Pubns.
--How to Raise & Train a Bull Terrier. (Orig.). pap. 2.00 (ISBN 0-87666-261-0, DS1066). TFH Pubns.
--How to Raise & Train a Staffordshire Terrier. (Orig.). pap. 2.00 (ISBN 0-87666-399-4, DS1123). TFH Pubns.
Rosenblum, Joseph, ed. The Plays of Thomas Holcroft, 2 vols. LC 78-66630. (Eighteenth Century English Drama Ser.). 1980. Set. lib. bdg. 50.00 (ISBN 0-8240-3594-1). Garland Pub.
Rosenblum, Leonard, jt. ed. see Lewis, Michael.
Rosenblum, Leonard A., ed. Primate Behavior: Developments in Field & Laboratory Research, 4 vols. Vol. 2, 1971. 40.50 (ISBN 0-12-534002-8); Vol. 3, 1974. 32.50 (ISBN 0-12-534003-6); Vol. 4, 1975. 49.00 (ISBN 0-12-534004-4). Acad Pr.
Rosenblum, Martin J. Divisions-Two. LC 77-95158. (Orig.). 1981. pap. 8.00 (ISBN 0-89018-006-7). Lionhead Pub.
--Free Verse Self. 1977. pap. text ed. 4.00 o.p. (ISBN 0-89018-005-9). Lionhead Pub.
--Scattered on: Omens & Curses. LC 74-33057. (Illus.). 80p. (Orig.). 1975. pap. 5.00x (ISBN 0-915316-04-8). Pentagram.
Rosenblum, Martin J., ed. & frwd. by. Brewing: Twenty Milwaukee Poets. LC 72-89435. 6.95 (ISBN 0-89018-008-3); soft 6.00x (ISBN 0-89018-007-5). Pentagram.
Rosenblum, Morris, jt. auth. see Nurnberg, Maxwell.
Rosenblum, Mort. Coups & Earthquakes: Reporting the World to America. LC 79-1680. 240p. 1981. pap. 4.95 (ISBN 0-06-090856-4, CN 856, CN). Har-Row.
Rosenblum, Ralph & Karen, Robert. When the Shooting Stops...the Cutting Begins: A Film Editor's Story. 1980. pap. 4.95 (ISBN 0-14-005698-X). Penguin.
Rosenblum, Richard. Wings: The Early Years of Aviation. LC 79-26363. (Illus.). 64p. (gr. 3-7). 1980. 7.95 (ISBN 0-590-07576-4, Four Winds). Schol Bk Serv.
Rosenblum, Robert. Cubism & Twentieth Century Art. 1976. pap. 13.95 (ISBN 0-13-195065-7). P-H.
--The Good Thief. 1976. pap. 1.75 o.p. (ISBN 0-345-25219-5). Ballantine.
--The International Style of Eighteen Hundred: A Study in Linear Abstraction. LC 75-23813. (Outstanding Dissertations in the Fine Arts - 18th Century). (Illus.). 1976. lib. bdg. 37.50 (ISBN 0-8240-2006-5). Garland Pub.
--The Sweetheart Deal. 1977. pap. 1.95 o.p. (ISBN 0-345-25620-4). Ballantine.
Rosenblum, Robert, ed. see De La Chavignerie, Emile B. & Auvray, Louis.
Rosenblum, Victor G. & Castberg, A. Didrick, eds. Cases on Constitutional Law: Political Roles of the Supreme Court. 1973. pap. text ed. 19.95x (ISBN 0-256-01165-6). Dorsey.
Rosenbluth, Sally. A Feast of Ashes. LC 80-13195. 1980. 12.95 (ISBN 0-689-11071-5). Atheneum.
Rosenburg, Amye, illus. One, Two, Buckle My Shoe. (Floppies Ser.). (Illus.). 6p. (ps-k). Date not set. 3.95 (ISBN 0-671-42532-3, Little Simon). S&S.
Rosencwaig, Allan. Photoacoustics & Photoacoustic Spectroscopy. LC 80-17286. (Chemical Analysis Ser.). 352p. 1980. 35.00 (ISBN 0-471-04495-4, Pub. by Wiley-Interscience). Wiley.
Rose-Neil, Sidney. Acupuncture & the Life Energies. 160p. 1981. pap. 8.95 (ISBN 0-88231-121-2). ASI Pubs Inc.
Rosenfeld, A. The Quintescence of Irving Langmuir. 1966. 15.00 (ISBN 0-08-011049-5); pap. 7.50 (ISBN 0-08-011048-7). Pergamon.
Rosenfeld, Albert. Prolongevity. 1977. pap. 2.50 (ISBN 0-380-01786-5, 35303, Discus). Avon.
Rosenfeld, Alvin H. Double Dying: Reflections on Holocaust Literature. LC 79-3006. 224p. 1980. 17.50x (ISBN 0-253-13337-8). Ind U Pr.
Rosenfeld, Anne H. Psychiatric Education: Prologue to the 1980's. Busse, Ewald W., et al, eds. 544p. 1976. 15.00 (ISBN 0-685-84651-2, P235-0). Am Psychiatric.
Rosenfeld, Arthur H., jt. ed. see Baltay, Charles.
Rosenfeld, Azriel. An Introduction to Algebraic Structures. LC 68-13895. 1968. 18.95x (ISBN 0-8162-7304-9). Holden-Day.
Rosenfeld, Clare, ed. see Chitrabkanu, Gurudev S.
Rosenfeld, Erwin & Geller, Harriet. Afro-Asian Culture Studies. rev. ed. LC 76-16066. (gr. 7-12). 1976. text ed. 9.75 o.p. (ISBN 0-8120-5122-X); pap. text ed. 5.50 o.p. (ISBN 0-8120-0648-8). Barron.
Rosenfeld, Isadore. Second Opinion. 1981. 14.95 (ISBN 0-686-68757-4, Linden). S&S.
Rosenfeld, Joseph, jt. auth. see Klotter, John C.
Rosenfeld, Lawrence. Now That We're All Here...Relations in Small Groups. (Interpersonal Communication Ser.). (Illus.). 1976. pap. text ed. 5.95x (ISBN 0-675-08642-6). Merrill.
Rosenfeld, Lulla. Bright Star of Exile: Jacob Adler & the Yiddish Theater. 1977. 12.95 o.p. (ISBN 0-690-01446-5, TYC-T). T Y Crowell.
--Death & I Ching: A/Mystery Novel. Southern, Carol, ed. 192p. 1981. 9.95 (ISBN 0-517-54029-0). Potter.
Rosenfeld, Oscar. The Phony War. Date not set. 8.95 (ISBN 0-533-04782-X). Vantage.
Rosenfeld, Sam. Story of Coins. LC 67-16903. (Story of Science Ser). (Illus.). (gr. 5 up). 1968. PLB 7.29 (ISBN 0-8178-3922-4). Harvey.
Rosenfeld, Sidney, tr. see Amery, Jean.
Rosenfeld, Stella P., tr. see Amery, Jean.
Rosenfield, A. R., et al, eds. What Does the Charpy Test Really Tell Us? 1978. 32.00 (ISBN 0-87170-027-1). ASM.
Rosenfield, Coleman R. Law of Franchising. LC 78-118362. 1970. 45.00 o.p. (ISBN 0-686-14483-X). Lawyers Co-Op.
Rosenfield, John, tr. see Noma, Seiroku.
Rosenfield, John M. The Dynastic Arts of the Kushans. (California Studies in the History of Art: No. V). 1967. 60.00x (ISBN 0-520-01091-4). U of Cal Pr.
Rosenfield, John M. & Ten Grotenhuis, Elizabeth. Journey of the Three Jewels: Japanese Buddhist Paintings from Western Collections. LC 79-15072. (Illus.). 1979. 19.95 (ISBN 0-87848-054-4). Asia Soc.
Rosenfield, John M., ed. Song of the Brush: Japanese Paintings from the Sanso Collection. (Illus.). 87p. 1979. text ed. 22.95 (ISBN 0-932216-02-1); pap. text ed. 14.95 (ISBN 0-932216-03-X). Seattle Art.
Rosenfield, Lawrence, et al. The Communicative Experience. 464p. 1976. text ed. 17.95x (ISBN 0-205-05419-6); instr's manual free (ISBN 0-205-05420-X). Allyn.
Rosenfield, Nancy S. The Radiology of Childhood Leukemia & Its Therapy. (Illus.). 164p. 1981. 17.50 (ISBN 0-87527-173-1). Green.
Rosengarten, Frederick. The Book of Spices. rev. ed. 1973. pap. 1.95 (ISBN 0-515-03220-4, Y3220). Jove Pubns.
Rosenhack, S. B. The American Government. (gr. 10-12). 1972. pap. text ed. 9.00 each incl 2 texts, tchrs' manual, & tests (ISBN 0-8449-0800-2). Learning Line.
Rosenhead, L., tr. see Prandtl, Ludwig & Tietjens, O. G.
Rosenkrantz, Barbara G. & Koelsch, William A., eds. The American Habitat: A Historical Perspective. LC 72-90281. (Illus.). 1973. 10.00 o.s.i. (ISBN 0-02-927290-4). Free Pr.
Rosenman, Martin F. Loving Styles: A Guide for Increasing Intimacy. 1979. 10.95 (ISBN 0-13-541052-5, Spec); pap. 4.95 (ISBN 0-13-541045-2). P-H.
Rosenman, Samuel I. Working with Roosevelt. LC 75-168391. (FDR & the Era of the New Deal Ser.). (Illus.). 1972. Repr. of 1952 ed. lib. bdg. 49.50 (ISBN 0-306-70328-9). Da Capo.
Rosenmeyer, Thomas G. The Green Cabinet: Theocritus & the European Pastoral Lyric. LC 78-82376. 1969. 18.50x (ISBN 0-520-01381-6); pap. 5.95x (ISBN 0-520-02362-5, CAMPUS90). U of Cal Pr.
Rosenne, S. Documents in International Court Justice. 2nd ed. 1979. 50.00 (ISBN 0-379-20460-6). Oceana.
Rosenoer, V. & Rothschild, M. A., eds. Controversies in Patient Management. LC 80-21593. (Illus.). 312p. text ed. 30.00 (ISBN 0-89335-121-0). Spectrum Pub.
Rosenoer, Victor, et al, eds. Albumin: Structure, Function & Uses. 1977. text ed. 57.00 (ISBN 0-08-019603-9). Pergamon.
Rosenof, Theodore. Dogma, Depression, and the New Deal: The Debate of Political Leaders Over Economic Recovery. 1975. 13.50 (ISBN 0-8046-9113-4, Natl U). Kennikat.
Rosenow, Frank. Manual Art: A Practical Guide to Drawing & Painting. (Illus.). 1980. 9.95 (ISBN 0-393-01398-7). Norton.
Rosenow, John E. & Pulsipher, Gerreld L. Tourism: The Good, the Bad, & the Ugly. (Illus.). 1979. 17.95 (ISBN 0-933400-44-6). Century Three.
Rosenquist, Carl M. & Megargee, Edwin I. Delinquency in Three Cultures. (Hogg Foundation Research Ser). (Illus.). 1969. 17.50 (ISBN 0-292-78415-5). U of Tex Pr.
Rosenquist, Glenn C. & Bergsma, Daniel, eds. Morphogenesis & Malinformation of the Cardiovascular System. LC 78-14527. (Alan R. Liss Ser.: Vol. 14, No. 7). 1978. 46.00 (ISBN 0-8451-1023-3). March of Dimes.
Rosenquist, Glenn C., ed. see International Workshop on Morphogenesis & Malformation, 4th, Grand Canyon, Ariz., 1977.
Rosensaft, Menachem Z. Moshe Sharett. LC 66-25854. 1966. 4.95 (ISBN 0-88400-019-2). Shengold.
Rosensfit, Gail R. Great Expectations. (Living Literature Workbook Ser.). (Orig.). (gr. 7). Date not set. pap. 1.50 (ISBN 0-671-09249-9). Monarch Pr. Postponed.
--Huckleberry Finn. (Living Literature Workbook Ser.). (Orig.). (gr. 7). Date not set. pap. 1.50 (ISBN 0-671-09248-0). Monarch Pr. Postponed.
Rosenstein, E., ed. Diccionario De Especialidades Farmaceuticas. 26th mexican ed. (Span.). 1980. pap. 35.00 (ISBN 0-914768-37-9). Drug Intl Pubns.
Rosenstein, Ira. Left on the Field to Die: Timothy Richardson, No. 1. 27p. (Orig.). 1980. pap. 2.00 (ISBN 0-9605438-0-5). Starlight Pr.
Rosenstein, Joseph & MacGinitie, Walter. Verbal Behavior of the Deaf Child: Studies of Word Meanings & Associations. LC 68-59116. 1969. pap. text ed. 4.75x (ISBN 0-8077-1720-7). Tchrs Coll.
Rosenstein, Joseph G. Linear Orderings. LC 80-2341. (Pure & Applied Mathematics Ser.). 1981. write for info. (ISBN 0-12-597680-1). Acad Pr.
Rosenstein, Neil. The Unbroken Chain. LC 75-2648. 1976. 18.95 (ISBN 0-88400-043-5). Shengold.
Rosenstein, Solomon N. Dentistry in Cerebral Palsy & Related Handicapping Conditions. (American Lecture in Cerebral Palsy Ser.). (Illus.). 184p. 1978. 18.50 (ISBN 0-398-03710-8). C C Thomas.
Rosenstein-Rodan, P. N., ed. Capital Formation & Economic Development. (Studies in the Economic Development of India). 1964. text ed. 10.95x o.p. (ISBN 0-04-330082-0). Allen Unwin.
Rosenstiehl, A. Drole d'alphabet. (Illus.). 1978. 14.75 (ISBN 2-03-051423-3, 3804). Larousse.
--Mon Premier Alphabet. (Illus.). 1978. 14.25 (ISBN 2-03-051422-5, 3803). Larousse.
Rosenstiel, Helen Von see Von Rosenstiel, Helene.
Rosenstock-Huessy, Eugen. Christian Future. pap. 3.50 (ISBN 0-912148-10-1). Argo Bks.
Rosenstock-Huessy, Eugen & Battles, Ford L. Magna Carta Latina: The Privilege of Singing, Articulating & Reading a Language & Keeping It Alive. 2nd ed. LC 75-23378. (Pittsburgh Reprint Ser.: No. 1). 1975. pap. text ed. 5.25 (ISBN 0-915138-07-7). Pickwick.
Rosenstone, Robert A. Protest from the Right. Krinsky, Fred & Boskin, Joseph, eds. (Insight Series: Studies in Contemporary Issues). 128p. 1968. pap. text ed. 4.95x (ISBN 0-02-477250-X, 47725). Macmillan.
Rosenstone, Robert A., jt. ed. see Boskin, Joseph.
Rosenthal & Rudman. Business Letter Writing Made Simple. (Span.). pap. 7.95 o.p. (ISBN 0-88332-136-X). Larousse.
Rosenthal, Alan. The Documentary Conscience: A Casebook in Film-Making. (Illus.). 1980. 19.50 (ISBN 0-520-03932-7); pap. 8.95 (ISBN 0-520-04022-8, CAL. NO. 436). U of Cal Pr.
--The New Documentary in Action: A Casebook in Film Making. 1972. 15.95 (ISBN 0-520-01888-5); pap. 2.95 (ISBN 0-520-02254-8, CAL249). U of Cal Pr.
Rosenthal, Alan S., ed. see Leukocyte Culture Conference, 9th.
Rosenthal, Alan S., jt. ed. see Unanue, Emil R.
Rosenthal, Barbara & Rosenthal, Nadia. Christmas: New Ideas for an Old-Fashioned Celebration. 1980. 12.95 (ISBN 0-517-53695-1). Potter.
Rosenthal, Bernard. Critical Essays on Charles Brockden Brown. (Critical Essays on American Literature). 1981. lib. bdg. 25.00 (ISBN 0-8161-8255-8). Twayne.
Rosenthal, Bert. Larry Bird: Cool Man on the Court. LC 80-27094. (Sport Stars Ser.). (Illus.). 48p. (gr. 2-8). 1981. PLB 7.35 (ISBN 0-516-04312-9). Childrens.
Rosenthal, Daniel. Resistance & Deformation of Solid Media. LC 72-10583. 372p. 1975. text ed. 23.00 (ISBN 0-08-017100-1). Pergamon.
Rosenthal, David. Materialism & the Mind-Body Problem. LC 77-157186. (Central Issues in Philosophy Ser). (Illus.). 1971. pap. 9.00 ref. ed. (ISBN 0-13-560177-0). P-H.
Rosenthal, David, jt. auth. see Hansen, James C.
Rosenthal, Donald B. The Expansive Elite: District Politics & State Policy-Making in India. 1977. 22.75x (ISBN 0-520-03160-1). U of Cal Pr.
Rosenthal, Donald B., ed. Urban Revitalization. LC 79-27881. (Urban Affairs Annual Reviews: Vol. 18). (Illus.). 308p. 1980. 20.00 (ISBN 0-8039-1190-4); pap. 9.95 (ISBN 0-8039-1191-2). Sage.
Rosenthal, Edwin I., ed. Averroe's Commentary on Plato's Republic. (University of Cambridge Oriental Pubns.: No. 1). 1966. 51.00 (ISBN 0-521-06130-X). Cambridge U Pr.
Rosenthal, Erwin I. Studia Semitica, 2 vols. Incl. Vol. 1. Jewish Themes. 57.00 (ISBN 0-521-07958-6); Vol. 2. Islamic Themes. 45.00 (ISBN 0-521-07959-4). (Oriental Publications Ser.: Nos. 16 & 17). Cambridge U Pr.
Rosenthal, Franz. The Classical Heritage in Islam. Marmorstein, Emile, tr. LC 69-12476. 1975. 25.75x (ISBN 0-520-01997-0). U of Cal Pr.
--History of Muslim Historiography. 1968. text ed. 93.50x (ISBN 90-04019-06-5). Humanities.
Rosenthal, Franz, ed. An Aramaic Handbook, 4 vols. LC 67-111051. 377p. 1967. Set. 52.50x (ISBN 3-447-00693-5). Intl Pubns Serv.
Rosenthal, Gary. Spalding Guide to Fitness for the Weekend Athlete. 7.95 (ISBN 0-916752-08-9). Green Hill.
Rosenthal, Gertrude, ed. Italian Paintings from the Fourteenth to the Eighteenth Century in the Collection of the Baltimore Museum of Art. LC 80-66714. 1981. pap. write for info. (ISBN 0-912298-51-0). Baltimore Mus.
Rosenthal, Harold. Covent Garden. (Folio Miniature Ser.). 1979. 4.95 (ISBN 0-7181-1474-4, Pub. by Michael Joseph). Merrimack Bk Serv.
--Five Hundred Five Football Questions Your Friends Can't Answer. 192p. 9.95 (ISBN 0-8027-0661-4); pap. 5.95 (ISBN 0-8027-7163-7). Walker & Co.
--The Ten Best Years of Baseball: An Informal History of the Fifties. 184p. 1981. pap. 5.95 (ISBN 0-442-27063-1). Van Nos Reinhold.
--The Ten Best Years of Baseball: An Informal History of the 50's. 1979. 8.95 o.p. (ISBN 0-8092-7362-4). Contemp Bks.
Rosenthal, Harold & Warrack, John, eds. The Concise Oxford Dictionary of Opera. 2nd ed. (Out-of-Ser. Paperback). 576p. 1981. pap. 11.95 (ISBN 0-19-311321-X). Oxford U Pr.
Rosenthal, Irving & Rudman, Harry W. Business Letter Writing Made Simple. rev. ed. pap. 3.50 (ISBN 0-385-01206-3, Made). Doubleday.

Rosenthal, Jean & Wertenbaker, Lael. Magic of Light. LC 72-6465. (Illus.). 1973. 15.00 (ISBN 0-87830-075-9, Co-Pub by Little). Theatre Arts.
Rosenthal, Joan. The Lord Is My Strength. (Orig.). pap. 1.25 (ISBN 0-89129-086-9). Jove Pubns.
--Lord Is My Strength. 1976. pap. 1.25 (ISBN 0-89129-086-9). Jove Pubns.
Rosenthal, Joseph H. The Neuropsychopathology of Written Language. LC 77-2825. 1977. 16.95 (ISBN 0-88229-382-6). Nelson-Hall.
Rosenthal, Kristine M. & Keshet, Harry F. Fathers Without Partners: A Study of Fathers & the Family After Marital Separation. 1981. 15.95x (ISBN 0-8476-6281-0). Rowman.
Rosenthal, Linda, jt. auth. see McKay, Sandra.
Rosenthal, Lois. Buy It for Less (Cincinnati) 144p. 1980. pap. 3.95 (ISBN 0-89879-033-6). Writers Digest.
--Buy It for Less (Detroit) 144p. 1980. pap. 3.95 (ISBN 0-89879-037-9). Writers Digest.
--Buy It for Less (Pittsburgh) 120p. 1980. pap. 3.95 (ISBN 0-89879-038-7). Writers Digest.
Rosenthal, M. L. Poetry & the Common Life. 1974. 12.95 (ISBN 0-19-501838-9). Oxford U Pr.
--The View from the Peacock's Tail: Poems. 64p. 1972. 12.95 (ISBN 0-19-501593-2). Oxford U Pr.
Rosenthal, Marvin J. Not Without Design. (Illus.). 1980. pap. 2.95 (ISBN 0-915540-27-4). Friends Israel-Spearhead Pr.
Rosenthal, Michael. Hogarth. (Oresko-Jupiter Art Bks). (Illus.). 96p. 1981. 17.95 (ISBN 0-933516-81-9, Pub. by Oresko-Jupiter England). Hippocrene Bks.
--Virginia Woolf. LC 79-12161. 1979. 20.00x (ISBN 0-231-04848-3). Columbia U Pr.
Rosenthal, Murray P. How to Select & Use Hi-Fi & Stereo Equipment. 1979. pap. 9.85 (ISBN 0-8104-0424-9). Hayden.
--How to Select & Use Hi-Fi & Stereo Equipment, Vol. 2. (Illus.). 1969. pap. 4.55 o.p. (ISBN 0-8104-0341-2). Hayden.
--How to Select & Use Record Players. 1979. pap. 6.50 (ISBN 0-8104-0833-3). Hayden.
--Mini-Micro Soldering & Wire Wrapping. 1978. pap. 4.75 (ISBN 0-8104-0864-3). Hayden.
--Understanding Integrated Circuits. (Illus.). 128p. 1975. pap. text ed. 5.95 (ISBN 0-8104-5526-9). Hayden.
Rosenthal, Nadia, jt. auth. see Rosenthal, Barbara.
Rosenthal, R. & Rosnow, R. L., eds. Artifact in Behavioral Research. (Social Psychology Ser). 1969. 15.50 (ISBN 0-12-597750-6). Acad Pr.
Rosenthal, Raymond, tr. see Chastel, Andre.
Rosenthal, Robert & Rosnow, Ralph L. The Volunteer Subject. LC 74-16378. (Personality Processes Ser). 288p. 1975. 23.95 (ISBN 0-471-73670-8, Pub. by Wiley-Interscience). Wiley.
Rosenthal, Robert, et al. Different Strokes: Pathways to Maturity in the Boston Ghetto. LC 76-7952. 1976. 27.50x (ISBN 0-89158-036-0); pap. 11.00x (ISBN 0-89158-047-6). Westview.
--PONS (Profile of Nonverbal Sensitivity) Test Manual. (Illus.). 1979. pap. text ed. 8.95x (ISBN 0-89197-647-7). Irvington.
Rosenthal, S., et al, eds. see FEBS Meeting, 12th, Dresden, 1978.
Rosenthal, Sandra. The Pragmatic a Priori. LC 75-41707. 104p. 1975. 10.00 (ISBN 0-87527-142-1). Fireside Bks.
Rosenthal, Sandra & Bourgeois, Patrick L. Pragmatism & Phenomenology: A Philosophic Encounter. 199p. 1980. text ed. 23.00x (ISBN 90-6032-179-0). Humanities.
Rosenthal, Sylvia. Cosmetic Surgery: A Consumers Guide. LC 76-58921. (Illus.). 1977. 10.95 o.p. (ISBN 0-397-01211-X). Lippincott.
--Live High on Low Fat. new rev. enlarged ed. LC 75-8938. 1975. 9.95 o.s.i. (ISBN 0-397-01060-5). Lippincott.
Rosenthall, David, tr. see Rodoreda, Merce.
Rosenthal-Schneider, Ilse. Reality & Scientific Truth: Discussions with Einstein, Von Laue, & Planck. Braun, Thomas, ed. (Illus.). 150p. 1981. 9.95 (ISBN 0-8143-1650-6). Wayne St U Pr.
Rosenvold, Lloyd. Drop Your Blood Pressure. 176p. (Orig.). 1980. pap. 2.50 (ISBN 0-515-05721-5). Jove Pubns.
Rosenwald, G. C., jt. auth. see Riegel, K. F.
Rosenwald, Henry, ed. see Mann, Thomas.
Rosenwater, Irving. Sir Donald Bradman: A Biography. 1978. 35.00 (ISBN 0-7134-0664-X, Pub. by Batsford England). David & Charles.
Rosenweig, Efraim M. We Jews: Invitation to a Dialogue. LC 77-81359. 1978. 7.95 (ISBN 0-8015-8428-0, Hawthorn). Dutton.
Rosenzweig, Franz. Star of Redemption. Hallo, William W., tr. 464p. 1972. pap. 3.95 o.p. (ISBN 0-8070-1129-0, BP441). Beacon Pr.
Rosenzweig, James, jt. auth. see Kast, Fremont.
Rosenzweig, James, jt. auth. see Kast, Fremont E.
Rosenzweig, Mark, jt. auth. see Mussen, Paul.
Rosenzweig, Mark R. & Brown, T. A., eds. Intelligence & Affectivity: Their Relationship During Child Development. Brown, T. A. & Kaegi, C. E., trs. (Illus.). 1981. 8.00 (ISBN 0-8243-2901-5). Annual Reviews.
Rosenzweig, Mark R. & Porter, Lyman W., eds. Annual Review of Psychology, Vol. 32. LC 50-13143. (Illus.). 1981. text ed. 20.00 (ISBN 0-8243-0232-X). Annual Reviews.
Rosenzweig, Norman. Psychopharmacology & Psychotherapy: Synthesis or Antithesis? LC 78-4088. 1978. text ed. 22.95 (ISBN 0-87705-354-5). Human Sci Pr.
Rosenzweig, Saul. Aggressive Behavior & the Rosenzweig Picture-Frustration Study. LC 78-18200. (Praeger Special Studies). 1978. 22.95 (ISBN 0-03-045656-8). Praeger.
--Freud & the Kingmaker: The Visit to America - The Letters of Sigmund Freud & G. S. Hall, 1908 to 1923 & Freud's Five Lectures at Clark University. LC 78-65156. 1981. 13.50 (ISBN 0-930172-03-5). Rana Hse.
--The Rosenzweig Picture-Frustration (P-F) Study--Basic Manual. LC 77-95428. 1978. 8.00 (ISBN 0-930172-02-7); pap. 3.50 o.p. (ISBN 0-685-06633-9). Rana Hse.
Rosenzweig, Victor M., jt. auth. see Frome, Robert L.
Roser, Nancy, jt. auth. see Farr, Roger.
Roseveare, Helen. Living Faith. (Orig.). 1981. pap. 3.95 (ISBN 0-8024-4941-7). Moody.
Roseveare, Henry. Treasury: The Evolution of a British Institution. 1970. 17.50x (ISBN 0-231-03405-9). Columbia U Pr.
Rosewall & Wilson. Diet Training for Sportsmen. pap. 1.00x (ISBN 0-392-07230-0, SpS). Soccer.
Rosewall, Ken. Ken Rosewall on Tennis. LC 78-18730. (Illus.). 1978. 9.95 (ISBN 0-8119-0334-6); pap. 4.95 (ISBN 0-8119-0386-9). Fell.
Roshal, A., jt. auth. see Karpov, Anatoly.
Roshko, Anatol, et al see Heat Transfer & Fluid Mechanics Institute.
Rosichan, R. H. Stamps & Coins. LC 73-90498. (Spare Time Guides Ser.: No. 5). 225p. 1974. lib. bdg. 13.50 o.p. (ISBN 0-87287-071-5). Libs Unl.
Rosier, John De see De Rosier, John.
Rosier, M. J. Changes in Secondary School Mathematics in Australia, 1964-1978. (ACER Research Monographs: No. 8). 1980. pap. 20.00 (ISBN 0-85563-208-9). Verry.
Rosier, Paul & Holm, Wayne. The Rock Point Experience: A Longitudinal Study of a Navajo School Program (Saad Naaki Bee Na'nitin) LC 80-19695. (Bilingual Education Ser.: No. 8). 95p. (Orig.). 1980. pap. text ed. 6.50 (ISBN 0-87281-119-0). Ctr Appl Ling.
Rosignoli, Guido. Army Badges & Insignia of World War II: Great Britain, Poland, Belgium, Italy, USSR, Germany. (Illus.). 228p. 1980. 10.95 (ISBN 0-7137-0697-X, Pub. by Blandford Pr England). Sterling.
--Army Badges & Insignia of World War 2, Book 2. LC 72-85765. (Illus.). 208p. 1976. 8.95 (ISBN 0-02-605080-3, 60508). Macmillan.
--Army Badges & Insignia Since 1945. (Illus.). 218p. 1980. 9.95 (ISBN 0-7137-0648-1, Pub. by Blandford Pr England). Sterling.
Rosine, L. L., ed. Advances in Electronic Circuit Packaging, Vol. 5. 297p. 1965. 25.00 (ISBN 0-686-64908-7, Plenum Pr). Plenum Pub.
Rosing, Kenneth E., jt. auth. see Odell, Peter R.
Rositzke, Harry. KGB: The Eyes of Russia. LC 80-2063. 288p. 1981. 14.95 (ISBN 0-385-15390-2). Doubleday.
Roskamp, Karl W., ed. see International Institute of Public Finance, 35th Congress, 1979.
Roskies, David G, jt. auth. see Roskies, Diane K.
Roskies, Diane K. & Roskies, David G. The Shtetl Book. pap. 8.95x (ISBN 0-685-56215-8). Ktav.
Roskill, Mark, ed. The Letters of Vincent Van Gogh. LC 63-13089. 1963. pap. 4.95 (ISBN 0-689-70167-5). Atheneum.
Roskill, Stephen. Admiral of the Fleet, Earl Beatty: The Last Naval Hero. LC 80-19778. 1981. 19.95 (ISBN 0-689-11119-3). Atheneum.
--Churchill & the Admirals. LC 78-57070. (Illus.). 1978. 12.95 o.p. (ISBN 0-688-03364-4). Morrow.
Roskill, Stephen W. The Strategy of Sea Power: Its Development & Application. LC 80-27028. (Lees-Knowles Lecture Ser., Cambridge, 1961). 287p. 1981. Repr. of 1962 ed. lib. bdg. 27.50x (ISBN 0-313-22801-9, ROSSP). Greenwood.
Roskin, Michael. Other Governments of Europe: Sweden, Spain, Italy, Yugoslavia, E. Germany. 1977. pap. text ed. 7.95 (ISBN 0-13-642959-9). P-H.
Rosland, Margaret, tr. see Linhart, Robert.
Rosler, Lee. Opportunities in Life Insurance Selling. LC 65-19433. 1965. pap. 4.95 (ISBN 0-89022-006-9). Farnswth Pub.
Roslin-Williams, Mary. All About the Labrador. (All About Ser.). (Illus.). 1980. 16.95 (ISBN 0-7207-1218-1, Pub. by Michael Joseph). Merrimack Bk Serv.
Rosman, Abraham & Rubel, Paula G. Feasting with Mine Enemy: Rank & Exchange Among Northwest Coast Societies. LC 74-133033. 1971. 17.50x (ISBN 0-231-03483-0). Columbia U Pr.
--The Tapestry of Culture. 1981. pap. text ed. 10.95x (ISBN 0-673-15281-2). Scott F.
Rosmond, Babette. Monarch. 1980. pap. 2.25 o.p. (ISBN 0-425-04147-6). Berkley Pub.
Rosner, Bernard & Beckerman, Jay. Inside the World of Miniatures & Dollhouses: A Comprehensive Guide to Collecting & Creating. LC 76-16458. (Illus.). 256p. 1976. 17.95 o.p. (ISBN 0-679-50617-9); pap. 9.95 (ISBN 0-679-50620-9). McKay.
Rosner, Jerome. Auditory Analysis Skillsbook. (gr. k-3). 1981. 17.50 (ISBN 0-8027-9127-1). Walker & Co.
--Basic Decoding Skillsbook. (gr. k-3). 1981. 10.80 (ISBN 0-8027-9128-X). Walker & Co.
--Helping Children Overcome Learning Difficulties: A Step-by-Step Guide for Parents & Teachers. 2nd, rev. ed. (Illus.). 377p. pap. 98.95 (ISBN 0-8027-7178-5). Walker & Co.
--Perceptual Skills Curriculum, 4 programs. Incl. Introductory Guide. LC 73-83888. 96p. tchr's ed. 7.50 (ISBN 0-8027-8025-3); Prog. 1. Visual-Motor Skills. 327p. pap. text ed. 24.90 (ISBN 0-8027-8026-1); Prog. 2. Auditory Motor Skills. 304p. pap. text ed. 15.95 (ISBN 0-8027-8027-X); Prog. 3. General Motor Skills. 144p. pap. text ed. 7.95 (ISBN 0-8027-8028-8); Prog. 4. Introducing Letters & Numerals, Pts. 1 & 2. 562p. pap. text ed. 46.90 (ISBN 0-8027-8029-6). 1973. Walker Educ.
--Visual Perceptual Skillsbook. (gr. k-3). 1981. 11.70 (ISBN 0-8027-9126-3). Walker & Co.
Rosner, Jonathon L., tr. see Novozhilov, Yuri V.
Rosner, Martic C. Hormones & Hyacinths. LC 79-82087. 1980. 5.95 (ISBN 0-87212-126-7). Libra.
Rosner, Menachem, tr. see Leviatan, Uri.
Rosner, Roy D. Packet Switching: Tomorrow's Communications Today. (Illus.). 1981. text ed. 31.50. Lifetime Learn.
Rosner, Ruth, jt. auth. see Durrell, Julie.
Rosner, Stanley & Abt, Lawrence. Essays in Creativity. LC 74-11096. 214p. 1974. 15.00x (ISBN 0-88427-012-2); pap. 6.95 o.p. (ISBN 0-88427-013-0, Dist. by Caroline Hse). North River.
Rosnow, R. L., jt. ed. see Rosenthal, R.
Rosnow, Ralph, ed. see Goldstein, Jeffrey H.
Rosnow, Ralph L. Paradigms in Transition: The Methodology of Social Inquiry. 176p. 1981. text ed. 12.00x (ISBN 0-19-502876-7); pap. text ed. 5.95 (ISBN 0-19-502877-5). Oxford U Pr.
Rosnow, Ralph L., jt. auth. see Rosenthal, Robert.
Rosof, Patricia J. & Zeisel, William, eds. Urban History: Reviews of Recent Research. (Trends in History Ser.: Vol. 2, No. 1). 112p. 1980. write for info. (ISBN 0-917724-26-7). Haworth Pr.
Rosoff, Arnold J. Informed Consent: A Guide for Health Care Providers. 300p. 1981. text ed. 37.50 (ISBN 0-89443-293-1). Aspen Systems.
Rosoff, Betty, jt. ed. see Tobach, Ethel.
Rosovsky, Henry, jt. ed. see Patrick, Hugh.
Rosow, I. Social Integration of the Aged. LC 67-15059. 1967. 17.95 (ISBN 0-02-927350-1). Free Pr.
Rosow, James M., ed. Productivity: Prospects for Growth. (Work in America Ser.). 288p. 1981. text ed. 19.95 (ISBN 0-442-29326-7). Van Nos Reinhold.
Rosow, Jerome M., ed. The Worker & the Job: Coping with Change. LC 74-765. (An American Assembly Bk.). (Illus.). 224p. 1974. 7.95 (ISBN 0-13-965350-3, Spec); pap. 2.95 (ISBN 0-13-965350-3, Spec). P-H.
Ross & Sellmeyer. School Publications: A Guidebook. 11.95x o.p. (ISBN 0-205-04195-7, 5141958). Allyn.
Ross, Al. Cartooning Fundamentals. LC 77-1201. (Illus.). 1977. 11.95 (ISBN 0-87396-080-7). Stravon.
Ross, Alan O. Learning Disability: The Unrealized Potential. (McGraw-Hill Paperbacks). 228p. 1980. pap. 4.95 (ISBN 0-07-053878-6, P&RB). McGraw.
Ross, Alec. Words for Work: Writing Fundamentals for Technical-Vocational Students. (Illus., Orig.). 1970. pap. text ed. 8.50 (ISBN 0-395-05333-1). HM.
Ross, Alexander. Mystagogus Poeticus, or the Muses Interpreter. 2nd ed. Orgel, Stephen, ed. LC 75-27875. (Renaissance & the Gods Ser.: Vol. 30). (Illus.). 1976. Repr. of 1648 ed. lib. bdg. 73.00 (ISBN 0-8240-2079-0). Garland Pub.
--Red River Settlement. Repr. 12.50 o.p. (ISBN 0-87018-055-X). Ross.
Ross, Alf. On Guilt, Responsibility & Punishment. LC 73-94446. 1975. 17.50x (ISBN 0-520-02717-5). U of Cal Pr.
--On Law & Justice. (California Library Repr). 1975. Repr. of 1959 ed. 23.75x (ISBN 0-520-02851-1). U of Cal Pr.
Ross, Allan. Techniques for Beginning Conductors. 1976. pap. text ed. 16.95x (ISBN 0-534-00403-2). Wadsworth Pub.
Ross, Angus. The Ampurias Exchange. 1977. 6.95 o.s.i. (ISBN 0-8027-5364-7). Walker & Co.
--The Hamburg Switch. 192p. 1980. 9.95 o.s.i. (ISBN 0-8027-5418-X). Walker & Co.
Ross, Ann. The Murder Cure. 1978. pap. 1.50 o.p. (ISBN 0-380-40915-1, 40915). Avon.
Ross, Anne. The Folklore of the Scottish Highlands. (Folklore of the British Isles Ser.). (Illus.). 174p. 1976. 11.50x (ISBN 0-87471-836-8). Rowman.
--Pagan Celtic Britain: Studies in Iconography & Tradition. LC 67-16099. (Illus.). 1967. 30.00x (ISBN 0-231-03058-4). Columbia U Pr.
Ross, Anne, jt. auth. see Place, Robin.
Ross, Bernard H., ed. Urban Management: A Guide to Information Sources. LC 78-10310. (The Urban Studies Information Guide Ser.: Vol. 8). 1979. 30.00 (ISBN 0-8103-1430-4). Gale.
Ross, Bette M. Our Special Child: A Guide to Successful Parenting of Handicapped Children. LC 80-54815. 192p. 1981. 12.95 (ISBN 0-8027-0678-9). Walker & Co.
Ross, Betty, tr. see Maser, Werner.
Ross, Betty, tr. see Schoeck, Helmut.
Ross, Bob L. Killing Effects of Calvinism. 1980. pap. 1.25. Pilgrim Pubns.
--Pictorial Biography of C. H. Spurgeon. 1976. 3.95 (ISBN 0-686-16830-5); pap. 2.25 (ISBN 0-686-16831-3). Pilgrim Pubns.
Ross, Carole D. & Kennedy, Aileen. Introductory Biology Laboratory Manual. 1979. pap. text ed. 6.95 o.p. (ISBN 0-8403-2086-8). Kendall-Hunt.
Ross, Caroline. Miss Nobody. 256p. 1981. 10.95 (ISBN 0-312-92536-0). St Martin.
Ross, Charles. Edward the Fourth. LC 74-79771. (English Monarchs Ser). (Illus.). 1975. 35.00x (ISBN 0-520-02781-7). U of Cal Pr.
--The Inner Sanctuary. 1967. pap. 2.45 (ISBN 0-686-12520-7). Banner of Truth.
Ross, Charles P. & Rouse, T. L. Early Day History of Wilbarger County. 7.95 o.p. (ISBN 0-685-48811-X). Nortex Pr.
Ross, Clarissa. Beloved Scoundrel. 1980. pap. 1.95 (ISBN 0-8439-0710-X, Leisure Bks). Nordon Pubns.
--Eternal Desire. 1979. pap. 2.50 (ISBN 0-515-04818-6). Jove Pubns.
--The Jade Princess. 1977. pap. 1.95 o.s.i. (ISBN 0-515-04033-9). Jove Pubns.
--Kashmiri Passions. (Orig.). 1978. pap. 2.25 o.s.i. (ISBN 0-446-82839-4). Warner Bks.
--A Scandalous Affair. 1977. pap. 1.50 (ISBN 0-505-51213-0). Tower Bks.
--Tangier Nights. 288p. (Orig.). 1981. pap. 2.75 (ISBN 0-515-05368-6). Jove Pubns.
--Venetian Moon. (Original Historical Romance Ser.). 288p. 1980. pap. 2.75 (ISBN 0-515-04817-8, Jove). BJ Pub Group.
Ross, Cleon. Plant Physiology Laboratory Manual. 1974. 10.95x (ISBN 0-534-00351-6). Wadsworth Pub.
Ross, Cleon W., jt. ed. see Salisbury, Frank B.
Ross, Corinne. To Market to Market. (Illus.). 1980. pap. 4.50 (ISBN 0-89182-022-1). Charles River.
Ross, Corinne M. The New England Guest House Book. LC 79-4899. (Illus.). 192p. 1979. lib. bdg. 10.25 o.p. (ISBN 0-914788-15-9). East Woods.
--The Southern Guest House Book. (Illus.). 192p. 1981. pap. 6.95 (ISBN 0-914788-35-3). East Woods.
Ross, Corinne M. & Woodward, Ralph. New England: Off the Beaten Path, a Guide to Unusual Places. (Illus.). 128p. 1981. pap. 4.95 (ISBN 0-914788-40-X). East Woods.
Ross, D. Aristote. (Publications Gramma Ser.). 1971. 26.50x (ISBN 0-685-33030-3). Gordon.
--Energy from the Waves. 2nd rev. ed. LC 80-41076. (Illus.). 160p. 1981. 21.00 (ISBN 0-08-026715-7); pap. 9.00 (ISBN 0-686-68875-9). Pergamon.
--Energy from the Waves. (Illus.). 1979. text ed. 23.00 (ISBN 0-08-023271-X); pap. text ed. 8.25 (ISBN 0-686-67668-8). Pergamon.
Ross, D. B. & Guder, W. G., eds. Biochemical Aspects of Renal Function: Proceedings of a Symposium Held in Honour of Professor Sir Hans Krebs FRS, at Merton College, Oxford, 16-19 September 1979. (Illus.). 340p. pap. 55.00 (ISBN 0-08-025517-5). Pergamon.
Ross, D. F. & Spencer, S. H. Aphasia Rehabilitation. (Illus.). 272p. 1980. 19.50 (ISBN 0-398-04031-1); pap. 14.75 (ISBN 0-398-04024-9). C C Thomas.
Ross, D. O. Backgrounds to Augustan Poetry, Gallus, Elegy & Rome. LC 74-31782. 260p. 1975. 32.00 (ISBN 0-521-20704-5). Cambridge U Pr.
Ross, D. W., et al, eds. Automation in Hematology: What to Measure & Why. (Illus.). 730p. 1981. pap. 46.00 (ISBN 0-387-10225-6). Springer-Verlag.

Ross, Dana F. California! (Wagons West Ser.). 384p. (Orig.). 1981. pap. 2.95 (ISBN 0-553-14260-7). Bantam.
--Texas! (The Wagons West Ser.). 368p. (Orig.). 1980. pap. 2.75 (ISBN 0-553-13980-0). Bantam.
Ross, Dave. How to Keep Warm in Winter. LC 79-6838. (Illus.). 32p. (Orig.). 1980. PLB 6.89 (ISBN 0-690-04077-6, TYC-J); pap. 3.95 (ISBN 0-690-04060-1). T Y Crowell.
--Making Robots. (gr. 1-3). 1980. PLB 7.90 (ISBN 0-531-04142-5). Watts.
--Making Space Puppets. (gr. 1-3). 1980. PLB 7.90 (ISBN 0-531-04143-3). Watts.
--Making UFOs. (gr. 1-3). 1980. PLB 7.90 (ISBN 0-531-04144-1). Watts.
--Space Monster. (Illus.). 32p. (gr. 2-5). 1981. PLB 6.85 (ISBN 0-8027-6415-0). Walker & Co.
Ross, Dave & Wilson, Jeanne. Mr. Terwilliger's Secret. (Easy-Read Story Bk.). (Illus.). 32p. (gr. k-3). 1981. 3.95 (ISBN 0-531-02472-5). Watts.
Ross, David. Introduction to Oceanography. 2nd ed. LC 76-17838. (Illus.). 1977. text ed. 19.95 (ISBN 0-13-491332-9). P-H.
Ross, David H., jt. ed. see Loh, Horace H.
Ross, David P., Jr., ed. see Adams, Russell L.
Ross, David R., et al, eds. Nation in Crisis 1828-1865. LC 78-101951. (AHM Structure of American History Ser: Vol. 3). 1970. pap. 4.95x (ISBN 0-88295-757-0). AHM Pub.
--Progress, War & Reaction: 1900-1933. LC 78-101951. (Structure of American History Ser: Vol. 5). 1970. pap. 4.95x (ISBN 0-88295-759-7). AHM Pub.
Ross, Davis R. Preparing for Ulysses: Politics & Veterans During World War Two. (Contemporary American History Ser). 1969. 22.50x (ISBN 0-231-03222-6). Columbia U Pr.
Ross, Diana. I Love My Love with an A. (Illus.). (ps-5). 1972. 6.95 (ISBN 0-571-09340-X, Pub. by Faber & Faber). Merrimack Bk Serv.
--Little Red Engine & the Rocket. (gr. k-2). 12.50 (ISBN 0-571-05256-8). Transatlantic.
--Little Red Engine & the Taddlecombe Outing. (gr. 1-3). 1969. 7.95 (ISBN 0-571-08697-7). Transatlantic.
--Little Red Engine Goes Carolling. (gr. 1-3). 1971. 7.95 (ISBN 0-571-09775-8). Transatlantic.
--Little Red Engine Goes to Market. (Illus.). (gr. k-2). 7.95 (ISBN 0-571-06330-6). Transatlantic.
--Little Red Engine Goes to Town. (Illus.). (gr. k-2). 7.95 (ISBN 0-571-06420-5). Transatlantic.
--Old Perisher. (Illus.). (ps-5). 1965. 6.95 (ISBN 0-571-06162-1, Pub. by Faber & Faber). Merrimack Bk Serv.
Ross, Donald H. The Writing Performance. LC 73-463. 240p. 1973. pap. text ed. 3.95 o.p. (ISBN 0-397-47284-6). Lippincott.
Ross, Donald M., jt. auth. see Sutton, George A.
Ross, Dorothea M. & Ross, Sheila A. Fundamental Skills & Concepts 1: Language Arts Lessons for Grades 1-3. (Makemaster Bk.). 1980. pap. 14.95 (ISBN 0-8224-0291-2). Pitman Learning.
--Fundamental Skills & Concepts 2: Arithmetic Lessons for Grades 1-3. (Makemaster Bk.). 1980. pap. 14.95 (ISBN 0-8224-0292-0). Pitman Learning.
--Hyperactivity: Research, Theory & Action. LC 76-5227. (Personality Processes Ser.). 480p. 1976. 29.95 (ISBN 0-471-73678-3, Pub. by Wiley-Interscience). Wiley.
Ross, Dorothy, jt. auth. see Driscole, Dee.
Ross, Douglas A., jt. auth. see Mueller, Peter G.
Ross, E. D., tr. see Haidar, Mirza M.
Ross, E. Denison. This English Language. LC 73-167147. 266p. 1973. Repr. of 1939 ed. 18.00 (ISBN 0-8103-3184-5). Gale.
Ross, E. Denison, Jr. The Persians. 142p. 1980. Repr. lib. bdg. 30.00 (ISBN 0-89987-713-3). Darby Bks.
Ross, E. K. On Death & Dying. 1969. 9.95 (ISBN 0-685-44001-X); pap. 1.95 (ISBN 0-02-089130-X, 08913). Macmillan.
Ross, Edward D. Islam. LC 79-2880. 127p. 1981. Repr. of 1931 ed. 14.50 (ISBN 0-8305-0048-0). Hyperion Conn.
Ross, Edyth L., ed. Black Heritage in Social Welfare: 1860-1930. LC 78-8403. 1978. 24.00 (ISBN 0-8108-1145-6). Scarecrow.
Ross, Elaine, jt. auth. see Elkon, Juliette.
Ross, Elizabeth. The Three Little Pigs. (Illus.). (ps-1). 1973. PLB 5.00 (ISBN 0-307-61544-8, Golden Pr). Western Pub.
Ross, Elizabeth D. The Kindergarten Crusade: The Establishment of Preschool Education in the United States. LC 75-36986. ix, 119p. 1976. 9.00x (ISBN 0-8214-0206-4); pap. 4.25 o.s.i. (ISBN 0-8214-0228-5). Ohio U Pr.
Ross, Eric. Beyond the River & the Bay: The Canadian Northwest in 1811. LC 71-486954. (Illus.). 1970. pap. 4.50 (ISBN 0-8020-6188-5). U of Toronto Pr.
Ross, Eric B., ed. Beyond the Myths of Culture: Essays in Cultural Materialism. LC 79-6772. (Studies in Anthropology Ser.). 1980. 31.00 (ISBN 0-12-598180-5). Acad Pr.
Ross, Eulalie S., ed. Lost Half-Hour: A Collection of Stories. LC 65-23537. (Illus.). (gr. 4-6). 1963. 5.95 o.p. (ISBN 0-15-249360-3, HJ). HarBraceJ.
Ross, Floyd H. & Hills, Tynette. Great Religions By Which Men Live. Orig. Title: Questions That Matter Most Asked by the World's Religions. 1977. pap. 2.50 (ISBN 0-449-30825-1, Prem). Fawcett.
Ross, Frank. Dead Runner. 1978. pap. 1.75 o.p. (ISBN 0-449-23454-1, Crest). Fawcett.
--The Shining Day. LC 80-69394. 1981. 12.95 (ISBN 0-689-11111-8). Atheneum.
--The Sixty-Fifth Tape. 304p. 1980. pap. 2.50 (ISBN 0-553-13747-6). Bantam.
Ross, Frank, Jr. Arabs & the Islamic World. LC 78-13219. (Illus.). (gr. 7 up). 1979. 10.95 (ISBN 0-87599-220-X). S G Phillips.
--Historic Plane Models: Their Stories & How to Make Them. LC 72-9361. (Illus.). 160p. (gr. 5-12). 1973. PLB 7.92 o.p. (ISBN 0-688-50046-3); pap. 2.95 (ISBN 0-688-45046-6). Lothrop.
--The Metric System: Measures for All Mankind. LC 74-14503. (Illus.). 128p. (gr. 7-10). 1974. 10.95 (ISBN 0-87599-198-X). S G Phillips.
--Racing Cars & Great Races. LC 74-177329. (Illus.). 192p. (gr. 5-12). 1972. 8.25 o.p. (ISBN 0-688-41634-9); PLB 7.92 (ISBN 0-688-51634-3). Lothrop.
--Stories of the States: A Reference Guide to the Fifty States & the U. S. Territories. LC 68-24585. (Illus.). (gr. 5 up). 1969. 12.95 (ISBN 0-690-77849-X, TYC-J). T Y Crowell.
--The Tin Lizzie: A Model-Making Book. LC 80-14482. (Illus.). (gr. 5 up). 1980. 8.95 (ISBN 0-688-41931-3); PLB 8.59 (ISBN 0-688-51931-8). Lothrop.
--Undersea Vechicles & Habitats: The Peaceful Uses of the Ocean. LC 76-106577. (Illus.). (gr. 5-8). 1970. 10.95 (ISBN 0-690-84416-6, TYC-J). T Y Crowell.
Ross, G. R., ed. see Descartes, Rene.
Ross, Gordon N., ed. see Markham, Gervase & Sampson, Willliam.
Ross, Gregory A. Grounds for Grammar. 1976. pap. text ed. 7.50x (ISBN 0-8191-0063-3). U Pr of Amer.
Ross, H. K., ed. Great Story Poems - Collection. (Illus.). 160p. 1981. PLB 6.95. Lion.
Ross, H. L. Settled Out of Court. 2nd ed. 1980. 14.95 (ISBN 0-686-65269-X); pap. 7.95 class lots of twenty or more (ISBN 0-202-30296-2). Aldine Pub.
--Wonderful Window Word Book. LC 79-1910. (Illus.). (ps-k). 1979. 1.95 (ISBN 0-525-69018-2, Gingerbread Bks); PLB 5.95 o.p. (ISBN 0-525-69019-0). Dutton.
Ross, Harold R., jt. auth. see Fluharty, George.
Ross, Harold R., jt. auth. see Fluharty, George W.
Ross, Harriet, compiled by. Exciting Western Stories. (Illus.). 160p. (gr. 4-7). 1981. PLB 7.21 (ISBN 0-87460-312-9). Lion.
Ross, Harriet, ed. Great Adventure Stories. LC 60-6579. (Illus.). 160p. (YA) 1979. PLB 6.99 (ISBN 0-87460-180-0); pap. 1.95 (ISBN 0-87460-181-9). Lion.
--Great Detective Stories. LC 64-24881. (Illus.). 160p. (YA) 1981. PLB 6.99 (ISBN 0-87460-186-X); pap. 1.95 (ISBN 0-87460-187-8). Lion.
--Great Horror Stories. new ed. LC 64-24882. (Illus.). 160p. (YA) 1981. PLB 6.99 (ISBN 0-87460-188-6); pap. 1.95 (ISBN 0-87460-189-4). Lion.
--Great Humorous Stories. LC 64-24883. (Illus.). 160p. (YA) 1979. PLB 6.99 (ISBN 0-87460-190-8); pap. 1.95 (ISBN 0-87460-191-6). Lion.
--Great Suspense Stories. new ed. LC 61-5152. (Illus.). 160p. (YA) 1981. PLB 6.99 (ISBN 0-87460-206-8); pap. 1.95 (ISBN 0-87460-207-6). Lion.
Ross, Harriet, compiled by. Heroes & Heroines of Many Lands. (Illus.). 160p. 1981. PLB 7.95 (ISBN 0-87460-214-9). Lion.
--Myths & Legends of Many Lands. new ed. LC 60-8670. (Illus.). 160p. (YA) (gr. 5 up). 1981. PLB 6.87 (ISBN 0-87460-214-9). Lion.
--Myths of Ancient Greece. (Illus.). 160p. 1981. PLB 7.95 (ISBN 0-87460-383-8). Lion.
Ross, Harvey. Fighting Depression. 221p. (Orig.). 1975. pap. 1.95. Larchmont Bks.
Ross, Heather L. & Sawhill, Isabel V. Time of Transition: The Growth of Families Headed by Women. 1975. 10.00 (ISBN 0-87766-149-9, 12800); pap. 4.95 (ISBN 0-87766-148-0, 12600). Urban Inst.
Ross, Hebert H. Biological Systematics. LC 73-2141. 1974. text ed. 17.95 (ISBN 0-201-06531-2). A-W.
Ross, Helen S. & Mico, Paul. Theory & Practice in Health Education. LC 80-82564. (Illus.). 338p. 1980. text ed. 14.95 (ISBN 0-87484-406-1). Mayfield Pub.
Ross, Herbert H. Understanding Evolution. (Orig.). 1967. pap. 2.45 o.p. (ISBN 0-13-935890-0, Spec). P-H.
Ross, Ian S. Lord Kames & the Scotland of His Day. (Illus.). 420p. 1972. 39.95x (ISBN 0-19-822361-7). Oxford U Pr.
Ross, Ian S., ed. see Smith, Adam.
Ross, J. L., jt. ed. see Satz, Paul.
Ross, J. M. & Chanan, G. Comprehensive Schools in Focus. (Exploring Education Ser.). 1972. pap. text ed. 3.00x (ISBN 0-85633-014-0, NFER). Humanities.
Ross, J. M., et al. A Critical Appraisal of Comprehensive Education. (Research Reports Ser). 240p. (Orig.). 1972. pap. text ed. 18.25x (ISBN 0-901225-95-9, NFER). Humanities.
Ross, James. Fuel Alcohol: How to Make It, How to Use It. 160p. 1981. 9.95 (ISBN 0-312-30932-5); pap. 4.95 (ISBN 0-312-30933-3). St Martin.
--How to Buy a Car. 160p. 1981. pap. 3.95 (ISBN 0-312-39546-9); prepack 39.50 (ISBN 0-312-39547-7). St Martin.
--Whisky. (Illus.). 1970. 12.00 (ISBN 0-7100-6685-6). Routledge & Kegan.
Ross, James F. Philosophical Theology. LC 68-17707. 326p. 1980. 17.50 (ISBN 0-915144-67-0); pap. text ed. 9.95 (ISBN 0-915144-68-9). Hackett Pub.
--Philosophical Theology. 1969. text ed. 24.50x (ISBN 0-8290-0335-5). Irvington.
Ross, Janet, jt. auth. see Doty, Gladys G.
Ross, Jean R., jt. ed. see Glenister, T. W.
Ross, Jessica, illus. Ms. Klondike. 1977. PLB 6.50 o.p. (ISBN 0-670-49510-7). Viking Pr.
Ross, Joe. Productivity, People & Profits. 150p. 1981. text ed. 17.95 (ISBN 0-8359-5473-0); pap. 10.95 (ISBN 0-8359-5472-2). Reston.
Ross, Joel, jt. auth. see Ross, Pat.
Ross, Joel E. Managing Productivity. (Illus.). 192p. 1977. text ed. 16.95 (ISBN 0-87909-459-1). Reston.
--Modern Management & Information Systems. (Illus.). 288p. 1976. 15.95 (ISBN 0-87909-499-0). Reston.
Ross, Joel E., jt. auth. see Murdick, Robert C.
Ross, Joel E., jt. auth. see Murdick, Robert G.
Ross, John & Romano, Clare. The Complete New Techniques in Printmaking. LC 74-2695. 1974. pap. text ed. 9.95 (ISBN 0-02-927410-9). Free Pr.
--The Complete Relief Print. LC 74-2694. 1974. pap. text ed. 9.95 (ISBN 0-02-927390-0). Free Pr.
--The Complete Screen Print & the Lithograph. LC 74-2696. 1974. pap. text ed. 9.95 (ISBN 0-02-927380-3). Free Pr.
Ross, John, jt. auth. see Peck, William.
Ross, John, jt. auth. see Romanoo, Clare.
Ross, John D. Story of the Kilmarnock Burns. LC 76-153519. Repr. of 1933 ed. 12.50 (ISBN 0-404-08978-X). AMS Pr.
Ross, John F. Handbook for Radio Engineering Managers. 1000p. 1980. text ed. 94.95 (ISBN 0-408-00424-X). Butterworths.
Ross, John, Jr., jt. auth. see O'Rourke, Robert A.
Ross, Jonathan. I Know What It's Like to Die. 1978. 8.95 o.s.i. (ISBN 0-8027-5386-8). Walker & Co.
--Murder Makers. 1977. 6.95 o.s.i. (ISBN 0-8027-5371-X). Walker & Co.
Ross, Josephine. The Winter Queen: A Biography of Elizabeth of Bohemia. 1979. 16.95x (ISBN 0-312-88232-7). St Martin.
Ross, Judith & Acton, Susan. Beauty Makeover Guide. LC 78-19956. 190p. 1981. pap. 6.95 (ISBN 0-8128-6113-2). Stein & Day.
Ross, Karen. The New Manual of Yoga. LC 74-75398. (Illus.). 1977. pap. 2.95 o.p. (ISBN 0-668-04347-4). Arco.
Ross, Laura. Finger Puppets: Easy to Make, Fun to Use. LC 78-155752. (Illus.). (gr. k-3). 1971. PLB 6.96 o.p. (ISBN 0-688-51613-0). Lothrop.
Ross, Lawrence J., ed. see Tourneur, Cyril.
Ross, Lee, jt. auth. see Nisbett, Richard.
Ross, Lee, jt. ed. see Flavell, John.
Ross, Leonard, jt. auth. see Passell, Peter.
Ross, Leonard Q. Education of Hyman Kaplan. LC 38-6588. (gr. 10 up). 1968. pap. 1.95 (ISBN 0-15-627811-1, HPL29, HPL). HarBraceJ.
Ross, Lillian. Moments with Chaplin. LC 80-80828. (Illus.). 64p. 1980. 8.95 (ISBN 0-396-07829-X). Dodd.
--Reporting. 442p. 1981. 12.94 (ISBN 0-396-07948-2); pap. 8.95 (ISBN 0-396-07949-0). Dodd.
Ross, Louis. In the Peanut Butter Colony. (Illus.). (ps-3). 1979. 1.95 (ISBN 0-525-69022-0, Gingerbread Bks); PLB 5.95 (ISBN 0-525-69023-9, Gingerbread Bks). Dutton.
--Puddle Duck. (Illus.). (ps-2). 1979. 1.95 (ISBN 0-525-69020-4, Gingerbread Bks); PLB 5.95 (ISBN 0-525-69021-2). Dutton.
Ross, Lynne N. Metric Measurement in Food Preparation & Service. (Illus.). 1978. pap. 3.95 (ISBN 0-8138-0985-1). Iowa St U Pr.
Ross, Lynne N., jt. auth. see Jernigan, Anna K.
Ross, M. Rheumatoid Arthritis: It Roughs up All the Edges. 4.50 o.p. (ISBN 0-8062-1220-9). Carlton.
Ross, M., jt. ed. see Goodman, G.
Ross, Macye. The Will-God's Way: The True Autobiography of an Orphan. 1981. 8.95 (ISBN 0-533-04846-X). Vantage.
Ross, Malcolm. The Creative Arts. LC 78-324078. (Organization in Schools Ser.). 1978. text ed. 27.95x (ISBN 0-435-80780-3); pap. text ed. 14.95x (ISBN 0-435-80781-1). Heinemann Ed.
--The Dukes. Date not set. 13.95 (ISBN 0-671-25111-2). S&S.
Ross, Malcolm, ed. The Arts & Personal Growth. LC 80-40260. (Curriculum Issues in Arts Education Ser.: Vol. 1). (Illus.). 136p. 1980. 14.75 (ISBN 0-08-024714-8). Pergamon.
Ross, Marc H. Grass Roots in an African City: Political Behavior in Nairobi. LC 74-34263. 192p. 1975. text ed. 22.50x (ISBN 0-262-18074-X). MIT Pr.
Ross, Marc H. & Williams, Robert H. Our Energy-Regaining Control. (Illus.). 320p. 1980. 16.95 (ISBN 0-07-053894-8, P&RB). McGraw.
Ross, Marilyn. Cellars of the Dead. (Stewarts of Stormhaven Ser.: No. 2). 1976. pap. 1.25 o.p. (ISBN 0-445-00410-X). Popular Lib.
--The Curse of Black Charlie. (Stewarts of Stormhaven Ser.: No. 1). 256p. 1976. pap. 1.25 o.p. (ISBN 0-445-00396-0). Popular Lib.
--Death's Dark Music. (Stewarts of Stormhaven Ser.: No. 4). 1977. pap. 1.50 o.p. (ISBN 0-445-03182-4). Popular Lib.
--Delta Flame. 1978. pap. 1.95 o.p. (ISBN 0-445-04157-9). Popular Lib.
--Fog Island. 1977. pap. 1.50 o.p. (ISBN 0-445-04105-6). Popular Lib.
--A Garden of Ghosts. 256p. (Orig.). 1974. pap. 1.25 o.p. (ISBN 0-445-00227-1). Popular Lib.
--Ghost Ship of Fog Island. 256p. (Orig.). 1975. pap. 1.25 o.p. (ISBN 0-445-00285-9). Popular Lib.
--Haiti Circle. 256p. 1976. pap. 1.25 o.p. (ISBN 0-445-00397-9). Popular Lib.
Ross, Mark. Principles of Aural Rehabilitation. LC 78-183116. (Studies in Communicative Disorders Ser.). 1972. pap. 2.50 (ISBN 0-672-61283-6). Bobbs.
Ross, Mark, jt. auth. see Ross, Raymond S.
Ross, Marvin. Economic Opportunity & Crime. 1977. pap. text ed. 12.20x o.p. (ISBN 0-685-87412-5). Renouf.
Ross, Marvin C., ed. George Catlin: Episodes from "Life Among the Indians" & "Last Rambles". LC 59-7959. 1979. 25.00 (ISBN 0-8061-0442-2); pap. 12.50 (ISBN 0-8061-1693-5). U of Okla Pr.
Ross, Marvin C., ed. see Catlin, George.
Ross, Marvin C., ed. see Miller, Alfred J.
Ross, Max. Double-Agent Fugitive. 1978. 10.00 o.p. (ISBN 0-682-48972-7). Exposition.
Ross, Michael H., jt. auth. see Reith, Edward J.
Ross, Michael J., jt. auth. see Goldbach, John.
Ross, Mitchell S. Literary Politicians. LC 76-52222. 1978. 10.00 o.p. (ISBN 0-385-13077-5). Doubleday.
Ross, Nathaniel, jt. ed. see Frosch, John.
Ross, Norman A. Index to the Briefs, Transcripts & GAO Reports Before the Indian Claims Commission. (Library of American Indian Affairs). 192p. 1981. 18.00x (ISBN 0-88354-108-4). Clearwater Pub.
Ross, Norman A., ed. Index to the Decisions of the Indian Claims Commission, 1948-1972. LC 72-13850. (Library of American Indian Affairs). 168p. 1973. lib. bdg. 18.00 (ISBN 0-88354-101-7). Clearwater Pub.
--Index to the Expert Testimony Presented Before the Indian Claims Commission. LC 72-13851. (Library of American Indian Affairs). 112p. 1973. lib. bdg. 18.00 (ISBN 0-88354-102-5). Clearwater Pub.
Ross, Pat. M & M & the Haunted House Game. (An I Am Reading Bk.). (Illus.). (gr. 1-4). 1980. 4.95 (ISBN 0-394-84185-9); PLB 5.99 (ISBN 0-394-94185-3). Pantheon.
--Young & Female. (Illus.). 108p. Date not set. pap. 2.95 (ISBN 0-394-70808-3, Vin). Random.
Ross, Pat & Ross, Joel. Your First Airplane Trip. 1981. 7.95 (ISBN 0-688-41989-5). Lothrop.
--Your First Airplane Trip. LC 80-22642. (Illus.). 40p. (gr. k-2). 1981. 7.95 (ISBN 0-688-41989-5); PLB 7.63 (ISBN 0-688-51989-X). Morrow.
Ross, Patricia F. Mexico. rev. ed. LC 73-90742. (American Neighbors Ser.). (Illus.). 208p. (gr. 5 up). 1975. text ed. 9.95, 5 or more copies 7.96 o.p. (ISBN 0-88296-096-2); tchrs'. guide 6.96 o.p. (ISBN 0-686-67148-1). Fideler.
Ross, Paul B. Fast Break. 1979. pap. 1.75 o.p. (ISBN 0-345-28128-4). Ballantine.
Ross, Peter, tr. see Maser, Werner.
Ross, Philip. Government as a Source of Union Power: The Role of Public Policy in Collective Bargaining. LC 65-10155. 320p. 1965. 12.50x (ISBN 0-87057-085-4, Pub. by Brown U Pr). Univ Pr of New England.

Ross, R. Adam Kok's Griquas. (African Studies: No. 21). (Illus.). 1977. 24.95 (ISBN 0-521-21199-9). Cambridge U Pr.

--Essentials of Speech Communication. 1979. pap. 10.95 (ISBN 0-13-289314-2). P-H.

Ross, Raymond S. Speech Communication: Fundamentals & Practice. 4th ed. 1977. text ed. 14.95 (ISBN 0-13-827485-1). P-H.

Ross, Raymond S. & Ross, Mark. Understanding Persuasion. (P-H Speech Communication Ser.). (Illus.). 224p. 1981. pap. text ed. 10.95 (ISBN 0-13-936484-6). P-H.

Ross, Regina. The Devil Dances for Gold. 1977. pap. 1.95 o.p. (ISBN 0-345-25256-X). Ballantine.

--Falls the Shadow. 248p. 1974. 6.95 o.p. (ISBN 0-440-02642-3). Delacorte.

Ross, Richard D., jt. auth. see Conway, Richard A.

Ross, Robert, jt. auth. see Cohen, Sanford I.

Ross, Robert, ed. see Wilde, Oscar.

Ross, Robert B. Metallic Materials Specification Handbook. 3rd ed. LC 79-40761. 1980. cancelled o.p. (ISBN 0-470-26757-7). Halsted Pr.

Ross, Robert D. The Management of Public Relations: Analysis & Planning External Relations. LC 77-9288. (Marketing Management Ser.). 1977. 23.95 (ISBN 0-471-03109-7). Ronald Pr.

Ross, Robert H., ed. see Tennyson, Alfred L.

Ross, Robert R. & McKay, Hugh B. Self-Mutilation. (Illus.). 1979. 21.00 (ISBN 0-669-02116-4). Lexington Bks.

Ross, Robert W. So It Was True: The American Protestant Press & the Nazi Persecution of the Jews. LC 80-196. 1980. 20.00x (ISBN 0-8166-0948-9); pap. 9.95x (ISBN 0-8166-0951-9). U of Minn Pr.

Ross, Rodger J. Color Film for Color Television. (Library of Image & Sound Technology). Date not set. 12.50 o.p. (ISBN 0-8038-1137-3). Hastings.

Ross, Ronald, tr. see Bergey, Alyce.

Ross, Ronald, tr. see Hill, Dave.

Ross, Ronald, tr. see Latourette, Jane.

Ross, Ronald, tr. see Prior, Brenda G.

Ross, Ronald G. Data Dictionaries & Data Administration: Concepts & Practices for Data Resource Management. 549p. 1981. 25.95 (ISBN 0-8144-5596-4). Am Mgmt.

Ross, Ruth, jt. ed. see Iglitzin, Lynne B.

Ross, Sam. Ready for the Tiger. 1964. 3.95 o.p. (ISBN 0-374-24760-9). FS&G.

Ross, Scott, et al. Scott Free. 1976. 5.95 o.p. (ISBN 0-912376-15-5). Chosen Bks Pub.

Ross, Sheila A., jt. auth. see Ross, Dorothea M.

Ross, Sheldon. Solutions Manual for Introduction to Probability Models. 2nd ed. (Probability & Mathematical Statistics Ser.). 1980. 2.00 (ISBN 0-12-598462-6). Acad Pr.

Ross, Sheldon M. Applied Probability Models with Optimization Applications. LC 73-111376. 1970. text ed. 19.95x (ISBN 0-8162-7336-7). Holden-Day.

--Introduction to Probability Models. (Probability & Mathematical Statistics Ser.). 1972. text ed. 20.95 (ISBN 0-12-598450-2). Acad Pr.

Ross, Shepley L. Differential Equations. 2nd ed. LC 73-84447. 1974. text ed. 21.95 (ISBN 0-471-00930-X). Wiley.

Ross, Stan. World of Drafting. (gr. 7-9). 1971. text ed. 15.16 (ISBN 0-87345-078-7). McKnight.

Ross, Stanley R., jt. ed. see Erb, Richard D.

Ross, Stephen D. Literature & Philosophy: An Analysis of the Philosophical Novel. LC 69-11284. (Century Philosophy Ser.). (Orig.). 1969. pap. text ed. 5.95x (ISBN 0-89197-278-1). Irvington.

Ross, Stephen V. Spelling Made Simple. LC 61-9566. 1958. pap. 2.50 (ISBN 0-385-01223-3, Made). Doubleday.

Ross, Steven. From Flintlock to Rifle: Infantry Tactics, 1740-1866. LC 77-74397. (Illus.). 1979. 15.00 (ISBN 0-8386-2051-5). Fairleigh Dickinson.

Ross, Steven M., jt. ed. see Upper, Dennis.

Ross, Thomas. A Book of Elizathan Magic: Thomas Hill's Naturall & Artificial Conclusions. 84p. 1974. 15.00 (ISBN 3-4180-0204-8). Adler.

--The Mordida Man. 1981. 13.95 (ISBN 0-671-42186-7). S&S.

Ross, Timothy A. Chiang Kuei. LC 74-2172. (World Authors Ser.: China: No. 320). 1974. lib. bdg. 12.50 (ISBN 0-8057-2214-9). Twayne.

Ross, Timothy A., jt. ed. see Lau, Joseph S.

Ross, Tony. The Greedy Little Cobbler. LC 79-56766. 24p. (gr. 1-6). 1980. 4.95 (ISBN 0-8120-5389-3). Barron.

--Jack & the Beanstalk. LC 80-67493. (Illus.). 32p. (gr. k-2). 1981. 8.95 (ISBN 0-440-04168-6); PLB 8.44 (ISBN 0-440-04174-0). Delacorte.

Ross, Tweed W., Jr. The Best Way to Destroy a Ship: The Evidence of European Naval Operations in World War II. 1980. pap. 23.00 (ISBN 0-89126-069-2). Military Aff Aero.

Ross, W. Nurse at the Ritz. 1979. 5.95 (ISBN 0-686-66185-0, Avalon). Bouregy.

--Phantom of Edgewater Hall. 1980. 5.95 (ISBN 0-686-59799-0, Avalon). Bouregy.

Ross, W. David, ed. see Aristotle.

Ross, W. E. The Music Room. 1978. pap. 1.50 (ISBN 0-505-51223-8). Tower Bks.

--Return to Barton. (YA) 1978. 5.95 (ISBN 0-685-86411-1, Avalon). Bouregy.

Ross, W. E. D. House on Lime Street. 192p. (YA) 1976. 5.95 (ISBN 0-685-64245-3, Avalon). Bouregy.

Ross, W. M., jt. auth. see Wall, J. S.

Ross, William M. Oil Pollution as an International Problem: A Study of Puget Sound & the Strait of Georgia. LC 73-5610. (Illus.). 296p. 1973. 15.00 (ISBN 0-295-95275-X). U of Wash Pr.

Rossand, Colette & Herman, Jill H. A Mostly French Food Processor Cookbook. rev. ed. 1980. pap. 2.50 (ISBN 0-451-09537-5, E9537, Sig). NAL.

Rossbach, Ed. The New Basketry. 128p. 1980. pap. 7.95 (ISBN 0-442-23996-3). Van Nos Reinhold.

Ross-Bryant, Lynn. Imagination & the Life of the Spirit: An Introduction to the Study of Religion & Literature. LC 79-28464. (Scholars Press General Ser.: Vol. 2). 13.50x (ISBN 0-89130-377-4, 00 03 02); pap. 9.00x (ISBN 0-89130-378-2). Scholar Pr CA.

--Theodore Roethke: Poetry of the Earth, Poet of the Spirit. (National University Publications, Literary Criticism Ser.). 1981. 15.00 (ISBN 0-8046-9270-X). Kennikat.

Ross-Craig, Stella. Drawings of British Plants, 8 vols. Incl. Vol. 1 (ISBN 0-7135-1137-0); Vol. 2 (ISBN 0-7135-1138-9); Vol. 3 (ISBN 0-7135-1139-7); Vol. 4; Vol. 5 (ISBN 0-7135-1141-9); Vol. 6 (ISBN 0-7135-1142-7); Vol. 7 (ISBN 0-7135-1143-5); Vol. 8. (Illus.). 1980. 256.25 set (ISBN 0-7135-1110-9); 32.50 ea. Lubrecht & Cramer.

Rossdale, P. D. & Ricketts, S. W. The Practice of Equine Stud Medicine. 2nd ed. (Illus.). 425p. 1980. text ed. write for info. (ISBN 0-8121-0750-0). Lea & Febiger.

Rossdale, Peter D. The Horse: From Conception to Maturity. 21.00 (ISBN 0-85131-198-9, Dist. by Sporting Book Center). J A Allen.

Rosse, Rebecca. The Unsuspected Isle. (Orig.). 1980. pap. 1.95 (ISBN 0-532-23323-9). Manor Bks.

Rosseau, Ann M. Shopping Bag Ladies. (Illus.). 244p. 1981. 16.95 (ISBN 0-8298-0413-7). Pilgrim NY.

Rossel, Seymour. Family. (gr. 4 up). 1980. PLB 6.45 (ISBN 0-531-04102-6). Watts.

--Judaism. LC 75-31561. (First Bks. Ser.). (Illus.). 72p. (gr. 4-8). 1976. PLB 6.45 (ISBN 0-531-00841-X). Watts.

Rossel, Sven H., tr. see Andersen, Hans C.

Rosselet, Joan, jt. auth. see Daix, Pierre.

Rosselin, G., et al, eds. Hormone Receptors in Digestion & Nutrition: Proceedings of the 2nd Int'l Symposium, France 797. 520p. 1979. 66.00 (ISBN 0-444-80155-3, North Holland). Elsevier.

Rossell, James H. & Frasure, William. Financial Accounting Concepts. 2nd ed. (Business Ser.). 1974. 19.95 (ISBN 0-675-08860-7); instructor's manual 3.95 (ISBN 0-686-67215-1). Merrill.

Rossen, Howard M., et al. Smith's Review of Federal Income Taxation. LC 79-4396. (Legal Gem Ser.). 364p. 1979. pap. text ed. 8.95 (ISBN 0-8299-2036-6). West Pub.

Rosser, Fred, jt. auth. see Ivison, Stuart.

Rosser, J. B., ed. see American Mathematical Society.

Rosser, James M. & Mossberg, Howard E. An Analysis of Health Care Delivery. LC 80-11611. 188p. 1980. Repr. of 1977 ed. lib. bdg. write for info. (ISBN 0-89874-158-0). Krieger.

Rosser, W. G. & McCulloch, R. K. Relativity & High Energy Physics. (Wykeham Science Ser.: No. 7). 1969. 9.95x (ISBN 0-8448-1109-2). Crane-Russak Co.

Rossetti, Christina. Doves & Pomegranates. Powell, David, ed. LC 74-146624. (Illus.). (gr. 5 up). 1971. 5.95 (ISBN 0-02-777760-X). Macmillan.

--Goblin Market. LC 76-115984. (gr. 1 up). 1970. PLB 7.95 o.p. (ISBN 0-525-30744-3). Dutton.

--Selected Poems of Christina Rossetti. Zaturenska, Marya, ed. LC 77-95183. 1970. pap. 9.95 (ISBN 0-02-633400-3). Macmillan.

--Sing-Song, Repr. Of 1872 Ed. Bd. with Speaking Likenesses. Repr. of 1874 ed; Goblin Market. Repr. of 1893 ed. LC 75-32176. (Classics of Children's Literature, 1621-1932: Vol. 39). (Illus.). 1977. PLB 38.00 (ISBN 0-8240-2288-2). Garland Pub.

--What Is Pink. LC 71-152289. (Illus.). (ps-3). 1971. 6.95 (ISBN 0-685-00251-9). Macmillan.

Rossetti, Dante G. Letters of Dante Gabriel Rossetti. Doughty, O. & Wahl, J. R., eds. 1965-67. Vols. 3 & 4. 75.00x (ISBN 0-19-811462-1). Oxford U Pr.

Rossi, Aldo, jt. auth. see Eisenman, Peter D.

Rossi, Alfred. Astonish Us in the Morning: Tyrone Guthrie Remembered. 1981. 13.95 (ISBN 0-8143-1669-7); pap. 5.95 (ISBN 0-8143-1670-0). Wayne St U Pr.

--Minneapolis Rehearsals: Tyrone Guthrie Directs Hamlet. LC 70-115496. 1970. 23.75x (ISBN 0-520-01719-6). U of Cal Pr.

Rossi, Alice S., ed. The Feminist Papers: From Adams to De Beauvoir. 600p. 1973. 22.50x (ISBN 0-231-03795-3). Columbia U Pr.

Rossi, Alice S., et al, eds. The Family. 1978. 10.95 (ISBN 0-393-01167-4); pap. 6.95x (ISBN 0-393-09064-7). Norton.

Rossi, B. E., ed. Experimental Mechanics, Vol. 1: Proceedings, International Congress on Experimental Mechanics - 1st. 1963. 60.00 (ISBN 0-08-013346-0). Pergamon.

Rossi, Bruno. A Dirty Way to Die. (Sharpshooter Ser). (Orig.). 1975. pap. 1.25 o.p. (ISBN 0-685-53129-5, LB276ZK, Leisure Bks). Nordon Pubns.

--Las Vegas Vengeance. (Sharpshooter Ser: No. 14). (Orig.). 1975. pap. 1.25 o.p. (ISBN 0-685-52940-1, LB261ZK, Leisure Bks). Nordon Pubns.

--Mafia Death Watch. (Sharpshooter Ser). (Orig.). 1975. pap. 1.25 o.p. (ISBN 0-685-53903-2, LB286ZK, Leisure Bks). Nordon Pubns.

--Triggerman. (Sharpshooter Ser: No. 11). 1975. pap. 0.95 o.p. (ISBN 0-685-51411-0, LB229NK, Leisure Bks). Nordon Pubns.

Rossi, Claude J. De see De Rossi, Claude J.

Rossi, Ernest E. & Plano, Jack C. The Latin American Political Dictionary. 263p. 1980. 25.25 (ISBN 0-87436-302-0). ABC Clio.

Rossi, Ernest L. Dreams & the Growth of Personality: Expanding Awareness in Psychotherapy. 232p. 1972. text ed. 19.00 (ISBN 0-08-016787-X). Pergamon.

Rossi, Ernest L., jt. auth. see Erickson, Milton.

Rossi, Ernest L., jt. auth. see Erickson, Milton H.

Rossi, G., jt. auth. see Zorgniotti, A. W.

Rossi, I., et al. Anthropology Full Circle. LC 74-33027. 444p. (Orig.). 1977. pap. text ed. 10.95 (ISBN 0-03-038926-7, HoltC); aval. instructor's manual (ISBN 0-03-036236-9). HR&W.

Rossi, Ino, ed. The Logic of Culture: Advances in Structural Theory & Methods. 320p. 1981. text ed. 24.95x (ISBN 0-89789-015-9). J F Bergin.

--The Unconscious in Culture: The Structuralism of Claude Levi-Strauss in Perspective. 1974. pap. 6.95 o.p. (ISBN 0-525-47358-0). Dutton.

Rossi, Ino, et al. People in Culture: A Survey of Cultural Anthropology. LC 79-11842. (Praeger Special Studies). 640p. 1980. 32.50 (ISBN 0-03-752235-0); pap. 15.95 student ed. (ISBN 0-03-051021-X). Praeger.

Rossi, Nick & Rafferty, Sadie. Music Through the Centuries. LC 80-9066. (Illus.). 760p. 1981. lib. bdg. 27.00 (ISBN 0-8191-1498-7); pap. text ed. 16.75 (ISBN 0-8191-1499-5). U Pr of Amer.

Rossi, Peter H. Why Families Move. 2nd ed. LC 79-25370. (Illus.). 243p. 1980. 18.00 (ISBN 0-8039-1348-6); pap. 8.95x (ISBN 0-8039-1349-4). Sage.

Rossi, Peter H. & Williams, Walter, eds. Evaluating Social Programs: Theory, Practice, & Politics. LC 75-183473. (Quantitative Studies in Social Relations). 320p. 1972. text ed. 23.00 (ISBN 0-12-785739-7). Acad Pr.

Rossi, Peter H., et al. Money, Work & Crime: A Field Experiment in Reducing Recidivism Through Postrelease Financial Aid to Prisoners. LC 80-512. (Quantitative Studies in Social Relations Ser.). 1980. 29.00 (ISBN 0-12-598240-2). Acad Pr.

Rossi, Vinio. Andre Gide. LC 68-54458. (Columbia Ser.: No. 35). (Orig.). 1968. pap. 2.00 (ISBN 0-231-02960-8, MW35). Columbia U Pr.

Rossides, Daniel. The History & Nature of Sociological Theory. (Illus., LC 77-074382). 1978. text ed. 18.50 (ISBN 0-395-25059-5). HM.

Rossignol, J. N. Le see Le Rossignol, J. N. & Holliday, C. B.

Rossing, Thomas D. Science of Sound: Musical, Electronic, Environmental. LC 80-12028. (Chemistry Ser.). (Illus.). 512p. 1981. text ed. price not set (ISBN 0-201-06505-3). A-W.

Rossini, F. P., ed. Slide Atlas of Coloscopy. Ferrari, A. (Illus.). 58p. 1980. Repr. of 1979 ed. text ed. 110.00x (ISBN 88-212-0791-9, Pub. by Piccin Italy). J K Burgess.

Rossini, Gioachino. Guillaume Tell, 2 vols. Gossett, Phillip & Rosen, Charles, eds. LC 76-49192. (Early Romantic Opera Ser.: No. 17). 1980. lib. bdg. 82.00 (ISBN 0-8240-2916-X). Garland Pub.

--Moise. Rosen, Charles & Gossett, Philip, eds. LC 76-49190. (Early Romantic Opera Ser.: Vol. 15). 1980. lib. bdg. 82.00 (ISBN 0-8240-2914-3). Garland Pub.

--Mose in Egitto, 2 vols. Gossett, Phillip & Rosen, Charles, eds. LC 76-49183. (Early Romantic Opera Ser.: No. 9). 1979. lib. bdg. 82.00 (ISBN 0-8240-2908-9). Garland Pub.

--Otello, 2 vols. Gossett, Philip & Rosen, Charles, eds. LC 76-49182. (Early Romantic Opera Ser.: Vol. 8). 1979. Set. lib. bdg. 164.00 (ISBN 0-8240-2907-0); lib. bdg. 82.00 ea. Garland Pub.

--Ricciardo E Zoraide, 2 vols. Gossett, Phillip & Rosen, Charles, eds. LC 76-49184. (Early Romantic Opera Ser.: No. 10). 1980. Set. lib. bdg. 82.00 (ISBN 0-8240-2909-7). Garland Pub.

--Semiramide. Gossett, Philip & Rosen, Charles, eds. LC 76-49188. (Early Romantic Opera Ser.: Vol. 13). 1978. lib. bdg. 82.00 (ISBN 0-8240-2912-7). Garland Pub.

--Le Siege De Corinthe. Gossett, Phillip & Rosen, Charles, eds. LC 76-49189. (Early Romantic Opera Ser.: No. 14). 1980. lib. bdg. 82.00 (ISBN 0-8240-2913-5). Garland Pub.

Rossiter, Anthony. Pendulum. LC 67-27440. 1967. 7.50 o.p. (ISBN 0-912326-22-0). Garrett-Helix.

Rossiter, B. see Weissberger, A.

Rossiter, B. W. Techniques of Chemistry: Vol. 9, Chemical Experimentation Under Extreme Conditions. 369p. 1980. 28.50 (ISBN 0-471-93269-8). Wiley.

Rossiter, Charles M. & Pearce, W. B., Jr. Communicating Personally: A Theory of Interpersonal Communication and Human Relationships. LC 74-23546. (SC Ser: No. 21). 286p. 1975. pap. 6.50 (ISBN 0-672-61352-2). Bobbs.

Rossiter, Clare. The White Rose. LC 77-12260. 1978. 7.95 o.p. (ISBN 0-312-86789-1). St Martin.

Rossiter, Clinton. American Presidency. rev. ed. LC 60-5436. 1960. pap. 2.95 o.p. (ISBN 0-15-605598-8, HB35, Harv). HarBraceJ.

--American Quest. LC 76-142095. (Fund for the Republic Ser.). 1971. 9.50 o.p. (ISBN 0-15-106110-6). HarBraceJ.

--Supreme Court & the Commander in Chief. LC 76-98182. 1970. Repr. of 1951 ed. lib. bdg. 17.50 (ISBN 0-306-71832-4). Da Capo.

Rossiter, Clinton L. Conservatism in America: The Thankless Persuasion. 2nd, rev. ed. LC 80-27937. xii, 306p. 1981. Repr. of 1962 ed. lib. bdg. 27.50x (ISBN 0-313-22720-9, ROCN). Greenwood.

Rossiter, Henry P. M. & M. Karolik Collection of American Watercolors & Drawings, 1800-1875, 2 vols. (Illus.). 1962. Set. boxed 30.00 (ISBN 0-87846-173-6). Mus Fine Arts Boston.

Rossiter, John. Dark Flight. LC 80-69380. 1981. 9.95 (ISBN 0-686-69530-5). Atheneum.

--The Deadly Gold. 1977. pap. 1.25 o.p. (ISBN 0-445-04077-7). Popular Lib.

Rossiter, John R., jt. auth. see Percy, Larry.

Rosskopf, Myron F., ed. Children's Mathematical Concepts: Six Piagetian Studies in Mathematical Education. LC 75-12872. 1975. text ed. 14.95x (ISBN 0-8077-2447-5). Tchrs Coll.

Rossland, Edmond C. The Utterly Irrational United States Monetary Policies & the Absolute Inevitability of a Major World Economic & Financial Crisis, 2 vols. in 1. (Illus.). 1979. deluxe ed. 61.85 (ISBN 0-930008-37-5). Inst Econ Pol.

Ross-Larson. Aborigines. LC 75-190188. (Illus.). (gr. 5-12). 1972. PLB 5.95 o.p. (ISBN 0-87191-210-4). Creative Ed.

--Bajun & the Sea. LC 77-190183. (Illus.). (gr. 4-8). 1972. PLB 6.95 (ISBN 0-87191-208-2). Creative Ed.

--Kenya's Nomads. LC 71-190187. (Illus.). (gr. 4-8). 1972. PLB 5.95 o.p. (ISBN 0-87191-209-0). Creative Ed.

Rossman, Charles & Friedman, Alan W., eds. Mario Vargas Llosa: A Collection of Critical Essays. 1978. 10.95 (ISBN 0-292-75039-0). U of Tex Pr.

Rossman, Isadore. Sex, Fertility & Birth Control. (Illus.). 1967. 9.95 (ISBN 0-87396-022-X). Stravon.

Rossman, Isadore & Obeck, Victor. Isometrics: The Static Way to Physical Fitness. LC 66-24095. (Illus.). 1966. 7.95 (ISBN 0-87396-017-3); pap. 3.95 (ISBN 0-87396-018-1). Stravon.

Rossman, Isidore, ed. see Parents Magazine Enterprises.

Rossman, Parker. Sexual Experience Between Men & Boys. 1976. 10.95 o.p. (ISBN 0-8096-1911-3, Assn Pr). Follett.

Ross-Molloy, Lynn, jt. auth. see Levy, Howard.

Rossner, John. Toward Recovery of the Primordial Tradition: Ancient Insights & Modern Discoveries, 2 bks, Vol. 1. Incl. Bk. 1. From Ancient Magic to Future Technology. LC 79-66892 (ISBN 0-8191-0861-8); Bk. 2. Toward a Parapsychology of Religion: from Ancient Religion to Future Science. LC 79-66893 (ISBN 0-8191-0862-6). 1979. pap. text ed. 11.25 ea. U Pr of Amer.

Rossner, Judith. Emmeline. 1980. 12.95 (ISBN 0-671-22938-9). S&S.

Rossof, Arthur H. & Robinson, William A., eds. Lithium Effects of Granulopiesis & Immune Function. (Advances in Experimental Medicine & Biology Ser.: Vol. 127). 470p. 1980. 47.50 (ISBN 0-306-40359-5). Plenum Pub.

Rossos, Andrew. Russia & the Balkans: Inter-Balkan Rivalries & Russian Foreign Policy 1908-1914. 320p. 1981. 35.00x (ISBN 0-8020-5516-8). U of Toronto Pr.

Rossotti, Hazel. Introducing Chemistry. 1975. pap. 3.95 (ISBN 0-14-021864-5, Pelican). Penguin.

Ross-Robertson, David, tr. see Smith, Agnes.

Rossum, Ralph A. & McDowell, Gary L., eds. The American Founding: Politics, Statesmanship, & the Constitution. (National University Publications, Political Science Ser.). 1981. 17.50 (ISBN 0-8046-9283-1). Kennikat.

Rossvaer, Viggo. Kant's Moral Philosophy: An Interpretation of the Categorical Imperative. 1979. pap. 23.00x (ISBN 82-00-01881-4, Dist. by Columbia U. Pr.). Universitet.

Rost, H. T. The Brilliant Stars: The Baha'i Faith & the Education of Children. 1979. 8.95 (ISBN 0-85398-082-9, 7-32-45, Pub. by G Ronald England); pap. 3.95 (ISBN 0-85398-083-7, 7-32-46, Pub. by G Ronald England). Baha'i.

Rost, Thomas L., et al. Botany: A Brief Introduction to Plant Biology. LC 78-5433. 1979. text ed. 20.95 (ISBN 0-471-02114-8); tchrs. manual avail. (ISBN 0-471-03758-3). Wiley.

Rosta, Paul, tr. see Valentinov, Nikolay.

Rostand, Claude. French Music Today. LC 73-4333. 146p. 1973. Repr. of 1955 ed. lib. bdg. 18.50 (ISBN 0-306-70578-8). Da Capo.

Rostand, Edmond. Cyrano de Bergerac. 18th ed. (French Texts Ser.). 1976. pap. text ed. 9.95x (ISBN 0-631-00550-1, Pub. by Basil Blackwell). Biblio Dist.

Rostand, Jean. Error & Deception in Science: Essays on Biological Aspects of Life. 1960. text ed. 3.50x (ISBN 0-391-01976-7). Humanities.

Rosten, Leo. King Silky! LC 79-3413. 352p. 1980. 11.95 (ISBN 0-06-013684-7, HarpT). Har-Row.

--Leo Rosten's Treasury of Jewish Quotations. 672p. 1980. pap. 3.95 (ISBN 0-553-14331-X). Bantam.

--Silky! 240p. 1980. pap. 2.25 (ISBN 0-553-13547-3). Bantam.

Rosten, Norman. Marilyn: An Untold Story. pap. 1.50 (ISBN 0-451-08880-8, W8880, Sig). NAL.

--Over & Out. LC 72-80735. 224p. 1972. 5.95 o.s.i. (ISBN 0-8076-0661-8). Braziller.

Rostenberg, Leona. The Minority Press & the English Crown: A Study in Repression, 1558-1625. 1971. text ed. 45.75x (ISBN 90-6004-271-9). Humanities.

Rostenberg, Leona & Stern, Madeleine B. Old & Rare: Thirty Years in the Book Business. (Illus.). 256p. 1975. 12.00 o.p. (ISBN 0-8390-0131-2). Allanheld & Schram.

Rostoker, N., jt. ed. see Reiser, M.

Roston, Murray. The Soul of Wit: A Study of John Donne. 250p. 1974. text ed. 29.00x (ISBN 0-19-812053-2). Oxford U Pr.

Rostov, Mara. Eroica. 1978. pap. 1.95 (ISBN 0-515-04469-5). Jove Pubns.

Rostovtzeff, Michael I. Out of the Past of Greece & Rome. LC 63-18047. (Illus.). 1960. 9.00x (ISBN 0-8196-0126-8). Biblo.

Rostovtzeff, Mikhail I. Rome. Bickerman, Elias J., ed. Duff, J. D., tr. 1960. pap. 5.95x (ISBN 0-19-500224-5). Oxford U Pr.

Rostow, W. W. Pre-Invasion Bombing Strategy: General Eisenhower's Decision of March 25, 1944. 176p. 1981. text ed. 18.00 (ISBN 0-292-76470-7); pap. 8.95 (ISBN 0-686-69545-3). U of Tex Pr.

--Stages of Economic Growth. 2nd ed. (Illus.). 1971. 32.95 (ISBN 0-521-08100-9); pap. 7.95x (ISBN 0-521-09650-2). Cambridge U Pr.

--Why the Poor Get Richer & the Rich Slow Down. (Illus.). 456p. 1980. text ed. 19.95 (ISBN 0-292-73012-8). U of Tex Pr.

--The World Economy: History & Prospect. 877p. 1980. pap. text ed. 20.00 (ISBN 0-292-79016-3). U of Tex Pr.

Rostron, Hilda L. Animals, Birds & Plants of the Bible. (Ladybird Ser). (Illus.). (gr. 1-5). 1964. bds. 1.49 (ISBN 0-87508-830-9). Chr Lit.

--Baby Jesus. (Ladybird Ser). (Illus.). 1961. bds. 1.49 (ISBN 0-87508-832-5). Chr Lit.

--Book of Prayers. (Ladybird Ser). (Illus.). (gr. 1-3). 1964. bds. 1.49 (ISBN 0-87508-834-1). Chr Lit.

--Lord's Prayer & Other Prayers. (Ladybird Ser.). (Illus.). (gr. 1-2). 1961. bds. 1.49 (ISBN 0-87508-848-1). Chr Lit.

--Stories About Children of the Bible. (Ladybird Ser). (Illus.). (gr. k-1). 1962. bds. 1.49 (ISBN 0-87508-860-0). Chr Lit.

--Stories About Jesus the Friend. (Ladybird Ser). (Illus.). (gr. k-1). 1961. bds. 1.49 (ISBN 0-87508-862-7). Chr Lit.

--Stories About Jesus the Helper. (Ladybird Ser). (Illus.). (gr. k-1). 1961. bds. 1.49 (ISBN 0-87508-864-3). Chr Lit.

Rostron, Michael, jt. auth. see Hutton, Geoffrey.

Rostvig, Maren Sofie. The Happy Man: Studies in the Metamorphoses of a Classical Ideal, 1600-1700, Vol. 1. 2nd ed. 1962. text ed. 17.00x (ISBN 0-685-84008-5, Dist. by Columbia U Pr). Universitet.

--The Happy Man: Studies in the Metamorphoses of a Classical Ideal, 1700-1760, Vol. 2. 2nd ed. 1971. text ed. 17.00x (ISBN 0-391-00218-X, Dist. by Columbia U Pr). Universitet.

Roszak, Betty & Roszak, Theodore, eds. Masculine Feminine: Readings in Sexual Mythology & the Liberation of Women. (Orig.). 1970. pap. 4.95x (ISBN 0-06-131952-X, TB 1952, Torch). Har-Row.

Roszak, Theodore. Making of a Counter Culture. LC 69-15215. pap. 2.50 (ISBN 0-385-07329-1, A697, Anch). Doubleday.

--Person-Planet: The Creative Disintegration of Industrial Society. 1978. 10.95 o.p. (ISBN 0-385-00063-4). Doubleday.

--The Unfinished Animal. LC 75-9333. (Illus.). 288p. 1975. 4.95 (ISBN 0-06-067016-9, CN 537, HarpR). Har-Row.

--Where the Wasteland Ends: Politics & Transcendence in Post-Industrial Society. 480p. 1973. pap. 2.95 (ISBN 0-385-02738-9, Anch). Doubleday.

Roszak, Theodore, jt. ed. see Roszak, Betty.

Roszkowiak, Lawrence R. Under the Rainbow. LC 80-68893. 94p. (Orig.). 1980. pap. 3.95 (ISBN 0-9604986-0-5). Brandywine Bks.

Rotberg, Robert I. Black Heart: Gore-Browne & the Politics of Multiracial Zambia. (Perspectives on Southern Africa Ser: Vol. 20). 1978. 20.00x (ISBN 0-520-03164-4). U of Cal Pr.

Rotberg, Robert I. & Barratt, John, eds. Conflict & Compromise in South Africa. LC 79-7712. 224p. 1980. 23.50 (ISBN 0-669-03205-0). Lexington Bks.

Rote, Kyle. Beyond the Goal. 1976. pap. 1.25 o.p. (ISBN 0-425-03261-2). Berkley Pub.

Rotenstreich, Nathan. Basic Problems of Marx's Philosophy. 1965. pap. 5.55 o.p. (ISBN 0-672-61210-0, LLA164). Bobbs.

Rotenstreich, Nathan, ed. Essays on Zionism & the Contemporary Jewish Condition. 1981. price not set. Herzl Pr.

Rotenstreich, Nathan, jt. ed. see Bauer, Yehuda.

Rotering, Robert, ed. Yesterday, Today & Tomorrow. (Illus.). 48p. (Orig.). 1971. pap. 4.95 o.p. (ISBN 0-88489-038-4). St Marys.

Roth, A. Vacuum Sealing Techniques. 1966. 120.00 (ISBN 0-08-011587-X). Pergamon.

Roth, Alexander D., jt. ed. see Turn, Rein.

Roth, Arthur. The Caretaker. LC 80-66249. 224p. (gr. 7 up). 1980. 9.95 (ISBN 0-590-07631-0, Four Winds). Schol Bk Serv.

--The Iceberg Hermit. LC 74-7435. 208p. (gr. 7 up). 1974. 7.95 (ISBN 0-590-07301-X, Four Winds). Schol Bk Serv.

Roth, B. Narcolepsy & Hypersomnia. Broughton, Roger, ed. Schierlova, Margaret, tr. Orig. Title: Czech. (Illus.). xiv, 304p. 1980. pap. 58.75 (ISBN 3-8055-0490-X). S Karger.

Roth, Bernhard A. The Complete Beginner's Guide to Archery. LC 75-26942. 192p. (gr. 6 up). 1976. PLB 7.95 (ISBN 0-385-07356-9). Doubleday.

--The Complete Beginner's Guide to Canoeing. LC 76-42391. (gr. 7 up). 1977. PLB 7.95 (ISBN 0-385-07297-X). Doubleday.

Roth, Bob. International Advertising. 1981. price not set (ISBN 0-87251-058-1). Crain Bks.

Roth, Cecil. Gleanings: Essays in Jewish History, Letters & Art. 1967. 7.95 (ISBN 0-8197-0178-5). Bloch.

--A History of the Jews in England. 3rd ed. 1979. 13.50x (ISBN 0-19-822488-5). Oxford U Pr.

--Spanish Inquisition. (Orig.). 1964. pap. 4.95 (ISBN 0-393-00255-1, Norton Lib). Norton.

Roth, Charles H. Fundamentals of Logic Design. 2nd ed. (Electrical Engineering Ser.). (Illus.). 1979. pap. 20.95 (ISBN 0-8299-0226-0); instrs. manual avail. (ISBN 0-8299-0572-3). West Pub.

Roth, David. The Hermit of Fog Hollow Station. LC 80-22241. 160p. (gr. 7 up). 1980. 7.95 (ISBN 0-8253-0012-6). Beaufort Bks NY.

Roth, David A. & Roach, Dale E. Missouri Supplement for Modern Real Estate Practice. 128p. (Orig.). 1980. pap. 7.95 (ISBN 0-88462-333-5). Real Estate Ed Co.

Roth, Edward S., ed. Gaging: Practical Design & Application. LC 80-53424. (Manufacturing Update Ser.). (Illus.). 289p. 1981. 29.00 (ISBN 0-87263-064-1). SME.

Roth, Ernest, ed. Plants for the Home. LC 77-82737. (Illus.). 1977. 7.95 (ISBN 0-8467-0370-X, Pub. by Two Continents). Hippocrene Bks.

Roth, George J. Slaying the Law School Dragon. LC 80-16974. 284p. 1980. 10.95 (ISBN 0-396-07880-X); pap. 7.95 (ISBN 0-396-07879-6). Dodd.

Roth, Guenther & Schluchter, Wolfgang. Max Weber's Vision of History: Ethics & Methods. LC 77-20328. 1979. 17.50x (ISBN 0-520-03604-2). U of Cal Pr.

Roth, H. W. & Roth-Wittig, M. Contact Lenses: A Handbook for Patients. MacKeen, D. L., tr. (Illus.). 75p. 1980. pap. text ed. 7.95 (ISBN 0-06-142301-7, Harper Medical). Har-Row.

Roth, Henry, jt. auth. see Applebaum, Samuel.

Roth, Jack J. The Cult of Violence: Sorel & the Sorelians. 1980. 27.50x (ISBN 0-520-03772-3). U of Cal Pr.

Roth, Jane, jt. auth. see Mannerberg, Donald.

Roth, John K. American Dreams: Meditations on Life in the United States. LC 76-26877. 194p. 1976. pap. 6.95 (ISBN 0-88316-527-9). Chandler & Sharp.

Roth, Jordon T., jt. auth. see Downey, Robert J.

Roth, Julius A. Timetables: Structuring the Passage of Time in Hospital Treatment & Other Careers. (Orig.). 1963. pap. 4.95 (ISBN 0-672-60851-0). Bobbs.

Roth, June. The Economy Cookbook: Lower Cost Foods & How to Prepare Them. (Berkley-Dorison House Bks.). (Illus.). (YA) 1978. 7.95 o.p. (ISBN 0-685-85769-7, Dist. by Putnam). Berkley Pub.

--Freeze & Please Home Freezer Cookbook. LC 63-21654. 1968. 5.95 (ISBN 0-8119-0063-0); pap. 4.95 (ISBN 0-8119-0372-9). Fell.

Roth, L. O., et al. An Introduction to Agricultural Engineering. (Illus.). 1975. pap. text ed. 19.50 (ISBN 0-87055-302-X). AVI.

Roth, Lillian. I'll Cry Tomorrow. 1977. pap. 4.95 (ISBN 0-8119-0385-0). Fell.

Roth, Lillian, et al. Corrosion of Pulp & Paper Mill Equipment. LC 76-21187. (Bibliographic: No. 269, Supplement I, Part 2). 1980. pap. 45.00 (ISBN 0-87010-055-6). Inst Paper Chem.

--Corrosion of Pulp & Paper Mill Equipment, Suppl. 1. LC 76-21187. (Bibliographic Ser.: No. 269, Suppl. 1). 1979. pap. 45.00 (ISBN 0-87010-056-4). Inst Paper Chem.

Roth, Martin. Comedy & America: The Lost World of Washington Irving. (Literary Criticism Ser.). 1976. 15.00 (ISBN 0-8046-9132-0, Natl U). Kennikat.

Roth, Mike & Eldred, Michael. Guide to Marx's "Capital". 1978. pap. text ed. 5.25x (ISBN 0-906336-11-2). Humanities.

Roth, Oscar & Galton, Lawrence. Heart Attack: A Question & Answer Book. (Illus.). 1978. 8.95 o.s.i. (ISBN 0-397-01263-2). Lippincott.

Roth, Philip. A Philip Roth Reader. 1980. 17.50 (ISBN 0-374-23170-2); pap. 7.95 (ISBN 0-374-51604-9). FS&G.

--Zuckerman Unbound. 1981. 10.95 (ISBN 0-374-29945-5). FS&G.

Roth, Robert A. Individualized Staff Development Programs for Competency Development: A Systematic Approach. LC 80-8258. 123p. 1980. pap. text ed. 7.50 (ISBN 0-8191-1326-3). U Pr of Amer.

Roth, Russell. Muddy Glory: America's Indian Wars in the Phillipines, 1899 to 1935. 1981. 12.95 (ISBN 0-8158-0402-4). Chris Mass.

Roth, Sid & Harrell, Irene. Something for Nothing. LC 75-31396. 1976. pap. 1.95 o.p. (ISBN 0-88270-258-0). Logos.

Roth, William. The Handicapped Speak. LC 80-20297. 240p. 1981. lib. bdg. write for info (ISBN 0-89950-022-6). McFarland & Co.

Roth, Wolfgang, jt. auth. see Hoyer, George W.

Rothafel, Roxy. Roxy's Ski Guide to New England. LC 78-61682. (Illus.). 192p. 1978. lib. bdg. 9.25 o.p. (ISBN 0-914788-08-6). East Woods.

Rothaus, Jim. Houston Oilers. (NFL Today Ser.). (gr. 3-12). 1980. PLB 6.45 (ISBN 0-87191-796-3); pap. 2.95 (ISBN 0-89812-248-1). Creative Ed.

--Seattle Seahawks. (NFL Today Ser.). (gr. 3-12). 1980. PLB 6.45 (ISBN 0-87191-795-5); pap. 2.95 (ISBN 0-89812-247-3). Creative Ed.

Rothbard, Murray. For a New Liberty: The Libertarian Manifesto. 1978. pap. 6.95 (ISBN 0-02-074690-3, Collier). Macmillan.

Rothbard, Murray N. America's Great Depression. rev. ed. (Studies in Economic Theory). 361p. 1975. 12.00; pap. 4.95. NYU Pr.

--Individualism & the Philosophy of the Social Sciences. (Cato Papers Ser.: No. 4). 1979. pap. 2.00 (ISBN 0-932790-03-8). Cato Inst.

--Man, Economy, & State: A Treatise on Economic Principles. 1978. write for info. NYU Pr.

--Man, Economy & State: A Treatise on Economic Principles, 2 vols. 2nd ed. LC 76-167504. (Studies in Economic Theory). 1979. 30.00; pap. 10.00. NYU Pr.

--Power & Market: Government & the Economy. 1977. write for info. NYU Pr.

--Power & Market: Government & the Economy. LC 70-111536. (Studies in Economic Theory). 304p. 1977. 15.00; pap. 4.95. NYU Pr.

Rothbard, Murray N., jt. auth. see Garrett, Garet.

Rothbard, Murray N., ed. see Fetter, Frank A.

Rothbard, Murray N., ed. & intro. by see Fetter, Frank A.

Rothbaum, Donald A., jt. auth. see Noble, R. Joe.

Rothberg, Michael. The Cat's-Eye. 12p. (Orig.). 1980. pap. 2.00 (ISBN 0-938370-00-6). Wildflower.

Rothberg, Robert R., ed. Corporate Strategy & Product Innovation. LC 75-32369. (Illus.). 1976. text ed. 17.75 o.s.i. (ISBN 0-02-927500-8). Free Pr.

--Corporate Strategy & Product Innovation. 2nd ed. LC 80-1857. (Illus.). 1981. text ed. 17.95 (ISBN 0-02-927520-2). Free Pr.

Rothblat, George H. & Christofalo, Vincent J., eds. Growth, Nutrition & Metabolism of Cells in Culture. Vol. 1, 1972. 51.50 (ISBN 0-12-598301-8); Vol. 2, 1972. 51.50 (ISBN 0-12-598302-6); Vol. 3, 1977. 39.00 (ISBN 0-12-598303-4); Set. 122.50. Acad Pr.

Rothblatt, Donald N., ed. National Policy for Urban & Regional Development. LC 73-11672. (Illus.). 224p. 1974. 21.50 (ISBN 0-669-85043-8). Lexington Bks.

Rothblatt, Donald N., et al. The Suburban Environment & Women. LC 78-19797. (Praeger Special Studies). 210p. 1979. 25.95 (ISBN 0-03-041031-2). Praeger.

Rothblatt, Henry, jt. auth. see Bailey, F. Lee.

Rothblatt, Henry B., jt. auth. see Bailey, F. Lee.

Rothchild, Donald & Curry, Robert L., Jr. Scarcity, Choice, & Public Policy in Middle Africa. LC 76-50255. 1978. 20.00x (ISBN 0-520-03378-7); pap. 6.95x (ISBN 0-520-03534-8). U of Cal Pr.

Rothchild, Sylvia, ed. Voices from the Holocaust. 1981. 14.95 (ISBN 0-453-00396-6, H396). NAL.

Rothe, Robert. Acadia: The Story Behind the Scenery. DenDooven, Gweneth R., ed. LC 78-78121. (Illus.). 1979. 7.95 (ISBN 0-916122-58-1); pap. 3.00 (ISBN 0-916122-57-3). K C Pubns.

Rothel, David. The Great Showbusiness Animals. LC 80-16891. 1980. 19.95 (ISBN 0-498-02519-5). A S Barnes.

--The Singing Cowboys. LC 77-89646. (Illus.). 272p. (Orig.). 1981. pap. 10.95 (ISBN 0-498-02523-3). A S Barnes.

--Who Was That Masked Man? The Story of the Lone Ranger. rev. ed. LC 80-27237. (Illus.). 290p. 1981. 19.90 (ISBN 0-498-02538-1). A S Barnes.

Rothenberg, Eleanore. Regulation & Expansion of Health Facilities. LC 76-7381. (Special Studies). (Illus.). 130p. 1976. text ed. 22.95 (ISBN 0-275-23080-5). Praeger.

Rothenberg, G. B. Refractory Materials. LC 76-17943. (Chemical Technology Review: No. 76). (Illus.). 1977. 39.00 o.p. (ISBN 0-8155-0635-X). Noyes.

Rothenberg, Gunther E. Art of Warfare in the Age of Napoleon. LC 77-86495. (Illus.). 288p. 1978. 15.00 (ISBN 0-253-31076-8). Ind U Pr.

Rothenberg, Gunther E., jt. ed. see Kiraly, Bela K.

Rothenberg, J. & Heggie, I. G. Transport & the Urban Environment: Proceedings of a Conference Held by the International Economic Assoc. at Lyngby. LC 73-15142. (International Economic Association Ser.). 273p. 1974. 20.95 (ISBN 0-470-73969-X). Halsted Pr.

Rothenberg, J. G. & Heggie, I. G., eds. The Management of Water Quality & the Environment: Proceedings of a Conference Held by the International Economic Assoc. at Lyngby. LC 74-7584. (International Economic Association Ser.). 1974. 36.95 (ISBN 0-470-73960-6). Halsted Pr.

Rothenberg, Jacob. Descensus As Terram: The Acquisition & Reception of the Elgin Marbles. LC 76-23716. (Outstanding Dissertations in the Fine Arts Ser.). 1977. lib. bdg. 70.00x (ISBN 0-8240-2726-4). Garland Pub.

Rothenberg, Jerome. Economic Evaluation of Urban Renewal. (Studies of Government Finance). 1967. 12.95 (ISBN 0-8157-7592-X); pap. 4.95 (ISBN 0-8157-7591-1). Brookings.

--Pre-Faces & Other Writings. LC 80-24031. 224p. 1981. 14.95 (ISBN 0-8112-0785-4); pap. 6.95 (ISBN 0-8112-0786-2, NDP511). New Directions.

Rothenberg, Jerome, ed. Shaking the Pumpkin: Traditional Poetry of the Indian North Americas. LC 74-171317. 1972. pap. 4.95 (ISBN 0-385-01296-9, Anch). Doubleday.

--Technicians of the Sacred: A Range of Poetries from Africa, America, Asia & Oceania. LC 67-15391. 1969. pap. 4.95 (ISBN 0-385-07597-9, A456, Anch). Doubleday.

Rothenberg, Jerome, ed. see Estrada, Alvaro.

Rothenberg, Jerome, ed. see Mac Low, Jackson.

Rothenberg, P. L., jt. auth. see Horowitz, Israel A.

Rothenberg, Robert. The Plain-Language Law Dictionary. 1981. pap. 7.95 (ISBN 0-14-051109-1). Penguin.

Rothenberg, Robert E. The Complete Book of Breast Care. 228p. 1976. pap. 1.95 o.p. (ISBN 0-345-25114-8). Ballantine.

Rothenbuehler, Mary L., ed. Family Secrets: Recipes from Grandma Fowler's Kitchen. (Illus., Orig.). 1981. pap. 2.25 (ISBN 0-939010-00-3). Zephyr.

Rothenstein, John & Butlin, Martin. Turner. LC 64-23604. (Illus.). 1964. 22.50 o.s.i. (ISBN 0-8076-0280-9). Braziller.

Rotherham, E. R., jt. auth. see Cady, Leo.

Rotherham, Joseph B. Studies in Psalms, Vol. I. DeWelt, Don, ed. (The Bible Study Textbook Ser.). (Illus.). 1970. Repr. 13.50 (ISBN 0-89900-016-9). College Pr Pub.

Rothermich, John A., jt. ed. see Howe, Florence.

Rothermund, D., et al, eds. Urban Growth & Rural Stagnation: Studies in the Economy of an Indian Coalfield & Its Hinterland. 1980. 36.00x (ISBN 0-8364-0662-1, Pub. by Manohar India). South Asia Bks.

Rothfeld, Benjamin, ed. Nuclear Medicine: Endocrinology. LC 78-3773. (Illus.). 1978. 43.50 (ISBN 0-397-50392-X). Lippincott.

--Nuclear Medicine: Hepatolineal. (Illus.). 288p. 1980. text ed. 45.00 (ISBN 0-397-50412-8). Lippincott.

Rothgarber, Herbert. Let's Folk Dance. 1980. pap. 3.00 (ISBN 0-918812-10-0). Magnamusic.

Rothkopf, Carol. Austria. (First Bk. Ser). (Illus.). 72p. (gr. 5 up). 1976. PLB 4.90 o.p. (ISBN 0-531-00842-8). Watts.

--The First Book of the Red Cross. LC 70-134498. (First Bks). (Illus.). (gr. 4-6). 1971. PLB 4.90 o.p. (ISBN 0-531-00736-7). Watts.

Rothkopf, Carol & Rothkopf, David. The Common Market: Uniting the European Community. (gr. 7 up). 1977. PLB 6.90 s&l (ISBN 0-531-01272-7). Watts.

Rothkopf, Carol Z. Czechoslovakia. LC 73-14703. (First Bks). (Illus.). 72p. (gr. 5-8). 1974. PLB 4.90 o.p. (ISBN 0-531-00814-2). Watts.

--East Europe. LC 78-184357. (First Bks). (Illus.). 96p. (gr. 7-9). 1972. PLB 4.90 o.p. (ISBN 0-531-00758-8). Watts.

--The Opening of the Suez Canal, November, 1869: A Water Gateway Joins East & West. LC 72-6893. (World Focus Bks.). (Illus.). 96p. (gr. 7 up). 1973. PLB 4.90 o.p. (ISBN 0-531-02166-1). Watts.

Rothkopf, David, jt. auth. see Rothkopf, Carol.

Rothman. Conscience & Convenience: The Asylum & Its Alternatives in Progressive America. (Orig.). 1980. pap. text ed. 8.95 (ISBN 0-316-75775-6). Little.

Rothman, David & Wheeler, Stanton, eds. Social History & Social Policy. LC 80-1772. (Studies in Social Discontinuity). 1981. price not set (ISBN 0-12-598680-7). Acad Pr.

Rothman, David, et al. Humanitarianism or Control? A Symposium on Nineteenth-Century Social Reform in Britain & America. Wiener, Martin, ed. (Rice University Studies: Vol. 67, No. 1). (Orig.). 1981. pap. 5.50x (ISBN 0-89263-248-8). Rice Univ.

Rothman, David J. Conscience & Convenience: The Asylum & Its Alternatives in Progressive America. 1980. 17.50 (ISBN 0-316-75774-8); pap. 8.95 (ISBN 0-316-75775-6). Little.

Rothman, David J. & Rothman, Sheila M. On Their Own: The Poor in Modern America. LC 76-183669. 1972. pap. text ed. 6.95 (ISBN 0-201-06527-4). A-W.

Rothman, Esther P., jt. auth. see Berkowitz, Pearl H.

Rothman, Harry, et al, eds. Biotechnology: A Review & Annotated Bibliography. 1980. 25.00 (ISBN 0-08-027177-4). Pergamon.

Rothman, J., et al. Promoting Innovation & Change in Organizations & Communities: A Planning Manual. LC 75-19454. 1976. 14.95x o.p. (ISBN 0-471-73967-7). Wiley.

Rothman, Jack. Planning & Organizing for Social Change. LC 74-4434. 1974. text ed. 27.00x (ISBN 0-231-03774-0); pap. text ed. 12.00x (ISBN 0-231-08335-1). Columbia U Pr.

Rothman, Jack, ed. Issues in Race & Ethnic Relations. LC 76-9544. 1977. pap. text ed. 9.95 (ISBN 0-87581-193-0). Peacock Pubs.

Rothman, Joel. At Last to the Ocean: The Story of the Endless Cycle of Water. LC 70-129753. (Illus.). (gr. k-3). 1971. 7.95 (ISBN 0-02-777800-2, CCPr). Macmillan.

--How to Play Drums. Rubin, Caroline, ed. LC 76-39937. (Music Involvement Series). (Illus.). 48p. (gr. 4-6). 1977. 6.50 (ISBN 0-8075-3420-X). A Whitman.

--Which One Is Different? LC 74-5. 32p. (ps-1). 1975. PLB 6.95 (ISBN 0-385-11017-0). Doubleday.

Rothman, Joel & Palacios, Argentina. This Can Lick a Lollypop: Body Riddles for Kids. LC 77-80911. (ps-3). 1979. 6.95a (ISBN 0-385-13071-6); PLB (ISBN 0-385-13072-4). Doubleday.

Rothman, Lynn. The Ball Book. (Golden Bk. for Early Childhood). (Illus.). 24p. (gr. k-1). 1979. PLB 5.38 (ISBN 0-307-68887-9, Golden Pr). Western Pub.

Rothman, Milton. Energy & the Future. LC 74-11447. (Illus.). 128p. (gr. 7 up). 1975. PLB 5.90 o.p. (ISBN 0-531-02796-1). Watts.

Rothman, Milton A. The Cybernetic Revolution: Thought & Control in Man & Machine. LC 7C-185691. (International Library). (Illus.). 128p. (gr. 7-12). 1972. text ed. 6.90 o.p. (ISBN 0-531-02106-8). Watts.

Rothman, Richard H. & Simeone, Frederick A., eds. The Spine, 2 vols. LC 74-4584. (Illus.). 922p. 1975. Vol. 1. 32.00 (ISBN 0-7216-7719-3); Vol. 2. 32.00 (ISBN 0-7216-7720-7); Set. 64.00 (ISBN 0-686-67075-2). Saunders.

Rothman, Robert A. Inequality & Stratification in the U. S. (P-H Ser. in Sociology). (Illus.). 1978. pap. 10.95 ref. ed. (ISBN 0-13-464305-4). P-H.

Rothman, Sandy, ed. see Ohsawa, George.

Rothman, Sheila M., jt. auth. see Rothman, David J.

Rothman, Stanley & Mosmann, Charles. Computers & Society. 2nd ed. LC 75-31622. (Illus.). 416p. 1976. text ed. 16.95 (ISBN 0-574-21055-5, 13-4055); instr's guide avail. (ISBN 0-574-21056-3, 13-4056). SRA.

Rothman, Tony. The World Is Round. (Del Rey Bks.). 1978. pap. 1.95 o.p. (ISBN 0-345-27213-7). Ballantine.

Rothnberg, Ronald I. Linear Programming. 1979. 22.95 (North Holland). Elsevier.

Rothschild, Eric. The Federalist Years: The Years in Review Seventeen Eighty-Nine to Eighteen Hundred. 109p. (gr. 9-12). 1980. pap. text ed. 25.00 (ISBN 0-667-00576-5). Microfilming Corp.

Rothschild, Eric & Brilliant, Livia. Forging a More Perfect Union: The Years in Review 1784-1788. 160p. (gr. 9-12). 1980. pap. text ed. 25.00 (ISBN 0-667-00575-7). Microfilming Corp.

Rothschild, Jeffrey, ed. see Nurbaksh, Javad.

Rothschild, Jon, jt. ed. see Camiller, Patrick.

Rothschild, Lincoln. Forms & Their Meaning in Western Art. LC 74-9298. (Illus.). 320p. 1976. 15.00 o.p. (ISBN 0-498-01608-0). A S Barnes.

--Susan Kahn. LC 79-5388. (Illus.). 180p. 1980. 25.00 (ISBN 0-87982-031-4). Art Alliance.

Rothschild, M. A., jt. ed. see Rosenoer, V.

Rothschild, M. A., et al, eds. Alcohol & Abnormal Protein Biosynthesis, Biochemical & Clinical. 550p. 1976. text ed. 46.00 (ISBN 0-08-017708-5). Pergamon.

Rothschild, Marcus A. The Physiologic Basis of Abdominal Organ Imaging. LC 78-55281. (Illus.). 1979. 24.50 (ISBN 0-88416-193-5). PSG Pub.

Rothschild, William E. Putting It All Together: A Guide to Strategic Thinking. LC 76-10535. (Illus.). 224p. 1976. 17.95 (ISBN 0-8144-5405-4). Am Mgmt.

--Strategic Alternatives: Selection, Development & Implementation. 1979. 15.95 (ISBN 0-8144-5514-X). Am Mgmt.

Rothstein, A. The Enzymology of the Cell Surface. Bd. with Tension at the Cell Surface. Harvey, E. N. (Protoplasmatologia: Vol. 2e, Pts. 4-5). (Illus.). iv, 116p. 1954. 24.80 o.p. (ISBN 0-387-80345-9). Springer-Verlag.

--The Soldier's Strikes of Nineteen Nineteen. 1980. text ed. 27.00x (ISBN 0-333-27693-0). Humanities.

Rothstein, Arthur. The American West in the Thirties: One Hundred Twenty-Two Photographs by Arthur Rothstein. (Illus.). 128p. (Orig.). 1981. pap. price not set (ISBN 0-486-24106-8). Dover.

Rothstein, Arthur, et al. A Vision Shared: The Words & Pictures of the Fsa Photographers, 1935-1943. LC 76-5381. (Illus.). 1976. 39.95 o.p. (ISBN 0-312-85015-8); prepub. 35.00 o.p. (ISBN 0-685-67163-1). St Martin.

Rothstein, Eric. Restoration & Eighteenth-Century Poetry 1660-1780. (Routledge Histort of English Poetry Ser.). 350p. 1981. price not set (ISBN 0-7100-0660-8). Routledge & Kegan.

--Systems of Order & Inquiry in Later Eighteenth-Century Fiction. LC 74-16716. 284p. 1975. 17.50x (ISBN 0-520-02862-7). U of Cal Pr.

Rothstein, Paul F. Evidence in a Nutshell, State & Federal Rules. 2nd ed. (Nutshell Ser.). 401p. 1981. pap. text ed. 6.95 (ISBN 0-8299-2131-1). West Pub.

Rothstein, Raphael. The Story of Masada. (Illus.). 296p. 1981. 10.95 (ISBN 0-89961-012-9). SBS Pub.

Rothstein, Raphael, ed. see Tadmor, S.

Rothstein, Robert, jt. auth. see Lamberg, Stanley L.

Rothstein, Robert, jt. auth. see Scimone, John.

Rothstein, Robert L. Alliances & Small Powers. LC 68-28401. (Institute of War & Peace Studies). 1968. 20.00x (ISBN 0-231-03113-0). Columbia U Pr.

--The Walk in the World of the Strong. 378p. 1980. pap. 8.50x (ISBN 0-231-04339-2). Columbia U Pr.

--The Weak in the World of the Strong: The Third World in the International System. LC 77-7889. (Institute of War & Peace Studies). 1977. 18.00x (ISBN 0-231-04338-4). Columbia U Pr.

Rothweiler, Paul R. Blood Sports. (Orig.). pap. 2.25 (ISBN 0-515-05410-0). Jove Pubns.

Rothwell, A. B. & Gray, J. Malcolm, eds. Welding of HSLA (Microalloyed) Structural Steels. 1978. 42.00 (ISBN 0-87170-005-0). ASM.

Rothwell, Evelyn. Oboe Technique. rev. ed. (YA) (gr. 9 up). 1962. 7.75 (ISBN 0-19-318602-0). Oxford U Pr.

Rothwell, Helene F. de. Canadian Selection: Filmstrips. 516p. 1980. 25.00 (ISBN 0-8020-4586-3). U of Toronto Pr.

Rothwell, J. Dan & Costigan, James I. Interpersonal Communications: Influences & Alternatives. new ed. (Speech & Drama Ser.). 288p. 1975. pap. text ed. 8.95x o.p. (ISBN 0-675-08764-3); instructors manual 3.95 o.p. (ISBN 0-685-50547-2). Merrill.

Rothwell, Naomi & Doniger, Joan. The Psychiatric Halfway House: A Case Study. 284p. 1966. pap. 11.00 spiral (ISBN 0-398-01615-1). C C Thomas.

Rothwell, Norman V. Human Genetics. (Illus.). 1977. text ed. 19.95 (ISBN 0-13-445080-9). P-H.

Rothwell, Roy & Zegveld, Walter. Technological Innovation & Public Policy. LC 81-493. (Contributions in Economics & Economic History Ser.: No. 42). 400p. 1981. lib. bdg. 35.00 (ISBN 0-313-22989-9, RTE/). Greenwood.

Rothwell, V. H. British War Aims & Peace Diplomacy Nineteen-Fourteen to Nineteen-Eighteen. 1971. 33.00x (ISBN 0-19-822349-8). Oxford U Pr.

Roth-Wittig, M., jt. auth. see Roth, H. W.

Rotkovich, Rachel, ed. Quality Patient Care & the Role of the Clinical Nurse Specialist. LC 76-5393. 1976. 18.50 (ISBN 0-471-74015-2, Pub. by Wiley Medical). Wiley.

Rotman, Joseph J. The Theory of Groups: An Introduction. 2nd ed. 352p. 1973. text ed. 25.15x (ISBN 0-205-03655-4, 5636558). Allyn.

Rotmans, Elmer A., et al. Basic Drafting Technology. 2nd ed. LC 78-50424. (gr. 8). 1980. pap. text ed. 18.00 (ISBN 0-8273-1293-8); instr's. guide 2.25 (ISBN 0-8273-1294-6). Delmar.

Roto-Vision Editors. Art Director's Index to Photographer: American Section, No. 7. (Illus., Orig.). 1981. pap. 17.50 (ISBN 2-88046-010-7, Pub. by Roto-Vision Switzerland). Norton.

--Art Director's Index to Photographers. (Art Directors Index Ser.: No. 7). (Illus.). 1981. 80.00 (ISBN 2-88046-005-0, Pub. by Roto-Vision Switzerland); pap. 17.50. Norton.

Rotoli, Nicholas J., jt. auth. see Arata, Esther S.

Rotondo, Joe, ed. Rotondo on Racing Pigeons. (Illus.). 330p. 1981. 35.00. North Am Fal Hunt.

Rotroff, Susan I. Hellenistic Pottery: Athenian & Imported Moldmade Bowls. (The Athenian Agora: Results of Excavations Conducted by the American School of Classical Studies at Athens: Vol. XXII). 1981. price not set (ISBN 0-87661-222-2). Am Sch Athens.

Rotsel, R. W., tr. see Bakhtin, M. M.

Rotsler, William, jt. auth. see Benford, Gregory.

Rotsstein, Aaron N. Judgement in St. Peters. 256p. 1981. pap. 2.50 (ISBN 0-445-04651-1). Popular Lib.

Rotstein, Abraham, ed. Beyond Industrial Growth. LC 76-7440. 1976. pap. 4.95 (ISBN 0-8020-6286-5). U of Toronto Pr.

Rottensteiner, Franz. View from Another Shore. 1978. pap. 1.75 o.s.i. (ISBN 0-515-04557-8). Jove Pubns.

Rottensteiner, Franz, ed. View from Another Shore. LC 73-78082. 1976. pap. 3.95 o.p. (ISBN 0-8164-9273-5). Continuum.

--View from Another Shore: European Science Fiction. LC 73-78082. 252p. (Translation from several languages). 1973. 6.95 o.p. (ISBN 0-8164-9151-8). Continuum.

Rotter, Jerome I., et al, eds. The Genetics & Heterogeneity of Common Gastrointestinal Disorders. 1980. 35.00 (ISBN 0-12-598760-9). Acad Pr.

Rotter, Joseph C., jt. auth. see McFadden, Johnnie.

Rotter, Joseph C., et al. Significant Influence People: A Sip of Discipline & Encouragement. LC 80-69233. 110p. 1981. perfect bdg. 8.95 (ISBN 0-86548-055-9). Century Twenty One.

Rotter, Julian B. Clinical Psychology. 2nd ed. LC 74-110493. (Foundations of Modern Psychology Ser). (Illus.). 1971. pap. 7.95x ref. ed. (ISBN 0-13-137836-8). P-H.

Rotterdam, Heidrun Z. & Sommers, Sheldon C. Biopsy Diagnosis of the Digestive Tract. (Biopsy Interpretation Ser.). 1981. text ed. price not set (ISBN 0-89004-541-0). Raven.

Rottger, Ernst. Creative Paper Craft. 1973. pap. 11.95 (ISBN 0-7134-2805-8, Pub. by Batsford England). David & Charles.

Rottman, Fran. Easy to Make Puppets & How to Use Them. Incl. Children & Youth. pap. 4.95 (ISBN 0-8307-0560-0, 52-022-05); Early Childhood. pap. 3.95 (ISBN 0-8307-0559-7, 52-021-08). 1978. Regal.

Rottschaefer, Henry. The Constitution & Socio-Economic Change. LC 77-173667. (American Constitutional & Legal History Ser.). 253p. 1971. Repr. of 1948 ed. lib. bdg. 29.50 (ISBN 0-306-70410-2). Da Capo.

Rotunda, Ronald D. Modern Constitutional Law: Cases & Notes. (American Casebook Ser.). 1058p. 1981. text ed. price not set (ISBN 0-8299-2136-2). West Pub.

Rotwein, Eugene, ed. David Hume: Writings on Economics. LC 55-12064. 1970. pap. 7.95 (ISBN 0-299-01324-3). U of Wis Pr.

Rotz, Anna O. Heritage Hill Farm Cookbook. 96p. 1980. 6.00 (ISBN 0-9605108-0-X). Rotz.

Rotz, Robert A., jt. auth. see Pearman, William A.

Rouard, Marguerite, jt. auth. see Simon, Jacques.

Rouault, Georges. Miserere. LC 63-21914. (Illus.). 87p. 1963. 30.00 (ISBN 0-912158-46-8, Pub. by Boston Bk & Art Shop). Hennessey.

Roubiczek, Paul. Existentialism: for & Against. (Orig.). 32.95x (ISBN 0-521-06140-7); pap. 8.95 (ISBN 0-521-09243-4). Cambridge U Pr.

Roucek, Joseph S. Unusual Child. LC 62-9772. 1962. 6.00 o.p. (ISBN 0-8022-1398-7). Philos Lib.

Rouch, Mark. Competent Ministry: A Guide to Effective Continuing Education. LC 73-22309. 192p. 1974. pap. 3.75 o.p. (ISBN 0-687-09318-X). Abingdon.

Rouch, Roger L. & Birr, Shirley. Diagnostic-Language Development Approach to Individualized Reading Instruction. 1976. 11.95 o.p. (ISBN 0-13-208553-4). P-H.

Rouder, Susan. American Politics: Playing the Game. LC 76-13962. Orig. Title: Game of American Politics: How to Play. (Illus.). 1977. pap. text ed. 12.50 (ISBN 0-395-24971-6); inst. manual 1.00 (ISBN 0-395-24972-4). HM.

Roudiez, Leon S. French Fiction Today: A New Direction. LC 70-185392. 1972. 28.00 (ISBN 0-8135-0724-3). Rutgers U Pr.

Roudiez, Leon S., ed. Contemporary French Literature: Essays by Justin O'Brien. LC 77-127052. 1971. 21.00 (ISBN 0-8135-0661-1). Rutgers U Pr.

Roudiez, Leon S., ed. see Kristeva, Julia.

Roudybush, Alexandra. Female of the Species. LC 77-12872. 1978. 7.95 o.p. (ISBN 0-385-13652-8). Doubleday.

Roudybush, Alezandra. Blood Ties. LC 80-1852. (Crime Club Ser.). 192p. 1981. 9.95 (ISBN 0-385-17339-3). Doubleday.

Roueche, Berton. The Last Enemy. LC 75-6375. (Harper Novel of Suspense). 224p. 1975. 6.95 o.p. (ISBN 0-06-013687-1, HarpT). Har-Row.

--The River World & Other Explorations. LC 78-4738. 1978. 9.95 o.s.i. (ISBN 0-06-013686-3, HarpT). Har-Row.

Roueche, John E. & Kirk, R. Wade. Catching Up: Remedial Education. LC 73-1851. (Higher Education Ser.). 1973. 9.95x o.p. (ISBN 0-87589-170-5). Jossey-Bass.

Roueche, John E. & Pitman, John C. A Modest Proposal: Students Can Learn. LC 73-184956. (Higher Education Ser.). 1972. 9.95x o.p. (ISBN 0-87589-116-0). Jossey-Bass.

Roueche, N. E. & Mink, B. Washburn. The Language of Mathematics: An Individualized Introduction. LC 78-13397. 1979. 17.95 (ISBN 0-13-522920-0). P-H.

Roueche, Nelda W. Fundamentals of Business Mathematics. (Illus.). 1979. pap. 12.95 (ISBN 0-13-334441-X). P-H.

Rouge Et Noir. Gambling World. LC 68-22047. 1968. Repr. of 1898 ed. 20.00 (ISBN 0-8103-3551-4). Gale.

Rougemont, Denis de see De Rougemont, Denis.

Roughsey, Dick. The Giant Devil-Dingo. LC 75-14210. (Illus.). 36p. (gr. k-3). 1975. 6.95 o.s.i. (ISBN 0-02-777840-1, 77784). Macmillan.

Rougier, Harry & Stockum, E. K. Getting Started: A Preface to Writing. (Orig.). 1970. pap. text ed. 3.95x (ISBN 0-393-09900-8, NortonC). Norton.

Rougier, Louis. The Genius of the West. LC 76-93466. (Principles of Freedom). 1976. 10.00x o.p. (ISBN 0-916054-36-5). Green Hill.

Rouiller, C. & Muller, A., eds. The Kidney: Morphology, Biochemistry, Physiology. Incl. Vols. 1-2. 1969. 65.00. Vol. 1 (ISBN 0-12-598801-X). Vol. 2. 68.00 (ISBN 0-12-598802-8); Vols. 3-4. 1971. 52.00 ea. Vol. 3 (ISBN 0-12-598803-6). Vol. 4 (ISBN 0-12-598804-4). Set. 196.00 (ISBN 0-686-66787-5). Acad Pr.

Roulac, Stephen E., jt. auth. see Maisel, Sherman J.

Roulet, E. Linguistic Theory, Linguistic Description & Language Teaching. LC 75-326964. 112p. 1975. pap. text ed. 9.00x (ISBN 0-582-55075-0). Longman.

Roulston, Robert. James Norman Hall. (United States Authors Ser.: No. 323). 1978. 12.50 (ISBN 0-8057-7255-3). Twayne.

Roulstone, Michael. Taverns in Town. (Travel in England Ser.). (Illus.). 96p. 1975. 7.95 (ISBN 0-85944-001-X). Transatlantic.

Round, F. E. The Biology of the Algae. 2nd ed. LC 73-89991. 288p. 1974. 19.95 (ISBN 0-312-07875-7); pap. 14.95 (ISBN 0-312-07910-9). St Martin.

Rounds, David, jt. auth. see Edmonson, Madeleine.

Rounds, Glen. The Day the Circus Came to Lone Tree. LC 73-78458. (Illus.). (gr. k-3). 1973. reinforced bdg. 6.95 (ISBN 0-8234-0232-0). Holiday.

--The Day the Circus Came to Lone Tree. (gr. k-6). 1980. pap. 1.25 (ISBN 0-440-41769-4, YB). Dell.

--Mr. Yowder & the Lion Roar Capsules. (gr. k-6). 1980. pap. 1.25 (ISBN 0-440-45726-2, YB). Dell.

--Mr. Yowder & the Steamboat. (gr. k-6). 1980. pap. 1.25 (ISBN 0-440-45727-0, YB). Dell.

--Ol' Paul, the Mighty Logger. LC 75-22163. 96p. (gr. 4-6). 1976. 9.95 (ISBN 0-8234-0269-X). Holiday.

--Once We Had a Horse. LC 76-151758. (Illus.). (ps-3). 1971. 5.95 (ISBN 0-8234-0193-6). Holiday.

--Wild Orphan. (Illus.). (gr. 4-6). 1961. 7.95 (ISBN 0-8234-0147-2). Holiday.

Rouner, Leroy, jt. ed. see Howie, John.

Rountree, B. Seebohm. Poverty: A Study of Town Life, London Nineteen Ten. 2nd ed. LC 79-56969. (The English Working Class Ser.). 1980. lib. bdg. 38.00 (ISBN 0-8240-0120-6). Garland Pub.

Rountree, B. Seebohm & Lasker, Bruno. Unemployment: A Social Study, London, 1911. LC 79-56970. (The English Workinh Class Ser.). 1980. lib. bdg. 28.00 (ISBN 0-8240-0121-4). Garland Pub.

Rountree, B. Seebohm & Pigou, A. C. Lectures on Housing, Manchester, 1914. LC 79-56971. (The English Working Class Ser.). 1980. lib. bdg. 12.00 (ISBN 0-8240-0122-2). Garland Pub.

Rouquerol, J. & Sabbah, R., eds. Chemical Thermodynamics - 4: Proceedings. LC 76-44615. 1977. text ed. 27.00 (ISBN 0-08-021366-9). Pergamon.

Rourke, C. P. & Sanderson, B. J. Introduction to Piecewise-Linear Topology. LC 72-85229. (Ergebnisse der Mathematik und Ihrer Grenzgebiete: Vol. 69). (Illus.). 140p. 1972. 17.60 o.p. (ISBN 0-387-05800-1). Springer-Verlag.

Rourke, Constance. American Humor: A Study of the National Character. LC 31-7953. 1971. pap. 3.95 o.p. (ISBN 0-15-605590-2, HB213, Harv). HarBraceJ.

--Charles Sheeler: Artist in the American Tradition. LC 70-87603. (Library of American Art Ser). 1969. Repr. of 1938 ed. lib. bdg. 22.50 (ISBN 0-306-71634-8). Da Capo.

Rourke, Elizabeth M. Forest Home. 1980. 5.50 (ISBN 0-8233-0314-4). Golden Quill.

Rourke, Margaret. Lampshades, Simple & Advanced. 1973. 2.95 o.p. (ISBN 0-263-51376-9). Transatlantic.

Rourke, Robert E., jt. auth. see Mosteller, F. R.

Rous, John. The Rous Roll. (Illus.). 144p. 1980. text ed. 31.50x (ISBN 0-904387-43-7). Humanities.

Rouse, tr. Great Dialogues of Plato. pap. 5.95 (ISBN 0-452-25234-2, Z5234, Plume). NAL.

Rouse, C. A., ed. Progress in High Temperature Physics & Chemistry, 5 vols. 1967-1973. Vols. 1 & 5. 62.00 ea.; Vol. 2-4. 58.00 ea. Vol. 1, 1967 (ISBN 0-08-012123-3). Vol. 2, 1968 (ISBN 0-08-012640-5). Vol. 3. 1969 (ISBN 0-08-013959-0). Vol. 4. 1971 (ISBN 0-08-016439-0). Vol. 5. 1973 (ISBN 0-08-017240-7). Pergamon.

Rouse, C. C. Montana Bullwhacker. LC 69-17694. 1969. pap. 4.95 (ISBN 0-8163-0122-0, 13644-0). Pacific Pr Pub Assn.

Rouse, Doris & Waldrop, Sybil. Moral & Spiritual Development for the Young Child. LC 79-55850. 1981. perfect bdg - 3 hole punch 6.95 (ISBN 0-8054-4923-X). Broadman.

Rouse, Hunter, ed. Engineering Hydraulics. 1950. 52.50 (ISBN 0-471-74283-X, Pub. by Wiley-Interscience). Wiley.

Rouse, John E. World Cattle, 2 Vols. LC 69-10620. (Illus.). 1970. Set. 42.50 (ISBN 0-8061-0864-9). U of Okla Pr.

Rouse, John E., Jr., ed. Public Administration in American Society: A Guide to Information Sources. (American Government & History Information Guide Ser.: Vol. 11). 300p. 1980. 30.00 (ISBN 0-8103-1424-X). Gale.

Rouse, Parke. Dining in Philadelphia. (Dining in-Ser.). 200p. 1981. pap. 7.95 (ISBN 0-89716-039-8). Peanut Butter.

Rouse, Parke, Jr. Beautiful Virginia. Shangle, Robert D., ed. LC 80-11162. (Illus.). 72p. 1980. 14.95 (ISBN 0-89802-077-8); pap. 7.95 (ISBN 0-89802-076-X). Beautiful Am.

Rouse, Richard H., ed. Serial Bibliographies for Medieval Studies. LC 68-31637. (UCLA Center for Medieval & Renaissance Studies). 1969. 17.50x (ISBN 0-520-01456-1). U of Cal Pr.

Rouse, Sandra H., jt. auth. see Rouse, William B.

Rouse, T. L., jt. auth. see Ross, Charles P.

Rouse, W. H., tr. see Homer.

Rouse, William B. & Rouse, Sandra H. Management of Library Networks: Policy Analysis, Implementation, & Control. LC 80-12644. (Information Sciences Ser.). 288p. 1980. 25.95 (ISBN 0-471-05534-4, Pub. by Wiley Interscience). Wiley.

Rousey, Clyde L. Psychiatric Assessment by Speech & Hearing Behavior. (Illus.). 392p. 1974. text ed. 26.75 (ISBN 0-398-03034-0). C C Thomas.

Roush, jt. auth. see Kim.

Roush, John H., Jr. Management Audits of Subordinate Claims Offices of National Insurance Companies. LC 74-31546. 197p. 17.00. J H Roush.

Rousmaniere, John. A Glossary of Modern Sailing Terms. LC 75-31504. (Illus.). 254p. 1976. 6.95 (ISBN 0-396-07006-X). Dodd.

Rousmaniere, Peter F. The Federal Challenge: S.1236. (Government Auditing Ser.). 52p. 1979. pap. 6.00 (ISBN 0-916450-30-9). Coun on Municipal.

--State Level Disclosure Guidelines. (Municipal Securities Regulation Ser.). 233p. 1980. pap. 40.00 (ISBN 0-916450-20-1). Coun on Municipal.

--The Way Back: Toward Accountability in America's Cities. (Municipal Securities Regulation Ser.). 231p. 1979. pap. 25.00x (ISBN 0-916450-21-X). Coun on Municipal.

Rousmaniere, Peter F., et al, eds. Local Government Auditing: A Manual for Public Officials. Olenick, Arnold & Pirnicory, Vincent. 90p. 1979. pap. 14.95 (ISBN 0-916450-27-9). Coun on Municipal.

Rousmaniere, Peter F. K, et al. Selling Your City: A Primer for Government Officials on Communicating with the Investment Community. 70p. 1978. pap. 8.00 (ISBN 0-916450-22-8). Coun on Municipal.

Roussakkis, Emmanuel N. Managing Commercial Banks. LC 77-4380. (Special Studies). 1977. text ed. 24.95 (ISBN 0-03-021966-3). Praeger.

Roussas, G. G. Contiguity of Probability Measures: Some Applications in Statistics. LC 71-171682. (Cambridge Tracts in Mathematics & Mathematical Physics: No. 63). 1972. 44.50 (ISBN 0-521-08354-0). Cambridge U Pr.

Roussas, George G. A First Course in Mathematical Statistics. LC 71-183673. 1973. text ed. 24.95 (ISBN 0-201-06522-3). A-W.

Rousseas, S. Capitalism & Catastrophe. LC 78-11996. (Illus.). 1979. 18.95 (ISBN 0-521-22333-4). Cambridge U Pr.

Rousseau, G. S. Organic Form: The Life of an Idea. 1972. 8.00x (ISBN 0-7100-7246-5). Routledge & Kegan.

Rousseau, G. S. & Bouce, P. G., eds. Tobias Smollett: Bicentennial Essays Presented to Lewis M. Knapp. 1971. 14.95 (ISBN 0-19-501370-0). Oxford U Pr.

Rousseau, G. S. & Porter, R., eds. The Ferment of Knowledge: Studies in the Historiography of Eighteenth-Century Science. LC 80-40001. 550p. 1980. 39.50 (ISBN 0-521-22599-X). Cambridge U Pr.

Rousseau, Jean J. Annotated Social Contract. Sheroner, Charles M., ed. pap. 3.95 (ISBN 0-452-00369-5, FM369, Mer). NAL.

Rousseau, Jean-Jacques. Confessions, 2 vols. 1960. Vol. I. 5.00 ea. (ISBN 0-460-00859-5). Vol. II (ISBN 0-460-00860-9). Dutton.

--Dialogues. Bd. with Reveries. (Documentation thematique). pap. 2.95 (ISBN 0-685-24456-3, 292). Larousse.

--Du Contrat Social. Grimsley, Ronald, ed. 264p. (Fr.). 1972. 22.50x (ISBN 0-19-815710-X). Oxford U Pr.

--Emile, Julie & Other Writings. abr. ed. Archer, R. L., tr. from Fr. & intro. by. LC 52-18638. 1964. pap. 3.50 (ISBN 0-8120-0062-5). Barron.

--Emile: Or, Education. 1955. 10.50x (ISBN 0-460-00518-9, Evman); pap. 3.95 (ISBN 0-460-01518-4). Dutton.

--The Government of Poland. Kendall, Willmoore, tr. LC 70-167692. 1972. pap. text ed. 3.95 (ISBN 0-672-60391-8, LLA165). Bobbs.

--Nouvelle Heloise, 2 Vols. (Documentation thematique). (Fr). pap. 2.95 ea. Larousse.

--The Social Contract. 227p. 1980. Repr. of 1893 ed. lib. bdg. 30.00 (ISBN 0-89987-716-8). Darby Bks.

--Social Contract. Incl. Discourses. 1976. pap. 3.25 (ISBN 0-460-01660-1, Evman). Dutton.

--Social Contract & Discourse on the Origin of Inequality. Crocker, Lester G., ed. (Orig.). 1971. pap. 2.95 (ISBN 0-671-47864-8). WSP.

Rousseau, M. & Mathieu, Jean P. Problems in Optics. 376p. 1973. text ed. 32.00 (ISBN 0-08-016980-5). Pergamon.

Rousseau, Phillip. Ascetics, Authority, & the Church in the Age of Jerome & Cassian. (Historical Monographs). 1978. 36.00x (ISBN 0-19-821870-2). Oxford U Pr.

Rousseau, Richard W. Disclosure of the Ultimate: Fundamental Theology Reconsidered. LC 80-8259. 399p. 1980. lib. bdg. 21.50 (ISBN 0-8191-1284-4); pap. 13.25 (ISBN 0-8191-1285-2). U Pr of Amer.

Rousseau, Viateur, jt. auth. see Murphy, Daniel B.

Roussel, Hubert. The Houston Symphony Orchestra 1913-1971. (Illus.). 1972. 12.50 (ISBN 0-292-73000-4). U of Tex Pr.

Roussel, Raymond. How I Wrote Certain of My Books. 2nd rev. ed. Winkfield, Trevor & Koch, Kenneth, trs. from Fr. LC 77-3630. 1977. pap. 4.00 (ISBN 0-915342-05-7). SUN.

--Impressions of Africa. 1967. 17.95x (ISBN 0-520-01096-5). U of Cal Pr.

Rousselet-Blanc, Pierre, ed. Larousse du cheval. new ed. (Larousse des animaux familiers). (Illus.). 260p. (Fr.). 1975. 43.95x (ISBN 2-03-014855-5). Larousse.

--Larousse du chien. (Decouvrir les animaux). (Illus.). 480p. (Fr.). 1975. 64.50x (ISBN 2-03-014850-4). Larousse.

Rousset, David. The Legacy of the Bolshevik Revolution: A Critical History of the USSR. (Allison & Busby Motive Ser.). 416p. 1981. pap. 12.95 (ISBN 0-8052-8091-X, Pub. by Allison & Busby England). Schocken.

Roustan, Marius. The Pioneers of the French Revolution. LC 68-9659. 1970. Repr. of 1926 ed. 15.75 (ISBN 0-86527-150-X). Fertig.

Rout, L. B. The African Experience in Spanish America: 1502 to the Present Day. LC 75-9280. (Latin American Studies: No. 23). (Illus.). 276p. 1976. 39.50 (ISBN 0-521-20805-X); pap. 9.95x (ISBN 0-521-29010-4). Cambridge U Pr.

Rout, Leslie B., Jr. Politics of the Chaco Peace Conference, 1935-1939. (Latin American Monographs: No. 19). (Illus.). 1970. 12.50 (ISBN 0-292-70049-0). U of Tex Pr.

Routh, E. J. Stability of Motion. Fuller, A. T., ed. LC 75-8772. 228p. 1975. Repr. of 1877 ed. 22.95 o.p. (ISBN 0-470-74350-6). Halsted Pr.

Routh, F. Organ. (Teach Yourself Ser.). 1974. pap. 2.95 o.p. (ISBN 0-679-10372-4). McKay.

Routh, Guy. Occupation & Pay in Great Britain. 2nd, rev. ed. 269p. 1981. text ed. 37.50x (ISBN 0-333-28417-8, Pub. by Macmilla, England); pap. text ed. 20.00x (ISBN 0-333-28653-7). Humanities.

Routh, Jane & Wolff, Janet, eds. The Sociology of Literature: Theoretical Approaches. (Sociological Review Monograph: No. 25). 180p. 1977. pap. 18.50x (ISBN 0-8476-2298-3). Rowman.

Routh, Robert. Photographics. LC 76-15436. (Petersen's How-to Photographic Library). (Illus.). 80p. 1976. pap. 3.95 o.p. (ISBN 0-8227-4001-X). Petersen Pub.

Routh, Thomas A. Choosing a Nursing Home: The Problems & Their Solutions. 172p. 1970. text ed. 11.75 (ISBN 0-398-01617-8). C C Thomas.

Routledge Associates, compiled by. Index to the Diaries of Beatrice Webb 1873-1943. 1978. lib. bdg. 60.00x (ISBN 0-914146-60-2). Somerset Hse.

Routledge, Linda. Only Child's Play: Developing the Capicities of Handicapped Children. (Illus.). 1978. pap. 11.95x (ISBN 0-433-28350-5). Intl Ideas.

Routley, Erik. Conversion. LC 77-20298. 64p. 1978. pap. 1.75 (ISBN 0-8006-1327-9, 1-1327). Fortress.

--The English Carol. LC 73-9129. (Illus.). 272p. 1973. Repr. of 1959 ed. lib. bdg. 22.25x (ISBN 0-8371-6989-5, ROEC). Greenwood.

--Twentieth Century Church Music. 1964. 5.75x o.p. (ISBN 0-19-519067-X). Oxford U Pr.

Routley, R., jt. auth. see Goddard, L.

Routtenberg, Aryeh, ed. Biology of Reinforcement: Facet of Brain Stimulation Reward. (Behavioral Biology Ser.). 1980. 16.00 (ISBN 0-12-599350-1). Acad Pr.

Rouverol, Jean. Juarez, a Son of the People. LC 72-81071. (Illus.). 192p. (gr. 7 up). 1973. 4.95g o.s.i. (ISBN 0-02-777820-7, CCPr). Macmillan.

Roux, Edward. Time Longer Than Rope: A History of the Black Man's Struggle for Freedom in South Africa. 2nd ed. 1964. pap. 7.95x (ISBN 0-299-03204-3). U of Wis Pr.

Roux, Georges. Ancient Iraq. rev. ed. 480p. 1980. pap. 5.95 (ISBN 0-14-020828-3, Pelican). Penguin.

Roux, H. see Serratrice, G.

Roux, Jacques. Discours Sur les Moyens De Sauver la France et la Liberte. 49p. (Fr.). 1977. lib. bdg. 15.00x o.p. (ISBN 0-8287-0742-1); pap. text ed. 5.00x o.p. (ISBN 0-685-75622-X). Clearwater Pub.

Rovelstad, James M., jt. auth. see Goodwin, John R.

Rover, Michelle. French for Business Studies. 95p. (Fr.). 1979. pap. text ed. 4.50 (ISBN 0-582-35900-7). Longman.

Rovere, Richard H. The American Establishment & Other Reports, Opinions, & Speculations. LC 80-22247. x, 308p. 1981. Repr. of 1962 ed. lib. bdg. 27.50x (ISBN 0-313-22646-6, ROAE). Greenwood.

--The True & Scandalous History of Howe & Hummel. (Illus.). 190p. 1979. pap. 5.95 (ISBN 0-89062-093-8, Pub. by Hughes Press). Pub Ctr Cult Res.

Rovetch, Emily, ed. Like It Is: Arthur E. Thomas Interviews Leaders on Black America. 1981. text ed. 9.95 (ISBN 0-525-93193-7); pap. 5.95 (ISBN 0-525-93194-5); tchr's. guide 3.95 (ISBN 0-525-93195-3). Dutton.

Rovin, Jeff. The Films of Charlton Heston. (The Films of...Ser.). (Illus.). 256p. 1980. pap. 7.95 (ISBN 0-8065-0741-1). Citadel Pr.

--Star Trek. (Orig.). 1979. pap. text ed. write for info. o.p. (ISBN 0-685-96937-1). Berkley Pub.

Rovit, Earl H. Ernest Hemingway. (U. S. Authors Ser.: No. 41). 1963. lib. bdg. 9.95 (ISBN 0-8057-0364-0). Twayne.

Rovner-Pieczník, Roberta. The Criminal Court. LC 76-42854. (Illus.). 1978. 14.95 (ISBN 0-669-01056-1). Lexington Bks.

--Pretrial Intervention Strategies: An Evaluation of Policy-Related Research & Policymaker Perceptions. LC 75-43473. (Illus.). 1976. 18.95 (ISBN 0-669-00566-5). Lexington Bks.

Row, H. J., ed. see Anderson, George B.

Row, T. Subba. Notes on the Bhagavad-Gita. LC 77-88628. 1978. 6.00 (ISBN 0-911500-81-2); softcover 3.50 (ISBN 0-911500-82-0). Theos U Pr.

Rowan, A. J., jt. ed. see Meinardi, H.

Rowan, Adriana. Trancas. 288p. Date not set. pap. 2.75 (ISBN 0-445-04641-4). Popular Lib. Postponed.

Rowan, Archibald H. The Autobiography of Archibald H. Rowan, Esq. 476p. 1972. Repr. of 1840 ed. 19.00x (ISBN 0-7165-0011-6, Pub. by Irish Academic Pr Ireland). Biblio Dist.

Rowan, Betty, et al. The Learning Match: A Developmental Guide to Teaching Young Children. (Ser. in Early Childhood). (Illus.). 1980. text ed. 16.95 (ISBN 0-13-527044-8). P-H.

Rowan, Bonnie. Scholars' Guide to Washington D. C. Film & Video Collections. (Scholars' Guide to Washington D. C. Ser.: No. 6). 282p. 1980. text ed. 25.00x (ISBN 0-87474-818-6); pap. text ed. 8.95x (ISBN 0-87474-819-4). Smithsonian.

Rowan, David. Australian Monetary Policy. (Illus.). 313p. 1981. text ed. 22.50x (ISBN 0-86861-360-6, 2318); pap. text ed. 13.95x (ISBN 0-86861-368-1, 2319). Allen Unwin.

Rowan, Deidre. Time of the Burning Mask. 1978. pap. 1.50 o.p. (ISBN 0-449-14048-2, GM). Fawcett.

Rowan, Frances P. Chronically-Distressed Client: A Model for Intervention in the Community. LC 79-22475. 1980. pap. 10.00 (ISBN 0-8016-4204-3). Mosby.

Rowan, John. Ordinary Ecstasy: Humanistic Psychology in Action. (Orig.). 1976. pap. 10.00 (ISBN 0-7100-8344-0). Routledge & Kegan.

Rowan, John, jt. auth. see Reason, Peter.

Rowan, Lilian & Laiken, D. S. Speedwalking: The Exercise Alternative. 1980. 9.95 (ISBN 0-686-68357-9). Putnam.

Rowan, Patricia. What Sort of Life? 138p. 1981. pap. text ed. 15.25x (ISBN 0-85633-200-3, NFER). Humanities.

Rowan, Richard L. Readings in Labor Economics & Labor Relations. 4th ed. 1980. pap. 11.95x (ISBN 0-256-02367-0). Irwin.

Rowan, Richard L. & O'Brien, Rae A. Multinational Union Organizations in the Public Service & White-Collar Industries. 1980. pap. 15.00 (ISBN 0-89546-022-X). Indus Res Unit-Wharton.

Rowan, Richard L., ed. Readings in Labor Economics & Labor Relations. 3rd ed. 1976. pap. text ed. 12.50x o.p. (ISBN 0-256-01829-4). Irwin.

Rowan, Richard L., et al. Multinational Union Organizations in the Manufacturing & Processing Industries. LC 80-53989. (Multinational Industrial Relations Ser.). 213p. (Orig.). 1980. pap. 15.00 (ISBN 0-89546-021-1). Indus Res Unit-Wharton.

Rowan, Robert L. Men & Their Sex. (Illus.). 159p. 1979. 12.50 (ISBN 0-934200-01-7); pap. 6.95. Irvington.

Rowan, William H., jt. auth. see Graham, Walter W.

Rowat, Donald C., ed. Administrative Secrecy in Developed Countries. LC 78-16376. (International Institute of Administrative Sciences Ser.). 1979. 21.50x (ISBN 0-231-04596-4). Columbia U Pr.

--International Handbook on Local Government Reorganization: Contemporary Developments. LC 79-54063. (Illus.). xv, 626p. 1980. lib. bdg. 45.00 (ISBN 0-313-21269-4, RHL/). Greenwood.

Rowbotham, John R. Troubadours & Courts of Love. LC 68-22048. 1969. Repr. of 1895 ed. 15.00 (ISBN 0-8103-3840-8). Gale.

Rowbotham, Theodore. The Art of Landscape Painting with a Detailed Analysis of the Colours to Use in Watercolouring. 1979. deluxe ed. 39.35 (ISBN 0-930582-21-7). Gloucester Art.

Rowbottom, R. W., et al. Hospital Organization. 1973. 19.50x o.p. (ISBN 0-8448-0684-6). Crane-Russak Co.

Rowe. Biographical Sketch: Writings of Benjamin Franklin. 6.95 (ISBN 0-89315-003-7). Lambert Bk.

--Los Dinosaurios Gigantes (Giant Dinosaurs) (ps-3). 1980. pap. 1.95 (ISBN 0-590-30928-5, Schol Pap). Schol Bk Serv.

Rowe, A. J., jt. auth. see Patz, Alan L.

Rowe, Albert H. & Rowe, Albert, Jr. Food Allergy, Its Manifestations & Control, & the Elimination Diets - a Compendium: With Important Consideration of Inhalant, Drug, & Infectant Allergy. (Illus.). 696p. 1972. text ed. 27.75 (ISBN 0-398-02395-6). C C Thomas.

Rowe, Albert, Jr., jt. auth. see Rowe, Albert H.

Rowe, David N., jt. auth. see Montagu, Ashley.

Rowe, Ednor, ed. see Kapitza, S. P. & Melekhin, V. N.

Rowe, Elizabeth S. Friendship in Death: In Twenty Letters from the Dead to the Living. LC 70-170576. (Foundations of the Novel Ser.: Vol. 53). lib. bdg. 50.00 (ISBN 0-8240-0565-1). Garland Pub.

Rowe, Francis W., jt. auth. see Clark, Ailsa M.

Rowe, James E. Industrial Plant Location. (Public Administation Ser.: Bibliography P-575). 52p. 1980. pap. 5.50. Vance Biblios.

Rowe, Jane. Parents, Children & Adoption. 1966. text ed. 23.50x (ISBN 0-7100-2055-4). Humanities.

--Yours by Choice: A Guide for Adoptive Parents. rev ed. 1971. pap. 6.00 (ISBN 0-7100-6369-5). Routledge & Kegan.

Rowe, Jeanne A. Album of Martin Luther King Jr. LC 73-110474. (Picture Albums Ser). (Illus.). 1970. PLB 7.90 (ISBN 0-531-01509-2). Watts.

Rowe, John. A Sounding of Storytellers. LC 79-2418. 1980. 13.95 o.p. (ISBN 0-397-31882-0). Lippincott.

--Tragi-Comoedia. LC 70-170430. (The English Stage Ser.: Vol. 16). lib. bdg. 50.00 (ISBN 0-8240-0599-6). Garland Pub.

Rowe, John W. Primary Commodities in International Trade. (Orig.). 1966. 41.50 (ISBN 0-521-06144-X); pap. 14.95x (ISBN 0-521-09277-9). Cambridge U Pr.

Rowe, Kenneth E., ed. Methodist Union Catalog Pre-1976 Imprints, 20 vols, Vol. I, A-bj. LC 75-33190. 1975. 25.00 (ISBN 0-8108-0880-3). Scarecrow.

--Methodist Union Catalog: Pre-1976 Imprints, Vol. II: Bl-cha. LC 75-33190. 1976. 25.00 (ISBN 0-8108-0920-6). Scarecrow.

--Methodist Union Catalog: Pre-1976 Imprints, Che-Dix, Vol. 3. LC 75-33190. 1978. 25.00 (ISBN 0-8108-1067-0). Scarecrow.

--Methodist Union Catalog: Pre-1976 Imprints: Volume IV, Do-Fy. LC 75-33190. 436p. 1979. 25.00 (ISBN 0-8108-1225-8). Scarecrow.

--The Place of Wesley in the Christian Tradition: Essays Delevered at Drew University in Celebration of the Commencement of the Publication of the Oxford Edition of the Works of John Wesley. LC 76-27659. 1976. 10.00 (ISBN 0-8108-0981-8). Scarecrow.

Rowe, Leo S. United States & Puerto Rico. LC 74-14249. (A Puerto Rican Experience Ser). 290p. 1975. Repr. 16.00x (ISBN 0-405-06235-4). Arno.

Rowe, M. B. & DeTure, L. A Summary of Research in Science Education, 1973. LC 75-21655. 85p. (Orig.). 1975. pap. 7.95 (ISBN 0-470-74354-9). Halsted Pr.

Rowe, Mary B., ed. What Research Says to the Science Teacher. 1978. pap. 3.50 (ISBN 0-87355-009-9). Natl Sci Tchrs.

--What Research Says to the Science Teacher, Vol. 2. (Orig.). 1979. pap. 4.00 (ISBN 0-87355-013-7). Natl Sci Tchrs.

Rowe, Mike. Chicago Breakdown. (The Roots of Jazz Ser.). (Illus.). 1979. Repr. of 1974 ed. lib. bdg. 21.50 (ISBN 0-306-79532-9). Da Capo.

Rowe, Nicholas. Fair Penitent. Goldstein, Malcolm, ed. LC 69-10354. (Regents Restoration Drama Ser). 1969. 5.95x (ISBN 0-8032-0367-5); pap. 1.65x (ISBN 0-8032-5367-2, BB 270, Bison). U of Nebr Pr.

--The Fair Penitent & Jane Shore. 254p. 1980. Repr. of 1907 ed. lib. bdg. 30.00 (ISBN 0-89987-714-1). Darby Bks.

--The Tragedy of Jane Shore. Pedicord, Harry W., ed. LC 73-85439. (Regents Restoration Drama Ser.). 1974. 8.95x (ISBN 0-8032-0381-0); pap. 1.85x (ISBN 0-8032-5381-8, BB 277, Bison). U of Nebr Pr.

--Tragedy of Lady Jane Gray. Sherry, Richard J., tr. (SSEL Poetic Drama Ser.: No. 59). (Orig.). 1980. pap. text ed. 25.00x (ISBN 0-391-01955-4). Humanities.

Rowe, R. E. Concrete Bridge Design. 1972. Repr. of 1966 ed. text ed. 52.20x (ISBN 0-85334-110-9, Pub. by Applied Science). Burgess-Intl Ideas.

Rowe, Richard D., et al. The Neonate with Congenital Heart Disease. 2nd ed. (Illus.). 450p. 1981. text ed. 42.50 (ISBN 0-7216-7775-4). Saunders.

Rowe, Stephen, ed. Living Beyond Crisis: Essays on Discovery & Being in the World. LC 80-18135. 261p. 1980. pap. 8.95 (ISBN 0-8298-0402-1). Pilgrim NY.

Rowe, Thomas, tr. see Chomei, Kano N.

Rowe, Violet A. Sir Henry Vane the Younger: A Study in Political & Administrative History. (Univ. of London on Historical Studies: No. 28). 1970. text ed. 15.25x (ISBN 0-485-13128-5, Athlone Pr). Humanities.

Rowe, W. Woodin. Nabokov's Spectral Dimension. 1981. 15.00 (ISBN 0-88233-641-X). Ardis Pubs.

Rowe, William. Exotic Alphabets & Ornaments. (Illus.). 80p. (Orig.). 1974. pap. 3.50 (ISBN 0-486-22989-0). Dover.

--Flora & Fauna Design Fantasies. (Pictorial Archive Ser.). (Illus.). 80p. (Orig.). 1976. 4.00 (ISBN 0-486-23289-1). Dover.

--Original Art Deco Designs. (Pictorial Archive Ser.). (Illus., Orig.). 1973. pap. 4.00 (ISBN 0-486-22567-4). Dover.

Rowe, William, ed. Jose M. Arguedas: Los Rios profundos. LC 73-4524. 288p. 1973. text ed. 19.50 (ISBN 0-08-017014-5); pap. text ed. 12.75 (ISBN 0-08-017015-3). Pergamon.

Rowe, William L. Philosophy of Religion: An Introduction. 1978. pap. text ed. 10.95x (ISBN 0-8221-0208-0). Dickenson.

Rowe, William T., jt. ed. see Fogel, Joshua A.

Rowe, William Woodin. Nabokov's Deceptive World. LC 76-158968. 1971. 12.00x (ISBN 0-8147-7353-2). NYU Pr.

Rowell, G. The Victorian Theatre: 1792-1914. 2nd ed. LC 78-2900. (Illus.). 1979. 36.00 (ISBN 0-521-22070-X); pap. 10.95 (ISBN 0-521-29346-4). Cambridge U Pr.

Rowell, Galen. Many People Come, Looking, Looking. LC 80-19394. (Illus.). 182p. 1980. 30.00 (ISBN 0-916890-86-4). Mountaineers.

Rowell, Galen A., ed. The Vertical World of Yosemite. LC 73-85908. (Illus.). 224p. 1974. 16.95 o.p. (ISBN 0-911824-28-6); pap. 11.95 (ISBN 0-911824-87-1). Wilderness.

Rowell, Henry T. Rome in the Augustan Age. (Centers of Civilization Ser.: No. 5). 1971. pap. 4.95x (ISBN 0-8061-0956-4). U of Okla Pr.

Rowell, John W. Yankee Artillerymen: Through the Civil War with Eli Lilly's Indiana Battery. LC 75-5918. (Illus.). 320p. 1975. 15.50x (ISBN 0-87049-171-7). U of Tenn Pr.

Rowell, Margit. New Images from Spain. Flint, Lucy, tr. LC 79-92992. (Illus.). 144p. (Orig.). 1980. soft cover 8.50 (ISBN 0-89207-023-4). S R Guggenheim.

Rowell, Thelma. Social Behavior of Monkeys. (Education Ser.). 1973. pap. 2.95 o.p. (ISBN 0-14-080706-3). Penguin.

Rowell, Unni H. Geological Survey of Norway, No. 361, Bulletin 58. 1981. pap. 12.00x (ISBN 82-00-31430-8). Universitet.

Rowen, Henry S., jt. auth. see Imai, Ryukichi.

Rowen, Herbert H. History of Early Modern Europe, 1500-1815. 1960. pap. 12.95 (ISBN 0-672-60697-6). Bobbs.

--The King's State: Proprietary Dynasticism in Early Modern France. 256p. 1980. 19.50 (ISBN 0-8135-0893-2). Rutgers U Pr.

Rowen, Joseph R. NRMA's Advertising & Sales Promotion Budget Book. 100p. 1981. text ed. 13.75 (ISBN 0-686-60193-9, 266780). Natl Ret Merch.

Rowen, R. Music Through Sources & Documents. 1979. pap. 15.95 (ISBN 0-13-608331-5). P-H.

Rowen, Ruth H. Early Chamber Music. 2nd ed. LC 68-8144. (Music Reprint Ser). 1969. Repr. of 1949 ed. lib. bdg. 22.50 (ISBN 0-306-71160-5). Da Capo.

Rowes, Barbara. Rock Talk. (YA) (gr. 7-12). 1977. pap. 1.25 (ISBN 0-590-10417-9, Schol Pap). Schol Bk Serv.

Roweton, William E. My Reflections on Educational Psychology, Science & American Schools. LC 80-8262. 124p. 1980. lib. bdg. 15.75 (ISBN 0-8191-1329-8); pap. text ed. 7.50 (ISBN 0-8191-1330-1). U Pr of Amer.

Roweton, William E., ed. Revitalizing Educational Psychology: Readings in Method & Substance. LC 76-20603. 384p. 1976. 18.95 (ISBN 0-88229-195-5). Nelson-Hall.

Rowinski, Ludwig J., jt. auth. see Naske, Claus M.

Rowland, Amy, ed. see Cohen, Maurice.

Rowland, Beatrice, jt. auth. see Rowland, Howard.

Rowland, Beatrice L., jt. auth. see Rowland, Howard S.

Rowland, Benjamin M., ed. Balance of Power or Hegemony: The Interwar Monetary System. LC 75-27423. 266p. 1976. 15.00x (ISBN 0-8147-7368-0). NYU Pr.

Rowland, Beryl. Birds with Human Souls: A Guide to Bird Symbolism. LC 77-4230. (Illus.). 1978. 15.00x (ISBN 0-87049-215-2). U of Tenn Pr.

--Medieval Woman's Guide to Health: The First English Gynecological Handbook. Rowland, Beryl, tr. Robbins, Rossell H. LC 80-82201. (Illus.). 194p. 1981. 17.50x (ISBN 0-87338-243-9). Kent St U Pr.

Rowland, Daniel B. Mannerism - Style & Mood. 1964. 29.50x (ISBN 0-685-69860-2). Elliots Bks.

Rowland, George, jt. auth. see Smith, David B.

Rowland, Harry F. & Rowland, Paul. Pasternak's "Doctor Zhivago". (Crosscurrents-Modern Critiques Ser.). 1968. pap. 6.95 (ISBN 0-8093-0293-4). S Ill U Pr.

Rowland, Howard & Rowland, Beatrice. Nursing Administration Handbook. LC 80-11857. 600p. 1980. text ed. 42.50 (ISBN 0-89443-275-3). Aspen Systems.

Rowland, Howard S. & Rowland, Beatrice L. The Nurse's Almanac. LC 78-311. (Illus.). 1978. 32.95 (ISBN 0-89443-031-9); pap. 21.95 (ISBN 0-89443-040-8). Aspen Systems.

Rowland, Leon. Santa Cruz: The Early Years. Gant, Michael S., ed. (Illus.). 260p. 1980. cancelled (ISBN 0-934136-03-3, Paper Vision); pap. 7.95 (ISBN 0-934136-04-1). Western Tanager.

Rowland, Lewis P., ed. Immunological Disorders of the Nervous System. LC 72-139827. (ARNMD Research Publications Ser: Vol. 49). 1971. 31.50 (ISBN 0-683-00243-0). Raven.

Rowland, Lorna. Growing Herbs. (Practical Gardening Ser.). (Illus.). 112p. (Orig.). 1979. pap. 10.50 (ISBN 0-589-01244-4, Pub. by Reed Bks Australia). C E Tuttle.

Rowland, Malcolm & Tozer, Thomas N. Clinical Pharmacokinetics: Concepts & Applications. LC 79-10735. (Illus.). 330p. 1980. text ed. 29.50 (ISBN 0-8121-0681-4). Lea & Febiger.

Rowland, Mark. The Ed King Kommemorative Kalender Nineteen Eighty-One. 1980. pap. 4.95. World Food.

Rowland, Mary F. & Rowland, Paul. Pasternak's "Doctor Zhivago". LC 68-10000. (Crosscurrents-Modern Critiques Ser.). 232p. 1967. 10.95 (ISBN 0-8093-0266-7). S Ill U Pr.

Rowland, Michael. Hypertension of Adults Twenty-Five to Seventy-Four Years of Age: United States, 1971-1975. Shipp, Audrey, ed. (Ser. 11, No. 221). 50p. Date not set. text ed. price not set (ISBN 0-8406-0207-3). Natl Ctr Health Stats.

Rowland, P. Last Liberal Governments. 1969. 8.95 o.s.i. (ISBN 0-02-605580-5). Macmillan.

Rowland, Paul, jt. auth. see Rowland, Harry F.

Rowland, Paul, jt. auth. see Rowland, Mary F.

Rowland, Peter. David Lloyd George: A Biography. (Illus.). 896p. 1976. 20.00 o.s.i. (ISBN 0-02-605590-2). Macmillan.

Rowland, Pleasant. Addison-Wesley Reading Program: Placement Tests. (Addison-Wesley Reading Program Ser.). (gr. k-3). 1979. 8.36 (ISBN 0-201-20870-9, Sch Div). A-W.

--Adventures of the Superkids, Bk. 1. (Addison-Wesley Reading Program). (gr. 1). 1979. pap. text ed. 6.40 (ISBN 0-201-20600-5, Sch Div); six skillbks 4.72 (ISBN 0-201-20601-3); tchr. guides in binder 38.50 (ISBN 0-201-20602-1); end-of-level tests 20.32. A-W.

--Happily Ever After: Readiness Teacher's Guide (Visual, Listening, Conceptual Development) (Addison-Wesley Reading Program Ser.). (ps-1). 1979. pap. text ed. 40.00 (ISBN 0-201-20389-8, Sch Div); dupe masters avail. (ISBN 0-201-20399-5). A-W.

--More Adventures of the Superkids, Bk. 2. (Addison-Wesley Reading Program). (gr. 1). 1979. pap. text ed. 6.72 (ISBN 0-201-20650-1, Sch Div); reader, 3 skills bks. 3.12 (ISBN 0-201-20651-X); binder with 3 tchr. guides, tape incl. 38.52; pretest pkg. of dup. masters, gr. 1 38.52 (ISBN 0-201-20657-9); dupe masters avail. A-W.

--The Nitty Gritty, Rather Pretty, City: Test Package. (Addison-Wesley Reading Program). (gr. 2). 1979. 28.76 (ISBN 0-201-20770-2, Sch Div); avail. tchr's man. progress & pretests 1.24 (ISBN 0-201-20760-5); pretest pkg. 28.76 (ISBN 0-201-20758-3); tchr's man. & class record form & ans. key 1.24 (ISBN 0-201-20768-0). A-W.

--The Nitty-Gritty, Rather Pretty, City, 1st to 12th Streets. (Addison-Wesley Reading Program). (gr. 2). 1979. text ed. 7.32 (ISBN 0-201-20700-1, Sch Div); tchr's. guides in binder (6 booklets) 23.40 (ISBN 0-201-20702-8); student skills books 2-1 2.52 (ISBN 0-201-20701-X); tchr. skills bks. 3.32 (ISBN 0-201-20709-5). A-W.

--The Nitty Gritty, Rather Pretty, City: 13-24th Streets. (Addison-Wesley Reading Program). (gr. 2). 1979. text ed. 7.32 (ISBN 0-201-20750-8, Sch Div); skills bk., s.e. 2.52 (ISBN 0-201-20751-6); tchr's. guides in binder (6 booklets) 23.40 (ISBN 0-201-20752-4). A-W.

Rowland, Ralph S. & Rowland, Star W. Clary Genealogy: Four Early American Lines & Related Families. LC 80-54651. 1980. write for info. R & S Rowland.

--Clary Genealogy: Four Early American Lines & Related Families. 1980. 17.50. R & S Rowland.

Rowland, Richard H., jt. auth. see Lewis, Robert A.

Rowland, Roy V. The Psychological Search for God. (Illus.). 1980. 34.75 (ISBN 0-89920-003-6). Am Inst Psych.

Rowland, Stanley P., ed. Water in Polymers. LC 80-13860. (ACS Symposium Ser.: No. 127). 1980. 48.00 (ISBN 0-8412-0559-0). Am Chemical.

Rowland, Star W., jt. auth. see Rowland, Ralph S.

Rowland-Entwistle, A. T. & Cooke, Joan. Animal Worlds. LC 76-13655. (Modern Knowledge Library). (Illus.). 48p. (gr. 9 up). 1976. 3.95 o.p. (ISBN 0-531-02441-5); PLB 5.90 o.p. (ISBN 0-531-01196-8). Watts.

Rowland-Entwistle, Theodore. Exploring Animal Homes. (Explorer Bks). (Illus.). (gr. 3-5). 1978. 2.95 (ISBN 0-531-09093-0); PLB 6.45 s&l (ISBN 0-531-09106-6). Watts.

--Exploring Animal Journeys. (Explorer Bks.). (Illus.). (gr. 3-5). 1978. 2.95 (ISBN 0-531-09094-9); PLB 6.45 s&l (ISBN 0-531-09100-7). Watts.

Rowlands & Humern, eds. Recent Advances in Cardiology, No. 8. (R-A in Cardiology Ser.). (Illus.). 1981. text ed. price not set. Churchill.

Rowlands, Avril J. Script Continuity & the Production Secretary. (Media Manuals Ser.). Date not set. pap. 6.95 o.p. (ISBN 0-8038-6737-9). Hastings.

Rowlands, Derek J., jt. auth. see Hamer, John.

Rowlands, Henry. Mona Antiqua Restaurata. Feldman, Burton & Richardson, Robert D., eds. LC 78-60894. (Myth & Romanticism Ser.: Vol. 21). 399p. 1979. lib. bdg. 60.00 (ISBN 0-8240-3570-4). Garland Pub.

Rowlands, John. Rubens: Drawings & Sketches. (Illus.). 1978. 17.50 o.p. (ISBN 0-684-15649-0, ScribT). Scribner.

Rowlands, Richard. A Restitution of Decayed Intelligence: In Antiquities, Concerning the...English Nation. by the Studie & Travaile of R. Verstagen. Dedicated Unto the Kings Most Excellent Majestie. LC 79-84134. (English Experience Ser.: No. 952). 380p. 1979. Repr. of 1605 ed. lib. bdg. 35.00 (ISBN 90-221-0952-6). Walter J Johnson.

Rowlands, Samuel. Uncollected Poems, 1604-1617. Incl. Humors Ordinairie; Theater of Delightful Recreation; Humors Antique Faces; The Bride. LC 78-119867. 210p. 1970. 21.00x (ISBN 0-8201-1074-4). Schol Facsimiles.

Rowlands, W. Cambrian Bibliography: Containing an Account of Books Printed in the Welsh Language, or Relating to Wales, Evans, Silvan D., ed. 1970. Repr. of 1869 ed. text ed. 51.50x (ISBN 90-6041-080-7). Humanities.

Rowledge, J. W., jt. auth. see Reed, Brian.

Rowles, Graham D. Prisoners of Space? Exploring the Geographical Experience of Older People. (Replica Edition Ser.). 216p. 1980. pap. text ed. 10.00x (ISBN 0-86531-072-6). Westview.

Rowlett, Elsebet S., jt. auth. see Feldman, Lawrence H.

Rowlett, Elsebet S., et al. Neolithic Levels on the Titelberg, Luxembourg. LC 76-623772. (Museum Brief: No. 18). iii, 61p. 1976. pap. write for info. (ISBN 0-913134-83-X). Mus Anthro Mo.

Rowlett, Elsebet S., et al, eds. Annual Report of the Museum of Anthropology, University of Missouri, Columbia, Missouri, 1975-1976. (Illus.). 1977. pap. 2.50x o.p. (ISBN 0-913134-93-7). Mus Anthro Mo.

Rowley, C. K. & Peacock, A. T. Welfare Economics: A Liberal Restatement. LC 75-22430. 198p. 1975. 24.95 (ISBN 0-470-74362-X). Halsted Pr.

Rowley, Charles K. Readings in Industrial Economics, 2 vols. LC 73-76642. 1973. Vol. 1. pap. 11.50x (ISBN 0-8448-0207-7); Vol. 2. pap. 11.50x (ISBN 0-8448-0208-5). Crane-Russak Co.

Rowley, G. Principles of Chinese Painting. rev ed. (Monographs in Art & Archaeology: No. 24). 1959. 26.50x (ISBN 0-691-03834-1); pap. 7.50 (ISBN 0-691-00300-9). Princeton U Pr.

Rowley, Gill. The Book of Music: A Visual Guide to Musical Appreciation. LC 78-53427. 1978. 19.95 o.p. (ISBN 0-13-079988-2). P-H.

Rowley, H. H. New Century Bible Commentary on Job. rev. ed. Clements, Ronald E., ed. 304p. 1980. pap. 7.95 (ISBN 0-8028-1838-2). Eerdmans.

--The Relevance of Apocalyptic. 3rd ed. LC 64-12221. 240p. pap. text ed. 7.95 (ISBN 0-87921-061-3). Attic Pr.

Rowley, J. C. Econometric Estimation. Corry, Bernard & Henry, Brian, eds. LC 72-7811. (Handbooks in Economic Analysis Ser). 234p. 1973. text ed. 19.95 (ISBN 0-470-74360-3). Halsted Pr.

Rowley, J. E. & Turner, C. M. The Dissemination of Information. LC 78-6138. (Grafton Library of Information Science). 1978. lib. bdg. 29.50x (ISBN 0-89158-830-2). Westview.

Rowley, J. W. & Stanbury, W. T. Competition Policy in Canada: Stage II, Bill C-13. 311p. 1978. pap. text ed. 12.95x (ISBN 0-920380-02-6, Pub. by Inst Res Pub Canada). Renouf.

Rowley, Jennifer E. Mechanized In-House Information Systems. 1979. 19.50 (ISBN 0-89664-404-9, Pub. by K G Saur). Shoe String.

Rowley, R. T., ed. The Origins of Open Field Agriculture. 288p. 1981. 26.50x (ISBN 0-389-20102-2). B&N.

Rowley, Trevor, jt. auth. see Astor, Michael.

Rowley, William, jt. auth. see Middleton, Thomas.

Rowlings, Cherry. Social Work with Elderly People. (Studies in the Personal Social Services: No. 3). 144p. (Orig.). 1981. text ed. 19.95x (ISBN 0-04-362036-1, 2603); pap. text ed. 7.95x (ISBN 0-04-362037-X, 2604). Allen Unwin.

Rowls, Michael D., jt. auth. see Friedman, Myles I.

Rowney, J. M., et al, eds. Thick Plate Working, Vol. 2. (Engineering Craftsmen: No. D21). (Illus.). 1969. spiral bdg. 15.50x (ISBN 0-85083-047-8). Intl Ideas.

Rowntree, Derek. Educational Technology in Curriculum Development. 2nd ed. 1981. text ed. 18.95 (ISBN 0-06-318169-X, IntlDept); pap. text ed. 10.25 (ISBN 0-06-318170-3). Har-Row.

--International Dictionary of Education. 1980. text ed. 15.70 (ISBN 0-06-318157-6, IntlDept). Har-Row.

Rowse, A. L. The Elizabethan Renaissance: The Life of the Society. (Illus.). 320p. 1972. lib. rep. ed. 20.00x (ISBN 0-684-15656-3, ScribT). Scribner.

--England of Elizabeth. LC 78-53293. 1978. 25.00 (ISBN 0-299-07720-9); pap. 8.95 (ISBN 0-299-07724-1). U of Wis Pr.

--Jonathan Swift: A Biography. LC 75-37779. (Encore Edition). 1976. 2.95 o.p. (ISBN 0-684-15447-1, ScribT). Scribner.

--Peter: The White Cat of Trenarren. 1974. 4.95 o.p. (ISBN 0-7181-1228-8, Pub. by Michael Joseph). Merrimack Bk Serv.

Rowse, A. L., jt. auth. see Betjeman, John.

Rowsey, Katheryn, jt. auth. see Knox, Carol.

Rowsome, Frank, Jr. Verse by the Side of the Road: Burma-Shave Signs & Jingles. LC 65-24618. 1965. 6.95 (ISBN 0-8289-0038-8). Greene.

Rowton, Frederic, ed. The Female Poets of Great Britain. (Illus.). 600p. 1981. 18.95 (ISBN 0-8143-1664-6). Wayne St U Pr.

Roxburgh, Edwin, jt. auth. see Goosens, Leon.

Roxburgh, Toby, ed. see Clissold, Stephen.

Roy, et al. Pediatric Clinical Gastroenterology. 2nd ed. LC 75-22272. (Illus.). 1975. 41.50 (ISBN 0-8016-4613-8). Mosby.

Roy, A. B. & Trudinger, P. Biochemistry of Inorganic Compounds of Sulphur. LC 78-79056. (Illus.). 1970. 57.50 (ISBN 0-521-07581-5). Cambridge U Pr.

Roy, A. E. & Clarke, D. Astronomy: Principles & Practice. LC 76-51875. 1977. 34.50x (ISBN 0-8448-1071-1); pap. 19.50x (ISBN 0-8448-1073-8). Crane-Russak Co.

Roy, Archie E. & Clarke, David. Astronomy: The Structure of the Universe. LC 76-51877. 1977. 24.50x. Crane-Russak Co.

Roy, Callista & Roberts, Sharon. Theory Construction in Nursing: An Adaptation Model. (Illus.). 352p. 1981. text ed. 17.95 (ISBN 0-13-913657-6). P-H.

Roy, Sr. Callista. Introduction to Nursing: An Adaptation Model. LC 75-43612. (Illus.). 400p. 1976. ref. ed. 16.95 (ISBN 0-13-491290-X). P-H.

Roy, Dilip K. & Devi, Indira. Pilgrims of the Stars. LC 72-93632. 324p. 1973. 7.95 o.s.i. (ISBN 0-02-605660-7). Macmillan.

Roy, Dilipkumar. Bhagavad Gita, a Revelation: Mahabharata Bhagavad Gita. 190p. 1975. 12.50 (ISBN 0-88253-698-2). Ind-US Inc.

Roy, E. P. Cooperatives: Development, Principles & Management. 1981. 11.95 o.p. (ISBN 0-8134-2143-8, 2143); pap. text ed. 8.95x o.p. (ISBN 0-685-73357-2). Interstate.

Roy, Ewell P. Collective Bargaining in Agriculture. LC 79-113823. 1970. pap. text ed. 7.50x (ISBN 0-8134-1161-0, 1161). Interstate.

--Cooperatives: Development, Principles & Management. 4th ed. 1981. 11.95 (ISBN 0-8134-2143-8, 2143); pap. text ed. 8.95x. Interstate.

--Exploring Agribusiness. 3rd ed. (Illus.). (gr. 9-12). 1980. 15.35 (ISBN 0-8134-2098-9, 2098); text ed. 11.50x (ISBN 0-685-64700-5). Interstate.

Roy, Ewell P., et al. Economics: Applications to Agriculture & Agribusiness. 3rd ed. x, 455p. 1981. 17.00 (ISBN 0-8134-2113-6, 2113); text ed. 12.75x. Interstate.

--Economics: Applications to Agriculture & Agribusiness. 2nd ed. x, 455p. 1981. 18.00 o.p. (ISBN 0-8134-2113-6, 2113); text ed. 13.50x o.p. (ISBN 0-685-64698-X). Interstate.

Roy, F. Hampton, jt. auth. see Fraunfelder, F. T.

Roy, G. Ross, ed. Studies in Scottish Literature, Vol. 13. LC 73-138822. 1978. lib. bdg. 14.95x (ISBN 0-87249-368-7). U of SC Pr.

Roy, Gregor. Monarch Notes on Cervantes' Don Quixote. (Orig.). pap. 1.95 (ISBN 0-671-00553-7). Monarch Pr.

--Monarch Notes on Graham Greene's Major Novels. (Orig.). pap. 1.95 (ISBN 0-671-00838-2). Monarch Pr.

--Monarch Notes on Kafka's the Trial, the Castle & Other Works. (Orig.). pap. 1.95 (ISBN 0-671-00847-1). Monarch Pr.

Roy, J. H. The Calf. 4th ed. LC 79-42840. (Studies in the Agricultural & Food Sciences). 1980. text ed. 79.95 (ISBN 0-408-70941-3). Butterworths.

Roy, Joaquin. El Gobierno y los Presidentes De los Estados Unidos De America. (Illus.). 96p. (Orig., Span.). (gr. 8 up). 1980. pap. 7.95 (ISBN 0-89196-073-2, Domus Bks). Quality Bks IL.

Roy, John F. A Guide to Barsoom. 1976. pap. 1.75 o.p. (ISBN 0-345-24722-1). Ballantine.

Roy, Jules. Battle of Dienbienphu. LC 64-25121. (Illus.). 1965. 15.00 o.p. (ISBN 0-06-013715-0, HarpT). Har-Row.

Roy, K. P. Introduction to Heat Engines, Vol. 1. 2nd ed. pap. 7.50x (ISBN 0-210-31186-X). Asia.

Roy, Kristina. The Heiress. Tenjack, Martha, tr. LC 79-56301. 1979. pap. 3.95 o.p. (ISBN 0-89107-176-8). Good News.

Roy, Linda, ed. see Lively, Jeanne.

Roy, M. Aaron. Species Identity & Attachment: A Phylogenic Evaluation. 1979. lib. bdg. 37.50 (ISBN 0-8240-7052-6). Garland Pub.

Roy, P. C. The Coin Age of Northern India. 1980. 27.50x (ISBN 0-8364-0641-9, Pub. by Abhinav India). South Asia Bks.

Roy, Paul S. The Faith Experience: Communal Spirituality for Justice. 240p. (Orig.). 1981. pap. 8.95 (ISBN 0-8091-2380-0). Paulist Pr.

Roy, Probir. Theory of Lepton-Hadron Processes at High Energies: Partons, Scale Invariance & Light-Cone Physics. (Oxford Studies in Physics). (Illus.). 188p. 1975. 33.50x (ISBN 0-19-851452-2). Oxford U Pr.

Roy, Prodipto, jt. ed. see Hursh-Cesar, Gerald.

Roy, R., jt. auth. see Henisch, H. K.

Roy, Ramashray. The Uncertain Verdict: A Study of the 1969 Elections in Four Indian States. (Illus.). 1975. 18.50x (ISBN 0-520-02475-3). U of Cal Pr.

Roy, Rammohun. The Complete Songs of Rammohun Roy. Guha, Nikhiles, tr. from Bengali. (Safronbird Bk.). 72p. (Eng.). 1975. 12.00 (ISBN 0-89253-544-X); pap. 4.80 (ISBN 0-88253-710-5). Ind-US Inc.

Roy, Robert H. The Cultures of Management. LC 76-47385. (Illus.). 512p. 1977. 19.95x (ISBN 0-8018-1875-3); pap. text ed. 9.95 (ISBN 0-8018-2524-5). Johns Hopkins.

Roy, Robert L. Cordwood Masonry Houses: A Practical Guide for the Owner-Builder. LC 80-52325. (Illus.). 168p. 1980. 14.95 (ISBN 0-8069-5418-3); lib. bdg. 13.29 (ISBN 0-8069-5419-1); pap. 7.95 (ISBN 0-8069-8944-0). Sterling.

--How to Build Log End Houses. LC 77-72392. (Illus.). 1977. 12.95 o.p. (ISBN 0-8069-8828-2); PLB 10.39 o.p. (ISBN 0-8069-8829-0). Sterling.

--Underground Houses: How to Build a Low-Cost Home. LC 79-64505. (Illus.). 1979. pap. 5.95 o.p. (ISBN 0-8069-8856-8). Sterling.

Roy, Ron. Awful Thursday. LC 78-14049. (An I Am Reading Bk.). (Illus.). (gr. 1-4). 1979. 3.95 (ISBN 0-394-84003-8); PLB 5.99 (ISBN 0-394-94003-2). Pantheon.

--The Great Frog Swap. LC 79-21966. (Illus.). 48p. (gr. 1-4). 1981. 7.95 (ISBN 0-394-84432-7); PLB 7.99 (ISBN 0-394-94432-1). Pantheon.

--Nightmare Island. LC 80-23526. (Illus.). 80p. (gr. 3-7). 1981. 7.95 (ISBN 0-525-35905-2). Dutton.

--Three Ducks Went Wandering. LC 78-12629. (Illus.). (gr. 1-3). 1979. 8.95 (ISBN 0-395-28954-8, Clarion). HM.

Roy, Rustrum. Experimenting with Truth: The Fusion of Religion with Technology Needed for Humanity's Survival. (The Hibbert Lectures: 1979). (Illus.). 228p. 1981. 29.00 (ISBN 0-08-025820-4); pap. 14.50 (ISBN 0-08-025819-0). Pergamon.

Roy, S. N., et al. Analysis & Design of Certain Quantitative Multiresponse Experiments. 314p. 1971. 25.00 (ISBN 0-08-006917-7). Pergamon.

Roy, Tarapada. Where to, Tarapada-Babu? Devi, Shyamasree & Lal, P., trs. from Bengali. (Saffronbird Bk.). 51p. 1975. 10.00 (ISBN 0-88253-839-X); pap. 4.80 (ISBN 0-88253-840-3). Ind-US Inc.

Roy, Willy & Walker, Jim. Coaching Winning Soccer. 1979. 12.95 o.p. (ISBN 0-8092-7458-2); pap. 6.95 (ISBN 0-8092-7457-4). Contemp Bks.

Royal Aeronautical Society. A List of the Books, Periodicals & Pamphlets in the Library of the Royal Aeronautical Society: With Which Is Incorporated the Institution of Aeronautical Engineers. Gilbert, James, ed. LC 79-7295. (Flight: Its First Seventy-Five Years Ser.). 1979. Repr. of 1941 ed. lib. bdg. 21.00x (ISBN 0-405-12202-0). Arno.

Royal Barry Wills Assoc. More Houses for Good Living. Date not set. 13.95 (ISBN 0-8038-0162-9). Hastings.

Royal College of Psychiatrists. Alcohol & Alcoholism. LC 79-20712. 1979. 15.95 (ISBN 0-02-927510-5). Free Pr.

Royal Entomological Society of London, Ninth. Diversity of Insect Faunas: Symposium. Mound, L. A. & Waloff, N., eds. 1979. 43.95 (ISBN 0-470-26544-2). Halsted Pr.

Royal Geographical Society. The Country of Turkomans, an Anthology of Exploration. 1977. text ed. 32.50x (ISBN 0-905820-01-0). Humanities.

Royal Geographical Society, Symposium, London, 1974. Racial Variations in Man: Proceedings. Ebling, F. J., ed. LC 75-12803. 1976. 39.95 (ISBN 0-470-22955-1). Halsted Pr.

Royal Institute of International Affairs. British Yearbook of Internaional Law. Incl. Vol. 3. 1965. 15.95x (ISBN 0-19-214625-4); Vol. 7. 1965. 15.95x (ISBN 0-19-214629-7); Vol. 39, 1963. Waldock, H. & Jennings, R. Y., eds. 1965. 24.95x (ISBN 0-19-214622-X); Vol. 40, 1964. Waldock, H. & Jennings, R. Y., eds. 1966. 24.95x (ISBN 0-19-214623-8); Vol. 41, 1965-66. Waldock, H. & Jennings, R. Y., eds. 1968. 24.95x (ISBN 0-19-214657-2); Waldock, H. & Jennings, R. Y., eds. 1969. 24.95x (ISBN 0-19-214658-0); Vol. 44. Waldcock, H. & Jennings, R. Y., eds. 1970. 24.95x (ISBN 0-19-214660-2); Vol. 45. Waldock, H. & Jennings, R. Y., eds. 1973. 59.50x (ISBN 0-19-214661-0). (Royal Institute of International Affairs Ser.). Oxford U Pr.

Royal Institute of International Affairs, London. Index to Periodical Articles, Nineteen Seventy-Three to Nineteen Seventy-Eight, in the Library of the Royal Institute of International Affairs. (Library Catalogs-Bib. Guides). 1979. lib. bdg. 125.00 (ISBN 0-8161-0281-3). G K Hall.

Royal Institute Of International Affairs. Problem of International Investment. LC 67-55858. Repr. of 1937 ed. 30.00x (ISBN 0-678-05195-X). Kelley.

Royal Institute of the Architects of Ireland. Dublin: A City in Crisis. LC 76-369270. 108p. 1975. pap. 10.50x o.p. (ISBN 0-9504628-0-2). Intl Pubns Serv.

Royal Institution Library of Science. Astronomy, 2 vols. LC 75-132808. 1970. Set. 45.95 (ISBN 0-470-74388-3). Halsted Pr.

--Earth Sciences, 3 vols. Bragg, W. L. & Runcorn, S. K., eds. LC 74-169065. 1592p. 1971. Set. 79.95 (ISBN 0-470-74389-1). Halsted Pr.

Royal Institution of Naval Architects & Institute of Marine Engineering, eds. Prevention & Control of Fires in Ships. (Illus.). 1976. 15.00 (ISBN 0-686-16691-4, Pub. by Inst Marine Eng). Intl Schol Bk Serv.

Royal Norwegian Ministry of Justice, ed. Administration of Justice in Norway. 96p. 1981. pap. 12.00x (ISBN 82-00-05501-9). Universitet.

Royal Shakespeare Company. Royal Shakespeare Company, Nineteen Eighty. 124p. 1980. pap. text ed. 8.95x (ISBN 0-904844-33-1, Pub. by TQ & Royal Shakespeare England). Advent Bk.

Royal Shakespeare Theatre. The Sonnets of William Shakespeare. 1980. 30.00x (ISBN 0-85683-013-5, Pub. by Shepheard-Walwyn England). State Mutual Bk.

Royal Society. Assessment of Sublethal Effects of Pollutants in the Sea. Cole, H. A., ed. (Illus.). 1979. text ed. 53.60 (ISBN 0-85403-112-X, Pub. by Royal Soc. London). Scholium Intl.

Royal Society, et al. The Middle Atmosphere As Observed from Baloons, Rockets & Satellites. (Royal Society Ser.). (Illus.). 268p. 1980. lib. bdg. 71.00x (ISBN 0-85403-137-5, Pub. by Royal Soc London). Scholium Intl.

--Influenza: Proceedings. (Royal Society Ser.). (Illus.). 172p. 1980. lib. bdg. 50.00x (ISBN 0-85403-138-3, Pub. by Royal Soc London). Scholium Intl.

Royal Society Discussion, March 7 & 8, 1979. The Psychology of Vision. Longuet-Higgins, H. C. & Sutherland, N. S., eds. (Illus.). 218p. 1980. text ed. 61.00x (ISBN 0-85403-141-3, Pub. by Royal Soc London). Scholium Intl.

Royal Society of London. Long-Term Hazards from Environmental Chemicals. Doll, Richard & McClean, A. E., eds. 1979. 25.00x (ISBN 0-85403-110-3, Pub. by Royal Soc London). Scholium Intl.

--The Terrestrial Ecology of Aldabra. Stoddart, D. R. & Westoll, T. S., eds. (Illus.). 1979. lib. bdg. 61.00x (ISBN 0-85403-111-1, Pub. by Royal Soc London). Scholium Intl.

Royal Society of London, et al. Theoretical & Practical Aspects of Uranium Geology. Bowie, S. H. & Fyfe, W. S., eds. (Illus.). 1979. lib. bdg. 46.00x (ISBN 0-85403-106-5, Pub. by Royal Soc London). Scholium Intl.

Royal Society of London, Study Group on Pollution in the Atmosphere, 1977. Pathways of Pollutants in the Atmosphere. (Proceedings of the Royal Society). (Illus.). 170p. 1979. 37.00x (ISBN 0-85403-107-3, Pub by Royal Soc London). Scholium Intl.

Royal United Services Institute for Defence Studies, London, ed. Defence Yearbook 1980. 90th ed. LC 75-614843. (Illus.). 355p. 1979. 40.00x (ISBN 0-904609-37-5). Intl Pubns Serv.

Royal United Services Institute for Defence Studies, ed. International Weapon Developments: A Survey of Current Developments in Weapon Systems. 4th ed. (Illus.). 203p. 1980. pap. 13.25 (ISBN 0-08-027028-X). Pergamon.

Royal United Services Institute for Defense Studies, ed. Rusi & Brassey's Defence Yearbook, 1977-78. LC 75-29923. 1978. lib. bdg. 37.50x (ISBN 0-89158-823-X). Westview.

Royal United Services Institute for Defence Studies, ed. RUSI Brassey's Defence Yearbook: 1981. 91st ed. 376p. 1980. 45.00 (ISBN 0-08-027006-9). Pergamon.

Royal, William R. & Burgess, Robert F. The Man Who Rode Sharks. LC 78-1854. (Illus.). 1978. 8.95 (ISBN 0-396-07537-1). Dodd.

Royall, Anne N. Letters from Alabama, 1817-1822. Griffith, Lucille, ed. LC 70-76584. (Southern Historical Ser: Vol. 14). 233p. 1969. 11.50 o.p. (ISBN 0-8173-5219-8). U of Ala Pr.

Royall, Vanessa. Firebrand's Woman. (Orig.). 1980. pap. 2.95 o.s.i. (ISBN 0-440-12597-9). Dell.

--Flames of Desire. 1978. pap. 2.25 o.s.i. (ISBN 0-440-14637-2). Dell.

Royan, Van P. see Van Royan, P.

Royce & Zook. Read English, Book One. 80p. (Orig.). 1980. pap. text ed. 4.95 (ISBN 0-88499-675-1). Inst Mod Lang.

Royce, Anya P. Anthropology of Dance. LC 77-74428. (Illus.). 256p. 1980. pap. 6.95 (ISBN 0-253-20235-3). Ind U Pr.

Royce, Charles. The Cherokee Nation of Indians. LC 75-20708. (Illus.). 272p. 1975. 12.50x (ISBN 0-87474-814-3); pap. 5.95x (ISBN 0-87474-815-1). Smithsonian.

Royce, J. R. & Mos, L. P., eds. Theoretical Advances in Behavior Genetics. (NATO Advanced Study Institute Ser.). 722p. 1980. 75.00x (ISBN 90-286-0569-X). Sijthoff & Noordhoff.

Royce, Kenneth. The Masterpiece Affair. 1974. pap. 1.25 o.p. (ISBN 0-380-00106-3, 20420). Avon.

Royce, Pat. Dinghy Sailing Illustrated: The Dinghy Sailor's Bible. (Illus.). 1974. pap. 2.50 o.p. (ISBN 0-930030-07-9). Western Marine Ent.

Royce, Sarah. A Frontier Lady: Recollections of the Gold Rush & Early California. Gabriel, Ralph H., ed. LC 76-44263. (Illus.). 1977. 10.95x (ISBN 0-8032-0909-6); pap. 2.45 (ISBN 0-8032-5856-9, BB 634, Bison). U of Nebr Pr.

Royce, William F. Introduction to Fishery Sciences. 351p. 1972. text ed. 22.50 (ISBN 0-12-600950-3). Acad Pr.

Royer, D., jt. auth. see Dieulesaint, E.

Royer, King. The Construction Manager in the Nineteen Eighties. (Illus.). 496p. 1981. text ed. 32.00 (ISBN 0-13-168690-9). P-H.

Royer, Pierre, et al. Pediatric Nephrology. LC 74-4585. (Major Problem in Clinical Pediatrics Ser.: Vol. 11). (Illus.). 415p. 1974. text ed. 25.00 (ISBN 0-7216-7776-2). Saunders.

Royer-Collard, F. B. Skeleton Clocks. 2nd ed. (Illus.). 1977. 24.00x (ISBN 0-7198-0110-9). Intl Ideas.

Royle, Trevor, ed. Jock Tamson's Bairns: Essays on a Scots Childhood. 1978. 19.95 (ISBN 0-241-89638-X, Pub. by Hamish Hamilton England). David & Charles.

Roys, Ralph L., tr. Ritual of the Bacabs. (Civilization of the American Indian Ser.: No. 77). 1965. 10.95 o.p. (ISBN 0-8061-0662-X). U of Okla Pr.

Royster, Charles. Light-Horse Harry Lee: The Legacy of the American Revolution. LC 80-2706. (Illus.). 320p. 1981. 15.00 (ISBN 0-394-51337-1). Knopf.

Royston, Michael G. Pollution Prevention Pays. 1979. 28.00 (ISBN 0-08-023597-2); pap. 8.50 (ISBN 0-08-023572-7). Pergamon.

Rozanov, Y. A. Probability Theory: A Concise Course. rev. ed. Silverman, Richard A., tr. from Russian. LC 77-78592. 1977. pap. text ed. 3.00 (ISBN 0-486-63544-9). Dover.

Rozanov, Yu A. Stationary Random Processes. LC 66-29909. 1967. 19.95x (ISBN 0-8162-7354-5). Holden-Day.

Rozella, et al. Your Youth Can Be Restored. 1978. 6.95 o.p. (ISBN 0-533-02792-6). Vantage.

Rozen, Marvin E. Comparative Economic Planning. Novack, David E., ed. (Studies in Economics). 1967. pap. text ed. 2.95x o.p. (ISBN 0-669-46557-7). Heath.

Rozenberg, L. D., ed. Physical Principles of Ultrasonic Technology, 2 vols. Incl. Vol. 1. 515p. 49.50 (ISBN 0-306-35041-6); Vol. 2. 544p. 47.50 (ISBN 0-306-35042-4). (Ultrasonic Technology Monographs Ser.). (Illus.). 1973 (Plenum Pr). Plenum Pub.

Rozenberg, Paul. Le Romantisme anglais: Le Defi des vulnerables. new ed. (Collection L). 287p. (Orig., Fr.). 1973. pap. 13.95 (ISBN 2-03-036010-4). Larousse.

Rozencweig, Marcel, jt. ed. see Muggia, Franco.

Rozendal, Nancy & Fallon, Patricia. Psychiatric Nursing: PreTest Self-Assessment & Review. LC 78-50596. (Nursing: Pretest Self-Assessment & Review Ser.). 1978. pap. 6.95 (ISBN 0-07-051569-7). McGraw-Pretest.

Rozental, D. E. Modern Russian Usage. James, C. V., ed. 1963. 11.75 o.p. (ISBN 0-08-009811-8). Pergamon.

Rozman, Deborah, ed. see Hills, Christopher.

Rozov, B. Kh, jt. auth. see Mishchenko, E. F.

Rozovsky, Lorne E. Canadian Patient's Book of Rights. LC 79-8942. 176p. 1980. 14.95 (ISBN 0-385-15377-5); pap. 8.95 (ISBN 0-385-15383-X). Doubleday.

Rozsa, Gyorgy. Selected Paintings of the Historical Gallery, Budapest. Halapy, Lili, tr. from Hungarian. LC 78-369118. (The Treasures of the Hungarian National Museum Ser.). (Illus.). 1977. 13.50x (ISBN 963-13-0081-1). Intl Pubns Serv.

Rozwenc, Edwin C., jt. auth. see Sandler, Martin W.

Rozzoli, R., ed. see Stringer, T.

Rse, Barbara. Claes Oldenburg. 224p. 1979. 12.50 (ISBN 0-87070-509-1). NYGS.

Ruark, Gibbons. Program for Survival: Poems. LC 74-151089. 1971. pap. 3.95x (ISBN 0-8139-0325-4). U Pr of Va.

Ruark, Robert. Honey Badger. 1976. pap. 2.25 o.p. (ISBN 0-449-22924-6, 2924, Crest). Fawcett.

--Old Man & the Boy. 1977. pap. 1.95 o.p. (ISBN 0-449-23151-8, Crest). Fawcett.

--Uhuru. 1977. pap. 2.25 o.p. (ISBN 0-449-23241-7, Crest). Fawcett.

Ruark, Robert C. Poor No More. 1978. pap. 2.50 o.p. (ISBN 0-449-23218-2, Crest). Fawcett.

Rubel, Macmillan. Marx Chronology. 226p. 1981. lib. bdg. 22.50 (ISBN 0-87196-516-X). Facts on File.

Rubel, Maximilien. Rubel on Karl Marx: Five Essays. O'Malley, Joseph & Algozin, Keith, eds. LC 80-21734. 272p. Date not set. price not set (ISBN 0-521-23839-0); pap. price not set (ISBN 0-521-28251-9). Cambridge U Pr.

Rubel, Nicole. Sam & Violet Are Twins. 32p. (gr. 1-3). 1981. pap. 1.95 (ISBN 0-380-76919-0, Camelot). Avon.

--Sam & Violet Go Camping. 32p. (gr. 1-3). 1981. pap. 1.95 (ISBN 0-380-76927-1, Camelot). Avon.

Rubel, Paula G., jt. auth. see Rosman, Abraham.

Rubel, Robert J. The Unruly School: Disorders, Disruptions, & Crimes. LC 77-3837. (Illus.). 1977. 19.95 (ISBN 0-669-01668-3). Lexington Bks.

Rubel, Tobert J., jt. auth. see Baker, Keith.

Ruben, Brent. Human Communication Handbook: Simulations & Games, Vol. 2. 1978. pap. text ed. 10.75 (ISBN 0-8104-5765-2). Hayden.

Ruben, Brent D. Interact 2. 1977. wkbk. 7.95x (ISBN 0-89529-025-1). Avery Pub.

Ruben, Brent D. & Budd, Richard W. Human Communication Handbook: Simulations & Games, Vol. 1. (Illus.). 1975. pap. text ed. 10.75 (ISBN 0-8104-5524-2). Hayden.

--Interdisciplinary Approaches to Human Communication. (gr. 12 up). 1979. pap. text ed. 8.50x (ISBN 0-8104-5125-5). Hayden.

Ruben, Brent D., jt. auth. see Budd, Richard W.

Ruben, David. Marxism & Materialism. rev. ed. (Marxist Theory & Contemporary Capitalism Ser.). 1978. text ed. 27.50x (ISBN 0-391-00966-4); pap. text ed. 11.00x (ISBN 0-391-00965-6). Humanities.

Ruben, H., jt. auth. see Resnik, H.

Ruben, Harvey L. C.I.-Crisis Intervention. 1976. pap. 1.75 o.p. (ISBN 0-445-08522-3). Popular Lib.

Ruben, Montague. Soft Contact Lenses: Clinical & Applied Technology. LC 77-26918. (Clinical Ophthalmology Ser.). 1978. 44.50 (ISBN 0-471-74430-1, Pub. by Wiley Medical). Wiley.

--Understanding Contact Lenses. 1976. pap. 10.00x (ISBN 0-685-83938-9). Intl Ideas.

Ruben, Patricia. What Is New? What Is Missing? What Is Different? LC 78-8109. (Illus.). (gr. k-2). 1978. 8.95 (ISBN 0-397-31816-2). Lippincott.

Ruben, Paula, jt. auth. see Dodson, Fitzhugh.

Ruben, Samuel. The Evolution of Electric Batteries in Response to Industrial Needs. (Illus.). 100p. 1978. 7.95 (ISBN 0-8059-2455-8). Dorrance.

Rubenfeld, Seymour. Family of Outcasts. LC 65-20000. 1965. 12.95 (ISBN 0-02-927580-6). Free Pr.

Rubens, Jeff. The Secrets of Winning Bridge. 241p. 1981. pap. 4.00 (ISBN 0-486-24076-2). Dover.

Rubens, Paul, tr. see Reck-Malleczewen, Friedrich P.

Rubenstein, Alvin Z. Foreign Policy of the Soviet Union. 3rd ed. 448p. 1972. pap. text ed. 9.95 (ISBN 0-394-31699-1). Random.

Rubenstein, Ben, jt. ed. see Levitt, Morton.

Rubenstein, Ben, ed. see Meeting of the American Orthopsychiatric Assoc., 47th.

Rubenstein, Carol. The Honey Tree Song: Poems, Chants & Epics of Sarawak Dayaks. (Illus.). 700p. 1981. 26.95x (ISBN 0-8214-0413-X); pap. 14.95 (ISBN 0-8214-0425-3). Ohio U Pr.

Rubenstein, Daryl R. Max Weber: A Catalogue Raisonne of His Graphic Work. LC 80-13883. (Illus.). 200p. 1980. incl. fiche 38.50x (ISBN 0-226-69598-0). U of Chicago Pr.

Rubenstein, David. Marx & Wittgenstein. 240p. 1981. write for info. (ISBN 0-7100-0688-8). Routledge & Kegan.

Rubenstein, Harvey M. Central City Malls. LC 78-7536. 1978. 27.50 (ISBN 0-471-03098-8, Pub. by Wiley-Interscience). Wiley.

--A Guide to Site & Environmental Planning. 2nd ed. LC 79-16142. 1980. 27.50 (ISBN 0-471-04729-5, Pub. by Wiley-Interscience). Wiley.

Rubenstein, Hilary. Europe's Wonderful Little Hotels & Inns. (Illus.). 512p. 1981. 12.95 (ISBN 0-312-92188-8); pap. 8.95 (ISBN 0-312-92189-6). St Martin.

Rubenstein, Irwin, et al, eds. Genetic Improvement of Crops: Emergent Techniques. 232p. 1980. 22.50x (ISBN 0-8166-0966-7). U of Minn Pr.

Rubenstein, Nancy, ed. see Stein, Charlotte M.

Rubenstein, Reuven Y. Simulation & the Monte Carlo Method. (Probability & Mathematical Statistics Ser.). 300p. 1981. 30.00 (ISBN 0-471-08917-6, Pub. by Wiley-Interscience). Wiley.

Rubenstein, Richard. The Cunning of History. 1978. pap. 3.50 (ISBN 0-06-090597-2, CN 597, CN). Har-Row.

Rubenstein, Richard J. After Auschwitz: Essays in Contemporary Judaism. (Orig.). pap. 6.95 (ISBN 0-672-61150-3). Bobbs.

Rubenstone, Jessie. Crochet for Beginners. LC 74-4462. (Illus.). 64p. (gr. 3-4). 1974. 7.95 (ISBN 0-397-31547-3); pap. 2.95 o.p. (ISBN 0-397-31548-1). Lippincott.

Rubert De Ventos, Xavier. Self-Defeated Man: Personal Identity & Beyond. 192p. (Orig.). 1975. pap. 2.95 o.p. (ISBN 0-06-090354-6, CN354, CN). Har-Row.

Ruberte, Ruth, jt. auth. see Martin, Franklin W.

Rubin, A., ed. see P-H Staff.

Rubin, Alvan D., jt. auth. see Efron, Benjamin.

Rubin, Amy K. Children of the Seventh Prophecy. LC 80-23522. 192p. (gr. 4-7). 1981. 8.95 (ISBN 0-7232-6200-4). Warne.

Rubin, Arnold P. The Evil That Men Do: The Story of the Nazis. LC 77-22722. (gr. 7 up). 1977. PLB 8.29 o.p. (ISBN 0-671-32852-2). Messner.

Rubin, Audrey, ed. see Heller, Jack.

Rubin, Barry. The Great Powers in the Middle East Nineteen Forty-One to Nineteen Forty-Seven: The Road to the Cold War. 264p. 1980. 26.00x (ISBN 0-7146-3141-8, F Cass Co). Biblio Dist.

--Paved with Good Intentions: The American Experience & Iran. (Illus.). 320p. 1980. 17.50 (ISBN 0-19-502805-8). Oxford U Pr.

Rubin, Barry M. & Spiro, Elizabeth P. Human Rights & U. S. Foreign Policy. 1979. lib. bdg. 26.50x (ISBN 0-89158-476-5). Westview.

Rubin, Bernard. Big Business & the Mass Media. LC 77-2516. 1977. 17.95 o.p. (ISBN 0-669-01517-2). Lexington Bks.

Rubin, Bernard, ed. Questioning Media Ethics. 1978. 25.95 (ISBN 0-03-046131-6); pap. 10.95 student ed. (ISBN 0-03-046126-X). Praeger.

--Small Voices & Great Trumpets: Minorities & the Media. 295p. 1980. 24.95 (ISBN 0-03-056973-7); pap. 9.95 (ISBN 0-03-056972-9). Praeger.

Rubin, Caroline, ed. see Bishop, Ann.

Rubin, Caroline, ed. see Brown, Fern.

Rubin, Caroline, ed. see Bunting, Eve.

Rubin, Caroline, ed. see Corey, Dorothy.

Rubin, Caroline, ed. see Fleishman, Seymour.

Rubin, Caroline, ed. see Goldman, Susan.

Rubin, Caroline, ed. see Heide, Florence P. & Heide, Roxanne.

Rubin, Caroline, ed. see Hopkins, Lee B.

Rubin, Caroline, ed. see Katz, Bobbi.

Rubin, Caroline, ed. see Lapp, Eleanor.

Rubin, Caroline, ed. see Litchfield, Ada B.

Rubin, Caroline, ed. see Neigoff, Mike.

Rubin, Caroline, ed. see Raynor, Dorka.

Rubin, Caroline, ed. see Rothman, Joel.

Rubin, Caroline, ed. see Schlein, Miriam.

Rubin, Caroline, ed. see Simon, Norma.

Rubin, Caroline, ed. see Stanton, Elizabeth & Stanton, Henry.

Rubin, Caroline, ed. see Udry, Janice M.

Rubin, Caroline, ed. see Vigna, Judith.

Rubin, Caroline, ed. see Warner, Gertrude C.

Rubin, Caroline, ed. see Warshaw, Jerry.

Rubin, Caroline, ed. see Wold, Joanne.

Rubin, Cynthia & Rubin, Jerome. Mission Furniture: Making It, Decorating with It, Its History & Place in the Antique Market. LC 79-24376. (Illus.). 160p. (Orig.). 1980. pap. 8.95 (ISBN 0-87701-169-9). Chronicle Bks.

--The New Fruit Cookbook. LC 76-42442. 1977. 12.95 o.p. (ISBN 0-8092-7892-8); pap. 4.95 o.p. (ISBN 0-8092-7890-1). Contemp Bks.

--The Oster Every Day a Gourmet Cookbook. 7.95 (ISBN 0-916752-29-1). Green Hill.

Rubin, Daniel, jt. ed. see Krippner, Stanley.

Rubin, David, ed. see Napier, John T.

Rubin, David, tr. A Season on the Earth: Selected Poems of Nirala. LC 76-40026. 1977. 15.00x (ISBN 0-231-04160-8); pap. 6.00x (ISBN 0-231-04161-6). Columbia U Pr.

Rubin, Don. What's the Big Idea? And Thirty-Five Other Unusual Puzzles. 1979. pap. 3.95 (ISBN 0-685-93958-8). Lippincott.

Rubin, Eli H. & Siegelman, Stanley S. Lungs in Systemic Diseases. (Illus.). 334p. 1969. 28.50 (ISBN 0-398-01626-7). C C Thomas.

Rubin, Estelle, jt. auth. see Atkin, Edith.

Rubin, Ira, jt. auth. see Frieden, Julian.

Rubin, Isaac I. A History of Economic Thought. Filtzer, Don, tr. 448p. 1980. text ed. 33.00x (ISBN 0-906133-16-5); pap. text ed. 15.50x (ISBN 0-906133-17-3). Humanities.

Rubin, James H. Realism & Social Vision in Courbet & Proudhon. LC 80-17559. (Essays on the Arts: No. 10). (Illus.). 270p. 1980. 17.50x (ISBN 0-691-03960-7); pap. 8.95x (ISBN 0-691-00327-0). Princeton U Pr.

Rubin, Jeffrey. Economics, Mental Health, & the Law. LC 78-19571. (Illus.). 1978. 17.95 (ISBN 0-669-02629-8). Lexington Bks.

Rubin, Jeffrey, jt. auth. see Raven, Bertran.

Rubin, Jeffrey, jt. ed. see LaPorte, Valerie.

Rubin, Jerome, jt. auth. see Rubin, Cynthia.

Rubin, Jerry. Growing (up) at 37. 1977. pap. 1.95 o.s.i. (ISBN 0-446-89315-3). Warner Bks.

Rubin, Jonathan. The Barking Deer. LC 73-88042. 1974. 7.95 o.s.i. (ISBN 0-8076-0727-4). Braziller.

Rubin, Lillian. Busing & Backlash: White Against White in an Urban School District. 1972. 16.95x (ISBN 0-520-02198-3); pap. 3.85 (ISBN 0-520-02257-2, CAL252). U of Cal Pr.

--Women of a Certain Age: The Midlife Search for Self. LC 79-1681. 320p. 1981. pap. 4.95 (ISBN 0-06-090833-5, CN 833, CN). Har-Row.

Rubin, Louis. Curriculum Handbook: The Disciplines, Current Movements, Instructional Methodology, Administration & Theory. abr. ed. 1977. pap. 13.95 (ISBN 0-205-05910-4). Allyn.

--The In-Service Education of Teachers: Trends, Processes & Prescriptions. 1978. text ed. 19.95 (ISBN 0-205-06022-6). Allyn.

Rubin, Louis, ed. see Research for Better Schools, Inc.

Rubin, Louis D. The Boll Weevil & the Triple Play. 1979. 5.00 (ISBN 0-937684-00-7). Tradd St Pr.

Rubin, Louis D., Jr. The Literary South. LC 78-24221. 1979. text ed. 19.95x (ISBN 0-471-04659-0). Wiley.

--Virginia: A History. (States & the Nation Ser.). (Illus.). 1977. 12.95 (ISBN 0-393-05630-9, Co-Pub. by AASLH). Norton.

Rubin, Louis D., Jr., ed. The Comic Imagination in American Literature. (Illus.). 448p. 1973. 29.00 (ISBN 0-8135-0758-8). Rutgers U Pr.

Rubin, Louis D., Jr. & Jacobs, Robert D., eds. Southern Renascence: The Literature of the Modern South. 456p. 1953. 20.00x (ISBN 0-8018-0568-6); pap. 4.95x (ISBN 0-8018-0569-4). Johns Hopkins.

Rubin, Louis J. Critical Issues in Educational Policy: An Administrator's Overview. 492p. 1980. text ed. 19.95 (ISBN 0-205-06815-4). Allyn.

--Facts & Feelings in the Classroom. LC 77-186190. 224p. 1973. 8.95 (ISBN 0-8027-0382-8); pap. 4.50 o.s.i. (ISBN 0-8027-7087-8). Walker & Co.

--Improving In-Service Education: Proposals & Procedures for Change. 1971. text ed. 12.95x o.s.i. (ISBN 0-205-03126-9, 2231263). Allyn.

Rubin, Lucille S., ed. Movement for the Actor. (Illus.). 1980. pap. 7.95x (ISBN 0-89676-010-3). Drama Bk.

Rubin, Marilyn. Neurologic Nursing. LC 76-6218. 300p. 1980. cancelled (ISBN 0-87527-250-9). Green.

Rubin, Martin L. Handbook of Data Processing Management, 6 vols. 1971. Set. 175.00 (ISBN 0-442-80343-5). Van Nos Reinhold.

Rubin, Melvin L. & Walls, Gordon L. Fundamentals of Visual Science. (Illus.). 460p. 1972. text ed. 21.50 (ISBN 0-398-01625-9). C C Thomas.

--Studies in Physiological Optics. (Illus.). 144p. 1965. 10.50 (ISBN 0-398-01624-0). C C Thomas.

Rubin, Neville & Warren, William M., eds. Dams in Africa. LC 68-19216. 1968. 25.00x (ISBN 0-678-05196-8). Kelley.

Rubin, Richard, jt. auth. see Goldberg, Philip.

Rubin, Richard L. Party Dynamics: The Democratic Coalition & the Politics of Change. LC 75-32352. 180p. 1976. 13.95x (ISBN 0-19-502036-7); pap. 5.95x (ISBN 0-19-502035-9). Oxford U Pr.

Rubin, Rick, jt. auth. see Byerly, Greg.

Rubin, Ronald. The Annulment. 1978. pap. 1.50 o.s.i. (ISBN 0-515-04453-9). Jove Pubns.

Rubin, S. G., ed. see Symposium on Computers in Aerodynamics at the Aerodynamics Laboratories Polytechnic Institute of New York, 1979.

Rubin, Seymour J. & Graham, Thomas R., eds. Environment & Trade: The Relation of International Trade & Environmental Policy. 380p. 1981. text ed. 28.50 (ISBN 0-86598-032-2). Allanheld.

Rubin, Stephen E. The New Met in Profile. (Illus.). 368p. 1974. 9.95 o.s.i. (ISBN 0-02-605800-6). Macmillan.

Rubin, Steven J. Combat Films: American Realism, Nineteen Forty-Five to Nineteen Seventy. LC 80-17022. (Illus.). 245p. 1981. lib. bdg. 15.95x (ISBN 0-89950-013-7); pap. 11.95x (ISBN 0-89950-014-5). McFarland & Co.

Rubin, Sylvia P. It's Not Too Late for a Baby: For Men & Women Over Thirty Five. (Illus.). 272p. 1980. 14.95 (ISBN 0-13-507046-5, Spec); pap. 6.95 (ISBN 0-13-507038-4). P-H.

Rubin, Ted. Standards Relating to Court Organization & Administration. (Juvenile Justice Standards Project Ser.). 1980. softcover 7.95; casebound 16.50 (ISBN 0-88410-231-9). Ballinger Pub.

--Standards Relating to Court Organization and Administration. LC 76-14413. (Juvenile Justice Standards Project Ser.). 1977. soft cover 5.95 o.p. (ISBN 0-88410-777-9); 12.50, casebound o.p. Ballinger Pub.

Rubin, Theodore I. Angry Book. 1969. pap. 3.95 (ISBN 0-02-077820-1). Macmillan.

--Compassion & Self-Hate. 228p. 1976. pap. 2.50 (ISBN 0-345-29475-0). Ballantine.

Rubin, Vera & Schaedel, Richard, eds. The Haitian Potential: Research & Resources of Haiti. LC 73-78672. 1975. text ed. 15.75x (ISBN 0-8077-2377-0). Tchrs Coll.

Rubin, Vitaly A. Individual & State in Ancient China: Essays on Four Chinese Philosophers. Levine, Steven I., tr. from Rus. 200p. 1976. 15.00x (ISBN 0-231-04064-4). Columbia U Pr.

Rubin, Wallace & Norris, Charles. Electronystagmography: What Is ENG? 116p. 1974. pap. 16.25 spiral (ISBN 0-398-03098-7). C C Thomas.

Rubin, William. Anthony Caro. LC 74-21725. (Illus.). 196p. 1975. 17.50 (ISBN 0-87070-275-0); pap. 7.95 (ISBN 0-87070-276-9). Museum Mod Art.

Rubin, William, ed. Cezanne: The Late Work. LC 77-77287. (Illus.). 1977. 45.00 (ISBN 0-87070-278-5, 134619, Pub. by Museum of Modern Art). NYGS.

--Pablo Picasso: A Retrospective. (Illus.). 1981. pap. 25.00 (ISBN 0-686-69217-9). NYGS.

Rubin, William & Bozo, Dominique, eds. Pablo Picasso: A Retrospective. (Illus.). 1980. 50.00 (ISBN 0-87070-528-8, 707023, Pub. by Museum Mod Art); prepub. 45.00 (ISBN 0-686-65854-X). NYGS.

Rubin, Zick & McNeil, Elton B. Psychology of Being Human: Brief Edition. 504p. 1979. pap. text ed. 15.50 scp (ISBN 0-06-044386-3, HarpC). Har-Row.

Rubincam, David P. & Rubincam, John. Diet with Vitamins. LC 77-73140. 1977. 8.95 o.p. (ISBN 0-89479-007-2). A & W Pubs.

Rubincam, John, jt. auth. see Rubincam, David P.

Rubinfeld, Daniel, ed. Essays on the Law & Economics of Local Governments. (Papers on Public Econmics Ser.: Vol. 3). 253p. (Orig.). 1980. pap. text ed. 7.50 (ISBN 0-87766-262-2, 27200). Urban Inst.

Rubington, Earl & Weinberg, Martin S., eds. The Study of Social Problems: Five Perspectives. 2nd ed. 1977. pap. text ed. 6.95x (ISBN 0-19-502146-0). Oxford U Pr.

--The Study of Social Problems: Five Perspectives. 3rd ed. 256p. 1981. pap. text ed. 7.95x (ISBN 0-19-502825-2). Oxford U Pr.

Rubington, Norman. Street Hustler. 1975. pap. 1.50 o.p. (ISBN 0-685-57552-7, LB301DK, Leisure Bks). Nordon Pubns.

Rubinow, S. I. Introduction to Mathematical Biology. LC 75-12520. 386p. 1975. 34.50 (ISBN 0-471-74446-8, Pub. by Wiley-Interscience). Wiley.

Rubinson, Ann. Heart Attacks: Is Your Family a Risk Factor? 1981. 8.95 (ISBN 0-533-04217-8). Vantage.

Rubinstein, Alvin Z. Soviet & Chinese Influence in the Third World. LC 74-11604. (Special Studies). 246p. 1976. 22.95 o.p. (ISBN 0-275-09640-8); pap. text ed. 9.95 o.p. (ISBN 0-275-64690-4). Praeger.

--Soviet Foreign Policy Since World War II: Imperial & Global. (Political Science Ser.). (Illus.). 354p. 1981. text ed. 15.00 (ISBN 0-87626-810-6); pap. text ed. 9.95 (ISBN 0-87626-809-2). Winthrop.

Rubinstein, Alvin Z, ed. see Ginsburgs, George.

Rubinstein, David & Simon, Brian. Evolution of the Comprehensive School 1926-1966. (Students Library of Education). 1970. text ed. 5.25x (ISBN 0-7100-6357-1). Humanities.

Rubinstein, E. Filmguide to The General. LC 72-88637. (Filmguide Ser: No. 5). 96p. 1973. 5.00x (ISBN 0-253-39309-4); pap. 1.75x (ISBN 0-253-39310-8). Ind U Pr.

Rubinstein, Elaine, jt. auth. see Sauber, Mignon.

Rubinstein, Helena. Food for Beauty. rev. ed. 256p. 1977. pap. 1.95 (ISBN 0-915962-19-5). Larchmont Bks.

Rubinstein, Hilary, ed. Europe's Wonderful Little Hotels & Inns. 3rd rev. ed. (Illus.). 512p. 1981. 14.95 (ISBN 0-86553-038-6); pap. 8.95 (ISBN 0-312-92189-6). Congdon & Lattes.

--Europe's Wonderful Little Hotels & Inns: 1979-1980. (Illus.). 1979. 10.95 o.p.; pap. 5.95 (ISBN 0-525-03383-1). Dutton.

Rubinstein, Jonathan. City Police. 1973. 12.95 (ISBN 0-374-12411-6); pap. 8.95 (ISBN 0-374-51555-7). FS&G.

--City Police. 480p. 1975. pap. 2.25 (ISBN 0-345-28409-7). Ballantine.

Rubinstein, Lucien J., jt. auth. see Earle, Kenneth M.

Rubinstein, Lucien J., tr. see Escourolle, Raymond & Poirier, Jacques.

Rubinstein, M. F., jt. auth. see Hurty, Walter C.

Rubinstein, Mark & Cox, John J. Options Markets. (Illus.). 432p. 1981. 29.95 (ISBN 0-13-638205-3). P-H.

Rubinstein, Mashe F. Patterns of Problem Solving. LC 74-20721. (Illus.). 640p. 1975. text ed. 22.95 ref. ed. (ISBN 0-13-654251-4). P-H.

Rubinstein, Moshe & Pfeiffer, Kenneth. Concepts in Problem Solving. (Illus.). 1980. pap. text ed. 10.95 (ISBN 0-13-166603-7). P-H.

Rubinstein, Moshe F. Matrix Computer Analysis of Structures. (Illus.). 1966. 26.95 (ISBN 0-13-565481-5). P-H.

Rubinstein, Nicolai. Florentine Studies. (Illus.). 1969. 15.95 o.p. (ISBN 0-571-08477-X, Pub. by Faber & Faber). Merrimack Bk Serv.

Rubinstein, Paul. Feasts for Two. 256p. 1975. pap. 1.50 o.p. (ISBN 0-445-03099-2). Popular Lib.

--Feasts for Two: A Cookbook of Menus & Recipes for Fifty Fabulous Meals. LC 72-92453. 256p. 1973. 9.95 (ISBN 0-02-605830-8). Macmillan.

--Just Good Food. (Illus.). 1978. 9.95 o.p. (ISBN 0-684-15526-5, ScribT). Scribner.

Rubinstein, Paul, jt. auth. see Tanous, Peter.

Rubinstein, Robert E. When Sirens Scream. LC 80-2788. 160p. (gr. 6 up). 1981. PLB 7.95 (ISBN 0-396-07937-7). Dodd.

Rubinstein, Ronald A., jt. auth. see Fry, Patricia B.

Rubinstein, Zalman. Course in Ordinary & Partial Differential Equations. 1969. text ed. 22.95 (ISBN 0-12-601550-3). Acad Pr.

Rubio, Antonio, jt. auth. see Jackson, Eugene.

Rubio, Pascal O., 3rd, ed. see Unibook Staff.

Ruble, Blair A., jt. auth. see Kahan, Arcadius.

Rublowsky, John. After the Crash: America in the Great Depression. LC 73-9019. (Illus.). (gr. 7-12). 1970. 4.95g o.s.i. (ISBN 0-02-777930-0, CCPr). Macmillan.

--Born in Fire: A Geological History of Hawaii. LC 79-2001. (Illus.). 96p. (gr. 5 up). 1981. 9.95 (ISBN 0-06-025088-7, HarpJ); PLB 9.89g (ISBN 0-06-025089-5). Har-Row.

Rubright, Bob & MacDonald, Dan. Marketing Human Services. 300p. 1981. text ed. price not set (ISBN 0-89443-338-5). Aspen Systems.

Rubsamen, Gisela. The Orsini Inventories. 224p. (Orig.). 1980. pap. 44.00 (ISBN 0-89236-010-0). J P Getty Mus.

Rubsamen, Walter A., ed. Court Intrigue & Scandal, Two: With the Fox Uncased, the Court Legacy, the Court Medley, the Fortunate Prince, the Wedding. (The Ballad Opera Ser.). 1974. lib. bdg. 50.00 (ISBN 0-8240-0918-5). Garland Pub.

Rubsamen, Walter H. Literary Sources of Secular Music in Italy: 1500. LC 72-4482. (Music Ser.). 82p. 1972. Repr. of 1943 ed. lib. bdg. 15.00 (ISBN 0-306-70496-X). Da Capo.

Rubsamen, Walter H., ed. American Ballad Operas. LC 74-4466. (The Ballad Opera Ser.). 1974. lib. bdg. 50.00 (ISBN 0-8240-0927-4). Garland Pub.

--The Beggar's Opera, Imitated & Parodied. (The Ballad Opera Ser.). 1974. lib. bdg. 50.00 (ISBN 0-8240-0900-2). Garland Pub.

--Classical Subjects 1: Satire & Burlesque. (The Ballad Opera Ser.). 1974. lib. bdg. 50.00 (ISBN 0-8240-0906-1). Garland Pub.

--Classical Subjects 2: Pastoral & Comedy. (Ballad Opera Ser.). 1974. lib. bdg. 50.00 (ISBN 0-8240-0907-X). Garland Pub.

--Country Operas, One: Romantic Intrigue & Deception with Southwark Fair, the Village Opera, the Chamber Maid, the Gentleman Gardiner, the Country Coquet, an Opera Called Westmeon Village. (The Ballad Opera Ser.). 1974. lib. bdg. 50.00 (ISBN 0-8240-0914-2). Garland Pub.

--Country Operas, Three: Sentimental & Moral Comedies with Sylvia, the Jovial Crew, Lucinda, the Reapers. (The Ballad Opera Ser.). 1974. lib. bdg. 50.00 (ISBN 0-8240-0916-9). Garland Pub.

--Country Operas, Two: Farcial Humor & Stratagem Wth Country Wedding, the Wedding (Hawker), Flora, a Sequel to Flora, the Livery Rake, the Whim, the Deceit, the Country-Wedding. (The Ballad Opera Ser.). 1974. lib. bdg. 50.00 (ISBN 0-8240-0915-0). Garland Pub.

--Court Intrigue & Scandal, One: With Calista, Vanelia, the Humours of the Court, the Intriguing Courtiers. (The Ballad Opera Ser.). 1974. lib. bdg. 50.00 (ISBN 0-8240-0917-7). Garland Pub.

--Farce: Amorous Intrigue & Deception 1. (The Ballad Opera Ser.). 1974. lib. bdg. 50.00 (ISBN 0-8240-0911-8). Garland Pub.

--Farce: Amorous Intrigue & Deception 2. (The Ballad Opera Ser.). 1974. lib. bdg. 50.00 (ISBN 0-8240-0912-6). Garland Pub.

--Farce, Broad or Satirical. (The Ballad Opera Ser.). 1974. lib. bdg. 50.00 (ISBN 0-8240-0910-X). Garland Pub.

--Farce: Magical Transformation & Necromancy. (The Ballad Opera Ser.). 1974. lib. bdg. 50.00 (ISBN 0-8240-0909-6). Garland Pub.

--Harlots, Rakes, & Bawds. (The Ballad Opera Ser.). 1974. lib. bdg. 50.00 (ISBN 0-8240-0902-9). Garland Pub.

--Historical & Patriotic Subjects. (The Ballad Opera Ser.). 1974. lib. bdg. 50.00 (ISBN 0-8240-0901-0). Garland Pub.

--The Influence of Pantomime & Harlequinade. (The Ballad Opera Ser.). 1974. lib. bdg. 50.00 (ISBN 0-8240-0908-8) Garland Pub.

--Irish Ballad Operas & Burlesques 1. (The Ballad Opera Ser.). 1974. lib. bdg. 50.00 (ISBN 0-8240-0921-5). Garland Pub.

--Irish Ballad Operas & Burlesques 2. (The Ballad Opera Ser.). 1974. 50.00 (ISBN 0-8240-0922-3). Garland Pub.

--The Medical & Legal Professions. (The Ballad Opera Ser.). 1974. lib. bdg. 50.00 (ISBN 0-8240-0903-7). Garland Pub.

--Political Operas 2: Attack Upon Excise. (The Ballad Opera Ser.). 1974. lib. bdg. 50.00 (ISBN 0-8240-0920-7). Garland Pub.

--Satire, Burlesque, Protest & Ridicule 1. (The Ballad Opera Ser.). 1974. lib. bdg. 50.00 (ISBN 0-8240-0904-5). Garland Pub.

--Satire, Burlesque, Protest, & Ridicule 2. (The Ballad Opera Ser.). 1974. lib. bdg. 50.00 (ISBN 0-8240-0905-3). Garland Pub.

--Scottish Ballad Operas, One: Pastoral Comedies. (The Ballad Opera Ser.). 1974. lib. bdg. 50.00 (ISBN 0-8240-0923-1). Garland Pub.

--Scottish Ballad Operas, Three: Farce & Satire. (The Ballad Opera Ser.). 1974. lib. bdg. 50.00 (ISBN 0-8240-0925-8). Garland Pub.

--Scottish Ballad Operas, Two: History & Politics. (The Ballad Opera Ser.). 1974. lib. bdg. 50.00 (ISBN 0-8240-0924-X). Garland Pub.

--Topical & Nautical Operas. (The Ballad Opera Ser.). 1974. lib. bdg. 50.00 (ISBN 0-8240-0913-4). Garland Pub.

--York Ballad Operas & Yorkshiremen. (The Ballad Opera Ser.). 1974. lib. bdg. 50.00 (ISBN 0-8240-0926-6). Garland Pub.

Ruby, Lois. Arriving at a Place You Never Left. (YA) (gr. 7-12). 1980. pap. 1.50 (ISBN 0-440-90254-1, LFL). Dell.

--What Do You Do in Quicksand? 224p. 1981. pap. 1.95 (ISBN 0-449-70004-6, Juniper). Fawcett.

Ruby, Robert H. & Brown, John A. The Cayuse Indians: Imperial Tribesmen of Old Oregon. LC 74-177345. (Civilization of the American Indian Ser.: Vol. 120). (Illus.). 320p. 1972. 16.95 (ISBN 0-8061-0995-5); pap. 7.95 (ISBN 0-8061-1316-2). U of Okla Pr.

--Indians of the Pacific Northwest: A History. LC 80-5946. (Civilization of the American Indian Ser.: Vol. 158). (Illus.). 400p. 1981. 24.95 (ISBN 0-8061-1731-1). U of Okla Pr.

--The Spokane Indians: Children of the Sun. LC 79-108797. (The Civilization of the American Indian Ser.: Vol. 104). (Illus.). 346p. 1981. 19.95 (ISBN 0-8061-0905-X); pap. 9.95 (ISBN 0-8061-1757-5). U of Okla Pr.

Ruchelman, Leonard, ed. Who Rules the Police? LC 72-96430. 288p. 1973. 15.00x (ISBN 0-8147-7354-0). NYU Pr.

Ruchlin, H., jt. auth. see Rogers, D.

Ruchlis, Hy. Science Puzzle Pictures. (Illus.). 8p. (Orig.). (gr. 4-8). 1972. pap. 4.00 set of twenty, with Tchr's Manual o.p. (ISBN 0-87594-048-X, 1300). Book-Lab.

Ruchpaul, Eva. Hatha Yoga. LC 68-23738. (Funk & W Bk.). 1969. 7.95 o.s.i. (ISBN 0-308-70418-5, TYC-T). T Y Crowell.

Ruck, Ruth J. Along Came a Llama. (Illus.). 1978. 13.95 (ISBN 0-571-11277-3, Pub. by Faber & Faber). Merrimack Bk Serv.

--Place of Stones. (Orig.). 1970. pap. 5.95 (ISBN 0-571-09392-2, Pub. by Faber & Faber). Merrimack Bk Serv.

Ruck, S. K., jt. auth. see Rhodes, Gerald.

Ruckdeschel, Fred. Basic Scientific Subroutines, Vol. I. Deubofsky, T. J., ed. 1980. 19.95 (ISBN 0-07-054201-5, BYTE Bks). McGraw.

Ruckebusch, Y. & Thivend, P. Digestive Physiology & Metabolism in Ruminants. (Illus., American ed.). 1980. pap. text ed. 54.00 (ISBN 0-87055-359-3). AVI.

Rucker, Bryce W. First Freedom. LC 68-11651. (Arcturus Books Paperbacks). 340p. 1971. pap. 9.95 (ISBN 0-8093-0498-8). S Ill U Pr.

Rucker, Marion E. & LaPidus, Anne. Ohio Magazine's Offical Guide to Columbus & Central Ohio. rev. ed. LC 80-53248. (Illus.). 272p. (Orig.). 1980. pap. 5.95 (ISBN 0-938040-00-6). Ohio Mag.

Rucker, Rudolf V. Geometry, Relativity & the Fourth Dimension. LC 76-22240. (Illus.). 1977. pap. text ed. 2.75 (ISBN 0-486-23400-2). Dover.

Rucker, Rudolf V., ed. see Hinton, Charles H.

Rucker, T. D., ed. Pharmacy: Career Planning & Professional Opportunities. (Illus.). 360p. 1981. pap. write for info. (ISBN 0-914904-52-3). Health Admin Pr.

Ruckerl, Adalbert. The Investigation of Nazi Crimes, Nineteen Forty-Five to Nineteen Seventy-Eight: A Documentation. 145p. 1980. 15.00 (ISBN 0-208-01883-2, Archon). Shoe String.

Rudd, Andrew & Clasing, Henry K., Jr. Modern Portfolio Theory. 1981. 21.50 (ISBN 0-87094-191-7). Dow Jones-Irwin.

Rudd, Anthony. Misogonus. Barber, Lester E. & Orgel, Stephen, eds. LC 78-66756. (Renaissance Drama Ser.). 1979. lib. bdg. 41.00 (ISBN 0-8240-9751-3). Garland Pub.

Rudd, Dale F., et al. Petrochemical Technology Assessment. 325p. 1981. 32.95 (ISBN 0-471-08912-5, Pub. by Wiley-Interscience). Wiley.

--Process Synthesis. LC 73-3331. (International Ser. in Physical & Chemical Engineering). (Illus.). 320p. 1973. ref. ed. 25.95 (ISBN 0-13-723353-1). P-H.

Rudd, Ernest. The Highest Education: A Study of Graduate Education in Britain. 1975. 14.00x (ISBN 0-7100-8307-6). Routledge & Kegan.

Rudd, Kenneth D., et al. Dental Laboratory Procedures: Removable Partial Dentures, Vol. III. (Illus.). 612p. 1981. text ed. 37.50 (ISBN 0-8016-3516-0). Mosby.

Rudd, Margaret T. & Taylor, Martin C. Gabriela Mistral; Poet & Humanitarian: The Chilean Years, 1889-1922. LC 79-2310. (Illus.). Date not set. cancelled o.p. (ISBN 0-8263-0519-9). U of NM Pr.

Rudd, N. Lines of Inquiry. LC 75-12467. 280p. 1976. 36.00 (ISBN 0-521-20993-5). Cambridge U Pr.

Rudd, Rebecca S., jt. auth. see Sizer, Nancy F.

Rudd, Robert L. Environmental Toxicology: A Guide to Information Sources. LC 73-17540. (Man & the Environmrnt Information Guide Ser.: Vol. 7). 1977. 30.00 (ISBN 0-8103-1342-1). Gale.

--Pesticides & the Living Landscape. 1964. pap. 7.95x (ISBN 0-299-03214-0). U of Wis Pr.

Rudd, Walter G. Assembly Language Programming & the IBM 360 & 370 Computers. 1976. 21.95 (ISBN 0-13-049536-0); wkbk. 6.95 (ISBN 0-13-049510-7). P-H.

Rudd, William see O'Neal, William B.

Ruddell, R. Reading-Language Instruction: Innovative Practices. 1973. 19.95 (ISBN 0-13-753285-7). P-H.

Ruddell, Robert B., jt. ed. see Singer, Harry.

Ruddell, Robert B., et al. Free Rein. (Pathfinder - Allyn & Bacon Reading Program: Level 16). (gr. 4-5). 1978. text ed. 9.12 (ISBN 0-205-05188-X, 5451884); 14.60 (ISBN 0-205-05190-1, 5451906); wkbk. 3.88. Allyn.

--Handstands. (Pathfinder - Allyn & Bacon Reading Program: Level 14). (gr. 3-4). 1978. text ed. 8.40 (ISBN 0-205-05168-5, 545168X); tchr's ed. 12.20 (ISBN 0-205-05169-3, 5451698); 2.60. Allyn.

--High Wires & Wigs. (Pathfinder - Allyn & Bacon Reading Program: Level 7). (gr. 1). 1978. pap. text ed. 3.28 (ISBN 0-205-05112-X, 5451124); 8.80 (ISBN 0-205-05127-8, 5451272). Allyn.

--Inside & Out. (Pathfinder - Allyn & Bacon Reading Program: Level 10). (gr. 1-2). 1978. text ed. 7.20 (ISBN 0-205-05115-4, 5451159); tchr's ed. 10.88 (ISBN 0-205-05130-8, 5451302); 3.28. Allyn.

--Majesty & Mystery. (Pathfinder - Allyn & Bacon Reading Program: Level 17). (gr. 5). 1978. text ed. 8.80 (ISBN 0-205-05208-8, 5452082); tchr's guide 14.60 (ISBN 0-205-05210-X, 5452104); 3.88. Allyn.

--Moon Magic. (Pathfinder - Allyn & Bacon Reading Program: Level 11). (gr. 2). 1978. text ed. 8.20 (ISBN 0-205-05145-6, 5451450); tchr's guide 12.20 (ISBN 0-205-05146-4, 5451469); 3.60. Allyn.

--Person to Person. (Pathfinder - Allyn & Bacon Reading Program: Level 15). (gr. 4). 1978. text ed. 9.12 (ISBN 0-205-05187-1, 5451876); tchrs. ed. 14.60 (ISBN 0-205-05189-8, 5451892). Allyn.

--Rides & Races. (Pathfinder - Allyn & Bacon Reading Program: Level 6). (gr. 1). 1978. pap. text ed. 3.28 (ISBN 0-205-05111-1, 5451116); tchr's ed. 8.80 (ISBN 0-205-05127-8, 5451272); 3.28. Allyn.

--Riding Rainbows. (Pathfinder - Allyn & Bacon Reading Program: Level 12). (gr. 2-3). 1978. text ed. 8.20 (ISBN 0-205-05147-2, 5451477); tchr's ed. 12.20 (ISBN 0-205-05148-0, 5451485); 3.60. Allyn.

--Sunshine Days. (Pathfinder - Allyn & Bacon Reading Program: Level 13). (gr. 3). 1978. text ed. 8.40 (ISBN 0-205-05166-9, 5451663); tchr's ed. 12.20 (ISBN 0-205-05167-7, 5451671); 3.60. Allyn.

--Surprises & Prizes. (Pathfinder - Allyn & Bacon Reading Program: Level 8). (gr. 1). 1978. pap. text ed. 3.28 (ISBN 0-205-05113-8, 5451132); 8.80 (ISBN 0-205-05128-6, 5451280); 3.28. Allyn.

--Time & Beyond. (Pathfinder - Allyn & Bacon Reading Program: Level 20). (gr. 6). 1978. text ed. 9.56 (ISBN 0-205-05230-4, 5452309); tchr's ed. 14.60 (ISBN 0-205-05232-0, 5452325); 3.88. Allyn.

--Upside & Down. (Pathfinder - Allyn & Bacon Reading Program: Level 9). (gr. 1). 1978. text ed. 6.92 (ISBN 0-205-05114-6, 5451140); tchr's ed. 10.88 (ISBN 0-205-05129-4, 5451299). Allyn.

--The Widening Path. (Pathfinder - Allyn & Bacon Reading Program: Level 19). (gr. 6). 1978. text ed. 9.56 (ISBN 0-205-05229-0, 5452295); tchr's ed. 14.60 (ISBN 0-205-05231-2, 5452317). Allyn.

Ruddell, Robrt B., et al. Standing Strong. (Pathfinder - Allyn & Bacon Reading Program: Level 18). (gr. 5-6). 1978. text ed. 9.12 (ISBN 0-205-05209-6, 5452090); tchr's ed. 14.60 (ISBN 0-205-05211-8, 5452112); 3.88. Allyn.

Rudden, M. N. & Wilson, J. Elements of Solid State Physics. LC 79-41730. 208p. 1980. 40.00 (ISBN 0-471-27750-9, Pub. by Wiley-Interscience); pap. 17.00 (ISBN 0-471-27749-5). Wiley.

Rudder, Robert S., tr. see Serrano-Plaja, Arturo.

Rudderham, Judith M. Peaceful Poems & Photography: Including the Veiled Reef of Saudi Arabia. 1981. 4.95 (ISBN 0-8062-1716-2). Carlton.

Ruddick, Sara & Daniels, Pamela, eds. Working It Out: 23 Women Writers, Artists, Scientists, & Scholars Talk About Their Lives & Work. LC 76-54624. 1978. pap. 5.95 (ISBN 0-394-73557-9). Pantheon.

Ruddle, John. Collectors' Guide to Britains Model Soldiers. (Illus.). 158p. 1980. 17.50x (ISBN 0-85242-568-6). Intl Pubns Serv.

Ruddle, Kenneth. The Yukpa Cultivation System: A Study of Shifting Cultivation in Columbia & Venezuela. (Publications in Ibero-Americana Ser: Vol. 52). 1976. pap. 14.50x (ISBN 0-520-09497-2). U of Cal Pr.

Ruddle, Kenneth & Chesterfield, Ray. Education for Traditional Food Procurement in the Orinoco Delta. (University of California Publications in Ibero-Americana Ser.: Vol. 53). 1977. pap. 14.50x (ISBN 0-520-09551-0). U of Cal Pr.

Ruddle, Kenneth, jt. auth. see Rondinelli, Dennis A.

Ruddock, E. C. Arch Bridges & Their Builders, 1735-1835. LC 77-82514. (Illus.). 1979. 82.50 (ISBN 0-521-21816-0). Cambridge U Pr.

Ruddock, Ralph. Roles & Relationships. (Library of Social Work). 1970. pap. text ed. 7.75x (ISBN 0-7100-6634-1). Humanities.

Ruddock, Ralph, ed. & pref. by. Six Approaches to the Person. 224p. 1972. 18.00x (ISBN 0-7100-7335-6); pap. 8.95 (ISBN 0-7100-7382-8). Routledge & Kegan.

Rudduck, J. & Kelly, P. The Dissemination of Curriculum Development. Wrigley, Jack & Sparrow, Freddie, eds. (Council of Europe Trend Reports). (Orig.). 1976. pap. text ed. 13.75 (ISBN 0-85633-092-2, NFER). Humanities.

Rudduck, L., jt. auth. see Crip, H.

Ruddy, F. American International Law Cases, Vols. 21-22. 1980. 45.00 ea. (ISBN 0-379-20400-2). Vol. 21. Vol. 22 (ISBN 0-379-20401-0). Oceana.

Rude, George. Hanoverian London, 1714-1808. LC 69-10590. (History of London Series). (Illus.). 1971. 20.00x (ISBN 0-520-01778-1). U of Cal Pr.

--Protest & Punishment: The Story of the Social & Political Protesters Transported to Australia, 1788-1868. 1978. 29.95x (ISBN 0-19-822430-3). Oxford U Pr.

Rude, George, jt. auth. see Hobsbawm, Eric.

Rudeanu, S., tr. see Tomescu, Ioan.

Rudebeck, Lars. Guinea-Bissau: A Study of Political Mobilization. (Illus.). 277p. 1974. pap. text ed. 15.00x o.p. (ISBN 0-8419-9715-2). Holmes & Meier.

Rudeen, Anne. American Royal. (Orig.). 1977. pap. 2.50 (ISBN 0-446-81827-5). Warner Bks.

--Summerblood. (Orig.). 1978. pap. 2.25 o.s.i. (ISBN 0-446-82535-2). Warner Bks.

Rudeen, Kenneth. Jackie Robinson. LC 75-139100. (Biography Ser). (Illus.). (gr. 2-5). 1971. PLB 7.89 (ISBN 0-690-45650-6, TYC-J); pap. 2.95 crocodile paperback ser. (ISBN 0-690-00208-4). T Y Crowell.

--Muhammad Ali. LC 76-12093. (Biography Ser.). (Illus.). 40p. (gr. 1-4). 1976. 7.89 (ISBN 0-690-01128-8, TYC-J). T Y Crowell.

--Roberto Clemente. LC 73-12794. (Biography Ser.). (Illus.). (gr. 1-5). 1974. PLB 7.89 (ISBN 0-690-00322-6, TYC-J). T Y Crowell.

--Wilt Chamberlain. LC 74-94800. (Biography Ser.). (Illus.). (gr. 2-5). 1970. 7.95 (ISBN 0-690-89458-9, TYC-J); PLB 7.89 (ISBN 0-690-01134-2). T Y Crowell.

Rudell, Fredrica. Consumer Food Selection & Nutrition Information. LC 79-10149. (Praeger Special Studies). 188p. 1979. 21.95 (ISBN 0-03-047596-1). Praeger.

Rudeng, Erik & Holm, Hans-Henrik, eds. Social Science Research: Prospects & Purposes. 210p. 1981. 36.00x (ISBN 82-00-05521-3). Universitet.

Rudenstine, Angelica Z. The Guggenheim Museum Collection: Paintings 1880-1945, 2 vols. LC 75-37356. (Illus.). 1976. Set. 85.00x (ISBN 0-89207-002-1); pap. 40.00x (ISBN 0-685-70089-5). S R Guggenheim.

Ruder. Developmental Language Intervention: Psycholinguistic Application. Date not set. 16.50 (ISBN 0-8391-1632-2). Univ Park.

Ruder, Emil. Typography: A Manual of Design. (Visual Communication Bks.). (Illus.). 1967. 42.50 o.p. (ISBN 0-8038-7086-8). Hastings.

--Typography: A Manual of Design. 2nd ed. (Illus.). 128p. 1981. pap. text ed. 12.95 (ISBN 0-8038-7223-2, Visual Communication). Hastings.

Ruder, William & Nathan, Raymond. The Businessman's Guide to Washington. 320p. 1975. 8.95 o.s.i. (ISBN 0-02-605910-X). Macmillan.

--The Businessman's Guide to Washington. 320p. 1975. pap. 4.50 o.s.i. (ISBN 0-02-008660-1, Collier). Macmillan.

Rudestam, Kjell. Methods of Self-Change: An ABC Primer. LC 79-25306. 1980. text ed. 10.95 (ISBN 0-8185-0362-9). Brooks-Cole.

Rudhyar, Dane. The Astrological Houses: The Spectrum of Individual Experience. LC 74-180105. pap. 3.95 (ISBN 0-385-03827-5). Doubleday.

--Astrology & the Modern Psyche: An Astrologer Looks at Depth Psychology. LC 76-21583. 1976. pap. 5.95 (ISBN 0-916360-05-9). CRCS Pubns NV.

--Fire Out of the Stone. 2nd ed. LC 79-89943. Date not set. cancelled (ISBN 0-89793-020-7). Hunter Hse.

--The Lunation Cycle. rev. ed. 1971. pap. 5.95 (ISBN 0-394-73020-8). Shambhala Pubns.

Rudhyar, Dane, jt. auth. see Rael, Leyla.

Rudick, Elliott, jt. auth. see Meier, August.

Rudig, Doug. Zion Adventure Guide. 32p. 1978. 1.95. Zion.

Rudin, A. James & Rudin, Marcia R. Prison or Paradise? The New Religious Cults? LC 80-10210. 168p. 1980. 8.95 (ISBN 0-8006-0637-X, 1-637). Fortress.

Rudin, Jacob. Haggadah for Children. 1973. 2.25x (ISBN 0-8197-0032-0). Bloch.

Rudin, Marcia R., jt. auth. see James, A.

Rudin, Marcia R., jt. auth. see Rudin, A. James.

Rudin, W. Fourier Analysis on Groups. (Pure & Applied Mathematics Ser.). 1962. 30.50 (ISBN 0-470-74481-2). Wiley.

Rudinger, Joel. Firelands Art Review 1977. (Anthology of the Arts Ser.: No. 2). 1977. pap. 3.00x o.p. (ISBN 0-918342-04-X). Cambric.

Rudkin, Margaret. Margaret Rudkin Pepperidge Farm Cookbook. (Illus.). 1963. 17.95 (ISBN 0-689-00027-8). Atheneum.

Rudkin, Mark, tr. see Billetdoux, Francois.

Rudler, G., ed. see Moliere.

Rudler, Gustave, ed. see Racine, Jean.

Rudley, Stephen. The Abominable Snowcreature. (Illus.). (gr. 5 up). 1978. PLB 7.45 s&l (ISBN 0-531-02212-9). Watts.

--Construction Industry Careers. LC 77-3051. (Career Concise Guides Ser.). (gr. 6 up). 1977. PLB 6.45 (ISBN 0-531-01301-4). Watts.

Rudman, jt. auth. see Rosenthal.

Rudman, Daniel, ed. Take It to the Hoop. (Illus.). 300p. (Orig.). 1980. 25.00; pap. 8.95 (ISBN 0-913028-76-2). North Atlantic.

Rudman, Harry W., jt. auth. see Rosenthal, Irving.

Rudman, Jack. Adult Nursing. (College Proficiency Examination Ser.: CLEP-35). (Cloth bdg. avail. on request). pap. 9.95 (ISBN 0-8373-5435-8). Natl Learning.

--African & Afro-American History. (College Proficiency Examination Ser.: CLEP-36). (Cloth bdg. avail. on request). pap. 9.95 (ISBN 0-8373-5436-6). Natl Learning.

--Anatomy & Physiology. (College Proficiency Examination Ser.: CLEP-37). (Cloth bdg. avail. on request). pap. 9.95 (ISBN 0-8373-5437-4). Natl Learning.

--Art History. (Undergraduate Program Field Test Ser.: UPFT-1). (Cloth bdg. avail. on request). pap. 9.95 (ISBN 0-8373-6001-3). Natl Learning.

--Associate Medical Examiner. (Career Examination Ser.: C-2722). (Cloth bdg. avail on request). 1980. pap. 14.00 (ISBN 0-8373-2722-9). Natl Learning.

--Biology. (Undergraduate Program Field Test Ser.: UPFT-2). (Cloth bdg. avail. on request) (ISBN 0-8373-6002-1). pap. 9.95 (ISBN 0-686-68259-9). Natl Learning.

--Business. (Undergraduate Program Field Test Ser.: UPFT-3). (Cloth bdg. avail. on request). pap. 9.95 (ISBN 0-8373-6003-X). Natl Learning.

--Certified Professional Social Worker (CPSW) (Admission Test Ser.: AT-88). (Cloth bdg. avail. on request). pap. 17.95 (ISBN 0-8373-5088-3). Natl Learning.

--Chief Multiple Residence Inspector. (Career Examination Ser.: C-2844). (Cloth bdg. avail. on request). 1980. pap. 14.00 (ISBN 0-8373-2844-6). Natl Learning.

--Diagnosis & Remediation of Reading Problems. (College Proficiency Examination Ser: CLEP-38). (Cloth bdg. avail. on request). pap. 9.95 (ISBN 0-8373-5438-2). Natl Learning.

--Director of Maintenance. (Career Examination Ser.: C-2812). (Cloth bdg. avail. on request). 1980. pap. 14.00 (ISBN 0-8373-2812-8). Natl Learning.

--Drama & Theatre. (Undergraduate Program Field Test Ser.: UPFT-5). (Cloth bdg. avail. on request). pap. 9.95 (ISBN 0-8373-6005-6). Natl Learning.

--Economics. (Undergraduate Program Field Test Ser.: UPFT-6). (Cloth bdg. avail. on request). pap. 9.95 (ISBN 0-8373-6006-4). Natl Learning.

--Education. (Undergraduate Program Field Test Ser.: UPFT-7). (Cloth bdg. avail. on request). pap. 9.95 (ISBN 0-8373-6007-2). Natl Learning.

--Engineering. (Undergraduate Program Field Test Ser.: UPFT-8). (Cloth bdg. avail. on request). pap. 9.95 (ISBN 0-8373-6008-0). Natl Learning.

--Evidence Technician. (Career Examination Ser.: C-2748). (Cloth bdg. avail. on request). 1980. pap. 10.00 (ISBN 0-8373-2748-2). Natl Learning.

--French. (Undergraduate Program Field Test Ser.: UPFT-9). (Cloth bdg. avail. on request). pap. 9.95 (ISBN 0-8373-6009-9). Natl Learning.

--Fundamentals of Nursing. (ACT Proficiency Examination Program: PEP-36). (Cloth bdg. avail. on request). pap. 14.95 (ISBN 0-8373-5536-2). Natl Learning.

--Geography. (Undergraduate Program Field Test Ser.: UPFT-10). (Cloth bdg. avail. on request). pap. 9.95 (ISBN 0-8373-6010-2). Natl Learning.

--Geology. (Undergraduate Program Field Test Ser.: UPFT-11). (Cloth bdg. avail. on request). pap. 9.95 (ISBN 0-8373-6011-0). Natl Learning.

--German. (Undergraduate Program Field Test Ser.: UPFT-12). (Cloth bdg. avail. on request). pap. 9.95 (ISBN 0-8373-6012-9). Natl Learning.

--Golf Course Supervisor. (Career Examination Ser.: C-2774). (Cloth bdg. avail. on request). 1980. pap. 12.00 (ISBN 0-8373-2774-1). Natl Learning.

--Health Restoration: Area I. (ACT Proficiency Examination Program Ser.: PEP-51). pap. 9.95 (ISBN 0-8373-5901-5). Natl Learning.

--Health Restoration: Area II. (ACT Proficiency Examination Program Ser.: PEP-52). (Cloth bdg. avail. on request). pap. 9.95 (ISBN 0-8373-5902-3). Natl Learning.

--History. (Undergraduate Program Field Test Ser.: UPFT-13). (Cloth bdg. avail. on request). pap. 9.95 (ISBN 0-8373-6013-7). Natl Learning.

--Hospital Administration Consultant. (Career Examination Ser.: C-2768). (Cloth bdg. avail. on request). 1980. pap. 12.00 (ISBN 0-8373-2768-7). Natl Learning.

--Incinerator Plant Maintenance Foreman. (Career Examination Ser.: C-2773). (Cloth bdg. avail. on request). 1980. pap. 12.00 (ISBN 0-8373-2773-3). Natl Learning.

--Laundry Worker. (Career Examination Ser.: C-435). (Cloth bdg. avail. on request). pap. 12.00 (ISBN 0-8373-0435-0). Natl Learning.

--Literature. (Undergraduate Program Field Test Ser.: UPFT-14). (Cloth bdg. avail. on request). pap. 9.95 (ISBN 0-8373-6014-5). Natl Learning.

--Mathematics. (Undergraduate Program Field Test Ser.: UPFT-15). (Cloth bdg. avail. on request). pap. 9.95 (ISBN 0-8373-6015-3). Natl Learning.

--Medical Sciences Knowledge Profile Examination (MSKP) (Admission Test Ser.: AT-86). (Cloth bdg. avail. on request). pap. 17.95 (ISBN 0-686-68260-2). Natl Learning.

--Multiple Residence Inspector. (Career Examination Ser.: C-2842). (Cloth bdg. avail. on request). 1980. pap. 10.00 (ISBN 0-8373-2842-X). Natl Learning.

--Music. (Undergraduate Program Field Test Ser.: UPFT-16). (Cloth bdg. avail. on request). pap. 9.95 (ISBN 0-8373-6016-1). Natl Learning.

--National Dental Assistant Boards (NDAB) (Admission Test Ser.: AT-87). (Cloth bdg. avail. on request). 17.95 (ISBN 0-8373-5087-5). Natl Learning.

--National Psychology Boards (NPsyB) (Admission Test Ser.: AT-89). (Cloth bdg. avail. on request). pap. 19.95 (ISBN 0-8373-5089-1). Natl Learning.

--National Veterinary Boards (NVB) (Admission Test Ser.: ATS-50). (Cloth bdg. avail. on request). pap. 25.95 (ISBN 0-8373-5050-6). Natl Learning.

--Oceanographer. (Career Examination Ser.: C-550). (Cloth bdg. avail. on request). pap. 10.00 (ISBN 0-8373-0550-0). Natl Learning.

--Philosophy. (Undergraduate Program Field Test Ser.: UPFT-17). (Cloth bdg. avail. on request). pap. 9.95 (ISBN 0-8373-6017-X). Natl Learning.

--Physical Education. (Undergraduate Program Field Test Ser.: UPFT-18). (Cloth bdg. avail. on request). pap. 9.95 (ISBN 0-8373-6018-8). Natl Learning.

--Physics. (Undergraduate Program Field Test Ser.: UPFT-19). (Cloth bdg. avail. on request). pap. 9.95 (ISBN 0-8373-6019-6). Natl Learning.

--Political Science. (Undergraduate Program Field Test Ser.: UPFT-20). (Cloth bdg. avail. on request). pap. 9.95 (ISBN 0-8373-6020-X). Natl Learning.

--Principal Drug & Alcohol Counselor. (Career Examination Ser.: C-2743). (Cloth bdg. avail. on request). 1980. pap. 16.00 (ISBN 0-8373-2743-1). Natl Learning.

--Psychology. (Undergraduate Program Field Test Ser.: UPFT-21). (Cloth bdg. avail. on request). pap. 9.95 (ISBN 0-8373-6021-8). Natl Learning.

--Purchasing Agent: Medical. (Career Examination Ser.: C-2733). (Cloth bdg. avail. on request). 1980. pap. 10.00 (ISBN 0-8373-2733-4). Natl Learning.

--Purchasing Agent: Printing. (Career Examination Ser.: C-2734). (Cloth bdg. avail. on request). 1980. pap. 10.00 (ISBN 0-8373-2734-2). Natl Learning.

--Scholastic Philosophy. (Undergraduate Program Field Test Ser.: UPFT-22). (Cloth bdg. avail. on request). pap. 9.95 (ISBN 0-8373-6022-6). Natl Learning.

--Senior Engineering Inspector. (Career Examination Ser.: C-2808). (Cloth bdg. avail. on request). 1980. pap. 12.00 (ISBN 0-8373-2808-X). Natl Learning.

--Senior Forestry Technician. (Career Examination Ser.: C-2715). (Cloth bdg. avail. on request). 1980. pap. 12.00 (ISBN 0-8373-2715-6). Natl Learning.

--Senior Medical Services Specialist. (Career Examination Ser.: C-2747). (Cloth bdg. avail. on request). 1980. pap. 14.00 (ISBN 0-8373-2747-4). Natl Learning.

--Senior Micrographics Technician. (Career Examination Ser.: C-2762). (Cloth bdg. avail. on request). 1980. pap. 12.00 (ISBN 0-8373-2762-8). Natl Learning.

--Senior Multiple Residence Inspector. (Career Examination Ser.: C-2843). (Cloth bdg. avail. on request). 1980. pap. 12.00 (ISBN 0-8373-2843-8). Natl Learning.

--Senior Research Assistant. (Career Examination Ser.: C-2717). (Cloth bdg. avail. on request). 1980. pap. 14.00 (ISBN 0-8373-2717-2). Natl Learning.

--Senior Title Searcher. (Career Examination Ser.: C-2086). (Cloth bdg. avail. on request). 1977. write for info. (ISBN 0-8373-2086-0). Natl Learning.

--Senior Zoning Inspector. (Career Examination Ser.: C-2856). (Cloth bdg. avail. on request). 1980. pap. 12.00 (ISBN 0-8373-2856-X). Natl Learning.

--Sociology. (Undergraduate Program Field Test Ser.: UPFT-23). (Cloth bdg. avail. on request). pap. 9.95 (ISBN 0-8373-6023-4). Natl Learning.

--Spanish. (Undergraduate Program Field Test Ser.: UPFT-24). (Cloth bdg. avail. on request). pap. 9.95 (ISBN 0-8373-6024-2). Natl Learning.

--Speech Pathology & Audiology. (Undergraduate Program Field Test Ser.: UPFT-25). (Cloth bdg. avail. on request). pap. 9.95 (ISBN 0-8373-6025-0). Natl Learning.

--State Policewoman. (Career Examination Ser.: C-1692). (Cloth bdg. avail. on request). pap. write for info. (ISBN 0-8373-1692-8). Natl Learning.

--Supervising Building Inspector. (Career Examination Ser.: C-2840). (Cloth bdg. avail. on request). 1980. Natl Learning.

--Undergraduate Program Field Test Series. (Cloth bdg. avail. on request). pap. 9.95 ea. (ISBN 0-8373-6000-5). Natl Learning.

--Unemployment Insurance Hearing Representative. (Career Examination Ser.: C-2728). (Cloth bdg. avail. on request). 1980. pap. 10.00 (ISBN 0-8373-2728-8). Natl Learning.

Rudman, Masha. Children's Literature: An Issues Approach. 1976. text ed. 11.95x o.p. (ISBN 0-669-00322-0); pap. text ed. 9.95x (ISBN 0-669-93203-5). Heath.

Rudner, Richard S. Philosophy of Social Science. (Orig.). 1966. pap. 7.95x ref. ed. (ISBN 0-13-664300-0). P-H.

Rudner, Richard S. & Scheffler, Israel, eds. Logic & Art: Essays in Honor of Nelson Goodman. LC 76-140799. 1971. 13.95 (ISBN 0-672-51639-X). Bobbs.

Rudner, Ruth. Off & Walking: A Hiker's Guide to American Places. LC 76-29913. (Illus.). 1977. pap. 4.95 o.p. (ISBN 0-03-015591-6). HR&W.

Rudnick, Dorothea, tr. see Baltzer, Fritz.

Rudnicki, Stefan, ed. Classical Monologues 2: Shakespeare & Friends. LC 79-16079. 1980. pap. 3.95x (ISBN 0-89676-022-7). Drama Bk.

--Classical Monologues 3: The Age of Style. 128p. (Orig.). 1981. pap. 3.95x (ISBN 0-89676-036-7). Drama Bk.

--Classical Monologues 4: Shakespeare & Friends Encore. 144p. (Orig.). 1981. pap. text ed. 4.95x (ISBN 0-89676-037-5). Drama Bk.

--Classical Monologues 5: Warhorses. 96p. (Orig.). 1981. pap. text ed. 4.95x (ISBN 0-89676-038-3). Drama Bk.

Rudnik, Maryka, tr. see Pelgrom, Els.

Rudnik, Raphael, tr. see Pelgrom, Els.

Rudnitsky, Alan N., jt. auth. see Posner, George J.

Rudnitsky, Konstantin. Meyerhold: The Director. Petrov, George, tr. from Rus. (Illus.). 1981. 42.50 (ISBN 0-88233-313-5). Ardis Pubs.

Rudoff, Alvin. Work Furlough & the County Jail. 212p. 1975. 17.25 (ISBN 0-398-03437-0). C C Thomas.

Rudofsky, Bernard. Architecture Without Architects: A Short Introduction to Non-Pedigreed Architecture. LC 64-8755. 1969. pap. 5.95 (ISBN 0-385-07487-5). Doubleday.

--Now I Lay Me Down to Eat: Notes & Footnotes on the Lost Art of Living. LC 80-714. (Illus.). 196p. 1980. pap. 10.95 (ISBN 0-385-15716-9, Anch). Doubleday.

--Now I Lay Me Down to Eat: Notes & Footnotes on the Lost Art of Living. LC 80-714. (Illus.). 160p. 1980. 19.95 (ISBN 0-385-15715-0, Anchor Pr); pap. 10.95 (ISBN 0-385-15716-9). Doubleday.

--Streets for People. LC 76-78735. 1969. 14.95 o.p. (ISBN 0-385-04231-0). Doubleday.

--The Unfashionable Human Body. LC 74-160871. 288p. 1974. pap. 5.95 (ISBN 0-385-07818-8, Anch). Doubleday.

Rudolf, Anthony, jt. ed. see Schwartz, Howard.

Rudolf, Max. The Grammar of Conducting: A Practical Guide to Baton Technique & Orchestral Interpretation. 2nd ed. LC 79-7634. (Illus.). 1980. text ed. 17.50 (ISBN 0-02-872220-5). Schirmer Bks.

Rudolph. Pediatrics. 16th ed. (Illus.). 1977. 42.95 (ISBN 0-8385-7794-6). ACC.

Rudolph, Erwin P. John Bunyan & Pilgrim's Progress. 1977. pap. 1.25 o.p. (ISBN 0-88207-505-5). Victor Bks.
--The John Donne Treasury. 1978. pap. 1.50 o.p. (ISBN 0-88207-514-4). Victor Bks.
--The John Wesley Treasury. 1979. pap. 1.95 (ISBN 0-88207-517-9). Victor Bks.
Rudolph, Erwin P., ed. The Martin Luther Treasury. 1979. pap. 1.95 (ISBN 0-88207-518-7). Victor Bks.
Rudolph, Frederick. American College & University. 1965. pap. 4.95 (ISBN 0-394-70288-3, Vin). Random.
Rudolph, Jack. Allergies: What They Are & What to Do About Them. 1973. pap. 1.75 (ISBN 0-515-05142-X, V3101). Jove Pubns.
Rudolph, Joachim. Chemistry for the Modern Mind. Grinter, H. C., tr. LC 73-6202. (Science for the Modern Mind Ser.). (Illus.). 358p. 1974. 12.95 (ISBN 0-02-605850-2). Macmillan.
Rudolph, Lee. The Country Changes. LC 78-60470. 72p. 1978. pap. 4.95 (ISBN 0-914086-23-5). Alicejamesbooks.
--Curses, & Songs & Poems. LC 74-81380. 72p. 1974. pap. 4.95 (ISBN 0-914086-04-9). Alicejamesbooks.
Rudolph, Lloyd & Rudolph, Susanne. The Regional Imperative: The Administration of U. S. Policy Towards the South Asian States Under Presidents Johnson & Nixon. 1980. text ed. 16.50x (ISBN 0-391-02178-8). Humanities.
Rudolph, Marguerita, jt. auth. see Cohen, Dorothy H.
Rudolph, Nancy. Workyards-Playgrounds Planned for Adventure. LC 74-5187. (Illus.). 1974. pap. 7.50x (ISBN 0-8077-2423-8). Tchrs Coll.
Rudolph, R. L. Finance & Industrialization in the Austro-Hungarian Empire, 1873-1914. LC 75-2736. (Illus.). 350p. 1976. 47.50 (ISBN 0-521-20878-5). Cambridge U Pr.
Rudolph, Susanne, jt. auth. see Rudolph, Lloyd.
Rudolph, Wilma. Wilma Rudolph on Track. (gr. 4-9). Date not set. pap. cancelled (ISBN 0-671-33064-0). Wanderer Bks.
Rudorf, E. Hugh, jt. auth. see Hodges, R. E.
Rudorff, Ray. The Venice Plot. (YA) 1976. 7.95 o.p. (ISBN 0-399-11803-9, Dist. by Putnam). Berkley Pub.
Rudorff, Raymond. War to the Death: The Sieges of Saragossa, 1808-1809. LC 73-21293. 304p. 1974. 8.95 o.s.i. (ISBN 0-02-605940-1). Macmillan.
Rudovsky, David, et al. The Rights of Prisoners. 1972. pap. 1.50 (ISBN 0-380-01387-8, 35436, Discus). Avon.
Rudrum, Alan, ed. Henry Vaughan: The Complete Poems. LC 80-53979. 718p. 1981. text ed. 30.00x (ISBN 0-300-02680-3); pap. 7.95x (ISBN 0-300-02687-0). Yale U Pr.
Rudwick, Elliott, jt. auth. see Meier, August.
Rudwick, M. J. Living & Fossil Brachiopods. 1970. pap. text ed. 7.50x (ISBN 0-09-103081-1, Hutchinson U Lib). Humanities.
Rudy, Ellen & Gray, Ruth. Handbook of Health Assessment. (Illus.). 184p. 1981. pap. text ed. 9.95 (ISBN 0-87619-843-4). R J Brady.
Rudy, Peter, et al. Russian: A Complete Elementary Course. 1970. 15.95x (ISBN 0-393-09871-0, NortonC); text & tape set o.p. 90.00 (ISBN 0-686-66509-0); tapes for duplication by school free (ISBN 0-393-99126-1). Norton.
Rue, Leonard L. Sportsman's Guide to Game Animals. LC 68-12140. (Illus.). 1968. 13.95 o.p. (ISBN 0-06-071715-7, HarpT). Har-Row.
--World of the White-Tailed Deer. LC 62-11348. (Living World Book Ser). 1962. 10.95 (ISBN 0-397-00254-8). Lippincott.
Rue, Leonard L., 3rd. Pictorial Guide to the Mammals of North America. (gr. 7 up). 1967. 11.95 o.s.i. (ISBN 0-690-62371-2, TYC-T). T Y Crowell.
--World of the Red Fox. LC 69-16165. (Living World Books Ser). 1969. 7.95 o.s.i. (ISBN 0-397-00627-6); PLB 7.82 o.s.i. (ISBN 0-397-00628-4). Lippincott.
--The World of the Ruffled Grouse. Terres, John, ed. LC 72-748. (Living World Bks). (Illus.). 291p. 1972. 8.95 (ISBN 0-397-00817-1). Lippincott.
Rue, Leslie W. & Byars, Lloyd L. Management: Theory & Application. rev. ed. 1980. 18.95x (ISBN 0-256-02346-8). Irwin.
--Management: Theory & Application. 1977. 15.95x o.p. (ISBN 0-256-01885-5). Irwin.
Rueff, Jacques. The Gods & the Kings: A Glance at Creative Power. LC 72-94011. 228p. 1973. Repr. 8.95 o.s.i. (ISBN 0-02-605880-4). Macmillan.
Ruehlmann, William. Saint with a Gun: The Unlawful American Private Eye. LC 74-11490. 155p. 1974. 12.00 (ISBN 0-8147-7355-9). NYU Pr.
Ruelas, Miguel, ed. see Altamirano, Ignacio M.
Ruesch, Hans. Back to the Top of the World. 1974. pap. 1.50 o.p. (ISBN 0-345-23884-2). Ballantine.
Ruesch, Jurgen. Disturbed Communication. 1972. pap. 4.95 o.p. (ISBN 0-393-00634-4, Norton Lib). Norton.
Rueschhoff, Norlin G. International Accounting & Financial Reporting. LC 76-12871. (Special Studies). 1976. 24.95 (ISBN 0-275-23110-0). Praeger.
Rueschhoff, Phil H. & Swartz, M. Evelyn. Teaching Art in the Elementary School: Enhancing Visual Perception. (Illus.). 1969. 19.95 (ISBN 0-8260-7655-6). Wiley.
Ruether, Rosemary & Keller, Rosemary. Women & Religion in America: Vol 1, the Nineteenth Century. LC 80-8346. (Illus.). 352p. 1981. 15.00 (ISBN 0-06-066829-6, HarpR). Har-Row.
Rueveni, Uri. Networking Families in Crisis. LC 78-8024. 1979. 16.95 (ISBN 0-87705-374-X). Human Sci Pr.
Ruff, Howard J. How to Prosper During the Coming Bad Years. rev. ed. 1981. pap. 3.50 (ISBN 0-446-96952-4). Warner Bks.
Ruff, James L. Shelley's the Revolt of Islam. (Salzburg Studies in English Literature, Romantic Reassessment: No.10). 1972. pap. text ed. 25.00x (ISBN 0-391-01512-5). Humanities.
Ruffell, Ann. Blood Brothers. (gr. 7 up). 1980. PLB 7.90 (ISBN 0-531-04177-8). Watts.
Ruffer, J. E. The Art of Good Shooting. (Illus.). 125p. 1976. 6.95 o.p. (ISBN 0-7153-5521-X). David & Charles.
--Good Shooting. LC 79-56044. (Illus.). 208p. 1980. 22.50x (ISBN 0-7153-7917-8). David & Charles.
Ruffier, Jonathan G. The Big Shots: Edwardian Shooting Parties. (Illus.). 1978. 17.50 o.p. (ISBN 0-670-16376-7, Debrett's Peerage, Ltd.). Viking Pr.
Ruffins, Reynold. My Brother Never Feeds the Cat. (Illus.). 32p. (gr. k-1). 1979. 7.95 (ISBN 0-684-16211-3). Scribner.
Ruffins, Reynold, jt. auth. see Sarnoff, Jane.
Ruffner, Budge. Shot in the Ass with Pesos: A Collection of Frontier Tales. (Illus.). 112p. (Orig.). 1979. pap. 4.95 (ISBN 0-918080-11-8). Treasure Chest.
Ruffner, James, rev. by. The Climates of the States, 2 vols. LC 76-11672. 1400p. 1978. 59.00 o.p. (ISBN 0-8103-1042-2). Gale.
Ruffner, James & Bair, Frank, eds. Weather Almanac: A Reference Guide to Weather & Climate of the United States & Its Key Cities. (Illus.). 700p. 1981. 42.00 (ISBN 0-8103-1053-8). Gale.
--Weather Almanac: A Reference Guide to Weather & Climate of the U.S. & Its Key Cities. 2nd ed. LC 73-9342. 1977. 42.00 (ISBN 0-8103-1043-0). Gale.
Ruffner, James, et al, eds. Eponyms Dictionaries Index: A Compilation of Terms Based on Names of Actual or Legendary Persons. LC 76-20341. 1977. 68.00 (ISBN 0-8103-0688-3). Gale.
Ruffo, Vinnie. Trapped in Death Valley. LC 72-76832. 121p. 1972. pap. 4.95 (ISBN 0-8163-0050-X, 20608-6). Pacific Pr Pub Assn.
Ruge, Daniel. Spinal Cord Injuries. 236p. 1969. pap. 16.25 spiral (ISBN 0-398-01630-5). C C Thomas.
Rugg, Tom & Feldman, Phil. Thirty-Two Basic Programs for the Apple Computer. 300p. 1981. pap. 17.95 (ISBN 0-918398-34-7). Dilithium Pr.
--Thirty-Two Basic Programs for the PET (8k) Computer. LC 78-24837. 1979. pap. 16.95 (ISBN 0-918398-25-8). Dilithium Pr.
--Thirty-Two Basic Programs for the Trs-Eighty (Level 2) Computer. LC 79-56399. 290p. 1980. pap. 16.95 (ISBN 0-918398-27-4). Dilithium Pr.
Rugg, Tom, et al. Thirty-Two BASIC Programs for the Exidy Sorcerer. 290p. 1981. pap. 16.95 (ISBN 0-918398-35-5). Dilithium Pr.
Ruggieri, George D. & Rosenberg, Norman D. The Healing Sea. LC 78-7333. (Illus.). 1978. 7.95 (ISBN 0-396-07449-9). Dodd.
Ruggieri, Lorraine. Woman's Day Book of No-Pattern Sewing. 128p. (Orig.). 1981. pap. 6.95 (ISBN 0-449-90053-3, Columbine). Fawcett.
Ruggiero. Art of Writing. 1981. 11.95 (ISBN 0-88284-118-1); manuel free (ISBN 0-88284-129-7). Alfred Pub.
Ruggiero, Vincent R. Beyond Feelings: A Guide to Critical Thinking. LC 74-34569. 191p. 1975. pap. text ed. 7.95x (ISBN 0-88284-020-7). Alfred Pub.
--The Moral Imperative: Ethical Issues for Discussion & Writing. LC 73-78659. (Illus.). 225p. (Orig.). 1973. pap. text ed. 7.95x (ISBN 0-88284-007-X). Alfred Pub.
Ruggiers, Paul G. Florence in the Age of Dante. (Centers of Civilization Ser.: No. 15). 1968. Repr. of 1964 ed. 5.95x o.p. (ISBN 0-8061-0617-4). U of Okla Pr.
--Versions of Medieval Comedy. LC 77-6384. 1977. pap. 5.95 (ISBN 0-8061-1438-X). U of Okla Pr.
Ruggiers, Paul G., ed. see Chaucer, Geoffrey.
Ruggles, Philip K. Printing Estimating. LC 79-13008. 1979. text ed. 16.95 (ISBN 0-534-00747-3, Breton Pubs). Wadsworth Pub.
Rugh, William A. The Arab Press: News Media & Political Process in the Arab World. (Illus.). 224p. 1979. 18.00x (ISBN 0-8156-2191-4); pap. 6.95s (ISBN 0-8156-0159-X). Syracuse U Pr.
Rugman, Alan M. International Diversification & the Multinational Enterprise. (Illus.). 160p. 1979. 16.95 (ISBN 0-669-02772-3). Lexington Bks.
Ruhe, Robert. Geomorphology. 1975. text ed. 20.95 (ISBN 0-395-18553-X). HM.
Ruhen, Olaf. Harpoon. 1975. pap. 1.25 o.p. (ISBN 0-685-61046-2, LB316, Leisure Bks). Nordon Pubns.
Ruhen, Olaf, jt. auth. see Collings, Lawrence.
Ruhe-Schoen, Janet. Organizing & Operating Profitable Workshop Classes. LC 80-25466. 1981. pap. 2.50 (ISBN 0-87576-092-9). Pilot Bks.
Ruhl, J. Mark. Colombia: Armed Forces & Society. LC 80-18762. (Latin American Ser.: Vol. 1). iv, 52p. (Orig.). 1980. pap. 4.50x (ISBN 0-915984-92-X). Syracuse U Foreign Comp.
Ruhl, Kathleen. Universal Supplementary Exercisebook. 1981. pap. text ed. 6.95x (ISBN 0-673-15453-X). Scott F.
Ruhl, Werner, ed. Field Theoretical Methods in Particle Physics. (NATO Advanced Study Institutes Ser., Ser. B: Physics: Vol. 55). 608p. 1980. 69.50 (ISBN 0-306-40444-3, Plenum Pr). Plenum Pub.
Ruhleder, Karl H., jt. ed. see Kurz, Edmund P.
Ruhm, Herbert, ed. see James, Henry.
Ruhman, Ruth. Chicken Little. (Illus.). (ps-2). 1974. PLB 5.38 (ISBN 0-307-68924-7, Golden Pr). Western Pub.
Ruhmer, Eberhardt. Cosimo Tura: Paintings & Drawings. (Illus.). 45.00 (ISBN 0-912158-47-6). Hennessey.
Ruhnau, Helena E. Light on a Mountain. (Illus.). 1975. 7.95 (ISBN 0-686-14460-0); pap. 4.50 (ISBN 0-686-28553-0). Colleasius Pr.
Ruhumbika, Gabriel. Village in Uhuru. (Orig.). 1969. pap. text ed. 3.00x (ISBN 0-582-64011-3). Humanities.
Ruigquist, Delbert, jt. auth. see Davis, James W.
Ruitenbeek, Hendrik. Psychotherapy: What It's All About. 1976. pap. 1.95 o.p. (ISBN 0-380-00811-4, 30858). Avon.
Ruiz, Mary & Amend, Karen S. The Complete Book of Handwriting Analysis. 1980. pap. 9.95 (ISBN 0-87877-050-X). Newcastle Pub.
Ruiz, Mary S. & Amend, Karen. The Complete Book of Handwriting Analysis. LC 80-8672. (Illus.). 196p. 1980. Repr. of 1980 ed. lib. bdg. 17.95 (ISBN 0-89370-650-7). Borgo Pr.
Ruiz, Pedro, jt. auth. see Lowinson, Joyce.
Ruiz, Ramon. The Treat Rebellion. 1980. write for info. Norton.
Ruiz, Ramon E. The Great Rebellion: Mexico Nineteen Hundred & Five to Nineteen Twenty-Four. 1980. 24.95 (ISBN 0-393-01323-5). Norton.
Ruiz, Roberto, jt. auth. see Bijou, Sidney W.
Ruiz, Roberto, jt. ed. see Bijou, Sidney W.
Ruiz-Fornells, Enrique, jt. auth. see Chatham, James R.
Ruiz-P-Ceretti, E., jt. auth. see Schanne, Otto F.
Ruiz Torres, F. Spanish-English & English-Spanish Medical Dictionary. 3rd ed. 1965. 25.00 o.p. (ISBN 8-4205-0455-6). Heinman.
Rukert, Norman G. Federal Hill: A Baltimore National Historic District. Robinson, Max, ed. LC 80-65865. (Illus.). 128p. (Orig.). 1980. 12.95 (ISBN 0-910254-14-1); pap. 6.95 (ISBN 0-910254-15-X). Bodine.
Rukeyser, Louis. How to Make Money in Wall Street. 288p. 1976. pap. 4.95 (ISBN 0-385-04652-9, Dolp). Doubleday.
Rukeyser, Muriel. More Night. LC 79-2680. (Illus.). 32p. (gr. k-3). 1981. 8.95 (ISBN 0-06-025127-1, HarpJ); PLB 8.79g (ISBN 0-06-025128-X). Har-Row.
--Traces of Thomas Hariot. 1971. 12.50 o.p. (ISBN 0-394-44923-1). Random.
Rukeyser, Muriel, et al, trs. see Paz, Octavio.
Rukl, Antonin. Moon, Mars & Venus. (Concise Guides Ser.). (Illus.). 1979. 7.95 (ISBN 0-600-36219-1). Transatlantic.
Ruland, Richard. The Native Muse: Theories of American Literature from Bradford to Whitman. 1976. pap. 6.95 o.p. (ISBN 0-525-47412-9). Dutton.
Ruland, Richard, ed. Twentieth Century Interpretations of Walden. 1968. pap. 8.95 (ISBN 0-13-944306-1, Spec). P-H.
Rule, Ann. Beautiful San Juans Island & Puget Sound. Shangle, Robert D., ed. LC 79-1204. (Illus.). 80p. 1980. 14.95 (ISBN 0-89802-081-6); pap. 7.95 (ISBN 0-89802-080-8). Beautiful Am.
--Beautiful Seattle. Shangle, Robert D., ed. LC 79-23392. (Illus.). 80p. 1979. 14.95 (ISBN 0-89802-071-9); pap. 7.95 (ISBN 0-89802-070-0). Beautiful Am.
--The Stranger Beside Me. (Illus.). 1981. pap. 3.50 (ISBN 0-451-09888-9, E9888, Sig). NAL.
Rule, James B. Private Lives & Public Surveillance: Social Control in the Computer Age. LC 73-90685. 1974. 8.00x (ISBN 0-8052-3542-6). Schocken.
Rule, Jane. Outlander. LC 80-84221. 220p. (Orig.). 1981. pap. 6.95 (ISBN 0-930044-17-7). Naiad Pr.
Rule, John. The Experience of Labour in Eighteenth Century Industry. 1980. 25.00 (ISBN 0-312-27664-8). St Martin.
Rule, La Reina & Hammond, William K. What's in a Name? Surnames of America. 1977. pap. 1.95 o.s.i. (ISBN 0-515-04460-1). Jove Pubns.
Rule, Leonard. Fire. LC 73-161698. (New Citizen Books). (Illus.). 80p. 1973. 10.50x (ISBN 0-85340-229-9). Intl Pubns Serv.
Rule, Wilfred P. Programacion Fortran IV. (Orig.). 1976. text ed. 7.20x (ISBN 0-06-316996-7, IntlDept). Har-Row.
Ruley, M. J. Practical Metal Projects. (gr. 9 up). text ed. 13.28 (ISBN 0-87345-137-6). McKnight.
--Projects in General Metalwork. (gr. 9 up). 1969. text ed. 13.28 (ISBN 0-87345-135-X). McKnight.
Ruley, M. J., jt. auth. see McGinnis, Harry.
Rulfo, Juan. Burning Plain & Other Stories. Schade, George D., tr. LC 67-25698. (Pan American Paperback Ser.: No. 6). (Illus.). 1957. 8.95x (ISBN 0-292-73685-1); pap. 3.95 (ISBN 0-292-70132-2). U of Tex Pr.
Rulla, Luigi M. Depth Psychology & Vocation: A Psycho-Social Perspective. LC 70-146938. 1971. 12.50 o.p. (ISBN 0-8294-0210-1). Loyola.
Rullo, Thomas A. The Manager's Standard Manual. LC 77-10033. (Illus.). 1977. text ed. 12.00 (ISBN 0-89433-000-4); pap. text ed. 10.00 (ISBN 0-89433-018-7). Petrocelli.
Rullo, Thomas A., ed. Advances in Data Communications Management, Vol. 1. 225p. 1980. 29.50 (ISBN 0-85501-605-1). Heyden.
--Advances in Data Processing Management, Vol. 1. 225p. 1980. 27.50 (ISBN 0-85501-601-9). Heyden.
--Advances in Distributed Processing Management, Vol. 1. 225p. 1980. 32.50 (ISBN 0-85501-604-3). Heyden.
--The Heyden Advances Library in EDP Management in Six Volumes. 1980. 159.00 (ISBN 0-85501-600-0). Heyden.
Rumaker, Michael. My First Satyrnalia. 180p. 1981. 12.95 (ISBN 0-912516-50-X); pap. 4.95 (ISBN 0-912516-51-8). Grey Fox.
Rumbaut, Ruben D. John of God: His Place in the History of Psychiatry & Medicine. LC 77-91668. 1978. pap. 5.95 (ISBN 0-89729-198-0). Ediciones.
Rumbelow, Donald, jt. auth. see Hindley, Judy.
Rumble, Greville, jt. ed. see Kay, Anthony.
Rumbold, Algernon. Watershed in India 1914-1922. 1979. text ed. 40.00x (ISBN 0-485-11182-9, Athlone Pr). Humanities.
Rumelhart, David E., jt. auth. see Norman, Donald A.
Rumford, Beatrix T., ed. American Folk Portraits: Paintings & Drawings from the Abbey Aldrich Rockefeller Folk Art Center. 1981. 35.00 (ISBN 0-686-69213-6). NYGS.
Rumi, Jalal A. Mystical Poems of Rumi. Arberry, A. J., tr. from Persian. LC 68-29935. vi, 202p. 1974. 12.50x o.s.i. (ISBN 0-226-73150-2); pap. 3.95 (ISBN 0-226-73151-0, P584, Phoen). U of Chicago Pr.
Rumi, Jalal Al-Din. Rumi: Mystical Poems: Poems 201-400. Arberry, A. J., tr. (Bibliotheca Persica: Persian Heritage Ser.: No. 23). 1979. lib. bdg. 22.50x (ISBN 0-89158-477-3). Westview.
Rummel, R. J. Dimensions of Nations, Vol. 1. LC 72-84054. 416p. 1972. 25.00x (ISBN 0-8039-0170-4). Sage.
--National Attributes & Behavior. LC 76-50501. (Dimensions of Nations Ser.: Vol. 3). 1979. 27.50x (ISBN 0-8039-0392-8). Sage.
--Peace Endangered: The Reality of Detente. LC 76-17372. (Illus.). 1976. 17.50x (ISBN 0-8039-0387-1); pap. 7.95x (ISBN 0-8039-0828-8). Sage.
Rummel, Rudolph J. Understanding Conflict & War, 2 vols. Incl. Vol. 1. 342p. 18.95 (ISBN 0-470-74501-0); Vol. 2. The Conflict Helix. 17.50 (ISBN 0-470-15123-4). LC 74-78565. 1975-76. Halsted Pr.
Rummel, W., jt. ed. see Forth, W.
Rumsey, Helen, jt. auth. see Clure, Beth.
Rumsey, Marian. Beaver of Weeping Water. LC 69-11542. (Illus.). (gr. 3-7). 1969. PLB 6.00 o.p. (ISBN 0-688-31074-5). Morrow.
--Carolina Hurricane. LC 77-5622. (Illus.). (gr. 3-7). 1977. 7.75 (ISBN 0-688-22128-9); PLB 7.44 (ISBN 0-688-32128-3). Morrow.
--Danger on Shadow Mountain. (Illus.). (gr. 5-9). 1970. 7.25 o.p. (ISBN 0-688-21208-5). Morrow.
--Devil's Doorstep. (Illus.). (gr. 3-7). 1966. 7.25 (ISBN 0-688-21235-2). Morrow.

--Lion on the Run. LC 72-7880. (Illus.). 160p. (gr. 3-7). 1973. 7.75 (ISBN 0-688-21770-2); PLB 7.44 (ISBN 0-688-31770-7). Morrow.

Rumshiskii, L. Z. Elements of Probability Theory. 1965. 26.00 (ISBN 0-08-010534-3); pap. 12.75 (ISBN 0-08-013609-5). Pergamon.

Rumyantsev, P. I., jt. auth. see Stanislavski, Constantin.

Runcie, John F. Experiencing Social Research. rev. ed. 1980. pap. 8.95x (ISBN 0-256-02304-2). Dorsey.

--Experiencing Social Research. 1980. pap. text ed. 7.95 o.p. (ISBN 0-256-02304-2). Dorsey.

Runcie, Robert, ed. Cathedral & City: St. Albans Ancient & Modern. 1977. text ed. 13.00x (ISBN 0-85422-149-2). Humanities.

Runciman, S. The Byzantine Theocracy. LC 76-47405. (Weil Lectures Ser.). 1977. 23.95 (ISBN 0-521-21401-7). Cambridge U Pr.

Runciman, Steven. Byzantine Civilization. 1933. 18.75 (ISBN 0-312-11165-7). St Martin.

--Fall of Constantinople, Fourteen Fifty-Three. LC 65-10383. (Illus.). 1969. 32.50 (ISBN 0-521-06165-2); pap. 9.95x (ISBN 0-521-09573-5). Cambridge U Pr.

--The First Crusade. LC 80-40228. (Illus.). 224p. 1980. 19.95 (ISBN 0-521-23255-4). Cambridge U Pr.

--Great Church in Captivity. LC 68-29330. 1968. 42.50 (ISBN 0-521-07188-7). Cambridge U Pr.

--History of the Crusades, 3 vols. 65.00 ea.; Vol. 1. (ISBN 0-521-06161-X); Vol.2. (ISBN 0-521-06162-8); Vol. 3. (ISBN 0-521-06163-6); 165.00 set (ISBN 0-521-20554-9). Cambridge U Pr.

--A History of the First Bulgarian Empire. LC 80-2369. 1981. Repr. of 1930 ed. 48.50 (ISBN 0-404-18916-4). AMS Pr.

--Last Byzantine Renaissance. (Wiles Lectures 1968-69). 1970. 15.50 (ISBN 0-521-07787-7). Cambridge U Pr.

--Sicilian Vespers. 1958. 35.50 (ISBN 0-521-06167-9). Cambridge U Pr.

Runciman, W. G. Relative Deprivation & Social Justice. (Reports of the Institute of Community Studies). 1980. Repr. pap. 35.00 (ISBN 0-7100-3923-9). Routledge & Kegan.

Runciman, W. G., ed. Max Weber: Selections in Translation. Matthews, E., tr. LC 77-80846. 1978. 39.00 (ISBN 0-521-21757-1); pap. 9.95x (ISBN 0-521-29268-9). Cambridge U Pr.

Runciman, Walter G. Social Science & Political Theory. 1963. 19.95 (ISBN 0-521-07474-6); pap. 7.50x (ISBN 0-521-09562-X, 562). Cambridge U Pr.

Runck, Bette, et al. Families Today: A Research Sampler on Families & Children, 2 vols. LC 79-66976. (Science Monographs: No. 1). (Illus., Orig.). 1980. Vol. 1. pap. 8.50 (ISBN 0-686-27076-2); Vol. 2. pap. 8.00 (ISBN 0-686-27077-0). Gov Printing Office.

Runck, Robert R., ed. Premachining Planning & Tool Presetting. LC 67-28208. (Manufacturing Data Ser). (Illus.). 1967. pap. 8.25x (ISBN 0-87263-008-0). SME.

Runcorn, S. K., ed. International Dictionary of Geophysics, 2 vols. 1968. Set. 300.00 (ISBN 0-08-011834-8). Pergamon.

Runcorn, S. K., ed. see Royal Institution Library of Science.

Rund, Douglas A. & Rausch, Tondra S. Triage. (Illus.). 256p. 1981. pap. text ed. 13.95 (ISBN 0-8016-4221-3). Mosby.

Rund, Hanno, jt. auth. see Lovelock, David.

Rundall, Thomas G., jt. ed. see Battistella, Roger M.

Rundle, Bede. Perception, Sensation & Verification. 1972. 22.50x (ISBN 0-19-824390-1). Oxford U Pr.

Rundle, R. N. International Affairs, Eighteen Ninety to Nineteen Thirty Nine. LC 79-12170. (Illus.). 1980. text ed. 27.75x (ISBN 0-8419-0516-9); pap. text ed. 12.95x (ISBN 0-8419-0601-7). Holmes & Meier.

Runeckles, V. C., ed. Recent Advances in Phytochemistry: Vol. 9, Phytochemistry in Disease & Medicine. LC 67-26242. 299p. 1975. 32.50 (ISBN 0-306-34709-1, Plenum Pr). Plenum Pub.

Runeckles, V. C., ed. see Phytochemical Society of North America.

Runeckles, V. C., ed. see Phytochemical Society of North American Symposium.

Runeckles, Victor C., jt. ed. see Finkle, Bernard J.

Runes, Dagobert & Schrickey, Harry G., eds. Encyclopedia of the Arts, 2 vols. Date not set. Repr. of 1946 ed. Set. 42.00 (ISBN 0-8103-4162-X). Gale.

Runes, Dagobert D., ed. Dictionary of Philosophy. rev., enl. ed. 1981. Repr. 25.00 (ISBN 0-8022-2388-5). Philos Lib.

Runes, Richard N., jt. auth. see Baskin, Wade.

Runge, Carl see Sierpinski, Waclaw, et al.

Runge, Senta M. Face Lifting by Exercise. 9th ed. LC 56-6321. (Illus.). 1977. Repr. of 1961 ed. 16.00 (ISBN 0-9601042-1-6). Allegro Pub.

Rungeling, Brian, et al. Employment, Income, & Welfare in the Rural South. LC 77-10612. (Praeger Special Studies). 1977. 33.95 (ISBN 0-03-023041-1). Praeger.

Runk, Wesley T. Object Lessons from the Bible. (Object Lessons Ser.). 96p. 1980. pap. 2.95 (ISBN 0-8010-7698-6). Baker Bk.

Runkel, Philip, et al, eds. The Changing College Classroom. LC 70-92896. (Higher Education Ser.). 1969. 14.95x o.p. (ISBN 0-87589-047-4). Jossey-Bass.

Runkel, Philip J. & Burr, Ann M. Bibliography on Organizational Change in Schools, Selected & Annotated. 1977. 4.00 (ISBN 0-936276-10-X). Ctr Educ Policy Mgmt.

Runkel, Philip J., et al. Organizational Renewel in a School District: Self-Help Through a Cadre of Organizational Specialists. LC 79-57252. 168p. (Orig.). 1980. pap. 7.50 (ISBN 0-936276-12-6). Ctr Educ Policy Mgmt.

Runner Magazine. The Runners: How the Champions Train, Race & Persevered--a Success Formula for All Runners. (Orig.). 1979. pap. 2.75 (ISBN 0-515-05857-2). Jove Pubns.

Runner's World Magazine Editors. The Complete Runner. 1978. pap. 4.95 (ISBN 0-380-01885-3, 37127). Avon.

Running Press, ed. The Scrabble Trade Mark Crossword Games Scorebook. 128p. (Orig.). 1980. lib. bdg. 12.90 (ISBN 0-89471-104-0); pap. 3.95 (ISBN 0-89471-105-9). Running Pr.

Runser, Dennis J. Maintaining & Troubleshooting HPLC Systems: A Users Guide. 208p. 1981. 22.50 (ISBN 0-471-06479-3, Pub. by Wiley Interscience). Wiley.

Runte, Roseann, ed. Studies in Eighteenth-Century Culture, Vol. 8. 1979. 25.00 (ISBN 0-299-07740-3). U of Wis Pr.

--Studies in Eighteenth-Century Culture, Vol. 9. LC 74-25572. 1980. 25.00 (ISBN 0-299-08020-X). U of Wis Pr.

Runyan, Lawrence P. Precalculus Mathematics with Elementary Functions. 1977. text ed. 18.85 o.p. (ISBN 0-205-05573-7); instr's manual avail. o.p. (ISBN 0-205-05574-5). Allyn.

Runyan, Paul & Aultman, Dick. The Short Way to Lower Scoring. LC 79-52549. (Illus.). 175p. 1980. 13.50 (ISBN 0-914178-27-X, 24921-5). Golf Digest.

Runyon. Consumer Behavior. 2nd ed. (Marketing & Management Ser.). 504p. 1980. text ed. 19.95 (ISBN 0-675-08159-9). Merrill.

Runyon, Catherine. Too Soon, Mr. Bear. (ps-5). 1979. pap. 1.95 (ISBN 0-8024-8788-2). Moody.

Runyon, Charles. I, Weapon. pap. 1.50 o.p. (ISBN 0-445-04127-7). Popular Lib.

--Kiss the Girls & Make Them Die. 1977. pap. 1.50 o.s.i. (ISBN 0-515-03963-2). Jove Pubns.

Runyon, Charles, Jr. Gypsy King. 1979. pap. 2.25 o.s.i. (ISBN 0-515-04041-X). Jove Pubns.

Runyon, Kenneth E. Advertising & the Practice of Marketing. (Marketing & Management Ser.). 1979. text ed. 19.95 (ISBN 0-675-08311-7); instructor's manual 3.95 (ISBN 0-686-67275-5); transparencies 3.95 (ISBN 0-686-67276-3). Merrill.

Runyon, Leilah. I Learn to Read About Jesus: Primer. (Basic Bible Readers Ser.). (Illus.). (gr. k-1). 1962. pap. 3.50 (ISBN 0-87239-257-0, 2754). Standard Pub.

Runyon, Mary B. Echoes of Marching Feet. Lawrence, Joseph, ed. LC 79-64729. 1979. 9.95 (ISBN 0-89144-083-6); pap. 4.95 (ISBN 0-686-68514-8). Crescent Pubns.

Runyon, Poke. Night Jump--Cuba. 1978. 1.75 o.s.i. (ISBN 0-515-04819-4). Jove Pubns.

Runyon, R. & Haber, A. Fundamentals of Behavioral Statistics. 4th ed. 1980. 16.95 (ISBN 0-201-06375-1); write for info. (ISBN 0-201-06378-6); students' wkbk. 5.95 (ISBN 0-201-06376-X); test item booklet 2.50 (ISBN 0-201-06377-8); PSI study guide 6.95 (ISBN 0-201-06633-5); PSI instrs manual 2.75 (ISBN 0-201-06632-7). A-W.

Runyon, Richard P. Descriptive & Inferential Statistics: A Contemporary Approach. LC 76-52668. (Statistiics Ser.). 1977. 13.95 (ISBN 0-201-06655-6). A-W.

--Descriptive Statistics: A Contemporary Approach. LC 76-15467. (Statistics Ser.). 1977. pap. text ed. 9.95 (ISBN 0-201-06652-1); test book avail. 2.75 (ISBN 0-201-06635-1). A-W.

--How Numbers Lie: A Consumer's Guide to Numerical Hocus Pocus. (Illus.). 192p. 1981. 7.95 (ISBN 0-86616-000-0). Lewis Pub Co.

--Inferential Statistics: A Contemporary Approach. LC 76-23991. (Illus.). 1977. pap. 7.95 (ISBN 0-201-06653-X). A-W.

--Nonparametric Statistics: A Contemporary Approach. LC 76-55635. 1977. pap. text ed. 9.95 (ISBN 0-201-06547-9); avail test book 2.75 (ISBN 0-201-06548-7). A-W.

--Winning with Statistics: A Painless First Look at Numbers, Ratios, Percentages, Means & Inference. (Statistics Ser.). (Illus.). 1977. pap. text ed. 8.95 (ISBN 0-201-06654-8). A-W.

Runyon, Richard P., jt. auth. see Haber, Audrey.

Runyon, Theodore H., ed. Santification & Liberation: Liberation Theologies in Light of the Wesleyan Tradition. LC 80-20287. 1981. 6.95 (ISBN 0-687-36810-3). Abingdon.

Ruoff, James E. Crowell's Handbook of Elizabethan & Stuart Literature. LC 73-22097. 576p. 1975. 14.95 o.s.i. (ISBN 0-690-22661-6, TYC-T). T Y Crowell.

Ruoff, Norman D., ed. Evan Fry's Illustrations from Radio Sermons. LC 74-84763. 1975. 6.50 o.p. (ISBN 0-8309-0131-0). Herald Hse.

--The Writings of President Frederick M. Smith, Vol. III: The Zionic Enterprise. 1981. pap. price not set (ISBN 0-8309-0300-3). Herald Hse.

Ruoss, Martin. A Policy & Procedure Manual for Church & Synagogue Libraries: A Do-It-Yourself Guide. LC 79-28676. 1980. pap. 3.75 (ISBN 0-915324-17-2). CSLA.

Rupert, Milan & Todd, O. J. Chinese Bronze Mirrors. (Illus.). 1966. 15.00 o.p. (ISBN 0-8188-0077-1). Paragon.

Ruperti, Alexander. Cycles of Becoming: The Planetary Pattern of Growth. LC 77-84029. 1978. pap. 7.95 (ISBN 0-916360-07-5). CRCS Pubns NV.

Ruple, Joelyn. Antonio Buero Vallejo: The First Fifteen Years. 1971. 12.95 (ISBN 0-88303-006-3); pap. 8.95 (ISBN 0-685-73210-X). E Torres & Sons.

Rupp, George. Beyond Existentialism & Zen: Religion in a Pluralistic World. 1979. 10.95x (ISBN 0-19-502462-1). Oxford U Pr.

--Culture-Protestantism: German Liberal Theology at the Turn of the Twentieth Century. LC 77-13763. (American Academy of Religion. Studies in Religion: No. 15). 1977. pap. 7.50 (ISBN 0-89130-197-6, 010015). Scholars Pr Ca.

Rupp, R. F., jt. auth. see Wujek, E. D.

Ruppel, Gregg. Manual of Pulmonary Function Testing. 2nd ed. LC 78-21100. (Illus.). 1979. pap. text ed. 12.50 (ISBN 0-8016-4209-4). Mosby.

Ruppert, Peter, et al, eds. see Florida State University Conference on Literature & Films, Fourth.

Ruprecht, J., jt. auth. see Alter, G.

Ruprecht, Theodore K. Rapid Population Growth & Macro Economic Development: The Philippines Case. (Illus.). 1975. pap. text ed. 5.00 o.p. (ISBN 0-89249-004-7). Intl Development.

Ruprecht, Theodore K. & Jewett, Frank I. The Micro-Economics of Demographic Change: Family Planning & Economic Wellbeing. LC 75-57. (Illus.). 176p. 1975. text ed. 25.00 (ISBN 0-275-05530-2). Praeger.

Rusalem, Herbert. Guiding the Physically Handicapped College Student. LC 62-14646. (Orig.). 1962. pap. 4.25x (ISBN 0-8077-2071-2). Tchrs Coll.

Rusalem, Herbert, jt. ed. see Malikin, David.

Rusbuldt, Richard E. Basic Leader Skills: Handbook for Church Leaders. 64p. 1981. pap. 4.95 (ISBN 0-8170-0920-5). Judson.

--Basic Teacher Skills: Handbook for Church School Teachers. 144p. 1981. pap. 4.95 (ISBN 0-8170-0919-1). Judson.

Rusbuldt, Richard E., et al. Medidas Principales En la Planificacion De la Iglesia Local: Key Steps in Local Church Planning. Rodriguez, Oscar E., tr. from Eng. 134p. (Span.). 1981. pap. 5.95 (ISBN 0-8170-0933-7). Judson.

Rusch, H. P., jt. ed. see Dove, W. F.

Rusch, William G., jt. ed. see Norris, Richard A., Jr.

Rusco, Elmer. Voting Behavior in Nevada. LC 66-63499. (History & Political Science Ser.: No. 9). ix, 78p. 1966. pap. 1.75x (ISBN 0-87417-014-1). U of Nev Pr.

Ruscoe, G. C. Conditions for Success in Educational Planning. 1969. pap. 6.00 (ISBN 92-803-1031-3, U116, UNESCO). Unipub.

Rush, Anne K. Getting Clear. 1973. 10.00 o.p. (ISBN 0-394-48382-0). Random.

Rush, Benjamin. Two Essays on the Mind. 1972. 7.50 (ISBN 0-87630-061-1). Brunner-Mazel.

Rush, Catharine, tr. see Farre, Henry.

Rush, Cathy & Mifflin, Lawrie. Women's Basketball. 1976. pap. 4.95 (ISBN 0-8015-8794-8, Hawthorn). Dutton.

Rush, David, et al. Diet in Pregnancy: A Randomized Controlled Trial of Nutritional Supplements, Vol.xvi,no.3. LC 79-3846. (Birth Defects: Original Article Series: Vol. XVI, No. 3). 188p. 1980. 26.00x (ISBN 0-8451-1037-3). A R Liss.

Rush, David, et al, eds. Diet in Pregnancy: A Randomized Controlled Trail of Nutritional Supplements. LC 79-3846. (Alan R. Liss Ser.: Vol. 16, No. 3). 1980. 26.00 (ISBN 0-8451-1037-3). March of Dimes.

Rush, Florence. The Best Kept Secret: Sexual Abuse of Children. LC 80-19525. 296p. 1980. 11.95 (ISBN 0-13-074781-5). P-H.

Rush, Gary B. & Denisoff, R. Serge, eds. Social & Political Movements. LC 72-146365. 1971. 34.50x (ISBN 0-89197-411-3). Irvington.

Rush, George E. Dictionary of Criminal Justice. (Criminal Justice Ser.). 1977. text ed. 13.95 o.p. (ISBN 0-205-05815-9, 825814-7); pap. text ed. 9.50 (ISBN 0-686-68522-9, 825815-5). Allyn.

Rush, John A. Witchcraft & Sorcery: An Anthropological Perspective of the Occult. (Illus.). 176p. 1974. 14.75 (ISBN 0-398-02981-4); pap. 11.25 (ISBN 0-398-03019-7). C C Thomas.

Rush, Joseph H. New Directions in Parapsychological Research. LC 64-22612. (Parapsychological Monograph No. 4). 1964. pap. 2.00 (ISBN 0-912328-07-X). Parapsych Foun.

Rush, Michael. Parliamentary Government in Britain. 260p. 1981. pap. text ed. 30.00x (ISBN 0-8419-0680-7). Holmes & Meier.

Rush, Michael, jt. auth. see Althoff, Phillip.

Rush, Myron. Political Succession in the U.S.S.R. LC 65-14778. xv, 223p. 1965. 17.50x (ISBN 0-231-02825-3); pap. 5.00x (ISBN 0-231-08585-0). Columbia U Pr.

Rush, N. Orwin. Diversions of a Westerner: With Emphasis Upon Owen Wister's & Frederic Remington's Books & Libraries. LC 78-53134. (Illus.). 224p. 1979. 10.00 (ISBN 0-932068-05-7). South Pass Pr.

Rush, Peter. Papier Mache. 1980. pap. 8.95 (ISBN 0-374-51611-1). FS&G.

Rush, Ralph E., jt. auth. see Matesky, Ralph.

Rush, Theressa G., et al. Black American Writers Past & Present: A Biographical & Bibliographical Dictionary, 2 vols. LC 74-28400. 1975. Set. 35.00 (ISBN 0-8108-0785-8). Scarecrow.

Rushby, N. J. Introduction to Educational Computing. 224p. 1980. 30.00x (Pub. by Croom Helm England). State Mutual Bk.

Rushby, Nicholas J. Computers in the Teaching Process. LC 79-10138. 123p. 1979. 19.95 (ISBN 0-470-26699-6). Halsted Pr.

Rushdie, Salman. Midnight's Children. LC 80-2712. 448p. 1981. 13.95 (ISBN 0-394-51470-X). Knopf.

Rusher, William A. How to Win Arguments. LC 79-6874. 264p. 1981. 10.95 (ISBN 0-385-15255-8). Doubleday.

Rushing, Jane G. The Raincrow. 1978. pap. 1.95 (ISBN 0-380-41749-9, 41749). Avon.

Rushing, Kenneth L. The Intimate Psychology of Stock Market Action. (Illus.). 1980. deluxe ed. 49.75 (ISBN 0-918968-55-0). Inst Econ Finan.

Rushmer, jt. auth. see Sitnick.

Rushmer, R. F. National Priorities for Health: Past, Present, & Projected. LC 79-25313. (Wiley Series in Health Service). 1980. 24.95 (ISBN 0-471-06472-6, Pub. by Wiley Med). Wiley.

Rushmer, Robert F. Humanizing Health Care: Alternative Future for Medicine. LC 75-1399. (Illus.). 211p. 1975. 15.50x (ISBN 0-262-18075-8); pap. 4.95x (ISBN 0-262-68032-7). MIT Pr.

Rushmore, Robert. Life of George Gershwin. (Illus.). (gr. 9 up). 1968. 6.95 (ISBN 0-02-777890-8, CCPr). Macmillan.

--Singing Voice. (Apollo Eds.). 1971. pap. 2.25 o.s.i. (ISBN 0-8152-0307-1, A307, TYC-T). T Y Crowell.

Rusho, W. L. Powell's Canyon Voyage. LC 70-64908. (Wild & Woolly West Ser., No. 11). (Illus., Orig.). 1969. 7.00 (ISBN 0-910584-86-9); pap. 2.00 (ISBN 0-910584-12-5). Filter.

Rushton, J. Philippe. Altruism, Socialization, & Society. (P-H Ser. in Social Learning Theory). (Illus.). 1980. text ed. 17.95 (ISBN 0-13-023408-7). P-H.

Rushton, Julian. W. A. Mozart: Don Giovanni. (Cambridge Opera Handbooks Ser.). (Illus.). Date not set. price not set (ISBN 0-521-22826-3); pap. price not set (ISBN 0-521-29663-3). Cambridge U Pr.

Rushton, William. Pigsticking. (Illus.). 14.95x o.p. (ISBN 0-8464-0719-1). Beekman Pubs.

Rushton, William F. The Cajuns: From Acadia to Louisiana. 1980. pap. 8.95 (ISBN 0-374-51555-7, N 632). FS&G.

Rusinow, Dennison. The Yugoslav Experiment 1948-1974. 1978. 28.50x (ISBN 0-520-03730-8, CAMPUS 215); pap. 7.95x (ISBN 0-520-03730-8). U of Cal Pr.

Rusk, Howard A., ed. Rehabilitation Medicine. 4th ed. LC 76-30550. (Illus.). 1977. 44.50 (ISBN 0-8016-4213-2). Mosby.

Rusk, Katherine. Renovating the Victorian House: A Guide for Aficionados of Old Houses. (Illus.). 250p. (Orig.). 1981. pap. 8.95 (ISBN 0-89286-187-8). One Hurd One Prods.

Rusk, Tom & Read, Randy. I Want to Change, but I Don't Know How. rev. & enl. 2nd ed. 367p. 1980. pap. 7.95 (ISBN 0-915520-19-2). Comm Creat.

--I Want to Change, but I Don't Know How. 1979. pap. 7.95 (ISBN 0-915520-19-2). Ross-Erikson.

Ruskin, Ariane. History in Art. LC 73-5673. (Illus.). 320p. (gr. 7 up). 1974. PLB 14.90 o.p. (ISBN 0-531-01988-8). Watts.

Ruskin, Ariane & Batterberry, Michael. Greek & Roman Art. (Discovering Art). (Illus.). (gr. 7 up). 1969. 9.95 o.p. (ISBN 0-07-054294-5, GB); pap. 4.95 o.p. (ISBN 0-07-054295-3). McGraw.

Ruskin, Arthur. Classics in Arterial Hypertension. (Amer. Lec. Classics in Science & Medicine Ser.). (Illus.). 400p. 1956. pap. 36.00 spiral (ISBN 0-398-01633-X). C C Thomas.

Ruskin, John. The Art of England: Lectures Given in Oxford by John Ruskin During His Second Tenure of the Slade Professorship. Freedberg, Sydney J., ed. LC 77-25769. (Connosseurship, Criticism, & Art History Ser.: Vol. 23). 292p. 1979. lib. bdg. 21.00 (ISBN 0-8240-3281-0). Garland Pub.

--The King of the Golden River. LC 77-22976. (Illus.). (gr. 7-9). 1978. 9.50 (ISBN 0-688-80122-6); PLB 9.12 (ISBN 0-688-84122-8). Greenwillow.

--The King of the Golden River, Repr. Of 1851 Ed. Bd. with A Holiday Romance. Dickens, Charles. (Illus.). Repr. of 1868 ed; Petsetilla's Posy. Hood, Tom. (Illus.). Repr. of 1870 ed. LC 75-32165. (Classics of Children's Literature, 1621-1932: Vol. 29). (Illus.). 1977. PLB 38.00 (ISBN 0-8240-2278-5). Garland Pub.

--Lectures on Architecture & Painting: Delivered at Edinburgh in November 1853. Freedberg, Sydney J., ed. LC 77-25766. (Connoisseurship Criticism & Art History Ser.: Vol. 21). (Illus.). 189p. 1979. lib. bdg. 22.00 (ISBN 0-8240-3279-9). Garland Pub.

--Lectures on Art Delivered Before the University of Oxford in Hilary Term, 1870. Freedberg, Sydney J., ed. LC 77-25767. (Connossieurship Critism & Art History: Vol. 22). 155p. 1979. lib. bdg. 14.00. Garland Pub.

--Letters of John Ruskin to Bernard Quaritch. 125p. 1980. Repr. of 1938 ed. lib. bdg. 25.00 (ISBN 0-8495-4637-0). Arden Lib.

--Literary Criticism. Bloom, Harold, ed. 8.50 (ISBN 0-8446-1691-5). Peter Smith.

--The Nature of Gothic: A Chapter from the Stones of Venice. Morris, William, ed. LC 76-17747. (Aesthetic Movement & the Arts & Crafts Movement Ser.: Vol. 1). 1977. Repr. of 1892 ed. lib. bdg. 44.00 (ISBN 0-8240-2450-8). Garland Pub.

--Sesame & Lillies. 1919. 2.95 o.p. (ISBN 0-04-824008-7). Allen Unwin.

--Seven Lamps of Architecture. 210p. 1961. pap. 5.95 (ISBN 0-374-50188-2, N215). FS&G.

--The Stones of Venice, 3 vols. Freedberg, Sydney J., ed. Incl. Vol. I. The Foundation; Vol. II. The Sea-Stories; Vol. III. The Fall. LC 77-25765. (Connoisseurship, Criticism & Art History Ser.: Vol. 20). 1979. Set. lib. bdg. 100.00 (ISBN 0-8240-3278-0). Garland Pub.

Russ, Charles V. Historical German Phonology & Morphology. (History of the German Language Ser.). (Illus.). 1979. 27.00 (ISBN 0-19-815727-4). Oxford U Pr.

Russ, Flint. The Caterpillar & the Cross. new ed. LC 74-81137. (Illus.). (gr. 1-6). 1979. cancelled (ISBN 0-914850-47-4, MO520). Impact Tenn.

Russ, Frederick A., jt. auth. see Kirkpatrick, Charles A.

Russ, Jennifer. Customs & Festivals in Germany. (Illus.). 1980. text ed. write for info. (ISBN 0-85496-365-0). Humanities.

Russ, Joanna. And Chaos Died. 1979. pap. 1.95 (ISBN 0-425-04135-2). Berkley Pub.

--On Strike Against God. pap. 3.50 (ISBN 0-918314-13-5). Out & Out.

--The Two of Them. LC 77-26137. (YA) 1978. 8.95 o.p. (ISBN 0-399-12149-8, Dist. by Putnam). Berkley Pub.

Russ, Lavinia. Over the Hills & Far Away. LC 68-13371. (gr. 5-9). 1968. 5.50 o.p. (ISBN 0-15-258946-5, HJ). HarBraceJ.

Russ-Eft, Darlene F., et al. Issues in Adult Basic Education & Other Adult Education: An Annotated Bibliography & Guide to Research. LC 80-16926. (Garland Bibliographies in Contemporary Educations, Vol. 1; Garland Reference Library of Social Science). 200p. 1981. 25.00 (ISBN 0-8240-9551-0). Garland Pub.

Russel, Robert A. The Electronic Briefcase: The Office of the Future. 52p. 1978. pap. text ed. 3.00x (ISBN 0-920380-05-0, Pub. by Inst Res Pub Canada). Renouf.

Russel, Valerie. Judging Horses & Ponies. (Pelham Horsemaster Ser.). (Illus.). 1979. 14.00 (ISBN 0-7207-1099-5). Transatlantic.

Russell, A. Clear Thinking for All. 1967. pap. text ed. 2.00 o.p. (ISBN 0-08-012281-7). Pergamon.

Russell, A. J. The Devalino Caper. 1977. pap. 1.75 o.p. (ISBN 0-345-25106-7). Ballantine.

--God at Eventide. 1975. pap. 1.25 (ISBN 0-89129-069-9, PV069). Jove Pubns.

Russell, A. J., ed. God Calling. (Spire Bk). 1972. pap. 2.50 (ISBN 0-8007-8096-5). Revell.

--God Calling. 1972. pap. 1.95 (ISBN 0-515-05618-9). Jove Pubns.

Russell, Amanda. A Woman Once Loved. (Orig.). 1979. pap. 2.50 (ISBN 0-515-04598-5). Jove Pubns.

Russell, Ann. From Clay to Art: A Complete Guide to the Craft of Ceramics. (Illus.). 118p. 1978. 8.95 (ISBN 0-8059-2514-7). Dorrance.

Russell, Bertrand. ABC of Relativity. 3rd ed. 1969. text ed. 7.50x o.p. (ISBN 0-04-521001-2, 2041). Allen Unwin.

--Authority & the Individual. (Unwin Paperbacks). 1949. pap. 3.95 (ISBN 0-04-170030-9). Allen Unwin.

--Bertrand Russell: An Introduction: Edited Selections from His Writings. Carr, E. H., ed. 1975. text ed. 12.50x (ISBN 0-04-192032-5); pap. text ed. 6.50x (ISBN 0-04-192033-3). Allen Unwin.

--Bertrand Russell Speaks His Mind. LC 74-3626. (Illus.). 173p. 1974. Repr. of 1960 ed. lib. bdg. 17.50x (ISBN 0-8371-7445-7, RUBR). Greenwood.

--Education & the Social Order. (Unwin Paperbacks). 1980. pap. 4.50 (ISBN 0-04-370080-2). Allen Unwin.

--Has Man a Future? 1961. 8.95 (ISBN 0-04-327015-8). Allen Unwin.

--Human Society in Ethics & Politics. 1954. text ed. 18.50x (ISBN 0-04-172004-0). Allen Unwin.

--Inquiry into Meaning & Truth. 1940. text ed. 18.00x (ISBN 0-04-121007-7). Humanities.

--Introduction to Mathematical Philosophy. (Muirhead Library of Philoaophy Ser.). Repr. of 1963 ed. text ed. 19.50x (ISBN 0-04-510020-9). Humanities.

--Mysticism & Logic & Other Essays. 2nd ed. 1980. pap. 5.95x. B&N.

--An Outline of Philosophy. 1927. text ed. 17.95x (ISBN 0-04-192017-1). Allen Unwin.

--The Practice & Theory of Bolshevism. (Unwin Books). 1962. text ed. 5.50x (ISBN 0-04-335017-8); pap. 3.95 (ISBN 0-04-335018-6). Allen Unwin.

--Principles of Social Reconstruction. (Unwin Bks.). 1960. pap. 3.95 (ISBN 0-04-320073-7). Allen Unwin.

--The Problem of China. 1922. text ed. 9.95x (ISBN 0-04-951009-6). Allen Unwin.

--Problems of Philosophy. 1959. pap. 3.95 (ISBN 0-19-500212-1, GB). Oxford U Pr.

--Prospects of Industrial Civilisation. 1959. text ed. 16.95x (ISBN 0-04-300013-4). Allen Unwin.

--Sceptical Essays. (Unwin Paperbacks). 1960. text ed. 9.50x o.p. (ISBN 0-04-104001-5); pap. 4.50 (ISBN 0-04-104003-1). Allen Unwin.

Russell, Bertrand, jt. auth. see Whitehead, Alfred N.

Russell, Betrand. Unarmed Victory. 1963. text ed. 12.50x (ISBN 0-04-327024-7). Allen Unwin.

Russell, Bill. Go up for Glory. 1980. pap. 2.25 o.p. (ISBN 0-425-04676-1). Berkley Pub.

Russell, C. A. History of Valency. 1971. text ed. 18.00x (ISBN 0-391-00033-0, Leicester). Humanities.

Russell, C. E. Social Problems of the North: London & Oxford, 1913. LC 79-56944. (The English Working Class Ser.). 1980. lib. bdg. 20.00 (ISBN 0-8240-0123-0). Garland Pub.

Russell, C. R. Reactor Safeguards. 1962. 40.00 (ISBN 0-08-009706-5); pap. 15.00 (ISBN 0-08-013610-9). Pergamon.

Russell, C. V. Post O-Level Studies in Modern Languages. 1971. 17.25 (ISBN 0-08-016194-4). Pergamon.

Russell, Charles. Five on the Black Hand Side: A Play. LC 73-82643. 1973. pap. 6.95 (ISBN 0-89388-092-2). Okpaku Communications.

Russell, Charles M. Trails Plowed Under. 1953. 12.95 (ISBN 0-385-04494-1). Doubleday.

Russell, Clifford S., ed. Safe Drinking Water; Current & Future Problems: Proceedings of a Natonal Conference in Washngton D. C. LC 78-19840. pap. 12.00x (ISBN 0-8018-2181-9). Johns Hopkins.

Russell, Conrad, jt. auth. see Melville, T. H.

Russell, D. H. & Durie, G. M. Polyamines As Biochemical Markers of Normal & Malignant Growth. LC 75-43340. (Progress in Cancer Research & Therapy Ser.: Vol. 8). 1978. 21.50 (ISBN 0-89004-116-4). Raven.

Russell, D. S. Between the Testaments. LC 77-74742. 176p. 1960. pap. 3.95 (ISBN 0-8006-1856-4, 1-1856). Fortress.

Russell, Dale A. A Vanished World: The Dinosaurs of Western Canada. (Illus.). 1977. 15.00 (ISBN 0-660-00011-3, 56545-9, Pub. by Natl Mus Canada). U of Chicago Pr.

Russell, Dan. Jack Russell & His Terriers. 1978. 10.35 (ISBN 0-85131-276-4, Dist. by Sporting Book Center). J A Allen.

Russell, Dan M. Dove Shooter's Handbook. 1974. 9.95 (ISBN 0-87691-135-1). Winchester Pr.

Russell, David, et al. Reading Aids Through the Grades: A Guide to Materials & 501 Activities for Individualizing Reading Instruction. 4th rev. ed. LC 75-15639. 320p. 1981. pap. text ed. 11.50x (ISBN 0-8077-2609-5). Tchrs Coll.

Russell, David H. & Russell, Elizabeth F. Listening Aids Through the Grades: Two Hundred Thirty-Two Listening Activities. rev ed. Hennings, Dorothy G., ed. LC 79-607. 1979. pap. text ed. 5.95x (ISBN 0-8077-2558-7). Tchrs Coll.

Russell, Diane H., ed. Polyamines in Normal & Neoplastic Growth. LC 72-96336. (Illus.). 1973. 34.50 (ISBN 0-911216-44-8). Raven.

Russell, Don. Bowling Now. LC 78-75333. (Illus.). 1980. 9.95 (ISBN 0-498-02311-7). A S Barnes.

Russell, Donald E., et al. Chiroptera & Dermoptera of the French Early Eocene. (U. C. Publ. in Geological Sciences: Vol. 95). 1973. pap. 7.50x (ISBN 0-520-09423-9). U of Cal Pr.

Russell, Donald S. & Collins. Elementary Algebra. 4th ed. 1971. text ed. 13.95x o.p. (ISBN 0-205-03282-6, 563282X); study guide 5.95x o.p. (ISBN 0-205-03283-4, 5632838). Allyn.

Russell, Dorothy, ed. Jokes on You. (Pal Paperbacks Ser., Kit A). (Illus., Orig.). (gr. 7-12). 1974. pap. text ed. 1.25 (ISBN 0-8374-3479-3). Xerox Ed Pubns.

Russell, Douglas A. Period Style for the Theatre. 1980. text ed. 23.95 (ISBN 0-205-06450-7, 4864506). Allyn.

--Stage Costume Design: Theory, Technique & Style. 1973. 22.95 (ISBN 0-13-840322-8). P-H.

Russell, Douglas A., ed. & intro. by. An Anthology of Austrian Drama. LC 76-19836. 400p. 1981. 22.50 (ISBN 0-8386-2003-5). Fairleigh Dickinson. Postponed.

Russell, E. W. Soil Conditions & Plant Growth. 10th ed. LC 74-168964. (Illus.). 867p. 1974. text ed. 33.00x (ISBN 0-582-44048-3). Longman.

Russell, Elbert W., et al. Assessment of Brain Damage: A Neuropsychological Key Approach. LC 73-121914. (Personality Disorders Ser). 1970. 25.95 (ISBN 0-471-74550-2, Pub. by Wiley-Interscience). Wiley.

Russell, Elizabeth F., jt. auth. see Russell, David H.

Russell, Elizabeth S., ed. see Symposium in Honor of the Jackson Laboratory's Fiftieth Anniversary, Bar Harbor, Maine, July 1979.

Russell, Ellen. Last Fix: Dan Russell & the World That Lost Him. LC 70-160409. 256p. 1971. 7.95 o.p. (ISBN 0-15-148480-5). HarBraceJ.

Russell, F. H. The Just War in the Middle Ages. LC 74-25655. (Studies in Medieval Life & Thought). 360p. 1975. 51.00 (ISBN 0-521-20690-1); pap. 13.95 (ISBN 0-521-29276-X). Cambridge U Pr.

Russell, F. S., ed. Advances in Marine Biology. Incl. Vol. 12. 1974. 62.00 (ISBN 0-12-026112-X); Vol. 13. 1976. 62.00 (ISBN 0-12-026113-8); Vol. 14. Cushing, D. H., ed. 1976. 66.50 (ISBN 0-12-026114-6). (Serial Publication). Acad Pr.

Russell, Frances T. One Word More on Browning. 157p. 1980. Repr. of 1927 ed. text ed. 28.00 (ISBN 0-8492-7709-4). R West.

Russell, Francis. Lexington, Concord & Bunker Hill. LC 63-10834. (American Heritage Junior Library). (Illus.). 153p. 1963. 6.95 (ISBN 0-06-024976-5, Dist. by Har-Row). Am Heritage.

--The Okefenokee Swamp. LC 73-78582. (American Wilderness Ser). (Illus.). (gr. 6 up). 1973. lib. bdg. 11.97 (ISBN 0-8094-1181-4, Pub. by Time-Life). Silver.

--The Secret War. (World War II). 208p. 1980. 12.95 (ISBN 0-8094-2546-7). Time-Life.

--World of Durer. (Library of Art). (Illus.). 1967. 15.95 (ISBN 0-8094-0241-6). Time-Life.

--World of Durer. LC 67-29856. (Library of Art Ser.). (Illus.). (gr. 6 up). 1967. 12.96 (ISBN 0-8094-0270-X, Pub. by Time-Life). Silver.

Russell, Frank D. Picasso's Guernica: The Labyrinth of Narrative and Vision. LC 79-52472. 350p. 1980. text ed. 35.00 (ISBN 0-8390-0243-2). Allanheld.

Russell, Franklin. The Okefenokee Swamp. (The American Wilderness Ser.). (Illus.). 1973. 12.95 (ISBN 0-8094-1201-2). Time-Life.

--Sea Has Wings. 1973. 10.00 (ISBN 0-87690-097-X). Dutton.

--Watchers at the Pond. 1981. pap. 8.95 (ISBN 0-87923-390-7). Godine.

Russell, Frederick S. Medusae of the British Isles II. 1970. 75.00 (ISBN 0-521-07293-X). Cambridge U Pr.

Russell, G. K. Marihuana Today: A Compilation of Medical Findings for the Layman. 3rd, rev. ed. LC 77-79477. (Illus.). 80p. 1979. pap. 3.45 (ISBN 0-08-025509-4). Pergamon.

Russell, George D. The Gas Guzzler to Gas Sipper Manual: The Motorist's Complete Step-by-Step Do-It-Yourself Guide for Converting Your V-8 Car Engine to a V-4, Plus More Than 100 Other Ways to Save Gas & Money. LC 79-92199. (Illus.). 110p. 1979. pap. 5.95 spiral bdg. (ISBN 0-935850-00-7). Rosetta Pub Co.

Russell, George E., ed. see Coldham, Peter W.

Russell, George H. & Black, Kenneth. Human Behavior & Life Insurance. 1963. ref. ed. 10.95 (ISBN 0-13-444687-9). P-H.

Russell, George K. Laboratory Investigations in Human Physiology. (Illus.). 1978. pap. text ed. 8.50 (ISBN 0-02-404680-9). Macmillan.

--Vivisection & the True Aims of Education in Biology. 3rd ed. 11p. (gr. 8-12). pap. 0.75 (ISBN 0-913098-30-2). Myrin Institute.

Russell, George W. E. Sydney Smith. LC 79-156929. 1971. Repr. of 1905 ed. 15.00 (ISBN 0-8103-3720-7). Gale.

Russell, H. D. Notes on Methods for the Narcotization, Killing, Fixation, & Preservation of Marine Organisms. 1963. 6.00 (ISBN 0-685-52861-8). Marine Bio.

Russell, Mrs. Hal. Settler Mac & the Charmed Quarter-Section. 159p. 1956. 4.95 (ISBN 0-8040-0271-1, SB). Swallow.

Russell, Harold & Ferullo, Dan. The Best Years of My Life. (Illus.). 224p. 1981. 12.95 (ISBN 0-8397-1026-7). Eriksson.

Russell, Hugh & Black, Kenneth. Understanding & Influencing Human Behavior. (Illus.). 240p. 1981. text ed. 12.95 (ISBN 0-13-936674-1, Spec). P-H.

Russell, J. G. B. & Fisher, A. S. Radiography in Obstetrics. 1975. 7.95 (ISBN 0-407-00009-7). Butterworths.

Russell, James. Marx-Engels Dictionary. LC 80-786. (Illus.). xxv, 140p. 1981. lib. bdg. 19.95 (ISBN 0-313-22035-2, RME/). Greenwood.

--Matilda: Or the Indian Captive. a Canadian Tale Founded on Fact. LC 75-7073. (Indian Captivities Ser.: Vol. 51). 1976. Repr. of 1833 ed. lib. bdg. 44.00 (ISBN 0-8240-1675-0). Garland Pub.

Russell, James A., jt. auth. see Mehrabian, Albert.

Russell, James E. Garages & Carports. Horowitz, Shirley M., ed. (Illus.). 144p. (Orig.). 1981. pap. 6.95 (ISBN 0-932944-32-9). Creative Homeowner.

--Walks, Walls & Fences. Horowitz, Shirley M. & Auer, Marilyn M., eds. (Illus., Orig.). 1981. pap. 6.95 (ISBN 0-932944-36-1). Creative Homeowner.

Russell, Jeffrey B. A History of Witchcraft: Sorcerers, Heretics & Pagans. (Illus.). 1980. 15.95 (ISBN 0-500-01225-3). Thames Hudson.

Russell, John. Francis Bacon. (World of Art Ser.). (Illus.). 1979. 17.95 (ISBN 0-19-520113-2); pap. 9.95 (ISBN 0-19-520114-0). Oxford U Pr.

--The Meanings of Modern Art. LC 80-8217. (Illus.). 384p. 1981. 29.95 (ISBN 0-06-013701-0, HarpT). Har-Row.

--Seurat. (World of Art Ser.). (Illus.). 1965. pap. 9.95 (ISBN 0-19-519954-5). Oxford U Pr.

--World of Matisse. (Library of Art). (Illus.). 1969. 15.95 (ISBN 0-8094-0249-1). Time-Life.

--World of Matisse. LC 69-19503. (Library of Art Ser.). (Illus.). (gr. 6 up). 1969. 12.96 (ISBN 0-8094-0278-5, Pub. by Time-Life). Silver.

--Yachtmaster Offshore. LC 77-89374. 1977. 11.95 (ISBN 0-7153-7465-6). David & Charles.

Russell, John, tr. see Martin Du Gard, Roger.

Russell, John, intro. by. Vuillard: Drawings 1855-1930. LC 78-65873. (Illus.). 1978. pap. 9.60 (ISBN 0-917418-59-X). Am Fed Arts.

Russell, John B. General Chemistry. (McGraw-Hill Series in Chemistry). (Illus.). 832p. 1980. text ed. 19.95 (ISBN 0-07-054310-0); instr's manual 5.95 (ISBN 0-07-054312-7); study guide 6.95 (ISBN 0-07-054313-5); study guide 5.95 (ISBN 0-07-054311-9); solutions manual 5.95 (ISBN 0-07-054314-3). McGraw.

Russell, John M. Giving & Taking: Across the Foundation Desk. LC 77-4865. 1977. pap. text ed. 4.95 (ISBN 0-8077-2526-9). Tchrs Coll.

Russell, John R., jt. auth. see Rosenbloom, Richard S.

Russell, Joyce, ed. Preservation of Library Materials. 1980. pap. write for info. (ISBN 0-87111-270-1). SLA.

Russell, Keith C. The Duck-Huntingest Gentleman. (Illus.). 312p. 1980. 14.95 (ISBN 0-87691-328-1). Winchester Pr.

Russell, Ken, jt. auth. see Tooke, Joan.

Russell, Kenneth L. How in Parliamentary Procedure. 3rd ed. LC 76-6837. (Illus.). (gr. 9-12). 1976. pap. text ed. 1.00x o.p. (ISBN 0-8134-1804-6, 1804). Interstate.

Russell, Kenneth L., ed. How in Parlimentary Procedure. 4th ed. (Illus.). (gr. 9-12). 1981. pap. text ed. 1.95 (ISBN 0-8134-2171-3, 2171). Interstate.

Russell, Leslie T., jt. auth. see Bowes, W. H.

Russell, Lester F. Black Baptist Secondary Schools in Virginia, 1887-1957: A Study in Black History. LC 80-22414. 218p. 1981. 12.50 (ISBN 0-8108-1373-4). Scarecrow.

Russell, Marian. Land of Enchantment: Memoirs of Marian Russell Along the Santa Fe Trail. 176p. 1981. write for info. (ISBN 0-8263-0571-7). U of NM Pr.

Russell, Martin. Death Fuse. 196p. 1981. 9.95 (ISBN 0-312-18698-3). St Martin.

Russell, Mercer P., jt. auth. see Hartman, Margaret.

Russell, N. J., et al. Blood Biochemistry. 128p. 1980. 24.00x (Pub. by Croom Helm England). State Mutual Bk.

Russell, Norman. Introduction to Plant Science: A Humanistic & Ecological Approach. LC 75-1445. (Illus.). 302p. 1975. pap. text ed. 12.95 (ISBN 0-8299-0043-8); instrs.' manual avail. (ISBN 0-8299-0603-7). West Pub.

Russell, Norman, jt. tr. see Ward, Benedicta.

Russell, O. Ruth. Freedom to Die: Moral & Legal Aspects of Euthanasia. rev. ed. LC 77-3383. 1977. 24.95 (ISBN 0-87705-311-1). Human Sci Pr.

Russell, Osborne. Journal of a Trapper. Haines, Aubrey L., ed. LC 56-52. (Illus.). 1965. 13.50x (ISBN 0-8032-0897-9); pap. 3.50 (ISBN 0-8032-5166-1, BB 316, Bison). U of Nebr Pr.

Russell, P., ed. Electron Microscopy & X-Ray Applications, Vol.2. 200p. 1981. text ed. write for info. (ISBN 0-250-40379-X). Ann Arbor Science.

Russell, Pamela R. The Woman Who Loved John Wilkes Booth. 1979. pap. 2.25 (ISBN 0-515-04869-0). Jove Pubns.

Russell, Paul L. History of Western Oil Shale. (Illus.). 176p. 1980. 49.50 (ISBN 0-686-61811-4). Ctr Prof Adv.

Russell, Peter. The Brain Book. 1979. 12.95 (ISBN 0-8015-0886-X, Hawthorn). Dutton.

--The TM Technique: A Skeptic's Guide to the TM Program. 1977. pap. 6.95 (ISBN 0-7100-8672-5). Routledge & Kegan.

Russell, Phillips. Emerson, the Wisest American. LC 80-2544. 1981. Repr. of 1929 ed. 37.00 (ISBN 0-404-19269-6). AMS Pr.

Russell, R. R. & Wilkinson, M. Microeconomics: A Synthesis of Modern & Neoclassical Theory. (Economics Ser.). 1979. text ed. 26.95 (ISBN 0-471-94652-4). Wiley.

Russell, R. T., jt. auth. see Cartwright, Ralph.

Russell, Ray. Incubus. Date not set. pap. price not set (ISBN 0-440-14129-X). Dell.

Russell, Raymond. The Harpsichord & Clavichord. (Illus.). 1980. 30.00 (ISBN 0-684-16466-3, ScribT). Scribner.

Russell, Renny, jt. auth. see Russell, Terry.

Russell, Richard. Paperbag. 1979. pap. 1.75 (ISBN 0-505-51427-3). Tower Bks.

--Point of Reference. 1979. pap. 1.50 (ISBN 0-505-51394-3). Tower Bks.

Russell, Richard J. River Plains & Sea Coasts. 1967. 19.50x (ISBN 0-520-01107-4). U of Cal Pr.

Russell, Robert. Act of Loving. LC 67-19287. 1967. 9.95 (ISBN 0-8149-0195-6). Vanguard.

--The Island. LC 72-83352. 368p. 1972. 9.95 (ISBN 0-8149-0721-0). Vanguard.

Russell, Robert, jt. auth. see Pease, Jack G.

Russell, Robert A., jt. auth. see Cook, Thomas M.

Russell, Robert B. Attractive & Easy-to-Build Wood Projects. (Illus.). 64p. (Orig.). 1980. pap. 3.00 (ISBN 0-486-23965-9). Dover.

Russell, Robert W. To Catch an Angel: Adventures in the World I Cannot See. LC 62-11209. (gr. 7 up). 1962. 9.95 (ISBN 0-8149-0194-8). Vanguard.

Russell, Ronald. Guide to British Topographical Prints. LC 79-53737. (Illus.). 1979. 32.00 (ISBN 0-7153-7810-4). David & Charles.

--Rivers. 1978. 14.95 (ISBN 0-7153-7473-7). David & Charles.

--Waterside Pubs: Pubs of the (British) Inland Waterways. LC 74-81057. 1975. 10.50 (ISBN 0-7153-6743-9). David & Charles.

Russell, Ronald, jt. auth. see Boyes, John.

Russell, Ross. Jazz Style in Kansas City & the Southwest. 1971. 18.95x (ISBN 0-520-01853-2); pap. 3.45 o.p. (ISBN 0-520-02363-3, CAL258). U of Cal Pr.

Russell, S. P. Animales Que Ayudan. Orig. Title: Four Legged Helpers. 1979. 0.85 (ISBN 0-311-38510-9). Casa Bautista.

Russell, Scott. Karate: The Energy Connection. 1976. 7.95 o.s.i. (ISBN 0-440-04386-7). Delacorte.

Russell, Solveig. From Footpaths to Freeways: The Story of Roads. LC 78-135528. (Finding-Out Bks.). (Illus.). (gr. 1-4). 1971. PLB 6.95 (ISBN 0-8193-0442-5). Enslow Pubs.

Russell, Solveig P. Bible ABC Book. LC 67-27153. (Illus.). 1981. laminated bdg. 5.50 (ISBN 0-570-03418-3, 56-1065). Concordia.

--One, Two, Three, & More. LC 66-18230. (ps). 1966. bds. 5.50 laminated (ISBN 0-570-03410-8, 56-1062). Concordia.

--What's the Time, Starling? A First Look at Nature's Clocks. (Illus.). (gr. 2-5). 1977. 6.95 o.p. (ISBN 0-679-20420-2). McKay.

Russell, Stanley. Plants & Flowers for Your Garden. (Illus.). 1978. 12.95 o.p. (ISBN 0-688-03332-6). Morrow.

Russell, Terry & Russell, Renny. On the Loose. (Sierra Club Ser). (Illus.). 1975. pap. 4.95 o.p. (ISBN 0-345-24307-2). Ballantine.

Russell, Thomas. The Economics of Bank Credit Cards. LC 73-9383. (Special Studies). 150p. 1975. text ed. 25.00 (ISBN 0-275-09390-5). Praeger.

Russell, W. C., jt. ed. see Burke, D. C.

Russell, W. M., jt. ed. see Porter, J. R.

Russell, W. Ritchie & Dewar, A. J. Explaining the Brain. (Illus.). 180p. 1975. 11.50x (ISBN 0-19-217650-1); pap. text ed. 5.95x (ISBN 0-19-289079-4). Oxford U Pr.

Russell, Wallace A., ed. Milestones in Motivation: Contributions to the Psychology of Drive & Purpose. 1970. 20.95 (ISBN 0-13-581686-6). P-H.

Russell, Wilfred T. The Role of Violence in History & the Metaphysics of War. (Illus.). 1979. deluxe ed. 47.50 (ISBN 0-930008-42-1). Inst Econ Pol.

Russell, Sir William O. A Treatise on Crimes & Misdemeanors, 6 vols. Berkowitz, David S. & Thorne, Samuel E., eds. LC 77-86641. (Classics of English Legal History in the Modern Era Ser.: Vol. 94). 1979. Set. lib. bdg. 55.00 ea. (ISBN 0-8240-3081-8). Garland Pub.

Russell, Wrio, jt. auth. see Fukushima, Sho.

Russell-Wood, A. J. Fidalgos & Philanthropists: The Santa Casa de Misericordia of Bahia, 1550-1755. 1968. 27.50x (ISBN 0-520-01108-2). U of Cal Pr.

Russett, Bruce M. Progress in Arms Control? Readings from Scientific American. LC 78-31864. (Illus.). 1979. text ed. 18.95x (ISBN 0-7167-1060-9); pap. text ed. 9.95x (ISBN 0-7167-1061-7). W H Freeman.

Russo, Anthony. Filling Gaps: An Interpersonal Skills Approach. 1978. pap. 6.95 (ISBN 0-89529-044-8). Avery Pub.

Russo, Barbara A. Gastroenterology Nursing Continuing Education Review. 1976. spiral bdg. 8.00 o.p. (ISBN 0-87488-373-3). Med Exam.

--Neurology & Neurosurgical Nursing: Continuing Education Review. 1974. spiral bdg. 8.00 o.p. (ISBN 0-87488-357-1). Med Exam.

Russo, David J. Families & Communities: A New View of American History. LC 74-11389. 1974. 7.00x (ISBN 0-910050-29-5). AASLH.

Russo, Eva M. & Shyne, Ann W. Coping with Disruptive Behavior in Group Care. LC 79-23739. (Orig.). 1980. 5.50 (ISBN 0-87868-137-X). Child Welfare.

Russo, Eva M., jt. auth. see Shyne, Ann W.

Russo, J. Robert. Serving & Surviving As a Human Service Worker. LC 80-18016. 170p. (Orig.). 1980. pap. text ed. 7.95 (ISBN 0-8185-0383-1). Brooks-Cole.

Russo, J. Robert, ed. Amphetamine Abuse. (Illus.). 176p. 1972. photocopy ed. spiral 17.50 (ISBN 0-398-01635-6). C C Thomas.

Russo, John. Limb to Limb. (Orig.). 1981. pap. price not set (ISBN 0-671-41690-1). PB.

--Midnight. 1980. pap. 2.25. PB.

Russo, Joseph S. Salvation Is a Necessary Evil. Bd. with The Science of Human Existence. LC 74-11822. 1981. pap. 5.95 (ISBN 0-932742-01-7). World Action.

Russo, Monica & Dewire, Robert. The Complete Book of Bird Houses & Feeders. LC 75-36155. (Illus.). 1976. pap. 5.95 (ISBN 0-8069-8224-1). Sterling.

Russo, Nancy F. Motherhood Mandate: Special Issue of Psychology of Women Quarterly. LC 79-88275. 148p. 1979. pap. text ed. 7.95x (ISBN 0-87705-463-0). Human Sci Pr.

Russo, Philip A., Jr., jt. ed. see Paul, Ellen F.

Russo, Raymond, et al, eds. Practical Points in Pediatrics. 3rd ed. LC 80-20380. 1980. write for info. (ISBN 0-87488-727-5). Med Exam.

Russo, Robert, ed. see Sullivan, David J.

Russo, Vito. The Celluloid Closet: Homosexuality in the Movies. LC 79-1682. (Illus.). 256p. 1981. 15.00 (ISBN 0-06-013704-5, HarpT). Har-Row.

--The Celluloid Closet: Homosexuality in the Movies. LC 79-1682. (Illus.). 256p. 1981. pap. 7.95 (ISBN 0-06-090871-8, CN). Har-Row.

Russo, William. Secrets of the Research Paper: An Easy Guide to Success. 1980. pap. 1.95 (ISBN 0-931660-03-3). R Oman Pubns.

Russo-Alesi, Anthony I. Martyrology Pronouncing Dictionary. LC 79-167151. 1973. Repr. of 1939 ed. 15.00 (ISBN 0-8103-3272-8). Gale.

Russon, Robb. Letters to a New Elder: The Melchizedek Priesthood, Its Duty Fulfillment. pap. 2.95 (ISBN 0-89036-144-4). Hawkes Pub Inc.

Russsell, James A., jt. auth. see Mehrabian, Albert.

Rust, Art, Jr. Get That Nigger off the Field. 1976. 7.95 o.p. (ISBN 0-440-02791-8). Delacorte.

Rust, Brian. Brian Rust's Guide to Discography. LC 79-6827. (Discographies: No. 4). (Illus.). x, 133p. 1980. lib. bdg. 19.95 (ISBN 0-313-22086-7, RGD/). Greenwood.

Rust, Claude. The Burning of the General Slocum. (Illus.). 160p. (YA) 1981. 8.95 (ISBN 0-525-66715-6). Elsevier-Nelson.

Rust, Doris. Donkey Tales. (Illus.). (ps-5). 1972. 6.50 (ISBN 0-571-09867-3, Pub. by Faber & Faber). Merrimack Bk Serv.

--Secret Friends. (Illus.). (ps-5). 1962. 3.95 o.p. (ISBN 0-571-05182-0, Pub. by Faber & Faber). Merrimack Bk Serv.

--Simple Tales for the Very Young. (Illus.). (ps-5). 1960. 4.95 o.p. (ISBN 0-571-03842-5, Pub. by Faber & Faber). Merrimack Bk Serv.

--Tales from the Australian Bush. (Illus.). (ps-5). 1968. 5.95 (ISBN 0-571-08358-7, Pub. by Faber & Faber). Merrimack Bk Serv.

Rust, Kenn, ed. see Matt, Paul, et al.

Rust, Kenn C. The Tenth Air Force Story. (World War II Forces History). (Illus.). 64p. 1980. pap. 7.50 (ISBN 0-911852-87-5). Hist Aviation.

--Tenth Air Force Story. (Illus.). 1980. pap. 7.50 (Pub. by Hist. Avn. Album). Aviation.

Rust, Kenn C. & Matt, Paul. Aero Album, 8 vols. Incl. Vol. 5. 1968. pap. o.p. (ISBN 0-8168-0104-5); Vol. 6. 1968. (ISBN 0-8168-0105-3); Vol. 7. 1968. (ISBN 0-8168-0106-1); Vol. 8. 1968. pap. (ISBN 0-8168-0107-X). 1.50 ea. Aero.

Rust, Kenn C. & Muth, Stephen. Fourteenth Air Force Story. (Illus.). 1977. 7.50 (ISBN 0-685-83159-0, Pub. by Hist Aviation). Aviation.

Rust, Zad. Teddy Bare: The Last of the Kennedy Clan. LC 79-25329. 1971. 7.00 o.p. (ISBN 0-88279-221-0); pap. 4.95 (ISBN 0-88279-109-5). Western Islands.

Rustamji, R. F. Introduction to the Law of Industrial Disputes. 1968. pap. 7.25x (ISBN 0-210-98198-9). Asia.

--Law of Industrial Disputes in India. 1965. 25.00x (ISBN 0-210-27087-X). Asia.

Rustin, Bayard. Strategies for Freedom: The Changing Pattern of Black Protest. 100p. 1976. 10.00x (ISBN 0-231-03943-3). Columbia U Pr.

Rustow, Alexander. Freedom & Domination: A Historical Critique of Civilization. Attanasio, Salvator, tr. from Ger. LC 80-10575. 700p. 1980. 35.00x (ISBN 0-691-05304-9). Princeton U Pr.

Rustow, Dankwart A. A World of Nations: Problems of Political Modernization. 1967. pap. 5.95 (ISBN 0-8157-7641-1). Brookings.

Rustow, Dankwart A. & Mugno, John F. OPEC: Success & Prospects. LC 75-29526. 179p. 1976. uKE 12.50x (ISBN 0-8147-7369-9); pap. 5.00x uke (ISBN 0-8147-7379-6). NYU Pr.

Rustow, Dankwart A., ed. Philosophers & Kings: Studies in Leadership. LC 77-7778. (Daedalus Library Ser). 1970. 7.50 o.s.i. (ISBN 0-8076-0540-9); pap. 3.75 (ISBN 0-8076-0539-5). Braziller.

Rustow, Dankwart A., jt. ed. see Czempiel, Ernst-Otto.

Ruswa, Mirza. The Courtesan of Lucknow. Singh, Khushwant & Husaini, M. A., trs. 240p. 1970. pap. 4.00 (ISBN 0-88253-076-3). Ind-US Inc.

Rusz, Joe. Porsche Sport 72. LC 72-97717. 1973. 4.95 (ISBN 0-87880-015-8). Norton.

--Porsche Sport 73. LC 73-89096. 1974. 5.95 (ISBN 0-87880-023-9). Norton.

Ruszkiewicz, John J. Well-Bound Words: A Rhetoric. 1981. text ed. 11.95x (ISBN 0-673-15355-X). Scott F.

Rutan, Al, jt. auth. see Dennis, Brad.

Rutberg, Sidney. The Joy of Expense Account Living (& the Pleasures of Executive Perks) LC 79-50990. 1979. 9.95 o.p. (ISBN 0-8092-7400-0). Contemp Bks.

Rutenber, Ralph D. How to Bring Up Two Thousand Teenagers. LC 78-24060. 1979. 11.95 (ISBN 0-88229-550-0). Nelson-Hall.

Rutgers, A. Budgerigars in Color - Their Care & Breeding. rev. ed. (Color Ser.). (Illus.). 1976. 9.95 (ISBN 0-7137-0813-1, Pub by Blandford Pr England). Sterling.

--The Handbook of Foreign Birds, Volumes 1 & 2. Incl. Vol. 1. The Small Seed-& Insect-Eating Birds. rev. ed. 1977. Repr. of 1964 ed (ISBN 0-7137-0815-8); Vol. 2. Larger Birds, Including Parrots & Parakeets. rev. ed. 1969. Repr. of 1965 ed (ISBN 0-7137-0769-0). (Color Ser.). (Illus.). 9.95 ea. (Pub. by Blandford Pr England). Sterling.

Rutgers, A. & Norris, K. A., eds. The Encyclopedia of Aviculture, 3 vols. Incl. Vol. 1. 1970 (ISBN 0-7137-0800-X); Vol. 2. 1973 (ISBN 0-7137-0801-8); Vol. 3. 1977 (ISBN 0-7137-0802-6). (Illus.). 37.50 ea. (Pub. by Blandford Pr England). Sterling.

Rutgers Symposium on Drug Abuse. Drugs & Youth: Proceedings. Wittenborn, J. R., et al, eds. (Illus.). 500p. 1969. text ed. 29.00 o.p. (ISBN 0-398-02097-3). C C Thomas.

Rutgers Symposium on Drug Abuse, 2nd. Communication & Drug Abuse: Proceedings. Wittenborn, J. R., et al, eds. (Illus.). 556p. 1970. 29.50 o.p. (ISBN 0-398-02099-X). C C Thomas.

Ruth, Beryl. Home Economics. 1974. pap. text ed. 4.95x o.p. (ISBN 0-435-42262-6). Heinemann Ed.

--Home Economics Assignments. 1969. pap. text ed. 2.50 o.p. (ISBN 0-435-42701-6). Heinemann Ed.

--Learning Home Economics, 4 bks. Incl. Bk 1. About the Kitchen. 1972. pap. text ed. 2.95x o.p. (ISBN 0-435-42252-9); Bk 2. About the Home. 1973. pap. text ed. 2.95x o.p. (ISBN 0-435-42261-8); Bk 3. You & Your Family. 1971. pap. text ed. 2.95x o.p. (ISBN 0-435-42260-X); Bk 4. You & the Community. 1977. pap. text ed. 2.95x o.p. (ISBN 0-435-42249-9). Heinemann Ed.

--One Hundred One Basic Recipes. 1973. pap. text ed. 4.95x o.p. (ISBN 0-435-42703-2). Heinemann Ed.

Ruth, Eddie. How Do the Ducks Know. 1980. pap. 3.00. Am Atheist.

Ruth, H., et al. Challenge of Crime in a Free Society. LC 79-152126. (Symposia on Law & Society Ser). 1971. Repr. of 1968 ed. lib. bdg. 19.50 (ISBN 0-306-70124-3). Da Capo.

Ruth, Henry. Research Priorities for Crime Reduction Efforts. (An Institute Paper). 140p. 1977. pap. 3.50 (ISBN 0-87766-183-9, 17200). Urban Inst.

Ruth, Linda. Real Life Mysteries. (gr. 2-3). 1977. pap. text ed. 2.95x (ISBN 0-933892-10-1). Child Focus Co.

Ruth, Rod, illus. Humpty Dumpty & Other Nursery Rhymes. (Tell-a-Tale Reader). 32p. (ps-3). 1980. PLB 4.77 (ISBN 0-307-68415-6, Golden Pr). Western Pub.

Ruth, W., jt. auth. see Stidger, Howe C.

Ruthberg, Helen. The Book of Miniatures: Furniture & Accessories. LC 76-451. (Creative Crafts Ser.). 1976. 13.95 (ISBN 0-8019-6366-4); pap. 7.95 (ISBN 0-8019-6365-6). Chilton.

Ruthenberg, Hans. Farming Systems in the Tropics. 3rd ed. 400p. 1980. 89.00 (ISBN 0-19-859481-X). Oxford U Pr.

Rutherford, Andrew & Cohen, Fred. Standards Relating to Corrections Administration. (Juvenile Justice Standards Project Ser.). 1980. softcover 7.95 (ISBN 0-88410-821-X); casebound 16.50 (ISBN 0-88410-750-7). Ballinger Pub.

--Standards Relating to Corrections Administration. LC 77-3375. (Juvenile Justice Standards Project Ser.). 1977. casebound 16.50 o.p.; softcover 7.95 o.p. (ISBN 0-88410-778-7). Ballinger Pub.

Rutherford, Andrew, ed. Kipling Short Stories, 2 vols. 1977. Vol. 1. pap. 2.95 (ISBN 0-14-003281-9); Vol. 2. pap. 3.95 (ISBN 0-14-003282-7). Penguin.

Rutherford, Anna & Hannah, Donald, eds. Commonwealth Short Stories. 245p. 1980. text ed. 19.50x (ISBN 0-8419-5075-X); pap. text ed. 9.50x (ISBN 0-686-62972-8). Holmes & Meier.

Rutherford, Bonnie & Rutherford, Bill, illus. The Gingerbread Man. 32p. (ps-3). 1972. 1.95 (ISBN 0-307-10460-5, Golden Pr); PLB 7.62 (ISBN 0-307-60460-8). Western Pub.

--Mother Goose. (ps-1). 1973. PLB 5.38 (ISBN 0-307-68970-0, Golden Pr). Western Pub.

Rutherford, D. L. Tanker Cargo Handling. 128p. 1979. 69.50x (ISBN 0-85264-256-3, Pub. by Griffin England). State Mutual Bk.

Rutherford, Don, jt. auth. see Creek, F. N.

Rutherford, Douglas. Turbo. 224p. 1980. 9.95 (ISBN 0-312-82332-0). St Martin.

Rutherford, Jean, jt. auth. see Rutherford, Robert.

Rutherford, John. Mexican Society During Revolution. 352p. 1971. 29.95x (ISBN 0-19-827183-2). Oxford U Pr.

Rutherford, Livingstone. John Peter Zenger. LC 80-29427. (American Men & Women of Letters Ser.). (Illus.). 275p. 1981. pap. 4.95 (ISBN 0-87754-150-7). Chelsea Hse.

Rutherford, Margaret, ed. see Sirrocco, Al & Koch, Hugo.

Rutherford, Mark. Autobiography & Deliverance. 2nd ed. (Victorian Library). 1970. Repr. of 1888 ed. text ed. 10.00x (ISBN 0-7185-5000-5, Leicester). Humanities.

Rutherford, Meg & Warren-Davis, Ann. A Pattern of Herbs. (Illus.). 150p. 1975. 9.50 (ISBN 0-04-635009-8). Allen Unwin.

Rutherford, Peggy, ed. African Voices: An Anthology of Native African Writings. LC 60-9719. 1959. 8.95 (ISBN 0-8149-0196-4). Vanguard.

Rutherford, Phoebe. Laboratory Manual for Mammalian Anatomy. 1973. text ed. 7.95 spiral bdg. (ISBN 0-8087-1883-5). Burgess.

Rutherford, Robert & Rutherford, Jean. Doctor Discusses Family Problems. (Illus.). 1969. pap. 2.50 (ISBN 0-910304-17-3). Budlong.

Rutherford, Robert B. & Edgar, Eugene. Teachers & Parents: A Guide to Interaction & Cooperation. new ed. 1979. text ed. 18.95 (ISBN 0-205-06578-3). Allyn.

Rutherford, Robert B., Jr. & Edgar, Eugene. Teachers & Parents: A Guide to Interaction & Cooperation. abr. ed. 1979. pap. text ed. 9.95 (ISBN 0-205-06671-2, 2466716). Allyn.

Rutherford, Robert D. Just in Time: The Inner Game of Time Management. 186p. 1981. 13.95 (ISBN 0-471-08434-4, Pub. by Wiley-Interscience). Wiley.

Rutherford, Samuel. Letters of Samuel Rutherford. 1973. pap. 2.45 (ISBN 0-85151-163-5). Banner of Truth.

Rutherford, Ward. Jersey. LC 75-31326. (Island Ser). (Illus.). 1976. 13.50 (ISBN 0-7153-7075-8). David & Charles.

--Russian Army in World War One. 1975. 15.95 o.p. (ISBN 0-86033-002-8). Gordon-Cremonesi.

Ruthven, John. The Earl of Gowries Conspiracie Against the Kings Maiestie of Scotland. LC 76-26080. (English Experience Ser.: No. 182). 1969. Repr. of 1600 ed. 7.00 (ISBN 90-221-0182-7). Walter J Johnson.

Ruthven, John A. & Zimmerman, William. Top Flight: Speed Index to Waterfowl of North America. 1976. pap. 5.95 o.p. (ISBN 0-684-14752-1, SL675, ScribT). Scribner.

Ruthven, K. K. Critical Assumptions. LC 78-57760. 1979. 28.50 (ISBN 0-521-22257-5). Cambridge U Pr.

--A Guide to Ezra Pound's "Personae" 1926. 1969. 17.95x (ISBN 0-520-01526-6). U of Cal Pr.

Rutkowski, ed. Advances in Smoking of Foods. 1977. text ed. 27.00 (ISBN 0-08-022002-9). Pergamon.

Rutkowski, G., jt. auth. see Olesky, J.

Rutkowski, George B. Solid State Electronics. 2nd ed. 1980. 19.95 (ISBN 0-672-97315-4); instructors guide 6.67 (ISBN 0-672-97317-0); lab manual 6.95 (ISBN 0-672-97316-2). Bobbs.

--Solid-State Electronics. LC 77-131132. 1972. 17.90 o.p. (ISBN 0-672-20801-6). Bobbs.

Rutkowski, George B. & Olesky, Jerome E. Microprocessor & Digital Computer Technology. (Illus.). 416p. 1981. text ed. 22.95 (ISBN 0-13-581116-3). P-H.

Rutkowski, Katherine, ed. Videotex Services. (NCTA Executive Seminar Ser.: No. 1). (Orig.). 1980. pap. 40.00 (ISBN 0-686-28867-X). Natl Cable.

Rutland. See Inside a Submarine. (gr. 5 up). 1980. PLB 6.90 (ISBN 0-531-09172-4, G16). Watts.

Rutland, Jonathan. Exploring the Planets. (Explorer Bks). (Illus.). (gr. 3-5). 1978. 2.95 o.p. (ISBN 0-531-09092-2); PLB 4.90 s&l o.p. (ISBN 0-531-09103-1). Watts.

--Exploring the Violent Earth. (gr. 3-5). 1980. 2.95 (ISBN 0-531-09177-5); PLB 6.45 (ISBN 0-531-09167-8). Watts.

--Exploring the World of Robots. (Explorer Books). (Illus.). (gr. 3-5). 1979. 2.95 (ISBN 0-531-09130-9); PLB 6.45 s&l (ISBN 0-531-09115-5). Watts.

--Exploring the World of Speed. (Explorer Books). (Illus.). (gr. 3-5). 1979. 2.95 (ISBN 0-531-09129-5); PLB 6.45 s&l (ISBN 0-531-09114-7). Watts.

--Exploring UFOs. (gr. 3-5). 1980. 2.95 (ISBN 0-531-09176-7); PLB 6.45 (ISBN 0-531-09166-X). Watts.

--Human Body. LC 77-917. (Illus.). (gr. 5-12). 1977. PLB 4.90 s&l o.p. (ISBN 0-531-09057-4). Watts.

--Photography & Film. LC 78-64659. (Fact Finders Ser.). (Illus.). 1979. lib. bdg. 3.96 (ISBN 0-686-51129-8). Silver.

--Plant Kingdom. LC 76-13651. (Modern Knowledge Library). (Illus.). 48p. (gr. 5 up). 1976. 3.95 o.p. (ISBN 0-531-02445-8); PLB 5.90 o.p. (ISBN 0-531-01194-1). Watts.

--See Inside a Galleon. (See Inside Bks.). (Illus.). (gr. 4-6). 1978. PLB 5.90 s&l o.p. (ISBN 0-531-09062-0). Watts.

--See Inside a Roman Town. (See Inside Bks.). (Illus.). (gr. 4-6). 1978. PLB 5.90 s&l o.p. (ISBN 0-531-09063-9). Watts.

--Ships. LC 76-15007. (Modern Knowledge Library). (Illus.). 48p. (gr. 5 up). 1976. 3.95 (ISBN 0-531-02447-4); PLB 6.90 (ISBN 0-685-67488-6). Watts.

Rutland, Joseph. See Inside an Airport. (See Inside Bks.). (Illus.). (gr. 5 up). 1978. PLB 6.90 s&l (ISBN 0-531-09065-5). Watts.

Rutland, Robert A. & Hobson, Charles F., eds. The Papers of James Madison, Vol. 13: Twenty January Seventeen Ninety to Thirty-One March Seventeen Ninety-One. LC 62-9144. (Papers of James Madison). 1981. 20.00x (ISBN 0-8139-0861-2). U Pr of Va.

Rutledge, Albert J. A Visual Approach to Park Design. 1981. lib. bdg. 21.50 (ISBN 0-8240-7258-8). Garland Pub.

Rutledge, Ann L. World Without Sex. 1981. 6.50 (ISBN 0-8062-1668-9). Carlton.

Rutledge, Don & Furlow, Elaine S. The Human Touch. LC 75-2365. (Human Touch Ser.). (Illus.). 1975. 5.95 (ISBN 0-937170-13-5). Home Mission.

Rutledge, Felix, et al. Gynecologic Oncology. LC 75-30951. 272p. 1976. 32.50 (ISBN 0-471-74720-3, Pub. by Wiley Medical). Wiley.

Rutledge, Harley D. Project Identification: The First Scientific Field Study of UFO Phenomena. (Illus.). 1981. 12.95 (ISBN 0-13-730713-6); pap. 7.95 (ISBN 0-13-730705-5). P-H.

Rutledge, I., jt. ed. see Duncan, K.

Rutledge, Kenneth R. The Thoughts of Robert Jacques Turgot As They Apply to the Economic Complexities of Our Present Age. (The Living Thoughts of the Great Economists Ser.). (Illus.). 93p. 1981. 17.55 (ISBN 0-918968-86-0). Inst Econ Finan.

Rutledge, Wiley. Declaration of Legal Faith. LC 74-114563. (American Constitutional & Legal History Ser). 1970. Repr. of 1947 ed. lib. bdg. 14.95 (ISBN 0-306-71921-5). Da Capo.

Rutman, Darrett B. Morning of America. LC 77-131289. (Illus., Orig.). 1971. pap. text ed. 7.25 (ISBN 0-395-04333-6). HM.

Rutman, Leonard. Planning Useful Evaluations: Evaluability Assessment. LC 79-24116. (Sage Library of Social Research: Vol. 96). (Illus.). 1980. 18.00x (ISBN 0-8039-1252-8); pap. 8.95x (ISBN 0-8039-1253-6). Sage.

Rutman, Leonard, jt. auth. see Jones, Andrew.

Rutman, Leonard, ed. Evaluation Research Methods: A Basic Guide. LC 77-17264. (Sage Focus Editions: Vol. 3). 1977. 18.95x (ISBN 0-8039-0907-1); pap. 9.95x (ISBN 0-8039-0908-X). Sage.

Rutman, Roanne, ed. The Aspen Manual of Transfusion Therapy. 250p. 1981. text ed. write for info. (ISBN 0-89443-281-8). Aspen Systems.

Rutsala, Vern. The Journey Begins. LC 76-12681. (Contemporary Poetry Ser.). 64p. 1977. 7.50 (ISBN 0-8203-0406-9). U of Ga Pr.

--Paragraphs. LC 77-20145. (Wesleyan Poetry Program: Vol. 91). 1978. 10.00x (ISBN 0-686-67967-9, Pub. by Wesleyan U Pr); pap. 4.95 (ISBN 0-685-86688-2). Columbia U Pr.

--Walk Home from the Ice-House. LC 80-70566. (Poetry Ser.). 1980. 9.95 (ISBN 0-915604-47-7); pap. 4.95 (ISBN 0-915604-48-5). Carnegie-Mellon.

--The Window. LC 64-22374. (Wesleyan Poetry Program: Vol. 24). (Orig.). 1964. 10.00x (ISBN 0-686-66568-6, Pub. by Wesleyan U Pr); pap. 4.95x (ISBN 0-8195-1024-6). Columbia U Pr.

Rutstein, David. A Blueprint for Medical Care. 245p. 1974. 12.00x (ISBN 0-262-18065-0); pap. 5.95 (ISBN 0-262-68033-5). MIT Pr.

Rutstein, J. B. Ancillary Ocular Studies. 1975. 12.95 (ISBN 0-407-00002-X). Butterworths.

Rutstrum, Calvin. Backcountry. LC 80-22052. (Illus.). 200p. 1981. pap. 10.00 (ISBN 0-934802-07-6). Ind Camp Supply.

--Chips from a Wilderness Log. LC 77-20847. 256p. 1981. pap. 6.95 (ISBN 0-8128-6124-8). Stein & Day.

--A Columnist Looks at Life. 133p. (Orig.). 1981. pap. 5.95 (ISBN 0-931714-10-9). Nodin Pr.

--Hiking Back to Health. LC 80-19803. (Illus.). 136p. (Orig.). 1980. pap. 5.95 (ISBN 0-934802-06-8). Ind Camp Supply.

--Once Upon a Wilderness. LC 72-91260. (Illus.). 208p. 1973. 9.95 (ISBN 0-02-606330-1). Macmillan.

--Wilderness Life. 256p. 1975. 10.95 (ISBN 0-02-606390-5). Macmillan.

Rutt. Surgery of the Leg & Foot. (Hackenbroch Ser.). 1980. text ed. write for info. (ISBN 0-7216-4446-5). Saunders.

Rutt, Richard. The Bamboo Grove: An Introduction to Sijo. LC 70-84785. (Center for Japanese & Korean Studies, UC Berkeley). 1971. 14.50x (ISBN 0-520-01611-4). U of Cal Pr.

Ruttan, Vernon W., et al, eds. Agricultural Policy in an Affluent Society. (Problems of the Modern Economy Ser.). 1969. 7.50x (ISBN 0-393-05274-5, NortonC); pap. text ed. 5.95x (ISBN 0-393-09839-7). Norton.

Ruttenber, E. M. & Clark, L. H. History of Orange County, New York: 1683-1881, 2 vols. 1112p. 1980. Repr. of 1881 ed. 45.00 (ISBN 0-932334-33-4). Heart of the Lakes.

Ruttencutter, Helen D. Pianist's Progress. LC 78-22464. 1979. 9.95 (ISBN 0-690-01761-8, TYC-T). T Y Crowell.

Rutter, Laurence. The Essential Community: Local Government in the Year 2000. Moore, Barbara, ed. LC 80-16901. (Municipal Management Ser.). (Illus.). 170p. (Orig.). 1980. pap. 15.00 (ISBN 0-87326-994-2). Intl City Mgt.

Rutter, M., et al, eds. Education, Health & Behavior. 390p. 1981. Repr. of 1970 ed. text ed. price not set (ISBN 0-89874-268-4). Krieger.

Rutter, Michael. Maternal Deprivation Reassessed. rev. ed. 1981. pap. 3.95 (ISBN 0-14-080561-3). Penguin.

Rutter, Michael & Martin, J. A. The Child with Delayed Speech. (Clinics in Developmental Medicine Ser.: Vol. 43). 1972. 29.00 (ISBN 0-685-34615-3). Lippincott.

Rutter, Michael & Schopler, Eric, eds. Autism: A Reappraisal of Concepts & Treatment. LC 77-26910. (Illus.). 562p. 1978. 24.50 (ISBN 0-306-31096-1, Plenum Pr). Plenum Pub.

Rutter, Russell J. & Pimlott, Douglas H. World of the Wolf. LC 67-16919. (Living World Books Ser). (gr. 4-9). 1968. 10.95 (ISBN 0-397-00570-9). Lippincott.

Rutter, Vicki. Your Book of Puppetry. 1969. 5.95 (ISBN 0-571-08291-2, Pub. by Faber & Faber). Merrimack Bk Serv.

Ruud, Even. Music Therapy & Its Relationship to Current Treatment Theories. rev ed. 1980. pap. 6.50 (ISBN 0-918812-14-3). Magnamusic.

Ruud, Ivar, jt. auth. see Maxwell, A. E.

Ruud, J. Teaching for Changed Attitudes & Values. LC 71-187577. 1972. pap. 2.50 (ISBN 0-686-14993-9, 265-08378). Home Econ Educ.

Ruuth, Marianne. Journey into Fear. 1977. pap. 1.50 (ISBN 0-505-51193-2). Tower Bks.

Ruvalds, J., jt. ed. see Dash, J. G.

Ruwet, Nicolas. Problems in French Syntax: Transformational - Generative Studies. Robins, Sheila M., tr. from Fr. (Linguistics Library). 1976. text ed. 22.00x (ISBN 0-582-55058-0). Longman.

Ruxton, G. F. Life in the Far West, 1846-47: Among the Indians & the Mountain Men. LC 72-11539. (Beautiful Rio Grande Classics Ser). lib. bdg. 12.00 o.p. (ISBN 0-87380-098-2). Rio Grande.

Ruxton, George F. Life in the Far West. Hafen, LeRoy R., ed. (Illus.). 1951. 9.95 (ISBN 0-8061-0221-7); pap. 4.95 (ISBN 0-8061-1534-3). U of Okla Pr.

--Ruxton of the Rockies. Hafen, LeRoy R., ed. (American Exploration & Travel Ser.: Vol. 13). (Illus.). 326p. 1979. pap. 7.95 (ISBN 0-8061-1603-X). U of Okla Pr.

--Ruxton of the Rockies. Hafen, LeRoy R., ed. (Illus.). 1980. 15.95 (ISBN 0-8061-1591-2); pap. 7.95 (ISBN 0-8061-1603-X). U of Okla Pr.

Ruzek, Sheryl B. The Women's Health Movement: Feminist Alternatives to Medical Control. LC 78-15483. (Praeger Special Studies). 1978. 29.95 (ISBN 0-03-041436-9); pap. 10.95 (ISBN 0-03-056236-8). Praeger.

Ruzicka, J. & Stary, J. Substoichiometry in Radiochemical Analysis. 1968. 27.00 (ISBN 0-08-012442-9). Pergamon.

Ruzicka, Jaromir & Hansen, Elo H. Flow Injection Analysis. 250p. 1981. 32.50 (ISBN 0-471-08192-2, Pub. by Wiley-Interscience). Wiley.

Ryabchikov, D. I. & Ryabukhin, V. A. Analytical Chemistry of Yttrium & the Lanthanide Elements. (Analytical Chemistry of the Elements Ser.). 1971. 23.95 o.p. (ISBN 0-470-74786-2). Halsted Pr.

Ryabukhin, V. A., jt. auth. see Ryabchikov, D. I.

Ryall, A. L. & Pentzer, Wilbur T. Handling, Transportation & Storage of Fruits & Vegetables: Fruits & Tree Nuts, Vol. No. 2. (Illus.). 1974. lib. bdg. 45.00 (ISBN 0-87055-165-5). AVI.

Ryall, A. Lloyd & Lipton, Werner J. Handling, Transporation & Storage of Fruits & Vegetables, Vol. 1. 2nd ed. (Illus.). 1979. text ed. 45.00 (ISBN 0-87055-264-3). AVI.

Ryall, R. W. Mechanisms of Drug Action on the Nervous System. LC 78-5965. (Cambridge Texts in the Physiological Sciences Ser.: No. 1). (Illus.). 1979. 24.95 (ISBN 0-521-22125-0); pap. 7.95x (ISBN 0-521-29364-2). Cambridge U Pr.

Ryalls, Alan. Modern Camping. LC 75-7. 1975. 2.95 o.p. (ISBN 0-7153-6996-2). David & Charles.

Ryalls, Alan & Marchant, Roger. Better Camping. (Better Ser.). (Illus.). 96p. (gr. 7 up). 1979. 14.50x (ISBN 0-7182-0494-8, SpS). Soccer.

Ryals, Clyde de L. Browning's Later Poetry, 1881-1889. LC 75-16927. 288p. 1975. 18.50x (ISBN 0-8014-0964-0). Cornell U Pr.

Ryals, Clyde De L., ed. see Ward, Mrs. Humphrey.

Ryan. The Social Studies Sourcebook: Ideas for Teaching in the Elementary & Middle School. new ed. 320p. 1980. pap. text ed. 10.45 (ISBN 0-205-06802-2, 2368021). Allyn.

Ryan, ed. see Walker Art Center & Minneapolis Institute of Arts.

Ryan, Adrian. Still Life Painting Techniques. 1978. 22.50 (ISBN 0-7134-0635-6). David & Charles.

Ryan, Alan. J. S. Mill. (Routledge Author Guides). 1974. 18.00x (ISBN 0-7100-7954-0); pap. 10.95 (ISBN 0-7100-7955-9). Routledge & Kegan.

--Panther! 1981. pap. 2.25 (ISBN 0-451-09726-2, E9726, Sig). NAL.

Ryan, Alan, ed. The Idea of Freedom: Essays in Honour of Isaiah Berlin. 1979. 17.95x (ISBN 0-19-215859-7). Oxford U Pr.

Ryan, Allan J. The Physician & Sportsmedicine Guide to Running. (Physician & Sportsmedicine Guides). (Illus.). 1980. 7.95 (ISBN 0-07-054358-5). McGraw.

Ryan, Anne, jt. auth. see Sluzas, Raymond.

Ryan, Bernard. How to Help Your Child Start School. 1980. 9.95. Caroline Hse.

Ryan, Bernard, Jr. How to Help Your Child Start School. Longman, Harold S., ed. LC 80-50170. 180p. 1980. 9.95 (ISBN 0-934924-01-5). Soundview Bks.

--How to Help Your Child Start School: A Practical Guide for Parents & Teachers of Four to Six Year Olds. 166p. 1981. pap. 4.95 (ISBN 0-399-50539-3, Perigee). Putnam.

Ryan, Betsy. Search the Silence: Poems of Self-Discovery. (Illus.). (gr. 10-12). 1975. pap. 1.25 (ISBN 0-590-09828-4, Schol Pap). Schol Bk Serv.

Ryan, Bruce P. Programmed Therapy for Stuttering in Children & Adults. (Illus.). 200p. 1980. text ed. 12.50 (ISBN 0-398-03104-5); pap. text ed. 9.75 (ISBN 0-398-03100-2). C C Thomas.

Ryan, Charles C. Starry Messenger: The Best of Galileo. LC 79-16604. 1979. 9.95 (ISBN 0-312-75599-6). St Martin.

Ryan, Charles J. H. P. Blavatsky & the Theosophical Movement. 2nd,rev. ed. Knoche, Grace F., ed. LC 75-4433. (Illus.). 1975. 9.00 (ISBN 0-911500-79-0); softcover 6.00 (ISBN 0-911500-80-4). Theos U Pr.

Ryan, Charles W. Basic Electricity. LC 76-4031. (Self-Teaching Guides Ser.). 1976. pap. text ed. 7.95 (ISBN 0-471-74787-4). Wiley.

Ryan, Cheli D. Hildilid's Night. LC 75-146627. (Illus.). (gr. k-3). 1971. 4.50g o.s.i. (ISBN 0-02-777990-4). Macmillan.

--Paz. LC 73-139444. (Illus.). (gr. 1-3). 1971. 4.95 o.s.i. (ISBN 0-02-777980-7). Macmillan.

Ryan, Cornelius. The Longest Day. 352p. 1975. pap. 2.75 (ISBN 0-445-08380-8). Popular Lib.

Ryan, Craig A. Beautiful New Mexico. Shangle, Robert D., ed. LC 79-16748. (Illus.). 80p. 1979. 14.95 (ISBN 0-89802-073-5); pap. 7.95 (ISBN 0-89802-072-7). Beautiful Am.

Ryan, Dennis. The Religious Element in Life. LC 77-18568. 1978. pap. text ed. 7.50x (ISBN 0-8191-0405-1). U Pr of Amer.

Ryan, Dennis P., ed. A Salute to Courage. 1979. 19.95 (ISBN 0-231-04230-2). Columbia U Pr.

Ryan, Desmond & Shurkin, Joel. Helix. 1981. pap. 2.75 (ISBN 0-671-41006-7). PB.

Ryan, Desmond, ed. The Nineteen Sixteen Poets. LC 79-18768. 224p. 1980. Repr. of 1963 ed. lib. bdg. 17.50x (ISBN 0-313-22100-6, RYNI). Greenwood.

Ryan, Frances R., tr. see Fulcher Of Chartres.

Ryan, Sr. Frances R., tr. see Fink, Henry S.

Ryan, Frank. Sports & Psychology. 224p. 1981. 9.95 (ISBN 0-13-837856-8). P-H.

Ryan, Frank L. Exemplars for the New Social Studies: Instruction in the Elementary Schools. LC 70-137484. (Illus.). 1971. pap. text ed. 9.95x (ISBN 0-13-294686-6). P-H.

--The Immediate Critical Reception of Ernest Hemingway. LC 79-6026. 77p. 1980. text ed. 12.75 (ISBN 0-8191-0970-3); pap. text ed. 6.50 (ISBN 0-8191-0971-1). U Pr of Amer.

Ryan, Gerald D. Radiographic Positioning of Small Animals. LC 80-26069. (Illus.). 147p. 1981. text ed. write for info. (ISBN 0-8121-0774-8). Lea & Febiger.

Ryan, Gerard R., jt. auth. see House, Peter W.

Ryan, James W., jt. auth. see Carisella, P. J.

Ryan, Joan. Contributions of Women: Sports. LC 74-32058. (Contributions of Women Ser.). (Illus.). 135p. (gr. 6 up). 1975. PLB 8.95 (ISBN 0-87518-082-5). Dillon.

Ryan, Joanne E., jt. auth. see Gunter, Laurie M.

Ryan, John. Captain Pugwash: A Pirate Story. (Illus.). (gr. k-3). 1979. 7.50 (ISBN 0-370-00706-9, Pub. by Chatto Bodley Jonathan). Merrimack Bk Serv.

--The Captain Pugwash: Cartoon Bk. (Illus.). (gr. 1 up). 1979. 7.50 (ISBN 0-370-30030-0, Pub. by Chatto Bodley Jonathan). Merrimack Bk Serv.

--Pugwash & the Ghost Ship. LC 68-23218. (Illus.). (gr. k-3). 1968. 8.95 (ISBN 0-87599-146-7). S G Phillips.

--Pugwash in the Pacific. LC 73-929. (Illus.). 32p. (gr. k-3). 1973. 8.95 (ISBN 0-87599-199-8). S G Phillips.

Ryan, John Augustine. Declining Liberty & Other Papers. LC 73-159802. (Civil Liberties in American History Ser). 350p. 1972. Repr. of 1927 ed. lib. bdg. 35.00 (ISBN 0-306-70253-3). Da Capo.

Ryan, John P., et al. American Trial Judges: Their Work Styles & Performance. LC 80-756. (Illus.). 1980. 19.95 (ISBN 0-02-927620-9). Free Pr.

Ryan, Kenneth J., jt. auth. see Tulchinsky, Dan.

Ryan, Kevin & Cooper, James M. Kaleidoscope: A Book of Readings. 2nd ed. 1975. pap. text ed. 9.00 o.p. (ISBN 0-395-18623-4); learning guide 6.75 o.p. (ISBN 0-395-19859-3). HM.

--Kaleidoscope: Readings in Education. 3rd ed. LC 79-90056. (Illus.). 1980. pap. text ed. 9.50 (ISBN 0-395-28498-8). HM.

--Those Who Can, Teach. 2nd ed. (Illus.). 500p. 1975. text ed. 14.95 o.p. (ISBN 0-395-18622-6); instructor's manual 1.50 o.p. (ISBN 0-395-18790-7). HM.

--Those Who Can, Teach. 3rd ed. LC 79-89788. (Illus.). 1980. text ed. 16.50 (ISBN 0-395-28495-3); instrs'. manual 0.80 (ISBN 0-395-28496-1); learning guide 6.25 (ISBN 0-395-28497-X). HM.

Ryan, Kevin, jt. ed. see Purpel, David.

Ryan, Kevin, jt. ed. see Purpel, David E.

Ryan, L., jt. auth. see Schubert, R.

Ryan, Marleigh G., tr. Japan's First Modern Novel. LC 67-15896. 1971. 7.50x (ISBN 0-231-08666-0). Columbia U Pr.

Ryan, Martha. Weather. (Easy-Read Fact Bks.). (Illus.). 48p. (gr. 2-4). 1976. PLB 4.47 o.p. (ISBN 0-531-00361-2). Watts.

Ryan, Mary P. Cradle of the Middle Class: The Family in Oneida County, New York, 1780-1865. LC 80-18460. (Interdisciplinary Perspectives on Modern History Ser.). (Illus.). 336p. Date not set. price not set (ISBN 0-521-23200-7). Cambridge U Pr.

--How Sacraments Celebrate Our Story. LC 78-53635. (Journeys Ser). 1978. pap. text ed. 4.20x (ISBN 0-88489-104-6); tchrs. guide 2.60x (ISBN 0-88489-108-9). St Mary's.

--Womanhood in America: From Colonial Times to the Present. 1975. 15.00 o.p. (ISBN 0-531-05365-2); pap. 5.95 o.p. (ISBN 0-531-05568-X). Watts.

Ryan, Michael. The Organization of Soviet Medical Care. (Aspects of Social Policy). 1978. 24.50x (ISBN 0-631-18140-7, Pub. by Basil Blackwell). Biblio Dist.

Ryan, Michael, jt. auth. see Penoyre, John.

Ryan, Michael D., ed. Dimensions of the Holocaust: Perpetrators, Victims, Bystanders & Resisters--Then & Now; Papers of the 1979 Bernhard E. Olson Scholar's Conference on the Church Struggle & the Holocaust Sponsored by the National Conference of Christians & Jews. (Texts & Studies in Religion: Vol. 9). 300p. 1981. soft cover 24.95x (ISBN 0-88946-902-4). E Mellen.

Ryan, Michael K. In Winter. LC 80-19799. (The National Poetry Ser.). 64p. 1981. 8.95 (ISBN 0-03-058942-8); pap. price not set (ISBN 0-03-058941-X). HR&W.

Ryan, Michael P. The Contemporary Explosion of Theology: Ecumenical Studies in Theology. LC 74-34125. 1975. 10.00 (ISBN 0-8108-0794-7). Scarecrow.

Ryan, Mick. Radical Alternatives to Prison & the Penal Lobby. LC 78-58895. 1975. 20.95 (ISBN 0-03-046351-3). Praeger.

Ryan, Mildred G. The Complete Encyclopedia of Stitchery. 1981. pap. 8.95 (ISBN 0-452-25264-4, Z5264, Plume). NAL.

--The Complete Encyclopedia of Stitchery: More Than 1400 Illustrations & 1000 Entries. LC 77-16942. (Illus.). 1979. 14.95 (ISBN 0-385-12385-X). Doubleday.

Ryan, N. J. The Cultural Heritage of Malaya. 2nd ed. Orig. Title: The Cultural Background of the Peoples of Malaya. (Illus.). 184p. 1971. pap. text ed. 3.25x (ISBN 0-582-72417-1). Humanities.

Ryan, Paul B. First Line Defense: The U. S. Navy Since 1945. (Publication Ser.: No. 237). 336p. 1981. 14.95 (ISBN 0-8179-7371-0). Hoover Inst Pr.

--The Panama Canal Controversy: U. S. Diplomacy & Defense Interests. LC 77-20643. (Publications Ser.: No. 187). (Illus.). 1977. pap. 5.95 (ISBN 0-8179-6872-5). Hoover Inst Pr.

Ryan, Paul B., jt. auth. see Bailey, Thomas A.

Ryan, Peter J., jt. auth. see Henin, Claude G.

Ryan, Ray. Basic Digital Electronics: Understanding Number Systems, Boolean Algebra & Logical Circuits. LC 74-14326. (Illus.). 1975. pap. 7.95 (ISBN 0-8306-3728-1, 728). TAB Bks.

Ryan, Regina S. & Travis, John W. Wellness Workbook: A Guide to Attaining High Level Wellness. 15.95 (ISBN 0-89815-033-7); pap. 9.95 (ISBN 0-89815-032-9). Ten Speed Pr.

Ryan, Richard. Ravenswood. (Orig.). 1974. pap. text ed. 3.25x (ISBN 0-85105-255-X, Dolmen Pr). Humanities.

Ryan, Robert M., jt. auth. see Klenk, Robert W.

Ryan, Selwyn. Race & Nationalism in Trinidad & Tobago. 1972. 25.00x (ISBN 0-8020-5256-8). U of Toronto Pr.

Ryan, Sheila A. & Clayton, Bruce D. Handbook of Practical Pharmacology. 2nd ed. LC 79-26035. (Illus.). 1980. pap. text ed. 10.95 (ISBN 0-8016-4240-X). Mosby.

Ryan, Thomas. Fasting Rediscovered: A Guide to Health & Wholeness for Your Body-Spirit. LC 80-81581. 176p. (Orig.). 1981. pap. 5.95 (ISBN 0-8091-2323-1). Paulist Pr.

--Recollections of an Old Musician. (Music Reprint Ser.). 1979. Repr. of 1899 ed. lib. bdg. 29.50 (ISBN 0-306-79521-3). Da Capo.

Ryan, Thomas J. Adolescence of P One. 1977. 10.95 (ISBN 0-02-606500-2). Macmillan.

Ryan, Thomas R. Orestes Brownson. 1976. text ed. 29.95x (ISBN 0-8290-0333-9). Irvington.

Ryan, Tom K. Let'er Rip Tumbleweeds. (Illus.). 128p. 1977. pap. 1.50 (ISBN 0-449-13894-1, GM). Fawcett.

--Ride on Tumbleweeds! 1978. pap. 1.25 o.p. (ISBN 0-449-14040-7, GM). Fawcett.

--Tumbleweed Express. 128p. (Orig.). 1981. pap. 1.75 (ISBN 0-449-14407-0, GM). Fawcett.

--Tumbleweeds, No. 3. (Tumbleweed Ser.). (Illus.). 1979. pap. 1.50 (ISBN 0-449-13672-8, GM). Fawcett.

--Tumbleweeds & Company. (Tumbleweed Ser.). (Illus.). 1979. pap. 1.50 (ISBN 0-449-14198-5, GM). Fawcett.

--Tumbleweeds, No. 5. (Tumbleweed Ser.). (Illus.). 1977. pap. 1.50 (ISBN 0-449-13789-9, GM). Fawcett.

Ryan, W. Properties of Ceramic Raw Materials: In SI Units. 2nd ed. 1978. text ed. 15.00 (ISBN 0-08-022113-0); pap. text ed. 5.75 (ISBN 0-08-022114-9). Pergamon.

Ryan, Will G., jt. ed. see Schwartz, Theodore B.

Ryan, William. Equality. 1981. 15.95 (ISBN 0-394-50493-3). Pantheon.

Ryans, John K., Jr., ed. Marketing Doctoral Dissertation Abstracts, 1979. (Bibliography Ser.: No. 38). 142p. 1980. 15.00 (ISBN 0-87757-146-5). Am Mktg.

Ryavec, Karl W. Implementation of Soviet Economic Reforms: Political, Organizational & Social Processes. LC 75-3627. (Special Studies). (Illus.). 380p. 1975. text ed. 34.50 (ISBN 0-275-05240-0). Praeger.

Rybach, L. & Muffler, L. J., eds. Geothermal Systems: Principles & Case Histories. LC 80-40290. 328p. 1981. 70.00 (ISBN 0-471-27811-4, Pub. by Wiley-Interscience). Wiley.

Ryback, Ralph S., et al. The Problem-Oriented Record in Psychiatry & Mental Health Care. 2nd ed. 1981. write for info. (ISBN 0-8089-1308-5). Grune.

Rybak, B. Principles of Zoophysiology, Vol. 1. 1969. 79.00 (ISBN 0-08-012158-6). Pergamon.

Rybak, B., ed. Advanced Technobiology. 712p. 1979. 56.00x (ISBN 90-286-0299-2). Sijthoff & Noordhoff.

Rybakov, Anatoli. Heavy Sand. Shukman, Harold, tr. from Rus. 384p. 1981. 13.95 (ISBN 0-670-36499-1). Viking Pr.

Ryberg, J., jt. ed. see Choppin, G.

Rycenga, J. A., jt. ed. see Schwartz, Joseph.

Rychlak, Joseph F. Discovering Free Will & Personal Responsibility. LC 78-31709. 1979. 13.95 (ISBN 0-19-502687-X); pap. text ed. 5.95x (ISBN 0-686-66190-7). Oxford U Pr.

--A Philosophy of Science for Personality Theory. 2nd ed. 528p. 1981. Repr. of 1968 ed. write for info. (ISBN 0-88275-889-6). Krieger.

--The Psychology of Rigorous Humanism. LC 76-54838. 1977. 28.95 (ISBN 0-471-74796-3, Pub. by Wiley-Interscience). Wiley.

Rycroft, M. J. Space Research, Vol. 20: Proceedings of the Open Meetings of the Working Groups on Physical Sciences of the Twenty-Second Plenary Meeting of the Committee on Space Research, Bangalore, India, 29 May--9 June 1979. LC 79-41359. (Illus.). 294p. 1980. 58.00 (ISBN 0-08-024437-8). Pergamon.

Rycroft, Michael J., ed. Space Research, Vols. 13-19. 1977. Vol. 13, 1977. text ed. 96.00 (ISBN 0-08-021787-7); Vol. 14, 1977. text ed. 115.00 (ISBN 0-08-021788-5); Vol. 15, 1977. text ed. 96.00 (ISBN 0-08-021789-3); Vol. 16, 1977. text ed. 96.00 (ISBN 0-08-021795-8); Vol. 17, 1977. text ed. 96.00 (ISBN 0-08-021636-6); Vol. 18, 1978. text ed. 115.00 (ISBN 0-08-022021-5); Vol. 19, 1979. text ed. 115.00 (ISBN 0-08-023417-8). Pergamon.

Rycroft, P. V., ed. Corneo-plastic Surgery. LC 68-58885. 1969. 97.00 (ISBN 0-08-013013-5). Pergamon.

Rydberg, Per A. Flora of the Prairies & Plains of Central North America. LC 79-166434. (Illus.). 1971. pap. 5.00 ea.; Vol. I. pap. o.p. (ISBN 0-486-22584-4); Vol. II. pap. (ISBN 0-486-22585-2). Dover.

--Flora of the Rocky Mountains & Adjacent Plains. 2nd ed. 1954. Repr. of 1922 ed. 24.00 o.s.i. (ISBN 0-02-851250-2). Hafner.

Ryde, Peter, ed. Mostly Golf: A Bernard Darwin Anthology. 1977. 15.00 (ISBN 0-7136-1687-3). Transatlantic.

Ryden, George H. Letters to & from Caesar Rodney. LC 75-107417. (Era of the American Revolution Ser). 1970. Repr. of 1933 ed. lib. bdg. 49.50 (ISBN 0-306-71881-2). Da Capo.

Ryden, Hope. Mustangs: A Return to the Wild. (Large Format Ser.). (Illus.). 1978. pap. 6.95 o.p. (ISBN 0-14-004838-3). Penguin.

Ryder, A. & Malcolmson, E. The Engineers' Computer Handbook. 336p. 1980. 95.00x (ISBN 0-7277-0078-2, Pub. by Telford England). State Mutual Bk.

Ryder, A. J. German Revolution of Nineteen Eighteen. 1967. 41.95 (ISBN 0-521-06176-8). Cambridge U Pr.

--Twentieth-Century Germany. 300p. 1972. 22.50x (ISBN 0-231-03692-2); pap. 10.00x (ISBN 0-231-08350-5). Columbia U Pr.

Ryder, Alan. Benin & the Europeans, Fourteen Eighty-Five to Eighteen Ninety-Seven. LC 68-54523. (Ibadan History Ser). 1969. text ed. 11.25x (ISBN 0-582-64514-X). Humanities.

--The Kingdom of Naples Under Alfonso the Magnanimous: The Making of a Modern State. 1976. 49.50x (ISBN 0-19-822535-0). Oxford U Pr.

Ryder, Beatrice. Astrology: Your Personal Sun Sign Guide. 1970. pap. 1.25 o.s.i. (ISBN 0-446-76700-X). Warner Bks.

Ryder, Edward J. Leafy Salad Vegetables. (Illus.). 1979. text ed. 26.00 (ISBN 0-87055-323-2). AVI.

Ryder, F. G. & McCormick, E. A. Lebendige Literatur: Deutsches Lesebuch Fur Anfanger. 1974. pap. text ed. 9.15 (ISBN 0-395-13826-4). HM.

Ryder, G. H., ed. Gates' Jigs, Fixtures, Tools & Gauges. 6th ed. (Illus.). 1973. 17.50x (ISBN 0-291-39432-9). Intl Ideas.

Ryder, Joanne. The Spiders Dance. LC 78-22495. (Illus.). 48p. (gr. 1-4). 1981. 8.95 (ISBN 0-06-025133-6, HarpJ); PLB 8.79 (ISBN 0-06-025134-4). Har-Row.

Ryder, John D. Electronic Fundamentals & Applications: Integrated & Discrete Systems. 5th ed. (Illus.). 640p. 1975. 25.95 (ISBN 0-13-251371-4). P-H.

--Introduction to Circuit Analysis. (Illus.). 400p. 1973. ref. ed. 26.95 (ISBN 0-13-481101-1). P-H.

--Networks, Lines, & Fields. 2nd ed. 1955. ref. ed. 23.95 (ISBN 0-13-611251-X); ans. 0.35 (ISBN 0-13-611269-2). P-H.

Ryder, Marion C. Scuttle Watch. LC 79-91988. (Illus.). 286p. (gr. 4-12). 1979. pap. 4.95 (ISBN 0-88492-034-8). W S Sullwold.

Ryder, T. A. Portrait of Gloucestershire. LC 66-73378. (Portrait Bks.). (Illus.). 1966. 10.50x (ISBN 0-7091-3318-9). Intl Pubns Serv.

Ryder, Verdene. Contemporary Living. LC 78-23516. (Illus.). 1979. text ed. 13.20 (ISBN 0-87006-266-2); wkbk. 3.20 (ISBN 0-87006-280-8). Goodheart.

Rydholm, Sven A. Pulping Processes. LC 65-18412. 1965. 80.00 (ISBN 0-471-74793-9, Pub. by Wiley-Interscience). Wiley.

Ryding, William, jt. auth. see Sareil, Jean.

Rydjord, John. Indian Place-Names: Their Origin, Evolution, & Meanings, Collected in Kansas from the Siouan, Algonquian, Shoshonean, Caddoan, Iroquoian, & Other Tongues. LC 68-10303. (Illus.). 380p. 1981. 19.95 (ISBN 0-8061-0801-0). U of Okla Pr.

Rye, Owen S. Pottery Technology: Principles & Reconstruction. LC 80-53439. (Manuals on Archeology Ser.: No. 4). (Illus.). 1981. 18.00x (ISBN 0-9602822-2-X). Taraxacum.

Rye, Walter. Chaucer: A Norfolk Man. 104p. 1980. Repr. of 1915 ed. lib. bdg. 20.00 (ISBN 0-8495-4636-2). Arden Lib.

--Records & Record Searching. LC 68-30663. 1969. Repr. of 1897 ed. 20.00 (ISBN 0-8103-3133-0). Gale.

Ryel, D., jt. auth. see Dahlstrom, J.

Ryen, Dag. This Trembling Land. 176p. (gr. 5-9). pap. 8.95 (ISBN 0-938578-01-4). How-to Pr.

Ryerse, Phyllis. A Guide to the History & Restoration of Antique Trunks. (Illus.). 34p. 1974. pap. 2.50 o.p. (ISBN 0-9603388-0-2). Ryerse.

Ryerson, Albert W. The Ryerson Genealogy: Genealogy & History of the Knickerbocker Families of Ryerson, Ryerse, Ryerss, Also Adriane & Martense Families All Descendants of Martin & Adriane Reyersz (Reyerszen) of Amsterdam, Holland. Holman, Alfred L., ed. 85.00x (ISBN 0-685-88555-0). Elliots Bks.

Ryerson, Ellen. The Best-Laid Plans: America's Juvenile Court Experiment. 1978. 8.95 o.p. (ISBN 0-8090-2905-7); pap. 4.95 (ISBN 0-8090-0135-7). Hill & Wang.

Ryerson, Margery A., ed. see Henri, Robert.

Ryerson, Martin. The Quick Badge. 1981. pap. 1.95 (ISBN 0-8439-0863-7, Leisure Bks). Nordon Pubns.

Ryf, Robert S. Henry Green. LC 67-27360. (Columbia Ser.: No. 29). 1968. pap. 2.00 (ISBN 0-231-02897-0, MW29). Columbia U Pr.

--Joseph Conrad. LC 74-110599. (Columbia Ser.: No. 49). (Orig.). 1970. pap. 2.00 (ISBN 0-231-03264-1, MW49). Columbia U Pr.

Ryffel, Henry H., ed. see Amiss, John M. & Jones, Franklin D.

Ryffell, Henry, jt. auth. see Jones, Franklin D.

Rykalin, N., et al. Laser Machinig and Welding. (Illus.). 1979. 48.00 (ISBN 0-08-022724-4). Pergamon.

Ryken, Leland, ed. The Christian Imagination: Essays on Literature & the Arts. 344p. (Orig.). 1981. pap. 9.95 (ISBN 0-8010-7702-8). Baker Bk.

Ryland, Frederick. Chronological Outlines of English Literature. LC 68-30587. 1968. Repr. of 1914 ed. 22.00 (ISBN 0-8103-3223-X). Gale.

Ryland, Hobart, tr. see De Sade, Marquis.

Ryle, Gilbert. Concept of Mind. 1975. 22.00x (ISBN 0-06-496042-0); pap. 3.95 o.p. (ISBN 0-06-463251-2). B&N.

--Dilemmas. 1954-1960. 19.95 (ISBN 0-521-06177-6); pap. 6.95x (ISBN 0-521-09115-2). Cambridge U Pr.

--On Thinking. 148p. 1980. 18.00x (ISBN 08476-6203-9). Rowman.

Ryle, J. C. Christian Leaders of the Eighteenth Century: Includes Whitefield, Wesley, Grimshaw, Romaine, Rowlands, Berridge, Venn, Walker, Harvey, Toplady, & Fletcher. 1978. pap. 5.45 (ISBN 0-85151-268-2). Banner of Truth.

--Nueva Vida. 1.50 o.p. (ISBN 0-686-12557-6). Banner of Truth.

--Practical Religion. (Summit Bks). 1977. pap. 3.95 (ISBN 0-8010-7657-9). Baker Bk.

--El Secreto De la Vida Cristiana. 3.50 (ISBN 0-686-12553-3). Banner of Truth.

--The Upper Room. 1977. 11.95 (ISBN 0-85151-017-5). Banner of Truth.

Ryle, John C. Charges & Addresses. 1978. 14.95 (ISBN 0-85151-267-4). Banner of Truth.

Ryle, Martin, tr. see Castoriadis, Cornelius.

Ryle, Michael, jt. ed. see Walkland, S. A.

Ryles, A. P., et al. Essential Organic Chemistry for Students of the Life Sciences. LC 78-31504. 1980. 40.95 (ISBN 0-471-27582-4, Pub. by Wiley-Interscience); pap. 14.00 (ISBN 0-471-27581-6, Pub. by Wiley-Interscience). Wiley.

Ryley, Thomas W. A Little Group of Willful Men. 1975. 13.95 (ISBN 0-8046-9088-X, Natl U). Kennikat.

Rymer, Alta M. Captain Zomo. LC 79-67651. (Tales of Planet Artembo Ser.: Bk. 2). (Illus.). (gr. 4-7). Date not set. pap. 6.95 (ISBN 0-9600792-2-X). Rymer Bks. Postponed.

Rymer, Marilyn P., et al. Medicaid Eligibility: Problems & Solutions. (Westview Replica Edition: an Urban Systems Research Report). 1979. lib. bdg. 28.50x (ISBN 0-89158-478-1). Westview.

Rymer, Thomas. The Tragedies of the Last Age Consider'd & Examin'd. Bd. with A Short View of Tragedy. (The English Stage Ser.: Vol. 18). lib. bdg. 50.00 (ISBN 0-8240-0601-1). Garland Pub.

Ryn, August Van see Van Ryn, August.

Rynin, David, ed. see Johnson, Alexander B.

Ryrie, Charles. We Believe in Biblical Innerancy. 61p. 1981. pap. 0.35 (ISBN 0-937396-53-2). Walterick Pubs.

--We Believe in Creation. 62p. 1981. pap. 0.35 (ISBN 0-937396-54-0). Walterick Pubs.

Ryrie, Charles C. The Best Is Yet to Come. 128p. 1981. pap. 2.95 (ISBN 0-8024-4938-7). Moody.

--The Bible & Tomorrow's News. LC 69-17068. 190p. 1969. pap. 1.95 o.p. (ISBN 0-88207-017-7). Victor Bks.

--Holy Spirit. (Bible Doctrine Handbook Ser). (Orig.). 1965. pap. 2.95 (ISBN 0-8024-3565-3); pap. 2.95 leader's guide (ISBN 0-8024-3564-5). Moody.

--The Truth, the Whole Truth, Nothing but the Truth. 96p. 1981. pap. 2.95 (ISBN 0-8024-8785-8). Moody.

--What You Should Know About the Rapture. (What You Know Ser.). 128p. 1981. pap. 2.95 (ISBN 0-8024-9416-1). Moody.

--You Mean the Bible Teaches That. 1974. pap. 2.50 (ISBN 0-8024-9828-0). Moody.

Ryshik, I. M., jt. auth. see Gradshteyn, I. S.

Ryskamp, Charles & Vliegenthart, A. W. William & Mary & Their House. (Illus.). 266p. 1980. 59.00x (ISBN 0-19-520185-X). Oxford U Pr.

Ryskamp, Charles, pref. by. Flowers in Books & Drawings, Nine Forty to Eighteen Forty. LC 80-83208. (Illus.). 84p. 1980. pap. 6.95 (ISBN 0-87598-072-4). Pierpont Morgan.

Ryskamp, Charles, ed. & pref. by. Seventeenth Report to the Fellows of the Pierpont Morgan Library: 1972-1974. (Illus.). 1976. 25.00 (ISBN 0-87598-064-3). Pierpont Morgan.

Ryskamp, Charles, ed. see Adams, Frederick B.

Ryskamp, Charles, ed. see Cooper, William.

Ryskamp, Charles, jt. ed. see King, James.

Ryskamp, Charles, pref. by. The Pierpont Morgan Library: Gifts in Honor of the Fiftieth Anniversary. 1974. pap. 6.00 (ISBN 0-87598-048-1). Pierpont Morgan.

Ryssel, Fritz H. Thomas Wolfe. Sebba, Helen, tr. LC 78-190352. (Modern Literature Ser.). 1972. 10.95 (ISBN 0-8044-2749-6). Ungar.

Ryterband, Edward C., jt. auth. see Bass, Bernard M.

Ryves, Thomas. The Poore Vicars Plea. Declaring That a Competencie of Means Is Due to Them Out of the Tithes..Notwithstanding the Impropriations. LC 79-84135. (English Experience Ser.: No. 953). 164p. 1979. Repr. of 1620 ed. lib. bdg. 17.00 (ISBN 90-221-0953-4). Walter J Johnson.

Rywell, Martin. Wild Game Cook Book. 74p. 1952. pap. 3.95 (ISBN 0-917420-05-5). Buck Hill.

Rywlin, Arkadi M. Histopathology of the Bone Marrow. LC 75-41570. (Series in Laboratory Medicine). 229p. 1976. text ed. 22.50 (ISBN 0-316-76369-1). Little.

Ryzin, Lani Van see Van Ryzin, Lani.

Ryzin, Lani van see Van Ryzin, Lani.
Ryzin, Lani Van see Van Ryzin, Lani.
Rzoska, J., ed. Euphrates & Tigris: Mesopotamian Ecology & Destiny. (Monographiae Biologicae: No. 38). (Illus.). 122p. 1980. lib. bdg. 31.50 (ISBN 90-6193-090-1). Kluwer Boston.

S

S. E. Haugan Consulting. Fish Versus Oil. 1980. 50.00x (Pub. by Norwegian Info Norway). State Mutual Bk.
S Karger AG, ed. Das Manuskript. (Illus.). 1980. pap. 9.00 (ISBN 3-8055-0182-X). S Karger.
SAA College & University Archives Committee. Forms Manual. 236p. 1973. pap. 11.00 o.p. (ISBN 0-931828-04-X). Soc Am Archivists.
Saab, Ann P. & Baumgart, Winfried, eds. The Peace of Paris Eighteen Fifty Six. 1981. write for info. (ISBN 0-87436-309-8). Abc-Clio.
Saad, M. N., jt. auth. see Barron, J. N.
Saad, M. N., jt. ed. see Barron, J. B.
Saad, Michel A. see Heat Transfer & Fluid Mechanics Institute.
Saada, Adel S. Elasticity: Theory & Applications. LC 72-86670. 1974. text ed. 41.00 (ISBN 0-08-017053-6); pap. text ed. 27.50 (ISBN 0-08-017972-X); solutions manual 0.50 (ISBN 0-686-66891-X). Pergamon.
Saake, Thomas F. Business & Consumer Mathematics. (gr. 9-12). 1977. text ed. 14.68 (ISBN 0-201-06775-7, Sch Div); tchr's ed. 18.64 (ISBN 0-201-06776-5). A-W.
Saakyan, G. S. Equilibrium Configurations of Degenerate Gaseous Masses. Hall, C. F., tr. from Rus. LC 74-13583. 294p. 1974. 52.95 (ISBN 0-470-74805-2). Halsted Pr.
Saalbach, Robert Palmer, ed. see Dreiser, Theodore.
Saalman, Howard. The Bigallo: The Oratory & Residence of the Compagnia Del Bigallo Della Misericordia in Florence. LC 69-18285. (College Art Association Monographs: Vol. 19). (Illus.). 1969. 18.50x (ISBN 0-8147-0370-4). NYU Pr.
--Filippo Brunelleschi: The Cupola of Santa Maria Del Fiore. (Studies in Architecture). (Illus.). 391p. 1980. 140.00 (ISBN 0-8390-0268-8). Allanheld & Schram.
--Medieval Cities. LC 68-24702. (Planning & Cities Ser). (Illus., Orig.). 1968. pap. 5.95 o.s.i. (ISBN 0-8076-0471-2). Braziller.
Saarinen, Thomas. Environmental Planning: Perception & Behavior. LC 75-19533. (Illus.). 288p. 1976. pap. text ed. 10.50 (ISBN 0-395-20618-9). HM.
Saariste, R. & Ligtelijn, V. J. M. Jujol Architect. (Archives d'Architecture Moderne). 150p. (Orig., Fr. & Eng.). 1980. write for info. (ISBN 0-8150-0923-2). Wittenborn.
Saaty, Thomas L. & Alexander, Joyce M. Thinking with Models: Mathematical Models in the Physical, Biological & Social Sciences. (I S Modern Applied Mathematics & Computer Science: Vol. 2). (Illus.). 208p. 1981. 35.00 (ISBN 0-08-026475-1); pap. 20.00 (ISBN 0-08-026474-3). Pergamon.
Saba, Bonaventura. The Sinful, the Intimate, & the Mysterious Life of Mary Magdalene, 2 vols. (Illus.). 1978. Set. 79.75 (ISBN 0-89266-133-X). Am Classical Coll Pr.
Saba, Thomas M., ed. see Papers from the Second Annual Conference on Shock, Williamsburg, Va. June 1979.
Sabady, P. The Solar House. 1978. 21.95 (ISBN 0-408-00290-5). Butterworths.
Sabanes De Plou, Dafne, tr. see Simmons, Paul D. & Crawford, Kenneth.
Sabaneyeff, Leonid. Modern Russian Composers. Joffe, Judah A., tr. from Rus. LC 75-14232. (Music Reprint Ser). 253p. 1975. Repr. of 1927 ed. lib. bdg. 25.00 (ISBN 0-306-70673-3). Da Capo.
Sabaroff, Rose & Hanna, Mary A. The Open Classroom: A Practical Guide for the Teacher of the Elementary Grades. LC 74-6442. (Illus.). 1974. 10.00 (ISBN 0-8108-0726-2). Scarecrow.
Sabath, L. D. & Finland, M., eds. A Comprehensive Guide to the Therapeutic Use of Cefsulodin. (Pharmanual: Vol. 1). (Illus.). vi, 94p. 1980. pap. 14.50 (ISBN 3-8055-1042-X). S Karger.
Sabatier, Paul, jt. ed. see Mazmanian, Daniel.
Sabatier, Paul A., jt. ed. see Mazmanian, Daniel.
Sabatier, Robert. Three Mint Lollipops. Southgate, Patsy, tr. 1974. 7.95 o.p. (ISBN 0-525-21855-6). Dutton.
Sabatini, Rafael. The Black Swan. 224p. 1976. pap. 1.50 o.p. (ISBN 0-345-24864-3). Ballantine.
--Master-at-Arms. 1977. pap. 1.95 o.p. (ISBN 0-685-75020-5, 345-25302-7-195). Ballantine.
--Mistress Wilding. 272p. 1976. pap. 1.50 o.p. (ISBN 0-345-25062-1). Ballantine.
--The Writings of Rafael Sabatini, 21 vols. 1981. Repr. of 1924 ed. Set. lib. bdg. 500.00 (ISBN 0-89987-766-4). Darby Bks.
Sabatino, David, jt. ed. see Mann, Lester.
Sabatino, David, et al. Learning Disabilities: Systemizing Teaching & Service Delivery. 350p. 1981. text ed. price not set (ISBN 0-89443-361-X). Aspen Systems.
Sabatino, David A. & Mauser, August J. Intervention Strategies for Specialized Secondary Education. new ed. 1978. text ed. 19.95 (ISBN 0-686-52747-X). Allyn.
--Specialized Education in Today's Secondary Schools. new ed. 1978. text ed. 19.95 (ISBN 0-205-06043-9). Allyn.
Sabato, Ernesto. On Heroes & Tombs. 1981. 17.95 (ISBN 0-87923-381-8). Godine.
Sabato, Larry. Goodbye to Good-Time Charlie. LC 78-333. (Illus.). 1978. 21.95 (ISBN 0-669-02161-X). Lexington Bks.
Sabbah, R., jt. ed. see Rouquerol, J.
Sabbath, Dan & Hall, Mandel. End Product: The First Taboo. 1977. pap. 4.95 (ISBN 0-916354-76-8). Urizen Bks.
Sabbe, Herman, et al, eds. Report on the International Conference on New Musical Notation Organized by the Index of New Musical Notation (New York) & the Seminar of Musicology (Ghent) 120p. 1975. pap. text ed. 25.50 (ISBN 90-265-0221-4, Pub. by Swets Pub Serv Holland). Swets North Am.
Sabek, Jerwan. English-French-Arabic Trilingual Dictionary. 35.00 (ISBN 0-686-63569-8). Intl Bk Ctr.
Sabel, W. Basic Techniques of Preparative Organic Chemistry. 1967. pap. 7.00 (ISBN 0-08-012307-4). Pergamon.
Sabelli, H., ed. Chemical Modulation of Brain Function. LC 72-96825. (Illus.). 331p. 1973. 24.50 (ISBN 0-685-92920-5). Raven.
Saben-Clare, E. E., et al, eds. Health in Tropical Africa During the Colonial Period. (Illus.). 256p. 1980. 42.00 (ISBN 0-19-858165-3). Oxford U Pr.
Saberhagen, Fred. Thorn. 1980. pap. 2.75 (ISBN 0-441-80744-5). Ace Bks.
Sabet, Huschmand. The Heavens Are Cleft Asunder. rev. ed. Coburn, Oliver, tr. from Ger. Orig. Title: Gespaltene Himmel. (Eng.). 1975. 6.25 (ISBN 0-85398-055-1, 7-32-14, Pub. by G Ronald England); pap. 4.90 o.s.i. (ISBN 0-85398-056-X, 7-32-15). Baha'i.
Sabia, Michael L., ed. see Members of the American Academy of Podiatric Sports Medicine.
Sabia, Michael L., Jr., ed. see American Academy of Podiatric Sports Medicine.
Sabin, A. Ross, ed. Automatic Dishwasher, Disposer, Trash Masher Compactor. (Illus.). 168p. (gr. 11). 1978. 20.00 (ISBN 0-938336-07-X). Whirlpool.
--Automatic Dryers. (Illus.). 160p. (gr. 11). 20.00 (ISBN 0-938336-05-3). Whirlpool.
--Automatic Washers. (Illus.). 200p. (gr. 11). 1975. 20.00 (ISBN 0-938336-04-5). Whirlpool.
--Basic Electricity for Appliances. (Illus.). 255p. (gr. 11). 1973. 20.00 (ISBN 0-938336-00-2). Whirlpool.
--Central Air Conditioning Service. (Illus.). 218p. (gr. 11). 1974. 20.00 (ISBN 0-938336-03-7). Whirlpool.
--Commercial Ice Makers. (Illus.). 273p. (gr. 11). 1980. 20.00 (ISBN 0-938336-08-8). Whirlpool.
--Range Service (Gas, Electric, Microwave) (Illus.). 253p. (gr. 11). 1979. 20.00 (ISBN 0-938336-06-1). Whirlpool.
--Refrigeration, Pt. I. (Illus.). 144p. (gr. 11). 1974. 20.00 (ISBN 0-938336-01-0). Whirlpool.
--Refrigeration, Pt. II. (Illus.). 203p. (gr. 11). 1974. 20.00 (ISBN 0-938336-02-9). Whirlpool.
Sabin, A. Ross, ed. see Brittan, John.
Sabin, Arthur J. All About Suing & Being Sued. LC 80-23991. (Illus.). 128p. (Orig.). 1981. pap. 12.95 (ISBN 0-89037-185-7); handbk. 15.00 (ISBN 0-89037-188-1). Anderson World.
Sabin, Joseph. Dictionary of Books Relating to America, 29 Vols. in 2. LC 66-31865. 1966. Repr. Set. 147.50 (ISBN 0-8108-0033-0). Scarecrow.
Sabin, Lou. Hot Shots of Pro Basketball. LC 74-4932. (Pro Basketball Library). (Illus.). 160p. (gr. 5 up). 1974. 2.50 o.p. (ISBN 0-394-82901-8); PLB 3.69 (ISBN 0-394-92901-2). Random.
Sabin, Lou & Sendler, Dave. Stars of Pro Basketball. LC 73-117546. (Pro Basketball Library: No. 4). (Illus.). (gr. 5-9). 1970. PLB 3.69 (ISBN 0-394-90621-7); pap. 0.95 (ISBN 0-394-82203-X). Random.
Sabin, Tracy. Getting the Type You Want. (Illus.). 1980. pap. 7.95 (ISBN 0-930904-01-X). Graphic Dimens.
Sabine, George H, tr. see Cicero.
Sabines, Jaime. Tarumba: The Selected Poems of Jaime Sabines. Levine, Philip & Trejo, Ernesto, trs. from Span. 88p. 1979. pap. 6.00 (ISBN 0-918786-21-5). Lost Roads.
Sabini, John. Armies in the Sand: The Struggle for Mecca & Medina. (Illus.). 224p. 1981. 16.95 (ISBN 0-500-01246-6). Thames Hudson.
Sabins, Floyd F., Jr. Remote Sensing: Principles & Interpretation. LC 77-27595. (Earth Sciences Ser.). (Illus.). 1978. text ed. 31.95x (ISBN 0-7167-0023-9). W H Freeman.
Sabinus, Georg. Metamorphosis, Seu Fabulae Poeticae. LC 75-27857. (Renaissance & the Gods Ser.: Vol. 14). (Illus.). 1976. Repr. of 1589 ed. lib. bdg. 73.00 (ISBN 0-8240-2063-4). Garland Pub.
Sabiston, David C., Jr., jt. auth. see Wolfe, Walter G.
Sable, Martin H. International & Area Studies Librarianship: Case Studies. LC 73-5547. 1973. 10.00 (ISBN 0-8108-0622-3). Scarecrow.
--Latin American Agriculture: A Bibliography. LC 70-628991. (Center Special Study Ser.: No. 1). 1970. pap. 6.00 (ISBN 0-930450-02-7). Univ of Wis Latin Am.
--Latin American Studies in the Non-Western World & Eastern Europe: A Bibliography on Latin America in the Languages of Africa, Asia, the Middle East, & Eastern Europe. LC 73-13114. 1970. 21.00 (ISBN 0-8108-0344-5). Scarecrow.
Sabloff, Jeremy A., jt. auth. see Willey, Gordon R.
Sabloff, Jeremy A., ed. Simulations in Archaeology. (School of American Research Advanced Seminar Ser.). (Illus.). 440p. 1981. 29.95x (ISBN 0-8263-0576-8). U of NM Pr.
Sabloff, Jeremy A. & Rathje, William L., eds. A Study of Changing Pre-Columbian Commercial Systems: Cozumel, Mexico. LC 75-20624. (Peabody Museum Monographs: No. 3). 1975. pap. 12.00 (ISBN 0-87365-902-3). Peabody Harvard.
Sabol, Andrew J., ed. Four Hundred Songs & Dances from the Stuart Masque. LC 77-6686. 661p. 1978. 100.00x (ISBN 0-87057-146-X, Pub. by Brown U Pr). Univ Pr of New England.
Sabol, Andrew J., ed. see Jonson, Ben.
Sabol, Andrew J., jt. ed. see Lewalski, Barbara K.
Sabolovic, D., jt. ed. see Preece, A. W.
Sabor, Peter, ed. see Richardson, Samuel.
Sabot, R. H., ed. Migration & the Labor Market in Developing Countries. (Westview Special Studies in Social, Political, & Economic Development). 350p. 1981. lib. bdg. 30.00x (ISBN 0-89158-763-2). Westview.
Sabourin, Conrad. Adverbs & Comparatives: An Analytical Bibliography. (Library & Information Sources in Linguistics: No. 2). 1979. text ed. 31.50x (ISBN 0-391-01647-4). Humanities.
Sabourin, Leopold. The Bible & Christ: The Unity of the Two Testaments. LC 80-14892. 208p. (Orig.). 1980. pap. 6.95 (ISBN 0-8189-0405-4). Alba.
Saccheri, Girolamo. Euclides Vindicatus. 2nd ed. Halstead, George B., tr. from Lat. 1980. text ed. 12.95 (ISBN 0-8284-0289-2). Chelsea Pub.
Sacchi, C. A., jt. ed. see Pratesi, R.
Sacchi, Louise. Ocean Flying. (McGraw-Hill Ser. in Aviation). (Illus.). 240p. 1979. 16.50 (ISBN 0-07-054405-0). McGraw.
Saccomanno, Geno. Diagnostic Pulmonary Cytology. LC 78-8285. (Illus.). 1978. text ed. 45.00 (ISBN 0-89189-050-5, 16-3-003-00). Am Soc Clinical.
Sachar, Edward J., ed. Hormones, Behavior, & Psychopathology. LC 75-16660. (American Psychopathological Association Ser.). 1976. 32.00 (ISBN 0-89004-094-X). Raven.
Sacharow, Stanley. Handbook of Packaging Materials. (Illus.). 1976. text ed. 26.50 (ISBN 0-87055-207-4). AVI.
--Packaging Regulations. (Illus.). 1979. lib. bdg. 25.50 (ISBN 0-87055-274-0). AVI.
Sacharow, Stanley & Griffin, Roger C. Principles of Food Packaging. 2nd ed. (Illus.). 1980. lib. bdg. 28.00 (ISBN 0-87055-347-X). AVI.
Sacharow, Stanley & Griffin, Roger C., Jr. Basic Guide to Plastics in Packaging. LC 72-91986. 1973. 21.95 (ISBN 0-8436-1208-8). CBI Pub.
--Food Packaging. (Illus.). 1970. 25.50 o.p. (ISBN 0-87055-070-5). AVI.
Sacharow, Stanley, jt. auth. see Griffin, Roger.
Sachchidananda. The Changing Munda. 1979. text ed. 25.00x (ISBN 0-391-01932-5). Humanities.
Sachchidananda & Lal. Elite & Development. 286p. 1980. text ed. 15.75x (ISBN 0-391-02129-X). Humanities.
Sacher, G. A., jt. ed. see Lindop, Patricia J.
Sachet, Marie-Helene & Fosberg, F. Raymond. Island Bibliographies Supplement. LC 55-60007. 448p. 1971. text ed. 11.00 (ISBN 0-309-01932-X). Natl Acad Pr.
Sachs. The U F O Encyclopedia. 1980. 14.95 (ISBN 0-399-12365-2). Putnam.
Sachs, A., jt. auth. see Neugebauer, O.
Sachs, Albie. Justice in South Africa. (Perspectives on Southern Africa Ser., No. 12). 1973. 17.50x (ISBN 0-520-02417-6); pap. 3.25 (ISBN 0-520-02624-1). U of Cal Pr.
Sachs, Albie & Wilson, Joan H. Sexism & the Law: Male Beliefs & Legal Bias in Britain & the United States. LC 78-63402. 1979. 15.95 (ISBN 0-02-927640-3). Free Pr.
Sachs, B. F. United States Constitutions Subject Index, Release 1. 1980. 35.00 (ISBN 0-379-20413-4). Oceana.
Sachs, Bonnie L. Renal Transplantaton - A Nursing Perspective. 1977. spiral bdg. 9.50 (ISBN 0-87488-358-X). Med Exam.
Sachs, Ernest, Jr., tr. see Bischoff, Ernst P.
Sachs, H. K., ed. Proceedings of the First International Conference on Vehicle Mechanics, Detroit, 16-18 July, 1968. 735p. 1969. text ed. 80.00 (ISBN 90-265-0101-3, Pub. by Swets Pub Serv Holland). Swets North Am.
--Proceedings of the Third International Conference on Vehicle System Dynamics, Blacksburg, VA, 12-15 August 1974. 324p. 1975. text ed. 54.00 (ISBN 90-265-0197-8, Pub. by Swets Pub Serv Holland). Swets North Am.
Sachs, H. K. & Rapin, P., eds. Proceedings of the Second International Conference on Vehicle Mechanics, Paris, 6-10 September, 1971. 500p. 1973. text ed. 54.00 (ISBN 90-265-0166-8, Pub. by Swets Pub Serv Holland). Swets North Am.
Sachs, Harvey. Toscanini. (Da Capo Quality Paperbacks Ser.). (Illus.). 380p. 1981. pap. 8.95 (ISBN 0-306-80137-X). Da Capo.
Sachs, Herbert L. Dynamic Personal Adjustment. LC 74-8053. 364p. 1975. 9.95 (ISBN 0-87705-165-8). Human Sci Pr.
Sachs, Ignacy. Studies in Political Economy of Development. LC 79-40488. 1980. 45.00 (ISBN 0-685-97187-2) (ISBN 0-685-97188-0). Pergamon.
Sachs, Judith, tr. see Sagan, Francoise.
Sachs, Margaret & Jahn, Ernest. Celestial Passengers: UFOs & Space Travel. (Orig.). 1977. pap. 2.95 o.p. (ISBN 0-14-004483-3). Penguin.
Sachs, Marilyn. Bears' House. LC 76-157621. (gr. 4-7). 1971. 6.95a (ISBN 0-385-03363-X); PLB (ISBN 0-385-06632-5). Doubleday.
--Bus Ride. LC 79-23596. (Illus.). (gr. 7 up). 1980. PLB 7.95 (ISBN 0-525-27325-5, Skinny Book); pap. 2.50 (ISBN 0-525-45048-3, Skinny Book). Dutton.
--Class Pictures. LC 80-390. 144p. (gr. 4-7). 1980. PLB 9.95 (ISBN 0-525-27985-7). Dutton.
--A December Tale. LC 76-7697. (gr. 5-9). 1976. PLB 5.95a (ISBN 0-385-12315-9). Doubleday.
--Fleet Footed Florence. LC 76-56330. (Illus.). 48p. (gr. 2). 1981. 8.95a (ISBN 0-385-12745-6); PLB (ISBN 0-385-12746-4). Doubleday.
--A Secret Friend. LC 77-25606. (gr. 4-7). 1978. 7.95a (ISBN 0-385-13569-6); PLB (ISBN 0-385-13570-X). Doubleday.
--A Summer's Lease. (gr. 7-12). Date not set. pap. 1.75 (ISBN 0-440-97787-8, LE). Dell.
--The Truth About Mary Rose. LC 72-89128. 160p. (gr. 4-7). 1973. PLB 5.95 (ISBN 0-385-09449-3). Doubleday.
--Veronica Ganz. (Illus.). (gr. 4-6). 1970. pap. 1.25 (ISBN 0-671-29774-0). PB.
Sachs, Marvin L., jt. auth. see Miller, Marian E.
Sachs, Mendel. Solid State Theory. LC 74-78777. (Illus.). 384p. 1974. pap. text ed. 4.50 o.p. (ISBN 0-486-61772-6). Dover.
Sachs, Moshe, ed. see Worldmark Press Ltd.
Sachs, Robert G., ed. National Energy Issues: How Do We Decide? Plutonium As a Test Case. LC 79-18341. (American Academy of Arts & Sciences Ser.). 360p. 1980. reference 25.00 (ISBN 0-88410-620-9). Ballinger Pub.
Sachs, Rudolf. British American Business Terms. 144p. (Orig.). 1975. pap. text ed. 10.00x (ISBN 0-7121-0242-6, Pub. by Macdonald & Evans England). Intl Ideas.
Sachs, Stanley L., jt. auth. see Gammage, Allen Z.
Sachse, W. L., ed. see Lowe, Roger.
Sachse, William L. English History in the Making: Readings from the Sources from 1689, 2 vols. LC 67-10154. 1970. Vol. 1. pap. text ed. 13.95x (ISBN 0-471-00494-4); Vol. 2. pap. text ed. 12.95 o.p. (ISBN 0-471-00497-9). Wiley.
--Lord Somers: A Political Portrait. LC 75-885. 336p. 1975. 30.00x (ISBN 0-299-06890-0). U of Wis Pr.
--Restoration England, 1660-1689. (Conference on British Studies, Bibliographical Handbks). 1971. 17.50 (ISBN 0-521-08171-8). Cambridge U Pr.
Sachsenmeier, Peter, ed. see First All-European Conference for Directors of National Research Institutions in Education, Hamburg 26-29 April 1976.
Sack, John & Gabriel, Judy M. Entering BASIC. 2nd ed. 160p. 1980. pap. text ed. 7.95 (ISBN 0-574-21270-1, 13-4270). SRA.

Sack, Robert D. Conceptions of Space in Social Thought: A Geographic Perspective. (Illus.). 240p. 1981. 27.50x (ISBN 0-8166-1012-6); pap. 9.95x (ISBN 0-8166-1015-0). U of Minn Pr.
--Libel, Slander, & Related Problems. 700p. 1980. text ed. 50.00 (ISBN 0-686-68826-0, G1-0658). PLI.
Sack, Saul. History of Higher Education in Pennsylvania, 2 vols. LC 65-7193. 1963. 13.00 (ISBN 0-911124-32-2). Pa Hist & Mus.
Sack, Steven M. & Steinberg, Howard J. The Salesperson's Legal Guide. LC 80-22647. 144p. 1981. 12.95 (ISBN 0-13-788190-8); pap. 5.95 (ISBN 0-13-788182-7). P-H.
Sacker, Hugh. Introduction to Wolfram's Parzival. 1963. 42.50 (ISBN 0-521-06180-6). Cambridge U Pr.
Sacker, Hugh, ed. see Musil, Robert.
Sacker, Hugh, jt. ed. see Richey, Margaret F.
Sackerville, Wellington De see De Sackerville, Wellington.
Sackett, Patrick L. The Power of Autosuggestion & How to Master It. (Illus.). 1979. deluxe ed. 37.55 (ISBN 0-930582-61-6). Gloucester Art.
Sackett, S. J. Edgar Watson Howe. (U. S. Authors Ser.: No. 195). lib. bdg. 10.95 (ISBN 0-8057-0383-7). Twayne.
Sackheim, Gertrude. The Practice of Clinical Casework. LC 73-19787. 212p. 1974. text ed. 14.95 (ISBN 0-87705-141-0). Human Sci Pr.
Sackman, Harold & Boehm, Barry W., eds. Planning Community Information Utilities. LC 72-83727. (Illus.). viii, 501p. 1972. 15.00 (ISBN 0-88283-000-7). AFIPS Pr.
Sackman, Harold & Nie, Norman, eds. The Information Utility & Social Choice. LC 78-129364. (Illus.). 310p. 1970. 9.00 (ISBN 0-88283-019-8). AFIPS Pr.
Sackner. Diagnostic Techniques in Pulmonary Disease, Pt. 1. 746p. 1980. 49.50 (ISBN 0-8247-1059-2). Dekker.
Sackrey, Charles. The Political Economy of Urban Poverty. 172p. 1972. pap. 4.95x (ISBN 0-393-09410-3, NortonC). Norton.
Sacks. Welding: Principles & Practices. rev. ed. (gr. 10-12). 1981. text ed. 24.40 (ISBN 0-87002-321-7). Bennett IL.
Sacks, Elizabeth. Shakespeare's Images of Pregnancy. 1980. 16.95 (ISBN 0-312-71595-1). St Martin.
Sacks, G. E. Saturated Model Theory. (Mathematics Lecture Series: No. 52). 1972. pap. text ed. 12.50 (ISBN 0-8053-8381-6, Adv Bk Prog). Benjamin Cummings.
Sacks, Howard R., jt. auth. see Silver, Theodore.
Sacks, Michael P. Women's Work in Soviet Russia: Continuity in the Midst of Change. LC 75-19813. (Special Studies). 1976. 19.95 o.p. (ISBN 0-275-55790-1). Praeger.
Sacks, Michael P., jt. ed. see Pankhurst, Jerry.
Sacks, Paul M., jt. ed. see Maisel, Louis.
Sacks, Raymond. Welding: Principles & Practice. (gr. 10-12). 1976. text ed. 23.32 (ISBN 0-87002-073-0); student guide 4.40 (ISBN 0-87002-193-1); tchr's guide 3.60 (ISBN 0-87002-198-2). Bennett IL.
Sacks, S., jt. auth. see Campbell, A. K.
Sackson, Marian, jt. auth. see Gustavson, Frances.
Sackson, Sid. Beyond Words: Exciting New Word Games. LC 76-54201. (Illus.). 1977. pap. 2.95 o.p. (ISBN 0-394-83444-5). Pantheon.
Sackville, Thomas & Norton, Thomas. Gorboduc, or Ferrex & Porrex. Cauthen, Irby B., Jr., ed. LC 74-88095. (Regents Renaissance Drama Ser.). 1970. 6.50x (ISBN 0-8032-0288-1); pap. 1.85x (ISBN 0-8032-5289-7, BB 235, Bison). U of Nebr Pr.
Sackville-West, V. A Joy of Gardening. LC 76-39685. (Illus.). 1977. 9.95 o.s.i. (ISBN 0-06-013741-X, HarpT). Har-Row.
--V. Sackville-West's Garden Book. 1968. 13.95 o.p. (ISBN 0-7181-0536-2, Pub. by Michael Joseph). Merrimack Bk Serv.
Sacranie, Raj. Charlie Chaplin. (Profiles Ser.). (Illus.). 64p. (gr. 3-6). 1981. 7.95 (ISBN 0-241-10481-5, Pub. by Hamish Hamilton England). David & Charles.
Sadacca, Robert, et al. The Development of a Prototype Equation for Public Housing Operating Expenses. (An Institute Paper). 111p. 1975. pap. 3.00 (ISBN 0-87766-144-8, 11900). Urban Inst.
Sadan, Simcha, jt. auth. see Ronen, Joshua.
Sadananda. Vedantasara of Sadananda. pap. 1.95 o.s.i. (ISBN 0-87481-073-6). Vedanta Pr.
Sadat, Anwar. In Search of Identity: An Autobiography. LC 77-3767. (Illus.). 1979. pap. 5.95 (ISBN 0-06-090705-3, CN705, CN). Har-Row.
Sadava, David, jt. auth. see Chrispeels, Maarten J.
Sadd, Susan, jt. auth. see Tavris, Carol.
Saddhatissa, H. Buddhist Ethics: Essence of Buddhism. LC 72-138436. 1971. 6.50 o.p. (ISBN 0-8076-0598-0); pap. 2.95 o.p. (ISBN 0-8076-0597-2). Braziller.
Saddler, Hugh. Energy in Australia. 215p. 1981. text ed. 19.95x (ISBN 0-86861-298-7, 2646). Allen Unwin.
Sade, De see De Sade, Marquis.
Sade, Marquis De. One Hundred Twenty Days of Sodom & Other Writings. Wainhouse, Austryn & Seaver, Richard, eds. (Illus.). 1966. pap. 7.95 (ISBN 0-394-17119-5, B138, BC). Grove.
Sade, Marquis De see Sade, Marquis De.
Sadee, Wolfgang & Beelen, Geertruida C. Drug Level Monitoring: Analytical Techniques, Metabolism, & Pharmacokinetics. LC 79-22652. 1980. 35.00 (ISBN 0-471-04881-X, Pub. by Wiley-Interscience). Wiley.
Sadhu, Mouni. Theurgy. 1965. 12.75 o.p. (ISBN 0-04-133003-X). Allen Unwin.
Sadhu, S. L. Folk Tales from Kashmir. 4.75x o.p. (ISBN 0-210-33861-X). Asia.
Sadick, Tamah L. & Pueschal, Siegfried M., eds. Genetic Diseases & Developmental Disabilities: Aspects of Detection & Prevention. (AAAS Selected Symposium: No. 33). 1979. lib. bdg. 16.00x (ISBN 0-89158-367-X). Westview.
Sadie, Julie A. The Bass Viol in French Baroque Chamber Music. Buelow, George, ed. (Studies in Musicology). 250p. 1981. 29.95 (ISBN 0-8357-1116-1, Pub. by UMI Res Pr). Univ Microfilms.
Sadie, Stanley. Beethoven. (Great Composers Ser.). (Illus.). 1967. 7.95 o.p. (ISBN 0-571-08094-4, Pub. by Faber & Faber). Merrimack Bk Serv.
Sadie, Stanley, ed. The New Grove Dictionary of Music & Musicians, 20 vols. 1980. 1900.00 (ISBN 0-333-23111-2). Groves Dict Music.
Sadist, Golem N. Cruel & Unusual Punishments: From the Here & the Hereafter. (Odd Books for Odd Moments Ser.). (Illus.). 72p. (Orig.). 1980. pap. 3.95 (ISBN 0-938338-03-X). Winds World Pr.
Sadleir, Michael. Excursions in Victorian Bibliography. 240p. 1980. Repr. of 1922 ed. lib. bdg. 35.00 (ISBN 0-8492-8205-5). R West.
Sadler, A. L. The Maker of Modern Japan: The Life of Shogun Tokugawa Ieyasu. LC 78-54935. (Illus.). 1978. pap. 8.50 (ISBN 0-8048-1297-7). C E Tuttle.
Sadler, Alfred M., Jr., et al. Physician's Assistant: Today & Tomorrow: Issues Confronting New Health Practitioners. LC 75-22407. 1975. 16.50 (ISBN 0-88410-125-8); pap. text ed. 8.95 (ISBN 0-88410-124-X). Ballinger Pub.
Sadler, C., jt. auth. see Eisenbach, S.
Sadler, George G., ed. see MacDonald, George.
Sadler, Glenn, ed. The Fantasy Stories of George Macdonald, 4 vols. 1980. pap. 12.95 set (ISBN 0-8028-1858-7); pap. 2.95 ea. (ISBN 0-686-68801-5). Eerdmans.
Sadler, Glenn G., ed. see MacDonald, George.
Sadler, Jacqueline D., jt. auth. see Sadler, Julius T., Jr.
Sadler, Julius T., Jr. & Sadler, Jacqueline D. American Stables: An Architectural Tour. 1981. 29.95 (ISBN 0-8212-1105-6). NYGS.
Sadler, Lynn. John Bunyan. (English Authors Ser.: No. 260). 1979. lib. bdg. 10.95 (ISBN 0-8057-6757-6). Twayne.
--Thomas Carew. (English Authors Ser.: No. 214). 1979. lib. bdg. 10.95 (ISBN 0-8057-6683-9). Twayne.
Sadler, Lynn V. Consolation in Samson Agonistes. (Salzburg Institute for English Literature: No. 82). (Orig.). 1979. pap. text ed. 25.00x (ISBN 0-391-01707-1). Humanities.
Sadler, M. T. The Law of Population: A Treatise in Six Books, 2 vols. 138p. 1971. Repr. of 1830 ed. Set. 72.00x (ISBN 0-7165-1579-2, Pub. by Irish Academic Pr Ireland). Biblio Dist.
Sadler, M. T., tr. & intro. by see Kandinsky, Wassily.
Sadler, Robert & Chapian, Marie. The Emancipation of Robert Sadler. LC 75-14063. (Illus.). 256p. 1975. 7.95 (ISBN 0-87123-132-8, 230132). Bethany Fell.
--Emanicipation of Robert Sadler. LC 75-14063. 1976. pap. 3.95 (ISBN 0-87123-133-6, 210133). Bethany Fell.
Sadler, Robert, jt. auth. see Chapian, Marie.
Sadler, William A., jt. ed. see Midgley, A. Rees.
Sadler, William A., Jr. Existence & Love: A New Approach in Existential Phenomenology. LC 68-17052. 1970. pap. 3.95 o.p. (ISBN 0-684-71883-9, SL235, ScribT). Scribner.
Sadler, William S., Jr. Appendices to a Study of the Master Universe. LC 75-21657. 1975. 21.00 (ISBN 0-686-17215-9). Second Soc Foun.
Sadlier, Paul, jt. auth. see Sadlier, Ruth.
Sadlier, Ruth & Sadlier, Paul. Fifty Hikes in Vermont. rev. ed. LC 79-92572. (Fifty Hike Ser.). (Illus.). 1981. pap. 7.95 (ISBN 0-89725-013-3). NH Pub Co.
--Short Walks Along the Maine Coast. LC 76-51125. (Illus.). 1977. pap. 3.50 (ISBN 0-87106-077-9). Globe Pequot.
--Short Walks on Cape Cod. LC 75-34252. (Illus.). 896p. 1976. pap. 4.95 (ISBN 0-87106-066-3). Globe Pequot.
Sadock, Benjamin J., jt. auth. see Kaplan, Harold I.
Sadoff, Robert L. Forensic Psychiatry: A Practical Guide for Lawyers & Psychiatrists. (American Lectures in Behavioral Science & Law Ser.). 272p. 1975. 19.75 (ISBN 0-398-03412-5). C C Thomas.
Sadoul, Georges. Dictionary of Film Makers. Morris, Peter, tr. from Fr. LC 78-136028. 1972. 22.95x (ISBN 0-520-01862-1); pap. 5.95 (ISBN 0-520-02151-7, CAL241). U of Cal Pr.
--Dictionary of Films. Morris, Peter, tr. from Fr. LC 78-136028. 1972. 22.95x (ISBN 0-520-01864-8); pap. 8.95 (ISBN 0-520-02152-5, CAL240). U of Cal Pr.
Sadoul, P., ed. Muscular Exercise in Chronic Lung Disease: Proceedings of Meeting on Factors Limiting Exercise, Nancy, France, 13-15 Sept. 1978. LC 79-40806. (Special Issue of the Bulletin Europeen De Physiopathologie Respiratoire). (Illus.). 1980. 50.00 (ISBN 0-08-024930-2). Pergamon.
Sadouski, Mary, tr. see Wrangell, Ferdinand P.
Sadow, Janet, et al. Human Reproduction. 224p. 1980. 50.00x (ISBN 0-85664-878-7, Pub. by Croom Helm England). State Mutual Bk.
Sadoway, Margaret W. Owls: Hunters of the Night. LC 80-27541. (Nature Books for Young Readers). (Illus.). (gr. 3-8). 1981. PLB 5.95g (ISBN 0-8225-0293-3). Lerner Pubns.
Sadowski, Karen & Gadbois, Robert. Where's Hodgey? LC 77-1999. (Books by Children for Children). (gr. 2-5). 1977. PLB 6.45 (ISBN 0-87191-610-X). Creative Ed.
Sadowsky, George. MASH: A Computer System for Microanalytic Simulation for Policy Exploration. 158p. 1977. pap. 9.00 (ISBN 0-87766-190-1, 17600). Urban Inst.
Sadun, Elvio H., jt. auth. see Cohen, Sydney.
Saegart, Susan, ed. Crowding in Real Environments. LC 75-42756. (Sage Contemporary Social Science Issues: Vol. 25). 1976. 4.95x (ISBN 0-8039-0583-1). Sage.
Saeger, Glen. String Designs. LC 74-31703. (Little Craft Book Ser.). (Illus.). 48p. (gr. 5 up). 1975. 5.95 (ISBN 0-8069-5320-9); PLB 6.69 (ISBN 0-8069-5321-7). Sterling.
Saeks, Richard. Generalized Networks. LC 76-162146. 1972. 34.50x (ISBN 0-03-085195-5); pap. text ed. 16.50x (ISBN 0-89197-767-8). Irvington.
Saenger, Gustave, ed. see Rode, Pierre.
Saeter, Martin. The Federal Republic, Europe & the World: Perspectives in West Germany Foreign Policy. 120p. 1980. text ed. 15.00x (ISBN 82-00-05315-6). Universitet.
Safa, Helen I. Familias De Arrabal: Un Estudio Sobre Desarrollo y Desigualdad. LC 80-19853. ix, 191p. Date not set. pap. price not set (ISBN 0-8477-2455-7). U of PR Pr.
Safa, Helen I., jt. ed. see Nash, June.
Safai, Bijan & Good, Robert A., eds. Immunodermatology. (Comprehensive Immunology Ser.: Vol. 7). (Illus.). 625p. 1981. 49.50 (ISBN 0-306-40380-3, Plenum Pr). Plenum Pub.
Safar, Peter & Grenvik, Ake. Brain Failure & Resuscitation. (Clinics in Critical Care Medicine). (Illus.). 256p. 1981. lib. bdg. 22.50 (ISBN 0-443-08143-3). Churchill.
Safer, Arnold E. International Oil Policy. LC 79-7185. 192p. 1979. 14.95 (ISBN 0-669-02959-9). Lexington Bks.
Safer, D. School Programs for Disruptive Adolescents. 1981. 22.95 (ISBN 0-685-32554-7). Univ Park.
Safer, P., jt. ed. see Frey, R.
Saferstein, Richard. Criminalistics: An Introduction to Forensic Science. 2nd ed. (Criminal Justice Ser.). 1981. 18.95 (ISBN 0-686-63386-5). P-H.
Saffady, William. Micrographics. LC 78-1309. (Library Science Text Ser.). 1978. 22.50x (ISBN 0-87287-175-4). Libs Unl.
Saffell, David C. The Politics of American National Government. 4th ed. (Illus.). 560p. 1981. pap. text ed. 12.95 (ISBN 0-87626-641-3). Winthrop.
--State & Local Government: Politics & Public Policies. LC 77-76119. (Political Science Ser.). 1978. pap. text ed. 11.95 (ISBN 0-201-06806-0); instr's manual & tests 1.50 (ISBN 0-201-06809-5). A-W.
Saffen, Wayne, jt. auth. see Malte, Paul R.
Saffon, M. J. The Fifteen Minute-a-Day Natural Face Lift. 112p. 1981. pap. 3.95 (ISBN 0-446-97788-8). Warner Bks.
Safford, E. L., Jr. Radio Control Manual: Systems, Circuits, Construction. 3rd ed. (Illus.). 1979. pap. 7.95 (ISBN 0-8306-1135-5, 1135). TAB Bks.
Safford, Ed. Aviation Electronics Handbook. LC 72-97217. (Illus.). 406p. 1975. pap. 8.95 (ISBN 0-8306-4631-0, 631). TAB Bks.
Safford, Edward L. Flying Model Airplanes & Helicopters by Radio Control. (Illus.). 1977. pap. 5.95 (ISBN 0-8306-6825-X, 825). TAB Bks.
Safford, Edward L., Jr. Advanced Radio Control. LC 65-22390. (Illus., Orig.). 1965. 7.95 (ISBN 0-8306-4122-X, 122); pap. 4.95 (ISBN 0-8306-5122-5). TAB Bks.
--Electrical Wiring & Lighting for Home & Office. LC 73-86765. (Illus.). 204p. 1974. 7.95 o.p. (ISBN 0-8306-3671-4); pap. 4.95 (ISBN 0-8306-2671-9, 671). TAB Bks.
Safford, Frank. The Ideal of the Practical: Colombia's Struggle to Form a Technical Elite. (Latin American Monographs: No. 39). 290p. 1975. 20.00 (ISBN 0-292-73803-X). U of Tex Pr.
Safford, Jeffrey J. Wilsonian Maritime Diplomacy: 1913-1921. 1978. 20.00 (ISBN 0-8135-0850-9). Rutgers U Pr.
Safford, Philip L. & Arbitman, Dena C. Developmental Intervention with Young Physically Handicapped Children. (Illus.). 336p. 1975. 28.75 (ISBN 0-398-03326-9). C C Thomas.
Saffron, Morris H. Surgeon to Washington: Dr. John Cochran (1730-1807) LC 77-2675. 1977. 20.00x (ISBN 0-231-04186-1). Columbia U Pr.
Saffron, Robert. The Demon Device. 288p. 1981. pap. 2.50 (ISBN 0-441-14255-9). Charter Bks.
Safilios-Rothschild, Constantina. Love, Sex & Sex Roles. LC 76-44439. 1977. 9.95 (ISBN 0-13-540948-9, Spec); pap. 5.95 (ISBN 0-13-540930-6). P-H.
--Women & Social Policy. (P-H Series in Social Policy). 224p. 1974. pap. 8.95 ref. ed. (ISBN 0-13-961680-2). P-H.
Safilios-Rothschild, Constantina, ed. Toward a Sociology of Women. LC 70-168398. (Illus., Orig.). 1972. pap. text ed. 12.95 (ISBN 0-471-00685-8). Wiley.
Safir, Aran. Refraction & Clinical Optics. (Illus.). 565p. 1980. text ed. 37.50 (ISBN 0-06-142318-1, Harper Medical). Har-Row.
Safire, William. The New Language of Politics. rev ed. 544p. 1972. pap. 4.95 o.s.i. (ISBN 0-02-074700-4, Collier). Macmillan.
--On Language. 1980. 13.95 (ISBN 0-8129-0937-2). Times Bks.
--Safire's Washington. 416p. 1980. 15.00 (ISBN 0-8129-0919-4). Times Bks.
Safonov, jt. auth. see Dodge.
Safran, Nadav. From War to War: The Arab-Israeli Confrontation 1948-1967. LC 68-27991. 1969. 10.00 o.p. (ISBN 0-672-53540-8); pap. 9.95 (ISBN 0-672-63540-2). Pegasus.
Safran, Rose. Don't Go Dancing Mother. LC 79-64288. (Illus.). 1979. pap. 4.95 (ISBN 0-9602786-1-3). Tide Bk Pub Co.
--Woman Ahead of Her Time. 1981. pap. 5.95 (ISBN 0-9602786-2-1). Tide Bk Pub Co.
Safran, William. French Polity. LC 76-58487. (Comparative Studies of Political Life Ser.). 1977. pap. 9.95x (ISBN 0-582-28102-4, Pub. by MacKay). Longman.
Safran, William, jt. auth. see Codding, George A., Jr.
Safrit, Margaret J. Evaluation in Physical Education. 2nd ed. (Illus.). 1980. text ed. 15.95 (ISBN 0-13-292250-9). P-H.
--Evaluation in Physical Education: Assessing Motor Behavior. LC 72-5427. (Illus.). 336p. 1973. text ed. 15.95x (ISBN 0-13-292227-4). P-H.
Sagafi-nejad, Tagi & Belfield, Robert. Transnational Corporations, Technology Transfer & Development: A Bibliographic Sourcebook. LC 80-36887. (Pergamon Policy Studies on International Development). 150p. Date not set. 25.00 (ISBN 0-08-026299-6). Pergamon.
Sagafi-Nejad, Tagi, jt. auth. see Perlmutter, Howard V.
Sagafi-nejad, Tagi, et al, eds. Controlling International Technology Transfer: Issues, Perspectives, & Policy Implications. LC 80-28329. (PPS on International Development Ser.). 525p. 1981. 55.00. Pergamon.
Sagal, Paul T. Skinner's Philosophy. LC 80-5737. 132p. 1981. lib. bdg. 15.75 (ISBN 0-8191-1432-4); pap. text ed. 7.50 (ISBN 0-8191-1433-2). U Pr of Amer.
Sagan, Carl. Broca's Brain. 384p. 1980. pap. 2.95 (ISBN 0-345-28823-8). Ballantine.
--Cosmic Connection: An Extraterrestrial Perspective. LC 80-1867. (Illus.). 288p. 1980. pap. 5.95 (ISBN 0-385-17365-2, Anch). Doubleday.
--The Dragons of Eden. 1978. pap. 2.50 (ISBN 0-345-28153-5). Ballantine.
Sagan, Carl & Shklovskii, I. S. Intelligent Life in the Universe. LC 64-18404. 1978. pap. text ed. 12.50x (ISBN 0-8162-7913-6). Holden-Day.
Sagan, Francois. Lost Profile. 192p. 1976. 6.95 o.s.i. (ISBN 0-440-05017-0). Delacorte.
Sagan, Francoise. Brigitte Bardot: Woman from 30 to 40. Sachs, Judith, tr. from Fr. 1977. pap. 6.95 o.s.i. (ISBN 0-440-00609-0, E Friede). Delacorte.

--Nightbird. (Clarkson N. Potter Bks.). (Illus.). 1980. 9.95 (ISBN 0-517-54224-2). Crown.

--Silken Eyes. Kilmartin, Joanna, tr. from French. 1977. 6.95 o.s.i. (ISBN 0-440-08308-7, E Friede). Delacorte.

--The Unmade Bed. 1978. 9.95 o.s.i. (ISBN 0-440-09212-4, E Friede). Delacorte.

Sagan, Hans. Beat the Odds: Microcomputer Simulations of Casino Games. 192p. 1980. pap. 7.95 (ISBN 0-8104-5181-6). Hayden.

Sagan, Hans & Meyer, Carl D., Jr. Ten Easy Pieces: Creative Programming for Fun & Profit. 192p. 1980. pap. 7.95 (ISBN 0-8104-5160-3). Hayden.

Sagan, Leonard A., ed. Human & Ecologic Effects of Nuclear Power Plants. (Illus.). 560p. 1974. 47.75 (ISBN 0-398-02929-6). C C Thomas.

Sagar, K. The Art of D. H. Lawrence. 279p. 1976. 42.00 (ISBN 0-521-06181-4); pap. 10.95 (ISBN 0-521-09387-2). Cambridge U Pr.

--The Art of Ted Hughes. 2nd ed. LC 77-90217. 1978. 44.00 (ISBN 0-521-21954-X); pap. 10.95 (ISBN 0-521-29321-9). Cambridge U Pr.

Sagarin, Edward, ed. Criminology: New Concerns. LC 79-14116. (Focus Editions Ser.: Vol. 10). (Illus.). 1979. 18.95x (ISBN 0-8039-1275-7); pap. 9.95x (ISBN 0-8039-1276-5). Sage.

--Other Minorities: Nonethnic Collectivities Conceptualized As Minority Groups. LC 77-126631. (Orig.). 1971. pap. text ed. 10.50 (ISBN 0-471-00498-7). Wiley.

--Taboos in Criminology. LC 80-18175. (Sage Research Progress Ser. in Criminology: Vol. 15). 152p. 1980. 12.95 (ISBN 0-8039-1513-6); pap. 6.50 (ISBN 0-8039-1514-4). Sage.

Sagarin, Edward, jt. ed. see Balsam, M. S.

Sagarin, Edward, jt. ed. see Thornberry, Terence P.

Sagarra, Eda. An Introduction to Nineteenth Century Germany. (Illus.). 1981. text ed. 14.95x (ISBN 0-582-35138-3); pap. text ed. 6.95x (ISBN 0-582-35137-5). Longman.

Sagasti, Francisco R. Technology, Planning & Self-Reliant Development: A Latin American View. LC 78-26010. (Praeger Special Studies). 1979. 22.95 (ISBN 0-03-047221-0). Praeger.

Sagay, J. O. & Wilson, D. A. Africa, A Modern History: Eighteen Hundred to Nineteen Seventy Five. LC 79-16594. (Illus.). 1980. text ed. 22.50x (ISBN 0-8419-0542-8, Africana); pap. text ed. 13.95x (ISBN 0-8419-0543-6, Africana). Holmes & Meier.

Sage, Andrew P. & White, Chelsea C. Optimum Systems Control. 2nd ed. (Illus.). 1977. ref. ed. 26.95 (ISBN 0-13-638296-7). P-H.

Sage, Andrew P., jt. auth. see Melsa, James L.

Sage, Daniel D., jt. auth. see Burrello, Leonard C.

Sage, Daniel D., ed. New Special Education Administrative Training Simulator (NSEATS) (Illus.). 1980. Data Bank, 1-9. 9.00 (ISBN 0-685-82631-7); 10-24 8.00 (ISBN 0-685-82632-5); 25 & over 7.00 (ISBN 0-685-82633-3); participants consumable booklet 11.00 (ISBN 0-8156-8103-8); inst. manual 9.00 (ISBN 0-8156-8104-6); package of 25 participant's booklets, 25 sets of data bank, 1 inst. manual 400.00. Syracuse U Pr.

Sage, George, jt. ed. see Luschen, Gunther.

Sage, George H. Introduction to Motor Behavior: A Neuro-Psychological Approach. 2nd ed. LC 76-14660. (A-W Physical Ed Ser.). 1977. text ed. 21.95 (ISBN 0-201-06766-8). A-W.

--Sport & American Society: Selected Readings. 3rd ed. LC 79-25573. (Physical Education Ser.). 1980. text ed. 9.50 (ISBN 0-201-06717-X). A-W.

Sage, Jacquelyn, jt. auth. see Grimm.

Sage, Jacquelyn, tr. see Grimm & Sage, Jacquelyn.

Sagen, Leda V., tr. see Konovalov, S. M.

Sager, Alan. Planning Home Care for the Elderly. Date not set. pns professional reference (ISBN 0-88410-725-6). Ballinger Pub.

Sager, G. R., jt. ed. see Cherrett, J. M.

Sager, J. C., jt. auth. see Mason, K. L.

Sager, J. C., ed. Standardization of Nomenclature: International Journal of the Sociology of Language, No. 23. 1980. pap. text ed. 21.95x (ISBN 90-279-3028-7). Mouton.

Sager, Naomi. Natural Language Information Processing: A Computer Grammmar of English & Its Applications. 1980. text ed. 37.50 (ISBN 0-201-06769-2). A-W.

Saggs, H. W. The Encounter with the Divine in Mesopotamia & Israel. (Jordan Lectures in Comparative Religion, 12th Ser). 1978. text ed. 31.25x (ISBN 0-485-17412-X, Athlone Pr). Humanities.

Sagnier, Thierry. Bike! Motorcycles & the People Who Ride Them. LC 72-9151. (Illus.). 208p. 1974. 10.95 o.p. (ISBN 0-06-013736-3, HarpT); pap. 3.95 o.s.i. (ISBN 0-06-013743-6, TD-199, HarpT). Har-Row.

Sagstetter, Brad. The Venison Handbook. LC 80-84354. (Illus., Orig.). 1981. 5.95 (ISBN 0-89896-075-4). Larksdale.

Sagstetter, Brad, jt. auth. see Viner, Jim.

Sagstetter, Brad. Conceived in Liberty: American Individual Rights Today. LC 77-18506. 1978. pap. 6.95 (ISBN 0-87872-162-2). Duxbury Pr.

Sagstetter, Karen. Lobbying. (American Government Ser.). (Illus.). (gr. 7 up). 1978. PLB 6.90 s&l (ISBN 0-531-01413-4). Watts.

Sagues, Paul, jt. auth. see Auslander, David.

Saha, P. & Farukhi, N. M., eds. Scaling in Two-Phase Flows. (HTD: Vol. 14). 53p. 1980. 12.00 (G00187). ASME.

Saha, P. K. Blue Magic. 80p. 1975. 14.00 (ISBN 0-88253-825-X); pap. 8.00 (ISBN 0-88253-826-8). Ind-US Inc.

--Poems from the Fifties. 8.00 (ISBN 0-89253-726-4). Ind-US Inc.

Saha, S. C. The Ruins of the Morning. 8.00 (ISBN 0-89253-729-9); flexible cloth 4.00 (ISBN 0-89253-730-2). Ind-US Inc.

--The Unseen Bird. 6.75 (ISBN 0-89253-727-2); flexible cloth 4.00 (ISBN 0-89253-728-0). Ind-US Inc.

Saha, Subhas C. Down the Silent Night Road. (Writers Workshop Redbird Book Ser.). 72p. 1975. 12.00 (ISBN 0-88253-530-7); pap. text ed. 4.80 (ISBN 0-88253-529-3). Ind-US Inc.

--Insights. (Writers Workshop Greybird Ser.). 109p. 1975. 8.00 (ISBN 0-88253-568-4); pap. text ed. 4.00 (ISBN 0-88253-567-6). Ind-US Inc.

--Modern Indo-Anglian Love Poetry. (Writer's Workshop Greybird Ser.). 46p. 1975. 5.00 (ISBN 0-88253-578-1); pap. text ed. 4.00 (ISBN 0-88253-577-3). Ind-US Inc.

--The Other Side. (Redbird Ser). 35p. 1975. 8.00 (ISBN 0-88253-598-6); pap. text ed. 4.00 (ISBN 0-88253-597-8). Ind-US Inc.

--The Under World. (Redbird Ser.). 1975. 8.00 (ISBN 0-88253-666-4); pap. text ed. 4.00 (ISBN 0-88253-665-6). Ind-US Inc.

Sahade, J. & Wood, F. Interacting Binary Stars. 1978. text ed. 30.00 (ISBN 0-08-021656-0). Pergamon.

Sahadi, Lou. The Steeler Gang. (gr. 7-12). 1977. pap. 1.25 o.p. (ISBN 0-590-10321-0, Schol Pap). Schol Bk Serv.

--Super Steelers: The Making of a Dynasty. 256p. 1980. 14.95 (ISBN 0-8129-0950-X). Times Bks.

--Super Sundays -- One to Thirteen. LC 79-50991. (Illus.). 1979. pap. 7.95 o.p. (ISBN 0-8092-7445-0). Contemp Bks.

Sahagun, Fray B. De see De Sahagun, Bernardino.

Sahai, Bhagwant. Iconography of Minor Hindu & Buddhist Deities. LC 75-904218. (Illus.). 1975. 26.00x o.p. (ISBN 0-88386-610-2). South Asia Bks.

Sahakian, Mabel, jt. auth. see Sahakian, William.

Sahakian, Mabel L. & Sahakian, William S. John Locke. (World Leaders Ser.: No. 40). 1975. lib. bdg. 9.95 (ISBN 0-8057-3539-9). Twayne.

Sahakian, Mabel L., jt. auth. see Sahakian, William S.

Sahakian, William & Sahakian, Mabel. Plato. (World Leaders Ser.: No. 66). 1977. lib. bdg. 9.95 (ISBN 0-8057-7690-7). Twayne.

Sahakian, William S. Ethics: An Introduction to Theories & Problems. 272p. (Orig.). 1974. pap. 3.95 (ISBN 0-06-460139-0, CO 139, COS). Har-Row.

--History & Systems of Social Psychology. 2nd ed. LC 80-2137. (Illus.). 624p. Date not set. text ed. 24.50 (ISBN 0-89116-179-1); pap. text ed. 16.95 (ISBN 0-89116-191-0). Hemisphere Pub.

--History of Philosophy. (Orig.). 1968. pap. 4.95 (ISBN 0-06-460002-5, 2, COS). Har-Row.

Sahakian, William S. & Sahakian, Mabel L. Ideas of the Great Philosophers. (Orig.). 1966. pap. 3.95 (ISBN 0-06-463218-0, EH 218, EH). Har-Row.

Sahakian, William S., jt. auth. see Sahakian, Mabel L.

Saham, Junid. British Industrial Investment in Malaysia, Nineteen Sixty-Three to Nineteen Seventy-One. (East Asian Social Science Monographs). 366p. 1981. 37.00 (ISBN 0-19-580418-X). Oxford U Pr.

Sahay, Arun. Sociological Analysis. (International Library of Sociology). 220p. 1972. 17.50x (ISBN 0-7100-7363-1). Routledge & Kegan.

Sahgal, Nayantara. This Time of Morning. 221p. 1969. pap. 1.95 (ISBN 0-88253-079-8). Ind-US Inc.

Sahi, Jyoti. The Child & the Serpent: Refelctions on Popular Indian Symbols. (Illus.). 192p. (Orig.). 1980. pap. 18.50 (ISBN 0-7100-0704-3). Routledge & Kegan.

Sahler, Olle J. The Child & Death. LC 78-18239. (Illus.). 1978. pap. text ed. 14.95 (ISBN 0-8016-4288-4). Mosby.

--The Child from Three to Eighteen. (Illus.). 260p. 1981. softcover 12.50 (ISBN 0-8016-4290-6). Mosby.

Sahlins, Marshall. Culture & Practical Reason. LC 75-27899. (Illus.). 1978. pap. 5.95 (ISBN 0-226-73361-0, P773, Phoen). U of Chicago Pr.

Sahlins, Marshall D. Tribesmen. (Illus., Orig.). 1968. pap. 6.95 ref. ed. (ISBN 0-13-930925-X). P-H.

Sahni, Bhisham. The Boss Came to Dinner & Other Stories. Ratan, Jai, et al, trs. from Hindi. (Greenbird Book). 95p. 1975. 14.00 (ISBN 0-88253-264-2); pap. 6.75 (ISBN 0-88253-720-2). Ind-US Inc.

Sahni, Chaman L. E. M. Forster: The Religious Dimension. 160p. 1981. text ed. write for info. (ISBN 0-391-02201-6). Humanities.

Sahni, Julie. Classic Indian Cooking. LC 80-19475. (Illus.). 320p. 1980. 15.95 (ISBN 0-688-03721-6). Morrow.

Sahni, Kalpana, ed. Reminiscences of Tolstoy. 144p. 1981. text ed. 10.00 (ISBN 0-391-02021-8). Humanities.

Sahs, A. L., et al, eds. Stroke: Cause, Prevention, Treatment & Rehabilitation. (Illus.). 1978. 36.00x o.p. (ISBN 0-7194-0003-1). Intl Ideas.

Sahs, Adolph L., et al. Aneurysmal Subarachnoid Hemorrhage: Report of the Cooperative Study. (Illus.). write for info. (ISBN 0-8067-1861-7). Urban & S.

Sahtouris, Miltos. With Face to the Wall. Friar, Kimon, tr. 1980. 7.50 (ISBN 0-685-54466-4). Charioteer.

Sahukar, Mani. Sai Baba, the Saint of Shirdi. LC 75-29273. 1977. 3.95 o.p. (ISBN 0-913922-11-0). Dawn Horse Pr.

Saibel, Bob. Iran: A People in Revolution. (Illus.). 352p. 1981. 21.95 (ISBN 0-916650-14-6); pap. 6.95 (ISBN 0-916650-15-4). Banner Pr IL.

Said, Abdul A. & Lerche, Charles Q. Concepts of International Politics: A Global Perspective. 3rd ed. 1979. text ed. 16.95 (ISBN 0-13-166033-0). P-H.

Said, Abdul A., ed. Ethnicity & U. S. Foreign Policy. LC 77-7812. (Praeger Special Studies). 1978. 22.95 (ISBN 0-03-021806-3). Praeger.

--Human Rights & World Order. LC 78-62438. 1978. 22.95 (ISBN 0-03-046341-6). Praeger.

Said, Edward. Covering Islam: How the Media & the Experts Determine How We See the Rest of the World. 1981. 10.95 (ISBN 0-394-51319-3); pap. 3.95 (ISBN 0-394-74808-5). Pantheon.

Said, Edward W. Orientalism. LC 79-10497. 1979. pap. 5.95 (ISBN 0-394-74067-X, Vin). Random.

Said, Marie-Bernard, tr. see Bernard Of Clairvaux.

Saide, Julie. New Grammar of the Arabic Language, 4 vols. pap. text ed. 22.00x (ISBN 0-686-63573-6). Intl Bk Ctr.

Saidi, F. Surgery of Hydatid Disease. LC 74-4587. (Illus.). 1976. text ed. 50.00 (ISBN 0-7216-7900-5). Saunders.

Saidin, Ahmad, jt. auth. see Gladwin, Thomas.

Saidman, Lawrence J. & Smith, N. Ty. Monitoring in Anesthesia. LC 77-12506. (Anesthesiology Ser.). 1977. 33.50 (ISBN 0-471-74980-X, Pub. by Wiley Medical). Wiley.

Saigado, Gamini, ed. D. H. Lawrence: Sons & Lovers. (Casebook Ser.). 1970. 2.50 o.s.i. (ISBN 0-87695-041-1). Aurora Pubs.

Saiger, Lydia. The Junk Food Cookbook. (Orig.). 1979. pap. 2.50 (ISBN 0-515-05740-1). Jove Pubns.

Saigusa, Mitsuyoshi, tr. Studien Zum Mahaprajnaparamita (Upadesa) Sastra. (Ger.). 1969. 39.50 o.p. (ISBN 0-89346-097-4, Pub. by Hokuseido Pr). Heian Intl.

Saila, Saul B., ed. Coastal & Offshore Environmental Inventory: Cape Hatteras to Nantucket Shoals. LC 72-619712. (Marine Publications Ser.). 1973. No. 2. pap. 10.00 (ISBN 0-938412-04-3); No. 3. pap. 5.00, complementary vol. (ISBN 0-686-09595-2). URI MAS.

--Fisheries & Energy Production. LC 74-32513. 1975. 18.95 (ISBN 0-669-98467-1). Lexington Bks.

Sailaja, P. & Rao, K. R. Experimental Studies of the Differential Effect in Life Setting. LC 72-84013. (Parapsychological Monograph No. 13). 1973. pap. 3.50 (ISBN 0-912328-20-7). Parapsych Foun.

Sailor, Wayne, ed. Methods of Instruction for Severely Handicapped Students. LC 80-16668. (Illus.). 352p. (Orig.). 1980. pap. text ed. 16.95 (ISBN 0-933716-06-0). P H Brookes.

Sain, Michael K. Introduction to Algebraic System Theory. LC 80-522. (Mathematics in Science & Engineering Ser.). 1981. write for info. (ISBN 0-12-614850-3). Acad Pr.

Saindower, Charles R. The Metaphysics of American Civilization. (An American Culture Library Book). (Illus.). 1979. 37.75 (ISBN 0-89266-201-8). Am Classical Coll Pr.

Saine, Thomas, jt. auth. see Burgoon, Judee K.

Saine, Thomas P. Georg Forster. (World Authors Ser.: Germany: No. 215). lib. bdg. 10.95 (ISBN 0-8057-2316-1). Twayne.

Sainer, Elliot A., jt. ed. see Hyman, Andrew A.

Saini, Balwant S. Building in Hot Dry Climates. LC 79-41777. 176p. 1980. 44.00 (ISBN 0-471-27764-9, Pub. by Wiley-Interscience). Wiley.

Sainsaulieu, Renaud. L' Identite au Travail: Les effets culturels de l'organisation. 1977. lib. bdg. 40.00x (ISBN 2-7246-0386-9); pap. text ed. 32.50x (ISBN 2-7246-0385-0). Clearwater Pub.

Sainsbury, David & Sainsbury, Peter. Livestock Health & Housing. 2nd ed. 388p. 1979. pap. 27.50 (ISBN 0-8121-0751-9). Lea & Febiger.

Sainsbury, Eric. Social Work with Families. (Library of Social Work). 1975. 15.00x (ISBN 0-7100-8039-5); pap. 7.45 (ISBN 0-7100-8040-9). Routledge & Kegan.

Sainsbury, Isobel S. The Milk-Free & Milk-Free, Egg-Free Cookbook. 160p. 1974. pap. text ed. 14.75 (ISBN 0-398-03108-8). C C Thomas.

Sainsbury, John. Sainsbury's Woodturning Projects for Dining. LC 80-54347. (Illus.). 160p. 1981. 14.95 (ISBN 0-8069-5436-1). Sterling.

Sainsbury, John C. Commercial Fishing Methods: An Introduction to Vessels & Gear. (Illus.). 120p. 13.75 (ISBN 0-85238-076-3, FN). Unipub.

Sainsbury, Mark. Russell. (The Arguments of the Philosophers Ser.). 1979. 36.00x (ISBN 0-7100-0155-X). Routledge & Kegan.

Sainsbury, Peter, jt. auth. see Sainsbury, David.

Sainsbury, Sally. Measuring Disability. 125p. 1973. pap. text ed. 6.25x (ISBN 0-7135-1899-5, Pub. by Bedford England). Renouf.

--Registered As Disabled. 205p. 1970. pap. text ed. 6.25x (ISBN 0-7135-1619-4, Pub. by Bedford England). Renouf.

St. Alphonsus de Liguori. The Glories of Mary. LC 79-112485. 1977. pap. 10.00 (ISBN 0-89555-021-0, 187). TAN Bks Pubs.

Saint, Andrew. Richard Norman Shaw. LC 75-43333. (Studies in British Art Ser.). 1976. 55.00x (ISBN 0-300-01955-6). Yale U Pr.

St. Aubyn, F. C. Arthur Rimbaud. (Twayne's World Authors Ser.: France: No. 369). 1975. lib. bdg. 12.50 (ISBN 0-8057-6192-6). Twayne.

St. Augustine. The City of God. LC 58-5717. 4.50 (ISBN 0-385-02910-1). Doubleday.

Saint, Avice M. Learning at Work: Human Resources & Organizational Development. LC 73-81275. 1974. 19.95 (ISBN 0-911012-22-2); pap. 10.95x (ISBN 0-88229-575-6). Nelson-Hall.

St. Basil The Great. On the Holy Spirit. Anderson, David, tr. from Gr. (Orig.). 1980. pap. 3.95 (ISBN 0-913836-74-5). St Vladimirs.

St. Bernard de Clairvaux. Letters. James, Bruno S., tr. LC 78-63344. (Crusades Ser.). 552p. 1980. Repr. of 1953 ed. 47.50 (ISBN 0-404-17004-8). AMS Pr.

St. Catherine Of Siena. The Dialogue of St. Catherine of Siena. Thorold, Algar, tr. from It. & intro. by. 1976. pap. 4.00 (ISBN 0-89555-037-7, 150). TAN Bks Pubs.

St. Clair, Leonard. The Seadon Fortune. 1979. pap. 2.25 o.p. (ISBN 0-425-03865-3). Berkley Pub.

St. Clair, William. Trelawny: The Incurable Romancer. LC 77-84020. (Illus.). 1978. 12.95 (ISBN 0-8149-0792-X). Vanguard.

St. Claire, Jessica. Cerissa. Date not set. pap. 2.25 (ISBN 0-686-66186-9, Leisure Bks). Nordon Pubns.

St. Denis, Albert, ed. Success Oriented Supervision. rev. ed. 1980. 44.15 (ISBN 0-87771-019-8). Grad School.

St. Etienne, Galerie. Kaethe Kollwitz. (Illus.). 1976. pap. 7.00 (ISBN 0-910810-18-4). Johannes.

St. George, Edith. West of the Moon. 192p. 1981. pap. 1.50 (ISBN 0-671-57069-2). S&S.

St. George, George. Soviet Deserts & Mountains. (The World's Wild Places Ser.). (Illus.). 184p. 1974. 12.95 (ISBN 0-8094-2012-0). Time-Life.

--Soviet Deserts & Mountains. (The World's Wild Places Ser.). (Illus.). 1978. lib. bdg. 11.97 (ISBN 0-686-51024-0). Silver.

St. George, Judith. Call Me Margo. 156p. (gr. 10 up). 1981. 7.95 (ISBN 0-399-20790-2). Putnam.

--Haunted. 156p. (YA) (gr. 7-12). 1980. 7.95 (ISBN 0-399-20736-8). Putnam.

St. Germain. Studies in Alchemy. (Alchemy Ser.). (Illus.). 92p. 1974. pap. 3.95 (ISBN 0-916766-00-4). Summit Univ.

St. James, Blakely. Christina's Desire. LC 77-88263. (Christina Van Bell Ser.: No. 7). 1978. pap. 2.25 (ISBN 0-87216-734-8). Playboy Pbks.

--Christina's Ecstasy. LC 80-82855. (Christina Ser.). 256p. (Orig.). 1981. pap. 2.50 (ISBN 0-87216-782-8). Playboy Pbks.

--Christina's Nights. LC 77-72969. (Christina Van Bell Ser.: No. 6). (Orig.). 1977. pap. 2.25 (ISBN 0-87216-739-9). Playboy Pbks.

--Christina's Obsession. LC 81-80095. 256p. (Orig.). 1981. pap. 2.75 (ISBN 0-87216-853-0). Playboy Pbks.

--Christina's Sins. LC 80-81522. (Christina Ser.). 256p. 1980. pap. 2.25 (ISBN 0-87216-729-1). Playboy Pbks.

--A Kiss for Christina. LC 80-83597. 256p. (Orig.). 1981. pap. 2.50 (ISBN 0-87216-793-3). Playboy Pbks.

St. James, Ian. Balfour Conspiracy. LC 80-69378. 1981. 10.95 (ISBN 0-689-11140-1). Atheneum.
--The Money Stones. LC 80-65984. 1980. 9.95 (ISBN 0-689-11104-5). Atheneum.
St. James, Warren. NAACP: Triumphs of a Pressure Group 1909-1980. (Biblio. Index Notes Ser.). (Illus.). 288p. 1980. 11.95 (ISBN 0-682-49605-7, University). Exposition.
St. Jerome, tr. Douay-Rheims New Testament. LC 77-80634. 1977. pap. 5.50 (ISBN 0-89555-001-6). TAN Bks Pubs.
St. John, Christopher, ed. Ellen Terry & Bernard Shaw: A Correspondence. LC 78-76887. 3.25 (ISBN 0-87830-043-0). Theatre Arts.
St. John, Gladys. Listening Across the Border. 1981. 8.95 (ISBN 0-533-04797-8). Vantage.
St. John, Michael. From Arithmetic to Algebra. 132p. (Orig.). 1980. pap. text ed. 4.50 (ISBN 0-937354-00-7, TX-334-207). Delta Systems.
St. John, Nancy H. School Desegregation: Outcomes for Children. LC 74-18492. 192p. 1975. 20.95 o.p. (ISBN 0-471-82633-2, Pub. by Wiley-Interscience). Wiley.
St. John, Nicole. Guinevere's Gift. 1979. pap. 1.95 (ISBN 0-446-89881-3). Warner Bks.
--The Medici Ring. 1975. 6.95 o.p. (ISBN 0-394-49342-7). Random.
St. John, Patricia. Treasures of the Snow. (gr. 5-8). 1950. pap. 2.50 (ISBN 0-8024-0008-6). Moody.
--Twice Freed. pap. 1.95 (ISBN 0-8024-8979-6). Moody.
St. John, Patricia M. Rainbow Garden. (gr. 2-5). pap. 2.50 (ISBN 0-8024-0028-0). Moody.
--Star of Light. (gr. 5-8). 1953. pap. 2.50 (ISBN 0-8024-0004-3). Moody.
--The Tanglewoods' Secret. (gr. 5-8). 1951. pap. 2.50 (ISBN 0-8024-0007-8). Moody.
St. John, Wylly F. The Ghost Next Door. (Illus.). (gr. 4-7). 1980. pap. 1.75 (ISBN 0-671-56084-0). Archway.
--The Mystery of the Gingerbread House. (Illus.). (YA) (gr. 9-12). 1977. pap. 1.95 (ISBN 0-380-01731-8, 45716, Camelot). Avon.
--The Mystery of the Other Girl. 1977. pap. 1.50 (ISBN 0-380-01926-4, 48207, Camelot). Avon.
--The Secret of the Seven Crows. (Illus.). (gr. 3-5). 1975. pap. 1.75 (ISBN 0-380-00433-X, 51763, Camelot). Avon.
--The Secrets of Hidden Creek. 1976. pap. 1.75 (ISBN 0-380-00746-0, 51359, Camelot). Avon.
--Uncle Robert's Secret. 1978. pap. 1.50 (ISBN 0-380-00909-9, 46326, Camelot). Avon.
St. Johns, Adela R. Final Verdict. pap. 2.50 (ISBN 0-451-07994-9, E7994, Sig). NAL.
St. Johns, Adela Rogers. Love, Laughter & Tears. LC 76-50786. 1978. 10.00 o.p. (ISBN 0-385-12054-0). Doubleday.
St. John-Stevas, Norman. Obscenity & the Law. LC 74-8011. (Civil Liberties in American History Ser.). 289p. 1974. Repr. of 1956 ed. lib. bdg. 27.50 (ISBN 0-306-70602-4). Da Capo.
St. John Thomas, David. The Breakfast Book. LC 80-69350. (Illus.). 96p. 1981. 11.95x (ISBN 0-7153-8094-X). David & Charles.
--A Regional History of the Railways of Great Britian: Volume I, The West Country. LC 80-70296. (Illus.). 256p. 1981. 28.00 (ISBN 0-7153-8152-0). David & Charles.
St. John Thomas, David, ed. Good Books Come from Devon. LC 80-70289. (Illus.). 108p. 1981. pap. 5.95 (ISBN 0-7153-8139-3). David & Charles.
St. John Williams, Guy & Hyland, Francis. The Irish Derby: Eighteen Sixty-Six to Nineteen Seventy-Nine. (Illus.). 432p. 1980. 40.00 (ISBN 0-85131-358-2). J A Allen.
St. Lawrence, Patricia, et al. The Experimental Geneticist: An Introductory Laboratory Manual. (Illus.). 1974. pap. 7.95x (ISBN 0-7167-0588-5); lab separates 0.50 ea. (ISBN 0-685-39560-X); instr's guide avail. W H Freeman.
St. Leger-Gordon, Douglas. Portrait of Devon. LC 66-4363. (Portrait Bks.). (Illus.). 192p. 1966. 10.50x (ISBN 0-7091-1858-9). Intl Pubns Serv.
St. Leonard. The Hidden Treasure: Holy Mass. 1971. pap. 2.00 (ISBN 0-89555-036-9, 111). TAN Bks Pubs.
St. Louis Public Library. Heraldry Index of the St. Louis Public Library. 1980. lib. bdg. 475.00 (ISBN 0-8161-0311-9). G K Hall.
St. Maur, Suzan & Streep, Norbert. The Jewelry Book. (Illus.). 198p. 1981. 9.95 (ISBN 0-312-44230-0). St Martin.
St. Omer, Garth. J-Black Bam & the Masquerades. 1972. 3.95 o.p. (ISBN 0-571-09102-4, Pub. by Faber & Faber). Merrimack Bk Serv.
St. Paul Technical Vocational Institute Curriculum Commitee. Mathematics for Careers: Measurement & Geometry. LC 80-67549. (General Mathematics Ser.). 176p. 1981. pap. text ed. 7.40 (ISBN 0-8273-2058-2); price not set instr's. guide (ISBN 0-8273-2059-0). Delmar.
St. Paul's Greek Orthodox Church Women. Art of Greek Cookery. LC 63-18214. 8.95 (ISBN 0-385-03793-7). Doubleday.
Saint, Phil. Amazing Saints: The Story of a Family of Christian Evangelists. 224p. 1972. pap. 2.50 o.p. (ISBN 0-912106-40-9). Logos.
Saint, Phil, tr. Cataclimo. (Spanish Bks.). (Span.). 1978. 1.00 (ISBN 0-8297-0435-3). Life Pubs Intl.
St. Pierre, Brian & Moose, Mary E. The Flavor of North Beach: The Insider's Guide to San Francisco's Historic Italian District. 160p. (Orig.). 1981. pap. 5.95 (ISBN 0-87701-157-5). Chronicle Bks.
St. Sauver, Dennis. Lightening Round. (Tromp It Ser.). (gr. 4-8). 1973. PLB 4.95 (ISBN 0-912022-40-X); pap. 2.95 (ISBN 0-685-93058-0). EMC.
--The Tough Decision. LC 73-8190. (Illus.). 32p. (gr. 3-5). 1973. PLB 4.95 o.p. (ISBN 0-87191-231-7). Creative Ed.
--The Two That Count. LC 73-8192. (Illus.). 32p. (gr. 3-5). 1973. PLB 4.95 o.p. (ISBN 0-87191-232-5). Creative Ed.
Saint-Alban, Dominique. Deja-Vu. LC 77-15341. 1978. 7.95 o.p. (ISBN 0-312-19183-9). St Martin.
St. Auby, Fiona, jt. auth. see Ager, Stanley.
Saint Augustine. On Christian Doctrine. 1981. pap. 3.95 (ISBN 0-89526-887-6). Regnery-Gateway.
Saint Augustine, Saint The Confessions of Saint Augustine. LC 60-13725. 4.50 (ISBN 0-385-02955-1, Im). Doubleday.
Saint-Denis, Michel. Theatre: The Rediscovery of Style. LC 60-10492. 1968. pap. 4.25 (ISBN 0-87830-523-8, 23). Theatre Arts.
Sainte-Beuve, Charles A. Memoirs of Madame Desbordes-Valmore: With a Selection from Her Poems. Preston, Harriet W., tr. from Fr. LC 77-11483. (Symbolists Ser.). 240p. 1980. Repr. of 1873 ed. 27.50 (ISBN 0-404-16344-0). AMS Pr.
Sainte Colombe, Paul De see De Sainte Colombe, Paul.
Saint-Exupery, Antoine De. The Little Prince. Woods, Katherine, tr. from Fr. LC 67-1144. (Illus.). 95p. (gr. 4-6). 1943. pap. 1.95 (ISBN 0-15-246507-3, VoyB). HarBraceJ.
--Little Prince. Woods, Katherine, tr. LC 67-1144. (Illus.). (gr. 3-7). 1943. 5.95 (ISBN 0-15-246503-0, HJ). HarBraceJ.
--Petit Prince. rev. ed. Miller, John R., ed. LC 47-151. (Fr). (gr. 11). 1975. pap. 5.00 (ISBN 0-395-24005-0). HM.
--Petit Prince. LC 43-5812. (Illus., Fr.). (gr. 3-7). 1943. 7.95 (ISBN 0-15-243818-1, HJ); pap. 1.95 (ISBN 0-15-650300-X). HarBraceJ.
Saint-Exupery, Antoine De see De Saint-Exupery, Antoine.
Saint-Gaudens, Homer & Weinberg, H. Barbara, eds. The Reminiscences of Augustus Saint-Gaudens, 2 vols. LC 75-28890. (Art Experience in Late 19th Century America Ser.: Vol. 23). (Illus.). 1976. Repr. of 1913 ed. Set. lib. bdg. 72.50 (ISBN 0-8240-2247-5). Garland Pub.
Saint-Germain, C. De see De Saint-Germain, C.
Saint-Jacques, Bernard, jt. auth. see Giles, Howard.
Saint-James, D., et al. Type Two Superconductivity. LC 67-27491. 1970. 42.00 (ISBN 0-08-012392-9). Pergamon.
St. John, Barclay, jt. auth. see Siracusa, Joseph M.
St. John, David, jt. auth. see Wright, Charles.
St. Johnston, Valerie, jt. auth. see Eccleshare, Elizabeth.
St. Joseph, J. K., jt. auth. see Beresford, M. W.
St. Louis, Patricia, jt. auth. see Leach, Joan.
Saint-Marcoux. Light. LC 58-8068. (gr. 9 up). 6.95 (ISBN 0-8149-0382-7). Vanguard.
St. Martin, Hardie, tr. see Donoso, Jose.
Saint-Phalle, Therese de. The Clearing. 1978. pap. 1.75 o.p. (ISBN 0-445-04234-6). Popular Lib.
Saint Phalle, Thibaut De see De Saint Phalle, Thibaut.
Saint-Pierre, Jacques H. Bernardin De see Bernardin De Saint-Pierre, Jacques H.
Saint-Pierre, Leland De see De Saint-Pierre, Leland.
Saint-Saens, Camille. Musical Memories. LC 70-93980. (Music Reprint Ser). 1969. Repr. of 1919 ed. lib. bdg. 29.50 (ISBN 0-306-71821-9). Da Capo.
Saintsbury, G. The Earlier Renaissance. LC 68-9660. 1968. Repr. of 1901 ed. 16.00 (ISBN 0-86527-047-3). Fertig.
Saintsbury, George. East India Slavery. 52p. 1972. Repr. of 1829 ed. text ed. 5.75x (ISBN 0-7165-1816-3). Humanities.
--East India Slavery. 52p. 1972. Repr. of 1929 ed. 15.00x (ISBN 0-7165-1816-3, Pub. by Irish Academic Pr Ireland). Biblio Dist.
Saintsbury, George E. Dryden. LC 67-23875. 1968. Repr. of 1881 ed. 20.00 (ISBN 0-8103-3053-9). Gale.
St. Thomas Aquinas, see Thomas Aquinas, St.
St. Vincent, Edna Millay see Millay, Edna St. Vincent.
Sainty, J. C., ed. & intro. by. Officials of the Boards of Trade 1660-1870. (Office-Holders in Modern Britain Ser: No. 3). 126p. 1974. text ed. 15.00x (ISBN 0-485-17143-0, Athlone Pr). Humanities.
Sainty, J. C., compiled by. Admiralty Officials Sixteen Sixty-Eighteen Seventy. (No. 4). 159p. 1975. text ed. 19.50x (ISBN 0-485-17144-9, Athlone Pr). Humanities.
Saisse, Louis. Dictionnaire Francais-Arabe. 1980. pap. 7.95x. Intl Bk Ctr.
Saisselin, Remy G. Taste in Eighteenth Century France: Critical Reflections on the Origins of Aesthetics, or An Apology for Amateurs. LC 65-23460. 1965. 9.00x o.p. (ISBN 0-8156-2083-7). Syracuse U Pr.
Sait, Talat, tr. see Barkan, Stanley H.
Saix, Guillot de see De Saix, Guillot.
Saiyidain, K. G. Man in the New World. 1964. 3.75x o.p. (ISBN 0-210-31216-5). Asia.
Saiyidain, Khwaja G. Faith of an Educationist. 1966. 10.25x o.p. (ISBN 0-210-26986-3). Asia.
Sajkovic, Miriam. F. M. Dostoevsky: His Image of Man. LC 62-20690. 1962. 8.00x o.p. (ISBN 0-8122-7368-0). U of Pa Pr.
Sakade, Florence. Origami, Japanese Paper Folding, 3 Vols. LC 57-10685. (Illus., Orig.). (gr. 2 up). pap. 2.50 ea. Vol. 1 (ISBN 0-8048-0454-0). Vol. 2 (ISBN 0-8048-0455-9). Vol. 3 (ISBN 0-8048-0456-7). C E Tuttle.
--Peach Boy & Other Stories. (Illus.). (gr. 1-5). 1958. pap. 5.25 (ISBN 0-8048-0469-9). C E Tuttle.
--Picture Play: The Japanese Twins' Lucky Day. LC 64-20367. (Illus.). 3.50 o.p. (ISBN 0-8048-0322-6). C E Tuttle.
Sakade, Florence & Sono, Kazuhiko. Fold-And-Paste Origami Storybook. LC 64-22899. (gr. 1-4). 1964. bds. 4.95 o.p. (ISBN 0-8048-0189-4). C E Tuttle.
Sakagami, Ryusho & Sakagami, Setsumei. Nunchaku & Sai: Ancient Okinawan Martial Arts. (Okinawan Combat Arts Ser.). (Illus.). 180p. 1974. pap. 9.95 (ISBN 0-87040-333-8). Japan Pubns.
Sakagami, Setsumei, jt. auth. see Sakagami, Ryusho.
Sakalys, Jurate A., jt. auth. see Bergersen, Betty S.
Sakatani, Baron Y. Manchuria: A Survey of Its Economic Development. LC 78-74315. (The Modern Chinese Economy Ser.). 305p. 1980. lib. bdg. 33.00 (ISBN 0-8240-4279-4). Garland Pub.
Sakharou, Andrei D. Sakharov Speaks. Salisbury, Harrison E., intro. by. 1974. pap. 1.65 (ISBN 0-394-71302-8, Vin). Random.
Sakharov, Andrei D. My Country & the World. 1975. pap. 1.65 o.p. (ISBN 0-394-72067-9, Vin). Random.
--Progress, Coexistence & Intellectual Freedom. 1968. 3.95 (ISBN 0-393-05362-8); pap. text ed. 3.95x (ISBN 0-393-09822-2, Norton C). Norton.
Sako, Sydney, jt. auth. see Finocchiaro, Mary.
Sakoian, Frances & Acker, Louis S. The Astrologer's Handbook. LC 78-160647. (Illus.). 480p. (YA) 1973. 13.95 (ISBN 0-06-013734-7, HarpT). Har-Row.
Sakol, Jeanne. Flora Sweet. 1977. pap. 1.95 o.p. (ISBN 0-345-25055-9). Ballantine.
Sakol, Jeannie. Hot Thirty. 1981. pap. 3.75 (ISBN 0-440-13429-3). Dell.
Sakran, Frank. Palestine, Still a Dilemma. 6.95. New World Press NY.
Saks, Michael J. Jury Verdicts: The Role of Group Size & Social Decision Rule. LC 76-44569. 1977. 16.95 (ISBN 0-669-01100-2). Lexington Bks.
Sala, Andre & Duxler, Margot. Expectations: A Completely Unexpected Guide to Planned & Unplanned Parenthood. (Illus.). 100p. 1981. pap. 2.95 (ISBN 0-399-50516-4, Perigee). Putnam.
Sala, Harold. Science, God & the 80's. 160p. (Orig.). 1980. pap. 2.25 (ISBN 0-89081-255-1). Harvest Hse.
Saladin, H. & Migeon, G. Manuel d'Art Musulman, 2 vols. Incl. Vol. I. Architecture. xxii, 596p; Vol. II. Les Arts Plastiques. iii, 477p. (Illus., Fr.). 1981. Repr. of 1907 ed. Set. lib. bdg. 160.00x (ISBN 0-89241-155-4). Caratzas Bros.
Saladin, Thomas A., jt. auth. see Sodeman, William A., Jr.
Saladino, Salvatore. Italy from Unification to 1919: Growth & Decay of a Liberal Regime. LC 75-101945. (AHM Europe Since 1500 Ser.). 1970. pap. text ed. 5.95x (ISBN 0-88295-762-7). AHM Pub.
Salaff, Janet W. Working Daughters of Hong Kong: Female Piety or Power in the Family? LC 80-23909. (ASA Rose Monographs). (Illus.). 304p. Date not set. price not set (ISBN 0-521-23679-7); pap. price not set (ISBN 0-521-28148-2). Cambridge U Pr.
Salam, A. & Wigner, E. P., eds. Aspects of Quantum Theory. LC 72-75298. (Illus.). 300p. 1972. 40.95 (ISBN 0-521-08600-0). Cambridge U Pr.
Salaman. Dictionary of Tools. 1974. 47.50 (ISBN 0-87002-912-6). Bennett IL.
Salaman, G. & Thompson, K. People & Organizations. 384p. 1974. text ed. 10.95x (ISBN 0-582-48669-6). Longman.
Salaman, Graeme & Thompson, Kenneth, eds. Control & Ideology in Organizations. 350p. (Orig.). 1980. pap. 12.50 (ISBN 0-262-69069-1). MIT Pr.
Salaman, Graeme, jt. ed. see Esland, Geoff.
Salaman, Malcolm C. British Book Illustration Yesterday & Today, with Commentary. Holme, Geoffrey, ed. LC 73-175758. (Illus.). viii, 175p. 1974. Repr. of 1923 ed. 26.00 (ISBN 0-8103-3977-3). Gale.
Salamanazar, George, tr. see Ledda, Gavino.
Salamini, Heather F. Agrarian Radicalism in Veracruz, 1920-38. LC 77-26106. (Illus.). 1978. 15.00x (ISBN 0-8032-0952-5). U of Nebr Pr.
Salamon, G. & Huang, Y. P. Computed Tomography of the Brain Atlas of Normal Anatomy. (Illus.). 160p. 1980. 116.90 (ISBN 0-387-08825-3). Springer-Verlag.
Salamon, George. Arnold Zweig. LC 75-12736. (World Author Ser.: Germany: No. 361). 1975. lib. bdg. 12.50 (ISBN 0-8057-6212-4). Twayne.
Salamon, Lester M. Welfare the Elusive Consensus: Where We Are, How We Got There, & What's Ahead. LC 78-12163. (Praeger Special Studies). 1978. 24.95 (ISBN 0-03-045601-0). Praeger.
Salamone, Rosa Maria, tr. see Oberto, Martino.
Salanave, Leon E. Lightning & Its Spectrum: An Atlas of Photographs. LC 80-18882. (Illus.). 1980. 25.00x (ISBN 0-8165-0374-5). U of Ariz Pr.
Salancik, Gerald R., jt. ed. see Staw, Barry M.
Salanki, J., et al, eds. Physiology of Non-Excitable Cells: Proceedings of the 28th International Congress of Physiological Sciences, Budapest, 1980. LC 80-41874. (Advannces in Physiological Sciences: Vol. 3). (Illus.). 350p. 1981. 40.00 (ISBN 0-08-026815-3). Pergamon.
--Physiology of Excitable Membranes: Proceedings of the 28th International Congress of Physiological Sciences, Budapest, 1980. LC 80-41853. (Advances in Physiological Sciences: Vol. 4). (Illus.). 350p. 1981. 40.00 (ISBN 0-08-026816-1). Pergamon.
Salant, Nathan. Superstars, Stars, & Just Plain Heroes. LC 79-3877. 288p. 1981. 14.95 (ISBN 0-8128-2716-3). Stein & Day.
Salant, Walter S. & Vaccara, Beatrice N. Import Liberalization & Employment: The Effects of Unilateral Reductions in U.S. Import Barriers. 1961. 12.95 (ISBN 0-8157-7696-9). Brookings.
Salant, Walter S., jt. ed. see Krause, Lawrence B.
Salas, C. G., jt. auth. see Salas, S. L.
Salas, Charles G., jt. auth. see Salas, Saturnino L.
Salas, F., et al. New Writers Ten. (New Writing & Writers Ser.). 1971. text ed. 13.00x (ISBN 0-7145-0751-2). Humanities.
Salas, Floyd, et al. New Writers Ten. 1980. pap. 6.00 (ISBN 0-7145-0752-0). Riverrun NY.
Salas, Luis. Social Control & Deviance in Cuba. LC 79-19597. (Praeger Special Studies). (Illus.). 416p. 1979. 32.95 (ISBN 0-03-052471-7). Praeger.
Salas, Nichole. Night of the Kachina. LC 78-16066. (Pacesetters Ser.). (Illus.). (gr. 4 up). 1978. PLB 7.95 (ISBN 0-516-02157-5). Childrens.
Salas, R. M. People: An International Choice. LC 76-11610. (Span.). 1979. 13.75 (ISBN 0-08-021952-7); pap. 8.25 (ISBN 0-08-021951-9). Pergamon.
Salas, Rafael M. International Population Assistance: the First Decade. 1979. 45.00 (ISBN 0-08-024701-6); pap. 21.00 (ISBN 0-08-024700-8). Pergamon.
--Population: un choix international: Approche multilaterale au probleme demographique. LC 71-11610. 1977. text ed. 26.00 (ISBN 0-08-021818-0); pap. text ed. 16.50 (ISBN 0-08-021819-9). Pergamon.
Salas, S. L. Calculus: One & Several Variables, 2 pts. 3rd ed. LC 77-11630. 1978. text ed. 28.95 (ISBN 0-471-74983-4); Pt. 1. text ed. 20.95 (ISBN 0-471-03285-9); Pt. 2. text ed. 20.95 (ISBN 0-471-03286-7); solutions manual 5.95 (ISBN 0-471-04282-X); student supplement 9.95 (ISBN 0-471-02882-7). Wiley.
Salas, S. L. & Salas, C. G. Precalculus: A Short Course. 250p. 1975. text ed. 15.95x (ISBN 0-471-01049-9). Wiley.
Salas, Saturnino L. & Hille, Einar. Calculus, 2 pts. 2nd ed. LC 73-79299. 1974. Pt. 1. text ed. 16.75x o.p. (ISBN 0-471-00888-5); Pt. 2. text ed. 18.95x (ISBN 0-471-01060-X). Wiley.

--Calculus: One & Several Variables. 2nd ed. LC 73-79299. 1974. text ed. 22.95x (ISBN 0-471-00956-3). Wiley.
Salas, Saturnino L. & Salas, Charles G. Precalculus. 2nd ed. LC 78-23236. 1979. text ed. 18.95x (ISBN 0-471-03124-0); solutions manual avail. (ISBN 0-471-05515-8). Wiley.
Salassi, Otto. On the Ropes. LC 80-20399. 224p. (gr. 5-7). 1981. 8.95 (ISBN 0-688-80313-X). Greenwillow.
Salat, Barbara & Copperfield, David, eds. Well-Being. LC 78-1219. 1979. pap. 5.95 (ISBN 0-385-14221-8, Anch). Doubleday.
Salaz, Fernando. Un Dia y una Vida. (Span. & Eng.). (gr. 7-8). 1977. pap. text ed. 3.00x o.p. (ISBN 0-87108-201-2). Pruett.
Salazar, Jose L., jt. auth. see Harpe, Shideler.
Salcher, Peter. From Cape Mystery to Cape of No Return: The Saga of Men at Sea. 1978. 6.95 o.p. (ISBN 0-533-03486-8). Vantage.
Salcido, Craig. Malago's Visit. (Orig.). 1980. pap. 1.75 (ISBN 0-505-51488-5). Tower Bks.
Salcman, Michael. Neurologic Emergencies: Recognition & Management. 1980. text ed. 27.00 (ISBN 0-89004-409-0). Raven.
Saldern, Axel Von see Von Saldern, Axel.
Saldich, Anne. Electronic Democracy: Television's Impact on the American Political Process. LC 79-18592. (Praeger Special Studies). 142p. 1979. 21.95 (ISBN 0-03-052146-7). Praeger.
Sale, Alura M. Marine Mammals. LC 78-16859. (Illus.). 272p. 1979. 26.50 (ISBN 0-914718-35-5); pap. text ed. 16.95 (ISBN 0-914718-48-7). Pacific Search.
Sale, Chic. I'll Tell You Why. 1975. Repr. 5.00 (ISBN 0-911416-01-3). Specialist.
--Specialist. 1974. 5.00 (ISBN 0-911416-00-5, 911416). Specialist.
Sale, Gilbert, tr. see Beyle, Marie H.
Sale, J. Russell. Filippino Lippi's Strozzi Chapel in Santa Maria Novella. Freedberg, Sydney J., ed. LC 78-74376. (Outstanding Dissertations in the Fine Arts Ser.). (Illus.). 1979. lib. bdg. 47.00 (ISBN 0-8240-3963-7). Garland Pub.
Sale, Larry L. Introduction to Middle School Teaching. 1979. text ed. 15.95 (ISBN 0-675-08279-X). Merrill.
Sale, Randall D. & Karn, Edwin D. American Expansion: A Book of Maps. LC 78-24508. (Illus.). 1979. pap. 3.95x (ISBN 0-8032-9104-3, BB 698, Bison). U of Nebr Pr.
Sale, Roger. Modern Heroism: Essays on D. H. Lawrence, William Empson, & J. R. R. Tolkien. LC 73-186106. 1973. 20.00x (ISBN 0-520-02208-4). U of Cal Pr.
--On Not Being Good Enough: Writings of a Working Critic. 1979. 14.95 (ISBN 0-19-502559-8). Oxford U Pr.
Sale, Suzanne, tr. see Beyle, Marie H.
Sale, William M., Jr., ed. see Bronte, Emily.
Saleh, Dennis. Typefoundry. 1978. 4.00 o.p. (ISBN 0-686-63955-3). Bieler.
Salem, H. & Aviado, D. M. Anti-Tussive Agents, 3 vols. 1970. Set. text ed. 130.00 (ISBN 0-08-013340-1). Pergamon.
Salem, James M. Drury's Guide to Best Plays. 3rd ed. LC 77-18139. 1978. 19.50 (ISBN 0-8108-1097-2). Scarecrow.
--A Guide to Critical Reviews, Part I: American Drama, 1909-1969. 2nd ed. LC 73-3120. 1973. 20.50 (ISBN 0-8108-0608-8). Scarecrow.
--A Guide to Critical Reviews, Part II: The Musical, 1909-1974. 2nd ed. LC 73-3120. 1976. 25.00 (ISBN 0-8108-0959-1). Scarecrow.
--A Guide to Critical Reviews: Part III. 2nd ed. LC 73-3120. 448p. 1979. 22.50 (ISBN 0-8108-1226-6). Scarecrow.
--A Guide to Critical Reviews, Part IV: The Screenplay from the Jazz Singer to Dr. Strangelove, 2 Vols. LC 66-13733. 1971. Set. 39.50 (ISBN 0-8108-0367-4). Scarecrow.
--A New Generation of Essays. 1972. pap. text ed. 6.95x o.p. (ISBN 0-697-03816-5); instructor's manual 1.00 o.p. (ISBN 0-686-28510-7). Wm C. Brown.
Salem, Luis. El Dios de Nuestros Libertadores. LC 77-165. (Illus.). 172p. (Orig., Span.). 1977. pap. 2.75 (ISBN 0-89922-093-2). Edit Caribe.
--Hogares de la Biblia. 107p. (Orig., Span.). pap. 1.95 (ISBN 0-89922-079-7). Edit Caribe.
--La Nota Biblica en la Literatura Castellana. LC 77-163. 186p. (Orig., Span.). 1977. pap. 3.25 (ISBN 0-89922-086-X). Edit Caribe.
--Por Eso Me Gustas. LC 77-17649. 78p. (Orig., Span.). 1978. pap. 1.95 (ISBN 0-89922-107-6). Edit Caribe.
--Rimas del Pesebre. LC 77-82265. 86p. (Orig., Span.). (gr. 4 up). 1978. pap. 1.50 (ISBN 0-89922-118-1). Edit Caribe.
--Sol de mi Infancia. 80p. (Orig., Span.). 1980. pap. 1.95 (ISBN 0-89922-166-1). Edit Caribe.
Salem, Luis D. Romancero Biblico. 144p. (Orig., Spanish.). 1980. pap. 3.50 (ISBN 0-89922-203-X). Edit Caribe.
Salem, Mahmound. Organizational Survival in the Performing Arts: The Making of the Seattle Opera. LC 74-15422. (Special Studies). (Illus.). 1976. text ed. 19.95 o.p. (ISBN 0-275-05670-8). Praeger.
Salerno, Charles. Police at the Bargaining Table. 1981. write for info (ISBN 0-398-04462-7). C C Thomas.
Salerno, Elizabeth M., jt. auth. see Blair, Carole L.
Salerno, Henry F., ed. English Drama in Transition, 1880-1920. Incl. Liars. Jones, Henry A; Second Mrs. Tanqueray. Pinero, Arthur W; Importance of Being Earnest. Wilde, Oscar; Major Barbara. Shaw, George B; Admirable Crichton. Barrie, James M; Silver Box. Galsworthy, John; Deirdre. Yeats, William B; Playboy of the Western World. Synge, John M; Our Betters. Maugham, W. Somerset. LC 67-25504. 512p. (Orig.). 1968. pap. 9.50 (ISBN 0-685-23230-1). Pegasus.
Salerno, M. Constance, jt. auth. see Ingalls, A. Joy.
Salerno, Nan & Vanderburgh, Rosamund. Shaman's Daughter. 1981. pap. 3.25 (ISBN 0-440-17863-0). Dell.
Salert, Barbara & Sprague, John. The Dynamics of Riots. Hannan, Michael, ed. LC 80-18546. (Methodology Monograph Ser.). (Illus.). 126p. (Orig.). 1980. pap. 9.25 (ISBN 0-89138-956-3, IS-00114, Pub. by ICPSR). Univ Microfilms.
Sales, Bruce D., ed. The Trial Process. (Perspectives in Law & Psychology Ser.: Vol. 2). 530p. 1981. 39.50 (ISBN 0-306-40491-5, Plenum Pr). Plenum Pub.
Sales, David. Jaguar Service - Repair Handbook: All 3.8 & 4.2 E-Types. Robinson, Jeff, ed. (Illus.). 240p. 1975. pap. text ed. 10.95 (ISBN 0-89287-055-9, A225). Clymer Pubns.
--John Deere Snowmobile Service-Repair: 1972-1977. Jorgenson, Eric, ed. (Illus.). 1977. pap. 8.95 (ISBN 0-89287-163-6, X950). Clymer Pubns.
--Ski-Doo Snowmobile Service-Repair: 1970-1979. Jorgensen, Eric, ed. (Illus.). 1977. pap. 8.95 (ISBN 0-89287-178-4, X953). Clymer Pubns.
--Suzuki DS80-185 Singles, 1978-1979: Service, Repair, Maintenance. Jorgensen, Eric, ed. (Illus.). 142p. (Orig.). 1980. pap. text ed. 9.95 (ISBN 0-89287-316-7, M363). Clymer Pubns.
--Suzuki GS1000 Fours: 1978-1979 Service-Repair-Performance. Jorgensen, Eric, ed. (Illus.). 216p. (Orig.). 1980. pap. text ed. 9.95 (ISBN 0-89287-315-9, M375). Clymer Pubns.
--Suzuki: GS400 Twins 1977-1978--Service, Repair, Performance. Jorgensen, Eric, ed. (Illus.). 1978. pap. 9.95 (ISBN 0-89287-237-3, M372). Clymer Pubns.
--Suzuki: GS550 Fours, 1977-1978--Service, Repair, Performance. Jorgensen, Eric, ed. (Illus.). 1978. pap. 9.95 (ISBN 0-89287-273-X, M373). Clymer Pubns.
--Suzuki GS850 Fours, 1979-1980: Service, Repair, Maintenance. Jorgensen, Eric, ed. (Illus.). 295p. (Orig.). 1980. pap. text ed. 9.95 (ISBN 0-89287-305-1, M376). Clymer Pubns.
--Suzuki SP-DR Three Hundred Seventy & Four Hundred Singles Nineteen Seventy-Eight to Nineteen Eighty: Service, Repair, Performance. Jorgensen, Eric, ed. (Illus.). 224p. (Orig.). 1980. pap. text ed. 9.95 (ISBN 0-89287-327-2, M374). Clymer Pubns.
--Suzuki: 50-120cc Singles 1964-1979--Service, Repair, Maintenance Handbook. 3rd ed. Jorgensen, Eric, ed. (Illus.). 1978. pap. 9.95 (ISBN 0-89287-292-6, M367). Clymer Pubns.
--Suzuki 50-400cc RM Series Singles, 1975-79: Service, Repair, Performance. Jorgensen, Eric, ed. (Illus.). 1977. pap. 9.95 (ISBN 0-89287-196-2, M371). Clymer Pubns.
--Yamaha Service-Repair Handbook: 90-200cc Twins, 1966-1977. Jorgensen, Eric, ed. (Illus.). 1978. pap. 9.25 (ISBN 0-89287-179-2, M400). Clymer Pubns.
Sales Meeting Magazine Research Staff. Directory of Conventions: With Supplement. (Annual). Date not set. pap. 60.00x (ISBN 0-89047-045-6). Herman Pub.
--Exhibits Schedule-Annual Directory of Trade & Industrial Shows. 300p. (Annual). 65.00x (ISBN 0-89047-047-2). Herman Pub.
Saleska, E. J. Be of Good Courage. 1948. 0.85 (ISBN 0-570-03678-X, 74-1004). Concordia.
--Strength from Above. 1946. 0.85 (ISBN 0-570-03677-1, 74-1002). Concordia.
Saleska, Edward J., jt. ed. see Gockel, Herman W.
Saleske, Theodore E. Easter. (Living Values Ser.). (Illus.). 64p. (Orig.). 1980. pap. 3.95 (ISBN 0-89107-206-3). Good News.
Saletore, R. N. Indian Pirates. 200p. 1980. pap. text ed. 11.25x (ISBN 0-391-02183-4, Pub. by Concept India). Humanities.
Saletu, B., et al, eds. see Collegium Internationale Neuro-Psychopharmacologium 11th Congress, Vienna, July 9-14 1978.
Salfelder, Karlhanns. Atlas of Deep Mycoses. LC 79-67221. (Illus.). 140p. 1980. text ed. 47.50 (ISBN 0-7216-7898-X). Saunders.
Salgado, Gamini. English Drama: A Critical Introduction. 1981. write for info. (ISBN 0-312-25429-6). St Martin.
Salgado, Gamini, ed. Othello. (New Swan Shakespeare Advanced Ser.). (Illus.). 1976. pap. text ed. 5.50x (ISBN 0-582-52748-1). Longman.
Salgado, Gamini, ed. see Lawrence, D. H.
Salgado, Maria A. Rafael Arevalo Martinez. (World Authors Ser.: No. 544). 1979. lib. bdg. 14.50 (ISBN 0-8057-6387-2). Twayne.
Salhab. Fi Khota Ali: Christian & Islamic Teaching. (Arabic.). 12.00x (ISBN 0-686-63563-9). Intl Bk Ctr.
Salhar. Nahj-Albalagha: Islamic Teachings. (Arabic.). 16.00x (ISBN 0-686-63564-7). Intl Bk Ctr.
Saliba, David R. A Psychology of Fear: The Nightmare Formula of Edgar Allan Poe. LC 80-8267. 277p. 1980. lib. bdg. 18.50 (ISBN 0-8191-1269-0); pap. text ed. 10.25 (ISBN 0-8191-1270-4). U Pr of Amer.
Salibi, Kamal S. History of Arabia. LC 80-11919. 1980. write for info. (ISBN 0-88206-036-8). Caravan Bks.
Saliers, Don E. The Soul in Paraphrase: Prayer & the Religious Affections. 160p. 1980. 8.95 (ISBN 0-8164-0121-7). Seabury.
Salignac De La Mothe, Francois De see Fenelon & De Salignac De La Mothe, Francois.
Salih, K., jt. ed. see Lo Fu-Chen.
Salih, Tayeb. Season of Migration to the North. Johnson-Davies, Denys, tr. from Arabic. 168p. 1978. 9.00 (ISBN 0-89410-198-6); pap. 5.00 (ISBN 0-89410-199-4). Three Continents.
--The Wedding of Zein. Johnson-Davies, Denys, tr. from Arabic. 120p. (Orig.). 1978. 9.00 (ISBN 0-89410-200-1); pap. 5.00 (ISBN 0-89410-201-X). Three Continents.
Salimbene Di Adam. From Saint Francis to Dante: Translations from the Chronicle of the Franciscan Salimbene (1221-88) Coulton, G. G., ed. & tr. from It. LC 68-10910. 462p. 1972. 15.00x o.p. (ISBN 0-8122-7672-8); pap. 5.95x (ISBN 0-8122-1053-0, Pa Paperbks). U of Pa Pr.
Salimbene Ognibene Di Guido Di Adamo. Chronik: Des Salimbene Von Parma Nach der Ausgabe der Monuments Germaniae, 2 Vols. Doren, A., ed. Repr. of 1914 ed. pap. 36.50 set (ISBN 0-384-53125-3). Johnson Repr.
Salinas, Carlos F. & Jorgenson, Ronald J., eds. Dentistry in the Interdisciplinary Treatment of Genetic Diseases. (Birth Defects: Original Article Ser.: Vol. XVI, No. 5). 216p. 1980. 26.00 (ISBN 0-8451-1039-X). A R Liss.
Salincourt, Ernest De see Wordsworth, William.
Salingar, L. G. Shakespeare & the Traditions of Comedy. LC 73-91617. 368p. 1974. 60.00 (ISBN 0-521-20384-8); pap. 12.95x (ISBN 0-521-29113-5). Cambridge U Pr.
Salinger, Gerhard L., jt. auth. see Sears, Francis W.
Salinger, Herman, tr. see Henisch, Peter.
Salinger, Herman, tr. see Krolow, Karl.
Salinger, Pierre, et al, eds. Honorable Profession: A Tribute to Robert F. Kennedy. LC 68-55381. (Illus.). 1968. (ISBN 0-385-07159-0). Doubleday.
Salinger, Richard, tr. see Melitz, Leo L.
Salinger, Wendy. Folly River. 1980. 7.95 (ISBN 0-525-10760-6). Dutton.
Salins, Peter D. The Ecology of Housing Destruction: Economic Effects of Public Intervention in the Housing Market. LC 79-3845. 176p. 1980. 12.50x (ISBN 0-8147-7811-9); pap. 6.00x (ISBN 0-8147-7812-7). NYU Pr.
Salis, Richard & Larsen, Egon, eds. Motives. Larsen, Egon, tr. from Ger. 228p. 1975. text ed. 10.00x (ISBN 0-85496-056-2). Humanities.
Salisbury, Allen. The Civil War & the American System: America's Battle with Britain 1860-76, Vol. 2. Stevens, Kathy, ed. (American History Ser.). 1978. pap. 5.95 (ISBN 0-918388-02-3, E469S24, Univ Edns). New Benjamin.
Salisbury, Carola. Count Vronsky's Daughter. LC 80-2065. 312p. 1981. 12.95 (ISBN 0-385-15918-8). Doubleday.
--Dark Inheritance. 1979. pap. 1.75 o.p. (ISBN 0-449-23888-1, Crest). Fawcett.
--Dolphin Summer. 1978. pap. 1.75 o.p. (ISBN 0-449-23415-0, Crest). Fawcett.
--The Pride of the Trevallions. 240p. 1978. pap. 1.75 o.p. (ISBN 0-449-23722-2, Crest). Fawcett.
Salisbury, Charlotte. Tibetan Diary: Travels Along the Ancient Silk Route. LC 80-54816. 1981. 9.95 (ISBN 0-8027-0683-5). Walker & Co.
Salisbury, E. J. see Jackson, B. D., et al.
Salisbury, Eugene W. Manual of Procedure for Town & Village Courts (N.Y., 2 vols. (Both volumes supplemented annually). 1978. Vol. 1. looseleaf 12.50 (ISBN 0-87526-180-9); Vol. 2. looseleaf 12.50 (ISBN 0-87526-181-7). Gould.
Salisbury, Frank B. & Ross, Cleon W., eds. Plant Physiology. 2nd ed. 1978. text ed. 22.95x (ISBN 0-534-00562-4). Wadsworth Pub.
Salisbury, G. W., et al. Physiology of Reproduction & Artificial Insemination of Cattle. 2nd ed. LC 77-13598. (Animal Science Ser.). (Illus.). 1978. text ed. 37.95x (ISBN 0-7167-0025-5). W H Freeman.
Salisbury, Harrison. Without Fear or Favor: An Uncompromising Look at the New York Times. 640p. 1981. pap. 8.95 (ISBN 0-345-29711-3). Ballantine.
Salisbury, Harrison E. Black Night, White Snow: Russia's Revolutions 1905-1917. LC 74-18830. 1978. 14.95 o.p. (ISBN 0-385-00844-9). Doubleday.
--Orbit of China. LC 67-11331. (Illus.). 1967. 10.00 o.s.i. (ISBN 0-06-013731-2, HarpT). Har-Row.
Salisbury, Harrison E., ed. Soviet Union: The Fifty Years. LC 67-26001. (New York Times Bk). (Illus.). 1967. 10.00 o.p. (ISBN 0-15-184605-7). HarBraceJ.
Salisbury, Harrison E., intro. by see Sakharou, Andrei D.
Salisbury, Hugh. Through Sorrow into Joy. LC 77-13329. (Illus.). 1977. pap. 2.95 (ISBN 0-87123-559-5, 210559). Bethany Fell.
Salisbury, J. K. see Kent, R. T.
Salisbury, Oliver M. The Bitter Root: The Pursuit of Freedom by a Man. (Illus.). 275p. 1980. pap. 8.95 (ISBN 0-87564-825-8). Superior Pub.
Salisbury, Rachel, jt. auth. see Henry, Ralph L.
Salisbury, Richard F. Vunamami: Economic Transformation in a Traditional Society. LC 70-79062. 1970. 22.75x (ISBN 0-520-01647-5). U of Cal Pr.
Salisbury, Roger E. & Bevin, A. Griswold. Atlas of Reconstructive Burn Surgery. 1981. text ed. price not set (ISBN 0-7216-7903-X). Saunders.
Salisbury, Roger E. & Pruitt, Basil A. Burns of the Upper Extremity. LC 75-14786. (Major Problems in Clinical Surgery Ser.: Vol. 19). (Illus.). 175p. 1976. text ed. 17.00 (ISBN 0-7216-7902-1). Saunders.
Salisbury, William T. & Theberge, James D., eds. Spain in the 1970s: Economics, Social Structure, Foreign Policy. LC 75-19816. (Special Studies). 1976. text ed. 32.95 (ISBN 0-275-55800-2). Praeger.
Salk, Lee. Dear Dr. Salk: Answers to Your Questions About Your Family. 1980. pap. 2.50 (ISBN 0-446-91486-X). Warner Bks.
--What Every Child Would Like His Parents to Know. 224p. 1973. pap. 2.50 (ISBN 0-446-91705-2). Warner Bks.
Salkever, David. Hospital Sector Inflation. (Illus.). 208p. 1979. 22.95 (ISBN 0-669-00704-8). Lexington Bks.
Salkever, David & Bice, Thomas. Hospital Certificate-of-Need Controls: Impact on Investment, Costs, & Use. 1979. pap. 5.25 (ISBN 0-8447-3325-3). Am Enterprise.
Salkever, Louis K., jt. auth. see Uppal, J. S.
Salkin, Harvey M. Integer Programming. (Illus.). 450p. 1975. text ed. 21.95 (ISBN 0-201-06841-9). A-W.
Salkin, J. Body Ego Technique: An Educational & Therapeutic Approach to Body Image & Self Identity. (Amer. Lec. in Special Education Ser.). (Illus.). 224p. 1973. 16.50 (ISBN 0-398-02826-5). C C Thomas.
Salkind, A. J., jt. auth. see Falk, S. Uno.
Salkind, Alvin J., jt. ed. see Yeager, Ernest.
Salkind, N., jt. auth. see Eliot, J.
Salkind, Neal. Theories of Human Development. (Orig.). 1980. pap. text ed. 13.95 (ISBN 0-442-25859-3). D Van Nostrand.
Sall, Dallas A. A Breath of Spring. (Illus.). 72p. (Orig.). 1980. pap. 4.95 (ISBN 0-9604344-1-0). Sunrise Pub OR.
Sall, Millard. Faith, Psychology & Christian Maturity. 1977. pap. 4.95 (ISBN 0-310-32431-9). Zondervan.
Salle, Innocent De La see De La Salle, Innocent.
Sallenave, Jean-Paul. Experience Analysis in Industrial Planning. LC 76-7164. (Illus.). 1976. 17.95 (ISBN 0-669-00658-0). Lexington Bks.
Sallese & Dominicis. Desarrollando Destrezas En Preparacion Para el Examen Equivalencia De Escuela Superior En Espanol: Ciencia. Date not set. pap. 2.75 (ISBN 0-8120-0989-4). Barron.
--Desarrollando Destrezas En Preparacion Para el Examen Equivalencia De Escuela Superior En Espanol: Estudios Sociales. Date not set. pap. 2.75 (ISBN 0-8120-0988-6). Barron.
Sallese, Nicolas F., et al. Desarrollando Destrezas En Preparacion Para el Examen Equivalencia De Escuela Superior En Espanol: Lectura: Developing Skills in Reading for the H.S. Equivalency Test in Spanish. (gr. 11-12). Date not set. pap. text ed. 2.75 (ISBN 0-8120-0990-8). Barron.
Salles Gomes, P. E. Jean Vigo. Francovich, Allan, tr. 1972. 17.95x (ISBN 0-520-01676-9); pap. 5.95 (ISBN 0-520-02332-3, CAL252). U of Cal Pr.
Sallis, John. The Gathering of Reason. LC 80-14485. (Continental Thought Ser.: Vol. 2). xii, 196p. 1981. 14.00x (ISBN 0-8214-0439-3). Ohio U Pr.

--Research in Phenomenology, Vol. 9. (Orig.). 1979. pap. text ed. 10.00x (ISBN 0-391-01297-5). Humanities.
Sallis, John, ed. Studies in Phenomenology & Human Science. 1980. text ed. 7.50 (ISBN 0-391-01702-0). Humanities.
Sallis, Susan. Only Love. LC 79-2686. 256p. (YA) (gr. 7 up). 1980. 8.95 (ISBN 0-06-025174-3, HarpJ); PLB 8.79 (ISBN 0-06-025175-1). Har-Row.
Salloum. Concession et Leg. Petrolieres Pays Arabe. (Fr.). 13.00x (ISBN 0-685-77134-2). Intl Bk Ctr.
Salloway, J. C. Health Care Delivery Systems. (Behavioral Sciences for Health Care Professionals Ser.). 128p. (Orig.). 1981. lib. bdg. 15.00x (ISBN 0-86531-016-5); pap. text ed. 6.00x (ISBN 0-86531-017-3). Westview.
--Introduction to Social Epidemiology. (Behavioral Science for Health Care Professionals Ser.). 128p. (Orig.). 1981. lib. bdg. 15.00x (ISBN 0-86531-014-9); pap. text ed. 6.00x (ISBN 0-86531-015-7). Westview.
Salloway, Nancy. Wipeoff Multiplication Table Quiz Book. 12p. (gr. 3 up). 1980. pap. 1.50 (ISBN 0-937518-05-0). Hartley Hse.
Sallust. Cataline. Merivale, C., ed. (Classical Ser). (Lat). 1870. pap. text ed. 7.95 (ISBN 0-312-12460-0). St Martin.
Sally, H. L. Irrigation Planning for Intensive Cultivation. 8.00x o.p. (ISBN 0-210-22610-2). Asia.
Salm, Peter. Three Modes of Criticism: The Literary Theories of Scherer, Walzel, & Staiger. 1968. 15.00 (ISBN 0-8295-0128-2). UPBS.
Salm, Thomas J. Vander see Vander Salm, Thomas J., et al.
Salm, Walter G. Auto Audio: How to Select & Install Stereo Equipment. 144p. 1980. pap. 7.70 (ISBN 0-8104-0759-0). Hayden.
--Remodeling Your Kitchen or Bathroom. LC 68-2130. (Illus.). 1967. Repr. of 1967 ed. lib. bdg. 3.50 o.p. (ISBN 0-668-01781-3). Arco.
Salman, Sydney E., ed. Cloning of Human Tumor Stem Cells. LC 80-19600. (Progress in Clinical & Biological Research: Vol. 48). 366p. 1980. 44.00 (ISBN 0-8451-0048-3). A R Liss.
Salmela, J. H. Competitive Behaviors of Olympic Gymnasts. (Illus.). 164p. 1980. 19.75 (ISBN 0-398-04019-2); pap. 14.50 (ISBN 0-398-04021-4). C C Thomas.
Salmela, John. The Advanced Study of Gymnastics. (Illus.). 288p. 1976. 27.50 (ISBN 0-398-03438-9). C C Thomas.
Salmen, S. Duties of Administrators in High Education. (Studies of the Modern Corporation Ser.). 1971. 9.95 o.s.i. (ISBN 0-02-927760-4). Macmillan.
Salmon, Arthur E. Alex Comfort. (English Authors Ser.: No. 237). 1978. lib. bdg. 12.50 (ISBN 0-8057-6708-8). Twayne.
Salmon, E. T. Samnium & the Samnites. 1967. 49.50 (ISBN 0-521-06185-7). Cambridge U Pr.
Salmon, Eliahi J., jt. auth. see Bentz, Edward J., Jr.
Salmon, Elizabeth G. Good in Existential Metaphysics. (Aquinas Lecture). 1952. 6.95 (ISBN 0-87462-117-8). Marquette.
Salmon, George. Conic Sections. 6th ed. LC 55-3390. 4.95 (ISBN 0-8284-0099-7); pap. 3.95 (ISBN 0-8284-0098-9). Chelsea Pub.
Salmon, James H. & Pearson, Donald H. Self-Assessment of Current Knowledge in Neurological Surgery. 1976. spiral bdg. 14.50 (ISBN 0-87488-247-8). Med Exam.
Salmon, Jaslin U. Black Executives in White Businesses. LC 79-66859. 1979. pap. text ed. 7.75 (ISBN 0-8191-0860-X). U Pr of Amer.
Salmon, Jill. The Goatkeeper's Guide. LC 80-69354. (Illus.). 152p. 1981. 14.95 (ISBN 0-7153-8055-9). David & Charles.
Salmon, John H. The French Religious Wars in English Political Thought. LC 80-24621. vii, 202p. 1981. Repr. of 1959 ed. lib. bdg. 22.50x (ISBN 0-313-22221-5, SAFR). Greenwood.
Salmon, Margaret B. Diabetic Diet Exchange Lists for Low Sodium Diets. (Illus.). 1979. pap. 1.50 (ISBN 0-918662-06-0). Techkits.
--Diabetic Diet Handbook. (Illus.). 1977. pap. 1.50 (ISBN 0-918662-02-8). Techkits.
--Dieta Siabetica Para Buena Salud. (Illus.). 1979. pap. 1.50 (ISBN 0-918662-06-0). Techkits.
--Joy of Breastfeeding. 2nd ed. LC 77-73690. (Illus.). 1979. 8.95 (ISBN 0-918662-04-4); pap. 5.95 (ISBN 0-918662-03-6). Techkits.
Salmon, Margaret B. & Quigley, Althea E., eds. Enjoying Your Restricted Diet. (Illus.). 328p. 1972. 15.75 (ISBN 0-398-02396-4). C C Thomas.
Salmon, Phillida, ed. Coming to Know. 180p. 1980. pap. 17.50 (ISBN 0-686-65610-5). Routledge & Kegan.
Salmon, Vivian. The Study of Language in Seventeenth Century England. (Studies in the History of Linguistics: No. 17). 1978. text ed. 37.25x (ISBN 0-391-01645-8). Humanities.
--The Works of Francis Lodwick: A Study of His Writings in the Intellectual Context of the Seventeenth Century. (The Classics of Linguistics Ser.). (Illus.). 263p. 1972. text ed. 24.00x (ISBN 0-582-52494-6). Longman.
Salmon, Wesley C. Logic. 2nd ed. (Foundations of Philosophy Ser). (Illus.). 160p. 1973. pap. 7.95 ref. ed. (ISBN 0-13-540104-6). P-H.
--Space, Time, & Motion: A Philosophical Introduction. 2nd rev. ed. LC 80-18423. (Illus.). 160p. 1981. pap. 8.95x (ISBN 0-8166-1004-5). U of Minn Pr.
Salmona, M., et al, eds. Insolubilized Enzymes. LC 74-80537. 1974. 27.00 (ISBN 0-911216-60-X). Raven.
Salmone, Anthony. Arabic-English Advanced Learners Dictionary. 30.00x (ISBN 0-685-89874-1). Intl Bk Ctr.
Salmonson, R. F., et al. A Survey of Basic Accounting. 3rd ed. 1981. text ed. 19.95x (ISBN 0-256-02471-5). Irwin.
Salmonson, Roland F., jt. auth. see Edwards, James D.
Salmore, Stephen A. see East, Maurice A., et al.
Salny, Roslyn W. Hobby Collections A-Z. LC 65-18701. (Illus.). (gr. 5-9). 1965. 6.95 o.p. (ISBN 0-690-39508-6, TYC-J). T Y Crowell.
Salo, Mauno A., tr. see Luukkanen, Eino.
Saloma, John S. & Sontag, Frederick H. Parties: The Real Opportunity for Effective Citizen Politics. 1972. 7.95 o.p. (ISBN 0-394-48097-X). Knopf.
Salomaa, Arto. Jewels of Formal Language Theory. (Illus.). 1981. text ed. 24.95 (ISBN 0-914894-69-2). Computer Sci.
Saloman, Erich. Portrait of an Age. (Illus.). 216p. 1975. pap. 7.50 o.s.i. (ISBN 0-02-000820-1, Collier). Macmillan.
Salomon, Brownell, ed. see Heywood, Thomas.
Salomon, C. R. Hacia la Felicidad: Como Vivir una Vida Victoriosa y Practicar la Terapia Espiritual. 1979. 2.50 (ISBN 0-311-42060-5). Casa Bautista.
Salomon, Erich, illus. Erich Salomon, No. 10. LC 77-80021. (Aperture History of Photography Ser.). (Illus.). 1978. paper over boards 8.95 (ISBN 0-89381-023-1). Aperture.
Salomon, Louis B. Devil Take Her: A Study of the Rebellious Lover in English Poetry. pap. 1.95 o.p. (ISBN 0-498-04058-5, Prpta). A S Barnes.
Salomon, M. Silver Azide, Cyanide, Cyanamides, Cyanate, Selenocyanate & Thiocyanate: Solubilities of Solids. (Solubility Data Ser.: Vol. 3). 1979. 100.00 o.p. (ISBN 0-08-022353-2). Pergamon.
Salomon, Rosalie K. Fashion Design for Moderns. 2nd ed. LC 76-14535. 144p. 1976. 10.00 (ISBN 0-87005-162-8). Fairchild.
Salomone-Marino, Salvatore. Customs & Habits of the Sicilian Peasants. Norris, Rosalie N., ed. & tr. from It. LC 80-65583. (Illus.). 256p. 1981. 19.50 (ISBN 0-8386-3010-3). Fairleigh Dickinson.
Salomonovich, A. E., jt. auth. see Kuzmin, A. D.
Salomonsky, Verna C. Masterpieces of Furniture in Photographs & Measured Drawings. rev. ed. (Illus.). 1953. pap. 5.00 (ISBN 0-486-21381-1). Dover.
Saloom, Pamela, jt. auth. see Stoltz, Berdine.
Saloutos, Theodore. The American Farmer & the New Deal. 312p. 1981. text ed. 17.50 (ISBN 0-8138-1760-9). Iowa St U Pr.
Salsbury, Stephen. Inside the Penn Central Crisis. (Illus.). 352p. 1980. 14.95 (ISBN 0-07-054483-2). McGraw.
Salser, Barbara H. The Democratization of Clothing in America: Student Syllabus. (gr. 10-12). 1979. pap. text ed. 6.95 (ISBN 0-89420-062-3, 165021); cassette recordings 88.10 (ISBN 0-89420-204-9, 165000). Natl Book.
Salser, Carl W. Letter Writing for the Office: Syllabus. 2nd ed. 1975. pap. text ed. 7.65 (ISBN 0-89420-026-7, 216720); cassette recordings 193.70 (ISBN 0-89420-160-3, 110800). Natl Book.
--Timings for Typing. 1969. 3.95 (ISBN 0-89420-013-5, 296955). Natl Book.
Salser, Carl W. & Yerian, Theo. Personal Shorthand, 3 pts. Incl. Pt. 1. pap. text ed. 6.85 (ISBN 0-89420-106-9, 241050); Cassette Recordings. 314.05 (ISBN 0-89420-167-0, 241000); Pt. 2. pap. text ed. 7.50 (ISBN 0-89420-107-7); cassette recordings 311.45 (ISBN 0-89420-168-9); Pt. 3. pap. text ed. (ISBN 0-89420-108-5). Cassette Recordings (ISBN 0-89420-169-7). (Personal Shorthand Cardinal Ser.). 1980. Set. text ed. write for info (ISBN 0-89420-105-0). cassette recordings 936.00 (ISBN 0-89420-170-0). Natl Book.
--Personal Shorthand: 70 Lesson Edition. 1968. text ed. 7.45 (ISBN 0-89420-047-X, 216707); cassette recordings 241.35 (176700). Natl Book.
Salser, Carl W. & Yerian, Theodore. Personal Shorthand: Thirty Lesson Edition. 1967. pap. text ed. 4.95 (ISBN 0-89420-004-6, 216701); cassette recordings 241.35 (ISBN 0-686-67952-0, 176700). Natl Book.
Salser, Carl W., jt. auth. see Yerian, Theodore.
Salsig, Doyen, ed. Parole-Quebec, Countersign-Ticonderoga: Second New Jersey Regimental Orderly Book, 1776. LC 77-74398. (Illus.). 1980. 24.50 (ISBN 0-8386-1793-X). Fairleigh Dickinson.
Salsini, Paul. Second Start. LC 79-92442. 168p. (Orig.). 1980. pap. 4.95 (ISBN 0-87973-525-2, 525). Our Sunday Visitor.
Salstrom, Paul. Manual on Peace Walks. 27p. 1967. pap. 1.00 (ISBN 0-934676-11-9). Greenlf Bks.
Salt, B. Programmes in Animation: Handbook for Animation Technicians. 1978. 150.00 (ISBN 0-08-023153-5). Pergamon.
Salt, Brian G. Basic Animation Stand Techniques. LC 76-40298. 1977. text ed. 26.00 (ISBN 0-08-021368-5). Pergamon.
Salt, F. B. Timetabling Models for Secondary Schools: A Practical Handbook. (General Ser.). (Illus.). 1978. pap. text ed. 20.75x (ISBN 0-85633-138-4, NFER). Humanities.
Salt, George. Cellular Defence Reactions of Insects. LC 71-118067. (Monographs in Experimental Biology: No. 16). (Illus.). 1970. 24.95 (ISBN 0-521-07936-5). Cambridge U Pr.
Salt, Henry S. Animals' Rights: Considered in Relation to Social Progress. rev. ed. LC 80-50160. 1980. 9.95 (ISBN 0-9602632-0-9). Soc Animal Rights.
Salt, John & Clout, Hugh, eds. Migration in Post-War Europe: Geographical Essays. (Illus.). 1976. 29.95x (ISBN 0-19-874027-1). Oxford U Pr.
Salta, Romeo. Pleasures of Italian Cooking. 1962. 12.95 (ISBN 0-02-606790-0). Macmillan.
Salten, Felix. Florian: The Lippizaner. Date not set. 8.75 (ISBN 0-85131-127-X, Dist. by Sporting Book Center). J A Allen.
Salter, Andrew. What Is Hypnosis? 106p. 1973. pap. 3.95 (ISBN 0-374-51038-5, N439). FS&G.
Salter, Brian, jt. auth. see Tapper, Ted.
Salter, C. H. Good Little Thomas Hardy. 236p. 1981. 26.50x (ISBN 0-389-20126-X). B&N.
Salter, Christopher & Lloyd, William. Landscape in Literature. Natoli, Salvatore J., ed. LC 76-29268. (Resource Papers for College Geography Ser.). 1977. pap. text ed. 4.00 (ISBN 0-89291-118-2). Assn Am Geographers.
Salter, Christopher L., jt. ed. see Pannell, Clifton W.
Salter, Debbie. One Is More Than un. 111p. 1978. pap. 2.50 (ISBN 0-8341-0548-9, Beacon). Nazarene.
Salter, Elizabeth. Helpmann: The Authorised Biography. (Illus.). 247p. 1981. text ed. 18.50x (ISBN 0-87663-349-1). Universe.
Salter, J. Query Languages. 1980. write for info. (ISBN 0-85501-494-6). Heyden.
Salter, John Thomas. Public Men in & Out of Office. LC 76-39131. (FDR & the Era of the New Deal Ser). (Illus.). 514p. 1972. Repr. of 1946 ed. lib. bdg. 49.50 (ISBN 0-306-70457-9). Da Capo.
Salter, P. J. & Bleasdale, J. K., eds. Know & Grow Vegetables. (Illus.). 1979. 14.50x (ISBN 0-19-857563-7). Oxford U Pr.
Salter, W. E. Productivity & Technical Change. (Cambridge Department of Applied Economies Monographs: No. 6). (Illus.). 1969. 35.50 (ISBN 0-521-06186-5); pap. 12.95x (ISBN 0-521-09568-9). Cambridge U Pr.
Salter, Walter L. Floors & Floors Maintenance. LC 74-11222. (Illus.). 360p. 1974. 29.95 (ISBN 0-470-74992-X). Halsted Pr.
Salthouse, J. A. & Ware, M. J. Point Group Character Tables & Related Data. (Illus.). 64p. 1972. 10.95 (ISBN 0-521-08139-4). Cambridge U Pr.
Salti, Danielle, tr. see Cueva, Agustin.
Saltman, Jules & Zimering, Stanley. Abortion Today. 192p. 1973. pap. 10.50 (ISBN 0-398-02672-6). C C Thomas.
Saltman, Juliet. Open Housing. LC 78-19464. 1978. 31.95 (ISBN 0-03-022376-8). Praeger.
Salton, Gerald. Automatic Information Organization & Retrieval. LC 68-25664. (Illus.). 1968. text ed. 25.95 o.p. (ISBN 0-07-054485-9, C). McGraw.
Salton, Gerard. Dynamic Information & Library Processing. (Illus.). 416p. 1975. ref. ed. 26.95 (ISBN 0-13-221325-7). P-H.
Salton, Milton R., ed. Immunochemistry of Enzymes & Their Antibodies. 240p. 1980. Repr. of 1977 ed. lib. bdg. write for info. (ISBN 0-89874-165-3). Krieger.
Saltonsall. Your Environment. 6.95 o.s.i. (ISBN 0-8027-0320-8). Walker & Co.
Saltykov-Shchedrin, Mikhail. The History of a Town: Or, the Chronicle of Foolov. Brownsberger, Susan, tr. from Rus. (Illus.). 204p. 1981. 16.50 (ISBN 0-88233-610-X); pap. 8.50 (ISBN 0-88233-611-8). Ardis Pubs.
Saltz, Daniel. A Short Calculus. 3rd ed. 1980. text ed. 17.95 (ISBN 0-87620-820-0); answers to even-numbered problems free (ISBN 0-8302-8201-7). Goodyear.
Saltz, Daniel & Bryant, Steven. College Algebra. 1980. 17.95 (ISBN 0-87620-198-2); write for info. (ISBN 0-8302-1983-8). Goodyear.
Saltz, Eli. The Cognitive Bases of Human Learning. 325p. 1971. pap. text ed. 17.95x (ISBN 0-256-01180-X). Dorsey.
Saltzberg, Barney. Utter Nonsense. (McGraw-Hill Paperbacks Ser.). (Illus.). 80p. (Orig.). 1980. pap. 3.95 (ISBN 0-07-054486-7). McGraw.
Saltzburg, Stephen A. Introduction to American Criminal Procedure. abr. ed. LC 80-52110. (American Casebook Ser.). 725p. 1980. pap. text ed. 13.95 (ISBN 0-8299-2106-0). West Pub.
Saltzburg, Stephen A. & Redden, Kenneth R. Federal Rules of Evidence Manual. 2nd ed. 1977. with 1979 suppl 50.00 (ISBN 0-87215-200-6); 1980 suppl. 22.50 (ISBN 0-87215-338-X). Michie.
Saltzman, Barry, ed. Advances in Geophysics: Vol. 22 Estuarine Physics & Chemistry-Studies in Long Island Sound. 1980. 44.50 (ISBN 0-12-018822-8); lib. ed. 58.00 (ISBN 0-12-018880-5); microfiche 31.00 (ISBN 0-12-018881-3). Acad Pr.
Saltzman, Elliot, jt. ed. see Pick, Herbert L., Jr.
Saltzman, Marvin L. & Muileman, Kathryn S. Eurail Guide: How to Travel Europe & All the World by Train 1981. 11th ed. LC 72-83072. 816p. 1981. pap. 9.95 (ISBN 0-912442-11-5). Eurail Guide.
Saltzman, Max, jt. auth. see Billmeyer, Fred W., Jr.
Saltzman, Stephen Arthur, ed. Energy Technology & Global Policy: A Selection of Contributing Papers to the Conference on Energy Policies & the International System. LC 76-49648. 276p. 1977. text ed. 21.15 (ISBN 0-87436-243-1). ABC-Clio.
Salu, Mary, ed. Essays on Troilus & Criseyde. (Chaucer Studies: No. III). 143p. 1979. 23.75x (ISBN 0-8476-6236-5). Rowman.
Salunkhe, D. K., jt. auth. see Haard, Norman F.
Salus, Peter H. Linguistics. LC 69-13632. (Speech Communication Ser). 1969. pap. 8.95 (ISBN 0-672-61084-1, SC14). Bobbs.
Salvador, Mari L. Yer Dailege! Kuna Women's Art. (Illus.). 103p. (Orig.). 1978. pap. 10.95 (ISBN 0-8263-0539-3, Pub. by Maxwell Mus Anthropology). U of NM Pr.
Salvadori, Giuseppina, jt. auth. see Madrigal, Margarita.
Salvadori, James A. Famous Architectural Illustrations from Distant Lands. (Illus.). 137p. 1981. 59.45 (ISBN 0-930582-96-9). Gloucester Art.
Salvadori, Mario. Why Buildings Stand Up: The Strength of Architecture from the Pyramid to the Skyscraper. (Illus.). 1980. cancelled (ISBN 0-393-01401-0). Norton.
Salvadori, Mario G. Statics & Strength of Structures. LC 70-138821. 1971. 21.95 (ISBN 0-13-844548-6). P-H.
Salvadori, Mario G. & Heller, Robert. Structure in Architecture: Building of Buildings. 2nd ed. (Illus.). 336p. 1975. 21.95 (ISBN 0-13-854109-4). P-H.
Salvadori, Massimo, ed. Modern Socialism. LC 68-27381. (Documentary History of Western Civilization Ser). 1968. 15.00x o.s.i. (ISBN 0-8027-2015-3). Walker & Co.
Salvan, Albert J., ed. see Zola, Emile.
Salvati, M. J. Build Your Own High-Quality, Low-Cost Test Equipment. (Illus.). 1976. pap. 7.25 (ISBN 0-8104-5664-8). Hayden.
--How to Custom Design Your Solid-State Equipment. (Illus.). 160p. 1974. pap. 7.75 (ISBN 0-8104-5585-4). Hayden.
Salvato, Sharon. Scarborough House. 1977. pap. 1.95 o.p. (ISBN 0-685-75033-7, 345-25168-7-195). Ballantine.
Salvatore, Francesco, et al, eds. The Biochemistry of Adenosylmethionine. LC 76-25565. 1977. 38.50x (ISBN 0-231-03895-X). Columbia U Pr.
Salvemini, Gaetano. La Dignita Cavalleresca Nel Comune Di Firenze. LC 80-2005. 1981. Repr. of 1896 ed. 22.00 (ISBN 0-404-18589-4). AMS Pr.
--The Fascist Dictatorship in Italy. 1967. 18.50 (ISBN 0-86527-063-5). Fertig.
--Under the Axe of Fascism. LC 68-9589. 1970. Repr. of 1936 ed. 18.00 (ISBN 0-86527-201-8). Fertig.
Salverson, Laura G. Confessions of an Immigrant's Daughter. (Social History of Canada Ser.). 400p. 1981. 30.00x (ISBN 0-8020-2424-6); pap. 15.00 (ISBN 0-8020-6434-5). U of Toronto Pr.
Salvia, John & Ysseldyke, James. Assessment in Special & Remedial Education. LC 77-72891. (Illus.). 1977. pap. text ed. 18.95 (ISBN 0-395-25073-0); inst. manual 0.50 (ISBN 0-395-25072-2). HM.
Salvia, John & Ysseldyke, James E. Assessment in Special & Remedial Education. 2nd ed. (Illus.). 576p. 1981. text ed. write for info. (ISBN 0-395-29694-3). HM.
Salvini, Roberto. The Hidden Michelangelo. LC 78-50815. (Illus.). 1978. 19.95 o.p. (ISBN 0-528-81043-X). Rand.
Salvo, Louis J. De see De Salvo, Louis J.

Salvo, Louise De see De Salvo, Louise.
Salvste, Guillaume de see De Saluste, Guillaume & Du Bartas, Sieur.
Salwak, Dale. John Wain. (English Authors Ser.: No. 316). 1981. lib. bdg. 11.95 (ISBN 0-8057-6806-8). Twayne.
Salway, Peter. Frontier People of Roman Britain. (Cambridge Classical Studies). 1965. 34.00 (ISBN 0-521-06187-3). Cambridge U Pr.
Salz, Kay, compiled by. Film Service Profiles. LC 80-10394. 56p. (Orig.). 1980. pap. 5.00 (ISBN 0-935654-00-3, Pub. by Ctr for Arts Info). Pub Ctr Cult Res.
Salz, Victor. Between Husband & Wife. LC 72-83634. 282p. (Orig.). 1972. pap. 2.95 o.p. (ISBN 0-8091-1727-4, Deus). Paulist Pr.
Salzberger-Wittenberg, Isca. Psycho-Analytic Insight & Relationships: A Kleinian Approach. (Library of Social Work). 1970. cased 12.50 (ISBN 0-7100-6835-2). Routledge & Kegan.
--Psycho-Analytic Insight & Relationships: A Kleinian Approach. (Library of Social Work). 1973. pap. 7.45 (ISBN 0-7100-7623-1). Routledge & Kegan.
Salzburg, Joseph S. Vietnam, Beyond the War. LC 75-10622. 1975. 12.50 o.p. (ISBN 0-682-48258-7, Banner). Exposition.
Salzer, Felix. Structural Hearing: Tonal Coherence in Music, 2 Vols. (Illus.). 1952. text ed. 7.50 ea.; Vol. 1. text ed. (ISBN 0-486-22275-6); Vol. 2. text ed. (ISBN 0-486-22276-4). Dover.
Salzer, Felix, ed. The Music Forum, Vol. 4. LC 67-16204. 1977. 22.50x (ISBN 0-231-03934-4). Columbia U Pr.
Salzer, Felix, jt. ed. see Mitchell, William J.
Salzer, Feliz, ed. The Music Forum, Vol. V. 384p. 1981. 27.50x (ISBN 0-231-04720-7). Columbia U Pr.
Salzinger, Kurt. Schizophrenia: Behavioral Aspects. LC 73-1276. (Approaches to Behavior Pathology Ser.). 192p. 1973. pap. text ed. 11.50x (ISBN 0-471-75090-5). Wiley.
Salzinger, Kurt & Feldman, Richard S. Studies in Verbal Behavior: An Empirical Approach. LC 76-179073. 474p. 1974. 26.00 (ISBN 0-08-016926-0). Pergamon.
Salzinger, Kurt, jt. ed. see Rieber, Robert W.
Salzinger, Suzanne, et al, eds. The Ecosystem of the "Sick" Child: Implications for Classification & Intervention for Disturbed & Mentally Retarded Children. 1980. 25.00 (ISBN 0-12-617250-1). Acad Pr.
Salzman, Ed, ed. California Environment & Energy. LC 80-66476. (Illus.). 96p. (Orig.). 1980. pap. text ed. 4.95 (ISBN 0-930302-23-0). Cal Journal.
Salzman, Jack. Albert Maltz. (United States Authors Ser.: No. 311). 1978. lib. bdg. 12.50 (ISBN 0-8057-7228-6). Twayne.
Salzman, Jack & Wallenstein, Barry, eds. Years of Protest: A Collection of American Writings of the 1930's. LC 67-13489. (Illus., Orig.). 1967. pap. 8.50 (ISBN 0-672-63614-X). Pegasus.
Salzman, Jack & Zanderer, Leo, eds. Social Poetry of the '30s: An Anthology. 1978. lib. bdg. 17.85 (ISBN 0-89102-046-2); pap. 5.95 o. p. (ISBN 0-686-68047-2). B Franklin.
Salzman, Jack, ed. see Dreiser, Theodore.
Salzman, Jerome. Catnip Re. LC 79-20289. (Illus.). 1980. 6.00 (ISBN 0-916906-24-8). Konglomerati.
Salzman, Louis F. English Life in the Middle Ages. (Illus.). 1926. 24.95x (ISBN 0-19-821251-8). Oxford U Pr.
Salzman, Philip C. When Nomads Settle. (Praeger Special Studies Ser.). 192p. 1980. 18.95 (ISBN 0-03-052501-2). Praeger.
Salzman, Stanley A. & Miller, Charles D. Mathematics for Business: In a Consumer Age. 1978. 14.95x (ISBN 0-673-15092-5). Scott F.
Salzman, Stanley A., jt. auth. see Miller, Charles D.
Salzmann, Zdenek, jt. auth. see Pi-Sunyer, Oriol.
Sam, Heron A. The Disposable People. LC 79-66268. 133p. 1980. 7.95 (ISBN 0-533-04374-3). Vantage.
Samaha, M. A., et al, eds. see Training Workshop on Water Management for Arid Regions, Ministry of Irrigation, Government of Egypt, in Cooperation with the United Nations Environment Programme, Cairo, Egypt.
Samanin, R., jt. ed. see Garattini, S.
Samant, D. R. Inflation & Development: Some Reflections. 128p. 1976. 7.50 o.p. (ISBN 0-89253-056-1). InterCulture.
Samantha, Lester. The Brash American. (Orig.). 1981. pap. 1.50 (ISBN 0-440-10945-0). Dell.
Samaras, Demetrios G. Theory of Ion Flow Dynamics. LC 78-153896. 1971. pap. text ed. 7.50 (ISBN 0-486-60309-1). Dover.
Samaras, Thomas T. & Czerwinski, Frank L. Fundamentals of Configuration Management. LC 75-127668. 1971. 35.95 (ISBN 0-471-75100-6, Pub. by Wiley-Interscience). Wiley.
Samarian, Sergiu. Queen's Gambit Declined. 1975. 18.95 (ISBN 0-7134-2865-1, Pub. by Batsford England). David & Charles.
Samarraie, Husam. Agriculture in Iraq During the Third Century. (Arab Background Ser.). 1972. 14.00x (ISBN 0-685-77104-0). Intl Bk Ctr.
Sambhi, Piara S., jt. auth. see Cole, W. Owen.
Sambrook, J. see Maniatis, T., et al.
Sambrook, James. William Cobbett. (Routledge Author Guides Ser). 236p. 1973. 13.50x (ISBN 0-7100-7560-X); pap. 8.95 (ISBN 0-7100-7561-8). Routledge & Kegan.
Sambursky, S. Physical World of the Greeks. Dagut, Merton, tr. 1956. pap. 8.95 (ISBN 0-7100-4637-5). Routledge & Kegan.
Samecl, E. see Von Wiesner, J. & Von Regel, C.
Samek, Robert A. Meta Phenomenon. LC 80-81699. 1981. 15.00 (ISBN 0-8022-2372-9). Philos Lib.
Samelson. English As a Second Language: Phase Zero Plus, Let's Begin. (Illus.). 288p. 1980. text ed. 13.95 (ISBN 0-8359-1725-8); pap. text ed. 10.95 (ISBN 0-8359-1724-X). Reston.
Samelson, William. English As a Second Language: Phase Four: Let's Continue. (Illus.). 1979. text ed. 13.95 (ISBN 0-8359-1727-4); pap. text ed. 10.95 (ISBN 0-8359-1726-6); instrs'. manual avail. (ISBN 0-8359-1728-2). Reston.
--English As a Second Language Phase I: Let's Converse. (Illus.). 1980. text ed. 13.95 (ISBN 0-8359-1730-4); pap. text ed. 10.95 (ISBN 0-8359-1729-0); free instrs' manual. Reston.
Sametz, Arnold, ed. Securities Activities of Commercial Banks. LC 80-8339. 1981. write for info. (ISBN 0-669-04031-2). Lexington Bks.
Sametz, Arnold W. Prospects for Capital Formation & Capital Markets. LC 76-55113. (Illus.). 1978. 15.95 (ISBN 0-669-01505-9). Lexington Bks.
Samhain, ed. see Yeats, W. B.
Sami, A. Intra Urban Market Geography: A Case Study of Patna. 219p. 1980. text ed. 15.75x (ISBN 0-391-02121-4). Humanities.
Saminsky, Lazare. Essentials of Conducting. (Student's Music Library). 1957. 6.95 (ISBN 0-234-77403-7). Dufour.
Samitz, M. H. & Dana, Alan S., Jr. Cutaneous Lesions of the Lower Extremities. LC 75-152141. (Illus.). 1971. 30.00 o.p. (ISBN 0-397-50280-X). Lippincott.
Samli, A. Coskun. Marketing & Distribution Systems in Eastern Europe. LC 78-19754. 1978. 22.95 (ISBN 0-03-046486-2). Praeger.
Sammartini, Giovanni B. Giovanni Batista Sammartini Sonate a Tre Stromenti. Churgin, Bathia D., ed. LC 80-12339. (Early Musical Masterworks Ser.). 80p. 1981. 20.00x (ISBN 0-8078-1446-6). U of NC Pr.
Sammartino, Peter. I Dreamed a College. LC 76-1140. 9.95 (ISBN 0-498-01926-8). A S Barnes.
Sammes, P. G. Topics in Antibiotic Chemistry, Vol. 5. LC 80-41091. 312p. 1980. 87.50 (ISBN 0-470-27050-0). Halsted Pr.
--Topics in Antibiotic Chemistry: Mechanisms of Action of Nalidixic Acid & Its Cogeners & New Synthetic B-Lactam Antibiotics, Vol. 3. LC 79-42955. 1980. 59.95x (ISBN 0-470-26882-4). Halsted Pr.
Sammes, P. G., ed. Topics in Antibiotic Chemistry: Vol. 2, Antibiotic from Marine Organisms, Oligosaccharides, Anthnacyclines and Their Biological Receptors. LC 78-40228. 1978. 49.95 (ISBN 0-470-26365-2). Halsted Pr.
--Topics in Antibiotic Chemistry, Vol. 4: The Chemistry & Antimicrobial Activity of New Synthetic B-Lactam Antibiotics. 278p. 1980. 75.00x (ISBN 0-470-26936-7). Halsted Pr.
Sammet, George, Jr. & Kelley, Clifton G. Subcontract Management Handbook. 370p. 1981. 24.95 (ISBN 0-8144-5639-1). Am Mgmt.
Sammons, Martha C. A Guide Through C. S. Lewis' Space Trilogy. LC 80-68329. 1980. pap. 4.95 (ISBN 0-89107-185-7, Cornerstone Bks). Good News.
Samoiloff, Louise C. Portrait of Puerto Rico. 1981. text ed. price not set. Schenkman.
Samora, Julian. Los Mojados: The Wetback Story. LC 71-148190. (Illus.). 1971. text ed. 8.95x o.p. (ISBN 0-268-00442-0); pap. text ed. 3.95 o.p. (ISBN 0-268-00445-5). U of Notre Dame Pr.
Samore, Theodore. Acquisition of Foreign Materials for U.S. Libraries. LC 73-4314. 1973. 13.00 (ISBN 0-8108-0614-2). Scarecrow.
Samovar, Larry A., et al. Understanding Intercultural Communication. 240p. 1980. pap. text ed. 8.95x (ISBN 0-534-00862-3). Wadsworth Pub.
Sampath, R. K. & Ganesan, Jayalakshmi. Economics of Dry Farming in Tamil Nadu. 128p. 1974. 4.50 (ISBN 0-88253-431-9). Ind-US Inc.
Sampayo, Carlos. Karate Within Your Grasp. LC 76-1170. (Illus.). 160p. (YA) 1976. 5.95 o.p. (ISBN 0-8069-4102-2); PLB 6.69 o.p. (ISBN 0-8069-4103-0). Sterling.
Sampere, Alberto, jt. auth. see Ortega, Wenceslao.
Samphan, Khieu. Cambodia's Economy & Industrial Development, Data Paper No. 113. Summers, Laura, tr. 129p. 1979. 6.00 (ISBN 0-87727-111-9). Cornell SE Asia.
Samples, Gordon. The Drama Scholars Index to Plays & Filmscripts. LC 73-22165. 1974. 15.00 (ISBN 0-8108-0699-1). Scarecrow.
--How to Locate Reviews of Plays & Films: A Bibliography of Criticism from the Beginnings to the Present. LC 76-3509. 124p. 1976. 10.00 (ISBN 0-8108-0914-1). Scarecrow.
Samples, Robert E., et al. Whole School Book: Teaching & Learning Late in the Twentieth Century. 1977. pap. text ed. 8.95 (ISBN 0-201-06699-8). A-W.
Sampley, J. Paul. And the Two Shall Become One Flesh, a Study of Traditions in Ephesians 5: 1-33. LC 77-152644. (New Testament Studies: No. 16). 1971. 26.50 (ISBN 0-521-08131-9). Cambridge U Pr.
--Pauline Partnership in Christ: Christian Community & Commitment in Light of Roman Law. LC 79-8895. 144p. 1980. 9.95 (ISBN 0-8006-0631-0, 1-631). Fortress.
Sampley, J. Paul, jt. ed. see Francis, Fred O.
Sampliner, Richard E. Preventing Viral Hepatitis. 300p. 1981. 22.50 (ISBN 0-87527-229-0). Green. Postponed.
Sampson. Introducing Social Psychology. 1980. 12.95 (ISBN 0-531-05413-6, BB02); pap. 9.95 (ISBN 0-531-05627-9, BB11, New Viewpoints). Watts.
Sampson, Alistair. Waiting with Abstain. (Illus.). 172p. 1978. 9.95 (ISBN 0-916838-14-5). Schiffer.
Sampson, Carlene, jt. auth. see Velten, Emmett C., Jr.
Sampson, Diane, ed. see Mary, Donnis, et al.
Sampson, Edward C. E. B. White. (U. S. Authors Ser.: No. 232). 1974. lib. bdg. 10.95 (ISBN 0-8057-0787-5). Twayne.
Sampson, Edward E. Social Psychology & Contemporary Society. 2nd ed. LC 75-30225. 592p. 1976. text ed. 22.95x (ISBN 0-471-75116-2); instructor's manual avail. (ISBN 0-471-01609-8). Wiley.
Sampson, Edward E. & Korn, Harold A. Student Activism & Protest: Alternatives for Social Change. LC 77-92898. (Higher Education Ser.). 1970. 14.95x o.p. (ISBN 0-87589-052-0). Jossey-Bass.
Sampson, Edward E. & Marthas, Marya S. Group Processes for the Health Professions. LC 77-23013. 1977. pap. 11.95 (ISBN 0-471-01987-9, Pub. by Wiley Medical). Wiley.
Sampson, Edward E. & Sampson, Marya. Group Process for the Health Professions. 2nd ed. 352p. 1981. pap. 12.95 (ISBN 0-471-08279-1, Pub. by Wiley Med). Wiley.
Sampson, Geoffrey. Liberty & Language. 1979. 17.95 (ISBN 0-19-215951-8). Oxford U Pr.
--Making Sense. 224p. 1980. text ed. 16.95x (ISBN 0-19-215950-X). Oxford U Pr.
--Schools of Linguistics. LC 80-81140. 272p. 1980. 23.50x (ISBN 0-8047-1084-8). Stanford U Pr.
Sampson, George. Concise Cambridge History of English Literature. rev. 3rd ed. LC 69-16287. 1970. 42.00 (ISBN 0-521-07385-5); pap. 17.95x (ISBN 0-521-09581-6). Cambridge U Pr.
--English for the English. Thompson, D., ed. LC 70-108111. (Studies in the Tests & History of Education). 1970. 14.95 (ISBN 0-521-07848-2); pap. 5.95 (ISBN 0-521-09964-1). Cambridge U Pr.
Sampson, Henry. History of Advertising from the Earliest Times. LC 68-22049. 1974. Repr. of 1874 ed. 30.00 (ISBN 0-8103-3515-8). Gale.
Sampson, Henry T. Blacks in Black & White: A Source Book on Black Films. LC 77-637. 1977. 15.50 (ISBN 0-8108-1023-9). Scarecrow.
Sampson, Marya, jt. auth. see Sampson, Edward E.
Sampson, Olive. Remedial Education. (Special Needs in Education Ser.). 1975. 11.50x (ISBN 0-7100-8141-3); pap. 6.00 (ISBN 0-7100-8142-1). Routledge & Kegan.
Sampson, Patricia. A Star to Steer by: Success Through Positive Experiencing. rev. ed. LC 77-18064. 1979. 9.95 (ISBN 0-8119-0301-X). Fell.
Sampson, R. J., et al. The American Economy. 1975. 15.36 (ISBN 0-395-19780-5); 7.16 (ISBN 0-395-20467-4). HM.
Sampson, Roy & Farris, Martin T. Domestic Transportation: Practice, Theory, & Policy. 4th ed. LC 78-69576. (Illus.). 1978. text ed. 19.50 (ISBN 0-395-26793-5); inst. manual 0.65 (ISBN 0-395-26794-3). HM.
Sampson, Roy J. & Calmus, Thomas W. Economics: Concepts, Applications, Analysis. 425p. 1974. text ed. 18.50 (ISBN 0-395-17812-6); instructors' manual 1.25 (ISBN 0-395-17856-8); study guide 6.95 (ISBN 0-395-17804-5). HM.
Sampson, Roy J., jt. auth. see Farris, Martin T.
Sampson, T. Cultivating the Presence. 1977. 8.95 o.p. (ISBN 0-690-01205-5, TYC-T); pap. 3.95 o.p. (ISBN 0-690-01206-3, TYC-T). T Y Crowell.
Sampson, William. The Catholic Question in America. LC 73-22105. (Civil Liberties in American History Ser.). 122p. 1974. Repr. of 1813 ed. lib. bdg. 17.50 (ISBN 0-306-70600-8). Da Capo.
Sampson, Willliam, jt. auth. see Markham, Gervase.
Samra, C. S. India & Anglo-Soviet Relations. 1959. 4.50x o.p. (ISBN 0-210-33665-X). Asia.
Samson. A Guide & Manual for History 17B at Imperial Valley College. 1976. pap. text ed. 3.95 o.p. (ISBN 0-8403-0721-7). Kendall-Hunt.
Samson, E. Progressive Practice in Dentistry. 1956. 7.50 o.p. (ISBN 0-8022-1475-4). Philos Lib.
Samson, J. A. Tropical Fruits. LC 74-40498. (Tropical Agriculture Ser.). (Illus.). 288p. 1980. lib. bdg. 38.00 (ISBN 0-582-46032-8). Longman.
Samson, Jim. Music in Transition: A Study of Tonal Expansion & Atonality, 1900-1920. 1977. 12.95x o.p. (ISBN 0-393-02193-9). Norton.
Samson, John G., ed. see Seton, Ernest T.
Samsonov, Gregory & Vinitskii, I. M. Handbook of Refractory Compounds. 550p. 1980. 75.00 (ISBN 0-306-65181-5). IFI Plenum.
Samtur, Susan J. & Tuleja, Tad. Cashing in at the Checkout. 1980. pap. 1.95 (ISBN 0-446-90585-2). Warner Bks.
Samuda, Ronald J. Psychological Testing of American Minorities: Issues & Consequences. LC 74-26165. 232p. (Orig.). 1975. text ed. 12.95 scp (ISBN 0-06-045696-5, HarpC). Har-Row.
Samuel, Christian M. The Rights of the Students & the Responisibilities of the Schools. (Illus.). 1980. deluxe ed. 39.75 (ISBN 0-89266-222-0). Am Classical Coll Pr.
Samuel, D. N. The Evangelical Succession. 144p. pap. 7.95 (ISBN 0-227-67834-6). Attic Pr.
Samuel, Edith, ed. Unlocking the Beauty of the Bible: A Study Guide by Alan D. Bennett. Incl. The Book of Praise: Dialogues Between Mark Van Doren & Maurice Samuel. 5.00 o.p. (ISBN 0-685-89266-2). UAHC.
Samuel, Geoffrey, tr. see Heissig, Walther.
Samuel, Herbert. Grooves of Change: A Book of Memoirs. (Return to Zion Ser.). (Illus.). 378p. 1980. Repr. of 1946 ed. lib. bdg. 25.00x (ISBN 0-87991-137-9). Porcupine Pr.
Samuel, Herbert L. Grooves of Change: A Book of Memoirs. LC 80-1913. 1981. Repr. of 1946 ed. 39.50 (ISBN 0-404-18985-7). AMS Pr.
Samuel, Irene, ed. see Tasso, Torquato.
Samuel, Mark A., jt. auth. see Swamy, N. V.
Samuel, Maurice. Certain People of the Book. 1977. pap. 7.50 (ISBN 0-8074-0082-3, 388350). UAHC.
Samuel, Raphael, ed. East End Underworld, Vol. 2: The Life of Arthur Harding. (History Workshop Ser.). (Illus.). 400p. 1981. price not set (ISBN 0-7100-0725-6); pap. price not set (ISBN 0-7100-0726-4). Routledge & Kegan.
--Miners, Quarrymen & Saltworkers. (History Workshop Ser.). (Illus.). 1977. 22.00 (ISBN 0-7100-8353-X); pap. 12.50 (ISBN 0-7100-8354-8). Routledge & Kegan.
--People's History & Socialist Theory. (History Workshop Ser.). 425p. 1981. price not set (ISBN 0-7100-0765-5); pap. price not set (ISBN 0-7100-0652-7). Routledge & Kegan.
--Village Life & Labour. (History Workshop Ser.). 1975. 22.50x (ISBN 0-7100-7499-9); pap. 9.95 (ISBN 0-7100-7500-6). Routledge & Kegan.
Samuel, William. Awareness of Self Discovery. 1981. pap. write for info. (ISBN 0-916108-13-9). Seed Center.
--The Awareness of Self Discovery. 1970. 7.00 o.p. (ISBN 0-916108-52-X). Seed Center.
Samuel, William S. Contemporary Social Psychology: An Introduction. 512p. 1975. text ed. 19.95 (ISBN 0-13-170621-7). P-H.
--Personality: Searching for the Sources of Human Behavior. (Illus.). 544p. 18.95 (ISBN 0-07-054520-0); instr's manual 4.95 (ISBN 0-07-054521-9). McGraw.
Samuel-Hool, Leonie. To All My Grandchildren: Lessons in Indonesian Cooking. Hool, Sherman, ed. LC 80-84766. (Illus.). 120p. 1981. 12.95 (ISBN 0-936016-50-7); pap. 7.95 (ISBN 0-936016-75-2). Liplop.
Samuels, Barbara. Copycat. LC 80-66640. 64p. 1980. 5.95 (ISBN 0-396-07862-1). Dodd.
Samuels, C. L., jt. auth. see Brejcha, M. F.

Samuels, Clifford L. Automotive Air Conditioning. (Illus.). 288p. 1981. text ed. 17.95 o.p. (ISBN 0-13-054213-X); pap. text ed. 13.95 (ISBN 0-13-054205-9). P-H.
Samuels, Ernest. Henry Adams. Incl. The Major Phase. LC 64-21790. xv, 687p. 1964. 22.50x (ISBN 0-674-38751-1); The Middle Years. LC 58-12975. xiv, 514p. 1958. o.p. (ISBN 0-674-38753-8); The Young Henry Adams. LC 48-10525. xvi, 378p. 1948. 17.50x (ISBN 0-674-96630-9). Belknap Pr). Harvard U Pr.
Samuels, Frederick. The Durable Group: Thoughts on Human Identity. 1977. pap. text ed. 7.50x (ISBN 0-8191-0087-0). U Pr of Amer.
Samuels, Gertrude. Adam's Daughter. LC 77-101. (gr. 7 up). 1977. 8.95 (ISBN 0-690-01322-1, TYC-J). T Y Crowell.
Samuels, J. M. Readings on Mergers & Takeovers. 1972. 39.95 (ISBN 0-236-17619-6, Pub. by Paul Elek). Merrimack Bk Serv.
Samuels, M. Screen Greats: Bogart. 1980. pap. 2.95 (ISBN 0-931064-31-7). O'Quinn Studio.
--Screen Greats: Hollywood Nostalgia. 1980. pap. 2.00 (ISBN 0-931064-30-9). O'Quinn Studio.
--Screen Greats: Monroe. 1980. pap. 2.95 (ISBN 0-931064-32-5). O'Quinn Studio.
Samuels, M. L. Linguistic Evolution with Special Reference to English. LC 72-176255. (Cambridge Studies in Linguistics: No. 5). (Illus.). 256p. 1973. 32.50 (ISBN 0-521-08385-0); pap. 9.95x (ISBN 0-521-09913-7). Cambridge U Pr.
Samuels, M. R., jt. auth. see Balzhiser, R. E.
Samuels, Marilyn S. Writing the Research Paper. 1978. pap. text ed. 5.67 (ISBN 0-87720-965-0). AMSCO Sch.
Samuels, Maurice. You Gentiles. pap. 3.00x (ISBN 0-911038-08-6). Noontide.
Samuels, Melvin L., jt. ed. see Johnson, Douglas E.
Samuels, Michael, jt. auth. see Bennett, Hal.
Samuels, Michael A. Education in Angola 1878-1914. LC 70-122747. (Illus.). 1970. pap. text ed. 9.75x (ISBN 0-8077-2087-9). Tchrs Coll.
Samuels, Michael A., et al. Implications of Soviet & Cuban Activities in Africa for U. S. Policy, Vol. 1. LC 79-90797. (Significant Issues Ser.: No. 5). 73p. 1979. write for info. (ISBN 0-89206-010-7). CSI Studies.
Samuels, Richard J. Political Generations & Political Development. LC 77-168. 1977. 16.95 (ISBN 0-669-01463-X). Lexington Bks.
Samuels, Robert J. Structured Polymer Properties. LC 73-21781. 288p. 1974. 29.95 (ISBN 0-471-75155-3, Pub. by Wiley-Interscience). Wiley.
Samuels, S. Jay, ed. What Research Has to Say About Reading Instruction. 1978. pap. text ed. 6.25 (ISBN 0-685-59434-3). Intl Reading.
Samuels, Shirley C. Enhancing Self-Concept in Early Childhood: Theory & Practice. LC 76-58348. 1977. text ed. 24.95 (ISBN 0-87705-316-2); pap. 11.95 (ISBN 0-87705-353-7). Human Sci Pr.
Samuels, Warren & Wade, Larry, eds. Taxing & Spending Policy. (Orig.). 1980. pap. 5.00 (ISBN 0-918592-41-0). Policy Studies.
Samuels, Warren J. & Wade, Larry L., eds. Taxing & Spending Policy. LC 79-3689. (A Policy Studies Organization Book). 1980. 19.95 (ISBN 0-669-03469-X). Lexington Bks.
Samuelson, David. Motion Picture Camera & Lighting Equipment. (Media Manuals Ser.). Date not set. pap. 8.95 (ISBN 0-8038-4685-1). Hastings.
Samuelson, Larry, jt. auth. see Baer, Werner.
Samuelson, Paul A. Economics. 11th ed. (Illus.). 1980. text ed. 18.95 (ISBN 0-07-054595-2); instructor's manual 6.95 (ISBN 0-07-054596-0); study guide 7.95 (ISBN 0-07-053271-0); test bank 10.95 (ISBN 0-07-054597-9); transparency masters 20.00 (ISBN 0-07-054598-7); overhead transparencies 225.00 (ISBN 0-07-075000-9). McGraw.
Samuelson, Paul A., jt. ed. see Bicksler, James L.
Samuelson, William. English As a Second Language Phase Two: Let's Read. (Illus.). 464p. 1975. text ed. 13.95 (ISBN 0-87909-258-0); pap. text ed. 8.95 (ISBN 0-87909-257-2); instrs'. manual avail. Reston.
Samuelsson, B. & Paoletti, R., eds. Advances in Prostaglandin & Thromboxane Research, 2 vols. LC 75-14588. 1976. Vol. 1. 52.00 (ISBN 0-89004-050-8); Vol. 2. 53.50 (ISBN 0-89004-074-5). Raven.
Samuelsson, Bengt, et al, eds. Advances in Prostaglandin & Thromboxane Research, Vols. 6-8. 1980. Set. text ed. 173.00 (ISBN 0-89004-452-X); text ed. 59.50 ea. Vol. 6 (ISBN 0-89004-452-X). Vol. 7 (ISBN 0-89004-513-5). Vol. 8 (ISBN 0-89004-514-3). Raven.
Samuelsson, G., jt. auth. see Grubb, R.
Samway, Patrick H. Faulkner's Intruder in the Dust: A Critical Study of the Typescripts. LC 79-57439. 408p. 1980. 28.50x (ISBN 0-87875-186-6). Whitston Pub.
San Antonio Bicentennial Heritage Committee. San Antonio in the Eighteenth Century. 2nd ed. (Illus.). 154p. 1976. pap. 7.95 (ISBN 0-933164-22-X). U of Tex Inst Tex Culture.
San Diego Police Dept. Police Tactics in Hazardous Situations. (Criminal Justice Ser.). 1976. pap. text ed. 8.95 (ISBN 0-8299-0628-2). West Pub.
San Francisco State College Staff, ed. Laboratory Exercises for Biology. 1967. 4.25 (ISBN 0-917962-07-9). Peek Pubns.
Sanadi, D. Rao, ed. Current Topics in Bioenergetics, Vol. XI. (Serial Publications). 1981. write for info. (ISBN 0-12-152511-2). Acad Pr.
Sanadi, S. Rao. Current Topics in Bioenergetics, Vol. 10. LC 66-28678. (Serial Pub). 1980. 34.50 (ISBN 0-12-152510-4). Acad Pr.
Sanberg, A. A. The Chromosomes in Human Cancer & Leukemia. LC 79-22474. 776p. 1979. 97.50 (ISBN 0-444-00289-8, North Holland). Elsevier.
Sanborn, Charlotte J., jt. ed. see Barton, Walter E.
Sanborn, F. B., ed. see Channing, William E.
Sanborn, F. B., ed. see Thoreau, Henry D.
Sanborn, Frank B. Henry David Thoreau. LC 80-23945. (American Men & Women of Letters Ser.). 330p. 1981. pap. 5.95 (ISBN 0-87754-155-8). Chelsea Hse.
Sanborn, Franklin B. A Concord Notebook: Selections from the Critic, 1905-1906. LC 80-2514. 1981. 27.50 (ISBN 0-404-19062-6). AMS Pr.
--Henry D. Thoreau. LC 80-2515. 1981. Repr. of 1910 ed. 37.50 (ISBN 0-404-19063-4). AMS Pr.
--The Personality of Thoreau. LC 80-2516. 1981. Repr. of 1901 ed. 18.50 (ISBN 0-404-19064-2). AMS Pr.
--Recollections of Seventy Years. LC 67-23889. 1967. Repr. of 1909 ed. 24.00 (ISBN 0-8103-3045-8). Gale.
Sanborn, Franklin B. & Harris, William T. A. Bronson Alcott: His Life & Philosophy, 2 Vols. LC 65-23481. 1893. Set. 15.00x (ISBN 0-8196-0161-6). Biblo.
Sanborn, Franklin B., ed. Life of Henry David Thoreau, Including Many Essays Hitherto Unpublished & Some Accounts of His Family & Friends. LC 67-23890. 1968. Repr. of 1917 ed. 20.00 (ISBN 0-8103-3047-4). Gale.
Sanborn, Franklin B., ed. see Thoreau, Henry D.
Sanborn, Hugh W. Mental-Spiritual Health Models: An Analysis of the Models of Boisen, Hiltner & Clinebell. LC 79-65295. 1979. pap. text ed. 8.75 (ISBN 0-8191-0784-0). U Pr of Amer.
Sanborn, Patricia F. Existentialism. LC 68-27983. (Traditions of Philosophy Ser). (Orig.). 1968. pap. 4.95 (ISBN 0-672-63535-6). Pegasus.
Sancher, Amir, ed. see Bragg, William, Jr.
Sanchez, David A. Ordinary & Differential Equations & Stability Theory: An Introduction. 1979. pap. text ed. 3.00 (ISBN 0-486-63828-6). Dover.
Sanchez, Florencio. La Gringa & Barranca Abajo. LC 72-6355. 186p. 1973. 12.50 o.p. (ISBN 0-8386-1264-4). Fairleigh Dickinson.
Sanchez, Irene, et al. The California Worker's Compensation Rehabilitation System. LC 80-70211. (Illus.). 360p. 1981. 35.00 (ISBN 0-02-927670-5). Macmillan.
Sanchez, Jose, ed. Nineteenth Century Spanish Verse. LC 79-18739. 1979. pap. text ed. 12.95x (ISBN 0-89197-538-1). Irvington.
Sanchez, Jose, ed. see Buero Vallejo, Antonio.
Sanchez, Jose M., tr. see Kerfoot, H. F.
Sanchez, Luis R. Macho Camacho's Beat. Rabassa, Gregory, tr. 1981. 10.95 (ISBN 0-394-50976-5). Pantheon.
Sanchez, Rene, tr. see Cowles, Kathleen.
Sanchez, Rene, tr. see Crawford, Mel.
Sanchez, Rene, tr. see Disney, Walt.
Sanchez, Rene, tr. see Ottun, Bob.
Sanchez, Rene, tr. see Parsons, Virginia.
Sanchez, Rene, tr. see Pfloong, Jan.
Sanchez, Roberto G., ed. see Laforet, Carmen.
Sanchez, Rosaura & Cruz, Rosa M., eds. Essays on la Mujer. (Anthology Ser.: No. 1). 200p. (Orig.). 1977. pap. 6.35 (ISBN 0-89551-020-0). Ucla Chicano Stud.
Sanchez, Soma. Sound Investment. 1980. pap. 2.95 (ISBN 0-88378-048-8). Third World.
Sanchez, Thomas. Zoot-Suit Murders. 1978. 9.95 o.p. (ISBN 0-525-24060-8, Henry Robbins). Dutton.
Sanchez-Albornoz, Nicolas. The Population of Latin America. 1974. 28.50x (ISBN 0-520-01766-8); pap. 6.95x (ISBN 0-520-02745-0). U of Cal Pr.
Sanchez-Albornoz y Menduina, Claudio. En Torno a los Origenes del Feudalismo, 3 vols. LC 80-2004. 1981. Repr. of 1942 ed. Set. 110.00 (ISBN 0-404-18590-8). Vol. 1 (ISBN 0-404-18591-6). Vol. 2 (ISBN 0-404-18592-4). Vol. 3 (ISBN 0-404-18593-2). AMS Pr.
Sanchez-Boudy, Jose. Niquin el Cesante. LC 78-74694. (Coleccion Caniqui). (Illus.). 157p. (Orig., Span.). 1980. pap. 5.95 (ISBN 0-89729-217-0). Ediciones.
--La Rebelion De los Negros. LC 79-56654. (Coleccion Teatro Ser.). 78p. (Orig., Span.). Date not set. pap. 5.95 (ISBN 0-89729-247-2). Ediciones.
Sanchez-Camara, Florencio & Ayala, Felipe, eds. World Anthropology Ser. (World Antropology Ser.). 1979. text ed. 24.75x (ISBN 90-279-7860-3). Mouton.
Sand, George. Consuelo: A Romance of Venice. 799p. 1979. pap. 8.95 (ISBN 0-686-68924-0). Da Capo.
--The Country Waif (Francois le Champi) Collis, Eirene, tr. from Fr. LC 76-14125. 1977. 10.95x (ISBN 0-8032-0888-X); pap. 2.95 (ISBN 0-8032-5850-X, BB 627, Bison). U of Nebr Pr.
--Indiana. Ives, G. B., tr. from Fr. LC 75-25896. xxi, 327p. 1975. Repr. of 1900 ed. 17.00 (ISBN 0-86527-260-3). Fertig.
Sand, L. B. & Mumpton, F. A., eds. Natural Zeolites: Occurrence, Properties, Use. LC 77-30439. 1978. text ed. 115.00 (ISBN 0-08-021922-5). Pergamon.
Sand, Leonard B., jt. ed. see Flanigen, E. M.
Sandage, Allan. The Hubble Atlas of Galaxies. LC 60-16568. (Illus.). 141p. 1961. pap. 17.00 (ISBN 0-87279-629-9, 618). Carnegie Inst.
Sandage, Allan & Tammann, G. A. A Revised Shapley-Ames Catalog of Bright Galaxies. 1981. 29.00 (ISBN 0-87279-646-9). Carnegie Inst.
Sandage, Charles H., et al. Advertising: Theory & Practice. 10th ed. 1979. text ed. 18.95 (ISBN 0-256-02174-0). Irwin.
Sandak, Cass R. Christmas. (gr. 2-4). 1980. PLB 7.90 (ISBN 0-531-04147-6). Watts.
--Easter. (gr. 2-4). 1980. PLB 7.90 (ISBN 0-531-04148-4). Watts.
--Halloween. (gr. 2-4). 1980. PLB 7.90 (ISBN 0-531-04149-2). Watts.
--Valentine's Day. (gr. 2-4). 1980. PLB 7.90 (ISBN 0-531-04151-4). Watts.
Sandal, M. L., tr. Mimansa Sutras of Jaimini, 2 vols. 1022p. 1980. text ed. 60.00 (ISBN 0-8426-1651-9). Verry.
Sandars, John. Introduction to Wargaming. 11.95 (ISBN 0-7207-0861-3, Pub. by Michael Joseph). Merrimack Bk Serv.
Sandars, Mary F. The Life of Christina Rossetti. LC 74-141488. (Illus.). 291p. 1980. Repr. of 1930 ed. lib. bdg. 27.50x (ISBN 0-8371-5874-5). Greenwood.
Sanday, Peggy R. Female Power & Male Dominance: On the Origins of Sexual Inequality. LC 80-18461. (Illus.). 256p. Date not set. text ed. price not set (ISBN 0-521-23618-5); pap. text ed. price not set (ISBN 0-521-28075-3). Cambridge U Pr.
Sanday, W. Divine Overruling. 112p. Repr. of 1920 ed. 2.95 (ISBN 0-567-02225-0). Attic Pr.
--Outlines of the Life of Christ. 2nd ed. 285p. Repr. of 1906 ed. 4.95 (ISBN 0-567-02224-2). Attic Pr.
Sanday, W. & Headlam, A. C. Romans. 5th ed. (International Critical Commentary Ser.). 568p. Repr. of 1977 ed. 23.00x (ISBN 0-567-05026-2). Attic Pr.
Sandbach, F. H., jt. auth. see Gomme, A. W.
Sandbach, Francis. Environment, Ideology & Policy. LC 80-65192. 254p. 1980. text ed. 26.50 (ISBN 0-916672-53-0). Allanheld.
Sandbank, C. P. Optical Fibre Communications. LC 79-40822. 1980. 49.00 (ISBN 0-471-27667-7, Pub. by Wiley-Interscience). Wiley.
Sandberg, Alvin, jt. auth. see Fawcett, Susan.
Sandberg, Alvin, jt. auth. see Fawcett, Susan C.
Sandberg, Berent. Brass Diamonds. 1980. 8.95 (ISBN 0-453-00383-4, H383). NAL.
--Brass Diamonds. 1981. pap. 2.50 (ISBN 0-451-09665-7, E9665, Sig). NAL.
Sandberg, E. W., jt. auth. see Fowler, Frank P.
Sandberg, Inger. Boy with Many Houses. LC 76-84907. (Illus.). (ps-3). 1970. 4.95 o.s.i. (ISBN 0-440-00772-0, Sey Lawr). Delacorte.
--Come on Out, Daddy. LC 70-122771. (Illus.). (ps-3). 1971. 4.95 (ISBN 0-440-01522-7, Sey Lawr); PLB 4.58 (ISBN 0-440-01523-5). Delacorte.
--Little Ghost Godfrey. Leupold, Nancy S., tr. LC 69-16928. (Illus.). (ps-3). 1968. 4.95 o.s.i. (ISBN 0-440-04864-8, Sey Lawr). Delacorte.
--Where Does All That Smoke Come from? LC 72-1445. (Illus.). 32p. (ps-3). 1972. 4.95 o.s.i. (ISBN 0-440-09651-0, Sey Lawr); PLB 4.58 (ISBN 0-440-09652-9, 9652, Sey Lawr). Delacorte.
Sandberg, Karl C. & Tatham, Eddison C. French for Reading: A Programmed Approach for Graduate Degree Requirements. 1972. text ed. 13.95 (ISBN 0-13-331603-3). P-H.
Sandberg, Karl C. & Wende, John R. German for Reading: A Programmed Approach. 1973. pap. text ed. 14.95 (ISBN 0-13-354019-7). P-H.
Sandberg, Karl C., ed. Lectures et Conversations. (Fr.). 1970. pap. text ed. 6.95x (ISBN 0-89197-272-2). Irvington.
Sandbrook, Richard & Cohen, Robin. The Development of an African Working Class. 1976. pap. 9.00. U of Toronto Pr.
Sandburg, Carl. Abraham Lincoln, the Prairie Years & the War Years, 3 Vols. Set. pap. 6.95 (ISBN 0-440-30008-8, LE). Dell.
--Honey & Salt. LC 63-9836. 1967. pap. 2.95 (ISBN 0-15-642165-8, HPL15, HPL). HarBraceJ.
--Rootabaga Stories, Repr. Of 1922 Ed. Incl. Rootabaga Pigeons. Repr. of 1923 ed. LC 75-32204. (Classics of Children's Literature, 1621-1932: Vol. 65). (Illus.). 1976. PLB 38.00 (ISBN 0-8240-2314-5). Garland Pub.
Sandeen, Eric J. The Letters of Randolph Bourne: A Comprehensive Edition. 466p. 1981. 30.00 (ISBN 0-87875-190-4). Whitston Pub.
Sandeen, Ernest R. & Hale, Frederick, eds. American Religion & Philosophy: A Guide to Information Sources. LC 73-17562. (American Studies Information Guide Ser.: Vol. 5). 1978. 30.00 (ISBN 0-8103-1262-X). Gale.
Sander, August, illus. August Sander. LC 77-70069. (The Aperture Historie of Photography Ser.). (Illus.). 1978. bds. 8.95 (ISBN 0-89381-007-X). Aperture.
Sander, B. An Introduction to the Study of Fabrics of Geological Bodies. 1970. 94.00 (ISBN 0-08-006660-7). Pergamon.
Sander, K. F. & Reed, G. A. Transmission & Propagation of Electromagnetic Waves. LC 77-87390. (Illus.). 1978. 80.50 (ISBN 0-521-21924-8); pap. 17.50x (ISBN 0-521-29312-X). Cambridge U Pr.
Sander, Reinhard W., ed. From Trinidad: An Anthology of Early West Indian Writing. LC 77-20785. 1979. text ed. 37.50x (ISBN 0-8419-0352-2, Africana). Holmes & Meier.
Sander, Reinhard W., ed. see Ogali, Ogali.
Sander, Volkmar, ed. see Brecht, Bertold.
Sanderlin, David. Spelling for the Aviation Technician. 75p. (Orig.). 1980. write for info. (ISBN 0-89100-180-8). Aviation Maintenance.
Sanderlin, Owenita. Match Point. (gr. 3 up). 1979. pap. 1.25 (ISBN 0-307-21518-0, Golden Pr). Western Pub.
--Tennis Rebel. (gr. 7-12). 1980. pap. 1.25 (ISBN 0-440-98752-0, LFL). Dell.
--Tennis Rebel. (Triumph Bks.). (Illus.). (gr. 5 up). 1978. PLB 5.90 s&l o.p. (ISBN 0-531-01466-5). Watts.
Sanders. The Arrow Book of Good "N" Easy Cooking. (gr. 3-5). 1980. pap. 1.25 (ISBN 0-590-30066-0, Schol Pap). Schol Bk Serv.
--Fundamentals of Social Work Practice. 1981. pap. text ed. price not set. Duxbury Pr.
Sanders, C. Gordon, et al. Engineering Graphics Problem Book. 1977. perfect bdg. 9.95 (ISBN 0-8403-8004-6). Kendall-Hunt.
Sanders, Charles. The Scope of Satire. 1971. pap. 5.95x o.p. (ISBN 0-673-05887-5). Scott F.
Sanders, Charles R., ed. The Collected Leters of Thomas & Jane Welsh Carlyle, Vols. 8 & 9. 1980. 30.00 ea.; 59.75 set (ISBN 0-686-64383-6). Vol. 8 (ISBN 0-8223-0433-3). Vol. 9 (ISBN 0-8223-0434-1). Duke.
Sanders, Charles R. & Fielding, Kenneth J., eds. The Collected Letters of Thomas & Jane Welsh Carlyle, Vols. 8-9. LC 71-101132. (Illus., Consolidated Index in Vol. 9). 1981. Vol. 8, 1835-1836. 30.00 (ISBN 0-8223-0433-3); Vol. 9, 1836-1837. 30.00 (ISBN 0-8223-0434-1); Set. 59.75 (ISBN 0-686-69104-0). Duke.
Sanders, D. G. The Brasspounder. LC 77-72820. (Illus.). 1978. 8.95 o.p. (ISBN 0-8015-0881-9). Dutton.
Sanders, David C., jt. auth. see Otto, Henry J.
Sanders, Deidre, et al. Would You Believe This Too. LC 76-19815. (Illus.). (gr. 3 up). 1976. 5.95 o.p. (ISBN 0-8069-0098-9); PLB 5.89 o.p. (ISBN 0-8069-0099-7). Sterling.
--Would You Believe...? Useless Information You Can't Afford to Be Without. LC 74-82321. (Illus.). 128p. (gr. 7 up). 1974. 5.95 o.p. (ISBN 0-8069-0084-9); PLB 5.89 o.p. (ISBN 0-8069-0085-7). Sterling.
Sanders, Derek A. Auditory Perception of Speech: An Introduction to Principles & Problems. LC 76-27320. (Illus.). 1977. text ed. 16.95 (ISBN 0-13-052787-4). P-H.
Sanders, Donald H. Computers in Society. 3rd ed. 536p. 1981. text ed. 16.95 (ISBN 0-07-054672-X, C); instructor's manual 4.95 (ISBN 0-07-054673-8); study guide 7.95 (ISBN 0-07-054674-6); test bank 5.95 (ISBN 0-07-054675-4). McGraw.
Sanders, E. P., ed. Jewish & Christian Self-Definition, Vol. 1: The Shaping of Christianity in the Second & Third Centuries. LC 79-7390. 336p. 1980. 15.95 (ISBN 0-8006-0578-0, 1-578). Fortress.
Sanders, E. P., et al, eds. Jewish & Christian Self-Definition, Vol. 2: Aspects of Judaism in the Greco-Roman Period. LC 80-2391. 450p. 1981. 17.95 (ISBN 0-8006-0660-4, 1-660). Fortress.

Sanders, Ed. Fame & Love in New York. (New World Writing Ser.: No. 17). (Illus.). 320p. 1980. 17.95 (ISBN 0-913666-31-9); pap. 7.95 (ISBN 0-913666-32-7). Turtle Isl Foun.
--The Family. 1972. pap. 1.95 (ISBN 0-380-00771-1, 24802). Avon.
Sanders, Gladys, jt. auth. see Wisely, Rae.
Sanders, Gordon, jt. auth. see Wass, Alonzo.
Sanders, Helen F., ed. see Beidler, John X.
Sanders, Herbert H. & Tomimoto, Kenkichi. The World of Japanese Ceramics. LC 67-16771. (Illus.). 267p. 1981. 27.50 (ISBN 0-87011-042-X). Kodansha.
Sanders, I. T. The Community: An Introduction to a Social System. 3rd ed. 1975. 19.95 (ISBN 0-8260-7821-4). Wiley.
Sanders, Irwin, et al. East European Presantries: Social Reflections-an Annotated Bibliography of Periodical Articles, Vol.2. (Reference Books Ser.). 1981. 16.00 (ISBN 0-8161-8488-7). G K Hall.
Sanders, Ivor J. Feudal Military Service in England: A Study of the Constitutional & Military Powers of the Barones in Medieval England. LC 80-23778. (Oxford Historical Ser., British Ser.). xv, 173p. 1980. Repr. of 1956 ed. lib. bdg. 19.25x (ISBN 0-313-22725-X, SAFM). Greenwood.
Sanders, J. M. The Velocity of Light. 1965. 15.00 (ISBN 0-08-011315-X); pap. 7.50 (ISBN 0-08-011314-1). Pergamon.
Sanders, J. Oswald. Consider Him. 2nd ed. 1979. pap. write for info. (ISBN 0-85363-123-9). OMF Bks.
--Effective Prayer. pap. 3.50 (ISBN 0-8024-2322-1). Moody.
--Enjoying Intimacy with God. 218p. 1980. pap. 4.95 (ISBN 0-8024-2346-9). Moody.
--For Believers Only. LC 76-15347. Orig. Title: Real Discipleship. 1977. pap. 1.95 (ISBN 0-87123-161-1, 200161). Bethany Fell.
--Holy Spirit & His Gifts. (Contemporary Evangelical Perspectives Ser). kivar 4.95 (ISBN 0-310-32481-5). Zondervan.
--Just the Same Today. 1979. pap. 2.50 (ISBN 0-85363-105-0). OMF Bks.
--Mighty Faith. 1980. pap. 0.90 (ISBN 0-85363-030-5). OMF Bks.
--Problems of Christian Discipleship. 1977. pap. 2.10 o.p. (ISBN 0-85363-046-1). OMF Bks.
--Spiritual Lessons. 440p. 1980. pap. 2.95 (ISBN 0-8024-0106-6). Moody.
--Spiritual Maturity. (Orig.). 1969. pap. 1.95 (ISBN 0-8024-0103-1). Moody.
Sanders, J. T., jt. ed. see Irvine, S. H.
Sanders, Jack T. Ethics in the New Testament: Change & Development. LC 74-26342. 160p. 1975. 8.95 (ISBN 0-8006-0404-0, 1-404). Fortress.
Sanders, James B., ed. Information Market Place, 1978-1979: A Directory of Information Products & Services. 1978. pap. 21.50 o.p. (ISBN 0-8352-1079-0, Pub. by Learned Information, Europe Ltd.). Bowker.
Sanders, Jay H. & Gardner, Laurence B. Handbook of Medical Emergencies. 2nd ed. LC 78-50127. 1978. pap. 12.75 (ISBN 0-87488-635-X). Med Exam.
Sanders, Jennings B. Evolution of Executive Departments of the Continental Congress, 1774-1789. 6.00 (ISBN 0-8446-0888-2). Peter Smith.
--Presidency of the Continental Congress 1774-89: A Study in American Institutional History. 6.00 (ISBN 0-8446-0889-0). Peter Smith.
Sanders, John, ed. Photography Yearbook 1978. 1977. 21.95 o.p. (ISBN 0-85242-552-X, Pub. by Fountain). Morgan.
Sanders, John E. Principles of Physical Geology. 608p. 1981. text ed. 19.95 (ISBN 0-471-08424-7). Wiley.
Sanders, John E., et al. Physical Geology. 1976. text ed. 21.50 scp (ISBN 0-06-163403-4, HarpC); instr. manual & test bank avail. (ISBN 0-06-361160-0). Har-Row.
Sanders, John T. The Ethical Argument Against Government. LC 80-488. 271p. 1980. text ed. 18.25 (ISBN 0-8191-1015-9); pap. text ed. 9.25 (ISBN 0-8191-1016-7). U Pr of Amer.
Sanders, Kamala. Tempestuous Heights. 176p. 1981. 8.50 (ISBN 0-682-49741-X). Exposition.
Sanders, Lawrence. The First Deadly Sin. 1980. pap. 2.95 (ISBN 0-425-04692-3). Berkley Pub.
--The Marlow Chronicles. 1979. pap. text ed. 2.50 (ISBN 0-425-04390-8). Berkley Pub.
--The Sixth Commandment. 1980. pap. 2.75 (ISBN 0-425-04271-5). Berkley Pub.
--The Tangent Factor. 1979. pap. 2.75 (ISBN 0-425-04858-6). Berkley Pub.
--The Tenth Commandment. 1980. 12.95 (ISBN 0-686-64422-0). Putnam.
--The Third Deadly Sin. 480p. 1981. 13.95 (ISBN 0-399-12614-7). Putnam.
--The Tomorrow File. 1976. pap. 2.95 (ISBN 0-425-04994-9). Berkley Pub.
Sanders, Leonard. The Hamlet Warning. 1977. pap. 1.95 o.s.i. (ISBN 0-446-89370-6). Warner Bks.
Sanders, Lloyd C. Celebrities of the Century: Being a Dictionary of Men & Women of the Nineteenth Century. LC 68-27185. 1971. Repr. of 1887 ed. 54.00 (ISBN 0-8103-3774-6). Gale.
Sanders, Marion. Clinical Assessment of Learning Problems: Model, Process & Remedial Planning. new ed. 1978. text ed. 18.95 (ISBN 0-205-06149-4). Allyn.
Sanders, P. B., jt. ed. see Damane, M.
Sanders, P. B., tr. see Damane, M. & Sanders, P. B.
Sanders, Peter, jt. auth. see Beyersdorff, Gerald.
Sanders, Peter, jt. auth. see Bledsoe, Terry.
Sanders, Peter, jt. auth. see Byers, Stephen.
Sanders, Peter, jt. auth. see Kupper, Mike.
Sanders, Peter, jt. auth. see Mack, Nancy.
Sanders, Peter, jt. auth. see Milverstedt, Van.
Sanders, Peter, jt. auth. see Moses, Sam.
Sanders, Peter, jt. auth. see Reardon, Maureen.
Sanders, Peter, jt. auth. see Stokes, Bill.
Sanders, Peter, jt. auth. see Vonier, Dick.
Sanders, Peter, jt. auth. see Zavoral, Nolan.
Sanders, Rhea. The Fire Gardens of Maylandia. 1980. 10.00 (ISBN 0-937684-10-4). Tradd St Pr.
Sanders, Ron. Broadcasting in Guyana. (Case Studies on Broadcasting Systems). (Orig.). 1978. pap. 14.00 (ISBN 0-7100-0025-1). Routledge & Kegan.
Sanders, Ronald, jt. ed. see Fried, Albert.
Sanders, Rosanne. The Remembering Garden. (Clarkson N. Potter Bks.). (Illus.). 1980. 17.95 (ISBN 0-517-54169-6). Crown.
Sanders, Ruth M. A Book of Cats & Creatures. LC 80-70012. (gr. 2-6). 1981. PLB 8.95 (ISBN 0-525-26773-5). Dutton.
Sanders, Shirley F. Search for Enchantment. (YA) 1978. 5.95 (ISBN 0-685-86142-2, Avalon). Bouregy.
Sanders, Steven & Cheny, David. The Meaning of Life: Questions, Answers & Analysis. 1980. pap. text ed. 7.95 (ISBN 0-13-567438-7). P-H.
Sanders, Thomas E. Currents: Concerns & Composition. 1971. pap. text ed. 9.95x (ISBN 0-02-477600-9, 47760). Macmillan.
--Speculations: Fantasy - Science Fiction. LC 72-86794. 608p. 1973. pap. text ed. 8.95x (ISBN 0-02-477630-0). Macmillan.
Sanders, Thomas E. & Peek, Walter W. Literature of the American Indian. LC 72-89050. 480p. 1973. text ed. 15.95x (ISBN 0-02-477640-8). Macmillan.
--Literature of the American Indian. abridged ed. 1976. pap. 7.95x (ISBN 0-02-477650-5). Macmillan.
Sanders, Toby. How to Be a Compleat Clown. LC 78-7520. (Illus.). 288p. 1980. pap. 7.95 (ISBN 0-8128-6090-X). Stein & Day.
Sanders, Wilbur. Dramatist & the Received Idea. 1968. 58.00 (ISBN 0-521-06924-6). Cambridge U Pr.
--John Donne's Poetry. LC 75-149436. 1971. 29.95 (ISBN 0-521-07968-3); pap. 8.95x (ISBN 0-521-09909-9). Cambridge U Pr.
Sanders, William B. Detective Work: A Study of Criminal Investigations. LC 77-72687. (Illus.). 1979. pap. text ed. 7.95 (ISBN 0-02-927590-3). Free Pr.
--Detective Work: A Study of Criminal Investigations. LC 77-72687. (Illus.). 1977. 15.95 (ISBN 0-02-927660-8). Free Pr.
--Rape & Woman's Identity. LC 80-13346. (Sage Library of Social Research: Vol. 106). (Illus.). 184p. 1980. 18.00x (ISBN 0-8039-1449-0); pap. 8.95x (ISBN 0-8039-1450-4). Sage.
Sanders, William T. & Marino, Joseph P. New World Pre-History: Archaeology of the American Indians. 1970. pap. 6.95 ref. ed. (ISBN 0-13-616185-5). P-H.
Sanderson, A. E. Current Researches in Education & Educational Psychology: 1968-69. (General Ser.). 1970. text ed. 20.00x (ISBN 0-901225-29-0, NFER). Humanities.
Sanderson, Allen R., ed. DRI-McGraw-Hill Readings in Macroeconomics. (Illus.). 480p. 1981. pap. text ed. 7.95 (ISBN 0-07-054659-2). McGraw.
Sanderson, B. J., jt. auth. see Rourke, C. P.
Sanderson, Fred. Japan's Food Prospects & Policies. 1979. pap. 3.95 (ISBN 0-8157-7701-9). Brookings.
Sanderson, Fred & Cleveland, Harold. Finance & Trade. LC 74-78422. (Policy Papers Ser.: The Washington Papers, No. 14). 1974. 3.50x (ISBN 0-8039-0443-6). Sage.
Sanderson, Glen C., ed. Management of Migratory Shore & Upland Game Birds in North America. LC 79-23802. (Illus.). 1980. pap. 10.95 (ISBN 0-8032-9117-5, BB725, Bison). U of Nebr Pr.
Sanderson, Ivan T. Investigating the Unexplained: A Compendium of Mysteries of the Natural World. LC 78-157765. (Illus.). 1972. pap. 4.95 (ISBN 0-13-503169-9). P-H.
--Science in Culture: A Study of Values & Institutions. LC 79-57289. 1980. 10.95 (ISBN 0-89754-007-7); pap. 3.50 (ISBN 0-89754-006-9). Dan River Pr.
--Uninvited Visitors: A Biologist Looks at UFO's. (Illus.). 1967. 6.95 o.p. (ISBN 0-8092-9225-4). Contemp Bks.
Sanderson, James L. Sir John Davies. (English Authors Ser.: No. 175). 1975. lib. bdg. 10.95 (ISBN 0-8057-1141-4). Twayne.
Sanderson, James L. & Gordon, Walter K., eds. Exposition & the English Language: Introductory Studies. 2nd ed. (Orig.). 1969. pap. text ed. 15.50 (ISBN 0-13-298026-6). P-H.
Sanderson, James L., ed. see Shakespeare, William.
Sanderson, Jeppesen. Aviation-Aerospace Fundamentals Student Exercise Book. (Illus.). 1979. pap. text ed. 4.85 (ISBN 0-88487-041-3, SA325952). Jeppesen Sanderson.
--Jeppesen Instrument Rating Course (Mach 2) (Illus.). 1978. 35.95 (ISBN 0-88487-022-7, JE304907). Jeppesen Sanderson.
--Jeppesen Instrument Rating Manual. (Flight Instruction Manuals Ser.). (Illus.). 1978. pap. text ed. 17.95 o.p. (ISBN 0-88487-021-9, JE314923). Jeppesen Sanderson.
--Jeppesen Sanderson Aerospace Fundamentals Textbook. (Illus.). 1977. lib. bdg. 11.80 (ISBN 0-88487-043-X, SA315253). Jeppesen Sanderson.
Sanderson, Jeppesen, ed. see Lyon, Thoburn C.
Sanderson, John W. The Fruit of the Spirit. 144p. 1976. pap. 2.95 (ISBN 0-310-32542-0). Zondervan.
Sanderson, Kenneth M, ed. see Blair, Walter.
Sanderson, M. H. Scottish Rural Society in the Sixteenth Century. 1980. text ed. 27.75x (ISBN 0-85976-027-8). Humanities.
Sanderson, Marie C. & Schroeder, Rosella J. It's Not Really Magic: Microwave Cooking for Young People. LC 79-24795. (Doing & Learning Bks.). (Illus.). 104p. (gr. 5 up). 1981. PLB 7.95 (ISBN 0-87518-196-1). Dillon.
Sanderson, Michael. Sea Battles: A Reference Guide. LC 74-21917. (Illus.). 216p. 1975. 14.95x (ISBN 0-8195-4080-3, Pub. by Wesleyan U Pr). Columbia U Pr.
--Sucessful Problem Management. LC 78-21050. 1978. 19.95 (ISBN 0-471-04871-2, Pub. by Wiley-Interscience). Wiley.
--Universities in the Nineteenth Century. 1975. 20.00x (ISBN 0-7100-8061-1). Routledge & Kegan.
Sanderson, P. C. Minicomputers. text ed. 12.95 (ISBN 0-408-00213-1). Butterworths.
Sanderson, Richard N. The Islamic Movement & the Threat to Western Civilization. (Illus.). 141p. 1980. deluxe ed. 47.45 (ISBN 0-930008-59-6). Inst Econ Pol.
Sanderson, Sharon T., jt. auth. see Reed, Kathlyn L.
Sanderson, Steven E. Agrarian Populism & the Mexican State: The Struggle for Land in Sonora. 1981. 18.50x (ISBN 0-520-04056-2). U of Cal Pr.
Sandford, C. T. Economics of Public Finance. 1969. pap. 7.70 o.p. (ISBN 0-08-013468-8); pap. 7.00 o.p. (ISBN 0-08-013467-X). Pergamon.
--Economics of Public Finance. 2nd ed. LC 77-6680. 1977. text ed. 27.00 (ISBN 0-08-021843-1); pap. text ed. 14.00 (ISBN 0-08-021842-3). Pergamon.
Sandford, Christine. The Lion of Judah Hath Prevailed: Being the Biography of His Imperial Majesty Haile Selassie I. LC 73-135611. (Illus.). 192p. 1972. Repr. of 1955 ed. lib. bdg. 20.25x (ISBN 0-8371-5198-8, SLJ&). Greenwood.
Sandford, Christopher, jt. ed. see Chambers, David.
Sandford, D. M. Using Sophisticated Models in Resolution Theorem Proving. (Lecture Notes in Computer Science Ser.: Vol. 90). (Illus.). 239p. 1981. pap. 14.00 (ISBN 0-387-10231-0). Springer Verlag.
Sandford, J. C. The Domestic Rabbit. 3rd ed. LC 78-11915. 1979. 17.95 (ISBN 0-470-26526-4). Halsted Pr.
Sandford, Jeremy. Down & Out in Britain. (Illus.). 1971. text ed. 9.25x (ISBN 0-7206-0341-2). Humanities.
Sandford, John. The New German Cinema. (Illus.). 180p. 1980. 25.75x (ISBN 0-389-20015-8). B&N.
Sandford, Rick. Heroes Die Young. 1979. pap. 1.75 (ISBN 0-505-51361-7). Tower Bks.
Sandhu, Harjit S. Modern Corrections: The Offenders, Therapies & Community Reintegration. (Illus.). 368p. 1977. 14.00 (ISBN 0-398-03031-6); pap. 11.50 (ISBN 0-398-03032-4). C C Thomas.
Sandhu, Harpreet & Bukkila, Laura. Guide to Publishers & Distributors Serving Minority Languages. rev. ed. 176p. 1980. pap. 4.50 (ISBN 0-89763-051-3). Natl Clearinghse Bilingual Ed.
Sandhu, Harpreet K. & Barone, Jory H. Guide to Publishers & Distributors Serving Minority Languages. 171p. (Orig.). 1979. pap. 4.50 o.p. (ISBN 0-89763-012-2). Natl Clearinghouse Bilingual Ed.
Sandhu, J. Singh & Hendriks-Jansen, Horst. Environmental Designs for Handicapped Children. (Illus.). 1976. 24.95 (ISBN 0-685-81670-2, 00709-9, Pub. by Saxon Hse). Lexington Bks.
Sandifer, Frank H., jt. auth. see Mushkin, Selma J.
Sandilands, Roger J. Monetary Correction & Housing Finance in Colombia, Brazil & Chile. 182p. 1980. text ed. 41.00x (ISBN 0-566-00355-4, Pub. by Gower Pub Co England). Renouf.
Sandison, A. T., jt. auth. see Brothwell, Don.
Sandler. Amniotic Fluid & Its Clinical Significance. Date not set. price not set (ISBN 0-8247-1346-X). Dekker.
Sandler, Bernard & Posner, Steve. In Front of the Camera. 1981. 12.95 (ISBN 0-525-93176-7); pap. 7.95 (ISBN 0-525-93177-5). Dutton.
Sandler, Irving. The New York School: The Painters & Sculptors of the Fifties. LC 77-82357. (Icon Editions). (Illus.). 1978. 29.95 (ISBN 0-06-438505-1, HarpT); pap. 14.95 (ISBN 0-06-430094-3, HarpT). Har-Row.
--Twenty Artists: Yale School of Art, 1950-1970. LC 80-54616. (Illus.). 64p. 1981. pap. write for info. (ISBN 0-89467-016-6). Yale Art Gallery.
Sandler, M. & Gessa, G. L., eds. Sexual Behavior: Pharmacology & Biochemistry. LC 74-14478. 364p. 1975. 34.50 (ISBN 0-89004-005-2). Raven.
Sandler, M., jt. ed. see Costa, E.
Sandler, Martin W. This Was America. 1980. 19.95 (ISBN 0-316-77022-1). Little.
Sandler, Martin W. & Rozwenc, Edwin C. The People Make a Nation. (gr. 10). 1975. text ed. 17.20 (ISBN 0-205-04236-8, 7842368); tchrs. guide 3.20 (ISBN 0-205-04237-6, 7842376). Allyn.
Sandler, Martin W., et al. Founders & Forefathers: Who Were the People Who Made America? (The People Make a Nation Ser.). (gr. 7-12). 1971. pap. text ed. 4.80 (ISBN 0-205-03437-3, 7834373). Allyn.
--Modern Politics in America: How Did It Come About? (People Make a Nation Ser.). (gr. 7-12). 1971. pap. text ed. 4.40 (ISBN 0-205-03438-1, 7834381). Allyn.
--The People Make a Nation, Vols. 1 & 2. (Orig.). (gr. 7-12). 1971. pap. text ed. 9.60 ea. Vol. 1 (ISBN 0-205-03227-3, 7832273). Vol. 2 (ISBN 0-205-03228-1, 7832281). tchrs'. ed. 5.12 (ISBN 0-205-02701-6, 7827016); activity bk. 5.12 (ISBN 0-205-02700-8, 7827008). Allyn.
--Race, Poverty, & Youth: Can This Generation Build a Better America? (People Make a Nation Ser.). (gr. 7-12). 1971. pap. text ed. 5.20 (ISBN 0-205-03440-3, 7834403). Allyn.
--Slavery & Segregation: Did the Civil War Change America? (The People Make a Nation Ser.). (gr. 7-12). 1971. pap. text ed. 5.20 (ISBN 0-205-03439-X, 783439X). Allyn.
Sandler, Merton, ed. Mental Illness in Pregnancy & the Puerperium. (Illus.). 1979. text ed. 21.95x (ISBN 0-19-261150-X). Oxford U Pr.
--Psychopharmacology of Aggression. 1979. 34.50 (ISBN 0-89004-392-2). Raven.
Sandler, Michael, jt. auth. see Sandler, Richard.
Sandler, P. L., jt. auth. see Bolitho, A. R.
Sandler, Richard & Sandler, Michael. Daily Management of Youth - Onset Diabetes Mellitus: An Integrated Guide for Patients & Physicians. (Illus.). 102p. 1977. 12.25 (ISBN 0-398-03631-4). C C Thomas.
Sandler, S. Gerald & Nusbacher, Jacob, eds. Immunobiology of the Erythrocyte. LC 80-81465. (Progress in Clinical & Biological Research Ser.: Vol. 43). 360p. 1980. 40.00 (ISBN 0-8451-0043-2). A R Liss.
Sandler, Sheldon S. Picture Processing & Reconstruction: Dimensional & Structural Analysis. LC 74-25087. (Illus.). 128p. 1975. 22.95 (ISBN 0-669-97683-0). Lexington Bks.
Sandler, Stanley I. Chemical & Engineering Thermodynamics. LC 77-1312. 1977. text ed. 29.95x (ISBN 0-471-01774-4); solutions manual avail. (ISBN 0-471-02736-7). Wiley.
Sandler, Stanley R. & Karo, Wolf. Organic Functional Group Preparations, 4 vols. (Organic Chemistry Ser.: Vol. 12). Vol.1. 1969. 50.00 (ISBN 0-12-618550-6); Vol.2. 1971. 48.00 (ISBN 0-12-618552-2); Vol. 3. 1972. 48.00 (ISBN 0-12-618553-0); 120.05 set (ISBN 0-686-66355-1). Acad Pr.
Sandmaier, Marian. The Invisible Alcoholics: Women & Alcohol Abuse in America. 324p. 1981. pap. 4.95 (ISBN 0-07-054661-4). McGraw.
Sandman, Larry, ed. A Guide to Greeting Card Writing. LC 80-19737. 256p. 1980. 10.95 (ISBN 0-89879-022-0). Writers Digest.
Sandman, Peter. Students & the Law. 1971. pap. 1.95 o.s.i. (ISBN 0-02-081470-4, Collier). Macmillan.
Sandman, Peter & Goldenson, Dan. Unabashed Career Guide. 1969. pap. 1.95 o.s.i. (ISBN 0-02-081490-9, Collier). Macmillan.
Sandman, Peter M., ed. see Philpot, Frank A.

Sandman, Peter M., et al. Media: An Introductory Analysis of American Mass Communication. 2nd ed. 1976. 16.95x (ISBN 0-13-572586-0); pap. text ed. 12.95x (ISBN 0-13-572578-X). P-H.

Sandman, Wm. E. & Hayes, John P. How to Win Productivity in Manufacturing. (Illus.). 224p. (Orig.). 1980. pap. 14.95 (ISBN 0-9604612-0-5). Yellow Bk PA.

Sandmel, Samuel. The Hebrew Scriptures: An Introduction to Their Literature & Religious Ideas. 1978. pap. 9.95x (ISBN 0-19-502369-2). Oxford U Pr.

--Judaism & Christian Beginnings. 25.00 (ISBN 0-19-502281-5); pap. 7.95x (ISBN 0-19-502282-3). Oxford U Pr.

--A Little Book on Religion: For People Who Are Not Religious. LC 75-1831. 1975. pap. 3.95 (ISBN 0-89012-002-1). Anima Pubns.

--Philo of Alexandria: An Introduction. 1979. 13.95 (ISBN 0-19-502514-8); pap. 5.95 (ISBN 0-19-502515-6). Oxford U Pr.

Sandmeyer, Louise, jt. auth. see Bartsch, Karl.

Sandmo, Agnar, ed. Essays in Public Economics. LC 77-7. 1978. 31.95 (ISBN 0-669-01424-9). Lexington Bks.

Sandner, Donald. Navajo Symbols of Healing: Essays, Aphorisms, Autobiographical Writings. 1979. pap. 8.95 (ISBN 0-15-665445-8, Harv). HarBraceJ.

Sandon, Henry. Royal Worcester Porcelain from 1862 to the Present Day. 1979. 29.95 o.p. (ISBN 0-214-20106-6, 8070, Dist. by Arco). Barrie & Jenkins.

Sandor, Bela I. Experiments in Strengths of Materials. (Illus.). 1980. pap. text ed. 9.95 (ISBN 0-13-295329-3). P-H.

--Fundamentals of Cyclic Stress & Strain. LC 70-176415. (Illus.). 204p. 1972. text ed. 17.50x (ISBN 0-299-06100-0). U of Wis Pr.

--Strength of Materials. (Illus.). 1978. ref. ed. 24.95 (ISBN 0-13-852418-1). P-H.

Sandor, Richard S., tr. Bernheim's New Studies in Hypnotism. 1980. 27.50 (ISBN 0-8236-0496-9). Intl Univs Pr.

Sandorvan, Lee W. A Negative Critique of the Philosophy of Johann Gottlieb Fichte. (Essential Library of the Great Philosophers). (Illus.). 141p. 1980. deluxe ed. 49.85 (ISBN 0-89266-268-9). Am Classical Coll Pr.

Sandoval, Ruben & Strick, David. Games, Games, Games, Juegos, Juegos, Juegos: Chicano Children at Play--Games & Rhymes. (gr. 1 up). 1977. PLB 6.95 (ISBN 0-385-05438-6). Doubleday.

Sandoval-Groce. Mundo Con Palabras. (Illus.). (gr. k-3). 1976. pap. 6.99 (ISBN 0-87892-886-3); tchr's handbook 3.99 (ISBN 0-87892-885-5); tapes 144.30 (ISBN 0-87892-883-9); dup. masters 4.59 (ISBN 0-87892-882-0). Economy Co.

Sandoz, Mari. Beaver Men. (American Procession Ser). (Illus.). 1975. Repr. of 1964 ed. 9.95 (ISBN 0-8038-0674-4). Hastings.

--The Beaver Men: Spearheads of Empire. LC 77-14081. (Illus.). 1978. pap. 5.95 (ISBN 0-8032-5884-4, BB 658, Bison). U of Nebr Pr.

--The Buffalo Hunters: The Story of the Hide Men. LC 77-14079. 1978. pap. 4.50 (ISBN 0-8032-5883-6, BB 659, Bison). U of Nebr Pr.

--Cattlemen. 1975. Repr. 11.95 (ISBN 0-8038-1087-3). Hastings.

--The Cattlemen: From the Rio Grande across the Far Marias. LC 77-14078. 1978. pap. 7.95 (ISBN 0-8032-5882-8, BB 660, Bison). U of Nebr Pr.

--Cheyenne Autumn. 1969. pap. 2.95 (ISBN 0-380-01094-1, 52621, Discus). Avon.

--Cheyenne Autumn. 1975. Repr. 9.95 (ISBN 0-8038-1094-6). Hastings.

--Crazy Horse. 1975. Repr. 10.95 (ISBN 0-8038-1119-5). Hastings.

--Crazy Horse, the Strange Man of the Oglalas. LC 42-50340. (Illus.). 1961. pap. 4.50 (ISBN 0-8032-5171-8, BB 110, Bison). U of Nebr Pr.

--Love Song to the Plains. LC 61-6441. (Illus.). 1966. pap. 3.50 (ISBN 0-8032-5172-6, BB 349, Bison). U of Nebr Pr.

--Old Jules. LC 35-27361. 1962. pap. 4.95 (ISBN 0-8032-5173-4, BB 100, Bison). U of Nebr Pr.

--Slogum House. LC 80-22077. 336p. 1981. 17.95x (ISBN 0-8032-4126-7); pap. 5.95 (ISBN 0-8032-9123-X, BB 756, Bison). U of Nebr Pr.

--Son of the Gamblin' Man: The Youth of an Artist. LC 76-17066. 1976. 14.95x (ISBN 0-8032-0895-2); pap. 3.95 (ISBN 0-8032-5833-X, BB 626, Bison). U of Nebr Pr.

--These Were the Sioux. 1975. Repr. 6.95 (ISBN 0-8038-7060-4). Hastings.

Sandreuter, William O. Whitewater Canoeing. 1976. 10.95 (ISBN 0-87691-223-4). Winchester Pr.

Sandroff, Ronni. Fighting Back. 1979. pap. 1.95 o.s.i. (ISBN 0-515-05120-9). Jove Pubns.

Sandry, Esther. Clerical Office Practice Set. 2nd ed. (gr. 9-12). 1973. pap. 2.96 (ISBN 0-8224-1741-3); supplies 6.20 (ISBN 0-8224-2082-1); tchrs'. manual 1.72 (ISBN 0-8224-2081-3). Pitman Learning.

--Transcription Office Practice Set. 3rd ed. (gr. 9-12). 1973. pap. 6.20 (ISBN 0-8224-2076-7); key 3.16 (ISBN 0-8224-2077-5). Pitman Learning.

--Typewriting Office Practice Set. 2nd ed. (gr. 9-12). pap. 3.32 (ISBN 0-8224-2083-X); supplies 6.20 (ISBN 0-8224-2084-8); tchr's. man. & key 1.72 (ISBN 0-8224-2085-6). Pitman Learning.

Sands, Bill. Beginning Gymnastics. (Illus.). 1981. 14.95 (ISBN 0-8092-5948-6); pap. 6.95 (ISBN 0-8092-5947-8). Contemp Bks.

--My Shadow Ran Fast. 1964. 6.95 o.p. (ISBN 0-13-608984-4). P-H.

Sands, Gary & Bower, Lewis L. Housing Turnover & Housing Policy: Case Studies of Vacancy Chains in New York State. LC 76-12619. (Special Studies). (Illus.). 1976. text ed. 23.95 (ISBN 0-275-56690-0). Praeger.

Sands, Harry & Minters, Frances C. The Epilepsy Fact Book. (Illus.). 1979. pap. 8.95 (ISBN 0-684-16823-5, ScribT). Scribner.

Sands, Howard, jt. ed. see Hamet, Pavel.

Sands, Leo G. CBers' How-to Book. rev., 2nd ed. (Illus.). Date not set. pap. cancelled (ISBN 0-8104-0828-7). Hayden.

--Easy Way to Service Radio Receivers. LC 68-16049. 1968. 7.95 o.p. (ISBN 0-8306-8429-8, 429). TAB Bks.

--Most Often Asked Questions & Answers About Amateur Radio. 1979. pap. 5.50 (ISBN 0-8104-0852-X). Hayden.

--Sound Systems Installers Handbook. 3rd ed. LC 73-79074. Orig. Title: Commercial Sound Installers Handbook. (Illus.). 1973. pap. 5.95 o.p. (ISBN 0-672-20980-2, 20980). Sams.

Sands, Leo G., jt. auth. see Burns, Robert F.

Sands, Leo G., jt. auth. see Leon, George.

Sands, Melissa. The Making of the American Mistress. (Orig.). 1981. pap. 2.50 (ISBN 0-425-04751-2). Berkley Pub.

Sands, Norma. Standard American Bridge Updated. pap. 4.95 (ISBN 0-686-28759-2). Rocky Mtn Bks.

Sandstroem, Yvonne, tr. see Gustafsson, Lars.

Sandstrom, G. E. Man the Builder. 1970. 19.50 o.p. (ISBN 0-07-054663-0, P&RB). McGraw.

Sandum, Howard, ed. see Moorcock, Michael.

Sandusky, Jerry. Developing Linebackers the Penn State Way. LC 80-84214. (Fitness America Ser.). (Illus.). 160p. (Orig.). 1981. pap. text ed. 5.95 (ISBN 0-918438-64-0). Leisure Pr.

Sandved, Kjell B. & Abbott, R. Tucker. Shells in Color. (Illus.). 1976. pap. 4.95 o.p. (ISBN 0-14-004237-7). Penguin.

Sandven, Johs. Projectometry. 1975. text ed. 26.00 (ISBN 8-200-04844-6, Dist. by Columbia U Pr). Universitet.

Sandver, Marcus H. & Blaine, Harry R. TEACHNEG: A Collective Bargaining Simulation in Public Education. 1980. pap. text ed. 3.95 (ISBN 0-88244-209-0). Grid Pub.

Sandweiss, Martha A., jt. auth. see Corpron, Carlotta.

Sandwell, Beryl & Atkinson, Jon. Writing for Cash. 1975. 6.95 (ISBN 0-236-31140-9, Pub. by Paul Elek). Merrimack Bk Serv.

Sandy, Stephen. The Raveling of the Novel: Studies in Romantic Fiction from Walpole to Scott. rev. ed. Varma, Devendra P., ed. LC 79-8476. (Gothic Studies & Dissertations Ser.). 1980. lib. bdg. 25.00x (ISBN 0-405-12660-3). Arno.

Sandys, Charles. A History of Gavelkind & Other Remarkable Customs in the County of Kent. xvi, 352p. 1981. Repr. of 1851 ed. lib. bdg. 35.00x (ISBN 0-8377-1117-7). Rothman.

Sandys, Elspeth. The Burning Dawn. (Orig.). Date not set. pap. 3.25 (ISBN 0-440-10882-9). Dell.

Sandys, George, jt. auth. see Ovid.

Sandys, J. E., ed. see Cope, E. M.

Sandywell, B. & Silverman, D. Problems of Reflexivity & Dialectics in Sociological Inquiry: Language Theorizing Difference. 1975. 15.00x (ISBN 0-7100-8304-1). Routledge & Kegan.

Sandzen, S. C., Jr. Atlas of Acute Hand Injuries. LC 79-21848. (Illus.). 456p. 1980. 95.00 (ISBN 0-88416-030-0, Dist. by McGraw). PSG Pub.

Sanecki, Kay N. The Complete Book of Herbs. (Illus.). 252p. 1974. 12.95 (ISBN 0-02-606890-7). Macmillan.

Saner, Gunay, ed. Chromium in Nutrition & Disease. LC 80-81854. (Current Topics in Nutrition & Disease: Vol. 2). 146p. 1980. 16.00 (ISBN 0-8451-1601-0). A R Liss.

Saner, Reg. Climbing into the Roots. LC 75-7953. 96p. 1976. 7.95 o.p. (ISBN 0-06-013762-2, HarpT); pap. 3.50 (ISBN 0-06-013763-0, TD233, HarpT). Har-Row.

Sanesi, P., jt. ed. see Franzosini, P.

Sanford, Agnes. Healing Gifts of the Spirit. 1976. pap. 1.75 (ISBN 0-89129-188-1). Jove Pubns.

--Healing Power of the Bible. 1976. pap. 1.75 (ISBN 0-89129-192-X). Jove Pubns.

--Route One. LC 74-25139. 1976. pap. 3.95 o.p. (ISBN 0-88270-155-X). Logos.

Sanford, Aubrey. Human Relations: The Theory & Practice of Organizational Behavior. 2nd ed. (Business Ser.). 1977. text ed. 18.95 (ISBN 0-675-08505-5); instructor's manual 3.95 (ISBN 0-685-74283-0). Merrill.

Sanford, Aubrey, jt. auth. see Bracey, Hyler J.

Sanford, Aubrey, et al. Communication Behavior in Organizations. new ed. 1976. text ed. 16.95x (ISBN 0-675-08601-9). Merrill.

Sanford, Bob. Riding the Dirt. 1973. 10.95 (ISBN 0-87880-012-3). Norton.

Sanford, Don. Prayers for Every Occasion. (Orig.). pap. 2.50 (ISBN 0-310-32582-X). Zondervan.

Sanford, Harry, jt. auth. see Lamb, Max.

Sanford, John. Invisible Partners. LC 79-56604. (Orig.). 1980. pap. 5.95 (ISBN 0-8091-2277-4). Paulist Pr.

--To Feed Their Hopes: A Book of American Women. LC 80-16505. 275p. 1980. 12.95 (ISBN 0-252-00804-9). U of Ill Pr.

Sanford, John A. Dreams: God's Forgotten Language. LC 60-29727. 1968. 9.95 (ISBN 0-397-10056-6). Lippincott.

--Evil: The Shadow Side of Reality. 176p. 1981. 10.95 (ISBN 0-8245-0037-7). Crossroad NY.

--The Kingdom Within. LC 80-82087. 232p. 1980. pap. 5.95 (ISBN 0-8091-2329-0). Paulist Pr.

--Kingdom Within: A Study of the Inner Meaning of Jesus' Sayings. LC 77-105548. 1970. 10.95 (ISBN 0-397-10101-5). Lippincott.

--The Man Who Wrestled with God. 144p. 1981. pap. 6.95 (ISBN 0-8091-2367-3). Paulist Pr.

Sanford, Linda T. Silent Children: A Parent's Guide to the Prevention of Child Abuse. LC 79-6284. 312p. 1980. 12.95 (ISBN 0-385-15142-X, Anchor Pr). Doubleday.

Sanford, Mollie D. Mollie: The Journal of Mollie Dorsey Sanford in Nebraska & Colorado Territories, 1857-1866. LC 75-8764. (Pioneer Heritage Series: Vol. 1). xii, 199p. 1976. pap. 3.95 (ISBN 0-8032-5826-7, BB 607, Bison). U of Nebr Pr.

Sanford, Nancy, jt. auth. see Parsons, Virgil.

Sanford, Nevitt. Learning After College. 264p. 1980. 14.50 (ISBN 0-917430-04-2); pap. 9.95 (ISBN 0-917430-03-4). Montaigne.

--Where Colleges Fail: A Study of the Student As a Person. LC 67-13279. (Higher Education Ser). 1967. 12.95x o.p. (ISBN 0-87589-003-2). Jossey-Bass.

Sanford, Nevitt & Comstock, Craig. Sanctions for Evil: Sources of Social Destructiveness. LC 79-129769. (Social & Behavioral Science Ser.). 1971. 17.95x o.p. (ISBN 0-87589-077-6). Jossey-Bass.

Sanford, R. Nevitt & Comstock, Craig. Learning After College. new ed. 277p. (Orig.). 1980. 14.50 (ISBN 0-917430-04-2); pap. 9.95 (ISBN 0-917430-03-4). Montaigne.

Sanford, Terry. Danger of Democracy: The Presidential Nominating Process. 160p. 1981. 15.00 (ISBN 0-86531-159-5). Westview.

Sanford, Trent E. The Architecture of the Southwest: Indian, Spanish, American. 1st ed. LC 76-100242. (Illus.). 1971. Repr. of 1950 ed. lib. bdg. 28.25x (ISBN 0-8371-4012-9, SAAS). Greenwood.

Sanford, William R. & Green, Carl R. Basic Principles of American Government. (gr. 10-12). 1977. text ed. 14.92 (ISBN 0-87720-622-8); pap. text ed. 8.50 (ISBN 0-87720-619-8). AMSCO Sch.

Sang, Bob. Sally & Joe. 288p. (Orig.). 1981. pap. 2.75 (ISBN 0-932844-04-9). R H Sang & Son.

Sang, Bob & Sang, Dusty. Deadly Companions. 1978. pap. 1.50 (ISBN 0-505-51243-2). Tower Bks.

Sang, Dusty. Hopes & Promises. 384p. (Orig.). 1981. pap. 2.95 (ISBN 0-932844-03-0). R H Sang & Son.

Sang, Dusty, jt. auth. see Sang, Bob.

Sangduk Kim, jt. auth. see Paik, Woon Ki.

Sanger, Donald B. & Hay, Thomas R. James Longstreet: Soldier, Politician, Officeholder, & Writer. 10.00 (ISBN 0-8446-0890-4). Peter Smith.

Sanger, Margaret. An Autobiography. 10.00 (ISBN 0-8446-0241-8). Peter Smith.

--What Every Girl Should Know. LC 80-16988. 96p. 1980. pap. 3.95 (ISBN 0-87754-219-8). Chelsea Hse.

--Works, 8 vols. Incl. Vol. 1. Margaret Sanger, an Autobiography. Guttmacher, A., intro. by. 33.00 (ISBN 0-08-018730-7); Vol. 2. Happiness in Marriage. 18.00 (ISBN 0-08-018731-5); Vol. 3. Motherhood in Bondage. 33.00 (ISBN 0-08-018732-3); Vol. 4. My Fight for Birth Control. 24.00 (ISBN 0-08-018733-1); Vol. 5. The New Motherhood. 18.00 (ISBN 0-08-018734-X); Vol. 6. The Pivot of Civilization. 21.00 (ISBN 0-08-018735-8); Vol. 7. What Every Boy & Girl Should Know. 13.50 (ISBN 0-08-018736-6); Vol. 8. Woman & the New Race. 18.00 (ISBN 0-08-018737-4). Repr. 200.00 set (ISBN 0-08-020244-6). Pergamon.

Sanger, Sirgay, jt. auth. see Petrillo, Madeline.

Sangster, Dess L., jt. auth. see Sangster, Tom.

Sangster, Tom & Sangster, Dess L. Alabama's Covered Bridges. LC 80-68408. (Illus.). 100p. (Orig.). 1980. pap. 20.00 (ISBN 0-938252-00-3); includes 13 lithographs 29.50, 1st 500 numbered & signed by artist Tom Sangster (ISBN 0-686-69146-6). Coffeetable.

Sangster, W. E. Teach Me to Pray. 1959. pap. 1.25x (ISBN 0-8358-0125-X). Upper Room.

Sani, Guelfo & Kos, Leon. Atlas of Vaginal Surgery. LC 76-55407. 1977. 66.50 (ISBN 0-471-02275-6, Pub. by Wiley Medical). Wiley.

Sanjian, Avedis K., ed. see Eghihse.

San Juan Cafferty, Pastora & Rivera-Martinez, Carmen. The Politics of Language: The Dilemma of Bilingual Education for Puerto Ricans. (Replica Edition Ser.). 200p. 1981. lib. bdg. 20.00x (ISBN 0-86531-170-6). Westview.

Sankar, D. Siva. Quantitative Problems in Physical & Chemical Biology: A Work Book. Date not set. price not set (ISBN 0-685-77285-3). PJD Pubns.

Sankaracarya. A Discourse on the Real Nature of Self. Das, Deb K., tr. from Sanskrit. (Writers Workshop Redbird Ser.). 1977. flexible bdg. 4.80 (ISBN 0-89253-618-7); lib. bdg. 8.00 (ISBN 0-89253-617-9). Ind-US Inc.

Sankaracharya. Atma-Bodhi, Self Knowledge. Mahadevan, T. M., tr. lib. bdg. 8.50 (ISBN 0-89253-043-X); pap. text ed. 2.00 (ISBN 0-89253-044-8). Ind-US Inc.

Sankaracharya, Srngeri. The Call of the Jagadguru. Aiyar, R. Krishnaswami, ed. 1961. pap. 1.75 o.p. (ISBN 0-89744-128-1, Pub. by Ganesh & Co India). Auromere.

Sankawulo, Wilton. The Marriage of Wisdom & Other Tales. (Secondary Readers Ser.). 1974. pap. text ed. 2.50x (ISBN 0-435-92820-1). Heinemann Ed.

Sankey, Alice. Basketballs for Breakfast. LC 63-20350. (Pilot Book Ser). (Illus.). (gr. 3-5). 1963. 6.95g (ISBN 0-8075-0583-8). A Whitman.

--Hit the Bike Trail. LC 73-7315. (Pilot Book Ser.). (Illus.). 128p. (gr. 4-7). 1974. 6.95 (ISBN 0-8075-3320-3). A Whitman.

--Judo Yell. LC 74-165819. (Pilot Book Ser). (Illus.). (gr. 4-8). 1971. 6.95 (ISBN 0-8075-4095-1). A Whitman.

Sankey, Benjamin. A Companion to William Carlos Williams' Paterson. LC 72-121193. (Illus.). 1971. 21.50x (ISBN 0-520-01742-0). U of Cal Pr.

Sankey, Ira D., et al. Gospel Hyms, 6 vols, No. 1-6. facsimile ed. LC 70-171076. (Earlier American Music Ser.: No. 5). 512p. 1972. Repr. of 1895 ed. lib. bdg. 25.00 (ISBN 0-306-77305-8). Da Capo.

Sankey, J. P. & Savory, T. H. British Harvestment: Arachniad: Opilidnes: Keip and Notes for the Indentification of the Species. 1974. 9.50 (ISBN 0-12-619050-X). Acad Pr.

Sankoff, Gillian. The Social Life of Language. LC 79-5048. (Conduct & Communication Ser.). 352p. 1980. 35.00x (ISBN 0-8122-7771-6); pap. 12.00x. U of Pa Pr.

Sanks, T. Howland. Authority in the Church: A Study in Changing Paradigms. LC 74-16565. (American Academy of Religion. Dissertation Ser.). 1974. pap. 7.50 (ISBN 0-88420-119-8, 010102). Scholars Pr Ca.

Sann, Paul. Kill the Dutchman! 352p. 1972. pap. 1.25 o.p. (ISBN 0-445-00138-0). Popular Lib.

--Trial in the Upper Room. Michaelman, Herbert, ed. 1981. price not set (ISBN 0-517-54284-6, Michaelman Books). Crown.

Sano, T., jt. ed. see Lieberman, M.

San Pedro, Diego de. The Castle of Love. LC 51-634. Repr. of 1549 ed. 23.00x (ISBN 0-8201-1217-8). Schol Facsimiles.

San Pedro, Diego De see San Pedro, Diego de.

San Severino, B. Quaranta Di see Mussolini, Benito.

Sansom, Basil. The Camp at Wallaby Cross: Aboriginal Fringe Dwellers in Darwin. 280p. 1980. text ed. 17.00x (ISBN 0-391-01696-2, Pub. by Australian Inst Australia); pap. text ed. 9.75x (ISBN 0-391-01697-0). Humanities.

Sansom, George. Japan: A Short Cultural History. rev. ed. LC 77-76152. (Illus.). 1952. 18.75x (ISBN 0-8047-0952-1); pap. 8.95 (ISBN 0-8047-0954-8, SP141). Stanford U Pr.

Sansom, William. The Ulcerated Milkman. 1979. 7.95 (ISBN 0-7012-0220-3, Pub. by Chatto Bodley Jonathan). Merrimack Bk Serv.
--A Young Wife's Tale. 1979. 7.95 (ISBN 0-7012-0396-X, Pub. by Chatto Bodley Jonathan). Merrimack Bk Serv.

San Souci, Robert. The Legend of Scarface: A Blackfeet Indian Tale. LC 77-15170. (gr. 1-3). 1978. 8.95a (ISBN 0-385-13247-6); PLB (ISBN 0-385-13248-4). Doubleday.

Sans Souci, Daniel, jt. auth. see Sans Souci, Robert.

Sans Souci, Robert & Sans Souci, Daniel. Song of Sedna. LC 80-627. (Illus.). 32p. (gr. 3). 1981. 8.95a (ISBN 0-385-15866-1); PLB (ISBN 0-385-15867-X). Doubleday.

Sansweet, S. Toys & Games. 1980. pap. 3.95 (ISBN 0-931064-27-9). Starlog Pr.

Sansweet, Stephen. Science Fiction Toys & Models, Vol. I. 1980. pap. 3.95 (ISBN 0-931064-27-9). O'Quinn Studio.

Sant, M. E. Industrial Movement & Regional Development: The British Case. 268p. 1975. text ed. 23.00 (ISBN 0-08-017965-7). Pergamon.

Santa Barbara Third Ward Relief Society, Church of Jesus Christ of Latter Day Saints. Blessings from the Kitchen. 1972. 6.00 (ISBN 0-686-17209-4). Sandollar Pr.

Santa, George F. A Modern Study in the Book of Proverbs: Charles Bridges Classic Revised for Today's Reader. LC 78-7667. 1978. kiver bdg. 17.95 (ISBN 0-915134-27-6); incl. study guide (ISBN 0-915134-49-7). Mott Media.

Santa Ana, Julio De see De Santa Ana, Julio.

Santana, Jorge A. Spanish for the Professions. 256p. 1981. pap. text ed. 7.95 (ISBN 0-394-32652-0). Random.

Santa Pinter, Jose J. Curso basico de Ciencias Sociales: Con especial interes para Puerto Rico. LC 79-15841. (Illus.). 500p. (Sp.). 1980. pap. text ed. write for info. (ISBN 0-8477-2449-2). U of PR Pr.

Santa-Pinter, Julio J. Interpretacion De los Derechos Civiles En Puerto Rico. LC 77-25835. 1978. pap. 9.00 (ISBN 0-8477-3015-8). U of PR Pr.

Santas, Constantine. Aristotelis Valaoritis. LC 76-10673. (World Author Ser.: No. 406). 1976. lib. bdg. 12.50 (ISBN 0-8057-6246-9). Twayne.

Santa Vicca, Edmund F. Four French Dramatists: A Bibliography of Criticism of the Works of Eugene Brieux, Francois De Curel, Emile Fabre, Paul Hervieu. LC 74-7495. (Author Bibliographies Ser.: No. 17). 1974. 10.00 (ISBN 0-8108-0755-6). Scarecrow.

SantaVicca, Edmund F. Reference Work in the Humanities. LC 80-18783. 173p. 1980. 10.00 (ISBN 0-8108-1342-4). Scarecrow.

Santayana, George. Dominations & Powers: Reflections on Liberty, Society & Government. LC 75-158153. Repr. of 1954 ed. lib. bdg. 19.50x (ISBN 0-678-02775-7). Kelley.
--Interpretations of Poetry & Religion. 8.25 (ISBN 0-8446-0893-9). Peter Smith.
--Last Puritan: A Memoir in the Form of a Novel. 1936. 10.00 o.p. (ISBN 0-684-13132-3, ScribT). Scribner.
--The Life of Reason: Volume One, Reason in Common Sense. 1980. pap. text ed. 4.00 (ISBN 0-486-23919-5). Dover.
--The Life of Reason: Volume Two, Reason in Society. 224p. 1980. pap. 3.50 (ISBN 0-486-24003-7). Dover.
--Scepticism & Animal Faith: Introduction to a System of Philosophy. 1955. pap. text ed. 5.00 (ISBN 0-486-20236-4). Dover.
--Selected Critical Writings, 2 Vols. Henfrey, Norman, ed. (Orig.). 1968. Vol. 1. 42.00 (ISBN 0-521-07103-8); Vol. 2. 35.50 o.p. (ISBN 0-521-07104-6); Vol. 1. pap. 13.95 (ISBN 0-521-09463-1); Vol. 2. pap. 10.50 (ISBN 0-521-09464-X). Cambridge U Pr.
--Sense of Beauty. 1896. pap. text ed. 2.50 (ISBN 0-486-20238-0). Dover.
--Winds of Doctrine & Platoism & the Spiritual Life. 1958. 8.25 (ISBN 0-8446-0242-6). Peter Smith.

Santayana, Manuel J., tr. see Inclan, Josefina.

Sante, Daniel P. Automatic Control System Technology. (Illus.). 1980. text ed. 19.95 (ISBN 0-13-054627-5). P-H.

Santee, Ross. Apache Land. LC 47-11035. (Illus.). 1971. pap. 4.25 (ISBN 0-8032-5737-6, BB 534, Bison). U of Nebr Pr.
--Cowboy. LC 77-7271. (Illus.). 1977. 11.95x (ISBN 0-8032-0931-2); pap. 3.50 (ISBN 0-8032-5867-4, BB 645, Bison). U of Nebr Pr.
--Lost Pony Tracks. LC 53-12239. (Illus.). vi, 303p. 1972. pap. 5.95 (ISBN 0-8032-5740-6, BB 521, Bison). U of Nebr Pr.
--Men & Horses. LC 76-57158. (Illus.). 1977. 11.95x (ISBN 0-8032-0919-3); pap. 3.50 (ISBN 0-8032-5859-3, BB 639, Bison). U of Nebr Pr.
--Rummy Kid Goes Home & Other Stories of the Southwest. (Illus.). 1965. 6.95 (ISBN 0-8038-6306-3). Hastings.

Santeford, H., ed. see U. S. National Committee for the International Hydrological Decade.

Santer, M., jt. ed. see Wiles, M.

Santesson, R. & Kaerre, Karl K. Swedish-English, English-Swedish Dictionary, 2 vols. 1976. Set. cancelled (ISBN 9-1241-9070-5). Heinman.

Santeusanio, Richard P. Developing Reading Skills for Business & Industry. LC 80-23463. 330p. 1980. pap. 9.95 (ISBN 0-8436-0792-0). CBI Pub.

Santhanam, K. Satyagraha & the State. 2.75x o.p. (ISBN 0-210-33743-5). Asia.
--Transition in India & Other Essays. 1964. 7.00x o.p. (ISBN 0-210-27002-0). Asia.
--Union State Relations in India. 3.25x o.p. (ISBN 0-210-33973-X). Asia.

Santhi, S. Arangetral. (Indian Poetry Ser.). 66p. 1974. lib. bdg. 6.95 (ISBN 0-88253-463-7). Ind-US Inc.
--Lamplight in the Sun. 4.80 (ISBN 0-89253-766-3); flexible cloth 4.00 (ISBN 0-89253-767-1). Ind-US Inc.
--Rhyme & Punishment: Random & Not So Academic Graffiti. (Indian Poetry Ser.). 80p. 1975. 6.00 (ISBN 0-89253-015-4). Ind-US Inc.
--Whispers Near Niagara. 5.00 (ISBN 0-89253-731-0); flexible cloth 4.00 (ISBN 0-89253-732-9). Ind-US Inc.

Santholzer, R. W. Five Language Dictionary of Surface Coatings, Platings, Product Finishing, Plastics & Rubber. 1969. 60.00 (ISBN 0-08-012336-8). Pergamon.

Santi, Bruno. Leonardo Da Vinci. (Scala Art Book). (Illus.). 1978. pap. 7.95 o.p. (ISBN 0-8467-0454-4, Pub. by Two Continents). Hippocrene Bks.

Santi, Paul & Hill, Richard, eds. The Europeans in the Sudan Eighteen Thirty Four to Eighteen Seventy Eight. (Illus.). 352p. 1980. 45.00 (ISBN 0-19-822718-3). Oxford U Pr.

Santiago Romero, Basilio. Tratado De Instrumentos Negociables. 2nd, enl.,rev. ed. LC 79-22321. (Illus.). 1980. write for info. (ISBN 0-8477-2636-3). U of PR Pr.

Santibanez, jt. auth. see Ludwig.

Santillana, Giorgio De see De Santillana, Giorgio.

Santini, Maurizo, ed. see Golgi Centennial Symposium, September 1973.

Santini, Rosemarie. Agnes Nixon's All My Children Book III: The Lovers. (Orig.). pap. 2.50 (ISBN 0-515-04896-8). Jove Pubns.
--Agnes Nixon's All My Children: Erica, Bk. II. 224p. (Orig.). 1980. pap. 2.25 (ISBN 0-515-04895-X). Jove Pubns.
--The Lovers. (Book III of Agnes Nixon's All My Children Ser.). 240p. (Orig.). 1981. pap. 2.50 (ISBN 0-515-04896-8). Jove Pubns.

Santini, Rosmarie. Agnes Nixon's All My Children: Tara & Philip, Bk. 1. 250p. (Orig.). 1980. pap. 2.25 (ISBN 0-515-04892-5). Jove Pubns.

Santis, Vincent De see De Santis, Vincent.

Santley, Charles. Reminiscences of My Life. LC 80-2297. 1981. Repr. of 1909 ed. 37.50 (ISBN 0-404-18865-6). AMS Pr.
--Student & Singer. 1981. Repr. of 1892 ed. 39.50 (ISBN 0-404-18866-4). AMS Pr.

Santo, Louise del see Del Santo, Louise.

Santon, Fredrick. MGM Ziegfeld Trilogy: A Literary & Pictorial Treasury. LC 78-75335. (Illus.). cancelled (ISBN 0-498-02330-3). A S Barnes.

Santoni, Ronald & Somerville, John, eds. Social & Political Philosophy: Readings from Plato to Gandhi. LC 63-18039. 1963. pap. 4.95 (ISBN 0-385-01238-1, A370, Anch). Doubleday.

Santore, Ron. Eighty-Eighty Machine Language Programming for Beginners. LC 78-53003. 1978. pap. 7.95 (ISBN 0-918398-14-2). Dilithium Pr.

Santore, Ron, et al. H-Eight Programming for Beginners. 175p. 1981. pap. 8.95 (ISBN 0-918398-17-7). Dilithium Pr.

Santoro, Caterina, ed. Documents of Milanese Ambassadors in France & Burgundy, 1450-1483, Vol. 3. LC 68-20933. 508p. 1980. 50.00x o.p. (ISBN 0-87580-069-6). N Ill U Pr.

Santos, Bienvenido N. Scent of Apples: A Collection of Stories. LC 79-4857. 250p. 1979. 12.95 (ISBN 0-295-95683-6); pap. 6.95 (ISBN 0-295-95695-X). U of Wash Pr.

Santos, Mary G. Math Can Be Easy. 90p. (Orig.). 1980. pap. 6.00 (ISBN 0-914562-10-X). Merriam-Eddy.

Santos, Nelly E. Espanol Comerclal. (Illus.). 410p. 1981. text ed. 17.50 scp (ISBN 0-06-045725-2, HarpC). Har-Row.

Santos, W. J., et al, eds. Nutrition & Food Science: Present Knowledge & Utilization, 3 vols. 1980. 195.00 set (Plenum Pr); Vol. 1, 850p. 75.00 (ISBN 0-306-40342-0); Vol. 2, 900p. 79.50 (ISBN 0-306-40343-9); Vol. 3, 760p. 69.50 (ISBN 0-306-40344-7). Plenum Pub.

Santostefano, Sebastiano. A Biodevelopmental Approach to Clinical Child Psychology: Cognitive Controls & Cognitive Control Therapy. LC 78-18485. (Wiley Ser. on Personality Processes). 1978. 45.00 (ISBN 0-471-75380-7, Pub. by Wiley-Interscience). Wiley.

Santrock, John W. Adolescence: An Introduction. 600p. 1981. pap. text ed. write for info. (ISBN 0-697-06635-5); instrs.' manual avail. (ISBN 0-697-06640-1). Wm C Brown.

Santschi, R. J. Treasure Trails. (Doodlebug Edition Ser.). 1974. plastic bag 6.00 (ISBN 0-89316-612-X); pap. 4.00 (ISBN 0-89316-601-4). Exanimo Pr.

Santucci, James A. An Outline of Vedic Literature. Bradford, M. Gerald, ed. LC 76-27859. (American Academy of Religion. Aids for the Study of Religion Ser.). 1976. pap. 6.00 (ISBN 0-89130-085-6, 010305). Scholars Pr Ca.

Santuccio, Mario, jt. auth. see Acquaviva, Sabino.

Santucho, Oscar J. George Gordon, Lord Byron: A Comprehensive Bibliography of Secondary Materials in English, 1807-1974. LC 76-41006. (Author Bibliographies Ser.: No. 30). 1977. 27.50 (ISBN 0-8108-0982-6). Scarecrow.

Santvoord, George Van see Harris, Joel C.

Sanyal, B. S. Culture - an Introduction. 1962. 10.00x (ISBN 0-210-34097-5). Asia.

Sanyal, Modhusudan. A Rumour of the Flesh & Soul. (Writers Workshop Redbird Ser.). 1975. 8.00 (ISBN 0-88253-620-6); pap. text ed. 4.00 (ISBN 0-88253-619-2). Ind-US Inc.

Sanzone, John G., jt. auth. see Reagan, Michael D.

Sanzotta, Donald. Manager's Guide to Interpersonal Relations. (Illus.). 1979. 12.95 (ISBN 0-8144-5508-5). Am Mgmt.
--Motivational Theories & Applications for Managers. new ed. LC 76-41732. 1977. 11.95 (ISBN 0-8144-5430-5). Am Mgmt.

Saoben, Marten & Ward, Janet. Pattern Cutting & Making up: Volume 2, Cutting & Making Skirts & Sleeves. 192p. 1980. 45.00 (ISBN 0-7134-3559-3, Pub. by Batsford England); pap. 30.00 (ISBN 0-7134-3560-7). David & Charles.

Sapeika, N. Food Pharmacology. 200p. 1969. pap. 12.00 spiral (ISBN 0-398-01648-8). C C Thomas.

Saper, Joel R. Migraine: Classification, Diagnosis & Treatment. 1981. write for info. (ISBN 0-88416-282-6, 282). PSG Pub.

Saperstein, Marc, jt. auth. see Brickner, Balfour.

Sapery, Elizabeth, jt. ed. see Alexander, Rodney.

Sapienza, D., et al. Readings on Managing Hotels-Restaurants-Institutions. 1977. pap. text ed. 12.95x (ISBN 0-8104-9469-8); net instructor's manual 1.95 (ISBN 0-8104-9473-6). Hayden.

Sapio, Rodolfo De see De Sapio, Rodolfo.

Sapio, Victor A. Pennsylvania & the War of Eighteen Twelve. LC 70-94070. (Illus.). 216p. 1970. 11.00x (ISBN 0-8131-1193-5). U Pr of Ky.

Sapir. Language. 1980. text ed. 10.50x (ISBN 0-246-11074-0). Humanities.

Sapir, E. Notes on Chasta Costa Phonology & Morphology. (Anthropological Publications Ser.: Vol. 2-2). (Illus.). 1914. 2.00 (ISBN 0-686-24092-8). Univ Mus of U.

Sapir, Edward. Culture, Language, & Personality: Selected Essays. Mandelbaum, David G., ed. 1949. pap. 5.95x (ISBN 0-520-01116-3, CAL5). U of Cal Pr.
--Language. 2nd ed. 1979. 11.95x (ISBN 0-8464-0059-6). Beekman Pubs.
--Selected Writings of Edward Sapir in Language, Culture, & Personality. Mandelbaum, David G., ed. 1949. 30.00x (ISBN 0-520-01115-5). U of Cal Pr.

Sapir, J. David & Crocker, J. Christopher, eds. The Social Use of Metaphor: Essays on the Anthropology of Rhetoric. LC 76-53200. 1977. 16.00x (ISBN 0-8122-7725-2). U of Pa Pr.

Sapir, Richard & Murphy, Warren. The Destroyer, No. 11: Kill or Cure. (Orig.). 1974. pap. 1.95 (ISBN 0-523-41226-6). Pinnacle Bks.

Sapire, K. E., jt. auth. see Philpott, R. H.

Sapolsky, Harvey M., jt. ed. see Altman, Stuart.

Saporetti, C. Assur 114446: La Famiglia "a". Bucellati, G., ed. (Cybernetica Mesopotamia Ser.). 139p. 1979. pap. 9.50 soft only (ISBN 0-89003-036-7). Undena Pubns.

Saporetti, Claudio. Le Leggi Medioassire. Buccellati, Giorgio, ed. (Illus.). 181p. (Orig., Ital.). 1979. pap. 9.50 (ISBN 0-89003-036-7). Undena Pubns.

Sapori, Armando. Italian Merchant in the Middle Ages. 1970. pap. text ed. 3.95x (ISBN 0-393-09956-3, NortonC). Norton.

Saposnik, Irving S. Robert Louis Stevenson. (English Authors Ser.: No. 167). 168p. 1974. lib. bdg. 10.95 (ISBN 0-8057-1517-7). Twayne.

Sapp, Allen. A Cree Life: The Art of Allen Sapp. (Illus.). 1977. 24.95 (ISBN 0-295-95684-4, Pub. by Douglas & McIntyre Canada). U of Wash Pr.

Sappho. Memoir. 4th ed. Wharton, H. T., tr. 217p. 1974. Repr. of 1898 ed. text ed. 21.75x (ISBN 90-6090-002-2). Humanities.
--Poems of Sappho. Groden, Suzy Q., tr. LC 65-26542. (Orig.). 1966. pap. 4.95 (ISBN 0-672-60464-7, LLA214). Bobbs.

Sappington, Roger. The Brethren in the New Nation. (Illus.). 1976. 13.95 (ISBN 0-87178-113-1). Brethren.

Sapronova, I., tr. see Balalaev, G. A.

Sapse, Anne-Marie, et al. Computer Applications in the Private Security Business. LC 80-36754. (Praeger Special Studies). 154p. 1980. 18.95 (ISBN 0-03-057031-X). Praeger.

Sapsford, David. Labour Market Economics. (Illus.). 240p. 1981. text ed. 30.00x (ISBN 0-04-331082-6, 2621/2); pap. text ed. 14.95x3210-04-331083-4 (ISBN 0-04-331083-4). Allen Unwin.

Sarabhai, Mrinalini. Indian Dancing. 1967. pap. 2.00 (ISBN 0-88253-334-7). Ind-US Inc.

Saracino, Dan. Abstract Algebra: A First Course. LC 79-18692. (Illus.). 1980. text ed. 17.95 (ISBN 0-201-07391-9). A-W.

Saradananda, Swami. Sri Ramakrishna: The Great Master, Part I. new, rev. ed. Swami Jagadananda, tr. (Illus.). 563p. pap. 8.50x (ISBN 0-87481-495-2). Vedanta Pr.
--Sri Ramakrishna: The Great Master, Pt. 2. rev. ed. Jagadananda, Swami, tr. from Bengali. 1980. pap. 8.50x (ISBN 0-87481-496-0). Vedanta Pr.

Saraf, B., ed. Physics Through Experiment: Mechanical Systems, Vol. II. 1980. text ed. 17.50x (ISBN 0-7069-0771-X, Pub. by Vikas India). Advent Bk.

Saraf, B., et al. Physics Through Experiment, Vol. 1. 1978. 10.00 (ISBN 0-7069-0643-8, Pub. by Vikas India). Advent Bk.

Saraf, D. N. Crafts of India. (Illus.). 380p. 1980. 40.00x (ISBN 0-7069-0735-3, Pub. by Croom Helm Ltd England). Biblio Dist.

Saran, Paramatma. The Provincial Government of the Mughals, 1526-1658. 2nd ed. (Illus.). 464p. 1973. lib. bdg. 12.95x (ISBN 0-210-22690-0). Asia.

Saran, Parmatma & Eames, Edwin, eds. The New Ethnics: Asian Indians in the U. S. 410p. 1980. 29.95 (ISBN 0-03-051121-6). Praeger.

Sarason, Barbara R., jt. auth. see Sarason, Irwin G.

Sarason, I. G. Abnormal Psychology: Problem of Maladaptive Behavior. 2nd ed. (Illus.). 1976. 21.95 o.p. (ISBN 0-13-001123-1); pap. 7.50 readings o.p. (ISBN 0-13-756759-6). P-H.

Sarason, Irwin G. Personality: An Objective Approach. 2nd ed. LC 79-175797. 1972. text ed. 21.95 (ISBN 0-471-75406-4). Wiley.

Sarason, Irwin G. & Sarason, Barbara R. Abnormal Psychology: The Problem of Maladaptive Behavior. 3rd ed. (Century Psychology Ser.). (Illus.). 1980. text ed. 21.95 (ISBN 0-13-001107-X). P-H.

Sarason, Irwin G. & Spielberger, Charles D., eds. Stress & Anxiety, Vol. 7. LC 74-28292. (Clinical & Community Psychology Ser.). (Illus.). 384p. 1980. text ed. 25.50 (ISBN 0-89116-183-X). Hemisphere Pub.

Sarason, Seymour. Culture of the School & the Problem of Change. 1971. pap. text ed. 9.95x (ISBN 0-205-02840-3, 2228408). Allyn.

Sarason, Seymour B. Psychology Misdirected. LC 80-69283. 1981. 16.95 (ISBN 0-02-928100-8). Free Pr.
--Work, Aging, & Social Change: Professionals & the One Life-One Career Imperative. LC 76-27224. 1979. pap. text ed. 7.95 (ISBN 0-02-927930-5). Free Pr.

Saraswati, Swami K. Yogic Ways to Happiness. (Illus., Orig.). 1981. pap. 5.95 (ISBN 0-89407-039-8). Strawberry Hill.

Sarat, Austin, jt. auth. see Feely, Malcolm.

Sarat, Austin, jt. ed. see Goldman, Sheldon.

Sarbaugh, L. E. Intercultural Communication. (gr. 10 up). 1978. pap. text ed. 8.50x (ISBN 0-8104-6090-4). Hayden.

Sarbaugh, Larry E. Teaching Speech Communication. (General Education Ser.). 1979. text ed. 15.95 (ISBN 0-675-08300-1). Merrill.

Sarbin, Theodore R. & Coe, William C. Hypnosis: A Social Psychological Analysis of Influence Communication. LC 72-185784. 1980. Repr. of 1972 ed. 21.00x (ISBN 0-8290-0388-6). Irvington.

Sarbin, Theodore R. & Mancuso, James C. Schizophrenia: Medical Diagnosis or Moral Verdict? (Pergamon General Psychology Ser.). 25.00 (ISBN 0-08-024613-3); pap. 9.50 (ISBN 0-08-024612-5). Pergamon.

Sarbin, Theodore R. & Adelson, Daniel, eds. Challenges to the Criminal Justice System: The Perspectives of Community Psychology. LC 78-32181. (Community Psychology Ser.: Vol. V). 166p. 1979. 14.95 (ISBN 0-87705-380-4). Human Sci Pr.

Sarchet, Bernard R., jt. auth. see Amos, John M.

Sardar, Ziauddin. The Future of Muslim Civilization. 224p. 1979. 37.00x (ISBN 0-85664-800-0, Pub. by Croom Helm Ltd England). Biblio Dist.
--Islam: Outline of a Classification Scheme. 1979. 12.50 (ISBN 0-89664-408-1, Pub. by K G Saur). Shoe String.

Sardar, Ziauddin & Badawi, M. Zaki, eds. Hajj Studies, Vol. 1. (Illus.). 168p. 1978. 22.00x (ISBN 0-85664-681-4, Pub. by Croom Helm Ltd England). Biblio Dist.

SarDesai, D. R. Indian Foreign Policy in Cambodia, Laos & Vietnam, 1947-1964. 1969. 21.75x (ISBN 0-520-01119-8). U of Cal Pr.

SarDesai, D. R., jt. ed. see Chawla, Sudershan.

Sardinas, Joseph & Burch, John G. EDP Auditing: A Primer. 200p. 1981. pap. text ed. 10.95 (ISBN 0-471-12305-6). Wiley.

Sardinas, Joseph L., Jr., jt. auth. see Burch, John G., Jr.

Sardinias, Joseph L., Jr. Computing Today: An Introduction to Business Data Processing. 512p. 1981. text ed. 17.95 (ISBN 0-686-69273-X); pap. 5.95 student guide (ISBN 0-13-165100-5). P-H.

Sardou see Stanton, Stephen S.

Sareil, Jean & Ryding, William. Au Jour le Jour: A French Review. 2nd ed. LC 73-18083. 240p. 1974. text ed. 12.95 (ISBN 0-13-052977-X). P-H.

Sarel, S., ed. Organic Synthesis Two: Second IUPAC Symposium on Organic Synthesis, Jerusalem & Haifa, Israel, 10-15 September, 1978. (IUPAC Symposia Ser.). (Illus.). 1979. 35.00 (ISBN 0-08-022363-X). Pergamon.

Saretsky. Resolving Treatment Impasses. 1981. 19.95x (ISBN 0-87705-088-0). Human Sci Pr.

Sargant, Rose. Easy ABC Shorthand. 1964. pap. 3.00 o.s.i. (ISBN 0-910458-00-6). Select Bks.

Sargeant, J. A. Sumo: The Sport & the Tradition. LC 59-5993. (Illus.). 1959. pap. 4.25 (ISBN 0-8048-0556-3). C E Tuttle.

Sargeant, Ralph, ed. see Shakespeare, William.

Sargeant, Winthrop. Jazz, Hot & Hybrid. new 3rd ed. LC 74-20823. (Roots of Jazz Ser). 302p. 1975. lib. bdg. 22.50 (ISBN 0-306-70656-3); pap. 3.45 (ISBN 0-306-80001-2). Da Capo.

Sargeaunt, M. J. Operational Research for Management. 1965. 16.95x (ISBN 0-685-83666-5). Intl Ideas.

Sargen, Nicholas P. Tractorization in the United States & Its Relevance for the Developing Counteries. LC 78-75050. (Outstanding Dissertations in Economics Ser.). 1979. lib. bdg. 30.00 (ISBN 0-8240-4128-3). Garland Pub.

Sargent, Alice G. The Androgynous Manager. 240p. 1981. 12.95 (ISBN 0-8144-5568-9). Am Mgmt.

Sargent, Ben. Texas Statehouse Blues. 144p. 1980. pap. 5.95 (ISBN 0-932012-11-6). Texas Month Pr.

Sargent, Betsye. The Integrated Day in an American School. (Illus.). 1972. pap. 5.75 (ISBN 0-934338-25-6). NAIS.

Sargent, Bill. Shallow Waters: A Year of Cape Cod's Pleasant Bay. (Illus.). 144p. 1981. 17.95 (ISBN 0-395-29481-9). HM.

Sargent, C. S., ed. see Rehder, A.

Sargent, Carl L. Exploring Psi in the Ganzfeld. LC 80-82752. (Parapsychological Monograph Ser.: No. 17). (Illus.). 1980. pap. text ed. 6.00 (ISBN 0-912328-33-9). Parapsych Foun.

--Exploring the Ganzfeld. LC 80-82752. (Parapsychological Monograph: No. 17). 1980. pap. 6.00 (ISBN 0-912328-33-9). Parapsych Foun.

Sargent, Charles S. Manual of the Trees of North America, 2 Vols. 2nd ed. (Illus.). 1922. pap. text ed. 5.00 ea.; Vol. 1. pap. text ed. (ISBN 0-486-20277-1); Vol. 2. pap. text ed. (ISBN 0-486-20278-X). Dover.

Sargent, Daniel. Thomas More. 299p. 1980. Repr. of 1933 ed. lib. bdg. 30.00 (ISBN 0-89984-412-X). Century Bookbindery.

Sargent, E. C., jt. auth. see Plummer, F. B.

Sargent, Elizabeth O., jt. auth. see Prentice, T. Merrill.

Sargent, G. W., ed. Saikaku's the Japanese Family Storehouse. (University of Cambridge Oriental Pubns.). 1959. 48.00 (ISBN 0-521-06182-2). Cambridge U Pr.

Sargent, Howard. Fishbowl Management: A Participative Approach to Systematic Management. LC 77-27924. 1978. 19.95 (ISBN 0-471-03574-2, Pub. by Wiley-Interscience). Wiley.

Sargent, J. Society, Schools & Progress in India. LC 68-21106. 1968. 22.00 (ISBN 0-08-012840-8); pap. 11.25 (ISBN 0-08-012839-4). Pergamon.

Sargent, J. R., jt. auth. see Malins, D. C.

Sargent, Jean V. An Easier Way: A Handbook for the Elderly & Handicapped. (Illus.). 216p. 1981. pap. 9.95 (ISBN 0-686-69403-1). Iowa St U Pr.

Sargent, L. Manlius, Jr., et al. Individualized Mathematics Algebra 1: A Versatile Approach. (gr. 8-10). 1974. pap. text ed. 10.00x o.p. (ISBN 0-88334-064-X). Ind Sch Pr.

Sargent, Linda, jt. auth. see Martin, Betty.

Sargent, Lyman T. Contemporary Political Ideologies: A Comparative Analysis. 5th ed. 1981. pap. text ed. 8.95x (ISBN 0-256-02545-2). Dorsey.

--New Left Thought. 1972. pap. text ed. 9.50x (ISBN 0-256-01203-2). Dorsey.

Sargent, Michael. Mycenae. (Aspects of Greek Life). (Illus.). 1972. pap. text ed. 2.95x (ISBN 0-582-34401-8). Longman.

Sargent, Murray, III, et al. Laser Physics. LC 74-5049. (Illus.). 1974. text ed. 30.50 (ISBN 0-201-06912-1, Adv Bk Prog); pap. text ed. 18.50 (ISBN 0-201-06913-X, Adv Bk Prog). A-W.

Sargent, Nathan. Public Men & Events, 2 vols. LC 79-106496. (American Public Figures Ser). 1970. Repr. of 1875 ed. lib. bdg. 69.50 (ISBN 0-306-71873-1). Da Capo.

Sargent, Rodney. Christian in the Making. (Orig.). 1981. pap. price not set. NavPress.

Sargent, S. Stansfeld & Stafford, Kenneth R. Basic Teachings of the Great Psychologists. rev. ed. LC 62-15320. pap. 3.50 (ISBN 0-385-03006-1, C397, Dolp). Doubleday.

Sargent, S. Stansfeld & Smith, Marion, eds. Culture & Personality. LC 73-76142. (Illus.). 219p. 1975. Repr. of 1949 ed. lib. bdg. 11.50x (ISBN 0-8154-0488-3). Cooper Sq.

Sargent, Sarah. Weird Henry Bird. 128p. (gr. 4-6). 1980. 7.95 (ISBN 0-517-54137-8). Crown.

Sargent, Shirley, ed. see Hutchings, James M.

Sargent, Thelma, tr. The Homeric Hymns: A Verse Translation. 96p. 1975. pap. 3.95 (ISBN 0-393-00788-X, Norton Lib). Norton.

Sargent, Thomas J., jt. ed. see Lucas, Robert E., Jr.

Sargious, Michael. Pavements & Surfacings for Highways & Airports. LC 75-11891. 619p. 1975. 54.95 (ISBN 0-470-75418-4). Halsted Pr.

Sarhadi, Ajit S. India's Security in Resurgent Asia. viii, 338p. 1980. text ed. 22.50x (ISBN 0-86590-003-5). Apt Bks.

Sarin, Prem S. & Gallo, Robert C., eds. Inhibitors of DNA & RNA Polymerases. (International Encyclopedia of Pharmacology & Therapeutics: Section 103). (Illus.). 1980. 69.00 set (ISBN 0-08-024932-9). Pergamon.

Sarjeant, W. A. Fossil & Living Dinoflagellates. 1975. 25.00 (ISBN 0-12-619150-6). Acad Pr.

Sarkar, A. D. Mould & Core Material for the Steel Industry. 1967. 22.00 (ISBN 0-08-012486-0); pap. 9.75 (ISBN 0-08-012487-9). Pergamon.

--Wear of Metals. 1976. 23.00 (ISBN 0-08-019738-8); pap. 11.25 (ISBN 0-08-019737-X). Pergamon.

Sarkar, Chanchal. Challenge & Stagnation: The Indian Mass Media. 1969. 5.00x o.p. (ISBN 0-8426-1501-6). Verry.

Sarkar, Himansu B. Literary Heritage of Southeast Asia. 1980. 11.50x (ISBN 0-8364-0606-0, Pub. by Mukhopadhyay India). South Asia Bks.

Sarkar, Nihar, ed. Foreign Investment & Economic Development in Asia. LC 76-901639. 1976. 17.50x o.p. (ISBN 0-88386-819-9, Orient Longman). South Asia Bks.

Sarkar, S., ed. Hindustan Yearbook, 1979. 47th ed. 180p. 1979. plastic cover 12.50x (ISBN 0-8002-2212-1). Intl Pubns Serv.

Sarkesian, Sam C. American Military Professionalism. LC 80-27027. (Pergamon Policy Studies on International Politics). 1981. 25.00 (ISBN 0-08-027178-2). Pergamon.

--The Professional Army Officer in a Changing Society. LC 74-10917. 230p. 1974. 17.95 (ISBN 0-911012-62-1). Nelson-Hall.

Sarkesian, Sam C. & Buck, James H. Introduction to Comparative Politics. Stout, John, ed. LC 78-12083. (Illus.). 1979. text ed. 15.95 (ISBN 0-88284-067-3). Alfred Pub.

Sarkesian, Sam C & Nanda, Krish. Politics & Power in American Government: An Introductory Text with Readings. LC 75-1244. (Illus.). 555p. 1976. pap. text ed. 11.50x (ISBN 0-88284-026-6). Alfred Pub.

Sarkesian, Sam C., ed. Combat Effectiveness: Cohesion, Stress, & the Volunteer Military. LC 80-17486. (Sage Research Progress Ser. on War, Revolution, & Peacekeeeping: Vol. 9). (Illus.). 305p. 1980. 20.00 (ISBN 0-8039-1440-7). Sage.

--Combat Effectiveness: Cohesion, Stress, & the Volunteer Military. LC 80-17486. (Sage Research Progress Ser. on War, Revolution, & Peacekeeping: Vol. 9). (Illus.). 305p. 1980. pap. 9.95 (ISBN 0-8039-1441-5). Sage.

--Defense Policy & the Presidency, Carter's First Years. (Special Studies in National Security & Defense Policy). 1979. lib. bdg. 26.50x (ISBN 0-89158-273-8). Westview.

--Non-Nuclear Conflicts in the Nuclear Age. 360p. 1980. 29.95 (ISBN 0-03-056138-8). Praeger.

--U. S. Policy & Low-Intensity Conflict: Potentials for Military Struggles in the 1980s. 224p. (Orig.). 1981. pap. 9.95 (ISBN 0-87855-851-9). Transaction Bks.

Sarkissian, Adele. Writers for Young Adults: Biographies Master Index. LC 79-13228. (Gale Biographical Index Ser.: Vol. 6). 1979. 36.00 (ISBN 0-8103-1083-X). Gale.

Sarkissian, Adele, ed. Children's Authors & Illustrators: An Index to Biographical Dictionaries. 3rd, rev. ed. (Gale Biographical Index Ser.: No. 2). 1981. 85.00 (ISBN 0-8103-1084-8). Gale.

Sarkissian, Henry A. Tales of One Thousand & One Iranian Days. 1981. 8.95 (ISBN 0-533-04476-6). Vantage.

Sarkissian, Wendy, et al. The Design of Medical Environments for Children & Adolescents: An Annotated Bibliography. (Archtecture Ser.: Bibliography A-261). 65p. 1980. pap. 7.00. Vance Biblios.

Sarkozy, Balazs, jt. auth. see Portisch, Lajos.

Sarles, John D. ABC's of Italian Wines. LC 80-51642. (Illus.). 200p. (Orig.). Date not set. 10.95 (ISBN 0-9604488-1-0); pap. 9.95 (ISBN 0-9604488-0-2). Wine Bks. Postponed.

Sarlette, Ralph. Practical Course in Modern Shoe Repairing. Orig. Title: Shoe Repairing Course. 1956. 13.95 (ISBN 0-911012-44-3). Nelson-Hall.

Sarma, Jyotimoyee. Caste Dynamics Among the Bengali Hindus. 1980. 11.50x (ISBN 0-8364-0633-8, Pub. by Mukhopadhyay India). South Asia Bks.

Sarma, M. V. The Eagle & the Phoenix. 108p. 1980. pap. text ed. 3.00x (ISBN 0-391-01914-7). Humanities.

Sarma, Ramaswamy H. Nucleic Acid Geometry & Dynamics. LC 80-10620. (Illus.). 424p. 1980. 55.00 (ISBN 0-08-024631-1); pap. 24.50 (ISBN 0-08-024630-3). Pergamon.

--Stereodynamics of Molecular Systems. 1979. 66.00 (ISBN 0-08-024629-X). Pergamon.

Sarmiento, A. & Latta, L. Closed Functional Treatment of Fractures. (Illus.). 650p. 1981. 148.00 (ISBN 0-387-10384-8). Springer-Verlag.

Sarna, Gregory P., ed. Practical Oncology. (UCLA Postgraduate Medicine Ser.). 1980. text ed. 18.00 (ISBN 0-89289-350-8). HM Prof Med Div.

Sarna, Jonathan D. Jacksonian Jew: The Two Worlds of Mordecai Noah. LC 79-24379. 1981. text ed. 24.50x (ISBN 0-8419-0567-3). Holmes & Meier.

Sarnat, Harvey B. & Netsky, Martin G. Evolution of the Nervous System. 2nd ed. (Illus.). 425p. 1981. text ed. 19.50x (ISBN 0-19-502775-2); pap. text ed. 13.95x (ISBN 0-19-502776-0). Oxford U Pr.

Sarnat, M., jt. auth. see Levy, H.

Sarnat, Marshall, jt. auth. see Levy, Haim.

Sarner. Plastic-Packed Trickling Filters. new ed. 1980. text ed. 12.50 (ISBN 0-250-40371-4, Butterworths). Ann Arbor Science.

Sarno, Art. Academy Awards. (Illus.). 1980. lib. bdg. 14.95 (ISBN 0-912076-37-2); pap. 9.95 (ISBN 0-912076-38-0). ESE Calif.

--Academy Awards Nineteen Eighty-One Oscar Annual. (Illus.). 1981. lib. bdg. 14.95 (ISBN 0-912076-43-7); pap. 9.95 (ISBN 0-912076-44-5). ESE Calif.

Sarno, Martha T. & Hook, Olle, eds. Aphasia: Assessment & Treatment. LC 80-80488. (Illus.). 288p. 1980. 34.50 (ISBN 0-89352-086-1). Masson Pub.

Sarno, Ronald, jt. auth. see Badia, Leonard F.

Sarnoff, Charles. Latency. LC 75-42548. 400p. 1981. Repr. of 1976 ed. 25.00 (ISBN 0-686-69588-7). Aronson.

Sarnoff, Jane. Words?! A Book About the Origins of Everyday Words & Phrases. (Illus.). 48p. (gr. 4-7). 1981. 8.95 (ISBN 0-686-69286-1). Scribner.

Sarnoff, Jane & Ruffins, Reynold. The Code & Cipher Book. LC 74-24419. (Illus.). 40p. (gr. 1-5). 1975. reinforced bdg. 8.95 (ISBN 0-684-14246-5, ScribJ); pap. 2.95 (ISBN 0-684-16219-9, SL 869, ScribJ). Scribner.

--Riddle Calendar, 1980. (Illus.). (gr. 1 up). 1979. 4.95 o.p. (ISBN 0-684-16209-1, ScribT). Scribner.

Sarnoff, Paul. Silver Bulls. (Illus.). 265p. 1980. 12.95 (ISBN 0-87000-480-8). Arlington Hse.

--Trading in Financial Futures. 144p. 1980. 30.00x (ISBN 0-85941-133-8, Pub. by Woodhead-Faulkner England). State Mutual Bk.

--Trading in Gold. 144p. 1981. limeted professional ed. 22.50 (ISBN 0-89047-039-1). Herman Pub.

Sarolea, Charles. Cardinal Newman & His Influence on Religious Life & Thought. 182p. Repr. of 1908 ed. 3.50 (ISBN 0-567-04523-4). Attic Pr.

Sarotte, Georges-Michel. Like a Brother, Like a Lover: Male Homosexuality in the American Novel & Theatre from Herman Melville to James Baldwin. LC 77-80912. 1978. 10.00 o.p. (ISBN 0-385-12765-0, Anchor Pr). Doubleday.

Saroyan, William. Human Comedy. rev. ed. LC 43-51036. (Illus.). (gr. 10 up). 1944. 10.95 (ISBN 0-15-142299-0). HarBraceJ.

--My Name Is Aram. LC 40-34075. (Modern Classic Ser.). (Illus.). 1940. 4.95 (ISBN 0-15-163827-6). HarBraceJ.

--Two Short Paris Summertime Plays of Nineteen Seventy-Four. (Santa Susana Press Ser.). 1979. numbered 50.00 (ISBN 0-937048-17-8); lettered 75.00 (ISBN 0-937048-26-7); with laid-in block print 100.00 (ISBN 0-937048-17-8). CSUN.

Sarper, R. M., jt. auth. see Karcioglu, Z. A.

Sarpkaya, Turgut see Heat Transfer & Fluid Mechanics Institute.

Sarraute, Nathalie. Between Life & Death. Jolas, Maria, tr. from Fr. 1980. pap. 11.95 (ISBN 0-7145-0122-0); pap. 4.95 (ISBN 0-7145-0123-9). Riverrun NY.

--Do You Hear Them? Jolas, Maria, tr. from Fr. LC 72-86680. 178p. 1973. 5.95 o.p. (ISBN 0-8076-0663-4); pap. 2.95 o.p. (ISBN 0-8076-0739-8). Braziller.

--The Golden Fruits. Jolas, Maria, tr. from Fr. 1980. 11.95 (ISBN 0-7145-0258-8); pap. 4.95 (ISBN 0-7145-0259-6). Riverrun NY.

--Martereau. 1959. 4.50 o.s.i. (ISBN 0-8076-0071-7). Braziller.

--The Planetarium. Jolas, Maria, tr. from Fr. 1980. pap. 4.95 (ISBN 0-7145-0444-0). Riverrun NY.

--Portrait of a Man Unknown. Jolas, Maria, tr. 1958. 4.50 o.p. (ISBN 0-8076-0061-X). Braziller.

--Theater: Five Plays: Silence, It Is Beautiful, Izzum, the Lie, It Is There. LC 78-7111. 176p. 1979. 10.00 (ISBN 0-8076-0939-0); pap. 4.95 o.p. (ISBN 0-8076-0940-4). Braziller.

--What Words Can Wield. LC 80-19957. 144p. 1980. 10.00 (ISBN 0-8076-0978-1); pap. 5.95 (ISBN 0-8076-0979-X). Braziller.

Sarre, Friedrich & Sarre, Trenkwald. Oriental Carpet Designs in Full Color. (Illus.). 1980. pap. 6.00 (ISBN 0-486-23835-0). Dover.

Sarre, Trenkwald, jt. auth. see Sarre, Friedrich.

Sarrel, Lorna J. & Sarrel, Philip M. Sexual Unfolding: Sexual Development & Sex Therapies in Late Adolescence. 1979. text ed. 15.95 (ISBN 0-316-77100-7). Little.

Sarrel, Philip M., jt. auth. see Sarrel, Lorna J.

Sarris, Andrew. American Cinema: Directors & Directions: 1929-1968. 1969. pap. 5.50 (ISBN 0-525-47227-4). Dutton.

--The History of the Cannes Film Festival, 1946-1979. (Illus.). 450p. 1981. 14.95 (ISBN 0-87754-224-4). Chelsea Hse.

--John Ford Movie Mystery. LC 75-37286. (Cinema One Ser.: No. 27). (Illus.). 192p. 1976. 8.95x (ISBN 0-253-33167-6). Ind U Pr.

Sarris, Shirley. Simply Stews. 1973. pap. 1.25 (ISBN 0-451-07805-5, Y7805, Sig). NAL.

Sarshik, Steve & Szykitka, Walter. Without a Lawyer. (Orig.). 1980. pap. 5.95 (ISBN 0-452-25226-1, Z5226, Plume). NAL.

Sartain, E. M. Jajal Al-Din Al-Suywti, 2 vols. Incl. Vol. 1. Biography & Background. 230p. 44.00 (ISBN 0-521-20547-6); Vol. 2. Al-Tahadduth bini'mat allah. 370p. 51.00 (ISBN 0-521-20546-8). LC 74-82226. (Oriental Publications Ser.: Nos. 23 & 24). 1975. Set. 86.00 (ISBN 0-521-20633-2). Cambridge U Pr.

Sarti, Roland. Fascism & the Industrial Leadership in Italy, 1919-1940: A Study in the Expansion of Private Power Under Fascism. LC 79-138636. 1971. 21.50x (ISBN 0-520-01855-9). U of Cal Pr.

Sarton, George. Ancient Science & Modern Civilization. LC 54-10992. 1964. pap. 1.65x o.p. (ISBN 0-8032-5228-5, 302, Bison). U of Nebr Pr.

--History of Science, Two: Hellenistic Science & Culture in the Last Three Centuries B.C. 1970. pap. 5.95 o.p. (ISBN 0-393-00526-7, Norton Lib). Norton.

Sarton, May. The Fur Person. 1973. pap. 1.50 (ISBN 0-451-08942-1, W8942, Sig). NAL.

--Journal of a Solitude. 1977. pap. 3.95 (ISBN 0-393-00853-3, N853, Norton Lib). Norton.

--Mrs. Stevens Hears the Mermaids Singing. 240p. 1974. 6.95 (ISBN 0-393-08695-X, Norton Lib); pap. 3.95 1975 (ISBN 0-393-00762-6). Norton.

--Poet & the Donkey. LC 72-80024. (Illus.). 1969. 4.50 o.p. (ISBN 0-393-08590-2). Norton.

--Writings on Writing. Hunting, Constance, ed. 55p. 1980. pap. 3.50 (ISBN 0-913006-20-3); pap. text ed. 3.50 (ISBN 0-913006-21-1); tchr.'s ed. 3.50 (ISBN 0-913006-22-X). Puckerbrush.

Sartorelli, A. C., et al, eds. Molecular Actions & Targets for Cancer Chemotherapeutic Agents. (Bristol-Myers Cancer Symposia Ser.). 1981. 45.00 (ISBN 0-12-619280-4). Acad Pr.

Sartre, J. & Storer, M., eds. Les Jeux Sont Faits. 1952. pap. 7.95 o.p. (ISBN 0-13-530675-2). P-H.

Sartre, J. & Stover, M., eds. Les Jeax Sont Faits. 1952. pap. 7.95 (ISBN 0-13-530675-2). P-H.

Sartre, Jean-Paul. Being & Nothingness. Barnes, Hazel E., tr. pap. 4.95 (ISBN 0-671-41890-4). WSP.

--The Communists & Peace. LC 68-17390. 1968. 6.95 o.s.i. (ISBN 0-8076-0451-8). Braziller.

--The Ghost of Stalin. LC 67-19872. 1968. 4.50 o.p. (ISBN 0-8076-0437-2). Braziller.

--Imagination: A Psychological Critique. Williams, Forrest, tr. from Fr. 1972. pap. 5.95 (ISBN 0-472-06185-2, 185, AA). U of Mich Pr.
--Imagination: A Psychological Critique. Williams, Forrest, tr. LC 62-7235. 1962. 3.95 o.p. (ISBN 0-472-80666-1). U of Mich Pr.
--Life Situations: Essays Written & Spoken by Jean-Paul Sartre. 1977. 8.95 o.p. (ISBN 0-394-40845-4). Pantheon.
--Literature & Existentialism. 1980. pap. 3.95 (ISBN 0-8065-0685-7). Lyle Stuart.
--Les Mouches. (Fr). 1962. pap. 1.00 o.p. (ISBN 0-685-13996-4, 3607). Larousse.
--Nausea. Alexander, Lloyd, tr. LC 49-8942. 1959. pap. 3.95 (ISBN 0-8112-0188-0, NDP82). New Directions.
--No Exit & Three Other Plays. 1955. pap. 2.95 (ISBN 0-394-70016-3, Vin). Random.
--Psychology of Imagination. 1980. pap. 4.95 (ISBN 0-8065-0305-X). Lyle Stuart.
--Saint Genet: Actor & Martyr. 8.50 o.s.i. (ISBN 0-8076-0243-4). Braziller.
--Situations. LC 65-14602. 1965. 5.95 o.s.i. (ISBN 0-8076-0292-2). Braziller.
--The Wall: Intimacy. 3rd ed. Alexander, Lloyd, tr. LC 73-88731. 1969. pap. 3.75 (ISBN 0-8112-0190-2, NDP272). New Directions.
--What Is Literature. 7.50 (ISBN 0-8446-2867-0). Peter Smith.
--The Words. 160p. 1977. pap. 1.50 o.p. (ISBN 0-449-30803-0, Prem). Fawcett.
Sartwell. Maxcy-Rosenau Preventive Medicine & Public Health Medicine. 10th ed. 1973. 45.00 o.p. (ISBN 0-8385-6186-1). ACC.
Sartwell, Philip E. & Nathanson, Neal, eds. Epidemiologic Reviews: 1980, Vol. 2. LC 79-7564. (Epidemiologic Reviews Ser.). (Illus.). 240p. 1980. text ed. 13.50x (ISBN 0-8018-2404-4). Johns Hopkins.
Sarup, Madan. Marxism & Education: A Study of Phenomenological & Marxist Approaches to Education. (Education Bks). 1978. 18.50x (ISBN 0-7100-8944-9); pap. 7.95 (ISBN 0-7100-8945-7). Routledge & Kegan.
Sarviel, E. Building Estimator's Reference Manual. 288p. (Orig.). 1981. pap. 14.75 (ISBN 0-910460-76-0). Craftsman.
Sarvis, Betty & Rodman, Hyman. The Abortion Controversy. 2nd ed. 200p. 1974. 17.50x (ISBN 0-231-03871-2); pap. 6.00x (ISBN 0-231-03865-8). Columbia U Pr.
Sarwar, Mohammad, et al. Basic Neuroradiology. (Illus.). 500p. 1981. 47.50 (ISBN 0-87527-230-4). Green.
Sarwar, Mohammed, et al. Computed Tomography of Congenital Malformations of the Brain. (Illus.). 300p. 1981. 45.00 (ISBN 0-87527-231-2). Green.
SAS Institute Inc. SAS-GRAPH User's Guide, 1980 Edition. (Illus.). 72p. (Orig.). 1980. pap. 9.95 o.s.i. (ISBN 0-686-62125-5). SAS Inst.
SAS Institute Inc., ed. SAS Applications Guide, 1980. (Illus.). 204p. (Orig.). 1980. pap. 9.95. SAS Inst.
--SAS-ETS User's Guide, 1980. 342p. 1980. pap. 14.95. Sas Inst.
--SAS Programmer's Guide, Nineteen Eighty-One Edition. (SAS Programmer's Guide). 208p. (Orig.). 1980. pap. 9.95. SAS Inst.
--SAS Views: Statistics, 1980 Edition. 322p. 1980. pap. 40.00 (ISBN 0-686-62786-5). SAS Inst.
--Sas Views, 1980 Edition. 424p. 1980. pap. 40.00 (ISBN 0-686-62785-7). SAS Inst.
Sas, Ted. Human Pax. LC 79-67757. 1981. 5.95 (ISBN 0-533-04481-2). Vantage.
Sasa, Manabu, ed. Recent Advances in Researches on Filariasis & Schistosomiasis in Japan. (Illus.). 1970. 39.50 (ISBN 0-8391-0032-9). Univ Park.
Sasaki, Naoto. Management & Industrial Structure in Japan. (Illus.). 160p. 1981. 24.00 (ISBN 0-08-024056-9); pap. 13.00 (ISBN 0-08-024057-7). Pergamon.
Sasamori, Junzo, jt. auth. see Warner, Gordon.
Sasek, Miroslav. This Is Australia. LC 79-117960. (Illus.). (gr. 4-6). 1971. 4.95g o.s.i. (ISBN 0-02-778160-7). Macmillan.
--This Is Edinburgh. (Illus.). (gr. 3 up). 1961. 5.95g o.s.i. (ISBN 0-02-778180-1). Macmillan.
--This Is Hong Kong. (Illus.). (gr. 3 up). 1965. 5.95g o.s.i. (ISBN 0-02-778190-9). Macmillan.
--This Is Ireland. (Illus.). (gr. 3 up). 1965. 6.95g (ISBN 0-02-778350-2). Macmillan.
--This Is Israel. (Illus.). (gr. 3 up). 1962. 4.95g o.s.i. (ISBN 0-02-778340-5). Macmillan.
--This Is London. (Illus.). (gr. 3 up). 1959-62. 4.95g o.s.i. (ISBN 0-02-778510-6); It. Ed. 3.00 o.s.i. (ISBN 0-685-16098-X). Macmillan.
--This Is New York. (Illus.). (gr. 3 up). 1960. 5.95g o.s.i. (ISBN 0-02-779530-6). Macmillan.
--This Is San Francisco. (Illus.). (gr. 3 up). 1962. 7.95 (ISBN 0-02-780830-0). Macmillan.
--This Is Texas. (Illus.). (gr. 3 up). 1967. 5.95g o.s.i. (ISBN 0-02-780740-1). Macmillan.
--This Is Venice. (Illus.). (gr. 3 up). 1961. 4.95g o.s.i. (ISBN 0-02-781050-X). Macmillan.
--This Is Washington, D. C. LC 69-13394. (Illus.). (gr. 3 up). 1969. 4.95 o.s.i. (ISBN 0-02-778240-9). Macmillan.
Sashkin, Marshal, jt. auth. see Morris, William C.
Saslaw, William C. & Jacobs, Kenneth C., eds. The Emerging Universe: Essays on Contemporary Astronomy. LC 72-188526. 120p. 1972. 9.95x (ISBN 0-8139-0397-1). U Pr of Va.
Saslow, Joan, ed. see Weiss, Edda.
Saslow, Richard & Straw Dog. Slide Guitar: A Book/Record Guide to Electric Lead & Traditional Slide & Bottleneck Styles with Special Chapters on Improvising Blues & Country & Western Lead Guitar Plus a Riff on Open Tunings. LC 72-76529. (Contemporary Guitar Styles Ser.). (Illus.). 82p. (Orig., Prog. Bk.). 1972. pap. 8.95 (ISBN 0-912910-02-X). Green Note Music.
Saslow, Richard, jt. auth. see Straw Dog.
Sasmor, Jeanette L. Childbirth Education: A Nursing Perspective. LC 78-32177. 1979. 14.95 (ISBN 0-471-75490-0, Pub. by Wiley Medical). Wiley.
Sasmor, Jeannette L. What Every Husband Should Know About Having a Baby: The Psychoprophlactic Way. LC 72-75633. 1972. 14.95 (ISBN 0-911012-18-4); pap. 7.95 (ISBN 0-88229-496-2). Nelson-Hall.
Sasnett, Martena & Sepmeyer, Inez. Educational Systems of Africa. 1966. 65.00x (ISBN 0-520-01122-8). U of Cal Pr.
Sass, C. Joseph. BASIC Programming & Applications. 368p. 1976. pap. text ed. 15.95x (ISBN 0-205-05422-6); ans. bk. 2.50 (ISBN 0-205-05423-4). Allyn.
--COBOL Programming & Applications. 1978. text ed. 15.95x (ISBN 0-205-06550-3); solutions man. avail. (ISBN 0-205-06552-X). Allyn.
--FORTRAN Four Programming & Applications. LC 72-93537. 328p. 1974. pap. text ed. 12.95x (ISBN 0-8162-7473-8). Holden-Day.
--A Structured Approach to BASIC Programming. 1980. pap. text ed. 15.95 (ISBN 0-205-06726-3, 2067269); solutions manual free (ISBN 0-205-06727-1). Allyn.
Sass, Lorna J. To the King's Taste: Richard the Second's Book of Feasts and Recipes Adapted for Modern Cooking. LC 75-17859. (Illus.). 136p. 1975. 5.95 o.p. (ISBN 0-87099-133-7). Metro Mus Art.
--To the Queen's Taste: Elizabethan Feasts & Recipes Adapted for Modern Cooking. LC 76-23242. 1976. 6.95 (ISBN 0-87099-151-5). Metro Mus Art.
Sasscer, Harrison, jt. ed. see Hartzell, Karl D.
Sasscer, Ruth V., et al. Exploraciones Chicano-Riquenas. 224p. 1981. pap. text ed. 7.95 (ISBN 0-394-32651-2). Random.
Sasse. Person to Person. (gr. 9-12). 1978. text ed. 10.60 (ISBN 0-87002-266-0); student's guide 5.12 (ISBN 0-87002-202-4); tchr's guide 7.96 (ISBN 0-87002-209-1). Bennett IL.
Sasse, Christoph, et al. Decision Making in the European Community. LC 77-1258. (Special Studies). 1977. text ed. 37.95 (ISBN 0-275-23900-4). Praeger.
Sasse, Connie R. Discovering Food. 1978. pap. 3.84 student guide o.p. (ISBN 0-87002-278-4). Bennett IL.
--Discovering Food Teacher's Guide: Discovering Food. 1978. pap. 7.36 tchr's guide o.p. (ISBN 0-87002-280-6). Bennett IL.
Sasse, F. H. Theme on a Pipedream. 7.35 (ISBN 0-85131-027-3, Dist. by Sporting Book Center). J A Allen.
Sassen, Georgia & Avrin, Cookie. Corporations & Child Care: Profit-Making Day Care, Workplace Day Care & a Look at the Alternatives. LC 76-17319. (Illus.). 1974. pap. 3.50 (ISBN 0-685-85529-5). Womens Research Act.
Sasser, W. Earl, jt. auth. see Wyckoff, D. Daryl.
Sasser, W. Earl, et al. Management of Service Operations. 1978. text ed. 23.95 (ISBN 0-205-06104-4, 0861049); instr's man. avail. (ISBN 0-205-06105-2, 0861057). Allyn.
Sassine, Williams. Wirriyannu. Reed, John & Wake, Clive, trs. (African Writers Ser.). 148p. 1980. pap. 5.50 (ISBN 0-435-90199-0). Heinemann Ed.
Sasso, Wilma R. La see La Sasso, Wilma R.
Sassoon, Donald, ed. see Togliatti, Palmiro.
Sassoon, Siegfried. The Complete Memoirs of George Sherston. 320p. 1980. 23.95 (ISBN 0-571-06146-X, Pub by Faber & Faber); pap. 13.95 (ISBN 0-571-09913-0). Merrimack Bk Serv.
--Memoirs of a Fox-Hunting Man. 313p. 1980. pap. 6.95 (ISBN 0-571-06454-X, Pub. by Faber & Faber). Merrimack Bk Serv.
--Selected Poems. 1968. pap. 4.95 (ISBN 0-571-08540-7, Pub. by Faber & Faber). Merrimack Bk Serv.
Sassouni, Viken. Orthodontics in Dental Practice. LC 70-141939. (Illus.). 1971. text ed. 37.50 o.p. (ISBN 0-8016-4300-7). Mosby.
Sassouni, Viken & Sotereanos, George C. Diagnosis & Treatment of Dento-Facial Abnormalities. (Illus.). 512p. 1974. 39.75 (ISBN 0-398-02888-5). C C Thomas.
Sastri, G. A Study in the Dialectics of Sphota. 106p. 1980. text ed. 10.50 (ISBN 0-8426-1653-5). Verry.
Sastri, K. Nilakanta. The Pandyan Kingdom. 2nd ed. 252p. 1974. text ed. 7.50 (ISBN 0-88253-426-2). Ind-US Inc.
Sastri, P. S. Ananda K. Coomaraswamy. Narasimhaiah, C. D., ed. (Indian Writers Ser.). 203p. 1975. 6.50 (ISBN 0-88253-700-8). Ind-US Inc.
--The Margin of a Stream. (Redbird Book). 59p. 1975. 14.00 (ISBN 0-88253-712-1); pap. 4.80 (ISBN 0-88253-844-6). Ind-US Inc.
Sastry, Alladi M., tr. Taittiriya Upanishad. 93p. 1980. 28.50 (ISBN 0-89744-145-1, Pub. by Samata Bks India). Auromere.
Sastry, D. U., jt. auth. see Dhar, Prithvi N.
Sastry, K. S. Performance Budgeting for Planned Development. (Illus.). 235p. 1980. text ed. 12.50x (ISBN 0-391-02170-2). Humanities.
Sastry, N. S. & Thomas, C. K. Farm Animal Management. 1976. text ed. 17.50 (ISBN 0-7069-0454-0, Pub. by Vikas India). Advent Bk.
Sastry, P. V. Vaiyakarana Siddhanta Kaumudi of Bhattoji Diksita, Vol. I. 1974. 11.50 (ISBN 0-8426-0582-7). Orient Bk Dist.
Satake, Ichiro. Algebraic Structures of Symmetric Domains. LC 80-7551. (Publications of the Mathematical Society of Japan Ser.: No. 14). 315p. 1981. 39.50x (ISBN 0-691-08271-5). Princeton U Pr.
Sataloff, Joseph & Michael, Paul. Hearing Conservation. (Illus.). 376p. 1973. 21.75 (ISBN 0-398-02822-2). C C Thomas.
Satcher, Buford. Blacks in Mississippi Politics 1865-1900. LC 78-53792. 1978. pap. text ed. 9.50x (ISBN 0-8191-0513-9). U Pr of Amer.
Satchidananda Murty, K., et al. Science, Philosophy & Culture. 12.50x (ISBN 0-210-22678-1). Asia.
Satchler, George R., jt. auth. see Brink, David M.
Sater, William F. The Heroic Image in Chile: Arturo Prat, Secular Saint. LC 70-189221. 1973. 17.95x (ISBN 0-520-02235-1). U of Cal Pr.
Sather, June. Spotty & Skunky Kitty Stories. 4.00 o.p. (ISBN 0-8062-1193-8). Carlton.
Sathre-Eldon, et al. Let's Talk: An Introduction to Interpersonal Communication. 3rd ed. 1980. pap. text ed. 7.95x (ISBN 0-673-15376-2). Scott F.
Satir, P. Structure & Function in Cilia & Flagella. Alfert, M., et al, eds. Bd. with Trichocystoides. Corps Trichocystoides. Cnidocystes & Colloblastes. Horvasse, R. (Illus.). 57p. 1965. (Protoplasmatologia: Vol. 3, Pt. E). (Illus.). iv, 52p. 1965. pap. 34.90 o.p. (ISBN 0-387-80732-2). Springer-Verlag.
Satir, Virginia, et al. Helping Families to Change. LC 75-29697. 296p. 1976. 20.00x (ISBN 0-87668-238-7). Aronson.
Satkowski, Leon. Studies on Vasari's Architecture. LC 78-74377. (Fine Arts Dissertations, Fourth Ser.). 1980. lib. bdg. 38.00 (ISBN 0-8240-3964-5). Garland Pub.
Sato, Hiroaki & Watson, Burton, eds. From the Country of Eight Islands: An Anthology of Japanese Poetry. 480p. 1981. 17.50 (ISBN 0-295-95798-0). U of Wash Pr.
Sato, Hiroaki & Watson, Burton, trs. From the Country of Eight Islands. LC 80-1077. 480p. 1981. pap. 9.95 (ISBN 0-385-14030-4, Anch). Doubleday.
Sato, Masahiko. Kyoto Ceramics. Towle, Anne V. & Coolidge, Usher, trs. from Japanese. LC 72-92256. (Arts of Japan Ser: No. 2). (Illus.). 128p. (Orig.). 1973. 12.50 o.p. (ISBN 0-8348-2701-8). Weatherhill.
Sato, Masayasu, jt. auth. see Katsuki, Yasuji.
Satow, Michael & Desmond, Ray. Railways of the Raj. (Illus.). 120p. 1980. 29.95 (ISBN 0-8147-7816-X). NYU Pr.
Satpathi, Nandini. Song of the Evening. Mohanty, J. B., tr. from Oriya. 110p. (Orig.). 1975. pap. 1.50 (ISBN 0-88253-770-9). Ind-US Inc.
Satryb, Ronald P., jt. ed. see Kemerer, Frank R.
Sattelmair, R. Oberammergau, Its Environment & Tradition. (Illus.). 1970. 6.00 o.p. (ISBN 0-911268-12-X). Rogers Bk.
Satterfield, Archie. After the Gold Rush. LC 76-13642. (Illus.). 1976. 8.95 o.p. (ISBN 0-397-01142-3). Lippincott.
--Lewis & Clark Country. LC 78-8324. (Illus.). 144p. 1978. 27.50 (ISBN 0-915796-12-0). Beautiful Am.
Satterfield, Charles N. Mass Transfer in Heterogeneous Catalysis. LC 80-23432. 286p. 1981. Repr. of 1970 ed. text ed. write for info. (ISBN 0-89874-198-X). Krieger.
Satterly, David. Assessment in Schools. (Theory & Practice in Education Ser.: Vol. 1). 320p. 1981. 40.00x (ISBN 0-631-11151-4, Pub. by Basil Blackwell England); pap. 19.95x (ISBN 0-631-12564-7). Biblio Dist.
Satterthwaite, David, jt. auth. see Hardoy, Jorge E.
Satterthwaite, Edwin H., Jr. Source Language Debugging Tools. LC 79-50820. (Outstanding Dissertations in the Computer Sciences). 1980. lib. bdg. 32.00 (ISBN 0-8240-4416-9). Garland Pub.
Satterthwaite, M. The Labrador Retriever: Its Care & Training. 100p. 1980. 3.95 (ISBN 0-903264-34-X, 4947-2, Pub. by K & R Bks England). Arco.
Sattler, F. P., et al, eds. Veterinary Critical Care. LC 80-27880. (Illus.). 450p. 1981. text ed. write for info. (ISBN 0-8121-0702-0). Lea & Febiger.
Sattler, Helen R. Dinosaurs of North America. (Illus.). 160p. (gr. 2 up). 1981. 10.95 (ISBN 0-688-51952-0); pap. 5.95 o.p. (ISBN 0-688-41952-6). Morrow.
--The Eggless Cookbook. LC 77-169071. 224p. 1972. 8.95 o.p. (ISBN 0-498-01049-X). A S Barnes.
--No Place for a Goat. (Illus.). 32p. (ps-3). 1981. 5.95 (ISBN 0-525-66723-7). Elsevier-Nelson.
Sattler, Martin J., jt. ed. see Sullivan, David S.
Sattler, Rolf. Organogenesis of Flowers: Photographic Text-Atlas. LC 73-185736. (Illus.). 1973. 35.00x (ISBN 0-8020-1864-5). U of Toronto Pr.
Sattler, William M. & Miller, W. Discussion & Conference. 2nd ed. 1968. text ed. 16.95 (ISBN 0-13-216135-4). P-H.
Satty. Illustrated Edgar Allan Poe. (Illus.). 1977. pap. 7.95 o.s.i. (ISBN 0-446-87203-2). Warner Bks.
Satyamurti, Carole. Occupational Survival: The Case of the Local Authority Social Worker. (Practice of Social Work Ser.: No. 5). 208p. 1981. 25.00x (ISBN 0-631-12441-1, Pub. by Basil Blackwell England); pap. 12.50x (ISBN 0-631-12595-7). Biblio Dist.
Satyanarayana, J. Incentives & Productivity in Public Enterprises. 153p. 1975. 11.00 o.p. (ISBN 0-89253-007-3). InterCulture.
Satyanarayanan, M. Multiprocessors: A Comparative Study. (Illus.). 208p. 1980. text ed. 22.95 (ISBN 0-13-605154-5). P-H.
Satz, Paul & Ross, J. L., eds. The Disabled Learner, Early Detection & Intervention. (Modern Approaches to the Diagnosis & Instruction of Multi-Handicapped Children Ser.: Vol. 8). 298p. 1973. text ed. 34.25 (ISBN 90-237-4107-2, Pub. by Swets Pub Serv Holland). Swets North Am.
Satz, Paul, jt. ed. see Bakker, Dirk J.
Saubel, Katherine S. & Galloway, Anne. I'Isniyatam. 1978. 2.00 (ISBN 0-686-25514-3). Malki Mus Pr.
Sauber, Mignon & Corrigan, Eileen M. The Six-Year Experience of Unwed Mothers As Parents: A Continuing Study of These Mothers & Their Children. 1970. pap. 3.50 (ISBN 0-86671-007-8). Comm Coun Great NY.
Sauber, Mignon & Rubinstein, Elaine. Experiences of the Unwed Mother As a Parent: A Longitudinal Study of Unmarried Mothers Who Keep Their First Born. 1965. pap. 3.50 (ISBN 0-86671-001-9). Comm Coun Great NY.
Sauber, Mignon & Taittonen, Edith. A Guide for Determining the Ability of an Absent Parent to Pay Child Support. 1977. 1.50 (ISBN 0-86671-037-X). Comm Coun Great NY.
Saucier, Gene A. Woodwinds: Fundamental Performance Techniques. LC 80-5223. (Illus.). 300p. 1981. pap. text ed. 12.95 (ISBN 0-02-872300-7). Schirmer Bks.
Saucier, Weems A. & Wendel, Robert L. Toward Humanistic Teaching in High School. 384p. 1974. pap. text ed. 6.95x o.p. (ISBN 0-669-90381-7). Heath.
Saucy, Robert L. The Bible: Breathed from God. 1978. pap. 3.95 (ISBN 0-88207-778-3). Victor Bks.
Sauer, Carl O. The Early Spanish Main. 1969. pap. 8.95 (ISBN 0-520-01415-4, CAL182). U of Cal Pr.
--Land & Life: A Selection from the Writings of Carl Ortwin Sauer. Leighly, John, ed. (California Library Reprint Ser.). 1974. 24.50x (ISBN 0-520-02633-0); pap. 3.95 (ISBN 0-520-01124-4, CAL 132). U of Cal Pr.
--Man in Nature: America Before the Days of the Whiteman. (New World Writing Ser.). (Illus.). 1975. 17.50 (ISBN 0-913666-28-9); pap. 9.95 (ISBN 0-913666-01-7). Turtle Isl Foun.
--Northern Mists. (Illus.). 1968. 17.50x (ISBN 0-520-01126-0). U of Cal Pr.
--Seventeenth Century North America: French & Spanish Accounts. (New World Writing Ser.). (Illus.). 1977. 19.95 (ISBN 0-913666-23-8); pap. 9.95 (ISBN 0-913666-22-X). Turtle Isl Foun.
--Sixteenth-Century North America: The Land & People As Seen by Europeans. LC 75-138635. 1971. 21.95x (ISBN 0-520-01854-0); pap. 4.95 (ISBN 0-520-02777-9). U of Cal Pr.

Sauer, Charles & Chandy, Mani K. Contemporary Systems Performance Modeling. (Illus.). 384p. 1981. text ed. 18.95 (ISBN 0-13-165175-7). P-H.

Sauer, E. E., tr. see Koehler, J.

Sauer, G. C. Teen Skin. (Illus.). 80p. 1973. pap. 4.75 (ISBN 0-398-02942-3). C C Thomas.

Sauer, Jonathan D. Plants & Man on the Seychelles Coast: A Study in Historical Biogeography. (Illus.). 1967. 15.00x (ISBN 0-299-04300-2). U of Wis Pr.

Sauer, Julia. Fog Magic. (Illus.). (gr. 3-6). 1977. pap. 1.25 (ISBN 0-671-29817-8). PB.

Sauer, Norman J. & Phenice, Terrell W. Hominid Fossils. 2nd ed. 1977. wire coil bdg. 5.95x (ISBN 0-697-07552-4). Wm C Brown.

Sauerbier, Charles L. Marine Cargo Operations. 1956. 39.50 (ISBN 0-471-75504-4, Pub. by Wiley-Interscience). Wiley.

Sauerland, B. A., jt. auth. see Sauerland, E. K.

Sauerland, E. K. & Sauerland, B. A. Human Anatomical Dissections: Laboratory Exercises for the Health Professions. (Illus.). 152p. 1980. pap. 13.95 (ISBN 0-683-07558-6). Williams & Wilkins.

Sauerland, Karl. Einfuehrung in Die Aesthetik Adornos. (De Gruyter Studienbuch). 1979. pap. text ed. 16.50x (ISBN 3-11-007167-3). De Gruyter.

Sauerland, Karol. Diltheys Erlebnisbegriff: Entstehung, Glanzzeit und Verkuemmerung eines literaturhistorischen Begriffs. 182p. 1972. 39.45x (ISBN 3-11-003599-5). De Gruyter.

Saufley, William H., Jr., jt. auth. see Keppel, Geoffrey.

Saul, Arthur. The Famous Game of Chesse-Play. LC 74-80216. (English Experience Ser.: No. 691). 1974. Repr. of 1614 ed. 5.00 (ISBN 90-221-0691-8). Walter J Johnson.

Saul, Eric & DeNevi, Don. The Great San Francisco & Fire, 1906. LC 80-83616. (Illus.). 176p. 25.00 (ISBN 0-89087-288-0). Celestial Arts.

Saul, Frank P. The Human Skeletal Remains of Altar De Sacrificios: An Osteobiographic Analysis. LC 72-91442. (Peabody Museum Papers: Vol. 63, No. 2). 1972. pap. text ed. 15.00 (ISBN 0-87365-181-2). Peabody Harvard.

Saul, George B. Adam Unregenerate: Selected Lyric Poems. LC 77-23070. 1977. 11.95 (ISBN 0-916144-13-5); pap. 5.95 (ISBN 0-916144-14-3). Stemmer Hse.

Saul, John. Comes the Blind Fury. (Orig.). 1980. pap. 2.75 o.s.i. (ISBN 0-440-11428-4). Dell.

Saul, LouElla. The North Pacific Cretaceous Trigoniid Genus Yaadia. (Publications in Geological Science Ser.: Vol. 119). 1978. pap. 10.50x (ISBN 0-520-09582-0). U of Cal Pr.

Saul, LouElla R. Evidence for the Origin of the Mactridae (Bivalvia) in the Cretaceous. (U. C. Publ. in Geological Sciences: Vol. 97). 1973. pap. 9.00x (ISBN 0-520-09426-3). U of Cal Pr.

Saul, S. B., jt. auth. see Milward, Alan S.

Saul, Wendy. Butcher, Baker, Cabinetmaker: Photographs of Women at Work. LC 77-27668. (Illus.). (gr. k-2). 1978. 7.95 (ISBN 0-690-03899-2, TYC-J); PLB 8.79 (ISBN 0-690-03900-X). T Y Crowell.

Saulex, William H. The Romance of the Hebrew Language. 243p. Date not set. Repr. of 1913 ed. lib. bdg. 25.00 (ISBN 0-8482-6303-0). Norwood Edns.

Saulnier, Louis. Repertoire De la Cuisine. 239p. 1970. text ed. 14.95x thumb indexed (ISBN 0-685-04746-6). Radio City.

--Le Repertoire De la Cuisine. 1976. text ed. 9.95 (ISBN 0-8120-5108-4); text ed. 14.95 deluxe ed. (ISBN 0-8120-5109-2). Barron.

Saulniers, Suzanne S. & Rakowski, Cathy A. Women in the Development Process: A Select Bibliography on Women in Sub-Saharan Africa & Latin America. 1978. pap. 6.95x (ISBN 0-292-79010-4). U of Tex Pr.

Sauls, Lynn. TM or CM? 1978. pap. 0.75 (ISBN 0-8163-0298-7, 20480-0). Pacific Pr Pub Assn.

Saum, Lewis O. The Popular Mood of Pre-Civil War America. LC 79-8281. (Contributions in American History: No. 46). xxiv, 336p. 1980. lib. bdg. 29.95 (ISBN 0-313-21056-X, SPM/). Greenwood.

Saunders. Edible & Useful Wild Plants of the United States & Canada. LC 75-46193. (Illus.). 320p. 1976. pap. 4.00 (ISBN 0-486-23310-3). Dover.

Saunders, jt. auth. see Wass, Alonzo.

Saunders, Albert C. Working with the Oscilloscope. LC 68-29175. (Illus., Orig.). 1968. 8.95 o.p. (ISBN 0-8063-8472-7); pap. 5.95 (ISBN 0-8306-7472-1, 472). TAB Bks.

Saunders, Ashley. The Night of the Lionhead. 67p. 1979. 2.95 (ISBN 0-8059-2571-6). Dorrance.

--Searching for Atlantis. 32p. 1980. 2.95 (ISBN 0-8059-2741-7). Dorrance.

Saunders, B. John Evelyn & His Times. 1976. 21.00 (ISBN 0-08-007118-X). Pergamon.

Saunders, Beatrice. Chekhov the Man. 1961. 13.95 (ISBN 0-900000-66-X). Dufour.

Saunders, Blanche, jt. auth. see Cross, Jeannette W.

Saunders, Brigitte. Mathematics Workbook for the SAT (College Entrance Examinations) 1980. pap. 5.00 (ISBN 0-668-04820-4). Arco.

Saunders, Brigitte, et al, eds. Scholastic Aptitude Test (SAT) LC 80-88. 512p. (Orig.). 1980. lib. bdg. 12.00 (ISBN 0-668-04916-2, 4916); pap. 6.95 (ISBN 0-668-04920-0, 4920-0). Arco.

Saunders, C. T., ed. Industrial Policies & Technology Transfers Between East & West. (East-West European Economic Interaction,Workshop Paper: Vol 3). (Illus.). 1978. pap. 33.70 o.p. (ISBN 0-387-81456-6). Springer-Verlag.

Saunders, D. S. Insect Clocks. 292p. 1976. text ed. 37.00 (ISBN 0-08-018211-9); pap. text ed. 13.75 (ISBN 0-08-024402-5). Pergamon.

Saunders, David C. An Introduction to Biological Rhythms. (Tertiary Level Biology Ser). 1978. text ed. 17.95 (ISBN 0-470-99019-8). Halsted Pr.

Saunders, Dennis, ed. Magic Lights & Streets of Shining Jet. LC 76-20519. (Illus.). (gr. 3-7). 1978. 8.95 (ISBN 0-688-80065-3); PLB 8.59 (ISBN 0-688-84065-5). Greenwillow.

Saunders, E. Dale. Buddhism in Japan: With an Outline of Its Origins in India. LC 64-10900. (Illus.). 1964. 9.00x o.p. (ISBN 0-8122-7411-3); pap. 4.95x (ISBN 0-8122-1006-9, Pa Paperbks). U of Pa Pr.

Saunders, E. Dale, tr. see Abe, Kobo.

Saunders, Ernest W. I Thessalonians, II Thessalonians, Philippians, Philomen. Hayes, John H., ed. (Preaching Guides Ser.). (Orig.). 1981. pap. 4.50 (ISBN 0-8042-3241-5). John Knox.

Saunders, George, tr. see Medvedev, Roy.

Saunders, Grady F., ed. Cell Differentiation & Neoplasia. LC 77-17694. (M.D. Anderson Symposia on Fundamental Cancer Research). 1978. 49.00 (ISBN 0-89004-200-4). Raven.

Saunders, Hal M. When Are We Ever Gonna Have to Use This? (Illus.). viii, 88p. (Orig.). (gr. 5-12). 1980. pap. text ed. 6.95 (ISBN 0-9604812-0-6). HMS Pubns.

Saunders, Hal M., jt. auth. see Carman, Robert A.

Saunders, Hale, jt. auth. see Carman, Robert A.

Saunders, Helen E. Modern School Library. 2nd ed. LC 75-20377. 1975. 10.00 (ISBN 0-8108-0864-1). Scarecrow.

Saunders, J. B., ed. see Vesalius, Andreas.

Saunders, J. J. A History of Medieval Islam. 1966. Repr. of 1965 ed. 20.00x (ISBN 0-7100-2077-5). Routledge & Kegan.

--A History of Medieval Islam. (Illus.). 1978. pap. 8.95 (ISBN 0-7100-0050-2). Routledge & Kegan.

--The History of the Mongol Conquests. 1971. 25.00 (ISBN 0-7100-7073-X). Routledge & Kegan.

Saunders, Jack. Screed. LC 80-53288. 250p. 1981. 12.95x (ISBN 0-912824-23-9); pap. 5.95 (ISBN 0-912824-24-7). Vagabond Pr.

Saunders, Jason L., ed. Greek & Roman Philosophy After Aristotle. LC 66-12892. (Orig.). 1966. pap. text ed. 6.95 (ISBN 0-02-927730-2). Free Pr.

Saunders, John, et al. Rural Electrification & Development: Social & Economic Impact in Costa Rica & Columbia. 1978. lib. bdg. 22.50x (ISBN 0-89158-274-6). Westview.

Saunders, K. J. Identification of Plastics & Rubbers. 1966. pap. 2.95 o.p. (ISBN 0-470-75511-3). Halsted Pr.

Saunders, Keith. So You Want to Be an Airline Stewardess. new rev. ed. (Illus.). 176p. 1973. pap. 1.50 o.p. (ISBN 0-668-02936-6). Arc Bks.

Saunders, L. The Absorption & Distribution of Drugs. (Illus.). 1974. text ed. 14.95 o.s.i. (ISBN 0-02-859150-X). Macmillan.

Saunders, Laura. Strange Exile. (YA) 1972. 5.95 (ISBN 0-685-28624-X, Avalon). Bouregy.

Saunders, Laurence. A Trewe Mirrour of Glase Wherin We Maye Beholde the Wofull State of Thys Our Realme of Englande. LC 74-28884. (English Experience Ser.: No. 761). 1975. Repr. of 1556 ed. 3.50 (ISBN 90-221-0761-2). Walter J Johnson.

Saunders, Leon Z. Evolution of Veterinary Pathology in Russia, Eighteen Sixty to Nineteen Thirty. LC 79-52502. (Illus.). 1980. 25.00x o.p. (ISBN 0-8014-1191-2). Cornell U Pr.

Saunders, M. Health Visiting Practice. 1968. 11.25 (ISBN 0-08-012899-8); pap. 5.75 (ISBN 0-08-012898-X). Pergamon.

Saunders, Mary. The Whitman Massacre. 1978. 5.50 (ISBN 0-87770-188-1); pap. 2.95 (ISBN 0-685-87578-4). Ye Galleon.

Saunders, N. F. Factory Organization & Management. 24.50x (ISBN 0-392-07812-0, SpS). Soccer.

Saunders, P. T. An Introduction to Catastrophe Theory. LC 79-54172. (Illus.). 1980. 27.50 (ISBN 0-521-23042-X); pap. 8.95 (ISBN 0-521-29782-6). Cambridge U Pr.

Saunders, Peter. Social Theory & the Urban Question. LC 80-21654. 302p. 1981. text ed. 28.50x (ISBN 0-8419-0622-X); pap. text ed. 11.95x (ISBN 0-8419-0623-8). Holmes & Meier.

Saunders, Rubie. Baby-Sitting: A Concise Guide. (YA) (gr. 7-9). 1979. pap. 1.50 (ISBN 0-671-56012-3). PB.

--Calling All Girls Party Book. LC 66-10017. (Illus.). (gr. 3-8). 1966. 5.95 o.s.i. (ISBN 0-8193-0131-0, Four Winds); PLB 5.41 o.s.i. (ISBN 0-8193-0132-9). Schol Bk Serv.

--The Franklin Watts Concise Guide to Babysitting. LC 71-188479. (Career Concise Guides Ser.). (Illus.). 72p. (gr. 5 up). 1972. PLB 4.90 o.p. (ISBN 0-531-02563-2). Watts.

--The Franklin Watts Concise Guide to Good Grooming for Boys. LC 72-1361. (Career Concise Guides Ser.). (Illus.). 72p. (gr. 5 up). 1972. PLB 5.45 o.p. (ISBN 0-531-02256-0). Watts.

--Quick & Easy House Keeping! LC 77-1078. (Concise Guides Ser.). (gr. 6-9). 1977. PLB 6.45 (ISBN 0-531-01277-8). Watts.

--Smart Shopping & Consumerism. LC 72-11707. (Career Concise Guides Ser.). (Illus.). 72p. (gr. 5 up). 1973. PLB 5.90 (ISBN 0-531-02608-6). Watts.

Saunders, Rubie, tr. see Le Paillot, Jean.

Saunders, Rudie. Good Grooming for Girls. (Career Concise Guides Ser.). (Illus.). 72p. (gr. 5-9). 1976. PLB 4.90 o.p. (ISBN 0-531-02902-6). Watts.

Saunders, S. J., ed. see South African International Liver Conference, 1973.

Saunders, V. T., jt. auth. see Cook, A. H.

Saunders, W. & Gardier, R. Pharmacotherapy in Otolaryngology. LC 76-1858. (Illus.). 1976. 19.50 o.p. (ISBN 0-8016-4310-4). Mosby.

Saunders, William. Carl Maria Von Weber. 2nd ed. LC 69-11670. (Music Reprint Ser). 1969. Repr. of 1940 ed. lib. bdg. 29.50 (ISBN 0-306-71200-8). Da Capo.

Saunders, William, et al. Nursing Care in Eye, Ear, Nose & Throat Disorders, Nineteen Seventy-Nine. LC 79-499. (Illus.). 1979. text ed. 19.95 (ISBN 0-8016-2113-5). Mosby.

Saunders, William H., jt. auth. see Deweese, David D.

Saunders, William H., et al. Atlas of Ear Surgery. 3rd ed. LC 79-5235. (Illus.). 1979. text ed. 52.50 (ISBN 0-8016-4318-X). Mosby.

Sauneron, Serge. The Priests of Ancient Egypt. LC 59-10792. (Illus.). 192p. 1980. pap. 3.50 (ISBN 0-394-17410-0, B433, BC). Grove.

Saunt. Revision Notes on Building Measurement. 1981. text ed. price not set. Butterworth.

Saurman, Judith & Pierce, Judith. Ready-to-Use Marbelized Papers. 1979. pap. 3.50 (ISBN 0-486-23901-2). Dover.

Sauser, Jean & Shay, Arthur. Beginning Racquetball Drills. (Illus., Orig.). 1981. pap. 3.95 (ISBN 0-8092-5928-1). Contemp Bks.

--Intermediate Racquetball Drills. (Illus., Orig.). 1981. pap. 3.95 (ISBN 0-8092-5926-5). Contemp Bks.

Saussure, Eric De. The Secret of Hell's Kitchen: A Parable for Young People. (Illus.). 112p. 1980. 8.95 (ISBN 0-8164-0460-7). Seabury.

Saussure, Ferdinand De see De Saussure, Ferdinand.

Sautter, Frederic J. & Glover, John A. Behavior, Development, & Training of the Dog: A Primer of Canine Psychology. LC 77-7582. 1978. lib. bdg. 8.95 o.p. (ISBN 0-668-04336-9); pap. 4.95 o.p. (ISBN 0-668-04491-8). Arco.

--Behavior, Development & Training of the Horse: A Primer of Equine Psychology. LC 80-23654. 176p. 1980. lib. bdg. 9.95 (ISBN 0-668-04809-3, 4809). Arco.

Sautter, H., jt. auth. see Marchesani, O.

Sauvageau, Juan. Stories That Must Not Die, Vol. 1. LC 75-36692. (Illus., Eng. & Span.). 1975. pap. 3.00 (ISBN 0-916378-00-4). PSI Res.

--Stories That Must Not Die, Vol. 2. (Illus., Eng. & Span.). 1976. pap. 3.00 (ISBN 0-916378-01-2). PSI Res.

--Stories That Must Not Die, Vol. 3. (Illus.). 1976. pap. 3.00 (ISBN 0-916378-02-0). PSI Res.

--Stories That Must Not Die, Vol. 4. (Illus.). (gr. k-12). 1978. pap. text ed. 3.00 (ISBN 0-916378-11-X). PSI Res.

Sauvageot, A. Francais ecrit, francais parle. (Langue vivante). (Fr). pap. 8.25 (ISBN 0-685-13928-X, 3623). Larousse.

--Portrait du vocabulaire francais. (Langue vivante). (Fr). pap. 8.25 (ISBN 0-685-14055-5, 3627). Larousse.

Sauvageot, Claude, jt. auth. see Donze, Marie-Ange.

Sauvain, Harry C. Investment Management. 4th ed. 592p. 1973. ref. ed. 19.95x (ISBN 0-13-503094-3). P-H.

Sauvant, K. & Hasenpflug, H. The New International Economic Order: Conflict or Cooperation Between North & South? LC 76-26623. 1977. lib. bdg. 28.75x o.p. (ISBN 0-89158-139-1); pap. 13.50 o.p. (ISBN 0-89158-288-6). Westview.

Sauvant, K. P. The Third World Without Superpowers, Vols. 1-4. 1978. 42.50 ea. Oceana.

Sauvant, Karl P., ed. Changing Priorities on the International Agenda: The New International Economic Order. (Systems Science & World Order Library: Explorations of World Order). (Illus.). 272p. 1981. 52.00 (ISBN 0-08-023117-9). Pergamon.

Sauver, Dennis St. see St. Sauver, Dennis.

Sauvigny, Guillaume De see De Sauvigny, Guillaume.

Sauvigny Guillaume De, Bertier De see De Bertier De Sauvigny, Guillaume.

Savage. Basic Engineering Craft Activities. 1980. pap. text ed. write for info. (ISBN 0-408-00568-8). Butterworths.

Savage, A. W. Personnel Management. Wilson, A., ed. (Management Pamphlet Ser.). 1977. pap. 3.95x (ISBN 0-85365-580-4, Pub. by Lib Assn England). Oryx Pr.

Savage, C. R. Vascular Surgery. (Pitman Nursing Books Ser.). (Illus.). 200p. 1970. 12.50x o.p. (ISBN 0-8464-0951-8). Beekman Pubs.

Savage, C. Wade. The Measurement of Sensation: A Critique of Perceptual Psychophysics. LC 69-15941. 1970. 29.50x (ISBN 0-520-01527-4). U of Cal Pr.

Savage, Christina. Dawn Wind. (Orig.). 1980. pap. 2.50 o.s.i. (ISBN 0-440-11792-5). Dell.

Savage, Christopher I. Economic History of Transport in Britain. 3rd ed. 1974. text ed. 16.50x (ISBN 0-09-121470-X, Hutchinson U Lib). Humanities.

Savage, Christopher I. & Small, John R. Introduction to Managerial Economics. 1967. text ed. 6.50x (ISBN 0-09-084092-5, Hutchinson U Lib). Humanities.

Savage, D. E., et al. Ceratomorpha & Ancylopoda (Perissodactyla) from the Lower Eocene Paris Basin, France. (U. C. Publ. in Geological Sciences: Vol. 66). 1966. pap. 5.00x (ISBN 0-520-09167-1). U of Cal Pr.

--European Eocene Equidae (Perissodactyla) (U. C. Publ. in Geological Sciences: Vol. 56). 1965. pap. 7.00x (ISBN 0-520-09157-4). U of Cal Pr.

Savage, David. Education Laws Nineteen Seventy-Eight: A Guide to New Directions in Federal Aid. 120p. 1979. pap. 11.95 (ISBN 0-87545-015-6). Natl Sch PR.

Savage, Dean, ed. see Mallet, Serge.

Savage, Denis, tr. see Ricoeur, Paul.

Savage, Donald T. Money & Banking. LC 76-56134. 1977. text ed. 23.50x (ISBN 0-471-75519-2); tchrs. manual avail. (ISBN 0-471-02578-X). Wiley.

Savage, E. Lynn & Biren, Helen A. A Study Guide to Putnam's Geology. 208p. (Orig.). 1978. pap. text ed. 6.95x (ISBN 0-19-502385-4). Oxford U Pr.

Savage, Elizabeth. Last Night at the Ritz. 208p. 1974. pap. 1.25 o.p. (ISBN 0-445-00232-8). Popular Lib.

--Willow Wood. 1979. pap. 2.25 o.p. (ISBN 0-425-04166-2). Berkley Pub.

Savage, Elizabeth, ed. see Donne, Sr. John.

Savage, Eric, jt. auth. see Wallace, Frank R.

Savage, Ernest. Pastels for Beginners. LC 79-56680. (Start to Paint Ser.). (Illus.). 1980. pap. 3.95 (ISBN 0-8008-6238-4, Pentalic). Taplinger.

Savage, Ernest A. Old English Libraries. LC 68-26177. (Illus.). 1968. Repr. of 1912 ed. 22.00 (ISBN 0-8103-3179-9). Gale.

Savage, G. J. & Roe, P. H., eds. Large Engineering Systems, Two: Proceedings of the Second Symposium on Large Engineering Systems, University of Waterloo, Waterloo, Ontario, May 15, 1978. (Illus.). 1979. 88.00 (ISBN 0-08-025090-4). Pergamon.

Savage, George. Art & Antique Restorers Handbook. 1978. 8.50 o.p. (ISBN 0-214-20268-2, 8008, Dist. by Arco). Barrie & Jenkins.

Savage, Helen, ed. Library of Congress Classification Schedules: A Cumulation of Additions & Changes Through 1978, 32 bound cumulations. 1979. Set. pap. 1350.00 (ISBN 0-8103-1150-X). Gale.

Savage, Henry, Jr. Discovering American Seventeen Hundred to Eighteen Seventy-Five. LC 78-20113. (New American Nation Ser.). (Illus.). 1980. pap. 6.95 (ISBN 0-06-090740-1, CN 740, CN). Har-Row.

Savage, Hughley. How to Find True Peace & Hapiness-Plus Inherit Eternal Life. (Orig.). 1980. pap. 2.00 (ISBN 0-9605150-0-3). Savage.

Savage, James E., ed. see Overbury, Thomas.

Savage, Jeanne. Remember to Remember. 1981. 7.95 (ISBN 0-533-04462-6). Vantage.

Savage, John. The Biodynamics of Hair Growth. 1980. 17.50x (ISBN 0-686-64691-6, Pub. by Daniel Co England). State Mutual Bk.
--The Biodynamics of Hair Growth. 88p. 1977. pap. 6.50x (ISBN 0-8464-0996-8). Beekman Pubs.
--The Gay Astrologer. 1981. 7.95. Ashley Bks.

Savage, John F. & Mooney, Jean F. Teaching Reading to Children with Special Needs. 1978. pap. text ed. 11.95 (ISBN 0-205-06130-3, 2361302). Allyn.

Savage, Mary. Addicted to Suicide: A Woman Struggling to Live. 1980. text ed. 12.50x (ISBN 0-87073-906-9); pap. text ed. 5.95x (ISBN 0-87073-907-7). Schenkman.

Savage, P. E. Disasters: Hospital Planning. 1979. 28.00 (ISBN 0-08-024914-0); pap. 12.75 (ISBN 0-08-024913-2). Pergamon.

Savage, Richard. Poetical Works. Tracy, C., ed. 1962. 58.00 (ISBN 0-521-06197-0). Cambridge U Pr.

Savage, Stephen P. The Theories of Talcott Parsons. LC 80-13828. 1980. write for info. (ISBN 0-312-79699-4). St Martin.

Savage, Thomas. Her Side of It. Date not set. price not set. Little.

Savage, W. Sherman. Blacks in the West. LC 75-44657. (Contributions in Afro-American & African Studies: No.23). 288p. (Orig.). 1976. lib. bdg. 17.50 (ISBN 0-8371-8775-3, SBW/). Greenwood.

Savage, William G., jt. auth. see Johnson, H. Webster.

Savage, William W., Jr., ed. Cowboy Life: Reconstructing an American Myth. (Illus.). 1975. 10.95 (ISBN 0-8061-1218-2); pap. 6.95 (ISBN 0-8061-1592-0). U of Okla Pr.

Savaiano, Eugene & Winget, Lynn W. Two Thousand & One Modismos Espanoles e Ingleses. (Barron's Educational Ser.). 336p. 1981. pap. 3.95 (ISBN 0-8120-2314-5). Barron.

Savant, C. J., Jr. Control System Design. 2nd ed. 1964. text ed. 25.50 o.p. (ISBN 0-07-054959-1, C). McGraw.

Savarin, Julian J. Waiters on the Dance. LC 78-2997. 1978. 8.95 o.p. (ISBN 0-312-85416-1). St Martin.

Savary, Louis, jt. auth. see James, Muriel.

Savary, Louis M., jt. auth. see Linde, Shirley M.

Savas, E. S. The Organization & Efficiency of Solid Waste Collection. LC 76-43606. 1977. 17.95 (ISBN 0-669-01095-2). Lexington Bks.

Savas, E. S., ed. Alternatives for Delivering Public Services: Toward Improved Performance. LC 77-6335. 1977. lib. bdg. 18.50x (ISBN 0-89158-306-8). Westview.

Savas, Savas J. Hymnology of the Eastern Orthodox Church. 1977. pap. text ed. 9.00x (ISBN 0-8191-0161-3). U Pr of Amer.

Savas, Steven E. Decision-Related Research on the Organization of Service Delivery Systems in Metropolitan Areas: Solid Waste Management. LC 79-83822. 1979. codebook 30.00 (ISBN 0-89138-982-2). ICPSR.

Savasini, Jose A. Export Promotion: The Case of Brazil. LC 78-16883. (Praeger Special Studies). 1978. 21.95 (ISBN 0-03-041616-7). Praeger.

Savastano, S. Total Knee Replacement. 256p. 1980. 22.50x (ISBN 0-8385-8690-2). ACC.

Saveland, Robert N., ed. Handbook of Environmental Education with International Case Studies. LC 76-4659. 1976. 29.75 (ISBN 0-471-75535-4, Pub. by Wiley-Interscience). Wiley.

Savell, Isabelle K. The Tonetti Years at Snedens Landing. (Illus.). 1977. 11.50 o.p. (ISBN 0-686-00570-8); pap. 7.95 o.p. (ISBN 0-686-00571-6). Rockland County Hist.
--Wine & Bitters. (Illus.). 1975. pap. 2.45 (ISBN 0-89062-008-3). Rockland County Hist.

Save-Soderbergh, Torgny, ed. see Hellstrom, Pontus & Langballe, Hans.

Save-Soderbergh, Torgny, ed. see Marks, Anthony E.

Saveson, John E. Conrad, the Later Moralist. 129p. (Orig.). 1976. pap. text ed. 14.25x (ISBN 90-6203-248-6). Humanities.
--Joseph Conrad: The Making of a Moralist. LC 72-83547. 195p. (Orig.). 1972. pap. text ed. 20.00x (ISBN 0-391-01998-8). Humanities.

Saveth, Edward N. American History & the Social Sciences. LC 64-20308. 1964. 15.95 (ISBN 0-02-927750-7). Free Pr.

Saviano, Eugene & Winget, Lynn W. Two Thousand & One Spanish & English Idioms: 2001 Modismos Espanoles E Ingleses. LC 75-11955. 1977. pap. text ed. 6.50 (ISBN 0-8120-0438-8). Barron.

Savides, Margaret. Bride & Bear. 1980. pap. 2.00. Quixote.

Savidis, George, tr. see Elytis, Odysseus.

Saville, jt. auth. see Miliband.

Saville, Anthony & Kavina, George. The Will of the People: Education in Nevada. 1977. pap. text ed. 10.00x (ISBN 0-8191-0162-1). U Pr of Amer.

Saville, John, jt. auth. see Miliband, Ralph.

Saville, John, jt. ed. see Bellamy, Joyce M.

Saville, John, jt. ed. see Miliband, Ralph.

Saville, Jonathan. The Medieval Erotic Alba: Structure As Meaning. LC 77-190191. 320p. 1972. text ed. 22.50x (ISBN 0-231-03569-1). Columbia U Pr.

Saville, Marshall H. Bibliographic Notes on Xochioalco, Mexico. (INM Ser.: Vol. 11, No.6). 1928. pap. 1.00 (ISBN 0-934490-28-7). Mus Am Ind.

Saville, P. & Blinkhorn, S. Undergraduate Personality by Factored Scales: A Large Scale Study on Cattell's 16PF & the Eysenck Personality Inventory. (NFER General Ser.). 1976. pap. text ed. 21.25x (ISBN 0-85633-104-X, NFER). Humanities.

Saville-Troike, Muriel. Foundations for Teaching English As a 2nd Language: Theory & Method for Multicultural Education. 200p. 1976. pap. 8.95 (ISBN 0-13-329946-5). P-H.
--A Guide to Culture in the Classroom. LC 78-61039. 67p. 1978. pap. 4.50 (ISBN 0-89763-000-9). Natl Clearinghse Bilingual Ed.

Savin, J. A., jt. ed. see Rook, Arthur.

Savin, Maynard. Thomas William Robertson: His Plays & Stagecraft. (Brown University Studies: No. 13). (Illus.). 146p. 1950. 6.50x (ISBN 0-87057-029-3, Pub. by Brown U Pr). Univ Pr of New England.

Savitch, H. V. Urban Policy & the Exterior City: Federal, State & Corporate Policies. (Pergamon Policy Studies). 1979. 39.00 (ISBN 0-08-023390-2). Pergamon.

Saviter, Mark H. The Awakening of Nationalistic Drives & the Tragic Dilemma of the Soviet Leadership. (The Major Currents in Contemporary World History Library). (Illus.). 113p. 1981. 67.75 (ISBN 0-930008-83-9). Inst Econ Pol.

Savitski, V. M., jt. auth. see Bassiouni, M. Cherif.

Savitt, Sam. The Dingle Ridge Fox & Other Stories. LC 78-7739. (Illus.). (gr. 5 up). 1978. 5.95 (ISBN 0-396-07614-9). Dodd.
--Draw Horses with Sam Savitt. LC 80-21812. (Illus.). 96p. 1981. 14.95 (ISBN 0-670-28259-6, Studio). Viking Pr.
--One Horse, One Hundred Miles, One Day: The Story of the Tevis Cup Endurance Ride. LC 80-2777. (Illus.). 96p. (gr. 7 up). 1981. PLB 7.95 (ISBN 0-396-07935-0). Dodd.
--Wild Horse Running. (Illus.). (gr. 4-6). 1976. pap. 1.50 (ISBN 0-590-00092-6, Schol Pap). Schol Bk Serv.

Savitt, Sam, jt. auth. see Steinkraus, William.

Savitt, Todd L. Medicine & Slavery: The Health Care of Blacks in Antebellum Virginia. LC 78-8520. (Blacks in the New World Ser.). (Illus.). 321p. 1981. pap. 7.50 (ISBN 0-252-00874-X). U of Ill Pr.

Savitz, Harriet M. Run, Don't Walk. 1980. pap. 1.50 (ISBN 0-451-09421-2, W9421, Sig). NAL.
--Wait Until Tomorrow. (Orig.). 1981. pap. 1.75 (ISBN 0-451-09780-7, E9780, Sig). NAL.

Savitz, Leonard D. & Johnston, Norman. Crime in Society. LC 78-806. 1978. pap. text ed. 19.95 (ISBN 0-471-03385-5). Wiley.

Savoca, Nick & Schneider, Dick. Road Block to Moscow. (Illus.). 160p. 1974. 4.95 o.p. (ISBN 0-8007-0658-7); pap. 2.95 o.p. (ISBN 0-8007-0659-5). Revell.
--Roadblock to Moscow. LC 77-89445. 1977. pap. 1.95 (ISBN 0-87123-489-0, 200489). Bethany Fell.

Savoie, Donald J. Federal-Provincial Collaboration: The Canada-New Brunswick General Development Agreement. (Institute of Public Administration of Canada (IPAC) Ser.). 220p. 1981. 25.00x (ISBN 0-7735-0373-0); pap. 11.95x (ISBN 0-7735-0374-9). McGill-Queens U Pr.

Savory, H., ed. see Elgood, John H.

Savory, Phyllis. Lion Outwitted by Hare & Other African Tales. LC 74-126432. (Folklore Ser). (Illus.). (gr. 3 up). 1971. 5.95g o.p. (ISBN 0-8075-4556-2). A Whitman.

Savory, R. M., ed. Introduction to Islamic Civilization. LC 74-25662. 220p. 1976. 36.00 (ISBN 0-521-20777-0); pap. 9.95 (ISBN 0-521-09948-X). Cambridge U Pr.

Savory, Roger M. Iran Under the Safavids. LC 78-73817. (Illus.). 300p. 1980. 34.50 (ISBN 0-521-22483-7). Cambridge U Pr.

Savory, T. H., jt. auth. see Sankey, J. P.

Savory, Ted, tr. see Hanh, Nhat & Vo-Dinh.

Savory, Teo. A Clutch of Fables. 4th ed. LC 73-76686. (Illus.). 80p. 1976. 12.00 (ISBN 0-87775-043-2); pap. 4.00 (ISBN 0-87775-104-8). Unicorn Pr.

Savory, Teo, tr. see Queneau, Raymond.

Savostin, A. P., jt. auth. see Dymov, A. M.

Savoy, Gene. The Decoded New Testament, Authorized Version: An Authoritative Translations of the Sacred Teachings of Light As Contained in the Encoded Writings of the Gospels, Acts, & Epistles. LC 73-90340. (Sacred Teachings of Light, Codex II: Vol. 1). xix, 118p. 1975. text ed. 39.50 (ISBN 0-936202-01-7). Intl Comm Christ.

Savvas, Minas, tr. see Ritsos, Yannis.

Sawai, Y., ed. Animal Plant & Microbial Toxins. 1976. pap. text ed. 16.25 (ISBN 0-08-019965-8). Pergamon.

Sawamura, Kaichi, ed. Graphic Arts Japan, Vol. 21, 1979-80. LC 64-43886. (Illus.). 190p. (Orig.). 1980. pap. 35.00x (ISBN 0-8002-2728-X). Intl Pubns Serv.

Saward, Blanche C., jt. auth. see Caulfield, Sophia F.

Saward, E. W., ed. The Regionalization of Personal Health Services. rev. ed. 1976. text ed. 15.00 o.p. (ISBN 0-88202-067-6); pap. text ed. 6.95 o.p. (ISBN 0-686-67234-8). N Watson.

Sawatsky, Rodney, jt. ed. see Quebedeaux, Richard.

Sawatsky, Walter. Soviet Evangelicals Since World War II. LC 81-94121. (Illus.). 560p. 1981. 19.95 (ISBN 0-8361-1238-5); pap. 14.95 (ISBN 0-8361-1239-3). Herald Pr.

Sawatzky, Harry L. They Sought a Country: Mennonite Colonization in Mexico. LC 78-92673. 1971. 24.50x (ISBN 0-520-01704-8). U of Cal Pr.

Sawatzky, Jasper J. & Chen, Shu-Jen. Programming in Basic-Plus. LC 80-27869. 336p. 1981. pap. 13.95 (ISBN 0-471-07729-1). Wiley.

Sawhill, Isabel V., jt. auth. see Ross, Heather L.

Sawhill, Isabel V., et al. Income Transfers & Family Structure. (An Institute Paper). 211p. 1975. pap. 8.50 (ISBN 0-87766-156-1, 13100). Urban Inst.

Sawicki, James A. Infantry Regiments of the US Army. LC 80-53362. (Illus.). 500p. 1981. 24.95 (ISBN 0-9602404-3-8); pap. 16.95 (ISBN 0-9602404-4-6). Wyvern.

Sawicki, Stanislaw J. Soviet Land & Housing Law: A Historical & Comparative Study. LC 77-3016. (Special Studies). 1977. text ed. 22.95 o.p. (ISBN 0-275-24480-6). Praeger.

Sawin, Douglas B., et al, eds. Exceptional Infant: Psychosocial Risks in Infant-Environment Transactions, Vol. 4. LC 80-14270. (Exceptional Infant Ser.). 1980. 32.50 (ISBN 0-87630-222-3). Brunner-Mazel.

Sawin, Dwight H. Microprocessors & Microcomputer Systems. 1977. 21.95 (ISBN 0-669-00564-9). Lexington Bks.

Sawko, F., ed. Developments in Prestressed Concrete, Vol. 1. (Illus.). 1978. text ed. 45.50x (ISBN 0-85334-790-5, Pub. by Applied Science). Burgess-Intl Ideas.
--Developments in Prestressed Concrete, Vol. 2. (Illus.). 1978. text ed. 28.50x (ISBN 0-85334-811-1, Pub. by Applied Science). Burgess-Intl Ideas.

Sawmill Clinic, 5th, Portland, Oregon, March 1975. Modern Sawmill Techniques Vol. 5: Proceedings. White, Vernon S., ed. LC 73-88045. (Sawmill Clinic Library: A Forest Industries Bk.). (Illus.). 1975. 35.00 (ISBN 0-87930-047-7). Miller Freeman.
--Modern Sawmill Techniques Vol. 6: Proceedings. White, Vernon S., ed. LC 73-88045. (Sawmill Clinic Library: A Forest Industries Bk.). (Illus.). 1976. 35.00 (ISBN 0-87930-052-3). Miller Freeman.

Sawmill Clinic, 8th, Portland, Oregon Mar. 1978. Modern Sawmill Techniques, Vol. 8: Proceedings. LC 73-88045. (Sawmill Clinic Library: A Forest Industries Bk.). (Illus.). 1978. pap. 29.50 (ISBN 0-87930-103-1). Miller Freeman.

Sawrey, James, jt. auth. see Telford, Charles W.

Sawrey, James M. & Telford, Charles W. Adjustment & Personality. 4th ed. 608p. 1975. text ed. 14.95x o.p. (ISBN 0-205-04642-8, 7946422). Allyn.

Sawtell, Lucille. All About the Golden Retriever. (All About Ser.). (Illus.). 1980. 16.95 (ISBN 0-7207-1217-3, Pub. by Michael Joseph). Merrimack Bk Serv.
--All About the Golden Retriever. 1975. 14.95 o.p. (ISBN 0-7207-0449-9, Pub. by Michael Joseph). Merrimack Bk Serv.

Sawtell, Vanda. Astrology & Biochemistry. 1980. lib. bdg. 15.95 (ISBN 0-85032-174-3, Pub. by Daniel Co England). State Mutual Bk.

Sawvel, Franklin R., ed. see Jefferson, Thomas.

Sawyer, Alex. In a Time Meant for Love. LC 80-65678. 1980. 9.95 (ISBN 0-89754-017-4); pap. 2.95 (ISBN 0-89754-016-6). Dan River Pr.

Sawyer, Charles. The Arrival of B. B. King: The Authorized Biography. LC 79-6085. (Illus.). 288p. 1980. 14.95 (ISBN 0-385-15929-3). Doubleday.

Sawyer, George. Business & Society: Managing Corporate Social Impact. LC 78-69570. (Illus.). 1978. text ed. 18.50 (ISBN 0-395-26541-X); instr's. manual o.p. (ISBN 0-395-26534-7). HM.

Sawyer, J. O. English-Wappo Vocabulary. (U. C. Publ. in Linguistics: Vol. 43). 1965. pap. 7.50x (ISBN 0-520-09238-4). U of Cal Pr.

Sawyer, J. O., jt. auth. see Smith, J. P.

Sawyer, Jesse. Studies in American Indian Languages. (California Library Reprint). 1974. 20.00x (ISBN 0-520-02525-3). U of Cal Pr.

Sawyer, John F. A Modern Introduction to Biblical Hebrew. (Orig.). 1976. pap. 12.50 (ISBN 0-85362-159-4, Oriel). Routledge & Kegan.

Sawyer, John W. & Hallberg, Kurt, eds. Sawyer's Turbomachinery Maintenance Handbook, 3 vols. LC 80-63559. (Illus.). 1060p. 1981. Set. 115.50 (ISBN 0-937506-03-6). Busn Journals.
--Sawyer's Turbomachinery Maintenance Handbook: Gas Turbines - Turbocompressors. LC 80-52103. (Illus.). 375p. 1980. 38.50 (ISBN 0-937506-01-X). Busn Journals.
--Sawyer's Turbomachinery Maintenance Handbook: Steam Turbines - Power Recovery Turbines. LC 80-52104. (Illus.). 350p. 1981. 38.50 (ISBN 0-937506-00-1). Busn Journals.
--Sawyer's Turbomachinery Maintenance Handbook, Vol. III: Support Services & Equipment. LC 80-53539. (Illus.). 340p. 1981. 38.00 (ISBN 0-937506-02-8). Busn Journals.

Sawyer, L. A. & Mitchell, W. H. The Liberty Ships. 2nd ed. LC 70-124469. (Illus.). 1973. 12.75 (ISBN 0-87033-152-3). Cornell Maritime.

Sawyer, Newell W. The Comedy of Manners from Sheridan to Maugham. 1961. pap. 1.95 o.p. (ISBN 0-498-04057-7, Prpta). A S Barnes.

Sawyer, P. H., ed. Medieval Settlement: Continuity & Change. LC 77-71251. 1977. 47.50x o.p. (ISBN 0-8448-1092-4). Crane-Russak Co.

Sawyer, Paul. Mom's New Job. LC 77-27982. (Moods & Emotions Ser.). (Illus.). (gr. k-3). 1978. PLB 8.95 (ISBN 0-8172-1150-0). Raintree Pubs.
--New Neighbors. LC 77-27974. (Moods & Emotions Ser.). (Illus.). (gr. k-3). 1978. PLB 8.95 (ISBN 0-8172-1156-X). Raintree Pubs.
--There Once Was a Book of Limericks. LC 77-27109. (Games & Activities Ser.). (Illus.). (gr. k-3). 1978. PLB 9.30 (ISBN 0-8172-1168-3). Raintree Pubs.

Sawyer, Philip L. A Neural Systemic Theory of Emotion: An Outline of a New Methodological Approach to Psychology & a Theory of Emotion & the Mind. LC 66-29400. 57p. 1966. 2.95 o.p. (ISBN 0-911308-00-8); pap. 1.75 o.p. (ISBN 0-911308-01-6). P Sawyer.
--Sudden Insurrection: Twelve Short Stories. LC 75-126427. 1970. pap. 2.75 o.p. (ISBN 0-911308-02-4). P Sawyer.

Sawyer, Philip N., jt. auth. see Stillman, Richard M.

Sawyer, Thomas E. The Jewish Minority in the Soviet Union. (Special Studies on the Soviet Union & Eastern Europe). 1979. lib. bdg. 27.50x (ISBN 0-89158-480-3). Westview.

Sawyer, W. W. A Concrete Approach to Abstract Algebra. 1978. pap. text ed. 4.00 (ISBN 0-486-63647-X). Dover.

Sax, Gilbert. Foundations of Educational Research. 2nd ed. 1979. 19.95 (ISBN 0-13-329300-9). P-H.
--Principles of Educational & Psychological Measurement & Evaluation. 2nd ed. 704p. 1980. text ed. 19.95x (ISBN 0-534-00832-1); wkbk 7.95x (ISBN 0-534-00833-X). Wadsworth Pub.
--Principles of Educational Measurement & Evaluation. 1974. 16.95x o.p. (ISBN 0-534-00338-9); study guide 6.95x o.p. (ISBN 0-534-00384-2). Wadsworth Pub.

Sax, Joseph L. Mountains Without Handrails: Reflections on the National Parks. 160p. 1980. 10.00x (ISBN 0-472-09324-X); pap. 5.95 (ISBN 0-472-06324-3). U of Mich Pr.

Sax, Saville, jt. auth. see Harmin, Merrill.

Saxberg, Borje O., jt. auth. see Knowles, Henry P.

Saxby, Graham. Holograms: How to Make & Use Them. (Illus.). 184p. 1980. 24.95 (ISBN 0-240-51054-2). Focal Pr.

Saxe, Richard. Educational Administration Today: An Introduction. LC 79-91196. 1980. 18.50 (ISBN 0-8211-1858-7); text ed. 16.50 10 or more copies (ISBN 0-686-65584-2). McCutchan.
--Opening the Schools: Alternative Ways of Learning. LC 78-190056. 1972. 19.50 (ISBN 0-8211-1851-X); text ed. 17.50x (ISBN 0-685-24961-1). McCutchan.
--School Community Interaction. LC 74-13595. 288p. 1975. 17.50x (ISBN 0-685-52301-2); text ed. 15.75x (ISBN 0-685-52302-0). McCutchan.

Saxe, Richard W., jt. auth. see Dickson, George E.

Saxena, R. K., jt. auth. see Mathai, A. M.

Saxon, David S. Elementary Quantum Mechanics. LC 68-16996. (Illus.). 1968. text ed. 24.95x (ISBN 0-8162-7562-9). Holden-Day.

Saxon, Edgar J. A Sense of Wonder. 64p. 1980. pap. 3.25x (ISBN 0-8464-1048-6). Beekman Pubs.

Saxon, Grant T. The Happy Hustler. (Illus.). 192p. (Orig.). 1975. pap. 1.95 o.s.i. (ISBN 0-446-89613-6). Warner Bks.

Saxon, J. & Englander, W. ANS COBOL Programming. 2nd ed. 1978. pap. text ed. 12.95 (ISBN 0-13-037770-8). P-H.
Saxon, James A. Cobol: A Self-Instructional Manual. 2nd ed. 1971. pap. 13.95 ref. ed. (ISBN 0-13-139469-X). P-H.
Saxon, John H., Jr. Algebra: An Incremental Approach, Vol. I. (Illus.). 1980. pap. 15.95 ref. (ISBN 0-13-021600-3). P-H.
Saxton, Alexander. The Indispensable Enemy: Labor & the Anti-Chinese Movement in California. 1971. 21.50x (ISBN 0-520-01721-8); pap. 3.95 (ISBN 0-520-02905-4). U of Cal Pr.
Saxton, Dolores F. & Haring, Phyllis W. Care of Patients with Emotional Problems. 3rd ed. LC 78-31641. (Illus.). 1979. pap. text ed. 8.50 (ISBN 0-8016-4341-4). Mosby.
Saxton, Dolores F. & Hyland, Patricia A. Planning & Implementing Nursing Intervention: Stress & Adaptation Applied to Patient Care. 2nd ed. LC 78-31818. (Illus.). 1979. pap. 10.50 (ISBN 0-8016-4337-6). Mosby.
Saxton, Dolores F., et al. Programmed Instruction in Arithmetic, Dosages, & Solutions. 4th ed. LC 76-51283. 1977. pap. 7.00 (ISBN 0-8016-4329-5). Mosby.
Saxton, Dolores F., et al, eds. Mosby's Comprehensive Review of Nursing. 9th ed. Nugent, Patricia M. & Pelikan, Phyllis K. 1977. text ed. 13.95 (ISBN 0-8016-3529-2). Mosby.
--Mosby's Comprehensive Review of Nursing. 10th ed. (Illus.). 1981. text ed. cancelled (ISBN 0-8016-3530-6). Mosby.
Saxton, Lloyd. Individual, Marriage & the Family. 4th ed. 672p. 1980. text ed. 17.95x (ISBN 0-534-00799-6); study guide 5.95x (ISBN 0-534-00800-3). Wadsworth Pub.
Saxton, Martha. Louisa May. 1978. pap. 3.50 (ISBN 0-380-48868-X, 48868, Discus). Avon.
Saxton, R. G., jt. auth. see Fray, G. I.
Saxtorph, Niels. Warriors & Weapons of Early Times in Color. (Illus.). 260p. 1980. 9.95 (ISBN 0-7137-0735-6, Pub. by Blandford Pr England). Sterling.
Say, M. G. Alternating Current Machines. 4th ed. LC 76-15265. 1976. 19.95 (ISBN 0-470-15133-1). Halsted Pr.
Say, M. G. & Taylor, E. O. Direct Current Machines. LC 79-19519. 1980. pap. text ed. 19.95x (ISBN 0-470-26838-7). Halsted Pr.
Sayasithsena, Souksomboun, tr. Delta's Effective English As a Second Language for the 21st Century Laotian Supplement. 104p. (Orig.). 1980. pap. 4.95 (ISBN 0-937354-02-3). Delta Systems.
Sayce, R. A., ed. see Corneille, Pierre.
Sayce, Roderick U. Primitive Arts & Crafts. (Illus.). 1963. Repr. of 1933 ed. 10.50x (ISBN 0-8196-0124-1). Biblo.
Saydah, J. Roger. The Ethical Theory of Clarence Irving Lewis. LC 68-20935. 1969. 10.00 o.p. (ISBN 0-8214-0050-9). Ohio U Pr.
Saye, Albert B. American Constitutional Law: Cases & Text. 2nd ed. LC 78-20883. 597p. 1979. text ed. 12.95 (ISBN 0-8299-2028-5). West Pub.
Saye, Albert B. & Allums, John F. Principles of American Government. 8th ed. (Illus.). 1978. pap. 12.50 ref. (ISBN 0-13-701128-8). P-H.
Saye, Albert B., jt. auth. see Pound, Merritt B.
Sayegh, Lily. Arabic Handwriting Workbook. 1979. 4.50x (ISBN 0-917062-03-5). Intl Bk Ctr.
Sayer, James E. Argumentation & Debate. LC 79-24519. 1980. 13.50 (ISBN 0-88284-102-5). Alfred Pub.
Sayer, James E., jt. auth. see Gaw, Beverly.
Sayer, Michael, ed. see Abbott, A. F. & Nelkon, M.
Sayers, Dorothy. Lord Peter. 1972. pap. 5.95 o.p. (ISBN 0-380-01694-X, 42606). Avon.
--Lord Peter. 1980. pap. 6.95 (ISBN 0-380-51672-1, 51672). Avon.
Sayers, Dorothy L. Busman's Honeymoon. LC 60-9116. 1960. 12.95 o.s.i. (ISBN 0-06-013765-7, HarpT). Har-Row.
--Five Red Herrings. 1968. pap. 2.25 (ISBN 0-380-01187-5, 51219). Avon.
--The Five Red Herrings. (Large Print Bks.). 1980. lib. bdg. 15.95 (ISBN 0-8161-3044-2). G K Hall.
--Gaudy Night. 1968. pap. 2.50 (ISBN 0-380-01207-3, 42457). Avon.
--Hangman's Holiday. 1970. pap. 1.95 (ISBN 0-380-01240-5, 48959). Avon.
--Have His Carcase. LC 59-10623. 1959. 12.95 o.s.i. (ISBN 0-06-013785-1, HarpT). Har-Row.
--Have His Carcase. (Large Print Bks.). 1980. lib. bdg. 17.95 (ISBN 0-8161-3043-4). G K Hall.
--In the Teeth of the Evidence. pap. 1.50 (ISBN 0-380-01280-4, 35998). Avon.
--Mind of the Maker. Repr. of 1941 ed. lib. bdg. 20.50x (ISBN 0-8371-3372-6, SAMM). Greenwood.
--The Mind of the Maker. LC 78-19503. 1979. pap. 4.95 (ISBN 0-06-067071-1, RD 295, HarpR). Har-Row.
--Murder Must Advertise. (Large Print Bks.). 1980. lib. bdg. 15.95 (ISBN 0-8161-3045-0). G K Hall.
--Strong Poison. (Large Print Bks.). 1980. lib. bdg. 15.95 (ISBN 0-8161-3042-6). G K Hall.
--Unpleasantness at the Bellona Club. LC 56-8786. 1957. 12.95 o.p. (ISBN 0-06-013805-X, HarpT). Har-Row.
--The Whimsical Christian: Eighteen Essays. 1978. 10.95 (ISBN 0-02-606930-X). Macmillan.
--Whose Body? 1961. pap. 1.95 (ISBN 0-380-00897-1, 51888). Avon.
--Wimsey Set II, 4 bks. Incl. Have His Carcase; Strong Poison; The Five Red Herrings; Murder Must Advertise. (Large Print Bks.). 1980. lib. bdg. 60.00 set (ISBN 0-8161-3136-8). G K Hall.
Sayers, Frances C. Oscar Lincoln Busby Stokes. LC 69-13778. (Illus.). (gr. 1-4). 1970. 4.50 o.p (ISBN 0-15-258814-0, HJ). HarBraceJ.
Sayers, Isabelle S. Annie Oakley & Buffalo Bill's Wild West: One Hundred & Two Illustrations. (Illus.). 96p. (Orig.). 1981. pap. price not set (ISBN 0-486-24120-3). Dover.
Sayers, R. S. The Bank of England: 1891-1944. LC 75-46116. 1976. 165.00 set (ISBN 0-521-21475-0); Vol. 1. (ISBN 0-521-21067-4); Vol. 2. (ISBN 0-521-21068-2); Vol. 3 (appendixes) (ISBN 0-521-21066-6). Cambridge U Pr.
Sayers, Richard S., ed. Banking in Western Europe. 1962. 22.500 (ISBN 0-19-828143-9). Oxford U Pr.
Sayers, Stanley E. The Tragedy of Sin. 1974. 4.50 o.p. (ISBN 0-89137-510-4); pap. 2.50 o.p. (ISBN 0-89137-509-0). Quality Pubns.
Sayers, William T. Body, Soul & Blood: Recovering the Human in Medicine. LC 79-56194. 112p. 1980. pap. 4.95 (ISBN 0-935718-00-1). Asclepiad.
Sayles, Ann. Stitchery, Step by Step. (Step by Step Craft Ser.). 1976. pap. 2.95 (ISBN 0-307-42018-3, Golden Pr). Western Pub.
Sayles, Leonard & Strauss, G. Human Behavior in Organizations. 1966. ref. ed. 19.95 (ISBN 0-13-444703-4). P-H.
Sayles, Leonard & Strauss, George. Sayles' & Strauss' Behavioral Stategies for Managers. 304p. 1980. text ed. 17.95 (ISBN 0-13-791459-8). P-H.
Sayles, Leonard, jt. auth. see Wegner, Robert.
Sayles, Myron A., et al. Oceanographic Atlas of the Bering Sea Basin. LC 76-49165. (Illus.). 170p. 1980. 25.00 (ISBN 0-295-95545-7). U of Wash Pr.
Saylor, David J. Jackson Hole, Wyoming: In the Shadow of the Tetons. (Illus.). 1971. pap. 4.95 (ISBN 0-8061-1424-X). U of Okla Pr.
Saylor, Dennis. And You Visited Me. LC 79-88403. 1979. pap. 6.95 (ISBN 0-933350-21-X). Morse Pr.
Saypol, Judyth R. & Wikler, Madeline. My Very Own Sukkot Book. (Illus.). 40p. (Orig.). (gr. k-6). 1980. pap. 2.95 (ISBN 0-930494-09-1). Kar Ben.
Sayre, Eleanor A. Albrecht Duerer: Master Printmaker. LC 77-183708. (Illus.). 320p. 1972. 27.50 (ISBN 0-87846-005-5); pap. 10.00 o.p. (ISBN 0-685-24672-8). Mus Fine Arts Boston.
Sayre, Joan M. Handbook for the Hearing-Impaired Older Adult. (Illus.). 80p. 1980. pap. 3.95x (ISBN 0-8134-2121-7). Interstate.
--Helping the Older Adult with an Acquired Hearing Loss. (Illus.). 72p. 1980. pap. 3.95x (ISBN 0-8134-2120-9). Interstate.
--Teaching Language Through Sight & Sound - Set 1. 1980. 29.75x (ISBN 0-8134-2077-6). Interstate.
Sayre, Joel & Faulkner, William. The Road to Glory: A Screenplay. Bruccoli, Matthew J., ed. (Illus.). 168p. 1981. price not set (ISBN 0-8093-0995-5); pap. price not set (ISBN 0-8093-0996-3). S Ill U Pr.
Sayre, John L. & Hamburger, Roberta. Tools for Theological Research. 6th ed. 100p. (Orig.). 1981. pap. price not set (ISBN 0-912832-20-7). Seminary Pr.
Sayre, John L. & Hamburger, Roberta. Illustrated Guide to the International Standard Bibliographic Description for Monographs. (Illus., Orig.). 1975. pap. 6.50x o.p. (ISBN 0-912832-12-6). Seminary Pr.
Sayre, Kenneth M. Cybernetics & the Philosophy of Mind. (International Library of Philosophy & Scientific Method). 350p. 1976. text ed. 18.25x (ISBN 0-391-00594-4). Humanities.
--Plato's Analytic Method. LC 69-15496. 1969. 12.50x (ISBN 0-226-73555-9). U of Chicago Pr.
Sayre, Lombard. Celestial Shaggy Dog Joke, No.2. (Illus.). 51p. (Orig.). 1980. pap. 3.95 (ISBN 0-89260-194-9). Hwong Pub.
Sayre, Rose, ed. Pig Iron, Number 7: Special Woman Issue. (Literary & Art Anthology Ser.). 1980. pap. 4.95 (ISBN 0-917530-15-2). Pig Iron Pr.
Sayre, Rose, jt. ed. see Villani, Jim.
Sayre, W. S., ed. see Syracuse University. Maxwell Graduate School of Citizenship & Public Affairs.
Sayre, Wallace S. & Kaufman, Herbert. Governing New York City. 1965. pap. 11.95x (ISBN 0-393-09657-2, NortonC). Norton.
Sayre, Wallace S. & Parris, Judith H. Voting for President: The Electoral College & the American Political System. (Studies in Presidential Selection). 169p. 1970. pap. 4.95 (ISBN 0-8157-7719-1). Brookings.
Saywell, John. The Rise of Parti Quebecois 1967-1976. 1977. pap. 5.95 (ISBN 0-8020-6317-9). U of Toronto Pr.
Sbarra, Anthony J. & Strauss, Robert, eds. The Reticuloendothelial System: A Comprehensive Treatise, 2 vols. Incl. Vol. 1. Morphology. Carr, Ian & Daems, W. T., eds. 700p. 49.50 (ISBN 0-306-40291-2); Vol. 2. Sbarra, Anthony J. & Strauss, Robert, eds. 560p. 45.00 (ISBN 0-306-40292-0). 1980 (Plenum Pr). Plenum Pub.
Scacco, Anthony M., Jr. Rape in Prison. (Amer. Lectures in Behavioral Science & Law Ser.). 144p. 1975. 14.75 (ISBN 0-398-03314-5). C C Thomas.
Scaduto, Anthony. Bob Dylan. 320p. (RL 7). 1973. pap. 2.50 (ISBN 0-451-09289-9, E9289, Sig). NAL.
Scaer, David P. What Do You Think of Jesus? LC 72-97341. 144p. 1973. pap. 3.75 (ISBN 0-570-03153-2, 12-2538). Concordia.
Scagel, Robert F., et al. Plant Diversity: An Evolutionary Approach. 1969. 19.95x o.p. (ISBN 0-534-00677-9). Wadsworth Pub.
Scaglione, Aldo. The Theory of German Word Order from the Renaissance to the Present. LC 80-16619. 275p. 1981. 22.50x (ISBN 0-8166-0980-2); pap. 9.95 (ISBN 0-8166-0983-7). U of Minn Pr.
Scagliotta, Edward G. An L D Program That Works. LC 75-13492. 1979. pap. 9.95 (ISBN 0-87804-319-5). Mafex.
Scagnetti, Jack, jt. auth. see Barris, George.
Scaife, B. K. Studies in Numerical Analysis. 1974. 38.50 (ISBN 0-12-621150-7). Acad Pr.
Scaife, Lawrence. Spotlight on the Card Sharp. (Gambler's Book Shelf). (Illus.). 1977. pap. 2.95 (ISBN 0-89650-575-8). Gamblers.
Scalapino, Robert A. Asia & the Road Ahead: Issues for the Major Powers. LC 75-15219. 1975. 15.95 (ISBN 0-520-03066-4); pap. 4.95 (ISBN 0-520-03173-3). U of Cal Pr.
--Democracy & the Party Movement in Pre-War Japan: The Failure of the First Attempt. (California Library Repr. Ser). 1975. Repr. of 1953 ed. 30.00x (ISBN 0-520-02914-3). U of Cal Pr.
--The Foreign Policy of Modern Japan. (Campus Ser.: No. 196). 1977. 21.50 (ISBN 0-520-03196-2); pap. 6.95x (ISBN 0-520-03499-6). U of Cal Pr.
--The Japanese Communist Movement, 1920-1966. (Center for Japanese & Korean Studies, UC Berkeley). 1967. 17.50x o.p. (ISBN 0-520-01134-1). U of Cal Pr.
--The United States & Korea: Looking Ahead. LC 79-54241. (The Washington Papers: No. 69). 88p. 1979. pap. 3.50 (ISBN 0-8039-1374-5). Sage.
Scalapino, Robert A. & Lee, Chong-Sik. Communism in Korea, Vols. 1 & 2. Incl. Vol. 1. The Movement. 38.50x (ISBN 0-520-02080-4); Vol. 2. The Society. 40.00x (ISBN 0-520-02274-2). LC 79-165236. 1500p. 1973. U of Cal Pr.
Scalapino, Robert A. & Yu, George T. The Chinese Anarchist Movement. LC 80-23499. (University of California Institute of International Studies, Center for Chinese Studies, Research Ser.). vi, 81p. 1980. Repr. of 1961 ed. lib. bdg. 19.75x (ISBN 0-313-22586-9, SCCM). Greenwood.
Scales, Susan. Retriever Training. LC 76-40806. (Illus.). 1977. 14.95 (ISBN 0-7153-7246-7). David & Charles.
Scaletta, Phillip, et al. Student Workbook to Accompany Lusk's Business Law. 4th ed. 1978. pap. text ed. 6.95 (ISBN 0-256-02022-1). Irwin.
Scalf, Henry P. Kentucky's Last Frontier. 565p. 1972. Repr. of 1966 ed. 12.00. Pikeville Coll.
Scalf, Sue. Devil's Wine. LC 76-41420. 1978. 5.95 (ISBN 0-916624-04-8). TSU Pr.
Scalf, Susan. Devil's Wine. LC 76-41420. 1976. pap. 3.95 (ISBN 0-916624-05-6). TSU Pr.
Scally, John, jt. ed. see Kakonis, Tom E.
Scalo, James V. The Complete Credits & Collection Starter Success Kit. rev. ed. 150p. 1981. pap. 29.50 (ISBN 0-914306-55-3). Intl Wealth.
Scalzi, John B., jt. auth. see Podolny, Walter, Jr.
Scalzo, Joe. Speedway. 192p. 1981. pap. 1.95 (ISBN 0-448-17200-3, Tempo). G&D.
Scamehorn, Richard G., jt. auth. see Beatty, James W.
Scammacca, Nat. La Raccomandazione. Barkan, Stanley H., ed. (Cross-Cultural Review Chapbook 1). 24p. (Ital. & Eng.). 1980. pap. 2.50 (ISBN 0-89304-800-3). Cross Cult.
Scammacca, Nat, ed. A Meeting with Nicolo D'Alessandro & Nat Scammacca. (Sicilian Antigruppo Ser.: No. 1). (Illus.). 4.00 o.p. (ISBN 0-89304-501-2); signed ltd. ed. o.p. 6.00 (ISBN 0-89304-502-0); pap. 3.00 (ISBN 0-89304-500-4); pap. 6.00 signed ltd. ed. (ISBN 0-89304-503-9). Cross Cult.
Scammacca, Nat, ed. & tr. see Axelrod, David B.
Scammacca, Nat, ed. see Cali, Santo.
Scammacca, Saverio A., jt. ed. see Barkan, Stanley H.
Scammell, W. M. International Monetary Policy. LC 74-26769. 1976. pap. 14.95 (ISBN 0-470-15197-8). Halsted Pr.
Scammon, Richard. The Odds: On Virtually Everything. 1980. 12.95 (ISBN 0-399-12483-7). Putnam.
Scandinavian Institute of Maritime Law. Norwegian Petroleum Law. 500p. 1980. 135.00x (Pub. by Norwegian Info Norway). State Mutual Bk.
Scandone, Thomas. Emphasis: Natural History. 1979. coil binging 12.95 (ISBN 0-88252-098-9). Paladin Hse.
Scandura, Joseph M. Structural Learning & Concrete Operations: An Approach to Piagetian Conservation. LC 80-16153. 218p. 1980. 21.95 (ISBN 0-03-056697-5). Praeger.
Scandure, Alice M., jt. auth. see Lowerre, George F.
Scanlan, Burt & Keys, J. Bernard. Management & Organizational Behavior. LC 78-15477. (Management Ser.). 1979. text ed. 21.95 (ISBN 0-471-02484-8); tchrs. manual (ISBN 0-471-04774-0); study guide (ISBN 0-471-04773-2). Wiley.
Scanlan, James P., tr. see Lavrov, Peter.
Scanlan, Michael. The Power in Penance. 64p. 1972. pap. 0.75 (ISBN 0-87793-092-9). Ave Maria.
Scanlan, Michael & Shields, Ann T. And Their Eyes Were Opened. 1976. pap. 2.50 (ISBN 0-89283-035-2). Servant.
Scanlon, Charles L., jt. auth. see Scanlon, Cora C.
Scanlon, Cora C. & Scanlon, Charles L. Latin Grammar: Grammar Vocabularies & Exercises in Preparation for the Reading of the Missal & Breviary. Thompson, Newton, ed. LC 79-112494. 1976. pap. text ed. 6.00 (ISBN 0-89555-002-4, 168). TAN Bks Pubs.
--Second Latin. LC 48-748. 1976. pap. 6.00 (ISBN 0-89555-003-2). TAN Bks Pubs.
Scanlon, David G. Traditions of African Education. LC 60-14305. (Orig.). 1964. text ed. 8.75 (ISBN 0-8077-2107-7); pap. text ed. 4.00x (ISBN 0-8077-2104-2). Tchrs Coll.
Scanlon, David G., ed. International Education: A Documentary History. LC 64-12575. (Orig.). 1960. text ed. 8.75 (ISBN 0-8077-2098-4); pap. 4.00x (ISBN 0-8077-2095-X). Tchrs Coll.
Scanlon, Henry. You Can Sell Your Photos. LC 80-7854. (Illus.). 256p. 1980. 16.95 (ISBN 0-690-01902-5, HarpT); pap. 7.95 (ISBN 0-690-01903-3, HarpT). Har-Row.
Scanlon, John. Young Adulthood. 1979. pap. 5.00 (ISBN 0-89492-005-7, Pub. by Acad Ed Dev). Interbk Inc.
Scanlon, Lynne W., jt. auth. see Mandell, Marshall.
Scanlon, Mark, jt. auth. see Grill, Tom.
Scanlon, Pat, jt. auth. see Broccoletti, Peter P.
Scanlon, William, jt. auth. see Holahan, John.
Scanlow, William, et al. Long Term Care: Experience & a Framework for Analysis. (Health Policy & the Elderly Ser.). 162p. 1979. pap. 7.00 (ISBN 0-87766-246-0, 25300). Urban Inst.
Scannell, Dale & Tracy, Dick. Testing & Measurement in the Classroom. 1975. pap. text ed. 9.75 (ISBN 0-395-18608-0). HM.
Scannell, Edward, jt. auth. see Donaldson, Les.
Scanu, Angelo M. & Landsberger, Frank R., eds. Lipoprotein Structure. (N.Y. Academy of Sciences Annals: Vol. 348). 436p. 1980. 76.00x (ISBN 0-89766-082-X). NY Acad Sci.
Scanzoni, John. Opportunity & the Family. LC 70-84935. 1970. 10.95 o.s.i. (ISBN 0-02-927800-7). Free Pr.
--Sex Roles, Women's Work, & Marital Conflict. LC 78-58981. (Illus.). 1978. 17.95 (ISBN 0-669-02400-7). Lexington Bks.
Scanzoni, John & Szinovacz, Maximiliane. Family Decision-Making: Sex Roles & Change Over the Life Cycle. LC 80-18243. (Sage Library of Social Research: Vol. 111). (Illus.). 312p. 1980. 18.00 (ISBN 0-8039-1533-0); pap. 8.95 (ISBN 0-8039-1534-9). Sage.
Scanzoni, John, jt. auth. see Scanzoni, Letha D.
Scanzoni, John H. The Black Family in Modern Society: Patterns of Stability & Security. 1977. pap. 9.00x (ISBN 0-226-73341-6, Phoen). U of Chicago Pr.

--Sex Roles, Life Styles & Childbearing: Changing Patterns in Marriage & the Family. LC 74-28939. (Illus.). 1975. 17.95 (ISBN 0-02-927720-5). Free Pr.
Scanzoni, Letha. Sex Is a Parent Affair. LC 72-77114. 1973. pap. 3.50 o.p. (ISBN 0-8307-0160-5, 54-065-01). Regal.
Scanzoni, Letha & Mollenkott, Virginia R. Is the Homosexual My Neighbor? Another Christian View. LC 77-20445. 176p. 1980. pap. 4.95 (ISBN 0-06-067076-2, RD 337, HarpR). Har-Row.
Scanzoni, Letha D. & Scanzoni, John. Men, Women, & Change. (Illus.). 576p. 1981. 18.95 (ISBN 0-07-055054-9); instr's manual 5.95 (ISBN 0-07-055055-7). McGraw.
Scapagnini, Umberto, jt. ed. see MacLeod, Robert.
Scarborough, G., jt. auth. see Robertson, B.
Scarborough, Gerald. Military Modelling. (Illus.). 64p. 1974. 4.95 o.p. (ISBN 0-85059-177-5). Aztex.
--Modelling RAF Vehicles. (Illus.). 1978. 6.50 o.p. (ISBN 0-85059-261-5). Aztex.
Scarborough, Hollis, jt. auth. see Haviland, Jeannette.
Scarborough, John. Facets of Hellenic Life. LC 75-29704. (Illus.). 320p. 1976. pap. text ed. 14.25 (ISBN 0-395-20368-6). HM.
Scarburough, G., jt. auth. see Robertson, B.
Scarcella, Robin C. & Krashen, Stephen D., eds. Research in Second Language Acquisition: Selected Papers of the Los Angeles Second Language Acquisition Research Forum. (Issues in Second Language Research Ser.). 1981. pap. 13.95 (ISBN 0-88377-143-8). Newbury Hse.
Scarf, Maggi. Antarctica: Exploring the Frozen Continent. (Illus.). (gr. 3-6). 1970. PLB 4.39 o.p. (ISBN 0-394-90799-X). Random.
Scarfe, Herbert. Advanced Lapidary Techniques. 1979. 27.00 (ISBN 0-7134-0398-5, Pub. by Batsford England). David & Charles.
--Collecting & Polishing Stones. (Illus.). 12.95 (ISBN 0-7134-2283-1). Dufour.
--Cutting & Setting Stones. 1972. 17.95 (ISBN 0-7134-2302-1, Pub. by Batsford England). David & Charles.
Scarfe, Norman. Essex. (Shell Guide Ser.). (Illus.). 1968. 13.95 (ISBN 0-571-08868-6, Pub. by Faber & Faber). Merrimack Bk Serv.
Scarfe, W. Shadow & Flowers. 8.00 (ISBN 0-89253-733-7). Ind-US Inc.
Scarff, R. W. & Torloni, H. Histological Typing of Breast Tumours. (World Health Organization: International Histological Classification of Tumours Ser.). 1977. 9.50 (ISBN 0-685-77229-2, 70-1-002-20). Am Soc Clinical.
Scargall, Jeanne. One Thousand & One Ways to Have Fun with Children. rev. ed. LC 72-12174. (Illus.). 160p. 1978. pap. 4.95 o.p. (ISBN 0-684-15926-0, SL815, ScribT). Scribner.
Scarinci, Tom. After the Last Heartbeat. LC 79-55679. 1980. 8.95 (ISBN 0-915684-55-1). Christian Herald.
Scaringi, Joyce W., jt. auth. see Scaringi, Louis T.
Scaringi, Louis T. & Scaringi, Joyce W. A Guide to Money for College. LC 79-83587. 132p. 1979. pap. 2.95 (ISBN 0-9602432-1-6). Anchorage.
Scarisbrick, J. J. Henry VIII. (English Monarchs Series). (Illus.). 1968. 20.00x (ISBN 0-520-01129-5); pap. 6.95 (ISBN 0-520-01130-9, CAL195). U of Cal Pr.
Scarlett, James D. How to Weave Fine Cloth. 208p. 1981. 14.95 (ISBN 0-8359-2987-6); pap. 7.95 (ISBN 0-8359-2986-8). Reston.
Scarne, John. Scarne on Cards. 1973. pap. 2.25 (ISBN 0-451-08559-0, E8559, Sig). NAL.
--Scarne on Dice. rev. ed. LC 62-7251. (Illus.). 1974. 12.95 o.p. (ISBN 0-8117-1516-7). Stackpole.
Scarne, John & Walsh, Audley V. Three Card Monte. (Gambler's Book Shelf). (Illus.). 1967. pap. 2.95 (ISBN 0-89650-505-7). Gamblers.
Scarpa, Ioannis S., et al, eds. Sourcebook on Food & Nutrition. 2nd ed. LC 79-91584. 500p. 1980. 39.50 (ISBN 0-8379-4502-X). Marquis.
Scarpelli, Emile M. & Cosmi, Ermelando V., eds. Reviews in Perinatal Medicine, Vol. 2. LC 77-74616. 1978. 34.50 (ISBN 0-89004-195-4). Raven.
--Reviews in Perinatal Medicine, Vol. 3. LC 77-74616. 1979. text ed. 45.50 (ISBN 0-89004-249-7). Raven.
Scarpelli, Emilie & Cosmi, Ermelando, eds. Reviews in Perinatal Medicine, Vol. 4. 550p. 1981. 39.00 (ISBN 0-89004-364-7). Raven.
Scarpitti, Frank R. & McFarlane, Paul T. Deviance-Action, Reaction, Interaction: Studies in Positive & Negative Deviance. LC 74-4719. 1975. text ed. 9.95 (ISBN 0-201-06721-8). A-W.
Scarpitti, Frank R. see Datesman, Susan K.
Scarpitti, Frank R. & Datesman, Susan K., eds. Drugs & the Youth Culture. LC 80-11613. (Sage Annual Reviews of Drug & Alcohol Abuse: Vol. 4). (Illus.). 320p. 1980. 20.00x (ISBN 0-8039-1103-3); pap. 9.95x (ISBN 0-8039-1104-1). Sage.
Scarr, J. R. Present Day Spanish. Vol. 1. 1966. 4.39 (ISBN 0-08-011551-9). Pergamon.
Scarr, Sandra W. IQ: Race, Social Class & Individual Differences. 500p. 1981. profess. & reference 30.00 (ISBN 0-89859-055-8). L Erlbaum Assocs.
Scarritt, James R., ed. Analyzing Political Change in Africa. (A Westview Replica Edition). 344p. 1980. lib. bdg. 26.50x (ISBN 0-89158-275-4). Westview.
Scarron, Paul. Scarrons Novels. Davies, John, tr. LC 80-2497. 1981. Repr. of 1694 ed. 69.50 (ISBN 0-404-19133-9). AMS Pr.
--The Whole Comical Works of Monsr. Scarron, Part One. LC 78-170503. (Foundations of the Novel Ser.: Vol. 2). lib. bdg. 50.00 (ISBN 0-8240-0514-7). Garland Pub.
--The Whole Comical Works of Monsr. Scarron, Parts Two & Three. LC 78-170503. (Foundations of the Novel Ser.: Vol. 3). lib. bdg. 50.00 (ISBN 0-8240-0515-5). Garland Pub.
Scarry, Huck. Huck Scarry's Steam Train Press-Outs. (Illus.). 32p. (Orig.). (gr. 2-5). 1980. pap. 4.95 (ISBN 0-529-05588-0). Philomel.
Scarry, Patricia. Corky. (Illus.). 24p. (gr. k-3). 1976. PLB 5.00 (ISBN 0-307-60086-6, Golden Pr). Western Pub.
--Just for Fun. (Illus.). (ps-1). 1977. PLB 5.00 (ISBN 0-307-60264-8, Golden Pr). Western Pub.
--Rags. (Illus.). (ps-3). 1970. PLB 5.00 (ISBN 0-307-60586-8, Golden Pr). Western Pub.
--The Wait-for-Me Kitten. (Illus.). (ps-2). 1962. PLB 4.57 o.p. (ISBN 0-307-60643-0, Golden Pr). Western Pub.
Scarry, Patsy. The Bunny Book. (Illus.). (ps-3). 1955. PLB 4.57 o.p. (ISBN 0-307-60215-X, Golden Pr). Western Pub.
Scarry, Richard. About Animals. (Golden Look-Look Bks.). (Illus.). 1976. limp bdg. 0.95 (ISBN 0-307-11822-3, Golden Pr); PLB 5.38 (ISBN 0-307-61822-6). Western Pub.
--All Day Long. (Golden Look-Look Book Ser). (Illus.). 1976. limp bdg. 0.95 (ISBN 0-307-11825-8, Golden Pr); PLB 5.38 (ISBN 0-307-61825-0). Western Pub.
--All Year Long. (Golden Look-Look Bks.). (Illus.). (ps-1). 1976. PLB 5.38 (ISBN 0-307-61826-9, Golden Pr); pap. 0.95 (ISBN 0-307-11826-6). Western Pub.
--At Work. (Golden Look-Look Ser.). (Illus.). 24p. 1976. limp bdg. 0.95 (ISBN 0-307-11824-X, Golden Pr); PLB 5.38 (ISBN 0-307-61824-2). Western Pub.
--The Bunny Book. (Illus.). 24p. (gr. k-1). 1976. PLB 5.38 (ISBN 0-307-68979-4, Golden Pr). Western Pub.
--Early Bird. (Illus.). (ps-1). 1968. 2.95 (ISBN 0-394-81138-0); PLB 3.99 (ISBN 0-394-91138-5). Random.
--In My Town. (Golden Look-Look Bks.). (Illus.). (ps-1). 1976. PLB 5.38 (ISBN 0-307-61828-5, Golden Pr); pap. 0.95 (ISBN 0-307-11828-2). Western Pub.
--Laugh & Learn Library, 4 bks. (Illus.). (ps-1). 1977. pap. 3.95 o.p. (ISBN 0-394-83336-8, BYR). Random.
--Learn to Count. (Golden Look-Look Bks.). (Illus.). (ps-1). 1976. PLB 5.38 (ISBN 0-307-61829-3, Golden Pr); pap. 0.95 (ISBN 0-307-11829-0). Western Pub.
--Little Bedtime Book. LC 78-55298. (Richard Scarry's Best Little Books Ever). (Illus.). (ps-2). 1978. pap. 0.95 (ISBN 0-394-83967-6, BYR). Random.
--My House. (Golden Look-Look Ser.). (Illus.). 1976. PLB 5.38 (ISBN 0-307-61820-X, Golden Pr); pap. 0.95 (ISBN 0-307-11820-7). Western Pub.
--On the Farm. (Golden Look-Look Ser.). (Illus.). 1976. PLB 5.38 (ISBN 0-307-61821-8, Golden Pr); pap. 0.95 (ISBN 0-307-11821-5). Western Pub.
--On Vacation. (Golden Look-Look Ser.). (Illus.). 1976. PLB 5.38 (ISBN 0-307-61823-4, Golden Pr); pap. 0.95 (ISBN 0-307-11823-1). Western Pub.
--Rabbit & His Friends. (Illus.). (ps-2). 1953. PLB 5.00 (ISBN 0-307-60169-2, Golden Pr). Western Pub.
--Richard Scarry's Best Word Book Ever. (Illus.). (ps-3). 1963. 4.95 (ISBN 0-307-15510-2, Golden Pr); PLB 12.23 (ISBN 0-307-65510-5). Western Pub.
--Richard Scarry's Busy Busy World. (Illus.). (gr. k-5). 5.95 (ISBN 0-307-15511-0, Golden Pr); PLB 12.23 (ISBN 0-307-65539-3). Western Pub.
--Richard Scarry's Cars & Trucks & Things That Go. 1974. 4.95 (ISBN 0-307-15785-7, Golden Pr); PLB 12.23 (ISBN 0-307-65785-X). Western Pub.
--Richard Scarry's Color Book. LC 75-36465. (Illus.). 14p. (ps-1). 1976. 2.95 (ISBN 0-394-83237-X, BYR). Random.
--Richard Scarry's Lowly Worm Word Book. LC 80-53103. (Chunky Bks.). (Illus.). 28p. (ps). 1981. pap. 2.50 board (ISBN 0-686-69031-1). Random.
--Richard Scarry's Nicky Goes to the Doctor. (Look-Look Bks.). (gr. k-1). 1978. PLB 5.38 (ISBN 0-307-61842-0, Golden Pr); pap. 0.95 (ISBN 0-307-11842-8). Western Pub.
--Richard Scarry's Peasant Pig & the Terrible Dragon. LC 80-5086. (Illus.). 48p. (ps-3). 1980. bds. 4.95 (ISBN 0-394-84567-6); PLB 5.99 (ISBN 0-394-94567-0). Random.
--Richard Scarry's Toy Book. (Illus.). (ps-3). 1978. pap. 3.95 (ISBN 0-394-83962-5, BYR). Random.
--Short & Tall. (Golden Look-Look Bks.). (Illus.). (ps-1). 1976. PLB 5.38 (ISBN 0-307-61827-7, Golden Pr); pap. 0.95 (ISBN 0-307-11827-4). Western Pub.
--Six Golden Look-Look Books, 6 bks. (Illus.). Date not set. pap. 5.70 boxed set (ISBN 0-307-15524-2, Golden Pr). Western Pub.
Scarry, Richard, illus. Great Big Car & Truck Book. (ps-2). 1951. 1.95 (ISBN 0-307-10473-7, Golden Pr); PLB 7.62 (ISBN 0-307-60473-X). Western Pub.
--Richard Scarry's Best Mother Goose Ever. (Illus.). (ps-1). 1970. 5.95 (ISBN 0-307-15578-1, Golden Pr); PLB 12.23 (ISBN 0-307-65578-4). Western Pub.
Scarry, S., jt. auth. see Kirby, L.
Scarth, Alwyn, tr. see Boillot, G.
Scary, Richard. Mi Primer Gran Libro Fabulas. 12.95 o.p. (ISBN 0-686-65647-4). Larousse.
Scase, Richard & Goffee, Robert. The Real World of the Small Business Owner. 166p. 1980. 27.50x (ISBN 0-7099-0452-5, Pub. by Croom Helm Ltd England). Biblio Dist.
Scase, Richard, ed. Readings in the Swedish Class Structure. 1976. text ed. 42.00 (ISBN 0-08-016663-6); pap. 16.25 (ISBN 0-08-020633-6). Pergamon.
Scataglini, Alberto, et al, trs. Brujula Para el Ministro. (Spanish Bks.). 1979. 3.75 (ISBN 0-8297-0877-4). Life Pubs Intl.
Scates, Allen & Ward, Jane. Volleyball. 2nd ed. 1975. 6.50x (ISBN 0-205-04817-X). Allyn.
Scates, Allen E. Winning Volleyball. 2nd ed. 304p. 1976. text ed. 18.95x (ISBN 0-205-04875-7). Allyn.
Scattergood, Pat & Scattergood, Terry. Lost Art of Handfinishing Furniture. 1980. 4.00 (ISBN 0-8062-1324-8). Carlton.
Scattergood, Terry, jt. auth. see Scattergood, Pat.
Scavnicky, Gary E. Dialectologia Hispanoamericana: Estudios Actuales. 127p. (Orig., Span.). 1980. pap. text ed. 6.95 (ISBN 0-87840-080-X). Georgetown U Pr.
Scaylea, Josef. Moods of the Mountain II. (Illus.). 64p. 1981. 24.95 (ISBN 0-87564-017-6). Superior Pub.
Sceve, Maurice. Delie. McFarlane, I. D., ed. 1966. 75.00 (ISBN 0-521-05628-4). Cambridge U Pr.
Schaad, R., jt. auth. see Laszt, L.
Schaaf, Dick, jt. auth. see Lane, Jim.
Schaaf, Peter. An Apartment House Close Up. LC 80-11301. (Illus.). 32p. (ps-3). 1980. 7.95 (ISBN 0-590-07670-1, Four Winds). Schol Bk Serv.
--The Violin Close up. LC 79-6337. (Illus.). 32p. (gr. 1 up). 1980. 6.95 (ISBN 0-590-07655-8, Four Winds). Schol Bk Serv.
Schaaf, William L. Carl Friedrich Gauss: Prince of Mathematicians. LC 64-11913. (Biography Ser). (Illus.). (gr. 7 up). 1964. PLB 5.90 o.p. (ISBN 0-531-00877-0). Watts.
Schaaf, William L., ed. Our Mathematical Heritage. 1963. pap. 1.50 o.s.i. (ISBN 0-02-093960-4, Collier). Macmillan.
Schaafsma, Polly. Rock Art in New Mexico. LC 75-5496. (Illus.). 209p. 1975. pap. 10.95 o.p. (ISBN 0-8263-0372-2). U of NM Pr.
--The Rock Art of Utah. Flint, Emily, ed. LC 72-173663. (Papers of the Peabody Museum Ser.: Vol.65). (Illus.). 1976. pap. 15.00 (ISBN 0-87365-186-3). Peabody Harvard.
Schaal, Wilbert. Written Communication Skills. rev. ed. 114p. 1980. pap. 6.60 (ISBN 0-87771-022-8). Grad School.
Schaap, Walter, tr. see Goffin, Robert.
Schaar, John H. Legitimacy in the Modern State. 341p. 1981. 15.95 (ISBN 0-87855-337-1). Transaction Bks.
Schabacker, Joseph & Schroeder, Paul. Accounting Problems & How to Solve Them. (Orig.). 1952. pap. 2.95 (ISBN 0-06-460085-8, CO 85, COS). Har-Row.
Schaber, Will, ed. Weinberg der Freiheit. Date not set. 10.50 (ISBN 0-8044-2763-1). Ungar.
Schach, Paul, ed. Languages in Conflict: Linguistic Acculturation on the Great Plains. LC 80-12710. xii, 186p. 1981. 17.50x (ISBN 0-8032-2106-1). U of Nebr Pr.
Schach, Paul, ed. see Sveinsson, Einar Ol.
Schach, Paul, tr. from Old Norse. & intro. by. The Saga of Tristram & Isond. LC 73-76351. (Illus.). xxiv, 148p. 1973. 9.50x (ISBN 0-8032-0832-4); pap. 2.25x (ISBN 0-8032-5847-X, BB 608, Bison). U of Nebr Pr.
Schach, Paul, tr. see Hallberg, Peter.
Schach, Paul, tr. see Sveinsson, Einar Ol.
Schachenmayr. The Book of Knitting & Crochet. Nye, ed. 300p. 1973. 11.25 (ISBN 0-8231-5031-3). Branford.
Schacht, Hjalmar. The End of Reparations. Gannett, Lewis, tr. LC 79-1590. 1981. Repr. of 1931 ed. 19.75 (ISBN 0-88355-895-5). Hyperion Conn.
Schacht, Jochen, jt. ed. see DeRobertis, Eduardo.
Schacht, Joseph. Introduction to Islamic Law. 1964. 24.95x (ISBN 0-19-825161-0). Oxford U Pr.
Schacht, Joseph & Bosworth, C. E., eds. The Legacy of Islam. 2nd ed. (Legacy Ser). (Illus.). 583p. 1974. text ed. 29.50x (ISBN 0-19-821913-X). Oxford U Pr.
Schacht, Richard. Alienation. LC 70-116252. 1971. pap. 1.95 o.p. (ISBN 0-385-04791-6, Anch). Doubleday.
Schacht, Wilhelm. Rock Gardens. (Illus.). 190p. Repr. 17.50 (ISBN 0-87663-354-8, Pica Pr). Universe.
Schachter, E. Neil, jt. auth. see Lehnert, Bruce E.
Schachter, G. & Dale, E. Economist Looks at Society. 1973. pap. 11.95x o.p. (ISBN 0-471-00951-2). Wiley.
Schachter, Howard & Kirsner, Joseph B. Crohn's Disease of the Gastrointestinal Tract. LC 80-10339. (Clinical Gastroenterology Monographs). 1980. 28.50 (ISBN 0-471-48896-8, Pub. by Wiley Medical). Wiley.
Schachter, M., ed. Histamine & Antihistamines. LC 72-10535. 196p. 1973. text ed. 31.00 (ISBN 0-08-016390-4). Pergamon.
Schachter, Oscar. Sharing the World's Resources. LC 76-28422. 1977. 12.50x (ISBN 0-231-04110-1). Columbia U Pr.
Schachter, Paul & Otanes, Fe T. A Tagalog Reference Grammar. LC 73-122946. 1972. pap. 19.50x (ISBN 0-520-01776-5). U of Cal Pr.
Schact, Joseph. The Origins of Muhammadan Jurisprudence. 364p. 1979. pap. text ed. 12.50x (ISBN 0-19-825357-5). Oxford U Pr.
Schad, Tennyson, jt. auth. see Shapiro, Ira.
Schad, Tennyson & Shapiro, Ira, eds. American Showcase, Vol.1. (Illus.). 226p. pap. 19.95 (ISBN 0-931144-01-9). Am Showcase.
--American Showcase, Vol. 2. (Illus.). 266p. 35.00 (ISBN 0-931144-04-3); pap. 22.50 (ISBN 0-931144-03-5). Am Showcase.
--American Showcase, Vol.4. (Illus.). 40.00 (ISBN 0-931144-08-6); pap. 27.50 (ISBN 0-931144-07-8). Am Showcase.
Schade, D., jt. auth. see Busch, G.
Schade, George D., tr. see Arreola, Juan J.
Schade, George D., tr. see Rulfo, Juan.
Schaechter, Moselio see Bourne, G. H. & Danielli, J. F.
Schaeck, Elisabeth, jt. auth. see Koch, Walter A.
Schaedel, Richard, jt. ed. see Rubin, Vera.
Schaef, Anne W. Woman's I View. Orig. Title: Another Reality: the Female System & White Male System. 180p. (Orig.). 1981. 12.95 (ISBN 0-03-059061-2); pap. 6.95 (ISBN 0-03-059061-2). Winston Pr.
Schaefer, Charles E. & Millman, Howard L. How to Help Children with Common Problems. 445p. 1980. 15.95 (ISBN 0-442-24506-8). Van Nos Reinhold.
Schaefer, Charles E. & Mellor, Kathleen, eds. Young Voices. (gr. 5 up). 1972. pap. 0.95 o.s.i. (ISBN 0-02-044960-7, Collier). Macmillan.
Schaefer, Cornelia, tr. see Signoret, Simone.
Schaefer, David L. Justice or Tyranny? A Critique of John Rawls's "Theory of Justice". (National Univ. Pubns. Political Science. Ser.). 1979. 12.50 (ISBN 0-8046-9221-1, National Univ. Pubns.). Kennikat.
Schaefer, David L., ed. The New Egalitarianism: Questions & Challenges. (National Univ. Pubns. Political Science Ser.). 1979. 17.50 (ISBN 0-8046-9220-3). Kennikat.
Schaefer, Don. Lightweight Equipment for Hiking, Camping & Mountaineering. 13th ed. 1972. pap. 1.00 o.p. (ISBN 0-915746-04-2). Potomac Appalach.
Schaefer, Elizabeth & Benson, Jim. Energy & Power in Your Community: How to Analyze Where It Comes from, How Much It Costs, & Who Controls It. (Illus.). 140p. (Orig.). 1980. pap. text ed. 6.00 (ISBN 0-937786-03-9). Inst Ecological.
Schaefer, F. P., ed. Dye Lasers. LC 73-11593. (Topics in Applied Physics: Vol. 1). (Illus.). xi, 285p. 1974. 37.80 o.p. (ISBN 0-387-06438-9). Springer-Verlag.
Schaefer, Florence. Interactive Audio-Visual Programming: The Learning Wall Concept. (Illus.). 172p. 1975. 15.50 (ISBN 0-398-03328-5). C C Thomas.

Schaefer, George & Graber, Edward A., eds. Complications in Obstetric & Gynecologic Surgery. (Illus.). 650p. 1981. text ed. write for info. (ISBN 0-06-142330-0, Harper Medical). Har-Row.

Schaefer, H. H. Topological Vector Spaces. LC 65-24692. (Graduate Texts in Mathematics: Vol. 3). 1971. text ed. 24.00 (ISBN 0-387-90026-8); pap. text ed. 9.50 (ISBN 0-387-05380-8). Springer-Verlag.

Schaefer, Henry F. The Electronic Structure of Atoms & Molecules: A Survey of Rigorous Quantum Mechanical Results. 1972. text ed. 12.95 (ISBN 0-201-06726-9). A-W.

Schaefer, Jack. Monte Walsh. LC 80-25036. x, 442p. 1981. 21.50x (ISBN 0-8032-4124-0); pap. 7.50 (ISBN 0-8032-9121-3, BB 755, Bison). U of Nebr Pr.

--Shane. (Literature Ser). (gr. 9-12). 1949. pap. text ed. 3.58 (ISBN 0-87720-757-7). AMSCO Sch.

--Shane. (Illus.). (gr. 7 up). 1954. 9.95 (ISBN 0-395-07090-2). HM.

Schaefer, Johanna. A Walk Toward Peace. 1977. 4.50 o.p. (ISBN 0-682-48798-8). Exposition.

Schaefer, Nicola. Does She Know She's There? LC 78-52115. 1978. 7.95 o.p. (ISBN 0-385-14413-X). Doubleday.

Schaefer, Patricia S., jt. auth. see Preksto, Peter W., Jr.

Schaefer, Robert J. School As a Center of Inquiry. (John Dewey Society Lectureship Ser.). 1967. 10.00x o.s.i. (ISBN 0-06-035814-9, HarpT). Har-Row.

Schaefer, Udo. The Light Shineth in Darkness: Five Studies in Revelation After Christ. Neri, Helene M. & Coburn, Oliver, trs. LC 78-320332. 1977. pap. 4.95 (ISBN 0-85398-072-1, 7-32-28, Pub. by G Ronald England). Baha'i.

Schaefer, Vincent J. & Day, John A. A Field Guide to the Atmosphere. (Illus.). 384p. 1981. 13.95 (ISBN 0-395-24080-8). HM.

Schaefer, William D. James Thomson, (B. V.): Beyond "The City". (Perspectives in Criticism: No. 17). 1965. 19.50x (ISBN 0-520-01138-4). U of Cal Pr.

Schaefer, William D., ed. The Speedy Extinction of Evil & Misery: Selected Prose of James Thomson (B. V.) 1967. 22.75x (ISBN 0-520-01139-2). U of Cal Pr.

Schaefer-Simmern, Henry. The Unfolding of Artistic Activity: Its Basis, Processes, & Implications. (Illus.). 1948. 18.50x (ISBN 0-520-01141-4). U of Cal Pr.

Schaefer-Simmern, Henry, tr. see Fiedler, Conrad.

Schaeffer, A. C. & Spencer, D. C. Coefficient Regions for Schlicht Functions. Bd. with The Region of Values of the Derivative of a Schlicht Function. Grad, Arthur. LC 51-944. (Colloquium Pubns. Ser.: Vol. 35). 1950. 12.80 (ISBN 0-8218-1035-9, COLL-35). Am Math.

Schaeffer, Benson, et al. Total Communication: A Signed Speech Program for Nonverbal Children. LC 80-51545. (Illus.). 260p. 1980. pap. text ed. 9.95 (ISBN 0-87822-218-9, 2189). Res Press.

Schaeffer, Charles E., ed. Therapeutic Use of Child's Play. LC 75-9556. 684p. 1981. Repr. of 1977 ed. 30.00 (ISBN 0-87668-209-3). Aronson.

Schaeffer, Edith. Christianity Is Jewish. 1975. pap. 2.95 (ISBN 0-8423-0242-5). Tyndale.

Schaeffer, Emil, ed. Goethes Aussere Erscheinung. (Illus.). 120p. 1980. text ed. 31.20 (ISBN 3-458-04925-8, Pub. by Insel Verlag Germany). Suhrkamp.

Schaeffer, Francis A. Art & the Bible. LC 73-75891. 64p. 1973. pap. 1.95 (ISBN 0-87784-443-7). Inter-Varsity.

--Church Before the Watching World. LC 76-166121. (Orig.). 1971. pap. 1.95 o.p. (ISBN 0-87784-542-5). Inter-Varsity.

--Genesis in Space & Time. LC 72-78406. 144p. 1972. pap. 3.50 (ISBN 0-87784-636-7). Inter-Varsity.

--New Super-Spirituality. pap. 0.95 o.p. (ISBN 0-87784-318-X). Inter-Varsity.

--No Little People. LC 74-78675. 276p. 1974. pap. text ed. 5.95 (ISBN 0-87784-765-7). Inter-Varsity.

Schaeffer, Franky. Addicted to Mediocrity. (Illus.). 128p. 1981. pap. 4.95 (ISBN 0-89107-214-4). Good News.

Schaeffer, Heinz. U-Boat Nine Hundred Seventy-Seven. (War Book). 208p. 1981. pap. 2.50 (ISBN 0-553-14591-6). Bantam.

Schaeffer, Richard L., jt. auth. see Mendenhall, William.

Schaeffer, Riley S., jt. auth. see Cordes, Eugene.

Schaeffer, Susan F. Anya. LC 73-20990. 520p. 1974. 8.95 o.s.i. (ISBN 0-02-607020-0). Macmillan.

--Anya. 1975. pap. 2.95 (ISBN 0-380-00573-5, 48645, Bard). Avon.

--Falling. 288p. 1973. 6.95 o.s.i. (ISBN 0-686-66747-6). Macmillan.

--Granite Lady: Poems. 150p. 1974. pap. 3.95 o.s.i. (ISBN 0-02-070750-9, Collier). Macmillan.

--Rhymes & Runes of the Toad. Fleuret, Sebastian, ed. LC 75-15927. (Illus.). 72p. 1975. 6.95 o.s.i. (ISBN 0-02-607040-5). Macmillan.

--Time of the King & Queen. (Illus.). Date not set. pap. cancelled (ISBN 0-916300-20-X). Gallimaufry.

Schaefler, G. F. Introducing Computers. LC 73-14925. 121p. 1974. 10.50x o.p. (ISBN 0-471-75695-4). Wiley.

Schaer, M. Kompendium der Schutzimpfungen. (Illus.). 1979. pap. 11.50 (ISBN 3-8055-2994-5). S Karger.

Schaerf, C., ed. Perspectives of Fundamental Physics. (Studies in High Energy Physics: Vol. 1). 470p. 1979. lib. bdg. 40.75 flexicover (ISBN 3-7186-0007-2). Harwood Academic.

Schaerf, C., jt. ed. see Carlton, D.

Schaerf, Carlo, jt. auth. see Carlton, David.

Schaerf, Carlo, jt. ed. see Carlton, David.

Schaetzle. Thermal Energy Storage in Aquifiers. (Design & Applications). 275p. 1980. text ed. 24.50 (ISBN 0-08-025977-4). Pergamon.

Schaf, Frank, Jr., jt. auth. see Blackstock, Paul W.

Schafer, Ann. Canoeing Western Waterways, 2 vols. Incl. The Mountain States. LC 74-1851. (Arizona, Colorado, Idaho, Montana, Nevada, New Mexico, Utah & Wyoming). 10.95 o.p. (ISBN 0-06-013797-5); pap. 5.95 (ISBN 0-06-013799-1, TD-281); The Coastal States. LC 76-54410. (California, Oregon, Washington & Hawaii). 10.95 o.p. (ISBN 0-06-013798-3); pap. 5.95 (ISBN 0-06-013806-8, TD-280). (Illus.). 1978 (HarpT). Har-Row.

Schafer, Edward. Ancient China. LC 67-30847. (Great Ages of Man). (Illus.). (gr. 6 up). 1967. PLB 11.97 (ISBN 0-8094-0379-X, Pub. by Time-Life). Silver.

Schafer, Edward H. Ancient China. (Great Ages of Man Ser). (Illus.). 1967. 12.95 (ISBN 0-8094-0357-9). Time-Life.

--The Divine Woman: Dragon Ladies & Rain Maidens in T'ang Literature. 250p. 1980. pap. 7.50 (ISBN 0-86547-009-X). N Point Pr.

--The Golden Peaches of Samarkand: A Study of T'ang Exotics. 1981. 35.00x (ISBN 0-520-01144-9). U of Cal Pr.

--Pacing the Void: T'ang Approaches to the Stars. 1978. 34.50x (ISBN 0-520-03344-2). U of Cal Pr.

--Shore of Pearls: Hainan Island in Early Times. LC 78-94990. (Illus.). 1970. 18.50x (ISBN 0-520-01592-4). U of Cal Pr.

--Tu Wan's Stone Catalogue of Cloudy Forest: A Commentary & Synopsis. (Illus.). 1961. 14.50x (ISBN 0-520-01143-0). U of Cal Pr.

--The Vermilion Bird: T'ang Images of the South. 1967. 22.75x (ISBN 0-520-01145-7). U of Cal Pr.

Schafer, Joseph. Helicopter Fundamentals. (Aviation Technician Training Course Ser.). (Illus.). 400p. 1980. pap. text ed. 8.95 (ISBN 0-89100-118-2). Aviation Maintenance.

--Social History of American Agriculture. LC 70-99471. (American Scene Ser). 1970. Repr. of 1936 ed. lib. bdg. 32.50 (ISBN 0-306-71857-X). Da Capo.

Schafer, Joseph, ed. see Schurz, Carl.

Schafer, Jurgen. Documentation in the O. E. D. Shakespeare & Nashe As Test Cases. (Illus.). 186p. 1980. text ed. 29.50x (ISBN 0-19-811938-0). Oxford U Pr.

Schafer, Murray. Creative Music Education. LC 75-30286. (Illus.). 1976. pap. text ed. 9.95 (ISBN 0-02-872330-9). Schirmer Bks.

Schafer, R. C., ed. Chiropractic Physical & Spinal Diagnosis. (Illus.). 578p. 1980. text ed. 30.00 (ISBN 0-936948-00-0). Am Chiro Acad.

Schafer, R. Murray. The Rhinoceros in the Classroom. 1975. pap. 5.00 (ISBN 0-900938-44-7, 50-26922). Eur-Am Music.

--The Tuning of the World: Toward a Theory of Soundscape Design. 1980. write for info.; pap. text ed. 11.50x (ISBN 0-8122-1109-X). U of Pa Pr.

Schafer, R. W. & Markel, J. D., eds. Speech Analysis. LC 78-65706. (IEEE Press Selected Reprint Ser.). 1979. 33.95 (ISBN 0-471-05830-0); pap. 22.00 (ISBN 0-471-05832-7, Pub. by Wiley-Interscience). Wiley.

Schafer, Ronald W., jt. auth. see Oppenheim, Alan V.

Schafer, Ronald W., jt. auth. see Rabiner, Lawrence R.

Schafer, Stephen. Introduction to Criminology. 352p. 1976. 14.95 (ISBN 0-87909-390-0). Reston.

Schafer, Stephen & Knudten, Richard D., eds. Criminological Theory. LC 76-18488. 1977. 22.95 (ISBN 0-669-00795-1). Lexington Bks.

Schafer, Stephen, et al. Social Problems in a Changing Society: Issues & Deviances. 272p. 1975. pap. 10.50 o.p. (ISBN 0-87909-771-X). Reston.

Schaff, Adam. Alienation As a Social Phenomenon. Date not set. 48.00 (ISBN 0-08-021807-5). Pergamon.

Schaff, Mary E., jt. auth. see Siebring, B. Richard.

Schaff, Philip. History of the Christian Church, 8 vols. Incl. Vol. 1. Apostolic Christianity. 14.95 (ISBN 0-8028-8047-9); Vol. 2. Ante-Nicene. 100-325. 14.95 (ISBN 0-8028-8048-7); Vol. 3. Nicene & Post-Nicene. 311-600. 14.95 (ISBN 0-8028-8049-5); Vol. 4. Medieval Christianity. 590-1073. 14.95 (ISBN 0-8028-8050-9); Vol. 5. Middle Ages. 1049-1294. 14.95 (ISBN 0-8028-8051-7); Vol. 6. Middle Ages. 1295-1517. 14.95 (ISBN 0-8028-8052-5); Vol. 7. German Reformation. 14.95 (ISBN 0-8028-8053-3); Vol. 8. Swiss Reformation. 14.95 (ISBN 0-8028-8054-1). 1960. Repr. 14.95 ea.; 119.60 (ISBN 0-8028-8046-0). Eerdmans.

--The Principle of Protestantism. Thompson, Bard & Bricker, George H., eds. 1964. pap. 6.95 (ISBN 0-8298-0348-3). Pilgrim NY.

Schaff, Phillip. History of the Christian Church, 3 vols. Set. 49.95 (ISBN 0-8254-3708-3, RBDH). Kregel.

Schaffarcick, Jon & Hampson, David. Strategies for Curriculum Development. LC 75-24652. 250p. 1975. 16.60x (ISBN 0-8211-0756-9); text ed. 15.00x (ISBN 0-685-57429-6). McCutchan.

Schaffarzick, Jon & Sykes, Gary, eds. Value Conflicts & Curriculum Issues. LC 79-88125. 1980. 17.90 (ISBN 0-685-96793-X); in copies of ten 16.20 (ISBN 0-685-96794-8). McCutchan.

Schaffer, Bernard, ed. Administrative Training & Development: A Comparative Study of East Africa, Zambia, Pakistan, & India. LC 73-21501. 456p. 1974. text ed. 29.95 o.p. (ISBN 0-275-28736-X). Praeger.

Schaffer, Edy G., jt. auth. see Tuazon, Redentor M.

Schaffer, Evelyn B. Community Policing. 145p. 1980. 25.00x (ISBN 0-85664-939-2, Pub. by Croom Helm Ltd England). Biblio Dist.

Schaffer, H. R. Child Care & the Family. 88p. 1968. pap. text ed. 5.00x (ISBN 0-7135-1511-2, Pub. by Bedford England). Renouf.

Schaffer, Jeff P., et al. Pacific Crest Trail, Vol. 2: Oregon & Washington. rev ed. Winnett, Thomas, ed. LC 72-96122. (Illus., Orig.). 1979. pap. 9.95 (ISBN 0-911824-82-0). Wilderness.

Schaffer, Jeffrey P. Lassen Volcanic National Park. Winnett, Thomas, ed. LC 80-53681. (Illus.). 224p. (Orig.). 1981. pap. 9.95 (ISBN 0-89997-004-4). Wilderness Pr.

--The Tahoe Sierra. rev. ed. Winnett, Thomas, ed. LC 78-65937. (Trail Guide Ser). (Illus., Orig.). 1979. pap. 9.95 (ISBN 0-911824-75-8). Wilderness.

Schaffer, Kay F. Sex-Role Issues in Mental Health. LC 79-53872. (Clinical & Professional Psychology Ser.). 1980. pap. text ed. 7.95 (ISBN 0-201-06762-5). A-W.

Schaffer, Kay R. Sex Roles & Human Behavior. (Psychology Ser.). 448p. 1981. text ed. 14.95 (ISBN 0-87626-807-6). Winthrop.

Schaffer, Ulrich. Love Reaches Out. LC 75-70810. (A Jubilee Bk). 96p. (Orig.). 1976. pap. 1.95 (ISBN 0-06-067080-0, HJ24, HarpR). Har-Row.

--Surprised by Light. LC 80-7751. (Illus.). 80p. 1980. 22.95 (ISBN 0-06-067086-X, HarpR); pap. 9.95 (ISBN 0-06-067087-8, RD 335). Har-Row.

--Zilya's Secret Plan. 1979. 3.95 o.p. (ISBN 0-8028-3514-7). Eerdmans.

Schaffert, R. M. Electrophotography. rev, 2nd ed. LC 75-20099. 989p. 1975. 94.95 (ISBN 0-470-75696-9). Halsted Pr.

Schaffner, Betty. Designs to Color, 6 bks. (ps-2). 1968. 2.50; Bk. 1. 1.95 (ISBN 0-8431-0005-2); Bk. 2. 2.50 (ISBN 0-8431-0006-0); Bk. 3. 1.95 (ISBN 0-8431-0007-9); Bk. 4. 1.95 (ISBN 0-8431-0008-7); Bk. 5. 2.50 (ISBN 0-8431-0104-0); Bk. 6. 1.95 (ISBN 0-8431-0218-7). Price Stern.

Schaffner, Elizabeth, jt. auth. see Schaffner, Nicholas.

Schaffner, Kenneth F. Nineteenth Century Aether Theories. 288p. 1972. text ed. 26.00 (ISBN 0-08-015674-6). Pergamon.

Schaffner, Nicholas & Schaffner, Elizabeth. Five Hundred & Five Rock & Roll Questions Your Friends Can't Answer. LC 80-54484. 160p. 1981. 9.95 (ISBN 0-8027-0674-6); pap. 5.95 (ISBN 0-8027-7171-8). Walker & Co.

Schaffner, Val. Algonquin Cat. (Illus.). 1980. 9.95 (ISBN 0-440-00073-4). Delacorte.

Schaffter, Dorothy. War & Military Courts: Judicial Interpretation of Its Meaning. 1980. 20.00 (ISBN 0-682-49570-0, Universtiy). Exposition.

Schaffter, Dorothy & Mathews, Dorothy. The Powers of the President As Commander-in-Chief of the Army & Navy of the United States. LC 76-172099. (American Constitution & Legal History Ser.). xi, 145p. 1974. Repr. of 1956 ed. lib. bdg. 19.50 (ISBN 0-306-70615-6). Da Capo.

Schafly, Phyllis. Power Ideas for a Happy Family. (Orig.). pap. 1.75 (ISBN 0-515-05104-7). Jove Pubns.

Schaible, P. J., jt. auth. see Patrick, Homer.

Schaie, Warner K., et al. Developmental Human Behavior Genetics: Nature-Nurture Redefined. LC 75-733. 320p. 1975. 21.50 (ISBN 0-669-99515-0). Lexington Bks.

Schain, George M. Estates, Gifts & Fiducuaries: Planning & Taxation. 3rd ed. Gold, Jeffrey S., ed. 444p. 1980. 29.95 (ISBN 0-07-055120-0, P&RB); wkbk. & 10 cassettes 195.00 (ISBN 0-07-079056-6). McGraw.

Schain, Martin, jt. ed. see Cerny, Philip.

Schainblatt, Alfred H. Monitoring the Outcomes of State Chronic Disease Control Programs: Some Initial Suggestions. (An Institute Paper). 60p. 1977. pap. 4.00 (ISBN 0-87766-205-3, 19800). Urban Inst.

--Monitoring the Outcomes of State Mental Health Treatment Programs: Some Initial Suggestions. (An Institute Paper). 86p. 1977. pap. 4.00 (ISBN 0-87766-202-9, 19400). Urban Inst.

Schajowicz, F. Tumors & Tumor Like Lesions of Bone & Joints. (Illus.). 650p. 65.00 (ISBN 0-387-90492-1). Springer-Verlag.

Schajowicz, F., et al. Histological Typing of Bone Tumours. (World Health Organization: International Histological Classification of Tumours Ser.). 1972. incl. slides 119.00 (ISBN 0-685-77236-5, 70-1-006-00). Am Soc Clinical.

Schajowicz, Ludwig. Los Nuevos Sofistas: La Subversion Cultural de Nietzche a Beckett. LC 78-9541. 1979. 12.00 (ISBN 0-8477-2823-4); pap. 10.00 (ISBN 0-8477-2817-X). U of PR Pr.

Schaleben-Lewis, Joy. Careers in a Hospital. LC 76-12487. (Whole Works Ser.). (Illus.). 48p. (gr. 3-7). 1976. PLB 9.65 (ISBN 0-8172-0709-0). Raintree Pubs.

--Careers in a Supermarket. LC 76-44915. (Whole Works Ser). (Illus.). 48p. (gr. 3-7). 1977. PLB 9.65 (ISBN 0-8172-0713-9). Raintree Pubs.

--The Dentist & Me. LC 76-46533. (Moods & Emotions Ser.). (Illus.). (gr. k-3). 1977. PLB 8.95 (ISBN 0-8172-0064-9). Raintree Pubs.

Schalet, Lilian Lee. Do You Know. (Illus.). 39p. 1979. 4.50 o.p. (ISBN 0-533-03765-4). Vantage.

Schalk, E. Mansfield. German Shepherds. rev. ed. (Illus.). 128p. 1974. pap. 2.95 o.p. (ISBN 0-87666-297-1, HS1043). TFH Pubns.

Schalkwijk, Bob & Lincoln, Nina. Ninos, Children of Mexico. (Illus.). 1980. 395.00 (ISBN 0-915998-08-4). Lime Rock Pr.

Schall, James V. Christianity & Life. LC 79-89759. 130p. (Orig.). 1981. pap. write for info. (ISBN 0-89870-004-3). Ignatius Pr.

Schall, Larry, jt. auth. see Haley, Charles W.

Schall, Maxine. Limits. Southern, Carol, ed. 320p. 1981. 11.95 (ISBN 0-517-54143-2). Potter.

Schaller, Agnes P. & Kinney, Analee. Seasonal Parties for Convalescents. 1981. write for info (ISBN 0-398-04452-X). C C Thomas.

Schaller, Friedrich. Soil Animals. (Ann Arbor Science Library Ser). (Illus.). 1968. pap. 1.95 o.p. (ISBN 0-472-05016-8, 516, AA). U of Mich Pr.

Schaller, George B. The Mountain Gorilla: Ecology & Behavior. LC 63-11401. (Illus.). 1976. pap. 9.00x (ISBN 0-226-73636-9, P684, Phoen). U of Chicago Pr.

--The Serengeti Lion: A Study of Predator-Prey Relations. LC 78-180043. (Wildlife Behavior & Ecology Ser.). (Illus.). 472p. 1976. pap. 12.95 (ISBN 0-226-73640-7, P661, Phoen). U of Chicago Pr.

Schaller, Lyle E. Local Church Looks to the Future. (Orig.). 1968. pap. 4.50 (ISBN 0-687-22524-8). Abingdon.

--Parish Planning. (Orig.). 1971. pap. 5.95 (ISBN 0-687-30102-5). Abingdon.

--Survival Tactics in the Parish. LC 76-54751. (Orig.). 1977. pap. 6.95 (ISBN 0-687-40757-5). Abingdon.

Schaller, Michael. The United States & China in the Twentieth Century. (Illus.). 1980. pap. text ed. 3.95x (ISBN 0-19-502599-7). Oxford U Pr.

--The U. S. Crusade in China, Nineteen Thirty-Eight to Nineteen Forty-Five: The United States & China, 1938-1945. 1979. 17.50 (ISBN 0-231-04454-2). Columbia U Pr.

Schaller, W., jt. auth. see Worick, W.

Schallert, William F. & Clark, Carol R. Programming in FORTRAN. LC 78-74039. 1979. pap. text ed. 13.95 (ISBN 0-201-06716-1). A-W.

Schally, Andrew V., jt. ed. see Locke, William.

Scham, Alan. Lyautey in Morocco: Protectorate Administration, 1912-1925. LC 74-92680. 1970. 21.75x (ISBN 0-520-01602-5). U of Cal Pr.

Schambra, William A., jt. ed. see Goldwin, Robert A.

Schambye, Per, ed. Proceedings: FEBS Meeting, 11th, 9 vols. (Illus.). 1978. Set. text ed. 295.00 (ISBN 0-08-021527-0). Pergamon.

Schamroth, Leo. Diagnostic Pointers in Electrocardiology, Vol. 2. LC 79-51385. (Cardiology & Critical Care Ser.). (Illus.). 248p. 1979. text ed. 24.95 (ISBN 0-89303-004-X). Charles.

Schandl, Charles W. Theory of Auditing. LC 78-17862. 1978. text ed. 13.00 (ISBN 0-914348-23-X). Scholars Bk.

Schandler, Herbert. The Unmaking of a President: Lyndon Johnson & Vietnam. (Illus.). 1977. text ed. 22.00 (ISBN 0-691-07586-7). Princeton U Pr.

Schane, Sanford A. Generative Phonology. (Foundations of Modern Linguistics Ser.). 176p. 1973. ref. ed. 10.95 (ISBN 0-13-350967-2); pap. text ed. 7.95 (ISBN 0-13-350959-1); wkbk. 6.50 (ISBN 0-13-350942-7). P-H.

Schank, Kenneth, jt. auth. see Graham, Frank.

Schank, Kenneth, jt. ed. see Arnold, Joseph.

Schank, Roger C. & Riesbeck, Christopher K. Inside Computer Understanding: Five Programs Plus Miniatures. LC 80-18314. (Artificial Intelligence Ser.). 368p. 1981. profess. & reference 24.95 (ISBN 0-89859-071-X). L Erlbaum Assocs.

Schank, Roger C. & Colby, Kenneth M., eds. Computer Models of Thought & Language. LC 73-11064. (Psychology Ser.). (Illus.). 1973. text ed. 29.95x (ISBN 0-7167-0834-5). W H Freeman.

Schanne, Otto F. & Ruiz-P-Ceretti, E. Impedance Measurements in Biological Cells. LC 77-17434. 1978. 36.95 o.p. (ISBN 0-471-76530-9, Pub. by Wiley-Interscience). Wiley.

Schansberg, Dave. Alex in Wonderland. (Illus.). 64p. (Orig.). (gr. 1-6). 1980. pap. 3.95 (ISBN 0-89542-941-1). Ideals.

Schansberg, David. Alex in Wonderland. (Illus.). 1980. 7.95g (ISBN 0-516-09201-4). Childrens.

Schantz, Enid, ed. see Allan, Grant.

Schantz, Enid, ed. see Post, Melville D.

Schantz, Maria E. & Brynner, Joseph F., eds. Reading in American Schools: A Guide to Information Sources. LC 79-23770. (Education Information Guide Ser.: Vol. 5). 1980. 30.00 (ISBN 0-8103-1456-8). Gale.

Schantz, Tom, ed. see Allan, Grant.

Schantz, Tom, ed. see Phillpotts, Eden.

Schantz, Tom, ed. see Post, Melville D.

Schantz, William T. & Jackson, Janice E. Review Outlines & Materials for Business Law & CPA Law Review. LC 80-13096. 997p. 1980. pap. text ed. write for info. (ISBN 0-8299-2071-4). West Pub.

Schantz, William T. & Robertson, Leonard F. Essentials of Business Law. 1977. text ed. 11.28 (ISBN 0-02-478190-8). Macmillan.

Schanz, John P. A Theology of Community. 1977. pap. text ed. 11.25x (ISBN 0-8191-0177-X). U Pr of Amer.

Schanz, John T., jt. auth. see Frank, Helmut.

Schanzer, Stephan N., jt. auth. see Brown, Herbert P.

Schaper, Eva. Prelude to Aesthetics. 1969. Repr. of 1949 ed. text ed. 7.50x (ISBN 0-04-160006-1). Humanities.

Schaper, Robert N. Why Me, God? 2nd ed. LC 73-82763. 1977. pap. 3.50 (ISBN 0-8307-0452-3, S273-1-28). Regal.

Schaper, W. A. Sectionalism & Representation in South Carolina. LC 68-31582. (American Scene Ser). (Illus.). 1968. Repr. of 1901 ed. lib. bdg. 25.00 (ISBN 0-306-71158-3). Da Capo.

Schapera, I. Tribal Innovators: Tswana Chiefs & Social Change 1795-1940. (Monographs on Social Anthropology Ser: No. 43). (Illus.). 1970. text ed. 25.00x (ISBN 0-391-00115-9, Athlone). Humanities.

Schapera, I., ed. & intro. by see Livingstone, David.

Schapera, Isaac. Handbook of Tswana Law & Custom. 328p. 1970. Repr. 28.50x (ISBN 0-7146-2481-0, F Cass Co). Biblio Dist.

Schapera, Isaac, ed. Western Civilization & the Natives of South Africa: Studies in Culture Contact. 1967. text ed. 14.00x (ISBN 0-7100-2083-X). Humanities.

Schapira, Karl, jt. auth. see Joel, David.

Schapiro. Guernica: Studies - Postscripts. Date not set. 20.00 (ISBN 0-8076-0983-8). Braziller.

Schapiro, Boris. Bridge Analysis. LC 76-1167. (Illus.). 192p. (YA) 1976. 6.95 o.p. (ISBN 0-8069-4928-7); PLB 6.69 o.p. (ISBN 0-8069-4929-5). Sterling.

Schapiro, Leonard & Godson, Joseph, eds. The Soviet Worker: Illusion & Realities. Date not set. price not set (ISBN 0-312-74923-6). St Martin.

Schapiro, Meyer. Cezanne. (Library Great Painters Ser). (Illus.). 1952. 35.00 (ISBN 0-8109-0052-1). Abrams.

--Late Antique, Early Christian & Mediaeval Art: Selected Papers. Date not set. 25.00 (ISBN 0-686-68085-5). Braziller.

Schapiro, Robert, jt. auth. see Feinberg, Gerald.

Schapiro, Ruth G., ed. Tax Shelters. 2nd ed. LC 80-81333. 425p. 1980. text ed. 40.00 (ISBN 0-686-62638-9, J1-1430). PLI.

Schapsmeier, Edward L. & Schapsmeier, Frederick H. Henry A. Wallace of Iowa: The Agrarian Years, 1910-1940. (Illus.). 1969. 8.95 o.p. (ISBN 0-8138-1741-2). Iowa St U Pr.

Schapsmeier, Frederick H., jt. auth. see Schapsmeier, Edward L.

Scharf, C. Particle Accelerators & Their Uses. Lepa, E., tr. from Polish. (Accelerators & Storage Rings Ser.: Vol. 3). 500p. 1981. lib. bdg. 100.00 (ISBN 3-7186-0034-X). Harwood Academic.

Scharf, Charles A. Guide to Employee Stock Ownership Plans: A Revolutionary Method for Increasing Corporate Profits. 1976. 27.95 o.p. (ISBN 0-13-369447-X). P-H.

Scharf, Peter. Moral & Psychological Education. 1976. pap. text ed. 10.25x (ISBN 0-8191-0027-7). U Pr of Amer.

Scharf, Peter, ed. Readings in Moral Education. 1978. pap. 9.95 (ISBN 0-03-021346-0). Winston Pr.

Scharf, Robert. Standard Handbook of Salt-Water Fishing. rev. ed. (Illus.). 1966. 9.95 o.s.i. (ISBN 0-690-76926-1, TYC-T). T Y Crowell.

Scharf, Thomas J. History of Maryland from the Earliest Period to the Present Day, 3 vols. LC 67-5141. (Illus.). 1967. Repr. of 1879 ed. incl. index 74.00 (ISBN 0-8103-5037-8); index only 5.00 (ISBN 0-8103-5038-6). Gale.

Scharfe, Norman. Suffolk: A Shell Guide. 1976. 14.95 (ISBN 0-571-04901-X, Pub. by Faber & Faber). Merrimack Bk Serv.

Scharfetter, C. General Psychopathology. Marshall, Helen, tr. from Ger. LC 79-52853. (Illus.). 1980. 54.50 (ISBN 0-521-22812-3); pap. 15.95x (ISBN 0-521-29655-2). Cambridge U Pr.

Scharff, Robert. First Aid for Your Car. 1980. pap. 2.50 (ISBN 0-451-09416-6, E9416, Sig). NAL.

--Golf. (Quick & Easy Ser). (Orig.). 1968. pap. 2.95 o.s.i. (ISBN 0-02-081500-X, Collier). Macmillan.

--Home & Shop Math. LC 76-48585. (Popular Science Ser). (Illus.). 425p. 1981. 14.95 (ISBN 0-06-013784-3, HarpT). Har-Row.

--How to Build Your Garage, or Carport. LC 80-5207. (Popular Science Skill Bks.). (Illus.). 192p. (Orig.). 1980. pap. 4.95 (ISBN 0-06-090822-X, CN 822, CN). Har-Row.

--Successful & Masonry. Case, Virginia A., ed. (Successful Ser.). 144p. 1981. 18.95 (ISBN 0-89999-023-1); pap. 8.95 (ISBN 0-89999-024-X). Structures Pub.

--Successful Plumbing. LC 80-24212. (Successful Ser.). (Illus.). 144p. 1980. 15.95 (ISBN 0-89999-014-2); pap. 6.95 (ISBN 0-89999-015-0). Structures Pub.

--Successful Putting It All Together. Diefenderfer, Hope, ed. LC 79-67828. (Successful Ser.). (Illus.). 1980. 14.95 (ISBN 0-912336-95-1); pap. 7.95 (ISBN 0-912336-96-X). Structures Pub.

Scharnhorst, Gary. Horatio Alger, Jr. (United States Author Ser.: No. 363). 1980. lib. bdg. 9.95 (ISBN 0-8057-7252-9). Twayne.

Scharp, Hal & Scharp, Mary. Shark Wanted! Dead or Alive. LC 75-29700. (Illus.). 256p. 1976. 12.00 o.p. (ISBN 0-498-01832-6). A S Barnes.

Scharp, Mary, jt. auth. see Scharp, Hal.

Schary, Dore. Heyday. 1981. pap. 2.95 (ISBN 0-425-04805-5). Berkley Pub.

Schary, Dore, jt. auth. see Lewis, Sinclair.

Scharzenberger, Georg, jt. ed. see Keeton, George W.

Schatborn, Peter & Van Hasselt, Carlos. Dutch Genre Drawings. LC 72-86013. (Illus.). 162p. (Orig.). 1972. pap. 7.50. Intl Exhibit Foun.

Schatt, S., jt. auth. see Agnos, T. J.

Schatt, Stanley. Kurt Vonnegut, Jr. (U.S. Authors Ser.: No. 276). 1976. lib. bdg. 12.50 (ISBN 0-8057-7176-X). Twayne.

Schatt, Stanley, ed. Kurt Vonnegut, Jr. LC 76-41754. (Twayne's U. S. Authors Ser.). 174p. 1976. pap. text ed. 4.95 (ISBN 0-672-61510-X). Bobbs.

Schattke, Rudolph W. & Jensen, Howard G. Financial Accounting: Concepts & Uses. 2nd ed. 1978. text ed. 19.95 (ISBN 0-205-05901-5); transparencies avail. (ISBN 0-205-05902-3); checklist avail. (ISBN 0-205-05903-1); practice set 5.95 (ISBN 0-205-05904-X); sol. man. avail. (ISBN 0-205-05905-8); study guide 6.95 (ISBN 0-205-05906-6); working papers 6.95 (ISBN 0-205-05907-4); tests avail. (ISBN 0-205-05908-2); sample pkg. avail. (ISBN 0-205-05909-0). Allyn.

Schattke, Rudolph W., et al. Managerial Accounting: Concepts & Uses. 2nd ed. 656p. 1981. text ed. 19.95 (ISBN 0-205-07319-0, 0543268); avail. tchrs guide (ISBN 0-205-06073-0); avail. study guide (ISBN 0-205-07322-0). Allyn.

Schattle, Margaret, tr. see Brentano, Franz.

Schattle, Margarete, tr. see Wittgenstein, Ludwig.

Schattner, Gertrud & Courtney, Richard, eds. Drama in Therapy, 2 vols. Incl. Vol. I. Drama in Therapy for Children. 1981. text ed. 15.00x (ISBN 0-89676-013-8); Vol. II. Drama in Therapy for Adults. 1981. text ed. 15.00x (ISBN 0-89676-014-6). LC 80-15680. Drama Bk.

Schatz, jt. auth. see Church.

Schatz, Anne E. & Funk, Berverley M. Transcription Skills for Information Processing, Module 2. 112p. 1981. pap. text ed. 2.92 (ISBN 0-07-055201-0). McGraw.

Schatz, Anne E. & Funk, Beverley M. Transcription Skills for Information Processing, Module 1. 96p. 1981. pap. text ed. 2.92 (ISBN 0-07-055200-2). McGraw.

Schatz, Gail, jt. auth. see Forkner, Jerry.

Schatz, Howard, et al. Interpretation of Fundus Fluorescein Angiography. new ed. LC 77-19094. (Illus.). 1977. text ed. 84.50 (ISBN 0-8016-4343-0). Mosby.

Schatz, John. Spaces by a Spaceman. LC 79-91038. (Illus., Orig.). 1979. pap. 4.65 (ISBN 0-9603546-0-3). Spaceman Pr.

Schatz, Letta. Banji's Magic Wheel. (Picture Bk). (Illus.). 32p. (gr. k-3). 1974. 5.95 o.p. (ISBN 0-695-80441-3); PLB 5.97 o.p. (ISBN 0-695-40441-5). Follett.

Schatz, Mary A. Love Thy Teen-Ager. (Uplook Ser.). 32p. 1973. pap. 0.75 (ISBN 0-8163-0014-3, 12693-8). Pacific Pr Pub Assn.

Schatz, Pauline. Manual in Clinical Dietetics. 2nd ed. 1978. spiral bdg. 6.95x (ISBN 0-916434-31-1). Plycon Pr.

Schatz, Sayre P. Nigerian Capitalism. LC 74-16718. 1978. 27.50x (ISBN 0-520-02859-7). U of Cal Pr.

Schatz, Thomas. Hollywood Genres. 320p. 1981. pap. text ed. 9.95 (ISBN 0-394-32255-X). Random.

Schatzker, J., et al, trs. see Mueller, M. E., et al.

Schatzki, Walter, ed. Old & Rare Children's Books Offered for Sale by Walter Schatzki, Dealer in Rare Books, Prints & Autographs. LC 73-16044. (Illus.). 46p. 1974. Repr. of 1941 ed. 15.00 (ISBN 0-8103-3878-5). Gale.

Schatzman, Evry & Biermann, Ludwig. Cosmic Gas Dynamics. LC 73-16025. 291p. 1974. 23.00 (ISBN 0-471-75720-9, Pub. by Wiley). Krieger.

Schatzman, Leonard & Strauss, Anselm L. Field Research: Strategies for a Natural Society. (Methods of Social Science Ser). 176p. 1973. pap. text ed. 9.95 (ISBN 0-13-314351-1). P-H.

Schaub, E. L., tr. see Wundt, Wilhelm M.

Schaub, Thomas H. Pynchon: The Voice of Ambiguity. LC 80-11944. 175p. 1981. 13.50 (ISBN 0-252-00816-2). U of Ill Pr.

Schauber, Ellen. The Syntax & Semantics of Questions in Navajo. Hankamer, Jorge, ed. LC 78-66568. (Outstanding Dissertations in Linguistics Ser.). 1979. lib. bdg. 35.00 (ISBN 0-8240-9676-2). Garland Pub.

Schaudinischky, L. H. Sound, Man, & Building. (Illus.). 1976. 74.50x (ISBN 0-85334-655-0, Pub. by Applied Science). Burgess-Intl Ideas.

Schaum, Konrad, ed. Deutsche Lyrik. (Orig., Ger.). 1963. pap. 2.95x (ISBN 0-393-09612-2, NortonC). Norton.

Schaumburg, Herbert, jt. auth. see Spencer, Peter S.

Schaumburg, Herbert H. & Scheinberg, Labe C., eds. Neurology Specialty Board Review. 2nd ed. 1972. spiral bdg. 16.50 (ISBN 0-87488-306-7). Med Exam.

Schaupp, Dietrich L. A Cross-Cultural Study of a Multinational Company: Attitudinal Responses to Participative Management. LC 78-8453. (Praeger Special Studies). 1978. 21.95 (ISBN 0-03-022871-9). Praeger.

Schauss, Hayyim. Jewish Festivals: From Their Beginnings to Our Own Day. rev. ed. (Illus.). (YA) 1969. 8.00 (ISBN 0-8074-0095-5, 383202); course syll. 1.25 (ISBN 0-686-66555-4, 247330). UAHC.

--Lifetime of a Jew: Throughout the Ages of Jewish History. rev. ed. (Illus.). (YA) (gr. 9 up). 1976. pap. 5.50 (ISBN 0-8074-0096-3, 383473). UAHC.

Schebera, Richard L. Christian, Non-Christian Dialogue: The Vision of Robert C. Zaehner. LC 78-64369. 1978. pap. text ed. 9.00 (ISBN 0-8191-0629-1). U Pr of Amer.

Schechner, Richard, ed. Dionysus in Sixty-Nine. 114p. 1970. 10.00 (ISBN 0-374-14004-9). FS&G.

Schechter, Harold. The New Gods: Psyche & Symbol in Popular Art. LC 79-92848. 1980. 13.95 (ISBN 0-87972-168-5); pap. 6.95 o.p. (ISBN 0-686-64303-8). Bowling Green.

Schechter, Harold & Semeiks, Jonna G. Patterns in Popular Culture: A Sourcebook for Writers. (Illus.). 1980. pap. text ed. 10.95 scp (ISBN 0-06-045761-9, HarpC); instructor's manual free. Har-Row.

Schechtman, Joseph B. Fighter & Prophet: The Vladimir Jabotinsky Story-the Later Years. (Return to Zion Ser.). (Illus.). 643p. 1981. Repr. of 1961 ed. lib. bdg. 35.00x (ISBN 0-87991-142-5). Porcupine Pr.

--Postwar Population Transfers in Europe, 1945-1955. LC 62-7200. 1962. 12.50x o.p. (ISBN 0-8122-7298-6). U of Pa Pr.

--The United States & the Jewish State Movement: The Crucial Decade 1939-1949. (Return to Zion Ser.). (Illus.). 474p. 1980. Repr. of 1963 ed. lib. bdg. 27.50x (ISBN 0-87991-123-9). Porcupine Pr.

Schechtman, Joseph E. Rebel & Statesman: The Vladimir Jabotinsky Story-the Early Years. (Return to Zion Ser.). (Illus.). 467p. 1980. Repr. of 1956 ed. lib. bdg. 27.50x (ISBN 0-87991-143-3). Porcupine Pr.

Scheck, Joann. El Hombre que se Bano Siete Veces. Lockward, J. Alfonso, tr. from Eng. (Libros Arco). (Illus.). 32p. (Orig., Span.). (gr. 1-3). 1975. pap. 0.95 o.s.i. (ISBN 0-89922-038-X). Edit Caribe.

Scheckman, Claudia S. The Perfect Chocolate Chip Cookie. LC 80-67918. (Illus.). 44p. (ps-6). Date not set. pap. 4.95 (ISBN 0-916634-09-4). Double M Pr. Postponed.

Schecter, Arnold J., ed. Drug Dependence & Alcohol, 2 vols. Incl. Biomedical Issues. 1350p (ISBN 0-306-40323-4); Vol. 2. Social & Behavioral Issues. 996p (ISBN 0-306-40324-2). 1981. 47.50 ea. (Plenum Pr). Plenum Pub.

Schecter, David & Yukoff, George. The Structured COBOL Report Writer. 1981. text ed. 17.95 (ISBN 0-8359-7097-3). Reston.

Schedelmann, Hans. Vienna Kunsthistorisches Die Grossen Buchsenmacher. (Illus.). 1976. 225.00 o.p. (ISBN 0-686-15688-9). Arma Pr.

Schedler, George. Behavior Modification & "Punishment" of the Innocent: Towards a Justification of the Institution of Legal Punishment. 1977. pap. text ed. 17.25x (ISBN 90-6032-084-0). Humanities.

Scheel, Joegen. Rivulins of the Old World. 14.95 (ISBN 0-87666-137-1, PS660). TFH Pubns.

Scheele, Adele M. Skills for Success. 208p. 1981. pap. 2.95 (ISBN 0-345-29484-X). Ballantine.

Scheele, Carl H. A Short History of the Mail Service. LC 69-12675. (Illus.). 250p. 1970. 8.95x o.p. (ISBN 0-87474-090-8). Smithsonian.

Scheele, Godfrey & Scheele, Margart. The Prince Consort. 1977. 15.95 (ISBN 0-8467-0321-1, Pub. by Two Continents); pap. 9.95 (ISBN 0-8467-0322-X). Hippocrene Bks.

Scheele, Margart, jt. auth. see Scheele, Godfrey.

Scheele, Ronald V. & Wakley, Jack. Elements of Radiation Protection. (Illus.). 112p. 1980. pap. 10.25 (ISBN 0-398-03267-X). C C Thomas.

Scheer, Arnold H. & Juergenson, E. M. Approved Practices in Fruit & Vine Production. 2nd ed. (Illus.). 550p. 1976. 14.00 (ISBN 0-8134-1704-X, 1704); text ed. 10.50x (ISBN 0-685-55573-9). Interstate.

Scheer, George F., ed. see Martin, J. P.

Scheer, James F., jt. auth. see Pinkley, Virgil.

Scheer, Linda & Ramirez, Miguel, eds. Anthology of Mexican Modern Poetry. 170p. Date not set. 13.50 (ISBN 0-931556-06-6); pap. 4.50 (ISBN 0-931556-07-4). Translation Pr. Postponed.

Scheer, Samuel, jt. auth. see Schultz, Donald.

Scheer, Steven C. Kalman Mikszath. (World Authors Ser.: Hungary: No. 462). 1977. lib. bdg. 11.95 (ISBN 0-8057-6299-X). Twayne.

Scheerenberger, R. C. Deinstitutionalization & Institutional Reform. (Illus.). 272p. 1976. 23.75 (ISBN 0-398-03552-0). C C Thomas.

--Managing Residential Facilities for the Developmentally Disabled. (Illus.). 320p. 1975. 22.75 (ISBN 0-398-03199-1). C C Thomas.

Scheerer, Penelope & Schwanbeck, John. The Traveling Runner's Guide: Where to Run in 21 Cities Around the U. S. 1978. pap. 5.95 o.p. (ISBN 0-525-47530-3). Dutton.

Scheer-Schaezler, Brigitte. Saul Bellow. LC 70-178167. (Modern Literature Ser.). 128p. 1972. 10.95 (ISBN 0-8044-2765-8). Ungar.

Scheetz, George. Philip Jose Farmer: The Authorized Bibliography. 112p. 1981. pap. 11.95 (ISBN 0-933180-16-0). Ellis Pr.

Scheff, Thomas J. Being Mentally Ill: A Sociological Theory. LC 66-15207. 210p. 1966. pap. text ed. 5.95x (ISBN 0-202-30252-0). Aldine Pub.

--Catharsis in Healing, Ritual & Drama. 1980. 14.95x (ISBN 0-520-03710-3); pap. 4.95x (ISBN 0-520-04125-9, CAMPUS NO. 249). U of Cal Pr.

Scheffe, Henry. Analysis of Variance. LC 59-14994. (Wiley Series in Probability & Mathematical Statistics). (Illus.). 1959. 31.95 (ISBN 0-471-75834-5). Wiley.

Scheffer, Victor B. The Amazing Sea Otter. (Illus.). 192p. (gr. 7 up). 1981. 10.95 (ISBN 0-684-16878-2). Scribner.

Scheffler, Israel. The Anatomy of Inquiry: Philosophical Studies in the Theory of Science. 390p. 1982. lib. bdg. 19.50 (ISBN 0-915144-97-2); pap. text ed. 8.50 (ISBN 0-915144-98-0). Hackett Pub. Postponed.

--Beyond the Letter. (International Library of Philosophy & Scientific Method). (Illus.). 1979. 18.00x (ISBN 0-7100-0315-3). Routledge & Kegan.
--Language of Education. (American Lectures in Philosophy Ser.). 128p. 1978. 8.75 (ISBN 0-398-01656-9). C C Thomas.
--Reason & Teaching. LC 72-86641. 1973. pap. text ed. 8.95 (ISBN 0-672-61253-4). Bobbs.
--Science & Subjectivity. LC 67-27839. (Orig.). 1967. pap. 4.95 (ISBN 0-672-60724-7). Bobbs.
Scheffler, Israel, jt. ed. see Rudner, Richard S.
Scheffler, Wolfgang. Goldschmiede Rheinland-Westfalens. Daten. Zeichen. Werke, 2 vols. LC 72-81568. 1200p. 1973. 267.65x (ISBN 3-11-003842-0). De Gruyter.
Scheffman, D. T., jt. auth. see Frankena, M. W.
Scheflen, Albert E. Body Language & the Social Order. (Illus.). 192p. 1973. 13.95 (ISBN 0-13-079590-9, Spec); pap. 4.25 (ISBN 0-13-079582-8, Spec). P-H.
--Levels of Schizophrenia. LC 80-21030. 200p. 1981. 17.50 (ISBN 0-87630-252-5). Brunner-Mazel.
Scheflen, Albert E., jt. auth. see Ashcraft, Norman.
Schefler, William C. Biology: Principles & Issues. LC 75-28725. (Life Sciences Ser.). (Illus.). 384p. 1976. text ed. 17.95 (ISBN 0-201-06764-1); instructor's manual 2.00 (ISBN 0-201-06763-3). A-W.
--Statistics for the Biological Sciences. 2nd ed. LC 78-55830. (Illus.). 1979. text ed. 14.95 (ISBN 0-201-07500-8). A-W.
Scheib, Ida & Welker, Carole E. The First Book of Food. rev. ed. LC 73-12477. (First Bks). (Illus.). 72p. (gr. 4-6). 1974. PLB 4.90 o.p. (ISBN 0-531-00534-8). Watts.
Scheibe, E. The Logical Analysis of Quantum Mechanics. 1973. 46.00 (ISBN 0-08-017158-3). Pergamon.
Scheibe, Karl E. Mirrors, Masks, Lies, Secrets & the Limits of Human Predictability. LC 78-19791. 192p. 1979. 19.95 (ISBN 0-03-046661-X). Praeger.
Scheiber, Harry N., et al. American Economic History. (Illus.). 432p. 1976. text ed. 24.50 scp (ISBN 0-06-042001-4, HarpC). Har-Row.
Scheick, William J. The Half-Blood: A Cultural Symbol in Nineteenth Century American Fiction. LC 79-4012. 128p. 1979. 10.50x (ISBN 0-8131-1390-3). U Pr of Ky.
--The Slender Human Word: Emerson's Artistry in Prose. LC 77-27020. 1978. 10.50x (ISBN 0-87049-222-5). U of Tenn Pr.
Scheidemandel, P. L., jt. auth. see Kanno, C. K.
Scheidemandel, Patricia, et al. Health Insurance for Mental Illness. 89p. 1968. pap. 3.00 (ISBN 0-685-24845-3, P195-0). Am Psychiatric.
Scheidemandel, Patricia L., jt. auth. see Kanno, Charles.
Scheidemandel, Patricia L., jt. auth. see Kanno, Charles K.
Scheider, Meg, ed. see Tallarico, Tony.
Scheidlinger, Saul. Focus on Group Psychotherapy. 1981. write for info. (ISBN 0-8236-1990-7). Intl Univs Pr.
Scheidt, David L., tr. see Lubkoll, Hans-Georg & Wiesnet, Eugen.
Scheidt, David L., tr. see Zickgraf, Cordula.
Scheier, Michael. What to Do with the Rocks in Your Head. (gr. 5 up). 1980. pap. 7.90 (ISBN 0-531-04174-3, G34). Watts.
Scheimann, Eugene & Neimark, Paul. Doctor's Sensible Approach to Dieting & Weight Control. (Illus.). 1976. pap. 2.50 (ISBN 0-910304-19-X). Budlong.
Scheimann, Eugene, jt. auth. see Mariken, Gene.
Schein, Bruce E. Following the Way: The Setting of John's Gospel. LC 79-54121. 224p. 1980. 12.50 (ISBN 0-8066-1758-6, 10-2348). Augsburg.
Schein, Clarence J. Introduction to Abdominal Surgery: Fifty Clinical Studies. (Illus.). 416p. 1981. pap. text ed. write for info. (ISBN 0-06-142381-5, Harper Medical). Har-Row.
Schein, Edgar, ed. see Carnegie Commission on Higher Education.
Schein, Edgar, et al, eds. see Beckhard, Richard.
Schein, Edgar, et al, eds. see Bennis, Warren G.
Schein, Edgar, et al, eds. see Blake, Robert R. & Mouton, Jane S.
Schein, Edgar G. Organizational Psychology. 3rd ed. (Foundations of Modern Psychology Ser.). (Illus.). 1980. text ed. 14.95 (ISBN 0-13-641340-4); pap. text ed. 8.95 (ISBN 0-13-641332-3). P-H.
Schein, Edgar H. Career Dynamics: Matching Individual & Organizational Needs. 1978. pap. text ed. 7.50 (ISBN 0-201-06834-6). A-W.
--Process Consultation: Its Role in Organization Development. LC 76-91149. (Organization Development Ser.). (Orig.). 1969. pap. text ed. 6.50 (ISBN 0-201-06733-1). A-W.
Schein, Jerome. Model State Plan for Vocational Evaluation of Deaf Clients. 1977. pap. 2.50 o.p. (ISBN 0-913072-28-1). Natl Assn Deaf.
Schein, Jerome, jt. auth. see Kates, Linda.
Schein, Martin, jt. ed. see Goodman, Irving.
Schein, Richard D., jt. auth. see Zadoks, Jan C.
Scheina, Robert L., jt. auth. see Reilly, John C.
Scheinberg, Labe C., jt. ed. see Schaumburg, Herbert H.
Scheinberg, Labe C., et al. Neurology Handbook. 1972. spiral bdg. 11.00 (ISBN 0-87488-604-X). Med Exam.
Scheinberg, Peritz. Modern Practical Neurology. 2nd ed. 360p. 1981. 26.00 (ISBN 0-89004-521-6); pap. 14.95 (ISBN 0-686-69137-7). Raven.
Scheinberg, Peritz, ed. Modern Practical Neurology: An Introduction to Diagnosis & Management of Common Neurological Disorders. LC 76-49718. 1977. 22.00 (ISBN 0-685-71561-2); pap. 13.00 (ISBN 0-685-71562-0). Raven.
Scheinberg, Peritz, ed. see Princeton Conferences on Cerebrovascular Diseases, 10th.
Scheiner, Albert P. & Abroms. The Practical Management of the Developmentally Disabled Child. LC 80-13725. (Illus.). 1980. text ed. 37.50 (ISBN 0-8016-0061-8). Mosby.
Scheiner, Irwin. Christian Converts & Social Protest in Meiji Japan. LC 74-94981. (Center for Japanese & Korean Studies, UC Berkeley). 1970. 18.50x (ISBN 0-520-01585-1). U of Cal Pr.
Scheinfeld, Amram. Heredity in Humans. rev. ed. (Illus.). 1972. 9.95 (ISBN 0-397-00820-1). Lippincott.
Scheingold & Wagner. Sex and the Aging Heart. 1975. pap. 1.50 (ISBN 0-515-03663-3). Jove Pubns.
Scheinmann, F. An Introduction to Spectroscopic Methods for the Identification of Organic Compounds, Vol. 1. LC 76-99991. 1970. text ed. 18.75 (ISBN 0-08-006661-5); pap. text ed. 9.25 (ISBN 0-08-006662-3). Pergamon.
--An Introduction to Spectroscopic Methods for the Identification of Organic Compounds, Vol. 2. LC 76-99991. 368p. 1974. text ed. 25.00 (ISBN 0-08-016719-5); pap. text ed. 12.75 (ISBN 0-08-016720-9). Pergamon.
Scheinmann, F., jt. ed. see Roberts, S. M.
Scheit, Karl H. Nucleotide Analogs: Synthesis & Biological Function. LC 79-25445. 1980. 29.50 (ISBN 0-471-04854-2, Pub. by Wiley-Interscience). Wiley.
Schelchter, R. Beitraege zur Orchideenkunde von Zentralamerika, 2 vols. in one. (Feddes Repertorium: Beiheft 17 & 18). 402p. (Ger.). 1980. Repr. of 1922 ed. lib. bdg. 70.20x (ISBN 3-87429-181-2, Pub. by Koeltz Germany). Lubrecht & Cramer.
Schele, Linda & Mat, Peter. The Bodeoa of Palenque, Chiapas Mexico. LC 79-63728. (Illus.). 166p. 1978. pap. 20.00 (ISBN 0-88402-085-1, Ctr Pre-Columbian). Dumbarton Oaks.
Schell, Catherine, jt. auth. see Kunz, Marilyn.
Schell, F. Practical Problems in Mathematics--Metric System. LC 78-73133. 1975. pap. text ed. 5.00 (ISBN 0-8273-1418-3); instructor's guide 1.60 (ISBN 0-8273-1419-1). Delmar.
Schell, Frank R. Welding Procedures: Electric Arc. LC 76-14084. (gr. 10-12). 1977. pap. text ed. 5.00 (ISBN 0-8273-1603-8); instr's manual 1.60 (ISBN 0-8273-1697-6). Delmar.
--Welding Procedures: Oxyacetylene. LC 76-4306. 1977. pap. text ed. 5.00 (ISBN 0-8273-1600-3); instr's manual 1.60 (ISBN 0-8273-1697-6). Delmar.
Schell, Frank R. & Matlock, Bill. Industrial Welding Procedures. LC 77-80481. 1979. text ed. 12.00 (ISBN 0-8273-1696-8); instructor's guide 1.60 (ISBN 0-8273-1697-6). Delmar.
Schell, Frank R. & Matlock, Bill J. Practical Problems in Mathematics for Welders. LC 74-24810. 1975. pap. text ed. 6.60 (ISBN 0-8273-0262-2); instructor's guide 1.60 (ISBN 0-8273-0263-0). Delmar.
--Welding Procedures: MIG & TIG. LC 76-62715. 1978. pap. text ed. 8.80 (ISBN 0-8273-1646-1); instr's manual 1.60 (ISBN 0-8273-1697-6). Delmar.
Schell, Hal B., ed. Reader on the Library Building. LC 73-93967. (Reader Ser in Librarianship & Information Science: Vol. 15). (Illus.). 1975. 22.00 (ISBN 0-910972-11-7). IHS-PDS.
Schell, Herbert S. History of South Dakota. 3rd, rev ed. LC 74-18431. (Illus.). xiv, 445p. 1975. pap. 6.50 (ISBN 0-8032-5820-8, BB 603, Bison). U of Nebr Pr.
Schell, Orville. Brown. 1978. 10.00 (ISBN 0-394-41043-2). Random.
--Watch Out for the Foreign Guests! China Encounters the West. 1981. 8.95 (ISBN 0-394-51331-2). Pantheon.
Schell, Rolfe F. Floridas Fascinating Everglades. LC 63-8861. (Illus.). 1974. 4.50 (ISBN 0-87208-004-8); pap. 2.00 (ISBN 0-87208-032-3). Island Pr.
Schell, William G. Biblical Trace of the Church. 173p. pap. 1.50. Faith Pub Hse.
--The Ordinances of the New Testament. 67p. pap. 0.50. Faith Pub Hse.
Schellenberg, Theodore R. Management of Archives. LC 65-14409. (Studies in Library Service: No. 14). 1965. 25.00x (ISBN 0-231-02812-1). Columbia U Pr.
Schellenberg, Walter. Hitler's Secret Service. 1977. pap. 2.25 o.s.i. (ISBN 0-515-04481-4). Jove Pubns.
Schellenberger, Robert E. & Boseman, Glenn F. Policy Formulation & Strategy Management. LC 77-2758. (Wiley Series in Management & Administration). 1978. text ed. 22.95 (ISBN 0-471-75903-1); tchrs. manual avail. (ISBN 0-471-03725-7). Wiley.
Scheller, William. Successful Home Greenhouses. LC 76-51747. (Illus.). 134p. 1977. 13.95 (ISBN 0-912336-40-4); pap. 6.95 (ISBN 0-912336-41-2). Structures Pub.
Scheller, William G. Train Trips: Exploring America by Rail. (Illus.). 270p. (Orig.). 1981. pap. 6.95 (ISBN 0-914788-34-5). East Woods.
Schellie, Don. Kidnapping Mr. Tubbs. LC 78-6153. 192p. (gr. 7 up). 1978. 7.95 (ISBN 0-590-07542-X, Four Winds). Schol Bk Serv.
--Maybe Next Summer. LC 79-6338. 256p. (gr. 7-12). 1980. 8.95 (ISBN 0-590-07585-3, Four Winds). Schol Bk Serv.
Schelling, F. W., tr. see Marti, Fritz.
Schelling, Friedrich. On University Studies. Guterman, Norbert, ed. Morgan, E. S., tr. LC 65-15086. xxii, 166p. 1966. 10.00x (ISBN 0-8214-0015-0). Ohio U Pr.
Schelling, Friedrich W. Of Human Freedom. Gutmann, James, tr. 128p. 1936. 10.95 (ISBN 0-87548-024-1); pap. 3.95 (ISBN 0-87548-025-X). Open Court.
Schelling, Thomas C. Arms & Influence. (Henry L. Stimson Lectures Ser.). 1967. pap. 5.45x (ISBN 0-300-00221-1, Y190). Yale U Pr.
--Strategy of Conflict. LC 60-11560. (Illus.). 1960. 15.00x (ISBN 0-674-84030-5); pap. text ed. 6.95 (ISBN 0-674-84031-3). Harvard U Pr.
Schellmann, Jorg & Kluser, Bernd, eds. Joseph Beuys, Multiples: Catalog Raisonne. LC 80-11593. (Illus.). 246p. 1981. 22.50x (ISBN 0-8147-7813-5); pap. 14.95 (ISBN 0-8147-7814-3). NYU Pr.
Scheltema, J. F., tr. Lebanon in Turmoil: Syria & the Powers in 1860. (Yale Oriental Researches Ser.: No. VII). 1920. 29.50x (ISBN 0-685-69861-0). Elliots Bks.
Schemmel, Rachel. Nutrition, Physiology & Obesity. 256p. 1980. 64.95 (ISBN 0-8493-5471-4). CRC Pr.
Schemmer, Kenneth E. Between Faith & Tears. 1981. pap. 3.95 (ISBN 0-8407-5770-0). Nelson.
Schemnitz, Sanford D., ed. see Wildlife Society.
Schenck, Carl A. The Birth of Forestry in America. LC 74-84457. 1974. 10.95 (ISBN 0-89030-001-1); pap. 4.50 (ISBN 0-89030-002-X). Appalach Consortium.
Schenck, Jeanne M. & Cordova, F. David. Introductory Biomechanics. 2nd ed. (Illus.). 173p. 1980. 13.95 (ISBN 0-8036-7733-2). Davis Co.
Schenck, P. A. Advances in Organic Geochemistry: Proceedings. 1969. 96.00 (ISBN 0-08-006628-3). Pergamon.
Schenck, Walter J., Jr. Reign of the Madman: The Birdcatcher. LC 80-81523. (Illus.). 1980. 14.95 (ISBN 0-936978-01-5); pap. 6.95 (ISBN 0-936978-00-7). Schenck Pubns.
Schendelen, M. P. van see Herman, V. & Van Schendelen, M. P.
Schenk, et al. Introduction to Analytical Chemistry. 2nd ed. 540p. 1981. text ed. 21.95 (ISBN 0-205-07236-4, 6872360); student's manual. Allyn.
Schenk, G. H. Organic Functional Group Analysis, Theory & Development. LC 67-28668. 1968. 16.50 (ISBN 0-08-012626-X); pap. 7.75 (ISBN 0-08-012625-1). Pergamon.
Schenk, George. Absorption of Light & Ultraviolet Radiation: Fluorescence & Phosphorescence Emission. (Instrumentation Ser., Vol. 4). 324p. 1973. pap. text ed. 11.95x o.p. (ISBN 0-205-03720-8). Allyn.
Schenk, George H., et al. Quantitative Analytical Chemistry: Principles & Life Science Applications. 1977. text ed. 19.95 (ISBN 0-205-05700-4, 6857000); instr's manual o.p. free (ISBN 0-205-05701-2). Allyn.
Schenk, George H., Jr., jt. auth. see Fritz, James S.
Schenk, H., jt. ed. see Schwemmler, W.
Schenk, Hans G. The Aftermath of the Napoleonic Wars. 1968. 16.50 (ISBN 0-86527-000-7). Fertig.
Schenk, Joyce. Caves of Darkness. (YA) 1977. 5.95 (ISBN 0-685-73814-0, Avalon). Bouregy.
Schenkel, R. & Schenkel-Hulliger, L. Ecology & Behavior of the Black Rhinoceros (Diceros Bicornis L.) A Field Study. (Illus.). 100p. (Orig.). 1969. pap. text ed. 16.50. Parey Sci Pubs.
Schenkel-Hulliger, L., jt. auth. see Schenkel, R.
Schenker, Alexander M. Beginning Polish, 2 vols. rev ed. LC 72-91305. 1973. Vol. 1. text ed. o.p. (ISBN 0-685-29210-X); Vol. 2. text ed. 22.50 (ISBN 0-300-01670-0); Vol. 1. pap. text ed. 8.00 (ISBN 0-300-01653-0); Vol. 2. pap. text ed. 10.00 (ISBN 0-300-01671-9). Yale U Pr.
--Spoken Polish. (Spoken Language Ser.). 487p. 1981. pap. 10.00x (ISBN 0-87950-040-9); cassettes, 17 oval track 115.00 (ISBN 0-87950-041-7); cassettes & bk. 120.00x (ISBN 0-87950-042-5). Spoken Lang Serv.
Schenker, Eric & Brockel, Harry C., eds. Port Planning & Development As Related to Problems of US Ports & US Coastal Environment. LC 74-22183. (Illus.). 1974. 12.50x (ISBN 0-87033-196-5). Cornell Maritime.
Schenker, Heinrich. Five Graphic Music Analyses. LC 69-15902. Orig. Title: Five Analyses in Sketch Form. 1969. pap. 3.50 (ISBN 0-486-22294-2). Dover.
--Free Composition-der Freie Satz, 2 vols. Oster, Ernst, tr. from Ger. LC 78-4420. (Music Ser.). 1979. Set. lib. bdg. 33.95x (ISBN 0-582-28073-7). Longman.
--Harmony. Jonas, Oswald, ed. Borgese, Elizabeth M., tr. LC 54-11213. 396p. 1980. pap. 8.95 (ISBN 0-226-73734-9, P894, Phoen). U of Chicago Pr.
Schenker, Heinrich, ed. see Beethoven, Ludwig Van.
Schenkkan, Robert, ed. see Ibsen, Henrik.
Schenkkan, Robert, tr. see Ibsen, Henrik.
Schenkkan, Robert F., et al. Case Studies in Institutional Licensee Management. 75p. 1980. pap. 4.00 (Pub Telecom). NAEB.
Schep, J. A. Baptism in the Spirit According to Scripture: The Report of a Reformed Church Theologian. pap. 2.50 o.p. (ISBN 0-912106-78-6). Logos.
Schepartz, B. Dimensional Analysis in the Biomedical Sciences. (Illus.). 184p. 1980. 19.75 (ISBN 0-398-03991-7). C C Thomas.
Schepman, F., jt. auth. see Cole, J.
Scheppach, Raymond C., Jr. State Projection of the Gross National Product, 1970, 1980, LC 72-8038. (Multiregional Input-Output Study: Vol. 3). (Illus.). 320p. 1972. 28.95 (ISBN 0-669-84996-0). Lexington Bks.
Scher, Anna & Verrall, Charles. Hundred Plus Ideas for Drama. 1975. pap. text ed. 4.50x (ISBN 0-435-18799-6). Heinemann Ed.
Scher, Helene, tr. see Scher, Helene, et al.
Scher, Helene, et al, eds. Four Romantic Tales from 19th Century German. Brentano, Clemens & Von Arnim, Achim. Scher, Helene, tr. from Ger. LC 75-1428. 1975. 7.50 (ISBN 0-8044-2769-0); pap. 3.95 (ISBN 0-8044-6804-4). Ungar.
Scher, Jordan. Theories of the Mind. LC 62-11860. 1962. 14.95 o.s.i. (ISBN 0-02-927870-8). Free Pr.
Scher, Jordan M. Drug Abuse in Industry: Growing Corporate Dilemma. (Illus.). 336p. 1973. 16.50 (ISBN 0-398-02809-5). C C Thomas.
Scher, Paula. The Honeymoon Book: A Tribute to the Last Ritual of Sexual Innocence. Graver, Fred, ed. (Illus.). 200p. (Orig.). 1981. pap. 9.95 (ISBN 0-87131-339-1). M Evans.
Scherchen, Herman. Handbook of Conducting. Calvocoressi, M. D., tr. LC 77-26270. (Music Reprint, 1978). 1978. Repr. of 1935 ed. lib. bdg. 22.50 (ISBN 0-306-77564-6). Da Capo.
Scherer, Donald, et al. Introduction to Philosophy: From Wonder to World View. (Illus.). 1979. text ed. 17.95 (ISBN 0-13-491860-6). P-H.
Scherer, Felicia. For the Shape of Your Life. 1976. pap. text ed. 2.50 (ISBN 0-918734-14-2). Reymont.
Scherer, George A., ed. Selected German Ballads. (Heath Visible Vocabulary German Ser). 1951. pap. text ed. 1.95x o.p. (ISBN 0-669-29728-3). Heath.
Scherer, Jeanne. Introductory Clinical Pharmacology. LC 75-4606. 300p. 1975. pap. 11.95 o.p. (ISBN 0-397-54168-6). Lippincott.
Scherer, John L. Complete Handbook of Home Painting. LC 74-33625. (Illus.). 210p. 1975. pap. 4.95 o.p. (ISBN 0-8306-4762-7, 762). TAB Bks.
Scherer, John L., ed. China Facts & Figures Annual (CHIFFA, Vol. 3, 1981. 37.00 (ISBN 0-87569-036-X). Academic Intl.
--U S S R Facts & Figures Annual (UFFA, Vol. 4 1980. 42.50 (ISBN 0-87569-035-1). Academic Intl.
--USSR Facts & Figures Annual. (UFFA: Vol. 3). 1979. 40.00 (ISBN 0-685-92202-2); Vol. 4. 1980 41.00 (ISBN 0-686-67545-2). Academic Intl.
--USSR Facts & Figures Annual, Vol. 1. (UFFA: Vol. 1). 1977. 36.00 (ISBN 0-685-82329-6). Academic Intl.
Scherer, K., jt. ed. see DeVore, R. A.

Scherer, Klaus R. & Giles, Howard, eds. Social Markers in Speech. LC 79-4080. (Illus.). 1980. 49.50 (ISBN 0-521-22321-0); pap. 12.95 (ISBN 0-521-29590-4). Cambridge U Pr.

Scherer, Ross P., ed. American Denominational Organization: A Sociological View. LC 80-13859. 378p. 1980. pap. 14.95x (ISBN 0-87808-173-9, Ecclesia). William Carey Lib.

Scherer, W., et al. A History of German Literature: From the Accession of Frederick the Great to the Death of Goethe. Muller, F. M., ed. Conybeare, Mrs. F. C., tr. 335p. 1980. Repr. of 1981 ed. lib. bdg. 45.00 (ISBN 0-8495-4898-5). Arden Lib.

Scherman, Katharine. The Flowering of Ireland: Saints, Scholars & Kings. (Illus.). 320p. 1981. 15.95 (ISBN 0-316-77284-4). Little.

Scherman, Nosson. Siddur: Sabbath Eve Service. 1980. 8.95 (ISBN 0-686-68764-7); pap. 5.95 (ISBN 0-686-68765-5). Mesorah Pubns.

Schermer, Irwin E. Automobile Liability Insurance. LC 73-82715. 1979. looseleaf with 1978 rev. pages 110.00 (ISBN 0-87632-102-3). Boardman.

Schertl, Albrecht. Abbreviations in Medicine. 204p. 1977. pap. 20.00 (ISBN 3-7940-7017-8, Pub. by K G Saur). Gale.

Schertle, Alice. The April Fool. LC 80-21435. (Illus.). 32p. (gr. k-3). 1981. 7.95 (ISBN 0-688-41990-9); PLB 7.63 (ISBN 0-688-51990-3). Morrow.

--Cathy & Company & Hank, the Horse. LC 79-19179. (Cathy & Company Ser.). (Illus.). 48p. (gr. 2 up). 1980. PLB 7.95 (ISBN 0-516-07725-2, Elk Grove Bks.). Childrens.

Schertzer, Bruce. Teacher's Guide to Group Vocational Guidance. LC 79-146112. (Guidance Information Ser). 74p. 1971. pap. 5.55 o.p. (ISBN 0-87442-021-0). Bellman.

Schery, Robert W. Plants for Man. 2nd ed. (Illus.). 608p. 1972. ref. ed. 25.95 (ISBN 0-13-681254-6). P-H.

Scherz, Frances H., jt. auth. see Feldman, Frances L.

Scherzer, Cathy C., jt. auth. see Barron, Cheryl C.

Schetzen, Martin. The Volterra & Weiner Theories of Nonlinear Systems. LC 79-13421. 1980. 32.50 (ISBN 0-471-04455-5, Pub. by Wiley-Interscience). Wiley.

Scheub, Harold. Xhosa Ntsomi. (Oxford Library of African Literature Ser.). 1974. 45.00x (ISBN 0-19-815140-3). Oxford U Pr.

Scheuer, jt. auth. see Wakin.

Scheuer, P. Liver Biopsy Interpretation. 3rd ed. 1980. text ed. 65.00 (ISBN 0-02-859180-1). Macmillan.

Scheuer, Paul J., ed. Marine Natural Products: Chemical & Biological Perspectives, Vol. 4. 1981. price not set (ISBN 0-12-624004-3). Acad Pr.

Scheuer, Sidney H. The Ethics of International Economics: An Innovative Approach to World Affairs. 192p. 1980. 8.50 (ISBN 0-682-49653-7). Exposition.

Scheuer, Steven H. TV: The Television Annual, 1979-80. (Illus.). 352p. Date not set. 19.95 (ISBN 0-02-607080-4). Macmillan. Postponed.

Scheuerle, William H., ed. see Kingsley, Henry.

Scheuerman, Richard & Trafzer, Clifford. The Volga Germans: Pioneers in the Pacific Northwest. LC 80-52314. (GEM Books-Historical Ser.). (Illus.). 240p. (Orig.). 1981. 18.95; pap. 7.95 (ISBN 0-89301-073-1). U Pr of Idaho.

Scheuerman, Richard V., jt. auth. see Barner, Herbert E.

Scheuermann, Mona. The Novels of William Godwin & Those of His Contemporaries. Varma, Devendra P., ed. LC 79-8477. (Gothic Studies & Dissertations Ser.). 1980. lib. bdg. 25.00x (ISBN 0-405-12678-6). Arno.

Scheurig, Bodo. Free Germany: The National Committee & the League of German Officers. Arnold, Herbert, tr. from Ger. LC 75-82540. 1969. 20.00x (ISBN 0-8195-4010-2, Pub. by Wesleyan U Pr). Columbia U Pr.

Scheuring, Lynn, jt. auth. see Scheuring, Tom.

Scheuring, Tom & Scheuring, Lynn. Two for Joy: Reflections for a Husband & Wife on Their Spirit Led Journey Through Jesus to the Father. LC 76-28274. 1976. pap. 4.95 (ISBN 0-8091-1985-4). Paulist Pr.

Schevill, James. The Arena of Ants: A Novel. (Illus., Orig.). 1977. pap. 7.50 (ISBN 0-914278-11-8). Copper Beech.

--Breakout: In Search of New Theatrical Environments. LC 77-189192. (Illus.). 411p. 1972. 15.00x (ISBN 0-8040-0574-5); pap. 4.95x o.s.i. (ISBN 0-8040-0640-7). Swallow.

--Lovecraft's Follies: A Play. LC 77-150761. 90p. 1971. 5.00 (ISBN 0-8040-0501-X); pap. 2.95 (ISBN 0-8040-0502-8). Swallow.

--The Mayan Poems. (Illus., Orig.). 1978. pap. 4.50 (ISBN 0-914278-16-9). Copper Beech.

--Pursuing Elegy: A Poem About Haiti. (Illus., Orig.). 1974. pap. 3.50 (ISBN 0-914278-01-0). Copper Beech.

--Stalingrad Elegies. LC 64-16113. 53p. (Orig.). 1964. pap. 2.25 (ISBN 0-8040-0281-9, 59). Swallow.

--Violence & Glory: Poems, Nineteen-Sixty-Two to Nineteen-Sixty-Eight. LC 76-75733. 1969. 7.95 o.p. (ISBN 0-8040-0313-0); pap. 5.95 (ISBN 0-8040-0314-9). Swallow.

Scheving, Lawrence E. & Halberg, Franz. Chronobiology: Principles & Applications to Shifts in Schedules. (NATO Advanced Study Institute: Behavioral Social Sciences, No. 3). 597p. 1980. 65.00x (ISBN 90-286-0940-7). Sijthoff & Noordhoff.

Schewe, Donald B., ed. see Roosevelt, Franklin D.

Schey, Harry M. Div, Grad, Curl & All That: An Informal Text on Vector Calculus. (Illus.). 150p. 1973. pap. text ed. 5.95x (ISBN 0-393-09367-0). Norton.

Schey, John A. Metal Deformation Processes: Friction & Lubrication. (Illus.). 824p. 110.00 (ISBN 0-08-024658-3); soft cover 95.00 (ISBN 0-08-024657-5); microfiche x 58.00 (ISBN 0-08-024656-7); microfilm xx 35.00 (ISBN 0-08-024655-9). Pergamon.

Schiari, Michael. Athletic Trainers Guide to Injuries of Young Athletes. (Illus.). 224p. 1981. 12.00 (ISBN 0-87460-317-X). Lion.

Schiavi, Michael R. The Athletic Trainers Guide: Prevention, Care - Treatment of Sports Injuries to Young Athletes. (Illus.). 1981. 11.95 (ISBN 0-87460-317-X). Lion.

Schiavi, Raul C. Assessment of Sexual & Marital Function: Special Issue of Journal of Sex & Marital Therapy. 1979. pap. 7.95x (ISBN 0-87705-468-1). Human Sci Pr.

Schiavone, James. Help Your Child to Read Better. LC 76-29055. 1977. 11.95 (ISBN 0-88229-221-8); pap. 6.95 (ISBN 0-88229-464-4). Nelson-Hall.

--Springboards: A College Reader. 1977. pap. text ed. 7.00 (ISBN 0-87720-955-3). AMSCO Sch.

Schick, Alice & Schick, Joel. Just This Once. LC 77-28871. (I-Like-to-Read Bks). (gr. k-2). 1978. 6.95 (ISBN 0-397-31803-0). Lippincott.

Schick, Alice, jt. auth. see Schick, Joel.

Schick, Alice, ed. see Shelley, Mary.

Schick, Alice, ed. see Stoker, Bram.

Schick, Allen. Congress & Money: Budgeting, Spending & Taxing. LC 80-53322. 600p. 1980. 27.50 (ISBN 0-87766-278-9). Urban Inst.

Schick, Allen & Pfister, Adrienne. American Government: Continuity & Change. (Illus.). 629p. (gr. 10-12). 1975. 17.44 (ISBN 0-395-18825-3); instrs' guide & key 6.72 (ISBN 0-395-18816-4); student's wk. guide 5.96 (ISBN 0-395-18824-5). HM.

Schick, Barbara A., jt. auth. see Rose, Allen J.

Schick, C. Dennis & Book, Albert C. Fundamentals of Creative Advertising. 1981. write for info. (ISBN 0-87251-035-2). Crain Bks.

Schick, Edwin A. Revelation-The Last Book of the Bible. LC 76-62602. 80p. (Orig.). 1977. pap. 2.75 (ISBN 0-8006-1253-1, 1-1253). Fortress.

Schick, Eleanor. City Green. LC 73-8574. (Illus.). 40p. (ps-3). 1974. 4.95g o.s.i. (ISBN 0-02-781170-0). Macmillan.

--City in Summer. LC 69-11306. (Illus.). (gr. k-2). 1969. 5.95g o.s.i. (ISBN 0-02-781270-7). Macmillan.

--City in the Winter. LC 69-18237. (Illus.). (gr. k-3). 1973. 5.95g o.s.i. (ISBN 0-02-781280-4). Macmillan.

--City Sun. (Illus.). 40p. (gr. 1-3). 1974. 4.95g o.s.i. (ISBN 0-02-781200-6). Macmillan.

--I'm Going to the Ocean. (gr. k-1). 1966. 3.95g o.s.i. (ISBN 0-02-781190-5). Macmillan.

--One Summer Night. LC 76-25199. (Illus.). (gr. k-3). 1977. PLB 7.92 (ISBN 0-688-84072-8). Greenwillow.

--Peggy's New Brother. LC 70-99124. (Illus.). (gr. k-2). 1970. 4.95g o.s.i. (ISBN 0-02-781140-9). Macmillan.

--Peter & Mr. Brandon. LC 75-165105. (Illus.). 32p. (ps-2). 1973. 5.95g o.s.i. (ISBN 0-02-781120-4). Macmillan.

--Rainy Sunday. LC 80-11596. (Easy-to-Read Ser.). (Illus.). 56p. (ps-3). 1981. PLB 5.99 (ISBN 0-8037-7369-2); pap. 2.50 (ISBN 0-8037-7371-4). Dial.

Schick, George B., jt. auth. see Raygor, Alton L.

Schick, Harold L., ed. Thermodynamics of Certain Refractory Compounds, 2 vols. Incl. Vol. 1. Discussion of Theoretical Studies. 56.00 (ISBN 0-12-624501-0); Vol. 2. Thermodynamic Tables, Bibliography & Property File. 56.00 (ISBN 0-12-624502-9). 1966. Set. 83.00 (ISBN 0-12-624566-5). Acad Pr.

Schick, Joel & Schick, Alice. Santaberry & the Snard. LC 78-23796. (Lippincott I-Like-to-Read Books). (Illus.). (gr. k-2). 1979. 6.95 (ISBN 0-397-31824-3). Lippincott.

Schick, Joel, jt. auth. see Schick, Alice.

Schick, Joel, ed. see Shelley, Mary.

Schick, Joel, ed. see Stoker, Bram.

Schickedanz, H. Ruth & Mayhall, Pamela D. Restorative Nursing in a General Hospital. (Illus.). 232p. 1975. 19.75 (ISBN 0-398-03312-9); pap. 14.75 (ISBN 0-398-03313-7). C C Thomas.

Schickel, Richard. Singled Out. LC 80-54080. 128p. 1981. 9.95 (ISBN 0-670-64710-1). Viking Pr.

--World of Goya. (Library of Art). (Illus.). 1968. 15.95 (ISBN 0-8094-0247-5). Time-Life.

--World of Goya. LC 68-56432. (Library of Art Ser.). (Illus.). (gr. 6 up). 1968. 12.96 (ISBN 0-8094-0276-9, Pub. by Time-Life). Silver.

Schieber, George J., jt. auth. see Kelly, Terence F.

Schiedermair, Ludwig. Die Deutche Oper: Grundzuge Ihres Werdens & Wesens. LC 80-2299. 1981. Repr. of 1930 ed. 38.50 (ISBN 0-404-18868-0). AMS Pr.

Schiefelbusch, R. Nonspeech Language & Communication. 1979. 24.95 (ISBN 0-8391-1558-X). Univ Park.

Schiefelbusch, R. L., jt. auth. see Haring, Norris G.

Schieffermann, Vance A. The Art of Successful Entrepreneurship & How to Get It. (Illus.). 1981. 49.95 (ISBN 0-918968-82-8). Inst Econ Pol.

Schieler, Leroy & Pauze, Denis. Hazardous Materials. LC 75-19526. 1976. pap. 9.20 (ISBN 0-8273-0593-1); instructor's guide 1.60 (ISBN 0-8273-0594-X). Delmar.

Schier, Steven E. The Rules & the Game: Democratic National Convention Delegate Selection in Iowa & Wisconsin. LC 79-5495. 1980. text ed. 24.00 (ISBN 0-8191-0891-X); pap. text ed. 15.00 (ISBN 0-8191-0892-8). U Pr of Amer.

Schierlova, Margaret, tr. see Roth, B.

Schiesl, Martin. The Politics of Efficiency: Municipal Administration & Reform in America, 1880-1920. LC 75-17285. 1977. 18.50x (ISBN 0-520-03067-2); pap. 6.95x (ISBN 0-520-04086-4). U of Cal Pr.

Schiesser, Frank J., jt. auth. see Beresin, Victor E.

Schieve, William C. & Allen, Peter M., eds. Self-Organization & Dissipative Structures: Applications in the Physical & Social Sciences. (Illus.). 472p. 1981. text ed. 50.00x (ISBN 0-292-70354-6). U of Tex Pr.

Schiewe, March, jt. auth. see Berg, Patty.

Schiff, Gert. Images of Horror & Fantasy. (Illus.). 160p. 1980. 19.95 (ISBN 0-8109-1062-4, 1062-4); pap. 9.95 (ISBN 0-8109-2192-8, 2192-8). Abrams.

Schiff, Irwin A. The Kingdom of Moltz. LC 80-14628. 1980. pap. 3.95 (ISBN 0-930374-02-9). Freedom Bks.

Schiff, Jacqui L. & Cathexis Institute. Cathexis Reader: Transactional Analysis Treatment of Psychosis. 1975. text ed. 13.95 scp (ISBN 0-06-045773-2, HarpC). Har-Row.

Schiff, Jacqui L. & Day, Beth. All My Children. LC 78-126389. 240p. 1970. 8.95 (ISBN 0-87131-036-8). M Evans.

Schiff, Jacqui L. & Day, Betty. All My Children. rev. ed. 1977. pap. 1.95 (ISBN 0-515-05422-4). Jove Pubns.

Schiff, Leon, ed. Diseases of the Liver. 4th ed. LC 75-20047. (Illus.). 1450p. 1975. text ed. 87.50 (ISBN 0-397-50319-9). Lippincott.

Schiff, Lillian. Getting Started in Film-Making. LC 77-79504. (Illus.). (gr. 6 up). 1977. 7.95 (ISBN 0-8069-5382-9); PLB 7.49 (ISBN 0-8069-5383-7). Sterling.

Schiff, Martin M. Docto Schiff's One-Day-at-a-Time Weight-Loss Plan. 1980. 9.95 (ISBN 0-8128-2692-2). Stein & Day.

Schiff, Roselyn L., et al. Communication Strategy: A Guide to Speech Preparation. 1980. pap. text ed. 6.95x (ISBN 0-673-15437-8). Scott F.

Schiff, S. O. & Griffith, D. A. Twenty-One Afternoons of Biology: A Laboratory Manual. Houston, ed. 155p. 1975. lab manual 6.95x o.p. (ISBN 0-205-04572-3); instr's manual free o.p. (ISBN 0-685-52902-9). Allyn.

Schiff, S. O., et al. Twenty-One Afternoons of Biology: A Laboratory Manual. 2nd ed. 1979. pap. text ed. 10.95x (ISBN 0-205-06132-X, 6761321); instr's man. o.p. avail. o.p. (ISBN 0-205-06193-1). Allyn.

Schiff, Stefan O. Buttons: Art in Miniature. (Lancaster-Miller Art Ser.). (Illus.). 1980. 9.95 (ISBN 0-89581-013-1). Lancaster-Miller.

Schiff, William. Perception: An Applied Approach. LC 79-88717. 1980. text ed. 18.50 (ISBN 0-395-27054-5). HM.

Schiffer, Don. The First Book of Basketball. rev ed. LC 77-3219. (First Bks.). (Illus.). (gr. 4-6). 1977. lib. bdg. 6.45 s&l (ISBN 0-531-01289-1). Watts.

Schiffer, H., et al. Chinese Export Porcelain: Standard Patterns & Forms, 1780-1880. 256p. 1980. 59.85x (ISBN 0-903485-96-6, Pub. by Allan Pubs England). State Mutual Bk.

Schiffer, Herbert & Schiffer, Peter. China for America: Export Porcelain of the 18th & 19th Centuries. LC 79-88254. 1979. 27.50 (ISBN 0-916838-23-4). Schiffer.

Schiffer, Herbert F. Early Pennsylvania Hardware. (Illus.). 64p. 1966. pap. 3.75 (ISBN 0-916838-42-0). Schiffer.

Schiffer, Irvine. Charisma: A Psychoanalytic Look at Mass Society. LC 72-95816. 1973. pap. 4.00 (ISBN 0-8020-6221-0). U of Toronto Pr.

Schiffer, Judith. School Renewal Through Staff Development. 1980. pap. 11.95x (ISBN 0-8077-2582-X). Tchrs Coll.

Schiffer, Leo. Johann Ladislaus Dussek: Seine Sonaten und Seine Konzerte. LC 79-168672. 136p. 1972. Repr. of 1914 ed. lib. bdg. 17.50 (ISBN 0-306-70266-5). Da Capo.

Schiffer, Margaret B. Arts & Crafts of Chester County, Pa. (Illus.). 356p. Date not set. cancelled (ISBN 0-916838-35-8). Schiffer.

Schiffer, Michael. Lessons of the Road. 1980. 10.95 (ISBN 0-686-68922-4, Kenan Pr). S&S.

Schiffer, Michael, jt. ed. see Gould, Richard A.

Schiffer, Michael B., ed. Advances in Archaeological Methods & Theory, Vol. 3. (Serial Publication). 1980. 39.50 (ISBN 0-12-003103-5). Acad Pr.

Schiffer, Peter, jt. auth. see Schiffer, Herbert.

Schiffer, Peter B. The Chester County Historical Society. (Illus.). 70p. 1970. pap. 3.50. Schiffer.

Schiffer, Robert L., ed. see Stevenson, Adlai.

Schiffer, Selma, ed. see Stevenson, Adlai.

Schifferes, Justus J. & Peterson, Louis J. Healthier Living Highlights. 2nd ed. LC 74-24339. (Illus.). 289p. 1975. text ed. 15.50x (ISBN 0-471-76071-4); thcrs. manual avail. (ISBN 0-471-76072-2). Wiley.

Schifferes, Justus J., jt. ed. see Moulton, Forest R.

Schiffhorst, Gerald J., jt. auth. see Fear, David E.

Schiffman, H. R. Sensation & Perception: An Integrated Approach. LC 76-185. 1976. text ed. 23.95 (ISBN 0-471-76091-9). Wiley.

Schiffman, Leon G., et al. Consumer Behavior. LC 77-25032. (Illus.). 1978. ref. 19.95x (ISBN 0-13-169201-1). P-H.

Schiffman, Muriel. Gestalt Self Therapy. LC 73-75228. 240p. (Orig.). 1980. pap. 4.95 (ISBN 0-914640-02-X, Pub. by Self Therapy Pr). Wingbow Pr.

--Self Therapy. LC 73-75227. 176p. (Orig.). 1980. pap. 3.95 (ISBN 0-914640-01-1, Pub. by Self Therapy Pr). Wingbow Pr.

Schiffmann, Gerard, jt. auth. see Rallis, Stephen.

Schiffrin, Harold Z. Sun Yat-sen & the Origins of the Chinese Revolution. (Center for Chinese Studies, UC Berkeley). 1968. 18.50x (ISBN 0-520-01142-2). U of Cal Pr.

Schijatscky, Milan. Life-Threatening Emergencies in the Dental Practice. (Illus.). 163p. 1975. 24.50. Quint Pub Co.

Schikaneder, Emanuel, jt. auth. see Gieseke, Carl L.

Schild, jt. auth. see Synge.

Schild, E. O., jt. ed. see Boocock, Sarane S.

Schild, Erich, et al. Structural Failure in Residential Buildings, 3 vols. Incl. Vol. 1. Flat Roofs, Roof Terraces & Balconies. 24.50x (ISBN 0-470-26305-9); Vol. 2. External Walls & Openings. 27.95x (ISBN 0-470-26789-5); Vol. 3. 154p. 29.95x (ISBN 0-470-26846-8). LC 77-28647. 1978-80. Set. 85.85x (ISBN 0-470-26898-0). Halsted Pr.

Schild, H. O. Applied Pharmacology. 12th ed. (Illus.). 500p. 1981. pap. text ed. 32.00 (ISBN 0-443-02199-6). Churchill.

Schilder, Klass. The Trilogy, 3 vols. 1978. 48.00 (ISBN 0-686-12940-7). Klock & Klock.

Schildknecht, C. E. & Skeist, I., eds. Polymerization Processes. LC 76-17108. (High Polymer Ser.: Vol. 29). 1977. 53.50 (ISBN 0-471-39381-9, Pub. by Wiley-Interscience). Wiley.

Schildt, Goran, ed. see Aalto, Alvar.

Schill, Michael H. Neighborhood Reinvestment & Displacement: A Working Paper. LC 80-85160. 64p. 1981. pap. 2.50x (ISBN 0-938882-01-5). PURRC.

Schillebeeck, Edward. Christ: The Christian Experience in the Modern World. 900p. 1980. 29.50 (ISBN 0-8245-0136-5). Crossroad NY.

Schillebeeck, Edward & Iersel, Van B., eds. Heaven. (Concilium Ser.: Vol. 123). 1979. pap. 4.95 (ISBN 0-8164-2231-1). Crossroad NY.

Schillebeeck, Edward & Van Iersel, B., eds. Revelation & Experience. (Concilium Ser.: Vol. 113). 1979. pap. 4.95 (ISBN 0-8164-2609-0). Crossroad NY.

Schillebeeckx, E. & Van Iersel, B., eds. Truth & Certainty. (Concilium Ser.: Religion in the Seventies: Vol. 83). 144p. 1973. pap. 4.95 (ISBN 0-8164-2539-6, 73613). Crossroad NY.

Schillebeeckx, Edward. Interim Report on the Books Jesus & Christ. 160p. 1980. 12.95 (ISBN 0-8245-0477-1). Crossroad NY.

--Jesus: An Experiment in Christology. 1979. 24.50. Crossroad NY.

--Ministry. 160p. (Dutch.). 1981. 12.95 (ISBN 0-8245-0030-X). Crossroad NY.
--Mission of the Church. 250p. 1973. 9.75 (ISBN 0-8164-1144-1). Crossroad NY.
--Understanding of Faith: Interpretation & Criticism. 1974. 8.95 (ISBN 0-8164-1185-9). Crossroad NY.
--Unifying Role of the Bishop. LC 70-168651. (Concilium Ser.: Religion in the Seventies: Vol. 71). 1972. pap. 4.95 (ISBN 0-8164-2527-2). Crossroad NY.
Schillebeeckx, Edward, ed. Dogma & Pluralism. (Concilium Ser.: Religion in the Seventies: Vol. 51). pap. 4.95 (ISBN 0-8164-2507-8). Crossroad NY.
--Sacramental Reconciliation. LC 76-129760. (Concilium Ser.: Religion in the Seventies: Vol. 61). 1971. pap. 4.95 (ISBN 0-8164-2517-5). Crossroad NY.
Schillebeeckx, Edward & Metz, Johann B., eds. The Right of the Community to a Priest, Concilium 133. (New Concilium 1980). 128p. 1980. pap. 5.95 (ISBN 0-8164-4766-7). Crossroad NY.
Schillebeeckx, Edward & Van Iersel, B., eds. Jesus Christ & Human Freedom. LC 73-17908. (Concilium Ser.: Religion in the Seventies: Vol. 93). 1974. pap. 4.95 (ISBN 0-8164-2577-9). Seabury.
Schillebeecky, E. & Van Iersel, B., eds. A Personal God. (Concilium Ser.: Vol. 103). 1977. pap. 4.95 (ISBN 0-8164-2149-8). Crossroad NY.
Schiller, B. R. The Economics of Poverty & Discrimination. 2nd ed. (Illus.). 224p. 1976. pap. 9.95 o.p. (ISBN 0-13-232009-6). P-H.
Schiller, Ely, ed. The First Photographs of Jerusalem: The Old City. (Illus.). 252p. (Eng. & Heb.). 1978. 30.00x (ISBN 0-8002-2455-8). Intl Pubns Serv.
Schiller, Francis. Paul Broca, Eighteen Twenty-Four to Eighteen Eighty: Founder of French Anthropoogy, Explorer of the Brain. 1979. 27.50x (ISBN 0-520-03744-8). U of Cal Pr.
Schiller, Francis, jt. auth. see Haymaker, Webb.
Schiller, Friedrich Von see Von Schiller, Friedrich.
Schiller, Johann. Die Rauber. 2nd ed. Magill, C. P. & Willoughby, L. A., eds. (Blackwell's German Text Ser.). 1974. pap. 4.50x o.p. (ISBN 0-631-01850-6, Pub. by Basil Blackwell). Biblio Dist.
Schiller, Judith D. Child Care Alternatives & Emotional Well-Being. 204p. 1980. 21.95 (ISBN 0-03-056139-6). Praeger.
Schiller, Justin G., ed. see Ballantyne, Robert.
Schiller, Justin G., ed. see Boreman, Thomas.
Schiller, Justin G., ed. see Charlesworth, Maria L.
Schiller, Justin G., ed. see D'Aulnoy, Marie C.
Schiller, Justin G., ed. see Finley, Martha.
Schiller, Justin G., ed. see Harris, Benjamin.
Schiller, Justin G., ed. see Kilner, Mary J.
Schiller, Justin G., jt. ed. see Lurie, Alison.
Schiller, Justin G., ed. see Newbery, F.
Schiller, Justin G., ed. see Perrault, Charles.
Schiller, Justin G., ed. see Wilde, Oscar.
Schiller, Marc, jt. auth. see Moffat, Anne.
Schiller, Nelson B., jt. auth. see Kleid, Jack J.
Schiller, Patricia. The Sex Profession. 252p. 1981. pap. 8.00 (ISBN 0-88416-340-7). PSG Pub.
--The Sex Profession: What Sex Therapy Can Do. 250p. (Orig.). 1980. 11.00 (ISBN 0-937532-00-2); pap. 8.00 (ISBN 0-937532-01-0). Chilmark Hse.
Schiller, Patricia, jt. auth. see Miller, Mary S.
Schilling, A. Automobile Engine Lubrication. (Illus.). 480p. 1972. text ed. 45.00x (ISBN 0-900645-00-8). Scholium Intl.
Schilling, Bernard M. Dryden & the Conservative Myth. 1961. 37.50x (ISBN 0-685-69862-9). Elliots Bks.
Schilling, Bernard N. The Comic Spirit: Boccaccio to Thomas Mann. LC 65-21652. (Waynebooks Ser: No. 26). 1965. 10.95x (ISBN 0-8143-1271-3); pap. 4.95x (ISBN 0-8143-1272-1). Wayne St U Pr.
Schilling, Harold K. The New Consciousness in Science & Religion. LC 72-13792. 1973. 10.95 (ISBN 0-8298-0247-9). Pilgrim NY.
Schilling, Irene A. A Manual of AACR 2 Examples for Liturgical Works & Sacred Scripture. Swanson, Edward & McClaskey, Marilyn J., eds. 50p. 1980. pap. 6.00 (ISBN 0-936996-06-4). Soldier Creek.
Schilling, Otto F. & Piper, W. Stephen. Basic Abstract Algebra. 416p. 1975. text ed. 20.95x o.p. (ISBN 0-205-04273-2, 5642736). Allyn.
Schilling, R. S., ed. Occupational Health Practice. 2nd ed. LC 80-41044. (Illus.). 512p. 1981. text ed. 49.00 (ISBN 0-407-33701-6). Butterworths.
Schilling, W. R. American Arms Changing Europe. 1973. 15.00x (ISBN 0-231-03704-X); pap. 7.50x (ISBN 0-231-03705-8). Columbia U Pr.
Schilling, Warner R, jt. ed. see Fox, William T.
Schilling, Warner R., et al. Strategy, Politics & Defense Budgets. LC 62-17353. (Institute of War & Peace Studies). 1962. 22.50x (ISBN 0-231-02556-4). Columbia U Pr.
Schillingburg, Herbert, et al. Fundamentals of Fixed Prosthodontics. 2nd ed. (Illus.). 454p. 1981. write for info. Quint Pub Co.
Schillinger, Brent, jt. auth. see Annexton, May.
Schillinger, Frances. Joseph Schillinger: A Memoir. LC 76-7575. (Music Reprint Ser.). 1976. Repr. of 1949 ed. lib. bdg. 22.50 (ISBN 0-306-70780-2). Da Capo.
Schillinger, Joseph. Encyclopedia of Rhythms: Instrumental Forms of Harmony. LC 76-10326. (Music Rerint Ser.). 1976. Repr. of 1966 ed. lib. bdg. 35.00 (ISBN 0-306-70782-9). Da Capo.
--The Schillinger System of Musical Composition. LC 77-21709. (Music Reprint Ser.). 1977. Repr. Vol. 1. lib. bdg. 85.00 (ISBN 0-306-77521-2); Vol. 2. lib. bdg. 37.50 (ISBN 0-306-77522-0). Set. lib. bdg. 75.00 (ISBN 0-306-77552-2). Da Capo.
Schilpp, Paul A. Kant's Pre-Critical Ethics. 2nd ed. Beck, Lewis W., ed. LC 75-32043. (The Philosophy of Immanuel Kant Ser.: Vol. 6). 1977. Repr. of 1960 ed. lib. bdg. 24.00 (ISBN 0-8240-2330-7). Garland Pub.
Schilpp, Paul A., ed. Albert Einstein Autobiographical Notes: A Centennial Edition. LC 78-13925. 1979. 10.95 (ISBN 0-87548-352-6). Open Court.
Schimel, David, jt. auth. see Brafman, Morris.
Schimke, R. Neil, jt. auth. see Jackson, Laird G.
Schimke, R. Neil, ed. see Birth Defects Conference, Kansas City, Mo., May 1975.
Schimke, R. Neil, ed. see Birth Defects Conference, 1975, Kansas City, Missouri.
Schimmel & Fischer. The Rights of Parents in the Education of Their Children. LC 77-90016. 1977. pap. text ed. 4.95 (ISBN 0-934460-05-1). NCCE.
Schimmel, jt. auth. see Lieberman.
Schimmel, Annemarie. The Triumphal Sun: A Study of the Works of Jalaloddin Rumi. (Illus.). 1978. 27.50 (ISBN 0-87773-750-9). Great Eastern.
Schimmel, David & Fischer, Louis. The Civil Rights of Students. (Critical Issues in Education Ser.). 347p. 1975. pap. text ed. 9.50 scp (ISBN 0-06-045776-7, HarpC). Har-Row.
Schimmel, Harold, tr. see Yeshurun, Avoth.
Schimmel, Paul R., jt. auth. see Cantor, Charles R.
Schindeler, Fred F. Responsible Government in Ontario. LC 70-390334. 1969. pap. 6.00 (ISBN 0-8020-6189-3). U of Toronto Pr.
Schindler. How to Live Three Hundred Sixty-Five Days a Year. pap. 3.95 (ISBN 0-13-416792-9, Parker). P-H.
Schindler, George. Magic with Everyday Objects. (Illus.). 1980. pap. 4.95 (ISBN 0-8128-6030-6). Stein & Day.
Schindler, John A. How to Live Three Hundred and Sixty-Five Days a Year. 192p. 1978. pap. 2.25 (ISBN 0-449-23922-5, Crest). Fawcett.
Schindler, Max. Microprocessor Software Design. 304p. 1980. pap. 13.25 (ISBN 0-8104-5190-5). Hayden.
Schindler, Regine. The Lost Sheep. LC 80-68546. Orig. Title: Das Verlorene Shaf. 32p. (gr. k-3). 1981. Repr. 5.95 (ISBN 0-687-22780-1). Abingdon.
Schindler-Rainman, Eva & Lippitt, Ronald. Taking Your Meetings Out of the Doldrums. LC 75-41890. (Illus.). 100p. 1975. 9.50 (ISBN 0-88390-136-6). Univ Assocs.
--The Volunteer Community: Creative Uses of Human Resources. 2nd ed. LC 75-18516. 176p. 1975. pap. 9.50 (ISBN 0-88390-140-4). Univ Assocs.
Schink, Christopher. Mastering Color & Design in Watercolor. 144p. 1981. 22.50 (ISBN 0-8230-3015-6). Watson-Guptill.
Schinke, Steven P., ed. Behavioral Methods in Social Work: Helping Children, Adults, & Families in Community Settings. (Modern Applications of Social Work Ser.). 448p. 1980. 24.95 (ISBN 0-202-36026-1). Aldine Pub.
Schinnelen, James A. Art Search & Self Discovery. LC 67-12110. (Illus.). (gr. 7-12). 1975. 18.95 (ISBN 0-87192-070-0). Davis Mass.
Schinnerer, Otto P., ed. see Kaestner, Erich.
Schinzinger, Robert, tr. see Nishida, Kitaro.
Schioeppe, Frederick. How to Raise & Train a Kerry Blue Terrier. (Illus., Orig.). pap. 1.79 o.p. (ISBN 0-87666-327-7, DS1092). TFH Pubns.
Schiotz, Arne. A Guide to Aquarium Fishes & Plants. Vevers, Gwynne, tr. LC 75-38541. 1977. pap. 3.95 o.s.i. (ISBN 0-397-01210-1). Lippincott.
Schiotz, Askel. Singer & His Art. LC 69-15259. (Illus.). 1970. 10.95 o.p. (ISBN 0-06-035817-3, HarpT). Har-Row.
Schiotz, Eiler H. & Cyriax, James. Manipulation: Past & Present. (Illus.). 1975. 18.95x (ISBN 0-433-07010-2). Intl Ideas.
Schipf, Robert G. Automotive Repair & Maintenance. LC 73-84413. (Spare Times Guides: No. 1). 1973. lib. bdg. 7.50 o.p. (ISBN 0-87287-066-9). Libs Unl.
--Home Repair & Improvement. LC 73-88698. (Spare Time Guides Ser.: No. 3). 1974. lib. bdg. 7.50 o.p. (ISBN 0-87287-078-2). Libs Unl.
--Outdoor Recreation. LC 75-30958. (Spare Time Guides Ser.: No. 9). 1976. 12.50x o.p. (ISBN 0-87287-123-1). Libs Unl.
Schire, Robert, jt. auth. see Weinstein, Warren.
Schirmer, R. H., jt. auth. see Schulz, G. E.
Schiro, George J., jt. auth. see Katsaros, Thomas.
Schirokauer, Conrad, tr. see Miyazaki, Ichisada.
Schissel, Marvin. Dentistry & Its Victims. 336p. 1981. 11.95 (ISBN 0-312-19391-2). St Martin.
Schittkowski, K. Nonlinear Programming Codes. (Lecture Notes in Economics & Mathematical Systems Ser.: Vol. 183). 242p. 1981. pap. 19.00 (ISBN 0-387-10247-7). Springer-Verlag.
Schiwetz, E. M. The Schiwetz Legacy: An Artist's Tribute to Texas, 1910-1971. (Illus.). 152p. 1972. 29.95 (ISBN 0-292-77502-4). U of Tex Pr.
Schjeide, O. A., jt. auth. see Morrison, L. M.
Schjeldahl, Peter. Since Nineteen Sixty-Four: New & Selected Poems. LC 78-15572. 1978. pap. 4.00 (ISBN 0-915342-26-X). SUN.
Schla, jt. auth. see Barish.
Schlachter, Gail & Thomison, Dennis. Library Science Dissertations 1925-1972: An Annotated Bibliography. LC 73-90497. (Research Studies in Library Science Ser.: No. 12). 293p. 1974. lib. bdg. 12.50 o.p. (ISBN 0-87287-074-X). Libs Unl.
Schlachter, Gail, ed. see Bell, Robert E.
Schlachter, Gail A. Directory of Financial Aids for Women. LC 77-78149. 16.95 (ISBN 0-918276-02-0). Ref Serv Pr.
Schlachter, Gail M. A Guide to the Reference Literature on Women in the Social Sciences, Humanities, and Sciences. (Clio Reference Guide Ser.). 1982. price not set (ISBN 0-87436-313-6). ABC Clio. Postponed.
Schlafly, Phyllis. The Power of the Christian Woman. (Orig.). 1981. pap. 3.50 (ISBN 0-87239-457-3, 2972). Standard Pub.
--Power of the Positive Women. 1978. pap. 2.95 (ISBN 0-515-05840-8). Jove Pubns.
Schlag, John D., jt. ed. see Petre-Quadens, Olga.
Schlagenhauff, Reinhold E., jt. auth. see Warfel, John H.
Schlaich, Joan, jt. auth. see Arnheim, Daniel D.
Schlaich, Joan & Dupont, Betty, eds. Dance: The Art of Production. LC 76-26583. (Illus.). 1977. pap. text ed. 7.75 o.p. (ISBN 0-8016-4346-5). Mosby.
Schlaifer, R. & Heron, S. D. Development of Aircraft Engines & Fuels. 1970. Repr. of 1950 ed. 54.00 (ISBN 0-08-018740-4). Pergamon.
Schlaifer, Robert. Introduction to Statistics for Business Decisions. 1961. text ed. 20.95 (ISBN 0-07-055308-4, C); solutions manual 4.95 (ISBN 0-07-055305-X). McGraw.
--Probability & Statistics for Business Decisions. 1959. text ed. 22.95 (ISBN 0-07-055309-2, C); tchr's manual 5.95 (ISBN 0-07-055313-0); student's manual 7.95 (ISBN 0-07-055314-9). McGraw.
--Probability & Statistics for Business Decisions. LC 79-23042. 744p. 1980. Repr. of 1959 ed. lib. bdg. write for info. (ISBN 0-89874-029-0). Krieger.
Schlanger, Bernard. Mental Retardation. LC 73-9613. (Studies in Communicative Disorders Ser.). 1973. 2.50 (ISBN 0-672-61289-5). Bobbs.
Schlanoff, Althea, tr. see Farmigier, Andre.
Schlant, Ernestine, tr. see Habermann, Gerhard.
Schlappi, Elizabeth. Roy Acuff: The Smoky Mountain Boy. Calhoun, James, ed. LC 77-11649. (Illus.). 1978. 13.95 (ISBN 0-88289-144-8). Pelican.
Schlebecker, John T. Whereby We Thrive: A History of American Farming 1607-1972. 342p. 1975. 15.50 (ISBN 0-8138-0090-0). Iowa St U Pr.
Schlechter, R. Beitraege zur Orchideenkunde von Colombia. (Feddes Repertorium: Beiheft 27). 183p. (Ger.). 1980. Repr. of 1924 ed. lib. bdg. 40.55x (ISBN 3-87429-182-0, Pub. by Koeltz Germany). Lubrecht & Cramer.
--Orchideenflora von Rio Grande do Sul. (Feddes Repertorium: Beiheft 35). 108p. (Ger.). 1980. Repr. of 1925 ed. lib. bdg. 30.70x (ISBN 3-87429-185-5, Pub. by Koeltz Germany). Lubrecht & Cramer.
--Orcidaceae Perrierianae zur Orchideenkunde der Insel Madagascar. (Feddes Repertorium: Beiheft 33). 391p. (Ger.). 1980. Repr. of 1925 ed. lib. bdg. 59.80x (Pub. by Koeltz Germany). Lubrecht & Cramer.
Schlechty, Phillip C. Teaching & Social Behavior: Toward an Organizational Theory of Instruction. 348p. 1976. pap. text ed. 7.95x o.p. (ISBN 0-205-05494-3). Allyn.
Schlegel, Alice, ed. Sexual Stratification: A Cross-Cultural View. LC 77-2742. 1977. 22.50x (ISBN 0-231-04214-0); pap. 10.00x (ISBN 0-231-04215-9). Columbia U Pr.
Schlegel, H. G. Microbial Energy Conversion. LC 76-56894. 1977. pap. text ed. 81.00 (ISBN 0-08-021791-5). Pergamon.
Schlegel, John P. The Deceptive Ash: Bilingualism & Canadian Policy in Africa, 1957-1971. LC 78-64827. 1978. pap. text ed. 15.00 (ISBN 0-8191-0637-2). U Pr of Amer.
Schlegel, Joseph R. The Growth & Decline of American Philosophy. (Illus.). 1980. 33.45 (ISBN 0-89266-225-5). Am Classical Coll Pr.
Schlegel, Richard. Superposition & Interaction: Coherence in Physics. LC 80-11119. (Illus.). 1980. lib. bdg. 22.50x (ISBN 0-226-73841-8). U of Chicago Pr.
Schlegel, Stuart A. Tiruray-English Lexicon. (U. C. Publ. in Linguistics: Vol. 67). 1971. pap. 10.00x (ISBN 0-520-09359-3). U of Cal Pr.
--Tiruray Justice: Traditional Tiruray Law & Morality. LC 72-107660. 1970. 17.50x (ISBN 0-520-01686-6). U of Cal Pr.
Schleicher, August. Die Sprachen Europas in Systematischer Ubersicht. (Amsterdam Classics in Linguistics Ser.: No. 4). 325p. (Ger.). 1980. Repr. text ed. 40.00x (ISBN 90-272-0875-1). Humanities.
Schleicher, E. M. Bone Marrow Morphology & Mechanics of Biopsy. (Illus.). 210p. 1974. 22.75 (ISBN 0-398-02838-9). C C Thomas.
Schleicher, Robert. Building & Displaying Model Aircraft. LC 80-70385. 176p. 1981. 13.95 (ISBN 0-686-69512-7); pap. 8.95 (ISBN 0-686-69513-5). Chilton.
--Building Plastic Models. LC 76-10915. (Orig.). 1976. 4.75 (ISBN 0-89024-527-4). Kalmbach.
--Miniature Dollhouses & Dioramas. LC 80-961. 176p. Date not set. 14.95 (ISBN 0-8019-6905-0); pap. 8.95 (ISBN 0-8019-6906-9). Chilton.
--Tyco Model Railroad Manual. LC 78-14628. (Chilton's Creative Crafts Ser.). Date not set. pap. 7.95 (ISBN 0-8019-6785-6). Chilton.
Schleicher, Robert & Barr, James R. Building & Flying Model Aircraft. LC 79-8312. (Illus.). 192p. 1980. 13.95 (ISBN 0-8019-6903-4); pap. 6.95 (ISBN 0-8019-6904-2). Chilton.
Schleier, Curt. The Team Behind Your Airline Flight. LC 80-27174. (gr. 5-8). 1981. 9.95 (ISBN 0-664-32678-1). Westminster.
Schleiermacher, Friedrich. Brief Outline on the Study of Theology. Tice, Terrence N., tr. LC 66-10301. (Orig.). 1966. pap. 3.95 (ISBN 0-8042-0485-3). John Knox.
--The Life of Jesus. new ed. Verheyden, Jack C. & Keck, Leander E., eds. MacLean, Gilmour, tr. from Ger. LC 72-87056. (Lives of Jesus Ser.). 542p. 1975. pap. 14.95 (ISBN 0-8006-1272-8, 1-1073). Fortress.
--On the Glaubenslehre: Two Letters to Dr. Lucke. Massey, James A., ed. Duke, James & Fiorenza, Francis S., trs. from Ger. LC 80-20717. (American Academy of Religion, Texts & Translations Ser.: No. 3). Orig. Title: Sendschreiben Uber Seine Glaubenslehre an Lucke. 1981. write for info. (ISBN 0-89130-419-3); pap. write for info. (ISBN 0-89130-420-7). Scholars Pr CA.
Schleifer, Abdullah. The Fall of Jerusalem. LC 79-178713. (Illus.). 256p. 1972. 7.50 o.p. (ISBN 0-85345-204-0, CL2040); pap. 3.45 (ISBN 0-85345-249-0, PB2490). Monthly Rev.
Schleifer, Herbert B., jt. auth. see Hill, Marnesba.
Schleifer, Jay. The Chopper Bunch. Mooney, Thomas J., ed. (Pal Paperbacks Ser., Kit A). (Illus., Orig.). (gr. 7-12). 1976. pap. text ed. 1.25 (ISBN 0-8374-3492-0). Xerox Ed Pubns.
--The Danger Angels. Mooney, Thomas J., ed. (Pal Paperbacks, Pal Skills Ser.). (Illus., Orig.). (gr. 7-12). 1978. pap. text ed. 1.25 (ISBN 0-8374-6706-3). Xerox Ed Pubns.
--Going Wild. Mooney, Thomas J., ed. (Beginning Pal Paperbacks Ser.). (Illus., Orig.). (gr. 7-12). 1977. pap. text ed. 1.25 (ISBN 0-8374-3454-8). Xerox Ed Pubns.
--The Vette (Corvette) McCarthy, Patricia, ed. (Pal Paperbacks Kit A Ser.). (Illus., Orig.). (gr. 7-12). 1974. pap. text ed. 1.25 (ISBN 0-8374-3470-X). Xerox Ed Pubns.
--Voice on the CB. Mooney, Thomas J., ed. (Beginning Pal Paperbacks Ser.). (Illus., Orig.). (gr. 7-12). 1977. pap. text ed. 1.25 (ISBN 0-8374-3463-7). Xerox Ed Pubns.
Schleifer, Ronald, ed. The Genres of the Irish Literary Revival. 190p. 1980. 16.95 (ISBN 0-937664-53-7). Pilgrim Bks OK.
Schleiffer, Hedwig. Narcotic Plants of the Old World, Used in Rituals & Everyday Life: An Anthology of Texts from Ancient Times to the Present. (Illus., Orig.). 1979. lib. bdg. 12.50x (ISBN 0-934454-01-9); pap. text ed. 7.95x (ISBN 0-934454-00-0). Lubrecht & Cramer.
--Sacred Narcotic Plants of the New World Indians: An Anthology of Texts from the 16th Century to Date. (Orig.). 1974. pap. 6.50 o.s.i. (ISBN 0-02-851780-6). Hafner.

Schlein, Miriam. Giraffe: The Silent Giant. LC 76-7922. (Illus.). 64p. (gr. 2-5). 1976. 6.95 (ISBN 0-590-07421-0, Four Winds). Schol Bk Serv.
--I Hate It. Rubin, Caroline, ed. LC 78-1744. (Self-Starter Bks.). (Illus.). (ps-2). 1978. 6.50 (ISBN 0-8075-3505-2). A Whitman.
--I, Tut: The Boy Who Became Pharaoh. LC 78-15603. (Illus.). 48p. 1979. 8.95 (ISBN 0-590-07571-3, Four Winds). Schol Bk Serv.
--Juju Sheep & the Python's Moonstone. LC 72-83686. (Folklore Ser.). (Illus.). 128p. (gr. 8-12). 1973. 5.95g o.p. (ISBN 0-8075-4050-1). A Whitman.
--Lucky Porcupine! LC 79-19673. (Illus.). 48p. (gr. 2-6). 1980. 7.95 (ISBN 0-590-07543-8, Four Winds). Schol Bk Serv.
--On the Track of the Mystery Animal: The Story of the Discovery of the Okapi. LC 78-5387. (Illus.). 64p. (gr. 3-7). 1978. 7.95 (ISBN 0-590-07488-1, Four Winds). Schol Bk Serv.
--Way Mothers Are. LC 63-13332. (Concept Bks.). (Illus.). (ps-2). 1963. 6.95g (ISBN 0-8075-8692-7). A Whitman.
--What's Wrong with Being a Skunk? LC 73-88078. (Illus.). 40p. (gr. k-3). 1974. 6.95 (ISBN 0-590-07305-2, Four Winds). Schol Bk Serv.
Schleiner, Winfried. Imagery of John Donne's Sermons. LC 70-91655. 254p. 1970. 10.00x (ISBN 0-87057-116-8, Pub. by Brown U Pr). Univ Pr of New England.
Schleirmacher, Friedrich. On Religion: Speeches to Its Cultured Despisers. 1959. 9.00 (ISBN 0-8446-2878-6). Peter Smith.
Schlemmer, Oskar. The Letters & Diaries of Oskar Schlemmer. Schlemmer, Tut, ed. Winston, Krishna, tr. from Ger. LC 77-184362. Orig. Title: Briefe und Tagebucher. (Illus.). 368p. 1972. 30.00x (ISBN 0-8195-4047-1, Pub. by Wesleyan U Pr). Columbia U Pr.
Schlemmer, Tut, ed. see Schlemmer, Oskar.
Schlenker, B. R. An Introduction to Materials Science: S. I. Edition. LC 73-16682. 364p. 1974. 22.95 (ISBN 0-471-76177-X). Wiley.
Schlenker, Barry R. Impression Management: The Self-Concept, Social Identity, & Interpersonal Relations. LC 80-15047. 250p. 1980. text ed. 14.95 (ISBN 0-8185-0398-X). Brooks-Cole.
Schlepp, Wayne. San-Ch'u: Its Technique & Imagery. 1970. 15.00x (ISBN 0-299-05540-X). U of Wis Pr.
Schlereth, Hewitt. Commonplace Coastal Navigation. (Illus.). 1981. 18.95 (ISBN 0-393-03224-8). Norton.
--Commonsense Sailboat Buying. LC 76-42443. 1977. 9.95 o.p. (ISBN 0-8092-8205-4). Contemp Bks.
Schlereth, Thomas J. Artifacts & the American Past: Techniques for the Teaching Historian. 300p. 1981. pap. 13.95 (ISBN 0-910050-47-3). AASLH.
--The University of Notre Dame: A Portrait of Its History & Campus. LC 74-27890. 1976. text ed. 25.00 o.p. (ISBN 0-268-01906-1); pap. text ed. 7.95x (ISBN 0-268-01905-3). U of Notre Dame Pr.
Schlerman, Gene. Schlerman in the Kitchen. 240p. 1980. 12.95 (ISBN 0-914842-56-0). Madrona Pubs.
Schlesinger, Arthur M. In Retrospect: The History of a Historian. LC 63-15318. 1963. 4.50 o.p. (ISBN 0-15-144490-0). HarBraceJ.
--Prelude to Independence: The Newspaper War on Britain 1764-1776. LC 80-22830. 340p. 1980. pap. text ed. 8.95x (ISBN 0-930350-13-8). NE U Pr.
Schlesinger, Arthur M., Jr. & Israel, F. L. History of American Presidential Elections, 4 vols. 1971. 150.00 o.p. (ISBN 0-07-079786-2, P&RB). McGraw.
Schlesinger, Arthur M., Jr., ed. American Statesmen, 41 vols. 1981. Set. pap. 180.00 (ISBN 0-87754-199-X). Chelsea Hse.
--Dynamics of World Power: A Documentary History of U. S. Foreign Policy, 1945-73. LC 78-150208. 5075p. 1981. pap. 80.00 (ISBN 0-87754-259-7). Chelsea Hse.
--History of U. S. Political Parties, 4 vols. LC 72-8682. 3600p. 1981. Repr. of 1973 ed. pap. 75.00 (ISBN 0-87754-134-5). Chelsea Hse.
Schlesinger, Arthur M., Jr. & Bruns, Roger, eds. Congress Investigates: A Documented History, 1792-1974, 5 vols. LC 74-34005. 1981. pap. 85.00 (ISBN 0-87754-132-9). Chelsea Hse.
Schlesinger, Arthur M., Jr. & Israel, Fred L., eds. The Coming to Power: Critical Presidential Elections in American History. LC 70-39588. 570p. 1981. pap. 8.95 (ISBN 0-87754-217-1). Chelsea Hse.
--History of American Presidential Elections, 5 vols. 4000p. 1981. pap. write for info. (ISBN 0-87754-124-8). Chelsea Hse.
Schlesinger, Benjamin. Sexual Behaviour in Canada: Patterns & Problems. 1977. pap. 6.95 (ISBN 0-8020-6314-4). U of Toronto Pr.
Schlesinger, G. Testing Machine Tools: For the Use of Machine Tool Makers, Users Inspectors & Plant Engineers. 8th ed. 1977. text ed. 18.00 (ISBN 0-08-021685-4). Pergamon.
Schlesinger, I. M. Steps to Language. 448p. 1981. text ed. 24.95 (ISBN 0-89859-045-0). L Erlbaum Assocs.
Schlesinger, Kurt, et al. Psychology: A Dynamic Science. 740p. 1976. text ed. 15.95x (ISBN 0-697-06620-7); study guide 8.95x (ISBN 0-697-06621-5); instructor's manual 3.00 (ISBN 0-686-67227-5); test item file 10.00x (ISBN 0-697-06660-6). Wm C Brown.
Schlesinger, Philip. Putting "Reality" Together: BBC News. LC 79-89074. (Communication & Society: Vol. 9). (Illus.). 1979. 22.00x (ISBN 0-8039-1357-5); pap. 12.50x (ISBN 0-8039-1358-3). Sage.
Schlesinger, R. Walter, ed. The Togaviruses. 1980. 58.00 (ISBN 0-12-625380-3). Acad Pr.
Schlesinger, Rudolph B. Comparative Law Cases-Text-Materials. 4th ed. LC 80-13375. (University Casebook Ser.). 894p. 1980. text ed. write for info. (ISBN 0-88277-007-1). Foundation Pr.
Schlessinger, David, ed. Microbiology Nineteen Eighty. (Illus.). 1980. text ed. 22.00 (ISBN 0-914826-23-9). Am Soc Microbio.
--Microbiology, Nineteen Eighty-One. (Illus.). 1981. 22.00 (ISBN 0-914826-31-X). Am Soc Microbio.
--Microbiology Nineteen Seventy-Nine. (Illus.). 1979. text ed. 22.00 (ISBN 0-914826-20-4). Am Soc Microbio.
--Microbiology 1974. LC 74-33538. (Annual Microbiology Ser.). 1975. 22.00 (ISBN 0-914826-02-6). Am Soc Microbio.
--Microbiology 1975. LC 74-33538. (Annual Microbiology Ser.). 1975. 22.00 (ISBN 0-914826-05-0). Am Soc Microbio.
--Microbiology 1976. LC 74-33538. (Annual Microbiology Ser.). 1976. 22.00 (ISBN 0-914826-11-5). Am Soc Microbio.
--Microbiology 1977. LC 74-33538. (Annual Microbiology Ser.). 1977. 22.00 (ISBN 0-914826-13-1). Am Soc Microbio.
--Microbiology 1978. LC 74-33538. (Illus.). 1978. text ed. 22.00 (ISBN 0-914826-15-8). Am Soc Microbio.
Schlichting, Hermann T. & Truckenbrodt, Erich A. Aerodynamics of the Airplane. (Illus.). 1979. text ed. 54.50 (ISBN 0-07-055341-6). McGraw.
Schlichting, Marvin. Basic Algebra. 400p. 1980. text ed. 14.95 (ISBN 0-442-25765-1); instr's. manual 2.95 (ISBN 0-442-25767-8). Van Nos Reinhold.
--Intermediate Algebra. Date not set. text ed. price not set (ISBN 0-442-21214-3). D Van Nostrand.
Schlieper, Carl, ed. Research Methods in Marine Biology. LC 72-6089. (Biology Ser.). (Illus.). 300p. 1972. 16.00 (ISBN 0-295-95234-2). U of Wash Pr.
Schliephake, Konrad. Oil & Regional Development: Examples from Algeria & Tunisia. LC 76-24367. (Praeger Special Studies). 1977. text ed. 25.95 (ISBN 0-275-23910-1). Praeger.
Schlierf, G. Langzeitstudie zum Ernaehrungs- und Gesundheitszustand einer Repraesentativen Stichprobe Heidelberger Frauen und Maenner. (Beitraege zu Infusionstherapie und Klinische Ernaehrung: Band 7). viii, 250p. 1981. pap. 18.00 (ISBN 3-8055-2384-X). S Karger.
Schlinger, Evert L., jt. auth. see Cole, Frank R.
Schlink, Basilea. Father of Comfort. 1971. pap. 2.95 (ISBN 0-87123-156-5, 200156). Bethany Fell.
--For Jerusalem's Sake I Will Not Rest. 1.45 (ISBN 0-551-00741-9). Evang Sisterhood Mary.
--More Precious Than Gold. 1978. pap. 3.95 (ISBN 0-88419-178-8). Creation Hse.
--My All for Him. 1971. pap. 2.95 (ISBN 0-87123-370-3, 200370). Bethany Fell.
--Praying Our Way Through Life. 1970. pap. 0.79 (ISBN 0-87123-455-6, 260455). Bethany Fell.
--Ruled by the Spirit. 1970. pap. 1.95 (ISBN 0-87123-483-1, 200483). Bethany Fell.
--Sinai- a Mountain Speaks. 1.25 o.p. (ISBN 0-686-12674-2). Evang Sisterhood Mary.
--Those Who Love Him. 96p. 1981. pap. 2.50 (ISBN 0-87123-609-5, 210609). Bethany Fell.
--You Will Never Be the Same. 192p. 1972. pap. 2.95 (ISBN 0-87123-661-3, 200661). Bethany Fell.
Schlink, M. Basilea. The Blessings of Illness. LC 76-51103. 1977. pap. 1.95 (ISBN 0-88419-023-4). Creation Hse.
--I Found the Key to the Heart of God. LC 75-23920. 416p. 1975. pap. 3.95 (ISBN 0-87123-239-1, 200239). Bethany Fell.
--A Matter of Life & Death. LC 73-10827. 96p. 1973. pap. 1.25 (ISBN 0-87123-359-2, 200359). Bethany Fell.
--Realities. 128p. 1972. pap. 2.50 (ISBN 0-310-32602-8). Zondervan.
--Repentance - the Joy-Filled Life. pap. 1.95 (ISBN 0-310-32612-5). Zondervan.
Schlissel, Lillian, jt. ed. see Reichart, Walter A.
Schlitt, Dorothy M., et al. Life: A Question of Survival. (Illus., Orig.). (gr. 7-11). 1972. pap. text ed. 6.64x (ISBN 0-913688-03-7); teacher's guide 5.32x (ISBN 0-913688-04-5). Pawnee Pub.
Schlitt, W. J., ed. Leaching & Recovering Copper from As-Mined Materials. LC 79-57347. (Illus.). 124p. 1980. pap. 15.00x (ISBN 0-89520-272-7). Soc Mining Eng.
Schlitt, W. J. & Shock, D. A., eds. In Situ Uranium Mining & Ground Water Restoration. LC 79-52217. (Illus.). 137p. 1979. pap. 15.00x (ISBN 0-89520-267-0). Soc Mining Eng.
Schloat, G. Warren, Jr. Adventures of a Letter. (Illus.). 48p. (gr. 3-7). 1949. reinforced bdg. 5.95 o.p. (ISBN 0-684-13479-9, ScribJ). Scribner.
Schlobin, Roger C., ed. see Brizzi, Mary T.
Schlobin, Roger C., ed. see Diskin, Lana.
Schlobin, Roger C., ed. see Gordon, Joan.
Schlobin, Roger C., ed. see Miller, David M.
Schlobin, Roger C., ed. see Wendell, Carolyn.
Schloss, Ezekiel. Ancient Chinese Ceramic Sculpture: From Han Through T'ang, 2 vols. 1977. Set. 300.00 (ISBN 0-686-25749-9). Castle Pub Co.
Schloss, Malcolm & Purdom, Charles. Three Incredible Weeks with Meher Baba. Frederick, Filis, ed. (Illus.). 1979. pap. 5.95 (ISBN 0-913078-36-0). Sheriar Pr.
Schlossberg, Allan. Adult Tooth Movement in General Dentistry. LC 74-4588. (Illus.). 244p. 1975. text ed. 22.50 o.p. (ISBN 0-7216-7957-9). Saunders.
Schlossberg, Edwin & Brockman, John. Pocket Calculator Game Book, No. 2. LC 77-7054. (Illus.). 1977. 6.95 (ISBN 0-688-03234-6); pap. 3.95 (ISBN 0-688-08234-3). Morrow.
Schlossberg, Julian & Yellen, Barry, eds. Inside the Movie Business. LC 79-93082. 224p. Date not set. cancelled (ISBN 0-8069-0188-8); lib. bdg. cancelled (ISBN 0-8069-0189-6). Sterling.
Schlott, W., jt. ed. see Birau, N.
Schlotter, Lowanna, ed. Nursing & the Nephrology Patient: A Symposium on Current Trends & Issues. 1973. spiral bdg. 9.50 (ISBN 0-87488-376-8). Med Exam.
Schlotterback, Thomas. Five-Thousand Years of Art: An Exhibition from the Collections of the Metropolitan Museum of Art. LC 76-50228. (Whatcom Museum Ser.). (Illus.). 1976. pap. 10.00 (ISBN 0-295-95575-9). U of Wash Pr.
Schlottmen, Alan M. Environmental Regulation & the Allocation of Coal: A Regional Analysis. LC 76-56841. (Special Studies). 1977. text ed. 21.95 (ISBN 0-275-24090-8). Praeger.
Schluchter, Wolfgang. Rationalismus der Weltbeherrschung. (Suhrkamp Taschenbuecher Wissenschaft). 336p. pap. text ed. 9.10 (ISBN 3-518-07922-0, Pub. by Insel Verlag Germany). Suhrkamp.
--Verhalten, Handeln und System. (Suhrkamp Taschenbuecher Wissenschaft: Vol. 310). 176p. (Orig.). 1980. pap. text ed. 6.50 (ISBN 3-518-07910-7, Pub. by Insel Verlag Germany). Suhrkamp.
Schluchter, Wolfgang, jt. auth. see Roth, Guenther.
Schlueter, June. Metafictional Characters in Modern Drama. LC 79-4207. 1979. 17.50x (ISBN 0-231-04752-5). Columbia U Pr.
Schlumberger, Jean. Madeleine & Andre Gide. Akeroyd, Richard H., tr. (Illus.) 1980. 12.00 (ISBN 0-916620-45-X). Portals Pr.
Schlunegger, U. P. Advanced Mass Spectrometry: Applications in Organic & Analytical Chemistry. (Illus.). 150p. 1980. 32.00 (ISBN 0-08-023842-4). Pergamon.
Schmaehl, Dietrich. Risk Assessment of N-Nitroso Compounds for Human Health: Oncology. (Oncology Journal: Vol. 37). (Illus.). 120p. 1980. pap. 36.75 (ISBN 3-8055-1137-X). S Karger.
Schmal, Henk, ed. Patterns of European Urbanisation Since 1500. 400p. 1981. 31.00x (ISBN 0-7099-0365-0, Pub. by Croom Helm LTD England). Biblio Dist.
Schmalenbach, Paul. German Raiders: A History of Auxiliary Cruisers of the German Navy 1895-1945. LC 78-71801. (Illus.). 144p. 1980. 15.95 (ISBN 0-87021-824-7). Naval Inst Pr.
Schmalenbach, Werner. Leger. LC 75-5520. (Library of Great Painters). (Illus.). 1976. 35.00 (ISBN 0-8109-0252-4). Abrams.
Schmalenberg, Claudia, jt. auth. see Kramer, Marlene.
Schmalensee, Richard. The Control of Natural Monopolies. LC 78-6061. 1979. 18.95 (ISBN 0-669-02322-1). Lexington Bks.
Schmalz, Larry C. & Sippl, Charles J. Computer Glossary for Students & Teachers. (Apollo Eds.). pap. 3.25 o.p. (ISBN 0-8152-0411-6, TYC-T). T Y Crowell.
Schmalzried, H. Solid State Reactions. rev. ed. (Monographs in Modern Chemistry: Vol. 12). Date not set. price not set. Verlag Chemie.
Schmandt, Henry J., jt. ed. see Bloomberg, Warner, Jr.
Schmandt, Jurgen, et al, eds. Nutrition Policy in Transition. LC 79-9628. (Illus.). 320p. 1980. 22.95x (ISBN 0-669-03596-3). Lexington Bks.
Schmeckebier, Laurence. A New Handbook of Italian Renaissance Painting. rev. ed. LC 79-50409. 1980. lib. bdg. 40.00 (ISBN 0-87817-253-X). Hacker.
Schmeckebier, Laurence E. The Art of A. Henry Nordhausen. LC 80-20077. (Illus.). 168p. 1980. 45.00 (ISBN 0-914016-73-3). Phoenix Pub.
Schmeckel, Carl D. The Piano-Owner's Guide. LC 74-7362. (Illus.). 120p. 1974. 6.95 o.p. (ISBN 0-684-13869-7, ScribT); pap. 3.95 (ISBN 0-684-13872-7, SL548, ScribT). Scribner.
Schmeid, Wieland. Fantasy Art. (Alpine Fine Arts Collection). (Illus.). 475p. 1981. 65.00 (ISBN 0-686-64751-3, Pub by Alpine Fine Arts). Hippocrene Bks.
Schmeidler, Gertrude. ESP in Relation to Rorschach Test Evaluation. LC 60-2760. (Parapsychological Monograph No. 2). 1960. pap. 2.00 (ISBN 0-912328-04-5). Parapsych Foun.
Schmeidler, Gertrude R., ed. Parapsychology: Its Relation to Physics, Biology, Psychology, & Psychiatry. LC 76-916. 291p. 1976. 13.50 (ISBN 0-8108-0909-5). Scarecrow.
Schmeling, Gareth L. Chariton. (World Authors Ser.: Greece: No. 295). 1974. lib. bdg. 10.95 (ISBN 0-8057-2207-6). Twayne.
Schmeller, Kurt R., ed. see Hall & Davis.
Schmelter, Harvey B. & Aslanian, Carol B., eds. Adult Access to Education & New Careers: A Handbook for Action. 141p. (Orig.). 1980. pap. 9.75 (ISBN 0-87447-125-7, 001257). College Bd.
Schmelzel, Carol. Church School Teaching Can Be Fun! Proven Ways to Make Your Class More Interesting. 1979. pap. 6.95 (ISBN 0-8164-2190-0); wkbk. avail. (ISBN 0-685-59465-3). Crossroad NY.
Schmemann, Alexander. Introduction to Liturgical Theology. LC 66-69197. 170p. 1966. pap. 5.95 (ISBN 0-913836-18-4). St Vladimirs.
--Of Water & the Spirit: A Liturgical Study of Baptism. LC 74-30061. 170p. 1974. pap. 4.95 (ISBN 0-913836-10-9). St Vladimirs.
Schmenner, Roger W. Production - Operations Management. 480p. 1980. text ed. 17.95 (ISBN 0-574-19500-9, 13-2500); instr's. guide avail. (ISBN 0-574-19501-7, 13-2501). SRA.
Schmid, A. Allan. Property, Power & Public Choice: An Inquiry into Law & Economics. LC 78-5930. (Praeger Special Studies). 1978. 24.95 (ISBN 0-03-042956-0). Praeger.
Schmid, Andrea B., jt. auth. see Drury, Blanche J.
Schmid, Calvin F. & Schmid, Stanton E. Handbook of Graphic Presentation. 2nd ed. LC 78-13689. 1979. 16.50 (ISBN 0-471-04724-4, Pub. by Wiley-Interscience). Wiley.
Schmid, Carol L. Conflict & Consensus in Switzerland. 1981. 18.50x (ISBN 0-520-04079-1). U of Cal Pr.
Schmid, E. W. & Ziegelmann, H. The Quantum Mechanical Three-Body Problem. 222p. 1974. text ed. 40.00 (ISBN 0-08-018240-2). Pergamon.
Schmid, Hermann. Decimal Computation. LC 74-10798. 304p. 1974. 27.50 o.p. (ISBN 0-471-76180-X, Pub. by Wiley-Interscience). Wiley.
--Decimal Computation. 280p. 1981. Repr. of 1974 ed. lib. bdg. write for info. (ISBN 0-89874-318-4). Krieger.
Schmid, Stanton E., jt. auth. see Schmid, Calvin F.
Schmid-Burleson, Bonny. The Technique of Macrame. LC 73-17335. (Illus.). 1974. 9.50 o.p. (ISBN 0-8231-7034-9). Branford.
Schmidek, Henry H. Pineal Tumors. LC 77-78560. 152p. 1977. 36.25 (ISBN 0-89352-007-1). Masson Pub.
Schmidgall, Gary. Shakespeare & the Courtly Aesthetic. (Illus.). 344p. 1981. 22.50x (ISBN 0-520-04130-5). U of Cal Pr.
Schmidgall-Tellings, A. Ed. & Stevens, Alan. Contemporary Indonesian-English Dictionary. LC 80-20994. 460p. 1981. 24.95x (ISBN 0-8214-0424-5); pap. 11.95 (ISBN 0-8214-0435-0). Ohio U Pr.
Schmidhauser, John & Berg, Larry. The Supreme Court & Congress: Conflict & Interaction, 1945-1968. LC 77-160068. 1972. pap. text ed. 4.50 o.s.i. (ISBN 0-02-927900-3). Free Pr.
Schmidhauser, John R. & Totten, George O., III, eds. The Whaling Issue in U.S.-Japan Relations. 1978. lib. bdg. 26.50x (ISBN 0-89158-176-6). Westview.
Schmidl, Fritz. On Applied Psychoanalysis. LC 79-92435. 1981. 15.00 (ISBN 0-8022-2364-8). Philos Lib.
Schmidt. Exploring Religion. 1980. text ed. 12.95 (ISBN 0-87872-244-0). Duxbury Pr.
Schmidt, jt. auth. see Andraeson, Tjalve.

Schmidt, Alexander. Shakespeare Lexicon & Quotation Dictionary, 2 vols. 8.95 ea. Vol. 1 (ISBN 0-486-22726-X). Vol. 2 (ISBN 0-486-22727-8). Dover.

Schmidt, Alvin J. Fraternal Organizations. LC 79-6187. (Greenwood Encyclopedia of American Institutions). xxxiii, 410p. 1980. lib. bdg. 35.00 (ISBN 0-313-21436-0, SFR/). Greenwood.

Schmidt, Arno. The Egghead Republic. LC 80-670270. 164p. 1980. 12.00 (ISBN 0-7145-2591-X, Pub. by M. Boyars). Merrimack Bk Serv.

--Evening Edged in Gold. LC 79-3373. (Helen & Kurt Wolff Bk.). 224p. 1980. 74.95 (ISBN 0-15-129376-7). HarBraceJ.

Schmidt, Arno B. The Banquet Book. 256p. 1980. 19.95 (ISBN 0-8436-2147-8). CBI Pub.

--Notes from the Chef's Desk. LC 77-3005. 1977. 13.95 o.p. (ISBN 0-8436-2158-3). CBI Pub.

Schmidt, B. GPSS Fortran. (Computing Ser.). 544p. 1981. write for info. (ISBN 0-471-27881-5, Pub. by Wiley-Interscience). Wiley.

Schmidt, Benno C., Jr. Freedom of the Press Vs. Public Access. LC 75-19818. (Special Studies). 1976. text ed. 26.95 (ISBN 0-275-01620-X); pap. text ed. 11.95 (ISBN 0-275-89430-4). Praeger.

Schmidt, Carl T. American Farmers in the World Crisis. LC 79-1591. 1981. Repr. of 1941 ed. 23.50 (ISBN 0-88355-896-3). Hyperion Conn.

Schmidt, Cynthia E. The Story of Colorado, 6 units. Incl. Unit 1. Colorado - Land & Animals (ISBN 0-913688-50-9); Unit 2. Prehistoric People (ISBN 0-913688-51-7); Unit 3. Tribes & Trailblazers (ISBN 0-913688-52-5); Unit 4. Gold Fever (ISBN 0-913688-53-3); Unit 5. Early Statehood (ISBN 0-913688-54-1); Unit 6. Twentieth Century Colorado (ISBN 0-913688-55-X). (Illus.). Set. 350.00 (ISBN 0-913688-56-8); 65.00 ea.; each set contains a tchr's manual, 2 film strips, 2 cassette tapes, 10 spirit duplications masters, 8 learning center cards, 2 color posters (ISBN 0-685-33322-1). Pawnee Pub.

Schmidt, Darlene. Scientific Approach to Women's Gymnastics. (Brighton Ser. in Health & Physical Education). 1980. text ed. 12.95x (ISBN 0-89832-011-9). Brighton Pub Co.

Schmidt, Donald H., jt. auth. see Pollock, Michael L.

Schmidt, Elizabeth. Decoding Corporate Camouflage: U. S. Business Support for Apartheid. 127p. 1980. pap. 4.95 (ISBN 0-89758-022-2). Inst Policy Stud.

Schmidt, Emerson P. Union Power & the Public Interest. LC 72-95239. (Illus.). 204p. 1973. 10.00x o.p. (ISBN 0-8402-5004-5). Nash Pub.

--Union Power & the Public Interest. LC 72-95239. (Principles of Freedom Ser.). 1976. pap. 6.95x (ISBN 0-916054-88-8, Caroline Hse Inc). Green Hill.

Schmidt, Frances & Weiner, Harold M., eds. Public Relations in Health & Welfare. LC 66-19480. 1966. 20.00x (ISBN 0-231-02911-X). Columbia U Pr.

Schmidt, Frank W. & Willmott, A. John. Thermal Energy Storage & Regeneration. (Illus.). 352p. 1981. 35.50 (ISBN 0-07-055346-7). McGraw.

Schmidt, Garfield C. Basic Linear Algebra with Applications. LC 79-16225. (Applied Mathematics Ser.). 536p. 1980. text ed. 34.50 (ISBN 0-89874-000-2). Krieger.

Schmidt, Gerald D. & Roberts, Larry S. Foundations of Parasitology. 2nd ed. (Illus.). 672p. 1981. pap. text ed. 24.95 (ISBN 0-8016-4344-9). Mosby.

--Foundations of Parasitology. LC 76-30335. (Illus.). 1977. text ed. 23.50 o.p. (ISBN 0-8016-4339-2); pap. 19.95 o.p. (ISBN 0-8016-4345-7). Mosby.

Schmidt, Gerd. Die Struktur Des Dramas Bei T. S. Eliot. (Salzburg Studies in English Literature, Poetic Drama & Poetic Theory Ser.: No. 38). 1978. pap. text ed. 25.00x (ISBN 0-391-01516-8). Humanities.

Schmidt, Glen H. & Van Vleck, L. Dale. Principles of Dairy Science. LC 73-2860. (Animal Science Ser.). (Illus.). 1974. text ed. 25.95x (ISBN 0-7167-0830-2). W H Freeman.

Schmidt, H. & Morike, K. Radiomographic Anatomic Atlas. (Illus.). 1971. 27.50 o.s.i. (ISBN 0-02-851830-6). Hafner.

Schmidt, Hans R., Jr. The United States Occupation of Haiti, 1915-1934. 1971. 22.00 (ISBN 0-8135-0690-5). Rutgers U Pr.

Schmidt, Herman. Liturgy, Self-Expression of the Church. LC 77-168650. (Concilium Ser.: Religion in the Seventies: Vol. 72). 1972. pap. 4.95 (ISBN 0-8164-2528-0). Crossroad NY.

Schmidt, Herman & Power, David. Liturgy & Cultural Religious Tradition. (Concilium Ser.: Vol. 102). 1977. pap. 4.95 (ISBN 0-8164-2146-3). Crossroad NY.

Schmidt, Herman, ed. Liturgy in Transition. LC 70-129761. (Concilium Ser.: Religion in the Seventies: Vol. 62). 1971. pap. 4.95 (ISBN 0-8164-2518-3). Crossroad NY.

--Prayer & Community. (Concilium Ser.: Religion in the Seventies: Vol. 52). pap. 4.95 (ISBN 0-8164-2508-6). Crossroad NY.

Schmidt, Herman & Power, David, eds. The Liturgical Experience of Faith. (Concilium Ser.: Religion in the Seventies: Vol. 82). 156p. 1973. pap. 4.95 (ISBN 0-8164-2538-8). Crossroad NY.

--Politics & Liturgy. LC 73-17912. (Concilium Ser.: Religion in the Seventies: Vol. 92). 1974. pap. 4.95 (ISBN 0-8164-2576-0). Crossroad NY.

Schmidt, Hugo, ed. see Von Hofmannsthal, Hugo.

Schmidt, I., et al, eds. Optometry Examination Review Book, Vol. 1. 2nd ed. 1978. spiral bdg. 12.00 o.s.i. (ISBN 0-87488-469-1). Med Exam.

Schmidt, J. Dictionnaire mythologie grecque et romaine. (Illus., Fr.). pap. 8.50 (ISBN 2-03-075408-0, 3728). Larousse.

Schmidt, J. D. Yang Wan-Li. LC 76-18839. (World Authors Ser: No. 413). 1976. lib. bdg. 12.50 (ISBN 0-8057-6255-8). Twayne.

Schmidt, J. E. Analyzer of Medical-Biological Words: A Clarifying Dissection of Medical Terminology, Showing How It Works, for Medics, Paramedics, Students, & Visitors from Foreign Countries. 224p. 1973. 10.75 (ISBN 0-398-02682-3). C C Thomas.

--English Idioms & Americanisms for Foreign Students, Professionals & Physicians. 544p. 1972. text ed. 26.50 (ISBN 0-398-02400-6). C C Thomas.

--English Word Power for Physicians & Other Professionals: A Vigorous & Cultured Vocabulary. 240p. 1971. 19.75 (ISBN 0-398-01666-6). C C Thomas.

--Index of Paramedical Vocabulary. (Illus.). 324p. 1974. pap. 10.75 (ISBN 0-398-02833-8). C C Thomas.

--Narcotics: Lingo & Lore. 216p. 1959. 7.50 (ISBN 0-398-01671-2). C C Thomas.

--Paramedical Dictionary: A Practical Dictionary for the Semi-Medical & Ancillary Medical Professions. 1974. 14.25 (ISBN 0-398-01672-0); pap. 10.75 (ISBN 0-398-02902-4). C C Thomas.

--Police Medical Dictionary. 256p. 1968. 19.75 (ISBN 0-398-01673-9). C C Thomas.

--Practical Nurses' Medical Dictionary: A Cyclopedic Medical Dictionary for Practical Nurses, Vocational Nurses, & Nurses' Aides. 300p. 1968. 11.75 (ISBN 0-398-01675-5). C C Thomas.

--Structural Units of Medical & Biological Terms: A Convenient Guide, in English, to the Roots, Stems, Prefixes, Suffixes, & Other Combining Forms Which Are the Building Blocks of Medical & Related Scientific Words. 180p. 1969. text ed. 11.75 (ISBN 0-398-01676-3). C C Thomas.

--Visual Aids for Paramedical Vocabulary. (Illus.). 196p. 1973. 10.75 (ISBN 0-398-02609-2). C C Thomas.

Schmidt, J. William. Mathematical Foundations for Management Science & Systems Analysis. (Operations Research & Industrial Engineering Ser.). 1974. text ed. 22.95 (ISBN 0-12-627050-3). Acad Pr.

Schmidt, J. William & Davis, Robert P. Foundation of Analysis in Operations Research. LC 80-987. (Operations Research & Industrial Engineering Ser.). 1981. 27.00 (ISBN 0-12-626850-9). Acad Pr.

Schmidt, Janet. Demystifying Parole. LC 76-48375. (Illus.). 1977. 21.95 (ISBN 0-669-01145-2). Lexington Bks.

Schmidt, Jay, jt. auth. see Neimark, Paul G.

Schmidt, Jay H. & Neimark, Paul. Good-Bye Loneliness. LC 77-16766. (Illus.). 192p. 1981. pap. 6.95 (ISBN 0-8128-6095-0). Stein & Day.

Schmidt, John A. The Gardens of Lucullus. 1980. 10.95 (ISBN 0-533-04588-6). Vantage.

Schmidt, John C. The Life & Works of John Knowles Paine. Buelow, George, ed. (Studies in Musicology). 597p. 1981. 49.95 (ISBN 0-8357-1126-9, Pub. by UMI Res Pr). Univ Microfilms.

Schmidt, Joseph D., jt. auth. see Buchsbaum, Herbert J.

Schmidt, K. O. The Message of the Grail. Muller, Leone, tr. from Ger. LC 75-1994. 1975. 4.95 o.p. (ISBN 0-87707-153-5); text ed. 4.95 o.p. (ISBN 0-685-53509-6). CSA Pr.

Schmidt, Lewis A. The Engine-Ear: Fifty Years of Engineering. (Illus.). 1977. 6.95 o.p. (ISBN 0-533-02937-6). Vantage.

Schmidt, Lewis D., jt. auth. see Prince, John R.

Schmidt, M., et al. The Chemistry of Sulphur, Selenium, Tellurium & Polonium. (Pergamon Texts in Inorganic Chemistry: Vol. 15). 214p. 1975. text ed. 32.00 (ISBN 0-08-018856-7); pap. text ed. 17.50 (ISBN 0-08-018855-9). Pergamon.

Schmidt, Margaret Fox, jt. auth. see Norman, James.

Schmidt, Marjorie G. Growing California Native Plants. 400p. 1980. 15.95 (ISBN 0-520-03761-8). U of Cal Pr.

Schmidt, Martin. John Wesley: A Theological Biography, Vol. 2, Pt. 1. Goldhawk, Norman, tr. from Ger. 312p. 1973. 12.95 o.p. (ISBN 0-687-20481-X). Abingdon.

Schmidt, Michael. A Reader's Guide to Fifty British Poets: 1300-1900. (A Reader's Guide Ser.). 430p. 1980. 16.50x (ISBN 0-389-20137-5). B&N.

--A Reader's Guide to Fifty Modern British Poets. LC 79-53438. (Reader's Guide Ser.). 1979. 18.50x (ISBN 0-06-496110-9). B&N.

Schmidt, Michael, ed. Ten English Poets: An Anthology. (Poetry Ser.). 1979. pap. 5.95 o.s.i. (ISBN 0-85635-167-9, Pub. by Carcanet New Pr England). Persea Bks.

Schmidt, Mike & Walder, Barbara. Always on the Offense. LC 80-69764. 1981. 12.95 (ISBN 0-689-11165-7). Atheneum.

Schmidt, Nancy J. Children's Fiction About Africa in English. LC 80-18491. 300p. 1981. 35.00 (ISBN 0-914970-63-1). Conch Mag.

Schmidt, Paul, ed. Meyerhold at Work. Levin, Ilya & McGee, Vern, trs. from Rus. LC 80-15265. (Slavic Ser.: No. 2). 263p. Date not set. text ed. 19.95x (ISBN 0-292-75058-7). U of Tex Pr.

--Meyerhold at Work, Vol2. (University of Texas Press Slavic Ser: Vol. 2). 340p. Date not set. 19.95x (ISBN 0-292-75058-7). U of Tex Pr.

Schmidt, Paul, tr. from Fr. Arthur Rimbaud: Complete Works. LC 74-1853. 336p. 1975. 15.00 o.s.i. (ISBN 0-06-013834-3, HarpT). Har-Row.

Schmidt, Paul F. Fuel Oil Manual. 3rd ed. LC 69-10507. (Illus.). 1969. 21.00 (ISBN 0-8311-3014-8). Indus Pr.

--Perception & Cosmology in Whitehead's Philosophy. 1967. 13.00 (ISBN 0-8135-0557-7). Rutgers U Pr.

--Temple Reflections. LC 80-80346. (Illus.). 112p. 1980. 16.50 (ISBN 0-912998-04-0); pap. 6.50 (ISBN 0-912998-05-9). Hummingbird.

Schmidt, Peggy J. Making It on Your First Job: When You're Young, Inexperienced & Ambitious. 288p. 1981. pap. 2.95 (ISBN 0-380-77354-6). Avon.

Schmidt, Peter R. Historical Archaeology: A Structural Approach in an African Culture. LC 77-84758. (Contributions in Intercultural & Comparative Studies: No. 3). (Illus.). 1978. lib. bdg. 29.95 (ISBN 0-8371-9849-6, SSA/). Greenwood.

Schmidt, R. F., ed. Fundamentals of Sensory Physiology. (Illus.). 1978. 18.50 (ISBN 0-387-08801-6). Springer-Verlag.

Schmidt, R. F., et al. Fundamentals of Neurophysiology. 2nd rev. ed. LC 74-18500. (Springer Study Ed.). (Illus.). x, 294p. 1975. pap. 12.40 o.p. (ISBN 0-387-06871-6). Springer-Verlag.

Schmidt, R. F., et al, eds. Fundamentals of Neurophysiology: Springer Study Edition. 2nd ed. Jordan, D. & Jordan, I., trs. from Ger. 1978. pap. 15.50 (ISBN 0-387-08188-7). Springer-Verlag.

Schmidt, R. Marilyn. The Simply Seafood Cookbook of East Coast Fish. (Illus.). 150p. (Orig.). 1980. pap. 7.95 (ISBN 0-937996-00-9). Barnegat.

--The Simply Seafood Cookbook of East Coast Shellfish. (Illus.). 150p. (Orig.). 1980. pap. 7.95 (ISBN 0-937996-01-7). Barnegat.

Schmidt, R. R., jt. auth. see Lemmerz, A. H.

Schmidt, Richard A. Motor Skills. (Scientific Perspectives of Physical Education). 192p. 1975. pap. text ed. 9.50 scp (ISBN 0-06-045784-8, HarpC). Har-Row.

Schmidt, Richard E., et al. Serving the Federal Evaluation Market: Strategic Alternatives for Managers & Evaluators. (An Institute Paper). 93p. 1976. pap. 4.50 o.p. (ISBN 0-685-99532-1, 17400). Urban Inst.

Schmidt, Robert M., ed. Handbook in Clinical Laboratory Science, CRC: Section I-Hematology. 1979-80. 67.95 (ISBN 0-8493-7091-4). CRC Pr.

Schmidt, Robert P. Autobody Repair & Refinishing. 350p. 1981. text ed. 18.95 (ISBN 0-8359-0247-1); instr's. manual free (ISBN 0-8359-0248-X). Reston.

Schmidt, Rudolf, jt. auth. see Brinkman, Karl-Heinz.

Schmidt, Stanley. Lifeboat Earth. 1978. pap. 1.75 o.p. (ISBN 0-425-03820-3, Dist. by Putnam). Berkley Pub.

Schmidt, Stanley, ed. Analog's Golden Anniversary Anthology. 384p. 1980. 10.95 (ISBN 0-8037-0217-5). Davis Pubns.

Schmidt, Steffen W., et al. Friends, Followers & Factions: A Reader in Political Clientelism. 1977. 32.50x (ISBN 0-520-02696-9); pap. 9.95x (ISBN 0-520-03156-3). U of Cal Pr.

Schmidt, Terry D., jt. auth. see Holtz, Herman R.

Schmidt, W. H. Child Development: The Human, Cultural, & Educational Context. (Holtzman Series). 191p. 1973. pap. text ed. 9.50 scp (ISBN 0-06-045781-3, HarpC). Har-Row.

Schmidt, W. J. & Keil, A. Polarization Microscopy of Dental Tissues. Middle, P., tr. 604p. 1971. 87.00 (ISBN 0-08-010787-7). Pergamon.

Schmidt, Wallace V. & Graham, Jo-Ann. The Public Forum. LC 78-23604. (Illus.). 1979. text ed. 10.95 (ISBN 0-88284-068-1). Alfred Pub.

Schmidt, Werner H. Einfuehrung in das Altet Estament. (De Gruyter Lehrbuch Ser.). 1979. text ed. 28.25x (ISBN 3-11-002445-4). De Gruyter.

Schmidt, Werner J. & Philbin, Janis. Solar Installer's Training Program: California Ed. 1981. Repr. of 1980 ed. 35.00 (ISBN 0-89934-084-9). Solar Energy Info.

Schmidt, Wilson. The U. S. Balance of Payments & the Sinking Dollar. LC 78-65582. 1979. 10.00x (ISBN 0-8147-7797-X); pap. 5.00x (ISBN 0-8147-7798-8). NYU Pr.

Schmidt, Winsor C., et al. Public Guardianship & the Elderly. 300p. 1981. 19.00 (ISBN 0-88410-596-2). Ballinger Pub.

Schmidt-Nielsen, K. How Animals Work. LC 77-174262. (Illus.). 100p. 1972. 17.95 (ISBN 0-521-08417-2); pap. 5.75x (ISBN 0-521-09692-8). Cambridge U Pr.

Schmidt-Nielsen, Knut. Animal Physiology. 3rd ed. (Biological Science & Foundations of Modern Biology Ser). 1970. ref. ed. 13.95x (ISBN 0-13-037390-7); pap. 9.95x ref. ed. (ISBN 0-13-037382-6). P-H.

--Animal Physiology. 2nd ed. LC 78-56822. (Illus.). 1978. 24.95x (ISBN 0-521-22178-1). Cambridge U Pr.

Schmiermann, W., jt. auth. see Pecher, R.

Schmincke-Ott, Eva, jt. ed. see Bisswanger, Hans.

Schminke, C. W., jt. auth. see Dumas, Enoch.

Schmirler, Otto. Art of Wrought Metalwork for House & Garden. Date not set. 60.00 (ISBN 0-8038-0018-5). Hastings.

Schmit, William. Sailmaking. rev ed. LC 76-21094. (Illus.). 136p. 1976. Repr. 10.95 (ISBN 0-8069-8634-4); PLB 9.29 (ISBN 0-8069-8635-2). Sterling.

Schmithals, Walter, jt. auth. see Gunneweg, Antonius H.

Schmitt, Barton D. Pediatric Telephone Advice. 1980. pap. write for info. (ISBN 0-316-77386-7). Little.

Schmitt, Bernadotte E. Annexation of Bosnia, Nineteen Eight to Nineteen Nine. LC 71-80588. 1971. Repr. of 1937 ed. 13.75 (ISBN 0-86527-002-3). Fertig.

--The Coming of the War, 1914. 2 Vols. 1968. Set. 48.50 (ISBN 0-86527-030-9). Fertig.

--England & Germany, 1740-1914. 1967. Repr. 16.50 o.p. (ISBN 0-685-09545-2). Fertig.

Schmitt, Bernard. Protein, Calories & Development: Nutritional Variables in the Economics of Developing Nations. (Westview Special Studies in Society, Politics & Economics Development). 1979. lib. bdg. 24.50x (ISBN 0-89158-185-5). Westview.

Schmitt, Conrad, jt. auth. see Germano, Joseph.

Schmitt, Conrad J. Espanol, Comencemos: Pupil's Edition. 3rd ed. Chimienti, Teresa, ed. LC 80-13033. (Illus.). 280p. (Span.). (gr. 7). 1980. text ed. 10.60 (ISBN 0-07-055573-7, W); tchr's ed. 11.96 (ISBN 0-07-055574-5); wkbk. 3.80 (ISBN 0-07-055575-3); tests 66.00 (ISBN 0-07-055576-1); filmstrips 93.32 (ISBN 0-07-098991-5); test replacements 39.60 (ISBN 0-07-055577-X). McGraw.

--Espanol: Sigamos, Pupil's Edition. 3rd ed. Chimienti, Teresa, ed. LC 80-13032. (Illus.). 282p. (Span.). (gr. 8). 1980. text ed. 11.64 (ISBN 0-07-055578-8, W); tchrs. ed. 13.16 (ISBN 0-07-055579-6); wkbk. avail. (ISBN 0-07-055575-3); filmstrips 93.92 (ISBN 0-07-098994-X). McGraw.

Schmitt, Conrad J; see Jones, George F.

Schmitt, Conrad J., jt. auth. see Okin, Josee.

Schmitt, D., jt. auth. see Thivolet, J.

Schmitt, Dotty. The Delight of Being His Daughter. 1981. pap. 4.95 (ISBN 0-88270-509-1). Logos.

Schmitt, E. William, Jr., jt. auth. see Hilt, Nancy E.

Schmitt, F. O., ed. Neurosciences: Second Study Program. LC 78-136288. (Illus.). 1088p. (Charts, Photos, Micrographs, Tabs). 1970. ref. ed. 60.00 (ISBN 0-87470-014-0); prof. ed. 30.00 (ISBN 0-685-04785-7). Rockefeller.

Schmitt, F. O., et al, eds. The Cerebral Cortex: Proceedings of a Neurosciences Research Program Colloquium. (Illus.). 576p. 1981. text ed. 50.00x (ISBN 0-262-19189-X). MIT Pr.

Schmitt, Francis P. Church Music Transgressed: Reflections on Reform. LC 77-9424. 1977. 7.95 (ISBN 0-8164-0355-4). Crossroad NY.

Schmitt, Gladys. Boris, the Lop-Sided Bear. (Illus.). (gr. 1-3). 1966. 2.95 o.s.i. (ISBN 0-02-781250-2, CCPr); PLB 3.95 o.s.i. (ISBN 0-02-781240-5, CCPr). Macmillan.

--Rembrandt. 1961. 12.95 o.p. (ISBN 0-394-44252-0). Random.

Schmitt, Hans A., ed. U. S. Occupation in Europe After World War II. LC 78-51611. 1978. 11.00x (ISBN 0-7006-0178-3); pap. text ed. 6.95x (ISBN 0-7006-0179-1). Regents Pr KS.

Schmitt, Karl M., jt. auth. see Leiden, Carl.

Schmitt, Martin F., jt. auth. see Brown, Dee.

Schmitt, Waldo L. Crustaceans. 4.95 (ISBN 0-472-05014-1). U of Mich Pr.

Schmitter, Peter, jt. ed. see Bulow, Edeltraud.

Schmitter, Philippe C. & Lehmbruch, Gerhard, eds. Trends Toward Corporatist Intermediation. LC 79-63824. (Contemporary Political Sociology: Vol. 1). 328p. 1979. 20.00x (ISBN 0-8039-9836-8); pap. 9.95x (ISBN 0-8039-9837-6). Sage.

Schmittroth, John, Jr. & Kruzas, Anthony T., eds. Encyclopedia of Information Systems & Services. 4th ed. 1500p. 1980. 175.00 (ISBN 0-8103-0942-4). Gale.

Schmitz, Andrew, jt. ed. see Hillman, Jimmye S.

Schmitz, Dennis. String. LC 79-9444. (The American Poetry Ser.: Vol. 19). 80p. 1981. pap. 4.95 (ISBN 0-912946-69-5). Ecco Pr.

Schmitz, Dorothy C. Chris Evert: Women's Tennis Champion. LC 77-70891. (Pros Ser.). (Illus.). (gr. 2). 1977. PLB 6.45 (ISBN 0-913940-64-X). Crestwood Hse.

--Dorothy Hamill: Skate to Victory. LC 77-70888. (Pros Ser.). (Illus.). (gr. 2). 1977. PLB 6.45 (ISBN 0-913940-62-3). Crestwood Hse.

--Evel Knievel: Motorcycle Daredevil. LC 77-70889. (Pros Ser.). (Illus.). (gr. 2). 1977. PLB 6.45 (ISBN 0-913940-61-5). Crestwood Hse.

--Fran Tarkenton: Master of the Gridiron. LC 77-70890. (Pros Ser.). (Illus.). (gr. 2). 1977. PLB 6.45 (ISBN 0-913940-63-1). Crestwood Hse.

Schmitz, James H. A Pride of Monsters. LC 72-85788. 248p. 1973. pap. 1.25 o.s.i. (ISBN 0-02-024860-1, Collier). Macmillan.

--The Universe Against Her. (Science Fiction Ser.). 1981. PLB 13.50 (ISBN 0-8398-2597-8). Gregg.

Schmitz, Kurt. Langfristplanung in der Energiewirtschaft eine Computersimulation Fur Die BRD. (Interdisciplinary Systems Research Ser.: No. 65). 264p. (Ger.). 1979. pap. 24.00 (ISBN 3-7643-1068-5). Birkhauser.

Schmitz, Walter J. Pocket Liturgikon: Pastoral Ministrations. abr. ed. LC 80-81346. 96p. 1980. 4.95 (ISBN 0-87973-674-7, 674). Our Sunday Visitor.

Schmoegner, Walter. Der Traum Vom Rueckenwind. (Illus.). 64p. (Ger.). 1980. text ed. 26.00 (ISBN 3-458-04939-8, Pub. by Insel Verlag Germany). Suhrkamp.

Schmoger, Carl E. The Life of Anne Catherine Emmerich, 2 vols. 1976. Vol.1. pap. 9.00 o.p. (ISBN 0-89555-059-8, 338-I); Vol.2. pap. 9.00 o.p. (ISBN 0-89555-060-1, 338-I*I); Set. pap. 18.00 o.p. (ISBN 0-89555-062-8). TAN Bks Pubs.

Schmoger, E. & Kelsey, J. H., eds. Visual Electrodiagnosis in Systematic Diseases. (Documenta Opthalmologica Ser.: No. 23). 290p. 1980. lib. bdg. 68.50 (ISBN 90-6193-163-0, Pub by Dr. W. Junk). Kluwer Boston.

Schmokel, Wolfe W. Dream of Empire: German Colonialism, 1919-1945. LC 80-15400. (Yale Historical Publications: Miscellany 78). xiv, 204p. 1980. Repr. of 1964 ed. lib. bdg. 22.50x (ISBN 0-313-22437-4, SCDE). Greenwood.

Schmoller, A, ed. Handkonkordanz Zum Grieschischen Neuen Testament. 15th ed. 1973. 12.85 (ISBN 3-438-05131-1, 56850). United Bible.

Schmorak, Hannah, tr. see Eldad, Israel.

Schmorak, J., tr. see Myshlyaeva, L. V. & Krasnoshchekov, V. V.

Schmuck, Philip, jt. auth. see Eberhart, Perry.

Schmucker, U., ed. Electromagnetics Induction in the Earth & Moon. (Advances in Earth & Planetary Sciences Ser.: No. 9). 200p. 1980. lib. bdg. 26.50 (ISBN 90-277-1131-3, Pub. by D. Reidel). Kluwer Boston.

Schmudde, Theodore H., jt. auth. see Harper, Robert A.

Schmugge, Ludwig, ed. Radulfus Niger "De Re Militari et Triplici Via Peregrinationis Ierosolimitane" (1187 88) (Beitraege Zur Geschichte und Quellenkunde des Mittelalters: Vol. 6). 1976. 72.25x (ISBN 3-11-006827-3). De Gruyter.

Schmuller, Alan, jt. auth. see Mortensen, Donald.

Schmultzhart, Berthold. The Handmade Furniture Book. (Illus.). 144p. 1981. 13.95 (ISBN 0-13-383638-X); pap. 5.95 (ISBN 0-13-383620-7). P-H.

Schmutzler, et al. Hemodynamics & Ventricular Function During Exercise. Heiss, ed. (Advances in Clinical Cardiology: Vol. 2). 290p. 1980. pap. 23.00x (ISBN 0-933682-01-8). G Witzstrock Pub Hse.

Schnabel, Artur. Music & the Line of Most Resistance. LC 69-12690. (Music Ser). 1969. Repr. of 1942 ed. lib. bdg. 15.00 (ISBN 0-306-71224-5). Da Capo.

Schnabel, Ernst. Anne Frank: A Portrait in Courage. LC 58-12702. (Illus.). 7.50 o.p. (ISBN 0-15-107527-1). HarBraceJ.

Schnabel, John F. Study Guide to Accompany Sociology: Human Society. 3rd ed. 1981. pap. text ed. 4.95x (ISBN 0-673-15479-3). Scott F.

Schnabel, T., jt. auth. see Fox, M.

Schnackenburg, Rudolf. The Gospel According to St. John, 2 vols. 1980. 29.50 ea. Vol. 1 (ISBN 0-8164-1210-3). Vol. 2 (ISBN 0-8164-0213-2). Crossroad NY.

--Moral Teaching of the New Testament. pap. 7.95 (ISBN 0-8164-2557-4). Crossroad NY.

Schnackenburg, Rudolph. Church in the New Testament. pap. 5.95 (ISBN 0-8164-2585-X). Crossroad NY.

Schnall, David. Radical Dissent in Contemporary Israeli Politics: Cracks in the Wall. (Praeger Special Studies). 1978. 24.95 (ISBN 0-03-047096-X). Praeger.

Schnapp, John B. Corporate Strategies of the Automotive Manufacturers. LC 79-2788. 224p. 1979. 22.95 (ISBN 0-669-03243-3). Lexington Bks.

Schneberg, Willa & Warren, Larkin. Box Poems & Old Sheets. LC 78-74231. 88p. 1979. pap. 4.95 (ISBN 0-914086-25-1). Alicejamesbooks.

Schneck, D. J., ed. Biofluid Mechanics, Vol. 2. 530p. 1980. 59.50 (ISBN 0-306-40426-5, Plenum Pr). Plenum Pub.

Schneck, Eleanor M. Reading America. (Illus.). 288p. 1978. pap. text ed. 9.95 (ISBN 0-13-753293-8). P-H.

Schneck, Paul D. Mork & Mindy. (TV-Movie Tie-Ins Ser.). 32p. (gr. 4-8). 1980. PLB 5.95 (ISBN 0-87191-754-8); pap. 2.95 (ISBN 0-89812-223-6). Creative Ed.

--Why Do We Have Skeletons? (Creative Questions & Answers Ser.). (Illus.). 32p. (gr. 3-4). Date not set. PLB 5.65 (ISBN 0-87191-750-5); pap. 2.75 (ISBN 0-89812-219-8). Creative Ed. Postponed.

Schnede, Brenda, ed. Chicago Performs: A Guide to Theatre & Dance. LC 77-87358. (Illus.). 93p. (Orig.). 1977. pap. 5.95 (ISBN 0-8040-0795-0). Swallow.

Schnee, Jerome E., et al. The Progress of Management: Process & Behavior in a Changing Environment. 3rd ed. (Illus.). 1977. pap. text ed. 12.95 (ISBN 0-13-730622-9). P-H.

Schneeberger, Kenneth, jt. auth. see Osburn, Donald.

Schneeberger, Kenneth C., jt. auth. see Osburn, Donald O.

Schneeberger, Pierre-F. Chinese Jades & Other Hardstones. Watson, Katherine, tr. from Fr. (Illus.). 1976. 225.00 (ISBN 0-7100-0455-9). Routledge & Kegan.

Schneede. Rene Magritte. 1981. pap. 3.50 (ISBN 0-8120-2187-8). Barron.

Schneede, Uwe M. George Grosz. (Illus.). 220p. 1981. pap. 3.75 (ISBN 0-8120-2184-3). Barron.

--Max Ernst. Last, R. W., tr. from Ger. (World of Art Ser.). (Illus.). 1972. pap. 9.95 (ISBN 0-19-520004-7). Oxford U Pr.

Schneer, Cecil J., ed. Two Hundred Years of Geology in America: Proceedings of the New Hampshire Bicentennial Conference. LC 78-63149. (Illus.). 401p. 1979. text ed. 22.50x (ISBN 0-87451-160-7). U Pr of New Eng.

Schneersohn, Y. Y. Notations on the Arrest. Levin, Moshe Chaim, ed. Gurevich, David A., tr. from Hebrew. LC 80-21987. (Illus.). 226p. (Orig.). 1980. 11.75 (ISBN 0-86639-100-2). Friends Refugees.

Schneewind, E., tr. see Brentano, Franz.

Schneidau & Duewer, Lawrence A., eds. Vertical Coordination in the Pork Industry: Symposium. (Illus.). 300p. 1972. text ed. 25.50 o.p. (ISBN 0-87055-114-0). AVI.

Schneidau, Herbert, ed. see Pound, Ezra.

Schneider & Bruell. Advanced Programming & Problem Solving with Pascal. 480p. 1981. text ed. 22.95 (ISBN 0-471-07876-X). Wiley.

Schneider, A. F. Power Packed Pronouncements. (Anthology of Familiar Quotes Ser.). 88p. (Orig.). 1980. pap. 1.75 (ISBN 0-938784-00-5). Dicul Pub.

Schneider, Albert J. Self-Instructional Guide to Federal Income Taxation, 1973 Edition. (Illus.). 400p. 1973. pap. text ed. 6.95 o.p. (ISBN 0-13-803510-5). P-H.

Schneider, Andrea, jt. auth. see Fingland, Randy.

Schneider, Anne & Schneider, Steven. The Climber's Sourcebook. LC 75-21251. 321p. 1976. pap. 4.95 (ISBN 0-385-11081-2, Anch). Doubleday.

Schneider, Barry, jt. auth. see Calhoun, Robert.

Schneider, Ben R., Jr. The Ethos of Restoration Comedy. LC 70-140670. 1971. 10.00 (ISBN 0-252-00151-6). U of Ill Pr.

Schneider, Ben R., Jr., compiled by. Index to the London Stage, 1660-1800. 960p. 1979. 60.00x (ISBN 0-8093-0907-6). S Ill U Pr.

Schneider, Bernard. Your Money - Going or Growing? (Illus.). (gr. 7 up). 1978. wkbk 2.25 (ISBN 0-912486-33-3). Finney Co.

Schneider, Carl & Vinovskis, Maris A., eds. The Law & Politics of Abortion. LC 79-3134. 320p. 1980. 15.95x (ISBN 0-669-03386-3). Lexington Bks.

Schneider, Claire. A Slice of Life - Reflections. 48p. (Orig.). pap. 2.95 (ISBN 0-9601982-1-0). Greenwood Hse.

Schneider, Clarence E. Syntax & Style. LC 72-97330. 342p. 1974. pap. 7.95x (ISBN 0-88316-019-6). Chandler & Sharp.

Schneider, Coleman. Embroidery Schiffli Multi Head. (Illus.). 1978. Repr. of 1968 ed. 35.00 (ISBN 0-9601662-1-1). C Schneider.

Schneider, Daniel E. The Psychoanalyst & the Artist. rev. ed. 1978. pap. text ed. write for info. o.p. (ISBN 0-391-00889-7). Humanities.

Schneider, David J. Introduction to Social Psychology. LC 75-18160. (Social Psychology Ser.). (Illus.). 656p. 1976. text ed. 18.95 (ISBN 0-201-06728-5); instr's manual 2.75 (ISBN 0-201-06724-2). A-W.

Schneider, David J., et al. Person Perception. 2nd ed. LC 78-67455. (Topics in Social Psychology). (Illus.). 1979. pap. text ed. 9.50 (ISBN 0-201-06768-4). A-W.

Schneider, David M. & Gough, Kathleen, eds. Matrilineal Kinship. (California Library Reprint Ser.). 1974. 35.00x (ISBN 0-520-02587-3); pap. 9.95x (ISBN 0-520-02529-6, CAMPUS 103). U of Cal Pr.

Schneider, Diana, jt. ed. see Bradshaw, Ralph.

Schneider, Diana J., et al, eds. Proteins of the Nervous System. LC 73-79287. 300p. 1973. 24.50 (ISBN 0-911216-54-5). Raven.

Schneider, Diana S., ed. Reviews of Neuroscience, Vol. 4. 1979. text ed. 20.50 (ISBN 0-89004-282-9). Raven.

Schneider, Dick, jt. auth. see Hughes, Harold.

Schneider, Dick, jt. auth. see Savoca, Nick.

Schneider, Dick, jt. auth. see Warren, Rita.

Schneider, Donald D. The Works & Doctrine of Jacques Hittorff (1792-1867) LC 76-23721. (Outstanding Dissertations in the Fine Arts Ser.). 1977. lib. bdg. 133.00x (ISBN 0-8240-2727-2). Garland Pub.

Schneider, Duane, jt. auth. see Franklin, Benjamin.

Schneider, Earl. All About Aquariums. (Illus., Orig.). pap. 4.95 (ISBN 0-87666-003-0, PS601). TFH Pubns.

Schneider, Edward L., ed. The Aging Reproductive System. LC 77-83693. (Aging Ser: Vol. 4). 1978. 34.50 (ISBN 0-89004-176-8). Raven.

Schneider, Edward W. & Bennion, Junius. Videodiscs. Duane, James E., ed. LC 80-23563. (The Instructional Media Library: Vol. 16). (Illus.). 128p. 1981. 13.95 (ISBN 0-87778-176-1). Educ Tech Pubns.

Schneider, Elisabeth. The Dragon in the Gate: Studies in the Poetry of G. M. Hopkins. LC 68-31434. (Perspectives in Criticism: No. 20). 1968. 19.50x (ISBN 0-520-01150-3). U of Cal Pr.

Schneider, Elizabeth W. T. S. Eliot: The Pattern in the Carpet. LC 73-90655. 1975. 16.50x (ISBN 0-520-02648-9). U of Cal Pr.

Schneider, F. Richard. Orthopaedics in Emergency Care. LC 80-12233. (Illus.). 1980. pap. text ed. 11.95 (ISBN 0-8016-4348-1). Mosby.

Schneider, Fred W., jt. auth. see Carlson, Steve.

Schneider, G. M., et al, eds. Extraction with Supercritical Gases. 1980. 48.80 (ISBN 3-527-25854-X). Verlag Chemie.

Schneider, G. Michael, et al. An Introduction to Programming & Problem Solving with Pascal. 394p. 1978. 16.95 (ISBN 0-471-02542-9). Wiley.

Schneider, G. W. Export-Import Financing: A Practical Guide. 1974. 29.95 (ISBN 0-8260-7915-6). Ronald Pr.

Schneider, Gotthard. Die Flechtengattung Psora Sensu Zahlbruckner. (Bibliotheca Lichenologica: 13). (Illus.). 308p. (Ger.). 1980. lib. bdg. 40.00x (ISBN 3-7682-1257-2). Lubrecht & Cramer.

Schneider, H. The Africans: An Ethnological Account. 1981. pap. 9.95 (ISBN 0-13-018648-1). P-H.

Schneider, H. J., jt. ed. see Knoedel, W.

Schneider, H. W., tr. see Dante.

Schneider, Harold. Solving Math Word Problems for Students & Adults. 1965. 4.50 (ISBN 0-911642-01-3); pap. 1.95 (ISBN 0-911642-02-1). Word-Fraction.

Schneider, Harold K. Economic Man: The Anthropolgy of Economics. LC 73-8493. (Illus.). 1974. 12.95 (ISBN 0-02-927940-2). Free Pr.

Schneider, Herbert W. A History of American Philosophy. LC 63-14114. 1963. 12.50x (ISBN 0-231-08612-1). Columbia U Pr.

--Making the Fascist State. LC 67-24597. 1968. Repr. 16.50 (ISBN 0-86527-121-6). Fertig.

--Religion in Twentieth Century America. LC 52-8219. (The Library of Congress Ser. in American Civilization). (Illus.). 1952. 10.00x (ISBN 0-674-75700-9). Harvard U Pr.

Schneider, Herbert W., ed. see Franklin, Benjamin.

Schneider, Herbert W., ed. see Hobbes, Thomas.

Schneider, Herman, jt. ed. see Prestol, Sack.

Schneider, Ilya I. Isadora Duncan: The Russian Years. Magarshack, David, tr. from Rus. (Da Capo Qauality Paperbacks Ser.). (Illus.). 221p. 1981. pap. 6.95 (ISBN 0-306-80142-6). Da Capo.

Schneider, Isidore, tr. see Gorky, Maxim.

Schneider, J. W., ed. From Nine to Twelve: Europe's Destiny. LC 80-50459. 256p. 1980. 47.50x (ISBN 90-286-0280-1). Sijthoff & Noordhoff.

Schneider, John C. Detroit & the Problem of Order, 1830-1880. LC 79-16492. xvi, 171p. 1980. 13.50x (ISBN 0-8032-4113-5). U of Nebr Pr.

Schneider, Joseph W., jt. auth. see Conrad, Peter.

Schneider, Joyce A. Flora Tristan: Feminist, Socialist & Free Spirit. LC 80-20067. 256p. (gr. 7-9). 1980. 8.95 (ISBN 0-688-22250-1); PLB 8.59 (ISBN 0-688-32250-6). Morrow.

Schneider, Laurence A. Ku Chieh-kang & China's New History: Nationalism & the Quest for Alternative Traditions. LC 73-129608. (Center for Chinese Studies, UC Berkeley). 1971. 22.75x (ISBN 0-520-01804-4). U of Cal Pr.

Schneider, Leo. Long Life to You: Modern Medicine at Work. LC 68-25195. (Illus.). (gr. 7 up). 1968. 4.95 o.p. (ISBN 0-15-248632-1, HJ). HarBraceJ.

--Microbes in Your Life. LC 66-13796. (Illus.). (gr. 7 up). 1966. 6.50 o.p. (ISBN 0-15-253574-8, HJ). HarBraceJ.

--You & Your Cells. LC 64-71496. (Illus.). (gr. 7-9). 1964. 5.95 o.p. (ISBN 0-15-299840-3, HJ). HarBraceJ.

--You & Your Senses. LC 56-5875. (gr. 5-9). 1960. 6.50 o.p. (ISBN 0-15-299857-8, HJ). HarBraceJ.

Schneider, Leo & Ames, Maurice U. Wings in Your Future: Aviation for Young People. rev. ed. LC 55-5966. (Illus.). (gr. 7-9). 1955. 4.95 o.p. (ISBN 0-15-297855-0, HJ). HarBraceJ.

Schneider, Lewis M. Future of United States Domestic Air Freight Industry. 1973. text ed. 11.00 (ISBN 0-87584-106-6). Harvard U Pr.

Schneider, Madelin S., jt. auth. see Tucker, Gina.

Schneider, Mark, jt. ed. see Kraft, Michael E.

Schneider, Maxine. Jackpot: To the Casino by Bus. (Gambler's Bookshelf). (Illus.). 1977. pap. 2.95 (ISBN 0-89650-577-4). Gamblers.

Schneider, Maxine S. Science Projects for the Intermediate Grades. LC 70-132146. (Illus.). 1971. pap. 4.50 (ISBN 0-8224-6310-5). Pitman Learning.

Schneider, Meg, ed. see Phillips, Louis.

Schneider, Meg, ed. see Phillips, Louis & Markoe, Karen.

Schneider, Meg, ed. see Tallarico, Tony.

Schneider, Michele, tr. see LaHaye, Beverly.

Schneider, Nina. The Woman Who Lived in a Prologue. 384p. 1981. pap. 2.75 (ISBN 0-445-04631-7). Popular Lib.

--The Woman Who Lived in a Prologue. 1980. 13.95 (ISBN 0-395-28211-X). HM.

Schneider, Pierre. World of Manet. (Library of Art). (Illus.). 1968. 15.95 (ISBN 0-8094-0248-3). Time-Life.

--World of Manet. LC 68-58484. (Library of Art Ser.). (Illus.). (gr. 6 up). 1968. 12.96 (ISBN 0-8094-0277-7, Pub. by Time-Life). Silver.

--World of Watteau. (Library of Art). (Illus.). 1967. 15.95 (ISBN 0-8094-0238-6). Time-Life.

--World of Watteau. LC 67-20332. (Library of Art Ser.). (Illus.). (gr. 6 up). 1967. 12.96 (ISBN 0-8094-0267-X, Pub. by Time-Life). Silver.

Schneider, R. Guten Tag: A German Language Course for Television. 1974. pap. text ed. 6.50x (ISBN 0-685-47484-4). Schoenhof.

Schneider, R. & Dickey, W. Reinforced Masonry Design. 1980. 36.00 (ISBN 0-13-771733-4). P-H.

Schneider, R. C. Correlative Neurosurgery, 2 vols. 3rd ed. (Illus.). 1808p. 1981. Set. 190.00 (ISBN 0-398-04037-0). C C Thomas.

Schneider, Raymond K. HVAC Control Systems. 400p. 1981. text ed. 19.95 (ISBN 0-471-05180-2). Wiley.

--Systematic Commercial Refrigeration Service. LC 78-14464. (Illus.). 192p. 1979. 15.95x (ISBN 0-912524-18-9). Busn News.

Schneider, Reinhold. Hohenzollern: Tragik & Koenigtum. (Suhrkamp Taschenbuecher: No. 590). 218p. 1980. pap. text ed. 5.85 (ISBN 3-518-37090-1, Pub. by Insel Verlag Germany). Suhrkamp.

--Lektuere Fuer Minuten. Meyer, Pirmin, ed. 200p. 1980. pap. 6.50 quality paper (ISBN 3-458-04918-5, Pub. by Insel Verlag Germany). Suhrkamp.

Schneider, Rex. The Wide-Mouthed Frog. LC 80-13449. (Illus.). 32p. (gr. k up). 1980. 9.95 (ISBN 0-916144-58-5); pap. 5.95 (ISBN 0-916144-59-3). Stemmer Hse.

Schneider, Rolf. November. LC 80-22770. 240p. 1981. 11.95 (ISBN 0-394-51440-8). Knopf.

Schneider, Ronald. Brazil: Foreign Relations of a Future World Power. new ed. LC 76-28345. 1977. lib. bdg. 21.00 o.p. (ISBN 0-89158-200-2). Westview.
Schneider, Ronald M. The Political System of Brazil. LC 75-154860. 431p. 1973. 22.50x (ISBN 0-231-03506-3); pap. text ed. 10.00x (ISBN 0-231-08324-6). Columbia U Pr.
Schneider, Stephen H. & Morton, Lynne. The Primordial Bond: Exploring Connections Between Man & Nature Through the Humanities & Sciences. (Illus.). 200p. 1981. 15.95 (ISBN 0-306-40519-9, Plenum Pr). Plenum Pub.
Schneider, Steven, jt. auth. see Schneider, Anne.
Schneider, Susan G., et al. Outstanding Dissertations in Bilingual Education. LC 8-80120. 127p. 1980. pap. 4.85 (ISBN 0-89763-020-3). Natl Clearinghse Bilingual Ed.
Schneider, Tom. The Moveable Nest. (Orig.). 1981. pap. write for info. (ISBN 0-440-56383-6, Delta). Dell. Postponed.
Schneider, Volker, tr. see Schondorf, Hubert.
Schneider, W., Jr., jt. ed. see Holst, J. J.
Schneider, William. Food, Foreign Policy & Raw Materials Cartels. LC 76-492. (Strategy Papers Ser.: No. 28). 1975. 6.50x (ISBN 0-8448-0921-7); pap. 2.95x (ISBN 0-8448-0922-5). Crane-Russak Co.
Schneider, William S., Jr., et al. U. S. Strategic-Nuclear Policy & Ballistic Missile Defense: The 1980s & Beyond. LC 79-3296. (Special Reports). 61p. 1980. 6.50 (ISBN 0-89549-018-8). Inst Foreign Policy Anal.
Schneidermeyer, Wilma, jt. auth. see Tominaga, Thomas T.
Schneider-Sickert, F. R., jt. auth. see Blauth, W.
Schneier, Craig E. & Beatty, Richard W. Personnel Administration Today. 1978. pap. text ed. 10.95 (ISBN 0-201-00503-4). A-W.
Schneier, Craig E., jt. auth. see Beatty, Richard W.
Schneirla, T. C. Army Ants: A Study in Social Organization. Topoff, Howard R., ed. LC 70-149408. (Illus.). 1971. text ed. 19.95x (ISBN 0-7167-0933-3). W H Freeman.
Schnell, J. D. Zytologie und Mikrobiologie der Vagina. 3rd ed. (Illus.). 92p. 1980. 35.50 (ISBN 3-8055-1428-X). S Karger.
Schnell, William J. Thirty Years a Watchtower Slave. (Direction Bks). pap. 1.95 (ISBN 0-8010-7933-0). Baker Bk.
Schneller, Eugene S. The Physician's Assistant. LC 76-11974. 1978. 18.95 (ISBN 0-669-00715-3). Lexington Bks.
Schnessel, Michael. I Cart. West, Jane, ed. 1981. 12.95 (ISBN 0-517-54399-0). Potter.
Schnessel, S. Michael. Icart. (Illus.). 1976. 25.00 (ISBN 0-517-52498-8, Dist. by Crown). Potter.
--Jessie Willcox Smith. LC 77-3530. (Illus.). 1977. 22.95 o.s.i. (ISBN 0-690-01493-7, TYC-T). T Y Crowell.
Schnidman, Frank & Silveman, Jane A., eds. Management & Control of Growth: Updating the Law. LC 80-50920. (Management & Control of Growth Ser.: Vol. V). 352p. 1980. pap. text ed. 19.50 (ISBN 0-87420-592-1, M12). Urban Land.
Schnidman, Frank, et al. Management & Control of Growth: Techniques in Application. LC 78-73139. (Management & Control of Growth Ser.: Vol. 4). 352p. 1978. pap. text ed. 19.50 (ISBN 0-87420-578-6). Urban Land.
Schnittker Assocs. Ethanol: Farm & Fuel Issues. 160p. 1981. pap. 19.50 (ISBN 0-89934-096-2). Solar Energy Info.
Schnitzer, Bertram, jt. auth. see Kass, Lawrence.
Schnitzer, Martin. Role of U. S. Multinationals in East-West Trade. LC 78-19794. (Praeger Special Studies Ser.). 168p. 1980. 19.95 (ISBN 0-03-043026-7). Praeger.
Schnitzer, Martin, jt. auth. see Fox, Harrison W., Jr.
Schnitzer, Robert J. & Hawking, F., eds. Experimental Chemotherapy, 5 vols. 1963-68. Vol. 1. 91.00 (ISBN 0-12-628401-6); Vol. 2. 65.00 (ISBN 0-12-628402-4); Vol. 3. 65.00 (ISBN 0-12-628403-2); Vol. 4. 65.00 (ISBN 0-12-628404-0); Vol. 5. 65.00 (ISBN 0-12-628405-9); Set. 271.00 (ISBN 0-685-23205-0). Acad Pr.
Schnitzer, Robert J., et al, eds. Advances in Pharmacology & Chemotherapy, Vol. 17. 1980. 36.00 (ISBN 0-12-032917-4); lib. ed. 47.00 (ISBN 0-12-032984-0); microfiche ed. 25.00 (ISBN 0-12-032985-9). Acad Pr.
Schnitzlein, H. N., jt. ed. see Crosby, Elizabeth C.
Schnitzler see Bentley, Eric.
Schnitzler, Arthur. Liebelei, Leutnant Gustl, Die Letzten Masken. Stern, J. P., ed. 1966. text ed. 7.50x (ISBN 0-521-06201-2). Cambridge U Pr.
--Undiscovered Country. Stoppard, Tom, tr. 94p. 1981. pap. 8.50 (ISBN 0-571-11575-6, Pub. by Faber & Faber). Merrimack Bk Serv.
Schnorr, Emil. Japanese Sword Guards. (Illus.). Date not set. pap. cancelled (ISBN 0-8048-1186-5). C E Tuttle.
Schnur, Harry C., ed. see Apuleius, Lucius.
Schnurre. Die Tat. (Easy Reader, C). pap. 3.75 (ISBN 0-88436-040-7, GEA201052). EMC.
Schobert, Geri. Books Are Fun. (Golden Books for Early Childhood). (Illus.). (ps-1). 1975. PLB 5.38 (ISBN 0-307-68956-5, Golden Pr). Western Pub.
Schoch, Henry A. Theodore Roosevelt: The Story Behind the Scenery. DenDooven, Gweneth R., ed. LC 74-77575. (Illus.). 1974. 7.95 (ISBN 0-916122-38-7); pap. 2.50 (ISBN 0-916122-13-1). K C Pubns.
Schochet, Gordon J., jt. ed. see Wilson, Richard W.
Schochet, Sydney S., Jr. & McCormick, William F. Essentials of Neuropathology. (Illus.). 1979. pap. 13.95 (ISBN 0-8385-2269-6). ACC.
--Neuropathology Case Studies. 2nd ed. 1979. pap. 16.50 (ISBN 0-87488-046-7). Med Exam.
Schochet, Victoria & Silbersack, John, eds. The Berkley Showcase, Vol. 4. 1981. pap. 2.25 (ISBN 0-425-04804-7). Berkley Pub.
--The Berkley Showcase: New Writings in Science Fiction, Vol. II. (Orig.). 1980. pap. 2.25 (ISBN 0-425-04553-6). Berkley Pub.
Schodde, tr. Book of Jubilees. LC 80-53467. 96p. 1980. pap. 3.00 (ISBN 0-934666-08-3). Artisan Sales.
Schoder, Judy, jt. auth. see Shebar, Sharon.
Schoderbek, Peter P., et al. Management Systems: Conceptual Considerations. rev. ed. 1980. pap. 11.95x (ISBN 0-256-02275-5). Business Pubns.
Schoeck, Helmut. Envy: A Theory of Social Behaviour. Glenny, Michael & Ross, Betty, trs. LC 69-14842. (Helen & Kurt Wolff Bk). Orig. Title: Der Neid. 408p. 1972. pap. 3.95 o.p. (ISBN 0-15-628798-6, HB241, Harv). HarBraceJ.
--Envy: A Theory of Social Behaviour. Glenny, Michael & Ross, Betty, trs. from Ger. LC 69-14842. 1966. 28.50x (ISBN 0-15-128952-2). Irvington.
Schoeck, R. J., ed. Editing Sixteenth Century Texts. (Conference on Editorial Problems Ser). 1976. lib. bdg. 16.50 (ISBN 0-8240-2400-1). Garland Pub.
Schoedinger, Andrew B. Wants, Decisions & Human Action: A Praxeological Investigation. LC 78-62705. 1978. pap. text ed. 9.50 (ISBN 0-8191-0591-0). U Pr of Amer.
Schoeffler, James D. IBM Series 1: Small Computer Concept. 1980. pap. text ed. 10.95 (ISBN 0-574-21330-9, 13-4330). SRA.
Schoelcher, Victor. The Life of Handel. (Music Reprint Ser.). 1979. Repr. of 1857 ed. lib. bdg. 35.00 (ISBN 0-306-79572-8). Da Capo.
Schoen, Cathy, jt. auth. see Davis, Karen.
Schoen, Juliet P. Silents to Sound: A History of the Movies. LC 76-16092. (Illus.). 192p. (gr. 7 up). 1976. 7.95 (ISBN 0-590-07337-0, Four Winds). Schol Bk Serv.
Schoen, Kenneth F., jt. auth. see Ward, David A.
Schoen, Linda A., ed. The AMA Book of Skin & Hair Care. (Illus.). 1976. 8.95 o.s.i. (ISBN 0-397-01157-1); pap. 4.95 (ISBN 0-397-01158-X). Lippincott.
Schoen, Sterling H. & Durand, Douglas E. Supervision: The Management of Organizational Resources. (Illus.). 1979. ref. 15.95 (ISBN 0-13-876235-X). P-H.
Schoen, Sterling H. & Hilgert, Raymond L. Cases in Collective Bargaining & Industrial Relations: A Decisional Approach. 3rd ed. 1978. pap. text ed. 10.95 (ISBN 0-256-02002-7). Irwin.
Schoenauer, Norbert. Six Thousand Years of Housing, 3 vols. Incl. Vol. 31. The Pre-Urban House. lib. bdg. 17.50 (ISBN 0-8240-7172-7); Vol. 2. The Oriental Urban House. lib. bdg. 17.50 (ISBN 0-8240-7173-5); Vol. 3. The Occidental Urban House. lib. bdg. 17.50 (ISBN 0-8240-7174-3). 250p. 1980. Garland Pub.
--Six Thousand Years of Housing, 3 vols. LC 79-20303. 250p. 1980. lib. bdg. 19.50 ea. Vol. 1, The Pre-urban House (ISBN 0-8240-7172-7). Vol. 2, The Oriental Urban House (ISBN 0-8240-7173-5). Vol. 3, The Occidental Urban House (ISBN 0-8240-7174-3). Garland Pub.
Schoenbaum, S. William Shakespeare: Records & Images. (Illus.). 316p. 1981. 98.00 (ISBN 0-19-520234-1). Oxford U Pr.
Schoenbaum, S., jt. auth. see Muir, K.
Schoenbaum, S., ed. see Harbage, Alfred.
Schoenbaum, Samuel. Shakespeare's Lives. LC 74-118290. 1970. 27.50 (ISBN 0-19-501243-7). Oxford U Pr.
Schoenberg, Arnold. Arnold Schoenberg Letters. Stein, E., ed. (Illus.). 1958. 8.75 o.p. (ISBN 0-685-20371-9). St Martin.
--Theory of Harmony. Carter, Roy E., tr. 1978. 49.50x (ISBN 0-520-03464-3). U of Cal Pr.
Schoenberg, Bernard & Gerber, Irwin, eds. Bereavement: It's Psychological Aspects. new ed. 368p. 1975. 20.00x (ISBN 0-231-03974-3). Columbia U Pr.
Schoenberg, Bernard, et al. Anticipatory Grief. (Thanatology Ser.). 336p. 1974. 20.00x (ISBN 0-231-03770-8). Columbia U Pr.
Schoenberg, Bernard, et al, eds. Teaching Psychosocial Aspects of Patient Care. LC 68-19757. 1968. 22.50x (ISBN 0-231-03162-9). Columbia U Pr.
--Psychosocial Aspects of Terminal Care. LC 73-184747. 385p. 1972. 22.50x (ISBN 0-231-03614-0). Columbia U Pr.
--Loss & Grief: Psychological Management in Medical Practice. LC 75-118356. 398p. 1973. 22.50x (ISBN 0-231-03329-X, CP165); pap. 10.00x (ISBN 0-231-08331-9). Columbia U Pr.
--Terminal Patient: Oral Care. LC 72-9892. 1973. 20.00x (ISBN 0-88238-701-4). Columbia U Pr.
Schoenberg, Bruce S., ed. Neurological Epidemiology: Principles & Clinical Applications. LC 77-72796. (Advances in Neurology Ser.: Vol. 19). 1978. 63.50 (ISBN 0-89004-212-8). Raven.
Schoenberg, Robert J. Art of Being a Boss: Inside Intelligence from Top-Level Business Leaders & Young Executives on the Move. 1978. 11.95 (ISBN 0-397-01291-8). Lippincott.
Schoenberger, Walter S. Decision of Destiny. LC 70-81452. viii, 330p. 1969. 14.00x (ISBN 0-8214-0068-1). Ohio U Pr.
Schoenborn, Charlotte A., jt. auth. see Danchik, Kathleen M.
Schoeneman, Charles W., jt. auth. see Jacobs, Vernon K.
Schoenfeld, Clarence A. & Zillman, Donald N. American University in Summer. 1967. 20.00x (ISBN 0-299-04520-X). U of Wis Pr.
Schoenfeld, H., ed. Antiparasitic Chemotherapy. (Antibiotics & Chemotherapy. Ser.: Vol. 30). (Illus.). 200p. 1981. 72.00 (ISBN 3-8055-2160-X). S Karger.
--Pharmacokinetics 1981. (Antibiotics & Chemotherapy Ser.: Vol. 31). (Illus.). 200p. 1981. 72.00 (ISBN 3-8055-2448-X). S Karger.
Schoenfeld, Hanns-Martin, jt. auth. see Sommer, Werner.
Schoenfeld, Hugh J. The Jesus Party. 320p. 1974. 7.95 o.s.i. (ISBN 0-02-607280-7). Macmillan.
Schoenfeld, Susan & Beniner, Winifred. Pattern Design for Needlepoint & Patchwork. 200p. 1981. pap. 9.95 (ISBN 0-442-20671-2). Van Nos Reinhold.
Schoenfield, Leslie J. Diseases of the Gallbladder & Biliary System. LC 77-5695. (Clinical Gastroenterology Monographs). 1977. 41.50 (ISBN 0-471-76246-6, Pub. by Wiley Medical). Wiley.
Schoenhals, Lawrence R. Companion to Hymns of Faith & Life. (Orig.). 1980. pap. 9.95 (ISBN 0-89367-040-5). Light & Life.
Schoenheimer, R. The Dynamic State of Body Constituents. 1964. Repr. of 1942 ed. 5.25 o.s.i. (ISBN 0-02-851800-4). Hafner.
Schoenhof, Jacob. The Economy of High Wages. (The Neglected American Economists Ser.). 1974. lib. bdg. 50.00 (ISBN 0-8240-1030-2). Garland Pub.
Schoenhofer, Peggy J. Fiddlin' Around. 1977. 4.50 o.p. (ISBN 0-682-48724-4). Exposition.
Schoening, Niles, jt. auth. see Quindry, Kenneth E.
Schoeninger, Douglas A., jt. auth. see Insko, Chester A.
Schoenly, Steven B., jt. auth. see Morrow, Carolyn C.
Schoenstadt, A. L., et al, eds. Information Linkage Between Applied Mathematics & Industry II. LC 80-17975. 1980. 20.00 (ISBN 0-12-628750-3). Acad Pr.
Schoenstein, Ralph. Yes, My Darling Daughters: Adventures in Fathering. 1976. 6.95 (ISBN 0-374-29360-0). FS&G.
Schoep, Arthur & Harris, Daniel. Word-by-Word Translations of Songs & Arias, Pt. 2: Italian. LC 66-13746. (A Companion to The Singer's Repertoire). 1972. 21.00 (ISBN 0-8108-0463-8). Scarecrow.
Schoepfer, G. R. River of Miracles. Schoepfer, Virginia B., ed. (Illus.). (gr. 1-11). 1978. pap. text ed. 2.75 (ISBN 0-931436-01-X, Children's Books). G R Schoepfer.
Schoepfer, Virginia B., ed. see Schoepfer, G. R.
Schofer, Lawrence. The Formation of a Modern Labor Force: Upper Silesia 1865-1914. LC 73-90658. 1975. 19.50x (ISBN 0-520-02651-9). U of Cal Pr.
Schoffeleers, Matthews & Meijers, Daniel. Religion, Nationalism & Economic Action Critical Questions on Durkheim & Weber. 1978. pap. text ed. 9.25x (ISBN 90-232-1614-8). Humanities.
Schoffeniels, E. & Neumann, E., eds. Molecular Aspects of Bioelectricity: Proceedings of the Symposium in Honour of David Nachmansohn, Liege, May 19-20, 1980. (Illus.). 360p. 1980. 72.00 (ISBN 0-08-026371-2). Pergamon.
Schoffeniels, E., et al, eds. Dynamic Properties of Glia Cells: An Interdisciplinary Approach to Their Study in the Central & Peripheral Nervous System. LC 78-40218. 1978. text ed. 69.00 (ISBN 0-08-021555-6). Pergamon.
Schofield, A. N., ed. see Malushitsky, Yu N.
Schofield, B. B. The Loss of the Bismarck. LC 75-187003. (Sea Battles in Close-up Ser: No. 3). (Illus.). 1972. 6.75 o.s.i. (ISBN 0-87021-840-9). Naval Inst Pr.
Schofield, C. W. Basic Mathematics for Technicians. (Illus.). 1977. pap. text ed. 11.00x (ISBN 0-7131-3379-1). Intl Ideas.
--Mathematics for Construction Students. 3rd ed. (Illus.). 1975. pap. text ed. 11.00x (ISBN 0-7131-3333-3). Intl Ideas.
Schofield, C. W., jt. auth. see Pollard, A. B.
Schofield, D. A., jt. auth. see Barnes, V. E.
Schofield, Diane. Beginning with Tropicals. pap. 2.00 (ISBN 0-87666-165-7, M523). TFH Pubns.
Schofield, Edmund, ed. Earthcare: Global Protection of Natural Areas; Proceedings of the Fourteenth Biennial Walderness Conference. LC 76-29358. (14th Biennial Wilderness Conference). 1978. 40.00x (ISBN 0-89158-034-4). Westview.
Schofield, Harry. The Philosophy of Education: An Introduction. (Unwin Education Bks.). text ed. 18.95x (ISBN 0-04-370039-X); pap. text ed. 8.95x (ISBN 0-04-370040-3). Allen Unwin.
Schofield, Henry. Essays on Constitutional Laws & Equity. LC 79-38814. (American Constitutional & Legal History Ser). (Illus.). 1972. Repr. lib. bdg. 75.00 (ISBN 0-306-70450-1). Da Capo.
Schofield, K. Aromatic Nitration. (Illus.). 350p. Date not set. 67.50 (ISBN 0-521-23362-3). Cambridge U Pr.
Schofield, K., et al. Heteroaromatic Nitrogen Compounds: The Azoles. LC 74-17504. (Illus.). 500p. 1976. 85.00 (ISBN 0-521-20519-0). Cambridge U Pr.
Schofield, M. An Essay on Anaxagoras. LC 79-10348. (Cambridge Classical Studies). 1980. 24.50 (ISBN 0-521-22722-4). Cambridge U Pr.
Schofield, Malcolm, et al, eds. Doubt & Dogmatism: Studies in Hellenistic Epistemology. 354p. 1980. text ed. 37.50x (ISBN 0-19-824601-3). Oxford U Pr.
Schofield, Maria, ed. Decorative Art & Modern Interiors: Environments for People. LC 80-81603. (Decorative Art & Modern Interiors, Theme Changes Annually). (Illus.). 192p. 1980. 35.00 (ISBN 0-688-03480-2). Morrow.
Schofield, R. E., jt. auth. see Allan, D. G.
Schofield, W. Engineering Surveying, Vol. 1. 2nd ed. (Illus.). 1978. pap. 15.95 (ISBN 0-408-00333-2). Butterworths.
Scholberg, Diana E., jt. auth. see Scholberg, Kenneth R.
Scholberg, Henry & Divien, Emmanuel. Bibliographie des Francais dans l'Inde. 216p. 1975. lib. bdg. 12.50 (ISBN 0-88253-738-5). Ind-US Inc.
Scholberg, Kenneth R. & Scholberg, Diana E. Aqui Mismo. (Illus., Orig.). 1980. pap. text ed. 6.95 (ISBN 0-88377-148-9). Newbury Hse.
Scholbin, Roger C., ed. see Frane, Jeff.
Scholefield, Alan. Point of Honour. LC 79-51250. 1979. 9.95 (ISBN 0-688-03454-3). Morrow.
--Point of Honour. 208p. 1980. pap. 2.25 (ISBN 0-345-28713-4). Ballantine.
Scholem, Gershom. Kabalah. 1978. pap. 5.95 (ISBN 0-452-00483-7, F483, Mer). NAL.
Scholen, Kenneth & Yung-Ping Chen, eds. Unlocking Home Equity for the Elderly. 1980. 27.50 (ISBN 0-88410-595-4). Ballinger Pub.
Scholes, France V., et al. Maya Chontal Indians of Acalan-Tixchel: A Contribution to the History & Ethnography of the Yucatan Peninsula. LC 68-15677. (Civilization of the American Indian Ser.: Vol. 91). (Illus.). 1968. 22.50x (ISBN 0-8061-0813-4). U of Okla Pr.
Scholes, Paul A. Bendigo Pottery. (Illus.). 281p. 1980. 34.95 (4040, Pub. by Lowden Pub Co Australia). Bks Australia.
Scholes, Percy A. The Life & Activities of Sir John Hawkins: Musician, Magistrate & Friend of Johnson. LC 77-26652. (Music Reprint Ser., 1978). (Illus.). 1978. Repr. of 1953 ed. lib. bdg. 27.50 (ISBN 0-306-77571-9). Da Capo.
--Listener's Guide to Music: With a Concert-Goer's Glossary. 10th ed. (Illus.). (YA) (gr. 9 up). 1961. pap. 4.95x (ISBN 0-19-284002-9). Oxford U Pr.
--Puritans & Music in England & New England: A Contribution to the Cultural History of 2 Nations. 1934. 34.50x (ISBN 0-19-816117-4). Oxford U Pr.
Scholes, Robert. Elements of Poetry. (Orig.). 1969. pap. text ed. 2.95x (ISBN 0-19-501047-7). Oxford U Pr.
--Structural Fabulation: An Essay on Fiction of the Future. LC 74-30167. 104p. 1975. text ed. 2.95 (ISBN 0-268-00570-2). U of Notre Dame Pr.
--Structural Fabulation: An Essay on Fiction of the Future. LC 74-30167. 111p. 1975. 2.95x o.p. (ISBN 0-268-00571-0). U of Notre Dame Pr.
Scholes, Robert & Kellogg, Robert. Nature of Narrative. 1968. pap. 5.95 (ISBN 0-19-500773-5, GB). Oxford U Pr.

Scholes, Robert & Rabkin, Eric. Science Fiction: History-Science-Vision. 1977. pap. 4.95 (ISBN 0-19-502174-6, 498, GB). Oxford U Pr.

Scholes, Robert, ed. Elements of Fiction: An Anthology. 984p. 1981. pap. text ed. 9.95x (ISBN 0-19-502881-3). Oxford U Pr.

--Learners & Discerners: A Newer Criticism. LC 64-13303. 1964. 10.95x (ISBN 0-8139-0213-4). U Pr of Va.

Scholes, Robert, et al, eds. Elements of Literature: Essay, Fiction, Poetry, Drama, Film. (Illus.). 1978. pap. text ed. 10.95x (ISBN 0-19-502265-3). Oxford U Pr.

Scholes, S. Glass Ceramic Technology. 1978. text ed. 16.70 o.p. (ISBN 0-08-019900-3). Pergamon.

Scholes, Walter V., ed. United States Diplomatic History: Readings for the Twentieth Century, Vol. 2. LC 72-6699. 1973. pap. text ed. 8.25 (ISBN 0-395-14057-9, 3-50121). HM.

Scholey, A. Sallinka & the Golden Bird. 1979. 6.95 (ISBN 0-13-789487-2). P-H.

Scholl, Geraldine T. Self Study & Evaluation Guide for Day School Programs for Visually Handicapped Pupils: A Guide for Program Improvement. LC 80-68282. 128p. 1980. pap. 14.50 (ISBN 0-86586-111-0). Coun Exc Child.

Scholl, Inge. Students Against Tyranny: The Resistance of the White Rose, Munich, 1942-1943. rev. ed. Schultz, Arthur R., tr. from Ger. LC 73-105504. Orig. Title: Weisse Rose. (Illus.). 1970. 12.50x (ISBN 0-8195-4021-8, Pub. by Wesleyan U Pr). Columbia U Pr.

Scholl, Lisette. Visionetics: The Holistic Way to Better Eyesight. LC 77-12882. 1978. pap. 4.95 (ISBN 0-385-13279-4, Dolp). Doubleday.

Scholl, Richard. Baseball Language: A Running Press Glossary. LC 77-410. (Orig.). 1977. lib. bdg. 12.90 o.p. (ISBN 0-914294-79-2); pap. 2.95 o.p. (ISBN 0-914294-80-6). Running Pr.

Schollhammer, Hans, jt. ed. see Boarman, Patrick M.

Schollick, Nigel & Bloxsom, Peter. Staff Appraisal-Self Appraisal: A Programmed Guide to Interviews. (Illus.). 1972. 17.95x (ISBN 0-7114-4919-8). Intl Ideas.

Scholt, Grayce, jt. ed. see Bingham, Jane.

Scholten, Robert, jt. ed. see De Jong, Kees A.

Scholtissek, C., et al. Chemistry & Cytochemistry of Nucleic Acids & Nuclear Proteins. (Protoplasmatologia: Vol. 5, Pt. 3A-D). (Illus.). 1966. pap. 57.90 o.p. (ISBN 0-387-80782-9). Springer-Verlag.

Scholtz, P. L., et al. Race Relations at the Cape of Good Hope, Sixteen Fifty-Two to Seventeen Ninety-Five: A Bibliography. (Reference Bks.). 1981. lib. bdg. 27.50 (ISBN 0-8161-8500-X). G K Hall.

Scholz, Charles B., jt. auth. see Glenn, George D.

Scholz, Jackson. Dugout Tycoon. (gr. 7 up). 1963. 6.75 o.p. (ISBN 0-688-21248-4). Morrow.

Scholz, Nellie, et al. How to Decide: A Workbook for Women. 1978. pap. 4.95 (ISBN 0-380-18985-2, 37309). Avon.

Scholz-Peters, Ruth. Indian Bead Stringing & Weaving. LC 75-14524. (Illus.). 64p. 1975. 5.95 o.p. (ISBN 0-8069-5334-9); lib. bdg. 6.69 o.p. (ISBN 0-8069-5335-7). Sterling.

Schomaekers, G. American Civil War. (Illus.). 1979. 14.95 (ISBN 0-7137-0872-7, Pub. by Blandford Pr England). Sterling.

Schoman, Kenneth E., Jr. The BASIC Workbook: Creative Techniques for Beginning Programmers. (gr. 10 up). 1977. pap. text ed. 7.15x (ISBN 0-8104-5104-2). Hayden.

Schomas, Rhonda. My Book of Gospel Treasures. (Illus.). 63p. (Orig.). 1980. pap. 3.95 (ISBN 0-87747-839-2). Deseret Bk.

Schomburgk, Robert H. Description of British Guiana. LC 67-16358. Repr. of 1840 ed. 17.50x (ISBN 0-678-05002-3). Kelley.

--History of Barbados. LC 68-21443. Repr. of 1848 ed. 35.00x (ISBN 0-678-05003-1). Kelley.

Schomerus, H. W. Der Caiva Siddhanta: Leipzig, 1912. LC 78-74268. (Oriental Religions Ser.: Vol. 9). 455p. 1981. lib. bdg. 50.00 (ISBN 0-8240-3906-8). Garland Pub.

Schon, Donald A., jt. auth. see Argyris, Chris.

Schon, Fritz. Teamwork in the Dental Practice. (Illus.). 88p. 1971. 27.50. Quint Pub Co.

Schon, Fritz, jt. auth. see Singer, Fritz.

Schon, Isabel. A Bicultural Heritage: Themes for the Exploration of Mexican & Mexican-American Culture in Books for Children & Adolescents. LC 78-4332. 1978. 10.00 (ISBN 0-8108-1128-6). Scarecrow.

--Books in Spanish for Children & Young Adults: An Annotated Guide. LC 78-10299. (Libros Infantiles y Juveniles en Espanol: Una Guia Anotada). 1978. 10.00 (ISBN 0-8108-1176-6). Scarecrow.

--A Hispanic Heritage: A Guide to Juvenile Books About Hispanic People & Cultures. LC 80-10935. 178p. 1980. lib. bdg. 10.00 (ISBN 0-8108-1290-8). Scarecrow.

Schonauer, Betty, jt. auth. see Wilkerson, Gwen.

Schonbach, Michael, jt. auth. see Herrel, Stephen.

Schonberg, Harold C. Facing the Music. 1981. 14.95 (ISBN 0-671-25406-5). Summit Bks.

--Grandmasters of Chess. (Illus.). 1981. 17.95 (ISBN 0-393-01403-7). Norton.

Schonberger, Martin. The Hidden Key to Life. 1978. pap. 7.95 (ISBN 0-88231-023-2). ASI Pubs Inc.

Schonborn, Karl L. Dealing with Violence: The Challenge Faced by Police & Other Peacekeepers. (Illus.). 376p. 1975. 22.75 (ISBN 0-398-03333-1); pap. 16.75 (ISBN 0-398-03334-X). C C Thomas.

Schondorf, Hubert. Aspiration Cytology of the Breast. Schneider, Volker, tr. LC 77-24004. (Illus.). 1978. text ed. 32.00 (ISBN 0-7216-8013-5). Saunders.

Schone, Virginia. Penny Tales. LC 76-17827. (Illus.). (ps-3). 1977. 5.95 o.s.i. (ISBN 0-8193-0850-1, Four Winds); PLB 5.41 o.s.i. (ISBN 0-8193-0851-X). Schol Bk Serv.

Schoner, Bertram & Uhl, Kenneth P. Marketing Research: A Short Course for Professionals. (Wiley Professional Development Programs). 1976. 23.95 (ISBN 0-471-01701-9). Wiley.

Schonert, H., jt. auth. see Haase, T.

Schonert, K., et al, eds. see European Federation of Chemical Engineering, European Symposium, Amsterdam, Holland, June 3-5, 1980.

Schonfeldt, N. Surface Active Ethylene Oxide Adducts. LC 69-19089. 1970. 115.00 (ISBN 0-08-012819-X). Pergamon.

Schonfield, Hugh. After the Cross. LC 80-27856. 128p. 1981. 7.95 (ISBN 0-498-02549-7). A S Barnes.

Schonzeler, Hans-Hubert. Bruckner. rev ed. (Illus.). 1978. pap. 7.95 (ISBN 0-7145-0145-X, Pub. by M Boyars). Merrimack Bk Serv.

--Dvorak. 192p. Date not set. 13.95 (ISBN 0-7145-2575-8, Pub. by M. Boyars). Merrimack Bk Serv.

School of Oriental & African Studies, University of London. Library Catalogue of the School of Oriental & African Studies: Third Supplement, 19 vols. 1979. Set. lib. bdg. 1990.00 (ISBN 0-8161-0203-1). G K Hall.

School of Social Work, Columbia University. Dictionary Catalog of the Whitney M. Young, Jr., Memorial Library of Social Work. (Library Catalogs & Supplements Ser.). 1980. lib. bdg. 1275.00 (ISBN 0-8161-0307-0). G K Hall.

Schoolboys Of Barbiana. Letter to a Teacher. 1971. Repr. of 1970 ed. 5.95 o.p. (ISBN 0-394-43294-0, Vin). Random.

Schoolbred, C. F. A Guide to Recent Criminal Legislation. LC 68-22498. 1968. 15.00 (ISBN 0-08-012895-5); pap. 7.00 (ISBN 0-08-012894-7). Pergamon.

Schoolbred, C. F., jt. auth. see Vick, R. W.

Schoolcraft, Henry R. The American Indians: Their History, Condition & Prospects from Original Notes & Manuscripts... Together with an Appendix Containing Thrilling Narratives, Daring Exploits, Etc. LC 75-7083. (Indian Captivities Ser.: Vol. 60). 1977. Repr. of 1851 ed. lib. bdg. 44.00 (ISBN 0-8240-1684-X). Garland Pub.

Schooler, D. Science, Scientists & Public Policy. LC 70-122274. 1971. 8.95 o.s.i. (ISBN 0-02-928000-1); pap. text ed. 4.50 o.s.i. (ISBN 0-02-928010-9). Free Pr.

Schoolland, M. Llevando los Pequenitos a Dios, 2 vols, Vols. 2 & 3. Vol. 2. 1.40 o.p. (ISBN 0-686-12555-X); Vol. 3. 1.30 o.p. (ISBN 0-686-12556-8). Banner of Truth.

Schoolland, Marian, tr. see Norel, K.

Schoolland, Marian M. Leading Little Ones to God: A Child's Book of Bible Teaching. rev., 2nd ed. (Illus.). 96p. 1981. 9.95 (ISBN 0-8028-4035-3). Eerdmans.

Schoolman, Morton. The Imaginary Witness: The Critical Theory of Herbert Marcuse. LC 80-640. 1980. 19.95 (ISBN 0-02-928040-0). Free Pr.

Schools Council. Project Technology Handbook, Book 14: Simple Computer & Control Logic. (gr. 12). 1974. pap. text ed. 5.25x (ISBN 0-435-75913-2). Heinemann Ed.

Schools Council History 13-16 Project. Arab-Israeli Conflict. (Modern World Problems Ser.). (Illus.). 1979. Repr. of 1977 ed. lib. bdg. 9.95 (ISBN 0-912616-68-7); pap. text ed. 4.45 (ISBN 0-912616-67-9). Greenhaven.

--The Rise of Communist China. (Modern World Problems Ser.). (Illus.). 1979. lib. bdg. 9.95 (ISBN 0-912616-70-9); pap. text ed. 4.45 (ISBN 0-912616-69-5). Greenhaven.

Schools Council Sixth Form Mathematics Project. Mathematics Applicable: Introductory Probability. 1975. pap. text ed. 3.95x (ISBN 0-435-51698-1). Heinemann Ed.

Schools Councils History 13-16 Project. The Irish Question. (Modern World Problems Ser.). (Illus.). 1979. lib. bdg. 9.95 (ISBN 0-912616-72-5); pap. text ed. 4.45 (ISBN 0-912616-71-7). Greenhaven.

Schoonenberg, Piet. The Christ. LC 74-127873. 1971. 8.95 (ISBN 0-8164-1006-2). Crossroad NY.

Schooneveld, C. H., jt. ed. see Armstrong, Daniel.

Schoonmaker, Ann. Me, Myself & I: Every Woman's Journey to Her Self. LC 76-62958. 1977. 7.95 o.p. (ISBN 0-06-067120-3, HarpR). Har-Row.

Schoonover, Shirley. Mountain of Winter. 192p. 1980. pap. 2.25 (ISBN 0-380-76513-6, 76513). Avon.

Schoor, Gene. Babe Didrikson: The World's Greatest Woman Athlete. LC 77-16944. (gr. 4-7). 1978. 7.95a (ISBN 0-385-13031-7); PLB (ISBN 0-385-13032-5). Doubleday.

--Bart Starr: A Biography. LC 76-56332. (gr. 4-7). 1977. PLB 6.95 (ISBN 0-385-11695-0). Doubleday.

--Football's Greatest Coach, Vince Lombardi. (Illus.). 240p. (gr. 6-7). 1974. 4.95 o.p. (ISBN 0-385-08513-3). Doubleday.

Schopenhauer, Arthur. Essay on the Freedom of the Will. Kolenda, Konstantin, tr. LC 59-11675. 1960. pap. 3.95 (ISBN 0-672-60248-2, LLA70). Bobbs.

--On the Basis of Morality. Payne, E. F., tr. LC 65-26525. (Orig.). 1965. pap. 5.50 (ISBN 0-672-60445-0, LLA203). Bobbs.

--Parerga & Paralipomena: Short Philosophical Essays, 2 vols. Payne, E. F., tr. from Ger. 1201p. 1974. Vol. 1. 56.00x (ISBN 0-19-824508-4); Vol. 2. 63.00x (ISBN 0-19-824527-0); Vol. 1. pap. 18.50x (ISBN 0-19-824634-X); Vol. 2. pap. 21.00x (ISBN 0-19-824635-8); Set. 115.00x (ISBN 0-19-519813-1). Oxford U Pr.

--Will to Live: Selected Writings of Arthur Schopenhauer. Taylor, Richard, ed. LC 67-17822. pap. 4.95 (ISBN 0-8044-6847-8). Ungar.

--World As Will & Representation, 2 vols. Payne, E. F., tr. Set. 22.00 (ISBN 0-8446-2885-9). Peter Smith.

--World As Will & Representation, 2 Vols. Payne, E. F., tr. 1966. pap. text ed. 6.50 ea.; Vol. 1. pap. text ed. (ISBN 0-486-21761-2); Vol. 2. pap. text ed. (ISBN 0-486-21762-0). Dover.

Schopler, E. Individualized Assessment & Treatment for Autistic & Developmentally Disabled Children. Incl. Vol. I. Psycho-Educational Profile. 1978. 29.50 (ISBN 0-8391-1521-0); Vol. II. Teaching Strategies for Parents & Professionals. 1979. 19.95 (ISBN 0-685-97001-9). Univ Park.

Schopler, Eric, jt. ed. see Rutter, Michael.

Schor, Amy. Line by Line. 256p. 1981. 11.95 (ISBN 0-399-90083-7). Marek.

Schor, Edith, jt. auth. see Danzig, Alan.

Schor, Linda. Appetites. 256p. 1975. pap. 1.50 o.s.i. (ISBN 0-446-78812-0). Warner Bks.

Schor, Sandra & Fishman, Judith. The Random House Guide to Writing. 2nd ed. 464p. 1981. pap. text ed. 10.95 (ISBN 0-394-32608-3). Random.

Schorer, Mark. Pieces of Life. 1977. 8.95 o.p. (ISBN 0-374-23280-6). FS&G.

--The World We Imagine, Selected Essays. LC 68-14917. 1968. pap. 2.95 o.p. (ISBN 0-374-50712-0, N350). FS&G.

Schorer, Mark & Lawrence, D. H., eds. Sons & Lovers: A Facsimile of the Manuscript. LC 75-46037. 1978. 95.00x (ISBN 0-520-03190-3). U of Cal Pr.

Schories, Pat. Let's Pretend. (Peggy Cloth Bks.). (Illus.). (ps-1). 1980. pap. 3.50 (ISBN 0-448-40026-X). G&D.

Schorr, Alan E., ed. Directory of Special Libraries in Alaska. LC 75-29043. 1975. 5.00 o.p. (ISBN 0-87111-239-6). SLA.

--Government Reference Books 76-77: A Biennial Guide to U.S. Government Publications. LC 76-146307. 1978. lib. bdg. 25.00x (ISBN 0-87287-192-4). Libs Unl.

Schorr, Alvin L., ed. Jubilee for Our Times: A Practical Program for Income Equality. LC 76-41824. 1977. 17.50x (ISBN 0-231-04056-3). Columbia U Pr.

Schorsch, Anita. The Warner Collector' Guide to American Clocks: 0the/Collectors' Guide to American Clocks. (Orig.). 1981. pap. 9.95 (ISBN 0-446-97633-4). Warner Bks.

Schorsch, Ismar. Jewish Reactions to German Anti-Semitism, 1870-1914. LC 74-190193. (Studies in Jewish History, Culture & Institutions). 288p. 1972. 20.00x (ISBN 0-231-03643-4). Columbia U Pr.

Schoshinski, Robert. American Law of Landlords & Tenant, Vol. 1. LC 80-81653. 1980. 60.00. Lawyers Co-Op.

Schotland, Donald L. Diseases of the Motor Unit. (Illus.). 1981. price not set (ISBN 0-89289-410-5). HM.

Schott, Joseph L. No Left Turns. 192p. 1976. pap. 1.50 o.p. (ISBN 0-345-25013-3). Ballantine.

Schott, Max. Up Where I Used to Live. LC 78-11619. (Illinois Short Fiction Ser.). 1978. 10.00 (ISBN 0-252-00719-0); pap. 3.95 (ISBN 0-252-00720-4). U of Ill Pr.

Schottelius, Byron A. & Schottelius, Dorothy D. Textbook of Physiology. 18th ed. LC 77-17844. (Illus.). 1978. text ed. 19.95 (ISBN 0-8016-4356-2). Mosby.

Schottelius, Byron A., et al. Physiology Laboratory Manual. (Illus.). 1978. pap. text ed. 9.50 (ISBN 0-8016-4354-6). Mosby.

Schottelius, Dorothy D., jt. auth. see Schottelius, Byron A.

Schottenfeld, David, ed. Cancer Epidemiology & Prevention: Current Concepts. (Illus.). 592p. 1975. 59.75 (ISBN 0-398-03173-8). C C Thomas.

Schotter, Andrew. The Economic Theory of Social Institutions. (Illus.). 240p. Date not set. 29.50 (ISBN 0-521-23044-6). Cambridge U Pr.

Schottland, Charles I. Social Security Program in the United States. 2nd ed. (YA) 1970. text ed. 10.95 (ISBN 0-13-818278-7). P-H.

Schou, M. Lithium Treatment of Manic-Depressive Illness. (Illus.). viii, 72p. 1980. pap. 14.50 (ISBN 3-8055-0392-X). S Karger.

Schoude, Lee E., jt. auth. see Cope, Dwight W.

Schouler, J. Constitutional Studies: State & Federal. LC 76-124894. (American Constitutional & Legal History Ser.). 1971. Repr. of 1897 ed. lib. bdg. 29.50 (ISBN 0-306-71993-2). Da Capo.

Schouls, P. Insight Authority & Power. 1972. pap. 1.95 o.p. (ISBN 0-686-11990-8). Wedge Pub.

--Man in Communication. 1968. pap. 1.50 o.p. (ISBN 0-686-11991-6). Wedge Pub.

Schouls, Peter A. The Imposition of Method: A Study of Descartes & Locke. 282p. 1980. text ed. 37.50x (ISBN 0-19-824613-7). Oxford U Pr.

Schoultz, Lars, jt. auth. see Martz, John D.

Schouten, Jan. The Pentagram As a Medical Symbol: An Iconological Study. 1979. text ed. 17.25x (ISBN 90-6004-166-6). Humanities.

Schouten, Jan A. & Van Der Kulk, W. Pfaff's Problem & Its Generalizations. LC 75-77140. 1969. Repr. of 1949 ed. 19.50 (ISBN 0-8284-0221-3). Chelsea Pub.

Schowalter, William R. Mechanics of Non-Newtonian Fluids. LC 76-51440. 1977. text ed. 52.00 (ISBN 0-08-021778-8). Pergamon.

Schrade, Leo. Bach: The Conflict Between the Sacred & the Secular. LC 73-4331. 1974. Repr. of 1955 ed. lib. bdg. 16.50 (ISBN 0-306-70581-8). Da Capo.

--Beethoven in France. LC 77-16533. (Music Reprint Ser.: 1978). 1978. lib. bdg. 35.00 (ISBN 0-306-77538-7). Da Capo.

--Monteverdi, Creator of Modern Music. (Music Reprint Ser.). 1979. Repr. of 1950 ed. lib. bdg. 32.50 (ISBN 0-306-79565-5). Da Capo.

Schrader, Alvin M., jt. auth. see Houser, L.

Schrader, B. & Meier, W., eds. Raman-IR Atlas of Organic Compounds. 1974-1976. Set. 467.70. Vol. 1,345p (ISBN 3-527-25539-7). Vol. 2,386p (ISBN 3-527-25541-9). Vol. 3,507p (ISBN 3-527-25542-7). Verlag Chemie.

Schrader, Constance. Nine to Five: The Complete Looks, Clothes & Personality Handbook for the Working Woman. (Illus.). 200p. 1981. 13.95 (ISBN 0-13-622555-1); pap. 6.95 (ISBN 0-13-622563-2). P-H.

Schrader, Constance, jt. auth. see Livingston, Lida.

Schrader, Halwart. BMW: A History. Wakefield, Ron, tr. from Ger. LC 78-71792. (Illus.). 1979. 69.95 (ISBN 0-915038-15-3); leather edition 6.95 (ISBN 0-915038-21-8). Princeton Pub.

Schrader, Halwart & Demand, Carlo. The Supercharged Mercedes. Tubbs, D. B., tr. (Illus.). 96p. 1979. 37.50 (ISBN 0-85059-417-0, Pub. by Edita Switzerland). Motorbooks Intl.

Schrader, Monika. Mimesis und Poiesis Poetologische Zum Bildungsroman. (Quellen und Forschungen zur Sprach-und Kulturgeschichte der germanischen). 367p. (Ger.). 1975. 44.70x (ISBN 3-11-005904-5). De Gruyter.

Schrader, Paul. Transcendental Style in Film: Ozu-Bresson-Dreyer. 1972. 14.95 (ISBN 0-520-02038-3). U of Cal Pr.

Schrader, Robert W. The Nature of Theological Argument: A Study of Paul Tillich. LC 75-43784. (Harvard Dissertations in Religion). 1975. pap. 7.50 (ISBN 0-89130-071-6, 020104). Scholars Pr Ca.

Schrader, William J., et al. Financial Accounting: An Events Approach. 520p. 1981. text ed. 18.95x (ISBN 0-931920-29-9). Dame Pubns.

Schraer, Harald, ed. Biological Calcification: Cellular & Molecular Aspects. LC 69-12161. 462p. 1970. 35.00 (ISBN 0-306-50073-6, Plenum Pr). Plenum Pub.

Schraff, Anne, jt. auth. see Schraff, Francis.

Schraff, Francis & Schraff, Anne. Jesus Our Brother. 1968. pap. 1.95 o.p. (ISBN 0-89243-030-3, 46525). Liguori Pubns.

Schraff, Francis, et al. Learning About Jesus. rev. ed. 80p. (gr. 2-4). 1980. pap. 1.95 (ISBN 0-89243-129-6). Liguori Pubns.

Schraffenberger, Nancy, jt. auth. see Herrick, Joy F.

Schraffenberger, Nancy, ed. Woman's Day Decorative Needlework for the Home. (Illus.). 176p. 1981. 15.95 (ISBN 0-8069-5442-6, Columbia Hse). Sterling.

Schrag, Adele F. How to Dictate. LC 80-26747. (Illus.). 96p. 1981. pap. text ed. 3.60 (ISBN 0-07-055601-6). McGraw.

Schrage, Alice. Birth of the King. LC 80-53874. 128p. 1981. pap. 1.95 (ISBN 0-8307-0765-4). Regal.

Schrage, Linus. Linear Programming Models: With Illustrations Using LINDO. (Illus.). 288p. (Orig.). 1981. pap. text ed. 16.00x (ISBN 0-89426-031-6); tchrs'. ed. 16.00x (ISBN 0-89426-033-2). Scientific Pr.

--User's Manual for LINDO. (Orig.). 1981. pap. text ed. 10.00x (ISBN 0-89426-032-4). Scientific Pr.

Schrage, Rainer. Speaking of: Family Planning. Heyden, Fransosis, tr. from Ger. LC 80-68765. (Medical Adviser Ser.). (Illus.). 1980. pap. 3.95 (ISBN 0-8326-2245-1, 7458). Delair.

Schrager, O., jt. auth. see De Quiros, J.

Schram, Joseph. Successful Bathrooms. 2nd rev. ed. Horowitz, Shirley M. & Frohn, Peggy, eds. LC 80-183. (Successful Series). (Illus.). 1980. 14.95 (ISBN 0-912336-97-8); pap. 6.95 (ISBN 0-912336-98-6). Structures Pub.

--Successful Children's Rooms. Horowitz, Shirley, ed. LC 79-11967. (Successful Ser.). (Illus.). 1979. 13.95 (ISBN 0-912336-89-7); pap. 6.95 (ISBN 0-912336-90-0). Structures Pub.

--Successful Garages & Carports. Case, Virginia, ed. LC 80-23515. (Successful Ser.). (Illus.). 128p. 1980. 15.95 (ISBN 0-89999-017-7); pap. 6.95 (ISBN 0-89999-018-5). Structures Pub.

Schram, Joseph F. Book of Successful Bathrooms. LC 75-31489. (Illus.). 160p. 1975. 12.00 o.p. (ISBN 0-912336-16-1); pap. 5.95 o.p. (ISBN 0-912336-17-X). Structures Pub.

--Finding & Fixing the Older Home. LC 76-25112. (Illus.). 1976. 13.95 (ISBN 0-912336-32-3); pap. 6.95 (ISBN 0-912336-33-1). Structures Pub.

--Improving the Outside of Your Home. LC 77-28008. 1978. 13.95 (ISBN 0-912336-64-1); pap. 6.95 (ISBN 0-912336-65-X). Structures Pub.

--Successful Home Additions. LC 77-8872. (A Successful Book). (Illus.). 1977. 13.95 (ISBN 0-912336-46-3); pap. 6.95 (ISBN 0-912336-47-1). Structures Pub.

Schram, S. T., ed. Authority, Participation & Cultural Change in China. (Contemporary China Institute Publications). (Illus.). 260p. 1973. 47.50 (ISBN 0-521-20296-5); pap. 14.50x (ISBN 0-521-09820-3). Cambridge U Pr.

Schramel, P., ed. Trace Elements: Analytical Chemistry in Medicine & Biology. 1000p. 1980. text ed. 113.00x (ISBN 3-11-008357-4). De Gruyter.

Schramm, Carl J., et al. Workers Who Drink. LC 76-58248. 1978. 18.95 (ISBN 0-669-01342-0). Lexington Bks.

Schramm, Carol, jt. auth. see Highberger, Ruth.

Schramm, G. M. The Graphemes of Tiberian Hebrew. (U. C. Publ. in Near Eastern Studies: Vol. 2). 1964. pap. 6.00x (ISBN 0-520-09294-5). U of Cal Pr.

Schramm, Sarah S. Plow Women Rather Than Reapers: An Intellectual History of Feminism in the United States. LC 78-10907. 1979. lib. bdg. 19.00 (ISBN 0-8108-1183-9). Scarecrow.

Schramm, Tim. Der Markus-Stoff Bei Lukas. LC 79-96099. (New Testament Studies Monographs: No. 14). (Ger). 1971. 32.50 (ISBN 0-521-07743-5). Cambridge U Pr.

Schramm, Wilbur. Big Media, Little Media: Tools & Technologies for Instruction. LC 76-30522. (People & Communication: Vol. 2). 1977. 20.00x (ISBN 0-8039-0740-0); pap. 9.95x (ISBN 0-8039-0745-1). Sage.

Schramm, Wilbur, jt. auth. see Chu, Godwin C.

Schramm, Wilbur, et al. Bold Experiment: The Story of Educational Television in American Samoa. LC 79-67777. (Illus.). 264p. 1981. text ed. 17.50x (ISBN 0-8047-1090-2). Stanford U Pr.

Schrammn, Wilbur L. The Story Workshop. 458p. 1980. Repr. of 1938 ed. lib. bdg. 20.00 (ISBN 0-89984-423-5). Century Bookbindery.

Schrand, Heinrich, jt. auth. see Dunlop, Ian.

Schrank, Barbara & Supino, David J., eds. The Famous Miss Burney: The Diaries & Letters of Fanny Burney. LC 75-25622. (John Day Bk.). 1976. 9.95 o.s.i. (ISBN 0-381-98285-8, TYC-T). T Y Crowell.

Schranz, Karl. The Karl Schranz 7-Day Ski System. Casewit, Curtis W., tr. (Illus.). 112p. 1974. 6.95 o.s.i. (ISBN 0-02-607300-5). Macmillan.

Schreck, Everett M. Principles & Styles of Acting. (Speech & Drama). 1970. text ed. 19.95 (ISBN 0-201-06765-X). A-W.

Schrecker, Anne, tr. see Leibniz, Gottfried.

Schrecker, Paul, tr. see Leibniz, Gottfried.

Schreeder & Huisman. The Chromatography of Hemoglobin. 320p. 1980. 29.75 (ISBN 0-8247-6941-4). Dekker.

Schreiber, Albert N. Cases in Manufacturing Management. (Management Ser.). (Illus.). 1965. text ed. 16.95 o.p. (ISBN 0-07-055608-3, C). McGraw.

Schreiber, Arthur C., et al. Economics of Urban Problems. 2nd ed. LC 75-31004. (Illus.). 480p. 1976. text ed. 18.50 (ISBN 0-395-20619-7). HM.

Schreiber, E. G., tr. see Bernardus Silvestris.

Schreiber, Elizabeth A. Wonders of Terns. LC 77-16862. (Wonders Ser.). (Illus.). (gr. 5 up). 1978. 5.95 (ISBN 0-396-07549-5). Dodd.

Schreiber, Flora R. Sybil. (Illus.). 464p. 1974. pap. 3.50 (ISBN 0-446-96903-6). Warner Bks.

Schreiber, Harvey K. The Eagle & the Sword. 1979. pap. 1.75 o.p. (ISBN 0-445-04346-6). Popular Lib.

Schreiber, Jose G. Small Business Development in Brazil: A Study of the UNO Program. 64p. (Orig.). 1976. pap. 3.00 (ISBN 0-89192-119-2). Interbk Inc.

Schreiber, K., ed. see FEBS Meeting, 12th, Dresden, 1978.

Schreiber, M. H. Introduction to Diagnostic Radiology. (Illus.). 368p. 1980. 29.50 (ISBN 0-398-04026-5). C C Thomas.

Schreiber, Martin H. Bodyscapes. LC 79-92484. (Illus.). 1980. pap. 14.95 (ISBN 0-89659-105-0). Abbeville Pr.

Schreiber, Melvyn H. Indications & Alternatives in X-Ray Diagnosis: A Guide to the Effective Employment of Roentgenologic Studies in the Solution of Diagnostic Problems. 2nd ed. (Illus.). 192p. 1974. pap. 16.75 (ISBN 0-398-03027-8). C C Thomas.

Schreiber, Meyer, ed. Social Work & Mental Retardation. LC 78-101462. (John Day Bk.). 1970. 18.00 o.s.i. (ISBN 0-381-97035-3, A72700, TYC-T). T Y Crowell.

Schreiber, Michael. Training to Run the Perfect Marathon. LC 80-82638. (Illus.). 181p. (Orig.). 1980. pap. 7.50 (ISBN 0-912528-19-2). John Muir.

Schreiber, Ron. False Clues. LC 77-88109. (Illus.). 1978. pap. 3.50 (ISBN 0-930762-01-0). Calamus Bks.

--Moving to a New Place. LC 74-26380. 72p. 1974. pap. 4.95 (ISBN 0-914086-07-3). Alicejamesbooks.

Schreiber, Ron, jt. auth. see Schwartz, Jeffrey.

Schreiber, W. G. A Bullet or a Rope. 192p. (YA) 1976. 5.95 (ISBN 0-685-64244-5, Avalon). Bouregy.

--The Mansville Brand. (YA) 1978. 5.95 (ISBN 0-685-84749-7, Avalon). Bouregy.

--Massacre at Fort Caid. (YA) 1977. 5.95 (ISBN 0-685-74265-2, Avalon). Bouregy.

--Revenge at Blue Valley. (YA) 1978. 5.95 (ISBN 0-685-86412-X, Avalon). Bouregy.

Schreibman, Walt, jt. auth. see Magid, Ken.

Schreier, Konrad F., Jr. Marbles, Knives & Axes. LC 78-15942. 70p. 1978. pap. 4.50 (ISBN 0-917714-19-9). Beinfeld Pub.

Schreier, Otto & Sperner, Emanuel. Projective Geometry of N Dimensions. 11.95 (ISBN 0-8284-0126-8). Chelsea Pub.

Schreier, Stefan. Compressible Flow. 768p. 1981. 40.00 (ISBN 0-471-05691-X, Pub. by Wiley-Interscience). Wiley.

Schreiner, G. E. Controversies in Nephrology. (Illus.). 722p. 1979. 49.50. Masson Pub.

Schreiner, Olive. The Story of an African Farm. Wolff, Robert L., ed. LC 75-1530. (Victorian Fiction Ser). 1975. Repr. of 1883 ed. lib. bdg. 66.00 (ISBN 0-8240-1602-5). Garland Pub.

Schreiner, Richard L., ed. Care of the Newborn. 318p. 1980. text ed. 24.00 (ISBN 0-89004-518-6). Raven.

Schreiner, Samuel A., Jr. Pleasant Places. 1978. pap. 1.95 o.p. (ISBN 0-449-23769-9, Crest). Fawcett.

--The Possessors & the Possessed. LC 79-54009. 1980. 12.95 (ISBN 0-87795-229-9). Arbor Hse.

--The Van Alens: First Family of a Nation's First City. LC 80-70222. 448p. 1981. 12.95 (ISBN 0-87795-311-2). Arbor Hse.

Schreuder, D. M. The Scramble for Southern Africa: 1877-1895. LC 78-58800. (Cambridge Commonwealth Ser.). 1980. 29.50 (ISBN 0-521-20279-5). Cambridge U Pr.

Schriber, T. J. Simulation Using GPSS. LC 73-21896. 608p. 1974. 29.95 (ISBN 0-471-76310-1). Wiley.

Schrickey, Harry G., jt. ed. see Runes, Dagobert.

Schrieber, Peter, ed. see Shugart, Cooksey.

Schrier, Allan M., et al, eds. Behavior of Non-Human Primates: Modern Research Trends. 1965-74. Vol. 1. 35.00 (ISBN 0-12-629101-2); Vol. 2. 32.50 (ISBN 0-12-629102-0); Vol. 3. 32.50 (ISBN 0-12-629103-9); Vol. 4. 32.50 (ISBN 0-12-629104-7). Acad Pr.

Schrier, Robert W. Renal & Electrolyte Disorders. LC 75-30300. 1976. text ed. 18.50 o.p. (ISBN 0-316-77475-8). Little.

Schrier, Robert W., ed. Renal & Electrolyte Disorders. 2nd ed. 500p. 1980. text ed. 22.95 (ISBN 0-316-77476-6). Little.

Schrier, William. Contest Oratory: A Handbook for High School & College Contestants & Coaches. LC 71-171595. 1971. 10.00 (ISBN 0-8108-0416-6). Scarecrow.

Schriesheim, Chester A., jt. auth. see Behling, Orlando.

Schriever, B. A., jt. ed. see Seifert, William W.

Schrils, Rudolph, jt. ed. see Kennedy, Hugh P.

Schrire, Robert A., jt. ed. see Van der Merwe, Hendrik.

Schriver, Peter, ed. see Curtiss, Richard A.

Schrock, Miriam M. Holistic Assessment of the Healthy Aged. LC 80-10198. 1980. pap. 10.95 (ISBN 0-471-05597-2, Pub. by Wiley Med). Wiley.

Schroder, Walter K. Defenses of Narragansett Bay in World War II. (Illus.). 133p. (Orig.). 1980. pap. 5.95 (ISBN 0-917012-22-4, 80-51763). RI Pubns Soc.

Schrodinger, Erwin. What Is Life? Bd. with Mind & Matter. pap. 8.95x (ISBN 0-521-09397-X). Cambridge U Pr.

Schroeder, Albert H. Apache Indians I: A Study of the Apache Indians. (American Indian Ethnohistory Ser: Indians of the Southwest). lib. bdg. 42.00 (ISBN 0-8240-0715-8). Garland Pub.

--Apache Indians IV. Horr, David A., ed. (American Indian Ethnohistory Ser.). 1978. lib. bdg. 42.00 (ISBN 0-8240-0719-0). Garland Pub.

Schroeder, Colin, jt. auth. see Cane, Brian.

Schroeder, Don & Lare, Gary. Audiovisual Equipment & Materials: A Basic Repair & Maintenance Manual. LC 79-384. 172p. 1979. pap. text ed. 10.00 (ISBN 0-8108-1206-1). Scarecrow.

Schroeder, Edward H., tr. see Elert, Werner.

Schroeder, Ernst. Algebra der Logik, 5 vols. in 3. 2nd ed. LC 63-11315. 2192p. (Ger.). 1980. Set. 75.00 (ISBN 0-8284-0171-3). Chelsea Pub.

Schroeder, H. E. Differentiation of Human Oral Stratified Epithelia. (Illus.). 310p. 1980. 90.00 (ISBN 3-8055-1462-X). S Karger.

Schroeder, Henry A. Poisons Around Us: Toxic Metals in Food, Air, & Water. LC 73-15283. 160p. 1974. 8.50x (ISBN 0-253-16675-6). Ind U Pr.

Schroeder, Howard, jt. auth. see Nentl, Jerolyn.

Schroeder, Howard, ed. see Abels, Harriette S.

Schroeder, Howard, ed. see East, Ben & Nentl, Jerolyn.

Schroeder, Howard, ed. see Fenton, Don & Fenton, Barb.

Schroeder, Howard, ed. see Hahn, James & Hahn, Lynn.

Schroeder, Howard, ed. see Nentl, Jerolyn.

Schroeder, Howard, ed. see Zelaznak, Shirley.

Schroeder, Howard, ed. see Zeleznak, Shirley.

Schroeder, Ira. Listener's Handbook: A Guide to Music Appreciation. 3rd ed. (Illus.). (gr. 9-12). 1966. text ed. 3.95x o.p. (ISBN 0-8138-1010-8). Iowa St U Pr.

Schroeder, J. W., jt. ed. see Berman, I.

Schroeder, John H. Mr. Polk's War: American Opposition & Dissent, 1846-1848. 224p. 1973. 17.50x (ISBN 0-299-06160-4). U of Wis Pr.

Schroeder, John S., jt. auth. see Daily, Elaine K.

Schroeder, Joseph J., ed. see Editors of Gun Digest.

Schroeder, L. Bonnetty A. Juan y Hechos: Tomo II. Cativiela, A., tr. 1977. Repr. of 1975 ed. 9.95 (ISBN 0-311-03051-3). Casa Bautista.

Schroeder, Larry D. & Sjoquist, David L. The Property Tax & Alternative Local Taxes: An Economic Analysis. LC 75-3751. (Special Studies). (Illus.). 128p. 1975. text ed. 22.95 (ISBN 0-275-07480-3). Praeger.

Schroeder, Lelah Crabbs, jt. auth. see McCall, William A.

Schroeder, Lynn, jt. auth. see Ostrander, Sheila.

Schroeder, Paul, jt. auth. see Schabacker, Joseph.

Schroeder, R. Operations Management. (Management Ser.). (Illus.). 736p. 1981. text ed. 19.95 (ISBN 0-07-055612-1, C); instr's manual 5.95 (ISBN 0-07-055613-X). McGraw.

Schroeder, Richard G., jt. auth. see McCullers, Levi D.

Schroeder, Rosella J., jt. auth. see Sanderson, Marie C.

Schroeder, Theodore A. Constitutional Free Speech Defined & Defended. LC 72-106497. (Civil Liberties in American History Ser). 1970. Repr. of 1919 ed. lib. bdg. 45.00 (ISBN 0-306-71872-3). Da Capo.

--Obscene Literature & Constitutional Law. LC 72-116913. (Civil Lib. in Am. Hist. Ser.). 440p. 1972. Repr. of 1911 ed. lib. bdg. 25.00 (ISBN 0-306-70156-1). Da Capo.

Schroeder, W. Widick & Davis, Keith A. Where Do I Stand? Living Theological Options for Contemporary Christians. 3rd ed. LC 78-59809. (Studies in Ministry & Parish Life). 1978. 13.50x (ISBN 0-913552-12-7); pap. 6.00x (ISBN 0-913552-13-5). Exploration Pr.

Schroeder, W. Widick, jt. ed. see Cobb, John B., Jr.

Schroeder, William C., jt. auth. see Hildebrand, Samuel F.

Schroeer, Dietrich. Physics & Its Fifth Dimension: Society. LC 75-184158. 1972. pap. text ed. 9.95 (ISBN 0-201-06767-6). A-W.

Schroeppel, Tom. The Bare Bones Camera Course for Film & Video. 2nd ed. LC 79-92048. (Illus.). 89p. (Orig.). 1980. pap. 5.95 (ISBN 0-9603718-0-X). Schroeppel.

Schroeter, Bob, jt. auth. see Kaufman, Hal.

Schroeter, L. C. Ingredient X. 1970. 17.25 (ISBN 0-08-015866-8). Pergamon.

Schroeter, Leonard. The Last Exodus. LC 79-4922. 444p. (Orig.). 1979. pap. 7.95 (ISBN 0-295-95685-2). U of Wash Pr.

Schroetter, Hilda N. Foxe's Book of English Martyrs. 360p. 1981. 10.95 (ISBN 0-8499-0152-9). Word Bks.

Schrotenboer, P. Motices of Ecumenism. 1967. pap. 1.25 o.p. (ISBN 0-686-11992-4). Wedge Pub.

Schroth, Marvin L. & Sue, Derald W. Introductory Psychology. 1975. pap. text ed. 12.95x (ISBN 0-256-01710-7). Dorsey.

Schruben, Francis W. Kansas in Turmoil, 1930-1936. LC 76-93048. 1969. 10.00x o.p. (ISBN 0-8262-0080-X). U of Mo Pr.

Schryver, Alice. Chinese Cooking for Beginners. LC 73-11986. (gr. 7 up). 1974. 6.95 (ISBN 0-396-06875-8). Dodd.

--Italian Cooking for Beginners. LC 76-53442. (gr. 7 up). 1977. 6.95 (ISBN 0-396-07428-6). Dodd.

Schubert, Delwyn G. & Torgerson, Theodore L. Improving the Reading Program. 5th ed. 1981. pap. text ed. 8.95x (ISBN 0-697-06186-8). Wm C Brown.

Schubert, E. D. Hearing: Its Function & Dysfunction. (Disorders of Human Communications: Vol. 1). (Illus.). 200p. 1980. 29.50 (ISBN 0-387-81579-1). Springer-Verlag.

Schubert, Earl D., jt. ed. see Tobias, Jerry V.

Schubert, Franz. Complete Chamber Music for Strings. pap. 8.95 (ISBN 0-486-21463-X). Dover.

--Complete Song Cycles. Mandyczewski, Euseblus, ed. Drinker, Henry S., tr. LC 74-116821. Orig. Title: Lieder & Gesange. 1970. pap. 6.00 (ISBN 0-486-22649-2). Dover.

--Schubert Symphony in B Minor (Unfinished) Chusid, Martin, ed. 1971. 7.95x (ISBN 0-393-02170-X); pap. 4.95x (ISBN 0-393-09731-5). Norton.

--Shorter Works for Pianoforte Solo. 199p. 1970. pap. 6.50 (ISBN 0-486-22648-4). Dover.

Schubert, Glendon. Dispassionate Justice: A Synthesis of the Judicial Opinions of Robert H. Jackson. LC 69-13634. 1969. 28.50x (ISBN 0-672-51138-X). Irvington.

--Human Jurisprudence: Public Law As Political Science. LC 74-78862. 416p. 1975. text ed. 16.00x (ISBN 0-8248-0294-2). U Pr of Hawaii.

--The Judicial Mind Revisited: Psychometric Analysis of Supreme Court Ideology. (Science & Engineering Policy Ser). (Illus.). 208p. 1974. text ed. 10.95x (ISBN 0-19-501754-4); pap. text ed. 5.95x (ISBN 0-19-501753-6). Oxford U Pr.

Schubert, Glendon A. The Presidency in the Courts. LC 72-8122. (American Constitutional & Legal History Ser). 408p. 1973. Repr. of 1957 ed. lib. bdg. 35.00 (ISBN 0-306-70529-X). Da Capo.

Schubert, Glendon A., ed. Judicial Decision-Making. LC 63-8422. 1963. 14.95 (ISBN 0-02-928230-6). Free Pr.

Schubert, Gottfried. Cure & Recognize Aquarium Fish Diseases. (Illus.). 128p. 1974. pap. 4.95 (ISBN 0-87666-033-2, PS-210). TFH Pubns.

Schubert, Margot, jt. auth. see Herwig, Rob.

Schubert, Paul B., ed. Die Methods: Design, Fabrication, Maintainance & Application, Bk. 1. LC 66-19984. (Illus.). 464p. 1966. 18.00 (ISBN 0-8311-1013-9). Indus Pr.

Schubert, Paul B., ed. see Oberg, Erik, et al.

Schubert, R. & Ryan, L. Fundamentals of Solar Heating. 1981. 23.95 (ISBN 0-13-344457-0). P-H.

Schubert, Robert P., jt. auth. see Davis, Albert J.

Schubnel, Henri-Jean. Gems & Jewels: Uncut Stones & Objets d'Art. (Illus.). (gr. 8 up). 1972. PLB 8.46 o.p. (ISBN 0-307-64313-1, Golden Pr). Western Pub.

Schubring, Walther. The Doctrine of the Jainas. Buerlen, Wolfgang, tr. 1978. Repr. 12.50 (ISBN 0-89684-005-0, Pub. by Motilal Banarsidass India). Orient Bk Dist.

Schuchardt, Hugo. The Ethnography of Variation: Selected Writings on Pidgins & Creoles. Markey, T. L., ed. & tr. from Ger, Fr. (Linguistica Extranea: Studia 3). 174p. 1979. lib. bdg. 7.50 (ISBN 0-89720-003-9); pap. 5.50 (ISBN 0-89720-004-7). Karoma.
Schuchart, Max. The Netherlands. LC 74-183927. (Nations & Peoples Library). 288p. 1972. 8.50x o.s.i. (ISBN 0-8027-2126-5). Walker & Co.
Schuchert, Richard, tr. see Endo, Shusaku.
Schuchhardt, Walter-Herwig. Greek Art. LC 70-175860. (History of Art Ser.). (Illus.). 192p. 1972. 8.95x (ISBN 0-87663-169-3). Universe.
Schuck, Victoria, jt. auth. see Cummings, Bernice.
Schuckers, J. W. Life & Public Services of Salmon Portland Chase. LC 76-118202. (American Constitutional & Legal History Ser). 1970. Repr. of 1874 ed. lib. bdg. 59.50 (ISBN 0-306-71934-7). Da Capo.
Schuckit, Marc A. Psychiatry Specialty Board Review. 2nd ed. Feighner, John P., ed. 1977. spiral bdg. 16.50 (ISBN 0-87488-312-1). Med Exam.
Schudson, Michael. Discovering the News: A Social History of American Newspapers. LC 78-54997. 288p. 1981. pap. 5.95 (ISBN 0-465-01666-9). Basic.
Schueler, Donald G. Incident at Eagle Ranch: Man & Predator in the American West. LC 80-13588. 320p. 1980. 12.95 (ISBN 0-87156-230-8). Sierra.
Schuerger, James M. & Watterson, David G. Using Tests & Other Information in Counseling: A Decision Model for Practitioners. LC 77-17888. 1977. 7.95 (ISBN 0-918296-08-0). Inst Personality & Ability.
Schuerger, James M., jt. auth. see Cattell, Raymond B.
Schuerman, D. W., ed. Light Scattering by Irregularly Shaped Particles. 345p. 1980. 39.50 (ISBN 0-306-40421-4, Plenum Pr). Plenum Pub.
Schuessler, Karl F., ed. Sociological Methodology 1979. LC 78-62564. (Social & Behavioral Science Ser.). (Illus.). 1978. text ed. 17.95x (ISBN 0-87589-387-2). Jossey-Bass.
Schuettinger, Robert. Saving Social Security. 1977. pap. 10.00 (ISBN 0-685-79966-2). Coun Am Affairs.
Schuettinger, Robert, ed. South Africa: The Vital Link. 1977. pap. 10.00 (ISBN 0-685-79964-6). Coun Am Affairs.
Schuetz, Robert D., jt. auth. see Hart, Harold.
Schuetze, A. Basic Doctrines of the Bible. 1969. pap. 2.50 (ISBN 0-8100-0016-4). Northwest Pub.
Schuetze, Armin W. & Habezk, Irwin J. The Shepherd Under Christ. LC 74-81794. 1974. text ed. 12.00 (ISBN 0-8100-0046-6, 15N0351). Northwest Pub.
Schugart, Gary L., et al. A Survey of Accounting. LC 80-67776. 600p. 1981. text ed. 18.95x (ISBN 0-931920-25-6); study guide 5.95 (ISBN 0-686-68565-2); practice problem 4.95 (ISBN 0-686-68566-0); working papers 6.95 (ISBN 0-686-68567-9). Dame Pubns.
Schuh, Fred. The Master Book of Mathematical Puzzles & Recreations. O'Beirne, T. H., ed. Gobel, F., tr. LC 68-28064. Orig. Title: Wonderlijke Problemen Leerzaam Tijoverdrijf Door Puzzle En Spel. (Illus.). 430p. 1969. pap. 4.95 (ISBN 0-486-22134-2). Dover.
Schuh, Nita. After Winter, Spring. 1978. pap. 2.95 o.p. (ISBN 0-88270-284-X). Logos.
Schuhardt, Vernon T. Pathogenic Microbiology: The Biology & Prevention of Selected Bacterial, Fungal, Rickettsial, & Viral Diseases of Clinical Importance. 1978. 23.75x o.p. (ISBN 0-397-47373-7); pap. text ed. 15.25x (ISBN 0-397-47370-2). Lippincott.
Schuhmann, R. Metallurgical Engineering Vol. 1. Engineering Principles. (Illus.). 1952. 22.95 (ISBN 0-201-06770-6). A-W.
Schuit, G. G. & Prins, R., eds. Chemistry & Chemical Engineering of Catalytic Processes. (NATO-Advanced Study Institute Ser.). 660p. 1980. 75.00x (ISBN 9-0286-0730-7). Sijthoff & Noordhoff.
Schuknecht, Harold F. Stapedectomy. 119p. 1971. 28.50 o.p. (ISBN 0-316-77511-8). Little.
Schul, Bill & Pettit, Ed. The Psychic Power of Pyramids. 1978. pap. 3.95 (ISBN 0-449-90001-0, Columbine). Fawcett.
Schul, Bill D. How to Be an Effective Group Leader. LC 74-31420. 208p. 1975. 13.95 (ISBN 0-911012-61-3); pap. 7.95 (ISBN 0-88229-497-0). Nelson-Hall.
Schulberg, Budd. Moving Pictures: Memories of a Hollywood Prince. LC 80-9055. 448p. 1981. 16.95 (ISBN 0-8128-2817-8). Stein & Day.
--Swan Watch. 160p. 1975. 8.95 o.p. (ISBN 0-440-06016-8). Delacorte.
Schulberg, Herbert C. & Baker, Frank, eds. Program Evaluation in the Health Fields, Vol. II. LC 78-102679. 1979. text ed. 29.95x (ISBN 0-87705-339-1). Human Sci Pr.
Schulberg, Herbert C. & Jerrell, Jeanette M., eds. The Evaluator & Management. LC 79-19458. (Sage Research Progress Ser. in Evaluation: Vol. 4). (Illus.). 1979. 12.95x (ISBN 0-8039-1304-4); pap. 6.50x (ISBN 0-8039-1305-2). Sage.
Schuld, Frank P. The Simple Squeeze in Bridge. LC 74-6305. (Illus.). 1977. 10.95 (ISBN 0-8069-8662-X); PLB 9.29 (ISBN 0-8069-8663-8); pap. 5.95 (ISBN 0-8069-8664-6). Sterling.
Schule, Cliff, illus. Golden Prize. (Illus.). (gr. 3 up). 1979. pap. 1.25 (ISBN 0-307-21508-3, Golden Pr). Western Pub.
Schuler & Hull. Coal Heat. (Illus.). 128p. 10.95 (ISBN 0-916838-34-X); pap. 5.95 (ISBN 0-916838-37-4). Schiffer.
Schuler, Charles A., ed. see Palmore, Phyllis & Andre, Nevin.
Schuler, Elizabeth. Raising Puppies for Pleasure & Profit. Harris, Dianne F., ed. 1970. 8.95 (ISBN 0-02-607430-3). Macmillan.
Schuler, Michael. The Utilization & Recycle of Agricultural Wastes & Residues. 304p. 1980. 69.95 (ISBN 0-8493-5569-9). CRC Pr.
Schuler, Randall S. Personnel & Human Resource Management. (Management Ser.). (Illus.). 600p. 1981. text ed. 15.96 (ISBN 0-8299-0406-9). West Pub.
Schuler, Randall S. & Huse, Edgar F. Case Problems in Management. (Management Ser.). (Illus.). 1979. pap. text ed. 9.50 (ISBN 0-8299-0242-2); instrs.' manual avail. (ISBN 0-8299-0604-5). West Pub.
Schuler, Randall S., et al. Applied Readings in Personnel & Human Resource Management. (Management Ser.). (Illus.). 300p. 1981. pap. text ed. 6.36 (ISBN 0-8299-0408-5). West Pub.
Schuler, Robert. The Red Cedar Scroll. 1980. pap. 3.00 (ISBN 0-930600-14-2). Uzzano Pr.
Schuler, Stanley. Complete Terrace Book. 1974. pap. 5.95 o.s.i. (ISBN 0-02-063710-1, Collier). Macmillan.
--The Complete Terrace Book. LC 73-22529. (Illus.). 256p. 1974. 8.95 o.s.i. (ISBN 0-02-607380-3). Macmillan.
--Gardens Are for Eating. (Illus.). 340p. 1975. pap. 3.95 o.s.i. (ISBN 0-02-063700-4, Collier). Macmillan.
--Handyman's Guide to Home Remodeling. 1978. 14.95 (ISBN 0-8359-2773-3). Reston.
--How to Build Fences, Gates & Walls. (Illus.). 192p. 1976. pap. 6.95 o.s.i. (ISBN 0-02-000840-6, Collier). Macmillan.
--How to Design & Build a Fireplace. LC 77-3331. (Illus.). 1977. 14.95 (ISBN 0-02-607360-9): Macmillan.
--How to Design & Build a Fireplace. LC 77-3331. (Illus.). 1977. pap. 6.95 o.s.i. (ISBN 0-02-081860-2, Collier). Macmillan.
--How to Redesign Your Yard & Garden. 1977. pap. 4.95 o.p. (ISBN 0-8015-3746-0). Dutton.
Schulke, Flip. Underwater Photography for Everyone. 1978. 17.95 (ISBN 0-13-936450-1). P-H.
Schull, Joseph. Battle for the Rock: The Story of Wolfe & Montcalm. (Illus.). (gr. 4-6). 1960. 4.95 o.p. (ISBN 0-685-20372-7). St Martin.
Schuller, Gunther. Horn Technique. (YA) (gr. 9 up). 1962. 7.75 (ISBN 0-19-318701-9). Oxford U Pr.
Schuller, Robert. It's Possible. 1978. 6.95 o.p. (ISBN 0-8007-0927-6). Revell.
--Power Ideas for a Happy Family. 1976. pap. 1.50 (ISBN 0-89129-111-3). Jove Pubns.
--Turning Your Stress into Strength. 1979. pap. 1.95 o.p. (ISBN 0-449-14262-0, GM). Fawcett.
Schuller, Robert, tr. Pensamento Da Possiblilidade, O. (Portugese Bks.). (Port.). 1979. 1.50 (ISBN 0-8297-0727-1). Life Pubs Intl.
--Seras Lo Que Quieras Ser. (Spanish Bks.). (Span.). 1978. 1.90 (ISBN 0-8297-0514-7). Life Pubs Intl.
Schuller, Robert A., ed. Robert Schuller's Life Changers. 1981. 7.95 (ISBN 0-8007-1182-3). Revell.
Schuller, Robert H. Daily Power Thoughts. LC 77-68012. 1978. 8.95 (ISBN 0-89081-131-8); kivar 5.95 (ISBN 0-89081-123-7). Harvest Hse.
--Discover Courage to Face Your Future. (Orig.). 1978. pap. 1.25 (ISBN 0-89081-156-3). Harvest Hse.
--Discover Freedom. (Orig.). 1978. pap. 1.25 (ISBN 0-89081-155-5). Harvest Hse.
--Discover Health & Happiness. (Orig.). 1978. pap. 1.25 (ISBN 0-89081-143-1). Harvest Hse.
--Discover How Life Can Be Beautiful. (Orig.). 1978. pap. 1.25 (ISBN 0-89081-153-9). Harvest Hse.
--Discover How to Bloom Where You Are Planted. 1978. pap. 1.25 (ISBN 0-89081-154-7). Harvest Hse.
--Discover How to Get Your Priorities Straight. (Orig.). 1978. pap. 1.25 (ISBN 0-89081-137-7). Harvest Hse.
--Discover How to Turn Activity into Energy. (Orig.). 1978. pap. 1.25 (ISBN 0-89081-135-0). Harvest Hse.
--Discover Self-Love. (Orig.). 1978. pap. 1.25 (ISBN 0-89081-134-2). Harvest Hse.
--Discover the Miracles in Your Life. (Orig.). 1978. pap. 1.25 (ISBN 0-89081-136-9). Harvest Hse.
--Discover the Power for Overcoming Defeat. (Orig.). 1978. pap. 1.25 (ISBN 0-89081-141-5). Harvest Hse.
--Discover Your Opportunities. (Orig.). 1978. pap. 1.25 (ISBN 0-89081-142-3). Harvest Hse.
--Discover Your Possibilities. 1979. pap. 2.25 (ISBN 0-345-29455-6). Ballantine.
--Discover Your Possibilities. (Orig.). 1980. pap. 2.25 (ISBN 0-89081-214-4). Harvest Hse.
--Discover Your Self-Confidence. (Orig.). 1978. pap. 1.25 (ISBN 0-89081-144-X). Harvest Hse.
--It's Possible. 1979. pap. 1.75 o.p. (ISBN 0-449-14094-6, GM). Fawcett.
--Move Ahead with Possibility Thinking. (Spire Bk). 1973. pap. 2.50 (ISBN 0-8007-8105-8). Revell.
--Peace of Mind Through Possibility Thinking. 1978. pap. 2.25 (ISBN 0-515-05671-5). Jove Pubns.
--Peace of Mind Through Possibility Thinking. LC 72-76203. 1977. 7.95 (ISBN 0-385-00673-X). Doubleday.
--The Peak to Peek Principle. LC 80-1693. 192p. 1980. 9.95 (ISBN 0-385-17319-9). Doubleday.
--Power Ideas for a Happy Family. 128p. 1972. 5.95 o.p. (ISBN 0-8007-0525-4). Revell.
--Reach Out for a New Life. 1977. 9.95 (ISBN 0-8015-6247-3, Hawthorn). Dutton.
--Self-Love. (Spire Bks). 1975. pap. 2.50 (ISBN 0-8007-8195-3). Revell.
--Self-Love. (Orig.). pap. 1.95 (ISBN 0-515-05829-7). Jove Pubns.
--Self Love: The Dynamic Force of Success. 1969. 6.95 (ISBN 0-8015-6714-9, Hawthorn); pap. 3.50 (ISBN 0-8015-6720-3, Hawthorn). Dutton.
--You Can Become the Person You Want to Be. 224p. 1973. 10.95 (ISBN 0-8015-9048-5, Hawthorn); pap. 3.95 (ISBN 0-8015-9049-3, Hawthorn). Dutton.
--You Can Become the Person You Want to Be. 1976. pap. 2.50 (ISBN 0-8007-8235-6, Spire Bks). Revell.
--You Can Become the Person You Want to Be. (Orig.). pap. 2.25 (ISBN 0-515-05970-6). Jove Pubns.
Schullery, Paul, ed. The Grand Canyon: Early Impressions. LC 80-66185. 130p. 1981. 15.00 (ISBN 0-87081-086-3); pap. 6.95 (ISBN 0-87081-087-1). Colo Assoc.
Schullery, Paul D. The Bears of Yellowstone. LC 79-65734. (Illus.). 180p. (Orig.). 1980. 10.95 (ISBN 0-934948-01-1); pap. 5.95 (ISBN 0-934948-00-3). Yellowstone Lib.
Schulman. Focus on the Retarded Adult: Programs & Services. LC 79-17181. 1979. pap. 18.95 (ISBN 0-8016-4367-8). Mosby.
Schulman, Estella F. Now Listen Good: A Collection of Authentic West Indian Recipes. 6.95 (ISBN 0-88427-037-8). Green Hill.
--Now Listen Good! A Collection of Authentic West Indian Recipes. LC 79-19954. 1979. 6.95 (ISBN 0-88427-037-8, Dist. by Caroline Hse). North River.
Schulman, Eveline D. Intervention in Human Services. 2nd ed. LC 77-15488. (Illus.). 1978. pap. text ed. 13.95 (ISBN 0-8016-4369-4). Mosby.
Schulman, Grace, tr. see Cuadra, Pablo A.
Schulman, Ivan A., jt. ed. see Moreno, Cesar F.
Schulman, Janet. The Big Hello. (gr. k-6). 1980. pap. 0.95 (ISBN 0-440-40484-3, YB). Dell.
--The Great Big Dummy. (gr. k-6). Date not set. pap. price not set (ISBN 0-440-43072-0, YB). Dell.
--Jenny & The Tennis Nut. (gr. k-6). 1981. pap. price not set (ISBN 0-440-44211-7, YB). Dell.
--The Nutcracker. LC 79-11223. (Illus.). (gr. 1-5). 1979. 7.95 (ISBN 0-525-36245-2). Dutton.
Schulman, Jerome L. & Kupst, Mary J. The Child with Cancer: Clinical Approaches to Psychosocial Care - Research in Psychosocial Aspects. (Illus.). 232p. 1980. text ed. 19.50 (ISBN 0-398-03944-5). C C Thomas.
Schulman, Jonas. Handbook for the Differential Diagnosis of Infectious Diseases. (Illus.). 1980. pap. 14.50 (ISBN 0-8385-3616-6). ACC.
Schulman, Joseph D. & Simpson, Joe L., eds. Genetic Diseases in Pregnancy: Maternal Effects & Fetal Outcome. 1981. write for info. (ISBN 0-12-630940-X). Acad Pr.
Schulman, L. M., ed. Cracked Looking Glass: Stories of Other Realities. LC 78-138302. (gr. 9 up). 1971. 4.95 o.s.i. (ISBN 0-02-781400-9). Macmillan.
--Loners: Short Stories About the Young & Alienated. (gr. 7 up). 1970. 5.95g o.s.i. (ISBN 0-02-781390-8). Macmillan.
--Travelers: Stories of Americans Abroad. (gr. 9 up). 1972. 5.95 o.s.i. (ISBN 0-02-781410-6). Macmillan.
--Winners & Losers. LC 68-24106. (gr. 7 up). 1968. 5.95 o.s.i. (ISBN 0-02-781380-0). Macmillan.
Schulman, L. S. Techniques & Applications of Path Integration. LC 80-19129. 350p. 1981. 25.00 (ISBN 0-471-76450-7, Pub. by Wiley-Interscience). Wiley.
Schulman, Martin. The Ascendant: Your Karmic Doorway. 1981. pap. 6.95 (ISBN 0-87728-507-1). Weiser.
--The Astrology of Sexuality. 1981. pap. 7.95 (ISBN 0-87728-481-4). Weiser.
--Celestial Harmony: A Guide to Horoscope Interpretation. 1980. pap. 7.95 (ISBN 0-87728-495-4). Weiser.
--Karmic Astrology: The Karma of the Now, Vol. 4. 1978. pap. 4.95 (ISBN 0-87728-288-9). Weiser.
--Karmic Relationships. 1981. pap. 6.951311 (ISBN 0-686-69318-3). Weiser.
--Student Handbook: A Review Guide, Activities Manual & Reader for "Understanding Psychology". 2nd ed. 1977. wkbk. 6.95 (ISBN 0-394-32022-0). Random.
Schulman, Michael & Mekler, Eva, eds. Contemporary Scenes for Student Actors. (Orig.). 1980. pap. 3.95 (ISBN 0-14-048153-2). Penguin.
Schulmerich, Alma A. Josie Pearl. 1966. 4.95 (ISBN 0-913814-13-X). Nevada Pubns.
Schulte, Rainer, jt. ed. see Mitchell, Edward.
Schulte, Renee K., ed. The Young Nixon: An Oral Inquiry. 1978. 13.95 (ISBN 0-930046-02-1); pap. 7.95 (ISBN 0-930046-01-3). CSUF Oral Hist.
Schulte, Terry T. Well, I Don't Know. 167p. (Orig.). 1980. pap. 4.95. Schulte.
Schulterbrandt, Joy G. & Raskin, Allen, eds. Depression in Childhood: Diagnosis, Treatment & Conceptual Models. LC 76-47122. 1977. 15.50 (ISBN 0-89004-147-4); pap. 11.00 (ISBN 0-685-74515-5). Raven.
Schultes, Richard E. & Hofmann, Albert. The Botany & Chemistry of Hallucinogens. 2nd ed. (Amer. Lec Living Chemistry). (Illus.). 464p. 1980. text ed. 29.75 (ISBN 0-398-03863-5). C C Thomas.
Schultheiss, Tom. A Day in the Life: The Beatles Day-by-Day 1960-1970. LC 79-91185. 1980. 11.95 (ISBN 0-87650-120-X). Pierian.
Schults, Dorothy, jt. auth. see Sturman, Julie.
Schultz, Arthur R., tr. see Scholl, Inge.
Schultz, Barbara, jt. ed. see Schultz, Mark.
Schultz, Bill. Blue Thumb Guide to Working on Your House. LC 78-1992. (Illus.). 1978. pap. 5.95 o.p. (ISBN 0-87701-111-7, Prism Editions). Chronicle Bks.
Schultz, Birl E., jt. auth. see Beard, Charles A.
Schultz, Claire K. Thesaurus of Information Science Terminolgy. rev. ed. LC 78-16878. 1978. 11.50 (ISBN 0-8108-1156-1). Scarecrow.
Schultz, D. O. & Scott, S. K. The Subversive. (Illus.). 120p. 1973. 8.75 (ISBN 0-398-02660-2). C C Thomas.
Schultz, D. O. & Slepecky, M. Police Unarmed Defense Tactics. 102p. 1973. pap. 7.50 (ISBN 0-398-02666-1). C C Thomas.
Schultz, Dodi, jt. auth. see Blau, Sheldon Paul, M.D.
Schultz, Don E. Essentials of Creative Advertising. LC 80-70203. 1981. pap. text ed. 9.95 (ISBN 0-87251-045-X). Crain Bks.
Schultz, Donald & Scheer, Samuel. Crime Scene Investigation. LC 76-7559. (Criminal Justice Ser.). (Illus.). 1977. 15.95x (ISBN 0-13-192864-3). P-H.
Schultz, Donald O. Critical Issues in Criminal Justice. (Illus.). 304p. 1975. 18.75 (ISBN 0-398-03331-5). C C Thomas.
Schultz, Donald O., jt. auth. see Bopp, William J.
Schultz, Douglas G. & Fry, Edward F., eds. Piero Dorazio: A Retrospective. LC 79-55355. (Illus.). 1979. pap. 15.00 (ISBN 0-914782-30-4). Buffalo Acad.
Schultz, Duane. A History of Modern Psychology. 3rd ed. LC 80-616. 1980. lib ed 18.95 (ISBN 0-12-633060-3); write for info. (ISBN 0-12-633065-4). Acad Pr.
--Sabers in the Wind. 448p. 1981. pap. 2.50 (ISBN 0-449-14380-5, GM). Fawcett.
--Theories of Personality. 2nd ed. LC 80-26414. 384p. 1981. text ed. 17.95 (ISBN 0-8185-0439-0). Brooks-Cole.
--Theories of Personality. 2nd ed. 384p. 1981. text ed. 16.95 o.p. (ISBN 0-8185-0439-0). Brooks-Cole.
Schultz, Ernst B. Essentials of American Government. rev. ed. LC 75-2476. (gr. 9 up). 1975. pap. text ed. 5.95 (ISBN 0-8120-0642-9). Barron.
Schultz, G. & Moss, T. S., eds. High-Resolution Infrared & Submillimetre Spectroscopy: A Selection of Papers Presented at a Workshop Held in Bonn, 1977. 1977. pap. text ed. 23.00 (ISBN 0-08-021675-7). Pergamon.
Schultz, George J., ed. Foreign Trade Marketplace. LC 76-20342. 1977. 70.00 (ISBN 0-8103-0981-5). Gale.
Schultz, Gwen. Icebergs & Their Voyages. LC 75-9958. (Illus.). 96p. (gr. 7-9). 1975. PLB 6.96 (ISBN 0-688-32047-3). Morrow.

Schultz, Harold J. English Liberalism & the State: Individualism or Collectivism. LC 70-158945. (Problems in European Civilization Ser.). 1972. pap. text ed. 4.95x o.p. (ISBN 0-669-73361-X). Heath.

--History of England. 3rd ed. LC 79-153052. 1979. pap. 5.95 (ISBN 0-06-460188-9, CO 188, COS). Har-Row.

Schultz, Harold W. Food Law Handbook. (Illus.). 1981. lib. bdg. 79.50 (ISBN 0-87055-372-0). AVI.

Schultz, Harry. Bear Market Investment Strategies. LC 80-70618. 235p. 1981. 13.95 (ISBN 0-87094-224-7). Dow Jones-Irwin.

Schultz, Harry D. Financial Tactics & Terms for the Sophisticated International Investor. LC 72-9152. (Illus.). 184p. 1974. 10.00 o.p. (ISBN 0-06-013808-4, HarpT). Har-Row.

--Panics & Crashes: How You Can Make Money from Them. rev. ed. 256p. 1980. 12.95 (ISBN 0-87000-491-3). Arlington Hse.

Schultz, Harry D., jt. auth. see Sinclair, James E.

Schultz, Howard L. see Marton, L.

Schultz, J. S. Comparative Statutory Sources. 2nd ed. LC 78-60176. 1978. 19.50 (ISBN 0-930342-62-3). W S Hein.

Schultz, J. W. My Life As an Indian. 208p. 1975. pap. 1.25 o.p. (ISBN 0-449-30678-X, P678, Prem). Fawcett.

Schultz, James E. Mathematics for Elemenatry School Teachers. (Mathematics Ser.). 1977. text ed. 17.50 (ISBN 0-675-08509-8); instructor's manual 3.95 (ISBN 0-685-74286-5). Merrill.

Schultz, James W. Blackfeet & Buffalo. Seele, Keith C., ed. 384p. pap. 7.95 (ISBN 0-8061-1700-1). U of Okla Pr.

--Why Gone Those Times? Silliman, Lee, ed. LC 72-9262. (Civilization of the American Indian Ser.: Vol. 127). 271p. 1974. 12.95 (ISBN 0-8061-1068-6). U of Okla Pr.

Schultz, Janet L. Biology & Man Laboratory Guide. 80p. 1980. pap. text ed. 5.95 (ISBN 0-8403-2351-4). Kendall-Hunt.

Schultz, Jerelyn & Ralston, Penny. Decision to Parent: A Teaching Guide. 164p. (gr. 7-12). 1980. pap. 7.95 (ISBN 0-8138-1595-9). Iowa St U Pr.

Schultz, Jerold. Polymer Materials Science. (P-H Int'l Series in the Physical & Chemical Engineering Sciences). (Illus.). 496p. 1973. ref. ed. 29.95 (ISBN 0-13-687038-4). P-H.

Schultz, John R. & Cleaves, A. B. Geology in Engineering. LC 55-7317. 1955. text ed. 28.95x (ISBN 0-471-76461-2). Wiley.

Schultz, Joseph P. Judaism & the Gentile Faiths: Comparative Studies in Religion. LC 75-5250. 405p. 1981. 19.50 (ISBN 0-8386-1707-7). Fairleigh Dickinson.

Schultz, Joseph P., jt. auth. see Klausner, Carla L.

Schultz, Konrad F., jt. auth. see Kaynor, Richard S.

Schultz, LeRoy G. Rape Victimology. 424p. 1975. 37.75 (ISBN 0-398-03183-5). C C Thomas.

--The Sexual Victimology of Youth. (Illus.). 432p. 1980. text ed. 19.75 (ISBN 0-398-03925-9). C C Thomas.

Schultz, Leroy G., jt. ed. see Gochros, Harvey L.

Schultz, Mark & Schultz, Barbara, eds. Bicycles & Bicycling: A Guide to Information Sources. LC 79-22839. (Sports, Games, & Pastimes Information Guide Ser.: Vol. 6). 1979. 30.00 (ISBN 0-8103-1448-7). Gale.

Schultz, Mort J. One Thousand One Questions About Your Car. LC 73-9815. (Illus.). 224p. 1973. 11.00 o.p. (ISBN 0-07-055645-8, P&RB). McGraw.

Schultz, Neil. The Complete Guide to Motorcycle Repair & Maintenance. LC 76-2820. 1977. pap. 4.95 o.p. (ISBN 0-385-11510-5). Doubleday.

Schultz, Owen. The Blue Valentine. LC 78-12184. (Illus.). (gr. k-3). 1979. Repr. of 1965 ed. 6.50 (ISBN 0-688-22176-9); lib. bdg. 6.24 (ISBN 0-688-32176-3). Morrow.

Schultz, Pearle H. Sir Walter Scott: Wizard of the North. LC 66-28884. (Illus.). (gr. 7-10). 1967. 5.95 (ISBN 0-8149-0383-5). Vanguard.

Schultz, Renate A., jt. auth. see Benseler, David P.

Schultz, Richard J. Federalism & the Regulatory Process. 91p. 1979. pap. text ed. 1.50x (ISBN 0-686-68857-0, Pub. by Inst Res Pub Canada). Renouf.

--Federalism, Bureaucracy, & Public Policy: The Politics of Highway Transport Regulation. (IPAC Ser.). 237p. 1980. 20.95x (ISBN 0-7735-0360-9); pap. 10.95x (ISBN 0-7735-0362-5). McGill-Queens U Pr.

Schultz, Robert C. & Lehmann, Helmut T., eds. Luther's Works: The Christian in Society III, Vol. 46. LC 55-9893. 1967. 15.95 (ISBN 0-8006-0346-X, 1-346). Fortress.

Schultz, Robert C., ed. see Earthday X Colloquium, University of Denver, April 21-24, 1980.

Schultz, Robert J., et al, eds. Geothermal: Energy for the Eighties. (Transactions: Vol. 4). (Illus.). 835p. 1980. 28.00 (ISBN 0-934412-54-5). Geothermal.

Schultz, Russel R. Blueprint Reading for the Machine Trades. (Illus.). 304p. 1981. text ed. 16.95 (ISBN 0-13-077727-7). P-H.

Schultz, Russell E. A Milwaukee Transport Era: The Trackless Trolley Years. Sebree, Mac, ed. (Interurbans Special Ser.: 74). (Illus.). 160p. (Orig.). 1980. pap. 13.95 (ISBN 0-916374-43-2). Interurban.

Schultz, Samuel. Ley e Historia del Antiguo Testamento. Villalobos, Fernando P., tr. from Eng. (Curso Para Meastros Cristianos Ser.: No. 1). Orig. Title: Old Testament Survey - Law & History. (Illus.). 122p. (Span.). 1972. pap. 2.50 (ISBN 0-89922-008-8); instructor's manual 1.50 (ISBN 0-89922-009-6). Edit Caribe.

Schultz, Samuel J. The Old Testament Speaks. 3rd ed. LC 80-7740. (Illus.). 448p. 1980. 11.95x (ISBN 0-06-067134-3, HarpR). Har-Row.

--Old Testament Speaks: Old Testament History & Literature. (Illus.). 1970. 10.50x o.p. (ISBN 0-06-067130-0, HarpR). Har-Row.

Schultz, Stanley G. Principles of Membrane Transport. LC 79-54015. (IUPAB Biophysics Ser.: No. 2). (Illus.). 1980. 22.50 (ISBN 0-521-22992-8); pap. 8.50x (ISBN 0-521-29762-1). Cambridge U Pr.

Schultz, Stanley K. The Culture Factory: Boston Public Schools, 1789-1860. (Illus.). 352p. 1973. 17.95 (ISBN 0-19-501668-8). Oxford U Pr.

Schultz, T. W. Investment in Human Capital. LC 77-122273. 1971. 14.95 (ISBN 0-02-928220-9). Free Pr.

Schultz, Terri. Bittersweet: Surviving & Growing from Loneliness. LC 76-9797. 1976. 8.95 o.p. (ISBN 0-690-01180-6, TYC-T). T Y Crowell.

--Women Can Wait: The Pleasures of Motherhood After Thirty. 1979. pap. 4.95 (ISBN 0-385-14040-1, Dolp). Doubleday.

Schultz, Theodore W. Economic Value of Education. LC 63-15453. 1963. 12.00x (ISBN 0-231-02640-4). Columbia U Pr.

Schultze, Charles L. The Distribution of Farm Subsidies: Who Gets the Benefits? 1971. pap. 2.00 (ISBN 0-8157-7753-1). Brookings.

Schultze, Charles. L. The Politics & Economics of Public Spending. 1969. pap. 4.95 (ISBN 0-8157-7751-5). Brookings.

Schultze, Charles L., jt. auth. see Kneese, Allen V.

Schultze, Charles L., jt. ed. see Fried, Edward R.

Schultze, Charles L., jt. ed. see Owen, Henry.

Schultze, Charles L., et al. Setting National Priorities: B the 1971 Budget. 1970. 11.95 (ISBN 0-8157-7750-7); pap. 4.95 (ISBN 0-8157-7749-3). Brookings.

--Setting National Priorities: C the 1972 Budget. 1971. 14.95 (ISBN 0-8157-7756-6); pap. 5.95 (ISBN 0-8157-7755-8). Brookings.

--Setting National Priorities: D the 1973 Budget. 350p. 1972. 14.95 (ISBN 0-8157-7758-2); pap. 5.95 (ISBN 0-8157-7757-4). Brookings.

Schultze, Donald E. All About Teaching: An Introduction to a Profession. 1977. pap. text ed. 7.50 (ISBN 0-8191-0205-9). U Pr of Amer.

Schultze, Sidney. The Structure of "Anna Karenina". 1981. 15.00 (ISBN 0-88233-587-1). Ardis Pubs.

Schultze, Walter. Die Quellen der Hamburger Oper Sixteen Seventy Eight to Seventeen Thirty Eight. LC 80-2300. 1981. Repr. of 1938 ed. 25.50 (ISBN 0-404-18869-9). AMS Pr.

Schulz. It Was a Short Summer, Charlie Brown. (gr. 3-5). 1980. pap. 1.95 (ISBN 0-590-30059-8, Schol Pap). Schol Bk Serv.

Schulz, Ann T. Local Politics & Nation-States: Case Studies in Politics & Policy. LC 79-11416. (Studies in International & Comparative Politics: No. 12). 234p. 1980. text ed. 21.50 (ISBN 0-87436-289-X). ABC-Clio.

Schulz, Ann T., ed. International & Regional Politics in the Middle East & North Africa: A Guide to Information Sources. LC 74-11568. (International Relations Information Guide Ser.: Vol. 6). 1977. 30.00 (ISBN 0-8103-1326-X). Gale.

Schulz, Charles. The Beagle Has Landed, Vol. II. 128p. 1981. pap. 1.75 (ISBN 0-449-24373-7, Crest). Fawcett.

--It Was a Short Summer, Charlie Brown. pap. 1.25 (ISBN 0-451-07958-2, Y7958, Sig). NAL.

--It's Show Time, Snoopy: Selected Cartoons from "Speak Softly & Carry a Beagle", Vol. II. (Peanuts Ser.). (Illus.). 1978. pap. 1.50 (ISBN 0-449-23602-1, Crest). Fawcett.

--Sing for Your Supper, Snoopy. 128p. 1981. pap. 1.75 (ISBN 0-449-24403-2, Crest). Fawcett.

--Stay with It Snoopy. 128p. 1980. pap. 1.50 (ISBN 0-449-24310-9, Crest). Fawcett.

--Summers Fly, Winters Walk, Vol. III. 128p. 1980. Repr. cancelled (ISBN 0-449-24310-9, Crest). Fawcett.

--Take It Easy Charlie Brown: Selected Cartoons from "You'll Flip, Charlie Brown," Vol. Ii. (Peanuts Ser.). (Illus.). 1978. pap. 1.50 (ISBN 0-449-23955-1, Crest). Fawcett.

--That's Life Snoopy: Selected Cartoons from "Thompson Is in Trouble, Charlie Brown," Vol. II. (Peanuts Ser.). (Illus.). 128p. (YA) 1978. pap. 1.50 (ISBN 0-449-23876-8, Crest). Fawcett.

Schulz, Charles M. All This & Snoopy, Too: Selected Cartoons from "You Can't Win, Charlie Brown", Vol. 2. (Peanuts Ser.). (Illus.). (gr. 5 up). 1978. pap. 1.50 (ISBN 0-449-23824-5, Crest). Fawcett.

--The Beagle Has Landed. LC 78-53776. (New Peanuts Parade Ser). 1978. pap. 2.95 (ISBN 0-03-044781-X). HR&W.

--Boy Named Charlie Brown. (Illus.). 144p. (gr. 5-7). 1981. pap. 2.25 (ISBN 0-449-23217-4, Crest). Fawcett.

--Charlie Brown & Snoopy: Selected Cartoons from "As You Like It", Charlie Brown, Vol. 1. (Illus.). 1978. pap. 1.50 (ISBN 0-449-24049-5, Crest). Fawcett.

--Charlie Brown Dictionary. (Illus.). (ps-3). 1973. text ed. 11.52 (ISBN 0-13-084269-9). P-H.

--Charlie Brown's Second Super Book of Questions & Answers: About the Earth & Space from Plants to Planets. LC 77-74455. (Illus.). (gr. 3-6). 1977. 6.95 (ISBN 0-394-83491-7, BYR); PLB 7.39 (ISBN 0-394-93491-1). Random.

--Charlie Brown's Third Super Book of Questions & Answers: About All Kinds of Boats & Trains, Cars & Planes & Other Things That Move! LC 78-7404. (Illus.). (gr. 4-7). 1978. 6.95 (ISBN 0-394-83729-0, BYR); PLB 7.39 (ISBN 0-394-93729-5). Random.

--Good Grief, Charlie Brown: Selected Cartoons from "Good Grief, More Peanuts", Vol. 1. (Peanuts Ser.). (Illus.). 1978. pap. 1.50 (ISBN 0-449-23801-6, Crest). Fawcett.

--Good Ol' Snoopy: Selected Cartoons from "Snoopy", Vol. 2. (Peanuts Ser.). (Illus.). 1978. pap. 1.50 (ISBN 0-449-23709-5, Crest). Fawcett.

--Here Comes Charlie Brown: Selected Cartoons from "Good Ol' Charlie Brown", Vol. 2. (Peanuts Ser.). (Illus.). 1978. pap. 1.50 (ISBN 0-449-23710-9, Crest). Fawcett.

--Here Comes Snoopy: Selected Cartoons from "Snoopy", Vol. 1. (Peanuts Ser.). (Illus.). 1978. pap. 1.50 (ISBN 0-449-23947-0, Crest). Fawcett.

--Here's to You, Charlie Brown: Selected Cartoons from "You Can't Win, Charlie Brown", Vol. 1. (Peanuts Ser.). (Illus.). 1978. pap. 1.50 (ISBN 0-449-23708-7, Crest). Fawcett.

--It's for You, Snoopy: Selected Cartoons from "Sunday's Fun Day, Charlie Brown", Vol. 1. (Peanuts Ser.). (Illus.). 1978. pap. 1.50 (ISBN 0-449-23807-5, Crest). Fawcett.

--Keep Up the Good Work, Charlie Brown. (Peanuts Ser.). (Illus.). 1979. pap. 1.50 (ISBN 0-449-23748-6, Crest). Fawcett.

--Play Ball, Snoopy: Selected Cartoons from "Win a Few, Lose a Few, Charlie Brown", Vol. I. (Peanuts Ser.). 1979. pap. 1.50 (ISBN 0-449-23222-0, Crest). Fawcett.

--Play It Again, Charlie Brown. 1972. pap. 1.50 (ISBN 0-451-09217-1, W9217, Sig). NAL.

--She's a Good Skate, Charlie Brown. LC 80-20285. (A Charlie Brown TV Special). (Illus.). 48p. 1981. PLB 4.99 (ISBN 0-394-94495-X); pap. 4.95 boards (ISBN 0-394-84495-5). Random.

--Snoopy's Facts & Fun Book About Farms. LC 79-22307. (Snoopy's Facts & Fun Bks.). (Illus.). 40p. (ps-1). 1980. bds. 2.50 (ISBN 0-394-84300-2); PLB 2.99 (ISBN 0-394-94300-7). Random.

--Snoopy's Facts & Fun Book About Nature. LC 79-22307. (Snoopy's Facts & Fun Bks.). (Illus.). 40p. (ps-1). 1980. bds. 2.50 (ISBN 0-394-84299-5); PLB 2.99 (ISBN 0-394-94299-X). Random.

--Snoopy's Facts & Fun Book About Seashores. LC 79-23362. (Snoopy's Facts & Fun Bks.). (Illus.). 40p. (ps-1). 1980. 2.50 (ISBN 0-394-84298-7); PLB 2.99 (ISBN 0-394-94298-1). Random.

--Snoopy's Facts & Fun Book About Trucks. LC 79-23616. (Snoopy's Facts & Fun Bks.). (Illus.). 40p. (ps-1). 1980. 2.50 (ISBN 0-394-84273-1); PLB 2.99 (ISBN 0-394-94273-6). Random.

--Things I Learned After It As Too Late: (& Other Minor Truths) (Illus.). 1981. pap. 4.95 (ISBN 0-686-69128-8). HR&W.

--Think Thinner, Snoopy. 1979. pap. 1.50 (ISBN 0-449-24042-8, Crest). Fawcett.

--This Is Your Life, Charlie Brown: Selected Cartoons from "It's a Dog's Life, Charlie Brown", Vol. 1. (Peanuts Series). (Illus.). 1978. pap. 1.50 (ISBN 0-449-23918-7, Crest). Fawcett.

--Very Funny, Charlie Brown: Selected Cartoons from "You're Out of Your Mind, Charlie Brown", Vol. 1. (Peanuts Ser.). (Illus.). 1978. pap. 1.50 (ISBN 0-449-23730-3, Crest). Fawcett.

--We Love You, Snoopy: Selected Cartoons from "Snoopy, Come Home". (Peanuts Ser.). (Illus.). 1979. pap. 1.50 (ISBN 0-449-23958-6, Crest). Fawcett.

--Who Do You Think You Are, Charlie Brown: Selected Cartoons from "Peanuts Every Sunday", Vol. 1. (Peanuts Ser.). (Illus.). 1978. pap. 1.50 (ISBN 0-449-23948-9, Crest). Fawcett.

--You're a Brave Man, Charlie Brown: Selected Cartoons from "You Can Do It, Charlie Brown", Vol. II. (Peanuts Ser.). (Illus.). 1977. pap. 1.50 (ISBN 0-449-23878-4, Crest). Fawcett.

--You're a Good Sport, Charlie Brown. (gr. 1 up). 1977. pap. 1.95 (ISBN 0-590-08502-6, Schol Pap). Schol Bk Serv.

--You're Not Elected, Charlie Brown. (Illus.). 96p. (gr. 3-7). 1980. pap. 1.95 (ISBN 0-590-08820-3, Schol Pap). Schol Bk Serv.

--You're the Greatest, Charlie Brown. (Illus.). 96p. (gr. 3-7). 1980. pap. 1.95 (ISBN 0-590-31504-8, Schol Pap). Schol Bk Serv.

--You're the Greatest, Charlie Brown. LC 79-4622. (Illus.). (gr. 1 up). 1979. 3.50 (ISBN 0-394-84260-X, BYR); PLB 4.99 (ISBN 0-394-94260-4). Random.

--You've Come a Long Way, Snoopy: Selected Cartoons from "Thompson Is in Trouble", Vol. I. (Peanuts Ser.). (Illus.). 1979. pap. 1.50 (ISBN 0-449-24004-5, Crest). Fawcett.

--You've Got a Friend, Charlie Brown: Selected Cartoons from "You'll Flip, Charlie Brown", Vol. I. 1979. pap. 1.50 (ISBN 0-449-23887-3, Crest). Fawcett.

Schulz, Charles M. & Kiliper, R. Smith. Charlie Brown, Snoopy & Me & All the Other Peanuts Characters. LC 80-923. (Illus.). 128p. 1980. 7.95a (ISBN 0-385-15805-X); PLB (ISBN 0-385-15806-8). Doubleday.

Schulz, Charles M., illus. Tubby Book Featuring Snoopy. (Tubby Bks.). (Illus.). 10p. (ps). 1980. vinyl book 2.95 (ISBN 0-671-41335-X, Pub. by Windmill). S&S.

Schulz, David A. The Changing Family: Its Function & Future. 2nd ed. (Illus.). 432p. 1976. 17.95 (ISBN 0-13-127977-7). P-H.

--Human Sexuality. (Illus.). 1979. pap. 15.95 ref. ed. (ISBN 0-13-447557-7). P-H.

Schulz, David A. & Rogers, Stanley F. Marriage, the Family & Personal Fulfillment. 2nd ed. (P-H Ser. in Sociology). (Illus.). 1980. text ed. 17.95 (ISBN 0-13-559385-9). P-H.

Schulz, David A., jt. auth. see Wilson, Robert A.

Schulz, Donald E. Political Participation in Communist Systems. (Pergamon Policy Studies). 1981. 32.51 (ISBN 0-08-024665-6). Pergamon.

Schulz, Dora & Griesbach, Heinz. Deutsche Sprachlehre Fuer Auslaender. Incl. Grundstufe in einem Band. 5.80x o.p. (ISBN 0-685-47471-2); pap. text ed. 7.80x (ISBN 0-685-47472-0); glossar deutsch-englisch 4.10x (ISBN 0-685-47473-9); leseheft 1, by roland hils. 3.25x (ISBN 0-685-47474-7); grammar german-english 4.55xschuelerheft.contrastive (ISBN 0-685-47475-5); Grundstufe. Ausgabe in zwei Baenden. pap. text ed. 4.00xGrundstufe 1. teil (ISBN 0-685-47476-3); pap. text ed. 7.15x grundstufe 2. teil (ISBN 0-685-47477-1); teaching supplement-phraseological glossary-key 5.20x (ISBN 0-685-47478-X); 2 tonbaender, aufnahme der lesetexte des buches und von uebungen, 9.5 cm/s, tapes 52.00x (ISBN 0-685-47479-8); Mittelstufe; Moderner Deutscher Sprachgebrauch.Ein Lehrgang Fuer Fortgeschrittene. pap. text ed. 12.25x (ISBN 0-685-47480-1); lehrerheft 4.90x (ISBN 0-685-47481-X); schuelerheft mit schluessel zuden uebungen 7.15x (ISBN 0-685-47482-8); 1 tonband, aufnahme von 28 lesetexten des lehrbuchs, 9.5 cm/s, tapes 31.20x (**ISBN 0-685-47483-6). Schoenhof.**

Schulz, Dora, et al. Deutsche Sprachlehre Amerikaner. LC 77-96479. 1970. pap. text ed. 14.95 (ISBN 0-684-41465-1, Scribner-C). Scribner.

Schulz, Erich J. Diesel Equipment I, Workbook: Lubrication, Hydraulics, Brakes, Wheels, Tires. Gilmore, D. E., ed. (Illus.). 56p. 1980. 5.95 (ISBN 0-07-055716-0, G); instructor's guide avail. (ISBN 0-07-055718-7); wkbk. avail. (ISBN 0-07-055717-9). McGraw.

--Diesel Equipment II, Workbook: Design, Electronic Controls, Frames, Suspensions, Steering, Transmissions, Drive Lines, Air Conditioning. Gilmore, D. E., ed. (Illus.). 64p. 1980. 5.95 (ISBN 0-07-055708-X, G); instructor's guide avail. (ISBN 0-07-055711-X); wkbk. avail. (ISBN 0-07-055709-8). McGraw.

Schulz, G. E. & Schirmer, R. H. Principles of Protein Structure. LC 78-11500. (Springer Advanced Texts in Chemistry). (Illus.). 1979. 29.80 o.p. (ISBN 0-387-90386-0); pap. 14.80 (ISBN 0-387-90334-8). Springer-Verlag.

Schulz, Heinrich E., et al, eds. see Institute for the Study of the U. S. S. R.

Schulz, James, et al. Providing Adequate Retirement Income: Pension Reform in the United States & Abroad. LC 74-82592. (Illus.). 350p. 1974. text ed. 20.00x (ISBN 0-87451-100-3). U Pr of New Eng.

Schulz, James H. The Economics of Aging. 2nd ed. 208p. 1979. pap. text ed. 8.95x (ISBN 0-534-00772-4). Wadsworth Pub.

Schulz, Jane B., jt. auth. see Turnbull, Ann P.

Schulz, Juergen. Venetian Painted Ceilings of the Renaissance. (California Studies in the History of Art: No. VIII). (Illus.). 1968. 57.50x (ISBN 0-520-01154-6). U of Cal Pr.

Schulz, Max F. Black Humor Fiction of the Sixties: A Pluralistic Definition of Man & His World. LC 72-85538. xi, 156p. 1973. 12.00x (ISBN 0-8214-0125-4). Ohio U Pr.

--Black Humor Fiction of the Sixties: A Pluralistic Definition of Man & His World. LC 72-85538. 156p. 1980. pap. 5.95x (ISBN 0-8214-0574-8). Ohio U Pr.

--Bruce Jay Friedman. (U. S. Authors Ser.: No. 219). 1974. lib. bdg. 10.95 (ISBN 0-8057-0290-3). Twayne.

--Radical Sophistication: Studies in Contemporary Jewish-American Novelists. LC 69-15914. xvi, 224p. 1969. 12.00 o.s.i. (ISBN 0-8214-0045-2); pap. 5.50 (ISBN 0-8214-0106-8). Ohio U Pr.

Schulz, Phillip S. Extravagant Things: A Catalog of Indulgences. (Illus.). 450p. (Orig.). 1980. pap. cancelled (ISBN 0-8092-7044-7). Contemp Bks.

Schulz, Richard. Psychology of Death, Dying & Bereavement. LC 77-83030. (Illus.). 1978. pap. text ed. 8.50 (ISBN 0-201-07328-5). A-W.

Schulz, T. Paul. Population Economics. LC 80-36830. (Perspectives in Economics Ser.). 224p. 1981. pap. text ed. price not set (ISBN 0-201-08371-X). A-W.

Schulz-Behrend, George, tr. see Grimmelshausen, Johann.

Schulze, David L., jt. auth. see Roberts, Blaine.

Schulze, Gene. Third Face of War. LC 76-94463. (Illus.). 1969. 9.50 (ISBN 0-8363-0097-1). Jenkins.

--Yesterday's Seasons: Memoirs of a Medical Practice in Rural Texas. LC 78-53481. 1978. 10.95 o.p. (ISBN 0-8015-0301-9). Dutton.

Schulzinger, Robert D. The Making of the Diplomatic Mind: The Training Outlook & Style of United States Foreign Service Officers 1908-31. LC 75-15790. 260p. 1975. 20.00x (ISBN 0-8195-4086-2, Pub. by Wesleyan U Pr). Columbia U Pr.

Schulz-Schaeffer, J. Cytogenetics: Plants, Animals, Humans. (Illus.). 460p. 1980. 32.80 (ISBN 0-387-90467-0). Springer-Verlag.

Schum, David A., jt. ed. see Pfeiffer, Paul E.

Schumach, Muarry. The Diamond People. (Illus.). 1981. 12.95 (ISBN 0-393-01404-5). Norton.

Schumach, Murray. The Face on the Cutting Room Floor: The Story of Music & Television Censorship. LC 73-19776. (Civil Liberties in American History Ser.). (Illus.). 306p. 1974. Repr. of 1956 ed. lib. bdg. 19.50 (ISBN 0-306-70603-2). Da Capo.

Schumacher, Claire W. Ore Dust in Her Shoes. (Illus.). 194p. (Orig.). 5.00. Schumacher Pubns.

--This Is Our St. Rose Church in Proctor Minnesota. (Illus.). 100p. 1976. pap. 3.00 (ISBN 0-917378-02-4). Schumacher Pubns.

--The Whiteside Island Story-Merald Isle of St. Louis Bay. LC 74-29021. 65p. 1980. 2.50 (ISBN 0-917378-04-0). Schumacher Pubns.

Schumacher, Craig. Bee Gees. (Rock'n Roll Stars Ser.). 32p. (gr. 4-12). 1979. PLB 5.95 (ISBN 0-87191-697-5); pap. 2.95. Creative Ed.

--Happy Days. (T.V. & Movie Tie-Ins Ser.). (Illus.). (gr. 4-12). 1979. PLB 5.95 (ISBN 0-87191-702-5); pap. 2.95 (ISBN 0-89812-034-9). Creative Ed.

--John Travolta. (Rock 'n Pop Stars Ser.). (Illus.). (gr. 4-12). 1979. PLB 5.95 (ISBN 0-87191-698-3); pap. 2.95 (ISBN 0-89812-094-2). Creative Ed.

--Nancy Lopez. (Sports Superstars Ser.). (Illus.). (gr. 3-9). 1979. PLB 5.95 (ISBN 0-87191-694-0); pap. 2.95 (ISBN 0-89812-164-7). Creative Ed.

--Shaun Cassidy. (Rock 'n Pop Stars Ser.). (Illus.). (gr. 4-12). 1979. PLB 5.95 (ISBN 0-87191-717-3); pap. 2.95 (ISBN 0-89812-097-7). Creative Ed.

Schumacher, E. F. A Guide for the Perplexed. 1978. pap. 3.95 (ISBN 0-06-090611-1, CN 611, CN). Har-Row.

--Small Is Beautiful: Economics As If People Mattered. 1973. pap. 5.95 (ISBN 0-06-090432-1, CN432, CN). Har-Row.

Schumacher, Edward J. Politics, Bureaucracy, & Rural Development in Senegal. 1975. 29.50x (ISBN 0-520-02087-1). U of Cal Pr.

Schumacher, F. Practical Problems in Mathematics for Sheet Metal Technicians. LC 71-74885. 1973. pap. text ed. 5.20 (ISBN 0-8273-0287-8); instructor's guide 1.60 (ISBN 0-8273-0288-6). Delmar.

Schumacher, F. W., jt. auth. see Zinngrabe, C. J.

Schumacher, Gary M., jt. auth. see Moates, Danny R.

Schumacher, George, jt. auth. see Whitford, L. A.

Schumacher, H. Ralph, Jr. Gout & Pseudogout. (Discussions in Patient Management Ser.). 1978. spiral 9.50 (ISBN 0-87488-888-3). Med Exam.

Schumacher, M. M., ed. Enhanced Oil Recovery: Secondary & Tertiary Methods. LC 77-15224. (Chemical Technology Review No. 103; Energy Technology Review No. 22). (Illus.). 1978. 32.00 o.p. (ISBN 0-8155-0692-9). Noyes.

--Enhanced Recovery of Residual & Heavy Oils. 2nd ed. LC 80-19812. (Energy Tech. Rev. 59; Chemical Tech. Rev. 174). (Illus.). 378p. 1981. 48.00 (ISBN 0-8155-0816-6). Noyes.

Schumacher, Margaret, jt. auth. see Boyd, Rogene.

Schumacher, Walter. Voice Therapy & Voice Improvement: A Simple & Practical Approach Through Correct Muscle Usage. (Illus.). 144p. 1974. 11.75 (ISBN 0-398-02920-2). C C Thomas.

Schumaker, John A., jt. auth. see Weinberg, George M.

Schumaker, L. L., tr. see Meinardus, Guenter.

Schumaker, Larry L. Spline Functions: Basic Theory. LC 80-14448. (Pure & Applied Mathematics: a Wiley-Interscience Ser. of Texts, Monographs, & Tracts). 500p. 1981. 35.00 (ISBN 0-471-76475-2, Pub. by Wiley Interscience). Wiley.

Schuman, Beatrice Chernuchin. Am I Greedy If I Want More? (Illus.). 179p. 1979. 9.95 (ISBN 0-8119-0329-X). Fell.

Schuman, Bernard M., jt. auth. see Sugawa, Choichi.

Schuman, David. The Ideology of Form. LC 77-15815. 1978. 19.90 (ISBN 0-669-02059-1). Lexington Bks.

--A Preface to Politics. 2nd ed. 1977. pap. 5.95x o.p. (ISBN 0-669-00348-4). Heath.

Schuman, Donna & Roche, Judy. Matinee. 1980. pap. 2.75 (ISBN 0-440-15223-2). Dell.

Schuman, Jo M. Art from Many Hands: Multicultural Art Projects for Home & School. (Illus.). 320p. 1980. 22.95 (ISBN 0-13-047217-4, Spec); pap. 10.95 (ISBN 0-13-047217-4). P-H.

Schuman, Julian. China: An Uncensored Look. rev. ed. LC 79-63789. 1979. 15.95 (ISBN 0-933256-01-9); pap. 7.95 (ISBN 0-933256-04-3). Second Chance.

Schuman, Leonard M., jt. ed. see Mortimer, James A.

Schuman, Patricia G. Materials for Occupational Education: An Annotated Source Guide. 2nd ed. (Neal-Schuman Sourcebook Ser.). 1980. 24.95x (ISBN 0-918212-17-0). Neal-Schuman.

Schuman, Samuel. Cyril Tourneur. (English Author Ser.: No. 221). 1977. lib. bdg. 12.50 (ISBN 0-8057-6690-1). Twayne.

Schuman, Verne B. Washington University Papyri I: Non-Literary Texts, Nos. 1-16. LC 79-14199. (American Society of Papyrologists Ser.: No. 17). 15.00 (ISBN 0-89130-286-7). Scholars Pr CA.

Schumann, Clara. Selected Piano Music. (Music Reprint Ser.). 1979. Repr. of 1846 ed. lib. bdg. 18.95 (ISBN 0-306-79554-X). Da Capo.

Schumann, Clara, ed. see Schumann, Robert.

Schumann, Donna N. Living with Plants: A Guide to the Practical Application of Botany. (Illus.). 328p. (Orig.). 1980. pap. 14.20 (ISBN 0-916422-20-8). Mad River.

Schumann, G. Berry & Weiss, Mark. Atlas of Renal & Urinary Tract Cytology & Its Histopathologic Bases. (Illus.). 240p. 1980. text ed. 55.00 (ISBN 0-397-50443-8). Lippincott.

Schumann, John H. & Stenson, Nancy. New Frontiers in Second Language Learning. 1975. pap. 9.95 (ISBN 0-912066-84-9). Newbury Hse.

Schumann, Marguerite. The Living Land: An Outdoor Guide to North Carolina. (Illus.). 200p. Date not set. pap. 7.50 (ISBN 0-914788-29-9). East Woods.

Schumann, Robert. Complete Symphonies in Full Score. 1980. pap. 11.95 (ISBN 0-486-24013-4). Dover.

--Piano Music of Robert Schumann: Series III. Schumann, Clara, ed. 1980. Repr. of 1887 ed. 6.50 (ISBN 0-486-23906-3). Dover.

Schumann, Walter. Gemstones of the World. Tennissen, Anthony T., ed. LC 77-79503. (Illus.). 1977. 17.95 (ISBN 0-8069-3088-8); lib. bdg. 16.79 (ISBN 0-8069-3089-6). Sterling.

Schumer, William, ed. see Third Annual Conference on Shock, Lake of the Ozarks, Missouri, June 1980, et al.

Schumer, William, et al, eds. see Papers from the First Annual Conference on Shock, Airlie, Va. June 1978.

Schumm, Stanley A., ed. River Morphology. LC 72-78310. (Benchmark Papers in Geology Ser.). 1972. pap. 32.00 (ISBN 0-12-787440-2). Acad Pr.

Schumpeter, Joseph A. Capitalism, Socialism & Democracy. pap. 4.95x (ISBN 0-06-133008-6, TB 3008, Torch). Har-Row.

--The Theory of Economic Development. Opie, Redvers, tr. 1961. pap. 6.95x (ISBN 0-19-500461-2). Oxford U Pr.

Schumway, Dwight, ed. see Miller, Harlan B.

Schuon, Frithjot. Understanding Islam. Matheson, D. M., tr. (Mandala Bks.). 1976. pap. 5.25 (ISBN 0-04-297035-0). Allen Unwin.

Schuon, Karl. First Book of Bowling. LC 66-1218. (First Bks). (Illus.). (gr. 4-6). 1966. PLB 4.90 o.p. (ISBN 0-531-00487-2). Watts.

Schupack, Andrew L. Formula Vee: Racing, History & Chassis-Engine Prep. (Orig.). 1980. 12.95 (ISBN 0-8306-9952-X); pap. 6.95 (ISBN 0-8306-2063-X, 2063). TAB Bks.

Schuppli, R., ed. Schweizerische Gesellschaft Fuer Dermatologie und Venerologie, 61. Jahresversammlung, Lausanne, Oktober 1979. (Illus.). viii, 68p. 1981. pap. 6.75 (ISBN 3-8055-2353-X). S Karger.

Schur, Edwin M. The Politics of Deviance: Stigma Contests & the Uses of Power. 256p. 1980. text ed. 11.95 (ISBN 0-13-684753-6, Spec); pap. text ed. 5.95 (ISBN 0-13-684746-3). P-H.

Schur, Norman W. English English: A Descriptive Dictionary. LC 77-20390. 1980. 24.95 (ISBN 0-930454-05-7). Verbatim.

Schur, Norman W., ed. English English. 2nd ed. 300p. 1980. 28.00 (ISBN 0-8103-1096-1). Verbatim.

Schur, Sylvia. The Tappan Creative Cookbook for Microwave Ovens & Ranges. LC 75-24994. 1976. 10.00 o.p. (ISBN 0-03-016806-6). HR&W.

--The Tappan Creative Cookbook for Microwave Ovens & Ranges. 1981. pap. 2.95 (ISBN 0-451-09742-4, Sig). NAL.

Schur, Sylvia, ed. Recipes for Busy People. (Orig.). 1980. pap. 2.50 (ISBN 0-446-91542-4). Warner Bks.

Schure, Alexander. Basic Transistors. rev.,2nd ed. 152p. 1976. pap. text ed. 8.95 (ISBN 0-8104-0860-0); exam 0.50 (ISBN 0-8104-0597-0); final exam 0.20 (ISBN 0-8104-0598-9). Hayden.

Schurer, Emil. History of the Jewish People in the Age of Jesus Christ (175 B.C.-A.D. 135, 2 vols. Vermes, Geza, et al, eds. Vol. 1, Repr. Of 1973 Ed., 632p. 42.00x (ISBN 0-567-02242-0); Vol. 2, Repr. Of 1979 Ed., 608p. 43.75x (ISBN 0-567-02243-9). Attic Pr.

Schurer, Ernst. Georg Kaiser. (World Authors Ser.: Germany: No. 196). lib. bdg. 10.95 (ISBN 0-8057-2480-X). Twayne.

Schurer, John, jt. auth. see Foy, Elizabeth.

Schurer, Marcia L., jt. auth. see Mutkoski, Stephen A.

Schurmann, Franz. Ideology & Organization in Communist China. 2nd enl ed. LC 68-26124. (Center for Chinese Studies, UC Berkeley). (Illus.). 1968. 25.00x (ISBN 0-520-01151-1); pap. 7.95 (ISBN 0-520-01153-8, CAL172). U of Cal Pr.

--The Logic of World Power: An Inquiry into the Origins, Currents & Contradictions of World Politics. LC 73-18732. 1974. 15.00 o.s.i. (ISBN 0-394-48481-9). Pantheon.

Schurmann, Franz, jt. auth. see Levenson, Joseph R.

Schurr. Poetry Pack Rat. (Choose-a-Card Ser.). (gr. 2-6). 1979. pap. text ed. 5.95 (ISBN 0-913916-86-2, IP86-2). Incentive Pubns.

Schurr, Evelyn L. Movement Experience for Children: A Humanistic Approach to Elementary School Physical Education. 3rd ed. 1980. text ed. 16.95 (ISBN 0-13-604553-7). P-H.

Schurz, Carl. Henry Clay. LC 80-18659. (American Statesmen Ser.). 815p. 1981. Set. pap. 10.95 (ISBN 0-87754-180-9). Chelsea Hse.

--Intimate Letters of Carl Schurz, 1841-1869. Schafer, Joseph, ed. LC 73-106989. (American Public Figures Ser). 1970. Repr. of 1928 ed. lib. bdg. 49.50 (ISBN 0-306-71876-6). Da Capo.

Schusky, Ernest & Culbert, T. Patrick. Introducing Culture. 3rd ed. (P-H Anthropology Ser.). (Illus.). 1978. pap. 9.95 ref. (ISBN 0-13-477240-7). P-H.

Schusky, Ernest L. The Forgotten Sioux: An Ethnohistory of the Lower Brule Reservation. LC 75-503. (Illus.). 272p. 1975. 16.95 (ISBN 0-88229-138-6); pap. 8.95 (ISBN 0-88229-501-2). Nelson-Hall.

--Introduction to Social Science. (Illus.). 512p. 1981. pap. text ed. 15.95 (ISBN 0-13-496703-8). P-H.

Schusky, Ernest L., ed. Political Organization of Native North Americans. LC 79-3715. 1980. text ed. 18.25 (ISBN 0-8191-0909-6); pap. text ed. 11.25 (ISBN 0-8191-0910-X). U Pr of Amer.

Schuss, Zeev. Theory & Applications of Stochastic Differential Equations. LC 80-14767. (Wiley Ser. in Probability & Mathematical Statistics: Applied Probability & Statistics). 375p. 1980. 25.95 (ISBN 0-471-04394-X). Wiley.

Schussler, Theodore. Federal Courts: Jurisdiction & Practice. 152p. 1980. 5.50 (ISBN 0-87526-036-5). Gould.

--Torts. 1981 ed. 171p. Date not set. 7.50 (ISBN 0-87526-166-3). Gould.

Schuster, Clara & Ashburn, Shirley. The Process of Human Development: A Holistic Approach. LC 79-91938. 1980. text ed. 19.95 (ISBN 0-316-77535-5). Little.

Schuster, E. H. Words Are Important: Primary Level (Tan) Bk. (gr. 4). 1975. pap. 1.48x (ISBN 0-8437-7983-7). Hammond Inc.

--Words Are Important Series. Incl. Level A (Blue) Bk. (gr. 5) (ISBN 0-8437-7985-3); Level B (Red) Bk. (gr. 6) (ISBN 0-8437-7991-8); Level C (Green) Bk. (gr. 7) (ISBN 0-8437-7980-2); Level D (Orange) Bk. (gr. 8) (ISBN 0-8437-7950-0); Level E (Purple) Bk. (gr. 9) (ISBN 0-8437-7955-1); Level F (Brown) Bk. (gr. 10) (ISBN 0-8437-7960-8); Level G (Pink) Bk. (gr. 11) (ISBN 0-8437-7965-9); Level H (Grey) Bk. (gr. 12) (ISBN 0-8437-7970-5). 1979. pap. 1.48x ea. Hammond Inc.

Schuster, Edgar H. Sentence Mastery: A & B. Weeden, Hester E., ed. (Sentence Mastery Ser.). (Illus.). 160p. (gr. 7). 1980. A. 3.96 (ISBN 0-07-055621-0, W); B. 3.96 (ISBN 0-07-055622-9). McGraw.

--Sentence Mastery B: Pupil's Edition. (Sentence Mastery Ser.). (Illus.). 160p. (gr. 8). 1980. 3.96 (ISBN 0-07-055622-9, W). McGraw.

Schuster, Edgar H., jt. auth. see Guth, Hans P.

Schuster, Edward J. Human Rights Today: Evolution or Revolution? LC 80-84737. 1981. 12.00 (ISBN 0-686-68868-6). Philos Lib.

Schuster, Fred E. Contemporary Issues in Human Resources Management. (Illus.). 496p. 1980. text ed. 21.95 (ISBN 0-8359-1005-9). Reston.

Schuster, George S., jt. auth. see Burnett, George W.

Schuster, H. Experimentele Untersuchungen Zur Schwermetallresistenz Von Sumersen Makrophyten. (Dissertationes Botanica 50 Ser.). (Illus., Ger.). 1980. pap. text ed. 20.00x (ISBN 3-7682-1229-7). Lubrecht & Cramer.

Schuster, H. J. Analyse und Bewertung Von Pflanzengesell-Schaften Im Noerdliche Frankenjura - ein Beitrag Zum Problem der Quantifizierung Unter-Schiedlich Anthropogen Beeinflusster Oekosystems. (Dissertationes Botanicae: No. 53). (Illus.). 482p. (Ger.). 1981. pap. text ed. 40.00x (ISBN 3-7682-1264-5, Pub. by Cramer Germany). Lubrecht & Cramer.

Schuster, Mel. The Contemporary Greek Cinema. LC 78-20969. 1979. lib. bdg. 16.50 (ISBN 0-8108-1196-0). Scarecrow.

--Motion Picture Directors: A Bibliography of Magazine & Periodical Articles, 1900-1972. LC 73-780. 1973. 16.50 (ISBN 0-8108-0590-1). Scarecrow.

--Motion Picture Performers: A Bibliography of Magazine & Periodical Articles, Supp. No. 1, 1970-74. LC 70-154300. 1976. 32.50 (ISBN 0-8108-0879-X). Scarecrow.

Schuster, R. O., jt. auth. see Grigarick, A. A.

Schuster, Robert L. Israel, The Middle East & the Moral Conscience of the Western World. (The Major Currents in Contemporary World History). (Illus.). 133p. 1981. 47.85 (ISBN 0-89266-301-4). Am Classical Coll Pr.

Schuster, Robert O., jt. auth. see Grigarick, Albert A.

Schuster, Rudolf M. Hepaticae & Anthocerotae of North America East of the Hundredth Meridian, 3 vols, Vols. 1, 2 & 3. LC 66-14791. 1966-74. 45.00x ea. Vol. 1 (ISBN 0-231-08981-3). Vol. 2 (ISBN 0-231-08982-1). Vol. 3 (ISBN 0-231-03567-5). Columbia U Pr.

Schuster, Slade. The Slade Short Course in Grammar. 54p. (Orig.). (gr. 8-11). 1978. pap. text ed. 2.25x (ISBN 0-88334-111-5). Ind Sch Pr.

Schuter, Hans & Magar, Kurt. Index Libycus: A Cumlative Index to Bibliography of Libya,Nineteen Fifteen to Nineteen Seventy-Five. (Reference Books Ser.). 1981. 25.00 (ISBN 0-8161-8534-4). G K Hall.

Schuth, H. Wayne. Mike Nichols. (Theatrical Arts Ser.). 1978. lib. bdg. 12.50 (ISBN 0-8057-9255-4). Twayne.

Schutte, William M. & Steinberg, Erwin R., eds. Personal Integrity. (Illus., Orig.). 1961. pap. 3.95x (ISBN 0-393-09571-1, NortonC). Norton.

Schutz, Albert. Call Adonoi: Manual of Practical Cabalah & Gestalt Mysticism. 114p. 1980. pap. 8.95. Ross-Erikson.

Schutz, Albert L. Call Adonoi: Manual of Practical Cabalah & Gestalt Mysticism. Lowenkopf, Anne N., ed. LC 80-50264. 200p. (Orig.). 1980. 11.95 (ISBN 0-936596-01-5); pap. 8.95 (ISBN 0-936596-00-7). Quantal.

--Exodus--Exodus: The Cabalistic Bible. Lowenkopf, Anne N., ed. (Orig.). Date not set. 15.50 (ISBN 0-686-69116-4); pap. 8.95 (ISBN 0-936596-04-X). Quantal.

--Love & Religion: A Study of Sexual Delusion. Lowenkopf, Anne N., ed. (Illus., Orig.). 1981. 14.50 (ISBN 0-936596-02-3); pap. 9.95 (ISBN 0-936596-02-3). Quantal.

Schutz, Alexander H., jt. ed. see Cabeen, David C.

Schutz, B. Geometrical Methods of Mathematical Physics. LC 80-40211. (Illus.). 300p. 1980. 39.95 (ISBN 0-521-23271-6); pap. 16.95 (ISBN 0-521-29887-3). Cambridge U Pr.

Schutz, Howard, et al. Lifestyles & Consumer Behavior of Older Americans. LC 79-13212. 276p. 1979. 23.95 (ISBN 0-03-049821-X). Praeger.

Schutz, J. H. Paul & the Anatomy of Apostolic Authority. LC 74-76573. (Society for New Testament Studies, Monographs: No. 26). 1975. 47.50 (ISBN 0-521-20464-X). Cambridge U Pr.

Schutz, John. Dawning of America. LC 80-68812. (Orig.). 1981. pap. text ed. 7.95x (ISBN 0-88273-109-2). Forum Pr MO.

Schutz, John A. & Kirkendall, Richard S. The American Republic. LC 77-9346. (Illus.). 1978. text ed. 16.95x (ISBN 0-88273-250-1). Forum Pr MO.

Schutz, John A. & Adair, Douglass, eds. The Spur of Fame: Dialogues of John Adams & Benjamin Rush 1805 to 1813. LC 66-15694. (Illus.). 301p. 1980. pap. 5.00 (ISBN 0-87328-025-3). Huntington Lib.

Schutz, Noel W., Jr. & Derwing, Bruce L. Essentials of Aviation Technology: Aviation Mechanics. LC 80-51692. (The ALA ESP Ser.). (Illus.). xii, 180p. (Orig.). 1980. pap. text ed. 10.00 (ISBN 0-934270-10-4). Am Lang Acad.

Schutz, Prior of Taize. Festival. LC 73-17913. (Orig.). 1974. pap. 2.95 (ISBN 0-8164-2583-3). Crossroad NY.

--Struggle & Contemplation. 1974. pap. 2.95 (ISBN 0-8164-2106-4). Crossroad NY.

Schutz, Roger. Dare to Live: The Taize Youth Experience. LC 73-17912. 1974. pap. 2.95 (ISBN 0-8164-2582-5). Crossroad NY.

--Rule of Taize. LC 74-10118. 1974. pap. 2.95 (ISBN 0-8164-2564-7). Crossroad NY.

Schutz, Susan P., ed. I Promise You My Love. (Illus.). 64p. (Orig.). 1981. pap. 4.95 (ISBN 0-88396-129-6). Blue Mtn Pr CO.

--One Day at a Time: Making the Most Out of Life. (Illus., Orig.). 1981. pap. 4.95 (ISBN 0-88396-131-8). Blue Mtn Pr CO.

--Thank You for Being My Parents. LC 80-70743. (Illus.). 64p. (Orig.). 1981. pap. 4.95 (ISBN 0-88396-137-7). Blue Mtn Pr CO.

Schutz, Walter E. Getting Started in Candlemaking. 104p. 1972. pap. 2.95 o.s.i. (ISBN 0-02-011900-3, Collier). Macmillan.

Schutz, William C. Here Comes Everybody: Bodymind & Encounter Culture. 1981. Repr. of 1971 ed. text ed. 16.50x (ISBN 0-8290-0044-5). Irvington.

--Joy: Expanding Human Awareness. 1981. Repr. of 1967 ed. text ed. 18.50x (ISBN 0-8290-0050-X). Irvington.

Schutze, Alfred. Enigma of Evil. 1978. pap. 7.95 (ISBN 0-903540-10-X, Pub by Floris Books). St George Bk Serv.

Schutze, Frieda, tr. see Stresau, Hermann.

Schutze, Gertrude. Documentation Source Book. LC 65-13551. 1965. 18.50 (ISBN 0-8108-0271-6). Scarecrow.

--Information & Library Science Source Book: Supplement to Documentation Source Book. LC 72-1157. 1972. 16.50 (ISBN 0-8108-0466-2). Scarecrow.

Schuurman & Egbert. Technology & the Future: A Philosophical Challenge. 1980. 19.95x (ISBN 0-88906-111-4). Radix Bks.

Schuurman, C. J. Intrance: Fundamental Psychological Problems of the Inner & Outer World. Boer-Hoff, Louise E., tr. from Dutch. LC 78-70618. (Illus.). 1981. pap. 6.95 (ISBN 0-89793-023-1). Hunter Hse.

Schuyler, James. The Morning of the Poem. 1981. pap. 6.95 (ISBN 0-374-51622-7). FS&G.

Schuyler, Jane. Florentine Busts: Sculpted Portraiture in the Fifteenth Century. LC 75-23814. (Outstanding Dissertations in the Fine Arts - 15th Century). (Illus.). 1976. lib. bdg. 41.00 (ISBN 0-8240-2007-3). Garland Pub.

Schuyt, jt. auth. see Eiffeis.

Schuzy, Georg. Philosophic Researches for Advancement of Science & Technology. 1980. 6.95 (ISBN 0-8062-1469-4). Carlton.

Schwaab, Eugene L., ed. Travels in the Old South, 1783-1860, Selected from Periodicals of the Times, 2 vols. LC 70-119814. (Illus.). 600p. 1973. Set. 35.00 (ISBN 0-8131-1229-X). U Pr of Ky.

Schwab, Donald P. The Manual for the Course Evaluation Instrument. (Wisconsin Business Monographs: No. 10). (Orig.). 1976. pap. 4.50 (ISBN 0-86603-002-6). Bureau Busn Res U Wis.

Schwab, Donald P., jt. ed. see Heneman, Herbert G.

Schwab, G. O., et al. Soil & Water Conservation Engineering. 2nd ed. LC 66-14131. 1966. 30.00 (ISBN 0-471-76520-1). Wiley.

Schwab, George, ed. Eurocommunism: The Ideological & Political-Theoretical Foundations. LC 80-26864. (Contributions in Political Science: No. 60). 352p. 1981. lib. bdg. 25.00 (ISBN 0-313-22908-2). Greenwood.

--Eurocommunism: The Ideological & Political-Theoretical Foundations. (Contributions in Political Science: No. 60). (Illus.). 352p. 1981. lib. bdg. 25.00 (ISBN 0-313-22908-2, SEU/). Greenwood.

--Eurocommunism: Theoretical, Political & Ideological Foundations. 300p. 1980. cancelled (ISBN 0-935764-03-8). Ark Hse NY.

--Ideology & Foreign Policy: A Global Perspective. 226p. 1981. Repr. of 1978 ed. pap. text ed. 10.95x (ISBN 0-8290-0393-2). Irvington.

Schwab, Karen, jt. auth. see Foner, Anne.

Schwab, Peter. Haile Selassie I: Ethiopia's Lion of Judah. LC 79-9897. (Illus.). 1979. 14.95 (ISBN 0-88229-342-7). Nelson-Hall.

Schwab, Peter & Shneidman, J. Lee. John F. Kennedy. (World Leaders Ser: No. 28). 1974. lib. bdg. 9.95 (ISBN 0-8057-3696-4). Twayne.

Schwab, Peter, jt. ed. see Pollis, Adamantia.

Schwab, Richard, tr. see D'Alembert, Jean L.

Schwab, Rick. Stuck on the Cubs. 192p. (Orig.). 1977. pap. 1.95 (ISBN 0-930528-01-8). Sassafras Pr.

Schwab, V. A. How to Write Advertisements. 230p. 1981. 28.50 o.p. (ISBN 0-686-68303-X). Porter.

Schwab, Victor O. How to Write a Good Advertisement. 1962. 9.95x o.p. (ISBN 0-06-111560-6, HarpT). Har-Row.

Schwabe, Calvin W. Veterinary Medicine & Human Health. 2nd ed. (Illus.). 1969. 31.00 o.p. (ISBN 0-683-07595-0). Williams & Wilkins.

Schwach, Howard. Wild Tales. McCarthy, Patricia, ed. (Pal Paperbacks Kit A Ser.). (Illus., Orig.). (gr. 7-12). 1974. pap. text ed. 1.25 (ISBN 0-8374-3473-4). Xerox Ed Pubns.

Schwager, Coleen & Schwager, Dirk. Lesotho. 1975. text ed. 20.00x o.p. (ISBN 0-620-01444-X). Verry.

Schwager, Dirk, jt. auth. see Schwager, Coleen.

Schwaig, Robert. Odessy of the Blithe Spirit II. 200p. (Orig.). pap. 6.95 (ISBN 0-86629-024-9). Sunrise MO.

Schwaiger, Konrad, jt. auth. see Kirchner, Emil.

Schwalb, Bobbie, jt. auth. see Jameson, Dee Dee.

Schwalbach, James A., jt. auth. see Schwalbach, Mathilda V.

Schwalbach, Mathilda V. & Schwalbach, James A. Silk-Screen Printing for Artists & Craftsmen. (Illus.). 150p. Date not set. pap. write for info. (ISBN 0-486-24046-0). Dover.

Schwalbery, Carol. Light & Shadow. LC 74-174587. (Finding-Out Book). 64p. (gr. 2-4). 1972. PLB 6.95 (ISBN 0-8193-0538-3). Enslow Pubs.

Schwalje, Marjory. Raggedy Andy's Treasure Hunt. (Tell-a-Tale Readers). (Illus.). (gr. k-3). 1979. PLB 4.77 (ISBN 0-307-68420-2, Whitman). Western Pub.

Schwaljie, Marjorie. Raggedy Andy & the Jump-up Contest. (Tell-a-Tale Readers). (Illus.). (gr. k-3). 1978. PLB 4.77 (ISBN 0-307-68641-8, Whitman). Western Pub.

--Raggedy Ann's Cooking School. (Tell-a-Tale Readers). (Illus.). (gr. k-3). 1974. PLB 4.77 (ISBN 0-307-68498-9, Whitman). Western Pub.

Schwaller, Anthony E. Energy: Sources of Power. LC 79-57017. (Technology Series). (Illus.). 446p. 1980. text ed. 15.95 (ISBN 0-87192-122-7, 000-4). Davis Pubns.

Schwaller De Lubicz, Isha. Her-Bak Egyptian Initiate. Fraser, Ronald, tr. from Fr. (Illus.). 1978. pap. 8.95 (ISBN 0-89281-002-5). Inner Tradit.

--Her-Bak, the Living Face of Ancient Egypt. Spague, Charles E., tr. from Fr. (Illus.). 1978. pap. 8.95 (ISBN 0-89281-003-3). Inner Tradit.

Schwaller de Lubicz, R. A. Esoterism & Symbol. (Illus.). 1981. 5.95 (ISBN 0-89281-014-9). Inner Tradit.

--The Sacred Science: The King of Pharaonic Theocracy. Vandenbroeck, A. & Vandenbroeck, G., trs. (Illus.). 1981. 12.95 (ISBN 0-89281-007-6). Inner Tradit.

Schwalm, M. A. Johannes Schwalm Historical Assn., Inc. (Le Monde D'outre-Mer Passe et Present: Etudes 38). (Illus.). 1972. 64.00x (ISBN 90-2797-052-1); pap. 50.00x (ISBN 0-686-21243-6). Mouton.

Schwan, Eduard. Die Altfranzosischen Liederhandschriften Ihr Verhaltniss, Ihre/Entstehung & Ihre Bestimmung. LC 80-2169. Repr. of 1886 ed. 39.50 (ISBN 0-404-19033-2). AMS Pr.

Schwan, Kas, et al. The Living Together Book. LC 79-67611. (Illus.). 64p. (Orig.). 1980. pap. 4.95 (ISBN 0-87223-601-3, Dist. by Har-Row). Wideview Bks.

Schwan, W. C., jt. ed. see Richter, H. P.

Schwanauer, Francis. No Many Is Not a One (For the Case Is a Comparison) LC 80-6173. 66p. (Orig.). 1981. pap. text ed. 5.00 (ISBN 0-8191-1455-3). U Pr of Amer.

--Wahrheit Ist eine Nachbarschaft, Die Nichts Trennt. 196p. (Ger.). 1980. pap. text ed. 9.50 (ISBN 0-8191-0995-9). U Pr of Amer.

Schwanbeck, John, jt. auth. see Scheerer, Penelope.

Schwandt, Med P. Preventing Arterial Lipidoses. 300p. 1981. 27.50 (ISBN 0-87527-232-0). Green.

Schwandt, P. Risk & Prevention of Arterial Lipidoses. 1981. 27.50 (ISBN 0-87527-232-0). Green.

Schwantes, Dave. Taming Your TV & Other Media. LC 79-16848. (Orion Ser.). 1979. pap. 2.95 (ISBN 0-8127-0246-8). Southern Pub.

Schware, Robert. Quantification in the History of Political Thought: Toward a Qualitative Approach. LC 80-1704. (Contributions in Political Science Ser.: No. 55). 184p. 1981. lib. bdg. 25.00 (ISBN 0-313-22228-2, SPT/). Greenwood.

Schware, Robert, jt. auth. see Kellogg, William W.

Schwark, Bryan L., jt. auth. see Camp, William L.

Schwarsenneger, Arnold. Arnold's Bodybuilding for Men. 1981. 14.95 (ISBN 0-671-25613-0). S&S.

Schwartz. Perscription Drugs in Short Supply. 144p. 1980. 17.50 (ISBN 0-686-60253-6). Dekker.

Schwartz, A., jt. auth. see Friedman, M.

Schwartz, A. J., jt. auth. see Friedman, M.

Schwartz, A. Truman. Chemistry. 1973. text ed. 18.50 (ISBN 0-12-632950-8). Acad Pr.

Schwartz, Alfred I., et al. Employing Civilians for Police Work. 1975. pap. 3.50 o.p. (ISBN 0-87766-139-1, 11700). Urban Inst.

Schwartz, Alvin. The Cat's Elbow & Other Secret Languages. (Illus.). 96p. (gr. 3 up). Date not set. 8.95 (ISBN 0-374-31224-9). FS&G.

--Central City - Spread City: The Metropolitan Regions Where More & More of Us Spend Our Lives. LC 72-81068. (Illus.). 160p. (gr. 5-9). 1973. PLB 4.95 o.s.i. (ISBN 0-02-781320-7). Macmillan.

--Cross Your Fingers, Spit in Your Hat. LC 73-21912. (Illus.). 160p. (gr. 4 up). 1974. 8.95 (ISBN 0-397-31530-9); pap. 2.95 (ISBN 0-397-31531-7). Lippincott.

--Kickle Snifters & Other Fearsome Critters. LC 75-29048. (gr. k-4). 1976. 8.95 (ISBN 0-397-31645-3). Lippincott.

--Stores. LC 76-47451. (Illus.). (gr. 3 up). 1977. 8.95 (ISBN 0-02-781310-X, 78131). Macmillan.

--A Twister of Twists, a Tangler of Tongues. LC 72-1434. (Illus.). 126p. (gr. 6 up). 1972. 8.95 (ISBN 0-397-31387-X); pap. 1.95 (ISBN 0-397-31412-4, LSC-22). Lippincott.

--Whoppers: Tall Tales & Other Lies. LC 74-32024. (gr. 4-7). 1975. 8.95 (ISBN 0-397-31575-9); pap. 2.95 (ISBN 0-397-31612-7). Lippincott.

--Witcracks: Jokes & Jests from American Folklore. LC 73-7630. (Illus.). (gr. 4 up). 1973. 8.95 (ISBN 0-397-31475-2); pap. 2.50 (ISBN 0-397-31476-0). Lippincott.

Schwartz, Arnold, jt. auth. see Bresnick, Edward.

Schwartz, Arthur, et al. Social Casework: A Behavioral Approach. new ed. LC 75-2298. 336p. 1975. 15.00x (ISBN 0-231-03778-3). Columbia U Pr.

Schwartz, Arthur J., jt. auth. see Goldberg, Jack L.

Schwartz, Arthur N. & Mensh, Ivan N. Professional Obligations & Approaches to the Aged. (Illus.). 392p. 1974. 22.50 (ISBN 0-398-02922-9). C C Thomas.

Schwartz, Arthur P., jt. auth. see Frishman, Austin M.

Schwartz, B. Clinical Venereology. 1965. pap. 9.75 (ISBN 0-08-011601-9). Pergamon.

Schwartz, Barry. Vertical Classification: A Study in Structuralism & the Sociology of Knowledge. LC 80-24207. (Chicago Original Paperback Ser.). 232p. 1981. lib. bdg. 17.00x (ISBN 0-226-74208-3). U of Chicago Pr.

Schwartz, Barry, ed. Human Connection & the New Media. (Human Futures Ser). (Illus.). 1973. pap. 2.45 o.p. (ISBN 0-13-444745-X). P-H.

Schwartz, Bernard. Administrative Law Casebook. 1977. 21.50 (ISBN 0-316-77563-0). Little.

--The American Heritage History of the Law in America. LC 74-8264. (Illus.). 379p. 1981. pap. 12.95 (ISBN 0-8281-0426-3, Dist. by Scribner). Am Heritage.

--Roots of the Bill of Rights: An Illustrated Sourcebook of American Freedom, 5 vols. rev. ed. LC 80-22931. (Illus.). 1500p. 1981. Set. pap. 64.95 (ISBN 0-87754-207-4). Chelsea Hse.

Schwartz, Bernard & Pugh, James M. How to Get Your Children to Be Good Students-How to Get Your Students to Be Good Children. LC 80-27826. 150p. 1981. 8.95 (ISBN 0-13-409862-5). P-H.

Schwartz, Bernard & Wade, H. W. Legal Control of Government: Administrative Law in Britain & the United States. 1972. 45.00x (ISBN 0-19-825315-X). Oxford U Pr.

Schwartz, Bernard, jt. auth. see Wood, Paul.

Schwartz, Bernice S., jt. auth. see Schwartz, George I.

Schwartz, C. M., jt. auth. see Kirkpatrick, E. M.

Schwartz, Charles W. & Schwartz, E. R. Wild Mammals of Missouri. (Illus.). 1959. 15.00x o.p. (ISBN 0-8262-0001-X). U of Mo Pr.

Schwartz, Charles W. & Schwartz, Elizabeth R. Wild Mammals of Missouri. rev. ed. 384p. 1981. text ed. 35.00 (ISBN 0-8262-0324-8). U of Mo Pr.

Schwartz, Dale J. The B's & B's. (Illus.). 116p. (Orig.). 1980. 2.95 (ISBN 0-935854-00-2). Baskin Pubs.

Schwartz, David C. & Schwartz, Sandra K., eds. New Directions in Political Socialization. LC 74-2653. (Illus.). 1975. 17.95 (ISBN 0-02-928180-6). Free Pr.

Schwartz, David J. The Magic of Thinking Big. 1962. pap. 3.95 (ISBN 0-346-12292-9). Cornerstone.

Schwartz, Dorothy T. & Aldrich, Dorothy, eds. Give Them Roots & Wings. 163p. 1972. pap. 7.50, ATA members 5.00 (ISBN 0-686-13195-9). Am Theatre Assoc.

Schwartz, Douglas W., jt. auth. see Palkovich, Ann M.

Schwartz, E. R., jt. auth. see Schwartz, Charles W.

Schwartz, Edmund I. & Landovitz, Leon F. Funk & Wagnalls Crossword Puzzle Word Finder. (Funk & W Bk.). 768p. 1974. 8.95 o.p. (ISBN 0-308-10126-X, TYC-T). T Y Crowell.

Schwartz, Eli, jt. ed. see Aronson, J. Richard.

Schwartz, Elias. The Mortal Worm: Shakespeare's Master Theme. (National University Pubns. Literary Criticism Ser.). 1977. 11.00 (ISBN 0-8046-9137-1). Kennikat.

Schwartz, Elizabeth R., jt. auth. see Schwartz, Charles W.

Schwartz, Elliot & Childs, Barney, eds. Contemporary Composers on Contemporary Music. (Music Reprint Ser., 1978). 1978. Repr. of 1967 ed. lib. bdg. 32.50 (ISBN 0-306-77587-5). Da Capo.

Schwartz, Elliot S. The Symphonies of Ralph Vaughan Williams. LC 64-24402. (Illus.). 1965. 12.00x o.p. (ISBN 0-87023-004-2). U of Mass Pr.

Schwartz, Eugene. How to Double Your Child's Grades in School. rev. ed. LC 64-17293. 1975. 8.95 (ISBN 0-8119-0081-9). Fell.

--The Sound of One Mind Thinking. (Illus.). 1981. pap. 6.95 (ISBN 0-89407-040-1). Strawberry Hill.

Schwartz, Federico. El Corazon Del Comunismo. Moore, Cecil, tr. from English. 1977. pap. 0.60 o.p. (ISBN 0-311-14204-4, Edit Mundo). Casa Bautista.

Schwartz, Gail G. & Choate, Pat. Being Number One: Rebuilding the U. S. Economy. 1980. 14.95 (ISBN 0-669-04308-7). Lexington Bks.

Schwartz, Gary, et al. Love & Commitment. LC 79-25460. (Sociological Observations: Vol. 9). (Illus.). 271p. 1980. 18.95 (ISBN 0-8039-1419-9); pap. 8.95 (ISBN 0-8039-1420-2). Sage.

Schwartz, George. Food Power. 204p. 1981. pap. 4.95 (ISBN 0-07-055674-1). McGraw.

Schwartz, George I. & Schwartz, Bernice S. Food Chains & Ecosystems: Ecology for Young Experimenters. LC 73-15171. (gr. 5-7). 1974. 4.95 o.p. (ISBN 0-385-08000-X). Doubleday.

Schwartz, Grace H. Monarch Notes on Wilde's Plays. (Orig.). pap. 1.95 (ISBN 0-671-00881-1). Monarch Pr.

Schwartz, Hans-Peter, jt. ed. see Kaiser, Karl.

Schwartz, Harry W. Bands of America. LC 74-23385. (Illus.). 320p. 1975. Repr. of 1957 ed. lib. bdg. 29.00 (ISBN 0-306-70672-5). Da Capo.

Schwartz, Helene. Justice by the Book. new ed. 1977. pap. 2.75x. Bloch.

Schwartz, Henry. Kit Carson's Long Walk & Other True Tales of Old San Diego. LC 80-68570. 112p. (Orig.). 1980. pap. 3.95 (ISBN 0-933362-03-X). Assoc Creative Writers.

Schwartz, Hillel. The French Prophets: The History of a Millenarian Group in Eighteenth-Century England. (Illus.). 1980. 27.50x (ISBN 0-520-03815-0). U of Cal Pr.

--Knaves, Fools, Madmen & That Subtile Effluvium: A Study of the Opposition to the French Prophets in England, 1706-1710. LC 78-1692. (U of Fla. Social Science Monographs: No. 62). 1978. pap. 5.50 (ISBN 0-8130-0505-1). U Presses Fla.

Schwartz, Howard & Rudolf, Anthony, eds. Voices Within the Ark. 1980. pap. 14.95 (ISBN 0-380-76109-2, 76109). Avon.

--Voices Within the Ark: The Modern Jewish Poets. 1980. 39.50 (ISBN 0-916366-11-1); slipcased ed. 50.00. Pushcart Pr.

Schwartz, Howard D. & Kart, Cary S. Dominant Issues in Medical Sociology. LC 77-76118. (Sociology Ser.). 1978. pap. text ed. 14.95 (ISBN 0-201-06781-1). A-W.

Schwartz, Irving L. General Physiological Processes. 225p. 1973. pap. 9.50 (ISBN 0-686-65355-6). Krieger.

Schwartz, J. Colloquial Czech. 2nd ed. (Tribner's Colloquial Manuals). 1945. 15.00 (ISBN 0-7100-8346-7); pap. 9.75 (ISBN 0-7100-4335-X). Routledge & Kegan.

Schwartz, J., jt. auth. see Schwartz, L.

Schwartz, J. T., ed. Mathematical Aspects of Computer Science: Proceedings of a Symposium, New York City, Apr. 1966. LC 67-16554. 1978. Repr. of 1967 ed. 12.80 (ISBN 0-8218-1319-6, PSAPM-19). Am Math.

Schwartz, Jacob T., jt. auth. see Dunford, Nelson.

Schwartz, Jeffrey & Schreiber, Ron. Contending with the Dark & Against That Time. LC 77-93269. 88p. 1978. pap. 4.95 (ISBN 0-914086-22-7). Alicejamesbooks.

Schwartz, Jerome L., jt. ed. see Nolan, Robert L.

Schwartz, Joel J., jt. ed. see Katz, William A.

Schwartz, Joseph & Rycenga, J. A., eds. The Province of Rhetoric. 4th ed. 1965. 11.95 (ISBN 0-8260-7955-5). Wiley.

Schwartz, Judy J. Teaching the Linguistically Diverse. (New York State English Council Monographs). 1980. text ed. 8.50 (ISBN 0-930348-08-7). NY St Eng Coun.

Schwartz, Jules J. Corporate Policy: A Casebook. (Illus.). 1978. 21.95 (ISBN 0-13-174813-0). P-H.

Schwartz, Kessel, jt. auth. see Chandler, Richard E.

Schwartz, L. & Schwartz, J. Psychodynamics of Patient Care. 448p. 1972. pap. 13.95 (ISBN 0-13-732578-9). P-H.

Schwartz, Lagar M. & Azar, Miguel M., eds. Advanced Cell Biology. 1168p. 1981. text ed. 39.50 (ISBN 0-442-27471-8). Van Nos Reinhold.

Schwartz, Lazar M. & Schwartz, Paula. An Excersise Manual in Immunology. LC 75-14774. 324p. 1975. 15.00 (ISBN 0-686-65368-8). Krieger.

Schwartz, Leland. Survey of Electronics. 2nd ed. (Electronics Technology Ser.). 1977. pap. text ed. 12.50 (ISBN 0-675-08554-3). Merrill.

Schwartz, Leni. The Life of the Unborn: Nurturing Your Child Before Birth. 312p. 1981. 12.95 (ISBN 0-399-90090-X). Marek.

Schwartz, Leon. Diderot & the Jews. LC 78-73304. 220p. 1981. 14.50 (ISBN 0-8386-2377-8). Fairleigh Dickinson.

Schwartz, Lester J. Choosing the Right College. 128p. Date not set. pap. 4.95 (ISBN 0-553-01276-2). Bantam.

Schwartz, Lewis M. Keats Reviewed by His Contemporaries: A Collection of Notices for the Years 1816-1821. LC 72-12779. 1973. 13.50 (ISBN 0-8108-0577-4). Scarecrow.

Schwartz, Lita. Exceptional Child. 2nd ed. 1979. pap. text ed. 8.95x (ISBN 0-534-00633-7). Wadsworth Pub.

Schwartz, Lita L. American Education: A Problem-Centered Approach. 3rd ed. LC 78-62182. 1978. pap. text ed. 13.75 (ISBN 0-8191-0508-2). U Pr of Amer.

Schwartz, Lynne S. Balancing Acts. LC 80-8366. 224p. 1981. 9.95 (ISBN 0-06-013702-9, HarpT). Har-Row.

--Rough Strife. LC 80-85111. 240p. 1981. pap. 2.75 (ISBN 0-87216-846-8). Playboy Pbks.

Schwartz, Malcolm, jt. auth. see Maher, Tom.

Schwartz, Martin. Extra Class Radio Amateur License Guide. LC 79-54856. 1980. pap. 1.50 (ISBN 0-912146-11-7). AMECO.

Schwartz, Martin F. Stuttering Solved. LC 75-42456. (Illus.). 1976. 9.95 (ISBN 0-397-01134-2). Lippincott.

Schwartz, Marvin. Physiological Psychology. 2nd ed. LC 77-17438. (Century Psychology Ser.). (Illus.). 1978. ref. ed. 20.95 (ISBN 0-13-674895-3). P-H.

Schwartz, Marvin D. Collector's Guide to Antique American Glass. LC 68-27138. 1969. 5.95 o.p. (ISBN 0-385-00889-9). Doubleday.

Schwartz, Mildred A. Public Opinion & Canadian Identity. 1967. 20.00x (ISBN 0-520-01156-2). U of Cal Pr.

Schwartz, Morris S. Social Approaches to Mental Patient Care. LC 64-13736. 1964. 20.00x (ISBN 0-231-02698-6). Columbia U Pr.

Schwartz, Morris S. & Shockley, Emmy L. Nurse & the Mental Patient: A Study of Interpersonal Relations. 1956. pap. 9.95 (ISBN 0-471-76610-0, Pub. by Wiley-Medical). Wiley.

Schwartz, Mortimer. Environmental Law: A Guide to Information Sources. LC 73-17541. (Man & the Environment Information Guide Series: Vol. 6). 1977. 30.00 (ISBN 0-8103-1339-1). Gale.

Schwartz, Mortimer D. & Henke, Dan F., eds. Combined Catalog Anglo-American Law Collections University of California Law Libraries Berkeley & Davis with Library of Congress Class K Added, 9 vols. 1970. text ed. 750.00x (ISBN 0-8377-0423-5). Rothman.

Schwartz, Mortimer D., ed. see Colloquium on the Law of Outer Space - International Institute of Space Law of the International Astronautical Federation, 20th, 1977.

Schwartz, Mortimer D., ed. see Conference on Space Science & Space Law.

Schwartz, Morton. The Foreign Policy of the USSR: Domestic Factors. 1975. pap. 7.95x (ISBN 0-8221-0145-9). Dickenson.

--Soviet Perceptions of the United States. 1978. 15.95x (ISBN 0-520-03234-9). U of Cal Pr.

Schwartz, Morton K., jt. ed. see Latner, A. L.

Schwartz, Murray. Law & the American Future: An American Assembly Book. 1976. 9.95 (ISBN 0-13-526061-2, Spec); pap. 4.95 (ISBN 0-13-526053-1, Spec). P-H.

Schwartz, Nancy & Schwartz, Sheila. The Hollywood Writers' Wars. LC 80-2728. (Illus.). 448p. 1981. 16.95 (ISBN 0-394-41140-4). Knopf. Postponed.

Schwartz, Narda Lacey. Articles on Women Writers, 1960-1975: A Bibliography. LC 77-9071. 236p. 1977. text ed. 24.95 (ISBN 0-87436-252-0). ABC-Clio.

Schwartz, Paula, jt. auth. see Schwartz, Lazar M.

Schwartz, Peter J., et al, eds. Neural Mechanisms in Cardiac Arrhythmias. LC 77-77962. (Perspectives in Cardiovascular Research Ser.: Vol. 2). 1978. 41.00 (ISBN 0-89004-209-8). Raven.

Schwartz, Philip J. Coalition Bargaining. (Key Issues Ser.: No. 5). 1970. pap. 2.00 (ISBN 0-87546-241-3). NY Sch Indus Rel.

Schwartz, Richard B. Samuel Johnson & the New Science. 1971. 20.00x (ISBN 0-299-06010-1). U of Wis Pr.

Schwartz, Robert, jt. auth. see Condemi, John J.

Schwartz, Robert N., ed. see Kevan, Larry.

Schwartz, Ronald. Jose Maria Gironella. (World Authors Ser.: Spain: No. 164). lib. bdg. 10.95 (ISBN 0-8057-2372-2). Twayne.

--Nomads, Exiles, & Emigres: The Rebirth of the Latin American Narrative, 1960-80. LC 80-20669. 168p. 1980. 10.00 (ISBN 0-8108-1359-9). Scarecrow.

Schwartz, Ronald A., jt. ed. see Browman, David L.

Schwartz, Ronald A., jt. ed. see Cordwell, Justine.

Schwartz, Sandra K., jt. ed. see Schwartz, David C.

Schwartz, Seymour I. & Ehrenberg, Ralph E. The Mapping of America. (Illus.). 360p. 1980. 60.00 (ISBN 0-686-62687-7, 1307-0). Abrams.

Schwartz, Seymour I., et al, eds. Principles of Surgery PreTest Self-Assessment & Review. (Illus., Orig.). 1981. pap. 25.00 (ISBN 0-07-051649-9). McGraw-PreTest.

Schwartz, Sheila. Teaching Adolescent Literature: A Humanistic Approach. LC 79-2042. 1979. pap. text ed. 9.50x (ISBN 0-8104-6036-X). Hayden.

Schwartz, Sheila, jt. auth. see Schwartz, Nancy.

Schwartz, Sidney. Housing Careers. (Home Economics Careers Ser.). (gr. 10-12). 1977. 6.36 (ISBN 0-13-392811-X); pap. text ed. 5.12 (ISBN 0-13-392803-9). P-H.

Schwartz, Stephen, jt. auth. see Hirson, Roger O.

Schwartz, Steven & Johnson, James H. Psychopathology of Childhood: A Clinical-Experimental Approach. (Pergamon General Psychology Ser.). 400p. Date not set. 19.51 (ISBN 0-08-023885-8). Pergamon.

Schwartz, Steven J. & Ferrarone, Stephen F. Community Mental Health & the Law: An Annotated Bibliography. LC 80-18872. 256p. 1981. 22.50x (ISBN 0-8290-0239-1). Irvington.

Schwartz, Stuart B. Sovereignty & Society in Colonial Brazil: The High Court of Bahia & Its Judges, 1609-1751. 1973. 28.50x (ISBN 0-520-02195-9). U of Cal Pr.

Schwartz, Theodore, ed. Socialization As Cultural Communication. LC 75-17282. 1976. 15.00x (ISBN 0-520-03061-3); pap. 6.95x (ISBN 0-520-03955-6). U of Cal Pr.

Schwartz, Theodore B. & Ryan, Will G., eds. Year Book of Endocrinology, 1980. 400p. 1980. 31.50 (ISBN 0-8151-7608-2). Year Bk Med.

Schwartz, Toby D. Mercy, Lord! My Husband's in the Kitchen & Other Equal Opportunity Conversations with God. LC 80-715. (Illus.). 96p. 1981. 6.95 (ISBN 0-385-17058-0). Doubleday.

Schwartz, Tony. The Responsive Chord. LC 73-81420. 192p. 1974. pap. 2.95 (ISBN 0-385-08895-7, Anch). Doubleday.

Schwartz, Warren C., jt. ed. see Martin, Donald L.

Schwartz, Wendy C., ed. see Council on Economic Priorities & Buchsbaum, Steven.

Schwartz, William & Zalba, Serapio R., eds. Practice of Group Work. LC 75-127101. 1971. 17.50x (ISBN 0-231-03241-2); pap. 5.00x (ISBN 0-231-08674-1). Columbia U Pr.

Schwartzman. Reform Judaism in the Making. 1959. 7.50 (ISBN 0-8074-0192-7, 183542). UAHC.

Schwartzman, Edward. Campaign Craftsmanship: A Professional's Guide to Campaigning for Elective Office. LC 72-91198. (Illus.). 272p. 1973. 10.00x (ISBN 0-87663-173-1); pap. 3.95x o.s.i. (ISBN 0-87663-906-6). Universe.

Schwartzman, Paulette. Collector's Guide to European & American Art Pottery. (Illus.). 1978. pap. 9.95 o.p. (ISBN 0-89145-072-6). Collector Bks.

Schwartzman, Steven. Hill Country Women. (Illus., Orig.). 1980. pap. 9.00 (ISBN 0-937710-02-4). SunShine.

--Stereo Infrared Landscapes. (Illus., Orig.). 1980. pap. 9.00 (ISBN 0-937710-01-6). SunShine.

Schwartzman, Sylvan D. Reform Judaism - Then & Now. (Illus.). (gr. 10). 1971. text ed. 7.50 (ISBN 0-8074-0191-9, 161900). UAHC.

Schwartzman, Sylvan D. & Spiro, Jack D. Living Bible: A Topical Approach to the Jewish Scriptures. (Illus.). (gr. 8-10). 1962. text ed. 5.00 (ISBN 0-8074-0097-1, 161751); tchrs'. guide o.p. 2.75. UAHC.

Schwartzman, Sylvan D., jt. auth. see Miller, Milton G.

Schwartz-Nobel, Loretta. Starving in the Shadow of Plenty. 256p. 1981. 12.95 (ISBN 0-399-12522-1). Putnam.

Schwarz & Goldberg. New York State in Story, Pts. 1 & 2. 1962. comb. 7.95x (ISBN 0-88323-099-2, 280); wkbk. 2.25x (ISBN 0-88323-100-X, 283). Richards Pub.

--New York State in Story, Pt. 1. rev. ed. 1962. pap. 3.00x (ISBN 0-88323-096-8, 281). Richards Pub.

--The Story of New York State. 1962. pap. 3.00x (ISBN 0-88323-098-4, 282). Richards Pub.

Schwarz, Berthold E. Parent-Child Telepathy: A Study of the Telepathy of Everyday Life. LC 70-155052. 7.95 o.p. (ISBN 0-912326-24-7). Garrett-Helix.

Schwarz, Daniel R. Conrad: "Almayer's Folly" to "Under Western Eyes". LC 79-48012. 1980. 23.50x (ISBN 0-8014-1311-7). Cornell U Pr.

--Disraeli's Fiction. 1979. text ed. 24.00x (ISBN 0-06-496124-9). B&N.

Schwarz, David. Naming & Referring: The Semantics & Pragmatics of Singular Terms. (Foundations of Communication Ser.). 194p. 1979. text ed. 45.00x (ISBN 3-11-007610-1). De Gruyter.

Schwarz, Edward W. How to Use Interest Rate Futures Contracts. LC 79-51781. 1979. 19.95 (ISBN 0-87094-180-1). Dow Jones-Irwin.

Schwarz, Egon. Joseph von Eichendorff. (World Authors Ser.: Germany: No. 163). lib. bdg. 10.95 (ISBN 0-8057-2296-3). Twayne.

--Poetry & Politics in the Work of Rainer Maria Rilke. Wellbery, David E., tr. from Ger. LC 80-53704. 160p. 1981. 9.95 (ISBN 0-8044-2811-5). Ungar.

Schwarz, Eugene. Dragon. Hapgood, Elizabeth R., tr. (Orig.). 1969. pap. 1.65x (ISBN 0-87830-512-2, 12). Theatre Arts.

Schwarz, G. S., jt. auth. see Grashey, R.

Schwarz, H. J., et al, eds. Laser Interaction & Related Plasma Phenomena, Vol. 5. 800p. 1981. 75.00 (ISBN 0-306-40545-8, Plenum Pr). Plenum Pub.

Schwarz, Hans. Colour for the Artist. LC 79-56605. (Start to Paint Ser.). (Illus.). 104p. 1980. pap. 3.95 (ISBN 0-8008-1726-5, Pentalic). Taplinger.

--Painting in Towns & Cities. LC 79-56606. (Start to Paint Ser.). (Illus.). 1980. pap. 3.95 (ISBN 0-8008-6204-X, Pentalic). Taplinger.

Schwarz, Harold, jt. auth. see Weston, Ralph.

Schwarz, Henry G., ed. Mongolian Short Stories. LC 74-620031. (Program in East Asian Studies Occasional Papers Ser: No. 8). (Illus.). 190p. 1974. pap. 5.00 o.p. (ISBN 0-914584-08-1). West Wash Univ.

Schwarz, Hermann A. Gesammelte Mathematische Abhandlungen, 2 vols. in 1. 2nd ed. LC 70-113147. (Ger). text ed. 39.50 (ISBN 0-8284-0260-4). Chelsea Pub.

Schwarz, Jack. The Path of Action. LC 77-2247. 1977. pap. 4.95 (ISBN 0-525-47466-8). Dutton.

Schwarz, Jeanne. Student Guide to Richards Atlas of New York State. 1976. pap. 6.95x ea. (ISBN 0-88323-108-5, 304). Richards Pub.

Schwarz, John I. Police Roadblock Operations. (Police Science Ser.). (Illus.). 96p. 1962. 9.75 (ISBN 0-398-01700-X). C C Thomas.

Schwarz, Jordan A. Ordeal of Twentieth-Century America: Interpretive Readings. 464p. 1974. pap. text ed. 7.95 (ISBN 0-395-14519-8). HM.

--The Speculator: Bernard M. Baruch in Washington, 1917-1965. LC 80-17386. (Illus.). 688p. 1981. 27.50 (ISBN 0-8078-1396-6). U of NC Pr.

Schwarz, Marvin, et al. Furniture of John Henry Belter & the Rococo Revival. 1981. 24.95 (ISBN 0-525-93170-8). Dutton.

Schwarz, Otto B., jt. auth. see Grafstein, Paul.

Schwarz, Richard A. & Yaffe, Sumner J., eds. Drug & Chemical Risks to the Fetus & Newborn. LC 79-26191. (Progress in Clinical & Biological Research Ser.: Vol. 36). 166p. 1980. 20.00 (ISBN 0-8451-0036-X). A R Liss.

Schwarz, Richard H., ed. Handbook of Obstetric Emergencies. 2nd ed. 1977. 11.00 (ISBN 0-87488-634-1). Med Exam.

Schwarz, S. Knowledge & Concepts in Future Studies. LC 76-54238. (Westview Replica Edition Ser.). 1977. lib. bdg. 24.50x (ISBN 0-89158-123-5). Westview.

Schwarz, Ted. Careers in Photography. 1981. 12.95 (ISBN 0-8092-7019-6); pap. 5.95 (ISBN 0-8092-7018-8). Contemp Bks.

--The Hillside Strangler: A Murderer's Mind. LC 80-2435. 264p. 1981. 12.95 (ISBN 0-385-17337-7). Doubleday.

--Practical Photographic Lighting. (Popular Photography Workshop Ser.). (Illus.). 128p. 1980. 10.95 (ISBN 0-87165-056-8). Ziff-Davis Pub.

Schwarz, Ted, jt. auth. see Green, Bernard.

Schwarz, Urs. The Eye of the Hurricane: Switzerland in World War Two. 150p. 1980. lib. bdg. 18.00 (ISBN 0-89158-766-7). Westview.

Schwarz, Victor. A Clinical Companion to Biochemical Studies. LC 77-17132. (Illus.). 1978. 19.95x (ISBN 0-7167-0078-6); pap. text ed. 9.95x (ISBN 0-7167-0077-8). W H Freeman.

Schwarz, Wolfgang, tr. see Kant, Immanuel.

Schwarz-Bart, Andre. The Last of the Just. Becker, Stephen, tr. from Fr. LC 79-24071. 1981. Repr. of 1960 ed. lib. bdg. 12.50x (ISBN 0-8376-0456-7). Bentley.

Schwarzenbach, J. & Gill, K. F. System Modeling & Control. LC 78-40537. 1978. pap. 19.95 (ISBN 0-470-26457-8). Halsted Pr.

Schwarzenberger, G., jt. auth. see Keeton, G. W.

Schwarzenberger, Georg, jt. ed. see Keeton, George W.

Schwarzenberger, George. International Constitutional Law: International Law As Applied by International Courts & Tribunals, Vol. 3. LC 57-59355. 1976. lib. bdg. 97.50x (ISBN 0-89158-542-7). Westview.

Schwarzrock, Shirley & Wrenn, C. Gilbert. Alcohol As a Crutch. (Coping with Ser.). (Illus.). (gr. 7-12). 1971. pap. text ed. 1.30 (ISBN 0-913476-17-X). Am Guidance.

--Can You Talk with Someone Else? (Coping with Ser.). (Illus.). 36p. (gr. 7-12). 1970. pap. text ed. 1.30 (ISBN 0-913476-22-6). Am Guidance.

--Changing Roles of Men & Women. (Coping with Ser.). (Illus.). 31p. (gr. 7-12). 1970. pap. text ed. 1.30 (ISBN 0-913476-29-3). Am Guidance.

--Coping with Cliques. (Coping with Ser.). (Illus.). 31p. (gr. 7-12). 1971. pap. text ed. 1.30 (ISBN 0-913476-30-7). Am Guidance.

--The Coping with Series. (Illus., Orig.). (gr. 7-12). 1970-73. pap. text ed. 26.00 complete ref. set (ISBN 0-913476-10-2); manual 3.50 (ISBN 0-913476-11-0). Am Guidance.

--Crises Youth Face Today. (Coping with Ser.). (Illus.). 64p. (gr. 7-12). 1973. pap. text ed. 1.30 (ISBN 0-913476-28-5). Am Guidance.

--Do I Know the "Me" Others See? (Coping with Ser.). (Illus.). 55p. (gr. 7-12). 1973. pap. text ed. 1.30 (ISBN 0-913476-27-7). Am Guidance.

--Easing the Scene. (Coping with Ser.). (Illus.). (gr. 7-12). 1970. pap. text ed. 1.30 (ISBN 0-913476-23-4). Am Guidance.

--Facts & Fantasies About Alcohol. (Coping with Ser.). (Illus.). (gr. 7-12). 1971. pap. text ed. 1.30 (ISBN 0-913476-13-7). Am Guidance.

--Facts & Fantasies About Drugs. (Coping with Ser.). (Illus.). (gr. 6-9). 1970. pap. text ed. 1.30 (ISBN 0-913476-12-9). Am Guidance.

--Facts & Fantasies About Smoking. (Coping with Ser.). (Illus.). 40p. (gr. 7-12). 1971. pap. text ed. 1.30 (ISBN 0-913476-14-5). Am Guidance.

--Food As a Crutch. (Coping with Ser.). (Illus.). (gr. 7-12). 1971. pap. text ed. 1.30 (ISBN 0-913476-18-8). Am Guidance.

--Grades, What's So Important About Them, Anyway? (Coping with Ser.). (Illus.). 33p. (gr. 7-12). pap. text ed. 1.30 (ISBN 0-913476-34-X). Am Guidance.

--I'd Rather Do It Myself, If You Don't Mind. (Coping with Ser.). (Illus.). 39p. (gr. 7-12). 1970. pap. text ed. 1.30 (ISBN 0-913476-31-5). Am Guidance.
--In Front of the Table & Behind It. (Coping with Ser.). (Illus.). 41p. (gr. 7-12). 1971. pap. text ed. 1.30 (ISBN 0-913476-24-2). Am Guidance.
--Living with Differences. (Coping with Ser.). (gr. 7-12). 1973. pap. text ed. 1.30 (ISBN 0-913476-19-6). Am Guidance.
--Living with Loneliness. (Coping with Ser.). (Illus.). 31p. (gr. 7-12). 1970. pap. text ed. 1.30 (ISBN 0-913476-32-3). Am Guidance.
--The Mind Benders. (Coping with Ser.). (gr. 10 up). 1971. pap. text ed. 1.30 (ISBN 0-913476-16-1). Am Guidance.
--My Life - What Shall I Do with It? (Coping with Ser.). (Illus.). 50p. (gr. 7-12). 1973. pap. text ed. 1.30 (ISBN 0-913476-26-9). Am Guidance.
--Parents Can Be a Problem. (Coping with Ser.). (Illus.). (gr. 7-12). 1970. pap. text ed. 1.30 (ISBN 0-913476-33-1). Am Guidance.
--Some Common Crutches. (Coping with Ser.). (Illus.). 43p. (gr. 7-12). pap. text ed. 1.30 (ISBN 0-913476-15-3). Am Guidance.
--To Like & Be Liked. (Coping with Ser.). (Illus.). 37p. (gr. 7-12). 1970. pap. text ed. 1.30 (ISBN 0-913476-25-0). Am Guidance.
--Understanding the Law of Our Land. (Coping with Ser.). (Illus.). 51p. (gr. 7-12). 1973. pap. text ed. 1.30 (ISBN 0-913476-21-8). Am Guidance.
--You Always Communicate Something. (Coping with Ser.). (Illus.). 58p. (gr. 7-12). 1973. pap. text ed. 1.30 (ISBN 0-913476-20-X). Am Guidance.
Schwarzweller, Harry K., jt. ed. see Photiadis, John D.
Schwebach, Gerhard H. A Practical Guide to Microbial & Parasitic Diseases. (Illus.). 256p. 1980. lexotone 19.75 (ISBN 0-398-03980-1). C C Thomas.
Schwebel, Andrew I., et al. The Student Teacher's Handbook: A Step-by-Step Guide Through the Term. LC 79-2239. 1979. pap. 3.95 (ISBN 0-06-460186-2, CO 186, COS). Har-Row.
Schwebke, Phyllis & Dorfmeister, Margery. Sewing with the New Knits: Techniques for Today's New Fabrics. LC 72-11675. (Illus.). 480p. 1974. 14.95 o.s.i. (ISBN 0-02-607780-9). Macmillan.
Schwed, Peter. Peter Schwed's Tennis Quiz. (Illus.). 224p. (Orig.). 1981. pap. 8.95 (ISBN 0-914178-46-6, 42907-8). Tennis Mag.
--Sinister Tennis-How to Play Against & with Left Handers. LC 73-20530. 96p. 1975. 4.95 o.p. (ISBN 0-385-06706-2); pap. 2.50 Softbound (ISBN 0-385-06368-7). Doubleday.
--Test Your Tennis I.Q. LC 80-84954. (Illus.). 224p. 1981. pap. 8.95 (ISBN 0-914178-46-6, 42907-8). Golf Digest Bks.
Schweer, Jean E. Creative Teaching in Clinical Nursing. 3rd ed. LC 75-31627. (Illus.). 316p. 1976. pap. 10.95 (ISBN 0-8016-4377-5). Mosby.
Schweer, Kathryn D., jt. auth. see Warner, Steven D.
Schweibert, Ernest G., Jr. Matching the Hatch. (Illus.). 1978. pap. 6.95 o.p. (ISBN 0-695-80924-5). Follett.
Schweickart, David. Capitalism or Worker Control: An Ethical & Economic Appraisal. 266p. 1980. 22.95 (ISBN 0-03-056724-6). Praeger.
Schweid, Richard. Hot Peppers: Cajuns & Capsicum in New Iberia, la. LC 80-23160. 200p. 1980. 9.95 (ISBN 0-914842-50-1); pap. 6.95 (ISBN 0-914842-51-X). Madrona Pubs.
Schweiger, H. G., ed. International Cell Biology 1980 - 1981. (Illus.). 1180p. 1981. 68.00 (ISBN 0-387-10475-5). Springer-Verlag.
Schweiger, Joyce F. Nurse As Manager. LC 80-17456. 194p. 1980. 11.95 (ISBN 0-471-04343-5, Pub. by Wiley Med). Wiley.
Schweik, Robert C. & Riesner, Dieter. Reference Sources in English & American Literature: An Annotated Bibliography. 1977. 12.95x (ISBN 0-393-04484-X); pap. 7.95x (ISBN 0-393-09104-X). Norton.
Schweinitz, Karl De see De Schweinitz, Karl.
Schweitzer, Albert. Indian Thought & Its Development. 1962. 8.25 (ISBN 0-8446-2893-X). Peter Smith.
--J. S. Bach, 2 Vols. (Illus.). 1962. Set. pap. 9.95 (ISBN 0-8283-1733-X, 64); pap. 4.95 ea. Branden.
--J. S. Bach, 2 vols. Newman, Ernest, tr. Set. 22.00 (ISBN 0-8446-0902-1). Peter Smith.
--Light Within Us. LC 75-139151. 1971. Repr. of 1959 ed. lib. bdg. 11.75x (ISBN 0-8371-5767-6, SCLW). Greenwood.
--Mysticism of Paul the Apostle. LC 68-28707. 1968. pap. 5.95 (ISBN 0-8164-2049-1, SP51). Crossroad NY.
--Out of My Life & Thought. pap. 1.50 o.p. (ISBN 0-451-61456-9, MW1456, Ment). NAL.
--Out of My Life & Thought. 1972. pap. 2.95 o.p. (ISBN 0-03-091483-3). HR&W.
--The Philosophy of Civilization. Campion, C. T., tr. from Ger. LC 80-27122. xvii, 347p. 1981. pap. 6.00 (ISBN 0-8130-0694-5). U Presses Fla.
--Psychiatric Study of Jesus. 7.50 (ISBN 0-8446-2894-8). Peter Smith.
--Thoughts for Our Times. Anderson, Erica, ed. (Illus.). 64p. 1981. Repr. of 1975 ed. 3.95 (ISBN 0-8298-0448-X). Pilgrim NY.
--A Treasury of Albert Schweitzer. LC 65-20328. 352p. 1965. 6.00 (ISBN 0-8022-1518-1). Philos Lib.
Schweitzer, Byrd B. Amigo. (gr. 1-3). 1963. 5.95g o.s.i. (ISBN 0-02-781300-2). Macmillan.
--One Small Blue Bead. (Illus.). (gr. k-3). 1965. 7.95 (ISBN 0-02-781330-4). Macmillan.
Schweitzer, Christoph E., ed. see Goes, Albrecht.
Schweitzer, Darrell. Essays Lovecraftian. LC 80-19213. 120p. 1980. Repr. lib. bdg. 9.95x (ISBN 0-89370-096-7). Borgo Pr.
--Science Fiction Voices, No. 5: Interviews with Science-Fiction Writers. (The Milford Series: Popular Writers of Today: Vol. 35). 64p. 1981. lib. bdg. 8.95 (ISBN 0-89370-151-3); pap. text ed. 2.95x (ISBN 0-89370-251-X). Borgo Pr.
Schweitzer, F. History of the Jew Since the First Century A.D. 1971. 7.95 o.p. (ISBN 0-02-608160-1); pap. 1.95 (ISBN 0-02-089260-8). Macmillan.
Schweitzer, Gerald. Basics of Fractional Horsepower Motors & Repair. (Illus.). 1960. pap. 7.65 (ISBN 0-8104-0418-4). Hayden.
Schweitzer, Iris, jt. auth. see Hildick, E. W.
Schweitzer, Martin, jt. auth. see Collins, Lawrence.
Schweitzer, Philip. A Handbook of Valves. 258p. 1972. 22.00 o.p. (ISBN 0-8311-3026-1). Indus Pr.
Schweitzer, Philip A. Handbook of Corrosion Resistant Piping. (Illus.). 1969. 35.00 o.p. (ISBN 0-8311-3016-4). Indus Pr.
Schweitzer, Sidney C. Cyclopedia of Trial Practice, 10 vols. 2nd ed. Incl. Vols 1-4. 1970. 240.00 (ISBN 0-686-14519-4, 745A); Vols. 5 & 5a. Dollar Verdicts. 1968. 80.00 (ISBN 0-686-14520-8); Vols. 6-10. Proof of Traumatic Injuries. 1972. 160.00 (ISBN 0-686-14521-6). LC 70-123204. Set. 375.00 (ISBN 0-686-14518-6). Lawyers Co-Op.
Schweizer Aircraft Corporation. Start Soaring. 1978. pap. 3.25x (ISBN 0-911721-75-4). Aviation.
Schweizer, Barbara, jt. ed. see Iglehart, Susan.
Schweizer, Eduard. Good News According to Matthew. Green, David E., tr. LC 74-3717. 1975. 15.00 (ISBN 0-8042-0251-6). John Knox.
--The Holy Spirit. LC 79-8892. 144p. 1980. 9.95 (ISBN 0-8006-0629-9, 1-629). Fortress.
--Jesus. LC 76-107322. 1979. pap. 4.95 (ISBN 0-8042-0331-8). John Knox.
Schweizer, W. Basel. 1975. bds. 7.50 (ISBN 0-911268-27-8). Rogers Bk.
Schwemmler, W. & Schenk, H., eds. Endosymbiosis & Cell Research. 900p. 1980. text ed. 107.00x (ISBN 3-11-008299-3). De Gruyter.
Schwengel, Jeanne S., jt. auth. see Perry, Louise M.
Schweninger, Ann. On My Way to Grandpa's. LC 80-22729. (Illus.). 32p. (ps-2). 1981. 7.50 (ISBN 0-8037-6741-2); PLB 7.28 (ISBN 0-8037-6752-8). Dial.
Schwenkhagen, Hans F. Dictionary of Electrical & Electronic Engineering: German-English & English-German. 2nd ed. LC 67-74452. 909p. 1967. 105.00x (ISBN 3-7736-5072-8). Intl Pubns Serv.
Schwenn, Donald C., jt. auth. see Malawicki, Douglas J.
Schwerdtfeger, Don. The Secret Truth About Fat People. LC 80-82369. (Illus.). 204p. Date not set. 11.95 (ISBN 0-8119-0409-1, Pegasus Rex). Fell.
Schwerdtfeger, Hans. Geometry of Complex Numbers. LC 79-52529. 1980. pap. text ed. 4.00 (ISBN 0-486-63830-8). Dover.
Schwerin, Horace S. & Newell, Henry H. Persuasion in Marketing: The Dynamics of Marketing's Great Untapped Resource. 280p. 1981. 23.95 (ISBN 0-471-04554-3, Pub. by Wiley-Interscience). Wiley.
Schwerin, Kurt. A Bibliography of German. (Language Legal Monograph Ser.). 383p. 1977. text ed. 58.00 (ISBN 3-7940-7037-2, Pub. by K G Saur). Gale.
Schwert, George W. & Winer, Alfred D., eds. The Mechanism of Action of Dehydrogenases: A Symposium in Honor of Hugo Theorell. LC 73-80094. (Illus.). 272p. 1970. 11.00x (ISBN 0-8131-1188-9). U Pr of Ky.
Schwicker, Angelo C. International Dictionary of Building Construction: English-French-German-Italian. 1280p. 1975. lib. bdg. 60.00x (ISBN 0-87936-004-6). Scholium Intl.
Schwidetzky, Ilse, et al, eds. Physical Anthropology of European Populations. (World Anthropology Ser.). 1979. text ed. 54.00x (ISBN 90-279-7900-6). Mouton.
Schwiebert, Ernest. Death of a Riverkeeper: And Other Stories. (Illus.). 288p. 1981. 14.95 (ISBN 0-525-08947-0). Dutton.
--Nymphs. LC 73-188596. (Illus.). 339p. 1973. 17.95 (ISBN 0-87691-074-6). Winchester Pr.
Schwieters, Elsa S., tr. see Watson, David.
Schwimmer, Erik, ed. Maori People in the Nineteen-Sixties: A Symposium. (Illus.). 1968. text ed. 11.00x (ISBN 0-900966-00-9). Humanities.
Schwimmer, Martin J. & Malca, Edward. Pension & Institutional Portfolio Management. LC 76-6473. (Special Studies). (Illus.). 120p. 1976. text ed. 22.95 (ISBN 0-275-56730-3). Praeger.
Schwimmer, Sigmund. Source Book of Food Enzymology. (Illus.). 1981. lib. bdg. 79.50 (ISBN 0-87055-369-0). AVI.
Schwind, Phil. Cape Cod Fisherman. LC 74-19999. (Illus.). 1974. 12.50 (ISBN 0-87742-045-9). Intl Marine.
Schwind-Belkin, Johanna & Caley, Earle R., eds. Eucharius Rosslin in the Younger: On Minerals & Mineral Products. (Arts Medica, Abeilung IV: Landessprachliche und Mittelalterliche Medizin I). 415p. 1978. text ed. 150.00x (ISBN 3-11006-907-5). De Gruyter.
Schwinger, Julian. Particles, Sources & Fields, Vol. 1. LC 73-119670. (Physics Ser). 1970. text ed. 28.50 (ISBN 0-201-06782-X, Adv Bk Prog). A-W.
--Particles, Sources & Fields, Vol. 2. (Physics Ser.). 1973. 28.50 (ISBN 0-201-06783-8, Adv Bk Prog). A-W.
Schwinger, Julian, ed. Selected Papers on Quantum Electrodynamics. 1958. pap. text ed. 6.00 (ISBN 0-486-60444-6). Dover.
Schwinn, Monika & Diehl, Bernhard. We Came to Help. LC 76-13882. (Helen & Kurt Wolff Bk.). (Illus.). 1976. 8.95 o.p. (ISBN 0-15-195595-6). HarBraceJ.
Schwitzgebel, R. Kirkland, jt. auth. see Schwitzgebel, Robert L.
Schwitzgebel, Robert L. & Schwitzgebel, R. Kirkland. Law & Psychological Practice. LC 79-20112. 1980. text ed. 16.50 (ISBN 0-471-76694-1). Wiley.
Schwoebel, Robert. The Shadow of the Crescent: The Renaissance Image of the Turk, 1453-1517. 1979. text ed. 42.75x (ISBN 90-6004-169-0). Humanities.
Schworck, Ernest. Go-West Guide - Los Angeles. (Illus.). 48p. 1978. pap. 2.45 English version o.p. (ISBN 0-912076-27-5); pap. 2.45 Japanese Version o.p. (ISBN 0-912076-28-3). ESE Calif.
Schwoyer, William E., ed. Polyelectrolytes for Water & Wastewater Treatment. 304p. 1981. 74.95 (ISBN 0-8493-5439-0). CRC Pr.
Schwyzer, H. R., ed. see Plotinus.
Sciacchetano, Larry & McCallum, Jack. Sports Illustrated Wrestling. 1979. 5.95 (ISBN 0-397-01275-6); pap. 2.95 (ISBN 0-397-01276-4). Lippincott.
Sciarra, Dorothy J. & Dorsey, Anne G. Developing & Administering a Child Care Center. LC 78-69564. (Illus.). 1978. 15.95 (ISBN 0-395-26263-1). HM.
Sciarra, John J. & Stoller, Leonard, eds. The Science & Technology of Aerosol Packaging. 736p. 1974. 62.50 (ISBN 0-471-76693-3, Pub. by Wiley-Interscience). Wiley.
Sciascia, Leonardo. Candido or, Dream Dreamed in Sicily. Wolff, Helen, ed. Foulke, Adrienne, tr. LC 79-1842. (Helen & Kurt Wolff Bk.). 1979. 7.95 (ISBN 0-15-115380-9). HarBraceJ.
--One Way or Another. Foulke, Adrienne, tr. from It. LC 76-26274. (Illus.). 1977. 7.95 o.s.i. (ISBN 0-06-013804-1, HarpT). Har-Row.
Scibor-Rylski, A. J. Road Vehicle Aerodynamics. LC 74-26859. 213p. 1975. 34.95 (ISBN 0-470-75920-8); pap. 18.95x (ISBN 0-470-26655-4). Halsted Pr.
Science Action Coalition. A Consumer's Guide to Cosmetics. LC 79-7193. (Illus.). 384p. 1980. pap. 3.95 (ISBN 0-385-13503-3, Anch). Doubleday.
Science & Public Policy Comm., Comm. on the Survey of Materials Science & Engineering. Materials & Man's Needs. LC 74-2118. (Illus.). 246p. 1974. pap. 8.00 (ISBN 0-309-02220-7). Natl Acad Pr.
Science Book Associates Editors, jt. auth. see McLeod, Sterling.
Science Council of Japan, ed. see International Seaweed Symposium, 7th, Sappora, Japan, Aug. 1971.
Scientific American Editors. The Biosphere: A Scientific American Book. LC 78-140849. (Illus.). 1970. pap. text ed. 8.95x (ISBN 0-7167-0945-7). W H Freeman.
--The Brain: A Scientific American Book. LC 79-21012. (Illus.). 1979. text ed. 15.95x (ISBN 0-7167-1150-8); pap. text ed. 7.95x (ISBN 0-7167-1151-6). W H Freeman.
--Communication: A Scientific American Book. LC 72-10100. (Illus.). 1972. text ed. 14.95x (ISBN 0-7167-0866-3); pap. text ed. 7.95x (ISBN 0-7167-0865-5). W H Freeman.
--Economic Development: A Scientific American Book. LC 80-22326. (Illus.). 1980. text ed. 13.95x (ISBN 0-7167-1273-3); pap. text ed. 6.95x (ISBN 0-7167-1274-1). W H Freeman.
--Energy & Power: A Scientific American Book. LC 75-180254. (Illus.). 1971. pap. text ed. 7.95x (ISBN 0-7167-0938-4). W H Freeman.
--Evolution: A Scientific American Book. LC 78-10747. (Illus.). 1978. text ed. 15.95x (ISBN 0-7167-1065-X); pap. text ed. 7.95x (ISBN 0-7167-1066-8). W H Freeman.
--Food & Agriculture: A Scientific American Book. (Illus.). 1976. 16.95x (ISBN 0-7167-0382-3); pap. 8.95x (ISBN 0-7167-0381-5). W H Freeman.
--The Human Population: A Scientific American Book. LC 74-19465. (Illus.). 147p. 1974. 15.95x (ISBN 0-7167-0515-X); pap. text ed. 7.95x (ISBN 0-7167-0514-1). W H Freeman.
--Information: A Scientific American Book. LC 66-29386. (Illus.). 1966. 14.95x (ISBN 0-7167-0967-8); pap. text ed. 7.95x (ISBN 0-7167-0966-X). W H Freeman.
--Life, Death & Medicine: A Scientific American Book. LC 73-16097. (Illus.). 1973. pap. text ed. 7.95x (ISBN 0-7167-0891-4). W H Freeman.
--Microelectronics: A Scientific American Book. LC 77-13955. (Illus.). 1977. pap. text ed. 8.95x (ISBN 0-7167-0066-2). W H Freeman.
--The Ocean: A Scientific American Book. LC 71-102897. (Illus.). 1969. pap. text ed. 7.95x (ISBN 0-7167-0997-X). W H Freeman.
--Scientific American Resource Library: Readings in Psychology, 3 vols. LC 73-80078. (Illus.). 1973. lib. bdg. 60.00x set (ISBN 0-7167-0990-2). W H Freeman.
--Scientific American Resource Library: Readings in the Earth Sciences, 3 vols. (Illus.). 1973. Set. lib. bdg. 60.00x (ISBN 0-7167-0988-0). W H Freeman.
--Scientific American Resource Library: Readings in the Life Sciences, 3 vols, Vols. 8-10. 1967-1973. Set. 60.00x set (ISBN 0-7167-0989-9). W H Freeman.
--Scientific American Resource Library: Readings in the Social Sciences, 2 vols. LC 78-8722. (Illus.). 1973. lib. bdg. 40.00x set (ISBN 0-7167-0992-9). W H Freeman.
--The Solar System: A Scientific American Book. LC 75-28113. (Illus.). 1975. text ed. 15.95x (ISBN 0-7167-0551-6); pap. text ed. 7.95x (ISBN 0-7167-0550-8). W H Freeman.
Scientific Personnel Office. The Science Committee. Parsons, Carole W., ed. (Illus.). 1972. pap. 5.25 (ISBN 0-309-02031-X). Natl Acad Pr.
Scigiano, John A., jt. auth. see Tedeschi, Frank P.
Scigliano, R. Supreme Court & the Presidency. LC 76-128475. 1971. pap. text ed. 4.50 o.s.i. (ISBN 0-02-928280-2). Free Pr.
Sciglimpaglia, Donald, jt. auth. see Vinson, Donald E.
Sciller, Justin G., ed. see Bunyan, John.
Scimecca, Joseph A. The Sociological Theory of C. Wright Mills. (National University Pubns. Series in American Studies). 1976. 11.50 (ISBN 0-8046-9155-X). Kennikat.
Scimone, John & Rothstein, Robert. Clinical Chemistry: Functional Medical Laboratory Manual. (Illus.). 1978. lab. manual 10.00 (ISBN 0-87055-271-6). AVI.
Scimone, John, ed. Clinical Bacteriology. (Functional Medical Laboratory Manual). (Illus.). 1978. pap. 10.00 (ISBN 0-87055-267-8). AVI.
Scindler, D. & Toman, J. The Laws of Armed Conflicts. rev. ed. 904p. 1980. 105.00x (ISBN 90-286-0199-6). Sijthoff & Noordhoff.
Scioli, Frank P. & Cook, Thomas J. Methodologies for Analyzing Public Policies. LC 75-8152. (Policy Studies Organization Policy Study Ser.). 160p. 1975. 17.95 (ISBN 0-669-00596-7). Lexington Bks.
Scism, Carol K. Secret Emily. (Illus.). (gr. 4-6). 1975. pap. 0.95 o.p. (ISBN 0-590-09944-2, Schol Pap). Schol Bk Serv.
Scithers, George, ed. Isaac Asimov's Adventures of Science Fiction. 1980. 9.95 (ISBN 0-8037-3533-2). Dial.
Scithers, George A., ed. Isaac Asimov's Worlds of Science Fiction. 288p. 1980. 9.95 (ISBN 0-8037-4192-8). Davis Pubns.
Scitt, Authur F. America Grows. 1981. 10.95 (ISBN 0-533-04906-7). Vantage.
Sclafani, R. J., jt. auth. see Dickie, George.
Sclossberg, Edwin, et al. The Home Computer Handbook. LC 77-95272. (Illus.). 1978. 12.95 (ISBN 0-8069-3096-9); lib. bdg. 11.69 (ISBN 0-8069-3097-7). Sterling.
Sclove, Stanley L., jt. auth. see Anderson, T. W.
Scneider, Bill. The Dakota Image. LC 80-83707. (Illus.). 96p. 1980. 20.00 (ISBN 0-934318-02-6). Falcon Pr MT.
Scnmelzer, R., jt. auth. see Raygor, A.

Scobel, Don N. Creative Worklife. 1980. 12.95x (ISBN 0-87201-905-5). Gulf Pub.
Scobey, Jan. He Rambled! 'til Cancer Cut Him Down. LC 76-54444. (Illus.). 1976. 35.00 (ISBN 0-918104-01-7). Pal Pub.
Scobey, Joan, jt. auth. see Myers, Norma.
Scobie, G. E. Psychology of Religion. LC 74-21832. 189p. 1975. text ed. 16.95 (ISBN 0-470-76712-X); pap. text ed. 7.95 (ISBN 0-470-26689-9). Halsted Pr.
Scobie, James R. Argentina: A City & a Nation. 2nd ed. (Latin American Histories Ser). 1971. 14.95 (ISBN 0-19-501479-0); pap. text ed. 4.95x (ISBN 0-19-501480-4). Oxford U Pr.
--Revolution on the Pampas: A Social History of Argentine Wheat. (Latin American Monograph: No. 1). 1964. 9.95 (ISBN 0-292-73352-6). U of Tex Pr.
Scobie, Stephen. Leonard Cohen. 294p. (Orig.). 1978. pap. 4.95 (ISBN 0-295-95686-0, Pub. by Douglas & McIntyre Canada). U of Wash Pr.
Scoble, Harry M., jt. auth. see Wiseberg, Laurie S.
Scoder, Judy. Funny Bunny. Wasserman, Dan, ed. (Ten Word Bks.). (Illus.). (gr. k-1). 1979. PLB 4.50 (ISBN 0-89868-069-7); pap. 1.95 (ISBN 0-89868-080-8). ARO Pub.
Scofield, C. I. Rightly Dividing the Word of Truth. 72p. (Orig.). 1974. pap. 1.95 (ISBN 0-310-32662-1, 6364P). Zondervan.
Scofield, Jonathan. Guns at Twilight. (Freedom Fighters Ser.: No. 4). (Orig.). 1981. pap. 2.75 (ISBN 0-440-02919-8). Dell.
--The King's Cannon. 1981. pap. 2.75 (ISBN 0-440-04292-5). Dell.
--Muskets of Seventy-Six. 1981. pap. 2.75 (ISBN 0-440-05756-6). Dell.
--Tomahawks & Long Rifles. 1981. pap. 2.75 (ISBN 0-440-09119-5). Dell.
Scofield, Martin. The Ghosts of Hamlet. LC 79-21297. 180p. 1981. 39.50 (ISBN 0-521-22735-6). Cambridge U Pr.
Scofield, William E. Northwest Heritage. (gr. 7-9). 1978. pap. text ed. 5.83 (ISBN 0-87720-623-6). AMSCO Sch.
Scoles, C. A. & Kirk, R. Gear Metrology. 166p. 1969. 15.00x o.p. (ISBN 0-8464-0443-5). Beekman Pubs.
Scoles, G. Handbook of Rectifier Circuits. LC 79-41814. (Ellis Horwood Series in Electrical & Electronic Engineering). 238p. 1980. 69.95x (ISBN 0-470-26950-2). Halsted Pr.
Scoles, Graham J. Handbook of Electronic Circuits. LC 74-13558. 370p. 1975. 49.95 (ISBN 0-470-76715-4). Halsted Pr.
Scollen, Christine M., ed. see De Ronsard, Pierre.
Scoones, William B., ed. Four Centuries of English Letters. LC 79-142558. 1971. Repr. of 1893 ed. 22.00 (ISBN 0-8103-3638-3). Gale.
Scopes, John. World's Most Famous Court Trail: State of Tennessee V. John T. Scopes. LC 78-121106. (Civil Liberties in American History Ser). 1971. Repr. of 1925 ed. lib. bdg. 29.50 (ISBN 0-306-71975-4). Da Capo.
Scopes, Nigel, jt. auth. see Machin, Barrie.
Scopes, Nigel, ed. Pest & Disease Control Handbook. 250p. 1979. 35.00x (ISBN 0-901436-42-9, Pub. by Brit Crop Protection England). Intl Schol Bk Serv.
Scopes, P. G. Mathematics in Secondary Schools. LC 72-78894. (Illus.). 128p. 1973. pap. text ed. 6.95x (ISBN 0-521-09728-2). Cambridge U Pr.
Scopp, Irwin W. Oral Medicine: A Clinical Approach with Basic Science Correlation. 2nd ed. LC 73-1275. 1973. text ed. 26.50 o.p. (ISBN 0-8016-4402-X). Mosby.
Scoppetone, Sandra. Trying Hard to Hear You. 324p. (gr. 7-9). 1981. pap. 1.95 (ISBN 0-553-13852-9). Bantam.
Scora, Rainer W. Interspecific Relationships in the Genus Monarda (Labiatae) (U. C. Publ. in Botany: Vol. 41). 1967. pap. 6.50x (ISBN 0-520-09014-4). U of Cal Pr.
Scorer, C. G. & Farrington, G. H. Congenital Deformities of the Testis & Epididymis. 1971. 16.20 (ISBN 0-407-13891-9). Butterworths.
Scorer, R. S. Air Pollution. 1968. 27.00 (ISBN 0-08-013345-2); pap. 13.25 (ISBN 0-08-012275-2). Pergamon.
--The Clever Moron. 1977. 15.00 (ISBN 0-7100-8552-4). Routledge & Kegan.
--Environmental Aerodynamics. LC 77-23909. (Mathematics & Its Applications Ser.). 1978. 69.95 (ISBN 0-470-99270-0). Halsted Pr.
--Pollution in the Air: Problems, Policies & Priorities. 156p. 1973. 12.00 (ISBN 0-685-30197-4). Routledge & Kegan.
Scorer, R. S. & Wexler, H. A Colour Guide to Clouds. 1976. 15.00 (ISBN 0-08-010375-8); pap. 7.00 (ISBN 0-08-010374-X). Pergamon.
Scorer, Richard. Clouds of the World: A Complete Color Encyclopedia. 42.50 o.p. (ISBN 0-7153-5485-X). David & Charles.
Scorseby, Lynn A. Marriage Dialogue. LC 76-45150. 1977. text ed. 6.95 (ISBN 0-201-06789-7). A-W.
Scortia, Thomas N. & Robinson, Frank M. The Gold Crew. LC 79-23066. 444p. 1980. 11.95 (ISBN 0-446-51202-8); pap. 2.95 (ISBN 0-446-83522-6). Warner Bks.
--The Nightmare Factor. LC 77-11760. 1978. 10.00 o.p. (ISBN 0-385-11462-1). Doubleday.
Scott. Window on the Wild. 8.95 (ISBN 0-399-20722-8). Putnam.
Scott & Smith. Dictionary of Waste & Water Treatment. 1981. text ed. price not set (ISBN 0-408-00495-9). Butterworth.
Scott, A. C. Chinese Costume in Transition. (Illus., Orig.). 1960. pap. 3.25 (ISBN 0-87830-017-1). Theatre Arts.
--Puppet Theatre of Japan. LC 63-21179. (Illus.). 1973. pap. 4.95 (ISBN 0-8048-1116-4). C E Tuttle.
--The Theatre in Asia. (Illus.). 304p. 1973. 12.95 (ISBN 0-02-608650-6). Macmillan.
Scott, A. C., ed. Traditional Chinese Plays, 3 vols. Incl. Vol. 1. Ssu Lang Visits His Mother; the Butterfly Dream. (Illus.). 1967. pap. 5.95x (ISBN 0-299-04134-4); Vol. 2. Longing for Worldly Pleasures; Fifteen Strings of Cash. (Illus.). 1969. 15.00x (ISBN 0-299-05370-9); pap. 5.95x (ISBN 0-299-05374-1); Vol. 3. Picking up the Jade Bracelet; a Girl Setting Out for Trial. LC 66-22854. 1975. 10.00x (ISBN 0-299-06630-4). U of Wis Pr.
Scott, A. F. The Early Hanoverian Age: 1714-1760 Commentaries of an Era. (Illus.). 175p. 1980. 20.00x (ISBN 0-7099-0145-3, Pub. by Croom Helm Ltd England). Biblio Dist.
--The Norman Age - Commentaries of an Era. Incl. The Norman Age. (Illus.). 336p. 1976. 16.00x (ISBN 0-8476-6000-1); The Plantagenet Age. (Illus.). 328p. 1976. 13.50x (ISBN 0-8476-6001-X); The Stuart Age. (Illus.). 328p. 1974. 12.00x (ISBN 0-8476-6003-6); The Tudor Age. (Illus.). 291p. 1975. 13.50x (ISBN 0-8476-6002-8). (Everyone a Witness Ser). (Illus.). Rowman.
--The Plantagenet Age. LC 75-4880. (Everyone a Witness Ser.). (Illus.). 328p. 1976. 9.95 (ISBN 0-690-01002-8, TYC-T); pap. 4.95 o.p. (ISBN 0-8152-0393-4, A-393). T Y Crowell.
--The Saxon Age: Commentaries of an Era. (Illus.). 182p. 1979. 20.00x (ISBN 0-85664-905-8, Pub. by Croom Helm Ltd England). Biblio Dist.
Scott, A. F., ed. Current Literary Terms. 324p. Repr. of 1980 ed. lib. bdg. 14.95x (ISBN 0-312-17956-1). St Martin.
Scott, A. G. Childmare. (Orig.). 1981. pap. 2.25 (ISBN 0-451-09807-2, E9807, Signet Bks). NAL.
Scott, A. I., jt. auth. see Devon, T. K.
Scott, A. J. An Introduction to Spatial Allocation Analysis. LC 71-173661. (CCG Resource Papers Ser.: No. 9). (Illus.). 1971. pap. text ed. 4.00 (ISBN 0-89291-056-9). Assn Am Geographers.
--The Urban Land Nexus & the State. 256p. 1980. 24.00 (ISBN 0-85086-079-2, 6390). Methuen Inc.
Scott, Alan, jt. auth. see Newsom, Doug.
Scott, Alice. How to Raise & Train a Pekingese. (Illus.). pap. 2.00 (ISBN 0-87666-346-3, DS1028). TFH Pubns.
Scott, Alwyn C. Neurophysics. LC 77-2762. 1977. 33.95 o.p. (ISBN 0-471-02998-X, Pub. by Wiley-Interscience). Wiley.
Scott, Ann H. Census, U. S. A. Fact Finding for the American People, 1790-1970. LC 68-24734. (Illus.). (YA) (gr. 9 up). 1968. 8.95 (ISBN 0-395-28924-6, Clarion). HM.
Scott, Anne F. Southern Lady: From Pedestal to Politics, 1830-1930. LC 73-123750. 1970. 10.00x o.s.i. (ISBN 0-226-74346-2). U of Chicago Pr.
Scott, Arthur F., ed. Survey of Progress in Chemistry, 8 vols. Incl. Vol. 1. 1963. 40.50 (ISBN 0-12-610501-4); Vol. 2. 1965. 40.50 (ISBN 0-12-610502-2); Vol. 3. 1966. 40.50 (ISBN 0-686-62064-X); Vol. 4. 1968. 40.50 (ISBN 0-12-610504-9); Vol. 5. 1969. 40.50 (ISBN 0-12-610505-7); Vol. 6. 1974. 51.50 (ISBN 0-12-610506-5); Vol. 7. 1976. 40.00 (ISBN 0-12-610507-3); lib. ed 50.50 (ISBN 0-12-610574-X); microfiche 29.00 (ISBN 0-12-610575-8); Vol. 8. 1978. 43.00 (ISBN 0-12-610508-1); lib. ed. 55.50 (ISBN 0-12-610576-6); microfiche 31.50 (ISBN 0-12-610577-4); Vol. 9. 1980. 35.00 (ISBN 0-12-610509-X); lib. bdg. 45.50 (ISBN 0-12-610578-2); microfiche 24.50 (ISBN 0-12-610579-0). Acad Pr.
Scott, Austin W. The Law of Trusts, 6 Vols. 3rd ed. 1980. Set. with 1980 supplement 275.00 (ISBN 0-316-77686-6). Little.
Scott, Austin W. & Kent, Robert B. Cases & Other Materials on Civil Procedure. 1117p. 1967. 18.50 o.p. (ISBN 0-316-77642-4). Little.
Scott, Beth & Norman, Michael. Haunted Wisconsin. LC 80-22151. (Illus.). 256p. (Orig.). 1980. pap. 9.95 (ISBN 0-88361-082-5). Stanton & Lee.
Scott, Bill. Darkness Under the Hills. (Illus.). 149p. (gr. 7 up). 1980. 9.95 (ISBN 0-19-554275-4). Oxford U Pr.
Scott, C. Initiate in the New World. pap. 4.95 (ISBN 0-87728-363-X). Weiser.
Scott, C. R., ed. Developments in Soil Mechanics, Vol. 1. (Illus.). 1978. text ed. 79.80x (ISBN 0-85334-771-9, Pub. by Applied Science). Burgess-Intl Ideas.
Scott, Carole E. Your Financial Plan: A Consumer's Guide. 1979. text ed. 19.50 scp (ISBN 0-06-045844-5, HarpC); inst. manual avail. (ISBN 0-685-63499-X). Har-Row.
Scott, Charles E., jt. ed. see Lachs, John.
Scott, Charles R., Jr. & Strickland, Alonzo J., III. Tempomatic IV: A Management Simulation. 2nd ed. LC 79-89182. (Illus.). 1980. pap. text ed. 9.50 (ISBN 0-395-28731-6); instrs'. manual 0.80 (ISBN 0-395-28732-4); computer centers manual 1.75 (ISBN 0-395-28733-2); punched card deck avail. (ISBN 0-395-28734-0). HM.
Scott, Charles T., jt. ed. see Rauch, Irmengard.
Scott, Christina, jt. ed. see Oliver, James.
Scott, Clifford H. Lester Frank Ward. LC 76-16539. (U.S. Authors Ser.: No. 275). 1976. lib. bdg. 12.50 (ISBN 0-8057-7175-1). Twayne.
Scott, Clive. The French Verse-Art. LC 79-50508. 1980. 37.50 (ISBN 0-521-22689-9). Cambridge U Pr.
Scott, Cyril. Cider Vinegar. 1980. pap. 1.95 (ISBN 0-87904-011-4). Lust.
--Crude Black Molasses. 1980. pap. 1.95 (ISBN 0-87904-010-6). Lust.
--Good Sleep Without Drugs. 1980. pap. 1.95 (ISBN 0-87904-012-2). Lust.
Scott, D. F., Jr., et al. Cases in Finance. (Illus.). 1977. pap. 10.95x ref. ed. (ISBN 0-13-115337-4). P-H.
Scott, D. R. Cultural Significance of Accounts. (Lucas Text Ser). 1978. Repr. text ed. 5.95x perfect bdg. (ISBN 0-87543-041-4). Lucas.
Scott, Daphne H., jt. auth. see Hoenig, Stuart A.
Scott, David. The Japanese Cookbook. (Illus.). 1978. 9.95 o.p. (ISBN 0-214-20576-2, 8069, Dist. by Arco). Barrie & Jenkins.
Scott, David H., ed. see Miller, Madeleine S. & Miller, J. Lane.
Scott, David L. Financing the Growth of Electric Utilities. LC 75-25024. (Illus.). 1976. text ed. 22.95 (ISBN 0-275-56460-6). Praeger.
--Security Investments. (Illus.). 1981. 17.95x (ISBN 0-8476-6971-8). Rowman.
--Security Investments. (Littlefield, Adams Quality Paperbacks: No. 352). (Illus., Orig.). 1981. pap. 7.95 (ISBN 0-8226-0352-7). Littlefield.
Scott, Diane, jt. auth. see Fuller, Millard.
Scott, Dick. Ask That Mountain. 1977. text ed. 19.95x (ISBN 0-435-32803-4). Heinemann Ed.
Scott, Donald M. From Office to Profession: The New England Ministry, 1750-1850. LC 77-20304. 1978. 16.00x (ISBN 0-8122-7737-6). U of Pa Pr.
Scott, Donald M., ed. see O'Hara, Betsy.
Scott, Dorothea H. Chinese Popular Literature & the Child. LC 80-10412. 192p. 1980. 15.00 (ISBN 0-8389-0289-8). ALA.
Scott, Ed. Batuvus Moped Owner Service-Repair. Jorgensen, Eric, ed. (Illus.). 104p. (Orig.). 1978. pap. 6.00 (ISBN 0-89287-199-7, M438). Clymer Pubns.
--Chevy Luv: 1972-1980--Service, Repair Handbook. Jorgensen, Eric, ed. (Illus.). 1978. pap. 10.95 (ISBN 0-89287-274-8, A145). Clymer Pubns.
--Garelli Moped Owner Service-Repair: 1976-1978. Jorgensen, Eric, ed. (Illus.). 1978. pap. 6.00 (ISBN 0-89287-200-4, M435). Clymer Pubns.
--Honda CB Seven Fifty DOHC Fours: 1979-1980. Jorgensen, Eric, ed. (Illus.). 318p. (Orig.). 1980. pap. text ed. 9.95 (ISBN 0-89287-304-3, M337). Clymer Pubns.
--Honda CX Five Hundred Twins 1978-1979 Service Repair Maintenance. Jorgesen, Eric, ed. (Illus.). 200p. (Orig.). 1979. pap. text ed. 9.95 (ISBN 0-89287-295-0, M335). Clymer Pubns.
--Honda Odyssey: 1977-1979 Service-Repair-Performance. Jorgensen, Eric, ed. (Illus.). 224p. (Orig.). 1980. pap. 9.95 (ISBN 0-89287-308-6, M316). Clymer Pubns.
--Honda XR-Seventy Five Singles: Service, Repair, Performance, 1975-78. Jorgensen, Eric, ed. (Illus.). 1978. pap. 9.95 (ISBN 0-89287-215-2, M312). Clymer Pubns.
--Honda XR-XL 250 & 500 Singles: 1978-1979 Service-Repair-Maintenance. Jorgensen, Eric, ed. (Illus.). 251p. (Orig.). 1980. pap. text ed. 9.95 (ISBN 0-89287-310-8, M319). Clymer Pubns.
--Peugeot Moped Owners Service-Repair, 1976-1978. Jorgensen, Eric, ed. (Illus.). 1978. pap. 6.00 (ISBN 0-89287-202-0, M436). Clymer Pubns.
--Puch Moped Owner Service-Repair: 1976-1977. Jorgensen, Eric, ed. (Illus.). pap. 6.00 (ISBN 0-89287-213-6, M437). Clymer Pubns.
--Yamaha XS Seven-Fifty Triples Nineteen Seventy-Six to Nineteen Seventy-Nine Service, Repair, Performance. (Illus.). 1979. pap. 9.95 (ISBN 0-89287-243-8, M40A). Clymer Pubns.
--Yamaha XS1100 Fours: 1978-1979 Service-Repair-Performance. Jorgensen, Eric, ed. (Illus.). 224p. (Orig.). 1980. pap. text ed. 9.95 (ISBN 0-89287-309-4, M411). Clymer Pubns.
--Yamaha YZ One Hundred to Four Hundred Sixty-Five Monoshock Nineteen Seventy-Five to Nineteen Eighty: Service, Repair, Performance. Jorgensen, Eric, ed. (Illus.). 293p. (Orig.). 1980. pap. text ed. 9.95 (ISBN 0-89287-329-9, M413). Clymer Pubns.
Scott, Edna see Lyman, Edna, pseud.
Scott, Edward. Honda Hawk: Four Hundred cc Twins 1978-1980--Service, Repair, Performance. Jorgensen, Eric, ed. (Illus.). 1978. pap. 9.95 (ISBN 0-89287-234-9, M334). Clymer Pubns.
--Honda Twinstar Nineteen Seventy-Eight to Nineteen Eighty: Service, Repair, Maintenance. Jorgensen, Eric, ed. (Illus.). 242p. (Orig.). 1980. pap. text ed. 9.95 (ISBN 0-89287-325-6, M324). Clymer Pubns.
Scott, Edward M. The Adolescent Gap: Research Findings on Drug Using & Non-Drug Using Teens. (Illus.). 160p. 1972. 9.75 (ISBN 0-398-02403-0). C C Thomas.
Scott, Edward M. & Scott, Kathryn L., eds. Criminal Rehabilitation - Within & Without the Walls: With Contributions from Experts Within the Field. 236p. 1973. 11.75 (ISBN 0-398-02730-7). C C Thomas.
Scott, Elizabeth A. Rim of the Tub. 1970. 5.95 o.p. (ISBN 0-688-02392-4). Morrow.
Scott, Ernest. Working in Wood. 1980. 25.00 (ISBN 0-686-68362-5). Putnam.
--Working in Wood: An Illustrated Encyclopedia. (Illus.). 272p. 1980. 25.00 (ISBN 0-399-12550-7). Putnam.
Scott, Eugene L. The Tennis Experience. LC 79-7519. (Illus.). 1979. 19.95 o.p. (ISBN 0-88332-119-X). Larousse.
Scott, Evelyn. Background in Tennessee. facsimile ed. LC 80-15703. (Tennesseana Editions). 324p. 1980. Repr. of 1937 ed. 11.50 (ISBN 0-87049-297-7). U of Tenn Pr.
Scott, Frank, jt. ed. see Martin, Cliff.
Scott, Frank R. Essays on the Constitution: Aspects of Canadian Law & Politics. 1977. 27.50x (ISBN 0-8020-2238-3); pap. 8.50 (ISBN 0-8020-6297-0). U of Toronto Pr.
Scott, Franklin D. Sweden: The Nation's History. LC 76-51159. (Illus.). 1979. 30.00x (ISBN 0-8166-0804-0); pap. 10.95x (ISBN 0-8166-0880-6). U of Minn Pr.
Scott, G. R. Rabbit Keeping. LC 78-65764. 1979. 11.95 (ISBN 0-7153-7643-8). David & Charles.
Scott, Gail R., ed. see Hartley, Marsden.
Scott, Gavin. A Flight of Lies. 224p. 1981. 9.95 (ISBN 0-312-29614-2). St Martin.
Scott, Geoffrey. The Architecture of Humanism: A Study in the History of Taste. (Illus.). 224p. 1974. pap. 5.95 (ISBN 0-393-00734-0). Norton.
--Egyptian Boats. LC 80-27676. (A Carolrhoda on My Own Bk). (Illus.). 48p. (gr. k-3). 1981. PLB 5.95 (ISBN 0-87614-138-6). Carolrhoda Bks.
Scott, George. Practical Arabic. 13.00x (ISBN 0-685-77113-X). Intl Bk Ctr.
--The Rise & Fall of the League of Nations. LC 73-20179. (Illus.). 432p. 1974. 9.95 o.s.i. (ISBN 0-02-608630-1). Macmillan.
Scott, George G. Personal & Professional Recollections. LC 77-1202. (Architecture & Decorative Arts Ser.). 1977. Repr. of 1879 ed. lib. bdg. 35.00 (ISBN 0-306-70873-6). Da Capo.
Scott, George P. & McMillin, J. M. Dissipative Structures & Spatiotemporal Organization Studies in Biomedical Research. (Illus.). 271p. 1980. pap. text ed. 9.95. Iowa St U Pr.
Scott, George P. & McMillan, J. Michael, eds. Dissipative Structures in Biomedical Research. 1980. 9.95 (ISBN 0-8138-1620-3). Iowa St U Pr.
Scott, George R. The History of Corporal Punishment: A Survey of Flagellation in Its Historical, Anthropological & Sociological Aspects. LC 74-1088. (Illus.). 261p. 1974. Repr. of 1938 ed. 18.00 (ISBN 0-8103-3978-1). Gale.
Scott, Gerald, ed. Developments in Polymer Stabilisation - Two. (Illus.). x, 245p. 1980. 45.00x (ISBN 0-85334-885-5). Burgess-Intl Ideas.
--Developments in Polymer Stabilisation, Vol. 1. (Illus.). 1979. 70.00x (ISBN 0-85334-838-3, Pub. by Applied Science). Burgess-Intl Ideas.
--Developments in Polymer Stabilisation, No. 3. (Illus.). ix, 195p. 1981. 38.00x (ISBN 0-85334-890-1). Intl Ideas.
Scott, Grahame, ed. see Gaydar, Arkadiy.
Scott, Guy. Introducing Finger Painting. 1973. 17.95 (ISBN 0-7134-2432-X, Pub. by Batsford England). David & Charles.

Scott, Gwendolyn D. & Carlo, Mona. Learning, Feeling, Doing: Designing Creative Learning Experiences for Elementary Health Education. (Illus.). 1978. ref. ed. 14.95 (ISBN 0-13-527689-6). P-H.

Scott, Harriet & Scott, William. The Armed Forces of the USSR. (Illus.). 1979. lib. bdg. 30.00 (ISBN 0-89158-276-2); pap. 12.50 (ISBN 0-86531-087-4). Westview.

Scott, Harriet F. & Scott, William F. The Armed Forces of the USSR. rev. ed. 440p. 1981. lib. bdg. 27.50x (ISBN 0-86531-194-3); pap. text ed. 12.50x (ISBN 0-86531-087-4). Westview.

Scott, Harriet F., tr. see Sokolovskiy, V. D.

Scott, Harry J. Portrait of Yorkshire. LC 66-4438. (Portrait Bks.). (Illus.). 1965. 10.50x (ISBN 0-7091-1842-2). Intl Pubns Serv.

Scott, Hildreth. Alone, Again! (Uplook Ser.). 1976. pap. 0.75 (ISBN 0-8163-0251-0, 01496-9). Pacific Pr Pub Assn.

--I'm Free. (Uplook Ser.). 31p. 1973. pap. 0.75 (ISBN 0-8163-0073-9, 09340-1). Pacific Pr Pub Assn.

Scott, Hugh. The Best of Quincy Scott. LC 80-83078. (Illus.). 216p. 1980. pap. 7.95 (ISBN 0-87595-087-6). Oreg Hist Soc.

Scott, J. F. The Scientific Work of Rene Descartes. LC 76-40683. 1976. 19.50x (ISBN 0-8448-1030-4). Crane-Russak Co.

Scott, J. F., ed. see Newton, Isaac.

Scott, J. M., jt. auth. see Theobald, Robert.

Scott, J. T. Arthritis & Rheumatism: The Facts. (The Facts Ser.). (Illus.). 126p. 1980. 11.95x (ISBN 0-19-261168-2). Oxford U Pr.

Scott, Jack. Athletic Revolution. LC 71-155098. 1971. 12.95 (ISBN 0-02-928330-2). Free Pr.

--Bill Walton: On the Road with the Portland Trail Blazers. LC 77-11569. (Illus.). 1978. 10.95 o.p. (ISBN 0-690-01694-8, TYC-T). T Y Crowell.

Scott, Jack, jt. auth. see Lowder, Hughston E.

Scott, Jack D. The Book of the Pig. (Illus.). 64p. (ps up). 1981. 8.95 (ISBN 0-399-20718-X). Putnam.

--The Sea File. 288p. 1981. 10.95 (ISBN 0-07-056110-9, GB). McGraw.

Scott, Jack D., jt. auth. see Scott, Maria L.

Scott, Jack L. Pewter Wares from Sheffield. LC 80-68670. (Illus.). 260p. 1980. 28.00 (ISBN 0-937864-00-5). Antiquary Pr.

Scott, Jack S. A Clutch of Vipers. 192p. 1981. pap. 1.95 (ISBN 0-445-04632-5). Popular Lib.

--The View from Deacon Hill. 192p. 1981. 9.95 (ISBN 0-89919-033-2). Ticknor & Fields.

Scott, James. Palaentology & Introduction. 160p. 1980. 15.00x (ISBN 0-89771-000-2). State Mutual Bk.

Scott, James D. Cable Television: Strategy for Penetrating Key Urban Markets. (Michigan Business Reports: No. 58). 1976. pap. 5.50 o.p. (ISBN 0-87712-172-9). U Mich Busn Div Res.

--Investigative Methods. (Illus.). 1978. ref. ed. 14.95 (ISBN 0-87909-392-7); instrs'. manual avail. Reston.

Scott, Jane. Cross Fox. LC 80-13515. 144p. (gr. 4-7). 1980. 8.95 (ISBN 0-689-50183-8, McElderry Bk). Atheneum.

Scott, Jane H., jt. auth. see Mooberry, F. M.

Scott, Jeanette, ed. Desalination of Seawater by Reverse Osmosis. LC 80-26421. (Pollution Tech. Rev. Ser.: No. 75). 431p. 1981. 39.00 (ISBN 0-8155-0837-9). Noyes.

--Membrane & Ultrafiltration Technology: Recent Advances. LC 79-24503. (Chemical Tecnology Review Ser.: No. 147). (Illus.). 1980. 48.00 (ISBN 0-8155-0784-4). Noyes.

--Zeolite Technology & Applications: Recent Advances. LC 80-19308. (Chemical Tech. Rev. 170). (Illus.). 381p. 1981. 64.00 (ISBN 0-8155-0817-4). Noyes.

Scott, Jeremy. Hunted. 1981. 13.95 (ISBN 0-671-42187-5, Wyndham Bks). S&S.

Scott, Joanna. Dusky Rose. 192p. (Orig.). 1980. pap. 1.50 (ISBN 0-671-57050-1). S&S.

--The Marriage Bargain. 192p. 1981. pap. 1.50 (ISBN 0-671-57068-4). S&S.

Scott, Jody. Passing for Human. (Science Fiction Ser.). (Orig.). 1977. pap. 1.50 o.p. (ISBN 0-87997-330-7, UW1330). DAW Bks.

Scott, John. Basic Computer Logic. LC 80-5074. (The Lexington Books Series in Computer Science). 1981. write for info. (ISBN 0-669-03706-0). Lexington Bks.

--Behind the Urals: An American Worker in Russia's City of Steel. LC 72-88916. (Classics in Russian Studies: No. 3). 288p. 1973. pap. 3.95x (ISBN 0-253-10600-1). Ind U Pr.

Scott, John & Miller, Nicholas, eds. Crime & the Responsible Community. 160p. 1980. pap. 6.95 (ISBN 0-8028-1831-5). Eerdmans.

Scott, John, tr. see Campert, Remco.

Scott, John, tr. see Wolkers, Jan.

Scott, John A. Fanny Kemble's America. LC 72-7557. (Women of America Ser). (Illus.). 168p. (gr. 5-9). 1973. 8.95 (ISBN 0-690-28911-1, TYC-J). T Y Crowell.

--Unity of Homer. LC 65-15246. 1921. 10.50x (ISBN 0-8196-0152-7). Biblo.

Scott, John A., tr. see Olschki, Leonardo.

Scott, John D. Pretty Penny. LC 64-22672. 1964. 3.95 o.p. (ISBN 0-15-173951-X). HarBraceJ.

Scott, John F. Danzantes of Monte Alban, 2 vols. LC 79-63725. (Studies in Pre-Columbian Art & Archaeology: No. 19). (Illus.). 238p. 1978. pap. 10.00 (ISBN 0-88402-079-7, Ctr Pre-Columbian). Dumbarton Oaks.

Scott, John M. The Senses: Seeing, Hearing, Tasting, Touching & Smelling. LC 75-2189. (Finding-Out Books for Science & Social Studies, Grades 1-4). (Illus.). 64p. (gr. 2-4). 1975. PLB 5.41 o.p. (ISBN 0-8193-0821-8). Enslow Pubs.

--What Is Science? LC 70-179362. (Finding-Out Books for Science & Social Studies, Grades 1-4). (Illus.). 64p. (gr. 2-4). 1972. PLB 6.95 (ISBN 0-8193-0539-1, Pub. by Parents). Enslow Pubs.

Scott, John S. Dictionary of Civil Engineering. 3rd ed. LC 80-24419. 308p. 1980. 19.95 (ISBN 0-470-27087-X). Halsted Pr.

Scott, Jonathan. Piranesi. LC 74-81701. (Illus.). 400p. 1975. 29.98 (ISBN 0-312-61355-5). St Martin.

Scott, Joseph E. & Dinitz, Simon, eds. Criminal Justice Planning. LC 76-14129. (Praeger Special Studies). 1977. 22.95 (ISBN 0-03-040896-2). Praeger.

Scott, Kathryn L., jt. ed. see Scott, Edward M.

Scott, Kenneth. Marriages & Deaths from the New Yorker: Double Quatro Edition 1836-1841. LC 80-80958. 308p. Date not set. price not set (ISBN 0-915156-46-6, SP46). Natl Genealogical.

Scott, Kenneth E., jt. auth. see Posner, Richard A.

Scott, Latayne C. The Mormon Mirage. 1980. 11.95 (ISBN 0-310-38910-0). Zondervan.

Scott, Leroy & Weih, Starr. Biology Laboratory Manual. 1980. coil binding 8.95 (ISBN 0-88252-106-3). Paladin Hse.

Scott, Louise B. & Thompson, Jesse J. Talking Time. 2nd ed. 1966. text ed. 12.40 o.p. (ISBN 0-07-055818-3, W). McGraw.

Scott, Margaret. Gothic Europe Fourteen Hundred to Fifteen Hundred: The History of Dress. (The History of Dress Ser.: Vol. 1). (Illus.). 1980. text ed. 62.50 (ISBN 0-391-02148-6). Humanities.

Scott, Maria L. & Scott, Jack D. Cook Like a Peasant, Eat Like a King. 1927p. 1976. 7.95 o.p. (ISBN 0-695-80592-4). Follett.

Scott, Mary. Forgetting's No Excuse. 1973. 6.95 o.p. (ISBN 0-571-09875-4, Pub. by Faber & Faber). Merrimack Bk Serv.

Scott, Mel. American City Planning Since 1890. (California Studies in Urbanization & Environmental Design). 1969. 39.50x (ISBN 0-520-01382-4); pap. 12.95x (ISBN 0-520-02051-0, CAL235). U of Cal Pr.

Scott, Michael. Hypnosis in Skin & Allergic Diseases. (Illus.). 164p. 1960. pap. 8.00 spiral (ISBN 0-398-01703-4). C C Thomas.

--Tom Cringle's Log. 1969. 5.00x (ISBN 0-460-00710-6, Evman); pap. 2.25 o.p. (ISBN 0-460-01710-1). Dutton.

Scott, Michael D. & Powers, William G. Interpersonal Communication: A Question of Needs. LC 77-76342. (Illus.). 1978. text ed. 12.95 (ISBN 0-395-25055-2); inst. manual 0.60 (ISBN 0-395-25056-0). HM.

Scott, Michael W. The Rakehell Dynasty: China Bride, No. 2. 544p. 1981. pap. 2.75 (ISBN 0-446-95201-X). Warner Bks.

Scott, Miriam M. & Stratton, Carol. The Art of Sukhothai. (Illus.). 200p. 1980. 35.95x (ISBN 0-19-580434-1). Oxford U Pr.

Scott, Nancy. Ponds & Streams. LC 76-511006. (Pegasus Books: No. 26). (Illus.). 1969. 10.50x (ISBN 0-234-77188-7). Intl Pubns Serv.

--Seashore. LC 68-2032. (Pegasus Books: No. 3). (Illus.). 1965. 7.50x (ISBN 0-234-77837-7). Intl Pubns Serv.

Scott, Nancy J. Vincenzo Vela (Eighteen Twenty to Ninety-One) LC 78-74378. (Fine Arts Dissertations, Fourth Ser.). (Illus.). 1980. lib. bdg. 66.00 (ISBN 0-8240-3965-3). Garland Pub.

Scott, Natalie. Mandy's Favorite Louisiana Recipes. 64p. 1978. pap. 2.25 (ISBN 0-88289-142-1). Pelican.

Scott, Natalie V. & Jones, Caroline M. Gourmet's Guide to New Orleans. 112p. 1976. pap. 2.95 o.p. (ISBN 0-88289-124-3); spiral bdg. 3.95 (ISBN 0-88289-079-4). Pelican.

Scott, Nathan A., Jr. Mirrors of Man in Existentialism. LC 78-69971. 1978. 7.95 (ISBN 0-529-05641-0, RB5641, Pub. by Collins Pubs); pap. 4.95 (ISBN 0-529-05487-6, FT5487). Abingdon.

--Mirrors of Man in Existentialism. 1980. pap. text ed. 7.95 (ISBN 0-687-27073-1). Abingdon.

Scott, P. A Coloured Key to the Wildfowl of the World. rev. ed. (Illus.). 1972. 15.00 (ISBN 0-685-12001-5). Heinman.

Scott, P. H. & Davis, A. C., eds. The Age of MacDiarmid: Essays on Hugh MacDiarmid & His Influence on Contemporary Scotland. 268p. 1981. 22.50x (ISBN 0-389-20199-5). B&N.

Scott, P. R. Introducing Data Communications Standards. (Illus.). 226p. 1979. pap. 25.00x (ISBN 0-85012-220-1). Intl Pubns Serv.

Scott, P. R. & Bainbridge, A., eds. Plant Disease Epidemiology. LC 78-15056. 1978. 30.95 (ISBN 0-470-26505-1). Halsted Pr.

Scott, Patrick, ed. Victorian Poetry 1830-1870. (Longman English Ser.). 1971. pap. text ed. 4.95x (ISBN 0-582-34178-7). Longman.

Scott, Paul. Staying on. 1979. pap. 2.25 (ISBN 0-380-46045-9, 46045). Avon.

Scott, Peter. Strategies for Postsecondary Education. LC 75-3372. 161p. 1975. 21.95 (ISBN 0-470-76860-6). Halsted Pr.

Scott, Peter C. Study Guide for College Chemistry: An Introduction to Inorganic, Organic, & Biochemistry. (Orig.). 1980. pap. text ed. 8.95 (ISBN 0-8185-0405-6). Brooks-Cole.

--Study Guide for Foundations of College Chemistry: Alternate Edition. (Orig.). 1980. pap. text ed. 6.95 (ISBN 0-8185-0404-8). Brooks-Cole.

Scott, Peter D., et al. The Assassinations: Dallas & Beyond - a Guide to Coverups & Investigations. 1976. 15.00 (ISBN 0-394-40107-7). Random.

Scott, R., ed. Contemporary Liquid Chromotography. LC 74-15553. (Techniques of Chemistry Ser.: Vol. XI). 1976. 34.00 (ISBN 0-471-92900-X, Pub. by Wiley-Interscience). Wiley.

Scott, R. B. Relevance of the Prophets. rev. ed. 1969. 9.95 (ISBN 0-02-608780-4); pap. 2.95 (ISBN 0-02-089270-5). Macmillan.

Scott, R. C. & Sondak, N. E. PL-One for Programmers. 1970. pap. 11.95 (ISBN 0-201-07081-2). A-W.

Scott, R. W. Handy Medical Guide for Seafarers: Fishermen, Trawlermen & Yachtsmen. (Illus.). 96p. 7.50 (ISBN 0-35238-007-0, FN). Unipub.

Scott, Ralph C. Clinical Cardiology & Diabetes: Clinical Pharmacology & Use of Selected Drugs, Vol. 2. LC 79-91228. (Illus.). 1980. 42.00 (ISBN 0-87993-136-1). Futura Pub.

Scott, Ralph C., ed. Clinical Manifestations--Medical Management, Vol. III, Pt. I. (Clinical Cardiology & Diabetes Monographs). (Illus.). 448p. 1981. 39.50 (ISBN 0-87993-137-X). Futura Pub.

--Diagnostic Procedures. (Clinical Cardiology & Diabetes: Vol. I, Part II). (Illus.). 352p. 1981. 32.00 (ISBN 0-87993-142-6). Futura Pub.

--Fundamental Consicerations in Cardiology & Diabetes. (Clinical Cardiology & Diabetes Ser.: Vol. I Part I). (Illus.). 384p. 1981. 36.00 (ISBN 0-87993-135-3). Futura Pub.

--Surgery, Renal Disease, & Special Problems, Vol. III, Pt. II. (Clinical Cardiology & Diabetes Monographs). (Illus.). 192p. 1981. 27.00 (ISBN 0-87993-138-8). Futura Pub.

Scott, Ralph W. A New Look at Biblical Crime. LC 78-27535. 1979. 15.95 (ISBN 0-88229-416-4). Nelson-Hall.

Scott, Randall W., ed. Management & Control of Growth: Issues, Techniques, Problems, Trends, 3 vols. LC 74-83560. 1800p. 1975. Set. pap. text ed. 36.50 (ISBN 0-87420-565-4). Urban Land.

Scott, Robert, jt. auth. see Liddell, Henry G.

Scott, Robert, jt. ed. see Liddell, H. G.

Scott, Robert, jt. ed. see Liddell, Henry G.

Scott, Robert A. The Making of Blind Men. 160p. 1981. pap. 4.95 (ISBN 0-87855-687-7). Transaction Bks.

Scott, Robert F., ed. Shooter's Bible 1981, No. 72. 35th ed. 576p. 1980. pap. 9.95 (ISBN 0-695-81450-8). Stoeger Pub Co.

Scott, Robert H. Problems in National Income Analysis & Forecasting. rev. ed. 1972. pap. 6.95x (ISBN 0-673-07793-4). Scott F.

Scott, Robert I. What Odd Expedients & Other Poems by Robinson Jeffers. 1981. 14.50 (ISBN 0-208-01885-9, Archon). Shoe String.

Scott, Robert J. Fiberglass Boat Design & Construction. LC 72-83719. 1973. 12.50 (ISBN 0-8286-0059-7). De Graff.

Scott, Robert L., jt. ed. see Brock, Bernard L.

Scott, Ronald B. Cancer: The Facts. 1980. text ed. 11.95x (ISBN 0-19-261149-6). Oxford U Pr.

Scott, Ronald E. Elements of Linear Circuits. 1965. 20.95 (ISBN 0-201-06842-7). A-W.

--Linear Circuits, Complete. Incl. Pt. 2. Frequency-Domain Analysis. 1961. Set. 25.95 (ISBN 0-201-06820-5). A-W.

Scott, Ronald E., jt. auth. see Cayford, John E.

Scott, Ronald F. Foundation Analysis. (Civil Engineering & Engineering Mechanics Ser.). (Illus.). 496p. 1981. text ed. 27.95 (ISBN 0-13-329169-3). P-H.

Scott, Ronald M., jt. auth. see Anderson, Kim E.

Scott, Rosemary. The Female Consumer. LC 75-31648. 300p. 1976. 22.95 (ISBN 0-470-76789-8). Halsted Pr.

Scott, Russell. The Body As Property. 1981. 14.95 (ISBN 0-670-17743-1). Viking Pr.

Scott, Russell, Jr., et al, eds. Current Controversies in Urologic Management. LC 70-173342. (Illus.). 391p. 1972. 20.00 (ISBN 0-7216-8043-7). Saunders.

Scott, Ruth K. & Hrebenar, Ronald J. Parties in Crisis: Party Politics in America. LC 78-14362. 1979. text ed. 15.95x (ISBN 0-471-01796-5). Wiley.

Scott, S. H. The Observer's Book of Cacti & Other Succulents. (Illus.). 1977. 2.95 (ISBN 0-684-14942-7, ScribT). Scribner.

Scott, S. K., jt. auth. see Schultz, D. O.

Scott, Sally. Brand New Kitten. LC 56-8355. (Illus.). (gr. 1-5). 1956. 4.95 o.p. (ISBN 0-15-211419-X, HJ). HarBraceJ.

--Judy's Summer Adventure. LC 60-6211. (Illus.). (gr. 1-5). 1960. 3.95 o.p. (ISBN 0-15-241133-X, HJ). HarBraceJ.

--What Susan Wanted. LC 56-5235. (Illus.). (gr. 1-4). 1956. 3.95 o.p. (ISBN 0-15-295528-3, HJ). HarBraceJ.

Scott, Samuel H., jt. ed. see Soderlund, G. F.

Scott, Sarah. A Description of Millenium Hall, & the Country Adjacent, 1762. (The Flowering of the Novel, 1740-1775 Ser: Vol. 62). 1974. lib. bdg. 50.00 (ISBN 0-8240-1161-9). Garland Pub.

--The History of Cornelia, 1750. (The Flowering of the Novel, 1740-1775 Ser: Vol. 29). 1974. lib. bdg. 50.00 (ISBN 0-8240-1128-7). Garland Pub.

Scott, Sheila. Barefoot in the Sky. LC 73-8350. (Illus.). 324p. 1974. 7.95 o.s.i. (ISBN 0-02-608660-3). Macmillan.

Scott, Shirley. The Thoughts of Giants & Other Poems. 60p. (Orig.). 1980. pap. 2.50 (ISBN 0-931846-16-1). Wash Writers Pub.

Scott, Shirley C. Myths of Consciousness in the Novels of Charles Maturin. Varma, Devendra P., ed. LC 79-8479. (Gothic Studies & Dissertations Ser.). 1980. lib. bdg. 22.00x (ISBN 0-405-12661-1). Arno.

Scott, Stuart D., Jr., jt. auth. see Cazeau, Charles J.

Scott, Thomas. The Interpreter, Wherein Three Principal Terms of State Are Clearly Unfolded. LC 74-80194. (English Experience Ser.: No. 673). 1974. Repr. of 1624 ed. 3.50 (ISBN 90-221-0281-5). Walter J Johnson.

Scott, Thomas, jt. auth. see Henry, Matthew.

Scott, Thomas G. & Wasser, Clinton H. Checklist of North American Plants for Wildlife Biologists. LC 79-89208. 58p. (Orig.). 1979. pap. 4.50 (ISBN 0-933564-07-4). Wildlife Soc.

Scott, Timothy Van see Van Scott, Timothy & Weiss, Sidney J.

Scott, Tom. Observer's Book of Golf. (Observer Bks.). (Illus.). 1977. 2.95 (ISBN 0-684-15212-6, ScribT). Scribner.

Scott, W. & Croker, J. W. Thoughts on the Proposed Change of Currency. 1971. Repr. of 1826 ed. 24.00x (ISBN 0-7165-0306-9, Pub. by Irish Academic Pr Ireland). Biblio Dist.

Scott, W. Richard. Organizations: Rationale, Natural, & Open Systems. (Ser. in Sociology). (Illus.). 320p. 1981. text ed. 16.95 (ISBN 0-13-641977-1). P-H.

Scott, Waldron. Bring Forth Justice. LC 80-15992. 304p. 1980. pap. 11.95 (ISBN 0-8028-1848-X). Eerdmans.

Scott, Waldron, ed. Serving Our Generation: Evangelical Strategies for the Eighties. 281p. (Orig.). 1980. pap. 5.95 o.s.i. (ISBN 0-936444-03-7). World Evang Fellow.

--The Task Before Us: Audio-Visual Presentation. (Illus.). 1976. 34.95 (ISBN 0-87808-600-5). William Carey Lib.

Scott, Walter. Abbot. 1969. 5.00x o.p. (ISBN 0-460-00124-8, Evman). Dutton.

--Bride of Lammermoor. 1955. 6.00x (ISBN 0-460-00129-9, Evman); pap. 3.50 (ISBN 0-460-01129-4, Evman). Dutton.

--The Evangelist: Eighteen Thirty-Two to Eighteen Forty-Two, 10 vols. 1980. Repr. text ed. 99.95 (ISBN 0-89900-226-9). College Pr Pub.

--Exposition of the Revelation of Jesus Christ. LC 79-88736. 1979. Repr. 14.50 (ISBN 0-8254-3731-8). Kregel.

--Guy Mannering. 1954. 6.00x o.p. (ISBN 0-460-00133-7, Evman). Dutton.

--Heart of Midlothian. 1956. 10.50x (ISBN 0-460-00134-5, Evman); pap. 3.95 o.p. (ISBN 0-460-01134-0, EP1134). Dutton.

--Ivanhoe. (Literature Ser). (gr. 7-12). 1970. pap. text ed. 3.83 (ISBN 0-87720-729-1). AMSCO Sch.

--Ivanhoe. 1962. pap. 0.95 o.s.i. (ISBN 0-02-053760-3, Collier). Macmillan.

--Kenilworth. 1955. 12.95x (ISBN 0-460-00135-3, Evman). Dutton.

--Minstrelsy of the Scottish Border, 4 Vols. Henderson, T. F., ed. LC 67-23924. 1968. Repr. of 1902 ed. Set. 90.00 (ISBN 0-8103-3418-6). Gale.

--Monastery. 1969. 11.50x (ISBN 0-460-00136-1, Evman). Dutton.

--Rob Roy. 1973. 11.50x (ISBN 0-460-00142-6, Evman); pap. 5.50 (ISBN 0-460-01142-1). Dutton.
--Waverly. 1969. 15.50x (ISBN 0-460-00075-6, Evman); pap. 8.95 (ISBN 0-460-01075-1). Dutton.
--Woodstock. 1969. 11.50x (ISBN 0-460-00072-1, Evman). Dutton.
Scott, Walter A., et al, eds. Mobilization & Reassembly of Genetic Information: Vol. 17 of the Miami Winter Symposia. LC 80-18845. 1980. 35.00 (ISBN 0-12-633360-2). Acad Pr.
Scott, Sir Walter. Fortunes of Nigel. Link, Frederick M., ed. LC 65-18715. 1965. pap. 3.25x (ISBN 0-8032-5176-9, BB 321, Bison). U of Nebr Pr.
--Life of John Dryden. Kreissman, Bernard, ed. LC 63-8121. 1963. pap. 2.95x (ISBN 0-8032-5177-7, BB 157, Bison). U of Nebr Pr.
--Waverley: Or 'Tis Sixty Years Since. Lamont, Claire, ed. 512p. 1981. 58.00 (ISBN 0-19-812643-3). Oxford U Pr.
Scott, William. An Essay on Drapery, 1635. (Kress Library of Business & Economics: No. 9). 1953. pap. 5.00x (ISBN 0-678-09904-9, Baker Lib). Kelley.
Scott, William, jt. auth. see Scott, Harriet.
Scott, William E. Alliance Against Hitler: The Origins of the Franco-Soviet Pact. LC 62-20214. 1962. 14.75 o.p. (ISBN 0-686-66403-5). Duke.
Scott, William E. & Cummings, L. L. Readings in Organizational Behavior & Human Performance. rev ed. 1973. pap. text ed. 13.95 (ISBN 0-256-01398-5). Irwin.
Scott, William F. Soviet Sources of Military Doctrine & Strategy. LC 75-18537. 64p. 1975. 6.50x (ISBN 0-8448-0709-5); pap. 2.75x (ISBN 0-8448-0710-9). Crane-Russak Co.
Scott, William F., jt. auth. see Scott, Harriet F.
Scott, William G. & Mitchell, Terence. Organization Theory: A Structural & Behavioral Analysis. 3rd ed. 1976. text ed. 18.95 (ISBN 0-256-01788-3). Irwin.
Scott, William R., et al. Atlas of the Human Brain & the Orbit for Computed Tomography. 2nd ed. (Illus.). 124p. 1980. 32.50 (ISBN 0-87527-155-3). Green.
Scotten, R. B. & Ferber, Helen. Public Expenditures & Social Policy in Australia. Vol. 1. text ed. 28.50 (ISBN 0-582-71084-7); Vol. 2. text ed. 26.00 (ISBN 0-582-71086-3). Longman.
Scott-Fox, L., tr. see Descombes, Vincent.
Scott-Giles, C. W. The Wimsey Family. LC 78-2074. (Illus.). 1978. 6.95 o.s.i. (ISBN 0-06-014001-1, HarpT). Har-Row.
Scotti, Paul. Seaports: Ships, Piers, & People. LC 80-21655. (Illus.). 64p. (gr. 4-6). 1980. PLB 7.29 (ISBN 0-671-34032-8). Messner.
Scotti, Thomas M., jt. auth. see Anderson, W. A. D.
Scotti, W. A., jt. auth. see Anderson, W. A.
Scottish Classics Group. Versiculi: A Companion in Verse. 1976. pap. text ed. 2.50x (ISBN 0-05-002897-9); tchr's notes 1.50x (ISBN 0-05-002898-7). Longman.
Scottish Rite Schizophrenia Research Program, Conference, Rochester, 2-6 May 1976. Attention & Information Processing in Schizophrenia: Proceedings. Matthyse, S., ed. 1979. text ed. 99.50 (ISBN 0-08-023126-8). Pergamon.
Scottish Schools Science Equipment Research Centre, ed. Hazardous Chemicals: A Manual for Schools & Colleges. 1979. pap. 12.95xlab. manual (ISBN 0-05-003204-6). Longman.
Scottish Tourist Board. Scotland: Bed & Breakfast. rev. ed. (Illus.). 252p. 1981. pap. price not set (ISBN 0-85419-170-4, Pub. by Auto Assn-British Tourist Authority England). Merrimack Bk Serv.
--Scotland: Hotels & Guesthouses. rev. ed. (Illus.). 328p. 1981. pap. price not set (ISBN 0-85419-169-0, Pub. by Auto Assn-British Tourist Authority England). Merrimack Bk Serv.
Scott-James, Anne & Lancaster, Osbert. The Pleasure Garden. LC 77-84332. 1980. pap. 5.95 (ISBN 0-87645-109-1). Gambit.
Scott-Kilvert, Ian see Henderson, Philip.
Scott-Kilvert, Ian, ed. British Writers, Vol. IV. LC 78-23483. 1981. lib. bdg. 55.00 (ISBN 0-684-16635-6). Scribner.
--British Writers, Vol. V. LC 78-23483. 1981. lib. bdg. 55.00 (ISBN 0-684-16636-4). Scribner.
--British Writers, Vol. III. LC 78-23483. 1980. lib. bdg. 55.00 (ISBN 0-684-16408-6). Scribner.
Scott-Kilvert, Ian & British Council, eds. British Writers, Vol. II. LC 78-23483. (British Council Pamphlet Ser.). 1979. lib. bdg. 55.00 (ISBN 0-684-16407-8). Scribner.
Scott-Kilvert, Ian, tr. see Plutarch.
Scott-Martin, Sue, jt. auth. see Boyd, Margaret A.
Scott-Morgan, John. The Colonel Stephens Railways. LC 77-91737. 1978. 17.95 (ISBN 0-7153-7544-X). David & Charles.
Scott-Morton, Michael S., jt. auth. see Keen, Peter F.
Scott-Morton, Michael S., jt. auth. see McCosh, Andrew M.
Scott-Washburn, Mildred. The Charm of Your Children. (Illus.). 176p. 1980. 8.00 (ISBN 0-682-49615-4). Exposition.
Scotus, John Duns see Duns Scotus, John.
Scouten, Arthur, intro. by. Restoration & Eighteenth Century Drama. 160p. 1981. pap. 5.95 (ISBN 0-312-67787-1). St Martin.
Scouten, Arthur H. London Stage, 1729-1747: A Critical Introduction. LC 60-6539. (Arcturus Books Paperbacks). (Illus.). 206p. 1968. pap. 6.95 (ISBN 0-8093-0338-8). S Ill U Pr.
Scouten, Arthur H., jt. auth. see Avery, Emmett L.
Scouten, Arthur H., ed. see Teerink, H.
Scouten, William H. Affinity Chromatography. (Chemical Analysis Ser.). 344p. 1981. 39.50 (ISBN 0-471-02649-2, Pub. by Wiley-Interscience). Wiley.
Scovel, Myra & Ragland, Phillda. Don't Just Sit There Reading: A Fun-To-Do Book on the Americas. (Orig.). (gr. 1-4). 1970. pap. 2.25 o.p. (ISBN 0-377-10751-4). Friend Pr.
Scoville, Herbert, Jr. Toward a Strategic Arms Limitation Agreemet. 1970. pap. 1.50 (ISBN 0-87003-025-6). Carnegie Endow.
Scoville, Ogden D. The Small Investor's Handbook for Long-Term Security or Quick Profit. 1971. pap. 3.95 (ISBN 0-06-463324-1, EH 324, EH). Har-Row.
Scoville, Warren C. & Laforce, J. Clayburn. Economic Development of Western Europe, 4 vols. Incl. Vol. 1. Middle Ages & the Renaissance. pap. text ed. 2.95x o.p. (ISBN 0-669-26906-9); Vol. 2. The Sixteenth & Seventeenth Centuries. pap. text ed. o.p. (ISBN 0-669-26914-X); Vol. 3. The Eighteenth & Early Nineteenth Centuries. pap. text ed. o.p. (ISBN 0-669-26922-0); Vol. 4. The Late Nineteenth & Early Twentieth Centuries. pap. text ed. 2.95x o.p. (ISBN 0-669-26930-1). 1969. Heath.
Scowen, Gerda. Figaro. 1981. 4.95 (ISBN 0-8062-1604-2). Carlton.
Scowen, Kenneth. Unknown England. Niall, Ian. (Illus.). 128p. 1980. 24.00 (ISBN 0-7134-1843-5, Pub. by Batsford England). David & Charles.
Scoy-Mosher, M. V. Chemotherapy: A Manual for Patients & Their Families. Date not set. Set Of 100. pap. 40.00. Masson Pub.
Scragg, D. G. see Gordon, E. V.
Scragg, Walter R. Directions: A Look at the Paths of Life. LC 77-78101. (Horizon Ser.). 1977. pap. 4.50 (ISBN 0-8127-0136-4). Southern Pub.
Screech, M. A. Ecstasy & "the Praise of Folly". 267p. 1980. 49.50x (ISBN 0-7156-1361-8, Pub. by Duckworth England). Biblio Dist.
Screen, J. E., jt. ed. see Walford, Alberto J.
Scriabine, Alexander, ed. The Pharmacology of Antihypertensive Drugs. 1980. text ed. 39.50 (ISBN 0-89004-329-9). Raven.
Scriabine, Helene. It Happened in Russia. (Illus.). 140p. (Orig.). 1980. pap. 7.00x (ISBN 0-935090-02-9, Dist. by Almanac Press). Maxims Bks.
Scribbs, Buck. The Adventures of Herbilee & Harbilee Hitlow. Garner, Sam, ed. 72p. (Orig.). 1980. pap. 2.95 (ISBN 0-935440-00-3). October Pr.
Scribe see Stanton, Stephen S.
Scribe, Eugene & Delestre-Poirson, Charles-Gaspard. Le Comte Ory. Gossett, Philip & Rosen, Charles, eds. LC 76-49191. (Early Romantic Opera Ser.: Vol. 16). 1978. lib. bdg. 82.00 (ISBN 0-8240-2915-1). Garland Pub.
Scriber, Robert L. & Tarter, Brent, eds. Revolutionary Virginia, the Road to Independence, Vol. 4: The Committee of Safety & the Balance of Forces, 1775 a Documentary Record. LC 72-96023. 1978. 25.00x (ISBN 0-8139-0748-9). U Pr of Va.
Scribner, Bob & Benecke, Gerhard. German Peasant War Fifteen Twenty-Five: New Viewpoints. (Illus.). 1979. text ed. 22.50x (ISBN 0-04-900031-4); pap. text ed. 8.95x (ISBN 0-04-900032-2). Allen Unwin.
Scribner, Robert L. & Tarter, Brent, eds. Revolutionary Virginia: The Road to Independence, Clash of Arms & the Fourth Convention, 1775-1776, a Documentary Record, Vol. V. LC 72-96023. 1980. 30.00x (ISBN 0-8139-0806-X). U Pr of Va.
--The Time for Decision, 1776: A Documentary Record. LC 72-96023. (Revolutionary Virginia Ser.: The Road to Independence, Vol. VI). 1981. write for info. (ISBN 0-8139-0880-9). U Pr of Va.
Scribner, S., jt. auth. see Cole, M.
Scrimgeour, James R. Sean O'Casey. (English Authors Ser.: No. 245). 1978. 12.50 (ISBN 0-8057-6735-5). Twayne.
Scripien, Gladys, et al. Comprehensive Pediatric Nursing. (Illus.). 992p. 1975. text ed. 21.95 o.p. (ISBN 0-07-055787-X, HP). McGraw.
Scripture Union. The Boy Who Shared. 1978. pap. 0.49 (ISBN 0-87508-930-5). Chr Lit.
--David, the Shepherd Boy. (New Owl Ser.). 1978. pap. 0.49 (ISBN 0-87508-928-3). Chr Lit.
--God Made the World (Creation) (New Owl Ser.). 1978. pap. 0.49 (ISBN 0-87508-925-9). Chr Lit.
--The Good Friends. 1978. pap. 0.49 (ISBN 0-87508-929-1). Chr Lit.
--Man up a Tree (Zacchaeus) 1978. pap. 0.49 (ISBN 0-87508-932-1). Chr Lit.
--The Wedding Party (at Cana) 1978. pap. 0.49 (ISBN 0-87508-931-3). Chr Lit.
Scriven, Carl & Stevens, James. Food Equipment Facts. new ed. LC 80-67617. (First Ser.). 429p. (Orig.). 1980. pap. 9.95 (ISBN 0-9604902-0-5). Concept Design.
Scriven, Charles. The Demons Have Had It. LC 76-2926. 128p. 1976. pap. 4.95 (ISBN 0-8127-0111-9). Southern Pub.
Scriven, F. B. Sports Facilities for Schools in Developing Countries. LC 72-96367. (Educational Studies & Documents). (Illus.). 39p. (Orig.). 1973. pap. 2.50 (ISBN 92-3-101049-2, U629, UNESCO). Unipub.
Scriven, Michael. Evaluation Thesaurus. 2nd ed. LC 80-68775. 149p. 1980. pap. text ed. 6.95x (ISBN 0-918528-08-9). Edgepress.
Scrivens, Steven. Interior Planting in Large Buildings: A Handbook for Architects Interior Designers & Horticulturists. LC 80-23565. 200p. 1981. 44.95 (ISBN 0-470-27067-5). Halsted Pr.
Scriver, Charles R. & Rosenberg, Leon E. Amino Acid Metabolism & Its Disorders. LC 72-90726. (Major Problems in Clinical Pediatrics Ser.: Vol. 10). (Illus.). 510p. 1973. text ed. 22.00 (ISBN 0-7216-8044-5). Saunders.
Scrivner, C. L. & Baker, James C. Soil Systems: A Guide for Assisted Learning in Soil Science. 1976. pap. text ed. 6.95 o.p. (ISBN 0-8403-1434-5). Kendall-Hunt.
Scroggie, Robert J., jt. auth. see Moyer, Frank A.
Scroggie, W. Graham. How to Pray. rev. ed. LC 80-8076. (W. Graham Scroggie Library). 112p. 1981. pap. 2.95 (ISBN 0-8254-3736-9). Kregel.
--Know Your Bible. 1965. 14.95 (ISBN 0-8007-0169-0). Revell.
--Salvation & Behavior. LC 80-8075. (W. Graham Scroggie Library). 104p. 1981. pap. 2.50 (ISBN 0-8254-3735-0). Kregel.
--The Study Hour Series. Incl. 192p. kivar o.p. 3.95 (ISBN 0-310-32671-0); Gospel of John. 144p. kivar o.p. 3.95 (ISBN 0-310-32681-8); Gospel of Mark. 288p. kivar 6.95 (ISBN 0-310-32691-5). 1976. Zondervan.
Scroggins, Clara J. Silver Christmas Ornaments: A Collector's Guide. LC 79-15323. (Illus.). 208p. 1980. 25.00 (ISBN 0-498-02385-0). A S Barnes.
Scroggle, W. Graham. Joshua in the Light of the New Testment. LC 80-8074. (W. Graham Scroggie Library). 1981. pap. 2.50 (ISBN 0-8254-3734-2). Kregel.
--Paul's Prison Prayers. LC 80-8077. 124p. 1981. pap. 2.95 (ISBN 0-8254-3737-7). Kregel.
Scroggs, James. Letting Love in. LC 77-27268. 1978. 10.95 (ISBN 0-13-531566-2, Spec); pap. 5.95 (ISBN 0-13-531558-1, Spec). P-H.
Scrogin, Michael. When God Intrudes. 112p. 1981. pap. 4.95 (ISBN 0-8170-0903-5). Judson.
Scruggs, Rachel I. Come, Follow Me. 1981. 7.95 (ISBN 0-533-04769-2). Vantage.
Scrupski, Stephen E., ed. see Electronics Magazine.
Scruton, Roger. The Meaning of Conservatism. 205p. 1980. 26.50x (ISBN 0-389-20082-4). B&N.
Scrutton, D. R. & Gilbertson, M. P. Physiotherapy in Pediatric Practice. (Postgraduate Pediatric Ser.). 1975. 19.95 (ISBN 0-407-00017-8). Butterworths.
Scudder, Horace E. Noah Webster. LC 80-20031. (American Men & Women of Letters Ser.). 310p. 1981. pap. 4.95 (ISBN 0-87754-158-2). Chelsea Hse.
Scudder, Robers V., jt. auth. see Jenney, Charles, Jr.
Scudder, Rogers, jt. auth. see Jenney, Charles.
Scudder, Rogers V., jt. auth. see Jenney, Charles, Jr.
Scudder, Thayer. The Ecology of the Gwembe Tonga. 1962. pap. text ed. 9.75x (ISBN 0-7190-1276-7). Humanities.
Scudder, Thayer & Colson, Elizabeth. Secondary Education & the Formation of an Elite: The Impact of Education on Gwembe District, Zambia. (Studies in Anthropology). 1980. 24.50 (ISBN 0-12-634280-6). Acad Pr.
Scudder, Townshend. The Lonely Wayfaring Man: Emerson & Some Englishmen. LC 80-2545. 1981. Repr. of 1936 ed. 32.50 (ISBN 0-404-19270-X). AMS Pr.
Scullard, H. H., ed. see Toynbee, J. M.
Scullion, John J., tr. see Westermann, Claus.
Scully, J. C. The Fundamentals of Corrosion. 2nd ed. 252p. 1975. text ed. 23.00 (ISBN 0-08-018081-7); pap. text ed. 11.25 (ISBN 0-08-018080-9). Pergamon.
Scully, J. C., ed. Ion Implantation & Ion Beam Analysis Techniques in Corrosion Studies. 1977. pap. text ed. 16.00 (ISBN 0-08-021420-7). Pergamon.
--Ion Implementation & Ion Beam Analysis Techniques in Corrosion: Selected Papers Presented at the Conference at the Corrosion & Protection Centre, UMIST, Manchester, 28-30 June 1978. 148p. 1980. 16.00 (ISBN 0-08-026135-3). Pergamon.
Scully, James. May Day. LC 80-80653. 72p. (Orig.). 1980. pap. 3.00 (ISBN 0-936484-00-4). Minn Rev Pr.
--Scrap Book. LC 77-89528. 1977. pap. 3.50 (ISBN 0-917488-03-2). Ziesing Bros.
Scully, James, tr. see Aeschylus.
Scully, Michael F. & Kakkar, Vijay V. Chromogenic Peptide Substrates. (Illus.). 1979. text ed. 37.50 o.s.i. (ISBN 0-443-01840-5). Churchill.
Scully, R. F., jt. auth. see Serov, S. F.
Scully, Vincent. Modern Architecture. rev ed. LC 61-13689. (Illus.). 128p. 1974. 12.50 (ISBN 0-8076-0159-4); pap. 5.95 (ISBN 0-8076-0334-1). Braziller.
--Shingle Style & the Stick Style: Architectural Theory & Design from Richardson to the Origins of Wright. rev. ed. (Publications in the History of Art Ser.: No. 20). (Illus.). 1971. 25.00x (ISBN 0-300-01434-1); pap. 10.95 (ISBN 0-300-01519-4). Yale U Pr.
Scully, Vincent, Jr. Frank Lloyd Wright. LC 60-6075. (Masters of World Architecture Ser). (Illus.). 128p. 1960. pap. 7.95 (ISBN 0-8076-0221-3). Braziller.
--Louis I. Kahn. LC 62-16265. (Makers of Contemporary Architecture Ser). (Illus., Orig.). 1962. 4.95 o.p. (ISBN 0-8076-0198-5); pap. 3.95 o.p. (ISBN 0-8076-0390-2). Braziller.
--The Shingle Style Today, or the Historian's Revenge. LC 74-79058. (Illus.). 112p. 1974. 12.50 (ISBN 0-8076-0759-2); pap. 5.95 (ISBN 0-8076-0760-6). Braziller.
Sculthorpe, William J. Design of High Pressure Steam & High Temperature Water Plants. 128p. 1972. 25.00 o.p. (ISBN 0-8311-1075-9). Indus Pr.
Scurfield, Cecelia & Scurfield, George. Home Baked. (Illus., Orig.). 1971. pap. 3.95 (ISBN 0-571-09844-4, Pub. by Faber & Faber). Merrimack Bk Serv.
--Home-Made Cakes and Biscuits. 2nd ed. (Orig.). 1975. pap. 3.95 (ISBN 0-571-10699-4, Pub. by Faber & Faber). Merrimack Bk Serv.
Scurfield, Cecila, jt. auth. see Scurfield, Georgia.
Scurfield, George, jt. auth. see Scurfield, Cecelia.
Scurfield, Georgia & Scurfield, Cecila. Home Baked: A Little Book of Bread Recipes. 1972. 8.95 (ISBN 0-571-06614-3); pap. 2.95 (ISBN 0-571-09844-4). Transatlantic.
Scuro, Vincent. Wonders of Cattle. LC 80-1019. (Wonders Ser.). (Illus.). 64p. (gr. 4 up). 1980. PLB 6.95 (ISBN 0-396-07892-3). Dodd.
Scuro, Vincent, jt. auth. see Lavine, Sigmund A.
Scurra, John, ed. see Kim, Richard.
Scurra, John, ed. see Kong, Bucksam & Ho, Eugene H.
Scutchfield, F., jt. auth. see Pieroni, Robert E.
Scutt, R. W. B. & Gotch, Christopher. Art, Sex & Symbol: The Mystery of Tatooing. LC 73-10526. (Illus.). 320p. 1974. 20.00 o.p. (ISBN 0-498-01343-X). A S Barnes.
Scwalb, Ann W., ed. see Hunt, Tamara & Renfro, Nancy.
Scwartz, Ronald A. see Browman, David L.
Scyoc, Sydney J. Van see Van Scyoc, Sydney J.
S. D. de Lerin, Olivia, tr. see Sutton, Joan L. & Watson de Barros, Leda.
Seaberg, Albin G. Menu Design, Merchandising & Marketing. 2nd ed. LC 72-149403. 1973. 22.95 (ISBN 0-8436-0572-3). CBI Pub.
Seaborg, Glenn T. Transuranium Elements. 1958. 42.50x o.p. (ISBN 0-685-69863-7). Elliots Bks.
Seaborne & Lowe. The English School: Its Architecture & Organization, Vol. 2. (Illus.). 1977. 50.00x (ISBN 0-7100-8408-0). Routledge & Kegan.
Seaborne, Malcolm, ed. & intro. by see Robson, E. R.
Seabourne, Malcolm. Recent Education from Local Sources. 1967. text ed. 5.50x (ISBN 0-7100-4204-3); pap. text ed. 3.00x (ISBN 0-7100-4208-6). Humanities.
Seabourne, P. L., tr. see Dienes, Z. P.
Seabrook. Bridge: From Average to Expert. 1979. 17.95 (ISBN 0-7134-1623-8, Pub. by Batsford England). David & Charles.
Seabrook, Peter. The Complete Vegetable Gardener. (Illus.). 128p. 1981. 17.95 (ISBN 0-686-69382-5); pap. 7.95 (ISBN 0-686-69383-3). A & W Pubs.
Seabrooke, Brenda. The Best Burglar Alarm. LC 78-7455. (Illus.). (gr. k-3). 1978. 7.95 (ISBN 0-688-22165-3); PLB 7.63 (ISBN 0-688-32165-8). Morrow.

Seabury, David. Art of Selfishness. 1979. pap. 3.95 (ISBN 0-346-12258-9). Cornerstone.
--How to Live with Yourself. 104p. 1972. pap. 3.95 (ISBN 0-911336-39-7). Sci of Mind.
--Pull Yourself Together. 1967. pap. 3.95 (ISBN 0-911336-14-1). Sci of Mind.
--Release from Your Problems. 1966. pap. 3.95 (ISBN 0-911336-15-X). Sci of Mind.
--Self-Mastery. Kinnear, Willis, ed. 96p. (Orig.). 1974. pap. 3.95 (ISBN 0-911336-58-3). Sci of Mind.
--Stop Being Afraid. 1965. pap. 3.95 (ISBN 0-911336-19-2). Sci of Mind.
--Your Four Great Emotions. 1969. pap. 3.95 (ISBN 0-911336-22-2). Sci of Mind.
Seabury, Samuel. Letters of a Westchester Farmer, 1774-1775. Vance, Clarence H., ed. LC 70-103943. (Era of the American Revolution Ser). 1970. Repr. of 1930 ed. lib. bdg. 22.50 (ISBN 0-306-71868-5). Da Capo.
Seader, J. D., jt. auth. see Henley, Ernest J.
Seager, Elizabeth, ed. The Countryman Book of Village Trades & Crafts. LC 77-91719. (Countryman Bks.). (Illus.). 1978. 16.95 (ISBN 0-7153-7493-1). David & Charles.
Seager, Robin. Pompey: A Political Biography. 1980. 27.50x (ISBN 0-520-03909-2). U of Cal Pr.
--Tiberius. LC 74-185511. (Illus.). 1972. 21.50x (ISBN 0-520-02212-2). U of Cal Pr.
Seager, Spencer L. & Slabaugh, Michael R. Introductory Chemistry: General, Organic, Biological. 1979. text ed. 19.95x (ISBN 0-673-15026-7); study guide 6.95x (ISBN 0-673-15215-4). Scott F.
Seager, Spencer L., jt. auth. see Stoker, H. Stephen.
Seagle, Janet, jt. ed. see Murdoch, Joseph S.
Seago, Eugene. A Practical Guide to Preparation of Partnership & Partner's Tax Returns. 2nd ed. 1978. pap. 9.50 (ISBN 0-88450-061-6, 1707-B). Lawyers & Judges.
Seagraves, Kelly L. Sons of God Return. 192p. 1975. pap. 1.50 o.p. (ISBN 0-8007-8190-2, Spire Bks). Revell.
Seagren, Daniel R. Couples in the Bible. (Contemporary Discussion Ser). 1972. pap. 2.50 (ISBN 0-8010-7971-3). Baker Bk.
Seal, Anil. Emergence of Indian Nationalism. (Political Change in Modern Asia: No. 1). (Illus.). 1968. 39.95 (ISBN 0-521-06274-8); pap. 11.50x (ISBN 0-521-09652-9). Cambridge U Pr.
Seal, Anna L. Cardiogenic Shock. (Myocardial Infarction Ser.). 100p. 1980. pap. 6.95x (ISBN 0-8385-1056-6). ACC.
Seale, Barbara. Writing Efficiently: A Step-by-Step Composition Course. (Illus.). 1978. pap. text ed. 8.95 (ISBN 0-13-970160-5). P-H.
Seale, Ervin. Learn to Live. 1966. pap. 5.95 (ISBN 0-911336-08-7). Sci of Mind.
--Take off from Within. LC 71-150974. 1971. 5.95 o.p. (ISBN 0-06-067198-X, HarpR). Har-Row.
--Ten Words That Will Change Your Life. 188p. 1972. pap. 5.95 (ISBN 0-911336-38-9). Sci of Mind.
Seale, Nancy. The Little Princess, Sara Crewe. (Orig.). 1981. playscript 2.00 (ISBN 0-87602-231-X). Anchorage.
Seale, William. A Tasteful Interlude: American Interiors Through the Camera's Eye, 1860 to 1917. (Illus.). 288p. 1981. pap. 12.95 (ISBN 0-910050-49-X). AASLH.
Sealey, Leonard G. & Gibbon, Vivian. Communication & Learning in the Primary School. rev. ed. 1963. text ed. 4.00x (ISBN 0-631-97120-3). Humanities.
Sealey, Raphael. A History of the Greek States, 700-388 BC. 1977. 22.75x (ISBN 0-520-03125-3); pap. 9.95x (ISBN 0-520-03177-6, CAMPUS 165). U of Cal Pr.
Sealey, Richard. How to Keep Your VW Rabbit Alive, a Manual of Step by Step Procedures for the Compleat Idiot. LC 79-91278. (Illus.). 416p. (Orig.). 1980. pap. 12.00 (ISBN 0-912528-17-6). John Muir.
Seals in Fluid Power Symposium. Proceedings. 1973. pap. 29.00 (ISBN 0-900983-31-0, Dist. by Air Science Co.). BHRA Fluid.
Sealts, Merton M., Jr. The Early Lives of Melville: Nineteenth-Century Biographical Sketches & Their Authors. LC 74-5906. 320p. 1975. 25.00x (ISBN 0-299-06570-7). U of Wis Pr.
Sealts, Merton M., Jr. & Ferguson, Alfred R., eds. Emerson's "Nature". Origin, Growth, Meaning. 2nd, enl. ed. LC 78-13945. (Illus.). 236p. 1979. 12.95x o.p. (ISBN 0-8093-0891-6); pap. 6.95 (ISBN 0-8093-0900-9). S Ill U Pr.
Sealy, Adrienne V. The Color Your Way into Black History Book. (Illus.). 78p. 1980. wkbk. 4.00 (ISBN 0-9602670-6-9). Assn Family Living.
Sealy, Lloyd G., jt. auth. see Fink, Joseph.
Seaman, Barbara. The Doctors' Case Against the Pill. 264p. 1980. pap. 6.50 (ISBN 0-385-14575-6, Dolp). Doubleday.
Seaman, David, jt. auth. see Buttimer, Anne.
Seaman, Don, ed. see Boyle, Patrick G.
Seaman, Donald. The Duel. 220p. 1981. pap. 2.50 (ISBN 0-445-04601-5). Popular Lib.
--Working Effectively with Task Force Oriented Groups. Pardoen, Alan, ed. (Adult Education Association Professional Development Ser.). (Illus.). 144p. 1981. text ed. 12.95x (ISBN 0-07-000554-0, C). McGraw.
Seaman, Florence & Lorimer, Anne. Winning at Work. 192p. 1980. pap. 2.95 (ISBN 0-553-14244-5). Bantam.
Seaman, L. C. Life in Victorian London. 1973. 19.95 (ISBN 0-7134-1465-0, Pub. by Batsford England). David & Charles.
Seamands, David A. Healing of Our Damaged Emotions. 1981. pap. 3.95 (ISBN 0-88207-228-5). Victor Bks.
Seamans, Eldon L. Studies in American Minority Life. 1976. pap. text ed. 7.50x (ISBN 0-8191-0092-7). U Pr of Amer.
Seamon, John G., ed. Human Memory: Contemporary Readings. (Illus.). 464p. 1980. text ed. 19.95x (ISBN 0-19-502738-8); pap. text ed. 11.95x (ISBN 0-19-502739-6). Oxford U Pr.
Seanor, D. A., jt. auth. see Patsis, A. V.
Searby, Ellen. The Inside Passage Traveler. 3rd ed. (Illus.). 112p. 1980. 3.95 o.p. (ISBN 0-686-27648-5). Windham Bay.
--The Inside Passage Traveler: Getting Around in Southeastern Alaska. 4th ed. (Illus.). 128p. 1981. pap. 5.50 (ISBN 0-9605526-0-X). Windham Bay.
Searby, Peter, jt. auth. see Digby, Anne.
Searl, C., jt. auth. see Irving, J.
Searle, A. G. & De Boer, P., eds. Workshops on Chromosomal Aspects of the Male Sterility in Mammals: Abstracts. (Journal; Cytogenetics & Cell Genetics: Vol. 27; No. 4). (Illus.). 84p. 1980. pap. 6.75 (ISBN 3-8055-1610-X). S Karger.
Searle, Campbell L., jt. auth. see Gray, Paul E.
Searle, Chris. Mainland. LC 76-365792. 1979. 9.95 (ISBN 0-7145-1069-6, Pub. by M Boyars); pap. 5.95 (ISBN 0-7145-0480-7). Merrimack Bk Serv.
--We're Building a New School! Diary of a Teacher in Mozambique, 1977-1978. (Illus.). 240p. (Orig.). 1981. 16.95 (ISBN 0-905762-87-8, Pub. by Zed Pr); pap. cancelled (ISBN 0-905762-88-6). Lawrence Hill.
Searle, G. R. The Quest for National Efficiency: A Study in British Politics & Political Thought, 1899-1914. LC 75-126758. 1971. 20.00x (ISBN 0-520-01794-3). U of Cal Pr.
Searle, G. R., ed. see White, Arnold.
Searle, Humphrey, tr. see Kolneder, Walter.
Searle, J. R. Expression & Meaning. LC 79-12271. 1979. 19.95 (ISBN 0-521-22901-4). Cambridge U Pr.
Searle, John R. Speech Acts. LC 68-24484. 1970. 29.95 (ISBN 0-521-07184-4); pap. 7.95x (ISBN 0-521-09626-X). Cambridge U Pr.
Searle, Mark. Christening: The Making of Christians. 185p. (Orig.). 1980. pap. text ed. 6.50 (ISBN 0-8146-1183-4). Liturgical Pr.
Searle, Mark, ed. Liturgy & Social Justice. 1980. pap. write for info (ISBN 0-8146-1209-1). Liturgical Pr.
Searle, Ronald. The Situation Is Hopeless. LC 80-15868. (Illus.). 64p. 1981. 12.95 (ISBN 0-670-64731-4, Studio). Viking Pr.
--The Square Egg. (Illus.). 96p. (Orig.). 1981. pap. 2.95 (ISBN 0-14-005467-7). Penguin.
Searle, Ronald, jt. auth. see Willans, Geoffrey.
Searle, S. R. Matrix Algebra for the Biological Sciences: Including Applications in Statistics. LC 66-11528. (Quantitative Methods for Biologists & Medical Statistics Ser.). 1966. 25.95 (ISBN 0-471-76930-4, Pub. by Wiley-Interscience). Wiley.
Searle, S. R. & Hausman, W. H. Matrix Algebra for Business & Economics. LC 66-11528. 1970. 31.95 (ISBN 0-471-76941-X, Pub. by Wiley-Interscience). Wiley.
Searle, Verna. Reach for Tomorrow. (Orig.). 1980. pap. 4.95 (ISBN 0-88270-449-4). Logos.
Searle, William. The Saint & the Skeptics: Joan of Arc in the Work of Mark Twain, Anatole France, & Bernard Shaw. LC 75-26709. 178p. 1976. text ed. 12.50x (ISBN 0-8143-1541-0). Wayne St U Pr.
Searles, Baird, et al. A Reader's Guide to Science Fiction. 1979. pap. 2.95 (ISBN 0-380-46128-5, 46128). Avon.
Searles, Herbert L. Logic & Scientific Methods: An Introductory Course. 3rd ed. LC 68-13474. (Illus.). 1968. 13.95x o.p. (ISBN 0-8260-7970-9). Wiley.
Searles, Richard B. Morphological Studies of Red Algae of the Order Gigartinales. (U. C. Publ. in Botany: Vol. 43). 1968. pap. 7.50x (ISBN 0-520-09016-0). U of Cal Pr.
Searls, Courtney, tr. see Petschull, Jurgen.
Searls, Hank. Firewind. LC 80-648. 384p. 1981. 12.95 (ISBN 0-385-17084-X). Doubleday.
Sears, C., jt. auth. see Stanitski, Conrad L., Jr.
Sears, Curtis T., jt. auth. see Stanitski, Conrad L.
Sears, Curtis T., jt. auth. see Turner, A. Mason.
Sears, David O., jt. auth. see Lane, Robert E.
Sears, Donald A. John Neal. (United States Authors Ser.). 1978. lib. bdg. 12.50 (ISBN 0-8057-7230-8). Twayne.
Sears, Francis W. Electricity & Magnetism. (Illus.). 1951. 17.95 (ISBN 0-201-06900-8). A-W.
--Mechanics, Heat, & Sound. 2nd ed. (Illus.). 1950. 17.95 (ISBN 0-201-06905-9). A-W.
--Optics. 3rd ed. 1949. 17.95 (ISBN 0-201-06915-6). A-W.
Sears, Francis W. & Brehme, Robert W. Introduction to the Theory of Relativity. 1968. 16.95 (ISBN 0-201-06890-7). A-W.
Sears, Francis W. & Salinger, Gerhard L. Thermodynamics, the Kinetic Theory of Gases & Statistical Mechanics. 3rd ed. 464p. 1975. text ed. 23.95 (ISBN 0-201-06894-X). A-W.
Sears, Francis W., jt. auth. see Lee, John E.
Sears, Francis W., et al. College Physics. 5th ed. LC 79-20729. (Physics Ser.). 1980. text ed. 22.95 (ISBN 0-201-07681-0). A-W.
--University Physics, 2 pts. 5th ed. LC 75-20989. (Physics Ser.). (Illus.). 804p. 1976. Set. text ed. 24.95 (ISBN 0-201-06936-9); Pt. 1. text ed. 15.95 (ISBN 0-201-06937-7); Pt. 2. text ed. 15.95 (ISBN 0-201-06938-5). A-W.
Sears, J. Kern & Darby, Joseph R. The Technology of Plasticizers. LC 80-10225. (SPE Monographs). 1981. 75.00 (ISBN 0-471-05583-2, Pub. by Wiley-Interscience). Wiley.
Sears, Lillian, tr. see Lozano, Argentina D.
Sears, M. & Merriman, D., eds. Oceanography: The Past. (Illus.). 812p. 1980. 37.50 (ISBN 0-387-90497-2). Springer-Verlag.
Sears, M. & Warren, Bruce, eds. Progress in Oceanography, Vols. 1 & 4-6. LC 63-15353. text ed. 76.00 ea. Vol. 1 1963 (ISBN 0-08-010199-2). Vol. 4 1963 (ISBN 0-08-012124-1). Vol. 5 1968. (ISBN 0-08-012631-6). Vol. 6, 1974 (ISBN 0-08-017707-7). Pergamon.
Sears, Martin V., ed. see Carosso, Vincent P.
Sears, Mason. Years of High Purpose: From Trusteeship to Nationhood. LC 80-5161. (Illus.). 205p. 1980. text ed. 15.00 (ISBN 0-8191-1052-3); pap. text ed. 8.25 (ISBN 0-8191-1053-1). U Pr of Amer.
Sears, P. Lands Beyond the Forest. LC 68-8126. 1968. 7.95 o.p. (ISBN 0-13-522698-8). P-H.
Sears, Paul B. This Is Our World. (Illus.). 1937. 8.95x (ISBN 0-8061-0932-7); pap. 4.95x (ISBN 0-8061-0933-5). U of Okla Pr.
Sears, Pauline S., ed. Intellectual Development. new ed. LC 73-146672. (Readings in Educational Research Ser.). 1971. 10 or more copies 25.00 19.50 (ISBN 0-471-76975-4); text ed. 22.50 (ISBN 0-686-67150-3). McCutchan.
Sears, Peter. The Lady Who Got Me to Say So Long Mom. LC 78-59482. 40p. 1979. pap. 3.00 (ISBN 0-932264-21-2). Trask Hse Bks.
Sears, Richard S. V-Discs: A History & Discography. LC 80-1022. (Discographies: No. 5). (Illus.). xciii, 1166p. 1980. lib. bdg. 67.50 (ISBN 0-313-22207-X, SHD/). Greenwood.
Sears, Robert R. & Feldman, S. Shirley, eds. The Seven Ages of Man: A Survey of Human Development. LC 73-12029. 145p. 1973. 8.95 o.p. (ISBN 0-913232-07-6); pap. 5.50 (ISBN 0-913232-06-8). W Kaufmann.
Sears, Robert S. see Hetherington, E. Mavis.
Sears, Ruth M. Heir of Grangerfjord Castle. (Orig.). 1975. pap. 0.95 o.p. (ISBN 0-685-53126-0, LB273NK, Leisure Bks). Nordon Pubns.
--In the Shadow of the Tower. 1975. pap. 0.95 o.p. (ISBN 0-685-52179-6, LB251NK, Leisure Bks). Nordon Pubns.
--A Lonely Place. (Orig.). 1976. pap. 1.25 o.p. (ISBN 0-685-64013-2, LB343ZK, Leisure Bks). Nordon Pubns.
--The Solitary Heart. 192p. (YA) 1976. 4.95 o.p. (ISBN 0-685-62629-6, Avalon). Bouregy.
--Wind in the Cypress. 1975. pap. 1.25 o.p. (ISBN 0-685-57554-3, LB302ZK, Leisure Bks). Nordon Pubns.
Sears, Ruth McCarthy. Dr. Sara's Vigil. (YA) 1978. 5.95 (ISBN 0-685-84746-2, Avalon). Bouregy.
--Ordeal of Love. (YA) 1977. 5.95 (ISBN 0-685-73815-9, Avalon). Bouregy.
--Tiger by the Tail. (YA) 1978. 5.95 (ISBN 0-685-85783-2, Avalon). Bouregy.
Sears, Stephen W. The American Heritage History of the Automobile in America. LC 77-23047. (Illus.). 352p. 1977. 12.95 (ISBN 0-8281-0200-7, Dist.by Scribner); deluxe ed. 39.95 slipcased (ISBN 0-8281-0201-5, Dist. by Scribner). Am Heritage.
Sears, Stephen W. & Marshall, S. L. A. Battle of the Bulge. LC 74-78441. (American Heritage Junior Library). (Illus.). 154p. (gr. 5 up). 1969. 9.95 (ISBN 0-06-025252-9, Dist. by Har-Row); PLB 6.89 o.p. (ISBN 0-06-025253-7). Am Heritage.
Sears, William. God Loves Laughter. 1960. 7.50 o.s.i. (ISBN 0-85398-018-7, 7-31-73); pap. 3.95 (ISBN 0-85398-019-5, 7-31-74, Pub. by G Ronald England). Baha'i.
--Release the Sun. rev. ed. LC 60-8220. 1960. 10.00 (ISBN 0-87743-027-6, 7-31-27); pap. 5.00 (ISBN 0-87743-003-9, 7-31-28). Baha'i.
--Thief in the Night. 1961. 6.50 (ISBN 0-85398-096-9, 7-31-60, Pub. by George Ronald England); pap. 2.50 (ISBN 0-85398-008-X). Baha'i.
--The Wine of Astonishment. 1963. pap. 1.95 o.s.i. (ISBN 0-85398-009-8, 7-31-64, Pub. by George Ronald England). Baha'i.
Sears, William & Quigley, Robert. The Flame. 1972. 3.95 (ISBN 0-85398-031-4, 7-31-81, Pub. by G Ronald England); pap. 1.95 (ISBN 0-85398-030-6, 7-31-82, Pub. by G Ronald England). Baha'i.
Seary, Susan, jt. auth. see Seavy, Marguita.
Seashore, Carl E. In Search of Beauty in Music: A Scientific Approach to Musical Esthetics. LC 80-25447. (Illus.). xvi, 389p. 1981. Repr. of 1947 ed. lib. bdg. 29.50x (ISBN 0-313-22758-6, SEIS). Greenwood.
Seashore, Marjorie J. & Haberfeld, Steven. Prisoner Education: Project Newgate & Other College Programs. LC 75-23991. (Special Studies). (Illus.). 1976. 23.95 o.p. (ISBN 0-275-56040-6). Praeger.
Seasoltz, R. Kevin. New Liturgy, New Laws. 1980. pap. 7.95 (ISBN 0-8146-1077-3). Liturgical Pr.
Seaton, Albert. Stalin As Warlord. 1976. 27.00 (ISBN 0-7134-3078-8, Pub. by Batsford England). David & Charles.
Seaton, Bruce. Study Guide for Modern Marketing. 1978. pap. 4.95x (ISBN 0-673-15128-X). Scott F.
Seaton, Donald C., et al. Physical Education Handbook. 6th ed. (Illus.). 438p. 1974. text ed. 17.95 (ISBN 0-13-667501-8); pap. text ed. 11.95 (ISBN 0-13-667493-3). P-H.
Seaton, Douglas P. Catholics & Radicals: The Association of Catholic Trade Unionists & the American Labor Movement, from Depression to Cold War. 300p. 1981. 18.50 (ISBN 0-8387-2193-1). Bucknell U Pr.
Seaton, Jack. The Five Points of Calvinism. 1979. pap. 0.95. Banner of Truth.
Seaton, Paul & Emery, David. Waterskiing. 1979. 10.95 (ISBN 0-571-11325-7, Pub. by Faber & Faber); pap. 6.95 (ISBN 0-571-11222-6). Merrimack Bk Serv.
Seaton, S. L. Sun Sight Sailing. 1980. 9.95 (ISBN 0-679-51363-9). McKay.
Seattle City Light. Power Generation Alternatives. 2nd ed. (Illus.). 180p. 1974. pap. 5.00 o.p. (ISBN 0-686-05739-2). Cone-Heiden.
Seaver, David-Linn. Mini-Bike Racing. LC 76-38615. (Speed Sports Ser.). (Illus.). (gr. 9 up). 1972. 6.50 o.p. (ISBN 0-397-31293-8). Lippincott.
Seaver, G. Edward Wilson of the Antarctic. 14.50 (ISBN 0-685-91531-X). Transatlantic.
Seaver, James E. A Narrative of the Life of Mrs. Mary Jamison Who Was Taken by the Indians in the Year 1755 When Only About 12 Years of Age & Has Continued to Reside Amongst Them to the Present Time, Repr. Of 1824 Ed. Bd. with enl. ed. Morgan, Lewis H., ed. Repr. of 1856 ed. LC 75-7063. (Indian Captivities Ser.: Vol. 41). 1977. lib. bdg. 44.00 (ISBN 0-8240-1665-3). Garland Pub.
Seaver, Jeannette, tr. see Petitjean, Pierre.
Seaver, Richard, ed. see Sade, Marquis De.
Seaver, Richard, tr. see Ionesco, Eugene.
Seaver, Richard, tr. see Petitjean, Pierre.
Seaver, Richard, tr. see Semprun, J.
Seaver, Tom, jt. auth. see Drucker, Malka.
Seavey, George L. Rhode Island's Coastal Natural Areas: Priorities for Protection & Management. (Marine Technical Report Ser.: No. 43). 1975. pap. 2.00 (ISBN 0-938412-13-2). URI MAS.
Seavey, George R. & Pratt, S. D. Disposal of Dredged Material in Rhode Island: An Evaluation of Past Practices & Future Options. (Marine Technical Report Ser.: No. 72). write for info. (ISBN 0-938412-06-X). URI MAS.
Seavy, Marguita & Seary, Susan. The Kindling of the Flame. (gr. 6 up). 1980. PLB 8.90 (ISBN 0-531-04161-1, E32). Watts.
Seaward, Eileen, jt. auth. see Ardiff, Martha B.
Seawell, L. Vann. Hospital Financial Accounting Theory & Practice. LC 74-27241. (Illus.). 569p. 1975. text ed. 19.95x (ISBN 0-930228-00-6, 1454); instr's manual 39.90. Hospital Finan.
--Introduction to Hospital Accounting. rev. ed. LC 77-74543. (Illus.). 508p. 1977. text ed. 14.95x (ISBN 0-930228-05-7); Practice Set (1978) 7.00 (ISBN 0-930228-08-1); Solutions Manual (1977) 29.90 (ISBN 0-930228-06-5). Hospital Finan.
Seay, Albert. Music in the Medieval World. 2nd ed. (Illus.). 202p. 1975. 12.95 (ISBN 0-13-608133-9); pap. text ed. 10.95 (ISBN 0-13-608125-8). P-H.
Seay, Bill M. & Gottfried, Nathan. The Development of Behavior: A Synthesis of Developmental & Comparative Psychology. LC 78-50639. (Illus.). 1978. text ed. 19.95 (ISBN 0-395-24747-0); inst. manual 0.65 (ISBN 0-395-24746-2). HM.

Seay, David R., jt. auth. see Bell, Gary.
Seay, Davin R., jt. auth. see Bell, Gary.
Seay, Earl. Small Airports - Managers Handbook. (Aviation Maagement Ser.). 1980. write for info. (ISBN 0-89100-140-9). Aviation Maintenance.
Seay, James. Let Not Your Hart. LC 71-105509. (Wesleyan Poetry Program: Vol. 50). 1970. 10.00x (ISBN 0-8195-2050-0, Pub. by Wesleyan U Pr); pap. 4.95x (ISBN 0-8195-1050-5). Columbia U Pr.
--Water Tables. LC 73-15014. (Wesleyan Poetry Program: Vol. 72). 72p. 1974. pap. 4.95 (ISBN 0-8195-1072-6, Pub. by Wesleyan U Pr). Columbia U Pr.
Sebald, Hans. Adolescence: A Social Psychological Analysis. 2nd ed. 1977. pap. text ed. 15.95 (ISBN 0-13-008599-5). P-H.
--Momism: The Silent Disease of America. LC 75-45223. 386p. 1976. 14.95 (ISBN 0-88229-275-7). Nelson-Hall.
Sebald, William J., tr. Selection of Japan's Emergency Legislation. (Studies in Japanese Law & Government). 177p. 1979. Repr. of 1937 ed. 16.00 (ISBN 0-89093-219-0). U Pubns Amer.
Sebaly, Kim, jt. auth. see Poffenberger, Thomas.
SeBastian, Margaret. Bow Street Brangle. 1977. pap. 1.50 (ISBN 0-445-04040-8). Popular Lib.
--Dilemma in Duet. (Regency Love Story). 1979. pap. 1.75 (ISBN 0-449-50003-9, Coventry). Fawcett.
--Lord Orlando's Protegee. 224p. 1981. pap. 1.95 (ISBN 0-515-05810-6). Jove Pubns.
--Meg Miller. 208p. 1981. pap. 1.95 (ISBN 0-515-05811-4). Jove Pubns.
--Meg Miller. large type ed. pap. 1.50 o.p. (ISBN 0-425-03191-8). Berkley Pub.
--The Plight of Pamela Pollworth. 224p. (Orig.). 1980. pap. 1.75 (ISBN 0-449-50119-1, Coventry). Fawcett.
Sebba, Helen, tr. see Frenz, Horst.
Sebba, Helen, tr. see Ryssel, Fritz H.
Sebba, Leslie, jt. auth. see Landau, Simha F.
Sebek, O. K. & Laskin, A. I., eds. Genetics of Industrial Microorganisms. (Illus.). 1979. 12.00 (ISBN 0-914826-19-0). Am Soc Microbio.
Sebeok, Thomas A. Cheremis Literary Reader: With Glossary. (Indiana University Uralic & Altaic Ser.: Vol. 132). 120p. 1978. 17.00 (ISBN 2-8017-0096-7). Ind U Res Inst.
--Sight, Sound, & Sense. LC 77-21520. (Advances in Semiotics Ser.). 320p. 1978. 17.50x (ISBN 0-253-35230-4). Ind U Pr.
--Spoken Finnish. Incl. Book, Units 1-30. xv, 487p. pap. 15.00x (ISBN 0-87950-070-0); Records, Three 12-Inch LP (33.3 rpm) o.p. (ISBN 0-87950-073-5); Record Course-Book & Records. o.p. (ISBN 0-87950-074-3); Cassettes, Three Dual Track. 40.00x (ISBN 0-87950-075-1); Cassette Course-Book & Cassettes. 45.00x (ISBN 0-87950-076-X). LC 74-164345. (Spoken Language Ser.). (Prog. Bk.). 1977. Spoken Lang Serv.
Sebeok, Thomas A. & Umiker-Sebeok, Jean. You Know My Method: A Juxtaposition of Charles S. Peirce & Sherlock Holmes. LC 79-55658. (Sherlock Holmes Monograph Ser.). (Illus.). 86p. 1980. 8.95x (ISBN 0-934468-01-X). Gaslight.
Sebeok, Thomas A., ed. Native Languages of the Americas, 2 vols. Incl. Vol. 1. 630p. 1976. 47.50 (ISBN 0-306-37157-X); Vol. 2. 535p. 1977. 47.50 (ISBN 0-306-37158-8). LC 76-28216 (Plenum Pr). Plenum Pub.
--Perfusion of Signs. LC 76-29318. (Advance in Semiotics Ser.). 224p. 1977. 15.00x (ISBN 0-253-34352-6). Ind U Pr.
Sebeok, Thomas A. & Umiker-Sebeok, D. J., eds. Speaking of Apes: A Critical Anthology of Two-Way Communication with Man. (Illus.). 500p. 1980. 37.50 (ISBN 0-306-40279-3, Plenum Pr). Plenum Pub.
Seber, G. A. The Linear Hypothesis: A General Theory. 2nd ed. LC 79-67711. (Griffin's Statistical Monographs & Courses: No. 19). 1981. 21.50 (ISBN 0-02-852000-9). Macmillan.
Seber, George A. Estimation of Animal Abundance. 2nd ed. 1981. 55.00 (ISBN 0-02-852010-6). Macmillan.
Sebert, L. M., jt. auth. see Nicholson, N. L.
Sebestyen, Gyula. Lightweight Building Construction. LC 77-21902. 1978. 47.95 (ISBN 0-470-99166-6). Halsted Pr.
Sebestyen, Ouida. Far from Home. 192p. (gr. 7 up). 1980. 8.95g (ISBN 0-316-77932-6, Pub. by Atlantic-Little Brown). Little.
Sebold, F. D., jt. auth. see Venieris, Y. P.
Sebolt, Don R. & McCubbin, William E. Scientific Bowling. rev. ed. (Illus.). 1976. pap. text ed. 2.95 o.p. (ISBN 0-8403-0685-7). Kendall-Hunt.
Sebranek, Patrick & Meyer, Verne. Basic English Revisited: A Student Handbook. 4th ed. (Illus.). (gr. 7-12). 1980. pap. text ed. 3.00 (ISBN 0-686-27693-0). Basic Eng Rev.
Sebree, Mac, ed. see Carlson, Steve & Schneider, Fred W.
Sebree, Mac, ed. see Chandler, Allison.
Sebree, Mac, ed. see Ford, Robert S.
Sebree, Mac, ed. see Forty, Ralph.
Sebree, Mac, ed. see Hamm, Edward, Jr.
Sebree, Mac, ed. see Keilty, Ed.
Sebree, Mac, ed. see Schultz, Russell E.
Sebree, Mac, ed. see Swett, Ira L.
Sebrell, W. H., Jr. & Harris, Robert S., eds. The Vitamins: Chemistry, Physiology, Pathology, Methods. Incl. Vol. 1. 2nd ed. 1967. 55.25 (ISBN 0-12-633761-6); Vol. 2. 1968. 52.25 (ISBN 0-12-633762-4); Vol. 3. 1971. 62.50 (ISBN 0-12-633763-2); Vol. 5. 1972. 48.50 (ISBN 0-12-633765-9); Vols. 6-7. Gyorgy, Paul & Pearson, W. N., eds. 1968. Vol. 6. 36.00 (ISBN 0-12-633706-3); Vol. 7. 37.50 (ISBN 0-12-633707-1). Acad Pr.
Sebrell, William H., Jr., jt. auth. see Haggerty, James J.
Secchi, Nicolo. Self-Interest (L'Interesse) Kaufman, Helen A., ed. Reymes, William, tr. LC 53-13162. (Illus.). 136p. 1953. pap. 4.00 (ISBN 0-295-73930-4). U of Wash Pr.
Secher, Bjorn. Your Appointment with Success. rev. ed. LC 75-135747. 1980. pap. 4.95 (ISBN 0-8119-0354-0). Fell.
Sechler, E. E. & Fung, Y. C., eds. Thin Shell Structures: Theory, Experiment & Design. ref. ed. 1974. 34.95 (ISBN 0-13-918193-8). P-H.
Sechrest, Lee, et al, eds. Evaluation Studies Review Annual, Vol. 4. rev. ed. LC 76-15865. (Illus.). 766p. 1979. 35.00 (ISBN 0-8039-1329-X). Sage.
Sechrist, Edward L. Amateur Beekeeping. LC 55-11865. (Illus.). 148p. 1981. pap. 4.95 (ISBN 0-8159-5001-2). Devin.
Sechrist, Elsie. Dreams Your Magic Mirror: With Interpretations of Edgar Cayce. 256p. 1974. pap. 2.25 (ISBN 0-446-92688-4, 9508-3). Warner Bks.
--Meditation - Gateway to Light. rev. ed. 53p. 1972. pap. 1.95 (ISBN 0-87604-062-8). ARE Pr.
--Meditation: Der Weg Zum Licht. Kronberger, Helge F., tr. from Eng. (Illus.). 53p. (Ger.). 1980. pap. 6.00 (ISBN 0-87604-131-4). ARE Pr.
Seckel, Edward. Stability & Control of Airplanes & Helicopters. 1964. text ed. 23.95 (ISBN 0-12-634450-7). Acad Pr.
Seckler, David, ed. California Water: A Study in Resource Management. LC 76-139773. 1971. 35.00x (ISBN 0-520-01884-2); pap. 7.95 o.p. (ISBN 0-520-02778-7). U of Cal Pr.
Secombe, Harry. Goon for Lunch. LC 75-24747. 1976. 7.95 o.p. (ISBN 0-312-34020-6). St Martin.
Second Conference, 1962 see Conferences on Brain & Behavior, los Angeles.
Second Cranfield Fluidics Conference. Proceedings. 1967. text ed. 39.00 (ISBN 0-685-85166-4, Dist. by Air Science Co.). BHRA Fluid.
Second European Conference on Mixing. Proceedings. Stephens, H. S. & Clarke, J. A., eds. 1978. pap. 68.00 (ISBN 0-900983-69-8, Dist. by Air Science Co.). BHRA Fluid.
Second Fluid Power Symposium. Proceedings. 1971. text ed. 47.00 (ISBN 0-900983-11-6, Dist. by Air Science Co.). BHRA Fluid.
Second International Conference on Dredging Technology. Proceedings, 2 vols. Stephens, H. S., ed. 1979. Set. pap. 71.00 (ISBN 0-900983-76-0, Dist. by Air Science Co). BHRA Fluid.
Second International Conference on Drag Reduction. Proceedings. pap. 60.00 (ISBN 0-900983-71-X, Dist. by Air Science Co.). BHRA Fluid.
Second International Conference on Pressure Surges. Proceedings. 1977. text ed. 65.00 (ISBN 0-900983-65-5, Dist. by Air Science Co.). BHRA Fluid.
Second International Conference on the Internal & External Protection of Pipes. Proceedings. Stephens, H. S. & Clarke, Jenny, eds. 1978. pap. 68.00 (ISBN 0-900983-73-6, Dist. by Air Science Co.). BHRA Fluid.
Second International Symposium on the Aerodynamics & Ventilation of Vehicle Tunnels. Proceedings. 1977. text ed. 68.00 (ISBN 0-900983-51-5, Dist. by Air Science Co.). BHRA Fluid.
Second International Symposium on Wind Energy Systems. Proceedings, 2 vols. Stephens, H. S. & Fantom, I., eds. (Illus.). 1979. Set. pap. text ed. 78.00 (ISBN 0-906085-03-9, Dist. by Air Science Co.). BHRA Fluid.
Secor, R. J. Mexico's Volcanoes: A Climbing Guide. (Illus.). 96p. (Orig.). 1981. pap. 6.95 (ISBN 0-89886-016-4). Mountaineers.
Secord, Paul F., jt. auth. see Harre, R.
Secrest, Meryle. Being Bernard Berenson. (Illus.). 1980. pap. 7.95 (ISBN 0-14-005697-1). Penguin.
Secrest, William, ed. I Buried Hickok, the Memoirs of White Eye Anderson. LC 80-65455. 300p. 1980. 17.50 (ISBN 0-932702-07-4); collector's edition 75.00 (ISBN 0-932702-08-2). Creative Texas.
Secretariat for Futures Studies, Stockholm. Energy & Society: The Solar Nuclear Alternative. 1980. 40.00 (ISBN 0-08-024758-X); pap. 18.00 (ISBN 0-08-024759-8). Pergamon.
Secretariat for Futures Studies, Stockholm, Sweden. Sweden in World Society: Thoughts About the Future. LC 80-40321. (Illus.). 228p. 1980. 33.00 (ISBN 0-08-025456-X); pap. 16.25 (ISBN 0-08-025455-1). Pergamon.
Security Through Science & Engineering, Nineteen Eighty International Conference, September 23-26, 1980. Proceedings. 1980. 33.50 (ISBN 0-89779-042-1). U of Ky OES Pubns.
Seda, Eduardo. Social Change & Personality in a Puerto Rican Agrarian Reform Community. LC 72-76262. 216p. 1973. text ed. 10.95x o.s.i. (ISBN 0-8101-0394-X). Northwestern U Pr.
Sedano, H. O., et al. Oral Manifestations of Inherited Disorders. 1977. 22.95 (ISBN 0-409-95050-5). Butterworths.
Sedano, Heddie O., jt. auth. see Young, William G.
Sedding, John. Art & Handicraft. Stansky, Peter & Shewan, Rodney, eds. LC 76-17777. (Aesthetic Movement & the Arts & Crafts Movement Ser.). 1977. Repr. of 1893 ed. lib. bdg. 44.00x (ISBN 0-8240-2482-6). Garland Pub.
Seddon, Edmund. Modern Economic History. (Illus.). 384p. 1979. pap. text ed. 11.95x (ISBN 0-7121-1286-3, Pub. by Macdonald & Evans England). Intl Ideas.
Seddon, George & Burrow, Jackie. The Natural Food Book. LC 77-77527. (Illus.). 1977. 14.95 o.s.i. (ISBN 0-528-81002-2). Rand.
Sedeen, Magaret, jt. auth. see Gallant, Roy A.
Sederberg, Arelo. The Power Players. 480p. 1981. pap. 2.75 (ISBN 0-553-14141-4). Bantam.
Sederberg, Peter C., jt. ed. see Rosenbaum, H. Jon.
Sedgewick, Robert. Quicksort. LC 79-50821. (Outstanding Dissertations in the Computer Sciences Ser.: Vol. 18). 350p. 1980. lib. bdg. 32.00 (ISBN 0-8240-4417-7). Garland Pub.
Sedgwick, Adam. Discourse on the Studies of the University. (Victorian Library). 1969. Repr. of 1833 ed. text ed. 8.00x (ISBN 0-7185-5004-8, Leicester). Humanities.
Sedgwick, Alexander. Third French Republic, 1870-1914. LC 68-13384. (AHM Europe Since 1500 Ser. 4). (Orig.). 1969. pap. 5.95x (ISBN 0-88295-763-5). AHM Pub.
Sedgwick, Cornelius E. & Cady, Blake. Surgery of the Thyroid & Parathyroid Glands. 2nd ed. (Major Problems in Clinical Surgery Ser.: No. XV). (Illus.). 200p. 1980. text ed. 21.50 (ISBN 0-7216-8054-2). Saunders.
Sedgwick, Ellery. Thomas Paine. 150p. 1980. Repr. of 1899 ed. lib. bdg. 20.00 (ISBN 0-8482-6306-5). Norwood Edns.
Sedgwick, Eve K. The Coherence of Gothic Conventions. Varma, Devendra P., ed. LC 79-8462. (Gothic Studies & Dissertations Ser.). 1980. lib. bdg. 17.00x (ISBN 0-405-12650-6). Arno.
Sedgwick, Jeffery L. Deterring Criminals: Policy Making & the American Political Tradition. 1980. pap. 4.25 (ISBN 0-8447-3385-7). Am Enterprise.
Sedgwick, Joan, jt. auth. see Mitchell, Marge.
Sedgwick, John P. Rhythms of Western Art. LC 73-170648. (Illus.). 1972. 14.50 (ISBN 0-8108-0449-2). Scarecrow.
Sedgwick, John P., Jr. Art Appreciation Made Simple. pap. 3.95 (ISBN 0-385-01222-5, Made). Doubleday.
Sedgwick, Michael. The Motor Car, Nineteen Forty-Six to Fifty-Six. (Illus.). 272p. 1980. 42.50 (ISBN 0-7134-1271-2, Pub. by Batsford England). David & Charles.
--Passenger Cars: 1924-42. LC 75-17949. (Illus.). 172p. 1976. 9.95 o.s.i. (ISBN 0-02-609000-7, 60900). Macmillan.
Sedgwick, Peter, tr. see Serge, Victor.
Sedgwick, Rae. Family Mental Health: Theory & Practice. LC 80-20160. (Illus.). 296p. 1980. pap. text ed. 9.95 (ISBN 0-8016-4447-X). Mosby.
Sedgwick, Robert P., et al. Cerebral Degenerations in Childhood. 1975. spiral bdg. 12.00 (ISBN 0-87488-759-3). Med Exam.
Sedgwick, Theodore. A Treatise on the Rules Which Govern the Interpretation & Construction of Statutory & Constitutional Law. 2nd ed. Pomeroy, John N., ed. xlviii, 692p. 1981. Repr. of 1874 ed. lib. bdg. 49.50x (ISBN 0-8377-1115-0). Rothman.
Sedivec, V. & Flek, J. The Handbook of Analysis of Organic Solvents. Sommernitz, Harry, tr. LC 75-44239. (Ser. in Analytical Chemistry). 1976. 61.95 (ISBN 0-470-15010-6). Halsted Pr.
Sedlacek, William E. & Brooks, Glenwood C., Jr. Racism in American Education: A Model for Change. LC 76-6909. 236p. 1976. 17.95 (ISBN 0-88229-136-X); pap. 8.95 (ISBN 0-88229-585-3). Nelson-Hall.
Sedlak, Michael W., jt. ed. see Walch, Timothy.
Sedlar, Jean W. India & the Greek World: A Study in the Transmission of Culture. (Illus.). 381p. 1980. 30.00x (ISBN 0-8476-6173-3). Rowman.
Sedley, Dorothy. College Writer's Workbook. 240p. 1981. pap. text ed. 7.95 (ISBN 0-675-08022-3); instr's. manual 3.95 (ISBN 0-686-69486-4). Merrill.
Sedley, Dorothy, jt. auth. see Bramer, George R.
Sedore, Marva J. To Walk & Not Faint. LC 80-65433. 160p. (Orig.). 1980. pap. 5.95 (ISBN 0-915684-65-9). Christian Herald.
Sedore, Stephen, jt. auth. see Bowers, James C.
Sedunov, Yu. S. Physics of Drop Formation in the Atmosphere. Greenberg, P., ed. Lederman, D., tr. from Rus. LC 74-8198. 234p. 1974. 29.95 (ISBN 0-470-77111-9). Halsted Pr.
Sedvall, G., et al, eds. Antipsychotic Drugs: Pharmacodynamics & Pharmacokinetics. 286p. 1976. text ed. 64.00 (ISBN 0-08-019688-8). Pergamon.
Sedway-Cooke. Land & the Environment: Planning in California Today. Planning & Conservation Foundation, ed. LC 75-19409. 160p. 1975. pap. 14.95 o.p. (ISBN 0-913232-21-1). W Kaufmann.
Sedwick, jt. auth. see Gallo.
Sedwick, jt. auth. see Paolozzi.
Sedwick, Frank. Conversation in Spanish: Points of Departure. 3rd ed. (Orig.). 1981. pap. text ed. write for info. (ISBN 0-442-24467-3). D Van Nostrand.
--Spanish for Careers: Conversational Perspectives. (Orig.). 1980. pap. text ed. 8.95 (ISBN 0-442-20562-7). D Van Nostrand.
Sedwick, Frank, jt. auth. see Bonnell, Peter.
Sedwick, Frank, jt. auth. see Dobson, Julia M.
Sedwick, Robert C. Interaction: Interpersonal Relationships in Organizations. (Illus.). 240p. 1974. pap. 9.95 (ISBN 0-13-469155-5). P-H.
See, Henri E. Les Classes Rurales et le Regime Domanial En France Au Moyen Age. LC 80-2003. 1981. Repr. of 1901 ed. 61.50 (ISBN 0-404-18594-0). AMS Pr.
Seebeck, jt. auth. see Hummel.
Seeber, S., et al, eds. Cisplatin Derzeitiger Stand und Neue Entwicklungen in der Chemotherapie Maligner Neoplasien. (Beitraege zur Onkologie: Band 3). (Illus.). 184p. 1980. pap. 21.00 (ISBN 3-8055-1364-X). S Karger.
Seebold, Herman. Old Louisiana Plantation Homes & Family Trees, Vol. 1. (Illus.). 1971. Repr. of 1941 ed. 30.00 (ISBN 0-911116-34-6). Pelican.
Seed, Alice, compiled by. Toothed Whales: In Eastern North Pacific & Arctic Waters. 2nd ed. LC 70-173350. (Sea Mammal Ser.). (Illus.). 40p. (Orig.). 1971. pap. 1.75 o.p. (ISBN 0-914718-00-2). Pacific Search.
Seed, David. Stream Runner. LC 78-21769. 192p. (gr. 5 up). 1979. 7.95 (ISBN 0-590-07568-3, Four Winds). Schol Bk Serv.
Seed, M. L., jt. auth. see Hodge, S. E.
Seedor, Marie M. Aids to Nursing Diagnosis. 3rd ed. (Nursing Education Monograph: No. 6). 1980. pap. 8.95 (ISBN 0-397-54120-1, Pub. by Columbia U Pr). Lippincott.
--Aids to Nursing Diagnosis: A Programmed Unit in Fundamentals of Nursing. 3rd ed. 378p. (Orig.). 1980. pap. text ed. 8.50 (ISBN 0-8077-2630-3). Tchrs Coll.
--Aids to Nursing Judgement: A Programed Unit in Fundamentals of Nursing. LC 76-189024. 401p. 1972. pap. text ed. 8.00x (ISBN 0-8077-2126-3). Tchrs Coll.
--Aids to Nursing Judgment. 2nd ed. (Nursing Education Monograph Ser, No. 6). 1972. pap. 7.25 o.p. (ISBN 0-397-54120-1, Pub. by Columbia U Pr). Lippincott.
--Body Mechanics & Patient Positioning: A Programmed Unit of Study for Nurses. LC 73-85804. 1977. pap. 8.75x (ISBN 0-8077-2524-2). Tchrs Coll.
--Introduction to Asepsis: A Programmed Unit in Fundamentals of Nursing. 2nd ed. (Nursing Education Monograph Ser No. 3). 1969. pap. 5.95 o.p. (ISBN 0-397-54095-7, Pub. by Columbia U Pr). Lippincott.
--A Nursing Guide to Oxygen Therapy: Unit in Fundamentals of Nursing. 3rd rev. ed. (Nursing Education Monograph: No. 10). (Illus.). 1980. pap. 8.50 (Pub. by Columbia U Pr). Lippincott.
--The Physical Assessment: A Programmed Unit in the Fundamantals of Nursing. LC 73-85804. (Illus.). 301p. 1974. pap. text ed. 7.50x (ISBN 0-8077-2424-6). Tchrs Coll.
--Therapy with Oxygen & Other Gases: A Programed Unit in Fundamentals. rev. ed. LC 66-25981. (Orig.). 1971. pap. 8.00x (ISBN 0-8077-2136-0). Tchrs Coll.
Seedor, Marie M., ed. The Nursing Process: Proceedings. LC 73-85353. 51p. 1973. pap. text ed. 3.50x (ISBN 0-8077-2405-X). Tchrs Coll.
Seeds, Harice L. Programming RPG II. LC 79-127669. 1971. pap. 17.50 (ISBN 0-471-77113-9). Wiley.

--Structured Fortran Seventy-Seven for Business & General Applications. 496p. 1981. text ed. 15.95 (ISBN 0-471-07836-0). Wiley.

Seefeldt, Carol. A Curriculum for Preschools. 2nd ed. (Early Childhood Education Ser.: No. C24). 368p. 1980. text ed. 14.95 (ISBN 0-675-08137-8); instructor's manual 3.95 (ISBN 0-686-63183-8). Merrill.

--Social Studies for the Preschool-Primary Child. (Elementary Education Ser.). (Illus.). 1977. pap. text ed. 12.95 (ISBN 0-675-08593-4). Merrill.

Seefeldt, Carol, ed. Curriculum for the Preschool-Primary Child: A Review of the Research. new ed. (Elementary Education Ser.). 352p. 1976. text ed. 15.95x (ISBN 0-675-08678-7). Merrill.

Seeger, C. Ronald. Problems for Exploration Geophysics. LC 78-62263. 1978. pap. text ed. 4.25 (ISBN 0-8191-0573-2). U Pr of Amer.

Seeger, Charles. Studies in Musicology, 1935-1975. LC 76-19668. 1977. 25.95x (ISBN 0-520-02000-6). U of Cal Pr.

Seeger, Charles, jt. auth. see Seeger, Pete.

Seeger, Francis M. Until My Last Breath. 1981. 5.95 (ISBN 0-932194-06-0). Green Hill.

Seeger, Peggy, jt. auth. see MacColl, Ewan.

Seeger, Pete & Seeger, Charles. The Foolish Frog. LC 73-2121. (Illus.). 40p. (gr. k-3). 1973. 7.95 (ISBN 0-02-781480-7). Macmillan.

Seeger, Raymond J. Benjamin Franklin. LC 73-7981. 200p. 1973. 16.50 (ISBN 0-08-017648-8). Pergamon.

--Galileo Galilei, His Life & Work. (Men of Physics Ser.). 1966. 16.50 (ISBN 0-08-012025-3); pap. 7.75 (ISBN 0-08-012024-5). Pergamon.

--Josiah Willard Gibbs-American Physicist Par Excellance. (Men of Physics Ser.). 1975. 34.00 (ISBN 0-08-018013-2). Pergamon.

Seeger, W. Microsurgery of the Brain, 2 vols. (Illus.). 750p. 1980. Set. 215.00 (ISBN 0-387-81573-2). Springer-Verlag.

Seeland, Irene & Kutscher, A. H. Hospital House Staff & Thanatology. (Thanatology Service Ser.). 125p. 1980. pap. 6.95 o.p. (ISBN 0-686-64836-6). Highly Specialized.

See-Lasley, Kay & Ignoffo, Robert. Manual of Oncology Therapeutics. 300p. 1981. pap. text ed. 19.95 (ISBN 0-8016-4448-8). Mosby.

Seele, Keith C., ed. see Schultz, James W.

Seeley, David. Mediating Structures & Education. 300p. Date not set. 16.50 (ISBN 0-88410-825-2). Ballinger Pub. Postponed.

Seeley, Harry W., Jr. & Van Demark, Paul J. Microbes in Action: A Laboratory Manual of Microbiology. 2nd ed. (Illus.). 1972. lab manual 9.95x (ISBN 0-7167-0689-X); tchr's manual avail. W H Freeman.

Seeley, Harry W., Jr. & VanDemark, Paul J. Microbes in Action: A Laboratory Manual of Microbiology. 3rd ed. (Illus.). 1981. write for info. (ISBN 0-7167-1259-8); instrs'. manual avail. W H Freeman.

Seeley, Harry W., Jr. & Van Demark, Paul J. Selected Exercises from Microbes in Action: A Laboratory Manual of Microbiology. 2nd ed. (Illus.). 1972. lab manual 8.95x (ISBN 0-7167-0690-3); teacher's manual avail. W H Freeman.

Seeley, Harry W., Jr. & VanDemark, Paul J. Selected Exercises from Microbes in Action: A Laboratory Manual of Microbiology. 3rd ed. (Illus.). 1981. price not set (ISBN 0-7167-1260-1). W H Freeman.

Seeley, J. High Contrast: Creative Imagemaking for Photographers, Designers & Graphic Artists. 1980. 24.95 (ISBN 0-442-23888-6). Van Nos Reinhold.

Seeley, John R., et al. Crestwood Heights: A North American Suburb. LC 56-9099. (Illus.). 1956. pap. 7.50 (ISBN 0-8020-6021-8). U of Toronto Pr.

Seeley, Robert T. Calculus of One & Several Variables. 1973. 16.95x o.p. (ISBN 0-673-07779-9). Scott F.

--Calculus of Several Variables: An Introduction. 1970. 15.95x (ISBN 0-673-07543-5). Scott F.

Seelig, Michael. The Architecture of Self-Help Communities. LC 77-15116. (Illus.). 1978. 25.00 o.p. (ISBN 0-07-056045-5, P&RB). McGraw.

Seelig, Mildred S., ed. Magnesium Deficiency in the Pathogenesis of Disease. (Topics in Bone & Mineral Disorders Ser.). 500p. 1980. 39.50 (ISBN 0-306-40202-5, Plenum Pr). Plenum Pub.

Seelig, Sharon C. The Shadow of Eternity: The Poetry of Herbert, Vaughan, & Traherne. LC 80-51018. 1981. price not set (ISBN 0-8131-1444-6). U Pr of Ky.

Seelig, Steven A., jt. auth. see Jessee, Michael A.

Seeliger, Heinz P. Listeriosis. 2nd ed. 1961. 15.50 (ISBN 0-02-852020-3). Hafner.

Seely. Elements of Thermal Technology. Date not set. price not set (ISBN 0-8247-1174-2). Dekker.

Seely, Clinton B., tr. see Bose, Buddladeva.

Seely, Rebecca, jt. auth. see Roberts, Carey.

Seely, Samuel. Introduction to Engineering Systems. 548p. 1972. text ed. 31.00 (ISBN 0-08-016821-3); pap. text ed. 15.50 (ISBN 0-08-018998-9). Pergamon.

Seelye, E. Data Book for Civil Engineers, 3 vols. Incl. Vol. 1. Design. 3rd ed. 670p. 1960. 57.95 (ISBN 0-471-77286-0); Vol. 2. Specifications & Costs. 3rd ed. 566p. 1957. 55.00 (ISBN 0-471-77319-0); Vol. 3. Field Practice. 2nd ed. 394p. 1954. 29.95 (ISBN 0-471-77352-2). LC 57-5932 (Pub. by Wiley-Interscience). Wiley.

Seeman, Ernest. American Gold. 1979. pap. 2.50 (ISBN 0-380-43679-5, 43679). Avon.

Seeman, Mark F., ed. see Prufer, Olaf.

Seemann, Caroline, tr. see Hobsley, M.

Seers, Dudley, et al, eds. Underdeveloped Europe: Studies in Core-Periphery Relations. (Harvester Studies in Development: No. 1). 1979. text ed. 30.00x (ISBN 0-391-00962-1). Humanities.

--Integration & Unequal Development. (Studies in the Integration of Western Europe). 1981. write for info. (ISBN 0-312-41890-6). St Martin.

Seerveld, C. A Christian Critique of Art & Literature. 1976. pap. 3.95 (ISBN 0-88958-004-9). Wedge Pub.

--For God's Sake Run with Joy. LC 72-81234. 1973. pap. 4.95x (ISBN 0-686-00489-2). Wedge Pub.

--Rainbows for the Fallen World. 1980. 14.95x (ISBN 0-919071-00-7); pap. 9.95x (ISBN 0-919071-01-5). Radix Bks.

Seerveld, Calvin. Balaam's Apocalyptic Prophecies: A Study in Reading Scripture. pap. 3.95 (ISBN 0-88906-110-6). Wedge Pub.

Seerveld, Calvin G. The Greatest Song: In Critique of Solomon. LC 69-27706. 1967. 12.95x (ISBN 0-686-27477-6). Radix Bks.

Seese, William S. & Daub, Grudo H. Basic Chemistry. 2nd ed. (Illus.). 1977. text ed. 18.95 (ISBN 0-13-057513-5); students guide 6.95 (ISBN 0-13-057539-9); lab. experiments 8.95 (ISBN 0-13-057547-X). P-H.

Seese, William S. & Daub, Guido H. Basic Chemistry. 3rd ed. 608p. 1981. text ed. 19.95 (ISBN 0-13-057679-4). P-H.

--In Preparation for College Chemistry. 2nd ed. (Illus.). 1980. pap. text ed. 9.95 (ISBN 0-13-453670-3). P-H.

Seethalakshami, K. A. Folk Tales of Himachal Pradesh. (Folk Tales of India Ser.: No. 8). 120p. 1972. 3.75x (ISBN 0-8002-0633-9). Intl Pubns Serv.

Seevers, James A. Space. LC 77-18976. (Read About Science Ser.). (Illus.). (gr. k-3). 1978. PLB 9.95 (ISBN 0-8393-0076-X). Raintree Child.

Seevers, James A., jt. auth. see Ciupik, Larry A.

Seferis, George. A Poet's Journal: Days of 1945-1951. Angnostopoulos, Athan, tr. from Gr. LC 73-92634. 208p. 1974. 8.95 (ISBN 0-674-68040-5, Belknap Pr); pap. 3.95 (ISBN 0-674-68041-3). Harvard U Pr.

Sefton, Frances. Complete Dog Guide. 6.98 o.p. (ISBN 0-385-01604-2). Doubleday.

--Pekingese Guide. 6.98 o.p. (ISBN 0-385-01580-1). Doubleday.

Sefton, James E. Andrew Johnson & the Uses of Constitutional Power. (Library of American Biography). 1980. 9.95 (ISBN 0-316-77990-3); pap. 4.95 (ISBN 0-316-77989-X). Little.

--The United States Army & Reconstruction, 1865-1877. LC 80-15136. (Illus.). xx, 284p. 1980. Repr. of 1967 ed. lib. bdg. 26.50x (ISBN 0-313-22602-4, SEUS). Greenwood.

Segal, Aaron, jt. auth. see Allen, Philip M.

Segal, Abraham, jt. auth. see Essrig, Harry.

Segal, Bernard, et al. Drugs, Daydreaming, & Personality: A Study of College Youth. LC 80-10094. 256p. 1980. 19.95 (ISBN 0-89859-042-6). L Erlbaum Assocs.

Segal, Brenda L. Aliya. 1979. pap. 1.95 (ISBN 0-515-04773-2). Jove Pubns.

--The Tenth Measure. 1981. pap. 3.25 (ISBN 0-425-05095-5). Berkley Pub.

Segal, Charles. Tragedy & Civilization: An Interpretation of Sophocles. LC 80-19765. (Modern Classical Lectures: No. 26). 544p. 1981. text ed. 30.00 (ISBN 0-674-90206-8). Harvard U Pr.

Segal, David. Urban Economics. 1977. 18.95x (ISBN 0-256-00547-8). Irwin.

Segal, Dimitri, jt. ed. see Jason, Heda.

Segal, E. Mathematical Cosmology & Extragalactic Astronomy. (Pure & Applied Mathematics Ser.: Vol. 68). 1976. 32.00 (ISBN 0-12-635250-X). Acad Pr.

Segal, Eric. Love Story. (Arabic.). pap. 6.95x (ISBN 0-686-63552-3). Intl Bk Ctr.

Segal, Erich. Love Story. 1977. pap. 1.75 (ISBN 0-380-01760-1, 34934). Avon.

--Man, Woman & Child. 192p. 1981. pap. 2.95 (ISBN 0-345-29318-5). Ballantine.

--Man, Woman & Child. (Large Print Bks.). 1980. lib. bdg. 10.95 (ISBN 0-8161-3124-4). G K Hall.

Segal, Erich, tr. Plautus: Three Comedies. 1969. pap. 5.95x (ISBN 0-06-131932-5, TB1932, Torch). Har-Row.

Segal, G., ed. New Development in Topology. LC 73-84323. (London Mathematical Society Lecture Notes Ser.: No. 11). 120p. 1973. 14.50 (ISBN 0-521-20354-6). Cambridge U Pr.

Segal, Herman, jt. auth. see Warner, Richard.

Segal, Jeanne S. Feeling Fine: Enhancing Your Well-Being. (Orig.). 1980. pap. 7.95 (ISBN 0-913300-51-9). Unity Pr.

Segal, Judah B. Hebrew Passover from the Earliest Times to A.D. 70. 1963. 24.95x (ISBN 0-19-713529-3). Oxford U Pr.

Segal, L., jt. auth. see Bikales, N. M.

Segal, M., jt. auth. see Danby, H.

Segal, M. H. A Grammar of Mishnaic Hebrew. 1979. pap. text ed. 12.95x (ISBN 0-19-815454-2). Oxford U Pr.

Segal, Marilyn. From Birth to One Year. LC 80-13831. (The Play & Learn Ser.: Vol. 1). (Illus.). 96p. pap. 3.95 (ISBN 0-916392-50-3). Oak Tree Pubns.

Segal, Marilyn, jt. auth. see Adcock, Don.

Segal, Nelly, tr. see Poochoo.

Segal, Patrick. The Man Who Walked in His Head. Stephens, John, tr. from Fr. LC 79-21426. 1980. Repr. 10.95 (ISBN 0-688-03529-9). Morrow.

Segal, Ryna A. New York City Department of Cultural Affairs, 1976-1973: A Record of Government's Involvement in the Arts. LC 76-22386. 88p. 1976. pap. 1.75x (ISBN 0-89062-037-7, Pub. by NYC Cultural). Pub Ctr Cult Res.

Segal, S. J. & Winikoff, B., eds. Health & Population in Developing Countries: Selected Papers from the 5th Bellagio Populaion Conference, Rockefeller Foundation, Bellagio, 1979. 100p. 1980. 20.00 (ISBN 0-08-026101-9). Pergamon.

Segal, S. S. No Child Is Ineducable. 2nd ed. LC 73-21571. 412p. 1974. text ed. 18.75 (ISBN 0-08-017815-4). Pergamon.

Segal, S. S., compiled by. Mental Handicap: A Select Annotated Bibliography. (Bibliographic Ser.). (Orig.). 1972. pap. text ed. 3.75x (ISBN 0-901225-90-8, NFER). Humanities.

Segal, Sheldon J., ed. Chorionic Gonadotropin. 485p. 1981. 42.50 (ISBN 0-306-40563-6, Plenum Pr). Plenum Pub.

Segal, Steven P. & Aviram, Uri. The Mentally Ill in Community-Based Sheltered Care: A Study of Community Care & Social Integration. (Health, Medicine & Society Ser.). 26.50 (ISBN 0-471-77400-6, Pub. by Wiley-Interscience). Wiley.

Segal, Thomas D. Men in Space. LC 75-28519. (Illus.). 225p. 1975. 19.95 (ISBN 0-87364-033-0). Paladin Ent.

Segall, Ascher, et al. Systematic Course Design for the Health Fields. LC 75-20398. 171p. 1975. 20.95 o.p. (ISBN 0-471-77410-3, Pub. by Wiley Med). Wiley.

Segall, B. Z. Electrical Code Diagrams. 7th ed. LC 61-10921. (Illus.). 1978. 55.00 (ISBN 0-930234-01-4). Peerless.

Segall, Harold F., jt. auth. see Dunbar, Robert E.

Segall, Helen, tr. see Mayakovsky, Vladimir & Brik, Lily.

Segall, M. H. Human Behavior & Public Policy - Political Psychology. 1977. 27.50 (ISBN 0-08-017087-0); pap. 12.50 (ISBN 0-08-017853-7). Pergamon.

Segall, Marshall & Ulin, Priscilla, eds. Traditional Health Care Delivery in Contemporary Africe. (Foreign & Comparative Studies - African Ser.: No. 35). 100p. 1980. pap. 8.00x (ISBN 0-915984-57-1). Syracuse U Foreign Comp.

Segall, Marshall, jt. ed. see Ulin, Priscilla.

Segall, Marshall H., et al. Influence of Culture on Visual Perception. LC 64-16721. (Illus., Orig.). 1966. pap. 6.95 (ISBN 0-672-60825-1). Bobbs.

--Political Identity: A Case Study from Uganda. LC 76-21273. (Foreign & Comparative Studies-Eastern Africa: No. 24). 179p. 1976. pap. text ed. 5.50x (ISBN 0-915984-21-0). Syracuse U Foreign Comp.

Segalman, Ralph & Basu, Asoke. Poverty in America: The Welfare Dilemma. LC 79-6568. (Contributions in Sociology: No. 39). (Illus.). 446p. 1981. lib. bdg. 35.00 (ISBN 0-313-20751-8, BPO/). Greenwood.

Segel, Harold B. Twentieth-Century Russian Drama from Gorky to the Present. LC 79-11673. (Illus.). 1979. 30.00x (ISBN 0-231-04576-X); pap. 15.00x (ISBN 0-231-04577-8). Columbia U Pr.

Segel, L. A., ed. Mathematical Models in Molecular & Cellular Biology. LC 79-52854. (Illus.). 600p. Date not set. 100.00 (ISBN 0-521-22925-1). Cambridge U Pr.

Segel, W. & Wheelis, M. Laboratory Manual to Introduction to the Microbial World. 1980. pap. 8.95 (ISBN 0-13-488031-5). P-H.

Segel, Yonny. Drafting Made Simple. LC 61-9550. pap. 3.50 (ISBN 0-385-01348-5, Made). Doubleday.

Segeler, C. George, ed. see American Gas Association.

Segelstein, Sidney, jt. auth. see Brandon, Dick H.

Seger, Gerhart H. Germany. rev. ed. LC 77-83909. (World Cultures Ser.). (Illus.). 188p. (gr. 6 up). 1978. text ed. 9.95 ea. 1-4 copies (ISBN 0-88296-180-2); text ed. 7.96 ea. 5 or more copies; tchrs'. guide 8.94 (ISBN 0-88296-369-4). Fideler.

Seger, Imogen. Sociology for the Modern Mind. (Modern Mind Ser.). 336p. 1973. 7.95 o.s.i. (ISBN 0-02-609090-2). Macmillan.

Seger, John H. Early Days Among the Cheyenne & Arapahoe Indians. Vestal, Stanley, ed. (Illus.). 1934. 8.95 (ISBN 0-8061-0344-2); pap. 4.95 (ISBN 0-8061-1533-5). U of Okla Pr.

Segerstedt, T., ed. Ethics for Science Policy: Proceedings. (Illus.). 35.00 (ISBN 0-08-024464-5); pap. 13.75 (ISBN 0-08-024463-7). Pergamon.

Segerstrom, Jane. Look Like Yourself & Love It! The 4-T Guide to Personal Style. LC 80-50836. (Illus.). 168p. (Orig.). 1980. pap. 14.95 (ISBN 0-936740-06-X). Triad Pr TX.

Segev, Eli, jt. auth. see Ein-Dor, Phillip.

Segger, S. W. Version & Themes Models. 1973. pap. text ed. 7.50x (ISBN 0-521-06276-4). Cambridge U Pr.

Segilman, E. R. The Social Evil, with Special Reference to Conditions Existing in the City of New York. Winick, Charles, ed. LC 78-60871. (Prostitution Ser.: Vol. 3). 188p. 1979. lib. bdg. 20.00 (ISBN 0-8240-9725-4). Garland Pub.

Segler, Franklin M. A Pailful of Stars. LC 75-178065. 128p. 1972. 2.95 o.p. (ISBN 0-8054-8224-5). Broadman.

--Theology of Church & Ministry. LC 60-14146. 1960. bds. 7.50 (ISBN 0-8054-2506-3). Broadman.

Seglow, Peter. Trade Unionism in Television. 1978. text ed. 23.00x (ISBN 0-566-00203-5, Pub. by Gower Pub Co England). Renouf.

Segno, A. Victor. Thought Vibrations. LC 80-23853. 208p. 1980. Repr. of 1973 ed. lib. bdg. 10.95x (ISBN 0-89370-625-6). Borgo Pr.

Segoloni, Giulio, jt. auth. see Bardeschi, Marco D.

Segonzac, Catherine de see De Segonzac, Catherine.

Segovia, Andres. Segovia: An Autobiography of the Years 1893-1920. (Illus.). 1976. 14.95 (ISBN 0-02-609080-5, 60908). Macmillan.

Segrave, Jeffrey & Chu, Donald, eds. Olympism. 1981. text ed. 17.95x (ISBN 0-931250-20-X). Human Kinetics.

Segraves, Kelly L. Pride Is for Peacocks, Young Readers Ser. (Young Readers Ser.). (Illus.). Date not set. pap. 2.95 (ISBN 0-89293-078-0). Beta Bk.

Segre, E., et al, eds. Annual Review of Nuclear Science, Vol. 22. LC 53-995. (Illus.). 1972. text ed. 19.50 (ISBN 0-8243-1522-7). Annual Reviews.

--Annual Review of Nuclear Science, Vol. 23. LC 53-995. (Illus.). 1973. text ed. 19.50 (ISBN 0-8243-1523-5). Annual Reviews.

--Annual Review of Nuclear Science, Vol. 26. LC 53-995. (Illus.). 1976. text ed. 19.50 (ISBN 0-8243-1526-X). Annual Reviews.

Segre, Emilio. From X-Rays to Quarks: Modern Physicists & Their Discoveries. LC 80-466. (Illus.). 1980. text ed. 21.95x (ISBN 0-7167-1146-X); pap. text ed. 10.95x (ISBN 0-7167-1147-8). W H Freeman.

Segre, Emilio, et al, eds. Annual Review of Nuclear Science, Vol. 25. LC 53-995. (Illus.). 1975. text ed. 19.50 (ISBN 0-8243-1525-1). Annual Reviews.

--Annual Review of Nuclear Science, Vol. 27. LC 53-995. (Illus.). 1977. text ed. 19.50 (ISBN 0-8243-1527-8). Annual Reviews.

Segre, Roberto & Katz, Fernando K., eds. Latin America in Its Architecture. Grossman, Edith, tr. from Span. LC 79-27695. (Latin America in Its Culture). Orig. Title: America Latina En Su Cultura. 300p. 1980. text ed. 25.00x (ISBN 0-8419-0532-0). Holmes & Meier.

Segreti, Mario M., jt. auth. see Simi, Gino J.

Seguin, Hubert, jt. auth. see Charbonneau, Gerard.

Segur, Comtesse de see De Segur, Comtesse.

Seguy, E. A. Seguy's Decorative Butterflies & Insects in Full Color. LC 77-83361. (Illus., Orig.). 1977. pap. 6.00 (ISBN 0-486-23552-1). Dover.

Segy, Ladislas. Masks of Black Africa. 11.50 (ISBN 0-8446-5455-8). Peter Smith.

Sehested, Ove H. The Basics of Astrology, 3 vols. LC 73-90440. 1973. Set. 3 vols. bound in 1 14.95 (ISBN 0-9601080-4-1). Vol. 1. pap. 4.95 (ISBN 0-9601080-1-7); Vol. 2. pap. 4.95 (ISBN 0-9601080-2-5); Vol. 3. pap. 3.95 (ISBN 0-9601080-3-3). Uranus Pub.

Sehgal, Lalit. The Verdict. Kohli, Suresh, tr. (Translated from Hindi). 8.00 (ISBN 0-89253-656-X); flexible cloth 3.00 (ISBN 0-89253-657-8). Ind-US Inc.

Sehgal, V. N. Clinical Leprosy. (Illus.). 1980. text ed. 13.50x (ISBN 0-7069-0785-X, Pub. by Vikas India). Advent Bk.

--A Textbook of Venereal Diseases. (Illus.). 1979. text ed. 15.00x (ISBN 0-7069-0639-X, Pub. by Vikas India). Advent Bk.

Sehlin, Gunhild. Mary's Little Donkey. (Illus.). 1979. 7.95 (ISBN 0-903540-29-0, Pub. by Floris Books). St George Bk Serv.

Sehlinger, Bob & Underwood, Wes. A Guide to the Float Fishing Streams of Kentucky. (Illus., Orig.). 1980. pap. 9.95 (ISBN 0-89732-006-9). Thomas Pr.

Seib, Philip M., jt. auth. see Brown, James.

Seibel, H. Dieter. The Dynamics of Achievement: A Radical Perspective. LC 73-13502. (Studies in Sociology Ser). 1974. pap. text ed. 2.50 (ISBN 0-672-61335-2). Bobbs.

Seibel, Hugo & Guyer, Kenneth E. Barron's How to Prepare for the New Medical College Admission Test (MCAT) LC 80-15470. 1981. pap. text ed. 6.50 (ISBN 0-8120-2190-8). Barron.

--Barron's How to Prepare for the New Medical College Admission Test MCAT. LC 77-24613. 1977. pap. text ed. 6.50 o.p. (ISBN 0-8120-0821-9). Barron.

Seiber, Marilyn J., jt. auth. see Franko, Lawrence G.

Seibert, Helen K., ed. see Hershey, Ronald A.

Seibert, J. J., jt. auth. see Ferris, Ernest J.

Seibert, Joseph C. Concepts of Marketing Management. Sheth, Jagdish, ed. (Marketing Management Ser). (Illus.). 1973. text ed. 20.50 scp o.p. (ISBN 0-06-045878-X, HarpC); tchrs' manual avail. o.p. (ISBN 0-685-02864-X); scp study guide 6.50 o.p. (ISBN 0-06-044015-5). Har-Row.

Seibert, Louise C. & Crocker, Lester G., eds. Le Fils Du Fauconnier. (Fr.). 1963. pap. text ed. 6.95x (ISBN 0-684-41431-7, ScribC). Scribner.

--Histoire D'une Revanche. (Orig., Fr.). 1963. pap. text ed. 6.95x (ISBN 0-684-41430-9, ScribC). Scribner.

Seibert-Shook, Mavis, jt. auth. see Beveridge-Wavering, Agnes.

Seid, jt. auth. see Cotton.

Seide, Diane. Careers in Health Sciences. 160p. Date not set. 7.95 (ISBN 0-525-66679-6). Elsevier-Nelson. Postponed.

Seide, Diane, jt. auth. see Traynor, Mark.

Seidel, Alison P., compiled by. Literary Criticism & Authors' Biographies: An Annotated Index. LC 78-11857. 1978. 11.00 (ISBN 0-8108-1172-3). Scarecrow.

Seidel, Anna, jt. ed. see Welch, Holmes.

Seidel, Beverly L. & Resnick, Matthew C. Physical Education: An Overview. 2nd ed. LC 77-79453. (Physical Education Ser.). (Illus.). 1978. text ed. 13.50 (ISBN 0-201-06988-1). A-W.

Seidel, George. Being, Nothing & God. 1970. text ed. 15.00x (ISBN 90-232-0061-6). Humanities.

Seidel, Linda. Romanesque Sculpture from the Cathedral of Saint-Etienne, Toulouse. LC 76-23646. (Outstanding Dissertations in the Fine Arts). (Illus.). 1977. Repr. of 1965 ed. lib. bdg. 52.00 (ISBN 0-8240-2729-9). Garland Pub.

Seidelman, James E. & Mintonye, Grace. Rub Book. (Illus.). (gr. k-3). 1968. 3.50g o.s.i. (ISBN 0-02-781590-0, CCPr). Macmillan.

Seiden, Hank. Advertising Pure & Simple. (AMACOM Executive Bks). 1978. pap. 5.95 (ISBN 0-8144-7510-8). Am Mgmt.

Seiden, Margaret. Practical Management of Chronic Neurologic Problems. 1981. 25.00 (ISBN 0-8385-7871-3). ACC.

Seiden, Martin H. Cable Television U. S. A. An Analysis of Government Policy: An Analysis of Government Policy. LC 72-76453. (Special Studies in U. S. Economic, Social, & Political Issues). 1972. 28.00x (ISBN 0-275-28634-7). Irvington.

Seiden, Melvin. The Revenge Motive in Websterian Tragedy. (Salzburg Studies in English Literature, Jacobean Drama Studies: No.15). 1973. pap. text ed. 25.00x (ISBN 0-391-01517-6). Humanities.

Seiden, O. J. The Capuchin. Emmet, Bob, ed. 240p. 1980. 12.95 (ISBN 0-917224-08-6). Gregory Pubns.

Seidenbaum, Art. Los Angeles Two Hundred: A Bicentennial Celebration. (Illus.). 320p. 1980. 30.00 (ISBN 0-686-62686-9, 1257-0). Abrams.

Seidenberg, Bernard, ed. Social Psychology. Snadowsky, Alvin. LC 75-9236. (Illus.). 1976. text ed. 15.95 (ISBN 0-02-928050-8). Free Pr.

Seidensticker, E. G., jt. ed. see Murakami, Hyoe.

Seidensticker, Edward G., tr. see Kawabata, Yasunari.

Seidensticker, Edward G., tr. see Tanizaki, Junichiro.

Seidensticker, Edward T., tr. see Tanizaki, Junichiro.

Seider, W., jt. auth. see Myers, A.

Seidl, Jennifer & McMordie, W. English Idioms: And How to Use Them. 4th ed. 1978. pap. text ed. 5.95x (ISBN 0-19-432764-7). Oxford U Pr.

Seidl, Jennifer, jt. auth. see Mackin, Ronald.

Seidle, Ronald. Air Time. 1977. text ed. 17.95 (ISBN 0-205-05602-4, 485602-3). Allyn.

Seidler, Armond. Defend Yourself: Scientific Personal Defense. LC 77-79405. (Illus.). 1978. pap. text ed. 8.25 (ISBN 0-395-25822-7). HM.

Seidler, Babara. The Legend of King Piast. Kedron, Jane, tr. (Young People's Ser.). (Illus.). (gr. 2-8). 1977. pap. 1.00 (ISBN 0-917004-08-6). Kosciuszko.

Seidler, Barbara. King Popiel & the Mice. (Young Peoples Ser.). 1976. pap. text ed. 1.00x (ISBN 0-917004-07-8). Kosciuszko.

Seidler, G. L. The Emergence of the Eastern World. 1968. 28.00 (ISBN 0-08-012637-5). Pergamon.

Seidler, Lee J. Social Accounting: Theory, Issues & Cases. LC 74-12116. (Management, Accounting & Information Systems Ser). 547p. 1975. 26.50 (ISBN 0-471-77488-X). Wiley.

Seidler, Lee J. & Carmichael, Douglas R. Accountants' Handbook. 6th ed. 1700p. 1981. 75.00 (ISBN 0-471-05505-0). Ronald Pr.

Seidler, Lee J., et al. The Equity Funding Papers: The Anatomy of a Fraud. LC 77-9921. (Accounting & Information Systems Ser.). 1977. text ed. 24.95x (ISBN 0-471-02273-X). Wiley.

Seidler, Rosalie. Panda Cake. LC 78-6109. (Illus.). 40p. (ps-3). 1978. 4.95 (ISBN 0-590-17706-0, Four Winds); lib. bdg. 4.95 (ISBN 0-590-07706-6). Schol Bk Serv.

Seidl-Hohenveldern. American-Austrian Private International Law. 1963. 9.00 (ISBN 0-379-11411-9). Oceana.

Seidl-Hohenveldern, Ignaz. The Austrian-German Arbitral Tribunal, Vol. 11. 1972. 10.00x (ISBN 0-8156-2159-0). U Pr of Va.

Seidman, Ann & Makgetla, Neva S. Outposts of Monopoly Capitalism: Southern Africa in the Changing Global Economy. 384p. (Orig.). 1980. 16.95 (ISBN 0-88208-114-4); pap. 8.95 (ISBN 0-88208-115-2). Lawrence Hill.

Seidman, Ann, ed. Natural Resources & National Welfare: The Case of Copper. LC 75-60. (Illus.). 476p. 1975. text ed. 27.50 (ISBN 0-275-05450-0). Praeger.

Seidman, Arthur, jt. auth. see Prensky, Sol.

Seidman, Arthur H. & Waintraub, Jack L. Electronics: Devices, Discrete & Integrated Circuits. (Electronics Technology Ser.). 1977. text ed. 22.95 (ISBN 0-675-08494-6); instr's manual 3.95 (ISBN 0-685-75491-X). Merrill.

Seidman, Arthur H., jt. auth. see Loveday, George C.

Seidman, Dolores. Stories of Here & Now. (gr. 9 up). 1978. pap. text ed. 4.33 (ISBN 0-87720-309-1). AMSCO Sch.

Seidman, Eric, ed. Wanted! 1980. pap. 8.95 (ISBN 0-553-01224-X). Bantam.

Seidman, Hillel. The Glory of the Jewish Holidays. 2nd ed. LC 68-58504. (Illus.). 1980. 13.95 (ISBN 0-88400-065-6). Shengold.

Seidman, J. Seidman's Legislative History of Excess Profit Tax Laws: 1917-1946. 1959. 15.00. P-H.

--Seidman's Legislative History of Federal Income & Excess Profits Tax Laws: 1939-1953, 2 vols. 1959. 50.00 (ISBN 0-13-799742-6). P-H.

--Seidman's Legislative History of Federal Income Tax Laws: 1851-1938. 25.00 (ISBN 0-13-799767-1). P-H.

Seidman, Joel, et al. Worker Views His Union. LC 58-5686. 1958. 10.50x o.s.i. (ISBN 0-226-74529-5). U of Chicago Pr.

Seidman, Robert B., jt. auth. see Chambliss, William J.

Seidman, Steve. The Film Career of Billy Wilder. Gottesman, Ronald, ed. (Three Director Set). 1978. pap. 7.80 (ISBN 0-913178-58-6). Redgrave Pub Co.

Seidman, Theodore R. & Albert, Marvin H. Becoming a Mother. 240p. 1980. pap. 1.95 (ISBN 0-686-69184-9, Crest). Fawcett.

Seidner, Constance J., jt. ed. see Dukes, Richard L.

Seifert, Elizabeth. The Problems of Doctor A. LC 79-11017. 1979. 7.95 (ISBN 0-396-07686-6). Dodd.

Seifert, Herbert & Threlfall, W. Lehrbuch Der Topologie. (Ger). 13.95 (ISBN 0-8284-0031-8). Chelsea Pub.

Seifert, Lois. Our Family Night in: Workbook of Convant Living. 200p. (Orig.). pap. 3.95x (ISBN 0-8358-0420-8). Upper Room.

Seifert, Ralph T., jt. auth. see Gucker, Frank T.

Seifert, Shirley. Waters of the Wilderness. 1976. Repr. of 1941 ed. lib. bdg. 9.95 (ISBN 0-89190-142-6). Am Repr-Rivercity Pr.

Seifert, William W. & Schriever, B. A., eds. Air Transportation Nineteen Seventy-Five & Beyond: A Systems Approach. 1968. 23.00x (ISBN 0-262-19042-7). MIT Pr.

Seiffer, Samuel, jt. auth. see Birenbaum, Arnold.

Seiffert, Dorothy. Beauty Mature Woman. (Illus.). 1977. 8.95 o.p. (ISBN 0-8015-3100-4). Dutton.

Seiffert, Karl. Damp Diffusion & Buildings. Phillips, A. B. & Turner, F. H., trs. from Ger. (Illus.). 1970. text ed. 37.30x (ISBN 0-444-20073-8, Pub. by Applied Science). Burgess-Intl Ideas.

Seifritz, W., ed. see World Hydrogen Energy Conference, 2nd, Zurich, Aug. 1978.

Seigfried, Charlene H. Chaos & Context: A Study in William James. LC 77-86346. xiii, 137p. 1978. 12.00x (ISBN 0-8214-0378-8). Ohio U Pr.

Seighman, Ruth. A Taste of Quality: Favorite Recipes from the Merillat Kitchens of America. 1980. write for info. (ISBN 0-937304-01-8). Impressions.

Seigle, Cecilia S., tr. see Kaiko, Ken.

Seigle, Cecilia S., tr. see Kaiko, Takeshi.

Seike, Kiyoshi & Kudo, Masanobu. A Japanese Touch for Your Garden. LC 79-66238. (Illus.). 80p. 1980. 14.95 (ISBN 0-87011-391-7). Kodansha.

Seiler, Hansjakob & Hioki, Kojiro. Cahuilla Dictionary. 1979. pap. 15.00 (ISBN 0-686-25243-8). Malki Mus Pr.

Seiler, Thomas H., jt. ed. see Sommerfeldt, John R.

Seippel. Opto Electronics. 1981. text ed. 21.95 (ISBN 0-8359-5255-X). Reston.

Seiss, Joseph. Gospel in Leviticus. LC 80-8078. 408p. 1981. 10.95 (ISBN 0-8254-3743-1). Kregel.

--The Great Pyramid: A Miracle in Stone. LC 72-81590. (Illus.). 256p. 1973. pap. 2.95 (ISBN 0-8334-1735-5). Steinerbks.

Seiss, Joseph A. Apocalpyse. 14.95 (ISBN 0-310-32760-1). Zondervan.

--The Great Pyramid: A Miracle in Stone. LC 80-8341. (Harper's Library of Spiritual Wisdom). 256p. 1981. pap. 5.95 (ISBN 0-06-067211-0, HarpR). Har-Row.

--Holy Types: The Gospel in Leviticus. Repr. of 1972 ed. 5.95 (ISBN 0-686-05045-2). St Thomas.

Seitel, Peter. See So That We May See: Performances & Interpretations of Traditional Tales from Tanzania. LC 79-3036. 320p. 1980. 32.50x (ISBN 0-253-15917-2); pap. 12.50x (ISBN 0-253-20242-6). Ind U Pr.

Seitelberger, F., ed. see International Symposium on Malignant Lymphomas of the Nervous System.

Seiter, William J. Studies in Niuean Syntax. Hankamer, Jorge, ed. LC 79-55857. (Outstanding Dissertations in Linguistics Ser.). 367p. 1980. lib. bdg. 41.00 (ISBN 0-8240-4560-2). Garland Pub.

Seitz, Clifford P., jt. auth. see Castellano, Carmine C.

Seitz, Don C. Artemus Ward: Charles Farrar Browne. 338p. 1980. Repr. of 1919 ed. lib. bdg. 40.00 (ISBN 0-89760-824-0). Telegraph Bks.

--The James Gordon Bennetts, Father & Son: Proprietors of the New York Herald. (American Newspapermen 1790-1933). (Illus.). 405p. 1974. Repr. of 1928 ed. 20.00x o.s.i. (ISBN 0-8464-0008-1). Beekman Pubs.

--Under the Black Flag. LC 78-167167. 1971. Repr. of 1925 ed. 20.00 (ISBN 0-8103-3805-X). Gale.

Seitz, Frederick & Nichols, Rodney W. Research & Development & the Prospects for International Security. LC 73-90816. 88p. 1974. 6.50x (ISBN 0-8448-0261-1); pap. 2.75x (ISBN 0-8448-0262-X). Crane-Russak Co.

Seitz, Heribert. Blankwaffen, 2 vols. (Illus.). 1976. Set. 90.00 o.p. (ISBN 0-686-14976-9). Arma Pr.

Seitz, Marianne. Creating Silver Jewelry with Beads. LC 75-180455. (Little Craft Bk.). (Illus.). 48p. (gr. 9 up). 1972. 4.95 o.p. (ISBN 0-8069-5196-6); PLB 5.89 o.p. (ISBN 0-8069-5197-4). Sterling.

Seitz, Martin, jt. auth. see Kaplan, Bert L.

Seitz, Neil & Yeager, Frederick. Financial Institution Management. 450p. 1982. text ed. 18.95 (ISBN 0-8359-2022-4); instr's. manual free (ISBN 0-8359-2023-2). Reston.

Seitz, Nick. Improve Your Game (and Learn About) the Superstars of Golf. 192p. 1981. pap. 4.95 (ISBN 0-346-12477-8). Cornerstone.

--Quick Tips from the Golf Spot. (Illus.). 208p. 1981. pap. 6.95 (ISBN 0-914178-43-1, 42903-5). Golf Digest Bks.

--Superstars of Golf. LC 77-92910. (Illus.). 192p. 1977. 10.95 (ISBN 0-914178-13-X, 22975). Golf Digest.

Seitz, Steven T. Bureaucracy Policy & the Public. new ed. LC 77-26656. (Illus.). 1978. pap. text ed. 4.95 (ISBN 0-8016-4482-8). Mosby.

Seitz, Victoria, jt. auth. see Yando, Regina.

Seitz, William C. Monet. LC 60-7800. (Library of Great Painters Ser). (Illus.). 1960. 35.00 (ISBN 0-8109-0326-1). Abrams.

Seitzinger, Jack M. & Kelley, Thomas M. Police Terminology: Programmed Manual for Criminal Justice Personnel. (Illus.). 152p. 1974. pap. 11.75 (ISBN 0-398-02947-4). C C Thomas.

Seixas, Cid. O Signo Selvagem. (Bi-Lingual Port.-Eng.). 1981. pap. 1.50. Ghost Dance.

Seixas, John R. Tax Havens & Offshore Companies. (Illus.). 159p. (Orig.). 1979. pap. 9.95 (ISBN 0-937456-00-4). Dragon Co.

Seixas, Judith S. Alcohol -- What It Is, What It Does. LC 76-43344. (Read-Alone Bk.). (Illus.). 56p. (gr. 1-3). 1981. pap. 2.95 (ISBN 0-688-00462-8). Greenwillow.

--Living with a Parent Who Drinks Too Much. LC 78-11108. (gr. 3-6). 1979. 7.50 (ISBN 0-688-80196-X); PLB 7.20 (ISBN 0-688-84196-1). Greenwillow.

Sekers, David. Popular Staffordshire Pottery. (Folio Miniature Ser.). (Illus.). 1978. 6.95 (ISBN 0-7181-1590-2, Pub. by Michael Joseph). Merrimack Bk Serv.

Sekers, Simone. Pates, Terrines & Potted Meats. 1978. 24.00 (ISBN 0-7134-0679-8, Pub. by Batsford England). David & Charles.

Sekiguchi, Sueo. Japanese Direct Foreign Investment. LC 78-59177. (Atlantic Institute for International Affairs Research Studies: Vol. 1). 171p. 1979. text ed. 20.00 (ISBN 0-916672-17-4). Allanheld.

Sekler, Mary P. The Early Drawings of Charles Edouard Jeanneret le Corbusier 1902-1908. LC 76-23726. (Outstanding Dissertations in the Fine Arts Ser.). 1978. lib. bdg. 80.00x (ISBN 0-8240-2728-0). Garland Pub.

Sekowsky, Jo Anne. Praise the Lord, I'm Under Construction. 112p. 1978. pap. 2.95 (ISBN 0-930756-40-1, 4230-SE3). Women's Aglow.

Sekowsky, Jo Anne, jt. auth. see Dull, Elaine.

Sekowsky, JoAnne, jt. auth. see Collingridge, Ruth.

Sela, M. & Prywes, M., eds. Topics in Basic Immunology. 1969. 32.50 (ISBN 0-12-635550-9). Acad Pr.

Sela, Michael, ed. The Antigens. 1974. Vol. 1. 52.50 (ISBN 0-12-635501-0). Acad Pr.

--The Antigens, Vol. 5. 1979. 38.00 (ISBN 0-12-635505-3); 32.75, by subscription. Acad Pr.

Sela, Owen. The Petrograd Consignment. 1980. pap. 2.50 o.s.i. (ISBN 0-440-16885-6). Dell.

Selakovich, Daniel. The Supreme Court: Does It Protect or Limit Our Liberties? Fraenkel, Jack R., ed. (Crucial Issues in American Government Ser.). (gr. 9-12). 1976. pap. text ed. 4.96 (ISBN 0-205-04911-7, 7649118). Allyn.

Selander, R. K. Speciation in Wrens of the Genus Campylorhynchus. (U. C. Publ. in Zoology: Vol. 74). 1964. pap. 10.00x (ISBN 0-520-09329-1). U of Cal Pr.

Selavan, Ida C., jt. ed. see Shiloh, Ailon.

Selber, Charles, jt. auth. see Lowe, Jacqueline.

Selber, Lillian P. A Little Quiet Dreaming, a Little Time to Think. LC 73-85884. (Illus.). 63p. 1973. 2.95 (ISBN 0-88415-450-5). Pacesetter Pr.

Selberg, Charles A. Foil. LC 74-30701. 224p. 1975. text ed. 9.95 (ISBN 0-201-06943-1). A-W.

Selbie, W. B. Belief & Life: Studies in the Thought of the Fourth Gospel. (Short Course Ser.). 151p. 1916. text ed. 2.95 (ISBN 0-567-08314-4). Attic Pr.

Selbo, M. L. Adhesive Bonding of Wood. LC 77-88958. (Drake Home Craftsman Ser.). (Illus.). 1978. pap. 5.95 (ISBN 0-8069-8104-0, 000900). Sterling.

Selby, Curt. Blood County. 1981. pap. 2.25 (ISBN 0-87997-622-5, UE1622, Daw Bks). NAL.

Selby, Edward B., Jr., jt. auth. see Timerlake, Richard H., Jr.

Selby, Elliot, jt. auth. see Gee, John.

Selby, Henry & Garretson, Lucy. Cultural Anthropology. 432p. 1981. pap. text ed. write for info. (ISBN 0-697-07562-1); instr's manual avail. (ISBN 0-697-07563-X). Wm C Brown.

Selby, Henry A. Zapotec Deviance: The Convergence of Folk & Modern Sociology. LC 73-22480. 214p. 1974. 10.00x o.p. (ISBN 0-292-79800-8). U of Tex Pr.

Selby, James W., et al. Psychological & Human Reproduction. LC 80-1641. 1980. 19.95 (ISBN 0-02-928690-5). Free Pr.

Selby, Peter H. Using Graphs & Tables. LC 78-25962. (Self-Teaching Guides Ser.). 1979. pap. text ed. 6.95 (ISBN 0-471-05413-5). Wiley.

Selby-Bigge, L. A., ed. see Hume, David.

Selcher, Wayne A. The Afro-Asian Dimension of Brazilian Foreign Policy, 1956-1972. LC 73-19968. (Latin American Monographs 2: No. 13). 1974. 11.00 (ISBN 0-8130-0384-9). U Presses Fla.

--Brazil's Multilateral Relations Between First & Third Worlds. LC 77-25273. (A Westview Replica Edition Ser.). 1978. lib. bdg. 23.50 o.p. (ISBN 0-89158-088-3). Westview.

Selcher, Wayne A., ed. Brazil in the International System. (Special Studies on Latin America & the Caribbean). 300p. 1981. lib. bdg. 26.50x (ISBN 0-89158-907-4). Westview.

Selden, George. Chester Cricket's Pigeon Ride. LC 80-20326. (gr. 1 up). 1981. 9.95 (ISBN 0-374-31239-7). FS&G.

--Cricket in Times Square. (Illus.). (gr. 2-7). 1970. pap. 1.50 (ISBN 0-440-41563-2, YB). Dell.

--Heinrich Schliemann: Discoverer of Buried Treasure. (Illus.). (gr. 1-5). 1964. 3.50 o.s.i. (ISBN 0-02-781770-9). Macmillan.

--Tucker's Countryside. (gr. 3-7). 1972. pap. 1.50 (ISBN 0-380-01584-6, 55046, Camelot). Avon.

Selden, John. Table-Talk. large type ed. Arber, Edward, ed. 1972. Repr. of 1869 ed. 7.50x (ISBN 0-87556-314-7). Saifer.

Selden, Raman. English Verse Satire, Fifteen Ninety to Seventeen Sixty-Five. 1978. text ed. 22.50x (ISBN 0-04-827016-4). Allen Unwin.

Selden, Samuel. Stage in Action. LC 67-21040. (Arcturus Books Paperbacks). (Illus.). 367p. 1967. pap. 9.95 (ISBN 0-8093-0275-6). S Ill U Pr.

Selden, Samuel & Sellman, Hunton D. Stage Scenery & Lighting. 3rd ed. (Illus.). 1959. 17.95 o.p. (ISBN 0-13-840470-4). P-H.

Selden, Samuel, Jr. & Rezzuto, Thomas. Essentials of Stage Scenery. LC 70-182307. (Illus.). 1972. 16.95 (ISBN 0-13-289215-4). P-H.

Seldes, G. Freedom of the Press. LC 73-146159. (Civil Liberties in American History Ser). 1971. Repr. of 1935 ed. lib. bdg. 35.00 (ISBN 0-306-70125-1). Da Capo.

--You Can't Do That. LC 70-37287. (Civil Liberties in American History Ser). 308p. 1972. Repr. of 1938 ed. lib. bdg. 27.50 (ISBN 0-306-70201-0). Da Capo.

Seldes, Gilbert. The Years of the Locust: America, 1929-1932. LC 72-2384. (FDR & the Era of the New Deal Ser). vi, 355p. 1973. Repr. of 1933 ed. lib. bdg. 35.00 (ISBN 0-306-70471-4). Da Capo.

Seldes, Lee. The Legacy of Mark Rothko. 1978. 14.95 o.p. (ISBN 0-03-014751-4). HR&W.

Seldin, Maury. Real Estate Investment for Profit Through Appreciation. 1980. text ed. 16.95 (ISBN 0-8359-6526-0). Reston.

Seldis, Anna. La Dolce Cucina: The Italian Dessert Cookbook. (Illus.). 256p. 1974. pap. 2.95 o.s.i. (ISBN 0-02-010300-X, Collier). Macmillan.

Seldon, Arthur & Pennance, F. G. Everyman's Dictionary of Economics. 2nd ed. LC 65-5820. 516p. 1976. 16.50x (ISBN 0-460-03028-0). Intl Pubns Serv.

Seldon, Arthur, ed. see Plant, Sir Arnold.

Seldon, Eric. The God of the Present Age. LC 80-26149. 1981. pap. price not set (ISBN 0-8309-0305-4). Herald Hse.

Seldon, Philip. How to Buy Wine. LC 79-8504. (Illus., Orig.). 1981. pap. 8.95 (ISBN 0-385-14961-1, Dolp). Doubleday.

Seldon, Robert. Life Cycle Costing: A Better Method for Government Procurement. (Westview Special Studies in Public Policy & Public Management). 1979. lib. bdg. 32.00x (ISBN 0-89158-277-0). Westview.

SeLegue, Roger. The Wayward Winds. LC 80-52064. 464p. (Orig.). 1980. pap. 3.95x (ISBN 0-9604600-0-4). Rooney Pubns.

Seler, Eduard. Codex Fejervary-Mayer. Young, Karl, ed. (Fourth Sun Ser.). (Illus.). lib. bdg. cancelled (ISBN 0-932282-40-7); pap. cancelled (ISBN 0-932282-39-3). Caledonia Pr.

Selesnick, Herbert, jt. auth. see Dinkelspiel, John R.

Selesnick, Herbert L. Rent Control: A Case for. LC 75-312990. 1976. 15.95 (ISBN 0-669-00338-7). Lexington Bks.

Seletz, Jeanette. Jone Brent: Neurosurgeon. LC 78-50163. 1981. 12.50 (ISBN 0-87527-136-7). Green.

Selevan, Ida C., jt. ed. see Shiloh, Ailon.

Self, Carolyn S. Confident Entertaining. LC 76-41764. 1976. 6.95 o.p. (ISBN 0-8407-4055-7). Nelson.

Self, Charles. Bathroom Remodeling. (Illus.). 224p. 1980. 12.95 (ISBN 0-8359-0436-9); pap. 4.95 (ISBN 0-8359-0435-0). Reston.

Self, Charles R. The Brickworker's Bible. (Illus.). 378p. (Orig.). 1980. 15.95 (ISBN 0-8306-9942-2, 1204); pap. 8.95 (ISBN 0-8306-1204-1). Tab Bks.

--Do-It-Yourselfer's Guide to Chainsaw Use & Repair. LC 77-1731. (Illus.). 1977. pap. 5.95 (ISBN 0-8306-6892-6, 892). TAB Bks.

--Western Horsemanship. (Illus.). 1979. 11.95 (ISBN 0-87691-291-9). Winchester Pr.

Self, Charles R., Jr. The Brazer's Handbook. LC 78-56960. (Home Craftsman Ser.). (Illus.). 1978. pap. 5.95 (ISBN 0-8069-8178-4). Sterling.

Self, Huber, jt. auth. see Socolofsky, Homer.

Self, Margaret C. Henrietta. LC 66-24003. (Illus.). (gr. 3-6). 1966. 5.95 (ISBN 0-8149-0385-1). Vanguard.

--Sky Rocket: The Story of a Little Bay Horse. LC 78-111913. (gr. 8 up). 1970. 5.95 (ISBN 0-396-06207-5). Dodd.

--World of Horses. 1961. 8.95 o.p. (ISBN 0-07-056108-7, GB). McGraw.

Self, Margaret M. Effective Year-Round Bible Ministries. LC 80-52962. Orig. Title: Effective Summer Bible Ministries. 160p. 1981. pap. 3.95 (ISBN 0-8307-0751-4, 5414318). Regal.

--How to Plan & Organize Year-Round Bible Ministries. (Orig.). 1976. pap. 2.95 o.p. (ISBN 0-8307-0413-2, 54-029-05). Regal.

Self, Margaret M., ed. How to Plan & Organize Year-Round Bible Ministries. pap. 2.25 o.p. (ISBN 0-8307-0751-4). Regal.

Self, Peter & Storing, Herbert J. The State & the Farmer: British Agricultural Policies & Politics. 1963. 20.00x (ISBN 0-520-01159-7). U of Cal Pr.

Self, Robert T. Barrett Wendell. LC 75-12735. (U. S. Authors Ser.: No. 261). 1975. lib. bdg. 12.50 (ISBN 0-8057-7160-3). Twayne.

Self, Timothy H., et al. Systematic Patient Medication Record Review: A Manual for Nurses. LC 80-12481. 1980. pap. text ed. 8.95 (ISBN 0-8016-4479-8). Mosby.

Selfridge, Oliver. A Primer for FORTRAN IV: On-Line. 1972. 7.95x (ISBN 0-685-27126-9). MIT Pr.

Selfridge-Field, Eleanor. Venetian Instrumental Music from Gabrieli to Vivaldi. 1975. 48.50x (ISBN 0-631-15440-X, Pub by Basil Blackwell England). Biblio Dist.

Seliger, M. The Marxist Conception of Ideology. LC 76-11092. (International Studies). 1977. 29.50 (ISBN 0-521-21229-4); pap. 10.50x (ISBN 0-521-29625-0). Cambridge U Pr.

Seligman, Alice B., tr. see Lehmann, Lilli.

Seligman, Ben B. Most Notorious Victory. 1966. 8.95 o.s.i. (ISBN 0-02-928310-8). Free Pr.

Seligman, Dee, compiled by. Doris Lessing: An Annotated Bibliography of Criticism. LC 80-24540. 160p. 1981. lib. bdg. 25.00 (ISBN 0-313-21270-8, SDL/). Greenwood.

Seligman, Gustav L., jt. auth. see Jones, Robert.

Seligman, Martin E. Helplessness: On Depression, Development, & Death. LC 74-23125. (Psychology Ser.). (Illus.). 1975. text ed. 17.95x (ISBN 0-7167-0752-7); pap. text ed. 9.95x (ISBN 0-7167-0751-9). W H Freeman.

--Helplessness: On Depression, Development & Death. 1980. Repr. of 1975 ed. text ed. 20.00x o.p. (ISBN 0-8290-0048-8). Irvington.

Seligman, Martin E., jt. ed. see Garber, Judy.

Seligman, Martin E., jt. ed. see Maser, Jack D.

Seligman, Milton. Group Counseling & Group Psychotherapy with Rehabilitation Clients. (Illus.). 352p. 1977. 22.00 (ISBN 0-398-03585-7); pap. 17.00 (ISBN 0-398-03588-1). C C Thomas.

Seligman, Milton & Baldwin, Norman F., eds. Counselor Education & Supervision: Readings in Theory, Practice, & Research. (Illus.). 436p. 1972. 19.75 (ISBN 0-398-02406-5). C C Thomas.

Seligmann, Herbert J., ed. Alfred Stieglitz Talking: Notes on Some of His Conversations, 1925-1931 with a Foreward. 161p. 1981. text ed. 15.00x (ISBN 0-300-03510-1, 66-20942). Yale U Pr.

Seligmann, Jean & Levine, Milton. Tommy Visits the Doctor. (Illus.). (ps-1). 1962. PLB 4.57 o.p. (ISBN 0-307-60480-2, Golden Pr). Western Pub.

Seligmann, Nancy. Homesteading in the City-a Survival Manual for Young People Living in Town or off Campus. (Illus.). 224p. 1975. pap. 5.95 o.p. (ISBN 0-695-80513-4). Follett.

Seligson, David see Reiner, Miriam, et al.

Seligson, Jane. Red Acre's Titan. 8.75 (ISBN 0-8062-1687-5). Carlton.

Seligson, Mitchell A., jt. ed. see Booth, John A.

Selin, W. E., ed. see Jonson, Ben.

Selincourt, Aubrey De see Livy.

Selincourt, Ernest De see Spenser, Edmund.

Selinker, Larry, et al, eds. English for Academic & Technical Purposes: Studies in Honor of Louis Trimble. (Orig.). 1981. pap. 13.95 (ISBN 0-88377-178-0). Newbury Hse.

Selitzer, Ralph. The Dairy Industry in America. LC 76-21921. 1976. 45.00 (ISBN 0-89451-001-0). Mag Indus.

Seljeskog, Edward L., jt. ed. see Chou, Shelley N.

Selko, Daniel. The Federal Financial System. LC 75-8891. (FDR & the Era of the New Deal Ser.). xii, 606p. 1975. Repr. of 1940 ed. lib. bdg. 59.50 (ISBN 0-306-70708-X). Da Capo.

Selkurt, Ewald E. Physiology. 4th ed. LC 75-36762. 1976. text ed. 18.50 o.p. (ISBN 0-316-78039-1); pap. text ed. 15.95 (ISBN 0-316-78040-5). Little.

Sell, Betty, jt. ed. see Sell, Kenneth D.

Sell, Charles M. Family Ministry: Family Life Through the Church. 272p. 11.95 (ISBN 0-310-42580-8). Zondervan.

Sell, Francis E. Art of Successful Deer Hunting. 1980. pap. 5.95 (ISBN 0-932558-13-5). Willow Creek.

Sell, George R., jt. auth. see Miller, Richard K.

Sell, Irene L. Dying & Death: An Annotated Bibliography. LC 76-58052. 1977. casebound 9.00 o.s.i. (ISBN 0-913292-36-2). Tiresias Pr.

Sell, Kenneth D. Bibliography on Divorce. 1981. price not set (ISBN 0-912700-81-5). Oryx Pr.

Sell, Kenneth D. & Sell, Betty, eds. Divorce in the United States, Canada, & Great Britain: A Guide to Information Sources. LC 78-15894. (Social Issues & Social Problems Information Guide Ser.: Vol. 1). 1978. 30.00 (ISBN 0-8103-1396-0). Gale.

Sell, Stewart. Immunología Inmunopatología. (Span.). 1980. pap. text ed. 16.50 (ISBN 0-06-317151-1, Pub. by HarLA Mexico). Har-Row.

--Immunology, Immunopathology & Immunity. 3rd ed. (Illus.). 600p. 1980. pap. text ed. 25.00 (ISBN 0-06-142369-6, Harper Medical). Har-Row.

Sell, Stewart, ed. Cancer Markers: Diagnostic & Developmental Significance. LC 79-91071. (Contemporary Biomedicine Ser.). 1980. 49.50 (ISBN 0-89603-009-1). Humana.

Sella, Amnon. Soviet Political & Military Conduct in the Middle East. 1980. write for info. (ISBN 0-312-74845-0). St Martin.

Sellar, Robert. Tragedy of Quebec: The Expulsion of Its Protestant Farmers, 1916. LC 73-90925. (Social History of Canada Ser.). 1974. pap. 6.50 (ISBN 0-8020-6195-8). U of Toronto Pr.

Sellar, William Y. Roman Poets of the Augustan Age. Incl. Bk. 1. Horace & the Elegiac Poets. Lang, Andrew, memoir by. LC 65-23488. (Illus.). xviii, 362p. Repr. of 1892 ed. o.p. (ISBN 0-8196-0165-9); Bk. 2. Virgil. 3rd ed. LC 65-23489. xiv, 423p. Repr. of 1908 ed. 15.00x (ISBN 0-8196-0162-4). Biblo.

Sellards, E. H., et al. The Geology of Texas: Vol.I, Stratigraphy. (Illus.). 1007p. 1978. Repr. of 1932 ed. 8.00 (BULL 3232). Bur Econ Geology.

Sellari, Carlo & Sellari, Dot. Official Price Guide to Bottles, Old & New. 4th ed. (Collector Ser.). (Illus.). 400p. 1980. pap. 8.95 (ISBN 0-87637-106-3, 106-03). Hse of Collectibles.

Sellari, Dot, jt. auth. see Sellari, Carlo.

Sellars, Wilfred. Science, Perception & Reality. (International Library of Philosophy & Scientific Method). 1963. text ed. 24.75x (ISBN 0-7100-3619-1). Humanities.

Sellars, Wilfred, ed. see Feigl, Herbert.

Sellars, Wilfrid. Naturalism & Ontology. 1980. lib. bdg. 22.00 (ISBN 0-917930-36-3); pap. text ed. 7.50x (ISBN 0-917930-16-9). Ridgeview.

--Philosophical Perspectives: History of Philosophy. 1979. lib. bdg. 21.00 (ISBN 0-917930-24-X); pap. text ed. 6.50x (ISBN 0-917930-04-5). Ridgeview.

--Philosophical Perspectives: Metaphysics & Epistemology. 1979. lib. bdg. 21.00 (ISBN 0-917930-25-8); pap. text ed. 6.50x (ISBN 0-917930-05-3). Ridgeview.

--Pure Pragmatics & Possible Worlds: The Early Essays of Wilfrid Sellars. Sicha, Jeffrey, ed. LC 78-65271. (Orig.). 1980. lib. bdg. 22.00 (ISBN 0-917930-26-6); pap. text ed. 8.50x (ISBN 0-917930-06-1). Ridgeview.

--Science & Metaphysics: Variations on Kantian Themes. LC 68-12258. (International Library of Philosophy & Scientific Method). 1968. text ed. 21.00x (ISBN 0-7100-3501-2). Humanities.

Sellars, Wilfrid & Hospers, John, eds. Readings in Ethical Theory. 2nd ed. 1970. text ed. 21.95 (ISBN 0-13-756007-9). P-H.

Sellars, Wilfrid, jt. ed. see Feigl, Herbert.

Sellassie, Sahle. Firebrands. (Orig.). 9.00 (ISBN 0-89410-103-X); pap. 5.00 (ISBN 0-89410-102-1). Three Continents.

Selleck, Henry B. & Whittaker, Albert H. Occupational Health in America. LC 61-16777. (Illus.). 1962. 14.00x o.p. (ISBN 0-8143-1121-0). Wayne St U Pr.

Sellekaerts, Willy, ed. Economic Development & Planning: Essays in Honour of Jan Tinbergen. LC 73-92712. 288p. 1974. 22.50 o.p. (ISBN 0-87332-055-7). M E Sharpe.

Sellens, Alvin. The Stanley Plane: A History & Descriptive Inventory. LC 75-9509. (Illus.). 1975. 11.95 (ISBN 0-686-27737-6). Sellens.

Seller, Charles E., jt. auth. see Werevka, Robert, Jr.

Seller, Maxine S., ed. Immigrant Women. 325p. 1980. 17.50x (ISBN 0-87722-190-1); pap. text ed. 8.95 (ISBN 0-87722-191-X). Temple U Pr.

Sellers, Charles C. Mr. Peale's Museum: Charles Willson Peale & the First Popular Museum of Natural Science. (Barra Bks.). (Illus.). 1980. 14.95 (ISBN 0-393-05700-3). Norton.

--Patience Wright: American Artist & Spy in George III's London. LC 76-7193. 1976. 17.50x (ISBN 0-8195-5001-9, Pub. by Wesleyan U Pr). Columbia U Pr.

Sellers, Con. Last Flower. 1980. pap. write for info. PB.

Sellers, Frank. Sharp's Firearms. LC 77-71186. 358p. 1978. 34.95 (ISBN 0-917714-12-1). Beinfeld Pub.

Sellers, Gene. Elementary Algebra. LC 80-23171. 475p. (Orig.). 1981. pap. text ed. 17.95 (ISBN 0-8185-0434-X). Brooks-Cole.

--Understanding Algebra & Trigonometry. 1979. text ed. 17.95 (ISBN 0-675-08306-0); instructor's manual 3.95 (ISBN 0-685-96157-5); test 3.95 (ISBN 0-686-67369-7). Merrill.

Sellers, Gene R. Understanding College Algebra. 1979. text ed. 14.95 (ISBN 0-675-08294-3); instructor's manual 3.95 (ISBN 0-686-67292-5); tests 3.95 (ISBN 0-686-67293-3). Merrill.

Sellers, James. Warming Fires: The Quest for Community in America. 224p. 1975. 7.95 (ISBN 0-8164-0273-6). Crossroad NY.

Sellers, James H. & Milam, Edward E. Ethics: Accounting Student Perceptions. 50p. (Orig.). 1980. pap. 4.50 (ISBN 0-938004-00-X). U MS Bus Econ.

Sellers, Kay, jt. auth. see Robison, Joleen.

Sellers, Kenneth C., jt. auth. see Leech, Frederick B.

Sellers, L. Cooking with Love. LC 77-99864. (Illus.). 1970. 11.25 (ISBN 0-08-006908-8); pap. 4.45 (ISBN 0-08-006907-X). Pergamon.

--The Simple Subs Book. 1968. 21.00 (ISBN 0-08-013042-9); pap. 12.75 (ISBN 0-08-013041-0). Pergamon.

Sellers, Leonard & Rivers, William R. Mass Media Issues: Articles & Commentaries. (Illus.). 432p. 1977. pap. text ed. 12.95 (ISBN 0-13-559500-2). P-H.

Sellers, Robert C., ed. Armed Forces of the World: A Reference Handbook. 4th ed. LC 76-12874. (Special Studies). 1977. text ed. 32.50 (ISBN 0-275-23200-X). Praeger.

Sellers, Thomas. Throwing on the Potter's Wheel. 4.95 (ISBN 0-934706-03-4). Prof Pubns Ohio.

Sellers, Thomas, ed. Ceramic Projects. 2.95 (ISBN 0-934706-08-5). Prof Pubns Ohio.

--Potter's Wheel Projects. 2.95 (ISBN 0-934706-04-2). Prof Pubns Ohio.

Sellers, William D. Physical Climatology. LC 65-24983. 1965. 15.00x (ISBN 0-226-74699-2). U of Chicago Pr.

Sellery, J'nan M, jt. ed. see Vickery, John B.

Selley, N. J. Experimental Approach to Electro-Chemistry. LC 77-7914. 1977. 24.95 (ISBN 0-470-99204-2). Halsted Pr.

Sellick, Bud. The Wild, Wonderful World of Parachutes & Parachuting. LC 80-20506. 1981. 17.95 (ISBN 0-13-959577-5). P-H.

Sellick, Roger. The West Somerset Mineral Railway: And the Story of the Brendon Hills Iron. 2nd ed. (Illus.). 126p. 1970. 10.50 (ISBN 0-7153-4662-8). David & Charles.

Sellin, Don & Birch, Jack. Educating Gifted & Talented Learners. LC 80-19565. 372p. 1980. text ed. 24.50 (ISBN 0-89443-295-8). Aspen Systems.

--Nature & Needs of the Gifted Child. 350p. 1981. text ed. price not set (ISBN 0-89443-362-8). Aspen Systems.

Sellin, Donald F. Mental Retardation: Nature, Needs, & Advocacy. 1979. text ed. 19.95 (ISBN 0-205-05989-9, 2459892); tests avail. (ISBN 0-205-05990-2, 2459906). Allyn.

Sellin, Henry, ed. see New York University, Division of General Education.

Sellman, Hunton D. Essentials of Stage Lighting. LC 75-187988. (Illus.). 1972. 16.95 (ISBN 0-13-289207-3). P-H.

Sellman, Hunton D., jt. auth. see Selden, Samuel.

Sellmeyer, jt. auth. see Ross.

Sells, A. L. Thomas Gray: His Life & Works. (Illus.). 320p. 1980. text ed. 29.50x (ISBN 0-04-928043-0, 2411). Allen Unwin.

Sells, Iris, tr. see Mireaux, Emile.

Sells, Robert L., jt. auth. see Weidner, Richard T.

Sellwood, Arthur & Sellwood, Mary. The Victorian Railway Murders. (Illus.). 1979. 14.95 (ISBN 0-7153-7650-0). David & Charles.

Sellwood, Mary, jt. auth. see Sellwood, Arthur.

Selman, Joseph. The Basic Physics of Radiation Therapy. 2nd ed. (Illus.). 768p. 1976. 34.75 (ISBN 0-398-03247-5). C C Thomas.

Selman, L. H. Collectors' Paperweights-Price Guide & Catalogue. LC 79-87448. (Illus.). 1979. pap. 5.00 o.p. (ISBN 0-933756-00-3). Paperweight Pr.

Selman, LaRue. Boots, Two. Jordan, Alton, ed. (Buppet Series). (Illus.). (gr. k-3). 1981. PLB 4.50 (ISBN 0-89868-094-8, Read Res); pap. text ed. 1.95 (ISBN 0-89868-105-7). ARO Pub.

--The Hero, Two. Jordan, Alton, ed. (Buppet Series). (Illus.). (gr. k-3). 1981. PLB 4.50 (ISBN 0-89868-089-1, Read Res); pap. text ed. 1.95 (ISBN 0-89868-100-6). ARO Pub.

--JD & the Bee. Jordan, Alton, ed. (Buppet Series). (Illus.). (gr. k-3). 1981. PLB 4.50 (ISBN 0-89868-093-X, Read Res); pap. text ed. 1.95 (ISBN 0-89868-104-9). ARO Pub.

--Rain Frog. Jordan, Alton, ed. (Buppet Series). (Illus.). (gr. k-3). 1981. PLB 4.50 (ISBN 0-89868-091-3, Read Res); pap. text ed. 1.95 (ISBN 0-89868-102-2). ARO Pub.

--Sammy Skunk Plays the Clown. Jordan, Alton, ed. (Buppet Series). (Illus.). (gr. k-3). 1981. PLB 4.50 (ISBN 0-89868-097-2, Read Res); pap. text ed. 1.95 (ISBN 0-89868-108-1). ARO Pub.

Selman, Lawrence H. Collectors' Paperweights-Price Guide & Catalogue. (Illus.). 1981. pap. 5.00 (ISBN 0-933756-02-X). Paperweight Pr.

Selman, Lawrence H. & Pope-Selman, Linda. Paperweights for Collectors. rev. ed. 1981. price not set (ISBN 0-933756-03-8). Paperweight Pr.

--Paperweights for Collectors. 2nd ed. LC 75-37108. 1975. 27.50 o.p. (ISBN 0-686-53122-1). Paperweight Pr.

Selman, Peter, jt. auth. see Potts, Malcolm.

Selmanowitz, Victor J. & Pereira, Frederick A. Dermatology Specialty Board Review. 3rd ed. 1978. spiral bdg. 16.50 (ISBN 0-87488-311-3). Med Exam.

Selmer, Knut S., jt. auth. see Bing, Jon.

Selmier, Dean & Kram, Mark. Blow Away. 1979. 9.95 o.p. (ISBN 0-670-17447-5). Viking Pr.

Selowsky, Marcello. Who Benefits from Government Expenditure? A Case Study of Columbia. (World Bank Research Publication Ser.). 1979. 14.95x (ISBN 0-19-520098-5); pap. 5.95x (ISBN 0-19-520099-3). Oxford U Pr.

Selsam, Howard & Martel, Harry, eds. Reader in Marxist Philosophy. LC 63-14262. (Orig.). 1963. 7.50 (ISBN 0-7178-0168-3); pap. 4.50 (ISBN 0-7178-0167-5). Intl Pub Co.

Selsam, Howard, et al, eds. Dynamics of Social Change: A Reader in Marxist Social Science. LC 77-120820. 1970. 10.00 (ISBN 0-7178-0242-6); pap. 4.50 (ISBN 0-7178-0264-7). Intl Pub Co.

Selsam, J. P. Pennsylvania Constitution of 1776. LC 77-124925. (American Constitutional & Legal History Ser.). 1971. Repr. of 1936 ed. lib. bdg. 29.50 (ISBN 0-306-71994-0). Da Capo.

Selsam, Millicent. Animals of the Sea. LC 75-27447. (Illus.). 40p. (gr. k-3). 1976. 6.95 (ISBN 0-590-07458-X, Four Winds). Schol Bk Serv.

--How Kittens Grow. LC 74-13162. (Illus.). 32p. (gr. k-3). 1975. 5.95 (ISBN 0-590-07409-1, Four Winds). Schol Bk Serv.

--How Kittens Grow. (gr. k-3). 1977. pap. 1.25 (ISBN 0-590-04794-9, Schol Pap). Schol Bk Serv.

--Questions & Answers About Horses. LC 73-88073. (Illus.). 64p. (gr. k-3). 1974. 6.95 (ISBN 0-590-07352-4, Four Winds). Schol Bk Serv.

Selsam, Millicent & Hunt, Joyce. A First Look at Dogs. Springer, Harriett, tr. (A First Look at Ser.). 32p. (gr. 1-4). 1981. 7.95 (ISBN 0-8027-6409-6); lib. bdg. 8.85 (ISBN 0-8027-6421-5). Walker & Co.

--A First Look at Fish. LC 72-81377. (First Look at Ser). 32p. (gr. 2-4). 1972. 4.50 o.s.i. (ISBN 0-8027-6119-4); PLB 5.39 (ISBN 0-8027-6120-8). Walker & Co.

Selsam, Millicent, ed. see Asimov, Isaac.

Selsam, Millicent, et al. A First Look at Sharks. (A First Look at Ser.). (Illus.). (gr. k-3). 1979. 7.95 o.s.i. (ISBN 0-8027-6372-3); PLB 7.85 (ISBN 0-8027-6373-1). Walker & Co.

Selsam, Millicent E. Bulbs, Corms & Such. LC 74-5939. (Illus.). 48p. (gr. 2-5). 1974. 7.75 o.p. (ISBN 0-688-21822-9); PLB 7.92 (ISBN 0-688-31822-3). Morrow.

--A First Look at Leaves. Selsam, Millicent E. & Hunt, Joyce, eds. LC 72-81376. (First Look at Ser). (Illus.). 32p. (gr. 2-4). 1972. 5.39 o.s.i. (ISBN 0-8027-6117-8); PLB 5.39 (ISBN 0-8027-6118-6). Walker & Co.

--Harlequin Moth: Its Life Story. LC 75-17862. (Illus.). 48p. (gr. 2-5). 1975. 8.25 (ISBN 0-688-22049-5); PLB 7.92 (ISBN 0-688-32049-X). Morrow.

--How Animals Tell Time. (Illus.). (gr. 5-9). 1967. PLB 7.92 (ISBN 0-688-31407-4). Morrow.

--How Puppies Grow. LC 72-77803. (Illus.). 40p. (gr. k-3). 1972. 7.95 (ISBN 0-590-07190-4, Four Winds). Schol Bk Serv.

--How to Grow House Plants. (Illus.). (gr. 5-9). 1960. PLB 7.44 o.p. (ISBN 0-688-31410-4). Morrow.

--Land of the Giant Tortoise: The Story of the Galapagos. LC 77-4897. (Illus.). 64p. (gr. 1-5). 1977. 7.95 (ISBN 0-590-07416-4, Four Winds). Schol Bk Serv.

--Maple Tree. LC 68-25933. (Illus.). (gr. 2-5). 1968. PLB 7.92 (ISBN 0-688-31496-1). Morrow.

--Microbes at Work. (Illus.). (gr. 5-9). 1953. PLB 7.92 (ISBN 0-688-31497-X). Morrow.

--Mimosa, the Sensitive Plant. (Illus.). (gr. 4-6). 1978. 7.95 (ISBN 0-688-22167-X); PLB 7.63 (ISBN 0-688-32167-4). Morrow.

--Night Animals. LC 80-13465. (Illus.). 40p. (gr. 1-5). 1980. 7.95 (ISBN 0-590-07755-4, Four Winds). Schol Bk Serv.

--Peanut. LC 70-81886. (Illus.). (gr. 2-5). 1969. PLB 7.92 (ISBN 0-688-31803-7). Morrow.

--The Plants We Eat. (Illus.). (gr. 2-5). 1955. PLB 6.96 (ISBN 0-688-31567-4). Morrow.

--Play with Plants. rev. ed. LC 78-8509. (Illus.). (gr. 4-6). 1978. PLB 7.63 (ISBN 0-688-32167-4). Morrow.

--Play with Seeds. (Illus.). (gr. 5-9). 1957. PLB 6.96 (ISBN 0-688-31489-9). Morrow.

--Popcorn. (Illus.). (gr. 2-5). 1976. 7.25 (ISBN 0-688-22083-5); PLB 6.96 (ISBN 0-688-32083-X). Morrow.

--Questions & Answers About Ants. LC 67-25033. (Illus.). (gr. 2-5). 1967. 6.95 o.s.i. (ISBN 0-590-07054-1, Four Winds). Schol Bk Serv.

--Sea Monsters of Long Ago. LC 78-5385. (Illus.). 32p. (gr. k-3). 1978. 6.95 (ISBN 0-590-07567-5, Four Winds). Schol Bk Serv.

--Sea Monsters of Long Ago. (gr. k-3). 1977. pap. 1.95 (ISBN 0-590-10419-5, Schol Pap). Schol Bk Serv.

--Vegetables from Stems & Leaves. (Illus.). 48p. (gr. 2-5). 1972. 7.44 o.p. (ISBN 0-688-30117-7). Morrow.

Selsam, Millicent E. & Hunt, Joyce. First Look at Cats. LC 80-7673. (First Look at Ser.). (Illus.). 32p. (gr. 1-4). 1981. 7.95 (ISBN 0-8027-6398-7); PLB 8.85 (ISBN 0-8027-6399-5). Walker & Co.

--A First Look at Flowers. LC 76-57063. (First Look at Ser.). (Illus.). (gr. k-3). 1977. 5.95 o.s.i. (ISBN 0-8027-6281-6); PLB 6.85 (ISBN 0-8027-6282-4). Walker & Co.

--A First Look at Frogs, Toads & Salamanders. (First Look at Ser.). (Illus.). 32p. (gr. 2-4). 1976. 5.50 o.s.i. (ISBN 0-8027-6243-3); PLB 6.85 (ISBN 0-8027-6244-1). Walker & Co.

--A First Look at Insects. LC 73-92451. (First Look at Ser). (Illus.). 32p. (gr. 2-4). 1974. 5.50 o.s.i. (ISBN 0-8027-6181-X); PLB 5.39 (ISBN 0-8027-6182-8). Walker & Co.

--A First Look at Snakes, Lizards & Other Reptiles. LC 74-26315. (Illus.). 32p. (gr. 1-4). 1975. 5.50 o.s.i. (ISBN 0-8027-6212-3); PLB 5.39 (ISBN 0-8027-6211-5). Walker & Co.

--A First Look at Whales. (First Look at Ser.). (gr. k-3). 1980. 7.95 o.s.i. (ISBN 0-8027-6387-1); PLB 8.85 (ISBN 0-8027-6388-X). Walker & Co.

Selsam, Millicent E. & Wexler, Jerome. The Amazing Dandelion. (Illus.). (gr. 2-5). 1977. 7.25 (ISBN 0-688-22129-7); PLB 6.96 (ISBN 0-688-32129-1). Morrow.

Selters, Andrew. High Sierra Hiking Guide to Triple Divide Peak. Winnett, Thomas, ed. LC 79-57596. (High Sierra Hiking Guide Ser.: No. 20). (Illus., Orig.). 1980. pap. 3.95 (ISBN 0-911824-94-4). Wilderness.

Seltman, Charles. Masterpieces of Greek Coinage. (Illus.). 128p. 1980. 20.00 (ISBN 0-916710-72-6). Obol Intl.

Seltman, Charles T. Women in Antiquity. LC 78-20490. 1981. Repr. of 1956 ed. 23.50 (ISBN 0-88355-867-X). Hyperion Conn.

Seltz, David, ed. How to Get Started in Your Own Franchise Business. rev. ed. LC 79-27945. 1980. 19.95 (ISBN 0-87863-172-0). Farnswth Pub.

Seltz, David D. Handbook of Innovative Marketing Techniques. LC 79-27415. 320p. 1981. text ed. 19.95 (ISBN 0-201-07617-9). A-W.

--A Handbook of Retail Promotion Ideas. 1970. 19.95 (ISBN 0-910580-20-0). Farnswth Pub.

--How to Prepare Effective Business Program Blueprints: A Management Handbook. 1981. text ed. price not set (ISBN 0-201-07618-7). A-W.

--MESBIC: An Exciting New Financial Concept with Great Growth Potential for Business. 1981. 15.00 (ISBN 0-87863-197-6). Farnswth Pub.

--Treasury of Business Opportunities...Featuring Over 400 Ways to Make a Fortune Without Leaving Your House. LC 76-47103. 1976. 15.00 (ISBN 0-87863-097-X). Farnswth Pub.

Seltz, David D. & Leslie, Mary. New Businesses Women Can Start & Successfully Operate. LC 77-608270. 1977. 9.95 (ISBN 0-87863-129-1). Farnswth Pub.

Seltz, David D. & Modica, Alfred J., Jr. Negotiate Your Way to Success: Intenious Strategies & Techniques for Succeeding in Any Business or Personal Negotiations. LC 80-24058. 1980. 10.95 (ISBN 0-87863-182-8). Farnswth Pub.

Seltzer, Charles A. Ferguson's Trail. 1979. pap. 1.25 (ISBN 0-505-51357-9). Tower Bks.

--Silver Spurs. 277p. 1975. Repr. of 1935 ed. lib. bdg. 12.25 (ISBN 0-88411-109-1). Amereon Ltd.

Seltzer, Daniel, ed. see Greene, Robert.

Seltzer, Leon F. The Vision of Melville & Conrad. LC 78-108735. 1970. 10.00x (ISBN 0-8214-0065-7). Ohio U Pr.

Seltzer, Mildred, et al. Gerontology in Higher Education. 1978. text ed. 23.95x (ISBN 0-534-00582-9). Wadsworth Pub.

Seltzer, Mildred M., et al. Social Problems of the Aging: Readings. 1978. pap. 10.95x (ISBN 0-534-00484-9). Wadsworth Pub.

Seltzer, Samuel & Bender, I. B. The Dental Pulp. 2nd ed. LC 75-22039. (Illus.). 356p. 1975. text ed. 25.95 (ISBN 0-397-52068-9). Lippincott.

Seltzer, Sandford. Jews & Non-Jews Falling in Love. 1976. 4.00 (ISBN 0-8074-0098-X, 164050). UAHC.

Seltzer, T., tr. see Hauptmann, Gerhart.

Selver, Paul, tr. see Capek, Karel.

Selvi, A. M., et al. Folklore of Other Lands: Folk Tales, Proverbs, Songs, Rhymes & Games of Italy, France, the Hispanic World & Germany. 1956. 9.75 o.p. (ISBN 0-913298-24-7). S F Vanni.

Selvi, Arthur S; see Kellenberger, Hunter.

Selvidge, James N. Hold Your Horses. 2nd ed. (Illus.). 176p. 1976. pap. 6.95. Jacada Pubns.

--Hold Your Horses. (Illus.). 176p. 1976. pap. 6.95 (ISBN 0-915700-01-8). Jacada Pubns.

Selvik, Arne, jt. ed. see Summers, Gene F.

Selvin, Hanan C., jt. auth. see Hirschi, Travis.

Selvon, Samuel. A Brighter Sun. 215p. 1979. 9.00 (ISBN 0-89410-111-0); pap. 5.00 (ISBN 0-89410-110-2). Three Continents.

--The Lonely Londoners. 126p. (Orig.). 1979. 9.00 (ISBN 0-89410-113-7); pap. 5.00 (ISBN 0-89410-112-9). Three Continents.

--Ways of Sunlight. 188p. (Orig.). 1979. 9.00 (ISBN 0-89410-109-9); pap. 5.00 (ISBN 0-89410-108-0). Three Continents.

Selwyn, Edward G. The First Epistle of St. Peter. 2nd ed. (Thornapple Commentaries Ser.). 517p. 1981. pap. 10.95 (ISBN 0-8010-8199-8). Baker Bk.

Selwyn, Victor, et al, eds. Return to Oasis. 256p. 1980. 25.00x (ISBN 0-85683-047-X, Pub by Shepheard-Walwyn England). State Mutual Bk.

Selye, Hans. Stress Without Distress. LC 74-1314. (Illus.). 1974. 10.95 (ISBN 0-397-01026-5). Lippincott.

Selz, Jean. Modern Sculpture: Origins & Evolution. LC 63-14802. 20.00 o.s.i. (ISBN 0-8076-0245-0). Braziller.

Selz, Peter. German Expressionist Painting. (Illus.). 1957. 38.50x (ISBN 0-520-01161-9); pap. 10.95 (ISBN 0-520-02515-6). U of Cal Pr.

Selzer, Arthur. The Heart: Its Function in Health & Disease. rev. ed. (Perspectives in Medicine: No. 1). (YA) (gr. 9 up). 1968. 14.50 (ISBN 0-520-01162-7). U of Cal Pr.

Selzer, Michael. Terrorist Chic. 1979. 9.95 (ISBN 0-8015-7534-6, Hawthorn). Dutton.

Selznick, Joyce. Blue Roses. 336p. 1980. pap. 2.50 (ISBN 0-553-13463-9). Bantam.

Selznick, Philip. T. V. A. & the Grass Roots: A Study in the Sociology of Formal Organization. (California Library Reprint Ser.: No. 103). 1980. 18.50x (ISBN 0-520-03979-3). U of Cal Pr.

Selznick, Philip, jt. auth. see Broom, Leonard.

Selznick, Philip, jt. auth. see Nonet, Phillippe.

Semanov, V. I. Lu Hsun & His Predecessors. Alber, Charles A., tr. from Rus. LC 80-50885. 1980. 25.00 (ISBN 0-87332-153-7). M E Sharpe.

Semb, George, jt. auth. see Ramp, Eugene.

Sembene, Ousmane. God's Bits of Wood. LC 75-133620. 1970. pap. 2.95 o.p. (ISBN 0-385-04430-5, Anch). Doubleday.

Semeiks, Jonna G., jt. auth. see Schechter, Harold.

Semel, Eleanor, jt. auth. see Wiig, Elisabeth.

Semel, Eleanor M., jt. auth. see Wiig, Elisabeth H.

Semenko, Irina M. Vasily Zhukovsky. LC 75-23419. (World Authors Ser.: Russia: No. 271). 1976. lib. bdg. 12.50 (ISBN 0-8057-2995-X). Twayne.

Semenov, N. N. Some Problems in Chemical Kinetics & Reactivity, Vol. 2. Boudart, M., tr. 1959. 19.00x o.p. (ISBN 0-691-08037-2). Princeton U Pr.

Semenza, G. Of Oxygen, Energy & Nutrients, Vol. 1, Pt. 1. (Evolving Life Sciences Ser: First-Hand Accounts of Scientific Ideas & Events). 440p. 1981. 90.00 (ISBN 0-471-27923-4, Pub. by Wiley-Interscience). Wiley.

Semin, G. K., et al. Nuclear Quadrupole Resonance in Chemistry. Shelnitz, P., tr. from Rus. 517p. 1975. 64.95 (ISBN 0-470-77580-7). Halsted Pr.

Seminar on Aacr-Two, Univ. of Nottingham, 1979. Proceedings. 1980. pap. 17.50x (ISBN 0-85365-593-6, Pub. by Lib Assn England). Oryx Pr.

Seminar on Engineering Equipment for Foundries & Advanced Methods of Producing Such Equipment, Geneva, 1977. Engineering Equipment for Foundries: Proceedings. United Nations Economic Commission for Europe, Geneva, ed. (Illus.). 1979. text ed. 81.00 (ISBN 0-08-022421-0). Pergamon.

Seminario De Estudios Hispanicos & Onis, Federico de. Luis Llorens Torres En Su Centenario. LC 80-21479. (Coleccion UPREX, 57 Ser.: Estudios Literarios). 1981. pap. write for info. (ISBN 0-8477-0057-7). U of PR Pr.

Semken, Holmes, jt. ed. see Anderson, Duane C.

Semler, Isabel P. Horatio Parker. LC 72-8291. (Music Ser). 332p. 1973. Repr. of 1942 ed. lib. bdg. 32.50 (ISBN 0-306-70538-9). Da Capo.

Semmel, Bernard. Rise of Free Trade Imperialism. LC 71-112473. 1970. 41.50 (ISBN 0-521-07725-7). Cambridge U Pr.

Semmel, Bernard, ed. Marxism & the Science of War. 288p. 1981. 37.50 (ISBN 0-19-876112-0); pap. 17.95 (ISBN 0-19-876113-9). Oxford U Pr.

Semmens, James P. & Lamers, William M., Jr. Teen-Age Pregnancy: Including Management of Emotional & Constitutional Problems. 132p. 1968. pap. 9.75 spiral (ISBN 0-398-01722-0). C C Thomas.

Semmler, Clement. Douglas Stewart. LC 74-7389. (World Authors Ser.: Australia: No. 327). 176p. 1974. lib. bdg. 12.50 (ISBN 0-8057-2863-5). Twayne.

Semniuk, Bazyli, jt. ed. see Kryt, Dobromila.

Sempangi, F. Kefa. A Distant Grief. LC 79-50394. 1979. pap. 4.95 (ISBN 0-8307-0684-4, 5411807). Regal.

Semple, J. G., jt. auth. see Tyrrell, J. A.

Semple, Jean. Hearing-Impaired Preschool Child: A Book for Parents. 104p. 1970. pap. 7.50 spiral (ISBN 0-398-01724-7). C C Thomas.

Semprevivo, Philip C. Systems Analysis: Definition Process & Design. LC 75-30539. (Illus.). 352p. 1976. text ed. 16.95 (ISBN 0-574-21045-8, 13-4045); instr's guide avail. (ISBN 0-574-21046-6, 13-4046). SRA.

--Teams in Development Information Systems. LC 80-50608. (Orig.). 1980. pap. 16.75 (ISBN 0-917072-20-0). Yourdon.

Semprun, J. La Guerre Est Finie. Seaver, Richard, tr. (Illus., Text for the film by Alain Resnais. Film editor Robert Hughes.). 5.75 (ISBN 0-8446-2906-5). Peter Smith.

Semrad, Alice. Comprehensive Review for Medical Technologists. 2nd ed. LC 78-31823. 1979. pap. text ed. 12.95 (ISBN 0-8016-4487-9). Mosby.

Sen, Amartya. Employment, Technology & Development. (Economic Development Ser.). 204p. 1975. text ed. 22.50x (ISBN 0-19-877052-9); pap. text ed. 3.50x (ISBN 0-19-877053-7). Oxford U Pr.

Sen, Bandhudas. The Green Revolution in India: A Perspective. LC 74-11066. 118p. 1974. 11.95 (ISBN 0-470-77590-4). Halsted Pr.

Sen, Chitrabhanu. Dictionary of Vedic Rituals. 1978. 22.50x o.p. (ISBN 0-8364-0278-2). South Asia Bks.

Sen, P. C. Thyristor DC Drives. LC 80-21226. 350p. 1981. 30.00 (ISBN 0-471-06070-4, Pub. by Wiley-Interscience). Wiley.

Sen, P. K. Sequential Nonparametrics: Invariance Principles & Statistical Inference. (Probability & Mathematical Statistics Ser.). 350p. 1981. 30.00 (ISBN 0-471-06013-5, Pub. by Wiley-Interscience). Wiley.

Sen, P. K., jt. auth. see Puri, M. L.

Sen, Pradip. And Then the Sun. 8.00 (ISBN 0-89253-734-5); flexible cloth 4.80 (ISBN 0-89253-735-3). Ind-US Inc.

Sen, Pranab K. Logic, Induction & Ontology, Vol. 2. (Jadavpur Studies in Philosophy). 1980. text ed. write for info. (ISBN 0-391-01765-9). Humanities.

Sen, R. N. & Weil, C., eds. Statistical Mechanics & Field Theory. LC 72-4108. 1972. 44.95 (ISBN 0-470-77595-5). Halsted Pr.

Sen, Samar. The Complete Poems of Samar Sen. Nandy, Pritish, tr. (Writers Workshop Saffronbird Ser.). 1975. 11.00 (ISBN 0-88253-514-5); pap. text ed. 4.80 (ISBN 0-88253-513-7). Ind-US Inc.

Sen, Samar R. Strategy for Agricultural Development & Other Essays on Economic Policy & Planning. 2nd ed. 1966. 6.50x o.p. (ISBN 0-210-34027-4). Asia.

Senay, James J. U. S. Government Surplus: A Complete Buyer's Manual. LC 80-18466. 120p. (Orig.). 1981. 12.95 (ISBN 0-936218-00-2); pap. 7.95 (ISBN 0-936218-01-0). Rainbow Pub Co.

Senayake, Pramilla, ed. see International Planned Parenthood Federation.

Sendak, Maurice. Outside Over There. LC 79-2682. (An Ursula Nordstrom Bk). (Illus.). 48p. (gr. k up). 1981. 12.95 (ISBN 0-06-025523-4, HarpJ); PLB 12.89 (ISBN 0-06-025524-2). Har-Row.

Sender. Requiem por un Campesino. (Easy Reader, C). pap. 3.75 (ISBN 0-88436-055-5, SPA201052). EMC.

Sender, Ramon J. Seven Red Sundays. 1961. pap. 0.95 o.s.i. (ISBN 0-02-024870-9, Collier). Macmillan.

Sendler, Dave, jt. auth. see Sabin, Lou.

Seneca. Medea. Hadas, Moses, tr. LC 56-1501. 1956. pap. 1.45 o.p. (ISBN 0-672-60228-8, LLA55). Bobbs.

--Medea. Costa, C. D., ed. 179p. 1973. 17.95x (ISBN 0-19-814451-2). Oxford U Pr.

--Oedipus. Hadas, Moses, tr. LC 55-13616. 1955. pap. 2.50 (ISBN 0-672-60210-5, LLA44). Bobbs.

--Stoic Philosophy of Seneca: Essays & Letters. Hadas, Moses & Hadas, Moses, eds. 1968. pap. 4.95 (ISBN 0-393-00459-7, Norton Lib). Norton.

--Thyestes. Hadas, Moses, tr. LC 57-14639. 1957. pap. 1.95 (ISBN 0-672-60258-X, LLA76). Bobbs.

Seneca, Joseph J. & Taussig, Michael K. Environmental Economics. 2nd ed. (Illus.). 1979. ref. ed. 18.95 (ISBN 0-13-283291-7). P-H.

Senecal, Jean-Michel, jt. auth. see Jacquemard, Yves.

Senecki, jt. auth. see Hewer.

Senefelder, Alois. A Complete Course of Lithography. LC 68-27721. (Graphic Art Ser). (Illus.). 1968. Repr. of 1819 ed. lib. bdg. 35.00 (ISBN 0-306-71155-9). Da Capo.

Senelick, Laurence, et al. British Music Hall 1840-1923: A Bibliography & Guide to Sources with a Supplement on European Music-Hall. (Archon Books on Popular Entertainments Ser.). 1981. 37.50 (ISBN 0-208-01840-9, Archon). Shoe String.

Senese, Donald J. Modernizing the Chinese Dragon: The Prospective Impact of Western Aid & Technology on Mainland China. pap. 10.00 (ISBN 0-686-64115-9). Coun Am Affairs.

Seneviratne, H. L. Rituals of the Kandyan State. LC 77-80842. (Studies in Social Anthropology: No. 22). (Illus.). 1978. 27.50 (ISBN 0-521-21736-9). Cambridge U Pr.

Seng, Roger W. The Skills of Selling. (Illus.). 1978. 14.95 (ISBN 0-8144-5458-5). Am Mgmt.

Seng, You-Poh, jt. ed. see Hughes, Helen.

Sengel, P. Morphogenesis of Skin. LC 74-25659. (Developmental & Cell Biology Ser.: No. 2). (Illus.). 300p. 1975. 69.00 (ISBN 0-521-20644-8). Cambridge U Pr.

Sengstock, Mary C. Chaldean-Americans Changing Conceptions of Ethnic Identity. (Illus.). 220p. Date not set. 7.95x (ISBN 0-913256-42-0). Ctr Migration.

Sen Gupta, Bhabani. Communism in Indian Politics. LC 73-190190. (Southern Asian Inst. Ser). 390p. 1972. 22.50x (ISBN 0-231-03568-3). Columbia U Pr.

--Soviet-Asian Relations in the 1970s & Beyond: An Interperceptional Study. LC 76-24368. 1976. text ed. 32.50 (ISBN 0-275-23740-0). Praeger.

Sengupta, Jati K., jt. auth. see Tintner, Gerhard.

Sen Gupta, N. N. Heredity in Mental Traits. 207p. 1980. Repr. of 1941 ed. lib. bdg. 50.00 (ISBN 0-89984-409-X). Century Bookbindery.

Sengupta, Nirmal. Destitutes & Development. 1979. text ed. 9.00x (ISBN 0-391-01864-7). Humanities.

Sengupta, Padmini. Sarojini Naidu: A Biography. (Illus.). 1966. 10.00 o.p. (ISBN 0-210-27023-3). Asia.

Sengupta, Surajit. Business Law in India. 894p. (Orig.). 1979. pap. text ed. 9.95x (ISBN 0-19-560658-2). Oxford U Pr.

Senick, Gerard J., ed. Children's Literature Review: Excerpts from Critical Commentaries on Juvenile & Young People's Authors & Their Books, 3 vols. Incl. Vol. 1. 1976 (ISBN 0-8103-0077-X); Vol. 2. 1976 (ISBN 0-8103-0078-8); Vol. 3 (ISBN 0-8103-0079-6). LC 75-34953. (Children's Literature Review Ser.). 44.00 ea. Gale.

Senior, Donald. First & Second Peter. (New Testament Message Ser.). 9.95 (ISBN 0-89453-143-3); pap. 4.95 (ISBN 0-89453-208-1). M Glazier.

--Invitation to Matthew: A Commentary on the Gospel of Matthew with Complete Text from the Jerusalem Bible. LC 77-73337. 1977. pap. 2.95 (ISBN 0-385-12211-X, Im). Doubleday.

Senior, Donald, ed. see Collins, Adela Y.

Senior, Donald, ed. see Crowe, Jerome.

Senior, Donald, ed. see Harrington, Daniel J.

Senior, Donald, ed. see Harrington, Wilfrid.

Senior, Donald, ed. see Karris, Robert J.

Senior, Donald, ed. see McPolin, James.

Senior, Donald, ed. see Maly, Eugene H.

Senior, Donald, ed. see Reese, James M.

Senior, Elinor K. British Regulars in Montreal: An Imperial Garrison, 1832-1854. (Illus.). 300p. 1981. 29.95 (ISBN 0-7735-0372-2). McGill-Queens U Pr.

Senior, Nassau W. Journals Kept in France & Italy from 1848 to 1852. LC 70-126608. (Europe 1815-1945 Ser.). 654p. 1973. Repr. of 1871 ed. lib. bdg. 59.50 (ISBN 0-306-70055-7). Da Capo.

Senn, Alfred E. Russian Revolution in Switzerland, 1914-1917. LC 76-143766. 1971. 25.00x (ISBN 0-299-05941-3). U of Wis Pr.

Senn, J. A. The Deadly Dinner. Verdick, Mary, ed. (Pal Paperbacks, Pal Skills Ser.). (Illus., Orig.). (gr. 7-12). 1978. pap. text ed. 1.25 (ISBN 0-8374-6711-X). Xerox Ed Pubns.

--The Wolf King. Verdick, Mary, ed. (Pal Paperbacks - Pal Skills Ser.). (Illus., Orig.). (gr. 7-12). 1978. pap. text ed. 1.25 (ISBN 0-8374-6707-1). Xerox Ed Pubns.

Senn, James A. Information Systems in Management. 1978. text ed. 22.95x (ISBN 0-534-00563-2). Wadsworth Pub.

Senn, Milton J. Speaking Out for America's Children. LC 76-49756. (Fastback Ser.: No. 17). 1977. 15.00x (ISBN 0-300-02107-0); pap. 4.95x (ISBN 0-300-02113-5). Yale U Pr.

Senn, Steve. The Double Disappearance of Walter Fozbek. new ed. 128p. (gr. 8-12). 1980. 8.95 (ISBN 0-8038-1571-9). Hastings.

--Spacebread. LC 80-18326. 224p. (gr. 7 up). 1981. PLB 9.95 (ISBN 0-689-30830-2, Argo). Atheneum.

Senna & Siegel. Cases & Comments on Juvenile Law. (Criminal Justice Ser.). 600p. 1976. pap. text ed. 17.95 (ISBN 0-8299-0629-0). West Pub.

Senna, Joseph J. & Siegel, Larry J. Introduction to Criminal Justice. 2nd ed. (Criminal Justice Ser.). (Illus.). 550p. 1981. text ed. 16.95 (ISBN 0-8299-0409-3). West Pub.

--Introduction to Criminal Justice. (Criminal Justice Ser.). (Illus.). 1978. text ed. 16.95 (ISBN 0-8299-0170-1); instrs.' manual avail. (ISBN 0-8299-0600-2). West Pub.

Senna, Joseph J., jt. auth. see Siegel, Larry J.

Sennett, Richard, ed. Classic Essays on the Culture of Cities. (Orig.). 1969. pap. text ed. 10.95 (ISBN 0-13-135194-X). P-H.

Sennett, Ted. Masters of Menace: Greenstreet & Lorre. 1979. pap. 8.95 o.p. (ISBN 0-525-47533-8). Dutton.

Sennett, Ted, ed. The Movie Buff's Book. (Orig.). 1975. pap. 3.95 o.p. (ISBN 0-515-03649-8, 3649, Harv). HarBraceJ.

Sennewald, Charles A. Effective Security Management. LC 78-6058. (Illus.). 1978. 15.95 (ISBN 0-913708-30-5). Butterworths.

--The Process of Investigation: Concepts & Strategies for the Security Professional. 255p. 1981. text ed. 21.95 (ISBN 0-409-95018-1). Butterworths.

Senning, Hillyer, jt. auth. see Brown, Doris S.

Seno, S., jt. auth. see Cowdry, E. V.

Senseney, Dan. Scanlon of the Sub Service. LC 63-11210. (gr. 6-9). 5.95 o.p. (ISBN 0-385-05149-2). Doubleday.

Sensoir, Jean-Jacques. The Ninth Decade: Secret Plans for the Coming Communist Takeovers. 1977. 7.50 o.p. (ISBN 0-682-48801-1). Exposition.

Sentell, Perry R. The Law of Municipal Tort Liability in Georgia. 3rd ed. LC 79-24276. 184p. 1980. pap. text ed. 15.00x (ISBN 0-89854-053-4). U of GA Inst Govt.

Senter, Ruth. So You're the Pastor's Wife. 1979. 6.95 (ISBN 0-310-38820-1). Zondervan.

--Unhappy Secrets of the Christian Life: Study Guide. 80p. 1980. pap. 1.50 (ISBN 0-310-35463-3). Zondervan.

Senterfitt, Arnold D. Airports of Mexico & Central America. (Illus.). 1980. pap. 24.95 (Pub. by Senterfitt). Aviation.

Senter Fitt, Arnold D. Airports of Mexico & Centro America. 15th ed. (Illus.). 560p. (Orig.). 1980. pap. 24.95 (ISBN 0-937260-00-2). Senterfitt.

Senterfitt, Arnold D. Baja Chart. 1980. plastic coated 9.50 (Pub. by Senterfitt). Aviation.

Sentlowitz, Michael & Trivisone, Margaret. College Algebra. (Math - Remedial & Precalculus Ser.). 576p. 1981. text ed. 14.95 (ISBN 0-201-06626-2). A-W.

--College Algebra & Trigonometry. (Math-Remedial & Precalculus Ser.). 576p. 1981. text ed. 14.95 (ISBN 0-201-06676-9). A-W.

Sentlowitz, Michael, jt. auth. see Brett, William.

Sentman, Everett, jt. auth. see Alderson, George.

Seo, K. K. & Winger, Bernard J. Managerial Economics. 5th ed. 1979. 19.00 (ISBN 0-256-02177-5). Irwin.

Seo, K. K., jt. auth. see Long, William A.

Sepamla, Sipho. The Soweto I Love. (Orig.). 1977. pap. 5.00 (ISBN 0-686-64551-0). Three Continents.

Sepharial. The Kabala of Numbers. LC 80-53342. 423p. 1980. Repr. of 1974 ed. lib. bdg. 12.95x (ISBN 0-89370-627-2). Borgo Pr.

--Manual of Astrology. 263p. 1981. pap. 10.00 (ISBN 0-89540-065-0). Sun Pub.

--A Manual of Occultism. LC 80-53345. 356p. 1980. Repr. of 1979 ed. lib. bdg. 11.95x (ISBN 0-89370-646-9). Borgo Pr.

Sepmeyer, Inez, jt. auth. see Sasnett, Martena.

Septier, A., ed. Focusing of Charged Particles, 2 Vols. 1967. Vol. 1. 55.25 (ISBN 0-12-636901-1); Vol. 2. 52.25 (ISBN 0-12-636902-X); Set. 87.25 (ISBN 0-685-05127-7). Acad Pr.

Sequeira, M. S. Motorcycles. LC 78-5963. (Easy-Read Fact Bks). (Illus.). (gr. 2-4). 1978. PLB 6.45 s&l (ISBN 0-531-01373-1). Watts.

Ser-Vo-Tel Institute. Dishwashing Procedures. (Foodservice Career Education Ser.). 1975. pap. 4.95 (ISBN 0-8436-2026-9). CBI Pub.

--Host-Hostess. (Foodservice Career Education Ser.). 1974. pap. 4.95 (ISBN 0-8436-2024-2). CBI Pub.

--Salad Preparation. (Foodservice Career Education Ser.). 1975. pap. 4.95 (ISBN 0-8436-2019-6). CBI Pub.

--Sandwich Preparation. (Foodservice Career Education Ser.). 1975. pap. 4.95 (ISBN 0-8436-2015-3). CBI Pub.

--Waiter-Waitress. (Foodservice Career Education Ser.). 1974. pap. text ed. 4.95 (ISBN 0-8436-2022-6). CBI Pub.

Ser-Vol-Tel Institute. Breakfast Preparation. (Foodservice Career Education Ser.). 1974. pap. 4.95 (ISBN 0-8436-2030-7). CBI Pub.

--Busing Attendant. (Foodservice Career Education Ser.). 1974. pap. 4.95 (ISBN 0-8436-2018-8). CBI Pub.

--Cashiering. (Foodservice Career Education Ser.). 1974. pap. 4.95 (ISBN 0-8436-2011-0). CBI Pub.

--Cleaning & Sanitation. (Foodservice Career Education Ser.). 1974. pap. 4.95 (ISBN 0-8436-2009-9). CBI Pub.

--Counter Service. (Food Service Career Education Ser.). 1974. pap. 4.95 (ISBN 0-8436-2020-X). CBI Pub.

--Customer-Employee Relationship. (Foodservice Career Education Ser.). 1974. pap. 4.95 (ISBN 0-8436-2013-7). CBI Pub.

--Food Care & Food Storage. (Foodservice Career Education Ser.). 1974. pap. 4.95 (ISBN 0-8436-2014-5). CBI Pub.

--Foodservice Safety. (Foodservice Career Education Ser.). 1974. pap. 4.95 (ISBN 0-8436-2008-0). CBI Pub.

--Foodservice Vocabulary. (Foodservice Career Education Ser.). 1975. pap. 4.95 (ISBN 0-8436-2007-2). CBI Pub.

--Fry Cooking. (Foodservice Career Education Ser.). 1974. pap. 4.95 (ISBN 0-8436-2028-5). CBI Pub.

--Grill Cooking. (Foodservice Career Education Ser.). 1974. pap. 4.95 (ISBN 0-8436-2029-3). CBI Pub.

--Kitchen Sanitation. (Foodservice Career Education Ser.). 1974. pap. 4.95 (ISBN 0-8436-2005-6). CBI Pub.

--Luncheon Cooking. (Foodservice Career Education Ser.). 1974. pap. 4.95 (ISBN 0-8436-2031-5). CBI Pub.

Serafetinides, E. A. Psychiatric Research in Practice: Biobehavioral Themes. (Seminars in Psychology Ser.). 1981. 24.50 (ISBN 0-8089-1316-6). Grune.

Serafin, Donald & Buncke, Harry. Microsurgical Composite Tissue Transplantation. LC 78-12279. (Illus.). 1978. text ed. 55.50 (ISBN 0-8016-0882-1). Mosby.

Serafine, Mary L., ed. see Galuppi, Baldassare.

Serafini, Aldo, jt. auth. see Guter, Marvin.

Seranne, Ann. Complete Book of Freezer Cookery. 7.95 o.p. (ISBN 0-385-03994-8). Doubleday.

--Complete Book of Home Preserving. 7.95 o.p. (ISBN 0-385-06608-2). Doubleday.

--The Home Canning & Preserving Book. 1975. pap. 4.95 (ISBN 0-06-463424-8, EH). Har-Row.

Seranne, Ann & Gaden, Eileen. The Blender Cookbook. LC 61-11228. 7.95 o.p. (ISBN 0-385-07978-8). Doubleday.

Seranne, Ann, ed. Midwestern Junior League Cookbook. 1978. 12.95 (ISBN 0-679-51204-7). McKay.

Seranne, Anne. The Joy of Breeding Your Own Show Dog. LC 80-16081. (Illus.). 272p. 1980. 11.95 (ISBN 0-87605-413-0). Howell Bk.

Serapiao, Luis B. & El-Khawas, Mohamed A. Mozambique in the Twentieth Century: From Colonialism to Independence. LC 79-64964. 1979. pap. text ed. 12.00 (ISBN 0-8191-0502-3). U Pr of Amer.

Serban, William, jt. ed. see Brady, Darlene.

Serbo, V. G., jt. auth. see Kotkin, G. I.

Sercarz, Eli, ed. Regulatory Genetics of the Immune System. 1977. 38.00 (ISBN 0-12-637160-1). Acad Pr.

Sercarz, Eli E. & Cunningham, Alastair J., eds. Strategies of Immune Regulation. LC 79-28392. 1980. 39.50 (ISBN 0-12-637140-7). Acad Pr.

Serebriakoff, Victor. How Intelligent Are You? 128p. 1974. pap. 1.50 (ISBN 0-451-09295-3, E9295, Sig). NAL.

Sered, Joan B. Oral Communication. 1978. pap. text ed. 7.95x (ISBN 0-02-471260-4). Macmillan.

Sereno, Kenneth & Bodaken, Edward. Trans-per: Understanding Human Communication. 1975. 14.95 (ISBN 0-395-18701-X); teaching strategies guide 1.50 (ISBN 0-395-18783-4). HM.

Serfass, Robert, jt. auth. see Papers Presented Before the College of Sports Medicine.

Serfaty, Simon. Fading Partnership, America & Europe After Thirty Years. LC 78-19755. 128p. 1979. 19.95 (ISBN 0-03-041816-X). Praeger.

--The United States, Western Europe, & the Third World: Allies & Adversaries, Vol. II. LC 80-50588. (Significant Issues Ser.: No. 4). 53p. 1980. 5.95 (ISBN 0-89206-018-2). CSI Studies.

Serfaty, Simon, ed. The Foreign Policies of the French Left. LC 79-53137. (Westview Special Studies in West European Politics & Society). 1979. lib. bdg. 16.50x (ISBN 0-89158-652-0). Westview.

Serfaty, Simon & Gray, Lawrence, eds. The Italian Communist Party: Yesterday, Today, & Tomorrow. LC 79-6833. (Contributions in Political Science: No. 46). (Illus.). xiii, 256p. 1980. lib. bdg. 29.95 (ISBN 0-313-20995-2, GIT/). Greenwood.

Serfaty, Simon, ed. see Braga de Macedo, Jorge.

Serfling, Robert J. Approximation Theorems of Mathematical Statistics. LC 80-13493. (Wiley Ser. in Probability & Statistics: Probability & Mathematical Statistics). 400p. 1980. 34.95 (ISBN 0-471-02403-1). Wiley.

Serge, Victor. Memoirs of a Revolutionary, 1901-1944. Sedgwick, Peter, tr. (Oxford Paperbacks Ser). (Orig.). 1967. pap. 8.95x (ISBN 0-19-281037-5). Oxford U Pr.

Sergeant, Elizabeth S. Willa Cather: A Memoir. LC 52-13732. (Illus.). 1963. pap. 1.95 (ISBN 0-8032-5179-3, BB 159, Bison). U of Nebr Pr.

Sergeant, Howard, ed. The Two Continents Book of Childrens Verse. 1977. Repr. of 1972 ed. 7.95 (ISBN 0-8467-0238-X, Pub. by Two Continents). Hippocrene Bks.

Sergeant, Philip W. Witches & Warlocks. LC 72-164055. (Illus.). 290p. 1975. Repr. of 1936 ed. 20.00 (ISBN 0-8103-3979-X). Gale.

Sergeant, Philip W., tr. see Znosko-Borovsky, Eugene.

Sergeeva, L. M., jt. auth. see Lipatov, Yu. S.

Sergio, Lisa. Jesus & Woman: An Exciting Discovery of What He Offered Her. LC 75-4365. 139p. 1980. pap. 4.95 (ISBN 0-914440-44-6). EPM Pubns.

Sergiovanni, Thomas J. & Carver, Fred D. The New School Executive: A Theory of Administration. 2nd ed. (Illus.). 1980. text ed. 16.50 scp (ISBN 0-06-045906-9, HarpC). Har-Row.

Sergrovanni, T., et al. Educational Governance & Administration. 1980. 18.95 (ISBN 0-13-236653-3). P-H.

Serif, Med. How to Manage Yourself. LC 65-23870. (gr. 9 up). 1965. 9.95 (ISBN 0-8119-0098-3). Fell.

Serig, Joseph A., jt. ed. see Hughes, Richard.

Serio, Mario & Martini, Luciano, eds. Animal Models in Human Reproduction. 499p. 1980. text ed. 45.00 (ISBN 0-89004-522-4). Raven.

Seriwaza, Katsusuke. Massage: The Oriental Method. LC 73-188762. (Illus.). 80p. 1972. 6.95 o.p. (ISBN 0-87040-080-0); pap. 6.95 (ISBN 0-87040-168-8). Japan Pubns.

Serizawa, Katsusuke. Tsubo: Vital Points for Oriental Therapy. (Illus.). 256p. 1976. 22.00 (ISBN 0-87040-350-8). Japan Pubns.

Serjeant, E. P. & Dempsey, B., eds. Ionisation Constants of Organic Acids in Aqueous Solution. (Chemical Data Ser.: Vol. 23). (Illus.). 1979. text ed. 190.00 (ISBN 0-08-022339-7). Pergamon.

Serjeant, R. B. & Bidwell, R. L., eds. Arabian Studies-One. (Illus.). 200p. 1974. 21.50x o.p. (ISBN 0-87471-482-6). Rowman.

Serman, Ilya Z. Konstantin Batyushkov. (World Authors Ser.: Russia: No. 287). 1974. lib. bdg. 12.50 (ISBN 0-8057-2118-5). Twayne.

Sernak, Cyril W. Trademark Register of the United States: 1881-1981. rev. ed. LC 73-86256. 1981. pap. 97.00 (ISBN 0-685-76665-9, 0082-5786). Trademark Reg.

Sernett, Milton C. Black Religion & American Evangelicalism: White Protestants, Plantation Missions, & the Flowering of Negro Christianity, 1787-1865. LC 75-4754. (ATLA Monograph: No. 7). (Illus.). 320p. 1975. 15.00 (ISBN 0-8108-0803-X). Scarecrow.

Seroff, Victor. Hector Berlioz. (gr. 7 up). 1967. 4.95g o.s.i. (ISBN 0-02-781910-8). Macmillan.

Seronde, Joseph, jt. ed. see Peyre, Henri.

Serote, Mongane W. Yakhal' Inkomo. 1974. pap. 5.00 o.s.i. (ISBN 0-685-80780-0, Pub by Ravan Press). Three Continents.

Serov, S. F. & Scully, R. F. Histological Typing of Ovarian Tumours. (World Health Organization: International Histological Classification of Tumours Ser.). 1973. 36.50 (ISBN 0-685-77242-X, 70-1-009-20); incl. slides 112.00 (ISBN 0-685-77243-8, 70-1-009-00). Am Soc Clinical.

Serpell, Christopher & Serpell, Jean. The Travellers' Guide to Elba & the Tuscan Archipelago. (Travellers' Guide Ser.). (Illus.). 1979. 9.95 (ISBN 0-224-01352-1, Pub. by Chatto Bodley Jonathan). Merrimack Bk Serv.

Serpell, Jean, jt. auth. see Serpell, Christopher.

Serraillier, Ian. Silver Sword. LC 59-6556. (Illus.). (gr. 7-9). 1959. 9.95 (ISBN 0-87599-104-1). S G Phillips.

Serraillier, Ian, jt. auth. see Ridout, Ronald.

Serrane, Ann, ed. The Southern Junior League Cookbook. 640p. 1981. pap. 7.95 (ISBN 0-345-29518-8). Ballantine.

Serrano, Antonio, jt. auth. see Cowman, Charles E.

Serrano, Irma Garcia De see Garcia de Serrano, Irma.

Serrano, M. J., tr. see Valera, Juan.

Serrano-Plaja, Arturo. Magic Realism in Cervantes: Don Quixote As Seen Through Tom Sawyer and The Idiot. Rudder, Robert S., tr. LC 71-94991. 1970. 15.75x (ISBN 0-520-01591-6). U of Cal Pr.

Serratrice, G., ed. Peroneal Atrophy & Related Disorders. Roux, H. LC 78-62593. (Illus.). 376p. 1979. 45.50 (ISBN 0-89352-028-4). Masson Pub.

Serre, J. P. Trees. 140p. 1980. 29.80 (ISBN 0-387-10103-9). Springer-Verlag.

Serres, Jean, jt. auth. see Wood, John R.

Serteant. Islamic Textiles. 1972. 35.00x (ISBN 0-685-77132-6). Intl Bk Ctr.

Sertillanges, A. D. The Intellectual Life. pap. 5.95 (ISBN 0-87061-053-8). Chr Classics.

Sertorio, L., jt. ed. see Cabibbo, N.

Serullaz, Maurice. The French Drawings: Great Drawings of the Louvre. LC 68-23040. (Illus.). 20.00 o.s.i. (ISBN 0-8076-0472-0). Braziller.

Serumaga, Robert. Return to the Shadows. (African Writers Ser.). 1969. pap. text ed. 4.95x (ISBN 0-435-90054-4). Heinemann Ed.

SerVaas, Cory, et al. The Saturday Evening Post Fiber & Bran Better Health Cookbook. LC 77-7804. (Illus.). 1977. 12.95 (ISBN 0-89387-008-0). Sat Eve Post.

--The Saturday Evening Post Fiber & Bran Better Health Cookbook. LC 80-67052. (Illus.). 1977. pap. 6.50 (ISBN 0-89387-048-X). Sat Eve Post.

Servadio, Emilio. Psychology Today. LC 65-27637. 7.50 o.p. (ISBN 0-912326-16-6). Garrett-Helix.

Servadio, Emilio, jt. auth. see Cavanna, Roberto.

Servadio, Gaia. Melinda. Conrad, L. K., tr. from It. LC 68-14913. 1968. 6.95 (ISBN 0-374-20588-4). FS&G.

Servagna. The Offsprings of Servagna. (Translated rom Kannada). 12.00 (ISBN 0-89253-609-8); flexible cloth 6.75 (ISBN 0-89253-610-1). Ind-US Inc.

Servan-Schreiber, J. J. American Challenge. 1976. pap. 1.65 (ISBN 0-380-01016-X, 11965, Discus). Avon.

Servan-Schreiber, Jean-Jacques. The World Challenge. 1981. 14.95 (ISBN 0-671-42524-2). S&S.

Serven, James E. Colt Firearms from Eighteen Thirty-Six. LC 54-8380. (Illus.). 416p. 1979. 29.95 (ISBN 0-8117-0400-9). Stackpole.

--Conquering the Frontiers. LC 74-75583. 1974. 19.95 (ISBN 0-910618-39-9). Foun Pubns.

Serventy, Vincent. Zoo Walkabout. 160p. 1980. 17.95x (ISBN 0-00-216420-5, Pub. by W Collins Australia). Intl Schol Bk Serv.

Servey, Richad W. Elementary Social Studies: A Skills Emphasis. 600p. 1981. text ed. 17.95 (ISBN 0-205-07213-5, 2372134). Allyn.

Service, Alastair. Architects of London. 1979. 22.95 (ISBN 0-8038-0017-7). Hastings.

--Edwardian Architecture: A Handbook. (World of Art Ser.). (Illus.). 1978. 17.95 (ISBN 0-19-519979-0); pap. 9.95 (ISBN 0-19-519982-0). Oxford U Pr.

Service, Elman R. The Hunters. (Illus.). 1966. pap. 3.95 ref. ed. o.p. (ISBN 0-13-448076-7). P-H.

--Origins of the State & Civilization: The Process of Cultural Evolution. 1975. pap. text ed. 7.95 (ISBN 0-393-09224-0). Norton.

Service, M. W. Mosquito Ecology: Field Sampling Methods. 1976. 87.95 (ISBN 0-470-15191-9). Halsted Pr.

Service, Robert. Collected Poems of Robert Service. LC 63-11542. 1944. 10.00 (ISBN 0-396-01356-2). Dodd.

--More Selected Verse of Robert Service. LC 71-171047. pap. 2.50 (ISBN 0-396-06562-7). Dodd.

--The Shooting of Dan McGrew & Other Favorite Poems. LC 80-16040. 1980. pap. 3.95 (ISBN 0-396-07897-4). Dodd.

--The Song of the Campfire. LC 78-15108. (Illus.). 1978. 6.95 (ISBN 0-396-07623-8). Dodd.

Serville, Paul De. Port Philip Gentlemen. (Illus.). 256p. 1980. 49.00x (ISBN 0-19-554212-6). Oxford U Pr.

Servin, Manuel P. Mexican Americans. 2nd ed. LC 73-8357. Orig. Title: An Awakened Minority. 320p. 1974. pap. text ed. 7.95x (ISBN 0-02-477940-7, 47794). Macmillan.

Serviss, Garrett P. The Second Deluge. 1976. lib. bdg. 12.95x (ISBN 0-89968-172-7). Lightyear.

Sesame Street. Cookie Monster's Book of Cookie Shapes. (A Tell-a-Tale Reader Ser.). (gr. k-3). 1979. PLB 4.77 (ISBN 0-307-68403-2, Golden Pr). Western Pub.

--The King on a Swing. (Sesame Street Pop-up Ser: No. 6). (Illus.). (ps-2). 1972. 4.95 (ISBN 0-394-82461-X, BYR). Random.

--More Posters from Sesame Street. (Illus.). 12p. (gr. 2-5). 1975. pap. 2.50 (ISBN 0-394-83176-4). Random.

--Sesame Street Storybook. (Illus.). (ps-4). 1971. 4.95 (ISBN 0-394-82332-X, BYR); PLB 5.99 (ISBN 0-394-92332-4). Random.

--Sherlock Hemlock: Great Twiddlebug Mystery. (Tell-a-Tale Readers). (Illus.). (gr. k-3). 1972. PLB 4.77 (ISBN 0-307-68564-0, Whitman). Western Pub.

--What Happens Next. (Sesame Street Pop-up Ser: No. 4). (Illus.). (ps-2). 1971. 4.95 o.p. (ISBN 0-394-82336-2). Random.

Seshadri, K. Agricultural Administration in Andhra Pradesh: A Study of the Process of Implementation of Intensive Agricultural Development Programmes. (Illus.). 302p. 1974. lib. bdg. 13.50 o.p. (ISBN 0-88253-490-4). InterCulture.

Seshadri, S. R. Fundamentals of Transmission Lines & Electromagnetic Fields. LC 77-128908. (Engineering Science Ser). 1971. text ed. 25.95 (ISBN 0-201-06722-6). A-W.

Seskin, Jane, jt. auth. see Mandel, Loring.

Sesonske, Alexander, jt. auth. see Glasstone, Samuel.

Sessions, Bruce. The Complete Dog Training Manual. (Illus.). 1978. pap. 6.95 (ISBN 0-8306-7983-9, 983). TAB Bks.

Sessions, Keith. Vanner's How-to Guide to Murals, Painting & Pinstriping. (Illus.). 1978. 8.95 (ISBN 0-8306-9888-4); pap. 5.95 (ISBN 0-8306-1032-4, 1032). TAB Bks.

Sessions, Ken. Second Class FCC Encyclopedia: Complete Study Guide to the Commercial Radio Telephone Exam. LC 74-75219. 602p. 1975. pap. 12.95 (ISBN 0-8306-4652-3, 652). TAB Bks.

Sessions, Ken, ed. Master Handbook of One Thousand and One Practical Electronic Circuits. LC 75-31458. 602p. 1975. pap. 13.95 (ISBN 0-8306-4800-3, 800). TAB Bks.

Sessions, Kendall W. The Homeowner's Handbook of Plumbing & Repair. LC 77-2133. 1978. text ed. 23.95x (ISBN 0-471-02550-X). Wiley.

Sessions, Kendall Webster. Discrete-Transistor Circuit Sourcemaster. LC 78-6774. 1978. text ed. 33.95 (ISBN 0-471-02626-3). Wiley.

Sessions, Kenneth W. Amateur FM Conversion & Construction Projects. LC 74-79584. (Illus.). 256p. 1974. 8.95 o.p. (ISBN 0-8306-4722-8); pap. 5.95 o.p. (ISBN 0-8306-3722-2, 722). TAB Bks.

--How to Be a Ham; Including Latest FCC Rules. LC 73-86768. 192p. 1974. 7.95 o.p. (ISBN 0-8306-4673-6); pap. 3.95 o.p. (ISBN 0-8306-3673-0, 673). TAB Bks.

Sessions, Ron. Hydra-Matic Transmissions. (Orig.). 1981. pap. 9.95 (ISBN 0-89586-051-1). H P Bks.

Sessler, Gloria J. Strokes: How to Prevent It-How to Survive. 256p. 1980. 14.95 (ISBN 0-13-852913-2, Spec); pap. 6.95 (ISBN 0-686-63391-1). P-H.

Sessoms, jt. auth. see Stein.

Sessoms, H. Douglas, et al. Leisure Services: The Organized Recreation & Parks System. rev. 5th ed. (Illus.). 416p. 1975. text ed. 15.95 (ISBN 0-13-530105-X). P-H.

Sestrap, Betsy, jt. auth. see Gault, Lila.

Setai, Bethuel. The Political Economy of South Africa: The Making of Poverty. 1977. pap. text ed. 9.50x (ISBN 0-8191-0171-0). U Pr of Amer.

Setalvad, C. Role of the United Nations in the Maintenance of World Peace. 1968. 3.50x o.p. (ISBN 0-210-22686-2). Asia.

Setek, William M., Jr. Fundamentals of Mathematics. 1976. text ed. 14.95x (ISBN 0-02-478370-6). Macmillan.

Seth, Andrew. The Development from Kant to Hegel, with Chapters on the Philosophy of Religion. Beck, Lewis W., ed. LC 75-32044. (The Philosophy of Immanuel Kant Ser.: Vol. 7). 1977. Repr. of 1882 ed. lib. bdg. 20.00 (ISBN 0-8240-2331-5). Garland Pub.

Seth, S. Up Against the Corporate Wall: Modern Corporations & Social Issues of the 80's. 4th ed. 1981. pap. 11.95 (ISBN 0-13-938308-5); 14.95 (ISBN 0-13-938316-6). P-H.

Sethares, George C., jt. auth. see Bent, Robert J.

Sethi, A. S. Universal Sikhism. 1972. 5.95 (ISBN 0-88253-767-9). Ind-US Inc.

Sethi, J. D. Gandhi Today. 2nd ed. 1979. text ed. 20.00 (ISBN 0-7069-0831-7, Pub. by Vikas India). Advent Bk.

Sethi, N. K. The World Is Split. 8.00 (ISBN 0-89253-736-1). Ind-US Inc.

Sethi, Narendra. Song-Lines of a Day. 8.00 (ISBN 0-89253-737-X); flexible cloth 4.80 (ISBN 0-89253-738-8). Ind-US Inc.

Sethi, Prakash, jt. auth. see Votaw, Dow.

Sethi, S. P. & Thompson, G. L. Optimal Control Theory: Applications to Management Science. (International Series in Management Science - Operations Research: Vol. 1). 1981. lib. bdg. 25.00 (ISBN 0-89838-061-8, Pub. by Martinus Nijhoff). Kluwer Boston.

Sethi, S. Prakash. Advocacy Advertising & Large Corporations: Social Conflict, Big Business Image, the News Media, and Public Policy. LC 76-6770. 1976. 25.95 o.p. (ISBN 0-669-00678-5). Lexington Bks.

--Promises of the Good Life. 1979. pap. 11.95 (ISBN 0-256-02230-5). Irwin.

--Up Against the Corporate Wall: Modern Corporations & Social Issues of the Seventies. 3rd ed. (Illus.). 1977. pap. text ed. 12.95 (ISBN 0-13-938217-8). P-H.

Sethi, S. Prakash & Swanson, Carl L. Private Enterprise & Public Purpose. (Management & Administration Ser.). 480p. 1981. pap. text ed. 12.95 (ISBN 0-471-07697-X). Wiley.

Sethi, S. Prakash & Holton, Richard H., eds. Management of the Multinationals: Policies, Operations, & Research. LC 73-17644. (Illus.). 1974. 19.95 (ISBN 0-02-928410-4). Free Pr.

Sethna, K. D. The Spirituality of the Future: A Search Apropos of R. C. Zaehner's Study in Sri Auribindo & Teilhard de Chardin. LC 76-14764. 400p. 1981. 22.50 (ISBN 0-8386-2028-0). Fairleigh Dickinson.

Seth-Smith, David. Small Parrots: Parrakeets. (Illus.). 1979. 9.95 (ISBN 0-87666-978-X, H-1017). TFH Pubns.

Seth-Smith, Michael. The Long Haul: A Social History of the British Commercial Vehicle Industry. (Illus.). 1975. text ed. 15.00x (ISBN 0-09-124440-4). Humanities.

--Steve: The Life & Times of Steve Donoghue. (Illus.). 1974. 8.95 o.p. (ISBN 0-571-10141-0, Pub. by Faber & Faber). Merrimack Bk Serv.

Setlow, Jane K. & Hollaender, Alexander, eds. Genetic Engineering: Principles & Methods, Vol. 1. 277p. 1979. 29.50 (ISBN 0-306-40154-1, Plenum Pr). Plenum Pub.

--Genetic Engineering: Principles & Methods, Vol. 2. 298p. 1980. 32.50 (ISBN 0-306-40447-8, Plenum Pr). Plenum Pub.

Setlowe, Rick. The Brink. 1977. pap. 1.50 o.s.i. (ISBN 0-515-04307-9). Jove Pubns.

Setnicka, Timothy J. Wilderness Search & Rescue: A Complete Handbook. Andrasko, Kenneth, ed. (Illus., Orig.). 1981. pap. 12.95 (ISBN 0-910146-21-7). Appalach Mtn.

Seton, Anya. Dragonwyck. 1977. pap. 1.95 o.p. (ISBN 0-449-23341-3, Crest). Fawcett.

--The Hearth & Eagle. 1978. pap. 2.50 (ISBN 0-449-23641-2, Crest). Fawcett.

--Katherine. 640p. 1978. pap. 2.75 (ISBN 0-449-24052-5, Crest). Fawcett.

--The Mistletoe & Sword. 1974. pap. 1.25 (ISBN 0-380-00583-2, 27672). Avon.

--The Mistletoe & Sword. 1976. lib. bdg. 11.40 (ISBN 0-89190-442-5). Am Repr-Rivercity Pr.

--My Theodosia. 1977. pap. 1.95 o.p. (ISBN 0-449-23034-1, Crest). Fawcett.

--The Turquoise. 1977. pap. 1.95 o.p. (ISBN 0-449-23088-0, Crest). Fawcett.

--The Winthrop Woman. 1975. pap. 1.75 o.s.i. (ISBN 0-515-03442-8). Jove Pubns.

Seton, Ernest T. The Arctic Prairies. (Nature Library Ser.). (Illus.). 320p. 1981. pap. 5.95 (ISBN 0-06-090841-6, CN 841, CN). Har-Row.

--King of the Grizzlies. Orig. Title: Biography of a Grizzly. (Illus.). (gr. 4-6). 1970. pap. 1.25 (ISBN 0-590-08786-X, Schol Pap); pap. 3.50 bk. & record (ISBN 0-590-20750-4). Schol Bk Serv.

--Wild Animals I Have Known. LC 77-7918. (Illus.). (gr. 5 up). 1977. pap. 4.95 o.s.i. (ISBN 0-87905-033-0). Peregrine Smith.

--The Worlds of Ernest Thompson Seton. Samson, John G., ed. 1976. 25.00 o.p. (ISBN 0-394-49547-0). Knopf.

Seton, Ernest Thompson. Animal Tracks & Hunter Signs. LC 58-7366. 1958. 6.95 o.p. (ISBN 0-385-06862-X). Doubleday.

Seton-Watson, Christopher, jt. auth. see Seton-Watson, Hugh.

Seton-Watson, H. Nations & States: An Inquiry into the Origins of Nations & the Politics of Nationalism. LC 77-4237. 1977. lib. bdg. 32.50x (ISBN 0-89158-227-4). Westview.

Seton-Watson, Hugh. Russian Empire, 1801-1917. (Oxford History of Modern Europe Ser). 1967. 45.00x (ISBN 0-19-822103-7). Oxford U Pr.

Seton-Watson, Hugh & Seton-Watson, Christopher. The Making of a New Europe: R. W. Seton-Watson & the Last Years of Austria-Hungary. 528p. 1981. 50.00 (ISBN 0-295-95792-1). U of Wash Pr.

Seton-Watson, R. W. Britain & the Dictators. 1968. Repr. of 1938 ed. 19.75 (ISBN 0-86527-015-5). Fertig.

--Racial Problems in Hungary. 540p. 1973. Repr. of 1908 ed. 23.50 (ISBN 0-86527-163-1). Fertig.

--The Southern Slav Question & the Hapsburg Monarchy. LC 68-9666. 1969. Repr. of 1911 ed. 21.50 (ISBN 0-86527-185-2). Fertig.

Seton-Weston, R. W. A History of the Czechs & Slovaks. 413p. 1980. Repr. of 1943 ed. lib. bdg. 50.00 (ISBN 0-8492-2974-X). R West.

Seton-Williams, M. V. Britain & the Arab States: A Survey of Anglo-Arab Relations, 1920-1948. LC 79-2881. (Illus.). 330p. 1981. Repr. of 1948 ed. 26.50 (ISBN 0-8305-0049-9). Hyperion Conn.

Setright, L. J. Motorcycling Facts & Feats. 258p. 1980. 17.95 (ISBN 0-8069-9232-8, Pub. by Guinness Superlatives England). Sterling.

Setright, Leonard. Mercedes-Benz Roadsters. (AutoHistory Ser.). (Illus.). 1979. 12.95 (ISBN 0-85045-325-9, Pub. by Osprey England). Motorbooks Intl.

Settar, G. Worldwide Medical Interpreter: English, Vol. 1. 1976. pap. 12.00 (ISBN 0-87489-101-9). Med Economics.

--Worldwide Medical Interpreter: Greek, Vol. 12. 1977. pap. 12.00 (ISBN 0-87489-112-4). Med Economics.

--Worldwide Medical Interpreter: Italian, Vol. 6. 1977. pap. 12.00 (ISBN 0-87489-106-X). Med Economics.

Settel, Irving, jt. ed. see Kleppner, Otto.

Settel, T. S. Faith of Billy Graham. 1970. pap. 1.25 o.p. (ISBN 0-451-07104-2, Y7104, Sig). NAL.

Setterington, R. E., jt. ed. see Randeraat, J. Van.

Setti, Giancarlo, jt. ed. see Giacconi, Richard.

Setti, Ginancarlo, jt. auth. see Brecher, Kenneth.

Settle, Elkanah. A Defence of Dramatick Poetry. Incl. A Farther Defence of Dramatick Poetry. LC 79-170450. (The English Stage Ser.: Vol. 25). lib. bdg. 50.00 (ISBN 0-8240-0608-9). Garland Pub.

Settle, Mary L. O Beulah Land. 304p. 1981. pap. 3.50 (ISBN 0-345-29311-8). Ballantine.

--Prisons. 244p. 1981. pap. 3.50 (ISBN 0-345-29312-6). Ballantine.

Settle, Mary L., jt. auth. see Settle, Raymond W.

Settle, Mary Lee. The Scopes Trial. LC 73-181449. (Illus.). 128p. (gr. 7 up). 1972. PLB 5.88 o.p. (ISBN 0-531-02027-4). Watts.

Settle, Raymond W. & Settle, Mary L. Saddles & Spurs: The Pony Express Saga. LC 55-10776. x, 217p. 1972. pap. 2.95 (ISBN 0-8032-5765-1, BB 556, Bison). U of Nebr Pr.

Settle, Russell F., jt. auth. see Anderson, Lee G.

Settle, William A., Jr. Jesse James Was His Name, or Fact & Fiction Concerning the Careers of the Notorious James Brothers of Missouri. LC 65-22965. (Illus.). 1966. 11.00x o.p. (ISBN 0-8262-0052-4). U of Mo Pr.

--Jesse James Was His Name: or, Fact & Fiction Concerning the Careers of the Notorious James Brothers of Missouri. LC 76-56786. (Illus.). 1977. pap. 5.95 (ISBN 0-8032-5860-7, BB 640, Bison). U of Nebr Pr.

Settlemire, C. Thomas & Hughes, William. Microbiology for Health Students. (Illus.). 1978. text ed. 15.95 case (ISBN 0-8359-4360-7); instrs'. manual avail. Reston.

Setton, Kenneth M. Athens in the Middle Ages. 270p. 1980. 60.00x (ISBN 0-902089-84-6, Pub. by Variorum England). State Mutual Bk.

Setton, Kenneth M., jt. auth. see Hazard, Harry W.

Setton, Kenneth M., ed. History of the Crusades, 2 vols. 2nd ed. Incl. Vol. 1. The First Hundred Years. Baldwin, Marshall W., ed. (Illus.). 740p. Repr. of 1955 ed (ISBN 0-299-04831-4); Vol. 2. The Later Crusades, 1189 to 1311. 2nd ed. Wolff, Robert L. & Hazard, Harry W., eds. (Illus.). 896p. Repr. of 1962 ed (ISBN 0-299-04841-1). 1969. 40.00 ea. U of Wis Pr.

Setton, Kenneth M., jt. ed. see Hazzard, Harry W.

Setty, K. Umapathy. Information Soures: An International Selective Guide. 1978. 12.50 (ISBN 0-7069-0628-4, Pub. by Vikas India). Advent Bk.

Setzekorn, William D. Formerly British Honduras: A Profile of the New Nation of Belize. (Illus.). 295p. pap. 7.95x (ISBN 0-8214-0568-3). Ohio U Pr.

--Formerly British Honduras: A Profile of the New Nation of Belize. LC 74-31640. (Illus.). 300p. 1976. 7.95 (ISBN 0-9600822-1-2); pap. 3.95 (ISBN 0-685-73559-1). Ohio U Pr.

Seufert, Francis A. Wheels of Fortune. Vaughan, Thomas, ed. LC 80-81719. (Illus.). 304p. 1981. 19.95 (ISBN 0-87595-083-3); pap. 12.95 (ISBN 0-87595-069-8). Oreg Hist Soc.

Seur, Jean Le see Le Seur, Jean F.

Sevareid, Eric. Canoeing with the Cree. LC 68-63520. (Illus.). 1980. Repr. of 1935 ed. 7.75 (ISBN 0-87351-038-0); pap. 4.50 (ISBN 0-87351-152-2). Minn Hist.

--Not So Wild a Dream. LC 76-11538. 1978. 15.00 (ISBN 0-689-10741-2); pap. 8.95 (ISBN 0-689-70578-6, 235). Atheneum.

Sevastopoulos, Julie W. Keys to Spelling: Sounds & Syllables. 80p. (Orig.). 1981. pap. text ed. 5.95 (ISBN 0-88499-541-0). Inst Mod Lang.

Seve, Lucien. Man in Marxist Theory & the Psychology of Personality. (Marxist Theory & Contemporary Capitalism Ser.). 1978. text ed. 42.00x (ISBN 0-391-00743-2); pap. text ed. 17.00x, 1980 (ISBN 0-391-01913-9). Humanities.

--Man in the Marxist Theory & the Psychology of Personality. (Marxist Theory & Contemporary Capitalism Ser.). 508p. 1980. text ed. 42.00x o.p. (ISBN 0-391-00743-2); pap. text ed. 15.50x o.p. (ISBN 0-391-01913-9). Humanities.

Seventeenth National Conference on School Finance. Futures in School Finance: Working Toward a Common Goal. Jordan, K. Forbis & Alexander, Kern, eds. LC 75-8465. 221p. 1975. 5.50 (ISBN 0-87367-757-9). Phi Delta Kappa.

Sever, John L., et al. Handbook of Perinatal Infections. 1979. pap. text ed. 16.95 (ISBN 0-316-78170-3). Little.

Severance, Gordon, ed. see Hoeber, Ralph, et al.

Severance, Jane. When Megan Went Away. LC 79-90437. 32p. (gr. k-2). 1979. pap. 2.50 (ISBN 0-914996-22-3). Lollipop Power.

Severens, Kenneth. Southern Architecture: An Architectural & Cultural History of the South from the Colonization of America to the 20th Century. 1981. 18.95 (ISBN 0-525-20692-2). Dutton.

Severianin, Igor. Solovei (Poezy) (Rus.). 1981. pap. 5.95 (ISBN 0-89830-011-8). Russica Pubs.

Severin, Timothy. The Horizon Book of Vanishing Primitive Man. Josephy, Alvin M., Jr., ed. LC 73-7781. (Illus.). 384p. 1973. 22.00 (ISBN 0-8281-0273-2, Dist. by Scribner); deluxe ed. 25.00 slipcased (ISBN 0-8281-0274-0, Dist. by Scribner). Am Heritage.

Severinghaus, Sheldon R., et al. A New Guide to the Birds of Taiwan. 222p. 1980. 7.50 (ISBN 0-89955-185-8, Spub. by Mei Ya China). Intl Schol Bk Serv.

Severn, Bill. Bill Severn's Big Book of Magic. 160p. (gr. 7 up). 1973. 8.95 o.p. (ISBN 0-679-20022-3). McKay.

--Fifty Ways to Have Fun with Old Newspapers. (Illus.). (gr. 3-7). 1977. 7.95 o.p. (ISBN 0-679-20402-4); pap. 3.50 o.p. (ISBN 0-679-20630-2). McKay.

--Magic As a Hobby. (Illus.). 1979. 14.95 o.p. (ISBN 0-679-51201-2); pap. 9.95 (ISBN 0-679-51202-0). McKay.

--Magic from Your Pocket. (Illus.). 1965. 5.50 (ISBN 0-571-06357-8, Pub. by Faber & Faber). Merrimack Bk Serv.

Severn, David. The Wishing Bone. (Illus.). (gr. 3-6). 1977. 10.95 (ISBN 0-04-823141-X). Allen Unwin.

Severn, Gillian E. Miniature Trees in the Japanese Style. (Illus.). 1967. 6.95 (ISBN 0-571-08624-1, Pub. by Faber & Faber). Merrimack Bk Serv.

Severn, Jill. Growing Vegetables in the Pacific Northwest. LC 77-29260. (Illus.). 1978. pap. 4.95 (ISBN 0-914842-25-0). Madrona Pubs.

Severn, John K. A Wellesley Affair: Richard Marquess Wellesley & the Conduct of Anglo-Spanish Diplomacy, 1809-1812. LC 80-25416. x, 294p. 1980. 21.50 (ISBN 0-8130-0684-8). U Presses Fla.

Severn, R. T., et al, eds. Tidal Power & Estuary Management. (Colston Paper Ser.: No. 30). (Illus.). 296p. 1979. 65.00 (ISBN 0-85608-023-3). Transatlantic.

Severns, William H. & Fellows, Julian R. Air Conditioning & Refrigeration. LC 58-7908. 1958. text ed. 28.95x (ISBN 0-471-77781-1). Wiley.

Severo, Emoke de Papp see De Papp Severo, Emoke.

Severs, Burke, jt. ed. see Hartung, Albert E.

Severson, Bedford A., ed. see Avens, Robert.

Severy, Larry, ed. Crowding: Theoretical & Research Implications for Population - Environment Psychology. LC 78-61527. 1979. pap. 6.95x (ISBN 0-87705-376-6). Human Sci Pr.

Sevier, John. Commission Book of Governor John Sevier, 1796-1801. Tennessee Historical Commission, ed. 1957. 5.00x o.p. (ISBN 0-87402-008-5). U of Tenn Pr.

Sevious, Edward, jt. auth. see Dixon, Conrad.

Sevitt, Simon. Bone Repair & Fracture Healing in Man. (Current Problems in Orthopaedics Ser.). (Illus.). 300p. 1981. lib. bdg. 62.00 (ISBN 0-443-01806-5). Churchill.

Sevrey, O. Irene. First Book of the Earth. LC 67-26379. (First Bks). (Illus.). (gr. 4-6). 1958. PLB 4.90 o.p. (ISBN 0-531-00519-4). Watts.

Seward, Desmond. Prince of the Renaissance: The Life of Francois I. LC 73-2331. (Illus.). 264p. 1973. 14.95 o.s.i. (ISBN 0-02-609700-1). Macmillan.

Seward, Rudy R., ed. The American Family: A Demographic History. LC 78-19609. (Sage Library of Social Research: Vol. 70). 1978. 18.00x (ISBN 0-8039-1112-2); pap. 8.95x (ISBN 0-8039-1113-0). Sage.

Sewell, Anna. Black Beauty. (Illus.). (gr. 3-6). 1962. 3.95g o.s.i. (ISBN 0-02-782070-X). Macmillan.

--Black Beauty. Vance, Eleanor G., ed. (Illus.). (gr. k-3). 1949. 3.95 (ISBN 0-394-80637-9, BYR); PLB 4.99 (ISBN 0-394-90637-3). Random.

--Black Beauty. LC 78-3823. (Raintree's Illustrated Classics). (Illus.). (gr. 5-8). 1978. PLB 9.65 (ISBN 0-8393-6209-9). Raintree Child.

Sewell, Elizabeth M. Margaret Percival, 1847. Bd. with The Experience of Life; or, Aunt Sarah, 1852. (Victorian Fiction Ser). 1975. lib. bdg. 66.00 (ISBN 0-8240-1550-9). Garland Pub.

Sewell, Ernestine & Rogers, Billi M., eds Confronting Crisis: Teachers in America. (Illus.). 220p. 1980. 12.95 (ISBN 0-87706-111-4). U of Tex Arlington Pr.

Sewell, George E. & Delacruz, Chester. A Gnome, a Candle, & Me: Reflections in a Candle on a Winter's Night. (Illus.). 60p. (Orig.). 1981. pap. 4.50 (ISBN 0-938012-00-2). Deluxe Co.

Sewell, H. & Bulfinch, T. Book of Myths. 1969. 9.95 (ISBN 0-02-782280-X). Macmillan.

Sewell, Helen. Blue Barns. (Illus.). (gr. k-3). 1933. 3.95g o.s.i. (ISBN 0-02-782150-1). Macmillan.

Sewell, James P. Functionalism & World Politics: A Study Based on United Nations Programs Financing Economic Development. 1966. 18.50x (ISBN 0-691-07508-5). Princeton U Pr.

Sewell, John & Overseas Development Council Staff. The United States & World Development: Agenda 1977. LC 76-30725. (Agenda Ser.). 272p. 1977. pap. 4.95. Overseas Dev Council.

Sewell, John W. The United States & World Development: Agenda 1980. 256p. 1980. 24.95 (ISBN 0-03-058993-2); pap. 6.95 (ISBN 0-03-058992-4). Praeger.

--The United States & World Development: Agenda 1977. LC 76-30725. (Special Studies). 1977. text ed. 24.95 (ISBN 0-275-24440-7); pap. 4.95 (ISBN 0-275-65000-6). Praeger.

Sewell, John W. & Overseas Development Council Staff. The United States & World Development: Agenda 1980. LC 80-82415. 242p. 1980. pap. 6.95. Overseas Dev Council.

Sewell, M. J., jt. ed. see Hopkins, H. G.

Sewell, Robert T. A Forgotten Empire-Vijayanagar: A Contribution to the History of India. (Illus.). 427p. 1972. Repr. of 1900 ed. 31.00x (ISBN 0-686-28323-6, Pub. by Irish Academic Pr). Biblio Dist.

Sewell, W. H., Jr. Work & Revolution in France. LC 80-12103. (Illus.). 336p. 1980. 35.95 (ISBN 0-521-23442-5); pap. 8.95 (ISBN 0-521-29951-9). Cambridge U Pr.

Sewell, W. R., jt. auth. see O'Riordan, Timothy.

Sewell, W. R., ed. Environmental Quality. LC 74-78558. (Sage Contemporary Social Science Issues: Vol. 13). 1974. 4.95x (ISBN 0-8039-0438-X). Sage.

Sewell, William. Hawkstone: A Tale of & for England in 184-, 1845. Wolff, Robert L., ed. LC 75-446. (Victorian Fiction Ser.). 1975. lib. bdg. 66.00 (ISBN 0-8240-1526-6). Garland Pub.

--Ordeal of Free Labour in the West Indies. 2nd ed. LC 67-31561. Repr. of 1862 ed. 19.50x (ISBN 0-678-05097-X). Kelley.

Sewell, Winifred. Guide to Drug Information. LC 75-17156. 180p. (Orig.). 1976. 13.00 (ISBN 0-914768-21-2). Drug Intl Pubns.

Sewing, K. F., et al, eds. Special Issue Dedicated to Dr. Bernard Brodie. (Pharmacology: Vol. 19, No. 5). (Illus.). 1979. cancelled soft cover o.p. (ISBN 3-8055-0408-X). S Karger.

Sewter, A. Charles. The Stained Glass of William Morris & His Circle: A Catalogue, Vol. 2. LC 72-91307. (Studies in British Art Ser.). 344p. 1975. 95.00x (ISBN 0-300-01836-3). Yale U Pr.

--The Stained Glass of William Morris & His Circle, Vol. 1. LC 72-91307. (Studies in British Art Ser.). (Illus.). 384p. 1974. 85.00x (ISBN 0-300-01471-6). Yale U Pr.

Sexton, M. L. The Way of Life. (Ser. Outlines). 2.95 (ISBN 0-89315-352-4). Lambert Bk.

Sexton, Michael. Illusions of Power: The Fate of a Reform Government. 1979. text ed. 21.00x (ISBN 0-86861-265-0); pap. text ed. 11.50x (ISBN 0-86861-273-1). Allen Unwin.

Sexton, Nancy N., et al. My Days As a Youngling, John Jacob Niles. (Orig.). 1981. playscript 2.50 (ISBN 0-87602-239-5). Anchorage.

Sexton, Robert F., ed. see Combs, Bert T.

Sexton, Robert F., ed. see Johnson, Keene.

Sexton, Virginia S. & Misiak, Henryk, eds. Psychology Around the World. LC 75-36017. 650p. 1976. text ed. 16.95x o.p. (ISBN 0-8185-0174-X). Brooks-Cole.

Sextus, Carl. Hypnotism. pap. 5.00 (ISBN 0-87980-076-3). Wilshire.

Seybold, John W. Fundamentals of Modern Photocomposition. (Illus.). 1979. text ed. 27.50 (ISBN 0-918514-03-7); pap. text ed. 22.50 (ISBN 0-918514-02-9). Seybold.

Seyd, Mary. Introducing Beads. 1973. 14.95 (ISBN 0-7134-2439-7, Pub. by Batsford England). David & Charles.

Seyer, Herman D. Millenialism. 68p. 1979. pap. 1.50. H D Seyer.

Seyer, Philip & Harmon, Paul. What Makes Music Work? Novick, Allan, ed. (Wiley Self-Teaching Guide Ser.). 300p. 1981. pap. text ed. 9.85 (ISBN 0-471-35192-X). Wiley.

Seyerstead, Per. Kate Chopin: A Critical Biography. LC 77-88740. (Southern Literary Ser.). (Illus.). 256p. 1980. pap. 5.95 (ISBN 0-8071-0678-X). La State U Pr.

Seyl, Susan. The Art Perfected: Portraiture from the Cronise Studio. LC 80-83177. (Illus.). 160p. 1980. pap. text ed. 10.95 (ISBN 0-87595-070-1). Oreg Hist Soc.

Seyler & Wilan. Introduction to Literature. 1981. 10.95 (ISBN 0-88284-113-0). Alfred Pub.

Seyler, Athene & Haggard, Stephen. Craft of Comedy. 1957. 5.95 (ISBN 0-87830-023-6). Theatre Arts.

Seyler, Dorothy U. & Sipple, M. Noel. Thinking for Writing. LC 77-22730. 1978. pap. text ed. 9.95 (ISBN 0-574-22035-6, 13-5035); instr's guide avail. (ISBN 0-574-22036-4, 13-5036). SRA.

Seymour, A. C; see Brooke, Charlotte.

Seymour, Charles see Johnson, Allen & Nevins, Allan.

Seymour, Charles, Jr., ed. & intro. by. Michelangelo: The Sistine Chapel Ceiling. (Critical Studies in Art History). (Illus.). 243p. 1972. pap. 6.95x (ISBN 0-393-09889-3). Norton.

Seymour, Dale & Gidley, Richard. Eureka. 1967. pap. 5.95 wkbk. o.p. (ISBN 0-88488-048-6). Creative Pubns.

Seymour, Eugene, ed. Psychosocial Needs of the Aged: A Health Care Perspective. rev. ed. LC 78-60818. 1978. pap. 5.00 (ISBN 0-88474-048-X). USC Andrus Geron.

Seymour, Forest W. Sitanka: The Full Story of Wounded Knee. 1981. 9.75 (ISBN 0-8158-0399-0). Chris Mass.

Seymour, Gerald. The Harrison Affair. 1981. pap. 2.95 (ISBN 0-440-13566-4). Dell.

--Harry's Game. 1977. pap. 1.95 o.p. (ISBN 0-449-23019-8, Crest). Fawcett.

--Kingfisher. 1979. pap. 2.25 (ISBN 0-380-40592-X, 40592). Avon.

Seymour, Harold. Baseball: The Early Years. 1960. 17.95 (ISBN 0-19-500100-1). Oxford U Pr.

--Baseball: The Golden Age. 1971. 18.95 (ISBN 0-19-501403-0). Oxford U Pr.

Seymour, Jeanette. Emmie. 1980. pap. write for info. (ISBN 0-671-83129-1). PB.

Seymour, John. The Fat of the Land. (Illus., Orig.). 1974. pap. 5.95 (ISBN 0-571-10532-7, Pub. by Faber & Faber). Merrimack Bk Serv.

--The Self-Sufficient Gardener: A Complete Guide to Growing & Preserving All Your Own Food. LC 78-19223. 1979. pap. write for info (ISBN 0-385-14671-X, Dolp). Doubleday.

Seymour, Miranda. Count Manfred. 1979. pap. 1.95 o.p. (ISBN 0-445-04377-6). Popular Lib.

Seymour, Nancy, ed. see Wachtel, Betsy & Powers, Brian.

Seymour, Raymond B. Modern Plastics Technology. (Illus.). 256p. 1975. 17.95 (ISBN 0-87909-500-8). Reston.

Seymour, Roger J. Heart Attack Survival Manual. 144p. 1981. 11.95 (ISBN 0-13-385740-9, Spec); pap. 5.95 (ISBN 0-13-385732-8). P-H.

Seymour, Thomas D. Life in the Homeric Age. LC 63-12451. (Illus.). 1907. 15.00x (ISBN 0-8196-0125-X). Biblo.

Seymour, Tryntje V. Acoma. portfolio 295.00 (ISBN 0-915998-05-X). Lime Rock Pr.

--Dylan Thomas' New York. LC 78-13286. (Illus.). 1978. pap. 5.95 (ISBN 0-916144-32-1). Stemmer Hse.

Seymour, William H. Story of Algiers. (Illus.). 143p. 1981. pap. 6.95 (ISBN 0-911116-33-8). Pelican.

Seymour-Smith, Martin. The Funk & Wagnalls Guide to Modern World Literature. LC 73-5931. (Funk & W Bk.). 1206p. 1975. 17.50 o.p. (ISBN 0-308-10079-4, TYC-T). T Y Crowell.

--A Reader's Guide to Fifty European Novels. (A Reader's Guide Ser.). 528p. 1980. 20.75x (ISBN 0-389-20138-3). B&N.

--Who's Who in Twentieth Century Literature. LC 75-21470. 1976. 12.95 o.p. (ISBN 0-03-013926-0). HR&W.

Seymour-Smith, Martin, jt. ed. see Reeves, James.

Seymour-Ure, Colin. The Political Impact of Mass Media. LC 73-90038. (Communication & Society: Vol. 4). 1974. 20.00x (ISBN 0-8039-0347-2); pap. 9.95x (ISBN 0-8039-0713-3). Sage.

Seyppel, Joachim. T. S. Eliot. LC 75-143187. (Modern Literature Ser.). 1971. 10.95 (ISBN 0-8044-2818-2). Ungar.

--William Faulkner. LC 74-134826. (Modern Literature Ser.). 120p. 10.95 (ISBN 0-8044-2820-4); pap. 3.45 (ISBN 0-8044-6858-3). Ungar.

Seyssel, Claude De. The Monarchy of France. Hexter, J. H. & Kelley, Donald H., trs. from Fr. LC 80-23554. 1981. text ed. 16.95x (ISBN 0-300-02516-5). Yale U Pr.

Sfeir-Younis, Alfredo & Bromley, Daniel W. Decision Making in Developing Countries: Multiobjective Formulation & Evaluation Methods. LC 77-9636. (Praeger Special Studies). 1977. text ed. 23.95 (ISBN 0-03-022286-9). Praeger.

Sgamozzi, Ottavio B. Le Fabriche E I Disegni Di Palladio. Date not set. 22.95 (ISBN 0-8038-0079-7). Hastings.

SGam po pa. The Jewel Ornament of Liberation. Guenther, Herbert V., tr. from Tibetan. LC 72-146507. (The Clear Light Ser.). 349p. 1981. pap. 9.95 (ISBN 0-87773-717-7). Great Eastern.

Sgarbi. Carpaccio. 1980. pap. cancelled (ISBN 0-8120-2304-8). Barron.

Sgontz, Larry G., jt. auth. see Pogue, Thomas F.

Sgro, Joseph A., ed. Virginia Tech Symposium on Applied Behavioral Science, Vol. I. LC 80-8614. 1981. 28.95 (ISBN 0-669-04332-X). Lexington Bks.

Sgro, Pasquale M. Wage Differentials & Economic Growth. 147p. 1980. 28.50x (ISBN 0-389-20002-6). B&N.

Sgroi, Peter. The Purchase of Alaska, March 30, 1867. LC 74-26677. (Focus Bks). (Illus.). 72p. (gr. 7-9). 1975. PLB 4.90 o.p. (ISBN 0-531-01089-9). Watts.

Shabad, Theodore. Basic Industrial Resources of the USSR. LC 75-101133. 1969. 27.50x (ISBN 0-231-03077-0). Columbia U Pr.

Shabalin, E. P. Fast Pulsed & Burst Reactors: A Comprehensive Account of the Physics of Both Single Burst & Repetitively Pulsed Reactors. (Illus.). 1979. 68.00 (ISBN 0-08-022708-2). Pergamon.

Shaban, M. A. The Abbasid Revolution. 1979. 32.00 (ISBN 0-521-07849-0); pap. 11.95 (ISBN 0-521-29534-3). Cambridge U Pr.

--Islamic History A. D. Six Hundred to Seven Fifty: New Interpretation I. LC 79-145604. 1971. 37.50 (ISBN 0-521-08137-8); pap. 11.95 (ISBN 0-521-29131-3). Cambridge U Pr.

--Islamic History: A.D. 750 to 1055, (A.H. 132 to 448) New Interpretation II, Vol. 2. LC 75-39390. (Illus.). 190p. 1976. 37.50 (ISBN 0-521-21198-0); pap. 11.95 (ISBN 0-521-29453-3). Cambridge U Pr.

Shabtai, Sabi. Five Minutes to Midnight. 1981. pap. 2.95 (ISBN 0-440-12534-0). Dell.

Shachtman, Tom. Edith & Woodrow. 288p. 1981. 12.95 (ISBN 0-399-12446-2). Putnam.

--Growing up Masai. LC 80-25017. (Illus.). 56p. (gr. 3-6). 1981. PLB 8.95 (ISBN 0-02-782550-7). Macmillan.

Shack, William A. & Cohen, Percy S., eds. Politics in Leadership: A Comparative Perspective. (Illus.). 310p. 1979. text ed. 29.95x (ISBN 0-19-823193-8). Oxford U Pr.

Shack, William A. & Skinner, Elliott P., eds. Strangers in African Society. LC 77-73501. (Campus Ser.: No. 220). 1979. 22.75x (ISBN 0-520-03458-9); pap. 6.95x (ISBN 0-520-03812-6). U of Cal Pr.

Shackburg, Richard. Yankee Doodle. (Illus.). (gr. 1-7). 1965. pap. 1.50 o.p. (ISBN 0-13-971879-6). P-H.

Shackel, B., ed. Man-Computer Interaction: Human Factors of Computers & People. (NATO Advanced Study Institute Ser.: Applied Sciences, No. 44). 550p. 1980. 60.00x (ISBN 90-286-0910-5). Sijthoff & Noordhoff.

Shackelford, Jean A., ed. Urban & Regional Economics: A Guide to Information Sources. LC 74-11556. (Economics Information Guide Ser.: Vol. 14). 190p. 1980. 30.00 (ISBN 0-8103-1303-0). Gale.

Shackelford, Richard T. & Zuidema, George D. Surgery of the Alimentary Tract, Vol. 2. 1981. text ed. price not set (ISBN 0-7216-8084-4). Saunders.

Shacket, Sheldon R. The Complete Book of Electric Vehicles. rev. ed. (Illus.). 224p. 1981. price not set (ISBN 0-89196-085-6, Domus Bks); pap. price not set (ISBN 0-89196-086-4). Quality Bks IL.

Shackle, G. L. An Economic Querist. LC 72-96679. 120p. 1973. 17.95 (ISBN 0-521-20188-8). Cambridge U Pr.

Shackle, George L. Decision Order & Time in Human Affairs. 2nd ed. 1970. 38.50 (ISBN 0-521-07711-7). Cambridge U Pr.

--Economics for Pleasure. 2nd ed. 1968. 38.50 (ISBN 0-521-06282-9); pap. 11.95x (ISBN 0-521-09507-7, 170). Cambridge U Pr.

--Epistemics & Economics: A Critique of Economic Doctrine. LC 72-76091. (Illus.). 400p. 1973. 54.00 (ISBN 0-521-08626-4). Cambridge U Pr.

--Expectations in Economics. LC 78-14143. (Illus.). 1979. Repr. of 1952 ed. 16.00 (ISBN 0-88355-816-5). Hyperion Conn.

--Nature of Economic Thought. 1966. 44.50 (ISBN 0-521-06278-0). Cambridge U Pr.

--Years of High Theory. 1967. 38.50 (ISBN 0-521-06279-9). Cambridge U Pr.

Shackleton, Basil. The Grape Cure. 1978. pap. 3.95 o.s.i. (ISBN 0-7225-0202-8). Newcastle Pub.

Shackleton, Elizabeth, jt. auth. see Shackleton, Robert.

Shackleton, M., ed. see Gide, Andre.

Shackleton, Robert. Montesquieu: A Critical Biography. 1961. 29.95x (ISBN 0-19-815339-2). Oxford U Pr.

Shackleton, Robert & Shackleton, Elizabeth. Quest of the Colonial. LC 72-99075. (Illus.). 1970. Repr. of 1907 ed. 20.00 (ISBN 0-8103-3574-3). Gale.

Shackleton-Bailey, D. R., ed. Cicero, Epistulae Ad Familiares: 47-43 B.C, Vol. II. LC 76-11079. (Classical Texts & Commentaries Ser.: No. 17). 1977. 82.00 (ISBN 0-521-21152-2). Cambridge U Pr.

--Cicero, Epistulae Ad Familiares: 62-47 B.C, Vol. 1. LC 76-11079. (Classical Texts & Commentaries Ser.: No. 16). 1977. 82.00 (ISBN 0-521-21151-4). Cambridge U Pr.

Shackley, Myra, jt. ed. see Davidson, Donald A.

Shackley, Myra L. Archaeological Sediments: A Survey of Analytical Methods. LC 75-1193. 159p. 1975. 27.95 (ISBN 0-470-77870-9). Halsted Pr.

Shadarevian, Sossy, jt. auth. see Pellet, P. L.

Shadburne, William, jt. auth. see Ascher, Scott.

Shade, William G., jt. auth. see Friedman, Jean E.

Shader, Richard, jt. ed. see DiMascio, Alberto.

Shadick, Harold & Liv Tieh-Yua. The Travels of Lao Ts'an. 1966. 15.00x o.p. (ISBN 0-8014-0376-6). Cornell U Pr.

Shadily, Hassan, jt. auth. see Echols, John M.

Shadman, Alonzo J. Who Is Your Doctor & Why? LC 80-82320. 446p. 1980. pap. 3.95 (ISBN 0-87983-227-4). Keats.

Shadwell, Thomas. The Virtuoso. Nicolson, Marjorie H. & Rodes, David S., eds. LC 65-19466. (Regents Restoration Drama Ser). 1966. 9.75x (ISBN 0-8032-0368-3); pap. 2.65x (ISBN 0-8032-5368-0, BB 254, Bison). U of Nebr Pr.

Shaefer, Jack. Great Endurance Horse Race. (Illus.). 112p. (Orig.). 1981. pap. 6.95 (ISBN 0-88496-165-6). Capra Pr.

Shaefer, Rudolph J. J. E. Buttersworth: Nineteenth Century Marine Painter. LC 74-82666. 1975. 75.00x (ISBN 0-913372-12-9, Pub. by Wesleyan U Pr England). Columbia U Pr.

Shaeffer, Ruth G. Nondiscrimination in Employment-& Beyond, Report No. 782. vi, 108p. (Orig.). 1980. pap. 30.00 (ISBN 0-8237-0218-9). Conference Bd.

Shaevel, M. Leonard, jt. auth. see Paul, Richard S.

Shafarevich, I. R., jt. auth. see Borevich, Z. I.

Shafer, Boyd C., et al. Historical Study in the West: France, Western Germany, Great Britain, the United States. LC 68-19485. 1968. 22.00x (ISBN 0-89197-212-9); pap. text ed. 6.95x (ISBN 0-89197-213-7). Irvington.

Shafer, Burr. Through More History with J. Wesley Smith. LC 53-10800. (Illus.). 1953. 6.95 (ISBN 0-8149-0200-6). Vanguard.

--Wonderful World of J. Wesley Smith. LC 60-15077. (Illus.). 1960. 5.95 (ISBN 0-8149-0199-9). Vanguard.

Shafer, Donald M. Manual on Retinal Detachment. 150p. 1981. write for info. (1550-8). Williams & Wilkins.

Shafer, Jack. Test Yourself: Find Your Hidden Talent. pap. 3.00 (ISBN 0-87980-259-6). Wilshire.

Shafer, Robert. Christianity & Naturalism: Essays in Criticism, Second Series. 1926. 11.50x (ISBN 0-686-51353-3). Elliots Bks.

Shafer, Robert J., ed. A Guide to Historical Method. 3rd ed. 1980. pap. 9.95x (ISBN 0-256-02313-1). Dorsey.

Shafer, Ronald G., jt. auth. see Sumichrast, Michael.

Shafer, Thomas. Real Estate & Economics. (Illus.). 320p. 1976. 15.95 (ISBN 0-87909-715-9). Reston.

Shaffer, Anthony. Murderer. 96p. 1979. 9.95 (ISBN 0-7145-2544-8, Pub. by M Boyars); pap. 5.95 (ISBN 0-7145-2545-6). Merrimack Bk Serv.

Shaffer, David & Dunn, Judy. The First Year of Life: Psychological & Medical Implications of Early Experience. LC 78-11237. (Studies in Psychiatry). 1980. 37.95 (ISBN 0-471-99734-X, Pub. by Wiley-Interscience). Wiley.

Shaffer, E. S. Kubla Kahn & the Fall of Jerusalem. LC 74-79141. 320p. 1975. 54.00 (ISBN 0-521-20478-X). Cambridge U Pr.

Shaffer, E. S., ed. Comparative Criticism: A Yearbook, Vol. 1. 1980. 32.50 (ISBN 0-521-22296-6). Cambridge U Pr.

--Comparative Criticism: A Yearbook, Vol. 2. 350p. 1980. 39.50 (ISBN 0-521-22756-9). Cambridge U Pr.

Shaffer, Harry G. Free Periodicals from Socialist Countries: An Annotated Bibliography. 1977. 0.60 (ISBN 0-89977-018-5). Am Inst Marxist.

--Periodicals on the Socialist Countries & on Marxism: A New Annotated Index of English Language Publications. LC 75-36907. 1977. text ed. 24.95 (ISBN 0-275-24010-X). Praeger.

--Women in the Two Germanies: A Comparative Study of a Socialist & a Non-Socialist Society. (Pergamon Policy Studies on Social Policy). (Illus.). 256p. 1981. 26.00 (ISBN 0-08-023862-9). Pergamon.

Shaffer, Harry G., ed. Communist World: Marxist & Non-Marxist Views. LC 67-21993. (Illus.). 1967. 28.00x (ISBN 0-89197-093-2); pap. text ed. 12.95x (ISBN 0-89197-094-0). Irvington.

--Soviet Agriculture: An Assessment of Its Contributions to Economic Development. LC 77-7512. (Praeger Special Studies). 1977. text ed. 22.95 (ISBN 0-03-021976-0). Praeger.

--Soviet Economy: A Collection of Western & Soviet Views. 2nd ed. LC 69-16223. (Illus., Orig.). 1969. pap. text ed. 5.95x (ISBN 0-89197-420-2). Irvington.

Shaffer, Howard & Burglass, Milton E., eds. Classic Contributions in the Addictions. 600p. 1981. 30.00 (ISBN 0-87630-260-6). Brunner-Mazel.

Shaffer, James H. Explorations in Psychological Experimentation. LC 79-65010. 1979. pap. text ed. 8.75 (ISBN 0-8191-0778-6). U Pr of Amer.

Shaffer, Jerome A. Philosophy of Mind. LC 68-24352. (Foundations of Philosophy Series). (Orig.). 1968. pap. 7.95x ref. ed. (ISBN 0-13-663724-8). P-H.

Shaffer, Joe. Just Because...I Needed to. Kulikowski, M. Karl, ed. (Gusto Press Poetry Discovery Ser.). (Orig.). 1979. pap. 4.25 (ISBN 0-933906-03-X). Gusto Pr.

Shaffer, John B. Humanistic Psychology. LC 77-15044. (Foundations of Modern Psychology Ser.). (Illus.). 1978. ref. ed. 15.95 (ISBN 0-13-447698-0); pap. text ed. 9.95 (ISBN 0-13-447680-8). P-H.

Shaffer, John B. & Galinsky, M. David. Models of Group Therapy & Sensitivity Training. (Personal, Clinical & Social Psychology Ser). 228p. 1974. 17.95 (ISBN 0-13-586081-4). P-H.

Shaffer, Kenneth, jt. auth. see Snyder, Graydon.

Shaffer, Lisa R., jt. auth. see Shaffer, Stephen M.

Shaffer, Peter. Amadeus. LC 79-3415. 128p. 1981. 10.95 (ISBN 0-06-014041-0, HarpT). Har-Row.

Shaffer, R. D., jt. auth. see Nanney, J. L.

Shaffer, Ray. A Guide to Places on the Colorado Prairie. (Illus.). 1978. 16.95x o.s.i. (ISBN 0-87108-513-5). Pruett.

Shaffer, Ron & Klose, Kevin. Surprise! Surprise. 1979. pap. 2.25 (ISBN 0-380-42853-9, 42853). Avon.

Shaffer, Stephen M. & Shaffer, Lisa R. The Politics of International Cooperation: A Comparison of U. S. Experience in Space & in Security. (Monograph Series in World Affairs). 73p. Date not set. pap. 4.00 (ISBN 0-87940-063-3). U of Denver Intl.

Shaffer, Stuart M., et al. Teaching in Schools of Nursing. xii, 110p. (Orig.). 1972. 6.95 o.p. (ISBN 0-8016-4531-X). Mosby.

Shaffer, William R. Computer Simulations of Voting Behavior. (Studies in Behavioral Political Science Ser). 1972. text ed. 9.00x o.p. (ISBN 0-19-501536-3); pap. text ed. 4.95x (ISBN 0-19-501521-5). Oxford U Pr.

Shaffrey, Patrick. The Irish Town: An Approach to Survival. (Illus.). 1976. 15.95 o.p. (ISBN 0-9502046-5-X). Irish Bk Ctr.

Shafritz, Jay, jt. ed. see Hyde, Albert C.

Shaftel, Fannie R. & Shaftel, G. Role-Playing for Social Values: Decision-Making in the Social Studies. (Illus.). 1967. pap. text ed. 17.95 (ISBN 0-13-782938-8). P-H.

Shaftel, G., jt. auth. see Shaftel, Fannie R.

Shagan, Steve. The Formula. 352p. 1980. pap. 2.75 (ISBN 0-553-13801-4). Bantam.

Shagass, Charles, et al, eds. Psychopathology & Brain Dysfunction. LC 76-55487. (American Psychopathological Association Ser). 1977. 28.00 (ISBN 0-89004-120-2). Raven.

Shah, A. M. The Household Dimension of the Family in India. LC 71-126757. 1974. 20.00x (ISBN 0-520-01790-0). U of Cal Pr.

Shah, Ali Ikbal. The Spirit of the East. 1975. pap. 2.95 o.p. (ISBN 0-525-47395-5). Dutton.

Shah, Amina. The Tale of Four Dervishes & Other Sufi Tales. LC 80-8895. 288p. (Orig.). 1981. pap. 5.95 (ISBN 0-06-067256-0). Har-Row.

Shah, Douglas. The Meditators. 1975. 5.95 o.p. (ISBN 0-88270-125-8); pap. 3.50 o.p. (ISBN 0-88270-126-6). Logos.

Shah, H., jt. auth. see Fischer, E.

Shah, Idries. Learning How to Learn: Psychology & Spirituality in the Sufi Way. LC 80-8892. 304p. 1981. pap. 6.95 (ISBN 0-06-067255-2). Har-Row.

--Way of the Sufi. 1970. pap. 3.95 (ISBN 0-525-47261-4). Dutton.

Shah, M. J. Engineering Simulation Using Small Scientific Computers. (Illus.). 336p. 1976. 23.95x (ISBN 0-13-279422-5). P-H.

Shah, N. M. Elementary Chemical Theory & Problems. pap. 2.50x o.p. (ISBN 0-210-22665-X). Asia.

Shah, N. S. Water Supply Engineering. 1972. 4.50x (ISBN 0-210-31171-1). Asia.

Shah, O. P. Education in India Today. 1980. 15.00x (ISBN 0-8364-0634-6, Pub. by Mukhopadhyay India). South Asia Bks.

Shah, Pravin. Cost Control & Information Systems: A Complete Guide to Effective Design & Implementation. (Illus.). 608p. 1981. 24.95 (ISBN 0-07-056369-1, P&RB). McGraw.

Shah, Sayed I., ed. Secret Lore of Magic. 1965. Repr. of 1957 ed. text ed. 11.50x (ISBN 0-584-10250-X). Humanities.

Shaha, Rishikesh. An Introduction to Nepal. (Illus.). 1976. 8.50x (ISBN 0-685-89510-6). Himalaya Hse.

Shahan, Robert W., jt. ed. see Kovach, Francis J.

Shahane, Vasant A. Approaches to E. M. Forester. 1981. 10.25 (ISBN 0-391-02200-8). Humanities.

--Ruth Prawer Jhabvala. new,enlarged ed. (Indian Writers Ser.: Vol. 11). 1981. 12.00 (ISBN 0-89253-074-X). Ind-US Inc.

Shaheen, Esber I. Basic Practice of Chemical Engineering. 1975. text ed. 27.50 (ISBN 0-395-17645-X); solutions manual 4.05 (ISBN 0-395-18791-5). HM.

Shaheen, Jack G., ed. Nuclear War Films. LC 78-17984. 213p. 1978. 12.95x (ISBN 0-8093-0843-6); pap. 6.95 (ISBN 0-8093-0879-7). S Ill U Pr.

Shaheen, Mahommad. George Meredith: A Reappraisal of the Novels. 1980. 19.50x (ISBN 0-389-20022-0). B&N.

Shahrani, M. Nazif Mohib. The Kirghiz & Wakhi of Afghanistan: Adaptation to Closed Frontiers. LC 79-11665. (Publications on Ethnicity & Nationality of the School of International Studies). (Illus.). 288p. 1979. 16.50 (ISBN 0-295-95669-0). U of Wash Pr.

Shaikh, Shafi. A Course in Spoken Arabic. 136p. (Orig.). 1978. pap. text ed. 3.95x (ISBN 0-19-561067-9). Oxford U Pr.

Shain, Henry. Legal First Aid. LC 75-12737. (Funk & W Bk.). (Illus.). 352p. 1975. 10.95 o.p. (ISBN 0-308-10201-0, TYC-T). T Y Crowell.

Shain, Martin, et al. Influence, Choice & Drugs: Toward a Systematic Approach to the Prevention of Substance Abuse. LC 77-5230. 1977. 16.95 (ISBN 0-669-01597-0). Lexington Bks.

Shain, Rochelle & Pauerstein, Carl J., eds. Fertility Control: Biologic & Behavioral Aspects. (Illus.). 500p. 1980. 35.00 (ISBN 0-06-142376-9, Harper Medical). Har-Row.

Shainberg, Lawrence. Brain Surgeon: An Intimate View of His World. 1979. 10.95 (ISBN 0-397-01310-8). Lippincott.

Shaine, Frederick, tr. see Pesce, Giovanni.

Shakarian, Demos & Sherrill, Elizabeth. The Happiest People on Earth. 1975. 6.95 o.p. (ISBN 0-912376-14-7); pap. 3.95 (ISBN 0-912376-18-X). Chosen Bks Pub.

Shaked, Haim, jt. ed. see Legum, Colin.

Shaked, Shaul, tr. Wisdom of the Sasanian Sages: Denkard Book Six. (Bibliotheca Persica: Persian Heritage Ser.: No. 36). 1979. lib. bdg. 50.00x (ISBN 0-89158-376-9). Westview.

Shakely, Lauren, tr. see Apollinaire, Guillaume.

Shaker. Nuclear Non-Proliferation Treaty, Vols. 1-3. 1980. 40.00 ea. Oceana.

Shaker, Mohamed I. The Nuclear Non-Proliferation Treaty: Origin & Implementation 1959 to 1979, 3 vols. LC 80-17359. 1980. lib. bdg. 40.00 ea. (ISBN 0-379-20470-3). Vol. 1 (ISBN 0-379-20470-3). Vol. 2 (ISBN 0-379-20471-1). Vol. 3 (ISBN 0-379-20472-X). Oceana.

Shakespeare. Julius Caesar. LC 80-16406. (Raintree Short Classics). (Illus.). 48p. (gr. 4 up). 1981. PLB 9.95 (ISBN 0-8172-1664-2). Raintree Pubs.

--Romeo & Juliet, with Reader's Guide. (Orig.). (gr. 10-12). 1974. pap. text ed. 4.92 (ISBN 0-87720-821-2); tchr's ed. s.p. 3.15 (ISBN 0-87720-921-9). AMSCO Sch.

Shakespeare, Edward O., et al. Understanding the Essay. 1978. pap. text ed. 4.50x (ISBN 0-88334-109-3). Ind Sch Pr.

Shakespeare Library, ed. see Lamb, Charles & Lamb, Mary.

Shakespeare, William. All's Well That Ends Well. Quiller-Couch, Arthur, et al, eds. (New Shakespeare Ser). 23.95 (ISBN 0-521-07525-4); pap. 4.50x (ISBN 0-521-09468-2). Cambridge U Pr.

--Antony & Cleopatra. Brown, John R., ed. LC 77-127584. (Casebook Ser). 1970. pap. text ed. 2.50 o.s.i. (ISBN 0-87695-046-2). Aurora Pubs.

--Antony & Cleopatra. Quiller-Couch, Arthur, et al, eds. (New Shakespeare Ser). 23.95 (ISBN 0-521-07526-2); pap. 4.50x (ISBN 0-521-09469-0). Cambridge U Pr.

--As You Like It. Quiller-Couch, Arthur, et al, eds. (New Shakespeare Ser). 1968. 23.95 (ISBN 0-521-07527-0); pap. 4.50x (ISBN 0-521-07527-0). Cambridge U Pr.

--As You Like It. Sargeant, Ralph, ed. (Shakespeare Ser.). 1959. pap. 2.25 (ISBN 0-14-071417-0, Pelican). Penguin.

--A Choice of Shakespeare's Verse. Hughes, Ted, ed. 1971. 7.95 (ISBN 0-571-09426-0, Pub. by Faber & Faber); pap. 3.95 o.p. (ISBN 0-571-09427-9). Merrimack Bk Serv.

--Comedy of Errors. rev. ed. Quiller-Couch, Arthur, et al, eds. (New Shakespeare Ser). 1968. 23.95 (ISBN 0-521-07528-9); pap. 4.50x (ISBN 0-521-09471-2). Cambridge U Pr.

--Comedy of Errors. Jorgensen, Paul A., ed. (Shakespeare Ser.). 1964. pap. 2.50 (ISBN 0-14-071432-4, Pelican). Penguin.

--Complete Works of Shakespeare. 2nd ed. Ribner, Irving, ed. 1971. 26.95 (ISBN 0-471-00553-3). Wiley.

--Complete Works of William Shakespeare. 1946. 15.95 (ISBN 0-385-00049-9). Doubleday.

--Coriolanus. Quiller-Couch, Arthur, et al, eds. (New Shakespeare Ser). 1969. 23.95 (ISBN 0-521-07529-7); pap. 4.50x (ISBN 0-521-09472-0). Cambridge U Pr.

--Coriolanus. rev. ed. Levin, Harry, ed. (Shakespeare Ser.). 1956. pap. 2.50 (ISBN 0-14-071402-2, Pelican). Penguin.

--Cymbeline. Quiller-Couch, Arthur, et al, eds. (New Shakespeare Ser). 1968. 23.95 (ISBN 0-521-07530-0); pap. 4.50x (ISBN 0-521-09473-9). Cambridge U Pr.

--Four Great Comedies. Incl. As You Like It; Midsummer Night's Dream; The Tempest; Twelfth Night. pap. 2.75 (ISBN 0-671-42463-7). WSP.

--Hamlet. Jump, John, ed. LC 78-127579. (Casebook Ser). 1970. pap. text ed. 2.50 o.s.i. (ISBN 0-87695-047-0). Aurora Pubs.

--Hamlet. Hoy, Cyrus, ed. (Critical Editions). (Annotated). (gr. 9-12). 1963. pap. text ed. 3.95x (ISBN 0-393-09591-6, 9591, NortonC). Norton.

--Hamlet. Quiller-Couch, Arthur, et al, eds. (New Shakespeare Ser). 23.95 (ISBN 0-521-07531-9); pap. 4.50x (ISBN 0-521-09474-7). Cambridge U Pr.

--Hamlet. Mack, Maynard & Boynton, Robert W., eds. (Shakespeare Ser). (Illus.). (gr. 10-12). 1972. pap. text ed. 0.95x (ISBN 0-8104-6016-5). Hayden.

--Hamlet. Bald, R. C., ed. LC 47-25585. (Crofts Classics Ser.). 1946. pap. text ed. 2.25x (ISBN 0-88295-073-8). AHM Pub.

--Hamlet, with Reader's Guide. (Literature Program Ser). (gr. 10-12). 1970. pap. text ed. 4.58 (ISBN 0-87720-801-8); tchrs ed. 2.95 (ISBN 0-87720-901-4). AMSCO Sch.

--Henry Eighth. Quiller-Couch, Arthur, et al, eds. (New Shakespeare Ser). 1969. 23.95 (ISBN 0-521-07538-6); pap. 2.95x o.p. (ISBN 0-521-09481-X). Cambridge U Pr.

--Henry Fifth. Quiller-Couch, Arthur, et al, eds. (New Shakespeare Ser). 23.95 (ISBN 0-521-07534-3); pap. 4.50x (ISBN 0-521-09477-1). Cambridge U Pr.

--Henry Fourth, Pt. 1. rev. ed. Sanderson, James L., ed. (Critical Editions Ser). (Annotated). (gr. 9-12). 1969. text ed. 5.00 (ISBN 0-393-04234-0); pap. text ed. 5.95x (ISBN 0-393-09554-1, 9554, NortonC). Norton.

--Henry Fourth, Pts. 1 & 2. (Shakespeare Ser). (gr. 10 up). pap. 1.25 ea. Pt. 1 (ISBN 0-8049-1018-9, S18). Pt. 2. pap. 0.60 (ISBN 0-8049-1019-7, S19). Airmont.

--Henry Fourth, Pt. 1. Quiller-Couch, Arthur, et al, eds. (New Shakespeare Ser). 23.95 (ISBN 0-521-07532-7); pap. 4.50x (ISBN 0-521-09475-5). Cambridge U Pr.

--Henry Fourth, Pt. 2. Quiller-Couch, Arthur, et al, eds. (New Shakespeare Ser). 23.95 (ISBN 0-521-07533-5); pap. 4.50x (ISBN 0-521-09476-3). Cambridge U Pr.

--Henry IV, Pt. I. Mack, Maynard & Boynton, Robert W., eds. (Shakespeare Ser). (Illus.). (gr. 10-12). 1972. pap. text ed. 0.95x (ISBN 0-8104-6017-3). Hayden.

--Henry Sixth, Pt. 1. Quiller-Couch, Arthur, et al, eds. (New Shakespeare Ser). 1968. 23.95 (ISBN 0-521-07535-1); pap. 4.50x (ISBN 0-521-09478-X). Cambridge U Pr.

--Henry Sixth, Pts. 1, 2 & 3. Bevington, S., et al, eds. 1966. Pt. 1. pap. 1.95 (ISBN 0-14-071434-0, Pelican); Pt.2&3. pap. 2.95 (ISBN 0-14-071435-9, Pelican). Penguin.

--Henry Sixth, Pt. 2. Quiller-Couch, Arthur, et al, eds. (New Shakespeare Ser). 1968. 23.95 (ISBN 0-521-07536-X); pap. 4.50x (ISBN 0-521-09479-8). Cambridge U Pr.

--Henry Sixth, Pt. 3. Quiller-Couch, Arthur, et al, eds. (New Shakespeare Ser). 1968. 23.95 (ISBN 0-521-07537-8); pap. 4.50x (ISBN 0-521-09480-1). Cambridge U Pr.

--Henry V. 1967. pap. text ed. 3.95x o.p. (ISBN 0-471-00519-3). Wiley.

--Julius Caesar. Quiller-Couch, Arthur, et al, eds. (New Shakespeare Ser). 1968. 23.95 (ISBN 0-521-07539-4); pap. 4.50x (ISBN 0-521-09482-8). Cambridge U Pr.

--Julius Caesar. Mack, Maynard & Boynton, Robert W., eds. (Shakespeare Ser). (Illus.). (gr. 10-12). 1972. pap. text ed. 0.95x (ISBN 0-8104-6014-9). Hayden.

--Julius Caesar, with Reader's Guide. (Literature Program). (gr. 10-12). 1970. pap. text ed. 4.00 (ISBN 0-87720-802-6); with model ans. s.p. 2.65 (ISBN 0-87720-902-2). AMSCO Sch.
--King John. Quiller-Couch, Arthur, et al, eds. (New Shakespeare Ser). 1969. 23.95 (ISBN 0-521-07540-8); pap. 2.95x o.p. (ISBN 0-521-09483-6). Cambridge U Pr.
--King Lear. Kerrmode, Frank, ed. LC 72-127580. (Casebook Ser). 1970. pap. text ed. 2.50 o.s.i. (ISBN 0-87695-050-0). Aurora Pubs.
--King Lear. Quiller-Couch, Arthur, et al, eds. (New Shakespeare Ser). 1968. 23.95 (ISBN 0-521-07541-6); pap. 4.50x (ISBN 0-521-09484-4). Cambridge U Pr.
--Love Poems & Sonnets of William Shakespeare. LC 57-11411. 6.95 (ISBN 0-385-01733-2). Doubleday.
--Love's Labor's Lost. Harbage, Alfred, ed. 1963. pap. 2.95 (ISBN 0-14-071427-8, Pelican). Penguin.
--Love's Labour's Lost. Quiller-Couch, Arthur, et al, eds. (New Shakespeare Ser). (Illus.). 1969. 23.95 (ISBN 0-521-07542-4); pap. 4.50x (ISBN 0-521-09485-2). Cambridge U Pr.
--Macbeth. Wain, John, ed. LC 78-127579. (Casebook Ser). 1970. pap. text ed. 2.50 o.s.i. (ISBN 0-87695-051-9). Aurora Pubs.
--Macbeth. Quiller-Couch, Arthur, et al, eds. (New Shakespeare Ser). 23.95 (ISBN 0-521-07543-2); pap. 4.50x (ISBN 0-521-09486-0). Cambridge U Pr.
--Macbeth. Mack, Maynard & Boynton, Robert W., eds. (Shakespeare Ser). (gr. 10-12). 1972. pap. text ed. 0.75 o.p. (ISBN 0-8104-6015-7). Hayden.
--Macbeth. Wright, Louis B. & LaMar, Virginia, eds. pap. 2.25 (ISBN 0-671-43294-X). PB.
--Macbeth, with Reader's Guide. (Literature Program). 1972. pap. text ed. 4.25 (ISBN 0-87720-803-4); tchr's ed. 2.75 (ISBN 0-87720-903-0). AMSCO Sch.
--Measure for Measure. Quiller-Couch, Arthur, et al, eds. (New Shakespeare Ser). 1969. 23.95 (ISBN 0-521-07544-0); pap. 4.50x (ISBN 0-521-09488-7). Cambridge U Pr.
--Measure for Measure. Bald, Robert C., ed. 1956. pap. 2.50 (ISBN 0-14-071403-0, Pelican). Penguin.
--Merchant of Venice. Quiller-Couch, Arthur, et al, eds. (New Shakespeare Ser). 23.95 (ISBN 0-521-07545-9); pap. 4.50x (ISBN 0-521-09488-7). Cambridge U Pr.
--Merchant of Venice. Wright, Louis B. & LaMar, Virginia A., eds. (Folger Library). (Illus.). (gr. 9 up). 1957. 2.25 o.p. (ISBN 0-671-43296-6). PB.
--Merry Wives of Windsor. Quiller-Couch, Arthur, et al, eds. (New Shakespeare Ser). 1969. 23.95 (ISBN 0-521-07546-7); pap. 4.50x (ISBN 0-521-09489-5). Cambridge U Pr.
--Merry Wives of Windsor. rev. ed. Kittredge, George L. & Ribner, Irving, eds. LC 69-15381. 1969. pap. 3.95x o.p. (ISBN 0-471-00533-9). Wiley.
--Midsummer Night's Dream. Quiller-Couch, Arthur, et al, eds. (New Shakespeare Ser). 23.95 (ISBN 0-521-07547-5); pap. 4.50x (ISBN 0-521-09490-9). Cambridge U Pr.
--A Midsummer Night's Dream. Wright, Louis B. & LaMar, Virginia, eds. (gr. 10 up). pap. 2.25 (ISBN 0-671-43297-4). PB.
--Midsummer Nights' Dream. LC 77-512. (Illus.). 1977. 32.50 (ISBN 0-913870-41-2). Abaris Bks.
--Much Ado About Nothing. Quiller-Couch, Arthur, et al, eds. (New Shakespeare Ser). 1969. 23.95 (ISBN 0-521-07548-3); pap. 4.50x (ISBN 0-521-09491-7). Cambridge U Pr.
--Norton Facsimile--William Shakespeare. 1969. academic ed. 75.00x (ISBN 0-393-09843-5). Norton.
--Othello. Quiller-Couch, Arthur, et al, eds. (New Shakespeare Ser). 1969. 23.95 (ISBN 0-521-07549-1); pap. 4.50x (ISBN 0-521-09492-5). Cambridge U Pr.
--Othello. Eccles, Mark, ed. LC 47-25793. (Crofts Classics Ser.). 1946. pap. text ed. 2.25x (ISBN 0-88295-079-7). AHM Pub.
--Othello, The Moor of Venice. LC 73-14771. (Shakespeare Ser). 1974. 9.85 o.p. (ISBN 0-672-51483-4); pap. 7.50 (ISBN 0-672-61106-6). Bobbs.
--Othello 1622. Hinman, Charlton, ed. (Shakespeare Quarto Facsimiles Ser: No. 16). 112p. 1975. 22.00x (ISBN 0-19-818147-7). Oxford U Pr.
--Pericles. Quiller-Couch, Arthur, et al, eds. (New Shakespeare Ser). 1969. 23.95 (ISBN 0-521-07550-5); pap. 4.50x (ISBN 0-521-09494-1). Cambridge U Pr.
--Pericles. 1969. pap. text ed. 3.50x o.p. (ISBN 0-471-00537-1). Wiley.
--Poems. Quiller-Couch, Arthur, et al, eds. (New Shakespeare Ser). 1969. 23.95 (ISBN 0-521-07551-3); pap. 4.50x (ISBN 0-521-09493-3). Cambridge U Pr.
--Richard III. 1968. pap. text ed. 3.95 (ISBN 0-471-00550-9). Wiley.
--Richard Second. Quiller-Couch, Arthur, et al, eds. (New Shakespeare Ser). 23.95 (ISBN 0-521-07552-1); pap. 4.50x (ISBN 0-521-09495-X). Cambridge U Pr.
--Richard Second. Black, Matthew W., ed. (Shakespeare Ser.). (YA) (gr. 9 up). 1957. pap. 2.25 (ISBN 0-14-071406-5, Pelican). Penguin.
--Richard Third. Quiller-Couch, Arthur, et al, eds. LC 68-133495. (New Shakespeare Ser). 1968. 23.95 (ISBN 0-521-07553-X); pap. 4.50x (ISBN 0-521-09496-8). Cambridge U Pr.
--The Riverside Shakespeare. Evans, G. Blakemore, et al, eds. 1728p. 1974. text ed. 22.50 (ISBN 0-395-04402-2). HM.
--Romeo & Juliet. (Illus.). (gr. 7 up). 1970. pap. 1.25 (ISBN 0-590-02921-5, Schol Pap). Schol Bk Serv.
--Romeo & Juliet. Quiller-Couch, Arthur, et al, eds. (New Shakespeare Ser). 1969. 23.95 (ISBN 0-521-07554-8); pap. 4.50x (ISBN 0-521-09497-6). Cambridge U Pr.
--Shakespeare's Complete Works. 1230p. 34.50 (ISBN 0-686-68309-9). Porter.
--Sonnets. Quiller-Couch, Arthur, et al, eds. (New Shakespeare Ser). 1969. 23.95 (ISBN 0-521-07555-6); pap. 4.50x (ISBN 0-521-09498-4). Cambridge U Pr.
--Sonnets. 1964. 2.25 o.p. (ISBN 0-212-35868-5). Dufour.
--Taming of the Shrew. Quiller-Couch, Arthur, et al, eds. (New Shakespeare Ser). 23.95 (ISBN 0-521-07556-4); pap. 4.50x (ISBN 0-521-09499-2). Cambridge U Pr.
--Tempest. Palmer, D. J., ed. LC 70-127577. (Casebook Ser). 1970. pap. text ed. 2.50 o.s.i. (ISBN 0-87695-053-5). Aurora Pubs.
--Tempest. Quiller-Couch, Arthur, et al, eds. (New Shakespeare Ser). 1969. 23.95 (ISBN 0-521-07557-2); pap. 4.50x (ISBN 0-521-09500-X). Cambridge U Pr.
--The Tempest. Harbage, Alfred, ed. LC 47-25589. (Crofts Classics Ser.). 1946. pap. text ed. 1.25x o.p. (ISBN 0-88295-083-5). AHM Pub.
--Timon of Athens. Quiller-Couch, Arthur, et al, eds. (New Shakespeare Ser). 23.95 (ISBN 0-521-07558-0); pap. 4.50x (ISBN 0-521-09501-8). Cambridge U Pr.
--Titus Andronicus. Quiller-Couch, Arthur, et al, eds. LC 68-133497. (New Shakespeare Ser). 1968. 23.95 (ISBN 0-521-07559-9); pap. 4.50x (ISBN 0-521-09502-6). Cambridge U Pr.
--Titus Andronicus. Cross, Gustav, ed. (Shakespeare Ser.). 1966. pap. 2.95 (ISBN 0-14-071433-2, Pelican). Penguin.
--Troilus & Cressida. Quiller-Couch, Arthur, et al, eds. (New Shakespeare Ser). 1969. 23.95 (ISBN 0-521-07560-2); pap. 4.50x (ISBN 0-521-09503-4). Cambridge U Pr.
--Troilus & Cressida. 1967. pap. text ed. 3.50x o.p. (ISBN 0-471-00542-8). Wiley.
--Twelfth Night. Quiller-Couch, Arthur, et al, eds. (New Shakespeare Ser). 1968. 23.95 (ISBN 0-521-07561-0); pap. 4.50x (ISBN 0-521-09504-2). Cambridge U Pr.
--Two Gentlemen of Verona. Quiller-Couch, Arthur, et al, eds. (New Shakespeare Ser). 1969. 23.95 (ISBN 0-521-07562-9); pap. 4.50x (ISBN 0-521-09505-0). Cambridge U Pr.
--Two Gentlemen of Verona. Jackson, Berners, ed. (Shakespeare Ser.). 1965. pap. 2.50 (ISBN 0-14-071431-6, Pelican). Penguin.
--Winter's Tale. Quiller-Couch, Arthur, et al, eds. (New Shakespeare Ser). 1968. 23.95 (ISBN 0-521-07563-7); pap. 4.50x (ISBN 0-521-09506-9). Cambridge U Pr.
Shakespeare, William, jt. auth. see Fletcher, John.
Shakibi, Jami G. & Liebson, Philip R., eds. Cardiology Review. 2nd. ed. 1976. spiral bdg. 14.00 (ISBN 0-87488-337-7). Med Exam.
Shakir, Moin. Politics of Minorities. 1980. 16.00x (ISBN 0-8364-0622-2, Pub. by Ajanta). South Asia Bks.
Shakman, Robert. Where You Live May Be Hazardous to Your Health. 1978. 14.95 (ISBN 0-8128-2506-3); pap. 5.95 (ISBN 0-8128-6001-2). Stein & Day.
Shakman, Robert A. Poison-Proof Your Body. 192p. 1980. 12.95 (ISBN 0-87000-478-6). Arlington Hse.
Shakow, David. Adaptation in Schizophrenia: The Theory of Segmental Set. LC 79-14979. (Personality Processes Ser.). 1979. 22.95 (ISBN 0-471-05756-8, Pub. by Wiley-Interscience). Wiley.
Shakum, Melvin F., jt. ed. see Lewin, Arie Y.
Shalaby, S. W., ed. Thermal Methods in Polymer Analysis. LC 78-8816. (Eastern Analytical Symposium Ser.). 1978. pap. text ed. 21.75 (ISBN 0-89168-016-0). Franklin Inst.
Shalhevet, J., et al, eds. Irrigation of Field & Orchard Crops Under Semi-Arid Conditions. (Illus.). 110p. 1980. pap. 10.50 (ISBN 0-08-025511-6). Pergamon.
Shalhope, Robert E. John Taylor of Caroline: Pastoral Republican. LC 80-12501. 314p. 1980. 19.50 (ISBN 0-87249-390-3). U of SC Pr.
Shalit, Nathan. Science Magic Tricks: Over 50 Fun Tricks That Mystify & Dazzle. LC 79-18645. (Illus.). 128p. (gr. 4-7). 1981. 8.95 (ISBN 0-03-047116-8); pap. 3.95 (ISBN 0-03-059269-0). HR&W.
Shalita, Richard A., jt. auth. see Sparks, Richard M.
Shallenberger, R. S. & Birch, G. G. Sugar Chemistry. 1975. lib. bdg. 24.50 (ISBN 0-87055-166-3). AVI.
Shallenberger, R. S., jt. ed. see Birch, G. G.
Shalom, Stephen R. The United States & the Philippines: A Study of Neocolonialism. (Illus.). 302p. 1981. 17.50 (ISBN 0-89727-014-2). Inst Study Human.
Shalom ben-Chorin. Martin Buber: A Living Memory. Herman, Judith M., tr. from Ger. LC 79-89933. Orig. Title: Zwiesprache mit Martin Buber. (Orig.). 1980. pap. cancelled (ISBN 0-89793-010-X). Hunter Hse.
Shalvi, Alice. The Relationship of Renaissance Concepts of Honour to Shakespeare's Problem Plays. (Salzburg Studies in English Literature, Jacobean Drama Studies: No.7). 1972. pap. text ed. 25.00x (ISBN 0-391-01519-2). Humanities.
Shaman, Margaret & Wilson, Derek. The Illustrated Book of World History. (Illus.). 1978. 14.95 (ISBN 0-8467-0532-X, Pub. by Two Continents). Hippocrene Bks.
Shambaugh, George E. & Glasscock, Michael E. Surgery of the Ear. 3rd ed. (Illus.). 784p. 1980. text ed. 70.00 (ISBN 0-7216-8142-5). Saunders.
Shambaugh, Irvin C., jt. auth. see Smith, Brenda H.
Shamblin, James E. & Stevens, G. T. Operations Research. (Illus.). 416p. 1974. text ed. 21.00 (ISBN 0-07-056378-0, C); instructor's manual 5.50 (ISBN 0-07-056379-9). McGraw.
Shames, George H. & Florance, Cheri L. Stutter-Free Speech: A Goal for Therapy. (Special Education Ser.). 184p. (Orig.). 1980. pap. text ed. 10.95 (ISBN 0-675-08178-5); recording forms 12.50 (ISBN 0-675-08174-2); media 195.00 (ISBN 0-675-08099-1). Merrill.
Shames, I. Engineering Mechanics, 2 vols. 3rd ed. 1980. Vol. 1, Statics. 21.95 (ISBN 0-13-279141-2); Vol. 2, Dynamics. 21.95 (ISBN 0-13-279158-7); combined ed. 27.95 (ISBN 0-13-279166-8). P-H.
Shames, Irving H. Introduction to Solid Mechanics. (Illus.). 688p. 1975. ref. ed. 25.95 (ISBN 0-13-497503-0). P-H.
Shames, Richard & Sterin, Chuck. Healing with Mind Power. 1980. 8.95 (ISBN 0-87857-210-4); pap. 6.95 (ISBN 0-87857-293-7). Rodale Pr Inc.
Shames, William H. Venture Management: The Business of the Inventor, Entrepreneur, Venture Capitalist, & Established Company. LC 73-17642. (Illus.). 1974. 10.00 o.s.i. (ISBN 0-02-928400-7). Free Pr.
Shamma, jt. auth. see Byrkit.
Shammas, jt. auth. see Al-Ani.
Shampaign, Charles E. Handbook on Percentages. (Gamblers Book Shelf). 1965. pap. 2.95 (ISBN 0-911996-02-8). Gamblers.
Shampine, Lawrence F. & Gordon, Marilyn K. Computer Solution of Ordinary Differential Equations: The Initial Value Problem. LC 74-23246. (Illus.). 1975. text ed. 28.95x (ISBN 0-7167-0461-7). W H Freeman.
Shampo, M. A., jt. auth. see Kyle, R. A.
Shamsie, Jalal, ed. New Directions in Children's Mental Health. new ed. LC 79-17844. 1979. text ed. 20.00 (ISBN 0-89335-083-4). Spectrum Pub.
Shamsuddin. Politics of Secularization in the USSR. 336p. 1980. text ed. 27.50x (ISBN 0-7069-1274-8, Pub. by Vikas India). Advent Bk.
Shamuyarira, Nathan. Crisis in Rhodesia. 1965. 9.95 (ISBN 0-685-20570-3). Transatlantic.
Shanabruch, Charles. Chicago's Catholics: An Evolution of an American Identity. LC 80-53071. (Studies in American Catholicism: Vol. 4). 288p. 1981. text ed. 18.95 (ISBN 0-268-01840-5). U of Notre Dame Pr.
Shanahan & Whisenand. Criminal Justice Planning. 444p. 1980. text ed. 16.95 (ISBN 0-205-06668-2, 8266689). Allyn.
Shanahan, Donald T. Patrol Administration: Management by Objectives. 2nd ed. 1978. pap. text ed. 17.95 (ISBN 0-205-06036-6, 8260362). Allyn.
Shanahan, William F. The College-Bound Student's Almanac. (Orig.). 1980. pap. 6.95 (ISBN 0-671-18431-8). Monarch Pr.
--College, Yes or No: The High School Student's Career Decision-Making Handbook. LC 80-11608. 272p. 1980. lib. bdg. 9.95 (ISBN 0-668-04907-3, 4911-1); pap. 6.95 (ISBN 0-668-04911-1). Arco.
--Essential Math, Science, & Computer Terms for College Freshmen. LC 79-3323. (Illus.). 1981. pap. 5.95 (ISBN 0-671-18435-0). Monarch Pr.
--International Student Guide to United States Colleges & Universities. LC 78-24772. 1981. pap. 5.95 (ISBN 0-671-18422-9). Monarch Pr.
--The Parent Student College Planning Guide. LC 80-24467. 224p. (Orig.). 1981. pap. 6.95 (ISBN 0-668-04996-0, 4996). Arco.
Shanahan, William O., jt. ed. see Palumbo, Michael.
Shanas, Ethel, ed. Aging in Contemporary Society. LC 73-89942. (Sage Contemporary Social Science Issues: No. 6). 1974. 4.95x (ISBN 0-8039-0338-3). Sage.
Shanas, Ethel & Sussman, Marvin B., eds. Family, Bureaucracy, & the Elderly. LC 76-44090. 1977. 12.75 (ISBN 0-8223-0381-7). Duke.
Shand, David D. Clinical Cardiovascular Pharmacology. (Monographs in Clinical Pharmacology). (Illus.). Date not set. text ed. price not set (ISBN 0-443-08040-2). Churchill. Postponed.
Shand, David G., jt. ed. see Turner, Paul.
Shand, Errol B. Glass Engineering Handbook. 2nd ed. 1958. 37.50 o.p. (ISBN 0-07-056395-0, P&RB). McGraw.
Shand, R. T., ed. Agricultural Development in Asia. LC 76-92678. 1969. 22.75x (ISBN 0-520-01554-1). U of Cal Pr.
Shandler, Michael & Shandler, Nina. The Complete Guide & Cookbook for Raising Your Child As a Vegetarian. 384p. 1981. 15.50x (ISBN 0-8052-3758-5); pap. 8.95. Schocken.
Shandler, Michael, jt. auth. see Shandler, Nina.
Shandler, Nina & Shandler, Michael. Homemade Natural Mixes. LC 80-51253. 256p. 1981. 12.95 (ISBN 0-89256-145-9); pap. 6.95 (ISBN 0-89256-150-5). Rawson Wade.
Shandler, Nina, jt. auth. see Shandler, Michael.
Shane, A. David. I'm Here for an Education...Really, I Am. 72p. (Orig.). 1980. pap. 2.50 (ISBN 0-9604862-0-8). Westlake.
Shane, Alex M. The Life & Work of Evgenij Zamjatin. LC 68-19643. 1968. 23.75x (ISBN 0-520-01164-3). U of Cal Pr.
Shane, Harold, jt. auth. see Shane, Ruth.
Shane, Harold D. Mathematics for Business Applications. new ed. (Mathematics Ser.). 432p. 1976. text ed. 19.95x (ISBN 0-675-08668-X). Merrill.
Shane, Harold G. Aladdin & the Wonderful Lamp. Clark, William, ed. (Hero Legends Bk). (Illus.). 16p. (gr. 3-5). 1980. pap. 22.00 ten bks & one cass. (ISBN 0-89290-080-6, BC15-3). Soc for Visual.
--Gulliver's Travels. Clark, William, ed. (Hero Legends Bk). (Illus.). 16p. (gr. 3-5). 1980. pap. 22.00 ten bks & one cass. (ISBN 0-89290-083-0, BC15-6). Soc for Visual.
--King Arthur & the Magic Sword. Clark, William, ed. (Hero Legends Bk.). (Illus.). 16p. (gr. 3-5). 1980. pap. 22.00 ten bks & one cass. (ISBN 0-89290-079-2, BC15-2). Soc for Visual.
Shane, Harold G., jt. ed. see Anderson, Robert H.
Shane, Paul G. Police & People: A Five Country Comparison. (Illus.). 1980. pap. text ed. 11.00 (ISBN 0-8016-4556-5). Mosby.
Shane, Ruth & Shane, Harold. The New Baby. LC 79-10844. (Illus.). (ps-k). 1979. PLB 7.62 (ISBN 0-307-60822-0, Golden Pr); pap. 1.95 (ISBN 0-307-10822-8). Western Pub.
Shane, S. M. Principles of Sedation, Local & General Anesthesia in Dentistry. (Illus.). 384p. 1975. 25.75 (ISBN 0-398-03387-0). C C Thomas.
Shaner, Madeleine. Goin' South. 1978. pap. 1.95 o.s.i. (ISBN 0-515-04623-X). Jove Pubns.
Shaner, W. W. Project Planning for Developing Economies. LC 79-13225. (Praeger Special Studies Ser.). 256p. 1979. 25.95 (ISBN 0-03-051126-7). Praeger.
Shang, Yung C. see Yung C. Shang.
Shange, Ntozake. For Colored Girls Who Have Considered Suicide When the Rainbow Is Enuf: A Choreopoem. 1977. 8.95 (ISBN 0-02-609840-7). Macmillan.
--Three Pieces. 160p. 1981. 12.95 (ISBN 0-312-80280-3). St Martin.
Shangle, Robert D., jt. auth. see Cook, Louis.
Shangle, Robert D., ed. Beautiful Monterey Peninsula & Big Sur. LC 80-20374. (Illus.). 72p. 1980. 14.95 (ISBN 0-89802-164-2); pap. 7.95 (ISBN 0-89802-163-4). Beautiful Am.
--Hawaii. LC 78-102325. (Illus.). 72p. 1976. 14.95 (ISBN 0-915796-16-3); pap. 7.95 (ISBN 0-915796-15-5). Beautiful Am.
--Volcano: Mt. St. Helens. (Illus.). 48p. 1980. pap. 4.95 (ISBN 0-89802-178-2). Beautiful Am.
Shangle, Robert D. & Shngle, Robert D., eds. Beautiful New York City. LC 79-27008. (Illus.). 72p. 1980. 14.95 (ISBN 0-89802-096-4); pap. 7.95 (ISBN 0-89802-095-6). Beautiful Am.
Shangle, Robert D., ed. see Atkeson, Ray.
Shangle, Robert D., ed. see Berger, Brian.
Shangle, Robert D., ed. see Carey, Robin.
Shangle, Robert D., ed. see Cook, Lewis.
Shangle, Robert D., ed. see Cook, Louis.
Shangle, Robert D., ed. see Curran, William.
Shangle, Robert D., ed. see Curran, William C.
Shangle, Robert D., ed. see Fagan, John M.

Shangle, Robert D., ed. see Fagan, Michael.
Shangle, Robert D., ed. see Foster, Lee.
Shangle, Robert D., ed. see Graetz, Rick.
Shangle, Robert D., ed. see Horn, Beth.
Shangle, Robert D., ed. see Kelso, Linda.
Shangle, Robert D., ed. see Kennet, Andrea.
Shangle, Robert D., ed. see Lewis, Paul M.
Shangle, Robert D., ed. see London, Duke.
Shangle, Robert D., ed. see Mitchell, Loren.
Shangle, Robert D., ed. see Peterson, Willis.
Shangle, Robert D., ed. see Radhuber, Stanley.
Shangle, Robert D., ed. see Rouse, Parke, Jr.
Shangle, Robert D., ed. see Rule, Ann.
Shangle, Robert D., ed. see Ryan, Craig A.
Shangle, Robert D., ed. see Sturholm, Larry & Howard, John.
Shangle, Robert D., ed. see Waesche, James F.
Shangle, Robert D., ed. see White, Sheryl.
Shangle, Robert D., jt. ed. see White, Sheryl.
Shangle, Robert D., ed. see Will, Robin.
Shangle, Robert D., ed. see Wrinkle, Ted.
Shangold, Helen. Cloze Stories for Reading Success. (gr. k-3). 1981. 13.50 (ISBN 0-8027-9124-7). Walker & Co.
--Crosswords for Reading Success. (gr. k-3). 1981. 13.60 (ISBN 0-8027-9125-5). Walker & Co.
Shan-Hse, Cheng. Selected Paintings of Cheng Shan-Shi. 220p. 1980. 39.95 (ISBN 0-89955-140-8, Pub. by Art Bk Co Taiwan). Intl Schol Bk Serv.
Shank, et al. Guide to Modern Meals. O'Neill, Martha, ed. (Illus.). 640p. (gr. 10-12). 1980. 17.28 (ISBN 0-07-056416-7, W); tchrs. resource guide avail. (ISBN 0-07-047514-8). McGraw.
Shank, Alan. American Politics, Policies & Priorities. 3rd ed. 350p. 1980. text ed. 13.60 (ISBN 0-205-07165-1, 767165-2). Allyn.
--Political Power & the Urban Crisis. 3rd ed. 570p. 1976. pap. text ed. 11.95 (ISBN 0-205-05491-9, 765491X). Allyn.
Shank, Alan, jt. ed. see Levin, Melvin R.
Shank, J. K. Matrix Methods in Accounting: An Introduction. 1972. pap. text ed. 6.50 (ISBN 0-201-07053-7). A-W.
Shank, John K. Contemporary Managerial Accounting: A Casebook. (Illus.). 352p. 1981. 14.95 (ISBN 0-13-170357-9). P-H.
Shank, Paul & McElroy, Wayne. Paraprofessionals or Teacher Aides. LC 70-107603. 1970. 8.00 o.p. (ISBN 0-87812-010-6). Pendell Pub.
Shank, W. H. Historic Bridges of Pennsylvania. 1980. 3.00 (ISBN 0-933788-17-7). Am Canal & Transport.
--History of York-Pullman Auto, 1903-1917. 1970. 2.50 (ISBN 0-933788-24-X). Am Canal & Transport.
--Vanderbilt's Folly: History of Pennsylvania Turnpike. 6th ed. 1979. 3.00 (ISBN 0-933788-05-3). Am Canal & Transport.
Shankar, Kripa. Concealed Tenancy & Its Implications for Economic Growth: A Case Study of Eastern Uttar Pradesh. 144p. 1980. text ed. 9.50x (ISBN 0-391-02137-0). Humanities.
Shankar, R. Principles of Quantum Mechanics. (Illus.). 630p. 1980. 29.50 (ISBN 0-306-40397-8, Plenum Pr). Plenum Pub.
Shankar, Vijay N. The Other Time & Other Poems. (Writers Workshop Redbird Ser.). 53p. 1975. 10.00 (ISBN 0-88253-602-8); pap. text ed. 4.80 (ISBN 0-88253-601-X). Ind-US Inc.
--Rusted Laughter. (Writers Workshop Redbird Ser.). 1975. 6.75 (ISBN 0-88253-622-2); pap. text ed. 4.00 (ISBN 0-88253-621-4). Ind-US Inc.
Shankara. Vivekachudamani of Shri Shankaracharya. Madhavananda, Swami, tr. (Sanskrit & Eng). pap. 3.25 o.s.i. (ISBN 0-87481-147-3). Vedanta Pr.
--Wisdom of Unity (Manisa-Pancakam) Mahadevan, T. M., tr. (Orig., Sanskrit & Eng.). pap. 1.25 o.p. (ISBN 0-89744-125-7, Pub. by Ganesh & Co. India). Auromere.
Shankaranarayanan, S. Glory of the Divine Mother. 1979. 7.50 o.p. (ISBN 0-89744-957-6). Auromere.
--Ten Great Cosmic Powers. 1979. 6.25 o.p. (ISBN 0-89744-956-8). Auromere.
Shanken, Marvin R. The Impact American Beer Market Review & Forecast: Nineteen-Eighty-One Edition. 2nd ed. (Illus.). 60p. 1981. pap. price not set (ISBN 0-918076-15-3). Tasco.
--The Impact American Beer Market Review & Forecast. (Illus.). 1980. pap. 75.00 (ISBN 0-918076-09-9). Tasco.
--The Impact American Distilled Spirits Market Review & Forecast. 4th ed. (Illus.). 1979. pap. 65.00 (ISBN 0-918076-04-8). Tasco.
--The Impact American Distilled Spirits Market Review & Forecast. 5th ed. (Illus.). 1980. pap. 75.00 (ISBN 0-918076-08-0). Tasco.
--The Impact American Distilled Spirits Market Review & Forecast: Nineteen-Eighty-One Edition. 6th ed. (Illus.). 60p. 1981. pap. price not set (ISBN 0-918076-14-5). Tasco.
--The Impact American Distilled Spirits Review & Forecast. 3rd ed. 1978. 50.00 (ISBN 0-918076-02-1). Tasco.
--The Impact American Wine Market Review & Forecast: Nineteen-Eighty-One Edition. 7th ed. (Illus.). 60p. 1981. pap. price not set (ISBN 0-918076-13-7). Tasco.
--The Impact American Wine Market Review & Forecast. (Illus.). 1975. 50.00 (ISBN 0-918076-12-9). Tasco.
--The Impact American Wine Market Review & Forecast. 6th ed. (Illus.). 1980. pap. 75.00 (ISBN 0-918076-07-2). Tasco.
--The Impact American Wine Market Review & Forecast. 4th ed. 1978. 50.00 (ISBN 0-918076-00-5). Tasco.
--The Impact American Wine Review & Forecast. 5th ed. (Illus.). 1979. pap. 50.00 (ISBN 0-918076-03-X). Tasco.
Shanken, Marvin R., ed. The Impact American Distilled Spirits Market Review & Forecast. (Illus.). 1976. 50.00 (ISBN 0-918076-10-2). Tasco.
--The Impact American Distilled Spirits Market Review & Forecast. 2nd ed. (Illus.). 1977. 75.00 (ISBN 0-918076-05-6). Tasco.
--The Impact American Wine Market Review & Forecast. 2nd ed. (Illus.). 1976. 50.00 (ISBN 0-918076-11-0). Tasco.
--The Impact American Wine Market Review & Forecast. 3rd ed. (Illus.). 1977. 50.00 (ISBN 0-918076-06-4). Tasco.
Shanks, Bernard. Wilderness Survival. LC 80-17508. (Illus.). 224p. 1980. text ed. 15.00x (ISBN 0-87663-343-2); pap. 5.95 (ISBN 0-87663-998-8). Universe.
Shanks, Merrill, et al. Pre-Calculus Mathematics. 4th ed. (gr. 11-12). 1981. text ed. 15.24 (ISBN 0-201-07684-5, Sch Div); tchr's ed. 7.12 (ISBN 0-201-07685-3); solution manual 13.08 (ISBN 0-201-07686-1). A-W.
Shanks, Michael. European Social Policy, Today & Tomorrow. 1977. text ed. 19.50 (ISBN 0-08-021444-4); pap. text ed. 7.75 (ISBN 0-08-021443-6). Pergamon.
--What's Wrong with the Modern World? Agenda for a New Society. 1979. 9.95 (ISBN 0-370-30101-3, Pub. by Chatto Bodley Jonathan). Merrimack Bk Serv.
Shanks, Royal E. & Sharp, Aaron J. Summer Key to Trees of Tennessee & the Great Smokies. (Illus.). 24p. 1963. pap. 1.50x (ISBN 0-87049-040-0). U of Tenn Pr.
Shanley, Diarmuid. Efficacy of Treatment Procedures in Periodontics. 340p. 1980. 68.00 (ISBN 0-931386-43-8). Quint Pub Co.
Shanmugam, K. Sam. Digital & Analog Communication Systems. LC 78-26191. 1979. text ed. 26.95 (ISBN 0-471-03090-2); solutions manual (ISBN 0-471-07832-8). Wiley.
Shanmugaratnam, K. Histological Typing of Upper Respiratory Tract Tumors. (World Health Organization: International Histological Classification of Tumours Ser.). (Illus.). 1978. text ed. 59.50 (ISBN 92-4-176019-2, 70-1-019-20); text & slides 182.00 (ISBN 0-685-96477-9, 70-1-019-00). Am Soc Clinical.
Shann, C. D. Pipeline Glossary & Directory. (Orig.). 1978. pap. 32.00 (ISBN 0-914082-05-1). Syentek Bks.
Shannon, Claude E. & Weaver, Warren. The Mathematical Theory of Communication. LC 49-11922. 1949. 6.00 o.p. (ISBN 0-252-72548-4); pap. 2.95 (ISBN 0-252-72548-4). U of Ill Pr.
Shannon, David, ed. see Webb, Beatrice.
Shannon, David A. Between the Wars: America, Nineteen Nineteen to Nineteen Forty-One. 2nd ed. LC 78-69558. (Illus.). 1978. pap. text ed. 8.25 (ISBN 0-395-26535-5). HM.
Shannon, Dell. Appearances of Death. 208p. 1980. pap. 1.95 (ISBN 0-553-13953-3). Bantam.
--Murder Most Strange. 224p. 1981. 9.95 (ISBN 0-688-00378-8). Morrow.
--Streets of Death. LC 80-24140. 315p. 1980. Repr. of 1976 ed. large print ed. 8.95 (ISBN 0-89621-250-5). Thorndike Pr.
Shannon, Doris. Cain's Daughters. LC 77-15323. 1978. 10.00 o.p. (ISBN 0-312-11390-0). St Martin.
Shannon, Fred. The Life & Agony of the Elephant Man. (Orig.). 1979. pap. 2.25 (ISBN 0-532-23280-1). Manor Bks.
Shannon, George. The Gang & Mrs. Higgins. LC 80-15957. (Read-Alone Bk.). (Illus.). 48p. (gr. 1-3). 1981. 5.95 (ISBN 0-688-80303-2); PLB 5.71 (ISBN 0-688-84303-4). Greenwillow.
Shannon, Ira L. Brand Name Guide to Sugar: Sucrose Content of Over 1,000 Common Foods & Beverages. LC 77-10902. (Illus.). 1977. 9.95 (ISBN 0-88229-454-7); pap. 1.95 (ISBN 0-88229-542-X). Nelson-Hall.
Shannon, Jasper B. Toward a New Politics in the South. 1949. 8.50x (ISBN 0-87049-006-0). U of Tenn Pr.
Shannon, Loren E., jt. auth. see Couger, Daniel.
Shannon, Loren E., jt. auth. see Couger, J. Daniel.
Shannon, Lytle. Golden Stallion. (YA) 1972. 5.95 (ISBN 0-685-02720-1, Avalon). Bouregy.
Shannon, Patrick, jt. auth. see Groebner, David.
Shannon, Patrick W., jt. auth. see Groebner, David F.
Shannon, R. R., ed. see International Commission on Optics International Congress, 9th.
Shannon, Robert E. Systems Simulation: The Art & Science. (Illus.). 368p. 1975. ref. ed. 19.95 (ISBN 0-13-881839-8). P-H.
Shannon, Thomas. Bioethics. rev. ed. LC 76-18054. 640p. 1980. pap. 11.95 (ISBN 0-8091-2326-6). Paulist Pr.
Shannon, Thomas A. & DiGiacomo, James. An Introduction to Bioethics. LC 79-66585. 1979. pap. 3.95 (ISBN 0-8091-2257-X). Paulist Pr.
Shannon, Thomas A., jt. ed. see O'Brien, David J.
Shannon, W. Wayne. Party, Constituency & Congressional Voting: A Study of Legislative Behavior in the United States House of Representatives. LC 80-25798. (Louisiana State University Studies, Social Science Ser.: No. 14). (Illus.). xii, 202p. 1981. Repr. of 1968 ed. lib. bdg. 23.50x (ISBN 0-313-22771-3, SHPV). Greenwood.
Shannon, William V. American Irish. rev. ed. 1966. 9.95 o.s.i. (ISBN 0-02-609950-0). Macmillan.
Shanor, Charles A. & Terrell, Timothy P. Military Law in a Nutshell. LC 80-165. (Nutshell Ser.). 418p. 1980. pap. text ed. 6.95 (ISBN 0-8299-2083-8). West Pub.
Shanskii, N. M. Russian Lexicology. 1969. 14.50 (ISBN 0-08-012842-4). Pergamon.
Shantz, Carolyn U. see Hetherington, E. Mavis.
Shao, Stephen. Statistics for Business & Economics. 2nd ed. 1973. 8.95 (ISBN 0-675-08898-4). Merrill.
Shapero, Lucy & Goodman, Anthony A. Never Say Die: A Doctor & Patient Talk About Breast Cancer. (Appleton Consumer Health Guides). 170p. 1980. 10.95 (ISBN 0-8385-6718-5). ACC.
Shapin, Betty & Coly, Lisette, eds. Communication & Parapsychology: Proceedings of an International Conference Held in Vancouver, Canada; August 9-10, 1979. LC 80-80486. 230p. 1980. 14.00 (ISBN 0-912328-32-0). Parapsych Foun.
--Education in Parapsychology: Proceedings, International Conference, San Francisco, 1975. LC 76-19467. 1976. 13.50 (ISBN 0-912328-28-2). Parapsych Foun.
--The Philosophy of Parapsychology: Proceedings of an International Conference, Copenhagen, 1976. LC 77-75663. 1977. 14.00 (ISBN 0-912328-29-0). Parapsych Foun.
Shapin, Betty, ed. see International Conference, Amsterdam, 1972.
Shapin, Betty, ed. see International Conference, France, 1971.
Shapin, Betty, ed. see International Conference, Montreal Canada, Aug. 24-25, 1978.
Shapin, Betty, ed. see Proceedings of an International Conference, France, 1969.
Shapin, Betty, ed. see Proceedings of the International Conference, Paris, France, 1977.
Shapin, Steven, jt. ed. see Barnes, Barry.
Shapira, Morris, ed. Selected Literary Criticism. 374p. 1981. pap. 7.95 o.p. (ISBN 0-8180-1130-0). Horizon.
Shapira, Rina, jt. auth. see Etzioni-Halevy, Eva.
Shapiro, Adrian M., et al. Carson McCullers: A/Descriptive Listing & Annotated Bibliography of Criticism. LC 79-7909. (Garland Reference Library of Humanities). 250p. 1980. lib. bdg. 35.00 (ISBN 0-8240-9534-0). Garland Pub.
Shapiro, Amy. Sun Signs: The Stars in Your Life. LC 77-21393. (Myth, Magic & Superstition Ser.). (Illus.). (gr. 4-5). 1977. PLB 9.65 (ISBN 0-8172-1028-8). Raintree Pubs.
Shapiro, Amy, ed. A Woman's Notebook: Being a Book of Women's Quotes with Space for Notes. (Illus.). 96p. (Orig.). 1980. lib. bdg. 12.90 (ISBN 0-89471-094-X); pap. 4.95 (ISBN 0-89471-095-8). Running Pr.
Shapiro, Andrew, jt. auth. see Striker, John M.
Shapiro, Arnold, jt. auth. see Kolman, Bernard.
Shapiro, Arthur K., et al, eds. Gilles de la Tourette Syndrome. LC 74-21986. 1978. 32.50 (ISBN 0-89004-057-5). Raven.
Shapiro, Ascher H. The Dynamics & Thermodynamics of Compressible Fluid Flow, 2 Vols. (Illus.). 1953-54. Vol. 1. 25.95 (ISBN 0-471-06845-4); Vol. 2. 23.95 (ISBN 0-8260-8075-8). Wiley.
Shapiro, Barbara J. John Wilkins, 1614-1672: An Intellectual Biography. LC 73-84042. 1969. 23.75x (ISBN 0-520-01396-4). U of Cal Pr.
Shapiro, Barbara S. Camille Pissarro: The Impressionist Printmaker. (Illus.). 1973. pap. 3.25 (ISBN 0-87846-075-6). Mus Fine Arts Boston.
Shapiro, Barry & Boericke, Arthur. Handmade Homes: The Natural Way to Build Houses. (Illus.). Date not set. 17.95 (ISBN 0-440-03340-3). Delacorte. Postponed.
Shapiro, Barry, jt. auth. see Shapiro, Evelyn.
Shapiro, Cecile & Mason, Lauris. Fine Prints: Collecting, Buying & Selling. LC 76-9200. (Illus.). 1976. 10.95 o.p. (ISBN 0-06-013853-X, HarpT). Har-Row.
Shapiro, Cecile, et al. Better Kitchens. Horowitz, Shirley M., ed. LC 80-67151. (Illus.). 160p. (Orig.). 1980. 12.95 (ISBN 0-932944-23-X); pap. 6.95 (ISBN 0-932944-24-8). Creative Homeowner.
Shapiro, Charles, ed. Contemporary British Novelists. LC 65-19772. (Crosscurrents-Modern Critiques Ser.). 182p. 1965. 10.95 (ISBN 0-8093-0176-8). S Ill U Pr.
--Contemporary British Novelists. LC 65-19772. (Arcturus Books Paperbacks). 185p. 1969. pap. 5.95 (ISBN 0-8093-0353-1). S Ill U Pr.
--Twelve Original Essays on Great English Novels. (Waynebooks Ser: No. 14). 1960. text ed. 7.95x o.p. (ISBN 0-8143-1126-1). Wayne St U Pr.
Shapiro, Constance H. Adolescent Pregnancy Prevention: School-Community Cooperation. (Illus.). 144p. 1981. price not set (ISBN 0-398-04463-5); pap. price not set (ISBN 0-398-04464-3). C C Thomas.
Shapiro, Dan, jt. auth. see Parsler, Ron.
Shapiro, David. Autonomy & Rigid Character. LC 80-68953. 167p. 1981. 12.95x (ISBN 0-465-00567-5). Basic.
--Chemistry of Sphingolipids. LC 70-451052. (Chemistry of Natural Products Ser.). 111p. 1969. 18.50x (ISBN 0-8002-0293-7). Intl Pubns Serv.
--John Ashbery: An Introduction to the Poetry. LC 79-4420. (Columbia Introductions to Twentieth-Century American Poetry Ser.). 1979. 15.00 (ISBN 0-231-04090-3). Columbia U Pr.
--Lateness. LC 76-47073. 1980. pap. 5.95 (ISBN 0-87951-111-7). Overlook Pr.
--Lateness: A Book of Poems. LC 76-47073. 96p. 1978. 10.00 (ISBN 0-87951-058-7). Overlook Pr.
Shapiro, David, et al, eds. Biofeedback & Behavioral Medicine: Therapeutic Applications & Experimental Foundations, 1979 to 1980. 1981. text ed. 39.95 (ISBN 0-202-25129-2). Aldine Pub.
--Biofeedback & Self-Control, 1972: An Aldine Annual on the Regulation of Bodily Processes & Consciousness. LC 73-75702. 513p. 1973. 34.95x (ISBN 0-202-25107-1). Aldine Pub.
Shapiro, David S. & Shapiro, Elaine S. The Search for Love & Achievement: Marriage & the Family in a Changing World. 2nd ed. 1980. pap. text ed. 10.95x (ISBN 0-917974-48-4). Waveland Pr.
Shapiro, Deane, Jr. Meditation: Self-Regulation Strategy & Altered States of Consciousness. 1980. 19.95 (ISBN 0-202-25132-2). Aldine Pub.
Shapiro, Deborah. Agencies & Children: A Child Welfare Network's Investment in Its Clients. 240p. 1976. text ed. 12.50x (ISBN 0-231-03578-0). Columbia U Pr.
Shapiro, Donald L., jt. auth. see Margolis, Carmi Z.
Shapiro, E. Donald, jt. auth. see Curran, William J.
Shapiro, Edna K. & Weber, Evelyn, eds. Cognitive & Affective Growth: Developmental Interaction. 240p. 1981. ref. 19.95 (ISBN 0-89859-092-2). L Erlbaum Assocs.
Shapiro, Elaine S., jt. auth. see Shapiro, David S.
Shapiro, Eli & Wolff, Charles R. The Role of Private Placements in Corporate Finance. 1972. text ed. 12.50 (ISBN 0-87584-099-X). Harvard U Pr.
Shapiro, Evelyn & Shapiro, Barry. The Women Say, the Men Say. 1979. postponed 14.95 (ISBN 0-440-09626-X). Delacorte.
Shapiro, Frank D. & Burchess, A. Understanding the Human Form: A Practical Study & Workbook for Surface Anatomy. (Illus.). 1980. 7.95 (ISBN 0-89529-024-3). Avery Pub.
Shapiro, H. L., jt. auth. see Alo, R. A.
Shapiro, Harry L. Race Mixture. (Orig.). 1958. pap. 2.50 (ISBN 92-3-100416-6, U509, UNESCO). Unipub.
Shapiro, Harvey. Battle Report. LC 66-23924. (Wesleyan Poetry Program: Vol. 32). (Orig.). 1966. pap. 10.00x (ISBN 0-8195-2032-2, Pub. by Wesleyan U Pr); pap. 4.95 (ISBN 0-8195-1032-7). Columbia U Pr.
--Faster Than Sound. LC 73-22610. (Illus.). 224p. 1975. 15.00 o.p. (ISBN 0-498-01507-6). A S Barnes.
--Lauds & Nightsounds. 2nd ed. LC 74-34539. 1978. 10.00 (ISBN 0-915342-07-3); pap. 4.00 (ISBN 0-915342-01-4). SUN.
--This World. LC 72-142725. (Wesleyan Poetry Program: Vol. 57). 1971. pap. 10.00x (ISBN 0-8195-2057-8, Pub. by Wesleyan U Pr); pap. 4.95x (ISBN 0-8195-1057-2). Columbia U Pr.
Shapiro, Henry D., ed. see Drake, Daniel.
Shapiro, Howard. The Birth Control Book. 1977. 10.00 o.p. (ISBN 0-312-08172-3). St Martin.

Shapiro, Ira & Schad, Tennyson. American Showcase, Vol. 3. 336p. 1980. 37.50 o.p. (ISBN 0-931144-06-X); pap. 25.00 o.p. (ISBN 0-931144-05-1). Am Showcase.
Shapiro, Ira, jt. ed. see Schad, Tennyson.
Shapiro, Irving J. Dictionary of Marketing Terms. 4th ed. (Littlefield, Adams Quality Paperback Ser.: No. 363). 276p. (Orig.). 1981. pap. 7.95 (ISBN 0-8226-0363-2). Littlefield.
--Dictionary of Marketing Terms. 4th ed. 276p. 1981. 19.50x (ISBN 0-8476-6967-X). Rowman.
Shapiro, Irwin. Heroes in American Folklore. LC 62-10205. (Illus.). (gr. 5 up). 1962. PLB 6.29 o.p. (ISBN 0-671-32054-8). Messner.
--Paul Revere. (Illus.). (gr. 1-3). 1957. PLB 5.00 (ISBN 0-307-60064-5, Golden Pr). Western Pub.
--Uncle Sam's Two Hundredth Birthday Parade. 1974. PLB 9.15 o.p. (ISBN 0-307-63745-X, Golden Pr). Western Pub.
Shapiro, Irwin, ed. see Bailey, Anne & Reit, Seymour.
Shapiro, Jack, jt. auth. see Fezler, William.
Shapiro, Jane P. & Potichnyj, Peter J., eds. Change & Adaptation in Soviet & East European Politics. LC 76-8415. (Special Studies). (Illus.). 275p. 1976. text ed. 27.95 (ISBN 0-275-56190-9). Praeger.
Shapiro, Jane P., jt. ed. see Potichnyj, Peter J.
Shapiro, Jeremy, tr. see Habermas, Jurgen.
Shapiro, Jeremy F. Mathematical Programming: Structures & Algorithms. LC 79-4478. 1979. 26.95 (ISBN 0-471-77886-9, Pub by Wiley-Interscience). Wiley.
Shapiro, Jerome H. & Hipona, Florencio A. Radiology. 2nd ed. (Medical Examination Review Book: Vol. 17). 1972. spiral bdg. 16.50 (ISBN 0-87488-117-X). Med Exam.
Shapiro, Jerrold L. Methods of Group Psychotherapy & Encounter: A Tradition of Innovation. LC 77-83390. 1978. text ed. 14.50 (ISBN 0-87581-229-5). Peacock Pubs.
Shapiro, Julius. Electrolysis, Key to a Beautiful Body. LC 80-24691. (Illus.). 246p. 1981. 8.95 (ISBN 0-396-07903-2). Dodd.
Shapiro, Karl. American Poetry. 1960. pap. 8.95 scp (ISBN 0-690-07664-9, HarpC). Har-Row.
--Poems of a Jew. 1958. 7.50 o.p. (ISBN 0-394-40412-2). Random.
Shapiro, Karl J. & Beum, R. Prosody Handbook. 1965. text ed. 11.50 scp (ISBN 0-06-045960-3, HarpC). Har-Row.
Shapiro, Larry. Pop-up Books. Incl. Pop-up Colors. (ISBN 0-525-61594-6); Pop-up Numbers. (ISBN 0-525-61591-1); Pop-Up Opposites. (ISBN 0-525-61593-8); Pop-Up Shapes (ISBN 0-525-61592-X). (Illus.). (gr. 3-7). 1979. 2.95 ea. (Pub. by Gingerbread Bks.). Dutton.
Shapiro, Lawrence E. Games to Grow On: Activities to Help Children Learn Self-Control. (Illus.). 176p. 1981. text ed. 13.95 (ISBN 0-13-346148-3, Spec); pap. text ed. 5.95 (ISBN 0-13-346130-0, Spec). P-H.
Shapiro, Lillian, ed. Fiction for Youth: A Recommended Guide to Books. 300p. 1981. 19.95 (ISBN 0-918212-34-0). Neal-Schuman.
Shapiro, Lillian L. Teaching Yourself in Libraries. 1978. 5.00 ea. (ISBN 0-8242-0628-2); 25 or more copies 4.00 ea. Wilson.
Shapiro, Marianne. Hieroglyph of Time: The Petrarchan Sestina. LC 80-10112. 344p. 1981. 22.50x (ISBN 0-8166-0945-4). U of Minn Pr.
Shapiro, Martin. Courts: A Comparative & Political Analysis. LC 80-18263. 1981. lib. bdg. 20.00x (ISBN 0-226-75042-6). U of Chicago Pr.
Shapiro, Max. The Penniless Billionaires. 1981. 15.00 (ISBN 0-8129-0923-2). Times Bks.
Shapiro, Max & Cadillac Publishing Company. Mathematics Encyclopedia: A Made Simple Book. LC 76-23817. 1977. pap. 5.95 (ISBN 0-385-12427-9, Made). Doubleday.
Shapiro, Max S. & Jaber, William, eds. The Cadillac Modern Encyclopedia. new ed. LC 73-81377. (Illus.). xiv, 1954p. 1973. 39.95 (ISBN 0-87445-000-4). Cadillac.
Shapiro, Max S., ed. see Hendricks, Rhoda A.
Shapiro, Meyer. Van Gogh. (Library of Great Painters Ser). (Illus.). 1950. 35.00 (ISBN 0-8109-0524-8). Abrams.
--Van Gogh. LC 80-646. (Illus.). 160p. 1980. 14.95 (ISBN 0-385-17168-4). Doubleday.
Shapiro, Michael. Children of the Revels: The Boy Companies of Shakespeare's Time and Their Plays. LC 76-47585. 1977. 20.00x (ISBN 0-231-04112-8). Columbia U Pr.
Shapiro, Michael H. & Spece, Roy G., Jr. Problems, Cases & Materials on Bioethics & Law. (American Casebook Ser.). 915p. 1981. text ed. 23.95 (ISBN 0-8299-2134-6). West Pub.
Shapiro, Milton. Ranger Battalion: American Rangers in World War Two. LC 79-9548. (Illus.). 192p. (gr. 8-12). 1979. PLB 8.29 (ISBN 0-671-32928-6). Messner.
Shapiro, Murray, et al. How to Prepare for American College Testing (ACT) rev. ed. LC 79-20856. (gr. 11-12). 1980. pap. text ed. 5.50 (ISBN 0-8120-0636-4). Barron.
Shapiro, Nat, ed. An Encyclopedia of Quotations About Music. (Da Capo Quality Paperbacks Ser.). 1981. pap. 7.95 (ISBN 0-306-80138-8). Da Capo.
Shapiro, Pamela, jt. auth. see Anderson, Barbara.
Shapiro, R., jt. auth. see Mehlman, M. A.
Shapiro, Ronald M., et al. Securities Regulation Forms - Compliance-Practice, 3 vols. LC 75-17451. 1975. with 1979 suppl. 165.00 (ISBN 0-87632-194-5). Boardman.
Shapiro, Stanley J. Exploring Careers in Science. (Careers in Depth Ser.). (Illus.). 140p. 1981. lib. bdg. 5.97 (ISBN 0-8239-0535-7). Rosen Pr.
Shapiro, Stanley J., jt. auth. see McCarthy, E. Jerome.
Shapiro, Stephen & Tyrka, Hilary. Trusting Yourself: Psychotherapy As a Beginning. 128p. 1975. pap. 2.45 (ISBN 0-13-931022-3, Spec). P-H.
Shapiro, Steven L. Supervision: An Introduction to Business Management. 1978. 12.50 (ISBN 0-87005-213-6); instructor's guide 2.50 (ISBN 0-87005-306-X). Fairchild.
Shapiro, Sue A. Contemporary Theories of Schizophrenia: Review & Synthesis. (Illus.). 1981. 18.95 (ISBN 0-07-056423-X). McGraw.
Shapiro, Warren. Miwuyt Marriage: The Cultural Anthropology of Affinity in Northeast Arnhem Land. (Illus.). 240p. 1981. text ed. 18.50x (ISBN 0-89727-021-5). Inst Study Hum.
Shapiro, William, ed. Lands & Peoples, 6 vols. LC 80-84474. (Illus.). 1981. write for info. (ISBN 0-7172-8008-X). Grolier Ed Corp.
Shapiro, William E., ed. Lands & Peoples, 6 vols. LC 79-3290. (Illus.). 1980. write for info o.p. (ISBN 0-7172-8007-1). Grolier Ed Corp.
--New Book of Knowledge, 21 vols. LC 80-82958. (Illus.). 1981. write for info. (ISBN 0-7172-0512-6). Grolier Ed Corp.
--New Book of Knowledge, 21 vols. LC 79-53915. (Illus.). 1980. write for info o.p. (ISBN 0-7172-0511-8). Grolier Ed Corp.
Shapiro, William E. & Mamberg, Fern, eds. New Book of Knowledge Annual, 1981. LC 79-26807. (Illus.). 1981. write for info. (ISBN 0-7172-0612-2). Grolier Ed Corp.
Shapiro, William E., ed. see C. B. S. News Staff.
Shapiro, Yonathan. The Formative Years of the Israeli Labour Party: The Organization of Power, 1919-1930. LC 74-22992. (Sage Studies in Twentieth Century History: Vol. 4). 1976. 17.50x (ISBN 0-8039-9936-4). Sage.
Shapland, D. G., jt. auth. see Sutton-Scott, Francis.
Shapo, Marshall S. Cases & Materials on Products Liability. LC 80-11639. (University Casebook Ser.). 906p. 1980. text ed. write for info. (ISBN 0-88277-001-2). Foundation Pr.
--Public Regulation of Dangerous Products. LC 80-13733. (University Casebook Ser.). 397p. 1980. write for info. (ISBN 0-88277-003-9). Foundation Pr.
Shapp, Charles & Shapp, Martha. Let's Find Out About Animal Homes. LC 68-10132. (Let's Find Out Bks). (Illus.). (gr. k-3). 1962. PLB 4.47 o.p. (ISBN 0-531-00003-6). Watts.
--Let's Find Out About Animals of Long Ago. LC 68-10132. (Let's Find Out Bks). (Illus.). (gr. k-3). 1968. PLB 5.90 (ISBN 0-531-00004-4). Watts.
--Let's Find Out About Birds. LC 67-13731. (Let's Find Out Bks). (Illus.). (gr. k-3). 1967. PLB 4.47 o.p. (ISBN 0-531-00006-0). Watts.
--Let's Find Out About Cavemen. LC 76-175800. (Let's Find Out Bks). (Illus.). 48p. (gr. k-3). 1972. PLB 4.47 o.p. (ISBN 0-531-00078-8). Watts.
--Let's Find Out About Daniel Boone. LC 67-15732. (Let's Find Out Bks). (Illus.). (gr. k-3). 1967. PLB 4.47 o.p. (ISBN 0-531-00008-7). Watts.
--Let's Find Out About Firemen. LC 65-24104. (Let's Find Out Bks). (Illus.). (gr. k-3). 1962. PLB 4.47 o.p. (ISBN 0-531-00023-0). Watts.
--Let's Find Out About Indians. (Let's Find Out Bks). (Illus.). (gr. k-3). 1962. PLB 4.47 o.p. (ISBN 0-531-00027-3). Watts.
--Let's Find Out About Policemen. (Let's Find Out Bks). (Illus.). (gr. k-3). 1962. PLB 4.47 o.p. (ISBN 0-531-00036-2). Watts.
--Let's Find Out About Snakes. LC 68-19238. (Let's Find Out Bks). (Illus.). (gr. k-3). 1968. PLB 4.47 o.p. (ISBN 0-531-00043-5). Watts.
--Let's Find Out About Space Travel. LC 70-131141. (Let's Find Out Bks). (Illus.). (gr. k-3). 1971. PLB 4.47 o.p. (ISBN 0-531-00068-0). Watts.
--Let's Find Out About Spring. (Let's Find Out Bks). (Illus.). (gr. k-3). 1963. PLB 4.47 o.p. (ISBN 0-531-00044-3). Watts.
--Let's Find Out About Thanksgiving. LC 64-18887. (Let's Find Out Bks). (Illus.). (gr. k-3). 1964. PLB 4.47 o.p. (ISBN 0-531-00049-4). Watts.
--Let's Find Out About the Sun. LC 74-2996. (Let's Find Out Bks). (Illus.). 48p. (gr. k-3). 1975. PLB 6.45 (ISBN 0-531-00104-0). Watts.
--Let's Find Out About Winter. (Let's Find Out Bks). (Illus.). (gr. k-3). 1963. PLB 4.47 o.p. (ISBN 0-531-00055-9). Watts.
Shapp, Charles, jt. auth. see Shapp, Martha.
Shapp, Martha & Shapp, Charles. Let's Find Out About Babies. LC 74-3503. (Let's Find Out Bks). (Illus.). 48p. (gr. k-3). 1975. PLB 6.45 (ISBN 0-531-00109-1). Watts.
--Let's Find Out About Houses. LC 74-3000. (Let's Find Out Bks). (Illus.). 48p. (gr. k-3). 1975. PLB 6.45 (ISBN 0-531-00100-8). Watts.
--Let's Find Out About Safety. LC 74-2998. (Let's Find Out Bks). (Illus.). 48p. (Color ed.). (gr. k-3). 1975. PLB 4.90 o.p. (ISBN 0-531-00102-4). Watts.
--Let's Find Out About the Moon. rev. ed. LC 72-4414. (Let's Find Out Bks). (Illus.). (gr. k-3). 1975. PLB 4.90 o.p. (ISBN 0-531-00101-6). Watts.
--Let's Find Out About Trees, Arbor Day. LC 74-100097. (Let's Find Out Bks). (Illus.). (gr. k-3). 1970. PLB 4.47 o.p. (ISBN 0-531-00057-5). Watts.
--Let's Find Out About Water. LC 74-2995. (Let's Find Out Bks). (Illus.). 48p. (gr. k-3). 1975. PLB 6.45 (ISBN 0-531-00108-3). Watts.
--Let's Find Out About What Electricity Does. LC 74-2993. (Let's Find Out Bks). (Illus.). 48p. (gr. k-3). 1975. PLB 6.45 (ISBN 0-531-00105-9). Watts.
--Let's Find Out About What's Big & What's Small. LC 74-2992. (Let's Find Out Bks). (Illus.). 48p. (gr. k-3). 1975. PLB 6.45 (ISBN 0-531-00106-7). Watts.
--Let's Find Out About What's Light & What's Heavy. LC 74-2991. (Let's Find Out Bks). (Illus.). 48p. (gr. k-3). 1975. PLB 6.45 (ISBN 0-531-00107-5). Watts.
Shapp, Martha, jt. auth. see Shapp, Charles.
Sharan, Shlomo, et al, eds. Cooperation in Education: Based on the Proceedings of the First International Conference on Cooperation in Education, Tel-Aviv, Israel. LC 80-20192. (Illus.). 420p. (Orig.). 1980. pap. text ed. 14.95x (ISBN 0-8425-1836-3). Brigham.
Sharar, Abdul H. Lucknow: The Last Phase of an Oriental Culture. Harcourt, E. S. & Hussain, Fakhir, trs. from Urdu. (Illus.). 1977. lib. bdg. 29.50 o.p. (ISBN 0-89158-640-7). Westview.
Sharat Chandra, G. S. Bharata Natyam Dancer. 2nd ed. (Redbird Bk.). 1976. 8.00 (ISBN 0-89253-129-0); flexible bdg. 4.80 (ISBN 0-89253-140-1). Ind-US Inc.
Sharer, Robert J. & Ashmore, Wendy A. Fundamentals of Archaeology. 1979. text ed. 17.95 (ISBN 0-8053-8760-9). Benjamin-Cummings.
Sharf, Frederic A. & Wright, John H. C. E. L. Green, Shore & Landscape Painter of Lynn & Newlyn. (Illus.). 49p. 1980. pap. 3.50 (ISBN 0-88389-080-1). Essex Inst.
Shargel, Leon & Yu, Andrew B. Applied Biopharmaceutics & Pharmacokinetics. 288p. 1980. pap. text ed. 18.50x (ISBN 0-8385-0206-7). ACC.
Sharif, Ja'Far. Islam in India. Crooke, William, ed. Herklots, G. A., tr. from Hindustani. (Illus.). 414p. 1972. Repr. of 1921 ed. text ed. 15.00x (ISBN 0-7007-0015-3). Humanities.
Sharkansky, Ira. Wither the State? Politics & Public Enterprise in Three Countries. 9.95 (ISBN 0-934540-01-2); pap. 7.95 (ISBN 0-934540-00-4). Chatham Hse Pubs.
Sharkansky, Ira, jt. auth. see Edwards, George C., 3rd.
Sharkawi, A. R. Egyptian Earth. Stewart, Desmond, tr. from Arabic. 255p. 1973. pap. 3.00 (ISBN 0-88253-121-2). Ind-US Inc.
Sharland, Ian. Woods Practical Guide to Noise Control. 3rd ed. LC 74-181675. (Illus.). 1979. 10.00x (ISBN 0-8002-0030-6). Intl Pubns Serv.
Sharlot, M. Michael, jt. auth. see Dix, George E.
Sharma & Sharma. Chromosome Techniques. 3rd ed. LC 79-41279. 1980. 135.00 (ISBN 0-408-70942-1). Butterworths.
Sharma, A. B., et al. Optical Fiber Systems & Their Components. (Springer Ser. in Optical Sciences: Vol. 24). (Illus.). 250p. 1981. 38.35 (ISBN 0-387-10437-2). Springer-Verlag.
Sharma, Arvind. The Hindu Scriptural Value System & the Economic Development of India. x, 113p. 1980. text ed. 15.00x (ISBN 0-86590-004-3). Apt Bks.
Sharma, B. Krishnamurti. Brahmasutras & Their Principal Commentaries. LC 72-901912. 275p. 1974. Vol. 2. 15.00x (ISBN 0-8002-0447-6). Intl Pubns Serv.
Sharma, B. L. Pakistan-China Axis. 7.50x (ISBN 0-210-98153-9). Asia.
Sharma, B. L. & Purohit, R. K. Semiconductor Heterojunctions. LC 73-18449. 1974. text ed. 45.00 (ISBN 0-08-017747-6). Pergamon.
Sharma, B. M. & Choudhry, L. P. Federal Polity. 15.00x (ISBN 0-210-26930-8). Asia.
Sharma, Brij L. Kashmir Story. 1967. 7.50x (ISBN 0-210-98107-5). Asia.
Sharma, Chandradhar D. Critical Survey of Indian Philosophy. 1964. 7.50x o.p. (ISBN 0-8426-1517-2). Verry.
Sharma, D. N. Afro-Asian Group in the U.N. 1969. 10.00x o.p. (ISBN 0-8426-1518-0). Verry.
Sharma, Govind N. Munshi Prem Chand. (World Author Ser.: No. 488). 1978. 14.95 (ISBN 0-8057-6329-5). Twayne.
Sharma, H. S. The Physiography of the Lower Chambal Valley & Its Agricultural Development. 1979. text ed. 15.00x (ISBN 0-391-01927-9). Humanities.
--Ravine Erosion in India. (Illus.). 100p. 1980. text ed. 11.25x (ISBN 0-391-02142-7). Humanities.
Sharma, J. P., jt. auth. see Tiwari, R. D.
Sharma, Jagdish. Mahatma Gandhi, Bibliography. 2nd ed. (National Bibliographies Ser No. 1). 1968. 12.50x o.p. (ISBN 0-8426-1521-0). Verry.
Sharma, Jagdish S. Substance of Library Science. 1966. 8.75x o.p. (ISBN 0-210-26952-9). Asia.
Sharma, Joseph see Zweig, Gunter.
Sharma, K. D. Fundamentals of Machine Design. 1971. 12.50x (ISBN 0-210-27015-2). Asia.
Sharma, K. K. & Sharma, L K. A Textbook of Physical Chemistry. 2nd rev. ed. 1980. text ed. 15.00x (ISBN 0-7069-0511-3, Pub. by Vikas India). Advent Bk.
Sharma, K. L. & Singh, Harnek. Entrepreneurial Growth & Development Programmes in Northern India: A Sociological Analysis. 1980. 12.50x (ISBN 0-8364-0649-4, Pub. by Abhinav India). South Asia Bks.
Sharma, K. N., jt. auth. see Dua-Sharma, Shushil.
Sharma, Krishan. The Konds of Orissa. 1979. text ed. 10.00x (ISBN 0-391-01816-7). Humanities.
--The Konds of Orissa: Anthropometric Study. (Illus.). 112p. 1979. 11.25x (ISBN 0-8002-2298-9). Intl Pubns Serv.
Sharma, L K., jt. auth. see Sharma, K. K.
Sharma, L. P. History of Ancient India. 400p. 1981. text ed. 22.50 (ISBN 0-7069-1113-X, Pub. by Vikas India). Advent Bk.
--History of Medieval India. 450p. 1981. text ed. 25.00x (ISBN 0-7069-1115-6, Pub. by Vikas India). Advent Bk.
Sharma, M. M. Folklore of Nepal. 1979. 11.50x o.p. (ISBN 0-8364-0317-7). South Asia Bks.
Sharma, Mukul. Hardpore Corn. 1976. 9.00 (ISBN 0-89253-817-1); flexible cloth 4.80 (ISBN 0-89253-818-X). Ind-US Inc.
Sharma, N. K., jt. auth. see Dandekar, M. M.
Sharma, Om P. Sarcoidosis: A Clinical Approach. (Illus.). 248p. 1975. 23.75 (ISBN 0-398-03303-X). C C Thomas.
Sharma, P. Men & Mules on a Mission of Democracy. 5.50x o.p. (ISBN 0-210-33704-4). Asia.
Sharma, P. D. The New Caribbean Man Poems-1972 to 1976. (Illus.). 72p. (Orig.). 1980. pap. 5.00 (ISBN 0-936378-00-X). Carib Hse.
Sharma, P. S. The Kalasamuddesa of Bhartrhari's Vakyapadiya. 1972. 4.50 (ISBN 0-8426-0414-6). Orient Bk Dist.
Sharma, P. S., ed. see Bhatt, Kjmarila.
Sharma, R. N., jt. auth. see Singh, Mohinder.
Sharma, R. R. A Marxist Model of Social Change. 256p. 1980. text ed. 14.50x (ISBN 0-391-01766-7). Humanities.
Sharma, R. S. Aspects of Political Ideas & Institutions in Ancient India. 2nd ed. rev. ed. & enl. ed. 1968. 6.75x o.p. (ISBN 0-8426-1523-7). Verry.
Sharma, Rameshwar K. & Criss, Wayne E., eds. Endocrine Control in Neoplasia. LC 77-72623. (Progress in Cancer Research & Therapy Ser.: Vol. 9). 1978. 41.00 (ISBN 0-89004-244-6). Raven.
Sharma, Savitri. Women Students in India. 1979. text ed. 12.50x (ISBN 0-391-01831-0). Humanities.
Sharma, T. C. & Continho, O. Economic & Commercial Geography of India. 2nd rev. ed. (Illus.). 400p. 1980. text ed. 22.50 (ISBN 0-7069-0546-6, Pub. by Vikas India). Advent Bk.
Sharma, T. N. Religious Thought in India. 1980. 11.00x (ISBN 0-8364-0619-2, Pub. by Ramneek). South Asia Bks.
Sharma, T. N., jt. auth. see Verma, M. K.
Sharma, T. R. S. Robert Frost's Poetic Style. 1980. text ed. write for info. (ISBN 0-391-01794-2). Humanities.
Sharma, Virendra. Studies in Victorian Verse Drama: An Appraisal of the Poetic Plays of Browning, Tennyson & Other Victorians. (SSEL Poetic Drama & Poetic Theory: No. 14). 1979. pap. text ed. 25.00x (ISBN 0-391-01621-0). Humanities.
Sharman, Campbell, jt. auth. see Holmes, Jean.
Sharman, D. F., tr. see Youdim, M. B. & Lovenberg, W.
Sharman, Nick. The Surrogate. (Orig.). 1980. pap. 2.50 (ISBN 0-451-09293-7, E9293, Sig). NAL.
Sharmat, Majorie W. Grumley the Grouch. LC 79-28290. (Illus.). 32p. (ps). 1980. PLB 7.95 (ISBN 0-8234-0410-2). Holiday.

Sharmat, Marjorie W. Chasing After Annie. LC 80-7906. (Illus.). 64p. (gr. 2-7). 1981. 7.95 (ISBN 0-06-025562-5, HarpJ); PLB 7.89g (ISBN 0-06-025567-6). Har-Row.
--Fifty-One Sycamore Lane. LC 73-129754. (Illus.). (gr. 3-7). 1971. 7.95 (ISBN 0-02-782340-7). Macmillan.
--Gila Monsters Meet You at the Airport. LC 80-12264. (Illus.). 32p. (gr. k-3). 1980. 8.95 (ISBN 0-02-782450-0). Macmillan.
--Griselda's New Year. LC 79-11375. (Ready-to-Read). (Illus.). (gr. 1-4). 1979. 7.95 (ISBN 0-02-782420-9). Macmillan.
--I Don't Care. LC 76-48251. (Illus.). (ps-1). 1977. 8.95 (ISBN 0-02-782290-7, 78229). Macmillan.
--I'm Terrific. LC 76-9094. (ps-3). 1977. reinforced bdg. 7.95 (ISBN 0-8234-0282-7). Holiday.
--The Lancelot Closes at Five. LC 75-31945. (Illus.). 128p. (gr. 3-6). 1976. 8.95 (ISBN 0-02-782320-2, 78232). Macmillan.
--Mitchell Is Moving. LC 78-6816. (Ready-to-Read Ser.). (Illus.). (gr. 1-4). 1978. 8.95 (ISBN 0-02-782410-1, 78241). Macmillan.
--Nate the Great & the Lost List. 1981. pap. 1.25 (ISBN 0-440-46282-7, YB). Dell.
--Nate the Great & the Missing Key. (Illus.). 48p. (gr. 7-10). 1981. PLB 6.99 (ISBN 0-698-30726-7). Coward.
--Nate the Great & the Phony Clue. (gr. k-6). 1981. pap. 1.25 (ISBN 0-440-46300-9, YB). Dell.
--Nate the Great & the Sticky Case. (gr. k-6). pap. 1.25 (ISBN 0-440-46289-4). Dell.
--Thornton the Worrier. LC 78-1286. (Illus.). (ps-3). 1978. PLB 7.95 (ISBN 0-8234-0328-9). Holiday.
--The Three Hundred Twenty Ninth Friend. LC 76-6454. (Illus.). 48p. (gr. k-3). 1979. 8.95 (ISBN 0-590-07558-6, Four Winds). Schol Bk Serv.
--Twitchwell the Wishful. LC 80-16845. (Illus.). 40p. (ps-3). 1981. PLB 7.95 (ISBN 0-8234-0379-3). Holiday.
Sharmat, Mitchell. Come Home Wilma. Tucker, Kathleen, ed. LC 80-18991. (Concept Bks.). (Illus.). 32p. (ps-2). 1980. 6.95 (ISBN 0-8075-1278-8). A Whitman.
--Gregory, the Terrible Eater. LC 79-19172. (Illus.). 32p. (gr. k-3). 1980. 7.95 (ISBN 0-590-07586-1, Four Winds). Schol Bk Serv.
Sharmat, Mitchell, jt. auth. see Weinman, Marjorie W.
Sharninghouse, Jane, jt. ed. see National Research & Appraisal Co.
Sharnoff, J. G. The Prevention of Venous Thrombosis & Pulmonary Thromboembolism. (Medical Publicatons Ser.). 1980. lib. bdg. 25.00 (ISBN 0-8161-2223-7). G K Hall.
Sharon, Mary B. Scenes from Childhood. (Illus.). (ps up). 1978. PLB 8.95 o.p. (ISBN 0-525-38820-6). Dutton.
Sharon, Richard K. Diary of a Lover. 272p. (Orig.). 1975. pap. 2.50 (ISBN 0-446-91703-6). Warner Bks.
Sharp & Muir. Comparative Anatomy of the Male Genital Tube in Coleoptera. (Illus.). 304p. 1969. 16.70 (ISBN 0-686-09300-3). Entomol Soc.
Sharp, Aaron J., jt. auth. see Shanks, Royal E.
Sharp, Abigail see Lee, Lorenzo P.
Sharp, Ann M., jt. auth. see Lipman, Matthew.
Sharp, Ann M., jt. ed. see Lipman, Matthew.
Sharp, Ansel M., jt. auth. see Leftwich, Richard H.
Sharp, Billy B., et al. Here's What's Stopping You. LC 79-64794. Date not set. pap. cancelled (ISBN 0-88453-020-5). Barrington.
Sharp, Buchanan. In Contempt of All Authority: Rural Artisans & Riot in the West of England. 1980. 19.50x (ISBN 0-520-03681-6). U of Cal Pr.
Sharp, C. J. New Training for Service. rev. ed. (Illus., Orig.). 1942. pap. 2.50 (ISBN 0-87239-334-8, 3059). Standard Pub.
Sharp, C. Martin, jt. auth. see Bowyer, Michael J.
Sharp, Cecil & Karpeles, Maud, eds. Eighty English Folk Songs from the Southern Appalachians. 1969. pap. 2.45 o.p. (ISBN 0-262-61006-X). MIT Pr.
Sharp, Cecil J. Insects, 2 vols. (Cambridge Natural History Ser.: Vols. 5 & 6). (Illus.). Set. 17.50 (ISBN 0-8446-0907-2). Peter Smith.
Sharp, Christopher. Bad Mouth Christopher. (gr. 1-4). 1980. pap. 3.50 (ISBN 0-570-03482-5, 56-1703). Concordia.
Sharp, Clifford & Jennings, Tony. Transport & the Environment. 1976. pap. text ed. 9.25x (ISBN 0-7185-1133-6, Leicester). Humanities.
Sharp, D. R. Concrete in Highway Engineering. LC 77-118319. 1970. 19.50 (ISBN 0-08-015845-5). Pergamon.
Sharp, David. Looking Inside the Wonders of Nature. LC 76-9914. (Illus.). 64p. (gr. 10 up). 1977. 4.95 o.p. (ISBN 0-528-82213-6). Rand.
--Ramblers' Ways. LC 79-56062. (Illus.). 192p. 1980. 19.95 (ISBN 0-7153-7972-0). David & Charles.
--Walking in the Countryside. LC 77-85013. 1978. 14.95 (ISBN 0-7153-7495-8). David & Charles.
Sharp, Dennis, ed. The Rationalists: Theory & Design in the Modern Movement. Date not set. 32.50 (ISBN 0-8038-0219-6). Hastings.
Sharp, Derrick. English at School: The Wood & the Trees. LC 79-40705. (Language Teaching Methodology Ser.). (Illus.). 128p. 1980. 13.95 (ISBN 0-08-024553-6); pap. 7.95 (ISBN 0-08-024552-8). Pergamon.
Sharp, Dolph. I'm OKay, You're Not So Hot. 1975. pap. 1.50 o.s.i. (ISBN 0-446-98176-1). Warner Bks.
Sharp, Eugene L., jt. auth. see Roebbelen, Gerhard.
Sharp, Francis M. The Poet's Madness: A Reading of George Trakl. (Illus.). 264p. 1981. 17.50x (ISBN 0-8014-1297-8). Cornell U Pr.
Sharp, Gene. Social Power & Political Freedom. LC 80-81479. (Extending Horizons Bks). 456p. 1980. 15.95 (ISBN 0-87558-091-2); pap. 8.95 (ISBN 0-87558-093-9). Porter Sargent.
Sharp, Gene, illus. The Three Bears. (Illus.). 24p. (gr. k-2). 1976. PLB 7.15 o.p. (ISBN 0-307-69058-X, Golden Pr). Western Pub.
Sharp, George, ed. see Hovey, Eddy.
Sharp, Granville. Declaration of the People's Natural Right to a Share in the Legislature. LC 74-119046. (Era of the American Revolution Ser). 1971. Repr. of 1774 ed. lib. bdg. 27.50 (ISBN 0-306-71955-X). Da Capo.
Sharp, H. M., jt. auth. see Kinzey, Bertram Y., Jr.
Sharp, Hal. Sportsman's Digest of Fishing. 1953. pap. 3.95 (ISBN 0-06-463247-4, EH 247, EH). Har-Row.
Sharp, Harold & Sharp, Marjorie Z. Index to Characters in the Performing Arts: Pt. 1. Non-Musical Plays, 2 vols. LC 71-189886. 1966. Set. 45.00 (ISBN 0-8108-0066-7). Scarecrow.
Sharp, Harold S. Footnotes to American History: A Bibliographic Source Book. LC 76-49967. 1977. 27.50 (ISBN 0-8108-0994-X). Scarecrow.
--Footnotes to World History: A Bibliographic Source Book. LC 78-23417. 1979. 32.50 (ISBN 0-8108-1185-5). Scarecrow.
--Handbook of Geographical Nicknames. LC 79-26860. 153p. 1980. lib. bdg. 10.00 (ISBN 0-8108-1280-0). Scarecrow.
--Handbook of Pseudonyms & Personal Nicknames: First Supplement, 2 vols. LC 71-189886. 1403p. 1975. Set. 40.00 (ISBN 0-685-55387-6). Vol 1: A-j. Vol. 2: K-Z. (ISBN 0-8108-0807-2). Scarecrow.
--Handbook of Pseudonyms & Personal Nicknames, 2 vols. LC 71-189886. 1972. Set. 35.00 (ISBN 0-8108-0460-3). Scarecrow.
Sharp, Harold S. & Sharp, Marjorie Z. Index to Characters in the Performing Arts: Pt. 2. Operas, & Musical Productions. LC 66-13744. 1969. 37.50 (ISBN 0-8108-0075-6). Scarecrow.
--Index to Characters in the Performing Arts: Pt. 3. Ballets A to Z & Symbols. 1972. 13.50 (ISBN 0-8108-0486-7). Scarecrow.
--Index to Characters in the Performing Arts: Pt. 4. Radio & Television. LC 66-13744. 1973. 20.50 (ISBN 0-8108-0605-3). Scarecrow.
Sharp, J. D. Elements of Steelmaking Practice. 1966. 14.50 (ISBN 0-08-011437-7); pap. 5.00 o.p. (ISBN 0-08-011436-9). Pergamon.
Sharp, J. J. Hydraulic Modelling. 1981. text ed. price not set (ISBN 0-408-00482-7). Butterworth.
--Hydraulic Modelling: Theory & Practice. 1981. text ed. price not set (Fnewnes-Butterworth). Butterworths.
Sharp, James R. Jacksonians Versus the Bank: Politics in the States After the Panic of 1837. LC 70-127783. 1970. 22.50x (ISBN 0-231-03260-9). Columbia U Pr.
Sharp, Margery. Miss Bianca & the Bridesmaid. (Illus.). (gr. 5 up). 1972. 6.95 o.p. (ISBN 0-316-78299-8). Little.
--Miss Bianca in the Antarctic. LC 75-158484. 1971. 6.95 (ISBN 0-316-78294-7). Little.
--Miss Bianca in the Orient. LC 79-119110. (Illus.). 1970. 6.95 o.p. (ISBN 0-316-78319-6). Little.
--The Turret. (Illus.). (gr. 7 up). 1963. 6.95 o.p. (ISBN 0-316-78318-8). Little.
Sharp, Marilyn. Marco Polo. 338p. 1981. 12.95 (ISBN 0-399-90106-X). Marek.
Sharp, Marjorie Z., jt. auth. see Sharp, Harold.
Sharp, Marjorie Z., jt. auth. see Sharp, Harold S.
Sharp, Mary. Point & Pillow Lace: A Short Account of Various Kinds, Ancient & Modern, & How to Recognize Them. LC 72-141752. (Tower Bks). (Illus.). 1971. Repr. of 1905 ed. 18.00 (ISBN 0-8103-3912-9). Gale.
Sharp, P. E., jt. auth. see Brichta, A.
Sharp, P. R., jt. auth. see Gosden, P. H.
Sharp, Paul F. Whoop-up Country: The Canadian-American West, 1865-1885. LC 73-3166. (Illus.). 368p. 1978. pap. 7.95 (ISBN 0-8061-1484-3). U of Okla Pr.
Sharp, R. Farquharson, ed. Dictionary of English Authors: Biographical & Bibliographical. LC 75-35577. 1978. Repr. of 1904 ed. 26.00 (ISBN 0-8103-4281-2). Gale.
Sharp, Rachel. Knowledge, Ideology & the Politics of Schooling: Towards a Marxist Analysis of Education. 176p. 1980. 25.00 (ISBN 0-7100-0526-1); pap. 12.50 (ISBN 0-7100-0527-X). Routledge & Kegan.
Sharp, Rachel & Green, Anthony. Education & Social Control. 1975. 19.50x (ISBN 0-7100-8160-X); pap. 10.00 (ISBN 0-7100-8161-8). Routledge & Kegan.
Sharp, Richard. The Best Games People Play. (Illus.). 12.95x (ISBN 0-8464-0188-6); pap. 5.95x (ISBN 0-8464-0194-0). Beekman Pubs.
Sharp, Richard M. & Mitzner, Seymour. Numero Magico, 4 bks. rev. ed. Editorial Turabo, Inc., ed. Incl. Libro Primero. 48p. (gr. 1-3) (ISBN 0-675-01038-1); Libro 2. 48p. (gr. 2-4) (ISBN 0-675-01039-X); Libra 3. 48p. (gr. 3-5) (ISBN 0-675-01040-3); Libra 4. 48p. (gr. 4-6) (ISBN 0-675-01041-1). (Span.). 1979. pap. 1.50 ea. Merrill.
Sharp, Ronald A. Keats, Skepticism, & the Religion of Beauty. LC 78-21463. 208p. 1979. 14.00x (ISBN 0-8203-0470-0). U of Ga Pr.
Sharp, Tony. The Wartime Alliance & the Zonal Division of Germany. (Illus.). 232p. 1975. 29.95x (ISBN 0-19-822521-0). Oxford U Pr.
Sharp, U. S. G. Strategy for Defeat: Vietnam in Retrospect. LC 78-17607. (Illus.). 1978. 12.95 (ISBN 0-89141-053-8). Presidio Pr.
Sharp, Walter R. United Nations Economic & Social Council. LC 72-87888. (Columbia Univ. Studies in International Organization: No. 5). 1969. 20.00x (ISBN 0-231-03239-0). Columbia U Pr.
Sharp, William F. Slavery on the Spanish Frontier: The Colombian Choco, 1680-1810. LC 76-18767. (Illus.). 253p. 1981. pap. 6.95 (ISBN 0-8061-1759-1). U of Okla Pr.
Sharp, William J. & Martin, Joseph. Wine: How to Develop Your Taste & Get Your Money's Worth. (Illus.). 192p. 1976. text ed. 9.95 (ISBN 0-13-957746-7, Spec); pap. 3.95 (ISBN 0-13-957738-6). P-H.
Sharpe. Barron's Practice Exercises for the TOEFL (Test of English As a Foreign Language) LC 79-65306. 1980. pap. 7.95 (ISBN 0-8120-2164-9). Barron.
Sharpe, A. G., jt. auth. see Emeleus, H. J.
Sharpe, A. G., jt. ed. see Emeleus, H. J.
Sharpe, A. N. Food Microbiology. (Illus.). 238p. 1980. 24.75 (ISBN 0-398-04017-6). C C Thomas.
Sharpe, Anthony N. & Clark, David S. Mechanizing Microbiology. (Amer. Lec. in Clinical Microbiology Ser.). (Illus.). 352p. 1978. 33.75 (ISBN 0-398-03658-6). C C Thomas.
Sharpe, Charles K. Historical Account of the Belief in Witchcraft in Scotland. LC 74-8196. 1974. Repr. of 1884 ed. 24.00 (ISBN 0-8103-3590-5). Gale.
Sharpe, D. W. & Vamos, P. Injective Modules. (Cambridge Tracts in Mathematics & Mathematical Physics: No. 63). (Illus.). 250p. 1972. 32.95 (ISBN 0-521-08391-5). Cambridge U Pr.
Sharpe, David J., et al. Cases & Materials on Law & Medicine. LC 78-12529. (American Casebook Ser.). 882p. 1978. text ed. 19.95 (ISBN 0-8299-2015-3). West Pub.
Sharpe, Deborah T. The Psychology of Color & Design. LC 73-91308. 184p. 1974. 14.95 (ISBN 0-88229-107-6). Nelson-Hall.
Sharpe, Eric J. Comparative Religion. LC 75-44614. 1976. text ed. 13.95x (ISBN 0-684-14675-4, ScribC). Scribner.
Sharpe, Glyn, ed. see Smith, Harold & Keiffer, Mildred.
Sharpe, Grant W., ed. Interpreting the Environment. LC 76-4564. 505p. 1976. 22.95 (ISBN 0-471-77896-6). Wiley.
Sharpe, Jon. Dakota Wild. (Trailsman: No. 6). (Orig.). 1981. pap. 1.95 (ISBN 0-451-09777-7, J9777, Sig). NAL.
--Trailsman No. Three: Mountain Man Kiel. (Orig.). 1980. pap. 1.75 (ISBN 0-451-09353-4, J9353, Sig). NAL.
--The Trailsman No. 4: The Sundown Searchers. (Orig.). 1980. pap. 1.75 (ISBN 0-451-09533-2, E9533, Sig). NAL.
--Trailsman No. 5. (Orig.). 1981. pap. 1.95 (ISBN 0-451-09615-0, J9605, Sig). NAL.
Sharpe, Kevin, ed. Faction & Parliament: Essays in Early Stuart History. LC 77-30635. 1978. 33.00x (ISBN 0-19-822468-0). Oxford U Pr.
Sharpe, L. J., ed. The Local Fiscal Crisis in Western Europe: Myths & Realities. (Sage Research Ser. in European Politics: Vol. 3). 300p. 1981. 20.00 (ISBN 0-8039-9813-9). Sage.
Sharpe, Mitchell R., jt. auth. see Ordway, Frederick I.
Sharpe, Robert & Lewis, David. The Success Factor. 1979. pap. 2.95 (ISBN 0-446-93980-3). Warner Bks.
Sharpe, Robert J. The Law of Habeas Corpus. 1976. 42.00x (ISBN 0-19-825332-X). Oxford U Pr.
Sharpe, Roger C. Pinball. LC 77-6283. 1977. 37.50 o.p. (ISBN 0-525-17975-5); pap. 8.95 o.p. (ISBN 0-525-47481-1). Dutton.
Sharpe, W. Investments. 2nd ed. 1981. 19.95 (ISBN 0-13-504613-0). P-H.
Sharpe, William F. Economics of Computers. LC 71-89567. 1969. 22.50x (ISBN 0-231-03266-8); pap. 10.00x (ISBN 0-231-08310-6). Columbia U Pr.
--Introduction to Managerial Economics. LC 73-7950. 128p. 1973. 15.00x (ISBN 0-231-03693-0); pap. 6.00x (ISBN 0-231-03786-4). Columbia U Pr.
--Investments. LC 77-8880. (Illus.). 1978. ref. ed. 21.00 (ISBN 0-13-504605-X). P-H.
Sharpe, William F. & Jacob, Nancy L. BASIC: An Introduction to Computer Programming Using the BASIC Language. 3rd ed. LC 78-72148. (Illus.). 1979. 14.95 (ISBN 0-02-928380-9); pap. text ed. 7.95 (ISBN 0-02-928390-6). Free Pr.
Sharpes, Donald K., jt. auth. see English, Fenwick W.
Sharples, Stephen P., jt. auth. see Morrison, Leonard A.
Sharples, Win, Jr., jt. auth. see Roberts, Kenneth H.
Sharrer, Harvey L. The Legendary History of Britain in Lope Garcia De Salazar's Libro De las Bienandanzas e Fortunas. LC 78-53334. (Haney Foundation Ser). 1978. 15.00x (ISBN 0-8122-7749-X). U of Pa Pr.
Sharrock, Roger, ed. see Bunyan, John.
Sharrock, Roger, ed. & intro. by see Bunyan, John.
Sharrock, Roger, ed. see Bunyan, John.
Shartel, Burke. Our Legal System & How It Operates. LC 73-173666. (American Constitutional & Legal History Ser.). 628p. 1972. Repr. of 1951 ed. lib. bdg. 59.50 (ISBN 0-306-70411-0). Da Capo.
Sharum, Abert, jt. auth. see Davey, Homer C.
Sharum, Albert, jt. auth. see Davey, Homer C.
Sharvelle, Eric. Plant Disease Control. (Illus.). 1979. text ed. 28.00 (ISBN 0-87055-335-6). AVI.
Shashi, S. S. Night Life of Indian Tribals. 1978. 11.00x o.p. (ISBN 0-8364-0440-8). South Asia Bks.
Shashower, Gloria. Careers in Management for the New Woman. (Choosing Careers & Life-Styles Ser.). (Illus.). (gr. 7 up). 1978. PLB 7.90 s&l (ISBN 0-531-01350-2). Watts.
Shastri, H. P., tr. The Ramayana of Valmiki, 3 vols. 3rd ed. 1976. Set. pap. 48.00 (ISBN 0-85424-016-0); Vol. 1. Vol. 2. (ISBN 0-85424-000-4); Vol. 3. (ISBN 0-85424-017-9). Orient Bk Dist.
Shastri, J. L., ed. Bhagavata Purana. Tagare, G. V., tr. (Ancient Indian Tradition & Mythology Ser.: Vols. 7, 8 & 9). 1976. 18.00x ea. Pt. 1 (ISBN 0-8426-0855-9). Pt. 2 (ISBN 0-8426-0882-6). Pt. 3 (ISBN 0-8426-0911-3). Verry.
--Bhagavata Purana: Part 4. (Ancient Indian Tradition & Mythology Ser.: Vol. 10). 1978. text ed. 18.00 (ISBN 0-8426-1079-0). Verry.
--Bhagavata Purana: Part 5. (Ancient Indian Tradition & Mythology Ser.: Vol. 11). (Contains index for vols. 1-5). 1979. text ed. 18.00x (ISBN 0-8426-1105-3). Verry.
--Garuda Purana, Pt. 1. (Ancient Indian Tradition & Mythology Ser.: Vol. 12). 1979. text ed. 18.00x (ISBN 0-8426-1106-1). Verry.
Shastri, P. N. & Lal, P. The Writers Workshop Handbook of Assamese Literature, Vol. 1: A-D. (Greybird Book Ser). 106p. 1975. text ed. 14.00 (ISBN 0-88253-702-4); pap. text ed. 8.00 (ISBN 0-88253-703-2). Ind-US Inc.
Shatalin, Stanislav S., jt. auth. see Cao-Pinna, Vera.
Shater, Safaa El see El Shater, Safaa.
Shatto, Gloria M., ed. Employment of the Middle-Aged: Papers from Industrial Gerontology Seminars. (Illus.). 232p. 1972. 15.75 (ISBN 0-398-02408-1). C C Thomas.
Shattuck, Roger. The Forbidden Experiment: The Story of the Wild Boy of Aveyron. 220p. 1980. 12.95 (ISBN 0-374-15755-3). FS&G.
Shattuck, Ruth R. Creative Cooking without Wheat, Milk & Eggs. LC 72-6392. 152p. 1973. 8.95 (ISBN 0-498-01157-7); large type o.p. 8.95 (ISBN 0-498-01856-3); pap. 5.95 (ISBN 0-498-02047-9). A S Barnes.
Shattuck, Warren L., jt. ed. see Doi, Teruo.
Shatz, Marshall S. Soviet Dissent in Historical Perspective. LC 80-13318. 240p. 1981. 19.95 (ISBN 0-521-23172-8). Cambridge U Pr.
Shatzman, Israel, jt. ed. see Avi Yonah, Michael.
Shatzman, Nancy, tr. see Suzuki, Kakichi.
Shauers, Margaret. Dark Knight. 192p. (YA) 1976. 5.95 (ISBN 0-685-61052-7, Avalon). Bouregy.

Shaughnessy, Edward J. & Trebbi, Diana. A Standard for Miller: A Community Response to Pornography. LC 80-5648. (Illus.). 256p. 1980. lib. bdg. 18.75 (ISBN 0-8191-1280-1); pap. text ed. 10.50 (ISBN 0-8191-1281-X). U Pr of Amer.

Shaughnessy, Patrick & Swingle, Diane. Hard Hunting. 1978. 11.95 (ISBN 0-87691-270-6). Winchester Pr.

Shaugnessy, Jim. The Rutland Road. rev. ed. LC 80-19534. (Illus.). 370p. 1980. 20.00 (ISBN 0-8310-7128-1). Howell-North.

Shaull, Richard, jt. auth. see Oglesby, Carl.

Shave, David W. Communication Breakdown: Cause & Cure. LC 73-377. 320p. 1975. 18.50 (ISBN 0-87527-125-1). Green.

--Psychodynamics of the Emotionally Uncomfortable. LC 79-50191. 489p. 1980. 27.75 (ISBN 0-87527-233-9). Green.

Shaver, James P. & Larkins, A. Guy. Analysis a Public Issues: Decision-Making in a Democracy. 232p. (gr. 9-12). 1973. pap. text ed. 10.88 (ISBN 0-395-13466-8); tchrs. guide & ans. key pap. 17.22 (ISBN 0-395-13467-6). HM.

Shaver, Kelly G. Principles of Social Psychology. 2nd ed. (Psychology Ser.). (Illus.). 656p. 1981. text ed. 19.95 (ISBN 0-87626-634-0). Winthrop.

Shaver, Larry G. Essentials of Exercise Physiology. (Orig.). 1980. pap. 14.95 (ISBN 0-8087-4200-0). Burgess.

Shaviv, G., ed. see International Conference, 7th, Tel Aviv, June 23-28, 1974.

Shaw, A. C., et al. Photomicrographs of Invertebrates. (Illus.). 1976. pap. text ed. 4.50x o.p. (ISBN 0-582-32279-0). Longman.

Shaw, A. G. Convicts and the Colonies. (Illus.). 1966. 9.95 (ISBN 0-571-06663-1, Pub. by Faber & Faber). Merrimack Bk Serv.

--The Story of Australia. 4th ed. (Story Ser.). (Illus., Orig.). 1973. pap. 6.95 (ISBN 0-571-04775-0, Pub. by Faber & Faber). Merrimack Bk Serv.

Shaw, A. M., ed. Handbook of Conversion Factors. 24p. 1978. 3.00x (ISBN 0-934366-01-2). Intl Research Serv.

--International Dictionary of Consulting & Environmental Engineers. 2nd rev. ed. 1981. 10.00. Intl Research Serv.

Shaw, Alan, jt. auth. see Pohl, Ira.

Shaw, Alan C. Logical Design of Operating Systems. (Illus.). 304p. 1974. 25.95 (ISBN 0-13-540112-7). P-H.

Shaw, Ann M. & Stevens, C. J., eds. Drama, Theatre & the Handicapped. 121p. 1979. 6.95; ATA members 4.95. Am Theatre Assoc.

Shaw, Arnold. Rock Revolution: What's Happening in Today's Music. LC 69-11109. (Illus.). (gr. 8 up). 1969. 9.95 (ISBN 0-02-782400-4, CCPr). Macmillan.

--The Rockin' Fifties. (Illus.). 256p. 1974. 13.50 (ISBN 0-8015-6432-8, Hawthorn); pap. 4.95 (ISBN 0-8015-6434-4, Hawthorn). Dutton.

Shaw, B. L. Inorganic Hydrides. 1967. 19.50 (ISBN 0-08-012110-1); pap. 9.75 (ISBN 0-08-012109-8). Pergamon.

Shaw, B. L. & Tucker, N. I. Organo-Transition Metal Compounds & Related Aspects of Homogenous Catalysis. (Pergamon Texts in Inorganic Chemistry: Vol. 23). 214p. 1975. text ed. 32.00 (ISBN 0-08-018872-9); pap. text ed. 17.50 (ISBN 0-08-018871-0). Pergamon.

Shaw, Barry, jt. auth. see Gartenberg, Michael.

Shaw, Bernard. Back to Methuselah. (Plays Ser.). 1972. pap. 2.95 (ISBN 0-14-048011-0). Penguin.

--Bernard Shaw's Nondramatic Literary Criticism. Weintraub, Stanley, ed. LC 70-149739. (Regents Critics Ser). xxviii, 246p. 1972. 12.50x (ISBN 0-8032-0466-3); pap. 3.95x (ISBN 0-8032-5466-0, BB 414, Bison). U of Nebr Pr.

--Doctor's Dilemma. (Play Ser). 1975. pap. 2.95 (ISBN 0-14-048001-3). Penguin.

--The Great Composers: Reviews & Bombardments. Crompton, Louis, ed. LC 76-14311. (Cal. Ser.: No. 351). 1978. 28.50x (ISBN 0-520-03253-5); pap. 6.95 (ISBN 0-520-03266-7). U of Cal Pr.

--Saint Joan, a Screenplay. Dukore, Bernard F., ed. LC 68-11039. (Illus.). 224p. 1968. 9.95 (ISBN 0-295-97885-6); pap. 2.45 (ISBN 0-295-95072-2, WP56). U of Wash Pr.

--Selected Plays: Bernard Shaw. 900p. 1981. 19.95 (ISBN 0-396-07905-9). Dodd.

Shaw, Bob. Pitching. (Illus.). 1981. pap. 6.95 (ISBN 0-8092-5913-3). Contemp Bks.

Shaw, Bradley & Del-Valle, Gonzalez. Luis Romero. (World Authors Ser.: No. 520). 1979. lib. bdg. 13.50 (ISBN 0-8057-6361-9). Twayne.

Shaw, Bryce R. Personalized Computational Skills Program. LC 79-90570. 544p. 1980. Set. pap. text ed. 14.75 (ISBN 0-395-29032-5); Mod. A. pap. text ed. 5.75 (ISBN 0-395-29033-3); Mod. B. pap. text ed. 5.75 (ISBN 0-395-29034-1); Mod. C. pap. text ed. 5.50 (ISBN 0-395-29035-X); pap. 1.00 inst. manual (ISBN 0-395-29036-8). HM.

Shaw, Catherine. Some Vanity of Mine Art: The Masque in English Renaissance Drama, Vols. 1, 2. (SSEL Jacobean Drama Ser.: No. 81). 1980. pap. text ed. 25.00x (ISBN 0-391-01938-4). Humanities.

Shaw, Charles R., ed. Prevention of Occupational Cancer. 256p. 1981. 72.95 (ISBN 0-8493-5625-3). CRC Pr.

Shaw, Charles R., ed. see Annual Symposium on Fundamental Cancer Research, No. 31.

Shaw, D. J. Introduction to Colloid & Surface Chemistry. 2nd ed. 248p. 1970. 12.95 (ISBN 0-408-70021-1). Butterworths.

--Introduction to Colloid & Surface Chemistry. 3rd ed. LC 80-49871. 256p. 1980. text ed. 14.95 (ISBN 0-408-71049-7). Butterworths.

Shaw, D. L., ed. Eduardo Mallea: Todo verdor perecera. 1968. 8.30 (ISBN 0-08-012868-8); pap. 5.75 (ISBN 0-08-012867-X). Pergamon.

Shaw, Darwin, ed. see Foster, Jeanne R.

Shaw, Dave & Eisman, Greg. Beyond Ideas into Information: A Writing Workbook. 192p. 1980. pap. text ed. 6.95 (ISBN 0-8403-2218-6). Kendall-Hunt.

Shaw, David. The Levy Caper. LC 74-10897. 324p. 1974. 6.95 o.s.i. (ISBN 0-02-610010-X). Macmillan.

Shaw, David, jt. auth. see Chamberlain, Wilt.

Shaw, David M., jt. auth. see Pierce, David G.

Shaw, David T. Fundamentals of Aerosol Science. LC 77-19331. 1978. 36.50 (ISBN 0-471-02949-1, Pub. by Wiley-Interscience). Wiley.

Shaw, Denis, jt. auth. see Pallot, Judith.

Shaw, E. R. London Money Market. 2nd ed. 1978. pap. text ed. 14.95x (ISBN 0-434-91832-6). Intl Ideas.

--London Money Market. 1st ed. 1975. 17.95x (ISBN 0-434-91830-X). Intl Ideas.

Shaw, Edward S. Financial Deepening in Economic Development. (Economic Development Ser.). 225p. 1973. text ed. 10.95x (ISBN 0-19-501633-5); pap. text ed. 4.95x (ISBN 0-19-501632-7). Oxford U Pr.

Shaw, Edward S., jt. auth. see Gurley, John G.

Shaw, Fran W. Thirty Ways to Help You Write. 192p. (Orig.). 1980. pap. 2.50 (ISBN 0-553-13924-X). Bantam.

Shaw, Frances J. The Northern & Western Islands of Scotland in the Seventeenth Century. (Illus.). 275p. 1980. text ed. 39.00x (ISBN 0-85976-059-6). Humanities.

Shaw, Frank R., jt. auth. see Eckert, John E.

Shaw, G. B. The Collected Screenplays of Bernard Shaw. Dukore, Bernard F., ed. LC 80-13320. (Illus.). 400p. 1980. 35.00 (ISBN 0-8203-0524-3). U of Ga Pr.

Shaw, G. K. An Introduction to the Theory of Macro-Economic Policy. 3rd ed. 208p. 1977. bds. 30.50x (ISBN 0-85520-183-5, Pub. by Martin Robertson England); pap. 12.50x (ISBN 0-85520-182-7). Biblio Dist.

Shaw, G. K., jt. auth. see Grant, R. M.

Shaw, G. W. Chromosome Studies. (Investigations in Biology Ser.). 1973. pap. text ed. 3.95x o.p. (ISBN 0-435-60286-1). Heinemann Ed.

Shaw, George B. Androcles & the Lion. (Penguin Plays Ser.). (Orig.). (YA) (gr. 9 up). 1963. pap. 2.95 (ISBN 0-14-048010-2, PL5). Penguin.

--Apple Cart. (Penguin Plays Ser.). 1956. pap. 2.50 (ISBN 0-14-048008-0). Penguin.

--Arms & the Man. (Penguin Plays Ser.). (YA) (gr. 9 up). 1950. pap. 2.75 (ISBN 0-14-048102-8). Penguin.

--Arms & the Man. Crompton, Louis, ed. LC 68-22306. 1969. pap. 5.50 (ISBN 0-672-61087-6). Bobbs.

--Arms & the Man. Jenckes, Norma, ed. LC 79-56802. (Bernard Shaw Early Texts: Play Manuscripts in Facsimile). 1981. lib. bdg. 45.00 (ISBN 0-8240-4578-5). Garland Pub.

--Back to Methuselah. rev. ed. 1947. 4.95x (ISBN 0-19-500181-8). Oxford U Pr.

--Bernard Shaw's Plays: Major Barbara, Heartbreak House, Saint Joan, Too Good to Be True. Smith, Warren S., ed. (Critical Editions Ser). 1970-71. pap. text ed. 5.95x (ISBN 0-393-09942-3). Norton.

--Caesar & Cleopatra: A History. Forter, Elizabeth T., ed. LC 65-14791. (Crofts Classics Ser.). 1965. pap. text ed. 2.95x (ISBN 0-88295-086-X). AHM Pub.

--Candida & How He Lied to Her Husband: Play Manuscripts in Facsimile. LC 79-56703. (Bernard Shaw Early Texts Ser.). 1981. lib. bdg. 45.00 (ISBN 0-8240-4579-3). Garland Pub.

--Captain Brassbound's Conversion. Weintraub, Rodelle, ed. LC 79-56711. (Bernard Shaw Early Texts: Play Manuscripts in Facsimile). 1981. lib. bdg. 45.00 (ISBN 0-8240-4586-6). Garland Pub.

--The Devil's Disciple. Whitman, Robert F., ed. LC 79-56706. (Bernard Shaw Early Texts: Play Manuscripts in Facsimile). 1981. lib. bdg. 45.00 (ISBN 0-8240-4581-5). Garland Pub.

--The Doctor's Dilemma. Morgan, Margery M., ed. LC 79-56709. (Bernard Shaw Early Texts: Play Manuscripts in Facsimile). 1981. lib. bdg. 55.00 (ISBN 0-8240-4584-X). Garland Pub.

--Dramatic Criticism: 1895-98; a Selection by John F. Matthews. LC 77-136084. 1971. Repr. of 1959 ed. lib. bdg. 23.00x (ISBN 0-8371-5234-8, S*H*D*R). Greenwood.

--Heartbreak House. Weintraub, Stanley & Wright, Anne, eds. LC 79-56710. (Bernard Shaw Early Texts: Play Manuscripts in Facsimile). 1981. lib. bdg. 50.00 (ISBN 0-8240-4585-8). Garland Pub.

--The Intelligent Woman's Guide to Socialism, Capitalism, Sovietism, & Fascism. 1981. pap. 3.95 (ISBN 0-14-040034-6). Penguin.

--Lady, Wilt Thou Love Me? Eighteen Love Poems for Ellen Terry. Werner, Jack, ed. LC 80-20009. (Illus.). 64p. 1980. 8.95 (ISBN 0-8128-2758-9). Stein & Day.

--Major Barbara. Forter, Elizabeth T., ed. LC 77-145842. (Crofts Classics Ser.). 1971. text ed. 5.95x (ISBN 0-88295-087-8); pap. text ed. 2.95x (ISBN 0-88295-088-6). AHM Pub.

--Major Barbara. Dukore, Bernard, ed. LC 79-56708. (Bernard Shaw Early Texts: Play Manuscripts in Facsimile). 1981. lib. bdg. 70.00 (ISBN 0-8240-4583-1). Garland Pub.

--The Man of Destiny & Caesar & Cleopatra: Play Manuscripts in Facsimile. LC 79-56707. (Bernard Shaw Early Ser.). 1981. lib. bdg. 70.00 (ISBN 0-8240-4582-3). Garland Pub.

--Millionairess. (Penguin Plays Ser.). 1961. pap. 2.50 (ISBN 0-14-048009-9). Penguin.

--Mrs. Warren's Profession. Peters, Margot, ed. LC 79-56701. (Bernard Shaw Early Texts: Play Manuscripts in Facsimile). 1981. lib. bdg. 50.00 (ISBN 0-8240-4577-7). Garland Pub.

--On Going to Church. 24p. pap. 1.00 (ISBN 0-934676-13-5). Greenlf Bks.

--The Philanderer. Novick, Julius, ed. LC 79-56700. (Bernard Shaw Early Texts: Play Manuscripts in Facsimile). 1981. lib. bdg. 85.00 (ISBN 0-8240-4576-9). Garland Pub.

--Plays Unpleasant. Incl. Widowers' Houses; Philanderer; Mrs. Warren's Profession. (Penguin Plays Ser.). 1950. pap. 2.75 (ISBN 0-14-048012-9). Penguin.

--Pygmalion. (gr. 9 up). 1973. pap. 2.25 (ISBN 0-671-43298-2). PB.

--Saint Joan. Weintraub, Stanley, ed. LC 76-134308. 1971. pap. 7.50 (ISBN 0-672-61091-4). Bobbs.

--Widowers' Houses. Bringle, Jerald, ed. LC 79-56699. (Bernard Shaw Early Texts: Play Manuscripts in Facsimile). 1981. lib. bdg. 50.00 (ISBN 0-8240-4575-0). Garland Pub.

--You Never Can Tell. Leary, Daniel J., ed. LC 79-56704. (Bernard Shaw Early Texts: Play Manuscripts in Facsimile). 1981. lib. bdg. 70.00 (ISBN 0-8240-4580-7). Garland Pub.

Shaw, George B; see Caputi, Anthony.

Shaw, George B; see Salerno, Henry F.

Shaw, George B; see Watson, E. Bradlee & Pressey, Benfield.

Shaw, George B., ed. Fabian Essays in Socialism. 1967. 7.00 (ISBN 0-8446-1403-3). Peter Smith.

Shaw, Graham, jt. auth. see Hebden, John.

Shaw, Graham W. Printing in Calcutta to Eighteen Hundred: A Description & Checklist. (Illus.). 144p. 1981. 79.00 (ISBN 0-19-721792-3). Oxford U Pr.

Shaw, Harold. Killing No Murder. 192p. 1981. 8.95 (ISBN 0-684-16884-7, ScribT). Scribner.

Shaw, Harry. Errors in English & Ways to Correct Them. 2nd ed. (gr. 7-12). 1970. pap. 3.95 (ISBN 0-06-463240-7, EH 240, EH). Har-Row.

--Punctuate It Right. (Orig.). 1963. pap. 2.95 (ISBN 0-06-463255-5, EH 255, EH). Har-Row.

--Spell It Right. 2nd ed. (Orig.). 1965. pap. 2.95 (ISBN 0-06-463279-2, EH 279, EH). Har-Row.

Shaw, Harry, jt. auth. see Wykoff, George S.

Shaw, Irwin. Nightwork. 384p. 1975. 8.95 o.s.i. (ISBN 0-440-05757-4). Delacorte.

--Top of the Hill. 1980. pap. 2.95 o.s.i. (ISBN 0-440-18976-4). Dell.

Shaw, J. Reactor Operation. 1969. 25.00 (ISBN 0-08-013325-8); pap. 12.25 (ISBN 0-08-013324-X). Pergamon.

Shaw, J. C., ed. see Cooper, R. & Osselton, J. W.

Shaw, J. M. The Resurrection of Jesus Christ. 223p. 1920. text ed. 4.95. Attic Pr.

Shaw, J. Martin. Rural Deprivation & Planning. 207p. 1980. 14.75x (ISBN 0-86094-020-9, Pub. by GEO Abstracts England); pap. 12.01x (ISBN 0-86094-019-5, Pub. by GEO Abstracts England). State Mutual Bk.

Shaw, James B., intro. by. Old Master Drawings from Christ Church, Oxford. LC 72-83826. (Illus.). 1972. pap. 5.95 o.p. (ISBN 0-88397-061-9). Intl Exhibit Foun.

Shaw, Jean. Second Cup of Coffee. 192p. (Orig.). 1981. pap. 2.95 (ISBN 0-310-43542-0). Zondervan.

Shaw, Jean M., jt. auth. see Cliatt, Mary J.

Shaw, Jeanne, ed. see Foster, Jeanne R.

Shaw, John. The Self in Social Work. (Library of Social Work). 1974. 12.50x (ISBN 0-7100-7920-6); pap. 6.95 (ISBN 0-7100-7921-4). Routledge & Kegan.

Shaw, John, jt. auth. see Fineberg, Marjorie.

Shaw, John A., jt. auth. see Leet, Don R.

Shaw, John M., ed. Childhood in Poetry: First Supplement, 3 Vols. LC 67-28092. (Illus.). 1972. Set. 130.00 (ISBN 0-8103-0476-7). Gale.

--Childhood in Poetry: Second Supplement-a Catalogue, with Biographical & Critical Annotations, of the Books of English & American Poets Comprising the Shaw Childhood in Poetry Collection in the Library of the Fla. St. U, 2 vols. LC 67-28092. 1500p. 1976. Set. 130.00 (ISBN 0-8103-0477-5); Vol. 1. 42.50 (ISBN 0-8103-0479-1); Vol. 2. index 58.00 (ISBN 0-686-67256-9). Gale.

--Childhood in Poetry: Third Supplement. LC 67-28092. (Childhood in Poetry Ser.). (Illus.). 75.00 (ISBN 0-8103-0480-5). Gale.

Shaw, John W., jt. auth. see Rohm, Robert.

Shaw, Josephine, jt. auth. see Stanwell, Sheila T.

Shaw, K. E., jt. auth. see Bloomer, M.

Shaw, L. Earl. Modern Competing Ideologies. 1973. pap. text ed. 7.95x o.p. (ISBN 0-669-81869-0). Heath.

Shaw, Lawrence & Ibanez, Carmen. Cartas De Zaragoza. (Illus.). (gr. 7-10). 1970. pap. text ed. 4.95 (ISBN 0-312-12285-3). St Martin.

Shaw, Leroy R. Playwright & Historical Change: Dramatic Strategies in Brecht, Hauptmann, Kaiser, & Wedekind. LC 75-106042. 1970. 17.00x (ISBN 0-299-05500-0). U of Wis Pr.

Shaw, Leroy R., ed. German Theater Today: A Symposium. (Dept of Germanic Languages Pubns). (Illus.). 1964. 10.00 (ISBN 0-292-73250-3). U of Tex Pr.

Shaw, M., et al. Using AACR2: A Diagrammatic Approach. 1980. text ed. 17.50 (ISBN 0-912700-88-2, Pub. by Lib Assn England); pap. text ed. 10.95 (ISBN 0-912700-89-0). Oryx Pr.

Shaw, Malcolm E., et al. Role Playing: A Practical Manual for Group Facilitators. LC 79-67712. 202p. 1980. pap. 15.50 (ISBN 0-88390-156-0). Univ Assocs.

Shaw, Mara L. How to Meet Men...and Be Successful with Them. 1981. 9.95 (ISBN 0-9605602-0-3). Shaw Inc.

Shaw, Margaret R., tr. see De Villehardouin, Geoffrey & De Joinville, Jean.

Shaw, Marvin. Group Dynamics. 3rd ed. (Illus.). 560p. 1980. 21.95 (ISBN 0-07-056504-X). McGraw.

Shaw, Merville C. School Guidance Systems: Objectives, Functions, Evaluation, & Change. LC 72-5248. 400p. 1973. text ed. 16.75 o.p. (ISBN 0-395-14058-7); instructor's manual. pap. 2.65 o.p. (ISBN 0-395-14059-5). HM.

Shaw, Nancy S. Forced Labor: Maternity Care in the United States. 1974. 18.50 (ISBN 0-08-017835-9); pap. text ed. 9.75 (ISBN 0-08-017834-0). Pergamon.

Shaw, Pat, jt. ed. see Karples, Maud.

Shaw, Pat, tr. see Askeland, Jan.

Shaw, Patick W. Literature: A College Anthology. LC 76-19905. (Illus.). 1976. text ed. 15.50 (ISBN 0-395-24841-8); instructors' manual 1.25 (ISBN 0-395-24842-6). HM.

Shaw, Patricia A. Theoretical Issues in Dakota Phonology & Morphology. Hankamer, Jorge, ed. LC 79-55856. (Outstanding Dissertations in Linguistics Ser.). 404p. 1980. lib. bdg. 44.00 (ISBN 0-8240-4562-9). Garland Pub.

Shaw, Paul. Black Letter Primer: An Introduction to Gothic Alphabets. LC 78-20699. (Illus.). 1981. pap. 4.95 (ISBN 0-8008-0808-8, Pentalic). Taplinger.

Shaw, Paul, jt. auth. see Reber, Jan.

Shaw, Peter & De Vet, Therese. Using Blackboard Drawing. (Practical Language Teaching Ser.). (Illus.). 112p. (Orig.). 1980. pap. text ed. 6.95x (ISBN 0-04-371075-1, 2559). Allen Unwin.

Shaw, Philip E., jt. ed. see Nagy, Steven.

Shaw, Priscilla W. Rilke, Valery & Yeats: The Domain of the Self. 1964. 16.00 (ISBN 0-8135-0454-6). Rutgers U Pr.

Shaw, R., et al, eds. Innovative Numerical Analysis for the Engineering Sciences. LC 80-14005. 1980. 40.00x (ISBN 0-8139-0867-1). U Pr of Va.

Shaw, Ralph R. & Shoemaker, R. H. American Bibliography, Eighteen Hundred & One to Eighteen -Nineteen, 22 vols. LC 58-7809. (Includes addenda, list of sources, library symbols, title index & author index). Set Vols. Prices For Separate Vols. On Request, 1958-1963. 225.50 (ISBN 0-8108-0192-2). Scarecrow.

Shaw, Ray & Zolotow, Charlotte. A Week in Lateef's World: India. (Face to Face Bks.). (gr. k-3). 1970. 7.95 (ISBN 0-02-782380-6, CCpr); text ed. 1.36 o.p. (ISBN 0-02-782360-1). Macmillan.

Shaw, Renata V., compiled by. Picture Searching: Tools & Techniques. LC 72-13234. (Bibliography Ser.: No. 6). 1973. pap. 2.25 (ISBN 0-87111-207-8). SLA.

Shaw, Richard. Call Me Al Raft. LC 75-16313. 160p. (YA) (gr. 6 up). 1975. 7.95 (ISBN 0-525-66464-5). Elsevier-Nelson.

--The Hard Way Home. LC 76-54132. (gr. 6 up). 1977. Repr. 6.95 o.p. (ISBN 0-525-66529-3). Elsevier-Nelson.
--The Kitten in the Pumpkin Patch. (Illus.). 40p. (gr. 2-5). 1973. 7.95 (ISBN 0-7232-6099-0). Warne.
Shaw, Richard, ed. The Bird Book. LC 74-81672. (Animal Art Anthology Ser). (Illus.). 48p. (gr. 3-6). 1974. PLB 4.95 o.p. (ISBN 0-7232-6107-5). Warne.
--Fox Book. LC 78-161068. (Animal Art Anthology Ser). (Illus.). (gr. 2-5). 1971. PLB 4.95 o.p. (ISBN 0-7232-6082-6). Warne.
--The Frog Book. LC 72-83128. (Animal Art Anthology Ser). (Illus.). 48p. (gr. 1 up). 1972. PLB 4.95 o.p. (ISBN 0-7232-6083-4). Warne.
--The Mouse Book. LC 75-8104. (Illus.). 48p. (gr. 4-7). 1975. PLB 4.95 o.p. (ISBN 0-7232-6119-9). Warne.
Shaw, Richard J. & On, Danny. Plants of Waterton-Glacier National Parks & the Northern Rockies. Orig. Title: Plants of Waterton-Glacier National Parks. 160p. 1981. pap. 6.95 (ISBN 0-87842-137-8). Mountain Pr.
Shaw, Robert. Comforting the Wilderness. LC 77-74603. (The Wesleyan Poetry Program: Vol. 87). 1977. pap. 4.95x (ISBN 0-8195-1087-4, Pub. by Wesleyan U Pr). Columbia U Pr.
Shaw, Robert B., ed. see Vaughan, Henry.
Shaw, Robert D'a see D'A. Shaw, Robert.
Shaw, Robert d'A see D'A. Shaw, Robert.
Shaw, Robert J. & Racina, Thom. Dynasty of Love. (Orig.). 1979. pap. 2.25 o.s.i. (ISBN 0-515-05180-2). Jove Pubns.
Shaw, Roy, jt. auth. see Goble, Ross.
Shaw, Royce Q. Regional Integration & National Policy Development. 1978. lib. bdg. 24.50 o.p. (ISBN 0-89158-278-9). Westview.
Shaw, Russell, jt. auth. see Grisez, Germain.
Shaw, S. J. History of the Ottoman Empire & Modern Turkey. LC 76-9179. (Illus.). 1977. Set. 82.00 (ISBN 0-521-08772-4); Vol. 1. 42.00 (ISBN 0-521-21280-4); Vol. 2. 54.00 (ISBN 0-521-21449-1); Set. pap. 27.50 (ISBN 0-521-08759-7); Vol. 1. pap. 15.95 (ISBN 0-521-29163-1); Vol. 2. pap. 17.95 (ISBN 0-521-29166-6). Cambridge U Pr.
Shaw, Samuel. Ernest Hemingway. LC 78-134827. (Modern Literature Ser.). 10.95 (ISBN 0-8044-2823-9). Ungar.
Shaw, Shiow-Jyu L. Early Ch'ing Imperial Printing. (Asian Library Ser.: No. 20). (Illus.). 1980. write for info. (ISBN 0-89644-621-2). Chinese Materials.
Shaw, Stan, et al. Responding to Drinking Problems. 272p. 1980. 40.00x (ISBN 0-85664-525-7, Pub. by Croom Helm England). State Mutual Bk.
Shaw, Stephen M. Surfboard Builders' Yearbook, Vols. 9 & 10. Morgan, Michael, et al, eds. (Illus.). 1973-75. Vol. 9. 4.00 o.p. (ISBN 0-912750-01-4); Vol.10. 5.00 o.p. (ISBN 0-912750-02-2). Transmedia.
Shaw, Stephen M. & Brown, Aileen, eds. Surfboard: How to Build Surfboards & How to Surf. (Illus.). 1980. 8.00 (ISBN 0-912750-03-0). Transmedia.
Shaw, Timothy M. & Anglin, Douglas G. Alternative Sources of Event Data on Zambian Foreign Policy. (Foreign & Comparative Studies Program, African Ser.: No. XXXVI). 1981. pap. text ed. price not set (ISBN 0-915984-60-1). Syracuse U Foreign Comp.
Shaw, Timothy M. & Heard, Kenneth A. Cooperation & Conflict in Southern Africa: Papers on a Regional Subsystem. 1976. pap. text ed. 14.55x o.p. (ISBN 0-8191-0005-6). U Pr of Amer.
Shaw, Timothy M., jt. auth. see Anglin, Douglas G.
Shaw, Timothy M., ed. Alternative Futures of Africa. (Westview Special Studies on Africa). (Illus.). 1981. lib. bdg. 26.50x (ISBN 0-89158-769-1). Westview.
Shaw, W. C. & Day, C. J. The Businessman's Complete Checklist. 1978. text ed. 24.50x (ISBN 0-220-66359-9, Pub. by Busn Bks England). Renouf.
Shaw, William. Legal Norms in a Confucian State. (Korea Research Monographs: No. 5). write for info. (ISBN 0-912966-32-7). IEAS Ctr Chinese Stud.
Shaw, William H. Presenting Entertainment Arts: Stage, Film, Television. 192p. 1980. pap. text ed. 9.95 (ISBN 0-8403-2226-7). Kendall-Hunt.
Shawchuck, Norman L., jt. auth. see Lindgren, Alvin J.
Shawcross, J. P. The Daily Biographer. 388p. 1980. Repr. of 1915 ed. lib. bdg. 50.00 (ISBN 0-8492-8118-0). R West.
Shawcross, John T., ed. The Complete Poetry of John Donne. LC 67-15386. pap. 5.95 (ISBN 0-385-05256-1, ACO11, Anch). Doubleday.
--Complete Poetry of John Milton. LC 72-150934. 1971. pap. 5.95 (ISBN 0-385-02351-0, Anch). Doubleday.
Shawcross, Mike. Antigua, Guatemala: City & Area Guide. (Illus.). 74p. 1979. pap. 4.95 (ISBN 0-933982-17-8). Bradt Ent.
--San Cristobal de las Casas, Chiapas: City & Area Guide. 3rd ed. (Illus.). 74p. 1980. pap. 4.95 (ISBN 0-933982-16-X). Bradt Ent.
Shawcross, William. Sideshow. rev. ed. 1981. price not set (ISBN 0-671-25414-6, Touchstone). S&S.
Shawker, Thomas H., jt. auth. see Brascho, Donn J.
Shawki, G. S. A. & Metwalli, S. M., eds. Current Advances in Mechanical Design & Production: Proceedings of the First International Conference, Cairo University, 27-29 December 1979. LC 80-41666. (Illus.). 500p. 1981. 75.00 (ISBN 0-08-027294-0). Pergamon.
Shawn, Wallace. Marie & Bruce. LC 80-991. 160p. 1980. pap. 4.95 (ISBN 0-394-17661-8, E-757, Ever). Grove.
Shawver, Donald L., ed. Marketing Doctoral Dissertation Abstracts, 1974-75. LC 76-21300. (Bibliography Ser.: No. 24). 1977. pap. 12.00 o.p. (ISBN 0-87757-079-5). Am Mktg.
--Marketing Doctoral Dissertation Abstracts 1976. LC 77-9426. 1978. 10.00 o.p. (ISBN 0-87757-099-X). Am Mktg.
Shawver, Donald L., jt. ed. see Littlefield, James E.
Shay, Arthur. Sports Photography: How to Take Great Action Shots. (Illus.). 1981. 14.95 (ISBN 0-8092-5962-1); pap. 7.95 (ISBN 0-8092-5961-3). Contemp Bks.
--What Happens at a Newspaper. LC 76-183835. (What Happens Ser.). (Illus.). 32p. (gr. 2-4). 1972. 5.95 o.p. (ISBN 0-8092-8612-2); PLB avail o.p. (ISBN 0-685-23702-8). Contemp Bks.
Shay, Arthur, jt. auth. see Sauser, Jean.
Shay, Frank. Judge Lynch: His First Hundred Years. LC 70-75359. 1969. Repr. of 1938 ed. 12.00x (ISBN 0-8196-0231-0). Biblo.
Shay, J. L. & Wernick, J. H. Ternary Chalcopyrite Semiconductors: Growth, Electronic Properties & Applications. LC 74-5763. 1975. text ed. 46.00 (ISBN 0-08-017883-9). Pergamon.
Shay, Robert P. & Dunkelberg, William C. Retail Store Credit Card Use in New York. new ed. (Studies in Consumer Credit, No. 4). 100p. 1975. pap. 6.00x (ISBN 0-231-03964-6). Columbia U Pr.
Shay, Sunny & Barbaresi, Sara M. How to Raise & Train an Afghan. (Orig.). pap. 2.00 (ISBN 0-87666-232-7, DS1001). TFH Pubns.
Shayer, David. The Teaching of English in Schools 1900-1970. 216p. 1972. 15.00 (ISBN 0-7100-7321-6). Routledge & Kegan.
Shazar, Yair, jt. auth. see Deegan, Paul J.
Shazly, Saad El see El Shazly, Saad.
She, Lao. Ma & Son. James, Jean M., tr. from Chinese. Orig. Title: Erh Ma. 1980. 21.60 (ISBN 0-89644-634-4). Chinese Materials.
Shea, Edward J. Ethical Decisions in Physical Education & Sport. (Illus.). 232p. 1978. 19.75 (ISBN 0-398-03787-6). C C Thomas.
Shea, George. Bears. LC 80-20367. (Creatures Wild & Free Ser.). (gr. 1-6). 1981. 5.95 (ISBN 0-88436-772-X). EMC.
--Big Cats. LC 80-23227. (Creatures Wild & Free). (gr. 1-6). 1981. text ed. 5.95 (ISBN 0-88436-774-6). EMC.
--Dolphins. LC 80-18259. (Creatures Wild & Free Ser.). (gr. 1-6). 1981. 5.95 (ISBN 0-88436-770-3). EMC.
--Snakes. LC 80-21294. (Creatures Wild & Free Ser.). (gr. 1-6). 1981. 5.95 (ISBN 0-88436-776-2). EMC.
--Strike Two. (Sportellers Ser.). (Illus.). 64p. (gr. 5 up). 1981. PLB 7.95 (ISBN 0-516-02267-9). Childrens.
--Whales. LC 80-18413. (Creatures Wild & Free Ser.). (gr. 1-6). 1981. 5.95 (ISBN 0-88436-768-1). EMC.
Shea, George E. Acting in Opera. (Music Reprint Ser.: 1980). (Illus.). 1980. Repr. of 1915 ed. lib. bdg. 14.50 (ISBN 0-306-76004-5). Da Capo.
Shea, J. G., ed. The Operations of the French Fleet Under the Count De Grasse. LC 75-167946. (The Era of the American Revolution Ser.). 206p. 1971. Repr. of 1864 ed. lib. bdg. 25.00 (ISBN 0-306-70246-0). Da Capo.
Shea, John. The Challenge of Jesus. 1977. pap. 2.45 (ISBN 0-385-12439-2, Im). Doubleday.
--Stories of Faith. 1980. 10.95 (ISBN 0-88347-112-4). Thomas More.
Shea, John C. The Pennsylvania Dutch & Their Furniture. 240p. 1980. 19.95 (ISBN 0-442-27546-3). Van Nos Reinhold.
Shea, John G. Antique Country Furniture of North America, & Details of Its Construction. 228p. 1980. pap. 9.95 (ISBN 0-442-25156-4). Van Nos Reinhold.
--Perils of the Ocean & Wilderness: Or, Narratives of Shipwreck & Indian Captivity, Gleaned from Early Missionary Annals. LC 75-7098. (Indian Captivities Ser.: Vol. 73). 1976. Repr. of 1857 ed. lib. bdg. 44.00 (ISBN 0-8240-1697-1). Garland Pub.
Shea, Robert. Last of the Zinja. (Shike Ser.: Bk. 2). 460p. (Orig.). 1981. pap. 2.95 (ISBN 0-515-05944-7). Jove Pubns.
--Time of the Dragons Shike, Bk. I. (Orig.). 1981. pap. 2.95 (ISBN 0-515-04874-7). Jove Pubns.
Shea, Robert J. & Wilson, Anton R. Leviathan. (Illuminatus 3). 256p. 1975. pap. 1.95 o.s.i. (ISBN 0-440-14742-5). Dell.
Shea, Robert J. & Wilson, Robert A. The Eye in the Pyramid. 304p. 1975. pap. 1.95 o.s.i. (ISBN 0-440-14688-7). Dell.
--The Golden Apple: Illuminatus 2. 1975. pap. 1.95 o.s.i. (ISBN 0-440-14691-7). Dell.
Shea, William R., jt. ed. see King-Farlow, John.
Shead, Herbert A. The History of the Emanuel Moor Double Keyboard Piano. LC 78-322797. (Illus.). 310p. (Orig.). 1978. pap. 37.50x (ISBN 0-9506023-0-2). Intl Pubns Serv.
Sheaffer, Billie C. A Manual for the Care of Wild Birds. (Illus.). 64p. 1980. 5.00 (ISBN 0-682-49617-0). Exposition.
Sheaffer, John R. & Brand, Raymond H. Whatever Happened to Eden? 1980. pap. 4.95 (ISBN 0-8423-7871-5). Tyndale.
Sheaffer, Robert. The UFO Verdict: Examining the Evidence. LC 80-84406. (Critiques of the Paranormal Ser.). 275p. 1981. 15.95 (ISBN 0-87975-146-0). Prometheus Bks.
Sheaffer, Thomas M. A Poem a Day. 58p. 1980. 3.50 (ISBN 0-8059-2721-2). Dorrance.
Sheafor, Bradford, jt. auth. see Morales, Armando.
Sheagren, John N. Financial Advice for Physicians. 132p. 1972. text ed. 11.75 (ISBN 0-398-02409-X). C C Thomas.
Sheahan, John. The Wage-Price Guideposts. (Studies in Wage-Price Policy). 1967. 11.95 (ISBN 0-8157-7842-2); pap. 4.95 (ISBN 0-8157-7841-4). Brookings.
Sheals, J. G., jt. auth. see Lincoln, R. J.
Shear, Lee & Reiners, Ed. The Los Angeles Runners Guide. LC 80-52538. 252p. (Orig.). 1980. pap. 6.95 (ISBN 0-87477-162-5). J P Tarcher.
Shear, T. Leslie, Jr. Kallias of Sphettos & the Revolt of Athens in 286 B.C. (Hesperia: Supplement 17). 1978. 10.00x (ISBN 0-87661-517-5). Am Sch Athens.
Shearer, Ann. Handicapped Children in Residential Care: A Study of Policy Failure. 114p. 1980. pap. text ed. write for info. (ISBN 0-7199-1035-8, Pub. by Bedford England). Renouf.
Shearer, Ann, tr. see Vanier, Vean.
Shearer, Helen. Invest in You. 1981. 5.75 (ISBN 0-8062-1600-X). Carlton.
Shearer, John. Billy Jo Jive & the Case of the Missing Pigeons. (gr. k-6). 1980. pap. 1.50 (ISBN 0-440-40669-2, YB). Dell.
--Billy Jo Jive & the Walkie-Talkie Caper: A Mystery. LC 80-17780. (Illus.). 48p. (gr. k-3). 1981. 7.95 (ISBN 0-440-00791-7); PLB 7.45 (ISBN 0-440-00792-5). Delacorte.
Shearer, L. S., et al. Introduction to System Dynamics. 1967. 24.95 (ISBN 0-201-07017-0). A-W.
Shearer, Marguerite R., jt. auth. see Shearer, Marshall L.
Shearer, Marshall L. & Shearer, Marguerite R. Rapping About Sex. (Orig.). 1972. pap. 1.75 o.p. (ISBN 0-06-463319-5, 319, EH). Har-Row.
Shearer, R. & Bond, D. Economics of the Canadian Financial System. 1972. 21.95 (ISBN 0-13-229781-7). P-H.
Shearer, William M. Illustrated Speech Anatomy. 3rd ed. (Illus.). 152p. 1979. 19.75 (ISBN 0-398-03817-1). C C Thomas.
Shearing, H., jt. auth. see Taylor, A. H.
Shearing, Joseph. So Evil My Love. 1961. pap. 0.95 o.s.i. (ISBN 0-02-025190-4, Collier). Macmillan.
Shearman, John, ed. see Wilde, Johannes.
Shears, Loyda M. & Bower, Eli M. Games in Education & Development. (Illus.). 392p. 1974. 27.75 (ISBN 0-398-02608-4). C C Thomas.
Shears, Sarah. Child of Gentle Courage. 1974. 8.95 (ISBN 0-236-31065-8, Pub. by Paul Elek). Merrimack Bk Serv.
--Courage in Darkness. 1974. 8.95 (ISBN 0-236-31066-6, Pub. by Paul Elek). Merrimack Bk Serv.
Shea-Simonds, Charles. Sport Parachuting. 3rd. ed. (Illus.). 206p. 1975. 18.00 (ISBN 0-7136-1929-5). Transatlantic.
Shebar, Jonathan & Shebar, Sharon. Sigmond. (gr. 3-6). 1981. write for info. (ISBN 0-671-34003-4). Messner.
Shebar, Jonathan M. & Shebar, Sharon S. Animal Dads Take Over. (Illus.). 64p. (gr. 3-5). 1981. PLB 6.97 (ISBN 0-671-34003-4). Messner.
Shebar, Sharon. Milk. Wasserman, Dan, ed. (Illus.). (gr. k-1). 1979. PLB 4.50 (ISBN 0-89868-067-0); pap. 1.95 (ISBN 0-89868-078-6). ARO Pub.
--Night Monsters. Wasserman, Dan, ed. (Ten Word Bks.). (Illus.). (gr. k-1). 1979. PLB 4.50 (ISBN 0-89868-068-9); pap. 1.95 (ISBN 0-89868-079-4). ARO Pub.
Shebar, Sharon & Schoder, Judy. Groundog Day. Jordan, Alton, ed. (Holdays Ser.). (Illus.). (gr. k-3). 1977. PLB 3.50 (ISBN 0-89868-027-1, Read Res); pap. text ed. 1.75 (ISBN 0-89868-060-3). ARO Pub.
Shebar, Sharon, jt. auth. see Shebar, Jonathan.
Shebar, Sharon S., jt. auth. see Shebar, Jonathan M.
Shebbeare, John. The History of the Excellence & Decline of the Constitution, Religion, Laws, Manners, & Genius of the Sumatrans, 1763, 2 vols. in 1. (The Flowering of the Novel, 1740-1775 Ser: Vol. 66). 1974. lib. bdg. 50.00 (ISBN 0-8240-1165-1). Garland Pub.
--Lydia; or, Filial Piety, Seventeen Fifty-Five, 4 vols. in 2. LC 74-17448. (Novel in England, 1700-1775 Ser). 1974. Set. lib. bdg. 90.00 (ISBN 0-8240-1143-0); lib. bdg. 50.00 ea. Garland Pub.
--The Marriage Act, 2 vols. in 1. LC 74-17449. (Novel in England, 1700-1775 Ser). 1974. Repr. of 1754 ed. lib. bdg. 50.00 (ISBN 0-8240-1139-2). Garland Pub.
Shechner, Mark. Joyce in Nighttown: A Psychoanalytic Inquiry into Ulysses. 1974. 14.50x (ISBN 0-520-02398-6). U of Cal Pr.
Sheckles, Mary. Building Children's Science Concepts Through Experience. LC 58-8243. 1958. pap. text ed. 4.25x (ISBN 0-8077-2149-2). Tchrs Coll.
Shecter, Ben. The Hiding Game. LC 80-15291. (Illus.). 40p. (ps-3). 1980. Repr. of 1977 ed. 7.95 (ISBN 0-590-07765-1, Four Winds). Schol Bk Serv.
Shed, Rosemarie, tr. see Kunz-Bircher, Ruth.
Shedd, Charles W. Grandparents: Then God Created Grandparents & It Was Very Good. LC 75-42892. (Illus.). 144p. 1976. 7.95 (ISBN 0-385-11067-7); pap. 4.95 (ISBN 0-385-13115-1). Doubleday.
Shedd, Charlie & Shedd, Martha. Celebration in the Bedroom. 128p. 1981. pap. 2.50 (ISBN 0-553-14436-7). Bantam.
Shedd, Charlie, ed. You Are Somebody Special. 224p. 1980. pap. 2.25 (ISBN 0-553-12803-5). Bantam.
Shedd, Charlie W. Letters to Karen: On Keeping Love in Marriage. (YA) (gr. 9 up). 1965. 7.95 (ISBN 0-687-21568-4). Abingdon.
--Letters to Karen: On Keeping Love in Marriage. 1968. pap. 1.25 (ISBN 0-380-00207-8, 30148). Avon.
--Letters to Philip. (Orig.). pap. 1.95 (ISBN 0-515-05827-0). Jove Pubns.
--Letters to Philip. 1976. pap. 1.50 (ISBN 0-89129-117-2). Jove Pubns.
--Stork Is Dead. 1976. pap. 1.50 (ISBN 0-89129-134-2). Jove Pubns.
--Talk to Me! (A Spire Bk). 1976. pap. 1.50 o.p. (ISBN 0-8007-8244-5). Revell.
--Talk to Me. 1976. pap. 1.50 (ISBN 0-89129-112-1). Jove Pubns.
Shedd, Donald P. & Weinberg, Bernd. Surgical-Prosthetic Approaches to Speech Rehabilitation. (Medical Publications Ser.). 1980. lib. bdg. 32.50 (ISBN 0-8161-2186-9). G K Hall.
Shedd, Joe. White Workers & Black Trainees: An Outline of Some of the Issues Raised by Special Training Programs for the Disadvantaged. (Key Issues Ser.: No. 13). 1973. pap. 2.00. NY Sch Indus Rel.
Shedd, Martha, jt. auth. see Shedd, Charlie.
Shedd, Robert, jt. ed. see Block, Haskell.
Shedd, W. G. Sermons to the Natural Man. 1977. 11.95 (ISBN 0-85151-260-7). Banner of Truth.
Shedd, William G. Dogmatic Theology, 4 vols. 1979. Repr. of 1889 ed. 49.50 (ISBN 0-686-25156-3); text ed. 44.95 (ISBN 0-686-25157-1). Klock & Klock.
--History of Christian Doctrine, 2 vols. 1978. 30.25 (ISBN 0-686-12956-3). Klock & Klock.
Shedd, William G. T. Critical & Doctrinal Commentary on Romans. 1978. 15.75 (ISBN 0-686-12955-5). Klock & Klock.
Shedley, Ethan I. Earth Ship & Star Song. 224p. 1981. pap. 1.95 (ISBN 0-445-04639-2). Popular Lib.
--Medusa Conspiracy. LC 79-56261. 372p. 1980. 13.95 (ISBN 0-670-46571-2). Viking Pr.
Shedlock, J. S. Pianoforte Sonata: Its Origin & Development. 2nd ed. LC 64-18993. (Music Ser). 1964. Repr. of 1895 ed. lib. bdg. 19.50 (ISBN 0-306-70900-7). Da Capo.
Shee, Mary-Venner. Jacques Hurtubise: Recent Works - Oeuvres Recentes. (Illus.). 64p. (Fr. & Eng.). 1981. pap. 10.00 (ISBN 0-936270-16-0). Art Mus Gall.
Sheed, Charlie. How to Know If You're Really in Love. 1981. pap. 2.25 (ISBN 0-671-82841-X). PB.
Sheed, F. The Lord's Prayer: The Prayer of Jesus. (Illus., Orig.). 1976. pap. 4.95 (ISBN 0-8164-2597-3). Crossroad NY.
Sheed, F. J. Our Hearts Are Restless: The Prayer of St. Augustine. 1976. pap. 4.95 (ISBN 0-8164-2127-7). Crossroad NY.
Sheed, Rosemary, tr. see Gattegno, Jean.

Sheehan, Angela. The Butterfly. LC 76-49994. (Illus.). (gr. 2-4). 1977. 2.50 (ISBN 0-531-09081-7); PLB 6.45 (ISBN 0-531-09056-6). Watts.

--The Duck. (First Look at Nature Bks). (Illus.). (gr. 2-4). 1979. 2.50 (ISBN 0-531-09098-1); PLB 6.45 s&l (ISBN 0-531-09074-4). Watts.

--The Frog. (First Look at Nature Books). (Illus.). (gr. 2-4). 1977. 2.50 (ISBN 0-531-09080-9); pap. 6.45 s&l (ISBN 0-531-09055-8). Watts.

--The Hedgehog. LC 76-49574. (Illus.). (gr. 2-4). 1977. 6.45 (ISBN 0-531-09079-5); PLB 3.50 (ISBN 0-531-09054-X). Watts.

--The Otter. (First Look at Nature Bks.). (Illus.). (gr. 2-4). 1979. 2.50 (ISBN 0-531-09099-X); PLB 6.45 s&l (ISBN 0-685-65721-3). Watts.

--The Penguin. LC 78-68537. (First Look at Nature Ser.). (Illus.). (gr. 2-4). 1979. 2.50 (ISBN 0-531-09142-2, Warwick Press); PLB 6.45 s&l (ISBN 0-531-09153-8, Warwick Pr). Watts.

Sheehan, Angela, ed. Discovering Nature. LC 77-6206. (Illus.). (gr. 3-12). 1977. PLB 15.95 (ISBN 0-8393-0025-5). Raintree Child.

Sheehan, Bernard. Savagism & Civility. LC 79-18189. 1980. 35.50 (ISBN 0-521-22927-8); pap. 7.50 (ISBN 0-521-29723-0). Cambridge U Pr.

Sheehan, Denza C. & Hrapchak, Barbara B. Theory & Practice of Histotechnology. 2nd ed. LC 80-11807. 1980. text ed. 29.95 (ISBN 0-8016-4573-5). Mosby.

Sheehan, George. This Running Life. 1980. 10.95 (ISBN 0-671-25608-4). S&S.

Sheehan, John & Valzey, John. Resources for Education. 1974. pap. text ed. 9.50x (ISBN 0-04-370022-5). Allen Unwin.

Sheehan, John F. Let the People Cry Amen! An Inquiry into the Oral History of the Old Testament. LC 76-45676. 1977. pap. 5.95 (ISBN 0-8091-2003-8). Paulist Pr.

--The Threshing Floor. LC 72-81574. 224p. 1972. pap. 5.95 (ISBN 0-8091-1731-2). Paulist Pr.

Sheehan, Larry, jt. auth. see Gilbertie, Sal.

Sheehan, Larry, jt. auth. see Kramer, Jack.

Sheehan, Larry, jt. auth. see Williams, Evan.

Sheehan, Larry, ed. Great Golf Humor. LC 79-52547. (Illus.). 1979. 9.95x (ISBN 0-914178-31-8, 25166-X). Golf Digest.

Sheehan, Larry, ed. see Ashe, Arthur, et al.

Sheehan, Patrick A. The Triumph of Failure, Repr. Of 1899 Ed. Bd. with A Flower of Asia. Dennehy, Henry E. Repr. of 1901 ed. LC 75-467. (Victorian Fiction Ser.). 1975. lib. bdg. 66.00 (ISBN 0-8240-1545-2). Garland Pub.

Sheehan, Thomas J. An Introduction to the Evaluation of Measurement Data in Physical Education. LC 78-137837. (Physical Education Ser). 1971. text ed. 14.95 (ISBN 0-201-07007-3). A-W.

Sheehan, Valerie H., ed. Unmasking: Ten Women in Metamorphosis. LC 72-96163. 286p. 1973. 11.95 (ISBN 0-8040-0626-1). Swallow.

Sheehey, Ann. Crimean Tartars & Volga Germans. (Minority Rights Group: No. 6). 1971. pap. 2.50 (ISBN 0-89192-095-1). Interbk Inc.

Sheehy, Emma D. Children Discover Music & Dance. LC 68-24571. 1968. pap. text ed. 7.25x (ISBN 0-8077-2150-6). Tchrs Coll.

Sheehy, Eugene P., ed. Guide to Reference Books: Supplement. 9th ed. LC 79-20541. 316p. 1980. pap. 15.00 (ISBN 0-8389-0294-4). ALA.

Sheeler, W. D. & Markley, R. W. Words, Words, Words, Bk. 1. 128p. (gr. 9-12). 1981. pap. text ed. 6.95 (ISBN 0-88345-419-X, 18829). Regents Pub.

--Words, Words, Words, Bk 2. (Words, Words, Words). 128p. (gr. 9-12). 1981. pap. text ed. 6.95 (ISBN 0-88345-449-1). Regents Pub.

Sheeler, W. D., et al. Foundations for Reading & Writing: Workbooks 1 & 2. Evans, A. R., ed. (Welcome to English Ser.). (Illus.). 1977. No. 1. wkbk 2.50 ea. (ISBN 0-89285-033-7). No. 2 (ISBN 0-89285-034-5). English Lang.

Sheeler, Willard D. Extra Drills & Practices. 1978. 4.25 (ISBN 0-89285-039-6). English Lang.

--Grammar & Drillbook. 1978. 4.25 (ISBN 0-89285-037-X). English Lang.

--Welcome to English: Introductory Teacher's Manual. (Illus.). 1977. pap. text ed. 2.50x (ISBN 0-19-502219-X). Oxford U Pr.

--Welcome to English Teacher's Guide. (Welcome to English Ser.). 1978. pap. text ed. 4.50x ea. Bks 1 & 2 (ISBN 0-19-520020-9). Bks 3 & 4 (ISBN 0-19-520021-7). Bks 5 & 6 (ISBN 0-19-520022-5). Oxford U Pr.

Sheeler, Willard D., jt. auth. see Dale, Jean N.

Sheeler, Willard D., jt. ed. see Dale, Jean N.

Sheeler, Williard D., jt. auth. see Dale, Jean N.

Sheen, Fulton J. God Love You. LC 80-23085. 224p. 1981. pap. 4.50 (ISBN 0-385-17486-1, Im). Doubleday.

--Guide to Contentment. 1970. pap. 1.95 (ISBN 0-385-02527-0, Im). Doubleday.

--Jesus, Son of Mary: A Book for Children. (Illus.). 32p. 1980. 7.95 (ISBN 0-8164-0470-4). Seabury.

--Life Is Worth Living. 1978. pap. 3.95 (ISBN 0-385-14510-1, Im). Doubleday.

--Lift up Your Heart. 280p. 1975. pap. 2.45 (ISBN 0-385-09001-3, Im). Doubleday.

--Peace of Soul. 1954. pap. 1.95 (ISBN 0-385-02871-7, D8, Im). Doubleday.

--Power of Love. 1968. pap. 1.95 (ISBN 0-385-01090-7, D235, Im). Doubleday.

--Treasure in Clay: The Autobiography of Fulton J. Sheen. (Illus.). 384p. 1980. 15.95 (ISBN 0-385-15985-4). Doubleday.

--The World's Great Love: The Prayer of the Rosary. (Classic Prayer Ser.). (Illus.). 1978. pap. 4.95 (ISBN 0-8164-2182-X). Crossroad NY.

Sheen, Jack H. Aesthetic Rhinoplasty. LC 78-27554. (Illus.). 1978. text ed. 87.50 (ISBN 0-8016-4575-1). Mosby.

Sheer, Bradley T., jt. ed. see Florkin, Marcel.

Sheeran, James. How to Skyrocket Your Income: The Businessman's Guide to Making Money. LC 75-45137. 192p. 1976. 9.95 (ISBN 0-8119-0263-3). Fell.

Sheeter, Sean. The Unified Model of the Universe: The Geometrically Unified Field Solution. (The Unified Theory of Process: Vol. 1). (Illus.). 150p. 1981. 18.98 (ISBN 0-9605378-0-5); pap. 9.50 (ISBN 0-9605378-1-3). Process Pr.

Sheets, Boyd. Anatomy & Physiology of the Speech Mechanism. LC 72-81499. (Studies in Communicative Disorders Ser.). 1973. pap. text ed. 4.50 (ISBN 0-672-61275-5). Bobbs.

Sheets, Hal & Morris, Roger. Disaster in the Desert: Failures of International Relief in the West African Drought. LC 74-76361. 1974. pap. 2.00 (ISBN 0-87003-027-2). Carnegie Endow.

Shefer, Daniel, jt. auth. see Guldmann, Jean-Michel.

Sheff, Alexander L. Bookkeeping Made Easy. (Orig.). 1971. pap. 3.50 (ISBN 0-06-463235-0, EH 235, EH). Har-Row.

Sheff, Donald A. Secretarial English. (gr. 9-12). 1964. pap. text ed. 4.25 (ISBN 0-88345-144-1, 17512). Regents Pub.

Sheffer, Gabriel, jt. ed. see Leitenberg, Milton.

Sheffield, Edward, et al. Systems of Higher Education: Canada. 1978. pap. 8.00 o.s.i. (ISBN 0-89192-204-0). Interbk Inc.

Sheffield, J. Riley, Jr. Floating Drilling: Equipment & Its Use. (Illus.). 260p. 1980. 21.95 (ISBN 0-87201-289-1). Gulf Pub.

Sheffield, James R. Education in Kenya: An Historical Study. LC 72-88639. (Illus.). 126p. 1973. pap. text ed. 5.25x (ISBN 0-8077-2419-X). Tchrs Coll.

Sheffield, James R. & Diejomack, Victor P. Non-Formal Education in African Development. 258p. 1972. pap. 3.00 o.p. (ISBN 0-89192-070-6). Interbk Inc.

Sheffield, James R., ed. Road to the Village: Case Studies in African Community Development. 152p. 1974. pap. 1.50 o.p. (ISBN 0-89192-075-7, Pub by African-American Institute). Interbk Inc.

Sheffield, James R., et al. Agriculture in African Secondary Schools. 124p. 1976. pap. 3.50 (ISBN 0-89192-125-7). Interbk Inc.

--Agriculture in Secondary Schools: Case Studies of Botswana, Kenya & Tanzania. LC 76-11330. 124p. (Orig.). 1976. pap. 1.75 (ISBN 0-686-66072-2). AAI.

Sheffield, Riley, jt. auth. see Goins, W. C.

Shefler, Oscar. I'd Rather Be in Philadelphia. 304p. (Orig.). 1981. pap. 2.75 (ISBN 0-523-41152-9). Pinnacle Bks.

Shefner, Jeremy M., jt. auth. see Levine, Michael W.

Shefner, Vadim. The Unman-Kovrigin's Chronicles. Bouis, Antonina, et al, trs. from Rus. (Best of Soviet Science Fiction Ser.). 192p. 1981. 3.95 (ISBN 0-02-025230-7). Macmillan.

Shefter, Harry. Faster Reading Self-Taught. rev. ed. 1981. pap. write for info. (ISBN 0-671-83230-1). PB.

Shefter, Harry, et al, eds. see Dickens, Charles.

Sheikh, Ahmed. International Law & National Behavior: A Behavioral Interpretation of Contemporary International Law & Politics. LC 73-19922. 352p. 1974. pap. text ed. 13.95x (ISBN 0-471-78230-0). Wiley.

Sheinhold, Patricia F. The Jolly Time Party Book. 6.95 (ISBN 0-916752-21-6). Green Hill.

Sheinkin, David. Self-Understanding: An Introduction to Transactional Analysis. 86p. 1973. pap. text ed. 4.00x (ISBN 0-89039-061-4); instructor's guide 1.50x (ISBN 0-89039-062-2). Ann Arbor Pubs.

Sheinwold, Alfred. Bridge Play for Beginners. (Orig.). 1970. 4.95 o.p. (ISBN 0-571-09528-3, Pub. by Faber & Faber). Merrimack Bk Serv.

--Duplicate Bridge. pap. 2.50 (ISBN 0-486-22741-3). Dover.

--First Book of Bridge. 1962. pap. 2.95 (ISBN 0-06-463242-3, EH 242, EH). Har-Row.

--First Book of Bridge. (Illus., Orig.). 1966. pap. 3.95 o.p. (ISBN 0-571-06717-4, Pub. by Faber & Faber). Merrimack Bk Serv.

Sheinwold, Pat. Successful Bridge Partnerships. 208p. 1981. 4.95 (ISBN 0-686-69323-X). Cornerstone.

Shek, B. Z., jt. ed. see Keith, W. J.

Shekelle, R. B., jt. ed. see Lauer, R. M.

Shekleton, Maureen E., jt. auth. see Groer, Maureen E.

Shelbourne, Cecily. Stage of Love. 1978. pap. 1.95 o.p. (ISBN 0-425-03879-3, Dist. by Putnam). Berkley Pub.

Shelby, C. A. Heavy Minerals in the Wellborn Formation, Lee & Burleson Counties, Texas. (Illus.). 54p. 1965. 1.25 (RI 55). Bur Econ Geology.

Shelby, David S. Anterior Restoration, Fixed Bridgework, & Esthetics. (Illus.). 416p. 1976. 38.75 (ISBN 0-398-03322-6). C C Thomas.

Shelby, Graham. The Cannaways. LC 76-56335. 1978. 8.95 o.p. (ISBN 0-385-09424-8). Doubleday.

Shelby, Peggy, jt. auth. see Yochem, Barbara.

Sheldon, jt. auth. see Lockwood.

Sheldon, Ann. Linda Craig: The Clue on the Desert Trail. Barish, Wendy, ed. (Linda Craig Ser.). 192p. (gr. 3-7). 1981. 7.95 (ISBN 0-671-42651-6, Wanderer); pap. 1.95 (ISBN 0-671-42652-4). S&S.

--Linda Craig: The Mystery in Mexico. Barish, Wendy, ed. (Linda Craig Ser.). 192p. (gr. 3-7). Date not set. Repr. of 1964 ed. 7.95 (ISBN 0-671-42649-4). Wanderer Bks.

--Linda Craig: The Mystery or Horseshoe Canyon. Barish, Wendy, ed. (Linda Craig Ser.). 192p. (gr. 3-7). 1981. 7.95 (ISBN 0-671-42653-2, Wanderer); pap. 1.95 (ISBN 0-671-42654-0). S&S.

--Linda Craig: The Secret of Rancho Del Sol. Barish, Wendy, ed. (Linda Craig Ser.). 192p. (gr. 3-7). 1981. 7.95 (ISBN 0-671-42647-8, Wanderer); pap. 1.95 (ISBN 0-671-42648-6). S&S.

Sheldon, Aure. Of Cobblers & Kings. LC 77-24725. (Illus.). 40p. (ps-3). 1978. lib. bdg. 6.95 (ISBN 0-590-07728-7, Four Winds); PLB 5.41 o.p. (ISBN 0-8193-0832-3). Schol Bk Serv.

Sheldon, Charles. In His Steps. (Family Library). 1973. pap. 1.25 o.s.i. (ISBN 0-89129-178-4). Jove Pubns.

--In His Steps. deluxe ed. 4.95 o.p. (ISBN 0-8007-0501-7); pap. 1.75 (ISBN 0-8007-8022-1, Spire Bks). Revell.

Sheldon, Charles, et al, eds. Supreme Court: Politicians in Robes. (Insight Ser). 1970. pap. text ed. 4.95x (ISBN 0-02-478150-9, 47815). Macmillan.

Sheldon, Charles H., jt. auth. see Baker, Donald G.

Sheldon, Charles M. En Sus Pasos. Reuben, Ruth, tr. from Eng. Orig. Title: In His Steps. 92p. (Span.). 1980. pap. 1.50 (ISBN 0-311-37011-X). Casa Bautista.

Sheldon, Della, ed. Dimensions of Detente. LC 78-6041. (Praegerspecial Studies). 1978. 24.95 (ISBN 0-03-044246-X). Praeger.

Sheldon, Eleanor B. Family Economic Behavior. LC 73-10458. 400p. 1973. 15.00 o.p. (ISBN 0-397-59058-X). Lippincott.

Sheldon, Eric, jt. auth. see Marmier, Pierre.

Sheldon, G. W. Hours with Art & Artists. Weinberg, H. Barbara, ed. LC 75-28873. (Art Experience in Late 19th Century America Ser.: Vol. 9). (Illus.). 1976. Repr. of 1882 ed. lib. bdg. 58.00 (ISBN 0-8240-2233-5). Garland Pub.

Sheldon, George W. Recent Ideals of American Art. LC 75-28882. (Art Experience in Late 19th Century America Ser.: Vol. 16). (Illus.). 1976. Repr. of 1890 ed. lib. bdg. 87.00 (ISBN 0-8240-2240-8). Garland Pub.

Sheldon, George W., ed. Artistic Country Seats, 2 vols, Vols. I & II. LC 78-17476. (Architecture & Decorative Arts: 1978). (Illus.). 1978. Repr. of 1887 ed. Set. lib. bdg. 125.00 (ISBN 0-306-70829-9); lib. bdg. 70.00 ea. Vol. I (ISBN 0-306-77598-0). Vol. II (ISBN 0-306-77599-9). Da Capo.

Sheldon, Huntington, jt. auth. see Boyd, William.

Sheldon, Margaret & Lockwood, Barbara. All About Crossbreeds & Mongrels. 1971. 3.95 o.p. (ISBN 0-7207-0478-2, Pub. by Michael Joseph). Merrimack Bk Serv.

--All About Poodles. 1970. 8.95 (ISBN 0-7207-0320-4, Pub. by Michael Joseph). Merrimack Bk Serv.

Sheldon Memorial Gallery. A Catalog of the Photographs in the Collection of the Sheldon Memorial Gallery at the University of Nebraska-Lincoln. LC 77-89862. (Illus.). 1977. 27.50 o.p. (ISBN 0-8032-7644-3); pap. 17.50 o.p. (ISBN 0-8032-5877-1). U of Nebr Pr.

Sheldon, Robert A. Roadside Geology of Texas. (Illus.). 180p. 1980. pap. 6.95. Corona Pub.

Sheldon, Sidney. The Other Side of Midnight. 1974. 12.95 (ISBN 0-688-00220-X). Morrow.

--Rage of Angels. 1981. pap. 3.50 (ISBN 0-446-36007-4). Warner Bks.

--A Stranger in the Mirror. 1977. pap. 2.95 (ISBN 0-446-93814-9). Warner Bks.

Sheldon, Stephen. Pediatric Differential Diagnosis: A Problem-Oriented Approach. 1979. softcover 7.50 (ISBN 0-89004-351-5). Raven.

Sheldon, Stephen H. Manual of Ambulatory Pediatrics. 275p. 1981. 9.50 (ISBN 0-89004-632-8). Raven.

Sheldon, Susanna. Susie's Girls. 1975. pap. 1.50 o.p. (ISBN 0-685-61050-0, LB314DK, Leisure Bks). Nordon Pubns.

Sheldon, William & Wheelock, Warren H. Over the Edge. (Orig.). (RL 3). 1972. pap. text ed. 4.96 (ISBN 0-205-03340-7, 5233402); tchrs'. guide 2.40 (ISBN 0-205-03338-5, 5233380). Allyn.

--Way Out. (Orig.). (RL 3). 1972. pap. text ed. 4.96 (ISBN 0-205-03337-7, 5233372); tchrs'. guide 2.40 (ISBN 0-205-03338-5, 5233380); activities 20.00 (ISBN 0-205-03339-3, 5233399). Allyn.

--Where It's At. (Orig.). (RL 4). 1973. pap. text ed. 4.96 (ISBN 0-205-03344-X, 5233445); tchrs'. guide 2.40 (ISBN 0-205-03342-3, 5233429); dup. masters 20.00 (ISBN 0-205-03343-1, 5233437). Allyn.

Sheldon, William & Woessner, Nina C. Coming Through. (Orig.). (RL 5). 1972. pap. text ed. 4.96 (ISBN 0-205-03096-3, 5230969); tchrs' guide 2.40 (ISBN 0-205-03094-7, 5230942); reading skills activities dupl. master 20.00 (ISBN 0-205-03095-5, 5230950). Allyn.

--How It Is. (Orig.). (RL 5). 1972. pap. text ed. 4.96 (ISBN 0-205-03093-9, 5230934); tchrs'. manual 2.40 (ISBN 0-205-03094-7, 5230942). Allyn.

--Making the Scene. (Orig.). (RL 6). 1972. pap. text ed. 4.96 (ISBN 0-205-03100-5, 5231000); tchrs'. guide 2.40 (ISBN 0-205-03098-X, 5230985); dup. masters 20.00 (ISBN 0-205-03099-8, 5230993). Allyn.

--On the Spot. (Breakthrough Ser). (Orig.). (RL 6). 1972. pap. text ed. 4.96 (ISBN 0-205-03097-1, 5230977); tchrs'. guide 2.40 (ISBN 0-205-03098-X, 5230985); dup. masters 20.00 (ISBN 0-205-03099-8, 5230993). Allyn.

Sheldon, William, et al. This Cool World. (Breakthrough Ser.). (gr. 7-12). 1979. pap. text ed. 4.96 (ISBN 0-205-05693-8, 5256933); tchrs'. ed. 2.40 (ISBN 0-205-06412-4, 526412X). Allyn.

--The Time Is Now. (gr. 7-12). 1972. pap. text ed. 3.80 (ISBN 0-205-02919-1, 5229197); tchrs'. guide 2.40 (ISBN 0-205-02920-5, 5229200). Allyn.

--On the Move. (Breakthrough Ser.). (gr. 7-12). 1979. pap. text ed. 4.96 (ISBN 0-205-06072-2, 5260728); tchrs'. guide 2.40 (ISBN 0-205-06073-0). Allyn.

--Under the Wire. (Breakthrough Ser.). (gr. 7-12). 1979. pap. text ed. 4.96 (ISBN 0-205-06072-2, 5260728); tchrs'. ed. 2.40 (ISBN 0-205-06075-7, 5260752). Allyn.

Sheldon, William D. Al Bate! Phipps, Nancy, tr. from Eng. (Breakthrough Ser.). (gr. 7-12). 1976. pap. text ed. 4.80 (ISBN 0-205-04873-0, 5248736); tchrs'. guide 2.40 (ISBN 0-205-05635-0, 5256356). Allyn.

Sheldon, William D. & Wheelock, Warren. Out of Sight. (Breakthrough Ser.). (gr. 6-12,RL 4). 1973. pap. text ed. 4.96 (ISBN 0-205-03341-5, 5233410); tchrs'. guide 2.40 (ISBN 0-205-03342-3, 5233429); dup. masters 20.00 (ISBN 0-205-03343-1, 5233437). Allyn.

Sheldon, William D. & Woessner, Nina. Play It Again. (Breakthrough Ser.). (gr. 7-12). 1976. pap. text ed. 5.12 (ISBN 0-205-04109-4, 524109X); dup. masters 22.00 (ISBN 0-205-02921-3, 5254396). Allyn.

--Point in Time. (Breakthrough Ser.). (gr. 9-12). 1976. pap. text ed. 4.96 (ISBN 0-205-04502-2, 5245028); tchrs'. ed. 2.40 (ISBN 0-205-04503-0, 5245036). Allyn.

Sheldon, William D., jt. auth. see Mason, George.

Sheldon, William D., et al. With It. (Breakthrough Ser). (gr. 7-12). 1972. pap. text ed. 3.80 (ISBN 0-205-03092-0, 5230926); tchrs'. guide 2.40 (ISBN 0-205-02920-5, 5229200). Allyn.

--Arrivals & Departures. (gr. 6). 1973. text ed. 11.20 (ISBN 0-205-03562-0, 5235626); tchrs'. guide 11.20 (ISBN 0-205-03563-9, 5235634); activity bk. 3.96 (ISBN 0-205-03564-7, 5235642); tchrs'. ed. 3.96 (ISBN 0-205-03565-5, 5235650); activities' masters 28.00 (ISBN 0-205-03566-3, 5235669). Allyn.

--At Home. new ed. (preprimer 1). 1973. pap. text ed. 3.92 (ISBN 0-205-03515-9, 5235154). Allyn.

--Believe & Make-Believe. new ed. (gr. 4). 1973. text ed. 10.80 (ISBN 0-205-03552-3, 5235529); tchrs' guide 10.80 (ISBN 0-205-03553-1, 5235537); activity bk. 3.96 (ISBN 0-205-03554-X, 5235545); activities' masters 28.00 (ISBN 0-205-03556-6, 5235561); tchrs'. ed. activity bk. 3.96 (ISBN 0-205-03555-8, 5235553). Allyn.

--Fields & Fences. new ed. (gr. 2). 1973. text ed. 7.96 (ISBN 0-205-03532-9, 5235324); tchrs'. guide 7.96 (ISBN 0-205-03533-7, 5235332); activity bk. 3.92 (ISBN 0-205-03534-5, 5235340); tchr's activity bk. 3.92 (ISBN 0-205-03535-3, 5235359); activities masters 28.00 (ISBN 0-205-03536-1, 5235367). Allyn.

--Finding the Way. new ed. (gr. 5). 1973. text ed. 10.80 (ISBN 0-205-03557-4, 523557X); tchrs'. guide 10.30 (ISBN 0-205-03558-2, 5235588); activity bk. 3.96 (ISBN 0-205-03559-0, 5235596); tchrs' activity bk 3.96 (ISBN 0-205-03560-4, 523560X); activities masters 28.00 (ISBN 0-205-03561-2, 5235618). Allyn.

--Here & Away. new ed. (Sheldon Reading Ser). (preprimer 3). 1973. pap. text ed. 3.92 (ISBN 0-205-03517-5, 5235170); tchr's. guide 8.20 (ISBN 0-205-03518-3, 5235189); activity bk. 3.92 (ISBN 0-205-03519-1, 5235197); tchrs'. ed. activity bk. 3.92 (ISBN 0-205-03520-5, 5235200); independent activ. 28.00 (ISBN 0-205-03521-3, 5235219). Allyn.

--Magic Windows. new ed. (gr. 3). 1973. text ed. 9.20 (ISBN 0-205-03542-6, 5235421); tchrs'. guide 9.20 (ISBN 0-205-03543-4, 523543X); tchrs'. activity bk. 3.92 (ISBN 0-205-03544-2, 5235448); tchr's activity bk. 3.92 (ISBN 0-205-03545-0, 5235456); activities masters 28.00 (ISBN 0-205-03546-9, 5235464). Allyn.

--Our School. (gr. 1). 1973. text ed. 7.96 (ISBN 0-205-03522-1, 5235227); tchrs'. guide 3.96 (ISBN 0-205-03523-X, 5235235); activity bk. 3.92 (ISBN 0-205-03524-8, 5235243); tchr's ed. 3.96 (ISBN 0-205-03525-6, 5235251); activ. masters 28.00 (ISBN 0-205-03526-4, 523526X). Allyn.

--Our Town. new ed. (gr. 1). 1973. text ed. 7.96 (ISBN 0-205-03527-2, 5235278); tchrs'. guide 7.96 (ISBN 0-205-03528-0, 5235286); activity bk. 3.92 (ISBN 0-205-03529-9, 5235294); tchrs'. ed. activity 3.92 (ISBN 0-205-03530-2, 5235308); independent activ. masters 28.00 (ISBN 0-205-03531-0, 5235316); word cards 88.00 (ISBN 0-205-03898-0, 5238986). Allyn.

--Picture Stories & Words. new ed. (Sheldon Reading Ser.). (gr. k-1). 1973. pap. text ed. 3.92 (ISBN 0-205-03512-4, 523512X); tchrs'. guide 8.20 (ISBN 0-205-03513-2, 5235138). Allyn.

--Story Caravan. new ed. (Sheldon Reading Ser). (gr. 3). 1973. text ed. 9.20 (ISBN 0-205-03547-7, 5235472); tchrs'. guide 9.20 (ISBN 0-205-03548-5, 5235480); activity bk. 3.92 (ISBN 0-205-03549-3, 5235499); tchrs'. ed. 3.92 (ISBN 0-205-03550-7, 5235502); independent activ. masters 28.00 (ISBN 0-205-03551-5, 5235510). Allyn.

--Town & Country. new ed. (gr. 2). 1973. text ed. 8.60 (ISBN 0-205-03537-X, 5235375); tchrs'. guide 8.60 (ISBN 0-205-03538-8, 5235383); activity bk. 3.92 (ISBN 0-205-03539-6, 5235391); tchrs.' ed. 3.92 (ISBN 0-205-03540-X, 5235405); independent activities masters 28.00 (ISBN 0-205-03541-8, 5235413). Allyn.

--From the Top. (Breakthrough Ser.). (gr. 7-12). 1976. pap. text ed. 5.12 (ISBN 0-205-04110-8, 5241103); tchrs'. ed. 2.40 (ISBN 0-205-04111-6, 5241111); dup masters 22.00 (ISBN 0-205-05439-0, 5254396). Allyn.

--Over & Out. (Breakthrough Ser.). (gr. 7-12). 1976. pap. text ed. 5.12 (ISBN 0-205-04622-3, 5246229); tchrs'. ed. 2.40 (ISBN 0-205-04620-7, 5246202); dup. masters 22.00 (ISBN 0-205-04621-5, 5246210). Allyn.

--Prime Time. (Breakthrough Ser.). (gr. 7-12). 1976. pap. text ed. 5.12 (ISBN 0-205-04619-3, 5246199); tchrs'. ed. 2.40 (ISBN 0-205-04620-7, 5246202); dup. masters 22.00 (ISBN 0-205-04621-5, 5246210). Allyn.

Sheldon, Wilmon H. Agapology: The Rational Love Philosphy, Guide of Life. 1965. 4.95 o.p (ISBN 0-8158-0184-X). Chris Mass.

--Woman's Mission to Humanity. LC 68-8815. 1968. 3.95 o.p. (ISBN 0-8158-0008-8). Chris Mass.

--Young Offer a New Step. 1970. 3.95 o.p. (ISBN 0-8158-0249-8). Chris/Mass.

Sheldon-Wildgen, Jan, jt. auth. see Vanbieryliet, Alan.

Sheldon-Wildgen, Jan, jt. auth. see Van Bieryliet, Alan.

Sheldrake, Peter & Berry, Stewart. Looking at Innovation - Two Approaches to Educational Research. (General Ser.). 152p. 1975. pap. text ed. 13.25x (ISBN 0-85633-055-8, NFER). Humanities.

Sheleff, Leon. Generations Apart: Adult Hostility to Youth. 352p. 1981. 18.95 (ISBN 0-07-056540-6, P&RB). McGraw.

Sheleff, Leon S. The Bystander: Behavior, Law & Ethics. LC 77-18577. 1978. 18.95 (ISBN 0-669-02110-5). Lexington Bks.

Sheleg, A. V., jt. auth. see Kuntsevich, I. M.

Shelgren, Margaret, jt. auth. see Lauderdale, Beverly.

Shelgren, Olaf W., Jr., et al. Cobblestone Landmarks of New York State. 1978. 12.95 o.p. (ISBN 0-8156-2201-5); pap. 7.95 o.p. (ISBN 0-8156-0149-2). Syracuse U Pr.

Shelhamer, E. E., ed. see Finney, Charles G.

Shelikhov, Grigorii I. Voyage to America, 1783-1786, Rus. Pierce, Richard A., ed. Ramsey, Marina, tr. (Materials for the Study of Alaska History Ser.: No. 19). (Illus.). 1981. 15.50x (ISBN 0-919642-67-5). Limestone Pr.

Sheline, Glenn E., et al. Pituitary Adenomas. (Oncologic Multidisciplinary Decisions in Onology Ser.). (Illus.). 248p. 1981. pap. 50.00 (ISBN 0-08-027463-3). Pergamon.

Shell, Adeline G. & Reynolds, Kay. Brown Bagging It: The Lunch Box Idea Book. LC 78-10945. 1979. 8.95 (ISBN 0-671-18414-8); pap. 3.95 (ISBN 0-671-18342-7). Sovereign Bks.

--Working Parent Food Book. 1979. 9.95 (ISBN 0-671-18439-3); pap. 4.95 (ISBN 0-346-12421-2). Cornerstone.

Shell, Joy. The Ministry of Angels. 1977. pap. 3.95 (ISBN 0-8065-0586-9). Citadel Pr.

Shell, Karl, jt. auth. see Fisher, Franklin M.

Shell, Karl, jt. ed. see Cass, David.

Shell, R. L. & Jeffries, N. P. Engineering Fundamentals. new ed. LC 74-32613. 150p. 1975. 10.50x (ISBN 0-87263-032-3). SME.

Shell UK Exploration & Production Ltd. Winning Supply & Service Business in Offshore Oil & Gas Markets. 112p. 1976. 77.00x (ISBN 0-86010-025-1, Pub. by Graham & Trotman England). State Mutual Bk.

Shellabarger, Samuel. Chevalier Bayard. LC 76-156738. (Illus.). 1971. Repr. of 1928 ed. 15.00x (ISBN 0-8196-0272-8). Biblo.

--Lord Chesterfield & His World. LC 72-156737. 1971. Repr. of 1951 ed. 15.00x (ISBN 0-8196-0271-X). Biblo.

Shellenberger, J. A., jt. auth. see Pomeranz, Y.

Shelley, Bruce. The Church: God's People. 1978. pap. 3.95 (ISBN 0-88207-770-8). Victor Bks.

Shelley, Bruce L. Four Marks of a Total Christian. 1978. pap. 1.95 (ISBN 0-88207-512-8). Victor Bks.

Shelley, Eugenie. ERA: Equality in Bondage. pap. 1.75 (ISBN 0-918700-08-6). Duverus Pub.

Shelley, Florence D., jt. auth. see Otten, Jane.

Shelley, John, tr. see Soelle, Dorothee.

Shelley, Joseph F. Engineering Mechanics: Statics & Dynamics, 2 vols. (Illus.). 1980. Set. text ed. 28.95 (ISBN 0-07-056555-4). Statics Vol. text ed. 19.95 (ISBN 0-07-056551-1); Dynamics Vol. text ed. 18.95 (ISBN 0-07-056553-8); solutions manual 11.95. Statics Vol (ISBN 0-07-056552-X). Dynamics Vol (ISBN 0-07-056554-6). McGraw.

Shelley, Louise I. Crime & Modernization: The Impact of Industrialization & Urbanization on Crime. LC 80-24044. (Science & International Affairs Ser.). 216p. 1981. 22.50x (ISBN 0-8093-0983-1). S Ill U Pr.

Shelley, Louise I., ed. Readings in Comparative Criminology. LC 80-19533. (Science & International Affairs). 312p. 1981. 25.00x (ISBN 0-8093-0938-6). S Ill U Pr.

Shelley, Mary. Frankenstein. 1959. 11.50x (ISBN 0-460-00616-9, Evman); pap. 2.95 (ISBN 0-460-01616-4). Dutton.

--Frankenstein. Schick, Alice & Schick, Joel, eds. LC 80-385. (Illus.). 48p. (gr. 3 up). 1980. PLB 8.44 (ISBN 0-440-02693-8); pap. 4.95 (ISBN 0-440-02692-X). Delacorte.

--Last Man. Luke, Hugh J., Jr., ed. LC 65-19465. 1965. 10.95x (ISBN 0-8032-0173-7); pap. 1.95 (ISBN 0-8032-5182-3, BB 323, Bison). U of Nebr Pr.

Shelley, Mary, jt. auth. see Stoker, Bram.

Shelley, Mary W. Frankenstein: Or, the Modern Prometheus. Rieger, James H., ed. LC 72-80409. (LL Ser). 333p. 1974. pap. text ed. 5.50 o.p. (ISBN 0-672-61020-5). Bobbs.

Shelley, Percy. Shelley's Poetry & Prose. Reiman, Donald H., ed. LC 76-26929. (Norton Critical Editions). 1977. 15.95 (ISBN 0-393-04436-X); pap. text ed. 10.95x (ISBN 0-393-09164-3). Norton.

Shelley, Percy B. Cenci. Duerksen, Roland A., ed. (Library of Liberal Arts Ser). 1970. 6.95 o.p. (ISBN 0-672-51322-6, LLA170); pap. 3.80 o.p. (ISBN 0-672-60398-5). Bobbs.

--The Complete Poetical Works of Percy Bysshe Shelley: 1814-1817, Vol. 2. (Oxford English Texts Ser.). 1974. 45.00x (ISBN 0-19-812707-3). Oxford U Pr.

--Shelley's Critical Prose. McElderry, B. R., Jr., ed. LC 66-19856. (Regents Critics Ser). 1967. 9.95x (ISBN 0-8032-0461-2); pap. 2.95x (ISBN 0-8032-5462-8, BB 407, Bison). U of Nebr Pr.

Shelley, Percy Bysshe. Poetical Works. Hutchinson, Thomas & Matthews, G. M., eds. (Oxford Standard Authors Ser). 948p. 1971. 26.00 (ISBN 0-19-254143-9); pap. 11.50x (ISBN 0-19-281069-3, OPB); leather bd. 45.00 (ISBN 0-19-192852-6). Oxford U Pr.

Shelley, Walter B. Consultations in Dermatology. LC 70-168599. (Illus.). 1972. 16.00 (ISBN 0-7216-8213-8). Saunders.

--Consultations in Dermatology Two. LC 73-88979. (Illus.). 289p. 1974. 17.00 (ISBN 0-7216-8214-6). Saunders.

Shelley, Walter B. & Crissey, John T. Classics in Clinical Dermatology: With Biographical Sketches. (Illus.). 496p. 1970. 20.75 (ISBN 0-398-01741-7). C C Thomas.

Shelly, Bruce. The Miracle of Anne. 96p. 1974. pap. 3.50 (ISBN 0-911336-55-9). Sci of Mind.

Shelly, Gary B. & Cashman, Thomas J. Advanced Ansi,COBOL Disk-Tape Programming Efficiencies. LC 74-21838. 1975. pap. text ed. 11.95x (ISBN 0-88236-105-8). Anaheim Pub Co.

--Business Systems Analysis & Design. LC 74-77398. 1975. 14.95x (ISBN 0-88236-043-4). Anaheim Pub Co.

--Computer Programming, Rpg II. LC 76-19352. 1976. pap. text ed. 14.95x (ISBN 0-88236-226-7). Anaheim Pub Co.

--Introduction to Computer Programming Structured Cobol. LC 77-89824. 1977. pap. 14.95x (ISBN 0-88236-111-2). Anaheim Pub Co.

--Introduction to Computers & Data Processing. (Illus.). 1980. pap. text ed. 15.95x (ISBN 0-88236-115-5); wkbk 5.95x (ISBN 0-88236-116-3). Anaheim Pub Co.

Shelly, Judith A. Dilemma: A Nurse's Guide for Making Ethical Decisions. (Orig.). 1980. pap. text ed. 4.95 (ISBN 0-87784-666-9). Inter-Varsity.

Shelly, Mary V. & Munro, Sandra H. Harriet Lane, First Lady of the White House. LC 80-20151. (Illus.). 48p. (gr. 4-6). 1980. 6.95 (ISBN 0-915010-29-1). Sutter House.

Shelly, Rubel. What Shall We Do with the Bible? 1975. 6.95 (ISBN 0-934916-42-X). Natl Christian Pr.

--Whom God Hath Joined. 3.50 (ISBN 0-89315-354-0). Lambert Bk.

Shelmire, Bedford. The Doctor's Overnight Beauty Program. (Illus.). 192p. 1981. 12.95 (ISBN 0-312-21489-8). St Martin.

Shelnitz, P., ed. see Ginzburg, S. I., et al.

Shelnitz, P., tr. see Brainina, K. Z.

Shelnitz, P., tr. see Geilikman, B. T. & Kresin, V. Z.

Shelnitz, P., tr. see Pshezhetsky, S. Ya., et al.

Shelnitz, P., tr. see Semin, G. K., et al.

Shelnutt, Eve. The Love Child. 1979. pap. 4.50 (ISBN 0-87685-384-X); pap. 4.50 (ISBN 0-87685-384-X). Black Sparrow.

Shelp, Earl E. & Sunderlan, Ronald, eds. A Biblical Basis for Ministry. Achtmeier, Paul J., et al. (Orig.). 1981. pap. price not set (ISBN 0-664-24371-1). Westminster.

Shelton, Austin J., Jr., ed. African Assertion: A Critical Anthology of African Literature. LC 67-18742. (Orig.). (gr. 9-12). 1968. pap. 5.00 o.p. (ISBN 0-672-63004-4). Odyssey Pr.

Shelton, Bill see Hart, R. S., pseud.

Shelton, Brenda, jt. auth. see Gardner, Eric K.

Shelton, Gilbert & Sheridan, Dave. The Best of the Rip off Press: More Fabulous Furry Freak Brothers, Vol. 4. (The Best of the Rip off Press Ser.). (Illus.). 96p. (Orig.). (YA) 1980. pap. 5.95 (ISBN 0-89620-086-8). Rip off.

Shelton, Glenn. Groundhog up a Tree. 6.95 (ISBN 0-685-48817-9). Nortex Pr.

Shelton, J. L. & Ackerman, J. M. Homework in Counseling & Psychotherapy. (Illus.). 308p. 1976. pap. 17.75 (ISBN 0-398-03076-6). C C Thomas.

Shelton, Jay. The Woodburner's Encyclopedia. (Orig.). 1980. pap. write for info. (ISBN 0-440-59652-1). Dell.

Shelton, John S. Geology Illustrated. LC 66-16380. (Illus.). 1966. 24.95x (ISBN 0-7167-0229-0). W H Freeman.

Shelton, Margaret R., et al. First Aid for Your Dog. Foyle, Christina, ed. 1972. 3.95 (ISBN 0-685-55804-5). Palmetto Pub.

Shelton, Ralph L., jt. auth. see Skinner, Paul H.

Shelton, Suzanne. Divine Dancer: Abiography of Ruth St. Denis. LC 80-2442. (Illus.). 312p. 1981. 14.95 (ISBN 0-385-14159-9). Doubleday.

Shelton, W. G. Dean Tucker & Eighteenth Century Economic & Political Thought. LC 79-29742. 1980. write for info. (ISBN 0-312-18538-3). St Martin.

Shelton, William & Kennedy, Ann. Houston. LC 76-57516. 1978. pap. 2.95 o.p. (ISBN 0-385-11405-2, Dolp). Doubleday.

Shely, Patricia. Party Ideas. (Ideas Ser). (Illus.). 1977. pap. text ed. 1.75 (ISBN 0-87239-121-3, 7961). Standard Pub.

Shely, Patricia, compiled by. All Occasion Finger Plays for Young Children. (Standard Ideas Ser.). (Illus.). 1978. pap. 1.75 (ISBN 0-87239-211-2, 2812). Standard Pub.

--Bible Finger Plays for Young Children. (Standard Ideas Ser.). (Illus.). 1978. pap. 1.75 (ISBN 0-87239-212-0, 2813). Standard Pub.

--Easy Games for Young Children. (Standard Ideas Ser.). (Illus.). 1978. pap. 1.75 (ISBN 0-87239-213-9, 2814). Standard Pub.

--Simple Songs for Young Children. (Standard Ideas Ser.). (Illus.). 1978. pap. 1.75 (ISBN 0-87239-214-7, 2815). Standard Pub.

Shely, Patricia, ed. see Brown, Francis, et al.

Shem, Samuel. House of God. 1980. pap. 2.95 (ISBN 0-440-13368-8). Dell.

Shemberg, Kenneth M., jt. auth. see Doherty, Michael E.

Shem-Ur, Ora. The Challenges of Israel. LC 80-52915. 80p. 1980. 4.95 (ISBN 0-88400-071-0). Shengold.

Shen, H. W., ed. Applications of Stochastic Processes to Sediment Transport: Sedimentation Process in Rivers & Coastal Environments. Kikkawa, H. LC 79-67693. 1979. 27.50 (ISBN 0-686-64297-X). WRP.

Shen, Hsieh W. Modeling of Rivers. LC 79-3913. 1979. 45.00 (ISBN 0-471-05474-7, Pub. by Wiley-Interscience). Wiley.

Shen, Jerome T. Clinical Practice of Adolescent Medicine. 750p. 1979. 36.50x (ISBN 0-8385-1148-1). ACC.

Shenfelt, R. D. Hymenopterorum Catalogus. (Hymenopterorum Catalogus Ser.: No. 16). 573p. 1980. pap. 137.00 (ISBN 0-686-28664-2, Pub. by Dr. W. Junk). Kluwer Boston.

Shenk, Robert. The Sinner's Progress: A Study of Madness in Elizabethan Renaissance Drama. (Salzburg Elizabethan & Renaissance Studies: No. 74). 1978. pap. text ed. 25.00x (ISBN 0-391-01520-6). Humanities.

Shenkel, William M. Marketing Real Estate. (Illus.). 1980. text ed. 19.95 (ISBN 0-13-557488-9). P-H.

--Modern Real Estate Principles. rev. ed. 1980. 17.95x (ISBN 0-256-02291-7); study guide 5.50x (ISBN 0-256-02292-5). Business Pubns.

--The Real Estate Professional. rev. ed. LC 78-52950. 1978. 14.95 (ISBN 0-87094-159-3). Dow Jones-Irwin.

Shennan, J. H. The Origins of the Modern European State, Fourteen Fifty to Seventeen Twenty-Five. 1980. text ed. 14.50x (ISBN 0-09-119030-4, Hutchinson U Pr); pap. text ed. 9.25x (ISBN 0-09-119031-2). Humanities.

Shenson, Howard L. How to Strategically Negotiate the Consulting Contract. 107p. 1980. pap. text ed. 24.00 (ISBN 0-930686-10-1). Bermont Bks.

Shenton, Eileen, jt. auth. see Fernald, Mary.

Shenton, James P. & Meckler, Alan. Plaid for U. S. History Since Eighteen Sixty-Five. 1975. pap. 5.50 (ISBN 0-256-01274-1, 06-0643-00). Learning Syst.

--Plaid for U. S. History to Eighteen Seventy-Seven. 1973. pap. 5.50 (ISBN 0-256-01273-3, 06-0641-00). Learning Syst.

Shenton, James P., et al. American Cooking: The Melting Pot. (Foods of the World Ser). (Illus.). 1971. 14.95 (ISBN 0-8094-0055-3). Time-Life.

Shepard, Anna O. Ceramics for the Archaeologist. (Illus.). 1980. pap. 11.00 (ISBN 0-87279-620-5, 609). Carnegie Inst.

Shepard, Barnett. Sailors Snug Harbor Eighteen Hundred & One to Nineteen Seventy-Six. LC 79-16979. (Illus.). 105p. (Orig.). 1979. 11.95 (ISBN 0-9604254-1-1); pap. 7.95 (ISBN 0-9604254-0-3). Snug Harbor NY.

Shepard, Dennis D., ed. Intraocular Lens Manual. rev. 3rd ed. LC 80-51743. 464p. 1980. 40.00 (ISBN 0-9601234-2-3). D D Shepard.

Shepard, Edward M. Martin Van Buren. LC 80-25465. (American Statesmen Ser.). 1981. pap. 6.95 (ISBN 0-87754-189-2). Chelsea Hse.

Shepard, Francis P. Geological Oceanography. LC 76-54533. 1977. 19.50x (ISBN 0-8448-1064-9). Crane-Russak Co.

--Submarine Geology. 3rd ed. (Harper's Geoscience Ser.). 1973. text ed. 31.50 scp (ISBN 0-06-046091-1, HarpC). Har-Row.

Shepard, J. M. & Stewart. Sociology & Social Problems: A Conceptual Approach. (Illus.). 336p. 1976. pap. text ed. 11.95 (ISBN 0-13-821652-5). P-H.

Shepard, John, jt. auth. see Painter, Desmond.

Shepard, John S. Shepard's Handbook of Wine Cocktails & Non-Alcoholic Drinks: A Guide for Foodservice & Bar Managers. (Foodservice Guides Ser.). 1981. 20.00 (ISBN 0-89047-031-6); spiral bdg. 20.00 (ISBN 0-89047-032-4). Herman Pub.

--Shepard's Wine & Liquor Pricing Guide. (Foodservice Guides Ser.). 1981. spiral bdg. 15.00 (ISBN 0-89047-034-0). Herman Pub.

Shepard, Jon M. Sociology. (Illus.). 600p. 1980. text ed. 16.95 (ISBN 0-8299-0412-3). West Pub.

Shepard, Leslie. Encyclopedia of Occultism & Parapsychology: A Compedium of Information on the Occult Sciences, Magic, Demonology, Superstitions, Spiritism, Mysticism, Metaphysics, Psychical Science & Parapsycholgy. 2nd ed. (Illus.). 400p. 1981. 125.00 (ISBN 0-8103-0196-2). Gale.

Shepard, Leslie, ed. The Dracula Book of Great Vampire Stories. 1978. pap. 1.95 o.s.i. (ISBN 0-515-04506-3). Jove Pubns.

--Encyclopedia of Occultism & Parapsychology: A Compendium of Information on the Occult Sciences, Magic, Demonology, Superstition, Spiritism, Mysticism, Metaphysics, Psychical Science & Parapsychology, 2 vols. LC 77-92. (Illus., Supplemented by Occultism update). 1978. Set. 90.00 (ISBN 0-8103-0185-7); pap. 45.00 occultism update: a periodical supplement (4 issues subscription) (ISBN 0-685-79636-1). Gale.

Shepard, Leslie A. Encyclopedia of Occultism & Parapsychlogy: Vols. 1 & 2. 1980. pap. 19.90 boxed set (ISBN 0-380-50112-0). Vol. 1 (ISBN 0-380-48835-3, 48835). Vol. 2 (ISBN 0-380-48975-9, 48975). Avon.

Shepard, Martin. Beyond Sex Therapy. LC 75-162. 1975. 7.95 o.p. (ISBN 0-89110-001-6). Penthouse Pr.

--The Do-It-Yourself Psychotherapy Book. LC 76-11881. 1976. pap. 3.95 o.p. (ISBN 0-8415-0447-4). Dutton.

--Fritz. LC 80-50243. 256p. 1980. 15.95 (ISBN 0-933256-14-0); pap. 7.95 (ISBN 0-933256-15-9). Second Chance.

--Fritz. LC 80-50243. 256p. 1981. Repr. of 1975 ed. 7.95 (ISBN 0-933256-15-9). Second Chance.

--A Question of Values. 1976. 7.95 o.p. (ISBN 0-8415-0449-0). Dutton.

--The Seducers. 218p. 1981. Repr. of 1976 ed. 11.95 (ISBN 0-932966-12-8). Permanent Pr.

Shepard, Odell. The Lore of the Unicorn. 1967. 12.95 o.p. (ISBN 0-04-291004-8). Allen Unwin.

Shepard, Paul. Thinking Animals: Animals & the Development of Human Intelligence. 1978. 14.95 o.p. (ISBN 0-670-70061-4). Viking Pr.

Shepard, Paul & McKinley, Daniel, eds. Subversive Science: Essays Toward an Ecology of Man. LC 69-15029. (Illus., Orig.). 1969. pap. text ed. 11.50 (ISBN 0-395-05399-4). HM.

Shepard, Roger N. & Cooper, Lynn A. Mental Images & Their Transformations. (Illus.). 1981. text ed. write for info. (ISBN 0-89706-008-3). Bradford Bks.

Shepard, Sam. Chicago & Other Plays. LC 80-27628. 1981. 15.00 (ISBN 0-89396-042-X); pap. 6.95 (ISBN 0-89396-043-8). Urizen.

--Twelve One Act Plays. Date not set. cancelled (ISBN 0-89396-018-7); pap. cancelled (ISBN 0-89396-019-5). Urizen Bks.

--The Unseen Hand & Other Plays. LC 80-27628. 1981. 15.00 (ISBN 0-89396-040-3); pap. 7.95 (ISBN 0-89396-041-1). Urizen Bks.

Shepard, Susan & Levering, Robert. In the Neighborhoods. (Orig.). 1981. pap. 6.95 (ISBN 0-87701-144-3). Chronicle Bks.

Shepard, Tim. Peaches Point. LC 76-4521. (Illus.). 1976. 8.95 o.s.i. (ISBN 0-690-01168-7, TYC-T). T Y Crowell.

Shepardson, Mary & Hammond, Blodwen. The Navajo Mountain Community: Social Organization & Kinship Terminology. LC 70-97233. 1970. 18.50x (ISBN 0-520-01570-3). U of Cal Pr.

Sheperak, Rita & DeBruin, Jerry. Metric Math Book. (gr. k-8). 1976. 11.95 (ISBN 0-916456-08-0, GA63). Good Apple.

Sheperd, D. Homoeopathy in Epidemic Diseases. 1980. text ed. 5.75 o.p. (ISBN 0-8464-1022-2). Beekman Pubs.

Sheperd, Dorothy. Homeopathy for the First Aider. 1980. text ed. 4.75x (ISBN 0-8464-1021-4). Beekman Pubs.

--The Magic of the Minimum Dose. 214p. 1964. text ed. 15.50x (ISBN 0-8464-1030-3). Beekman Pubs.

Shephard, Eugene, jt. auth. see Davis, Grant M.

Shephard, G. C. Vector Spaces of Finite Dimension. (University Mathematical Texts Ser.). 1966. 5.95 o.p. (ISBN 0-471-78324-2). Halsted Pr.

Shephard, J. Edward. Preventive Dentistry for the Patient. (Illus.). 136p. 1972. pap. 3.75 (ISBN 0-398-02480-4). C C Thomas.

Shephard, Roy J. The Fit Athlete. (Illus.). 1978. 16.50x (ISBN 0-19-217549-1). Oxford U Pr.

--Men at Work: Applications of Ergonomics to Performance & Design. (Illus.). 408p. 1974. 32.75 (ISBN 0-398-02965-2). C C Thomas.

Shephard, Roy J. & Lavallee, Hugues. Physical Fitness Assessment: Principles, Practice & Application. (Illus.). 320p. 1978. 33.75 (ISBN 0-398-03701-9). C C Thomas.

Shepherd. Instructions to Young Anglers. (Illus.). 9.75x (ISBN 0-392-06451-0, SpS). Soccer.

Shepherd, Anne-Mariel & Shepherd, Don. Embrace My Scarlet Heart. 1977. pap. 1.75 o.s.i. (ISBN 0-515-04268-4). Jove Pubns.

Shepherd, C. Jonathan, jt. auth. see Roberts, Ronald J.

Shepherd, C. W. A Thousand Years of London Bridge. Date not set. 7.95 o.p. (ISBN 0-8038-5368-8). Hastings.

Shepherd, D. Essentials of Homoeopathic Prescribing. 78p. 1970. pap. 3.00x (ISBN 0-8464-1008-7). Beekman Pubs.

Shepherd, David L. Comprehensive High School Reading Methods. 2nd ed. Heilman, Arthur W., ed. (Secondary Education Ser.). 1978. text ed. 16.95 (ISBN 0-675-08426-1). Merrill.

Shepherd, Don, jt. auth. see Shepherd, Anne-Mariel.

Shepherd, Donald & Slatzer, Robert. Bing Crosby. (Illus.). 320p. 1981. 13.95 (ISBN 0-312-07866-8). St Martin.

Shepherd, Dorothy. More Magic of the Minimum Dose. 1980. text ed. 7.00x (ISBN 0-8464-1033-8). Beekman Pubs.

--A Physician's Posy. 1980. text ed. 7.95 o.p. (ISBN 0-8464-1037-0). Beekman Pubs.

Shepherd, F. A. Engineering Surveying: Problems & Solutions. (Illus.). 1977. pap. text ed. 21.00x (ISBN 0-7131-3370-8). Intl Ideas.

Shepherd, Geoffrey, ed. Ancrene Wisse, Pts. 6 & 7. (Old & Middle English Texts). 116p. 1972. pap. 6.95x (ISBN 0-06-496228-8). B&N.

Shepherd, Geoffrey, ed. see Sidney, Philip.

Shepherd, George W., Jr. Anti-Apartheid: Transnational Conflict & Western Policy in the Liberation of South Africa. LC 77-71868. (Studies in Human Rights: No. 3). 1977. lib. bdg. 17.50x (ISBN 0-8371-9537-3, SHA/). Greenwood.

Shepherd, Irma L., jt. ed. see Fagan, Joen.

Shepherd, J. Barrie. A Diary of Prayer: Daily Meditations on the Parables of Jesus. (Orig.). 1981. pap. 5.95 (ISBN 0-664-24352-5). Westminster.

Shepherd, J. F. & Walton, G. Shipping, Maritime Trade & the Economic Development of Colonial America. LC 76-176256. (Illus.). 350p. 1972. 29.95 (ISBN 0-521-08409-1). Cambridge U Pr.

Shepherd, J. F., jt. auth. see Walton, G. M.

Shepherd, J. T. & Vanhoutte, P. M., eds. The Human Cardiovascular System: Facts & Concepts. 1979. 27.00 (ISBN 0-89004-367-1); softcover 15.95 (ISBN 0-686-52359-8). Raven.

Shepherd, J. W., ed. Srygley-Hall Debate on the Church. pap. 3.50 (ISBN 0-89225-169-7). Gospel Advocate.

Shepherd, J. W., et al. A Social Atlas of London. (Illus.). 100p. 1975. 29.95x (ISBN 0-19-874026-3). Oxford U Pr.

Shepherd, Jack. Cannibals of the Heart: A Personal Biography of Louisa Catherine & John Quincy Adams. (Illus.). 300p. 1981. 15.00 (ISBN 0-07-056730-1). McGraw.

--The Politics of Starvation. LC 75-40831. 101p. 1975. 3.00 o.p. (ISBN 0-87003-002-7). Carnegie Endow.

Shepherd, James F. College Vocabulary Skills. LC 78-69548. (Illus.). 1978. pap. text ed. 7.95 (ISBN 0-395-26851-6); inst. manual 0.30 (ISBN 0-395-26852-4). HM.

--Reading Skills for College Study. LC 79-89520. (Illus.). 1979. pap. text ed. 9.50 (ISBN 0-395-28503-8); instrs.' manual 0.65 (ISBN 0-395-28504-6). HM.

--RSVP: The Houghton Mifflin Reading, Study, & Vocabulary Program. LC 80-82698. (Illus.). 352p. 1981. pap. text ed. 8.50 (ISBN 0-395-29342-1); instr's manual avail. (ISBN 0-395-29343-X). HM.

--RSVP: The Houghton Mifflin Reading, Study, & Vocabulary Program. (Illus.). 352p. 1981. pap. text ed. 8.50 (ISBN 0-395-29342-1); write for info. instr's manual (ISBN 0-395-29343-X). HM.

Shepherd, Jean. The Phantom of the Open Hearth. LC 77-76280. 1978. pap. 4.95 o.p. (ISBN 0-385-12976-9, Dolp). Doubleday.

--Wanda Hickey's Night of Golden Memories & Other Diasters. LC 72-161317. (Illus.). 1971. 6.95 o.p. (ISBN 0-385-04870-X). Doubleday.

Shepherd, John T. & Vanhoutte, Paul M. Veins & Their Control. LC 75-15353. (Illus.). 269p. 1975. text ed. 22.00 (ISBN 0-7216-8220-0). Saunders.

Shepherd, K. R. & Richter, H. V., eds. Forestry in National Developments: Production Systems, Conservation, Foreign Trade & Aid. (Development Studies Centre - Monograph: No. 17). (Orig.). 1980. pap. 13.95 (ISBN 0-7081-1822-4, 0414, Pub. by ANUP Australia). Bks Australia.

Shepherd, Massey H., Jr. Worship of the Church. (Orig.). 1952. pap. 3.95 (ISBN 0-8164-2071-8, SP4). Crossroad NY.

Shepherd, P. J., jt. auth. see Poole, R. H.

Shepherd, P. J., ed. see Patashinskii, A. Z., et al.

Shepherd, P. J., ed. & tr. see Sitenko, A. G.

Shepherd, Roberta, jt. auth. see Carr, Janet.

Shepherd, Stella. Like a Mantle, the Sea. LC 73-85450. (Illus.). 184p. 1971. 9.50x (ISBN 0-8214-0133-5). Ohio U Pr.

Shepherd, W. & Zand, P. Energy Flow & Power Factor in Nonsinusoidal Circuits. LC 78-51684. (Illus.). 1979. 59.50 (ISBN 0-521-21990-6). Cambridge U Pr.

Shepherd, Walter. Let's Look at Insects. Date not set. price not set (ISBN 0-392-08023-0, SpS). Soccer.

Shepherd, William C. Symbolical Consciousness: A Commentary on Love's Body. LC 76-26582. (American Academy of Religion. Aids for the Study of Religion Ser.). 1976. pap. 6.00 (ISBN 0-89130-083-X, 010304). Scholars Pr Ca.

Shepherd, William G. The Economics of Industrial Organization. LC 78-6285. 1979. 19.95 (ISBN 0-13-231464-9). P-H.

--The Treatment of Market Power: Antitrust Regulation & Public Enterprise. 272p. 1975. 20.00x (ISBN 0-231-03773-2). Columbia U Pr.

Shepherd, William G. & Clair, Wilcox. Public Policies Toward Business. 6th ed. 1979. 19.95x (ISBN 0-256-02183-X). Irwin.

Shepherd, William G., ed. Public Enterprise: Economic Analysis of Theory & Practice. LC 75-41926. (Illus.). 256p. 1976. 18.95 (ISBN 0-669-00477-4). Lexington Bks.

--Public Policies Toward Business: Readings & Cases. rev ed. 1979. pap. 11.95 (ISBN 0-256-02236-4). Irwin.

Shepherd, William R. Shepherd's Historical Atlas. 9th rev. ed. (Illus.). (gr. 7 up). 1976. 28.50x (ISBN 0-06-013846-7). B&N.

--Shepherd's Historical Atlas. 9th ed. (Illus.). 368p. (YA) 1973. Repr. of 1964 ed. 22.50x (ISBN 0-06-013846-7, HarpT). Har-Row.

Shepherd, William R see Johnson, Allen & Nevins, Allan.

Shepherd-Moore, Marie. To Strive to Search, to Find. 1976. 6.50 o.p. (ISBN 0-682-48568-3). Exposition.

Shepherd-Thorn, E. R. see Bowen, D. Q.

Sheppard, David I. & Glickman, Albert S. Police Careers: Constructing Career Paths for Tomorrow's Police Force. (Illus.). 164p. 1973. 11.75 (ISBN 0-398-02811-7). C C Thomas.

Sheppard, Donna C. Williamsburg Christmas. LC 80-7487. (Illus.). 84p. (Orig.). 1980. 9.95 (ISBN 0-87935-053-9); pap. 4.95 (ISBN 0-87935-054-7). Williamsburg.

Sheppard, F. H., ed. Grosvenor Estate in Mayfair: The Buildings, Pt. 2. (Survey of London Ser.: Vol. 40). 429p. 1980. text ed. 143.00x (ISBN 0-485-48240-1, Athlone Pr). Humanities.

Sheppard, Francis. London, Eighteen Eight Eighteen Seventy: The Infernal Wen. (History of London Series). (Illus.). 1971. 24.50x (ISBN 0-520-01847-8). U of Cal Pr.

Sheppard, Georgie M., jt. auth. see Liebers, Arthur.

Sheppard, Harold L. & Herrick, Neal Q. Where Have All the Robots Gone? Worker Dissatisfaction in the Seventies. LC 72-77285. 1972. 7.95 (ISBN 0-02-928600-X); pap. text ed. 3.95 (ISBN 0-02-928590-9). Free Pr.

Sheppard, Harold L & Rix, Sara E. The Graying of Working America: The Coming Crisis in Retirement-Age Policy. LC 77-2528. (Illus.). 1979. pap. text ed. 6.95 (ISBN 0-02-928720-0). Free Pr.

Sheppard, Judith, jt. ed. see Sheppard, Roger.

Sheppard, K. The Treatment of Cats by Homoeopathy. 62p. 1960. 3.50x (ISBN 0-8464-1055-9). Beekman Pubs.

--The Treatment of Dogs by Homoeopathy. 1980. 4.00 (ISBN 0-8464-1056-7). Beekman Pubs.

Sheppard, Leslie & Axelrod, R. Herbert. Paganini. (Illus.). 704p. 1980. 20.00 (ISBN 0-87666-618-7, Z-28). Paganiniana Pubns.

Sheppard, P. A. see Landsberg, H. E.

Sheppard, P. M., ed. Practical Genetics. LC 73-9709. 337p. 1973. text ed. 44.95 (ISBN 0-470-78360-5). Halsted Pr.

Sheppard, Philip M. Natural Selection & Heredity. 4th ed. 1975. text ed. 10.75x (ISBN 0-09-036801-0, Hutchinson U Lib); pap. text ed. 7.50x (ISBN 0-09-036802-9). Humanities.

Sheppard, Roger & Sheppard, Judith, eds. International Directory of Book Collectors 1978-1980: A Directory of Book Collectors in Britain, America & the Rest of the World. 2nd ed. cancelled o.s.i. (ISBN 0-904929-18-3, Pub. by Trigon Press England). Bowker.

Sheppard, Sally. The First Book of Brazil. rev. ed. (First Bks). (Illus.). 72p. (gr. 4-7). 1972. PLB 4.90 o.p. (ISBN 0-531-00488-0). Watts.

--Indians of the Eastern Woodlands. LC 74-13609. (Illus.). 96p. (gr. 5 up). 1975. PLB 3.90 o.p. (ISBN 0-531-00825-8). Watts.

--Indians of the Plains. (First Bks. Ser.). (Illus.). 72p. (gr. 5 up). 1976. PLB 6.45 (ISBN 0-531-00847-9). Watts.

Sheppard, Trish, jt. auth. see Finlay, Iain.

Sheppard, William. Of Corporations, Fraternities, & Guilds, or a Discourse Wherein the Learning of the Law Touching Bodies-Politique Is Unfolded...with Forms & Presidents of Charters of Corporations. Berkowitz, David & Thorne, Samuel, eds. LC 77-86635. (Classics of English Legal History in the Modern Era Ser.: Vol. 88). 1979. Repr. of 1659 ed. lib. bdg. 55.00 (ISBN 0-8240-3075-3). Garland Pub.

Sheppard, William A. Organic Syntheses. LC 21-17747. (Organic Syntheses Ser.: Vol. 58). 1978. 16.95 (ISBN 0-471-04739-2, Pub. by Wiley-Interscience). Wiley.

Shepperd, M. J., jt. auth. see Minski, L.

Sheppherd, J. L., tr. see Maissin, Eugene.

Sher, Hanan, ed. Facts About Israel. 2nd ed. LC 55-19995. (Illus.). 232p. (Orig.). 1978. pap. 5.00x (ISBN 0-8002-2247-4). Intl Pubns Serv.

Sher, Jonathan P., ed. Rural Education in Urbanized Nations: Issues & Innovations. (Special Studies in Education). 425p. 1981. lib. bdg. 27.50x (ISBN 0-89158-964-3). Westview.

Sher, Jonathon P. Education in Rural America: A Reassessment of Conventional Wisdom. LC 76-57184. 1977. lib. bdg. 26.00x (ISBN 0-89158-201-0); pap. text ed. 10.50x (ISBN 0-89158-203-7). Westview.

Sher, Lisa, jt. ed. see Miller, Thomas E.

Sher, R., jt. ed. see Williams, M. M.

Sher, Richard B. Church, University, Enlightenment: The Moderate Literati of Edinburgh, 1720-1793. 1980. text ed. write for info. (ISBN 0-391-01208-8). Humanities.

Sher, Richard K., jt. auth. see Colburn, David R.

Shera, Jesse H. An Introduction to Library Science: Basic Elements of Library Services. LC 76-21332. (Library Science Text Ser.). 1976. lib. bdg. 13.50x (ISBN 0-87287-173-8). Libs Unl.

Sherali, H. D. & Shetty, C. M. Optimization with Disjunctive Constraints. (Lecture Notes in Economics & Mathematical Systems: Vol. 181). (Illus.). 156p. 1980. pap. 15.00 (ISBN 0-387-10228-0). Springer-Verlag.

Sherar, Mariam G. Shipping Out. LC 72-78239. 1973. pap. 6.00x (ISBN 0-87033-173-6). Cornell Maritime.

Sherard, Ethel C. Double List Word Book. 306p. (Orig.). 1981. pap. 9.95 (ISBN 0-9605288-0-6). Gwethine Pub Co.

Sherard, James L., et al. Earth & Earth-Rock Dams: Engineering Problems of Design & Construction. LC 63-14068. 1963. 49.95 (ISBN 0-471-78547-4, Pub. by Wiley-Interscience). Wiley.

Sheraton, Mimi. From My Mother's Kitchen: Recipes & Reminiscences. LC 75-6360. (Illus.). 1979. 12.95 (ISBN 0-06-013846-7, HarpT). Har-Row.

--The New York Times Guide to Dining Out in New York. 352p. 1981. pap. 6.95 (ISBN 0-8129-0930-5). Times Bks.

Sheraton, Thomas. The Cabinet-Maker & Upholsterer's Drawing Book. (Illus.). 13.50 (ISBN 0-8446-4637-7). Peter Smith.

Sherbet, G. V., ed. Phenomenon of Control of Growth in Neoplastic & Differentiative Systems. (Illus.). xii, 184p. 1981. 58.75 (ISBN 3-8055-2305-X). S Karger.

Sherbinin, Michael de, ed. Nineteen Eighty-One World Refugee Survey. (Illus.). 64p. 1981. 5.00 (ISBN 0-936548-02-9). US Comm Refugees.

Sherbiny, Naiem A. Arab Oil: Impact on Arab Countries & Global Implications. Tessler, Mark A., ed. LC 75-19820. (Special Studies). (Illus.). 340p. 1976. text ed. 34.95 (ISBN 0-275-55810-X). Praeger.

Sherbon, Florence B. The Child: His Origin, Development & Care. 707p. 1980. Repr. of 1934 ed. lib. bdg. 50.00 (ISBN 0-89984-422-7). Century Bookbindery.

Sherbourne, Julia F. Toward Reading Comprehension. 2nd ed. 1977. pap. text ed. 9.95x (ISBN 0-669-91371-5). Heath.

Sherburn, George. Roehenstart: A Late Stuart Pretender. LC 60-8402. 1960. 7.50x o.s.i. (ISBN 0-226-75294-1). U of Chicago Pr.

Sherburn, George & Bond, Donald F. Literary History of England: The Restoration & Eighteenth Century 1660-1789. 2nd ed. LC 66-26100. 1967. pap. text ed. 14.95x (ISBN 0-89197-277-3). Irvington.

Sherburne, Zoa. Almost April. (gr. 7 up). 1956. PLB 7.44 (ISBN 0-688-31013-3). Morrow.

--Girl in the Mirror. (gr. 7 up). 1966. 7.75 (ISBN 0-688-21344-8). Morrow.

--The Girl Who Knew Tomorrow. (gr. 7 up). 1970. PLB 7.44 (ISBN 0-688-31347-7). Morrow.

--Jennifer. (gr. 7 up). 1959. 8.25 (ISBN 0-688-21744-3). Morrow.

--Leslie. 192p. (gr. 7 up). 1972. 6.25 o.p. (ISBN 0-688-21814-8); PLB 6.96 (ISBN 0-688-31814-2). Morrow.

--Too Bad About the Haines Girl. (gr. 9-12). 1967. PLB 7.44 (ISBN 0-688-31646-8); pap. 2.95 (ISBN 0-688-26646-0). Morrow.

--Why Have the Birds Stopped Singing? 192p. (gr. 7 up). 1974. PLB 6.96 (ISBN 0-688-30111-8). Morrow.

Shercliff, J. A. Vector Fields. LC 76-8153. (Illus.). 1977. 63.50 (ISBN 0-521-21306-1); pap. 12.95x (ISBN 0-521-29092-9). Cambridge U Pr.

Shere, Waris. Miracles of Survival: Canada & French Canada. 160p. 1981. 7.50 (ISBN 0-682-49730-4). Exposition.

Sherer, George see Bottiglia, William F.

Shereshefsky, Pauline M. & Yarrow, Leon J. Psychological Aspects of a First Pregnancy & Early Postnatal Adaptation. LC 73-87877. 350p. 1973. 20.50 (ISBN 0-911216-65-0). Raven.

Sheridan, Adora. The Signet Ring. 1979. pap. 1.75 o.p. (ISBN 0-345-27785-6). Ballantine.

Sheridan, Alan, tr. see Green, Andre.

Sheridan, Anne-Marie. Far off Rhapsony. LC 76-54898. 1977. 8.95 (ISBN 0-671-22601-0). S&S.

Sheridan, Dave, jt. auth. see Shelton, Gilbert.

Sheridan, Frances see Boswell, James.

Sheridan, James E. China in Disintegration: The Republican Era in Chinese History, 1912-1949. LC 74-28940. (Transformation of Modern China Ser.). 1977. 15.95 (ISBN 0-02-928610-7); pap. text ed. 7.95 (ISBN 0-02-928650-6). Free Pr.

Sheridan, James F. Psyche: Lectures on Psychology & Philosophy. LC 79-66579. 1979. pap. text ed. 8.75 (ISBN 0-8191-0843-X). U Pr of Amer.

Sheridan, James F., Jr. Once More from the Middle: A Philosophical Anthropology. LC 72-85543. ix, 157p. 1973. 9.50x (ISBN 0-8214-0108-4). Ohio U Pr.

Sheridan, Jane. Damaris. 1980. pap. 2.75 (ISBN 0-425-04482-3). Berkley Pub.

--My Lady Hoyden. 378p. 1981. 13.95 (ISBN 0-312-55776-0). St Martin.

Sheridan, M. D. Children's Developmental Progress from Birth to Five Years: The Stycar Sequences. (General Ser). (Illus.). 72p. 1975. pap. text ed. 6.25x (ISBN 0-85633-018-3, NFER). Humanities.

Sheridan, Mary. Spontaneous Play in Early Childhood. (Orig.). 1977. pap. text ed. 4.25x (ISBN 0-85633-123-6, NFER). Humanities.

Sheridan, Mary S. To Michael with Love. (YA) 1977. 4.95 o.p. (ISBN 0-685-74271-7, Avalon). Bouregy.

Sheridan, Michael. The Fifth Season. LC 78-7507. 52p. 1978. 7.50 (ISBN 0-8214-0405-9); pap. 4.00 (ISBN 0-8214-0407-5). Ohio U Pr.

Sheridan, P. H. Outline Descriptions of the Posts in the Military Division of the Missouri. (Illus.). 1972. Repr. of 1182 ed. 10.95 o.p. (ISBN 0-88342-004-X). Old Army.

Sheridan, Richard B. Letters of Richard Brinsley Sheridan, 3 Vols. Price, Cecil, ed. 1966. 79.00x (ISBN 0-19-811438-9). Oxford U Pr.

--Sheridan: Six Plays. Kronenberger, Louis, ed. & intro. by. Incl. The Rivals; St. Patrick's Day; The Duenna; A Trip to Scarborough; The School for Scandal; The Critic. 359p. (Orig.). 1957. pap. 4.95 (ISBN 0-8090-0705-3, Mermaid). Hill & Wang.

Sheridan, T. Mindful Militants. LC 74-17503. 352p. 1976. 35.50 (ISBN 0-521-20680-4). Cambridge U Pr.

Sheridan, T. J. Seven Chinese Stories. (Oxford Progressive English Readers Ser.). (Illus.). 1975. pap. 2.95x (ISBN 0-19-638230-0). Oxford U Pr.

Sheridan-Smith, A. M., tr. see Foucault, Michel.

Sherif, Muzafer & Hovland, Carl I. Social Judgment: Assimilation & Contrast Effects in Communication & Attitude Change. LC 80-21767. (Yale Studies in Attitude & Communication: Vol. 4). xii, 218p. 1981. Repr. of 1961 ed. lib. bdg. 25.00x (ISBN 0-313-22438-2, SHSO). Greenwood.

Sheriff, D. W., jt. auth. see Meidner, Hans.

Sherington, Geoffrey. Australia's Immigrants. (Australian Experience Ser.). 216p. 1981. text ed. 16.95x (ISBN 0-86861-010-0, 2511); pap. text ed. 9.95x (ISBN 0-86861-018-6, 2512). Allen Unwin.

Sherk, Bill. More Brave New Words. LC 80-1729. (Illus.). 240p. 1981. pap. 6.95 (ISBN 0-385-17250-8). Doubleday.

Sherlock, jt. auth. see Smith.

Sherlock, Basil J. & Morris, Richard T. Becoming a Dentist: A Longitudinal Study of Dental Students. (Illus.). 152p. 1972. text ed. 12.75 (ISBN 0-398-02411-1). C C Thomas.

Sherlock, F. E. Home Carpentry. (Illus.). 1980. 14.50 (ISBN 0-7207-1243-2, Pub. by Michael Joseph). Merrimack Bk Serv.

--Machine Woodworking Technology for Hand Woodworkers. (Illus.). 222p. 1975. pap. 16.50x (ISBN 0-408-00113-5). Transatlantic.

Sherlock, Philip K. Anansi, the Spider Man. LC 54-5619. (Illus.). (gr. 3-7). 1954. 9.95 (ISBN 0-690-08905-8, TYC-J). T Y Crowell.

Sherlock, Thomas. The Tryal of the Witnesses of the Resurrection of Jesus, 1973 & the Use & Extent of Prophecy, 1728. Wellek, Rene, ed. LC 75-25131. (British Philosophers & Theologians of the 17th & 18th Centuries Ser.). 1978. lib. bdg. 42.00 (ISBN 0-8240-1761-7). Garland Pub.

Sherma, Joseph, jt. ed. see Zweig, Gunter.

Sherman. The Babysitter's Guide. (Illus.). (gr. 7-12). 1980. pap. 1.25 (ISBN 0-590-31342-8, Schol Pap). Schol Bk Serv.

Sherman, jt. auth. see Libow, Leslie S.

Sherman, A. J. Island Refuge: Britain & Refugees from the Third Reich 1933-1939. 1974. 20.00x (ISBN 0-520-02595-4). U of Cal Pr.

Sherman, A. J., jt. auth. see Rosenbaum, E.

Sherman, Alan & Sherman, Sharon J. The Elements of Life: Approach to Chemistry for the Health Sciences. (Illus.). 1980. text ed. 19.95 (ISBN 0-13-266130-6); lab. man. 8.95 (ISBN 0-13-266148-9). P-H.

Sherman, Alan, et al. Basic Concepts of Chemistry. 2nd ed. LC 79-88447. (Illus.). 1980. text ed. 18.25 (ISBN 0-395-28153-9); instrs' manual 1.00 (ISBN 0-395-28154-7); study guide 6.25 (ISBN 0-395-28702-2); lab experiments 9.50 (ISBN 0-395-28155-5). HM.

Sherman, B. Pilot's Radio Communications Manual. 1977. pap. 6.95 (ISBN 0-911721-26-6, Pub. by Mease Assocs). Aviation.

Sherman, Barbara H., jt. auth. see Sherman, James E.

Sherman, Barrie, jt. auth. see Jenkins, Clive.

Sherman, Barry, jt. auth. see Jenkins, Clive.

Sherman, Charles E., jt. auth. see Johnson, R. Charles.

Sherman, Charles L., ed. see Locke, John.

Sherman, Claire R. & Holcomb, Adele M., eds. Women As Interpreters of the Visual Arts, 1820-1979. LC 80-785. (Contributions in Women's Studies: No. 18). (Illus.). 512p. 1981. lib. bdg. 35.00 (ISBN 0-313-22056-5, SWS/). Greenwood.

Sherman, Dan. Dynasty of Spies. LC 79-54012. 1980. 11.95 (ISBN 0-87795-255-8). Arbor Hse.

--The Mole. 1978. pap. 1.75 o.p. (ISBN 0-449-23531-9, Crest). Fawcett.

--Riddle. 1978. pap. 1.95 o.p. (ISBN 0-449-23765-6, Crest). Fawcett.

Sherman, Dorothy, jt. ed. see Spriestersbach, C.

Sherman, Edmund A., et al. Service to Children in Their Own Homes: Its Nature & Outcome. LC 72-92326. 1973. pap. text ed. 2.25 o.p. (ISBN 0-87868-106-X). Child Welfare.

Sherman, Eileen. The Celtic Heart. LC 80-50889. 328p. (YA) 1980. 12.95 (ISBN 0-9604382-0-3); pap. 4.00. Resolute Pr.

Sherman, Ernest, jt. auth. see Gill, Richard.

Sherman, Florence J. How to Raise & Train a West Highland White Terrier. (Orig.). pap. 2.00 (ISBN 0-87666-408-7, DS1133). TFH Pubns.

Sherman, Franklin & Lehman, Helmut T., eds. Luther's Works: The Christian in Society IV, Vol. 47. LC 55-9893. 1971. 8.00 (ISBN 0-8006-0347-8, 1-347). Fortress.

Sherman, Franklin, ed. see Elert, Werner.

Sherman, Franklin, ed. see Moberly, Walter.

Sherman, Franklin, ed. see Temple, William.

Sherman, George, jt. auth. see Carey, Mary.

Sherman, George B., jt. auth. see Duffy, Gerald G.

Sherman, H. J. Sociology: Traditional & Radical Perspectives. 1981. pap. text ed. 15.70 (ISBN 0-06-318190-8, Pub. by Har-Row Ltd Eng). Har-Row.

Sherman, H. J., jt. auth. see Edginton, J. K.

Sherman, Harold. How to Picture What You Want. 1978. pap. 1.75 o.p. (ISBN 0-449-14003-2, GM). Fawcett.

--How to Take Yourself Apart & Put Yourself Together Again. 1979. pap. 1.75 o.p. (ISBN 0-449-14182-9, GM). Fawcett.

--Know Your Own Mind. 1978. pap. 1.50 o.p. (ISBN 0-449-13932-8, GM). Fawcett.

--The New TNT - Miraculous Power Within You! rev. ed. 1979. Repr. of 1966 ed. 3.95 (ISBN 0-346-12383-6). Cornerstone.

--You Live After Death. 1949. 7.95 (ISBN 0-910140-16-2). Anthony.

Sherman, Harold & Pollard, Al. Extra Success Potential: The Art of Out-Thinking & Out-Sensing Others in Business & Everyday Life. 200p. 1981. pap. 5.95 (ISBN 0-13-298109-2). P-H.

Sherman, Helene. Common Elements in New Mathematics Programs: Their Origins & Evolution. LC 72-75560. (Illus.). 1972. pap. text ed. 7.25x (ISBN 0-8077-2151-4). Tchrs Coll.

Sherman, Howard. Estanflacion. (Span.). 1980. pap. text ed. 7.60 (ISBN 0-06-317152-X, Pub. by HarLA Mexico). Har-Row.

Sherman, Irwin W. & Sherman, Vilia G. Biology: A Human Approach. 2nd ed. (Illus.). 636p. 1979. text ed. 18.95 o.p. (ISBN 0-19-502439-7). Oxford U Pr.

Sherman, Jacques L., Jr. & Fields, Sylvia K., eds. Guide to Patient Evaluation. 3rd ed. LC 78-50128. 1978. 17.50 (ISBN 0-87488-985-5); pap. 12.75. Med Exam.

Sherman, James E. & Sherman, Barbara H. Ghost Towns & Mining Camps of New Mexico. LC 72-9525. (Illus.). 270p. 1975. 13.95 (ISBN 0-8061-1066-X); pap. 6.95x (ISBN 0-8061-1106-2). U of Okla Pr.

Sherman, James R. How to Overcome a Bad Back. LC 79-90870. (Illus., Orig.). 1980. pap. 5.95 (ISBN 0-935538-00-3). Pathway Bks.

--Stop Procrastinating--Do It! LC 80-82893. (Orig.). 1981. pap. 1.75 (ISBN 0-935538-01-1). Pathway Bks.

Sherman, Jane. Soaring: The Diary & Letters of a Denishawn Dancer in the Far East, 1925-1926. LC 75-34445. (Illus.). 1976. 16.95 (ISBN 0-8195-4093-5, Pub. by Wesleyan U Pr). Columbia U Pr.

Sherman, Jean, tr. see Nin, Anais.

Sherman, Jerry, jt. auth. see Hertz, Eric.

Sherman, Jory. Blood Justice. (Gunn Ser.: No. 4). 256p. (Orig.). 1980. pap. 1.95 (ISBN 0-89083-670-1). Zebra.

--Death's-Head Trail. (Gunn Ser.: No. 3). 240p. (Orig.). 1980. pap. 1.95 (ISBN 0-89083-648-5). Zebra.

--House of Scorpions. (Chill Ser.: No. 6). 192p. 1980. pap. 1.95 (ISBN 0-523-40699-1). Pinnacle Bks.

--Winter Hell. (Gunn Ser.: No. 5). 256p. (Orig.). 1981. pap. 1.95 (ISBN 0-89083-708-2). Zebra.

Sherman, Julia A. On the Psychology of Woman: A Survey of Empirical Studies. 320p. 1975. 15.50 (ISBN 0-398-01744-1); pap. 9.75 (ISBN 0-398-02762-5). C C Thomas.

Sherman, Lawrence W. Scandal & Reform: Controlling Police Corruption. LC 77-79236. 1978. 17.50x (ISBN 0-520-03523-2). U of Cal Pr.

Sherman, Lawrence W. & Lambert, Richard D., eds. Police & Violence. (The Annals of the American Academy of Political & Social Science Ser.: No. 452). 1980. 7.00 (ISBN 0-87761-256-0); pap. text ed. 6.00 (ISBN 0-87761-257-9). Am Acad Pol Soc Sci.

Sherman, Leona F. Ann Radcliffe & the Gothic Romance: A Psychoanalytic Approach. Varma, Devendra P., ed. LC 79-8480. (Gothic Studies & Dissertations Ser.). 1980. lib. bdg. 22.00x (ISBN 0-405-12679-4). Arno.

Sherman, Lucille. Lady on the Run. LC 80-83999. 1981. pap. 4.95 (ISBN 0-89081-278-0). Harvest Hse.

Sherman, Mark. Personality: Inquiry & Application. LC 78-13540. (Pergamon General Psychology Ser.: Vol. 74). 560p. 1979. 18.50 (ISBN 0-08-019585-7). Pergamon.

Sherman, P. Industrial Rheology. 1970. 58.50 o.s.i. (ISBN 0-12-639950-6). Acad Pr.

Sherman, Patricia J. Sleep off the Highway. (Orig.). 1979. pap. 1.95 (ISBN 0-686-68910-0). Manor Bks.

Sherman, Ralph W., jt. auth. see Hungate, Lois A.

Sherman, Richard B. The Republican Party & Black America: From McKinley to Hoover, 1896-1933. LC 72-96714. 1973. 12.95x (ISBN 0-8139-0467-6). U Pr of Va.

Sherman, Robert M. & Sherman, Ruth W. Vital Records of Marshfield, Massachusetts to the Year 1850. LC 73-85851. 491p. 1969. Repr. of 1969 ed. 13.00x (ISBN 0-930272-04-8). RI Mayflower.

--Vital Records of Yarmouth, Mass. to Eighteen Fifty, 2 vols. LC 79-189435. 1975. Set. 20.00x (ISBN 0-930272-00-5). RI Mayflower.

Sherman, Roger. The Shermans: A Sketch of Family History & a Genealogical Record, 1570-1890 with Some Account of Families Intermarried. 1946. pap. 24.50x (ISBN 0-685-89781-8). Elliots Bks.

Sherman, Ruth W., jt. auth. see Sherman, Robert M.

Sherman, Sharon J., jt. auth. see Sherman, Alan.

Sherman, Steve. A B C's of Library Promotion. 2nd ed. LC 79-24232. 252p. 1980. 12.00 (ISBN 0-8108-1274-6). Scarecrow.

--Home Heating with Coal. (Illus.). 192p. 1980. pap. 8.95 (ISBN 0-8117-2081-0). Stackpole.

Sherman, Steve, jt. auth. see Older, Julia.

Sherman, Susan. With Anger-with Love. pap. 3.50 (ISBN 0-913142-05-0). Out & Out.

Sherman, T. D. O & M in Local Government. 1969. 22.00 (ISBN 0-08-013317-7); pap. 11.25 (ISBN 0-08-013309-6). Pergamon.

Sherman, Theodore A. & Johnson, Simon. Modern Technical Writing. 3rd ed. (Illus.). 480p. 1975. 15.95 (ISBN 0-13-598763-6). P-H.

Sherman, Vilia G., jt. auth. see Sherman, Irwin W.

Sherman, William L., jt. auth. see Meyer, Michael C.

Shern, Mary. Real Estate: A Woman's World. 1979. 10.95 (ISBN 0-88462-373-4). Real Estate Ed Co.

Shernington, Kathleen B., jt. auth. see Gaman, Pamela D.

Sheron, Carole. The Rise & Fall of Superwoman. LC 79-26704. (Orion Ser.). 96p. 1980. pap. 2.50 (ISBN 0-8127-1270-6). Southern Pub.

Sheroner, Charles M., ed. see Rousseau, Jean J.

Sherover, Charles M., ed. The Human Experience of Time: The Development of Its Philosophic Meaning. LC 74-21659. 1975. 25.00x (ISBN 0-8147-7759-7); pap. 12.50x (ISBN 0-8147-7766-X). NYU Pr.

Sherr, Paul. Short Story & the Oral Tradition. LC 70-101314. 1970. pap. text ed. 6.95x o.p. (ISBN 0-87835-002-0). Boyd & Fraser.

Sherrard, D. G. To Antarctica with the Royal Navy. LC 79-67138. 122p. 1980. 7.95 (ISBN 0-533-04448-0). Vantage.

Sherrard, Philip. Byzantium. LC 66-28334. (Great Ages of Man Ser). (Illus.). (gr. 6 up). 1966. PLB 11.97 (ISBN 0-8094-0372-2, Pub. by Time-Life). Silver.

Sherrard-Smith, Barbara, jt. auth. see Moss, Elaine.

Sherratt & Urry. International Construction. 160p. 1980. 38.00 (ISBN 0-86095-847-7, Construction Pr). Longman.

Sherratt, A. F., jt. auth. see Orchard, W. R.

Sherratt, A. F., ed. Energy Conservation & Energy Management in Buildings. (Illus.). 1976. text ed. 74.50x (ISBN 0-85334-684-4, Pub. by Applied Science). Burgess-Intl Ideas.

--Integrated Environment in Building Design. LC 74-22250. 281p. 1975. 44.95 (ISBN 0-470-78575-6). Halsted Pr.

Sherratt, A. F., jt. ed. see Croome, D. J.

Sherrell, Carl. Arcane. (Orig.). 1978. pap. 1.95 o.s.i. (ISBN 0-515-04466-0). Jove Pubns.

--Raum. 1977. pap. 1.50 o.p. (ISBN 0-380-01646-X, 33043). Avon.

Sherrer, jt. auth. see Nadel.

Sherrer, Arthur, jt. auth. see Nadel, Max.

Sherrer, Arthur, Jr., jt. auth. see Nadel, Max.

Sherrick, Joseph C., jt. auth. see Elias, H.

Sherril, John L. They Speak with Other Tongues. 1976. pap. 1.50 (ISBN 0-685-84387-4). Jove Pubns.

Sherrill, Anne H., jt. auth. see Kushner, Howard I.

Sherrill, Claudine. Adapted Physical Education & Recreation: A Multidisciplinary Approach. 2nd ed. 1981. 15.95x (ISBN 0-697-07176-6). Wm C Brown.

Sherrill, Elizabeth, jt. auth. see Shakarian, Demos.

Sherrill, John L. My Friend the Bible. 1978. 5.95 (ISBN 0-912376-37-6). Chosen Bks Pub.

Sherrill, Rowland A. The Prophetic Melville. LC 78-20436. 227p. 1979. 17.00x (ISBN 0-8203-0455-7). U of Ga Pr.

Sherrill, W. A. & Chu, W. K. An Anthology of I Ching. 1978. 22.00 (ISBN 0-7100-8590-7). Routledge & Kegan.

Sherring, M. A. Benares: The Sacred City of the Hindus. LC 75-906423. 1975. Repr. 17.00x o.p. (ISBN 0-88386-668-4). South Asia Bks.

Sherrington, Charles S. Man on His Nature. 1951. 39.95 (ISBN 0-521-06436-8); pap. 11.95x (ISBN 0-521-09203-5). Cambridge U Pr.

Sherrington, K. B., jt. auth. see Gaman, P. M.

Sherrington, P. J. & Oliver, R. Granulation: Monographs in Powder Science & Technology. 1980. write for info. (ISBN 0-85501-177-7). Heyden.

Sherrington, R. J. Three Novels by Flaubert: A Study of Techniques. 1970. 29.99x (ISBN 0-19-815398-8). Oxford U Pr.

Sherrod, H. Floyd, ed. Environment Law Review: Annual. Incl. 1970 (ISBN 0-87632-042-6); 1971 (ISBN 0-87632-048-5); 1972 (ISBN 0-87632-082-5); 1973 (ISBN 0-87632-090-6); 1974 (ISBN 0-87632-115-5). 39.50 ea. o.p. Boardman.

Sherrod, Lonnie R., jt. ed. see Lamb, Michael E.

Sherrod, Robert. History of Marine Corps Aviation in World War Two. 496p. 1980. Repr. 16.95 (ISBN 0-89141-111-9). Presidio Pr.

--Tarawa: The Story of a Battle. LC 73-84464. (Illus.). 207p. 1973. 9.00 (ISBN 0-686-05675-2); ltd. presentation vol. 75.00 (ISBN 0-686-05676-0); pap. 1.95 (ISBN 0-686-05677-9). Adm Nimitz Foun.

Sherron, R. H. & Lumsden, D. B., eds. Introduction to Educational Gerontology. new ed. LC 78-13292. (Illus.). 1978. pap. text ed. 17.00 (ISBN 0-89116-101-5). Hemisphere Pub.

Sherry, Norman. Charlotte & Emily Bronte. LC 73-101773. (Literary Critiques Ser.). (Illus., Orig.). 1970. lib. bdg. 4.95 o.p. (ISBN 0-668-02184-5). Arco.

--Conrad & His World. LC 77-77381. (Illus.). 1977. 9.95 o.p. (ISBN 0-684-15300-9, ScribT). Scribner.

--Conrad's Eastern World. 1966. 49.50 (ISBN 0-521-06437-6); pap. 14.95x (ISBN 0-521-29120-8). Cambridge U Pr.

--Conrad's Western World. LC 70-130910. (Illus.). 1971. 49.50 (ISBN 0-521-07972-1). Cambridge U Pr.

Sherry, Norman, ed. Conrad: The Critical Heritage. (The Critical Heritage Ser.). 1973. 34.00x (ISBN 0-7100-7388-7). Routledge & Kegan.

--Joseph Conrad: A Commemoration Papers from 1974 International Conference on Conrad. LC 76-24069. 1979. Repr. of 1976 ed. text ed. 18.50x (ISBN 0-06-496233-4). B&N.

Sherry, Patrick. Religion, Truth & Language-Games. LC 75-41579. (Library of Philosophy & Religion Ser.). 234p. 1977. text ed. 18.50x (ISBN 0-06-496236-9). B&N.

Sherry, Pearl A., jt. auth. see Vidaver, Doris.

Sherry, Richard J., tr. see Rowe, Nicholas.

Sherster, Joyce. OJT File Clerk Resource Materials. 2nd ed. (Gregg Office Job Training Program). (Illus.). 104p. (gr. 11-12). soft-cover 4.80 (ISBN 0-07-056640-2, G). McGraw.

Shertzer, Bruce. Career Planning: Freedom to Choose. 2nd ed. LC 80-81846. (Illus.). 416p. 1981. pap. text ed. 9.25 (ISBN 0-395-29738-9); 0.80 (ISBN 0-395-29739-7). HM.

Shertzer, Bruce & Linden, James D. Fundamentals of Individual Appraisal: Assessment Techniques for Counselors. LC 78-69542. (Illus.). 1978. text ed. 18.95 (ISBN 0-395-26536-3); inst. manual 0.60 (ISBN 0-395-26537-1). HM.

Shertzer, Bruce & Stone, Shelley C. Fundamentals of Guidance. 4th ed. LC 80-81917. (Illus.). 576p. 1981. text ed. 18.95 (ISBN 0-395-29712-5); write for info. instr's manual (ISBN 0-395-29713-3). HM.

Shertzer, Bruce, jt. auth. see Peters, Herman J.

Shertzer, Bruce, jt. auth. see Stone, Shelley C.

Shertzer, Bruce E. & Stone, Shelley C. Fundamentals of Counseling. 2nd ed. 544p. 1974. text ed. 17.75 o.p. (ISBN 0-395-17580-1); instructors' manual pap. 2.00 o.p. (ISBN 0-395-17803-7). HM.

--Fundamentals of Counseling. 3rd ed. LC 79-88448. (Illus.). 1980. text ed. 17.95 (ISBN 0-395-28580-1); instrs'. manual 1.00 (ISBN 0-395-28579-8). HM.

--Fundamentals of Guidance. 3rd ed. LC 75-31026. (Illus.). 576p. 1976. text ed. 18.95 (ISBN 0-395-20621-9); inst. manual 2.00 (ISBN 0-395-20614-6). HM.

Shervatov, V. G. Hyperbolic Functions. (Topics in Mathematics Ser). 1963. pap. text ed. 2.95x o.p. (ISBN 0-669-19620-7). Heath.

Sherwell-Cooper, W. E. Vegetables: Growing & Cooking the Natural Way. 1975. pap. 8.95 o.p. (ISBN 0-04-641027-9). Allen Unwin.

Sherwin, Byron. Abraham Joshua Herschel. LC 78-71051. (Makers of Contemporary Theology Ser.). 1979. pap. 3.45 (ISBN 0-8042-0466-7). John Knox.

Sherwin, E. & Weston, G. J. Chemistry of the Non-Metallic Elements. 1966. 15.00 (ISBN 0-08-011296-X); pap. 7.00 (ISBN 0-08-011295-1). Pergamon.

Sherwin, J. Stephen. A Word Index to Walden, Turth Textual Notes. LC 80-2517. 1981. Repr. of 1960 ed. 24.50 (ISBN 0-404-19065-0). AMS Pr.

Sherwin, Keith. To Fly Like a Bird: The Story of Man-Powered Aircraft. (Illus.). 1977. 8.95 o.p. (ISBN 0-8069-0114-4); lib. bdg. 8.29 o.p. (ISBN 0-8069-0115-2). Sterling.

Sherwin, Mary, jt. auth. see Patten, Marion.

Sherwin, W. K., et al, trs. see Mahaney, William E. & Sherwin, Walter K.

Sherwin, Walter K., jt. auth. see Mahaney, William E.

Sherwin, Walter K., jt. ed. see Mahaney, William E.

Sherwin, Walter K., tr. see Mahaney, William E. & Sherwin, Walter K.

Sherwin-White, A. N. The Roman Citizenship. 2nd ed. 496p. 1980. pap. 24.95x (ISBN 0-19-814847-X). Oxford U Pr.

Sherwin-White, Adrian N. Racial Prejudice in Imperial Rome. 1967. 19.95 (ISBN 0-521-06438-4). Cambridge U Pr.

Sherwood, Charles S., jt. auth. see Davis, Grant M.

Sherwood, Dennis H. Crystals, X-Rays, & Protein. LC 73-7098. 1976. 44.95 (ISBN 0-470-78590-X). Halsted Pr.

Sherwood, Don, jt. auth. see Newell, Gordon.

Sherwood, E. M., jt. auth. see Campbell, Ivor E.

Sherwood, Eva R., jt. ed. see Stern, Curt.

Sherwood, F., jt. auth. see Pfiffner, John M.

Sherwood, George, jt. auth. see Sherwood, Ruth.

Sherwood, Hugh C. How Corporate & Municipal Debt Is Rated: An Inside Look at Standard & Poor's Rating System. LC 76-12099. 1976. 29.95 (ISBN 0-471-78585-7, Pub by Wiley-Interscience). Wiley.

--How to Invest in Bonds. LC 74-81543. 192p. 1974. 7.95 o.s.i. (ISBN 0-8027-0466-2). Walker & Co.

Sherwood, John J., jt. ed. see Fromkin, Howard L.

Sherwood, John J., jt. ed. see Pasmore, William A.

Sherwood, John R. & Wagner, John C. Sources & Shapes of Power. LC 80-28125. (Into Our Third Century Ser.). (Orig.). 1981. pap. 3.95 (ISBN 0-687-39142-3). Abingdon.

Sherwood, M. C., jt. auth. see Roe, A. K.

Sherwood, Mary. The History of the Fairchild Family. LC 75-32157. (Classics of Children's Literature, 1621-1932: Vol. 22). 1976. Repr. of 1818 ed. lib. bdg. 38.00 (ISBN 0-8240-2271-8). Garland Pub.

Sherwood, Mary C., jt. auth. see Roe, Anne K.

Sherwood, Morgan, ed. The Cook Inlet Collection: Two Hundred Years of Selected Alaskan History. LC 74-24638. (Illus.). 222p. (Orig.). 1974. 8.95 o.p. (ISBN 0-88240-051-7); pap. 4.95 o.p. (ISBN 0-88240-044-4). Alaska Northwest.

Sherwood, Nancy & Timiras, Paola. A Stereotaxic Atlas of the Developing Rat Brain. LC 70-103674. (Illus., Fr. & Ger.). 1970. 45.00x (ISBN 0-520-01656-4). U of Cal Pr.

Sherwood, P. M. Vibrational Spectroscopy of Solids. LC 79-185566. (Cambridge Monographs in Physical Chemistry: No. 1). (Illus.). 256p. 1972. 45.00 (ISBN 0-521-08482-2). Cambridge U Pr.

Sherwood, Rae. The Psychodynamics of Race: Vicious & Benign Spirals. 608p. 1980. text ed. 55.00x (ISBN 0-391-01804-3). Humanities.

Sherwood, Ruth & Sherwood, George. Homes, Today & Tomorrow. rev. ed. (gr. 9-12). 1976. text ed. 15.92 (ISBN 0-87002-173-7); trans. master 13.32 (ISBN 0-685-65670-5); student guide 5.80 (ISBN 0-87002-127-3); trans. master 11.56 (ISBN 0-87002-151-6). Bennett IL.

Sherwood, S. Tendencies in American Economic Thought. Repr. of 1897 ed. pap. 7.00 (ISBN 0-384-55110-6). Johnson Repr.

Sherwood, Sylvia & Mor, Vincent. The Hidden Patient. Date not set. price not set prof. reference (ISBN 0-88410-722-1). Ballinger Pub. Postponed.

Sherwood, Sylvia, et al. An Alternative to Institutionalization: The Highland Heights Experiment. Kastenbaum, Robert & Barber, Theodore, eds. (Cushing Hospital Ser. on Aging). 1981. write for info. (ISBN 0-88410-720-5). Ballinger Pub.

Sherwood, Valerie. Her Shining Splendor. (Orig.). 1980. pap. 2.75 (ISBN 0-446-85487-5). Warner Bks.

--These Golden Pleasures. (Orig.). 1977. pap. 2.75 (ISBN 0-446-95744-5). Warner Bks.

--This Loving Torment. (Orig.). 1977. pap. 2.75 (ISBN 0-446-95745-3). Warner Bks.

Sherwood, William & Cohen, Alan, eds. Transfusion Therapy in Infancy & Childhood: The Fetus, Infant, & Child. LC 80-80304. (Masson Monographs in Pediatrics). (Illus.). 232p. 1980. text ed. 34.50 (ISBN 0-89352-074-8). Masson Pub.

Shestack, Alan, jt. ed. see Marrow, James H.

Shestov, Lev. All Things Are Possible & Penultimate Words & Other Essays. LC 76-8303. xiii, 239p. 1977. 13.50x (ISBN 0-8214-0237-4). Ohio U Pr.

--Athens & Jerusalem. Martin, Bernard, tr. LC 66-18480. 447p. 1966. 16.00x o.s.i. (ISBN 0-8214-0022-3). Ohio U Pr.

--Dostoevsky, Tolstoy & Nietzsche. Martin, Bernard & Roberts, Spencer E., trs. LC 74-78504. xxx, 322p. 1969. 16.00x (ISBN 0-8214-0053-3). Ohio U Pr.

--In Job's Balances: On the Sources of the Eternal Truths. Coventry, Camilla & Macartney, C. A., trs. from Ger. LC 73-92902. l, 379p. (Eng.). 1975. 16.00x (ISBN 0-8214-0143-2). Ohio U Pr.

--Kierkegaard & the Existential Philosophy. Hewitt, Elinor, tr. LC 68-29656. vii, 314p. 1969. 16.00 (ISBN 0-8214-0060-6). Ohio U Pr.

--Potestas Clavium. Martin, Bernard, tr. LC 67-24282. 1968. 16.00 (ISBN 0-8214-0040-1). Ohio U Pr.

--Turgenev. 110p. (Rus.). 1981. 12.50 (ISBN 0-88233-504-9); pap. 4.00 (ISBN 0-88233-505-7). Ardis Pubs.

Shetelig, Hakon, jt. auth. see Brogger, W. W.

Sheth, Jagdish, ed. see Seibert, Joseph C.

Shetty, C. M., jt. auth. see Bazaraa, M. S.

Shetty, C. M., jt. auth. see Bazaraa, Mokhtar S.

Shetty, C. M., jt. auth. see Sherali, H. D.

Shetty, Y. Krishna, jt. auth. see Prasad, S. Benjamin.

Shevelov, George Y. & Holling, Fred, eds. Reader in the History of the Eastern Slavic Languages: Russian, Belorussian, Ukranian. (Columbia Slavic Studies). 1958. pap. 6.00x (ISBN 0-231-02273-5). Columbia U Pr.

Shevin, Jann, jt. auth. see Hutcheson, John D., Jr.

Shevitz, jt. auth. see Berman.

Shewan, Rodney see Stansky, Peter.

Shewan, Rodney, ed. see Ashbee, C. R.

Shewan, Rodney, ed. see Cobden-Sanderson, et al.

Shewan, Rodney, ed. see Cobden-Sanderson, T. J.

Shewan, Rodney, ed. see Crane, Walter.

Shewan, Rodney, ed. see Cust, M. M.

Shewan, Rodney, ed. see Day, Lewis F.

Shewan, Rodney, ed. see Day, Lewis F. & Buckle, Mary.

Shewan, Rodney, ed. see Dresser, Christopher.

Shewan, Rodney, ed. see Godwin, E. W.

Shewan, Rodney, ed. see Haweis, E.

Shewan, Rodney, ed. see Lethaby, et al.

Shewan, Rodney, ed. see Loftie, M. J., et al.

Shewan, Rodney, ed. see Loftie, W. J., et al.

Shewan, Rodney, ed. see Rational Dress Association.

Shewan, Rodney, ed. see Sedding, John.

Shewan, Rodney, jt. ed. see Stansky, Peter.

Shewan, Rodney, ed. see Sylvia's Home Help Series.

Shewan, Rodney, ed. see Wilde, Oscar.

Shewell-Cooper, W. E. Basic Book of Greenhouse Growing. (Illus.). 1978. 15.00 (ISBN 0-214-20499-5). Transatlantic.

--Complete Vegetable Grower. 1973. pap. 5.50 (ISBN 0-571-04797-1, Pub. by Faber & Faber). Merrimack Bk Serv.

--The Compost Fruit Grower. 1975. 13.95 (ISBN 0-7207-0757-9, Pub. by Michael Joseph). Merrimack Bk Serv.

Shewmake, Georgia M. Balcony of Evil. 192p. (YA) 1976. 5.95 (ISBN 0-685-62023-9, Avalon). Bouregy.

--The Curse of the Rebellars. 192p. (YA) 1975. 5.95 (ISBN 0-685-52654-2, Avalon). Bouregy.

--The Shadow of Dolores. (YA) 1978. 5.95 (ISBN 0-685-86413-8, Avalon). Bouregy.

Shewmaker, Stan. Tonga Christianity. 1971. pap. 3.45. William Carey Lib.

Shewring, Walter, tr. see Homer.

Shey, Thomas H. Danish Communes: An Analysis of Collective Families in Contemporary Danish & American Society. LC 78-60793. (Illus.). 1978. pap. text ed. 8.50 o.p. (ISBN 0-8191-0322-5). U Pr of Amer.

Shi, David. Matthew Josephson, Bourgeois Bohemiam. LC 80-24493. (Illus.). 328p. 1981. 19.95 (ISBN 0-300-02563-7). Yale U Pr.

Shibamoto, Takayuki, jt. auth. see Jennings, Walter.

Shibata, H. & Ariman, T., eds. Recent Advances in Lifeline Earthquake Engineering in Japan. (PVP: No. 43). 158p. 1980. 24.00 (H00170). ASME.

Shibata, Shingo. Lessons of the Vietnam War: Philosophical Considerations on the Vietnam Revolution. (Philosophical Currents Ser: No. 6). 229p. 1973. pap. text ed. 24.00x (ISBN 90-6032-016-6). Humanities.

Shibayama, Zenkei. Flower Does Not Talk: Zen Essays. LC 79-109494. (Illus.). 1970. pap. 6.75 (ISBN 0-8048-0884-8). C E Tuttle.

--Zen Comments on the Mumonkan. 1975. pap. 2.25 o.p. (ISBN 0-451-61403-8, ME1403, Ment). NAL.

Shibel, Elaine & Moser, Kenneth M. Respiratory Emergencies. LC 77-8139. (Illus.). 1977. pap. text ed. 24.50 (ISBN 0-8016-4583-2). Mosby.

Shibutani, Tamotsu. The Derelicts of Company K: A Sociological Study of Demoralization. LC 77-79237. 1978. 17.95 (ISBN 0-520-03524-0). U of Cal Pr.

--Improvised News: A Sociological Study of Rumor. (Orig.). 1966. pap. 6.50 (ISBN 0-672-60823-5). Bobbs.

--Improvised News: A Sociological Study of Rumor. LC 66-29399. 1966. 24.50x (ISBN 0-672-51148-7). Irvington.

--Society & Personality: An Interactionist Approach to Social Psychology. 1961. text ed. 19.95 (ISBN 0-13-820019-X). P-H.

Shichor, Y. The Middle East in China's Foreign Policy: 1949-1977. LC 78-58801. (International Studies). (Illus.). 1979. 29.95 (ISBN 0-521-22214-1). Cambridge U Pr.

Shick, Blair C. & Plotkin, Irving H. Torrens in the United States. 18.95 (ISBN 0-669-02666-2). Lexington Bks.

Shickel, Richard. Another I, Another You. 1979. pap. 2.25 o.p. (ISBN 0-345-28098-9). Ballantine.

Shideler, Ross. Voices Under the Ground: Themes & Images in the Early Poetry of Gunnar Ekelof. (U. C. Publ. in Modern Philology: Vol. 104). 1973. pap. 8.00x (ISBN 0-520-09415-8). U of Cal Pr.

Shideler, Ross, tr. see Enquist, Per Olov.

Shiefman, Vicky. M Is for Move. LC 80-23526. (Illus.). (ps-2). 1981. PLB 7.95 (ISBN 0-525-35905-2). Dutton.

Shieh, Francis. A Glimpse of Chinese Language: Peking's Language Reforms & the Teaching of Chinese in the U.S. pap. 6.50 (ISBN 0-686-09053-5, AD612722); microfiche 3.50 (ISBN 0-686-09054-3). Natl Tech Info.

Shieh, Francis, jt. auth. see Elliot, Jeffrey M.

Shieh, Paulinus S. & Inam-Ur-Rahman. Introduction to Thermonuclear Engineering. LC 80-13153. Date not set. text ed. cancelled o.p. (ISBN 0-88275-973-6). Krieger.

Shiel, M. P. The Purple Cloud. lib. bdg. 14.95x (ISBN 0-89966-228-5). Buccaneer Bks.

--Shapes in the Fire: London Eighteen Ninety-Five. Fletcher, Ian & Stokes, John, eds. LC 76-20072. (Decadent Consciousness Ser.). 1977. lib. bdg. 38.00 (ISBN 0-8240-2771-X). Garland Pub.

Shields, jt. auth. see O'Reilly, P H.

Shields, Ann T., jt. auth. see Scanlan, Michael.

Shields, Conal & Parris, Leslie. John Constable. (Tate Gallery: Little Art Book Ser.). (Illus.). 1977. pap. 1.95 (ISBN 0-8120-0860-X). Barron.

Shields, Currin V., ed. see Mill, James.

Shields, Currin V., ed. see Mill, John S.

Shields, Donald C., jt. auth. see Cragan, John F.

Shields, Edward D. see Melnick, Michael.

Shields, Gerald, jt. auth. see Robotham, John.

Shields, Harry, jt. auth. see Shields, Joan.

Shields, J. Adhesive Bonding. (Engineering Design Guides Ser.). (Illus.). 1974. pap. 9.95x (ISBN 0-19-859130-6). Oxford U Pr.

Shields, J. B. The Gifted Child. (Exploring Education Ser.). 1968. pap. text ed. 5.00x (ISBN 0-901225-42-8, NFER). Humanities.

Shields, J. H. To Handmake a Saddle. (Illus.). pap. 7.70 (ISBN 0-85131-222-5, Dist. by Sporting Book Center). J A Allen.

Shields, James, jt. auth. see Gottesman, Irving I.

Shields, James J. & Greer, Colin, eds. Foundations of Education: Dissenting Views. LC 73-16438. 208p. 1974. text ed. 11.50x (ISBN 0-471-78635-7). Wiley.

Shields, Joan & Shields, Harry. The Modern Dairy Goat. Date not set. 5.00 (ISBN 0-686-26683-8). Dairy Goat.

Shields, John P. Novel Experiments with Electricity. LC 78-122966. (Illus.). 1970. pap. 3.50 o.p. (ISBN 0-672-20794-X, 20794). Sams.

Shields, Joyce F. Make It: An Index to Projects & Materials. LC 74-17114. 1975. 18.50 (ISBN 0-8108-0772-6). Scarecrow.

Shields, Laurie. Displaced Homemakers: Organizing for a New Life. (McGraw-Hill Paperback Ser.). 256p. (Orig.). 1980. pap. 5.95 (ISBN 0-07-056802-2). McGraw.

Shields, Mary L. Sea Run. LC 80-52406. 352p. 1981. 11.95 (ISBN 0-87223-665-X). Seaview Bks.

Shields, Mike, tr. see Gotze, Hans.

Shields, Paul C. Elementary Linear Algebra. 3rd rev. ed. (Illus.). 1980. text ed. 17.95x (ISBN 0-87901-121-1). Worth.

Shields, Phyllis G. Guide to Flower Arranging. (Illus.). 1967. 4.00 o.p. (ISBN 0-8231-6017-3). Branford.

Shields, Steven L. No Greater Sacrifice. LC 80-83864. 250p. 1980. 6.95 (ISBN 0-88290-166-4, 1059). Horizon Utah.

Shields, Thomas W. Bronchial Carcinoma. (American Lectures in Surgery Ser.). (Illus.). 200p. 1974. text ed. 17.50 (ISBN 0-398-03095-2). C C Thomas.

Shiels, Frederick L. America, Okinawa, & Japan: Case Studies for Foreign Policy Theory. LC 79-5496. 1980. text ed. 18.50 (ISBN 0-8191-0893-6); pap. text ed. 11.25 (ISBN 0-8191-0894-4). U Pr of Amer.

--Tokyo & Washington: Dilemmas of a Mature Alliance. LC 79-3339. 1980. 20.50 (ISBN 0-669-03378-2). Lexington Bks.

Shiels, Larry, Jr. Mortgage Credit & Closing. 1972. pap. 45.00 (ISBN 0-686-04915-2). Home Equity.

Shiers, George. Bibliography of the History of Electronics. LC 72-3740. 1972. 11.50 (ISBN 0-8108-0499-9). Scarecrow.

--Electronic Drafting Techniques & Excercises. (Illus.). 1963. pap. text ed. 12.95 (ISBN 0-13-250605-X). P-H.

Shiffrin, Nancy, jt. auth. see Netherton, Morris.

Shifreen, Lawrence J. Henry Miller: A Bibliography of Secondary Sources. LC 78-12518. (Scarecrow Author Bibliographies: No. 38). 1979. lib. bdg. 22.50 (ISBN 0-8108-1171-5). Scarecrow.

Shigley, Joseph E. & Uiker, John J. Theory of Machines & Mechanisms. (Mechanical Engineering Ser.). (Illus.). 576p. 1980. text ed. 27.95x (ISBN 0-07-056884-7); solutions manual 13.95 (ISBN 0-07-056885-5). McGraw.

Shih, C. T. A Guide to the Jellyfish of Canadian Atlantic Waters. (Illus.). 1977. pap. text ed. 5.00x (ISBN 0-660-00017-2, 56366-9, Pub. by Natl Mus Canada). U of Chicago Pr.

Shih, Chung-Wen. Injustice to Tou O Yuan: A Study & Translation. LC 74-155585. (Princeton-Cambridge Studies in Chinese Linguistics, No. 4). 480p. 1973. 49.50 (ISBN 0-521-08228-5); pap. 19.95x (ISBN 0-521-09739-8). Cambridge U Pr.

Shih, Vincent Y. The Taiping Ideology: Its Sources, Interpretations & Influences. LC 66-19571. (Publications on Asia of the School of International Studies: No. 15). 576p. 1967. 16.00 (ISBN 0-295-73957-6, PAI15); pap. 4.95 (ISBN 0-295-95243-1). U of Wash Pr.

Shih-Chun Wang. Physiology & Pharmacology of the Brain Stem. LC 79-89753. (Illus.). 320p. 1980. 29.50 (ISBN 0-87993-127-2). Futura Pub.

Shiigi, Stanley M., jt. ed. see Mishell, Barbara B.

Shikes, Ralph E. & Harper, Paula. Pissarro: His Life & Work. 1980. 30.00 (ISBN 0-8180-0128-3). Horizon.

Shillaber, Carol see O'Neal, William B.

Shillea, Tom, jt. auth. see Hafey, John.

Shillif, Karl A., jt. auth. see Litka, Michael P.

Shilliff, Karl, jt. auth. see Deitzer, Bernard.

Shilliff, Karl A., jt. auth. see Deitzer, Bernard A.

Shilling. Acceptance Sampling in Quality Control. Date not set. price not set (ISBN 0-8247-1347-8). Dekker.

Shilling, N. A. Doing Business in Saudi Arabia & the Arab Gulf States. LC 75-37251. (Doing Business in the Middle East Ser.). 185.00 (ISBN 0-916400-01-8); supplement 65.00 (ISBN 0-685-83461-1); 40.00 (ISBN 0-916400-01-8); 55.00 (ISBN 0-916400-01-8). Inter-Crescent.

Shillingburg, Herbert. Preparations for Cast Gold Restorations. (Illus.). 168p. 1974. 48.50. Quint Pub Co.

Shillingburg, Herbert, et al. Fundamentals of Fixed Prosthodontics. (Illus.). 339p. 1978. 32.50 (ISBN 3-87652-641-8). Quint Pub Co.

Shillinglaw, Gordon. Managerial Cost Accounting: Analysis & Control. 4th ed. 1977. text ed. 20.50 (ISBN 0-256-01905-3). Irwin.

Shillinglaw, Gordon, et al. Accounting: A Management Approach. 6th ed. 1979. 20.95 (ISBN 0-256-02175-9). Irwin.

Shiloh, Ailon, ed. Studies in Human Sexual Behavior: The American Scene. (Illus.). 488p. 1970. text ed. 23.00 (ISBN 0-398-01746-8). C C Thomas.

Shiloh, Ailon & Selavan, Ida C., eds. Ethnic Groups of America; Their Morbidity, Mortality & Behavior Disorders, Vol. 2: The Blacks. (Illus.). 312p. 1974. 24.50 (ISBN 0-398-03022-7); pap. 17.50 (ISBN 0-398-03023-5). C C Thomas.

Shiloh, Ailon & Selevan, Ida C., eds. Ethnic Groups of America; Their Morbidity, Mortality & Behavior Disorders, Vol. 1. The Jews. (Illus.). 446p. 1973. text ed. 24.50 (ISBN 0-398-02610-6); pap. text ed. 17.50 (ISBN 0-398-02619-X). C C Thomas.

Shilov, G. Y. Mathematical Analysis: A Special Course. 1965. 37.00 (ISBN 0-08-010796-6); pap. 21.00 (ISBN 0-08-013616-8). Pergamon.

Shilov, V. N., jt. auth. see Dukhin, S. S.

Shils, Edward. Tradition. LC 80-21643. 320p. 1981. lib. bdg. price not set (ISBN 0-226-75325-5). U of Chicago Pr.

Shils, Edward, tr. see Mannheim, Karl.

Shilts, Dick. Teaching Basketball Fundamentals. 1977. 4.95 (ISBN 0-932826-13-X). New Issues MI.

Shim, Chang, jt. auth. see Williams, Henry M., Jr.

Shim, Jae K., jt. auth. see Geller, Louis.

Shimahara, Mobuo. Adaptation & Education in Japan. LC 79-9929. 1979. 22.95 (ISBN 0-03-049206-8). Praeger.

Shimer, Dorothy B. Bhabani Bhattacharya. (World Authors Ser.: India: No. 343). 1975. lib. bdg. 12.50 (ISBN 0-8057-2151-7). Twayne.

Shimer, John A. This Sculptured Earth: The Landscape of America. LC 59-10628. (Illus.). 1959. 22.50x (ISBN 0-231-02331-6). Columbia U Pr.

Shimizu, Hamoru, tr. see Kawamoto, Shigeo, et al.

Shimizu, Kay. Asian Flavors. LC 70-164869. 1971. 7.00 o.p. (ISBN 0-682-47305-7, Banner). Exposition.

Shimizu, Mamoru, tr. see Kawamoto, Shigeo & Nishiwaki, Junzaburo.

Shimony, Abner, ed. see Carnap, Rudolf.

Shin, Kilman. Death Penalty & Crime: Empirical Studies. LC 77-84025. 1978. text ed. 20.00 (ISBN 0-686-12042-6). Ctr Econ Analysis.

--Inflation, Stock Price, & Housing Cost: Empirical Studies. LC 77-84026. 1978. text ed. 20.00 (ISBN 0-686-12043-4). Ctr Econ Analysis.

Shinagel, Michael, ed. see Defoe, Daniel.

Shinar, David. Psychology on the Road: The Human Factor in Traffic Safety. LC 78-18219. 1978. text ed. 20.95 (ISBN 0-471-03997-7). Wiley.

Shindler, Colin. Hollywood Goes to War. (Cinema & Society Ser.). (Illus.). 1979. 23.50 (ISBN 0-7100-0290-4). Routledge & Kegan.

Shine, Frances L. Conjuror's Journal. LC 78-17869. 1978. 8.95 (ISBN 0-396-07598-3). Dodd.

Shine, I. Serendipity in St. Helena. 1970. 34.00 (ISBN 0-08-012794-0). Pergamon.

Shiner, Reva P., jt. auth. see Norris, Dorothy E.

Shiner, Roger A. Knowledge & Reality in Plato's Philebus. 64p. 1974. pap. text ed. 10.00x (ISBN 90-232-1170-7). Humanities.

Shingi, P. M., et al. Rural Youth: Education, Occupation & Social Outlook. 1980. 10.00x (ISBN 0-8364-0663-X, Pub. by Abhinav India). South Asia Bks.

Shingleton, John D. Trout, the Whole Trout, & Nothing but the Trout: Solemnly Sworn Testimony on America's No. 1 Gamefish & How to Hook Him. (Illus.). 144p. 1974. 7.95 (ISBN 0-87691-138-6). Winchester Pr.

Shinkarev, Leonid. Siberia: The Land Beyond the Mountains. 352p. 1973. 7.95 o.s.i. (ISBN 0-02-610520-9). Macmillan.

Shinn, Bev & Shinn, Duane. One Hundred & One Ways to Get Free Publicity for Yourself, Your Product or Your Organization. 1978. pap. 9.95 (ISBN 0-912732-37-7); spiral bdg. 19.95. Duane Shinn.

--Thirty-Three Mail Order Business You Can Operate from Your Home. 1978. pap. 9.95 o.p. (ISBN 0-912732-38-5). Duane Shinn.

--You Are the Greatest: How to Get from Where You Are to Where You Want to Be. 1978. pap. 9.95 o.p. (ISBN 0-912732-52-0). Duane Shinn.

Shinn, Byron M., jt. auth. see Jackson, John M.

Shinn, Charles H. The Story of the Mine. LC 79-23102. (Vintage Nevada Ser.). Orig. Title: Story of the Mine. (Illus.). xiv, 277p. 1980. pap. 6.50 (ISBN 0-87417-059-1). U of Nev Pr.

Shinn, Duane. How to Sell Your Product to Mail Order Houses by the Thousands. 1976. 19.95 (ISBN 0-912732-23-7). Duane Shinn.

--Piano Breakthrough: How to Revolutionize Your Playing Through Chords & Broken Chords. 1978. pap. 25.00 (ISBN 0-912732-44-X). Duane Shinn.

Shinn, Duane, jt. auth. see Brown, Max.

Shinn, Duane, jt. auth. see Shinn, Bev.

Shinn, Eugene, jt. auth. see Fanshel, David.

Shinn, George. The Miracle of Motivation. 1981. text ed. 8.95 (ISBN 0-8423-4353-9). Tyndale.

Shinn, Larry D., jt. auth. see Amore, Roy C.

Shinners, Lloyd H. Shinners' Spring Flora of the Dallas-Ft. Worth Area. 2nd rev. ed. Mahler, William F., ed. Orig. Title: Spring Flora of the Dallas-Ft. Worth Area. (Illus.). 1972. pap. 8.50x (ISBN 0-934786-01-1). G Davis.

Shinners, Stanley M. A Guide to Systems Engineering & Management. LC 76-7289. (Illus.). 1976. 21.95 (ISBN 0-669-00680-7). Lexington Bks.

--Modern Control, System Theory & Application. 2nd ed. LC 78-52497. (Electrical Engineering Ser.). 1978. text ed. 24.95 (ISBN 0-201-07494-X); instr's man. 3.00 (ISBN 0-201-07495-8). A-W.

Shinnie, P. L. African Iron Age. 1971. 29.00x (ISBN 0-19-813158-5). Oxford U Pr.

Shinskey, F. Greg. Distillation Control: For Productivity & Energy Conservation. 1976. 23.95 (ISBN 0-07-056893-6, P&RB). McGraw.

Shioda, Gozo. Dynamic Aikido. Hamilton, Geoffrey, tr. LC 68-31356. (Illus.). 1968. 9.95 o.p. (ISBN 0-87011-096-9). Kodansha.

Shipes, Ellen A. & Lehr, Sally T. Sexual Counseling for Ostomates: A Resource Book for Health Care Professionals. (Illus.). 118p. 1980. text ed. 8.50 lexotone (ISBN 0-398-03950-X). C C Thomas.

Shipherd, Jacob R. History of the Oberlin-Wellington Rescue. LC 77-127261. (Civil Liberties in American History Ser). 280p. 1972. Repr. of 1859 ed. lib. bdg. 32.50 (ISBN 0-306-71241-5). Da Capo.

Shiphorst, Albert. The Hilarious Saints. 1981. 5.75 (ISBN 0-8062-1640-9). Carlton.

Shipigler, B., jt. auth. see Beraha, E.

Shipka, Thomas A., jt. auth. see Minton, Arthur J.

Shiplett, Gary R. Worship & Hymnody. (Illus.). 122p. (Orig.). 1980. pap. text ed. 5.95 (ISBN 0-916260-08-9). A Meriwether.

Shiplett, June. The Raging Winds of Heaven. (Orig.). 1978. pap. 2.50 (ISBN 0-451-09439-5, E9439, Sig). NAL.

Shiplett, June L. Defy the Savage Winds. (Orig.). 1980. pap. 2.50 (ISBN 0-451-09337-2, E9337, Sig). NAL.

Shipley, Kenneth G. & Banis, Carolyn S. Teaching Morphology Developmentally: Methods & Materials for Teaching Bound Morphology. 1981. manual 50.00 (ISBN 0-88450-728-9). Communication Skill.

Shipley, Peter. Revolutionaries in Modern Britain. 256p. 1976. 16.95 (ISBN 0-370-11311-X). Transatlantic.

--Revolutionaries in Modern Britain. 1979. 12.95 (ISBN 0-370-11311-X, Pub. by Chatto Bodley Jonathan). Merrimack Bk Serv.

Shipley, T., ed. The Beginnings of Visual Photochemistry: Translations & Biographies in Honor of F. Boll & F. W. Kuhne. 1978. text ed. 30.00 (ISBN 0-08-021534-3). Pergamon.

Shipley, Thorne. Sensory Integration in Children: Evoked Potentials & Intersensory Functions in Pediatrics & Psychology. (Illus.). 176p. 1980. 15.75 (ISBN 0-398-03869-4). C C Thomas.

Shipman, Carl. Canon SLR Cameras. LC 76-50430. (Illus.). 1977. pap. 9.95 (ISBN 0-912656-56-5). H P Bks.

--How to Select & Use Minolta SLR Cameras. (Orig.). 1980. pap. 9.95 (ISBN 0-89586-044-9). H P Bks.

--How to Select & Use Nikon SLR Cameras. LC 78-52274. (Illus.). 1978. pap. 9.95 (ISBN 0-912656-77-8). H P Bks.

--How to Select & Use Olympus Slr Cameras. LC 79-84702. (Illus.). 1979. pap. 9.95 (ISBN 0-89586-015-5). H P Bks.

--Pentax SLR Cameras. LC 76-51908. (Illus.). 1977. pap. 9.95 (ISBN 0-912656-57-3). H P Bks.

Shipman, Harry L. Black Holes, Quasars, & the Universe. 2nd ed. (Illus.). 1980. 14.95 o.p. (ISBN 0-395-24374-2); pap. text ed. 8.95 (ISBN 0-395-28499-6). HM.

--The Restless Universe: An Introduction to Astronomy. LC 77-78584. (Illus.). 1978. text ed. 20.50 (ISBN 0-395-25392-6); inst. manual 0.45 (ISBN 0-395-25393-4). HM.

Shipman, Homer D. Historical Models & the Anticipation of the Future. (Illus.). 1979. deluxe ed. 47.50 (ISBN 0-930008-43-X). Inst Econ Pol.

Shipman, James T., et al. An Introduction to Physical Science. 3rd ed. 1979. text ed. 19.95x (ISBN 0-669-01720-5); inst. manual free (ISBN 0-669-01723-X); lab. manual 6.95x (ISBN 0-669-01722-1); student guide 6.95x (ISBN 0-669-01721-3). Heath.

Shipman, Marten. Childhood: A Sociological Perspective. (Exploring Education Ser.). 115p. (Orig.). 1972. pap. text ed. 5.00x (ISBN 0-85633-006-X, NFER). Humanities.

Shipman, Natalie. Follow Your Heart. (YA) 1971. 5.95 (ISBN 0-685-03336-8, Avalon). Bouregy.

Shipman, S. S., jt. auth. see Bogen, J. I.

Shipman, Thomas. Carolina. LC 80-17666. 1980. Repr. of 1683 ed. 30.00x (ISBN 0-8201-1355-7). Schol Facsimiles.

Shipman, William D. An Inquiry into the High Cost of Electricity in New England. LC 62-18344. (Illus.). 1962. 17.50x (ISBN 0-8195-3031-X, Pub. by Wesleyan U Pr). Columbia U Pr.

Shipmen, Marten, ed. Organisation & Impact of Social Research: Six Original Case Studies in Education & Behavioural Sciences. 1976. 12.00 (ISBN 0-7100-8320-3). Routledge & Kegan.

Shipp, Audrey, jt. auth. see Plateris, Alexander A.

Shipp, Audrey, ed. Serun Cholesterol Levels of Persons Aged 4-74 Years by Socioeconomic Characteristics United States, 1971-74. (Series 11: No. 217). 1979. pap. text ed. 1.75 (ISBN 0-8406-0180-8). Natl Ctr Health Stats.

--Utilization of Short-Stay Hospitals: Annual Summary for the United States, 1975. (Series 13: No. 31). 1977. pap. 1.95 (ISBN 0-8406-0092-5). Natl Ctr Health Stats.

Shipp, Audrey, ed. see Bloom, Barbara.

Shipp, Audrey, ed. see Gardocki, Gloria J. & Pokras, Robert.

Shipp, Audrey, ed. see Harvey, Clair & Kelly, James E.

Shipp, Audrey, ed. see Klebba, A. Joan.

Shipp, Audrey, ed. see Lewis, Frank.

Shipp, Audrey, ed. see Rowland, Michael.

Shipp, Audrey, ed. see Young, Harben B., et al.

Shipp, Audrey M., ed. see Ranofsky, Abraham L.

Shipp, Audrey M., ed. see Wilder, Charles S.

Shipp, G. P. Studies in the Language of Homer. 2nd ed. LC 76-149439. (Cambridge Classical Studies). 1972. 42.00 (ISBN 0-521-07706-0). Cambridge U Pr.

Shipp, James F. Russian-English Dictionary of Surnames: Important Names from Science & Technology. xvi, 317p. (Orig.). 1981. pap. 30.00x (ISBN 0-917564-10-3). Translation Research.

--Russian-English Index to Scientific Apparatus Nomenclature. (Orig.). 1977. pap. 10.00x o.p. (ISBN 0-917564-03-0). Translation Research.

Shipp, Ralph D. Retail Merchandising: Principles & Applications. LC 75-31040. (Illus.). 352p. 1976. text ed. 17.75 (ISBN 0-395-20271-X); inst. manual 1.75 (ISBN 0-395-20270-1). HM.

Shipp, Ralph D., Jr. Practical Selling. LC 79-88039. 1980. text ed. 15.50 (ISBN 0-395-28181-4); instrs'. manual 1.10 (ISBN 0-395-28182-2); dialogue tape 1.50 (ISBN 0-395-29303-0). HM.

Shipp, Thomas, jt. auth. see Dedo, Herbert H.

Shippee, Lester B., ed. see Whipple, Bishop.

Shippen, J. M., et al. Basic Farm Machinery. 3rd ed. (Illus.). 1980. 52.00 (ISBN 0-08-024912-4); pap. 16.00 (ISBN 0-08-024911-6). Pergamon.

Shippey, T. A. Old English Verse. 1972. text ed. 14.50x (ISBN 0-09-111030-0, Hutchinson U Lib); pap. text ed. 7.50x (ISBN 0-09-111031-9). Humanities.

Shipton, Clifford K. New England Life in the Eighteenth Century: Representative Biographies from Sibley's Harvard Graduates. LC 63-9562. (Illus.). 1963. 25.00x (ISBN 0-674-61250-7, Belknap Pr). Harvard U Pr.

Shipton, Clifford K. & Mooney, James E., eds. National Index of American Imprints Through 1800: The Short-Title Evans. xxv, 1028p. 1969. 50.00x (ISBN 0-8271-6908-6, Dist. by U Pr of Va). Am Antiquarian.

Shipton, E., et al. Maturing in a Changing World. 1971. text ed. 5.60 o.p. (ISBN 0-13-566166-8). P-H.

Shipton, Eric. Tierra Del Fuego: The Fatal Lodestone. (Illus.). 175p. 1974. 24.00 (ISBN 0-85314-194-0). Transatlantic.

Shipton, Eric & Washburn, Bradford. Mountain Conquest. LC 66-15087. (Horizon Caravel Bks). (Illus.). 153p. (gr. 6 up). 1966. 9.95 (ISBN 0-06-025642-7, Dist. by Har-Row); PLB 12.89 (ISBN 0-06-025643-5, Dist. by Har-Row). Am Heritage.

Shipton, Nathaniel N. & Swain, David. Rhode Islanders Record the Revolution: The Journals of William Humphrey & Zuriel Waterman. LC 78-68840. (Rhode Island Revolutionary Heritage Ser.: Vol. 4). (Illus.). 125p. 1981. 10.95 (ISBN 0-917012-03-8). RI Pubns Soc.

Shipway, V. C. & Shipway, W. Decorative Design in Mexican Homes. Date not set. 18.95 (ISBN 0-8038-0058-4). Hastings.

--Mexican Homes of Today. Date not set. 18.95 (ISBN 0-8038-0157-2). Hastings.

--The Mexican House: Old & New. Date not set. 18.95 (ISBN 0-8038-0158-0). Hastings.

Shipway, Verna C. & Shipway, Warren. Decorative Design in Mexican Homes. (Illus.). 1966. 16.95 (ISBN 0-8038-0058-4). Architectural.

--Houses of Mexico: Origins & Traditions. 16.95 (ISBN 0-8038-0104-1). Architectural.

--Mexican Interiors. Date not set. 18.95 (ISBN 0-8038-0159-9). Hastings.

Shipway, W., jt. auth. see Shipway, V. C.

Shipway, Warren, jt. auth. see Shipway, Verna C.

Shirah, A. Jason. For Children Mainly: Story Talks for Use in Church. (Orig.). 1980. pap. 3.95 (ISBN 0-8272-1010-8). Bethany Pr.

Shirahata, Shiro. The Alps. LC 80-50658. (Illus.). 220p. 1980. 75.00 (ISBN 0-8478-0316-3). Rizzoli Intl.

Shiraki, H., jt. ed. see Roizin, L.

Shirani Kali, Natari. Passions, Realms & Visions. 1979. 4.00 o.p. (ISBN 0-682-49406-2). Exposition.

Shir-Cliff, J., et al. Chromatic Harmony. LC 64-23079. 1965. text ed. 10.95 (ISBN 0-02-928630-1); wkbk. 9.95 (ISBN 0-02-928640-9). Free Pr.

Shire, Ellen. Adventures of Miss Bigley & Her Little Store. (gr. k-3). 1971. 4.95 o.s.i. (ISBN 0-8027-6003-1); PLB 4.85 o.s.i. (ISBN 0-8027-6004-X). Walker & Co.

Shire, Helena. A Preface to Spenser. Hussey, Maurice, ed. & frwd. by. (Preface Books). (Illus.). 1979. text ed. 11.95x (ISBN 0-582-31511-5); pap. text ed. 7.50x (ISBN 0-582-31512-3). Longman.

Shire, John G. Genetic Variation in Hormone Systems, 2 vols. 1979. Vol. 1, 208p. 54.95 (ISBN 0-8493-5283-5); Vol. 2, 192p. 49.95 (ISBN 0-8493-5284-3). CRC Pr.

Shirer, William. Gandhi: A Memoir. 1981. 6.95 (ISBN 0-671-25080-9, Touchstone). S&S.

--The Rise & Fall of the Third Reich. 1981. price not set (ISBN 0-671-42813-6, Touchstone). S&S.

Shirer, William L. Ghandhi: A Memoir. 1981. pap. 4.95 (ISBN 0-671-25080-9, Touchstone Bks). S&S.

Shires, David B. Computer Technology in the Health Sciences. (Illus.). 160p. 1974. text ed. 14.75 (ISBN 0-398-03005-7). C C Thomas.

Shires, G. Tomas, et al. Shock. LC 73-85076. (Major Problems in Clinical Surgery Ser.: Vol. 13). (Illus.). 175p. 1973. text ed. 14.00 (ISBN 0-7216-8250-2). Saunders.

Shires, H. Bess & March, Rita N. Adventures in Pennsylvania. (gr. 5-6). 1976. pap. 3.50 (ISBN 0-931992-12-5). Penns Valley.

Shiridharani, Krishnalal. War Without Violence. LC 79-147633. (Library of War & Peace; Non-Resis. & Non-Vio.). lib. bdg. 38.00 (ISBN 0-8240-0409-4). Garland Pub.

Shirk, Evelyn, jt. ed. see Kronovet, Esther.

Shirkey, Harry C. Pediatric Dosage Handbook. 1980. 18.00 (ISBN 0-917330-05-6). Am Pharm Assn.

--Pediatric Therapy. 6th ed. LC 80-14601. (Illus.). 1321p. 1980. text ed. 57.50 (ISBN 0-8016-4596-4). Mosby.

Shirlaw, Matthew. Theory of Harmony. LC 72-87348. (Music Reprint Ser). 1969. Repr. of 1917 ed. lib. bdg. 29.50 (ISBN 0-306-71658-5). Da Capo.

Shirley, Carl R., tr. Two Plays by Wilberto Canton. 99p. 1980. 5.95 (ISBN 0-8059-2706-9). Dorrance.

Shirley, Glenn. Last of the Real Badmen: Henry Starr. LC 75-38554. xiv, 208p. 1976. 11.95x (ISBN 0-8032-0871-5); pap. 2.95 (ISBN 0-8032-5837-2, BB 617, Bison). U of Nebr Pr.

--Law West of Fort Smith: A History of Frontier Justice in the Indian Territory, 1834-1896. LC 57-6193. (Illus.). 1968. pap. 4.25 (ISBN 0-8032-5183-1, BB 392, Bison). U of Nebr Pr.

--Pawnee Bill: A Biography of Major Gordon W. Lillie. LC 58-6870. (Illus.). 1965. pap. 5.95 (ISBN 0-8032-5185-8, BB 331, Bison). U of Nebr Pr.

--Temple Houston: Lawyer with a Gun. 1980. 14.95 (ISBN 0-8061-1627-7). U of Okla Pr.

Shirley, Grace. Shirley's Twentieth Century Lovers' Guide. 160p. (Orig.). 1981. pap. 2.50 (ISBN 0-523-40868-4). Pinnacle Bks.

Shirley, James. The Bird in a Cage: Edited from the Quarto of 1633 with Introduction and Notes. Orgel, Stephen, ed. LC 79-3121. (Renaissance Drama Second Ser.). 220p. 1980. lib. bdg. 24.00 (ISBN 0-8240-4486-X). Garland Pub.

--The Gentlemen of Venice. Engel, Wilson F., ed. (Salzburg Studies in English Literature, Jacobean Drama Studies: No. 62). 199p. 1976. pap. text ed. 25.00x (ISBN 0-391-01521-4). Humanities.
--The Humorous Courtier. Morillo, Marvin & Orgel, Stephen, eds. LC 78-66821. (Renaissance Drama Ser.). 1979. lib. bdg. 25.00 (ISBN 0-8240-9738-6). Garland Pub.
--The Lady of Pleasure. Thorensen, Marilyn J. & Orgel, Stephen, eds. LC 79-54328. (Renaissance Drama Second Ser.). 335p. 1980. lib. bdg. 37.50 (ISBN 0-8240-4478-9). Garland Pub.
--Love's Cruelty: Edited from the Quarto of 1640 with Introduction & Notes. Orgel, Stephen, ed. LC 79-54354. (Renaissance Drama Second Ser.). 220p. 1980. lib. bdg. 24.00 (ISBN 0-8240-4471-1). Garland Pub.
--The Maid's Revenge: Edited from the Quarto of 1639 with Introduction and Notes. Orgel, Stephen, ed. LC 79-3100. (Renaissance Drama Second Ser.). 185p. 1980. lib. bdg. 22.00 (ISBN 0-8240-4485-1). Garland Pub.
--Traitor. Carter, John S., ed. LC 65-11520. (Regents Renaissance Drama Ser). 1965. 7.95x (ISBN 0-8032-0282-2); pap. 1.65x (ISBN 0-8032-5283-8, BB 212, Bison). U of Nebr Pr.
--The Wedding. Flavin, Martin & Orgel, Stephen, eds. LC 79-54338. (Renaissance Drama Second Ser.). 330p. 1980. lib. bdg. 36.00 (ISBN 0-8240-4456-8). Garland Pub.
Shirley, James, et al. The Young Admiral. Ericksen, Kenneth J. & Orgel, Stephen, eds. LC 78-66752. (Renaissance Drama Ser.). 1979. lib. bdg. 20.00 (ISBN 0-8240-9746-7). Garland Pub.
Shirley, Janet, ed. Garnier's Becket: Translated from the 12th Century Vie Saint Thomas le Martyr de Cantorbire of Gannier of Pont-Sainte Maxence. (Illus.). 191p. 1975. 20.00x (ISBN 0-87471-798-1). Rowman.
Shirley, John. The Brigade. 256p. 1981. pap. 2.25 (ISBN 0-380-77156-X, 77156). Avon.
--Three-Ring Psychus. 240p. (Orig.). 1980. pap. 1.95 (ISBN 0-89083-674-4). Zebra.
Shirley, John. M. Dartmouth College Causes & the Supreme Court of the United States. LC 79-124904. (American Constitutional & Legal History Ser). (Illus.). 1971. Repr. of 1895 ed. lib. bdg. 45.00 (ISBN 0-306-71995-9). Da Capo.
Shirley, John W. Thomas Harriott: Renaissance Scientist. (Illus.). 1974. 29.50x (ISBN 0-19-858140-8). Oxford U Pr.
Shirley, Peggy F. Serious & Tragic Elements in the Comedy of Thomas Dekker. (Salzburg Studies in English Literature, Jacobean Drama Studies: No. 50). 132p. 1975. pap. text ed. 25.00x (ISBN 0-391-01522-2). Humanities.
Shirley, Robert C., et al. The Study of Strategy & Policy Formation: A Multifunctional Orientation. LC 75-25814. 232p. 1976. text ed. 10.95x o.p. (ISBN 0-471-78643-8). Wiley.
Shirley, Robert W. End of Tradition: Cultural Change & Development in the Municipio of Cunha, Sao Paulo, Brazil. LC 76-129535. (Institute of Latin America Studies). 1971. 20.00x (ISBN 0-231-03193-9). Columbia U Pr.
Shirokogoroff, S. M. Social Organization of the Northern Tungus. LC 78-66515. (Classics of Anthropology Ser.: Vol. 28). (Illus.). 1979. lib. bdg. 63.00 (ISBN 0-8240-9620-7). Garland Pub.
Shirokogoroff, Sergei M. Anthropology of Northern China. (Orig.). 1966. Repr. of 1923 ed. text ed. 9.00x (ISBN 90-6234-039-3). Humanities.
Shirreffs, Gordon. Captain Cutlass. 1978. pap. 1.95 o.p. (ISBN 0-449-14001-6, GM). Fawcett.
Shirreffs, Gordon D. Arizona Justice. 1977. pap. 1.50 (ISBN 0-505-51195-9). Tower Bks.
--Five Graves to Boot Hill. 1977. pap. 1.25 (ISBN 0-505-51157-6). Tower Bks.
--Last Man Alive. 1977. pap. 1.25 (ISBN 0-505-51167-3, BT51167). Tower Bks.
--Legend of the Damned. 1979. pap. 1.75 o.p. (ISBN 0-449-14183-7, GM). Fawcett.
--The Lonely Gun. 1977. pap. 1.50 (ISBN 0-505-51175-4). Tower Bks.
--The Manhunter. 160p. 1981. pap. 1.75 (ISBN 0-449-13728-7, GM). Fawcett.
--The Nevada Gun. 1977. pap. 1.25 (ISBN 0-505-51166-5, BT51166). Tower Bks.
--The Proud Gun. 1977. pap. 1.25 (ISBN 0-505-51197-5). Tower Bks.
--Range Rebel. 1978. pap. 1.50 (ISBN 0-505-51226-2). Tower Bks.
--The Untamed Breed. 352p. 1981. pap. 2.75 (ISBN 0-449-14387-2, GM). Fawcett.
Shirts, Morris. Warm Up for Little League Baseball. LC 70-151708. (Illus.). 176p. (gr. 2 up). 1976. 7.95 (ISBN 0-8069-4044-1); PLB 7.49 (ISBN 0-8069-4045-X). Sterling.
Shirts, Morris A. Warm up for Little League Baseball. (Illus.). (gr. 3-6). 1977. pap. 1.75 (ISBN 0-671-41135-7). PB.
--Warm up for Little League Baseball. Date not set. pap. 1.95 (ISBN 0-671-42422-X). Archway.
Shirts, Morris A. & Kingsford, Thomas R. Playing with a Football. (Illus.). 128p. (gr. 4-8). 1973. 4.95 o.p. (ISBN 0-8069-4524-9); PLB 4.99 o.p. (ISBN 0-8069-4525-7). Sterling.
Shirts, Morris A. & Myers, Kent E. Call It Right! Umpiring in the Little League. LC 76-51169. (Illus.). 1977. 7.95 (ISBN 0-8069-4108-1); lib. bdg. 7.49 (ISBN 0-8069-4109-X). Sterling.
Shirvanzade, Alexandre. Evil Spirit. Parlakian, Nishan, tr. from Armenian. LC 78-65962. Orig. Title: Char Voki. (Illus.). xxxvi, 146p. 1980. 6.95 (ISBN 0-934728-00-3); pap. 4.95 (ISBN 0-934728-01-1). St Vartan.
Shisler, William, jt. auth. see Eisner, Vivien.
Shivananda, Swami. For Seekers of God: Spiritual Talks of Mahapurush Swami Shivananda. Vividishananda, Swami & Gambhirananda, Swami, trs. from Bengali. 186p. 1972. 5.79 (ISBN 0-87481-169-4); pap. 5.95 (ISBN 0-87481-130-9). Vedanta Pr.
Shively, Ann. Pedigrees. LC 80-7888. 408p. 1980. 12.95 (ISBN 0-690-02002-3). Lippincott & Crowell.
Shively, W. Phillips. The Craft of Political Research. 2nd ed. (Contemporary Comparative Politics Ser.). (Illus.). 1980. pap. text ed. 8.95 (ISBN 0-13-188748-3). P-H.
Shivers, Alfred S. Jessamyn West. (U. S. Authors Ser.: No. 192). lib. bdg. 10.95 (ISBN 0-8057-0784-0). Twayne.
--The Life of Maxwell Anderson. LC 80-5721. 356p. 1981. 16.95 (ISBN 0-8128-2789-9). Stein & Day.
--Maxwell Anderson. (U.S. Authors Ser: No. 279). 1976. lib. bdg. 10.95 (ISBN 0-8057-7179-4). Twayne.
Shivers, Jay S. & Fait, Hollis F. Recreational Service for the Aging. LC 80-360. (Illus.). 324p. 1980. text ed. 16.50 (ISBN 0-8121-0713-6). Lea & Febiger.
Shivers, Jay S. & Halper, Joseph W. The Crisis in Urban Recreational Services. LC 79-17414. 384p. 1981. 27.50 (ISBN 0-8386-3006-5, 3006). Fairleigh Dickinson.
Shivkumar, K. King's Choice. LC 76-81195. (Illus.). (gr. k-3). 1971. 5.95 o.s.i. (ISBN 0-8193-0364-X, Four Winds); PLB 5.41 o.s.i. (ISBN 0-8193-0365-8). Schol Bk Serv.
Shkhvatsabaya, Igor K. Ischemic Heart Disease. LC 78-31414. (Illus.). 1979. 37.50 (ISBN 0-8016-4624-3). Mosby.
Shklar, G. & McCarthy, P. Oral Manifestations of Systemic Disease. 1976. 22.95 (ISBN 0-409-95002-5). Butterworths.
Shklar, Gerald, jt. auth. see McCarthy, Philip L.
Shklovskii, I. S., jt. auth. see Sagan, Carl.
Shklovskii, Iosif S. Stars: Their Birth, Life, & Death. Rodman, Richard B., tr. LC 77-13889. (Illus.). 1978. text ed. 25.95x (ISBN 0-7167-0024-7). W H Freeman.
Shlaim, A. & Yannopoulos, G. N. The EEC & Eastern Europe. LC 78-51675. 1979. 45.00 (ISBN 0-521-22072-6). Cambridge U Pr.
Shlaim, A. & Yannopoulos, G., eds. The EEC & the Mediterranean Countries. LC 75-3858. (Illus.). 356p. 1976. 54.00 (ISBN 0-521-20817-3). Cambridge U Pr.
Shlaim, Avi, ed. International Organizations in World Politics Yearbook, 1975. 1976. 26.25x (ISBN 0-89158-608-3). Westview.
Shloming, Robert, jt. auth. see Carnevale, Thomas.
Shneiderman, Ben, ed. Database Management Systems. LC 76-41070. (Information Technology Ser.: Vol. I). (Illus.). 137p. 1976. pap. 15.00 (ISBN 0-88283-014-7). AFIPS Pr.
Shneidman, Edwin S., jt. auth. see Farberow, Norman L.
Shneidman, Edwin S., ed. Death: Current Perspectives. 2nd ed. LC 80-81360. 557p. 1980. pap. text ed. 12.95 (ISBN 0-87484-508-4). Mayfield Pub.
--Death: Current Perspectives. LC 75-21075. 1976. pap. 10.95 o.p. (ISBN 0-87484-332-4). Mayfield Pub.
Shneidman, Edwin S. & Farberow, Norman L., eds. Clues to Suicide. 1957. pap. 4.95 (ISBN 0-07-056981-9, SP). McGraw.
Shneidman, Edwin S., ed. see Murray, Henry A.
Shneidman, J. Lee, jt. auth. see Schwab, Peter.
Shneour, Elie A. The Malnourished Mind. LC 73-9175. 216p. 1974. 6.95 o.p. (ISBN 0-385-03909-3, Anchor Pr); pap. 2.95 o.p. (ISBN 0-385-00835-X, Anch). Doubleday.
Shngle, Robert D., jt. ed. see Shangle, Robert D.
Shnider, S., jt. ed. see Harnad, J. P.
Shnitka, T. K., ed. Gastric Secretions - Mechanism & Control. 1967. 75.00 (ISBN 0-08-012412-7). Pergamon.
Shnol, S. E. Physico-Chemical Factors of Biological Evolution. 327p. 1981. 65.50 (ISBN 3-7186-0044-7). Harwood Academic.
Shoate, Alec & Main, Barbara Y., eds. Summerland. 242p. 1980. 16.95x (ISBN 0-85564-166-5, Pub. by U of West Australia Pr Australia). Intl Schol Bk Serv.
Shoben, Edward J., Jr., jt. ed. see Milton, Ohmer.
Shoben, Martin & Ward, Janet. Pattern Cutting & Making up: Vol. 3, The Professional Approach. (Illus.). 192p. 1981. 53.00 (ISBN 0-7134-3561-5, Pub. by Batsford England); pap. 30.00 (ISBN 0-7134-3562-3). David & Charles.
Shobin, David. The Unborn. 1981. 11.95 (ISBN 0-671-25626-2, Linden). S&S.
Shock, D. A., jt. ed. see Schlitt, W. J.
Shockley, A. A., jt. ed. see Josey, E. J.
Shockley, Ann A. & Chandler, Sue P., eds. Living Black American Authors: A Biographical Directory. LC 73-17005. 220p. 1973. 15.95 o.p. (ISBN 0-8352-0662-9). Bowker.
Shockley, Emmy L., jt. auth. see Schwartz, Morris S.
Shockley, Norman. Back from the Edge. LC 79-56163. (Illus.). 96p. (Orig.). 1979. pap. 3.75x (ISBN 0-8358-0392-9). Upper Room.
Shoebridge, D. J., jt. auth. see Giggins, L. W.
Shoecraft, Paul. Arithmetic Primer. (gr. 4 up). 1979. pap. text ed. 11.50 (ISBN 0-201-07321-8, Sch Div); tchrs'. materials 4.90 (ISBN 0-201-07143-6, Sch Div). A-W.
Shoemaker, F., jt. auth. see Rogers, E.
Shoemaker, Helen S. The Exploding Mystery of Prayer. (Orig.). 1978. pap. 3.95 (ISBN 0-8164-2183-8). Crossroad NY.
--Secret of Effective Prayer. 1976. pap. 1.75 (ISBN 0-89129-211-X). Jove Pubns.
Shoemaker, James S. Small Fruit Culture. 5th ed. (Illus.). 1978. lib. bdg. 20.50 (ISBN 0-87055-248-1). AVI.
Shoemaker, James S., jt. auth. see Teskey, Benjamin J.
Shoemaker, Kathryn. Creative Christmas: Simple Crafts from Many Lands. 1978. pap. 7.95 (ISBN 0-03-045716-5). Winston Pr.
--Creative Classroom. 1980. pap. 7.95 (ISBN 0-03-053441-0). Winston Pr.
Shoemaker, Kathryn E., illus. Children, Go Where I Send Thee: An American Spiritual. (Illus.). 32p. (Orig.). 1980. pap. 6.95 (ISBN 0-03-056673-8). Winston Pr.
Shoemaker, Len. Roaring Fork Valley: An Illustrated Chronicle. (Illus.). 216p. 27.00 (ISBN 0-913582-06-9). Sundance.
--Roaring Fork Valley: An Illustrated Chronicle. 3rd ed. Collman, Russ, ed. (Illus.). 1979. 27.00 (ISBN 0-913582-06-9). Sundance.
Shoemaker, R. H., jt. auth. see Shaw, Ralph R.
Shoemaker, Richard H. Checklist of American Imprints, Vol. 1828. Cooper, Gayle, ed. 1971. 20.00 (ISBN 0-8108-0377-1). Scarecrow.
--Checklist of American Imprints, Vol. 1820. LC 64-11784. 1964. 12.50 (ISBN 0-8108-0153-1). Scarecrow.
--Checklist of American Imprints, Vol. 1825. LC 64-11784. 1969. 12.00 (ISBN 0-8108-0259-7). Scarecrow.
--Checklist of American Imprints, Vol. 1826. LC 64-11784. 1970. 16.00 (ISBN 0-8108-0323-2). Scarecrow.
--Checklist of American Imprints, Vol. 1829. LC 64-11784. 1971. 16.00 (ISBN 0-8108-0395-X). Scarecrow.
--Checklist of American Imprints, Vol. 1821. LC 64-11784. 1967. 12.00 (ISBN 0-8108-0154-X). Scarecrow.
--Checklist of American Imprints, Vol. 1822. LC 64-11784. 1967. 12.00 (ISBN 0-8108-0155-8). Scarecrow.
--Checklist of American Imprints, Vol. 1823. LC 64-11784. 1968. 12.00 (ISBN 0-8108-0156-6). Scarecrow.
Shoemaker, Richard H., ed. Checklist of American Imprints, Vol. 1827. LC 64-11784. 1970. 14.00 (ISBN 0-8108-0336-4). Scarecrow.
--Checklist of American Imprints, Vol. 1824. LC 64-11784. 1969. 15.50 (ISBN 0-8108-0246-5). Scarecrow.
Shoemaker, Ronald L., jt. auth. see Ballast, Daniel L.
Shoemaker, Silas H. Rhymes Without Reason. 59p. 1980. 3.95 (ISBN 0-8059-2744-1). Dorrance.
Shoemaker, Terry. Performance Activities in Mathematics, 6 bks. Incl. Bk. 1 (ISBN 0-913688-10-X); Bk. 2 (ISBN 0-913688-11-8); Bk. 3 (ISBN 0-913688-12-6); Bk. 4 (ISBN 0-913688-13-4); Bk. 5 (ISBN 0-913688-14-2); Bk. 6 (ISBN 0-913688-15-0). 1974. pap. 6.64x ea. Pawnee Pub.
Shoemaker, Thomas M., jt. auth. see Kurtz, Edwin B.
Shoemaker, William H. The Multiple Stage in Spain During the Fifteenth & Sixteenth Centuries. LC 78-137076. 150p. 1973. Repr. of 1935 ed. lib. bdg. 17.00x (ISBN 0-8371-5539-8, SHMS). Greenwood.
Shoemaker, William H., ed. see Casona, Alejandro.
Shoemaker, Willie & Smith, Daniel G. The Shoe: Willie Shoemaker's Illustrated Book of Racing. LC 76-46368. (Illus.). 208p. 1976. 14.95 o.p. (ISBN 0-528-81845-7). Rand.
Shoenberg, David. Superconductivity. 2nd ed. (Cambridge Monographs on Physics). (Illus.). 1960-1965. pap. 5.00 (ISBN 0-521-09254-X). Cambridge U Pr.
Shoenberg, Elisabeth. A Hospital Looks at Itself. 1972. 8.95 (ISBN 0-571-81004-7, Pub. by Faber & Faber). Merrimack Bk Serv.
Shoenfield, J. R. Mathematical Logic. 1967. text ed. 19.95 (ISBN 0-201-07028-6). A-W.
Shofer, Jack D. How to Raise & Train a Basenji. 1966. pap. 2.00 (ISBN 0-87666-239-4, DS1051). TFH Pubns.
Shoff, Janet see Corrigan, L. Luan.
Shofner, David. Soul Winning. (Illus.). 96p. (Orig.). 1980. pap. write for info. (ISBN 0-89957-051-8). AMG Pubs.
Shogan, Robert. Promises to Keep: Carter's First 100 Days. LC 77-22818. 1977. 8.95 o.p. (ISBN 0-690-01497-X, TYC-T). T Y Crowell.
Shogan, Robert & Craig, Tom. The Detroit Race Riot. LC 76-1011. (Fdr & the Era of the New Deal). 1976. Repr. of 1964 ed. lib. bdg. 22.50 (ISBN 0-306-70808-6). Da Capo.
Shoghi Effendi, tr. see Baha'u 'llah.
Shoghi Efferdi, tr. see Baha'u'llah.
Shogren, Linda. The Quilt Pattern Index. LC 79-63203. 50p. (Orig.). 1979. pap. 4.95 o.p. (ISBN 0-933758-06-5). L Shogren Quilt.
Shoham, S. Giora, ed. Israel Studies in Criminology, Vol. V. 228p. 1980. 20.00x (ISBN 965-20-0026-4, Pub. by Turtledove Pr Israel). Intl Schol Bk Serv.
Shoham, Shlomo, jt. ed. see Mednick, Sarnoff A.
Shohet, J. L. Plasma State. 1971. text ed. 22.95 (ISBN 0-12-640550-6). Acad Pr.
Shoji, Yoshiro. Systematic Endodontics. (Illus.). 126p. 1977. 22.00. Quint Pub Co.
Sholerar, G. P. Marriage Is a Family Affair. Date not set. text ed. price not set (ISBN 0-89335-120-2). Spectrum Pub.
Sholevar, G. Pirooz. Changing Sexual Values & the Family. (Illus.). 192p. 1977. 16.50 (ISBN 0-398-03519-9). C C Thomas.
--Self-Assessment of Current Knowledge in Child & Adolescent Psychiatry. 2nd. ed. LC 80-18727. 1980. pap. 15.00 (ISBN 0-87488-287-7). Med Exam.
Sholevar, Pirooz, et al, eds. Emotional Disorders in Children & Adolescents: Medical & Psychological Approaches to Treatment. new ed. LC 79-17849. 1980. text ed. 60.00 (ISBN 0-89335-084-2). Spectrum Pub.
Sholevar, Pirooz G., ed. Child & Adolescent Psychiatry Continuing Education Review. 1977. spiral bdg. 14.00 (ISBN 0-87488-343-1). Med Exam.
Sholinsky, Jane. The Challenge of Skiing. LC 74-3073. (gr. 5-8). 1974. PLB 4.47 o.p. (ISBN 0-531-02736-8). Watts.
Sholiton, Robert D. & Van Campen, Joseph A. Pattern Drills for Introductory Russian. 1968. pap. 3.95x (ISBN 0-393-09772-2, NortonC). Norton.
Sholl, Betsy. Appalachian Winter. LC 77-93267. 72p. 1978. pap. 4.95 (ISBN 0-914086-21-9). Alicejamesbooks.
--Changing Faces. LC 74-81379. 72p. 1974. pap. 4.95 (ISBN 0-914086-05-7). Alicejamesbooks.
Sholnick, Robert J. Edmund Clarence Stedman. (United States Authors Ser.: No. 286). 1977. lib. bdg. 12.50 (ISBN 0-8057-7188-3). Twayne.
Shoman, James. Nature Centers: The Pursuit of Environmental Awareness. 1980. 20.00 o.p. (ISBN 0-8424-0122-9). Caroline Hse.
Shonfield, Andrew. International Economic Relations. LC 76-54540. (The Washington Papers: No. 42). 1977. 3.50x (ISBN 0-8039-0790-7). Sage.
--Modern Capitalism: The Changing Balance of Public & Private Power. 1969. pap. 7.95 (ISBN 0-19-500298-9, GB). Oxford U Pr.
Shonfield, Andrew, ed. see Strange, Susan.
Shonfield, Andrew, et al. International Economic Relations of the Western World 1959-1971, Vol. 1. Shonfield, Andrew, ed. (Royal Institute of International Affairs Ser). 448p. 1976. 45.00x (ISBN 0-19-218314-1). Oxford U Pr.
Shonle, John I. Environmental Applications of General Physics. 1974. text ed. 7.95 (ISBN 0-201-07058-8). A-W.
Shook, Georg & Witt, Gary. Sharp Focus Watercolor Painting: Techniques for Hot-Pressed Surfaces. 144p. 1981. 21.95 (ISBN 0-8230-4794-6). Watson-Guptill.
Shook, Glenn. Mysticism, Science & Revelation. rev. ed. 1953. 6.75 o.s.i. (ISBN 0-85398-015-2, 7-31-83); pap. 3.50 o.s.i. (ISBN 0-85398-053-5, 7-31-84). Baha'i.
Shook, Robert & Bingaman, Ronald. Total Commitment. LC 75-12690. (Illus.). 256p. 1975. 9.95 (ISBN 0-8119-0232-3). Fell.
Shook, Robert L. The Entrepreneurs. LC 79-2735. (Illus.). 192p. 1981. pap. 3.95 (ISBN 0-06-464043-4, B*N 4043). Har-Row.
--The Entrepreneurs: Twelve Who Took Risks & Succeeded. LC 79-2735. 192p. 1981. pap. 3.95 (ISBN 0-06-464043-4, BN 4043, EH). Har-Row.
--Winning Images. 1977. 9.95 (ISBN 0-02-610540-3, 61054). Macmillan.
Shooter, Jim, et al. Superman & Spiderman. 160p. (Orig.). 1981. pap. 2.50 (ISBN 0-446-91757-5). Warner Bks.

Shoppee, Charles W., ed. Excited States of Matter. (Graduate Studies: No. 2). (Illus., Orig.). 1973. pap. 8.00 (ISBN 0-89672-009-8). Tex Tech Pr.

Shopsin, Baron, ed. Manic Illness. LC 78-66347. 1979. text ed. 21.00 (ISBN 0-89004-211-X). Raven.

Shor, R. E. & Orne, M. T., eds. The Nature of Hypnosis: Selected Basic Readings. 1981. Repr. of 1965 ed. 18.95x (ISBN 0-03-050965-3). Irvington.

Shor, Ronald E., jt. auth. see Fromm, Erika.

Shore, Barry. Introduction to Quantitative Methods for Business Decisions: Text & Cases. (Illus.). 1978. text ed. 19.95 (ISBN 0-07-057050-7, C); instructor's manual 6.95 (ISBN 0-07-057051-5). McGraw.

--Operations Management. (Management Ser.). (Illus.). 544p. 1973. text ed. 21.00 (ISBN 0-07-057045-0, C); instructor's manual 7.95 (ISBN 0-07-057046-9). McGraw.

Shore, Warren. Social Security: The Fraud in Your Future. 252p. 1975. 9.95 (ISBN 0-02-610550-0). Macmillan.

Shores, Christopher. Ground Attack Aircraft of World War II. (Illus.). 191p. 1979. 9.95 (ISBN 0-356-08338-1, Pub by Macdonald & Jane's England). Hippocrene Bks.

Shores, Christopher F. & Ward, Richard. North American Mustang Mk. 1-4. LC 73-88967. (Arco-Aircam Aviation Ser., No. 3). (Illus., Orig.). 1968. lib. bdg. 5.00 o. p. (ISBN 0-668-02098-9); pap. 2.95 (ISBN 0-668-02097-0). Arco.

Shores, Louis. Library Education. LC 74-187784. 178p. 1972. lib. bdg. 11.50x o.p. (ISBN 0-87287-043-X). Libs Unl.

--Reference As the Promotion of Free Inquiry. LC 76-6150. 189p. 1976. lib. bdg. 11.50x o.p. (ISBN 0-87287-156-8). Libs Unl.

Shorey, Kenneth P., ed. The Letters of John Randolph & John Brockenbrough. (Illus.). 1978. write for info o.p. (ISBN 0-916624-25-0). Troy State Univ.

Shorr, Joseph B., et al, eds. Imagery: Its Many Demensions & Applications. 405p. 1980. 32.50 (ISBN 0-306-40456-7, Plenum Pr). Plenum Pub.

Shorr, Joseph E. Go See the Movie in Your Head. 1977. pap. 1.95 o.p. (ISBN 0-445-04100-5). Popular Lib.

Shorris, Earl. The Oppressed Middle: The Politics of Middle Management. LC 80-717. 408p. 1981. 13.95 (ISBN 0-385-14564-0, Anchor Pr). Doubleday.

Shorrock, William I. French Imperialism in the Middle East: The Failure of Policy in Syria & Lebanon, 1900-1914. LC 75-32078. 264p. 1976. 25.00x (ISBN 0-299-07030-1). U of Wis Pr.

Shorrocks, B. Drosophila. (Illus.). 144p. 1980. 12.00 (ISBN 0-08-025941-3). Pergamon.

Shorrosh, Anis A. Jesus, Prophecy & the Middle East. 1981. pap. 3.95 (ISBN 0-8407-5764-6). Nelson.

Short, Andrew & Kinnibugh, William. Lightweight Concrete. 3rd ed. (Illus.). 1978. text ed. 71.30x (ISBN 0-85334-734-4). Intl Ideas.

Short, Andrew, ed. Lightweight Aggregate Concrete: Design & Technology. (Euro-International Concrete Committee). (Illus.). 1978. text ed. 38.00x (ISBN 0-904406-24-5). Longman.

Short, Anthony. The Communist Insurrection in Malaya 1948-1960. LC 73-93384. 513p. 1974. 32.50 (ISBN 0-8448-0306-5). Crane-Russak Co.

Short, Charles. Clinical Veterinary Anesthesia: A Guide for the Practitioner. LC 74-8001. 1974. 29.50 o.p. (ISBN 0-8016-4601-4). Mosby.

Short, Dan. Study Guide to Accompany Pyle & Larson's Financial Accounting. 1980. pap. 5.00x (ISBN 0-256-02331-X). Irwin.

Short, Douglas, jt. auth. see Dickie, D. E.

Short, Douglas D. Beowulf Scholarship: An Annotated Bibliography. LC 79-7924. 353p. 1980. lib. bdg. 38.00 (ISBN 0-8240-9530-8). Garland Pub.

Short, Eirian. Quilting: Technique, Design & Application. 1979. 24.00 (ISBN 0-7134-1540-1, Pub. by Batsford England). David & Charles.

Short, J. R. Urban Data Sources. LC 79-42888. (Sources & Methods in Geography Ser.). 1980. pap. text ed. 7.50 (ISBN 0-408-10640-9). Butterworths.

Short, J. Rodney & Dickerson, Beverly. The Newspaper: An Alternative Textbook. LC 79-54759. (gr. 6-11). 1980. pap. 5.50 (ISBN 0-8224-4661-8). Pitman Learning.

Short, James R., ed. see Washington, George.

Short, John. The Final Larval Instars of the Ichneumonidae. (Memoir Ser.: No. 25). (Illus.). 508p. 1978. 35.00 (ISBN 0-686-26663-3). Am Entom Inst.

Short, K. Microprocessors & Programmed Logic. 1980. 28.95 (ISBN 0-13-581173-2). P-H.

Short, Kenneth. The Dynamite War: Irish-American Bombers in Victorian Britain. (Illus.). 1979. text ed. 23.25x (ISBN 0-391-00964-8). Humanities.

Short, Kenneth, ed. Feature Films As History. LC 80-28715. 192p. 1981. price not set (ISBN 0-87049-314-0). U of Tenn Pr.

Short, Luke. Barren Land Showdown. 1981. pap. 1.75 (ISBN 0-449-14138-1, GM). Fawcett.

--Bold Rider. 1978. pap. 1.25 o.s.i. (ISBN 0-440-10683-4). Dell.

--Brand of Empire. 1977. pap. 1.25 o.s.i. (ISBN 0-440-10770-9). Dell.

--Dead Freight for Piute. 160p. (Orig.). 1981. pap. 1.95 (ISBN 0-553-13553-8). Bantam.

--Desert Crossing. 160p. (Orig.). 1980. pap. 1.75 (ISBN 0-553-13760-3). Bantam.

--A Man Could Get Killed. x ed. 192p. 1980. pap. 1.95 o.s.i. (ISBN 0-515-05558-1). Jove Pubns.

--Paper Sheriff. 176p. 1980. pap. 1.75 (ISBN 0-553-14181-3). Bantam.

--Play a Lone Hand. 160p. 1981. pap. 1.95 (ISBN 0-553-13751-4). Bantam.

--Saddle by Starlight. 176p. 1981. pap. 1.95 (ISBN 0-553-14531-2). Bantam.

Short, M. H., jt. auth. see Leech, G. N.

Short, Martin & McDermott, Anthony. The Kurds. (Minority Rights Group: No. 23). 1975. pap. 2.50 (ISBN 0-89192-109-5). Interbk Inc.

Short, Nicholas M. Planetary Geology. (Illus.). 384p. 1975. ref. ed. 28.95 (ISBN 0-13-679290-1). P-H.

Short, Philip. Banda. 358p. 1974. 20.00 (ISBN 0-7100-7631-2). Routledge & Kegan.

Short, R. V. & Baird, D. T. Contraceptives of the Future. LC 77-371447. (Illus.). 1977. text ed. 22.50x (ISBN 0-85403-087-5). Scholium Intl.

Short, R. V., jt. ed. see Austin, C. R.

Short, Robert L. Gospel According to "Peanuts". LC 65-11632. (Illus.). 1965. pap. 2.95 (ISBN 0-8042-1968-0). John Knox.

Short, Thayne, jt. auth. see Cornelius, Wanda.

Short, W., et al. Questions & Answers on Cutting Fuel Costs. 104p. 1975. 11.00x (ISBN 0-86010-019-7, Pub. by Graham & Trotman England). State Mutual Bk.

Shortall, Leonard. Ben on the Ski Trail. (Illus.). (ps-3). 1965. 7.25 o.p. (ISBN 0-688-31081-8). Morrow.

--The Hat Book. (Illus.). 24p. (gr. k-1). 1976. PLB 5.38 (ISBN 0-307-68976-X, Golden Pr). Western Pub.

--Jerry the Newsboy. LC 70-118273. (Illus.). (ps-3). 1970. PLB 7.44 (ISBN 0-688-31711-1). Morrow.

--Sam's First Fish. (Illus.). (ps-3). 1962. PLB 7.44 (ISBN 0-688-31658-1). Morrow.

--Tod on the Tugboat. LC 73-153186. (Illus.). (ps-3). 1971. 7.25 (ISBN 0-688-21804-0); PLB 6.96 (ISBN 0-688-31804-5). Morrow.

Shortell, Stephen M. & Richardson, William C. Health Program Evaluation. LC 78-4866. (Issues & Pr0blems in Health Care). 1978. pap. text ed. 8.95 (ISBN 0-8016-4595-6). Mosby.

Shorter, A. W. The Egyptian Gods: A Handbook. 1978. 12.00 (ISBN 0-7100-0037-5). Routledge & Kegan.

Shorter, Aylward. East African Societies. (Library of Man). 1974. 12.50x (ISBN 0-7100-7957-5); pap. 6.95 (ISBN 0-7100-7958-3). Routledge & Kegan.

Shorter, Clement K. Charlotte Bronte & Her Circle. LC 78-78241. 1969. Repr. of 1896 ed. 26.00 (ISBN 0-8103-3138-1). Gale.

Shorter, Roy G., ed. see Kirsner, Joseph B.

Shorthouse, Joseph H. John Inglesant. Wolff, Robert L., ed. (Victorian Fiction Ser.). 1975. Repr. of 1880 ed. lib. bdg. 66.00 (ISBN 0-8240-1557-6). Garland Pub.

Shortley, George & Williams, Dudley. Elements of Physics, 2 vols. 5th ed. (Illus.). 1971. Combined. text ed. 27.95 (ISBN 0-13-268383-0); Vol. 1. text ed. 17.95 (ISBN 0-13-268367-9); Vol. 2. text ed. 17.95 (ISBN 0-13-268375-X). P-H.

Shortley, George H., jt. auth. see Condon, Edward U.

Shortt, Joseph & Wilson, Thomas C. Problem Solving & the Computer: A Structured Concept with PL 1 (PLC) 2nd ed. 1979. pap. text ed. 13.95 (ISBN 0-201-06916-4). A-W.

Shortt, S. E., ed. Medicine in Canadian Society: Historical Perspectives. 400p. 1981. 23.95x (ISBN 0-7735-0356-0); pap. 11.95 (ISBN 0-7735-0369-2). McGill-Queens U Pr.

Shostak. How to Prepare for College Board Achievement Test in English. 1981. pap. 3.95 (ISBN 0-8120-2282-3). Barron.

Shostak, et al. How to Prepare for the LSAT: Canadian Edition. LC 77-80603. 1977. pap. text ed. 6.95 (ISBN 0-8120-0864-2). Barron.

Shostak, Arthur B. Our Sociological Eye: Personal Essays on Society & Culture. LC 76-30578. 1977. pap. text ed. 9.95x (ISBN 0-88284-048-7). Alfred Pub.

Shostak, Arthur B., et al. Privilege in America: An End to Inequality? 160p. 1974. pap. 6.95 (ISBN 0-13-711119-3, Spec). P-H.

Shostakovskii, M. F. The Chemistry of Diacetylenes. Lederman, N., ed. Mandel, N., tr. from Rus. Bogdanova, A. V., ed. LC 74-8274. 493p. 1974. 64.95 (ISBN 0-470-78854-2). Halsted Pr.

Shosteck, Patti. A Lexicon of Jewish Cooking. rev. ed. 1981. pap. 6.95 (ISBN 0-8092-5995-8). Contemp Bks.

Shostrum, Everett, jt. auth. see Brammer, L.

Shotski. Agro-Industrial Complexes & Types of Agriculture in Eastern Siberia. 1979. 14.00 (ISBN 0-9960016-2-X, Pub. by Kaido Hungary). Heyden.

Shotski, V. P. Agro-Industrial Complexes & Types of Agriculture in Eastern Siberia. Kecskes, Bela, tr. from Rus. (Geography of World Agriculture Ser.: Vol. 8). (Illus.). 131p. 1979. 13.50x (ISBN 963-05-1845-7). Intl Pubns Serv.

Shotter, jt. auth. see Gauld.

Shotter, David. Angekommen. 1975. pap. text ed. 8.95x o.p. (ISBN 0-435-38843-6); two tapes 54.00 o.p. (ISBN 0-435-38846-0). Heinemann Ed.

--Biberswald. 1973. pap. text ed. 5.95x o.p. (ISBN 0-435-38835-5); tchr's ed. 3.95x o.p. (ISBN 0-435-38836-3); four tapes 80.00 o.p. (ISBN 0-435-38837-1). Heinemann Ed.

--Unterwegs. 1974. pap. text ed. 7.95x o.p. (ISBN 0-435-38839-8); tchr's ed. 6.25x o.p. (ISBN 0-435-38840-1); four tapes 80.00 o.p. (ISBN 0-435-38841-X). Heinemann Ed.

Shotter, John, jt. auth. see Gauld, Alan.

Shotton, F. W. see Bowen, D. Q.

Shotwell, James T. The Story of Ancient History. LC 39-4448. 1961. pap. 6.00x (ISBN 0-231-08518-4, 18). Columbia U Pr.

Shouksmith, George. Intelligence, Creativity & Cognitive Style. 1970. 32.00 (ISBN 0-7134-0980-0, Pub. by Batsford England). David & Charles.

Shoumatoff, Alex. Florida Ramble. LC 72-9154. (Illus.). 196p. (YA) 1974. 7.95 o.p. (ISBN 0-06-013858-0, HarpT). Har-Row.

Shoup, Carl S., ed. Fiscal Harmonization in Common Markets, 2 Vols. Vol. 1. Theory, Vol. 2. Practice. LC 66-14789. 1966. Set. 50.00x (ISBN 0-231-08964-3). Columbia U Pr.

Shoup, Carls. Test Your Bible Knowledge. 1973. pap. 0.95 o.s.i. (ISBN 0-515-02725-1, N2725). Jove Pubns.

Shoup, Paul. Communism & the Yugoslav National Question. LC 68-19759. (East Central European Studies). 1968. 20.00x (ISBN 0-231-03125-4). Columbia U Pr.

Shoup, T. Practical Guide to Computer Methods for Engineers. 1979. 21.95 (ISBN 0-13-690651-6). P-H.

Shoup, T., et al. Introduction to Engineering Design with Design Projects. 1981. pap. 15.95 (ISBN 0-13-482364-8); pap. 8.95 wkbk. (ISBN 0-13-716274-X). P-H.

Shoup, T. E., jt. auth. see Fletcher, L. S.

Shoup, T. E., ed. International Conference on Medical & Sports Devices. 270p. 1980. 30.00 (H00160). ASME.

Shouppe, F. X. Purgatory: Explained by the Lives & Legends of the Saints. LC 79-112489. 1973. pap. 6.50 (ISBN 0-89555-042-3, 143). TAN Bks Pubs.

Shourds, Harry V. & Hillman, Anthony. Carving Duck Decoys, with Full-Size Patterns for Hollow Contruction. (Illus.). 64p. (Orig.). 1981. pap. price not set (ISBN 0-486-24083-5). Dover.

Shourie, Arun. Institutions in the Janata Phase. 300p. 1980. text ed. 18.00 (ISBN 0-8426-1678-0). Verry.

Shover, Neal. A Sociology of American Corrections. 1979. pap. text ed. 10.95x (ISBN 0-256-02216-X). Dorsey.

Showalter, Carol. Three-D. LC 77-90947. 144p. 1980. pap. 4.95 (ISBN 0-932260-04-7). Rock Harbor.

Showalter, Rachel. Home Fires Beneath the Northern Lights. 260p. 1970. 5.70 o.p. (ISBN 0-686-05598-5). Rod & Staff.

Showell, Ellen H. The Ghost of Tillie Jean Cassaway. LC 78-5353. (Illus.). 128p. (gr. 3-7). 1978. 6.95 (ISBN 0-590-07559-4, Four Winds). Schol Bk Serv.

Showers, Kay S., jt. auth. see Showers, Paul.

Showers, Paul. Baby Starts to Grow. LC 69-11827. (A Let's-Read-&-Find-Out Science Bk). (Illus.). (gr. k-3). 1969. PLB 7.89 (ISBN 0-690-11320-X, TYC-J); (ISBN 0-685-20467-7); filmstrip with record 11.95 (ISBN 0-690-11321-8); film with cassette 14.95 (ISBN 0-690-11323-4). T Y Crowell.

--Columbus Day. LC 65-16186. (Holiday Ser.). (Illus.). (gr. k-3). 1965. 7.89 (ISBN 0-690-19982-1, TYC-J). T Y Crowell.

--Drop of Blood. LC 67-23672. (A Let's-Read-&-Find-Out Science Bk). (Illus.). (gr. k-3). 1967. PLB 7.89 (ISBN 0-690-24526-2, TYC-J); filmstrip with record 11.95 (ISBN 0-690-24527-0); film with cassette 14.95 (ISBN 0-690-24529-7). T Y Crowell.

--Find Out by Touching. LC 60-13242. (A Let's-Read-&-Find-Out Science Bk). (Illus.). (gr. k-3). 1961. PLB 7.89 (ISBN 0-690-29782-3, TYC-J). T Y Crowell.

--Follow Your Nose. LC 63-15097. (A Let's-Read-&-Find-Out Science Bk). (Illus.). (gr. k-3). 1963. PLB 7.89 (ISBN 0-690-31273-3, TYC-J); filmstrip with record 11.95 (ISBN 0-690-31274-1); film with cassette 14.95 (ISBN 0-690-31276-8). T Y Crowell.

--Fortune Telling for Fun. LC 80-2549. 349p. 1980. Repr. of 1971 ed. lib. bdg. 10.95x (ISBN 0-89370-607-8). Borgo Pr.

--Hear Your Heart. LC 68-11067. (A Let's Read & Find Out Science Bk). (Illus.). (gr. k-3). 1968. bds. 6.95 (ISBN 0-690-37378-3, TYC-J); PLB 7.89 (ISBN 0-690-37379-1); filmstrip with record 11.95 (ISBN 0-690-37380-5); film with cassette 14.95 (ISBN 0-690-37382-1). T Y Crowell.

--Hear Your Heart. LC 68-11067. (Crocodile Paperbacks Ser.). (Illus.). 40p. (gr. k-3). 1975. pap. 2.95 (ISBN 0-690-00636-5, TYC-J). T Y Crowell.

--How Many Teeth. LC 62-11004. (A Let's-Read-&-Find-Out Science Bk). (Illus.). (gr. k-3). 1962. PLB 7.89 (ISBN 0-690-40716-5, TYC-J); filmstrip with record 11.95 (ISBN 0-690-40717-3); films with cassette 14.95 (ISBN 0-690-40719-X). T Y Crowell.

--How You Talk. LC 66-15766. (A Let's-Read-&-Find-Out Science Bk). (Illus.). (ps-3). 1967. 7.89 (ISBN 0-690-42136-2, TYC-J); filmstrip with record 11.95 (ISBN 0-690-42137-0); films with cassette 14.95 (ISBN 0-690-42139-7). T Y Crowell.

--In the Night. LC 61-6138. (A Let's-Read-&-Find-Out Science Bk). (Illus.). (gr. k-3). 1961. PLB 7.89 (ISBN 0-690-44621-7, TYC-J). T Y Crowell.

--Listening Walk. LC 61-10495. (A Let's-Read & Find-Out Science Bk). (Illus.). (gr. k-3). 1961. 7.89 (ISBN 0-690-49663-X, TYC-J). T Y Crowell.

--Look at Your Eyes. LC 62-12821. (A Let's-Read-&-Find-Out Science Bk). (Illus.). (gr. k-3). 1962. bds. 6.95 (ISBN 0-690-50727-5, TYC-J); PLB 7.89 (ISBN 0-690-50728-3); filmstrip with record 11.95 (ISBN 0-690-50731-3); film with cassette 14.95 (ISBN 0-690-50733-X). T Y Crowell.

--Me & My Family Tree. LC 77-26595. (A Let's-Read-&-Find-Out Science Bk). (Illus.). (gr. k-3). 1978. 7.95 (ISBN 0-690-03886-0, TYC-J); PLB 7.89 (ISBN 0-690-03887-9). T Y Crowell.

--Mirate Los Ojos. Palmer, Richard J., tr. LC 68-29617. (A Let's-Read-and-Find-Out Science Bk). Orig. Title: Look at Your Eyes. (Illus., Span.). (gr. k-3). 1968. bds. 7.95 (ISBN 0-690-50729-1, TYC-J). T Y Crowell.

--The Moon Walker. LC 73-17490. 48p. (ps-3). 1975. PLB 4.95 o.p. (ISBN 0-385-02042-2). Doubleday.

--No Measles, No Mumps for Me. LC 79-7106. (Let's-Read-&-Find-Out Science Book). (Illus.). 40p. (gr. k-3). 1980. 7.95 (ISBN 0-690-04017-2, TYC-J); PLB 7.89 (ISBN 0-690-04018-0). T Y Crowell.

--Sleep Is for Everyone. LC 72-83785. (A Let's Read-&-Find-Out Science Bk). (Illus.). (ps-3). 1974. 7.89 (ISBN 0-690-01118-0, TYC-J). T Y Crowell.

--Use Your Brain. LC 79-157646. (A Let's-Read-&-Find-Out Science Bk). (Illus.). (gr. k-3). 1971. 7.95 (ISBN 0-690-85410-2, TYC-J); PLB 7.89 (ISBN 0-690-85411-0); pap. 1.95 crocodile paperback ser. (ISBN 0-690-00204-1); filmstrip with record 11.95 (ISBN 0-690-85412-9); filmstrip with cassette 14.95 (ISBN 0-690-85414-5). T Y Crowell.

--What Happens to a Hamburger. LC 70-106578. (A Let's Read & Find Out Science Bk). (Illus.). (gr. k-3). 1970. bds. 7.95 (ISBN 0-690-87540-1, TYC-J); PLB 7.89 (ISBN 0-690-87541-X); filmstrip with record 11.95 (ISBN 0-690-87542-8); filmstrip with cassette 14.95 (ISBN 0-690-87544-4). T Y Crowell.

--Where Does the Garbage Go? LC 73-14881. (A Let's-Read-&-Find-Out Science Bk). (Illus.). (ps-3). 1974. 7.95 (ISBN 0-690-00392-7, TYC-J); PLB 7.89 (ISBN 0-690-00402-8). T Y Crowell.

--Your Skin & Mine. LC 65-16185. (A Let's-Read-&-Find-Out Science Bk). (Illus.). (gr. k-3). 1965. PLB 7.89 (ISBN 0-690-91127-0, TYC-J); pap. 2.95 crocodile paperback ser. (ISBN 0-690-00205-X); filmstrip with record 11.95 (ISBN 0-690-91130-0); filmstrip with cassette 14.95 (ISBN 0-690-91132-7). T Y Crowell.

Showers, Paul & Showers, Kay S. Before You Were a Baby. LC 68-13588. (A Let's-Read-&-Find-Out Science Bk). (Illus.). (gr. k-3). 1968. PLB 7.89 (ISBN 0-690-12882-7, TYC-J). T Y Crowell.

Showler, Brian. The Public Employment Service. LC 76-8923. 1976. text ed. 13.00x (ISBN 0-582-48541-X); pap. text ed. 9.00x (ISBN 0-582-48542-8). Longman.

Showler, Brian & Sinfield, Adrian. The Workless State: A Study of Unemployment. 252p. 1981. 20.00x (ISBN 0-85520-327-7, Pub. by Martin Robertson England); pap. 9.95x (ISBN 0-85520-340-4). Biblio Dist.

Showman, Richard K., jt. ed. see Freidel, Frank.

Shrader, Robert D. & Everden, Sue. Team Sports: A Competency Based Approach. 1977. pap. text ed. 10.25 o.p. (ISBN 0-8403-1807-3). Kendall-Hunt.

Shrader, Stephen R. Introductory Mass Spectrometry. 1971. pap. 10.95x o.p. (ISBN 0-205-02914-0, 6829147). Allyn.

Shrader-Frechette, K. S. Nuclear Power & Public Policy: The Social & Ethical Problems of Fission Technology. (Pallas Paperbacks Ser.: No. 15). 220p. 1980. lib. bdg. 19.95 (ISBN 90-277-1054-6); pap. 10.50 (ISBN 90-277-1080-5). Kluwer Boston.

Shrager, Arthur M. Elementary Metallurgy & Metallography. 2nd ed. (Illus.). 1961. pap. text ed. 5.00 (ISBN 0-486-60138-2). Dover.

Shrager, Sidney. Scatology in Modern Drama. 128p. 1981. text ed. 20.00x (ISBN 0-8290-0261-8). Irvington.

Shrake, Edwin. Peter Arbiter: The Adventures of a Young Man in Texas. (Illus.). 152p. 1973. 7.95 o.s.i. (ISBN 0-88426-030-5). Encino Pr.

Shreck. More Very First Stories with Hilary Hippo & Friends. 117p. pap. 8.95 (ISBN 0-02-037130-6). Macmillan.

--Very First Stories with Brian Badger & Friends. 121p. Date not set. pap. 8.95 (ISBN 0-02-037120-9). Macmillan.

Shreve, G. M. & Arewa, E. O. Genesis of Structures in African Narrative: Dahomean Narratives, Vol. 2. (Studies in African Semiotics Ser.). 1981. 30.00 (ISBN 0-914970-01-1). Conch Mag.

Shreve, R. Norris & Brink, Joseph. Chemical Process Industries. 4th ed. (Illus.). 1977. 28.50 (ISBN 0-07-057145-7, P&RB). McGraw.

Shreve, Susan. The Masquerade. LC 79-20073. 224p. 1980. 7.95 (ISBN 0-394-84142-5); PLB 7.99 (ISBN 0-394-94142-X). Knopf.

Shreve, Susan R. Children of Power. 1979. 8.95 o.s.i. (ISBN 0-02-610510-1). Macmillan.

Shrewsbury, J. F. History of Bubonic Plague in the British Isles. LC 69-10197. (Illus.). 1970. 75.00 (ISBN 0-521-07083-X). Cambridge U Pr.

Shribert, Lawrence D. & Kwiatkowski, Joan. Natural Process Analysis (NPA) A Procedure for Phonological Analysis of Continuous Speech Analysis. LC 80-51707. (Wiley Ser. on Communication Disorders). 175p. 1980. pap. 10.50x (ISBN 0-471-07893-X). Wiley.

Shrier, Linda, jt. auth. see Margolis, Clorinda.

Shriner, Charles A. Wit, Wisdom & Foibles of the Great. LC 68-30617. 1969. Repr. of 1918 ed. 22.00 (ISBN 0-8103-3297-3). Gale.

Shriner, D. S., et al, eds. Atmospheric Sulfur Deposition: Environmental Impact & Health Effects. 586p. 1980. 29.50 (ISBN 0-250-40380-3). Ann Arbor Science.

Shriner, Ralph, et al. The Systematic Identification of Organic Compounds: A Laboratory Manual. 6th ed. 1980. 22.95x (ISBN 0-471-78874-0). Wiley.

Shriner, Ralph L., et al. Systematic Identification of Organic Compounds. 5th ed. LC 64-15000. 1964. 17.95 o.p. (ISBN 0-471-78873-2). Wiley.

Shrivastava, B. K., jt. auth. see Venkataramani, M. S.

Shrivastava, B. K. & Casstevens, Thomas B., eds. American Government & Politics. 1980. text ed. 20.00x (ISBN 0-391-01798-5). Humanities.

Shrivastava, K. C. Mrs. Gaskell As Novelist. (Salzburg Studies in English Literature: Romantic Reassessment Ser.: No. 70). 1977. pap. text ed. 25.00x (ISBN 0-391-01523-0). Humanities.

Shrivastava, O. S. Demography. 500p. 1980. text ed. 25.00 (ISBN 0-7069-1109-1, Pub. by Vikas India). Advent Bk.

Shriver, D. F. The Manipulation of Air-Sensitive Compounds. LC 81-60. 320p. 1981. Repr. of 1969 ed. lib. bdg. price not set (ISBN 0-89874-323-0). Krieger.

Shriver, Donald W., Jr., ed. Medicine & Religion: Strategies of Care. LC 79-23420. (Contemporary Community Health Ser.). 1980. pap. 10.95 (ISBN 0-8229-3412-4). U of Pittsburgh Pr.

Shriver, H. C., ed. Justice Oliver Wendell Holmes: His Book Notices & Uncollected Letters & Papers. LC 72-10336. (American Constitutional & Legal History Ser). 300p. 1973. Repr. of 1936 ed. lib. bdg. 29.50 (ISBN 0-306-70557-5). Da Capo.

Shroff, Homai J. The Eighteenth Century Novel: The Idea of the Gentleman. 1978. text ed. 13.50x (ISBN 0-391-01067-0). Humanities.

Shrope, Wayne A. Speaking & Listening: A Contemporary Approach. 2nd ed. 305p. 1979. pap. text ed. 8.95 (ISBN 0-15-583182-8, HC); instructor's manual avail. (ISBN 0-15-583183-6). HarBraceJ.

Shry, Carroll L., Jr., jt. auth. see Reiley, H. Edward.

Shryack, Dennis, jt. auth. see Butler, Michael.

Shryock, Clifford. How to Raise & Train a Chow Chow. (Orig.). pap. 2.00 (ISBN 0-87666-268-8, DS1070). TFH Pubns.

Shtern, V. Y. The Gas-Phase Oxidation of Hydrocarbons. Mullins, B. P., ed. 1964. 37.50 o.p. (ISBN 0-08-010202-6). Pergamon.

Shtogren, John A., ed. Models for Management: The Structure of Competence. LC 79-93291. (Illus.). 1981. pap. 17.95 (ISBN 0-937932-00-0). Telecometrics.

Shuard, H. & Quadling, D. Teachers of Math. 1980. text ed. 18.35 (ISBN 0-06-318174-6, IntlDept); pap. text ed. 9.25 (ISBN 0-06-318175-4). Har-Row.

Shub, Anatole. New Russian Tragedy. 1970. pap. text ed. 2.95x (ISBN 0-393-09910-5, NortonC). Norton.

Shub, Elisabeth, tr. see Borchers, Elisabeth.

Shub, Elizabeth, tr. see Brothers Grimm.

Shub, Elizabeth, tr. see Fontane, Theodor.

Shub, Elizabeth, tr. see Grimm Brothers.

Shub, Elizabeth, tr. see Hauff, Wilhelm.

Shub, Elizabeth, adapted by. Clever Kate. LC 72-81063. (Ready-to-Read Ser.). (Illus.). 64p. (gr. 1-4). 1973. 7.95g (ISBN 0-02-782490-X). Macmillan.

Shuba, M. F., jt. ed. see Bulbring, E.

Shubik, Martin, jt. auth. see Whitman, Martin.

Shubin, John A. Business Management. rev. ed. (Orig.). 1957. pap. 3.95 (ISBN 0-06-460092-0, CO 92, COS). Har-Row.

Shubin, Penni. A Lonely Rose. LC 78-10136. Date not set. 11.95 (ISBN 0-87949-153-1). Ashley Bks.

Shubnikov, A. V. & Belov, N. V. Colored Symmetry. 1964. 37.00 (ISBN 0-08-010505-X); pap. 22.00 (ISBN 0-08-013790-3). Pergamon.

Shu Chao Hu. The Development of the Chinese Collection in the Library of Congress. LC 79-1741. (A Westview Replica Edition Ser.). (Illus.). 1979. lib. bdg. 25.50x (ISBN 0-89158-552-4). Westview.

Shuchman, Hedvah L. Information Transfer in Engineering. (Illus.). 300p. (Orig.). 1981. pap. 45.00 (ISBN 0-9605196-0-2). Futures Group.

Shuck, Victoria, jt. ed. see Milburn, Josephine.

Shuckburgh, E. S., ed. see Herodotus.

Shue, Henry, jt. ed. see Brown, Peter G.

Shue, Vivienne. Peasant China in Transition: The Dynamics of Development Toward Socialism 1949 to 1956. 500p. 1980. 25.75x (ISBN 0-520-03734-0). U of Cal Pr.

Shuecraft, Steven. Days Without Beginnings. 1981. 4.50 (ISBN 0-8062-1619-0). Carlton.

Shufeldt, H. H. Slide Rule for the Mariner. LC 74-188008. 1972. 8.00 o.s.i. (ISBN 0-87021-655-4). Naval Inst Pr.

Shufeldt, H. H. & Newcomer, Kenneth. The Calculator Afloat: A Mariner's Guide to the Electronic Calculator. LC 80-81091. 256p. 1980. 16.95 (ISBN 0-87021-116-1). Naval Inst Pr.

Shuffstall, Richard M. & Hemmaplardh, Brecharr. The Hospital Laboratory: Modern Concepts of Management, Operations, & Finance. LC 78-11877. (Illus.). 1979. 15.95 (ISBN 0-8016-4620-0). Mosby.

Shuford, Wade H. & Sybers, Robert G. The Aortic Arch & Its Malformations: With Emphasis on the Angiographic Features. (Illus.). 288p. 1973. 26.50 (ISBN 0-398-02854-0). C C Thomas.

Shufunotomo Editorial Staff, jt. ed. see Tetsuzo Tanikawa.

Shugar, D., jt. auth. see McLaren, A. D.

Shugar, D. & Shugar, D., eds. Enzymes & Isoenzymes: Structure, Properties & Function. 1970. 50.00 (ISBN 0-12-640860-2). Acad Pr.

Shugar, G., et al. Basic Mathematics for Allied Health. 1975. pap. 9.95x (ISBN 0-02-478500-8, 47850). Macmillan.

Shugar, G. J. & Bauman, R. S. Arithmetic: A Practical Approach. 1977. pap. text ed. 10.95x (ISBN 0-02-478520-2). Macmillan.

Shugar, Gershon, et al. Chemical Technicians' Ready Reference Handbook. 2nd ed. 864p. 1981. 39.50 (ISBN 0-07-057176-7, P&RB). McGraw.

Shugar, Gershon J., et al. How to Get into Medical & Dental School. rev. ed. LC 80-23397. 160p. 1981. lib. bdg. 8.00 (ISBN 0-668-05105-1); pap. 6.00 (ISBN 0-668-05112-4). Arco.

Shugarman, D., ed. Thinking About Change. LC 74-82285. 1974. pap. 4.95 (ISBN 0-8020-6251-2). U of Toronto Pr.

Shugart, Cecil G., ed. see Einstein Centennial Celebration, Memphis State University, March 14-16, 1979.

Shugart, Cooksey. The Complete Guide to American Pocket Watches 1981: Pocket Watches from 1809-1950. Schrieber, Peter, ed. 1981. pap. 8.95 (ISBN 0-517-54378-8, Harmony). Crown.

Shugrue, Michael, ed. see Burnet, Sir Thomas & Duckett, George.

Shugrue, Michael, ed. see Farquhar, George.

Shugrue, Michael F., ed. Adventures of a Cork-Screw, Seventeen Seventy-Five. (The Flowering of the Novel, 1740-1775 Ser: Vol. 107). 1974. lib. bdg. 50.00 (ISBN 0-8240-1206-2). Garland Pub.

--Adventures of a Jesuit, Seventeen Seventy-One, 2 vols. in 1. (The Flowering of the Novel, 1740-1775 Ser: Vol. 94). 1974. lib. bdg. 50.00 (ISBN 0-8240-1193-7). Garland Pub.

--Adventures of a Kidnapped Orphan, Seventeen Forty-Seven. (The Flowering of the Novel, 1740-1775 Ser: Vol. 21). 1974. lib. bdg. 50.00 (ISBN 0-8240-1120-1). Garland Pub.

--The Adventures of an Author: Written by Himself and a Friend, 2 vols. in 1. (The Flowering of the Novel, 1740-1775 Ser: Vol. 77). 1974. lib. bdg. 50.00 (ISBN 0-8240-1176-7). Garland Pub.

--The Adventures of Jack Wander, 1766. (The Flowering of the Novel, 1740-1775 Ser: Vol. 73). 1974. lib. bdg. 50.00 (ISBN 0-8240-1172-4). Garland Pub.

--The Adventures of Oxymel Classic, Esq., Once an Oxford Scholar, 1768. (The Flowering of the Novel, 1740-1775 Ser: Vol. 82). 1974. lib. bdg. 50.00 (ISBN 0-8240-1181-3). Garland Pub.

--The Adventures of Sylvia Hughes, Written by Herself 1761. (The Flowering of the Novel, 1740-1775 Ser: Vol. 56). 1974. lib. bdg. 50.00 (ISBN 0-8240-1155-4). Garland Pub.

--The Birmingham Counterfeit; or, Invisible Spectator, 1772, 2 vols. in 1. LC 74-16027. (The Flowering of the Novel, 1740-1775 Ser: Vol. 98). 1974. lib. bdg. 50.00 (ISBN 0-8240-1197-X). Garland Pub.

--Fatal Friendship: A Novel; by a Lady, 1771, 2 vols. in 1. (The Flowering of the Novel, 1740-1775 Ser: Vol. 95). 1974. lib. bdg. 50.00 (ISBN 0-8240-1194-5). Garland Pub.

--The Female American; or, the Adventures of Unca Eliza Winkfield, 1767, 2 vols. in 1. (The Flowering of the Novel, 1740-1775 Ser: Vol. 79). 1974. lib. bdg. 50.00 (ISBN 0-8240-1178-3). Garland Pub.

--Foundations of the Novel Series: Representative Early Eighteenth-Century Fiction, 71 vols. lib. bdg. 50.00 ea. Garland Pub.

--The Fruitless Repentance; or, the History of Kitty le Fever, 1769, 2 vols. in 1. (The Flowering of the Novel, 1740-1775 Ser: Vol. 86). 1974. lib. bdg. 50.00 (ISBN 0-8240-1185-6). Garland Pub.

--A Full and Particular Account of the Life and Transactions of Roger Johnson. Bd. with The Life and Adventures of Gilbert Langley. Repr. of 1740 ed; A True and Impartial History of the Life and Adventures of Somebody. Repr. of 1740 ed; An Apology for the Life of Mrs. Shamela Andrews. Fielding, Henry. Repr. of 1741 ed. (The Flowering of the Novel, 1740-1775 Ser: Vol. 3). 1974. Repr. of 1740 ed. lib. bdg. 50.00 (ISBN 0-8240-1102-3). Garland Pub.

--The History of the Human Heart; or, the Adventures of a Young Gentleman, 1749. (The Flowering of the Novel, 1740-1775 Ser: Vol. 26). 1974. lib. bdg. 50.00 (ISBN 0-8240-1125-2). Garland Pub.

--The History of Tom Jones the Foundling, in His Married State, 1750. (The Flowering of the Novel, 1740-1775 Ser: Vol. 28). 1974. lib. bdg. 50.00 (ISBN 0-8240-1127-9). Garland Pub.

--The Ladies Advocate; or, Wit & Beauty a Match for Treachery & Inconstancy, 1749. (Novel in England 1700-1775 Ser.). 1974. lib. bdg. 50.00 (ISBN 0-8240-1126-0). Garland Pub.

--The Lady's Drawing Room. (Novel in England 1700-1775). 1974. Repr. of 1744 ed. lib. bdg. 50.00 (ISBN 0-8240-1110-4). Garland Pub.

--The Life, Adventures, Intrigues & Amours of the Celebrated Jemmy Twitcher, 1770. Bd. with The Life, Adventures, & Amours of Sir Richard Perrot, 1770. LC 74-31492. (Novel in England, 1700-1775 Ser). 1974. lib. bdg. 50.00 (ISBN 0-8240-1191-0). Garland Pub.

--Memoirs of a Coquet, or the History of Miss Harriet Airy, 1765. (The Flowering of the Novel, 1740-1775 Ser: Vol. 70). 1974. lib. bdg. 50.00 (ISBN 0-8240-1169-4). Garland Pub.

--Memoirs...of Captain Mackheath, Repr. Of 1728. Bd. with A Trip to the Moon. Repr. of 1728 ed; The Adventures of Abdalla. Bignon, Jean P. Repr. of 1729 ed. LC 79-170573. (Foundations of a Novel Ser.). lib. bdg. 50.00 (ISBN 0-8240-0564-3). Garland Pub.

--Sophronia; or, Letters to the Ladies. (Flowering of the Novel Ser.: 1740-1775). Repr. of 1761 ed. lib. bdg. 50.00 (ISBN 0-8240-1158-9). Garland Pub.

--The Temple-Beau; or, the Town Coquets: A Novel, 1754. (The Flowering of the Novel, 1740-1775 Ser: Vol. 42). 1974. lib. bdg. 50.00 (ISBN 0-8240-1141-4). Garland Pub.

--The Theatre of Love: A Collection of Novels, 1759. (The Flowering of the Novel, 1740-1775 Ser: Vol. 52). 1974. lib. bdg. 50.00 (ISBN 0-8240-1151-1). Garland Pub.

--The Wanderer; or, Memoirs of Charles Searle, Esq., 1766: Containing His Adventures by Sea and Land, 2 vols. in 1. (The Flowering of the Novel, 1740-1775 Ser: Vol. 74). 1974. lib. bdg. 50.00 (ISBN 0-8240-1173-2). Garland Pub.

Shugrue, Michael F., ed. see Bicknell, Alexander.

Shugrue, Michael F., ed. see Boswell, James.

Shugrue, Michael F., ed. see Bridges, Thomas.

Shugrue, Michael F., ed. see Brooke, Frances.

Shugrue, Michael F., ed. see Burton, John.

Shugrue, Michael F., ed. see Coventry, Francis.

Shugrue, Michael F., ed. see Doddridge, Philip.

Shugrue, Michael F., ed. see Fielding, Sarah.

Shugrue, Michael F., ed. see Gentleman, Francis.

Shugrue, Michael F., ed. see Graffigny, Francoise.

Shugrue, Michael F., ed. see Graves, Richard.

Shugrue, Michael F., ed. see Guunning, Susannah Minnifie.

Shugrue, Michael F., ed. see Hawkesworth, John.

Shugrue, Michael F., ed. see Helvetius, Claude.

Shugrue, Michael F., ed. see Hill, John.

Shugrue, Michael F., ed. see Holberg, Ludwig.

Shugrue, Michael F., ed. see Jenner, Charles.

Shugrue, Michael F., ed. see Johnstone, Charles.

Shugrue, Michael F., ed. see Le Camus, A.

Shugrue, Michael F., ed. see Leland, Thomas.

Shugrue, Michael F., ed. see Lennox, Charlotte.

Shugrue, Michael F., ed. see Lyttleton, George.

Shugrue, Michael F., ed. see McCarthy, Charlotte.

Shugrue, Michael F., ed. see Marmontel, Jean Francois.

Shugrue, Michael F., ed. see Mouhy, Charles.

Shugrue, Michael F., ed. see Richardson, Samuel.

Shugrue, Michael F., ed. see Tencin, Claudine.

Shugrue, Michael F., ed. see Voltaire, Francois.

Shugrue, Michael F., ed. see Woodfin, Mrs. A.

Shugrue, Michael F., ed. see Young, Arthur.

Shugrve, Michael, ed. see Walker, Charles.

Shuilleabhain, Eibhlis Ni. Letters from the Great Blasket. (Illus.). 1978. pap. 3.95 (ISBN 0-85342-526-4). Irish Bk Ctr.

Shuja Ibn Aslam, Abukamil. The Algebra of Abu Kamil, in a Commentary by Mordecai Finzi. Levey, Martin, tr. (Publications in Medieval Science No. 10). 1966. 24.50x (ISBN 0-299-03800-9). U of Wis Pr.

Shukla, Ashok C. & Misra, Shital P. Essentials of Paleobotany. 1975. 15.00 (ISBN 0-7069-0381-1, Pub. by Vikas India). Advent Bk.

Shukla, K. S. Adolescent Thieves. 1979. text ed. 15.00x (ISBN 0-391-01925-2). Humanities.

Shukla, P. D. Towards the New Pattern of Education in India. 1976. text ed. 12.00x o.p. (ISBN 0-8426-0918-0). Verry.

Shukla, S. Social & Moral Ideas in the Plays of Galsworthy. (Salzburg Studies in English Literature: 48). 263p. 1979. text ed. 25.00x (ISBN 0-391-01780-2). Humanities.

Shukla, Shaligram. Bhojpuri Grammar. (Bhojpuri.). 1981. text ed. 10.00x (ISBN 0-87840-189-X). Georgetown U Pr.

Shukman, Harold, tr. see Rybakov, Anatoli.

Shula, Dorothy, et al. Souper Bowl of Recipes. 1980. 15.00 (ISBN 0-89002-164-3); pap. 7.95 (ISBN 0-89002-163-5). Northwoods Pr.

Shulberg, Lucille. Historic India. LC 68-22440. (Great Ages of Man Ser.). (gr. 6 up). 1968. PLB 11.97 (ISBN 0-8094-0381-1, Pub. by Time-Life). Silver.

Shuldener, Henry L. & Fullman, James B. Water & Piping Problems: A Troubleshooter's Guide for Large & Small Buildings. 275p. 1981. 19.95 (ISBN 0-471-08082-9, Pub. by Wiley-Interscience). Wiley.

Shuldner, Herbert. The Popular Science Guide to Ingenious Devices. Michaelman, Herbert, ed. Date not set. 12.95 (ISBN 0-517-54280-3, Michelman Books). Crown.

Shulevitz, Uri. Dawn. LC 74-9761. (Illus.). 32p. (ps-3). 1974. 8.95 (ISBN 0-374-31707-0). FS&G.

--The Magician. LC 72-85186. (Illus.). 32p. (gr. k-3). 1973. 8.95 (ISBN 0-02-782510-8). Macmillan.

Shull, Henry A. & Krause, Peter. The Complete Guide to Cibachrome Printing. LC 80-51937. (Illus.). 220p. 1980. 16.95 (ISBN 0-87165-057-6); pap. 11.95 (ISBN 0-87165-062-2). Ziff-Davis Pub.

Shull, Peg. Children of Appalachia. LC 79-81386. (Illus.). (gr. 3-6). 1969. PLB 3.64 o.p. (ISBN 0-671-32134-X). Messner.

Shulman, Albert M. Gateway to Judaism, 2 vols. LC 69-15777. 1971. Set. 30.00 o.p. (ISBN 0-498-06896-X, Yoseloff). A S Barnes.

Shulman, Bernard H. & Forgus, Ronald. Personality: A Cognitive View. 1979. text ed. 19.95 (ISBN 0-13-657882-9). P-H.

Shulman, Colette, ed. We the Russians: Voices from Russia. LC 78-83345. (Illus.). 320p. (gr. 9 up). 1971. pap. 2.95 o.p. (ISBN 0-275-88550-X). Praeger.

Shulman, Frank J. Doctoral Dissertations on South Asia, 1966-1970: An Annotated Bibliography Covering North America, Europe, & Australia. LC 78-186256. (Michigan Papers on South & Southeast Asia: No. 4). 223p. 1971. pap. 6.00x (ISBN 0-89148-004-8). Ctr S&SE Asian.

Shulman, Julius, jt. auth. see Gleve, Paul.

Shulman, Lawrence. The Skills of Helping Individuals & Groups. LC 78-71816. 1979. text ed. 14.95 (ISBN 0-87581-243-0). Peacock Pubs.

Shulman, Lee, ed. Review of Research in Education, Four, 1976. LC 72-89719. 1977. text ed. 15.00 o.p. (ISBN 0-87581-214-7). Peacock Pubs.

Shulman, Max. Barefoot Boy with Cheek. 1.95 o.p. (ISBN 0-686-67648-3). Doubleday.

Shulman, Morton. Anyone Can Make Big Money Buying Art. 1977. 7.95 o.s.i. (ISBN 0-02-610560-8). Macmillan.

--How to Invest Your Money & Profit from Inflation. 1981. pap. 2.50 (ISBN 0-345-29740-7). Ballantine.

Shulte, Rainer, jt. ed. see Troupe, Quincy.

Shults, Eric. Glass, Mosaics, & Plastic. (Encore Edition). (Illus.). 1979. 3.95 (ISBN 0-684-16924-X, ScribT). Scribner.

Shultz, George P., jt. auth. see Rees, Albert.

Shultz, George P. & Aliber, Robert Z., eds. Guidelines, Informal Controls, & the Market Place. LC 66-23699. (Orig.). 1966. 12.00x o.s.i. (ISBN 0-226-75597-5); pap. 3.95 o.s.i. (ISBN 0-226-75598-3). U of Chicago Pr.

Shultz, Richard H., Jr. & Sloan, Stephen, eds. Responding to the Terrorist Threat: Security & Crisis Management. (Policy Studies). 1981. 27.50 (ISBN 0-08-025106-4). Pergamon.

Shulz. What a Nightmare, Charlie Brown. pap. 1.95 (ISBN 0-590-12114-6, Schol Pap). Schol Bk Serv.

Shum, Annie W. Queueing Models for Computer Systems: With General Service Time Distributions. LC 79-50229. (Outstanding Dissertations in the Computer Sciences Ser.: Vol. 19). 290p. 1980. lib. bdg. 28.00 (ISBN 0-8240-4404-5). Garland Pub.

Shumaker, Arthur W. History of Indiana Literature: With Emphasis on the Authors of Imaginative Works Who Commenced Writing Prior to World War II. 624p. 1962. 15.00x (ISBN 0-253-37012-4). Ind U Pr.

Shumaker, Virginia O. The Alaska Pipeline. LC 79-13696. (Illus.). 64p. (gr. 3-5). 1979. PLB 7.29 (ISBN 0-671-32975-8). Messner.

Shumaker, Wayne. The Occult Sciences in the Renaissance: A Study in Intellectual Patterns. LC 70-153552. (Illus.). 1972. 24.50x (ISBN 0-520-02021-9); pap. 6.95 (ISBN 0-520-03840-1). U of Cal Pr.

Shumaker, Wayne & Heilbron, J. L. John Dee on Astronomy: Propaedeumata Aphoristica (1558 & 1568) LC 76-50254. 1978. 22.75x (ISBN 0-520-03376-0). U of Cal Pr.

Shuman, Bernard, jt. auth. see Gross, Barbara.

Shuman, Bruce A. Riverbend Casebook. 1981. lib. bdg. 14.95x (ISBN 0-912700-57-2). Oryx Pr.

Shuman, John. Art Glass Sampler. (Illus.). 1978. softbound 12.95 o.p. (ISBN 0-87069-171-6). Wallace-Homestead.

Shuman, Larry J., et al, eds. Operations Research in Health Care: A Critical Analysis. LC 74-24397. 440p. 1975. 20.00x o.p. (ISBN 0-8018-1642-4). Johns Hopkins.

Shuman, R. Baird, jt. auth. see Krejewski, Robert J.

Shuman, R. Baird, et al, eds. Educational Drama for Today's Schools. LC 78-15115. 1978. 11.00 (ISBN 0-8108-1166-9). Scarecrow.

Shumsky, Abraham & Shumsky, Adaia. Ahavat Chesed - Love Mercy: Reader. (Mah Tov Hebrew Teaching Ser.: Bk. 2). (Illus.). (gr. 4 up). 1970. text ed. 5.00 (ISBN 0-8074-0175-7, 405304); tchrs'. guide 3.50 (ISBN 0-8074-0176-5, 205305); wkbk. 3.50 (ISBN 0-8074-0177-3, 405303). UAHC.

--Asot Mishpat. (Mah Tov Hebrew Teaching Ser.: Bk. 1). (Illus.). (gr. 4-8). 1969. text ed. 5.00 (ISBN 0-8074-0178-1, 405301); tchrs'. guide 3.50 (ISBN 0-8074-0179-X, 205302); wkbk. 3.50 (ISBN 0-8074-0180-3, 405300). UAHC.

--Hatznea Lechet: Walk Humbly. Spiro, Jack D., ed. (Mah Tov Hebrew Teaching Ser.: Bk. 3). (Illus.). (gr. 4). 1971. text ed. 5.00 (ISBN 0-8074-0181-1, 405307); tchrs'. guide 3.50 (ISBN 0-8074-0182-X, 205308); wkbk. 3.50 (ISBN 0-8074-0183-8, 405306). UAHC.

--Olam Gadol, 2 bks. Incl. Alef: a Big World. (Preprimer). text ed. 5.00 o.p. (ISBN 0-8074-0184-6, 405250); Bet. (Primer). 1973. text ed. 5.00 o.p. (ISBN 0-8074-0185-4, 405252); wkbk. with record 4.25 o.p. (ISBN 0-8074-0186-2, 405253). (Mah Tov Hebrew Program Ser.). (gr. 1-2). tchrs'. guide 5.00 o.p. (ISBN 0-8074-0187-0, 205254). UAHC.

Shumsky, Adaia, jt. auth. see Shumsky, Abraham.

Shumway, Floyd. Seaport City: New York 1775. LC 75-3940. 1975. pap. 1.95 o.s.i. (ISBN 0-913344-20-6). Interbk Inc.

Shumway, George. Rifles of Colonial America, 2 vols. Incl. Vol. 1. 352p (ISBN 0-87387-079-4); Vol. 2. 318p (ISBN 0-87387-082-4). (Congrife Ser.). (Illus.). 352p. 1980. casebound ea. 49.50 (ISBN 0-686-65023-9). Shumway.

Shumway, R. J., jt. auth. see Larsen, M. D.

Shumway, Richard, ed. Research in Mathematics Education. National Council of Teachers of Mathematics. 1980. 27.00 (ISBN 0-87353-163-9). NCTM.

Shupak, Sidney, jt. auth. see Lasson, Robert.

Shupe. What Every Engineer Should Know About Economic Decision Making. 224p. 1980. 12.50 (ISBN 0-8247-1019-3). Dekker.

Shupe, Anson D., Jr. & Bromley, David G. The New Vigilantes: Deprogrammers, Anti-Cultists & the New Religions. LC 80-23276. (Sage Library of Social Research: Vol. 113). 272p. 1980. 18.00 (ISBN 0-8039-1542-X); pap. 8.95 (ISBN 0-8039-1543-8). Sage.

Shur, Irene G. & Littell, Franklin H. Reflection on the Holocaust. Lambert, Richard D., ed. LC 80-66618. (The Annals of the American Academy of Political & Social Science: No. 450). 250p. 1980. 5.50x (ISBN 0-87761-252-8); pap. text ed. 7.00x (ISBN 0-87761-253-6). Am Acad Pol Soc Sci.

Shura, Mary F. The Gray Ghosts of Taylor Ridge. LC 77-16861. (gr. 5 up). 1978. 5.95 (ISBN 0-396-07526-6). Dodd.

--Mister Wolf & Me. LC 78-22432. (Illus.). (gr. 5 up). 1979. 5.95 (ISBN 0-396-07666-1). Dodd.

--Riddle of Raven Hollow. (gr. 4-6). 1976. pap. 1.25 (ISBN 0-590-03568-1, Schol Pap). Schol Bk Serv.

Shurcliff, William A. Superinsulated Houses & Double-Envelope Houses. (Illus.). 228p. 1981. 19.95 (ISBN 0-931790-19-0); pap. 12.00. Brick Hse Pub.

--Thermal Shutters & Shades. LC 80-11574. 272p. 1980. pap. 12.95 (ISBN 0-931790-14-X). Brick Hse Pub.

Shurden, Walter B. The Sunday School Board: Ninety Years of Service. (Orig.). 1981. soft cover 5.95 (ISBN 0-8054-6558-8). Broadman.

--The Sunday School Board: Ninety Years of Service. (Orig.). pap. 5.95 (ISBN 0-8054-6558-8). Broadman.

Shu-Ren Lin, jt. auth. see Lee, K. Francis.

Shurkin, Joel, jt. auth. see Ryan, Desmond.

Shurley, Jay T., ed. Relating Environment to Mental Health & Illness: The Ecopsychiatric Base. (Task Force Reports: 16). 58p. 1979. pap. 5.00 (ISBN 0-685-95864-7, P147-0). Am Psychiatric.

Shurter, Robert L. Handy Grammar Reference. 1959. pap. 3.50 (ISBN 0-07-057345-X). McGraw.

Shurtgleff, William & Aoyagi, Akiko. The Book of Miso. 768p. 1981. pap. 3.50 (ISBN 0-345-29107-7). Ballantine.

Shurtleff, Harold R. The Log-Cabin Myth: A Study of the Early Dwellings of the English Colonists in North America. (Illus.). 1967. 8.50 (ISBN 0-8446-1404-1). Peter Smith.

Shurtleff, M. C. Compendium of Corn Diseases. 2nd ed. (Compendium Ser.: No. 1). (Illus.). 124p. 1980. 11.00 (ISBN 0-89054-029-2). Am Phytopathol Soc.

Shurtleff, William & Aoyagi, Akiko. Miso Production: The Book of Miso, Vol. II. rev. ed. LC 76-19599. (Soyfood Production Ser.: No. 1). (Illus.). 1979. pap. 9.95 (ISBN 0-933332-00-9). Soyfoods-New Age.

--Tempeh Production: The Book of Tempeh, Vol. II. LC 79-89281. (Soyfood Production Ser.: No. 3). (Illus.). 1980. 22.95 (ISBN 0-933332-04-1); pap. 15.95 (ISBN 0-933332-02-5). Soyfoods-New Age.

--Tofu & Soymilk Production: The Book of Tofu, Vol. II. LC 74-31629. (Soyfood Production Ser.: No. 2). (Illus.). 1979. 22.95 (ISBN 0-933332-03-3); pap. 17.95 (ISBN 0-933332-01-7). Soyfoods-New Age.

Shuster, Albert H., jt. auth. see Ploghoft, Milton E.

Shuster, George N. The Ground I Walked on. 1961. 4.50 o.p. (ISBN 0-374-16692-7). FS&G.

Shuster, M. R. The Public International Law of Money. (Illus.). 359p. 1973. 32.00x (ISBN 0-19-825308-7). Oxford U Pr.

Shuster, Sam. Dermatology in Internal Medicine. 1979. pap. 11.95x (ISBN 0-19-261142-9). Oxford U Pr.

Shuster, Sam & Marks, Janet. Systemic Effects of Skin Disease. (Illus.). 1969. 16.50x (ISBN 0-685-83926-5). Intl Ideas.

Shuster, Susan K., jt. auth. see Ochoa, Anna S.

Shusterman, David. C. P. Snow. LC 74-23949. (World Authors Ser.: No. 179). 1975. lib. bdg. 12.50 (ISBN 0-8057-1510-X). Twayne.

Shute, C. D. The McCollough Effect. LC 78-15609. (Illus.). 1979. 32.95 (ISBN 0-521-22395-4). Cambridge U Pr.

Shute, Gary B. On the Corner: Male Social Life in a Paramaribo Creole Neighborhood. (Studies of Developing Countries: No. 21). 1979. pap. text ed. 13.50x (ISBN 90-232-1605-9). Humanities.

Shute, Nevil. The Breaking Wave. LC 80-83020. (Great War Stories Ser.). 310p. 1980. Repr. of 1955 ed. 16.95 (ISBN 0-933852-16-9). Nautical & Aviation.

--Most Secret. 310p. 1976. Repr. of 1945 ed. lib. bdg. 13.95x (ISBN 0-89244-084-8). Queens Hse.

Shute, Wilfrid E. The Health Preserver. LC 77-14086. 1977. 8.95 (ISBN 0-87857-189-2). Rodale Pr Inc.

Shute, Wilfrid E. & Taub, Harald. Vitamin E for Ailing & Healthy Hearts. 1972. pap. 2.50 (ISBN 0-515-05724-X). Jove Pubns.

Shutler, M. E., jt. auth. see Shutler, Richard, Jr.

Shutler, Richard, Jr. & Shutler, M. E. Oceanic Prehistory. 1975. pap. text ed. 5.95 (ISBN 0-8465-1938-0). Benjamin-Cummings.

Shuttle, Penelope. The Orchard Upstairs. 64p. 1981. pap. 11.95 (ISBN 0-19-211938-9). Oxford U Pr.

Shuttlesworth, Dorothy E. A B C of Buses. (ps-1). PLB 4.95 o.p. (ISBN 0-385-01999-8). Doubleday.

--How Wild Animals Fight. LC 75-19144. 96p. (gr. 2-5). 1976. 5.95 o.p. (ISBN 0-385-08596-6); PLB write for info. o.p. (ISBN 0-385-08599-0). Doubleday.

--Story of Horses. LC 60-6355. (gr. 6-9). PLB 4.95 o.p. (ISBN 0-385-03570-5). Doubleday.

--Story of Spiders. LC 59-5441. (gr. 3-9). 1959. PLB 5.95 o.p. (ISBN 0-385-02286-7). Doubleday.

--Zoos in the Making. (gr. 4-6). 1977. PLB 8.50 (ISBN 0-525-43725-8, Henry Robbins Bks.). Dutton.

Shuttlewood, Arthur. UFO Prophecy. 266p. (Orig.). 1978. pap. 7.95 (ISBN 0-910122-42-3, Pub. by Global Commun). Amherst Pr.

Shuttleworth, Jack M., jt. ed. see Kiley, Frederick T.

Shuttleworth, K. E., et al. Benign Enlargement of the Prostate. (Illus.). 1974. 16.95x (ISBN 0-433-30270-4). Intl Ideas.

Shuy, Roger W., ed. Some New Directions in Linguistics. LC 73-76752. 149p. 1973. pap. 4.95 o.p. (ISBN 0-87840-202-0). Georgetown U Pr.

Shuy, Roger W., jt. ed. see Fasold, Ralph W.

Shvarts, V. V. The Concise Illustrated Russian-English Dictionary of Mechanical Engineering. (Illus.). 224p. 1981. pap. 30.00 (ISBN 0-08-027574-5). Pergamon.

Shwayder, David S. Stratification of Behavior. 1971. text ed. 14.25x (ISBN 0-391-00145-0). Humanities.

Shy, John. A People Numerous & Armed: Reflections on the Military Struggle for American Independence. LC 75-32353. 300p. 1976. 17.95 (ISBN 0-19-502012-X). Oxford U Pr.

--A People Numerous & Armed: Reflections on the Military Struggle for American Independence. 1976. pap. 5.95 (ISBN 0-19-502013-8, GB). Oxford U Pr.

Shy, John, compiled by. The American Revolution. LC 72-178292. (Goldentree Bibliographies in American History Ser.). 152p. (Orig.). 1973. pap. 6.95x (ISBN 0-88295-532-2). AHM Pub.

Shyer. Welcome Home, Jellybean. (gr. 3-5). 1980. pap. 1.25 (ISBN 0-590-30902-1, Schol Pap). Schol Bk Serv.

Shyer, Marlene F. My Brother, the Thief. LC 80-343. (gr. 6 up). 1980. 8.95 (ISBN 0-684-16434-5). Scribner.

--Welcome Home, Jellybean. LC 77-17970. 160p. (gr. 6-8). 1978. reinforced bdg. 8.95 (ISBN 0-684-15519-2, ScribJ). Scribner.

Shyne, Ann W. & Russo, Eva M. Disruptive Behavior in Group Care: Problems & Solutions. LC 79-23739. 80p. (Orig.). 1980. pap. text ed. write for info. o.p. (ISBN 0-87868-137-X). Child Welfare.

Shyne, Ann W., jt. auth. see Reid, William J.

Shyne, Ann W., jt. auth. see Russo, Eva M.

Shyrock, Henry & Siegel, Jacob. The Methods & Materials of Demography. (Studies in Population Ser.). 577p. 1976. text ed. 19.75 (ISBN 0-12-641150-6). Acad Pr.

Siafaca, Ekaterini. Investor-Owned Hospitals & Their Role in the Changing U. S. Health Care System. (Health Care Economics & Technology Ser.). 192p. 1981. 32.95x (ISBN 0-86621-000-8). F&S Pr.

Siann, Gerda & Ugwuegbu, Denis. Educational Psychology in a Changing World. (Illus.). 256p. (Orig.). 1980. text ed. 22.50x (ISBN 0-04-370099-3, 2587); pap. text ed. 11.50x (ISBN 0-04-370100-0, 2588). Allen Unwin.

Siao-Yu. Mao Tse-Tung & I Were Beggars. LC 59-15411. (Illus.). 320p. 1973. pap. 1.95 o.s.i. (ISBN 0-02-037000-8, Collier). Macmillan.

Sibbes, Richard. Exposition of St. Paul's Epistles. 1978. Repr. 14.95 (ISBN 0-85151-246-1). Banner of Truth.

--Works on Sibbes, Vol. 1. 1979. 14.95 (ISBN 0-85151-169-4). Banner of Truth.

Sibbett, Ed. Ready-to-Use Floral Designs. (Illus.). 64p. pap. 2.50 (ISBN 0-486-23976-4). Dover.

Sibbett, Ed, Jr. Art Deco Stained Glass Pattern Book. LC 77-77051. (Illus.). 1977. pap. 2.50 (ISBN 0-486-23550-5). Dover.

--Art Nouveau Stained Glass Pattern Book. LC 77-87497. (Pictorial Archives Ser.). (Illus.). 1978. pap. 2.75 (ISBN 0-486-23577-7). Dover.

--Easy-to-Make Stained Glass Lightcatchers: Sixty-Seven Designs for Small Ornaments, with Full-Size Templates. (Illus., Orig.). 1981. pap. price not set (ISBN 0-486-24081-9). Dover.

--Full-Size Stained Glass Templates: Sixteen Attractive & Easy Patterns. (Illus.). 1979. pap. 4.00 (ISBN 0-486-23744-3). Dover.

--Iron-On T-Shirt Transfers for Hand Coloring. (Illus., Orig.). 1976. pap. 1.75 (ISBN 0-486-23395-2). Dover.

--New Glass Stained Glass Pattern Book. (Illus.). 64p. (Orig.). 1980. pap. 3.00 (ISBN 0-486-24029-0). Dover.

--Victorian Stained Glass Pattern Book: 96 Designs for Workable Projects. 1979. pap. 3.00 (ISBN 0-486-23811-3). Dover.

Siberry, K. M. Instruments of Flight. LC 73-91533. (Illus.). 160p. 1974. 10.50x o.p. (ISBN 0-8448-0301-4). Crane-Russak Co.

Sibert, Edgar H. Railfan's Guide to Colorado. (Illus.). Date not set. pap. price not set o.s.i. (ISBN 0-87108-556-9). Pruett. Postponed.

Sibert, Jody, ed. The Incredible Shrinking Woman. 160p. (Orig.). 1981. pap. 2.50 (ISBN 0-515-05753-3). Jove Pubns.

Sibley, Agnes. May Sarton. (U. S. Authors Ser.: No. 213). lib. bdg. 10.95 (ISBN 0-8057-0656-9). Twayne.

Sibley, Celestine. Children, My Children. LC 80-8231. 210p. 1981. 9.95 (ISBN 0-06-014872-1, HarpT). Har-Row.

--Small Blessings. LC 76-42394. 1977. 7.95 (ISBN 0-385-12318-3). Doubleday.

Sibley, Celestine, jt. auth. see Middleton, Sallie.

Sibley, Hi. One Hundred & Two Bird Houses, Feeders You Can Make. (Illus.). 1980. pap. 4.80 (ISBN 0-87006-304-9). Goodheart.

--One Hundred Two Birdhouses Feeders You Can Make. (Illus.). 96p. 1980. pap. text ed. 4.80 (ISBN 0-87006-304-9). Goodheart.

Sibley, Jack R. & Gunter, Pete A., eds. Process Philosophy: Basic Writings. LC 78-57668. 1978. pap. text ed. 16.00 (ISBN 0-8191-0531-7). U Pr of Amer.

Sibley, Marilyn M. Port of Houston: A History. (Illus.). 1968. 15.00 (ISBN 0-292-73619-3). U of Tex Pr.

Sibley, Stanley D., jt. auth. see Michman, Ronald D.

Sibley, Susan K. Somebody Killed Reddy Fox. Bayes, Ronald H., ed. 160p. (Orig.). 1980. pap. 7.00x (ISBN 0-932662-33-1). St Andrews NC.

Sibree, J., tr. see Hegel, Georg W.

Sibson, R., jt. auth. see Jardine, N.

Sicat, Gerardo P., jt. auth. see Power, John H.

Sices, David, jt. auth. see Denoeu, Francois.

Sicha, Jeffrey, ed. see Sellars, Wilfrid.

Sichel, Kim, tr. see Tabart, Marielle & Monod-Fontaine, Isabelle.

Sichel, Marion. Costume of the Classical World. (Illus.). 72p. 1980. 17.95 (ISBN 0-7134-1511-8, Pub. by Batsford England). David & Charles.

--Costume Reference Nine: Nineteen Thirty-Nine to Nineteen Fifty. 1979. 17.95 (ISBN 0-7134-1507-X, Pub. by Batsford England). David & Charles.

--Costume Reference Ten: Nineteen Fifty to Present Day. 1979. 17.95 (ISBN 0-7134-1509-6, Pub. by Batsford England). David & Charles.

Sichel, Peter M. & Allen, Judy L. Which Wine? rev. ed. LC 77-71723. 1977. pap. 5.95 o.p. (ISBN 0-89104-075-7). A & W Pubs.

Sichel, Werner. Public Utility Rate Making in an Energy Conscious Environment. 1979. lib. bdg. 22.00x (ISBN 0-89158-180-4). Westview.

Sichel, Werner, ed. Economic Advice & Executive Policy: Recommendations from Past Members of the Council of Economic Advisers. LC 77-7807. (Praeger Special Studies). 1978. 20.95 (ISBN 0-03-022381-4). Praeger.

Sichel, Werner & Gies, Thomas G., eds. Applications of Economic Principles in Public Utility Industries. (Michigan Business Studies: Vol. 2, No. 3). (Illus.). 180p. 1981. price not set (ISBN 0-87712-211-3). U Mich Busn Div Res.

Sicher, Harry, jt. ed. see Bhasker, S. N.

Sicilia, Gail, compiled by. Hollywood Squares. (Illus.). 160p. 1974. pap. 1.25 o.p. (ISBN 0-445-00221-2). Popular Lib.

Sickel, John V. Van see Van Sickle, John V.

Sickels, Robert J. The Presidency: An Introduction. 1980. pap. text ed. 10.95 (ISBN 0-13-697433-3). P-H.

Sicker, Philip. Love & the Quest for Identity in the Fiction of Henry James. LC 79-17311. 1980. 16.00x (ISBN 0-691-06417-2); pap. 8.50 (ISBN 0-691-10092-6). Princeton U Pr.
Sickert, Bernhard. Whistler. 175p. 1980. Repr. lib. bdg. 25.00 (ISBN 0-8495-5039-4). Arden Lib.
Sickinghe, Jhr. W., jt. ed. see Kaempfer, H. M.
Sickle, Sylvia Van see Van Sickle, Sylvia.
Sickler, R. The Ritual of the Hearth. 1973. pap. 3.95 o.s.i. (ISBN 0-02-010350-6, Collier). Macmillan.
Siclen, Charles C. van see Habachi, Labib.
Sid-Ahmed, Mohamed. After the Guns Fall Silent. LC 76-24997. 1976. 19.95 (ISBN 0-312-01155-5). St Martin.
Sidar, Jean. George Hamell Cook: A Life in Agriculture & Geology, 1818-1889. 1976. 13.00 (ISBN 0-8135-0827-4). Rutgers U Pr.
Siddall, Abigail T., tr. see Corvisier, Andre.
Siddall, James. Analytical Decision Making in Engineering Design. (Illus.). 1972. ref. ed. 24.95 (ISBN 0-13-034538-5). P-H.
Sidders, Max. S. O. S. An Exposition of the Song of Solomon. 1981. 5.95 (ISBN 0-533-04640-8). Vantage.
Sidders, Peter. A Guide to World Screw Threads. 292p. 1972. 19.50 (ISBN 0-8311-1092-9). Indus Pr.
Siddiqi, I. W., jt. auth. see Johnson, R. M.
Siddiqi, R. A. Man, Reality & Values. 1964. 5.00x o.p. (ISBN 0-210-27048-9). Asia.
Siddiqui, M. I. Penal Law of Islam. 1980. 9.95 (ISBN 0-686-64662-2). Kazi Pubns.
Siddons, Anne R. Fox's Earth. 1981. 14.95 (ISBN 0-671-24962-2). S&S.
--The House Next Door. 1980. pap. 2.50 (ISBN 0-345-29330-4). Ballantine.
Siddons, Anne Rivers. Heartbreak Hotel. 1977. pap. 1.95 o.p. (ISBN 0-445-04027-0). Popular Lib.
Siddons, Arthur W., et al. New Calculus. 1950. Pt. 1. text ed. 5.95x (ISBN 0-521-06465-1). Cambridge U Pr.
Siddons, H. & Sowton, E. Cardiac Pacemakers. (Amer. Lec. in Living Chemistry Ser.). (Illus.). 352p. 1974. 18.50 (ISBN 0-398-03091-X). C C Thomas.
Siddons, Suzy. Cycling on Dizzy Duncan. (Illus.). 24p. (gr. 6 up). 1980. pap. 1.60 ea. (Pub. by Dinosaur Pubns); pap. in 5 pk. avail. (ISBN 0-85122-199-8). Merrimack Bk Serv.
Sidebotham, R. Accounting for Industrial Management. 1964. 25.00 (ISBN 0-08-009892-4); pap. 12.75 (ISBN 0-08-009891-6). Pergamon.
--Introduction to the Theory & Context of Accounting. 2nd ed. 1970. pap. 7.15 o.p. (ISBN 0-08-015620-7). Pergamon.
Sideman, Samuel & Chang, T. M., eds. Hemoperfusion: Kidney & Liver Support Detoxification, Pt. 2. 1982. text ed. price not set (ISBN 0-89116-211-9). Hemisphere Pub. Postponed.
Sider, J. W. & Orgel, Stephen, eds. The Troublesome Raigne of John King of England. LC 78-66778. (Renaissance Drama Ser.). 1979. lib. bdg. 31.00 (ISBN 0-8240-9733-5). Garland Pub.
Sider, Ronald J. Cry Justice: The Bible on Hunger & Poverty. LC 80-82133. 192p. 1980. pap. 2.45 (ISBN 0-8091-2308-8). Paulist Pr.
--Cry Justice: The Bible on Hunger & Poverty. 192p. (Orig.). 1980. pap. 2.95 (ISBN 0-87784-495-X). Inter-Varsity.
Sider, Ronald J., ed. Living More Simply. LC 79-3634. (Orig.). 1980. pap. 4.95 (ISBN 0-87784-808-4). Inter-Varsity.
Sideri, S. & Johns, S., eds. Mining for Development in the Third World: Multinationals, State Enterprises & the International Economy. LC 80-20930. (Pergamon Policy Studies on International Development). 376p. 1980. 35.00 (ISBN 0-08-026308-9). Pergamon.
Sidgwick, J. B. Amateur Astronomer's Handbook. (Illus.). 576p. 1981. pap. write for info. (ISBN 0-486-24034-7). Dover.
--Amateur Astronomer's Handbook. 4th, rev. ed. (Illus.). 568p. 1980. 24.95 (ISBN 0-89490-049-8). Enslow Pubs.
--Introducing Astronomy. 2nd ed. (Illus., Orig.). 1973. pap. 6.50 (ISBN 0-571-04823-4, Pub. by Faber & Faber). Merrimack Bk Serv.
--Observational Astronomy for Amateurs. (Illus.). 384p. 1981. pap. write for info. (ISBN 0-486-24033-9). Dover.
Sidgwick, Jean, tr. see Del Vasto, Lanza.
Sidhu, Jagjit S. Administration in the Federated Malay States: Eighteen Ninety-Six-Nineteen Twenty. (East Asian Historical Monographs). 250p. 1980. 25.00 (ISBN 0-19-580432-5). Oxford U Pr.
Sidi Ali Al-Jamal Of Fez. The Meaning of Man. Abd Al-Kabir Al Munawarra, ed. Aisha Abd Ar-Rahman At-Tarjumana, tr. from Arabic. Orig. Title: The Foundations of the Science of Knowledge. (Illus.). 455p. (Orig.). 1977. 20.00 (ISBN 0-9504446-6-9); pap. 12.00 (ISBN 0-9504446-5-0). Iqra.
Sidis, Boris. Psychopathological Researches. 329p. 1980. Repr. of 1902 ed. lib. bdg. 75.00 (ISBN 0-89984-411-1). Century Bookbindery.
Sidis, William J. Notes on the Collection of Transfers. LC 80-50701. 305p. 1981. Repr. of 1928 ed. lib. bdg. 40.00x (ISBN 0-88000-115-1). Quarterman.
Sidnell, R. G., jt. auth. see Reed, H. O.
Sidnell, Robert G., jt. auth. see Reed, H. Owen.
Sidney, Philip. An Apology for Poetry. Robinson, Forrest, ed. LC 73-122682. 1970. pap. 3.95 (ISBN 0-672-60254-7). Bobbs.
--An Apology for Poetry or the Defence of Poesy. Shepherd, Geoffrey, ed. (Old & Middle English Texts Ser.). 244p. 1979. pap. 8.95x (ISBN 0-686-63938-3). B&N.
--Complete Prose Works, 4 vols. Feuillerat, A., ed. Incl. Vol. 1. The Countesse of Pembroke's Arcadia. 65.00 (ISBN 0-521-06468-6); Vol. 2. The Last Part of Countesse of Pembroke's Arcadia & the Lady of May. 42.00 (ISBN 0-521-06469-4); Vol. 3. The Defence of Poesie, Political Discourses, Correspondence, Translations. 57.00 (ISBN 0-521-06470-8); Vol. 4. The Older Arcadia. 57.00 (ISBN 0-521-06471-6). 190.00 set (ISBN 0-521-08770-8). Cambridge U Pr.
--Poems of Sir Philip Sidney. Ringler, William A., Jr., ed. (Oxford English Texts Ser). 1962. 49.00x (ISBN 0-19-811834-1). Oxford U Pr.
Sidney, Phillip. Selected Poems. Duncan-Jones, Katherine, ed. 1973. pap. 8.95x (ISBN 0-19-871053-4). Oxford U Pr.
Sidran, Ben. Black Talk: Roots of Jazz. xvii, 201p. 1981. Repr. of 1971 ed. lib. bdg. 19.50 (ISBN 0-306-76056-8). Da Capo.
Sidwell, Duncan. Expedition Two Thousand Sixty-One. LC 73-145608. (Illus.). 1971. text ed. 2.95x (ISBN 0-521-08087-8). Cambridge U Pr.
Sidwell, Duncan & Sidwell, Margaret. Speaking French. 1974. pap. text ed. 1.95x o.p. (ISBN 0-435-37800-7); tchr's ed. 3.50x o.p. (ISBN 0-435-37801-5). Heinemann Ed.
Sidwell, Frederick H. The Artistic Reproduction of the Personality of the Human Figure. (Illus.). 1980. deluxe ed. 37.25 (ISBN 0-930582-62-4). Gloucester Art.
Sidwell, Margaret, jt. auth. see Sidwell, Duncan.
Siebel, Fritz, jt. auth. see Nodset, Joan L.
Sieben, Hermann J. Voces: Eine Bibliofraphie zu Woetern und Begriffen aus der Patristik (1918-1978) (Bibliographia Patristica). 461p. 1979. text ed. 81.25x (ISBN 3-11-007966-6). De Gruyter.
Sieben, Hubert. Tahiti. (Illus.). 1970. bds. 12.00 o.p. (ISBN 0-911268-28-6). Rogers Bk.
Siebenschuh, William R. Form & Purpose in Boswell's Biographical Works. 1972. 14.50x (ISBN 0-520-02246-7). U of Cal Pr.
Siebenschuh, William R., jt. auth. see Mundhenk, Robert T.
Sieber, Roy. African Furniture & Household Objects. LC 79-5340. (Illus.). 240p. 1980. 37.50x (ISBN 0-253-11927-8); pap. 20.00x (ISBN 0-253-28242-X). Ind U Pr.
Sieber, Sam D. & Wilder, David E., eds. The School in Society: Studies in the Sociology of Education. LC 72-80079. (Illus.). 1973. text ed. 14.95 (ISBN 0-02-928680-8). Free Pr.
Siebert, Dick & Vogel, Otto. Baseball. LC 68-18803. (Athletic Institute Ser). (Illus.). (gr. 7 up). 1968. 6.95 (ISBN 0-8069-4300-9); PLB 7.49 (ISBN 0-8069-4301-7). Sterling.
Siebert, Donald T. & Backscheider, Paula R., eds. The Plays of John Hoole. LC 78-66635. (Eighteenth-Century English Drama Ser.: Vol. 21). 1980. lib. bdg. 50.00 (ISBN 0-8240-3595-X). Garland Pub.
Siebert, Horst. Economics of the Environment. LC 80-7442. 1981. price not set (ISBN 0-669-03693-5). Lexington Bks.
Siebert, Rudolf J. From Critical Theory of Society to Theology of Communicative Praxis. LC 79-65296. 1979. pap. text ed. 9.50 (ISBN 0-8191-0783-2). U Pr of Amer.
--Hegel's Concept of Marriage & Family: The Origin of Subjective Freedom. LC 78-78401. 1979. pap. text ed. 7.50 (ISBN 0-8191-0710-7). U Pr of Amer.
--Hegel's Philosophy of History: Theological, Humanistic & Scientific Elements. LC 78-66279. 1979. pap. text ed. 9.00 (ISBN 0-8191-0689-5). U Pr of Amer.
--Horkheimer's Critical Sociology of Religion: The Relative & the Transcendent. LC 78-66280. 1979. pap. text ed. 7.50 (ISBN 0-8191-0688-7). U Pr of Amer.
Siebrand, J. C., jt. auth. see Lenderink, R. S.
Siebring, B. Richard & Schaff, Mary E. General Chemistry. 864p. 1980. text ed. 21.95x (ISBN 0-534-00802-X); lab manual 11.95x (ISBN 0-534-00838-0); study guide 7.95x (ISBN 0-534-00839-9); solutions manual 5.95x (ISBN 0-534-00859-3). Wadsworth Pub.
Sieburth, John M. Sea Microbes. (Illus.). 1979. text ed. 59.95x (ISBN 0-19-502419-2). Oxford U Pr.
Siedentop, Daryl. Developing Teacher Skills in Physical Education. LC 75-26084. (Illus.). 352p. 1976. pap. text ed. 12.25 (ISBN 0-395-20616-2). HM.
Siefert, Susan S. The Dilemma of the Talented Heroine: A Study in Nineteenth Century Fiction. 1978. 14.95 (ISBN 0-88831-018-8). EPWP.
Sieg, Theodore Le see Le Sieg, Theodore.
Siegal, Benjamin. Strangers, Healers. 352p. (Orig.). 1981. pap. 2.75 (ISBN 0-345-29439-4). Ballantine.
Siegal, Mordecal. The Good Dog Book: Loving Care. (Illus.). 1977. 11.95 (ISBN 0-02-610600-0). Macmillan.
Siegal, Vivian, jt. auth. see Mann, Peggy.
Siegan, Bernard. Other People's Property. LC 75-22884. 160p. 1976. 16.95 (ISBN 0-669-00187-2). Lexington Bks.
--Planning Without Prices. 160p. 1977. 16.95 (ISBN 0-669-00247-X). Lexington Bks.
Siegan, Bernard H. Economic Liberties & the Constitution. LC 80-15756. 1981. 19.50x (ISBN 0-226-75663-7). U of Chicago Pr.
--The Interaction of Economics & the Law. LC 76-1223. 352p. 1977. 15.95 (ISBN 0-669-01340-4). Lexington Bks.
--Regulation, Economics, & the Law. LC 77-11398. 144p. 1979. 15.95 (ISBN 0-669-02091-5). Lexington Bks.
Siegel, jt. auth. see Senna.
Siegel, Adrienne. The Image of the American City in Popular Literature: 1820 to 1870. (National University Publications, Interdisciplinary Urban Ser.). 210p. 1981. 15.00 (ISBN 0-8046-9271-8). Kennikat.
Siegel, Arthur, et al. Chicago's Famous Buildings: A Photographic Guide to the City's Architectural Landmarks & Other Notable Buildings. 2nd ed. LC 69-15367. (Illus.). 1970. pap. 3.25 o.s.i. (ISBN 0-226-75685-8). U of Chicago Pr.
Siegel, Arthur I., et al. Professional Police-Human Relations Training. (Illus.). 192p. 1970. 10.50 (ISBN 0-398-01753-0). C C Thomas.
Siegel, Beatrice. Fur Trappers & Traders: The Indians, the Pilgrims, & the Beaver. LC 80-7671. (Illus.). 64p. (gr. 3-7). 1981. 8.50 (ISBN 0-8027-6396-0); PLB 8.85 (ISBN 0-8027-6397-9). Walker & Co.
Siegel, Ben. The Controversial Sholem Asch: An Introduction to His Fiction. LC 76-43446. 1976. 12.95 (ISBN 0-87972-076-X); pap. 7.95 (ISBN 0-87972-170-7). Bowling Green Univ.
Siegel, Benjamin. Four Doctors. 288p. 1975. 7.95 o.p. (ISBN 0-440-04563-0). Delacorte.
Siegel, Bernard J., et al, eds. Annual Review of Anthropology, Vol. 9. LC 72-82136. (Illus.). 1980. text ed. 20.00 (ISBN 0-8243-1909-5). Annual Reviews.
Siegel, Betty. Lion in a Paper Tent. 42p. 1980. pap. 3.25 (ISBN 0-937308-03-X). Hearthstone.
Siegel, C. L. Topics in Complex Function Theory, 3 vols. Incl. Vol. 1. Elliptical Functions & Uniformization Theory. 1969. 26.95 (ISBN 0-471-79070-2); Vol. 2. Automorphic Functions & Abelian Integrals. 1972. 26.95 (ISBN 0-471-79080-X); Vol. 3. Abelian Functions & Modular Functions of Several Variables. Tretkoff, M. & Gottschling, E., trs. 244p. 1973. 29.95 (ISBN 0-471-79090-7). LC 69-19931. (Pure & Applied Mathematics Ser., Pub. by Wiley-Interscience). Wiley.
Siegel, Carole & Fischer, Susan K. Psychiatric Records in Mental Health Care. (Illus.). 250p. (Orig.). 1981. 15.00 (ISBN 0-87630-241-X). Brunner Mazel.
Siegel, Dorothy. Topics in English Morphology. Hankamer, Jorge, ed. LC 78-66592. (Outstanding Dissertations in Linguistics Ser.). 205p. 1980. lib. bdg. 24.00 (ISBN 0-8240-9675-4). Garland Pub.
Siegel, Eli. Self & World. LC 75-44647. 1981. pap. price not set (ISBN 0-910492-27-1); text ed. price not set (ISBN 0-910492-28-X). Definition. Postponed.
Siegel, Ernest. The Exceptional Child Grows Up: Guidelines for Understanding & Helping the Brain Injured Adolescent & Young Adult. 1978. 8.95 (ISBN 0-87690-112-7); pap. 4.95 (ISBN 0-87690-155-0). Dutton.
Siegel, Ernest, jt. auth. see Siegel, Rita.
Siegel, Esther, jt. auth. see Parker, David L.
Siegel, George J., et al. Basic Neurochemistry. 3rd ed. 1981. write for info (ISBN 0-316-79002-8). Little.
Siegel, Gilbert B. Breaking with Orthodoxy in Public Administration. LC 80-5081. 706p. 1980. text ed. 25.00 (ISBN 0-8191-1042-6). U Pr of Amer.
--The Vicissitudes of Governmental Reform in Brazil: A Study of the DASP. LC 78-62264. 1978. pap. text ed. 9.50 (ISBN 0-8191-0572-4). U Pr of Amer.
Siegel, Gonnie M., jt. auth. see Abarbanel, Karin.
Siegel, Gonnie M., jt. auth. see Abarbanol, Karin.
Siegel, H. H. Alcohol Detoxification Programs: Treatment Instead of Jail. (Illus.). 110p. 1973. 11.75 (ISBN 0-398-02820-6). C C Thomas.
Siegel, Hans. Guide to the Wines of Germany. 1979. pap. 2.95 (ISBN 0-346-12426-3). Cornerstone.
Siegel, Jacob, jt. auth. see Shyrock, Henry.
Siegel, James T. The Rope of God. (Library Reprint Ser.: Vol. 96). 1978. 18.50x (ISBN 0-520-03714-6). U of Cal Pr.
Siegel, Jonathan P. The Severus Scroll & 1Q1SA. LC 75-28372. (Society of Biblical Literature, Masoretic Studies). 1975. pap. 7.50 (ISBN 0-89130-028-7, 060502). Scholars Pr Ca.
Siegel, Larry & Torres, Angelo. The Mad Make-Out Book. 1979. pap. 1.50 (ISBN 0-446-88947-4). Warner Bks.
Siegel, Larry & Woodbridge, George. Mad's Cradle to Grave Primer. (Mad Ser.). (Illus.). 192p. (Orig.). 1973. pap. 1.75 (ISBN 0-446-94438-6). Warner Bks.
Siegel, Larry J. & Senna, Joseph J. Juvenile Delinquency: Theory, Practice & Law. (Criminal Justice Ser.). (Illus.). 550p. 1981. text ed. 17.95 (ISBN 0-8299-0414-X). West Pub.
Siegel, Larry J., jt. auth. see Senna, Joseph J.
Siegel, Laurence & Lane, Irving M. Psychology in Industrial Organizations. 3rd ed. 1974. text ed. 18.95x (ISBN 0-256-01563-5). Irwin.
Siegel, Lawrence J., jt. auth. see Melamed, Barbara G.
Siegel, Marcia B. The Shapes of Change. 400p. 1981. pap. 3.95 (ISBN 0-380-53892-X, 53892, Discus). Avon.
Siegel, Micki. Cops & Women. (Orig.). 1980. pap. 2.25 (ISBN 0-505-51524-5). Tower Bks.
Siegel, Miriam. Psychological Testing of Children from Pre-School Through Adolescence: A Psychodynamic Approach. 1981. write for info. (ISBN 0-8236-5615-2). Intl Univs Pr.
Siegel, Murray J. & Van Keuren, Dolores. Think Thin. LC 76-151435. (Illus.). 1971. 8.95 o.s.i. (ISBN 0-8397-7992-5); pap. 9.95 (ISBN 0-8397-7993-3). Eriksson.
Siegel, Murray J. & Van Kueren, Dolores. Think Thin. LC 76-151435. 288p. 1981. pap. 9.95 (ISBN 0-8397-7993-3). Eriksson.
Siegel, Paul S., jt. auth. see Miller, Howard L.
Siegel, R. K. & West, L. J., eds. Hallucinations: Behavior, Experience, & Theory. LC 75-12670. 322p. 1975. 43.95 (ISBN 0-471-79096-6, Pub. by Wiley Medical). Wiley.
Siegel, Richard L. & Weinberg, Leonard. Comparing Public Policies: United States, Soviet Union & Europe. 1977. pap. 12.50x (ISBN 0-256-01935-5). Dorsey.
Siegel, Rita & Siegel, Ernest. Help for the Lonely Child: Strengthening Social Perceptions. (Illus.). 1978. 9.95 o.p. (ISBN 0-87690-289-1). Dutton.
Siegel, Robert. Alpha Centauri. LC 80-68330. 256p. (gr. 4 up). 1980. 9.95 (ISBN 0-89107-180-6, Cornerstone Bks.). Good News.
--In a Pig's Eye. LC 80-13313. (University of Central Florida Contemporary Poetry Ser.). 73p. 1980. 6.95 (ISBN 0-8130-0679-1). U Presses Fla.
Siegel, Robert & Howell, John R. Thermal Radiation Heat Transfer. 2nd ed. LC 79-17242. (Thermal & Fluids Engineering Hemisphere Ser.). (Illus.). 928p. 1980. text ed. 32.00 (ISBN 0-07-057316-6, C); solutions manual 16.95 (ISBN 0-07-057317-4). McGraw.
Siegel, Scott. Gunfire & Flame. (Orig.). 1980. pap. 1.75 (ISBN 0-532-23137-6). Manor Bks.
Siegel, Stanley. The Poet President of Texas. new ed. 1977. 12.50 (ISBN 0-8363-0153-6). Jenkins.
Siegel, Steven A., compiled by. Archival Resources. (Jewish Immigrants of the Nazi Period in the USA). 1979. 42.00 (ISBN 0-89664-027-2, Pub. by K G Saur). Gale.
Siegel, W. L. People Management for Small Business. 130p. 1978. 5.95 (ISBN 0-471-04030-4, 1-382). Wiley.
Siegelaub, Seth, jt. ed. see Mattelart, Armand.
Siegele, H. H. Cabinets & Built-Ins. LC 80-52589. (Illus.). 104p. 1980. pap. 5.95 o.p. (ISBN 0-8069-8188-1). Sterling.
--Roof Framing. LC 74-25285. (Drake Home Craftsman Ser.). (Illus.). 176p. 1975. 7.95 o.p. (ISBN 0-8069-8624-7). Sterling.
Siegelman, Jim, jt. auth. see Conway, Flo.
Siegelman, Stanley S., jt. auth. see Rubin, Eli H.
Siegelstein, Sidney, jt. auth. see Brandon, Dick H.
Siegfried, A. France: A Study in Nationality. 122p. 1980. Repr. of 1930 ed. lib. bdg. 20.00 (ISBN 0-89760-826-7). Telegraph Bks.
Siegfried, Andre. America Comes of Age: A French Analysis. 2nd ed. Hemming, Doris & Hemming, H. H., trs. LC 68-16244. (American Scene Ser.). 368p. 1974. Repr. of 1927 ed. lib. bdg. 32.50 (ISBN 0-306-71025-0). Da Capo.
Siegfried, Joan C., jt. auth. see Prokopoff, Stephen S.
Siegfried, John J., jt. ed. see Andreano, Ralph.
Siegfried, Susan L., jt. auth. see Cohn, Marjorie B.

Siegle, Arthur. Basic Plane Surveying. LC 77-87883. 1979. pap. text ed. 7.20 (ISBN 0-8273-1698-4); instructor's guide 1.60 (ISBN 0-8273-1699-2). Delmar.

Siegle, Bernard. Marriage Today: A Commentary on the Code of Canon Law. 3rd ed. LC 79-18786. 1979. pap. 10.95 (ISBN 0-8189-0384-8). Alba.

Siegler, Miriam & Osmond, Humphrey. Models of Madness, Models of Medicine. 1976. pap. 5.95x (ISBN 0-06-131953-8, TB 1953, Torch). Har-Row.

Siegler, Miriam & Osmond, Humphry. Models of Madness, Models of Medicine. Huston, Paul, pref. by. 384p. 1974. 8.95 o.s.i. (ISBN 0-02-594000-7). Macmillan.

Siegman, Aron Wolfe & Pope, Benjamin. Studies in Dyadic Communication: Proceedings of a Research Conference on the Interview. 356p. 1972. text ed. 21.00 (ISBN 0-08-015867-6). Pergamon.

Siegman, Athilia E., jt. ed. see Elinson, Jack.

Siegmeister, Elie. Invitation to Music. LC 61-15658. (Illus.). (gr. 8-12). 1961. PLB 6.27 (ISBN 0-8178-3182-7). Harvey.

Siegmond, Warren E. In Search of a Stranger. Zola, Irene, et al, eds. LC 80-69803. 472p. (Orig.). 1981. pap. 5.95 (ISBN 0-937868-01-9). Cameo Pr.

Siegner, Otto. Oberammergau: The Passion-Play-Village & Its Text in German-English-French. (Illus.). 1978. 15.00x (ISBN 0-686-63526-4). Heinman.

Siegrist, J., jt. ed. see Halhuber, M. J.

Sieller, William L. Returning to a Dream. 1979. 6.50 (ISBN 0-8233-0308-X). Golden Quill.

Siemaszko, Frederick. Computing in Clinical Laboratories. LC 77-94061. 1978. 31.95 (ISBN 0-471-04321-4, Pub. by Wiley Medical). Wiley.

Siemens, Nicolai, et al. Operations Research: Planning, Operating & Information Systems. LC 70-184529. 1973. text ed. 19.95 (ISBN 0-02-928740-5). Free Pr.

Siemers, J. P., ed. European Integration: Select International Bibliography of Theses & Disserations 1957-1977. 240p. 1979. 47.50x (ISBN 90-286-0166-X). Sijthoff & Noordhoff.

Sienkiewicz, Henryk. Western Septet: Seven Stories of the American West. new ed. Coleman, Marion M., ed. LC 72-96321. (Illus.). 175p. 1973. pap. 5.00 (ISBN 0-910366-15-2). Alliance Coll.

Sienko, Michael J. Chemistry Problems. 2nd ed. LC 70-151306. (Chemistry Ser). 1972. pap. text ed. 8.95 (ISBN 0-8053-8808-7). Benjamin-Cummings.

Sienko, Michell J. & Plane, Robert A. Chemistry: Principles & Properties. 2nd ed. (Illus.). 736p. 1974. text ed. 19.00 o.p. (ISBN 0-07-057364-6, C); instructor's manual 6.50 o.p. (ISBN 0-07-057366-2); study guide 7.00 o.p. (ISBN 0-686-57683-7). McGraw.

Sieny, M. Syntax of Urban Hijazi Arabic. 12.00x (ISBN 0-685-89879-2). Intl Bk Ctr.

Sieper, Ernst, ed. see Lydgate, John.

Sierles, Frederick. Clinical Behavioral Science. 1981. text ed. write for info. (ISBN 0-89335-131-8). Spectrum Pub.

Sierpinski, Waclaw, et al. Congruence of Sets, & Other Monographs, 4 vols. in 1. Incl. On the Congruence of Sets. Sierpinski, Waclaw; Mathematical Theory of the Top. Klein, Felix; Graphical Methods. Runge, Carl; Algebraic Equations. Dickson, Leonard E. LC 67-17000. 14.95 (ISBN 0-8284-0209-4). Chelsea Pub.

Sierra, Gregorio M. Mama. 1937. pap. 2.95x (ISBN 0-393-09456-1, NortonC). Norton.

Sierra, Justo. Political Evolution of the Mexican People. Ramsdell, Charles, tr. LC 69-63009. (Pan American Paperbacks Ser.: No. 3). 1966. 17.50x (ISBN 0-292-78382-5); pap. 8.95 (ISBN 0-292-70071-7). U of Tex Pr.

Siers, James. Samoa in Colour. (Illus.). 1970. 11.95 o.p. (ISBN 0-589-00455-7, Dist. by C E Tuttle). Reed.

Sies, Luther F., jt. auth. see Goldstein, Susan B.

Siesjo, B. K. Brain Energy Metabolism. 607p. 1978. 79.50 (ISBN 0-471-99515-0). Wiley.

Siesler & Holland-Moritz. IR & Roman Spectoscopy of Polymers. 440p. 1980. 47.50 (ISBN 0-8247-6935-X). Dekker.

Siest, G., ed. Drug Effects on Laboratory Test Results. (Developments in Clinical Biochemistry: No. 2). (Illus.). 338p. 1981. PLB 49.50 (ISBN 0-686-28843-2, Pub. by Martinus Nijhoff). Kluwer Boston.

Siever, Norman L. Intermediate Algebra: A Clear Approach. 1981. write for info. (ISBN 0-8302-4206-6). Goodyear.

Siever, Raymond, jt. auth. see Press, Frank.

Siever, Raymond, commentary by. Energy & Environment: Readings from Scientific American. LC 79-21980. (Illus.). 1980. text ed. 19.95x (ISBN 0-7167-1052-8); pap. text ed. 9.95x (ISBN 0-7167-1053-6). W H Freeman.

Siever, Raymond see Press, Frank.

Sieverding, C. H., jt. auth. see Moore, M. J.

Sievers, Robert E. Nuclear Magnetic Resonance Shift Reagents. 1973. 23.00 (ISBN 0-12-643050-0). Acad Pr.

Sievers, W. David. Freud on Broadway. LC 76-141891. 1971. Repr. of 1955 ed. lib. bdg. 17.50x (ISBN 0-8154-0366-6). Cooper Sq.

Sievking, G., et al. Problems in Economic & Social Archaeology. LC 76-49652. 1977. lib. bdg. 60.00 o.p. (ISBN 0-89158-713-6). Westview.

Siewert, Carol H., et al. Basic Textiles: A Learning Package. 228p. 1973. 11.50 (ISBN 0-395-14220-2). HM.

Siewiorek, Daniel & Swarz, Robert. The Design & Evaluation of Reliable Computing Structures. 520p. Date not set. 35.00 (ISBN 0-932376-13-4). Digital Pr.

Siewiorek, Daniel, et al. Principles of Computer Structures. (Computer Science Ser.). (Illus.). 768p. 1981. text ed. 29.95 (ISBN 0-07-057302-6, C). McGraw.

Sifferlen, Thomas P. & Vartanian, Vartan. Digital Electronics with Engineering Applications. (Electrical Engineering Ser). 1970. ref. ed. 22.95 (ISBN 0-13-214304-6). P-H.

Sifford, Darrell. A Love of the Land. (Illus.). 288p. 1980. 11.95 (ISBN 0-89795-010-0). Farm Journal.

Sigafoos, Robert A. Corporate Real Estate Development: The Pursuit of America's Leading Corporations for Profit in Housing & Land Use. LC 76-3874. (Special Ser. in Real Estate & Urban Land Economics). (Illus.). 1976. 19.95 (ISBN 0-669-00644-0). Lexington Bks.

Sigal, Clancy. Going Away. 1978. pap. 2.25 o.p. (ISBN 0-445-04210-9). Popular Lib.

--Zone of the Interior. LC 76-4831. 288p. 1976. 8.95 o.p. (ISBN 0-690-01091-5, TYC-T). T Y Crowell.

Sigal, Janet, ed. see Gibbs, Margaret S. & Lachenmeyer, Juliana R.

Sigal, Leon V. Reporters & Officials: The Organization & Politics of New Making. LC 72-7014. (Illus.). 256p. 1973. 17.95 (ISBN 0-669-85035-7). Lexington Bks.

Sigal, Phillip. Emergence of Contemporary Judaism: The Foundation of Judaism from Biblical Origins to the Sixth Century A. D, Vol. 1, Pts. 1 & 2. Incl. Pt. 1. From the Origins to the Separation of Christianity. (Pittsburgh Theological Monographs: No. 29). pap. text ed. 17.50 (ISBN 0-686-64852-8); Pt. 2. Rabbinic Judaism. (Pittsburgh Theological Monographs: No. 29a). pap. text ed. 15.75 (ISBN 0-915138-46-8). 1980. pap. text ed. 31.25 set (ISBN 0-915138-46-8). Pickwick.

--Emergence of Contemporary Judaism: Vol. 1, the Foundations of Judaism from Biblical Origins to the Sixth Century A.D. Pt. 1 from the Origins to the Separation of Christianity. (Pittsburgh Theological Monographs: No. 29). 1980. pap. text ed. 17.50 (ISBN 0-915138-30-1). Pickwick.

Sigall, Michael W., jt. auth. see Reilly, Thomas A.

Sigband, Norman B. Communication for Management & Business. 2nd ed. 1976. 18.95x (ISBN 0-673-07884-1). Scott F.

Sigband, Norman B. & Bateman, David N. Communicating in Business. 1981. text ed. 16.95x (ISBN 0-673-15175-1); study guide 6.95x (ISBN 0-673-15429-7). Scott F.

Sigel. Metal Ions in Biological Systems, Vol. II. 448p. 1980. 55.00 (ISBN 0-8247-1004-5). Dekker.

Sigel, Bernard. Clinical Simulations in Surgery. Forman, Phillip M., ed. 352p. 1980. pap. 38.50 (ISBN 0-8385-1174-0). ACC.

Sigel, Efrem. The Kermanshah Transfer. 224p. 1973. 6.95 o.s.i. (ISBN 0-02-610630-2). Macmillan.

Sigel, Efrem, ed. Videotext: The Coming Revolution in Home-Office Information Retrieval. LC 79-18935. (Communications Library). 1979. 24.95x (ISBN 0-914236-41-5). Knowledge Indus.

Sigel, Efrem, et al. Video Discs: The Technology, the Applications & the Future. LC 80-23112. (Video Bookshelf Ser.). (Illus.). 183p. 1980. text ed. 29.95x (ISBN 0-914236-56-3). Knowledge Indus.

Sigel, I. E., et al, eds. New Directions in Piagetian Theory & Practice. 320p. 1981. ref. 19.95 (ISBN 0-89859-072-8). L Erlbaum Assocs.

Sigel, Irving E., jt. auth. see Forman, George E.

Sigel, Roberta S. & Hoskin, Marilyn. The Political Involvement of Adolescents. 320p. 1981. 22.00 (ISBN 0-8135-0897-5). Rutgers U Pr.

Sigerist, Henry E. Henry E. Sigerist on the Sociology of Medicine. Roemer, Milton I., ed. LC 60-6647. 1960. 6.75 o.p. (ISBN 0-910922-14-4). MD Pubns.

Sigford, Ann. Eight Words for Thirsty. LC 79-13892. (Story of Environmental Action Ser.). (Illus.). (gr. 7 up). 1979. PLB 8.95 (ISBN 0-87518-183-X). Dillon.

--Tall Grass & Trouble. LC 77-15560. (Story of Environmental Action Ser.). (Illus.). (gr. 7 up). 1978. PLB 8.95 (ISBN 0-87518-153-8). Dillon.

Siggaard-Andersen, Ole. The Acid-Base Status of the Blood. 4th ed. 230p. 1974. 22.50 (ISBN 87-16-01567-3). Krieger.

Siggia, Sidney, ed. Instrumental Methods of Organic Functional Group Analysis. LC 77-168642. 1972. 40.50 o.p. (ISBN 0-471-79110-5, Pub. by Wiley-Interscience). Wiley.

Siggins, Ian. Luther & His Mother. LC 80-2386. 96p. (Orig.). 1981. pap. 4.95 (ISBN 0-8006-1498-4, 1-1498). Fortress.

Sigham & Van Dihn, eds. From Bandung to Colombo: Conference of the Non-Aligned Countries. LC 76-162957. 1975. 7.95 (ISBN 0-89388-221-6). Okpaku Communications.

Sightler, Verna W. Reach for the Stars. (YA) 5.95 (ISBN 0-685-07456-0, Avalon). Bouregy.

Sigl, Rupert. In the Claws of the KGB: Memoirs of a Double Agent. 248p. 1978. 7.95 (ISBN 0-8059-2520-1). Dorrance.

Sigle, John D; see O'Neal, William B.

Sigler, Jay A. American Rights Policies. 1975. pap. text ed. 9.95x (ISBN 0-256-01700-X). Dorsey.

--Understanding Criminal Law. 1981. text ed. 16.95 (ISBN 0-316-79054-0); training manual free (ISBN 0-316-79055-9). Little.

Sigman, David S. & Brazier, Mary, eds. The Evolution of Protein Structure & Function: A Symposium in Honor of Prof. Emil L. Smith. LC 80-18140. (UCLA Forum in Medical Science Ser.: Vol. 21). 1980. 25.00 (ISBN 0-12-643150-7). Acad Pr.

Sigman, Marian, jt. ed. see Friedman, Sarah L.

Sigmon, Becky A. & Cybulski, Jerome S., eds. Homo Erectus: Essays in Honor of Davidson Black. 336p. 1981. 30.00x (ISBN 0-8020-5511-7). U of Toronto Pr.

Sigmon, D. L. A Framing Guide & Steel Square Book. rev. ed. 312p. 1958. 9.00 (ISBN 0-914760-01-7). Cline-Sigmon.

Sigmond, G. G. The Life of the Right Honourable Richard Brinsley Sheridan. 206p. 1980. Repr. of 1848 ed. lib. bdg. 30.00 (ISBN 0-8414-8049-4). Folcroft.

Sigmund, Janice, jt. auth. see Richards, Blair.

Sigmund, Paul E. Multinationals in Latin America: The Politics of Nationalization. 435p. 1980. 22.50 (ISBN 0-299-08260-1); pap. 6.75 (ISBN 0-299-08264-4). U of Wis Pr.

Signell, Karl. Makam: Modal Practice in Turkish Art Music. LC 74-76787. (D Monographs: No. 4). 1976. pap. text ed. 9.00x (ISBN 0-913360-07-4). Asian Music Pub.

Signitzer, Benno. Regulation of Direct Broadcasting from Satellites: The UN Involvement. LC 76-14372. (Special Studies). (Illus.). 175p. 1976. text ed. 23.50 (ISBN 0-275-56800-8). Praeger.

Signoret, Simone. Nostalgia Isn't What It Used to Be. Schaefer, Cornelia, tr. from French. LC 77-3773. 1978. 12.95 o.p. (ISBN 0-06-013986-2, HarpT). Har-Row.

Signy, F. C. History of the Queen's Park Rangers. 10.00x (ISBN 0-392-07910-0, SpS). Soccer.

Sigurdson, Joh S. Technology & Science in the People's Republic of China. 1980. 30.00 (ISBN 0-08-024288-X); pap. 12.01 (ISBN 0-686-66170-2). Pergamon.

Sigurdson, Jon, jt. ed. see Baark, Erik.

Sigurdsson, Angrimur & Bogason, Sigurdur O. Icelandic-English - English-Icelandic Dictionary, 2 vols. 3rd ed. 1980. Set. 130.00 (ISBN 0-686-68938-0). Vol. 1, Icelandic-Eng., 942pp. Vol. 2, Eng.-Icelandic, 862pp. Heinman.

Sih, G. C. & Tamus, V. P. Fracture of Composite Materials. 429p. 1979. 35.00x (ISBN 90-286-0289-5). Sijthoff & Noordhoff.

Sih, G. C., ed. Plates & Shells with Cracks: A Collection of Stress Intensity Factor Solutions for Cracks in Plates & Shells. (Mechanics of Fracture Ser.: No. 3). 352p. 1976. 62.50x (ISBN 90-286-0146-5). Sijthoff & Noordhoff.

--Stress Analysis of Notch Problems. (Mechanics of Fracture Ser.: No. 5). 312p. 1978. 45.00x (ISBN 90-286-0166-X). Sijthoff & Noordhoff.

Siirala, Aarne. The Voice of Illness. (A Study in Therapy & Prophecy). 1981. Repr. of 1964 ed. soft cover 19.95 (ISBN 0-88946-995-4). E Mellen.

Siiteri, Pentti K., ed. see Cshl Banbury Center Report 8 - Hormones & Breast Cancer, et al.

Sijben, J. J. Rational Expectations & Monetary Policies. LC 79-56565. 144p. 1980. 37.50x (ISBN 0-686-27288-9). Sijthoff & Noordhoff.

Sik, Ota. The Communist Power System. (Praeger Special Studies). 170p. 1980. 21.95 (ISBN 0-03-044106-4). Praeger.

--Plan & Market Under Socialism. LC 66-23896. 1967. 17.50 o.p. (ISBN 0-87332-012-3). M E Sharpe.

Sikat, Dorian. Filipino Immigrant. Date not set. 7.50 (ISBN 0-682-49405-4). Exposition. Postponed.

Sikes, Bette, ed. see Nimmer, Raymond T.

Sikes, Herschel M., et al, eds. The Letters of William Hazlitt. LC 78-54079. 1978. cOBE 22.50x (ISBN 0-8147-4986-0); pap. 9.00x cobe (ISBN 0-8147-4987-9). NYU Pr.

Sikes, Lewright B. The Public Life of Pierce Butler: South Carolina Statesman. LC 78-66122. 1979. pap. text ed. 8.00 (ISBN 0-8191-0683-6). U Pr of Amer.

Sikes, Walter W., et al. Renewing Higher Education from Within: A Guide for Campus Change Teams. LC 74-9113. (Higher Education Ser.). 1974. 12.95x o.p. (ISBN 0-87589-239-6). Jossey-Bass.

Sikiotis, Nicholas. Structures in Context. (Illus.). 1980. pap. text ed. 4.50x (ISBN 0-582-55884-0); key 1.75x (ISBN 0-582-55885-9). Longman.

Sikorowa, Ludwika, et al, eds. Salivary Gland Tumors. LC 80-14975. 200p. 1981. 9.50 (ISBN 0-08-025557-4). Pergamon.

Sikorski, Linda, jt. auth. see Zaltman, Gerald.

Sikorski, R. Advanced Calculus: Functions of Several Variables. 1969. 15.95 (ISBN 0-02-852280-X). Hafner.

Siksek, Simon G. The Legal Framework for Oil Concessions in the Arab World. LC 79-2882. 140p. 1981. Repr. of 1960 ed. 15.00 (ISBN 0-8305-0050-2). Hyperion Conn.

Siksek, Simon G., jt. auth. see Badr, Albirt Y.

Sikula, Andrew F. Management & Administration. LC 72-95954. 1973. text ed. 15.95x (ISBN 0-675-09000-8). Merrill.

--Personnel Administration & Human Resources Management. LC 75-8691. (Management & Administration Ser.). 456p. 1976. 21.95 (ISBN 0-471-79140-7). Wiley.

Sikula, Jaromir. Grasses. (Concise Guides Ser.). (Illus.). 1979. 7.95 (ISBN 0-600-34045-7). Transatlantic.

Sila, Nechistaia. Arkadii Averchenko. (Panteon Sovietov Molodym Liugiam, Deti). 1979. 7.95 (ISBN 0-89830-010-X). Russica Pubs.

Silbajoris, Rimvydas. Perfection of Exile: Fourteen Contemporary Lithuanian Writers. LC 72-108798. (Illus.). 1970. 15.95x (ISBN 0-8061-0907-6). U of Okla Pr.

Silbajoris, Rimvydas, ed. Russian Versification: The Theories of Trediakovsky, Lomonosov & Kantemir. LC 67-13777. (Russian Institute Occasional Papers Ser.). 1968. 15.00x (ISBN 0-231-03011-8). Columbia U Pr.

Silber, Bettina & Feldman, Clarice R., eds. U. S. Refinery Policy in the Nineteen Eighties: Security, Economics & Equity. LC 80-68123. (Energy Policy Ser.). (Orig.). 1980. 7.00 (ISBN 0-934458-02-2). Americans Energy Ind.

Silber, Bettina, jt. ed. see Feldman, Clarice.

Silber, Gordon R; see Eddy, Frederick D.

Silber, William L., jt. auth. see Ritter, Lawrence S.

Silberbauer, G. B. Hunter & Habitat in the Central Kalahari Desert. LC 80-16768. (Illus.). 288p. Date not set. 39.50 (ISBN 0-521-23578-2); pap. 14.95 (ISBN 0-521-28135-0). Cambridge U Pr.

Silberberg, Margaret C., jt. ed. see Silberberg, Norman E.

Silberberg, Norman E. & Silberberg, Margaret C., eds. Who Speaks for the Child? (Illus.). 226p. 1974. 16.75 (ISBN 0-398-03014-6); pap. 12.50 (ISBN 0-398-03015-4). C C Thomas.

Silberger, Allan J. Introduction to Harmonic Analysis on Reductive P-Adic Groups. LC 79-19020. (Mathematical Notes Ser.: 23). 376p. 1979. pap. 11.00x (ISBN 0-691-08246-4). Princeton U Pr.

Silberman, Adolph, jt. auth. see Blackham, Garth J.

Silberman, Charles E. Criminal Violence, Criminal Justice. LC 79-2318. 1980. pap. 3.75 (ISBN 0-394-74147-1, Vin). Random.

Silberman, Melvin, jt. auth. see Wheelan, Susan.

Silbernagel, S., ed. Abstracts of the International Conference on Renal Transport of Organic Substances Held in Innsbruck, July, 1980. (Journal: Renal Physiology: Vol. 2, No. 3). (Illus.). 62p. 1980. pap. 17.00 (ISBN 3-8055-1641-X). S Karger.

Silbersack, John, jt. ed. see Schochet, Victoria.

Silberstang, Edwin. Abandoned. LC 80-1071. 312p. 1981. 10.95 (ISBN 0-385-15978-1). Doubleday.

--Play Bridge Tonight. (Gamblers Book Shelf). 64p. 1976. pap. 2.00 o.p. (ISBN 0-911996-59-1). Gamblers.

--Play Chess Tonight. (Gambler's Book Shelf). (Illus.). 1976. pap. 2.95 (ISBN 0-911996-68-0). Gamblers.

--Play Pinochle Tonight. (Gambler's Book Shelf). 64p. 1976. pap. 2.95 (ISBN 0-89650-562-6). Gamblers.

--Playboy's Guide to Casino Gambling: Craps, Blackjack, Roulette, & Baccarat. LC 80-7727. (Playboy's Lifestyles Library). (Illus.). 512p. 1980. 15.95 (ISBN 0-87223-618-8, Dist. by Har-Row). Playboy.

--Smart Casino Play. (Gamblers Book Shelf). 64p. 1976. pap. 2.95 (ISBN 0-89650-560-X). Gamblers.

--Snake Eyes. 1977. 8.95 o.p. (ISBN 0-525-20625-6). Dutton.

Silberston, A., jt. auth. see Boehm, K. H.

Silberston, Z. A., jt. auth. see Taylor, C. T.

Silbert, Alvin, jt. auth. see Silbert, Linda P.

Silbert, Alvin J., jt. auth. see Silbert, Linda P.

Silbert, Jerry, et al. Direct Instruction Mathematics. (Illus., Orig.). 1981. pap. text ed. write for info. (ISBN 0-675-08047-9). Merrill.

Silbert, Linda P. & Silbert, Alvin. My Own Book of Feelings. (Little Twirps, TM Creative Thinking Workbooks). (Illus.). (gr. k-8). 1977. 2.25 (ISBN 0-89544-017-2, 017). Silbert Bress.

Silbert, Linda P. & Silbert, Alvin J. Agnes' Cardboard Piano. (Little Twirps, TM Understanding People Bks.). (Illus.). (gr. k-4). 1978. pap. 2.25 (ISBN 0-89544-054-7). Silbert Bress.

--Guess What I Am Thinking of... (Little Twirps, TM Creative Thinking Wkbks.). (Illus.). (gr. 2-6). 1977. wkbk. 2.25 (ISBN 0-89544-021-0, 021). Silbert Bress.

--I'll Be Your Best Friend. (Little Twirps, TM Understanding People Books). (Illus.). (gr. k-4). 1978. pap. 2.25 (ISBN 0-89544-056-3). Silbert Bress.

--Lost in the Cave. (Little Twirps, TM Understanding People Books). (Illus.). (gr. k-4). 1978. pap. 2.25 (ISBN 0-89544-057-1). Silbert Bress.

--My Own Book of Special Things. (Little Twirps, TM Creative Thinking Wkbks.). (Illus.). (ps-4). 1977. wkbk. 2.25 (ISBN 0-89544-019-9, 019). Silbert Bress.

--My Own Book of Wishes. (Little Twirps Creative Thinking Workbooks). (Illus.). (gr. k-6). 1976. wkbk. 2.25 (ISBN 0-89544-016-4). Silbert Bress.

--Penelope's Pen Pal. (Little Twirps, TM Understanding People Books). (Illus.). (gr. k-4). 1978. pap. 2.25 (ISBN 0-89544-053-9). Silbert Bress.

--This Is My Opinion About... (Little Twirps, TM Creative Thinking Wkbks.). (Illus.). (gr. 5-12). 1977. 2.25 (ISBN 0-89544-020-2, 020). Silbert Bress.

--Tiger, Take off Your Hat. (Little Twirps, TM Understanding People Books). (Illus.). (gr. k-4). 1978. pap. 2.25 (ISBN 0-89544-051-2). Silbert Bress.

--Tuffy's Bike Race. (Little Twirps, TM Understanding People Books). (Illus.). (gr. k-4). 1978. pap. 2.25 (ISBN 0-89544-058-X). Silbert Bress.

--Tyrone Goes Camping. (Little Twirps, TM Understanding People Books). (Illus.). (gr. k-4). 1978. pap. 2.25 (ISBN 0-89544-055-5). Silbert Bress.

--What Would Happen If... (Little Twirps, TM Creative Thinking Wkbks.). (Illus.). (gr. 3-9). 1976. wkbk. 2.25 (ISBN 0-89544-018-0, 018). Silbert Bress.

--Whitney's New Glasses. (Little Twirps, TM Understanding People Book). (Illus.). (gr. k-4). 1978. pap. 2.25 (ISBN 0-89544-052-0). Silbert Bress.

Silberton, A., jt. auth. see Cockerill, A.

Silbey, jt. auth. see Parker.

Silbey, J. & McSeveney, S. Voters, Parties & Elections: Quantitative Essays in the History of Popular American Voting Behaviour. 434p. 1972. pap. 9.95 o.p. (ISBN 0-471-00684-X). Krieger.

Silbey, Joel H. A Respectable Minority: The Democratic Party in the Civil War Era, 1860-1868. 1977. 12.95 (ISBN 0-393-05648-1); pap. 4.95x (ISBN 0-393-09087-6). Norton.

Silcock, T. H., tr. see Worakwinto, Thongyoy.

Silente, Douglas M. Half Man, Half Beast, & Other Fantastic Combinations. (Odd Books for Odd Moments Ser.). (Illus.). 72p. (Orig.). 1981. pap. 3.95 (ISBN 0-938338-02-1). Winds World Pr.

Silet, Charles L. The Writings of Paul Rosenfeld: An Annotated Bibliography. LC 79-7931. 250p. 1981. lib. bdg. 35.00 (ISBN 0-8240-9532-4). Garland Pub.

Silet, Charles L. P. Transition: An Author Index. LC 79-67477. 186p. 1979. 15.00x (ISBN 0-87875-168-8). Whitston Pub.

Silfen, Martin E. Counseling Clients in the Entertainment Industry 1980, 2 vols. LC 80-80021. (Patents, Copyrights, Trademarks, & Literary Property Course Handbook Ser.). 1433p. 1980. pap. text ed. 25.00 (ISBN 0-686-68822-8, G6-3666). PLI.

Silfen, Paul Harrison. Essays in English History: World History in Six Dimensions. LC 74-80691. 1975. 4.00 o.p. (ISBN 0-682-48047-9, University). Exposition.

--Essays in French & German History: World History in Six Dimensions. 1976. 6.50 o.p. (ISBN 0-682-48375-3, University). Exposition.

--Essays in Greek & Roman History: World History in Six Dimensions. 1975. 4.50 o.p. (ISBN 0-682-48279-X, University). Exposition.

--Essays in Russian History: World History in Six Dimensions. LC 74-80692. 1975. 4.00 o.p. (ISBN 0-682-48048-7, University). Exposition.

--Essays in World History from Antiquity to the Present. 1976. 17.50 o.p. (ISBN 0-682-48482-2, University). Exposition.

--The Influence of the Mongols of Russia: A Dimensional History. LC 74-76040. 1974. 7.00 o.p. (ISBN 0-682-47969-1, University). Exposition.

--The Volkisch Ideology & the Roots of Nazism: The Early Writings of Arthur Moeller van den Bruck. LC 73-86549. 1973. 5.00 o.p. (ISBN 0-682-47786-9, University). Exposition.

Silgalis, Eugene, jt. auth. see Taber, Margaret R.

Siliconix, Inc. Designing with Field Effect Transistors. (Illus.). 352p. 1981. 24.50 (ISBN 0-07-057449-9). McGraw.

Silinish, E. A. Organic Molecular Crystals: Their Electronic States. (Springer Series in Solid State Sciences: Vol. 16). (Illus.). 410p. 1980. 54.50 (ISBN 0-387-10053-9). Springer-Verlag.

Silitch, Clarissa, ed. Yankee Church Supper Cookbook. LC 80-612. 240p. 1980. pap. 9.95 (ISBN 0-686-68933-X, 3075). Yankee Bks.

--Yankee Church Suppers. LC 80-612. 1980. pap. 9.95 (ISBN 0-911658-14-9, 3075). Yankee Bks.

Siljander, R. P. Terrorist Attacks. (Illus.). 342p. 1980. 33.50 (ISBN 0-398-04028-1). C C Thomas.

Siljander, Raymond P. Applied Police & Fire Photography. (Illus.). 336p. 1976. 24.75 (ISBN 0-398-03566-0). C C Thomas.

--Applied Surveillance Photography. (Illus.). 120p. 1975. 14.50 (ISBN 0-398-03376-5). C C Thomas.

--Fundamentals of Physical Surveillance: A Guide for Uniformed & Plainclothes Personnel. (Illus.). 288p. 1978. 24.50 (ISBN 0-398-03660-8). C C Thomas.

Silk, Alvin J., jt. auth. see Davis, Harry L.

Silk, John. Statistical Concepts in Geography. (Illus.). 1979. text ed. 22.50x (ISBN 0-04-910065-3); pap. text ed. 9.95x (ISBN 0-04-910066-1). Allen Unwin.

Silk, Joseph. The Big Bang: The Creation & Evolution of the Universe. LC 79-19340. (Illus.). 1980. text ed. 18.00x (ISBN 0-7167-1084-6); pap. text ed. 9.95x (ISBN 0-7167-1085-4). W H Freeman.

Silk, Leonard & Silk, Mark. The American Establishment. LC 80-50533. 351p. 1980. 13.95 (ISBN 0-465-00134-3). Basic.

Silk, Leonard & Warner, Raleigh, Jr. Ideals in Collision. 1979. 7.50 (ISBN 0-915604-33-7). Columbia U Pr.

Silk, M. S. Interaction in Poetic Imagery. LC 73-90813. 304p. 1974. 42.00 (ISBN 0-521-20417-8). Cambridge U Pr.

Silk, M. S. & Stern, J. P. Nietzsche on Tragedy. LC 80-40433. 500p. Date not set. price not set (ISBN 0-521-23262-7). Cambridge U Pr.

Silk, Mark, jt. auth. see Silk, Leonard.

Silkin, Jon. Amana Grass. LC 71-153105. (Wesleyan Poetry Program: Vol. 59). 1971. 10.00x (ISBN 0-8195-2059-4, Pub. by Wesleyan U Pr); pap. 4.95 (ISBN 0-8195-1059-9). Columbia U Pr.

--Poems New & Selected. LC 66-14661. (Wesleyan Poetry Program: Vol. 30). (Orig.). 1966. 10.00x (ISBN 0-8195-2030-6, Pub. by Wesleyan U Pr); pap. 6.95x (ISBN 0-8195-1030-0). Columbia U Pr.

Silko, Leslie M. Storyteller. 320p. 1981. 16.95 (ISBN 0-394-51589-7); pap. 9.95 (ISBN 0-394-17795-9). Seaver Bks.

--Storyteller. LC 80-20251. (Illus.). 320p. 1981. 16.95 (ISBN 0-394-51589-7); pap. 9.95 (ISBN 0-394-17795-9). Seaver Bks.

Sill, Sterling W. The Law of the Harvest. 392p. 1980. 8.50 (ISBN 0-88290-142-7). Horizon Utah.

--The Laws of Success. LC 75-18818. 219p. 1975. 6.95 (ISBN 0-87747-556-3). Deseret Bk.

--Lessons from Great Lives. LC 80-84567. 300p. 1981. 7.95 (ISBN 0-88290-172-9, 2049). Horizon Utah.

--Principles, Promises & Powers. LC 73-87714. 352p. 1973. 5.95 o.p. (ISBN 0-87747-506-7). Deseret Bk.

--Thy Kingdom Come. LC 75-37275. 239p. 1975. 6.95 o.p. (ISBN 0-87747-602-0). Deseret Bk.

--The Upward Reach. LC 80-83863. 350p. 1980. 8.50 (ISBN 0-88290-167-2, 1060). Horizon Utah.

Sill, Webster H., Jr. Integrated Plant Protection. (Illus.). 328p. 1981. text ed. 25.00. Iowa St U Pr.

--The Plant Protection Discipline: Problems. LC 78-59171. 1978. text ed. 25.00x (ISBN 0-470-26443-8). Allanheld.

Sillamy, N. Dictionnaire psychologie. (Illus., Fr.). pap. 8.50 (ISBN 0-685-13883-6). Larousse.

Sillar, F. C. & Meyler, Ruth. Skye. (Islands Ser). (Illus.). 248p. pap. 10.50 (ISBN 0-7153-5751-4). David & Charles.

Sillars, Malcolm O., jt. auth. see Rieke, Richard D.

Silleck, Anne, jt. auth. see Reid, James M.

Silliman, Benjamin. Letters of Shahcoolen: A Hindu Residing in Philadelphia. LC 62-7013. 1962. Repr. of 1802 ed. 20.00x (ISBN 0-8201-1041-8). Schol Facsimiles.

Silliman, Lee, ed. see Schultz, James W.

Sillitoe, Alan. Second Chance. 1981. 12.95 (ISBN 0-671-42761-X). S&S.

--The Widower's Son. 1978. pap. 1.95 (ISBN 0-06-080465-3, P 465, PL). Har-Row.

--The Widower's Son. LC 76-52776. 1977. 8.95 o.s.i. (ISBN 0-06-013892-0, HarpT). Har-Row.

Sills, Beverly. Bubbles. (Illus.). 1978. pap. 2.50 o.s.i. (ISBN 0-446-81520-9). Warner Bks.

Sills, D. E., ed. International Encyclopedia of the Social Sciences, 17 vols. 1968. 55.00 ea. o.s.i. (89511-89527). Macmillan.

Sills, David L., ed. International Encyclopedia of the Social Sciences, 8 vols. LC 77-72778. (Illus.). 1977. 250.00 set (ISBN 0-02-895700-8). Free Pr.

Sills, David L., et al, eds. Accident at Three Mile Island: The Human Dimensions. 200p. (Orig.). 1981. lib. bdg. 20.00x (ISBN 0-86531-165-X); pap. text ed. 12.00x (ISBN 0-86531-187-0). Westview.

Sills, Stephanie, jt. ed. see Oliver, Clinton S.

Silman, James B., jt. auth. see Quintanilla, Guadalupe C.

Silo. The Look Within. 1980. pap. 3.95 (ISBN 0-87728-494-6). Weiser.

Silva, jt. auth. see Haswell.

Silva, D. M. De see De Silva, D. M.

Silva, Jose & Miele, Philip. The Silva Mind Control Method. 1978. pap. 2.95 (ISBN 0-671-43343-1). PB.

Silva, Ruth C. Rum, Religion, & Votes: Nineteen Twenty-Eight Re-Examined. LC 80-24997. ix, 76p. 1981. Repr. of 1962 ed. lib. bdg. 22.50x (ISBN 0-313-22768-3, SIRR). Greenwood.

--Rum, Religion, & Votes: Nineteen Twenty-Eight Re-Examined. LC 80-24997. 85p. 1981. Repr. of 1962 ed. lib. bdg. 22.50 (ISBN 0-313-22768-3, SIRR). Greenwood.

Silva, Sharon, ed. see Low, Jennie & Yee, Diane.

Silva, Sharon, ed. see Sun Yun Chiang, Cecilia & Carr, Allan.

Silva, Tony & Kotlar, Barbara. Conures. (Illus.). 96p. 1980. 2.95 (ISBN 0-87666-893-7, KW-121). TFH Pubns.

--Discus. (Illus.). 98p. 1980. 2.95 (ISBN 0-87666-535-0, KW-097). TFH Pubns.

Silva-Michelena, Jose A. The Illusion of Democracy in Dependent Nations: Vol. 3 of Politics of Change on Venezuela. 1971. 20.00x (ISBN 0-262-19069-9). MIT Pr.

Silva-Michelena, Jose A., jt. auth. see Bonilla, Frank.

Silvan, Matthew. Lazarus, Come Out! The Story of My Life. Moran, Hugh, ed. Giannini, Vera, tr. from It. LC 80-82599. Orig. Title: Quella Violenza Di Dio. 224p. (Orig.). 1981. pap. 5.95 (ISBN 0-911782-36-2). New City.

Silveman, Jane A., jt. ed. see Schnidman, Frank.

Silvennoinen, P. Reactor Core Fuel Management. 250p. 1976. text ed. 42.00 (ISBN 0-08-019853-8); pap. text ed. 18.75 (ISBN 0-08-019852-X). Pergamon.

Silver, A. David. The Radical New Road to Wealth. rev. ed. 1981. pap. 15.00 (ISBN 0-914306-53-7). Intl Wealth.

Silver, Abba H. Vision & Victory: A Collection of Addresses 1942-1948. (Return to Zion Ser.). (Illus.). 232p. 1980. Repr. of 1949 ed. lib. bdg. 17.50x (ISBN 0-87991-124-7). Porcupine Pr.

Silver, Archie A. & Hagin, Rosa A. Search Manual. LC 75-43437. 112p. (Orig.). 1975. pap. text ed. 11.80 (ISBN 0-8027-9035-6). Walker Educ.

Silver, Arnold. Bernard Shaw: The Darker Side. LC 79-92454. (Illus.). 384p. 1981. text ed. 25.00x (ISBN 0-8047-1091-0). Stanford U Pr.

Silver, B. L. Irreducible Tensor Methods: An Introduction for Chemists. 1976. 42.50 o.p. (ISBN 0-12-643650-9). Acad Pr.

Silver, Brian D., jt. ed. see McCagg, William O.

Silver, C. E. Surgery for Cancer of the Larynx. 1981. text ed. write for info. (ISBN 0-443-08064-X). Churchill.

Silver, Caroline. Eventing. LC 76-28058. 1977. 15.95 (ISBN 0-312-27090-9). St Martin.

--Guide to Horses of the World. (Illustrated Natural History Guides). (Illus.). 1977. pap. 4.95 (ISBN 0-8467-0365-3, Pub. by Two Continents). Hippocrene Bks.

Silver, Catherine B. Black Teachers in Urban Schools: The Case of Washington D.C. LC 72-92467. (Special Studies in U.S. Economic, Social, & Political Issues). 1973. 24.00x (ISBN 0-8290-0456-4); pap. text ed. 12.50x (ISBN 0-89197-682-5). Irvington.

Silver, Edward A., jt. auth. see Peterson, Rein.

Silver, Gary T. The Dope Chronicles: Eighteen Fifty to Nineteen Fifty. LC 78-15835. (Illus., Orig.). 1979. pap. 7.95 o.p. (ISBN 0-06-250790-7, RD 231, HarpR). Har-Row.

Silver, George A. Child Health: America's Future. LC 78-14217. 1978. text ed. 22.50 (ISBN 0-89443-043-2). Aspen Systems.

--A Spy in the House of Medicine. LC 76-2184. 1976. 21.75 (ISBN 0-912862-18-1). Aspen Systems.

Silver, Gerald. Graphic Layout & Design. LC 80-65062. (Graphic Arts Ser.). 216p. 1981. pap. text ed. 10.40 (ISBN 0-8273-1374-8); instructor's guide 1.60 (ISBN 0-8273-1375-6). Delmar.

Silver, Gerald A. Graphic Layout & Design. 320p. 1981. 13.95 (ISBN 0-442-26774-6). Van Nos Reinhold.

--Introduction to Management. (Illus.). 525p. 1981. text ed. 16.95 (ISBN 0-8299-0415-8). West Pub.

Silver, Gerald A. & Silver, J. Simplified Basic Programming. (Illus.). 320p. 1974. pap. 15.75 o.p. (ISBN 0-07-057387-5, G). McGraw.

Silver, Gerald A. & Silver, Joan B. Introduction to Systems Analysis. (Illus.). 1976. 17.95x (ISBN 0-13-498683-0). P-H.

Silver, H. T., jt. auth. see Dolan, Edward F., Jr.

Silver, Harold, jt. auth. see Silver, Pamela.

Silver, Harold, ed. Robert Owen on Education. LC 69-10432. (Cambridge Texts & Studies in Education). 1969. 27.50 (ISBN 0-521-07353-7). Cambridge U Pr.

Silver, Howard & Nydahl, John. Introduction to Engineering Thermodynamics. LC 76-3601. (Illus.). 500p. 1977. text ed. 22.95 (ISBN 0-8299-0053-5); solutions manual avail. (ISBN 0-8299-0573-1). West Pub.

Silver, Howard A. Intermediate Algebra. 512p. 1981. text ed. 17.95 (ISBN 0-13-469411-2). P-H.

--Mathematics: Contemporary Topics & Applications. (Illus.). 1979. text ed. 17.95 (ISBN 0-13-563304-4). P-H.

Silver, J., jt. auth. see Silver, Gerald A.

Silver, James W. Mississippi: The Closed Society. LC 66-15957. (Illus.). 1966. 5.75 o.p. (ISBN 0-15-118176-4). HarBraceJ.

Silver, Joan B., jt. auth. see Silver, Gerald A.

Silver, Morris. Affluence, Altruism, & Atrophy: The Decline of the Welfare State. LC 79-3528. 200p. 1980. 17.00x (ISBN 0-8147-7810-0). NYU Pr.

Silver, P. H., jt. auth. see Green, J. H.

Silver, Pamela & Silver, Harold. The Education of the Poor: The History of a National School 1824-1974. (Routledge Library in the History of Education). 208p. 1974. 22.00x (ISBN 0-7100-7804-8). Routledge & Kegan.

Silver, Pat, jt. auth. see Lasky, Jesse, Jr.

Silver, Pat, jt. auth. see Lasky, Jesse L.

Silver, Pat, jt. auth. see Lasky, Jesse L., Jr.

Silver, Philip. Ortega As Phenomenologist. LC 78-667. 1978. 15.00x (ISBN 0-231-04544-1). Columbia U Pr.

Silver, Philip W., tr. see Martinez-Bonati, Felix.

Silver, Robert S. & Watt, James. Introduction to Thermodynamics. LC 79-138380. (Illus.). 1971. 21.50 (ISBN 0-521-08064-9). Cambridge U Pr.

Silver, Stuart & Haiblum, Isidore. Faster Than a Speeding Bullet. LC 80-82221. 240p. (Orig.). 1980. pap. 2.25 (ISBN 0-87216-760-7). Playboy Pbks.

Silver, Sylvia. Anaerobic Bacteriology for the Clinical Laboratory. LC 79-23329. 1980. pap. 9.50 (ISBN 0-8016-4625-1). Mosby.

Silver, Theodore & Sacks, Howard R. Your Key to Success in Law School. (Orig.). 1981. pap. 5.95 (ISBN 0-671-09256-1). Monarch Pr.

Silvera, Alain, ed. see Halevy, Daniel.

Silverberg, James, jt. ed. see Barlow, George W.

Silverberg, R., ed. Science Fiction Hall of Fame, Vol. 1. 1971. pap. 2.50 (ISBN 0-380-00795-9, 44933). Avon.

Silverberg, Robert. Across a Billion Years. (Orig.). 1980. pap. 1.95 o.p. (ISBN 0-425-04627-3). Berkley Pub.

--Auk, the Dodo, & the Oryx: Vanished & Vanishing Creatures. LC 67-10476. (Illus.). (gr. 7 up). 1967. 10.95 (ISBN 0-690-11106-1, TYC-J). T Y Crowell.

--The Best of Robert Silverberg. 1980. pap. write for info. (ISBN 0-671-83497-5). PB.

--Clocks for the Ages: How Scientists Date the Past. (Illus.). (gr. 7 up). 1971. 6.95 o.s.i. (ISBN 0-02-782680-5). Macmillan.

--Ghost Towns of the American West. LC 68-17081. (Illus.). (gr. 7 up). 1968. 10.95 (ISBN 0-690-32621-1, TYC-J). T Y Crowell.

--Lord Valentine's Castle. 480p. 1981. pap. 2.95 (ISBN 0-553-14428-6). Bantam.

--The Man in the Maze. 1978. pap. 1.50 (ISBN 0-380-00198-5, 38539). Avon.

--Masks of Time. 1973. pap. 1.25 o.p. (ISBN 0-345-23446-4). Ballantine.

--Mound Builders. 1975. pap. 1.50 o.p. (ISBN 0-345-24846-5). Ballantine.

--Nightwings. 1978. pap. 1.50 (ISBN 0-380-00571-9, 41467). Avon.

--A Robert Silverberg Omnibus: Downward to Earth, the Man in the Maze, & Nightwings. LC 80-8232. 540p. 1981. 14.95 (ISBN 0-06-014047-X, HarpT). Har-Row.

--Seven Wonders of the Ancient World. LC 70-95298. (Illus.). (gr. 6-9). 1970. 8.95 (ISBN 0-02-782650-3, CCPr). Macmillan.

--Son of Man. (A Del Rey Bk.). 1977. pap. 2.25 o.p. (ISBN 0-345-28884-X). Ballantine.
--The Stochastic Man. 240p. 1977. pap. 1.50 o.p. (ISBN 0-449-13570-5, GM). Fawcett.
--Up the Line. 4th ed. (Del Rey Bks). 256p. 1978. pap. 2.50 (ISBN 0-345-29696-6). Ballantine.
Silverberg, Robert, ed. Earth Is the Strangest Planet. LC 76-55728. (Nelson's Science Fiction Ser.). (gr. 8 up). 1977. 7.95 o.p. (ISBN 0-525-66401-7). Elsevier-Nelson.
--Explorers of Space: Eight Stories of Science Fiction. LC 74-30399. (Science Fiction Ser.). 224p. 1975. 7.95 o.p. (ISBN 0-525-66439-4). Elsevier-Nelson.
--New Dimensions: Science Fiction No. 7. LC 76-26276. (Illus.). 1977. 8.95 o.p. (ISBN 0-06-013862-9, HarpT). Har-Row.
--New Dimensions: 8. LC 77-11774. 1978. 10.95 o.s.i. (ISBN 0-06-013792-4, HarpT). Har-Row.
Silverberg, Robert & Elwood, Roger, eds. Epoch. (YA) 1975. 10.95 o.p. (ISBN 0-399-11460-2, Dist. by Putnam). Berkley Pub.
Silverberg, Robert, ed. see McIntyre, Vonda N., et al.
Silverberg, Steven G. Surgical Pathology of the Uterus. LC 77-8569. (Surgical Pathology Ser.). 1977. 25.95 (ISBN 0-471-01476-1, Pub. by Wiley Medical). Wiley.
Silverberg, Steven G. & Major, Francis J. Estrogens & Cancer. LC 78-17275. 1978. 32.95 (ISBN 0-471-04172-6, Pub. by Wiley Medical). Wiley.
Silverleaf, Jane, jt. auth. see Bradley, Judy.
Silverman, Al. Foster & Laurie. 1975. pap. 1.75 o.p. (ISBN 0-445-08403-0). Popular Lib.
Silverman, Bertram & Yanowitch, Murray. The Worker in Post-Industrial Capitalism: Liberal & Radical Responses. LC 73-14431. (Illus.). 1974. pap. text ed. 8.95 (ISBN 0-02-928770-7). Free Pr.
Silverman, D., jt. auth. see Sandywell, B.
Silverman, David. Reading Castaneda: A Prologue to the Social Sciences. 1975. 15.00 (ISBN 0-7100-8145-6); pap. 7.95 (ISBN 0-7100-8146-4). Routledge & Kegan.
Silverman, Eleanor. One Hundred One Media Center Ideas. LC 80-17034. 213p. 1980. pap. 13.50 (ISBN 0-8108-1329-7). Scarecrow.
Silverman, F. Communication for the Speechless. 1980. 17.95 (ISBN 0-13-153361-4). P-H.
Silverman, Frank H. Research Design in Speech Pathology & Audiology: Asking & Answering Questions. (Illus.). 1977. text ed. 19.95 (ISBN 0-13-774117-0). P-H.
Silverman, Harold I., ed. Pride of the Wineries: The California Living Wine Report. LC 80-66282. (Illus.). 192p. (Orig.). 1980. pap. 5.95 (ISBN 0-89395-042-4). Cal Living Bks.
Silverman, Herb. Complex Variables. 1975. text ed. 21.50 (ISBN 0-395-18582-3). HM.
Silverman, Hirsch L., ed. Marital Therapy: Moral, Sociological, & Psychological Factors. (Illus.). 576p. 1972. 32.75 (ISBN 0-398-02415-4); pap. 19.75 (ISBN 0-398-03065-0). C C Thomas.
Silverman, Hugh. Piaget, Philosophy & the Human Sciences. 1980. text ed. 17.50 (ISBN 0-391-00958-3). Humanities.
Silverman, Hugh J. & Elliston, Frederick A., eds. Jean-Paul Sartre: Contemporary Approaches to His Philosophy. 425p. 1981. text ed. 22.50x (ISBN 0-391-01634-2); pap. 9.95x (ISBN 0-391-01635-0). Duquesne.
Silverman, J., ed. Energy Storage: Transactions of the First International Assembly on Energy Storage, Held in Dubrovnik, Yugoslavia, 1979. LC 80-40771. (Illus.). 512p. 1980. 100.00 (ISBN 0-08-025471-3). Pergamon.
Silverman, Jerry. How to Play the Guitar. LC 68-14557. 1968. pap. 5.95 (ISBN 0-385-09862-6, Dolp). Doubleday.
--Liberated Woman's Songbook. Markel, Robert, ed. (Illus.). 1971. 7.95 o.s.i. (ISBN 0-02-610780-5). Macmillan.
Silverman, Jerry, jt. ed. see Handy, W. C.
Silverman, Joseph & Van Dyken, A. R., eds. Radiation Processing: Transactions of the First International Meeting on Radiation Processing, 2 vols. LC 76-58383. 1977. Set. text ed. 165.00 (ISBN 0-08-021640-4). Pergamon.
Silverman, Joseph H., jt. auth. see Armistead, Samuel G.
Silverman, K. Literature in America: Founding of a Nation. LC 73-139984. 1971. pap. text ed. 7.95 (ISBN 0-02-928760-X). Free Pr.
Silverman, Louis. The Determination of Impurities in Nuclear Grade Sodium Metal & Related Sodium Compounds. 156p. 1971. 26.00 (ISBN 0-08-016165-0). Pergamon.
Silverman, Manuel S., jt. auth. see Kroll, Larry J.
Silverman, Milton. The Drugging of the Americas: How Multinational Drug Companies Say One Thing About Their Products to Physicians in the United States, & Another Thing to Physicians in Latin America. LC 75-27935. 1976. 14.95x (ISBN 0-520-03122-9). U of Cal Pr.
Silverman, Milton & Lee, Philip R. Pills, Profits, & Politics. 1974. 15.95 (ISBN 0-520-02616-0); pap. 4.95 (ISBN 0-520-03050-8). U of Cal Pr.
Silverman, Milton, et al. Pills & the Public Purse. 300p. 1981. 14.95 (ISBN 0-520-04381-2). U of Cal Pr.
Silverman, Milton J. & Winslow, Ron. Open & Shut. 1981. 15.95 (ISBN 0-393-01442-8). Norton.
Silverman, R. Essentials of Psychology. 1979. pap. 14.95 (ISBN 0-13-286658-7); study guide & wkbk. 6.95 (ISBN 0-13-286666-8). P-H.
Silverman, R., tr. see Gelfand, Izrail M. & Fomin, S. V.
Silverman, R. A., tr. see Kotelnikov, Vladimir A.
Silverman, Richard A., tr. see Rozanov, Y. A.
Silverman, Robert. Law & Urban Growth: Civil Litigation in the Boston Trial Courts, 1880-1900. LC 80-7553. 224p. 1981. 16.50 (ISBN 0-691-04677-8). Princeton U Pr.
Silverman, Robert A., jt. auth. see Henshel, Richard L.
Silverman, Robert E. Psychology. 3rd ed. (Illus.). 1978. text ed. 18.95 (ISBN 0-13-733022-7); pap. 6.95 study guide & wkbk. (ISBN 0-13-733048-0). P-H.
Silverman, Ronald H., ed. Art Education & the World of Work. 208p. 1980. 9.75 (ISBN 0-686-27490-3). Natl Art Ed.
Silverman, Ruth D. Idaho Supplement for Modern Real Estate Practice. 3rd ed. 140p. 1981. pap. 7.95 (ISBN 0-88462-291-6). Real Estate Ed Co.
--North Carolina Supplement for Modern Real Estate Practice. Hetrick, Patrick, ed. 130p. (Orig.). 1981. pap. 7.95 (ISBN 0-88462-301-7). Real Estate Ed Co.
Silverman, Shirley. Barclay's Bridge Teacher's Manual for Five-Card Majors. rev ed. 250p. 1980. loose leaf 28.95x (ISBN 0-87643-017-5). Barclay Bridge.
Silverman, Stephen. Public Spectales. 1981. 9.95 (ISBN 0-525-18605-0). Dutton.
Silverman, Sydel. Three Bells of Civilization. 1978. pap. 7.50x (ISBN 0-231-08365-3). Columbia U Pr.
--The Three Bells of Civilization: The Life of an Italian Hill Town. LC 75-15916. (Illus.). 304p. 1975. 17.50x (ISBN 0-231-03804-6). Columbia U Pr.
Silverman, Wade H. Community Mental Health: A Sourcebook for Professionals & Advisors. 450p. 1981. 39.95 (ISBN 0-03-057006-9). Praeger.
Silverman, William, jt. auth. see Kulash, Damian J.
Silverman, William B. Rabbinic Wisdom & Jewish Values. rev. ed. Orig. Title: Rabbinic Stories for Christian Ministers & Teachers. 1971. pap. 5.00 (ISBN 0-8074-0190-0, 383210). UAHC.
Silvern, Leonard C. Fundamentals of Teaching Machine & Programmed Learning Systems, 3 vols. LC 64-14098. (Illus., Prog. Bk.). 1964. Set. 50.00 (ISBN 0-685-09258-5). Ed & Training.
Silvers, Arthur & Crosson, Pierre R. Rural Development & Urban Bound Migration in Mexico. LC 80-8024. (Resources for the Future Research Ser.: Paper R-17). (Illus.). 160p. (Orig.). 1980. pap. text ed. 6.95x (ISBN 0-8018-2493-1). Johns Hopkins.
Silvers, Arthur L., jt. auth. see Krueckeberg, Donald A.
Silvers, John B. & Prahalad, C. K. Financial Management of Health Institutions. 339p. 1974. 17.95 (ISBN 0-686-68576-8, 14910). Hospital Finan.
Silvers, Ruth, jt. auth. see Goodwin, Irene.
Silverstein, et al. Spanish Now! A Level One Worktext. 2nd ed. Quinones, Nathan, ed. LC 75-40329. (gr. 7-12). 1977. 14.95 (ISBN 0-8120-5202-1); pap. text ed. 6.95 (ISBN 0-8120-0928-2); tchr's manual 1.25 (ISBN 0-8120-0951-7). Barron.
Silverstein, A. & Silverstein, V. The Skin: Coverings & Linings of Living Things. 1972. 5.95 (ISBN 0-13-812776-X, 812776). P-H.
Silverstein, Alvin. Human Anatomy & Physiology. LC 79-13053. 1980. text ed. 27.95x (ISBN 0-471-79166-0); tchrs.' manual avail. (ISBN 0-471-03121-6); experiments avail. (ISBN 0-471-79164-4) (ISBN 0-471-07781-X). Wiley.
Silverstein, Alvin & Silverstein, Virginia B. Alcoholism. LC 75-17938. 128p. (gr. 5-8). 1975. 7.95 (ISBN 0-397-31648-8); pap. 3.50 (ISBN 0-397-31649-6, LSC-39). Lippincott.
--Allergies. LC 77-1284. (gr. 4 up). 1977. 7.95 (ISBN 0-397-31758-1); pap. 2.95 (ISBN 0-397-31759-X). Lippincott.
Silverstein, Alvin & Silverstein, Virginia. Cancer. rev. ed. LC 76-4946. (Illus.). (gr. 3 up). 1976. PLB 7.89 (ISBN 0-381-99604-2, JD-J). John Day.
Silverstein, Alvin & Silverstein, Virginia B. Diabetes: The Sugar Disease. LC 78-11631. 1979. 7.95 (ISBN 0-397-31844-8). Lippincott.
--Epilepsy. LC 74-31382. (gr. 4-7). 1975. 5.95 (ISBN 0-397-31615-1); pap. 1.95 o.p. (ISBN 0-397-31624-0). Lippincott.
--The Genetics Explosion. LC 79-22651. (Illus.). 160p. (gr. 7 up). 1980. 8.95 (ISBN 0-590-07517-9, Four Winds). Schol Bk Serv.
--Gerbils. LC 75-34390. (gr. 3-6). 1976. 8.95 (ISBN 0-397-31660-7); pap. 3.95 (ISBN 0-397-31661-5). Lippincott.
Silverstein, Alvin & Silverstein, Virginia. Guinea Pigs, All About Them. LC 74-148487. (Illus.). 96p. (gr. 3-7). 1972. 7.25 o.p. (ISBN 0-688-41664-0); PLB 6.96 (ISBN 0-688-51664-5). Lothrop.
--Harold Urey. LC 74-125573. (Great Men of Science Ser). (gr. 7-10). 1971. 4.50 o.p. (ISBN 0-381-99705-7, A32700, JD-J). John Day.
--Itch, Sniffle & Sneeze: All About Asthma, Hay Fever & Other Allergies. LC 77-20791. (Illus.). 48p. (gr. 1-5). 1978. 7.95 (ISBN 0-590-07540-3, Four Winds). Schol Bk Serv.
--Mice: All About Them. LC 79-9621. (Illus.). 160p. (gr. 4up). 1980. 9.95 (ISBN 0-397-31922-3); PLB 9.79 (ISBN 0-397-31923-1). Lippincott.
--Sleep & Dreams. LC 73-13825. (Illus.). 160p. (gr. 7 up). 1974. 8.95 (ISBN 0-397-31325-X). Lippincott.
--The Story of Your Ear. (Illus.). 64p. (gr. 5-9). 1981. PLB 6.99 (ISBN 0-698-30704-6). Coward.
Silverstein, Arthur M. & O'Connor, G. Richard. Immunology & Immunopathology of the Eye. LC 79-84781. 416p. 1979. 57.25 (ISBN 0-89352-042-X). Masson Pub.
Silverstein, Charles. Man to Man: Gay Couples in America. LC 80-23566. 384p. 1981. 12.95 (ISBN 0-688-00041-X). Morrow.
Silverstein, Harry, jt. auth. see Rosenberg, Bernard.
Silverstein, Harvey. Superships & Nation-States: The Transnational Politics of the Intergovernmental Maritime Consultative Organization. LC 77-27662. (Illus.). 1978. lib. bdg. 24.50x (ISBN 0-89158-058-1). Westview.
Silverstein, Karen, jt. auth. see Silverstein, Mel.
Silverstein, Max. Psychiatric Aftercare: Planning for Community Mental Health Service. LC 68-21550. 1968. 6.00 o.p. (ISBN 0-8122-7565-9). U of Pa Pr.
Silverstein, Mel & Silverstein, Karen. Side Effects. LC 77-92231. 1978. 7.95 o.p. (ISBN 0-385-13632-3). Doubleday.
Silverstein, Mira. International Needlework Designs. LC 77-21189. (Encore Edition). (Illus.). 1978. 8.95 (ISBN 0-684-16925-8, ScribT). Scribner.
--Mira Silverstein's Guide to Upright Stitches. (Illus.). 1977. 9.95 o.p. (ISBN 0-679-50818-X); pap. 3.95 o.p. (ISBN 0-679-50784-1). McKay.
Silverstein, Norman, jt. auth. see Huss, Roy.
Silverstein, R. M., jt. ed. see Muller-Schwarze, D.
Silverstein, Robert M. & Bassler, G. Clayton. Spectrometric Indentification of Organic Compounds. 4th ed. Morrill, Terence C., ed. 704p. 1981. text ed. 20.95 (ISBN 0-471-02990-4). Wiley.
Silverstein, Shel. The Missing Piece Meets the Big O. LC 80-8721. (Illus.). 112p. (gr. 3 up). 1981. 8.95 (ISBN 0-06-025657-5, HarpJ); PLB 8.79 (ISBN 0-06-025658-3). Har-Row.
Silverstein, Solomon, jt. auth. see Malka, Sora.
Silverstein, Theodore, ed. see Auerbach, Erich.
Silverstein, V., jt. auth. see Silverstein, A.
Silverstein, Virginia, jt. auth. see Silverstein, Alvin.
Silverstein, Virginia B., jt. auth. see Silverstein, Alvin.
Silverstone, jt. auth. see Simon.
Silverstone, Leon. Preventive Dentistry. (Illus.). 1978. text ed. 12.50x (ISBN 0-906141-06-0, Pub. by Update Pubns. England). Kluwer Boston.
Silverstone, Lou & Rickard, Jack. Mad Book of Mysteries. (Mad Ser.). (Illus., Orig.). 1980. pap. 1.75 (ISBN 0-446-84843-3). Warner Bks.
--Politically Mad. (Mad Ser.). (Illus.). 1976. pap. 1.75 (ISBN 0-446-94601-X). Warner Bks.
Silverstone, Rosalie & Ward, Audrey, eds. Careers of Professional Women. 227p. 1980. 30.00x (ISBN 0-85664-923-6, Pub. by Croom Helm Ltd England). Biblio Dist.
Silverstone, Trevor & Turner, Paul. Drug Treatment in Psychiatry. rev. ed. (Social & Psychological Aspects of Medical Practice Ser.). 1978. 22.00 (ISBN 0-7100-8933-3); pap. 9.75 (ISBN 0-7100-8934-1). Routledge & Kegan.
Silverthorne, Jeanne, et al. Projects: Made in Philadelphia 4. LC 80-84522. (Illus.). 1979. pap. 4.00 (ISBN 0-88454-058-8). U of Pa Contemp Art.
Silverton, R. E., jt. auth. see Baker, F. J.
Silvestri, R., jt. auth. see Padovani, G.
Silvestrini De Pacheco, Blanca. Violencia y Criminalidad En Puerto Rico, 1898-1973: Apuntes para un Estudio De Historia Social. LC 79-15801. Orig. Title: Analisis Historico De la Violencia en Puerto Rico. (Illus.). x, 237p. (Sp.). 1980. pap. text ed. write for info. (ISBN 0-8477-2488-3). U of PR Pr.
Silvette, Herbert. Doctor on the Stage: Medicine & Medical Men in Seventeenth-Century England. Butler, Francelia, ed. LC 66-14775. 1967. 14.50x (ISBN 0-87049-074-5). U of Tenn Pr.
Silvey, Larry P., ed. see DeMers, Donald O., Jr. & Beilharz, Edwin A.
Silvey, Larry P., ed. see Engstrand, Iris W.
Silvey, Larry P., ed. see Garrett, Betty.
Silvey, Larry P., ed. see Kratt, Mary.
Silvey, Larry P., ed. see Lavender, David.
Silvey, Larry P., ed. see Noel, Thomas.
Silvey, Larry P., ed. see Pirtle, Caleb.
Silvius, G. Harold & Bohn, Ralph C. Planning & Organizing Instruction. rev. ed. Orig. Title: Organizing Course Materials for Industrial Education. 1976. text ed. 16.09 (ISBN 0-87345-720-X). McKnight.
Silvius, G. Harold & Curry, Estell H. Teaching Successfully in Industrial Education. rev. ed. 1967. text ed. 16.09 (ISBN 0-87345-451-0). McKnight.
Silvius, George H. & Curry, Estell H. Managing Multiple Activities in Industrial Education. new ed. 1971. text ed. 16.09 (ISBN 0-87345-456-1). McKnight.
Sim, Joe, jt. auth. see Fitzgerald, Mike.
Sim, Joseph M. Minor Tooth Movement in Children. 2nd ed. LC 77-24370. (Illus.). 1977. 47.50 (ISBN 0-8016-4616-2). Mosby.
Simai, M., jt. ed. see Vajda, Imre.
Simai, Mihaly & Garam, Katalin, eds. Economic Integration: Concepts, Theories & Problems. LC 78-308400. 423p. 1977. 30.00x (ISBN 963-05-1188-6). Intl Pubns Serv.
Simak, Clifford. Way Station. LC 79-20182. 1980. Repr. of 1963 ed. lib. bdg. 10.00x (ISBN 0-8376-0440-0). Bentley.
Simak, Clifford D. Enchanted Pilgrimage. LC 74-16617. 224p. 1975. 6.95 o.p. (ISBN 0-399-11477-7, Dist. by Putnam). Berkley Pub.
--The Fellowship of the Talisman. 1979. pap. 2.25 (ISBN 0-345-27592-6, Del Rey Bks). Ballantine.
--A Heritage of Stars. LC 76-53742. 1977. 7.95 o.p. (ISBN 0-399-11946-9, Dist. by Putnam). Berkley Pub.
--Shakespeare's Planet. LC 75-43651. (YA) 1976. 6.95 o.p. (ISBN 0-399-11729-6, Dist. by Putnam). Berkley Pub.
--Skirmish: The Great Short Fiction of Clifford D. Simak. LC 77-7176. 1977. 8.95 o.p. (ISBN 0-399-12032-7, Dist. by Putnam). Berkley Pub.
Simart, G., jt. auth. see Picard, Emile.
Simches, Seymour O; see Bird, Thomas E.
Simcich, Tina L., jt. auth. see Council on Economic Priorities.
Simco, Nancy D. & James, Gene G. Elementary Logic. 1976. text ed. 15.95x (ISBN 0-8221-0156-4). Dickenson.
Simcox, C. A Treasury of Quotations on Christian Themes. 1975. 12.95 (ISBN 0-8164-0274-4). Crossroad NY.
Simcox, Carroll E. Learning to Believe: A Meditation on the Christian Creed. LC 80-2372. 112p. 1981. pap. 5.95 (ISBN 0-8006-1497-6, 1-1497). Fortress.
--Notes to the Overworld. LC 72-81029. 128p. 1972. 4.50 (ISBN 0-8164-0242-6). Crossroad NY.
Simcox, G. A. Poems & Romances. Fletcher, Ian & Stokes, John, eds. LC 76-24392. (Decadent Consciousness Ser.). 1978. lib. bdg. 38.00 (ISBN 0-8240-2779-5). Garland Pub.
Simcox, Helen E., ed. Dear Dark Faces. (Illus.). 110p. (Orig.). 1980. pap. 6.00 perf. bound (ISBN 0-916418-23-5). Lotus.
Simcox, W. H. Language of the New Testament. Date not set. 8.95 (ISBN 0-88469-140-3). BMH Bks.
--Writers of the New Testament. Date not set. 8.95 (ISBN 0-88469-139-X). BMH Bks.
Sime. Read Your Child's Thoughts: Pre-School Learning Piaget's Way. 1980. 13.95 (ISBN 0-500-01217-2). Thames Hudson.
Sime, James. William Herschel & His Work. 272p. 1900. text ed. 3.50 (ISBN 0-567-04521-8). Attic Pr.
Simek, Thomas C. & O'Brien, Richard M. Total Golf: A Behavioral Approach to Lowering Your Score & Getting More Out of Your Game. LC 79-6086. (Illus.). 192p. 1981. 14.95 (ISBN 0-385-15404-6). Doubleday.
Simenon. Les Enigmes. (Easy Reader, B). pap. 3.75 (ISBN 0-88436-058-X, FRA201051). EMC.
--Maigret et le Clochard. (Easy Reader, B). pap. 3.75 (ISBN 0-88436-047-4, FRA201052). EMC.
Simenon, Georges. The Delivery. Ellenbogen, Eileen, ed. LC 80-8759. (Helen & Kurt Wolff Bk.). 1981. 10.95 (ISBN 0-15-124655-6). HarBraceJ.

--The Grandmother. Stewart, Jean, tr. LC 80-14918. (Helen & Kurt Wolff Bk.). 192p. 1980. Repr. of 1959 ed. 8.95 (ISBN 0-15-136738-8). HarBraceJ.
--The Little Doctor. Stewart, Jean, tr. from Fr. (Helen & Kurt Wolff Bk.). 1981. 10.95 (ISBN 0-15-152768-7). HarBraceJ.
--Maigret & the Apparition. LC 80-14212. 1980. pap. 2.95 (ISBN 0-15-655127-6, Harv). HarBraceJ.
--Maigret et le Fantome. (Easy Readers, B). (Illus.). 1977. pap. text ed. 3.75 (ISBN 0-88436-287-6). EMC.
--Maigret Loses His Temper. Eglesfield, Rbt, tr. LC 80-14212. (Helen & Kurt Wolff Bk.). 1980. pap. 2.95. HarBraceJ.
--Trois Nouvelles de Georges Simenon. Lindsay, Frank W. & Nazzaro, Anthony M., eds. (gr. 10-12). 1966. pap. text ed. 7.95 o.p. (ISBN 0-13-930917-9). P-H.
--When I Was Old. LC 70-153690. (Helen & Kurt Wolff Bk). (Illus.). 343p. 1971. 8.50 o.p. (ISBN 0-15-195950-1). HarBraceJ.
Simeon, Margaret. The History of Lace. (Illus.). 144p. 1979. 32.50x (ISBN 0-8476-6263-2). Rowman.
Simeone, Frederick A., jt. ed. see Rothman, Richard H.
Simeons, Albert T. Man's Presumptuous Brain: An Evolutionary Interpretation of Psychosomatic Diseases. 1962. pap. 4.50 o.p. (ISBN 0-525-47109-X). Dutton.
Simeons, C. Coal: It's Role in Tomorrow's Technology. 1978. text ed. 105.00 (ISBN 0-08-022712-0). Pergamon.
Simeons, Charles. Hydro-Power: The Use of Water As an Alternative Source. (Illus.). 560p. 1980. 89.00 (ISBN 0-08-023269-8). Pergamon.
Simes, Dimitri K., et al. Soviet Succession: Leadership in Transition. LC 78-62798. (Sage Policy Paper Ser.: Vol. 59). 80p. 1978. pap. 3.50 (ISBN 0-8039-1124-6). Sage.
Simi, Gino J. & Segreti, Mario M. St. Francis of Paola: God's Miracle Worker Supreme. LC 77-78097. 1977. pap. 3.00 (ISBN 0-89555-065-2, 200). TAN Bks Pubs.
Simic, Andrei, jt. ed. see Myerhoff, Barbara G.
Simic, Charles. Classic Ballroom Dances. LC 80-14470. 1980. 8.95 (ISBN 0-8076-0973-0); pap. 4.95 (ISBN 0-8076-0974-9). Braziller.
Simic, Charles, tr. see Popa, Vasko.
Simini, Joseph Peter. Accounting Made Simple. LC 66-12174. pap. 3.50 (ISBN 0-385-02032-5, Made). Doubleday.
Simionescu, C. I., jt. auth. see Vogl, O.
Simister, W. Home Aquarium. LC 76-20105. 1976. 8.95 (ISBN 0-7153-7255-6). David & Charles.
Simitses, George J. An Introduction to the Elastic Stability of Structures. (Illus.). 288p. 1976. 27.95 (ISBN 0-13-481200-X). P-H.
Simkin, Mark G., jt. auth. see Moscove, Stephen A.
Simkins, Michael. The Roman Army from Caesar to Trajan. LC 74-76629. (Men-at-Arms Ser). (Illus.). 40p. (Orig.). 1974. pap. 7.95 o.p. (ISBN 0-88254-229-X). Hippocrene Bks.
Simmel, Georg. Conflict & the Web of Group Affiliations. LC 54-10671. 1955. 12.95 (ISBN 0-02-928830-4); pap. text ed. 5.95 (ISBN 0-02-928840-1). Free Pr.
--Philosophy of Money. Bottomore, Tom & Frisby, David, trs. from Fr. 1978. 40.00x (ISBN 0-7100-8874-4). Routledge & Kegan.
--Sociology of Georg Simmel. Wolff, Kurt H., tr. 1964. pap. text ed. 7.95 (ISBN 0-02-928920-3). Free Pr.
Simmel, Johannes M. Love Is Just a Word. 448p. 1980. pap. 2.95 (ISBN 0-445-04622-8). Popular Lib.
Simmen, Edward, et al. A Comprehensive Chicano Bibliography, 1960-1972. Simmen, Edward, ed. LC 73-81559. 1973. 12.95 (ISBN 0-8363-0114-5). Jenkins.
Simmonds, A. B., jt. ed. see Harper, N. J.
Simmonds, D. M., ed. see Euripides.
Simmonds, J. D. China's World: The Foreign Policy of a Developing State. LC 75-126932. 1971. 18.50x (ISBN 0-231-03511-X). Columbia U Pr.
Simmonds, James D., ed. Milton Studies, Vol. XIV. LC 69-12335. (Milton Studies). (Illus.). 286p. 1981. 21.95x (ISBN 0-8229-3429-9). U of Pittsburgh Pr.
Simmonds, K. Multinational Corporations Law, Vols. 1-2. 1979. Set. 75.00 (ISBN 0-379-20373-1). Oceana.
--Multinational Corporations Law, Release 3. 1980. 50.00. Oceana.
Simmonds, Kenneth, jt. auth. see Leighton, David.
Simmonds, N. W. Principles of Crop Improvement. LC 78-40726. (Illus.). 1979. text ed. 32.00 (ISBN 0-582-45586-3); pap. text ed. 19.95 (ISBN 0-582-44630-9). Longman.
Simmonds, N. W., ed. Evolution of Crop Plants. LC 78-40509. (Illus.). 1979. pap. text ed. 18.95 (ISBN 0-582-44496-9). Longman.
Simmonds, W. H., jt. ed. see Linstone, Harold A.
Simmonite, W. J. The Arcana of Astrology. LC 80-19739. 426p. 1980. Repr. of 1974 ed. lib. bdg. 11.95x (ISBN 0-89370-626-4). Borgo Pr.
Simmons. California Prsonnel Managers Guide to EEO Laws. 1980. pap. 25.00 (ISBN 0-917386-40-X). Exec Ent.
--Nursing Research: A Survey & Assessment. 1964. 18.50 o.p. (ISBN 0-8385-7046-1). ACC.
Simmons, A. LeRoi. Ephemerides 1890-1950. 407p. 1970. text ed. 17.00 (ISBN 0-9605126-0-8). Aquarian Bk Pubs.
--Ephemeris Nineteen Fifty to Nineteen Seventy-Five. (Illus.). 375p. 1977. 14.00 (ISBN 0-9605126-1-6). Aquarian Bk Pubs.
--Twentieth Century Table of Houses. 202p. 1972. text ed. 6.00 (ISBN 0-9605126-2-4). Aquarian Bk Pubs.
Simmons, Adelma. Herb Gardens Delight. 1979. pap. 4.95 (ISBN 0-8015-3403-8, Hawthorn). Dutton.
--Herbs to Grow Indoors. 1969. pap. 4.50 (ISBN 0-8015-3416-X, Hawthorn). Dutton.
Simmons, Adelma G. Herb Gardening in Five Seasons. 1977. pap. 6.95 (ISBN 0-8015-3395-3, Hawthorn). Dutton.
--The Illustrated Herbal Handbook. 120p. 1972. pap. 2.95 (ISBN 0-8015-3960-9, Hawthorn). Dutton.
Simmons, Amelia. First American Cook Book. 1966. pap. 3.50 (ISBN 0-917420-00-4). Buck Hill.
Simmons, Arthur. Basic Hematology: An Introduction for Student Medical Technologists & Medical Assistants. (Illus.). 296p. 1973. text ed. 24.75 photocopy ed. spiral (ISBN 0-398-02536-3). C C Thomas.
--Self-Assessment of Current Knowledge in Medical Technology-Hematology. 1974. spiral bdg. 8.50 o.p. (ISBN 0-87488-273-7). Med Exam.
Simmons, Beatrice, ed. Paperback Books for Children. LC 72-86489. 130p. (Orig.). 1972. pap. 0.95 (ISBN 0-590-09542-0, Citation). Schol Bk Serv.
Simmons, Clifford, jt. ed. see Morpurgo, Michael.
Simmons, D. B., jt. auth. see Wigmore, John H.
Simmons, D. M. Nonlinear Programming for Operations Research. (International Ser. in Management). (Illus.). 480p. 1976. ref. ed. 21.95 (ISBN 0-13-623397-X). P-H.
Simmons, Daniel E. Current Pulmonology, Vol. 2. (Current Pulmonology Ser.). (Illus.). 1980. text ed. 40.00 (ISBN 0-89289-113-0). HM Prof Med Div.
Simmons, Daniel H., ed. Current Pulmonology, Vol. 1. (Illus.). 1979. 40.00 (ISBN 0-89289-102-5). HM Prof Med Div.
Simmons, David. Medical School Game. pap. 4.95 o.p. (ISBN 0-8473-1109-0). Sterling.
Simmons, Dawne L. Margaret Rutherford: A Blithe Spirit. (Illus., Orig.). 1981. pap. 7.95 (ISBN 0-89407-032-0). Strawberry Hill.
Simmons, Donald M. Linear Programming for Operations Research. LC 70-188129. 1972. text ed. 23.95x (ISBN 0-8162-7986-1). Holden-Day.
Simmons, Edward. From Seven to Seventy: Memoirs of a Painter & a Yankee. Weinberg, H. Barbara, ed. LC 75-28891. (Art Experience in Late 19th Century America Ser.: Vol. 24). (Illus.). 1976. Repr. of 1922 ed. lib. bdg. 37.00 (ISBN 0-8240-2248-3). Garland Pub.
Simmons, Ernest J. Feodor Dostoevsky. LC 77-76254. (Columbia Ser.: No. 40). (Orig., Pap). 1969. pap. 2.00 (ISBN 0-231-03205-6, MW40). Columbia U Pr.
--Pushkin. 8.50 (ISBN 0-8446-0259-0). Peter Smith.
--Through the Glass of Soviet Literature. LC 53-8757. (Studies of the Russian Institute of Col. Univ.). 1963. pap. 6.00x (ISBN 0-231-08527-3, 27). Columbia U Pr.
--Tolstoy. (Routledge Author Guides). 272p. 1973. 18.00x (ISBN 0-7100-7394-1); pap. 8.95 (ISBN 0-7100-7395-X). Routledge & Kegan.
Simmons, Frank G. & Coombes, Susan E. Cardiopulmonary Technology Examination Review Book, Vol. 1. 1980. pap. 12.50 (ISBN 0-87488-473-X). Med Exam.
Simmons, Frank G. & Coombs, Susan E. Cardiopulmonary Technology Examination Review Book, Vol. 1. 1971. spiral bdg. 8.50 o.p. (ISBN 0-87488-473-X). Med Exam.
Simmons, Geoffrey. The Adam Experiment. 1979. pap. 2.25 o.p. (ISBN 0-425-04492-0). Berkley Pub.
Simmons, George F. Precalculus Primer. (Illus.). 176p. (Orig.). Date not set. pap. 7.95 (ISBN 0-86576-009-8). W Kaufmann.
Simmons, Harold. The Psychosocial Origins of Mental Retardation. 1980. pap. 5.95 (ISBN 0-87312-011-6). Gen Welfare.
--The Side Effects of Estrogen Drug Therapy: Contraception & Menopause. 1979. pap. 4.95 (ISBN 0-87312-007-8). Gen Welfare.
Simmons, Harold E. The Psychogenic Biochemical Aspects of Cancer. 1979. pap. 9.95 (ISBN 0-87312-010-8). Gen Welfare.
Simmons, Ian. The Ecology of Natural Resources. LC 74-4812. 424p. 1974. pap. text ed. 14.95 (ISBN 0-470-79194-2). Halsted Pr.
Simmons, J. L. Shakespeare's Pagan World: The Roman Tragedies. LC 73-80126. 1973. 10.95x (ISBN 0-8139-0488-9). U Pr of Va.
Simmons, J. L., jt. auth. see McCall, George J.
Simmons, Jack. The Railway in England & Wales, 1830-1914, Vol. 1: The System & Its Working. (Illus.). 1978. text ed. 31.25x (ISBN 0-7185-1146-8, Leicester). Humanities.
--The Railway in England & Wales, 1830-1914. Incl. Vol. 2. Town & Country. text ed. write for info. (ISBN 0-391-01168-5); Vol. 3. Mind & Eve. text ed. write for info. (ISBN 0-391-01169-3); Vol. 4. The Community. text ed. price not set (ISBN 0-391-01170-7). (Illus.). 1981. text ed. (ISBN 0-685-51832-9, Leicester). Humanities.
Simmons, James G. How to Obtain Financing & Make Your Best Deal with Any Bank, Finance or Leasing Company. (Illus.). 380p. (Orig.). 1980. pap. 19.95 (ISBN 0-937700-00-2). Cambrian.
Simmons, James W., jt. ed. see Bourne, Larry S.
Simmons, Janet A. The Nurse-Client Relationship in Mental Health Nursing: Workbook Guides to Understanding & Management. LC 75-40639. 240p. 1978. pap. 8.95 (ISBN 0-7216-8286-3). Saunders.
Simmons, Joan. High Jumps & Dumbbells: The Adventures of an Obedience Dog. LC 79-55024. (Illus.). (gr. 6-12). 1979. 7.95 (ISBN 0-931866-04-9). Alpine Pubns.
Simmons, John. The Education Dilemma. (Illus.). 1980. 35.00 (ISBN 0-08-024304-5); pap. 17.25 (ISBN 0-08-024303-7). Pergamon.
--The Life of Plants. LC 77-88438. (Easy Reading Edition of Introduction to Nature Ser.). (Illus.). 1978. lib. bdg. 7.95 (ISBN 0-686-51144-1). Silver.
Simmons, John, ed. Cocoa Production: Economic & Botanical Perspectives. LC 75-19821. (Special Studies). 1976. text ed. 44.50 (ISBN 0-275-56030-9). Praeger.
Simmons, John S., et al. Decisions About the Teaching of English. 324p. 1976. text ed. 17.95x (ISBN 0-205-04542-1). Allyn.
Simmons, Leo W., ed. Sun Chief: The Autobiography of a Hopi Indian. rev. ed. (Illus.). 1942. 30.00x (ISBN 0-300-00949-6); pap. 5.95x 1963 (ISBN 0-300-00227-0, YW8). Yale U Pr.
Simmons, Marc. The Little Lion of the Southwest: A Life of Manuel Antonio Chaves. Cisneros, Jose, tr. LC 73-1500. 263p. 1974. 10.95 (ISBN 0-8040-0632-6, SB). Swallow.
--New Mexico. (States & the Nation Ser.). (Illus.). 1977. 12.95 (ISBN 0-393-05631-7, Co-Pub by AASLH). Norton.
Simmons, Mary Ann, jt. ed. see Knight, Allen W.
Simmons, Merle E., ed. Folklore Bibliography for Nineteen Seventy-Six. (Indiana University Folklore Institute Monograph Ser.: Vol. 33). 256p. 1981. text ed. 17.50 (ISBN 0-89727-023-1). Inst Study Hum.
Simmons, Norman. How to Go Railway Modelling. (Illus.). 216p. 1975. 17.95 o.p. (ISBN 0-85059-167-8). Aztex.
--How to Go Railway Modelling. 3rd ed. (Illus.). 216p. 1980. 31.95 (ISBN 0-85059-402-2). Aztex.
Simmons, Pamela J., jt. auth. see Clifton, Nancy A.
Simmons, Paul D. & Crawford, Kenneth. Mi Desarrollo Sexual. Sabanes De Plou, Dafne, tr. from Eng. (El Sexo En la Vida Cristiana). 96p. (Span.). (gr. 10-12). Date not set. Repr. pap. price not set (ISBN 0-311-46253-7, Edit Mundo). Casa Bautista.
Simmons, Peter J. Choice & Demand. LC 73-23035. 1974. text ed. 16.95 (ISBN 0-470-79179-9). Halsted Pr.
Simmons, Richard. Surgical Infectious Disease. 1981. 65.00 (ISBN 0-8385-8729-1). ACC.
Simmons, Richard A., jt. auth. see Lasker, Michael.
Simmons, Richard E. Managing Behavioral Processes: Applications of Theory & Research. Mackenzie, Kenneth D., ed. LC 77-86007. (Organizational Behavior Ser.). (Illus.). 1978. pap. text ed. 9.95x (ISBN 0-88295-454-7). AHM Pub.
Simmons, Robert H., jt. auth. see Dvorin, Eugene P.
Simmons, Roberta G., et al. Gift of Life: The Social & Psychological Impact of Organ Transplantation. LC 77-2749. (Health, Medicine & Society Ser.). 1977. 29.95 (ISBN 0-471-79197-0, Pub by Wiley-Interscience). Wiley.
Simmons, Roger A. Palca & Pucara: A Study of the Effects of Revolution on Two Bolivian Haciendas. (U. C. Publ. in Anthropology: Vol. 9). pap. 12.50x (ISBN 0-520-09440-9). U of Cal Pr.
Simmons, Ronald. Managing Special Programs in Higher Education. 160p. 1980. text ed. 16.50x (ISBN 0-87073-064-9). Schenkman.
Simmons, Sandra J., jt. auth. see Given, Barbara A.
Simmons, Steven J. The Fairness Doctrine & the Media. LC 77-85740. 1978. 15.95 (ISBN 0-520-03585-2). U of Cal Pr.
Simmons, Suzanne. The Tempestuous Lovers. (Orig.). 1981. pap. 1.50 (ISBN 0-440-18551-3). Dell.
Simmons, Ted. Magical Friday. LC 74-24635. (Illus.). 76p. 1975. text ed. 7.00 o.p. (ISBN 0-685-51344-0); pap. 1.95 o.p. (ISBN 0-912662-07-7). Fur Line Pr.
--Middlearth. LC 74-24634. (Illus.). 74p. 1975. 4.95 o.p. (ISBN 0-912662-06-9); pap. 3.95 o.p. (ISBN 0-912662-35-2). Fur Line Pr.
Simmons, W. T. & Lindsay, L. Brooks. Charlotte & Mecklenburg County: A Pictorial History. LC 77-12680. (Illus.). 1977. 15.95 (ISBN 0-915442-33-7). Donning Co.
Simmons, Walter J. Lapstrake Boatbuilding, Vol. 2. LC 78-55779. (Illus.). 1980. 17.50 (ISBN 0-87742-127-7). Intl Marine.
Simmons, William S. Cautantowwit's House: An Indian Burial Ground on the Island of Conanicut in Narragansett Bay. LC 77-111456. (Illus.). 1970. 10.00 (ISBN 0-87057-122-2, Pub. by Brown U Pr). Univ Pr of New England.
Simmoas-Martin, A. & Calvert, D. R. Parent-Infant Intervention: Communication Disorders. 1979. 12.00 (ISBN 0-8089-1185-6). Grune.
Simms, A. E., ed. Fish and Shellfish. rev. ed. (Illus.). 1973. 54.95 (ISBN 0-685-90327-3, Northwood Pub.). CBI Pub.
Simms, Carolynne. Letters from a Roman Catholic. 1976. pap. 3.00. Am Atheist.
Simms, Eric. Wildlife Sounds & Their Recording. (Illus.). 1980. 13.95 (ISBN 0-236-40134-3, Pub. by Paul Elek). Merrimack Bk Serv.
Simms, G. O. The Book of Kells: A Selection of Pages Reproduced with a Description & Notes. 1976. Repr. of 1961 ed. pap. text ed. 3.25x (ISBN 0-391-00608-8, Dolmen Pr). Humanities.
Simms, J. A. & Simms, T. H. From Three to Thirteen: Socialization & Achievement in School. (Longman Sociology of Education Ser.). 1969. text ed. 5.00x (ISBN 0-582-32436-X); pap. text ed. 3.00x (ISBN 0-582-32437-8). Humanities.
Simms, John D., jt. auth. see Logue, H. E.
Simms, Madeleine & Hindell, Keith. Abortion Law Reformed. (Contemporary Issues Ser: No. 3). 1971. text ed. 11.50x (ISBN 0-391-01941-4). Humanities.
Simms, T. H., jt. auth. see Simms, J. A.
Simms, Theodore F. Improving College Study Skills: A Guide & Workbook. (Illus., Orig.). 1970. pap. text ed. 5.95x (ISBN 0-02-478180-0, 47818). Macmillan.
Simo, Connie, et al. Sandtiquity. LC 78-20696. (Illus.). 1980. 10.95 (ISBN 0-8008-6989-3); pap. 4.95 (ISBN 0-8008-6990-7). Taplinger.
Simon. Necronomicon. 288p. 1979. pap. 2.75 (ISBN 0-380-75192-5, 75192). Avon.
Simon & Silverstone. Cancer of the Uterus. 1981. price not set (ISBN 0-89352-016-0). Masson Pub.
Simon, Alexander & Epstein, Leon J., eds. Aging in Modern Society. 1968. pap. 7.50 (ISBN 0-685-24866-6, P023-0). Am Psychiatric.
Simon, Alfred. Dictionnaire theatre francais contemporain. (Dict. de l'Homme du Vingtieme Siecle). (Illus., Fr.). 1970. 8.50 (ISBN 0-685-13885-2, 3740). Larousse.
Simon, Andre L. & Howe, Robin. Dictionary of Gastronomy. 2nd ed. LC 78-16260. (Illus.). 400p. 1979. 25.00 (ISBN 0-87951-081-1). Overlook Pr.
Simon, Andrew L. Basic Hydraulics. LC 80-15341. 256p. 1981. text ed. 18.95 (ISBN 0-471-07965-0). Wiley.
--Energy Resources. LC 74-28320. 176p. 1975. text ed. 23.00 (ISBN 0-08-018750-1); pap. text ed. 13.25 (ISBN 0-08-018751-X). Pergamon.
--Practical Hydraulics. 2nd ed. 416p. 1981. text ed. 18.95 (ISBN 0-471-05381-3); tchrs.' ed. 7.50 (ISBN 0-471-07783-6). Wiley.
Simon, Anne W. The Thin Edge. 1978. pap. 2.50 (ISBN 0-380-42754-0, 42754). Avon.
--The Thin Edge: Coast & Man in Crisis. LC 76-26253. 1978. 10.00 o.p. (ISBN 0-06-013890-4, HarpT). Har-Row.
Simon, Arthur B. Algebra & Trigonometry with Analytic Geometry. LC 78-23409. (Mathematical Sciences Ser.). (Illus.). 1979. text ed. 18.95x (ISBN 0-7167-1016-1); solutions manual avail. W H Freeman.
Simon, Arthur C. The Creative Way to Finding the Best Job for You. (Illus.). 1980. pap. 12.95 o.p. (ISBN 0-930490-22-3). Future Shop.
--How to Develop a Millionaire's Mind. LC 78-55990. (Illus.). 1978. softcover 12.95 o.p. (ISBN 0-686-66476-0). Future Shop.
--How to Invest in Diamonds, Metals & Collectibles for Maximum Profits. (Illus.). 1980. pap. 12.95 o.p. (ISBN 0-930490-23-1). Future Shop.

--How to Start a Business & Make It Grow. LC 78-55987. (Illus.). 1978. softcover 12.95 o.p. (ISBN 0-930490-04-5). Future Shop.
--A New Investor's Guide to Real Estate: An Apartment House Guide. LC 78-55988. (Illus.). 1978. softcover 12.95 o.p. (ISBN 0-930490-05-3). Future Shop.
--The Success Guide to Writing for TV & Motion Pictures: Learn the Business Side of Show Business. LC 78-55986. (Illus.). 1978. softcover 12.95 o.p. (ISBN 0-930490-03-7). Future Shop.
Simon, Barry. Functional Integration & Quantum Physics. (Pure & Applied Mathematics Ser.). 1979. 32.50 (ISBN 0-12-644250-9). Acad Pr.
--Trace Ideals & Their Applications. LC 78-20867. (London Mathematical Society Lecture Notes Ser.: No. 35). 1979. pap. 16.95x (ISBN 0-521-22286-9). Cambridge U Pr.
Simon, Barry, jt. auth. see Reed, Michael.
Simon, Barry, jt. ed. see Reed, Michael.
Simon, Bennett. Mind & Madness in Ancient Greece: The Classical Roots of Modern Psychiatry. LC 77-90911. (Cornell Paperback Ser.). (Illus.). 336p. 1980. pap. 6.95 o.p. (ISBN 0-8014-9202-5). Cornell U Pr.
--Mind & Madness in Ancient Greece: The Classical Roots of Modern Psychiatry. LC 77-90911. (Illus.). 1978. 19.50x (ISBN 0-8014-0859-8); pap. 9.95 1980 ed. (ISBN 0-8014-9202-5). Cornell U Pr.
Simon, Bert. Ham Radio Incentive Licensing Guide. 2nd ed. (Illus.). 1977. pap. 4.95 o.p. (ISBN 0-8306-7989-8, 989). TAB Bks.
Simon, Brian, jt. auth. see Galton, Maurice.
Simon, Brian, jt. auth. see Rubinstein, David.
Simon, Brian, ed. Education in Leicestershire, 1540-1940. 1968. text ed. 11.50x (ISBN 0-7185-1076-3, Leicester). Humanities.
--Education of the Eighties: A Central Issue. Taylor, William. 256p. 1981. 45.00 (ISBN 0-7134-3679-4, Pub. by Batsford England); pap. 14.95 (ISBN 0-7134-3680-8). David & Charles.
Simon, Charles E., jt. auth. see Kennedy, Tom.
Simon, Claude. The Battle of Pharsalus. Howard, Richard, tr. from Fr. LC 72-138436. Orig. Title: Bataille De Pharsale. 1971. 5.95 o.p. (ISBN 0-8076-0579-4). Braziller.
--The Flanders Road. 1961. 4.00 o.p. (ISBN 0-8076-0146-2). Braziller.
--The Grass. Howard, Richard, tr. LC 60-6241. 1960. 4.50 o.p. (ISBN 0-8076-0100-4). Braziller.
--Histoire. Howard, Richard, tr. LC 68-16109. 1968. 5.95 o.p. (ISBN 0-8076-0443-7). Braziller.
--The Palace. 4.50 o.s.i. (ISBN 0-8076-0234-5). Braziller.
Simon, David. BASIC from the Ground up. (Computer Programming Ser.). 1978. pap. 10.75 (ISBN 0-8104-5760-1); pap. text ed. 7.95x (ISBN 0-8104-5117-4). Hayden.
Simon, Douglas, jt. auth. see Lucier, Alvin.
Simon, Dyanne. The Barter Book. 1979. 8.95 o.p. (ISBN 0-87690-352-9); pap. 4.50 o.p. (ISBN 0-87690-290-5). Dutton.
Simon, Eckehard. Neidhart Von Reuenthal. LC 75-2067. (World Authors Ser.: Germany: No. 364). 1975. lib. bdg. 12.50 (ISBN 0-8057-6215-9). Twayne.
Simon, Edith. Reformation. (Great Ages of Man). (Illus.). (gr. 6 up). 1966. PLB 11.97 (ISBN 0-8094-0370-6, Pub. by Time-Life). Silver.
--Reformation. (Great Ages of Man Ser). (Illus.). 1966. 12.95 (ISBN 0-8094-0348-X); lib. bdg. avail. (ISBN 0-685-20549-5). Time-Life.
--The Saints. 1968. 4.50 o.s.i. (ISBN 0-440-07585-8). Delacorte.
Simon, Elliott M. Problem Play in British Drama, Eighteen Ninety to Nineteen Fourteen. (Salzburg Studies in English Literature, Poetic Drama & Poetic Theory: No. 40). 1978. pap. text ed. 25.00x (ISBN 0-391-01525-7). Humanities.
Simon, Ernest, tr. see Lizot, Jacques.
Simon, Ethelyn, et al. The First Hebrew Primer for Adults. (Orig.). 1981. pap. text ed. 12.95 (ISBN 0-939144-01-8). EKS Pub Co.
Simon, Frank A., jt. auth. see Howell, R. Rodney.
Simon, G. Principles of Bone X-Ray Diagnosis. 3rd ed. 1973. 49.95 (ISBN 0-407-36319-X). Butterworths.
--X-Ray Diagnosis for Clinical Students. 3rd ed. 1975. 37.50 (ISBN 0-407-00004-6). Butterworths.
Simon, George T. Big Bands. 1974. 14.95 (ISBN 0-02-610980-8). Macmillan.
--The Big Bands Songbook. LC 75-14419. (Illus.). 1976. pap. 8.95 o.s.i. (ISBN 0-690-01189-X, TYC-T). T Y Crowell.
Simon, Gerhard. Church, State & Opposition in U. S. S. R. 1974. 20.00x (ISBN 0-520-02612-8). U of Cal Pr.
Simon, H. A. Administrative Behavior. 2nd ed. 1957. 5.95 o.s.i. (ISBN 0-02-610990-5). Macmillan.
Simon, H. A., jt. ed. see Bugliarello, George.
Simon, Hansjorg, jt. auth. see Bloomfield, Dennis A.
Simon, Harold A. A Student's Introduction to Engineering Design. LC 74-19010. 1975. text ed. 28.00 (ISBN 0-08-017103-6); pap. text ed. 21.00 (ISBN 0-08-018234-8). Pergamon.
Simon, Henry W. One Hundred Great Operas & Their Stories. rev. ed. LC 68-27816. (Reference Bk.). 1968. pap. 3.95 (ISBN 0-385-05448-3, C100, Dolp). Doubleday.
Simon, Herbert. Introduction to Printing. 1968. 4.95 o.p. (ISBN 0-571-08408-7, Pub. by Faber & Faber). Merrimack Bk Serv.
--Introduction to Printing: The Craft of Letterpress. (Illus.). 1980. pap. 7.50 (ISBN 0-571-11528-4, Pub. by Faber & Faber). Merrimack Bk Serv.
--Sciences of the Artificial. 2nd, rev. ed. 192p. 1981. text ed. 15.00 (ISBN 0-262-19193-8); pap. 4.95 (ISBN 0-262-69073-X). MIT Pr.
Simon, Herbert, jt. auth. see Newell, Allen.
Simon, Herbert A. Administrative Behavior. 3rd ed. LC 75-18009. 1976. 17.95 (ISBN 0-02-928970-X); pap. text ed. 8.95 (ISBN 0-02-929000-7). Free Pr.
--The New Science of Management Decision. rev. ed. LC 76-40414. 1977. ref. ed. 15.95x (ISBN 0-13-616144-8); pap. text ed. 10.95 (ISBN 0-13-616136-7). P-H.
Simon, Herbert A., et al. Centralization vs. Decentralization in Organizing the Controller's Department. LC 77-90343. 1978. Repr. of 1954 ed. text ed. 10.00 (ISBN 0-914348-24-8). Scholars Bk.
Simon, Hilda. Bird & Flower Emblems of the United States. LC 78-7324. (gr. 5). 1978. 7.95 (ISBN 0-396-07581-9). Dodd.
--The Courtship of Birds. LC 77-3211. (Illus.). 1977. 12.95 (ISBN 0-396-07459-6). Dodd.
--The Date Palm. LC 77-14244. (gr. 7 up). 1978. 8.95 (ISBN 0-396-07523-1). Dodd.
--Easy Identification Guide to North American Snakes. LC 79-55263. (Illus.). 1979. flex. cover 8.95 (ISBN 0-396-07771-4). Dodd.
--Exploring the World of Social Insects. LC 74-178823. (Illus.). (gr. 6 up). 1962. 6.95 (ISBN 0-8149-0390-8). Vanguard.
--Milkweed Butterflies: Monarchs, Models, & Mimics. LC 68-56601. (Illus.). (gr. 4 up). 1968. 6.95 (ISBN 0-8149-0389-4). Vanguard.
--The Private Lives of Orchids. LC 74-18331. (Illus.). 1975. 15.00 o.p. (ISBN 0-397-01075-3). Lippincott.
--Snails of Land & Sea. LC 75-25140. (Illus.). (gr. k-3). 1977. 7.95 (ISBN 0-8149-0772-5). Vanguard.
Simon, Irving B. Story of Printing. LC 65-14386. (Story of Science Ser). (Illus.). (gr. 6-9). 1965. PLB 7.29 (ISBN 0-8178-3552-0). Harvey.
Simon, J. C., jt. ed. see Hralick, R. M.
Simon, J. Malcolm, jt. auth. see Reeves, John A.
Simon, Jacques & Rouard, Marguerite. Children's Play Spaces. LC 76-57882. (Illus.). 1977. 30.00 (ISBN 0-87951-056-0). Overlook Pr.
Simon, James F. Independent Journey: The Life of William O. Douglas. LC 79-2637. (Illus.). 464p. 1980. 16.95 (ISBN 0-06-014042-9, HarpT). Har-Row.
Simon, Jim. The Bionic Joke Book. 1976. pap. 1.25 o.p. (ISBN 0-685-72572-3, LB406, Leisure Bks). Nordon Pubns.
--The King Kong Joke Book. 1977. pap. 1.25 (ISBN 0-505-51124-X). Tower Bks.
Simon, Joan. Education & Society in Tudor England. LC 79-50915. 1979. 47.50 (ISBN 0-521-22854-9); pap. 14.95x (ISBN 0-521-29679-X). Cambridge U Pr.
Simon, John. Paradigms Lost: Essays on Literacy & Its Decline. (Illus.). 256p. 1980. 12.95 (ISBN 0-517-54034-7). Potter.
--Singularities: Essays on the Theater 1964-1974. LC 75-10260. 256p. 1976. 12.95 (ISBN 0-394-73118-2); pap. 4.95 (ISBN 0-394-73118-2). Random.
Simon, John O., jt. ed. see Kennedy, Sarah.
Simon, John Y., ed. see Grant, Ulysses S.
Simon, John Y., jt. ed. see Grant, Ulysses S.
Simon, Julian. Applied Managerial Economics. (Illus.). 560p. 1975. ref. ed. 20.95 (ISBN 0-13-041194-9). P-H.
Simon, Julian L. How to Start & Operate a Mail Order Business. 2nd ed. (Illus.). 448p. 1976. 23.50 o.p. (ISBN 0-07-057409-X, P&RB). McGraw.
--The Ultimate Resource. LC 80-8575. 336p. 1981. 14.50x (ISBN 0-691-09389-X). Princeton U Pr.
Simon, Julius. Ralph Waldo Emerson in Deutschland: 1851-1932. LC 80-2546. (Ger.). 1981. Repr. of 1936 ed. 25.50 (ISBN 0-404-19271-8). AMS Pr.
Simon, Kate. Mexico: Places & Pleasures. rev ed. LC 78-3317. (Illus.). 1979. 14.95 (ISBN 0-690-01653-0, TYC-T); pap. 5.95 (ISBN 0-690-01778-2, TYC-T). T Y Crowell.
--New York Places & Pleasures: An Uncommon Guidebook. rev. 4th ed. LC 70-138761. (Illus.). 1972. pap. 5.95 (ISBN 0-06-013876-9, CN-0818, HarpT). Har-Row.
Simon, Larry G., et al. Access Policy & Procedures & the Law in U. S. Higher Education. (Access to Higher Education Ser.: No. 6). 124p. 1978. pap. 6.00 (ISBN 0-89192-215-6, Pub. by Intl Coun Ed Dev). Interbk Inc.
Simon, Marcel. Jewish Sects at the Time of Jesus. Farley, James H., tr. from Fr. LC 66-25265. 192p. 1980. pap. 5.95 (ISBN 0-8006-0183-1, 1-183). Fortress.
Simon, Marvin K., jt. auth. see Lindsey, William C.
Simon, Maurice D., jt. auth. see Kanet, Roger E.
Simon, Myron. The Georgian Poetic. (Library Reprint Ser.: Vol. 89). 1978. 14.50x (ISBN 0-520-03618-2); pap. 5.95x o.p. (ISBN 0-520-09495-6). U of Cal Pr.
Simon, Myron, ed. see London, Jack.
Simon, Nathan, ed. The Psychological Aspects of Intensive Care Nursing. 295p. 1980. text ed. 16.95 (ISBN 0-87619-663-6). R J Brady.
Simon, Neil. The Collected Plays of Neil Simon, Vol. 2. 744p. 1980. pap. 7.95 (ISBN 0-380-51904-6, 51094). Avon.
Simon, Norma. All Kinds of Families. Rubin, Caroline, ed. LC 75-42283. (Concept Bks). (Illus.). 40p. (gr. k-2). 1975. 6.95 (ISBN 0-8075-0282-0). A Whitman.
--Cuando Me Enojo. Rubin, Caroline, ed. Ada, Alma F., tr. from Eng. LC 76-4932. (Concept Bks). (Illus.). 40p. (Span.). (gr. k-3). 1976. 6.50 (ISBN 0-8075-1371-7). A Whitman.
--Go Away, Warts! Tucker, Kathleen, ed. LC 79-28534. (Concept Bk.: Level 2). (Illus.). (gr. 3-6). 1980. 6.50g (ISBN 0-8075-2970-2). A Whitman.
--Hanukkah. LC 66-10065. (Holiday Ser.). (Illus.). (gr. k-3). 1966. PLB 7.89 (ISBN 0-690-36953-0, TYC-J). T Y Crowell.
--How Do I Feel. LC 77-126430. (Concept Bks.). (Illus.). (ps-2). 1970. 6.95g (ISBN 0-8075-3414-5). A Whitman.
--I Know What I Like. LC 76-165822. (Concept Bks.). (Illus.). (ps-2). 1971. 6.50g (ISBN 0-8075-3507-9). A Whitman.
--I Was So Mad! LC 73-22425. (Concept Bks.). (Illus.). 40p. (gr. k-2). 1974. 6.50g (ISBN 0-8075-3520-6). A Whitman.
--I'm Busy, Too. Tucker, Kathleen, ed. LC 79-18374. (Concept Bk.: Level I). (Illus.). (gr. k-1). 1980. 6.50g (ISBN 0-8075-3464-1). A Whitman.
--Nobody's Perfect. Tucker, Kathleen, ed. (Concept Bks.). (Illus.). 32p. (gr. k-3). 1981. 6.50 (ISBN 0-8075-5707-2). A Whitman.
--Passover. LC 65-11644. (Holiday Ser.). (Illus.). (gr. k-3). 1965. PLB 7.89 (ISBN 0-690-61094-7, TYC-J). T Y Crowell.
--We Remember Philip. Rubin, Caroline, ed. LC 78-11691. (Concept Bks). (Illus.). (gr. 2-4). 1978. 6.50g (ISBN 0-8075-8709-5). A Whitman.
--What Do I Do: English - Spanish Edition. LC 74-79544. (Concept Bks.). (Illus.). (ps-2). 1969. 6.95g (ISBN 0-8075-8823-7). A Whitman.
--What Do I Say. LC 67-17420. (Concept Bks.). (Illus.). (ps-2). 1967. 6.95g (ISBN 0-8075-8826-1). A Whitman.
--What Do I Say? English-Spanish Edition. LC 67-17420. (Concept Bks.). (Illus.). (ps-2). 6.95g (ISBN 0-8075-8828-8). A Whitman.
--Why Am I Different? Rubin, Caroline, ed. LC 76-41172. (Concept Books). (Illus.). 32p. 1976. 6.50g (ISBN 0-8075-9074-6). A Whitman.
Simon, Paul. One-Trick Pony. LC 80-7636. (Illus.). 224p. 1980. 15.95 (ISBN 0-394-51381-9); pap. 8.95 (ISBN 0-394-73961-2). Knopf.
Simon, Peter, jt. auth. see Davis, Stephen.
Simon, Philip J. Log of the Mayflower. LC 56-9513. 208p. 1980. Repr. of 1958 ed. 7.95 (ISBN 0-911180-02-8, Pub. by Priam Pr). Chicago Review.
Simon, Phillip J. Log of the Mayflower. LC 56-9513. 208p. 1980. pap. 7.95 (ISBN 0-911180-02-8). Priam Pr.
Simon, R. & Orlowski, S., eds. Radioactive Waste Management & Disposal. 703p. 1980. 82.00 (ISBN 3-7186-0056-0). Harwood Academic.
Simon, R. L., jt. auth. see Bowie, Norman E.
Simon, Raymond. Public Relations: Concepts & Practices. 2nd ed. LC 79-16160. (Grid Ser. in Advertising & Journalism). 1980. text ed. 19.50 (ISBN 0-88244-193-0). Grid Pub.
--Public Relations Management: Cases & Simulations. 2nd ed. LC 76-47362. (Advertising & Journalism). 1977. pap. text ed. 9.95 (ISBN 0-88244-148-5). Grid Pub.
--Publicity & Public Relations Work Text. 4th ed. LC 78-50047. (Public Relations Ser.). 1978. pap. text ed. 10.95 (ISBN 0-88244-165-5). Grid Pub.
Simon, Reeva S. The Modern Middle East: A Guide to Research Tools in the Social Sciences. LC 77-27319. (Westview Special Studies on the Middle East Ser.). 1978. lib. bdg. 26.50x (ISBN 0-89158-059-X); pap. text ed. 9.50x (ISBN 0-89158-158-8). Westview.
Simon, Rita J. Continuity & Change. LC 77-15090. (ASA Rose Monograph Ser.: No. 6). (Illus.). 1978. 19.95 (ISBN 0-521-21938-8); pap. 6.95x (ISBN 0-521-29318-9). Cambridge U Pr.
--Women & Crime. LC 74-25067. 128p. 1975. 15.95 (ISBN 0-669-97428-5). Lexington Bks.
Simon, Rita J. & Altstein, Howard. Transracial Adoption. LC 76-44817. 1977. 19.95 (ISBN 0-471-79208-X, Pub. by Wiley-Interscience). Wiley.
Simon, Rita J., jt. auth. see Adler, Freda.
Simon, Rita J., jt. auth. see O'Connell, Jeffrey.
Simon, Ruth B. Reading Seismograms: A Manual for the Interpretation of Earthquake Records. (Illus.). 200p. (Orig.). 1981. pap. text ed. 9.95 (ISBN 0-913232-81-5). W Kaufmann.
--Relax & Stretch. 1974. 7.95 o.s.i. (ISBN 0-8027-0410-7). Walker & Co.
Simon, S. Easy Models You Can Make. LC 75-134660. (Science at Work). (gr. 4-6). 1971. 4.90 o.p. (ISBN 0-531-01972-1, G-49). Watts.
--Projects in Oceanography. LC 75-190354. (Science at Work Ser). (gr. 5-8). 1972. 4.90 o.p. (ISBN 0-531-02580-2, C41). Watts.
--Projects in Space Science. LC 70-171900. (Science at Work Ser). (gr. 5-8). 1971. 4.90 o.p. (ISBN 0-531-01997-7, O40). Watts.
Simon, Sandor, tr. see Juhasz, Gyula.
Simon, Sandor, tr. see Kovacs, Ferenc.
Simon, Seymour. About the Food You Eat. Date not set. price not set. McGraw.
--Beneath Your Feet. LC 76-57066. (Illus.). (gr. 2-4). 1977. 5.95 o.s.i. (ISBN 0-8027-6293-X); PLB 5.85 (ISBN 0-8027-6294-8). Walker & Co.
--A Building on Your Street. LC 72-92583. (Illus.). 48p. (gr. k-3). 1973. reinforced bdg. 3.95 o.p. (ISBN 0-8234-0216-9). Holiday.
--Creatures from Lost Worlds. LC 78-25875. (Eerie Ser.). (Illus.). (gr. 2-4). 1979. 7.95 (ISBN 0-397-31834-0); PLB 7.89 (ISBN 0-397-31852-9). Lippincott.
--Danger from Below: Earthquakes - Past, Present, & Future. LC 78-22283. (Illus.). 96p. (gr. 3-7). 1979. 7.95 (ISBN 0-590-07514-4, Four Winds). Schol Bk Serv.
--Discovering What Crickets Do. LC 72-10078. (Illus.). 48p. (gr. 3-6). 1973. PLB 6.95 o.p. (ISBN 0-07-057438-3, GB). McGraw.
--Einstein Anderson Makes up for Lost Time. (Einstein Anderson, Science Sleuth Ser.). (Illus.). 96p. (gr. 3-7). 1981. 6.95 (ISBN 0-670-29067-X). Viking Pr.
--Everything Moves. LC 75-21069. (Illus.). 48p. (gr. 1-4). 1976. 5.95 o.s.i. (ISBN 0-8027-6239-5); PLB 5.85 o.s.i. (ISBN 0-8027-6238-7). Walker & Co.
--From Shore to Ocean Floor: How Life Survives in the Sea. LC 72-6248. (Living Things in Their Environment Ser). 72p. (gr. 4-5). 1973. PLB 5.90 (ISBN 0-531-02614-0). Watts.
--Life in the Dark: How Animals Survive at Night. LC 74-934. (Animal Environment Ser.). (Illus.). 72p. (gr. 4-6). 1974. PLB 4.90 o.p. (ISBN 0-531-02719-8). Watts.
--Life on Ice. LC 75-37512. (How Animals Survive in Their Environment Ser.). (Illus.). 96p. (gr. 4-6). 1976. PLB 4.90 o.p. (ISBN 0-531-01133-X). Watts.
--Meet the Giant Snakes. LC 78-74162. (gr. 1-4). 7.95 o.s.i. (ISBN 0-8027-6356-1); PLB 7.85 (ISBN 0-8027-6357-X). Walker & Co.
--Mirror Magic. LC 80-13038. (Illus.). 48p. (gr. 1-4). 1980. 7.95 (ISBN 0-688-41955-0); PLB 7.63 (ISBN 0-688-51955-5). Lothrop.
--The Optical Illusion Book. LC 75-33873. (Illus.). 80p. (gr. 2-6). 1976. 8.95 (ISBN 0-685-62042-5, Four Winds). Schol Bk Serv.
--Poisonous Snakes. LC 80-23938. (Illus.). 80p. (gr. 2-6). 1981. 11.95 (ISBN 0-590-07513-6, Four Winds). Schol Bk Serv.
--Projects with Air. LC 74-26651. (Science at Work Ser.). (Illus.). 96p. (gr. 4-6). 1975. PLB 4.90 o.p. (ISBN 0-531-02807-0). Watts.
--Projects with Plants. LC 73-5710. (Science at Work Ser). (Illus.). (gr. 4-6). 1973. PLB 4.90 o.p. (ISBN 0-531-02649-3). Watts.
--Silly Animal Jokes & Riddles. 64p. (gr. 1-3). 7.95 (ISBN 0-07-057397-2). McGraw.
--Space Monsters: From Movies, TV & Books. LC 77-3566. (gr. 4 up). 1977. 7.95 (ISBN 0-397-31765-4); pap. 2.95 o.p. (ISBN 0-397-31766-2). Lippincott.
--Strange Mysteries from Around the World. LC 79-6339. (Illus.). 64p. (gr. 3-7). 1980. 6.95 (ISBN 0-590-07639-6, Four Winds). Schol Bk Serv.
--Weather & Climate. (Science Library: No. 7). (gr. 4-6). 1969. PLB 4.99 (ISBN 0-394-80805-3); pap. 1.50 (ISBN 0-394-80805-3). Random.
--What Do You Want to Know About Guppies? LC 77-5930. (Illus.). 80p. (gr. 2-5). 1977. 7.95 (ISBN 0-590-07412-1, Four Winds). Schol Bk Serv.

Simon, Sheldon W., ed. The Military & Security in the Third World: Domestic & International Impacts. LC 77-29133. (A Westview Special Study Ser.). 1978. lib. bdg. 28.00x (ISBN 0-89158-424-2). Westview.

Simon, Sherry, tr. see Foucault, Michel.

Simon, Shirley. Best Friend. (gr. 4-6). 1979. pap. 1.75 (ISBN 0-671-56013-1). PB.

Simon, Sidney B. & O'Rourke, Robert. Developing Values with Exceptional Children. (Illus.). 160p. 1977. pap. text ed. 9.95 (ISBN 0-13-205310-1). P-H.

Simon, Sidney B., jt. auth. see Kirschenbaum, Howard.

Simon, Sidney B., jt. auth. see Read, Donald C.

Simon, Steven A. I Am Not Sure What You're Saying but I Can Relate. 1980. pap. 3.95 (ISBN 0-9605594-0-X). Monkey Man.

Simon, Ted. Jupiter's Travels. 360p. 1981. pap. 4.95 (ISBN 0-14-005410-3). Penguin.

Simon, W. M. Germany in the Age of Bismarck. (Historical Problems: Studies & Documents). 1968. text ed. 8.95x o.p. (ISBN 0-04-943010-6). Allen Unwin.

Simon, Walter M. The Failure of the Prussian Reform Movement, 1807-1819. LC 73-80591. 1971. Repr. 17.00 (ISBN 0-86527-062-7). Fertig.

Simon, Wilhelm. The Numerical Control of Machine Tools. 2nd rev. ed. LC 72-89494. 1972. 55.00x (ISBN 0-8448-0117-8). Crane-Russak Co.

Simon, William. A Time for Truth. 1979. pap. 2.95 (ISBN 0-425-05025-4). Berkley Pub.

Simon, Yves. Freedom of Choice. Wolff, Peter, ed. LC 75-75040. xx, 167p. 1969. 10.00 o.p. (ISBN 0-8232-0840-0). Fordham.

Simond, Ada D. Let's Pretend: Mae Dee & Her Family Ten Years Later. LC 78-62431. (National History Ser.). (Illus.). (gr. 5 up). Date not set. 8.95 (ISBN 0-89482-012-5); softcover 5.95 (ISBN 0-89482-013-3). Stevenson Pr.

Simonds, Charles Shea see Shea-Simonds, Charles.

Simonds, Rollin H., jt. auth. see Grimaldi, John V.

Simone, Donald De see De Simone, Donald.

Simonet, D. Glosario De Voces Ibericas y Latinas. (French-Arabic.). 1974. 18.00x (ISBN 0-685-82825-5). Intl Bk Ctr.

Simonett, David S., jt. ed. see Lintz, Joseph, Jr.

Simonett, Martha L. Descriptive List of the Map Collection in the Pennsylvania State Archives. Kent, Donald H. & Whipkey, Harry E., eds. 1976. 8.00 (ISBN 0-911124-83-7). Pa Hist & Mus.

Simonetti, Martha L., jt. auth. see Eddy, Henry H.

Simoni, Felix De see De Simoni, Felix.

Simonian, Charles. Fundamentals of Sports Biomechanics. (Illus.). 224p. 1981. text ed. 13.95 (ISBN 0-13-344499-6). P-H.

Simons & Menzies. Short Course in Foundation Engineering. 1977. 19.95 (ISBN 0-408-00295-6). Butterworths.

Simons, Barbara B. A Visit to the Mountains. LC 78-13562. (Adventures in Nature Ser). (Illus.). (gr. 2-6). 1980. PLB 6.95 (ISBN 0-916392-31-7); pap. 3.95 (ISBN 0-916392-30-9). Oak Tree Pubns.

--A Visit to the Prairies. LC 78-13738. (Adventures in Nature Ser). (Illus.). (gr. 2-6). 1978. PLB 6.95 (ISBN 0-916392-33-3); pap. 3.95 (ISBN 0-916392-32-5). Oak Tree Pubns.

--Volcanoes: Mountains of Fire. LC 76-15550. (Science Information Ser.). (Illus.). (gr. 4). 1976. PLB 8.65 (ISBN 0-8172-0350-8). Raintree Pubs.

Simons, C. J., jt. auth. see Ritchie, Robert L.

Simons, Eric N. Communication. LC 79-512663. (Pegasus Books: No. 28). (Illus.). 1970. 7.50x (ISBN 0-234-77317-0). Intl Pubns Serv.

--Dictionary of Ferrous Metals. (Illus.). 1971. 14.00 (ISBN 0-584-10059-0). Transatlantic.

Simons, Eugene, jt. ed. see Strasser, Gabor.

Simons, George F. Keeping Your Personal Journal. LC 77-99299. 1978. pap. 4.95 (ISBN 0-8091-2092-5). Paulist Pr.

Simons, Gerald. Barbarian Europe. LC 68-54209. (Great Ages of Man). (Illus.). (gr. 6 up). 1968. PLB 11.97 (ISBN 0-8094-0380-3, Pub. by Time-Life). Silver.

Simons, Gordon, jt. auth. see Cambanis, Stamatis.

Simons, Gustave. Coping with Crisis. LC 72-81081. 288p. 1973. 7.95 o.s.i. (ISBN 0-02-611180-2). Macmillan.

Simons, Herbert W. Persuasion: Understanding, Practice & Analysis. LC 75-9015. (Speech Communication Ser.). (Illus.). 400p. 1976. text ed. 15.50 (ISBN 0-201-07082-0). A-W.

Simons, Herbert W., jt. ed. see Miller, Gerald R.

Simons, Howard & Califano, Joseph A., eds. The Media & the Law. LC 75-19822. (Special Studies). 1976. text ed. 26.95 (ISBN 0-275-55820-7); pap. 11.95 (ISBN 0-275-89530-0). Praeger.

Simons, J. W., jt. ed. see Cleton, F. J.

Simons, Jim, et al. Texas Tenants' Handbook. 1980. pap. price not set (ISBN 0-201-08302-7). A-W.

Simons, Joseph. Living Together: Communication in the Unmarried Relationship. LC 78-972. 1978. 12.95 (ISBN 0-88229-274-9); pap. 6.95 (ISBN 0-88229-599-3). Nelson-Hall.

--The Search for Self: An Introduction to Personal Social Adjustment. 1980. pap. text ed. 12.95 (ISBN 0-669-02570-4); inst. manual cancelled (ISBN 0-669-02571-2). Heath.

Simons, Leon. The Basic Arts of Financial Management. 2nd ed. 249p. 1978. text ed. 25.75x (ISBN 0-220-66370-X, Pub. by Busn Bks England). Renouf.

Simons, M. Laird, ed. see Duyckinck, Evert A. & Duyckinck, George L.

Simons, R. H., jt. auth. see Bean, A. R.

Simons, Richard C. & Pardes, Herbert. Understanding Human Behavior in Health & Illness. 2nd ed. (Illus.). 760p. 1981. write for info. (7740-6). Williams & Wilkins.

Simons, Robin. Recyclopedia. (Illus.). (gr. 3-7). 1976. 9.95 (ISBN 0-395-24390-4). HM.

--Recyclopedia. (gr. 1 up). 1976. pap. 5.95 (ISBN 0-395-24380-7, Sandpiper). HM.

Simons, Rosemary. Collecting Original Prints. (The Christies International Collectors Ser.). (Illus.). 128p. 1980. 14.95 (ISBN 0-8317-1499-9). Mayflower Bks.

Simons, S. Vector Analysis for Mathematicians, Scientists & Engineers. 2nd ed. 1970. 15.00 (ISBN 0-08-006988-6); pap. 9.25 (ISBN 0-08-006895-2). Pergamon.

Simons, Thomas G. Blessings: A Reappraisal of Their Nature, Purpose, & Celebration. 1981. pap. 12.95 (ISBN 0-686-69223-3). Resource Pubns.

Simons, William B. The Soviet Codes of Law. (Law in Eastern Europe Ser.: No. 23). 1288p. 1980. 92.50x (ISBN 90-286-0810-9). Sijthoff & Noordhoff.

Simonsen, Clifford E. & Gordon, Marshall S. Juvenile Justice in America. 1979. text ed. write for info. (ISBN 0-02-478350-1). Macmillan.

Simonsen, Clifford E., jt. auth. see Allen, Harry E.

Simonsen, J. L. & Barton, D. H. Terpenes, Vol. 3 Sesquiterpenes & Diterpenes & Their Derivatives. 65.00 (ISBN 0-521-06476-7). Cambridge U Pr.

Simonsen, R., ed. Fourth Symposium on Recent & Fossil Marine Diatoms, Oslo 1976: Proceedings. (Beiheft zur Nova Hedwigia Ser.: No. 54). (Illus.). 1977. lib. bdg. 100.00x (ISBN 3-7682-5454-2). Lubrecht & Cramer.

Simonsen, Richard J. Clinical Applications of the Acid Etch Technique. (Illus.). 123p. 1978. 42.00 (ISBN 0-931386-01-2). Quint Pub Co.

Simonson, Harold P., ed. Quartet: A Book of Stories, Plays, Poems, & Critical Essays. 2nd ed. 1973. pap. text ed. 14.50 scp o.p. (ISBN 0-06-046184-5, HarpC); instructor's manual free o.p. (ISBN 0-06-366185-3). Har-Row.

Simonson, Harold P., ed. see Edwards, Jonathan.

Simonson, Lee. Stage Is Set. LC 62-12338. (Illus.). 1963. pap. 3.95 (ISBN 0-87830-508-4, 8). Theatre Arts.

Simonsuuri, K. Homer's Original Genius. LC 78-56758. (Illus.). 1979. 32.95 (ISBN 0-521-22198-6). Cambridge U Pr.

Simont, Marc & Boston Children's Medical Center Staff. A Child's Eye View of the World. (Illus.). 128p. 1972. 4.95 o.p. (ISBN 0-440-01221-X, Sey Lawr). Delacorte.

Simonton, Carl, et al. Getting Well Again. 256p. (Orig.). 1980. pap. 2.75 (ISBN 0-553-12268-1). Bantam.

Simonton, Dave. Directory of Engineering Document Sources. 2nd ed. 436p. 1974. perfect bnd. 39.95x (ISBN 0-912702-06-0). Global Eng.

Simonton, Wesley & Mannie, Phillip. A Manual of AACR 2 Examples for Musical Scores & Musical Sound Recordings. Swanson, Edward & McClasky, Marilyn J., eds. 1980. pap. 6.00 (ISBN 0-936996-05-6). Soldier Creek.

Simony, M., et al, eds. Traveler's Reading Guides: Background Books, Novels, Travel Literature & Articles, Vol. 1. Europe. new ed. LC 80-65324. 1981. pap. 11.95 (ISBN 0-9602050-1-2). Freelance Pubns.

Simonyi. Noninvasive Evaluation of Human Circulation. 1976. 17.00 (ISBN 0-9960008-0-1, Pub. by Kaido Hungary). Heyden.

Simonyi, K. Foundations of Electrical Engineering. 1964. 40.00 (ISBN 0-08-010204-2); pap. 18.50 (ISBN 0-08-019001-4). Pergamon.

Simoons, Elizabeth S., jt. auth. see Simoons, Frederick J.

Simoons, Frederick J. Eat Not This Flesh: Food Avoidances in the Old World. LC 80-22232. (Illus.). xiii, 241p. 1981. Repr. of 1967 ed. lib. bdg. 29.75x (ISBN 0-313-22772-1, SIEN). Greenwood.

Simoons, Frederick J. & Simoons, Elizabeth S. Ceremonial Ox of India: The Mithan in Nature, Culture, & History. LC 68-9023. (Illus.). 1968. 27.50x (ISBN 0-299-04980-9). U of Wis Pr.

Simosko, Vladimir & Tepperman, Barry. Eric Dolphy: A Musical Biography & Discography. LC 73-16248. (Illus.). 164p. 1974. 12.50 o.p. (ISBN 0-87474-142-4). Smithsonian.

Simper, Robert. British Sail. LC 76-58784. 1977. 24.00 (ISBN 0-7153-7263-7). David & Charles.

--Gaff Sail. LC 79-90907. (Illus.). 144p. 1980. 14.95 (ISBN 0-87021-827-1). Naval Inst Pr.

--Scottish Sail: A Forgotten Era. LC 74-81055. 1974. 8.95 (ISBN 0-7153-6703-X). David & Charles.

--Victorian & Edwardian Yachting. 1978. 17.95 (ISBN 0-7134-0914-2). David & Charles.

Simpkin, Brigadier R. Mechanized Infantry. (Illus.). 144p. 1980. 26.00 (ISBN 0-08-027030-1). Pergamon.

Simpkin, Richard. Cruising Yachtsman's Troubleshooter. 1979. 11.95 o.p. (ISBN 0-214-20384-0, 8028, Dist. by Arco). Barrie & Jenkins.

Simpkins, John. Investigations in Animal Physiology. (Investigations in Biology Ser.). 1973. pap. text ed. 3.95x o.p. (ISBN 0-435-60285-3). Heinemann Ed.

--Techniques of Biological Preparation. (Illus.). 1974. 16.50x (ISBN 0-216-89767-X). Intl Ideas.

Simpson, A. B. Days of Heaven & Earth. 371p. 1945. pap. 1.50 o.p. (ISBN 0-686-65444-7). Chr Pubns.

--Life of Prayer. 122p. 1975. pap. 2.00 (ISBN 0-87509-164-4). Chr Pubns.

Simpson, A. W. A History of the Common Law of Contract: The Rise of the Action of Assumpsit. 660p. 1975. 65.00x (ISBN 0-19-825327-3). Oxford U Pr.

Simpson, Alan & Simpson, Mary, eds. I Too Am Here. LC 76-11093. (Illus.). 1977. 26.50 (ISBN 0-521-21304-5). Cambridge U Pr.

Simpson, Albert B. The Christ Life. LC 80-69301. 96p. pap. 1.75 (ISBN 0-87509-291-8). Chr Pubns.

Simpson, Alfred W. Introduction to the History of the Land Law. 1961. 29.50x (ISBN 0-19-825150-5). Oxford U Pr.

Simpson, Alfred W., ed. Oxford Essays in Jurisprudence, Vol. 2. 315p. 1973. text ed. 39.95x (ISBN 0-19-825313-3). Oxford U Pr.

Simpson, B. Geological Maps. 1968. 13.75 (ISBN 0-08-012781-9); pap. 6.25 (ISBN 0-08-012780-0). Pergamon.

--Rocks & Minerals. 1966. 23.00 (ISBN 0-08-011744-9); pap. 9.00 (ISBN 0-08-011743-0). Pergamon.

Simpson, B. Mitchell, 3rd. War, Strategy & Maritime Power. 1977. 25.00 (ISBN 0-8135-0842-8). Rutgers U Pr.

Simpson, Bob, jt. auth. see Carol, Estelle.

Simpson, C. Adventures of Huckleberry Finn: Twentieth Century Interpretations. 1968. 7.95 o.p. (ISBN 0-13-013995-5, Spec). P-H.

Simpson, Catherine, jt. auth. see Simpson, Claude C.

Simpson, Charles R. Soho: The Artist in the City. LC 80-27083. 352p. 1981. 20.00 (ISBN 0-226-75937-7). U of Chicago Pr.

Simpson, Claude C. & Simpson, Catherine. North of the Narrows: Story of Priest Lake Country. LC 80-51781. (GEM Bks-Historical Ser.). (Illus.). 332p. (Orig.). 1981. pap. 11.95 (ISBN 0-89301-069-3). U Pr of Idaho.

Simpson, Colleen E. & Hirshman, S. Stalking the Seattle Bargain: A Complete Bargain Hunter's Catalogue & Consumer Education Guide. (Illus.). 160p. (Orig.). 1980. pap. 3.95 (ISBN 0-938406-00-0). Simpson-Hirshman.

Simpson, D. D., jt. ed. see Coles, J. M.

Simpson, D. D., jt. ed. see Megaw, J. V.

Simpson, David. General Equilibrium Analysis: An Introduction with Applications. LC 74-31814. 164p. 1975. text ed. 17.95 (ISBN 0-470-79209-4). Halsted Pr.

Simpson, Dick. Winning Elections: A Handbook in Participatory Politics. LC 78-171874. 1971. 10.00x o.p. (ISBN 0-8040-0541-9); pap. 4.95x o.p. (ISBN 0-8040-0542-7). Swallow.

--Winning Elections: A Handbook in Participatory Politics. rev. & enl. ed. (Illus.). 240p. 1981. 13.95x (ISBN 0-8040-0365-3); text ed. 7.95x (ISBN 0-8040-0366-1). Swallow.

Simpson, Dick & Beam, George. Strategies for Change: How to Make the American Political Dream Work. LC 75-43482. 258p. 1976. 12.00 (ISBN 0-8040-0696-2). Swallow.

Simpson, Dorothy. The Night She Died. 192p. 1981. 8.95 (ISBN 0-684-16869-3, ScribT). Scribner.

Simpson, Douglas. The Liberated People. 1981. pap. 3.95 (ISBN 0-89265-064-8). Randall Hse.

Simpson, Douglas B. & Podsakoff, Philip M. Workshop Management: A Behavioral & Systems Approach. (Illus.). 152p. 1975. 17.50 (ISBN 0-398-03364-1). C C Thomas.

Simpson, Duncan. C. F. A. Voysey: An Architect of Individuality. 160p. 1981. 19.95 (ISBN 0-8230-7483-8, Whitney Lib). Watson-Guptill.

Simpson, E. K. & Bruce, Frederick F. Epistles to the Ephesians & Colossians. (New International Commentary on the New Testament). 1958. 12.95 (ISBN 0-8028-2193-6). Eerdmans.

Simpson, Elizabeth L. Democracy's Stepchildren: A Study of Need & Belief. LC 73-146735. (Social & Behavioral Science Ser.). 1971. 12.95x o.p. (ISBN 0-87589-089-X). Jossey-Bass.

Simpson, Evelyn M., ed. & intro. by see Donne, John.

Simpson, F. Dale. Seven Steps Along the Way. 1981. pap. write for info. (ISBN 0-89137-527-9). Quality Pubns.

Simpson, Frank, tr. see Lem, Stanislaw.

Simpson, George E. Black Religions in the New World. (Illus.). 1978. 27.50x (ISBN 0-231-04540-9). Columbia U Pr.

--Melville J. Herskovitz. (Leaders of Modern Anthropology Ser.). 200p. 1973. 15.00x (ISBN 0-231-03385-0); pap. 6.00x (ISBN 0-231-03396-6). Columbia U Pr.

Simpson, George G. American Mesozoic Mammalia. (Illus.). 1929. 125.00x (ISBN 0-685-89733-8). Elliots Bks.

--Major Features of Evolution. LC 53-10263. (Columbia Biological Ser.: No. 17). 1953. 27.50 (ISBN 0-231-01821-5). Columbia U Pr.

--Mammals around the Pacific. (Thomas Burke Memorial Lecture Ser.: No. 2). 1966. pap. 4.00 (ISBN 0-295-74056-6). U of Wash Pr.

--Meaning of Evolution: A Study of the History of Life & of Its Significance for Man. rev. ed. (Terry Lectures Ser.). (Illus.). 1967. pap. 5.45x (ISBN 0-300-00229-7, Y23). Yale U Pr.

--Principles of Animal Taxonomy. LC 60-13939. (Columbia Biological Ser.: No. 20). (Illus.). 1961. 22.50x (ISBN 0-231-02427-4). Columbia U Pr.

--Why & How: Some Problems & Methods in Historical Biology. LC 79-42774. (Illus.). 270p. 1980. 44.00 (ISBN 0-08-025785-2); pap. 22.00 (ISBN 0-08-025784-4). Pergamon.

Simpson, George G. see Gidley, James W.

Simpson, Grant G., jt. auth. see Stones, E. L.

Simpson, Harold B. Cry Comanche. (Illus.). 1979. lib. bdg. 10.50 o.p. (ISBN 0-912172-25-8). Hill Jr. Coll.

--Hood's Texas Brigade: A Compendium, Vol. 4. new ed. LC 77-91396. (Illus.). 1977. 12.50 (ISBN 0-912172-22-3). Hill Jr Coll.

Simpson, Hassell A. Rumer Godden. (English Authors Ser.: No. 151). 1973. lib. bdg. 10.95 (ISBN 0-8057-1219-4). Twayne.

Simpson, Howard N. Invisible Armies: The Impact of Disease on American History. LC 80-682. 300p. 1980. 12.95 (ISBN 0-672-52659-X). Bobbs.

Simpson, I. M. Fieldwork in Geology. (Introducing Geology Ser.). (Illus.). 1977. pap. text ed. 5.50x (ISBN 0-04-550025-8). Allen Unwin.

Simpson, Ida. From Student to Nurse. LC 78-31933. (ASA Rose Monographs). 1979. 19.95 (ISBN 0-521-22683-X); pap. 6.95x (ISBN 0-521-29616-1). Cambridge U Pr.

Simpson, Jacqueline, ed. see Partridge, Eric.

Simpson, Jan. Citizens' Energy Directory. 2nd, rev. ed. (Illus.). 185p. 1980. pap. 11.00 (ISBN 0-89988-055-X). Citizens Energy.

Simpson, Jan, jt. auth. see Bossong, Ken.

Simpson, Jeffery, jt. auth. see Holme, Bryan.

Simpson, Joe L., jt. ed. see Schulman, Joseph D.

Simpson, John E. Georgia History: A Bibliography. LC 76-15642. 1976. 18.00 (ISBN 0-8108-0960-5). Scarecrow.

Simpson, Keith. Police: The Investigation of Violence. (Illus.). 240p. 1978. 17.95x (ISBN 0-7121-1689-3, Pub. by Macdonald & Evans England). Intl Ideas.

Simpson, Kieran, ed. The Canadian Who's Who, 1980. 15th ed. 1980. 75.00 (ISBN 0-8020-4579-0). U of Toronto Pr.

--Toronto Legal Directory (Metropolitan List) & Tariff Guide. 1980. 14.00 (ISBN 0-8020-4581-2). U of Toronto Pr.

--Who's What in Canadian Who's Who. 15th ed. 1980. pap. 15.00 (ISBN 0-8020-4584-7). U of Toronto Pr.

Simpson, Kiernan, ed. Canadian Who's Who 1979, Vol. 14. cancelled o.s.i. (ISBN 0-8020-4555-3). Bowker.

Simpson, L. Management Accounting: Techniques for Non-Financial Mangers. 246p. 1979. pap. 12.25x (ISBN 0-220-67023-4, Pub. by Busn Bks England). Renouf.

Simpson, L. L., ed. Drug Treatment of Mental Disorders. LC 74-14480. 400p. 1976. 22.00 (ISBN 0-89004-007-9). Raven.

Simpson, Lesley B. Many Mexicos, Silver Anniversary Edition. (YA) (gr. 9 up). 1966. 16.95x (ISBN 0-520-01179-1); pap. 4.65 (ISBN 0-520-01180-5, CAL29). U of Cal Pr.

Simpson, Lesley B., ed. & frwd. by see Chevalier, Francois.

Simpson, Lesley B., tr. The Poem of the Cid. (YA) (gr. 9 up). 1957. pap. 3.50 (ISBN 0-520-01176-7, CAL10). U of Cal Pr.

Simpson, Lesley B., tr. see Iglesia, Ramon.

Simpson, Lesley B., tr. see Ricard, Robert.

Simpson, Louis. A Dream of Governors. LC 59-12480. (Wesleyan Poetry Program: Vol. 3). (Orig.). 1959. 10.00x (ISBN 0-8195-2003-9, Pub. by Wesleyan U Pr). Columbia U Pr.

Simpson, M. A., ed. Dying, Death, & Grief: A Critically Annotated Bibliography & Source Book of Thanatology & Terminal Care. LC 78-27273. 300p. 1979. 21.95 (ISBN 0-306-40147-9, Plenum Pr). Plenum Pub.

Simpson, Margaret, jt. auth. see Driskill, Linda.

Simpson, Marianna S. Arab & Persian Painting in the Fogg Art Museum, Vol. II. Walsh, Peter & Kaliski, Andrea, eds. LC 80-10525. (Fogg Art Museum Handbooks). (Illus.). 125p. 1980. pap. 8.50 (ISBN 0-916724-10-7). Fogg Art.

--The Illustration of an Epic: The Earliest Shahnama Manuscripts. LC 78-74379. (Outstanding Dissertations in the Fine Arts, Fourth Ser.). (Illus.). 1979. lib. bdg. 47.00 (ISBN 0-8240-3966-1). Garland Pub.

Simpson, Mary, jt. ed. see Simpson, Alan.

Simpson, Michael A., ed. Psycholinguistics in Clinical Practice. LC 79-11813. 450p. 1980. text ed. 24.50x (ISBN 0-8290-0091-7). Irvington.

Simpson, N., ed. Training in Libraries: Report of the Library Association Working Party on Training. 1977. pap. 2.75x (ISBN 0-85365-339-9, Pub. by Lib Assn England). Oryx Pr.

Simpson, Norman T. Country Inns & Back Roads, North America. 16th ed. (Illus.). 450p. (Orig.). 1981. pap. 8.95 (ISBN 0-912944-65-X). Berkshire Traveller.

Simpson, Pamela H., jt. auth. see Lyle, Royster, Jr.

Simpson, Peggy. Hospitality: In the Spirit of Love. 1980. pap. 3.45 o.p. (ISBN 0-89137-416-7). Quality Pubns.

Simpson, Peggy, ed. see Associated Women's Organization, Mars Hill Bible School.

Simpson, Penny & Sodeoka, Kanji. The Japanese Pottery Handbook. LC 78-71314. 118p. 1979. pap. 8.95 (ISBN 0-87011-373-9). Kodansha.

Simpson, Peter & Levitt, Ruth. Going Home. (Illus.). 400p. 1981. pap. text ed. 20.00 (ISBN 0-443-01839-1). Churchill.

Simpson, Philip, tr. see Oz, Amos.

Simpson, Robert. Introductory Electronics for Scientists & Engineers. 600p. 1974. text ed. 25.95x (ISBN 0-205-03845-X, 7338457). Allyn.

Simpson, Robert H. & Riehl, Herbert. The Hurricane & Its Impact. LC 80-13911. (Illus.). 448p. 1981. 20.00 (ISBN 0-8071-0688-7). La State U Pr.

Simpson, Ronald D. & Anderson, Norman D. Science, Students, & Schools: A Guide for the Middle & Secondary Teacher. LC 80-23124. 400p. 1981. text ed. 16.95 (ISBN 0-471-02477-5). Wiley.

Simpson, S. R. Land Law & Registration. LC 74-16994. 700p. 1976. 90.00 (ISBN 0-521-20628-6); pap. 24.95 (ISBN 0-521-29419-3). Cambridge U Pr.

Simpson, Sandra I., ed. see Wilson, J. D.

Simpson, Stephen M., Jr. FORTRAN & FAP: A Program Library, Vol. 1. cancelled o.s.i. (ISBN 0-201-07022-7, Adv Bk Prog). A-W.

Simpson, Thomas. Money, Banking & Economic Analysis. (Illus.). 496p. 1976. 18.95 (ISBN 0-13-600247-1). P-H.

Simpson, W. Douglas. Portrait of Skye & the Outer Hebrides. LC 67-74411. (Portrait Bks.). 1967. 10.50x (ISBN 0-7091-0650-5). Intl Pubns Serv.

--Portrait of the Highlands. LC 75-376702. (Portrait Bks.). 1969. 10.50x (ISBN 0-7091-0415-4). Intl Pubns Serv.

Simpson, William. The Jonah Legend: A Suggestion of Interpretation. LC 72-177422. (Illus.). vi, 182p. 1971. Repr. of 1899 ed. 15.00 (ISBN 0-8103-3820-3). Gale.

Simpson, William F., jt. auth. see Broadwell, Martin M.

Simpson, William G. Which Way Western Man? LC 79-91738. 758p. 1980. pap. 7.00 (ISBN 0-937944-01-7). Natl Alliance.

Simpson, William K. Papyrus Reisner I: The Records of a Building Project in the Reign of Sesostris I. (Illus.). 1963. 35.00 (ISBN 0-87846-030-6). Mus Fine Arts Boston.

--Papyrus Reisner II: Accounts of the Dockyard Workshop at This in the Reign of Sesostris I. (Illus.). 1965. 35.00 (ISBN 0-87846-031-4). Mus Fine Arts Boston.

--Papyrus Reisner III: The Records of a Building Project N the Early Twelfth Dynasty. (Illus.). 1969. 35.00 (ISBN 0-87846-032-2). Mus Fine Arts Boston.

Simring, Marvin R., jt. auth. see Ward, Howard L.

Simrock, N. The N. Simrock Thematic Catalog of the Works of Johannes Brahms. LC 72-5954. (Music Reprint Ser.). 180p. 1973. Repr. of 1897 ed. lib. bdg. 35.00 (ISBN 0-306-70271-1). Da Capo.

Sims, jt. auth. see Wright.

Sims, Carolyn. Labor Unions in the United States. LC 72-172449. (First Bks). (Illus.). (gr. 4-6). 1971. PLB 4.90 o.p. (ISBN 0-531-00748-0). Watts.

Sims, Chester T. & Hagel, William C., eds. The Superalloys. LC 72-5904. (Science & Technology of Materials Ser.). 688p. 1972. 54.50 (ISBN 0-471-79207-1, Pub. by Wiley-Interscience). Wiley.

Sims, Clarence A., jt. auth. see Budzik, Janet K.

Sims, Dorothea S. Diabetes: Reach for Health & Freedom. LC 80-16065. (Illus.). 145p. 1980. pap. 5.95 (ISBN 0-8016-4657-X). Mosby.

Sims, E. H. Boatbuilding in Alluminum Alloy. 124p. 1980. 18.00x (ISBN 0-245-53128-9, Pub. by Nautical England). State Mutual Bk.

Sims, Edward H. Fighter Tactics & Strategy Nineteen Fourteen to Nineteen Seventy. 2nd ed. LC 80-68106. (Illus.). 266p. 1980. 12.95 (ISBN 0-8168-8795-0). Aero.

Sims, Edward R. A Season with the Savior: Meditations on Mark. 1979. 6.95 (ISBN 0-8164-0413-5); pap. 3.95 (ISBN 0-8164-2195-1). Crossroad NY.

Sims, Harold. Images & Reflections. 1981. 4.95 (ISBN 0-533-04370-0). Vantage.

Sims, J. & Peterson, P. Better Listening Skills. (Illus.). 128p. 1981. pap. 6.95 (ISBN 0-13-074815-3). P-H.

Sims, J. Marion. Story of My Life. LC 68-29603. (American Medicine Ser). 1968. Repr. of 1884 ed. lib. bdg. 39.50 (ISBN 0-306-71116-8). Da Capo.

Sims, Janet L., compiled by. Marian Anderson: An Annotated Bibliography & Discography. LC 80-1787. (Illus.). viii, 243p. 1981. lib. bdg. 29.95 (ISBN 0-313-22559-1, SIM/). Greenwood.

Sims, John A. Edward John Carnell: Defender of the Faith. LC 78-57980. 1978. pap. text ed. 9.00 (ISBN 0-8191-0658-5). U Pr of Amer.

Sims, Michael. United States Doctoral Dissertations in Third World Studies, 1869-1978. 436p. 1980. 60.00. African Studies Assn.

Sims, Nicholas, jt. auth. see Lloyd, Lorna.

Sims, P. K. & Morey, G. B., eds. Geology of Minnesota. LC 73-62334. 1972. pap. 12.00 (ISBN 0-934938-00-8). Minn Geol Survey.

Sims, Patsy. Cleveland Benjamin's Dead. LC 79-84669. (Illus.). cancelled (ISBN 0-8015-0586-0, Hawthorn). Dutton.

--The Klan. LC 77-2335. (Illus.). 384p. 1981. pap. 8.95 (ISBN 0-8128-6096-9). Stein & Day.

Sims, Phillip L., jt. ed. see Vallentine, John F.

Sims, R. W. Animal Identification: A Reference Guide, 2 vols. Incl. Vol. 1. Marine & Brackish Water Animals. 108p (ISBN 0-471-27765-7); Vol. 2. Land & Freshwater Animals. 108p (ISBN 0-471-27766-5). 1980. 25.00 ea. Wiley.

Sims, Victor, jt. auth. see Owen, George.

Sims, William E. Black Studies: Pitfalls & Potential. LC 77-18563. 1978. pap. text ed. 7.75 (ISBN 0-8191-0316-0). U Pr of Amer.

Simsar, Muhammed A., tr. see Nakhshabi, Ziya'U'D-Din.

Simson, Otto Von see Von Simson, Otto.

Simtek Inc. Business Games Directory. (Orig.). 1980. pap. 2.95 (ISBN 0-933836-15-5). Simtek.

Simundson, Danile J. Faith Under Fire: Biblical Interpretations of Suffering. LC 79-54119. 158p. 1980. pap. 4.95 (ISBN 0-8066-1756-X, 10-2195). Augsburg.

Sinaer, George, jt. auth. see Campbell, Frank.

Sinai, Anne, jt. auth. see Oesterreicher, John M.

Sinai, Ya G. Mathematical Problems in the Theory of Phase Transitions. 128p. 1981. 27.00 (ISBN 0-08-026469-7). Pergamon.

Sinaiko, H. Wallace, ed. Selected Papers on Human Factors in the Design & Use of Control Systems. (Illus., Orig.). 1961. pap. text ed. 6.00 (ISBN 0-486-60140-4). Dover.

Sinanian, Sylva, et al, eds. Eastern Europe in the 1970's. LC 72-85944. (Special Studies in International Politics & Government). 1972. 28.00x (ISBN 0-275-28632-0); pap. text ed. 12.50x (ISBN 0-89197-740-6). Irvington.

Sinanoglu, Paula A., jt. ed. see Maluccio, Anthony N.

Sinberg, Janet. Divorce Is a Grown up Problem. 1978. pap. 2.95 (ISBN 0-380-01901-9, 37333). Avon.

Sinclair. Der Fremde, Erzaehlung. (Edition Suhrkamp. Neue Folge: es. NF 7). 150p. (Orig., Ger.). 1980. pap. text ed. 4.55 (ISBN 3-518-11007-1, Pub. by Insel Verlag Germany). Suhrkamp.

Sinclair, A., et al. The Child's Conception of Language. (Springer Ser. in Language & Communication: Vol. 2). (Illus.). 1979. 22.50 (ISBN 0-387-09153-X). Springer-Verlag.

Sinclair, A. M. Automatic Continuity of Linear Operators. LC 74-31804. (London Mathematical Society Lecture Note Ser.: No. 21). 120p. 1976. 14.50x (ISBN 0-521-20830-0). Cambridge U Pr.

Sinclair, A. R. & Norton-Griffiths, M. Serengeti: Dynamics of an Ecosystem. LC 79-10146. (Illus.). 384p. 1979. lib. bdg. 32.00x (ISBN 0-226-76028-6). U of Chicago Pr.

Sinclair, Andrew. Corsair: The Life of J. Pierpont Morgan. 1981. 15.00 (ISBN 0-316-79240-3). Little.

Sinclair, Andrew, ed. see London, Jack.

Sinclair, Angus. Development of the Locomotive Engine. 1970. 6.95 o.p. (ISBN 0-262-19068-0). MIT Pr.

Sinclair, Bruce. A Centennial History of the American Society of Mechanical Engineers: 1880-1980. 256p. 1980. text ed. 15.00 (H0175H); pap. text ed. 10.00 (H0175P). ASME.

--A History of the American Society of Mechanical Engineers. 304p. 1980. 15.00x (ISBN 0-8020-2380-0). U of Toronto Pr.

Sinclair, Caroline B. Movement of the Young Child: Ages Two to Six. LC 72-96100. 1973. pap. text ed. 8.95 (ISBN 0-675-08975-1). Merrill.

Sinclair, Catherine. Beatrice; or, the Unknown Relatives, 1852. Wolff, Robert L., ed. LC 75-453. (Victorian Fiction Ser.). 1975. lib. bdg. 66.00 (ISBN 0-8240-1532-0). Garland Pub.

--Holiday House. LC 75-32159. (Classics of Children's Literature, 1621-1932: Vol. 24). 1976. Repr. of 1839 ed. lib. bdg. 38.00 (ISBN 0-8240-2273-4). Garland Pub.

Sinclair, D. J., jt. auth. see Jones, E.

Sinclair, Dale, ed. see Farrands, Barry J.

Sinclair, Donna M. The Pastor's Wife Today. LC 80-26076. (Creative Leadership Ser.). 128p. (Orig.). 1981. pap. 4.95 (ISBN 0-687-30269-2). Abingdon.

Sinclair, George. Satan's Invisible World Discovered. LC 68-17017. 1969. Repr. of 1685 ed. 31.00x (ISBN 0-8201-1068-X). Schol Facsimiles.

Sinclair, H. M. Progress in Food & Nutrition Science, Vol. 2, No. 11-12. LC 75-7734. (Illus.). 70p. 1979. pap. 23.00 (ISBN 0-08-023758-4). Pergamon.

Sinclair, H. M. & Howat, G. R., eds. World Nutrition & Nutrition Education. (Illus.). 272p. 1980. text ed. 42.50x (ISBN 0-19-261176-3). Oxford U Pr.

Sinclair, Ian, jt. auth. see Mattinson, Janet.

Sinclair, James. Warrior Queen. 1979. pap. 2.25 o.p. (ISBN 0-425-03947-1). Berkley Pub.

Sinclair, James, ed. see O'Neill, Jack.

Sinclair, James E. & Schultz, Harry D. How the Experts Buy & Sell Gold Bullion, Gold Stocks & Gold Coins. 1975. 8.95 o.p. (ISBN 0-87000-309-7). Arlington Hse.

Sinclair, John. Quarrying, Opencast, & Alluvial Mining. (Illus.). 1969. 59.60x (ISBN 0-444-20040-1). Intl Ideas.

Sinclair, John A. God vs We the People. 1977. 7.50 o.p. (ISBN 0-682-48746-5). Exposition.

Sinclair, John D. The Rest Principle: A Neurophysiological Theory of Behavior. LC 80-17396. 240p. 1981. text ed. 16.50 (ISBN 0-89859-065-5). L Erlbaum Assocs.

Sinclair, John L. Cousin Drewey & the Holy Twister. LC 80-177530. 1980. 14.95 (ISBN 0-914366-18-1). Columbia Pub.

--New Mexico: The Shining Land. 224p. 1980. 14.95 (ISBN 0-8263-0548-2). U of NM Pr.

Sinclair, Marti, et al. Prison Story. 1981. pap. 3.95 (ISBN 0-89191-110-3). Cook.

Sinclair, Robert L., ed. A Two-Way Street: Home-School Cooperation in Curriculum Decisionmaking. 92p. (Orig.). 1980. pap. 6.00 (ISBN 0-917754-16-6). Inst Responsive.

Sinclair, Stuart W., jt. auth. see Hallwood, C. Paul.

Sinclair, T. A. A History of Greek Political Thought. 1967. pap. 12.00 (ISBN 0-7100-4615-4). Routledge & Kegan.

Sinclair, Tracy. Paradise Island. 192p. (Orig.). 1980. pap. 1.50 (ISBN 0-671-57039-0). S&S.

Sinclair, Upton. Boston: A Documentary Novel of the Sacco-Vanzetti Case. LC 77-86279. 1978. Repr. of 1928 ed. 16.50x (ISBN 0-8376-0420-6). Bentley.

--The Jungle. LC 79-151835. 1971. Repr. of 1906 ed. lib. bdg. 12.50x (ISBN 0-8376-0400-1). Bentley.

--Jungle. (Literature Ser). (gr. 9-12). 1970. pap. text ed. 3.75 (ISBN 0-87720-730-5). AMSCO Sch.

--Mental Radio. rev. 2nd ed. (Illus.). 256p. 1962. 11.75 (ISBN 0-398-01766-2). C C Thomas.

--Oil! LC 79-24682. 1981. Repr. of 1927 ed. lib. bdg. 15.00x (ISBN 0-8376-0444-3). Bentley.

Sinclair, Upton B. King Coal: A Novel. LC 74-22813. (Labor Movement Ser.). 408p. 1980. Repr. of 1921 ed. 24.00 (ISBN 0-404-58469-1). AMS Pr.

Sinclair, William A., jt. auth. see Arnheim, Daniel D.

Sinclair, William A., jt. auth. see Pestolesi, Robert A.

Sinden, J. A. & Worrell, Albert C. Unpriced Values: Decisions Without Market Prices. LC 78-24183. 1979. 32.50 (ISBN 0-471-02742-1, Pub. by Wiley-Interscience). Wiley.

Sinding, Franey, tr. see Bernhardsen, Christian.

Sindler, Allan P. Bakke, DeFunis & Minority Admissions: The Quest for Equal Opportunity. 1978. pap. text ed. 10.95 (ISBN 0-582-28053-2). Longman.

--Unchosen Presidents: The Vice-President & Other Frustrations of Presidential Succession. (A Quantum Book). 1976. 11.95 (ISBN 0-520-03185-7); pap. 2.95 (ISBN 0-520-03493-7). U of Cal Pr.

Sindoni, E., ed. see Commission of the European Communities.

Sindoni, E., jt. ed. see Eubank, H.

Sine, Robert D., et al. Basic Rehabilitation Techniques: A Self-Instructional Guide. 2nd. ed. 250p. 1981. text ed. write for info. (ISBN 0-89443-342-3). Aspen Systems.

Sinek, Jeremy. Supercars. LC 79-10851. (Illus.). 128p. 1979. 14.95 (ISBN 0-89196-041-4, Domus Bks). Quality Bks IL.

Sinel, Allen. The Classroom & the Chancellery: State Educational Reform in Russia Under Count Dmitry Tolstoi. LC 72-95185. (Russian Research Center Studies: No. 72). 352p. 1973. text ed. 16.50x (ISBN 0-674-13481-8). Harvard U Pr.

Sinfield, Adrian, jt. auth. see Showler, Brian.

Sinfield, Alan. The Language of Tennyson's "In Memoriam". 1971. pap. 24.50x (ISBN 0-631-12980-4, Pub. by Basil Blackwell). Biblio Dist.

Singarimbun, Masri. Kinship, Descent & Alliance Among the Karo Batak. LC 73-93061. 1975. 22.75x (ISBN 0-520-02692-6). U of Cal Pr.

Singelmann, Jay & Longhurst, Jean. Business Programming Logic: A Structured Approach. (Illus.). 1978. pap. 12.95 ref. ed. (ISBN 0-13-107631-0). P-H.

Singelmann, Joachim. From Agriculture to Services: The Transformation of Industrial Employment. LC 78-19843. (Sage Library of Social Research: Vol. 69). 1978. 18.00x (ISBN 0-8039-1092-4); pap. 8.95x (ISBN 0-8039-1093-2). Sage.

Singer & Statsky. Rights of the Imprisoned, Cases, Materials, & Directions. 1265p. 1974. 24.00 (ISBN 0-672-81874-4, Bobbs-Merrill Law); 1979 suppl 7.50 (ISBN 0-672-84049-9). Michie.

Singer, Albert, jt. auth. see Lees, David H.

Singer, Albert, jt. ed. see Jordan, Joseph A.

Singer, Andre, ed. see Evans-Pritchard, Edward.

Singer, Armand. Paul Bourget. LC 76-2548. (World Authors Ser.: No. 393: France). 1976. lib. bdg. 10.95 (ISBN 0-8057-6235-3). Twayne.

Singer, Barnett. Modern France: Mind, Politics, Society, 1870-1970. LC 80-24177. 212p. 1981. 16.95 (ISBN 0-686-69480-5). U of Wash Pr.

Singer, Barry, jt. auth. see Abell, George D.

Singer, Barry, jt. auth. see Weil, Susanne.

Singer, Bertrand B. Mathematics at Work: Algebra. (Illus.). (gr. 9-12). 1977. pap. text ed. 12.95x (ISBN 0-07-057491-X, G); ans. key 1.95x (ISBN 0-07-057492-8); instructor's manual 5.95x (ISBN 0-07-057486-3). McGraw.

Singer, Beth J., ed. see Randall, John H., Jr.

Singer, Burns. Burns Singer: Selected Poems. Cluysenaar, Anne, ed. (Poetry Ser.). 1979. 7.95 o.s.i. (ISBN 0-85635-177-6, Pub. by Carcanet New Pr England). Persea Bks.

Singer, C. Gregg. The Unholy Alliance. 1975. 11.95 o.p. (ISBN 0-87000-327-5). Arlington Hse.

Singer, Charles. Short History of Anatomy & Physiology: From the Greeks to Harvey. Orig. Title: Evolution of Anatomy. (Illus.). 1957. pap. text ed. 4.50 (ISBN 0-486-20389-1). Dover.

--Short History of Scientific Ideas to 1900. 1959. pap. 9.95x (ISBN 0-19-881049-0). Oxford U Pr.

Singer, Daniel. The Road to Gdansk: Eastern Europe on the Move. LC 80-39914. 288p. 1981. 15.00 (ISBN 0-85345-567-8). Monthly Rev.

Singer, Dorothy & Singer, Jerome. Partners in Play. 1977. 10.95 o.p. (ISBN 0-06-013891-2, HarpT). Har-Row.

Singer, Dorothy G., jt. auth. see Singer, Jerome L.

Singer, Dorothy G., et al. Teaching Television: How to Use TV to Your Child's Advantage. (Illus.). 192p. 1981. 10.95 (ISBN 0-8037-8515-1). Dial.

Singer, Edgar A. Experience & Reflection. Churchman, C. West, ed. LC 57-11956. 1959. 15.00 o.p. (ISBN 0-8122-7039-8). U of Pa Pr.

Singer, Edwin J. Effective Management Coaching. 2nd ed. (Management in Perspective Ser.). 212p. 1979. pap. 11.50x (ISBN 0-85292-248-5). Intl Pubns Serv.

Singer, Eleanor D., jt. ed. see Hyman, Herbert H.

Singer, Eugene M. Antitrust Economics & Legal Analysis. LC 80-19847. (Economics Ser.). 200p. 1981. pap. 12.95 (ISBN 0-88244-227-9). Grid Pub.

Singer, Ferdinand L. Mecanica Para Ingenieros, Tomo Primero: Estatica. 1976. text ed. 10.00x (ISBN 0-06-316997-5, IntlDept). Har-Row.

Singer, Florence. Structuring Child Behavior Through Visual Art: A Therapeutic, Individualized Art Program to Develop Positive Behavior Attitudes in Children. (Illus.). 144p. 1980. text ed. 15.75. C C Thomas.

Singer, Fritz & Schon, Fritz. Partial Dentures. (Illus.). 207p. 1973. 42.00. Quint Pub Co.

Singer, Harry & Donlan, Dan. Reading & Learning from Text. 543p. 1980. text ed. 15.95 (ISBN 0-316-79274-8). Little.

Singer, Harry & Ruddell, Robert B., eds. Theoretical Models & Processes of Reading. rev., 2nd ed. 1976. text ed. 25.00 (ISBN 0-87207-436-6); pap. text ed. 18.50 (ISBN 0-87207-432-3). Intl Reading.

Singer, I. J. The Brothers Ashkenazi. LC 80-66017. 1980. 14.95 (ISBN 0-689-11102-9). Atheneum.

--Of a World That Is No More. LC 73-134665. 1970. 10.00 (ISBN 0-8149-0683-4). Vanguard.

Singer, Isaac B. A Crown of Feathers. 1981. pap. 6.95 (ISBN 0-374-51622-7). FS&G.

--A Crown of Feathers. 1979. pap. 2.95 (ISBN 0-449-23465-7, Crest). Fawcett.

--Enemies: A Love Story. 1977. pap. 2.95 (ISBN 0-449-24065-7, Crest). Fawcett.

--A Friend of Kafka & Other Stories. LC 70-115752. 311p. 1970. 12.95 (ISBN 0-374-15880-0); pap. 5.95 (ISBN 0-374-51538-7). FS&G.

--Gimpel the Fool & Other Stories. Bellow, Saul, et al, trs. 1957. 9.95 (ISBN 0-374-16244-1); pap. 4.95 (ISBN 0-374-50052-5). FS&G.

--An Isaac Bashevis Singer Reader. 586p. 1971. 12.95 (ISBN 0-374-17747-3); pap. 7.95 (ISBN 0-374-64030-0). FS&G.

--Joseph & Koza, or the Sacrifice to the Vistula. LC 78-106398. (ps-3). 1970. 4.95 o.p. (ISBN 0-374-33795-0). FS&G.

--Lost in America. LC 79-6037. 1981. 17.95 (ISBN 0-686-69069-9). Doubleday.

--The Manor & the Estate. 818p. 1979. 15.00 (ISBN 0-374-20225-7). FS&G.

--Old Love. 1980. pap. 2.50 (ISBN 0-449-24343-5, Crest). Fawcett.

--Passions. 1978. pap. 2.95 (ISBN 0-449-24067-3, Crest). Fawcett.

--The Power of Light: Eight Stories for Hanukkah. (Illus.). (gr. 1 up). 1980. 10.95 (ISBN 0-374-36099-5). FS&G.

--The Seance. 256p. 1981. pap. 2.75 (ISBN 0-449-24364-8, Crest). Fawcett.

--Shosha. 1979. pap. 2.95 (ISBN 0-449-23997-7, Crest). Fawcett.

--The Spinoza of Market Street. Gottleib, Elaine, et al, trs. 1961. 8.95 (ISBN 0-374-26776-6); pap. 4.95 (ISBN 0-374-50256-0). FS&G.

--A Young Man in Search of Love. LC 77-2538. (Illus.). 1978. 12.95 (ISBN 0-385-12357-4); limited ed. o.p. 50.00 (ISBN 0-385-13492-4). Doubleday.

Singer, J. D., ed. Quantitative International Politics. LC 66-23083. 1968. 14.95 o.s.i. (ISBN 0-02-928940-8). Free Pr.

Singer, J. David & Small, Melvin. Wages of War, Eighteen Sixteen to Nineteen Sixty-Five. 1974. codebk 8.00 (ISBN 0-89138-068-X). ICPSR.

Singer, J. David, jt. auth. see LaBarr, Dorothy F.

Singer, J. David & Wallace, Michael D., eds. To Augur Well: Early Warning Indicators in World Politics. LC 79-14277. (Sage Focus Editions: Vol. 11). (Illus.). 1979. 18.95x (ISBN 0-8039-1246-3); pap. 9.95x (ISBN 0-8039-1247-1). Sage.

Singer, James. Elements of Numerical Analysis. (Illus.). 1964. text ed. 21.95 (ISBN 0-12-646450-2). Acad Pr.

Singer, James, jt. auth. see Kress, John R.

Singer, Jerome, jt. auth. see Singer, Dorothy.

Singer, Jerome E., jt. ed. see Baum, Andrew.

Singer, Jerome L. & Singer, Dorothy G. Television, Imagination & Aggression: A Study of Preschoolers. LC 80-36810. 224p. 1981. text ed. 19.95 (ISBN 0-89859-060-4). L Erlbaum Assocs.

Singer, Jerome L. & Switzer, Ellen. Mind Play: The Creative Uses of Fantasy. 1980. 13.95 (ISBN 0-13-198069-6, Spec); pap. 4.95 (ISBN 0-13-198051-3, Spec). P-H.

Singer, Judith E., jt. auth. see Grob, Mollie C.

Singer, June. Androgyny: Toward a New Theory of Sexuality. LC 76-2825. 1977. pap. 3.95 (ISBN 0-385-11026-X, Anch). Doubleday.

Singer, Laura J. & Buskin, Judith. Sex Education on Film: A Guide to Visual Aids & Programs. LC 75-154694. 1971. pap. 5.25x (ISBN 0-8077-2160-3). Tchrs Coll.

Singer, Lester. Sociology: A Student's Introduction. LC 79-48092. 347p. 1980. pap. text ed. 11.25 (ISBN 0-8191-1011-6). U Pr of Amer.

Singer, Linda R. Standards Relating to Dispositions. (Junvenile Justice Standards Project Ser.). 1980. softcover 7.95 (ISBN 0-88410-816-3); casebound 16.50 (ISBN 0-88410-229-7). Ballinger Pub.

--Standards Relating to Dispositions. LC 76-14412. (Juvenile Justice Standards Project Ser.). 1977. soft cover 7.95 o.p. (ISBN 0-88410-779-5); 16.50, casebound o.p. Ballinger Pub.

Singer, Loren. The Parallax View. 192p. 1981. Repr. of 1970 ed. 15.95 (ISBN 0-933256-20-5). Second Chance.

Singer, M. Introduction to the DEC System Ten Assembler Language Programming. LC 78-8586. 1978. 12.95 (ISBN 0-471-03458-4). Wiley.

Singer, M., ed. see Meigs, Walter B. & Meigs, Robert F.

Singer, Marshall. Weak States in a World of Power: The Dynamics of International Relationships. LC 70-158070. 1972. 16.95 (ISBN 0-02-928900-9). Free Pr.

Singer, Michael. PDP-11 Assembler Language Programming & Machine Organization. 1980. text ed. 13.95 (ISBN 0-471-04905-0). Wiley.

Singer, Milton B., ed. Krishna: Myths, Rites, & Attitudes. LC 80-29194. xvii, 277p. 1981. Repr. of 1966 ed. lib. bdg. 27.50x (ISBN 0-313-22822-1, SIKR). Greenwood.

Singer, Morris. Growth, Equality, & the Mexican Experience. (Latin American Monographs: No. 16). (Illus.). 1969. 15.00 (ISBN 0-292-70011-3). U of Tex Pr.

Singer, P., jt. auth. see Regan, Tom.

Singer, Peter. Animal Liberation. 1977. pap. 3.50 (ISBN 0-380-01782-2, 35253, Discus). Avon.

--Democracy & Disobedience. 150p. 1974. pap. text ed. 3.95x (ISBN 0-19-519803-4). Oxford U Pr.

--The Expanding Circle: Ethics and Sociobiology. 1981. 10.95 (ISBN 0-374-15112-1). FS&G.

--Marx. 1980. 7.95 (ISBN 0-8090-7550-4); pap. 2.95 (ISBN 0-8090-1412-2). Hill & Wang.

--Practical Ethics. LC 79-52328. 1980. 32.95 (ISBN 0-521-22920-0); pap. 6.95 (ISBN 0-521-29720-6). Cambridge U Pr.

Singer, Philip. Road to Megiddo. LC 77-94858. 1978. softcover 7.00 (ISBN 0-89430-025-3). Morgan-Pacific.

Singer, Philip & Titus, Elizabeth A. Selected W.H.O. Documents Relating to Traditional Healing. (Traditional Healing Ser.: Vol. 3). 1981. text ed. 19.50x (ISBN 0-932426-02-6); pap. text ed. 10.00x (ISBN 0-932426-06-9). Trado-Medic.

Singer, Philip & Titus, Elizabeth M. Selected Readings in Traditional Healing. (Traditional Healing Ser.: Vol. 2). 1980. text ed. 15.75x (ISBN 0-932426-01-8); pap. text ed. 10.00x (ISBN 0-932426-05-0). Trado-Medic.

Singer, Philip, ed. see Johnson, O.

Singer, Phyllis, jt. auth. see Holden, Alan.

Singer, R. The Agaricales in Modern Taxonomy. 3rd & rev. ed. 1975. 125.00 o.s.i. (ISBN 3-7682-0143-0). Lubrecht & Cramer.

Singer, R. N. & Milne, C. Laboratory & Field Experiments in Motor Learning. (Illus.). 292p. 1975. 26.75 (ISBN 0-398-03262-9). C C Thomas.

Singer, Richard B. & Levinson, Louis, eds. Medical Risks: Patterns of Mortality & Survival. LC 74-31609. 1976. 37.95 (ISBN 0-669-98228-8). Lexington Bks.

Singer, Robert N. & Dick, Walter. Teaching Physical Education: A Systems Approach. 400p. 1974. text ed. 17.25 o.p. (ISBN 0-395-17770-7); instructors' manual pap. 2.45 o.p. (ISBN 0-395-17854-1); study guide 6.95 o.p. (ISBN 0-395-17788-X). HM.

--Teaching Physical Education: A Systems Approach. 2nd ed. LC 79-88450. (Illus.). 1980. text ed. 18.25 (ISBN 0-395-28359-0); instrs'. manual 0.75 (ISBN 0-395-28360-4). HM.

Singer, S. Fred, intro. by. Energy: Readings from Scientific American. LC 78-31979. (Illus.). 1979. text ed. 17.95x (ISBN 0-7167-1082-X); pap. text ed. 8.95x (ISBN 0-7167-1083-8). W H Freeman.

Singer, Sam. Human Genetics: An Introduction to the Principles of Heredity. LC 78-82. (Biology Ser.). (Illus.). 1978. pap. text ed. 7.95x (ISBN 0-7167-0054-9); tchr's resource bk. 2.95x. W H Freeman.

Singer, Sam & Hilgard, Henry R. The Biology of People. LC 77-17893. (Biology Ser.). (Illus.). 1978. text ed. 21.95x (ISBN 0-7167-0026-3); tchr's resource bk. 2.75x. W H Freeman.

Singer, Stuart R. & Weiss, Stanley. Foreign Investment in the United States: 1980 Course Handbook. LC 79-92658. 617p. 1980. pap. text ed. 25.00 (ISBN 0-686-68824-4, B4-6531). PLI.

Singer, Thomas P., et al, eds. Monoamine Oxidase: Structure, Function & Altered Functions. LC 79-24107. 1980. 39.00 (ISBN 0-12-646880-X). Acad Pr.

Singer, Walter, et al. Pharmacy Review. LC 74-80957. (Arco Medical Review Ser.). 288p. 1976. pap. 9.00 o.p. (ISBN 0-668-03611-7). Arco.

Singer, Werner, jt. auth. see Coffin, Berton.

Singh, A., jt. ed. see Gupta, K. C.

Singh, Ajit. Formation & Role of Excited States in Radiolysis: Special Issue of International Journal for Radiation Physics & Chemistry, Vol. 8, Nos. 1 & 2. pap. text ed. 42.00 (ISBN 0-08-019986-0). Pergamon.

--Takeovers: Their Relevance to the Stock Market & the Theory of the Firm. (Department of Applied Economics Monographs: No. 19). 1972. 31.50 (ISBN 0-521-08245-5). Cambridge U Pr.

Singh, Armitjit, et al, eds. Indian Literature: A Guide to Information Sources. LC 74-11532. (American Literature, English Literature & World Literatures in English Information Guide Ser.: Vol 36). 450p. 1981. 30.00 (ISBN 0-8103-1238-7). Gale.

Singh, B. N. Pathogenic & Non-Pathogenic Amoebae. LC 75-15788. 235p. 1975. 54.95 (ISBN 0-470-79305-8). Halsted Pr.

Singh, Balbir. Electric Machine Design. 464p. 1981. text ed. 27.50x (ISBN 0-7069-1111-3, Pub. by Vikas India). Advent Bk.

Singh, Baljit. Indian Foreign Policy: An Analysis. 111p. 1979. pap. 4.95 (ISBN 0-210-40570-8). Asia.

Singh, Baljit & Ko Wang Mei. Theory & Practice of Modern Guerilla Warfare. 1971. 5.75x o.p. (ISBN 0-210-98169-5). Asia.

Singh, Baljit & Vajpeyi, Dhirendra. Goverment & Politics in India. 130p. (Orig.). 1981. pap. text ed. 8.95 (ISBN 0-86590-006-X). Apt Bks.

--Government & Politics in India. 130p. 1980. text ed. 10.50 (ISBN 0-86590-008-6). Apt Bks.

Singh, Chanan & Dhillon, B. S. Engineering Reliability: New Techniques & Applications. LC 80-18734. (Systems Engineering & Analysis Ser.). 425p. 1981. 36.95 (ISBN 0-471-05014-8, Pub. by Wiley-Interscience). Wiley.

Singh, D. Bright. Inflationary Price Trends in India Since 1939. 2nd ed. 10.00x (ISBN 0-210-33682-X). Asia.

Singh, Darshan, intro. by. Portrait of Perfection: A Pictorial Biography of Kirpal Singh. LC 79-92472. (Illus.). 300p. 1981. 18.00 (ISBN 0-918224-08-X). Sawan Kirpal.

Singh, Devendra. Tulsidas. (National Biography Ser.). (Orig.). 1979. pap. 2.25 (ISBN 0-89744-207-5, Pub. by Natl Bk Trust India). Auromere.

Singh, Devendra & Avery, David D. Physiological Techniques in Behavioral Research. LC 74-82037. 1975. pap. text ed. 8.95x o.p. (ISBN 0-8185-0110-3). Brooks-Cole.

Singh, Devendra, jt. tr. see Thakar, Vimala.

Singh, Elen C. The Spitsbergen Question: United States Foreign Policy, Nineteen Seven to Nineteen Thirty-Five. 237p. 1981. pap. 18.00x (ISBN 8-20001-971-3). Universitet.

Singh, G., tr. see Montale, Eugenio.

Singh, Gopal. Religion of the Sikhs. 1971. 5.50x (ISBN 0-210-22296-4). Asia.

Singh, Harbans. Guru Nanak & the Origins of Sikh Faith. 1970. 10.00x (ISBN 0-210-22311-1). Asia.

Singh, Harnek, jt. auth. see Sharma, K. L.

Singh, I., jt. auth. see Day, R. H.

Singh, I. B., jt. auth. see Reineck, H. E.

Singh, Indera P. & Tiwari, S. C., eds. Man & His Environment. (International Conference of Anthropological & Ethnological Sciences Ser.: No. 10). 299p. 1980. text ed. 18.00x (ISBN 0-391-02140-0). Humanities.

Singh, Indra J. Indian Prison. 1979. text ed. 13.50x (ISBN 0-391-01849-3). Humanities.

Singh, J. Statistical Aids to Railway Operations. 8.75x o.p. (ISBN 0-210-27042-X). Asia.

Singh, J. P. Urban Land Use Planning in Hill Areas: A Case Study of Shillong. 192p. 1980. text ed. 18.00x (ISBN 0-391-02122-2). Humanities.

Singh, Jagjit. Great Ideas & Theories of Modern Cosmology. 1966. pap. text ed. 4.50 (ISBN 0-486-20925-3). Dover.

--Great Ideas in Information Theory, Language & Cybernetics. (Orig.). 1966. pap. text ed. 4.00 (ISBN 0-486-21694-2). Dover.

--Great Ideas of Modern Mathematics. (Illus.). 1959. pap. text ed. 4.00 (ISBN 0-486-20587-8). Dover.

--Great Ideas of Operations Research. (Illus., Orig.). 1968. pap. text ed. 3.50 (ISBN 0-486-21886-4). Dover.

--Memoirs of a Mathematician Manque. 176p. 1980. text ed. 15.00x (ISBN 0-7069-1128-8, Pub. by Vikas India). Advent Bk.

Singh, Jitendra. Management of Scientific Research in India: Administrative Staff College of India Occasional Papers. (Illus.). 311p. 1974. 15.00 o.p. (ISBN 0-88253-485-8). InterCulture.

Singh, John R. A Coronary Experience. 2nd ed. LC 80-82823. (Illus.). 128p. (Orig.). 1980. text ed. 9.95 (ISBN 0-9604672-0-3); pap. text ed. 4.95 (ISBN 0-9604672-1-1). Mid Am Pr.

Singh, Jyoti S. A New International Economic Order: Toward a Fair Redistribution of the World's Resources. LC 76-54508. (Special Studies). 1977. text ed. 20.95 (ISBN 0-275-24170-X). Praeger.

--World Population Policies. LC 78-19756. 1979. 22.95 (ISBN 0-03-044051-3). Praeger.

Singh, K. R. Iran: Quest for Security. 421p. 1980. text ed. 37.50x (ISBN 0-7069-1259-4, Pub. by Vikas India). Advent Bk.

Singh, K. Suresh see Suresh Singh, K.

Singh, Khushwant. A Bride for the Sahib & Other Stories. 168p. 1967. pap. 2.00 (ISBN 0-88253-087-9). Ind-US Inc.

--Indira Gandhi Returns. 1980. 10.00x (ISBN 0-8364-0655-9, Pub. by Vision India). South Asia Bks.

--Train to Pakistan (Mano Majra) LC 80-8920. (YA) (gr. 9 up). 1981. pap. 3.25 (ISBN 0-394-17887-4, B456, BC). Grove.

Singh, Khushwant & Singh, Suneet V. Homage to Guru Gobind Singh. 1970. pap. 2.30 (ISBN 0-88253-088-7). Ind-US Inc.

Singh, Khushwant, tr. see Bedi, Rajinder S.

Singh, Khushwant, tr. see Ruswa, Mirza.

Singh, Kirpal. The Light of Kirpal. LC 80-52537. 496p. 1980. pap. 12.00 (ISBN 0-89142-033-9). Sant Bani Ash.

Singh, M. G. & Titli, A. Systems: Decomposition, Optimisation & Control. 1978. text ed. 90.00 (ISBN 0-08-022150-5); pap. text ed. 28.00 (ISBN 0-08-023238-8). Pergamon.

Singh, M. G., jt. auth. see Titli, A.

Singh, M. G., et al. Applied Industrial Control--an Introduction. (International Ser. on Systems & Control: Vol. 1). (Illus.). 450p. 1980. 52.00 (ISBN 0-08-024764-4); pap. 21.00 (ISBN 0-08-024765-2). Pergamon.

Singh, M. M., et al. Special Agencies in Metropolitan Calcutta. 1968. 6.50x o.p. (ISBN 0-210-27119-1). Asia.

Singh, M. S., tr. see Wright, D.

Singh, Maharaja K. Varied Rhythms. 3.75x o.p. (ISBN 0-210-33791-5). Asia.

Singh, Manju S. The Spice Box: A Vegetarian Indian Cookbook. (Illus.). 224p. 1981. 12.95 (ISBN 0-89594-052-3); pap. 6.95 (ISBN 0-89594-053-1). Crossing Pr.

Singh, Mohinder & Sharma, R. N. A Cummulative Index to Public Administration: Journal of the Royal Institute of Public Administration, Vols. 1-55, 1928-1977, 1979. text ed. 17.50x (ISBN 0-391-01871-X). Humanities.

Singh, N. Human Rights & International Co-Operation. LC 70-904156. 1969. 12.50x (ISBN 0-8002-0907-9). Intl Pubns Serv.

Singh, N. Iqbal. The Andaman Story. (Illus.). 321p. 1978. 20.00x (ISBN 0-7069-0632-2, Pub. by Croom Helm Ltd. England). Biblio Dist.

Singh, Nagendra. Defense Mechanisms of the Modern State. 1964. 30.00x (ISBN 0-210-33832-6). Asia.

Singh, Narindar. Economics & the Crisis of Ecology. 2nd ed. 1979. pap. 3.95x (ISBN 0-19-561078-4). Oxford U Pr.

Singh, Pushpindar. Aircraft of the Indian Air Force, 1933-73. LC 74-903552. (Illus.). 186p. 1974. 21.00x (ISBN 0-8002-0433-6). Intl Pubns Serv.

Singh, R. P., jt. auth. see Heldman, D. R.

Singh, R. R., ed. Social Work Perspectives on Poverty. 1980. text ed. 12.50x (ISBN 0-391-01832-9). Humanities.

Singh, Raghubir, ed. Rajasthan: India's Enchanted Land. 1981. 27.50 (ISBN 0-500-54070-5). Thames Hudson.

Singh, Rudra P., et al. The Bleaching of Pulp. 3rd ed. LC 78-78362. (TAPPI PRESS Bks). (Illus.). 1979. 69.95 (ISBN 0-89852-043-6, 01-02-B043). TAPPI.

Singh, S. K. Development Economics: Theory and Findings. LC 72-1966. (Illus.). 320p. 1975. 23.95 (ISBN 0-669-83626-5). Lexington Bks.

Singh, S. P. Centre-State Relations in Agricultural Development. 1973. 15.00 (ISBN 0-7069-0182-7, Pub. by Vikas India). Advent Bk.

Singh, Sangat, tr. see Nanak, Guru.

Singh, Sheelendra, ed. Bangladesh Documents, 2 vols. 1972. Set. pap. 33.00 set (ISBN 0-8002-0445-X). Intl Pubns Serv.

Singh, Sheila U. Shelley & the Dramatic Form. (Salzburg Studies in English Literature, Romantic Reassessment: No. 1). 1972. pap. text ed. 25.00x (ISBN 0-391-01527-3). Humanities.

Singh, Sohan. Way of Education. 1968. 5.25x o.p. (ISBN 0-210-27171-X). Asia.

Singh, Sukhwant. India's Wars Since Independence: Defence of the Western Front, Vol. II. 350p. 1981. text ed. 35.00 (ISBN 0-7069-1277-2, Pub by Vikas India). Advent Bk.

Singh, Suneet V., jt. auth. see Singh, Khushwant.

Singh, Surendra. Engineering Materials. 2nd rev. ed. 1980. text ed. 12.50x (ISBN 0-7069-0789-2, Pub. by Vikas India). Advent Bk.

--Strength of Materials. 1980. text ed. 18.95x (ISBN 0-7069-0705-1, Pub. by Vikas India). Advent Bk.

Singha, M. M. Municipal Government in the Calcutta Metropolitan District. 4.25x o.p. (ISBN 0-210-27114-0). Asia.

Singha, Rina, jt. auth. see Massey, Reginald.

Singhal, Damodar P. Pakistan. (Modern Nations in Historical Perspective Ser.). (Illus.). 224p. 1972. pap. 2.95 (ISBN 0-13-648469-7, Spec). P-H.

Singhal, Radhey L. see Thomas, John A.

Singletary, Dasie. Parents: The Child's First Piano Teacher. (Illus.). 32p. (gr. k-4). 1980. PLB 5.95 (ISBN 0-89962-042-6). Todd & Honeywell.

Singletary, Ernest E., et al. Law Briefs on Litigation & the Rights of Exceptional Children, Youth, & Adults. 1977. pap. text ed. 16.75x (ISBN 0-8191-0188-5). U Pr of Amer.

Singletary, Milly. Hawaiian Quilting Made Easy. (Illus.). 64p. 1980. pap. 5.00 (ISBN 0-9601256-8-X). Singletary.

Singleton, et al. Business Law: Part Two Syllabus. 1973. pap. text ed. 7.35 (ISBN 0-89420-054-2, 146757); cassette recordings 470.00 (ISBN 0-89420-128-X, 146700). Natl Book.

--Business Law: Part One Syllabus. 1973. pap. text ed. 7.35 (ISBN 0-89420-042-9, 146755); cassette recordings 470.00 (ISBN 0-89420-128-X, 146700). Natl Book.

Singleton, Charles S., ed. see Toynbee, Paget J.

Singleton, Charles S., tr. see Dante Aligieri.

Singleton, Edward B., et al. Radiology of the Alimentary Tract in Infants & Children. LC 75-299. (Monograhs in Clinical Radiology: No. 10). (Illus.). 1977. text ed. 30.00 (ISBN 0-7216-8314-2). Saunders.

Singleton, Esther. The Shakespeare Garden: With Numerous Illustrations from Photographs & Reproductions of Old Wood Cuts. LC 74-8203. 1974. Repr. of 1922 ed. 22.00 (ISBN 0-8103-4048-8). Gale.

Singleton, Fred. Twentieth Century Yugoslavia. 340p. 1976. 22.50x (ISBN 0-231-04016-4); pap. 10.00x (ISBN 0-231-08341-6). Columbia U Pr.

Singleton, Fred, ed. Environmental Misuse in the Soviet Union. LC 75-19823. (Special Studies). (Illus.). 140p. 1976. text ed. 24.95 (ISBN 0-275-56210-7). Praeger.

Singleton, George M. Adventures with Aeneas. (Lat). (gr. 7-9). 1969. 4.95 (ISBN 0-312-00665-9). St Martin.

Singleton, Laurel R., ed. Data Book of Social Studies Materials & Resources, Vol. 6. (Data Bk.). (Orig.). 1981. pap. 10.00 (ISBN 0-89994-254-7). Soc Sci Ed.

Singleton, Mack H., tr. Celestina: A Play in Twenty-One Acts Attributed to Fernando De Rojas. 1958. pap. 7.95 (ISBN 0-299-01774-5). U of Wis Pr.

Singleton, Robert R. You'll Never Get Lost Again. (Illus.). 1979. 9.95 (ISBN 0-87691-294-3); pap. 6.95 (ISBN 0-87691-295-1). Winchester Pr.

Singleton, V. L. see Mrak, E. M. & Stewart, G. F.

Singleton, Val & Gilpin, Arthur. How About Birdwatching. (How About Paperback Ser.). (Illus.). 96p. 1980. pap. 3.95 (ISBN 0-8069-9078-3, Pub. by EP Publishing England). Sterling.

Singleton, Val & Mills, Dick. How About Keeping Fish. (How About Paperback Ser.). 96p. 1980. pap. 3.95 (ISBN 0-8069-9086-4, Pub. by EP Publishing England). Sterling.

Singleton, W. R. & Johansson, E. R. Advanced Accounting Part 1: Syllabus. 1977. pap. text ed. 8.55 (ISBN 0-89420-016-X, 352050); cassette recordings 255.10 (ISBN 0-89420-124-7, 352000). Natl Book.

--Advanced Accounting Part 2: Syllabus. 1977. pap. text ed. 8.55 (ISBN 0-89420-017-8, 352060); cassette recordings 257.20 (ISBN 0-89420-124-7, 352000). Natl Book.

Singleton, W. T., et al, eds. The Analysis of Social Skill. (NATO Conference Ser., Series III, Human Factors: Vol. II). 350p. 1980. 35.00 (ISBN 0-306-40337-4). Plenum Pub.

--Measurement of Man at Work. 1971. 24.00x (ISBN 0-85066-041-6); pap. 16.95x (ISBN 0-85066-071-8). Intl Ideas.

Singmaster, David. Rubik's Cube. 64p. 1981. pap. 5.95 (ISBN 0-89490-043-9). Enslow Pubs.

Sinha, Amarendro N. Law of Citizenship & Aliens in India. 15.00x (ISBN 0-210-33895-4). Asia.

Sinha, B. K., jt. auth. see Pandey, S. N.

Sinha, C. P. Eugene O'neill's Tragic Vision. 1981. text ed. 16.00 (ISBN 0-391-02203-2). Humanities.

Sinha, D. P. Culture Change in an Inter-Tribal Market. 7.50x (ISBN 0-210-27031-4). Asia.

Sinha, Dorothy. Facets. 8.00 (ISBN 0-89253-739-6); flexible cloth 4.80 (ISBN 0-89253-740-X). Ind-US Inc.

Sinha, H. S. Communism & Gita: A Philosophico-Ethical Study. 1979. text ed. 15.50x (ISBN 0-391-01869-8). Humanities.

Sinha, Jai B. The Nurturant Task Leader: A Model of the Effective Executive. 1980. text ed. 11.25x (ISBN 0-391-01823-X). Humanities.

Sinha, Krishna N. Wait Without Hope. (Greenbird Bk.). 1976. flexible bdg. 6.75 (ISBN 0-89253-149-5); flexible bdg. 6.50 (ISBN 0-685-69684-7). Ind-US Inc.

Sinha, M. M. The Impact of Urbanization on Land Use in the Rural-Urban Fringe: A Case Study of Patna. 258p. 1980. text ed. 18.00x (ISBN 0-391-02141-9). Humanities.

Sinha, Phulgenda. Yoga - Meaning, Values & Practice. 1973. pap. 2.50 (ISBN 0-88253-259-6). Ind-US Inc.

Sinha, R. Social Change in Indian Society. 1980. 11.25 (ISBN 0-391-02184-2). Humanities.

Sinha, R. N. & Muir, William E., eds. Grain Storage: Part of a System. (Illus.). 1973. text ed. 35.50 o.p. (ISBN 0-87055-123-X). AVI.

Sinha, Radha & Drabek, Gordon, eds. The World Food Problem: Consensus & Conflict. 1978. text ed. 32.00 (ISBN 0-08-022229-3); pap. text ed. 22.00 (ISBN 0-08-024318-5). Pergamon.

Sinha, S. K. Thackeray: A Study in Technique. (Salzburg Institute for English Literature: Studies in Romantic Reassessment: No. 86). (Orig.). 1979. pap. text ed. 25.00x (ISBN 0-391-01713-6). Humanities.

Sinha, S. K. & Kale, B. K. Life Testing & Reliability Estimation. 1980. 16.95x (ISBN 0-470-26911-1). Halsted Pr.

Sinha, S. N. The Sequential Novels of C.P. Snow: A Study of the Themes of Power & Morality. 242p. 1979. text ed. 15.00 (ISBN 0-8426-1655-1). Verry.

Sinha, Sunita, jt. auth. see Sinha, U.

Sinha, U. & Sinha, Sunita. Cytogenetics: Plant Breeding & Evolution. 1980. text ed. 25.00x (ISBN 0-7069-0469-9, Pub. by Vikas Indig). Advent Bk.

Sinha, U. & Srivastava, S. An Introduction to Bacteria. (Illus.). 180p. Date not set. text ed. 13.95x (ISBN 0-7069-1179-2, Pub. by Vikas India). Advent Bk.

Sinha, V. N., jt. ed. see Mandal, R. B.

Sinick, Daniel. Counselling Older Persons: Careers, Retirement, Dying, Vol.4. Walz, Garry R. & Benjamin, Libby, eds. LC 77-21963. (New Vistas in Counseling Ser.). 1977. 12.95 (ISBN 0-87705-312-X). Human Sci Pr.

Sink, John M. Political Criminal Trials: How to Defend Them. LC 73-89533. 1974. with 1978 rev. pages 40.00 (ISBN 0-87632-103-1). Boardman.

Sinkler, Lorraine. The Alchemy of Awareness. LC 76-62957. 1977. 6.95 o.p. (ISBN 0-06-067387-7, HarpR). Har-Row.

--The Spiritual Journey of Joel Goldsmith. LC 72-13190. 1973. pap. 3.95 o.p. (ISBN 0-06-067388-5, RD 243, HarpR). Har-Row.

Sinkler, Lorraine, ed. see Goldsmith, Joel S.

Sinkovics, Joseph G., jt. auth. see Harris, Jules E.

Sinks, Dwight B., jt. auth. see Tesitor, Irene A.

Sinks, Lucius F., ed. see Symposium, Roswell Park Memorial Institute, Buffalo, Sept. 1974.

Sinkula, jt. auth. see Yalkowsky.

Sinlyavsky, Andrei see Tertz, Abram, pseud.

Sinn, Gerald R. Cash Operations Management: Profit from Within. 1980. 19.00 (ISBN 0-89433-116-7). Petrocelli.

Sinnema, John R. Hendrik van Veldeke. (World Authors Ser.: Netherlands: No. 223). lib. bdg. 10.95 (ISBN 0-8057-2936-4). Twayne.

Sinnett, A. P. Occult World. 9th ed. 1969. 10.25 (ISBN 0-7229-5019-5). Theos Pub Hse.

Sinnett, E. Robert. Crisis Services for Campus & Community: A Handbook for the Volunteer. (Illus.). 260p. 1976. 17.50 (ISBN 0-398-03467-2). C C Thomas.

Sinnhuber, K. A. Germany: Its Geography & Growth. 1972. 14.00 (ISBN 0-7195-1286-7). Transatlantic.

Sinnott, Edmund G. Problem of Organic Form. 1963. 27.50x (ISBN 0-685-69864-5). Elliots Bks.

Sinnott, Loraine T., jt. auth. see Cline, Hugh F.

Sinor, Denis, ed. Studies in Finno-Ugric Linguistics: In Honor of Alo Raun. (Indiana University Uralic & Altaic Ser.: Vol. 131). 440p. 1977. 70.00 (ISBN 0-933070-00-4). Ind U Res Inst.

Sinor, Denis, ed. see Gronbech, Kaare.

Sinor, Denis, ed. see Gronbech, Vilhelm.

Sinor, Denis, ed. see Kwanten, Luc & Hesse, Susan.

Sinor, Denis, ed. see Permanent International Altaistic Conference, Indiana University, 1962.

Sinor, John. Small Escapes Under the Sun. 1981. pap. 4.95 (ISBN 0-935572-10-4). Alive Pubns.

Sinsberg, A. Mushroom in the Rain. LC 72-92438. (Illus.). 32p. (gr. k-2). 1974. 5.95g (ISBN 0-685-38979-0); PLB 8.95 (ISBN 0-02-736240-X). Macmillan.

Sinsheimer. The Book of Life. 1976. 1.50 (ISBN 0-201-07026-X). A-W.

Sinski, James T. Dermatophytes in Human Skin, Hair & Nails. (American Lectures in Clinical Microbiology Ser.). (Illus.). 64p. 1974. text ed. 10.75 (ISBN 0-398-03102-9). C C Thomas.

Sioli, P., ed. History of el Dorado County, California. facsimile ed. 272p. Repr. of 1883 ed. quarto 35.00. Holmes.

Sipay, Edward R., jt. auth. see Harris, Albert J.

Sipes, D. C. Bridgeport: First Hundred Years, 1873-1973. 8.95 (ISBN 0-685-48791-1). Nortex Pr.

Sipes, Richard G. Population Growth, Society & Culture: An Inventory of Cross-Culturally Tested Causal Hypotheses. LC 80-81242. (Comparative Studies Ser.). 1981. 12.00x (ISBN 0-87536-337-7); pap. 6.00 (ISBN 0-87536-338-5). HRAFP.

Sipes, Robert. Fast Freeze or Slow Squeeze. LC 80-51885. 1980. 8.95 (ISBN 0-533-04731-5). Vantage.

Sipherd, Ray. The Count's Poem. (Illus.). (gr. k-1). 1978. PLB 4.77 (ISBN 0-307-68653-1, Whitman). Western Pub.

--Ernie's Telephone Call. (Tell-a-Tale Readers). (Illus.). (gr. k-2). 1978. PLB 4.77 (ISBN 0-307-68652-3, Whitman). Western Pub.

Siposs, Allan J. Exporting: Practical Handbook for Entrepreneurs & Managers. rev. ed. (Illus.). 103p. (Orig.). 1978. pap. 25.00x (ISBN 0-935402-01-2). Intl Comm Serv.

--Importing: Practical Tips & Ideas. (Illus.). 1979. 25.00x (ISBN 0-686-59709-5). Intl Comm Serv.

Siposs, George G. Building & Racing Radio Control Cars & Motorcycles. Angle, Burr, ed. LC 80-84853. (Illus.). 80p. (Orig.). 1981. pap. price not set (ISBN 0-89024-556-8). Kalmbach.

Sipowicz, A. Edwin, tr. see Graham, Billy.

Sipowicz, Edwin, tr. see Palau, Luis.

Sipowicz, Edwin, tr. see Warren, Max.

Sippl, Charles J. & Dahl, Fred. Vider-Computers: How to Select, Mix, & Operate Personal Computers & Home Video Equipment. (Illus.). 256p. 1980. 15.95 (ISBN 0-13-941856-3, Spec); pap. 7.95 (ISBN 0-13-941849-0). P-H.

Sippl, Charles J. & Sippl, Roger J. Computer Dictionary. 3rd ed. LC 79-91696. 1980. pap. 12.95 (ISBN 0-672-21652-3, 21652). Sams.

--Computer Dictionary & Handbook. 3rd ed. LC 79-67133. 1980. text ed. 29.95 (ISBN 0-672-21632-9, 21632). Sams.

Sippl, Charles J., jt. auth. see Mayer, JoAnne C.

Sippl, Charles J., jt. auth. see Miller, Merl K.

Sippl, Charles J., jt. auth. see Schmalz, Larry C.

Sippl, Roger J., jt. auth. see Sippl, Charles J.

Sipple, M. Noel, jt. auth. see Seyler, Dorothy U.

Sipple, Thomas S., ed. see Klausmeier, Herbert J.

Sippy, Francis H., jt. auth. see Langland, Olaf E.

SIPRI. Chemical Weapons: Destruction & Conversion. LC 80-13956. 1980. pap. 19.50x (ISBN 0-8448-1349-4). Crane-Russak Co.

--Internationalization to Prevent the Spread of Nuclear Weapons. LC 80-14962. 220p. 1980. 24.50x (ISBN 0-8448-1378-8). Crane-Russak Co.

--The NPT: The Main Political Barrier to Nuclear Weapon Proliferation. LC 80-16984. 1980. pap. 8.95x (ISBN 0-8448-1380-X). Crane-Russak Co.

--Strategic Disarmament: Verification & National Security. LC 77-85318. 1977. 19.50x (ISBN 0-8448-1227-7). Crane-Russak Co.

--World Armaments & Disarmament: SIPRI Yearbook 1980. 1980. 49.50x (ISBN 0-8448-1375-3). Crane-Russak Co.

--World Armaments & Disarmament: SIPRI Yearbooks 1968-1979 Cumulative Index. LC 80-65479. 90p. 1980. 16.50x (ISBN 0-8448-1348-6). Crane-Russak Co.

Sir Ronald Prain Mining Journal Books Ltd. Copper: The Anatomy of an Industry. 300p. 1980. 20.25x (ISBN 0-900117-07-9, Pub. by Mining Journal England). State Mutual Bk.

Siracusa, Carl. A Mechanical People: Perceptions of the Industrial Order in Massachusetts, 1815-1880. LC 78-26715. 1979. 22.50x (ISBN 0-8195-5029-9, Pub. by Wesleyan U Pr). Columbia U Pr.

Siracusa, Joseph, jt. auth. see Laurenti, Joseph L.

Siracusa, Joseph M. The American Diplomatic Revolution: A Documentary History of the Cold War, 1941-1947. LC 76-54281. (National University Publications Ser. in American Studies). 1977. 12.50 (ISBN 0-8046-9174-6); pap. 6.95 (ISBN 0-8046-9180-0). Kennikat.

--New Left Diplomatic Histories & Historians: The American Revisionists. LC 73-75575. (National University Publications). 1973. 12.00 (ISBN 0-8046-9037-5). Kennikat.

Siracusa, Joseph M. & St. John, Barclay. The Impact of the Cold War: Reconsiderations. 12.50 (ISBN 0-8046-9158-4); pap. text ed. 6.95 (ISBN 0-8046-9182-7). Kennikat.

Siraisi, Nancy G. Taddeo Alderotti & His Pupils: Two Generations of Italian Medical Learning. LC 80-7554. 488p. 1981. 32.00x (ISBN 0-691-05313-8). Princeton U Pr.

Sirc, L. Outline of International Finance: Exchange Rates & Payments Between Countries. LC 74-3259. 1974. 14.95 (ISBN 0-470-79325-2). Halsted Pr.

Sircar, D. C. Grammar of the Prakrit Language. 2nd rev. ed. 6.50 (ISBN 0-89684-209-6). Orient Bk Dist.

Sircom, Geoffrey, tr. see Hediger, H.

Sircus, Wilfred & Smith, Adam N. Scientific Foundations of Gastroenterology. LC 80-5260. (Illus.). 650p. 1980. 90.00 (ISBN 0-7216-8319-3). Saunders.

Sire, James W. Jeremiah, Meet the Twentieth Century. LC 74-31846. 120p. 1975. pap. 2.50 o.p. (ISBN 0-87784-641-3). Inter-Varsity.

--Scripture Twisting: Twenty Ways the Cults Misread the Bible. LC 80-19309. 216p. (Orig.). 1980. pap. 4.95 (ISBN 0-87784-611-1). Inter-Varsity.

Siren, Osvald. History of Early Chinese Art, 4 vols. in 2. LC 74-78362. (Illus.). 1970. Repr. of 1929 ed. 150.00 o.p. (ISBN 0-87817-036-7). Hacker.

Sirico, Louis J., Jr. How to Talk Back to the Telephone Company: Playing Tthe Telephone Game to Win. pap. 20.00 (ISBN 0-9603466-0-0). NCCB.

Sirkin, Gerald, ed. Lexeconics: The Interaction of Law & Economics. (Social Dimensions of Economics, CCNY Ser.: Vol. 2). 272p. 1981. lib. bdg. 17.50 (ISBN 0-89838-053-7, Pub. by Martinus Nijhoff). Kluwer Boston.

Sirkin, Gerald, jt. ed. see Leiter, Robert D.

Sirkis, Susan B. Fashioning Miniatures - One More Time. (Wish Booklets: Vol. 23). (Illus.). 52p. 1980. pap. 5.50x (ISBN 0-913786-23-3). Wish Bklets.

--Men's Fashions: 1860-1970. (Wish Booklets Ser: Vol. 21). (Illus.). 52p. 1978. pap. 5.50x (ISBN 0-913786-21-7). Wish Bklets.

--La Petite Bebe Eighteen Eighty Three to Eighteen Eighty-Seven, Vol.2. (The Wish Booklets). 48p. 1973. pap. 5.50x (ISBN 0-913786-11-X). Wish Bklets.

Sirmans, C. F. & Jaffe, Austin J. Complete Real Estate Investment Handbook. (Illus.). 272p. 1981. 17.95 (ISBN 0-13-162321-4, Spectrum); pap. 8.95 (ISBN 0-13-162313-3). P-H.

Sirohi, R. S. Mechanical Measurements. LC 80-27233. 210p. 1981. 13.95 (ISBN 0-470-27107-8). Halsted Pr.

Siropolis, Nicholas C. Small Business Management: A Guide to Entrepreneurship. LC 76-13799. (Illus.). 1977. text ed. 17.95 (ISBN 0-395-24475-7); inst. manual 2.25 (ISBN 0-395-24476-5). HM.

Sirota, David. Essentials of Real Estate. (Illus.). 304p. 1980. ref. ed. 19.95; pap. 16.95 (ISBN 0-8359-1776-2). Reston.

--Essentials of Real Estate Finance. 2nd ed. 424p. 1979. pap. 22.95 (ISBN 0-88462-265-7). Real Estate Ed Co.

Sirota, Mike. Master of Boranga. (Ro-Lan Ser.: No. 1). 320p. (Orig.). 1980. pap. 1.95 (ISBN 0-89083-616-7). Zebra.

--The Shrouded Walls of Boranga. (Ro-Lan Ser.: No. 2). 304p. (Orig.). 1980. pap. 1.95 (ISBN 0-89083-677-9). Zebra.

--The Twentieth Son of Ornon. (Orig.). 1980. pap. 1.95 (ISBN 0-89083-685-X). Zebra.

Sirrocco, Al. Employees in Nursing Homes: National Nursing Home Survey, 1977. Cox, Klaudia, ed. (Ser. Fourteen: No. 25). 50p. 1981. pap. text ed. 1.50 (ISBN 0-8406-0213-8). Natl Ctr Health Stats.

Sirrocco, Al & Koch, Hugo. Nursing Homes in Profile: National Nursing Home Survey, 1973-74. (Ser. 14). 1976. pap. 1.50 (ISBN 0-8406-0084-4). Natl Ctr Health Stats.

--Nursing Homes in the United States: 1973-74 National Nursing Home Survey. Rutherford, Margaret, ed. (Ser. 14: No. 17). 1977. pap. 1.50 (ISBN 0-8406-0097-6). Natl Ctr Health Stats.

Sisam, Kenneth, ed. Fourteenth Century Prose & Verse. (Smith, D. N., Ser). 1921. pap. 13.50x (ISBN 0-19-871093-3). Oxford U Pr.

Sisco, John I., jt. auth. see Koehler, Jerry W.

Sisemore, J. T. Practiquemos la Visitacion. Gonzalez, Ananias, ed. Grijalva, Josue, tr. Orig. Title: The Ministry of Visitation. 1979. 1.95 (ISBN 0-311-11034-7). Casa Bautista.

Sisk, B. F. A Congressional Record: The Memoir of Bernie Sisk. Dickman, A. I., ed. LC 80-84208. (Illus.). 280p. 1980. 20.00 (ISBN 0-914330-36-5). Panorama West.

Siskin, Bernard R., jt. auth. see Johnson, Rodney D.

Siskind, Charles S. Electrical Circuits. 2nd ed. 1965. text ed. 17.95 o.p. (ISBN 0-07-057744-7, G). McGraw.

Siskind, Janet. To Hunt in the Morning. LC 73-82674. (Illus.). 224p. 1975. pap. 5.95 (ISBN 0-19-501891-5, GB430, GB). Oxford U Pr.
Sisler, M. David, Jr. Finished. 1978. pap. 2.50 (ISBN 0-87148-333-5). Pathway Pr.
Sisley, Emily. The Novel Writers. LC 80-81487. 78p. (Orig.). 1980. pap. 2.95 (ISBN 0-934696-01-2). Mosaic Pr.
Sissman, L. E. Innocent Bystander: Scene from the Seventies. LC 75-25144. 1975. 7.95 (ISBN 0-8149-0769-5). Vanguard.
Sisson. Sisson's Word & Expression Locater. 12.95 (ISBN 0-13-810671-1). P-H.
Sisson, A. F. Unabridged Crossword Puzzle Dictionary. 1963. 6.95 (ISBN 0-385-02843-1); thumb-indexed edition 8.95 (ISBN 0-385-01350-7). Doubleday.
Sisson, Barb. Elevation Sea Level. LC 79-67521. 1981. 5.95 (ISBN 0-533-04473-1). Vantage.
Sisson, C. H. The Case of Walter Bagehot. 140p. 1972. text ed. 10.50x (ISBN 0-571-09501-1). Humanities.
Sisson, C. H., ed. see Swift, Jonathan.
Sisson, C. J. The Boar's Head Theatre: An Inn-Yard Theatre of the Elizabethan Age. (Illus.). 1972. 15.00x (ISBN 0-7100-7252-X). Routledge & Kegan.
Sisson, Charles A. Tax Burdens in American Agriculture: An Intersectoral Comparison. 1981. write for info. (ISBN 0-8138-1680-7). Iowa St U Pr.
Sisson, James E. & Martens, Robert W. Jack London First Editions. LC 78-63374. (Illus.). 1978. 24.50 (ISBN 0-932458-00-9). Star Rover.
Sisson, Jim, ed. see London, Jack.
Sisson, Joseph A. Handbook of Clinical Pathology. LC 75-21273. (Illus.). 1976. pap. text ed. 21.50 o.p. (ISBN 0-397-50346-6). Lippincott.
Sisson, Keith. Industrial Relations in Fleet Street. 1975. 17.50x o.p. (ISBN 0-631-16530-4, Pub. by Basil Blackwell). Biblio Dist.
Sisson, Richard. The Congress Party in Rajasthan: Political Integration & Institution-Building in an Indian State. LC 70-129607. (Center for South & Southeast Asia Studies, UC Berkeley). 1972. 24.50x (ISBN 0-520-01808-7). U of Cal Pr.
Sisson, Rosemary A. Will in Love. (gr. 7 up). 1977. 9.25 (ISBN 0-688-22107-6); lib. bdg. 8.88 (ISBN 0-688-32107-0). Morrow.
Sissons, J. B. see Bowen, D. Q.
Sister Incarnata Marie. Nuclear Mysteries: Or Creation of the Parent Atoms. 1980. 9.95 (ISBN 0-533-03850-2). Vantage.
Sister Jean Daniel. Our Family Prepares for Mass. Orig. Title: Tomorrow Is Sunday. (Illus.). 216p. 1980. pap. 6.95 (ISBN 0-03-057842-6). Winston Pr.
Sit, Amy. Sing It! 1979. pap. 2.95 (ISBN 0-917726-39-1). Hunter Bks.
Sitchin, Zecharia. The Stairway to Heaven. 384p. 1981. 17.95 (ISBN 0-312-75505-8). St Martin.
SITE. Architecture As Art. (Illus.). 112p. 1981. pap. 14.95 (ISBN 0-312-04814-9). St Martin.
Sitenko, A. G. Fluctuations & Non-Linear Wave Interactions in Plasmas. Kocherga, O. D., tr. (International Series in Natural Philosophy: Vol. 107). (Illus.). 250p. 1981. 42.00 (ISBN 0-08-025051-3). Pergamon.
--Lectures in Scattering Theory. Shepherd, P. J., ed. & tr. 280p. 1972. text ed. 34.00 (ISBN 0-08-016574-5). Pergamon.
Sitenko, A. G. & Tartakovsky, V. K. Lectures on the Theory of the Nucleus. LC 74-10827. 312p. 1975. text ed. 37.00 (ISBN 0-08-017876-6). Pergamon.
Sites, George L. Boater's Guide to Biscayne Bay: Miami to Jewfish Creek. LC 75-173322. (Illus.). 1971. spiral bdg. 3.95 (ISBN 0-87024-233-4). U of Miami Pr.
Sith, Craig & Skjei, Eric. Getting Grants: A Creative Guide to the Grants System: How to Find Funders, Write Convincing Proposals, & Make Your Grants Work. LC 78-20187. 288p. pap. 4.95 (ISBN 0-06-090834-3, CN 834, CN). Har-Row.
Sithole, Ndabaningi. African Nationalism. 2nd ed. LC 68-133467. (Illus.). 1968. 10.50x (ISBN 0-19-215631-4); pap. 3.95x (ISBN 0-19-501053-1). Oxford U Pr.
Sitkoff, Harvard. A New Deal for Blacks: The Emergence of Civil Rights As a National Issue; the Depression Decade. 412p. 1981. pap. 6.95 (ISBN 0-19-502893-7, GB 627, OPB). Oxford U Pr.
--The Struggle for Black Equality, Nineteen Fifty-Four to Nineteen Eighty. Forer, Eric, ed. 1981. 10.95; pap. 4.95. FS&G.
--The Struggle for Black Equality, Nineteen Fifty-Four to Nineteen Eighty. Foner, Eric, ed. 1981. 10.95 (ISBN 0-8090-8925-4); pap. 4.95 (ISBN 0-8090-0144-6). Hill & Wang.
Sitney, P. Adams, ed. The Essential Cinema: Essays on Films in The Collection of Anthology Film Archives. LC 74-10371. (Anthology Film Archives Series). 380p. 1975. 20.00x (ISBN 0-8147-7767-8); pap. 9.00x (ISBN 0-8147-7768-6). NYU Pr.
Sitnick & Rushmer. Parent -Infant Communication. 250p. 1977. 29.95 (ISBN 0-86575-035-1). Dormac.
Sitomer, Harry & Sitomer, Mindel. Zero Is Not Nothing. LC 77-11562. (A Young Math Book). (gr. 1-3). 1978. PLB 7.89 (ISBN 0-690-03829-1, TYC-J). T Y Crowell.
Sitomer, Harry, jt. auth. see Sitomer, Mindel.
Sitomer, Mindel & Sitomer, Harry. Circles. LC 71-113856. (Young Math Ser.). (Illus.). (gr. 1-4). 1971. 6.95 (ISBN 0-690-19430-7, TYC-J); PLB 7.89 (ISBN 0-690-19431-5). T Y Crowell.
--How Did Numbers Begin? LC 75-11756. (Young Math Ser.). (Illus.). 40p. (gr. k-3). 1976. 7.89 (ISBN 0-690-00794-9, TYC-J). T Y Crowell.
--Spirals. LC 73-9874. (Young Math Ser.). (Illus.). (gr. 1-5). 1974. 7.89 (ISBN 0-690-00180-0, TYC-J). T Y Crowell.
Sitomer, Mindel, jt. auth. see Sitomer, Harry.
Sittig, M. How to Remove Pollutants & Toxic Materials from Air & Water: A Practical Guide. LC 77-71309. (Pollution Technology Review Ser.: No. 32). (Illus.). 1977. 48.00 o.p. (ISBN 0-8155-0654-6). Noyes.
--Pollution Detection & Monitoring Handbook. LC 74-75905. (Environmental Technology Handbook Ser: No. 1). (Illus.). 401p. 1974. 36.00 o.p. (ISBN 0-8155-0529-9). Noyes.
Sittig, Marshall. Organic & Polymer Waste Reclaiming Encyclopedia. LC 80-26007. (Chem. Tech. Rev. 180 Ser.: Pollution Tech. Rev. 73). (Illus.). 512p. 1981. 54.00 (ISBN 0-8155-0832-8). Noyes.
Sittig, Marshall, ed. Metal & Inorganic Waste Reclaiming Encyclopedia. LC 80-21669. (Pollution Tech. Rev. 70; Chem. Tech. Rev. 175). (Illus.). 591p. (Orig.). 1981. 54.00 (ISBN 0-8155-0823-9). Noyes.
--Pesticide Manufacturing & Toxic Materials Control Encyclopedia. LC 80-19373. (Chemical Tech. Rev. 168; Env. Health Rev. 3; Pollution Tech. Rev. 69). (Illus.). 810p. 1981. 96.00 (ISBN 0-8155-0814-X). Noyes.
--Priority Toxic Pollutants: Health Impacts & Allowable Limits. LC 80-311. (Environmental Health Review Ser.: No. 1). 370p. 1980. 54.00 (ISBN 0-8155-0797-6). Noyes.
Sittl, jt. auth. see Von Kardoff.
Sittler, Joseph. Ecology of Faith. LC 61-10278. 112p. 1970. pap. 0.50 (ISBN 0-8006-1882-3, 1-1882). Fortress.
Sittler, Joseph A. Grace Notes & Other Fragments. Herhold, Robert M. & Delloff, Linda M., eds. LC 80-8055. 128p. (Orig.). 1981. pap. 5.50 (ISBN 0-8006-1404-6, 1-1404). Fortress.
Sitwell, Edith. Bath. LC 78-14145. (Illus.). 1981. Repr. of 1932 ed. 26.00 (ISBN 0-88355-818-1). Hyperion Conn.
--Collected Poems. LC 67-31053. 1954. 15.00 (ISBN 0-8149-0203-0). Vanguard.
--Edith Sitwell: Selected Letters 1919-1964. LC 72-134662. 1970. 12.50 (ISBN 0-8149-0678-8). Vanguard.
--Music & Ceremonies. LC 63-13788. 1963. 6.95 (ISBN 0-8149-0205-7). Vanguard.
Sitwell, Nigel. The Roman Roads of Europe. (Illus.). 240p. 1981. 35.00 (ISBN 0-312-69080-0). St Martin.
Sitwell, Osbert. Left Hand, Right Hand. 7.00 (ISBN 0-8446-2949-9). Peter Smith.
Sitwell, Sacheverell. The Netherlands. 1974. 24.00 (ISBN 0-7134-2779-5, Pub. by Batsford England). David & Charles.
Sitzman, Marion. Indomitable Irishery: Paul Vincent Carroll: Study & Interviews. (Salzburg Studies in English Literature, Romantic Reassessment Ser.: No. 29). (Illus.). 180p. 1975. pap. text ed. 25.00x (ISBN 0-391-01528-1). Humanities.
Siu, Bobby. Women of China in Struggle. 240p. 1981. text ed. 18.95 (ISBN 0-905762-58-4, Pub. by Zed Pr); pap. text ed. 8.50 (ISBN 0-905762-63-0). Lawrence Hill.
Siu, R. G. The Master Manager. LC 80-13390. 341p. 1980. 17.50 (ISBN 0-471-07961-8). Wiley.
Siu, Ralph G. Transcending the Power Game: The Way to Executive Serenity. LC 79-25299. 1980. 14.95 (ISBN 0-471-06001-1, Pub. by Wiley-Interscience). Wiley.
Siuchninski, Mateusz. An Illustrated History of Poland. Tarnowski, Stanislaw, tr. from Pol. LC 80-460137. (Illus.). 228p. 1979. 13.50x (ISBN 0-8002-2293-8). Intl Pubns Serv.
Sivachev, Kolai V. & Yakovlev, Nikolai N. Russia & the United States. Titelbaum, Olga A., tr. LC 78-10554. xvi, 303p. 1980. pap. 5.95 (ISBN 0-226-76150-9, P902, Phoen). U of Chicago Pr.
Sivam, Avraham J. & Ikeda, Yutaka. Useful Expressions in Chinese. (Useful Expressions Ser.). 64p. (Orig.). 1981. pap. 1.50 (ISBN 0-86628-023-5). Ridgefield Pub.
Sivan, Avraham J. & Ikeda, Yutakada, eds. Useful Expressions in Japanese. (Useful Expressions Ser.). (Illus.). 64p. (Orig.). 1980. pap. 1.50 (ISBN 0-86628-011-1). Ridgefield Pub.
Sivan, Raphael, jt. auth. see Kwakernaak, Huibert.
Sivananda, Swami. Practice of Karma Yoga. 1974. 5.00 (ISBN 0-8426-0675-0); pap. 3.50 (ISBN 0-686-67764-1). Orient Bk Dist.
--Sadhana. 1978. 15.95 (ISBN 0-89684-345-9); pap. 11.50 (ISBN 0-89684-311-4). Orient Bk Dist.
Sivananda Radha, Swami. Kundalini Yoga for the West. LC 78-1857. (Illus.). 1978. 24.95 (ISBN 0-931454-01-8). Timeless Bks.
Sivaram, M. Death & Nachiketas. 192p. 1981. text ed. 15.00x (ISBN 0-7069-1284-5, Pub by Vikas India). Advent Bk.
Sivaramakrishnan, R. Principles & Applications of Electricity. 1967. pap. 10.00x (ISBN 0-210-22551-3). Asia.
Sivaramamurti, C. Album of Indian Sculpture. (Illus.). 1979. pap. 10.00 (ISBN 0-89744-194-X). Auromere.
Sive, Mary R. Selecting Instructional Media: A Guide to Audiovisual & Other Instructional Media Lists. 2nd ed. LC 77-27278. 1978. lib. bdg. 18.50x (ISBN 0-87287-181-9). Libs Unl.
Sive, Mary R., ed. Environmental Legislation: A Sourcebook. LC 75-61. 1976. text ed. 42.95 (ISBN 0-275-05470-5). Praeger.
Siver, Edward W. A Management Guide to Casualty & Property Insurance. 1981. write for info. (ISBN 0-87251-049-2). Crain Bks.
SI Version, ed. see Meriam, J. L.
Siverstone, Lou & Rickard, Jack. A Mad Look at the Future. (Mad Ser.). (Illus., Orig.). 1978. pap. 1.50 (ISBN 0-446-88174-0). Warner Bks.
Sivetz, Michael & Desrosier, Norman W. Coffee Technology. (Illus.). 1979. lib. bdg. 56.00 (ISBN 0-87055-269-4). AVI.
Sixth International Congress on Biblical Studies, Oxford, 3-7 April 1978. Studia Biblica Nineteen Seventy-Eight, I: Papers on Old Testament & Related Themes. Livingstone, E. A., ed. 272p. 1979. text ed. 36.95x (ISBN 0-905774-16-7, Pub. by JSOT Pr England); pap. text ed. 23.95x (ISBN 0-905774-17-5). Eisenbrauns.
Siy, jt. auth. see Bennett.
Sizemore, Chris C. & Pittillo, Elen S. I'm Eve. 1978. pap. 2.25 (ISBN 0-515-04656-6). Jove Pubns.
Sizemore, Helen. Teaching with Flannelgraph. (Illus.). 48p. 1976. pap. 1.75 (ISBN 0-87239-074-8, 3280). Standard Pub.
Sizer, Nancy F. & Rudd, Rebecca S. China: A Brief History. (Illus.). 210p. (Orig.). (gr. 9-12). 1979. pap. text ed. 4.50x (ISBN 0-88334-119-0). Ind Sch Pr.
Sizer, T., ed. see Trumbull, John.
Sjeklocha, Paul & Mead, Igor. Unofficial Art in the Soviet Union. (Illus.). 1967. 27.50x (ISBN 0-520-01181-3). U of Cal Pr.
Sjo, John. Economics for Agriculturalists: A Beginning Text in Agricultural Economics. LC 75-26011. (Agricultural Economics Ser.). 1976. text ed. 17.95 o.p. (ISBN 0-88244-072-1). Grid Pub.
Sjoback, H. Psychoanalytic Theory of Defensive Processes. 1973. 14.95 (ISBN 0-470-79370-8). Halsted Pr.
Sjoberg, Gideon, jt. ed. see Hancock, M. Donald.
Sjoberg, Leif. Columbia Essays on Modern Writers, No. 74: Par Lagerkvist. 1976. pap. 2.00 (ISBN 0-231-03103-3). Columbia U Pr.
Sjoberg, Leif, tr. see Lundkvist, Artur.
Sjoeqvist, Erik. Sicily & the Greeks: Studies in the Interrelationship between the Indigenous Populations & the Greek Colonists. LC 79-163625. (Jerome Lecture Ser: No. 9). (Illus.). 1972. 10.00x o.p. (ISBN 0-472-08795-9). U of Mich Pr.
Sjogren, Clifford F. Diversity, Accessibility & Quality: A Brief Introduction to American Education for Non-Americans. (Illus., Orig.). 1977. pap. 2.00 o.p. (ISBN 0-87447-036-6, 221620). College Bd.
Sjogren, Per-Olof. The Jesus Prayer. Linton, Sydney, tr. from Swedish. LC 75-18789. 96p. 1975. pap. 3.50 (ISBN 0-8006-1216-7, 1-1216). Fortress.
Sjoman, Vilgot. Diary with Ingmar Bergman. 243p. 1978. 9.95 (ISBN 0-89720-015-2, L136); pap. 5.50 (ISBN 0-89720-016-0). Karoma.
--I Am Curious (Yellow) 1969. pap. 1.75 (ISBN 0-394-17133-0, B184, BC). Grove.
Sjoquist, David L., jt. auth. see Schroeder, Larry D.
Sjoqvist, Folke & Tottie, Malcolm, eds. Abuse of Central Stimulants. LC 72-116704. (Illus.). 1969. 13.50 (ISBN 0-911216-28-6). Raven.
Sjostedt, Gunnar. The External Role of the European Community. 1977. 24.95 (ISBN 0-566-00172-1, 01455-9, Pub. by Saxon Hse England). Lexington Bks.
Sjostrand, Fritiof S. Electron Microscopy of Cells & Tissues. Vol. 1, 1967. 50.50, by subscription 41.00 (ISBN 0-12-647550-4). Acad Pr.
Sjostrand, Sven-Erik, jt. auth. see Westerlund, Gunnar.
Sjothun, I. J., jt. ed. see Alliger, G.
Sjovold, Thorleif. The Iron Age Settlement of Arctic Norway, Vol. II. 1974. pap. text ed. 27.00x (ISBN 82-00-06157-4, Dist. by Columbia U Pr). Universitet.
Sjowall, Maj & Wahloo, Per. The Laughing Policeman. 1977. pap. 1.65 (ISBN 0-394-72341-4, Vin). Random.
Sjurzynski, Gloria. Honest Andrew. (Let-Me-Read Ser.). (Illus.). (gr. k-3). 1980. pap. 1.95 (ISBN 0-15-642152-6, VoyB). HarBraceJ.
Skaare, Kolbjorn. Coins & Coinage in Viking-Age Norway. 1976. 36.00x (ISBN 8-200-01542-4, Dist. by Columbia U Pr). Universitet.
Skadden, Donald H. A New Tax Structure for the United States. LC 77-29249. (Key Issues Lecture Ser). 1978. 11.50 (ISBN 0-672-97222-0); pap. 5.50 (ISBN 0-672-97223-9). Bobbs.
Skaer, R. J., jt. auth. see Grimstone, A. V.
Skager, R. & Dave, Ravindra H. Curriculum Evaluation for Lifelong Education. 1977. text ed. 19.50 (ISBN 0-08-021816-4); pap. 9.00 o.p. (ISBN 0-08-021817-2). Pergamon.
Skagestad, Peter. Making Sense of History. 1975. pap. text ed. 10.50 (ISBN 8-200-01460-6, Dist. by Columbia U Pr). Universitet.
--The Road of Inquiry: C. S. Pierce's Pragmatic Realism. LC 80-25278. 296p. 1981. 20.00x (ISBN 0-231-05004-6). Columbia U Pr.
Skaife, Sydney H. African Insect Life. 2nd ed. Ledger, John, ed. (Illus.). 1980. 35.00 o.p. (ISBN 0-684-16335-7, ScribT). Scribner.
Skal, David J., ed. Graphic Commmunications for the Performing Arts. (Illus.). 200p. (Orig.). 1981. pap. 10.95x (ISBN 0-930452-11-9, Pub. by Theatre Comm). Pub Ctr Cult Res.
Skal, David J. & Finnegan, Michael, eds. Theatre Profiles Four: A Resource Book on Nonprofit Professional Theatres in the United States. rev. ed. (Illus.). 288p. 1979. pap. 12.95 (ISBN 0-930452-01-1, Pub. by Theatre Comm). Pub Ctr Cult Res.
--Theatre Profiles-Four: Resource Book of Nonprofit Professional Theatres in the United States. (Illus.). 276p. (Orig.). 1980. pap. 12.95x (ISBN 0-930452-07-0, Pub. by Theatre Comm). Pub Ctr Cult Res.
Skalka, Patricia. Skiing the Midwest. 1978. 14.95 o.p. (ISBN 0-8092-7610-0); pap. 7.95 (ISBN 0-8092-7609-7). Contemp Bks.
Skalka, Patricia, ed. see Gibson, Karon W., et al.
Skamene, Emil, ed. Genetic Control of Natural Resistance to Infection & Malignancy. (Perspectives in Immunology Ser.). 1980. 33.00 (ISBN 0-12-647680-2). Acad Pr.
Skandalakis, John E., jt. auth. see Gray, Stephen W.
Skard, Sigmund. American Myth & the European Mind: American Studies in Europe, 1776-1960. LC 61-15199. 1961. 7.00x o.p. (ISBN 0-8122-7323-0). U of Pa Pr.
--Classical Tradition in Norway. 204p. 1980. pap. 20.00x (ISBN 8-20001-972-1). Universitet.
--Trans-Atlantica: Memoirs of a Norwegian Americanist. 1978. 20.50x (ISBN 82-00-05224-9, Dist. by Columbia U Pr.). Universitet.
Skard, Sigmund, jt. auth. see Hollander, A. N.
Skarda, Patricia L. & Jaffe, Nora C. The Evil Image: Two Centuries of Gothic Short Fiction & Poetry. (Illus.). 1981. pap. 7.95 (ISBN 0-452-00549-3, F549, Meridan Bks). NAL.
Skardon, Mary A., ed. Yester Year in Clark County, Ohio, 2 vols. in one. (Annual Monograph Ser.). 76p. (Repr. of 1947 & 1948 eds.). 1978. pap. 3.00. Clark County Hist Soc.
Skeat, W. W., ed. see Milton, John.
Skeat, Walter W. Ryme Index to the Manuscript Texts of Chaucer's Minor Poems. 1887. 40.00 (ISBN 0-8274-3318-2). R West.
Skeat, Walter W., ed. Concise Etymological Dictionary of the English Language. 1911. 19.95x (ISBN 0-19-863105-7). Oxford U Pr.
--Etymological Dictionary of the English Language. rev. & enl. ed. 1910. 58.00x (ISBN 0-19-863104-9). Oxford U Pr.
Skeat, Walter W., ed. see Chaucer, Geoffrey.
Sked, Alan. The Survival of the Habsburg Empire: Radetzky, the Imperial Army & the Class War, 1848. (Illus.). 289p. 1979. lib. bdg. 35.00 (ISBN 0-582-50711-1). Longman.
Skedgell, Marian, ed. see Borges, Jorge L.
Skee, Stanley, jt. auth. see Chaney, Charles.
Skeen, C. Edward, ed. Description of Louisiana by Thomas Jefferys: From His "Natural & Civil History of the French Dominions in North & South America". (Mississippi Valley Collection Bulletin, No. 6). (Illus.). 50p. 1973. pap. 5.95x facsimile ed. (ISBN 0-87870-082-X). Memphis St Univ.
Skees, William D. Computer Software for Data Communications: An Introduction for Programmers. LC 80-24266. 190p. 1981. text ed. 21.00 (ISBN 0-534-97979-3). Lifetime Learn.
Skehel, J. J., jt. ed. see Carlile, M. J.
Skeist, I., jt. ed. see Schildknecht, C. E.

Skelcher, Derek. Word Processing Equipment Survey. 222p. (Orig.). 1980. pap. 125.00x (ISBN 0-903796-56-2, Pub. by Online Conferences England). Renouf.

Skelland, A. H. Diffusional Mass Transfer. LC 73-12976. 510p. 1974. 45.00 (ISBN 0-471-79374-4, Pub. by Wiley-Interscience). Wiley.

Skellern, Claire & Rogers, Paul. Basic Botany. (Illus.). 208p. (Orig.). 1977. pap. text ed. 9.95x (ISBN 0-7121-0255-8, Pub. by Macdonald & Evans England). Intl Ideas.

Skelley, Esther G. Medications & Mathematics for the Nurse. LC 76-5302. 1976. pap. 7.40 (ISBN 0-8273-1343-8); instructor's guide 1.60 (ISBN 0-8273-1344-6). Delmar.

Skelley, Esther G., jt. auth. see Ferris, Elvira.

Skelley, Jeffrey, ed. The General Strike 1926. 1976. text ed. 15.75x (ISBN 0-85315-337-X). Humanities.

Skellorn, James, ed. Off Watch: A Selection of Bunkside Reading. 1979. 21.95x (ISBN 0-8464-0069-3). Beekman Pubs.

Skelly, Herbert & Skelly, Margaret. An Advent Event. 32p. (Orig.). 1973. pap. 3.25 (ISBN 0-8192-1148-6); kit 13.95 (ISBN 0-8192-1283-0). Morehouse.

Skelly, James R., jt. auth. see Zim, Herbert S.

Skelly, James R., jt. ed. see Zim, Herbert S.

Skelly, Madge. Glossectomee Speech Rehabilitation. (Illus.). 180p. 1973. text ed. 14.75 (ISBN 0-398-02706-4). C C Thomas.

Skelly, Margaret, jt. auth. see Skelly, Herbert.

Skelsey, Alice. Orchids. new ed. Time-Life Books, ed. (The Encyclopedia of Gardening). (Illus.). 1978. 11.95 (ISBN 0-8094-2591-2). Time-Life.

Skelsy, Alice F., jt. auth. see Crockett, James U.

Skelton, C. L. Hardacre. 1977. pap. 2.25 o.p. (ISBN 0-445-04026-2). Popular Lib.

Skelton, Geoffrey, tr. see Frisch, Max.

Skelton, John. Ballade of the Scottysshe Kynge. LC 67-23927. 1969. Repr. of 1882 ed. 15.00 (ISBN 0-8103-3461-5). Gale.

Skelton, Marvin L. Callahan, the Last War Bird. 1980. pap. 19.00 (ISBN 0-89126-081-1). Military Aff Aero.

Skelton, Mary B., jt. auth. see McSwain, Norman, Jr.

Skelton, Mary L. & Rao, G. Gopal. South Indian Cookery. 115p. 1975. pap. 2.00 (ISBN 0-89253-030-8). Ind-US Inc.

Skelton, Mary L., ed. see Desikachar, T. K.

Skelton, Mollie. You & Your Poodle. 4.95 (ISBN 0-87666-362-5, PS641). TFH Pubns.

Skelton, Oscar D see Johnson, Allen & Nevins, Allan.

Skelton, Robin. Irish Album. 1969. 6.50 (ISBN 0-85105-003-4). Dufour.

Skelton, V., jt. auth. see Holley, B.

Skemp, B. J., tr. see Plato.

Skempton, A. W., jt. auth. see Hadfield, Charles.

Skendi, Stavro. Balkan Cultural Studies. (East European Monograph: No. 72). 256p. 1980. 20.00x (ISBN 0-914710-66-4). East Eur Quarterly.

Skene, Felicia. Use & Abuse, Repr. Of 1849 Ed. Wolff, Robert L., ed. Bd. with Hidden Depths. Repr. of 1866 ed. LC 75-474. (Victorian Fiction Ser.). 1975. lib. bdg. 66.00 (ISBN 0-8240-1552-5). Garland Pub.

Skene, Reg. The Cuchulain Plays of W. B. Yeats: A Study. 264p. 1974. 17.50x (ISBN 0-231-03930-1). Columbia U Pr.

Skene Melvin, Ann, jt. auth. see Skene Melvin, David.

Skene Melvin, David & Skene Melvin, Ann. Crime, Detective, Espionage, Mystery, & Thriller Fiction & Film: A Comprehensive Bibliography of Critical Writing Through 1979. LC 80-1194. 384p. 1980. lib. bdg. 29.95 (ISBN 0-313-22062-X, MCD/). Greenwood.

Skene Smith, N. Introductory Atlas: Economics, Commerce & Administration, a Visual Analysis, Vol. 1. 1966. 14.50 (ISBN 0-08-010966-7). Pergamon.

Skerman, V. B., ed. Abstracts of Microbiological Methods. LC 69-16128. 1969. 81.00 o.p. (ISBN 0-471-79385-X, Pub. by Wiley-Interscience). Wiley.

Sketchley, Rose E. English Book-Illustration of To-Day: Appreciations of the Work of Living English Illustrators with Lists of Their Books. LC 78-179655. (Illus.). xxx, 175p. 1974. Repr. of 1903 ed. 24.00 (ISBN 0-8103-4052-6). Gale.

Skeyne, Gilbert. Ane Breif Descriptioun of the Well of the Woman-Hill Besyde Abirdene. LC 72-233. (English Experience Ser.: No. 104). 1969. Repr. of 1580 ed. 7.00 (ISBN 90-221-0104-5). Walter J Johnson.

Skhi-Igumen, John. Christ Is in Our Midst: Letters from a Russian Monk. Williams, Esther, tr. from Rus. LC 80-10530. 168p. (Orig.). 1980. pap. 4.95 (ISBN 0-913836-64-8). St Vladimirs.

Ski Magazine Editors. Skier's Handbook. (Illus.). 1965. 13.95 (ISBN 0-06-111710-2, HarpT). Har-Row.

Ski Magazine Editors, jt. auth. see Lund, Morten.

Skidelsky, Robert, ed. The End of the Keynesian Era: Essays on the Disintegration of the Keynesian Political Economy. LC 77-8878. 1977. text ed. 21.00x (ISBN 0-8419-0329-8); pap. text ed. cancelled (ISBN 0-8419-0340-9). Holmes & Meier.

Skidmore, D., jt. auth. see Butterworth, C. A.

Skidmore, Ian. Escape from Singapore. LC 73-13242. 198p. 1974. 7.95 o.p. (ISBN 0-684-13638-4, ScribT). Scribner.

--Lifeboat: The Story of Coxwain Dick Evans & His Many Rescues. LC 78-66965. 1979. 14.95 (ISBN 0-7153-7691-8). David & Charles.

Skidmore, Max J. American Political Thought. LC 77-86296. 1978. text ed. 19.95 (ISBN 0-312-02894-6); pap. text ed. 7.95 (ISBN 0-312-02895-4). St Martin.

Skidmore, Max J. & Wanke, Marshall C. American Government: A Brief Introduction. 2nd ed. LC 76-41545. (Illus.). 1977. pap. text ed. 7.50x (ISBN 0-312-02485-1). St Martin.

Skidmore, R. A. & Thackeray, Milton G. Introduction to Social Work. 2nd ed. (Illus.). 464p. 1976. ref. ed. 17.95 (ISBN 0-13-497024-1). P-H.

Skidmore, Thomas E. Politics in Brazil, Nineteen Thirty - Nineteen Sixty-Four: An Experiment in Democracy. LC 67-20406. (YA) (gr. 9 up). 1969. pap. 6.95 (ISBN 0-19-500784-0, GB). Oxford U Pr.

Skidmore, William L. Theoretical Thinking in Sociology. 2nd ed. LC 78-74540. (Illus.). 1979. 27.50 (ISBN 0-521-22663-5); pap. 9.95x (ISBN 0-521-29606-4). Cambridge U Pr.

Skier, Kenneth. Beyond Games: System Software for Your 6502 Personal Computer. 200p. 1981. pap. 14.95 (ISBN 0-07-057860-5, BYTE Bks). McGraw.

Skillen, Anthony. Ruling Illusions: Philosophy & the Social Order. 1978. text ed. 22.25x (ISBN 0-391-00770-X); pap. text ed. 9.25x (ISBN 0-391-00775-0). Humanities.

Skillen, Charles R. & Williams, Mason. American Police Handgun Training. (Illus.). 216p. 1977. 14.75 (ISBN 0-398-03684-5). C C Thomas.

Skilleter, Paul. Jaguar E-Type Collector's Guide. (Collector's Guide Ser.). (Illus.). 1979. 17.50 (ISBN 0-900549-46-7, Pub. by Motor Racing Pubns. England). Motorbooks Intl.

Skillicorn, Stanley A. Quality & Accountability: A New Era in American Hospitals. (Illus.). 143p. 1980. 14.00 (ISBN 0-917636-03-1). Edit Consult.

Skilling, H. H. Fundamentals of Electric Waves. 2nd ed. LC 74-8930. 256p. 1974. Repr. of 1948 ed. 11.75 o.p. (ISBN 0-88275-180-8). Krieger.

Skilliter, Susan. William Harborne & the Trade with Turkey: Secret Agent, 1578-1581. (Illus.). 1978. 49.00x (ISBN 0-19-725971-5). Oxford U Pr.

Skillman, Thomas G., jt. auth. see Mazzaferri, Ernest L.

Skilton, John. The New Testament Student, the New Testament Student at Work, Vol. II. kivar 5.00 o.p. (ISBN 0-87552-434-6). Presby & Reformed.

Skilton, M. Deutsche Texte und Wortschatzuebungen. LC 76-93127. pap. 3.20 o.p. (ISBN 0-08-006462-0); pap. 3.20 o.p. (ISBN 0-08-006461-2); tchr's. ed. 4.40 o.p. (ISBN 0-08-015811-0). Pergamon.

Skimming, Anne. Eat, Drink & Be Slim. 1972. 4.95 o.p. (ISBN 0-571-09646-8, Pub. by Faber & Faber). Merrimack Bk Serv.

Skinner, A. E. Rowena Country. 11.95 (ISBN 0-685-48806-3). Nortex Pr.

Skinner, Andrew S. & Wilson, Thomas, eds. Essays on Adam Smith. 1976. 59.00x (ISBN 0-19-828191-9). Oxford U Pr.

Skinner, Andrew S., jt. ed. see Wilson, Thomas.

Skinner, B. Behavior of Organisms: Experimental Analysis. 1966. 18.95 (ISBN 0-13-073213-3). P-H.

--Earth Resources. 2nd ed. 1976. pap. 7.95 (ISBN 0-13-223008-9). P-H.

Skinner, B., jt. auth. see Ferster, C.

Skinner, B. F. Contingencies of Reinforcement: A Theoretical Analysis. 1969. pap. 14.95 (ISBN 0-13-171728-6). P-H.

--Notebooks. Epstein, Robert, ed. LC 80-20094. 1981. 15.95 (ISBN 0-13-624106-9). P-H.

--Reflections on Behaviorism & Society. (Century Psychology Ser.). (Illus.). 1978. ref. 17.95 (ISBN 0-13-770057-1). P-H.

--Technology of Teaching. (Orig.). 1968. pap. text ed. 9.95 (ISBN 0-13-902163-9). P-H.

--Verbal Behavior. 1957. 21.00 (ISBN 0-13-941591-2). P-H.

Skinner, B. F., ed. Cumulative Record: A Selection of Papers. 3rd ed. (Century Psychology Ser). (Illus.). 450p. 1961. 19.95 (ISBN 0-13-195305-2). P-H.

Skinner, Betty L. Daws: The Story of Dawson Trotman, Founder of the Navigators. 392p. 1975. pap. 6.95 (ISBN 0-310-32801-2). Zondervan.

Skinner, Bob & Finley, Richard. Guide to Rogallo Flight. 1974. pap. 2.50 (ISBN 0-911721-76-2). Aviation.

Skinner, Brian J., jt. auth. see Dietrich, Richard V.

Skinner, Brian J., jt. auth. see Emery, K. O.

Skinner, Brian J., jt. auth. see Flint, Richard F.

Skinner, Brian J., ed. Climates Past & Present. (The Earth & Its Inhabitants: Selected Readings from American Scientist Ser.). (Illus.). 200p. (Orig.). 1981. pap. 9.95 (ISBN 0-913232-91-2). W Kaufmann.

--Earth's Energy & Mineral Resources. (The Earth & Its Inhabitants: Selected Readings from American Scientist Ser.). (Illus.). 200p. 1980. pap. 8.95 (ISBN 0-913232-90-4). W Kaufmann.

--Earth's History, Structure, & Materials. (The Earth & Its Inhabitants: Selected Readings from American Scientist Ser.). (Illus.). 184p. (Orig.). 1980. pap. 8.95 (ISBN 0-913232-89-0). W Kaufmann.

--Paleontology & Paleoenvironments. (The Earth & Its Inhabitants: Selected Readings from American Scientist Ser.). (Illus.). 250p. (Orig.). 1981. pap. 8.95 (ISBN 0-913232-93-9). W Kaufmann.

--The Solar System & Its Strange Objects. (The Earth & Its Inhabitants: Selected Readings from American Scientist Ser.). (Illus.). 200p. (Orig.). 1981. pap. 9.95 (ISBN 0-913232-84-X). W Kaufmann.

--Use & Misuse of Earth's Surface. (The Earth & Its Inhabitants: Selected Readings from American Scientist Ser.). (Illus.). 200p. (Orig.). 1981. pap. 9.95 (ISBN 0-913232-95-5). W Kaufmann.

Skinner, Charles M. American Myths & Legends, 2 vols. LC 78-175743. (Illus.). 697p. 1975. Repr. of 1903 ed. Set. 40.00 (ISBN 0-8103-4036-4). Gale.

--Myths & Legends of Our Own Land, 2 Vols. LC 79-76999. 1969. Repr. of 1896 ed. Set. 24.00 (ISBN 0-8103-3851-3). Gale.

Skinner, Constance L. Becky Landers Frontier Warrior. (gr. 4-6). 1967. 3.95g o.s.i. (ISBN 0-02-782810-7); pap. 0.79 o.s.i. (ISBN 0-686-66480-9). Macmillan.

Skinner, Constance L. see Gabriel, Ralph H.

Skinner, Cornelia O. & Kimbrough, Emily. Our Hearts Were Young & Gay. LC 42-36388. (Illus.). 1942. 6.95 (ISBN 0-396-02401-7). Dodd.

Skinner, David E. Thomas George Lawson: African Historian & Administrator in Sierra Leone. LC 78-70393. (Publications Ser, No. 222: Hoover Colonial Studies). 1980. pap. 10.95 (ISBN 0-8179-7221-8). Hoover Inst Pr.

Skinner, David R. An Introduction to Petroleum Production Operations, Vol. 1. 200p. 1981. 12.95 (ISBN 0-87201-767-2). Gulf Pub.

Skinner, Edith & Monich, Timothy. Good Speech for the American Actor. 1980. text ed. 13.95x incl. cassette (ISBN 0-89676-039-1). Drama Bk.

Skinner, Elliott P., jt. ed. see Shack, William A.

Skinner, Hubert M. The Story of the Letters & Figures. LC 71-175744. (Illus.). 1971. Repr. of 1905 ed. 18.00 (ISBN 0-8103-3035-0). Gale.

Skinner, James S. Body Energy. LC 80-24094. (Illus.). 120p. (Orig.). 1981. pap. 5.95 (ISBN 0-89037-174-1). Anderson World.

Skinner, John. Genesis. (International Critical Commentary Ser.). 640p. 1930. text ed. 23.00x (ISBN 0-567-05001-7). Attic Pr.

Skinner, Louise. Motor Development in the Preschool Years. (Illus.). 128p. 1979. pap. 11.75 (ISBN 0-398-03835-X). C C Thomas.

Skinner, Orten C. Basic Microbiology. LC 74-78590. (Allied Health Ser). 1975. pap. 7.65 (ISBN 0-672-61390-5). Bobbs.

--Introduction to Diagnostic Microbiology. LC 75-78591. (Allied Health Ser). 1975. pap. 12.05 (ISBN 0-672-61391-3). Bobbs.

Skinner, Paul, jt. auth. see Hodgson, W. R.

Skinner, Paul H. & Shelton, Ralph L. Speech, Language & Hearing: Normal Processes & Disorders. LC 77-73956. (Speech Pathology & Audiology Ser.). 1978. text ed. 16.95 (ISBN 0-201-07461-3); instr's man. price not set (ISBN 0-201-07462-1). A-W.

Skinner, Q. The Foundations of Modern Political Thought: The Renaissance, 2 vols. LC 78-51676. 1978. Vol. 1. 39.50 (ISBN 0-521-22023-8); Vol. 1. pap. 10.95x (ISBN 0-521-29337-5); Vol. 2. 39.50 (ISBN 0-521-22284-2); Vol. 2. pap. 10.95x (ISBN 0-521-29435-5). Cambridge U Pr.

Skinner, Robert. How to Design & Make Wood Assemblages & Reliefs. (Illus.). 64p. (Orig.). Date not set. pap. price not set (ISBN 0-486-24057-6). Dover. Postponed.

Skinner, Stephen, jt. auth. see King, Francis.

Skinner, Thomas. How Black Is the Gospel? 1976. pap. 1.25 (ISBN 0-89129-185-7). Jove Pubns.

Skinner, Tom. If Christ Is the Answer, What Are the Questions? 192p. 1974. pap. 4.95 (ISBN 0-310-32821-7). Zondervan.

Skinner, W. B., et al. Peoples & Cultures of Early Florida. (Florida Social Studies Ser.). (Illus.). 90p. (gr. 4-9). 1971. pap. text ed. 1.50 (ISBN 0-913122-01-7); teacher's guide avail. (ISBN 0-913122-02-5); package of 25 texts & 1 tchrs' guide 24.70 (ISBN 0-913122-15-7). Mickler Hse.

Skinner, Wickham. Manufacturing in the Corporate Strategy. LC 78-602. (Manufacturing Management Ser.). 1978. 27.95 (ISBN 0-471-01612-8, Pub. by Wiley-Interscience). Wiley.

Skipp, V. Crisis & Development. LC 77-71426. (Illus.). 1978. 21.95 (ISBN 0-521-21660-5). Cambridge U Pr.

Skipper, G. C. Battle of Leyte Gulf. LC 80-27265. (World at War Ser.). (Illus.). 48p. (gr. 3-8). 1981. PLB 7.95 (ISBN 0-516-04788-4). Childrens.

--Benito Mussolini: A Dictator Dies. LC 80-25345. (World at War Ser.). (Illus.). 48p. (gr. 3-8). 1981. PLB 7.95 (ISBN 0-516-04790-6). Childrens.

--Sicily. (World at War Ser.). (Illus.). 48p. (gr. 3-8). PLB 7.95 (ISBN 0-516-04792-2). Childrens.

Skipper, Howard E. Cancer Chemotherapy, Vol. 10: Some Thoughts Regarding the Modes of Action of Drugs on Cells & on Application of Available Pharmacokinetic Data (Anticancer Drugs) LC 78-24299. (Illus.). 132p. (Orig.). 1980. pap. 14.25 (ISBN 0-8357-0557-9, SS-00140, Pub. by Southern Res Inst). Univ Microfilms.

--Cancer Chemotherapy: Vol. 5, Ridgway Osteogenic Sarcoma; Response at Different Stages to Surgery, Single Drugs, Combinatons of Drugs & Surgery - Chemotherapy. LC 78-24299. (Illus.). 272p. (Orig.). 1979. pap. 22.75 (ISBN 0-8357-0421-1, SS-00097, Pub. by Southern Res Inst). Univ Microfilms.

Skipper, W. E. Sermon Charts & Outlines, 3 vols. spiral bdg. 2.95 ea. (ISBN 0-685-70356-8). Vol. 1 (ISBN 0-89315-253-6). Vol. 2 (ISBN 0-89315-254-4). Vol. 3 (ISBN 0-89315-255-2). Lambert Bk.

Skirvanek, John J. Modern Conversational Czech, 2 bks. 2nd ed. Mendl, James, ed. 1977. pap. 7.25x ea. Bk. 1 (ISBN 0-934786-02-X). Bk. 2 (ISBN 0-934786-03-8). G Davis.

Skirvin, Charles E. Session One: Self-Awareness & the Counselor Within. LC 78-72500. 124p. 1979. pap. 4.95 (ISBN 0-8059-2578-3). Dorrance.

Skitok, J. & Marshall, R. Electromagnetic Concepts & Applications. 1981. 28.00 (ISBN 0-13-248963-5). P-H.

Skjei, Eric & Rabkin, Richard. The Male Ordeal: Role Crisis in a Changing World. 320p. 1981. 13.95 (ISBN 0-399-12575-2, Perigee). Putnam.

Skjei, Eric, jt. auth. see Sith, Craig.

Sklansky, David. Hold 'em Poker. (Gambler's Book Shelf). (Illus.). 64p. 1976. pap. 2.95 (ISBN 0-89650-567-7). Gamblers.

--Sklansky on Poker Theory. rev. ed. 176p. 1980. pap. 5.95 (ISBN 0-89650-918-4). Gamblers.

--Sklansky's Poker Theory. 1978. pap. 3.95 o.p. (ISBN 0-89650-917-6). Gamblers.

Sklansky, Gloria J. & Algazi, Linda. Helping Women: A Guide to Counseling Women and Girls. 192p. 1981. 12.95 (ISBN 0-916068-15-3). Groupwork Today.

Sklar, Dusty. Gods & Beasts: The Nazis & the Occult. LC 77-87197. (Illus.). 1977. 9.95 o.s.i. (ISBN 0-690-01232-2, TYC-T). T Y Crowell.

Sklar, Lawrence. Space, Time, & Spacetime. 1977. pap. 7.75x (ISBN 0-520-03174-1, CAMPUS164). U of Cal Pr.

Sklar, Morty. Riverside. (Outstanding Author Ser.: No. 1). 13p. 1974. pap. 2.25 (ISBN 0-930370-00-7). Spirit That Moves.

Sklar, Morty, intro. by. Cross-Fertilization: The Human Spirit As Place. (Contemporary Anthology Ser.: No. 3). (Illus.). 64p. 1980. pap. 2.50 (ISBN 0-930370-10-4) (ISBN 0-930370-10-4). Spirit That Moves.

Sklar, Morty & Mulac, Jim, eds. Editor's Choice: Literature & Graphics from the U. S. Small Press, 1965-1977. LC 79-64861. (Contemporary Anthology Ser.: No. 2). (Illus.). 501p. 1980. 14.50 (ISBN 0-930370-05-8); pap. 9.50 (ISBN 0-930370-04-X); signed, numbered ed. 25.00 (ISBN 0-930370-06-6). Spirit That Moves.

Sklar, Morty, ed. see Ray, David.

Sklar, Richard L. Corporate Power in an African State: The Political Impact of Multinational Mining Companies in Zambia. LC 74-81440. 1975. 24.50x (ISBN 0-520-02814-7). U of Cal Pr.

Sklar, Richard L., ed. see Wormuth, Francis D.

Sklar, Robert, ed. The Plastic Age. LC 70-104698. (American Culture Ser). 386p. 1970. 8.95 (ISBN 0-8076-0571-9); pap. 4.95 (ISBN 0-8076-0570-0). Braziller.

Sklare, Arnold. Technician Writes: A Guide to Basic Technical Writing. LC 72-141220. (Illus.). 1971. pap. text ed. 5.95x o.p. (ISBN 0-87835-013-6). Boyd & Fraser.

Sklarew, jt. auth. see Steckman.
Sklorz, Martin. Table Tennis. (Sports Library). (Illus.). 1979. 12.95 (ISBN 0-8069-9148-8); pap. 6.95 (ISBN 0-8069-9150-X). Sterling.
Skocpol, Theda. States & Social Revolutions. LC 78-14314. 1979. 34.95 (ISBN 0-521-22439-X); pap. 9.95 (ISBN 0-521-29499-1). Cambridge U Pr.
Skoda, J. & Langen, P., eds. Antimetabolites in Biochemistry, Biology & Medicine: Proceedings, Prague, 1978. (Federation of European Biochemical Societies Symposium: Vol. 57). (Illus.). 1979. text ed. 60.00 (ISBN 0-08-024384-3). Pergamon.
Skoggard, Bruno. China Hand. LC 79-522. 1979. 8.95 (ISBN 0-396-07662-9). Dodd.
--China Hand. LC 80-85112. 288p. 1981. pap. 2.95 (ISBN 0-87216-838-7). Playboy Pbks.
Skoglund, Elizabeth. Woman Beyond Roleplay. LC 75-893. 1975. pap. 1.25 o.p. (ISBN 0-912692-62-6). Cook.
--Your Troubled Children. LC 74-19440. 128p. 1975. pap. 1.50 o.p. (ISBN 0-912692-50-2). Cook.
Skoglund, John E. Manual of Worship. LC 68-20431. 1968. bds. 5.95 o.p. (ISBN 0-8170-0395-9). Judson.
Skogsberg, Bertil. Wings on the Screen. Bisset, George, tr. from Swedish. (Illus.). 192p. 1981. 25.00 (ISBN 0-498-02495-4). A S Barnes.
Skolbel'Tsyn, D. V., ed. Nuclear Physics & Interaction of Particles with Matter. LC 70-120025. (P. N. Lebedev Physics Institute Ser.: Vol. 44). 269p. 1971. 37.50 (ISBN 0-306-10851-8, Consultants). Plenum Pub.
--Quantum Field Theory & Hydrodynamics. LC 66-12629. (P. N. Lebedev Physics Institute Ser.: Vol. 29). 271p. 1967. 32.50 (ISBN 0-306-10768-6, Consultants). Plenum Pub.
--Theory of Interaction of Elementary Particles at High Energies. LC 73-83900. (P. N. Lebedev Physics Institute Ser.: Vol. 57). (Illus.). 258p. 1974. 42.50 (ISBN 0-306-10899-2, Consultants). Plenum Pub.
Skolem, Thoralf. Diophantische Gleichungen. LC 51-6891. (Ger). 8.95 (ISBN 0-8284-0075-X). Chelsea Pub.
Skoler, Daniel L. Organizing the Non-System. LC 76-27023. (Illus.). 1977. 19.50 (ISBN 0-669-00941-5). Lexington Bks.
Skoler, Martin E., ed. Health Care Labor Manual, 3 vols. (Updated bimonthly). 1974. loose-leaf metal binding 275.00 (ISBN 0-912862-11-4). Aspen Systems.
Skolimowski, H., tr. see Ajdukiewicz, K.
Skolimowski, Henryk. Polish Analytical Philosophy: A Survey & a Comparison with British Analytical Philosophy. 1967. text ed. 10.25x (ISBN 0-7100-3632-9). Humanities.
Skolimowsky, Henryk. Eco-Philosophy. LC 79-56846. (Ideas in Progress Ser.). 1980. 12.00 (ISBN 0-7145-2677-0, Pub. by M Boyars); pap. 6.95 (ISBN 0-7145-2676-2, Pub. by M. Boyars). Merrimack Bk Serv.
Skolnick. House of Cards: Legalization & Control of Casino Gambling. (Orig.). 1981. pap. text ed. 7.95 (ISBN 0-316-79708-1). Little.
Skolnick, Emanuel. Alford Waters. LC 80-17192. (The Story of an American Indian Ser.). (Illus.). 64p. (gr. 5 up). 1980. PLB 6.95 (ISBN 0-87518-201-1). Dillon.
Skolnik, Peter L. Jump Rope! LC 75-8811. (Illus.). 160p. (Orig.). (gr. 2 up). 1974. pap. 3.95 (ISBN 0-911104-47-X). Workman Pub.
Skolnik, Peter L., et al. Fads: America's Crazes, Fevers & Fancies from the 1890s to the 1970s. LC 77-886. (Illus.). 1978. 9.95 o.p. (ISBN 0-690-01215-2, TYC-T); pap. 5.95 o.p. (ISBN 0-690-01216-0, TYC-T). T Y Crowell.
Skolsky, Mindy W. Hannah Is a Palindrome. LC 79-2009. (Illus.). 128p. (gr. 3-6). 1980. 8.95 (ISBN 0-06-025726-1, HarpJ); PLB 8.79 (ISBN 0-06-025727-X). Har-Row.
Skoog, F., ed. Plant Growth Substances, Nineteen Seventy-Nine: Proceedings. (Proceedings in Life Sciences Ser.). (Illus.). 580p. 1981. 57.90 (ISBN 0-387-10182-9). Springer-Verlag.
Skorohod, A. V., jt. auth. see Gihman, I. I.
Skorokhod, A. V. Studies in the Theory of Random Processes. cancelled o.s.i. (ISBN 0-201-07021-9, Adv Bk Prog). A-W.
Skorov, G. E., ed. Science, Technology & Economic Growth in the Developing Countries. 1978. text ed. 27.00 (ISBN 0-08-022223-4). Pergamon.
Skorupski, J. Symbol & Theory. LC 76-3037. 1976. 32.95 (ISBN 0-521-21200-6). Cambridge U Pr.
Skorupski, Tadeusz, jt. auth. see Snellgrove, David L.
Skoss, Solomon, ed. Hebrew-Arabic Dictionary of the Bible Known As Kitab Jami-Al-Alfaz, 2 vols. (Yale Oriental Researches Ser.: No. XX, XXI). 1945. 50.00x ea.; 95.00x set (ISBN 0-686-57837-6). Elliots Bks.
Skotak, Robert & Holton, Scot. Fantastic Worlds. Zimmerman, Howard & Snelson, Robin, eds. (Illus.). (gr. 3 up). 1978. pap. 7.95 (ISBN 0-931064-03-1). Starlog.
Skotheim, Robert A. & McGiffert, Michael. American Social Thought: Sources & Interpretations, Vol. 2, Since the Civil War. LC 75-140946. (History Ser). 1972. pap. text ed. 8.50 (ISBN 0-201-07045-6). A-W.
Skousen, K. Fred, jt. auth. see Carey, John L.
Skousen, K. Fred, et al. Principles of Accounting. 1981. text ed. write for info. (ISBN 0-87901-137-8); write for info. study guide (ISBN 0-87901-147-5); write for info. practie set, vol. 1 (ISBN 0-87901-150-5); write for info. practice set, vol. 2 (ISBN 0-87901-151-3); write for info. practice set, vol. 3 (ISBN 0-87901-152-1); write for info. working papers, vol. 1 (ISBN 0-87901-148-3); write for info. working papers, vol. 2 (ISBN 0-87901-149-1). Worth.
--Financial Accounting. 1981. text ed. write for info. (ISBN 0-87901-156-4); write or info. study guide (ISBN 0-87901-157-2); write for info. practice set, vol. 2 (ISBN 0-87901-159-9); price not set practice set, vol. 2 (ISBN 0-87901-160-2); write for info. working papers (ISBN 0-87901-158-0). Worth.
Skousen, Mark. The Insider's Banking & Credit Almanac. 14.95 (ISBN 0-932496-01-6). Green Hill.
--Mark Skousen's Guide to Financial Privacy. 1979. 14.95 o.p. (ISBN 0-932496-02-4). Alexandria Hse.
Skousen, W. Cleon. The First Two Thousand Years. 1953. 7.50 (ISBN 0-685-48240-5). Bookcraft Inc.
--The Fourth Thousand Years. LC 66-29887. 1966. 13.95 (ISBN 0-685-48242-1). Bookcraft Inc.
--So You Want to Raise a Boy. LC 61-9555. 1962. 9.95 (ISBN 0-385-02408-8). Doubleday.
--The Third Thousand Years. 1964. 12.50 (ISBN 0-685-48241-3). Bookcraft Inc.
Skousgaard, Stephen. Language & the Existence of Freedom: A Study in Paul Ricoeur's Philosophy of Will. LC 79-63257. 1979. pap. text ed. 7.50 (ISBN 0-8191-0725-5). U Pr of Amer.
Skovholt, Thomas M., et al, eds. Counseling Men. LC 79-29722. (Counseling Psychology Ser.). (Orig.). 1980. pap. text ed. 9.95 (ISBN 0-8185-0372-6). Brooks-Cole.
Skowronski, Carl A., jt. auth. see Sloan, Robert E.
Skowronski, JoAnn. Women in American Music: A Bibliography. LC 77-26611. 1978. 10.00 (ISBN 0-8108-1105-7). Scarecrow.
Skoyles, John. A Little Faith. LC 80-70564. (Poetry Ser.). 1980. 9.95 (ISBN 0-915604-43-4); pap. 4.95 (ISBN 0-915604-44-2). Carnegie-Mellon.
Skrabanek, P. & Powell, D. Substance P, Vol. 1, 1977. 1978. 21.60 (ISBN 0-88831-019-6). Eden Med Res.
Skrabanek, Petr & Powell, David. Substance P, Vol. 2. Horrobin, D. F., ed. LC 80-646426. (Annual Research Reviews Ser.). 175p. 1980. 26.00 (ISBN 0-88831-073-0). Eden Med Res.
Skrapek, Wayne A., et al. Mathematical Dictionary for Economics & Business Administration. 1978. text ed. 29.95 o.p. (ISBN 0-205-05011-5). Allyn.
Skrebitski, G. A. Forest Echo. LC 66-21974. (gr. 2-4). PLB 4.35 o.s.i. (ISBN 0-8076-0414-3). Braziller.
Skrebneski, Victor. Skrebneski Portraits: A Matter of Record. LC 78-18566. 1978. 19.95 o.p. (ISBN 0-385-14623-X). Doubleday.
Skrjabin, K. I., et al. Essentials of Nematodology: Vol. 13, Oxyurata of Animals & Man. 1976. 69.95 (ISBN 0-470-98978-5). Halsted Pr.
Skrjabina, Elena. After Leningrad: From the Caucasus to the Rhine, August 9, 1942-March 25, 1945. Luxenburg, Norman, ed. LC 78-18872. (Illus.). 197p. 1978. 14.95 (ISBN 0-8093-0856-8). S Ill U Pr.
--The Allies on the Rhine, Nineteen Forty-Five to Nineteen-Fifty. Luxenburg, Norman, ed. & illus. LC 79-28187. (Illus.). 176p. 1980. 12.95 (ISBN 0-8093-0939-4). S Ill U Pr.
Skrodzki, Woljciech, jt. auth. see Osek, Andrzej.
Skrokov, M. Robert, ed. Mini & Microcomputer Control in Industrial Processes: Handbook of Systems Application & Strategies. 320p. 1980. text ed. 27.50 (ISBN 0-442-27643-5). Van Nos Reinhold.
Skrynnikov, R. G. Ivan the Terrible. Graham, Hugh F., ed. (Russian Ser.: No. 32). 1981. 15.00 (ISBN 0-87569-039-4). Academic Intl.
Skrzynska, Maria, jt. ed. see Czerni, Sergiusz.
Skudlarek, William. The Word in Worship. LC 80-25525. (Abingdon Preacher's Library). 128p. (Orig.). 1981. pap. 4.95 (ISBN 0-687-46131-6). Abingdon.
Skudrzyk, E. J. Foundations of Acoustics, Basic Mathematics & Basic Acoustics. LC 76-161480. (Illus.). 1972. 130.00 (ISBN 0-387-80988-0). Springer-Verlag.
Skulachev, V. P., ed. Soviet Scientific Review: Biology Review, Vol. 2, Section D. 1981. write for info. (ISBN 3-7186-0058-7). Harwood Academic.
--Soviet Scientific Reviews: Biology Reviews, Vol. 1, Section D. 476p. 1980. lib. bdg. 79.50 (ISBN 0-686-60585-3). Harwood Academic.
--Soviet Scientific Reviews: Biology Reviews, Vol. 2, Section D. 1981. write for info. (ISBN 3-7186-0058-7). Harwood Academic.
Skull, John. Sport & Leisure. pap. text ed. 2.95x o.p. (ISBN 0-435-14488-X); tchr's ed. 1.50x o.p. (ISBN 0-435-14489-8). Heinemann Ed.
Skully, Michael T., ed. International Business Education: A Curriculum Survey of Australia & New Zealand. LC 77-670090. (Illus.). 1977. pap. 5.95 o.p. (ISBN 0-909162-05-0). Australiana.
Skultans, Vieda. Intimacy & Ritual: A Study of Spiritualism, Mediums & Groups. 114p. 1974. 14.00x (ISBN 0-7100-7760-2). Routledge & Kegan.
--Madness & Morals: Ideas on Insanity in the Nineteenth Century. 1975. 20.00x (ISBN 0-7100-8022-0). Routledge & Kegan.
Skura, Meredith A. The Literary Use of the Psychoanalytic Process. LC 80-23390. 288p. 1981. 19.50x (ISBN 0-300-02380-4). Yale U Pr.
Skurdenis, Juliann V. & Smircich, Lawrence J. Walk Straight Through the Square: Walking Tours of Europe's Most Picturesque Cities. LC 76-3516. (Illus.). 1976. 8.95 o.p. (ISBN 0-679-50572-5); pap. 5.95 o.p. (ISBN 0-679-50628-4). McKay.
Skurnik, L. S., jt. auth. see Wood, R.
Skurnik, W. A. The Foreign Policy of Senegal. xx, 308p. 1972. 13.00x o.s.i. (ISBN 0-8101-0373-7). Northwestern U Pr.
Skurnik, W. A., ed. Sub-Saharan Africa: A Guide to Information Sources. LC 73-17513. (International Relations Information Guide Ser.: Vol. 3). 1977. 30.00 (ISBN 0-8103-1391-X). Gale.
Skurnowicz, Joan S. Romantic Nationalism & Liberalism: Joachim Lelewel & the Polish National Idea. (East European Monographs: No. 83). 224p. 1981. text ed. 16.00x (ISBN 0-914710-77-X). East Eur Quarterly.
Skurzynski, Gloria. Bionic Parts for People: The Real Story of Artificial Organs & Replacement Parts. LC 78-54678. (Illus.). 160p. (gr. 7 up). 1978. 8.95 (ISBN 0-590-07490-3, Four Winds). Schol Bk Serv.
--In a Bottle with a Cork on Top. LC 75-29466. (Illus.). (gr. 2-5). 1976. 5.95 (ISBN 0-396-07277-1). Dodd.
--Manwolf. 192p. (gr. 6 up). 1981. 9.95 (ISBN 0-395-30079-7, Clarion). HM.
--Safeguarding the Land. LC 80-8805. (Illus.). 192p. (gr. 7-12). 1981. pap. 3.95 (ISBN 0-15-269957-0, VoyB). HarBraceJ.
--Safeguarding the Land. LC 80-8805. (Illus.). 192p. (gr. 7 up). 1981. 9.95 (ISBN 0-15-269956-2, HJ). HarBraceJ.
Skutch, Alexander. A Naturalist on a Tropical Farm. LC 78-64474. (Illus.). 1980. 16.95; pap. 7.95 (ISBN 0-520-04149-6, CAL 461). U of Cal Pr.
Skutch, Alexander F. Life of the Hummingbird. 1973. 9.95 o.p. (ISBN 0-517-50572-X). Crown.
--The Life of the Hummingbird. (Illus.). 96p. 1980. 15.95 (ISBN 0-517-50572-X). Crown.
Skwire, David & Chitwood, Frances. Student's Book of College English. 2nd ed. 1978. pap. text ed. 7.95 (ISBN 0-02-478330-7). Macmillan.
Sky, Kathleen. Death's Angel. (Star Trek Ser.). 192p. (Orig.). 1981. pap. 2.25 (ISBN 0-553-14703-X). Bantam.
Skydell, Ruth H., jt. auth. see Belkin, Gary S.
Skyler, Jay S. & Cahill, George F., eds. Diabetes Mellitus. (Illus.). 400p. 1981. text ed. write for info. (ISBN 0-914316-23-0). Yorke Med.
Skyrme, Thomas. The Changing Image of the Magistracy: 1974-1977. 1979. text ed. 23.25x (ISBN 0-391-01123-5). Humanities.
Slaatte, Howard A. The Armenian Arm of Theology. 1977. 7.50 (ISBN 0-8191-0252-0). U Pr of Amer.
--The Dogma of Immaculate Perception: A Critique of Positivistic Thought. LC 79-66858. 1979. pap. text ed. 7.50 (ISBN 0-8191-0849-9). U Pr of Amer.
--Fire in the Brand: An Introduction to the Creative Work & Theology of John Wesley. 1963. 4.00 o.p. (ISBN 0-682-41125-6). Exposition.
--Pertinence of the Paradox: A Study of the Dialectics of Reason-In-Existence. LC 68-27100. 1967. text ed. 8.50x o.p. (ISBN 0-391-00469-7). Humanities.
Slaatten, Evelyn. The Good, the Bad & the Rest of Us. LC 80-15595. 160p. (gr. 4-6). 1980. 7.95 (ISBN 0-688-22251-X); PLB 7.63 (ISBN 0-688-32251-4). Morrow.
Slaba, D., jt. auth. see Kolafova, V.
Slabaugh, Michael R., jt. auth. see Seager, Spencer L.
Slabaugh, Michael R., jt. auth. see Stoker, H. Stephen.
Slabaugh, Wendell H. & Butler, Alfred B. College Physical Science. 3rd ed. (Illus.). 624p. 1973. text ed. 19.95 (ISBN 0-13-147371-9). P-H.
Slaby, Andrew & Tancredi, Lawrence. Collusion for Conformity. LC 75-5989. 1975. 20.00x (ISBN 0-87668-207-7). Aronson.
Slaby, Andrew E. & Wyatt, Richard J. Dementia in the Presenium. (Illus.). 244p. 1974. 18.50 (ISBN 0-398-02946-6). C C Thomas.
Slaby, Andrew E., et al. Handbook of Psychiatric Emergencies. 2nd. ed. 1981. pap. write for info. (ISBN 0-87488-645-7). Med Exam.
Slaby, Steve M. Engineering Descriptive Geometry. (Orig.). 1969. pap. 4.95 (ISBN 0-06-460101-3, CO 101, COS). Har-Row.
Slack, Adrian. Carnivorous Plants. (Illus.). 240p. 1980. 19.95 (ISBN 0-262-19186-5). MIT Pr.
Slack, Kathleen M. Old People & London Government. 82p. 1970. pap. text ed. 5.00x (ISBN 0-7135-1620-8, Pub. by Bedford England). Renouf.
Slack, Kenneth. The United Reformed Church. 1978. pap. 2.90 (ISBN 0-08-021414-2). Pergamon.
Slack, Robert C. & Cottrell, Beekman W. Writing: A Preparation for College Composition. 2nd ed. 1978. pap. text ed. 6.95x (ISBN 0-02-478250-5). Macmillan.
Slack, Walter H. The Grim Science: The Struggle for Power. (National Univ. Publications, Political Science Ser.). 200p. 1981. 20.00 (ISBN 0-8046-9260-2). Kennikat.
Slade, B. A. Complete Course in Short-Cut Mathematics: Combined with Simplified Mechanics for the Practical Man. 9.95 (ISBN 0-911012-11-7). Nelson-Hall.
Slade, Carole, jt. auth. see Cummins, Marsha Z.
Slade, E. R. Jornado. (Orig.). 1979. pap. 1.95 (ISBN 0-532-23270-4). Manor Bks.
Slade, Jack. The Badlanders. (Lassiter Ser.). 1978. pap. 1.50 (ISBN 0-505-50597-5). Tower Bks.
--Big Foot's Range. (Lassiter Ser.). 1979. pap. 1.75 (ISBN 0-505-51428-1). Tower Bks.
--Cattle Baron. (Lassiter Ser). 1977. pap. 1.25 (ISBN 0-505-51163-0). Tower Bks.
--Five Graves for Lassiter. 1979. pap. 1.50 (ISBN 0-505-51409-5). Tower Bks.
--Guerilla. (Lassiter Ser). 1976. pap. 1.25 (ISBN 0-505-51105-3). Tower Bks.
--Lassiter: Lust for Gold. 1977. pap. 1.25 (ISBN 0-505-51127-4). Tower Bks.
--The Man from Lordsburg. (Lassiter Ser.). 1978. pap. 1.25 (ISBN 0-505-51296-3). Tower Bks.
--The Man from Tombstone & Gunfight at Ringo Junction. (Lassiter Ser.). 1978. pap. 2.25 (ISBN 0-505-51285-8). Tower Bks.
Slade, K. A. Steel Boat Construction. (Questions & Answers Ser.). (Illus.). 115p. (Orig.). 1979. pap. 7.50 (ISBN 0-686-64487-5). Transatlantic.
Slade, P. Child Drama. 1979. pap. 25.00 (ISBN 0-340-20968-2). Verry.
Slade, Peter. Introduction to Child Drama. 1958. pap. 5.00x (ISBN 0-340-11881-4). Verry.
Slade, R. C., jt. auth. see Gerloch, M.
Slade, Richard. Patterns in Space. 1969. 8.50 (ISBN 0-571-08327-7, Pub. by Faber & Faber). Merrimack Bk Serv.
Slade, Ruth. Sarah-Christina: A Girl of Old Portland. Hunting, Constance, ed. (gr. 4-8). 1981. pap. text ed. 5.95 (ISBN 0-913006-19-X). Puckerbrush.
Sladecek, Vladimir. System of Water Quality from the Biological Point of View. Elster, H. & Ohle, W., eds. LC 74-170857. (Ergebnisse der Limnologie: Vol. 7). (Illus.). 218p. (Orig.). 1973. pap. 57.50x (ISBN 3-510-47005-2). Intl Pubns Serv.
Sladek, John. The Invisible Green. 1979. 7.95 o.s.i. (ISBN 0-8027-5404-X). Walker & Co.
Sladen, Douglas. Queer Things About Japan, to Which Is Added a Life of the Emperor of Japan. 4th ed. LC 68-26607. (Illus.). 1968. Repr. of 1913 ed. 20.00 (ISBN 0-8103-3500-X). Gale.
Sladky, Joseph F. & Klimas, Paul C. Surface Effect Vehicles: Principles & Applications. LC 75-27231. (Illus.). 620p. Date not set. cancelled (ISBN 0-271-01211-0). Pa St U Pr. Postponed.
Slaga, Thomas J., ed. Modifiers of Chemical Carcinogenesis. LC 77-504. (Carcinogenesis: a Comprehensive Survey Ser.: Vol. 5). 1979. text ed. 32.50 (ISBN 0-89004-232-2). Raven.
Slaga, Thomas J., et al, eds. Mechanisms of Tumor Promotion & Cocarcinogenesis. LC 77-17752. (Carcinogenesis: a Comprehensive Survey: Vol. 2). 1978. 56.00 (ISBN 0-89004-208-X). Raven.
Slagle, Uhlan & Anttila, Raimo. Dynamic Fields & the Structure of Language. (Current Issues in Linguistic Theory: No. 6). 1980. text ed. 37.25x (ISBN 0-391-01644-X). Humanities.
Slamecka, V. & Borka, H., eds. Planning & Organisation of National Research Programs in Information Science. (Illus.). 83p. 1980. pap. 27.50 (ISBN 0-08-026472-7). Pergamon.

Slamon, Geoffrey. Planning Your Office. (Design Centre Bks.). 1978. 15.95 o.p. (ISBN 0-8256-3100-9); pap. 8.95 o.p. (ISBN 0-685-88353-1). Music Sales.

Slane, B. MacGuckin. Ibn Khallikan's Biographical Dictionary: Wafayat Al-a Yan, 4 vols. 90.00x (ISBN 0-685-72046-2). Intl Bk Ctr.

Slaney, Brenda, ed. Occupational Health Nursing. 177p. 1980. 22.00x (ISBN 0-85664-779-9, Pub. by Croom Helm Ltd England). Biblio Dist.

Slappey, G. Sterling, ed. see Center for Strategic & International Studies, Georgetown University.

Slaten, Jeff, jt. auth. see Ellis, Albert C.

Slater & Smith. Basic Plumbing. LC 77-85751. 1979. pap. text ed. 6.40 (ISBN 0-8273-1204-0); instructor's guide 1.60 (ISBN 0-8273-1205-9). Delmar.

Slater, Abby. In Search of Margaret Fuller: A Biography. LC 77-86335. (gr. 7 up). 1978. 7.50 (ISBN 0-440-03944-4). Delacorte.

Slater, Barbara R., jt. auth. see Boehm, Ann E.

Slater, Charles C. & White, Phillip D., eds. Macromarketing, Vol. II: Distributive Processes from a Societal Perspective, an Elaboration of Issues. 477p. 1978. 10.00 (ISBN 0-686-69388-4). U CO Busn Res Div.

Slater, Charles C., et al. Kensim: A Systems Simulation of the Developing Kenyan Economy, 1970-1978. LC 77-4141. 1977. lib. bdg. 23.50x (ISBN 0-89158-346-7). Westview.

Slater, Charlotte. All the Things Your Mother Never Taught You. (Illus.). 294p. 1975. pap. 4.95 o.p. (ISBN 0-8362-0625-8). Andrews & McMeel.

Slater, Harry. Advanced Plumbing. LC 79-89242. (Construction Ser.). 1981. pap. text ed. 6.60 (ISBN 0-8273-1111-7); instructor's guide 1.60 (ISBN 0-8273-1112-5). Delmar.

Slater, Harry & Smith, Lee. Advanced Plumbing. 3rd ed. 198p. 1980. 8.95 (ISBN 0-442-23873-8). Van Nos Reinhold.

--Advanced Plumbing. LC 79-89242. 1981. pap. 6.60 (ISBN 0-8273-1106-0); instructor's guide 1.60 (ISBN 0-8273-1112-5). Delmar.

Slater, Herbert J., ed. see Burton, John H.

Slater, J. Man the Artist. 1976. 3.35 (ISBN 0-08-006899-5). Pergamon.

Slater, Jeffrey. Rx for Small Business Success: Accounting, Planning, & Recordkeeping Techniques for a Healthy Bottom Line. (Illus.). 256p. 1981. 18.95 (Spec); pap. 12.95 (ISBN 0-13-785006-9). P-H.

Slater, Jerome. Intervention & Negotiation: The United States & the Dominican Revolution. LC 70-95985. (Illus.). 1970. text ed. 22.50x (ISBN 0-06-013924-2). Irvington.

Slater, Jim. Big Snowy. LC 80-53066. (A. Mazing Monsters Ser.). (Illus.). 1981. pap. 1.25 (ISBN 0-394-84736-9). Random.

--Bignose. LC 80-53065. (A. Mazing Monsters Ser.). (Illus.). 1981. pap. 1.25 (ISBN 0-394-84739-3). Random.

--The Boy Who Saved Earth. LC 80-1662. (Illus.). 128p. (gr. 6-9). 1981. 8.95a (ISBN 0-385-17115-3); PLB (ISBN 0-385-17116-1). Doubleday.

--The Great Gulper. LC 80-53067. (A. Mazing Monsters Ser.). (Illus.). 1981. pap. 1.25 (ISBN 0-394-84737-7). Random.

--The Tricky Troggle. LC 80-53064. (A. Mazing Monsters Ser.). (Illus.). 1981. pap. 1.25 (ISBN 0-394-84738-5). Random.

Slater, John C. The Calculation of Molecular Orbitals. LC 78-323. 1979. 23.95 (ISBN 0-471-03181-X, Pub. by Wiley-Interscience). Wiley.

--Solid State & Molecular Theory: A Scientific Biography. LC 74-22367. 416p. 1975. text ed. 30.50 (ISBN 0-471-79681-6, Pub. by Wiley-Interscience). Wiley.

Slater, John C. & Frank, Nathaniel H. Electromagnetism. LC 69-17476. (Illus.). 1969. pap. text ed. 3.50 (ISBN 0-486-62263-0). Dover.

Slater, John H. Illustrated Sporting Books. LC 71-75800. 1969. Repr. of 1899 ed. 15.00 (ISBN 0-8103-3889-0). Gale.

Slater, Joseph, ed. see Emerson, Ralph W. & Carlyle, Thomas.

Slater, L. J. Gem, a General Econometric Matrix Program. LC 76-16920. (Applied Economics, Occasional Papers Ser.: No. 46). (Illus.). 1976. pap. 11.95x (ISBN 0-521-29114-3). Cambridge U Pr.

Slater, L. J., jt. auth. see Pesaran, M. H.

Slater, Lloyd E. & Levin, Susan K., eds. Climate's Impact on Food Supplies. (Selected Symposium Ser.: No. 62). 250p. 1981. lib. bdg. 20.00x (ISBN 0-86531-166-8). Westview.

Slater, Lucy J. More Fortran Programs for Economists. (Department of Applied Economics, Occasional Papers: No. 3). (Illus.). 150p. 1972. 15.95x (ISBN 0-521-09722-3). Cambridge U Pr.

Slater, Mariam K. The Caribbean Family: Legitimacy in Martinique. LC 76-28118. 1976. text ed. 15.95x (ISBN 0-312-12075-3); pap. text ed. 7.95x (ISBN 0-312-12110-5). St Martin.

Slater, Mary L. Future Maker in India: The Story of Sara Chakko. (Orig.). 1968. pap. 0.95 o.p. (ISBN 0-377-84121-8). Friend Pr.

Slater, Maya. Humour in the Works of Proust. (Oxford Modern Languages & Literature Monographs). 200p. 1979. text ed. 22.00x (ISBN 0-19-815534-4). Oxford U Pr.

Slater, Michael, ed. see Dickens, Charles.

Slater, Phil. Origin & Significance of the Frankfurt School: A Marxist Perspective. (International Library of Sociology). 1976. 22.50x (ISBN 0-7100-8438-2). Routledge & Kegan.

Slater, Phil, ed. Outlines of a Critique of Technology. 160p. 1980. text ed. 14.50x (ISBN 0-391-01889-2). Humanities.

Slater, Philip. Earthwalk. LC 73-83671. 240p. 1974. pap. 3.95 (ISBN 0-385-03286-2, Anch). Doubleday.

Slater, R. A. Engineering Plasticity: Theory & Its Application to Metal Forming, Processes. LC 73-10606. 1977. text ed. 43.95 (ISBN 0-470-79647-2). Halsted Pr.

Slater, Robert. Rabin of Israel: A Biography. (Illus.). 304p. 1977. 17.50x (ISBN 0-8476-3127-3). Rowman.

Slater, Robert H. World Religions & World Community. LC 63-9805. (Lectures on the History of Religions Ser.: No. 6). 1963. 17.50x (ISBN 0-231-02615-3). Columbia U Pr.

Slater, S. D. The Strategy of Cash: A Liquidity Approach to Maximizing the Company's Profits. LC 74-9811. (Systems & Controls for Financial Management Ser). 416p. 1974. 28.50 (ISBN 0-471-79640-9, Pub. by Wiley-Interscience). Wiley.

Slater, Scott & Solomita, Alec. Exits: Dying Words & Last Moments. 1980. 7.95 (ISBN 0-525-93070-1). Dutton.

Slatkes, Leonard. Rembrandt. LC 79-57583. (Abbeville Library of Art Ser.: No. 7). (Illus.). 112p. 1980. pap. 4.95 (ISBN 0-89659-134-4). Abbeville Pr.

Slatkes, Leonard, ed. Netherlandish Masters. LC 79-50679. (The Illustrated Bartsch: Vol. I). 1979. 120.00 (ISBN 0-89835-001-8). Abaris Bks.

Slatter, Douglas H. Fundamentals of Veterinary Opthtalmology. (Illus.). 400p. 1980. text ed. write for info. (ISBN 0-7216-8357-6). Saunders.

Slattery, John C. Momentum, Energy, & Mass Transfer in Continua. 2nd ed. LC 80-22746. 700p. 1980. text ed. 32.50 (ISBN 0-89874-212-9). Krieger.

Slattery, Kathryn S., jt. auth. see Prewitt, Cheryl.

Slattery, Thomas C. Percy Grainger: The Inveterate Innovator. (Illus.). 12.50 (ISBN 0-686-15893-8). Instrumentalist Co.

Slatzer, Robert, jt. auth. see Shepherd, Donald.

Slaughter, B. H., et al. The Hill-Shuler Local Faunas of the Upper Trinity River, Dallas & Denton Counties, Texas. (Illus.). 75p. 1962. 2.50 (RI 48). Bur Econ Geology.

Slaughter, C. Marxism Ideology & Literature. 1979. text ed. 20.00x (ISBN 0-391-01190-1); pap. text ed. 10.25x (ISBN 0-333-23217-8). Humanities.

Slaughter, Frank. Buccaneer Surgeon. 1976. Repr. of 1954 ed. lib. bdg. 13.20 (ISBN 0-89190-533-2). Am Repr-Rivercity Pr.

--Darien Venture. 1976. Repr. of 1955 ed. lib. bdg. 12.45 (ISBN 0-89190-532-4). Am Repr-Rivercity Pr.

--The Golden Ones. 1976. Repr. of 1957 ed. lib. bdg. 12.45 (ISBN 0-89190-531-6). Am Repr-Rivercity Pr.

Slaughter, Frank G. Gospel Fever. LC 80-25615. 475p. 1980. Repr. of 1980 ed. large print ed. 12.95 (ISBN 0-89621-256-4). Thorndike Pr.

--Gospel Fever: A Novel About America's Most Beloved TV Evangelist. LC 79-6094. (Illus.). 384p. 1980. 10.95 (ISBN 0-385-15308-2). Doubleday.

--In a Dark Garden. 1976. Repr. of 1946 ed. lib. bdg. 16.70 (ISBN 0-89190-289-9). Am Repr-Rivercity Pr.

Slaughter, Howard see Fitzmaurice, George.

Slaughter, Howard K. George Fitzmaurice & His Enchanted Land. (Irish Theatre Ser.: No. 2). (Illus., Orig.). 1972. pap. text ed. 3.25x (ISBN 0-85105-188-X, Dolmen Pr). Humanities.

Slaughter, J. C., jt. auth. see Duffus, C. M.

Slaughter, Jean. And It Came to Pass. LC 70-127471. (Illus.). (gr. k-3). 1971. 4.95 o.s.i. (ISBN 0-02-782900-6). Macmillan.

Slauson, Nedra, jt. auth. see Munz, Lucille T.

Slauson, Nedra, ed. Index to Illustrations of the Natural World: Where to Find Pictures of the Living Things of North America. 265p. 1981. 29.95 (ISBN 0-208-01911-1, Lib Prof Pubns). Shoe String.

Slauson, Nedra & Thompson, John W., eds. Index to Illustrations of the Natural World: Where to Find Pictures of the Living Things of North America. 265p. 1981. Repr. of 1980 ed. 29.95 (ISBN 0-208-01911-1, Lib Prof Pubns). Shoe String.

Slavens, Thomas P. Informational Interviews & Questions. LC 77-18502. 1978. 10.00 (ISBN 0-8108-1102-2). Scarecrow.

Slavin, Albert & Reynolds, Isaac. Basic Accounting. 3rd ed. LC 74-20045. 1975. text ed. 18.95 (ISBN 0-03-089468-9). Dryden Pr.

Slavin, Albert, et al. Financial Accounting: A Basic Approach. 756p. 1980. text ed. 19.95 (ISBN 0-03-048906-7). Dryden Pr.

Slavin, Arthur J. The Way of the West, 5 vols. 1973-1975. Vols. A & 1-3. pap. text ed. 14.95x ea. Vol. A (ISBN 0-471-00907-5). Vol. B. pap. text ed. 14.50x (ISBN 0-471-00908-3). Vol. 1 (ISBN 0-471-00788-9). Vol. 2 (ISBN 0-471-00789-7). Vol. 3 (ISBN 0-471-00891-5). Wiley.

Slavinsky, Ann T., jt. auth. see Krauss, Judith B.

Slavitt, David R. Jo Stern. LC 77-11548. 1978. 8.95 o.p. (ISBN 0-06-013994-3, HarpT). Har-Row.

--Vital Signs: New and Selected Poems. LC 74-18833. 6.95 o.p. (ISBN 0-385-01365-5). Doubleday.

Slavnov, A. A, jt. auth. see Faddeev, L. D.

Slavov, Atanas. The Thaw in Bulgarian Literature. (East European Monographs: No. 84). 200p. 1981. 15.00x (ISBN 0-914710-78-8). East Eur Quarterly.

Slavson, Samuel R. Re-Educating the Delinquent. 1961. pap. 1.50 o.s.i. (ISBN 0-02-078010-9, Collier). Macmillan.

Slawski, Carl J. Social Psychological Theories: A Comparative Handbook. 1980. pap. text ed. 8.95x (ISBN 0-673-15333-9). Scott F.

Slayden, John E., jt. ed. see Dalrymple, Glenn V.

Slaymaker, S. R., 2nd. Captives' Mansion. LC 72-9155. (Illus.). 256p. 1973. 10.95 o.p. (ISBN 0-06-013923-4, HarpT). Har-Row.

--Simplified Fly Fishing. LC 69-15262. (Illus.). 1969. 9.95 o.p. (ISBN 0-06-036061-5, HarpT). Har-Row.

Sleator, William. Among the Dolls. 80p. (gr. 2-5). 1975. PLB 8.95 (ISBN 0-525-25563-X). Dutton.

--The Green Futures of Tycho. LC 80-23020. (gr. 5-9). 1981. PLB 9.95 (ISBN 0-525-31007-X). Dutton.

--That's Silly. LC 80-21902. (Illus.). (gr. k-3). 1981. 7.95 (ISBN 0-525-40981-5). Dutton.

Slechte, C. H. The Hague in Pen & Pencil: Den Haag in Pen en Penseel. (Illus.). 120p. 1977. 25.00 (ISBN 90-247-2029-X). Heinman.

Slee, Shubha, tr. see Nagarkar, Kiran.

Sleeman, J. F. The Welfare State: Its Aims, Benefits & Costs. 1973. pap. text ed. 7.95x o.p. (ISBN 0-04-360029-8). Allen Unwin.

Sleeman, Phillip, jt. auth. see Zalatimo, Suleiman.

Sleeman, Phillip & Rockwell, D. M., eds. Designing Learning Environments. (Professional Books Ser.). (Illus.). 288p. 1980. lib. bdg. 22.50 (ISBN 0-582-28077-X). Longman.

Sleeper, C. Freeman. Black Power & Christian Responsibility. 1969. 4.50 o.p. (ISBN 0-687-03596-1). Abingdon.

Sleeper, C. Freeman & Spivey, Robert A. The Study of Religion in Two Year Colleges. LC 75-28158. (American Academy of Religion, Individual Volumes). 1975. pap. 4.50 (ISBN 0-89130-031-7, 010801). Scholars Pr CA.

Sleeper, Harold R. Building Planning & Design Standards for Architects, Engineers, Designers, Consultants, Building Committees, Draftsman & Students. 1955. 31.95 (ISBN 0-471-79761-8, Pub. by Wiley-Interscience). Wiley.

Sleeth, Charles. Studies in "Christ & Satan". (McMaster Old English Studies & Texts). 160p. 1981. 15.00x (ISBN 0-8020-5484-6). U of Toronto Pr.

Sleeth, Ronald E. & Donahue, John R. Pentecost 1. LC 73-88347. (Proclamation 1: Aids for Interpreting the Lessons of the Church Year, Ser. C). 64p. 1974. pap. 1.95 (ISBN 0-8006-4056-X, 1-4056). Fortress.

Sleffel, Linda. The Law & the Dangerous Criminal. LC 77-287. (Dangerous Offender Project Ser.). 1977. 17.95 (ISBN 0-669-01481-8). Lexington Bks.

Sleight, Jack & Hull, Raymond. The Home Book of Smoke Cooking, Meat, Fish & Game. 1975. pap. 1.50 (ISBN 0-515-03638-2). Jove Pubns.

Sleight, Jack, jt. auth. see Hull, Raymond.

Sleight, Peter, ed. Arterial Baroreceptors & Hypertension. (Illus.). 380p. 1981. text ed. 67.50x (ISBN 0-19-261259-X). Oxford U Pr.

Sleightholme, J. D. Cruising: A Manual for the Small Sailing Boat Owner. (Illus.). 238p. 1977. 21.95x (ISBN 0-8464-0305-6). Beekman Pubs.

--Old Harry's Bunkside Book. 1979. 4.95x (ISBN 0-8464-0068-5). Beekman Pubs.

Sleisenger, Lenore. Guidebook for the Volunteer Reading Teacher. LC 65-28685. (Orig.). 1965. pap. text ed. 3.00x (ISBN 0-8077-2167-0). Tchrs Coll.

Slemmer, Robert E. An Atlas of Gross Neuropathology. (Illus.). 236p. (Orig.). 1981. 42.50 (ISBN 0-87527-239-8). Green.

Slenczynska, Ruth. Music at Your Fingertips: Advice for the Artist & Amateur on Playing the Piano. LC 74-1018. (Music Ser.). 160p. 1974. lib. bdg. 19.50 (ISBN 0-306-70653-9); pap. 3.95 (ISBN 0-306-80034-9). Da Capo.

Slepecky, M., jt. auth. see Schultz, D. O.

Slepian, Jan. Lester's Turn. LC 80-29467. 144p. (gr. 6 up). 1981. PLB 8.95 (ISBN 0-02-782940-5). Macmillan.

Slesser, Malcolm & Lewis, Chris. Biological Energy Resources. LC 79-10255. (Energy Ser.). 250p. 1979. text ed. 23.50x (ISBN 0-419-11340-1, Pub. by E & FN Spon). Methuen Inc.

Sletmo, Gunnar K. & Williams, Ernest W., Jr. Liner Conferences in the Container Age: U. S. Policy at Sea. LC 80-70838. (Studies of the Modern Corporation). (Illus.). 1981. 29.95 (ISBN 0-02-929200-X). Free Pr.

Sletta, Yvonne, jt. auth. see Goeldner, C. R.

Slette, T. Norwegian-English Dictionary. 1977. 80.00x (ISBN 82-521-0692-7, N-537). Vanous.

Slevin, Dennis P., jt. auth. see Bomoma, Thomas V.

Slevin, Jeri S. Clown Book. (Golden Book for Early Childhood Ser.). 24p. (ps-3). 1980. PLB 4.60 o.p. (ISBN 0-307-68993-X, Golden Pr). Western Pub.

Slibar, A., ed. see IUTAM Symposium 5th, VSD-2nd, Held at Technical University, Vienna, Austria, Sept. 19-23, 1977.

Slichter, C. P. Principles of Magnetic Resonance. 2nd rev ed. (Springer Series in Solid State Science: Vol 1). 1978. pap. 24.80 (ISBN 0-387-08476-2). Springer-Verlag.

--Principles of Magnetic Resonance 1980: Second Corrected Printing of the Second Revised & Expanded Edition. (Springer Ser. in Solid-State Sciences: Vol. I). 397p. 1980. 24.80 (ISBN 0-387-08476-2). Springer-Verlag.

Slichter, Charles, jt. ed. see Fitzgerald, Anne.

Slichter, Sumner H., et al. The Impact of Collective Bargaining on Management. 1960. 18.95 (ISBN 0-8157-7984-4). Brookings.

Slide, Anthony. Aspects of American Film History Prior to 1920. LC 78-2912. 1978. 10.00 (ISBN 0-8108-1130-8). Scarecrow.

--The Big V. LC 76-21247. 1976. 10.00 (ISBN 0-8108-0967-2). Scarecrow.

--Films on Film History. LC 79-17662. 242p. 1979. 13.00 (ISBN 0-8108-1238-X). Scarecrow.

--The Kindergarten of the Movies: A History of the Fine Arts Company. LC 80-20391. 246p. 1980. 13.50 (ISBN 0-8108-1358-0). Scarecrow.

Slide, Anthony & Wagenknecht, Edward. Early Feature Films: A Pictorial Survey of Fifty American Classics, Nineteen Twelve to Nineteen Twenty. (Illus.). 176p. (Orig.). 1980. pap. 6.95 (ISBN 0-486-23985-3). Dover.

Slider, H. C. Practical Petroleum Reservoir Engineering Methods. LC 74-33712. 1976. 39.50 (ISBN 0-87814-061-1). Pennwell Pub.

S.L.I.G. Buyers Guide. Starting, Lighting, Ignition & Generating Systems. 7th ed. 1981. 7.00 IBMA Pubns.

Slights, Camille W. The Casuistical Tradition in Shakespeare, Donne, Herbert, & Milton. LC 80-8576. 352p. 1981. 26.50x (ISBN 0-691-06463-6). Princeton U Pr.

Slijper, E. J. Whales. LC 78-74217. (Illus.). 1979. Repr. 32.50x (ISBN 0-8014-1161-0). Cornell U Pr.

Sliker, Alan, jt. auth. see Summitt, Robert.

Sliney, David & Wolbarsht, Myron. Safety with Lasers & Other Optical Sources: A Comprehensive Handbook. 1060p. 1980. 49.50 (ISBN 0-306-40434-6, Plenum Pr). Plenum Pub.

Sling, Marian, tr. see Pachman, Ludek.

Slinger, Penny, jt. auth. see Douglas, Nik.

Slingerland, Aart, jt. auth. see Wilmot, Philip D.

Slingerland, H. Dixon. The Testaments of the Twelve Patriarchs: A Critical History of Research. LC 75-34233. (Society of Biblical Literature. Monograph). 1977. 9.00 (ISBN 0-89130-332-4, 060021); pap. 7.50 (ISBN 0-89130-062-7). Scholars Pr Ca.

Slinkman, John & Navy Times Editors, eds. Duel to the Death: Eyewitness Accounts of Great Battles at Sea. LC 69-13779. (Illus.). (gr. 4-7). 1969. 5.50 o.p. (ISBN 0-15-224290-2, HJ). HarBraceJ.

Slipp, Freude N. Joy of the Limerick Sex Manual: Sex for Sophisticates. 1979. 6.95 (ISBN 0-934622-01-9). Agora Pr.

Slipp, Samuel. Curative Factors in Dynamic Psychotherapy. (Illus.). 448p. 1981. 22.95 (ISBN 0-07-058190-8). McGraw.

Slisenko, A. O., ed. Studies in Constructive Mathematics & Mathematical Logic, Pt. 3. LC 69-12507. (Seminars in Mathematics Ser.: Vol. 16). 1971. 25.00 (ISBN 0-306-18816-3, Consultants). Plenum Pub.

Sloan, A. Elizabeth, jt. auth. see Labuza, T. P.

Sloan, A. W. Man in Extreme Environments. (Environmental Studies Ser.). (Illus.). 144p. 1979. text ed. 13.75 (ISBN 0-398-03941-0). C C Thomas.

Sloan, Alfred P., Jr. My Years with General Motors. LC 64-11306. 560p. 1972. pap. 3.50 (ISBN 0-385-04235-3, Anch.). Doubleday.

Sloan, Annette & Capaccio, Albert. High Marks. (Orig.). (gr. 9). 1981. pap. text ed. 4.75 (ISBN 0-87720-393-8). AMSCO Sch.

Sloan, Blanche C. & Swinburne, Bruce R. Campus Art Museums & Galleries: A Profile. LC 80-23418. 64p. (Orig.). 1981. pap. price not set (ISBN 0-8093-1005-8). S Ill U Pr.

Sloan Commission on Government & Higher Education. A Program for Renewed Partnership: A Report. Kaysen, Carl, ed. 1980. 18.50 (ISBN 0-88410-193-2). Ballinger Pub.

Sloan, David. The Pulitzer Prize Editorials: America's Best Editorial Writing, 1917-1979. 182p. 1980. text ed. 10.50 (ISBN 0-8138-1490-1). Iowa St U Pr.

Sloan, Douglas. The Great Awakening & American Education. LC 72-91270. 270p. 1973. pap. text ed. 5.25x (ISBN 0-8077-2381-9). Tchrs Coll.

--Scottish Enlightenment & the American College Ideal. LC 75-132938. 1971. text ed. 12.75x (ISBN 0-8077-2168-9). Tchrs Coll.

Sloan, Earl S. Treatise on the Horse. (Illus.). 1980. Repr. of 1897 ed. softcover 5.00 (ISBN 0-686-64453-0). S J Durst.

Sloan, Eric. Folklore of American Weather. 1976. pap. 3.50 (ISBN 0-8015-2719-8, Hawthorn). Dutton.

Sloan, Ethel. A Kangaroo in the Kitchen: And Other Adventures of an American Family Down Under. LC 77-15437. 1978. 7.95 (ISBN 0-672-52378-7). Bobbs.

Sloan, Frank, et al. Private Physicians & Public Programs. LC 77-18330. (Illus.). 1978. 18.95 (ISBN 0-669-02093-1). Lexington Bks.

Sloan, Frank A. & Bentkover, Judith D. Access to Ambulatory Care & the U. S. Economy. LC 78-19537. 1979. 17.95 (ISBN 0-669-02510-0). Lexington Bks.

Sloan, Glenna. The Child As Critic: Teaching Literature in the Elementary School. LC 75-23360. 1975. pap. text ed. 6.50x (ISBN 0-8077-2482-3). Tchrs Coll.

Sloan, I. Alcohol & Drug Abuse & the Law, Vol. 27. 1980. 5.95 (ISBN 0-379-11137-3). Oceana.

Sloan, Jacob. Generation of a Journey. 12.00 (ISBN 0-89253-675-6); flexible cloth 4.80 (ISBN 0-89253-676-4). Ind-US Inc.

Sloan, Larry, jt. auth. see Price, Roger.

Sloan, M. E. Computer Hardware. 2nd ed. 576p. Date not set. text ed. 19.95 (ISBN 0-686-63004-1); instr's guide avail. SRA. Postponed.

--Computer Hardware & Organization. LC 75-34109. (Illus.). 480p. 1976. text ed. 19.95 (ISBN 0-574-21065-2, 13-4065); instr's guide avail. (ISBN 0-574-21066-0, 13-4066). SRA.

Sloan, Martha E. Introduction to Minicomputers & Microcomputers. LC 78-74693. 1980. text ed. 23.95 (ISBN 0-201-07279-3). A-W.

Sloan, R. Bryan. Bell Is Phony. 1976. pap. 4.00 (ISBN 0-916378-08-X). Oasis Pr.

Sloan, Robert E. & Skowronski, Carl A. The Rainbow Route: An Illustrated History of the Silverton Railroad, the Silverton Northern Railroad & the Silverton, Gladstone & Northerly Railroad. Thode, Jackson C., et al, eds. (Illus.). 1975. 49.00 (ISBN 0-913582-12-3). Sundance.

Sloan, Samuel. City & Suburban Architect. LC 75-31711. (Architecture & Decorative Art Ser.). (Illus.). 1975. Repr. of 1859 ed. lib. bdg. 65.00 (ISBN 0-306-70745-4). Da Capo.

--Sloan's Victorian Buildings: Illustrations & Floor Plans for 60 Residences & Other Structures, 2 vols. in 1. (Illus.). 400p. 1981. pap. 12.95 (ISBN 0-486-24009-6). Dover.

Sloan, Stephen. Simulating Terrorism. LC 80-5937. (Illus.). 200p. 1981. 12.95 (ISBN 0-8061-1746-X); pap. 5.95 (ISBN 0-8061-1760-5). U of Okla Pr.

Sloan, Stephen, jt. ed. see Shultz, Richard H., Jr.

Sloan, Steve. A Whole New Ball Game. LC 75-24737. (Illus.). 168p. 1975. 5.95 (ISBN 0-8054-5559-0). Broadman.

Sloan, Thomas O. & Waddington, Raymond B., eds. The Rhetoric of Renaissance Poetry. LC 73-80824. 1974. 16.95x (ISBN 0-520-02501-6). U of Cal Pr.

Sloan, W. H. & Lerin, A. Concordancia Alfabetica De la Biblia. Date not set. pap. 9.95 (ISBN 0-311-42054-0). Casa Bautista.

Sloane, A. A. & Witney, F. Labor Relations. 3rd ed. 1977. text ed. 21.00 (ISBN 0-13-519595-0). P-H.

Sloane, Albert E. So You Have Cataracts: What You & Your Family Should Know. (Illus.). 112p. 1975. 9.50 (ISBN 0-398-01771-9). C C Thomas.

Sloane, Eric. A B C Book of Early Americana. LC 63-18657. (gr. 1 up). 1963. 4.95a (ISBN 0-385-04663-4); PLB o.p. (ISBN 0-385-05169-7). Doubleday.

--Diary of an Early American Boy. LC 62-18313. 1977. pap. 4.95 (ISBN 0-345-29451-3). Ballantine.

--The Do's & Don'ts of Yesterday. (Illus.). 1975. pap. 3.45 o.p. (ISBN 0-380-00429-1, 25858). Avon.

--Eric Sloane's Double Barrel. Incl. The Cracker Barrel; The Second Barrel. (Funk & W Bk.). 1969. boxed set 17.95 o.s.i. (ISBN 0-308-70111-9, 711100, TYC-T). T Y Crowell.

--Eric Sloane's Sketchbook Calender for 1979. (Funk & W Bk.). (Illus.). 1978. 3.95 o.s.i. (ISBN 0-308-10348-3, TYC-T). T Y Crowell.

--I Remember America. (Funk & W Bk.). (Illus.). 1971. 14.95 o.p. (ISBN 0-308-70041-4, TYC-T). T Y Crowell.

--A Museum of Early American Tools. 1973. pap. 2.95 o.p. (ISBN 0-345-24675-6). Ballantine.

--Return to Taos: A Sketchbook of Roadside Americana. LC 60-14499. (Funk & W Bk.). (Illus.). 1969. 11.95 o.s.i. (ISBN 0-308-70099-6, TYC-T). T Y Crowell.

--Reverence for Wood. LC 65-25668. (Funk & W Bk.). (Illus.). 12.95 (ISBN 0-308-70048-1, 710220, TYC-T). T Y Crowell.

--Reverence for Wood. 1975. pap. 2.95 o.p. (ISBN 0-345-24492-3). Ballantine.

--Second Barrel. (Funk & W Bk.). (Illus.). 1969. 10.95 o.s.i. (ISBN 0-308-70100-3, TYC-T). T Y Crowell.

--Sloan's Almanac & Weather Forecaster. 1977. pap. 3.50 (ISBN 0-8015-6877-3, Hawthorn). Dutton.

--Three by Sloane. Incl. Diary of an Early American Boy; A Museum of Early American Tools; A Reverence for Wood. (Funk & W Bk.). 1969. boxed set 29.95 o.p. (ISBN 0-308-70110-0, 711090, TYC-T). T Y Crowell.

Sloane, Ethel. Biology of Women. LC 79-15256. 1980. 16.95 (ISBN 0-471-02165-2, Pub. by Wiley-Medical). Wiley.

Sloane, Eugene A. The All New Complete Book of Bicycling. (Illus.). 1981. 19.95 (ISBN 0-671-24967-3). S&S.

Sloane, Howard N. Classroom Management: Remediation & Prevention. LC 75-35987. 1976. pap. text ed. 10.95 (ISBN 0-471-79857-6). Wiley.

Sloane, Irving. Classic Guitar Construction. (Illus.). 1966. 10.95 o.p. (ISBN 0-525-08200-X). Dutton.

Sloane, Irving, jt. auth. see Pollack, Richard.

Sloane, Joseph C. French Painting Between the Past & the Present: Artists, Critics, & Traditions from 1848 to 1870. (Monographs in Art & Archaeology: No. 27). (Illus.). 300p. 1973. 27.50x (ISBN 0-691-03817-1); pap. 7.50 (ISBN 0-691-00306-8). Princeton U Pr.

Sloane, Leonard, jt. auth. see Mahoney, Tom.

Sloane, Martin. The Nineteen Eighty-One Guide to Coupons & Refunds. 2nd rev. ed. (Orig.). 1981. pap. 2.95 (ISBN 0-553-14617-3). Bantam.

Sloane, Peter, ed. Women & Low Pay. 1980. text ed. 30.00x (ISBN 0-333-26817-2). Humanities.

Sloane, R. Bruce & Horvitz, Diana F. A General Guide to Abortion. LC 72-90556. 1973. 13.95 (ISBN 0-911012-30-3). Nelson-Hall.

Sloane, R. Bruce, jt. ed. see Birren, James E.

Sloane, Randy, jt. auth. see Carroll, Mary-Jo.

Sloane, William M. The Life of Napoleon Bonaparte, 4 vols. 1980. Repr. of 1910 ed. Set. lib. bdg. 125.00 (ISBN 0-8492-8128-8). R West.

Sloat, Clarence, et al. Introduction to Phonology. LC 77-23100. (Illus.). 1978. ref. 12.95 (ISBN 0-13-492207-7). P-H.

Slobin, Dan I. Psycholinguistics. 2nd ed. 1979. pap. text ed. 8.95x (ISBN 0-673-15140-9). Scott F.

Slobin, Mark. Kirgiz Instrumental Music. LC 70-93475. (D (Monographs), No. 2). (Illus.). xiv, 158p. (Orig.). 1969. pap. text ed. 6.00x (ISBN 0-913360-01-5). Asian Music Pub.

Slobodin, Richard. W. H. R. Rivers. LC 78-6393. (Leaders of Modern Anthropology Ser.). (Illus.). 1978. 22.50x (ISBN 0-231-03582-9). Columbia U Pr.

Slobodkin, Florence & Slobodkin, Louis. Io Sono (I Am) LC 62-11219. (Illus.). (gr. 3 up). 1962. 4.95 (ISBN 0-8149-0392-4). Vanguard.

--Mister Papadilly & Willy. LC 64-23322. (Illus.). (gr. 4-9). 4.95 (ISBN 0-8149-0391-6). Vanguard.

--Sara Somebody. LC 75-103162. (Illus.). (gr. 7 up). 1969. 5.95 (ISBN 0-8149-0663-X). Vanguard.

--Too Many Mittens. LC 58-12198. (Illus.). (gr. 1-4). 1958. 5.95 (ISBN 0-8149-0394-0). Vanguard.

Slobodkin, Florence, jt. auth. see Slobodkin, Louis.

Slobodkin, Lawrence B. Growth & Regulation of Animal Populations. (Illus.). 1980. pap. 6.00 (ISBN 0-486-63958-4). Dover.

Slobodkin, Louis. The Amazing Space Ship Adventures, 3 bks. Incl. The Space Ship Under the Apple Tree; The Space Ship Returns to the Apple Tree; The Three-Seated Space Ship. (Young Science Fiction Ser.). (Illus.). (gr. 3-5). 1981. Boxed Set. pap. 7.95 (ISBN 0-02-045220-9). Macmillan.

--Clear the Track. (gr. k-3). 1967. 4.95g o.s.i. (ISBN 0-02-783680-0). Macmillan.

--Excuse Me! Certainly! LC 59-15200. (Illus.). (gr. 1-3). 1959. 5.95 (ISBN 0-8149-0403-3). Vanguard.

--First Book of Drawing. (First Bks). (Illus.). (gr. 4-6). 1958. PLB 6.45 (ISBN 0-531-00516-X). Watts.

--Late Cuckoo. LC 62-19106. (Illus.). (ps-3). 5.95 (ISBN 0-8149-0400-9). Vanguard.

--Magic Michael. (gr. k-3). 1944. 7.95 (ISBN 0-02-784680-6). Macmillan.

--Read About the Policeman. LC 66-10582. (Read About Bks). (Illus.). (gr. k-3). 1966. PLB 4.47 o.p. (ISBN 0-531-01263-8). Watts.

--Round Trip Space Ship. LC 68-11007. (gr. 3-7). 1968. 4.95g o.s.i. (ISBN 0-686-66486-8). Macmillan.

--Sculpture: Principles & Practice. (Illus.). 256p. 1973. pap. 6.00 (ISBN 0-486-22960-2). Dover.

--The Space Ship in the Park. LC 70-187799. (Illus.). (gr. 3-7). 1972. 7.95 (ISBN 0-02-784700-4). Macmillan.

--Space Ship Under the Apple Tree. (gr. k-3). 1952. 7.95g (ISBN 0-02-785340-3). Macmillan.

--Thank You, You're Welcome. LC 57-12259. (Illus.). (gr. k-3). 5.95 (ISBN 0-8149-0404-1). Vanguard.

--Trick or Treat. (gr. k-3). 1967. 4.95g o.s.i. (ISBN 0-02-785690-9). Macmillan.

--Wide Awake Owl. (gr. 1-2). 1958. 4.50g o.s.i. (ISBN 0-02-785890-1). Macmillan.

--Wilbur the Warrior. LC 79-175537. (Illus.). (gr. 1-3). 5.95 (ISBN 0-8149-0713-X). Vanguard.

Slobodkin, Louis & Slobodkin, Florence. Cowboy Twins. LC 60-9731. (Illus.). (gr. 1-3). 1960. 5.95 (ISBN 0-8149-0393-2). Vanguard.

Slobodkin, Louis, jt. auth. see Slobodkin, Florence.

Slobodkin, Marvin. Inside Dope. 1971. 5.50 o.p. (ISBN 0-525-13355-0). Dutton.

Slobodkina, Esphyr. Billy, the Condominium Cat. LC 79-23402. (Illus.). 1980. 6.95 (ISBN 0-201-09204-2, 9204). A-W.

--Caps for Sale. (gr. k-3). 1976. pap. 1.50 (ISBN 0-590-31401-7, Schol Pap); pap. 3.50 bk. & record (ISBN 0-590-04418-4). Schol Bk Serv.

Slocombe, Walter. Controlling Strategic Nuclear Weapons. (Headline Ser.: 226). (Illus.). 1975. pap. 2.00 (ISBN 0-87124-031-9, 75-9293). Foreign Policy.

Slocum, D. W. & Hughes, O. R., eds. Transition Metal Mediated Organic Syntheses. LC 79-24735. (N.Y. Academy of Sciences Annals: Vol. 333). 301p. 1980. 55.00x (ISBN 0-89766-039-0). NY Acad Sci.

Slocum, John, jt. auth. see Hellriegel, Don.

Slocum, John W., Jr., jt. auth. see Hellriegel, Don.

Slocum, Joshua. Sailing Alone Around the World. (Illus.). 1956. pap. 3.50 (ISBN 0-486-20326-3). Dover.

Slocum, Keith. Business English: A Worktext with Programmed Reinforcement. 2nd ed. 1981. 7.95 (ISBN 0-672-97310-3); tchrs. manual 6.67 (ISBN 0-672-97311-1). Bobbs.

Slocum, Robert B. Sample Cataloguing Forms: Illustrations of Solutions to Problems of Description (with Particular Reference to Chapters 1-13 of the Anglo-American Cataloguing Rules, Second Edition) 3rd ed. LC 80-21507. (Illus.). 121p. 1980. 11.00 (ISBN 0-8108-1364-5). Scarecrow.

Slocum, Robert B., ed. Biographical Dictionaries & Related Works: An International Bibliography. LC 67-27789. 1967. 52.00 (ISBN 0-8103-0972-6); supplement no. 1 52.00 (ISBN 0-8103-0973-4); supplement no. 2 52.00 (ISBN 0-8103-0974-2). Gale.

Slocum, Victor. Capt. Joshua Slocum: The Life & Voyages of America's Best Known Sailor. LC 80-28585. (Illus.). 384p. 1981. Repr. of 1950 ed. 16.50 (ISBN 0-911378-04-9). Sheridan.

Slodowy, P. Simple Singularities & Simple Algebraic Groups. (Lecture Notes in Mathematics: Vol. 815). 175p. 1980. pap. 11.80 (ISBN 0-387-10026-1). Springer-Verlag.

Sloma, Richard S. No-Nonsense Management. 176p. 1981. pap. 3.50 (ISBN 0-553-20035-6). Bantam.

Sloman, Aaron. The Computer Revolution in Philosophy: Philosophy, Science & Models of Mind. (Harvester Studies in Cognitive Science). 1978. text ed. 27.25x (ISBN 0-391-00830-7); pap. text ed. 15.50x (ISBN 0-391-00831-5). Humanities.

Slonczewski, Joan. Still Forms on Foxfield. 1980. pap. 1.95 (ISBN 0-345-28762-2). Ballantine.

Slone, Verna M. What My Heart Wants to Tell. LC 78-31688. (Illus.). 1979. 8.95 o.p. (ISBN 0-915220-47-4). New Republic.

Sloniger, Jerry. Porsche: The Four-Cylinder, Four-Cam Sports & Racing Cars. (Illus.). 120p. (Orig.). 1977. pap. 10.95 (ISBN 0-914792-03-2, Pub. by DB Pubns). Motorbooks Intl.

--The VW Story. (Illus.). 216p. 1981. 37.95 (ISBN 0-85059-441-3). Aztex.

Slonim, Marc. Soviet Russian Literature: Writers & Problems, 1917-1977. 2nd ed. 1977. pap. 7.95 (ISBN 0-19-502152-5, GB184, GB). Oxford U Pr.

Slonimskii, Aleksandr L. Tekhnika Komicheskogo U Gogolia. LC 63-7523. (Slavic Reprint Ser., No. 2). 65p. (Rus.). 1969. pap. 1.50 (ISBN 0-87057-070-6, Pub. by Brown U Pr). Univ Pr of New England.

Slonimsky, Juri. Soviet Ballet. LC 77-107873. (Music Ser). (Illus.). 1970. Repr. of 1947 ed. lib. bdg. 29.50 (ISBN 0-306-71897-9). Da Capo.

Slonimsky, Nicholas. Thesaurus of Scales & Melodic Patterns. 1947. 27.50 (ISBN 0-684-10551-9, ScribT). Scribner.

Slonimsky, Nicolas. Lexicon of Musical Invective: Critical Assaults on Composers Since Beethoven's Time. 2nd ed. LC 65-26270. 331p. 1969. pap. 7.95 (ISBN 0-295-78579-9, WP52). U. of Wash Pr.

--The Road to Music. (Music Reprint Ser.). 1979. Repr. of 1966 ed. lib. bdg. 17.95 (ISBN 0-306-79566-3). Da Capo.

Sloper, Patricia, jt. auth. see Cunningham, Cliff.

Slosar, John A., Jr. Prisonization, Friendship & Leadership. LC 77-14698. (Illus.). 1978. 16.95 (ISBN 0-669-02023-0). Lexington Bks.

Slosberg, Paul S. Neurology. 6th ed. (Medical Examination Review Book Ser.: Vol. 8). 1977. spiral bdg. 8.50 (ISBN 0-87488-108-0). Med Exam.

Sloshberg, Willard. Contemporary Society. (Illus.). 1978. pap. text ed. 12.50 (ISBN 0-8299-0140-X); wkbk. avail. (ISBN 0-8299-0574-X). West Pub.

Sloss, D. J., ed. see Blake, William.

Sloss, L. L., jt. auth. see Krumbein, William C.

Sloss, V. & Dufty, J. H. Handbook of Bovine Obstetrics. (Illus.). 224p. 1980. lib. bdg. 29.95 (ISBN 0-683-07745-7). Williams & Wilkins.

Slosser, Bob. See How the Winds Blows. 1980. pap. 4.95 (ISBN 0-88270-398-6). Logos.

Slosser, Bob, jt. auth. see Fullam, Everett L.

Slosser, Bob, jt. auth. see Vaughan, Curry.

Slosson, Edwin E see Johnson, Allen & Nevins, Allan.

Slote, Alfred. The Biggest Victory. (gr. 3-7). 1977. pap. 1.95 (ISBN 0-380-00907-2, 31732, Camelot). Avon.

--Hang Tough, Paul Mather. (gr. 7 up). 1973. 8.95 (ISBN 0-397-31451-5). Lippincott.

--Hang Tough, Paul Mather. (gr. 3-5). 1975. pap. 1.75 (ISBN 0-380-00225-6, 54999, Camelot). Avon.

--The Hotshot. (Triumph Books). (Illus.). (gr. 4 up). 1977. PLB 6.90 s&l (ISBN 0-531-00330-2). Watts.

--Matt Gargan's Boy. LC 74-26669. (gr. 3-5). 1975. 8.79 (ISBN 0-397-31617-8). Lippincott.

--Matt Gargan's Boy. (gr. 3-7). 1977. pap. 1.95 (ISBN 0-380-01730-X, 34199, Camelot). Avon.

--My Father, the Coach. (gr. 3-7). 1977. pap. 1.75 (ISBN 0-380-01724-5, 49809, Camelot). Avon.

--My Robot Buddy. (Illus.). (gr. 2-7). 1978. pap. 1.75 (ISBN 0-380-40329-3, 52001, Camelot). Avon.

--My Robot Buddy. LC 75-9922. (Illus.). 96p. (gr. 2-4). 1975. 7.95 (ISBN 0-397-31641-0). Lippincott.

--My Trip to Alpha I. (Illus.). (gr. 2-5). 1980. pap. 1.95 (ISBN 0-380-51128-2, 51128, Camelot). Avon.

--My Trip to Alpha 1. LC 78-6463. (Illus.). (gr. 3-5). 1978. 7.95 (ISBN 0-397-31810-3). Lippincott.

--Termination: The Closing at Baker Plant. LC 69-13100. 360p. 1977. 11.50 (ISBN 0-87944-219-0). U of Mich Soc Res.

--Tony & Me. LC 74-5182. 160p. (gr. 4-6). 1974. 8.95 (ISBN 0-397-31507-4). Lippincott.

--Tony & Me. (gr. 3-5). 1975. pap. 1.25 (ISBN 0-380-00438-0, 45914, Camelot). Avon.

Slote, Bernice, jt. auth. see Miller, James E., Jr.

Slote, Bernice, ed. see Cather, Willa.

Slote, Bernice, ed. see Frye, Northrop, et al.

Slote, Stanley J. Weeding Library Collections. LC 74-23062. (Research Studies in Library Science: No. 14). 1975. lib. bdg. 20.00x (ISBN 0-87287-105-3). Libs Unl.

Sloterdijk, Peter, jt. ed. see Kreiler, Kurt.

Slotkin, Edgar M., tr. see Dubois, Jacques, et al.

Slotkin, Richard. The Crater. LC 80-65988. 1980. 17.95 (ISBN 0-689-11107-X). Atheneum.

Slotkin, Richard & Folsom, James K., eds. So Dreadful a Judgement: Puritan Responses to King Philip's War, 1676-1677. 1978. 25.00x (ISBN 0-8195-6058-8); pap. 10.00x. Wesleyan U Pr.

Slotkin, Richard S. Regeneration Through Violence: The Mythology of the American Frontier, 1600-1860. LC 72-3725. 670p. (Orig.). 1973. 27.50x (ISBN 0-8195-4055-2, Pub. by Wesleyan U Pr); pap. 8.95 (ISBN 0-8195-6034-0). Columbia U Pr.

Slotnick, Daniel L. & Slotnick, Joan L. Computers: Their Structure, Use, & Influence. (Illus.). 1979. ref. 18.95 (ISBN 0-13-165068-8). P-H.

Slotnick, Joan L., jt. auth. see Slotnick, Daniel L.

Slottman, William B., jt. ed. see Janos, Andrew C.

Slovenko, Ralph. Crime, Law & Corrections. (Illus.). 1966. 76.75 (ISBN 0-398-01774-3). C C Thomas.

Slover, Luella, ed. Life After Youth. 1981. pap. write for info. (ISBN 0-8309-0303-8). Herald Hse.

Slover, Luella H. Ministry with Young Adults. 1980. pap. 3.00 (ISBN 0-8309-0283-X). Herald Hse.

Slovin, M. B. & Sushka, M. E. Interest Rates on Savings Deposits: Theory, Estimation, & Policy. LC 74-16931. (Illus.). 192p. 1975. 18.95 (ISBN 0-669-96453-0). Lexington Bks.

Slovin, Myron B. & Sushka, Marie E. Money & Economic Activity. LC 76-20950. (Illus.). 1977. 21.00 o.p. (ISBN 0-669-00882-6). Lexington Bks.

Sloyan, Gerard S. Christ the Lord. pap. 0.95 (ISBN 0-385-00620-9, E6, Echo). Doubleday.

Sloyan, Gerard S. & Kee, Howard C. Pentecost 3. LC 73-88347. (Proclamation 1: Aids for Interpreting the Lessons of the Church Year, Ser. C). 64p. 1974. pap. 1.95 (ISBN 0-8006-4058-6, 1-4058). Fortress.

Sloyer, Clifford W. Algebra & Its Applications: A Problem Solving Approach. LC 72-10087. 1970. text ed. 11.95 (ISBN 0-201-07041-3). A-W.

Sloyer, Clifford W., jt. auth. see Baxter, Willard E.

Slugg, J. T. Reminiscences of Manchester Fifty Years Ago. (The Development of Industrial Society Ser.). 355p. 1980. Repr. 24.00x (ISBN 0-7165-1771-X, Pub. by Irish Academic Pr). Biblio Dist.

Slupecki, J. & Borkowski, L. Elements of Mathematical Logic & Set Theory. 1967. 32.00 o.p. (ISBN 0-08-011096-7). Pergamon.

Slurzberg, Morris & Osterheld, William. Essentials of Electricity-Electronics. 3rd ed. 1965. text ed. 17.95 (ISBN 0-07-058260-2, G); answers 1.50 (ISBN 0-07-058261-0). McGraw.

SLUSA, ed. see Hanriot, Hugo.

Slusser, George E. Frank Herbert: Prophet of Dune. LC 78-1310. (The Milford Ser: Popular Writers of Today: Vol. 14). Date not set. lib. bdg. 8.95x (ISBN 0-89370-119-X); pap. 2.95 (ISBN 0-89370-219-6). Borgo Pr. Postponed.

--I. Asimov: The Foundations of His Science Fiction. LC 78-1042. (Milford Ser.: Popular Writers of Today: Vol. 15). Date not set. lib. bdg. 8.95x (ISBN 0-89370-122-X); pap. 2.95 (ISBN 0-89370-222-6). Borgo Pr. Postponed.

Slusser, Robert M. & Ginsburgs, George. A Calendar of Soviet Treaties: 1958-1973. LC 80-50453. 990p. 1980. 125.00x (ISBN 90-286-0609-2). Sijthoff & Noordhoff.

Slusser, Robert M. & Triska, Jan F. Calendar of Soviet Treaties, 1917-1957. 1959. 25.00x (ISBN 0-8047-0587-9). Stanford U Pr.

Slutzkin, D., ed. see Emanuel', N. M. & Knorre, D. G.

Slutzkin, D., ed. see Gur'Yanova, E. N., et al.

Slutzkin, D., ed. see Kiselev, A. V. & Lygin, V. I.

Slutzkin, D., ed. see Lipatov, Yu. S & Sergeeva, L. M.

Slutzkin, D., ed. see Myasoedov, B. I., et al.

Slutzkin, D., ed. see Pshezhetsky, S. Ya., et al.

Slutzkin, D., tr. see Tugarinov, A. I.

Sluzar, jt. ed. see Bialer.

Sluzar, S., jt. ed. see Bialer, S.

Sluzar, Sophia, jt. ed. see Bialer, Seweryn.

Sluzas, Raymond & Ryan, Anne. A Graphic Guide to Industrialized Building Elements. LC 77-13121. (Illus.). 1977. 19.95 (ISBN 0-8436-0163-9); pap. 12.95 (ISBN 0-8436-0164-7). CBI Pub.

Sly, Michael R. Pediatric Allergy. 2nd ed. (Medical Outline Ser.). 1980. pap. price not set (ISBN 0-87488-624-4). Med Exam.

Slyke, Helen Van see Van Slyke, Helen.

Slyke, L. L. van see Van Slyke, L. L. & Price, W. V.

Slyke, Lyman P. Van see Marshall, George C.

Smail, R. C. Crusading Warfare, 1097-1193: A Contribution to Medieval Military History. LC 67-26956. (Cambridge Studies in Medieval Life & Thought Ser). (Cambridge U Pr Library Editions). 1967. 35.50 (ISBN 0-521-21315-0); pap. 11.50 (ISBN 0-521-09730-4). Cambridge U Pr.

Smail, Thomas A. The Forgotten Father. 1981. pap. 5.95 (ISBN 0-8028-1879-X). Eerdmans.

Smail, William M., ed. Quintilian on Education. LC 66-13554. 1966. text ed. 8.75 (ISBN 0-8077-2173-5); pap. text ed. 4.00x (ISBN 0-8077-2170-0). Tchrs Coll.

Smailes, Arthur E. Geography of Towns. (Orig.). 1966. pap. text ed. 2.50x (ISBN 0-09-028624-3, Hutchinson U Lib). Humanities.

Smakov, Gennady. Baryshnikov: From Russia to the West. (Illus.). 1981. 17.50 (ISBN 0-374-10908-7). FS&G.

Smaldone, Joseph P., ed. see Fetter, Bruce, et al.

Smale, S. The Mathematics of Time. (Illus.). 151p. 1981. pap. 16.00 (ISBN 0-387-90519-7). Springer-Verlag.

Smale, Stephen, jt. auth. see Hirsch, Morris.

Small, Arnold. Birds of California. 1974. 13.95 (ISBN 0-87691-119-X). Winchester Pr.

Small, Arnold M. Elements of Hearing Science: A Programmed Text. LC 77-20110. (Communications Disorders Ser.). 1978. 11.95 (ISBN 0-471-01732-9). Wiley.

Small, Beatrice. The Kadin. 1977. pap. 2.25 (ISBN 0-380-01699-0, 43190). Avon.

Small, Benjamin F. Workmen's Compensation Law of Indiana. 1950. with suppl. 35.00 o.p. (ISBN 0-672-82540-6, Bobbs-Merrill Law). Michie.

Small, Bertrice. Adora. (Orig.). 1980. pap. 2.50 (ISBN 0-345-28493-3). Ballantine.

--Skye O'Malley. 1980. 5.95 (ISBN 0-345-29256-1). Ballantine.

Small, Dwight H. After You've Said I Do. 1976. pap. 1.75 (ISBN 0-89129-213-6). Jove Pubns.

--Marriage As Equal Partnership. 1980. pap. 2.95 (ISBN 0-8010-8177-7). Baker Bk.

--The Right to Remarry. 1977. pap. 1.75 o.p. (ISBN 0-8007-8272-0, Spire). Revell.

Small, Dwight Hervey. Christian: Celebrate Your Sexuality. 224p. 1974. 7.95 o.p. (ISBN 0-8007-0661-7). Revell.

Small, George L. The Blue Whale. LC 76-134986. (Illus.). 1973. 17.50x (ISBN 0-231-03288-9); pap. 4.95 (ISBN 0-231-08322-X). Columbia U Pr.

Small, Harold A., ed. see Greenough, Horatio.

Small, HyDee. The Complete Bed Building Book. (Illus.). 1979. 12.95 o.p. (ISBN 0-8306-9822-1); pap. 7.95 (ISBN 0-8306-1124-X, 1124). TAB Bks.

Small, Ian. The Aesthetes: A Sourcebook. (Illus.). 1979. 21.00x (ISBN 0-7100-0145-2); pap. 9.95 (ISBN 0-7100-0146-0). Routledge & Kegan.

Small, Iver F., ed. Introduction to the Clinical History. 2nd ed. 1971. spiral bdg. 4.00 o.p. (ISBN 0-87488-729-1). Med Exam.

Small, J. The PH of Plant Cells. Bd. with The PH of Animal Cells. Wiercinski, F. J. (Protoplasmatologica: Vol. 2B, Pt. 2c). (Illus.). iv, 172p. 1955. pap. 40.20 o.p. (ISBN 0-387-80386-6). Springer-Verlag.

Small, John, ed. see Monkhouse, F. J.

Small, John R., jt. auth. see Savage, Christopher I.

Small, Leonard. Neuropsychodiagnosis in Psychotherapy. rev. ed. LC 80-19415. 480p. 1980. 25.00 (ISBN 0-87630-243-6). Brunner Mazel.

Small, M., ed. Buffets & Receptions. (Illus.). 1978. text ed. 99.95 (ISBN 0-685-47808-4). Radio City.

Small, Melvin. Was War Necessary? National Security & U. S. Entry into War. LC 80-13536. (Sage Library of Social Research: Vol. 105). (Illus.). 311p. 1980. 18.00 (ISBN 0-8039-1486-5); pap. 8.95 (ISBN 0-8039-1487-3). Sage.

Small, Melvin, jt. auth. see Singer, J. David.

Small, Michael, jt. ed. see Fuller, John.

Small, Miriam R. Oliver Wendell Holmes. (U. S. Authors Ser.: No. 29). 1962. lib. bdg. 10.95 (ISBN 0-8057-0380-2). Twayne.

Small, Norman J. Some Presidential Interpretations of the Presidency. LC 71-87353. (Politics & Law Ser). 1969. Repr. of 1932 ed. lib. bdg. 27.50 (ISBN 0-306-71663-1). Da Capo.

Small, R. J. The Study of Landforms. 2nd ed. LC 77-71427. 1978. 57.50 (ISBN 0-521-21634-6); pap. 23.95x (ISBN 0-521-29238-7). Cambridge U Pr.

Small, R. L. No Uncertain Sound. (Scholar As Preacher Ser.). 190p. 1963. text ed. 7.75 (ISBN 0-567-04431-9). Attic Pr.

Small, R. Leonard. No Other Name. 190p. 1966. text ed. 4.95 (ISBN 0-567-02257-9). Attic Pr.

Small, S. A., jt. auth. see Carmichael, H. T.

Small, Samuel & Pilot Books Staff. Directory of Franchising Organizations 1981. LC 62-39831. 1981. pap. 3.50 (ISBN 0-87576-000-7). Pilot Bks.

Smallbone, Douglas W. Practice of Marketing. (Illus.). 400p. 1972. 16.50x o.p. (ISBN 0-8464-0745-0). Beekman Pubs.

Smalley, Barbara. George Eliot & Flaubert: Pioneers of the Modern Novel. LC 73-85446. ix, 240p. 1974. 12.00x (ISBN 0-8214-0136-X). Ohio U Pr.

Smalley, Beryl. Historians in the Middle Ages. 1975. lib. rep. ed. 20.00x o.p. (ISBN 0-684-15879-5, ScribT). Scribner.

Smalley, Donald, ed. Anthony Trollope: The Critical Heritage. 1969. 40.00x (ISBN 0-7100-6153-6). Routledge & Kegan.

Smalley, Richard V., jt. auth. see Durant, John R.

Smalley, Ruth E. Theory for Social Work Practice. LC 67-14290. 1967. 20.00x (ISBN 0-231-02769-9); pap. 9.00x (ISBN 0-231-08327-0). Columbia U Pr.

Smalley, S. S., jt. auth. see Lindars, B.

Smalley, W. A., jt. auth. see De Waard, J.

Smalley, W. A., jt. ed. see Black, M.

Smalley, W. A., et al. Orthography Studies. 1964. 3.00 (ISBN 0-8267-0027-6, 08508). United Bible.

Smalley, Webster. The Boy Who Talked to Whales. (Orig.). 1981. playscript 2.00 (ISBN 0-87602-232-8). Anchorage.

Smalley, William A. Manual of Articulatory Phonetics. LC 73-14763. (Applied Cultural Anthropology Ser.). (Illus.). 522p. 1973. pap. text ed. 7.95x (ISBN 0-87808-139-9). William Carey Lib.

Smalley, William A., jt. auth. see Larson, Donald N.

Smalley, William A., ed. Readings in Missionary Anthropology II. 2nd rev. enl. ed. LC 78-6009. (Applied Cultural Anthropology Ser.). 1978. pap. text ed. 12.95x (ISBN 0-87808-731-1). William Carey.

Smalley, William A., ed. see Loewen, Jacob A.

Smallman, R. E. & Ashbee, K. H. Modern Metallography. 1966. 13.75 (ISBN 0-08-011571-3); pap. 6.25 (ISBN 0-08-011570-5). Pergamon.

Smallwood, jt. auth. see Corley.

Smallwood, Charles, et al. The Cable Car Book. LC 80-65238. (Illus.). 160p. 1980. 25.00 (ISBN 0-89087-280-5). Celestial Arts.

Smallwood, Charles A. The White Front Cars of San Francisco. Walker, Jim, ed. LC 78-71892. (Special Ser.: No. 44). 1978. 35.00 (ISBN 0-916374-32-7). Interurban.

Smallwood, Frank. Greater London: The Politics of Metropolitan Reform. LC 64-25258. 1965. 28.00x (ISBN 0-672-51145-2). Irvington.

Smallwood, James M. An Oklahoma Adventure: Of Banks & Bankers. LC 79-4745. (Illus.). 1979. 11.95 (ISBN 0-8061-1545-9). U of Okla Pr.

--Time of Hope, Time of Despair: Black Texans During Reconstruction. (National University Publications, Ethnic Studies). 1981. 17.50 (ISBN 0-8046-9273-4). Kennikat.

Smaridge, Nora. Raggedy Ann: A Thank You, Please & I Love You Book. (Illus.). (ps-1). 1970. 1.95 (ISBN 0-307-10487-7, Golden Pr); PLB 7.62 (ISBN 0-307-60487-X). Western Pub.

Smaridge, Norah. The Big Tidy-up. (Big Picture Bks.). (ps-3). 1970. PLB 7.62 (ISBN 0-307-60877-8, Golden Pr). Western Pub.

--Famous British Women Novelists. LC 67-22722. (Illus.). (gr. 7-9). 1967. 5.95 (ISBN 0-396-05612-1). Dodd.

--Famous Literary Teams for Young People. LC 76-53636. (Famous Biographies Ser). (gr. 7 up). 1977. 5.95 (ISBN 0-396-07407-3). Dodd.

--Litterbugs Come in Every Size. (Illus.). (ps-4). 1972. PLB 7.62 (ISBN 0-307-60455-1, Golden Pr). Western Pub.

--Neatos & Litterbugs: Mystery of the Missing Ticket. (Illus.). 24p. (ps-2). 1952. PLB 5.00 (ISBN 0-307-60515-9, Golden Pr). Western Pub.

--Only Silly People Waste. LC 75-15623. (Illus.). (gr. k-4). 1976. 5.50g (ISBN 0-687-28847-9). Abingdon.

--Raggedy Andy: The I Can Do It, You Can Do It Book. (Illus.). (gr. k-2). 1973. 1.95 (ISBN 0-307-10494-X, Golden Pr); PLB 7.62 (ISBN 0-307-60494-2). Western Pub.

Smarr, Larry. Sources of Gravitational Radiation. LC 79-50177. (Illus.). 1979. 24.95 (ISBN 0-521-22778-X). Cambridge U Pr.

Smart, Bath C. & Crofton, H. T. Dialect of the English Gypsies. 2nd ed. LC 68-22050. 1968. Repr. of 1875 ed. 18.00 (ISBN 0-8103-3292-2). Gale.

Smart, C. F. & Stanbury, W. T. Studies on Crisis Management. 195p. 1978. pap. text ed. 9.95x (ISBN 0-920380-03-4, Pub. by Inst Res Pub Canada). Renouf.

Smart, Carol. Women, Crime & Criminology: A Feminist Critique. 1976. 15.00 (ISBN 0-7100-8449-8). Routledge & Kegan.

--Women, Crime & Criminology: A Feminist Critique. 1978. pap. 7.95 (ISBN 0-7100-8833-7). Routledge & Kegan.

Smart, Christopher. The Poetical Works of Christopher Smart, Volume I: Jubilate Agno. Williamson, Karina, ed. (English Texts Ser.). (Illus.). 168p. 1980. 39.95 (ISBN 0-19-811869-4). Oxford U Pr.

--Selected Poems. Walsh, Marcus, ed. (Fyfield Ser.). 150p. (Orig.). 1979. pap. 3.95 (ISBN 0-85635-307-8, Pub. by New Pr England). Persea Bks.

Smart, D. R. Fixed Point Theorems. (Cambridge Tracts in Mathematics: No. 66). (Illus.). 100p. 1980. pap. 13.95x (ISBN 0-521-29833-4). Cambridge U Pr.

--Fixed Point Theorems. LC 73-79314. (Tracts in Mathematics Ser.: No. 66). (Illus.). 160p. 1974. 23.95 (ISBN 0-521-20289-2). Cambridge U Pr.

Smart, J. J. & Williams, B. Utilitarianism: For & Against. LC 73-80487. 180p. 1973. 23.95 (ISBN 0-521-20297-3); pap. 6.95x (ISBN 0-521-09822-X). Cambridge U Pr.

Smart, James R. Metric Math: The Modernized Metric System. LC 73-93954. (Contemporary Undergrad Math Ser). 1974. pap. text ed. 4.95x o.p. (ISBN 0-8185-0126-X). Brooks-Cole.

Smart, John J. Philosophy & Scientific Realism. 1963. text ed. 8.00x (ISBN 0-7100-3617-5). Humanities.

Smart, Margaret, jt. auth. see Lund, Charles.

Smart, Ninian. A Dialogue of Religions. LC 79-8730. (The Library of Philosophy & Theology). 142p. 1981. Repr. of 1960 ed. lib. bdg. 17.50x (ISBN 0-313-22187-1, SMDR). Greenwood.

--The Phenomenon of Religion. Hick, John, ed. (Philosophy of Religion Ser). 168p. 1973. 8.95 (ISBN 0-8164-1102-6). Crossroad NY.

--The Philosophy of Religion. 1979. 13.95 (ISBN 0-19-520138-8); pap. 4.50 (ISBN 0-19-520139-6). Oxford U Pr.

--Reasons & Faiths. 1958. text ed. 15.75x (ISBN 0-7100-3155-6). Humanities.

--Secular Education & the Logic of Religion: Heslington Lectures, University of York, 1966. 1969. text ed. 5.00x (ISBN 0-571-08284-X). Humanities.

Smart, Peter. The Vanitie & Downe-Fall of Superstitious Popish Ceremonies. LC 77-7428. (English Experience Ser.: No. 894). 1977. Repr. of 1628 ed. lib. bdg. 6.00 (ISBN 90-221-0894-5). Walter J Johnson.

Smart, Veronica, ed. Sylloge of Coins of the British Isles, Vol. 28. 164p. 1981. 74.00 (ISBN 0-19-726002-0). Oxford U Pr.

Smart, W. M. Textbook on Spherical Astronomy. 6th ed. LC 76-50643. (Illus.). 1977. 53.50 (ISBN 0-521-21516-1); pap. 16.95x (ISBN 0-521-29180-1). Cambridge U Pr.

Smart, William M. Riddle of the Universe. LC 68-25830. (Illus.). 1968. 9.95 (ISBN 0-471-79914-9). Halsted Pr.

Smartt, J. Tropical Pulses. (Tropical Agriculture Ser.). (Illus.). 1976. text ed. 36.00x (ISBN 0-582-46679-2). Longman.

Smartt, Steven S. Fact Book on Higher Education in the South: Nineteen Seventy-Nine & Nineteen Eighty. rev. ed. 1980. pap. 3.50. S Regional Ed.

Smeak, Ethel M., ed. see Chapman, George.

Smeaton, George. Doctrine of the Atonement According to the Apostles. Date not set. 17.95 (ISBN 0-88469-136-5). BMH Bks.

--Doctrine of the Holy Spirit. 1980. 12.95 (ISBN 0-85151-187-2). Banner of Truth.

Smedes, Susan D. Memorials of a Southern Planter. Green, Fletcher M., ed. 408p. pap. 8.95 (ISBN 0-87805-132-5). U Pr of Miss.

Smedley, Agnes. Battle Hymn of China. LC 74-32113. (China in the 20th Century Ser). xxiii, 528p. 1975. Repr. of 1943 ed. lib. bdg. 45.00 (ISBN 0-306-70693-8). Da Capo.

--Daughter of Earth. 416p. 1973. 10.00 (ISBN 0-912670-87-8); pap. 4.95 (ISBN 0-912670-10-X). Feminist Pr.

Smedley, Margaret. T'ang Pottery & Porcelain. (Illus.). 168p. 1981. 58.00 (ISBN 0-571-10957-8, Pub. by Faber & Faber). Merrimack Bk Serv.

Smedley, Ronald & Tether, John. Let's Dance-Country Style. 1975. 6.95 (ISBN 0-236-31061-5, Pub. by Paul Elek). Merrimack Bk Serv.

Smee, Alfred. Principles of the Human Mind. LC 80-68665. (Illus.). 96p. 1980. pap. 5.95 (ISBN 0-89708-030-0). And Bks.

Smeed, J. W., ed. see Paul, Jean.

Smeets, G. P., jt. ed. see Hunter, W. J.

Smeets, Rieks. Sept Histoires on Sapsag: Racontees Par Nazam Met et Suivies De Quelques Remarques Sur la Parler Du Conteur. (PDR Press Publication on North Caucasian Languages Ser.: No. 2). 1976. pap. text ed. 10.25x (ISBN 9-0316-0105-5). Humanities.

Smellie, Alexander. Men of the Covenant. 1975. 13.95 (ISBN 0-85151-212-7). Banner of Truth.

Smellie, W. A Treatise on the Theory & Practice of Midwifery. 480p. 1974. Repr. of 1752 ed. 29.50 o.p. (ISBN 0-88275-159-X). Krieger.

Smellie, William. The Philosophy of Natural History, 2 vols. LC 78-67541. Repr. 125.00 set (ISBN 0-404-17230-X, QL50). AMS Pr.

Smelser, Marshal L. Democratic Republic, 1801-1815. Commager, Henry S. & Morris, Richard S., eds. LC 68-28218. (New American Nation Series). (Illus.). 1968. 15.00 o.s.i. (ISBN 0-06-013927-7, HarpT). Har-Row.
Smelser, Marshall & Gundersen, Joan R. American History at a Glance. 4th ed. (Illus.). 1979. pap. text ed. 3.95 (ISBN 0-06-463475-2, EH 475, EH). Har-Row.
Smelser, Neil J. Sociology. (Ser. in Sociology). (Illus.). 640p. 1981. text ed. 18.95 (ISBN 0-13-820829-8). P-H.
--Theory of Collective Behavior. LC 62-15350. (Illus.). 1962. text ed. 12.95 (ISBN 0-02-929390-1); pap. text ed. 5.95 (ISBN 0-02-929400-2). Free Pr.
Smelser, Neil J., jt. auth. see Parsons, Talcott.
Smelser, Neil J. & Almond, Gabriel, eds. Public Higher Education in California. 1974. 24.95x (ISBN 0-520-02510-5). U of Cal Pr.
Smelser, Newt. Beginner's CB & Two-Way Radio Repairing. LC 80-23818. (Illus.). 232p. 1981. text ed. 29.95 (ISBN 0-88229-573-X); pap. text ed. 14.95 (ISBN 0-88229-763-5). Nelson-Hall.
Smelser, Ronald M. The Sudeten Problem, 1933-38: "Volkstumpolitik" & the Formulation of Nazi Foreign Policy. LC 74-5912. 296p. 1975. 20.00x (ISBN 0-8195-4077-3, Pub. by Wesleyan U Pr). Columbia U Pr.
Smeriglio, Vincent L., ed. Newborns & Parents: Parent-Infant Contact & Newborn Sensory Stimulation. 224p. 1981. text ed. 19.95 (ISBN 0-89859-041-8). L Erlbaum Assocs.
Smernoff, Richard. Andre Chenier. (World Author Ser.: France: No. 418). 1977. lib. bdg. 12.50 (ISBN 0-8057-6258-2). Twayne.
Smethurst, George. Basic Water Treatment -- for Application Worldwide. 228p. 1980. 40.00x (ISBN 0-7277-0071-5, Pub. by Telford England). State Mutual Bk.
Smethurst, Richard J. A Social Basic for Prewar Japanese Militarism: The Army & the Rural Community. (Center for Japanese & Korean Studies). 1974. 24.95x (ISBN 0-520-02552-0). U of Cal Pr.
Smetinoff, Olga. The Yogurt Cookbook. pap. 1.95 (ISBN 0-515-05693-6, N2417). Jove Pubns.
--Yogurt Cookbook. LC 65-23871. 1966. pap. 4.95 (ISBN 0-8119-0402-4). Fell.
Smialowski, Arthur & Currie, Donald J. Photography in Medicine. (Illus.). 340p. 1960. 20.50 (ISBN 0-398-01780-8). C C Thomas.
Smialowski, Arthur, jt. auth. see Currie, Donald J.
Smidt, J., ed. see Joint ISMAR-AMPERE International Conference on Magnetic Resonance.
Smil, V. & Knowland, W. E., eds. Energy in the Developing World: The Real Energy Crisis. 394p. 1980. 74.00x (ISBN 0-19-854425-1); pap. 34.95x (ISBN 0-19-854421-9). Oxford U Pr.
Smil, Vaclav. China's Energy: Achievements, Problems, Prospects. LC 75-44939. (Illus.). 1976. text ed. 26.95 (ISBN 0-275-23050-3). Praeger.
Smil, Vaclav & Nachman, Paul. Energy Analysis & Agriculture: An Application to U.S. Corn Production. (Special Studies in Agricultural Science & Policy). 175p. 1981. lib. bdg. 22.00x (ISBN 0-86531-167-6). Westview.
Smilansky, Moshe & Nevo, David. The Gifted Disadvantaged: A Ten Year Longitudinal Study of Compensatory Education in Israel. 356p. 1980. 26.50 (ISBN 0-677-04400-3). Gordon.
Smiles, Samuel. Josiah Wedgewood. LC 71-141603. 1971. Repr. of 1894 ed. 20.00 (ISBN 0-8103-3617-0). Gale.
--Self-Help. 1959. 15.00 (ISBN 0-7195-1294-8). Transatlantic.
Smiley, David. Lion of White Hall: The Life of Cassius M. Clay (1810-1903) 7.50 (ISBN 0-685-25623-5). Peter Smith.
Smiley, Jane. Barn Blind. LC 79-3417. 1980. 9.95 o.s.i. (ISBN 0-06-014016-X, HarpT). Har-Row.
Smiley, Nixon. Florida Gardening Month by Month. LC 78-125661. (Illus.). 1980. pap. 7.95 (ISBN 0-87024-302-0). U of Miami Pr.
Smiley, Sam. Playwriting: The Structure of Action. LC 78-125077. (Theatre & Drama Ser). 1971. pap. 11.95 ref. ed. (ISBN 0-13-684530-4). P-H.
Smiley, Virginia. Liza Hunt, Pediatric Nurse. 192p. (YA) 1976. 5.95 (ISBN 0-685-64248-8, Avalon). Bouregy.
Smilie, R. S. Sonoma Mission: San Francisco De Sonoma. LC 74-81641. (Illus.). 1975. 9.95 o.p. (ISBN 0-913548-24-3, Valley Calif). Western Tanager.
Smillie, Keith W. APL-360 with Statistical Examples. 1974. text ed. 11.95 (ISBN 0-201-07069-3). A-W.
Smircich, Lawrence J., jt. auth. see Skurdenis, Juliann V.
Smirnitsky, A. I., ed. Russian-English Dictionary. rev. ed. 1973. 19.95 o.p. (ISBN 0-525-19520-3). Dutton.

Smith & Elliott. Illustrations of Contra Costa County, California with Historical Sketch: 1879. (Illus.). 1979. Repr. 19.95 (ISBN 0-913548-68-5, Valley Calif). Western Tanager.
Smith & Sherlock. Surgery of the Gall Bladder & Bile Ducts. 2nd ed. 1981. price not set (ISBN 0-407-00118-2). Butterworths.
Smith, jt. auth. see Blowers.
Smith, jt. auth. see Kirby.
Smith, jt. auth. see Naifeh.
Smith, jt. auth. see Scott.
Smith, jt. auth. see Slater.
Smith, jt. auth. see Walker.
Smith, ed. History of Entomology. LC 73-76435. 517p. 1973. 18.25 (ISBN 0-686-09298-8). Entomol Soc.
Smith, ed. see Ballantyne, J.
Smith, ed. see Nixon, H. H.
Smith, ed. see Vogel, A. I.
Smith, tr. see Barthes, Roland.
Smith, et al. Smith's Guide to the Literature of the Life Sciences. 9th ed. 223p. 1980. pap. 12.95 (ISBN 0-8087-3576-4). Burgess.
Smith, A., jt. auth. see Carty, T.
Smith, A. Broxton. About Our Dogs. 17.50x (ISBN 0-392-06336-0, SpS). Soccer.
Smith, A. D. The Development of Rates of Postage. LC 77-77433. 1979. Repr. of 1917 ed. lib. bdg. 65.00x (ISBN 0-88000-110-0). Quarterman.
--Social Change. LC 75-42477. (Aspects of Modern Sociology, Social Processes Ser.). 1977. text ed. 9.50x o.p. (ISBN 0-582-48010-8). Longman.
Smith, A. D., et al. Commentaries in the Neurosciences. (Illus.). 702p. 1980. 72.00 (ISBN 0-08-025501-9). Pergamon.
Smith, A. G. & Briden, J. C. Mesozoic & Cenozoic Paleocontinental Maps. LC 76-114025. (Cambridge Earth Science Ser.). (Illus.). 1977. 7.95x (ISBN 0-521-29117-8). Cambridge U Pr.
Smith, A. G., et al. Phanerozoic Paleocontinental World Maps. LC 79-42669. (Cambridge Earth Science Ser.). 96p. Date not set. 29.50 (ISBN 0-521-23257-0); pap. 13.95 (ISBN 0-521-23258-9). Cambridge U Pr.
Smith, A. H. Chinese Characteristics. (Illus.). 344p. 1972. Repr. of 1900 ed. 29.00x (ISBN 0-7165-2043-5, Pub. by Irish Academic Pr Ireland). Biblio Dist.
Smith, A. Hassell. County & Court: Government & Politics in Norfolk 1558-1603. 392p. 1974. 48.00x (ISBN 0-19-822407-9). Oxford U Pr.
Smith, A. J. The Moss Flora of Britain & Ireland. LC 77-71428. (Illus.). 1978. 82.50 (ISBN 0-521-21648-6). Cambridge U Pr.
Smith, A. J., ed. John Donne: The Critical Heritage. (The Critical Heritage Ser.). 448p. 1975. 40.00x (ISBN 0-7100-8242-8). Routledge & Kegan.
Smith, A. Ledyard. Excavations at Altar De Sacrificios: Architecture, Settlement, Burials & Caches. LC 72-126638. (Peabody Museum Papers: Vol. 62, No. 2). 1972. pap. 25.00 (ISBN 0-87365-178-2). Peabody Harvard.
Smith, A. Ledyard, jt. auth. see Willey, Gordon R.
Smith, A. M., jt. auth. see Cebeci, Tuncer.
Smith, A. M., tr. see Foucault, Michel.
Smith, A. R., ed. Corporate Manpower Planning. 187p. 1980. text ed. 27.00x (ISBN 0-566-02167-6, Pub. by Gower Pub Co England). Renouf.
Smith, A. Robert & Giles, James V. An American Rape: A True Account of the Giles-Johnson Case. LC 75-17823. (Illus.). 300p. 1975. 10.00 o.p. (ISBN 0-915220-05-9); pap. 4.95 o.p. (ISBN 0-915220-32-6, 522967). New Republic.
Smith, Adam. The Correspondence of Adam Smith. Mossner, Ernest C. & Ross, Ian S., eds. 1977. 59.00x (ISBN 0-19-828185-4). Oxford U Pr.
--An Inquiry into the Nature & Causes of the Wealth of Nations, 2 vols. Campbell, R. H., ed. (Glasgow Edition of the Works & Correspondence of Adam Smith). 1976. 98.00x (ISBN 0-19-828184-6). Oxford U Pr.
--Lectures on Jurisprudence. Meek, R. L. & Raphael, D. D., eds. (The Glasgow Edition of the Works & Correspondence of Adam Smith Ser.). 1978. 75.00x (ISBN 0-19-828188-9). Oxford U Pr.
--Money Game. LC 68-14526. 1968. 10.00 o.p. (ISBN 0-394-43667-9). Random.
Smith, Adam, pseud. Paper Money. 288p. 1981. 13.95 (ISBN 0-671-44825-0). Summit Bks.
Smith, Adam. The Theory of Moral Sentiments. (Glasgow Edition of the Works & Correspondence of Adam Smith Ser.). (Illus.). 1976. 54.00x (ISBN 0-19-828189-7). Oxford U Pr.
--Wealth of Nations: Representative Selections. Mazlish, Bruce, ed. LC 60-12945. 1961. pap. 6.95 (ISBN 0-672-60327-6, LLA125). Bobbs.
--Wealth of Nations: Selections. Stigler, George J., ed. LC 57-12307. (Crofts Classics Ser.). 1957. pap. text ed. 2.75x (ISBN 0-88295-093-2). AHM Pub.

Smith, Adam N., jt. auth. see Sircus, Wilfred.
Smith, Adeline M. Free Magazines for Libraries. LC 80-15557. 280p. 1980. lib. bdg. 16.95x (ISBN 0-89950-021-8). McFarland & Co.
Smith, Agnes. The Bluegreen Tree. LC 76-50105. (Illus.). 108p. (Orig.). 1977. 9.00 (ISBN 0-686-28762-2). Westwind Pr.
--An Edge of the Forest. (Illus.). 202p. (gr. 7 up). 1974. 9.00 (ISBN 0-686-28761-4). Westwind Pr.
--Speaking As a Writer. Ross-Robertson, David, tr. LC 78-65831. (Illus.). 76p. (Orig.). 1979. 7.75 (ISBN 0-9602342-0-9); pap. 5.95 (ISBN 0-9602342-1-7). Westwind Pr.
Smith, Aileen M., jt. auth. see Smith, W. Eugene.
Smith, Al. Poker to Win. (Gambler's Book Shelf). 64p. 1975. pap. 2.95 (ISBN 0-89650-544-8). Gamblers.
Smith, Alan. Getting Started in Treasure Hunting. (Illus.). 192p. 1981. pap. 7.95 (ISBN 0-8117-2045-4). Stackpole.
Smith, Alan R. Systematics of the Neotropical Species of Thlypteris Section Cyclosorus. (U. C. Publ. in Botany: Vol. 59). 1971. pap. 10.50x (ISBN 0-520-09396-8). U of Cal Pr.
--Taxonomy of Thelypteris Subgenus Steiropteris (Including Glaphyropteris) (U. C. Publications in Botany Ser.: Vol. 76). 1980. pap. 6.00 (ISBN 0-520-09602-9). U of Cal Pr.
Smith, Albert A., Jr. The Coupling of External Electromagnetic Fields to Transmission Lines. LC 76-49504. 1977. 22.50 (ISBN 0-471-01995-X, Pub. by Wiley-Interscience). Wiley.
Smith, Alberta. I Lift My Lamp. 1938. Repr. 3.50 o.p. (ISBN 0-685-88271-3). Metaphysical.
Smith, Alex H., et al. How to Know the Non-Gilled Mushrooms. (Pictured Key Nature Ser). 440p. 1973. text ed. 9.95x (ISBN 0-697-04867-5); wire coil 7.95x (ISBN 0-697-04866-7). Wm C Brown.
Smith, Alexander. Memoirs of the Life & Times of the Famous Jonathan Wilde. LC 76-170567. (Foundations of the Novel Ser.: Vol. 48). lib. bdg. 50.00 (ISBN 0-8240-0560-0). Garland Pub.
Smith, Alexander B. & Berlin, Louis. Introduction to Probation & Parole. 2nd ed. (Criminal Justice Ser.). (Illus.). 1979. text ed. 14.95 (ISBN 0-8299-0235-X); instrs.' manual avail. (ISBN 0-8299-0601-0). West Pub.
Smith, Alexander H. & Weber, Nancy. The Mushroom Hunter's Field Guide: All Color & Enlarged. (Illus.). 336p. 1980. 14.95 (ISBN 0-472-85610-3). U of Mich Pr.
Smith, Alice K. & Weiner, Charles, eds. Robert Oppenheimer: Letters & Recollections. LC 80-10106. 1980. 20.00 (ISBN 0-674-52833-6). Harvard U Pr.
Smith, Alice L. Microbiology & Pathology. 12th ed. LC 79-27338. (Illus.). 756p. 1980. text ed. 19.95 (ISBN 0-8016-4673-1). Mosby.
--Microbiology Laboratory Manual & Workbook. 5th ed. (Illus.). 179p. 1981. paper perfect 9.95 (ISBN 0-8016-4707-X). Mosby.
--Microbiology Laboratory Manual & Workbook. 4th ed. LC 76-30332. (Illus.). 1977. pap. 8.95 (ISBN 0-8016-4706-1). Mosby.
--Principles of Microbiology. 8th ed. LC 76-30332. (Illus.). 1977. text ed. 18.95 (ISBN 0-8016-4681-2). Mosby.
--Principles of Microbiology. 9th ed. (Illus.). 816p. 1981. text ed. 19.95 (ISBN 0-8016-4682-0). Mosby.
Smith, Alison. Help! There's a Cat Washing in Here! LC 80-25522. (Illus.). (gr. 4-6). 1981. 9.95 (ISBN 0-525-31630-2). Dutton.
Smith, Allan G. The Analysis of Motives: Early American Psychology & Fiction. (Costerus Ser.). 189p. 1980. pap. text ed. 23.00x (ISBN 90-6203-861-1). Humanities.
Smith, Allan K. & Circle, Sydney. Soybeans: Chemistry & Technology, Vol. 1, Proteins. 2nd ed. 1978. text ed. 35.50 (ISBN 0-87055-262-7). AVI.
Smith, Allen W. Understanding Inflation & Unemployment. LC 75-29492. 176p. 1976. 11.95 (ISBN 0-88229-276-5); pap. 6.95 (ISBN 0-88229-492-X). Nelson-Hall.
Smith, Ann. Celebrity Exercise. LC 75-12188. (Illus.). 160p. 1976. 10.00 o.s.i. (ISBN 0-8027-0501-4). Walker & Co.
Smith, Ann P., ed. Orthopedic Nursing. (Nursing Outline Ser.). 1974. spiral bdg. 8.00 (ISBN 0-87488-381-4). Med Exam.
Smith, Ann S. Divorce. LC 78-10464. (First Bks.). (gr. 4 up). 1979. PLB 6.45 s&l (ISBN 0-531-02254-4). Watts.
Smith, Anna H. Africana Byways. (Illus.). 1976. 14.00 (ISBN 0-949937-19-3). Munger Africana Lib.
Smith, Anne, ed. The Art of Emily Bronte. LC 76-19859. (Barnes & Noble Critical Studies). 1976. text ed. 23.50x (ISBN 0-06-496376-4); pap. text ed. 9.95x (ISBN 0-389-20054-9). B&N.
--George Eliot: Centenary Essays & Unpublished Fragment. (Critical Studies Ser.). 221p. 1980. 27.50x (ISBN 0-389-20058-1). B&N.

--Lawrence & Women. LC 78-62592. (Critical Studies Ser.). 1978. 23.50x (ISBN 0-06-496377-2); pap. text ed. 8.95x (ISBN 0-389-20055-7). B&N.
--Obesity: A Bibliography 1974-1979. 340p. 1980. 55.00 (ISBN 0-904147-17-7). Info Retrieval.
Smith, Anthony. Blind White Fish in Persia. (Unwin Bks). 1953. pap. 2.95 o.p. (ISBN 0-04-915010-3). Allen Unwin.
--Goodbye Gutenberg: The Newspaper Revolution of the 1980's. LC 79-24263. (Illus.). 1980. 16.95 (ISBN 0-19-502709-4). Oxford U Pr.
--The Politics of Information: Problems of Policy of Modern Media. (Communication & Culture Ser.). 1978. text ed. 25.00x (ISBN 0-333-23610-6); pap. text ed. 10.50x (ISBN 0-333-23611-4). Humanities.
Smith, Anthony, ed. Newspapers & Democracy. 320p. 1980. text ed. 25.00x (ISBN 0-262-19184-9). MIT Pr.
Smith, Anthony D. The Concept of Social Change: A Critique of the Functionalist Theory of Social Change. (Monographs in Social Theory). 208p. 1973. 18.50x (ISBN 0-7100-7607-X); pap. 8.95 (ISBN 0-7100-7697-5). Routledge & Kegan.
--Nationalism in the Twentieth Century. LC 78-71404. 1979. cUSA 17.50x (ISBN 0-8147-7799-6); pap. 9.00x cusa (ISBN 0-8147-7803-8). NYU Pr.
Smith, April. Friends. (gr. 7-12). 1980. pap. 1.50 (ISBN 0-440-92666-1, LFL). Dell.
--James at Fifteen. (gr. 7-12). 1980. pap. 1.50 (ISBN 0-440-94389-2, LFL). Dell.
--James at Fifteen. 1977. pap. 1.50 o.s.i. (ISBN 0-440-14389-6). Dell.
Smith, Arthur. Game of Go. LC 56-12653. (Illus.). 1956. pap. 5.25 (ISBN 0-8048-0202-5). C E Tuttle.
Smith, Arthur C. Introduction to the Natural History of the San Francisco Bay Region. (California Natural History Guides: No. 1). (Illus.). 1959. 12.95x (ISBN 0-520-03099-0); pap. 3.95 (ISBN 0-520-01185-6). U of Cal Pr.
Smith, Arthur H. China in Convulsion, 2 vols. (Illus.). 770p. 1972. Repr. of 1901 ed. 70.00x (ISBN 0-686-28324-4, Pub. by Irish Academic Pr). Biblio Dist.
--Chinese Characteristics. 342p. 1980. Repr. of 1894 ed. lib. bdg. 40.00 (ISBN 0-89760-849-6). Telegraph Bks.
Smith, Arthur J., ed. Seven Centuries of Verse: English & American. 3rd & rev ed. 1967. text ed. 9.95x o.p. (ISBN 0-684-41441-4, ScribC). Scribner.
Smith, Asa P., jt. ed. see Farrell, John C.
Smith, B. Babington, ed. Training in Small Groups: A Study of Five Methods. rev. ed. Farrell, B. A. 114p. 1979. 23.00 (ISBN 0-08-023689-8). Pergamon.
Smith, B. C., jt. auth. see Pitt, D. C.
Smith, B. J. & Ingley, James M. The Last of the Generations. 1981. 8.95 (ISBN 0-533-04609-2). Vantage.
Smith, B. L. What Is Man? 1977. 4.00 o.p. (ISBN 0-682-48831-3). Exposition.
Smith, B. L. & Webb, J. P. The Inert Gases: Model Systems for Science. (Wykeham Science Ser: No. 16). 1971. 9.95x (ISBN 0-8448-1118-1). Crane Russak Co.
Smith, B. Othanel, ed. Research in Teacher Education: A Symposium. LC 73-138471. (Illus.). 1971. ref. ed. 12.95 (ISBN 0-13-774455-2). P-H.
Smith, Bailey E. Real Evangelistic Preaching. 1981. 6.95 (ISBN 0-8054-6229-5). Broadman.
Smith, Ballard, jt. auth. see Lawson, J. W.
Smith, Barbara. Toward a Black Feminst Criticism. (Out & Out Pamphlet Ser). pap. 1.00 (ISBN 0-918314-14-3). Out & Out.
--The Westminster Concise Bible Dictionary. LC 80-25771. 1981. pap. 5.95 (ISBN 0-664-24363-0). Westminster.
Smith, Barbara G. Although...Those Who Overcame. 1981. pap. 9.95 (ISBN 0-914598-03-1). Padre Prods.
Smith, Barbara H. Poetic Closure: A Study of How Poems End. LC 68-15034. 1971. pap. 6.95 (ISBN 0-226-76343-9, P381, Phoen). U of Chicago Pr.
Smith, Barbara L., et al. Political Research Methods: Foundations & Techniques. (Illus.). 352p. 1976. text ed. 16.95 (ISBN 0-395-20363-5). HM.
Smith, Barbara T. A Log Book. LC 81-65196. (Illus.). 100p. (Orig.). 1981. 15.00 (ISBN 0-937122-03-3). Astro Artz.
Smith, Bardwell L., ed. Religion & Legitimation of Power in Sri Lanka. LC 77-7449. 1978. pap. 7.95 (ISBN 0-89012-008-0). Anima Pubns.
--Religion & Legitimation of Power in Thailand, Laos & Burma. LC 77-7444. 1978. pap. 7.95 (ISBN 0-89012-009-9). Anima Pubns.

--The Two Wheels of Dhamma: Essays on the Theravada Tradition in India & Ceylon. LC 70-188906. (American Academy of Religion. Studies in Religion). 1972. pap. text ed. 7.50 (ISBN 0-89130-155-0, 010003). Scholars Pr Ca.

Smith, Bardwell L., et al. The Tenure Debate. LC 72-6058. (Higher Education Ser.). 1973. 13.95x o.p. (ISBN 0-87589-148-9). Jossey-Bass.

Smith, Bardwell Z., jt. ed. see Elison, George.

Smith, Barry M. & Spargo, Edward. Selective Reading. rev. ed. LC 73-9349. (The Powereading Program Ser., Bk. 4). 54p. 1974. pap. text ed. 3.95 (ISBN 0-913310-01-8). PAR Inc.

Smith, Barry M., ed. see Hodges, Raymond W., et al.

Smith, Barry M., et al. Powereading, 4 vols. rev. ed. (Powereading Program Ser.: Bk. 1). (Illus.). 1974. Set Of 3 Bks. pap. text ed. 21.30 set of 4 bks. (ISBN 0-913310-00-X). PAR Inc.

Smith, Beatrice S. The Babe: Mildred Didriksen Zaharias. LC 75-42046. (Sport Profiles Ser.). (Illus.). 49p. (gr. 4-11). 1976. PLB 8.50 (ISBN 0-8172-0136-X). Raintree Pubs.

--Don't Mention Moon to Me. 1974. 6.95 o.p. (ISBN 0-525-66397-5). Elsevier-Nelson.

--From Peanuts to President. LC 76-51267. (Illus.). (gr. 3-6). 1977. PLB 6.65 o.p. (ISBN 0-8172-0428-8). Raintree Pubs.

Smith, Bennett L., jt. ed. see Johnson, Helgi.

Smith, Bernard. Place, Taste, & Tradition: A Study of Australian Art Since Seventeen Eighty-Eight. 2nd ed. (Illus.). 304p. 1979. text ed. 39.50x (ISBN 0-19-550561-1). Oxford U Pr.

Smith, Bernard T. Focus Forecasting: Computer Techniques for Inventory Control. LC 78-6120. 1978. 19.95 (ISBN 0-8436-0761-0). CBI Pub.

Smith, Bernice D. Bonny Squirrel & Mrs. Boyette. (Illus.). 1980. 4.50 (ISBN 0-533-03079-X). Vantage.

Smith, Bertha. Our Lost World. LC 80-68537. 1981. pap. 3.95 (ISBN 0-8054-6324-0). Broadman.

Smith, Betsy. Breakthrough: Women in Television. LC 80-54704. (Illus.). 192p. 1981. 9.95 (ISBN 0-8027-6420-7). Walker & Co.

--A Day in the Life of a Firefighter. LC 80-54099. (Illus.). 32p. (gr. 4 up). 1980. PLB 5.89 (ISBN 0-89375-444-7); pap. 2.50 (ISBN 0-89375-445-5). Troll Assocs.

Smith, Betty. Joy in the Morning. 1976. pap. 1.75 (ISBN 0-06-080368-1, P368, PL). Har-Row.

Smith, Betty J. Anesthesia for Infants & Children. 4th ed. LC 79-18284. (Illus.). 1979. text ed. 52.50 (ISBN 0-8016-4699-5). Mosby.

--Fundamentals of Anesthesia Care. LC 72-86526. (Illus.). 145p. (Orig.). 1972. pap. text ed. 7.95 o.p. (ISBN 0-8016-4693-6). Mosby.

Smith, Billy A., jt. ed. see Bonneau, B. Lee.

Smith, Billy E. Managing the Information Systems Audit: A Case Study-Policies, Procedures, & Guidelines. (Illus.). 65p. 1980. pap. text ed. 22.50 (ISBN 0-89413-086-2); avail. wkbk. (ISBN 0-89413-087-0). Inst Inter Aud.

Smith, Bradford. Meditation: The Inward Art. LC 63-14633. 1968. pap. 3.95 o.s.i. (ISBN 0-397-10062-0, LP6). Lippincott.

Smith, Bradley. The Road to Nuremberg. LC 80-68174. 336p. 1980. 13.95 (ISBN 0-465-07056-6). Basic.

Smith, Bradley F. The American Road to Nuremberg: The Documentary Record, 1944-1945. LC 80-83830. 234p. 1981. price not set (ISBN 0-8179-7481-4). Hoover Inst Pr.

Smith, Brenda. Bridging the Gap: College Reading. 1981. pap. text ed. 6.95x (ISBN 0-673-15364-9). Scott F.

Smith, Brenda H. & Shambaugh, Irvin C. AIMS Information About Aptitudes. rev. ed. 201p. 1980. pap. 10.00 (ISBN 0-9602710-1-5). Aptitude Inventory.

Smith, Brian. Cotswolds. 1979. 17.95 (ISBN 0-7134-3058-3, Pub. by Batsford England). David & Charles.

--How to Prosper in Your Own Business: Getting Started & Staying on Course. 352p. 1980. 20.00 (ISBN 0-8289-0408-1). Greene.

--Pineapple Hold 'Em. (Gambler's Book Shelf). 1979. pap. 2.95 (ISBN 0-89650-827-7). Gamblers.

Smith, Brian & Stanyer, Jeffery. Administering Britain. 288p. 1976. 24.00x (ISBN 0-85520-139-8, Pub. by Martin Robertson England). Biblio Dist.

Smith, Brian C. Advising Ministers: A Case Study of the South West Economic Planning Council. (Library of Political Studies). 1969. text ed. 7.25x (ISBN 0-7100-6371-7). Humanities.

Smith, Brian C. & Stanyer, Jeffrey. Administering Britain: A Guidebook to Administrative Institutions. 288p. 1981. pap. 9.95x (ISBN 0-85520-374-9, Pub. by Martin Robertson England). Biblio Dist.

Smith, Brian J., jt. auth. see Lewis, Theodore.

Smith, Brian R. The Small Computer in Small Business. (Illus.). 160p. 1980. 12.50 (ISBN 0-8289-0407-3). Greene.

Smith, Brian S. History of Malvern. 1964. text ed. 6.75x (ISBN 0-7185-1041-0, Leicester). Humanities.

Smith, Bruce. Police Systems in the United States. rev. & enl. ed. Smith, Bruce, Jr., ed. LC 60-11498. 1960. 9.95x o.s.i. (ISBN 0-06-036090-9, HarpT). Har-Row.

Smith, Bruce A., ed. A Perspective on Energy Modeling. 1977. pap. text ed. 22.00 (ISBN 0-08-019985-2). Pergamon.

Smith, Bruce L. & Karlesky, Joseph J. State of Academic Science: Background Papers, Vol. 2. LC 77-72979. 1977. pap. 5.95 (ISBN 0-915390-13-2). Change Mag.

Smith, Bruce L., ed. The New Political Economy: The Public Use of Private Sector. 2nd ed. 1977. pap. 9.95 (ISBN 0-470-15157-9). Halsted Pr.

Smith, Brydon. Donald Judd. (Illus.). 1975. 20.00 o.s.i. (ISBN 0-88884-277-5, 56317-0, Pub. by Natl Gallery Canada). U of Chicago Pr.

Smith, C. A. O. Henry. LC 80-23470. (American Men & Women of Letters Ser.). 1981. pap. 4.95 (ISBN 0-87754-167-1). Chelsea Hse.

Smith, C. A. & Vernon, J. A., eds. Handbook of Auditory & Vestibular Research Methods. (Illus.). 610p. 1976. 57.50 (ISBN 0-398-03231-9). C C Thomas.

Smith, C. C. Human Diseases in Color. (Illus.). 1978. 32.95 (ISBN 0-87489-188-4). Med Economics.

Smith, C. C., ed. Internal Friction & Ultrasonic Attentuation in Solids: Proceedings of the 3rd European Conference 18-20 July 1979, University of Manchester, England. (Illus.). 400p. 1980. 50.00 (ISBN 0-08-024771-7); pap. 18.00 (ISBN 0-08-024770-9). Pergamon.

Smith, C. Carter. The Art of Mixing Drinks. (Orig.). 1981. pap. 7.95 (ISBN 0-446-97759-4). Warner Bks.

Smith, C. Colin, ed. Spanish Ballads. 1965. 8.75 (ISBN 0-08-010914-4); pap. 6.95 (ISBN 0-08-010913-6). Pergamon.

Smith, C. E. & Mink, Oscar G., eds. Foundations of Guidance & Counseling: Multidisciplinary Readings. LC 72-75026. 1969. pap. text ed. 5.50 o.p. (ISBN 0-397-47158-0). Lippincott.

Smith, C. Fox. Valiant Sailor. (Illus.). (gr. 6-10). 1957. 9.95 (ISBN 0-87599-105-X). S G Phillips.

Smith, C. N., ed. see De La Taille, Jean.

Smith, C. N., ed. see De Montchrestien, Antoine.

Smith, C. Ray & Theatre Craft Editors, eds. The Theatre Crafts Book of Costume. LC 72-80663. (Illus.). 1973. pap. 4.95 (ISBN 0-87857-016-0). Rodale Pr Inc.

Smith, C. Ray, ed. see Margolies, John.

Smith, C. U. The Problem of Life: An Essay of Biological Thought. LC 75-20106. 1976. 24.95 (ISBN 0-470-80188-3). Halsted Pr.

Smith, C. W. Country Music. 304p. 1976. pap. 1.95 o.p. (ISBN 0-345-25068-0). Ballantine.

--The Thin Men of Haddam. 1975. pap. 1.50 o.s.i. (ISBN 0-380-00422-4, 24943). Avon.

Smith, Carl & Fay, Leo. Getting People to Read: Volunteer Programs That Work. LC 73-7538. 256p. 1973. 8.95 o.p. (ISBN 0-440-02836-1). Delacorte.

Smith, Carlton G. Serial Discussions of the Human Brain. (Illus.). 100p. 1981. text ed. price not set (ISBN 0-8067-1811-0). Urban & S.

Smith, Carol. Auditory Discrimination Practice Exercises. 1981. pap. 3.95 (ISBN 0-8134-2168-3, 2168). Interstate.

Smith, Carol, jt. auth. see Danhof, Kenneth.

Smith, Carol A., ed. Regional Analysis, 2 vols. (Studies in Anthropology). 1976. 31.00 ea. Vol. 1 (ISBN 0-12-652101-8). Vol. 2 (ISBN 0-12-652102-6). Set. 49.00 (ISBN 0-686-57828-7). Acad Pr.

Smith, Carole, jt. auth. see Hooker, Ruth.

Smith, Carrie. Forget Harry. 1981. 11.95 (ISBN 0-671-42265-0). S&S.

Smith, Carter, jt. auth. see Novotny, Ann.

Smith, Catherine R., tr. see Sokolov, Yury M.

Smith, Cecil & Litton, Glenn. Musical Comedy in America: From the Black Crook Through Sweeney Todd. (Illus.). 1981. pap. 12.45 (ISBN 0-87830-564-5). Theatre Arts.

Smith, Cecil L., jt. auth. see Murrill, Paul W.

Smith, Cedric. Alcoholism Treatment, Vol. 2. Horrobin, D. F., ed. (Alcoholism Research Review Ser.). 107p. 1980. Repr. of 1978 ed. 14.95x (ISBN 0-87705-968-3). Human Sci Pr.

Smith, Charles. Lord Mountbatten: His Butler's Story. LC 80-51787. (Illus.). 224p. 1980. 12.95 (ISBN 0-8128-2751-1). Stein & Day.

--What If I Don't Go Overseas. 1981. pap. 0.50 (ISBN 0-87784-182-9). Inter-Varsity.

Smith, Charles B. A Guide to Business Research: Developing, Conducting & Writing Research Projects. LC 79-22991. 200p. 1981. text ed. 16.95 (ISBN 0-88229-546-2); pap. text ed. 8.95 (ISBN 0-88229-750-3). Nelson-Hall.

--Practical Word Choice in Business Writing. 4th ed. 1978. saddle stitch 2.95 o.p. (ISBN 0-8403-1867-7). Kendall-Hunt.

--Troy State University: Nineteen Thirty-Seven to Nineteen Seventy, Troy Alabama. (Illus.). 1972. pap. 3.50 (ISBN 0-916624-34-X). TSU Pr.

Smith, Charles E. Applied Mechanics. Incl. Dynamics (ISBN 0-471-80178-X); Statics (ISBN 0-471-80460-6). 1976. text ed. 18.95x ea. Wiley.

--Applied Mechanics - More Dynamics. LC 75-44021. 1976. text ed. 23.95x (ISBN 0-471-79996-3). Wiley.

Smith, Charles J. Synonyms Discriminated. Smith, Percy H., ed. LC 78-126007. 1970. Repr. of 1903 ed. 26.00 (ISBN 0-8103-3010-5). Gale.

Smith, Charles K. Styles & Structures: Alternative Approaches to College Writing. 340p. 1974. pap. text ed. 8.95x (ISBN 0-393-09273-9). Norton.

Smith, Charles M., ed. Pastor's Complete Workbook. 1958. 9.95 (ISBN 0-687-30140-8). Abingdon.

Smith, Charles O. Science of Engineering Materials. 2nd ed. (Illus.). 1977. text ed. 25.95 (ISBN 0-13-794990-1). P-H.

Smith, Charles P., ed. Achievement-Related Motives in Children. LC 75-81045. 1969. 8.75x (ISBN 0-87154-811-9). Russell Sage.

Smith, Charles W. Roger B. Taney: Jacksonian Jurist. LC 72-8802. (American Constitutional & Legal History Ser.). 252p. 1973. Repr. of 1936 ed. lib. bdg. 27.50 (ISBN 0-685-30417-5). Da Capo.

Smith, Charles W. & Koester, Helmut. Lent. LC 74-76925. (Proclamation 1: Aids for Interpreting the Lessons of the Church Year, Ser. A). 64p. 1974. pap. 1.95 (ISBN 0-8006-4063-2, 1-4063). Fortress.

Smith, Charlotte. Desmond: A Novel, 3 vols. Luria, Gina, ed. LC 73-22133. (The Feminist Controversy in England, 1788-1810 Ser.). 1974. lib. bdg. 50.00 ea. (ISBN 0-8240-0879-0). Garland Pub.

--Emmeline: The Orphan of the Castle. Ehrenpreis, Anne H., ed. (Oxford English Novels Ser). 1971. 16.95x (ISBN 0-19-255322-4). Oxford U Pr.

--The Old Manor House: A Novel, 4 vols. (The Feminist Controversy in England, 1788-1810 Ser.). 1974. lib. bdg. 50.00 ea. (ISBN 0-8240-0880-4). Garland Pub.

--The Young Philosopher: A Novel, 4 vols. (The Feminist Controversy in England, 1788-1810 Ser.). 1974. Set. lib. bdg. 154.00 (ISBN 0-8240-0881-2); lib. bdg. 60.50 ea. Garland Pub.

Smith, Chris & Hoath, David C. Law & the Underprivileged. 280p. 1975. 20.00x (ISBN 0-7100-8259-2). Routledge & Kegan.

Smith, Chris, jt. auth. see Riera, Russell S.

Smith, Christine. The Baptistery of Pisa. LC 77-94715. 1978. lib. bdg. 44.00 (ISBN 0-8240-3249-7). Garland Pub.

Smith, Christopher J. Geography & Mental Health. Natoli, Salvatore J., ed. LC 76-29269. 1977. pap. text ed. 4.00 (ISBN 0-89291-119-0). Assn Am Geographers.

Smith, Chuck. The Answer for Today, Vol. 1. 72p. (Orig.). 1980. pap. 1.95 (ISBN 0-936728-09-4). Word for Today.

--Effective Prayer Life. LC 78-27511. 96p. 1980. pap. 1.95 (ISBN 0-936728-03-5). Word for Today.

Smith, Clement A. & Nelson, Nicholas M., eds. Physiology of the Newborn Infant. 4th ed. (Illus.). 784p. 1976. 68.50 (ISBN 0-398-03232-7). C C Thomas.

Smith, Clifford T. An Historical Geography of Western Europe Before 1800. rev. ed. (Illus.). 1978. pap. text ed. 21.00x (ISBN 0-582-48986-5). Longman.

Smith, Clifton F. A Flora of the Santa Barbara Region, California. LC 76-9164. 331p. 1976. pap. text ed. 12.50 (ISBN 0-936494-00-X). Santa Barbara Mus Nat Hist.

Smith, Clinton L. The Boy Captives, Being the True Story of the Experiences & Hardships of Clinton L. Smith & Jeff D. Smith, Among the Comanche & Apache Indians During the Early Days. LC 75-7138. 1976. Repr. lib. bdg. 44.00 (ISBN 0-8240-1734-X). Garland Pub.

Smith, Clive, jt. auth. see Giles, Ken.

Smith, Clodus R. Planning & Paying Your Way to College. (Illus., Orig.). 1968. pap. 1.95 o.s.i. (ISBN 0-02-082050-X, Collier). Macmillan.

Smith, Clyde. Portrait of Maine. Pfeiffer, Douglas, ed. (Portrait of America Ser.). (Illus.). 80p. (Orig.). 1981. pap. 5.95 (ISBN 0-912856-71-8). Graphic Arts Ctr.

Smith, Clyde, photos by. Appalachian Mountains. LC 80-65134. (Belding Imprint Ser.). (Illus.). 160p. (Text by Wilma Dykeman & Stokley Dykeman). 1980. 29.50 (ISBN 0-912856-59-9). Graphic Arts Ctr.

--Pennsylvania. LC 78-51218. (Belding Imprint Ser.). (Illus.). 192p. (Text by Cronan Minton). 1978. 29.50 (ISBN 0-912856-40-8). Graphic Arts Ctr.

Smith, Colin. The Cut-Out. 1981. 10.95 (ISBN 0-670-25192-5). Viking Pr.

--The Palestinians. (Minority Rights Group Ser.: No. 24). 1975. pap. 2.50 (ISBN 0-89192-110-9). Interbk Inc.

Smith, Colin, tr. see Merleau-Ponty, Maurice.

Smith, Cordwainer. Space Lords. 1979. pap. 1.75 (ISBN 0-515-05122-5). Jove Pubns.

Smith, Craig B., jt. auth. see Fazzolare, Rocco A.

Smith, Craig B., ed. Efficient Electricity Use: A Reference Book on Energy Management for Engineers, Architects, Planners, & Managers. 2nd ed. 1978. 49.00 (ISBN 0-08-023227-2). Pergamon.

Smith, Craig R. & Hunsaker, David M. Bases of Argument: Ideas in Conflict. LC 72-173978. (Speech Communication Ser.: No. 17). 1972. pap. 4.50 (ISBN 0-672-61156-2). Bobbs.

Smith, Craig R., jt. auth. see Robertson, David H.

Smith, Curtis A., Jr. Help for the Bereaved. 2nd ed. 1972. pap. 1.50 (ISBN 0-686-09019-5). Ed Dev Assn.

Smith, Curtis S. Twentieth Century Science Fiction Writers. (Twentieth Century Writers Ser.). 1600p. 1981. 65.00x (ISBN 0-312-82420-3). St Martin.

Smith, Cushing. I Can Heal Myself & I Will. new ed. LC 62-14344. 1980. pap. 5.95 (ISBN 0-8119-0384-2). Fell.

Smith, Cynthia S. How to Get Big Results from a Small Advertising Budget. 1973. pap. 4.50 (ISBN 0-8015-3649-9, Hawthorn). Dutton.

Smith, Cyril S. From Art to Science: Seventy-Two Objects Illustrating the Nature of Discovery. (Illus.). 1980. 25.00 (ISBN 0-262-19181-4). MIT Pr.

--A Search for Structure: Selected Essays in Science, Art & History. (Illus.). 480p. 1981. 30.00 (ISBN 0-262-19191-1). MIT Pr.

Smith, Cyril S., tr. see Theophilus.

Smith, D. Rhodesia - The Problem. 1969. text ed. 14.50 (ISBN 0-08-007094-9). Pergamon.

--Rhodesia, the Problem. 1969. Repr. 14.50 (ISBN 0-08-007094-9). Pergamon.

Smith, D. A., ed. see Heinisch, K. F.

Smith, D. C. & Tiffon, Y., eds. Nutrition in the Lower Metazoa: Proceedings. (Illus.). 192p. 1980. 35.00 (ISBN 0-08-025904-9). Pergamon.

Smith, D. H. Confucius. (Encore Edition). (Illus.). 1973. 3.95 o.p. (ISBN 0-684-15706-3, ScribT). Scribner.

Smith, D. Howard. The Wisdom of the Taoists. LC 80-15629. (Wisdom Ser.). 96p. 1980. 4.95 (ISBN 0-8112-0777-3, NDP509). New Directions.

Smith, D. I. & Stopp, P. The River Basin. LC 77-85688. (Topics in Geography Ser.). (Illus.). 1979. 17.95 (ISBN 0-521-21900-0); pap. 7.95x (ISBN 0-521-29307-3). Cambridge U Pr.

Smith, D. I., ed. Editing Eighteenth-Century Texts. (Conference on Editorial Problems Ser.). 1976. lib. bdg. 16.50 (ISBN 0-8240-2402-8). Garland Pub.

--Editing Seventeenth Century Prose. (Conference on Editorial Problems Ser.). 1976. lib. bdg. 16.50 (ISBN 0-8240-2405-2). Garland Pub.

Smith, D. I. & Drew, D. P., eds. Limestones & Caves of the Mendip Hills. LC 74-76186. 1975. 22.50 (ISBN 0-7153-6572-X). David & Charles.

Smith, D. J. Collecting & Restoring Horse-Drawn Vehicles. 120p. 1981. 39.95 (ISBN 0-85059-429-4). Aztex.

--Collecting & Restoring Horse-Drawn Vehicles. (Illus.). 192p. 1981. 39.95 (ISBN 0-85059-429-4). Aztex.

Smith, D. K. Package Conveyors: Design & Estimating. 136p. 1972. 25.00x (ISBN 0-85264-213-X, Pub. by Griffin England). State Mutual Bk.

Smith, D. Moody. Interpreting the Gospels for Preaching. LC 79-8900. 132p. (Orig.). 1980. pap. 4.50 (ISBN 0-8006-1381-3, 1-1381). Fortress.

Smith, D. N. A Forgotten Sector: The Training of Ancillary Staff in Hospitals. 1969. text ed. 22.00 (ISBN 0-08-013379-7); pap. text ed. 10.75 (ISBN 0-08-013378-9). Pergamon.

Smith, D. N., ed. see Swift, Jonathan.

Smith, D. S., jt. auth. see Locke, Michael.

Smith, D. W., et al, eds. Correspondance generale d'helvetius, Vol. I: 1737-1756. (Romance Ser.). 384p. 1981. 35.00x (ISBN 0-8020-5517-6). U of Toronto Pr.

Smith, Dan see Kaldor, Mary, et al.

Smith, Daniel B. Inside the Great House: Planter Family Life in Eighteenth-Century Chesapeake Society. LC 80-14557. (Illus.). 368p. 1980. 17.50x (ISBN 0-8014-1313-3). Cornell U Pr.

Smith, Daniel G., jt. auth. see Shoemaker, Willie.

Smith, Daniel M. American Diplomatic Experience. LC 73-175171. (Illus., Orig.). 1972. pap. text ed. 10.95 (ISBN 0-395-12569-3). HM.

--Robert Lansing & American Neutrality, 1914-1917. LC 79-126610. (American Scene: Comments & Commentators Ser.). (Illus.). 254p. 1972. Repr. of 1958 ed. lib. bdg. 25.00 (ISBN 0-306-70057-3). Da Capo.

Smith, Datus C., Jr. A Guide to Book Publishing. LC 66-23133. 244p. 1966. Spanish ed. 14.25 (ISBN 0-8352-0055-8). Bowker.

Smith, Dave. Blue Spruce. (Illus.). 24p. 1980. 15.00 (ISBN 0-918092-17-5); pap. 4.00 (ISBN 0-918092-19-1); signed paper 8.00 (ISBN 0-918092-18-3). Tamarack Edns.

--The Fisherman's Whore. LC 73-85445. 74p. 1974. 6.50 (ISBN 0-8214-0137-8). Ohio U Pr.

Smith, David. Patterns in Human Geography. LC 75-21520. 1976. 19.50x (ISBN 0-8448-0764-8). Crane-Russak Co.

Smith, David & Williams, Gareth. Fields of Praise: The Official History of the Welsh Rugby Union, 1881-1981. (Illus.). 505p. 1981. text ed. 47.50 (ISBN 0-7083-0766-3). Verry.

Smith, David, jt. auth. see Francis, Hywel.

Smith, David, ed. Conrad's Manifesto, Preface to a Career: The History of the Preface to "The Nigger of the 'Narcissus'". facsimile ed. (Illus.). 1966. 27.50 (ISBN 0-686-28306-6). Rosenbach Mus and Lib.

Smith, David, tr. see Gunneweg, Antonius H. & Schmithals, Walter.

Smith, David, tr. see Kasper, Walter.

Smith, David A. Interface: Calculus & the Computer. LC 75-25016. (Illus.). 288p. 1976. pap. text ed. 10.25 (ISBN 0-395-21875-6); instructors manual 2.25 (ISBN 0-395-21876-4). HM.

Smith, David B. Long Term Care in Transition: Nursing Homes on the Cutting Edge. (Illus.). 350p. 1981. text ed. price not set (ISBN 0-914904-65-5). Health Admin Pr.

Smith, David B. & Kaluzny, Arnold D. The White Labyrinth: Understanding the Organization of Health Care. LC 75-7012. 250p. 1975. 23.50x (ISBN 0-8211-1854-4); text ed. 21.00x (ISBN 0-685-53678-5). McCutchan.

Smith, David B. & Rowland, George. Systems Engineering & Management. (Advances in Modern Engineering Ser). (Illus.). 150p. 1974. pap. text ed. 8.95 (ISBN 0-201-07079-0). A-W.

Smith, David E. History of Mathematics, 2 vols. Incl. Vol. 1. General Survey of the History of Elementary Mathematics. Repr. of 1923 ed (ISBN 0-486-20429-4); Vol. 2. Special Topics of Elementary Mathematics. Repr. of 1925 ed (ISBN 0-486-20430-8). pap. text ed. 7.50 ea. Dover.

--Number Stories of Long Ago. LC 70-167181. (Illus.). 150p. (gr. 1 up). 1973. Repr. of 1951 ed. 18.00 (ISBN 0-8103-3273-6). Gale.

--The Regional Decline of a National Party: Liberals on the Prairies. (Canadian Government Ser.). 184p. 1981. 14.00x (ISBN 0-8020-2421-1); pap. 6.50 (ISBN 0-8020-6430-2). U of Toronto Pr.

Smith, David E. & De Morgan, Augustus. Rara Arithmetica & Arithmetical Books, 2 vols. in 1. 4th ed. LC 74-113148. (Illus., Eng.). 1970. text ed. 29.50 (ISBN 0-8284-0192-6). Chelsea Pub.

Smith, David E., jt. auth. see Wesson, Donald R.

Smith, David E. & Gay, George R., eds. It's So Good, Don't Even Try It Once: Heroin in Perspective. 224p. 1972. pap. 2.45 o.p. (ISBN 0-13-506584-4). P-H.

Smith, David G. The Music Stops & the Waltz Continues. 256p. 1981. 10.95 (ISBN 0-8037-5719-0). Dial.

Smith, David H. & Hokelman, Robert A. Controversies in Child Health & Pediatrics. (Illus.). 480p. 1981. text ed. 29.95 (ISBN 0-07-058510-5, HP). McGraw.

Smith, David H., jt. auth. see Inkeles, Alex.

Smith, David H., et al. Participation in Social & Political Activities: A Comprehensive Analysis of Political Involvement, Expressive Leisure Time, & Helping Behavior. LC 80-16362. (Social & Behavioral Science Ser.). 1980. text ed. 27.95x (ISBN 0-87589-463-1). Jossey Bass.

Smith, David L. Legends of the Glasgow & South Western Railway: In LMS Days. LC 80-66093. (Illus.). 176p. 1980. 17.95 (ISBN 0-7153-7981-X). David & Charles.

--Locomotives of the Glasgow & Southwestern Railway. 1976. 13.95 (ISBN 0-7153-6960-1, Pub. by Batsford England). David & Charles.

Smith, David M. Industrial Location: An Economic Geographical Analysis. 2nd ed. LC 80-19231. 450p. 1981. text ed. 22.95 (ISBN 0-471-06078-X). Wiley.

--Who Rules the Universities? An Essay in Class Analysis. LC 73-90075. 224p. 1974. 7.95 o.p. (ISBN 0-85345-320-9, CL-3209). Monthly Rev.

Smith, David N. The Leo Conversion. LC 80-13316. (Illus.). 288p. 1980. 9.95 (ISBN 0-396-07854-0). Dodd.

Smith, David S. Self-Assessment of Current Knowledge in Pediatrics. 2nd ed. 1974. spiral bdg. 14.00 (ISBN 0-87488-256-7). Med Exam.

Smith, David W. Recognizable Patterns of Human Deformation: Identification & Management of Mechanical Effects on Morphogenesis. (Illus.). 240p. 1981. text ed. write for info. (ISBN 0-7216-8401-7). Saunders.

Smith, David W. & Wilson, Ann C. The Child with Down's Syndrome (Mongolism) LC 72-88852. (Illus.). 120p. 1973. pap. 7.95 (ISBN 0-7216-8420-3). Saunders.

Smith, Del & Cauthron, Michael. Bedrock: Images from the Wayside. LC 75-16938. (Illus.). 128p. 1975. 10.50 (ISBN 0-89052-015-1). Madrona Pr.

Smith, Denis. Freesias. 90p. 1980. pap. 9.95 (ISBN 0-901361-25-9, Pub. by Grower Bks England). Intl Schol Bk Serv.

Smith, Denis M., ed. Garibaldi. LC 69-15335. (Great Lives Observed Ser). 1969. pap. text ed. 1.95 o.p. (ISBN 0-13-346783-X). P-H.

Smith, Dennis. Glitter & Ash. 1981. pap. 2.95 (ISBN 0-451-09761-0, E9761, Sig). NAL.

Smith, Dennis & Freedman, Jill. Firehouse. (Illus.). 1978. pap. 7.95 o.p. (ISBN 0-385-12577-1, Dolp). Doubleday.

Smith, Dennis C. The Naked Child: The Long Range Effects of Family & Social Nudity. LC 80-69234. (Illus.). 180p. 1981. perfect bdg. 7.95 (ISBN 0-86548-056-7). Century Twenty One.

Smith, Dennis E. Report from Engine Company Eighty Two. LC 71-154259. 1972. 5.95 o.p. (ISBN 0-8415-0138-6). Dutton.

Smith, Denzell S., ed. see May, Thomas.

Smith, Dian G. Careers in the Visual Arts: Talking with Professionals. LC 80-17848. (Career Bks.). (Illus.). 224p. (gr. 7 up). 1980. PLB 9.29 (ISBN 0-671-33080-2). Messner.

Smith, Dinitia. The Hard Rain. 207p. 1980. 9.95 (ISBN 0-8037-3409-3). Dial.

Smith, Doc see Smith, E. E. & Goldin, Stephen.

Smith, Don. How Sports Began. (Illus.). (gr. 5 up). 1977. PLB 7.90 (ISBN 0-531-00093-1). Watts.

--The Strausser Transfer. (Secret Mission Ser.). 1978. pap. 1.95 (ISBN 0-441-77200-5). Charter Bks.

--Trials Bike Riding. (EP Sports Ser.). (Illus.). 112p. 1981. 12.95 (ISBN 0-8069-9050-3, Pub. by EP Publishing England). Sterling.

Smith, Don P. Page Systems. (Illus.). 1976. pap. 3.00 (ISBN 0-937514-08-X, New Era). World Merch Import.

--Retired Man's Way to Riches. 330p. 1980. pap. 15.00 (ISBN 0-937514-10-1, New Era). World Merch Import.

--Shadows of Chaos. rev. ed. 1981. pap. 5.00 (ISBN 0-937514-09-8). World Merch Import.

Smith, Donald. Under Cover of Darkness. 1981. pap. 2.50 (ISBN 0-8439-0903-X, Leisure Bks). Nordon Pubns.

Smith, Donald, et al. CAD-CAM International Delphi Forecast. LC 80-53001. (Illus.). 181p. 1980. pap. 24.00 (ISBN 0-87263-062-5). SME.

Smith, Donald A. & Mukerjee, Gitanjali, eds. Assuring Quality Ambulatory Health Care: The Martin Luther King, Jr. Health Center. (Westview Special Studies in Health Care Ser.). 1978. lib. bdg. 24.50x (ISBN 0-89158-409-9). Westview.

Smith, Donald E. India As a Secular State. 1963. 27.00 o.p. (ISBN 0-691-03027-8, 76). Princeton U Pr.

--Religion & Politics in Burma. 1965. 20.00 (ISBN 0-691-03054-5). Princeton U Pr.

--Religion, Politics & Social Change in the Third World. LC 73-143516. 1971. 12.95 (ISBN 0-02-929490-8); pap. text ed. 6.95 (ISBN 0-02-929460-6). Free Pr.

Smith, Donald E. & Fisher, Danial. More Than You Ever Wanted to Know About Measurement & Statistics: For Reading Specialists. (Michigan Learning Module: No. 7). (Orig.). 1978. pap. text ed. 2.95x (ISBN 0-914004-10-7). Ulrich.

Smith, Donald E., jt. auth. see Smith, Judith M.

Smith, Donald E., ed. see Bronzo, Mary L., et al.

Smith, Donald F. Lithium & Animal Behavior, Vol. I. (Lithium Research Review Ser.). 66p. 1980. Repr. of 1977 ed. 11.95x (ISBN 0-87705-961-6). Human Sci Pr.

Smith, Donald L. John Jay: Founder of a State & Nation. LC 68-57156. (gr. 12 up). 1968. text ed. 8.75x (ISBN 0-8077-2177-8). Tchrs Coll.

Smith, Donald M., jt. auth. see Mitchell, John, Jr.

Smith, Donald P. Congregations Alive. (Orig.). pap. write for info. (ISBN 0-664-24370-3). Westminster.

Smith, Donald R. Variational Methods in Optimization. (Illus.). 464p. 1974. 22.95 (ISBN 0-13-940627-1). P-H.

Smith, Doris B. Dreams & Drummers. LC 77-26590. (gr. 6 up). 1978. 6.95 (ISBN 0-690-01381-7, TYC-J); PLB 7.89 (ISBN 0-690-03843-7). T Y Crowell.

--Kick a Stone Home. LC 74-4209. (gr. 5 up). 1974. 8.95 (ISBN 0-690-00535-0, TYC-J). T Y Crowell.

--Last Was Lloyd. 144p. (gr. 3-7). 1981. 8.95 (ISBN 0-670-41921-4). Viking Pr.

--Salted Lemons. LC 80-66250. 240p. (gr. 3-7). 1980. 9.95 (ISBN 0-590-07666-3, Four Winds). Schol Bk Serv.

--Up & Over. 224p. (gr. 7 up). 1976. 7.92 (ISBN 0-688-22066-5); PLB 7.44 (ISBN 0-688-32066-X). Morrow.

Smith, Dorothy. In Our Own Interest: A Handbook for the Citizen Lobbyist in State Legislatures. LC 78-10625. 144p. 1979. pap. 4.95 (ISBN 0-914842-33-1). Madrona Pubs.

Smith, Dorothy & Germain, Carol P. Care of the Adult Patient. (Illus.). 1975. 21.75 o.p. (ISBN 0-397-54165-1); pap. 21.00 o.p. (ISBN 0-397-54171-6). Lippincott.

Smith, Dorothy H. The Tall Book of Christmas. LC 54-9002. (Tall Bks). (Illus.). 96p. (gr. k-3). 1980. 5.95 (ISBN 0-06-025700-8, HarpJ); PLB 6.89 (ISBN 0-06-025701-6). Har-Row.

Smith, Dorothy L. Medication Guide for Patient Counseling. LC 76-54361. (Illus.). 1977. pap. 12.00 o.p. (ISBN 0-8121-0586-9). Lea & Febiger.

Smith, Dorothy W., et al. Survival of Illness: Implications for Nursing. 1981. pap. text ed. 9.95 (ISBN 0-8261-2871-8). Springer Pub.

Smith, Douglas B. & Topp, William R. Activity Approach to Elementary Concepts of Mathematics. (Mathematics Ser.). (Illus.). 150p. 1981. pap. text ed. price not set (ISBN 0-201-07694-2). A-W.

Smith, Douglas C. & Gibbons, John T. The Real Estate Education Company Real Estate Exam Manual. (Orig.). 1980. pap. 14.95 (ISBN 0-88462-383-1). Real Estate Ed Co.

Smith, Duane & Vandenbusche, Duane. A Land Alone: Colorado's Western Slope. (Illus.). 300p. 1981. 16.95 (ISBN 0-87108-560-7). Pruett.

Smith, Duane A. Colorado Mining: A Photographic History. LC 76-46583. (Illus.). 176p. 1979. Repr. of 1977 ed. 17.50 (ISBN 0-8263-0437-0). U of Nm Pr.

--Rocky Mountain Mining Camps: The Urban Frontier. LC 67-24522. (Illus.). xii, 304p. 1974. pap. 3.50 (ISBN 0-8032-5792-9, BB 582, Bison). U of Nebr Pr.

Smith, Duane A. & Wieler, Hank. Secure the Shadow: Lachlan McLean, Colorado Mining Photographer. LC 80-10693. (Illus.). 100p. 1980. 13.50 (ISBN 0-918062-09-8). Colo Sch Mines.

Smith, Dwight. Above Timberline: A Wildlife Biologist's Rocky Mountain Journal. Anderson, Alan, Jr., ed. LC 80-7618. (Illus.). 1981. 13.95 (ISBN 0-394-40037-2). Knopf.

Smith, E. Alistair, jt. auth. see Mellor, Roy.

Smith, E. B., jt. auth. see Dymond, J. H.

Smith, E. Brian. Basic Chemical Thermodynamics. 2nd ed. (Oxford Chemistry Ser.). (Illus.). 1977. 13.95x (ISBN 0-19-855507-5); pap. 7.95x (ISBN 0-19-855508-3). Oxford U Pr.

Smith, E. D. Battle for Burma. 1979. 27.00 (ISBN 0-7134-0737-9, Pub. by Batsford England). David & Charles.

--Battles for Cassino. LC 75-12057. (Encore Edition). (Illus.). 1975. 3.95 o.p. (ISBN 0-684-15456-0, ScribT). Scribner.

Smith, E. Durham. Spina Bifida & the Total Care of Spinal Myelomeningocele. (Pediatric Surgical Monograph Ser). (Illus.). 168p. 1965. 16.75 (ISBN 0-398-01785-9). C C Thomas.

Smith, E. E. The Best of E. E. "Doc" Smith. (The Family D'alembert Ser.). (Orig.). pap. 1.75. Jove Pubns.

--First Lensman. 1973. pap. 1.75 (ISBN 0-515-05332-5). Jove Pubns.

--Galactic Patrol. 1973. pap. 1.75 (ISBN 0-515-05288-4, V3084). Jove Pubns.

--Gray Lensman. 1973. pap. 1.50 (ISBN 0-515-04589-6). Jove Pubns.

--Imperial Stars. (Family Lambert Ser.: No. 1). (Orig.). 1976. pap. 1.50 o.s.i. (ISBN 0-515-03839-3). Jove Pubns.

--Masters of Space. (The Family D'Alembert Ser.). (Orig.). 1979. pap. 1.75 (ISBN 0-515-04335-4). Jove Pubns.

--Masters of the Vortex. (The Lensman Ser.). pap. 1.75 (ISBN 0-515-05328-7). Jove Pubns.

--Second Stage Lensman. 1973. pap. 1.50 o.s.i. (ISBN 0-515-03172-0, V3172). Jove Pubns.

--Skylark DuQuesne. 1973. pap. 1.50 o.s.i. (ISBN 0-515-03050-3, N3050). Jove Pubns.

--Skylark of Valeron. 1973. pap. 1.50 o.s.i. (ISBN 0-515-03022-8, V3022). Jove Pubns.

--Skylark Three. 1973. pap. 1.50 o.s.i. (ISBN 0-515-03160-7, V3160). Jove Pubns.

--Spacehounds of IPC. 1974. pap. 1.50 o.s.i. (ISBN 0-515-03300-6, N3300). Jove Pubns.

Smith, E. E. & Goldin, Stephen. Appointment at Bloodstar. (The Family D'Alembert Ser: No. 5). 1978. pap. 1.50 (ISBN 0-515-04005-3). Jove Pubns.

--Getaway World, No. 4. (The Family D'alembert Ser.). (Orig.). pap. 1.75 (ISBN 0-515-04809-7). Jove Pubns.

Smith, E. Evelyn & Crusius, Vera C. Handbook on Quantity Food Management. 2nd ed. 1970. spiral bdg. 7.95 o.p. (ISBN 0-8087-1959-9). Burgess.

Smith, E. J., ed. Hospital Consumables: Reference for Medical Surgical Products. (Illus.). 652p. 1980. text ed. 145.00 (ISBN 0-87619-715-2). R J Brady.

Smith, E. Kinsey. Fluids & Electrolytes. Brain, Elizabeth, ed. (Illus.). 112p. 1980. pap. text ed. 9.00 (ISBN 0-443-08101-8). Churchill.

Smith, E. Peshine. A Manual of Political Economy. (The Neglected American Economists Ser.). 1974. lib. bdg. 50.00 (ISBN 0-8240-1010-8). Garland Pub.

Smith, Ed. Black Students in Interracial Schools: A Guide for Students, Teachers & Schools. LC 80-81701. 134p. (Orig.). 1980. pap. 7.95 (ISBN 0-686-69010-9). Garrett Pk.

Smith, Edith. Soundless Sound. 1980. 7.95 o.p. (ISBN 0-8062-1035-4). Carlton.

Smith, Edith K. How to Raise & Train a Great Pyrenees. (Orig.). pap. 2.00 (ISBN 0-87666-311-0, DS1084). TFH Pubns.

Smith, Edward, compiled by. The Frogs Who Wanted a King & Other Songs from La Fontaine. LC 77-5819. (Illus.). 64p. (gr. 1 up). 1977. 11.95 (ISBN 0-590-17294-8, Four Winds). Schol Bk Serv.

Smith, Edward C. The Constitution of the United States: With Case Summaries. 11th ed. LC 75-21722. 1979. pap. 3.50 (ISBN 0-06-460184-6, CO 184, COS). Har-Row.

Smith, Edward C. & Zurcher, Arnold J. Dictionary of American Politics. 2nd ed. LC 67-28530. (Orig., Maps). 1968. pap. 4.95 (ISBN 0-06-463261-X, EH 261, EH). Har-Row.

--Dictionary of American Politics. 2nd ed. (Illus.). 1968. pap. text ed. 12.50x (ISBN 0-06-480803-3). B&N.

Smith, Edward E. Children of the Lens. 1970. pap. 1.75 (ISBN 0-515-05326-0, V3251). Jove Pubns.

--Skylark of Space. 1970. pap. 1.50 o.s.i. (ISBN 0-685-19678-X, V2969). Jove Pubns.

--Triplanetary. (The Lensman Ser.). 1970. pap. 1.75 (ISBN 0-515-05331-7). Jove Pubns.

Smith, Edwin. Literacy Education for Adolescents & Adults: A Teacher's Resource Book. LC 74-101315. 1970. text ed. 6.00x o.p. (ISBN 0-87835-001-2). Boyd & Fraser.

Smith, Edwin, jt. auth. see Lewis, John.

Smith, Edwin W. Great Lion of Bechuanaland: The Life and Times of Roger Price, Missionary. 1957. text ed. 15.00x (ISBN 0-8401-2210-1). Allenson.

Smith, Elinor. Aviatrix. (Illus.). 32p. 1981. 12.95 (ISBN 0-15-110372-0). HarBraceJ.

Smith, Elizabeth. The Christmas Mice. 1979. 4.00 (ISBN 0-8062-1287-X). Carlton.

--The Irish Journals of Elizabeth Smith Eighteen Forty to Eighteen Fifty. Thomson, David & McGusty, Moyra, eds. (Illus.). 352p. 1980. 29.00x (ISBN 0-19-822471-0). Oxford U Pr.

Smith, Elizabeth & Huber, Barbara. Concepts in Leadership for the Licensed Practical Nurse. LC 73-4416. 1973. pap. text ed. 7.95 o.p. (ISBN 0-8016-4728-2). Mosby.

Smith, Elizabeth H., jt. ed. see Blocker, H. Gene.

Smith, Elizabeth S., jt. auth. see Corbett, J. Elliott.

Smith, Elliott L. & Hart, Andrew W. The Short Story: A Contemporary Looking Glass. 678p. 1981. pap. text ed. 9.95 (ISBN 0-394-32529-X). Random.

Smith, Elna N., jt. auth. see Melvin, Bruce L.

Smith, Elsdon C. The New Dictionary of Family Names. LC 72-79693. 512p. 1973. 17.50 (ISBN 0-06-013933-1, HarpT). Har-Row.

--Personal Names: A Bibliography. LC 66-31855. 1965. Repr. of 1952 ed. 15.00 (ISBN 0-8103-3134-9). Gale.

--Story of Our Names. LC 71-109181. 1970. Repr. of 1950 ed. 15.00 (ISBN 0-8103-3858-0). Gale.

Smith, Elton E. Louis MacNeice. (English Authors Ser.: No. 99). lib. bdg. 10.95 (ISBN 0-8057-1364-6). Twayne.

Smith, Elva B. A Long Look at Man: Who Is He? What Is He? Where Is He Going? 1981. 3.50 (ISBN 0-8059-2693-3). Dorrance.

Smith, Elva S. & Hodges, Margaret. The History of Children's Literature: A Syllabus with Selected Bibliographies. LC 79-28323. 312p. 1980. 40.00 (ISBN 0-8389-0286-3). ALA.

Smith, Emma. Emily the Traveling Guinea Pig. (gr. 1-5). 1960. 6.95 (ISBN 0-8392-3007-9). Astor-Honor.

Smith, Emory. Hilltop. 1977. pap. 2.95 (ISBN 0-918784-16-6). Legacy Pub Co.

Smith, Ernest A. Working in Precious Metals. (Illus.). 1978. 24.00x (ISBN 0-7198-0032-3). Intl Ideas.

Smith, Ernest Bramah see Bramah, Ernest, pseud.

Smith, Ervin. The Ethics of Martin Luther King, Jr. (Studies in American Religion: Vol. 2). 1981. soft cover 24.95x (ISBN 0-88946-974-1). E Mellen.

Smith, Erwin E. & Haley, J. E. Life on the Texas Range. LC 52-13181. (Illus.). 1973. 19.95 (ISBN 0-292-74605-9); pap. 9.95 (ISBN 0-292-74623-7). U of Tex Pr.

Smith, Eugene. Criminal Law in the United States. (Russell Sage Foundation Reprint Ser). Repr. of 1910 ed. lib. bdg. 24.50x (ISBN 0-697-00208-X). Irvington.

Smith, Everett L. & Stoedefalke, Karl. Aging & Exercise. 1981. pap. text ed. 8.95 (ISBN 0-89490-040-4). Enslow Pubs.

Smith, Evieline L. Tomorrow's Reality. LC 79-67224. 78p. 1980. 5.95 (ISBN 0-533-04452-9). Vantage.

Smith Experimental Fiction Project. The Novella Box. Incl. The Invisibles. Fox, Hugh. pap. 3.00 (ISBN 0-685-78301-4); The Same Thing Happened Over & Over. Chabrowe, Leonard. pap. 3.00 (ISBN 0-685-78302-2); Teak. Reinhold, Robert. pap. 2.00 (ISBN 0-685-78303-0). 1976. Boxed Set. pap. 5.00 (ISBN 0-912292-40-7). The Smith.

Smith, F. G. The Last Reformation. 256p. 5.00; pap. 3.50. Faith Pub Hse.

--Prophetic Lectures on Daniel & Revelations. 260p. pap. 3.50. Faith Pub Hse.

--Pulsars. LC 75-44569. (Cambridge Monographs on Physics). (Illus.). 1977. 39.50 (ISBN 0-521-21241-3). Cambridge U Pr.

--The Revelation Explained. 464p. 5.50. Faith Pub Hse.

--What the Bible Teaches. 576p. Repr. of 1914 ed. 5.50. Faith Pub Hse.

Smith, F. Leslie. Perspectives on Radio & Television: An Introduction to Broadcasting in the United States. (Illus.). 1979. text ed. 19.50 scp (ISBN 0-06-046309-0, HarpC); inst. manual avail. (ISBN 0-685-63493-0). Har-Row.

Smith, F. V. Purpose in Animal Behaviour. 1971. text ed. 7.75x (ISBN 0-09-109131-4, Hutchinson U Lib). Humanities.

Smith, F. Walton & Kalber, F. A., eds. Handbook in Marine Science, CRC: Section A, Oceanography. LC 73-88624. 640p. 1974. Vol. 1. 59.95 (ISBN 0-87819-389-8); Vol. 2, 390p. 53.95 (ISBN 0-87819-390-1). CRC Pr.

Smith, Forrest G. Dictionary of Freshman Composition. LC 70-78633. (Quality Paperback: No. 239). (Orig.). 1969. pap. 3.95 (ISBN 0-8226-0239-3). Littlefield.

Smith, Foster, jt. ed. see Chadwich, Philip.

Smith, Frances, jt. auth. see Briault, Eric.

Smith, Frances C. The First Book of Conservation. rev. ed. (First Bks). (Illus.). 72p. (gr. 4-6). 1972. PLB 4.90 o.p. (ISBN 0-531-00510-0). Watts.

--First Book of Swamps & Marshes. LC 69-10887. (First Bks). (Illus.). (gr. 4-6). 1969. PLB 4.90 o.p. (ISBN 0-531-00649-2). Watts.

Smith, Franceska, jt. auth. see Beder, Harold.

Smith, Francis G. Data Communications & the Systems Designer. Dufey, Gunter, ed. (Research for Business Decisions). 207p. 1980. 24.95 (ISBN 0-8357-1127-7, Pub. by UMI Res Pr). Univ Microfilms.

Smith, Frank. Dragon's Breath. LC 80-21818. 368p. 1980. 12.95 (ISBN 0-8253-0007-X). Beaufort Bks NY.

--Reading Without Nonsense. LC 79-11078. 1979. pap. text ed. 7.50x (ISBN 0-8077-2567-6). Tchrs Coll.

Smith, Frank & Smith, Ruth. Miniature Lamp. (Illus.). 288p. 1981. Repr. of 1968 ed. 18.95 (ISBN 0-916838-44-7). Schiffer.

Smith, Frank E. Conservation in the United States, 5 vols. 1971. Set. 150.00x (ISBN 0-442-37775-4). Van Nos Reinhold.

Smith, Frederick. The Early History of Veterinary Literature & Its British Development. limited ed. (Illus.). 140.00 (ISBN 0-85131-026-5, Dist. by Sporting Book Center). J A Allen.

Smith, Frederick E. The War God. 336p. (Orig.). 1981. pap. 2.75 (ISBN 0-553-13663-1). Bantam.

Smith, Frederick H. Nail-Biting: The Beatable Habit. LC 80-11687. (Illus., Orig.). 1980. pap. 7.95 (ISBN 0-8425-1806-1). Brigham.

Smith, Frederick R. The Minder: The Story of the Courtship, Call & Conflicts of John Ledger, Minder & Minister, 1900. Wolff, Robert L., ed. Bd. with The Coming of the Preachers: A Tale of the Rise of Methodism, 1901. (Victorian Fiction Ser). 1975. lib. bdg. 66.00 (ISBN 0-8240-1590-8). Garland Pub.

Smith, G., jt. auth. see Bolam, R.

Smith, G. Dallas. Outline of Bible Study. pap. 2.95 (ISBN 0-89225-192-1); pap. 2.95 (ISBN 0-89225-192-1). Gospel Advocate.

Smith, G. Henry. Forgotten Planet. (YA) 5.95 (ISBN 0-685-07434-X, Avalon). Bouregy.

Smith, G. Hubert. Omaha Indians. Horr, David A., ed. (American Indian Ethnohistory Ser. - Plains Indians). 1974. lib. bdg. 42.00 (ISBN 0-8240-0739-5). Garland Pub.

Smith, G. Kerry, ed. Agony & Promise: Current Issues in Higher Education 1969. LC 73-92897. (Higher Education Ser.). 1969. 12.95x o.p. (ISBN 0-87589-049-0). Jossey-Bass.

--New Teaching, New Learning: Current Issues in Higher Education 1971. LC 72-173856. (Higher Education Ser.). 1971. 12.95x o.p. (ISBN 0-87589-113-6). Jossey-Bass.

--Stress & Campus Response: Current Issues in Higher Education 1968. LC 73-92897. (Higher Education Ser.). 1968. 12.95x o.p. (ISBN 0-87589-025-3). Jossey-Bass.

--The Troubled Campus: Current Issues in Higher Education 1970. LC 71-128700. (Higher Education Ser.). 1970. 12.95x o.p. (ISBN 0-87589-078-4). Jossey-Bass.

--Twenty-Five Years: 1945 to 1970. LC 73-110640. (Higher Education Ser.). 1970. 14.95x o.p. (ISBN 0-87589-058-X). Jossey-Bass.

Smith, G. L. & Davis, P. E. Medical Terminology. 4th ed. 300p. 1980. pap. 11.95 (ISBN 0-471-05827-0, Pub. by Wiley Med). Wiley.

Smith, G. N. Introduction to Matrix & Finite Elements in Civil Engineering. (Illus.). 1971. text ed. 18.60x (ISBN 0-85334-502-3). Intl Ideas.

Smith, Gary. Windsinger. (Illus.). 176p. 1978. pap. 5.95 (ISBN 0-345-25677-8). Ballantine.

--Windsinger. (Illus.). 176p. 1976. 7.95 (ISBN 0-87156-192-1). Windsinger.

Smith, Gene. The Hayburners. LC 73-15677. (Illus.). 80p. (gr. 5-8). 1974. 5.95 o.s.i. (ISBN 0-440-03500-7); PLB 5.47 o.s.i. (ISBN 0-440-03501-5). Delacorte.

--High Crimes & Misdemeanors: The Impeachment & Trial of Andrew Johnson. LC 76-9838. 320p. 1976. 10.00 o.p. (ISBN 0-688-03072-6). Morrow.

--Where Are My Legions. LC 79-28277. 320p. 1980. 12.95 (ISBN 0-688-03645-7). Morrow.

Smith, Genevie L. Spelling by Principles. 1966. text ed. 7.95 (ISBN 0-13-834242-3). P-H.

Smith, Genevieve L. & Davis, Phyllis E. Quick Medical Terminology. LC 72-4193. (Wiley Self-Teaching Guides Ser). 248p. 1972. 6.95 (ISBN 0-471-80198-4). Wiley.

Smith, Geoffrey, jt. auth. see Polsby, Nelson W.

Smith, Geoffrey N. Elements of Soil Mechanics for Civil & Mining Engineers. 4th ed. (Illus.). 370p. 1978. text ed. 15.00x (ISBN 0-8464-0367-6); pap. 12.00x (ISBN 0-8464-0368-4). Beekman Pubs.

Smith, George. Dictionary of National Biography, 22 vols. Stephen, Leslie & Lee, Sidney, eds. 1882-1953. suppl. 1. 695.00x (ISBN 0-19-865101-5); suppl. 2. 65.00x (ISBN 0-19-865201-1); suppl. 3 65.00x (ISBN 0-19-865202-X); suppl. 4 65.00x (ISBN 0-19-865203-8); suppl. 5 65.00x (ISBN 0-19-865204-6); suppl. 6 65.00x (ISBN 0-19-865205-4). Oxford U Pr.

--The Firebrands. LC 80-82222. 384p. (Orig.). 1980. pap. 2.95 (ISBN 0-87216-765-8). Playboy Pbks.

--Flower Arranging in House & Garden. 15.95 (ISBN 0-7207-0958-X, Pub. by Michael Joseph). Merrimack Bk Serv.

Smith, George A. Four Psalms: Twenty-Three, Thirty-Seven, Fifty-Two & One Hundred Twenty-One. LC 80-82329. (Shepherd Classic Ser.). 1980. pap. 5.95 (ISBN 0-87983-235-5). Keats.

Smith, George A., Jr. & Matthews, John B., Jr. Business, Society, & the Individual. rev. ed. 1967. text ed. 19.50 (ISBN 0-256-00487-0). Irwin.

Smith, George H. Atheism: The Case Against God. LC 79-2726. (Skeptic's Bookshelf Ser.). 355p. 1979. pap. 6.95 (ISBN 0-87975-124-X). Prometheus Bks.

--Bayou Belle. LC 67-1512. (Illus.). (gr. 6-8). 1967. PLB 7.89 (ISBN 0-381-99704-9, A07200, JD-J). John Day.

Smith, George I. The Ghosts of Kampala: The Rise & Fall of Idi Amin. 208p. 1980. 10.95 (ISBN 0-312-32662-9). St Martin.

Smith, George O. The Complete Venus Equilateral. 1976. pap. 1.95 o.p. (ISBN 0-345-25551-8). Ballantine.

Smith, George V., ed. Material-Environment Interactions in Structural & Pressure Containment Service. (MPC: No. 15). 160p. 1980. 30.00 (G00188). ASME.

Smith, Gerald A., ed. see Marston, John.

Smith, Gerald B., jt. ed. see Mathews, Shailer.

Smith, Gerald W., ed. Engineering Economy: Analysis of Capital Expenditures. 3rd ed. 1979. text ed. 22.95 (ISBN 0-8138-0552-X). Iowa St U Pr.

Smith, Gerard. Doubletalk: The Story of the First Strategic Arms Limitation Talks. LC 76-50788. (Illus.). 576p. 1980. 17.95 (ISBN 0-385-11444-3). Doubleday.

Smith, Gilbert. Juan Pablo Forner. LC 75-33832. (World Authors Ser.,: Spain: No. 377). 1976. lib. bdg. 12.50 (ISBN 0-8057-6170-5). Twayne.

Smith, Glenn & Kniker, Charles R. Myth & Reality: A Reader in Education. 2nd ed. 500p. 1975. pap. text ed. 7.95x o.p. (ISBN 0-205-04777-7, 2247771). Allyn.

Smith, Glenn H. Langer of North Dakota. Freidel, Frank, ed. LC 78-62502. (Modern American History Ser.: Vol. 16). 1979. lib. bdg. 25.00 (ISBN 0-8240-3639-5). Garland Pub.

Smith, Glenna C. The Little Mouse Was a Grouch. Jordan, Alton, ed. (Buppet Series). (Illus.). (gr. k-3). 1981. PLB 4.50 (ISBN 0-89868-095-6, Read Res); pap. text ed. 1.95 (ISBN 0-89868-106-5). ARO Pub.

Smith, Goldwin. Canada & the Canadian Question. LC 70-163837. 236p. 1971. pap. 5.00 (ISBN 0-8020-6124-9). U of Toronto Pr.

Smith, Gordon. Politics in Western Europe. 3rd ed. LC 80-81211. 344p. 1980. 24.75 (ISBN 0-8419-0627-0); pap. 9.75 (ISBN 0-8419-0628-9). Holmes & Meier.

Smith, Gordon B., ed. Public Policy & Administration in the Soviet Union. 240p. 1980. 23.95 (ISBN 0-03-057726-8); pap. 9.95 (ISBN 0-03-057727-6). Praeger.

Smith, Gordon B., et al, eds. Soviet & East European Law & the Scientific-Technical Revolution. (Pergamon Policy Studies on International Politics). (Illus.). 330p. 1981. 34.00 (ISBN 0-08-027195-2). Pergamon.

Smith, Gordon D. Numerical Solution of Partial Differential Equations. 2nd ed. (Oxford Mathematical Handbooks Ser.). (Illus.). 1978. text ed. 29.95x (ISBN 0-19-859625-1); pap. text ed. 14.95x (ISBN 0-19-859626-X). Oxford U Pr.

Smith, Gordon W. The External Public Debt Prospects of the Non-Oil-Exporting Developing Countries. LC 77-90866. (Monographs: No. 10). 64p. 1977. 4.00 (ISBN 0-686-28685-5). Overseas Dev Council.

Smith, Graham E. The Latvian Nation. (Studies in Russian & East European History). (Illus.). 1981. 29.00x (ISBN 0-389-20025-5). B&N.

Smith, Grahame. Dickens, Money & Society. 1968. 19.50x (ISBN 0-520-01190-2). U of Cal Pr.

Smith, Gregory J., jt. ed. see Howes, Barbara.

Smith, Gregory W., jt. auth. see Naifeh, Steven W.

Smith, Grover, ed. see Huxley, Aldous.

Smith, Gusse T. Birds of the Southwestern Desert. LC 56-2505. (Illus.). Date not set. pap. 5.95 (ISBN 0-9603270-0-2). Doubleshoe.

Smith, Guy-Harold, ed. Conservation of Natural Resources. 4th ed. LC 71-129661. 1971. 21.95 (ISBN 0-471-80192-5). Wiley.

Smith, Guy N. Sleeping Beauty: Disney Classic. 1976. pap. 1.50 o.s.i. (ISBN 0-515-04165-3). Jove Pubns.

--Snow White & the Seven Dwarfs: Disney Classic. 1976. pap. 1.50 o.s.i. (ISBN 0-515-04164-5). Jove Pubns.

Smith, H. Strategies of Social Research. 2nd ed. 1980. 18.95 (ISBN 0-13-851154-3). P-H.

Smith, H., jt. auth. see Draper, N. R.

Smith, H., ed. Commentaries in Plant Science, Vol. 2. LC 80-41007. (Illus.). 250p. Date not set. 41.01 (ISBN 0-08-025898-0). Pergamon.

Smith, H. & Pearce, J. H., eds. Microbial Pathogenicity in Man & Animals: Proceedings. LC 75-177940. (Illus.). 1972. 50.50 (ISBN 0-521-08430-X). Cambridge U Pr.

Smith, H., et al, eds. Molecular Basis of Microbial Pathogenicity. (Dahlem Workshop Reports, Life Sciences Research Report Ser.: No. 16). (Illus.). 357p. (Orig.). pap. text ed. 27.50 (ISBN 0-89573-098-7). Verlag Chemie.

Smith, H. Allen. The Compleat Practical Joker. rev. ed. LC 80-20668. 288p. 1980. Repr. of 1953 ed. 12.95 (ISBN 0-688-03705-4). Morrow.

--The Life & Legend of Gene Fowler. 1977. 10.00 o.p. (ISBN 0-688-03188-9). Morrow.

Smith, H. Daniel. The Smith Agama Collection: Sanskrit Books & Manuscripts Relating to Pancaratra Studies- a Descrptive Catalog. LC 78-9149. (Foreign & Comparative Studies-South Asian Special Publications Ser.: No. 2). 1978. pap. text ed. 6.50x (ISBN 0-915984-79-2). Syracuse U Foreign Comp.

Smith, H. P. First & Second Samuel. LC 99-1607. (International Critical Commentary Ser.). 462p. 1899. text ed. 20.00x (ISBN 0-567-05005-X). Attic Pr.

Smith, H. Shelton, et al. American Christianity: An Historical Interpretation with Representative Documents. lib. rep. ed. 1960. Vol. I. 30.00x (ISBN 0-684-15744-6, ScribT); Vol. II. 30.00x (ISBN 0-684-15745-4). Scribner.

Smith, Halbert C., et al. Real Estate & Urban Development. rev ed. 1977. text ed. 19.50 (ISBN 0-256-01931-2). Irwin.

Smith, Hallett. Shakespeare's Romances: A Study of Some Ways of the Imagination. LC 72-79314. 1972. 10.00 (ISBN 0-87328-052-0); pap. 3.50 (ISBN 0-87328-053-9). Huntington Lib.

--The Tension of the Lyre: Poetry in Shakespeare's Sonnets. (Illus.). 180p. 1981. price not set (ISBN 0-87328-114-4). Huntington Lib.

Smith, Hannah W. God of All Comfort. 1956. pap. 2.50 (ISBN 0-8024-0018-3). Moody.

Smith, Hans, intro. by. Second Report of the Commissioners Appointed to Inquire into the Truck System (Shetland), 1892. 1980. pap. 10.95x (ISBN 0-906191-06-8, Pub. by Thule Pr England). Intl Schol Bk Serv.

Smith, Harmon L., jt. auth. see Gianturco, Daniel T.

Smith, Harold & Baker, William. The Administrative Manager. LC 78-6085. 1978. text ed. 16.95 (ISBN 0-574-20030-4, 13-3030); instr's guide avail. (ISBN 0-574-20031-2, 13-3031); study guide 6.50 (ISBN 0-574-20032-0, 13-3032). SRA.

Smith, Harold & Keiffer, Mildred. Pathways in Mathematics: Level II. 3rd ed. Sharpe, Glyn, ed. (Illus.). (gr. 8). 1980. pap. text ed. 6.64x (ISBN 0-913688-37-1); tchr's guide 6.00x (ISBN 0-913688-34-7). Pawnee Pub.

Smith, Harold, jt. auth. see Keiffer, Mildred.

Smith, Harold E. Historical & Cultural Dictionary of Thailand. (Historical & Cultural Dictionaries of Asia Ser.: No. 6). 1976. 10.00 (ISBN 0-8108-0926-5). Scarecrow.

Smith, Harold W. Approximate Analysis of Randomly Excited Non-Linear Controls. (Press Research Monographs: No. 34). 1966. 13.00x (ISBN 0-262-19027-3). MIT Pr.

Smith, Harry, ed. Commentaries in Plant Science. LC 76-7531. 272p. 1976. text ed. 46.00 (ISBN 0-08-019759-0). Pergamon.

Smith, Harry A. Principles & Methods of Pharmacy Management. 2nd ed. LC 80-17560. (Illus.). 413p. 1980. text ed. 19.50 (ISBN 0-8121-0765-9). Lea & Febiger.

Smith, Harry, Jr., jt. auth. see Kuebler, Roy R., Jr.

Smith, Hedrick, et al. Reagan. 1981. 9.95. Macmillan.

Smith, Helen M., jt. auth. see Marchant, Harold.

Smith, Helen R. Basic Story Techniques. 1964. pap. 5.95x (ISBN 0-8061-1170-4). U of Okla Pr.

Smith, Helena H. War on Powder River. LC 65-28734. (Illus.). 1967. pap. 5.25 (ISBN 0-8032-5188-2, BB 375, Bison). U of Nebr Pr.

Smith, Helena H., jt. auth. see Alderson, Nannie T.

Smith, Henry. A Preparative to Mariage: Whereunto Is Annexed a Treatise of the Lords Supper, & Another of Usurie. LC 74-28885. (English Experience Ser.: No. 762). 1975. Repr. of 1591 ed. 16.00 (ISBN 90-221-0762-0). Walter J Johnson.

Smith, Henry A., tr. see Kolmar, Gertrud.

Smith, Henry J. Collected Mathematical Papers, 2 Vols. LC 65-11859. 60.00 (ISBN 0-8284-0187-X). Chelsea Pub.

--Report on the Theory of Numbers. LC 64-8080. 1966. 14.95 (ISBN 0-8284-0186-1). Chelsea Pub.

Smith, Henry N. Democracy & the Novel: Popular Resistance to Classic American Writers. (A Galaxy Book: No. 633). 214p. 1981. pap. 5.95 (ISBN 0-19-502896-1). Oxford U Pr.

--Democracy & the Novel: Popular Resistance to Classic American Writers. 214p. 1981. pap. 5.95 (ISBN 0-19-502896-1, GB 633, OPB). Oxford U Pr.

Smith, Henry P. Glossary of Terms & Phrases. LC 79-175746. x, 521p. 1972. Repr. of 1889 ed. 26.00 (ISBN 0-8103-3816-5). Gale.

Smith, Herbert. Dreams of Natural Places: A New England Schooner Odyssey. LC 80-69529. (Illus.). 102p. 1981. 15.95 (ISBN 0-89272-107-3). Down East.

Smith, Herman W. Strategies of Social Research: The Methodological Imagination. (Methods of Social Science Ser.). (Illus.). 448p. 1975. text ed. 18.95 (ISBN 0-13-851147-0). P-H.

Smith, Herschel. Aircaft Piston Engines: From the Manly Baltzer to the Continental Tiara. (Aviation Ser.). (Illus.). 264p. 1981. 18.95 (ISBN 0-07-058472-9, P&RB). McGraw.

Smith, Hervey G. Marlinspike Sailor. rev. ed. LC 77-143856. (Illus.). 1969. 10.00 (ISBN 0-8286-0044-9). De Graff.

Smith, Hervey Garrett. The Small-Boat Sailor's Bible. rev ed. LC 73-82247. 144p. 1974. pap. 3.50 (ISBN 0-385-05527-7). Doubleday.

Smith, Hilary D. Preaching in the Spanish Golden Age: A Study of Some Preachers of the Reign of Philip III. (Modern Language & Literature Monographs). 1979. 29.95 (ISBN 0-19-815532-8). Oxford U Pr.

Smith, Hobart M. Amphibians of North America. (Golden Field Guide Ser.). (Illus.). 1978. 7.95 (ISBN 0-307-47008-3, Golden Pr); PLB 10.00 (ISBN 0-307-63662-3); pap. 4.95 (ISBN 0-307-13662-0). Western Pub.

Smith, Holly. Pidgey & P. J. 1981. 4.50 (ISBN 0-8062-1670-0). Carlton.

Smith, Horatio. Amarynthus...with Other Poems. Reiman, Donald H., ed. LC 75-31255. (Romantic Context Ser.: Poetry 1789-1830). 1977. Repr. of 1821 ed. lib. bdg. 47.00 (ISBN 0-8240-2202-5). Garland Pub.
Smith, Horatio, jt. auth. see Smith, James.
Smith, Horton, jt. auth. see Taylor, Dawson.
Smith, Howard, jt. auth. see Nelson, A. T.
Smith, Howard E., Jr. The Complete Beginner's Guide to Mountain Climbing. LC 76-18366. (gr. 7 up). 1977. 6.95 o.p. (ISBN 0-385-11428-1); PLB write for info. o.p. (ISBN 0-385-11429-X). Doubleday.
--From Under the Earth: America's Metals, Fuels, & Minerals. LC 67-18546. (Curriculum Related Bks). (Illus.). (gr. 5-9). 1967. 5.25 o.p. (ISBN 0-15-230270-0, HJ). HarBraceJ.
Smith, Howard G. Cattle Trails to Trenches. (Illus.). 8.95 (ISBN 0-8363-0020-3). Jenkins.
Smith, Howard P., et al. Performance Appraisal & Human Development. LC 76-52663. 1977. pap. text ed. 8.95 (ISBN 0-201-07455-9). A-W.
Smith, Huston. Forgotten Truth: The Primordial Tradition. LC 74-15850. (Illus.). 192p. 1976. 8.95 o.s.i. (ISBN 0-06-013902-1, HarpT). Har-Row.
--Forgotten Truth: The Primordial Tradition. 1977. pap. 3.95 (ISBN 0-06-090576-X, CN 576, CN). Har-Row.
--Religions of Man. pap. 4.95 (ISBN 0-06-090043-1, CN43, CN). Har-Row.
Smith, I. MacFarlane. Spatial Ability: Its Educational & Social Significance. LC 64-22822. 1964. text ed. 8.95 o.p. (ISBN 0-912736-04-6). EDITS Pubs.
Smith, I. W., ed. Physical Chemistry of Fast Reactions: Vol. 2: Reaction Dynamics. (Illus.). 290p. 1980. 32.50 (ISBN 0-306-40227-0, Plenum Pr). Plenum Pub.
Smith, Ian W. Kinetics & Dynamics of Elementary Gas Reactions. LC 79-40533. (Illus.). 1980. 72.95 (ISBN 0-408-70790-9). Butterworths.
Smith, Irving D., ed. Doane's Farm Management Guide. 14th ed. LC 79-56892. (Illus.). 1980. pap. 8.95 (ISBN 0-932250-09-2). Doane Agricultural.
Smith, Irving H., ed. Trotsky. (Great Lives Observed Ser). 192p. 1973. pap. 2.45 o.p. (ISBN 0-13-930966-7, Spec). P-H.
Smith, Irwin. Shakespeare's Globe Playhouse: A Modern Reconstruction. LC 56-6150. (Encore Edition). (Illus.). 1979. pap. 4.95 (ISBN 0-684-16926-6, ScribT). Scribner.
Smith, Ivan. Death of a Wombat. 1972. 14.95 (ISBN 0-85885-009-5). David & Charles.
Smith, Ivan C. & Carson, Bonnie L., eds. Cobalt, Vol. 6. LC 77-88486. (Trace Metals in the Environment Ser.). 1981. 49.50 (ISBN 0-250-40362-5). Ann Arbor Science.
Smith, J., ed. see Riviere, J.
Smith, J., ed. see U. S. National Committee for the International Hydrological Decade.
Smith, J., tr. see Riviere, J.
Smith, J., et al, eds. Ordered Groups. (Lecture Notes in Pure & Applied Mathematics). 192p. 1980. 25.50 (ISBN 0-8247-6943-0). Dekker.
Smith, J. Berwick, intro. by. Dod's Parliamentary (Pocket) Companion. 161st ed. LC 6-7438. (Illus.). 653p. 1980. 57.50x (ISBN 0-905702-04-2). Intl Pubns Serv.
Smith, J. C., ed. see Spenser, Edmund.
Smith, J. D. The Chemistry of Arsenic, Antimony & Bismuth. (Pergamon Texts in Inorganic Chemistry: Vol. 2). 138p. 1975. text ed. 27.00 (ISBN 0-08-018778-1); pap. text ed. 14.00 (ISBN 0-08-018777-3). Pergamon.
--The Visaladeuarasa: A Restoration of the Text. LC 75-30441. (Cambridge Oriental Publications Ser.: No. 26). 260p. 1977. 64.00 (ISBN 0-521-20815-7). Cambridge U Pr.
Smith, J. E. Integrated Injection Logic. 424p. 1980. 34.00 (ISBN 0-471-08675-4, Pub. by Wiley-Interscience); pap. 22.00 (ISBN 0-471-08676-2). Wiley.
Smith, J. E., ed. Integrated Injection Logic. LC 80-18841. 1980. 34.95 (ISBN 0-87942-137-1). Inst Electrical.
Smith, J. E., jt. ed. see Ashworth, J. M.
Smith, J. H., jt. ed. see Gould, Julius.
Smith, J. L., jt. auth. see Barnett, M. T.
Smith, J. Lawton. Neuro-Ophthalmology Update. LC 77-78562. (Illus.). 412p. 1977. 57.75 (ISBN 0-89352-005-5). Masson Pub.
Smith, J. Lawton, jt. auth. see Glaser, Joel S.
Smith, J. Lawton, ed. Neuro-Ophthalmology Focus, 1980. LC 79-87484. (Illus.). 472p. 1979. text ed. 57.75 (ISBN 0-89352-071-3). Masson Pub.
Smith, J. M. Advanced Analysis with the Sharp 5100 Scientific Calculator. LC 79-22505. 1979. 7.95 (ISBN 0-471-07753-4, Pub. by Wiley-Interscience). Wiley.
--Mathematical Modeling & Digital Simulation for Engineers & Scientists. LC 76-52419. 1977. 29.00 (ISBN 0-471-80344-8, Pub. by Wiley-Interscience). Wiley.
--Models in Ecology. (Illus.). 200p. 1974. 21.95 (ISBN 0-521-20262-0); pap. 8.50x (ISBN 0-521-29440-1). Cambridge U Pr.
Smith, J. M., et al. Micah, Zephaniah, Nahum, Habakkuk, Obadiah & Joel. (International Critical Commentary Ser.). 560p. 1911. text ed. 23.00x (ISBN 0-567-05019-X). Attic Pr.
Smith, J. Maynard. The Evolution of Sex. LC 77-85689. (Illus.). 1978. 35.50 (ISBN 0-521-21887-X); pap. 9.95x (ISBN 0-521-29302-2). Cambridge U Pr.
--Mathematical Ideas in Biology. LC 68-25088. (Illus.). 1968. 21.50 (ISBN 0-521-07335-9); pap. 7.95x (ISBN 0-521-09550-6). Cambridge U Pr.
Smith, J. P. & Sawyer, J. O. Keep to the Vascular Plants of Northwest California. 1981. pap. price not set. Mad River.
--Keys to the Vascular Plants of Northwest California. rev. ed. 160p. 1980. pap. text ed. write for info (ISBN 0-916422-23-2). Mad River.
--Keys to the Vascular Plants of Northwest California. 1978. pap. 3.75x o.p. (ISBN 0-916422-11-9). Mad River.
Smith, J. P., Jr. A Key to the Genera of Grasses of the Conterminous United States. 1981. pap. price not set. Mad River.
Smith, J. Robert. A Prairie Garden: Seventy Plants You Can Grow in Town or Country. 120p. 1980. 22.50 (ISBN 0-299-08300-4); pap. 9.95 (ISBN 0-299-08304-7). U of Wis Pr.
Smith, J. Sydney & Kiloh, L. G., eds. Psychosurgery & Society: A Symposium Organised by the Neuropsychiatric Institute, Sydney, Australia. 37.00 (ISBN 0-08-021836-9). Pergamon.
Smith, Jack. Jack Smith's L.A. LC 80-13127. 224p. 1980. 9.95 (ISBN 0-07-058471-0, GB). McGraw.
Smith, Jacqueline M. Dance Composition: A Practical Guide for Teachers. (Illus.). 1978. 14.00 (ISBN 0-86019-016-1). Transatlantic.
Smith, James. Handfuls on Purpose, 5 vols. 1943. 55.00 set (ISBN 0-8028-8139-4). Eerdmans.
Smith, James & Smith, Horatio. James Smith (Seventeen Seventy-Five to Eighteen Thirty-Nine) & Horatio (Horace) Smith (Seventeen Seventy-Nine to Eighteen Forty-Nine) Reiman, Donald H., ed. LC 75-31254. (Romantic Context Ser.: Poetry 1789-1830). 1978. lib. bdg. 47.00 (ISBN 0-8240-2201-7). Garland Pub.
Smith, James, jt. ed. see Roosevelt, Anna C.
Smith, James A. Basic Mathematics, 12 bks. 2nd ed. Incl. Bk. 1. Numbers & Numerals. 1.50 (ISBN 0-916780-00-7); Bk. 2. Addition of Whole Numbers & Subtraction of Whole Numbers. 3.95 (ISBN 0-916780-01-5); Bk. 3. Multiplication of Whole Numbers. 3.00 (ISBN 0-916780-02-3); Bk. 4. Division of Whole Numbers. 3.55 (ISBN 0-916780-03-1); Bk. 5. Fractions & Fractional Numbers. 1.80 (ISBN 0-916780-04-X); Bk. 6. Addition & Subtraction of Fractional Numbers & Multiplication & Division of Fractional Numbers. 3.55 (ISBN 0-916780-05-8); Bk. 7. Decimal Numerals: Addition & Subtraction with Decimals & Multiplication & Division with Decimals. 3.95 (ISBN 0-916780-06-6); Bk. 8. Percents & Applications. 2.45 (ISBN 0-916780-07-4); Bk. 9. Formulas & Applications. 3.30 (ISBN 0-916780-08-2); Bk. 10. Measurement & Applications. 3.70 (ISBN 0-916780-09-0); Bk. 11. Measurement in Geometry. 3.75 (ISBN 0-916780-10-4); Bk. 12. Units of Measure & the Metric System. 3.00 (ISBN 0-916780-11-2). (Illus.). 1974. pap. text ed. **30.00 set (ISBN 0-916780-12-0); tchr's. manual 3.20 (ISBN 0-916780-14-7); student test booklet 3.30 (ISBN 0-916780-13-9). CES.**
--Creative Teaching of Language Arts in the Elementary School, 2. 2nd ed. 384p. 1973. pap. text ed. 10.95x (ISBN 0-205-03834-4, 2238349). Allyn.
--Creative Teaching of Reading in the Elementary School. 2nd ed. (Series in Creative Teaching in the Elementary School). 350p. 1975. text ed. 14.95x (ISBN 0-205-04688-6); pap. text ed. 10.45x (ISBN 0-205-04687-8, 2246880). Allyn.
--Creative Teaching of the Social Studies in the Elementary School. (Orig.). 1967. pap. text ed. 10.95x o.p. (ISBN 0-205-00089-4, 2200899). Allyn.
--Setting Conditions for Creative Teaching in the Elementary School. 1966. 9.95x o.p. (ISBN 0-205-00132-7, 2201321). Allyn.
Smith, James A. & Park, Dorothy M. Word Music & Word Magic: Children's Literature Methods. 1977. text ed. 17.80 (ISBN 0-205-05587-7, 2255871). Allyn.
Smith, James A., jt. auth. see Westcott, Alvin M.
Smith, James B., et al. Real Estate in California. 11th ed. LC 79-55422. (Illus.). 1980. 19.95 (ISBN 0-914504-08-8). General Educ.
Smith, James D., ed. Modeling the Distribution & Intergenerational Transmission of Wealth. LC 80-15537. (National Bureau of Economic Research). 1981. lib. bdg. 28.00x (ISBN 0-226-76454-0). U of Chicago Pr.
Smith, James E. Divided We Fall. LC 79-67439. 96p. (Orig.). 1980. pap. 1.95 (ISBN 0-87239-381-X, 40086). Standard Pub.
--First & Second Kings. LC 78-300507. (The Bible Study Textbook Ser.). (Illus.). 1975. 16.50 (ISBN 0-89900-012-6). College Pr Pub.
Smith, James E., Jr. & Payne, James S. Teaching Exceptional Adolescents. (Special Education Ser.). 312p. 1980. pap. text ed. 16.95 (ISBN 0-675-08128-9). Merrill.
Smith, James F. Chrysanthemums. (Illus.). 224p. 1975. 16.50 o.s.i. (ISBN 0-7134-2936-4). Hippocrene Bks.
Smith, James G. Arctic Art: Eskimo Ivory. 127p. soft cover 19.95x (ISBN 0-934490-37-6). Mus Am Ind.
Smith, James G., ed. & intro. by. The New Liberty Bell: A Bicentennial Anthology of American Choral Music. LC 76-373. (Illus.). 1976. pap. 5.50 (ISBN 0-916656-00-4, MF276). Mark Foster Mus.
Smith, James H. History of Dutchess County, New York: 1683-1882. 720p. 1980. Repr. of 1882 ed. 35.00 (ISBN 0-932334-35-0). Heart of the Lakes.
Smith, James L. The Liverworts Pallavicinia & Symphyogyna & Their Conducting System. (U. C. Publ. in Botany: Vol. 39). 1966. pap. 6.50x (ISBN 0-520-09012-8). U of Cal Pr.
Smith, James L. & Kampine, John P. Circulatory Physiology: The Essentials. 344p. 1980. softcover 14.95 (ISBN 0-683-07885-2). Williams & Wilkins.
Smith, James P. Key to the Genera of Grasses of the Conterminous United States. (Illus.). 40p. 1975. pap. 2.00x o.p. (ISBN 0-916422-04-6). Mad River.
--Pete Rose. (Sports Superstars Ser.). (Illus.). (gr. 3-9). 1977. PLB 5.95 (ISBN 0-87191-540-5); pap. 2.95 (ISBN 0-89812-174-4). Creative Ed.
Smith, James P., Jr. A Key to the Genera of Grasses of the Coterminous United States. rev. ed. 80p. 1980. pap. write for info. (ISBN 0-916422-22-4). Mad River.
--Vascular Plant Families. (Illus.). 1977. pap. 9.10x (ISBN 0-916422-07-0). Mad River.
Smith, James R. English Linguistics. 1978. 2.50 (ISBN 0-8403-1436-1). Kendall-Hunt.
Smith, James W. Killer Colt. 1977. pap. 1.25 o.s.i. (ISBN 0-515-04376-1). Jove Pubns.
--The Loner. 1977. pap. 1.25 o.s.i. (ISBN 0-515-04377-X). Jove Pubns.
Smith, James W., ed. Blood & Tissue Parasites. (Atlases of Diagnostic Medical Parasitology: 1). (Illus.). 1976. 76.50 (ISBN 0-89189-065-3, 15-7-006-00); microfiche ed. 22.00 (ISBN 0-89189-046-7, 17-7-006-00). Am Soc Clinical.
--Intestinal Helminths. (Atlases of Diagnostic Medical Parasitology: 3). (Illus.). 1976. slide atlas 76.50 (ISBN 0-89189-066-1, 15-7-008-00); microfiche ed. 22.00 (ISBN 0-89189-048-3, 17-7-008-00). Am Soc Clinical.
--Intestinal Protozoa. (Atlases of Diagnostic Medical Parasitology: 2). (Illus.). 1976. 76.50 (ISBN 0-89189-067-X, 15-007-00); microfiche ed. 22.00 (ISBN 0-89189-047-5, 17-7-007-00). Am Soc Clinical.
Smith, Jane I. An Historical & Semantic Study of the Term "Islam" As Seen in a Sequence of Qur'an Commentaries. LC 75-22485. (Harvard Dissertations in Religion). 1975. 7.50 (ISBN 0-89130-020-1, 020101). Scholars Pr Ca.
Smith, Jane I., ed. The Precious Pearl: A Translation from the Arabic. LC 79-140. (Studies in World Religions: No. 1). 1979. 12.00 (ISBN 0-89130-278-6, 030001); pap. 7.50 (ISBN 0-89130-305-7). Scholars Pr Ca.
Smith, Janet. Play Environments for Movement Experience. (Illus.). 64p. 1980. pap. 9.50 (ISBN 0-398-04073-7). C C Thomas.
Smith, Janet A., ed. The Faber Book of Children's Verse. 1962. 8.95 (ISBN 0-571-05273-8, Pub. by Faber & Faber). Merrimack Bk Serv.
Smith, Jason W. Foundations of Archeology. 1976. pap. 14.95x (ISBN 0-02-478680-2). Macmillan.
Smith, Jay D. & Guffridge, Len. Jack Teagarden (Jazz) 208p. 21.50 (ISBN 0-306-70813-2). Da Capo.
Smith, Jay H. Baseball's Greatest Catcher: Johnny Bench. (The Allstars Ser.). (Illus.). (gr. 2-6). 1977. PLB 5.95 o.p. (ISBN 0-87191-589-8). Creative Ed.
--Bobby Orr. LC 74-8848. (Sports Superstars Ser.). (Illus.). 32p. (gr. 3-9). 1974. PLB 5.95 (ISBN 0-87191-368-2); pap. 2.95 (ISBN 0-686-67087-6). Creative Ed.
--Chris Evert. LC 75-8739. (New Creative Education Superstar Bks.). (Illus.). 32p. (gr. 3-9). 1975. PLB 5.95 (ISBN 0-87191-439-5); pap. 2.95 (ISBN 0-89812-176-0). Creative Ed.
--Defensive Linemen. LC 74-23193. (Stars of the NFL Ser.). (gr. 4-12). 1975. PLB 7.95 (ISBN 0-87191-420-4). Creative Ed.
--Fran Tarkenton. LC 74-9863. (Creative Education Sports Superstars Ser.). (Illus.). 32p. (gr. 3-6). 1974. PLB 5.95 o. p. (ISBN 0-87191-376-3); pap. 2.75 (ISBN 0-89812-167-1). Creative Ed.
--The Infielders. LC 76-8465. (Stars of the Nl & Al Ser.). (Illus.). (gr. 4-12). 1976. PLB 7.95 (ISBN 0-87191-517-0). Creative Ed.
--The Managers. LC 76-8905. (Stars of the Nl & Al Ser.). (Illus.). (gr. 4-12). 1976. PLB 7.95 (ISBN 0-87191-516-2). Creative Ed.
--Meet the Infielders. (Meet the Players: Baseball). (Illus.). (gr. 2-4). 1977. PLB 5.95 o.p. (ISBN 0-87191-578-2). Creative Ed.
--Meet the Managers. (Meet the Players: Baseball). (Illus.). (gr. 2-4). 1977. PLB 5.95 (ISBN 0-87191-577-4). Creative Ed.
--Meet the Pitchers. (Meet the Players: Baseball), (Illus.). (gr. 2-4). 1977. PLB 4.95 o.p. (ISBN 0-87191-576-6). Creative Ed.
--Olga Korbut. LC 74-19169. (Creative Education Sports Superstars Ser.). (Illus.). 32p. (gr. 3-6). 1974. PLB 5.95 (ISBN 0-87191-384-4); pap. 2.95 (ISBN 0-89812-190-6). Creative Ed.
--The Pitchers. LC 76-8485. (Stars of the NL & AL Ser.). (Illus.). (gr. 4-12). 1976. PLB 7.95 (ISBN 0-87191-518-9). Creative Ed.
--Receivers. LC 74-23400. (Stars of the NFL Ser.). (gr. 4-12). 1975. PLB 7.95 (ISBN 0-87191-418-2). Creative Ed.
Smith, Jay M. & Lusterman, Don-David. The Teacher As Learning Facilitator: Psychology & the Education Process. 1979. pap. text ed. 11.95x (ISBN 0-534-00587-X). Wadsworth Pub.
Smith, Jean E., ed. Papers of General Lucius D. Clay: Germany 1945-1949, 2 vols. LC 73-16536. 1216p. 1975. 40.00x (ISBN 0-253-34288-0). Ind U Pr.
Smith, Jean R., jt. ed. see Smith, Lacey B.
Smith, Jeanne G. Nature Walks in the Kikapoo Valley. (Illus.). 274p. 1977. 11.95x (ISBN 0-9604694-0-0); plastic bound 8.45x (ISBN 0-9604694-1-9). Jeannes Dreams.
Smith, Jeffery M. Preventing Legal Malpractice. 160p. 1981. pap. text ed. 7.95 (ISBN 0-8299-2118-4). West Pub.
Smith, Jeffrey, jt. auth. see Chapman, Joan.
Smith, Jeffrey A. American Presidential Elections: Trust & the Rational Voter. 224p. 1980. 20.95 (ISBN 0-03-056143-4). Praeger.
Smith, Jerald R. The Personnel Management Game. 1980. pap. text ed. 4.95 (ISBN 0-933836-14-7). Simtek.
Smith, Jerome & Miroff, Franklin I. You're Our Child: A Social-Psychological Approach to Adoption. LC 80-5957. 110p. (Orig.). 1981. lib. bdg. 15.75 (ISBN 0-8191-1416-2); pap. text ed. 7.25 (ISBN 0-8191-1417-0). U Pr of Amer.
Smith, Jerome F. The Coming Currency Collapse & What to Do About It! LC 80-66785. (Illus.). 250p. 1980. 13.95 (ISBN 0-916728-41-2). Bks in Focus.
Smith, Jessie C. Black Academic Libraries & Research Collections: An Historical Survey. LC 77-71857. (Contributions in Afro-American & African Studies: No. 34). 1977. lib. bdg. 16.95 (ISBN 0-8371-9546-2, SBA/). Greenwood.
Smith, Jim. Alphonse & the Stonehenge Mystery. (The Frog Band Ser.). (Illus.). 32p. (gr. 1-3). 1980. 7.95 (ISBN 0-316-80162-3). Little.
--Frog Band & Durrington. (The Frog Band Ser.). (Illus.). 32p. (gr. 1-3). 1980. pap. 3.95g (ISBN 0-316-80159-3). Little.
--The Frog Band & the Owlnapper. (Illus.). 32p. (ps-3). 1981. 8.95 (ISBN 0-316-80163-1). Little.
--Sex & the Single Teen. 31p. 1972. pap. 0.69 o.p. (ISBN 0-88207-365-6). Victor Bks.
Smith, Joan. Aurora. 224p. 1980. 10.95 o.s.i. (ISBN 0-8027-0651-7). Walker & Co.
--La Comtesse. (A Regency Romance Ser.). 1978. pap. 1.50 o.p. (ISBN 0-449-23490-8, Crest). Fawcett.
--Escapade. 1977. pap. 1.50 o.p. (ISBN 0-449-23232-8, Crest). Fawcett.
--Imprudent Lady. (A Regency Romance Ser.). 1978. pap. 1.75 o.p. (ISBN 0-449-23663-3, Crest). Fawcett.
--Lace for Milady. 201p. 1980. 11.95 (ISBN 0-8027-0659-2). Walker & Co.
--Perdita. 224p. 1981. pap. 1.95 (ISBN 0-449-50173-6, Coventry). Fawcett.
--Social Issues & Problems: The Contradictions of Capitalism. (Sociology Ser.). 416p. 1981. pap. text ed. 11.95 (ISBN 0-87626-813-0). Winthrop.
--Sweet & Twenty. 1979. pap. 1.75 o.p. (ISBN 0-449-23818-0, Crest). Fawcett.
--The Talk of the Town. (Regency Romance Ser.). 1979. pap. 1.75 o.p. (ISBN 0-449-24137-8, Crest). Fawcett.
Smith, Joan F. & Nachazel, Delbert P. Ophthalmologic Nursing. 1980. text ed. 14.95 (ISBN 0-316-80158-5). Little.

Smith, Joan M. Interviewing in Market & Social Research. 1972. 14.75 o.p. (ISBN 0-7100-7196-5). Routledge & Kegan.
Smith, Joe M. Chemical Engineering Kinetics. 2nd ed. (Chemical Engineering Ser.). 1970. text ed. 24.95 o.p. (ISBN 0-07-058693-4, C). McGraw.
Smith, John. Captain John Smith's History of Virginia. Hawke, David F., ed. LC 74-12083. (American History Landmarks Ser.). 1970. 5.50 (ISBN 0-672-60881-2). Bobbs.
--New England Trials. LC 70-171793. (English Experience Ser.: No. 416). 1971. Repr. of 1620 ed. 7.00 (ISBN 90-221-0416-8). Walter J Johnson.
--Select Discourses. Wellek, Rene, ed. LC 75-11252. (British Philosophers & Theologians of the 17th & 18th Centuries Ser.). 1978. Repr. of 1660 ed. lib. bdg. 42.00 (ISBN 0-8240-1803-6). Garland Pub.
--Select Discourses. LC 79-15690. 1979. Repr. of 1660 ed. 58.00x (ISBN 0-8201-1335-2). Schol Facsimiles.
Smith, John, jt. auth. see Lopez, Arcadia.
Smith, John C. Alger Hiss: The True Story. 1977. pap. 2.95 o.p. (ISBN 0-14-004427-2). Penguin.
--The Children of Master O'Rourke. LC 77-23278. 1977. 10.95 o.p. (ISBN 0-03-016916-X). HR&W.
Smith, John E. Experience & God. 1968. 9.95x (ISBN 0-19-501207-0). Oxford U Pr.
Smith, John E. & Berry, David, eds. Filamentous Fungi. Incl. Vol. 1. Industrial Mycology. LC 75-2101. 340p. 59.00 (ISBN 0-470-80187-5); Vol. 2. Biosynthesis & Metabolism. LC 75-41613. 79.50 (ISBN 0-470-15005-X); Vol. 3. Developmental Mycology. LC 75-2101. 54.95 (ISBN 0-470-99352-9). (Filamentous Fungi Ser.: Vols. 1-3). 1975-78. Halsted Pr.
Smith, John H. Death of Classical Paganism. 1977. 12.95 o.p. (ISBN 0-684-14449-2, ScribT). Scribner.
Smith, John H., ed. see Chapman, George.
Smith, John H., et al see Dryden, John.
Smith, John L. Another Song to Sing: An Illustrated Discography of Johnny Cash. (Illus.). 1981. pap. 5.95 (ISBN 0-915608-06-5). Country Music Found.
Smith, John Malcolm & Cotter, Cornelius P. Powers of the President During Crises. LC 71-39371. (American Constitutional & Legal History Ser). 1972. Repr. of 1960 ed. lib. bdg. 19.50 (ISBN 0-306-70462-5). Da Capo.
Smith, Johni. How to Be a Flight Stewardess or Steward. 3rd, rev. ed. LC 65-28387. 331p. 1978. 14.95 (ISBN 0-87219-009-9). Pan Am Nav.
Smith, Jon M. Financial Analysis & Business Decisions on the Pocket Calculator. LC 75-39752. (Systems & Controls for Financial Management Ser.). 320p. 1976. 21.50 (ISBN 0-471-80184-4, Pub. by Wiley-Interscience). Wiley.
Smith, Joseph. History of the Church, 8 vols. & Index. (Vol. 7 from the Manuscript History of Brigham Young). Set. pap. 12.95 (ISBN 0-87747-725-6); index 9.95 (ISBN 0-87747-291-2). Deseret Bk.
Smith, Joseph C. The Day the Music Died. LC 80-8914. 464p. 1981. 12.95 (ISBN 0-394-51951-5). Grove.
Smith, Joseph F. Teachings of the Prophet Joseph Smith. LC 76-111624. 437p. pap. 2.50 (ISBN 0-87747-778-7). Deseret Bk.
Smith, Joseph H., ed. Kierkegaard's Truth: The Disclosure of the Self. LC 80-27055. (Psychiatry & the Humanities: Vol. 5). (Illus.). 456p. 1981. 36.50x (ISBN 0-300-02621-8). Yale U Pr.
Smith, Joseph M. Chemical Engineering Kinetics. 3rd ed. (Chemical Engineering Ser.). (Illus.). 704p. 1980. text ed. 27.95 (ISBN 0-07-058710-8, C); solution manual 8.95 (ISBN 0-07-058711-6). McGraw.
Smith, Josephine M. Chronology of Librarianship. LC 67-12062. 1968. 10.00 (ISBN 0-8108-0024-1). Scarecrow.
Smith, Josiah W., ed. see Fearne, Charles.
Smith, Josie, tr. see Hill, Tomas.
Smith, Josie de see De Smith, Josie.
Smith, Joyce M. A Rejoicing Heart. 1979. pap. 1.75 (ISBN 0-8423-5418-2). Tyndale.
Smith, Judith M. & Smith, Donald E. Child Management: A Program for Parents & Teachers. LC 76-22829. 1976. pap. text ed. 5.95 (ISBN 0-87822-125-5); discussion guide 2.95 (ISBN 0-87822-126-3). Res Press.
Smith, Julia F. Slavery & Plantation Growth in Antebellum Florida, 1821-1860. LC 70-150656. 249p. 1972. 8.50 (ISBN 0-8130-0323-7). U Presses Fla.
Smith, Julian. Nevil Shute. LC 76-8018. (English Authors Ser.: No. 190). 1976. lib. bdg. 10.95 (ISBN 0-8057-6664-2). Twayne.
Smith, Juliet. Northamptonshire & the Soke of Peterborough: A Shell Guide. (Shell Guide Ser.). (Illus.). 1968. 12.95 (ISBN 0-571-08420-6, Pub. by Faber & Faber). Merrimack Bk Serv.
Smith, Justin. Our Struggle for the Fourteenth Colony: Canada & the American Revolution, 2 vols. LC 74-12272. (Era of the American Revolution Ser.). 1273p. 1974. Repr. of 1907 ed. lib. bdg. 95.00 (ISBN 0-306-70633-4). Da Capo.
Smith, K. M; see Luria, S. E.
Smith, Karen W. Constantin Guys: Crimean War Drawings 1854-1856. LC 78-14991. (Illus.). 84p. 1978. pap. 7.95x (ISBN 0-910386-43-9, Pub. by Cleveland Mus Art). Ind U Pr.
Smith, Karl J. Arithmetic for College Students. 400p. 1981. text ed. 16.95 (ISBN 0-8185-0422-6). Brooks-Cole.
--Basic Mathematics for College Students. LC 80-20492. 400p. (Orig.). 1981. pap. text ed. 15.95 (ISBN 0-8185-0419-6). Brooks-Cole.
--The Nature of Modern Mathematics. 2nd ed. LC 75-19937. (Contemporary Undergraduate Mathematics Ser.). (Illus.). 1976. text ed. 15.95 o.p. (ISBN 0-8185-0171-5); instructor's manual avail. o.p. (ISBN 0-685-55263-2). Brooks-Cole.
--The Nature of Modern Mathematics. 3rd ed. LC 79-20064. 1980. text ed. 16.95 (ISBN 0-8185-0352-1). Brooks-Cole.
--Precalculus Mathematics: A Functional Approach. Wisner, Robert J., ed. LC 78-6279. (Contemporary Undergraduate Mathematics Ser.). (Illus.). 1979. text ed. 16.95 (ISBN 0-8185-0269-X). Brooks-Cole.
--Trigonometry for College Students. LC 76-19454. (Contemporary Undergraduate Mathematics Ser.). (Illus.). 1977. text ed. 14.95 o.p. (ISBN 0-8185-0198-7). Brooks-Cole.
--Trigonometry for College Students. 2nd ed. LC 79-9122. 1980. text ed. 16.95 (ISBN 0-8185-0340-8). Brooks-Cole.
Smith, Karl J. & Boyle, Patrick J. Beginning Algebra for College Students. LC 76-46476. (Contemporary Undergraduate Mathematics Seri Es). (Illus.). 1976. text ed. 15.95 (ISBN 0-8185-0184-7); study guide 5.95 (ISBN 0-8185-0219-3). Brooks-Cole.
--Beginning Algebra for College Students. 2nd ed. LC 80-12572. 1980. text ed. 15.95 (ISBN 0-8185-0365-3). Brooks-Cole.
Smith, Kathleen, jt. auth. see Ulett, George A.
Smith, Kathryn. Hey Kids, Stay Well-Feel Good. LC 78-50432. 1979. pap. 3.95 (ISBN 0-8163-0236-7). Pacific Pr Pub Assn.
Smith, Keith. Principles of Applied Climatology. LC 74-20976. 233p. 1975. text ed. 24.95 (ISBN 0-470-80169-7). Halsted Pr.
Smith, Keith V. & Eiteman, David K. Essentials of Investing. 1974. text ed. 18.95 (ISBN 0-256-01554-6). Irwin.
Smith, Ken. Southern Home Landscaping. (Gardening Ser.). (Orig.). 1981. pap. 7.95 (ISBN 0-89586-063-5). H P Bks.
--Western Home Landscaping. LC 78-51897. (Illus.). 1978. pap. 5.95 (ISBN 0-89586-012-0). H P Bks.
--Work, Distances: Poems. LC 75-189189. 98p. 1972. pap. 5.00 o.s.i. (ISBN 0-8040-0588-5); pap. 5.00 (ISBN 0-8040-0589-3). Swallow.
Smith, Kendon R. Behavior & Conscious Experience: A Conceptual Analysis. LC 69-15918. 139p. 1969. 9.00x (ISBN 0-8214-0052-5). Ohio U Pr.
Smith, Kendric C., ed. Photochemical & Photobiological Reviews, Vols. 1-5. Incl. Vol. 1. 391p. 1976. 39.50 (ISBN 0-306-33801-7); Vol. 2. 329p. 1977. 29.50 (ISBN 0-306-33802-5); Vol. 3. 315p. 1978. 27.50 (ISBN 0-306-33803-3); Vol. 4. 343p. 1979. 35.00 (ISBN 0-306-40225-4); Vol. 5. 375p. 1980. 35.00 (ISBN 0-306-40360-9). LC 75-43689 (Plenum Pr). Plenum Pub.
Smith, Kenneth M. Virus-Insect Relationships. (Illus.). 1977. text ed. 30.00x (ISBN 0-582-46612-1). Longman.
--Viruses. 1962. pap. 8.50 (ISBN 0-521-06496-1). Cambridge U Pr.
Smith, Kussel & DePaula. Internal Control & Audit. 24.50x (ISBN 0-392-07955-0, SpS). Soccer.
Smith, L. Learning Can Be Fun. 4.00 o.p. (ISBN 0-8062-1184-9). Carlton.
--The Pathogenic Anaerobic Bacteria. 2nd ed. 444p. 1975. 35.75 (ISBN 0-398-03393-5). C C Thomas.
Smith, L. Neil. The Venus Belt. (Orig.). 1981. pap. 2.25 (ISBN 0-345-28721-5, Del Rey). Ballantine.
Smith, Lacey B. Elizabeth I. LC 79-54031. (Problems in Civilization Ser.). (Orig.). 1980. pap. text ed. 3.95x (ISBN 0-88273-407-5). Forum Pr MO.
Smith, Lacey B., jt. auth. see Williams, Jay.
Smith, Lacey B., ed. A History of England, 4 vols. 3rd ed. Incl. Vol. 1. The Making of England, 55 B.C.-1399. Hollister, C. W. pap. text ed. 7.95x (ISBN 0-685-56522-X); Vol. 2. This Realm of England, 1399-1688. Smith, Lacey B. pap. text ed. 7.95x (ISBN 0-669-97949-X); Vol. 3. The Age of Aristocracy, 1688-1830. Willcox, William B. pap. text ed. 7.95x (ISBN 0-669-97956-2); Vol. 4. Britain Yesterday & Today, 1830 to the Present. Arnstein, Walter L. (Illus.). pap. text ed. 8.95x (ISBN 0-669-97964-3). 1975. Heath.
Smith, Lacey B. & Smith, Jean R., eds. The Past Speaks: Sources & Problems in English History to 1688. 368p. 1981. pap. text ed. 7.95 (ISBN 0-669-02920-3). Heath.
Smith, Larry L. Crisis Intervention Theory & Practice: A Source Book. 1976. pap. text ed. 10.50x (ISBN 0-8191-0077-3). U Pr of Amer.
Smith, Larry R. Kenneth Patchen. (United States Authors Ser.: No. 292). 1978. lib. bdg. 12.50 (ISBN 0-8057-7195-6). Twayne.
Smith, Laura A. Music of the Waters. LC 69-16479. 1969. Repr. of 1888 ed. 20.00 (ISBN 0-8103-3552-2). Gale.
Smith, Laura L. & Minor, Lewis J. Food Service Science. (Illus.). 1974. pap. text ed. 19.00 (ISBN 0-87055-382-8). AVI.
Smith, Laurence J., jt. auth. see Frankel, Nat.
Smith, Lawrence R., ed. The New Italian Poetry: Nineteen Forty-Five to the Present. 400p. 1981. 16.95 (ISBN 0-520-03859-2). U of Cal Pr.
Smith, Ledyard. Excavations at Seibal: Major Architecture & Caches & Analysis of Fine Paste Ceramics. Subloff, Jeremy A., ed. (Peabody Museum Memoirs Ser.: Vol. 15, No. 1 & 2). 1981. pap. price not set (ISBN 0-87365-687-3). Peabody Harvard.
Smith, Lee, jt. auth. see Slater, Harry.
Smith, Lee A. Amedeo Amedei. (Greenbird Ser.). 1975. 12.00 (ISBN 0-88253-494-7); pap. text ed. 4.80 (ISBN 0-88253-493-9). Ind-US Inc.
Smith, Leial R. English for Careers Business Professionals & Technical. 2nd ed. 528p. 1981. pap. text ed. 13.95 (ISBN 0-471-08991-5). Wiley.
Smith, Leila R. English for Careers. LC 76-54780. (Read & Replay Ser). 1977. pap. text ed. 15.95x (ISBN 0-471-80176-3). Wiley.
Smith, Lendon. Feed Your Kids Right. 1980. pap. 4.95 (ISBN 0-440-52704-X, Dell Trade Pbks). Dell.
Smith, LeRoi. How to Fix Up Old Cars. rev. ed. LC 80-10614. (Illus.). 260p. 1980. 7.95x (ISBN 0-396-07830-3); pap. 3.95x (ISBN 0-396-07831-1). Dodd.
Smith, Leroy. Money-Savers' Do-It-Yourself Car Repair. LC 73-18509. (Illus.). 320p. 1975. 12.95 (ISBN 0-02-611940-4). Macmillan.
Smith, Leslie R. From Sunset to Dawn. 1945. 4.95 (ISBN 0-687-13664-4). Abingdon.
Smith, Lillian. Killers of the Dream. rev. ed. 1961. 12.95 (ISBN 0-393-06332-1, Norton Lib); pap. 3.95 1978 (ISBN 0-393-00884-3). Norton.
--Memory of a Large Christmas. (Illus.). 96p. 1980. pap. 2.95 (ISBN 0-393-00038-9). Norton.
--Our Faces, Our Words. (Illus.). 1964. pap. 1.95 o.p. (ISBN 0-393-00251-9, 4, Norton Lib). Norton.
Smith, Linda, et al. Actor Training 3. Brown, Richard, ed. LC 72-90200. 112p. 1976. pap. text ed. 3.95x o.p. (ISBN 0-910482-76-4). Drama Bk.
Smith, Linda H., jt. auth. see Dow, Clista.
Smith, Linda H., jt. auth. see Mathews, F. Neil.
Smith, Linda H., ed. see Ciabotti, Patricia.
Smith, Linda H., ed. see Johnson, Judith M.
Smith, Linell. Who's Who in the Zoo. (Illus.). 48p. (gr. k-1). 1981. pap. 5.95 (ISBN 0-916392-78-3). Oak Tree Pubns.
Smith, Lloyd H. & Thier, Samuel O. Pathophysiology: The Biological Principles of Disease. (International Textbook of Medical Science: Vol. 1). 1981. text ed. price not set (ISBN 0-7216-8400-9). Saunders.
Smith, Logan P. Words & Idioms. LC 77-148923. 1971. Repr. of 1925 ed. 22.00 (ISBN 0-8103-3651-0). Gale.
Smith, Logan P., et al. Needed Words. Commager, Steele, ed. Incl. The B.B.L.'s Recommendations for Pronouncing Doubtful Words; The Bull's Bellow; The Possibility of a Universal Language; Robert Bridges Recollections; Colloquial Language in Literature; Oxford English; Arabic Words in English; The Best English; Index to Tracts XXI-XXIX. (Society for Pure English Ser.: Vol. 4). 1979. lib. bdg. 42.00 (ISBN 0-8240-3668-9). Garland Pub.
Smith, Loren W. Home Gunsmithing: The Colt Single Action Revolvers. (Illus.). 1971. 7.95 o.p. (ISBN 0-686-15791-5). Ray Riling.
Smith, Lou. The Secret of MI6. LC 80-83570. 240p. 1981. pap. 2.50 (ISBN 0-87216-800-X). Playboy Pbks.
Smith, Louis. Botulism: The Organism, Its Toxins, the Disease. (Illus.). 256p. 1977. 25.75 (ISBN 0-398-03543-1). C C Thomas.
Smith, Louis A. & Barndt, Joseph R. Beyond Brokeness. (Orig.). 1980. pap. 2.95 (ISBN 0-377-00100-7). Friend Pr.
Smith, Lyn W. & Moure, Nancy D. Index to Reproductions of American Paintings. LC 77-14498. 1977. 50.00 (ISBN 0-8108-1084-0). Scarecrow.
Smith, Lynda, jt. auth. see TerHuen, Pat.
Smith, Lynette, jt. auth. see Milburn, Joyce.
Smith, M. A., jt. ed. see Haworth, J. T.
Smith, M. Brewster. Humanizing Social Psychology. LC 73-21076. (Social & Behavioral Science Ser.). 358p. 1974. 15.95x (ISBN 0-87589-229-9). Jossey-Bass.
Smith, M. Daniel. Educational Psychology & Its Classroom Applications. 2nd ed. 1978. pap. text ed. 16.95 (ISBN 0-205-06025-0); instr's man avail. (ISBN 0-205-06026-9); student guide avail. (ISBN 0-205-06028-5); tests avail. (ISBN 0-205-06027-7). Allyn.
Smith, M. G. The Affairs of Daura: History & Change in a Hausa State, 1800-1958. LC 73-80825. 1978. 35.00x (ISBN 0-520-02502-4). U of Cal Pr.
--The Plural Society in the British West Indies. (California Library Repr). 1975. Repr. of 1965 ed. 24.50x (ISBN 0-520-02853-8). U of Cal Pr.
Smith, M. H. The Writs of Assistance Case. 1978. 38.50x (ISBN 0-520-03349-3). U of Cal Pr.
Smith, M. I., jt. auth. see Yapp, W. B.
Smith, M. J. Materials & Structures. 2nd ed. (Illus.). 180p. 1980. pap. text ed. 13.95x (ISBN 0-7114-5639-9). Intl Ideas.
Smith, M. K. Professional Training in Mathematics. rev. ed. 1979. Repr. of 1976 ed. 0.80 (ISBN 0-685-91809-2, PT). Am Math.
Smith, M. L., ed. see I.A.U Symposium No. 78, Kiev, USSR, May 23-28, 1977, et al.
Smith, Malcolm. How I Learned to Meditate. 1977. pap. 3.95 o.p. (ISBN 0-88270-253-X). Logos.
Smith, Marcelle d'Argy, ed. British Art & Antiques Yearbook Nineteen Seventy-Nine. (Illus.). 1979. 36.00 (ISBN 0-900305-20-7, Natinal Magazine Co.). Gale.
Smith, Margaret. An Introduction to Mysticism. 1977. pap. 5.95 (ISBN 0-19-519956-1). Oxford U Pr.
--The Way of the Mystics: The Early Christian Mystics & the Rise of the Sufis. 1979. 14.95 (ISBN 0-19-520039-X). Oxford U Pr.
Smith, Margaret, ed. see Bronte, Charlotte.
Smith, Margaret K., tr. see Herbart, Johann F.
Smith, Margo L., jt. ed. see Damien, Yvonne M.
Smith, Marie, jt. auth. see Stanford, Gene.
Smith, Marilyn Z. Standard COBOL: A Problem-Solving Approach. 308p. 1974. pap. text ed. 14.25 (ISBN 0-395-17091-5). HM.
Smith, Marilyn Z., jt. auth. see Cooper, Laura G.
Smith, Marilyn Z., jt. auth. see Lewis, Theodore G.
Smith, Marion, jt. ed. see Sargent, S. Stansfeld.
Smith, Marion H., jt. auth. see Jennings, Jerry E.
Smith, Marion J. General William King. LC 79-67417. (Illus.). 182p. 1980. 11.95 (ISBN 0-89272-072-7). Down East.
Smith, Mark. The Death of the Detective. 1975. pap. 2.25 (ISBN 0-380-00549-2, 36897). Avon.
--The Middleman. 1977. pap. 1.95 (ISBN 0-380-01766-0, 34991). Avon.
--The Moon Lamp. 1976. 7.95 o.p. (ISBN 0-394-49888-7). Knopf.
Smith, Marsella, jt. auth. see Mummah, Hazel.
Smith, Martin. The Analog Bullet. 1978. pap. 1.50 (ISBN 0-505-51220-3). Tower Bks.
Smith, Martin C. Nightwing. 1978. pap. 2.50 (ISBN 0-515-05298-1). Jove Pubns.
Smith, Mary E. Love Kindling Fire: A Study Christopher Marlowe's the Tragedy of Dido Queen of Carthage. (Salzburg Studies in English Literature: Elizabethan & Renaissance: No.63). 1977. pap. text ed. 25.00x (ISBN 0-391-01529-X). Humanities.
Smith, Mary L., jt. auth. see Fischer, Pauline.
Smith, Mary L., et al. The Benefits of Psychotherapy. LC 80-11610. 320p. 1981. text ed. 22.50x (ISBN 0-8018-2352-8). Johns Hopkins.
Smith, Maury. A Practical Guide to Value Clarification. LC 76-20047. 322p. 1977. pap. 16.95 (ISBN 0-88390-124-2). Univ Assocs.
Smith, Maury, jt. auth. see Hall, Brian.
Smith, Maxwell A. Prosper Merimee. (World Authors Ser.: France: No. 249). lib. bdg. 10.95 (ISBN 0-8057-2612-8). Twayne.
Smith, Melvin H., jt. auth. see Niss, James F.
Smith, Merriman. Thank You Mr. President. LC 75-31769. (FDR & the Era of the New Deal Ser.). 1975. Repr. of 1946 ed. lib. bdg. 32.50 (ISBN 0-306-70740-3). Da Capo.
Smith, Merritt R. Harpers Ferry Armory & the New Technology: The Challenge of Change. 1980. 19.50 o.p. (ISBN 0-8014-0984-5); pap. 7.95 o.p. Cornell U Pr.

Smith, Michael. Everyday Home Repairs. pap. 2.95 (ISBN 0-7153-7553-9). David & Charles.

--Fine English Cookery. 1977. pap. 5.95 o.p. (ISBN 0-571-11128-9, Pub. by Faber & Faber). Merrimack Bk Serv.

--Secrets. 238p. 1981. 10.95 (ISBN 0-312-70913-7). St Martin.

--Times & Locations. 1972. text ed. 5.00x (ISBN 0-85105-219-3, Dolmen Pr). Humanities.

Smith, Michael, jt. ed. see Orzel, Nick.

Smith, Michael, et al, eds. Perspectives on World Politics. 224p. 1981. 32.50x (ISBN 0-7099-2302-3, Pub. by Croom Helm Ltd England). Biblio Dist.

Smith, Michael A. Landscapes 1975-1979, 2 vols. (Illus.). 120p. 1981. Set. 275.00 (ISBN 0-9605646-0-8). Vol. I (ISBN 0-9605646-1-6). Vol. II (ISBN 0-9605646-2-4). Lodima.

--Legacy of the Lake. 1980. pap. 2.25 (ISBN 0-686-69247-0, 75879). Avon.

Smith, Michael D. Poets & Poems of the First World War: The English. LC 78-65845. 1979. pap. text ed. 4.50 o.p. (ISBN 0-8191-0672-0). U Pr of Amer.

Smith, Michael H. & Persse, Mary K. Preparing for Confirmation: Program Outline. LC 72-92730. 80p. (Orig., Prog. Bk.). (gr. 6-8). 1972. pap. 1.95 (ISBN 0-87793-050-3). Ave Maria.

Smith, Michael H. & Joule, James, eds. Mammalian Population Genetics. 1981. 25.00 (ISBN 0-8203-0547-2). U of Ga Pr.

Smith, Michael L., jt. auth. see Bertin, John J.

Smith, Michael P. American Politics & Public Policy. 1972. pap. text ed. 5.95 (ISBN 0-394-31650-9). Random.

--The City & Social Theory. LC 77-86294. 1979. text ed. 14.95 (ISBN 0-312-14000-2); pap. text ed. 7.95 (ISBN 0-312-14035-5). St Martin.

Smith, Michael P., jt. ed. see Garson, G. David.

Smith, Mickey C. & Knapp, David A. Pharmacy, Drugs & Medical Care. 3rd ed. 345p. 1981. write for info. softcover (7761-9). Williams & Wilkins.

Smith, Mike. Success in Football (Soccer) (Illus.). 96p. 1974. 9.95 (ISBN 0-7195-2822-4). Transatlantic.

Smith, Milton. Money Today, More Tomorrow. 320p. 1981. 14.95 (ISBN 0-87626-593-X); pap. text ed. 9.95 (ISBN 0-87626-592-1). Winthrop.

Smith, Milton M. Play Production. (Illus.). 1948. 29.50x (ISBN 0-89197-345-1); pap. text ed. 16.95x (ISBN 0-89197-346-X). Irvington.

Smith, Miranda. Dorothy Hamill. (Sports Superstars Ser.). (Illus.). (gr. 3-9). 1977. PLB 5.95 (ISBN 0-87191-546-4); pap. 2.95 (ISBN 0-89812-194-9). Creative Ed.

--Pablo Picasso. LC 74-19319. (Illus.). 40p. (gr. 4-8). 1975. PLB 5.75 o.p. (ISBN 0-87191-411-5). Creative Ed.

Smith, Mont. What the Bible Says About the Covenant. (What the Bible Says Ser.). 400p. 1981. 13.50 (ISBN 0-89900-083-5). College Pr Pub.

Smith, Mortimer. My School the City. LC 80-51727. 190p. 1980. 9.95 (ISBN 0-89526-674-1). Regnery-Gateway.

Smith, Murphy D. Sherman Day: Artist, Engineer & Forty Niner. 30.00 (ISBN 0-89453-152-2). M Glazier.

Smith, Murray F. Selected Bibliography of German Literature in English Translation, 1956-1960: A Second Supplement to Bayard Quincy Morgan's - A Critical Bibliography of German Literature in English Translation. LC 76-157727. 1972. 14.50 (ISBN 0-8108-0411-5). Scarecrow.

Smith, Myron J. Cloak & Dagger Bibliography: An Annotated Guide to Spy Fiction, 1937-1975. 1975. 10.00 (ISBN 0-8108-0897-8). Scarecrow.

Smith, Myron J., Jr. Air War Southeast Asia, Nineteen Sixty-One to Nineteen Seventy-Three: An Annotated Bibliography & 16mm Film Guide. LC 79-21046. 316p. 1979. 16.50 (ISBN 0-8108-1261-4). Scarecrow.

--American Civil War Navies: A Bibliography. LC 72-6063. (American Naval Bibliography Ser.: Vol. 3). 1972. 13.50 (ISBN 0-8108-0509-X). Scarecrow.

--American Navy, Seventeen Eighty-Nineteen to Eighteen-Sixty: A Bibliography. LC 73-18464. (American Naval Bibliography Ser.: Vol. 2). 1974. 18.50 (ISBN 0-8108-0659-2). Scarecrow.

--The American Navy 1865-1918: A Bibliography. LC 74-11077. (American Naval Bibliography Ser.: Vol. 4). 1974. 15.00 (ISBN 0-686-67008-6). Scarecrow.

--The American Navy, 1918-1941: A Bibliography. LC 74-11077. (American Naval Bibliography Ser.: Vol. 5). 1974. 18.00 (ISBN 0-8108-0756-4). Scarecrow.

--Navies in the American Revolution: A Bibliography. LC 72-10995. (American Naval Bibliography Ser.: Vol. 1). 1973. 10.00 (ISBN 0-8108-0569-3). Scarecrow.

--The Secret Wars: A Guide to Sources in English: Vol. 1, Intelligence, Propaganda & Psychological Warfare, Resistance Movements & Secret Operations, 1939-1945. Burns, Richard D., ed. (War-Peace Bibliography Ser.: No. 12). 250p. 1980. 34.50 (ISBN 0-87436-271-7). ABC-Clio.

--The Secret Wars: A Guide to Sources in English: Vol. 2, Intelligence, Propaganda & Psychological Warfare, Covert Operations, 1945-1980. Burns, Richard D., ed. (War-Peace Bibliography Ser.: No. 13). 375p. 1981. 47.00 (ISBN 0-87436-303-9). ABC Clio.

--The Secret Wars: A Guide to Sources in English: Vol. 3, International Terrorism, 1968 to 1980. Burns, Richard D., ed. (War-Peace Bibliography Ser.: No. 14). 237p. 1980. 33.75 (ISBN 0-87436-304-7). ABC-Clio.

--The Soviet Air & Strategic Rocket Forces, 1939 to 1980: A Guide to Sources in English. Burns, Richard D., ed. (War-Peace Bibliography Ser.: No. 10). 1981. price not set (ISBN 0-87436-306-3). Abc-Clio.

--The Soviet Army: A Guide to Sources in English. Burns, Richard D., ed. (War-Peace Bibliography Ser.: No. 11). 1982. price not set (ISBN 0-87436-307-1). Abc-Clio. Postponed.

--The Soviet Navy, Nineteen Fourty-One to Nineteen Seventy Eight: A Guide to Sources in English. LC 79-26542. (War-Peace Bibliography Ser.: No. 9). 211p. 1980. text ed. 23.75 (ISBN 0-87436-265-2). ABC-Clio.

--World War I in the Air: A Bibliography & Chronology. LC 76-45461. (Illus.). 1977. 13.50 (ISBN 0-8108-0990-7). Scarecrow.

--World War Two at Sea: A Bibliography of Sources in English, 3 vols. Incl. Vol. 1. The European Theater. 15.00 (ISBN 0-8108-0884-6); Vol. 2. The Pacific Theater. 18.00 (ISBN 0-8108-0969-9); Vol. 3. 24.00 (ISBN 0-8108-0970-2). Pt. 1: Gen. Works, Naval Hardware, & The All Hands Chronology (1941-1945) Pt. 2: Home Fronts & Special Studies. LC 75-34098. 1976. Set. 39.50 o.p. (ISBN 0-685-73560-5). Scarecrow.

Smith, Myron J., Jr. & Weller, Robert C. Sea Fiction Guide. LC 76-7590. 1976. 12.00 (ISBN 0-8108-0929-X). Scarecrow.

Smith, N., jt. auth. see Robinson, H.

Smith, N. A. New Enlightenment. 1980. pap. 6.95 (ISBN 0-7145-3604-0). Riverrun NY.

Smith, N. A., jt. auth. see Wiggin, K. D.

Smith, N. D., tr. see Bockle, Franz.

Smith, N. D., tr. see Labat, Elisabeth-Paule.

Smith, N. D., tr. see Oosterhuis, Huub.

Smith, N. Ty, jt. auth. see Saidman, Lawrence J.

Smith, N. Ty, et al, eds. Drug Interactions in Anesthesia. LC 80-17454. (Illus.). 351p. 1981. text ed. write for info. (ISBN 0-8121-0683-0). Lea & Febiger.

Smith, N. V. The Acquisition of Phonology. LC 72-95409. 228p. 1973. 29.95 (ISBN 0-521-20154-3). Cambridge U Pr.

Smith, Nancy, jt. auth. see Bijur, Hilda.

Smith, Nancy A. All I Need Is Love. LC 77-6036. (Orig.). 1977. pap. 2.75 (ISBN 0-87784-723-1). Inter-Varsity.

Smith, Neil S. Materials on Japanese Social & Economic History: Tokugawa, Japan. (Studies in Japanese History & Civilization). 176p. 1979. Repr. of 1937 ed. 19.50 (ISBN 0-89093-262-X). U Pubns Amer.

Smith, Nelson C. The Art of Gothic: Ann Radcliffe's Major Novels. Varma, Devendra P., ed. LC 79-8481. (Gothic Studies & Dissertations Ser.). 1980. lib. bdg. 22.00x (ISBN 0-405-12680-8). Arno.

Smith, Nelson M. What Is This Thing Called Love. 1970. 6.65 (ISBN 0-89137-505-8); pap. 3.10 (ISBN 0-89137-504-X). Quality Pubns.

Smith, Nicholas D., jt. ed. see Miller, Fred D.

Smith, Nigel. Wood: An Ancient Fuel with a New Future. LC 80-54881. (Worlwatch Papers). 1981. pap. 2.00 (ISBN 0-916468-41-0). Worldwatch Inst.

Smith, Nigel J. Man, Fishes, & the Amazon. 176p. 1981. 20.00x (ISBN 0-231-05156-5). Columbia U Pr.

Smith, Nila B. Speed Reading Made Easy. 1977. pap. 1.95 (ISBN 0-445-08383-2). Popular Lib.

Smith, Nila B., et al. Best of Literature. Incl. Voyages in Reading. (gr. 7). text ed. 6.00 (ISBN 0-672-70565-6); tchrs' ed 6.00 (ISBN 0-685-23133-X); Challenges in Reading. (gr. 8). text ed. 6.40 (ISBN 0-672-70569-9); tchrs' ed 6.40 (ISBN 0-685-23134-8); Riches in Reading. (gr. 9). text ed. 6.76 (ISBN 0-672-70562-1). (Reading Literature Ser.). (gr. 7-9). 1969. tchrs' manuals o.p. 1.40. Bobbs.

--Best of Children's Literature. Incl. Sunny & Gay. (gr. 1). text ed. 3.12 (ISBN 0-672-70530-3); Foolish & Wise. (gr. 2). text ed. 3.32 (ISBN 0-672-70534-6); Fun All Around. (gr. 3). text ed. 3.56 (ISBN 0-672-70538-9); Shining Hours. (gr. 4). text ed. 3.76 (ISBN 0-672-70542-7); Time for Adventure. (gr. 5). text ed. 4.04 (ISBN 0-672-70546-X); Beyond the Horizon. (gr. 6). text ed. 4.16 (ISBN 0-672-70550-8). (gr. 1-6). 1968. tchrs' manuals o.p. 1.40. Bobbs.

Smith, Noel T., jt. auth. see Zeiss, P. Anthony.

Smith, Nora, jt. ed. see Wiggins, Kate.

Smith, Norman. Man & Water: A History of Hydro-Technology. LC 75-24865. 1976. 12.95 o.p. (ISBN 0-684-14522-7, ScribT). Scribner.

Smith, Norman A. Victorian Technology & Its Preservation in Modern Britain. (Orig.). 1970. pap. text ed. 4.00x (ISBN 0-7185-1098-4, Leicester). Humanities.

Smith, Norman F. Gliding, Soaring, & Skysailing. LC 79-27680. (Illus.). 160p. (gr. 9-12). 1980. PLB 7.79 (ISBN 0-671-32981-2). Messner.

--Michigan Trees Worth Knowing. rev., 5th ed. LC 78-61161. (Illus.). 1978. 9.95 (ISBN 0-910726-69-8); pap. 6.50 (ISBN 0-910726-72-8). Hillsdale Educ.

Smith, Norman K., ed. see Hume, David.

Smith, Ora. Potatoes: Production, Storing, Processing. 2nd ed. (Illus.). 1977. lib. bdg. 39.50 (ISBN 0-87055-224-4). AVI.

Smith, Ora, jt. ed. see Talburt, W. F.

Smith, P., jt. auth. see Brommelle, N. S.

Smith, P., jt. auth. see Jordan, D. W.

Smith, P., ed. The Historian & Film. LC 75-19577. 235p. 1976. 24.95 (ISBN 0-521-20992-7). Cambridge U Pr.

Smith, P., tr. see Palm, Goran.

Smith, P. J., ed. The Prairie Provinces. (Studies in Canadian Geography). 1972. pap. 5.50x (ISBN 0-8020-6161-3). U of Toronto Pr.

Smith, P. K. & Connolly, K. J. The Ecology of Preschool Behaviour. LC 79-42647. (Illus.). 400p. Date not set. 49.50 (ISBN 0-521-22331-8). Cambridge U Pr.

Smith, P. R. & Julian, W. G. Building Services. (Illus.). 1976. 52.20x (ISBN 0-685-90194-7, Pub. by Applied Science). Burgess-Intl Ideas.

Smith, Page. Religious Origins of the American Revolution. LC 76-13157. (American Academy of Religion, Aids for the Study of Religion). 1976. pap. 7.50 (ISBN 0-89130-121-6, 010303). Scholars Pr Ca.

Smith, Parker. Golf Techniques: How to Improve Your Game. LC 73-3048. (Concise Guide Ser). (Illus.). (gr. 5 up). 1973. PLB 4.90 o.p. (ISBN 0-531-02627-2). Watts.

Smith, Parker F. Exile's Odyssey: The Memoirs of an American Deserter. LC 78-75338. (Illus.). 1979. 12.00 o.p. (ISBN 0-498-02387-7). A S Barnes.

Smith, Patricia. China & Parian Dolls. (Illus.). 1980. pap. 9.95 (ISBN 0-89145-144-7). Collector Bks.

--German Dolls II. (Illus.). 1980. pap. 9.95 (ISBN 0-89145-151-X). Collector Bks.

--Modern Collector's Dolls: Second Ser. (Illus.). 1975. 17.95 (ISBN 0-517-52110-5). Collector Bks.

--Modern Collector's Dolls: Third Ser. (Illus.). 1976. 17.95 (ISBN 0-517-52666-2). Collector Bks.

--Price Guide to Madame Alexander Dolls. (No. 6). (Illus.). 1980. 3.95 o.p. (ISBN 0-89145-136-6). Collector Bks.

--Price Guide to Madame Alexander Dolls, No. 7. (Illus.). 1981. 3.95 (ISBN 0-89145-167-6). Collector Bks.

--The Real Estate Professional's Design-a-Day 1980. 1979. text ed. 15.95 o.p. (ISBN 0-8359-6583-X); pap. text ed. 10.95 o.p. (ISBN 0-8359-6584-8). Reston.

--Real Estate Professionals Design-A-Day: 1981 Edition. 1980. 18.00 (ISBN 0-8359-6587-2). Reston.

Smith, Patricia, jt. auth. see Barrow, Georgia.

Smith, Patti. Babel. 1979. pap. text ed. 2.75 (ISBN 0-425-04230-8). Berkley Pub.

Smith, Paul C. Know Your Oscilloscope. 3rd ed. Middleton, Robert G., ed. LC 74-15451. (Illus.). 1974. pap. 5.25 o.p. (ISBN 0-672-21102-5). Sams.

Smith, Paul F. Money & Financial Intermediation: The Theory & Structure of Financial Systems. LC 77-21636. (Illus.). 1978. 19.95 (ISBN 0-13-600288-9). P-H.

Smith, Paul I. Recycling Waste. 1976. text ed. 22.50x (ISBN 0-87936-011-9). Scholium Intl.

Smith, Paul T., Jr. Pacific Crusaders. (Illus.). 225p. 1981. 11.50 (ISBN 0-87881-094-3). Mojave Bks.

Smith, Pauline. The Little Karoo. 1978. 7.95 (ISBN 0-224-60699-9, Pub. by Chatto Bodley Jonathan). Merrimack Bk Serv.

Smith, Percy D. Deck Machinery. LC 73-12704. (Illus.). 1973. 7.00x (ISBN 0-87033-185-X, Pub. by Tidewater). Cornell Maritime.

--Modern Marine Electricity & Electronics. LC 66-20866. (Illus.). 1966. 16.00x (ISBN 0-87033-062-4). Cornell Maritime.

Smith, Percy H., ed. see Smith, Charles J.

Smith, Peter & Swann, Dennis. Protecting the Consumer: An Economic & Legal Analysis. 286p. 1980. 36.00x (ISBN 0-85520-259-9, Pub. by Martin Robertson England); pap. 12.50x (ISBN 0-85520-258-0). Biblio Dist.

Smith, Peter & Summerfield, Geoffrey, eds. Matthew Arnold & the Education of the New Order. LC 69-10433. (Cambridge Texts & Studies in Education: No. 3). 1969. 24.50 (ISBN 0-521-07341-3). Cambridge U Pr.

Smith, Peter B. Group Processes & Personal Change. 1980. text ed. 18.35 (ISBN 0-06-318146-0, IntlDept); pap. text ed. 10.45 (ISBN 0-06-318151-7). Har-Row.

Smith, Peter C. The Design & Construction of Stables. (Illus.). 18.35 (ISBN 0-85131-000-1, Dist. by Sporting Book Center). J A Allen.

Smith, Peter H. Argentina & the Failure of Democracy: Conflict Among the Political Elites, 1904-1955. LC 74-5907. 320p. 1974. 20.00 (ISBN 0-299-06600-2). U of Wis Pr.

--Upgrading Lecture Rooms. (Illus.). 1979. 38.90x (ISBN 0-85334-849-9, Pub. by Applied Science). Burgess-Intl Ideas.

Smith, Peter M. On the Hymm to Zeus in Aeschylus' Agamemnon. LC 80-11327. (American Classical Studies: No. 5). 12.00x (ISBN 0-89130-387-1); pap. 7.50x (ISBN 0-89130-388-X). Scholars Pr CA.

Smith, Phil D., ed. see Fryxell, Fritiof.

Smith, Philip. Total Breathing. (McGraw-Hill Paperbacks Ser.). 1980. pap. 6.95 (ISBN 0-07-058989-5). McGraw.

Smith, Philip, jt. auth. see McFarland, Wayne J.

Smith, Philip C. More Marine & Drawings in the Peabody Museum. (Illus.). 192p. 1979. 35.00 (ISBN 0-87577-064-9); boxed numbered 50.00 (ISBN 0-686-68319-6). Peabody Mus Salem.

Smith, Philip L. Sources of Progressive Thought in American Education. LC 80-8290. 217p. 1980. lib. bdg. 18.75 (ISBN 0-8191-1300-X); pap. text ed. 9.75 (ISBN 0-8191-1301-8). U Pr of Amer.

Smith, Philip M., ed. see Giles, Howard & Robinson, W. Peter.

Smith, Phillip E. Food Production & Its Consequences. new ed. LC 75-28640. (Cummings Modular Program in Anthropology). 1975. text ed. 7.50 o.p. (ISBN 0-8465-6718-0); pap. text ed. 5.50 o.p. (ISBN 0-8465-6719-9). Benjamin-Cummings.

Smith, R. Drawing. (Teach Yourself Ser.). 1975. pap. 2.95 o.p. (ISBN 0-679-10422-4). McKay.

Smith, R. & Beasley, N. Carter Glass: A Biography. LC 72-172012. (FDR & the Era of the New Deal Ser). (Illus.). 520p. 1972. Repr. of 1939 ed. lib. bdg. 49.50 (ISBN 0-306-70392-0). Da Capo.

Smith, R., ed. see Logue, Valentine.

Smith, R. A. Semiconductors. 2nd ed. LC 77-82515. 1978. 86.50 (ISBN 0-521-21824-1); pap. 25.95x (ISBN 0-521-29314-6). Cambridge U Pr.

Smith, R. A., ed. Fracture Mechanics, Current Status, Future Prospects: Proceedings of a Conference Held at Cambridge University, March 16, 1979. (Illus.). 128p. 1979. 55.00 (ISBN 0-08-024766-0). Pergamon.

Smith, R. A., jt. ed. see D'Urso, S.

Smith, R. Dennis & Williamson, L. Keith. Interpersonal Communication: Roles, Rules, Strategies & Games. 2nd ed. 370p. 1981. pap. text ed. write for info. (ISBN 0-697-04182-4); instrs.' manual 2.00 (ISBN 0-697-04188-3). Wm C Brown.

Smith, R. Douglas, jt. auth. see Cohen, Arthur M.

Smith, R. E. Sheet Metalwork. pap. 5.00 (ISBN 0-87345-111-2). McKnight.

Smith, R. F. Peasant Farming in Muscovy. LC 75-23843. (Illus.). 1977. 41.95 (ISBN 0-521-20912-9). Cambridge U Pr.

Smith, R. F. & Lawrence, J. F. Clarification of the Status of the Type Specimens of Diabroticites (Coleoptera, Chrysomelidae, Galerocinae) (U. C. Publ. in Entomology: Vol. 45). 1967. pap. 8.50x (ISBN 0-520-09117-5). U of Cal Pr.

Smith, R. Franklin. Edward R. Murrow: The War Years. (Orig.). 1978. pap. 5.95x (ISBN 0-932826-04-0). New Issues MI.

Smith, R. H. Acts. LC 70-98297. (Concordia Commentary Ser). 1970. 10.95 (ISBN 0-570-06283-7, 15-2059). Concordia.

Smith, R. Harris. OSS: The Secret History of America's First Central Intelligence Agency. LC 73-153553. (Illus.). 450p. 1972. 14.50 o.p. (ISBN 0-520-02023-5); pap. 6.95 o.p. (ISBN 0-520-04246-8). U of Cal Pr.

Smith, R. J. Electronics: Circuits & Devices. LC 72-12833. 1973. 23.95x o.p. (ISBN 0-471-80181-X). Wiley.

Smith, R. L., jt. auth. see Bababunmi, E. A.

Smith, R. L., jt. auth. see Parke, D. V.

Smith, R. Nelson. Chemistry: A Quantitative Approach. LC 71-75642. 639p. 1969. 24.50x o.p. (ISBN 0-8260-8300-5); lab. manual 9.95x o.p. (ISBN 0-8260-8301-3). Wiley.

Smith, R. Nelson & Pierce, Conway. Solving General Chemistry Problems. 5th ed. LC 79-23677. (Illus.). 1980. 8.95x (ISBN 0-7167-1117-6); answers to b group avail. W H Freeman.

Smith, R. P. Consumer Demand for Cars in the U. S. A. LC 74-31802. (Department of Applied Economics, Occasional Papers Ser.: No. 44). (Illus.). 200p. 1975. 19.95 (ISBN 0-521-20770-3); pap. 12.95x (ISBN 0-521-09947-1). Cambridge U Pr.

Smith, R. Payne. Compendious Syriac Dictionary Founded Upon the Thesaurus Syriacus of R. Payne Smith. Payne Smith, J., ed. 1903. 65.00x (ISBN 0-19-864307-1). Oxford U Pr.

Smith, R. R. & Robertson, J. T. Subarachnoid Hemorrhage & Cerebrovascular Spasm. (Illus.). 284p. 1975. 33.50 (ISBN 0-398-03230-0). C C Thomas.

Smith, Ralph C. A Biographical Index of American Artists. LC 79-167186. 1976. Repr. of 1930 ed. 18.00 (ISBN 0-8103-4251-0). Gale.

Smith, Ralph E. Women in the Labor Force in Nineteen Ninety. (An Institute Paper). 176p. 1979. pap. 7.00 (ISBN 0-685-99692-1, 24600). Urban Inst.

Smith, Ralph E., ed. The Subtle Revolution: Women at Work. 1979. 15.00 (ISBN 0-87766-259-2, 26800); pap. 7.50 (ISBN 0-87766-260-6, 26700). Urban Inst.

Smith, Ralph I. & Carlton, James T., eds. Light's Manual: Intertidal Invertebrates of the Central California Coast. 3rd ed. 1975. 26.50x (ISBN 0-520-02113-4). U of Cal Pr.

Smith, Ralph R., jt. auth. see Eisenberg, Abne M.

Smith, Ray. Permanent Fires: Reviews of Poetry 1958-1973. LC 74-22230. 1975. 10.00 (ISBN 0-8108-0757-2). Scarecrow.

--Till Hope Creates. 1981. price not set. Kirk Pr.

--Weathering. 1980. pap. 2.50 (ISBN 0-930600-13-4). Uzzano Pr.

Smith, Raymond G. Message Measurement Inventory: A Profile for Communication Analysis. LC 77-17677. 224p. 1978. 12.50x (ISBN 0-253-33750-X). Ind U Pr.

Smith, Raymond J. Charles Churchill. (English Authors Ser.: No. 197). 1977. lib. bdg. 10.95 (ISBN 0-8057-6669-3). Twayne.

Smith, Reed M. State Government in Transition: Reforms of the Leader Administration, 1955-1959. LC 63-7864. 1963. 9.00x o.p. (ISBN 0-8122-7399-0). U of Pa Pr.

Smith, Rex A. Moon of Popping Trees. LC 80-24863. (Illus.). xviii, 220p. 1981. 15.50x (ISBN 0-8032-4123-2); pap. 4.95 (ISBN 0-8032-9120-5, BB 750, Bison). U of Nebr Pr.

Smith, Richard A., ed. Thinking, Knowing, Living: An Introduction to Philosophy. LC 78-52290. 1978. pap. text ed. 7.75x (ISBN 0-8191-0492-2). U Pr of Amer.

Smith, Richard E. Richard Aldington. (English Authors Ser.: No. 222). 1977. lib. bdg. 12.50 (ISBN 0-8057-6691-X). Twayne.

Smith, Richard F. Chemistry for the Million. LC 77-37219. 1974. pap. 2.95 o.p. (ISBN 0-684-13692-9, SL507, ScribT). Scribner.

Smith, Richard J. & Barrett, Thomas C. Teaching Reading in the Middle Grades. 2nd ed. LC 78-18650. (Education Ser.). (Illus.). 1979. text ed. 9.50 (ISBN 0-201-07057-X). A-W.

Smith, Richard J. & Veley, Victor F. Practice FCC-Type Exams for Radiotelephone Operator's License-1st Class. (gr. 10 up). 1977. pap. 5.95 (ISBN 0-8104-5974-4). Hayden.

--Practice FCC-Type Exams for Radiotelephone Operator's License-2nd Class. (Illus.). 180p. 1975. pap. 7.25 (ISBN 0-8104-5965-5). Hayden.

Smith, Richard J., jt. auth. see Otto, Wayne.

Smith, Richard J., et al. The School Reading Program: A Handbook for Teachers, Supervisors, & Specialists. LC 77-77993. (Illus.). 1978. text ed. 17.95 (ISBN 0-395-25452-3). HM.

Smith, Richard K. First Across! The U. S. Navy's Transatlantic Flight of 1919. LC 72-85396. 1973. 11.00 (ISBN 0-87021-184-6). Naval Inst Pr.

--Forty-Nine & Holding. LC 75-11179. (Illus.). 1975. 7.95 (ISBN 0-89430-023-7). Morgan-Pacific.

Smith, Richard L. Emile Lessore, 1805-1876: His Life & Work. Bd. with The Sydney Cove Medallion. (Monographs in Wedgwood Studies: Nos. 3 & 4). 1979. 9.00 (ISBN 0-912014-52-0). Buten Mus.

Smith, Richard L., jt. auth. see Lewis, J. David.

Smith, Richard P. Deer Hunting. rev. ed. (Illus.). 256p. 1981. pap. 9.95 (ISBN 0-8117-2132-9). Stackpole.

Smith, Richard T. & Atkinson, Kenneth. Techniques in Pedology. 1975. 15.95 (ISBN 0-236-30939-0, Pub. by Paul Elek); pap. 8.95 (ISBN 0-236-31020-8). Merrimack Bk Serv.

Smith, Richard W., jt. auth. see Giannotti, John B.

Smith, Riley K & Tessina, Tina B. How to Be a Couple & Still Be Free. LC 80-8669. 1980. lib. bdg. 11.95x (ISBN 0-89370-651-5). Borgo Pr.

Smith, Riley K. & Tessina, Tina B. How to Be a Couple & Still Be Free. 1980. pap. 5.95 (ISBN 0-87877-051-8). Newcastle Pub.

Smith, Robert. Applied General Mathematics. LC 79-51586. (General Mathematics Ser.). (Illus.). 480p. 1981. text ed. price not set (ISBN 0-8273-1674-7); price not set instr's. guide (ISBN 0-8273-1675-5). Delmar.

--Guide to Air Traffic Control. 1963. pap. 3.95 o.p. (ISBN 0-8306-2213-6, 2213). TAB Bks.

--Hiking Hawaii. Winnett, Thomas, ed. LC 79-93247. (Wilderness Press Trail Guide Ser.). (Illus.). 112p. (Orig.). 1981. write for info. (ISBN 0-89997-000-1). Wilderness Pr.

--Hiking Oahu. 2nd ed. LC 80-53464. 122p. 1980. pap. 4.95 (ISBN 0-89997-006-0). Wilderness Pr.

--Massachusetts Colony. LC 69-19575. (Forge of Freedom Ser). (Illus.). (gr. 5-8). 1969. 8.95 (ISBN 0-02-785880-4, CCPr). Macmillan.

--Teacher Diagnosis of Educational Difficulties. LC 69-11433. 1969. text ed. 14.95 (ISBN 0-675-09550-6). Merrill.

Smith, Robert, photos by. Wildlife. LC 76-5667. (Illus.). 120p. (Text by Robert Storm). 1976. pap. 10.95 (ISBN 0-912856-27-0); 20.00 o.p. (ISBN 0-686-67420-0). Graphic Arts Ctr.

Smith, Robert, et al. By Any Means Necessary: The Revolutionary Struggle at San Francisco State. LC 75-128701. (Higher Education Ser.). 1970. 15.95x o.p. (ISBN 0-87589-075-X). Jossey-Bass.

Smith, Robert A. The Fox Trap. 1978. pap. 1.75 o.p. (ISBN 0-449-14073-3, GM). Fawcett.

--The Inner Way: With Prayers from Psalms. 1977. 5.50 (ISBN 0-912128-09-7); pap. 3.50 (ISBN 0-912128-10-0). Pubns Living.

--Prey. 1978. pap. 1.95 o.p. (ISBN 0-449-13923-9, GM). Fawcett.

--Science of Life: With Affirmations of Jesus Christ. 1970. 2.25 (ISBN 0-912128-07-0). Pubns Living.

--Seeking & Finding. 1974. 1.75 (ISBN 0-912128-08-9). Pubns Living.

--Sermons from the Bible. 1981. pap. 3.00 (ISBN 0-912128-21-6). Pubns Living.

--Spirit of Life. 1978. 5.50 (ISBN 0-912128-13-5); pap. 3.50 (ISBN 0-912128-14-3). Pubns Living.

--Thought for the Day. 1978. pap. 3.50 (ISBN 0-912128-41-0). Pubns Living.

Smith, Robert B. & Manning, Peter K., eds. Qualitative Methods. (Handbook of Social Science Methods Ser.: Vol. 1). (Illus.). 1981. text ed. 19.50x (ISBN 0-8290-0086-0). Irvington.

Smith, Robert D., jt. auth. see Burack, Elmer H.

Smith, Robert E. Discovering BASIC: A Problem Solving Approach. (Illus.). (gr. 10 up). 1970. pap. 8.25x (ISBN 0-8104-5783-0). Hayden.

--Forging & Welding. rev. ed. (Illus.). (gr. 7 up). 1956. text ed. 14.00 (ISBN 0-87345-120-1). McKnight.

--Machine Woodworking. rev. ed. (Illus.). (gr. 9-10). 1958. text ed. 13.28 (ISBN 0-87345-010-8). McKnight.

--Patternmaking & Founding. (gr. 9 up). 1959. pap. 5.00 (ISBN 0-87345-020-5). McKnight.

--The Pottery of Mayapan: Including Studies of Ceramic Material from Uxmal, Kabah, & Chichen Itza. LC 73-158899. (Peabody Museum Papers: Vol. 66, Nos. 1 & 2). 1971. pap. 40.00 (ISBN 0-87365-187-1). Peabody Harvard.

Smith, Robert E. & Johnson, Dora E. Fortran Autotester. (Prog. Bk.). 1962. pap. 10.95 (ISBN 0-471-80337-5, Pub. by Wiley-Interscience). Wiley.

Smith, Robert H. Patches of Godlight: The Pattern of Thought of C. S. Lewis. LC 80-14132. 287p. 1981. 18.00x (ISBN 0-8203-0528-6). U of Ga Pr.

--Pathological Physiology for the Anesthesiologist. (American Lecture Anestesiology Ser). (Illus.). 600p. 1974. pap. 24.75 (ISBN 0-398-03167-3). C C Thomas.

--Pella of the Decapolis, Vol. 1. LC 72-619700. (Illus.). 248p. 1973. 50.00 (ISBN 0-9604658-0-4). Coll Wooster.

Smith, Robert H., jt. auth. see Hay, Alan M.

Smith, Robert H., jt. ed. see Groh, John E.

Smith, Robert I. Men & Societies: Experimental Courses in the Humanities & Social Sciences. 1968. text ed. 6.50 o.p. (ISBN 0-435-80835-4). Heinemann Ed.

Smith, Robert K. Chocolate Fever. 1978. pap. 1.25 (ISBN 0-440-41369-9, YB). Dell.

--Jelly Belly: A Novel. LC 80-23898. (Illus.). 156p. (gr. 4-7). 1981. 8.95 (ISBN 0-440-04186-4); PLB 8.44 (ISBN 0-440-04190-2). Delacorte.

--Sadie Shapiro, Matchmaker. 192p. 1981. pap. 2.50 (ISBN 0-449-24406-7, Crest). Fawcett.

--Sadie Shapiro's Knitting Book. 224p. 1975. pap. 1.25 o.p. (ISBN 0-449-22318-3, P2318-125, Crest). Fawcett.

Smith, Robert L. Electrical Wiring-Industrial. LC 77-92083. 1978. pap. text ed. 10.20 (ISBN 0-8273-1414-0); instr's. guide 1.60 (ISBN 0-8273-1415-9). Delmar.

--Elements of Ecology & Field Biology. 1977. text ed. 19.50 scp (ISBN 0-06-046329-5, HarpC); instructor's manual avail. (ISBN 0-685-74055-2). Har-Row.

Smith, Robert L. & Alexander, Ann M. Counseling Couples in Groups: A Manual for Improving Troubled Relationships. (Illus.). 128p. 1974. 12.75 (ISBN 0-398-03191-6). C C Thomas.

Smith, Robert L., jt. auth. see Mullin, Ray C.

Smith, Robert M., jt. auth. see Neisworth, John T.

Smith, Robert M., ed. Handbook of Adult Education in the United States. 1970. 17.25 (ISBN 0-88379-003-3). Adult Ed.

Smith, Robert M., jt. ed. see Martell, Arthur E.

Smith, Robert M., et al. Handbook of Adult Education. 1970. 17.95 (ISBN 0-02-896110-2). Macmillan.

--Evaluating Educational Environments. 1978. pap. text ed. 7.95 (ISBN 0-675-08388-5); instructor's manual 3.95 (ISBN 0-686-67978-4). Merrill.

Smith, Robert S. The Lagos Consulate, 1851-1861. 1979. 21.50x (ISBN 0-520-03746-4). U of Cal Pr.

Smith, Robert T. Make a Wish Come True. LC 72-89459. 32p. (gr. 5-12). 1973. PLB 4.95 (ISBN 0-87191-224-4). Creative Ed.

--A New Day. LC 72-81449. (Illus.). 32p. (gr. 5-12). 1973. PLB 4.95 (ISBN 0-87191-213-9). Creative Ed.

--Put Them in Cages. LC 72-89460. 32p. (gr. 5-12). 1973. PLB 4.95 (ISBN 0-87191-223-6). Creative Ed.

--White Buses Can Fly. 32p. (gr. 5-12). 1973. PLB 4.95 (ISBN 0-87191-225-2). Creative Ed.

Smith, Robert W. & Draeger, Donn F. Asian Fighting Arts. LC 69-16366. (Illus.). 1969. 16.50 o.p. (ISBN 0-87011-079-9). Kodansha.

Smith, Robert W., jt. auth. see Draeger, Donn F.

Smith, Roberta K. Foraminiferal Studies in the Lower & Middle Tertiary of Soquel Creek, Santa Cruz County, California. (U. C. Publ. in Geological Sciences: Vol. 91). 1971. pap. 7.50x (ISBN 0-520-09389-5). U of Cal Pr.

Smith, Robin, jt. auth. see Willey, Keith.

Smith, Rodney, jt. ed. see Rob, Charles.

Smith, Rodney, ed. see Roberts, David W.

Smith, Rodney, ed. see Symon, Lindsay.

Smith, Roger. Trial by Medicine: The Insanity Defense in Victorian England. 280p. 1981. 33.00x (ISBN 0-85224-407-X, Pub.by Edinburgh U Pr Scotland). Columbia U Pr.

Smith, Roger & Apley, Alan. Biochemical Disorders of the Skeleton. (Postgraduate Orthopedic Ser.). (Illus.). 1979. text ed. 59.95 (ISBN 0-407-00122-0). Butterworths.

Smith, Roger H. Paperback Parnassus: The Birth, the Development, the Pending Crises of the Modern American Paperbound Book. 100p. 1976. 18.00x (ISBN 0-89158-007-7). Westview.

Smith, Roger T. Renaissance Architecture. (Illus.). 1979. 61.75 (ISBN 0-930582-46-2). Gloucester Art.

Smith, Ronald B. How to Plan, Design & Implement a Bad System. (Illus.). 1981. 12.00 (ISBN 0-89433-148-5). Petrocelli.

Smith, Ronald C. Landscape Contracting. LC 79-51504. 1979. pap. 15.00 (ISBN 0-918436-07-9). Environ Des VA.

--Principles & Practices of Light Construction. 2nd ed. LC 78-95754. (Engineering Technology Ser). (Illus.). 1970. 18.95 o.p. (ISBN 0-13-701961-0). P-H.

Smith, Ronald G. Martin Buber. LC 67-10206. (Makers of Contemporary Theology Ser). 1967. pap. 3.45 (ISBN 0-8042-0697-X). John Knox.

Smith, Ronald G., tr. see Ebeling, Gerhard.

Smith, Ross. Propane Conversion of Engines. rev. ed. (Applied Technology Ser.). (Illus.). 76p. 1980. pap. 8.45 (ISBN 0-938260-01-4). Smith & Assoc.

--Propane Conversion of Engines. rev. ed. (Applied Technology Ser.). (Illus.). 76p. 1980. pap. 9.15. Ashford.

--Texas Dew: Manual on Conversion of Engines to Propane (Lpg) (Applied Technology Ser.). (Illus.). 76p. (Orig.). 1979. pap. 8.45 (ISBN 0-938260-00-6). Ashford.

Smith, Rowland, jt. auth. see Fuoss, Donald E.

Smith, Roy M., et al. Atlas of Oral Pathology. (Illus.). 204p. 1981. text ed. 24.95 (ISBN 0-8016-4684-7). Mosby.

Smith, Ruth, jt. auth. see Smith, Frank.

Smith, Ruth S. Cataloging Made Easy: How to Organize Your Congregation's Library. (Orig.). 1978. pap. 4.95 (ISBN 0-8164-2191-9). Crossroad NY.

Smith, S. E. & Rawlins, M. D. Variability in Human Drug Response. 1976. 14.95 (ISBN 0-407-43301-5). Butterworths.

Smith, S. M. Battered Child Syndrome. 1976. 29.95 (ISBN 0-407-00046-1). Butterworths.

Smith, S. Stephenson. How to Double Your Vocabulary. rev. ed. (Funk & W Bk.). 352p. 1974. pap. 4.95 o.p. (ISBN 0-308-10099-9, F87, TYC-T). T Y Crowell.

Smith, S. Watson, jt. auth. see Gifford, James C.

Smith, Sally. Parachuting & Skydiving. (Illus.). 1978. 14.50 (ISBN 0-7207-1063-4). Transatlantic.

Smith, Sally L. No Easy Answers: The Learning Disabled Child. 352p. 1981. pap. 3.95 (ISBN 0-553-14138-4). Bantam.

Smith, Sally T. Never Leave Shadow Wood. (YA) 1977. 4.95 o.p. (ISBN 0-685-71791-7, Avalon). Bouregy.

--The Secret of Harpen's Landing. (YA) 1978. 5.95 (ISBN 0-685-86414-6, Avalon). Bouregy.

Smith, Sam. Builder's Detail Sheets. (Series 1). (Illus.). 1973. wirebound 15.95x (ISBN 0-7198-2540-7). Intl Ideas.

--Builder's Detail Sheets. (Series Two). (Illus.). 1977. wirebound 13.50x (ISBN 0-7198-2670-5). Intl Ideas.

Smith, Sam B., ed. Tennessee History: A Bibliography. LC 74-8504. 512p. 1974. 21.50x (ISBN 0-87049-158-X). U of Tenn Pr.

Smith, Sam B. & Owsley, Harriet C., eds. The Papers of Andrew Jackson: 1770-1803, Vol. 1. LC 79-15078. (Illus.). 656p. 1980. 25.00 (ISBN 0-87049-219-5). U of Tenn Pr.

Smith, Samuel. Read It Right, & Remember What You Read. (Orig.). 1970. pap. 3.50 (ISBN 0-06-463306-3, EH 306, EH). Har-Row.

Smith, Samuel, et al. Best Methods of Study. 4th ed. (Illus.). 1970. pap. 2.95 (ISBN 0-06-460028-9, CO 28, COS). Har-Row.

Smith, Sandra, tr. see Stehle, Hansjakob.

Smith, Scottie F., et al, eds. see Fitzgerald, F. Scott.

Smith, Selwyn M. & Koranyi, Erwin K. Self-Assessment of Current Knowledge in Forensic & Organic Psychiatry. 1978. spiral bdg. 15.00 (ISBN 0-87488-235-4). Med Exam.

Smith, Shea & Walsh, John E., Jr. Strategies in Business. LC 77-25091. (Systems & Controls for Financial Management Ser). 1978. 27.95 (ISBN 0-471-80002-3). Ronald Pr.

Smith, Sheila & Toye, John, eds. Trade & Poor Economies. 166p. 1979. 26.00x (ISBN 0-7146-3137-X, F Cass Co). Biblio Dist.

Smith, Sherwood. Thirteen Lessons on Romans, Vol. II. LC 81-65030. (Bible Student Study Guides Ser.). 180p. 1981. pap. 2.95 (ISBN 0-89900-170-X). College Pr Pub.

--Thirteen Lessons on Romans. LC 79-55509. (Bible Student Study Guides). 113p. (Orig.). 1980. pap. 2.95 (ISBN 0-89900-164-5). College Pr Pub.

Smith, Stan, et al. Teach Yourself Tennis! LaMarche, Robert J., ed. LC 80-66688. (Tennis Magazine Bks.). (Illus.). 184p. 1980. 12.95 (ISBN 0-914178-39-3, 41418-6). Golf Digest.

--Teach Yourself Tennis! LaMarche, Robert J., ed. LC 80-66688. (Illus.). 224p. Date not set. 12.95 (ISBN 0-914178-39-3). Tennis Mag.

Smith, Stanley B, tr. see Cicero.

Smith, Stephen. The City That Was. Bd. with The Report of the General Committee of Health, New York City, 1806. LC 73-1827. (History of Medicine Ser.: No. 36). 1973. Repr. of 1911 ed. 11.00 (ISBN 0-8108-0598-7). Scarecrow.

Smith, Steve L., jt. auth. see Taylor, Fred I.

Smith, Susan. Made in America. LC 71-145708. 1971. Repr. of 1929 ed. 15.00 (ISBN 0-8103-3396-1). Gale.

Smith, Susy. Confessions of a Psychic. (Illus.). 1971. 10.95 (ISBN 0-02-612120-4). Macmillan.

--Enigma of Out-Of-Body Travel. LC 65-18998. 1965. 4.95 o.p. (ISBN 0-912326-15-8). Garrett-Helix.

Smith, Sydney G. Collected Poems. (The Scottish Library Ser). 269p. 1975. text ed. 22.25x (ISBN 0-7145-3511-7). Humanities.

Smith, Sydney G., ed. see Burns, Robert.

Smith, T., jt. ed. see Barker, J.

Smith, T. Alexander. The Comparative Policy Process. LC 75-2373. (Studies in International & Comparative Politics: No. 8). 184p. 1975. 15.80 (ISBN 0-87436-210-5). ABC-Clio.

Smith, T. E. Commonwealth Migration: Flows & Policies. 1980. text ed. 40.00x (ISBN 0-333-27898-4). Humanities.

Smith, T. Lynn. Process of Rural Development in Latin America. LC 67-22199. (U of Fla. Social Sciences Monographs: No. 33). (Illus.). 1967. pap. 3.25 o.p. (ISBN 0-8130-0211-7). U Presses Fla.

Smith, T. Lynn & Zopf, Paul E., Jr. Demography: Principles & Methods. 2nd ed. LC 75-23243. (Illus.). 600p. 1976. text ed. 13.50x (ISBN 0-88284-033-9). Alfred Pub.

Smith, T. M. Multiengine Airplane Rating. 7th ed. LC 64-7947. (The Zweng Manuals). (Illus.). 1981. soft bdg. 6.95 (ISBN 0-87219-003-X). Pan Am Nav.

Smith, T. Roger. Gothic Architecture in England, Western & Southern Europe with an Illustrated Glossary of Technical Words. (Illus.). 1979. Repr. of 1880 ed. deluxe ed. 67.50 (ISBN 0-930582-19-5). Gloucester Art.

Smith, Terry. Images of Rural Texas. LC 80-54842. (Illus.). 128p. 1981. 18.95 (ISBN 0-938898-11-6). Red River.

Smith, Theresa B., jt. auth. see Gochnour, Elizabeth A.

Smith, Thomas. De Republica Anglorum: A Discourse on the Commonwealth of England. 210p. 1972. Repr. of 1583 ed. 23.00x (ISBN 0-686-28335-X, Pub. by Irish Academic Pr). Biblio Dist.

Smith, Thomas A. Discovering Discipleship: A Resource for Home Bible Studies. (Illus.). 64p. (Orig.). 1981. pap. 2.75 (ISBN 0-87239-438-7, 88570). Standard Pub.

Smith, Thomas J. Jesus Alive! The Mighty Message of Mark. LC 73-81824. 1973. pap. 4.90x (ISBN 0-88489-015-5); tchr ed 2.60x (ISBN 0-88489-117-8). St Marys.

Smith, Thomas M., jt. auth. see Redmond, Kent C.

Smith, Thorne. Topper. 208p. 1980. pap. 2.25 (ISBN 0-345-28722-3, Del Rey). Ballantine.

Smith, Thurman L. Investors Can Beat Inflation. LC 79-52816. 150p. 1980. pap. 5.95 (ISBN 0-89709-018-7). Liberty Pub.

--The Lazy Investor's Way to Beat Inflation. (Illus.). 1979. pap. 5.95 (ISBN 0-934410-00-3). Explorer Pub Co.

Smith, Tim D., jt. auth. see Fowler, Charles W.

Smith, Timothy. Revivalism & Social Reform: American Protestantism on the Eve of the Civil War. LC 80-8114. Orig. Title: Revivalism & Social Reform in Mid-Nineteenth Century America. 272p. 1980. pap. text ed. 5.95x (ISBN 0-8018-2477-X). Johns Hopkins.

Smith, Tom W. & Rich, Guy J. A Compendium of Trends on General Social Survey Questions. (National Opinion Research Center (NORC): No. 129). (Orig.). 1980. pap. text ed. 7.50x (ISBN 0-932132-24-3). NORC.

Smith, Tom W., jt. auth. see Davis, James A.

Smith, Tom W., et al. Compendium of Trends on General Social Survey Questions. 1980. pap. 7.50 (ISBN 0-932132-24-3). NORC.

Smith, Tony & Lee, Richard V. Accident Action: The Essential Family Guide to Home Safety & First Aid. Breckon, Bill, ed. (Illus.). 1979. 9.95 o.p. (ISBN 0-670-10206-7, Studio). Viking Pr.

Smith, Trevor. The Politics of the Corporate Economy. 229p. 1979. 30.50x (ISBN 0-85520-202-5, Pub by Martin Robertson England). Biblio Dist.

Smith, V. Jackson. Programming for Radio & Television. LC 80-5635. 141p. 1980. pap. text ed. 7.75 (ISBN 0-8191-1250-X). U Pr of Amer.

Smith, Valene L., ed. Hosts & Guests: The Anthropology of Tourism. LC 77-81447. 1977. 16.00 (ISBN 0-8122-7732-5). U of Pa Pr.

Smith, Valerie K. Lenny. pap. 1.75 o.s.i. (ISBN 0-440-15672-6). Dell.

Smith, Vearl R., jt. ed. see Larson, Bruce L.

Smith, Verity. Ramon del Valle-Inclan. (World Authors Ser.: Spain: No. 160). lib. bdg. 10.95 (ISBN 0-8057-2924-0). Twayne.

Smith, Vernon H., ed. Visual Disorders in Cerebral Palsy. (Clinics in Developmental Medicine Ser. No. 9). 62p. 1963. 3.25 o.p. (ISBN 0-685-24715-5). Lippincott.

Smith, Vian. Portrait of Dartmoor. LC 66-72759. (Portrait Bks.). (Illus.). 206p. 1966. 10.50x (ISBN 0-7091-0919-9). Intl Pubns Serv.

--Tall & Proud. (gr. 5-7). pap. 1.25 o.p. (ISBN 0-671-29787-2). Archway.

--Tall & Proud. (Illus.). (gr. 5-7). 1968. pap. 1.25 (ISBN 0-671-29787-2). PB.

Smith, Virgil E. Your Piano & Your Piano Technician. LC 80-82009. 1981. pap. write for info. (ISBN 0-8497-5078-4, WP71, Pub. by Kjos West). Kjos.

Smith, Vivian. Vance & Nettie Palmer. LC 74-9791. (World Authors Ser.: Australia: No. 332). 168p. 1974. lib. bdg. 10.95 (ISBN 0-8057-2667-5). Twayne.

Smith, W. Elementary Complex Variables. LC 43-87526. 352p. 1974. text ed. 16.95x (ISBN 0-675-08870-4). Merrill.

Smith, W., tr. see Fichte, Johann G.

Smith, W. E., jt. auth. see Halling, J.

Smith, W. Eugene & Smith, Aileen M. Minamata. LC 74-15467. (Illus.). 208p. 1975. 20.00 o.p. (ISBN 0-03-013631-8); pap. 10.00 o.p. (ISBN 0-03-013636-9). HR&W.

Smith, W. G. Gardening for Food. LC 71-37212. (Illus.). 192p. 1972. pap. 2.45 o.p. (ISBN 0-684-12836-5, SL427, ScribT). Scribner.

Smith, W. H. Air Pollution & Forests. (Springer Series on Environmental Management). (Illus.). 400p. 1981. 39.80 (ISBN 0-387-90501-4). Springer-Verlag.

Smith, W. H., tr. see Ribot, Theodule A.

Smith, W. L., ed. Remote-Sensing Applications for Mineral Exploration. 1977. 62.00 (ISBN 0-12-787477-1). Acad Pr.

Smith, W. Lynn, ed. Drugs, Development, & Cerebral Function. (Illus.). 424p. 1972. 31.75 (ISBN 0-398-02417-0). C C Thomas.

Smith, W. Lynn, jt. ed. see Kinsbourne, Marcel.

Smith, W. Novis & Larson, C. F., eds. Innovation & U. S. Research: Problems & Recommendations. LC 80-16192. (ACS Symposium Ser.: No. 129). 1980. 26.75 (ISBN 0-8412-0561-2). Am Chemical.

Smith, W. Stevenson. The Art & Architecture of Ancient Egypt. rev ed. 360p. 1981. pap. 19.95 (ISBN 0-14-056114-5). Penguin.

Smith, W. Thomas. Augustine: His Life & Thought. LC 79-92071. (Illus.). 190p. (Orig.). 1980. pap. 8.50 (ISBN 0-8042-0871-9). John Knox.

Smith, Waldemar R. The Fiesta System and Economic Change. LC 77-390. 1977. 16.00x (ISBN 0-231-04180-2). Columbia U Pr.

Smith, Walker C. The Everett Massacre. LC 72-151619. (Civil Liberties in American History Ser.). 1971. Repr. of 1920 ed. lib. bdg. 32.50 (ISBN 0-306-70150-2). Da Capo.

Smith, Wallace F. Housing: The Social & Economic Elements. LC 71-86372. (California Studies in Urbanization & Environmental Design). (Illus.). 1970. 18.50x (ISBN 0-520-01561-4). U of Cal Pr.

--Urban Development: The Process & the Problems. LC 74-79772. 320p. 1975. 20.00x (ISBN 0-520-02780-9); pap. 7.95x (ISBN 0-520-03956-4). U of Cal Pr.

Smith, Walter see Weinberg, H. Barbara.

Smith, Walter L. On the Cumulants of Cumulative Processes. 48p. 1959. pap. 1.60 (1257). U of NC Pr.

Smith, Walter S. & Stroup, Kala M. Science Career Exploration for Women. 1978. pap. 2.50 (ISBN 0-87355-010-2). Natl Sci Tchrs.

Smith, Warren S., ed. see Shaw, George B.

Smith, Warren T. Harry Hosier: United Methodist Circuit Rider. LC 80-54008. 64p. 1980. pap. 2.95x (ISBN 0-8358-0422-4). Upper Room.

Smith, Warren W., Jr., ed. see Hatada, Takashi.

Smith, Watson. Painted Ceramics of the Western Mound at Awatovi. LC 79-102785. (Peabody Museum Papers: Vol. 38). 1970. pap. text ed. 40.00 (ISBN 0-87365-114-6). Peabody Harvard.

--Prehistoric Kivas of Antelope Mesa, Northeastern Arizona. LC 72-92005. (Peabody Museum Papers: Vol. 39, No. 1). 1972. pap. text ed. 15.00 (ISBN 0-87365-115-4). Peabody Harvard.

--The Williams Site: A Frontier Mongollon Village in West-Central New Mexico. LC 73-86928. (Peabody Museum Papers: Vol. 39, No. 2). 1973. pap. text ed. 10.00 (ISBN 0-87365-190-1). Peabody Harvard.

Smith, Wilbur. Delta Decision. LC 79-6660. 408p. 1981. 12.95 (ISBN 0-385-13604-8). Doubleday.

--Eagle in the Sky. 1981. pap. 2.75 (ISBN 0-440-14592-9). Dell.

--The Eye of the Tiger. LC 75-14841. 312p. 1976. 7.95 o.p. (ISBN 0-385-11264-5). Doubleday.

--Hungry As the Sea. 1981. pap. 3.50 (ISBN 0-451-09599-5, E9599, Sig). NAL.

--Shout at the Devil. LC 77-87166. 1978. Repr. of 1968 ed. lib. bdg. 12.50x (ISBN 0-8376-0421-4). Bentley.

Smith, Wilbur M. The Biblical Doctrine of Heaven. 1980. text ed. 5.95 (ISBN 0-8024-0705-6). Moody.

Smith, Wilfred & Wise, M. J. A Historical Introduction to the Economic Geography of Great Britain. (Advanced Economic Geography Ser.). 1968. lib. bdg. 20.00x (ISBN 0-7135-1509-0). Westview.

Smith, Wilfred C. Belief & History. LC 75-50587. 1977. 12.95x (ISBN 0-8139-0670-9). U Pr of Va.

--Towards a World Theology: Faith & the Comparative History of Religion. 1980. write for info. (ISBN 0-664-21380-4). Westminster.

Smith, William. New Smith's Bible Dictionary. rev. ed. Lemmons, Reuel G., et al, eds. LC 66-20927. 1966. 8.95 (ISBN 0-385-04872-6); thumb-indexed 9.95 (ISBN 0-385-04869-6). Doubleday.

--Smith's Bible Dictionary. (Family Library). (YA) (gr. 7-12). 1967. pap. 2.50 (ISBN 0-515-05619-7). Jove Pubns.

--Smith's Bible Dictionary. Peloubet, F. N. & Peloubet, M. A., eds. 1979. 8.95 (ISBN 0-8407-5170-2); pap. 5.95 (ISBN 0-8407-5700-X). Nelson.

--The Vaudevillians. LC 75-28477. (Illus.). 288p. 1976. 9.95 o.s.i. (ISBN 0-02-611890-4, 61189). Macmillan.

--Wonders in Weeds. 187p. 1977. 13.00x (ISBN 0-8464-1062-1). Beekman Pubs.

Smith, William, tr. see Fichte, Johann G.

Smith, William A., jt. auth. see Anderson, David.

Smith, William C. Reactions to Delinquency. LC 78-70859. 1978. pap. text ed. 7.50 (ISBN 0-8191-0649-6). U Pr of Amer.

Smith, William D., et al, eds. Reflections on Black Psychology. LC 79-63256. 1979. pap. text ed. 15.25 (ISBN 0-8191-0722-0). U Pr of Amer.

Smith, William E. Francis Preston Blair Family in Politics. LC 70-87725. (American Scene Ser). Repr. of 1933 ed. lib. bdg. 75.00 (ISBN 0-306-71665-8). Da Capo.

Smith, William F. Noticiario: Primer Nivel-Sight Readings in Spanish. (Orig.). 1981. pap. text ed. 5.95 (ISBN 0-88377-161-6). Newbury Hse.

--The Shaping of the Earth. (Illus.). 128p. 1981. 7.00 (ISBN 0-682-49715-0). Exposition.

Smith, William F., tr. see Carducci, Giosue.

Smith, William H. Saint Clair Papers: The Life & Public Services of Arthur St. Clair, with His Correspondence & Other Papers, 2 Vols. LC 79-119058. (Illus.). 1970. Repr. of 1882 ed. lib. bdg. 95.00. Da Capo.

Smith, William J. Laughing Time: Nonsense Poems. LC 80-65839. (Illus.). 96p. (gr. 3 up). 1980. 9.95 (ISBN 0-440-05534-2). Delacorte.

--New & Selected Poems. 1970. 6.95 o.p. (ISBN 0-440-06371-X, Sey Lawr). Delacorte.

--The Traveler's Tree: New & Selected Poems. (Illus.). 200p. 1980. text ed. 13.95 (ISBN 0-686-64515-4); text ed. 13.95 (ISBN 0-89255-049-X). Persea Bks.

Smith, William Jay, tr. see Lundkvist, Artur.

Smith, William M., jt. ed. see Coward, Raymond T.

Smith, William P., jt. auth. see Harvey, John H.

Smith, William R. The Prophets of Israel. (Social Science Classics Ser.). 446p. 1982. 19.95 (ISBN 0-87855-318-5); text ed. 19.95 (ISBN 0-686-68059-6); pap. 7.95 (ISBN 0-87855-700-8); pap. text ed. 7.95 (ISBN 0-686-68060-X). Transaction Bks. Postponed.

Smith, William S. Ancient Egypt As Represented in the Museum of Fine Arts, Boston. 6th rev ed. LC 60-13944. (Illus.). 1968. Repr. of 1960 ed. 4.50 (ISBN 0-87846-004-7). Mus Fine Arts Boston.

Smith, William S. & Canty, Donald J. Method & Means of Public Speaking. (Orig.). 1962. pap. 5.95 (ISBN 0-672-60859-6). Bobbs.

Smith, Willie & Hoefer, George. Music on My Mind: The Memoirs of an American Pianist. LC 74-23406. (Roots of Jazz Ser). xvi, 318p. 1975. Repr. of 1964 ed. lib. bdg. 25.00 (ISBN 0-306-70684-9). Da Capo.

Smith, Willie Mae. One Step at a Time. 1979. 4.95 (ISBN 0-533-04046-9). Vantage.

Smith, Zay N. & Zekman, Pamela. The Mirage Bar. LC 79-47460. (Illus.). 1979. 8.95 (ISBN 0-394-50368-6). Random.

Smith-Blau, Zena see Blau, Zena S.

Smith-Burnett, G. C., jt. auth. see Jefferson, G.

Smithdeal, Judy. Quick & Easy Exercises for Figure Beauty. pap. 2.00 (ISBN 0-87980-381-9). Wilshire.

Smithells, C. J., ed. Metals Reference Book. 5th ed. 1976. 160.00 (ISBN 0-408-70627-9). Butterworths.

Smither, Graham B. Gymnastics. (Illus.). 128p. 1981. pap. 7.95 (ISBN 0-906071-36-4). Proteus Pub NY.

Smitherman, Colleen. Nursing Actions for Health Promotion. LC 80-17464. (Illus.). 415p. 1980. pap. text ed. 13.95 (ISBN 0-8036-7941-6). Davis Co.

Smitherman, Larry, ed. see Kennedy, John F.

Smithers, A. J. Wonder Aces of the Air. 1980. 19.95 (ISBN 0-86033-077-X). Gordon-Cremonesi.

Smithers, Alan G. Sandwich Courses: An Integated Education? (Orig.). 1976. pap. text ed. 13.75x (ISBN 0-85633-088-4, NFER). Humanities.

Smithers, C. D. Foundation. Understanding Alcoholism for the Patient, the Family, & the Employer. pap. 5.95 (ISBN 0-684-71891-X, SL200, ScribT). Scribner.

Smithers, D. W., et al. Cancer of the Breast. 1980. 10.00x (Pub. by Brit Inst Radiology England). State Mutual Bk.

Smithers, David. Dicken's Doctors. 1979. text ed. 17.25 (ISBN 0-08-023386-4). Pergamon.

Smithers, G. V., jt. ed. see Bennett, J. A.

Smithers, Jane, jt. auth. see Cane, Brian.

Smithers, Ray. Your Book of the Earth. (Your Book Ser.). (Illus.). 1966. 4.95 o.p. (ISBN 0-571-06703-4, Pub. by Faber & Faber). Merrimack Bk Serv.

Smithies, Frank. Integral Equations. (Cambridge Tracts in Mathematics & Mathematical Physics). 1958. 27.50 (ISBN 0-521-06502-X). Cambridge U Pr.

Smithies, Richard H. The Shoplifter. 1968. 4.95 o.s.i. (ISBN 0-8180-0601-3). Horizon.

Smithies, Richard H. & Cavanagh, Maura. Yeggs & the Yahbuts. (Illus.). (gr. 3-5). 1969. 3.95 (ISBN 0-394-80888-6); PLB 5.39 (ISBN 0-394-90888-0). Random.

Smithsonian. Fire of Life: The Smithsonian Book of the Sun. (Illus.). 1981. 24.95 (ISBN 0-89599-006-7). Smithsonian Expo.

Smithsonian Institute. A Zoo for All Seasons: The Smithsonian Animal World. (Illus.). 1979. 16.95 (ISBN 0-89577-003-2). Norton.

Smithsonian Institution. American Land. 1979. 21.95. Smithsonian Expo Bks.

--The American Land: The Smithsonian Book of the American Environment. (A Smithsonian Exposition Book). (Illus.). 1980. 21.95 (ISBN 0-89577-004-0). Norton.

--Every Four Years: The American Presidency. (Smithsonian Exposition Bk.). (Illus.). 1980. 21.95 (ISBN 0-89577-005-9). Norton.

--Magnificent Foragers: Smithsonian Explorations in the Natural Sciences. 1978. 16.95 (ISBN 0-89599-001-6). Smithsonian Expo Bks.

--Smithsonian Experience. 1977. 21.95. Smithsonian Expo Bks.

Smithsonian Institution, National Collection of Fine Arts (NCFA) Images of an Era: The American Poster 1945-1975. LC 75-34602. 1976. 29.95 o.p. (ISBN 0-685-69547-6); pap. 12.50 o.p. (ISBN 0-262-64015-5). MIT Pr.

Smithsonian Science Information Exchange Inc. Summary of International Energy Research & Development Activities 1974-1976. 1978. 61.00 (ISBN 0-08-023248-5). Pergamon.

Smith William, A., jt. ed. see Anderson, David.

Smits, Ted. Soccer for the American Boy. (Illus.). 1970. 4.95 o.p. (ISBN 0-13-815456-2); pap. 1.50 (ISBN 0-13-815282-9). P-H.

Smitten, Jeffrey R., jt. auth. see Kloesel, Christion J.

Smock, Audrey C., jt. auth. see Giele, Janet Z.

Smock, C. R. Your Left Hip Pocket. 4.95 o.p. (ISBN 0-8062-1071-0). Carlton.

Smock, David R. & Bentsi-Enchill, Kwamina. The Search for National Integration in Africa. LC 74-33090. 1976. 19.95 (ISBN 0-02-929560-2). Free Pr.

Smock, Martha. Listen, Beloved. LC 80-50624. 177p. 1980. 3.95 (ISBN 0-87159-101-4). Unity Bks.

Smock, Raymond W., jt. ed. see Harlan, Louis R.

Smodlaka, Vojin N., ed. see Mellerowicz, Harald.

Smolden, William L. The Music of the Medieval Church Drama. 1981. 120.00 (ISBN 0-19-316321-7). Oxford U Pr.

Smolderen, J. J., jt. auth. see Wirz, H. J.

Smole, William J. The Yanoama Indians: A Cultural Geography. (Texas Pan American Ser.). (Illus.). 478p. 1975. 15.00 (ISBN 0-292-71019-4). U of Tex Pr.

Smolen, Maxine. Wheelchair Recipes from the Collection of Momma Wheels. Hammond, Debbie, ed. 1980. 9.95 (ISBN 0-87949-171-X). Ashley Bks.

Smolensky, Jack & Bonvechio, Richard. Principles of School Health. 1966. text ed. 9.95x o.p. (ISBN 0-669-20198-7). Heath.

Smolensky, M. H. & Reinberg, A., eds. Recent Advances of the Chronobiology of Allergy & Immunology: Symposium on Chronobiology in Allergy & Immunology, Israel, 1979. LC 80-41028. (Illus.). 350p. 1980. 50.00 (ISBN 0-08-025891-3). Pergamon.

Smolin, Pauline & Clayton, Philip T. The Sentence. 1977. pap. text ed. 5.95x (ISBN 0-669-00783-8). Heath.

Smolinski, Richard, ed. see Verdick, Mary.

Smolira, M. Analysis of Structures by the Force-Displacement Method. xii, 389p. 1980. 62.50 (ISBN 0-85334-814-6, Pub. by Applied Science). Burgess-Intl Ideas.

--Analysis of Tall Buildings by the Force Displacement Method. LC 74-19011. 299p. 1975. 49.95 (ISBN 0-470-80620-6). Halsted Pr.

Smolka, Richard G., jt. auth. see Gosnell, Harold F.

Smolkin, Shelley, jt. auth. see Rivers, William L.

Smollet, Tobias. The Adventures of Ferdinand Count Fathom. Grant, Damian, ed. (Oxford English Novels Ser). 1971. 14.95x (ISBN 0-19-255321-6). Oxford U Pr.

Smollett, Eleanor W. Bulgaria: Textbook & Reality. (Occasional Papers: No. 28). 1978. 1.25 (ISBN 0-89977-014-2). Am Inst Marxist.

Smollett, Tobias. Tobias Smollett: Travels Through France & Italy. facsimile ed. Felsenstein, Frank, ed. 45.00x (ISBN 0-19-812611-5). Oxford U Pr.

Smollett, Tobias G. Roderick Random. 1958. 11.50x (ISBN 0-460-00790-4, Evman); pap. 2.95 (ISBN 0-460-01790-X). Dutton.

Smooha, Sammy. Israel: Pluralism & Conflict. LC 74-76390. 1978. 28.50x (ISBN 0-520-02722-1). U of Cal Pr.

Smoot, Dan. The Invisible Government. 3rd ed. 1977. pap. 3.95 o.p. (ISBN 0-88279-125-7). Western Islands.

Smoots, Vernon A., jt. auth. see Fletcher, Gordon A.

Smotherman, William F., jt. ed. see Bell, Robert W.

Smothermon, Ron. Winning Through Enlightenment. 1980. pap. 5.95 (ISBN 0-932654-01-0). Context Pubns.

Smout, T. C., jt. ed. see Flinn, M. W.

Smoyak, Shirley, ed. The Psychiatric Nurse As a Family Therapist. LC 75-5813. 251p. 1975. 14.50 (ISBN 0-471-80770-2, Pub. by Wiley Medical). Wiley.

Smulkstys, Julius. Karl Marx. (World Authors Ser.: Germany: No. 296). 1974. lib. bdg. 10.95 (ISBN 0-8057-2595-4). Twayne.
Smulow, Jerome B., jt. auth. see Glickman, Irving.
Smuslov, jt. auth. see Levenfish.
Smuts, J. C. Selections from the Smuts Papers, 4 vols. Hancock, William K. & Van Der Poel, Jean, eds. Vol. 1, 1886-1902. 85.50 (ISBN 0-521-05190-8); Vol. 2, From 1902-1910. 85.50 (ISBN 0-521-05191-6); Vol. 3, From 1910-1918. 85.50 (ISBN 0-521-05192-4); Vol. 4, From 1918-1919. 85.50 (ISBN 0-521-05193-2); Vol. 5. from 1945-1950 94.00 (ISBN 0-521-08604-3); Vol. 5, From 1919-1943. 93.50 (ISBN 0-521-08602-7); Vol. 6, From 1934-1945. 94.00 (ISBN 0-521-08603-5). Cambridge U Pr.
Smykla, John O. Cocorrections: A Case Study of a Coed Federal Prison. rev. ed. LC 79-64719. 1979. pap. text ed. 5.75 (ISBN 0-8191-0767-0). U Pr of Amer.
Smyser, Carol A. Nature's Design: A Practical Guide to Natural Landscaping. (Illus.). 416p. Date not set. 16.95 (ISBN 0-87857-343-7). Rodale Pr Inc. Postponed.
Smyser, W. R. The Independent Vietnamese: Vietnamese Communism Between Russia & China, 1959 to 1969. (Southeast Asia Ser., Ohio University Center for International Studies). 143p. (Orig.). 1980. pap. 12.75 (ISBN 0-89680-105-5, 80-18308). Ohio U Ctr Intl.
Smyser, W. R., ed. German-American Relations. LC 79-57535. (The Washington Papers: No. 74). 88p. 1980. pap. 3.50 (ISBN 0-8039-1451-2). Sage.
Smyth, Albert H. Philadelphia Magazines & Their Contributors 1741-1850. LC 77-140401. 1970. Repr. of 1892 ed. 24.00 (ISBN 0-8103-3596-4). Gale.
Smyth, Alfred P. Scandinavian Kings in the British Isles, 850-880. (Oxford Historical Monographs). 1978. 42.00x (ISBN 0-19-821865-6). Oxford U Pr.
--Scandinavian York & Dublin, No. 2. 1980. pap. text ed. 15.00x (ISBN 0-391-01049-2). Humanities.
Smyth, D. S. & Gordon, D. L. Chronic Ear Disease. (Monographs in Clinical Otolaryngology). (Illus.). 224p. 1980. text ed. 28.00x (ISBN 0-443-08071-2). Churchill.
Smyth, Daniel. Robert Frost Speaks. 158p. 18.95x (ISBN 0-8290-0203-0). Irvington.
Smyth, Frank. Modern Witchcraft. 128p. 1973. pap. 1.25 o.p. (ISBN 0-06-087038-9, HW). Har-Row.
Smyth, Frank & Ludwig, Myles. The Detectives: Crime & Detection in Fact & Fiction. (Illus.). 1978. 12.50 o.p. (ISBN 0-397-01253-5); pap. 7.95 o.p. (ISBN 0-397-01252-7). Lippincott.
Smyth, Henry D. Atomic Energy for Military Purposes: The Official Report on the Development of the Atomic Bomb Under the Auspices of the United States Government, 1940-1945. (The Politics & Strategy of World War II Ser: No. 2). 1976. Repr. of 1945 ed. lib. bdg. 25.00 (ISBN 0-306-70767-5). Da Capo.
Smyth, Herbert W. Aeschylean Tragedy. LC 67-19531. 1969. Repr. of 1924 ed. 8.50x (ISBN 0-8196-0235-3). Biblo.
Smyth, Howard M. Secrets of the Fascist Era: How Uncle Sam Obtained Some of the Top-Level Documents of Mussolini's Period. LC 74-31340. (Illus.). 336p. 1979. pap. 9.95 (ISBN 0-8093-0924-6). S Ill U Pr.
Smyth, J. D. The Physiology of Cestodes. (Illus.). 1969. 13.95x (ISBN 0-7167-0676-8). W H Freeman.
Smyth, Michael P. Linear Engineering Systems: Tools & Techniques. 386p. 1972. text ed. 28.00 (ISBN 0-08-016324-6). Pergamon.
--Mathematics: The Formal Tools of Engineering. (Advances in Modern Engineering Ser.). (Illus.). 160p. 1974. pap. text ed. 8.95 (ISBN 0-201-07078-2). A-W.
Smyth, Peter R. A Guide to Marine Photography. (Illus.). 144p. 1974. 12.50 o.p. (ISBN 0-393-03182-9). Norton.
Smyth, Piazzi. Our Inheritance in the Great Pyramid. LC 77-5284. (Spiritual Science Library). (Illus.). 672p. 1978. 20.00x (ISBN 0-8334-0720-1); pap. 15.00 (ISBN 0-8334-3503-5). Steinerbks.
Smythe. The Undisputed Andy Capp. 128p. 1976. pap. 1.50 (ISBN 0-449-13668-X, GM). Fawcett.
--You're Something Else, Andy Capp. 128p. (Orig.). 1981. pap. 1.75 (ISBN 0-449-14401-1, GM). Fawcett.
--You're the Boss, Andy Capp. (Andy Capp Cartoons Ser.). 1978. pap. 1.50 (ISBN 0-449-13631-0, GM). Fawcett.
Smythe, Colin, ed. see Gregory, Augusta.
Smythe, Dallas W. Dependency Road: Communications, Capitalism, Consciousness & Canada. 300p. 1981. text ed. price not set (ISBN 0-89391-067-8). Ablex Pub.
Smythe, Lewis. The Christian in Today's World: Inner City to World Community. 1974. 6.50 o.p. (ISBN 0-682-48055-X). Exposition.
Smythe, R. H. Healers on Horseback. pap. 8.75 (ISBN 0-85131-282-9). J A Allen.
--The Horse: Structure & Movement. 2nd ed. (Illus.). pap. 10.50 (ISBN 0-85131-242-X, Dist. by Sporting Book Center). J A Allen.
--The Mind of the Horse. (Illus.). 10.50 (ISBN 0-85131-150-4, Dist. by Sporting Book Center). J A Allen.
Smythe, Reginald H. How to Raise & Train a Shih Tzu. (Orig.). pap. 2.00 (ISBN 0-87666-388-9, DS1117). TFH Pubns.
Smythies, B. E., jt. auth. see Polunin, Oleg.
Smythies, J. R., ed. Science & E. S. P. (International Library of Philosophy & Scientific Method Ser.). 1967. text ed. 15.50x (ISBN 0-7100-3638-8). Humanities.
Smythies, John R. & Bradley, Ronald J. International Review of Neurobiology, Vol. 22. (Serial Publication). 1980. write for info. (ISBN 0-12-366822-0). Acad Pr.
Smythies, John R., ed. Brain & Mind. (International Library of Philosophy & Scientific Method Ser.). 1965. text ed. 23.50x (ISBN 0-7100-3624-8). Humanities.
Snadowsky, Alvin see Seidenberg, Bernard.
Snaer, Seymour. San Francisco Nineteen Thirty-Nine. 1980. pap. 9.95 (ISBN 0-9602462-5-8). Working Pr CA.
Snaith, Linton, jt. auth. see Szekely, Paul.
Snaith, N., ed. Torah Nebiim u Ketubim. 1958. 5.30 (ISBN 0-564-00029-9, 60679). United Bible.
Snaith, Philip. Clinical Neurosis. 240p. 1981. text ed. 16.95x. Oxford U Pr.
Snaith, V. P. Algebraic Cobordism & K-Theory. LC 79-17981. (Memoirs Ser.: No. 221). 1979. 7.60 (ISBN 0-8218-2221-7). Am Math.
Snape, W. H. How to Find Out About Local Government. 1969. 16.50 (ISBN 0-08-013957-4); pap. 7.75 (ISBN 0-08-013956-6). Pergamon.
Snapper, Ernst & Troyer, Robert J. Metric Affine Geometry. 435p. 1971. text ed. 20.95 (ISBN 0-12-653650-3). Acad Pr.
Snawder, Kenneth D. Handbook of Clinical Pedodontics. LC 79-19983. 1979. pap. text ed. 19.95 (ISBN 0-8016-2951-9). Mosby.
Snawsel, Robert. A Looking-Glasse for Married Folkes. LC 74-28886. (English Experience Ser.: No. 763). 1975. Repr. of 1631 ed. 7.00 (ISBN 90-221-0763-9). Walter J Johnson.
Snead, R. E. World Atlas of Geomorphic Features. LC 77-28009. 300p. 1980. 39.50 (ISBN 0-88275-272-3). Krieger.
Sneath, E. Hershey, ed. Evolution of Ethics. 1927. 42.50x (ISBN 0-685-69867-X). Elliots Bks.
Sneath, Peter H. & Sokal, Robert R. Numerical Taxonomy: The Principles & Practice of Numerical Classification. LC 72-1552. (Biology Ser.). (Illus.). 1973. 36.95x (ISBN 0-7167-0697-0). W H Freeman.
Sneddon, I. B. & Church, R. E. Skin Disorders in Clinical Practice. 3rd ed. 19.50 (ISBN 0-201-07705-1). A-W.
Snedecor, George W., jt. auth. see Cochran, William G.
Snedigar, Robert. Our Small Native Animals: Their Habits & Care. rev. ed. (Illus.). 8.00 (ISBN 0-8446-2961-8). Peter Smith.
--Our Small Native Animals: Their Habits & Care. (Illus.). 1963. pap. 4.00 (ISBN 0-486-21022-7). Dover.
Snelgrove, Dudley, jt. auth. see Egerton, Judy.
Snell, Bruno. Scenes from Greek Drama. (Sather Classical Lectures: No. 34). 1964. 18.50x (ISBN 0-520-01191-0). U of Cal Pr.
Snell, David. Lights, Camera...Murder. LC 79-16542. 1979. 10.95 (ISBN 0-312-48605-7). St Martin.
Snell, E. E., et al, eds. Chemical & Biological Aspects of Pyridoxal Catalysis. 1963. 45.00 (ISBN 0-08-010423-1). Pergamon.
Snell, Esmond E., ed. Annual Review of Biochemistry, Vol 50. LC 32-25093. (Illus.). 1218p. 1981. text ed. 21.00 (ISBN 0-8243-0850-6). Annual Reveiws.
Snell, Esmond E., et al, eds. Annual Review of Biochemistry, Vol. 49. LC 32-25093. (Illus.). 1980. text ed. 21.00 (ISBN 0-8243-0849-2). Annual Reviews.
Snell, Frank. How to Stand up & Speak Well in Business. 1968. 3.95 (ISBN 0-346-12307-0). Cornerstone.
--How to Win the Meeting. 1979. 8.95 (ISBN 0-8015-3896-3, Hawthorn); pap. 4.95 (ISBN 0-8015-3897-1, Hawthorn). Dutton.
Snell, H. Mental Disorder: An Introductory Textbook for Nurses. (Illus.). 1977. pap. text ed. 8.95x (ISBN 0-04-610005-9). Allen Unwin.
Snell, J. Laurie. Introduction to Probability Theory with Computing. (Illus.). 288p. 1975. pap. 13.95x ref. ed. (ISBN 0-13-493445-8). P-H.
Snell, J. Laurie, jt. auth. see Kindermann, Ross.
Snell, Joseph, ed. see Triplett, Frank.
Snell, Joseph W., jt. auth. see Miller, Nyle H.
Snell, K. S. & Morgan, J. B. Elementary Analysis, Vol. 2. 1966. 22.00 (ISBN 0-08-011777-5); pap. 10.75 (ISBN 0-08-011776-7). Pergamon.
Snell, M. M., tr. see Ribot, Theodule A.
Snell, Richard S. Clinical Anatomy for Medical Students. 2nd ed. 1981. text ed. price not set. Little.
--Clinical Neuroanatomy for Medical Students. 1980. text ed. 21.95 (ISBN 0-316-80213-1). Little.
Snellgrove, David. Himalayan Pilgrimage: A Study of Tibetan Religion. (Illus.). 326p. (Orig.). 1981. pap. 12.50 (ISBN 0-87773-720-7). Great Eastern.
Snellgrove, David, ed. The Image of the Buddha. LC 77-75964. (Illus.). 1978. 60.00 (ISBN 0-87011-302-X). Kodansha.
Snellgrove, David L. Hevajra Tantra, 2 Vols. 1959. 59.00x (ISBN 0-19-713516-1). Oxford U Pr.
Snellgrove, David L. & Richardson, Hugh E. The Cultural History of Tibet. LC 78-13032. (Illus.). 1980. pap. 12.50 (ISBN 0-87773-740-1, Prajna). Great Eastern.
Snellgrove, David L. & Skorupski, Tadeusz. The Cultural Heritage of Ladakh, Vol. 1. (Illus.). 1977. 30.00 (ISBN 0-87773-700-2, Prajna). Great Eastern.
Snellgrove, David L., ed. The Nine Ways of Bon: Excerpts from Gzi-brjid. LC 78-13010. (Illus.). 1980. pap. 12.50 (ISBN 0-87773-739-8, Prajna). Great Eastern.
Snellgrove, L. E., jt. auth. see Cootes, R. J.
Snelling, William J. Tales of the Northwest: On Sketches of Indian Life & Character. LC 75-7067. (Indian Captivities Ser.: Vol. 45). 1976. Repr. of 1830 ed. lib. bdg. 44.00 (ISBN 0-8240-1669-6). Garland Pub.
Snelling, William J. see Goodrich, Samuel G.
Snelson, Robin. Weapons. 1979. pap. 3.95 (ISBN 0-931064-13-9). Starlog.
Snelson, Robin, ed. see Skotak, Robert & Holton, Scot.
Snelson, Robin, ed. see Vallejo, Doris.
Snesrud, Janet E., ed. see Blixrud, Julia C.
Snethen, Donald. Expansive Soils, 2 vols. LC 66-140. 900p. 1981. pap. text ed. 46.00 (ISBN 0-87262-245-2). Am Soc Civil Eng.
Sneve, Virginia. They Led a Nation. Hunt, N. Jane, ed. LC 75-254. (Illus.). 1975. 5.95 (ISBN 0-88498-026-X); text ed. 3.95 o.p. (ISBN 0-685-52611-9); pap. 3.95 (ISBN 0-88498-027-8); pap. text ed. 2.66 o.p. (ISBN 0-685-52612-7). Brevet Pr.
Sneve, Virginia D., ed. South Dakota Geographic Names. new ed. LC 73-80523. 639p. 1973. 19.95 (ISBN 0-88498-008-1); text ed. 17.96 o.p. (ISBN 0-685-46504-7). Brevet Pr.
Snibbe, H. M., jt. auth. see Snibbe, J. R.
Snibbe, J. R. & Snibbe, H. M. The Urban Policeman in Transition. (Illus.). 628p. 1973. 24.75 (ISBN 0-398-02661-0); pap. 16.75 (ISBN 0-398-02741-2). C C Thomas.
Snidecor, John C., ed. Speech Rehabilitation of the Laryngectomized. 2nd ed. (Amer. Lec. in Speech & Hearing Ser). (Illus.). 288p. 1978. 16.75 (ISBN 0-398-01803-0). C C Thomas.
Snider, jt. auth. see Brody.
Snider, Arthur D., jt. auth. see Davis, Harry F.
Snider, Arthur D., jt. auth. see Soff, Edward B.
Snider, Arthur J. & Adatto, I. J. A Doctor Discusses Learning How to Live with Nervous Tension. (Illus.). 1980. pap. 2.50 (ISBN 0-685-58312-0). Budlong.
--A Doctor Discusses Learning to Live with Heart Trouble. (Illus.). 1980. pap. 2.50 (ISBN 0-685-35677-9). Budlong.
Snider, Arthur J. & Oparil, Suzanne. A Doctor Discusses Hypertension. (Illus.). 1981. pap. 2.50 (ISBN 0-685-79070-3). Budlong.
Snider, Clifton. Jesse Comes Back. 1980. 1.50 (ISBN 0-917554-05-1). Maelstrom.
Snider, Delbert A. Introduction to International Economics. 7th ed. 1979. text ed. 18.95x (ISBN 0-256-02176-7). Irwin.
Snider, Felix E., ed. History of Southeast Missouri. (Illus.). 1978. Repr. of 1888 ed. 35.00 o.p. (ISBN 0-911208-09-7). Ramfre.
Snider, Gordon, jt. ed. see Brody, Jerome S.
Snider, H. Wayne, ed. Employee Benefits Management. 240p. Date not set. price not set (ISBN 0-937802-00-X). Risk & Ins.
Snider, Nancy. The Professional Chef's Soy Protein Recipe Ideas. Wilkinson, Jule, ed. (Illus.). 80p. 1971. pap. 8.95 (ISBN 0-8436-0540-5). CBI Pub.
Snider, Patricia J., ed. Human Resources Planning: A Guide to Data. 2nd ed. LC 80-67468. 392p. 1980. pap. 21.00 (ISBN 0-937856-00-2). Equal Employ.
Sniderman, Florence M., jt. auth. see Breed, Paul F.
Sniderman, Paul M. Personality & Democratic Politics. 1975. 20.00x (ISBN 0-520-02324-2). U of Cal Pr.
Sniezko, S., et al. Diseases of Fishes: Bacteria. (Illus.). 12.95 (ISBN 0-87666-038-3, PS202). TFH Pubns.
Sniff, William F. A Curriculum for the Mentally Retarded Young Adult. 180p. 1973. 10.75 (ISBN 0-398-01804-9). C C Thomas.
Snitzer, Herb. Living at Summerhill. LC 64-17368. Orig. Title: Summerhill: A Loving World. (Illus.). 1968. pap. 1.95 o.s.i. (ISBN 0-02-015750-9, Collier). Macmillan.
Snodgrass, A. M. The Dark Age of Greece. 1972. 26.50x (ISBN 0-85224-089-9, Pub. by Edinburgh U Pr Scotland). Columbia U Pr.
Snodgrass, Anthony. Archaic Greece: The Age of Experiment. (Orig.). 1981. pap. price not set (ISBN 0-520-04373-1, CAL 505). U of Cal Pr.
Snodgrass, Donald R. Inequality & Economic Development in Malaysia. (East Asian Social Science Monographs). (Illus.). 340p. 1981. 34.95 (ISBN 0-19-580431-7); pap. 17.95 (ISBN 0-19-580442-2). Oxford U Pr.
Snodgrass, Joan G. The Numbers Game: Statistics in Psychology. 1977. 14.95x (ISBN 0-19-502301-3). Oxford U Pr.
Snodgrass, Milton M. & Wallace, Tim. Agriculture, Economics & Resource Management. 2nd ed. (Illus.). 1980. text ed. 18.95 (ISBN 0-13-018820-4). P-H.
Snodgrass, W. D. In Radical Pursuit. 1977. pap. 3.95 o.p. (ISBN 0-06-090575-1, CN 575, CN). Har-Row.
Snodgrass, W. D., tr. from Hungarian. Traditional Hungarian Songs. (Fine Press Poetry Ser.). (Illus.). 1978. ltd. signed ed. 60.00 (ISBN 0-931356-01-6). Seluzicki Poetry.
Snodin, David. A Mighty Ferment: Britain in the Age of Revolution, 1750-1850. LC 77-16482. (Illus.). (gr. 6 up). 1978. 8.95 (ISBN 0-395-28925-4, Clarion). HM.
Snoeyink, Vernon L. & Jenkins, David. Water Chemistry. (SPE Monographs). 1980. text ed. 27.95 (ISBN 0-471-05196-9); lab manual avail. (ISBN 0-471-06272-3). Wiley.
Snoock, T., et al. Report on the Programming Language PLZ-SYS. (Illus.). 1979. pap. 3.50 (ISBN 0-387-90374-7). Springer-Verlag.
Snook, Barbara. Costumes for Children. 1970. 5.25 o.p. (ISBN 0-8231-1020-6). Branford.
--Embroidery Stitches. 1975. pap. 13.50 (ISBN 0-7134-2611-X, Pub. by Batsford England). David & Charles.
--English Embroidery. (Illus.). 135p. 1975. 12.50 (ISBN 0-263-05579-5). Transatlantic.
--Fancy Dress for Children. 1975. 2.95 o.s.i. (ISBN 0-7134-2635-7). Hippocrene Bks.
--Puppets. (gr. 4 up). 1966. 5.95 o.p. (ISBN 0-8231-3027-4). Branford.
Snook, Donald. Hospitals: What They Are & How They Work. 250p. 1981. text ed. price not set (ISBN 0-89443-339-3). Aspen Systems.
Snook, H. J., jt. auth. see Johnson, Myrtle E.
Snook, I. A. Indoctrination & Education. (Students Library of Education). 1972. 15.00x (ISBN 0-7100-7222-8). Routledge & Kegan.
--Indoctrination & Education. (Students of Library Education). 1975. pap. 7.95 (ISBN 0-7100-8163-4). Routledge & Kegan.
Snook, I. A., ed. & intro. by. Concepts of Indoctrination: Philosophical Essays. (International Library of the Philosophy of Education). 224p. 1972. 15.00 (ISBN 0-7100-7279-1). Routledge & Kegan.
Snorra, S. Snnorra Sagas of Norse Kings. 1973. 25.00x (ISBN 82-09-00752-1, N-393). Vanous.
Snorri. Heimskringla: From the Sagas of the Norse Kings. Monsen, Erling, tr. (Illus.). 398p. 1980. 35.00 (ISBN 0-906191-39-4, Pub. by Thule Pr England). Intl Schol Bk Serv.
Snortland, jt. auth. see Pursley.
Snouffer, Gary H. Property & Casuality Insurance Agent. 224p. (Orig.). 1981. pap. 8.00 (ISBN 0-668-04308-3, 4308). Arco.
Snouffer, Robert W. A Retailer's Guide to Managing Communications Expenses. Date not set. cancelled (ISBN 0-686-25107-5). Telecom Lib.
Snow, C. P. The Affair. (Hudson River Edition). 1960. 17.50x (ISBN 0-684-15317-3, ScribT). Scribner.
--A Coat of Varnish. 1981. 5.95 (ISBN 0-684-16949-5). Scribner.
--Death Under Sail. 256p. 1981. 9.95 (ISBN 0-684-16735-2, ScribT). Scribner.
--The Homecoming. LC 56-10199. 1956. lib. rep. ed. 17.50x (ISBN 0-684-15133-2, ScribT). Scribner.
--The Light & the Dark. LC 76-29285. 1961. lib. rep. ed. 17.50x (ISBN 0-684-14841-2, ScribT). Scribner.
--The Masters. 1960. lib. rep. ed. 17.50x (ISBN 0-684-14744-0, ScribT, SL886, ScribT). Scribner.
--Strangers & Brothers. LC 60-12605. 1960. lib.rep.ed. 17.50x (ISBN 0-684-15367-X, ScribT). Scribner.
--Time of Hope. 1961. lib. rep. ed. 17.50x (ISBN 0-684-15315-7, ScribT). Scribner.
Snow, Catherine & Ferguson, C. Talking to Children. LC 76-11094. 1977. 35.00 (ISBN 0-521-21318-5); pap. 12.95x (ISBN 0-521-29513-0). Cambridge U Pr.

Snow, Charles E. Early Hawaiians: An Initial Study of Skeletal Remains from Mokapu, Oahu. LC 72-81317. (Illus.). 192p. 1974. 17.50x (ISBN 0-8131-1277-X). U Pr of Ky.

Snow, Charles E., jt. auth. see Webb, William S.

Snow, Charles P. Two Cultures: And a Second Look. LC 64-1425. 1969. 15.50 (ISBN 0-521-06520-8); pap. 3.95 (ISBN 0-521-09576-X). Cambridge U Pr.

Snow, D. W., ed. The Status of Birds in Britain & Ireland. (Illus.). 354p. 1971. 10.50 o.p. (ISBN 0-397-60204-9, Blackwell). Lippincott.

Snow, Dana A. The World's Worst Blank Book. 1976. 1.25 o.p. (ISBN 0-8431-0410-4); pap. 1.25 o.p. (ISBN 0-685-74201-6). Price Stern.

Snow, Dean. The Archaeology of North America: American Indians & Their Origins. (Illus.). 272p. 1980. pap. 12.95 (ISBN 0-500-27183-6). Thames Hudson.

Snow, Dean R. The Archaeology of New England. LC 80-982. (New World Archaeological Record Ser.). 1980. 32.50 (ISBN 0-12-653950-2). Acad Pr.

--Native American Prehistory: A Critical Bibliography. LC 79-2168. (Newberry Library Center for the History of the American Indian Bibliographical Ser.). 96p. 1980. pap. 3.95x (ISBN 0-253-33498-5). Ind U Pr.

Snow, Deborah, jt. auth. see Blue, Shelley.

Snow, Donald M. Introduction to World Politics: A Conceptual & Developmental Perspective. LC 80-5851. 230p. 1981. lib. bdg. 18.25 (ISBN 0-8191-1398-0); pap. text ed. 9.75 (ISBN 0-8191-1399-9). U Pr of Amer.

--Nuclear Strategy in a Dynamic World: American Policy in the Nineteen Eighties. LC 80-13634. 332p. 1981. 25.00 (ISBN 0-8173-0044-9); pap. 12.95 (ISBN 0-8173-0045-7). U of Ala Pr.

Snow, Dorothea. Donald Duck on Tom Sawyer's Island. (Tell-a-Tale Readers). (Illus.). (gr. k-3). 1978. PLB 4.77 (ISBN 0-307-68409-1, Whitman). Western Pub.

Snow, Edward R. Adventures, Blizzards & Coastal Calamities. LC 78-23316. (Illus.). 1978. 8.95 (ISBN 0-396-07634-3). Dodd.

--Boston Bay Mysteries & Other Tales. LC 77-10901. (Illus.). 1977. bds. 8.95 (ISBN 0-396-07505-3). Dodd.

--Marine Mysteries & Dramatic Disasters of New England. LC 76-28985. 1976. 8.95 (ISBN 0-396-07378-6). Dodd.

--The Romance of Casco Bay. LC 75-29352. (Illus.). 1975. 7.95 (ISBN 0-396-07214-3). Dodd.

--Sea Disasters & Inland Catastrophes. LC 80-23876. (Illus.). 288p. 1980. 9.95 (ISBN 0-396-07908-3). Dodd.

--Tales of Terror & Tragedy. LC 79-21872. (Illus.). 1979. 8.95 (ISBN 0-396-07775-7). Dodd.

Snow, Helen, pseud. Inside Red China. 1974. lib. bdg. 27.50 (ISBN 0-306-70622-9); pap. 7.95 (ISBN 0-306-80110-8). Da Capo.

Snow, James B., Jr., ed. Controversy in Otolaryngology. LC 79-64601. (Illus.). 561p. 1980. text ed. 45.00 (ISBN 0-7216-8433-5). Saunders.

Snow, Jimmy & Hefley, James. I Cannot Go Back. 1977. 5.95 o.p. (ISBN 0-88270-193-2); pap. 2.95 o.p. (ISBN 0-88270-194-0). Logos.

Snow, John. Secrets of a Salt Marsh. 64p. (Orig.). (gr. 4-10). pap. 5.95 (ISBN 0-930096-09-6). G Gannett.

Snow, John H. & Furnish, Victor P. Easter. LC 74-76927. (Proclamation 1: Aids for Interpreting the Lessons of the Church Year, Ser. A). 64p. 1975. pap. 2.50 (ISBN 0-8006-4065-9, 1-4065). Fortress.

Snow, Karen. Willo. 288p. 1981. pap. 2.95 (ISBN 0-523-41189-8). Pinnacle Bks.

Snow, Keith. Insects & Diseases. LC 73-15433. (Illus.). 208p. 1974. text ed. 16.95 (ISBN 0-470-81017-3). Halsted Pr.

Snow, Keith R. Arachnids. LC 70-109151. 1970. 15.00x (ISBN 0-231-03419-9). Columbia U Pr.

--Insects & Disease. LC 73-15433. 208p. 1974. 9.95 (ISBN 0-470-81017-3, Pub. by Wiley). Krieger.

Snow, Marcellus S. International Commercial Satellite Communications: Economic & Political Issues of the First Decade of Intelstat. LC 75-8410. (Special Studies). (Illus.). 192p. 1976. text ed. 23.95 (ISBN 0-275-01150-X). Praeger.

Snow, Marcellus S., jt. ed. see Pelton, Joseph N.

Snow, Michael. Cover to Cover. LC 75-27116. 1975. 20.00x (ISBN 0-8147-7769-4); pap. 12.95x (ISBN 0-8147-7770-8). NYU Pr.

Snow, Mike. Christian Pacifism. 1981. write for info. (ISBN 0-913408-67-0). Friends United.

Snow, Pegeen. Mrs. Periwinkle's Groceries. LC 80-22140. (Illus.). 48p. (gr. k-3). 1981. PLB 9.25 (ISBN 0-516-03556-4). Childrens.

Snow, Peter G. Political Forces in Argentina. rev ed. LC 78-19779. 1979. 17.95 (ISBN 0-03-043496-3); pap. 9.95 student ed. (ISBN 0-03-045316-X). Praeger.

Snow, Richard. The Iron Road: A Portrait of American Railroading. LC 78-5388. (Illus.). 96p. (gr. 5 up). 1978. 9.95 (ISBN 0-590-07523-3, Four Winds). Schol Bk Serv.

Snow, Richard E., jt. auth. see Cronbach, Lee J.

Snow, Richard E., et al, eds. Aptitude, Learning, & Instruction: Cognitive Process Analyses, Vol. 1. LC 80-18040. 368p. 1980. text ed. 29.95 (ISBN 0-89859-043-4). L Erlbaum Assocs.

--Aptitude, Learning, & Instruction: Cognitive Process Analyses, Vol. 2. LC 80-18039. 352p. 1980. text ed. 29.95 (ISBN 0-89859-046-9). L Erlbaum Assocs.

Snow, Robert J. The Extant Music of Rodrigo De Ceballos & Its Sources. LC 78-70024. (Detroit Studies in Music Bibliography Ser.: No. 44). 1980. 17.50 (ISBN 0-89990-001-1). Info Coord.

--The Sixteen-Thirteen Print of Juan Esquivel Barahona. LC 78-70021. (Detroit Monographs in Musicology: No. 7). 1978. 11.00 (ISBN 0-911772-92-8). Info Coord.

Snow, Robert J., jt. ed. see Reese, Gustave.

Snow, Toni A. Abigull. LC 80-82792. (Illus.). 48p. (Orig.). (gr. 1-6). 1980. pap. 2.95 (ISBN 0-932384-12-9). Tashmoo.

Snow, Wilbert. Codline's Child: The Autobiography of Wilbert Snow. LC 73-15008. (Illus.). 504p. 1974. 20.00x (ISBN 0-8195-4069-2, Pub. by Wesleyan U Pr). Columbia U Pr.

Snowden, M. Management of Engineering Projects. 1977. 19.95 (ISBN 0-408-00273-5). Butterworths.

Snowden, Philip see Hardie, James K.

Snowdon, photos by. Assignments. (Illus.). 136p. 1972. 12.50 o.p. (ISBN 0-688-00027-4). Morrow.

Snowdon, J. C. Vibration & Shock in Damped Mechanical Systems. 1968. 39.95 (ISBN 0-471-81000-2, Pub. by Wiley-Interscience). Wiley.

Snowdon, John C. & Ungar, Eric E., eds. Isolation of Mechanical Vibration Impact & Noise, AMD Vol. I. 270p. 1973. pap. text ed. 25.00 o.p. (ISBN 0-685-38862-X, G00047). ASME.

Snowman, Daniel. America Since Nineteen Twenty. LC 79-30076. (Studies in Modern History). 1978. 19.95x (ISBN 0-435-31775-X); pap. text ed. 7.95x (ISBN 0-435-31776-8). Heinemann Ed.

--Britain & America: An Interpretation of Their Culture 1945-1975. LC 76-56927. 1977. usa 17.50x (ISBN 0-8147-7778-3). NYU Pr.

Snowman, Kenneth J. Eighteenth Century Gold Boxes of Europe. (Illus.). 1966. 70.00 o.p. (ISBN 0-571-06800-6, Pub. by Faber & Faber). Merrimack Bk Serv.

Snuggs, Henry L., tr. see Giraldi Cinthio.

Snukal, R. Philosophical Poetry of W. B. Yeats. LC 72-87440. 240p. 1972. 44.00 (ISBN 0-521-20057-1). Cambridge U Pr.

Snustad, D. Peter, jt. auth. see Gardner, Eldon J.

Snyder, jt. auth. see Snyder, Bernhart R.

Snyder, A. B & Yost, Nellie S. Pinnacle Jake. LC 51-14574. (Illus.). 1962. pap. 2.95 (ISBN 0-8032-5189-0, BB 132, Bison). U of Nebr Pr.

Snyder, Al. How Our Universe Works. 150p. (Orig.). 1978. pap. 6.95 (ISBN 0-686-27926-3). Snyder Inst Res.

Snyder, Anne. First Step. LC 75-4867. 128p. (gr. 5-10). 1975. 5.95 o.p. (ISBN 0-03-014651-8). HR&W.

--My Name Is Davy: I'm an Alcoholic. LC 76-28457. (gr. 6 up). 1977. reinforced bdg. 5.95 o.p. (ISBN 0-03-017841-X). HR&W.

Snyder, Bascha, jt. auth. see Miller, Mildred.

Snyder, Bernhart R. & Snyder. Fundamentals of Individual Retirement Plans. 1980. 8.95 (ISBN 0-87863-206-9). Farnswth Pub.

Snyder, C. R. & Fromkin, Howard L. Uniqueness: The Human Pursuit of Difference. (Perspectives in Social Psychology Ser.). (Illus.). 250p. 1980. 16.95 (ISBN 0-306-40376-5, Plenum Pr). Plenum Pub.

Snyder, Carey H., ed. see Roberts, Cecil E.

Snyder, Charles M. The Jacksonian Heritage: Pennsylvania Politics, 1833-1848. LC 59-9122. 1958. 8.00 (ISBN 0-911124-28-4). Pa Hist & Mus.

--The Lady & the President: The Letters of Dorothea Dix & Millard Fillmore. LC 75-3551. (Illus.). 400p. 1976. 15.50x (ISBN 0-8131-1332-6). U Pr of Ky.

Snyder, Charles R. Alcohol & the Jews: A Cultural Study of Drinking & Sobriety. LC 77-24885. (Arcturus Books Paperbacks). 240p. 1978. pap. 6.95 (ISBN 0-8093-0846-0). S Ill U Pr.

Snyder, Charles R., jt. auth. see Pittman, David J.

Snyder, Charles R., jt. ed. see Pittman, David J.

Snyder, Donald L. Random Point Processes. LC 75-11556. 485p. 1975. 37.50 (ISBN 0-471-81021-5, Pub. by Wiley-Interscience). Wiley.

Snyder, Earl. Before You Invest: Questions & Answers on Real Estate. 1981. text ed. 12.95 (ISBN 0-8359-0453-9). Reston.

Snyder, Edwin K., et al. The Taiwan Relations Act & the Defense of the Republic of China. (Policy Papers in International Affairs Ser.: No. 12). 132p. 1980. pap. 3.95x (ISBN 0-87725-512-1). U of Cal Intl St.

Snyder, Eldon E. & Spreitzer, Elmer. Social Aspects of Sport. LC 77-26318. (P-H Ser. in Sociology). (Illus.). 1978. pap. 10.95 (ISBN 0-13-815399-X). P-H.

Snyder, Ernest E. Man and the Physical Universe. LC 75-30446. (Physical Science Ser.). 373p. 1976. text ed. 19.95 (ISBN 0-675-08631-0). Merrill.

Snyder, Eugene E. Early Portland Or, Stumptown Triumphant. (Illus.). 1970. 7.95 (ISBN 0-8323-0218-X); pap. 4.85 o.p. (ISBN 0-685-06924-9). Binford.

Snyder, F. G., ed. Symposium on Mineral Resources of the Southeastern United States. 1950. 14.50x (ISBN 0-87049-007-9). U of Tenn Pr.

Snyder, Gary. Regarding Wave. LC 72-122107. 1970. 6.00 (ISBN 0-8112-0386-7); pap. 4.95 (ISBN 0-8112-0196-1, NDP306). New Directions.

Snyder, Gerald S. Are There Alien Beings? The Story of UFOs. LC 80-10453. (Illus.). 160p. (gr. 7 up). 1980. PLB 7.79 (ISBN 0-671-33077-2). Messner.

Snyder, Glenn H. Deterrence & Defense: Toward a Theory of National Security. LC 75-18405. (Illus.). 294p. 1975. Repr. of 1961 ed. lib. bdg. 22.25x (ISBN 0-8371-8333-2, SNDD). Greenwood.

Snyder, Graydon & Shaffer, Kenneth. Texts in Transit. pap. 2.95 o.p. (ISBN 0-685-61334-8). Brethren.

Snyder, Helene A. Thoreau's Philosophy of Life, with Special Consideration of the Influence of Hindoo Philosophy. LC 80-2518. 1981. Repr. of 1900 ed. 18.50 (ISBN 0-404-19066-9). AMS Pr.

Snyder, Howard. The Radical Wesley. LC 80-18197. 180p. (Orig.). 1980. pap. 5.25 (ISBN 0-87784-625-1). Inter-Varsity.

Snyder, Howard A. The Problem of Wineskins: Church Renewal in Technological Age. LC 74-31842. (Illus.). 216p. 1975. pap. text ed. 4.95 (ISBN 0-87784-769-X); study guide 0.95 (ISBN 0-87784-460-7); study guide 0.95 (ISBN 0-87784-460-7). Inter-Varsity.

Snyder, J. Richard. William S. Culbertson: In Search of a Rendezvous. LC 79-6025. 156p. 1980. text ed. 16.75 (ISBN 0-8191-0972-X); pap. text ed. 8.75 (ISBN 0-8191-0973-8). U Pr of Amer.

Snyder, James C. Fiscal Management & Planning in Local Government. LC 76-43218. 1977. 18.95 (ISBN 0-669-01055-3). Lexington Bks.

Snyder, Jane. Puns & Poetry in Lucretius De Rerum Natura. 1980. text ed. 28.00 (ISBN 90-6032-124-3). Humanities.

Snyder, L. R. & Kirkland, J. J. Introduction to Modern Liquid Chromatography. 2nd ed. LC 79-4537. 1979. 33.95 (ISBN 0-471-03822-9, Pub. by Wiley-Interscience). Wiley.

Snyder, Laura. Homemaking Executive. pap. 3.95 (ISBN 0-89036-140-1). Hawkes Pub Inc.

Snyder, Laurence H. & David, Paul R. Principles of Heredity. 5th ed. (Illus.). text ed. 16.95x o.p. (ISBN 0-669-25312-X). Heath.

Snyder, LeMoyne. Homicide Investigation: Practical Information for Coroners, Police Officers, & Other Investigators. 3rd ed. (Illus.). 416p. 1977. 26.75 (ISBN 0-398-03632-2). C C Thomas.

Snyder, Leon C. Gardening in the Upper Midwest. LC 77-8650. (Illus.). 1978. 12.50 (ISBN 0-8166-0833-4). U of Minn Pr.

Snyder, Leslie. Justice or Revolution. LC 78-74594. 1979. 12.95 (ISBN 0-916728-20-X). Bks in Focus.

Snyder, Louis. First Book of World War One. (First Bks). (Illus.). (gr. 7 up). 1958. PLB 6.45 (ISBN 0-531-00675-1). Watts.

--First Book of World War Two. (First Bks). (Illus.). (gr. 7 up). 1958. PLB 6.45 (ISBN 0-531-00676-X); pap. 1.25 (ISBN 0-531-02319-2). Watts.

Snyder, Louis L. The First Book of the Soviet Union. rev. ed. (First Bks). (Illus.). 96p. (gr. 7 up). 1972. PLB 6.45 (ISBN 0-531-00638-7). Watts.

--Meaning of Nationalism. LC 68-8338. (Illus.). 1968. Repr. of 1954 ed. lib. bdg. 19.25x (ISBN 0-8371-0233-2, SNMN). Greenwood.

--The Soviet Union. 2nd rev. ed. LC 78-4842. (First Bks.). (Illus.). (gr. 5 up). 1978. PLB 6.45 s&l (ISBN 0-531-02230-7). Watts.

Snyder, Louis L. & Brown, Ida M. Frederick the Great: Prussian Warrior & Statesman. LC 68-24122. (Biography Ser). (Illus.). (gr. 7 up). 1968. PLB 5.90 o.p. (ISBN 0-531-00872-X). Watts.

Snyder, Mariah & Jackle, Mary. Neurologic Problems: A Critical Care Nursing Focus. (Critical Care Ser.). (Illus.). 352p. 1980. pap. text ed. 17.95 (ISBN 0-87619-713-6). R J Brady.

Snyder, Martha, et al. The Young Child As Person: Toward the Development of Healthy Conscience. 1980. 19.95 (ISBN 0-87705-466-5). Human Sci Pr.

Snyder, Nathan W., ed. Space Power Systems. (Progress in Astronautics & Aeronautics Ser.: Vol. 4). (Illus.). 1961. 20.00 (ISBN 0-12-535104-6). Acad Pr.

Snyder, Paul. Health & Human Nature. 256p. 1980. pap. 10.95 (ISBN 0-8019-6798-8). Chilton.

Snyder, Robert. Anais Nin Observed: Portrait of a Woman As Artist. LC 76-3123. (Illus.). 116p. 1976. pap. 9.95 (ISBN 0-8040-0708-X). Swallow.

--The Biology of Population Growth. 300p. 1980. 30.00x (Pub. by Croom Helm England). State Mutual Bk.

Snyder, Ross, ed. Openings into Ministry. LC 77-92707. (Studies in Ministry & Parish Life). 1977. 12.95x (ISBN 0-913552-10-0); pap. 5.50x (ISBN 0-913552-11-9). Exploration Pr.

Snyder, Solomon, jt. ed. see Usdin, Earl.

Snyder, Solomon H. Biological Aspects of Mental Disorder. (Illus.). 272p. 1981. pap. 8.95x (ISBN 0-19-502888-0). Oxford U Pr.

Snyder, Stephen. Pier Paolo Pasolini. (Theater Arts Ser.). 1980. lib. bdg. 13.95 (ISBN 0-8057-9271-6). Twayne.

Snyder, Virgil, et al. Selected Topics in Algebraic Geometry, 2 Vols in 1. 2nd ed. LC 78-113149. 1970. text ed. 13.95 (ISBN 0-8284-0189-6). Chelsea Pub.

Snyder, W. S., et al, eds. Radiation Protection: Proceedings of the First International Congress. LC 67-30114. 1968. 225.00 (ISBN 0-08-012413-5). Pergamon.

Snyder, William. Tory's. 384p. (Orig.). 1981. pap. 2.75 (ISBN 0-380-76547-0, 76547). Avon.

Snyder, William P., jt. auth. see Hambrick, Ralph S., Jr.

Snyder, William U. Thomas Wolfe: Ulysses & Narcissus. LC 78-141381. xxiv, 234p. 1971. 12.00x (ISBN 0-8214-0087-8). Ohio U Pr.

Snyder, Zilpha K. A Fabulous Creature. LC 80-18977. 252p. (gr. 5-9). 1981. PLB 9.95 (ISBN 0-689-30829-9). Atheneum.

So, Frank S., et al, eds. Practice of Local Government Planning, Vol. 1. LC 79-21380. (Municipal Management Ser.). (Illus.). 1979. text ed. 35.00 (ISBN 0-87326-020-1). Intl City Mgt.

Soames, Barbra. Keeping Domestic Geese. (Illus.). 128p. 1980. 13.95 (ISBN 0-7137-1070-5, Pub. by Blandford Pr England). Sterling.

Soames, Henry. The Anglo-Saxon Church: Its History, Revenues & General Character. 4th ed. LC 80-2212. 1981. Repr. of 1856 ed. 39.50 (ISBN 0-404-18786-2). AMS Pr.

Soames, Scott, jt. auth. see Perlmutter, David M.

Soare, M. Application of Finite Difference Equations to Shell Analysis. 1968. 71.00 (ISBN 0-08-010214-X). Pergamon.

Soaring Society of America. American Soaring Handbook. (Illus.). 1972. ring binder 27.50x o.p. (ISBN 0-911720-65-0, Pub. by Soaring Soc). Aviation.

Sobchack, Thomas & Sobchack, Vivian C. An Introduction to Film. (Illus.). 512p. 1980. pap. text ed. 11.95 (ISBN 0-316-80250-6); instructor's manual free (ISBN 0-316-80251-4). Little.

Sobchack, Vivian C., jt. auth. see Sobchack, Thomas.

Sobeck, Joan M., jt. auth. see Cyr, John.

Sobecka, Z., et al, eds. Dictionary of Chemistry & Chemical Technology in Six Languages. rev. ed. 1966. 120.00 (ISBN 0-08-011600-0). Pergamon.

Sobel. Cambodia: Holocaust in Asia. 200p. 1981. lib. bdg. 17.50 (ISBN 0-87196-209-8). Facts on File. Postponed.

Sobel, David J. Ways of Health: Holistic Approaches to Ancient & Contemporary Medicine. LC 78-14081. 1979. pap. 7.95 (ISBN 0-15-694992-X, Harv). HarBraceJ.

Sobel, Eli & Wagener, Hans, eds. Liebesspiele. (Orig.). 1970. pap. text ed. 3.95x (ISBN 0-19-501056-6). Oxford U Pr.

Sobel, Irwin Philip. Dr. Monte Cristo. LC 77-82773. 1978. 8.95 o.p. (ISBN 0-385-12085-0). Doubleday.

Sobel, Lester, ed. Castro's Cuba in the 1970's. 1977. lib. bdg. 17.50x (ISBN 0-87196-151-2). Facts on File.

--China Since Mao. 200p. 1980. lib. bdg. 17.50 (ISBN 0-87196-210-1). Facts on File.

Sobel, Lester A. Post-Watergate Morality. lib. bdg. 15.00x o.p. (ISBN 0-87196-261-6). Facts on File.

Sobel, Lester A., ed. Energy Crisis, Vol. 4. 1980. lib. bdg. 17.50 (ISBN 0-87196-284-5). Facts on File.

--Energy Crisis: Nineteen Seventy-Seven to Nineteen Seventy-Nine, Vol. 4. 1980. lib. bdg. 17.50 (ISBN 0-87196-284-5). Facts on File.

--Kissinger & Detente. 275p. 1975. lib. bdg. 17.50 (ISBN 0-87196-243-8). Facts on File.

--Media Controversies. 1980. 17.50 (ISBN 0-87196-242-X, Checkmark). Facts on File.
--Money & Politics 1970-74: Contributions, Campaign Abuses, & the Law. LC 74-81147. 225p. 1974. lib. bdg. 15.00x o.p. (ISBN 0-87196-262-4); pap. 4.95x o.p. (ISBN 0-87196-263-2). Facts on File.
--U. S. Military Dilemma. 200p. 1981. 17.50x (ISBN 0-87196-202-0, Checkmark). Facts on File.

Sobel, Max & Maletsky, Evan. Teaching Mathematics: A Source Book for Aids, Activities, & Strategies. (Illus.). 288p. 1975. pap. text ed. 11.95 (ISBN 0-13-894121-1). P-H.

Sobel, Max A. & Lerner, Norbert. Algebra & Triginometry: A Precalculus Approach. (Illus.). 1979. ref. ed. 17.95 (ISBN 0-13-021709-3). P-H.

Sobel, Max A., jt. auth. see Merserve, Bruce E.

Sobel, Max A., jt. auth. see Meserve, B. E.

Sobel, Max A., jt. auth. see Meserve, Bruce E.

Sobel, Nathan R. Eye-Witness Identification. LC 72-85036. 1972. 25.00 (ISBN 0-87632-083-3); 1979 supplement incl. (ISBN 0-685-99205-5). Boardman.

Sobel, Robert. The Age of Giant Corporations: A Microeconomic History of American Business, 1914-1970. LC 72-835. (Contributions in Economics & Economic History). 1972. lib. bdg. 15.00 (ISBN 0-8371-6404-4, SAB/); pap. 3.45 (ISBN 0-8371-7339-6). Greenwood.
--Complete Guide to American History. (Quick & Easy Ser). 1966. pap. 1.95 o.s.i. (ISBN 0-02-082060-7, Collier). Macmillan.
--For Want of a Nail: If Burgoyne Had Won at Saratoga. (Illus.). 384p. 1973. 12.95 o.s.i. (ISBN 0-02-612250-2). Macmillan.
--Great Bull Market: Wall Street in the 1920's. LC 68-19795. (Essays in American History). 1968. pap. 5.95x (ISBN 0-393-09817-6, NortonC). Norton.
--Monarch Notes on Machiavelli's the Prince. (Orig.). pap. 1.95 (ISBN 0-671-00565-0). Monarch Pr.
--They Satisfy: The Cigarette in American Life. LC 77-27681. 1978. 8.95 o.p. (ISBN 0-385-12956-4, Anchor Pr). Doubleday.

Sobel, Samuel. Intrepid Sailor. LC 80-13026. (Illus.). 1980. 12.95 (ISBN 0-936082-04-6). Cresset Pubs.

Sobel, Stuart, ed. see Urquidez, Benny.

Sobell, Linda C., ed. Evaluating Alcohol & Drug Abuse Treatment Effectiveness. 1979. 22.00 (ISBN 0-08-022997-2). Pergamon.

Sobel'man, I. I. Introduction to the Theory of Atomic Spectra. 632p. 1972. text ed. 81.00 (ISBN 0-08-016166-9). Pergamon.

Sobeloff, Jonathan & Weidenbruch, Peter P. Federal Income Taxation of Corporations & Stockholders in a Nutshell. 2nd ed. (Nutshell Ser.). 351p. 1981. pap. 6.95 (ISBN 0-8299-2122-2). West Pub.

Sober, Elliott. Simplicity. (Clarendon Library of Logic & Philosophy). (Illus.). 160p. 1975. 24.00x (ISBN 0-19-824407-X). Oxford U Pr.

Sobey, Francine. Nonprofessional Revolution in Mental Health. LC 71-118355. 1970. 15.00x (ISBN 0-231-03304-4). Columbia U Pr.

Sobieski, jt. auth. see Anderson.

Sobieszek, Barbara, jt. auth. see Webster, Murray, Jr.

Sobieszek, Robert A. & Appel, Odette M. The Daguerreotypes of Southworth & Hawes. (Illus.). 1980. pap. text ed. 6.95 (ISBN 0-486-23841-5). Dover.

Sobieszek, Robert A., ed. see Engrand, Bernard.

Sobin, Dennis P. Future of the American Suburbs: Survival or Extinction. LC 72-154034. 1971. 11.50 (ISBN 0-8046-9014-6, Natl U). Kennikat.

Sobin, J. M., jt. auth. see Kaplan, F. M.

Soble, Alan, ed. Philosophy of Sex: Contemporary Readings. 412p. 1980. 17.50x (ISBN 0-8476-6292-6). Rowman.

Sobol. Encyclopedia Brown Takes the Case. (gr. 3-6). pap. 1.50 o.p. (ISBN 0-671-56016-6, 56016). Archway.

Sobol, Donal J. Angie's First Case. LC 80-70011. (Illus.). 128p. (gr. 3-7). 1981. 8.95 (ISBN 0-590-07564-0, Four Winds). Schol Bk Serv.

Sobol, Donald. Disaster. (Orig.). (YA) (gr. 7-9). 1979. pap. 1.50 (ISBN 0-671-29939-5). PB.

Sobol, Donald J. Encyclopedia Brown & the Case of the Midnight Visitor, No. 13. (The Encyclopedia Brown Ser.). 96p. 1980. pap. 1.50 (ISBN 0-553-15076-6). Bantam.
--Encyclopedia Brown Carries on. LC 79-6340. (Illus.). 80p. (gr. 3-7). 1980. 6.95 (ISBN 0-590-07562-4, Four Winds). Schol Bk Serv.
--Encyclopedia Brown Finds the Clues. LC 66-10230. (Encyclopedia Brown Ser.: No. 3). (Illus.). (gr. 2-6). 1966. 5.95 o.p. (ISBN 0-525-67204-4); pap. 2.98 (ISBN 0-525-67802-6). Elsevier-Nelson.
--Encyclopedia Brown Shows the Way, No. 9. 96p. (gr. 3-6). 1981. pap. 1.50 (ISBN 0-553-15107-X). Bantam.
--Encyclopedia Brown Tracks Them Down, No. 8. 96p. (gr. 3-6). 1981. pap. 1.50 (ISBN 0-553-15093-6). Bantam.
--Encyclopedia Brown's Record Book of Weird & Wonderful Facts. (gr. k-6). 1981. pap. price not set (ISBN 0-440-42361-9, YB). Dell.

Sobol, Evelyn G. & Robischon, Paulette. Family Nursing: A Study Guide. 2nd ed. (Illus.). 182p. 1975. pap. 7.95 o.p. (ISBN 0-8016-4727-4). Mosby.

Sobol, Harriet L. Cosmo's Restaurant. LC 78-9685. (Illus.). (gr. 3-6). 1978. 8.95 (ISBN 0-02-785970-3, 78597). Macmillan.
--My Brother Steven Is Retarded. LC 76-46996. (Illus.). (gr. 3-6). 1977. 7.95 (ISBN 0-02-785990-8). Macmillan.
--My Other-Mother, My Other-Father. LC 78-24165. (Illus.). 48p. (gr. 3-7). 1979. 7.95 (ISBN 0-02-785960-6). Macmillan.
--Pete's House. LC 77-12564. (Illus.). (gr. 3-6). 1978. 8.95 (ISBN 0-02-785980-0, 78598). Macmillan.

Sobol, Max A. & Lerner, Norbert. Algebra for College Students: An Intermediate Approach. 2nd ed. 1980. text ed. 16.95 (ISBN 0-13-021584-8). P-H.

Sobolev, V. V. Light Scattering in Planetary Atmospheres. Irvine, W. M., tr. 1974. text ed. 46.00 (ISBN 0-08-017934-7). Pergamon.

Sobosan, Jeffrey. Act of Contrition. LC 79-54695. 128p. 1979. pap. 2.95 (ISBN 0-87793-189-5). Ave Maria.
--The Ascent to God. 1981. 9.95 (ISBN 0-88347-128-0). Thomas More.

Sobotta, Johannes. Atlas of Human Anatomy. Figge, Frank H. & Hild, Walter J., eds. Incl. Vol. 1. Regions, Bones, Ligaments & Muscles. text ed. 39.50 (ISBN 0-8067-1719-X); Vol. 2. Visceral Anatomy (Cardiovascular, Lymphatic, Digestive, Respiratory & Urogenital Systems) text ed. 39.50 (ISBN 0-8067-1729-7); Vol. 3. Central Nervous System, Autonómic Nervous System, Sense Organs & Skin, Peripheral Nerves & Vessels. text ed. 45.00 (ISBN 0-8067-1739-4). (Illus.). 1978. Repr. of 1974 ed. complete set 112.00 (ISBN 0-686-67832-X); Set. 112.00 (ISBN 0-686-67833-8). Urban & S.

Soboul, Albert. A Short History of the French Revolution, 1789-1799. Symcox, Geoffrey, tr. (Cal Ser.: No. 360). 1977. 18.50x (ISBN 0-520-02855-4); pap. 4.25x (ISBN 0-520-03419-8). U of Cal Pr.

Soboul, Albert, intro. by. Affiches De la Commune De Paris, 1793-1794. (Fr.). 1976. Repr. lib. bdg. 550.00x o.p. (ISBN 0-8287-1326-X). Clearwater Pub.

Soby, James T. Ben Shahn: His Graphic Art. LC 57-12840. 1957. 25.00 o.s.i. (ISBN 0-8076-0053-9). Braziller.
--Ben Shahn: Paintings. LC 63-18187. 1963. 35.00 o.p. (ISBN 0-8076-0241-8). Braziller.
--The School of Paris: Paintings from the Florene May Schoenbrorn & Samuel A. Marx Collection. LC 65-25727. (Illus.). 56p. 1965. pap. 7.95 (ISBN 0-87070-575-X). Museum Mod Art.

Sochen. Herstory. 2nd ed. 1981. 11.95 (ISBN 0-88284-115-7). Alfred Pub.

Sochen, June. Herstory: A Woman's View of American History. 2nd ed. Incl. Vol. 1. 1600-1880. 220p. 6.95x o.p. (ISBN 0-88284-046-0); Vol. 2. From 1861. 227p. 6.95x o.p. (ISBN 0-88284-047-9). LC 74-80471. (Illus.). 448p. 1974. Set. 12.50 o.p. (ISBN 0-88284-017-7); Complete. pap. text ed. 11.95x (ISBN 0-88284-115-7). Alfred Pub.
--The New Feminism in Twentieth Century America. LC 71-160664. (Problems in American Civilization Ser). 1971. pap. 4.25x o.p. (ISBN 0-669-63461-1). Heath.

Social Science Panel. Freedom of Choice in Housing. 80p. 1972. pap. 3.00 (ISBN 0-309-02025-5). Natl Acad Pr.

Social Science Panel of the Advisory Committee to HUD. Segregation in Residential Areas. LC 72-85593. 256p. 1973. pap. 7.25 (ISBN 0-309-02042-5). Natl Acad Pr.

Social Science Research Council. Civil-Military Relations, an Annotated Bibliography, 1940-1952. LC 75-3796. 140p. 1975. Repr. of 1954 ed. lib. bdg. 13.75x (ISBN 0-8371-8076-7, CIMR). Greenwood.

Social Science Research Council Conference on Social Experiments. Experimental Testing of Public Policy: Proceedings, 1974. Boruch, Robert F. & Riecken, Henry W., eds. LC 75-30613. 180p. 1976. 20.25x (ISBN 0-89158-004-2). Westview.

Social Security Administration. Survey of Low Income Aged & Disabled, 1973-1975. LC 79-67535. 1979. codebook 20.00 (ISBN 0-89138-965-2). ICPSR.

Social Studies Division of the Pennsylvania Department of Education. A Conceptual Approach to Teaching About Pennsylvania. LC 72-90894. 1973. pap. 7.50 (ISBN 0-931992-13-3). Penns Valley.

Social Systems, Inc., jt. auth. see Mayo, R. Britton.

Societe Jean Bodin Pour L'histoire Comparative Des Institutions. Recueils, 4 vols. Incl. Vol. 1. Les Liens De Vassalite et les Immunities (ISBN 0-404-18596-7); Vol. 2. Le Servage (ISBN 0-404-18597-5); Vol. 3. La Tenure (ISBN 0-404-18598-3); Vol. 4. Le Domaine (ISBN 0-404-18599-1). LC 80-2205. 1981. 139.50 set (ISBN 0-404-18595-9); 35.00 ea. AMS Pr.

Society for Hospital Social Work Directors of the American Hospital Association. Cost Accountability for Hospital Social Work. LC 80-12334. 48p. (Orig.). 1980. pap. 10.00 (ISBN 0-87258-278-7, 1330). Am Hospital.
--Documentation by Social Workers in Medical Records. 1978. pap. 6.00 (ISBN 0-87258-256-6, 1085). Am Hospital.
--Quality & Quantity Assurance for Social Workers in Health Care: A Training Manual. LC 80-26488. (Illus.). 96p. (Orig.). 1980. manual 27.50 (ISBN 0-87258-325-2, 2100). Am Hospital.
--Reporting System for Hospital Social Work. LC 78-5696. 1978. pap. 8.75 (ISBN 0-87258-237-X, 1562). Am Hospital.
--Social Work Staff Development for Health Care. LC 76-41793. 1976. pap. 7.25 (ISBN 0-87258-322-8, 2550). Am Hospital.

Society for Industrial & Applied Mathematics - American Mathematical Society Symposia - New York - March, 1971. Computers in Algebra & Number Theory: Proceedings, Vol. 4. Birkhoff, Garrett & Hall, Marshall, Jr., eds. LC 76-167685. 208p. 1980. Repr. of 1971 ed. 14.20 (ISBN 0-8218-1323-4, SIAMS-4). Am Math.

Society for Industrial & Applied Mathematics-American Mathematical Society Symposia-New York, March 1975. Nonlinear Programming: Proceedings, Vol. 9. Cottle, Richard W. & Lemke, C. E., eds. LC 75-47471. 1980. Repr. of 1976 ed. 14.00 (ISBN 0-8218-1329-3, SIAMS-9). Am Math.

Society for Industrial Microbiology. Developments in Industrial Microbiology, 11 vols. LC 60-13953. Vols. 5-15. 25.00 ea. Lubrecht & Cramer.

Society for Psychosomatic Research, 22nd, Royal College of Physicians, London, Nov. 27-28 1978. Psychosomatics in War & Peace: Proceedings. Williams, P., ed. 112p. 1980. pap. 22.00 (ISBN 0-08-026064-0). Pergamon.

Society for Technical Communication, ed. see International Technical Communication Conference, 27th, Minneapolis, May 14-17, 1980.

Society for Technical Communication, ed. International Technical Communication Conference, Dallas, 1978: Proceedings, Vol. 25. 1978. 25.00 (ISBN 0-914548-29-8). Univelt Inc.

Society For The Study Of Developmental Biology - 25th Symposium. Current Status of Some Major Problems in Developmental Biology: Proceedings. Locke, Michael, ed. 1967. 46.50 (ISBN 0-12-454162-3). Acad Pr.

Society For The Study Of Developmental Biology - 24th Symposium. Reproduction: Molecular, Subcellular & Cellular. Locke, M., ed. 1966. 43.50 (ISBN 0-12-454174-7). Acad Pr.

Society of Automotive Engineers. Accident Causation. 1980. 15.00. Soc Auto Engineers.
--Advanced Gas Turbine Systems for Automobiles. 1980. 18.00 (ISBN 0-89883-236-5). Soc Auto Engineers.
--Alcohols As Motor Fuels. 1980. 29.95 (ISBN 0-89883-107-5). Soc Auto Engineers.
--Automotive Aerodynamics. 1978. 22.00 (ISBN 0-89883-104-0). Soc Auto Engineers.
--Automotive Electronic Instrumentation: Displays & Sensors. 1980. 24.95 (ISBN 0-89883-228-4). Soc Auto Engineers.
--Automotive Electronic Systems. 1979. 24.95 (ISBN 0-89883-212-8). Soc Auto Engineers.
--Automotive Fuel Economy, No. 2. 1979. 18.95 (ISBN 0-89883-106-7). Soc Auto Engineers.
--Automotive Sensors. 1979. 16.95 (ISBN 0-89883-213-6). Soc Auto Engineers.
--Cumulative Index of SAE Technical Papers, 1965-1978. 1979. 39.95. Soc Auto Engineers.
--Current Trends in Truck Suspensions. 1980. 15.00 (ISBN 0-89883-246-2). Soc Auto Engineers.
--Diesel Combustion & Emissions. 1980. 30.00 (ISBN 0-89883-055-9). Soc Auto Engineers.
--Diesel Engineers, Combustion & Emissions Research in Japan. 1980. 25.00 (ISBN 0-89883-239-X). Soc Auto Engineers.
--Diesel Engines Noise Conference: Proceedings. 1979. 29.95 (ISBN 0-89883-050-8). Soc Auto Engineers.
--Diesel Engines Thermal Loading. 1979. 22.00 (ISBN 0-89883-220-9). Soc Auto Engineers.
--Energy Saving Ideas for Mobile Equipment Designers. 1980. 12.00 (ISBN 0-89883-240-3). Soc Auto Engineers.
--Engines, Fuels & Lubricants: Perspective on the Future. 1980. 15.00 (ISBN 0-89883-242-X). Soc Auto Engineers.
--Fatigue Resistance: Testing & Forecasting. 1979. 13.50 (ISBN 0-89883-219-5). Soc Auto Engineers.
--Historical Perspective of Farm Machinery. 1980. 12.50 (ISBN 0-89883-241-1). Soc Auto Engineers.
--Materials Availability for the Automotive Industries. 1980. 15.00 (ISBN 0-89883-233-0). Soc Auto Engineers.
--Measurement & Control of Diesel Particulate Emissions. 1979. 22.95 (ISBN 0-89883-105-9). Soc Auto Engineers.
--Multiple Engine Oils. 1980. 12.00 (ISBN 0-89883-243-8). Soc Auto Engineers.
--Ninth International Forum for Air Cargo Proceedings. 1979. 18.00 (ISBN 0-89883-049-4). Soc Auto Engineers.
--Past, Present & Future of Automotive Elastomer Applications. 1980. 15.00 (ISBN 0-89883-235-7). Soc Auto Engineers.
--Piston Engine: Meeting the Challenge of the 1980's. 1980. 8.95 (ISBN 0-89883-238-1). Soc Auto Engineers.
--Practical Treatise on Engine Crankshaft Torsional Vibration Control. 1979. pap. 7.50 (ISBN 0-89883-216-0). Soc Auto Engineers.
--Relationship Between Engine Oil Viscosity & Engine Performance, Pts. V & VI. 1980. 18.00. Soc Auto Engineers.
--Retained Austenite & Its Measurement by X-Ray Diffraction. 1980. 8.50 (ISBN 0-89883-224-1). Soc Auto Engineers.
--Sensors for Automotive Systems. 1980. 18.00 (ISBN 0-89883-229-2). Soc Auto Engineers.
--Topics on Contamination in Hydraulic Systems. 1979. 15.00 (ISBN 0-89883-218-7). Soc Auto Engineers.
--Turbochargers & Turbocharged Engines. 1979. 24.95 (ISBN 0-89883-214-4). Soc Auto Engineers.
--Twenty-Third Stamp Car Crash Conference. 1979. 35.00 (ISBN 0-89883-052-4). Soc Auto Engineers.
--Universal Joint & Driveshaft Design Manual. 1979. 37.95 (ISBN 0-89883-007-9). Soc Auto Engineers.
--Vehicle Noise Regulation & Reduction. 1980. 22.50 (ISBN 0-89883-227-6). Soc Auto Engineers.
--Vehicle Structured Mechanics, 3rd International Proceedings. 1979. 30.00 (ISBN 0-89883-053-2). Soc Auto Engineers.

Society of Automotive Engineers, jt. auth. see Bosch, Robert.

Society of Brothers & Swinger, Marlys, eds. Songs of Light: The Bruderhof Songbook. LC 77-1716. (Illus.). 1977. 12.75 o.p. (ISBN 0-87486-017-2). Plough.

Society of Education Officers. Educational Administration. Brooksbank, Kenneth, ed. 300p. (Orig.). 1981. pap. text ed. 16.95 (ISBN 0-900313-65-X). Longman.
--Management in the Education Service: Challenge & Response. (Open University Set Bk.). 128p. 1975. pap. 5.25 (ISBN 0-7100-8292-4). Routledge & Kegan.

Society of Mexican Architects, ed. Mexican Architecture. (Illus.). 1956. 60.00 (ISBN 0-685-39858-7). Heinman.

Society of North American Goldsmiths. Metalsmith Papers. 96p. (Orig.). 1980. pap. text ed. 12.00 (ISBN 0-9604446-0-2). SNAG.

Society of Paitent Representatives of the American Hospital Association. Essentials of Patient Representative Programs in Hospitals. LC 78-26889. 1978. pap. 8.75 (ISBN 0-87258-255-8, 1251). Am Hospital.

Society of Patient Representatives of the American Hospital Association. The Patient Representative's Participation in Risk Management. (Orig.). 1980. pap. 8.75 (ISBN 0-87258-315-5, 1532). Am Hospital.

Society of the Plastics Industry. Plastics Industry Safety Handbook. Rosato, D. V. & Lawrence, John R., eds. LC 72-91982. 1973. 17.95 (ISBN 0-8436-1207-X). CBI Pub.

Sociological Resources for the Social Studies. Crowd & Mass Behavior. (Readings in Sociology Ser.). (gr. 9-12). 1972. pap. text ed. 4.96 (ISBN 0-205-02578-1, 8125783). Allyn.
--Population Growth & the Complex Society. (Readings in Sociology Ser.). (gr. 9-12). 1972. pap. text ed. 4.96 (ISBN 0-205-02577-3, 8125775). Allyn.

Sockman, Ralph W. Easter Story for Children. (Illus.). (gr. 2-5). 1966. 6.95 (ISBN 0-687-11507-8). Abingdon.

Socolofsky, Homer & Self, Huber. Historical Atlas of Kansas. 1972. 11.95x (ISBN 0-8061-1022-8); pap. 7.95 (ISBN 0-8061-1032-5). U of Okla Pr.

Socolow, Susan M. Merchants of Buenos Aires, Seventeen Seventy-Eight to Eighteen Hundred & Ten. LC 77-85216. (Cambridge Latin American Studies: No. 30). (Illus.). 1979. 35.50 (ISBN 0-521-21812-8). Cambridge U Pr.

Socrates, G. Infrared Characteristic Group Frequencies. LC 79-1406. 1980. 72.00 (ISBN 0-471-27592-1, Pub. by Wiley-Interscience). Wiley.

Sodd, et al, eds. see International Symposium on Radiopharmaceuticals, 2nd.
Soddy, Frederick. The Story of Atomic Energy. 1949. 30.00 (ISBN 0-911268-29-4). Rogers Bk.
Sodee, D. Bruce & Early, Paul J. Mosby's Manual of Nuclear Medicine Procedures. 3rd ed. (Illus.). 574p. 1981. pap. text ed. 34.95 (ISBN 0-8016-4729-0). Mosby.
--Technology & Interpretation of Nuclear Medicine Procedures. 2nd ed. LC 75-15607. (Illus.). 544p. 1975. text ed. 31.95 (ISBN 0-8016-4732-0). Mosby.
Sodeman, Thomas M., jt. auth. see Sodeman, William A.
Sodeman, William A. & Sodeman, Thomas M. Sodeman's Pathologic Physiology: Mechanisms of Disease. 6th ed. LC 78-1790. (Illus.). 1145p. 1979. text ed. 39.50 (ISBN 0-7216-8473-4). Saunders.
Sodeman, William A., Jr. & Saladin, Thomas A. Gastroenterology Specialty Board Review. 1977. spiral bdg. 16.50 (ISBN 0-87488-316-4). Med Exam.
Soden, John V., jt. auth. see McLean, Ephraim R.
Soden, Michael Von see Von Soden, Michael.
Sodeoka, Kanji, jt. auth. see Simpson, Penny.
Soderberg, George A. Finishing Technology. rev. ed. (gr. 10-12). 1969. text ed. 15.96 (ISBN 0-87345-016-7). McKnight.
Soderberg, Percy M. Cat Diseases. (Orig.). pap. 2.50 (ISBN 0-87666-171-1, AP4800). TFH Pubns.
Soderholm, Marjorie. Prayers That Make a Difference. rev. ed. Orig. Title: A Study Guide to Bible Prayers. 96p. 1980. pap. 2.50 (ISBN 0-911802-49-5). Free Church Pubns.
Soderholm, Marjorie E. Understanding the Pupil, 3 pts. Incl. Pt. 1. The Pre-School Child. pap. 2.50 (ISBN 0-8010-7906-3); Pt. 2. The Primary & Junior Child. pap. 2.50 (ISBN 0-8010-7953-5); Pt. 3. The Adolescent. pap. 2.50 (ISBN 0-8010-7922-5). Baker Bk.
Soderlund, G. F. & Scott, Samuel H., eds. Examples of Gregorian Chant & Other Sacred Music of the 16th Century. LC 70-129090. (Orig.). 1971. 15.95 (ISBN 0-13-293753-0). P-H.
Soderman, Harry & O'Connell, John J. Modern Criminal Investigation. 5th ed. O'Hara, Charles E., ed. LC 62-9736. (Funk & W Bk.). (Illus.). 1962. 10.00 o.s.i. (ISBN 0-308-40080-1, TYC-T). T Y Crowell.
Soderstrom, Elisabeth. In My Own Key. (Illus.). 102p. 1980. 18.95 (ISBN 0-241-10318-5, Pub. by Hamish Hamilton England). David & Charles.
Soderstrom, Lori, jt. auth. see Hubbard, Irene.
Soderstrom, Lou. Primarily Time. (gr. k-3). 1978. 7.95 (ISBN 0-916456-28-5, GA92). Good Apple.
Sodha, M. S. & Ghatak, A. K. Inhomogeneous Optical Waveguides. (Optical Physics & Engineering Ser.). (Illus.). 281p. 1977. 35.00 (ISBN 0-306-30916-5, Plenum Pr). Plenum Pub.
Soeharjo, Mintari, jt. auth. see Copeland, Marks.
Soelen, Philip Van see Van Soelen, Philip.
Soelle, Dorothee. Political Theology. Shelley, John, tr. from Ger. LC 73-88349. 128p. 1974. pap. 3.50 (ISBN 0-8006-1065-2, 1-0165). Fortress.
Sofer, Cyril. Men in Mid-Career: A Study of British Managers & Technical Specialists. (Studies in Sociology: No. 4). 1970. 29.95 (ISBN 0-521-07788-5); pap. 14.95x (ISBN 0-521-09606-5). Cambridge U Pr.
Sofer, Eugene. From Pale to Pampa: The Jewish Immigrant Experience in Buenos Aires. 1981. text ed. 24.00x (ISBN 0-8419-0428-6). Holmes & Meier.
Soff, Edward B. & Snider, Arthur D. Fundamentals of Complex Analysis for Mathematics, Science & Engineering. (Illus.). 1976. 23.95 (ISBN 0-13-332148-7). P-H.
Soffer, Reba N. Ethics & Society in England: The Revolution in the Social Sciences, 1870-1914. 1978. 22.75x (ISBN 0-520-03521-6). U of Cal Pr.
Soffer, Richard L. Biochemical Regulation of Blood Pressure. 425p. 1981. 35.00 (ISBN 0-471-05600-6, Pub. by Wiley-Interscience). Wiley.
Sofge, Opal. From the Grass Roots. 3.95 o.p. (ISBN 0-685-48830-6). Nortex Pr.
Sofios, Nicholas, jt. auth. see Abramson, Harold J.
Sofr, Ota, tr. see Weisser, Otto & Landa, S.
Softly, Barbara. Lennon-Yellow Elephant Called Trunk. LC 71-115818. (Illus.). 48p. (gr. k-2). PLB 5.29 (ISBN 0-8178-4772-3). Harvey.
Sofu Teshigahara. Sofu Zokei (the Art of Sofu) (Illus.). 260p. (Japanese.). 1978. 200.00 (ISBN 0-8048-1344-2, Pub. by Shufunotomo Co Ltd Japan). C E Tuttle.
Sogaard, Viggo B. Everything You Need to Know for a Cassette Ministry. LC 74-20915. 224p. 1975. pap. 3.95 (ISBN 0-87123-125-5, 210125). Bethany Fell.
Soggin, J. Alberto. Judges: A Commentary. Bowden, John, tr. from Ital. (Old Testament Library). 1981. text ed. price not set (ISBN 0-664-21368-5). Westminster.
Soh, C. T. Korea. (Geomedical Monographs: Vol. 6). (Illus.). 270p. 1980. 57.90 (ISBN 0-387-09128-9). Springer-Verlag.
Sohl, Damian G., jt. auth. see Rehg, Kenneth L.
Sohl, Jerry. Underhanded Bridge. 128p. 1975. pap. 3.95 (ISBN 0-8015-8128-1, Hawthorn). Dutton.
--Underhanded Chess. 1973. pap. 3.50 (ISBN 0-8015-8130-3, Hawthorn). Dutton.
Sohl, Marcia & Dackerman, Gerald. Around the World in Eighty Days: Student Activity Book. (Now Age Illustrated Ser.). (Illus.). (gr. 4-12). 1976. wkbk. 0.95 (ISBN 0-88301-285-5). Pendulum Pr.
--The Best of O. Henry: Student Activity Book. (Now Age Illustrated Ser.). (Illus.). (gr. 4-12). 1976. wkbk. 0.95 (ISBN 0-88301-292-8). Pendulum Pr.
--The Best of Poe: Student Activity Book. (Now Age Illustrated Ser.). (Illus.). (gr. 4-12). 1976. wkbk. 0.95 (ISBN 0-88301-293-6). Pendulum Pr.
--Captains Courageous: Student Activity Book. (Now Age Illustrated Ser.). (Illus.). 1976. wkbk. 0.95 (ISBN 0-88301-286-3). Pendulum Pr.
--A Connecticut Yankee in King Arthur's Court: Student Activity Book. (Now Age Illustrated Ser.). (Illus.). (gr. 4-12). 1976. 0.95 (ISBN 0-88301-287-1). Pendulum Pr.
--The Hound of the Baskervilles: Student Activity Book. (Now Age Illustrated Ser.). (gr. 4-12). 1976. 0.95 (ISBN 0-88301-288-X). Pendulum Pr.
--The House of the Seven Gables: Student Activity Book. (Now Age Illustrated Ser.). (Illus.). (gr. 4-12). 1976. 0.95 (ISBN 0-88301-289-8). Pendulum Pr.
--Jane Eyre: Student Activity Book. (Now Age Illustrated Ser.). (Illus.). (gr. 4-12). 1976. wkbk. 0.95 (ISBN 0-88301-290-1). Pendulum Pr.
--The Last of the Mohicans: Student Activity Book. (Now Age Illustrated Ser.). (Illus.). (gr. 4-12). 1976. wkbk. 0.95 (ISBN 0-88301-291-X). Pendulum Pr.
--White Fang: Student Activity Book. (Now Age Illustrated Ser.). (Illus.). (gr. 4-12). 1976. wkbk. 0.95 (ISBN 0-88301-295-2). Pendulum Pr.
--Wuthering Heights: Student Activity Book. (Now Age Illustrated Ser.). (Illus.). (gr. 4-12). 1976. wkbk. 0.95 (ISBN 0-88301-296-0). Pendulum Pr.
Sohmer, Bernard, jt. auth. see Gondin, William R.
Sohn, David A. Good Looking. LC 75-27940. 1975. 8.95 (ISBN 0-912920-47-5). North Am Pub Co.
Sohner, Charles P. California Government & Politics Today. 3rd ed. 1979. pap. text ed. 4.95x (ISBN 0-673-15242-1). Scott F.
Sohner, Charles P. & Martin, Helen P. American Government & Politics Today. 3rd. ed. 1979. text ed. 12.95x (ISBN 0-673-15241-3); study guide 4.95x (ISBN 0-673-15243-X). Scott F.
Sohn-Rethel, Alfred. Economy & Class Structure of German Fascism. 1978. text ed. 15.50x (ISBN 0-906336-00-7, Trans. by M. Sohn-Rethel); pap. text ed. 7.75x (ISBN 0-906336-01-5). Humanities.
--Intellectual & Manual Labour: A Critique of Epistemology. LC 77-12975. (Critical Social Studies). 1978. text ed. 25.00x (ISBN 0-391-00774-2); pap. text ed. 10.25x (ISBN 0-333-23046-9). Humanities.
Sohns, Marvin L. & Buffington, Audrey V. El Libro De Medicion. (Illus.). 212p. (Span.). 1980. pap. 9.95 (ISBN 0-86582-029-5). Enrich.
--The Measurement Book. (Illus.). 1977. pap. 9.95 (ISBN 0-933358-00-8). Enrich.
Soil Chemistry, Soil Fertility & Soil Clay Mineralogy Commissions of the International Society of Soil Science, 13-18 July 1976, Jerusalem. Agrochemicals in Soils: Selected Papers. Banin, A. & Kafkafi, U., eds. LC 79-41750. 500p. 1980. 79.00 (ISBN 0-08-025914-6). Pergamon.
Soja, E. W. The Political Organization of Space. LC 70-135471. (CCG Resource Papers Ser.: No. 8). (Illus.). 1971. pap. text ed. 4.00 (ISBN 0-89291-055-0). Assn Am Geographers.
Sojka, G. Microbial Physiology. LC 77-11223. 1981. text ed. write for info. (ISBN 0-12-655250-9). Acad Pr.
Sokal, Michael M., ed. An Education in Psychology: James McKeen Cattell's Journal & Letters from Germany & England 1880-1888. 768p. 1980. text ed. 30.00x (ISBN 0-262-19185-7). MIT Pr.
Sokal, Robert R. & Rohlf, F. James. Biometry: The Principles & Practices of Statistics in Biological Research. 2nd ed. LC 81-4. 1981. text ed. price not set (ISBN 0-7167-1254-7). W H Freeman.
--Biometry, the Principles & Practice of Statistics in Biological Research. LC 68-16819. (Biology Ser.). (Illus.). 1969. text ed. 28.95x (ISBN 0-7167-0663-6). W H Freeman.
--Introduction to Biostatistics. LC 71-178257. (Illus.). 1973. text ed. 22.95x (ISBN 0-7167-0693-8). W H Freeman.
Sokal, Robert R., jt. auth. see Rohlf, F. James.
Sokal, Robert R., jt. auth. see Sneath, Peter H.
Sokel, Walter H. Franz Kafka. LC 66-26005. (Columbia Ser.: No. 19). (Orig.). 1966. pap. 2.00 (ISBN 0-231-02751-6, MW19). Columbia U Pr.
Sokkar, Jo A., jt. auth. see Soltow, Martha.
Sokol, David M. American Architecture & Art: A Guide to Information Sources. LC 73-17563. (American Studies Information Guide Ser.: Vol. 2). 480p. 1976. 30.00 (ISBN 0-8103-1255-7). Gale.
Sokolinsky, Martin, tr. see Gavoty, Bernard.
Sokoloff, A. The Biology of Tribolium: With Special Emphasis on Genetic Aspects, Vol. 3. 1978. 98.00x (ISBN 0-19-857512-2). Oxford U Pr.
--The Biology of Tribolium with Special Emphasis on Genetic Effects, Vol. 1. (Illus.). 1972. 45.00x (ISBN 0-19-857353-7). Oxford U Pr.
Sokoloff, Alexander. The Biology of Tribolium with Special Emphasis on Genetic Aspects, Vol. 2. (Illus.). 628p. 1975. 75.00x (ISBN 0-19-857381-2). Oxford U Pr.
Sokoloff, Alexander see Demerec, M.
Sokoloff, Natalie J. Between Love & Money: The Dialectics of Women, Work, & the Family. LC 80-17101. 300p. 1980. 26.95 (ISBN 0-03-055296-6). Praeger.
Sokolosky, Barbara A., ed. American Association of University Women Archives 1881-1976. 115p. 1980. pap. write for info. (ISBN 0-667-00651-6). Microfilming Corp.
Sokolov, A. A. Synchrotron Radiation. 1969. 50.00 (ISBN 0-08-012945-5). Pergamon.
Sokolov, E. N. & Vinogradova, O. S., eds. Neuronal Mechanisms of the Orienting Reflex. LC 75-23135. 302p. 1975. 19.95 (ISBN 0-470-92562-0, Pub. by Wiley). Krieger.
Sokolov, V., jt. auth. see Gligoric, S.
Sokolov, Yury M. Russian Folklore. Smith, Catherine R., tr. LC 79-134444. (Illus.). 1971. Repr. of 1966 ed. 30.00 (ISBN 0-8103-5020-3). Gale.
Sokolovskill. Statics of Granular Media. 1965. pap. 30.00 (ISBN 0-08-013624-9). Pergamon.
Sokolovskiy, V. D. Soviet Military Strategy. 3rd ed. Scott, Harriet F., tr. from Rus. LC 73-94042. (Illus.). 560p. 1975. pap. 29.50x (ISBN 0-8448-0311-1). Crane-Russak Co.
Sokolowska, Zofia, jt. auth. see Duleba, Wladyslaw.
Sokolyszyn, Aleksander & Wertsman, Vladimir, eds. Ukrainians in Canda & the United States: A Guide to Information Sources. (Ethnic Studies Information Guide Ser.: Vol. 7). 375p. 1981. 32.00 (ISBN 0-8103-1494-0). Gale.
Sola, Donald F. & Agard, Frederick B. Spanish Pocket Dictionary. 1954. 2.50 (ISBN 0-394-40064-X). Random.
Solan, Joseph M., et al, eds. A Moment of Vision. LC 80-68991. 80p. (Orig.). 1980. pap. 9.50 (ISBN 0-937968-00-5). Dark Sun.
Solar Age Magazine, ed. The Solar Age Resource Book: A Complete Guidebook for the Consumer to Harnessing the Power of Solar Energy, in Depth & up-to-Date. LC 78-74580. (Illus.). 1979. pap. 9.95 (ISBN 0-89696-050-1). SolarVision.
Solar Age Magazine, ed. see Solar Vision Inc.
Solar Cooling & Heating Forum, Dec. 13-15, 1976, Miami Beach. Solar Cooling & Heating: Architectural, Engineering & Legal Aspects, Proceedings, 3 vols. new ed. Veziroglu, T. N., ed. LC 77-28813. (Illus.). 1978. Set. text ed. 145.00 (ISBN 0-89116-165-1). Hemisphere Pub.
Solar Energy & Conservation Symposium-Workshop, Miami Beach, Florida, 1978. Solar Energy & Conservation: Technology, Commercialization, Utilization: Proceedings. Veziroglu, T. Nejat, ed. LC 79-19526. (Illus.). 2000p. 1980. 275.00 (ISBN 0-08-025551-5). Pergamon.
Solar Energy Conversion Course, 5th, University of Waterloo, Ontario, August 6-19, 1978. Solar Energy Conversion: An Introductory Course. Dixon, A. E. & Leslie, J. D., eds. LC 79-41159. (Illus.). 1979. 69.00 (ISBN 0-08-024744-X). Pergamon.
Solar Energy Group, Argonne National Laboratory. Design & Installation Manual for Thermal Storage. 2nd ed. 1981. 39.95 (ISBN 0-89934-009-1); pap. 24.95 (ISBN 0-89934-010-5). Solar Energy Info.
Solar Energy Group, Los Alamos Scientific Laboratory. Passive Solar Heating & Cooling Conference & Workshop Proceedings, 1976. 355p. 1980. pap. cancelled (ISBN 0-89934-021-0). Solar Energy Info.
Solar Energy Research Institute. Fuel from Farms. 161p. 1980. 20.95 (ISBN 0-89934-050-4, B947-PP); pap. 10.95 (ISBN 0-89934-051-2, B047-PP). Solar Energy Info.
--Solar Energy Information Locator - Nineteen Eighty. 60p. 1981. pap. 3.95 (ISBN 0-89934-089-X). Solar Energy Info.
Solar Energy Research Institute (SERI) Guide to Commercial-Scale Ethanol Production & Financing. 305p. 1981. 34.50 (ISBN 0-89934-118-7). Solar Energy Info.
Solar Vision Inc. Solar Age Catalog. Solar Age Magazine, ed. LC 79-79117. (Illus.). 232p. 1977. pap. 8.50 (ISBN 0-918984-00-9). Brick Hse Pub.
Solarex Corporation. Guide to Solar Electricity. 143p. 1979. pap. text ed. 6.95 (ISBN 0-686-65543-5). Solar Energy Info.
Solberg, Harry L., et al. Thermal Engineering. LC 60-11730. 1960. text ed. 26.95x (ISBN 0-471-81147-5). Wiley.
Solberg, William K. & Clark, Glenn T. Temporomandibular Joint Problems: Biological Diagnosis & Treatment. 177p. 1980. 39.00 (ISBN 0-931386-18-7). Quint Pub Co.
Solberg, Winton U. The University of Illinois, Eighteen Sixty-Seven to Eighteen Ninety-Four: An Intellectual & Cultural History. LC 68-11030. (Illus.). 1968. 17.50 o.p. (ISBN 0-252-72424-0). U of Ill Pr.
Solberg, Winton U., ed. The Federal Convention & the Formation of the Union of the American States. LC 58-9959. (YA) (gr. 9 up). 1958. pap. 10.95 (ISBN 0-672-60024-2, AHS19). Bobbs.
Solbrig, Otto T., ed. Demography & Evolution in Plant Populations. (Botanical Monographs Ser.: Vol. 15). 1980. monograph 32.50x (ISBN 0-520-03931-9). U of Cal Pr.
Solbrig, Otto T., et al, eds. Topics in Plant Population Biology. LC 78-27630. (Illus.). 1979. 27.50x (ISBN 0-231-04336-8). Columbia U Pr.
Soldati, Joseph A. Configurations of Faust: Three Studies in the Gothic (1798-1820) Varma, Devendra P., ed. LC 79-8482. (Gothic Studies & Dissertations Ser.). 1980. lib. bdg. 17.00x (ISBN 0-405-12662-X). Arno.
Sole, Carlos, jt. auth. see Sole, Yolanda.
Sole, William C. History of Irrigation in Adams County. 1969. pap. 1.95 (ISBN 0-934858-07-1). Adams County.
Sole, Yolanda & Sole, Carlos. Modern Spanish Syntax. 1977. text ed. 17.95x (ISBN 0-669-00193-7). Heath.
Soleillant, Claude. Activities & Projects: India in Color. LC 77-79499. (Activities & Projects Ser.). (Illus.). (gr. 2 up). 1977. 9.95 (ISBN 0-8069-4550-8); PLB 9.29 (ISBN 0-8069-4551-6). Sterling.
--Japan: Activities & Projects in Color. LC 79-91394. (Illus.). 96p. (gr. 2-12). 1980. 9.95 (ISBN 0-8069-4556-7); PLB 9.29 (ISBN 0-8069-4557-5). Sterling.
--Mexico: Activities & Projects in Color. LC 77-81955. (Activities & Projects Ser.). (Illus.). 96p. (English.). (gr. 3 up). 1978. 9.95 (ISBN 0-8069-4552-4); PLB 9.29 (ISBN 0-8069-4553-2). Sterling.
Soleillant, Claude, jt. auth. see Farnay, Josie.
Solem, jt. auth. see Hempel.
Solem, Alan. The Shell Makers: Introducing Mollusks. LC 73-20315. 304p. 1974. 16.95 (ISBN 0-471-81210-2, Pub. by Wiley-Interscience). Wiley.
Soleri, Paolo. Arcology: The City in the Image of Man. 1970. reduced size o.p. 27.50x (ISBN 0-262-19060-5); pap. 14.95 (ISBN 0-262-69041-1). MIT Pr.
--The Bridge Between Matter & Spirit Is Matter Becoming Spirit. LC 72-87501. 280p. 1973. pap. 2.95 (ISBN 0-385-02361-8, Anch). Doubleday.
Solesbury, William. Policy in Urban Planning: Structure Plans, Local Plans, & Urban Development. 1974. 18.00 (ISBN 0-08-017758-1). Pergamon.
Solga, Tim, jt. auth. see Rights, Mollie.
Solheim, B. Cell Wall Biochemistry Related to Specificity in Host-Plant Pathogen Interactions. 1977. pap. 43.00x (ISBN 82-00-05141-2, Dist. by Columbia U Pr). Universitet.
Soligo, Ronald see Berry, R. Albert.
Soliman, O., jt. auth. see Favez, G.
Solinas, PierNico. Ultimate Porno. LC 80-69871. 1981. 14.95 (ISBN 0-938112-00-7). Eyecontact.
Solinger, Dorothy J. Regional Government & Political Integration in Southwest China, 1949-1954: A Case Study. LC 75-22662. 1977. 27.50x (ISBN 0-520-03104-0). U of Cal Pr.
Solinger, Jacob. The Apparel Manufacturing Handbook. 800p. 1981. text ed. 60.00 (ISBN 0-442-21904-0). Van Nos Reinhold.
Solis, jt. auth. see Kozloff.
Solis, Leopoldo. Economic Policy Reform in Mexico: A Case Study for Developing Countries. LC 80-26937. (Pergamon Press Series on International Development). 225p. 1981. 25.00 (ISBN 0-08-026330-5). Pergamon.

Solis, M. Leopoldo, jt. auth. see Brothers, Dwight S.

Solis De Meras, Gonzalo. Pedro Menendez De Aviles. McAlister, Lyle N., ed. Connor, Jeannette T., tr. LC 64-19155. (Floridiana Facsimile & Reprint Ser). 1964. Repr. of 1567 ed. 16.00 (ISBN 0-8130-0214-1). U Presses Fla.

Solkey, Lee. Dummy up & Deal. 160p. (Orig.). 1980. pap. 3.95 (ISBN 0-89650-677-0). Gamblers.

Solkov, Arnold, jt. auth. see Buckley, Edmund H.

Solla Price, Derek J. De see Price, Derek J.

Sollertinsky, Dmitri & Sollertinsky, Ludmilla. Pages from the Life of Dmitri Shostakovich. Hobbs, Graham & Midgely, Charles, trs. LC 79-3364. 1980. 12.95 (ISBN 0-15-170730-8). HarBraceJ.

Sollertinsky, Ludmilla, jt. auth. see Sollertinsky, Dmitri.

Sollors, Werner. Amiri Baraka - Leroi Jones. 1978. 17.50 (ISBN 0-231-04226-4). Columbia U Pr.

Solly, Henry. Working Men's Social Clubs & Educational Institutes: London Nineteen Four. LC 79-56943. (The English Working Class Ser.). 1980. lib. bdg. 22.00 (ISBN 0-8240-0124-9). Garland Pub.

Solman, Joseph. The Monotypes of Joseph Solman. (Illus.). 1977. lib. bdg. 18.95 (ISBN 0-306-77425-9). Da Capo.

Solmen, Lewis C. & Gordon, Joanne J. The Characteristics & Needs of Adults in Postsecondary Education. 1981. 20.95 (ISBN 0-669-04361-3). Lexington Bks.

Solmon, Lewis C. Macroeconomics. 3rd ed. LC 79-25516. 480p. 1980. pap. text ed. 12.95 (ISBN 0-201-07217-3); student guide avail. (ISBN 0-201-07220-3). A-W.

--Male & Female Graduate Students: The Question of Equal Opportunity. LC 75-43725. (Special Studies). 1976. text ed. 25.95 (ISBN 0-275-22870-3). Praeger.

--Microeconomics. 3rd ed. LC 79-25515. 528p. 1980. pap. text ed. 12.95 (ISBN 0-201-07218-1); student guide avail. (ISBN 0-201-07221-1). A-W.

Solmon, Lewis C., et al. College As a Training Ground for Jobs. LC 77-2939. (Special Studies). 1977. text ed. 22.95 (ISBN 0-275-24450-4). Praeger.

Solmsen, Friedrich. Intellectual Experiments of the Greek Enlightenment. LC 74-25629. 296p. 1975. 34.00x (ISBN 0-691-07201-9). Princeton U Pr.

Solnick, Robert L. Sexuality & Aging. rev. ed. LC 78-51932. 1978. pap. 5.50 (ISBN 0-88474-023-4). USC Andrus Geron.

Solnit, Albert, jt. auth. see Jones, Warren W.

Solnit, Albert J., et al, eds. The Psychoanalytic Study of the Child, Vol. 35. LC 80-5398. (Illus.). 544p. 1980. 27.50x (ISBN 0-300-02607-2). Yale U Pr.

Solo, Len. Alternative, Innovative & Traditional Schools: Some Personal Views. LC 80-7950. 232p. 1980. lib. bdg. 17.25 (ISBN 0-8191-1087-6); pap. text ed. 9.50 (ISBN 0-8191-1088-4). U Pr of Amer.

Solo, Robert. Across the High Technology Threshold: The Case of Synthetic Rubber. 130p. 1980. Repr. of 1959 ed. lib. bdg. 17.50 (ISBN 0-8482-6222-0). Norwood Edns.

Solodow, Joseph B. The Latin Particle Quidem. (American Philological Association, American Classical Studies). 1978. pap. 6.00 (ISBN 0-89130-252-2, 400404). Scholars Pr Ca.

Soloff, Mordecai, et al. Your Siddur. (Sacred Hebrew Ser.). (Illus.). 175p. 1981. pap. 3.50 (ISBN 0-86628-001-4). Ridgefield Pub.

--Jewish Life. (Sacred Hebrew Ser.). (Illus.). 112p. (Orig.). 1980. pap. 3.50 (ISBN 0-86628-000-6). Ridgefield Pub.

Soloman, J. B., ed. Developmental & Comparative Immunology I: First Congress of Developmental & Comparative Immunology, 27 July-1 August 1980, Aberdeen. (Illus.). 580p. 1980. 90.00 (ISBN 0-08-025922-7). Pergamon.

Solomita, Alec, jt. auth. see Slater, Scott.

Solomon. Arise, My Love. LC 75-4077. (Illus.). 56p. (From King James Version - Song of Songs). 1975. 15.95 (ISBN 0-570-03253-9, 15-2161); pap. 6.95 (ISBN 0-570-03712-3, 12-2614). Concordia.

Solomon, Arthur, et al. Interpersonal Communication: A Cross-Disciplinary Approach. 120p. 1970. 12.75 (ISBN 0-398-01810-3). C C Thomas.

Solomon, Barbara. Black Empowerment. LC 76-36972. 1976. 17.50x (ISBN 0-231-04086-5). Columbia U Pr.

Solomon, Barbara H., ed. Ain't We Got Fun: Essays, Lyrics, & Stories of the Twenties. 1980. pap. 2.95 (ISBN 0-451-61846-7, ME 1846, Ment). NAL.

Solomon, Ben & Bowers, Ethel M. You Can Be a Leader. 140p. (Orig.). 1981. pap. 4.95 (ISBN 0-936626-03-8). Leadership Pr.

Solomon, Brad. Jake & Katie. 304p. (Orig.). 1980. pap. 2.50 (ISBN 0-380-52969-6, 52969). Avon.

--The Open Shadow. LC 78-13486. 1979. 10.00 (ISBN 0-671-40057-6). Summit Bks.

Solomon, Charles R. Counseling with the Mind of Christ: The Dynamics of Spirituotherapy. 1977. pap. 4.95 (ISBN 0-8007-0889-X). Revell.

Solomon, Daniel & Kendall, Arthur J. Children in Classrooms: An Investigation of Person-Environment Interaction. (Praeger Special Studies). 1979. 25.95 (ISBN 0-03-047071-4). Praeger.

Solomon, David. Inside the Australian Parliament. LC 77-78557. 1978. text ed. 15.95x (ISBN 0-86861-344-4); pap. text ed. 8.95x (ISBN 0-86861-352-5). Allen Unwin.

Solomon, Erwin, jt. auth. see Alexander, Kern.

Solomon, Erwin S., jt. ed. see Abbott, Earl L.

Solomon, Ezra. Theory of Financial Management. LC 63-8405. (Illus.). 1963. 12.50x (ISBN 0-231-02604-8). Columbia U Pr.

Solomon, Hannah. Bake Bread. LC 76-18807. (Illus.). (gr. 5-12). 1976. 7.95 (ISBN 0-397-31670-4); pap. 3.95 o.p. (ISBN 0-397-31671-2). Lippincott.

Solomon, Hassim M. Community Corrections. (Criminal Justice Ser.). 442p. 1976. text ed. 16.50 (ISBN 0-205-04996-6, 824996-2); instr's manual free (ISBN 0-205-04997-4, 824997-0). Allyn.

Solomon, Herbert & Zinn, Walter. The Complete Guide to Eye Care, Eyeglasses & Contact Lenses. LC 77-8753. 1977. 9.95 (ISBN 0-8119-0281-1). Fell.

Solomon, J. Structure of Space. LC 73-8543. (Illus.). 219p. 1974. 15.95 (ISBN 0-470-81221-4). Halsted Pr.

Solomon, Jerome. Financial & Accounting Handbook for the Service Industries. 560p. 1981. 29.95 (ISBN 0-8436-0854-4). CBI Pub.

Solomon, Joan. Science Teaching. 224p. 1981. 25.00x (ISBN 0-7099-2304-X, Pub. by Croom Helm Ltd England). Biblio Dist.

Solomon, Joel & Keeley, Kim. Alcohol & Drugs: Similarities & Differences. 1981. write for info. (ISBN 0-88416-306-7). PSG Pub.

Solomon, Lawrence. The Conserver Solution. LC 78-19216. 1979. 12.50 o.p. (ISBN 0-385-14533-0); pap. 6.95 (ISBN 0-385-14534-9). Doubleday.

--Energy Shock: After the Oil Runs Out. LC 80-1072. 224p. 1981. 17.95 (ISBN 0-385-17160-9); pap. 9.95 (ISBN 0-385-17161-7). Doubleday.

Solomon, Lawrence M., et al. Adolescent Dermatology. LC 77-78574. (Major Problems in Clinical Pediatrics Ser.: Vol. 19). (Illus.). 1978. text ed. 39.50 (ISBN 0-7216-8492-0). Saunders.

Solomon, Lewis C. Economics. LC 79-25514. 832p. 1980. text ed. 18.95 (ISBN 0-201-07635-7); avail. student guide 8.95 (ISBN 0-201-07637-3). A-W.

Solomon, Lois & Reitman, Anita. Calico Pantry Cookbook. 320p. 1980. pap. 6.95 (ISBN 0-346-12475-1). Cornerstone.

Solomon, M. E., jt. ed. see Price-Jones, D.

Solomon, Martin B., jt. auth. see Kennedy, Michael.

Solomon, Martin B., Jr. & Lovan, Nora G. Annotated Bibliography of Films in Automation, Data Processing, & Computer Science. LC 67-23778. 1967. pap. 4.50x (ISBN 0-8131-1145-5). U Pr of Ky.

Solomon, Miriam L., ed. see Art Directors Club of New York.

Solomon, Morton B., et al. Main Hurdman & Cranston Guide to Preparing Financial Reports, 1981. 272p. 1981. 75.00 (ISBN 0-471-09104-9, Pub. by Wiley-Interscience). Wiley.

Solomon, Nathan A., ed. Nuclear Medicine. 2nd. ed. (Medical Examination Review Bk. Ser.: Vol. 25). 1977. spiral bdg. 16.50 (ISBN 0-87488-133-1). Med Exam.

Solomon, Neil. Family Therapy & Social Change. 1981. text ed. 22.50x (ISBN 0-8290-0088-7); audio cassette incl. Irvington.

--Stop Smoking, Lose Weight. 320p. 1981. 11.95 (ISBN 0-399-12600-7). Putnam.

Solomon, Neil & Knudson, Mary. Doctor Solomon's Easy, No Risk Diet. 240p. 1976. pap. 1.95 o.s.i. (ISBN 0-446-89012-X). Warner Bks.

Solomon, P. & Glueck, B. C., eds. Recent Research on Schizophrenia. 1964. pap. 4.00 o.p. (ISBN 0-685-24874-7, 019). Am Psychiatric.

Solomon, P. M. & Edmunds, M. G. Giant Molecular Clouds in the Galaxy. (Illus.). 348p. 1980. 48.00 (ISBN 0-08-023068-7). Pergamon.

Solomon, Pearl C. Dickens & Melville in Their Time. LC 74-13307. 1975. 12.50x (ISBN 0-231-03889-5). Columbia U Pr.

Solomon, Peter H., Jr. Soviet Criminologists & Criminal Policy. LC 77-3357. (Studies of the Russian Institute Ser.). 1978. 17.50x (ISBN 0-231-04316-3). Columbia U Pr.

Solomon, Philippa H., jt. auth. see Nakanishi, Koji.

Solomon, Richard H. Mao's Revolution & the Chinese Political Culture. (Center for Chinese Studies, Univ. of Michigan). 1971. 28.50x (ISBN 0-520-01806-0); pap. 5.95 (ISBN 0-520-02250-5, CAL246). U of Cal Pr.

--A Revolution Is Not a Dinner Party: A Feast of Images of the Maoist Transformation of China. LC 74-25123. 1978. 6.95 o.p. (ISBN 0-385-09926-6, Anch). Doubleday.

Solomon, Robert. From Rationalism to Existentialism: The Existentialist & Their Nineteenth Century Backgrounds, 1972. 1978. pap. text ed. 7.95x (ISBN 0-391-00850-1). Humanities.

Solomon, Robert C. Introducing the Existentialists. (Philosophical Dialogues Ser.). 80p. 1981. lib. bdg. 9.50 (ISBN 0-915145-00-6); pap. text ed. 2.50 (ISBN 0-915145-01-4). Hackett Pub.

--Introducing the German Idealists. (Philosophical Dialogue Ser.). 80p. 1981. lib. bdg. 9.50 (ISBN 0-915145-02-2); pap. text ed. 2.50 (ISBN 0-915145-03-0). Hackett Pub.

--The Passions. LC 74-33691. 1977. pap. 3.95 (ISBN 0-385-12220-9, Anch). Doubleday.

Solomon, Robert C., ed. Phenomenology & Existentialism. LC 79-66420. 1979. pap. text ed. 10.50 (ISBN 0-8191-0826-X). U Pr of Amer.

Solomon, Ruth F. The Candlestick & the Cross. 416p. 1980. pap. 2.75 (ISBN 0-515-05249-3). Jove Pubns.

--The Eagle & the Dove. 512p. 1980. pap. 2.75 (ISBN 0-515-05248-5). Jove Pubns.

--Two Lives, Two Lands. 384p. 1980. pap. 2.75 (ISBN 0-515-05250-7). Jove Pubns.

Solomon, Shirl. Scryptics. (Orig.). 1977. pap. 1.75 o.p. (ISBN 0-451-07555-2, E7555, Sig). NAL.

Solomon, Steve. The Complete Guide to Organic Gardening West of the Cascades. 192p. 1981. pap. 9.95 (ISBN 0-914718-58-4). Pacific Search.

Solomon, Susan G. Soviet Agrarian Debate: A Controversy in Social Science, 1923-1929. LC 77-21555. (Special Studies on the Soviet Union & Eastern Europe Ser.). (Illus.). 1978. lib. bdg. 26.50x (ISBN 0-89158-339-4). Westview.

Solomon, Susan G., jt. ed. see Lubrano, Linda L.

Solomons, David. Divisional Performance: Measurement & Control. 1968. pap. text ed. 10.50 (ISBN 0-256-00529-X). Irwin.

Solomons, T. W., jt. auth. see Truitt, Willis H.

Solomons, T. W. Graham. Organic Chemistry. 2nd ed. 1980. text ed. 28.95 (ISBN 0-471-04213-7); solutions manual avail. (ISBN 0-471-05770-3); tests avail. (ISBN 0-471-05137-3). Wiley.

Solovier, S. M., ed. History of Russia: Vol. 24, the Character of Old Russia. Muller, Alexander V., tr. 1980. 20.00 (ISBN 0-87569-034-3). Academic Intl.

Soloviev, Sergei M. History of Russia: Peter the Great: the Great Reforms Being, Vol. 16. Papmehl, K. A., tr. 1981. 20.00 (ISBN 0-87569-042-4). Academic Intl.

Soloviev, V. G. Theory of Complex Nuclei. 1976. 67.00 (ISBN 0-08-018053-1). Pergamon.

Solow, Robert M. Growth Theory: An Exposition. (Illus.). 1970. 8.95x (ISBN 0-19-501295-X). Oxford U Pr.

Solow, Robert M., jt. auth. see Blinder, Alan S.

Solrac, Odelot. Tortola Valencia & Her Times. 1981. 11.95 (ISBN 0-533-04563-0). Vantage.

Solt, David L., jt. auth. see Naiman, Robert J.

Soltau, Henry W. Holy Vessels & Furniture of the Tabernacle. LC 74-85428. (Illus.). 1973. 8.95 (ISBN 0-8254-3707-5). Kregel.

--Tabernacle, Priesthood & the Offerings. Enlarged type ed. LC 72-88590. 1974. 9.95 (ISBN 0-8254-3703-2). Kregel.

Soltis, Andrew. The Art of Defense in Chess. LC 74-25728. 1975. 9.95 o.p. (ISBN 0-679-13043-8). McKay.

Soltis, Andy, jt. auth. see Bisquier, Arthur.

Soltis, Andy, jt. auth. see McCormick, Gene H.

Soltis, Andy, jt. auth. see Reinfeld, Fred.

Soltis, Jonas, ed. Philosophy & Education. LC 80-83743. (National Society for the Study of Education 80th Yearbooks: Pt. I). 288p. 1981. lib. bdg. price not set. U of Chicago Pr.

Soltis, Jonas F. An Introduction to the Analysis of Educational Concepts. 2nd rev. ed. LC 77-79465. (Education Ser.). (Illus.). 1978. pap. text ed. 6.95 (ISBN 0-201-06989-X). A-W.

Soltow, Martha & Sokkar, Jo A. Industrial Relations & Personnel Management: Selected Information Sources. LC 78-31795. 294p. 1979. lib. bdg. 12.00 (ISBN 0-8108-1203-7). Scarecrow.

Soltow, Martha J. & Wery, Mary K. American Women & the Labor Movement, 1825-1974: An Annotated Bibliography. LC 76-40169. 1976. 10.00 (ISBN 0-8108-0986-9). Scarecrow.

Soltz, Vicki, jt. auth. see Dreikurs, Rudolf.

Soltzberg, Len, et al. BASIC & Chemistry. 1975. pap. text ed. 9.75 (ISBN 0-395-21720-2). HM.

Solvit, Marie-Janine. Magnificent Macrame: 50 Projects You Can Create. LC 78-66295. (Illus.). 1979. 19.95 (ISBN 0-8069-5390-X); lib. bdg. 16.79 (ISBN 0-8069-5391-8). Sterling.

--Pictures in Patchwork. LC 76-51189. (Illus.). 120p. 1981. pap. 8.95. Sterling.

--Pictures in Patchwork. LC 76-51189. (Illus.). 1977. 16.95 (ISBN 0-8069-5380-2); lib. bdg. 14.99 (ISBN 0-8069-5381-0). Sterling.

Solymar, L. Lectures on Electromagnetic Theory: A Short Course for Engineers. (Illus.). 1976. text ed. 39.95x (ISBN 0-19-856126-1); pap. 17.95x (ISBN 0-19-856137-7). Oxford U Pr.

Solymar, L. & Walsh, D. Lectures on the Electrical Properties of Materials. 2nd ed. (Illus.). 1980. 36.50x (ISBN 0-19-851144-2); pap. 18.95x (ISBN 0-19-851145-0). Oxford U Pr.

Solzhenitsyn, A., et al. From Under the Rubble. 308p. 1981. pap. 6.95 (ISBN 0-89526-890-6). Regnery-Gateway.

Solzhenitsyn, Aleksandr. We Never Make Mistakes. Blackstock, Paul W., tr. from Rus. 1971. pap. 3.95 (ISBN 0-393-00598-4, Norton Lib). Norton.

Solzhenitsyn, Aleksandr I. East & West: The Nobel Lecture on Literature, a World Split Apart, Letter to the Soviet Leaders, & a BBC Interview with Aleksandr I. Solzhenitsyn. LC 79-5222. 1980. pap. 1.95 (ISBN 0-06-080508-0, P 508, PL). Har-Row.

Solzhenitsyn, Alexander. One Day in the Life of Ivan Denisovich. Gillon, Aitken, tr. from Rus. 174p. 1971. 15.00 (ISBN 0-374-22642-3); pap. 1.50 o.p. (ISBN 0-686-66696-8). FS&G.

Solzhenitsyn, Alexandr I. First Circle. Whitney, Thomas P., tr. from Rus. LC 68-54547. 1968. 20.00 o.p. (ISBN 0-06-013949-8, HarpT). Har-Row.

Solzman, David M. Waterway Industrial Sites: A Chicago Case Study. LC 66-29231. (Research Papers Ser.: No. 107). 138p. 1967. pap. 8.00 (ISBN 0-89065-016-0). U Chicago Dept Geog.

Solzman, E. Twentieth Century Music: An Introduction. 2nd ed. 1974. pap. 10.95 (ISBN 0-13-935007-1). P-H.

Som, Ranjan K. A Manual of Sampling Techniques. 390p. 1973. 27.50x o.p. (ISBN 0-8448-0785-0). Crane-Russak Co.

Soma, John T. The Computer Industry: An Economic-Legal Analysis of Its Technology & Growth. LC 76-2989. (Illus.). 1976. 21.50 (ISBN 0-669-00643-2). Lexington Bks.

Soman, Robert. Natural Foods Ice Cream Book. (Orig.). 1975. pap. 1.50 o.s.i. (ISBN 0-515-03575-0, A3575). Jove Pubns.

Somanath, V. S., jt. ed. see Brada, Josef C.

Somasundaran, P., ed. Fine Particles Processing, 2 vols. LC 79-57344. (Illus.). 1865p. 1980. text ed. 45.00x (ISBN 0-89520-275-1). Soc Mining Eng.

Somasundaran, P. & Arbiter, N., eds. Beneficiation of Mineral Fines. LC 79-91945. (Illus.). 406p. (Orig.). 1979. pap. text ed. 21.00x (ISBN 0-89520-259-X). Soc Mining Eng.

Sombart, Werner. The Quintessence of Capitalism. 1967. 22.50 (ISBN 0-86527-162-3). Fertig.

Somekh, Emile. Allergy & Your Child. LC 73-14291. 288p. 1974. 9.95 o.s.i. (ISBN 0-06-013969-2, HarpT). Har-Row.

Somer, John L. & Cooper, Barbara E. American & British Literature Nineteen Forty Five to Nineteen Seventy Five: An Annotated Bibliography of Contemporary Scholarship. LC 79-19299. 1980. 20.00x (ISBN 0-7006-0195-3). Regents Pr KS.

Somerlott, Robert. Writing of Modern Fiction. text ed. 8.95 (ISBN 0-87116-068-4). Writer.

Somers, Anne R. & Fabian, Dorothy R. The Geriatric Imperative: An Introduction to Gerontology & Clinical Geriatrics. 320p. 1981. pap. 14.95 (ISBN 0-686-69606-9). ACC.

Somers, Anne R. & Somers, Herman M. Health & Health Care: Policies in Perspective. LC 77-76921. 1977. 29.95 (ISBN 0-912862-45-9); pap. text ed. 15.95 (ISBN 0-912862-49-1). Aspen Systems.

Somers, Anne R., jt. auth. see Somers, Herman M.

Somers, David J. Learning Functional Words & Phrases for Everyday Living. Bk. 1, 1977. pap. 2.25x (ISBN 0-88323-135-2, 223); Bk. 2, 1980. pap. 2.25x (ISBN 0-88323-159-X, 249). Richards Pub.

Somers, Gerald G., ed. Labor, Management, & Social Policy: Essays in the John R. Commons Tradition. 1963. 27.50 (ISBN 0-299-02870-4). U of Wis Pr.

--Retraining the Unemployed. 1968. 29.50x (ISBN 0-299-04820-9). U of Wis Pr.

Somers, Herman M. & Somers, Anne R. Doctors, Patients, & Health Insurance: The Organization & Financing of Medical Care. 1961. 15.95 (ISBN 0-8157-8036-2). Brookings.

Somers, Herman M., jt. auth. see Somers, Anne R.

Somers, John & Jacob, Giles. Judgment of Whole Kingdoms & Nations. Berkowitz, David S. & Thorne, Samuel E., eds. LC 77-86589. (Classics of English Legal History in the Modern Era Ser.: Vol. 19). 467p. 1979. lib. bdg. 40.00 (ISBN 0-8240-3069-9). Garland Pub.

Somers, John, jt. auth. see Williams, Thomas.

Somerscales, Euan F. & Knudsen, James G., eds. Fouling of Heat Transfer Equipment: International Conference 1979. LC 80-28694. (Illus.). 700p. 1981. text ed. 75.00 (ISBN 0-89116-199-6). Hemisphere Pub.

Somerset, J. A., ed. Four Tudor Interludes. (Renaissance Library). 192p. 1974. text ed. 18.75x (ISBN 0-485-13602-3, Athlone Pr); pap. text ed. 10.00x (ISBN 0-485-12602-8, Athlone Pr). Humanities.

Somers-Heidhues, Mary. Southeast Asia's Chinese Minorities. (Studies in Contemporary South Asia). 160p. 1974. pap. text ed. 4.50x o.p. (ISBN 0-582-71039-1). Longman.

Somervill, John W., jt. auth. see Rimm, David C.

Somerville, Christopher. Walking Old Railways. LC 78-74078. 1979. 14.95 (ISBN 0-7153-7681-0). David & Charles.

Somerville, James M. Total Commitment: Blondel's L'Action. 1979. 9.50 (ISBN 0-89012-015-3). Anima Pubns.

Somerville, John. Critical. 4.50 o.p. (ISBN 0-8062-1230-6). Carlton.

Somerville, John, jt. ed. see Santoni, Ronald.

Somerville, Robert. Pope Alexander III & the Council of Tours (1163) A Study of Ecclesiastical Politics & Institutions in the Twelfth Century. (UCLA Center for Medieval & Renaissance Studies: Vol. 12). 1978. 14.50x (ISBN 0-520-03184-9). U of Cal Pr.

Somerville, Rose M., ed. Intimate Relationships: Marriage, Family & Lifestyles Through Literature. (Family & Consumer Science Ser.). (Illus.). 480p. 1975. ref. ed. 16.95 (ISBN 0-13-476861-2); pap. 10.95 (ISBN 0-13-476879-5). P-H.

Sominskii, I. S., jt. auth. see Faddeev, D. K.

Somit, Albert & Tanenhaus, Joseph. Development of American Political Science: From Burgess to Behavioralism. enl. ed. 1981. 21.00x (ISBN 0-8290-0122-0); pap. text ed. 10.95x (ISBN 0-8290-0123-9). Irvington.

Somjee, A. H. Political Theory of John Dewey. LC 67-19028. 1968. text ed. 14.65x (ISBN 0-8077-2191-3). Tchrs Coll.

--Politics of a Periurban Community in India. 1966. 2.50x o.p. (ISBN 0-210-27091-8). Asia.

Somjen, George. Sensory Coding in the Mammalian Nervous System. LC 75-31519. 286p. 1975. softcover 7.95 (ISBN 0-306-20020-1, Rosetta). Plenum Pub.

Sommer, Armand & Kedzie, Daniel P. Your Future in Insurance. LC 70-114117. (Career Guidance Ser). 1971. pap. 3.50 (ISBN 0-668-02249-3). Arco.

Sommer, Carol, jt. ed. see Wilgus, D. K.

Sommer, Elyse & Sommer, Mike. The Two-Boss Business. Lawson, K., ed. (Illus.). 160p. 1980. 12.95 (ISBN 0-88421-071-5). Butterick Pub.

Sommer, John G. Beyond Charity: U. S. Voluntary Aid for a Changing Third World. LC 77-89276. 192p. 1977. pap. 3.95 (ISBN 0-686-28706-1). Overseas Dev Council.

--U. S. Voluntary Aid to the Third World: What Is Its Future? LC 75-43481. (Development Papers: No. 20). 68p. 1975. pap. 1.50 (ISBN 0-686-28677-4). Overseas Dev Council.

Sommer, Margaret F. The Shaker Seed Industry. (Illus., Orig.). 1972. lib. bdg. 6.50 (ISBN 0-937942-05-7); pap. text ed. 3.00 (ISBN 0-937942-06-5). Shaker Mus.

Sommer, Mike, jt. auth. see Sommer, Elyse.

Sommer, Robert. The Mind's Eye. 1978. 9.95 o.p. (ISBN 0-440-03950-9). Delacorte.

Sommer, Werner & Schoenfeld, Hanns-Martin. Management Dictionary. 5th rev. enl. ed. 621p. 1979. text ed. 34.25x. De Gruyter.

Sommerfeld, Arnold. Lectures on Theoretical Physics. Incl. Vol. 1. Mechanics. 1952. text ed. 19.95 (ISBN 0-12-654668-1); pap. 9.95 (ISBN 0-12-654670-3); Vol. 2. Mechanics of Deformable Bodies. 1950. text ed. 19.95 (ISBN 0-12-654650-9); pap. text ed. 9.95 (ISBN 0-12-654652-5); Vol. 3. Electrodynamics. 1952. text ed. 19.95 (ISBN 0-12-654662-2); pap. 9.95 (ISBN 0-12-654664-9); Vol. 4. Optics. 1954. text ed. 19.95 (ISBN 0-12-654674-6); pap. 9.95 (ISBN 0-12-654676-2); Vol. 5. Thermodynamics & Statistical Mechanics. 1956. text ed. 19.95 (ISBN 0-12-654680-0); pap. 9.95 (ISBN 0-12-654682-7); Vol. 6. Partial Differential Equations in Physics. 1949. 19.95 (ISBN 0-12-654656-8); pap. text ed. 9.95 (ISBN 0-12-654658-4). Acad Pr.

Sommerfeld, Ray M. The Dow Jones-Irwin Guide to Tax Planning. 3rd ed. 364p. 1981. pap. 9.95 (ISBN 0-87094-233-6). Dow Jones-Irwin.

--The Dow Jones-Irwin Guide to Tax Planning. rev. ed. LC 77-83537. 1978. 17.50 o.p. (ISBN 0-87094-155-0). Dow Jones-Irwin.

--Federal Taxes & Management Decisions. rev. ed. 1978. pap. text ed. 12.95 (ISBN 0-256-02069-8). Irwin.

Sommerfeldt, John R., ed. Abba: Guides to Wholeness & Holiness East & West. (Cistercian Studies Ser.: No. 38). 1981. price not set (ISBN 0-87907-838-3). Cistercian Pubns.

Sommerfeldt, John R. & Elder, E. Rozanne, eds. Studies in Medieval Culture, Vols. 6 & 7. combined ed. 1976. write for info. Medieval Inst.

Sommerfeldt, John R. & Elder, Rozanne E., eds. Studies in Medieval Culture, Vols. 8 & 9. combined ed. 1976. write for info. Medieval Inst.

Sommerfeldt, John R. & Seiler, Thomas H., eds. Studies in Medieval Culture, Vol. 1. 1977. write for info. Medieval Inst.

--Studies in Medieval Culture, Vol. 10. 1977. write for info. Medieval Inst.

--Studies in Medieval Culture, Vol. 12. 1978. write for info. Medieval Inst.

Sommerfeldt, John R., jt. ed. see Elder, E. Rozanne.

Sommerfeldt, John R., ed. see Studies in Medieval Culture, IIII.

Sommerfeldt, John R., ed. see Studies in Medieval Culture I,Kalamazoo.

Sommerfeldt, John R., et al, eds. see Studies in Medieval Culture, IV 2, Kalamazoo.

Sommerfeldt, John R., et al, eds. see Studies in Medieval Culture, V.

Sommerfeldt, John R., et al, eds. see 1.

Sommerfeldt, John R., et al, eds. see 3,Kalamazoo.

Sommerfield, Sylvia F. Rebel Pride. 512p. (Orig.). 1980. pap. 2.75 (ISBN 0-89083-691-4). Zebra.

Sommerfield, Sylvie F. Erin's Ecstasy. 320p. (Orig.). 1980. pap. 2.50 (ISBN 0-89083-656-6). Zebra.

--Tazia's Torment. 416p. (Orig.). 1980. pap. 2.50 (ISBN 0-89083-669-8). Zebra.

Sommerlad, Lloyd E. National Communications Systems: Some Policy Issues & Options. (Reports & Papers on Mass Communication Ser: No. 74). 35p. 1975. pap. 2.50 (ISBN 92-3-101248-7, U398, UNESCO). Unipub.

Sommernitz, Harry, tr. see Sedivec, V. & Flek, J.

Sommers. Pathology Annual: 1975, Vol. 10. (Illus.). 1975. 25.50 o.p. (ISBN 0-8385-7744-X). ACC.

--Pathology Annual: 1976, Vol. 11. (Illus.). 1976. 27.50 o.p. (ISBN 0-8385-7745-8). ACC.

--Pathology Annual: 1977, Vol. 12, Pt. 2. (Illus.). 1977. 32.50 (ISBN 0-8385-7749-0). ACC.

--Pathology Annual: 1977, Vol. 12, Pt. 1. (Illus.). 1977. 28.50 (ISBN 0-8385-7748-2). ACC.

Sommers, ed. Pathology Decennials 1966-1975, 7 vols. Incl. Cardiovascular Pathology Decennial 1966-1975. (Illus.). 22.50 o.p. (ISBN 0-8385-1050-7); Endocrine Pathology Decennial 1966-1975. (Illus.). 26.50 o.p. (ISBN 0-8385-2201-7); Gastrointestinal & Hepatic Pathology Decennial 1966-1975. (Illus.). 24.75 o.p. (ISBN 0-8385-3092-3); Genital & Mammary Pathology Decennial 1966-1975. (Illus.). 24.75 o.p. (ISBN 0-8385-3123-7); Hematologic & Lymphoid Pathology Decennial 1966-1975. (Illus.). 26.50 o.p. (ISBN 0-8385-3683-2); Kidney Pathology Decennial 1966-1975. (Illus.). 27.00 o.p. (ISBN 0-8385-5192-0); Pulmonary Pathology Decennial 1966-1975. (Illus.). 25.50 o.p. (ISBN 0-8385-7952-3). 1975. 137.00 set o.p. (ISBN 0-8385-7746-6). ACC.

Sommers, Helen. The Married Single. 1981. 4.95 (ISBN 0-8062-1548-8). Carlton.

Sommers, J. & Ybarra-Frausto, T. Modern Chicano Writers: A Collection of Critical Essays. 1979. 10.95 (ISBN 0-13-589721-1); pap. 3.45 (ISBN 0-13-589713-0). P-H.

Sommers, Montrose S., jt. ed. see Kernan, Jerome B.

Sommers, Richard J. & Vandiver, Frank E. Richmond Redeemed: The Seige at Petersburg. LC 79-7844. (Illus.). 648p. 1981. 22.50 (ISBN 0-385-15626-X). Doubleday.

Sommers, Sheldon C., jt. auth. see Rotterdam, Heidrun Z.

Sommers, Sheldon C. & Rosen, Paul P., eds. Pathology Annual: Cumulative Index 1966-1979. (Pathology Annual Ser.). 208p. 1980. 13.50x (ISBN 0-8385-7766-0). ACC.

--Pathology Annual 1978, Pt. 2. (Illus.). 1978. 32.50 (ISBN 0-8385-7752-0). ACC.

--Pathology Annual: 1979, Vol. 14, Pt. 1. (Illus.). 451p. 1979. 33.50x (ISBN 0-8385-7756-3). ACC.

--Pathology Annual 1979, Vol. 15, Pt. 2. (Illus.). 384p. 1979. 35.00x (ISBN 0-8385-7759-8). ACC.

--Pathology Annual 1980, Pt. 1. (Pathology Annual Ser.). 482p. 1980. 35.00x (ISBN 0-8385-7761-X). ACC.

--Pathology Annual 1980, Pt. 2. (Pathology Annual Ser.). 432p. 1980. 33.50x (ISBN 0-8385-7762-8). ACC.

--Pathology Annual,1981: Part 1. (Pathology Annual Series). 1981. 35.00 (ISBN 0-8385-7763-6). ACC.

Sommerville, Duncan Y. Bibliography of Non-Euclidean Geometry. 2nd ed. LC 72-113150. 1960. text ed. 18.50 (ISBN 0-8284-0175-6). Chelsea Pub.

Somner, William. The Antiquities of Canterbury. (Classical Town Histories Ser.). 1977. Repr. of 1703 ed. 57.50x (ISBN 0-8476-6120-2). Rowman.

Somogyi, J. C., ed. Foreign Substances & Nutrition. Tarjan, R. (Bibliotheca Nutritio et Dieta: No. 29). (Illus.). 1980. pap. 49.75 (ISBN 3-8055-0621-X). S Karger.

Somogyi, J. C. & Varela, G., eds. Nutritional Deficiencies in Industrialized Countries. (Bibliotheca Nutritic et Dieta Ser.: Vol. 30). (Illus.). 1981. soft cover 48.00 (ISBN 3-8055-1994-X). S Karger.

Somorjai, jt. ed. see Templeton.

Somorjai, Gabor A. Chemistry in Two Dimensions: Surfaces. LC 80-21443. (George Fisher Baker Non-Resident Lectureship in Chemistry at Cornell University Ser.). (Illus.). 552p. 1981. 48.50 (ISBN 0-8014-1179-3). Cornell U Pr.

Somoza, Anastasio. Nicaragua Betrayed. 1980. 15.00 (ISBN 0-88279-235-0). Western Islands.

--Nicaragua Traicionada. 1980. pap. 7.95 (ISBN 0-88279-128-1). Western Island.

Son, Duk S. & Clark, R. Korean Karate: The Art of Tae Kwan Do. LC 68-17527. 1968. 11.95 (ISBN 0-13-516815-5). P-H.

Sondak, N. E., jt. auth. see Scott, R. C.

Sonde, B. S. Introduction to System Design Using Integrated Circuits. 261p. 1981. 24.95 (ISBN 0-470-27110-8). Halsted Pr.

Sondel, Bess. Everyday Speech: How to Say What You Mean. 1950. pap. 3.50 (ISBN 0-06-463239-3, EH 239, EH). Har-Row.

Sonderegger, Stefan. Grundzuege deutscher Sprachgeschichte: Band 1. 1979. text ed. 52.00x (ISBN 3-11-003570-7). De Gruyter.

Sonderegger-Kummer, Irene. Transparenz der Wirklichkeit: Edzard Schaper und die innere Spannung in der christlichen Literatur des zwanzigstes Jahrhunderts (Quellen und Forschungen zur Sprach- und Kulturgeschichte der germanischen Voelker, No. 37). (Ger). 1971. 60.60x (ISBN 3-11-001845-4). De Gruyter.

Sondheim, Stephen, jt. auth. see Wheeler, Hugh.

Sondheim, Stephen, et al. Pacific Overtures. LC 76-55020. 1977. 6.95 (ISBN 0-396-07414-6). Dodd.

Sondheimer, Janet, tr. see Bloch, Marc.

Sondheimer, Janet, tr. see Ganshof, F. L.

Sondrup, Steven P., ed. Arts & Inspiration: Mormon Perspectives. LC 80-21927. (Illus.). 240p. 1980. pap. 8.95 (ISBN 0-8425-1845-2). Brigham.

Sone, Monica. Nisei Daughter. LC 79-4921. (Orig.). 1979. pap. 5.95 (ISBN 0-295-95688-7). U of Wash Pr.

Sonenblick, Jerry & Sowerwine, Martha. The Legality of Love. 480p. (Orig.). 1981. pap. 3.95 (ISBN 0-515-05491-7). Jove Pubns.

Song, Bang-Song. An Annotated Bibliography of Korean Music. LC 75-163013. (A (Bibliographies), No. 2). xiv, 251p. (Orig.). 1971. pap. text ed. 11.75x (ISBN 0-913360-04-X). Asian Music Pub.

Song, Joseph. Pathology of Sickle Cell Disease. (Illus.). 472p. 1971. photocopy ed. spiral 47.50 (ISBN 0-398-01812-X). C C Thomas.

Song, Minako I. & Matsui, Masato, eds. Japanese Sources on Korea in Hawaii. LC 79-55927. (Occassional Papers Ser.: No. 10). 251p. (Orig.). 1980. pap. 8.00 (ISBN 0-917536-14-2). Ctr Korean U HI at Manoa.

Songe, Alice H. American Universities & Colleges: A Dictionary of Name Changes. LC 78-5497. 1978. lib. bdg. 12.00x (ISBN 0-8108-1137-5). Scarecrow.

Songe, Alice H., jt. auth. see Fang, Josephine R.

Song Pill-Soon, ed. Symposium on Photomorphogenesis. 1978. pap. text ed. 21.00 (ISBN 0-08-022677-9). Pergamon.

Soniat, Leon. La Bouche Creole. LC 80-23178. (Illus.). 1981. spiral bdg. 3.95 (ISBN 0-88289-242-8). Pelican.

Sonnack, Iver, ed. see Corbit, Julia.

Sonne, Niels H. Liberal Kentucky, 1780-1828. LC 39-20412. 300p. 1968. pap. 5.00x (ISBN 0-8131-0119-0). U Pr of Ky.

Sonneborn, Ruth A. Seven in a Bed. LC 68-27564. (Illus.). (gr. k-2). 1968. PLB 3.95 o.p. (ISBN 0-670-63507-3). Viking Pr.

Sonneck, O. G. Early Concert-Life in America: 1731-1800. LC 78-2580. (Music Reprint, 1978 Ser.). 1978. Repr. of 1907 ed. lib. bdg. 29.50 (ISBN 0-306-77591-3). Da Capo.

Sonneck, O. G., jt. auth. see Whittlesey, W. R.

Sonneck, Oscar G. Bibliography of Early Secular American Music: Eighteenth Century. 3rd ed. LC 64-18992. (Music Ser). 1964. Repr. of 1945 ed. lib. bdg. 45.00 (ISBN 0-306-70902-3). Da Capo.

--Catalogue of First Editions of Edward MacDowell. LC 72-155232. (Music Ser). 1971. Repr. of 1917 ed. lib. bdg. 15.00 (ISBN 0-306-70161-8). Da Capo.

--Dramatic Music: Catalogue of Full Scores. LC 69-12619. (Music Ser). 1969. Repr. of 1908 ed. lib. bdg. 25.00 (ISBN 0-306-71229-6). Da Capo.

--Francis Hopkinson, the First American Poet-Composer, & James Lyon, Patriot, Preacher, Psalmodist. 2nd ed. LC 65-23393. (Music Ser). 1967. Repr. of 1905 ed. lib. bdg. 19.50 (ISBN 0-306-70918-X). Da Capo.

--Miscellaneous Studies in the History of Music. LC 68-9192. (Music Reprint Ser). 1968. Repr. of 1921 ed. lib. bdg. 35.00 (ISBN 0-306-71163-X). Da Capo.

--Orchestral Music Catalog: Scores. LC 69-12692. (Music Reprint Ser). 1969. Repr. of 1912 ed. lib. bdg. 55.00 (ISBN 0-306-71228-8). Da Capo.

--Star-Spangled Banner. LC 68-16245. (Music Ser). (Illus.). 1969. Repr. of 1914 ed. lib. bdg. 25.00 (ISBN 0-306-71108-7). Da Capo.

Sonnedecker, Glenn, jt. auth. see Stieb, Ernst W.

Sonnenberg, David E. & Birnbaum, Michael. Pacemakers: A Patient's Guide. Groom, Kathe, ed. (Illus.). 200p. 1980. write for info. (ISBN 0-935576-04-5); pap. write for info. (ISBN 0-935576-05-3). Kesend Pub Ltd.

Sonnenberg, G. J. Radar & Electronic Navigation. 5th ed. LC 77-30476. 1978. 34.95 (ISBN 0-408-00272-7). Butterworths.

Sonnenfeld, Albert, ed. Thirty-Six French Poems. 1960. pap. text ed. 4.75 o.p. (ISBN 0-395-05420-6). HM.

Sonnenfeld, Jeffrey A. Corporate Views of the Public Interest: The Perceptions of the Forest Products Industry. 200p. 1981. 19.95 (ISBN 0-86569-060-X). Auburn Hse.

Sonnenschein, W. A., ed. see Plautus.

Sonnenschein, William S. Best Books, 6 Vols. 3rd ed. LC 68-58760. 1969. Repr. of 1935 ed. Set. 220.00 (ISBN 0-8103-3362-7). Gale.

Sonnenschmidt, Fredric H. & Nicolas, Jean F. The Professional Chef's Art of Garde Manger. 2nd ed. LC 72-92377. 1976. 22.95 (ISBN 0-8436-2067-6). CBI Pub.

Sonnenwirth, A. C. Bacteremia: Laboratory & Clinical Aspects. (Amer. Lec. in Clinical Microbiology Ser.). (Illus.). 120p. 1973. 11.75 (ISBN 0-398-02829-X). C C Thomas.

Sonnenwirth, Alex C. & Jarett, Leonard. Gradwohl's Clinical Laboratory Methods & Diagnosis. 8th ed. LC 79-26398. (Illus.). 1980. text ed. 115.00 (ISBN 0-8016-4741-X). Mosby.

Sonnershein, Richard, ed. see Marmion, Shakerly.

Sonnerup, B. V. An Introduction to Distributed Systems & Fields. 1978. 25.00 o.p. (ISBN 0-08-017101-X). Pergamon.

Sonnett, Sherry. Smoking. (First Bks.). (Illus.). (gr. 4-6). 1977. PLB 6.45 (ISBN 0-531-01299-9). Watts.

Sonnichsen, C. L. Outlaw: Bill Mitchell, Alias Baldy Russell: His Life & Times. LC 65-25798. 1965. 9.95 (ISBN 0-8040-0238-X, SB). Swallow.

--Pass of the North, Vol. I. 1980. 20.00 (ISBN 0-87404-013-2). Tex Western.

--Pass of the North, Vol. II. 1980. 15.00 (ISBN 0-87404-066-3). Tex Western.

--Tularosa--Last of the Frontier West. 356p. 1980. 14.95x (ISBN 0-8263-0563-6); pap. 7.95 (ISBN 0-8263-0561-X). U of NM Pr.

--Tularosa: Last of the Frontier West. rev. ed. (Illus.). 1971. 10.00 o.s.i. (ISBN 0-685-40705-5). Devin.

Sonnichsen, Charles L. Cowboys & Cattle Kings: Life on the Range Today. LC 80-12743. (Illus.). xviii, 316p. 1980. Repr. of 1950 ed. lib. bdg. 30.00x (ISBN 0-313-22472-2, SOCO). Greenwood.

Sonnino, Paul, tr. Louis the Fourteenth: Memoires for the Instruction of the Dauphin. 1970. 12.95 (ISBN 0-02-930130-0). Free Pr.

Sonnino, Paul, tr. see Frederick Of Prussia.

Sonnino, Sidney. Carteggio (Political Correspondence), 1916-1922. Pastorelli, Pietro, ed. (Complete Works of Sidney Sonnino Ser). (It.). 1976. 15.00x o.p. (ISBN 0-7006-0150-3). Regents Pr KS.

Sonnleitner, A. T. Cave Children. Bell, Anthea, tr. from Ger. LC 70-120785. (Illus.). (gr. 8 up). 1971. 9.95 (ISBN 0-87599-169-6). S G Phillips.

Sonntag, H. & Strenge, K. Coagulation & Stability of Disperse Systems. 139p. 1972. 27.95 (ISBN 0-470-81350-4). Halsted Pr.

Sonntag, Linda. Butterflies. (The Leprechaun Library). (Illus.). 64p. 1980. 3.95 (ISBN 0-399-12546-9). Putnam.

--Frogs. (The Leprechaun Library). (Illus.). 64p. 1981. 3.95 (ISBN 0-399-12611-2). Putnam.

Sonntag, R. E. & Van Wylen, G. J. Fundamentals of Statistical Thermodynamcis. LC 65-27654. 1966. text ed. 26.95x (ISBN 0-471-81360-5). Wiley.

Sonntag, Richard E., jt. auth. see Van Wylen, Gordon J.

Sono, Kazuhiko, jt. auth. see Sakade, Florence.

Sonquist, John A. & Dunkelberg, William C. Survey & Opinion Research: Procedures for Processing & Analysis. (Illus.). 1977. 28.95 (ISBN 0-13-878264-4). P-H.

Sonquist, John A., et al. Searching for Structure. rev. ed. LC 73-620236. 236p. 1974. cloth 10.00 (ISBN 0-87944-110-0); pap. 6.50 (ISBN 0-87944-109-7). U of Mich Soc Res.

Sonsino, Rifat. Motive Clauses in Hebrew Law: Biblical Forms & Near Eastern Parallels. LC 79-15024. (Society of Biblical Literature Dissertation Ser.: No. 45). 13.50x (ISBN 0-89130-317-0, 060145); pap. 9.00x. Scholars Pr CA.

Sonstroem, David. Rossetti & the Fair Lady. LC 70-105506. (Illus.). 1970. 17.50x (ISBN 0-8195-4019-6, Pub. by Wesleyan U Pr). Columbia U Pr.

Sontag, Frederick. A Kierkegaard Handbook. LC 79-87741. 1980. pap. 6.95 (ISBN 0-8042-0654-6). John Knox.

--Sun Myung Moon & the Unification Church: An in-Depth Investigation of the Man & the Movement. LC 77-9075. (Illus.). 1977. 8.95 o.p. (ISBN 0-687-40622-6). Abingdon.

Sontag, Frederick H., jt. auth. see Saloma, John S.

Sontag, Raymond J. Broken World, 1919-1939. LC 77-156572. (Rise of Modern Europe Ser). (Illus.). 1971. 15.00x o.s.i. (ISBN 0-06-013954-4, HarpT). Har-Row.

Sontag, Susan. Brother Carl. LC 72-82949. (Illus.). 192p. 1974. pap. 4.95 o.p. (ISBN 0-374-11700-4); pap. 4.95 (ISBN 0-374-51026-1). FS&G.

--Under the Sign of Saturn. 300p. 1980. 10.95 (ISBN 0-374-28076-2). FS&G.

Sontag, Susan, ed. see Barthes, Roland.

Sontheimer, Kurt. Government & Politics of West Germany. 1972. text ed. 8.00x (ISBN 0-09-111130-7, Hutchinson U Lib). Humanities.

Sood, Mohan K. Modern Igneous Petrology. 250p. 1981. 22.50 (ISBN 0-471-08915-X, Pub. by Wiley-Interscience). Wiley.

Soohoo, Ronald F. Microwave Electronics. LC 75-127893. (Engineering Ser). 1971. text ed. 19.95 (ISBN 0-201-07086-3). A-W.

Soong, Stephen C., ed. Song Without Music: Chinese Tz'u Poetry. (Renditions Ser). (Illus.). 286p. 1981. 20.00 (ISBN 0-295-95811-1, Pub. by Chinese Univ Hong Kong). U of Wash Pr.

Soonja Lee Koh, Gertrude. The Semantic Problems of Translated Subject Headings. 1979. write for info. (ISBN 0-686-25169-5). CHCUS Inc.

Soons, Alan. Alonso De Castillo Solorzano. (World Author Ser.: No. 457). 1978. 12.95 (ISBN 0-8057-6294-9). Twayne.

Soothill, W. E. The Three Religions of China: The Interrelationship Between Confucianism, Buddhism & Taoism. new ed. 1973. text ed. 9.50x o.p. (ISBN 0-7007-0031-5). Humanities.

Sootin, Harry. Gregor Mendel: Father of the Science of Genetics. LC 59-7933. (Illus.). (gr. 7-10). 1958. 7.95 (ISBN 0-8149-0409-2). Vanguard.

Sooy, Louise P., jt. auth. see Mackey, Margaret G.

Soper, Alexander, tr. see Akiyama, Terukazu & Matsubara, Saburo.

Soper, Davison E. Classical Field Theory. LC 75-37659. 300p. 1976. text ed. 30.95 (ISBN 0-471-81368-0, Pub. by Wiley-Interscience). Wiley.

Soper, Eunice. Red Wagons & Billy Goats. 1980. pap. 2.25 (ISBN 0-8280-0054-9, 18125-5). Review & Herald.

Soper, Gill, jt. auth. see Stuart, Monica.

Soper, James H. & Szczawinski, Adam F. Mount Revelstoke National Park Wild Flowers. (Illus.). 1976. pap. 2.95x (ISBN 0-660-00003-2, 56429-0, Pub. by Natl Mus Canada). U of Chicago Pr.

Soper, Kate, tr. see Chiodi, Pietro.

Soper, Robert T., jt. auth. see Liechty, Richard D.

Soper, Tony. The Bird Table Book in Colour. LC 77-89367. (Illus.). 1978. 11.95 (ISBN 0-7153-7404-4). David & Charles.

--Everyday Birds. LC 76-20134. 1976. 10.50 (ISBN 0-7153-7277-7). David & Charles.

--Wildlife Begins at Home. LC 75-10700. 1975. 11.95 (ISBN 0-7153-7111-8). David & Charles.

Sopher, Charles & Baird, Jack. Soils & Soil Management. 2nd ed. 1981. text ed. 16.95 (ISBN 0-8359-7031-0); instr's. manual free (ISBN 0-8359-7032-9). Reston.

Sopher, Charles D. & Baird, Jack V. Soils & Soil Management. (Illus.). 1978. text ed. 14.95 (ISBN 0-87909-801-5); instrs'. manual avail. Reston.

Sopher, Irvin M. Forensic Dentistry. (American Lectures in Forensic Pathology Ser.). (Illus.). 176p. 1976. 19.75 (ISBN 0-398-03474-5). C C Thomas.

Sophocles. Antigone. smaller ed. Jebb, ed. (Gr., Gr). 1971. text ed. 9.95x (ISBN 0-521-06525-9). Cambridge U Pr.

--Antigone. Braun, Richard, tr. (Greek Tragedy in New Translations Ser). 96p. 1973. 10.95x (ISBN 0-19-501741-2). Oxford U Pr.

--The Antigone. Murray, Gilbert, tr. 1924. pap. text ed. 3.95x (ISBN 0-04-882048-2). Allen Unwin.

--Electra. Jebb, Richard C., tr. 1950. pap. 1.80 o.p. (ISBN 0-672-60185-0, LLA25). Bobbs.

--Electra & Other Plays. Watling, E. F., tr. Incl. Women of Trachis; Philoctetes. (Classics Ser.). (YA) (gr. 9 up). 1953. pap. 2.95 (ISBN 0-14-044028-3). Penguin.

--Oedipus at Colonus. Murray, Gilbert, tr. 1948. pap. text ed. 3.95x (ISBN 0-04-882050-4). Allen Unwin.

--The Oedipus Cycle of Sophocles. Fitts, Dudley & Fitzgerald, Robert, trs. Incl. Oedipus Rex; Antigone; Oedipus at Colonus. 243p. 1955. pap. 2.95 (ISBN 0-15-683838-9, HB8, Harv). HarBraceJ.

--Oedipus, King of Thebes. Murray, Gilbert, tr. pap. text ed. 3.95x (ISBN 0-04-882052-0). Allen Unwin.

--Oedipus the King. Berg, Stephen & Clay, Diskin, trs. from Greek. (Greek Tragedy in New Translations Ser.). 1978. 10.95x (ISBN 0-19-502325-0). Oxford U Pr.

--Oedipus Tyrannus. (Norton Critical Editions Ser). (Orig.). 1970. text ed. 5.00 (ISBN 0-393-04307-X); pap. 4.95x (ISBN 0-393-09874-5). Norton.

--Oedipus Tyrannus. smaller ed. (Gr.). text ed. 8.95x (ISBN 0-521-06527-5). Cambridge U Pr.

--Philoctetes. Webster, ed. 1970. pap. 9.95x (ISBN 0-521-09890-4). Cambridge U Pr.

--The Wife of Heracles. Murray, Gilbert, tr. 1947. pap. text ed. 3.95x (ISBN 0-04-882054-7). Allen Unwin.

--Women of Trachis. Williams, C. K. & Dickerson, Gregory W., trs. from Gr. (Greek Texts in New Translations Ser.). 1978. text ed. 10.95x (ISBN 0-19-502050-2). Oxford U Pr.

Sopp, LaVerne. Personal Name Index to the Eighteen Fifty-Six City Directories of Iowa. (Genealogy & Local History Ser.: Vol. 13). 400p. 1980. 30.00 (ISBN 0-8103-1486-X). Gale.

Soppeland, Mark, ed. Word! (Illus.). 120p. (Orig.). 1980. pap. 6.95 (ISBN 0-913232-60-2). W Kaufmann.

Sor, F. Method for the Spanish Guitar. LC 77-158960. (Music Ser). 1971. Repr. lib. bdg. 17.50 (ISBN 0-306-70188-X). Da Capo.

Soraas, H., jt. ed. see Bjerke, L.

Sorabji, Richard. Aristotle on Memory. LC 72-79966. 122p. 1972. 6.50 (ISBN 0-87057-137-0, Pub. by Brown U Pr). Univ Pr of New England.

--Necessity, Cause & Blame: Perspectives on Aristotle's Theory. LC 79-2449. 1980. 38.50x (ISBN 0-8014-1162-9). Cornell U Pr.

Soracco, Lionel J., Jr. Math House Proficiency Review Tapes: Applications Involving Money, Unit D. (YA) (gr. 7 up). 1980. manual & cassettes 159.95 (ISBN 0-917792-06-8). Math Hse.

--Math House Proficiency Review Tapes: Operations with Decimals & Percent, Unit B. (YA) (gr. 7 up). 1980. manual & cassettes 159.95 (ISBN 0-917792-04-1). Math Hse.

Sorauf. Perspectives on Political Science. 1966. pap. text ed. 4.95 (ISBN 0-675-09714-2). Merrill.

SorBello, Marisa. Woman in Reformation Europe. Ide, Arthur F., ed. LC 79-19011. (Woman in History Ser.: Vol. 19). (Illus.). 80p. (Orig.). 1981. 16.95 (ISBN 0-86663-053-8); pap. 10.95 (ISBN 0-86663-054-6). Ide Hse.

Sorbom, Dag, jt. auth. see Joreskog, Karl G.

Sorcher, Melvin, jt. auth. see Goldstein, Arnold P.

Sordelli, F., jt. auth. see Jan, G.

Sordo, Enrique. Moorish Spain: Cordoba, Seville, Granada. 1971. 21.95 (ISBN 0-236-31091-7, Pub. by Paul Elek). Merrimack Bk Serv.

Sorel, Albert. The Eastern Question in the Eighteenth Century: The Partition of Poland & the Treaty of Kainardji. LC 68-9661. 1969. Repr. of 1898 ed. 15.75 (ISBN 0-86527-048-1). Fertig.

Sorel, Edward, jt. auth. see Miller, Warren.

Sorel, Georges. The Illusions of Progress. Stanley, John & Stanley, Charlotte, trs. LC 69-16511. 1969. 19.50x (ISBN 0-520-01531-2); pap. 3.25 (ISBN 0-520-02256-4, CAL251). U of Cal Pr.

Sorel, Julia. Dawn: Portrait of a Teenage Runaway. (Orig.). 1971. pap. 1.95 (ISBN 0-345-29610-9). Ballantine.

Sorell, Walter. Dance in Its Time. LC 80-913. (Illus.). 480p. 1981. 19.95 (ISBN 0-385-13418-5). Doubleday.

--Hanya Holm: The Biography of an Artist. LC 69-17796. 1979. 15.00x (ISBN 0-8195-3096-4, Pub. by Wesleyan U Pr); pap. 8.00 (ISBN 0-8195-6060-X). Columbia U Pr.

Sorell, Walter, ed. Dance Has Many Faces. 2nd ed. LC 66-25457. (Illus.). (YA) (gr. 9 up). 1966. 17.50x (ISBN 0-231-02968-3). Columbia U Pr.

Sorell, Walter, tr. see Wigman, Mary.

Soren, David. The Rise & Fall of the Horror Film. 1977. perfect bdg. 5.50x (ISBN 0-87543-136-4). Lucas.

--Unreal Reality: The Cinema of Harry Kumel. LC 78-71774. (Illus.). 1979. pap. text ed. 9.50x (ISBN 0-87543-145-3). Lucas.

Sorensen, Andrew A. Alcoholic Priests: A Sociological Study. 1977. 8.95 (ISBN 0-8164-0317-1). Crossroad NY.

Sorensen, Chris & Flying Magazine Editors. Antique Airplanes. LC 78-11272. (Encore Edition). (Illus.). 1979. 8.95 (ISBN 0-684-16927-4, ScribT). Scribner.

Sorensen, Lorin. The American Ford. (Fordiana Ser.). (Illus.). 263p. 1975. 49.50 (ISBN 0-87938-079-9). Silverado.

--The Ford Road. (Illus.). 191p. 1978. 16.95 (ISBN 0-87938-078-0). Silverado.

--The Ford Road. (Illus.). 1978. 19.95 (ISBN 0-87938-078-0, Pub. by Silverado Pubns Co). Motorbooks Intl.

--The Open Fords. (Fordiana Ser.). 1979. 49.50 o.p. (ISBN 0-87938-081-0). Motorbooks Intl.

Sorensen, Marlene. Legal Aspects of Life Insurance: Teaching, Pt. 3. (FLMI Insurance Education Program Ser.). 1978. instrs.' manual 8.00x (ISBN 0-915322-29-3). LOMA.

Sorensen, Robert. Shadow of the Past. Uhlich, Richard, ed. (Bluejeans Paperback Ser.). (Illus., Orig.). (gr. 7-12). 1978. pap. text ed. 1.25 (ISBN 0-8374-5003-9). Xerox Ed Pubns.

Sorensen, Robert M. Basic Coastal Engineering. LC 77-29256. (Ocean Engineering Ser.). 1978. 27.50 (ISBN 0-471-81370-2, Pub. by Wiley-Interscience). Wiley.

Sorensen, Theodore. Kennedy. LC 65-14660. 1965. 17.50 o.s.i. (ISBN 0-06-013950-1, HarpT). Har-Row.

--Watchmen in the Night: Presidential Accountability After Watergate. LC 75-1273. 1975. 12.00x (ISBN 0-262-19133-4); pap. 5.95 (ISBN 0-262-69055-1). MIT Pr.

Sorensen, Theodore C. Decision-Making in the White House: The Olive Branch or the Olives. LC 63-20465. 1963. 12.50x (ISBN 0-231-02673-0); pap. 5.00x (ISBN 0-231-08550-8). Columbia U Pr.

Sorensen, Virginia. Curious Missie. LC 53-7872. (Illus.). (gr. 3-6). 1963. 5.50 o.p. (ISBN 0-15-221085-7, HJ). HarBraceJ.

--Lotte's Locket. LC 64-17087. (Illus.). (gr. 4-6). 1964. 5.95 o.p. (ISBN 0-15-249457-X, HJ). HarBraceJ.

Sorenson. Parameter Estimation: Principles & Problems. 400p. 1980. 45.00 (ISBN 0-8247-6987-2). Dekker.

Sorenson, Grethe. Oriental Rug Designs in Needlepoint. (Illus.). 112p. 1980. cancelled (ISBN 0-684-16622-4, ScribT). Scribner.

Sorenson, J. H., jt. auth. see Bailey, Alfred M.

Sorenson, J. S., jt. auth. see Haney, R. E.

Sorenson, James A. & Phelps, Michael E. Physics in Nuclear Medicine. 1980. 39.50 (ISBN 0-8089-1238-0). Grune.

Sorenson, Stephen, jt. auth. see Kopp, Ruth.

Sorenson, Vernon. International Trade Policy: Agriculture & Development. LC 74-620204. xix, 290p. 1975. 11.00 (ISBN 0-87744-127-8); pap. 6.00 (ISBN 0-87744-168-5). Mich St U Busn.

Sorge, Bart W., jt. auth. see Weston, J. Fred.

Sorgenfrey, Robert H., jt. auth. see Dolciani, Mary P.

Sorger, T. J. The Computer Buyer's Attorney. (Illus., Orig.). pap. 39.95 (ISBN 0-9604072-0-0). Sorger Assocs.

Soria, Regina. The Dictionary of Nineteenth-Century American Artists in Italy, 1760-1914. LC 74-4986. 600p. 1981. 27.50 (ISBN 0-8386-1310-1). Fairleigh Dickinson.

Sorin, Gerald. Abolitionism: A New Perspective. LC 79-143981. (New Perspectives in American History). 187p. 1972. pap. 7.95 (ISBN 0-275-84140-5). Praeger.

Sorine, D. At Every Turn! It's Ballet. LC 80-19232. (Illus.). 49p. (ps-3). 1981. 8.95 (ISBN 0-394-84473-4); pap. 1.95 (ISBN 0-394-94473-9). Knopf.

--Imagine That! It's Modern Dance. LC 80-19232. (Illus.). 48p. (ps-3). 1981. PLB 4.99 (ISBN 0-394-84474-2); PLB 8.95 (ISBN 0-394-94474-7). Knopf.

Sork, David, et al. Growing & Sharing: The Catechist Formation Book. 128p. (Orig.). 1981. pap. 6.95 (ISBN 0-8091-2365-7). Paulist Pr.

Sorkin. Education, Unemployment & Economic Growth. LC 73-11656. 1974. 16.95 (ISBN 0-669-85498-0). Lexington Bks.

Sorkin, Alan. Health Economics: An Introduction. LC 73-11656. (Illus.). 160p. 1975. 16.95 (ISBN 0-669-93393-7). Lexington Bks.

--Health Economics in Developing Nations. LC 74-25059. 1976. 18.95 (ISBN 0-669-96875-7). Lexington Bks.

--Health Manpower: An Economic Perspective. LC 75-17335. 1977. 17.95 (ISBN 0-669-00086-8). Lexington Bks.

Sorkin, Alan L. American Indians & Federal Aid. (Studies in Social Economics). 231p. 1971. 10.95 (ISBN 0-8157-8044-3). Brookings.

--The Urban American Indian. LC 76-54459. (Illus.). 1978. 17.95 (ISBN 0-669-01296-3). Lexington Bks.

Sorkin, Michael. Hardy Holzman Pfeiffer. 136p. 1981. 18.95 (ISBN 0-8230-7264-9, Whitney Lib). Watson-Guptill.

Sorkin, R. B. Integrated Electronics: How Cowboys & Longhorns Opened the Mid-Continent. 1970. 23.50 o.p. (ISBN 0-07-059738-3, P&RB). McGraw.

Sorley, Imogene, jt. auth. see Carr, Jo.

Sorlien, Robert P., ed. see Manningham, John.

Sorlin, Pierre. The Film in History: Restaging the Past. (Illus.). 226p. 1980. 21.50x (ISBN 0-389-20130-8). B&N.

Sorm, Frantisek & Dolejs, Ladislaw. Guaianolides & Germacranolides. LC 66-16515. 1966. 20.00x (ISBN 0-8162-8261-7). Holden-Day.

Sorochan, Walter D. & Bender, Stephen J. Teaching Secondary Health Science. LC 78-1760. 1978. text ed. 21.50 (ISBN 0-471-81387-7). Wiley.

Soroka, I. Portland Cement Paste & Concrete. 1980. 48.00 (ISBN 0-8206-0281-7). Chem Pub.

Sorokin, Pitirim. Fads & Foibles in Modern Sociology & Related Sciences. LC 76-154. 357p. 1976. Repr. of 1956 ed. lib. bdg. 26.75x (ISBN 0-8371-8733-8, SOFF). Greenwood.

--Social & Cultural Dynamics. (Social Science Classics Ser.). 720p. 1982. 19.95 (ISBN 0-87855-363-0); pap. 7.95 (ISBN 0-87855-787-3). Transaction Bks. Postponed.

Sorokin, Pitirim A. Man & Society in Calamity, the Effects of War, Revolution, Famine, Pestilence Upon Human Mind, Behavior, Social Organization & Cultural Life. LC 69-10157. (Illus.). 1968. Repr. of 1942 ed. lib. bdg. 25.50x (ISBN 0-8371-0236-7, SOMS). Greenwood.

--Social & Cultural Mobility. LC 59-13122. 1959. 12.95 (ISBN 0-02-930270-6). Free Pr.

Soroko, L. M. Holography & Coherent Optics. (Illus.). 650p. 1978. 59.50 (ISBN 0-306-40101-0, Plenum Pr). Plenum Pub.

Sorosky, Marlene. Cookery for Entertaining. LC 78-71788. (Illus.). 1979. pap. 5.95 (ISBN 0-89586-019-8). H P Bks.

Sorracco, Lionel J., Jr. Math House Proficiency Review Tapes: Operations with Whole Numbers & Fractions, Unit A. (YA) (gr. 7 up). 1980. manual & cassettes 159.95 (ISBN 0-917792-03-3). Math Hse.

Sorrell, Alan. Reconstructing the Past. Sorrell, Mark, ed. (Illus.). 168p. 1981. 19.50x (ISBN 0-389-20196-0). B&N.

--Reconstructing the Past. Sorrell, Mark, ed. LC 79-56473. (Illus.). 168p. 1980. 24.00 (ISBN 0-7134-1588-6, Pub. by Batsford England). David & Charles.

--Roman Towns in Britain. 1976. 17.95 (ISBN 0-7134-3237-3). David & Charles.

Sorrell, Alan, jt. auth. see Hamilton, John.

Sorrell, Charles. Rocks & Minerals. (Golden Field Guide Ser). (Illus.). 280p. 1974. 7.95 (ISBN 0-307-47005-9, Golden Pr); pap. 4.95 (ISBN 0-307-13661-2). Western Pub.

Sorrell, Mark, ed. see Sorrell, Alan.

Sorrell, Neil. What Happens in Indian Music: A Practical Introduction. (Illus.). 1980. pap. 27.50x (ISBN 0-8147-7815-1). NYU Pr.

Sorrentino, Anthony. Organizing Against Crime: Redeveloping the Neighborhood. LC 76-21840. 1977. 22.95 (ISBN 0-87705-301-4). Human Sci Pr.

Sorrentino, Gilbert. Aberration of Starlight. 1981. pap. 3.95 (ISBN 0-14-005879-6). Penguin.

--Aberration of Starlight. LC 80-5280. 224p. 1980. 8.95 (ISBN 0-394-51189-1). Random.

--Selected Poems: 1958 to 1980. 225p. (Orig.). 1981. 14.00 (ISBN 0-87685-502-8); pap. 7.50 (ISBN 0-87685-501-X); signed ed. 20.00 (ISBN 0-87685-503-6). Black Sparrow.

Sors, L. Fatigue Design of Machine Components. 224p. 1971. text ed. 42.00 (ISBN 0-08-016138-3). Pergamon.

Sorsby, A. Clinical Genetics. 2nd ed. 1973. 77.95 (ISBN 0-407-13651-7). Butterworths.

--Diseases of the Fundus Oculi. 1976. 54.95 (ISBN 0-407-00023-2). Butterworths.

Sorsby, Arnold, ed. Modern Ophthalmology, 4 vols. 2nd ed. Incl. Vol. 1. Basic Aspects. (Illus.). 640p. 45.00 o.p. (ISBN 0-685-27023-8); Vol. 2. Systemic Aspects. (Illus.). 748p. 50.00 o.p. (ISBN 0-685-27024-6); Vols. 3 & 4. Topical Aspects. (Illus.). 1200p. Set. 95.00 o.p. (ISBN 0-685-27025-4). (Illus.). 2588p. 1972. Set. 190.00 o.p. (ISBN 0-685-27022-X). Lippincott.

Sorum, Boikess. How to Solve General Chemistry Problems. 5th ed. (Illus.). 320p. 1976. pap. text ed. 10.95 (ISBN 0-13-434100-7). P-H.

Sorum, C. Harvey, jt. auth. see Boikess, Robert S.

Sorum, Henry & Lagowski, Joseph J. Introduction to Semimicro Qualitative Analysis. 5th ed. LC 76-51795. (Illus.). 320p. 1977. pap. text ed. 11.95 (ISBN 0-13-496059-9). P-H.

Sosa, Michael, tr. see Tynyanov, Yury.

Soseki, Natsume. Botchan. Turney, Alan, tr. from Japanese. LC 71-174215. 173p. 1980. pap. 3.95 (ISBN 0-87011-367-4). Kodansha.

Sosin, Jack M. English America & the Restoration Monarchy of Charles II: Trans-Atlantic Politics, Commerce & Kinship. LC 80-16215. xii, 389p. 1981. 25.00x (ISBN 0-8032-4118-6). U of Nebr Pr.

--Whitehall & the Wilderness: The Middle West in British Colonial Policy, 1760 to 1775. LC 80-21061. (Illus.). xi, 307p. 1981. Repr. of 1961 ed. lib. bdg. 35.00x (ISBN 0-313-22678-4, SOWW). Greenwood.

Sosna, Morton. In Search of the Silent South: Southern Liberals & the Race Issue. LC 77-4965. (Contemporary American History Ser.). 1977. 17.50x (ISBN 0-231-03843-7). Columbia U Pr.

Sosne, Michael. Handbook of Adapted Physical Education Equipment & Its Use. (Illus.). 224p. 1973. text ed. 16.50 (ISBN 0-398-02782-X). C C Thomas.

Sosnoff, Martin T. Humble on Wall Street. 1975. 8.95 o.p. (ISBN 0-87000-330-5). Arlington Hse.

Sotereanos, George C., jt. auth. see Sassouni, Viken.

Sotheby, William. Oberon: A Poem from the German of Wieland. Reiman, Donald H., ed. LC 75-31258. (Romantic Context Ser.: Poetry 1789-1830). 1978. Repr. of 1798 ed. lib. bdg. 47.00 (ISBN 0-8240-2205-X). Garland Pub.

--William Sotheby (Seventeen Fifty-Seven to Eighteen Thirty-Three) Oberon & Orestes. Reiman, Donald H., ed. LC 75-31259. (Romantic Context Ser.: Poetry 1789-1830). 1978. Repr. of 1802 ed. lib. bdg. 47.00 (ISBN 0-8240-2206-8). Garland Pub.

--William Sotheby (Seventeen Fifty-Seven to Eighteen Thirty-Three) Poems 1790-1818. Reiman, Donald H., ed. LC 75-31256. (Romantic Context Ser.: Poetry 1789-1830). 1978. lib. bdg. 47.00 (ISBN 0-8240-2203-3). Garland Pub.

--William Sotheby (Seventeen Fifty-Seven to Eighteen Thirty-Three) Saul. Reiman, Donald H., ed. LC 75-31257. (Romantic Context Ser.: Poetry 1789-1830). 1978. Repr. of 1807 ed. lib. bdg. 47.00 (ISBN 0-8240-2204-1). Garland Pub.

Sottovagina, Hugh see Hugh The Chantor, pseud.

Soucek, Branko. Microprocessors & Microcomputers. LC 75-33123. 1976. 30.00 (ISBN 0-471-81391-5, Pub. by Wiley-Interscience). Wiley.

--Minicomputers in Data Processing & Simulation. LC 77-37436. 533p. 1972. 34.50 (ISBN 0-471-81390-7, Pub. by Wiley-Interscience). Wiley.

Souchal, Francois. French Sculptors, Vol. 2. (Illus.). 464p. 1981. 200.00 (ISBN 0-85181-063-2, Pub. by Faber & Faber). Merrimack Bk Serv.

--French Sculptors of the Seventeenth & Eighteenth Centuries: The Region of Louis XIV. (The Reign of Louis XIV Catalogue Raisonne Ser.: Vol. 1, A-F). (Illus.). 1977. 165.00 (ISBN 0-85181-062-4, Pub. by Faber & Faber). Merrimack Bk Serv.

Soucheray, Joe. Bruce Jenner. (Sports Superstars Ser.). (Illus.). (gr. 3-9). 1979. PLB 5.95 (ISBN 0-87191-723-8); pap. 2.95 (ISBN 0-89812-158-2). Creative Ed.

--Fred Lynn. (Sports Superstars Ser.). (Illus.). (gr. 3-9). 1977. PLB 5.95 (ISBN 0-87191-541-3); pap. 2.95 (ISBN 0-89812-175-2). Creative Ed.

--Walter Payton. (Sports Superstars Ser.). (Illus.). (gr. 3-9). 1979. PLB 5.95 (ISBN 0-87191-722-X); pap. 2.95 (ISBN 0-89812-160-4). Creative Ed.

Soucy, Robert. Fascist Intellectual: Drieu la Rochelle. 1979. 27.50x (ISBN 0-520-03463-5). U of Cal Pr.

Souerwine, Andrew H. Career Strategies: Planning for Personal Achievement. new ed. LC 77-28087. 1978. 15.95 (ISBN 0-8144-5454-2); pap. 6.95 (ISBN 0-8144-6963-9). Am Mgmt.

Soule, Dorothy F. Zoology Made Simple. LC 67-15392. 1967. pap. 3.50 (ISBN 0-385-08870-1, Made). Doubleday.

Soule, Gardner. Men Who Dared the Sea: The Ocean Adventures of the Ancient Mariners. LC 75-34451. 1976. 9.95 o.s.i. (ISBN 0-690-01095-8, TYC-T). T Y Crowell.

Soule, George, ed. The Theatre of the Mind. (P-H Series in English Literature). 640p. 1974. pap. text ed. 13.95 (ISBN 0-13-913020-9). P-H.

Soule, George H. Ideas of the Great Economists. 1955. pap. 1.25 o.p. (ISBN 0-451-61475-5, MY1475, Ment). NAL.

Soule, Jean C. Never Tease a Weasel. LC 64-12353. 48p. (gr. k-3). PLB 5.41 o.s.i. (ISBN 0-8193-0095-0, Four Winds). Schol Bk Serv.

Soule, Jean C. & Soule, Nancy J. Scuttle, the Stowaway Mouse. LC 68-21083. (Illus.). (gr. k-3). 1969. 5.95 o.s.i. (ISBN 0-8193-0253-8, Four Winds); PLB 5.41 o.s.i. (ISBN 0-8193-0254-6). Schol Bk Serv.

Soule, M. E., jt. auth. see Frankel, O. H.

Soule, Nancy J., jt. auth. see Soule, Jean C.

Soulen, Richard, tr. see Westermann, Claus.

Soulen, Richard N. Care for the Dying. LC 74-19968. 120p. 1975. pap. 4.95 (ISBN 0-8042-1098-5). John Knox.

--Handbook of Biblical Criticism. LC 76-12398. 1976. pap. 7.95 (ISBN 0-8042-0044-0). John Knox.

Soules, Eugene H. First Principles of Composition, 4 vols. Incl. Vol. 1-Using a Dictionary to Avoid Spelling Errors (ISBN 0-86589-001-3); Vol. 2 Editing & Revising for Correct Entence Structure (ISBN 0-86589-002-1); Vol. 3-Using Modifiers for Clarity & Effectiveness (ISBN 0-86589-003-X); Vol. 4-Analyzing Sentences for Consistency (ISBN 0-86589-004-8). 1975. Set. 11.00 (ISBN 0-86589-000-5). Individual Learn.

Soules, Eugene H., jt. auth. see Wilson, Sidney R.

Soules, Jim. How to Single Out Your Mate: A Guide for Twogetherness in the 80's. 140p. 1980. pap. 4.95 (ISBN 0-936890-05-3). Singles World.

Soulier, J. Steven. Real Objects & Models. Duane, James E., ed. LC 80-21450. (The Instructional Media Library: Vol. 12). (Illus.). 96p. 1981. 13.95 (ISBN 0-87778-172-9). Educ Tech Pubns.

Sounin, Leonie De see De Sounin, Leonie.

Souper. About to Teach: An Introduction to Method in Teaching. 1976. 16.00x (ISBN 0-7100-8311-4); pap. 8.95 (ISBN 0-7100-8315-7). Routledge & Kegan.

Sourian, Etienne, jt. auth. see MacAgy, Jermayne.

Sours, John A. Starving to Death in a Sea of Objects. LC 80-68043. 400p. 1980. 25.00 (ISBN 0-87668-426-6). Aronson.

Souryal, Sam. Police Administration & Management. (Criminal Justice Ser.). 1977. text ed. 17.50 (ISBN 0-8299-0141-8); instrs.' manual avail. (ISBN 0-8299-0371-2). West Pub.

Sousa, John P. National Patriotic & Typical Airs of All Lands. LC 76-52480. (Music Reprint Series). 1977. Repr. of 1890 ed. lib. bdg. 32.50 (ISBN 0-306-70861-2). Da Capo.

--Sousa's Great Marches in Piano Transcription. LC 74-93543. (Orig.). 1975. pap. 4.50 (ISBN 0-486-23132-1). Dover.

Sousa, Maria De see De Sousa, Maria.

Sousa, Ronald W. The Rediscoverers: Major Writers in the Portuguese Literature of National Regeneration. LC 80-21453. (Illus.). 208p. 1981. 17.50x (ISBN 0-271-00300-6). Pa St U Pr.

Sousa Sanchez, Mario. Las Colecciones Botanicas de C. A. Purpus En Mexico Periodo 1898-1925. (U. C. Publ. in Botany: Vol. 51). 1969. pap. 5.50x (ISBN 0-520-09024-1). U of Cal Pr.

Souter, Alexander, ed. Pocket Lexicon to the Greek New Testament. 1916. 14.95x (ISBN 0-19-864203-2). Oxford U Pr.

Souter, Gavin. Lion & Kangaroo. 344p. 1980. 8.95x (ISBN 0-00-634512-3, Pub. by W Collins Australia). Intl Schol Bk Serv.

Souter, Susan J. How to Be a Confident Woman: A Bible Study Guide for Women. LC 78-51904. 1978. pap. 2.50 (ISBN 0-89081-124-5, 1245). Harvest Hse.

South African International Liver Conference, 1973. Liver: Proceedings. Saunders, S. J. & Terblanche, John, eds. (Illus.). 432p. 1973. pap. text ed. 20.00x (ISBN 0-8464-0575-X). Beekman Pubs.

South, John B., jt. auth. see Bradley, Iver F.

South Penn School Study Council. Muslim Heartlands. 1963. text ed. 3.50x spiral bdg. o.p. (ISBN 0-8134-0150-X, 150). Interstate.

South Suburban Dietetic Association, jt. auth. see Chicago Dietetic Association.

Southall, Ivan. Ash Road. LC 77-15063. (gr. 5-9). 1978. 7.95 (ISBN 0-688-80135-8); PLB 7.63 (ISBN 0-688-84135-X). Greenwillow.

--Head in the Clouds. LC 72-85189. (Illus.). 108p. (gr. 3-7). 1973. 4.95 o.s.i. (ISBN 0-02-786100-7). Macmillan.

--Hills End. new ed. LC 63-15002. 192p. (gr. 6-8). 1974. 5.95g o.s.i. (ISBN 0-02-786120-1). Macmillan.

--Josh. LC 75-187795. 192p. (gr. 7 up). 1972. 7.95g (ISBN 0-02-786080-9). Macmillan.

--Journey into Mystery, Story of Explorers Burke & Wills. 10.00x (ISBN 0-392-08006-0). Soccer.

--A Journey of Discovery: On Writing for Children. LC 75-31547. 138p. 1976. 6.95 o.s.i. (ISBN 0-02-786150-3, 78615). Macmillan.

--King of the Sticks. LC 79-10473. (gr. 6 up). 1979. 6.95 (ISBN 0-688-80224-9); PLB 6.67 (ISBN 0-688-84224-0). Greenwillow.

Southall, Raymond. The Courtly Maker: An Essay on the Poetry of Wyatt & His Contemporaries. 1964. 16.50x o.p. (ISBN 0-631-08350-2, Pub. by Basil Blackwell). Biblio Dist.

Southam, B. C., ed. Critical Essays on Jane Austen. 1968. 14.00x (ISBN 0-7100-6243-5); pap. 6.50 (ISBN 0-7100-6904-9). Routledge & Kegan.

Southam, Brian, ed. Jane Austen's "Sir Charles Grandison". (Illus.). 128p. 1981. 24.00 (ISBN 0-19-812637-9). Oxford U Pr.

Southard, Doris. Bobbin Lacemaking. LC 77-2240. (Encore Edition). (Illus.). 1977. 4.95 (ISBN 0-684-16555-4, ScribT). Scribner.

Southard, Edna C. The Frescoes in Siena's Palazzo Pubblico, Twelve Eighty-Nine to Fifteen Thirty-Nine: Studies in Imagery & Relations to Other Communal Palaces in Tuscany. LC 78-74381. (Fine Arts Dissertations, Fourth Ser.). (Illus.). 1980. lib. bdg. 66.00 (ISBN 0-8240-3967-X). Garland Pub.

Southard, Helen. Sex Before Twenty: New Answers for Young People. rev. ed. 1971. 6.95 o.p. (ISBN 0-525-20099-1). Dutton.

Southard, Samuel. Comprehensive Pastoral Care: Enabling the Laity to Share in Pastoral Ministry. 128p. 1975. pap. 3.50 (ISBN 0-8170-0655-9); pap. 9.95 with casette (ISBN 0-8170-0692-3). Judson.

--Pastoral Evangelism. LC 80-82196. 192p. 1981. pap. 8.95 (ISBN 0-8042-2037-9). John Knox.

Southard, W. W. Season of Vengeance. 192p. 1981. pap. 1.95 (ISBN 0-553-14741-2). Bantam.

Southerington, F. R., ed. see Hardy, Thomas.

Southern Appalachian Regional Conference. Toward Nineteen Eighty-Four: The Future of Appalachia? LC 75-521. 1975. pap. 2.95 (ISBN 0-686-27853-4). Appalach Consortium.

Southern, Carol, ed. see Gilbert, Lynn & Moore, Gaylen.

Southern, Carol, ed. see Griffiths, Patricia B.

Southern, Carol, ed. see Penney, Alexandra.

Southern, Carol, ed. see Rosenfeld, Lulla.

Southern, Carol, ed. see Schall, Maxine.

Southern, Eileen. Music of Black Americans: A History. (Illus.). 1971. text ed. 15.00x (ISBN 0-393-02156-4); pap. text ed. 6.95x (ISBN 0-393-09899-0). Norton.

Southern Living Foods Staff. Southern Living Annual Recipes-1980. LC 79-88364. (Illus.). 352p. 1981. 14.95 (ISBN 0-8487-0516-5). Oxmoor Hse.

Southern Living Foods Staff, ed. Southern Living 1979: Annual Recipes. LC 79-88364. 1979. 14.95 (ISBN 0-8487-0513-0). Oxmoor Hse.

Southern Living Garden & Landscape Staff. Trees & Shrubs. 1980. cancelled (ISBN 0-8487-0512-2). Oxmoor Hse.

Southern Living Gardening Staff & Floyd, John A., Jr. Southern Living Garden Guide: Your Answer Book to Garden Questions. LC 80-84409. (Illus.). 224p. 198 . 17.95 (ISBN 0-8487-0518-1). Oxmoor Hse.

Southern Living Travel Editors, jt. auth. see Rand McNally & Company.

Southern, R., tr. see Gongora, M.

Southern, R. W., ed. & tr. see Eadmer.

Southern, Richard. The Staging of Plays Before Shakespeare. LC 73-76707. (Illus.). 1973. 19.95 (ISBN 0-87830-130-5). Theatre Arts.

Southern, Richard W. St. Anselm & His Biographer. 58.00 (ISBN 0-521-06532-1). Cambridge U Pr.

Southerton, Peter. Story of a Prison: History of Penal Practice, 16th Century to Modern Times. (Illus.). 1975. 11.95x o.p. (ISBN 0-8464-0885-6). Beekman Pubs.

Southey, E. G. Photographic Careers. 1978. pap. 7.95 o.p. (ISBN 0-85242-541-0, Pub. by Fountain). Morgan.

Southey, Robert. A Choice of Southey's Verse. Grigson, Geoffrey, ed. 1971. 4.95 o.p. (ISBN 0-571-09055-9, Pub. by Faber & Faber); pap. 3.95 (ISBN 0-571-09056-7). Merrimack Bk Serv.

--Essays, Moral & Political, 2 vols. 865p. 1971. Repr. of 1832 ed. 70.00x (ISBN 0-686-28336-8, Pub. by Irish Academic Pr). Biblio Dist.

--The Remains of Henry White, with an Account of His Life. Reiman, Donald H., ed. LC 75-31271. (Romantic Context Ser.: Poetry 1789-1830). 1978. lib. bdg. 47.00 (ISBN 0-8240-2217-3). Garland Pub.

Southgate, D. A. Determination of Food Carbohydrates (Illus.). 1976. 40.90x (ISBN 0-85334-693-3, Pub. by Applied Science). Burgess-Intl Ideas.

Southgate, Minoo, ed. Modern Persian Short Stories. LC 79-89930. 228p. (Orig.). 1980. 14.00x (ISBN 0-89410-032-7, 033-5); pap. 6.00x (ISBN 0-686-64484-0). Three Continents.

Southgate, Minoo S., tr. Iskandarnamah: A Persian Medieval Alexander-Romance. LC 77-27047. 1978. 17.50x (ISBN 0-231-04416-X). Columbia U Pr.

Southgate, Patsy, tr. see Sabatier, Robert.

Southwell, B. C. Making & Decorating Pottery Tiles. 1972. 9.95 (ISBN 0-571-09603-4, Pub. by Faber & Faber). Merrimack Bk Serv.

Southwell, Samuel B. Quest for Eros: Browning & "Fifine". LC 79-4945. 272p. 1980. 17.00x (ISBN 0-8131-1399-7). U Pr of Ky.

Southwell-Sander, Peter. Verdi, His Life & Times. expanded ed. (Illus.). 192p. Repr. of 1978 ed. 19.95 (ISBN 0-87666-639-X). Paganiniana Pubns.

--Verdi-His Life & Times. (Illustrated Lives & Times of the Composers). (Illus.). 1978. 16.95 (ISBN 0-8467-0421-8, Pub. by Two Continents); pap. 5.95 (ISBN 0-8467-0422-6). Hippocrene Bks.

Southwest Regional Laboratory for Education Research & Development. Instructional Product Research, 8 vols. Incl. Vol. 1. Classifying & Interpreting Educational Research Studies. pap. text ed. 1.95x (ISBN 0-442-27863-2); Vol. 2. Selecting Variables for Educational Research. pap. text ed. 1.95x (ISBN 0-442-27864-0); Vol. 3. Components of the Educational Research Proposal. pap. text ed. 1.50x (ISBN 0-442-27865-9); Vol. 4. pap. o.p.; Vol. 5. pap. o.p.; Vol. 6. Choosing an Appropriate Statistical Procedure. pap. text ed. 1.95x (ISBN 0-442-27868-3); Vol. 7. The Use of Library Computer Programs for Statistical Analysis. pap. text ed. 1.50x (ISBN 0-442-27869-1); Vol. 8. The Research Report. pap. text ed. 1.95x (ISBN 0-442-27870-5). 1972. Van Nos Reinhold.

Southwestern Law Enforcement Institute. Traffic Law Enforcement: A Guide for Patrolmen. (Illus.). 116p. 1971. 9.75 (ISBN 0-398-01816-2). C C Thomas.

Southwick, Albert P. Quizzism & Its Key. LC 68-22051. 1970. Repr. of 1884 ed. 15.00 (ISBN 0-8103-3094-6). Gale.

--Wisps of Wit & Wisdom, or Knowledge in a Nutshell. LC 68-30582. 1968. Repr. of 1892 ed. 15.00 (ISBN 0-8103-3095-4). Gale.

Southwick, Arthur F. The Law of Hospital & Health Care Administration. LC 78-4846. 1978. text ed. 29.50 (ISBN 0-914904-27-2). Health Admin Pr.

Southwick, Marcia. Build with Adobe. 2nd rev. & enl. ed. LC 73-1504. (Illus.). 225p. 1974. pap. 5.95 (ISBN 0-8040-0634-2, SB). Swallow.

Southwick, Selma I., jt. auth. see Jolles, Isaac.

Southworth, jt. auth. see Van Duyn, John.

Southworth, Franklin. Student's Hindi-Urdu Reference Manual. LC 71-164367. 256p. 1971. pap. 4.95x o.p. (ISBN 0-8165-0306-0). U of Ariz Pr.

Southworth, Franklin C. & Daswani, Chander J. Foundations of Linguistics. LC 73-9137. (Illus.). 1974. text ed. 14.95 (ISBN 0-02-930300-1). Free Pr.

Southworth, Franklin C., jt. auth. see Kavadi, Naresh B.

Southworth, H. N. & Hull, R. A. Introduction to Modern Microscopy. LC 74-32488. (Wykeham Science Ser.: No.34). 1975. 8.60x (ISBN 0-8448-1161-0). Crane-Russak Co.

Southworth, Herbert R. Guernica! Guernica! A Study of Journalism, Diplomacy, Propaganda, & History. LC 74-82850. 1977. 25.00x (ISBN 0-520-02830-9). U of Cal Pr.

Souviney, Randall. Solving Problems Kids Care About. (Illus.). 176p. (Orig.). 1981. pap. 10.95 (ISBN 0-8302-8653-5). Goodyear.

Souza, Anthony De see Vogeler, Ingolf & De Souza, Anthony.

Souza, F. Refugees: Viewpoints, Case Studies & Theoretical Considerations on the Care & Management of Refugees. (Illus.). 136p. 1980. 19.25 (ISBN 0-08-025460-8). Pergamon.

Souza, Harry E., jt. auth. see Holmes, Paul C.

Sova, Margaret, jt. auth. see Kreitner, Robert.

Sovani, N. V. Urbanization & Urban India. 7.50x (ISBN 0-210-22695-1). Asia.

Sovik, Nils. Developmental Cybernetics of Handwriting & Graphic Behavior: An Experimental System Analysis of Writing Readiness & Instruction. 1975. pap. text ed. 30.00x (ISBN 8-200-01476-2, Dist. by Columbia U Pr). Universitet.

Sowande, Bode. Farewell to Babylon. 179p. (Orig.). 1979. 9.00 (ISBN 0-89410-107-2); pap. 5.00 (ISBN 0-89410-106-4). Three Continents.

Soward, J. Kelley. Desiderius Erasmus. LC 74-23864. (World Authors Ser.: Netherlands: No. 353). 1975. lib. bdg. 12.50 (ISBN 0-8057-2302-1). Twayne.

Sowby, F. D., ed. Annals of the ICRP, Vol. 5, No. 1-6. (ICRP Publication: No. 30, Supplement to Part 2). 756p. 1980. 100.00. Pergamon.

--Radionuclide Release into the Environment: Assessment of Doses to Man. (International Commission on Radiological Protection Publications: No 29). (Illus.). pap. 18.25 (ISBN 0-08-022635-3). Pergamon.

Sowder, Barbara J. & Burt, Marvin R. Children of Heroin Addicts. 200p. 1980. 18.95 (ISBN 0-03-057033-6). Praeger.

Sowelem, R. A. Towards Financial Independence in a Developing Economy: An Analysis of the Monetary Experience of the Federation of Rhodesia & Nyasaland. (Charts). 1967. text ed. 11.00x (ISBN 0-04-332028-7). Humanities.

Sowell, Andrew J. Rangers & Pioneers of Texas. (Illus.). 1964. Repr. of 1884 ed. 20.00 (ISBN 0-87266-029-X). Argosy.

Sowell, Ellis. The Evolution of the Theories & Techniques of Standard Costs. LC 73-2027. 548p. 1973. 15.00 (ISBN 0-8173-8901-6). U of Ala Pr.

Sowell, Thomas. Ethnic America: A History. (Illus.). 336p. 1981. 16.95 (ISBN 0-465-02074-7). Basic.

--Race & Economics. LC 74-19982. 1975. pap. text ed. 9.95x (ISBN 0-582-28015-X). Longman.

Sowell, Thomas, ed. American Ethnic Groups. 254p. 1978. pap. 7.50 (ISBN 0-87766-210-X, 16100). Urban Inst.

--Essays & Data on American Ethnic Groups. 420p. 1978. 15.00 (ISBN 0-87766-211-8, 20800). Urban Inst.

Sowers, Robert. The Language of Stained Glass. (Illus.). 220p. 1981. 24.95 (ISBN 0-917304-61-6, Pub. by Timber Pr). Intl Schol Bk Serv.

Sowerwine, Martha, jt. auth. see Sonenblick, Jerry.

Sowinski, A. Musiciens Polonais & Slaves. LC 77-155149. (Music Ser). 1971. Repr. of 1857 ed. lib. bdg. 55.00 (ISBN 0-306-70166-9). Da Capo.

Sowls, Lyle K. Prairie Ducks: A Study of Their Behavior, Ecology & Management. LC 77-14153. (Illus.). 1978. 11.50x (ISBN 0-8032-0978-9); pap. 3.50 (ISBN 0-8032-5895-X, BB 665, Bison). U of Nebr Pr.

Sowter. Bridge: Improve Your Defence. 1979. 17.95 (ISBN 0-7134-1621-1, Pub. by Batsford England). David & Charles.

Sowton, E., jt. auth. see Siddons, H.

Soyer, Raphael. Diary of an Artist. LC 77-4798. (Illus.). 1977. 15.95 o.p. (ISBN 0-915220-29-6); deluxe ed. 200.00 o.p. (ISBN 0-915220-33-4). New Republic.

Soyinka, W. Myth, Literature & the African World. LC 75-38184. 180p. 1976. 27.50 (ISBN 0-521-21190-5); pap. 8.95 (ISBN 0-521-29394-4). Cambridge U Pr.

Soyinka, Wole. Camwood on the Leaves & Before the Blackout: Plays. LC 73-92792. 1973. 5.95 (ISBN 0-89388-150-3); pap. 2.95. Okpaku Communications.

--Idanre & Other Poems. LC 68-30761. 88p. 1968. 3.95 (ISBN 0-8090-5725-5); pap. 1.75 (ISBN 0-8090-1352-5). Hill & Wang.

--Ogun Abibiman. 24p. 1976. pap. 5.00x (ISBN 0-86036-031-8). Three Continents.

Sozu, Kate, tr. see Castoriadis, Cornelius.

Sozuki. East Asian Cooking. 1981. 8.95 (ISBN 0-8120-5401-6). Barron.

Space Science Board. Biology & the Exploration of Mars. 1965. 8.75 (ISBN 0-309-01296-1). Natl Acad Pr.

--Human Factors in Long-Duration Space Flight. LC 70-189063. (Illus.). 288p. 1972. pap. 6.75 (ISBN 0-309-01947-8). Natl Acad Pr.

--Planetary Astronomy: An Appraisal of Ground-Based Opportunities. 1968. pap. 4.75 (ISBN 0-309-01688-6). Natl Acad Pr.

--Priorities for Space Research 1971-1980. LC 75-610526. (Orig.). 1971. pap. text ed. 5.25 (ISBN 0-309-01872-2). Natl Acad Pr.

--Radiobiological Factors in Manned Space Flight. Langham, Wright H., ed. 1967. 8.75 (ISBN 0-309-01487-5). Natl Acad Pr.

--Space Research: Directions for the Future. 1966. pap. 8.75 o.p. (ISBN 0-309-01403-4). Natl Acad Pr.

Spache & Spache. Reading in the Elementary School. 4th ed. 1977. text ed. 17.95 o.p. (ISBN 0-205-05784-5); student guide avail. o.p. (ISBN 0-205-05797-7). Allyn.

Spache, Evelyn B. Reading Activities for Child Involvement. 2nd ed. 256p. 1976. pap. text ed. 9.40x (ISBN 0-205-04840-4). Allyn.

--Reproducible Skills & Concept Ideas: Reading Activities for Child Involvement. new ed. 1978. text ed. 18.95 (ISBN 0-205-06557-0). Allyn.

Spache, George D. Diagnosing & Correcting Reading Disabilities. 416p. 1976. pap. text ed. 15.95x o.s.i. (ISBN 0-205-04916-8). Allyn.

--Diagnosing & Correcting Reading Disabilities. 2nd ed. 480p. 1980. text ed. 18.95 (ISBN 0-205-07175-9, 2371758). Allyn.

Spache, George D., et al. Case Studies in Reading Disability. new ed. 250p. 1980. text ed. 13.50 (237258-4). Allyn.

Spack, Eliot G. Evaluating & Supervising Teachers: Research & Methods. 1978. pap. 10.00 o.p. (ISBN 0-686-00907-X, D-116). Essence Pubns.

Spackman, Robert R., Jr. Conditioning for Baseball: Pre-Season, Regular Season & Off-Season. (Illus.). 100p. 1967. 10.75 (ISBN 0-398-01818-9). C C Thomas.

--Conditioning for Football: Pre-Season, Regular Season & Off-Season. (Illus.). 112p. 1968. 11.50 (ISBN 0-398-01819-7). C C Thomas.

--Conditioning for Gymnastics: Pre-Season, Regular Season & Off-Season. (Illus.). 120p. 1970. 12.75 (ISBN 0-398-01820-0). C C Thomas.

--Exercise in the Office: Easy Ways to Better Health & Firmer Figures. LC 68-25554. (Arcturus Books Paperbacks). 112p. pap. 3.95 (ISBN 0-8093-0317-5). S Ill U Pr.

Spackman, Robert R., Jr. & Vincent, William F. Physical Fitness in Law Enforcement: A Guide to More Efficient Service. LC 70-83663. (Illus.). 123p. 1969. pap. 3.95 (ISBN 0-8093-0406-6). S Ill U Pr.

Spackman, W. M. A Presence with Secrets. LC 80-11406. 176p. 1980. 8.95 (ISBN 0-394-51279-0). Knopf.

Spada, James. Captain & Tennille. (Rock 'n Pop Stars Ser). (Illus.). (gr. 4-12). PLB 5.95 (ISBN 0-87191-615-0); pap. 2.95 (ISBN 0-89812-119-1). Creative Ed.

Spadaro, Louis M., ed. New Directions in Austrian Economics. LC 77-28611. (Studies in Economic Theory Ser.). 240p. 1978. 15.00; pap. 4.95. NYU Pr.

Spadone, Frank G. Major Variety & Oddity Guide of U. S. Coins. 8th ed. LC 80-84159. (Collector Ser.). (Illus.). 128p. 1981. pap. 4.95 (ISBN 0-87637-162-4, 162-04). Hse of Collectibles.

Spady, Richard H. Econometric Estimation of Cost Functions for the Regulated Transportation Industries. LC 78-75058. (Outstanding Dissertations in Economics Ser.). 1979. lib. bdg. 25.00 (ISBN 0-8240-4135-6). Garland Pub.

Spady, Richard H., jt. auth. see Friedlaender, Ann F.

Spae, Joseph J. Church & China: Toward Reconciliation? 168p. 1980. pap. 10.00 (ISBN 0-936078-01-4). Chicago Theology & Culture.

Spaeth, Harold J. Supreme Court Policy Making: Explanation & Prediction. LC 78-14493. (Illus.). 1979. text ed. 16.95x (ISBN 0-7167-1013-7); pap. text ed. 8.95x (ISBN 0-7167-1012-9). W H Freeman.

Spaeth, Harold J., jt. auth. see Rohde, David W.

Spaeth, Marcia J., jt. ed. see Zeigler, Earle F.

Spaeth, Sigmund. Read'em & Weep: The Songs You Forgot to Remember. (Music Reprint Ser.). 1979. Repr. of 1926 ed. lib. bdg. 22.50 (ISBN 0-306-79564-7). Da Capo.

--Weep Some More, My Lady. (Music Reprint 1980 Ser.). (Illus.). xv, 268p. 1980. Repr. of 1927 ed. lib. bdg. 22.50 (ISBN 0-306-76003-7). Da Capo.

Spaeth, Sigmund G. Milton's Knowledge of Music. LC 72-8052. (Music Ser). 186p. 1972. Repr. of 1913 ed. lib. bdg. 22.50 (ISBN 0-306-70535-4). Da Capo.

Spaethling, Robert & Weber, Eugene, eds. Literature Eins. 2nd ed. 1979. pap. 5.95x (ISBN 0-393-95041-7). Norton.

--Literature One: Supplementary Readings with Exercises. (Ger). 1972. pap. text ed. 4.95 (ISBN 0-19-501550-9); tapes set 29.95 (ISBN 0-19-501703-X). Oxford U Pr.

Spaey, Elizabeth, tr. see Von Emmichoven, J. E.

Spaggiari, Albert. Fric-Frac. 288p. 1981. pap. 2.50 (ISBN 0-445-04592-2). Popular Lib.

Spague, Charles E., tr. see Schwaller De Lubicz, Isha.

Spahn, Janet P., jt. auth. see Spahn, Theodore J.

Spahn, Mark, jt. auth. see Hadamitzky, Wolfgang.

Spahn, Theodore J. & Spahn, Janet P. From Radical Left to Extreme Right: A Bibliography of Current Periodicals of Protest, Controversy, Advocacy, or Dissent, with Dispassionate Content - Summaries to Guide Librarians & Other Educators, Vol. 3. 2nd. rev. enl. ed. LC 76-126558. 1976. 27.50 (ISBN 0-8108-0883-8). Scarecrow.

Spain, Carl. Letters of Paul to Timothy & Titus. Ferguson, Everett, ed. LC 75-133509. (Living Word New Testament Commentary Ser.: Vol. 14). 1970. 7.95 (ISBN 0-8344-0006-5). Sweet.

Spain, Daphne, jt. auth. see Laska, Shirley.

Spain, David H., ed. The Human Experience: Readings in Sociocultural Anthropology. 1975. pap. text ed. 9.95 o.p. (ISBN 0-256-01708-5). Dorsey.

Spalding. Life & Teaching of the Masters of the Far East, 5 vols. 25.00 set (ISBN 0-87516-088-3); pap. 15.00 set (ISBN 0-686-67590-8). R Collier.

Spalding, A., tr. see Arthus, Gothard.

Spalding, Albert. Rise to Follow: An Autobiography. LC 77-5563. (Music Reprint Ser.). 1977. Repr. of 1943 ed. lib. bdg. 27.50 (ISBN 0-306-77421-6). Da Capo.

Spalding, Arthur W. Who Is the Greatest. LC 41-11607. (Harvest Ser.). 1976. pap. 3.95 (ISBN 0-8163-0271-5, 23568-9). Pacific Pr Pub Assn.

Spalding, D. A., et al. Seminal Research Papers. (Contributions to the History of Psycholgy Ser.: No. 11, Pt. A Orientations). 1978. Repr. of 1873 ed. 30.00 (ISBN 0-89093-160-7). U Pubns Amer.

Spalding, D. Brian & Afgan, N., eds. Heat Transfer & Turbulent Buoyant Convection: Studies & Applications for Natural Environment, Buildings Engineering Systems, 2 vols. new ed. LC 77-1868. (Thermal and Fluids Engineering Ser.). (Illus.). 1977. text ed. 129.50 set (ISBN 0-89116-163-5, Co-Pub. by McGraw Intl). Hemisphere Pub.

Spalding, D. Brian & Afgan, Naim H., eds. Heat & Mass Transfer in Metallurgical Systems: Proceedings of the International Center for Heat & Mass Transfer. (Illus.). 800p. 1981. text ed. 85.50 (ISBN 0-89116-169-4). Hemisphere Pub.

Spalding, D. Brian, jt. ed. see Kakac, Sadik.

Spalding, Dudley B., ed. GENMIX: A General Computer Program for Two-Dimensional Parabolic Flow. LC 77-7978. 1977. text ed. 66.00 (ISBN 0-08-021708-7). Pergamon.

Spalding, Elizabeth C. How to Raise & Train a Cavalier King Charles Spaniel. (Orig.). pap. 1.79 o.p. (ISBN 0-87666-264-5, DS1142). TFH Pubns.

Spalding, Eugenia K. & Notter, Lucille E. Professional Nursing: Foundations, Perspectives & Relationships. 8th ed. LC 76-109946. (Illus.). 1970. text ed. 10.75 o.p. (ISBN 0-397-54109-0). Lippincott.

Spalding, Eugenia K., jt. auth. see Notter, Lucille E.

Spalding, Henry, ed. Joys of Italian Humor & Folklore. LC 80-13750. 360p. 1980. 16.95 (ISBN 0-8246-0255-2). Jonathan David.

Spalding, Hobart A., Jr. Organized Labor in Latin America: Historical Case Studies of Workers in Dependent Societies. LC 77-10203. 1977. 17.50x (ISBN 0-8147-7787-2). NYU Pr.

Spalding, R. W., jt. auth. see McFadden, A. Elisabeth.

Spalding, Walter R. Music at Harvard: A Historical Review of Men & Events. LC 76-58921. (Music Reprint Series). 1977. Repr. of 1935 ed. lib. bdg. 27.50 (ISBN 0-306-70871-X). Da Capo.

Spallato, Sonja L., jt. auth. see Psaltis, Cynthia D.

Spallholz, J. E., et al. Selenium in Biology & Medicine: Second International Symposium. (Illus.). 1981. lib. bdg. 45.00 (ISBN 0-87055-379-8). AVI.

Spangler, Charles W. Organic Chemistry: A Brief Contemporary Perspective. (Illus.). 1980. text ed. 19.95 (ISBN 0-13-640318-2); pap. 4.95 (ISBN 0-13-640342-5). P-H.

Spangler, David. Arithmetic Skills in Everyday Life: A Self-Correcting Competency Assessment. 112p. 1980. pap. text ed. 2.95x (ISBN 0-534-00917-4). Wadsworth Pub.

Spangler, Earl. Blacks in America. LC 71-150773. (In America Bks.). (Illus.). (gr. 5-11). 1980. PLB 5.95. Lerner Pubns.

--Negro in America. rev. ed. LC 71-150773. (In America Bks.). (Illus.). (gr. 5-11). 1971. PLB 5.95 o.p. (ISBN 0-8225-0207-0). Lerner Pubns.

Spangler, John, jt. auth. see Williams, Dudley.

Spangler, Richard, jt. auth. see Chow, David.

Spangler, Richard C. Arithmetic: The Essentials. 576p. (Orig.). 1981. pap. text ed. 15.95 (ISBN 0-675-08066-5); tchr's. ed. 5.95 (ISBN 0-675-09971-4). Merrill.

Spanier, John & Nogee, Joe, eds. Congress, the Presidency & American Foreign Policy. (Pergamon Policy Studies). Date not set. price not set (ISBN 0-08-025575-2); pap. price not set (ISBN 0-08-025574-4). Pergamon.

Spanke, Hans, ed. Eine Altfranzosische Liedersammlung, Deranonyme Teil der Liederhandschriften Knpx. LC 80-2161. 1981. Repr. of 1925 ed. 54.50 (ISBN 0-404-19025-1). AMS Pr.

Spann, Meno. Franz Kafka. LC 75-26548. (World Authors Ser.: Austria: No. 381). 1976. lib. bdg. 9.95 (ISBN 0-8057-6182-9). Twayne.

Spann, Nancie, jt. auth. see Spann, Owen.

Spann, Nancy, jt. auth. see Spann, Owen.

Spann, Owen & Spann, Nancie. The Last Meal on Earth. Stewart, Jay, ed. LC 78-75161. 1979. pap. 4.95 (ISBN 0-89395-022-X). Cal Living Bks.

Spann, Owen & Spann, Nancy. Your Child? I Thought It Was My Child. 1980. pap. write for info. (ISBN 0-671-83084-8). PB.

Spann, Sylvia & Culp, Mary B., eds. Thematic Units in Teaching English & the Humanities. 2nd ed. (Orig.). (gr. 6-12). 1980. pap. text ed. 6.00 (ISBN 0-8141-5376-3). NCTE.

Spannaus, Nancy B. & White, Christopher, eds. The Political Economy of the American Revolution. 1977. pap. text ed. 5.95 (ISBN 0-918388-01-5, Univ Edns). New Benjamin.

Spanner, D. C. Introduction to Thermodynamics. (Experimental Botany Ser.: Vol. 1). 1965. 23.50 o.p. (ISBN 0-12-656050-1). Acad Pr.

Spano, Pier F., et al, eds. Sulpiride & Other Benzamides. 326p. 1979. text ed. 27.00 (ISBN 0-89004-502-X). Raven.

Spanogle, John A., Jr. & Rohner, Ralph J. Consumer Law: Cases & Materials. LC 79-12301. (American Casebook Ser.). 693p. 1979. text ed. 18.95 (ISBN 0-8299-2046-3). West Pub.

Spanos, William V. Christian Tradition in Modern British Verse Drama: The Poetics of Sacramental Time. 1967. 22.00 o.p. (ISBN 0-8135-0554-2). Rutgers U Pr.

Spar, J. Earth, Sea & Air: A Survey of the Geophysical Sciences. 2nd ed. (gr. 9-12). 1965. pap. 8.50 (ISBN 0-201-07093-6). A-W.

Spar, Jerome. Way of the Weather. LC 66-30641. (Creative Science Ser). (gr. 4-9). 1967. PLB 7.95 (ISBN 0-87191-013-6). Creative Ed.

Sparagna, Aniceto. Personal Evangelism Among Roman Catholics. (Orig.). 1978. pap. 3.95 (ISBN 0-89900-122-X). College Pr Pub.

Sparano, Vin. Complete Outdoors Encyclopedia. LC 72-90934. 1980. 18.95 (ISBN 0-06-013955-2, HarpT). Har-Row.

Sparano, Vin T. The Complete Outdoors Encyclopedia. rev. ed. LC 72-90934. (An Outdoor Life Bk.). (Illus.). 634p. 1973. 16.95 (ISBN 0-06-013955-2, 0-06014033, HarpT). Har-Row.

--The Sportsman's Dictionary of Fishing & Hunting Lingo. (Illus.). 1980. 12.95 o.p. (ISBN 0-679-51360-4). McKay.

Sparano, Vin T., ed. The American Fisherman's Fresh & Salt Water Guide. 1976. 12.95 (ISBN 0-87691-214-5). Winchester Pr.

Sparberg, Marshall. Ileostomy Care. (Illus.). 176p. 1971. 14.50 (ISBN 0-398-02620-3). C C Thomas.

Sparberg, Marshall, jt. auth. see Goodman, Michael J.

Sparger, Celia. Anatomy & Ballet. 5th ed. LC 76-146051. (Illus.). 1970. 14.95 (ISBN 0-87830-006-6). Theatre Arts.

Spargo, Benjamin H., et al. Renal Biopsy Pathology with Diagnostic & Therapeutic Implications. 1979. 42.50 (ISBN 0-471-03119-4, Pub. by Wiley-Interscience). Wiley.

Spargo, Edward. The Now Student: Reading & Study Skills. rev ed. (Illus.). (gr. 12 up). 1977. pap. text ed. 4.80x (ISBN 0-89061-120-3); instructor's guide free (ISBN 0-89061-121-1). Jamestown Pubs.

Spargo, Edward & Harris, Raymond. Reading the Content Fields: English. (Content Skills Ser.-Middle Level). (Illus., Orig.). (gr. 6-8). 1978. pap. text ed. 2.40x (ISBN 0-89061-125-4, 551M). Jamestown Pubs.

--Reading the Content Fields: English. (Content Skills Ser.-Advanced Level). (Orig.). (gr. 9-12). 1978. pap. text ed. 2.40x (ISBN 0-89061-135-1, 551-A). Jamestown Pubs.

--Reading the Content Fields: Mathematics. (Content Skills Ser-Advanced Level). (Illus.). (gr. 9-12). 1978. pap. text ed. 2.40x (ISBN 0-89061-139-4, 553A). Jamestown Pubs.

--Reading the Content Fields: Mathematics. (Content Skills Ser.-Middle Level). (Illus.). (gr. 6-8). 1978. pap. text ed. 2.40x (ISBN 0-89061-129-7, 553M). Jamestown Pubs.

--Reading the Content Fields: Practical Arts. (Content Skills Ser.-Advanced Level). (Illus.). (gr. 9-12). 1978. pap. text ed. 2.40x (ISBN 0-89061-143-2, 555A). Jamestown Pubs.

--Reading the Content Fields: Practical Arts. (Contents Skills Ser.-Middle Level). (Illus.). (gr. 6-8). 1978. pap. text ed. 2.40x (ISBN 0-89061-133-5, 555M). Jamestown Pubs.

--Reading the Content Fields: Science. (Content Skills Ser.-Advanced Level). (Illus.). (gr. 9-12). 1978. pap. text ed. 2.40x (ISBN 0-89061-141-6, 554A). Jamestown Pubs.

--Reading the Content Fields: Science. (Content Skills Ser.-Middle Level). (Illus.). (gr. 6-8). 1978. pap. text ed. 2.40x (ISBN 0-89061-131-9, 554M). Jamestown Pubs.

--Reading the Content Fields: Social Studies. (Content Sskills Ser.-Middle Level). (Illus., Orig.). (gr. 6-8). 1978. pap. text ed. 2.40x (ISBN 0-89061-127-0, 552M). Jamestown Pubs.

--Reading the Content Fields: Social Studies. (Content Skills Ser.-Advanced Level). (Illus., Orig.). (gr. 9-12). 1978. pap. text ed. 2.40x (ISBN 0-89061-137-8, 552A). Jamestown Pubs.

Spargo, Edward, jt. auth. see Smith, Barry M.

Spargo, Edward, ed. Selections from the Black Brown Book. 2nd ed. (The College Reading Skills Ser). (Illus.). 176p. (gr. 12 up). 1974. pap. text ed. 4.80x (ISBN 0-89061-001-0). Jamestown Pubs.

--Selections from the Black Olive Book. 2nd ed. (The College Reading Skills Ser). (Illus.). 176p. (gr. 12 up). 1974. pap. text ed. 4.80x (ISBN 0-89061-000-2). Jamestown Pubs.
--Selections from the Black Purple Book. 2nd ed. (The College Reading Skills Ser). (Illus.). 176p. (gr. 12 up). 1974. pap. text ed. 4.80x (ISBN 0-89061-002-9). Jamestown Pubs.
--Topics for the Restless Brown Book. (The College Reading Skills Ser). (Illus.). 176p. (gr. 12 up). 1974. pap. text ed. 4.80x (ISBN 0-89061-007-X). Jamestown Pubs.
--Topics for the Restless Olive Book. (The College Reading Skills Ser). (Illus.). 176p. (gr. 12 up). 1974. pap. text ed. 4.80 (ISBN 0-89061-006-1). Jamestown Pubs.
--Topics for the Restless Purple Book. (The College Reading Skills Ser). (Illus.). 176p. (gr. 12 up). 1974. pap. text ed. 4.80x (ISBN 0-89061-008-8). Jamestown Pubs.
Spargo, Edward, ed. see Giroux, James A.
Spargo, Edward, ed. see Giroux, James A. & Twining, James E.
Spargo, Edward, ed. see Giroux, James A. & Williston, Glenn R.
Spargo, Edward, et al. Timed Readings. (Illus., Orig.). (gr. 4-5). 1979. Bk. 1, 120p. pap. text ed. 2.80 (ISBN 0-89061-198-X, 801); Bk. 2, 120p. pap. text ed. 2.80 (ISBN 0-89061-199-8, 802). Jamestown Pubs.
Spargo, Edward, et al, eds. Voices from the Bottom Brown Book. (The College Reading Skills Ser). (Illus.). 176p. (gr. 12 up). 1972. pap. text ed. 4.80x (ISBN 0-89061-004-5). Jamestown Pubs.
--Voices from the Bottom Olive Book. (The College Reading Skills Ser). (Illus.). 176p. (gr. 12 up). 1972. pap. text ed. 4.80x (ISBN 0-89061-003-7). Jamestown Pubs.
--Voices from the Bottom Purple Book. (The College Reading Skills Ser). (Illus.). 176p. (gr. 12 up). 1972. pap. text ed. 4.80x (ISBN 0-89061-005-3). Jamestown Pubs.
Spark, Muriel. The Abbess of Crewe. 1977. pap. 1.95 o.s.i. (ISBN 0-14-004074-9). Penguin.
--Girls of Slender Means. 1963. 4.95 o.p. (ISBN 0-394-42637-1). Knopf.
--Prime of Miss Jean Brodie. LC 62-7182. 1962. 3.95 o.p. (ISBN 0-397-00232-7). Lippincott.
Sparke, Archibald, ed. see Corns, Albert R.
Sparke, Edgar H. Cantus Firmus in Mass & Motet Fourteen Twenty to Fifteen Twenty. LC 74-31190. (Music Reprint Ser). (Illus.). xi, 504p. 1975. Repr. of 1963 ed. lib. bdg. 42.50 (ISBN 0-306-70720-9). Da Capo.
Sparkes, Ivan G., ed. A Dictionary of Collective Nouns & Group Terms. LC 75-4117. 213p. 1975. 28.00 (ISBN 0-8103-2016-9, Pub. by White Lion Publishers). Gale.
Sparkes, J. J. Transistor Switching & Sequential Circuits. 1969. 22.00 (ISBN 0-08-012982-X); pap. 10.75 (ISBN 0-08-012981-1). Pergamon.
Sparkes, John C. How to Master the Art of Pottery Painting. (Illus.). 101p. 1981. 39.75 (ISBN 0-930582-86-1). Gloucester Art.
Sparkes, Robert S., et al, eds. see ICN-UCLA Symposia on Molecular & Cellular Biology.
Sparkes, Roy. Exploring Materials with Young Children. 1975. pap. 13.50 (ISBN 0-7134-2926-7, Pub. by Batsford England). David & Charles.
--Painting Without a Brush. 1978. 16.95 (ISBN 0-7134-0189-3). David & Charles.
--Teaching Art Basics. 1973. 17.95 (ISBN 0-7134-2314-5, Pub. by Batsford England). David & Charles.
Sparkes, Vernone M. Theological Enterprise. LC 73-89842. 1969. pap. 6.50 o.p. (ISBN 0-8309-0020-9). Herald Hse.
Sparkia, Roy. The Dirty Rotten Truth. 1973. pap. 1.25 (ISBN 0-451-07721-0, Y7721, Sig). NAL.
--The Golden People. 1976. pap. 1.95 o.s.i. (ISBN 0-515-03974-8). Jove Pubns.
Sparks, Albert K. Invertebrate Pathology: Noncommunicable Diseases. 1972. 48.50 (ISBN 0-12-656450-7). Acad Pr.
Sparks, Beatrice. Voices. 1980. pap. 1.95 o.s.i. (ISBN 0-440-19024-X). Dell.
Sparks, George, ed. see Ashurst, Henry F.
Sparks, H. F. On Translations of the Bible. (Ethel M. Wood Lectures). 1973. pap. text ed. 2.50x (ISBN 0-485-14316-X, Athlone Pr). Humanities.
Sparks, Howard. Amazing Mail Order Business & How to Succeed in It. LC 66-17336. 1966. 9.95 (ISBN 0-8119-0005-3). Fell.
Sparks, J. E. & Johnson, C. E. Reading for Power & Flexibility. 1970. text ed. 6.95x (ISBN 0-02-478400-1, 47840). Macmillan.
Sparks, J. E. & Johnson, Carl E. Read Right: Comprehension Power. 1971. pap. text ed. 8.95x (ISBN 0-02-478390-0, 47839). Macmillan.
Sparks, Jack. The Mindbenders. LC 79-4290. 1977. pap. 4.95 (ISBN 0-8407-5686-0). Nelson.
Sparks, Jack, ed. The Apostolic Fathers: New Translations of Early Christian Writings. LC 78-14870. 1978. pap. 5.95 (ISBN 0-8407-5661-5). Nelson.
Sparks, James C. Mini & Trail Bikes: How to Build Them Yourself. (Illus.). 1976. 9.95 (ISBN 0-87690-184-4); pap. 5.95 (ISBN 0-87690-190-9). Dutton.
Sparks, James C., Jr., jt. auth. see McFarland, Kenton.
Sparks, Jerry D. Overhead Projection. Duane, James E., ed. LC 80-21334. (The Instructional Media Library: Vol. 10). (Illus.). 112p. 1981. 13.95 (ISBN 0-87778-170-2). Educ Tech Pubns.
Sparks, Judith, ed. Christman Programs for the Church, No. 14. 64p. (Orig.). 1981. pap. 2.75 (ISBN 0-87239-437-9, 8614). Standard Pub.
--Christmas Programs for the Church, No. 13. 64p. (Orig.). 1980. pap. 2.75 (ISBN 0-87239-392-5, 8613). Standard Pub.
Sparks, Judith, ed. see O'Rourke, Robert.
Sparks, Judy, ed. Spring Programs for the Church, No. 1. (Special-Day Program Bks). 64p. (Orig.). 1979. pap. 2.75 (ISBN 0-87239-253-8, 8731). Standard Pub.
Sparks, Laurence. Self-Hypnosis: A Conditioned - Response Technique. pap. 4.00 (ISBN 0-87980-139-5). Wilshire.
Sparks, Leroy, jt. auth. see Garber, A. Brent.
Sparks, Phillip D., et al. Study Notes for the Biological Sciences. 1973. pap. text ed. 4.95 o.p. (ISBN 0-8087-6033-5). Burgess.
Sparks, Richard, jt. auth. see Elstein, Max.
Sparks, Richard M. & Shalita, Richard A. Prostaglandin Abstracts: A Guide to the Literature, 1906-1970. Incl. Vol. 1. 497p. 1974 (ISBN 0-306-67011-9); Vol. 2. 451p. 1975 (ISBN 0-306-67012-7). LC 73-21780. 75.00 ea. IFI Plenum.
Sparlin, Don M., jt. auth. see Alexander, Ralph W.
Sparling, Joseph & Lewis, Isabelle. Learning Games for the First Three Years. 320p. 1981. pap. 2.95 (ISBN 0-425-04752-0). Berkley Pub.
--Learningames for the First Three Years. 1981. pap. 2.95 (ISBN 0-425-04752-0). Berkley Pub.
Sparnaay, M. J. The Electrical Double Layer. 427p. 1973. text ed. 64.00 (ISBN 0-08-016852-3). Pergamon.
Sparrow, E. M. & Cess, R. D. Radiation Heat Transfer: Augmented Edition. LC 77-24158. (McGraw-Hill Series in Thermal & Fluids Engineering). (Illus.). 1978. text ed. 25.95 (ISBN 0-07-059910-6, Hemisphere Pub. Corp.). McGraw.
Sparrow, Freddie, ed. see Rudduck, J. & Kelly, P.
Sparrow, Geoffrey. Foxes & Physic. (Illus.). 3.75 o.p. (ISBN 0-85131-067-2, Dist. by Sporting Book Center). J A Allen.
--The Terriers Vocation. (Illus.). pap. 4.35 (ISBN 0-85131-111-3, Dist. by Sporting Book Center). J A Allen.
Sparrow, Jane. Diary of a Delinquent Episode. (Orig.). 1976. pap. 7.95 (ISBN 0-7100-8340-8). Routledge & Kegan.
--Diary of a Student Social Worker. 1978. 14.00 (ISBN 0-7100-8857-4). Routledge & Kegan.
Sparrow, John. Half Lines & Repetitions in Virgil. Commager, Steele, ed. LC 77-70823. (Latin Poetry Ser.). 1978. lib. bdg. 15.50 (ISBN 0-8240-2979-8). Garland Pub.
--Visible Words: A Study of Inscriptions in Books As Works of Art. LC 68-10027. (Illus.). 1969. 75.00 (ISBN 0-521-06534-8). Cambridge U Pr.
Sparrow, Stephen, ed. Immunodeficient Animals for Cancer Research. (Illus.). 230p. 1980. text ed. 39.50 (ISBN 0-19-520220-1). Oxford U Pr.
Spate, O. H. Pacific Since Magellan: The Spanish Lake, Vol. 1. LC 78-23164. 1979. 39.50x (ISBN 0-8166-0882-2). U of Minn Pr.
Spath, H. Cluster Analysis Algorithms: For Data Reduction & Classification of Objects. (Computers & Their Applications). 226p. 1980. 56.95x (ISBN 0-470-26946-4). Halsted Pr.
Spatola, Anthony L. Mastering Medical Language. (Illus.). 464p. 1981. pap. text ed. 15.95 (ISBN 0-13-560151-7). P-H.
Spatt, Leslie & Koegler, Horst. Stuttgart Ballet. 1978. 14.95 (ISBN 0-903102-42-0). Dance Horiz.
Spatz, Chris & Johnston, James O. Basic Statistics: Tales of Distributions. 2nd ed. 1980. text ed. 16.95 (ISBN 0-8185-0384-X). Brooks-Cole.
Spatz, Chris, jt. auth. see Johnston, James O.
Spatz, Jacob. The Speaker's Bible. 200p. 1981. 12.95 (ISBN 0-8159-6841-8). Devin.
Spatz, Lois S. Aristophanes. (World Authors Ser.: No. 482). 1978. lib. bdg. 10.95 (ISBN 0-8057-6323-6). Twayne.
Spatz, M., et al, eds. Circulatory & Developmental Aspects of Brain Metabolism. 445p. 1980. 49.50 (ISBN 0-306-40542-3, Plenum Pr). Plenum Pub.
Spaulding, C. E. & Spaulding, Jackie. The Complete Care of Orphaned or Abandoned Baby Animals. (Illus.). 1979. 10.95 (ISBN 0-87857-266-X); pap. 7.95 (ISBN 0-87857-265-1). Rodale Pr Inc.
Spaulding, Clark & Spaulding, Jackie. Dr. Spaulding's Veterinary Answer Book. (Illus.). 1978. lib. bdg. 13.50 (ISBN 0-88930-026-7, Pub. by Cloudburst Canada); pap. 6.95 (ISBN 0-88930-025-9). Madrona Pubs.
Spaulding, J. G., jt. auth. see Pollock, T. C.
Spaulding, Jackie, jt. auth. see Spaulding, C. E.
Spaulding, Jackie, jt. auth. see Spaulding, Clark.
Spaulding, Karen L., ed. Alfred Jensen: Paintings & Diagrams from the Years 1957-1977. LC 77-83756. (Illus.). 1978. pap. 12.00 (ISBN 0-914782-15-0, Pub. by Albright-Knox Art Gallery). C E Tuttle.
Spaulding, Malcolm, jt. auth. see Gordon, Robert.
Spaulding, Robert K. How Spanish Grew. (YA) (gr. 9-12). 1943. pap. 5.95 (ISBN 0-520-01193-7, CAMPUS60). U of Cal Pr.
Spaulding, Ruth. The Improbable Puritan. (Illus.). 1975. 12.95 o.p. (ISBN 0-571-10626-9, Pub. by Faber & Faber). Merrimack Bk Serv.
Spaulding, Seth, et al. The World's Students in the United States: A Review & Evaluation of Research on Foreign Students. LC 75-23992. (Special Studies). (Illus.). 544p. 1976. text ed. 31.95 (ISBN 0-275-56130-5). Praeger.
Spaventa, Lou, ed. Towards the Creative Teaching of English. (Illus., Orig.). 1980. pap. text ed. 8.95x (ISBN 0-04-371074-3, 2558). Allen Unwin.
Speaight, G. The History of the Circus. LC 80-17376. 216p. 1980. 20.00 (ISBN 0-498-02470-9). A S Barnes.
Speak, P. & Carter, A. H. Map Reading & Interpretation. (Illus., New Edition with Metric Examples). 1974. pap. text ed. 6.50x (ISBN 0-582-31010-5). Longman.
Speake, George. Anglo-Saxon Animal Art & Its Germanic Background. (Illus.). 164p. 1980. text ed. 50.00x (ISBN 0-19-813194-1). Oxford U Pr.
Speakman, J. C., jt. auth. see Brand, J. C.
Spear, Brad. Cheyenne Payoff. 1981. pap. 2.25 (ISBN 0-440-01269-4). Dell.
--The Silver Mistress. 1981. pap. 2.25 (ISBN 0-440-07940-3). Dell.
Spear, Curtis V. Self-Assessment of Knowledge in Orthopedic Surgery. LC 80-80368. 1980. pap. 16.50 (ISBN 0-87488-225-X). Med Exam.
Spear, F. G., ed. Certain Aspects of the Action of Radiation on Living Cells. 1980. 10.00x (Pub. by Brit Inst Radiology England). State Mutual Bk.
Spear, George E., jt. ed. see Mocker, Donald W.
Spear, Hilda D., ed. see Calverley, C. S.
Spear, Percival. The Oxford History of Modern India: Seventeen Forty to Nineteen Seventy-Five. 2nd ed. 1979. pap. 6.95 (ISBN 0-19-561076-8). Oxford U Pr.
Spear, Percival, ed. The Nabobs. 1980. Repr. of 1963 ed. 17.00x (ISBN 0-8364-0659-1, Pub. by Curzon Pr). South Asia Bks.
Spear, Victor I. Sports Illustrated Racquetball. 1979. 8.95 (ISBN 0-685-93949-9); pap. 5.95 (ISBN 0-685-93950-2). Lippincott.
Speare, Elizabeth. The Witch of Blackbird Pond. 256p. (gr. 5-8). 1972. pap. 1.75 (ISBN 0-440-49569-5, YB). Dell.
Speare, Jean E., ed. The Days of Augusta. LC 75-13479. (Illus.). 1977. pap. 5.95 sewn binding (ISBN 0-914842-04-8). Madrona Pubs.
Spearing, A. C. Gawain-Poet. LC 72-112476. 1971. 42.00 (ISBN 0-521-07851-2); pap. 10.95x (ISBN 0-521-29119-4). Cambridge U Pr.
--Medieval Dream-Poetry. LC 75-46114. 1976. 42.00 (ISBN 0-521-21194-8); pap. 10.95x (ISBN 0-521-29069-4). Cambridge U Pr.
Spearing, A. C., ed. see Chaucer, Geoffrey.
Spearl, Alexander. Living with a Car. 12.50x (ISBN 0-392-05915-0, SpS). Soccer.
Spearman, jt. auth. see Miles, A. J.
Spearman, James E. United States Metallurgical Coal Industry. 209p. 1980. 12.50 (ISBN 0-937058-00-9). West Va U Lib.
Spearman, R. I. The Integument, a Textbook of Skin Biology. LC 72-88612. (Biological Structure & Function Ser.: No. 3). (Illus.). 200p. 1973. 40.00 (ISBN 0-521-20048-2). Cambridge U Pr.
Spears, Charleszine W. How to Wear Colors: With Emphasis on Dark Skins. 5th ed. LC 73-89010. 1974. pap. text ed. 5.50 o.p. (ISBN 0-8087-1927-0). Burgess.
Spears, Jack. The Civil War on the Screen & Other Essays. LC 75-5175. 1977. 17.50 o.p. (ISBN 0-498-01728-1). A S Barnes.
Spears, John R. The Fighting Whales As Whalers Knew Them. (American Culture Library Bk). (Illus.). 137p. 1981. 27.45 (ISBN 0-89266-289-1). Am Classical Coll Pr.
Spears, Stanley. Stop Dying & Live Forever. 1972. pap. 2.95 o.p. (ISBN 0-87516-122-7). De Vorss.
Speas, Jan C. Bride of the Machugh. 1977. pap. 1.95 (ISBN 0-380-01825-X, 36152). Avon.
--My Lord Monleigh. 1977. pap. 1.95 (ISBN 0-380-01847-0, 36442). Avon.
Spece, Roy G., Jr., jt. auth. see Shapiro, Michael H.
Spechler, Dina R. Domestic Influences on Soviet Foreign Policy. LC 78-61396. 1978. pap. text ed. 6.75 (ISBN 0-8191-0596-1). U Pr of Amer.
Specht, David I., jt. auth. see Bloch, Peter B.
Specht, H., jt. auth. see Gilbert, N.
Specht, Harry, jt. auth. see Brager, George.
Specht, Harry, jt. auth. see Gilbert, Neil.
Specht, Harry, jt. ed. see Kramer, Ralph M.
Special Consultative Committee On Security. Cultural Congress of Havana. (Eng. & Span.). 1968. 2.00 ea. o.p. OAS.
--Moscow Conference. (Eng. & Span.). 1968. pap. 1.00 ea. o.p. OAS.
Special Learning Corp., ed. Learning Disabilities: Reference Book. (Special Education Ser.). (Illus., Orig.). 1980. pap. text ed. 64.00 (ISBN 0-89568-116-1). Spec Learn Corp.
Special Learning Corp, ed. Mental Retardation. rev. ed. (Special Education Ser.). (Illus., Orig.). 1980. pap. text ed. write for info. (ISBN 0-89568-195-1). Spec Learn Corp.
Special Learning Corporation. Readings in Mainstreaming. rev. ed. Sullivan, John M., ed. (Special Education Ser.). (Illus.). 224p. 1981. pap. text ed. 9.95 (ISBN 0-89568-293-1). Spec Learn Corp.
Specialists Meeting Held at the Central Bureau for Nuclear Measurements, Geel, Belgium, 5-8 Dec. 1977. Neutron Data of Structural Materials for Fast Reactors: Proceedings. Bockhoff, K. H., ed. (Illus.). 1979. text ed. 120.00 (ISBN 0-08-023424-0). Pergamon.
Speck, Frank G. Naskapi: The Savage Hunters of the Labrador Peninsula. (Civilization of the American Indian Ser: Vol. 10). (Illus.). 1935. 12.50 (ISBN 0-8061-1412-6); pap. 5.95 (ISBN 0-8061-1418-5). U of Okla Pr.
Speck, S. L. & Riggle, H. M., eds. Bible Readings for Bible Students & for the Home & Fireside. 432p. 1902. 5.00. Faith Pub Hse.
Speckhart, Frank H. & Green, Walter L. A Guide to Using CSMP: The Continuous System Modeling Program - a Program for Simulating Physical Systems. 1976. 18.95 (ISBN 0-13-371377-6); solutions manual 4.50 (ISBN 0-13-371351-2). P-H.
Specter, Gerald & Claiborn, William, eds. Crisis Intervention. LC 73-4360. (Continuing Series in Community-Clinical Psychology: Vol. 2). 224p. 1973. text ed. 19.95 (ISBN 0-87705-118-6); pap. write for info. (ISBN 0-87705-124-0). Human Sci Pr.
Spector, Leo & Weiss, Richard. Chemistry Achievement Test. LC 65-23057. (College Board Ach. Test Ser.). 318p. 1966. lib. bdg. 4.50 o.p. (ISBN 0-668-01261-7). Arco.
Spector, Malcom & Kitsuse, John. Constructing Social Problems. LC 76-29487. 1977. pap. text ed. 7.95 (ISBN 0-8465-6725-3). Benjamin-Cummings.
Spector, Rachel E. Cultural Diversity in Health & Illness. (Illus.). 1979. pap. 13.85 (ISBN 0-8385-1394-8). ACC.
Spector, Robert D. Arthur Murphy. (English Authors Ser.: No. 258). 1979. lib. bdg. 13.50 (ISBN 0-8057-6751-7). Twayne.
--Par Lagerkvist. (World Authors Ser.: Spain: No. 267). 1973. lib. bdg. 10.95 (ISBN 0-8057-2509-1). Twayne.
--Tobias Smollett: A Reference Guide. (Scholarly Reference Publications). 1980. lib. bdg. 28.00 (ISBN 0-8161-7960-3). G K Hall.
Spector, Sherman D., ed. & tr. see Ristelhueber, Rene.
Spectre, Peter, jt. auth. see Lang, Steven.
Spectre, Peter, jt. ed. see Putz, Geo.
Spectre, Peter H. & Putz, George. Marine Art Clipbook. 160p. 1980. pap. 8.95 (ISBN 0-442-25190-4). Van Nos Reinhold.
Spedding, D. J. Air Pollution. (Oxford Chemistry Ser.). (Illus.). 90p. 1974. pap. text ed. 8.95x (ISBN 0-19-855464-8). Oxford U Pr.
Spedding, James, et al, eds. see Bacon, Francis.
Speed, F. Maurice. Film Review: 1979-1980. (Illus.). 1980. 8.95 (ISBN 0-8015-2632-9, Hawthorn). Dutton.
Speed, F. Maurice, ed. Film Review, Nineteen Seventy-Seven to Seventy-Eight. (Illus.). 1978. 15.00 (ISBN 0-491-02211-5). Transatlantic.
Speed, Peter. Social Problems of the Industrial Revolution. 160p. 1976. pap. 5.40 (ISBN 0-08-018883-4). Pergamon.
Speed, Roger D. Strategic Deterrence in the Nineteen Eighty's. LC 78-70887. (Publications Ser.: 214). (Illus.). 1979. pap. 7.95 (ISBN 0-8179-7142-4). Hoover Inst Pr.
Speedy, Andrew W. Sheep Production: Science into Practice. (Longman Handbooks in Agriculture Ser.). (Illus.), 208p. (Orig.). 1980. pap. text ed. 16.95 (ISBN 0-582-45582-0). Longman.
Speer, Albert. Infiltration: The SS & German Armament. Neugroschel, Joachim, tr. 604p. 1981. 15.00 (ISBN 0-02-612800-4). Macmillan.
--Inside the Third Reich. (Illus.). 624p. 1981. 8.95 (ISBN 0-02-037500-X). Macmillan.
--Inside the Third Reich: Memoirs of Albert Speer. (Illus.). 1970. 24.95 (ISBN 0-02-612820-9). Macmillan.

--Spandau: The Secret Diaries. 1981. pap. price not set (ISBN 0-671-42447-5). PB.

Speer, Dana C., jt. auth. see Dwight, John A.

Speer, David C., ed. Nonverbal Communication. LC 73-90714. (Sage Contemporary Social Science Issues: No. 10). 1974. 4.95x (ISBN 0-8039-0339-1). Sage.

Speer, David G. & Speer, Marilene B. Belle Etoile. (Illus.). 1970. text ed. 11.95 o.p. (ISBN 0-07-060031-7, C); pap. text ed. 8.95 o.p. (ISBN 0-07-060032-5). McGraw.

Speer, Frederic. Allergy of the Nervous System. (Illus.). 280p. 1970. text ed. 27.50 (ISBN 0-398-01822-7). C C Thomas.

--Migraine. LC 76-25172. (Illus.). 1977. 12.95 (ISBN 0-88229-301-X); pap. 6.95 (ISBN 0-88229-467-9). Nelson-Hall.

Speer, Frederic & Dockhorn, Robert J. Allergy & Immunology in Children. (Illus.). 780p. 1973. 54.50 (ISBN 0-398-02670-X). C C Thomas.

Speer, Laurel. A Bit of Wit. (Gusto Press Poetry Discovery Ser.). (Orig.). 1979. pap. 4.95 (ISBN 0-933906-04-8). Gusto Pr.

--A Different War Story. (Novella Discovery Ser.). 150p. (Orig.). pap. 5.00 (ISBN 0-933906-11-0). Gusto Pr.

--The Hundred Percent Black Steinway Grand. Kulikowski, M. Karl, ed. (Gusto Press Short Story Discovery Ser.). (Orig.). 1979. pap. 6.95 (ISBN 0-933906-10-2). Gusto Pr.

--The Self-Mutilation of an Aged Apple Woman. LC 79-22664. 1980. pap. 4.95 (ISBN 0-914974-21-1). Holmgangers.

Speer, Marilene B., jt. auth. see Speer, David G.

Speers, Joan A., ed. Art at Auction 1979-80: The Year at Sotheby Parke Bernet. (Illus.). 496p. 1980. 45.00 (ISBN 0-85667-010-3, Pub. by Sotheby Parke Bernet England). Biblio Dist.

Speeth, Kathleen, jt. ed. see Boorstein, Seymour.

Speeth, Kathleen R. & Friedlander, Ira. Gurdjieff Seeker of the Truth. LC 78-24696. (Illus.). 1979. pap. 5.95 (ISBN 0-06-090693-6, CN-693, CN). Har-Row.

Speh, Thomas W., jt. auth. see Hutt, Michael D.

Speicher, Klaus. Canary Varieties. Ahrens, Christa, tr. from Ger. Orig. Title: Kanarienrassen. (Illus.). 1979. 2.95 (ISBN 0-87666-993-3, KW-024). TFH Pubns.

Speidel, Hans. Invasion Nineteen Forty-Four: Rommel & the Normandy Campaign. LC 79-147223. (Illus.). 1971. Repr. of 1950 ed. lib. bdg. 18.75x (ISBN 0-8371-5988-1, SPIN). Greenwood.

Speidel, Michael P. Mithras-Orion: Greek Hero & Roman Army God. (Illus.). 56p. 1980. pap. text ed. 16.00x (ISBN 90-04-06055-3). Humanities.

Speier, Hans. From the Ashes of Disgrace: A Journal from Germany, 1945-1955. LC 80-21599. 336p. 1981. lib. bdg. 20.00x (ISBN 0-87023-135-9). U of Mass Pr.

Speigel, John, jt. auth. see Grinker, Roy R., Sr.

Speight, Charlotte F. Hands in Clay. LC 78-22715. 1979. pap. text ed. 14.50 (ISBN 0-88284-080-0). Alfred Pub.

Speight, P. A., jt. auth. see Hallett, F. R.

Speight, Phyllis. Arnica the Wonder Herb. 1977. text ed. 3.00x (ISBN 0-686-68090-1). Beekman Pubs.

--Before Calling the Doctor. 1976. pap. 3.00x (ISBN 0-8464-0994-1). Beekman Pubs.

--A Comparison of the Chronic Miasms. 56p. 1977. text ed. 15.50x (ISBN 0-8464-1002-8). Beekman Pubs.

--A Study Course in Homeopathy. 145p. 1979. text ed. 23.95x (ISBN 0-8464-1052-4). Beekman Pubs.

Speir, Jerry. Ross MacDonald. LC 78-4297. (Recognitions Ser.). 1978. 10.95 (ISBN 0-8044-2824-7); pap. 4.95 (ISBN 0-8044-6871-0). Ungar.

Speirs, Gill, jt. auth. see Koenig, Marion.

Speirs, John. Chaucer the Maker. 2nd ed. 1964. pap. text ed. 3.25x (ISBN 0-571-05814-0). Humanities.

--Medieval English Poetry. 1957. 9.95 (ISBN 0-571-06738-7, Pub. by Faber & Faber). Merrimack Bk Serv.

Speirs, Logan. Tolstoy & Chekov. 1972. 42.00 (ISBN 0-521-07950-0). Cambridge U Pr.

Speiser, Jean. Schools Are Where You Find Them. LC 70-135278. (Illus.). (gr. 2-4). 1971. PLB 9.89 (ISBN 0-381-99701-4, A67700, JD-J). John Day.

Speiser, Stuart & Krause, Charles. Aviation Tort Law, 3 vols. LC 78-55326. 1980. 180.00. Lawyers Co-Op.

Speiser, Stuart M. Attorney's Fees, 2 vols. LC 72-91431. 1973. 100.00 (ISBN 0-686-05453-9). Lawyers Co-Op.

--Lawsuit. 600p. 1980. 40.00 (ISBN 0-8180-2200-0); pap. 9.95 (ISBN 0-8180-2201-9). Horizon.

--The Negligence Case: Res Ipsa Loquitur, 2 vols. LC 72-84856. 1972. 85.00 (ISBN 0-686-14530-5). Lawyers Co-Op.

Spell, Jefferson R. Contemporary Spanish-American Fiction. LC 67-29553. 1968. Repr. of 1944 ed. 12.00x (ISBN 0-8196-0211-6). Biblo.

Speller, D. C. Anti Fungal Chemotherapy. LC 79-40524. 1980. 96.25 (ISBN 0-471-27620-0, Pub. by Wiley-Interscience). Wiley.

Spelling, Thomas C. A Treatise on Trusts & Monopolies, Containing an Exposition of the Rule of Public Policy Against Contracts & Combinations in Restraint of Trade, & a Review of Cases, Ancient & Modern. xxvii, 274p. 1981. Repr. of 1893 ed. lib. bdg. 27.50x (ISBN 0-8377-1116-9). Rothman.

Spellman, Shirley, jt. auth. see Davis, Judy.

Spellmann, Charles M. & Williams, Rachel. Pitching in: How to Teach Your Children to Work Around the House. (Illus.). 1981. pap. 4.95 (ISBN 0-915190-31-1). Jalmar Pr.

Speltz, Alexander. Styles of Ornament. (Illus.). 12.50 (ISBN 0-8446-2982-0). Peter Smith.

Spence. Basic Industrial Drafting. 1979. pap. text ed. 9.28 (ISBN 0-87002-297-0); worksheets 6.08 (ISBN 0-87002-142-7). Bennett IL.

--Drafting Technology & Practice. rev ed. (gr. 9-12). 1980. text ed. 22.60 (ISBN 0-87002-303-9); worksheets 10.00 (ISBN 0-87002-130-3). Bennett IL.

--Graphic Reproductions. 1980. text ed. 22.64 (ISBN 0-87002-285-7); student guide 2.60 (ISBN 0-87002-319-5). Bennett IL.

Spence & Atkins. Technical Drafting. (gr. 9-12). 1980. text ed. 18.60 (ISBN 0-87002-305-5). Bennett IL.

Spence, Alexander & Mason, Elliott. Human Anatomy & Physiology. LC 78-57266. (Illus.). 1979. text ed. 22.95 (ISBN 0-8053-6990-2); instr's resource package 150.00 (ISBN 0-8053-6991-0); transparencies 150.00 (ISBN 0-8053-6992-9). Benjamin-Cummings.

Spence, Alexander P. & Mason, Elliott B. Instructor's Resource Manual to Accompany Human Anatomy & Physiology. 150.00 (ISBN 0-8053-6993-7, 800F00). Benjamin Cummings.

Spence, Clark C. Montana: A History. (States & the Nation Ser.). (Illus.). 1978. 12.95 (ISBN 0-393-05679-1, Co-Pub by AASLH). Norton.

--The Rainmakers: American "Pluviculture" to World War II. LC 79-26022. xii, 181p. 1980. 15.95 (ISBN 0-8032-4117-8). U of Nebr Pr.

Spence, David. Shetland's Living Landscape. 160p. 1980. 17.95x (ISBN 0-906191-14-9, Pub. by Thule Pr England). Intl Schol Bk Serv.

Spence, Dennis R., ed. Army Vehicle Manuals. (Military Vehicle Reference Ser.: No. 1). 121p. 1980. pap. 15.00x (ISBN 0-938242-00-8). Portrayal.

Spence, Geoffrey, jt. auth. see Biddle, Gordon.

Spence, Gordon. Charles Dickens As a Familiar Essayist. (Salzburg Studies in English Literature: Romantic Reassessment Ser.: No. 71). 1977. pap. text ed. 25.00x (ISBN 0-391-01530-3). Humanities.

Spence, H. D. & Exell, T. S. The Pulpit Commentary, 23 vols. Incl. Old Testament only, 14 Vols. 260.00 (ISBN 0-8028-8056-8, 2209); New Testament only, 8 Vols. 165.00 (ISBN 0-8028-8057-6, 2210). 1959. Repr. Set. 425.00 (ISBN 0-8028-8055-X, 2208). Eerdmans.

Spence, J. C. Experimental High-Resolution Electron Microscopy. (Monographs on the Physics & Chemistry of Materials). (Illus.). 384p. 1981. 74.00 (ISBN 0-19-851365-8). Oxford U Pr.

Spence, J. D., jt. auth. see Teer, F.

Spence, J. T., et al. Elementary Statistics. 3rd ed. (Illus.). 288p. 1976. ref. ed. 14.95 (ISBN 0-13-260109-5); wkbk. 6.95 (ISBN 0-13-260091-9). P-H.

Spence, Jack. Search for Justice: Neighborhood Courts in Allende's Chile. 1979. lib. bdg. 22.50x (ISBN 0-89158-279-7). Westview.

Spence, Janet T. & Helmreich, Robert L. Masculinity & Femininity: Their Psychological Dimensions, Correlates & Antecedents. LC 77-10693. (Illus.). 1978. 14.95x o.p. (ISBN 0-292-76443-X). U of Tex Pr.

Spence, Jeffery. Victorian & Edwardian Railway Travel. 1977. 19.95 (ISBN 0-7134-0639-9). David & Charles.

Spence, Jeoffry. Surviving Steam Railways. 1979. pap. 5.95 (ISBN 0-7134-0641-0, Pub. by Batsford England). David & Charles.

--Victorian & Edwardian Railways. 1976. pap. 13.50 (ISBN 0-7134-3287-X, Pub. by Batsford England). David & Charles.

Spence, Jonathan & Wills, John E., Jr. From Ming to Ch'ing: Conquest, Region, & Continuity in Seventeenth-Century China. LC 78-15560. (Illus.). 437p. 1981. pap. 8.95x (ISBN 0-300-02672-2). Yale U Pr.

--From Ming to Ch'ing: Conquest, Region & Continuity in 17th Century China. LC 78-15560. (Illus.). 1979. 30.00x (ISBN 0-300-02218-2). Yale U Pr.

Spence, Joseph. Polymetis. LC 75-27886. (Renaissance & the Gods Ser.: Vol. 41). (Illus.). 1976. Repr. of 1747 ed. lib. bdg. 73.00 (ISBN 0-8240-2090-1). Garland Pub.

Spence, L. Myths & Legends of the North American Indian. LC 72-81598. (Illus.). 396p. pap. 6.50 (ISBN 0-8334-1745-2). Steinerbks.

Spence, Lewis. Atlantis Discovered. 1973. Repr. of 1924 ed. 18.00 (ISBN 0-685-70656-7). Gale.

--The Mysteries of Britain. 192p. 1980. pap. 7.95 o.s.i. (ISBN 0-85030-215-3). Newcastle Pub.

--Myths & Legends of Babylonia & Assyria. LC 77-167199. (Illus.). 414p. 1975. Repr. of 1916 ed. 28.00 (ISBN 0-8103-4089-5). Gale.

--Occult Sciences in Atlantis. LC 70-16446. 1970. pap. 5.00 (ISBN 0-87728-136-X). Weiser.

Spence, Martha I., jt. auth. see Vinsant, Marielle.

Spence, Mary L. & Jackson, Donald, eds. The Expeditions of John Charles Fremont, Supplement: Proceedings of the Court Martial. 1973. 17.50 (ISBN 0-252-00403-5). U of Ill Pr.

Spence, Michele. Shadow Play. (Orig.). 1981. pap. 2.75 (ISBN 0-440-17655-7). Dell.

Spence, Robert. Linear Active Networks. LC 73-88242. 1970. 32.95 (ISBN 0-471-81525-X, Pub. by Wiley-Interscience). Wiley.

Spence, William. Drafting Technology & Practice. (gr. 9-12). 1973. text ed. 19.96 o.p. (ISBN 0-87002-129-X); wksheets 8.68 o.p. (ISBN 0-87002-130-3). Bennett IL.

Spence, William P. Architecture: Design-Engineering-Drawing. rev. ed. (gr. 9-12). 1979. text ed. 18.60 (ISBN 0-87345-097-3); quizzes & problems 5.00 (ISBN 0-87345-098-1); ans. key avail. (ISBN 0-685-14523-9). McKnight.

Spencer, A. G., ed. Milling, Vol. 2. (Engineering Craftsmen: No. H29). (Illus.). 1969. spiral bdg. 14.95x (ISBN 0-85083-060-5). Intl Ideas.

Spencer, A. J. Deformations of Fibre-Reinforced Materials. (Oxford Science Research Papers). (Illus.). 140p. 1972. pap. 19.95x (ISBN 0-19-851939-7). Oxford U Pr.

Spencer, Arthur. The Lapps. LC 77-88165. (This Changing World Ser.). 1978. 14.50x (ISBN 0-8448-1263-3). Crane-Russak Co.

Spencer, B. P. Benefit-Cost Analysis of Data Used to Allocate Funds. (Lecture Notes in Statistics: Vol. 3). 296p. 1980. pap. 16.80 (ISBN 0-387-90511-1). Springer-Verlag.

Spencer, Bonnell. God Who Dares to Be Man: Theology of Prayer & Suffering. 128p. Date not set. 12.95 (ISBN 0-8164-0478-X). Seabury.

Spencer, Bud, jt. auth. see Jordan, Payton.

Spencer, Carol M. The Complete BioCycle Kit. (Illus.). 1974. 5.95 (ISBN 0-918882-01-X). PSI Rhythms.

Spencer, Charles. Erte. (Illus.). 192p. 1980. 25.00 (ISBN 0-517-54391-5); pap. 10.95 (543915). Potter.

--The World of Serge Diaghilev. (Illus.). 174p. 1979. 14.95 o.p. (ISBN 0-670-78783-3, Studio). Viking Pr.

Spencer, Charles & Dyer, Philip. The World of Serge Diaghilev. 1974. 9.95 o.p. (ISBN 0-236-31054-2, Pub. by Paul Elek). Merrimack Bk Serv.

Spencer, Christopher. Nahum Tate. (English Authors Ser.: No. 126). lib. bdg. 10.95 (ISBN 0-8057-1536-3). Twayne.

Spencer, D. C., jt. auth. see Schaeffer, A. C.

Spencer, D. C., ed. see Symposia in Pure Mathematics - Berkeley, Calif. - 1971.

Spencer, Dale R. Law for the Reporter. 5th ed. 1980. text ed. 12.95x (ISBN 0-87543-137-2). Lucas.

Spencer, Daniel L. India: Mixed Enterprise & Western Business: Experiments in Controlled Change for Growth & Profit. LC 79-1592. 1981. Repr. of 1959 ed. 21.00 (ISBN 0-88355-897-1). Hyperion Conn.

Spencer, David, et al. Contexts for Composition. 5th ed. 1979. pap. text ed. 9.95 (ISBN 0-13-171512-7). P-H.

Spencer, Donald. Problems for Computer Solution. 2nd ed. 128p. 1979. pap. 6.60 (ISBN 0-8104-5191-3). Hayden.

--Sixty Challenging Problems with BASIC Solutions. LC 79-50793. 1979. pap. 7.70 (ISBN 0-8104-5180-8). Hayden.

Spencer, Donald D. Computer Dictionary for Everyone. rev. ed. 1980. 9.95 (ISBN 0-684-16946-0, ScribT). Scribner.

--Computer Science Mathematics. (Mathematics Ser.). 320p. 1976. text ed. 18.95 (ISBN 0-675-08650-7). Merrill.

--Computers in Society: The Where's, Why's, & How's of Computer Use. (Illus.). 208p. 1974. 7.50 (ISBN 0-8104-5916-7); pap. 8.35 (ISBN 0-8104-5915-9). Hayden.

--Data Processing: An Introduction. (Business C11 Ser.). 1978. pap. text ed. 15.95 (ISBN 0-675-08416-4); instructor's manual 3.95 (ISBN 0-686-67973-3); transparencies 3.95 (ISBN 0-686-67974-1). Merrill.

--FORTRAN Programming. 1980. pap. 8.95 (ISBN 0-686-65745-4); tchr's manual 4.95 (ISBN 0-686-65746-2); wkbk 3.95 (ISBN 0-89218-018-8). Camelot Pub.

--Fun with Computers & Basic. LC 76-45411. 1977. pap. 6.95 (ISBN 0-89218-005-6). Camelot Pub.

--Game Playing with BASIC. 1977. pap. 9.50 (ISBN 0-8104-5109-3). Hayden.

--Game Playing with Computers. rev., 2nd ed. 320p. 1975. 19.95x (ISBN 0-8104-5103-4). Hayden.

--Guide to BASIC Programming. 2nd ed. 1975. text ed. 13.95 (ISBN 0-201-07106-1). A-W.

--Introduction to Information Processing. 3rd ed. 650p. 1981. text ed. 17.95 (ISBN 0-675-08073-8). Merrill.

--Introduction to Information Processing. 2nd ed. (Business Ser.). 1977. text ed. 17.95 (ISBN 0-675-08520-9); student guide 6.95 (ISBN 0-675-08519-5); instructor's manual 3.95 (ISBN 0-686-67522-3); transparencies 3.95 (ISBN 0-686-67523-1). Merrill.

--Problem Solving with FORTRAN. LC 76-26040. (Illus.). 1977. pap. text ed. 13.95 (ISBN 0-13-720094-3). P-H.

--Some People Just Won't Believe a Computer. 1978. pap. 3.95 (ISBN 0-89218-032-3). Camelot Pub.

--The Story of Computers. LC 77-7466. 1977. 7.95 o.p. (ISBN 0-89218-000-5); pap. 3.95 (ISBN 0-89218-001-3). Camelot Pub.

--Using Basic in the Classroom. LC 77-17539. 1977. pap. 9.95 (ISBN 0-89218-027-7). Camelot Pub.

--What Computers Can Do. LC 76-21227. 1977. pap. 5.95 (ISBN 0-89218-029-3). Camelot Pub.

Spencer, Donna E., jt. auth. see Moon, Parry.

Spencer, Elizabeth & Welty, Eudora. The Stories of Elizabeth Spencer. LC 79-6601. 456p. 1981. 14.95 (ISBN 0-385-15697-9). Doubleday.

Spencer, Elma D. Green Russell & Gold. 1966. 9.95 o.p. (ISBN 0-292-73623-1). U of Tex Pr.

Spencer, Francis M. & Monroe, Lee S. The Color Atlas of Intestinal Parasites. rev. ed. (Illus.). 176p. 1977. 23.50 (ISBN 0-398-03418-4). C C Thomas.

Spencer, Frank. Aspects of Human Biology: Theory Relevant to Medical Laboratory Sciences. (Illus.). 352p. 1972. 22.95 o.p. (ISBN 0-407-70400-0). Butterworths.

Spencer, Geoffrey. The Burning Bush. LC 74-84762. 1974. 6.50 (ISBN 0-8309-0129-9). Herald Hse.

Spencer, Harold. American Art: Readings from the Colonial Era to the Present. LC 80-12325. (Illus.). 1980. pap. text ed. 10.95x (ISBN 0-684-16608-9, ScribC). Scribner.

Spencer, Harold, ed. Readings in Art History, 2 Vols. 2nd ed. LC 76-7404. (Illus., Orig.). 1969. pap. text ed. 8.95x ea. (ScribC); Vol. 1 - Ancient Egypt Through The Middle Ages. pap. text ed. 9.95x (ISBN 0-684-14617-7, ScribC); Vol. 2 - The Renaissance To The Present. pap. text ed. (ISBN 0-684-14618-5, ScribC). Scribner.

Spencer, Hazelton, jt. auth. see Ornstein, Robert.

Spencer, Hazelton, et al. British Literature, 2 vols. 3rd ed. 1974. text ed. 16.95x ea.; Vol. 1. text ed. (ISBN 0-669-84129-3); Vol. 2. text ed. (ISBN 0-669-84137-4). Heath.

Spencer, Helen. Beginning Field Hockey. 1970. pap. 3.95x o.p. (ISBN 0-534-00640-X). Wadsworth Pub.

Spencer, Henry C., et al. Technical Drawing Problems: Series Three. 3rd ed. (Illus.). 1980. pap. text ed. 9.95 (ISBN 0-02-414360-X). Macmillan.

Spencer, Herbert. The Principles of Ethics, 2 vols, Vol. 2. LC 77-1274. 550p. 1980. 9.00 (ISBN 0-913966-76-2); Set. pap. 6.00 (ISBN 0-913966-75-4). Liberty Fund.

--Study of Sociology. 1961. pap. 3.25 o.p. (ISBN 0-472-06060-0, 60, AA). U of Mich Pr.

--Works: 1884-1917, 21 vols. LC 68-109116. 1966. Repr. Set. 999.00x (ISBN 3-535-00480-2). Intl Pubns Serv.

Spencer, Herbert see Haeckel, Ernst.

Spencer, Isobel. Walter Crane. LC 75-18567. (Illus.). 208p. 1976. 25.00 o.s.i. (ISBN 0-02-612930-2). Macmillan.

Spencer, Ivor D. Victor & the Spoils: A Life of William L. Marcy. LC 59-6898. (Illus.). 438p. 1959. 15.00x (ISBN 0-87057-056-0, Pub. by Brown U Pr). Univ Pr of New England.

Spencer, J. E. Shifting Cultivation in Southeastern Asia. (California Library Reprint Ser.). 1978. 20.00x (ISBN 0-520-03517-8). U of Cal Pr.

Spencer, J. E. & Thomas, W. L. Introducing Cultural Geography. 2nd ed. LC 77-20230. 1978. text ed. 20.95x (ISBN 0-471-81631-0); tchrs.' manual avail. (ISBN 0-471-03422-3). Wiley.

Spencer, James. When from Viet Nam. 1981. 6.00 (ISBN 0-8062-1681-6). Carlton.

Spencer, James H., et al. The Hospital Emergency Department. (Illus.). 388p. 1972. 29.75 (ISBN 0-398-02482-0). C C Thomas.

Spencer, John H. Ethiopia, the Horn of Africa, & U. S. Policy. LC 77-87562. (Foreign Policy Reports Ser.). 1977. 5.00 (ISBN 0-89549-005-6). Inst Foreign Policy Anal.

Spencer, John R., tr. see Filarete.

Spencer, Joseph E. Oriental Asia: Themes Toward a Geography. LC 73-5645. (Illus.). 160p. 1973. ref. ed. 9.95 (ISBN 0-13-642843-6); pap. text ed. 6.95 (ISBN 0-13-642835-5). P-H.

Spencer, Joseph E., jt. auth. see Wernstedt, Frederick L.

Spencer, Kevin, jt. ed. see Price, Christopher P.

Spencer, LaVyrle. The Fulfillment. 1979. pap. 2.25 (ISBN 0-380-47084-5, 47084). Avon.

Spencer, Leland & Blanford, Charles J. An Economic History of Milk Marketing, Vol. III. LC 77-90779. 1977. text ed. 30.00 o.p. (ISBN 0-88244-078-0). Grid Pub.

Spencer, Louise. Cake Decorating Ideas & Designs. LC 80-54334. (Illus.). 1981. 14.95 (ISBN 0-8069-0214-0); lib. bdg. 13.29 (ISBN 0-8069-0215-9); pap. 9.95 (ISBN 0-8069-7502-4). Sterling.

Spencer, M. Lyle. Editorial Writing, Ethics, Policy Practice. 362p. 1980. Repr. of 1924 ed. lib. bdg. 30.00 (ISBN 0-89984-419-7). Century Bookbindery.

--News Writing. 357p. 1980. Repr. of 1917 ed. lib. bdg. 30.00 (ISBN 0-89760-828-3). Telegraph Bks.

Spencer, Mary & Spencer, Mike. The Ultimate Soup Book. LC 75-9085. (Illus.). 128p. 1975. pap. 4.95 o.p. (ISBN 0-89087-057-8). Celestial Arts.

Spencer, Mike, jt. auth. see Spencer, Mary.

Spencer, Milton H. Contemporary Economics. 4th rev. ed. 1980. text ed. 18.95x (ISBN 0-87901-113-0); study guide 6.95 (ISBN 0-87901-109-2). Worth.

--Contemporary Macroeconomics. 4th ed. (Illus.). text ed. 11.95x (ISBN 0-87901-114-9); study guide 4.95 (ISBN 0-87901-110-6). Worth.

--Contemporary Microeconomics. 4th ed. 1980. text ed. 11.95x (ISBN 0-87901-115-7); study guide 4.95 (ISBN 0-87901-111-4). Worth.

Spencer, Peter S. & Schaumburg, Herbert. Experimental & Clinical Neurotoxicology. (Illus.). 952p. 1980. lib. bdg. 110.00 (ISBN 0-683-07854-2). Williams & Wilkins.

Spencer, Philip. Politics of Belief in Nineteenth-Century France. LC 77-80592. 284p. 1973. Repr. of 1954 ed. 16.00 (ISBN 0-86527-156-9). Fertig.

Spencer, Richard A., ed. Orientation by Disorientation: Studies on Literary Criticism & Biblical Literary Criticism Presented in Honor of William A. Beardslee. (Pittsburgh Theological Monograph Ser.: No. 35). 1980. pap. text ed. 13.50 (ISBN 0-915138-44-1). Pickwick.

Spencer, Richard E., et al, eds. MERMAC Manual: Test & Questionnaire Analysis Programs Written for the IBM System-360. LC 71-131006. 1971. pap. 4.95 (ISBN 0-252-00131-1); 3,500.00 (ISBN 0-252-00227-X); supplement to manual 4.95 (ISBN 0-252-00651-8). U of Ill Pr.

Spencer, Richard P. Nuclear Medicine - Focus on Clinical Diagnosis. 2nd ed. 1980. pap. 18.00 (ISBN 0-87488-825-5). Med Exam.

Spencer, Ross. The Radish River Caper. 144p. 1981. pap. 1.95 (ISBN 0-380-77248-5, 77248). Avon.

Spencer, Ross H. The Abu Wahab Caper. 1980. pap. 1.95 (ISBN 0-686-69269-1, 76356). Avon.

--The Dada Caper. 1977. pap. 1.75 (ISBN 0-380-01839-X, 36293). Avon.

--The Stranger City Caper. 1979. pap. 1.95 (ISBN 0-380-75036-8, 75036). Avon.

Spencer, Ruth. Aircraft Woodwork. 1972. pap. 3.95 o.p. (ISBN 0-8306-2204-7, 2204). TAB Bks.

Spencer, S. H., jt. auth. see Ross, D. F.

Spencer, Scott. Endless Love. 1980. pap. 2.75 (ISBN 0-686-69252-7, 50823). Avon.

--Preservation Hall. 1980. pap. 2.50 (ISBN 0-686-69266-7, 52209). Avon.

--Preservation Hall. 1978. pap. 2.50 (ISBN 0-380-01877-2, 49262). Avon.

Spencer, Sharon. Collage of Dreams: The Writings of Anais Nin. 1981. 5.95 (ISBN 0-15-618581-4, Harv). HarBraceJ.

--Collage of Dreams: The Writings of Anais Nin. LC 77-78781. 188p. 1977. 10.95 (ISBN 0-8040-0760-8). Swallow.

--Space, Time & Structure in the Modern Novel. LC 76-142375. 251p. 1971. pap. 5.95x (ISBN 0-8040-0334-3). Swallow.

Spencer, Sidney. Mysticism in World Religion. 8.00 (ISBN 0-8446-0927-7). Peter Smith.

Spencer, T. D. & Kass, N. Perspectives in Child Psychology: Research & Review. 1970. text ed. 17.95 o.p. (ISBN 0-07-060194-1, C). McGraw.

Spencer, T. J. & Wells, S., eds. A Book of Masques. (Illus.). 448p. 1981. pap. 19.95 (ISBN 0-521-29758-3). Cambridge U Pr.

Spencer, Virginia E., jt. auth. see Jett, Stephen C.

Spencer, Warren F., jt. auth. see Case, Lynn M.

Spencer, William. Algiers in the Age of the Corsairs. (The Centers of Civiization Ser.: Vol. 34). 184p. 1981. pap. 3.95 (ISBN 0-8061-1705-2). U of Okla Pr.

--Historical Dictionary of Morocco. LC 80-21328. (African Historical Dictionaries: No. 24). 195p. 1980. 11.00 (ISBN 0-8108-1362-9). Scarecrow.

Spencer, Zane, jt. auth. see Leech, Jay.

Spender, Dale, ed. Men's Studies Modified: The Impact of Feminism on the Academic Disciplines. (Athene Ser.: Vol. 1). 350p. 1981. 40.00 (ISBN 0-08-026770-X); pap. 18.90 (ISBN 0-08-026117-5). Pergamon.

Spender, Stephan. Selected Poems. 1965. pap. 4.95 (ISBN 0-571-06358-6, Pub. by Faber & Faber). Merrimack Bk Serv.

Spender, Stephen. Letters to Christopher: Stephen Spender's Letters to Christopher Isherwood 1929-1939, with "The Line of the Branch--Two Thirties Journals ". Bartlett, Lee, ed. (Illus.). 230p. (Orig.). 1980. 14.00 (ISBN 0-87685-470-6); pap. 7.50 (ISBN 0-87685-476-5). Black Sparrow.

--Selected Poems. 1964. pap. 6.95 (ISBN 0-394-40445-9). Random.

Spender, Stephen, ed. D. H. Lawrence: Novelist, Poet, Prophet. LC 73-2000. (Illus.). 288p. 1973. 17.50 o.s.i. (ISBN 0-06-013956-0, HarpT). Har-Row.

--World of W. H. Auden. (Illus.). 256p. 1975. 14.95 o.s.i. (ISBN 0-02-612940-X). Macmillan.

Spender, Stephen, tr. see Wedekind, Frank.

Spener, Philip J. Pia Desideria. Tappert, Theodore G., ed. & tr. LC 64-12995. 1964. pap. 4.50 (ISBN 0-8006-1953-6, 1-1953). Fortress.

Spengler, Barbara, jt. auth. see Pate, Ellen.

Spengler, Carol, jt. auth. see Grissum, Marlene.

Spengler, J. J., jt. auth. see Clark, R. L.

Spengler, Joseph J. Declining Population Growth Revisited. LC 80-23714. (Carolina Population Center Monograph: No. 14). (Illus.). 60p. 1980. Repr. of 1971 ed. lib. bdg. 13.75x (ISBN 0-313-22621-0, SPDE). Greenwood.

--Origins of Economic Thought & Justice. LC 79-27026. (Political & Social Economy Ser.). 192p. 1980. 15.00x (ISBN 0-8093-0947-5). S Ill U Pr.

Spenser, Benjamin. Vox Civitatis, or Londons Complaint Against Her Children in the Countrey. LC 79-84137. (English Experience Ser.: No. 954). 52p. (Eng.). 1979. Repr. of 1625 ed. lib. bdg. 8.00 (ISBN 90-221-0954-2). Walter J Johnson.

Spenser, Edmund. Faerie Queene, 2 Vols. Smith, J. C., ed. (Oxford English Texts Ser.). 1909. 89.00x (ISBN 0-19-811824-4). Oxford U Pr.

--Faerie Queene: The Mutability Cantos & Selections from the Minor Poems, Bks. 1 & 2. Kellogg, Robert L. & Steele, Oliver L., eds. LC 65-22702. (Orig.). 1965. pap. 9.95 (ISBN 0-672-63034-6). Odyssey Pr.

--Poetical Works. Smith, J. C. & De Selincourt, Ernest, eds. (Oxford Standard Authors Ser.). 1912. 24.95 (ISBN 0-19-254144-7); pap. 9.95x (ISBN 0-19-281070-7). Oxford U Pr.

Spenser, Jay P. Aeronca C-Two: The Story of the Flying Bathtub. LC 78-606098. (Famous Aircraft of the National Air & Space Museum Ser.: No. 2). (Illus.). 72p. 1978. pap. 5.95 (ISBN 0-87474-879-8). Smithsonian.

Sperb, Rene. Maximum Principles & Their Applications. (Mathematics in Science & Engineering). 1981. price not set (ISBN 0-12-656880-4). Acad Pr.

Sperber, D. Rethinking Symbolism. Morton, A. L., tr. from Fr. LC 75-18433. (Studies in Social Anthropology: No. 11). 164p. 1975. 19.95 (ISBN 0-521-20834-3); pap. 6.95x (ISBN 0-521-09967-6). Cambridge U Pr.

Sperber, Manes. Masks of Loneliness: Alfred Adler in Perspective. LC 73-13167. 250p. 1974. 7.95 o.s.i. (ISBN 0-02-612950-7). Macmillan.

Sperber, Milo. Zarabanda. 1972. pap. text ed. 13.50 (ISBN 0-912022-32-9). EMC.

Sperber, Murray. And I Remember Spain. 1974. pap. 3.95 o.s.i. (ISBN 0-02-054030-2, Collier). Macmillan.

--Literature & Politics. (Humanities Ser.). (gr. 12 up). 1978. pap. text ed. 7.45x (ISBN 0-8104-5878-0). Hayden.

Sperber, Murray, ed. And I Remember Spain: A Spanish Civil War Anthology. 368p. 1974. 7.95 o.s.i. (ISBN 0-02-612960-4). Macmillan.

Sperber, Paula & Pezzano, Chuck. Inside Bowling for Women. LC 77-75852. (Inside Ser.). (Illus.). 1977. 7.95 o.p. (ISBN 0-8092-7995-9); pap. 4.95 (ISBN 0-8092-7980-0). Contemp Bks.

Sperber, Perry A. Drugs, Doctors, Demons & Disease. LC 70-111808. 294p. 1973. 15.50 (ISBN 0-87527-127-8). Fireside Bks.

--Treatment of the Aging Skin & Dermal Defects. (Illus.). 116p. 1965. 11.75 (ISBN 0-398-01826-X). C C Thomas.

Sperber, Philip. Intellectual Property Management - Law - Business - Strategy. LC 74-21479. 1974. with 1978 rev. pages 60.00 (ISBN 0-87632-150-3). Boardman.

Sperka, Joshua S. Proverbs to Live by. Bd. with The Book of Proverbs. 246p. 1966. 4.95x (ISBN 0-8197-0183-1). Bloch.

Sperlich, Elizabeth K., jt. auth. see Sperlich, Norbert.

Sperlich, Norbert & Sperlich, Elizabeth K. Guatemalan Backstrap Weaving. LC 79-56663. (Illus.). 275p. 1980. 25.00 (ISBN 0-8061-1571-8). U of Okla Pr.

Sperline, Meredith E. Ordinary Differential Equations: Solutions & Applications. LC 80-6101. 584p. 1981. pap. text ed. 17.95 (ISBN 0-8191-1358-1). U Pr of Amer.

Sperling, A. P. Arithmetic Made Simple. pap. 3.50 (ISBN 0-385-00983-6, Made). Doubleday.

--How to Make Psychology Work for You. rev. ed. Orig. Title: Psychology for the Millions. 192p. 1975. pap. 1.25 o.p. (ISBN 0-449-30642-9, P642, Prem). Fawcett.

--Psychology Made Simple. 1957. pap. 3.50 (ISBN 0-385-01218-7, Made). Doubleday.

Sperling, A. P. & Stuart, Monroe. Mathematics Made Simple. rev. ed. LC 62-16025. pap. 3.50 (ISBN 0-385-02028-7, Made). Doubleday.

Sperling, Abraham I. Reasons for Jewish Customs & Traditions. Matts, Abraham, tr. LC 68-31711. 1975. 10.00x (ISBN 0-8197-0184-X); pap. 6.95x (ISBN 0-8197-0008-8). Bloch.

Sperling, John G. The South Sea Company: (Kress Library of Business & Economics: No. 17). (Illus.). 1962. pap. 5.00x (ISBN 0-678-09911-1, Baker Lib). Kelley.

Sperling, Melitta. Psychosomatic Disorders in Childhood. LC 76-22870. 1978. 25.00x (ISBN 0-87668-274-3). Aronson.

Sperling, Susan K. Tenderfeet & Ladyfingers: A Visceral Approach to Words & Their Origins. LC 80-51778. (Illus.). 160p. 1981. 9.95 (ISBN 0-670-69633-1). Viking Pr.

Sperlinger, David. Animals in Research: New Perspectives in Animal Experimentation. 384p. 1980. 49.50 (ISBN 0-471-27843-2, Pub. by Wiley-Interscience). Wiley.

Sperner, Emanuel, jt. auth. see Schreier, Otto.

Spero, Herbert & Davids, Lewis E. Money & Banking. 3rd ed. (Orig.). 1970. pap. 3.95 (ISBN 0-06-460069-6, CO 69, COS). Har-Row.

Spero, James. North American Mammmals: A Photographic Album for Artists & Designers. 1980. 9.00 (ISBN 0-8446-5667-4). Peter Smith.

Spero, Joan E. The Failure of the Franklin National Bank. LC 79-18851. 1980. 17.50 (ISBN 0-231-04788-6). Columbia U Pr.

Spero, Robert. The Duping of the American: Dishonesty & Deception in Presidential Television Advertising. 1980. 12.95 (ISBN 0-690-01884-3). Lippincott

Speroni, Charles. Wit & Wisdom of the Italian Renaissance. 1964. 20.00x (ISBN 0-520-01199-6). U of Cal Pr.

Sperounis, Frederick P. The Limits of Progressive School Reform in the Nineteen Seventies: A Case Study. LC 80-5063. 286p. 1980. pap. text ed. 10.25 (ISBN 0-8191-1031-0). U Pr of Amer.

Sperry, Armstrong. Call It Courage. (gr. 4-6). 1940. 8.95 (ISBN 0-02-786030-2). Macmillan.

--Pacific Islands Speaking. (Illus.). (gr. 7 up). 1955. 4.75g o.s.i. (ISBN 0-02-786130-9). Macmillan.

--Rain Forest. (Illus.). (gr. 7 up). 1947. 8.95 (ISBN 0-02-786230-5). Macmillan.

Sperry, Kip. Index to Genealogical Periodical Literature, 1960-1977. LC 79-9407. (Gale Genealogy & Local History Ser.: Vol. 9). 1979. 30.00 (ISBN 0-8103-1403-7). Gale.

Sperry, Kip, ed. Survey of American Genealogical Periodicals & Periodical Indexes. LC 78-55033. (Genealogy & Local History Ser.: Vol. 3). 1978. 30.00 (ISBN 0-8103-1401-0). Gale.

Sperry, Len & Hess, Lee R. Contact Counseling. (Illus.). 240p. 1974. text ed. 11.95 (ISBN 0-201-07116-9). A-W.

Sperry, Len, et al. You Can Make It Happen: A Guide to Self-Actualization & Organizational Change. LC 76-45156. (Illus.). 1977. pap. text ed. 8.95 (ISBN 0-201-07129-0). A-W.

Sperry, Sidney B. The Spirit of the Old Testament. LC 70-119330. (Classics in Mormon Literature Ser.). 246p. 1980. Repr. 5.95 (ISBN 0-87747-832-5). Deseret Bk.

Spessivtzeva, Olga. Technique for the Ballet Artists. (Illus.). 1978. pap. 6.95 (ISBN 0-584-10297-6). Transatlantic.

Spevack, Jerome M. Prison English. 180p. (Orig.). pap. 7.95 (ISBN 0-9604448-0-7). Spevack.

Speyer, A. James, jt. auth. see Art Institute of Chicago.

Spice, J. E. Chemical Binding & Structure. 1964. 9.35 (ISBN 0-08-010568-8); pap. 10.75 (ISBN 0-08-010567-X). Pergamon.

Spicer, Arnold, ed. Advances in Preconcentration & Dehydration of Foods. LC 74-9512. 526p. 1974. 69.95 (ISBN 0-470-81591-4). Halsted Pr.

--Bread: Social, Nutritional, & Agricultural Aspects of Wheaten Bread. (Illus.). 1975. 67.20x (ISBN 0-85334-627-2, Pub. by Applied Science). Burgess-Intl Ideas.

Spicer, Dorothy. Desert Adventure. (YA) 1968. 5.95 (ISBN 0-685-07428-5, Avalon). Bouregy.

--Humming Top. LC 68-31176. (gr. 7-11). 1968. 9.95 (ISBN 0-87599-147-5). S G Phillips.

--The Tower Room. 1973. pap. 0.75 o.s.i. (ISBN 0-380-01589-7, 14506). Avon.

Spicer, Dorothy G. Folk Festivals & the Foreign Community. LC 70-167201. 1976. Repr. of 1923 ed. 18.00 (ISBN 0-8103-4301-0). Gale.

Spicer, Edward H. The Yaquis: A Cultural History. LC 79-27660. 1980. 28.50x (ISBN 0-8165-0589-6); pap. 14.50x (ISBN 0-8165-0588-8). U of Ariz Pr.

Spicer, Edward H. & Thompson, Raymond H., eds. Plural Society in the Southwest. 380p. 1972. 5.95 (ISBN 0-913456-53-5). Interbk Inc.

Spicer, George W. Supreme Court & Fundamental Freedoms. 2nd ed. (Orig.). 1967. pap. 9.95 (ISBN 0-13-877852-3). P-H.

Spicer, Jack. The Collected Books of Jack Spicer. Blaser, Robin, ed. 382p. (Orig.). 1975. 14.00 (ISBN 0-87685-242-8); pap. 7.50 (ISBN 0-87685-241-X). Black Sparrow.

--Fifteen False Propositions About God. 1974. pap. 2.50 (ISBN 0-686-28709-6). Man-Root.

--One Night Stand & Other Stories. Allen, Donald, ed. LC 79-28053. 136p. 1980. 12.00 (ISBN 0-912516-45-3); pap. 4.95 (ISBN 0-912516-46-1). Grey Fox.

Spicer, Jerry. Outcome Evaluation: How to Do It. 1980. pap. 4.95 (ISBN 0-89486-112-3). Hazelden.

Spicer, Robert A., jt. auth. see Goodman, Robert B.

Spiegal, Murray R. Applied Differential Equations. 3rd ed. 1980. text ed. 23.95 (ISBN 0-13-040097-1). P-H.

Spiegel, Alan. Fiction & the Camera Eye: Visual Consciousness in Film & the Modern Novel. LC 75-22353. 1976. 12.95x (ISBN 0-8139-0598-2). U Pr of Va.

Spiegel, Allen. Medical Technology, Health Care & the Consumer. LC 79-25539. 352p. 1980. 29.95x (ISBN 0-87705-498-3). Human Sci Pr.

Spiegel, Allen D. The Medicaid Experience. LC 78-27669. (Illus.). 1979. text ed. 35.75 (ISBN 0-89443-088-2). Aspen Systems.

Spiegel, Allen D. & Hyman, Herbert Harvey. Basic Health Planning Methods. LC 78-10780. 1978. 37.95 (ISBN 0-89443-077-7). Aspen Systems.

Spiegel, Allen D. & Podair, Simon. Rehabilitating People with Disabilities into the Mainstream of Society. LC 80-16497. (Illus.). 350p. 1981. 28.00 (ISBN 0-8155-0839-5). Noyes.

Spiegel, Allen D. & Backhaut, Bernard, eds. Curing & Caring: A Review of the Factors Affecting the Quality & Acceptability of Health Care. (Health Systems Management Ser.: Vol. 13). 205p. 1980. text ed. 30.00 (ISBN 0-89335-099-0). Spectrum Pub.

Spiegel, Herbert J., jt. auth. see Burrus, Thomas L.

Spiegel, Janet. Stretching the Food Dollar: Practical Solutions to the Challenges of the 80's. (Urban Life Ser.). (Illus.). 96p. (Orig.). 1981. pap. 4.95 (ISBN 0-87701-172-9). Chronicle Bks.

Spiegel, John D., jt. ed. see Light, Donald, Jr.

Spiegel, John P., jt. auth. see Machotka, Pavel.

Spiegel, Murray R. Applied Differential Equations. 2nd ed. 1967. text ed. 21.95 (ISBN 0-13-040089-0). P-H.

Spiegel, Steven L. Dominance & Diversity: The International Hierarchy. LC 80-8295. 317p. 1980. lib. bdg. 19.00 (ISBN 0-8191-1331-X); pap. text ed. 10.50 (ISBN 0-8191-1332-8). U Pr of Amer.

Spiegelberg, Frederic, ed. see Chaudhuri, Haridas.

Spiegelberg, Nancy & Purdy, Dorothy. Fanfare: A Celebration of Belief. LC 80-25519. (Illus., Orig.). 1981. pap. 5.95 (ISBN 0-930014-56-1). Multnomah.

Spiegler, K. S., ed. Principles of Desalination. 1966. 51.00 o.p. (ISBN 0-12-656750-6). Acad Pr.

Spiegler, K. S. & Laird, A. D., eds. Principles of Desalination. 2nd ed. 1980. Pt. A. 41.00 (ISBN 0-12-656701-8); Pt. B. 52.00 (ISBN 0-12-656702-6); Set. 85.00. Acad Pr.

Spiegler, Michael D., jt. ed. see Liebert, Robert M.

Spiekerman, Joseph A., tr. see Hermans, Hubert J.

Spielberg, Franklin. Transportation Improvements in Madison, Wisconsin: Preliminary Analysis of Pricing Programs for Roads & Parking in Conjunction with Transit Changes. (An Institute Paper). 65p. 1978. pap. 5.00 (ISBN 0-87766-234-7, 22400). Urban Inst.

Spielberg, Steven. Close Encounters of the Third Kind. 1977. 8.95 o.s.i. (ISBN 0-440-01373-9): Delacorte.

--Close Encounters of the Third Kind. 1977. pap. 2.50 (ISBN 0-440-11332-6). Dell.

Spielberger, Charles D. Police Selection & Evaluation: Issues & Techniques. LC 78-9958. (Praeger Special Studies Ser.). 1979. 27.95 (ISBN 0-03-050976-9). Praeger.

Spielberger, Charles D. & Vagg, Peter R., eds. The Assessment & Treatment of Test Anxiety. (Clinical & Community Psychology Ser.). 352p. 1981. text ed. 25.00 (ISBN 0-89116-212-7). Hemisphere Pub. Postponed.
Spielberger, Charles D., jt. ed. see Sarason, Irwin G.
Spielberger, Charles D., et al, eds. Stress & Anxiety, Vol. 8. LC 74-28292. (Clinical & Community Psychology). (Illus.). 560p. 1981. text ed. 27.50 (ISBN 0-89116-184-8). Hemisphere Pub.
Spielberger, Walter J. & Feist, Uwe. Panzerkampfwagen IV. LC 68-56381. (Illus.). 1968. pap. 4.95 (ISBN 0-8168-7109-4). Aero.
--Panzerkampfwagen V. LC 68-22408. (Illus.). 1968. pap. 4.95 (ISBN 0-8168-7110-8). Aero.
--Panzerkampfwagen VI. LC 68-58102. (Illus.). 1968. pap. 5.95 (ISBN 0-8168-7111-6). Aero.
Spielhagen, Friedrich. Problematic Characters. DeVere, S., tr. from Ger. LC 76-28509. viii, 507p. 1977. Repr. of 1888 ed. 18.50 (ISBN 0-86527-296-4). Fertig.
Spielman, John see Chang, Raymond.
Spielman, John P. Leopold the First of Austria. 1977. 17.50 (ISBN 0-8135-0836-3). Rutgers U Pr.
Spielman, Katherine, ed. Outrage. LC 75-13420. 1976. 5.95 o.p. (ISBN 0-89110-010-5). Penthouse Pr.
Spielman, Patrick. Making Wood Signs. LC 80-54342. (Illus.). 144p. 1981. 10.95 (ISBN 0-8069-5434-5); lib. bdg. 9.89 (ISBN 0-8069-5435-3); pap. 6.95. Sterling.
--Working Green Wood with Peg. LC 79-91406. (Illus.). 160p. 1980. 14.95 (ISBN 0-8069-5416-7); lib. bdg. 13.29 (ISBN 0-8069-5417-5); pap. 7.95 (ISBN 0-8069-8924-6). Sterling.
Spielmann, M. H. History of Punch. LC 69-16069. 1969. Repr. of 1895 ed. 28.00 (ISBN 0-8103-3553-0). Gale.
Spier, Arthur. Comprehensive Hebrew Calendar. LC 75-32238. 1952. 14.95x (ISBN 0-87441-050-9). Behrman.
Spier, Peter. Crash Bang Boom. LC 70-157625. (Illus.). (ps-1). 1972. 7.95a (ISBN 0-385-06780-1); PLB (ISBN 0-385-02496-7). Doubleday.
--Erie Canal. LC 70-157625. (gr. 1-3). 1970. pap. 1.95 (ISBN 0-385-05234-0, Zephyr). Doubleday.
--Fast-Slow High-Low: A Book of Opposites. LC 72-76207. (Illus.). 48p. (gr. k-3). 1972. 8.95a (ISBN 0-385-06781-X); PLB (ISBN 0-385-02876-8). Doubleday.
--Fox Went Out on a Chilly Night. LC 60-7139. (Illus.). (gr. 1-3). pap. 1.49 (ISBN 0-385-01065-6, Zephyr). Doubleday.
--The Legend of New Amsterdam. LC 78-6032. (Illus.). 32p. 1979. 7.95a (ISBN 0-385-13179-8); PLB (ISBN 0-385-13180-1). Doubleday.
--Noah's Ark. 48p. (ps). 1981. pap. 3.95 (ISBN 0-385-17302-4, Zephyr). Doubleday.
--Noah's Ark. LC 76-43630. (gr. 1-3). 1977. 8.95a (ISBN 0-385-09473-6); PLB (ISBN 0-385-12730-8). Doubleday.
--Oh, Were They Ever Happy. LC 77-78144. (gr. k-3). 1978. 7.95a (ISBN 0-385-13175-5); PLB (ISBN 0-385-13176-3). Doubleday.
--People. (Illus.). 48p. (gr. 1-3). 1980. 10.00 (ISBN 0-385-13181-X); PLB (ISBN 0-385-13182-8). Doubleday.
Spierer, Howard. Major Transitions in the Human Life Cycle. 60p. 1977. pap. 5.00 (ISBN 0-89192-240-7). Interbk Inc.
Spiering, Frank. Berserker. 256p. 1981. pap. 2.75 (ISBN 0-515-05401-1). Jove Pubns.
--Prince Jack. 224p. 1980. pap. 2.25 (ISBN 0-515-05496-8). Jove Pubns.
Spiers, Antony & Stebbens, Derek. Chemistry by Concept. 1973. pap. text ed. 8.95x o.p. (ISBN 0-435-64830-6). Heinemann Ed.
Spiers, Maurice. Techniques & Public Administration: A Contextual Evaluation. 250p. 1975. 24.50x (ISBN 0-85520-108-8, Pub by Martin Robertson England). Biblio Dist.
Spies, Stewart M., et al. Nuclear Medicine Technology Examination Review. LC 79-17328. (Orig.). 1980. pap. text ed. 12.00 o.p. (ISBN 0-668-04724-0). Arco.
Spies, Werner. The Running Fence Project: Christo. LC 77-13109. (Illus.). 1978. pap. 9.95 o.p. (ISBN 0-8109-2080-8). Abrams.
Spiess, A. E., ed. Conservation Archaeology in the Northeast: Toward a Research Orientation, No. 3. LC 78-56049. 1978. pap. 8.00 (ISBN 0-87365-953-8). Peabody Harvard.
Spiess, Arthur E., ed. see Willoughby, Charles C.
Spigelgass, Leonard, jt. auth. see Robinson, Edward G.
Spight, Edwin & Spight, Jeanne. Eagles of the Pacific: Consairways Service During WW-II. (Illus.). 1980. 12.95 (ISBN 0-911852-88-3, Pub. by Hist Avn. Album). Aviation.
Spight, Jeanne, jt. auth. see Spight, Edwin.
Spigler, Iancu. Economic Reform in Rumanian Industry. (Economic Reforms in East European Industry Ser.). (Illus.). 194p. 1973. 15.95x o.p. (ISBN 0-19-215339-0). Oxford U Pr.
Spiker, Charles G see Reese, Hayne.
Spiker, Sina K. Indexing Your Book: A Practical Guide for Authors. 2nd ed. 1963. pap. 2.50x (ISBN 0-299-01173-9). U of Wis Pr.
Spilhaus, Athelstan. Ocean Laboratory. LC 66-246868. (Illus., Orig.). (gr. 6 up). 1967. PLB 7.95 (ISBN 0-87191-009-8). Creative Ed.
Spilka, Mark. Dickens & Kafka; a Mutual Interpretation. 7.50 (ISBN 0-8446-0928-5). Peter Smith.
--Virginia Woolf's Quarrel with Grieving. LC 80-11792. xii, 142p. 1980. 13.50x (ISBN 0-8032-4120-8). U of Nebr Pr.
Spilke, Francine S. The Family That Changed. (The Divorced Family Ser.). (Illus.). 32p. (ps). 1979. 6.95 (ISBN 0-517-53785-0, Michelman Bks). Crown.
--What About Me? (The Divorced Family Ser.). (Illus.). 80p. (gr. 3-9). 1979. 6.95 (ISBN 0-517-53784-2, Michelman Bks). Crown.
Spilker, J., Jr. Digital Communication by Satellite. 1976. 39.95 (ISBN 0-13-214155-8). P-H.
Spillane, Daniel. History of the American Pianoforte. 2nd ed. LC 68-16246. (Music Ser). 1968. Repr. of 1890 ed. lib. bdg. 22.50 (ISBN 0-306-71109-5). Da Capo.
Spillane, John D. The Doctrine of the Nerves: Chapters in the History of Neurology. (Illus.). 500p. 1981. text ed. 50.00x (ISBN 0-19-261135-6). Oxford U Pr.
Spillane, Mickey. Day of the Guns. pap. 1.50 (ISBN 0-451-07512-9, W9092, Sig). NAL.
--Day of the Guns. Bd. with The Death Dealers. 1981. pap. 2.95 (ISBN 0-451-09733-5, 9733, Sig). NAL.
--The Day the Sea Rolled by. 128p. 1981. pap. 1.75 (ISBN 0-553-14597-5). Bantam.
--I, the Jury. 1972. pap. 1.75 (ISBN 0-451-08309-1, E9067, Sig). NAL.
--One Lonely Night - The Twisted Thing. 1980. pap. 2.50 (ISBN 0-451-09465-4, E9465, Sig). NAL.
Spillard, Peter. Sales Promotion: Its Place in Marketing Strategy. 2nd ed. 1976. 27.50x o.p. (ISBN 0-8464-0811-2). Beekman Pubs.
Spiller, Burton. Drummer in the Woods. (Illus.). 240p. 1980. Repr. of 1962 ed. text ed. 13.95 (ISBN 0-8117-0528-5). Stackpole.
Spiller, Earl A., Jr. Financial Accounting: Basic Concepts. 3rd. ed. 1977. text ed. 19.50 (ISBN 0-256-01906-1). Irwin.
Spiller, James D., jt. auth. see Bernthal, Patricia J.
Spiller, Robert, ed. see Adams, Henry.
Spiller, Robert E. Cycle of American Literature. LC 68-7396. 1967. pap. 6.95 (ISBN 0-02-930420-2). Free Pr.
--Cycle of American Literature: An Essay in Historical Criticism. 1967. 5.95 o.s.i. (ISBN 0-02-613040-8). Macmillan.
--Late Harvest: Essays & Addresses in American Literature & Culture. LC 80-543. (Contributions to American Studies: No. 49). xi, 280p. 1981. lib. bdg. 25.00 (ISBN 0-313-22023-9, SLH/). Greenwood.
--Milestones in American Literary History. LC 76-47170. (Contributions in American Studies Ser.: No. 27). 1977. lib. bdg. 13.50 (ISBN 0-8371-9403-2, SMI/). Greenwood.
--Third Dimension. 5.95 o.s.i. (ISBN 0-02-613010-6). Macmillan.
Spiller, Robert E., ed. see Emerson, Ralph W.
Spillers, W. R. Automated Structural Analysis: An Introduction. 1972. 21.00 (ISBN 0-08-016782-9). Pergamon.
Spillman, Ronald. Darkroom Techniques. 1976. 12.95 o.p. (ISBN 0-85242-367-5, Pub. by Fountain). Morgan.
Spilsbury, W. J., tr. see Huxley, Anthony.
Spina, John F., jt. auth. see Weiner, Donald D.
Spinard, Norman. The Mind Game. (Orig.). pap. 2.50 (ISBN 0-515-04847-X). Jove Pubns.
Spinden, Herbert J. Ancient Civilizations of Mexico & Central America. 3rd rev. ed. LC 67-29554. (Illus.). 1968. Repr. of 1928 ed. 10.50x (ISBN 0-8196-0215-9). Biblo.
--A Study of Maya Art: Its Subject Matter & Historical Development. LC 74-20300. (Illus.). 352p. 1975. pap. text ed. 6.95 (ISBN 0-486-21235-1). Dover.
Spindler, George, ed. see Dozier, Edward P.
Spindler, George, ed. see Horowitz, Michael M.
Spindler, George, ed. see Lustig-Arecco, Vera.
Spindler, George, ed. see Ohnuki-Tierney, Emiko.
Spindler, George, ed. see Ward, Martha C.
Spindler, George, ed. see Warren, Richard L.
Spindler, George, ed. see Williams, Thomas R.
Spindler, George D., ed. The Making of Psychological Anthropology. LC 76-24597. 1978. 35.00x (ISBN 0-520-03320-5); pap. 10.75x (ISBN 0-520-03957-2). U of Cal Pr.
Spindler, Louise, ed. see Dozier, Edward P.
Spindler, Louise, ed. see Horowitz, Michael M.
Spindler, Louise, ed. see Lustig-Arecco, Vera.
Spindler, Louise, ed. see Ohnuki-Tierney, Emiko.
Spindler, Louise, ed. see Ward, Martha C.
Spindler, Louise, ed. see Warren, Richard L.
Spindler, Louise, ed. see Williams, Thomas R.
Spinelli, Emily. English Grammar for Students of Spanish. LC 79-90976. 1980. pap. 4.50 (ISBN 0-934034-01-X). Olivia & Hill.
Spinelli, Jackaline. Talking to God. (Color Us Wonderful Ser.). (ps). 1972. pap. 0.35 (ISBN 0-8091-6526-0). Paulist Pr.
Spinelli, Joseph S. & Enos, L. Reed. Drugs in Veterinary Practice. LC 78-7046. 1978. pap. text ed. 26.50 (ISBN 0-8016-4749-5). Mosby.
Spingarn, Joel E., ed. Critical Essays of the Seventeenth Century, 3 vols. Incl. Vol. 1. 364p. 12.50x (ISBN 0-253-31551-4); Vol. 2. 368p. 12.50x (ISBN 0-253-31552-2); Vol. 3. 384p. 12.50x (ISBN 0-253-31553-0). LC 57-10727. 1957. Set. 32.50x (ISBN 0-253-31554-9). Ind U Pr.
Spingarn, Lawrence P. Moral Tales. (Illus.). 80p. 1981. pap. 4.00 (ISBN 0-912288-17-5). Perivale Pr. Postponed.
Spingler, M., jt. ed. see Mernier, G.
Spink, Frank H., Jr. Dollars & Cents of Shopping Centers: 1978. 7th ed. LC 78-50885. (Triennial Report Ser.). (Illus.). 300p. 1978. pap. 55.00 (ISBN 0-87420-581-6). Urban Land.
Spink, Frank H., Jr., ed. see ULI Commercial & Office Development Council.
Spink, Frank H., Jr., ed. see ULI Industrial Council.
Spink, Martin S. & Lewis, Geoffrey, eds. Albucasis on Surgery & Instruments: A Definitive Edition of the Arabic Text, with English Translation & Commentary. LC 68-10498. (Welcome Institute of the History of Medicine & Near Eastern Center UCLA). (Illus.). 1973. 67.50x (ISBN 0-520-01532-0). U of Cal Pr.
Spink, Michael. The ABC Frieze. (Illus.). (ps-1). 1980. pap. 4.95 (ISBN 0-224-61538-6, Pub. by Chatto Bodley Jonathan). Merrimack Bk Serv.
Spink, R. Hans Christian Andersen: The Man & His Work. (Illus.). 64p. 1975. pap. 5.00x (ISBN 8-7142-7882-0, D-742). Vanous.
Spinka, Matthew, tr. John Hus at the Council of Constance. LC 65-11019. (Records of Civilzation, Sources & Studies: No. 73). 1965. 20.00x (ISBN 0-231-02742-7). Columbia U Pr.
Spinks, J. W., tr. see Herzberg, Gerhard.
Spinnanger, Ruthe. Better Than Divorce. 1978. pap. 3.95 o.p. (ISBN 0-88270-271-8). Logos.
Spinner, Stephanie, ed. Feminine Plural: Stories by Women About Growing up. LC 76-187798. (gr. 7 up). 1972. 8.95 (ISBN 0-02-786040-X). Macmillan.
Spinner, Stephanie, adapted by. Popeye: A Photo-Storybook Based on the Movie. LC 80-623. (Movie Storybooks Ser.). (Illus.). 64p. (gr. 6-9). 1981. PLB 6.99 (ISBN 0-394-94668-5); pap. 5.95 boards (ISBN 0-394-84668-0). Random.
Spinner, T. J., Jr. George Joachim Goschen: The Transformation of a Victorian Liberal. (Conference on British Studies Biographical Ser.). 268p. 1973. 39.00 (ISBN 0-521-20210-8). Cambridge U Pr.
Spino, Dyveke. New Age Training for Fitness & Health. LC 78-65254. 1980. pap. 7.95 (ISBN 0-394-17738-X, E766, Ever). Grove.
Spino, Michael. Running Home. 1978. pap. 2.25 o.p. (ISBN 0-425-04005-4, Dist. by Putnam). Berkley Pub.
Spinola, Edward, ed. & tr. see Tesio, Frederico.
Spinoza, Baruch. Earlier Philosophical Writings: The Cartesian Principles & Thoughts on Metaphysics. Hayes, Frank A., tr. from Latin. LC 63-12199. 1973. 29.50x (ISBN 0-672-51071-5); pap. text ed. 4.95x (ISBN 0-672-60389-6). Irvington.
--Letters to Friend & Foe. LC 66-22242. 1967. 2.75 o.p. (ISBN 0-8022-1620-X). Philos Lib.
Spinoza, Benedict. On the Improvement of the Understanding. 1977. pap. text ed. 4.50 (ISBN 0-486-20250-X). Dover.
--Theologico-Political Treatise: Political Treatise. Elwes, R. H., tr. pap. text ed. 4.50 (ISBN 0-486-20249-6). Dover.
Spinoza, Benedictus de see De Spinoza, Benedictus.
Spinrad, Norman. The Iron Dream. 1978. pap. 1.95 o.s.i. (ISBN 0-685-54629-2, 04741-4). Jove Pubns.
--A World Between. (Orig.). 1979. pap. 1.75 o.p. (ISBN 0-685-67757-5). Jove Pubns.
Spinrad, Norman, jt. auth. see Leiber, Fritz.
Spinrad, Norman, ed. Modern Science Fiction. LC 73-18782. 560p. 1974. pap. 3.50 (ISBN 0-385-02263-8, Anch). Doubleday.
Spira, Michael, jt. auth. see Irwin, Vincent.
Spirer, H. F., jt. auth. see Spirer, L. Z.
Spirer, Herbert F. Business Statistics. 1975. 18.95 (ISBN 0-256-01672-0). Irwin.
Spirer, Herbert F. & Dueker, Marilynn. Study Guide to Accompany Vazsonyi's Introduction to Data Processing. 3rd ed. 1980. pap. 6.50 (ISBN 0-256-02381-6). Irwin.
Spirer, L. Z. & Spirer, H. F. German Shorthaired Pointer. 1970. 9.95 (ISBN 0-87666-303-X, PS635). TFH Pubns.
Spires, Elizabeth. Globe. (Wesleyan Poetry Program Ser.: No. 101). 72p. 1981. 10.00 (ISBN 0-8195-2101-9); pap. 4.95 (ISBN 0-8195-1101-3). Wesleyan U Pr.
Spirey, W. Allen & Wrobleski, William J. Econometric Model Performance in Forecasting & Policy Assessment. 1979. pap. 4.25 (ISBN 0-8447-3327-X). Am Enterprise.
Spiritual Counterfeits Project, jt. auth. see Duddy, Neil T.
Spiro, Elizabeth P., jt. auth. see Rubin, Barry M.
Spiro, Herbert T. Finance for the Nonfinancial Manager. LC 76-56371. 1977. 19.95 (ISBN 0-471-01788-4, Pub. by Wiley-Interscience). Wiley.
--Finance for the Nonfinancial Manager, Student Edition. LC 76-56371. 1978. 19.95x (ISBN 0-471-04803-8, Pub. by Wiley-Interscience); tchr's manual avail. (ISBN 0-471-05952-8). Wiley.
--Financial Planning for the Independent Professional. LC 78-18179. 1978. 26.95 (ISBN 0-471-03111-9, Pub. by Wiley-Interscience). Wiley.
Spiro, Jack D. Time to Mourn: Judaism and the Psychology of Bereavement. 1968. 4.95 o.p. (ISBN 0-8197-0185-8). Bloch.
Spiro, Jack D., jt. auth. see Schwartzman, Sylvan D.
Spiro, Jack D., jt. auth. see Spong, John S.
Spiro, Jack D., ed. see Shumsky, Abraham & Shumsky, Adaia.
Spiro, Melford E. Kinship & Marriage in Burma: A Cultural & Psychodynamic Analysis. 1977. 21.50x (ISBN 0-520-03220-9). U of Cal Pr.
Spiro, Peter. Electroforming. 2nd rev. ed. 1971. 40.00x (ISBN 0-901994-34-0). Intl Pubns Serv.
Spiro, Rand J., et al, eds. Theoretical Issues in Reading Comprehension: Perspectives from Cognitive Psychology, Linguistics, Artificial Intelligence & Education. LC 80-20716. 608p. 1980. text ed. 39.95 (ISBN 0-89859-036-1). L Erlbaum Assocs.
Spiro, Socrates. Arabic-English Dictionary: Colloquial Arabic of Egypt. 1973. 25.00 (ISBN 0-685-77125-3). Intl Bk Ctr.
--English-Arabic Dictionary: Colloquial Arabic of Egypt. 1974. 20.00x (ISBN 0-685-77124-5). Intl Bk Ctr.
Spiro, Stanley R. Amnesia-Analgesia Techniques in Dentistry. (Amer. Lec. in Dentistry Ser.). (Illus.). 248p. 1973. 19.50 (ISBN 0-398-02638-6). C C Thomas.
Spiro, Stanley R., ed. Pain & Anxiety Control in Dentistry. (Illus.). 340p. 1981. text ed. 37.50 (ISBN 0-937218-66-9, Pub. by Piccin Italy). J K Burgess.
Spiro, Thomas G. Copper Proteins. (Metal Ions in Biology Ser.: Vol. 3). 356p. 1981. 37.50 (ISBN 0-471-04400-8, Pub. by Wiley Interscience). Wiley.
Spiro, Thomas G., ed. Metal Ion Activation of Dioxygen. LC 79-13808. (Metal Ions in Biology Ser.: Vol. 2). 1980. 29.50 (ISBN 0-471-04398-2, Pub. by Wiley-Interscience). Wiley.
Spirt, Diana L., jt. auth. see Gillespie, John T.
Spiteris, Tony P. Art of Cyprus. Burton, Thomas, tr. from Fr. LC 75-128117. (Illus.). 1970. 29.95 o.p. (ISBN 0-688-61003-X). Reynal.
Spitler, Sue & Culinary Arts Inst. Cooking French the New Way. Finnegan, Edward G., ed. LC 80-65527. (Adventures in Cooking Ser.). (Illus.). 1980. cloth cancelled (ISBN 0-8326-0610-3); pap. 3.95 (ISBN 0-8326-0609-X, 2519). Delair.
Spitsbergen, Judith. Seacoast Life: An Ecological Guide. LC 80-15282. (Illus.). 1980. 5.95 (ISBN 0-917134-03-6). NC Natl Hist.
Spitta, Philip, ed. see Frederick The Great.
Spittle, Denys see Lehmann, Karl & Lehmann, P. W.
Spittler, Russell P. The Church. LC 77-83982. (Radiant Life Ser.). 1977. pap. 1.50 (ISBN 0-88243-910-3, 02-0910); 2.50 (ISBN 0-88243-180-3, 32-0180). Gospel Pub.
--The Corinthian Correspondence. (Radiant Life Ser). 128p. 1976. pap. 1.25 (ISBN 0-88243-892-1, 02-0892, Radiant Books); teachers ed. 2.50 (ISBN 0-88243-166-8, 32-0166). Gospel Pub.
--God the Father. (Radiant Life). 1976. pap. 1.25 (ISBN 0-88243-898-0, 02-0898, Radiant Bks); teacher's ed 2.50 (ISBN 0-88243-170-6, 32-0170). Gospel Pub.
Spitz, Allan A. Developmental Change: An Annotated Bibliography. LC 69-19766. 328p. 1969. 16.00x (ISBN 0-8131-1179-X). U Pr of Ky.
Spitz, Bruce & Holashan, John. Modifying Medicaid Eligibility & Benefits. (Medicaid Cost Containment Ser.). 93p. 1977. pap. 3.00 (ISBN 0-87766-195-2, 17700). Urban Inst.
Spitz, David. Patterns of Anti-Democratic Thought: An Analysis & Criticism, with Special Reference to the American Political Mind in Recent Times. LC 80-22640. 347p. 1981. Repr. of 1965 ed. lib. bdg. 27.50x (ISBN 0-313-22392-0, SPPD). Greenwood.

Spitz, Edna H., jt. ed. see Herrmann, Elizabeth R.

Spitz, Leon. What the Liberty Bell Proclaimed. 1975. Repr. of 1951 ed. 4.95x (ISBN 0-8197-0033-9). Bloch.

Spitz, Lewis W. & Lehmann, Helmut T., eds. Luther's Works: Career of the Reformer IV, Vol. 34. LC 55-9893. 1960. 10.00 (ISBN 0-8006-0334-6, 1-334). Fortress.

Spitz, Mark & Herskowitz, Mickey. Seven Golds: Mark Spitz' Own Story. LC 80-1694. (Illus.). 256p. 1981. 10.95 (ISBN 0-385-12135-0). Doubleday.

Spitz, Mark & LeMond, Alan. The Mark Spitz Complete Book of Swimming. LC 75-42490. (Illus.). 192p. 1976. 10.00 o.s.i. (ISBN 0-690-00690-X, TYC-T). T Y Crowell.

Spitz, W. U. & Fisher, R. S. Medicolegal Investigation of Death. 2nd ed. 1980. 45.00 o.p. (ISBN 0-398-03973-9). C C Thomas.

Spitz, Werner U. & Fisher, Russell S., eds. Medicolegal Investigation of Death: Guidelines for the Application of Pathology to Crime Investigation. 2nd ed. (Illus.). 600p. 1980. 47.75 (ISBN 0-398-03973-9). C C Thomas.

Spitzbart, Abraham. Calculus with Analytic Geometry. 768p. 1975. 17.95x (ISBN 0-673-07907-4). Scott F.

--College Algebra. 3rd ed. LC 77-81200. (Illus.). 1978. text ed. 15.95 (ISBN 0-201-07482-6). A-W.

Spitzbarth, L. M. Basic COBOL Programming: Self-Instructional Manual & Text. 1970. pap. 13.95 (ISBN 0-201-07133-9). A-W.

Spitzberg, Irving J., Jr., ed. Universities & the International Distribution of Knowledge. LC 80-16569. 222p. 1980. 21.95 (ISBN 0-03-056976-1). Praeger.

Spitzberg, Irving R., Jr., ed. Exchange of Expertise: The Counterpart System in the New International Order. (Westview Replica Edition). 1978. lib. bdg. 20.25 o.p. (ISBN 0-89158-280-0). Westview.

Spitze, H. Choosing Techniques for Teaching & Learning. 2nd ed. LC 78-68514. 1979. pap. 2.50 (ISBN 0-686-14992-0, 261-08402). Home Econ Educ.

Spitze, H. & Griggs, M. Choosing Evaluation Techniques. LC 75-32848. 1976. pap. 3.50 (ISBN 0-686-15326-X, 261-08424). Home Econ Educ.

Spitzer, John J., ed. see Papers from the Second Annual Conference on Shock, Williamsburg, Va., June 1979.

Spitzer, John J., ed. see Third Annual Conference on Shock, Lake of the Ozarks, Missouri, June 1980, et al.

Spitzer, Judy A., ed. Physiology. 2nd ed. LC 79-83722. (Basic Sciences PreTest Self-Assessment & Review Ser.). (Illus.). 1980. 9.95 (ISBN 0-07-050962-X). McGraw-Pretest.

Spitzer, L. Physics of Fully Ionized Gases. 2nd ed. 1962. 14.50 (ISBN 0-470-81723-2). Wiley.

Spitzer, Leo. The Creoles of Sierra Leone: Responses to Colonialism, 1870-1945. LC 74-5908. 304p. 1974. 25.00x (ISBN 0-299-06590-1). U of Wis Pr.

Spitzer, Lyman, Jr. Physical Processes in the Interstellar Medium. LC 77-14273. 1978. 19.95 (ISBN 0-471-02232-2, Pub. by Wiley-Interscience). Wiley.

Spitzer, Mary E., et al. A Renal Failure Diet Manual Utilizing the Food Exchange System. 132p. 1976. pap. 11.75 (ISBN 0-398-03466-4). C C Thomas.

Spitzer, R. R. & Hoffman, Gregg. The American Challenge. (Illus.). 360p. 1980. 12.50 (ISBN 0-87319-019-X). C Hallberg.

Spitzer, Robert L. & Klein, Donald F., eds. Critical Issues in Psychiatric Diagnosis. LC 77-72812. (American Psychopathological Association Ser.). 1978. 31.50 (ISBN 0-89004-213-6). Raven.

Spitzing, G. Two Hundred Photo Tips. 1978. pap. 5.00 o.p. (ISBN 0-85242-507-4, Pub. by Fountain). Morgan.

--Two Hundred Slide Tips. 1978. pap. 5.00 o.p. (ISBN 0-85242-502-3, Pub. by Fountain). Morgan.

Spiva, Ulysses V. Legal Outlook: A Message to College & University People. LC 80-69232. 115p. 1981. perfect bdg. 9.95 (ISBN 0-86548-057-5). Century Twenty One.

Spivack, Bernard. Shakespeare & the Allegory of Evil: The History of a Metaphor in Relation to His Major Villains. LC 57-12758. 1958. 25.00x (ISBN 0-231-01912-2). Columbia U Pr.

Spivack, Kathleen. Swimmer in the Spreading Dawn. (Orig.). 1981. pap. 4.95 (ISBN 0-918222-24-9). Apple Wood.

Spivak, Jerry L. Fundamentals of Clinical Hematology. (Illus.). 405p. 1980. 25.00 (ISBN 0-06-142465-X, Harper Medical). Har-Row.

Spivak, Michael. Calculus. 2nd ed. 1980. text ed. 18.50 (ISBN 0-914098-77-2); pap. text ed. 5.75 (ISBN 0-914098-78-0). Publish or Perish.

Spivey, Donald. Schooling for the New Slavery: Black Industrial Education, 1868-1915. LC 77-87974. (Contributions in Afro-American & African Studies: No. 38). 1978. lib. bdg. 16.95x (ISBN 0-313-20051-3, SSN/). Greenwood.

Spivey, Richard L. Maria. LC 78-71373. (Illus.). 1979. 37.50 (ISBN 0-87358-181-4). Northland.

Spivey, Robert A., jt. auth. see Sleeper, C. Freeman.

Spivey, Ted R. Journey Beyond Tragedy: A Study of Modern Myth & Literature. LC 80-18348. 1980. 20.00 (ISBN 0-8130-0681-3). U Presses Fla.

Spjut, Harlan J., jt. auth. see Del Regato, Juan A.

Splaver, Bernard R. Successful Catering. LC 75-30645. 1975. 16.95 (ISBN 0-8436-2061-7). CBI Pub.

Splitter, Randolph. Proust's "Recherche". A Psychoanalytic Interpretation. 176p. 1981. 20.00 (ISBN 0-7100-0664-0). Routledge & Kegan.

Splittstoesser, D. F., jt. auth. see De Figueiredo, M. P.

Splittstoesser, Walter E. Vegetable Growing Handbook. (Illus.). 1979. text ed. 14.00 (ISBN 0-87055-319-4). AVI.

Spock, Marjorie. Eurythmy. (Illus.). 148p. (Orig.). 1980. pap. 9.95 (ISBN 0-910142-88-2). Anthroposophic.

--Fairy Worlds & Workers: A Natural History of the Middle Kingdom. 1980. pap. 5.95 (ISBN 0-916786-46-3). St George Bk Serv.

Spoczynska, Joy O. An Age of Fishes: The Development of the Most Successful Vertebrate, LC 75-18750. 1976. 10.00 o.p. (ISBN 0-684-14495-6, ScribT). Scribner.

Spodek, Bernard. Early Childhood Education. (Viewpoint & Alternatives Ser.). (Illus.). 288p. 1973. pap. text ed. 11.95 (ISBN 0-13-222414-3). P-H.

--Teaching in the Early Years. 2nd ed. (Early Childhood Ser.). (Illus.). 1978. ref. ed. 17.95 (ISBN 0-13-892562-3). P-H.

Spodek, Bernard & Walberg, Herbert J., eds. Early Childhood Education: Issues & Insights. LC 76-62804. 1977. 15.25 (ISBN 0-8211-1856-0); text ed. 13.75x 10 or more copies (ISBN 0-685-74999-1). McCutchan.

Spoehr, Alexander, ed. Maritime Adaptations: Essays on Contemporary Fishing Communities. LC 79-22486. 1980. 12.95x (ISBN 0-8229-1139-6). U of Pittsburgh Pr.

Spoel, S. Van der see Van der Spoel, S. & Pierrot-Bults, A. C.

Spoelstra, Nyle, jt. ed. see Morgan, Theodore.

Spofford, Walter O., Jr., et al, eds. Energy Development in the Southwest: Problems of Water, Fish & Wildlife in the Upper Colorado River Basin. LC 80-8020. (Resources for the Future Research Ser.: Paper R-18). 1980. Set Of 2 Vols. pap. text ed. 25.00x (ISBN 0-8018-2495-8). Johns Hopkins.

Spohler, Albert A. Stock Market & Me: An Independent Approach to Wall Street. LC 74-78226. 1974. 7.95 (ISBN 0-686-10560-5). A A Spohler.

Spohr, Louis. Autobiography, 2 vols. LC 69-12693. (Music Ser). (Ger). 1969. Repr. of 1878 ed. lib. bdg. 39.50 (ISBN 0-306-71222-9). Da Capo.

Spohr, Mark. Physician's Guide to Microcomputers. 1981. 18.95 (ISBN 0-8359-5548-6). Reston.

Spohrer, Zella R. The Spider's Silk of Time. (Contemporary Poets of Dorrance Ser.). 64p. 1981. 3.95 (ISBN 0-8059-2771-9). Dorrance.

Spolsky, Bernard, ed. Approaches to Language Testing. LC 78-62080. (Advances in Language Testing Ser.: No. 2). 1978. pap. text ed. 4.95x (ISBN 0-87281-075-5). Ctr Appl Ling.

--Some Major Tests. LC 78-60576. (Advances in Testing Ser.: No. 1). 1979. pap. text ed. 5.50x (ISBN 0-87281-074-7). Ctr Appl Ling.

Spolsky, Bernard, jt. ed. see Jones, Randall L.

Spolton, L. The Upper Secondary School. 1967. 25.00 (ISBN 0-08-012497-6); pap. 13.75 (ISBN 0-08-012496-8). Pergamon.

Spolton, L., jt. auth. see Riley, D.

Sponar, J., ed. see FEBS Symposium on DNA, Liblice, 24-29 September, 1979.

Spong, John S. The Easter Moment. 176p. 1980. 9.95 (ISBN 0-8164-0133-0). Crossroad NY.

--The Living Commandments. LC 77-8344. 1977. 6.95 (ISBN 0-8164-0356-2). Crossroad NY.

--This Hebrew Lord. 1976. pap. 3.95 (ISBN 0-8164-2133-1). Crossroad NY.

Spong, John S. & Spiro, Jack D. Dialogue: In Search of Jewish-Christian Understanding. LC 75-2192. 109p. 1975. pap. 3.50 (ISBN 0-8164-2115-3). Crossroad NY.

Sponsored by the Center for Blood Research. The Chemistry & Physiology of the Human Plasma Proteins: Proceedings of a Conference Held November 19-21 1978 in Boston, Massachusetts, USA. rev. ed. Bing, David H., ed. LC 79-10742. (Illus.). 416p. 1979. 44.00 (ISBN 0-08-023860-2). Pergamon.

Spontini, Gasparo. Fernand Cortez Ou la Conquete Du Mexique, 2 vols. Gossett, Phillip & Rosen, Charles, eds. LC 76-49226. (Early Romantic Opera Ser.: No. 43). 1980. lib. bdg. 82.00 (ISBN 0-8240-2942-9). Garland Pub.

--Olympie. Grossett, Philip & Rosen, Charles, eds. LC 76-49227. (Early Romantic Opera Ser.: Vol. 44). 1980. lib. bdg. 82.00 (ISBN 0-8240-2943-7). Garland Pub.

Spooner, Glenda. The Handbook of Showing. (Illus.). pap. 9.65 (ISBN 0-85131-240-3, Dist. by Sporting Book Center). J A Allen.

--Instructions in Ponymastership. (Illus.). 1977. 9.10 (ISBN 0-85131-241-1, Dist. by Sporting Book Center). J A Allen.

--Pony Trekking. (Illus.). pap. 4.35 (ISBN 0-85131-246-2, Dist. by Sporting Book Center). J A Allen.

Spooner, J. D. Ocular Anatomy. (Illus.). 1972. pap. 24.95 (ISBN 0-407-93412-X). Butterworths.

Spooner, L. Poverty: Its Illegal Causes & Legal Cure. LC 78-156804. (Studies in American History & Government Ser.). 108p. 1971. Repr. of 1846 ed. lib. bdg. 17.50 (ISBN 0-306-70207-X). Da Capo.

Spooner, Lysander. Essay on the Trial by Jury. LC 70-166097. (Civil Liberties in American History Ser). 1971. Repr. of 1852 ed. lib. bdg. 25.50 (ISBN 0-306-70320-3). Da Capo.

Spooner, M. F., ed. The Amoco Cadiz Oil Spill. (Illus.). 1979. pap. text ed. 7.75 (ISBN 0-08-023830-0). Pergamon.

Spooner, Maggie. Sunpower Experiments. LC 79-65077. (Illus.). (gr. 5 up). 1979. 8.95 (ISBN 0-8069-3110-8); PLB 8.29 (ISBN 0-8069-3111-6). Sterling.

Spoor, J. H., et al. Copies in Copyright. Jehoram, Herman C., ed. LC 80-50456. (Monographs on Industrial Property & Copyright Law: Vol. IV). 187p. 1980. 37.50x (ISBN 90-286-0350-6). Sijthoff & Noordhoff.

Sporakowski, Michael & Hicks, Mary W. Families, Individuals, & Marriage. 2nd ed. 1976. pap. text ed. 8.95 o.p. (ISBN 0-8403-0789-6). Kendall-Hunt.

Spore, Keith. Death of a Scavenger. 1980. pap. 1.95 (ISBN 0-505-51465-6). Tower Bks.

Sporne, K. R. Morphology of Gymnosperms: The Structure & Evolution of Primitive Seed Plants. 1967. text ed. 12.50x (ISBN 0-09-077151-6, Hutchinson U Lib); pap. text ed. 9.25x (ISBN 0-09-077152-4, Hutchinson U Lib). Humanities.

--Morphology of Pteridophytes: The Structure of Ferns & Allied Plants. 4th ed. 1975. pap. text ed. 9.25x (ISBN 0-09-123861-7, Hutchinson U Lib). Humanities.

Sporre, Dennis. Perceiving the Arts: An Introduction to the Humanities. (Illus.). 256p. 1981. text ed. 9.95 (ISBN 0-13-657031-3). P-H.

Sporre, Dennis J. Percieving the Arts: An Introduction. (Illus.). 1978. pap. text ed. 8.25 o.p. (ISBN 0-8403-1884-7). Kendall-Hunt.

Sports Illustrated Editors. Sports Illustrated Basketball. LC 76-168552. (Illus.). (gr. 7-9). 1971. 5.95 (ISBN 0-397-00881-3); pap. 2.95 (ISBN 0-397-00882-1, LP54). Lippincott.

--Sports Illustrated Dog Training. LC 72-3179. (Illus.). (YA) 1972. 5.95 (ISBN 0-397-00906-2); pap. 2.95 (ISBN 0-397-00907-0, LP-66). Lippincott.

--Sports Illustrated Horseback Riding. LC 74-161580. (Illus.). (gr. 7-9). 1971. 5.95 (ISBN 0-397-00736-1); pap. 2.95 (ISBN 0-397-00735-3, LP55). Lippincott.

--Sports Illustrated Ice Hockey. LC 78-156366. (Illus.). (gr. 7-9). 1971. 5.95 (ISBN 0-397-00835-X); pap. 2.95 (ISBN 0-397-00836-8). Lippincott.

--Sports Illustrated Small Boat Sailing. rev. ed. LC 76-37930. (Illus.). (YA) 1972. 4.95 o.s.i. (ISBN 0-397-00861-9); pap. 1.95 o.s.i. (ISBN 0-397-00860-0, LP-62). Lippincott.

--Sports Illustrated Squash. rev. ed. LC 70-161579. (Illus.). 1971. 4.95 o.s.i. (ISBN 0-397-00837-6); pap. 2.95 (ISBN 0-397-00838-4, LP58). Lippincott.

--Sports Illustrated Swimming & Diving. 1973. 5.95 (ISBN 0-397-01002-8); pap. 2.95 (ISBN 0-397-01003-6). Lippincott.

Sports Illustrated Editors & Allen, Barry. Sports Illustrated Skin Diving & Snorkeling. LC 72-14150. 1973. 5.95 (ISBN 0-397-00969-0); pap. 2.95 (ISBN 0-397-00970-4, LP79). Lippincott.

Sports Illustrated Editors & Dunaway, James O. Sports Illustrated Book of Track & Field: Running Events. rev. ed. LC 76-8268. (Illus.). (gr. 7-9). 1971. 5.95 (ISBN 0-397-01172-5); pap. 2.95 (ISBN 0-397-01171-7). Lippincott.

Sports Illustrated Editors & Jerome, John. Sports Illustrated Skiing. rev. ed. LC 71-146685. 1971. 5.95 (ISBN 0-397-00840-6); pap. 2.95 (ISBN 0-397-00839-2, LP57). Lippincott.

Sports Illustrated Editors, jt. auth. see Dunaway, James O.

Sports Illustrated Editors, jt. auth. see Gibbs, Tony.

Sports Illustrated Editors, jt. auth. see Hidy, Vernon S.

Sports Illustrated Editors, jt. auth. see Robison, Bonnie.

Sports Illustrated Editors, jt. auth. see Talbert, Bill.

Sports Illustrated Editors, jt. auth. see Wilkinson, Bud.

Sports in American Culture Conference, University of South Florida, May 8-9 1980. Sports in American Culture, 1980: Proceedings. Harkness, Don, ed. (Illus.). 50p. (Orig.). 1980. pap. 2.50 (ISBN 0-934996-09-1). Am Stud Pr.

Spoto, Donald. The Art of Alfred Hitchcock. LC 79-7672. (Illus.). 1979. pap. 9.95 (ISBN 0-385-15569-7, Dolp). Doubleday.

Spoto, T. Jane. Shamra, the Camera: A Story & Coloring Book for Children. (Illus.). 1981. 4.95 (ISBN 0-533-04739-0). Vantage.

Spotte, Stephen. Marine Aquarium Keeping: The Science, Animals & Art. LC 73-4425. (Illus.). 176p. 1973. 15.00 (ISBN 0-471-81759-7, Pub. by Wiley-Interscience). Wiley.

--Seawater Aquariums: The Captive Environment. LC 79-11038. 1979. 27.50 (ISBN 0-471-05665-0, Pub. by Wiley-Interscience). Wiley.

Spotts, Dean. Pop-Rock Crossword Puzzles. (gr. 7-12). 1972. pap. 0.95 o.p. (ISBN 0-590-04490-7, Schol Pap). Schol Bk Serv.

Spotts, Frederic. The Churches & Politics in Germany. LC 72-11050. 352p. 1973. 25.00x (ISBN 0-8195-4059-5, Pub. by Wesleyan U Pr). Columbia U Pr.

Spotts, Leon H. Wisdom Literature of the Bible: Proverbs, Job, Ecclesiates. 1967. pap. 1.25 (ISBN 0-8074-0198-6, 247310). UAHC.

Spotts, M. F. Design of Machine Elements. 5th ed. (Illus.). 1978. ref. ed. 27.95 (ISBN 0-13-200576-X). P-H.

Spouge, J. D. Oral Pathology. LC 72-86010. (Illus.). 640p. 1973. text ed. 20.00 o.p. (ISBN 0-8016-4736-3). Mosby.

Spouse, Mary. The Hammerword Technique. (Orig.). 1980. pap. 2.25 (ISBN 0-505-51496-6). Tower Bks.

Spove, Steen H., ed. see Brome, Richard.

SPR Charter. Man on Earth: A Preliminary Evaluation of the Ecology of Man. LC 78-75232. 1979. text ed. 8.00 (ISBN 0-89615-007-0); pap. 10.95 (ISBN 0-89615-051-8). Guild of Tutors.

Spracklen, Kathe. Z-Eighty & Eighty-Eighty Assembly Language Programming. (Computer Programming Ser.). 192p. 1979. pap. 8.85 (ISBN 0-8104-5167-0). Hayden.

Spradbery, J. Philip. Wasps: An Account of the Biology & Natural History of Social & Solitary Wasps. LC 73-7872. (Biology Ser). (Illus.). 424p. 1973. 22.50 (ISBN 0-295-95287-3). U of Wash Pr.

Spradley, Barbara W. Community Health Nursing: Concepts & Practice. 1981. text ed. price not set (ISBN 0-316-80748-6). Little.

Spradley, James P., jt. auth. see Veninga, Robert L.

Spradling, Mary M., ed. In Black & White, 2 vols. 3rd ed. 1980. Set. 65.00 (ISBN 0-8103-0438-4). Gale.

Spragens, Thomas A., Jr. The Politics of Motion: The World of Thomas Hobbes. LC 72-81318. 1973. 12.00x (ISBN 0-8131-1278-8). U Pr of Ky.

Spragens, William C. The Presidency & the Mass Media in the Age of Television. LC 78-51149. 1978. pap. text ed. 11.75x (ISBN 0-8191-0476-0). U Pr of Amer.

Spragg, S. P. The Physical Behavior of Macromolecules with Biological Functions. (Biophysics & Biochemistry Monographs). 208p. 1981. write for info. (ISBN 0-471-27784-3, Pub. by Wiley-Interscience). Wiley.

Spraggett, Allen. Ross Peterson: A New Edgar Cayce. 1978. pap. 2.25 (ISBN 0-515-04579-9). Jove Pubns.

Sprague, Charles E. The Philosophy of Accounts. LC 72-81869. 1972. Repr. of 1919 ed. text ed. 10.00 (ISBN 0-914348-09-4). Scholars Bk.

Sprague, Charles S. The Scientific Foundation of Man's Intimate Existence. (Illus.). 1980. deluxe ed. 37.45 (ISBN 0-89266-235-2). Am Classical Coll Pr.

Sprague, Elmer. Metaphysical Thinking. 1978. pap. 5.95x (ISBN 0-19-502263-7). Oxford U Pr.

Sprague, Howard B. Turf Management Handbook. 2nd ed. LC 74-19656. 1976. 14.65 (ISBN 0-8134-1692-2); text ed. 11.00x (ISBN 0-685-71186-2). Interstate.

Sprague, Howard B., ed. Hunger Signs in Crops. 3rd ed. LC 64-20015. 1977. 19.95x (ISBN 0-679-30106-2, Pub. by MacKay). Longman.

Sprague, James & Epstein, Alan, eds. Progress in Psychobiology & Physiological Psychology, Vol. 8. LC 66-29640. 1979. 38.00 (ISBN 0-12-542108-7); lib. ed. 49.50 (ISBN 0-12-542178-8); microfiche 30.50 (ISBN 0-12-542179-6). Acad Pr.

Sprague, James M. & Epstein, Alan N., eds. Progress in Psychobiology & Physiological Psychology, Vol. 9. 1980. 37.50 (ISBN 0-12-542109-5); lib. ed. 48.50 (ISBN 0-12-542180-X); microfiche 26.50 (ISBN 0-12-542181-8). Acad Pr.

Sprague, Janet, jt. auth. see Austin-Lett, Genelle.

Sprague, John, jt. auth. see Salert, Barbara.

Sprague, John D. Voting Patterns of the United States Supreme Court: Cases in Federalism, 1889-1959. LC 68-18392. 1968. 22.50x (ISBN 0-672-51175-4). Irvington.

Sprague, Ken. The Athlete's Body. 1981. 10.95 (ISBN 0-87477-140-4); pap. 7.95 (ISBN 0-87477-151-X). J P Tarcher.

--The Gold's Gym Book of Strength Training for the Dedicated Athlete. LC 78-65364. (Illus.). 1979. 13.50 o.p. (ISBN 0-312-90557-2); pap. 7.95 o.p. (ISBN 0-312-90556-4). St Martin.

Sprague, Kurth. The Promise Kept. new ed. (Illus.). 104p. 1975. 10.00 o.p. (ISBN 0-88426-043-7). Encino Pr.

Sprague, Marshall. Colorado: A Bicentennial History. (States & the Nation Ser.). (Illus.). 1976. 12.95 (ISBN 0-393-05599-X). Norton.

--The Great Gates: The Story of the Rocky Mountain Passes. LC 80-21994. (Illus.). x, 468p. 1981. 23.50x (ISBN 0-8032-4122-4); pap. 8.50 (ISBN 0-8032-9119-1, BB 742, Bison). U of Nebr Pr.

--Money Mountain: The Story of Cripple Creek Gold. LC 79-13838. (Illus.). 1979. 16.50x (ISBN 0-8032-4104-6); pap. 5.95 (ISBN 0-8032-9103-5, BB696, Bison). U of Nebr Pr.

--Newport in the Rockies: The Life & Good Times of Colorado Springs. rev. ed. 2nd ed. LC 79-150759. (Illus.). 1971. 7.95 o.p. (ISBN 0-8040-0540-0, SB). Swallow.

--Newport in the Rockies: The Life & Good Times of Colorado Spring. rev. ed. LC 80-52995. 1981. 15.95 (ISBN 0-8040-0412-9, SB); pap. 9.95 (ISBN 0-8040-0413-7). Swallow.

Sprague, Norman & Knatz, Hilary F. Finding a Job: A Resource Guide for the Middle Aged & Retired. 1978. pap. 9.25 o.p. (ISBN 0-685-62973-2). Adelphi Univ.

Sprague, R. H., Jr., jt. ed. see Fick, G.

Sprague, Rosamond K., ed. see Plato.

Sprague, Stuart & Perkins, Elizabeth. Frankfort: A Pictorial History. (Illus.). 1980. 16.95 (ISBN 0-89865-003-8); ltd. ed. 24.95 (ISBN 0-89865-001-1). Donning Co.

Sprague, William B. Lectures on Revivals. 1978. 12.95 (ISBN 0-85151-276-3). Banner of Truth.

Sprague de Camp, L. The Hostage of Zir. 1978. pap. 1.75 o.p. (ISBN 0-425-03870-X, Dist. by Putnam). Berkley Pub.

--The Tritonian King. (A Del Rey Bk.). 1977. pap. 1.50 (ISBN 0-345-25803-7, 345-25803-7-150). Ballantine.

Sprague de Camp, L. & Carter, Lin. Conan of the Isles, No. 12. 1977. pap. 2.25 (ISBN 0-441-11641-8). Ace Bks.

--Conan the Buccaneer, No. 6. 1977. pap. 2.25 (ISBN 0-441-11635-3). Ace Bks.

Sprague De Camp, L., jt. auth. see Howard, Robert E.

Sprague de Camp, L., jt. auth. see Howard, Robert E.

Sprague de Camp, L., ed. see Howard, Robert E.

Spratley, Richard D., jt. auth. see Pimentel, George C.

Spratt, John S. Road to Spindletop: Economic Change in Texas, 1875-1901. (Texas History Paperbacks Ser: No. 5). 1970. pap. 6.95 (ISBN 0-292-70030-X). U of Tex Pr.

Spratt, John S., Jr., et al. Exenterative Surgery of the Pelvis. LC 72-90729. (Major Problems in Clinical Surgery Ser.: No. 12). (Illus.). 177p. 1973. text ed. 9.95 (ISBN 0-7216-8523-4). Saunders.

Spray, Pauline E. Coping with Tension. (Direction Bks). 136p. 1981. pap. 2.95 (ISBN 0-8010-8189-0). Baker Bk.

Spray, Russell E. Easy-to-Use Sermon Outlines. (Sermon Outline Ser.). 1978. pap. 1.95 (ISBN 0-8010-8143-2). Baker Bk.

--Instant Sermons for Busy Pastors. (Sermon Outline Ser.). (Orig.). 1981. pap. 1.45 (ISBN 0-8010-8192-0). Baker Bk.

--Simple Outlines on the Christian Faith. (Dollar Sermon Library). 1977. pap. 1.45 (ISBN 0-8010-8120-3). Baker Bk.

--Soul Building Sermon Outlines. (Dollar Sermon Library). 1977. pap. 1.45 (ISBN 0-8010-8118-1). Baker Bk.

--Time-Saving Sermon Outlines. (Sermon Outline Ser.). (Orig.). 1981. pap. 1.45 (ISBN 0-8010-8193-9). Baker Bk.

--Why Sermon Outlines. (Sermon Outline Ser.). 48p. (Orig.). 1980. pap. 1.95 (ISBN 0-8010-8188-2). Baker Bk.

Spreadbury, P. J., jt. auth. see Ahmed, H.

Sprecher, C. Ronald. Essentials of Investments. LC 77-74380. (Illus.). 1977. text ed. 19.25 (ISBN 0-395-25454-X); inst. manual 0.70 (ISBN 0-395-25455-8). HM.

Sprecher, Daniel, ed. Guide to Government-Loan Film 16mm. 5th ed. 1978. pap. 12.95 o.p. (ISBN 0-685-73566-4). Serina.

Sprecher, R. Ronald. Introduction to Investment Management. 1975. text ed. 20.50 (ISBN 0-395-18706-0); instructor's manual pap. 1.50 (ISBN 0-395-18724-8). HM.

Spreckley, Val. Keeping a Cow. LC 78-74083. 1979. 11.95 (ISBN 0-7153-7655-1). David & Charles.

Spreiregen, Paul D. Urban Design: The Architecture of Towns & Cities. 1965. 29.50 o.p. (ISBN 0-07-060380-4, P&RB). McGraw.

Spreitzer, Elmer, jt. auth. see Snyder, Eldon E.

Sprencz, Margaret E., et al. Ohio Supplement for Modern Real Estate Practice. 5th ed. 128p. (Orig.). 1980. pap. 7.95 (ISBN 0-88462-283-5). Real Estate Ed Co.

Sprengelmeyer, James & Weisberger, Calvin L. Practical Nuclear Cardiology. (Illus.). 1979. text ed. 34.50 (ISBN 0-06-142470-6, Harper Medical). Har-Row.

Sprenkel, Sybille Van Der see Van Der Sprenkel, Sybille.

Sprent, Janet, jt. auth. see Stewart, W. D.

Spretnak, Charlene. Lost Goddesses of Early Greece: A Collection of Pre-Hellenic Mythology. LC 80-68169. (Illus.). 132p. 1981. pap. 5.95 (ISBN 0-8070-3239-5, BP 617). Beacon Pr.

Spriano, Paolo. Antonio Gramsci & the Party: The Prison Years. 1979. text ed. 18.25x (ISBN 0-85315-486-4). Humanities.

Spriegel, W. R., et al. Elements of Supervision. 2nd ed. LC 57-5934. 1957. 21.95 (ISBN 0-471-81774-0). Wiley.

Spriestersbach, C. & Sherman, Dorothy, eds. Cleft Palate & Communication. LC 68-18682. 1968. text ed. 20.50 (ISBN 0-12-658850-3). Acad Pr.

Sprigge, Cecil, tr. see Croce, Benedetto.

Sprigge, Cecil J. The Development of Modern Italy. 1969. 14.00 (ISBN 0-86527-043-0). Fertig.

Sprigge, Elizabeth, tr. see Cocteau, Jean.

Sprigge, L. S. Facts, Words & Beliefs. (International Library of Philosophy & Scientific Method). 1970. text ed. 15.00x (ISBN 0-391-00069-1). Humanities.

Sprigge, T. L., ed. see Bentham, Jeremy.

Sprigge, Timothy. Santayana: An Examination of His Philosophy. (Arguments of the Philosophers Ser). 1974. 19.00x (ISBN 0-7100-7721-1). Routledge & Kegan.

Spriggle, H. Kenwood, compiled by. Ninety Nine Advertising Layout Designs. (Illus.). 1980. write for info. H Spriggle.

Spriggle, Judith A., ed. An Apple a Day, in a Different Way: 365 Wholesome & Tasty Recipes. 1980. spiral bdg. 5.95 (ISBN 0-938686-02-X). H Spriggle.

Spriggle, Kenwood. Basic Advertising Layout Designs. wire-o bdg. 50.00 (ISBN 0-938686-05-4). H Spriggle.

Spriggle, Kenwood, ed. Consumer's Nineteen Seventy-Eight Guide to Wholesale Prescription Drug Prices. LC 77-92884. (First annual suppl. 1980). 1978. spiral bdg. 8.95x (ISBN 0-938686-00-3). H Spriggle.

Sprinchorn, Evert, tr. & intro. by see Strindberg, August.

Sprinchorn, Evert, et al, trs. see Strindberg, August.

Spring, David & Spring, Eileen, eds. Ecology & Religion in History. 1974. pap. 3.95x o.p. (ISBN 0-06-131829-9, TB1829, Torch). Har-Row.

Spring, Eileen, jt. ed. see Spring, David.

Spring, Elizbeth. Obadiah Comes Fourteen. (N. H.-Vermont Historiettes). (Illus.). 64p. (gr. 4-5). 1976. 4.95x (ISBN 0-915892-07-3); pap. 1.95x (ISBN 0-915892-16-2). Regional Ctr Educ.

Spring, Ira & Manning, Harvey. Mountain Flowers. LC 79-9284. (Illus.). 1979. pap. 3.95 (ISBN 0-916890-92-9). Mountaineers.

Spring, Joel. American Education: An Introduction to Social & Political Aspects. LC 77-17608. (Educational Policy, Planning, & Theory Ser.). 1978. pap. text ed. 8.95x (ISBN 0-582-28020-6). Longman.

--Educating the Worker-Citizen. (Educational Policy, Planning & Theory). 1980. pap. text ed. 9.95 (ISBN 0-582-28075-3). Longman.

--The Sorting Machine: National Education Policy Since 1945. LC 75-53801. (Educational Policy, Planning, & Theory Ser.). 1976. pap. 9.95 (ISBN 0-582-28127-X). Longman.

Spring, Michael, ed. The American Way of Working: A Collection of Writings from Henry David Thoreau to Joseph Heller. 272p. (Orig.). 1980. pap. 2.50 (ISBN 0-553-13925-8). Bantam.

Spring, Norma. Alaska, Travel Guide. LC 71-77497. (Illus.). 1970. 6.95 o.s.i. (ISBN 0-685-14593-X). Macmillan.

Spring Research Association, Sheffield, ed. Strip Spring Making & Forming. (Engineering Craftsmen: No. H7). (Illus.). 1977. spiral bdg. 18.95x (ISBN 0-85083-331-0). Intl Ideas.

Springall, W. Herbert, jt. auth. see Durbin, Richard L.

Springarn, Natalie D., ed. see Conference on Confidentiality of Health Records, Key Biscayne, Fla., Nov. 6-9, 1974.

Springborn, R. K., ed. Cutting & Grinding Fluids: Selection & Application. LC 67-17077. (Manufacturing Data Ser). 1967. pap. 8.75 (ISBN 0-87263-001-3). SME.

Springer, jt. auth. see Hahn.

Springer, Edward, ed. The Penthouse Letters. 1977. pap. 2.50 (ISBN 0-446-91329-4). Warner Bks.

--The Penthouse Letters. LC 75-10029. 1976. 8.95 o.p. (ISBN 0-89110-007-5). Penthouse Pr.

Springer, Eric W., ed. Automated Medical Records & the Law. LC 70-110587. 1971. 25.00 (ISBN 0-912862-02-5). Aspen Systems.

Springer, H., ed. see IUTAM Symposium 5th, VSD-2nd, Held at Technical University, Vienna, Austria, Sept. 19-23, 1977.

Springer, Harriett, tr. see Selsam, Millicent & Hunt, Joyce.

Springer, J. Fred, jt. auth. see Gable, Richard W.

Springer, J. Frederick, jt. auth. see Musolf, Lloyd D.

Springer, Jane, tr. see Bell, Ken & Major, Henriette.

Springer, Llewellyn W. Emergency Treatment of Accute Respiratory Disease. 3rd ed. (Illus.). 180p. 1981. pap. text ed. 11.95 (ISBN 0-87619-862-0). R J Brady.

Springer, Melvin D. The Algebra of Random Variables. LC 78-9315. (Wiley Ser. in Probability & Mathematical Statistics: Applied Section). 1979. 32.95 (ISBN 0-471-01406-0, Pub. by Wiley-Interscience). Wiley.

Springer, Nancy. The Sable Moon. 1981. pap. 2.50 (ISBN 0-671-83157-7). PB.

--The Silver Sun. (gr. 10-12). 1980. pap. write for info. (ISBN 0-671-83496-7). PB.

Springer, Otto. Langenscheidt's New Muret-Sanders German-English Encyclopedic Dictionary: Vol. 1 a-K, Pt. 2. 1014p. 1974. 80.00x (ISBN 3-468-01124-5). Hippocrene Bks.

Springer, Otto, ed. Langenscheidt's New Muret-Sanders English-German Dictionary, 2 vols, Part I. Incl. Vol. 1. A-M. 924p. 1962. 52.50x (ISBN 3-468-01120-2); Vol. 2. N-Z. 958p. 1963. 70.00x (ISBN 0-685-31317-4). (Eng. & Ger.). Hippocrene Bks.

--Langenscheidt's New Muret-Sanders German-English Encyclopedic Dictionary: Part 2, Vol. 2, L-Z. 1975. 80.00x (ISBN 3-468-01126-1). Hippocrene Bks.

Springer, Philipo. Makaha: The Legend of the Broken Promise. Tabrah, Ruth, ed. LC 74-80511. (Illus.). (gr. 1-7). 1974. 5.95 (ISBN 0-89610-008-1). Island Her.

Springer, Rebecca R. Intra Muros: My Dream of Heaven. LC 78-67820. 1980. pap. 1.75 (ISBN 0-932484-01-8). Book Searchers.

Springer, Sally P. & Deutsch, Georg. Left Brain, Right Brain. LC 80-25453. (Psychology Ser.). (Illus.). 1981. text ed. 11.95x (ISBN 0-7167-1269-5); pap. text ed. 6.95x (ISBN 0-7167-1270-9). W H Freeman.

Springfield Historical Society. The Battle of Springfield: June, 1780. LC 80-15765. (Illus.). 1980. 3.95x (ISBN 0-89490-041-2). Enslow Pubs.

Springford, Michael, ed. Electrons at the Fermi Surface. LC 79-50509. (Illus.). 496p. 1980. 85.00 (ISBN 0-521-22337-7). Cambridge U Pr.

Spring-Mills, E., jt. ed. see Hafez, E. S.

Spring-Mills, Elinor, jt. ed. see Hafez, E. S.

Springstubb, Tricia. Growing Things. 228p. (gr. 6). 1981. 8.95 (ISBN 0-686-69141-5, Pub. by Atlantic). Little.

--My Minnie Is a Jewel. LC 80-66712. (Carolrhoda on My Own Bks.). (Illus.). 48p. (gr. k-3). 1980. PLB 5.95g (ISBN 0-87614-131-9). Carolrhoda Bks.

Sprinkel, Beryl W. & Genetski, Robert J. Winning with Money. LC 76-47751. 1977. 10.95 o.p. (ISBN 0-87094-135-6). Dow Jones-Irwin.

Sprinthall, Normal, jt. auth. see Sprinthall, Richard.

Sprinthall, Norman A., jt. auth. see Sprinthall, Richard C.

Sprinthall, Richard & Sprinthall, Normal. Educational Psychology: A Developmental Approach. 3rd ec. LC 80-15223. (Illus.). 624p. 1981. pap. text ed. 14.95 (ISBN 0-201-06872-9). A-W.

Sprinthall, Richard C. & Sprinthall, Norman A. Educational Psychology: A Developmental Approach. 2nd ed. LC 76-17721. (Illus.). 1977. text ed. 15.50 o.p. (ISBN 0-201-06821-4); instr's manual o.p. 3.50 o.p. (ISBN 0-201-06822-2). A-W.

Sprintzen, Alice. Jewelry: Basic Technique & Design. 224p. Date not set. 15.95 (ISBN 0-8019-6828-3); pap. 9.95 (ISBN 0-8019-6830-5). Chilton.

Sprintzen, David A. The Drama of Thought: An Inquiry into the Place of Philosophy in Human Experience. LC 78-64821. 1978. pap. text ed. 9.00 (ISBN 0-8191-0640-2). U Pr of Amer.

Spritz, Kenneth. Theatrical Evolution: 1776-1976. LC 76-9774. (Illus.). 120p. 1976. 10.00 (ISBN 0-89062-021-0, Pub. by Hudson River Mus); pap. 6.95 (ISBN 0-89062-027-X). Pub Ctr Cult Res.

Sproat, Audrey T., jt. auth. see Learned, Edmund P.

Sprokel, Gerald J., ed. The Physics & Chemistry of Liquid Crystal Devices. (IBM Research Symposia Ser.). 362p. 1980. 42.50 (ISBN 0-306-40440-0, Plenum Pr). Plenum Pub.

Sprott, Julien C. Introduction to Modern Electronics. 512p. 1981. text ed. 22.95 (ISBN 0-471-05840-8). Wiley.

Sprott, Richard L., ed. Age, Learning Ability & Intelligence. 176p. 1980. text ed. 15.00 (ISBN 0-442-27895-0). Van Nos Reinhold.

Sprott, Walter J. Sociology. (Orig.). 1966. pap. text ed. 2.50x (ISBN 0-09-042622-3, Hutchinson U Lib). Humanities.

Sproul, R. C. Discovering the Intimate Marriage. 160p. 1981. pap. 2.95 (ISBN 0-87123-118-2, 200118). Bethany Fell.

--Discovering the Intimate Marriage. LC 75-23494. 1975. pap. 2.45 (ISBN 0-87123-249-9, 210249). Bethany Fell.

--If There Is a God, Why Are There Atheists? LC 74-13762. Orig. Title: Psychology of Atheism. 1974. pap. 2.95 (ISBN 0-87123-238-3, 200238). Bethany Fell.

Sproule, J. Michael. Communication Today. 1980. pap. text ed. 9.95x (ISBN 0-673-15168-9); wkbk. 4.95x (ISBN 0-673-15469-6). Scott F.

Sproule, John A. In Defense of Pretribulationism. 56p. (Orig.). 1980. pap. 2.95 (ISBN 0-88469-133-0). BMH Bks.

Sproull, R. L. & Phillips, W. A. Modern Physics. 3rd ed. LC 79-26680. 682p. 1980. text ed. 27.95 (ISBN 0-471-81840-2). Wiley.

Sproull, Robert L. Modern Physics. 2nd ed. LC 63-11452. 1963. text ed. 27.95x o.p. (ISBN 0-471-81845-3). Wiley.

Sprouse, Mary L. How to Survive a Tax Audit: What to Do Before & After You Hear from the IRS. LC 80-1127. (Illus.). 288p. 1981. 11.95 (ISBN 0-385-17260-5). Doubleday.

Sprouse, Robert T. & Swieringa, Robert J. The Essentials of Financial Statement Analysis. (Economics Ser). 480p. (Prog. Bk.). 1972. 12.95 (ISBN 0-201-07170-3). A-W.

Sprouse, Robert T., jt. auth. see Jaedicke, Robert K.

Sprout, Harold & Sprout, Margaret. The Rise of American Naval Power, Seventeen Seventy-Six to Nineteen Eighteen. LC 79-93093. 420p. 1980. 14.95x (ISBN 0-87021-534-5). Naval Inst Pr.

Sprout, Margaret, jt. auth. see Sprout, Harold.

Sprowls, James T. Discretion & Lawlessness: Compliance in Juvenile Court. LC 79-6735. 144p. 1980. 14.95x (ISBN 0-669-03540-8). Lexington Bks.

Sprowls, Joseph B., Jr., ed. Prescription Pharmacy: Dosage Formulation & Pharmaceutical Adjuncts. 2nd ed. LC 70-109958. (Illus.). 1970. text ed. 22.50 o.p. (ISBN 0-397-52050-6). Lippincott.

Sprowls, R. Clay. Management Data Bases. LC 76-6100. 1976. text ed. 24.95 (ISBN 0-471-81865-8, Pub. by Wiley Hamilton). Wiley.

Spruce, Everett. Everett Spruce: A Portfolio of Eight Paintings. (Blaffer Ser. of Southwestern Art: No. 1). 1958. 40.00 (ISBN 0-292-73387-9). U of Tex Pr.

Sprug, Joseph. Index to Nutrition & Health. (Useful Reference Ser. of Library Books: Vol. 119). 1981. write for info. (ISBN 0-87305-125-4). Faxon.

Sprug, Joseph, jt. auth. see Zelkind, Irving.

Spruill, Stephen G. The Psychopath Plague. 1979. pap. 1.75 o.s.i. (ISBN 0-440-17230-6). Dell.

Spruill, Steven G. The Psychopath Plague. LC 77-77661. 1978. 6.95 o.p. (ISBN 0-385-13147-X). Doubleday.

Sprung, Barbara, ed. Perspectives on Non-Sexist Early Childhood Education. LC 78-6251. 1978. pap. 9.50x (ISBN 0-8077-2547-1). Tchrs Coll.

Sprung, Mervyn, et al, trs. from Sanskrit. Lucid Exposition of the Middle Way: The Essential Chapters from the Prasannapada of Candrakirti. LC 79-13033. 1980. 17.50 (ISBN 0-87773-711-8, Prajna). Great Eastern.

Sprunger, W. Frederic. Tee in Japan: A Realistic Vision: the Feasibility of Theological Education by Extension for Churches in Japan. (Illus., Orig.). Date not set. pap. write for info. (ISBN 0-87808-434-7). William Carey Lib. Postponed.

Sprunt, James, et al. From Bondage to Freedom. (Orig.). 1968. pap. 4.50 (ISBN 0-8042-9020-2); tchrs' guide pap. 3.00. John Knox.

Spruth, W. C., jt. ed. see Hasselmeier, H.

Spry, A. Metamorphic Textures. 1969. 42.00 (ISBN 0-08-013316-9); pap. 19.25 (ISBN 0-08-013315-0). Pergamon.

Spufford, Margaret. Contrasting Communities. LC 73-83105. (Illus.). 1980. pap. 12.95 (ISBN 0-521-29748-6). Cambridge U Pr.

--Contrasting Communities: English Villagers in the Sixteenth & Seventeenth Centuries. LC 73-83105. (Illus.). 1974. 43.95 (ISBN 0-521-20323-6). Cambridge U Pr.

Spuhler, Friedrich. Islamic Carpets & Textiles. Wingfield Digby, George & Wingfield Digby, Cornelia, trs. from Xger. (Illus.). 1978. 92.00 (ISBN 0-571-09783-9, Pub. by Faber & Faber). Merrimack Bk Serv.

Spuhler, James N., ed. The Evolution of Man's Capacity for Culture. LC 59-10223. (Waynebooks Ser: No. 17). 1959. pap. text ed. 3.95x (ISBN 0-8143-1114-8). Wayne St U Pr.

Spulber, Nicholas. Organizational Alternatives in Soviet-Type Economies. LC 78-68378. 1979. 35.00 (ISBN 0-521-22393-8). Cambridge U Pr.

Spulber, Nicolas. Soviet Economy. rev. ed. 1969. 12.95x (ISBN 0-393-09860-5, NortonC). Norton.

Spulber, Nicolas & Horowitz, Ira. Quantitative Economic Policy & Planning: Theory & Models of Economic Control. new ed. (Illus.). 550p. 1976. text ed. 18.95x (ISBN 0-393-09181-3). Norton.

Spuler, Bertold. History of the Mongols: Based on Eastern & Western Accounts of the Thirteenth & Fourteenth Centuries. Drummond, Helga, tr. 1971. 21.75x (ISBN 0-520-01960-1). U of Cal Pr.

--The Muslim World: A Historical Survey, 2 vols. Incl. Vol. 1. Age of the Caliphs. text ed. 20.00x (ISBN 0-685-23328-6); Vol. 2. The Mongol Period. text ed. 10.00x (ISBN 0-685-23329-4). 1960. Humanities.

--The Muslim World: A Historical Survey, Vol. 4. 1981. text ed. write for info. (ISBN 0-391-01209-6). Humanities.

Spungin, Charlotte I., jt. auth. see Tallent, Norman.

Spunt, Georges. When Nature Speaks: The Life of Dr. Forrest Shaklee. LC 77-9916. 1977. 8.95 (ISBN 0-8119-0279-X). Fell.

Spurgeon, C. H. According to Promise. pap. 2.25 (ISBN 0-686-26192-5). Pilgrim Pubns.

--All of Grace. 128p. 1981. pap. 2.50 (ISBN 0-88368-097-1). Whitaker Hse.

--All Round Ministry. 1978. pap. 5.45 (ISBN 0-85151-277-1). Banner of Truth.

--Around the Wicket Gate. pap. 2.25 (ISBN 0-686-09098-5). Pilgrim Pubns.

--Election. 1978. pap. 1.25 (ISBN 0-686-00503-1). Pilgrim Pubns.

--The Golden Alphabet (on Psalm 119) pap. 3.95 (ISBN 0-686-09094-2). Pilgrim Pubns.

--The Gospel of the Kingdom (Matthew) 4.95 (ISBN 0-686-09110-8). Pilgrim Pubns.

--John Ploughman's Pictures. 1975. pap. 2.25 (ISBN 0-686-10526-5). Pilgrim Pubns.

--John Ploughman's Talk. 1976. pap. 2.25 (ISBN 0-686-16833-X). Pilgrim Pubns.

--Metropolitan Tabernacle Pulpit, 1861-1917, Vols. 7-63. (C. H. Spurgeon's Sermon Ser.). Repr. black or gold bdgs. (vols. 7-61) 11.95 ea.; (vols. 62-63 combined) 15.95. Pilgrim Pubns.

--Un Ministerio Ideal, 2 vols, Vols. 1 & 2. Vol. 1. 2.30 o.p. (ISBN 0-686-12558-4); Vol. 2. 2.60 o.p. (ISBN 0-686-12559-2). Banner of Truth.

Spurgeon, C H. New Park Street Pulpit 1855-1860, 6 vols, 1981. 60.00 (ISBN 0-686-16847-X). Pilgrim Pubns.

Spurgeon, C. H. Only a Prayer Meeting. pap. 3.95 (ISBN 0-686-09106-X). Pilgrim Pubns.

--Sermons in Candles. 3.95 (ISBN 0-686-09093-4). Pilgrim Pubns.

--Till He Come. 3.95 (ISBN 0-686-09089-6). Pilgrim Pubns.

--Words of Cheer for Daily Life. pap. 2.25 (ISBN 0-686-09101-9). Pilgrim Pubns.

--Words of Warning for Daily Life. pap. 2.25 (ISBN 0-686-09100-0). Pilgrim Pubns.

--Words of Wisdom for Daily Life. pap. 2.25 (ISBN 0-686-09099-3). Pilgrim Pubns.

Spurgeon, Carlos M. Discursos a Mis Estudiantes. 1980. pap. 4.50 (ISBN 0-311-42006-0). Casa Bautista.

Spurgeon, Caroline. Shakespeare's Imagery. 1952. 54.00 (ISBN 0-521-06538-0); pap. 9.95x (ISBN 0-521-09258-2). Cambridge U Pr.

Spurgeon, Charles H. All of Grace. pap. 1.50 (ISBN 0-8024-0001-9). Moody.

--All of Grace. (Summit Books). 1976. pap. text ed. 2.45 (ISBN 0-8010-8095-9). Baker Bk.

--Barbed Arrows. (Charles H. Spurgeon Library). 280p. 1980. pap. 3.95 (ISBN 0-8010-8185-8). Baker Bk.

--Charles Haddon Spurgeon: Autobiography, Vol. 1 The Early Years, 1834-1860. 1976. 14.95 (ISBN 0-85151-076-0). Banner of Truth.

--Charles Haddon Spurgeon: Autobiography, Vol. 2 The Full Harvest, 1861-1892. 1975. 14.95 (ISBN 0-85151-182-1). Banner of Truth.

--Counsel for Christian Workers. (Charles H. Spurgeon Library). 124p. 1975. pap. 2.50 o.p. (ISBN 0-8010-8039-8). Baker Bk.

--Daily Help. (Summit Ser.). 296p. 1981. pap. 3.95 (ISBN 0-8010-8195-5). Baker Bk.

--Faith's Checkbook. pap. 2.50 (ISBN 0-8024-0014-0, 35-14). Moody.

--Great Verses from the Psalms. 278p. 1981. pap. 6.95 (ISBN 0-310-32901-9). Zondervan.

--Great Verses from the Psalms. Hillyer, Norman, ed. 1977. 8.95 (ISBN 0-310-32900-0). Zondervan.

--Guide to Commentaries. Date not set. 0.30 (ISBN 0-686-28947-1). Banner of Truth.

--King's Highway. (Charles H. Spurgeon Library). 126p. 1975. pap. 2.50 o.p. (ISBN 0-8010-8040-1). Baker Bk.

--Metropolitan Tabernacle Pulpit, 12 vols, Vols. 28-31, 34-37. 1971. 11.95 ea. Banner of Truth.

--Morning & Evening. 1980. 10.95 (ISBN 0-310-32920-5); large print 8.95 (ISBN 0-310-32927-2). Zondervan.

--Morning by Morning. Incl. Evening by Evening. (Direction Bks). pap. 3.95 (ISBN 0-8010-8067-3). Baker Bk.

--Spurgeon's Gems. (Charles H. Spurgeon Ser.). 1980. pap. 3.95 (ISBN 0-8010-8186-6). Baker Bk.

--Spurgeon's Lectures to My Students. 1955. 10.95 o.p. (ISBN 0-310-32910-8). Zondervan.

--Spurgeon's Morning & Evening. 736p. 1980. Repr. 10.95 (ISBN 0-310-32940-X). Zondervan.

--Twelve Missionary Sermons. (Charles H. Sprugeon Library). 1978. pap. 2.95 (ISBN 0-8010-8135-1). Baker Bk.

--Twelve Sermons on Backsliding. (Charles H. Spurgeon Library). 1979. pap. 2.95 (ISBN 0-8010-8162-9). Baker Bk.

--Twelve Sermons on Hope. (Charles H. Spurgeon Library Ser.). 1979. pap. 2.95 (ISBN 0-8010-8145-9). Baker Bk.

--Twelve Sermons on the Prodigal Son & Other Texts in Luke 15. (Charles H. Spurgeon Library). 1976. pap. 2.95 (ISBN 0-8010-8084-3). Baker Bk.

Spurgeon, Charles H., et al. Ready Sermon Outlines. (Sermon Outline Ser.). 1974. pap. 1.95 (ISBN 0-8010-7985-3). Baker Bk.

Spurgeon, Sandra L., jt. auth. see Porter, John W.

Spurling, John. Shades of Heathcliffe & Death of Captain Doughty. 1978. 10.95 (ISBN 0-7145-2517-0, Pub. by M Boyars); pap. 5.95 (ISBN 0-7145-2518-9). Merrimack Bk Serv.

Spurling, Laurie. Phenomenology & the Social World: The Philosophy of Merleau-Ponty & Its Relation to the Social Sciences. (International Library of Sociology Ser.). 1978. 22.50x (ISBN 0-7100-8712-8). Routledge & Kegan.

Spurling, T. H., jt. auth. see Mason, E. A.

Spurlock, John H. He Sings for Us: A Sociolinguistic Analysis of the Appalachian Subculture & of Jesse Stuart As a Major American Author. LC 80-8297. (Illus.). 190p. 1980. lib. bdg. 16.50 (ISBN 0-8191-1271-2); pap. text ed. 8.75 (ISBN 0-8191-1272-0). U Pr of Amer.

Spurlock, Rae. Modern French Cooking. LC 79-23751. 208p. 1981. 16.95 (ISBN 0-88229-480-6). Nelson-Hall.

Spurr, R. T., jt. auth. see Newcomb, T. P.

Spurr, Stephen H. & Barnes, Burton V. Forest Ecology. 3rd ed. LC 79-10007. 1980. text ed. 24.95 (ISBN 0-471-04732-5). Wiley.

Spurr, William A. & Bonini, Charles P. Statistical Analysis for Business Decisions. rev. ed. 1973. text ed. 19.00 (ISBN 0-256-00491-9). Irwin.

Spurrier, Robert L. & Lawler, James J. American Government: A Modular Approach. 1978. pap. text ed. 12.95 (ISBN 0-8403-1903-7). Kendall-Hunt.

Spurrier, Robert L., Jr. Inexpensive Justice: Self Representation in the Small Claims Court. (National University Publications, Multi-Disciplinary Ser. in the Law). 1980. 9.95 (ISBN 0-8046-9262-9). Kennikat.

--To Preserve These Rights: Remedies for the Victims of Constitutional Deprivations. (National University Pubns. Multi-Disciplinary Studies in the Law). 1977. 12.95 (ISBN 0-8046-9199-1). Kennikat.

Spurzheim, Johann C. Observations on the Deranged Manifestations of the Mind, or Insanity. LC 78-81359. (Hist. of Psych. Ser.). (Illus.). 1970. Repr. of 1833 ed. 27.00x (ISBN 0-8201-1078-7). Schol Facsimiles.

Spuy, H. van der see Van Der Spuy, H. I.

Spyers-Duran, Peter & Mann, Thomas, Jr., eds. Shaping Library Collections for the Eighties. 1981. lib. bdg. 18.50 (ISBN 0-912700-58-0). Oryx Pr.

Spyker, John H. Little Lives. 1980. pap. 2.25 (ISBN 0-380-48322-X, 48322). Avon.

Spykman, E. C. The Wild Angel. (Children's Literature Ser.). 1981. PLB 9.95 (ISBN 0-8398-2624-9). Gregg.

Spykman, Gordon, et al. Society, State, & Schools: A Case for Structural & Confessional Pluralism. 224p. (Orig.). 1981. pap. 11.95 (ISBN 0-8028-1880-3). Eerdmans.

Spyri, Joanna. Heidi. (Illus.). 24p. (ps-3). 1954. PLB 5.00 (ISBN 0-307-60407-1, Golden Pr). Western Pub.

Spyri, Johanna. Heidi. (Illus.). (gr. 2-6). 1962. 4.95g o.s.i. (ISBN 0-02-786550-9). Macmillan.

--Heidi. LC 78-5489. (Raintree's Illustrated Classics). (Illus.). (gr. 5-8). 1978. PLB 9.65 (ISBN 0-8393-6206-4). Raintree Child.

Spyridakis, Stylianos. Ptolemaic Itanos & Hellenistic Crete. (U. C. Publ. in History: Vol. 82). 1970. pap. 7.00x (ISBN 0-520-09193-0). U of Cal Pr.

Squadrito, Kathleen. John Locke. (English Authors Ser.: No. 271). 1979. 10.95 (ISBN 0-8057-6772-X). Twayne.

Squadrito, Kathleen M. Locke's Theory of Sensitive Knowledge. LC 78-62265. 1978. pap. text ed. 9.25 (ISBN 0-8191-0571-6). U Pr of Amer.

Squier, Charles L. Sir John Suckling. (English Authors Ser.: No. 218). 1978. 12.50 (ISBN 0-8057-6721-5). Twayne.

Squier, E. G. see Bard, Samuel A., pseud.

Squiers, Granville. Secret Hiding-Places the Origins, Histories & Descriptions of English Secret Hiding-Places Used by Priests, Cavaliers, Jacobites & Smugglers. LC 70-157499. (Tower Bks). (Illus.). 1971. Repr. of 1934 ed. 20.00 (ISBN 0-8103-3920-X). Gale.

Squillante, Alphonse M. & Fonseca, John R. Williston on Sales: 1973-74, 3 vols. 4th ed. LC 73-88236. 1973. 150.00 (ISBN 0-686-14489-9). Lawyers Co-Op.

Squire, Aelred. Aelred of Rievaulx: A Study. (Cistercian Studies Ser.: No. 50). 192p. 1981. price not set (ISBN 0-87907-950-9); pap. price not set. Cistercian Pubns.

--Summer in the Seed. LC 79-52126. 1980. pap. 7.95 (ISBN 0-8091-2237-5). Paulist Pr.

Squire, Charles. Celtic Myth & Legend, Poetry & Romance. LC 80-53343. (Newcastle Mythology Library: Vol. 1). 450p. 1980. Repr. of 1975 ed. lib. bdg. 12.95x (ISBN 0-89370-630-2). Borgo Pr.

Squire, Elizabeth D. Heroes of Journalism. LC 76-161377. (Heroes of Ser.). (Illus.). 128p. (gr. 9 up). 1973. 7.95 (ISBN 0-8303-0114-3). Fleet.

Squire, Enid. Introducing Systems Design. LC 78-18651. 1979. pap. text ed. 13.95 (ISBN 0-201-07421-4). A-W.

Squire, Geoffrey & Baynes, Pauline. Observer's Book of European Costume. (Observer Bks.). (Illus.). 1977. 2.95 (ISBN 0-684-15213-4, ScribT). Scribner.

Squire, Jessie & Clayton, Bruce D. Basic Pharmacology for Nurses. 7th ed. 400p. 1981. pap. text ed. 13.95 (ISBN 0-8016-4743-6). Mosby.

Squire, Lyn & Van der Tak, Herman G. Economic Analysis of Projects. LC 75-40228. (A World Bank Research Publication Ser). (Illus.). 166p. 1976. 10.00x o.p. (ISBN 0-8018-1817-6); pap. 5.00x (ISBN 0-8018-1818-4). Johns Hopkins.

Squire, Norman. Beginner's Guide to Bridge. (Beginner's Guide Ser.). 6.95 (ISBN 0-7207-0468-5, Pub. by Michael Joseph). Merrimack Bk Serv.

Squire, P. S. Third Department: The Political Police in the Russia of Nicholas First. LC 69-10198. (Illus.). 1968. 33.50 (ISBN 0-521-07148-8). Cambridge U Pr.

Squire, Stan, jt. auth. see French, Brian.

Squires, David A., jt. auth. see Muse, Ivan D.

Squires, G. L. Introduction to the Theory of Thermal Neutron Scattering. LC 77-85682. (Illus.). 1978. 57.50 (ISBN 0-521-21884-5). Cambridge U Pr.

Squires, Harry A. Guide to Police Report Writing. (Illus.). 104p. 1976. pap. 10.50 (ISBN 0-398-01831-6). C C Thomas.

Squires, Michael. The Pastoral Novel: Studies in George Eliot, Thomas Hardy, & D. H.Lawrence. LC 74-75793. 1975. 9.75x (ISBN 0-8139-0530-3). U Pr of Va.

Squires, William T. The Metal Craftsman Handbook. 1981. 7.95 (ISBN 0-89606-050-0). Green Hill.

SRA Data Processing & Curriculum Group. Case Study in Business System Design. (Illus.). 1970. pap. text ed. 5.95 (ISBN 0-574-16094-9, 13-0782); instr's guide avail. (ISBN 0-574-16095-7, 13-0783). SRA.

Sraffa, P. Production of Commodities by Means of Commodities. (Illus.). 99p. 1975. pap. 10.95x (ISBN 0-521-09969-2). Cambridge U Pr.

Sraffa, P., ed. see Ricardo, David.

Srb, Adrian, et alintro. by. Facets of Genetics: Readings from Scientific American. LC 78-99047. 1970. pap. text ed. 9.95x (ISBN 0-7167-0949-X). W H Freeman.

Srb, Jozetta H. Communicating with Employees About Pension & Welfare Benefits. (Key Issues Ser.: No. 8). 1971. pap. 2.00 (ISBN 0-87546-244-8). NY Sch Indus Rel.

--Portable Pensions. (Key Issues Ser.: No. 4). 1969. pap. 3.00 (ISBN 0-87546-245-6). NY Sch Indus Rel.

SRI International. California Energy Futures: Two Alternative Societal Scenarios & Their Energy Implications - Consultant Report. 206p. 1981. pap. 24.50 (ISBN 0-89934-094-6). Solar Energy Info.

Sri Aurobindo. Bases of Yoga. 168p. 1979. pap. 1.75 (ISBN 0-89071-288-3, Pub. by Sri Aurobindo Ashram India). Matagiri.

--Isha Upanishad. Aurobindo, Sri, tr. 1979. pap. 2.00 (ISBN 0-89744-922-3). Auromere.

--Kena Upanishad. Sri Aurobindo, tr. 1979. pap. 2.50 (ISBN 0-89744-923-1). Auromere.

--The Life Divine. 1112p. 1980. 18.75 (ISBN 0-89071-290-5, Pub. by Sri Aurobindo Ashram India); pap. 14.00 (ISBN 0-89071-289-1). Matagiri.

--Lights on Yoga. 1979. pap. 2.00 (ISBN 0-89744-916-9). Auromere.

--The Mother. 1979. pap. 1.00 (ISBN 0-89744-914-2); pap. 1.00 (ISBN 0-89744-915-0). Auromere.

--Savitri: A Legend & a Symbol. 1978. lib. bdg. 20.00 (ISBN 0-89744-954-1); Two-Vol. Set. lib. bdg. 17.00 (ISBN 0-89744-953-3). Auromere.

--Sri Aurobindo & the Mother on Education. 6th ed. 1978. Fifth Ed. 1973. pap. 3.00 (ISBN 0-89744-955-X). Sixth Ed. 1978. Auromere.

Sri Chinmoy. Life-Tree Leaves. 63p. 1974. pap. 2.00 o.p. (ISBN 0-88497-166-X). Aum Pubns.

--Palmistry, Reincarnation & the Dream State. (Orig.). 1977. pap. 2.00 o.p. (ISBN 0-88497-378-6). Aum Pubns.

Srikantaiah, Taverekere & Hoffman, Herbert H. Introduction to Quantitative Research Methods for Librarians. 2nd ed. 223p. 1978. pap. 8.00x (ISBN 0-89537-002-6). Headway Pubns.

Srikantaiah, Taverekere, jt. auth. see Gough, Chester R.

Srinijasan, V. Applied Thermodynamics for Engineers. (Illus.). 400p. Date not set. text ed. 25.00 (ISBN 0-7069-1177-6, Pub. by Vikas India). Advent Bk.

Srinivas, M. N. The Remembered Village. 1977. 21.50x (ISBN 0-520-02997-6); pap. 6.95 (ISBN 0-520-03948-3). U of Cal Pr.

--Social Change in Modern India. (Rabindranath Tagore Memorial Lectures). (gr. 9-12). 1966. 17.507 (ISBN 0-520-01203-8); pap. 5.95x (ISBN 0-520-01421-9, CAMPUS21). U of Cal Pr.

Srinivas, M. N., et al. The Fieldworker & the Field: Problems & Challenges in Sociological Investigation. 300p. 1979. text ed. 13.95x (ISBN 0-19-561118-7). Oxford U Pr.

Srinivasadasa. Yatindramatadipika. Adidevananda, Swami, tr. (Sanskrit & Eng.). 2.75 o.s.i. (ISBN 0-87481-428-6). Vedanta Pr.

Srinivasan, B. Representations of Finite Chevalley Groups. (Lecture Notes in Mathematics: Vol. 764). 177p. 1980. pap. text ed. 11.80 (ISBN 0-387-09716-3). Springer-Verlag.

Srinivasan, B. & Parthasarathy, S. Some Statistical Applications in X-Ray Crystallography. LC 75-9676. 1976. text ed. 42.00 (ISBN 0-08-018046-9). Pergamon.

Srinivasan, Dobli, ed. Ocular Therapeutics. LC 80-80728. (Illus.). 248p. 1980. 42.25 (ISBN 0-89352-084-5). Masson Pub.

Srinivasan, K. Selections in Two Keys. 10.00 (ISBN 0-89253-548-2). Ind-US Inc.

Srinivasan, Krishnan. The Water's Edge & Other Stories. 120p. 1981. text ed. 10.50x (ISBN 0-86590-009-4, Pub. by Writers Workshop India). Apt Bks.

Srinivasan, R., jt. auth. see Ramachandran, G. N.

Srinivasan, S. K. & Mehata, K. M. Stochastic Processes. LC 77-20511. 1978. text ed. 18.95 (ISBN 0-07-096612-5, C); pap. text ed. 8.95 (ISBN 0-07-011548-6). McGraw.

Sri Ram, N. Life's Deeper Aspects. 1968. 2.00 o.p. (ISBN 0-8356-7172-0). Theos Pub Hse.

--Seeking Wisdom. 1969. 3.50 (ISBN 0-8356-7194-1). Theos Pub Hse.

Srivastava. Mother Goddess in Indian Art, Archaeology & Literature. 1980. 32.00x (ISBN 0-686-65576-1, Pub. by Agam India). South Asia Bks.

Srivastava, Dharma. The Province of Agra. 1979. text ed. 18.50x (ISBN 0-391-01814-0). Humanities.

Srivastava, Girish & Anand, Narender K. Paediatrics Diagnosis. 400p. 1980. text ed. 35.00 (ISBN 0-7069-1047-8, Pub. by Vikas India). Advent Bk.

Srivastava, H. M. & Buschman, R. G. Convolution Integral Equations with Special Function Kernals. LC 76-52979. 1977. 12.95 (ISBN 0-470-99050-3). Halsted Pr.

Srivastava, I. P. Dhrupada: A Study of Its Origin, Historical Development, Structure & Present State. (Illus.). 176p. 1980. text ed. 15.00x (ISBN 0-8426-1648-9). Verry.

Srivastava, Jane J. Area. LC 73-18057. (Young Math Ser.). (Illus.). (gr. 1-5). 1974. 7.95 (ISBN 0-690-00404-4, TYC-J); PLB 7.89 (ISBN 0-690-00405-2). T Y Crowell.

--Averages. LC 75-5927. (Young Math Ser.). (Illus.). 40p. (gr. 1-5). 1975. 7.95 (ISBN 0-690-00742-6, TYC-J); PLB 7.89 (ISBN 0-690-00743-4). T Y Crowell.

--Computers. LC 70-171009. (Young Math Ser.). (Illus.). (gr. 1-4). 1972. 7.95 (ISBN 0-690-20850-2, TYC-J); PLB 7.89 (ISBN 0-690-20851-0). T Y Crowell.
--Number Families. LC 78-19511. (Illus.). (gr. 2-5). 1979. PLB 7.89 (ISBN 0-690-03924-7, TYC-J). T Y Crowell.
--Statistics. LC 72-7559. (Young Math Ser.). (Illus.). (gr. 1-5). 1973. PLB 7.89 (ISBN 0-690-77300-5, TYC-J). T Y Crowell.
--Weighing & Balancing. LC 73-106579. (Young Math Ser.). (Illus.). (gr. 1-4). 1970. 7.95 (ISBN 0-690-87114-7, TYC-J); filmstrip with record 12.85 (ISBN 0-690-87116-3); filmstrip with cassette 15.85 (ISBN 0-690-87118-X). T Y Crowell.
Srivastava, Meera. Constitutional Crisis in the States in India. 220p. 1980. text ed. 12.50x (ISBN 0-391-02135-4). Humanities.
Srivastava, S., jt. auth. see Sinha, U.
Srivastava, S. B. Textbook of Mechanical Engineering. pap. 5.00x o.p. (ISBN 0-210-22550-5). Asia.
Srivastava, Shyam B., ed. Steam Tables & Mollier Chart M.K.S. System. 1966. pap. 1.00x o.p. (ISBN 0-210-22682-X). Asia.
Srivastva, Suresh, jt. auth. see Cummings, Thomas G.
Sroka, Barbara. One Is a Whole Number. 1978. pap. 3.95 (ISBN 0-88207-631-0). Victor Bks.
Sroog, C. E., jt. auth. see Berry, G. C.
Sroufe, Alan. Knowing & Enjoying Your Baby. LC 77-21703. (Illus.). 1977. 10.95 (ISBN 0-13-516690-X, Spec); pap. 3.95 (ISBN 0-13-516682-9, Spec). P-H.
Ssu Shu. Chinese Classical Work Commonly Called the Four Books, 1828. Collie, David, ed. LC 75-122487. 1970. Repr. of 1828 ed. 36.00x (ISBN 0-8201-1079-5). Schol Facsimiles.
Staal, Frits. Exploring Mysticism: A Methodological. LC 74-76391. 1975. 22.75x (ISBN 0-520-02726-4); pap. 4.95 (ISBN 0-520-03119-9, CAL 313). U of Cal Pr.
Staal, Fritz. Agni: The Vedic Ritual of the Fire Altar, 2 vols. (Illus.). 1982. 250.00 (ISBN 0-89581-450-1). Lancaster-Miller.
Staar, Richard F., ed. The Yearbook of International Communist Affairs: 1977. reference ed. LC 76-51879. (Publications Ser: No. 170). 1977. 30.00 (ISBN 0-8179-6701-X). Hoover Inst Pr.
--Yearbook on International Communist Affairs, 1980. (Publication Ser.: No. 235). 517p. 1980. 35.00 (ISBN 0-8179-7351-6). Hoover Inst Pr.
--Yearbook on International Communist Affairs 1979. LC 76-51879. (Publications Ser.: No.215). 1979. 35.00 (ISBN 0-8179-7151-3). Hoover Inst Pr.
--Yearbook on International Communist Affairs: 1981. 1981. 35.00 (ISBN 0-8179-7501-2). Hoover Inst Pr.
Staar, Richard F., ed. see De Weydenthal, Jan B.
Staar, Richard F., ed. see Douglass, Joseph D., Jr. & Hoeber, Amoretta M.
Staar, Richard F., ed. see Kovrig, Bennett.
Staar, Richard F., ed. see Noyes, James H.
Staar, Richard F., ed. see Wesson, Robert G.
Staats, Arthur W. Social Behaviorism. 1975. text ed. 18.95x (ISBN 0-256-01537-6). Dorsey.
Staats, Gregory R. Images of Deviants: Stereotypes & Their Importance for Labeling Deviant Behavior. LC 78-52338. 1978. pap. text ed. 7.25x o.p. (ISBN 0-8191-0489-2). U Pr of Amer.
Stabb, Martin S. Jorge Luis Borges. (World Authors Ser.: Argentina: No. 108). lib. bdg. 10.95 (ISBN 0-8057-2168-1). Twayne.
Stabile, Toni. Cosmetics: The Great American Skin Game. 1979. pap. 2.25 (ISBN 0-441-30246-7). Charter Bks.
Stableford, Brian M. The Castaways of Tangar. (Science Fiction Ser.). 1981. pap. 2.50 (ISBN 0-87997-609-8, UE1609). DAW Bks.
--Masters of Science-Fiction, No. 1: Essays on Science-Fiction Authors. LC 80-24116. (Milford Series: Popular Writers of Today: Vol. 32). 64p. (Orig.). 1981. lib. bdg. 8.95x (ISBN 0-89370-147-5); pap. text ed. 2.95x (ISBN 0-89370-247-1). Borgo Pr.
--Optiman. (Science Fiction Ser.). 1980. pap. 1.95 (ISBN 0-87997-571-7, UJ1571). DAW Bks.
Stabler, C. Norman. How to Read the Financial News. 10th ed. 239p. 1972. pap. 2.95 (ISBN 0-06-463327-6, EH 327, EH). Har-Row.
Stables, Mira. The Byram Succession. 1978. pap. 1.50 o.p. (ISBN 0-449-23558-0, Crest). Fawcett.
--Honey-Pot. 1979. pap. 1.75 o.p. (ISBN 0-449-23915-2, Crest). Fawcett.
--Lissa. (Regency Romance Ser.). 1979. pap. 1.75 o.p. (ISBN 0-449-24138-6, Crest). Fawcett.
--Miss Mouse. 224p. 1981. pap. 1.95 (ISBN 0-449-50178-7, Coventry). Fawcett.
--Swynden Necklace. 1977. pap. 1.50 o.p. (ISBN 0-449-23270-0, Crest). Fawcett.
Stabley, Don. Logical Programming with System 360. LC 75-96047. 1970. 29.95 (ISBN 0-471-81945-X). Wiley.
--System 360 Assembler Language. LC 67-30037. 1967. pap. 14.50 (ISBN 0-471-81950-6, Pub. by Wiley-Interscience). Wiley.
Stace, C. & Jones, P. V. Stilus Artifex. LC 78-164453. 1971. text ed. 5.25x (ISBN 0-521-08143-2). Cambridge U Pr.
Stace, Walter T. Concept of Morals. 8.50 (ISBN 0-8446-2990-1). Peter Smith.
--Philosophy of Hegel: A Systematic Exposition. 1923. pap. text ed. 6.00 (ISBN 0-486-20254-2). Dover.
--Religion & the Modern Mind. LC 52-7471. 1960. pap. 3.50 o.p. (ISBN 0-397-00142-8, KB21, Key). Lippincott.
--Religion & the Modern Mind. LC 80-24093. 285p. 1980. Repr. of 1952 ed. lib. bdg. 22.50x (ISBN 0-313-22662-8, STRM). Greenwood.
Stacey, C. P. Canada & the Age of Conflict: A History of Canadian External Policies, Vol. II; 1921-48--the Mackenzie King Era. 480p. 1981. 30.00x (ISBN 0-8020-2397-5); pap. 12.50 (ISBN 0-8020-6420-5). U of Toronto Pr.
Stacey, D. Fire in My Bones. 1976. pap. 4.30 (ISBN 0-08-018054-X). Pergamon.
Stacey, Frank. British Government 1966 to 1975: Years of Reform. 254p. 1975. 24.95x (ISBN 0-19-876035-3). Oxford U Pr.
Stacey, Frank D. Physics of the Earth. 2nd ed. LC 76-41891. 1977. text ed. 26.95 (ISBN 0-471-81956-5). Wiley.
Stacey, J. The Common People of the Old Testament. 1976. pap. 4.30 (ISBN 0-08-018101-5). Pergamon.
Stacey, M. Methods of Social Research. 1969. 13.75 (ISBN 0-08-013355-X); pap. 6.25 (ISBN 0-08-013354-1). Pergamon.
Stacey, Margaret. Power, Persistence & Change: A Second Study of Banbury. (International Library of Sociology Ser.). 1975. 20.00x (ISBN 0-7100-7995-8). Routledge & Kegan.
Stacey, Margaret, jt. ed. see Hall, David.
Stacey, Margaret, et al. Hospitals, Children & Their Families: The Report of a Pilot Study. (Medicine, Illness & Society Ser). 1970. 14.00x o.p. (ISBN 0-7100-6783-6). Routledge & Kegan.
Stacey, Nicholas A. & Aubrey, Wilson. The Changing Pattern of Distribution. 1965. 16.50 (ISBN 0-08-010654-4); pap. 7.75 (ISBN 0-08-010653-6). Pergamon.
Stacey, William A. Black Home Ownership: A Sociological Case Study of Metropolitan Jacksonville. LC 73-186201. (Special Studies in U.S. Economic, Social & Political Issues). 1972. 28.50x (ISBN 0-275-04810-1). Irvington.
Stachura, Peter D. Nazi Youth in the Weimar Republic. LC 74-14196. (Studies in International & Comparative Politics: No. 5). 301p. 1975. text ed. 18.80 (ISBN 0-87436-198-2); pap. text ed. 6.00 (ISBN 0-87436-199-0). ABC-Clio.
Stack, Carol B. All Our Kin: Strategies for Survival in a Black Community. 1975. pap. 3.95 (ISBN 0-06-090424-0, CN424, CN). Har-Row.
Stack, E. Le Pont Neuf. 3rd ed. (Fr.). 1978. 15.95 (ISBN 0-13-530394-X); wkbk. 4.95 (ISBN 0-13-530402-4). P-H.
Stack, Edward M. Language Laboratory & Modern Language Teaching. 3rd ed. 1971. text ed. 8.95x (ISBN 0-19-501388-3). Oxford U Pr.
--Reading French in the Arts & Sciences. 3rd ed. 265p. 1979. pap. text ed. 8.80 (ISBN 0-395-27505-9). HM.
Stack, Frank, jt. ed. see Bussabarger, Robert F.
Stack, Herbert & Elkow, J. D. Education for Safe Living. 4th ed. (Illus.). 1966. text ed. 15.95 (ISBN 0-13-239194-5). P-H.
Stack, John F., Jr., ed. Ethnic Identities in a Transnational World. LC 80-1199. (Contributions in Political Science Ser.: No. 52). 264p. 1981. lib. bdg. 27.50 (ISBN 0-313-21088-8, SEI/). Greenwood.
Stack, Louise & Morton, Don. Torment to Triumph in Southern Africa. (Orig.). 1976. pap. 2.75 o.p. (ISBN 0-377-00050-7). Friend Pr.
Stack, Nicolette. Corky's Hiccups. (Illus.). 24p. (ps-4). 1968. PLB 5.00 (ISBN 0-307-60513-2, Golden Pr). Western Pub.
Stack, Norman. U. S. Coins of Value. (Orig.). 1981. pap. 2.50 (ISBN 0-440-18759-1). Dell.
--U. S. Coins of Value. (Orig.). pap. 2.25 o.s.i. (ISBN 0-440-19102-5). Dell.
Stack, Richard. Warriors: A Parris Island Journal. (Illus.). 128p. (Orig.). 1975. pap. 4.95 o.p. (ISBN 0-06-090319-8, CN319, CN). Har-Row.
Stack, Robert & Evans, Mark. Straight Shooting. 1981. pap. 2.75 (ISBN 0-425-04757-1). Berkley Pub.
Stackelberg, Roderick. Idealism Debased: From Volkisch Ideology to National Socialism. LC 80-84663. (Illus.). 220p. 1981. 18.00x (ISBN 0-87338-252-8). Kent St U Pr.
Stackpole, Edouard, jt. auth. see Dreyer, Peter.
Stackpole, Edouard A. Scrimshaw at Mystic Seaport. 1958. 5.95 (ISBN 0-8286-0048-1). De Graff.
Stackpole, Renny A. American Whaling in Hudson Bay, Eighteen Sixty-One to Nineteen Nineteen. LC 79-110367. (Illus.). 68p. 1969. pap. 3.00 (ISBN 0-913372-01-3). Mystic Seaport.
Stacpoole, Henry D. The Blue Lagoon Omnibus. 210p. (Orig.). 1981. Repr. of 1908 ed. 3.95x (ISBN 0-9605338-0-X). Blue Lagoon.
Stacy, Don. Drawing & Painting from Imagination. (Illus.). 224p. 1980. 14.95 (ISBN 0-87396-083-1). Stravon.
Stacy, Ralph W. & Waxman, Bruce. Computers in Biomedical Research, 4 vols. 1965-1964. Vol. 1. 51.00 (ISBN 0-12-662301-5); Vol. 2. 46.50 (ISBN 0-12-662302-3); Vol. 3. 46.50 (ISBN 0-12-662303-1); Vol. 4. 1974. 43.50 (ISBN 0-12-662304-X). Acad Pr.
Staddon, John E. Limits to Action: The Allocation of Individual Behavior. LC 79-6794. 1980. 24.00 (ISBN 0-12-662650-2). Acad Pr.
Staddor, J., jt. ed. see Honig, Werner K.
Stade, George. Robert Graves. LC 67-16890. (Columbia: No. 25). (Orig.). 1967. pap. 2.00 (ISBN 0-231-02907-1, MW25). Columbia U Pr.
Stade, George, ed. Six Contemporary British Novelists. 1976. 20.00x (ISBN 0-231-04054-7). Columbia U Pr.
--Six Modern British Novelists. LC 74-6141. 336p. 1974. 17.50x (ISBN 0-231-03846-1). Columbia U Pr.
Stadelman, William J. & Cotterill, Owen J. Egg Science & Technology. 2nd ed. (Illus.). 1977. lib. bdg. 28.50 (ISBN 0-87055-261-9); pap. text ed. 19.50 (ISBN 0-87055-292-9). AVI.
Stadelmann, Rudolph. The Social & Political History of the German 1848 Revolution. Chastain, James G., tr. from Ger. LC 74-27711. Orig. Title: Soziale und Politis Che Geschichet der Revolution Von 1848. xvi, 218p. 1975. 14.00x (ISBN 0-8214-0177-7). Ohio U Pr.
Staden, Ann. Pepper Face & Other Stories. (Illus.). (ps-5). 1972. 4.95 (ISBN 0-686-24619-5, Pub. by Faber & Faber). Merrimack Bk Serv.
Staden, Wendelgard von see Von Staden, Wendelgard.
Stadler, E. M., jt. auth. see Gourevitch, D.
Stadler, John. Animal Cafe. LC 80-15072. (Illus.). 32p. (gr. k-2). 8.95 (ISBN 0-87888-166-2). Bradbury Pr.
--Rodney & Lucinda's Amazing Race. (Illus.). 32p. (ps-2). 1981. 8.95 (ISBN 0-87888-179-4). Bradbury Pr.
Stadler, Jozef, tr. see Lange, Oskar.
Stadt, Ronald & Gooch, Bill. Cooperative Education: Vocational, Occupational Career. LC 75-36971. 1977. 11.95 (ISBN 0-672-97110-0). Bobbs.
Stadt, Ronald & Nystrom, Dennis. Planning & Organizing Career Curricula. LC 72-92619. 1975. 13.95 (ISBN 0-672-97533-5). Bobbs.
Stadt, Ronald W., jt. auth. see Bailey, Larry J.
Stadtfield, Curtis K. From the Land & Back. LC 76-38946. (Illus.). 1974. pap. 2.95 o.p. (ISBN 0-684-13691-0, SL508, ScribT). Scribner.
Stadtman, Earl R., jt. ed. see Hoercker, Bernard L.
Stadtman, Verne, ed. see Carnegie Commission on Higher Education.
Stadtman, Verne A. Academic Adaptations: Higher Education Prepares for the 1980's & 1990's. LC 80-8000. (Carnegie Council Ser.). 1980. text ed. 15.95x (ISBN 0-87589-480-1). Jossey-Bass.
Stadtmauer, Saul. Visions of the Future: Magic Boards. LC 77-10735. (Myth, Magic & Superstition Ser.). (Illus.). (gr. 4-5). 1977. PLB 9.65 (ISBN 0-8172-1040-7). Raintree Pubs.
Staebler, Warren. Ralph Waldo Emerson. (World Leaders Ser: No. 25). 1973. lib. bdg. 9.95 (ISBN 0-8057-3674-3). Twayne.
Staelin, Richard, jt. auth. see Hinich, Melvin J.
Staff, Frank. The Transatlantic Mail. LC 79-67394. 192p. 1980. Repr. of 1956 ed. lib. bdg. 35.00x (ISBN 0-88000-113-5). Quarterman.
Staff of American Book Collector. Directory of Specialized American Bookdealers 1981-1982. 256p. 1981. lib. bdg. 19.95 (ISBN 0-668-05203-1). Arco.
Staff of Eastman Kodak Co., ed. Close-up Photography & Photomacrography. LC 77-88930. (Kodak Publication). (Illus.). 1977. pap. 8.00 (ISBN 0-87985-206-2, N-12). Eastman Kodak.
Staff of Innovation, ed. Managing Advancing Technology, 2 vols. LC 79-182225. 1972. Set. 27.50 o.p. (ISBN 0-8144-5283-3). AM Mgmt.
Staff of National Committee for Citizens in Education. Violence in Our Schools: What to Know About It - What to Do About It. new ed. 40p. (Orig.). 1975. pap. 3.50 (ISBN 0-934460-00-0). NCCE.
Staff of NCCE. Every Child Can Learn. 1980. pap. 0.50 (ISBN 0-934460-11-6). NCCE.
Staff of Ortho Books, ed. All About Roses. LC 76-29248. 1977. pap. 4.95 (ISBN 0-917102-23-1). Ortho.
--Gardening with Color. LC 77-89690. (Illus.). 1978. pap. 4.95 (ISBN 0-917102-58-4). Ortho.
--The World of Cactus & Succulents. LC 77-89689. (Illus.). 1978. pap. 4.95 (ISBN 0-917102-59-2). Ortho.
--The World of Trees. LC 77-89692. (Illus.). 1978. pap. 4.95 Midwest-Northeast ed. (ISBN 0-917102-60-6); pap. 4.95 South ed. (ISBN 0-917102-61-4); pap. 4.95 West ed. (ISBN 0-917102-62-2). Ortho.
Staff of the Culinary Arts Institute, jt. auth. see Magida, Phylis.
Staff of the TI Learning Center & Personal Computer Division. User's Reference Guide. LC 79-65511. (Texas Instruments Home Computer User-Educational Software Ser.). (Illus.). 1979. pap. text ed. 14.95 (ISBN 0-89512-029-1). Tex Instr Inc.
Staff of Vedanta Kesari, ed. Paths of Meditation. 241p. 1980. pap. write for info. o.s.i. (ISBN 0-87481-501-0). Vedanta Pr.
Staff of Workbasket Magazine. Aunt Ellen's Crochet Handbook: A Treasury of Techniques & Projects. LC 80-85484. (Illus., Orig.). 1981. pap. 2.95 (ISBN 0-86675-325-7, 3257). Mod Handicraft.
Staff of World Bank. World Tables: 1980. LC 79-3649. (World Bank Occasional Paper Ser.). (Illus.). 480p. 1980. text ed. 27.50x (ISBN 0-8018-2389-7); pap. text ed. 10.95x (ISBN 0-8018-2390-0). Johns Hopkins.
Staffeld, Jean, et al. Thirty-Eight Recipes for Bulletin Boards & Art Projects That Christian Kids Can Make. (Illus.). 1978. pap. 4.50 (ISBN 0-570-03774-3, 12-2721). Concordia.
Staffieri, Anthony, jt. auth. see Post, Elizabeth.
Staffieri, Anthony, jt. auth. see Post, Emily.
Stafford, Caroline. The House by Exmoor. 1977. pap. 1.50 o.p. (ISBN 0-449-23058-9, Crest). Fawcett.
--Moira. 1978. pap. 1.75 o.p. (ISBN 0-449-23530-0, Crest). Fawcett.
Stafford, Carolyn, jt. auth. see Stafford, Robert.
Stafford, D. A., et al, eds. Anaerobic Digestion. (Illus.). xii, 528p. 1980. 95.00x (ISBN 0-85334-904-5). Burgess-Intl Ideas.
Stafford, D. C., jt. auth. see Corner, D. C.
Stafford, David. Britain & European Resistance, Nineteen Forty to Nineteen Forty-Five: A Survey of the Special Operations Executive, with Documents. LC 79-19224. 1980. 25.00 (ISBN 0-8020-2361-4). U of Toronto Pr.
Stafford, Donald & Renner, John. The Physical Sciences: Inquiry & Investigation. 1977. text ed. 14.95x (ISBN 0-02-478900-3). Macmillan.
Stafford, E. M., jt. auth. see Ellison, A. P.
Stafford, Edward P. The Big E. 1976. pap. 2.75 (ISBN 0-345-28795-9). Ballantine.
Stafford, Eugene C. Modern Industrial Ceramics. LC 72-14907. 1979. 19.95 (ISBN 0-672-97129-1); pap. 4.95 student's manual (ISBN 0-672-97128-3); instructor's manual 3.33 (ISBN 0-672-97127-5). Bobbs.
Stafford, Harry C. Culture & Cosmology: Essays on the Birth of World View. LC 80-5642. 371p. 1981. lib. bdg. 21.25 (ISBN 0-8191-1371-9); pap. text ed. 12.50 (ISBN 0-8191-1372-7). U Pr of Amer.
Stafford, Howard A. Principles of Industrial Facility Location. LC 80-26737. (Illus.). 1980. pap. 25.00 (ISBN 0-910436-18-5). Conway Pubns.
Stafford, Irving, jt. auth. see Leventhal, Lance A.
Stafford, Jean. The Mountain Lion. 231p. (New preface by the author). 1972. 6.95 o.p. (ISBN 0-374-21402-6). FS&G.
Stafford, Kenneth R., jt. auth. see Sargent, S. Stansfeld.
Stafford, L. W. The Modern Economy: A Theoretical Debate & Its Practical Implications. LC 75-20322. (Illus.). 1976. text ed. 12.00x (ISBN 0-582-44357-1); pap. text ed. 7.95x (ISBN 0-582-44358-X). Longman.
Stafford, R. H. Digital Television: Bandwidth Reduction & Communication Aspects. LC 80-17542. 400p. 1980. 34.95 (ISBN 0-471-07857-3, Pub. by Wiley-Interscience). Wiley.
Stafford, Reid W. Ashes: A Collection of Poems. 1977. 4.50 o.p. (ISBN 0-533-02977-5). Vantage.
Stafford, Rick, jt. auth. see Wylie, Laurence.
Stafford, Robert & Stafford, Carolyn. The Parent Child Fun Kit. (Illus.). 318p. 1980. soft cover 10.00 (ISBN 0-933586-00-0). Book Promo Unltd.
Stafford, Roy L. Elementary Luo Grammar, with Vocabularies. 1967. pap. 2.00x o.p. (ISBN 0-19-639396-5). Oxford U Pr.
Stafford, Roy W., Jr., jt. auth. see Endicott, John E., Jr.
Stafford, Tim, jt. auth. see Kesler, Jay.
Stafford, William. Going Places. 1976. pap. 2.50 (ISBN 0-915596-05-9). West Coast.
--Writing the Australian Crawl. Hall, Donald, ed. LC 77-5711. (Poets on Poetry Ser.). pap. 5.95 (ISBN 0-472-87300-8). U of Mich Pr.

Stafford, William B. Schools Without Counselors: Guidance Practices for Teachers. LC 73-90567. 1974. 16.95 (ISBN 0-911012-52-4). Nelson-Hall.

Stafford, William S. Domesticating the Clergy: The Inception of the Reformation in Strasbourg 1522-1524. LC 76-15567. (American Academy of Religion, Dissertation Ser.). 1976. pap. 9.00 (ISBN 0-89130-109-7, 010117). Scholars Pr Ca.

Stafford, William T. Books Speaking to Books: A Contextual Approach to American Fiction. LC 80-25892. 224p. 1981. 16.50x (ISBN 0-686-69544-5). U of NC Pr.

Stafleu. Time & Again: A Systematic Analysis of the Foundations of Physics. 1981. 19.95x (ISBN 0-88906-108-4). Radix Bks.

Stage, Sarah. Female Complaints: Lydia Pinkham & the Business of Women's Medicine. (Illus.). 304p. 1981. pap. 4.95 (ISBN 0-393-00033-8). Norton.

Stagg, Frank. Galatians & Romans. (Knox Pereaching Guides Ser.). 160p. (Orig.). 1980. pap. 4.50 (ISBN 0-8042-3238-5). John Knox.

--Galatians & Romans. LC 79-92066. (Knox Preaching Guides Ser.). 128p. (Orig., John Hayes series editor). 1980. pap. 4.50 (ISBN 0-8042-3238-5). John Knox.

--Teologia Del Nuevo Testamento. Canclini, Arnoldo, tr. 1976. pap. 7.95 (ISBN 0-311-09077-X). Casa Bautista.

Stagner, Ross & Rosen, Hjalmar. Psychology of Union-Management Relations. (Behavioral Science in Industry Ser). (Orig.). 1966. pap. text ed. 6.95 o.p. (ISBN 0-8185-0315-7). Brooks-Cole.

Stahel, Walter R. The Potential for Substituting Manpower for Energy. Date not set. 12.50 (ISBN 0-533-04799-4). Vantage.

Stahl, Dulcelina A., jt. auth. see Baldonado, Ardelina A.

Stahl, E. L., ed. see Goethe, Johann W.

Stahl, E. L., ed. see Lessing, Gotthold.

Stahl, Ernest L., ed. Oxford Book of German Verse, Twelfth to Twentieth Century. 3rd ed. (Ger). 1967. 27.50 (ISBN 0-19-812132-6). Oxford U Pr.

Stahl, Franklin W. Genetic Recombination: Thinking About It in Phage & Fungi. LC 79-13378. (Biology Ser.). (Illus.). 1979. text ed. 28.95x (ISBN 0-7167-1037-4). W H Freeman.

--Mechanics of Inheritance. 2nd ed. Suskind, Sigmund & Hartman, Philip, eds. LC 69-19870. (Foundations of Modern Genetics Ser). 1969. pap. 10.95 ref. ed. (ISBN 0-13-571042-1). P-H.

Stahl, Friedrich J. The Present-Day Parties in the State & Church. Taylor, Timothy D., tr. LC 76-54054. 502p. 1976. 35.75 o.p. (ISBN 0-918288-01-0); pap. 26.75 lmt. ed. o.p. (ISBN 0-918288-08-8). Slavia Lib.

Stahl, Friedrich Julius. Roman Civil Law: Ueber As Aeltere Roemische Klagenrecht, Vol. 1 Of 2 Vol. Set. LC 77-74020. 1977. pap. text ed. 5.75 limited ed. o.p. (ISBN 0-918288-04-5). Slavia Lib.

--What Is the Revolution? Taylor, Timothy D., tr. from Ger. Orig. Title: Was Ist Die Revolution? 1977. pap. 3.55 limited ed. o.p. (ISBN 0-918288-06-1). Slavia Lib.

Stahl, Henri. Traditional Romanian Village Communities. Chirot, D. & Chirot, H. C., trs. LC 79-52855. (Studies in Modern Capitalism). (Illus.). 1980. 39.95 (ISBN 0-521-22957-X). Cambridge U Pr.

Stahl, Hilda. Elizabeth Gail & the Strange Birthday Party. (gr. 4-6). 1980. 1.95 (ISBN 0-8423-0724-9). Tyndale.

--Elizabeth Gail & the Terrifying News. (gr. 4-8). 1980. 1.95 (ISBN 0-8423-0725-7). Tyndale.

--Tina's Reluctant Friend. (gr. 4-7). 1981. pap. 2.25 (ISBN 0-8423-7216-4). Tyndale.

Stahl, Nancy. If It's Raining, This Must Be the Weekend. 1979. 7.95 o.p. (ISBN 0-8362-1114-6). Andrews & McMeel.

Stahl, S. Sigmund. Periodontal Surgery: Biological Basis & Technique. (American Lectures in Dentistry Ser.). (Illus.). 480p. 1976. 54.50 (ISBN 0-398-03431-1). C C Thomas.

Stahl, S. Sigmund, et al. What Dentists Do: A Patient's Guide to Modern Dentistry. (Appleton Consumer Health Guides). (Illus.). 226p. 1980. 12.95 (ISBN 0-8385-9712-2); pap. 5.95 (ISBN 0-8385-9711-4). ACC.

Stahl, Sidney M. & Hennes, James D. Reading & Understanding Applied Statistics: A Self-Learning Approach. 2nd ed. LC 79-29760. (Illus.). 1980. pap. text ed. 11.95 (ISBN 0-8016-4754-1). Mosby.

Stahl, W. H., tr. Commentary on the Dream of Scipio. LC 52-1644. 1952. 20.00x (ISBN 0-231-01737-5). Columbia U Pr.

Stahl, William H. Martianus Capella & the Seven Liberal Arts, Vol. 1. LC 76-121876. (Records of Civilization, Sources & Studies). 1971. 17.50x (ISBN 0-231-03254-4). Columbia U Pr.

Stahl, William H. & Johnson, Richard C., eds. Martianus Capella & the Seven Liberal Arts: The Marriage of Philology & Mercury, Vol. 2. LC 76-121876. 1977. 27.50x (ISBN 0-231-03719-8). Columbia U Pr.

Stahlberg, H., tr. see Hoffman, M., et al.

Stahle, J. Vestibular Function on Earth & in Space. 1970. 55.00 (ISBN 0-08-015592-8). Pergamon.

Stahlkopf, K. E., jt. ed. see Steele, L. E.

Stahmann, Mark C., ed. see International Symposium On Poly-A-Amino Acids - 1st - University Of Wisconsin - 1961.

Stahmann, Robert F. & Hiebert, William. Premarital Counseling: Education for Marriage. LC 78-19727. 192p. 1980. 19.95 (ISBN 0-669-02726-X). Lexington Bks.

Stahnke, A. A., jt. auth. see Ellsworth, J. W.

Stahr, Elvis J., jt. auth. see Boulding, Kenneth E.

Stahr, Jack. Tennis Umpire's Clinic Kit. 1975. 3.00 (ISBN 0-938822-11-X). USTA.

Staiger, Janet, ed. see Buscombe, et al.

Staiger, Janet, ed. see Glasser, et al.

Staimle, Fritz, jt. auth. see Von Cube, Hans L.

Stainback, Susan, jt. auth. see Healy, Harriet.

Stainback, Susan, jt. auth. see Stainback, William.

Stainback, Susan B. & Stainback, William C. Classroom Discipline: A Positive Approach. 180p. 1977. pap. 11.75 (ISBN 0-398-02814-1). C C Thomas.

Stainback, William & Stainback, Susan. Educating Children with Severe Maladaptive Behaviors. 1980. 24.50 (ISBN 0-8089-1269-0). Grune.

Stainback, William C., jt. auth. see Stainback, Susan B.

Stainer, John. Music of the Bible. LC 74-100657. (Music Ser). (Illus.). 1970. Repr. of 1914 ed. lib. bdg. 22.50 (ISBN 0-306-71862-6). Da Capo.

Staines, Bill. If I Were a Word, I'd Be a Song. 96p. 1980. pap. 6.95 (ISBN 0-686-27977-8). Folk-Legacy.

Staines, Brian. The Red Deer. (Mammal Society Ser.). (Illus.). 50p. 1980. 6.95 (ISBN 0-7137-0898-0, Pub. by Blandford Pr England). Sterling.

Stair, Lila B. Careers in Business: Selecting & Planning Your Career Path. 1980. 6.95x (ISBN 0-256-02368-9). Irwin.

Stair, Ralph M., Jr. Programming in BASIC. 1979. pap. 11.50x (ISBN 0-256-02145-7). Irwin.

Stair, Ralph M., Jr. & Render, Barry. Production & Operations Management: A Self-Correcting Approach. 1980. pap. text ed. 13.95 (ISBN 0-205-06715-8, 086715-2). Allyn.

Stair, Ralph M., Jr., jt. auth. see Render, Barry.

Stair, William K., ed. Student, Teacher, & Engineer: Selected Speeches & Articles of Nathan W. Dougherty. LC 76-186707. 1972. 13.50x (ISBN 0-87049-138-5). U of Tenn Pr.

Stairs, Denis & Munton, Don, eds. Perspectives on Canada's Foreign Policy. (Pergamon Policy Studies). 280p. Date not set. price not set (ISBN 0-08-025972-3). Pergamon.

Stajka, Nika. The Last Days of Freedom. 1981. 12.95 (ISBN 0-533-04637-8). Vantage.

Stakgold, Ivar. Green's Functions & Boundary Value Problems. LC 78-27259. (Pure & Applied Mathematics: Texts, Monographs & Tracts). 1979. 35.95 (ISBN 0-471-81967-0, Pub. by Wiley-Interscience). Wiley.

Stakkestad, James, jt. auth. see Wyant, Linsley.

Stalberg. Neurology: Clinical Neurophysiology, Vol. 1. (Butterworths International Medical Reviews Ser.). 1981. text ed. price not set (ISBN 0-407-02294-5). Butterworth.

Stalberg, Roberta & Nesi, Ruth. China's Crafts: The Story of How They're Made & What They Mean. 1980. pap. 10.95 (ISBN 0-8351-0740-X). China Bks.

Stalder, G. & Fliegel, C. P., eds. Praeventive Aspekte in der Paediatrie. (Paediatrische Fortbildungskurse Fuer Die Praxis Ser.: Vol. 52). (Illus.). 1981. soft cover 48.00 (ISBN 3-8055-1980-X). S Karger.

Staley, Allen. The Pre-Raphaelite Landscape. (Oxford Studies in the History of Art & Architecture Ser.). (Illus.). 1973. 54.00x (ISBN 0-19-817307-5). Oxford U Pr.

Staley, C. W. Unfair at Any Gridiron. LC 80-66404. 250p. 1981. 14.95 (ISBN 0-9604324-0-X, 8012 800326). CWS Group Pr.

Staley, James & Stryker, Jay. Modular Electronics: An Individualized Study Program. LC 73-91054. 1974. text ed. 11.95x o.p. (ISBN 0-675-08880-1); instructor's manual 3.95 o.p. (ISBN 0-686-66914-2). Merrill.

Staley, Jeffrey L. A Transportation Energy Use Forcasting Model: An Integrated Modal Approach. LC 78-75009. (Outstanding Dissertations on Energy Ser.). 1979. lib. bdg. 16.50 (ISBN 0-8240-3982-3). Garland Pub.

Staley, Thomas F. Dorothy Richardson. (English Authors Ser.: No. 187). 1976. lib. bdg. 12.50 (ISBN 0-8057-6662-6). Twayne.

Staley, Thomas F., jt. auth. see Baker, James R.

Stalin, Joseph. Economic Problems of Socialism in the U.S.S.R. pap. 1.25 (ISBN 0-8351-0068-5). China Bks.

--Marxism & the Problems of Linguistics. pap. 1.00 (ISBN 0-8351-0150-9). China Bks.

--On the Opposition. 1974. 6.95 (ISBN 0-8351-0549-0); pap. 4.95 (ISBN 0-8351-0214-9). China Bks.

Stalker, D. M., tr. see Bornkamm, Gunther.

Stalker, J. The Life of Jesus Christ. 2nd ed. (Handbooks for Bible Classes). 157p. 1891. text ed. 8.95 (ISBN 0-567-28130-2). Attic Pr.

--The Life of Saint Paul. (Handbooks for Bible Classes). 150p. 1967. pap. text ed. 3.50 (ISBN 0-567-28131-0). Attic Pr.

Stalker, James. The Example of Jesus Christ: Imago Christi. LC 80-82322. (Orig.). 1980. pap. 5.95 (ISBN 0-87983-231-2). Keats.

--Vida De Jesucristo. Orig. Title: Life of Jesus Christ. 177p. (Span.). 1973. pap. 2.95 (ISBN 0-89922-024-X). Edit Caribe.

--Vida De San Pablo. Orig. Title: Life of Saint Paul. 160p. (Span.). 1973. pap. 2.95 (ISBN 0-89922-025-8). Edit Caribe.

Stall, Chris, jt. auth. see Pandell, Karen.

Stallard, John. Four in a Wild Place. LC 79-152674. 1971. 6.95 o.p. (ISBN 0-393-08649-6). Norton.

Stallard, John J., jt. auth. see Terry, George R.

Stallard, Patricia Y. Glittering Misery. LC 77-94525. (Illus.). 1978. 10.95 o.p. (ISBN 0-88342-054-6); pap. 4.95 (ISBN 0-88342-239-5). Presidio Pr.

Stalley, Marshall, ed. Patrick Geddes: Spokesman for Man & the Environment. LC 75-163963. 1972. 27.50 (ISBN 0-8135-0697-2). Rutgers U Pr.

Stallings, Constance, jt. auth. see Murlless, Dick.

Stallings, J. H. Soil Conservation. 1957. 21.95 (ISBN 0-13-821819-6). P-H.

Stallings, Jane. Learning to Look: A Handbook on Classroom Observation. 1977. pap. 11.95x (ISBN 0-534-00522-5). Wadsworth Pub.

Stallman, R. W. The Houses That James Built and Other Literary Studies. LC 77-371844. 256p. 1977. 12.00x (ISBN 0-8214-0362-1); pap. 4.50x (ISBN 0-8214-0363-X). Ohio U Pr.

Stallman, Robert. The Captive. (Orig.). 1981. pap. 2.25 (ISBN 0-671-41382-1). PB.

Stallo, Johann B., et al. Bible in Public Schools. 2nd ed. LC 67-27464. (Law, Politics & History Ser). 1967. Repr. of 1870 ed. lib. bdg. 35.00 (ISBN 0-306-70963-5). Da Capo.

Stallone, Sylvester. Paradise Alley. LC 77-22926. (Illus.). (YA) 1977. 8.95 o.p. (ISBN 0-399-12080-7, Pub. by Berkley Pub). Berkley Pub.

Stallworth, Anne N. Where the Bright Lights Shine. LC 75-25145. 1978. 7.95 (ISBN 0-8149-0770-9). Vanguard.

Stallworthy, Jon, ed. A Book of Love Poetry. 385p. 1974. 17.95 (ISBN 0-19-519774-7). Oxford U Pr.

Stallybrass, Oliver, ed. see Forster, E. M.

Stalonas, Peter, jt. auth. see Johnson, William G.

Stam, Robert, jt. auth. see Johnson, Randal.

Stamatoyannopoulos, G. & Nienhuis, A., eds. Cellular & Molecular Regulation of Hemoglobin Switching. 1979. 68.50 (ISBN 0-686-63983-9). Grune.

Stamaty, Mark Alan. MacDoodle Street. 96p. 1981. pap. 6.95 (ISBN 0-312-92519-0). St Martin.

Stambaugh, Harriett, ed. Social Work on Pediatric Settings. (Social Work in Health Care Ser.: Vol. 1). 350p. 1981. text ed. 22.95 (ISBN 0-917724-29-1). Haworth Pr.

Stambaugh, Joan. Nietzsche's Thought of Eternal Return. LC 75-171553. 144p. 1972. 10.00x o.p. (ISBN 0-8018-1288-7). Johns Hopkins.

Stambaugh, John E., jt. auth. see Rice, David G.

Stambolian, George, ed. Twentieth-Century French Fiction: Essays for Germaine Bree. 1975. 20.00 (ISBN 0-8135-0786-3). Rutgers U Pr.

Stambolian, George & Marks, Elaine, eds. Homosexualities & French Literature: Cultural Contexts, Critical Texts. LC 78-25659. 1979. 22.50x (ISBN 0-8014-1186-6). Cornell U Pr.

Stambolis, C., ed. Solar Energy in the Eighties: Conference Proceedings, London, 14-51 Jan 1981. LC 80-41617. (Illus.). 232p. 1981. 60.00 (ISBN 0-08-026123-X). Pergamon.

Stamey, Thomas A. Pathogenesis & Treatment of Urinary Tract Infections. (Illus.). 624p. 1980. 54.00 (ISBN 0-683-07909-3). Williams & Wilkins.

Stamford, Paul, jt. auth. see Duff, Charles.

Stamford, Sarah. The Magnificent Duchess. 1975. 6.95 o.p. (ISBN 0-440-05252-1). Delacorte.

--The Marshal's Lady. 1981. 11.95 (ISBN 0-525-15320-9). Dutton.

Stamm, A. J. Wood & Cellulose Science. (Illus.). 1964. 30.50 (ISBN 0-8260-8495-8, Pub. by Wiley-Interscience). Wiley.

Stamm, Charles F., jt. auth. see Howell, James M.

Stamm, James R. A Short History of Spanish Literature: Revised & Updated Edition. LC 78-53803. (The Gotham Library). 1979. 16.00x (ISBN 0-8147-7791-0); pap. 7.00x (ISBN 0-8147-7792-9). NYU Pr.

Stamm, Laura, et al, eds. Power Skating the Hockey Way. LC 76-19759. (Illus.). 1978. pap. 5.95 (ISBN 0-8015-4435-1, Hawthorn). Dutton.

Stamm, Martin L. & Nissman, Blossom S. Improving Middle School Guidance: Procedures for Counselors, Teachers, & Administrators. new ed. 1979. text ed. 18.95 (ISBN 0-205-06449-3). Allyn.

Stamm, Sara B. Favorite New England Recipes. (Illus.). 304p. 1972. pap. 9.75 (ISBN 0-911658-87-4). Yankee Bks.

Stamm, Theo. Political Parties in Europe. 1981. 42.50 (ISBN 0-930466-28-4). Meckler Bks.

Stammen, Theo. Political Parties in Europe. 350p. 1980. 22.50x (ISBN 0-906237-08-4). Nichols Pub.

Stammers, Michael K. The Passage Makers. (Illus.). xx, 508p. 1980. 50.00 (ISBN 0-903662-06-X, Pub. by Teredo Bks England). McCartan & Root.

Stamp, A. H. A Social & Economic History of England from Seventeen Hundred to Nineteen Seventy. 334p. 1980. 22.50x (ISBN 0-7050-0070-2, Pub. by Skilton & Shaw England). State Mutual Bk.

Stamp, Don. Field Archery. (Illus.). 1980. 15.95 (ISBN 0-7136-1981-3). Transatlantic.

Stamp, Dudley & Clark, Audrey N. A Glossary of Geographical Terms. 3rd ed. 1979. text ed. 35.00 (ISBN 0-582-35258-4). Longman.

Stamp, E. International Auditing Standards. 1979. 21.95 (ISBN 0-13-470948-9). P-H.

Stamp, Edward, jt. auth. see Leach, Ronald.

Stamp, Elizabeth, ed. Growing Out of Poverty. (Illus.). 1977. 12.50x (ISBN 0-19-857529-7); pap. 8.95x (ISBN 0-19-857528-9). Oxford U Pr.

Stamp, L. Dudley. Our Developing World. 3rd ed. 1969. pap. 2.95 o.p. (ISBN 0-571-04639-8, Pub. by Faber & Faber). Merrimack Bk Serv.

Stamp, L. Dudley & Beaver, S. H. The British Isles. 6th ed. LC 70-17425. (Geographies for Advanced Studies). 1972. 35.00 (ISBN 0-312-10325-5). St Martin.

Stampe, David. A Dissertation on Natural Phonology. Hankamer, Jorge, ed. LC 78-66538. (Outstanding Dissertations in Linguistics Ser.). 1979. lib. bdg. 16.50 (ISBN 0-8240-9674-6). Garland Pub.

Stamper, Eugene & Koral, Richard L., eds. Handbook of Air Conditioning, Heating & Ventilating. 3rd ed. (Illus.). 1979. 59.00 (ISBN 0-8311-1124-0). Indus Pr.

Stamper, J. G. & Stamper, M. A. Chemistry for Biologists. 1971. pap. text ed. 5.95x (ISBN 0-04-540006-7). Allen Unwin.

Stamper, M. A., jt. auth. see Stamper, J. G.

Stampp, Kenneth M. And the War Came: The North and the Secession Crisis, 1860-1861. LC 80-15742. (Illus.). xvii, 331p. 1980. Repr. of 1950 ed. lib. bdg. 27.25x (ISBN 0-313-22566-4, STAN). Greenwood.

--Indiana Politics during the Civil War. LC 77-23629. 320p. 1978. Repr. of 1949 ed. 12.50x (ISBN 0-253-37022-1). Ind U Pr.

Stamps, Paula L. Ambulatory Care Systems, Vol. 3: Evaluation of Outpatient Facilities. LC 76-55865. (Illus.). 1978. 21.50 (ISBN 0-669-01325-0). Lexington Bks.

Stanaford, Penny. Contributing to Family Living: A Guide to Household Management. (Illus.). 99p. 1980. 7.95 (ISBN 0-9604850-1-5). Postscript.

--Create-A-Cookbook: Guide to Easy Meal Planning. (Illus.). 68p. 1980. 10.95 (ISBN 0-9604850-0-7). Postscript.

Stanard, Mary N. Colonial Virginia: Its People & Customs. LC 78-99055. (Social History Reference Ser.). (Illus.). 1970. Repr. of 1917 ed. 26.00 (ISBN 0-8103-0161-X). Gale.

Stanat, Kirby W. & Reardon, Patrick. Job Hunting Secrets & Tactics. LC 76-49663. 1977. lib. bdg. 10.95 (ISBN 0-8172-0509-8); pap. 4.95 (ISBN 0-8172-0508-X). Follett.

Stanback, Thomas M. & Knight, Richard V. Metropolitan Economy. LC 77-133492. 1970. 20.00x (ISBN 0-231-03426-1). Columbia U Pr.

Stanback, Thomas M., Jr. & Knight, Richard V. Suburbanization & the Ciy. LC 76-472. (Conservation of Human Resources Ser.: No. 2). 256p. 1976. text ed. 19.50 (ISBN 0-916672-01-8). Allanheld.

Stanbury, David. Living World, 2 bks. Elder, Joseph, ed. LC 76-126509. (Illus.). 224p. (gr. 7 up). 1973. pap. text ed. 2.50 ea. o.s.i. (CCPr). Bk. 1 (78672). Bk. 2 (78673). Macmillan.

Stanbury, John B., jt. auth. see DeGroot, Leslie J.

Stanbury, Percy & Carlisle, G. L. Shotgun & the Shooter. 1978. 11.95 o.p. (ISBN 0-214-66874-6, 8029, Dist. by Arco). Barrie & Jenkins.

--Shotgun Marksmanship. 1978. 11.95 o.p. (ISBN 0-214-20065-5, 8030, Dist. by Arco). Barrie & Jenkins.

Stanbury, Peter. Looking at Mammals. 1972. 14.95x o.p. (ISBN 0-435-60800-2). Heinemann Ed.

Stanbury, Peter & Phipps, Graeme. Australia's Animals Discovered. (Illus.). 120p. 1980. 23.40 (ISBN 0-08-024796-2). Pergamon.

Stanbury, W. T. Government Regulation: Scope, Growth, Process. 267p. 1980. pap. text ed. 10.95x (ISBN 0-920380-48-4, Pub. by Inst Res Pub Canada). Renouf.

--Studies on Regulation in Canada. 249p. 1978. pap. text ed. 9.95x (ISBN 0-920380-04-2, Pub. by Inst Res Pub Canada). Renouf.

Stanbury, W. T., jt. auth. see Gorecki, P. K.

Stanbury, W. T., jt. auth. see Rowley, J. W.

Stanbury, W. T., jt. auth. see Smart, C. F.

Stanbury, W. T., jt. auth. see Thompson, Fred.

Stanchfield, Jo. Driving Through the Clouds & Other Stories. LC 72-92846. (Highway Holidays Ser). 1973. pap. text ed. 3.54 (ISBN 0-8372-0798-3). Bowmar-Noble.

--Pablo, the Bullfighter & Other Stories. LC 72-92848. (Highway Holidays Ser). 1973. pap. text ed. 3.54 (ISBN 0-8372-0797-5). Bowmar-Noble.

--Wrong-Way Camper & Other Stories. LC 72-92847. (Highway Holidays Ser). (gr. 3-6). 1973. pap. text ed. 3.54 (ISBN 0-8372-0796-7). Bowmar-Noble.

Stancil, Deborah, jt. auth. see Batten, Peter.

Stancliff, Leon. Biblical Prophets in Outlined Notes. 1976. 8.50 (ISBN 0-89225-176-X); pap. 7.00 (ISBN 0-89225-190-5). Gospel Advocate.

Standard Education Corporation. New Standard Encyclopedia, 14 vols. Downey, Douglas W., ed. LC 80-19936. (gr. 9-12). 1981. Set. 349.50 (ISBN 0-87392-186-0). Standard Ed.

Standard, Stella, jt. auth. see Barr, Stringfellow.

Stander, Siegfried. Flight from the Hunter. LC 77-76653. 1977. 7.95 o.p. (ISBN 0-312-29598-7). St Martin.

Standing, Sue. Amphibious Weather. (Orig.). 1981. pap. 2.25 (ISBN 0-939010-02-X). Zephyr.

Standing Bear, Luther. Land of the Spotted Eagle. LC 77-14062. (Illus.). 1978. 12.95x (ISBN 0-8032-0964-9); pap. 4.50 (ISBN 0-8032-5890-9, BB 655, Bison). U of Nebr Pr.

--My People the Sioux. Brininstool, E. A., ed. LC 74-77394. (Illus.). 1975. 14.95x (ISBN 0-8032-0874-X); pap. 3.95 (ISBN 0-8032-5793-7, BB 578, Bison). U. of Nebr Pr.

Standingford, Oliver. Simplifying Office Work. 2nd ed. (Orig.). 1974. pap. 6.95x o.p. (ISBN 0-8464-0850-3). Beekman Pubs.

Standish, Bob, jt. auth. see Eberle, Bob.

Standish, John. A Lytle Treatise Composyd by Johan Stadysshe...Against the Protestacion of Robert Barnes at the Tyme of His Death. LC 79-85138. (English Experience Ser.: No. 955). 100p. 1979. Repr. of 1540 ed. lib. bdg. 8.00 (ISBN 90-221-0955-0). Walter J Johnson.

Standish, Marjorie. Cooking Down East. 1979. 8.95 (ISBN 0-930096-00-2). G Gannett.

--Cooking Down East. 12th ed. (Illus.). 260p. 1980. 8.95 (ISBN 0-930096-14-2). G Gannett.

--Keep Cooking: The Maine Way. 8.95 (ISBN 0-930096-02-9). G Gannett.

--Keep Cooking the Maine Way. 5th ed. (Illus.). 260p. 1980. 8.95 (ISBN 0-930096-15-0). G Gannett.

Standish, Thomas A. A Data Definition Facility for Programming Languages. LC 79-7307. (Outstanding Dissertations in the Computer Sciences). 1980. lib. bdg. 30.00 (ISBN 0-8240-4422-3). Garland Pub.

Standke, Klaus-Heinrich, ed. see International Colloquium on Science, Technology & Society, Vienna, 1979.

Standley, Fred L. Stopford Brooke. (English Authors Ser.: No. 135). lib. bdg. 10.95 (ISBN 0-8057-1060-4). Twayne.

Standley, K. J. Oxide Magnetic Materials. 2nd ed. (Monographs on the Physics & Chemistry of Materials). (Illus.). 265p. 1972. 34.95x (ISBN 0-19-851327-5). Oxford U Pr.

Standley, Paul C. Flora of Costa Rica, 4 vols. 1980. Set. lib. bdg. 595.00 (ISBN 0-8490-3181-8). Gordon Pr.

Stands In Timber, John & Liberty, Margot. Cheyenne Memories. LC 67-24515. (Illus.). 1972. pap. 3.95 (ISBN 0-8032-5751-1, BB 544, Bison). U of Nebr Pr.

Stands In Timber, John, et al. Cheyenne Memories. (Western Americana Ser.: No. 17). (Illus.). 1967. 22.00x o.p. (ISBN 0-300-00971-2). Yale U Pr.

Stanek, Carolyn. The Complete Guide to Women's College Athletics. (Illus.). 1981. 14.95 (ISBN 0-8092-5986-9); pap. 7.95 (ISBN 0-8092-5985-0). Contemp Bks.

Stanek, Muriel. Growl When You Say R. Pacini, Kathy, ed. LC 79-171. (Concept Bk.: Level II). (Illus.). (gr. k-3). 1979. 6.50g (ISBN 0-8075-3074-3). A Whitman.

--I Won't Go Without a Father. LC 78-188435. (Concept Bks.). (Illus.). 32p. (gr. 1-4). 1972. 6.50g (ISBN 0-8075-3524-9). A Whitman.

--Left, Right, Left, Right. LC 79-79548. (Concept Bks.). (Illus.). 40p. (gr. k-2). 1969. 6.95g (ISBN 0-8075-4421-3). A Whitman.

--New in the City. LC 65-23888. (Illus.). 128p. (gr. 3-5). 1965. 5.95g o.p. (ISBN 0-8075-5576-2). A Whitman.

--One, Two, Three for Fun. LC 67-26519. (Concept Bks.). (Illus.). 32p. (ps-2). 1967. 6.95g (ISBN 0-8075-6106-1). A Whitman.

--Starting School. Fay, Ann, ed. (Self-Starter Bks.). (Illus.). 32p. (ps-1). 1981. 6.50 (ISBN 0-8075-7617-4). A Whitman.

--Who's Afraid of the Dark? Tucker, Kathleen, ed. LC 80-19074. (Concept Bks.). (Illus.). 32p. (gr. 1-3). 1980. 6.50g (ISBN 0-8075-9011-8). A Whitman.

Stanfield, J. Paget, jt. auth. see Jelliffe, D. B.

Stanford, A. L., Jr. Foundations of Biophysics. 1975. text ed. 22.75 (ISBN 0-12-663350-9). Acad Pr.

Stanford, Barbara D. I, Too, Sing America: Black Voices in American Literature. (gr. 10). 1971. text ed. 6.85x o. p. (ISBN 0-8104-5864-0); pap. text ed. 5.95x (ISBN 0-8104-5863-2). Hayden.

Stanford, Barnara D. & Amin, Karima. Black Literature for High School Students. LC 78-16890. 1978. pap. text ed. 6.25x (ISBN 0-8077-2562-5, Pub. by Natl Coun Teach English). Tchrs Coll.

Stanford Cade Memorial Symposium, Royal Institute, London, Sept. 1976. Interaction of Radiation & Anti-Tumor Drugs. Hellmann, Kurt, ed. (International Journal of Radiation Oncology, Biology, Physics: Vol. 4, No. 1-2 78--Special Issue). (Illus.). 1978. pap. text ed. 48.00 (ISBN 0-08-022666-3). Pergamon.

Stanford, Derek. Muriel Spark. 10.00x (ISBN 0-87556-326-0). Saifer.

Stanford, Donald, ed. see Taylor, Edward.

Stanford, Gene. McGraw-Hill Vocabulary, Bk 1. 2nd ed. Weeden, Hester E., ed. (Illus.). 128p. (gr. 7-12). 1981. pap. text ed. 3.84 (ISBN 0-07-060771-0). McGraw.

--McGraw-Hill Vocabulary: Book 2. 2nd ed. (McGraw-Hill Vocabulary Ser.). Orig. Title: Vocab 2. (Illus.). 128p. 1981. pap. text ed. 4.24 (ISBN 0-07-060772-9). McGraw.

Stanford, Gene & Roark, Albert E. Human Interaction in Education. 320p. 1974. pap. text ed. 8.95 o.p. (ISBN 0-205-03854-9, 2238543). Allyn.

Stanford, Gene & Smith, Marie. A Guide Book for Teaching Composition. new ed. 1977. pap. text ed. 18.95 (ISBN 0-205-05872-8). Allyn.

--A Guide Book for Teaching Creative Writing. new ed. 1977. pap. text ed. 16.95 (ISBN 0-205-05873-6). Allyn.

Stanford, Gene, jt. auth. see Cormican, John.

Stanford, Gene, jt. auth. see Thompson, Richard A.

Stanford, Gene, jt. ed. see Editors of NCTE Committee.

Stanford, J. K. Awl-Birds. (Illus.). 1949. 4.95 (ISBN 0-8159-5016-0). Devin.

Stanford, Melvin J. Management Policy. (Illus.). 1979. ref. 21.00 (ISBN 0-13-548794-1). P-H.

Stanford Research Institute. Solar Energy in America's Future. 1980. pap. 10.00 (ISBN 0-89934-044-X). Solar Energy Info.

Stanford, Richard A., ed. Rural Development in Pakistan. LC 77-88663. (Illus.). 180p. 1980. pap. 7.95 (ISBN 0-686-60269-2). Carolina Acad Pr.

Stanford, Sandra. Long Winters Night. 192p. 1981. pap. 1.50 (ISBN 0-671-57058-7). S&S.

Stanford, Sondra. Bellefleur. (Harlequin Romances Ser.). 192p. 1980. pap. 1.25 o.p. (ISBN 0-373-02354-5, Pub. by Harlequin). PB.

--Golden Tide. 192p. (Orig.). 1980. pap. 1.50 (ISBN 0-671-57006-4). S&S.

--No Trespassing. 192p. (Orig.). 1980. pap. 1.50 (ISBN 0-671-57046-3). S&S.

--Shadow of Love. 192p. (Orig.). 1980. pap. 1.50 (ISBN 0-671-57025-0). S&S.

Stanford, Sondrs. Storm's End. 192p. (Orig.). 1980. pap. 1.50 (ISBN 0-671-57035-8). S&S.

Stanford, W. B. The Sound of Greek: Studies in the Greek Theory & Practice of Euphony. (Sather Classical Lectures: No. 38). (YA) (gr. 9 up). 1967. 21.50x (ISBN 0-520-01204-6). U of Cal Pr.

Stanforth, Deirdre. Romantic New Orleans. (Large Format Ser). (Illus.). 1979. pap. 7.95 o.p. (ISBN 0-14-005058-2). Penguin.

Stang, David. Introduction to Social Psychology. LC 80-19469. 570p. 1981. text ed. 17.95 (ISBN 0-8185-0427-7). Brooks-Cole.

Stang, David J. & Wrightman, Lawrence S. Dictionary of Social Behavior & Social Research Methods. LC 80-21511. 250p. 1980. pap. text ed. 6.95 (ISBN 0-8185-0243-6). Brooks-Cole.

Stang, Judy. The Pet in the Jar. (Eager Readers Ser.). (Illus.). (gr. k-3). 1975. PLB 5.00 (ISBN 0-307-60801-8, Golden Pr). Western Pub.

Stang, N. C. Edvard Munch. Knudsen, Carol J., tr. (Tokens of Norway Ser). (Illus.). 305p. (Orig.). 1972. pap. 15.00x (ISBN 82-518-0010-2). Intl Pubns Serv.

Stang, Ragna. Gustav Vigeland: The Sculptor & His Works. Grosjean, Ardis, tr. from Norwegian. LC 79-254352. (Tokens of Norway Ser.). (Illus.). 190p. (Orig.). 1965. pap. 11.25x (ISBN 82-518-0152-4). Intl Pubns Serv.

Stang, Richard, ed. George Eliot (Discussions of Literature). 1960. pap. text ed. 2.95x o.p. (ISBN 0-669-21865-0). Heath.

Stang, Sondra J. Ford Madox Ford. LC 77-41. (Modern Literature Ser.). 1977. 10.95 (ISBN 0-8044-2832-8). Ungar.

Stange, G. Robert, jt. auth. see Houghton, Walter E.

Stange, L. A., jt. auth. see Bohart, R. M.

Stange, L. A., jt. auth. see Grigarick, A. A.

Stangos, Nikos, ed. see Hockney, David.

Stanhope, Henry. The Soldiers: An Anatomy of the British Army. (Illus.). 372p. 1980. 30.00 (ISBN 0-241-10273-1, Pub. by Hamish Hamilton England). David & Charles.

Stanhope, Lavinia. Careers in a Department Store. LC 76-4836. (Whole Works Ser.). (Illus.). 48p. (gr. 3-7). 1976. PLB 9.65 (ISBN 0-8172-0703-1). Raintree Pubs.

Stanhope, P. H. Notes on Conversations with the Duke of Wellington 1831-1851. LC 72-126611. (Modern European History Ser). 1973. Repr. of 1888 ed. lib. bdg. 35.00 (ISBN 0-306-70056-5). Da Capo.

Stanier, R. Y. & Rogers, H. J., eds. Relations Between Structure & Function in the Prokaryotic Cell. LC 77-21093. (Society for General Microbiology Symposium: No. 28). (Illus.). 1978. 65.00 (ISBN 0-521-21909-4). Cambridge U Pr.

Stanier, Roger, et al. Introduction to the Microbial World. (Illus.). 1979. ref. ed. 19.95 (ISBN 0-13-488049-8); lab. manual 8.95 (ISBN 0-13-488031-5). P-H.

Staniford, Philip. Pioneers in the Tropics. (London School of Economics Monographs on Social Anthropology Ser: No. 45). (Illus.). 210p. 1973. text ed. 23.50x (ISBN 0-391-00267-8, Athlone Pr). Humanities.

Staniforth, Maxwell, tr. see Aurelius, Marcus.

Staniloae, Dumitru. Theology & the Church. Barry, Robert, tr. from Romanian. LC 80-19313. 240p. 1980. pap. 6.95 (ISBN 0-913836-69-9). St Vladimirs.

--Theology & the Church. Barringer, Robert, tr. from Romanian. LC 80-19313. 240p. (Orig.). 1980. pap. 6.95 (ISBN 0-913836-69-9, BS695.57 230.19498). St Martin.

Stanish, Bob. Sunflowering. (gr. 4-12). 1977. 7.95 (ISBN 0-916456-12-9, GA69). Good Apple.

Stanislavski, Constantin. Actor Prepares. 1948. 9.95 (ISBN 0-87830-001-5). Theatre Arts.

--Building a Character. 1977. 9.95 (ISBN 0-87830-012-0). Theatre Arts.

--My Life in Art. 1952. pap. 6.95 (ISBN 0-87830-550-5). Theatre Arts.

--Stanislavski's Legacy. rev. ed. Hapgood, Elizabeth R., tr. LC 68-16450. (Orig.). 1968. pap. 4.25 (ISBN 0-87830-504-1). Theatre Arts.

Stanislavski, Constantin & Rumyantsev, P. I. Stanislavski on Opera. LC 72-87119. (Illus.). 1975. 18.25 (ISBN 0-87830-132-1); pap. 8.45 (ISBN 0-87830-552-1). Theatre Arts.

Stanislavsky, Konstantin. Stanislavsky on the Art of the Stage. 1967. pap. 9.95 (ISBN 0-571-08172-X, Pub. by Faber & Faber). Merrimack Bk Serv.

Stanislawczyk, Irene E., jt. ed. see Gomez-Gil, Orlando.

Stanislawski, J. & Billip, K. Polish Practical Dictionary (English-Polish) 1976. 15.00x (ISBN 0-89918-533-9, P-533) Vanous.

Stanitski, Conrad L. & Sears, Curtis T. Chemistry for Health-Related Sciences: Concepts & Correlations. 1976. 19.95 (ISBN 0-13-129429-6); lab. manual 8.95 (ISBN 0-13-129437-7); student guide 6.95 (ISBN 0-13-129403-2). P-H.

Stanitski, Conrad L., Jr. & Sears, C. Aspects of Chemistry for Health-Related Sciences: Concepts & Correlations. 1979. 19.95 (ISBN 0-13-049262-0); study guide 6.95 (ISBN 0-13-049254-X). P-H.

Stankiewicz, Edward, tr. see Baudouin de Courtenay, Jan.

Stankiewicz, W. J. Approaches to Democracy: Philosophy of Government at the Close of the Twentieth Century. 1981. 25.00 (ISBN 0-312-04668-5). St Martin.

--Political Thought Since World War 2. LC 64-13234. 1964. text ed. 11.50 o.s.i. (ISBN 0-02-930630-2). Free Pr.

Stankovic, Slobodan. The End of the Tito Era: Yugoslavia's Dilemmas. (Publication Ser.: No. 236). 168p. 1981. 9.95 (ISBN 0-8179-7362-1). Hoover Inst Pr.

Stanley, Arthur P. Epistles of Paul to the Corinthians. Date not set. 20.95 (ISBN 0-86524-051-5). Klock & Klock.

Stanley, Autumn. The Enchanted Quill. 1978. pap. 1.00 o.p. (ISBN 0-931832-10-1). No Dead Lines.

Stanley, Burton, ed. Instrument Repair for the Music Teacher. LC 78-11832. 154p. (Orig.). 1978. pap. 9.95x (ISBN 0-88284-075-4); pap. text ed. 9.95x (ISBN 0-686-64875-7). Alfred Pub.

Stanley, C. S. The Adventures of Carlo Pittore. (Illus.). 18p. 1979. pap. 10.00 (ISBN 0-934376-01-8). Pittore Euforico.

Stanley, Charles F. A Man's Touch. 1977. pap. 2.95 (ISBN 0-88207-753-8). Victor Bks.

Stanley, Charlotte, tr. see Sorel, Georges.

Stanley, David M. Jesus in Gethsemane: The Early Church Reflects on the Suffering of Jesus. LC 80-80596. (Orig.). 1980. pap. 7.95 (ISBN 0-8091-2285-5). Paulist Pr.

Stanley, David T. Changing Administrations: The 1961 & 1964 Transitions in Six Departments. 1965. 8.95 (ISBN 0-8157-8100-8). Brookings.

--The Higher Civil Service: An Evaluation of Federal Personnel Practices. 1964. 8.95 (ISBN 0-8157-8104-0). Brookings.

--Managing Local Government Under Union Pressure. (Studies of Unionism in Government). 1972. pap. 5.95 (ISBN 0-8157-8101-6). Brookings.

Stanley, David T., et al. Bankruptcy: Problem, Process, Reform. LC 79-161592. 1971. 11.95 (ISBN 0-8157-8098-2). Brookings.

--Men Who Govern: A Biographical Profile of Federal Political Executives. 1967. 10.95 (ISBN 0-8157-8108-3). Brookings.

Stanley, Del & Black, John. Practical Accounting. 3rd ed. 1980. pap. text ed. write for info. (ISBN 0-8302-7305-0). Goodyear.

Stanley, Dennis K., et al. Physical Education Activities Handbook for Men & Women. 3rd ed. 352p. 1973. text ed. 18.95x o.p. (ISBN 0-205-03640-6, 6236405). Allyn.

Stanley, Dorothy E. How to Live Creatively. LC 79-17841. (Orig.). 1980. pap. 4.95 (ISBN 0-89865-016-X, Unilaw). Donning Co.

Stanley, Edwin J. Rambles in Wonderland: Or up the Yellowstone & Among the Geysers & Other Curiosities of the National Park. LC 75-7118. (Indian Captivities Ser.: Vol. 91). 1976. Repr. of 1878 ed. lib. bdg. 44.00 (ISBN 0-8240-1715-3). Garland Pub.

Stanley, George C., Jr. Transistor Basics: A Short Course. rev. 2nd ed. (Illus.). 128p. 1975. pap. 7.25 (ISBN 0-8104-5866-7). Hayden.

Stanley Gibbons Ltd., ed. Stamps of the World. (Illus.). 1979. write for info (ISBN 0-85259-001-6). StanGib Ltd.

Stanley Gibbons Ltd, ed. Stanley Gibbons British Commonwealth. (Illus.). write for info (ISBN 0-85259-086-5). StanGib Ltd.

Stanley, Hiram M. Essays on Literary Art: Tennyson, Wordsworth, Jane Austen, Thoreau. 164p. 1980. Repr. of 1897 ed. lib. bdg. 25.00 (ISBN 0-8414-8035-4). Folcroft.

Stanley, Jackson, jt. auth. see Kantar, Edwin B.

Stanley, John, jt. auth. see Toogood, Alan.

Stanley, John, tr. see Sorel, Georges.

Stanley, Julia P. & Wolfe, Susan J., eds. The Coming Out Stories. LC 79-27073. 286p. (Orig.). 1980. pap. text ed. 6.95 (ISBN 0-930436-03-2). Persephone.

Stanley, Julian, jt. auth. see Hopkins, Kenneth.

Stanley, Julian C., jt. auth. see Glass, Gene V.

Stanley, Julian C., et al, eds. The Gifted & the Creative: A Fifty Year Perspective. LC 77-4790. (Hyman Blumberg Symposium Ser.: No. 6). (Illus.). 1978. text ed. 17.50x o.p. (ISBN 0-8018-1974-1); pap. 4.95 (ISBN 0-8018-1975-X). Johns Hopkins.

Stanley, Leo L. San Miguel at the Turn of the Century. (Illus.). 1976. pap. 3.95 o.p. (ISBN 0-913548-33-2, Valley Calif). Western Tanager.

Stanley, Leon R. Easy to Make Electric Gadgets. LC 80-82003. (Easy to Make Ser.). (Illus.). 64p. (gr. 3-6). 1981. PLB 5.79 (ISBN 0-8178-0011-5). Harvey.

Stanley, Linda, ed. see Associated Women's Organization, Mars Hill Bible School.

Stanley, Linda, et al. Close-up on Composition. 464p. 1980. pap. text ed. 9.95x (ISBN 0-534-00745-7). Wadsworth Pub.

Stanley, Louis. Pelham Golf Year. 448p. 1981. 19.95 (ISBN 0-7207-1290-4). Merrimack Bk Serv.

Stanley, Lyn T. Practical Statistics for Petroleum Engineers. LC 72-95444. 150p. 1973. 14.00 (ISBN 0-87814-019-0). Pennwell Pub.

Stanley, Manfred. The Technological Conscience: Survival & Dignity in an Age of Expertise. LC 78-428. 1978. 17.95 (ISBN 0-02-930610-8). Free Pr.

Stanley, Marguerite. Life's Thundering Melodies. 66p. (Orig.). 1980. pap. text ed. 5.50 (ISBN 0-932218-12-1). Hall Pr.

Stanley, Michael. The Swiss Conspiracy. 1976. pap. 1.95 (ISBN 0-380-00492-5, 34082). Avon.

Stanley, P. Fracture Mechanics in Engineering Practice. (Illus.). 1977. 86.90x (ISBN 0-85334-723-9, Pub. by Applied Science). Burgess-Intl Ideas.

Stanley, P., ed. Non-Linear Problems in Stress Analysis. (Illus.). 1978. text ed. 96.80x (ISBN 0-85334-780-8). Intl Ideas.

Stanley., P., jt. ed. see Richards, T. H.

Stanley, Paul E., ed. Handbook of Hospital Safety. 416p. 1981. 59.95 (ISBN 0-8493-0751-1). CRC Pr.

Stanley, R. Promotion: Advertising, Publicity, Personal Selling, Sales Promotion. (Illus.). 1977. text ed. 18.95 (ISBN 0-13-730770-5). P-H.

Stanley, Richard & Neame, Alan. Exploration Diaries of H. M. Stanley. LC 62-11208. (Illus.). 1962. 10.00 (ISBN 0-8149-0212-X). Vanguard.

Stanley, Steven M. Macroevolution: Pattern & Process. LC 79-15464. (Illus.). 1979. text ed. 22.95x (ISBN 0-7167-1092-7). W H Freeman.

Stanley, Steven M., jt. auth. see Raup, David M.

Stanley, Thomas. A History of Philosophy, 3 vols. Wellek, Rene, ed. LC 75-11254. (British Philosophers & Theologians of the 17th & 18th Centuries Ser.). 1978. Repr. of 1687 ed. lib. bdg. 42.00 (ISBN 0-8240-1804-4). Garland Pub.

Stanley, Timothy W., jt. auth. see International Economic Studies Institute.

Stanley, William O. Education & Social Integration. 1953. text ed. 8.75x (ISBN 0-8077-2197-2). Tchrs Coll.

Stannage, Tom. Baldwin Thwarts the Opposition: The British General Election of 1935. 320p. 1980. 50.00x (ISBN 0-7099-0341-3, Pub. by Croom Helm Ltd England). Biblio Dist.

Stannard, David E. The Puritan Way of Death: A Study in Religion, Culture & Social Change. LC 76-42647. (Illus.). 1977. 14.95x (ISBN 0-19-502226-2). Oxford U Pr.

Stannard, David E., ed. Death in America. LC 75-10124. 1975. 13.95 (ISBN 0-8122-7695-7); pap. 5.95x (ISBN 0-8122-1084-0, Pa Paperbks). U of Pa Pr.

Stannard, Una. Mrs Man. LC 76-58834. (Illus.). 1977. 14.00 (ISBN 0-914142-02-X). Germainbooks.

Stannard-Friel, Don. Harassment Therapy: A Case Study of Psychiatric Violence. (University Books Ser.). 1981. lib. bdg. 16.95 (ISBN 0-8161-9030-5). G K Hall.

Stannett, V. & Jenkins, A. D., eds. Progress in Polymer Science, Vol. 6. (Illus.). 266p. 1981. 35.00 (ISBN 0-08-020335-3). Pergamon.

Stansbury, Arthur Joseph. Report of the Trial of James H. Peck. LC 70-38789. (Law, Politics & History Ser). 592p. 1972. Repr. of 1833 ed. lib. bdg. 59.50 (ISBN 0-306-70443-9). Da Capo.

Stansbury, Deborah. Moment a Day. 1980. 4.95 (ISBN 0-533-04420-0). Vantage.

Stansbury, E. E., ed. see Symposium on Corrosion Fundamentals.

Stansell, Gary, tr. see Wolff, Hans W.

Stansfield, Charles, jt. auth. see Zimolzak, Chester.

Stansfield, Kathy, jt. ed. see Clouston, Brian.

Stansfield, Richard H. The Best Ever How-to-Get-a-Job Book. LC 80-967. 176p. Date not set. 10.95 (ISBN 0-8019-6974-3); pap. 6.95 (ISBN 0-8019-6975-1). Chilton.

Stansky, Peter. Gladstone: A Progress in Politics. 224p. 1981. pap. 4.95 (ISBN 0-393-00037-0). Norton.

Stansky, Peter, ed. Churchill: A Profile. (World Profiles Ser.). 1973. 7.95 o.p. (ISBN 0-8090-3447-6). Hill & Wang.

--The Quarto, Eighteen Ninety-Six to Ninety-Eight, 4 vols. in 2. Shewan, Rodney. (Aesthetic Movement & the Arts & Crafts Movement Ser.: Periodicals: Vol. 6). 1979. Set. lib. bdg. 53.00 each (ISBN 0-8240-3622-0). Garland Pub.

--The Victorian Revolution: Government & Society in Victoria's Britain. (Modern Scholarship on European History Ser.). 419p. 1973. pap. 4.50 (ISBN 0-531-06482-4). Watts.

Stansky, Peter & Shewan, Rodney, eds. The Pageant, Eighteen Ninety-Six to Ninety-Seven, 2 vols. (Aesthetic Movement & the Arts & Crafts Movement Ser.: Periodicals: Vol. 5). (Illus.). 1979. Set. lib. bdg. 88.00 (ISBN 0-8240-3621-2); lib. bdg. 44.00 ea. Garland Pub.

--Transactions of the National Association for the Advancement of Art, & Its Application to Industry, 1889-91, 3 vols. (Aesthetic Movement & the Arts & Crafts Movement Ser.: Periodicals: Vol. 1). 1979. lib. bdg. 53.00 ea. (ISBN 0-8240-3617-4). Garland Pub.

Stansky, Peter, ed. see Ashbee, C. R.

Stansky, Peter, ed. see Cobden-Sanderson, et al.

Stansky, Peter, ed. see Cobden-Sanderson, T. J.

Stansky, Peter, ed. see Crane, Walter.

Stansky, Peter, ed. see Cust, M. M.

Stansky, Peter, ed. see Day, Lewis F.

Stansky, Peter, ed. see Day, Lewis F. & Buckle, Mary.

Stansky, Peter, ed. see Dresser, Christopher.

Stansky, Peter, ed. see Godwin, E. W.

Stansky, Peter, ed. see Haweis, E.

Stansky, Peter, ed. see Lethaby, et al.

Stansky, Peter, ed. see Loftie, M. J., et al.

Stansky, Peter, ed. see Loftie, W. J., et al.

Stansky, Peter, ed. see Rational Dress Association.

Stansky, Peter, ed. see Sedding, John.

Stansky, Peter, ed. see Sylvia's Home Help Series.

Stansky, Peter, ed. see Wilde, Oscar.

Stant, Margaret. The Young Child: His Activities & Materials. (Illus.). 160p. 1972. pap. text ed. 9.95 (ISBN 0-13-977157-3). P-H.

Stanton, Beryle, ed. Expanding Cooperative Horizons. (Illus.). 500p. 1980. 12.00; pap. 9.50. Am Inst Cooperation.

Stanton, David H. The String (Double) Bass. 8.00 (ISBN 0-686-15896-2). Instrumentalist Co.

Stanton, E. N., jt. auth. see Idleman, H. K.

Stanton, Elizabeth & Stanton, Henry. Sometimes I Like to Cry. Rubin, Caroline, ed. LC 77-19131. (Concept Bks.). (Illus.). 32p. (ps-2). 1978. 6.95g (ISBN 0-8075-7537-2). A Whitman.

--The Very Messy Room. Rubin, Caroline, ed. LC 78-1031. (Concept Bks.). (Illus.). 32p. (gr. 1-3). 1978. 6.95g (ISBN 0-8075-5077-9). A Whitman.

Stanton, Erwin S. Successful Personnel Recruiting & Selection: Within EEO-Affirmative Action Guidelines. new ed. LC 77-21384. 1977. 15.95 (ISBN 0-8144-5450-X). Am Mgmt.

Stanton, G. N. Jesus of Nazareth in New Testament Preaching. LC 73-92782. (Society of New Testament Studies: No. 27). 228p. 1975. 34.00 (ISBN 0-521-20465-8). Cambridge U Pr.

Stanton, H. U. Teaching of the Qur'An, with an Account of Its Growth & Subject Index. LC 74-90040. 1969. Repr. 12.50x (ISBN 0-8196-0253-1). Biblo.

Stanton, Harry E. Helping Students Learn: The Improvement of Higher Education. LC 78-70519. 1978. pap. text ed. 7.25 o.p. (ISBN 0-8191-0644-5). U Pr of Amer.

Stanton, Henry, jt. auth. see Stanton, Elizabeth.

Stanton, J. R. Theory & Practice of Propellers for Auxiliary Sailboats. LC 75-31778. (Illus.). 1975. pap. 4.00 (ISBN 0-87033-213-9). Cornell Maritime.

Stanton, Jim & Zerchykov, Ross. Overcoming Barriers to School Effectiveness. 153p. (Orig.). 1979. pap. 6.50 (ISBN 0-917754-10-7). Inst Responsive.

Stanton, Kenneth. Jazz Theory: A Creative Approach. LC 79-9651. 192p. (Orig.). Date not set. pap. 7.95 (ISBN 0-8008-4311-8, Crescendo). Taplinger.

Stanton, Marcie. Clem the Clam & His Friends. Date not set. 5.95 (ISBN 0-533-04852-4). Vantage.

Stanton, Maura. Molly Companion. 1978. pap. 1.95 (ISBN 0-380-40436-2, 40436). Avon.

Stanton, R. E. Analytical Methods for Use in Geochemical Exploration. LC 76-26050. 1976. pap. 6.95 o.p. (ISBN 0-470-98920-3). Halsted Pr.

Stanton, Robert J. Gore Vidal: A Primary & Secondary Bibliography. (Reference Publications). 1980. lib. bdg. 25.00 (ISBN 0-8161-8109-8). G K Hall.

Stanton, Robert J. & Vidal, Gore, eds. Views from a Window: Conversations with Gore Vidal. 320p. 1980. lib. bdg. 14.95 (ISBN 0-8184-0302-0). Lyle Stuart.

Stanton, Robert J., Jr., jt. auth. see Dodd, Robert J.

Stanton, Royal. Steps to Singing for Voice Classes. 2nd ed. 1976. pap. 12.95x (ISBN 0-534-00419-9). Wadsworth Pub.

Stanton, S. L. & Tanagho, E. A., eds. Surgery of Female Incontinence. (Illus.). 203p. 1980. 58.00 (ISBN 0-387-10155-1). Springer-Verlag.

Stanton, Shelby L. U. S. Army Order of Battle in Vietnam. (Illus.). 400p. 1980. cancelled (ISBN 0-88254-519-1). Hippocrene Bks.

Stanton, Stephen S., ed. & intro. by. Camille & Other Plays. Incl. Camille. Dumas, Alexandre, fils; A Peculiar Position. Scribe; The Glass of Water. Scribe; A Scrap of Paper. Sardou; Olympe's Marriage. Augier. 306p. (Orig.). 1957. pap. 5.95 (ISBN 0-8090-0706-1, Mermaid). Hill & Wang.

Stanton, William. The Great United States Exploring Expedition of 1838-1842. LC 73-84390. (Illus.). 1975. 18.95 (ISBN 0-520-02557-1). U of Cal Pr.

Stanton, William J. Fundamentals of Marketing. 6th ed. (Illus.). 704p. 1981. text ed. 19.95 (ISBN 0-07-060891-1, C); instrs. manual 10.95 (ISBN 0-07-060892-X); study guide 6.95 (ISBN 0-07-060893-8); test file 15.95 (ISBN 0-07-060894-6); transparency masters avail. (ISBN 0-07-060895-4). McGraw.

Stanton, William J. & Buskirk, Richard H. Management of the Sales Force. 5th ed. 1978. text ed. 19.95x (ISBN 0-256-02046-9). Irwin.

Stanwell, S. T., et al. Typewell Typewriting Course. Incl. Vol. 1. Keyboard Mastery. 1974. wire bound 11.00x (ISBN 0-685-85702-6); Vol. 2. Speed Development. 1975. wire bound 12.00x (ISBN 0-685-85703-4); Vol. 3. Intermediate Display. 1975. wire bound 12.00x (ISBN 0-685-85704-2). 1975. Intl Ideas.

--Typewell Typewriting Course: Advanced Display, Vol. 4. 1977. wire bound 13.00x (ISBN 0-7131-1842-3). Intl Ideas.

Stanwell, Sheila T. & Shaw, Josephine. Essential Secretarial Studies. 1974. pap. 17.50x (ISBN 0-7131-1788-5). Intl Ideas.

Stanwick, Kathy & Li, Christine. The Political Participation of Women in the United States: A Selected Bibliography, 1950-1976. LC 77-23036. 1977. 10.00 (ISBN 0-8108-1075-1). Scarecrow.

Stanwood, Donald. The Memory of Eva Ryker. 1979. pap. 2.50 o.s.i. (ISBN 0-440-15550-9). Dell.

Stanwood, Edward. American Tariff Controversies in the Nineteenth Century, 2 vols. (The Neglected American Economists Ser.). 1974. Set. lib. bdg. 76.00 (ISBN 0-8240-1033-7); lib. bdg. 50.00 ea. Garland Pub.

Stanworth, M. J. & Curran, J. Management Motivation in the Smaller Business. 1973. 17.95x o.p. (ISBN 0-8464-0591-1). Beekman Pubs.

Stanworth, P. & Giddens, A., eds. Elites & Power in British Society. LC 73-92788. (Studies in Sociology: No. 8). (Illus.). 280p. 1974. 29.95 (ISBN 0-521-20441-0); pap. 9.95x (ISBN 0-521-09853-X). Cambridge U Pr.

Stanyer, Jeffery, jt. auth. see Smith, Brian.

Stanyer, Jeffrey. County Government in England & Wales. (Library of Political Science). (Orig.). 1967. text ed. 6.00x (ISBN 0-7100-5116-6); pap. text ed. 2.75x (ISBN 0-391-01969-4). Humanities.

--Understanding Local Government. 320p. 1976. 30.50x (ISBN 0-85520-140-1, Pub. by Martin Robertson England). Biblio Dist.

--Understanding Local Government. 320p. 1981. pap. 9.95x (ISBN 0-85520-373-0, Pub. by Martin Robertson England). Biblio Dist.

Stanyer, Jeffrey, jt. auth. see Smith, Brian C.

Stapler, Harry. Your Future in Pro Sports. (Careers in Depth Ser). (Illus.). 160p. (gr. 7-12). 1977. PLB 5.97 (ISBN 0-8239-0372-9). Rosen Pr.

Staples, Frederick. Auditing Manual. 181p. 1980. pap. 9.50. Counting Hse.

Staples, R. C. & Kuhr, R. J., eds. Linking Research to Crop Production. LC 79-25737. 250p. 1980. 29.50 (ISBN 0-306-40331-5, Plenum Pr). Plenum Pub.

Staples, Robert. The Black Family. 2nd ed. 1978. pap. 9.95x (ISBN 0-534-00557-8). Wadsworth Pub.

--The Black Woman in America: Sex, Marriage & the Family. LC 72-95280. 1973. 15.95x (ISBN 0-911012-55-9); pap. 8.95x (ISBN 0-685-99065-6). Nelson-Hall.

--The World of Black Singles: Changing Patterns of Male-Female Relations. LC 80-1025. (Contributions in Afro-American & African Studies: No. 57). 288p. 1981. lib. bdg. 25.00 (ISBN 0-313-22478-1, SBS/). Greenwood.

Staples, W. R. Rhode Island in the Continental Congress, 1765-1790. LC 71-153373. (Era of the American Revolution Ser.). 726p. 1972. Repr. of 1870 ed. lib. bdg. 65.00 (ISBN 0-306-70203-7). Da Capo.

Stapleton, C. A., ed. see European Conference on Mixing, 3rd.

Stapleton, C. A., ed. see Fifth Fluid Power Symposium.

Stapleton, C. A., ed. see Fourth International Conference on the Pneumatic Transport of Solids in Pipes.

Stapleton, C. A., jt. ed. see Stephens, H. S.

Stapleton, Constance & Richman, Phyllis. Barter: How to Get Almost Anything Without Money. LC 77-21624. 1978. 9.95 o.p. (ISBN 0-684-15193-6, ScribT); pap. 4.95 (ISBN 0-684-15320-3, ScribT). Scribner.

Stapleton, Gerald. Beginner's Guide to Computer Logic. LC 70-155978. (Illus.). 1971. pap. 5.95 (ISBN 0-8306-0548-7, 548). TAB Bks.

Stapleton, John. How to Prepare a Marketing Plan. 2nd ed. 162p. 1975. 17.50 o.s.i. (ISBN 0-7161-0251-X). Herman Pub.

Stapleton, John F., jt. auth. see Sussex, Margie.

Stapleton, Margaret L. Sir John Betjeman: A Bibliography of Writings by & About Him. (Author Bibliographies Ser.: No. 21). 1974. 10.00 (ISBN 0-8108-0758-0). Scarecrow.

Stapleton, Mrs. C. A., jt. auth. see Stephens, H. S.

Stapleton, Richard C. Managing Creatively: Action Learning in Action. 1976. pap. text ed. 9.45 (ISBN 0-8191-0035-8). U Pr of Amer.

Stapleton, Richard J. De-Gaming Teaching & Learning: How to Motivate Learners & Invite OKness. LC 78-73696. (Illus., Orig.). 1979. pap. 15.00 (ISBN 0-933594-00-3). Effect Learning GA.

Stapleton, Ruth C. The Gift of Inner Healing. LC 75-36180. 1976. 5.95 (ISBN 0-87680-809-7, Key Word Bks.); pap. 1.75 (ISBN 0-686-67399-9, 91030). Word Bks.

Stapleton, Thomas. The Prevention of Psychiatric Disorders in Children. 244p. 1981. 16.00 (ISBN 0-87527-234-7). Green.

Stapley, Ray. The Car Owner's Handbook. LC 73-75166. 312p. 1973. pap. 3.95 (ISBN 0-385-05097-6, Dolp). Doubleday.

Stapp, Melinda M., jt. ed. see Caskey, Jefferson D.

Stapp, William B. & Liston, Mary D., eds. Environmental Education: A Guide to Information Sources. LC 73-17542. (Man & the Environment Information Guide Ser.: Vol. 1). 350p. 1975. 30.00 (ISBN 0-8103-1337-5). Gale.

Staquet, M., jt. ed. see Tagnon, H. J.

Staquet, Maurice J., ed. Cancer Therapy: Prognostic Factors & Criteria of Response. LC 74-14481. (European Organization for Research on Treatment of Cancer Ser.). 1975. 31.50 (ISBN 0-89004-008-7). Raven.

--Randomized Trials in Cancer: A Critical Review by Sites. LC 77-17753. (European Organization for Research on Treatment of Cancer Monograph: Vol. 4). 1978. 45.00 (ISBN 0-89004-264-0). Raven.

Staquet, Maurice J., jt. ed. see Klastersky, Jean.

Staquet, Maurice J., jt. ed. see Tagnon, Henri J.

Star, Robin R. We Can, Vol. 1. 88p. (gr. 4 up). 1980. PLB 5.00 (ISBN 0-88200-135-3, C2670). Alexander Graham.

--We Can, Vol. 2. 98p. (gr. 4 up). 1980. PLB 5.00 (ISBN 0-88200-136-1, C2786). Alexander Graham.

Starbird, Kaye. The Covered Bridge House & Other Poems. LC 79-11418. (Illus.). 64p. (gr. 3-7). 1979. 7.95 (ISBN 0-590-07544-6, Four Winds). Schol Bk Serv.

Starbird, William, jt. auth. see Oriti, Ronald.

Starbrook, Dave. Judo Starbrook Style: Champion's Method. (Illus.). 1978. pap. 9.95x (ISBN 0-8464-0540-7). Beekman Pubs.

Starchild, Adam. Everyman's Guide to Tax Havens. 112p. (Orig.). 1980. pap. 6.00 (ISBN 0-87364-203-1). Paladin Ent.

Starcke, Carl N. The Primitive Family in Its Origin & Development. Needham, Rodney, ed. LC 75-12232. 336p. pap. 14.00x (ISBN 0-226-77133-4, Midway). U of Chicago Pr.

Starcke, Walter. Ultimate Revolution. LC 73-85058. 1973. pap. 3.95 o.p. (ISBN 0-06-067524-1, RD65, HarpR). Har-Row.

Stare, Fredrick J. & McWilliams, Margaret. Nutrition for Good Health. LC 74-81644. 1974. 8.95x (ISBN 0-916434-11-7). Plycon Pr.

Stark, Ann B., jt. ed. see Cloherty, John P.

Stark, David C. & Roberts, R. B., eds. Practical Points in Anesthesiology. 2nd. ed. LC 79-89168. 1980. 13.50 (ISBN 0-87488-700-3). Med Exam.

Stark, E., et al, eds. Endocrinology, Neuroendocrinology, Neuropeptides- Part 1: Proceedings of the 28th International Congress of Physiological Sciences, Budapest, 1980. LC 80-42047. (Advances in Physiological Sciences: Vol. 13). (Illus.). 350p. 1981. 40.00 (ISBN 0-08-026827-7). Pergamon.

--Endocrinology, Neuroendocrinology, Neuropeptides-Part II: Proceedings of the 28th International Congress of Physiological Sciences, Budapest, 1980. LC 80-42046. (Advances in Physiological Sciences Ser.: Vol. 14). (Illus.). 350p. 1981. 40.00 (ISBN 0-08-026871-4). Pergamon.

Stark, Frederick. Phrase Dictionaries for the American Tourist, 6 bks. Incl. German for the American Tourist. pap. (ISBN 0-8326-2409-8, 6570); Spanish for the American Tourist. pap. (ISBN 0-8326-2410-1, 6571); French for the American Tourist. pap. (ISBN 0-8326-2411-X, 6572); Italian for the American Tourist. pap. (ISBN 0-8326-2412-8, 6573); Greek for the American Tourist. pap. (ISBN 0-8326-2413-6, 6574); Russian for the American Tourist. pap. (ISBN 0-8326-2414-4, 6575). 128p. (Orig.). 1981. pap. 1.95 ea. Delair.

Stark, Freya. Dust in the Lion's Paw. 1975. 22.00 (ISBN 0-7195-1334-0). Transatlantic.

--East Is West. (Illus.). 19.50 (ISBN 0-7195-1324-3). Transatlantic.

--Journey's Echo. 16.95 (ISBN 0-7195-1336-7). Transatlantic.

--Minaret of Djam: An Excursion in Afghanistan. (Illus.). 99p. 1972. 19.50 (ISBN 0-7195-2066-5). Transatlantic.

--A Peak in Darien. 1977. 12.00 (ISBN 0-7195-3291-4). Transatlantic.

--The Valleys of the Assassins. rev. ed. (Illus.). 1972. 20.00 (ISBN 0-7195-2429-6). Transatlantic.

Stark, Gary D. Entrepreneurs of Ideology: Neoconservative Publishers in Germany, 1890-1933. LC 80-14906. 384p. 1981. 26.50x (ISBN 0-8078-1452-0). U of NC Pr.

Stark, Harold E. A Revision of the Flea Genus Thrassis Jordan 1933 (Siphonaptera: Ceratophyllidae) With Observations on Ecology & Relationship to Plague. (U. C. Pub. in Entomology: Vol. 53). 1970. pap. 9.00x (ISBN 0-520-09126-4). U of Cal Pr.

Stark, Harry A., ed. Ward's Automotive Yearbook. 1980. 60.00 (ISBN 0-686-18833-0). Wards Comm.

Stark, Henry & Tuteru, Franz B. Modern Electrical Communications: Theory & Systems. (Illus.). 1979. ref. 27.95 (ISBN 0-13-593202-5). P-H.

Stark, Joan, jt. auth. see Stark, Tom.

Stark, Joan S., et al. The Many Faces of Educational Consumerism. LC 77-8722. 1977. 19.95 (ISBN 0-669-01631-4). Lexington Bks.

Stark, John O. Almanac of British & American Literature. LC 78-24249. 1979. lib. bdg. 20.00x (ISBN 0-87287-188-6). Libs Unl.

--Pynchon's Fictions: Thomas Pynchon & the Literature of Information. LC 79-28466. x, 183p. 1980. 13.95x (ISBN 0-8214-0419-9, 0419E). Ohio U Pr.

Stark, Jurgen K. Personal Names in Palmyrene Inscriptions. 1971. 19.25x o.p. (ISBN 0-19-815443-7). Oxford U Pr.

Stark, M., jt. auth. see Mostowski, J.

Stark, Myra, jt. ed. see Murray, Janet H.

Stark, Norman. The Formula Book. 1976. pap. 1.75 (ISBN 0-380-00840-8, 31047). Avon.

Stark, Raymond. The Book of Aphrodisiacs. LC 80-6206. 212p. 1981. 11.95 (ISBN 0-8128-2798-8). Stein & Day.

--Indian Herbs. Campbell, Margaret, ed. (Illus.). 50p. 1981. pap. 4.95 (ISBN 0-88839-077-7). Hancock Hse.

Stark, Richard & Dearholt, Donald W. Computer Concepts & Assembler Programming: 360-370 Systems. 1975. text ed. 20.95 (ISBN 0-12-664550-7); instr's manual 3.00 (ISBN 0-12-664552-3). Acad Pr.

Stark, Richard B., ed. Aesthetic Plastic Surgery. LC 80-80594. 1980. text ed. 55.00 (ISBN 0-316-81085-1). Little.

Stark, Rodney & Glock, Charles Y. American Piety: The Nature of Religious Commitment. (Patterns of Religious Commitment: No. 1). 1968. 17.50x (ISBN 0-520-01210-0); pap. 2.65 (ISBN 0-520-01756-0, CAL197). U of Cal Pr.

Stark, Thomas. Distribution of Personal Income in the United Kingdom, 1949-1963. LC 72-160099. (Illus.). 1972. 34.50 (ISBN 0-521-08258-7). Cambridge U Pr.

Stark, Tom & Stark, Joan. Guidance & God's Will. (Fisherman Bible Study Guide Ser.). 1978. saddle stitch 1.95 (ISBN 0-87788-324-6). Shaw Pubs.

Stark, Werner. Sociology of Knowledge: An Essay in Aid of a Deeper Understanding of the History of Ideas. (International Library of Sociology & Social Reconstruction Ser.). 1958. pap. text ed. 13.00x (ISBN 0-7100-6554-X). Humanities.

Starke, Frederick, jt. auth. see Gray, Jerry.

Starke, Frederick A., jt. auth. see Gray, Jerry L.

Starkes, M. Thomas. The Foundation for Missions. LC 80-67460. 1981. pap. 4.95 (ISBN 0-8054-6325-9). Broadman.

Starkey, Jane, ed. Horse Sense: Buying & Looking After Your First Horse. (Illus.). 128p. 1981. 9.95 (ISBN 0-8069-3746-7); lib. bdg. 9.29 (ISBN 0-8069-3747-5). Sterling.

Starkey, Marion L. Devil in Massachusetts: A Modern Enquiry into the Salem Witch Trials. LC 49-10395. 1969. pap. 2.95 (ISBN 0-385-03509-8, Anch). Doubleday.

Starkey, Ronald. Study Guide & Solutions Manual for an Introduction to Organic Chemistry. 1978. 11.50x (ISBN 0-8162-8391-5, 8162-8391). Holden-Day.

Starkie, Enid, ed. see Baudelaire, Charles.

Starkie, Walter. Scholars & Gypsies: An Autobiography. (Illus.). 1963. 20.00 (ISBN 0-520-01205-4). U of Cal Pr.

Starkloff, Carl. People of the Center: American Indian Religions & Christianity. 1974. 5.95 o.p. (ISBN 0-8164-9207-7). Continuum.

Starkweather, David. Hospital Mergers in the Making. (Illus.). 1981. text ed. write for info. (ISBN 0-914904-54-X). Health Admin Pr.

Starkweather, David see Hoffmann, William M.

Starling. The Changing Environment of Business. (Illus.). 1980. text ed. 16.95 (ISBN 0-87872-251-3). Duxbury Pr.

Starling, Grover. Managing the Public Sector. 1977. 17.95x (ISBN 0-256-01936-3). Dorsey.

--The Politics & Economics of Public Policy: An Introductory Analysis with Cases. 1979. 18.50x (ISBN 0-256-02067-1). Dorsey.

Starling, Thomas. The Garlic Kid. LC 77-91896. Orig. Title: Ringling Hall. 1978. pap. 3.95 (ISBN 0-914864-01-7). Spindrift.

--The King & the Cat. LC 74-82405. 1975. 6.95 (ISBN 0-914864-00-9). Spindrift.

Starn, Randolph, jt. auth. see Partridge, Loren.

Starnes, C., jt. auth. see Turner, J.

Starnes, George E. & Fernandez, Oscar. De Que Hablamos? (Orig., Span.). 1981. Repr. of 1952 ed. pap. text ed. 9.50x. Irvington.

Starnes, J. L., jt. auth. see Feray, D. E.

Starnes, Kathleen M. Peter Abelard: His Place in History. LC 80-8298. 161p. 1981. lib. bdg. 17.50 (ISBN 0-8191-1510-X); pap. text ed. 8.75 (ISBN 0-8191-1511-8). U Pr of Amer.

Starobin, Robert S. Industrial Slavery in the Old South. LC 72-112894. 1970. 14.95 (ISBN 0-19-500113-3). Oxford U Pr.

Starobin, Robert S., ed. Denmark Vesey: The Slave Conspiracy of 1822. (Great Lives Observed Ser). 1970. pap. 1.95 o.p. (ISBN 0-13-198432-2, Spec). P-H.

Starosciak, Kenneth. J. D. Salinger: A Thirty Year Bibliography,1938-1968. 1971. 6.95 (ISBN 0-87018-072-X). Ross.

Starr, Adaline. Psychodrama. LC 76-49045. 1977. 18.95x (ISBN 0-88229-224-2); pap. 10.95x (ISBN 0-685-99103-2). Nelson-Hall.

Starr, Albert, jt. auth. see Lefrak, Edward.

Starr, Bernard, jt. ed. see Eisdorfer, Carl.

Starr, Bernard D. & Weiner, Marcella B. The Starr-Weiner Report on Sex & Sexuality in the Mature Years. 1981. 12.95 (ISBN 0-8128-2750-3). Stein & Day.

Starr, Bill. The Treasure of Wonderwhat. pap. 1.95 (ISBN 0-345-28286-8). Ballantine.

Starr, C. Current Issues in Energy. 1979. text ed. 28.00 (ISBN 0-08-023243-4); pap. text ed. 12.75 (ISBN 0-08-023244-2). Pergamon.

Starr, Chauncey & Ritterbush, Philip C., eds. Science, Technology & the Human Prospect. (Pergamon Policy Studies). 1980. 66.00 (ISBN 0-08-024650-8); leather bdg. 350.00 (ISBN 0-685-97190-2) (ISBN 0-08-024652-4). Pergamon.

Starr, Chester G. Ancient Romans. (Illus.). 1971. 13.95x (ISBN 0-19-501455-3); pap. 8.95x (ISBN 0-19-501454-5). Oxford U Pr.

--The Beginnings of Imperial Rome: Rome in the Mid-Republic. 86p. 1980. 10.00x (ISBN 0-472-09317-7). U of Mich Pr.

Starr, G. Australian Political Parties. 1978. pap. text ed. 12.95x (ISBN 0-686-65414-5, 00513). Heinemann Ed.

Starr, George R., Jr. How to Make Working Decoys. (Illus.). 1978. 17.50 (ISBN 0-87691-260-9). Winchester Pr.

Starr, Hampton. Contemporary Illusions People Live by. (Essential Knowledge Library). 1979. spiral bdg. 21.45 (ISBN 0-89266-170-4). Am Classical Coll Pr.

Starr, Isidore. Great Ideas in the Law-Justice: Due Process of Law. 300p. 1981. pap. text ed. 6.50 (ISBN 0-8299-1020-4). West Pub.

Starr, John T., Jr. The Evolution of the Unit Train, 1960-1969. LC 73-92655. (Research Papers Ser.: No. 158). (Illus.). 233p. 1976. pap. 8.00 o.p. (ISBN 0-89065-065-9). U Chicago Dept Geog.

Starr, Kevin. Americans & the California Dream, 1850-1915. (Illus.). 512p. 1981. pap. 11.50 (ISBN 0-87905-083-7). Peregrine Smith.

--California! LC 80-51092. (Illus.). 296p. (gr. 4-9). 1980. text ed. 15.00x (ISBN 0-87905-100-0). Peregrine Smith.

Starr, Martin K. Systems Management of Operations. (Illus.). 1971. ref. ed. 18.95 (ISBN 0-13-881524-0). P-H.

Starr, Martin K. & Stein, Irving. The Practice of Management Science. (Illus.). 208p. 1976. 12.95 (ISBN 0-13-693630-X). P-H.

Starr, Martin K., jt. auth. see Dannebring, David D.

Starr, Martin K., jt. auth. see Miller, David W.

Starr, Mortimer P., et al, eds. Annual Review of Microbiology, Vol. 34. LC 49-432. (Illus.). 1980. text ed. 20.00 (ISBN 0-8243-1134-5). Annual Reviews.

Starr, Philip C. Economics: Principles in Action. 2nd ed. 1978. pap. 14.95x (ISBN 0-534-00588-8); wkbk. 7.95x (ISBN 0-534-00589-6). Wadsworth Pub.

Starr, R. H., ed. Child Abuse Predictions: Policy Implications. 1981. pns professional reference (ISBN 0-88410-378-1). Ballinger Pub.

Starr, S. Fredrick. Melnikov: Solo Architect in a Mass Society. LC 77-85566. (Illus.). 295p. 1981. pap. 9.95 (ISBN 0-691-00331-9). Princeton U Pr.

Starr, Walter A., Jr. Starr's Guide to the John Muir Trail & the High Sierra Region. 12th rev. ed. Robinson, Douglas, ed. LC 67-25840. (Totebook Ser.). (Illus.). 224p. 1974. pap. 4.95 (ISBN 0-87156-172-7); Starr's Map of the John Muir Trail 1.95 (ISBN 0-87156-173-5). Sierra.

Starr, William J. & Devine, George F., eds. Music Scores Omnibus. Incl. Pt. 2. Romantic & Impressionist Music. 1964. pap. text ed. 18.95 (ISBN 0-13-608216-5). 1964. P-H.

--Music Scores Omnibus, Vol. 1. 2nd ed. 430p. 1974. pap. text ed. 18.95 (ISBN 0-13-608349-8). P-H.

Starr, William T. French Six Bibliography: Critical & Biograpical References for the Study of Nineteenth Century French Literature, No. 1-7, 1954-1967. (Orig.). 1945-69. Set. pap. 25.00x (ISBN 0-933444-00-1). French Inst.

Starr, Wilmarth H; see Bree, Germaine.

Starr, Wilmarth H; see Eddy, Frederick D.

Starratt, Alfred B. Your Self, My Self & the Self of the Universe. LC 79-9971. 1979. 12.95 (ISBN 0-916144-38-0); pap. 7.95 (ISBN 0-916144-39-9). Stemmer Hse.

Starrett, Vincent. The Private Life of Sherlock Holmes. (Illus.). 224p. 1975. pap. 1.95 o.p. (ISBN 0-523-00695-0, 25-695-7). Pinnacle Bks.

Starshak, Thomas J. Preprosthetic Oral & Maxillofacial Surgery. LC 80-17921. (Illus.). 351p. 1980. 47.50 (ISBN 0-8016-4757-6). Mosby.

Start, A. The Gifted Child: An Annotated Bibliography. (Bibliographic Ser.). 1971. pap. text ed. 4.25x (ISBN 0-85633-003-5, NFER). Humanities.

Start, Clarissa. Second Song. 232p. (Orig.). 1980. pap. 5.95 (ISBN 0-86629-013-3). Sunrise MO.

--We Buy Junque - We Sell Antiques. 158p. (Orig.). 1979. pap. 5.95 (ISBN 0-86629-012-5). Sunrise MO.

--When You're a Widow. LC 73-78880. (Illus.). 1973. 4.95 (ISBN 0-570-03288-1, 15-2084). Concordia.

Start, K. B. & Wells, B. K. The Trend of Reading Standards. (General Ser.). 80p. (Orig.). 1972. pap. text ed. 5.00x (ISBN 0-901225-96-7, NFER). Humanities.

Start, K. B., jt. auth. see Hilsum, Sidney.

Startup, Richard. The University Teacher & His World. 1979. text ed. 34.00x (ISBN 0-566-00295-7, Pub. by Gower Pub Co England). Renouf.

Stary, J., jt. auth. see Ruzicka, J.

Stary, J., et al, eds. Critical Evaluation of Equilibrium Constants Involving Hydroxyquinoline & Its Metal Chelates: Critical Evaluation of Equilibrium Constants in Solutions: Pt. A: Stability Constants of Metal Complexes. (Chemical Data Ser.: Vol. 24). (Illus.). 1979. text ed. 16.50 (ISBN 0-08-023929-3). Pergamon.

Stasack, Edward, jt. auth. see Cox, Halley.

Stasio, D. L. Fate Stepped in. 256p. 1981. 10.50 (ISBN 0-682-49726-6). Exposition.

Stassinopoulos, Arianna. Maria Callas: The Woman Behind the Legend. 1981. 13.95 (ISBN 0-671-25583-5). S&S.

Stasz, Clarice. The American Nightmare: The Success Ideal & Work Discrimination. LC 80-6191. 192p. 1981. 14.95 (ISBN 0-8052-3765-8). Schocken.

Staszewski, Jerzy. Epidemiology of Cancer of Selected Sites. LC 74-1096. 300p. 1975. 25.00 o.p. (ISBN 0-88410-114-2). Ballinger Pub.

Staszkow, Ronald. Developmental Mathematics: Basic Arithmetic with a Brief Introduction to Algebra. 384p. 1980. pap. text ed. 14.95 (ISBN 0-8403-2213-5). Kendall-Hunt.

State, Frederick J. & McWilliams, Margaret. Living Nutrition. 3rd ed. 470p. 1981. text ed. 16.95 (ISBN 0-471-04940-9). Wiley.

State Industrial Directories. Nebraska State Industrial Directory, 1980. 1980. pap. 20.00 (ISBN 0-89910-005-8). State Indus Dir.

State Industrial Directories Corp. Arizona State Industrial Directory, 1980. 1980. pap. 35.00 (ISBN 0-89910-025-2). State Indus Dir.

--Arkansas State Industrial Directory, 1980. 1980. pap. 40.00 (ISBN 0-89910-000-7). State Indus Dir.

--Delaware State Industrial Directory, 1980. 1980. pap. 20.00 (ISBN 0-89910-032-5). State Indus Dir.

--Florida State Industrial Directory 1980. 1980. pap. 65.00 (ISBN 0-89910-039-2). State Indus Dir.

--Georgia State Industrial Directory, 1980. 1980. pap. 50.00 (ISBN 0-89910-021-X). State Indus Dir.

--Indiana State Industrial Directory, 1981. Date not set. pap. price not set (ISBN 0-89910-046-5). State Indus D.

--Kentucky State Industrial Directory, Nineteen Eighty-One. Date not set. pap. price not set (ISBN 0-89910-042-2). State Indus D.

--Louisiana State Industrial Directory, Nineteen Eighty-One. Date not set. pap. price not set (ISBN 0-89910-047-3). State Indus D.

--Maine State Industrial Directory, 1981. 1980. pap. write for info. (ISBN 0-89910-045-7). State Indus Dir.

--Maryland State Industrial Directory 1980. 1980. pap. 35.00 (ISBN 0-89910-040-6). State Indus Dir.

--Michigan State Industrial Directory, Nineteen Eighty-One. Date not set. pap. price not set (ISBN 0-89910-048-1). State Indus D.

--Minnesota State Industrial Directory, 1980. 1980. pap. 50.00 (ISBN 0-89910-003-1). State Indus Dir.

--Mississippi State Industrial Directory, Nineteen Eighty-One. Date not set. pap. price not set (ISBN 0-89910-050-3). State Indus D.

--Montana State Industrial Directory, 1980. 1980. pap. 25.00 (ISBN 0-89910-026-0). State Indus Dir.

--Nevada State Industrial Directory, 1980. 1980. pap. 15.00 (ISBN 0-89910-017-1). State Indus Dir.

--New Jersey Industrial Directory 1980. 1980. pap. 90.00 (ISBN 0-89910-027-9). State Indus Dir.

--New Mexico State Industrial Directory 1980. 1980. pap. write for info. (ISBN 0-89910-037-6). State Indus Dir.

--New York State Industrial Directory, 1980. 1980. 95.00 (ISBN 0-89910-023-6). State Indus Dir.

--North Carolina State Industrial Directory, 1980. 1980. pap. 60.00 (ISBN 0-89910-033-3). State Indus Dir.

--North Dakota State Industrial Directory, 1980. 1980. pap. 15.00 (ISBN 0-89910-034-1). State Indus Dir.

--Oklahoma State Industrial Directory 1981. 1980. pap. 35.00 (ISBN 0-89910-036-8). State Indus Dir.

--Oregon State Industrial Directory, 1980. 1980. pap. 30.00 (ISBN 0-89910-018-X). State Indus Dir.

--Pennsylvania State Industrial Directory, 1980. 1980. 90.00 (ISBN 0-89910-024-4). State Indus Dir.

--Rhode Island State Industrial Directory, 1980-81. 1979. pap. 20.00 (ISBN 0-89910-019-8). State Indus Dir.

--South Carolina State Directory, 1980. 1980. pap. write for info. (ISBN 0-89910-030-9). State Indus Dir.

--South Dakota State Industrial Directory, 1980. 1980. pap. 15.00 (ISBN 0-89910-035-X). State Indus Dir.

--Tennessee State Industrial Directory, Nineteen Eighty-One. Date not set. pap. price not set (ISBN 0-89910-049-X). State Indus D.

--Vermont State Industrial Directory, Nineteen Eighty-One. Date not set. pap. price not set (ISBN 0-89910-043-0). State Indus D.

--Virginia State Industrial Directory, Nineteen Eighty-One. Date not set. pap. price not set (ISBN 0-89910-044-9). State Indus D.

--Washington State Industrial Directory, 1981. Date not set. pap. price not set (ISBN 0-89910-007-4). State Indus Dir.

--West Virginia State Industrial Directory, 1980-81. 1980. pap. 25.00 (ISBN 0-89910-022-8). State Indus Dir.

--Wisconsin State Industrial Directory, 1980. 1979. pap. 50.00 (ISBN 0-89910-010-4). State Indus Dir.

State Industrial Directories Corp., ed. Utah State Industrial Directory, 1980-81. 1980. pap. 15.00 (ISBN 0-89910-020-1). State Indus Dir.

State Industrial Directory Corp. Kansas State Industrial Directory, 1980. 1980. pap. 35.00 (ISBN 0-89910-002-3). State Indus Dir.

State Library, Pretoria, ed. South African National Bibliography, 1977. 972p. 1977. 35.00x. Intl Pubns Serv.

--South African National Bibliography, 1978. 735p. 1978. 35.00x (ISBN 0-8002-2754-9). Intl Pubns Serv.

--South African National Bibliography, 1979. 747p. 1979. 66.50x (ISBN 0-8002-2755-7). Intl Pubns Serv.

State Research. Review of Security & the State Nineteen Seventy-Nine. 2nd ed. 154p. 1980. 27.50x (ISBN 0-905290-04-6). Nichols Pub.

Stateham, B. R. Banners of the Sa'yen. (Science Fiction Ser.). 1981. pap. 2.25 (ISBN 0-87997-636-5, UE1636). DAW Bks.

States, Bert O. The Shape of Paradox: An Essay on Waiting for Godot. (Quantum Bk.). 1978. 11.95x (ISBN 0-520-03549-6); pap. 2.65 (ISBN 0-520-03572-0). U of Cal Pr.

Statham, Daphne. Radicals in Social Work. (Radical Social Policy Ser.). 1978. 16.00 (ISBN 0-7100-8728-4); pap. 7.95 (ISBN 0-7100-8729-2). Routledge & Kegan.

Statham, Frances P. Flame of New Orleans. 416p. 1978. pap. 1.95 o.p. (ISBN 0-449-13720-1, GM). Fawcett.

Statham, Ian. Earth Surface Sediment Transport. (Contemporary Problems in Geography Ser.). (Illus.). 1977. 29.95x (ISBN 0-19-874076-X); pap. 6.95x (ISBN 0-19-874077-8). Oxford U Pr.

Statham, Ian & Finlayson, Brian. Hillslope Analysis. LC 80-40564. (Sources & Methods in Geography Ser.). 176p. 1980. pap. text ed. 8.95 (ISBN 0-408-10622-0). Butterworths.

Statham, Jane, jt. ed. see ReQua, Eloise.

Stathas, Thalia, ed. see Centlivre, Susannah.

Stathatos, Constantine C. & Teschner, Richard V., eds. En Onda. new ed. 250p. 1975. pap. text ed. 6.95x (ISBN 0-393-09284-4). Norton.

Statistical Office of the United Nations, ed. World Trade Annual 1972, 5 vols. LC 64-66238. Set. 209.00 o.s.i. (ISBN 0-8027-5914-9). Walker & Co.

Statistics Canada. Canada Handbook: The 48th Annual Handbook of Present Conditions & Recent Progress. LC 77-642536. (Illus.). 354p. 1980. pap. 8.95 (ISBN 0-295-95705-0). U of Wash Pr.

Statler, Oliver. Japanese Inn. (Arena Bks). 1972. pap. 1.95 o.s.i. (ISBN 0-515-02780-4, Y2780). Jove Pubns.

--Modern Japanese Prints: An Art Reborn. LC 59-8180. (Illus.). 1956. 17.50 (ISBN 0-8048-0406-0). C E Tuttle.

Staton, Julia. What the Bible Says About Women. LC 80-66128. (What the Bible Says Ser.). 400p. 1980. 13.50 (ISBN 0-89900-079-7). College Pr Pub.

Staton, Julia & Staton, Knofel. Check Your Character (Instructor) LC 80-199950. 132p. (Orig.). 1980. pap. 2.50 (ISBN 0-87239-421-2, 39992). Standard Pub.

Staton, Knofel. Check Your Character (Student) 116p. (Orig.). 1980. pap. 2.25 (ISBN 0-87239-422-0, 39993). Standard Pub.

--Check Your Lifestyle. LC 78-66436. (Illus.). 1978. instr's manual o.s.i. 2.50 (ISBN 0-87239-232-5, 39996); pap. 2.25 student (ISBN 0-87239-233-3, 39997). Standard Pub.

--Meet Jesus. LC 80-53674. 192p. (Orig.). 1981. pap. 3.50 (ISBN 0-87239-426-3, 40092). Standard Pub.

Staton, Knofel, jt. auth. see Staton, Julia.

Staton, Thomas F. How to Study. 1959. pap. text ed. 1.35 (ISBN 0-913476-07-2). Am Guidance.

Staton, Wesley M., jt. auth. see Cornacchia, Harold J.

Statsky, jt. auth. see Singer.

Statsky, William P. Domestic Relations: Law & Skills. LC 78-7303. (Paralegal Ser.). 537p. 1978. text ed. 18.95 (ISBN 0-8299-2007-2). West Pub.

Statt, D. Dictionary of Human Behavior. 1981. text ed. 15.70 (ISBN 0-686-69149-0, Pub. by Har-Row Ltd England). Har-Row.

Statt, David A. La Psicologia. Pulido, Mei Mei A. & Hernandez, Jose C., eds. Romero, Jose G., tr. 272p. 1980. pap. text ed. 6.00x (ISBN 0-06-316850-2, Pub. by HarLA Mexico). Har-Row.

Staub, Ervin, ed. Personality: Basic Aspects & Current Research. (Illus.). 1980. text ed. 20.95 (ISBN 0-13-657932-9). P-H.

Staub, George E. & Kent, Leona M. The Para-Professional in the Treatment of Alcoholism: A New Profession. 184p. 1979. 11.00 (ISBN 0-398-02860-5). C C Thomas.

Staubach, Roger & Luksa, Frank. Roger Staubach: Time Enough to Win. 256p. 1980. 9.95 (ISBN 0-8499-0274-6). Word Bks.

Staubus, George. Making Accounting Decisions. LC 77-73906. 1978. text ed. 20.00 (ISBN 0-914348-19-1). Scholars Bk.

Staubus, George J. Activity Costing & Input-Output Accounting. (Willard J. Graham Ser. in Accounting). 1971. pap. text ed. 6.95x o.p. (ISBN 0-256-00543-5). Irwin.

--A Theory of Accounting to Investors. LC 61-7516. 1971. Repr. of 1961 ed. text ed. 10.00 (ISBN 0-914348-10-8). Scholars Bk.

St Aubyn, F. C. Charles Peguy. (World Authors Ser.: France: No. 467). 1977. lib. bdg. 12.50 (ISBN 0-8057-6304-X). Twayne.

Stauderman, Albert P. Facts About Lutherans. 1959. pap. 0.65 (ISBN 0-8006-1832-7, 1-1832). Fortress.

Staudt, Thomas A. & Taylor, Donald. Managerial Introduction to Marketing. 3rd ed. (Illus.). 576p. 1976. 18.95x (ISBN 0-13-550186-5). P-H.

Staufenberger, Richard A., ed. see Police Foundation.

Stauffer, Donald B. A Short History of American Poetry. LC 69-13347. 1974. pap. 6.95 o.p. (ISBN 0-525-47318-1). Dutton.

Stauffer, Francis H. Queer, the Quaint, the Quizzical. LC 68-22052. 1968. Repr. of 1882 ed. 15.00 (ISBN 0-8103-3096-2). Gale.

Stauffer, George B. The Organ Preludes of Johann Sebastian Bach. Buelow, George, ed. (Studies in Musicology: Vol. 27). 274p. 1980. 34.95 (ISBN 0-8357-1117-X, Pub. by UMI Res Pr). Univ Microfilms.

Stauffer, Jay R., Jr., jt. ed. see Hocutt, Charles H.

Stauffer, Ted. Forever Is a Hell of a Long Time. LC 75-32995. 320p. 1976. 9.95 o.p. (ISBN 0-8092-8089-2). Contemp Bks.

Staugaard, Andrew C., Jr. How to Program & Interface the 6800. LC 80-50050. 1980. pap. 15.95 (ISBN 0-672-21684-1). Sams.

Staum, Martin S. Cabanis: Enlightenment & Medical Philosophy in the French Revolution. LC 79-3231. 1980. 27.50x (ISBN 0-691-05301-4). Princeton U Pr.

Staunford, William & Romilly, Samuel. Les Plees Del Coron. Berkowitz, David S. & Thorne, Samuel E., eds. LC 77-86634. (Classics of English Legal History in the Modern Era Ser.: Vol. 28). 484p. 1979. lib. bdg. 40.00 (ISBN 0-8240-3077-X). Garland Pub.

Staunton, George L., tr. see Tulisen.

Staunton, J. Primary Metabolism: A Mechanistic Approach. (Illus.). 1978. text ed. 24.00x (ISBN 0-19-855460-5). Oxford U Pr.

Stava, Pamela S. Handbook of Trees for the Midwest. (Illus.). 1978. pap. text ed. 14.95 (ISBN 0-8403-1851-0). Kendall-Hunt.

Stave, Bruce M. & Stave, Sondra A. Urban Bosses, Machines, & Progressive Reformers. rev. ed. 178p. (Orig.). 1981. pap. 5.95 (ISBN 0-89874-119-X). Krieger.

Stave, Bruce M., ed. Socialism & the Cities. (National University Publications Interdisciplinary Urban Ser.). 1975. 15.00 (ISBN 0-8046-9133-9, Natl U); pap. 8.95 (ISBN 0-8046-9189-4). Kennikat.

Stave, Sondra A., jt. auth. see Stave, Bruce M.

Stavearce, Tony, jt. auth. see Colin, Sid.

Staveley, A. L. Memories of Gurdjieff. 1978. 6.95 (ISBN 0-89756-025-6). Two Rivers.

Stavenhagen, Kurt. Absolute Stellungnahmen: Eine Ontologische Untersuchung Uber das Wesen der Religion. Natanson, Maurice, ed. LC 78-66740. (Phenomenology Ser.: Vol. 13). 234p. 1979. lib. bdg. 23.00 (ISBN 0-8240-9557-X). Garland Pub.

Stavig, Mark. John Ford & the Traditional Moral Order. 1968. 25.00x (ISBN 0-299-04680-X). U of Wis Pr.

Stavis, Barrie. Coat of Many Colors. LC 68-11075. 1968. 7.95 o.p. (ISBN 0-498-06819-6). A S Barnes.

--Harper's Ferry. LC 67-23982. 1967. 7.95 o.p. (ISBN 0-498-06728-9). A S Barnes.

--John Brown: The Sword & the Word. LC 76-81676. (Illus.). 1969. 8.95 o.p. (ISBN 0-498-07520-6). A S Barnes.

--Lamp at Midnight. (Illus.). 7.95 o.p. (ISBN 0-498-06488-3). A S Barnes.

--The Man Who Never Died: A Play About Joe Hill. LC 70-88295. (Illus.). 128p. 1972. 7.95 o.p. (ISBN 0-498-07538-9). A S Barnes.

Stavrianos, L. S. The Balkans: 1815-1914. (Berkshire Ser.). 144p. 1963. pap. 5.50 o.p. (ISBN 0-685-72303-8, Pub. by HR&W). Krieger.

--The Promise of the Coming Dark Age. LC 76-8232. (Illus.). 1976. pap. text ed. 8.95x (ISBN 0-7167-0496-X). W H Freeman.

Stavrianos, Leften. Epic of Modern Man: A Collection of Readings. 2nd ed. LC 77-138472. 1971. pap. text ed. 13.95 (ISBN 0-13-283333-6). P-H.

--Man's Past & Present: A Global History. 2nd ed. LC 74-28215. (Illus.). 576p. 1975. pap. text ed. 16.95 (ISBN 0-13-552091-6). P-H.

--The World Since Fifteen Hundred: A Global History. 3rd ed. LC 74-30161. (Illus.). 576p. 1975. pap. text ed. 16.95 (ISBN 0-13-968156-6). P-H.

--The World to Fifteen Hundred: A Global History. 2nd ed. (Illus.). 416p. 1975. pap. write for info. (ISBN 0-13-968198-1). P-H.

Stavrianos, Leften S., et al. A Global History of Man. (gr. 9-12). 1974. text ed. 17.40 (ISBN 0-205-03815-8, 7838158); tchrs'. guide 4.40 (ISBN 0-205-03816-6, 7838166); tests & dup. masters 44.00 (ISBN 0-205-02467-X, 782467X). Allyn.

--A Global History. rev. ed. 1979. text ed. 17.40 (ISBN 0-205-06113-3, 7861133); tchrs'. guide 4.40 (ISBN 0-205-06114-1, 7861141); tests 44.00 (ISBN 0-205-06115-X, 786115X). Allyn.

Stavropoulos, C. Partakers of Divine Nature. 1976. pap. 3.50 (ISBN 0-937032-09-3). Light & Life Pub Co MN.

Stavrou, Nikolaos A. Edvard Kardelj: The Historical Roots of Non-Alignment. LC 80-5251. 95p. 1980. pap. text ed. 6.00 (ISBN 0-8191-1066-3). U Pr of Amer.

Stavroulakis, P., ed. Interference Analysis of Communication. LC 80-18464. 1980. 34.95 (ISBN 0-87942-135-5). Inst Electrical.

Stavroulakis, Peter. Interference Analysis of Communication Systems. 472p. 1980. 38.00 (ISBN 0-471-08674-6, Pub. by Wiley-Interscience); pap. 25.75 (ISBN 0-471-08673-8). Wiley.

Staw, Barry M. & Salancik, Gerald R., eds. New Directions in Organizational Behavior. LC 76-47795. (Illus.). 250p. 1976. pap. text ed. 9.95 (ISBN 0-914292-06-4). Wiley.

Stawar, Terry L. Teaching Children Self-Control: A Fable Mod Manual for Dealing with Behavior Problems of Elementary School-Age Children. LC 78-71018. (Illus.). Date not set. pap. cancelled (ISBN 0-917476-12-3). Rational Living.

Stayer, James M. & Packull, Werner O. The Anabaptists & Thomas Muntzer. 176p. 1980. pap. text ed. 9.95 (ISBN 0-8403-2235-6). Kendall-Hunt.

Stcherbatsky, T. Papers of Th. Stcherbatsky. Chattopadhyaya, D., ed. Gupta, H. C., tr. from Rus. (Soviet Indology Ser.: No. 2). 136p. 1972. 7.50x o.p. (ISBN 0-8426-1552-0). Verry.

Stcherbatsky, Theodore. Buddhist Logic, 2 vols. 1930. pap. text ed. 6.00 ea.; Vol. 1. pap. text ed. (ISBN 0-486-20955-5); Vol. 2. pap. text ed. (ISBN 0-486-20956-3). Dover.

Stea, David, jt. ed. see Downs, Robert M.

Stead, Alfred, ed. Japan by the Japanese: A Survey by Its Authorities, 2 vols. (Studies in Japanese History & Civilization). 1979. Repr. of 1904 ed. 55.00 (ISBN 0-89093-264-6). U Pubns Amer.

Stead, Betty A. Women in Management. (Illus.). 1978. 15.95 (ISBN 0-13-961730-2); pap. text ed. 9.95 (ISBN 0-13-961722-1). P-H.

Stead, Christina. The Man Who Loved Children. LC 65-10128. 576p. 1980. 12.95 o.p. (ISBN 0-03-047265-2); pap. 7.95 (ISBN 0-03-057642-3). HR&W.

Stead, Evelyn S. & Warren, Gloria K. Low-Fat Cookery. LC 72-3329. 284p. 1972. pap. 1.45 o.p. (ISBN 0-668-02672-3). Arc Bks.

Stead, Robert J. The Homesteaders. LC 73-82583. (Literature of Canada Ser.). 1973. pap. 6.50 (ISBN 0-8020-6196-6). U of Toronto Pr.

Stead, William T. United States of Europe on the Eve of the Parliament of Peace. LC 70-147592. (Library of War & Peace; Int'l. Organization Arbitration & Law). lib. bdg. 38.00 (ISBN 0-8240-0353-5). Garland Pub.

Steadman, John M. Disembodied Laughter: Troilus & the Apotheosis Tradition. 1972. 17.50x (ISBN 0-520-02047-2). U of Cal Pr.

--The Lamb & the Elephant: Ideal Imitation & the Context of Renaissance Allegory. LC 73-93874. 1974. 18.50 (ISBN 0-87328-062-8). Huntington Lib.

Steadman, P. Energy, Environment & Building. LC 74-21715. (Urban & Architectural Studies: No. 3). (Illus.). 294p. 1975. 36.00 (ISBN 0-521-20694-4); pap. 11.95x (ISBN 0-521-09926-9). Cambridge U Pr.

--The Evolution of Designs. LC 78-18255. (Cambridge Urban & Architectural Studies: No. 5). 32.50 (ISBN 0-521-22302-4). Cambridge U Pr.

Steadman, Ralph. America. LC 74-82705. 1977. pap. 6.95 o.p. (ISBN 0-394-73307-X). Random.

--Dogs Bodies. 1971. pap. 1.95 o.p. (ISBN 0-200-71727-8). Transatlantic.

Steady, Filomina C., ed. The Black Woman Cross-Culturally. 400p. 1980. text ed. 24.95x (ISBN 0-87073-345-1); pap. text ed. 12.50x (ISBN 0-87073-346-X). Schenkman.

Stealingworth, Slim. Tom Wesselmann. (Illus.). 320p. 1980. 75.00 (ISBN 0-89659-072-0); limited ed. 2000.00 (ISBN 0-89659-160-3). Abbeville Pr.

Stean, Michael. Sicilian: Najdorf. 1976. pap. 10.95 o.p. (ISBN 0-7134-0099-4). David & Charles.

--Simple Chess. 1978. 9.50 o.p. (ISBN 0-571-11215-3, Pub. by Faber & Faber); pap. 4.95 (ISBN 0-571-11257-9). Merrimack Bk Serv.

Steane, J. B. Marlowe: A Critical Study. 1964. 54.00 (ISBN 0-521-06545-3); pap. 13.95x (ISBN 0-521-09624-3). Cambridge U Pr.

Steane, J. B., ed. see Jonson, Ben.

Stearn, Colin W., et al. Geological Evolution of North America. 3rd ed. LC 78-8124. 1979. text ed. 23.95x (ISBN 0-471-07252-4). Wiley.

Stearn, Jess. Dr. Thompson's New Way for You to Cure Your Aching Back. LC 72-96260. 216p. 1973. 7.95 o.p. (ISBN 0-385-00473-7). Doubleday.

--In Search of Taylor Caldwell. LC 80-6150. 224p. 1981. 12.95 (ISBN 0-8128-2791-0). Stein & Day.

--The Search for a Soul: Taylor Caldwell's Psychic Lives. 1978. pap. 2.25 (ISBN 0-449-23437-1, Crest). Fawcett.

Stearn, Jess & Geller, Larry. The Truth About Elvis. 288p. (Orig.). 1980. pap. 2.50 (ISBN 0-515-05154-3). Jove Pubns.

Stearn, Jess, jt. auth. see Caldwell, Taylor.

Stearns, Arthur A. The Law of Suretyship. Elder, James L., ed. LC 74-170608. 720p. 1973. Repr. lib. bdg. 58.25x (ISBN 0-8371-6030-8, STLS). Greenwood.

Stearns, Betty & Degen, Clara, eds. Careers in Music. rev. ed. LC 76-150516. (Illus.). 1980. pap. text ed. 2.00 (ISBN 0-918196-00-0). American Music.

Stearns, Bill. Anyone Here Know Right from Wrong? 1976. pap. 1.95 (ISBN 0-88207-724-4). Victor Bks.

--From Rock Bottom to Mountaintop. 1979. pap. 2.50 (ISBN 0-88207-580-2). Victor Bks.

Stearns, Frederic R. Anger: Psychology, Physiology, Pathology. 84p. 1972. photocopy ed. spiral 10.75 (ISBN 0-398-02612-2). C C Thomas.

Stearns, Harold T. Geology of the State of Hawaii. 2nd ed. (Illus.). Date not set. price not set (ISBN 0-87015-234-3). Pacific Bks.

Stearns, Marshall W. Story of Jazz. (Illus.). 1970. pap. 6.95 (ISBN 0-19-501269-0, GB). Oxford U Pr.

Stearns, Mary Lee. Haida Culture in Custody: The Masset Band. LC 80-50862. (Illus.). 315p. 1980. 24.50 (ISBN 0-295-95763-8). U of Wash Pr.

Stearns, Monroe. Charlemagne. LC 77-132069. (Biography Ser). (Illus.). (gr. 7 up). 1971. PLB 5.90 o.p. (ISBN 0-531-00960-2). Watts.

--Great Awakening, 1720-1760: Religious Revival Arouses America's Sense of Individual Liberties. LC 73-93224. (Focus Bks). (Illus.). (gr. 7 up). 1970. PLB 4.90 o.p. (ISBN 0-531-01008-2). Watts.

--Louis the Fourteenth of France: Pattern of Majesty. LC 77-137152. (Biography Ser). (Illus.). (gr. 7 up). 1971. PLB 5.90 o.p. (ISBN 0-531-00962-9). Watts.

--Mark Twain. LC 65-13679. (Biography Ser). (gr. 7 up). 1965. PLB 5.90 o.p. (ISBN 0-531-00927-0). Watts.

--Michelangelo. (Art Biography Ser). (Illus.). (gr. 7 up). 1970. PLB 5.88 o.p. (ISBN 0-531-00944-0). Watts.

--Shay's Rebellion 1786-87: Americans Take up Arms Against an Unjust Law. LC 68-17705. (Focus Bks). (Illus.). (gr. 7 up). 1968. PLB 4.47 o.p. (ISBN 0-531-01003-1). Watts.

--Story of New England. (Landmark Giant Ser). (Illus.). (gr. 5-10). 1967. 4.95 o.p. (ISBN 0-394-81894-6, BYR). Random.

--Wolfgang Amadeus Mozart, Master of Pure Music. (Biography Ser). (Illus.). (gr. 7 up). 1968. PLB 6.90 (ISBN 0-531-00906-8). Watts.

Stearns, Peter N. Revolutionary Syndicalism & French Labor. 1971. 13.00 (ISBN 0-8135-0688-3). Rutgers U Pr.

Stearns, Robert I., jt. auth. see Berndt, Alan F.

Stearns, Sam D. Digital Signal Analysis. 288p. 1975. text ed. 23.95x (ISBN 0-8104-5828-4). Hayden.

Stebbens, Derek. Chemistry by Inquiry. pap. text ed. 4.95x o.p. (ISBN 0-435-64841-1); tchr's guide 4.95x o.p. (ISBN 0-435-64842-X). Heinemann Ed.

Stebbens, Derek, jt. auth. see Spiers, Antony.

Stebbing, Rita. The Philosophy of Spiritual Activity As a Path to Self-Knowledge. 1980. pap. 2.95 (ISBN 0-916786-50-1). St George Bk Serv.

Stebbins, D. Multiple Choice Questions for A-Level Chemistry. LC 79-41510. (Illus.). 132p. 1980. pap. 8.95 (ISBN 0-408-10644-1). Butterworths.

Stebbins, G. Ledyard. Processes of Organic Evolution. 3rd ed. (Illus.). 1977. pap. text ed. 11.95 (ISBN 0-13-723452-X). P-H.

Stebbins, George L. Variations & Evolution in Plants. LC 50-9426. (Columbia Biological Ser.: No. 16). (Illus.). 1950. 40.00x (ISBN 0-231-01733-2). Columbia U Pr.

Stebbins, Lucy & Stebbins, Richard P. Enchanted Wanderer: The Life of Carl Maria Von Weber. LC 80-2301. 1981. Repr. of 1940 ed. 39.50 (ISBN 0-404-18870-2). AMS Pr.

Stebbins, Natalie & Barbaresi, Sara M. How to Raise & Train a Doberman Pinscher. (Illus.). pap. 2.00 (ISBN 0-87666-282-3, DS1013). TFH Pubns.

Stebbins, Richard P. & Adam, Elaine P. American Foreign Relations, 1975: A Documentary Record. LC 77-6093. 1977. 28.50x (ISBN 0-8147-7783-X). NYU Pr.

Stebbins, Richard P., jt. auth. see Stebbins, Lucy.

Stebbins, Richard P. & Adam, Elaine P., eds. American Foreign Relations, 1971: A Documentary Record. LC 75-13518. 658p. 1976. 28.50x (ISBN 0-8147-7763-5). NYU Pr.

--American Foreign Relations, 1972: A Documentary Record. LC 75-15127. 590p. 1976. 28.50x (ISBN 0-8147-7764-3). NYU Pr.

--American Foreign Relations, 1974: A Documentary Record. LC 76-47172. 1977. 28.50x (ISBN 0-8147-7776-7). NYU Pr.

Stebbins, Richard P. & Adams, Elaine P., eds. American Foreign Relations, 1973: A Documentary Record. LC 76-15891. 1976. 28.50x (ISBN 0-8147-7775-9). NYU Pr.

Stebbins, Robert C. Amphibians & Reptiles of California. LC 72-165229. (California Natural History Guides: No. 31). Orig. Title: Reptiles & Amphibians of the San Francisco Bay Area. (Illus.). 112p. 1972. pap. 5.95 (ISBN 0-520-02090-1). U of Cal Pr.

Stebel, S. L., jt. auth. see Thomas, Bill.

Stebel, Sid, jt. auth. see Thomas, Bill.

Steben, Ralph E. & Bell, Sam. Track & Field: An Administrative Approach to the Science of Coaching. LC 77-2001. 1978. text ed. 19.95 (ISBN 0-471-02546-1). Wiley.

Stec, W. J. Phosphorous Chemistry Directed Towards Biology: International Symposium on Phosphorus Chemistry Directed Towards Biology, Burzenin, Poland, 25-28 September 1979. (IUPAC Symposium Ser.). 240p. 1980. 69.00 (ISBN 0-08-023969-2). Pergamon.

Stech, et al. Integral & Functional Differential Equations. Date not set. price not set (ISBN 0-8247-1354-0). Dekker.

Stechow, Wolfgang. Dutch Landscape Painting of the Seventeenth Century. LC 79-91824. (Illus.). 494p. 1980. Repr. of 1966 ed. lib. bdg. 60.00 (ISBN 0-87817-268-8). Hacker.

Steck, Allen & Roper, Steve, eds. Ascent: The Mountaineering Experience in Word & Image. LC 80-13855. (Illus.). 272p. (Orig.). 1980. pap. 14.95 (ISBN 0-87156-240-5). Sierra.

--Ascent 1975-76: The Mountaineering Experience in Word & Image. (Illus.). 128p. 1976. pap. 8.95 (ISBN 0-87156-189-1). Sierra.

Stecker, Margaret L. Intercity Differences in Costs of Living in March, 1935 - 59 Cities. LC 79-165689. (FDR & the Era of the New Deal Ser). 1971. Repr. of 1937 ed. lib. bdg. 22.50 (ISBN 0-306-70344-0). Da Capo.

Steckin, S. B., ed. The Approximation of Functions by Polynomials & Splines. (Trudy Steklov: No. 145). Date not set. price not set o.p. (ISBN 0-8218-3049-X). Am Math.

Steckman & Sklarew. Amusettes. (Illus.). (gr. 7-9). 1973. pap. text ed. 3.50 (ISBN 0-88345-185-9, 18082). Regents Pub.

Stedman, Donald, jt. ed. see Caldwell, Bettye.

Stedman, James M., et al. Clinical Studies in Behavior Therapy with Children, Adolescents, & Their Families. (Illus.). 412p. 1973. 26.75 (ISBN 0-398-02736-6); pap. 20.50 (ISBN 0-398-02763-3). C C Thomas.
Stedman, Preston. The Symphony. (Illus.). 1979. ref. ed. 16.95 (ISBN 0-13-880062-6). P-H.
Stedman, Ray. Birth of the Body. 1975. pap. 2.95 o.p. (ISBN 0-88449-013-0). Vision Hse.
--Triumph of the Body. (Orig.). 1981. pap. 3.95 (ISBN 0-88449-041-6). Vision Hse.
Stedman, Ray C. Authentic Christianity. (Orig.). pap. 1.75 (ISBN 0-89129-249-7). Jove Pubns.
--What on Earth's Going to Happen? LC 73-104085. 1970. pap. 2.25 o.p. (ISBN 0-8307-0532-5, 5016002). Regal.
Stedman, Raymond W. The Serials. 2nd, rev. & enl. ed. (Suspense & Drama by Installment). 574p. 1980. pap. 9.95 (ISBN 0-8061-1695-1). U of Okla Pr.
Stedman, William. Guide to Public Speaking. LC 70-136283. (Illus.). 1971. pap. text ed. 9.95 (ISBN 0-13-370635-4). P-H.
--A Guide to Public Speaking. 2nd ed. (Illus.). 208p. pap. text ed. 9.95 (ISBN 0-13-370619-2). P-H.
Stedwell, Paki. Vaulting: Gymnastics on Horseback. LC 79-11556. (Illus.). 128p. (gr. 7-12). 1980. PLB 7.79 (ISBN 0-671-34023-9). Messner.
Steed, Freida R. A Special Picture Cookbook. 1974. 5.75 o.p. (ISBN 0-89079-041-8). H & H Ent.
Steed, Henry W. The Hapsburg Monarchy. 1969. 19.00 (ISBN 0-86527-091-0). Fertig.
Steedman, Ian. Trade Amongst Growing Economies. LC 78-73818. 1980. 24.95 (ISBN 0-521-22671-6). Cambridge U Pr.
Steedman, Marguerite C. South Carolina Colony. LC 74-95299. (Forge of Freedom Ser). (Illus.). (gr. 5-8). 1970. 7.95 (ISBN 0-02-786770-6, CCPr). Macmillan.
Steedman, W., et al. Chemistry for the Engineering & Applied Sciences: Second Edition of Chemistry for the Applied Sciences. 2nd ed. 1980. 69.00 (ISBN 0-08-022851-8); pap. 19.25 (ISBN 0-08-022852-6). Pergamon.
Steeds, D., jt. auth. see Nish, I.
Steeds, J. W. Introduction to Anisotropic Elasticity Theory of Dislocations. (Monographs on the Physics & Chemistry of Materials). (Illus.). 286p. 1973. 42.00x (ISBN 0-19-851341-0). Oxford U Pr.
Steefel, Lawrence D., Jr. The Position of Duchamp's Glass in the Development of His Art. LC 76-23647. (Outstanding Dissertations in the Fine Arts Ser.). 1977. lib. bdg. 63.00x (ISBN 0-8240-2730-2). Garland Pub.
Steeg, Clarence L. Ver see Ver Steeg, Clarence L.
Steegman, M. G., tr. see Da Foligno, Angela.
Steegmuller, Francis. Apollinaire: Poet Among the Painters. LC 80-67030. 392p. 1980. pap. 10.95 (ISBN 0-87923-352-4, Nonpareil Bks). Godine.
Steel, Daniel I. A Lincolnshire Village: The Parish of Corby Glen in Its Historical Context. (Illus.). 242p. 1979. lib. bdg. 22.00 (ISBN 0-582-50285-3). Longman.
Steel, Danielle. Love: Poems by Danielle Steel. (Orig.). 1981. pap. 2.50 (ISBN 0-440-15377-8). Dell.
--Palomino. (Orig.). 1981. pap. 6.95 (ISBN 0-440-56753-X, Dell Trade Pbks). Dell.
--A Perfect Stranger. (Orig.). Date not set. pap. 2.75 (ISBN 0-440-17221-7). Dell.
--The Ring. 1980. 10.95 (ISBN 0-440-07622-6). Delacorte.
Steel, David. Preaching Through the Year. LC 80-82191. 168p. 1980. pap. 6.50 (ISBN 0-8042-1801-3). John Knox.
Steel, Flora A. & Temple, R. C., eds. Tales of the Punjab. LC 73-175388. (Illus.). 310p. 1980. 10.95 (ISBN 0-370-01271-2, Pub. by Chatto, Bodley Head & Jonathan). Merrimack Bk Serv.
Steel, Flora Annie. Tattercoats. LC 76-9947. (Illus.). (gr. k-3). 1976. 9.95 (ISBN 0-87888-109-3). Bradbury Pr.
Steel, L. E. Neutron Irradiation Embrittlement of Reactor Pressure Vessel Steels. (Technical Report Ser.: No. 163). (Illus.). 235p. 1975. pap. 21.00 (ISBN 92-0-155075-8, IAEA). Unipub.
Steel, Mike. New & Used Car Gas Mileage & Price Guide for 1981. 160p. (Orig.). 1981. pap. 3.95 (ISBN 0-933474-23-7, Gabriel Bks). Minn Scholarly.
Steel, Rodney & Harvey, Anthony. The Encyclopedia of Pre-Historic Life. (Illus.). 1979. 24.95 (ISBN 0-07-060920-9). McGraw.
Steel, Ronald. Walter Lippmann & the American Century. (Illus.). 640p. 1980. 19.95 (ISBN 0-316-81190-4). Little.
Steel, Ronald, ed. Italy. (Reference Shelf Ser: Vol. 35, No. 6). 1963. 6.25 (ISBN 0-8242-0078-0). Wilson.
--North Africa. (Reference Shelf Ser: Vol. 38, No. 5). 1967. 6.25 (ISBN 0-8242-0092-6). Wilson.
Steel, William F. Small-Scale Employment & Production in Developing Countries: Evidence from Ghana. LC 75-44940. (Special Studies). 1977. text ed. 25.95 (ISBN 0-275-56330-8). Praeger.
Steel, William H. Interferometry. (Cambridge Monographs on Physics). 1967. 35.50 (ISBN 0-521-06547-X). Cambridge U Pr.
Steele. Child Health Nursing: Concepts & Management. 1981. price not set (ISBN 0-89352-035-7). Masson Pub.
--Gospel of the Comforter. pap. 5.95 (ISBN 0-686-12870-2). Schmul Pub Co.
--Half Hours with St. John. pap. 5.95 (ISBN 0-686-12871-0). Schmul Pub Co.
--Half Hours with St. Paul. pap. 4.95 (ISBN 0-686-12872-9). Schmul Pub Co.
Steele, Alexander. How to Spy on the U. S. 1974. 7.95 o.p. (ISBN 0-87000-278-3). Arlington Hse.
Steele, B., ed. Cues & Signals 1: A Self-Instruction Workbook for Visual Accuracy. reusable ed. (gr. 4). 1971. wkbk. 5.00 (ISBN 0-89039-023-1). Ann Arbor Pubs.
Steele, B. & Wehrli, K., eds. Cues & Signals 2: A Self-Instruction Workbook for Visual Accuracy. reusable ed. (gr. 4). 1971. wkbk. 5.00 (ISBN 0-89039-025-8). Ann Arbor Pubs.
--Cues & Signals 3: A Self-Instruction Workbook for Visual Accuracy. reusable ed. (gr. 4). 1971. wkbk. 5.00 (ISBN 0-89039-027-4). Ann Arbor Pubs.
--Cues & Signals 4: A Self-Instruction Workbook for Visual Accuracy. reusable ed. (gr. 4). 1971. wkbk. 5.00 (ISBN 0-89039-029-0). Ann Arbor Pubs.
Steele, Bill. The Need to Fail. 72p. 1974. pap. text ed. 3.50x (ISBN 0-89039-060-6). Ann Arbor Pubs.
Steele, Bonnie G. Self-Assessment of Current Knowledge in General Surgical Nursing. 1978. spiral bdg. 9.50 (ISBN 0-87488-290-7). Med Exam.
Steele, C. Hoy, jt. auth. see Yetman, Norman R.
Steele, D. Steele's Answers. 6.95 (ISBN 0-686-27781-3). Schmul Pub Co.
Steele, E. D. Irish Land & British Politics: Tenant-Right & Nationality, 1865-1870. LC 73-91618. (Illus.). 352p. 1974. 41.00 (ISBN 0-521-20421-6). Cambridge U Pr.
Steele, E. J. Somatic Selection & Adaptive Evolution. 100p. 1980. 30.00x (Pub. by Croom Helm England). State Mutual Bk.
Steele, F. I. Physical Settings & Organization Development. LC 70-172802. 1973. pap. text ed. 6.50 (ISBN 0-201-07211-4). A-W.
Steele, Fritz & Jenks, Stephen. The Feel of the Work Place: Understanding & Improving Organization Climate. LC 76-12802. (Illus.). 1977. pap. text ed. 8.95 (ISBN 0-201-07213-0). A-W.
Steele, Gerald L. Exploring the World of Plastics. LC 75-42964. (gr. 8-12). 1977. text ed. 15.72 (ISBN 0-87345-411-1). McKnight.
Steele, Henry B., jt. auth. see Griffin, James M.
Steele, James. I Have a Ghetto in My Heart. 1973. pap. 2.25 (ISBN 0-87148-428-5). Pathway Pr.
Steele, James H., jt. ed. see Arambulo, Primo.
Steele, James H., jt. ed. see Beran, George.
Steele, James W. Frontier Army Sketches. LC 73-99567. 1969. 7.95x (ISBN 0-8263-0159-2); pap. 2.95 o.p. (ISBN 0-8263-0233-5). U of NM Pr.
Steele, Jessica. The Magic of His Kiss. (Harlequin Romances). 192p. 1981. pap. 1.25 (ISBN 0-373-02394-4, Pub. by Harlequin). PB.
--Turbulent Covenent. (Harlequin Romances Ser.). 192p. 1980. pap. 1.25 o.p. (ISBN 0-373-02355-3, Pub. by Harlequin). PB.
Steele, Joan. Captain Mayne Reid. (English Authors Ser: No. 229). 1978. lib. bdg. 12.50 (ISBN 0-8057-6700-2). Twayne.
Steele, L. E. & Stahlkopf, K. E., eds. Assuring Structural Integrity of Steel Reactor Pressure Vessels. (Illus.). xii, 220p. 1980. 40.00x (ISBN 0-85334-906-1). Burgess-Intl Ideas.
Steele, Marion A. & Armstrong, Ronald M. I Had the Craziest Dream Last Night: A Psychiatrist Helps You Interpret Your Dreams. LC 73-169125. 1971. 11.95 (ISBN 0-911012-16-8). Nelson-Hall.
Steele, Mary Q. Because of the Sand Witches There. LC 75-5932. (Illus.). 192p. (gr. 3-7). 1975. 8.25 (ISBN 0-688-80001-7); PLB 7.92 (ISBN 0-688-84001-9). Greenwillow.
--The Fifth Day. (Illus.). (gr. 6-9). 1978. 8.25 (ISBN 0-688-80146-3); PLB 7.92 (ISBN 0-688-84146-5). Greenwillow.
--The First of the Penguins. LC 73-1964. (Illus.). 160p. (gr. 5-9). 1973. 4.95g o.s.i. (ISBN 0-02-786880-X). Macmillan.
--The Owl's Kiss: Three Stories. LC 78-1983. (gr. 5-9). 1978. 7.95 (ISBN 0-688-80174-9); PLB 7.63 (ISBN 0-688-84174-0). Greenwillow.
--The True Men. LC 76-5482. (gr. 5-9). 1976. 8.25 (ISBN 0-688-80052-1); PLB 7.92 (ISBN 0-688-84052-3). Greenwillow.
--Wish, Come True. LC 79-10321. (Illus.). (gr. 4-6). 1979. 7.95 (ISBN 0-688-80230-3); PLB 7.63 (ISBN 0-688-84230-5). Greenwillow.
Steele, Mike. The New & Used Car Gas Milage & Price Guide. (Orig.). 1981. pap. 3.95 (ISBN 0-933474-11-3, Gabriel Bks). Minn Scholarly.
Steele, Oliver L., ed. see Spenser, Edmund.
Steele, P. M., jt. auth. see Hamill, B. J.
Steele, Peter. Jonathan Swift: Preacher & Jester. 1979. 31.00x (ISBN 0-19-812088-5). Oxford U Pr.
--Medical Care for Mountain Climbers. 1976. pap. 11.00x (ISBN 0-433-31560-1). Intl Ideas.
Steele, Phillip. The Last of the Cherokee Warriors. 2nd ed. (Illus.). (gr. 6-12). 1978. pap. 3.95 (ISBN 0-88289-203-7); 5.95 (ISBN 0-911116-99-0). Pelican.
Steele, R. Delta Modulation Systems. LC 74-11299. 379p. 1975. 42.95 (ISBN 0-470-82104-3). Halsted Pr.
--Do-It-Yourself Conveyancing. LC 78-62481. 1978. 14.95 (ISBN 0-7153-7676-4). David & Charles.
Steele, R., ed. see Bartholomaeus, Anglicus.
Steele, Richard. The Conscious Lovers. Kenney, Shirley S., ed. LC 68-11409. (Regents Restoration Drama Series). 1968. 8.95x (ISBN 0-8032-0369-1); pap. 2.25x (ISBN 0-8032-5369-9, BB 268, Bison). U of Nebr Pr.
--Correspondence of Richard Steele. Blanchard, Rae, ed. 1941. 49.00x o.p. (ISBN 0-19-811499-0). Oxford U Pr.
--Tatler. 1953. 12.95x (ISBN 0-460-00993-1, Evman). Dutton.
--Tender Husband. Winton, Calhoun, ed. LC 66-25598. (Regents Restoration Drama Ser). 1967. 6.95x (ISBN 0-8032-0370-5); pap. 1.65x (ISBN 0-8032-5370-2, BB 261, Bison). U of Nebr Pr.
Steele, Richard, jt. auth. see Addison, Joseph.
Steele, Richard, et al, eds. Tatler, 4 Vols. Repr. of 1898 ed. Set. 163.00 o.p. (ISBN 0-685-05295-8). Adler.
Steele, Richard W. First Offensive, 1942: Roosevelt, Marshall, & the Making of American Strategy. LC 73-75792. 256p. 1973. 15.00x (ISBN 0-253-32215-4). Ind U Pr.
Steele, Robert R., ed. see Muhammad Ibn Zakariya.
Steele, Sara. Cost-Benefit Analysis & the Adult Educator. 1971. 2.30 (ISBN 0-88379-002-5). Adult Ed.
Steele, Stephen F., jt. ed. see Zinner, Ellen S.
Steele, William A. The Interaction of Gases with Solid Surfaces. LC 73-21747. 356p. 1974. text ed. 55.00 (ISBN 0-08-017724-7). Pergamon.
Steele, William O. Daniel Boone's Echo. LC 57-9741. (Illus.). (gr. k-3). 1957. 5.95 o.p. (ISBN 0-15-221980-3, HJ). HarBraceJ.
--Wilderness Journey. LC 55-9006. (Illus.). (gr. 4-6). 6.75 o.p. (ISBN 0-15-297318-4, HJ). HarBraceJ.
--Year of the Bloody Sevens. LC 63-16036. (Illus.). (gr. 4-6). 1963. 6.75 o.p. (ISBN 0-15-299800-4, HJ). HarBraceJ.
Steeley, G. C., jt. auth. see Cowling, T. M.
Steelman, Robert. Apache Wells. 160p. 1975. pap. 0.95 o.p. (ISBN 0-345-24755-8). Ballantine.
Steelman, Robert J. The Fox Dancer. 1976. pap. 0.95 o.p. (ISBN 0-685-69161-6, LB370NK, Leisure Bks). Nordon Pubns.
--Lord Apache. LC 76-53416. 1977. 6.95 o.p. (ISBN 0-385-12430-9). Doubleday.
--The Prairie Baroness. LC 80-2348. 192p. 1981. 9.95 (ISBN 0-385-17015-7). Doubleday.
Steely, John E., ed. see De Jonge, Marinus.
Steely, John E., tr. see Flesseman-Van Leer, E.
Steely, John E., tr. see Kaiser, Otto & Lohse, Eduard.
Steely, John E., tr. see Reitzenstein, Richard.
Steemers, Tc, jt. ed. see Palz, W.
Steen, Edwin B. Abbreviations in Medicine. 4th ed. 1978. pap. 10.95 (ISBN 0-02-859430-4). Macmillan.
Steen, Edwin B. & Ashley Montagu. Anatomy & Physiology, 2 vols. Incl. Cells, Tissues, Integument, Skeletal, Muscular & Digestive Systems, Blood, Lymph, Circulatory System (ISBN 0-06-460098-X, 98); Urinary, Respiratory & Nervous Systems, Sensations & Sense Organs, Endocrine & Reproductive Systems (ISBN 0-06-460099-8, CO 99). 1959. 4.50 ea. (COS). Har-Row.
Steen, Edwin B. & Price, James H. Human Sex & Sexuality: With a Dictionary of Sexual Terms. LC 76-21654. (Illus.). 1977. 17.95x (ISBN 0-471-82101-2). Wiley.
Steen, Frederick H. & Ballou, D. H. Analytic Geometry. 3rd ed. 1963. text ed. 17.95x (ISBN 0-471-00570-3). Wiley.
Steen, Lynn A. Mathematics Today. LC 80-10888. (Illus.). 384p. 1980. pap. 4.95 (ISBN 0-394-74503-5, Vin). Random.
Steen, Peter, jt. auth. see Lonnroth, Mans.
Steenrod, N., jt. auth. see Eilenberg, S.
Steensma, Robert C. Dr. John Arbuthnot. (English Authors Ser.: No. 256). 1979. lib. bdg. 13.95 (ISBN 0-8057-6749-5). Twayne.
Steenson, Gary P. Not One Man! Not One Penny! German Social Democracy, 1863-1914. LC 80-54058. (Illus.). 336p. 1981. 19.95 (ISBN 0-8229-3440-X); pap. 8.95 (ISBN 0-8229-5329-3). U of Pittsburgh Pr.
Steenstrup, Carl. Hojo Shigetoki (Eleven Ninety-Eight to Twelve Sixty-One) & His Role in the History of Political & Ethical Ideas in Japan. (Scandinavian Institute of Asian Studies Monographs: No. 41). (Orig.). 1980. pap. text ed. 16.50x (ISBN 0-7007-0132-X). Humanities.
Steenwyk, C. Van see Van Steenwyk, C.
Steenwyk, Elizabeth Van see Van Steenwyk, Elizabeth.
Steer,. Alvise Vivarini: His Art & Influence. (Illus.). 200p. Date not set. price not set (ISBN 0-521-23363-1). Cambridge U Pr.
Steer, M., jt. auth. see Gunning, B. E.
Steer, M. W. Understanding Cell Structure. (Illus.). 120p. Date not set. price not set (ISBN 0-521-23745-9); pap. text ed. price not set (ISBN 0-521-28198-9). Cambridge U Pr.
Steer, Roger. George Mueller: Delighted in God. LC 75-33488. 1979. pap. 5.95 (ISBN 0-87788-303-3). Shaw Pubs.
Steere, Bob F. The Teaching of Elementary Science. LC 80-13992. 174p. (Orig.). 1981. pap. text ed. write for info. (ISBN 0-89874-178-5). Krieger.
Steere, Daniel C. I Am - I Can. 128p. 1973. 4.95 o.p. (ISBN 0-8007-0618-8). Revell.
--I Am, I Can. 1976. pap. 1.50 (ISBN 0-89129-216-0). Jove Pubns.
Steere, Douglas V. Prayer & Worship. LC 78-70480. 1978. pap. 2.50 (ISBN 0-913408-44-1). Friends United.
--Prayer in the Contemporary World. LC 80-82942. 32p. Repr. of 1966 ed. pap. 1.25 (ISBN 0-87574-907-0). Pendle Hill.
Steers, J. A. The Coastline of Scotland. LC 72-86419. (Illus.). 384p. 1973. 74.50 (ISBN 0-521-08696-5). Cambridge U Pr.
Steers, J. A., ed. Applied Coastal Geomorphology. 1st u.s. ed. 1971. 17.50x (ISBN 0-262-19088-5). MIT Pr.
Steers, J. Alfred. Coastal Features of England & Wales: Eight Essays. (Illus.). 240p. 1980. 35.00 (ISBN 0-900891-70-X). Oleander Pr.
Steers, James A. Coast of England & Wales in Pictures. 1960. 26.95 (ISBN 0-521-06549-6); pap. 13.95 (ISBN 0-521-29274-3). Cambridge U Pr.
Steeves, Edna & Steeves, Harrison, eds. Friedrich Gerstacker: Wild Sports in the Far West. LC 68-16624. 1968. 14.75 (ISBN 0-8223-0167-9). Duke.
Steeves, Frank L. & English, Fenwick W. Secondary Curriculum for a Changing World. 1978. text ed. 15.95 (ISBN 0-675-08424-5); instructor's manual 3.95 (ISBN 0-686-67991-1). Merrill.
Steeves, Harrison, jt. ed. see Steeves, Edna.
Steeves, Paul. Getting to Know Your Faith. 1977. pap. 2.95 o.p. (ISBN 0-87784-629-4). Inter-Varsity.
Steeves, R. F. Pharmacist's Guide to Liability. 1974. pap. 3.50 (ISBN 0-87489-057-8). Med Economics.
Steeves, Taylor A. & Sussex, Ian M. Patterns in Plant Development. (Foundations of Developmental Biology Ser). (Illus.). 1972. ref. ed. 15.95x (ISBN 0-13-653998-X). P-H.
Stefan, Paul. Anton Dvorak. LC 79-146147. (Music Ser.). 1971. Repr. of 1941 ed. lib. bdg. 25.00 (ISBN 0-306-70105-7). Da Capo.
Stefan, Raymond J., jt. auth. see Klaus, Bille.
Stefani, S. & Hubbard, Lincoln B. Mathematics for Technologists in Radiology, Nuclear Medicine & Radiation Therapy. LC 78-32110. (Illus.). 1979. pap. text ed. 13.95 (ISBN 0-8016-4762-2). Mosby.
Stefanini, Mario & Benson, Ellis, eds. Progress in Clinical Pathology, Vol. 8. (Serial Publication Ser.). 1981. write for info. (ISBN 0-8089-1310-7). Grune.
Stefanis, et al, eds. Hashish: Studies of Long-Term Use. LC 76-19848. 1977. 15.50 (ISBN 0-89004-138-5). Raven.
Stefano, Johanna S. de see DeStefano, Johanna S.
Stefansson, Vilhjalmur. Adventures in Error. LC 71-121210. 1970. Repr. of 1936 ed. 15.00 (ISBN 0-8103-3838-6). Gale.
Steffan, Jack. Long Fellow: Story of the Great Irish Patriot, Eamon De Vallera. (gr. 7 up). 1966. 4.95 o.s.i. (ISBN 0-02-786930-X). Macmillan.
Steffanides, George F. Olives & Olive Oil for the Gourmet. LC 38-9182. (Illus.). iv, 49p. 1980. pap. 2.50 (ISBN 0-686-61076-8). Steffanides.
Steffek, Edwin, ed. see Hutchison, Frances.
Steffel, Edwin, ed. Home Growing. LC 77-256. (Illus.). 1977. 19.95 (ISBN 0-312-38836-5). St Martin.
Steffel, Victor L., jt. auth. see Henderson, Davis.
Steffen, Jerome O. Comparative Frontiers: A Proposal for Studying the American West. LC 79-20315. 128p. 1980. 10.95 (ISBN 0-8061-1617-X). U of Okla Pr.

Steffen, Jerome O., ed. The American West: New Perspectives, New Dimensions. LC 78-58097. 238p. 1981. pap. 6.95 (ISBN 0-8061-1744-3). U of Okla Pr.

Steffen, John, jt. auth. see Karoly, Paul.

Steffen, Roscoe T. & Kerr, Thomas R. Agency-Partnership - Cases & Materials. 4th ed. LC 79-28206. (American Casebook Ser.). 859p. 1980. text ed. 21.95 (ISBN 0-8299-2077-3). West Pub.

Steffens, Lincoln. Upbuilders. LC 68-19419. (Americana Library Ser: No. 6). (Illus.). 373p. 1968. 10.50 (ISBN 0-295-73991-6, AL6); pap. 2.95 (ISBN 0-295-95036-6). U of Wash Pr.

Steffensen, Arnold J. & Johnson, L. M. Algebra & Trigonometry. 1980. pap. text ed. 16.95 (ISBN 0-673-15371-1). Scott F.

--Intermediate Algebra. 1980. pap. text ed. 14.95 (ISBN 0-673-15369-X). Scott F.

Steffensen, Arnold R. & Johnson, L. Murphy. College Algebra. 1980. pap. text ed. 15.95x (ISBN 0-673-15370-3). Scott F.

--Introductory Algebra. 1980. pap. text ed. 14.95x (ISBN 0-673-15368-1). Scott F.

Steffensen, James L., Jr., ed. Great Scenes from the World Theater, Vol. 1. (Orig.). 1965. pap. 2.95 (ISBN 0-380-42705-2, 42705, Bard). Avon.

--Great Scenes from the World Theatre, Vol. 2. (Orig.). 1976. pap. 3.95 (ISBN 0-380-01220-0, 53157, Bard). Avon.

Steffensmeier, Darrell J. & Terry, Robert M. Examining Deviance Experimentally: Selected Readings. LC 74-32334. 311p. 1975. pap. text ed. 8.50x (ISBN 0-88284-021-5). Alfred Pub.

Steffes, Robert A., jt. auth. see Horrell, C. William.

Steffgen, Kent H. The Bondage of the Free. 380p. (Orig.). 1966. pap. 1.00 (ISBN 0-911038-74-4, Vanguard). Noontide.

Steffy, Karen, jt. auth. see Teleki, Geza.

Steffy, Robert E. The Dowser's Primer. 60p. 1980. pap. 4.50 (ISBN 0-935648-04-6). Halldin Pub.

Steg, L., ed. Should We Limit Science & Technology. 1976. pap. text ed. 16.25 (ISBN 0-08-019981-X). Pergamon.

Stegall, Donald P., et al. Managing the Small Business. rev ed. 1976. text ed. 18.50 (ISBN 0-256-01784-0). Irwin.

Stegemann, Jelle. Aspekte der kontrastiven Syntax am Beispiel des Niederlaendischen und Deutschen. (Studia Linguistica Germanica). 201p. 1979. text ed. 34.25x (ISBN 3-11-008017-6). De Gruyter.

Stegemayer, Ann. Who's Who in Fashion. (Illus.). 1980. text ed. 13.50 (ISBN 0-87005-257-8). Fairchild.

Stegman, Michael. Housing Investment in the Inner City: The Dynamics of Decline: a Study of Baltimore Maryland, 1968-1970. 320p. 1972. 18.00 (ISBN 0-262-19103-2). MIT Pr.

Stegman, Michael, ed. Housing & Economics: The American Dilemma. 1971. 19.95x o.p. (ISBN 0-262-19081-8). MIT Pr.

Stegner, Wallace. Angle of Repose. 1978. pap. 2.50 (ISBN 0-449-23796-6, Crest). Fawcett.

--The Big Rock Candy Mountain. 1973. Repr. of 1943 ed. 8.95 o.p. (ISBN 0-385-07905-2). Doubleday.

--Joe Hill. LC 80-10760. 381p. 1980. 19.50x (ISBN 0-8032-4116-X); pap. 5.95 (ISBN 0-8032-9115-9, BB 728, Bison). U of Nebr Pr.

--Recapitulation. 1980. pap. 2.50 o.p. (ISBN 0-449-24263-3, Crest). Fawcett.

--Sound of Mountain Water. LC 69-12196. 5.95 o.p. (ISBN 0-385-07138-8). Doubleday.

--The Women on the Wall. LC 80-22461. x, 277p. 1981. 16.50x (ISBN 0-8032-4111-9); pap. 5.50 (ISBN 0-8032-9110-8, BB-710, Bison). U of Nebr Pr.

Stegner, William R. An Introduction to the Parables Through Programmed Instruction. 1977. pap. text ed. 6.50x o.p. (ISBN 0-8191-0132-X). U Pr of Amer.

Stegun, Irene A., jt. ed. see Abramowitz, Milton.

Stehle, Hansjakob. Eastern Politics of the Vatican, 1917-1979. Smith, Sandra, tr. from Ger. LC 80-15236. Orig. Title: Die Ostpolitik Des Vatikans, 1917-1975. (Illus.). 1981. 20.00x (ISBN 0-8214-0367-2, 0367E); pap. 10.00 (ISBN 0-8214-0564-0, 0564E). Ohio U Pr.

Stehle, Matthias. Greek Word Building. LC 76-14405. (Society of Biblical Literature). 1976. pap. 6.00 (ISBN 0-89130-108-9, 060310). Scholars Pr Ca.

Stehlin, Hans G. Die Saugethiere des schweizerischen Eocaens. LC 78-72723. Repr. of 1912 ed. 67.50 (ISBN 0-404-18300-X). AMS Pr.

Stehling, Linda C. & Zauder, Howard L., eds. Anesthetic Implications of Congenital Anomalies in Children. 224p. 1980. 18.50x (ISBN 0-8385-0102-8). ACC.

Stehouwer, Gulle, jt. auth. see Bisgaard, Erling.

Steibel, Gerald L. Detente: Promises & Pitfalls. LC 74-33205. 1975. pap. 2.95x (ISBN 0-8448-0661-7). Crane-Russak Co.

Steichen, Edward. Life in Photography. LC 63-11119. 1968. 19.95 (ISBN 0-385-05571-4). Doubleday.

Steichen, Edward, photos by. Edward Steichen. LC 77-70071. (History of Photography Ser). (Illus.). 1978. 8.95 (ISBN 0-89381-006-1). Aperture.

Steidl, Paul M. The Earth, the Stars, & the Bible. 1979. pap. 5.95 (ISBN 0-8010-8169-6). Baker Bk.

Steidl, Rose E. & Bratton, Esther C. Work in the Home. LC 67-29007. 1968. 21.95 (ISBN 0-471-82085-7). Wiley.

Steier, Moshe. Self-Assessment of Current Knowledge in Pediatric Cardiology. 1977. spiral bdg. 15.00 (ISBN 0-87488-241-9). Med Exam.

Steif, Bill. What You've Got Coming in Social Security & Medicare. 101p. (Orig.). 1980. pap. 1.50 o.s.i. (ISBN 0-915106-16-7). Newspaper Ent.

Steif, William. What You've Got Coming in Social Security & Medicare. LC 79-87560. 1979. pap. 1.50 o.p. (ISBN 0-915106-15-9, Enterprise Pubns). Newspaper Ent.

Steig, Irwin. Play Gin to Win. rev. ed. 1971. 3.95 (ISBN 0-346-12172-8). Cornerstone.

Steig, William. Abel's Island. 128p. (gr. 4-6). 1981. pap. 1.95 (ISBN 0-553-15060-X, Skylark). Bantam.

--Abel's Island. LC 75-35918. (Illus.). 128p. (gr. 4 up). 1976. 7.95 (ISBN 0-374-30010-0). FS&G.

--Amos & Boris. LC 72-165403. (Illus.). 32p. (ps-3). 1971. 7.95 (ISBN 0-374-30278-2). FS&G.

--Drawings. 192p. 1979. 19.95 (ISBN 0-374-29031-8). FS&G.

--Gorky Rises. LC 80-68068. (Illus.). 32p. (ps-3). 1980. 10.95 (ISBN 0-374-32752-1). FS&G.

--Male - Female. LC 79-171491. (Illus.). 128p. 1972. 6.95 (ISBN 0-374-20092-0); pap. 3.95 (ISBN 0-374-51011-3, N430). FS&G.

Steiger, Brad. The Aquarian Revelations. (Orig.). 1980. pap. cancelled o.p. (ISBN 0-89407-029-0). Strawberry Hill.

--The Chindi. (Orig.). 1980. pap. 2.75 (ISBN 0-440-11119-6). Dell.

--Gods of Aquarius. 1981. pap. 2.50 (ISBN 0-425-04753-9). Berkley Pub.

--Medicine Talk: A Guide to Walking in Balance & Surviving on the Earth Mother. LC 74-1774. 216p. 1976. pap. 2.95 o.p. (ISBN 0-385-09734-4). Doubleday.

--Mysteries of Time & Space. LC 74-7288. (Illus.). 224p. 1974. 8.95 o.p. (ISBN 0-13-609040-0). P-H.

--Revelation: The Divine Fire. 1981. pap. 2.50 (ISBN 0-425-04615-X). Berkley Pub.

--Unknown Powers. 1981. pap. 2.50 (ISBN 0-425-05005-X). Berkley Pub.

Steiger, Brad & Steiger, Francie. The Star People. (Orig.). 1981. pap. 2.25 (ISBN 0-425-04823-3). Berkley Pub.

Steiger, Francie, jt. auth. see Steiger, Brad.

Steigmann, Frederick & Clowdus, Bernard F., 2nd. Hepatic Encephalopathy. (Illus.). 214p. 1971. text ed. 18.75 (ISBN 0-398-01841-3). C C Thomas.

Steila, Donal. Geography of Soils: Formation, Distribution & Management. (Illus.). 256p. 1976. 8.95x (ISBN 0-13-351734-9). P-H.

Steila, Donald, et al. Introduction to Earth & Man: A Systematic Geography. LC 80-19689. 600p. 1981. text ed. 19.95 (ISBN 0-471-04221-8). Wiley.

Steimann, I. & Nissen, M. Danish Modern for Udlaendinge. 1974. pap. 18.50x (ISBN 8-7008-1281-1, D-728). Vanous.

Stein. Basic Mathematics for College Students. 6th ed. 1980. text ed. 17.80 (ISBN 0-205-06814-6). Allyn.

Stein & Sessoms. Recreation & Special Populations. 2nd ed. 430p. 1977. text ed. 16.95 (ISBN 0-205-05690-3, 845690-9). Allyn.

Stein, jt. auth. see Johannes, Walter.

Stein, Aaron M. A Body for a Buddy. LC 80-2897. (Crime Club Ser.). 192p. 1981. 9.95 (ISBN 0-385-17583-3). Doubleday.

Stein, Aaron Marc. Chill Factor. LC 77-11754. 1978. 7.95 o.p. (ISBN 0-385-13556-4). Doubleday.

Stein, Agnes, ed. & tr. see Eich, Gunter, et al.

Stein, Aletha H. see Hetherington, E. Mavis.

Stein, Allen F. Cornelius Matthews. (U. S. Authors Ser.: No. 221). 1974. lib. bdg. 10.95 (ISBN 0-8057-0478-7). Twayne.

Stein, Allen F. & Walters, Thomas N. The Southern Experience in Short Fiction. 1971. pap. 6.95x (ISBN 0-673-07605-9). Scott F.

Stein, Arnold. The Art of Presence: The Poet & Paradise Lost. 1976. 16.75x (ISBN 0-520-03167-9). U of Cal Pr.

Stein, Arthur A. The Nation at War. LC 80-7994. 176p. 1981. text ed. 12.95x (ISBN 0-8018-2441-9). Johns Hopkins.

Stein, Aurel. Serindia, 5 vols. (Illus.). 500p. 1981. 75.00 ea. (Pub. by Motilal Banarsidass); Set. 350.00 (ISBN 0-686-69377-9); Vol. 1. (ISBN 0-89581-504-4); Vol. 2. (ISBN 0-89581-505-2); Vol. 3. (ISBN 0-89581-506-0); Vol. 4. (ISBN 0-89581-507-9); Vol. 5. (ISBN 0-89581-508-7). Lancaster-Miller.

Stein, Benjamin, jt. auth. see McGuinness, William J.

Stein, Bruno. Work & Welfare in Britain & the U. S. A. LC 75-44186. 1976. 14.95 (ISBN 0-470-15007-6). Halsted Pr.

Stein, Burton. Peasant State & Society in Medieval South India. (Illus.). 550p. 1980. text ed. 31.00x (ISBN 0-19-561065-2). Oxford U Pr.

Stein, Charlotte M. Communal Dialogue Programs. rev. ed. 1980. Vol. 1. 2.95 (ISBN 0-916634-21-3); Multi-volume Set. pap. write for info. (ISBN 0-916634-19-1). Double M Pr.

--The Pear Tree. Rubenstein, Nancy, ed. LC 79-54652. (Illus.). 200p. 1980. pap. 6.00 (ISBN 0-916634-03-5). Double M Pr.

--The Stained Glass Window. Date not set. price not set. Double M Pr.

Stein, Clem, Jr. The Joy of Home Winemaking. LC 72-6901. (Illus.). 96p. 1973. 7.95 (ISBN 0-87396-073-4). Stravon.

Stein, E., ed. see Schoenberg, Arnold.

Stein, E. P. Flight of the Vin Fiz. 1980. cancelled (ISBN 0-8129-0839-2). Times Bks.

Stein, Edwin I. First Course in Fundamentals of Mathematics. (gr. 7-12). 1978. text ed. 13.96 (ISBN 0-205-05540-0, 5655404); tchr's guide 2.00 (ISBN 0-205-05541-9, 5655412). Allyn.

--Fundamentals of Mathematics. (gr. 7-12). 1980. text ed. 15.80 (ISBN 0-205-06895-2, 5668956); tchrs'. guide 4.20 (ISBN 0-205-06896-0). Allyn.

--Fundamentals of Mathematics. (gr. 7-12). 1976. text ed. 15.80 (ISBN 0-205-05003-4, 5650038); tchrs'. ed. 4.20 (ISBN 0-205-05004-2, 5650046). Allyn.

--Practical Applications in Mathematics. new ed. Orig. Title: Refresher Workbook in Arithmetic. (gr. 7-12). 1972. 4.80 (ISBN 0-205-03385-7, 5633850); answer bk 2.40 (ISBN 0-205-03386-5, 5633869). Allyn.

--Refresher Mathematics. rev. ed. (gr. 7-12). 1974. text ed. 13.56 (ISBN 0-205-04306-2, 5643066); tchrs'. guide 5.12 (ISBN 0-205-04307-0, 5643074). Allyn.

--Refresher Mathematics. (gr. 7-12). 1980. text ed. 13.56 (ISBN 0-205-06160-5, 5661609); tchrs'. guide 5.12 (ISBN 0-205-06161-3, 5661617). Allyn.

--Second Course in Fundamentals of Mathematics. (gr. 7-12). 1978. text ed. 14.20 (ISBN 0-205-05538-9, 5655382); tchr's guide 2.40 (ISBN 0-205-05539-7, 5655390). Allyn.

Stein, Elizabeth P. David Garrick, Dramatist. 315p. 1980. Repr. of 1937 ed. lib. bdg. 40.00 (ISBN 0-89760-827-5). Telegraph Bks.

Stein, Emanuel. The Electrocardiogram: A Self-Study Course in Clinical Electrocardiography (a Tape Presentation) LC 75-8186. (Illus.). 1976. pap. text ed. 16.50 (ISBN 0-7216-8585-4); tapes 85.00 (ISBN 0-7216-9893-X). Saunders.

Stein, Emanuel, jt. auth. see Delman, Abner.

Stein, Frances P. & Udell, Rochelle. Hot Tips: One Thousand Real Life Fashion & Beauty Tricks. (Illus.). 224p. 1981. 12.95 (ISBN 0-399-12580-9). Putnam.

Stein, Gary see Prescott, David M.

Stein, Gertrude. Autobiography of Alice B. Toklas. 7.25 (ISBN 0-8446-3003-9). Peter Smith.

--The Geographical History of America or the Relation of Human Nature to the Human Mind. 224p. Date not set. pap. 1.95 (ISBN 0-394-71941-7). Random.

--How to Write. LC 74-17880. 416p. 1975. pap. text ed. 4.00 (ISBN 0-486-23144-5). Dover.

--Lectures in America. LC 74-17454. 1975. pap. 2.45 o.p. (ISBN 0-394-71477-6, Vin). Random.

--Lectures in America. 246p. Date not set. pap. 2.45 o.p. (ISBN 0-394-71477-6, Vin). Random.

--Picasso. (Illus.). 1959. pap. 3.95 o.p. (ISBN 0-8070-6687-7, BP90). Beacon Pr.

--Reflection on the Atomic Bomb: The Previously Uncollected Writings of Gertrude Stein, Vol. 1. Haas, Robert B., ed. 100p. (Orig.). 1975. 14.00 (ISBN 0-87685-166-9); pap. 5.00 (ISBN 0-87685-167-7). Black Sparrow.

--The Yale Gertrude Stein. LC 80-5398. 480p. 1980. text ed. 30.00x (ISBN 0-300-02574-2); pap. 6.95x (ISBN 0-300-02609-9). Yale U Pr.

Stein, Gertrude & Toklas, Alice B. Last Operas & Plays. 512p. Date not set. pap. 4.95 (ISBN 0-394-71695-7, Vin). Random.

Stein, Gordon. Freethought in the United Kingdom & the Commonwealth: A Descriptive Bibliography. LC 80-1792. 192p. 1981. lib. bdg. 35.00 (ISBN 0-313-20869-7, SFU/). Greenwood.

Stein, Gordon, jt. auth. see Brown, Marshall G.

Stein, Gordon, ed. An Anthology of Atheism & Rationalism. LC 80-81326. (Skeptic's Bookshelf Ser.). 354p. 1980. 16.95 (ISBN 0-87975-136-3). Prometheus Bks.

Stein, Guenther. The Challenge of Red China. LC 74-34407. (China in the 20th Century Ser). (Illus.). x, 490p. 1975. Repr. of 1945 ed. lib. bdg. 35.00 (ISBN 0-306-70736-5). Da Capo.

Stein, Harry. Salem: A Pictorial History. (Illus.). 205p. 1981. pap. price not set (ISBN 0-89865-125-5). Donning Co.

--Southern Africa: Angola, Botswana, Lesotho, Malawi, Mozambique, Namibia, Republic of South Africa, Rhodesia, Swaziland, Zambia. LC 74-11391. (Illus.). 96p. (gr. 5 up). 1975. PLB 3.90 o.p. (ISBN 0-531-00823-1). Watts.

Stein, Herbert M., jt. auth. see Ernest, John.

Stein, Herman D., ed. Organization & the Human Services: Cross-Disciplinary Reflections. 275p. 1981. 17.50x (ISBN 0-87722-209-6). Temple U Pr.

Stein, Herman D. & Cloward, R. A., eds. Social Perspectives on Behavior. LC 57-12960. 1958. text ed. 12.25 o.s.i. (ISBN 0-02-930830-5). Free Pr.

Stein, Irving, jt. auth. see Starr, Martin K.

Stein, Jacob A. Damages & Recovery: Personal Injury & Death Actions. LC 72-91244. 1972. 47.50 (ISBN 0-686-14531-3). Lawyers Co-Op.

Stein, Janet, ed. Handbook of Phycological Methods. (Illus.). 512p. 1973. 44.95 (ISBN 0-521-20049-0); pap. 15.95 (ISBN 0-521-29747-8). Cambridge U Pr.

Stein, Janet see Prescott, David M.

Stein, Janice G. & Tanter, Raymond. Rational Decision-Making: Israel's Security Choices, 1967. LC 80-13589. 414p. 1980. 25.00 (ISBN 0-8142-0312-4). Ohio St U Pr.

Stein, Jay H., jt. auth. see Brenner, Barry M.

Stein, Jay H., jt. ed. see Brenner, Barry M.

Stein, Jay W. Mass Media, Education, & a Better Society. LC 79-11517. 1979. 16.95 (ISBN 0-88229-310-9). Nelson-Hall.

Stein, Jerome L. Money & Capacity Growth. LC 73-160844. 1971. 17.50x (ISBN 0-231-03372-9). Columbia U Pr.

Stein, Jerome L., jt. auth. see Borts, George H.

Stein, Jess, ed. The Random House Dictionary. (Orig.). 1981. pap. 2.25 (ISBN 0-345-29096-8). Ballantine.

Stein, Joseph. Making Life Meaningful. LC 78-15347. 1979. 12.95 (ISBN 0-88229-375-3); pap. 6.95 (ISBN 0-88229-651-5). Nelson-Hall.

Stein, Joseph, tr. see Gal, Hans.

Stein, Joshua B. C. G. Montefiore on the Ancient Rabbis: The Second Generation on Reform Judaism in Britain. LC 77-13194. (Brown University. Brown Judaic Studies: No. 4). 1977. pap. 6.00 (ISBN 0-89130-190-9, 140004). Scholars Pr Ca.

Stein, Judith, jt. auth. see Holcombe, Marya.

Stein, Laszlo K., et al. Deafness & Mental Health. 1981. write for info. (ISBN 0-8089-1347-6). Grune.

Stein, Leon, ed. see Welford, A. T. & Birren, James E.

Stein, M. L. Your Career in Journalism. rev ed. LC 77-28141. (Messner Career Ser.). (Illus.). 1978. PLB 7.79 o.p. (ISBN 0-671-32840-9). Messner.

Stein, Mark. Good & Bad Feelings. LC 75-28353. (Illus.). 96p. (gr. 3-7). 1976. 6.25 o.p. (ISBN 0-688-22061-4); PLB 6.48 (ISBN 0-688-32061-9). Morrow.

Stein, Mark L. The T Factor. 192p. 1981. pap. 2.25 o.p. (ISBN 0-87216-761-5). Playboy Pbks.

--The T Factor: How to Make Time Work for You. LC 76-17275. 1977. pap. 2.25 (ISBN 0-87216-761-5). Playboy Pbks.

Stein, Maurice R., et al, eds. Identity & Anxiety. LC 60-7091. 1965. pap. text ed. 6.95 o.s.i. (ISBN 0-02-930920-4). Free Pr.

Stein, Max. Love Story of a Jewish Cat. (Illus.). 1979. pap. 3.95 (ISBN 0-8467-0582-6, Pub. by Two Continents). Hippocrene Bks.

Stein, Morris I., ed. Contemporary Psychotherapies. LC 61-13969. 1961. 14.95 (ISBN 0-02-930990-5). Free Pr.

Stein, Murray, tr. see Kerenyi, Karl.

Stein, Norman, jt. auth. see Goldstein, Arnold P.

Stein, Peter. Single. 1976. pap. text ed. 2.95x (ISBN 0-13-810564-2, Spec). P-H.

Stein, Peter J., et al. The Family: Functions, Conflicts & Symbols. (Sociology Ser.). 1977. pap. text ed. 12.95 (ISBN 0-201-07362-5). A-W.

Stein, Philip G., jt. auth. see Abrams, Marshall D.

Stein, R. Incest & Human Love. LC 73-82641. 1973. 8.95 (ISBN 0-89388-090-6). Okpaku Communications.

Stein, R. B. Nerve & Muscle: Membranes, Cells & Systems. (Illus.). 250p. 1980. 18.95 (ISBN 0-306-40512-1, Plenum Pr). Plenum Pub.

Stein, R. J. see Ordway, Frederick I., 3rd.

Stein, Richard. The Flight of the Vin Fin: The Wondrous Adventures of C.P. Rodgers & His Aero Machine in the Grand Coast-to-Coast 50,000 Dollar Race. LC 79-51432. (Illus.). 1979. 10.95 o.p. (ISBN 0-8129-0839-2, Dist. by Har-Row). Times Bks.

Stein, Rita, et al, eds. Major Modern Dramatists, 2 vols. LC 78-4310. (Library of Literary Criticism). 1100p. 1980. 65.00 (ISBN 0-8044-3270-8). Ungar.

Stein, Robert A. In Pursuit of Excellence. (Illus.). 545p. 1980. 24.50 (ISBN 0-917126-13-0). Mason Pub.

Stein, Robert A., ed. Stein on Probate, 2 vols. 1976. Set. text ed. 155.00 (ISBN 0-917126-14-9); Vol. I, 477 Pgs. text ed. 45.00 (ISBN 0-917126-15-7); Vol. II, 658 Pgs. text ed. 45.00 (ISBN 0-917126-16-5); Supplement, 523 Pgs. looseleaf text 35.00 (ISBN 0-917126-17-3); Supplement, 43 Pgs. looseleaf pgs. 15.00 (ISBN 0-917126-18-1). Mason Pub.

Stein, Robert E. & Johnson, Brian. Banking on the Biosphere? 1979. 22.95 (ISBN 0-669-02734-0). Lexington Bks.

Stein, Rose, tr. see Hajdu, Victor.

Stein, Sara. The Kids' Kitchen Takeover. LC 75-20382. (Parents & Children Together Ser.). (Illus.). 208p. (gr. 4 up). 1975. 9.95 (ISBN 0-911104-45-3); pap. 5.95 (ISBN 0-911104-46-1). Workman Pub.

Stein, Sherman & Crabill, Calvin. Elementary Algebra: A Guided Inquiry. LC 78-179131. 96p. (Orig.). 1972. text ed. 17.50 (ISBN 0-395-12669-X); instr. ed. 18.95 (ISBN 0-395-12670-3); solution key. pap. 2.15 (ISBN 0-395-13756-X). HM.

Stein, Sherman K. Mathematics, the Man-Made Universe: An Introduction to the Spirit of Mathematics. 3rd ed. LC 75-25950. (Mathematics Ser.). (Illus.). 1976. text ed. 19.95x (ISBN 0-7167-0465-X); tchrs manual avail. W H Freeman.

Stein, Sherman K. & Crabill, Calvin D. Algebra II - Trigonometry: Final Preliminary Edition. (Illus.). (gr. 11-12). 1976. text ed. 11.95x (ISBN 0-7167-0469-2); solutions key avail. (ISBN 0-685-65024-3). W H Freeman.

Stein, Stanley J. Vassouras: A Brazilian Coffee County, 1850-1900. LC 57-8627. (Studies in American Negro Life). 1970. pap. 5.95x (ISBN 0-689-70229-9, NL23). Atheneum.

Stein, Stanley J., jt. ed. see Cortes Conde, Roberto.

Stein, Steve. Populism in Peru: The Emergence of the Masses & the Politics of Social Control. LC 79-5415. (Illus.). 300p. 1980. 21.50 (ISBN 0-299-07990-2). U of Wis Pr.

Stein, Theodore J., et al. Children in Foster Homes: Achieving Continuity of Care. LC 78-16927. 1978. 28.95 (ISBN 0-03-046421-8). Praeger.

Stein, Vivian. Batik As a Hobby. LC 69-19491. (Illus.). (gr. 9 up). 1969. 6.95 o.p. (ISBN 0-8069-5132-X); PLB 6.69 o.p. (ISBN 0-8069-5133-8). Sterling.

Stein, Walter. Criticism As Dialogue. LC 69-12929. 1969. 42.00 (ISBN 0-521-07439-8). Cambridge U Pr.

Stein, William B., ed. Two Brahman Sources of Emerson & Thoreau, 1822-1832. LC 67-10340. 1967. 33.00x (ISBN 0-8201-1043-4). Schol Facsimiles.

Steinaker, Norman & Bell, M. Robert. The Experiential Taxonomy: A New Approach to Teaching & Learning. LC 79-1141. (Educational Psychology Ser.). 1979. 15.00 o.s.i. (ISBN 0-12-665550-2). Acad Pr.

Steinbeck, John. In Dubious Battle. 1979. pap. 2.95 (ISBN 0-14-004888-X). Penguin.

--Of Mice & Men. 1937. 9.95 (ISBN 0-670-52071-3); large type ed. 6.50 (ISBN 0-670-52073-X, LT1). Viking Pr.

--Portable Steinbeck. 2nd ed. Covici, Pascal, Jr., ed. (Portable Library: No. 2). 1971. 14.95 (ISBN 0-670-66960-1). Viking Pr.

Steinbeck, John & Ricketts, Edward F. Sea of Cortez: A Leisurely Journal of Travel & Research. (Illus.). 640p. Repr. of 1941 ed. 22.50 o.s.i. (ISBN 0-911858-08-3). Appel.

Steinberg, Alfred. The Bosses. 384p. 1974. pap. 1.95 o.p. (ISBN 0-451-61293-0, MJ1293, Ment). NAL.

Steinberg, Arnold. The Political Campaign Handbook. LC 75-43130. 1976. 21.95 (ISBN 0-669-00481-2). Lexington Bks.

--Political Campaign Management: A Systems Approach. LC 75-36014. 320p. 1976. 23.95 (ISBN 0-669-00374-3). Lexington Bks.

Steinberg, Arthur G. & Cook, Charles E. The Distribution of the Human Immunoglobulin Allotypes. (Illus.). 272p. 1981. text ed. 65.00x (ISBN 0-19-261181-X). Oxford U Pr.

Steinberg, Authur G., et al, eds. Progress in Medical Genetics, Vol. 4. (Genetics of Gastrointestinal Disease Ser.). (Illus.). 320p. 1980. text ed. 39.50 (ISBN 0-7216-8604-4). Saunders.

Steinberg, C. M. & Lefkovits, I., eds. The Immune System: Festschrift in Honor of Niels Kaj Jerne, on the Occasion of His 70th Birthday, Vol. 1. (Illus.). x, 390p. 1981. 118.75 (ISBN 3-8055-3407-8). S Karger.

--The Immune System: Festschrift in Honor of Niels Kaj Jerne, on the Occasion of His 70th Birthday, 2 vols, Vols. 1 & 2. (Illus.). xx, 780p. 1981. 237.50 set (ISBN 3-8055-3409-4). S Karger.

--The Immune System: Festschrift in Honor of Neils Kaj Jerne, on the Occasion of His 70th Birthday, Vol. 2. (Illus.). x, 390p. 1981. 118.75 (ISBN 3-8055-3408-6). S Karger.

Steinberg, Charles S., ed. Mass Media & Communication. 2nd rev. & enl. ed. (Studies in Public Communication). 650p. 1972. 14.00 o.s.i. (ISBN 0-8038-4664-9); pap. text ed. 8.50x (ISBN 0-8038-4663-0). Hastings.

Steinberg, Cobbett. Film Facts. 350p. 1980. 17.95 (ISBN 0-87196-313-2). Facts on File.

--TV Facts. 1980. 17.95 (ISBN 0-87196-312-4). Facts on File.

Steinberg, D. D. & Jakobovits, L. A. Semantics: An Interdisciplinary Reader in Philosophy, Linguistics & Psychology. LC 78-123675. (Illus.). 1971. 49.50 (ISBN 0-521-07822-9); pap. 14.95x (ISBN 0-521-20499-2). Cambridge U Pr.

Steinberg, Dave S. Cooling Techniques for Electronic Equipment. LC 80-14141. 425p. 1980. 26.50 (ISBN 0-471-04403-2, Pub. by Wiley Interscience). Wiley.

Steinberg, David J., et al. In Search of Southeast Asia: A Modern History. LC 70-121850. (Illus.). 522p. 1971. pap. 9.95x (ISBN 0-275-88390-6). Praeger.

Steinberg, Eleanor B. & Yager, Joseph A. New Means of Financing International Needs. LC 77-21275. 1978. 14.95 (ISBN 0-8157-8116-4); pap. 5.95 (ISBN 0-8157-8115-6). Brookings.

Steinberg, Erwin, jt. ed. see Gregg, Lee W.

Steinberg, Erwin R., jt. ed. see Schutte, William M.

Steinberg, Ffranz U. The Immobilized Patient. LC 79-25903. (Topics in Bone & Mineral Disorders Ser.). (Illus.). 160p. 1980. 16.50 (ISBN 0-306-40372-2, Plenum Pr). Plenum Pub.

Steinberg, H. Organoboron Chemistry, Vol. 1, Boron-Oxygen & Boron-Sulfur Compounds. LC 62-20337. 1964. 66.95 (ISBN 0-470-82093-4, Pub. by Wiley-Interscience). Wiley.

Steinberg, H. & McCloskey, A. L., eds. Progress in Boron Chemistry, 3 vols. LC 64-13501. Vol. 1, 1964. 62.00 (ISBN 0-08-010619-6); Vol. 2, 1970. 62.00 (ISBN 0-08-013079-8); Vol. 3, 1970. 62.00 (ISBN 0-08-013080-1). Pergamon.

Steinberg, Howard J., jt. auth. see Sack, Steven M.

Steinberg, Ira. Behaviorism & Schooling. 1980. 20.00 (ISBN 0-312-07253-8). St Martin.

Steinberg, J. Why Switzerland? LC 75-36024. (Illus.). 224p. 1976. 23.50 (ISBN 0-521-21139-5). Cambridge U Pr.

--Why Switzerland? LC 75-36024. (Illus.). 225p. 1981. pap. 9.50 (ISBN 0-521-28144-X). Cambridge U Pr.

Steinberg, J. Leonard & McEvoy, Donald, eds. The Police & the Behavioral Sciences. 176p. 1974. text ed. 16.75 (ISBN 0-398-02957-1). C C Thomas.

Steinberg, Jean, tr. see Bracher, Karl D.

Steinberg, Jean, tr. see Doerner, Klaus.

Steinberg, Jean, tr. see Hankel, Wilhelm.

Steinberg, Jules. Locke, Rousseau, & the Idea of Consent: An Inquiry into the Liberal-Democratic Theory of Political Obligation. LC 77-91094. (Contributions in Political Science: No. 6). 1978. lib. bdg. 16.50 (ISBN 0-313-20052-1, SLR/). Greenwood.

Steinberg, Leo. Borromini's San Carlo Alle Quattro Fontane: A Study in Multiple Form & Architectural Symbolism. LC 75-23815. (Outstanding Dissertations in the Fine Arts - 17th Century). (Illus.). 1976. lib. bdg. 41.00 (ISBN 0-8240-2008-1). Garland Pub.

Steinberg, Milton. Basic Judaism. LC 47-30768. (Modern Classic Ser.). 5.95 o.p. (ISBN 0-15-110697-5). HarBraceJ.

--A Partisan Guide to the Jewish Problem. (Return to Zion Ser.). 308p. 1980. Repr. of 1945 ed. lib. bdg. 20.00x (ISBN 0-87991-135-2). Porcupine Pr.

Steinberg, Peter, jt. auth. see Cantu, Connie.

Steinberg, Peter, jt. auth. see Vargoshe, Richard.

Steinberg, Rafael. Cooking of Japan. LC 75-84632. (Foods of the World Ser.). (Illus.). (gr. 6 up). 1969. PLB 14.94 (ISBN 0-8094-0067-7, Pub. by Time-Life). Silver.

--Cooking of Japan. (Foods of the World Ser.). (Illus.). 1969. 14.95 (ISBN 0-8094-0040-5). Time-Life.

--Island Fighting. LC 78-52847. (World War II Ser.). (Illus.). 1978. lib. bdg. 14.94 (ISBN 0-686-51047-X). Silver.

--Man & the Organization. (Human Behavior Ser). 176p. 1975. 9.95 (ISBN 0-8094-1912-2); lib. bdg. avail. (ISBN 0-685-52490-6). Time-Life.

--Pacific & Southeast Asian Cooking. (Foods of the World Ser). (Illus.). 1970. 14.95 (ISBN 0-8094-0045-6). Time-Life.

--Pacific & Southeast Asian Cooking. LC 70-114231. (Foods of the World Ser.). (Illus.). (gr. 6 up). 1970. PLB 14.94 (ISBN 0-8094-0072-3, Pub. by Time-Life). Silver.

--Return to the Philippines. (World War II Ser.). (Illus.). 1979. lib. bdg. 14.94 (ISBN 0-686-51052-6). Silver.

Steinberg, Rafael & Time-Life Books Editors. Island Fighting. (World War II Ser.). 1978. 12.95 (ISBN 0-8094-2486-X). Time-Life.

Steinberg, Rafael, jt. auth. see Javits, Jacob K.

Steinberg, Raphael. Man & the Organization. LC 74-23044. (Human Behavior Ser.). (Illus.). 176p. (gr. 5 up). 1975. PLB 9.99 o.p. (ISBN 0-8094-1913-0). Silver.

Steinberg, S. A Fairy Tale. 1981. pap. 2.50 (ISBN 0-440-10181-6). Dell.

Steinberg, Samuel. Seven Against Odds: Shapers of Our Democratic Heritage. Date not set. 7.95 (ISBN 0-533-04639-4). Vantage.

Steinberg, Sigfrid H. Thirty Years' War. (Foundations of Modern History Series). (Illus.). 1967. pap. 3.95x (ISBN 0-393-09752-8, NortonC). Norton.

Steinberg, Stephen. The Ethnic Myth: Race, Ethnicity & Class in America. LC 80-69377. 1981. 12.95 (ISBN 0-689-11151-7). Atheneum.

Steinberg, Stephen, ed. see Carnegie Commission on Higher Education.

Steinberg, Theodore L. Mendele Mocher Seforim. (World Authors Ser.: Yiddish: No. 405). 1977. lib. bdg. 12.50 (ISBN 0-8057-6308-2). Twayne.

Steinberger, Anna & Steinberger, Emil, eds. Testicular Development. 1979. text ed. 56.00 (ISBN 0-89004-397-3). Raven.

Steinberger, Emil, jt. ed. see Steinberger, Anna.

Steinberger, G. In the Footprints of the Lamb. Christensen, Bernard, tr. LC 78-73416. 1979. pap. 1.95 (ISBN 0-87123-237-5, 200237). Bethany Fell.

Steinbock, B. Killing & Letting Die. 239p. 1980. pap. 9.00 (ISBN 0-13-515361-1). P-H.

Steinbock, R. Ted. Paleopathological Diagnosis & Interpretation: Bone Diseases in Ancient Human Populations. (Illus.). 440p. 1976. 30.50 (ISBN 0-398-03512-1). C C Thomas.

Steinbruckner, Bruno F. Ludwig Thoma. (World Authors Ser.: No. 494). 1978. lib. bdg. 14.95 (ISBN 0-8057-6335-X). Twayne.

Steinbrueck, Victor. Market Sketchbook. LC 68-8513. (Illus.). 192p. 1968. limited ed. 100.00 (ISBN 0-295-95665-8); pap. 7.95 (ISBN 0-295-95631-3). U of Wash Pr.

Steinbrunner, Chris & Michaels, Norman. The Films of Sherlock Holmes. 1980. pap. 9.95 (ISBN 0-8065-0739-X). Lyle Stuart.

Steinburg, Sheldon, jt. auth. see Heptner, Angelo M.

Steindl, Josef. Random Processes & the Growth of Firms. 1965. 22.00 (ISBN 0-02-852950-2). Hafner.

Steindler, Arthur. Kinesiology: Of the Human Body Under Normal & Pathological Conditions. (Illus.). 736p. 1977. 33.75 (ISBN 0-398-01846-4). C C Thomas.

--Lectures on the Interpretation of Pain in Orthopedic Practice. (Illus.). 680p. 1959. pap. 34.75 spiral (ISBN 0-398-01847-2). C C Thomas.

Steindler, Geraldine. Game Cookbook. 1965. pap. 5.95 o.p. (ISBN 0-695-87906-5). Follett.

Steiner, Barry. Payless Tax Legally-1980: Edition for 1979 Tax Return. (Orig.). 1980. pap. cancelled o.p. (ISBN 0-451-82058-4, XE2058, Sig). NAL.

Steiner, Barry R. Pay Less Tax Legally: 1981 Edition. (Orig.). 1980. pap. 3.95 (ISBN 0-451-09522-7, E9522, Sig). NAL.

Steiner, Bradley. The Techniques & Psychology of Disarming for Law Enforcement Personnel. (Illus.). 248p. 1980. write for info. o.p. (ISBN 0-398-04039-7). C C Thomas.

Steiner, Bradley J. Subway Survival: The Art of Self Defense on American Public Transit Facility. 1980. pap. 7.95. Loompanics.

Steiner, Bruce E. Samuel Seabury, 1729-1796: A Study in the High Church Tradition. LC 78-181686. (Illus.). xiii, 508p. 1971. 17.50x (ISBN 0-8214-0098-3). Ohio U Pr.

Steiner, C., jt. auth. see Berne, Eric.

Steiner, Charles V., Jr. & Davis, Richard B. Caged Bird Medicine. (Illus.). 176p. 1981. pap. text ed. 17.50 (ISBN 0-8138-1715-3). Iowa St U Pr.

Steiner, Claude. Games Alcoholics Play. 1977. pap. 2.50 (ISBN 0-345-28470-4). Ballantine.

--The Other Side of Power. LC 80-8921. 192p. 1981. 16.50 (ISBN 0-394-51950-7, Ever); pap. 6.95 (ISBN 0-394-17926-9). Grove.

Steiner, Claude M. Healing Alcoholism. LC 79-2320. 208p. 1981. pap. 3.95 (ISBN 0-394-17923-4, BC). Grove.

--Scripts People Live. 1974. 8.95 (ISBN 0-394-49267-6, GP7480). Grove.

Steiner, Dale R., ed. Historical Journals: A Handbook for Writers & Reviewers. 1981. price not set (ISBN 0-87436-312-8). ABC-Clio.

Steiner, Dorothea. William Wordsworth und Die Romantische Paradieseskonzeption. (Salzburg Studies in English Literature, Romantic Reassessment: No.31). 1973. pap. text ed. 25.00x (ISBN 0-391-01532-X). Humanities.

Steiner, Dorothea, jt. auth. see Stokes, Penelope J.

Steiner, E. Determination & Interpretaion of Molecular Wave Functions. LC 75-78120. (Monographs in Physical Chemistry: No. 3). 250p. 1976. 44.50 (ISBN 0-521-21037-2). Cambridge U Pr.

Steiner, Elizabeth. Logical & Conceptual Analytic Techniques for Educational Researchers. LC 77-18575. 1978. pap. text ed. 5.75x (ISBN 0-8191-0406-X). U Pr of Amer.

Steiner, Frederick. The Politics of New Town Planning: The Newfields, Ohio, Story. LC 80-12783. (Illus.). xiv, 266p. 1981. 16.95 (ISBN 0-8214-0414-8, 0414E). Ohio U Pr.

Steiner, George. After Babel: Aspects of Language & Translation. 512p. 1975. 27.50 (ISBN 0-19-212196-0). Oxford U Pr.

--Anno Domini. LC 80-15345. 205p. 1980. Repr. of 1964 ed. 10.95 (ISBN 0-87951-113-3). Overlook Pr.

--Death of Tragedy. 1963. 13.95 (ISBN 0-571-05467-6, Pub. by Faber & Faber); pap. 8.95 (ISBN 0-571-05658-X). Merrimack Bk Serv.

--On Difficulty & Other Essays. 224p. 1980. pap. 3.95 (ISBN 0-19-520222-8, G-B613). Oxford U Pr.

Steiner, George & Lawrence, Patricia A. Educating Diabetic Patients. 1981. text ed. price not set (ISBN 0-8261-2760-6); pap. text ed. price not set (ISBN 0-8261-2761-4). Springer Pub.

Steiner, George A. Strategic Planning: What Every Manager Must Know. LC 78-20647. (Illus.). 1979. 14.95 (ISBN 0-02-931110-1). Free Pr.

Steiner, Gerald M. Home for Sale by Owner. LC 77-85358. (Illus.). 1978. pap. 8.95 (ISBN 0-8015-3529-8, Hawthorn). Dutton.

Steiner, Gilbert Y. The Children's Cause. 1976. 14.95 (ISBN 0-8157-8120-2); pap. 5.95 (ISBN 0-8157-8119-9). Brookings.

--The Futility of Family Policy. 250p. 1981. 15.95 (ISBN 0-8157-8124-5); pap. 5.95 (ISBN 0-8157-8123-7). Brookings.

--The State of Welfare. 1971. 14.95 (ISBN 0-8157-8122-9); pap. 5.95 (ISBN 0-8157-8121-0). Brookings.

Steiner, Henry M. Conflict in Urban Transportation. LC 78-2070. (Illus.). 1978. 15.95 (ISBN 0-669-02268-3). Lexington Bks.

Steiner, Irene H. The Year Growing Ancient. LC 77-16748. Date not set. cancelled (ISBN 0-312-89619-0). St Martin.

Steiner, Ivan D. Group Processes & Productivity. (Social Psychology Ser). 1972. 14.50 (ISBN 0-12-665350-X). Acad Pr.

Steiner, Joerg. Ein Messer Fuer Den Ehrlichen Finder. (Suhrkamp Taschenbuecher: 583). 208p. (Ger.). 1980. pap. text ed. 3.90 (ISBN 3-518-37083-9, Pub. by Insel Verlag Germany). Suhrkamp.

Steiner, Kurt, et al, eds. Political Opposition & Local Politics in Japan. LC 80-7555. 480p. 1980. 30.00 (ISBN 0-691-07625-1); pap. 9.95 (ISBN 0-691-10109-4). Princeton U Pr.

Steiner, Louis A. The Complete Diamond Book. (Illus.). 296p. 1981. cancelled 10.95 (ISBN 0-89961-015-3). SBS Pub.

Steiner, Ludwig, ed. Fibonacci's Secret Discoveries into the Occult Power of Numbers. (Illus.). 1979. 57.50 (ISBN 0-89266-150-X). Am Classical Coll Pr.

Steiner, M. E., jt. auth. see Harrower, M. R.

Steiner, Mark. Philosophy: Advanced Test for the G. R. E. LC 66-28209. (Orig.). 1966. lib. bdg. 5.50 o. p. (ISBN 0-668-01574-8); pap. 4.95 (ISBN 0-668-01472-5). Arco.

Steiner, Nancy H. Closer Look at Ariel. 128p. 1974. pap. 1.50 o.p. (ISBN 0-445-03020-8). Popular Lib.

Steiner, Ralph. A Point of View. LC 77-20513. (Illus.). 1978. 29.95 (ISBN 0-8195-5019-1, Pub. by Wesleyan U Pr); ltd. ed. o.p. 150.00 (ISBN 0-8195-8037-6). Columbia U Pr.

Steiner, Richard. Managing the Human Service Organization: From Survival to Achievement. LC 77-2150. (Sourcebooks for Improving Human Services: Vol. 1). (Illus.). 1977. 18.00x (ISBN 0-8039-0850-4); pap. 8.95x (ISBN 0-8039-8050-7). Sage.

Steiner, Robert. Passion. Peich, Michael, ed. (Penmaen Fiction Ser.: No. 2). 1980. 12.00 (ISBN 0-915778-33-5); ltd. signed ed. 40.00x (ISBN 0-915778-32-7). Penmaen Pr.

Steiner, Robert, et al. Chemistry of Living Systems. 1981. text ed. write for info. (ISBN 0-442-20052-8). D Van Nostrand.

Steiner, Rodney. Los Angeles: The Centrifugal City. 224p. 1981. pap. text ed. 12.95 (ISBN 0-8403-2333-6). Kendall-Hunt.

Steiner, Rodney, ed. Yearbook of the Association of Pacific Coast Geographers, Vol. 37, 1975. (Illus.). 144p. 1975. pap. 5.00 (ISBN 0-686-65495-1). Oreg St U Pr.

Steiner, Roger J. The New College French & English Dictionary. (gr. 7-12). 1972. pap. text ed. 7.17 (ISBN 0-87720-463-2). AMSCO Sch.

Steiner, Rudolf. An Autobiography. (Spiritual Science Library). (Illus.). 560p. 1980. 18.00x (ISBN 0-8334-0757-0). Multimedia.

--Background to the Gospel of St. Mark. 1968. 9.75 o.p. (ISBN 0-85440-191-1). Anthroposophic.

--Christianity & Occult Mysteries of Antiquity. LC 72-175057. (Illus.). 256p. 1972. pap. 6.95 (ISBN 0-8334-1719-3). Steinerbks.

--Christianity As Mystical Fact & the Mysteries of Antiquity. 1972. 9.75 (ISBN 0-85440-252-7); pap. 6.95 (ISBN 0-910142-04-1). Anthroposophic.

--Education As a Social Problem. LC 70-83525. 1969. 5.95 o.p. (ISBN 0-910142-08-4). Anthroposophic.

--Education As an Art. (Spiritual Science Library). 128p. 1980. 10.00x (ISBN 0-8334-0707-4); pap. 4.50 (ISBN 0-8334-1707-X). Steinerbks.

--Human Values in Education. 190p. 1971. 9.75 o.p. (ISBN 0-85440-250-0). Anthroposophic.

--Karmic Relationships, 8 vols. Incl. Vol. 1. o.p. (ISBN 0-685-36127-6); Vol. 2. 12.50 (ISBN 0-685-36128-4); Vol. 3. 9.75 (ISBN 0-685-36129-2); Vol. 4. o.p. (ISBN 0-685-36130-6); Vol. 5. o.p. (ISBN 0-685-36131-4); Vol. 6. 9.75 (ISBN 0-685-36132-2); Vol. 7. 8.50 (ISBN 0-685-36133-0); Vol. 8. 8.50 (ISBN 0-685-36134-9). Anthroposophic.

--The Kingdom of Childhood. 160p. 1974. 9.75 o.p. (ISBN 0-85440-058-3). Anthroposophic.

--Mystery Dramas, 4 vols. in 1. 1973. pap. 16.50 (ISBN 0-919924-08-5). Anthroposophic.

--Mysticism at the Dawn of the Modern. (Spiritual Science Library). 256p. 1980. 12.00x (ISBN 0-8334-0753-8); pap. 6.95 (ISBN 0-8334-1786-X). Steinerbks.

--Outline of Occult Science. 352p. 1972. 9.95 (ISBN 0-910142-26-2); pap. 5.50 (ISBN 0-910142-75-0). Anthroposophic.

--Philosophy of Spiritual Activity. (Spiritual Science Library). 304p. 1980. 13.00x (ISBN 0-8334-0728-7); pap. 6.95 (ISBN 0-8334-1786-X). Steinerbks.

--Reincarnation & Immortality. LC 79-3592. (Harper Library of Spiritual Wisdom). 208p. 1980. pap. 5.95 (ISBN 0-06-067571-3, RD 404). Har-Row.

--The Theory of Knowledge Implicit in Goethe's World Conception. 2nd ed. Wannamaker, Olin D., tr. from Ger. LC 70-76994. Orig. Title: Grundlinien Einer Erkenntnistheorie der Goetheschen Weltanschauung. 133p. 1978. 6.95 (ISBN 0-910142-94-7); pap. 3.95 (ISBN 0-910142-85-8). Anthroposophic.

--Threefold Social Order. rev. ed. Heckel, Frederick C., ed. LC 66-29676. Orig. Title: Threefold Commonwealth. (Orig.). 1966. pap. 3.50 o.p. (ISBN 0-910142-40-8). Anthroposophic.

--Waldorf Education for Adolescence. 1980. pap. 9.50x (ISBN 0-906492-37-8, Pub. by Kolisko Archives). St George Bk Serv.

--World History in the Light of Anthroposophy. new ed. Adams, George & Adams, Mary, trs. from Ger. 1978. pap. 5.50 o.p. (ISBN 0-85440-316-7). Anthroposophic.

Steiner, Stan. The Islands: The Worlds of the Puerto Ricans. LC 72-9157. (Illus.). 448p. (YA) 1974. 12.50 o.s.i. (ISBN 0-06-014079-8, HarpT). Har-Row.

--The Ranchers: A Book of Generations. LC 80-7646. (Illus.). 224p. 1980. 13.95 (ISBN 0-394-50193-4). Knopf.

--La Raza: The Mexican Americans. LC 77-83622. (Illus.). 1970. 12.50 o.p. (ISBN 0-06-014083-6, HarpT). Har-Row.

--The Tiguas: The Lost Tribe of City Indians. LC 77-189728. (Illus.). (gr. 5up). 1972. 4.95g o.s.i. (ISBN 0-02-787900-3, CCPr). Macmillan.

Steiner, Stan & Valdez, Luis, eds. Aztlan: An Anthology of Mexican-American Literature. 416p. Date not set. pap. 3.45 (ISBN 0-394-71770-8, Vin). Random.

Steiner, Stan, jt. ed. see Babin, Maria T.

Steiner, T. R. English Transition Theory, Sixteen Fifty to Eighteen Hundred. (Approaches to Translation Studies: No. 2). 159p. (Orig.). 1976. pap. text ed. 23.00x (ISBN 90-232-1276-2). Humanities.

Steiner, Wendy, ed. The Sign in Music & Literature. (Illus.). 264p. 1981. text ed. 25.00x (ISBN 0-292-77563-6). U of Tex Pr.

Steiner, Zara. Britain & the Origins of the First World War. LC 76-55861. (Making of the Twentieth Century Ser). 160p. 1978. 16.95x (ISBN 0-312-09818-9); pap. 6.95 (ISBN 0-312-09819-7). St Martin.

Steiner, Zara S. Foreign Office & Foreign Policy 1898-1914. LC 70-85739. (Illus.). 1970. 37.50 (ISBN 0-521-07654-4). Cambridge U Pr.

Steinfatt, Thomas. Human Communication: An Interpersonal Introduction. LC 76-18065. 1977. pap. 9.95 (ISBN 0-672-61359-X). Bobbs.

Steinfeld, Jeffrey I., ed. Laser-Induced Chemical Processes. 255p. 1981. 32.50 (ISBN 0-306-40587-3, Plenum Pr). Plenum Pub.

Steinfeld, Otto. Quasi-Ideals in Rings & Semi-Groups. LC 79-308570. (Illus.). 154p. 1978. 17.50x (ISBN 963-05-1696-9). Intl Pubns Serv.

Steinfels, Peter. The Neo-Conservatives. 1980. 5.95 (ISBN 0-686-62897-7, 41384, Touchstone). S&S.

Steinfield, M. Cracks in the Melting Pot. 2nd ed. 1973. pap. 7.95x (ISBN 0-02-478670-5, 47867). Macmillan.

Steinforth, Alex. Employee Benefits: A Guide for Hospitals. LC 80-12159. 124p. 1980. 22.50 (ISBN 0-89443-290-7). Aspen Systems.

Steingass, David. Body Compass. LC 76-78534. (Pitt Poetry Ser). 1969. 7.95 o.p. (ISBN 0-8229-3180-X); pap. 3.95 o.p. (ISBN 0-8229-5209-2). U of Pittsburgh Pr.

Steingass, F. Arabic-English Learners Dictionary. 1972. 30.00 (ISBN 0-685-77126-1). Intl Bk Ctr.

--A Comprehensive Persian-English Dictionary: Including the Arabic Words & Phrases to Be Met with in Persian Literature. 1977. 65.00 (ISBN 0-7100-2152-6). Routledge & Kegan.

--Comprehensive Persian-English Dictionary. 1975. 60.00x (ISBN 0-685-77128-8). Intl Bk Ctr.

--English-Arabic Learner's Dictionary. 1972. 18.00x (ISBN 0-685-77127-X). Intl Bk Ctr.

Steingraber, Jack. FORTRAN Fundamentals: A Short Course. (Computer Programming Ser.). (Illus.). 96p. 1975. pap. text ed. 5.95 (ISBN 0-8104-5860-8). Hayden.

Steinhardt, F., tr. see Laugwitz, D.

Steinhauer, Harry, ed. Das Deutsche Drama, Vol. 2. 1939. 6.95x (ISBN 0-393-09435-9, NortonC). Norton.

--Die Deutsche Novelle, 1880-1950. expanded ed. 1958. 7.50x o.p. (ISBN 0-393-09515-0, NortonC). Norton.

Steinhauer, Harry, tr. Twelve German Novellas. (Campus Ser.). 1977. 22.75x (ISBN 0-520-03002-8); pap. 8.95x (ISBN 0-520-03504-6). U of Cal Pr.

Steinhauer, Harry, tr. see Von Goethe, Johann W.

Steinhauer, Kurt, ed. Hegel: Bibliography. 894p. 1980. 129.50 (ISBN 3-598-03184-X). Bowker.

Steinhauer, Raleigh F. Fundamentals of Business Policy. 1978. pap. text ed. 7.50 (ISBN 0-8191-0370-5). U Pr of Amer.

Steinhaus, Edward A., ed. Insect Pathology: An Advanced Treatise, 2 Vols. 1963. 55.25 ea. Vol. 1 (ISBN 0-12-665801-3). Vol. 2. (ISBN 0-12-665802-1). Acad Pr.

Steinhaus, Hugo. Mathematical Snapshots. 3rd ed. (Illus.). 1969. 15.95 (ISBN 0-19-500117-6). Oxford U Pr.

Steinhilber, R. M. & Ulett, G. A., eds. Psychiatric Research in Public Service. 166p. 1962. pap. 3.00 (ISBN 0-685-24862-3, P015-0). Am Psychiatric.

Steinhoff, Carl R., jt. auth. see Owens, Robert G.

Steinhoff, Ernst A., ed. Organizing Space Activities for World Needs. 1971. 67.00 (ISBN 0-08-006851-0). Pergamon.

Steinhoff, Manfred. Prestige & Profit: The Development of Entrepreneurial Abilities in Taiwan 1880-1972. (Development Studies Centre Monograph: No. 20). (Illus.). 153p. (Orig.). 1980. pap. text ed. 11.95 (ISBN 0-909150-94-X, 0588). Bks Australia.

Steinhoff, William. George Orwell & the Origins of 1984. LC 74-78989. 1975. 12.50 o.p. (ISBN 0-472-87400-4); pap. 6.50x (ISBN 0-472-08802-5). U of Mich Pr.

Steinike, Otto A. Blueprint Reading, Checking & Testing, 2 Pts. 3rd ed. (Illus.). (gr. 9-10). 1956. Pt. 1. pap. text ed. 4.60 (ISBN 0-87345-080-9); Pt. 2. text ed. 3.96 s.p. (ISBN 0-87345-082-5). McKnight.

Steinitz, Ernst. Algebraische Theorie der Koerper. LC 51-10623. 1976. text ed. 9.95 (ISBN 0-8284-0077-6). Chelsea Pub.

Steinitz, Kate T. Kurt Schwitters: A Portrait from Life. 1968. 19.50x (ISBN 0-520-01219-4). U of Cal Pr.

Steinitz, Lucy Y. Living After the Holocaust: Reflections by the Post-War Generation in America. Szonyi, David M., ed. LC 76-8322. (Illus.). 1976. 6.95x; pap. 4.95 (ISBN 0-8197-0016-9). Bloch.

Steinke, Don C. Thirty Days to Metric Mastery: For People Who Hate Math. (Illus., Orig.). 1981. pap. 9.00x (ISBN 0-9605344-0-7). Hse of Charles.

Steinke, Peter. With Eyes Wide Open. LC 74-3735. 1974. pap. 2.50 (ISBN 0-570-03180-X, 12-2583). Concordia.

Steinkirchner, Albert V. Self Psychotherapy, Vol. 1. LC 75-760. 159p. 1974. 9.95 (ISBN 0-915352-00-1); pap. 4.95 (ISBN 0-915352-01-X). Aquin Pub.

Steinkoler, Ronnie. A Jewish Cookbook for Children. LC 80-17428. (Illus.). 96p. (gr. 4-7). 1980. PLB 7.79 (ISBN 0-671-33093-4). Messner.

Steinkraus, Warren E., jt. ed. see Beck, Robert N.

Steinkraus, William & Savitt, Sam. Great Horses of the U. S. Equestrian Team. LC 76-53434. (gr. 5 up). 1977. 6.95 (ISBN 0-396-07432-4). Dodd.

Steinkuehler, Pearl, jt. auth. see Nordtvedt, Matilda.

Steinlage, Ralph. College Algebra & Trigonometry. 1981. text ed. write for info. (ISBN 0-8302-1640-5). Goodyear.

Steinle, Paul, jt. auth. see Printz, Peggy.

Steinlen, Theophile-Alexandre. Steinlen Cats. (Illus.). 48p. 1980. pap. 2.00 (ISBN 0-486-23950-0). Dover.

--Steinlen's Lithographs: One Hundred Twenty-One Plates from "Gil Blas Illustre". (Illus.). 128p. 1980. pap. 6.50 (ISBN 0-486-23943-8). Dover.

Steinman, D. B. Songs of a Bridge Builder. 12.00 (ISBN 0-88253-762-8); flexible cloth 4.80 (ISBN 0-88253-761-X). Ind-US Inc.

Steinman, Michael. Energy & Environmental Issues: The Making & Implementation of Public Policy Issues. LC 78-13871. 224p. 1979. 19.95 (ISBN 0-669-02699-9). Lexington Bks.

Steinmetz, Alexander. Sea of Process. 1975. 5.00 o.p. (ISBN 0-87482-043-X). Wake-Brook.

Steinmetz, Charles P. Lectures in Electrical Engineering, Vol. 2, Electric Waves & Impulses. LC 70-137004. 1971. pap. text ed. 5.00 (ISBN 0-486-62515-X). Dover.

--Lectures in Electrical Engineering, Vol. 3. LC 70-137004. 1971. pap. text ed. 5.00 (ISBN 0-486-62516-8). Dover.

--Lectures on Electrical Engineering, Vol. 1, Elements Of Electrical Engineering. LC 70-137004. 1971. pap. text ed. 5.00 (ISBN 0-486-62514-1). Dover.

Steinmetz, David C. Luther & Staupitz: An Essay in the Intellectual Origins of the Protestant Reformation. LC 80-23007. (Duke Monographs in Medieval & Renaissance Studies: No. 4). 1981. 16.75 (ISBN 0-8223-0447-3). Duke.

Steinmetz, Ferdinand H., jt. auth. see Hyland, Fay.

Steinmetz, Lawrence L. Art & Skill of Delegation. LC 75-28727. (Illus.). 220p. 1976. pap. text ed. 8.95 (ISBN 0-201-07269-6). A-W.

--Interviewing Skills for Supervisory Personnel. (Business Ser). (Illus.). 1971. pap. text ed. 8.95 (ISBN 0-201-07280-7). A-W.

Steinmetz, Lawrence L. & Todd, H. Ralph, Jr. First-Line Management: Approaching Supervision Effectively. rev. ed. 1979. pap. 10.50x (ISBN 0-256-02213-5). Business Pubns.

Steinmetz, Leon. Pip Stories. (Illus.). 48p. (gr. k-2). 1980. 8.95 (ISBN 0-316-78738-8). Little.

Steinmetz, Suzanne K. Cycle of Violence: Assertive, Aggressive, & Abusive Family Interation. LC 77-24411. (Praeger Special Studies). 1977. text ed. 21.95 (ISBN 0-03-022876-X); pap. 9.95 (ISBN 0-03-046806-X). Praeger.

Steinmetz, Urban G. Strangers, Lovers, Friends. LC 80-69479. (Illus.). 176p. (Orig.). 1981. pap. 3.95 (ISBN 0-87793-217-4). Ave Maria.

Steinweg, Reiner. Der Gerechte Kriege: Christentum, Islam, Marxismus. (Edition Suhrkamp. Neue Folge: esNF 17). 250p. (Orig., Ger.). 1980. pap. text ed. 6.50 (ISBN 3-518-11017-9, Pub. by Insel Verlag Germany). Suhrkamp.

Steiss, Alan W. Local Government Finance: Capital Facilities Planning & Debt Administration in Local Government. 288p. 1975. 21.95 (ISBN 0-669-00126-0). Lexington Bks.

--Public Budgeting & Management. 1972. 16.95 (ISBN 0-669-82149-7). Lexington Bks.

Steitz, Edward S. Illustrated Basketball Rules. LC 75-44526. 2.50 (ISBN 0-385-11407-9, Dolp). Doubleday.

Stekl, William, jt. auth. see Hill, Evan.

Stekler, H. O. The Structure & Performance of the Aerospace Industry. 1965. 20.00x (ISBN 0-520-01214-3). U of Cal Pr.

Steklov Institute of Mathematics, Academy of Sciences, U S S R, No. 102. Boundary Value Problems of Mathematical Physics V: Proceedings. Ladyzenskaja, O. A., ed. 1979. Repr. of 1970 ed. 28.40 (ISBN 0-8218-3002-3, STEKLO-102). Am Math.

Steklov Institute of Mathematics, No. 126. Boundary Value Problems for Differential Equations III: Proceedings. Mihailhov, V. P., ed. LC 70-9052. 1975. 34.80 (ISBN 0-8218-3026-0, STEKLO-126). Am Math.

Steklov Institute of Mathematics, No. 117. Investigations on the Theory & Applications of Differentiable Functions of Several Variables, 4: Proceedings. Nikolsky, S. M., ed. LC 68-1677. 403p. 1974. 43.60 o.p. (ISBN 0-8218-3017-1, STEKLO-117). Am Math.

Stelczer, K. Theory & Practice of Bed-Load Transport. 1981. 22.00 (ISBN 0-918334-38-1). WRP.

Steley, Dennis. Walkabout Long Canoe. LC 78-59309. (Destiny Ser.). 1979. pap. 4.95 (ISBN 0-8163-0248-0). Pacific Pr Pub Assn.

Stell, P. M. & Maran, A. G. Head & Neck Surgery. 2nd ed. LC 78-66407. 1979. 35.00 (ISBN 0-397-58241-2). Lippincott.

Stella, Frank, jt. auth. see Crochetti, Gino.

Stella, Joseph G. The Graphic Work of Renoir: A Catalogue Raisonne. (Illus.). 112p. 1975. pap. 25.00 o.p. (ISBN 0-8390-0168-1). Allanheld & Schram.

Stellar, Eliot, jt. auth. see Dethier, Vincent G.

Stelle & Harrison. The Gunsmith's Manual: A Complete Handbook for the American Gunsmith. (Illus.). Repr. of 1883 ed. 12.95 (ISBN 0-88227-002-8). Gun Room.

Steller, Arthur W. Educational Planning for Educational Success. LC 80-82685. (Fastback Ser.: No. 152). (Orig.). 1980. pap. 0.75 (ISBN 0-87367-152-X). Phi Delta Kappa.

Stellingwerf, Johannes, jt. auth. see Koops, Willeur R.

Stelmok, Jerry. Building the Maine Guide Canoe. LC 80-80780. (Illus.). 272p. 1980. 20.00 (ISBN 0-87742-120-X). Intl Marine.

Stelson, Thomas E., jt. auth. see Au, Tung.

Stelter, Gayle A. & Kodet, Ambrose S. Accounting Simplified: An Inroductory Text. 1981. write for info. (ISBN 0-672-97177-1); tchrs. manual avail. (ISBN 0-672-97180-1); working papers avail. (ISBN 0-672-97179-8). Bobbs.

Steltzer, Ulli & Kerr, Catherine. Coast of Many Faces. LC 79-4916. (Illus.). 224p. 1979. 27.50 (ISBN 0-295-95689-5). U of Wash Pr.

Stelzer, Irwin M. Selected Antitrust Cases: Landmark Decisions. 6th ed. 1981. pap. text ed. 12.95x (ISBN 0-256-02339-5). Irwin.

Stelzer, Leigh & Banthin, Joanna. Teachers Have Rights, Too: What Educators Should Know About School Law. (Orig.). 1981. pap. write for info. (ISBN 0-89994-249-0). Soc Sci Ed.

Stemp, Robin. Guy & the Flowering Plum Tree. LC 80-67029. (Illus.). 32p. (ps-3). 1981. 8.95 (ISBN 0-689-50188-9, McElderry Bk). Atheneum.

Stempel, Guido H., III & Westley, Bruce H. Research Methods in Mass Communication. (Illus.). 480p. 1981. text ed. 19.95 (ISBN 0-13-774240-1). P-H.

Stempel, Tom. Screenwriter: The Life & Times of Nunnally Johnson. LC 78-75339. (Illus.). 1980. 12.00 (ISBN 0-498-02362-1). A S Barnes.

Stemple, David. High Ride Gobbler: The Story of the American Wild Turkey. LC 78-24200. (Illus.). 1979. 7.95 (ISBN 0-529-05524-4). Philomel.

Sten, Terje, jt. auth. see Marek, Julius.

Stenberg, Odin K. A Church Without Walls. LC 76-7702. 1976. pap. 2.45 (ISBN 0-87123-056-9, 200056). Bethany Fell.

Stendahl. Best Restaurants New York. rev. ed. LC 80-18846. 225p. 1980. pap. 3.95 (ISBN 0-89286-167-3). One Hund One Prods.

Stendahl, Krister. Holy Week. LC 74-76926. (Proclamation 1: Aids for Interpreting the Lessons of the Church Year, Ser. A: Ser. A). 64p. (Orig.). 1974. pap. 1.95 (ISBN 0-8006-4064-0, 1-4064). Fortress.

--Paul Among Jews & Gentiles & Other Essays. LC 75-36450. 144p. 1976. pap. 3.75 (ISBN 0-8006-1224-8, 1-1224). Fortress.

Stender-Petersen, Adolf, ed. Anthology of Old Russian Literature. LC 55-14251. (Columbia Slavic Studies). (Illus.). 1955. 27.50x (ISBN 0-231-01897-5). Columbia U Pr.

Stendhal, pseud. A Life of Napoleon. LC 76-13154. 1977. Repr. of 1956 ed. 15.00 (ISBN 0-86527-272-7). Fertig.

Stendhal. Life of Rossini. rev. ed. Coe, Richard N., ed. LC 71-121698. 592p. 1972. Repr. of 1824 ed. pap. 3.95 (ISBN 0-295-95189-3). U of Wash Pr.

--Red & Black: An Annotated Text with Critical Essays. Adams, Robert M., ed. (Norton Critical Editions Ser.). 1969. pap. 7.95x (ISBN 0-393-09821-4, NortonC). Norton.

--Red & the Black. Parks, Lloyd C., tr. (Orig.). 1970. pap. 1.95 (ISBN 0-451-51398-3, CJ1398, Sig Classics). NAL.

--Red & the Black. Tergie, Charles, ed. 1961. pap. 0.95 o.s.i. (ISBN 0-02-054080-9, Collier). Macmillan.

--Stendhal: Memoirs of an Egotist. Ellis, David, tr. from Fr. 1975. 6.95 o.p. (ISBN 0-8180-0224-7). Horizon.

Steneck, Nicholas H. Science & Creation in the Middle Ages: Henry of Langenstein (d. 1397) on Genesis. LC 75-19881. 256p. 1976. text ed. 14.95x (ISBN 0-268-01672-0); pap. write for info. (ISBN 0-268-01691-7). U of Notre Dame Pr.

Steneman, Shep, adapted by. Star Wars: The Empire Strikes Back Storybook. 4.95 (ISBN 0-515-05282-5). Random.

Stenesh, J. Dictionary of Biochemistry. LC 75-23037. 344p. 1975. 33.50 (ISBN 0-471-82105-5, Pub. by Wiley-Interscience). Wiley.

Stengel, Edmund, ed. Chronologisches Verzeichnis Franzosischer Grammatiken Vom Ende Des 14 Bis Zum Ausgange Des 18 Jahrhunderts, Nebst Angabe der Bisher Ermittelten Fundoret Derselben. (Studies in the History of Linguistics: No. 8). 1976. text ed. 34.25x (ISBN 0-391-01643-1). Humanities.

Stenhagen, E., et al, eds. Registry of Mass Spectral Data, 4 vols. LC 74-910. 3200p. 1974. Set. 450.00 (ISBN 0-471-82115-2, Pub. by Wiley-Interscience). Wiley.

Stenholm, Anne. Travel Agency: A How-to-Do-It Manual for Starting One of Your Own. 1981. price not set (ISBN 0-9602050-3-9). Freelance Pubns.

--Travel Agency: A How-to-Do-It Manual for Starting One of Your Own. LC 78-67643. 1979. 8.95 o.p. (ISBN 0-9602050-0-4). Freelance Pubns.

Stenhouse, N. S. Busselton Norms. 1980. pap. 8.50x (ISBN 0-85564-164-9, Pub. by U of West Australia Pr Australia). Intl Schol Bk Serv.

Stening, Malcolm. Cancer & Related Lesions of the Vulva. (Illus.). 184p. 1980. text ed. 45.00 (ISBN 0-909337-22-5). ADIS Pr.

Stenlake, J. B. Foundations of Molecular Pharmacology, 2 vols. Incl. Vol. 1. Medicinal & Pharmaceutical Chemistry. text ed. 90.00x (ISBN 0-485-11171-3); Vol. 2. The Chemical Basis of Drug Action. text ed. 46.25x (ISBN 0-485-11172-1). 1979 (Athlone Pr). Humanities.

Stenlake, J. B., jt. auth. see Beckett, A. H.

Stenning, E. H. Portrait of the Isle of Man. 3rd ed. LC 66-4371. (Portrait Bks.). (Illus.). 192p. 1975. 12.50x (ISBN 0-7091-5190-X). Intl Pubns Serv.

Stenning, Eiliah M. Cavalier King Charles Spaniels. Foyle, Christina, ed. (Foyle's Handbks). (Illus.). 1973. 3.95 (ISBN 0-685-55793-6). Palmetto Pub.

Stensbol, Ottar. Model Flying Handbook. LC 75-14507. (Illus.). 128p. (gr. 6 up). 1976. 9.95 (ISBN 0-8069-0088-1); PLB 9.29 (ISBN 0-8069-0089-X). Sterling.

Stenson, Janet S. Now I Have a Step-Parent, & It's Kind of Confusing. 1979. pap. 2.95 (ISBN 0-380-46516-7, 46516). Avon.

Stenson, Nancy, jt. auth. see Schumann, John H.

Stensrud, Rockwell, jt. auth. see Kirschenbaum, Howard.

Stensvold, Mike, ed. Available Light. LC 80-83130. (Petersen's Photographic Library). (Illus.). 160p. (Orig.). (gr. 8-12). 1980. pap. 8.95 (ISBN 0-8227-4042-7). Petersen Pub.

--Blueprint Series, Vol. 2. LC 73-82543. (Photography How-to Ser.). (Illus.). 1978. pap. 3.95 (ISBN 0-8227-4017-6). Petersen Pub.

--Photo Filters. LC 76-5980. (Petersen's How-to Photographic Library Ser.). (Illus.). 80p. 1976. pap. 3.95 o.p. (ISBN 0-8227-4012-5). Petersen Pub.

Stensvold, Mike, ed. see Buckner, Ken.

Stensvold, Mike, ed. see Jacobs, Lou, Jr.

Stent, Gunther S. & Calendar, Richard. Molecular Genetics: An Introductory Narrative. 2nd ed. LC 78-688. (Illus.). 1978. text ed. 27.95x (ISBN 0-7167-0048-4). W H Freeman.

Stent, Gunther S., ed. Function & Formation of Neural Systems, LSRR 6. (Dahlem Workshop Reports Ser.). 1977. pap. 33.90 (ISBN 0-89573-090-1). Verlag Chemie.

--Morality As a Biological Phenomenon, LSRR 9. (Dahlem Wporkshop Reports Ser.). 1978. pap. 25.60 (ISBN 0-89573-093-6). Verlag Chemie.

--Morality As a Biological Phenomenon: The Presuppositions of Sociobiological Research. 1980. 12.95 (ISBN 0-520-04028-7, CAL 482); pap. 6.95 (ISBN 0-520-04029-5). U of Cal Pr.

Stent, Gunther S., ed. see Watson, James D.

Stent, Madelon D. Cultural Pluralism in Education: A Mandate for Change. new ed. Hazard, William R. & Rivlin, Harry N., eds. LC 72-92109. 1973. 12.95 (ISBN 0-13-195461-X). P-H.

Stent, Madelon D., jt. auth. see Brown, Frank.

Stenton, Adrian, jt. auth. see DeJoia, Alex.

Stenton, Doris M., ed. see Stenton, Frank M.

Stenton, Frank. Anglo-Saxon England. 3rd ed. (Oxford History of England Ser.). 1971. 33.00x (ISBN 0-19-821716-1). Oxford U Pr.

Stenton, Frank M. Preparatory to Anglo-Saxon England: Being the Collected Papers of Frank Merry Stenton. Stenton, Doris M., ed. 1970. 29.95x (ISBN 0-19-822314-5). Oxford U Pr.

Stenton, Michael. Who's Who of British Members of Parliament: 1946-1978, Vol. 4. 1981. text ed. 86.50x (ISBN 0-391-01087-5). Humanities.

Stenzel, Franz. Cleveland Rockwell: Scientist & Artist, Eighteen Thirty-Seven to Nineteen Hundred & Seven. LC 72-80732. (Illus.). 168p. 1972. pap. 9.95 (ISBN 0-87595-037-X); 10.95. Oreg Hist Soc.

Stenzel, George, jt. auth. see Pearce, J. Kenneth.

Stenzel, H. B. The Geology of Henrys Chapel Quadrangle, Northeastern Cherokee County, Texas. (Illus.). 119p. 1953. 3.50 (PUB 5305). Bur Econ Geology.

Stenzel, H. B., et al. Pelecypoda from the Type Locality of the Stone City Beds (Middle Eocene) of Texas. (Illus.). 237p. 1957. 3.75 (PUB 5704). Bur Econ Geology.

Stepan, Alfred, ed. Authoritarian Brazil: Origins, Policies, & Future. LC 73-77167. (Illus.). 1973. 15.00x (ISBN 0-300-01622-0); pap. 5.95x (ISBN 0-300-01991-2). Yale U Pr.

Stepanek, Joseph F. Bangladesh: Equitable Growth? LC 78-16797. 1979. text ed. 22.00 (ISBN 0-08-023335-X). Pergamon.

Stepanek, Stephanie. Winslow Homer. 1977. pap. 2.00 (ISBN 0-87846-115-9). Mus Fine Arts Boston.

Stepanoff, A. J. Centrifugal & Axial Flow Pumps: Theory, Design & Application. 2nd ed. LC 57-10815. 462p. 1957. 36.50 (ISBN 0-471-82137-3, Pub. by Wiley-Interscience). Wiley.

Stepanov, Nikolai L. Ivan Krylov. (World Authors Ser.: Russia: No. 247). lib. bdg. 10.95 (ISBN 0-8057-2504-0). Twayne.

Stepford, John, jt. auth. see Dunning, John.

Stephan, H., et al. The Brain of the Common Marmoset (Callithrix Jacchus) (Illus.). 1980. 92.40 (ISBN 0-387-09782-1). Springer-Verlag.

Stephan, John J. The Kuril Islands: Russo-Japanese Frontier in the Pacific. (Illus.). 256p. 1975. 29.95x (ISBN 0-19-821563-0). Oxford U Pr.

--The Russian Facists: Tragedy & Farce in Exile, 1925-1945. LC 77-11804. (Illus.). 1978. 15.00 o.s.i. (ISBN 0-06-014099-2, HarpT). Har-Row.

Stephan, Leslie. Murder R.F.D. 1978. 8.95 o.p. (ISBN 0-684-15522-2, ScribT). Scribner.

Stephan, Walter G. & Feagin, Joe R., eds. School Desegregation: Past, Present, & Future. (Perspectives in Social Psychology Ser.). (Illus.). 370p. 1980. 21.50 (ISBN 0-306-40378-1, Plenum Pr). Plenum Pub.

Stephanou, Archimandrite E., tr. see Makrakis, Apostolos.

Stephanus, Charles. Dictionarium Historicum, Geographicum, Poeticum. LC 75-27859. (Renaissance & the Gods Ser.: Vol. 16). (Illus.). 1976. Repr. of 1596 ed. lib. bdg. 73.00 (ISBN 0-8240-2065-0). Garland Pub.

Stephen. Solubilities on Inorganic & Organic Compounds, Vol 3. 1979. 500.00 (ISBN 0-08-023570-0); pap. 400.00 (ISBN 0-08-023571-9). Pergamon.

Stephen, A. C. & Edmonds, S. J. The Phyla Sipuncula & Echiura. 1972. 62.50x (ISBN 0-565-00717-3, Pub. by Brit Mus Nat Hist England). Sabbot-Natural Hist Bks.

Stephen, Alberta, jt. auth. see Ashlock, Patrick.

Stephen, C. R., et al. Elements of Pediatric Anesthesia. 2nd ed. (American Lecture Anesthesiology Ser). (Illus.). 216p. 1970. 17.75 (ISBN 0-398-01855-3). C C Thomas.

Stephen, E. Residential Care for the Mentally Retarded. 64p. 1970. pap. 6.25 (ISBN 0-08-016106-5). Pergamon.

Stephen, George, jt. auth. see Vila, Robert.

Stephen, Henry J. New Commentaries on the Law of England, 4 vols. Berkowitz, David S. & Thorne, Samuel E., eds. LC 77-86571. (Classics of English Legal History in the Modern Era Ser.: Vol. 73). 1979. lib. bdg. 55.00 ea. (ISBN 0-8240-3060-5). Garland Pub.

Stephen, James F. Liberty, Equality, Fraternity. White, R. J., ed. (Cambridge Studies in the History & Theory of Politics). 1968. 36.00 (ISBN 0-521-06550-X). Cambridge U Pr.

Stephen, James F., jt. auth. see Best, William M.

Stephen, Sir James F. see Best, William M.

Stephen, Leslie. The Life of Sir James Fitzjames Stephen, a Judge of the High Court of Justice. LC 75-190291. (Illus.). x, 504p. 1972. Repr. of 1895 ed. lib. bdg. 27.50x (ISBN 0-8377-2606-9). Rothman.

Stephen, Leslie, ed. see Smith, George.

Stephen, W. J. An Analysis of Primary Medical Care. LC 77-83999. (Illus.). 1979. 37.50 (ISBN 0-521-21860-8). Cambridge U Pr.

Stephens. Probing the Past: A Guide to the Study & Teaching of History. 19.95 (ISBN 0-205-04196-5, 224196X). Allyn.

Stephens, jt. auth. see Bacon.

Stephens, A. Rainer Maria Rilke's Gedichte an Die Nacht: An Essay in Interpretation. LC 72-178284. (Anglica Germanica Ser.: No. 2). 288p. 1972. 47.00 (ISBN 0-521-08388-5). Cambridge U Pr.

Stephens, Alan. Sum. LC 58-13024. (New Poetry Ser.). 1958. 2.50 (ISBN 0-8040-0285-1). Swallow.

--Tree Meditation & Others. LC 70-132580. 53p. 1971. 6.00 (ISBN 0-8040-0296-7); pap. 3.75 (ISBN 0-8040-0622-9). Swallow.

Stephens, Alan, ed. see Googe, Barnabe.

Stephens, Bruce M. God's Last Metaphor: The Doctrine of the Trinity in New England Theology. LC 80-11421. (American Academy of Religion Studies in Religion). 12.00x (ISBN 0-89130-385-5, 01 00 24); pap. 7.50x (ISBN 0-89130-386-3). Scholars Pr CA.

Stephens, Casey. The Porterfield Legacy. (Orig.). 1980. pap. 1.95 (ISBN 0-89083-684-1, Kable News Co). Zebra.

--The Shadows of Fieldcrest Manor. 224p. (Orig.). 1980. pap. 1.95 (ISBN 0-89083-698-1). Zebra.

Stephens, Cleo M. Island Adventure. (YA) 5.95 (ISBN 0-685-07438-2, Avalon). Bouregy.

Stephens, D., ed. Contemporary Voices: The Short Story in Canada. 1973. pap. text ed. 6.95 o.p. (ISBN 0-13-171306-X). P-H.

Stephens, Donald. Bliss Carman. (World Authors Ser.: Canada: No. 8). 1966. lib. bdg. 10.95 (ISBN 0-8057-2200-9). Twayne.

Stephens, Ferris J. Personal Names from Cuneiform Inscriptions of Cappadocia. (Yale Oriental Researches Ser.: No. XIII). 1928. pap. 22.50x (ISBN 0-685-69868-8). Elliots Bks.

Stephens, Frederick J. Fighting Knives. LC 80-10699. (Illus.). 144p. 1980. 14.95 (ISBN 0-668-04955-3, 4955-3). Arco.

Stephens, Graham. Data Communications. 1981. text ed. price not set (ISBN 0-86103-046-X, Westbury Hse). Butterworth.

Stephens, H. S. & Radband, D. Papers Presented at the Sixth Fluid Power Symposium. (Orig.). 1981. pap. 78.00 library ed. (ISBN 0-686-69307-8). BHRA Fluid.

Stephens, H. S. & Stapleton, Mrs. C. A. Papers Presented at the Ninth International Conference on Fluid Sealing. (Illus., Orig.). 1981. pap. 78.00 library ed. (ISBN 0-686-69309-4). BHRA Fluid.

Stephens, H. S. & Gittins, L., eds. Hydrotransport Seven: Papers Presented at the Seventh International Conference on the Hydraulic Transport of Solids in Pipes. (Illus., Orig.). 1980. pap. 112.00. BHRA Fluid.

Stephens, H. S. & Jarvis, B., eds. Papers Presented at the Fifth International Symposium on Jet Cutting. (Illus.). 438p. (Orig.). 1980. pap. 99.00x (ISBN 0-906085-41-1). BHRA Fluid.

Stephens, H. S. & Priestley, G., eds. Papers Presented at the International Conference on Hydrocyclones. (Illus.). 247p. (Orig.). 1980. pap. 78.00 (ISBN 0-906085-48-9). BHRA Fluid.

--The Profitable Aeration of Waste Water. (Illus.). 98p. (Orig.). 1980. pap. 45.00x (ISBN 0-906085-44-6). BHRA Fluid.

Stephens, H. S. & Stapleton, C. A., eds. Papers Presented at the Third International Symposium on Wind Energy Systems. (Illus.). 579p. 1980. pap. 99.00 (ISBN 0-906085-47-0). BHRA Fluid.

Stephens, H. S., ed. see Eighth International Conference on Fluid Sealing.

Stephens, H. S., ed. see European Conference on Mixing, 3rd.

Stephens, H. S., ed. see Fifth Fluid Power Symposium.

Stephens, H. S., ed. see Fifth International Conference on the Hydraulic Transport of Solids in Pipes.

Stephens, H. S., ed. see First International Symposium on Wave & Tidal Energy.

Stephens, H. S., ed. see Fourth International Conference on Jet Cutting Technology.

Stephens, H. S., ed. see Fourth International Conference on the Pneumatic Transport of Solids in Pipes.

Stephens, H. S., ed. see International Conference on Pressure Surges, 3rd.

Stephens, H. S., ed. see International Conference on the Hydraulic Transport of Solids in Pipes, 6th.

Stephens, H. S., ed. see Second European Conference on Mixing.

Stephens, H. S., ed. see Second International Conference on Dredging Technology.

Stephens, H. S., ed. see Second International Conference on the Internal & External Protection of Pipes.

Stephens, H. S., ed. see Second International Symposium on Wind Energy Systems.

Stephens, H. S., ed. see Third International Symposium on Dredging Technology.

Stephens, Irlene R., jt. ed. see Tauber, Maurice F.

Stephens, Irving E. & Barnes, Dorothy L., eds. A Bibliography of Noise for Nineteen Seventy-Six. LC 72-87107. 202p. 1978. 12.50 (ISBN 0-87875-128-9). Whitston Pub.

Stephens, J. A., jt. auth. see Merewether, H. A.

Stephens, J. R. Censorship of English Drama, 1824-1901. LC 79-41601. (Illus.). 230p. Date not set. 39.50 (ISBN 0-521-23021-7). Cambridge U Pr.

Stephens, Jacquelyn W. A Practical Guide in the Use & Implementation of Bibliotherapy. 64p. 1981. PLB 6.95 (ISBN 0-89962-045-0). Todd & Honeywell.

Stephens, James. Crock of Gold. (Illus.). 1960. 5.95 o.p. (ISBN 0-02-614120-5). Macmillan.

--Deirdre. LC 23-12751. (Illus.). (gr. 7 up). 1970. 8.95 (ISBN 0-02-788020-6). Macmillan.

--Irish Fairy Tales. LC 20-21207. (Illus.). (gr. 4 up). 1968. Repr. of 1920 ed. 9.95g (ISBN 0-02-788000-1). Macmillan.

Stephens, Jeanne. Mexican Nights. 192p. (Orig.). 1980. pap. 1.50 (ISBN 0-671-57022-6). S&S.

Stephens, Jim & Woessner, Warren. Bright Moments: Jazzpoems & Poetry About Jazz. 1980. pap. 4.00 (ISBN 0-932868-03-7). Abraxas.

Stephens, John. Incidents of Travel in Central America, Chiapas & Yucatan, 2 Vols. (Illus.). 1969. pap. 5.00 (ISBN 0-685-09122-8); Vol. 1. pap. 5.00 ea. (ISBN 0-486-22404-X); Vol. 2. pap. (ISBN 0-486-22405-8). Dover.

Stephens, John, tr. see Segal, Patrick.

Stephens, John C. The Guardian. LC 79-57559. 112p. 1981. 13.50x (ISBN 0-8131-1422-5). U Pr of Ky.

Stephens, John D. The Transition from Capitalism to Socialism. (New Studies in Sociology). 1980. text ed. 25.00x (ISBN 0-391-01623-7); pap. text ed. 13.00x (ISBN 0-333-23407-3). Humanities.

Stephens, John F. Spirit Filled Family, No. 11. 48p. (Orig.). 1980. pap. 1.50 (ISBN 0-89841-008-8). Zoe Pubns.

Stephens, John L. Incidents of Travel in Yucatan. Von Hagen, Victor W., ed. LC 62-10771. (American Exploration & Travel Ser.: Vol. 37). (Illus.). 1962. 32.50 (ISBN 0-8061-0528-3). U of Okla Pr.

Stephens, Joyce. Loners, Losers, & Lovers: Elderly Tenants in a Slum Hotel. LC 75-40874. 138p. 1976. pap. 6.95 (ISBN 0-295-95762-X). U of Wash Pr.

Stephens, Ken. Discipleship Evangelism. LC 81-80258. 1981. pap. 6.95 (ISBN 0-89081-283-7). Harvest Hse.

--Study Guide for Discipleship Evangelism. 1981. pap. 2.50 (ISBN 0-89081-286-1). Harvest Hse.

Stephens, Kent. Matches, Flames & Rails: The Diamond Match Co. in the High Sierra. rev., 2nd ed. LC 80-51156. 1980. 17.95 (ISBN 0-87046-056-0). Trans-Anglo.

Stephens, Lester D. Historiography: A Bibliography. LC 75-17578. 1975. 11.00 (ISBN 0-8108-0856-0). Scarecrow.

Stephens, M. D., jt. auth. see Roderick, G. W.

Stephens, M. D. & Roderick, G. W., eds. Universities for a Changing World: The Role of the University in the Later Twentieth Century. LC 75-6567. 221p. 1975. 15.95 (ISBN 0-470-82209-0). Halsted Pr.

Stephens, Mark. Three Mile Island. (Illus.). 1981. 11.95 (ISBN 0-394-51092-5). Random. Postponed.

Stephens, Mary Jo. Witch of the Cumberlands. LC 73-22062. (Illus.). 240p. (gr. 4-9). 1974. 8.95 (ISBN 0-395-18509-2). HM.

Stephens, Michael D. & Roderick, Gordon W., eds. Higher Education Alternatives. LC 77-21407. 1978. text ed. 18.00x (ISBN 0-582-48915-6). Longman.

Stephens, Otis H. & Rathjen, Gregory. The Supreme Court & the Allocation of Constitutional Power. LC 79-26468. (Illus.). 1980. text ed. 21.95x (ISBN 0-7167-1154-0); pap. text ed. 13.95x (ISBN 0-7167-1218-0). W H Freeman.

Stephens, Otis H., Jr. The Supreme Court & Confessions of Guilt. LC 73-8777. 248p. 1973. 13.50x (ISBN 0-87049-147-4). U of Tenn Pr.

Stephens, P., ed. FIA Yearbook of Automobile Sport. (Illus.). 800p. 1981. pap. 43.95 (ISBN 0-85059-497-9). Aztex.

Stephens, Peter J. The Story of Fire Fighting. LC 66-14175. (Story of Science Ser.). (Illus.). (gr. 5-10). 1966. PLB 7.29 (ISBN 0-8178-3722-1). Harvey.

Stephens, R. C. Strength of Materials: Theory & Examples. (Illus.). 1970. pap. text ed. 16.50x (ISBN 0-7131-3211-6). Intl Ideas.

Stephens, R. C., jt. auth. see Hannah, John.

Stephens, R. E., jt. ed. see Inoue, S.

Stephens, R. W., ed. Sound: In Eight Languages. LC 74-16209. (International Dictionaries of Science & Technology Ser). 853p. 1974. 49.95 (ISBN 0-470-82200-7). Halsted Pr.

Stephens, Robert W. Texas Ranger Indian War Pensions. 1976. 6.95 (ISBN 0-89015-087-7). Nortex Pr.

--Walter Durbin: Texas Ranger & Sheriff. 8.95 (ISBN 0-685-48823-3). Nortex Pr.

Stephens, Roger B. & Stilwell, Donald L. Arteries & Veins of the Human Brain. (Illus.). 196p. 1969. 27.75 (ISBN 0-398-01857-X). C C Thomas.

Stephens, Thomas M. Directive Teaching of Children with Learning & Behavioral Handicaps. 2nd ed. 272p. 1976. pap. text ed. 9.95 (ISBN 0-675-08590-X). Merrill.

--Teaching Skills to Children with Learning & Behavioral Disorders. 1977. text ed. 18.50 (ISBN 0-675-08533-0). Merrill.

Stephens, Thomas M., et al. Teaching Children Basic Skills: A Curriculum Handbook for Directive Teaching. (Special Education Ser.). 1978. pap. text ed. 16.95 (ISBN 0-675-08399-0). Merrill.

Stephens, Thomas W. The United Nations Disaster Relief Office: The Politics & Administration of International Relief Assistance. LC 78-60792. 1978. pap. text ed. 13.25 o.p. (ISBN 0-8191-0414-0). U Pr of Amer.

Stephens, Virginia. Beauty Lost - Then Found. 1981. 6.95 (ISBN 0-8062-1574-7). Carlton.

Stephens, W. D. Holy Spirit in the Theology of Martin Bucer. LC 79-96100. Orig. Title: Martin Bucer, a Theologian of the Spirit. 1970. 51.00 (ISBN 0-521-07661-7). Cambridge U Pr.

Stephens, W. P. Traditions & Memories of American Yachting: Complete Edition. LC 80-83038. (Illus.). 384p. write for info. (ISBN 0-87742-132-3). Intl Marine.

Stephens, William N. Our Children Should Be Working. (Illus.). 228p. 1979. text ed. 13.75 (ISBN 0-398-03851-1). C C Thomas.

Stephensen, P. R., jt. auth. see Bisset, James.

Stephenson. Power Technology. LC 77-85745. 1979. 16.52 (ISBN 0-8273-1023-4); instructor's guide 1.50 (ISBN 0-8273-1024-2). Delmar.

Stephenson, Andrew M. The Wall of Years. (Orig.). 1980. pap. 2.75 (ISBN 0-440-19431-8). Dell.

Stephenson, D. Grier, jt. ed. see Mason, Alpheus T.

Stephenson, Dennis Q., tr. see Gerstner, Karl.

Stephenson, F. Douglas. Gestalt Therapy Primer: Introductory Readings in Gestalt Therapy. (Illus.). 232p. 1975. pap. 22.75 (ISBN 0-398-03233-5). C C Thomas.

Stephenson, Fairfax. Sit Down & Shape up: Sit & Exercise? Yes You Can. LC 78-6286. 1979. pap. 4.00 (ISBN 0-931490-04-9). Gotuit Ent.

Stephenson, G. M., jt. auth. see Morley, Ian.

Stephenson, Geoffrey M. Development of Conscience. (International Library of Sociology & Social Reconstruction). 1966. text ed. 8.50x (ISBN 0-7100-3460-1). Humanities.

Stephenson, George E. Drawing for Product Planning. (gr. 7-12). 1970. text ed. 7.96 (ISBN 0-87002-037-4); student guide 1.80 (ISBN 0-87002-087-0). Bennett IL.

--Small Gasoline Engines. LC 76-51117. 1978. pap. text ed. 6.80 (ISBN 0-8273-1026-9); instructor's guide 1.60 (ISBN 0-8273-1027-7). Delmar.

Stephenson, Gilbert T. & Wiggins, Norman A. Estates & Trusts. 5th ed. (Risk & Insurance Ser.). 480p. 1973. text ed. 18.95 (ISBN 0-13-289546-3). P-H.

Stephenson, Hugh E. & Kimpton, Robert S. Immediate Care of the Acutely Ill & Injured. 2nd ed. (Illus.). 1978. pap. text ed. 15.95 (ISBN 0-8016-4783-5). Mosby.

Stephenson, J. & Callander, R. A. Engineering Design. LC 73-5277. 705p. 1974. 39.95 (ISBN 0-471-82210-8, Pub. by Wiley-Interscience). Wiley.

Stephenson, J., jt. auth. see Ord-Smith, R. J.

Stephenson, Jill. The Nazi Organisation of Women. 246p. 1980. 23.50x (ISBN 0-389-20113-8). B&N.

Stephenson, John B., jt. ed. see Walls, David S.

Stephenson, Nathaniel W see Johnson, Allen & Nevins, Allan.

Stephenson, Ralph. The Animated Film. LC 72-1785. 208p. 1981. pap. 5.95 (ISBN 0-498-01202-6). A S Barnes.

Stephenson, Sherry, jt. auth. see Franko, Lawrence.

Stephenson, Vivian. Years Apart, Minds Away. (Illus.). 80p. 1979. 8.95 (ISBN 0-934444-01-3); pap. 5.95 (ISBN 0-934444-03-X). Aazunna.

Stephenson, W. A. Seaweed in Agriculture & Horticulture. 3rd ed. Bargyla & Rateaver, Gylver, eds. LC 74-12812. (Conservation Gardening & Farming Ser: Ser. C). 1974. pap. 7.00 (ISBN 0-9600698-3-6). Rateavers.

Stephenson, Wendell H. Alexander Porter, Whig Planter of Old Louisiana. LC 69-19761. (American Scene Ser.). 1969. Repr. of 1934 ed. lib. bdg. 17.50 (ISBN 0-306-71254-7). Da Capo.

Stephenson, William K. Concepts in Cell Biology. LC 77-16205. 1978. text ed. 12.95x (ISBN 0-471-03390-1). Wiley.

--Concepts in Neurophysiology. 1980. pap. text ed. 10.95x (ISBN 0-471-05585-9). Wiley.

Stepin, L. D. Quantum Radio Frequency Physics. 1965. 17.50x (ISBN 0-262-19016-8). MIT Pr.

Steppacher, Rolf, et al, eds. Economics in Institutional Perspective: Memorial Essays in Honor of K. William Kapp. LC 76-41116. 1977. 16.95 (ISBN 0-669-00977-6). Lexington Bks.

Steppat, Michael Von see Von Steppat, Michael.

Steptoe, Patrick, jt. auth. see Edwards, Robert.

Sterba, James P. Justice: Alternative Political Perspectives. 272p. 1979. pap. text ed. 8.95x (ISBN 0-534-00762-7). Wadsworth Pub.

Stericker, Anne, jt. auth. see Pringle, Mary Beth.

Sterin, Chuck, jt. auth. see Shames, Richard.

Sterin, K. E., et al. Raman Spectra of Hydrocarbons: A Data Handbook. LC 79-42704. 360p. 1980. 80.00 (ISBN 0-08-023596-4). Pergamon.

Sterling, Ada, ed. Belle of the Fifties: Memoirs of Mrs. Virginia Clay of Alabama. LC 79-84187. (American Scene Ser). 1969. Repr. of 1905 ed. lib. bdg. 39.50 (ISBN 0-306-71395-0). Da Capo.

Sterling, Bruce. Involution Ocean. (Orig.). 1978. pap. 1.50 o.s.i. (ISBN 0-515-04301-X). Jove Pubns.

Sterling, Carlos M. & Sterling, Manuel M. Historia De la Isla De Cuba. (Illus.). 392p. (Span.). (gr. 12 up). 1976. pap. 8.95 (ISBN 0-88345-251-0). Regents Pub.

Sterling, Charles. Still-Life Painting from Antiquity to the Present. rev. ed. LC 78-24827. (Icon Editions Ser.). (Illus.). 320p. 1981. 25.00 (ISBN 0-06-438530-2, HarpT). Har-Row.

Sterling, Christopher H. & Haight, Timothy. The Mass Media: Aspen Guide to Communication Industry Trends. LC 76-24370. (Special Studies). 1978. text ed. 34.95 (ISBN 0-275-24020-7). Praeger.

Sterling, Dorothy. Captain of the Planter. LC 58-5582. (gr. 8-12). 1958. 4.95 o.p. (ISBN 0-385-11394-3). Doubleday.

--Ellen's Blue Jays. LC 61-7823. (ps-5). pap. 1.49 (ISBN 0-385-08056-5). Doubleday.

Sterling, Dorothy, ed. Speak Out in Thunder Tones: Letters & Other Writings by Black Northerners, 1787-1865. LC 72-92245. 352p. (gr. 9 up). 1973. 5.95a o.p. (ISBN 0-385-02474-6); PLB (ISBN 0-385-01909-2). Doubleday.

Sterling, E. M. Trips & Trails, 2. 2nd ed. LC 67-26501. (Illus.). 228p. 1978. pap. 6.95 (ISBN 0-916890-13-9). Mountaineers.

--Western Trips & Trails. (Illus.). 350p. (Orig.). 1981. pap. 6.95 (ISBN 0-87108-584-4). Pruett.

Sterling Editors. Bolivia in Pictures. LC 73-93603. (Visual Geography Ser). (Illus.). 64p. (gr. 5 up). 1974. PLB 4.99 (ISBN 0-8069-1177-8); pap. 2.95 (ISBN 0-8069-1176-X). Sterling.

--Christmas Crafts Book. LC 79-65064. (Illus.). 1979. 16.95 (ISBN 0-8069-5396-9); lib. bdg. 13.99 (ISBN 0-8069-5397-7). Sterling.

--Easy Crafts Book. LC 75-14517. (Illus.). 112p. (gr. 4 up). 1975. 9.95 (ISBN 0-8069-5328-4); PLB 9.29 (ISBN 0-8069-5329-2). Sterling.

--Metal-Crafting Encyclopedia. LC 75-14518. (Illus.). 200p. 1975. 17.95 o.p. (ISBN 0-8069-5336-5); lib. bdg. 15.99 o.p. (ISBN 0-8069-5337-3). Sterling.

--Paraguay - in Pictures. LC 75-14513. (Visual Geography Ser.). (Illus.). 64p. (gr. 6 up). 1975. pap. 2.50 (ISBN 0-8069-1204-9). Sterling.

--The USA - in Pictures. LC 74-82329. (Visual Geography Ser.). (Illus.). 64p. (gr. 5 up). 1975. PLB 4.99 o.p. (ISBN 0-8069-1195-6); pap. 2.95 (ISBN 0-8069-1194-8). Sterling.

Sterling, Harold, et al. The Quick Neurological Screening Test. 1978. pap. 10.00 (ISBN 0-87879-185-X); 25 recording forms 5.00 (ISBN 0-685-85991-6). Acad Therapy.

Sterling, Julie, jt. auth. see Lampman, Linda.

Sterling, Manuel M., jt. auth. see Sterling, Carlos M.

Sterling, Martie & Sterling, Robin. Last Flight from Iran. 272p. (Orig.). 1981. pap. 2.50 (ISBN 0-553-20005-4). Bantam.

Sterling Publishing Company Editors. Alaska in Pictures. LC 58-13382. (Visual Geography Ser). (Orig.). (gr. 6 up). 1966. PLB 4.99 (ISBN 0-8069-1001-1); pap. 2.95 (ISBN 0-8069-1000-3). Sterling.

--Australia in Pictures. LC 66-16198. (Visual Geography Ser.). (Orig.). (gr. 4-12). PLB 4.99 o.p. (ISBN 0-8069-1041-0); pap. 2.95 (ISBN 0-8069-1040-2). Sterling.

--Austria in Pictures. LC 64-15115. (Visual Geography Ser). (Orig.). (gr. 5 up). PLB 4.99 (ISBN 0-8069-1063-1); pap. 2.95 (ISBN 0-8069-1062-3). Sterling.

--Belgium & Luxembourg in Pictures. (Visual Geography Ser). (Illus.). (gr. 5 up). 1966. PLB 4.99 o.p. (ISBN 0-8069-1065-8); pap. 2.95 o.p. (ISBN 0-8069-1064-X). Sterling.

--Brazil in Pictures. LC 67-16015. (Visual Geography Ser). (gr. 6 up). PLB 4.99 (ISBN 0-8069-1081-X); pap. 2.95 (ISBN 0-8069-1080-1). Sterling.

--Canada in Pictures. LC 66-16200. (Visual Geography Ser.). (Illus.). (gr. 6 up). 1966. PLB 4.99 (ISBN 0-8069-1067-4); pap. 2.95 (ISBN 0-8069-1066-6). Sterling.

--Caribbean, English Speaking Islands, in Pictures. LC 68-18795. (Visual Geography Series). (Illus., Orig.). (gr. 4-12). 1968. PLB 4.99 (ISBN 0-8069-1097-6); pap. 2.95 o.p. (ISBN 0-8069-1096-8). Sterling.

--China in Pictures. LC 73-83436. (Visual Geography Ser.). (Illus.). 64p. (gr. 6 up). 1973. PLB 4.99 (ISBN 0-8069-1171-9); pap. 2.95 (ISBN 0-8069-1170-0). Sterling.

--Denmark in Pictures. LC 61-10396. (Visual Geography Ser). (gr. 5 up). PLB 4.99 (ISBN 0-8069-1003-8); pap. 2.95 (ISBN 0-8069-1002-X). Sterling.

--El Salvador in Pictures. LC 73-93604. (Visual Geography Ser.). (Illus.). 64p. (gr. 5 up). 1974. PLB 4.99 (ISBN 0-8069-1181-6); pap. 2.95 (ISBN 0-8069-1180-8). Sterling.

--England in Pictures. LC 65-15825. (Visual Geography Ser.). (Illus., Orig.). (gr. 6 up). PLB 4.99 (ISBN 0-8069-1055-0); pap. 2.95 (ISBN 0-8069-1054-2). Sterling.

--Family Book of Crafts. LC 72-95199. (Illus.). 576p. (gr. 6 up). 1973. 20.00 (ISBN 0-8069-5250-4); PLB 17.59 (ISBN 0-8069-5251-2). Sterling.

--France in Pictures. LC 65-24384. (Visual Geography Ser). (Illus., Orig.). (gr. 5 up). 1965. PLB 4.99 (ISBN 0-8069-1057-7); pap. 2.95 (ISBN 0-8069-1056-9). Sterling.

--Greece in Pictures. rev. ed. LC 62-12596. (Visual Geography Ser). (Illus., Orig.). (gr. 6 up). PLB 4.99 (ISBN 0-8069-1023-2); pap. 2.95 (ISBN 0-8069-1022-4). Sterling.

--Holland in Pictures. LC 62-18637. (Visual Geography Ser). (Illus., Orig.). (gr. 6 up). 1962. PLB 4.99 (ISBN 0-8069-1033-X); pap. 2.95 (ISBN 0-8069-1032-1). Sterling.

--Ireland in Pictures. rev. ed. LC 62-12600. (Visual Geography Ser). (Illus., Orig.). (gr. 6 up). 1978. PLB 4.99 o.p. (ISBN 0-8069-1025-9); pap. 2.95 (ISBN 0-8069-1024-0). Sterling.

--Israel in Pictures. rev. ed. LC 62-12601. (Visual Geography Ser). (Illus.). 64p. (gr. 5 up). 1974. PLB 4.99 (ISBN 0-8069-1027-5); pap. 2.95 (ISBN 0-8069-1026-7). Sterling.

--Italy in Pictures. LC 66-16199. (Visual Geography Ser). (Illus., Orig.). (gr. 4-12). 1966. PLB 4.99 (ISBN 0-8069-1071-2); pap. 2.95 (ISBN 0-8069-1070-4). Sterling.

--Jamaica in Pictures. LC 67-16016. (Visual Geography Ser). (Illus.). (gr. 4-12). 1967. PLB 4.99 (ISBN 0-8069-1085-2); pap. 2.95 (ISBN 0-8069-1084-4). Sterling.

--Japan in Pictures. rev. ed. LC 60-14338. (Visual Geography Ser). (Orig.). (gr. 6 up). 1978. PLB 4.99 (ISBN 0-8069-1011-9); pap. 2.95 (ISBN 0-8069-1010-0). Sterling.

--Korea in Pictures. LC 68-8767. (Visual Geography Ser). (Illus., Orig.). (gr. 4-12). 1968. pap. 2.95 (ISBN 0-8069-1104-2). Sterling.

--Malawi in Pictures. LC 72-95206. (Visual Geography Ser.). (Illus.). 64p. (gr. 6 up). 1973. pap. 2.95 (ISBN 0-8069-1166-2). Sterling.

--Mexico in Pictures. rev. ed. LC 60-14339. (Visual Geography Ser). (Illus., Orig.). (gr. 4-12). 1961. PLB 4.99 (ISBN 0-8069-1013-5); pap. 2.95 o.p. (ISBN 0-8069-1012-7). Sterling.

--New Zealand in Pictures. LC 64-24690. (Visual Geography Ser.). (Orig.). (gr. 6 up). PLB 4.99 (ISBN 0-8069-1047-X); pap. 2.95 (ISBN 0-8069-1046-1). Sterling.

--Norway in Pictures. LC 67-16017. (Visual Geography Ser). (Orig.). (gr. 6 up). PLB 4.99 (ISBN 0-8069-1089-5); pap. 2.95 (ISBN 0-8069-1088-7). Sterling.

--Philippines in Pictures. LC 64-24692. (Visual Geography Ser). (Orig.). (gr. 6 up). pap. 2.95 (ISBN 0-8069-1048-8). Sterling.

--Poland in Pictures. LC 71-90811. (Visual Geography Ser). (Illus., Orig.). (gr. 6 up). 1969. PLB 4.99 (ISBN 0-8069-1127-1); pap. 2.95 (ISBN 0-8069-1126-3). Sterling.

--Puerto Rico in Pictures. LC 61-10399. (Visual Geography Ser). (gr. 6 up). PLB 4.99 (ISBN 0-8069-1015-1); pap. 2.95 (ISBN 0-8069-1014-3). Sterling.

--Russia in Pictures. LC 66-25201. (Visual Geography Ser.). (Illus., Orig.). (gr. 6 up). 1966. PLB 4.99 (ISBN 0-8069-1073-9); pap. 2.95 (ISBN 0-8069-1072-0). Sterling.

--Saudi Arabia in Pictures. rev. ed. LC 72-95213. (Visual Geography Ser.). (Illus.). 64p. (Orig.). (gr. 6 up). 1978. PLB 4.99 (ISBN 0-8069-1169-7); pap. 2.95 (ISBN 0-8069-1168-9). Sterling.

--Scotland in Pictures. rev. ed. LC 62-18638. (Visual Geography Ser). (Illus., Orig.). (gr. 6 up). 1978. PLB 4.99 (ISBN 0-8069-1051-8); pap. 2.95 (ISBN 0-8069-1050-X). Sterling.

--Spain in Pictures. LC 62-18639. (Visual Geography Ser). (Illus., Orig.). (gr. 6 up). 1962. PLB 4.99 (ISBN 0-8069-1029-1); pap. 2.95 (ISBN 0-8069-1028-3). Sterling.

--Sweden in Pictures. (Visual Geography Ser). (Illus., Orig.). (gr. 6 up). 1966. PLB 4.99 o.p. (ISBN 0-8069-1091-7); pap. 2.95 o.p. (ISBN 0-8069-1090-9). Sterling.

--Switzerland in Pictures. LC 60-14340. (Visual Geography Ser.). (Orig.). (gr. 6 up). PLB 4.99 (ISBN 0-8069-1017-8); pap. 2.95 (ISBN 0-8069-1016-X). Sterling.

--Thailand in Pictures. rev. ed. LC 63-11593. (Visual Geography Ser.). (Illus., Orig.). (gr. 6 up). 1978. PLB 4.99 (ISBN 0-8069-1037-2); pap. 2.95 (ISBN 0-8069-1036-4). Sterling.

--Tunisia in Pictures. LC 72-81053. (Visual Geography Ser.). (Illus.). 64p. (gr. 6 up). 1972. pap. 2.95 (ISBN 0-8069-1158-1). Sterling.

--Venezuela in Pictures. LC 65-24381. (Visual Geography Ser.). (Illus., Orig.). (gr. 5 up). 1965. PLB 4.99 o.p. (ISBN 0-8069-1075-5); pap. 2.95 (ISBN 0-8069-1074-7). Sterling.

--West Germany in Pictures. LC 67-16018. (Visual Geography Ser). (Illus., Orig.). (gr. 6 up). 1967. PLB 4.99 (ISBN 0-8069-1095-X); pap. 2.95 (ISBN 0-8069-1094-1). Sterling.

Sterling, Robert R. Theory of the Measurement of Enterprise Income. LC 79-11417. 1979. Repr. of 1970 ed. text ed. 20.00 (ISBN 0-914348-26-4). Scholars Bk.

--Toward a Science of Accounting. LC 80-14502. 247p. 1980. text ed. 13.00 (ISBN 0-914348-31-0). Scholars Bk.

Sterling, Robert R., ed. Asset Valuation & Income Determination: A Consideration of the Alternatives. LC 73-160580. 1971. text ed. 10.00 (ISBN 0-914348-11-6). Scholars Bk.

--Institutional Issues in Public Accounting. LC 73-86393. 1974. text ed. 20.00 (ISBN 0-914348-12-4). Scholars Bk.

--Research Methodology in Accounting. LC 72-77235. 1972. text ed. 10.00 (ISBN 0-914348-13-2). Scholars Bk.

Sterling, Robert R. & Bentz, William F., eds. Accounting in Perspective. LC 78-26732. 1979. text ed. 13.00 (ISBN 0-914348-25-6). Scholars Bk.

Sterling, Robert R. & Thomas, Arthur L., eds. Accounting for a Simplified Firm Owning Depreciable Assets: Seventeen Essays & a Synthesis Based on a Common Case. LC 79-18604. 1979. text ed. 15.00 (ISBN 0-914348-27-2). Scholars Bk.

Sterling, Robin, jt. auth. see Sterling, Martie.

Sterling Swift Publishing Co. Educational Software Directory: Apple II Edition. 104p. 1981. pap. 11.95 (ISBN 0-88408-141-9); Educational 9.95. Sterling Swift.

Sterling, Theodor D. & Pollack, Seymour V. Computers & the Life Sciences. LC 65-27765. (Illus.). 1965. 20.00x (ISBN 0-231-02744-3). Columbia U Pr.

Sterling, Thomas. The Evil of the Day. LC 80-8414. 224p. 1981. pap. 2.25 (ISBN 0-06-080529-3, P529, PL). Har-Row.

Sterling, Tom. The Amazon. (The World's Wild Places Ser). (Illus.). 1973. 12.95 (ISBN 0-8094-2003-1). Time-Life.

--The Amazon. (The World's Wild Places Ser.). (Illus.). 1978. lib. bdg. 11.97 (ISBN 0-686-51015-1). Silver.

Stermer, Dugald. Vanishing Creatures: Portraits of Endangered Species. (Illus.). 80p. 1980. 15.95 (ISBN 0-89581-019-0); pap. 8.95 (ISBN 0-89581-021-2). Lancaster-Miller.

Stermole, Franklin J. Economic Evaluation & Investment Decision Methods. 3rd ed. 1980. text ed. 22.50 (ISBN 0-9603282-0-3); solutions manual 6.50 (ISBN 0-9603282-3-8). Invest Eval.

Stern. Intensive Care in the Newborn, Vol. III. 1981. write for info (ISBN 0-89352-114-0). Masson Pub.

--Stage Management: A Guidebook of Practical Techniques. 19.50 (ISBN 0-205-04197-3, 4841972). Allyn.

Stern, A. Five Hundred Mail Order Ideas. 1978. 14.50 o.p. (ISBN 0-685-04997-3, 0-911156-27-5). Porter.

Stern, A. L. How Mail Order Fortunes Are Made. 1977. 12.50 o.p. (ISBN 0-685-80653-7). Porter.

Stern, A Z. & Reif, Joseph A. Useful Expressions Portuguese. (Useful Expressions Ser.). 64p. (Orig.). 1981. pap. 1.50 (ISBN 0-86628-022-7). Ridgefield Pub.

Stern, A. Z. & Reif, Joseph A., eds. Useful Expressions in Arabic. (Useful Expressions). 64p. (Orig.). 1980. pap. 1.50 (ISBN 0-86628-005-7); cassette 4.50 (ISBN 0-86628-015-4). Ridgefield Pub.

--Useful Expressions in Dutch. (Useful Expressions). 64p. 1980. pap. 1.50 (ISBN 0-86628-004-9). Ridgefield Pub.

--Useful Expressions in French. (Useful Expressions Ser.). 64p. (Orig.). 1980. pap. 1.50 (ISBN 0-86628-006-5). Ridgefield Pub.

--Useful Expressions in German. (Useful Expressions Ser.). 64p. (Orig.). 1980. pap. 1.50 (ISBN 0-86628-007-3). Ridgefield Pub.

--Useful Expressions in Greek. (Useful Expressions Ser.). 64p. (Orig.). 1980. pap. 1.50 (ISBN 0-86628-008-1). Ridgefield Pub.

--Useful Expressions in Hebrew. (Useful Expressions Ser.). 64p. (Orig.). 1980. pap. 1.50 (ISBN 0-86628-009-X); cassette 4.50 (ISBN 0-86628-014-6). Ridgefield Pub.

--Useful Expressions in Italian. (Useful Expressions Ser.). 64p. (Orig.). 1980. pap. 1.50 (ISBN 0-86628-010-3). Ridgefield Pub.

--Useful Expressions in Russian. (Useful Expressions Ser.). (Illus.). 64p. (Orig.). 1980. pap. 1.50 (ISBN 0-86628-012-X). Ridgefield Pub.

--Useful Expressions in Spanish. (Useful Expressions Ser.). 64p. (Orig.). 1980. pap. 1.50 (ISBN 0-86628-013-8). Ridgefield Pub.

Stern, Arthur C., et al. Fundamentals of Air Pollution. 1973. text ed. 21.50 (ISBN 0-12-666560-5). Acad Pr.

Stern, August. USSR Versus Dr. Mikhail Stern. Carynnk, Marco, tr. from Rus. 1977. 9.95 (ISBN 0-916354-61-X). Urizen Bks.

--The USSR Vs. Dr. Mikhail Stern: Soviet Justice Vs. Human Rights. Carynnyk, Marco & Lipson, Leon, trs. from Rus. Date not set. pap. 5.95 (ISBN 0-916354-62-8). Urizen Bks.

Stern, Beverly, jt. ed. see Eliot, Simon.

Stern, Cecily. A Different Kind of Gold. LC 80-8452. (Illus.). 128p. (gr. 5 up). 1981. 9.95 (ISBN 0-06-025770-9, HarpJ); PLB 9.89g (ISBN 0-06-025771-7). Har-Row.

Stern, Chaim. Gates of the House. 1977. 6.95 (ISBN 0-916694-35-6); lib. bdg. 7.50 o.s.i. (ISBN 0-916694-42-9). Central Conf.

Stern, Chaim, ed. Gates of Forgiveness: Selichot. 1980. pap. 2.00 ea. Eng. Ed (ISBN 0-916694-57-7). Hebrew Ed (ISBN 0-916694-74-7). Central Conf.

--Gates of Prayer: The New Union Prayerbook. 1975. English ed. 10.00 (ISBN 0-916694-01-1); Hebrew ed. 10.00 (ISBN 0-916694-00-3). Central Conf.

--Gates of Repentance. 1978. 10.00 (ISBN 0-916694-38-0); pulpit ed. 20.00 (ISBN 0-916694-40-2); Hebrew ed. 10.00 (ISBN 0-916694-39-9). Central Conf.

Stern, Clarence A. Golden Republicanism: The Crusade for Hard Money. 1964. pap. 1.50 (ISBN 0-9600116-1-7). Stern.

--Republican Heyday: Republicanism Through the McKinley Years. 1962. pap. 1.25 (ISBN 0-9600116-2-5). Stern.

--Resurgent Republicanism: The Handiwork of Hanna. 1963. pap. 1.25 (ISBN 0-9600116-3-3). Stern.

Stern, Curt. Principles of Human Genetics. 3rd ed. LC 72-4357. (Illus.). 315p. 1973. text ed. 25.95x (ISBN 0-7167-0597-4); answers to problems avail. (ISBN 0-685-27915-4). W H Freeman.

Stern, Curt & Sherwood, Eva R., eds. The Origin of Genetics: A Mendel Source Book. LC 66-27948. (Illus.). 1966. pap. text ed. 8.95x (ISBN 0-7167-0655-5). W H Freeman.

Stern, D. Nordlinger & Yaney, Joseph P. Cases in Labor Law. LC 76-5617. (Law Ser.). 1977. pap. text ed. 11.95 o.p. (ISBN 0-88244-110-8). Grid Pub.

Stern, Daniel. An Urban Affair. 1980. 12.95 (ISBN 0-671-41226-4). S&S.

Stern, David P. Math Squared: Graph Paper Activities for Fun & Fundamentals. LC 80-15932. 115p. 1981. pap. text ed. 5.50x (ISBN 0-8077-2585-4). Tchrs Coll.

Stern, Don. Backgammon. 1977. PLB 6.45 (ISBN 0-531-01298-0). Watts.

Stern, E. S., ed. The Chemist in Industry, One: Fine Chemicals for Polymers. (Oxford Chemistry Ser.). (Illus.). 96p. 1973. pap. text ed. 4.95x o.p. (ISBN 0-19-855415-X). Oxford U Pr.

Stern, Edward L., ed. & intro. by. Direct Marketing Market Place Nineteen Eighty. 1979. pap. 25.00 o.p. (ISBN 0-934464-01-4). Hilary Hse Pubs.

Stern, F. C. A Chalk Garden. (Illus.). 1974. 13.95 (ISBN 0-571-10189-5, Pub. by Faber & Faber). Merrimack Bk Serv.

Stern, Frances M., et al. Mind Trips to Help You Lose Weight. LC 76-44202. 192p. 1981. pap. 2.25 (ISBN 0-87216-786-0). Playboy Pbks.

Stern, Fritz, ed. The Varieties of History: From Voltaire to the Present. 1973. pap. 5.95 (ISBN 0-394-71962-X, Vin). Random.

Stern, Fritz R. The Politics of Cultural Despair: A Study in the Rise of the Germanic Ideology. (California Library Reprint Ser.). 1974. 21.50x (ISBN 0-520-02643-8); pap. 6.95x (ISBN 0-520-02626-8). U of Cal Pr.

Stern, Gary H., jt. auth. see DeRosa, Paul.

Stern, Gerald. The Red Coal. 96p. 1981. 10.95 (ISBN 0-686-69058-3); pap. 5.95 (ISBN 0-686-69059-1). HM.

Stern, H. H., tr. see Hoermann, H.

Stern, Hans H. Languages & the Young School Child. (Language & Language Learning Ser.). 1969. pap. 4.95x o.p. (ISBN 0-19-437035-6). Oxford U Pr.

Stern, Harold. The Couch: Its Use & Meaning in Psychotherapy. LC 77-15610. 1978. 19.95 (ISBN 0-87705-303-0). Human Sci Pr.

Stern, Henry L. Help from Beyond: How to Lead an Enriched Life Through Spiritual Communication. LC 73-90380. 192p. 1974. 7.95 o.s.i. (ISBN 0-8027-0444-1). Walker & Co.

Stern, J. P. Re-Interpretations: Seven Studies in Nineteenth Century German Literature. 370p. Date not set. price not set (ISBN 0-521-23983-4); pap. price not set (ISBN 0-521-28366-3). Cambridge U Pr.

--A Study of Nietzsche. LC 78-54328. (Major European Authors Ser.). 1979. 26.95 (ISBN 0-521-22126-9). Cambridge U Pr.

--A Study of Nietzsche. LC 78-54328. (Major European Authors Ser.). Date not set. pap. price not set (ISBN 0-521-28380-9). Cambridge U Pr.

--The World of Kafka. (Illus.). 256p. 1980. 18.95 (ISBN 0-03-051366-9). HR&W.

Stern, J. P., jt. auth. see Silk, M. S.

Stern, J. P., ed. see Schnitzler, Arthur.

Stern, J. P., tr. see Meyer, R. W.

Stern, James L., ed. see National Academy of Arbitrators, Annual Meeting.

Stern, Jane & Stern, Michael. Auto Ads. 1978. 12.95 (ISBN 0-394-50094-6). Random.

--Horror Holiday: Secrets of Vacation Survival. 144p. 1981. pap. 5.95 (ISBN 0-525-47655-5). Dutton.

Stern, Jean, jt. auth. see Rochester, J. Martin.

Stern, Jonathan P. Soviet Natural Gas Development to Nineteen Ninety: The Implications for the CMEA & the West. LC 79-2705. 208p. 1980. 21.95x (ISBN 0-669-03233-6). Lexington Bks.

Stern, Joseph J., jt. auth. see Roemer, Michael.

Stern, Joseph P. Thomas Mann. LC 67-16891. (Columbia Essays on Modern Writers Ser.: No. 24). 1967. pap. 2.00 (ISBN 0-231-02847-4, MW24). Columbia U Pr.

Stern, Judith & Denenberg, R. V. The Fast Food Diet. 160p. 1980. 9.95 (ISBN 0-13-307736-5); pap. 4.95 (ISBN 0-13-307728-4). P-H.

Stern, Karl. Love & Success. 1975. 8.95 o.p. (ISBN 0-374-19258-8); pap. 4.95 o.p. (ISBN 0-374-51386-4). FS&G.

Stern, Kurt, jt. auth. see Davidsohn, Israel.

Stern, Lawrence. School & Community Theater Management: A Handbook for Survival. new ed. 1979. text ed. 18.95 (ISBN 0-205-06174-5). Allyn.

Stern, Leo, jt. auth. see Denhoff, Eric.

Stern, Leo, et al. Intensive Care in the Newborn. LC 76-22262. 296p. 1977. 37.50 (ISBN 0-89352-000-4). Masson Pub.

--Intensive Care of the Newborn II. LC 78-63400. (Newborn Ser.). (Illus.). 418p. 1979. 45.50 (ISBN 0-89352-022-5). Masson Pub.

Stern, Leonard, jt. auth. see Price, Roger.

Stern, Lev, tr. see Melcuk, Igor A.

Stern, Louis W. & El-Ansary, Adel I. Marketing Channels. 1977. ref. ed. 20.95x (ISBN 0-13-557124-3). P-H.

Stern, Madeleine, intro. by see Alcott, Louisa May.

Stern, Madeleine B. Purple Passage: Life of Mrs Frank Leslie. (Illus.). 1970. Repr. of 1953 ed. 11.95 (ISBN 0-8061-0271-3); pap. 5.95 (ISBN 0-8061-0939-4). U of Okla Pr.

Stern, Madeleine B., jt. auth. see Rostenberg, Leona.

Stern, Michael. Douglas Sirk. (Theatrical Arts Ser.). 1979. lib. bdg. 10.95 (ISBN 0-8057-9269-4). Twayne.

Stern, Michael, jt. auth. see Stern, Jane.

Stern, Mikhail. Sex in the U.S.S.R. 384p. 1981. 12.95 (ISBN 0-8129-0942-9). Times Bks.

Stern, Milton, ed. see Melville, Herman.

Stern, Milton R. & Gross, Seymour L, eds. American Literature Survey. Incl. Vol. 1. Colonial & Federal to 1800. 672p. pap. text ed. 5.25 (ISBN 0-14-015085-4); Vol. 2. The American Romantics 1800-1860. Brooks, Van W., pref. by. 720p. pap. text ed. 4.95 (ISBN 0-14-015086-2); Vol. 3. Nation & Region 1860-1900. Jones, Howard M., pref. by. 736p. pap. text ed. 4.95 (ISBN 0-14-015087-0); Vol. 4. The Twentieth Century. Cowley, Malcolm, pref. by. 736p. pap. text ed. 5.95 (ISBN 0-14-015088-9). LC 74-3690. (Viking Portable Library). 1977. Penguin.

Stern, N. H., jt. auth. see Bliss, C. J.

Stern, Nancy. History of Computing: From ENIAC to UNIVAC. (Illus.). 280p. 1981. 21.00 (ISBN 0-932376-14-2). Digital Pr.

Stern, Nancy & Stern, Robert A. Structured Cobol Programming. 3rd ed. 571p. 1980. pap. 16.95 (ISBN 0-471-04913-1). Wiley.

Stern, Nancy, jt. auth. see Stern, Robert.

Stern, Nancy, et al. Three Seventy Three Sixty Assembler Language Programming. LC 78-10504. 1979. pap. text ed. 21.95 (ISBN 0-471-03429-0); tchrs. manual avail. (ISBN 0-471-05393-7). Wiley.

Stern, Norton B. California Jewish History: Descriptive Bibliography. 1967. 17.50 o.p. (ISBN 0-87062-056-8). A H Clark.

Stern, Peter S., tr. see Kriegel, Annie.

Stern, Richard. The Chaleur Network. 244p. 1981. Repr. of 1962 ed. 15.95 (ISBN 0-933256-18-3). Second Chance.

Stern, Richard M. Power. 352p. 1976. pap. 1.95 o.p. (ISBN 0-345-25003-6). Ballantine.

--The Will. 1977. pap. 1.95 o.p. (ISBN 0-345-25763-4). Ballantine.

Stern, Richard Martin. Snowbound Six. LC 77-77551. 1977. 7.95 o.p. (ISBN 0-385-12320-5). Doubleday.

Stern, Robert & Stern, Nancy. Principles of Data Processing. 2nd ed. LC 78-16178. 1979. text ed. 21.95x (ISBN 0-471-01696-9); tchrs.' manual avail. (ISBN 0-471-03143-7); study guide 8.50 (ISBN 0-471-05431-3). Wiley.

Stern, Robert A. New Directions in American Architecture. rev. ed. LC 70-81278. (New Directions in Architecture Ser). 1978. 9.95 (ISBN 0-8076-0523-9); pap. 5.95 (ISBN 0-8076-0527-1). Braziller.

Stern, Robert A., jt. auth. see Stern, Nancy.

Stern, Robert M. The Balance of Payments: Theory & Economic Policy. LC 72-78222. 488p. 1973. 27.95x (ISBN 0-202-06059-4). Aldine Pub.

Stern, Robert M. & Ray, William J. Biofeedfack: Potential & Limits. LC 79-18700. (Illus.). viii, 197p. 1980. pap. 3.95 (ISBN 0-8032-9114-0, BB721, Bison). U of Nebr Pr.

Stern, Robert M., et al. Psychophysiological Recording. (Illus.). 256p. 1980. text ed. 14.95x (ISBN 0-19-502695-0); pap. text ed. 8.95x (ISBN 0-19-502696-9). Oxford U Pr.

Stern, Samuel M. Hispano-Arabic Strophic Poetry. Harvey, L. P., ed. 268p. 1974. text ed. 29.95x (ISBN 0-19-815735-5). Oxford U Pr.

Stern, Simon. Mrs. Vinegar. (Illus.). (ps-2). 1979. 7.95g (ISBN 0-13-604488-3). P-H.

Stern, Steven, ed. see Institute for Paralegal Training.

Stern, Stuart. The Minotaur Factor. LC 76-49403. 1978. pap. 1.95 o.p. (ISBN 0-87216-370-9). Playboy Pbks.

--The Poison Tree. LC 78-51092. 1978. pap. 1.95 o.p. (ISBN 0-87216-463-2). Playboy Pbks.

Stern, Susan. Women Composers: A Handbook. LC 78-5505. 1978. 10.00 (ISBN 0-8108-1138-3). Scarecrow.

Stern, Virginia, jt. auth. see Wraight, A. D.

Stern, Walter. Stern's Handbook of Package Design Research. 704p. 1981. 42.50 (ISBN 0-471-05901-3, Pub. by Wiley-Interscience). Wiley.

Stern, William L. Psychological Methods of Testing Intelligence. Whipple, G. M., tr. from Ger. Bd. with Selected Essays. Binet, Alfred, et al.. (Contributions to the History of Psychology Ser., Vol. IV, Pt. B: Psychometrics & Educational Psychology). 1978. Repr. of 1914 ed. 30.00 (ISBN 0-89093-164-X). U Pubns Amer.

Stern, William L., jt. auth. see Tippo, Oswald.

Sternbach, George, ed. The Organization & Administration of Emergency Medical Care. LC 78-74611. 117p. 1979. 9.50 (ISBN 0-87762-269-8). Technomic.

Sternbach, L. Juridical Studies in Ancient Indian Law, 2 vols. 1967. 24.00 set (ISBN 0-89684-232-0). Orient Bk Dist.

Sternbach, Richard A., ed. The Psychology of Pain. LC 77-84554. 1978. 21.00 (ISBN 0-89004-278-0). Raven.

Sternberg, Barbara, jt. auth. see Sternberg, Eugene.

Sternberg, Betty J., jt. auth. see Clark, Clara E.

Sternberg, Cecilia. Masquerade. 1981. pap. 2.75 (ISBN 0-451-09603-7, E9603, Sig). NAL.

Sternberg, Charles. Basic Computer Programs for the Home. 336p. 1979. pap. 9.95 (ISBN 0-8104-5154-9). Hayden.

Sternberg, Eugene & Sternberg, Barbara. Community Centers & Student Unions. LC 70-151719. 1976. 31.50x (Van Nos Reinhold). Westview.

Sternberg, Jacques. Future Without Future. LC 73-6427. 256p. 1973. 6.95 o.p. (ISBN 0-8164-9170-4). Continuum.

Sternberg, Jacques & Chapelot, Pierre. Pin up. LC 74-83498. (Illus.). 104p. 1975. pap. 8.95 o.p. (ISBN 0-312-61215-X). St Martin.

Sternberg, Josef Von see Von Sternberg, Josef.

Sternberg, Martin L. American Sign Language Dictionary. LC 75-25066. (Illus.). 1981. 30.00 (ISBN 0-06-014097-6, HarpT). Har-Row.

Sternberg, R., jt. auth. see Anikouchine, W.

Sternberg, Richard, jt. auth. see Anikouchine, William.

Sternberg, Robert J. & Detterman, Douglas K., eds. Human Intelligence: Perspectives on Its Theory & Measurement. LC 79-17994. 1979. 14.95 (ISBN 0-89391-030-9). Ablex Pub.

Sternberg, Shlomo, jt. auth. see Loomis, Lynn H.

Sternberger, Adolf. Der Verstandene Tod: Eine Untersuchung Zu Martin Heideggers Existenzialontologie. Natanson, Maurice, ed. LC 78-66753. (Phenomenology Ser.: Vol. 14). 165p. 1979. lib. bdg. 17.00 (ISBN 0-8240-9556-1). Garland Pub.

Sternberger, Ludwig A. Immunocytochemistry. 2nd ed. LC 78-13263. (Basic & Clinical Immunology Ser.). 1979. 35.50 (ISBN 0-471-03386-3, Pub. by Wiley Medical). Wiley.

Sterne, Emma G. They Took Their Stand. (America in the Making Ser.). (Illus.). (gr. 7-12). 1968. 8.95 (ISBN 0-02-788130-X, CCPr). Macmillan.

Sterne, Harold E. Catalogue of Nineteenth Century Printing Presses. LC 78-63314. (Illus.). 384p. 1978. 19.95 (ISBN 0-932606-00-8). Ye Olde Print.

Sterne, Laurence. Letters. Curtis, L. P., ed. 1935. 33.00x o.p. (ISBN 0-19-811453-2). Oxford U Pr.

--A Sentimental Journey Through France & Italy by Mr. Yorick. rev. ed. Stout, Gardner D., Jr., ed. (Illus.). 1967. 22.75x (ISBN 0-520-01228-3). U of Cal Pr.

--Tristnam Shandy. pap. 1.95 (ISBN 0-451-51051-8, CJ1051, Sig Classics). NAL.

--Tristram Shandy. 1979. 7.00x (ISBN 0-460-00617-7, Evman); pap. 4.95 (ISBN 0-460-01617-2, Evman). Dutton.

Sterne, Laurence J. Tristram Shandy: The Life & Opinions of Tristram Shandy, Gentleman. Work, James A., ed. 1940. pap. 7.95 (ISBN 0-672-63128-8). Odyssey Pr.

Sterne, M. & Batty, I. Pathogenic Clostridia. 1975. 24.95 (ISBN 0-407-35350-X). Butterworths.

Sterner. Gaudi: The Architecture in Barcelona, Antoni. Date not set. pap. 3.50 (ISBN 0-8120-2293-9). Barron. Postponed.

Sterner, Gabriele. Antoni Gaudi: Architecture in Barcelona. (Illus.). 1981. pap. 3.50 (ISBN 0-8120-2293-9). Barron.

--Art Nouveau. (Pocket Art Ser.). (Illus.). 1981. pap. 3.50 (ISBN 0-8120-2105-3). Barron.

Sternfeld, F. W. Music in Shakespearean Tragedy. (Illus.). 1967. Repr. of 1963 ed. 30.00x (ISBN 0-7100-2153-4). Routledge & Kegan.

Sternfeld, F. W., et al, eds. Essays on Opera & English Music: In Honor of Sir Jack Westrup. (Illus.). 1975. 30.50x (ISBN 0-631-15890-1, Pub. by Basil Blackwell). Biblio Dist.

Sternfeld, Frederick. Goethe & Music. (Music Reprint Ser.). 176p. 1979. Repr. of 1954 ed. 19.50 (ISBN 0-306-79515-9). Da Capo.

Sternfeld, Frederick see Abraham, Gerald, et al.

Sternfeld, Robert, jt. auth. see Zyskind, Harold.

Sternfield, Jonathan, jt. auth. see Torbet, Laura.

Sternglass, Ernest. Secret Fallout: Low-Level Radiation from Hiroshima to Three-Mile Island. rev. ed. (McGraw-Hill Paperbacks Ser.). 300p. (Orig.). 1981. pap. 5.95 (ISBN 0-07-061242-0, GB). McGraw.

Sternheim see Bentley, Eric.

Sternheim, Carl. Carl Sternheim Plays: The Bloomers, The Snob, Paul Schiffel, 1913 & The Fossil. 1980. pap. 6.95 (ISBN 0-7145-0027-5). Riverrun NY.

Sternheim, Morton M., jt. auth. see Kane, Joseph W.

Sternheimer, Stephen. East-West Technology Transfers: Japan & the Communist Bloc. LC 80-50901. (The Washington Papers: No. 76). (Illus.). 88p. 1980. pap. 3.50 (ISBN 0-8039-1485-7). Sage.

Sternheimer, Stephen, jt. auth. see Lewis, Carol.

Sternhell, S., jt. auth. see Jackman, L. M.

Sternlicht, jt. auth. see Jameson.

Sternlicht, Sanford. John Masefield. (English Authors Ser.: No. 209). 1977. lib. bdg. 10.95 (ISBN 0-8057-6678-2). Twayne.

Sternlicht, Stanford. McKinley's Bulldog: The Battleship Oregon. LC 77-8603. 1977. text ed. 13.95 (ISBN 0-88229-263-3); pap. 6.95 (ISBN 0-88229-516-0). Nelson-Hall.

Sternlict, Manny & Hurwitz, Abraham. Games Children Play: Instructive & Creative Play Activities for the Mentally Retarded & Developmentally Disabled Child. 128p. 1980. 12.95 (ISBN 0-442-25857-7). Van Nos Reinhold.

Sternlieb, George. The Tenement Landlord. 1969. 15.00 (ISBN 0-8135-0604-2); pap. 3.25x (ISBN 0-8135-0605-0). Rutgers U Pr.

Sternloff, Robert E. & Warren, Roger M. Park & Recreation Maintenance Management. 388p. 1977. text ed. 16.95 (ISBN 0-205-05601-6, 845601-1). Allyn.

Sterns, Harvey L., et al. Gerontology in Higher Education: Developing Institutional & Community Strength. new ed. 1979. text ed. 23.95x (ISBN 0-534-00708-2). Wadsworth Pub.

Sterns, Indrikis. The Greater Medieval Historians: An Interpretation & a Bibliography. LC 80-5850. 260p. 1980. lib. bdg. 18.75 (ISBN 0-8191-1327-1); pap. text ed. 10.50 (ISBN 0-8191-1328-X). U Pr of Amer.

Sternsher, Bernard. Consensus, Conflict, & American Historians. LC 73-16531. (Illus.). 448p. 1975. 15.00x o.p. (ISBN 0-253-31410-0); pap. 8.95x (ISBN 0-253-28070-2). Ind U Pr.

Sternsher, Bernard, ed. The New Deal. LC 78-73287. (Orig.). 1979. pap. text ed. 3.95x (ISBN 0-88273-212-9). Forum Pr MO.

Stertz, Eda. Katie's Treasure. (Pathfinder Ser.). 144p. (gr. 2-6). 1980. pap. 2.50 (ISBN 0-310-37921-0, 0018P). Zondervan.

Sterzl, J. & Riha, I., eds. Developmental Aspects of Antibody Formation & Structure: Proceedings, Vols. 1 & 2. 1971. Vol. 1. 51.75 (ISBN 0-12-667901-0); Vol. 2. 51.75 (ISBN 0-12-667902-9). Acad Pr.

Steskal, T. J. Understanding Medicare. 93p. (Orig.). 1980. pap. 9.95 (ISBN 0-937978-00-0, MC-1). Info Prods.

Stessin, Lawrence. Product Liability Portfolio. 1977. 39.95. Busn Res Pubns.

Stetler, Charles. Roger, Karl, Rick, & Shane Are Friends of Mine. 1980. 2.00 (ISBN 0-917554-16-7). Maelstrom.

Stetler, Cheryl B., et al, eds. see Massachussetts General Hospital.

Stetler, Russell, ed. see Giap, Vo Nguyen.

Stetson. Hunting with Scenthounds. (Sportsman's Library off Gun Dogs Vol 5). 1965. pap. 1.79 o.p. (ISBN 0-87666-380-3, DS1140). TFH Pubns.

Stetson, Damon. Starting Over. Markel, Robert, ed. 1971. 5.95 o.s.i. (ISBN 0-02-614390-9). Macmillan.

Stetson, Joe. Handbook of Gundogs. (Sportsman's Library of Gun Dogs, Vol. 1). (Orig.). 1965. pap. 2.00 (ISBN 0-87666-315-3, DS1139). TFH Pubns.

--Hunting with Flushing Dogs. (Sportsman's Library of Gun Dogs, Vol. 2). (Orig.). 1965. pap. 2.00 (ISBN 0-87666-293-9, DS1137). TFH Pubns.

--Hunting with Pointing Dogs. (Sportsman's Library of Gun Dogs, Vol. 3). (Orig.). 1965. pap. 1.79 o.p. (ISBN 0-87666-351-X, DS1138). TFH Pubns.

--Hunting with Retrievers. (Sportsman's Library of Gun Dogs, Vol. 4). (Orig.). pap. 2.00 (ISBN 0-87666-371-4, DS1136). TFH Pubns.

Stetson, Milton, jt. auth. see Epple, August.

Stettler, H. Auditing Principles. 4th ed. 1977. text ed. 19.95 (ISBN 0-13-051706-2); practice case 10.95 (ISBN 0-13-694521-X); audit workpapers, 3rd ed. 7.95 (ISBN 0-13-052712-2). P-H.

Stettler, Howard F. Systems-Based Independent Audits. 2nd ed. 1974. 21.95 (ISBN 0-13-881375-2). P-H.

Stettner, Irving. Hurrah! Selected Poems. (Illus.). 124p. (Orig.). 1980. pap. 3.50 (ISBN 0-917402-13-8). Downtown Poets.

Stettner, N. Productivity, Bargaining & Industrial Change. 1969. 16.50 (ISBN 0-08-006756-5); pap. 7.75 (ISBN 0-08-006757-3). Pergamon.

Steuben, Norton L. Real Estate Planning: Cases, Materials, Problems, Questions & Commentary on the Planning of Real Estate Transactions. 2nd ed. LC 80-17983. (University Casebook Ser.). 1264p. 1980. text ed. write for info. (ISBN 0-88277-013-6). Foundation Pr.

Steuck, Jeanne, tr. Buenos Dias, Judy. (Spanish Bks.). (Span.). 1979. 1.75 (ISBN 0-8297-0496-5). Life Pubs Intl.

Steuding, Bob. Gary Snyder. LC 76-14938. (U.S. Authors Ser: No. 274). 1976. lib. bdg. 12.50 (ISBN 0-8057-7174-3). Twayne.

Steuer, M. D., jt. auth. see Holland, Janet.

Steurer, jt. auth. see Corley.

Stevans, C. M., jt. ed. see Daniels, Cora L.

Steven, Hugh. Never Touch a Tiger. 180p. 1980. pap. 4.95 (ISBN 0-8407-5737-9). Nelson.

Steven, Margaret. Merchant Campbell, 1769-1846. 1965. 11.25x o.p. (ISBN 0-19-550275-2). Oxford U Pr.

Stevens & Perillo. Growing Marijuana for Home Medical Use. (Illus.). 1981. perfect bdg. 5.95 (ISBN 0-686-26920-9). Pacific Pipeline.

Stevens, Alan, jt. auth. see Schmidgall-Tellings, A. Ed.

Stevens, Alan, jt. ed. see Bancroft, John D.

Stevens, Albert C. Cyclopaedia of Fraternities. 2nd rev. ed. LC 66-20332. 1966. Repr. of 1907 ed. 20.00 (ISBN 0-8103-3084-9). Gale.

Stevens, Ann, tr. see Eca de Queiroz.

Stevens, Ardis. Fun Is Therapeutic: A Recreation Book to Help Therapeutic Recreation Leaders by People Who Are Leading Recreation. 104p. 1972. 9.75 (ISBN 0-398-02421-9). C C Thomas.

Stevens, B. Teaching the Metric System in the Foreign Language Classroom. (Language in Education Ser.: No. 32). 1980. pap. 4.95 (ISBN 0-87281-131-X). Ctr Appl Ling.

Stevens, Barbara, ed. Delicate Art of Nursing Supervision & Leadership. LC 77-85309. 1977. pap. 6.95 o.s.i. (ISBN 0-913654-41-8). Nursing Res.

Stevens, Barbara J. First-Line Patient Care Management. LC 76-499. 192p. 1976. 13.25 o.s.i. (ISBN 0-913654-25-6); pap. 8.95 o.s.i. (ISBN 0-913654-26-4). Nursing Res.

Stevens, Beulah F. Dear Georgia. LC 78-13546. 1979. pap. 0.65 (ISBN 0-8127-0204-2). Southern Pub.

Stevens, Blaine. The Outlanders. pap. 2.50 (ISBN 0-515-04861-5). Jove Pubns.

Stevens, Bob. If You Read Me, Rock the Tower! LC 80-66159. (Illus.). 144p. 1980. write for info. (ISBN 0-8168-6505-1). Aero.

Stevens, C. A. Your Key to the Cockpit. (Illus.). 1980. pap. 3.00 (ISBN 0-911721-85-1, Pub. by Inflight). Aviation.

Stevens, C. J., jt. ed. see Shaw, Ann M.

Stevens, Carla. Bear's Magic & Other Stories. (gr. k-3). 1977. pap. 1.50 (ISBN 0-590-01506-0, Schol Pap); pap. 3.50 bk. & record (ISBN 0-590-20800-4). Schol Bk Serv.

--The Birth of Sunset's Kittens. LC 69-14569. (Illus.). (gr. k-5). 1969. PLB 7.95 (ISBN 0-685-21698-5, A-W Childrens). A-W.

--Hooray for Pig! LC 73-17074. (Illus.). (ps-3). 1974. 5.95 (ISBN 0-395-28824-X, Clarion). HM.

--How to Make Possum's Honey Bread. LC 75-28183. 40p. (gr. 2-6). 1976. 6.50 (ISBN 0-395-28882-7, Clarion). HM.

--Pig & the Blue Flag. LC 76-58384. (Illus.). (gr. k-3). 1977. 6.95 (ISBN 0-395-28825-8, Clarion). HM.

--Rabbit & Skunk & Spooks. (Illus.). (gr. 2-3). pap. 1.25 (ISBN 0-590-08087-3, Schol Pap); pap. 3.50 bk. & record (ISBN 0-590-20612-5). Schol Bk Serv.

--Rabbit & Skunk & the Big Fight. (gr. k-3). 1976. pap. 1.25 (ISBN 0-590-01311-4, Schol Pap). Schol Bk Serv.

--Rabbit & Skunk & the Scary Rock. (gr. k-3). 1970. pap. 1.25 (ISBN 0-590-00111-6, Schol Pap). Schol Bk Serv.

--Sara & the Pinch. (Illus.). 48p. (gr. k-3). 1980. 6.95 (ISBN 0-395-29435-5, Clarion). HM.

--Stories from a Snowy Meadow. LC 76-3542. 48p. (gr. 2-5). 1976. 6.95 (ISBN 0-395-28883-5, Clarion). HM.

--Your First Pet. LC 74-2267. (Ready-to-Read Ser). (Illus.). 128p. (gr. 1-4). 1974. 7.95g o.s.i. (ISBN 0-02-788200-4). Macmillan.

Stevens, Carolyn B. Special Needs of Long-Term Patients. 250p. 1974. pap. text ed. 5.90 o.p. (ISBN 0-397-54133-3). Lippincott.

Stevens, Charles F. & Tsien, Richard W., eds. Membrane Transport Processes, Vol. 3. LC 76-19934. 1979. text ed. 16.00 (ISBN 0-89004-224-1). Raven.

Stevens, Christine, ed. see Leavitt, Emily S., et al.

Stevens, Cindy. Public Assistance in France. 94p. 1973. pap. text ed. 5.00x (ISBN 0-7135-1846-4, Pub. by Bedford England). Renouf.

Stevens, D. & Robertson. Classical & Romantic. 1968. pap. 2.50 o.p. (ISBN 0-14-020494-6). Penguin.

Stevens, Denis. Letters of Claudio Monteverdi. LC 80-66219. 432p. 1980. 45.00 (ISBN 0-521-23591-X). Cambridge U Pr.

Stevens, Denis, ed. History of Song. rev. ed. (Illus.). 1970. pap. 7.95 (ISBN 0-393-00536-4, Norton Lib). Norton.

Stevens, Denis, ed. see Menuhin, Yehudi.

Stevens, Denis, ed. see Ottaway, Hugh & Hutchings, Arthur.

Stevens, Dennis. Tudor Church Music. LC 73-4335. 144p. 1973. Repr. of 1955 ed. lib. bdg. 19.50 (ISBN 0-306-70579-6). Da Capo.

Stevens, Diane. Labyrinth. 1977. pap. 1.50 o.p. (ISBN 0-445-04131-5). Popular Lib.

Stevens, Don E. Man's Search for Certainty. LC 80-15743. 288p. 1980. 9.95 (ISBN 0-396-07860-5). Dodd.

Stevens, Earl E. & Stevens, H. Ray, eds. John Galsworthy: An Annotated Bibliography of Writings About Him. LC 78-60456. (Annotated Secondary Bibliography Ser. on English Literature in Transition, 1880-1920). 496p. 1980. 30.00x o.p. (ISBN 0-87580-073-4). N Ill U Pr.

Stevens, Edmund, tr. see Nizan, Paul.

Stevens, Edward. Business Ethics. LC 79-91409. (Orig.). 1980. pap. 7.95 (ISBN 0-8091-2244-8). Paulist Pr.

Stevens, Elisabeth. Elisabeth Stevens Nineteen Eighty-One Guide to Baltimore's Inner Harbor. (Illus.). 64p. 1981. pap. 2.50 (ISBN 0-916144-86-0). Stemmer Hse.

Stevens, Elliot L., ed. CAR Yearbook: 1979, Vol. 89. 1980. 15.00. Central Conf.

Stevens, Elliot L. & Weber, Donald A., eds. CCAR Yearbook: 1978, Vol. 88. 1979. 15.00x o.p. (ISBN 0-916694-58-5). Central Conf.

Stevens, Floyd A. Complete Course in Electronic Piano Tuning. LC 73-92238. (Illus.). 216p. 1974. 37.95 (ISBN 0-911012-24-9). Nelson-Hall.

--Complete Course in Professional Piano Tuning, Repair & Rebuilding. LC 74-173598. (Illus.). 1972. 37.95 (ISBN 0-911012-07-9). Nelson-Hall.

Stevens, Franklin. Dance As Life. 1977. pap. 2.95 (ISBN 0-380-01711-3, 33860, Discus). Avon.

Stevens, G. B. The Theology of the New Testament. 2nd ed. (International Theological Library). 636p. Repr. of 1918 ed. text ed. 13.95x (ISBN 0-567-07215-0). Attic Pr.

Stevens, G. T., jt. auth. see Shamblin, James E.

Stevens, G. T., Jr. Economic & Financial Analysis of Capital Investments. 1979. text ed. 26.95 (ISBN 0-471-04851-8); solutions manual avail. (ISBN 0-471-05001-6). Wiley.

Stevens, Gigs. Free-Form Bargello. LC 77-5784. (Illus.). 1977. 14.95 o.p. (ISBN 0-684-15024-7, ScribT); pap. 7.95 o.p. (ISBN 0-684-15055-7, SL719, ScribT). Scribner.

Stevens, H. Ray, jt. ed. see Stevens, Earl E.

Stevens, Helen B. Lines & Fragments. 68p. 1980. 4.50 (ISBN 0-8059-2756-5). Dorrance.

Stevens, Henry. Dawn of British Trade to the East Indies. 331p. Repr. of 1967 ed. 27.50x (ISBN 0-7146-1105-0, F Cass Co). Biblio Dist.

Stevens, Henry B. Recovery of Culture. 1963. 5.95 o.p. (ISBN 0-686-00957-6). Wellington.

--The Recovery of Culture. 1980. text ed. 4.75 o.p. (ISBN 0-8464-1047-8). Beekman Pubs.

Stevens, J. & Grant, J. The Purchasing-Marketing Interface: Text & Cases. LC 75-9965. 1976. 19.95 (ISBN 0-470-82438-7). Halsted Pr.

Stevens, J. E. Medieval Romance: Themes & Approaches. 1973. text ed. 15.00x (ISBN 0-09-114000-5, Hutchinson U Lib). Humanities.

Stevens, J. E., ed. Music & Poetry in the Early Tudor Court. LC 77-90180. (Cambridge Studies in Music). (Illus.). 1979. 69.50 (ISBN 0-521-22030-0); pap. 17.95 (ISBN 0-521-29417-7). Cambridge U Pr.

Stevens, James. Paul Bunyan. 1975. pap. 1.75 o.p. (ISBN 0-345-24423-0). Ballantine.

Stevens, James, jt. auth. see Scriven, Carl.

Stevens, Janet, illus. Animal Fair. (Illus.). 32p. (ps-2). 1981. PLB 8.95 (ISBN 0-8234-0388-2). Holiday.

Stevens, John. Measuring Purchasing Performance. 254p. 1978. text ed. 23.50x (ISBN 0-220-66331-9, Pub. by Busn Bks England). Renouf.

--Sacred Calligraphy of the East. LC 80-53446. (Illus.). 176p. (Orig.). 1981. pap. 9.95 (ISBN 0-394-74832-7). Shambhala Pubn.

Stevens, John, tr. The Spanish Libertines. LC 80-2499. 1981. Repr. of 1707 ed. 83.50 (ISBN 0-404-19135-5). AMS Pr.

Stevens, John, tr. see Bede.

Stevens, John, tr. see Quevedo y Villegas, Francisco G. de.

Stevens, John, tr. see Taneda, Santoka.

Stevens, John D. & Garcia, Hazel D. Communication History. LC 80-11132. (Sage Commtext Ser.: No. 2). (Illus.). 159p. 1980. 12.50x (ISBN 0-8039-1256-0); pap. 5.95 (ISBN 0-8039-1257-9). Sage.

Stevens, John G. R., jt. auth. see Gunn, Donald L.

Stevens, Joseph L. Impact of Federal Legislation & Programs on Private Land in Urban & Metropolitan Development. LC 73-5229. (Special Studies in U.S. Economic, Social & Political Issues). 1973. 28.50x (ISBN 0-275-28728-9). Irvington.

Stevens, Karl K. Statics & Strength of Materials. (Illus.). 1979. ref. 24.95 (ISBN 0-13-844688-1). P-H.

Stevens, Kathy, ed. see LaRouche, Lyndon H., Jr.

Stevens, Kathy, ed. see Salisbury, Allen.

Stevens, Kim. The Bee Gees: A Photo-Bio. 1979. pap. 1.95 (ISBN 0-515-05158-6). Jove Pubns.

Stevens, L. Robert. Charles Darwin. (English Authors Ser.: No. 240). 1978. 12.50 (ISBN 0-8057-6718-5). Twayne.

Stevens, Laura J. & Stoner, Rosemary B. How to Improve Your Child's Behavior Through Diet. 1981. pap. 3.50 (ISBN 0-451-09812-9, E9812, Signet Bks). NAL.

Stevens, Leonard A. How a Law Is Made: The Story of a Bill Against Air-Pollution. LC 74-101934. (Illus.). (gr. 5-9). 1970. 7.95 (ISBN 0-690-40609-6, TYC-J). T Y Crowell.

--Neurons: Building Blocks of the Brain. LC 74-4399. (Illus.). 128p. (gr. 7 up). 1974. 7.95 (ISBN 0-690-00403-6, TYC-J). T Y Crowell.

--The Trucks That Haul by Night. LC 66-10066. (Illus.). (gr. k-3). 1966. 7.89 (ISBN 0-690-83743-7, TYC-J). T Y Crowell.

Stevens, Lucile V. Green Shadows. 192p. (YA) 1973. 5.95 (ISBN 0-685-32415-X, Avalon). Bouregy.

--Joni of Storm Hill. 192p. (YA) 1976. 4.95 o.p. (ISBN 0-685-61054-3, Avalon). Bouregy.

--Red Tower. (YA) 5.95 (ISBN 0-685-07457-9, Avalon). Bouregy.

Stevens, Malcolm P. Polymer Chemistry: An Introduction. 1975. text ed. 23.50 (ISBN 0-201-07312-9, Adv Bk Prog); pap. text ed. 21.50 (ISBN 0-201-07313-7, Adv Bk Prog). A-W.

Stevens, Maria, jt. auth. see Lane, Gary.

Stevens, Marion K. The Practical Nurse in Supervisory Roles. LC 73-80982. (Illus.). 160p. 1973. text ed. 7.50x (ISBN 0-7216-8591-9). Saunders.

Stevens, Mark. How to Play Five Point Pitch: A Card Game for Everyone. (Illus.). 51p. (Orig.). 1980. 10.95; pap. 5.95 (ISBN 0-686-28069-5). Clawson.

Stevens, Martin see Cawley, A. C.

Stevens, Mary O., jt. auth. see McNulty, Thomas F.

Stevens, Nola. God & You Unlimited. (Illus.). 144p. 1980. 7.00 (ISBN 0-682-49642-1). Exposition.

Stevens, Nora see Stevens, Norman.

Stevens, Norman, ed. Author's Guide to Journals in Library & Information Science. Stevens, Nora. (Author's Guide to Journals Ser.). 1981. 16.95 (ISBN 0-917724-13-5). Haworth Pr.

Stevens, Norman D. Library Humor: A Bibliothecal Miscellany to 1970. LC 76-149995. 1971. 13.50 (ISBN 0-8108-0379-8). Scarecrow.

Stevens, Norman D., ed. Essays for Ralph Shaw. LC 75-6664. 219p. 1975. 10.00 (ISBN 0-8108-0815-3). Scarecrow.

--Essays from the New England Academic Librarians' Writing Seminar. LC 80-21502. 230p. 1980. 12.50 (ISBN 0-8108-1365-3). Scarecrow.

Stevens, Norman D., jt. ed. see Durnell, Jane B.

Stevens, P. T., ed. see Euripides.

Stevens, Patricia B. God Save Ireland! The Irish Conflict in the Twentieth Century. LC 73-19067. 224p. (gr. 7 up). 1974. 10.95 (ISBN 0-02-788180-6). Macmillan.

--Merry Christmas! A History of the Holiday. LC 79-13762. (Illus.). (gr. 6 up). 1979. 9.95 (ISBN 0-02-788210-1). Macmillan.

Stevens, Peter, ed. Modern English Canadian Poetry: A Guide to Information Sources. LC 73-16994. (American Literature, English Literature, & World Literatures in English Information Guide Ser.: Vol. 15). 1978. 30.00 (ISBN 0-8103-1244-1). Gale.

Stevens, Peter, ed. see Knister, Raymond.

Stevens, Peter S. A Handbook of Regular Patterns: An Introduction to Symmetry in Two Dimensions. (Illus.). 384p. 1981. 37.50 (ISBN 0-262-19188-1). MIT Pr.

Stevens, R. H., tr. see Hoffmann, Heinrich.

Stevens, R. T. The Summer Day Is Done. 464p. 1977. pap. 2.50 (ISBN 0-446-91667-6). Warner Bks.

--Woman of Texas. 1981. pap. 2.95 (ISBN 0-440-19555-1). Dell.

Stevens, Richard G., jt. ed. see Frisch, Morton J.

Stevens, Richard P. Historical Dictionary of the Republic of Botswana. LC 75-16489. (African Historical Dictionaries Ser.: No. 5). 189p. 1975. 10.00 (ISBN 0-8108-0857-9). Scarecrow.

Stevens, Robert & Stevens, Rosemary. Welfare Medicine in America: A Case Study of Medicaid. LC 74-2870. 1974. 16.95 (ISBN 0-02-931520-4). Free Pr.

Stevens, Robert D., et al, eds. see Japan-U.S. Conference on Libraries & Information Science in Higher Education, 3rd, Kyoto, Japan, Oct. 28-31, 1975.

Stevens, Rosemary, jt. auth. see Stevens, Robert.

Stevens, Rosemary, et al. Alien Doctors: Foreign Medical Graduates in American Hospitals. LC 77-12934. (Health, Medicine & Society Ser.). 1978. 26.95 (ISBN 0-471-82455-0, Pub. by Wiley-Interscience). Wiley.

Stevens, Russell B. Plant Disease. (Illus.). 459p. 1974. 22.95 (ISBN 0-8260-8503-2). Wiley.

Stevens, S. K., et al. The Papers of Henry Bouquet. Incl. Vol. 1. 1756-1758. 470p. 1972 (ISBN 0-911124-66-7); Vol. 2. Forbes Expedition. 736p. 1951. LC 51-9537. 15.00 ea. Pa Hist & Mus.

Stevens, S. S. Psychophysics: Introduction to Its Perceptual, Neutral & Social Prospects. LC 74-13473. 1975. 30.95 (ISBN 0-471-82437-2, Pub. by Wiley-Interscience). Wiley.

Stevens, S. Smith, jt. auth. see Warshofsky, Fred.

Stevens, Sherrill, jt. auth. see Preuss, Angela.

Stevens, V. L., jt. auth. see Haglund, E.

Stevens, W. C. The Book of Daniel. 190p. 1915. pap. 2.50 (ISBN 0-87509-061-3). Chr Pubns.

Stevens, W. R. Building Physics: Lighting. 1969. 25.00 (ISBN 0-08-006370-5); pap. 13.25 (ISBN 0-08-006369-1). Pergamon.

Stevens, Wallace. Selected Poems. 1965. pap. 5.95 (ISBN 0-571-06384-5, Pub. by Faber & Faber). Merrimack Bk Serv.

Stevens, Wayne P. Using Structured Design: How to Make Programs Simple, Changeable, Flexible & Reusable. 232p. 1981. 21.95 (ISBN 0-471-08198-1, Pub. by Wiley-Interscience). Wiley.

Stevens, William O. Famous American Statesmen. (Illus.). (gr. 7-9). 1953. 5.95 o.p. (ISBN 0-396-03449-7). Dodd.

Stevensen, Robert L. Kidnapped. (Childrens Illustrated Classics Ser). (Illus.). 1974. Repr. of 1960 ed. 5.50x o.p. (ISBN 0-460-05045-1, Pub. by J. M. Dent England). Biblio Dist.

Stevenson, Adlai. Looking Outward: Years of Crisis at the United Nations. Schiffer, Robert L. & Schiffer, Selma, eds. 1963. 10.95 o.s.i. (ISBN 0-06-014115-8, HarpT). Har-Row.

Stevenson, Anne. Correspondences: A Family History in Letters. LC 74-2871. 104p. 1974. 10.00x (ISBN 0-8195-4073-0, Pub. by Wesleyan U Pr). Columbia U Pr.

--Reversals. LC 73-82545. (Wesleyan Poetry Program: Vol. 47). 1969. 10.00x (ISBN 0-8195-2047-0, Pub. by Wesleyan U Pr); pap. 4.95x (ISBN 0-8195-1047-5). Columbia U Pr.

Stevenson, Burton, ed. Home Book of Quotations. rev. ed. LC 67-13583. 1967. 40.00 (ISBN 0-396-02533-1). Dodd.
Stevenson, Burton E. The Home Book of Verse. 10th ed. 45.00 o.p. (ISBN 0-03-028035-4). HR&W.
Stevenson, C. E., et al. Progress in Nuclear Energy, Series 3. 1970. 97.00 (ISBN 0-08-013401-7). Pergamon.
Stevenson, C. H. Spanish Language Today. 1970. text ed. 6.00x (ISBN 0-09-104550-9, Hutchinson U Lib); pap. text ed. 4.75x (ISBN 0-09-104501-0, Hutchinson U Lib). Humanities.
Stevenson, Charles L. see Dewey, John.
Stevenson, D. Alasdair MacColla & the Highland Problem in the Seventeenth Century. 1980. text ed. 39.00x (ISBN 0-85976-055-3). Humanities.
Stevenson, D. E. Celia's House. LC 76-29915. 1977. 7.95 o.p. (ISBN 0-03-020441-0). HR&W.
--The English Air. LC 75-29720. 1976. 7.95 o.p. (ISBN 0-03-016841-4). HR&W.
Stevenson, David K., jt. auth. see Olsen, Stephen B.
Stevenson, Don & Blyth, Hugh. The Wonderlamp. (Illus.). 49p. 1981. text ed. price not set (ISBN 0-933770-19-7). Kalimat.
Stevenson, Dwight E. Monday's God. new ed. 128p. (Orig.). 1976. pap. 1.25 (ISBN 0-8272-2309-9). Bethany Pr.
Stevenson, Dwight W., jt. auth. see Mathes, J. C.
Stevenson, Dwight W., et al, eds. Courses, Components, & Exercises in Technical Communication. 1981. pap. price not set (ISBN 0-8141-0877-6). NCTE.
Stevenson, Edwina, jt. auth. see Stevenson, James.
Stevenson, Florence. The Curse of the Concullens. pap. 1.50 (ISBN 0-451-07228-6, W7228, Sig). NAL.
--The Golden Galatea. (Orig.). 1979. pap. 2.25 o.s.i. (ISBN 0-515-04338-9). Jove Pubns.
--House at Luxor. pap. 1.25 (ISBN 0-451-07156-5, Y7156, Sig). NAL.
--The Moonlight Variations. 224p. (Orig.). 1981. pap. 2.50 (ISBN 0-515-05655-3). Jove Pubns.
--A Shadow on the House. 1975. pap. 1.25 o.p. (ISBN 0-451-06520-4, Y6520, Sig). NAL.
Stevenson, Florence, jt. auth. see Halbert, Sara.
Stevenson, Frederick W. Projective Planes. LC 72-156824. (Illus.). 1972. text ed. 26.95x (ISBN 0-7167-0443-9); teacher's manual avail. W H Freeman.
Stevenson, G. S., jt. auth. see Pierson, R. H.
Stevenson, George A. Graphic Arts Encyclopedia. 2nd ed. (Illus.). 1979. 29.95 (ISBN 0-07-061288-9). McGraw.
Stevenson, Gordon. Rudolph Focke & the Theory of the Classified Catalog: (Occasional Papers: No. 145). 1980. pap. 3.00. U of Ill Lib Sci.
Stevenson, H. N. Economics of the Central Chin Tribes. (Illus.). 1969. Repr. of 1943 ed. text ed. 15.50x (ISBN 0-576-59276-5). Humanities.
Stevenson, Harold W. Children's Learning. (Illus.). 425p. 1972. 16.95 (ISBN 0-13-132472-1). P-H.
Stevenson, Ian. Cases of the Reincarnation Type: Twelve Cases in Lebanon & Turkey, Vol. 3. LC 74-28263. 1980. 25.00x (ISBN 0-8139-0816-7). U Pr of Va.
--Twenty Cases Suggestive of Reincarnation. 2nd rev. ed. LC 73-93627. Orig. Title: Proceedings of the American Society for Psychical Research, Vol. 26. xvi, 368p. 1974. 15.00x o.p. (ISBN 0-8139-0546-X). U Pr of Va.
Stevenson, J. F-Eighteen Hornet, Vol. 29. (Aero Ser.). 104p. 1981. 7.95 (ISBN 0-8168-0608-X). Aero.
Stevenson, J. W. Incredible Church. 2.50 o.p. (ISBN 0-227-67490-1). Attic Pr.
Stevenson, James. Could Be Worse! LC 76-28534. (gr. k-3). 1977. 8.25 (ISBN 0-688-80075-0); PLB 7.92 (ISBN 0-688-84075-2). Greenwillow.
--Let's Boogie! LC 78-17558. (Illus.). 1978. 8.95 (ISBN 0-396-07633-5). Dodd.
--Monty. LC 78-11409. (Illus.). (gr. k-3). 1979. 8.50 (ISBN 0-688-80209-5); PLB 8.16 (ISBN 0-688-84209-7). Greenwillow.
--Monty. (Illus.). 32p. 1980. Repr. pap. 1.95 (ISBN 0-590-30268-X, Schol Pap). Schol Bk Serv.
--The Sea View Hotel. LC 78-2749. (Illus.). (gr. k-3). 1978. 7.95 (ISBN 0-688-80168-4); PLB 7.63 (ISBN 0-688-84168-6). Greenwillow.
--That Terrible Halloween Night. LC 79-27775. (Illus.). 32p. (ps). 1980. 7.95 (ISBN 0-688-80281-8); PLB 7.63 (ISBN 0-688-84281-X). Greenwillow.
--Wilfred the Rat. LC 77-1091. (Illus.). (ps-3). 1977. 7.25 (ISBN 0-688-80103-X); PLB 6.96 (ISBN 0-688-84103-1). Greenwillow.
--The Wish Card Ran Out! (Illus.). 32p. (gr. k-4). 1981. 7.95 (ISBN 0-688-80305-9); PLB 7.63 (ISBN 0-688-84305-0). Greenwillow.
--The Worst Person in the World. LC 77-22141. (Illus.). (gr. k-3). 1978. 7.95 (ISBN 0-688-80127-7); PLB 7.63 (ISBN 0-688-84127-9). Greenwillow.
Stevenson, James & Stevenson, Edwina. Help, Yelled Maxwell. LC 77-21247. (Illus.). (gr. 3-5). 1978. 7.95 (ISBN 0-688-80133-1); PLB 7.63 (ISBN 0-688-84133-3). Greenwillow.
Stevenson, James P. McDonnell Douglas F-15 "Eagle". LC 78-17244. (Aero Ser.: Vol. 28). 1978. pap. 7.95 (ISBN 0-8168-0604-7). Aero.
Stevenson, Janet. Montgomery Bus Boycott, December, 1955: American Blacks Demand an End to Segregation. LC 78-161072. (Focus Bks). (Illus.). (gr. 7 up). 1971. PLB 4.90 o.p. (ISBN 0-531-00994-7). Watts.
--The School Segregation Cases: Brown Vs. Board of Education of Topeka & Others. LC 73-5722. (Focus Bks.). (gr. 7-12). 1973. PLB 4.90 o.p. (ISBN 0-531-01046-5). Watts.
--Spokesman for Freedom: The Life of Archibald Grimke. (Illus.). (gr. 5-8). 1969. 3.95g o.s.i. (ISBN 0-02-788240-3, CCPr). Macmillan.
--The Undiminished Man: A Political Biography of Robert Walker Kenny. LC 80-10889. (Illus.). 218p. 1980. 10.95 (ISBN 0-88316-538-4). Chandler & Sharp.
--Women's Rights. LC 74-182299. (First Bks). (Illus.). 96p. (gr. 5-7). 1972. PLB 4.90 o.p. (ISBN 0-531-00763-4). Watts.
Stevenson, John. Merchant of Menace. (Orig.). 1980. pap. 1.75 (ISBN 0-505-51507-5). Tower Bks.
Stevenson, John, jt. auth. see Cook, Christopher.
Stevenson, John, ed. London in the Age of Reform. 1977. 30.50x (ISBN 0-631-17820-1, Pub. by Basil Blackwell). Biblio Dist.
Stevenson, John P. Trout Farming Manual. 1980. 60.75x (ISBN 0-686-64739-4, Pub. by Fishing News England). State Mutual Bk.
--Trout Farming Manual. (Illus.). 1980. text ed. 26.50x (ISBN 0-85238-102-6). Scholium Intl.
Stevenson, Leslie. Seven Theories of Human Nature. 1974. text ed. 8.95 (ISBN 0-19-875033-1); pap. text ed. 3.95x (ISBN 0-19-875034-X). Oxford U Pr.
Stevenson, Leslie, ed. The Study of Human Nature. 352p. 1981. pap. text ed. 7.95x (ISBN 0-19-502827-9). Oxford U Pr.
Stevenson, Merritt R., et al. A Marine Atlas of the Pacific Coastal Waters of South America. LC 79-85448. (Illus.). 1970. 75.00x (ISBN 0-520-01616-5). U of Cal Pr.
Stevenson, Olive. Someone Else's Child: A Book for Foster Parents of Young Children. 2nd ed. 1977. pap. 6.50 (ISBN 0-7100-8706-3). Routledge & Kegan.
Stevenson, Peter. Braithwaite's Original Brass Band. LC 80-18065. (Illus.). 32p. (gr. 6-9). 1981. 8.95 (ISBN 0-7232-6193-8). Warne.
Stevenson, R. E., jt. ed. see Cowing, T. G.
Stevenson, Richard A. & Jennings, Edward H. Fundamentals of Investments. LC 75-42350. (Illus.). 580p. 1976. text ed. 16.95 (ISBN 0-8299-0077-2); instrs.' manual avail. (ISBN 0-8299-0575-8). West Pub.
--Fundamentals of Investments. 2nd ed. (Illus.). 608p. 1980. text ed. 15.95 (ISBN 0-8299-0299-6). West Pub.
Stevenson, Robert. Christmas Music from Baroque Mexico. (Illus.). 1974. 35.00x o.p. (ISBN 0-520-02036-7). U of Cal Pr.
--Music in Aztec & Inca Territory. (California Library Reprint Ser.: No. 64). 1977. Repr. of 1968 ed. 38.50x (ISBN 0-520-03169-5). UCDLA.
--Protestant Church Music in America: A Short Survey of Men & Movements from 1564 to the Present. (Illus.). 1970. pap. 2.95 o.p. (ISBN 0-393-00535-6, Norton Lib). Norton.
--Spanish Cathedral Music in the Golden Age. LC 76-1013. (Illus.). 523p. 1976. Repr. of 1961 ed. lib. bdg. 39.50x (ISBN 0-8371-8744-3, STSP). Greenwood.
--Spanish Music in the Age of Columbus. LC 78-20496. (Encore Music Editions Ser.). 1981. Repr. of 1960 ed. 29.50 (ISBN 0-88355-872-6). Hyperion Conn.
Stevenson, Robert A. The Complete Book of Salt-Water Aquariums: How to Equip & Maintain Your Marine Aquarium & Understand Its Ecology. (Funk & W Bk.). 224p. 1974. 9.95 (ISBN 0-308-10090-5, TYC-T). T Y Crowell.
Stevenson, Robert F. Population & Political Systems in Tropical Africa. LC 68-11435. (Illus.). 1968. 17.50x (ISBN 0-231-03052-5). Columbia U Pr.
Stevenson, Robert L. The Black Arrow. (Childrens Illustrated Classics Ser). (Illus.). 1967. Repr. of 1957 ed. 9.00x o.p. (ISBN 0-460-05040-0, Pub. by J. M. Dent England). Biblio Dist.
--Child's Garden of Verses. (Illus.). (gr. k-3). 1951. PLB 7.62 o.p. (ISBN 0-307-65557-1, Golden Pr). Western Pub.
--A Child's Garden of Verses. (Children's Library of Picture Bks.). (Illus.). 10p. (ps). 1979. 1.95 (ISBN 0-89346-178-4, TA60, Pub. by Froebel-Kan Japan). Heian Intl.
--Dr. Jekyl & Mr. Hyde. Incl. Merrymen & Other Tales. 1954. 10.50x (ISBN 0-460-00767-X, Evman); pap. 4.50 (ISBN 0-460-01767-5). Dutton.
--Dr. Jekyll & Mr. Hyde & Other Stories. Calder, Jenni, ed. 1981. pap. 2.95 (ISBN 0-14-005776-5). Penguin.
--Master of Ballantrae. Incl. Weir of Hermiston. 1956. 11.50x (ISBN 0-460-00764-5, Evman); pap. 3.25 (ISBN 0-460-01764-0). Dutton.
--Poems of Robert Louis Stevenson. Plotz, Helen, ed. LC 72-78282. (Poets Ser.). (Illus.). 128p. (gr. 7 up). 1973. 8.95 (ISBN 0-690-64395-0, TYC-J). T Y Crowell.
--Selected Prayers by Robert Louis Stevenson. (Illus.). 1980. Repr. of 1904 ed. 29.75 (ISBN 0-89901-004-0). Found Class Reprints.
--Strange Case of Dr. Jekyll & Mr. Hyde. (gr. 3 up). 1978. pap. 1.25 (ISBN 0-307-21633-0, Golden Pr). Western Pub.
--The Touchstone. LC 76-3412. (Illus.). 48p. (gr. 3 up). 1976. 8.25 (ISBN 0-688-80051-3); PLB 7.92 (ISBN 0-688-84051-5). Greenwillow.
--Travels with a Donkey in the Cevennes. 1980. 12.95 (ISBN 0-906223-17-2). Dufour.
--Treasure Island. abr. ed. Gray, Jenny, ed. LC 70-133537. (Pacemaker Classics Ser.). (Illus., Orig., Adapted to grade 2 reading level). (RL 2.5). 1970. pap. 3.80 (ISBN 0-8224-9230-X); tchrs' manual free (ISBN 0-8224-5200-6). Pitman Learning.
--Treasure Island. (Literature Ser). (gr. 7-12). 1969. pap. text ed. 3.50 (ISBN 0-87720-718-6). AMSCO Sch.
--Treasure Island. (Keith Jennison Large Type Bks). (Illus.). (gr. 9 up). 1964. PLB 7.95 o.p. (ISBN 0-531-00296-9). Watts.
--Treasure Island. (Tempo Classic Ser.). 1979. pap. 1.50 (ISBN 0-448-17121-X, Tempo). G&D.
--Treasure Island. LC 78-3553. (Raintree's Illustrated Classics). (Illus.). (gr. 5-8). 1978. PLB 9.65 (ISBN 0-8393-6211-0). Raintree Child.
Stevenson, Robert L., et al. Monster Masterpieces, 3 bks. 1980. pap. 3.75 boxed set (ISBN 0-307-13621-3, Golden Pr). Western Pub.
Stevenson, Robert Louis. Treasure Island with Reader's Guide. (Amsco Literature Program). (gr. 10-12). 1972. pap. text ed. 4.17 (ISBN 0-87720-817-4); model ans. bk. 2.70 (ISBN 0-87720-917-0). AMSCO Sch.
Stevenson, Ronald, ed. see Ziehn, Bernhard.
Stevenson, Russell B., Jr. Corporations & Information: Secrecy, Access & Disclosure. LC 79-3683. 212p. 1980. text ed. 17.95x (ISBN 0-8018-2344-7). Johns Hopkins.
Stevenson, Taloria, ed. see Glickman, Linda.
Stevenson, Taloria, ed. see Wilder, C. S.
Stevenson, Taylor, jt. auth. see Gibbs, Lee.
Stevenson, W. B. Crusaders in the East. 16.00x (ISBN 0-686-53119-1). Intl Bk Ctr.
--Portuguese of the Arabian Coast. (Arab Background Ser.). 1968. 14.00x (ISBN 0-685-77105-9). Intl Bk Ctr.
Stevenson, W. C. Making & Managing a Pub. LC 79-51101. (Making & Managing Ser.). (Illus.). 1980. 17.95 (ISBN 0-7153-7801-5). David & Charles.
Stevenson, W. H. The Poems of William Blake. (Longman Annotated English Poets Ser.). (Illus.). 1972. pap. text ed. 13.95x (ISBN 0-582-48459-6). Longman.
Stevenson, Warren. Divine Analogy: A Study of the Creation Motif in Blake & Coleridge. (Salzburg Studies in English Literature, Romantic Reassessment: No. 25). 403p. 1972. pap. text ed. 25.00x (ISBN 0-391-01534-6). Humanities.
Stevenson, Warren H., jt. ed. see Thompson, H. Doyle.
Stevenson, William. Golden Berg Who Wouldn't Dance. LC 80-7943. 576p. 1980. 8.95 (ISBN 0-15-135338-7). HarBraceJ.
--A Man Called Intrepid. (Illus.). 1979. pap. 3.50 (ISBN 0-345-28124-1). Ballantine.
--A Man Called Intrepid: The Secret War. Moore, John, tr. LC 75-29051. (Illus.). 512p. 1976. 15.95 (ISBN 0-15-156795-6). HarBraceJ.
Stevenson, William B. Grammar of Palestinian Jewish Aramaic. 2nd ed. (With an Appendix on the Numerals). 1962. 13.95x (ISBN 0-19-815419-4). Oxford U Pr.
Stever, H. Guyford & Haggerty, James J. Flight. LC 65-24362. (Life Science Library). (Illus.). (gr. 5 up). 1969. PLB 8.97 o.p. (ISBN 0-8094-0469-9, Pub. by Time-Life). Silver.
Steves, Rick. Europe - Through the Back Door. 2nd ed. 112p. 1981. pap. 5.95 (ISBN 0-686-28770-3). Steves Wide World.
Steveson, H. L., compiled by. Light Upon the Word. 1980. pap. 6.95 (ISBN 0-8007-1105-X). Revell.
Stevick, Daniel. Canon Law: A Handbook. rev. ed. 1979. 8.95 (ISBN 0-8164-0347-3). Crossroad NY.
Stevick, Daniel B. & Johnson, Ben. Holy Week. LC 73-79351. (Proclamation 1: Aids for Interpreting the Lessons of the Church Year, Ser. C). 64p. 1973. pap. 1.95 (ISBN 0-8006-4054-3, 1-4054). Fortress.
Stevick, E. W. & Aremu, Odaleye. Spoken Yoruba. (Spoken Language Ser.). 381p. 1980. pap. 10.00x (ISBN 0-87950-708-X); cassettes, 34 oval track 165.00 (ISBN 0-686-64676-2); text & cassettes 170.00x (ISBN 0-87950-712-8). Spoken Lang Serv.
Stevick, Earl & Aremu, Odaleye. Spoken Yoruba, Units 1-50. 381p. 1980. pap. 10.00x (ISBN 0-87950-708-X); cassettes 34 dual track 165.00 (ISBN 0-87950-710-1); bk. & cassettes 170.00x (ISBN 0-87950-712-8). Spoken Lang Serv.
Stevick, Earl W. Teaching Languages: A Way & Ways. (Orig.). 1980. pap. text ed. 11.95 (ISBN 0-88377-147-0). Newbury Hse.
Stevick, P. Anti-Story: An Anthology of Experimental Fiction. LC 78-131596. 1971. pap. text ed. 6.95 (ISBN 0-02-931500-X). Free Pr.
Stevick, Philip, ed. Theory of the Novel. LC 67-25335. 1967. pap. text ed. 8.95 (ISBN 0-02-931490-9). Free Pr.
Stevick, Robert D., ed. One Hundred Middle English Lyrics. LC 76-20862. (Orig.). 1964. pap. 5.50 (ISBN 0-672-60974-6, LL7). Bobbs.
Steward, Barbara & Steward, Dwight. Evermore. 1978. 7.95 o.p. (ISBN 0-688-03278-8). Morrow.
Steward, Dwight, jt. auth. see Steward, Barbara.
Steward, F. C. & Krikorian, A. D. Plants, Chemicals & Growth. 1971. text ed. 21.50 (ISBN 0-12-668662-9); pap. 8.95 (ISBN 0-12-668660-2). Acad Pr.
Steward, F. C., ed. Plant Physiology: A Treatise, 6 vols. Incl. Vol. 1A. Cellular Organization & Respiration. 1960. 41.00 (ISBN 0-12-668601-7); Vol. 1B. Photosynthesis & Chemosynthesis. 1960. 40.50 (ISBN 0-12-668641-6); Vol. 2. Plants in Relation to Water & Solutes. 1959. 59.00 (ISBN 0-12-668602-5); Vol. 3. Inorganic Nutrition of Plants. 1963. 59.00 (ISBN 0-12-668603-3); Vol. 4A. Metabolism: Organic Nutrition & Nitrogen Metabolism. 1965. 59.00 (ISBN 0-12-668604-1); Vol. 4B. Metabolism: Intermediary Metabolism & Pathology. 1966. 59.00 o.s.i. (ISBN 0-12-668644-0); Vol. 5A. Analysis of Growth: Behavior of Plants & Their Organs. 1969. 59.00 (ISBN 0-12-668605-X); Vol. 5B. Analysis of Growth: The Responses of Cells & Tissues in Culture. 1969. 47.00 (ISBN 0-12-668645-9); Vol. 6A. Physiology of Development: Plants & Their Reproduction. 1972. 59.00 (ISBN 0-12-668606-8); Vol. 6B. Physiology of Development: the Hormones. 1972. 48.00 (ISBN 0-12-668646-7); Vol. 6C. From Seeds to Sexuality. 1972. 47.00 (ISBN 0-12-668656-4). Set. 897.80 (ISBN 0-685-23211-5). Acad Pr.
Steward, Frederick C. About Plants: Topics in Plant Biology. LC 66-10506. (Biology Ser). (Orig.). 1966. pap. 7.95 (ISBN 0-201-07284-X). A-W.
--Plants at Work. (gr. 10-12). 1964. pap. 7.95 (ISBN 0-201-07286-6). A-W.
Steward, J. K., jt. auth. see Marsden, H. B.
Steward, Joyce S. Contemporary College Reader. 2nd ed. 1981. pap. 7.95x (ISBN 0-673-15404-1). Scott F.
Steward, Julian. Alfred Kroeber. LC 72-8973. (Leaders of Modern Anthropology Ser.). 225p. 1973. 15.00x (ISBN 0-231-03489-X); pap. 4.00x (ISBN 0-231-03490-3). Columbia U Pr.
Steward, Julian H. Basin-Plateau Aboriginal Sociopolitical Groups. 2nd ed. (Smithsonian Institution Bureau of Ethnology Ser.: Bulletin 120). 1975. pap. 8.00x (ISBN 0-87480-014-5). U of Utah Pr.
Steward, Julian H. & Wheeler-Voegelin, Erminie. Paiute Indians, Vol. Three: The Northern Paiute Indians. (American Indian Ethnohistory Ser: California & Basin - Plateau Indians). (Illus.). lib. bdg. 42.00 (ISBN 0-8240-0742-5). Garland Pub.
Steward, M. W. Immunochemistry. LC 74-4104. (Outline Studies in Biology). 64p. (Orig.). 1974. pap. 5.95x o.p. (ISBN 0-412-12450-5, Pub. by Chapman & Hall). Methuen Inc.
--Immunochemistry. LC 74-4104. (Outline Studies in Biology). (Orig.). 1974. pap. text ed. 4.95 o.p. (ISBN 0-470-82470-0). Halsted Pr.
Steward, M. W., ed. see Glynn, L. E.
Steward, M. W., jt. ed. see Glynn, L. E.
Steward, Robert M. Boatbuilding Manual. 2nd ed. LC 79-90479. (Illus.). 228p. 1980. 18.50 (ISBN 0-87742-130-7). Intl Marine.
Steward, Samuel M. Chapters from an Autobiography. LC 80-26602. 160p. 1981. 12.00 (ISBN 0-912516-59-3); pap. 5.95 (ISBN 0-912516-60-7). Grey Fox.
Stewart. Welcome the Birds. 7.95 (ISBN 0-392-07518-0, LTB). Soccer.
Stewart, jt. auth. see Shepard, J. M.
Stewart, A. C. Dark Dove. LC 74-14814. 192p. (gr. 6-9). 1974. 9.95 (ISBN 0-87599-203-X). S G Phillips.

--Elizabeth's Tower. LC 72-4063. 220p. (gr. 6-9). 1972. 9.95 (ISBN 0-87599-193-9). S G Phillips.
--Ossian House. LC 76-9645. (gr. 6 up). 1976. PLB 9.95 (ISBN 0-87599-219-6). S G Phillips.
Stewart, A. T. The Narrow Ground. (Illus.). 1977. 14.95 o.p. (ISBN 0-571-10325-1, Pub. by Faber & Faber). Merrimack Bk Serv.
--The Ulster Crisis. (Illus., Orig.). 1969. pap. 6.50 (ISBN 0-571-08066-9, Pub. by Faber & Faber). Merrimack Bk Serv.
Stewart, Alec, ed. see Positron Annihilation Conference - Wayne State University - 1965.
Stewart, Alexander, et al. Social Stratification & Occupations. Prandy, Ken & Blackburn, R. M., eds. LC 80-16282. 320p. 1980. text ed. 36.00x (ISBN 0-8419-0630-0); pap. text ed. 19.95x (ISBN 0-8419-0630-0). Holmes & Meier.
Stewart, Andrew. The American System: Speeches on the Tariff Question, & on Internal Improvements. (The Neglected American Economists Ser.). 1974. lib. bdg. 50.00 (ISBN 0-8240-1019-1). Garland Pub.
--Live to Ninety & Stay Young. 184p. 1968. 5.25x (ISBN 0-8464-1029-X). Beekman Pubs.
Stewart, Andrew, jt. auth. see Stewart, Valerie.
Stewart, Anne. What's a Wilderness Worth? LC 79-13781. (Story of Environmental Action Ser.). (Illus.). (gr. 7 up). 1979. PLB 8.95 (ISBN 0-87518-182-1). Dillon.
Stewart, Arvis, illus. Bible Studies for Children. LC 79-27811. (Illus.). 336p. (gr. 1-5). 1980. 12.95 (ISBN 0-02-554060-2). Macmillan.
Stewart, Barbara J. Washington, D.C. in Color. (Profiles of America Ser.). (Illus.). 1977. 6.95 (ISBN 0-8038-8083-9). Hastings.
Stewart, Bruce. A Disorderly Girl. 294p. 1981. 11.95 (ISBN 0-312-21265-8). St Martin.
--Science of Social Issues. 1971. 10.00 (ISBN 0-8108-0410-7). Scarecrow.
Stewart, C. C. & Stewart, E. K. Islam & Social Order in Mauritania: A Case Study from the Nineteenth Century. (Oxford Studies in African Affairs Ser.). 1973. 24.00x (ISBN 0-19-821688-2). Oxford U Pr.
Stewart, C. M., jt. auth. see Allport, J. A.
Stewart, C. P. & Stolman, A., eds. Toxicology: Mechanisms & Analytical Methods. 2 vols. 1960-61. Vol. 2. 67.25 o.s.i. (ISBN 0-12-669702-7). Acad Pr.
Stewart, Charles E., ed. see Philippakis, Andreas S. & Kazmier, Leonard.
Stewart, Charles E., ed. see Philippakis, Andreas S. & Kazmier, Leonard J.
Stewart, Charles E., ed. see Rice, John R.
Stewart, Charles E., ed. see Tremblay, Jean-Paul & Bunt, Richard B.
Stewart, Charles T. Air Pollution, Human Health, & Public Policy. LC 78-13818. 1979. 16.50 (ISBN 0-669-02670-0). Lexington Bks.
Stewart, Charles T., Jr. Low-Wage Workers in an Affluent Society. LC 73-78912. 1974. 15.95 (ISBN 0-88229-101-7). Nelson-Hall.
Stewart, Christina D., intro. by. Ann Taylor Gilbert's Album. LC 75-32206. 525p. 1977. lib. bdg. 38.00 (ISBN 0-8240-2316-1). Garland Pub.
Stewart Conference on Research in Nursing, Sixteenth. Perspectives on Nursing Leadership: Proceedings. Ketefian, Shake, ed. LC 80-27464. (Orig.). 1981. pap. text ed. 10.95 (ISBN 0-8077-2637-0). Tchrs Coll.
Stewart, D. L. Fathers Are People Too. (Illus.). 128p. (Orig.). 1980. pap. 4.95 (ISBN 0-938492-01-2). Journal Herald.
Stewart, Darryl. Canadian Endangered Species. 12.95 o.s.i. (ISBN 0-685-57292-7). Vanguard. Postponed.
Stewart, David, ed. see Ricoeur, Paul.
Stewart, David H., jt. auth. see Eckhardt, Caroline D.
Stewart, David S. Practical Design of Simple Steel Structures, 2 vols. Incl. Vol. 1. Shop Practice, Riveted Connections, Beams, Tables. 6.50 o.p. (ISBN 0-8044-4906-6); Vol. 2. Plate Girders, Columns, Trusses. 8.50 o.p. (ISBN 0-8044-4907-4). Set (ISBN 0-8044-4905-8). Ungar.
Stewart, Desmond. Early Islam. LC 67-27863. (Great Ages of Man Ser.). (gr. 6 up). 1967. PLB 11.97 (ISBN 0-8094-0377-3, Pub. by Time-Life). Silver.
--The Vampire of Mons. 1977. pap. 1.50 o.p. (ISBN 0-380-01681-8, 33522). Avon.
Stewart, Desmond, tr. see Ghanem, Fathy.
Stewart, Desmond, tr. see Sharkawi, A. R.
Stewart, Don. Miracle Happiness. (Orig.). 1981. pap. 2.95 (ISBN 0-88270-483-4). Logos.
--Miracle Success. 1980. pap. text ed. 2.95 (ISBN 0-88270-484-2). Logos.
Stewart, Don, jt. auth. see McDowell, Josh.
Stewart, Donald C. Handling Radioactivity: A Practical Approach for Scientists & Engineers. LC 80-19258. 416p. 1981. 38.00 (ISBN 0-471-04557-8, Pub. by Wiley-Interscience). Wiley.
Stewart, Dugald. Outlines of the Moral Philosophy. LC 75-11255. (British Philosophers & Theologians of the 17th & 18th Centuries: Vol. 54). 1976. Repr. of 1793 ed. lib. bdg. 42.00 (ISBN 0-8240-1805-2). Garland Pub.
Stewart, E. K., jt. auth. see Stewart, C. C.
Stewart, Ed. Here Comes Jesus. 1977. pap. 1.95 (ISBN 0-8307-0553-8, S101-1-57). Regal.
Stewart, Edgar I. Custer's Luck. (Illus.). 522p. 1955. 17.95 (ISBN 0-8061-0321-3); pap. 12.50 (ISBN 0-8061-1632-3). U of Okla Pr.
Stewart, Edith H. I, Me, My, We: From the Orient to a Kansas Ranch & Chick Hatchery, with Much Fun Along the Way. (Illus.). 151p. 1963. 3.95 (ISBN 0-8040-0084-0). Swallow.
Stewart, Edward. Great Los Angeles Fire. 1980. 11.95 (ISBN 0-671-25135-X). S&S.
--Launch. 1977. pap. 1.95 o.p. (ISBN 0-451-07743-1, J7743, Sig). NAL.
Stewart, Edward C. American Cultural Patterns: A Cross-Cultural Perspective. LC 70-26361. 1971. pap. text ed. 6.50 (ISBN 0-933662-01-7). Intercult Pr.
Stewart, Edward T., et al. An Atlas of Endoscopic Retrograde Cholangiopancreatography. LC 77-11169. (Illus.). 1977. text ed. 53.50 (ISBN 0-8016-4803-3). Mosby.
Stewart, Elbert W. The Human Bond: Introduction to Social Psychology. LC 77-9002. 1978. pap. text ed. 18.95x (ISBN 0-471-82479-8); tchrs. manual avail. (ISBN 0-471-82481-X). Wiley.
Stewart, Elinore P. Letters of a Woman Homesteader. LC 61-16191. 1961. pap. 3.50 (ISBN 0-8032-5193-9, BB 115, Bison). U of Nebr Pr.
--Letters on an Elk Hunt by a Woman Homesteader. LC 79-13840. (Illus.). 1978. 10.95x (ISBN 0-8032-4112-7); pap. 3.75 (ISBN 0-8032-9112-4, BB 703, Bison). U of Nebr Pr.
Stewart, Emily & Dean, Martha H. The Almost Whole Earth Catalog of Process Oriented Enrichment Materials. 1980. pap. 12.95 (ISBN 0-936386-12-6). Creative Learning.
Stewart, Ernest I. & Malfetti, James L. Rehabilitation of the Drunken Driver: A Corrective Course in Phoenix, Arizona for Persons Convicted of Driving Under the Influence of Alcohol. LC 73-137738. 1970. pap. 7.00x (ISBN 0-8077-1801-7). Tchrs Coll.
Stewart, Evelyn S., jt. auth. see Sullivan, Neil V.
Stewart, F. H., et al. My Body, My Health: The Concerned Woman's Guide to Gynecology. LC 78-31499. 1979. 15.95 (ISBN 0-471-04517-9); pap. 8.95 (ISBN 0-471-04515-2, Pub. by Wiley Medical). Wiley.
Stewart, Felicia & Hatcher, Robert. My Body, My Health. 592p. 1981. pap. 9.95 (ISBN 0-553-01299-1). Bantam.
Stewart, Fred M. Century. LC 80-22417. 576p. 1981. 13.95 (ISBN 0-688-00398-2). Morrow.
--A Rage Against Heaven. 1979. pap. 2.75 o.p. (ISBN 0-449-24037-1, Crest). Fawcett.
--A Rage Against Heaven. 1978. 10.95 o.p. (ISBN 0-670-58910-1). Viking Pr.
Stewart, G. A., et al. The Potential for Liquid Fuels from Agriculture & Forestry in Australia. 147p. 1980. pap. 7.50 (ISBN 0-643-00353-3, Pub. by SIRO Australia). Intl Schol Bk Serv.
Stewart, G. B. A New Mythos: The Novel of the Artist As Heroine, 1877-1977. LC 78-74840. 1979. 17.95 (ISBN 0-88831-030-7). EPWP.
Stewart, G. F., jt. ed. see Mrak, E. M.
Stewart, Gary K., jt. auth. see Hatcher, Robert A.
Stewart, George & Amerine, Maynard. Introduction to Food Science. (Food Science & Technology Ser). 1973. text ed. 18.95 (ISBN 0-12-670250-0). Acad Pr.
Stewart, George F., jt. ed. see Rockland, Louis B.
Stewart, George R. John Phoenix Esq., the Veritable Squibob, a Life of Captain George H. Derby, U. S. A. LC 75-87721. (American Scene Ser.). 1969. Repr. of 1937 ed. lib. bdg. 25.00 (ISBN 0-306-71669-0). Da Capo.
--Year of the Oath. LC 77-150422. (Civil Liberties in American History Ser). 1971. Repr. of 1950 ed. lib. bdg. 25.00 (ISBN 0-306-70103-0). Da Capo.
Stewart, Gordon T., ed. Trends in Epidemiology: Application to Health Service Research & Training. (Amer. Lec. Epidemiology Ser). (Illus.). 624p. 1972. 40.75 (ISBN 0-398-02422-7). C C Thomas.
Stewart, H. C., jt. auth. see Hughes, W. H.
Stewart, H. L., jt. auth. see Kifer, R. S.
Stewart, H. M. Egyptian Stelae, Relief & Printings from the Petrie Collection. (Modern Egyptology Ser.). 100p. 40.00x (ISBN 0-85668-171-7, Pub. by Aris & Phillips England). Intl Schol Bk Serv.
Stewart, Harris B., Jr. & Henderson, J. Welles, eds. Challenger Sketchbook: B. Shephard's Sketchbook of the H.M.S. Challenger Expedition 1872-1874. (Illus.). 34p. 1972. 25.00 (ISBN 0-913346-01-2). Phila Maritime Mus.
Stewart, Harry L. Hydraulics for off-the Road Equipment. LC 77-93790. 1978. 8.95 (ISBN 0-672-23306-1). Audel.
--Pneumatics & Hydraulics. 3rd ed. LC 75-36658. (Illus.). 1976. 10.95 (ISBN 0-672-23237-5, 23237). Audel.
--Pumps. 3rd ed. LC 77-75529. 1978. 10.95 (ISBN 0-672-23292-8). Audel.
Stewart, Harry L. & Storer, John M. Fluid Power. 3rd ed. LC 73-82160. 1980. 19.95 (ISBN 0-672-97224-7); instructor's manual 3.33 (ISBN 0-672-97226-3); student manual 8.95 (ISBN 0-672-97225-5). Bobbs.
Stewart, Harry L, jt. auth. see Storer, John M.
Stewart, Hilary. Indian Fishing: Early Methods on the Northwest Coast. LC 77-950. (Illus.). 136p. 1981. pap. 15.00 (ISBN 0-295-95803-0). U of Wash Pr.
--Wild Teas, Coffees, & Cordials. (Illus.). 128p. 1981. 7.95 (ISBN 0-295-95804-9). U of Wash Pr.
Stewart, Hugh B. Transitional Energy Policy 1980-2030: Alternative Nuclear Technologies. (Pergamon Policy Studies on Science & Technology). 266p. 1981. 30.00 (ISBN 0-08-027183-9); pap. 12.50 (ISBN 0-08-027182-0). Pergamon.
Stewart, I., jt. auth. see Amayo, R. K.
Stewart, I. N. & Tall, D. O. Algebraic Number Theory. LC 78-31625. 200p. 1979. pap. 14.95 (ISBN 0-412-16000-5, Pub. by Chapman & Hall). Methuen Inc.
Stewart, Ian. The Peking Payoff. 252p. 1975. 8.95 o.s.i. (ISBN 0-02-614700-9). Macmillan.
Stewart, Ian & Tall, David. The Foundations of Mathematics. (Illus.). 1977. 13.50x (ISBN 0-19-853164-8); pap. 10.95x (ISBN 0-19-853165-6). Oxford U Pr.
Stewart, Irene. A Voice in Her Tribe: A Navajo Woman's Own Story. (Ballena Press Anthropological Papers: No. 17). (Illus.). 91p. 1980. pap. 5.95 o.p. (ISBN 0-87919-088-4). Ballena Pr.
Stewart, J. Sir Godfrey Kneller. (Illus.). 10.00 (ISBN 0-685-26748-2). Newbury Bks Inc.
Stewart, Jack C. Counseling Parents of Exceptional Children. (Special Education Ser.). 1978. pap. text ed. 7.50 (ISBN 0-675-08386-9). Merrill.
Stewart, James S. The Gates of New Life. (Scholar As Preacher Ser.). 261p. Repr. of 1937 ed. pap. text ed. 10.00 (ISBN 0-567-24426-1). Attic Pr.
--Man in Christ. (James S. Stewart Library). 1975. pap. 5.95 (ISBN 0-8010-8045-2). Baker Bk.
--The Strong Name. (Scholar As Preacher). 268p. Repr. of 1940 ed. text ed. 7.75 (ISBN 0-567-04427-0). Attic Pr.
Stewart, Jane E. Home Health Care. LC 78-31116. (Illus.). 1979. pap. text ed. 10.95 (ISBN 0-8016-4801-7). Mosby.
Stewart, Janice S. The Folk Arts of Norway. 2nd enl. ed. (Illus.). 12.50 (ISBN 0-8446-4610-5). Peter Smith.
Stewart, Jay, ed. see Milne, Terry.
Stewart, Jay, ed. see Spann, Owen & Spann, Nancie.
Stewart, Jean. Careful Consumer. 2nd ed. 1978. pap. text ed. 3.00 o.p. (ISBN 0-435-42281-2). Heinemann Ed.
--Good Cooking. 1974. pap. text ed. 7.50x o.p. (ISBN 0-435-42713-X). Heinemann Ed.
Stewart, Jean, tr. see Butot, Michel.
Stewart, Jean, tr. see Diderot, Denis.
Stewart, Jean, tr. see Mauriac, Francois.
Stewart, Jean, tr. see Mosse, Claude.
Stewart, Jean, tr. see Simenon, Georges.
Stewart, Jeffrey R., jt. auth. see Huffman, Harry.
Stewart, Jeffrey R., Jr & Blockhus, Wanda A. Office Procedures. LC 79-9095. (Illus.). 1980. text ed. 12.95 (ISBN 0-07-061440-7); General Office Projects 5.20 (ISBN 0-07-061441-5); Administrative Projects 5.20 (ISBN 0-07-061442-3); tchrs. manual & key 5.50 (ISBN 0-07-061443-1). McGraw.
Stewart, Jeffrey R., Jr., et al. Filing Systems & Records Management. 3rd ed. LC 80-21605. (Illus.). 240p. 1981. text ed. 10.95 (ISBN 0-07-061471-7, G); instructor's manual & key avail. (ISBN 0-07-061473-3); practice materials avail. (ISBN 0-07-061472-5). McGraw.
Stewart, Jim, et al. Community Competencies for the Handicapped: School Graduation Requirements: A Basis for Curriculum & IEP Development. 208p. 1978. spiral bdg. 14.50 (ISBN 0-398-03765-5). C C Thomas.
Stewart, Jo. Run from Danger. LC 80-26611. (Prime Time Adventures Ser.). (Illus.). 64p. (gr. 4 up). 1981. PLB 7.95 (ISBN 0-516-02109-5). Childrens.
Stewart, John. Bridges Not Walls. 2nd ed. LC 76-46606. (Speech Communication Ser.). 1977. pap. 8.95 (ISBN 0-201-07227-0). A-W.
Stewart, John & D'Angelo, Gary. Together-Communicating Interpersonally. 2nd ed. LC 79-26426. (Speech Communication Ser.). (Illus.). 1980. pap. 11.50 (ISBN 0-201-07506-7). A-W.
Stewart, John, jt. auth. see Parker, Alan.
Stewart, John, compiled by. Filmarama: The Flaming Years, 1920-1929, Vol. 2. LC 75-2440. 1977. 30.00 (ISBN 0-8108-1008-5). Scarecrow.
--Filmarama: The Formidable Years, 1893-1919, Vol. 1. LC 75-2440. 401p. 1975. 18.00 (ISBN 0-8108-0802-1). Scarecrow.
Stewart, John F., ed. The Crime of Moscow in Vynnytsia. 2nd new ed. (Illus.). 48p. 1980. pap. 3.00 (ISBN 0-911038-90-6, 357). Noontide.
Stewart, John H. see Lefebvre, Georges.
Stewart, John I. Eight Modern Writers. (Oxford History of English Literature Ser.). 1963. 37.50x (ISBN 0-19-812207-1). Oxford U Pr.
Stewart, John J. Mormonism & the Negro. LC 78-52123. 1978. 4.50 (ISBN 0-88290-098-6). Horizon Utah.
Stewart, John P. Welders-Fitters Guide. LC 78-64873. 1979. pap. 7.95 (ISBN 0-672-23325-8). Audel.
--The Welder's Handbook. 1981. 25.95 (ISBN 0-8359-8605-5). Reston.
Stewart, Jon. Understanding Econometrics. 1980. text ed. 18.25x (ISBN 0-09-126230-5, Hutchinson U Pr); pap. text ed. 10.25x (ISBN 0-09-126231-3). Humanities.
Stewart, Joseph T. Dynamic Stock Option Trading. 184p. 1981. 31.95 (ISBN 0-471-08670-3). Ronald Pr.
Stewart, Joyce A. Methods of Media Preparation for the Biological Sciences. (Illus.). 108p. 1974. text ed. 10.75 (ISBN 0-398-02990-3). C C Thomas.
Stewart, Joyce L., jt. auth. see Campbell, Mary C.
Stewart, Kenneth. A Background to Racing. (Illus.). 12.25 (ISBN 0-85131-221-7, Dist. by Sporting Book Center). J A Allen.
Stewart, Kerry. The Concorde: Airport 79. (Orig.). pap. 2.25 (ISBN 0-515-05348-1). Jove Pubns.
Stewart, Lawrence D., jt. auth. see Jablonski, Edward.
Stewart, Louis. Life Forces: A Contemporary Guide to the Cult & Occult. (Illus.). 1980. 20.00 o.p. (ISBN 0-8362-7903-4); pap. 9.95 o.p. (ISBN 0-8362-7906-9). Andrews & McMeel.
Stewart, Lowell S. Public Land Surveys: History, Instructions, Methods. 1976. Repr. of 1935 ed. 14.00 (ISBN 0-686-18867-5, 610). CARBEN Survey.
Stewart, Margaret. Employment Conditions in Europe. (Illus.). 249p. 1976. 25.00 o.p. (ISBN 0-7161-0307-9, Gower). Unipub.
Stewart, Marjabelle Y. Marjabelle Stewart's Book of Modern Table Manners. (Illus.). 192p. 1981. 14.95 (ISBN 0-312-51525-1); pap. 7.95 (ISBN 0-312-51526-X). St Martin.
Stewart, Marjabelle Y. & Buchwald, Ann. What to Do - When & Why: At School, at Parties, at Home, in Your Growing World. LC 75-31840. (gr. 7 up). 1975. 7.95 (ISBN 0-679-50566-0). McKay.
Stewart, Mark B. & Kenneth, Wallis F. Introductory Econometrics. 2nd ed. 352p. 1981. 24.95 (ISBN 0-470-27132-9). Halsted Pr.
Stewart, Mary. The Gabriel Hounds. 256p. 1981. pap. 2.50 (ISBN 0-449-23946-2, Crest). Fawcett.
--The Ivy Tree. 1978. pap. 2.25 (ISBN 0-449-23976-4, Crest). Fawcett.
--The Little Broomstick. (Illus.). 192p. (gr. 3-7). 1972. PLB 7.44 (ISBN 0-688-31507-0). Morrow.
--Ludo & the Star Horse. LC 74-26662. (Illus.). 192p. (gr. 3-7). 1975. 7.75 (ISBN 0-688-22017-7); PLB 7.44 (ISBN 0-688-32017-1). Morrow.
--The Moon-Spinners. 1978. pap. 2.25 (ISBN 0-449-23941-1, Crest). Fawcett.
--My Brother Michael. (Keith Jennison Large Type Bks). (gr. 7 up). PLB 8.95 o.p. (ISBN 0-531-00243-8). Watts.
--My Brother Michael. 1978. pap. 2.25 (ISBN 0-449-24029-0, Crest). Fawcett.
--Nine Coaches Waiting. 1959. 9.95 o.p. (ISBN 0-688-02185-9). Morrow.
--This Rough Magic. 1979. pap. 2.25 (ISBN 0-449-24129-7, Crest). Fawcett.
--Thunder on the Right. 192p. 1981. pap. 2.25 (ISBN 0-449-23940-3, Crest). Fawcett.
--Thunder on the Right. 1978. pap. 2.25 o.p. (ISBN 0-449-23940-3, Crest). Fawcett.
Stewart, Mary J. El Intrepido Francisco: Vida y Ministerio de un Editor Evangelico. 1980. pap. 1.25 (ISBN 0-311-01069-5). Casa Bautista.

Stewart, Michael. The British Approach to Politics. 1966. pap. text ed. 14.95x (ISBN 0-04-320038-9). Allen Unwin.
--Politics & Economic Policy in the UK Since 1964: The Jekyll & Hyde Years. 1978. pap. 12.00 (ISBN 0-08-022469-5). Pergamon.
Stewart, N., et al. Systematic Counseling. LC 77-24374. (Illus.). 1978. 18.95 (ISBN 0-13-880252-1). P-H.
Stewart, P. R. & Letham, D. S., eds. The Ribonucleic Acids. LC 73-76335. (Illus.). xv, 268p. 1973. 26.20 o.p. (ISBN 0-387-06190-8). Springer-Verlag.
Stewart, Paul. Sports Illustrated Judo. LC 75-15827. (Sports Illustrated Ser). (Illus.). 1976. 5.95 (ISBN 0-397-01096-6); pap. 2.95 (ISBN 0-397-01104-0). Lippincott.
Stewart, Philip, tr. see Mahfouz, Naguib.
Stewart, Philip D. Political Power in the Soviet Union: A Study of Decision-Making in Stalingrad. LC 68-17706. 1968. pap. 5.50 (ISBN 0-672-60764-6). Bobbs.
--Political Power in the Soviet Union: A Study of Decision-Making in Stalingrad. LC 68-17706. 1968. 24.50x (ISBN 0-672-51163-0). Irvington.
Stewart, Philippa. Growing up in Ancient Greece. LC 79-56475. (Growing up Ser.). (Illus.). 72p. (gr. 7 up). 1980. text ed. 14.95 (ISBN 0-7134-3376-0, Pub. by Batsford England). David & Charles.
Stewart, Phyllis L. & Cantor, Muriel, eds. Varieties of Work Experience: The Social Control of Occupational Groups & Roles. LC 74-6158. 1974. text ed. 13.95x (ISBN 0-470-82477-8); pap. text ed. 5.95x o.p. (ISBN 0-470-82478-6). Halsted Pr.
Stewart, R. A., et al. Person - Perception & Stereotyping. 1979. 21.95 (ISBN 0-347-01072-5, 96768-8, Pub. by Saxon Hse). Lexington Bks.
--Person-Perception & Stereotyping. 1979. 21.95 (ISBN 0-566-00072-5, 96768-8, Pub. by Saxon Hse England). Lexington Bks.
Stewart, R. F. And Always a Detective: Chapters on the History of Detective Fiction. LC 79-56436. 352p. 1980. 36.00 (ISBN 0-7153-7922-4). David & Charles.
Stewart, R. W. Benjamin Disraeli: A List of Writings by & About Him. LC 72-3906. (Author Bibliographies Ser.: No. 7). 1972. 10.00 (ISBN 0-8108-0489-1). Scarecrow.
--Disraeli's Novels Reviewed, Eighteen Twenty-Six to Nineteen Sixty-Eight. LC 74-28454. 1975. 12.00 (ISBN 0-8108-0759-9). Scarecrow.
Stewart, Ramona. The Nightmare Candidate. Date not set. pap. 2.25 (ISBN 0-440-16062-6). Dell.
Stewart, Regina & Cosentino, Geraldine. Bottles. (Golden Handbook of Collectibles Ser.). (Illus.). 1977. pap. 3.95 o.p. (ISBN 0-307-43176-2, Golden Pr). Western Pub.
--Carnival Glass. (Handbook of Collectibles Ser.). (Illus.). 1977. pap. 3.95 o.p. (ISBN 0-307-43175-4, Golden Pr). Western Pub.
Stewart, Rex. Jazz Masters of the Thirties. (The Roots of Jazz Ser.). 223p. 1980. Repr. of 1972 ed. lib. bdg. 22.50 (ISBN 0-306-76030-4). Da Capo.
Stewart, Richard. Modern Design in Metal. (Illus.). 1979. 18.00 (ISBN 0-7195-3537-9). Transatlantic.
--Modern Design in Wood. (Illus.). 1979. 18.50 (ISBN 0-7195-3536-0). Transatlantic.
Stewart, Richard B. & Krier, James E. Environmental Law & Policy. 2nd ed. (Contemporary Legal Education Ser.). 1978. 25.00 (ISBN 0-672-82859-6, Bobbs-Merrill Law). Michie.
Stewart, Robert. The Foundation of the Conservative Party 1830-1867. (A History of the Conservative Party Ser.). (Illus.). 1978. text ed. 35.00x (ISBN 0-582-50712-X). Longman.
--Labrador. (The World's Wild Places Ser.). (Illus.). 1977. lib. bdg. 11.97 (ISBN 0-686-51020-8). Silver.
--Labrador. (World's Wild Places Ser.). (Illus.). 1977. 12.95 (ISBN 0-8094-2065-1). Time-Life.
--A Living from Lobsters. 2nd ed. (Illus.). 70p. 9.75 (ISBN 0-85238-099-2, FN). Unipub.
--Politics of Protection: Lord Derby & the Protectionist Party, 1841-1852. LC 77-152628. 1971. 35.50 (ISBN 0-521-08109-2). Cambridge U Pr.
Stewart, Rosemarie. The Best Days of Your Life. 1977. pap. 1.95 (ISBN 0-515-03660-9). Jove Pubns.
Stewart, Rosemarie see Hanson, Virginia.
Stewart, Rosemarie, ed. East Meets West: The Transpersonal Approach. LC 80-53952. 202p. 1981. pap. 5.25 (ISBN 0-8356-0544-2). Theos Pub Hse.
Stewart, Rosemary. Continously Under Review. 70p. 1967. pap. text ed. 5.00x (Pub. by Bedford England). Renouf.
Stewart, Stanley. The Expanded Voice: The Art of Thomas Traherne. LC 71-111800. 1970. 10.00 (ISBN 0-87328-045-8). Huntington Lib.
--The King James Version. 1977. 8.95 o.p. (ISBN 0-394-40042-9). Random.
Stewart, T. D. The People of America. LC 73-1371. (Illus.). 272p. 1973. 10.00 o.p. (ISBN 0-684-13539-6, ScribT). Scribner.
Stewart, T. H., jt. auth. see Ellinger, A. G.
Stewart, V. Lorne, ed. The Changing Faces of Juvenile Justice. LC 77-87578. 1978. 12.00x (ISBN 0-8147-7788-0). NYU Pr.
Stewart, V. Lorne, intro. by. Justice & Troubled Children Around the World, Vol. 1. LC 79-3154. 1981. 17.50 (ISBN 0-8147-7809-7). NYU Pr.
Stewart, V. Lorne, jt. ed. see Friday, Paul C.
Stewart, Valerie & Stewart, Andrew. Managing the Manager's Growth. 1979. 22.95 (ISBN 0-470-26561-2). Halsted Pr.
Stewart, W. A., jt. auth. see Mannheim, Karl.
Stewart, W. D. & Sprent, Janet. Nitrogen Fixation in Plants. 1980. cancelled (ISBN 0-485-11155-1, Athlone Pr). Humanities.
Stewart, W. D., ed. Nitrogen Fixation by Free-Living Micro-Organisms. LC 75-2731. (International Biological Programme Ser.: Vol. 6). (Illus.). 448p. 1976. 72.00 (ISBN 0-521-20708-8). Cambridge U Pr.
Stewart, Walter K. Time Structure in Drama, Goethe's Storm und Drgng Plays. (Amsterdamer Publikationen Zur Sprache und Literatur: No. 35). 1978. pap. text ed. 34.50x (ISBN 90-6203-682-1). Humanities.
Stewart, Warren E., et al, eds. Dynamics & Modeling of Reactive Systems. (Mathematics Research Center Ser.). 1980. 17.50 (ISBN 0-12-669550-4). Acad Pr.
Stewart, William C. Mathematics: With Applications. 1979. 16.95x (ISBN 0-256-02114-7). Business Pubns.
Stewart, William C., jt. auth. see Braverman, Jerome D.
Stewart, William D., et al. Dermatology: Diagnosis & Treatment of Cutaneous Disorders. 4th ed. LC 78-12789. (Illus.). 1978. text ed. 38.50 (ISBN 0-8016-4809-2). Mosby.
Stewart, William E. & Hadden, John, eds. The Lymphokines. LC 80-85521. (Contemporary Immunology Ser.). (Illus.). 1981. 59.50 (ISBN 0-89603-012-1). Humana.
--The Lympholsines. (Illus.). 500p. 1981. cancellrd (ISBN 0-89603-012-1). Humana.
Stewart, William T., et al. International Film Necrology. LC 80-17636. (Garland Reference Library of Humanities). 350p. 1981. 35.00 (ISBN 0-8240-9552-9). Garland Pub.
St-Exupery, Antoine De see De St-Exupery, Antoine.
Steyermark, Julian A. Spring Flora of Missouri. 1964. text ed. 7.95x (ISBN 0-87543-044-9). Lucas.
Steyert, Richard D., jt. ed. see American Society of Civil Engineers.
Steyn, P. S., ed. The Biosynthesis of Mycotoxins: A Study in Secondary Metabolism. LC 80-12013. 1980. 44.00 (ISBN 0-12-670650-6). Acad Pr.
Steyskal, G. C., et al. Taxonomy of North American Flies of the Genus Limnia (Diptera: Sciomyzidae) (Publications in Entomology Ser.: No. 83). 1978. pap. 10.00x (ISBN 0-520-09577-4). U of Cal Pr.
Stiansen, S., jt. auth. see Armen, H.
Stibbs, Alan M., ed. Search the Scriptures. rev. ed. 7.95 (ISBN 0-87784-856-4). Inter-Varsity.
Stibbs, Andrew. Assessing Children's Language: Guidelines for Teachers. 1980. pap. text ed. 4.25x (ISBN 0-7062-3853-2, Pub. by Ward Lock Educational England). Hayden.
Stich, Sidra. Joan Miro: The Development of a Sign Language. LC 80-80078. (Illus.). 72p. pap. 6.00x o.p. (ISBN 0-936316-00-4). Wash U Gallery.
Stich, Stephen P., ed. Innate Ideas. 1975. 18.50x (ISBN 0-520-02822-8); pap. 5.95x (ISBN 0-520-02961-5). U of Cal Pr.
Sticht, Frank D., jt. auth. see Wood, William B.
Stick, David. Dare County. (Illus.). 1975. pap. 2.00 (ISBN 0-86526-125-3). NC Archives.
Stick, David, jt. auth. see Robert, Bruce.
Stickel, D. L. The Brain Death Criterion of Human Death. (Illus.). 73p. 1981. 19.00 (ISBN 0-08-025814-X). Pergamon.
Stickells, Austin T. Federal Control of Business-Antitrust Laws. LC 72-84857. (Commercial Law Library). 930p. 1972. 55.00 (ISBN 0-686-02629-2). Lawyers Co-Op.
Stickgold, Bob. The California Coven Project. 192p. 1981. pap. 2.25 (ISBN 0-345-28677-4, Del Rey). Ballantine.
Stickle, Warren E., jt. ed. see Brownell, Blaine A.
Stickney, Trumbull. The Poems of Trumbull Stickney. Whittle, Amberys, ed. 368p. (Index of first lines). 1972. 17.50 o.p. (ISBN 0-374-23537-6). FS&G.
Stickter, Jim. The Little Man with Three Legs. LC 80-8771. (Illus.). 224p. (Orig.). 1980. 10.00 (ISBN 0-930770-17-X). Hemisphere Hse.
Stidger, Howe C. & Ruth, W. Inflation Management: One Hundred Practical Techniques for Business & Industry. LC 80-11271. 448p. 1980. Repr. of 1976 ed. lib. bdg. 19.95 (ISBN 0-89874-132-7). Krieger.
Stidger, Howe C. & Stidger, Ruth W. Inflation Management: 100 Practical Techniques for Business & Industry. LC 76-8927. 400p. 1976. 19.95 o.p. (ISBN 0-471-82485-2, Pub. by Wiley-Interscience). Wiley.
Stidger, Ruth W. The Compentence Game: How to Find, Use & Keep Competent Employees. LC 80-17657. (Illus.). 160p. 1980. 12.95 (ISBN 0-444-00453-X, Thomond Pr). Elsevier.
Stidger, Ruth W., jt. auth. see Stidger, Howe C.
Stieb, Ernst W. & Sonnedecker, Glenn. Drug Adulteration: Detection & Control in Nineteenth-Century Britain. (Illus.). 1966. 29.50x (ISBN 0-299-04150-6). U of Wis Pr.
Stieber, Jack. Public Employee Unionism: Structure, Growth, Policy. LC 73-1591. (Studies of Unionism in Government). 256p. 1973. 12.95 (ISBN 0-8157-8160-1); pap. 5.95 (ISBN 0-8157-8159-8). Brookings.
Stieber, Wilhelm J. The Chancellor's Spy: The Revelations of the Chief of Bismarck's Secret Service. Van Heurck, Jan, tr. from German. LC 79-52090. Orig. Title: Spion Des Kanzlers. 272p. 1981. 12.50 (ISBN 0-394-50869-6). Grove.
Stieber, Z. A. Historical Phonology of the Polish Language. (Illus.). 171p. 1973. 32.50 (ISBN 0-685-55680-8). Adler.
Stief, Carl. Studies in the Russian Historical Song. LC 79-3073. (Illus.). 274p. 1981. Repr. of 1953 ed. 23.50 (ISBN 0-8305-0092-8). Hyperion Conn.
Stiefbold, Annette E. The French Communist Party in Transition: PCF-CPSU Relations & the Challenge to Soviet Authority. LC 77-83477. (Praeger Special Studies). 1978. 22.95 (ISBN 0-03-040946-2). Praeger.
Stiefel, E. L. Introduction to Numerical Mathematics. Rheinboldt, W. C., tr. 1963. text ed. 18.95 (ISBN 0-12-671150-X); problem bklt. free (ISBN 0-685-05133-1). Acad Pr.
Stiefel, W. E., ed. see Alegria, Ciro.
Stieglitz, Alfred, ed. Camera Work: A Critical Anthology. LC 73-85257. (Illus.). 1975. 35.00 o.p. (ISBN 0-912334-47-9); pap. 20.00 o.p. (ISBN 0-912334-73-8). Aperture.
Stieglitz, Francine. Progressive Audio-Lingual Drills in English. (gr. 9-12). 1970. pap. 4.50 (ISBN 0-88345-125-5); cassettes 125.00 (ISBN 0-685-65047-2). Regents Pub.
Stiehl, Ruth, jt. auth. see Altheim, Franz.
Stiehl, Ulrich. Dictionary of Book Publishing. 538p. (Eng. & Ger.). 1977. text ed. 55.00 (ISBN 3-7940-4147-X, Pub. by K G Saur). Gale.
Stiehm, Judith H. Bring Me Men & Women: Mandated Changes at the U. S. Air Force Academy. 1981. 19.95 (ISBN 0-520-04045-7). U of Cal Pr.
Stiel, Beth, jt. auth. see Herman, Linda.
Stieper, Donald R. & Wiener, Daniel N. Dimensions of Psychotherapy: An Experimental & Clinical Approach. LC 65-22494. 1965. 24.50x (ISBN 0-89197-622-1). Irvington.
Stievater, Eric H. What Is Acuncture? How Does It Work? 48p. 1971. pap. 3.00x (ISBN 0-8464-1061-3). Beekman Pubs.
Stiff, M. J., ed. River Pollution Control. 300p. 1980. 99.95x (ISBN 0-470-27004-7). Halsted Pr.
Stifle, J. M. ABC Book About Christmas. 1981. pap. 2.95 (ISBN 0-570-04053-1, 56-1714). Concordia.
--ABC Book About Jesus. 1981. pap. 2.95 (ISBN 0-570-04054-X, 56-1715). Concordia.
--Set of ABC Books, 2 bks. 1981. pap. 5.25 (ISBN 0-570-04055-8, 56-1716). Concordia.
Stifter, Adalbert. Bergkristall und Andere Erzaehlungen. (Insel Taschenbuecher: It 438). 325p. (Ger.). 1980. pap. text ed. 5.85 (ISBN 3-458-32138-1, Pub. by Insel Verlag Germany). Suhrkamp.
Stigant, S. Austin & Franklin, A. C. The J & P Transformer Book. 10th ed. Worth, C. A., ed. 770p. 1973. 76.95 (ISBN 0-470-82505-7). Halsted Pr.
Stigen, Gail. Heartaches & Handicaps: An Irreverent Survival Manual for Parents. LC 74-74561. 1976. 5.95 o.p. (ISBN 0-8314-0040-4). Sci & Behavior.
Stigers, Harold G. A Commentary on Genesis. 320p. 1975. 15.95 (ISBN 0-310-36800-6). Zondervan.
Stigler, George J., ed. see Smith, Adam.
Stigum, Marcia. Money Market Calculations: Yields, Swaps, & Break-Even Prices. 1981. 27.50 (ISBN 0-87094-192-5). Dow Jones-Irwin.
Stigum, Marcia L. Problems in Microeconomics. 1975. pap. text ed. 10.95 (ISBN 0-256-01734-4). Irwin.
Stiles, jt. auth. see Higdon.
Stiles, jt. auth. see Higdon, A.
Stiles, David. Easy-to-Make Children's Furniture. (Illus.). 1980. 7.95 (ISBN 0-394-73871-3). Pantheon.
Stiles, Deirdre. Dangerford. 1977. pap. 1.75 (ISBN 0-505-51212-2). Tower Bks.
Stiles, George, et al. Laboratory Guide for Freshman Biology. 2nd ed. 1980. pap. text ed. 12.95 (ISBN 0-8403-2227-5). Kendall-Hunt.
Stiles, Harold, jt. auth. see Nichols, Talmage.
Stiles, Henry R. Bundling: Its Origin, Progress & Decline in America. LC 78-167211. 146p. Repr. of 1934 ed. 18.00 (ISBN 0-8103-3204-3). Gale.
Stiles, Norman. The Count's Number Parade. (Illus.). 24p. (ps-4). 1977. PLB 5.38 (ISBN 0-307-68876-3, Golden Pr). Western Pub.
--The Ernie & Bert Book. (Sesame Street Shape Bks.). (Illus.). (ps-1). 1977. PLB 5.38 (ISBN 0-307-68879-8, Golden Pr). Western Pub.
--Farmer Grover. (Illus.). 24p. (ps-4). 1977. PLB 5.38 (ISBN 0-307-68878-X, Golden Pr). Western Pub.
--Grover's Little Red Riding Hood. (Illus.). (gr. k-2). 1976. PLB 5.38 (ISBN 0-307-68934-4, Golden Pr). Western Pub.
Stiling, Marjorie. Famous Brand Names, Emblems and Trademarks. LC 80-69353. (Illus.). 64p. 1981. 8.95 (ISBN 0-7153-8098-2). David & Charles.
Stilkind, Jerry, jt. auth. see Todaro, Michael P.
Still, Bayrd. Mirror for Gotham: New York As Seen by Contemporaries from Dutch Days to the Present. LC 80-16246. (Illus.). xix, 417p. 1980. Repr. of 1956 ed. lib. bdg. 35.00x (ISBN 0-313-22439-0, STMG). Greenwood.
Still, Henry. Surviving the Male Mid-Life Crisis. 1977. 9.95 o.s.i. (ISBN 0-690-01445-7, TYC-T). T Y Crowell.
Still, James. Early Recollections & Life of Dr. James Still, 1812-1885. (Illus.). 288p. 1973. Repr. 19.50 (ISBN 0-8135-0769-3). Rutgers U Pr.
--Pattern of a Man & Other Stories. LC 76-45313. (YA) 1976. pap. 5.00 (ISBN 0-917788-01-X). Gnomon Pr.
--The Run for the Elbertas. LC 80-51019. 160p. 1980. 12.50 (ISBN 0-8131-1414-4); pap. 5.50 (ISBN 0-8131-0151-4). U Pr of Ky.
Still, R. R., et al. Sales Management: Decisions, Policies & Cases. 3rd ed. (Illus.). 544p. 1976. 21.00 (ISBN 0-13-788042-1). P-H.
Still, Richard & Harris, Clyde E., Jr. Cases in Marketing: Decision, Policies, Strategies. (Illus.). 304p. 1972. pap. text ed. 9.95 (ISBN 0-13-118877-1). P-H.
Still, Richard R. & Cundiff, Edward W. Essentials of Marketing. 2nd ed. LC 79-170644. 1972. ref. ed. 10.95 (ISBN 0-13-286468-1). P-H.
Still, Richard R., jt. auth. see Cundiff, Edward W.
Still, Steven. Herbaceous Plants. (Illus.). 210p. 1980. text ed. write for info. (ISBN 0-87563-185-1); pap. text ed. write for info. (ISBN 0-87563-184-3). Stipes.
Still, William N., Jr. American Sea Power in the Old World: The United States Navy in European and Near Eastern Waters, 1865-1917. LC 79-6572. (Contributions in Military History: No. 24). (Illus.). xi, 291p. 1980. lib. bdg. 29.95 (ISBN 0-313-22120-0, STA/). Greenwood.
Stille, G., ed. Psychotropic Agents Parti: Part I, Antipschotics & Antidepressants. (Handbook of Experimental Pharmacology: Vol. 55, Pt. 1). (Illus.). 800p. 1980. 172.00 (ISBN 0-387-09858-5). Springer-Verlag.
Stiller, Nikki. Eve's Orphans: Mothers & Daughters in Medieval English Literature. LC 79-8954. (Contributions in Women's Studies: No. 16). (Illus.). xii, 152p. 1980. lib. bdg. 19.95 (ISBN 0-313-22067-0, SEO/). Greenwood.
Stiller, Richard. Habits. 158p. 1980. pap. 3.95 (ISBN 0-346-12437-9). Cornerstone.
--Queen of Populists: The Story of Mary Elizabeth Lease. LC 78-94801. (Women of America Ser). (Illus.). (gr. 6-9). 1970. 6.95 o.p. (ISBN 0-690-66252-1, TYC-J). T Y Crowell.
Stillinger, Elizabeth. The Antiquers. LC 80-7625. (Illus.). 320p. 1980. 16.95 (ISBN 0-394-40329-0). Knopf.
--Antiques Guide to Decorative Arts in America 1600-1875. 1973. pap. 6.95 o.p. (ISBN 0-525-47334-3). Dutton.
Stillinger, Jack, ed. The Early Draft of John Stuart Mill's "Autobiography". LC 61-62769. 1961. 10.00 o.p. (ISBN 0-252-72386-4). U of Ill Pr.
Stillings, Frank S., tr. see Gasparini, Francesco.
Stillman, Damie. The Decorative Work of Robert Adam. 20.00 (ISBN 0-85458-160-X). Transatlantic.

Stillman, David M. & Gordon, Ronni L. Comunicando: A First Course in Spanish. 1979. text ed. 16.95x (ISBN 0-669-01359-5); instrs'. manual free (ISBN 0-669-02404-X); wkbk.-lab. manual 5.25x (ISBN 0-669-01708-6); reel tapeset 60.00 (ISBN 0-669-01711-6); cassette tapeset 60.00 (ISBN 0-669-01710-8). Heath.

Stillman, Deanne & Beatts, Anne. Titters: The First Collection of Humor by Women. (Illus.). 1976. 14.95 o.s.i. (ISBN 0-02-614680-0). Macmillan.

--Titters: The First Collection of Humor by Women. (Illus.). 1976. pap. 7.95 o.s.i. (ISBN 0-02-040700-9, Collier). Macmillan.

Stillman, Edmund. The American Heritage History of the Twenties & Thirties. LC 72-117350. 416p. 1970. deluxe ed. 25.00 slipcased (ISBN 0-8281-0093-4, Dist. by Scribner). Am Heritage.

Stillman, Frances, ed. see Whitfield, Jane S.

Stillman, Gordon P. Men & Milestones of the Middle Ages. (gr. 9-11). 1970. pap. text ed. 4.50x (ISBN 0-88334-029-1). Ind Sch Pr.

--Roman Rulers & Rebels. (gr. 8-11). 1972. pap. text ed. 4.50x (ISBN 0-88334-048-8). Ind Sch Pr.

Stillman, Irwin M., jt. auth. see Baker, Samm S.

Stillman, John M. Theophrastus Bombastus von Hohenheim Called Paracelsus. LC 79-8625. Repr. of 1920 ed. 25.00 (ISBN 0-404-18491-X). AMS Pr.

Stillman, Mildred W., tr. see Fenelon, Francois.

Stillman, Peter R. Introduction to Myth. (Literature Ser.). (gr. 10 up). 1977. pap. text ed. 6.40x (ISBN 0-8104-5890-X). Hayden.

Stillman, R. C. & Willette, R. E., eds. The Psychopharmacology of Hallucinogens. LC 78-14019. 1979. 40.00 (ISBN 0-08-021938-1). Pergamon.

Stillman, Richard. Guide to Personal Finance: A Lifetime Program of Money Management. 3rd ed. 1979. text ed. 19.95 (ISBN 0-13-370486-6). P-H.

--Public Administration: Concepts & Cases. LC 75-31022. (Illus.). 384p. 1976. pap. text ed. 9.95 o.p. (ISBN 0-395-20606-5). HM.

Stillman, Richard, jt. auth. see Henri, Florette.

Stillman, Richard J. Moneywise: The Prentice-Hall Book of Personal Money Management. LC 77-25493. (Illus.). 1978. 14.95 o.p. (ISBN 0-13-600734-1). P-H.

Stillman, Richard J., II. Public Administration: Concepts & Cases. 2nd ed. LC 79-89817. (Illus.). 1980. text ed. 10.50 (ISBN 0-395-28634-4). HM.

Stillman, Richard M. Surgery Review & Assessment: Tumor, Trauma, & Specialties. 1981. pap. 12.50 (ISBN 0-686-69608-5). ACC.

Stillman, Richard M. & Sawyer, Philip N. Surgical Resident's Manual. 192p. 1980. pap. 12.50x (ISBN 0-8385-8732-1). ACC.

Stillman, W. J. Construction Practices for Project Managers & Superintendents. (Illus.). 1978. text ed. 18.95 (ISBN 0-87909-164-9). Reston.

Stillwater, Maitreya. Windows of Nature. (Illus., Orig.). (gr. 1-12). 1978. pap. 2.25 (ISBN 0-912300-90-6, 90-6). Troubador Pr.

Stillwell, Agnes N. & Benson, J. L. The Potters' Quarter: The Pottery. (Corinth: Results of Excavations Conducted by the School of Classical Studies at Athens: Vol. XV, iii). 1981. price not set (ISBN 0-87661-153-6). Am Sch Athens.

Stillwell, Alexandra. Teneriffe Lace. (Illus.). 144p. 1980. 16.95 (ISBN 0-8231-5056-9). Branford.

Stillwell, J. Classical Topology & Combinatorial Group Theory. (Graduate Texts in Mathematics Ser.: Vol. 72). (Illus.). 301p. 1980. 32.00 (ISBN 0-387-90516-2). Springer-Verlag.

Stillwell, Lyda, jt. auth. see Heinig, Ruth B.

Stilman, Galina, et al. Introductory Russian Grammar. 2nd ed. LC 75-179421. (Illus.). 576p. (Rus.). 1972. text ed. 18.95x (ISBN 0-471-00738-2) (ISBN 0-471-00740-4). wkbk. 4.50x (ISBN 0-471-00906-7); o.p. (ISBN 0-685-99773-1); tapes avail. (ISBN 0-471-00741-2). Wiley.

Stilman, Leon. Graded Readings in Russian History: The Formation of the Russian State. LC 60-7695. (Columbia Slavic Studies). (Illus.). (gr. 9 up). 1960. pap. 6.00x (ISBN 0-231-02390-1). Columbia U Pr.

--Russian Alphabet & Phonetics. LC 51-4951. (Columbia Slavic Studies). (gr. 9 up). 1951. pap. 6.00x (ISBN 0-231-09922-3). Columbia U Pr.

--Russian Verbs of Motion. LC 51-7695. (Columbia Slavic Studies). 1951. pap. 6.00x (ISBN 0-231-09931-2). Columbia U Pr.

Stilson, Charles B. Polaris & the Immortals. (YA) 5.95 (ISBN 0-685-07455-2, Avalon). Bouregy.

Stilson, Max. Who? What? Where? Bible Quizzes. (Quiz & Puzzle Bks.). 96p. 1980. pap. 1.95 (ISBN 0-8010-8012-6). Baker Bk.

Stilwell, Anne & Stilwell, Hart. The Child Who Walks Alone: Case Studies of Rejection in the Schools. LC 79-38569. 218p. 1972. 10.00 (ISBN 0-292-71002-X). U of Tex Pr.

Stilwell, Donald L., jt. auth. see Stephens, Roger B.

Stilwell, Frank J. Economic Crisis, Cities & Regions: An Analysis of Current Urban & Regional Problems in Australia. 192p. 1980. 14.50 (ISBN 0-08-024810-1); pap. 8.95 (ISBN 0-08-024809-8). Pergamon.

--Normative Economics: An Introduction to Microeconomic Theory & Radical Critiques. 162p. 1975. pap. text ed. 10.75 (ISBN 0-08-018300-X). Pergamon.

Stilwell, Hart, jt. auth. see Stilwell, Anne.

Stimer, Lyn. Beware the Greeks. 256p. (Orig.). 1981. pap. 2.50 (ISBN 0-523-41115-4). Pinnacle Bks.

Stimmann, Michael. Pesticide Application & Safety Training. rev. ed. (Illus.). 98p. (Orig.). 1980. pap. text ed. 4.00. Ag Sci Pubns.

Stimmel, Barry. Cardiovascular Effects of Mood-Altering Drugs. LC 77-91582. 1979. text ed. 27.00 (ISBN 0-89004-287-X). Raven.

Stimpson, Catherine & Person, Ethel S., eds. Women-Sex & Sexuality. 384p. 1981. lib. bdg. 14.50x (ISBN 0-226-77476-7); pap. 5.95 (ISBN 0-226-77477-5, P 914, Phoen). U of Chicago Pr.

Stimpson, Catherine, et al, eds. Women & the American City. LC 80-53136. 280p. 1981. lib. bdg. 16.00x (ISBN 0-226-77478-3); pap. 5.95 (ISBN 0-226-77479-1). U of Chicago Pr.

Stimpson, George W. Nuggets of Knowledge. LC 75-109182. 1970. Repr. of 1928 ed. 22.00 (ISBN 0-8103-3860-2). Gale.

--Popular Questions Answered. LC 74-109601. 1970. Repr. of 1930 ed. 26.00 (ISBN 0-8103-3859-9). Gale.

Stimson, Gerry V. Heroin & Behaviour. LC 73-174. 246p. 1973. 17.95 (ISBN 0-470-82530-8). Halsted Pr.

Stimson, Henry L. The Far Eastern Crisis. 1975. Repr. of 1936 ed. 16.50 (ISBN 0-86527-327-8). Fertig.

Stimson, Russel L. Opthalmic Dispensing. 3rd ed. (Illus.). 720p. 1979. text ed. 33.75 (ISBN 0-398-03823-6). C C Thomas.

Stinchcomb, W. W., et al, eds. Mechanics of Nondestructive Testing. 415p. 1980. 47.50 (ISBN 0-306-40567-9). Plenum Pub.

Stinchcombe, Arthur L., et al. Crime & Punishment: Changing Attitudes in America. LC 80-8004. (Social & Behavioral Science Ser.). 1980. text ed. 15.95x (ISBN 0-87589-472-0). Jossey-Bass.

Stinchcombe, William. The XYZ Affair. LC 80-544. (Contributions in American History: No. 89). (Illus.). 167p. 1980. lib. bdg. 23.95 (ISBN 0-313-22234-7, SXY/). Greenwood.

Stine, ed. Weird Worlds, No. 3. (gr. 7-12). 1980. pap. 1.50 (ISBN 0-590-30036-9, Schol Pap). Schol Bk Serv.

Stine, Alan. Love Power: New Dimensions for Building Strong Families. LC 78-70360. 1978. 5.95 (ISBN 0-88290-105-2). Horizon Utah.

Stine, Bob. Gnasty Gnomes. (Illus.). 62p. (gr. 3-6). 1981. PLB 6.99 (ISBN 0-394-94686-3); pap. 5.95 (ISBN 0-394-84686-9). Random.

Stine, Bob & Stine, Jane. The Cool Kids' Guide to Summer Camp. LC 80-24172. (Illus.). 80p. (gr. 3-7). 1981. 7.95 (ISBN 0-590-07704-X, Four Winds). Schol Bk Serv.

Stine, Hank, ed. see Anderson, Poul.

Stine, Jane, jt. auth. see Stine, Bob.

Stine, Richard. Smile in a Mad Dog's I. 2nd ed. 1977. 6.95 (ISBN 0-916860-02-7); pap. 3.95 (ISBN 0-916860-01-9). Bean Pub.

Stine, Whitney, ed. see Hurrell, George.

Stineman, Esther. American Political Women: Comtemporary & Historical Profiles. LC 80-24478. 225p. 1980. lib. bdg. 19.50x (ISBN 0-87287-238-6). Libs Unl.

Stineman, Esther & Loeb, Catherine. Women's Studies: A Recommended Core Bibliography. LC 79-13679. 1979. lib. bdg. 35.00x (ISBN 0-87287-196-7). Libs Unl.

Stingley, James. Mother, Mother. 224p. 1981. 11.95 (ISBN 0-312-92543-3). St Martin.

--Mother, Mother. 224p. 1981. 11.95 (ISBN 0-312-92543-3). Congdon & Lattes.

Stinneford, Carol, jt. auth. see Whittenburg, Clarice.

Stinnett, Nick & Birdsong, Craig W. The Family & Alternate Life-Styles. LC 77-16593. 1978. text ed. 15.95 (ISBN 0-88229-208-0). Nelson-Hall.

Stinnett, Nick, et al, eds. Building Family Strengths: Blueprints for Action. LC 79-51329. 1979. 19.50x (ISBN 0-8032-4114-3); pap. 9.95x (ISBN 0-8032-9113-2). U of Nebr Pr.

--Family Strengths: Positive Models for Family Life. LC 80-50917. x, 518p. 1980. 21.50x (ISBN 0-8032-4125-9); pap. 9.95x (ISBN 0-8032-9122-1). U of Nebr Pr.

Stinnett, Roger, jt. auth. see Kirkman, Kay.

Stinnett, Ronald F. Democrats, Dinners, & Dollars: A History of the Democratic Party, Its Dinners, Its Ritual. 1967. 8.95 o.p. (ISBN 0-685-99404-X). Iowa St U Pr.

Stinnett, T. M., jt. auth. see Haberman, Martin.

Stinson, D. C. Intermediate Mathematics of Electromagnetics. (Illus.). 320p. 1976. ref. ed 24.95 (ISBN 0-13-470633-1). P-H.

Stinson, John E., jt. auth. see Johnson, Thomas W.

Stinson, Robert. Lincoln Steffens. LC 79-4831. (Modern Literature Ser.). 1980. 10.95 (ISBN 0-8044-2829-8). Ungar.

Stiny, George & Gips, James. Algorithmic Aesthetics: Computer Models for Criticism & Design in the Arts. 1979. 18.50x (ISBN 0-520-03467-8). U of Cal Pr.

Stipp, John, et al. The Rise & Development of Western Civilization, Pt. 1: Beginnings to 1500. 2nd ed. LC 72-2661. (Illus.). 640p. 1972. pap. text ed. 16.95x (ISBN 0-471-82601-4). Wiley.

--The Rise & Development of Western Civilization, Pt. 3: 1815 to Present. 2nd ed. LC 72-2661. (Illus.). 416p. 1972. pap. text ed. 12.95x o.p. (ISBN 0-471-82609-X). Wiley.

Stirewalt, Edward N., jt. auth. see Maycock, Paul D.

Stirewalt, Maurice R., jt. ed. see Leary, Helen F.

Stirk, S. D., ed. see Hauptmann, Gerhart.

Stirling, Brents. The Shakespeare Sonnet Order: Poems & Groups. 1968. 17.50x (ISBN 0-520-01221-6, CAMPUS 240); pap. 5.95x (ISBN 0-520-03958-0). U of Cal Pr.

Stirling, C. J. The Chemistry of Sulphoniom Group, Part 2. (Chemistry of Functional Group Ser.). 1400p. 1981. 130.00 (ISBN 0-471-27770-3, Pub.by Wiley-Interscience); Set. 240.00 (ISBN 0-471-27655-3). Wiley.

--The Chemistry of the Sulphonium Group, 2 pts. (Chemistry of Functional Groups). 1981. Pt. 1. 110.00 (ISBN 0-471-27769-X, Pub. by Wiley-Interscience); Pt. 2. write for info. (ISBN 0-471-27770-3). Wiley.

Stirling, David & Woodford, Jim. Birdwatching in Canada. 127p. 1975. pap. text ed. write for info. (ISBN 0-919654-28-2). Hancock Hse.

Stirling, J. F., ed. Handbook on University & Polytechnic Librarianship. 1980. 33.00x (ISBN 0-85365-621-5, Pub. by Lib Assn England). Oryx Pr.

Stirling, James. James Stirling: Buildings & Projects, 1950-1974. (Illus.). 184p. 1975. 30.00 o.p. (ISBN 0-19-519801-8). Oxford U Pr.

Stirling, Jessica. Call Home the Heart. LC 76-28059. 416p. 1977. 8.95 o.p. (ISBN 0-312-11427-3). St Martin.

--The Dark Pasture. LC 77-15325. 1978. 8.95 o.p. (ISBN 0-312-18257-0). St Martin.

--The Deep Well at Noon. 1980. 12.95 o.p. (ISBN 0-312-19090-5). St Martin.

--Strathmore. Orig. Title: Call Home the Heart. 1975. 8.95 o.s.i. (ISBN 0-440-05971-2). Delacorte.

Stirling, Norman. Introduction to Technical Drawing: Metric Edition. LC 79-56653. 370p. 1981. pap. text ed. 15.00 (ISBN 0-8273-1939-8). Delmar.

--Technical Drawing: An Introduction Metric. Edition. 370p. 1981. 18.95 (ISBN 0-442-23151-2). Van Nos Reinhold.

Stirrup, M. N. Geology: The Science of the Earth. LC 78-73233. (Illus.). 1980. pap. 11.95 (ISBN 0-521-22567-1). Cambridge U Pr.

Stirton, R. A. Relationships of the Protoceratid Artiodactyls, & Description of a New Genus. (U. C. Publ. in Geological Sciences: Vol. 72). 1967. pap. 6.00x (ISBN 0-520-09175-2). U of Cal Pr.

Stirton, R. A., et al. Australian Tertiary Deposits Containing Terrestrial Mammals. (U. C. Publ. in Geological Sciences: Vol. 77). 1968. pap. 6.00x (ISBN 0-520-09180-9). U of Cal Pr.

Stitch, Stephen P., jt. auth. see Jackson, David A.

Stitcher, Teresa L., jt. ed. see Blouet, Brian W.

Stites, Frances N. John Marshall: Defender of the Constitution. (Library of American Biography). (Orig.). 1981. 11.95 (ISBN 0-316-81669-8); pap. text ed. 4.95 (ISBN 0-316-81667-1). Little.

Stites, Francis. John Marshall: Defender of the Constitution. 208p. 1980. 11.95 (ISBN 0-316-81669-8). Little.

Stites, William H., jt. auth. see Pacilio, John, Jr.

Stitt, Fred A. Systems Drafting. (Illus.). 1980. 19.95 (ISBN 0-07-061550-0). McGraw.

Stitt, Milan. The Runner Stumbles. 1979. pap. 2.25 (ISBN 0-380-44719-3, 44719, Bard). Avon.

Stitzel, Thomas E., jt. auth. see Widicus, Wilbur W.

Stivala, S. S., jt. auth. see Reich, L.

Stivers, R. E. Privateers & Volunteers, 1766-1866. LC 75-20749. 502p. 1975. 17.00x (ISBN 0-87021-395-4). Naval Inst Pr.

Stivers, Richard, jt. ed. see Davis, F. James.

Stiverson, Gregory A. & Jacobsen, Phebe R. William Paca: A Biography. LC 76-17519. (Illus.). 1976. 7.95 (ISBN 0-938420-18-6); pap. 4.95 (ISBN 0-686-23680-7). Md Hist.

Stiverson, Gregory A., Jr., jt. ed. see Papenfuse, Edward C.

Stix, Hugh & Stix, Marguerite. Shell: Five Hundred Million Years of Inspired Design. LC 68-12922. (Illus.). 1968. 45.00 (ISBN 0-8109-0475-6); pap. 8.95 (ISBN 0-8109-2098-0). Abrams.

Stix, Marguerite, jt. auth. see Stix, Hugh.

Stob, Henry. Theological Reflections. 200p. (Orig.). 1981. pap. 11.95 (ISBN 0-8028-1881-1). Eerdmans.

Stobaugh, Robert & Yergin, Daniel, eds. Energy Future: The Report of the Energy Project at the Harvard Business School. 1980. pap. 2.95 (ISBN 0-345-29349-5). Ballantine.

Stobaugh, Robert B. Nine Investments Abroad & Their Impact at Home. 1976. text ed. 12.00 (ISBN 0-87584-113-9). Harvard U Pr.

Stobbs, John, jt. auth. see Cochran, Alastair.

Stobbs, William. Dilly Dally. (Illus.). 1975. 3.95 (ISBN 0-7207-0767-6, Pub. by Michael Joseph). Merrimack Bk Serv.

--Little Tiger. 1975. 3.95 (ISBN 0-7207-0769-2, Pub. by Michael Joseph). Merrimack Bk Serv.

--Sophie. 1974. 3.95 (ISBN 0-7207-0769-2, Pub. by Michael Joseph). Merrimack Bk Serv.

--Wheels. (Illus.). (ps). 1979. 1.25 (ISBN 0-370-02005-7, Pub. by Chatto Bodley Jonathan). Merrimack Bk Serv.

--Wild Animals. (Illus.). (ps). 1979. 1.25 (ISBN 0-370-10735-7, Pub. by Chatto Bodley Jonathan). Merrimack Bk Serv.

Stobbs, William, jt. auth. see Williams-Ellis, Amabel.

Stock, Albert E. & Hargrave, Bettyan. In Case I'm Found Unconscious, the Ups & Downs of Diabetes. (Illus.). 52p. (Orig.). 1972. 7.00 (ISBN 0-910584-26-5); pap. 2.00 (ISBN 0-910584-75-3). Filter.

Stock, Dennis. James Dean Revisited. (Large Format Ser.). (Illus.). 1978. pap. 5.95 o.p. (ISBN 0-14-004939-8); pap. 15.00 o.p. (ISBN 0-670-40481-0). Penguin.

Stock, Dennis & Johnson, Josephine W. Circle of Seasons. LC 73-20661. (Illus.). 108p. 1974. 16.95 o.p. (ISBN 0-670-22263-1, Studio). Viking Pr.

Stock, Dennis, photos by. A Haiku Journey. LC 74-24903. (Illus.). 111p. 1975. 22.50 (ISBN 0-87011-239-2). Kodansha.

Stock, G., jt. auth. see Conybeare, Frederick C.

Stock, Garfield R. Wisconsin Supplement for Real Estate Principles & Practices. (Business Ser.). 1977. pap. text ed. 4.95 (ISBN 0-675-08508-X). Merrill.

Stock, Garfield R., et al. Professional Real Estate Brokerage: A Guide for Real Estate Executives. LC 78-444. 1978. 11.95 o.p. (ISBN 0-87094-160-7). Dow Jones-Irwin.

Stock, R. D., ed. see Johnson, Samuel.

Stockard, James G. Career Development & Job Training: A Manager's Handbook. new ed. 1978. 24.95 (ISBN 0-8144-5449-6). Am Mgmt.

Stockard, Jean & Johnson, Miriam M. Sex Roles, Sex Inequality, & Sex Role Development. (Illus.). 1980. pap. text ed. 13.95 (ISBN 0-13-807560-3). P-H.

Stockdale, jt. auth. see Butterworth.

Stockdale, Connie R., jt. auth. see Neeson, Jean D.

Stocker, Claudell S. Listening for the Visually Impaired: A Teaching Manual. 192p. 1974. pap. 11.75 (ISBN 0-398-02936-9). C C Thomas.

Stocker, F. & Weber, J. W., eds. Neuere Aspekte Kinderkardiologie. (Paediatrische Fortbildungskurse Fuer Die Praxis: Vol. 51). (Illus.). vi, 130p. 1980. pap. 41.50 (ISBN 3-8055-0926-X). S Karger.

Stockhammer, M., ed. Thomas Aquinas Dictionary. LC 64-21468. 1965. 7.50 o.p. (ISBN 0-8022-1653-6). Philos Lib.

Stockhold, Henry F., tr. see Lefebvre, Georges.

Stockholm, H. K., jt. ed. see Colonell, J. M.

Stockholm International Peace Research Institute. Southern Africa: The Escalation of a Conflict. LC 76-4518. (Special Studies). 400p. 1976. text ed. 32.50 (ISBN 0-275-56840-7). Praeger.

Stocking, George W., Jr. Race, Culture & Evolution: Essays in the History of Anthropology. LC 69-10279. (Illus.). 1968. 12.95 (ISBN 0-02-931530-1). Free Pr.

Stocks, Broan, jt. auth. see Arnold, Eddie.

Stocks, Eleanor. Educational Methods & Materials. 1977. pap. text ed. 7.50x (ISBN 0-8191-0174-5). U Pr of Amer.

Stocks, J., jt. auth. see Down, C. G.

Stocks, John L. Aristotelianism. LC 63-10300. (Our Debt to Greece & Rome Ser). 1963. Repr. of 1930 ed. 16.50x (ISBN 0-8154-0220-1). Cooper Sq.

Stockton, David. The Gracchi. 1979. 28.50x (ISBN 0-19-872104-8); pap. 12.95x (ISBN 0-19-872105-6). Oxford U Pr.

Stockton, Doris S. Essential Algebra & Trigonometry. LC 77-76337. (Illus.). 1978. text ed. 18.75 (ISBN 0-395-25413-2); inst. manual 0.70 (ISBN 0-395-25414-0). HM.
--Essential College Algebra. LC 78-69526. (Illus.). 1979. text ed. 16.95 (ISBN 0-395-26544-4); inst. manual 0.90 (ISBN 0-395-26538-X). HM.
--Essential Precalculus. LC 77-75647. (Illus.). 1978. text ed. 18.75 (ISBN 0-395-25417-5); inst. manual 1.70 (ISBN 0-395-25418-3). HM.
--Essential Trigonometry. LC 78-69543. (Illus.). 1979. text ed. 15.95 (ISBN 0-395-26539-8); inst. manual 0.90 (ISBN 0-395-26545-2). HM.
Stockton, Frank R. Buccaneers & Pirates of Our Coasts. new ed. (Illus.). (gr. 5 up). 1967. 9.95 (ISBN 0-02-788520-8). Macmillan.
--Buccaneers & Pirates of Our Coasts. new ed. (Illus.). (gr. 5 up). 1967. pap. 0.79 o.s.i. (ISBN 0-02-045310-8, Collier). Macmillan.
--Storyteller's Pack. LC 67-23694. 384p. (gr. 6 up). 1968. 7.95 o.p. (ISBN 0-684-12825-X, ScribJ). Scribner.
Stockton, John M. Sales in a Nutshell. 2nd ed. LC 80-25579. (Nutshell Ser.). 358p. 1980. pap. text ed. write for info. (ISBN 0-8299-2116-8). West Pub.
Stockton, William. Altered Destinies. 1980. pap. 2.50 (ISBN 0-451-09460-3, E9460, Sig). NAL.
Stockum, E. K., jt. auth. see Rougier, Harry.
Stockum, Hilda Van see Broger, Achim.
Stockwell, Edward G. & Laidlaw, Karen A. Third World Development: Problems & Prospects. LC 79-24088. 362p. 1981. text ed. 21.95 (ISBN 0-88229-532-2); pap. text ed. 10.95 (ISBN 0-88229-751-1). Nelson-Hall.
Stockwell, Herbert G. How to Read a Financial Statement: Adapted Especially to Needs of Credit Men, Bankers & Investors. 443p. 1980. Repr. of 1925 ed. lib. bdg. 30.00 (ISBN 0-8495-5049-1). Arden Lib.
Stockwell, John & Holtje, Herbert, eds. The Photographer's Business Handbook. (Illus.). 320p. 1980. 14.95 (ISBN 0-07-061585-3, P&RB). McGraw.
Stockwell, Nancy. Out Somewhere & Back Again: The Kansas Stories. 1978. pap. write for info. (ISBN 0-9601714-0-1). Medusa.
Stockwell, P. B., jt. auth. see Foreman, J. K.
Stockwell, P. B., jt. ed. see Foreman, J. K.
Stockwell, R. A. Biology of Cartilage Cells. LC 78-67433. (Biological Structure & Function Ser.: No. 7). (Illus.). 1979. 63.50 (ISBN 0-521-22410-1). Cambridge U Pr.
Stockwell, Robert P. Foundations of Syntactic Theory. LC 76-8021. (Foundations of Modern Linguistics Ser.). 1977. 14.95 (ISBN 0-13-329987-2); pap. text ed. 9.95 (ISBN 0-13-329979-1); wkbk. 5.95 (ISBN 0-13-965202-7). P-H.
Stockwell, Robert P., et al. Grammatical Structures of English & Spanish. (Orig.). 1965. pap. 6.00x (ISBN 0-226-77504-6). U of Chicago Pr.
Stockwin, J. A. Japan: Divided Politics in a Growth Economy. (Comparative Modern Government Ser). 320p. 1975. text ed. 10.00x (ISBN 0-393-05544-2); pap. text ed. 6.95x (ISBN 0-393-09233-X). Norton.
Stoddard, Alan. Back-Relief from Pain. LC 78-24488. (Positive Health Guides Ser.). (Illus.). 1979. 8.95 (ISBN 0-668-04677-5, 4677-5); pap. 4.95 (ISBN 0-668-04684-8, 4684-8). Arco.
--Manual of Osteopathic Technique. 2nd ed. 1979. text ed. 32.50x (ISBN 0-09-051120-4, Hutchinson U Lib). Humanities.
Stoddard, Alexandra. Style for Living: How to Make Where You Live You. LC 73-82250. 320p. 1974. 12.50 o.p. (ISBN 0-385-08252-5). Doubleday.
Stoddard, Charles H. Essentials of Forestry Practice. 3rd ed. LC 78-6652. 1978. text ed. 17.95 (ISBN 0-471-07262-1). Wiley.
Stoddard, Darrell. The Hero. Jordan, Alton, ed. (I Can Read Underwater Bks). (Illus.). (gr. k-3). 1974. PLB 3.50 (ISBN 0-89868-001-8); pap. 1.75 (ISBN 0-89868-034-4). ARO Pub.
Stoddard, Edward. The First Book of Magic. (First Bks.). (Illus.). 72p. (gr. 4-6). 1977. PLB 6.45 (ISBN 0-531-00575-5). Watts.
--The First Book of Magic. 1980. pap. 1.75 (ISBN 0-380-49221-0, 49221, Camelot). Avon.
Stoddard, Elizabeth P., jt. ed. see Renzulli, Joseph S.
Stoddard, Herbert L. Memoirs of a Naturalist. LC 69-16713. (Illus.). 303p. (Orig.). 1969. 15.95 (ISBN 0-8061-0857-6); pap. 6.95 (ISBN 0-8061-1167-4). U of Okla Pr.
Stoddard, Richard, ed. Stage Scenery, Machinery, & Lighting: A Guide to Information Sources. LC 76-13574. (Performing Arts Information Guide Ser.: Vol. 2). 1977. 30.00 (ISBN 0-8103-1374-X). Gale.
--Theatre & Cinema Architecture: A Guide to Information Sources. LC 78-14820. (Performing Arts Information Guide Ser.: Vol. 5). 1978. 30.00 (ISBN 0-8103-1426-6). Gale.
Stoddard, Sandol. Five Who Found the Kingdom: New Testament Stories. LC 80-1663. (Illus.). 128p. (gr. 7). 1981. 8.95a (ISBN 0-385-17169-2); PLB (ISBN 0-385-17170-6). Doubleday.
Stoddard, Whitney S. Monastery & Cathedral in France: Medieval Architecture, Sculpture, Stained Glass, Manuscripts, the Art of the Church Treasuries. LC 66-23923. 1966. 40.00x (ISBN 0-8195-3071-9). Wesleyan U Pr.
Stoddart, D. M. see Ebling, F. J.
Stoddart, D. R., ed. Geography, Ideology & Social Concern. (Illus.). 1981. 26.50x (ISBN 0-389-20207-X). B&N.
Stoddart, D. R. & Yonge, Maurice, eds. The Northern Great Barrier Reaf. (Proceedings of the Royal Society). (Illus.). 364p. 1979. text ed. 95.75x (ISBN 0-85403-102-2, Pub. by Royal Soc London). Scholium Intl.
Stoddart, D. R., ed. see Royal Society of London.
Stoddart, R. W. Polysaccharide Metabolism. 224p. 1980. 35.00x (ISBN 0-85664-807-8, Pub. by Croom Helm England). State Mutual England.
Stodder, Joseph H. Moral Perspective in Webster's Major Tragedies. (Salzburg Studies in English Literature, Jacobean Drama Studies: No. 48). 1974. pap. text ed. 25.00x (ISBN 0-391-01536-2). Humanities.
--Satire in Jacobean Tragedy. (Salzburg Studies in English Literature, Jacobean Drama Studies: No. 35). 186p. 1974. pap. text ed. 25.00x (ISBN 0-391-01535-4). Humanities.
Stodelle, Ernestine. The Dance Technique of Doris Humphrey & Its Creative Potential. LC 78-5124. (Illus.). 279p. 1978. 14.95 o.p. (ISBN 0-916622-07-X). Princeton Bk Co.
Stoeber, Edward A. How to Use Life & Health Insurance in Business & Estate Planning. 2nd ed. LC 79-87867. 1979. pap. 15.00 o.p. (ISBN 0-87218-402-1). Natl Underwriter.
Stoeckel, H. & Omaya, T. Endocrinology in Anaesthesia & Surgery. (Anaesthesiology & Intensive Care Medicine Ser.: Vol. 132). (Illus.). 205p. 1981. pap. 55.60 (ISBN 0-387-10211-6). Springer-Verlag.
Stoecker, W. F. Design of Thermal Systems. 2nd ed. (Illus.). 1980. 29.95 (ISBN 0-07-061618-3). McGraw.
Stoeckl, Agnes De see De Stoeckl, Agnes.
Stoeckle, Bernard, ed. The Concise Dictionary of Christian Ethics. 1979. 19.50 (ISBN 0-8164-0357-0). Crossroad NY.
Stoedefalke, Karl, jt. auth. see Smith, Everett L.
Stoehr, Taylor, ed. see Goodman, Paul.
Stoenner, Herbert, et al, eds. Handbook Series in Zoonoses, CRR, Section A: Bacterial, Rickettsial & Mycotic Diseases, Vol. 2. 1980. 69.95 (ISBN 0-8493-2907-8). CRC Pr.
Stoerker, Fredrick C., jt. auth. see Thomas, Norman C.
Stoess, H. A., Jr. Pneumatic Conveying. LC 79-105393. 1970. 32.95 (ISBN 0-471-82680-4, Pub. by Wiley-Interscience). Wiley.
Stoessinger, John G. Nations in Darkness: China, Russia, & America. 3rd ed. 263p. 1981. pap. text ed. 6.95 (ISBN 0-394-32657-1). Random.
--Nations in Darkness: China, Russia, & America. 3rd ed. 1978. pap. text ed. 6.95x (ISBN 0-394-32126-X). Random.
Stoever, William A. Renegotiations in International Business Transactions: The Process of Dispute-Resolution Between Multinational Investors & Host Societies. LC 79-4727. 1981. 27.95 (ISBN 0-669-03057-0). Lexington Bks.
Stoever, William K. A Faire & Easie Way to Heaven: Covenant Theology & Antinomianism in Early Massachusetts. LC 77-14851. 1978. 20.00x (ISBN 0-8195-5024-8, Pub. by Wesleyan U Pr). Columbia U Pr.
Stoeving, Paul. Violin: Its Famous Makers & Players. (Illus.). Repr. of 1928 ed. lib. bdg. 14.25x (ISBN 0-8371-4346-2, STVI). Greenwood.
Stoffel, Ernest L. The Dragon Bound: Revelation Speaks to Our Times. 120p. (Orig.). 1981. pap. 4.50 (ISBN 0-8042-0227-3). John Knox.
Stoffel, Joseph. Explosives & Homemade Bombs. 2nd ed. (Illus.). 324p. 1977. 24.75 (ISBN 0-398-02424-3). C C Thomas.
Stoffel, R. & Lavalla, Patrick. Survival Sense for the Pilot. (Illus.). 160p. (Orig.). 1980. pap. 5.95 (ISBN 0-913724-24-6). Survival Ed Assoc.
Stoffer, Janet Y., ed. Science Fair Project Index: Nineteen Sixty to Nineteen Seventy-Two. LC 74-30269. 1975. 30.00 (ISBN 0-8108-0783-1). Scarecrow.
Stoffer, R. & Lavalla, Rick. Emergency Preparedness Education: An Overview. 74p. pap. 3.00 (ISBN 0-913724-23-8). Survival Ed Assoc.
Stofferahn, Curtis W. & Korsching, Peter F. Communication, Diffusion & Adoption of Innovations: A Bibliographical Update. (Public Administration Ser.: Bibliography P-433). 50p. 1980. pap. 5.50. Vance Biblios.
Stoffle, Carla J., jt. auth. see Harleston, Rebekah M.
Stogdill, Ralph M. Handbook of Leadership: A Survey of Theory & Research. LC 73-6494. (Illus.). 1974. 25.00 (ISBN 0-02-931660-X). Free Pr.
Stohl, Michael. War & Domestic Political Violence: The American Capacity for Repression & Reaction. LC 76-22799. (Sage Library of Social Research: Vol. 30). 1976. 18.00x (ISBN 0-8039-0575-0); pap. 8.95x (ISBN 0-8039-0576-9). Sage.
Stohr, W. B. Inter-Urban Systems & Regional Economic Development. LC 74-79829. (CCG Resource Papers Ser.: No. 26). (Illus.). 1974. pap. text ed. 4.00 (ISBN 0-89291-073-9). Assn Am Geographers.
Stohr, Walter & Taylor, D. R. Development from Above or Below? A Radical Reappraisal of Spatial Planning in Developing. 448p. 1981. 47.85 (ISBN 0-471-27823-8, Pub.by Wiley-Interscience). Wiley.
Stoia, Judith, jt. auth. see Bullard, Pamela.
Stoiber, Richard E. & Morse, Stearns A. Microscopic Identification of Crystals. 286p. 1981. Repr. of 1972 ed. lib. bdg. 16.50 (ISBN 0-89874-276-5). Krieger.
Stoica, L. Local Operator & Markow Processes. (Lecture Notes in Mathematics: Vol. 816). 104p. 1980. pap. 9.80 (ISBN 0-387-10028-8). Springer-Verlag.
Stoil, Michael J. Cinema Beyond the Danube: The Camera & Politics. LC 74-5274. 1974. 10.00 (ISBN 0-8108-0722-X). Scarecrow.
Stokell, Marjorie. A Visitor's Guide to L.A. Harper, Susan, ed. LC 80-67475. (Illus.). 224p. (Orig.). 1981. pap. 6.95 (ISBN 0-89395-061-0). Cal Living Bks.
Stoker, Bram. Dracula. Schick, Alice & Schick, Joel, eds. LC 80-13619. (Illus.). 48p. (gr. 3 up). 1980. PLB 8.44 (ISBN 0-440-01349-6); pap. 4.95 (ISBN 0-440-01348-8). Delacorte.
--Dracula. pap. 2.50 (ISBN 0-515-05347-3). Jove Pubns.
--Under the Sunset. Reginald, R. & Menville, Douglas, eds. LC 80-19564. (Newcastle Forgotten Library Ser.: Vol. 17). 190p. 1980. Repr. of 1978 ed. lib. bdg. 10.95x (ISBN 0-89370-516-0). Borgo Pr.
Stoker, Bram & Shelley, Mary. Dracula, Frankenstein, Dr. Jekyll & Mr. Hyde. 672p. (RL 7). Date not set. pap. 2.50 (ISBN 0-451-51290-1, CE1290, Sig Classics). NAL.
Stoker, H. Stephen & Seager, Spencer L. Environmental Chemistry: Air & Water Pollution. 2nd ed. 1976. pap. 7.95x (ISBN 0-673-07978-3). Scott F.
Stoker, H. Stephen & Slabaugh, Michael R. General, Organic & Biochemistry: A Brief Introduction. 1980. text ed. 18.95x (ISBN 0-673-15091-7); study guide 7.95x (ISBN 0-673-15501-3). Scott F.
Stoker, J. J. Nonlinear Vibrations in Mechanical & Electrical Systems Pure & Aplied Mechanics, Vol. 2. 1950. 29.95 (ISBN 0-470-82830-7). Wiley.
Stoker, James. Differential Geometry. (Pure & Applied Mathematics Ser.). 1969. 32.50 (ISBN 0-471-82825-4, Pub. by Wiley-Interscience). Wiley.
Stokes, Adrian. The Critical Writings of Adrian Stokes. Gowing, Lawrence, ed. 1978. 24.95 ea. (ISBN 0-685-87325-0); Vol. I. (ISBN 0-500-01175-3); Vol. II. (ISBN 0-500-01176-1); Vol. III. (ISBN 0-500-01177-X). Thames Hudson.
--The Image in Form: Selected Writings of Adrian Stokes. Wollheim, Richard, ed. LC 72-84750. (Icon Editions Ser.). (Illus.). 384p. 1972. 10.00 o.p. (ISBN 0-06-438540-X, HarpT); pap. 4.95x o.s.i. (ISBN 0-06-430028-5, IN-28, HarpT). Har-Row.
--With All the Views: Collected Poems. Robinson, Peter, ed. 160p. 1981. 17.50x (ISBN 0-933806-04-3). Black Swan CT.
Stokes, Allen W., jt. auth. see Price, Edward O.
Stokes, Antony, jt. auth. see Fennell, John.
Stokes, Arch. The Collective Bargaining Handbook for Hotels, Restaurants & Institutions. (The Stokes Employee Relations Ser.). 352p. 1981. spiral bdg. 39.95 (ISBN 0-8436-2149-4). CBI Pub.
--The Equal Opportunity Handbook for Hotels, Restaurants & Institutions. LC 79-859. 1979. 14.95 (ISBN 0-8436-2148-6). CBI Pub.
--The Wage & Hour Handbook for Hotels, Restaurants, & Institutions. LC 78-9278. 1978. 14.95 (ISBN 0-8436-2133-8). CBI Pub.
Stokes, Bill. You Can Catch Fish. LC 76-12478. (Games & Activities Ser.). 48p. (gr. k-3). 1976. 9.30 (ISBN 0-8172-0627-2). Raintree Pubs.
Stokes, Bill & Sanders, Peter. Slap Shot. LC 75-22001. (Venture Ser. a Reading Incentive Program). (Illus.). (gr. 7-12). 1975. text ed. 23.25 ea. pack of 5 (RL4, 5-6, 7). Follett.
Stokes, Bruce. Helping Ourselves: Local Responses to Global Problems. 1981. 12.95 (ISBN 0-393-01362-6); pap. 4.95 (ISBN 0-393-00054-0). Norton.
--Men & Family Planning. (Worldwatch Papers Ser.). 1980. pap. 2.00 (ISBN 0-916468-40-2). Worldwatch Inst.
Stokes, Charles J. & Fisher, Ernest M. Housing Market Performance in the United States. LC 74-11605. (Special Studies). (Illus.). 175p. 1976. text ed. 16.95 o.p. (ISBN 0-275-05720-8). Praeger.
Stokes, Donald. The Natural History of Wild Shrubs & Vines. LC 80-8219. (Illus.). 256p. 1981. 12.95 (ISBN 0-06-014163-8, HarpT). Har-Row.
Stokes, Durward T. Company Shops, North Carolina: The Town Built by a Railroad. 1981. 12.95 (ISBN 0-89587-016-9). Blair. Postponed.
Stokes, E. T. The Peasant & the Raj: Studies in Agrarian Society & Peasant Rebellion in Colonial India. LC 77-77731. (Cambridge South Asian Studies: No. 23). 304p. 1980. pap. 12.95x (ISBN 0-521-29770-2). Cambridge U Pr.
Stokes, Eric & Brown, Richard. Zambesian Past: Studies in Central African History. 1966. text ed. 10.25x (ISBN 0-7190-0261-3). Humanities.
Stokes, F. Joseph. Handguide to the Coral Reef Fishes of the Caribbean. LC 79-27224. (Illus.). 160p. 1980. 9.95 (ISBN 0-690-01919-X). Lippincott & Crowell.
Stokes, Frances K. My Father Owen Wister. 54p. (Orig.). 1952. pap. 5.00. South Pass Pr.
Stokes, Francis G. A Dictionary of the Characters & Proper Names in the Works of Shakespeare. Repr. of 1960 ed. 49.00 (ISBN 0-403-04029-9). Somerset Pub.
Stokes, G. S. & Mahony, J. H., eds. Hormones & the Kidney. (Progress in Biochemical Pharmacology: Vol. 17). (Illus.). 250p. 1980. 75.00 (ISBN 3-8055-1090-X). S Karger.
Stokes, Gale. Legitimacy through Liberalism: Vladimir Jovanovic & the Transformation of Serbian Politics. LC 75-1423. (Publications on Russia & Eastern Europe of the School of International Studies: No. 5). (Illus.). 296p. 1975. 13.50 (ISBN 0-295-95384-5). U of Wash Pr.
Stokes, Geoffrey. The Beatles. 256p. 1980. 29.95 (ISBN 0-8129-0928-3). Times Bks.
--Star-Making Machinery: Inside the Business of Rock & Roll. 1977. pap. 3.95 (ISBN 0-394-72432-1, Vin). Random.
Stokes, Gordon. Beginner's Guide to Woodturning. (Illus.). 124p. 1975. 18.00 (ISBN 0-7207-0637-8). Transatlantic.
--Cleared for Takeoff: Flying for Beginners. LC 78-595. (Illus.). 1978. 9.95 o.p. (ISBN 0-684-15787-X, ScribT). Scribner.
--Toy Making in Wood. (Pelham Craft Ser.). (Illus.). 1978. 16.50 (ISBN 0-7207-0999-7). Transatlantic.
--Woodturning for Pleasure. (Illus.). 128p. 1980. 12.95 (ISBN 0-13-962563-1, Spec); pap. 4.95 (ISBN 0-13-962555-0). P-H.
Stokes, I. N. & Haskell, Daniel C. American Historical Prints: Early Views of American Cities, Etc., from the Phelps Stokes & Other Collections. LC 77-180284. (Illus.). 235p. 1974. Repr. of 1933 ed. 28.00 (ISBN 0-8103-3950-1). Gale.
Stokes, Jack. Let's Be Nature's Friend! LC 76-15087. (Illus.). (gr. k-3). 1977. 6.95 o.p. (ISBN 0-679-20355-9). McKay.
--Loony Limericks: From Alabama to Wyoming. LC 77-10304. (gr. 3-7). 1978. PLB 4.95 (ISBN 0-385-12917-3). Doubleday.
--Monster Madness Outrageous Jokes About Weird Folks. LC 80-2068. (Illus.). 64p. (gr. 6). 1981. 8.95a (ISBN 0-385-15690-1); PLB (ISBN 0-385-15691-X). Doubleday.
--One Hundred Seven & Three Quarters Elephant Jokes. LC 78-1223. (Illus.). 1979. 6.95a (ISBN 0-385-14101-7); PLB (ISBN 0-385-14102-5). Doubleday.
Stokes, John, ed. see Adams, Francis.
Stokes, John, ed. see Allen, Grant.
Stokes, John, ed. see Brookfield, Charles & Glover, J. M.
Stokes, John, ed. see D'Arcy, Ella.
Stokes, John, ed. see Davidson, John.
Stokes, John, ed. see Dixon, R. W.
Stokes, John, ed. see Dowson, Ernest & Moore, Arthur.
Stokes, John, ed. see Egerton, George.
Stokes, John, jt. ed. see Fletcher, Ian.
Stokes, John, ed. see Gissing, George.
Stokes, John, ed. see Harland, Henry.
Stokes, John, ed. see Henniker, Florence.
Stokes, John, ed. see Hichens, Robert S.
Stokes, John, ed. see Lee, Vernon.
Stokes, John, ed. see Miall, A. B.
Stokes, John, ed. see Moore, George.
Stokes, John, ed. see O'Shaughnessy, Arthur.
Stokes, John, ed. see O'Sullivan, Vincent.
Stokes, John, ed. see Shiel, M. P.
Stokes, John, ed. see Simcox, G. A.
Stokes, John W. The Man Who Lived Two Lives. LC 79-57548. 1981. 6.75 (ISBN 0-533-04561-4). Vantage.
Stokes, Judy F. Cost-Effective Quality Food Service: An Institutional Guide. LC 78-25871. (Illus.). 1979. text ed. 29.75 (ISBN 0-89443-083-1). Aspen Systems.

Stokes, Mack B. The Bible in the Wesleyan Heritage. LC 80-23636. 96p. (Orig.). 1981. pap. 3.95 (ISBN 0-687-03100-1). Abingdon.

Stokes, Penelope J. & Steiner, Dorothea. The Quest for Maturity: A Study of William Wordsworth's "the Prelude". (Salzburg Studies in English Literature, Romantic Reassessment: No. 44). 1974. pap. text ed. 25.00x (ISBN 0-391-01537-0). Humanities.

Stokes, Peter J. Old Niagara on the Lake. LC 74-151393. 1971. pap. 10.95 (ISBN 0-8020-6318-7). U of Toronto Pr.

Stokes, R. H., jt. auth. see Guggenheim, E. A.

Stokes, Roy. Michael Sadleir Eighteen Eighty-Eight to Nineteen Fifty-Seven. LC 80-11419. (The Great Bibliographers Ser.: No. 5). 162p. 1980. 10.00 (ISBN 0-8108-1292-4). Scarecrow.

Stokes, Sylvia, jt. ed. see Reincke, Mary.

Stokes, Terry. Life in These United States. LC 78-13018. (A Raccoon Book). 1979. signed 4.95 (ISBN 0-918518-14-8); pap. 3.95 (ISBN 0-918518-11-3). St Luke TN.

Stokes, William L., et al. Introduction to Geology: Physical & Historical. 2nd ed. LC 77-21570. 1978. text ed. 20.95 (ISBN 0-13-484352-5). P-H.

Stokes, William N., Jr. Oil Mill on the Texas Plains: A Study in Agricultural Cooperation. LC 78-6372. (Illus.). 248p. 1979. 10.00 (ISBN 0-89096-059-3). Tex A&M Univ Pr.

Stokes, William T. Gems of Geometry. 1978. pap. text ed. 5.95 (ISBN 0-914534-02-5). Stokes.

--Notable Numbers. rev. ed. (Illus.). 1974. 5.95 (ISBN 0-914534-01-7). Stokes.

Stokesbury, James L. A Short History of World War I. LC 80-22206. (Illus.). 352p. 1981. 13.95 (ISBN 0-688-00128-9). Morrow.

--A Short History of World War I. LC 80-22207. (Illus.). 352p. 1981. pap. 7.95 (ISBN 0-688-00129-7, Quill). Morrow.

Stoklosa, Mitchell J. & Ansel, Howard C. Pharmaceutical Calculations. 7th ed. LC 80-10333. (Illus.). 385p. 1980. text ed. 15.00 (ISBN 0-8121-0725-X). Lea & Febiger.

Stokoe, John, jt. auth. see Bruce, John C.

Stokoe, W. J. The Observer's Book of Butterflies. (The Observer Bks). (Illus.). 1979. 2.95 (ISBN 0-684-16035-8, ScribT). Scribner.

Stokoe, William C. Dictionary of American Sign Language on Linguistic Principles. LC 65-28740. 1965. 9.00x (ISBN 0-932130-00-3). Linstok Pr.

--Sign Language Structure. rev. ed. 1978. pap. text ed. 4.00x (ISBN 0-932130-03-8). Linstok Pr.

Stolba, K. Marie. A History of Violin Etude to About Eighteen Hundred. (Music Reprint Ser.). 1968. Repr. of 1869 ed. lib. bdg. 25.00 (ISBN 0-306-79544-2). Da Capo.

Stoldt, Hans-Herbert. History & Criticism of the Marcan Hypothesis. Niewyk, Donald L., tr. from Ger. LC 80-82572. xvi, 302p. 1980. 18.95 (ISBN 0-86554-002-0). Mercer Univ Pr.

Stolear, Zaida. The Soviet Union As a Criminal System. 1981. 7.95 (ISBN 0-533-04601-7). Vantage.

Stoler, John A. Ann Radcliffe: The Novel of Suspense & Terror. Varmer, Devendra P., ed. LC 79-8483. (Gothic Studies & Dissertations Ser.). 1980. lib. bdg. 25.00x (ISBN 0-405-12670-0). Arno.

Stoler, Mark A. The Politics of the Second Front: American Military Planning & Diplomacy in Coalition Warfare, 1941-1943. LC 76-47171. (Contributions in Military History Ser.: No 12). 1977. lib. bdg. 18.95 (ISBN 0-8371-9438-5, SPF/). Greenwood.

Stolka, M., jt. auth. see Pearson, J. M.

Stoll, B. A., ed. Mind & Cancer Prognosis. LC 79-40643. 1980. 33.75 (ISBN 0-471-27644-8, Pub. by Wiley-Interscience). Wiley.

Stoll, Clarice, jt. auth. see Inbar, Michael.

Stoll, Clarice S., jt. auth. see Livingston, Samuel A.

Stoll, Clarice S., ed. Sexism: Scientific Debates. LC 72-11077. 1973. pap. text ed. 5.50 (ISBN 0-201-07308-0). A-W.

Stoll, Edgar E. Shakespeare Studies: Historical & Comparative in Method. 502p. 1980. lib. bdg. 50.00 (ISBN 0-89984-410-3). Century Bookbindery.

Stoll, Jack L., ed. The Man Who Took the Next Train. 365p. (Orig.). 1980. text ed. 14.95 (ISBN 0-918258-15-4); pap. text ed. 7.95 (ISBN 0-686-69212-8). New Earth.

Stoll, Robert R. Set Theory & Logic. 474p. 1979. pap. 6.50 (ISBN 0-486-63829-4). Dover.

Stoll, Robert R. & Wong, Edward T. Linear Algebra. 1968. text ed. 19.95 (ISBN 0-12-672150-5); answer bklt. 2.00 (ISBN 0-12-672152-1). Acad Pr.

Stollberg, Robert & Hill, Faith F. Physics: Fundamental & Frontiers. rev. ed. 1975. 18.20 (ISBN 0-395-18243-3); tchr's guide 9.32 (ISBN 0-395-18241-7); lab. supplement 2.64 (ISBN 0-395-18242-5). HM.

Stolle, Fred & Appel, Martin. Let's Play Tennis! (Illus.). Date not set. pap. cancelled (ISBN 0-671-33068-3). Wanderer Bks.

Stoller, Alan, jt. auth. see Krupinski, Jerzy.

Stoller, David S. Operations Research: Process & Strategy. 1964. 17.50x (ISBN 0-520-01222-4). U of Cal Pr.

Stoller, Leonard, jt. ed. see Sciarra, John J.

Stollman, Gerald H. Michigan: State Legislators & Their Work. LC 77-18633. 1978. text ed. 12.50x o.p. (ISBN 0-8191-0425-6). U Pr of Amer.

Stollo, Toni, ed. see Niehaus, Sandy I.

Stolman, A., jt. ed. see Stewart, C. P.

Stolten, Jane Henry. The Mental Health Worker. 1981. pap. text ed. price not set (ISBN 0-316-81744-9). Little.

Stoltenberg, Donald. The Artist & the Built Environment. LC 79-53779. (Illus.). 160p. 1980. 18.95 (ISBN 0-87192-118-9). Davis Mass.

--Collagraph Printmaking. LC 74-27699. (Illus.). 96p. 1975. 12.95 (ISBN 0-87192-067-0). Davis Mass.

Stoltman, James B. Groton Plantation: An Archaeological Study of a South Carolina Locality. LC 74-77556. (Peabody Museum Monographs: No. 1). 1974. pap. text ed. 12.00 (ISBN 0-87365-900-7). Peabody Harvard.

Stoltz, Berdine & Saloom, Pamela. Why, What & How of Interest Development Centers. 1978. pap. text ed. 3.95 (ISBN 0-936386-02-9). Creative Learning.

Stoltze, Herbert J., jt. auth. see Weinberg, Stanley L.

Stoltzfus, Doris. Self-Assessment of Current Knowledge in Mental Health Nursing. 1979. spiral bdg. 9.50 (ISBN 0-87488-264-8). Med Exam.

Stolz, Mary. What Time of Night Is It. LC 80-7917. (An Ursula Nordstrom Bk.). 224p. (gr. 6 up). 1981. 9.95 (ISBN 0-06-026061-0, HarpJ); PLB 9.89g (ISBN 0-06-026062-9). Har-Row.

Stolz, Matthew. Politics of the New Left. (Studies in Contemporary Issues). 1971. pap. text ed. 4.95x (ISBN 0-02-478700-0, 47870). Macmillan.

Stolze, Herbert J., jt. auth. see Weinberg, Stanley L.

Stolzenberg, Mark. Clown: For Circus & Stage. LC 80-54337. (Illus.). 1981. 12.95 (ISBN 0-8069-7034-0); lib. bdg. 11.69 (ISBN 0-8069-7035-9). Sterling.

--Exploring Mime. LC 79-65068. (Illus.). 1979. 10.95 (ISBN 0-8069-7028-6); lib. bdg. 9.89 (ISBN 0-8069-7029-4). Sterling.

Stommmel, Henry. The Gulf Stream: A Physical & Dynamical Description. (California Library Reprint Ser). 1977. Repr. of 1964 ed. 20.00x (ISBN 0-520-03307-8). U of Cal Pr.

Stone, jt. auth. see Rhodes.

Stone, A. Harris. Science Projects That Make Sense. LC 72-113737. (Illus.). (gr. 3-5). 1971. PLB 6.95 o.p. (ISBN 0-525-38825-7). Dutton.

Stone, A. Harris & Collins, Steven. Populations: Experiments in Ecology. LC 72-2303. (Illus.). 96p. (gr. 5 up). 1973. 6.45 (ISBN 0-531-02579-9). Watts.

Stone, A., Jr., ed. Ambassador: Twentieth Century Interpretations. 1969. 8.95 (ISBN 0-13-023937-2, Spec); pap. 1.25 (ISBN 0-13-023929-1, Spec). P-H.

Stone, Alan, jt. auth. see Knight, Kenneth L.

Stone, Alan, jt. auth. see Stone, Sue.

Stone, Alan, jt. ed. see Calloway, Barbara.

Stone, Alan, tr. see Radiquet, Raymond.

Stone, Alfred R. & Deluca, Stuart M. Investigating Crimes: An Introduction. LC 79-88446. (Illus.). 1980. text ed. 19.50 (ISBN 0-395-28525-9); inst. manual 1.00 (ISBN 0-395-28526-7). HM.

Stone, Andy. Song of the Kingdom. 256p. 1981. pap. 2.25 (ISBN 0-445-04654-6). Popular Lib.

Stone, Archie A. Careers in Agribusiness & Industry. 3rd ed. LC 76-106341. (Illus.). (gr. 9-12). 12.65 (ISBN 0-8134-2073-3); text ed. 9.50x. Interstate.

--Careers in Agribusiness & Industry. 2nd ed. LC 76-106341. (Illus.). (gr. 9-12). 1980. 12.65 o.p. (ISBN 0-8134-2073-3); text ed. 9.50x o.p. (ISBN 0-685-03875-0, 2073). Interstate.

Stone, Bailey S. Parlement of Paris, 1774-1789. LC 79-27732. xi, 227p. 1981. 19.00x (ISBN 0-8078-1442-3). U of NC Pr.

Stone, Bernard. Inspector Mouse. LC 80-83772. (Illus.). (gr. k-2). 1981. 9.95 (ISBN 0-03-059113-9). HR&W.

Stone, Clarence R. Eye & Ear Fun, 3 bks. 1946. 2.64 ea. o.p. Bk. 1 (ISBN 0-07-061701-5). Bk. 2 (ISBN 0-07-061702-3). Bk. 4 (ISBN 0-07-061703-1). McGraw.

Stone, Clifford. The Great Sunflower. LC 76-10020. 192p. 1976. 8.95 (ISBN 0-8149-0775-X). Vanguard.

Stone, Daniel, ed. see Rose, William J.

Stone, Daniel J., et al. Practical Points in Pulmonary Diseases. 1978. spiral bdg. 14.00 (ISBN 0-87488-724-0). Med Exam.

Stone, David. Viewing Your Career. new ed. Gall, Morris, ed. LC 73-83977. (Consumer Education Ser). (Illus., Orig.). (gr. 7-12). 1973. pap. text ed. 1.45 o.p. (ISBN 0-88301-117-4). Pendulum Pr.

Stone, Deborah A. The Limits of Professional Power: National Health Care in the Federal Republic of Germany. LC 80-16864. (Illus.). 244p. 1981. lib. bdg. 18.50x (ISBN 0-226-77553-4). U of Chicago Pr.

Stone, Donald, jt. auth. see Lambert, Charles E.

Stone, Donald B., et al. Elementary School Health Education: Ecological Perspectives. 2nd ed. 1980. pap. text ed. 12.95x (ISBN 0-697-07385-8); instructor's manual avail. (ISBN 0-697-07386-6). Wm C Brown.

Stone, Doris. Arqueologia de la Costa Norte De Honduras. (Peabody Museum Memoirs: Vol. 9, No. 1). 1975. pap. 12.00 (ISBN 0-87365-678-4). Peabody Harvard.

--Pre-Columbian Man Finds Central America. Flint, Emily, ed. LC 72-801668. (Peabody Museum Press Ser.). (Illus.). 1972. 18.00 (ISBN 0-87365-776-4); pap. 12.00 (ISBN 0-685-84984-8). Peabody Harvard.

--Pre-Columbian Man in Costa Rica. Flint, Emily, ed. LC 77-86538. (Peabody Museum Press Books). (Illus.). 1978. pap. 12.00 (ISBN 0-87365-792-6). Peabody Harvard.

Stone, E. Medicine Among the American Indians. (Illus.). 1962. Repr. of 1932 ed. pap. 7.50 o.s.i. (ISBN 0-02-853000-4). Hafner.

Stone, E., et al. Model Continuing Education Recognition System in Library & Information Science. 1979. 32.80 (ISBN 0-89664-145-7, Pub. by K G Saur). Shoe String.

Stone, Edward. Battle & the Books: Some Aspects of Henry James. LC 64-22886. xi, 234p. 1964. 12.95x (ISBN 0-8214-0002-9). Ohio U Pr.

Stone, Edward, ed. What Was Naturalism? Materials for an Answer. (Orig.). 1959. pap. text ed. 8.95 o.p. (ISBN 0-13-955179-4). P-H.

Stone, Elaine, jt. auth. see Troxell, Mary D.

Stone, Elaine M. Uganda: Fire & Blood. 1977. pap. 1.95 o.p. (ISBN 0-88270-237-8). Logos.

Stone, Elizabeth W. Factors Related to the Professional Development of Librarians. LC 75-7741. (Illus.). 1969. 10.00 (ISBN 0-8108-0274-0). Scarecrow.

Stone, Elna. Ghost at the Wedding. 1977. pap. 1.25 (ISBN 0-505-51145-2). Tower Bks.

Stone, Evelyn, ed. Bedtime Mother Goose. (Look-Look Ser.). (Illus.). 24p. (ps). 1980. pap. 0.95 (ISBN 0-307-11855-X, Golden Pr). Western Pub.

Stone, Frank A. The Rub of Cultures in Modern Turkey: Literary View of Education. (Uralic & Altaic Ser.: No. 123). 184p. 1973. pap. text ed. 42.50x (ISBN 0-686-27757-0). Mouton.

Stone, Fred H. Psychiatry & the Pediatrician. Apley, John, ed. (Postgraduate Pediatrics Ser). 1976. 15.95 (ISBN 0-407-00074-7). Butterworths.

Stone, Frederick B., jt. auth. see McMaster, John.

Stone, George K. Science Projects You Can Do. Orig. Title: One Hundred One Science Projects. (Illus.). (gr. 7-9). 1963. PLB 6.95 (ISBN 0-13-795377-1); pap. 1.95 (ISBN 0-13-795328-3). P-H.

Stone, George N. & Becker, Lawrence W. Relevant Mathematics. Incl. Algebra I. (gr. 9). 1970 (ISBN 0-88334-024-0); Geometry. (gr. 10). 1971 (ISBN 0-88334-043-7); Advanced Algebra & Trigonometry. (gr. 11-12). 1971 (ISBN 0-88334-044-5). pap. text ed. 5.75 ea. Ind Sch Pr.

Stone, George W., Jr. & Kahrl, George M. David Garrick: A Critical Biography. LC 79-9476. (Illus.). 791p. 1979. 60.00x (ISBN 0-8093-0931-9). S Ill U Pr.

Stone, George W., Jr., ed. The Stage & the Page: London's "Whole Show" in the Eighteenth Century Theatre. 1981. 14.95x (ISBN 0-520-04201-8). U of Cal Pr.

Stone, Gerald. Introduction to Polish. 128p. 1980. 11.50x (ISBN 0-19-815802-5). Oxford U Pr.

Stone, Gerald, jt. auth. see Comrie, Bernard.

Stone, Gerald C. The Smallest Slavonic Nation. (Illus.). 214p. 1972. text ed. 12.75x (ISBN 0-485-11129-2, Athlone Pr). Humanities.

Stone, Gerald L. A Cognitive-Behavioral Approach Psychology: Implications for Practice, Research, & Training. LC 80-21344. 256p. 1980. 21.95 (ISBN 0-03-055926-X). Praeger.

Stone, Gregory B., ed. In the Spirit of Enterprise from the Rolex Awards. LC 78-23479. (Illus.). 1978. pap. 9.95x (ISBN 0-7167-1034-X). W H Freeman.

Stone, Gregory P. & Farberman, Harvey A. Social Psychology Through Symbolic Interaction. 2nd ed. 450p. 1981. pap. text ed. 13.95 (ISBN 0-471-03029-5). Wiley.

Stone, Gregory P. & Farberman, Harvey A., eds. Social Psychology Through Symbolic Interaction. LC 79-83731. 1970. text ed. 17.95x o.p. (ISBN 0-471-00575-4). Wiley.

Stone, Harold S. Introduction to Computer Architecture. 2nd, rev. ed. 640p. 1980. text ed. 25.95 (ISBN 0-574-21225-6, 13-4225). SRA.

Stone, Howard. Short Bike Rides in Rhode Island. LC 78-73547. (Illus.). 224p. (Orig.). pap. 4.95 (ISBN 0-87106-021-3). Globe Pequot.

Stone, Howard E., ed. see Stone, Howard W.

Stone, Howard W. Suicide & Grief. LC 70-171506. 144p. 1972. pap. 3.50 o.p. (ISBN 0-8006-1402-X, 1-402). Fortress.

--Using Behavioral Methods in Pastoral Counseling. Clinebell, Howard J. & Stone, Howard E., eds. LC 79-2287. (Creative Pastoral Care & Counseling Ser.). 96p. 1980. pap. 3.25 (ISBN 0-8006-0563-2, 1-563). Fortress.

Stone, Howard W., ed. see Augsburger, David W.

Stone, Howard W., ed. see Clements, William M.

Stone, Howard W., ed. see Irwin, Paul B.

Stone, Howard W., ed. see Leas, Speed & Kittlaus, Paul.

Stone, Howard W., ed. see Oates, Wayne E.

Stone, Howard W., ed. see Pattison, E. Mansell.

Stone, Hoyt E. Of Course You Can! 1973. pap. 1.75 (ISBN 0-87148-654-7). Pathway Pr.

--Yet Will I Serve Him. 1976. pap. 2.25 (ISBN 0-87148-931-7). Pathway Pr.

Stone, Irving. Immortal Wife. 504p. 1972. pap. 2.50 (ISBN 0-451-08499-3, E8499, Sig). NAL.

--Lust for Life. 1981. pap. 3.50 (ISBN 0-451-09898-6, E9898, Sig). NAL.

--Men to Match My Mountains: The Story of the Opening of the Far West 1840-1900. LC 56-9405. 1956. 11.95 (ISBN 0-385-04662-6). Doubleday.

--The Origin: A Biographical Novel of Charles Darwin. LC 79-6655. 744p. 1980. 14.95 (ISBN 0-385-12064-8). Doubleday.

--The Passionate Journey. 10.95 (ISBN 0-385-17198-6). Doubleday.

--Passions of the Mind. LC 75-139064. 1971. 14.95 (ISBN 0-385-02396-0); Limited edition 35.00 (ISBN 0-385-02568-8). Doubleday.

--They Also Ran. rev. ed. LC 66-21914. 6.95 o.p. (ISBN 0-385-07409-3). Doubleday.

Stone, Irving, ed. Dear Theo: The Autobiography of Vincent Van Gogh. LC 46-4152. (Illus.). 12.95 (ISBN 0-385-17197-8). Doubleday.

Stone, J. & Philips, A. Contact Lenses, 2 vols. 2nd ed. LC 80-40981. 1980. Vol. I. 79.95 ea. (ISBN 0-407-93270-4). Vol.2 (ISBN 0-407-93271-2). Butterworths.

Stone, J., jt. auth. see Borden, G.

Stone, James C. Breakthrough in Teacher Education. LC 68-54945. (Higher Education Ser.). 1968. 11.95x o.p. (ISBN 0-87589-024-5). Jossey-Bass.

--Teachers for the Disadvantaged. LC 79-92893. (Higher Education Ser.). 1969. 13.95x o.p. (ISBN 0-87589-043-1). Jossey-Bass.

Stone, James C. & DeNevi, Donald P., eds. Portraits of the American University: 1890-1910. LC 72-146783. (Higher Education Ser.). (Illus.). 1971. 17.95x o.p. (ISBN 0-87589-087-3). Jossey-Bass.

Stone, James W. Van see Van Stone, James W.

Stone, Janet & Musset, Anthony. Contact Lens Design Tables. 1981. text ed. price not set. Butterworth.

Stone, Jeremy J. Strategic Persuasion: Arms Limitations Through Dialogue. LC 67-25591. 1967. 20.00x (ISBN 0-231-03090-8). Columbia U Pr.

Stone, Jim, ed. Darkroom Dynamics: An Introduction to Creative Printing. 208p. 1981. pap. 12.95 (ISBN 0-442-27927-2). Van Nos Reinhold.

Stone, John, jt. auth. see Palmquist, Al.

Stone, John C., ed. see Bendavid-Val, Leah, et al.

Stone, Jon. The Monster at the End of This Book. (Illus.). (gr. k-2). 1976. PLB 5.00 (ISBN 0-307-60316-4, Golden Pr). Western Pub.

--The Monster at the End of This Book. (Illus.). (ps-2). 1977. 1.95 (ISBN 0-307-10506-7, Golden Pr); PLB 7.62 (ISBN 0-307-60506-X). Western Pub.

Stone, Josephine R. The Mudhead. LC 80-11982. 156p. (gr. 5-9). 1980. 8.95 (ISBN 0-689-30787-X, Argo). Atheneum.

Stone, Julius. Social Dimensions of Law & Justice. LC 73-168258. 1971. Repr. lib. bdg. 50.00x (ISBN 0-912004-08-8). W W Gaunt.

Stone, Katharine, et al. Practice for the B.S.E. 170p. 1980. pap. text ed. 5.95 (ISBN 0-89892-037-X). Contemp Pub Co Raleigh.

Stone, Kurt. Music Notation in the Twentieth Century: A Practical Guidebook. (Illus.). 1981. text ed. 29.95x (ISBN 0-393-95053-0). Norton.

Stone, L. Joseph & Church, Joseph. Childhood & Adolescence: A Psychology of the Growing Person. 4th ed. LC 78-10730. 1979. text ed. 15.95x (ISBN 0-394-32086-7); study guide 5.95x (ISBN 0-394-32170-7). Random.

Stone, Lawrence. Crisis of the Aristocracy, 1558-1641. 1965. 49.00x (ISBN 0-19-821314-X). Oxford U Pr.

--Family & Fortune: Studies in Aristocratic Finance in the Sixteenth & Seventeenth Centuries. (Illus.). 1973. 29.95x (ISBN 0-19-822401-X). Oxford U Pr.

--Family, Sex & Marriage in England, Fifteen Hundred to Eighteen Hundred. abr. ed. LC 79-2028. (Illus.). 1980. pap. 8.95 (ISBN 0-06-090735-5, CN 735, CN). Har-Row.

--The Past & the Present. 288p. 1981. 15.95 (ISBN 0-7100-0628-4). Routledge & Kegan.

Stone, Lawrence D., jt. ed. see Haley, K. Brian.

Stone, Leo, jt. auth. see Langs, Robert.

Stone, Leroy O. Canadian Population Trends & Public Policy Through the 1980's. 1977. pap. text ed. 4.00x (ISBN 0-7735-0288-2, Pub. by Inst Res Pub Canada). Renouf.

Stone, Leroy O. & MacLean, Michael J. Future Income Prospects for Canada's Senior Citizens. 104p. 1979. pap. text ed. 7.95x (ISBN 0-920380-13-1, Pub. by Inst Res Pub Canada). Renouf.

Stone, Leslie F. Out of the Void. (YA) 5.95 (ISBN 0-685-07452-8, Avalon). Bouregy.

Stone, Linda, jt. auth. see Bracken, John.

Stone, M. H. Linear Transformations in Hilbert Space & Their Applications to Analysis. LC 33-2746. (Colloquium Pbns. Ser: Vol. 15). 1979. Repr. of 1974 ed. 36.90 (ISBN 0-8218-1015-4, COLL-15). Am Math.

Stone, Marie K., jt. auth. see Kahan, Jane.

Stone, Marilyn A., jt. auth. see Proctor, Tony.

Stone, Mark H., jt. auth. see Wright, Benjamin D.

Stone, Merlin. Ancient Mirrors of Womanhood, 2 vols. 224p. Vol. I. pap. 6.95 (ISBN 0-9603352-0-X); Vol. II. pap. 7.95 (ISBN 0-9603352-1-8). New Sibylline.

--Ancient Mirrors of Womanhood: Our Goddess & Heroine Heritage, Vol. 2. (Illus.). 224p. Date not set. pap. 7.95 (ISBN 0-9603352-1-8). New Sibylline.

--Product Planning: An Integrated Approach. LC 76-26335. 1976. 24.95 (ISBN 0-470-98915-7). Halsted Pr.

Stone, Michael E. The Testament of Abraham. LC 72-88770. (Society of Biblical Literature. Texts & Translation-Psuedepigrapha Ser.). 1972. pap. 6.00 (ISBN 0-89130-170-4, 060202). Scholars Pr Ca.

Stone, Michael E. & Strugnell, John. The Books of Elijah, Pts. 1 & 2. LC 79-15153. (Pseudepigrapha Ser.: No. 8). 1979. 10.50 (ISBN 0-89130-315-4, 060218); pap. 6.00 (ISBN 0-89130-316-2). Scholars Pr Ca.

Stone, Michael E., ed. The Armenian Version of IV Ezra. LC 78-17084. 1979. 15.00 (ISBN 0-89130-287-5); pap. 10.50 (ISBN 0-89130-255-7, 210201). Scholars Pr Ca.

Stone, Nancy & Grey, Robert W., eds. White Trash: An Anthology of Contemporary Southern Poets. nd ed. 135p. 1981. pap. 7.50 (ISBN 0-917990-06-4). New South Co.

Stone, Naomi B., ed. see Merton, Thomas.

Stone, Naomi B., et al, eds. see Merton, Thomas.

Stone, P. A. Structure, Size & Costs of Urban Settlements. LC 73-80480. (National Institute of Economic & Social Research Economic & Social Studies: No. 28). (Illus.). 300p. 1973. 38.50 (ISBN 0-521-20309-0). Cambridge U Pr.

--Urban Development in Britain: Measurement of Consumer's Expenditure in the United Kingdom, 1920-38. Vol. 1. 42.00 (ISBN 0-521-06932-7); Vol. 2. 42.00 (ISBN 0-521-06558-5). Cambridge U Pr.

Stone, P. W., tr. see Laclos, Choderlos de.

Stone, Peter. Gravel Pit Angling. LC 77-91759. (Illus.). 1978. 17.95 (ISBN 0-7153-7580-6). David & Charles.

Stone, Peter B. Did We Save the Earth at Stockholm? (Earth Island Ser). 1973. 5.95x o.p. (ISBN 0-85644-017-5); pap. 3.95 o.p. (ISBN 0-85644-023-X). Friends Earth.

Stone, R. H. A Basic Biology for the Tropics, 2 vols. (Illus.). (gr. 9). 1973. text ed. 6.95 ea. Vol. 1 (ISBN 0-521-08233-1). Vol. 2 (ISBN 0-521-08612-4). Cambridge U Pr.

--Tropical Nature Study. 9.95 (ISBN 0-521-06559-3). Cambridge U Pr.

Stone, Richard K., et al. Textbook Study Guide of Pediatrics. (Medical Examination Review Book: Vol. 11A). 1976. spiral bdg. 8.50 o.s.i. (ISBN 0-87488-157-9). Med Exam.

Stone, Robert. Dog Soldiers. 352p. 1975. pap. 2.75 (ISBN 0-345-27574-8). Ballantine.

Stone, Robert B., jt. auth. see Petrie, Sidney.

Stone, Robert B., jt. auth. see Stransky, Judith.

Stone, Robert T. & Berlin, Howard M. Design of VMOS Circuits, with Experiments. LC 79-5617. 1980. pap. 8.95 (ISBN 0-672-21686-8). Sams.

Stone, Rochelle. Boleslaw Lesmian: The Poet & His Poetry. LC 73-84382. 1976. 22.75x (ISBN 0-520-02549-0). U of Cal Pr.

Stone, Roland. The Presidents. (Orig.). 1979. pap. 1.95 (ISBN 0-532-23284-4). Manor Bks.

Stone, Ronald H. Realism & Hope. 1977. pap. text ed. 8.75x (ISBN 0-8191-0128-1). U Pr of Amer.

Stone, Ronald H., ed. & intro. by see Niebuhr, Reinhold.

Stone, Russell A., ed. OPEC & the Middle East: The Impact of Oil on Societal Development. LC 77-2920. (Special Studies). 1976. text ed. 28.95 (ISBN 0-275-24490-3). Praeger.

Stone, Sandra, et al, eds. Management for Nurses: A Multidisciplinary Approach. LC 75-15561. 1976. pap. 9.95 (ISBN 0-8016-4812-2). Mosby.

Stone, Scott C. Pearl Harbor: The Way It Was--December 7, 1941. LC 77-82234. (Illus.). 1977. pap. 4.95 (ISBN 0-89610-039-1). Island Her.

--Volcano!! (Illus.). 1978. pap. 4.95 (ISBN 0-89610-064-2). Island Her.

Stone, Scott C. & McGowan, John E. Wrapped in the Wind's Shawl: The Refugees of Southeast Asia. (Illus.). 138p. (Orig.). 1980. pap. 8.95 (ISBN 0-89141-107-0). Presidio Pr.

Stone, Shelley C. & Shertzer, Bruce. Careers in Counseling & Guidance. LC 72-185792. 160p. (Orig.). 1972. pap. text ed. 9.75 (ISBN 0-395-13494-3). HM.

Stone, Shelley C., jt. auth. see Shertzer, Bruce.

Stone, Shelley C., jt. auth. see Shertzer, Bruce E.

Stone, Sue & Stone, Alan. Abnormal Personality Through Literature. (Orig.). 1966. pap. text ed. 11.95 (ISBN 0-13-000786-2). P-H.

Stone, Tabor R. Beyond the Automobile: Reshaping the Transportation Environment. (Illus.). 1971. 5.95 o.p. (ISBN 0-13-076026-9, Spec). P-H.

Stone, W. L. Campaign of Lieut. Gen. John Burgoyne & the Expedition of Lieut. Col. Barry St. Leger. LC 75-114716. (Era of the American Revolution Ser). 1970. Repr. of 1877 ed. lib. bdg. 42.50 (ISBN 0-306-71925-8). Da Capo.

Stone, Wilfred & Hoopes, Robert, eds. Form & Thought in Prose. 4th ed. LC 77-73100. 1977. 11.95x (ISBN 0-8260-8556-3). Wiley.

Stone, William D. Earth Moving Machines. LC 78-26947. (Machine World Ser.). (Illus.). (gr. 2-4). 1979. PLB 9.95 (ISBN 0-8172-1329-5). Raintree Pubs.

Stone, William F. The Psychology of Politics. LC 73-17647. (Illus.). 1974. 14.95 (ISBN 0-02-931690-1); pap. text ed. 8.95 (ISBN 0-02-931680-4). Free Pr.

Stone, William J. & Kroll, William A. Sports Conditioning & Weight Training: Programs for Athletic Competition. new ed. 1978. pap. 15.95 (ISBN 0-205-06999-1). Allyn.

Stone, William L., ed. Letters of Brunswick & Hessian Officers During the American Revolution. LC 76-112706. (Era of the American Revolution). 1970. Repr. of 1891 ed. lib. bdg. 32.50 (ISBN 0-306-71919-3). Da Capo.

Stone, William T., jt. auth. see Hart, Jerrems C.

Stone, Williard E., ed. Theory Formulations. (U of Fla. Accounting Ser.: No. 6). 1970. pap. 2.00 (ISBN 0-8130-0341-5). U Presses Fla.

Stone, Witmer. The Plants of Southern New Jersey. LC 72-93855. (Illus.). 944p. 1973. Repr. of 1910 ed. 30.00x o.p. (ISBN 0-88000-011-2). Quarterman.

Stonecash, Jeffrey M., jt. auth. see Nardulli, Peter F.

Stonecipher, Harry W. & Trager, Robert. The Mass Media & the Law in Illinois. LC 76-25463. (New Horizons in Journalism Ser.). 256p. 1976. 14.95x (ISBN 0-8093-0788-X). S Ill U Pr.

Stonehill, Robert B., jt. auth. see Jay, Stephen J.

Stonehouse, Bernard. A Closer Look at Plant Life. (Closer Look at Ser.). (Illus.). (gr. 5-8). 1978. PLB 6.90 s&l (ISBN 0-531-01430-4). Watts.

--A Closer Look at Reptiles. LC 78-11539. (Closer Look at Ser.). (Illus.). (gr. 5-8). 1979. PLB 6.90 s&l (ISBN 0-531-03401-1). Watts.

--A Closer Look at Whales & Dolphins. (Closer Look at Ser.). (Illus.). (gr. 4 up). 1978. PLB 6.90 s&l (ISBN 0-531-01484-3); pap. 1.95 (ISBN 0-531-02489-X). Watts.

--Kangaroos. LC 77-60872. (Animals of the World Ser.). (Illus.). (gr. 4-8). 1978. PLB 10.65 (ISBN 0-8172-1079-2). Raintree Pubs.

Stonehouse, Frederick. The Wreck of the Edmund Fitzgerald. LC 77-93064. (Illus.). 1977. 4.95 o.p. (ISBN 0-685-87719-1). Avery Color.

Stoneking, Gary E. Minnesota Legal Forms-Personal Injury. Mason Publishing Staff, ed. 150p. 1981. ring binder 15.00 (ISBN 0-917126-93-9). Mason Pub.

Stonely, Jack. Scruffy. 1981. Repr. pap. 1.95 (ISBN 0-671-41304-X). Archway.

Stoneman, Milton. Easy to Make Wooden Sundials: Instructions & Plans for Five Projects. (Illus.). 64p. (Orig.). 1981. pap. price not set (ISBN 0-486-24141-6). Dover.

Stoneman, P. Technological Diffusion & the Computer Revolution. LC 75-12136. (Department of Applied Economics Monograph: No. 25). (Illus.). 1976. 38.50 (ISBN 0-521-20945-5). Cambridge U Pr.

Stoneman, William E. A History of the Economic Analysis of the Great Depression in America. Freidel, Frank, ed. LC 78-62514. (Modern American History Ser.: Vol. 17). 1979. lib. bdg. 30.00 (ISBN 0-8240-3640-9). Garland Pub.

Stoner, Carol, ed. see Corbett, Michael N.

Stoner, Carol, ed. see Sussman, Vic.

Stoner, Carol H. Producing Your Own Power: How to Make Nature's Energy Sources Work for You. LC 74-10765. (Illus.). 320p. 1974. 10.95 (ISBN 0-87857-088-8). Rodale Pr Inc.

--Stocking up. rev. ed. LC 77-3942. 1977. 13.95 (ISBN 0-87857-167-1); 13.95 (ISBN 0-87857-221-X); deluxe ed. 15.95 (ISBN 0-686-67634-3). Rodale Pr Inc.

Stoner, J. A. Management. (Illus.). 1978. text ed. 21.00 (ISBN 0-13-549303-X); study guide & wkbk 7.95 (ISBN 0-13-549329-3). P-H.

Stoner, Martha H., jt. auth. see Gutch, C. F.

Stoner, Peter W. Science Speaks. 1958. pap. 1.50 (ISBN 0-8024-7630-9). Moody.

Stoner, Rosemary B., jt. auth. see Stevens, Laura J.

Stones, E. Psychopedagogy: Psychological Theory & the Practice of Teaching. 490p. 1979. 21.95 (ISBN 0-416-71330-0, 2525); pap. 13.95 (ISBN 0-416-71340-8, 2526). Methuen Inc.

Stones, E. L. & Simpson, Grant G. Edward I & the Throne of Scotland 1290-1296: An Edition of the Record Sources for the Great Cause, 2 vols. 1979. 165.00x (ISBN 0-19-713308-8). Oxford U Pr.

Stonesifer, Richard J. W. H. Davies: A Critical Biography. 1965. 17.50x (ISBN 0-8195-3056-5, Pub. by Wesleyan U Pr). Columbia U Pr.

Stong, Clair L., jt. auth. see Hammesfahr, James E.

Stong, Phil. Honk the Moose. LC 35-27382. (Illus.). (gr. 4-6). 1935. PLB 6.95 (ISBN 0-396-07358-1). Dodd.

Stonier, T., jt. auth. see Braun, A. C.

Stoodley, Bartlett H., ed. Society & Self: A Reader in Social Psychology. LC 62-11864. 1962. 10.50 o.s.i. (ISBN 0-02-931630-8); pap. text ed. 5.50 o.s.i. (ISBN 0-02-931640-5). Free Pr.

Stookey, R. Yemen. LC 77-454. (Westview Special Studies on the Middle East). 1978. lib. bdg. 26.50x (ISBN 0-89158-300-9). Westview.

Stookey, Robert W. America & the Arab States: An Uneasy Encounter. LC 75-25874. (America & the World Ser). 298p. 1975. pap. text ed. 10.95x (ISBN 0-471-82976-5). Wiley.

Stoop, Dave. A Parent's Cry for Help. rev. ed. LC 78-62916. 144p. 1981. pap. 2.50 (ISBN 0-89081-270-5). Harvest Hse.

Stoops, Emery, et al. Handbook of Educational Administration: A Guide for the Practitioner. 912p. 1975. text ed. 35.95x o.p. (ISBN 0-205-04469-7, 2244691). Allyn.

Stopa, Roman. The Structure of Bushman & Its Traces in Indo-European. (Illus.). 216p. 1972. text ed. 11.75x (ISBN 0-7007-0017-X). Humanities.

Stopford, John, ed. see Association of Teachers of Management.

Stopher, Peter R. Urban Transportation Modeling & Planning. LC 74-21876. 224p. 1975. 24.95x (ISBN 0-669-96941-9). Lexington Bks.

Stopher, Peter R. & Meyberg, Arnim. Transportation Systems Evaluation. 1976. 18.95 (ISBN 0-669-96958-3). Lexington Bks.

Stopher, Peter R. & Mevburg, Arnim H., eds. Behavioral Travel-Demand Models. LC 76-14666. 1976. 27.95 (ISBN 0-669-00734-X). Lexington Bks.

Stopher, Peter R., et al, eds. New Horizons in Travel-Behavior Research. LC 78-24830. 1981. price not set (ISBN 0-669-02850-9). Lexington Bks.

Stopp, P., jt. auth. see Smith, D. I.

Stoppard, Tom. Night & Day. LC 78-73218. 1979. 10.00 (ISBN 0-394-50526-3, GP 825, Grove). Grove.

Stoppard, Tom, tr. see Schnitzler, Arthur.

Storandt, Martha, jt. auth. see Botwinick, Jack.

Storaska, Frederic. How to Say No to a Rapist - and Survive. 224p. 1976. pap. 1.95 o.s.i. (ISBN 0-446-89277-7). Warner Bks.

Storch, Janet L., jt. auth. see Meilicke, Carl A.

Storer, Doug. Encyclopedia of Amazing but True Facts. LC 79-91385. (Illus.). 448p. 1980. 9.95 (ISBN 0-8069-0184-5); lib. bdg. 9.89 (ISBN 0-8069-0185-3). Sterling.

Storer, Jay, ed. Basic Bodywork & Painting. 5th, rev. ed. LC 73-79967. (Illus.). 192p. (Orig.). 1981. pap. 4.95 (ISBN 0-8227-5057-0). Petersen Pub.

Storer, John H. Man in the Web of Life. (Orig.). (RL 8). 1968. pap. 0.95 o.p. (ISBN 0-451-03664-6, Q3664, Sig). NAL.

--The Web of Life. LC 53-12063. (Illus.). 142p. 1981. pap. 5.95 (ISBN 0-8159-7203-2). Devin.

Storer, John M & Stewart, Harry L. ABC's of Hydraulic Circuits. LC 73-83372. (Illus., Orig.). 1973. pap. 4.50 o.p. (ISBN 0-672-21003-7). Sams.

Storer, John M., jt. auth. see Stewart, Harry L.

Storer, M., jt. ed. see Sartre, J.

Storer, Malcolm. Numismatics of Massachusetts. LC 80-52820. 317p. 1981. Repr. of 1923 ed. 35.00x (ISBN 0-88000-117-8). Quarterman.

Storer, Norman W. Focus on Society: An Introduction to Sociology. 2nd ed. LC 79-26376. (Sociology Ser.). (Illus.). 1980. text ed. 13.95 (ISBN 0-201-07337-4). A-W.

Storer, Tracy I. & Usinger, Robert L. General Zoology. 5th ed. (Illus.). 864p. 1972. text ed. 17.50 o.p. (ISBN 0-07-061776-7). McGraw.

Storey, David. Pasmore. 1975. pap. 1.95 (ISBN 0-380-00276-0, 38547). Avon.

Storey, Del. Collision Course. 1977. pap. 2.95 o.p. (ISBN 0-88270-230-0). Logos.

Storey, Edward J. How to Kick a Football. (Illus.). 160p. (Orig.). 1981. pap. text ed. 5.95 (ISBN 0-918438-61-6). Leisure Pr.

Storey, Eric, jt. auth. see Dickens, Michael.

Storey, James R., et al. The Better Jobs & Income Plan: A Guide to President Carter's Welfare Reform Proposal & Major Issues. (Welfare Reform Policy Analysis Sr.: No. 1). 97p. 1978. pap. 4.00 (ISBN 0-87766-213-4, 21100). Urban Inst.

Storey, Joan. Running a Home. (Illus.). 1968. 5.95 (ISBN 0-571-08443-5, Pub. by Faber & Faber). Merrimack Bk Serv.

Storey, Joan & Reece, Daphne E. U. S. A. West: A Travel Guide to Hawaii, the Pacific States & the Southwest. (Illus.). 1981. pap. 6.95 (ISBN 0-908086-09-1). Hippocrene Bks.

Storey, John. Challenge to Management Control. 160p. 1980. 30.00x (ISBN 0-85038-187-8). Nichols Pub.

Storey, Margaret. Ask Me No Questions. (gr. 5 up). 1975. PLB 7.95 o.p. (ISBN 0-525-25972-4). Dutton.

--The Family Tree. LC 73-10040. (Illus.). 196p. (gr. 4-7). 1973. 5.95 o.p. (ISBN 0-525-66330-4). Elsevier-Nelson.

--The Mollyday Holiday. (Illus.). (ps-5). 1971. 6.95 (ISBN 0-571-09590-9, Pub. by Faber & Faber). Merrimack Bk Serv.

--A Quarrel of Witches. (Illus.). (ps-5). 1970. 7.95 o.p. (ISBN 0-571-09416-3, Pub. by Faber & Faber). Merrimack Bk Serv.

--A War of Wizards. (Illus.). (ps-5). 1976. 8.95 (ISBN 0-686-24629-2, Pub. by Faber & Faber). Merrimack Bk Serv.

Storey, Mark, ed. Clare: The Critical Heritage. (The Critical Heritage Ser). 474p. 1973. 38.00x (ISBN 0-7100-7389-5). Routledge & Kegan.

Storey, Moorfield. Charles Sumner. LC 80-25284. (American Statesmen Ser.). 470p. 1981. pap. 6.95 (ISBN 0-87754-197-3). Chelsea Hse.

Storey, R. L., jt. ed. see Bullough, D. A.

Storey, Reed K. The Search for Accounting Principles. LC 77-81833. 1977. Repr. of 1964 ed. text ed. 10.00 (ISBN 0-914348-20-5). Scholars Bk.

Storey, S. H., jt. auth. see Van Zeggeren, F.

Storey, William G., et al, eds. Morning Praise & Evensong. LC 72-91427. 200p. 1973. 8.00 o.p. (ISBN 0-8190-0601-7). Fides Claretian.

Stori, Mouse. I'll Eat Anything If I Can Make It Myself. (Illus.). 176p. spiral bdg. 7.95. Chicago Review.

Storing, Herbert J., jt. auth. see Self, Peter.

Stork, Charles W., ed. Modern Swedish Masterpieces. LC 79-53464. (Short Story Index in Reprint Ser.). Date not set. Repr. of 1923 ed. 22.50x (ISBN 0-8486-5012-3). Core Collection. Postponed.

Stork, F. C. So You Want to Learn a Language. (Illus., Orig.). 1976. pap. 4.95 (ISBN 0-571-10820-2, Pub. by Faber & Faber). Merrimack Bk Serv.

Stork, F. C. & Widdowson, J. D. Learning About Linguistics. 1980. pap. text ed. 8.50x (ISBN 0-09-118061-9, Hutchinson U Lib). Humanities.

Stork, F. C., jt. ed. see Hartmann, R. R.

Stork, Uwe. Der Sprachliche Rhythmus in Den Buhnenstucken John Millington Synges. (Salzburg Studies in Elizabethan Literature: Poetic Drama: No. 55). 1980. pap. text ed. 25.00x (ISBN 0-391-01876-0). Humanities.

Storm, Gerrit, ed. see Furst, Bruno.

Storm, Hyemyohsts. The Song of Hyemeyohsts: A Novel. LC 80-8359. (Native American Publishing Program). (Illus.). 224p. 1981. 12.95 (ISBN 0-06-452000-5, HarpR). Har-Row.

Storm, Theodor. Aquis Submersus. Boswell, Patricia M., ed. (Blackwell's German Text Ser.). 1974. pap. 9.95x (ISBN 0-631-01920-0, Pub. by Basil Blackwell). Biblio Dist.

--Immensee. Zeydel, E. H., ed. (Illus., Ger.). 1926. text ed. 11.95x (ISBN 0-89197-226-9); pap. text ed. 3.95x (ISBN 0-89197-227-7). Irvington.

--Viola Tricolor & Curator Carsten. LC 65-7498. 1956. 6.50 o.p. (ISBN 0-8044-2841-7); pap. 2.45 (ISBN 0-8044-6881-8). Ungar.

Stornetta, Ruth R. David's Real World. (Illus.). 1980. 6.00 (ISBN 0-682-49624-3). Exposition.

Storr, Anthony. The Art of Psychotherapy. 204p. 1980. 13.95 (ISBN 0-686-68763-9). S&S.

Storr, Catherine. Hugo & His Grandma. (Illus.). 24p. 1980. pap. 1.60 ea. (Pub. by Dinosaur Pubns); pap. in 5 pk. avail. (ISBN 0-85122-136-X). Merrimack Bk Serv.

--Kate & the Island. (Illus.). 1978. 8.95 (ISBN 0-571-10119-4, Pub. by Faber & Faber). Merrimack Bk Serv.

--The Painter & the Fish. (Illus.). (ps-5). 6.95 (ISBN 0-571-10475-4, Pub. by Faber & Faber). Merrimack Bk Serv.
--The Story of the Terrible Scar. (Illus.). (gr. 2-5). 1978. 7.50 (ISBN 0-571-10996-9, Pub. by Faber & Faber). Merrimack Bk Serv.
--Tales of Polly & the Hungry Wolf. (Illus.). 96p. (gr. 2-5). 10.95 (ISBN 0-571-11585-3, Pub. by Faber & Faber). Merrimack Bk Serv.
Storr, R. C., jt. auth. see Gilchrist, T. L.
Storr, Richard J., ed. see Carnegie Commission on Higher Education.
Storrer, Philip & Williams, Brian. The Nineteen Eighty-One Tax Fighter's Guide. 192p. 1981. pap. 6.95 (ISBN 0-936602-08-2). Harbor Pub CA.
--The Tax Fighter's Guide 1981. 192p. (Orig.). 1981. pap. 6.95 (ISBN 0-936602-08-2). Harbor Pub CA.
Stortz, Diane, et al, eds. Teaching Toddlers. Downs, Kathy & Grewell, Joy. (Illus.). 1978. pap. 3.50 (ISBN 0-87239-219-8, 7964). Standard Pub.
Story, D., ed. Liberty & the Struggle for the Franchise. (Themes in Modern History Ser.: Documentary Research Folder: No. 1). 1972. 4.25x (ISBN 0-7022-0788-8). U of Queensland Pr.
Story, Dale. Sectoral Clash & Industrialization in Latin America. LC 80-28553. (Latin American Foreign & Comparative Studies Program: No. 2). 1981. pap. text ed. 6.00x (ISBN 0-915984-93-8), Syracuse U Foreign Comp.
Story, G. M., ed. see Andrewes, Lancelot.
Story, Joseph. Commentaries of the Constitution of the United States with a Preliminary Review of the Constitutional History of the Colonies & States Before the Adoption of the Constitution. LC 69-11327. (American Constitutional & Legal History Ser). 1970. Repr. of 1833 ed. Set. lib. bdg. 125.00 (ISBN 0-306-71179-6). Da Capo.
--The Miscellaneous Writings of Joseph Story. Story, William W., ed. LC 79-75269. (American Constitutional & Legal History Ser). 828p. 1972. Repr. of 1852 ed. lib. bdg. 75.00 (ISBN 0-306-71314-4). Da Capo.
Story, Norah. Oxford Companion to Canadian History & Literature. 1967. 35.00 o.p. (ISBN 0-19-540115-8). Oxford U Pr.
Story, Ronald. The Forging of an Aristocracy. 1980. 16.00x (ISBN 0-8195-5044-2, Pub by Wesleyan U Pr England). Columbia U Pr.
--The Space-Gods Revealed. 160p. 1980. pap. 3.95 (ISBN 0-06-464040-X, BN 4040). Har-Row.
Story, Ronald D. UFO's & the Limits of Science. LC 80-25543. (Illus.). 224p. 1981. 10.95 (ISBN 0-688-00144-0). Morrow.
Story, William W., ed. see Story, Joseph.
Storz, Johannes. Chlamydia & Chlamydia-Induced Diseases. (Illus.). 376p. 1971. 26.75 (ISBN 0-398-01870-7). C C Thomas.
Storzer, jt. auth. see Gerber.
Storzer, Gerald, jt. auth. see Gerber, Barbara.
Stoskopf, Neal C. Understanding Crop Production. 420p. 1981. text ed. 16.95 (ISBN 0-8359-8027-8). Reston.
Stotesbury, Sidney D., jt. auth. see Tung Yen Lin.
Stotland, Ezra, jt. ed. see Geis, Gilbert.
Stott, D. Human Population Control Mechanisms. 1981. cancelled (ISBN 0-685-32564-4). Univ Park.
Stott, David, ed. see Thinley, Karma.
Stott, Deborah A. Jacques Lipschitz & Cubism. LC 77-94717. (Outstanding Dissertations in the Fine Arts Ser.). 1978. lib. bdg. 33.00x (ISBN 0-8240-3251-9). Garland Pub.
Stott, Douglas, tr. see Hermission, Hans-Jurgen & Lohse, Eduard.
Stott, Geraldine, jt. auth. see Cook, Bridget M.
Stott, J. R., jt. auth. see Munton, R.
Stott, J. R., ed. see Lucas, R. J.
Stott, John R. God's New Society. Motyer, J. A. & Stott, John R., eds. LC 79-3636. (The Bible Speaks Today Ser.). 1980. pap. text ed. 5.95 (ISBN 0-87784-587-5). Inter-Varsity.
--Johannine Epistles. (Tyndale Bible Commentaries). 1964. pap. 3.95 (ISBN 0-8028-1418-2). Eerdmans.
--Our Guilty Silence: The Church, the Gospel & the World. 1969. pap. 2.95 (ISBN 0-8028-1287-2). Eerdmans.
--Sed Llenos del Espiritu Santo. rev. ed. Cook, David A., tr. from Eng. LC 77-162. 112p. (Orig., Span.). 1977. pap. 2.50 (ISBN 0-89922-084-3). Edit Caribe.
Stott, John R., ed. see Stott, John R.
Stott, John R., ed. see Wilcock, Michael.
Stott, Philip. Historical Plant Geography. (Illus.). 192p. 1981. text ed. 30.00x (ISBN 0-04-580010-3, 2641-2); pap. text ed. 14.95x (ISBN 0-04-580011-1). Allen Unwin.
Stott, Wilfrid, jt. auth. see Beckwith, Roger T.
Stott, William. Documentary Expression & Thirties America. LC 73-82676. (Illus.). 441p. 1976. pap. 6.95 (ISBN 0-19-502099-5, 474, GB). Oxford U Pr.
Stouffer. The Stouffer Cookbook of Great American Food & Drink. 1974. 10.95 (ISBN 0-394-48810-5). Random.
Stough, Ada B. Life Is a Weaver. 1979. pap. 4.95 (ISBN 0-910286-59-0). Boxwood.
Stough, Charlotte L. Greek Skepticism: A Study in Epistemology. LC 76-82464. 1969. 18.50x (ISBN 0-520-01604-1). U of Cal Pr.
Stough, Furman C. & Holmes, Urban T., 3rd, eds. Realities & Visions: Contributions to the Church's Mission Today. 1976. pap. 3.95 (ISBN 0-8164-2130-7). Crossroad NY.
Stoughton, Donald M., jt. ed. see Reagen, Michael V.
Stout, Ann M., jt. auth. see Stout, James H.
Stout, David B. Sac, Fox & Iowa Indians, Vol. 2: Indians of E. Missouri, W. Illinois & S. Wisconsin, from the Proto-Historic Period to 1804. (American Indian Ethnohistory Ser: North Central & Northeastern Indians). (Illus.). lib. bdg. 42.00 (ISBN 0-8240-0790-5). Garland Pub.
Stout, David B; see Horr, David A.
Stout, Gardner D., Jr., ed. see Sterne, Laurence.
Stout, George F. Manual of Psychology. (Contributions to the History of Psychology Ser.: Orientations). 1978. Repr. of 1899 ed. write for info. U Pubns Amer.
Stout, George L., jt. auth. see Gettens, Rutherford J.
Stout, James H. & Stout, Ann M. Backpacking with Small Children. LC 74-23854. (Funk & W Bk.). (Illus.). 224p. 1975. 7.95 (ISBN 0-308-10182-0, TYC-T). T Y Crowell.
Stout, John, ed. see Sarkesian, Sam C. & Buck, James H.
Stout, John L. What the Bible Does Not Say. LC 80-84340. (Illus.). 208p. 1981. 10.95 (ISBN 0-8187-0042-4). Harlo Pr.
Stout, Joseph A., Jr., jt. ed. see Faulk, Odie B.
Stout, Marilyn, jt. auth. see Kunin, Madeleine.
Stout, Rex. And Four to Go. 208p. 1980. pap. 2.25 (ISBN 0-553-14452-9). Bantam.
--Black Orchids. 1976. pap. 1.75 (ISBN 0-515-05085-7). Jove Pubns.
--The Broken Vase. 1976. pap. 1.25 o.s.i. (ISBN 0-515-04065-7). Jove Pubns.
--Double for Death. 1973. pap. 0.95 o.s.i. (ISBN 0-515-03119-4, N3119). Jove Pubns.
--Double for Death. 1979. pap. 1.75 (ISBN 0-515-05277-9). Jove Pubns.
--Fer-De-Lance. 1979. pap. 1.75 o.s.i. (ISBN 0-515-05115-2). Jove Pubns.
--The Final Deduction. 144p. 1981. pap. 1.95 (ISBN 0-553-12205-3). Bantam.
--Gambit. 160p. 1981. pap. 2.25 (ISBN 0-553-14646-7). Bantam.
--The Hand in the Glove. 1976. pap. 1.25 o.s.i. (ISBN 0-515-04149-1). Jove Pubns.
--The League of Frightened Men. 1979. pap. 1.75 o.s.i. (ISBN 0-515-05116-0). Jove Pubns.
--Might As Well Be Dead. 160p. 1980. pap. 1.95 (ISBN 0-553-14447-2). Bantam.
--Murder by the Book. 208p. 1981. pap. 1.95 (ISBN 0-553-14450-2). Bantam.
--Not Quite Dead Enough. (Adventures of Nero Wolfe). pap. 1.75 (ISBN 0-515-05119-5). Jove Pubns.
--Over My Dead Body. 1979. pap. 1.75 (ISBN 0-515-04865-8, 04865-8). Jove Pubns.
--Please Pass the Guilt. 1979. pap. 6.95 (ISBN 0-8161-6737-0, Large Print Bks). G K Hall.
--The Red Box. pap. 1.75 (ISBN 0-515-05117-9). Jove Pubns.
--Red Threads. 1979. pap. 1.75 o.s.i. (ISBN 0-515-05280-9). Jove Pubns.
--The Rubber Band. 1979. pap. 1.75 o.s.i. (ISBN 0-515-04867-4). Jove Pubns.
--Second Confession. 208p. 1980. pap. 1.95 (ISBN 0-553-14448-0). Bantam.
--Some Buried Caeser. 1979. pap. 1.75 (ISBN 0-515-05118-7). Jove Pubns.
--The Sound of Murder. 1979. pap. 1.75 (ISBN 0-515-05281-7). Jove Pubns.
--Too Many Cooks. 1976. pap. 1.75 (ISBN 0-515-04866-6). Jove Pubns.
--Too Many Cooks. LC 75-46002. (Crime Fiction Ser). 1976. Repr. of 1938 ed. lib. bdg. 17.50 (ISBN 0-8240-2394-3). Garland Pub.
--Too Many Women. 176p. 1981. pap. 2.25 (ISBN 0-553-14595-9). Bantam.
Stout, Rex & Viking Press Eds. The Nero Wolfe Cookbook. 224p. 1981. pap. 3.95 (ISBN 0-14-005754-4). Penguin.
Stout, Rext. Three Witnesses. 192p. 1981. pap. 2.25 (ISBN 0-553-14451-0). Bantam.
Stout, Russell, Jr. Management or Control? The Organizational Challenge. LC 79-3302. 224p. 1980. 12.95x (ISBN 0-253-12082-9). Ind U Pr.
--Organizations, Management, & Control: An Annotated Bibliography. LC 79-3639. 256p. 1980. 15.00x (ISBN 0-253-14448-5). Ind U Pr.
Stout, Ruth. How to Have a Green Thumb Without an Aching Back. 160p. 1968. pap. 3.50 (ISBN 0-346-12126-4). Cornerstone.
Stout, Sandra. Depression Glass in Color. No. 1. plastic bdg. 6.95 (ISBN 0-87069-022-1); No. 2. plastic bdg. 6.95 (ISBN 0-87069-023-X). Wallace-Homestead.
--McKee Glass. (Illus.). 19.50 (ISBN 0-686-51456-4). Wallace-Homestead.
Stout, Sandra M. Depression Glass Book Three in Colors. (Illus.). 6.95 (ISBN 0-87069-181-3); price guide 1.50 (ISBN 0-87069-182-1). Wallace-Homestead.
Stoutenburg, Adrien. Where to Now, Blue? LC 78-4336. 192p. (gr. 3-7). 1978. 7.95 (ISBN 0-590-07518-7, Four Winds). Schol Bk Serv.
Stoutt, G. The First Month of Life. 1977. pap. 6.95 (ISBN 0-87489-067-5). Med Economics.
Stoutt, Glen R., Jr. The First Month of Life: A Parent's Guide to Care of the Newborn. 1981. pap. 1.95 (ISBN 0-451-09613-4, J9613, Sig). NAL.
Stovall, Floyd. The Foreground of 'Leaves of Grass' LC 73-87861. 288p. 1974. 17.50x (ISBN 0-8139-0523-0). U Pr of Va.
Stovall, Floyd, ed. see Poe, Edgar A.
Stovall, Floyd, ed. see Whitman, Walt.
Stovall, Ruth, jt. auth. see Boyd, Fannie L.
Stovall, Sidney T., et al. Composition: Skills & Models. 2nd ed. LC 77-77681. (Illus.). 1978. pap. text ed. 10.95 (ISBN 0-395-25749-2); inst. manual 0.25 (ISBN 0-395-25750-6). HM.
Stovall, Walter. Presidential Emergency. 1978. 8.95 o.p. (ISBN 0-525-18325-6). Dutton.
Stove, Betty & Adams, Susan. Tennis. (Burns Sports Ser.). 156p. Date not set. pap. cancelled (ISBN 0-695-81571-7). Follett.
Stove, David. Popper & After: Four Modern Irrationalists. 192p. 1981. 20.50 (ISBN 0-08-026792-0); pap. 10.75 (ISBN 0-08-026791-2). Pergamon.
Stove, J. D. & Phillips, K. A. A Modern Approach to Chemistry. 1971. pap. text ed. 9.50 o.p. (ISBN 0-435-64856-X). Heinemann Ed.
Stover, Annette A. & Culinary Arts Institute Staff. Cooking with Beer. Finnegan, Edward G., ed. LC 80-65528. (Adventures in Cooking Ser). (Illus.). 1980. cloth cancelled (ISBN 0-8326-0614-6); pap. 3.95 (ISBN 0-8326-0613-8, 2521). Delair.
Stover, Edgar M., jt. auth. see Kitson, Harry D.
Stover, John F. Iron Road to the West: American Railroads in the 1850's. LC 78-9588. (Illus.). 1978. 17.50x (ISBN 0-231-04046-6). Columbia U Pr.
Stover, Leon E. & Kraig, Bruce. Stonehenge: The Indo-European Heritage. LC 77-25255. 1978. 20.95 (ISBN 0-88229-482-2); pap. 10.95 (ISBN 0-88229-612-4). Nelson-Hall.
Stover, M., jt. ed. see Sartre, J.
Stover, Ruby E. Life's Golden Gleanings. 94p. pap. 1.00. Faith Pub Hse.
Stow, George B. Historia Vitae et Regni Ricardi Secundi. LC 76-19937. (Haney Foundation Ser). (Orig., Latin.). 1977. 9.00x (ISBN 0-8122-7711-2). U of Pa Pr.
Stow, Randolph. Visitants: A Novel. LC 80-53710. 192p. 1981. 9.95 (ISBN 0-8008-8018-8). Taplinger.
Stowe, Charles E. Life of Harriet Beecher Stowe. LC 67-23881. 1967. Repr. of 1889 ed. 20.00 (ISBN 0-8103-3046-6). Gale.
Stowe, Elaine, jt. auth. see Ransom, Grayce A.
Stowe, Harriet B. Uncle Tom's Cabin. LC 66-20534. (Illus.). (gr. 5 up). 1966. 7.95 o.s.i. (ISBN 0-8076-0377-5). Braziller.
Stowe, Keith S. Ocean Science. LC 78-11962. 1979. pap. text ed. 21.95x (ISBN 0-471-04261-7); tchrs' manual avail. (ISBN 0-471-08084-5). Wiley.
Stowe, Noel J. California Government: The Challenge of Change. 1975. pap. text ed. 5.95x (ISBN 0-02-478720-5, 47872); test bk. free (ISBN 0-685-52459-0, 47871). Macmillan.
Stowe, Richard S. Alexandre Dumas, Pere. (World Authors Ser.: No. 388). 1976. lib. bdg. 9.95 (ISBN 0-8057-6230-2). Twayne.
Stowell, Gordon. Abraham. Lerin, S. D. de, tr. from English. (Libros Pescaditos Sobre Perssonajes Biblicos). (Illus.). 1978. pap. 0.40 (ISBN 0-311-38511-7, Edit Mundo). Casa Bautista.
--Abraham. (Illus.). 24p. (Orig.). (ps-2). 1975. pap. 0.39 o.p. (ISBN 0-8307-0340-3, 56-009-01). Regal.
--Ana. Lerin, S. D. De, tr. from English. (Libros Pescaditos Sobre Personajes Biblicos). (Illus.). 1978. pap. 0.40 (ISBN 0-311-38512-5, Edit Mundo). Casa Bautista.
--Dorcas. Lerin, S. D. de, tr. from English. (Libros Pescaditos Sobre Personajes Biblicos). (Illus.). 1978. pap. 0.40 (ISBN 0-311-38517-6, Edit Mundo). Casa Bautista.
--Jonas. Lerin, S. D. de, tr. from English. (Libros Pescaditos Sobre Personajes Biblicos). (Illus.). 1978. pap. 0.40 (ISBN 0-311-38514-1, Edit Mundo). Casa Bautista.
--Juan el Bautista. Lerin, S. D. de, tr. from English. (Libros Pescaditos Sobre Personajes Biblicos). (Illus.). 1978. pap. 0.40 (ISBN 0-311-38515-X, Edit Mundo). Casa Bautista.
--Pablo. Lerin, S. D. de, tr. from English. (Libros Pescaditos Sobre Personajes Biblicos). (Illus.). 1978. pap. 0.40 (ISBN 0-311-38518-4, Edit Mundo). Casa Bautista.
--Pedro. Lerin, S. D. de, tr. from English. (Libros Pescaditos Sobre Personajes Biblicos). 1978. pap. 0.40 (ISBN 0-311-38516-8, Edit Mundo). Casa Bautista.
--Rut. Lerin, S. D. de, tr. from English. (Libros Pescaditos Sobre Personajes Biblicos). (Illus.). 1980. pap. 0.40 (ISBN 0-311-38513-3, Edit Mundo). Casa Bautista.
Stowell, H. Peter. Literary Impressionism, James & Chekhov. LC 78-23737. 286p. 1980. 17.00x (ISBN 0-8203-0468-9). U of Ga Pr.
Stowell, Jerald P. The Beginner's Guide to American Bonsai. LC 77-15372. 1978. 14.95 (ISBN 0-87011-326-7). Kodansha.
Stowell, John C. Carbanions in Organic Synthesis. LC 79-373. 1979. 24.50 (ISBN 0-471-02953-X, Pub. by Wiley-Interscience). Wiley.
Stowell, William H. Stowell Genealogy: A Record of the Descendants of Samuel Stowell of Hingham, Mass. LC 78-87789. (Illus.). 1969. Repr. 27.50 (ISBN 0-8048-0717-5). C E Tuttle.
Stoyva, Johann, et al, eds. Biofeedback & Self-Control: Nineteen Seventy-Seven to Nineteen Seventy-Eight. 1979. text ed. 34.95 (ISBN 0-202-25128-4). Aldine Pub.
--Biofeedback & Self-Control, 1971: An Aldine Annual on the Regulation of Bodily Processes & Consciousness. LC 74-151109. 350p. 1972. 34.95x (ISBN 0-202-25085-7). Aldine Pub.
Straaten, Zak Van, ed. Philosophical Subjects: Essays Presented to P. F. Strawson. 304p. 1980. 37.50 (ISBN 0-19-824603-X). Oxford U Pr.
Straatsma, Bradley R., et al, eds. The Retina: Morphology, Function, & Clinical Characteristics. (UCLA Forum in Medical Sciences: No. 8). (Illus.). 1969. 57.50x (ISBN 0-520-01533-9). U of Cal Pr.
Straayer, A. Christine. The Rock & Me Immediately. LC 79-84578. (Illus.). (ps-5). 1981. pap. 5.00 (ISBN 0-934816-05-0). Metis Pr Inc.
Straayer, John A. American State & Local Government. 2nd ed. (Political Science Ser.). 1977. pap. 11.50 (ISBN 0-675-08489-X). Merrill.
Straayer, John A. & Muessig, Raymond H. The Study & Teaching of Political Science. 2nd ed. (Social Science Seminar, Secondary Education Ser.: No. C28). 112p. 1980. pap. text ed. 5.95 (ISBN 0-675-08191-2). Merrill.
Strachan, C. The Theory of Beta-Decay. LC 72-86202. 1969. 22.00 (ISBN 0-08-006509-0). Pergamon.
Strachan, Harry W. Family & Other Business Groups in Economic Development: The Case of Nicaragua. LC 75-25025. (Special Studies). (Illus.). 160p. 1976. text ed. 21.95 (ISBN 0-275-56050-3). Praeger.
Strachan-Davidson, J. L., ed. see Appian.
Strache, Neil E. & Danky, James P. Hispanic Americans in the United States: A Union List of Periodicals & Newspapers Held by the Library of the State Historical Society of Wisconsin & the Libraries of the University of Wisconsin-Madison. LC 79-26240. 1979. pap. 2.50x (ISBN 0-87020-192-1). State Hist Soc Wis.
Strachey, Alix. Unconscious Motives of War. 1957. text ed. 5.75x (ISBN 0-391-02065-X). Humanities.
Strachey, Barbara. Journeys of Frodo. 128p. (Orig.). 1981. pap. 7.95 (ISBN 0-345-29633-8). Ballantine.
Strachey, James, ed. & tr. see Freud, Sigmund.
Strachey, Lytton. Eminent Victorians. 1969. pap. 3.50 (ISBN 0-15-628697-1, HPL40, HPL). HarBraceJ.
Strachey, Marjorie. The Fathers Without Theology. LC 58-6625. 1958. 4.00 o.p. (ISBN 0-8076-0056-3). Braziller.
Strack, Hermann L. Introduction to the Talmud & Midrash. LC 59-7191. (Temple Books). 1969. pap. text ed. 5.95x (ISBN 0-689-70189-6, T10). Atheneum.
Stracke, J. Richard, ed. The Laud Herbal Glossary. LC 72-93569. 208p. (Orig.). 1976. pap. text ed. 34.25x (ISBN 90-6203-497-7). Humanities.
Stradal, Marianne. Needlecraft with Beads & Crystals. (Illus.). 64p. 1975. 6.95 (ISBN 0-263-05005-X). Transatlantic.
Strader, Janet, jt. auth. see Cheney, Gay.
Strader, W. C. One for Paradise. LC 79-56873. 1981. 8.95 (ISBN 0-533-04542-8). Vantage.
Stradford, H. Todd. Orthopaedics. 4th ed. (Medical Examination Review Book: Vol. 13). 1976. spiral bdg. 16.50 (ISBN 0-87488-113-7). Med Exam.
Stradford, H. Todd, ed. Orthopaedics Review Book: Essay Questions & Answers. 1973. text ed. 12.00 o.p. (ISBN 0-87488-349-0). Med Exam.
Straetz, Ralph, et al, eds. Critical Perspectives & Issues in Health Policy. (Orig.). 1980. pap. 5.00 (ISBN 0-918592-42-9). Policy Studies.

Strage, Mark. The Durable Fig Leaf: A Historical, Cultural, Medical, Social, Literary, & Iconographic Account of Man's Relations with His Penis. 1979. 14.95 (ISBN 0-688-03582-5); pap. 7.95 (ISBN 0-688-08582-2, Quill). Morrow.

Strahan, Bradley R. Love Songs for an Age of Anxiety. (Black Buzzard Chapbook Ser.). (Illus.). 20p. (Orig.). 1981. pap. 1.50 (ISBN 0-938872-00-1). Black Buzzard.

Strahan, Edward. The Art Treasures of America, 3 vols. LC 75-28871. (Art Experience in Late 19th Century America Ser.: Vol. 7). (Illus.). 1976. Set. lib. bdg. 290.00 (ISBN 0-8240-2231-9). Garland Pub.

Strahan, Edward see Weinberg, H. Barbara.

Strahan, Geneviene W. Inpatient Health Facilities Statistics United States, 1978. Olmsted, Mary, ed. (Ser. 14, No. 24). 50p. 1980. pap. text ed. 1.75 (ISBN 0-8406-0204-9). Natl Ctr Educ Broker.

Strahan, William, tr. see Domat, Jean.

Strahler, Alan H., jt. auth. see Strahler, Arthur N.

Strahler, Arthur N. Exercises in Physical Geography. 2nd ed. 328p. 1975. pap. text ed. 10.95x (ISBN 0-471-83177-8); instructor's ed. avail. (ISBN 0-471-83157-3). Wiley.

--Physical Geography. 4th ed. LC 74-9994. 651p. 1975. text ed. 24.95x (ISBN 0-471-83160-3). Wiley.

Strahler, Arthur N. & Strahler, Alan H. Elements of Physical Geography. 2nd ed. LC 78-23776. 1979. text ed. 21.95x (ISBN 0-471-04459-8); tchrs. manual avail. (ISBN 0-471-05004-0); study guide 7.95x (ISBN 0-471-05005-9). Wiley.

--Environmental Geosciences: Interaction Between Natural Systems & Man. LC 72-10325. 1973. 24.95 (ISBN 0-471-83163-8). Wiley.

--Geography & Man's Environment. LC 76-30759. 1977. text ed. 21.95x (ISBN 0-471-01870-8). Wiley.

--Modern Physical Geography. LC 77-20242. 1978. text ed. 22.95x (ISBN 0-471-01871-6); tapes avail. (ISBN 0-471-04093-2); study guide 4.95x (ISBN 0-471-04310-9). Wiley.

Straight, Stephen H. The Acquisition of Maya Phonology: Variation in Yucatec Child Language. LC 75-25123. (American Indian Linguistics Ser.). 1976. lib. bdg. 42.00 (ISBN 0-8240-1973-3). Garland Pub.

Strain, Barbara & Wysong, Patricia. Communication Skills. LC 78-64356. (Speech Communication Ser.). (Illus.). 1979. pap. text ed. 9.95 (ISBN 0-201-07318-8); instr. resource guide avail. 2.50 (ISBN 0-201-07333-1). A-W.

Strain, Samuel F. From the Nolichucky to Memphis: Reminiscences of a Tennessee Doctor. LC 79-129552. (Twentieth Century Reminiscence Ser.: No. 2). (Illus.). 1979. 13.95 (ISBN 0-87870-064-1). Memphis St Univ.

Strait, Newton A., ed. Alphabetical List of Battles, 1754-1900. 1968. Repr. of 1905 ed. 15.00 (ISBN 0-8103-3339-2). Gale.

Strait, Raymond & Robinson, Terry. Lanza: His Tragic Life. LC 80-17281. 208p. 1980. 10.00 (ISBN 0-13-523407-7). P-H.

Strait, Raymond, jt. auth. see Clooney, Rosemary.

Strait, Treva A. The Price of Free Land. LC 78-24287. (Illus.). (gr. 4-6). 1979. 8.95 (ISBN 0-397-31836-7). Lippincott.

Straiton, Eddie. Animals Are My Life. (Illus.). 1979. pap. 15.75 (ISBN 0-85131-316-7, Dist. by Sporting Book Center). J A Allen.

Strakhovsky, Leonid I. Intervention at Archangel: Allied Intervention & Russian Counter-Revolution in North Russia, 1918-1920. LC 74-80594. 1971. Repr. 17.50 (ISBN 0-86527-105-4). Fertig.

Strakosch, G. R. Vertical Transportaion: Elevators & Escalators. 1967. 35.95 (ISBN 0-471-83167-0, Pub. by Wiley-Interscience). Wiley.

Stramesi, Annette. Creative Home Decorating. 7.95 (ISBN 0-916752-14-3). Green Hill.

Strand, Elenora. Ideas to Make Your Days Easier: A Potpourri of Helpful Hints. 1977. 4.00 o.p. (ISBN 0-682-48813-5). Exposition.

Strand, Kenneth A. Essays on the Sabbath in Early Christianity. 1979. pap. text ed. 4.80 (ISBN 0-89039-140-8). Ann Arbor FL.

--The Open Gates of Heaven: A Brief Introduction to Literary Analysis of the Book of Revelations. 1979. pap. text ed. 2.75 o.p. (ISBN 0-89039-119-X). Ann Arbor FL.

Strand, Marcella M. & Elmer, Lucille A. Clinical Laboratory Tests: A Manual for Nurses. 2nd ed. LC 79-29765. 1980. pap. text ed. 7.50 (ISBN 0-8016-4827-0). Mosby.

Strand, Mark. The Owl's Insomnia. LC 73-81724. 1973. pap. 4.95. Atheneum.

--Selected Poems. 1980. 10.95 (ISBN 0-689-11088-X); pap. 6.95 (ISBN 0-689-11089-8). Atheneum.

Strand, Mark, et al. Strand: A Profile. Maier, Carol, tr. (Profile Editions Ser.). (Illus.). 1979. pap. 4.00 o.p. (ISBN 0-931238-08-0); pap. 8.00 signed & lettered o. p. o.p. (ISBN 0-931238-09-9). Grilled Flowers Pr.

Strand, Stanley & Gruber, Edward C. Resumes for Better Jobs. pap. 3.95 (ISBN 0-671-18708-2). Monarch Pr.

Strandberg, Victor H. The Poetic Vision of Robert Penn Warren. LC 76-9503. 304p. 1977. 16.00x (ISBN 0-8131-1347-4). U Pr of Ky.

Strandholt, S. Norman. The Adventures of Dan & Mark. (gr. 1-4). 1978. 4.00 o.p. (ISBN 0-682-49070-9). Exposition.

Strandness, D. E. & Thiele, Brian L. Selected Topics in Venous Disorders: Pathophysiology & Treatment. LC 80-69527. (Illus.). 1981. 29.50 (ISBN 0-87993-154-X). Futura Pub.

Strandness, D. E., Jr. Collateral Circulation in Clinical Surgery. LC 68-23692. (Illus.). 1969. 18.50 o.p. (ISBN 0-7216-8610-9). Saunders.

Strang, Celia. This Child Is Mine. LC 80-28457. 160p. (gr. 6 up). 1981. 7.95 (ISBN 0-8253-0049-5). Beaufort Bks NY.

Strang, David M., jt. auth. see Wheeler, Gary L.

Strang, Gilbert. Linear Algebra & Its Applications. 1976. 17.50 o.p. (ISBN 0-12-673650-2). Acad Pr.

Strang, Paul. The Chinese Shar-Pei. 1980. 19.95 (ISBN 0-87714-072-3). Caroline Hse.

Strang, Paul D. & Olsen, Eve C. The Chinese Shari-Pei. 19.95 (ISBN 0-87714-072-3). Green Hill.

Strang, Roger A. The Promotion Planning Process: Sales Promotion Vs. Advertising. (Praeger Special Studies Ser.). 144p. 1980. 18.95 (ISBN 0-03-049101-0). Praeger.

Strang, W. Gilbert. Instructor's Manual for Linear Algebra & Its Applications. 2nd ed. 1980. 3.00 (ISBN 0-12-673662-6). Acad Pr.

--Linear Algebra & Its Applications. 2nd ed. LC 79-53993. 1980. 18.95 (ISBN 0-12-673660-X). Acad Pr.

Strang, William A. The Restaurant & Food Store Surveys 1979: Evaluating the Potential for a Small Business Information System in Wisconsin: Evaluating the Potential for a Small Business Information System in Wisconsin. (Wisconsin Economy Studies: No. 18). (Illus.). 101p. 1979. 5.00 (ISBN 0-86603-007-7). U Wis Grad Sch Bush.

--Restaurant & Food Store Surveys, 1979: Evaluating the Potential for a Small Business Information System in Wisconsin. (Wisconsin Economy Studies: No. 18). (Orig.). 1979. pap. 5.00 (ISBN 0-86603-007-7). Bureau Busn Res U Wis.

Strang, William A. & Feldman, Howard. Non-Resident Students & the U. W. Madison: Summer Session. (Wisconsin Economy Studies: No. 17). (Illus.). 52p. 1979. 2.50 (ISBN 0-86603-006-9). U Wis Grad Sch Bush.

--Non-Resident Students & the U. W. Madison Summer Session: An Evaluation of Demand & an Estimate of Local Economic Impact. (Wisconsin Economy Studies: No. 17). (Orig.). 1979. pap. 2.50. Bureau Busn Res U Wis.

Strange, Allen. Electronic Music: Systems, Techniques & Controls. 2nd ed. 1981. pap. text ed. 7.95x (ISBN 0-697-03602-2). Wm C Brown.

Strange, D. C. Nascent Marxist Christian Dialogue: 1961-1967-a Bibliography. (Bibliographical Ser.: No. 5). 0.75 o.p. (ISBN 0-89977-005-3). Am Inst Marxist.

Strange, Howard. How to Save Lots of Money on Your Phone Bill. 128p. (Orig.). 1981. pap. 1.95 (ISBN 0-345-29373-8). Ballantine.

Strange, Ian. The Bird Man. (Illus.). 1976. 12.95 o.p. (ISBN 0-86033-015-X). Gordon-Cremonesi.

Strange, James F., jt. auth. see Meyers, Eric M.

Strange, Jerry D. & Rice, Bernard J. Analytical Geometry & Calculus: With Technical Applications. 1970. text ed. 19.95 (ISBN 0-471-83190-5). Wiley.

Strange, Michael, jt. auth. see Allington, Richard.

Strange, Nicholas Le see Le Strange, Nicholas.

Strange, Susan. International Economic Relations of the Western World, 1959-71, Vol. 2: International Monetary Relations. Shonfield, Andrew, ed. 1976. 45.00x (ISBN 0-19-218317-6). Oxford U Pr.

Strange de Jim. The Strange Experience: How to Become the World's Second Greatest Lover. LC 80-69868. (Illus.). 94p. (Orig.). 1980. perfect bdg. 6.95 (ISBN 0-9605308-1-9). Ash-Kar Pr.

Stranger, Joyce. All About Your Pet Puppy. (All About Ser.). (Illus.). 1980. 16.95 (ISBN 0-7207-1216-5, Pub. by Michael Joseph). Merrimack Bk Serv.

Strangeways, A. H. Fox see Fox Strangeways, A. H.

Strangio, Christopher E. Digital Electronics: Fundamental Concepts & Applications. (Illus.). 1980. text ed. 25.95 (ISBN 0-13-212100-X). P-H.

Strangwayes-Booth, Joanna. Cricket in the Thorn Tree: Helen Suzman & the Progressive Party of South Africa. LC 76-486. 320p. 1976. 12.50x (ISBN 0-253-31483-6). Ind U Pr.

Stranks, D. R., et al. Chemistry: A Structural View. LC 74-31783. 500p. 1975. 41.50 (ISBN 0-521-20707-X); pap. 19.95x (ISBN 0-521-09928-5). Cambridge U Pr.

Stransky, E., jt. auth. see Baar, H. S.

Stransky, Judith & Stone, Robert B. The Alexander Technique: Joy in the Life of Your Body. LC 80-26380. (Illus.). 224p. 1981. 14.95 (ISBN 0-8253-0000-2). Beaufort Bks NY.

Stransky, Thomas & Anderson, Gerald H., eds. Mission Trends, No. 4: Liberation Theologies. LC 78-70827. (Mission Trend Ser.). 1979. pap. 3.45 (ISBN 0-8091-2185-9). Paulist Pr.

Stransky, Thomas F., jt. auth. see Anderson, Gerald H.

Stransky, Thomas F., jt. ed. see Anderson, Gerald H.

Strapac, Joseph A. Southern Pacific Review Nineteen Eighty. (Illus.). 1980. pap. 14.00 (ISBN 0-930742-04-4). Shade Tree.

--Southern Pacific Review 1978-1979. new ed. (Illus.). 1979. pap. 12.00 o.p. (ISBN 0-930742-03-6). Shade Tree.

Strapal, Joseph A. Southern Pacific Motive Power Annual, 1971. (Illus.). 1971. 9.95 (ISBN 0-89685-005-6). Chatham Pub CA.

Strasberg, Susan. Bittersweet. (Illus.). 1981. pap. 3.50 (ISBN 0-451-09760-2, E9760, Sig). NAL.

Strassburg, Gottfried Von see Von Strassburg, Gottfried.

Strassburg, M. & Knolie, G. Disease of the Oral Mucosa: A Color Atlas. (Illus.). 270p. 1972. 58.00. Quint Pub Co.

Strasser, Alex. The Work of the Science Film Maker. (Library of Film & Television Practice). Date not set. 18.95 (ISBN 0-8038-8051-0). Hastings.

Strasser, Daniel. The Finances of Europe. LC 77-24408. (Praeger Special Studies). 1977. text ed. 31.95 (ISBN 0-03-022386-5). Praeger.

Strasser, Gabor & Simons, Eugene, eds. Science & Technology Policies: Yesterday, Today & Tomorrow. LC 73-17229. 1973. text ed. 18.50 o.p. (ISBN 0-88410-013-8). Ballinger Pub.

Strasser, Hermann. The Normative Structure of Sociology: Conservative & Emancipatory Themes in Social Thought. (International Library of Sociology). 340p. 1976. 24.00x (ISBN 0-7100-8166-9); pap. 12.00 (ISBN 0-7100-8167-7). Routledge & Kegan.

Strasser, Todd. Angel Dust Blues. (gr. 7-12). 1981. pap. 1.75 (ISBN 0-440-90956-2, LE). Dell.

--Friends till the End: A Novel. LC 80-68738. 192p. (YA) (gr. 8-12). 1981. 8.95 (ISBN 0-440-02750-0). Delacorte.

Straszak, A. & Tuch, R., eds. The Shinkansen High-Speed Rail Network of Japan: Procceedings of a IIASA Conference, June 27-30 1977. (IIASA Proceedings Ser.: Vol. 7). 1980. 130.00 (ISBN 0-08-024444-0). Pergamon.

Strate, James W., jt. auth. see Christiansen, Larry K.

Strategy & Tactics Staff. War in the East. new ed. Dunnigan, James F., ed. (Illus.). 9.95 o.p. (ISBN 0-917852-00-1). Simul Pubns.

Stratemeyer, Florence, et al. Developing a Curriculum for Modern Living. 2nd ed. LC 57-11371. 1957. text ed. 12.95x (ISBN 0-8077-2221-9). Tchrs Coll.

Stratemeyer, Florence B. & Lindsey, M. Working with Student Teachers. LC 58-8555. 1958. pap. text ed. 9.50x (ISBN 0-8077-2222-7). Tchrs Coll.

Stratford, H. Alan. Air Transport Economics in the Supersonic Era. 2nd, new ed. LC 72-84866. 1973. 22.50 (ISBN 0-312-01610-7). St Martin.

Strathdee, Elizabeth D. & Young, Daniel G. Paediatric Surgery. (Modern Practical Nursing Ser: No. 3). (Illus.). 81p. 1971. pap. 9.95x (ISBN 0-433-31858-9). Intl Ideas.

Strathdee, Jean. The House That Grew. (Illus.). 32p. (ps-3). 1980. 8.95 (ISBN 0-19-558041-9). Oxford U Pr.

Strathern, Andrew. Rope of Moka. 26.95 (ISBN 0-521-07987-X); pap. 10.95x (ISBN 0-521-09957-9). Cambridge U Pr.

Strathern, Marilyn. Kinship at the Core: An Anthropology of Elmdon, a Village in North-West Essex. LC 80-40550. (Illus.). 336p. Date not set. price not set (ISBN 0-521-23360-7). Cambridge U Pr.

Strathern, Marilyn, jt. ed. see MacCormack, Carol.

Stratmann, Francis H. Middle-English Dictionary: Containing Words Used by English Writers from the Twelfth to the Fifteenth Century. Bradley, Henry, ed. 1891. 39.00x (ISBN 0-19-863106-5). Oxford U Pr.

Stratmann, William C. & Ullman, Ralph. Evaluating Hospital-Based Ambulatory Care: A Case Study. LC 77-11403. 1980. 24.95 (ISBN 0-669-02096-6). Lexington Bks.

Straton, George D. Theistic Faith for Our Time: An Introduction to the Process Philosophies of Royce & Whitehead. LC 78-65429. 1978. pap. text ed. 11.25 (ISBN 0-8191-0661-5). U Pr of Amer.

Stratton, Carol, jt. auth. see Scott, Miriam M.

Stratton, Clarence. Handbook of English. LC 74-19222. 1975. Repr. of 1940 ed. 26.00 (ISBN 0-8103-4112-3). Gale.

Stratton, Deborah. Mugs & Tankards: A Collector's Guide. LC 76-26359. (Illus.). 1977. 9.95 o.p. (ISBN 0-684-14831-5, ScribT). Scribner.

Stratton, George & Frank, Alan. Playing of Chamber Music. (Student's Music Library). 1951. 6.95 (ISBN 0-234-77197-6). Dufour.

Stratton, George Malcolm. Theophrastus & the Greek Physiological Psychology Before Aristotle. 227p. 1964. Repr. of 1917 ed. text ed. 27.75x (ISBN 90-6031-042-X). Humanities.

Stratton, John, jt. auth. see Montgomery, Michael.

Stratton, John R., jt. auth. see Leger, Robert G.

Stratton, Josephine. The Blind Child in the Regular Kindergarten. 64p. 1977. 9.75 (ISBN 0-398-03623-3). C C Thomas.

Stratton, L. W. Your Book of Shell Collecting. (Illus.). (gr. 7 up). 1968. 5.95 (ISBN 0-571-08211-4). Transatlantic.

Stratton, Lorum H. Emilio Rabasa: Life & Works. (Graduate Studies: No. 8). (Orig.). 1974. pap. 5.00 (ISBN 0-89672-015-2). Tex Tech Pr.

Stratton, Rebecca. The Inherited Bride. (Harlequin Romances). 192p. 1981. pap. 1.25 (ISBN 0-373-02399-5, Pub. by Harlequin). PB.

--The Leo Man. (Harlequin Romances Ser.). 192p. 1981. pap. 1.25 (ISBN 0-373-02405-3, Pub. by Harlequin). PB.

--The Tears of Venus. (Harlequin Romances Ser.). (Orig.). 1980. pap. text ed. 1.25 o.p. (ISBN 0-373-02339-1, Pub. by Harlequin). PB.

--Trader's Cat. (Harlequin Romances Ser.). 192p. 1980. pap. 1.25 (ISBN 0-373-02376-6, Pub. by Harlequin). PB.

Stratton, Royal. Life Among the Indians: Being an Interesting Narrative of the Captivity of the Oatman Girls, Among the Apache & Mohave Indians. LC 75-7096. (Indian Captivities Ser.: Vol. 71). (Bnd. with 2nd ed., changed 1857). 1977. Repr. of 1857 ed. lib. bdg. 44.00 (ISBN 0-8240-1695-5). Garland Pub.

Stratton, Russell J., jt. auth. see Johnson, Dean L.

Stratton, Stephen S., jt. auth. see Brown, James D.

Stratton, Tom. Buffalo Chips. (Illus.). 1979. pap. 1.95 (ISBN 0-930000-13-7). Mathom.

Straub, O. C. Bovine Hematology. (Illus.). 64p. (Orig.). 1981. pap. text ed. 18.00. Parey Sci Pub.

Straub, Ralph W. & Bolis, Liana, eds. Cell Membrane Receptors for Drugs & Hormones. LC 77-87454. 1978. 36.50 (ISBN 0-89004-227-6). Raven.

Straub, W., ed. Current Genetical, Clinical & Morphological Problems. (Developments in Ophthalmology: Vol. 3). (Illus.). 1981. 66.00 (ISBN 3-8055-2000-X). S Karger.

Straubing, H. The Nymphomaniac's Cookbook. (Illus.). 144p. 1980. 4.95 (ISBN 0-87786-003-3); pap. 2.97 (ISBN 0-686-69011-7). Gold Penny.

Strauch, K. P. & Brundage, D. J. Guide to Library Resources for Nursing. 509p. 1980. pap. 12.75 (ISBN 0-8385-3528-3). ACC.

Strauer, B. E. Hypertensive Heart Disease. (Illus.). 106p. 1980. pap. 16.60 (ISBN 0-387-10041-5). Springer-Verlag.

Straugham, R. & Wrigley, J. Values & Evaluation in Education. 1980. text ed. 21.00 (ISBN 0-06-318137-1, IntlDept); pap. text ed. 11.20 (ISBN 0-06-318158-4). Har-Row.

Straughan, B. P. & Walker, S., eds. Spectroscopy, 2 vols. 2nd ed. LC 75-45328. 1978. Vol. 1. pap. text ed. 16.50x o.p. (ISBN 0-412-13350-4, Pub. by Chapman & Hall England); Vol. 2. pap. text ed. 22.50x o.p. (ISBN 0-412-13370-9). Halsted Pr.

--Spectroscopy, 2 vols. 2nd ed. LC 75-45328. 1978. Vol. 1. 15.00 o.p. (ISBN 0-686-00608-9). Vol. 1 (ISBN 0-470-26322-9). Vol. 2. pap. 15.00 o.p. (ISBN 0-470-26323-7). Halsted Pr.

Strauli, Peter, et al, eds. Proteinases & Tumor Invasion, Vol. 6. (European Organization for Research on Treatment of Cancer (EORTC)). 227p. 1980. 22.50 (ISBN 0-89004-515-1). Raven.

Straus, Anselm L., jt. auth. see Glaser, Barney G.

Straus, Bernard. The Maladies of Marcel Proust. LC 80-11204. 175p. 1980. text ed. 24.50x (ISBN 0-8419-0546-0). Holmes & Meier.

Straus, Davis, jt. auth. see Doyle, Micheal.

Strauss, Allan R., Jr. A Critical Study of Freud's Concept of Unconscious Mental Processes with Special Reference to Candid Psychology. (Illus.). 1980. 12.50 (ISBN 0-682-49602-2, University). Exposition.

Strauss, Anselm, jt. auth. see Fagerhaugh, Shizuko.
Strauss, Anselm, et al. Psychiatric Ideologies & Institutions. 418p. 1981. 19.95 (ISBN 0-87855-361-4); pap. 7.95 (ISBN 0-87855-785-7). Transaction Bks.
Strauss, Anselm A. Chronic Illness & the Quality of Life. LC 75-2458. 1975. pap. text ed. 10.50 (ISBN 0-8016-4837-8). Mosby.
Strauss, Anselm L., jt. auth. see Glaser, Barney G.
Strauss, Anselm L., jt. auth. see Schatzman, Leonard.
Strauss, Anselm L., frwd. by. Organizational Scientist: Their Professional Careers. LC 63-12180. 1964. pap. 2.50 (ISBN 0-672-60835-9). Bobbs.
Strauss, David F. The Christ of Faith & the Jesus of History: A Critique of Schleiermacher's The Life of Jesus. Keck, Leander E., tr. & intro. by. LC 75-37152. (Lives of Jesus Ser.). 288p. 1976. pap. 9.95 (ISBN 0-8006-1273-6, 1-1273). Fortress.
Strauss, David P. & Worth, Fred L. Hollywood Trivia. 352p. (Orig.). 1981. pap. 2.75 (ISBN 0-446-95492-6). Warner Bks.
Strauss, Erwin S. Basement Nukes: The Consequences of Cheap Weapons of Mass Destruction. 1980. pap. 6.95. Loompanics.
--The Case Against a Liberatarian Political Party. 1980. pap. 4.50. Loompanics.
Strauss, G., jt. auth. see Sayles, Leonard.
Strauss, Gail, jt. auth. see Relis, Nurie.
Strauss, George, jt. auth. see Sayles, Leonard.
Strauss, H., tr. see Vogt, Hannah.
Strauss, H. William & Pitt, Bertram. Cardiovascular Nuclear Medicine. 2nd ed. LC 79-18410. (Illus.). 1979. text ed. 54.50 (ISBN 0-8016-2409-6). Mosby.
Strauss, James D. The Seer, the Saviour, & the Saved. rev. ed. (The Bible Study Textbook Ser.). (Illus.). 1972. 13.50 (ISBN 0-89900-048-7). College Pr Pub.
Strauss, Jennifer, jt. auth. see Bragg, Gordon M.
Strauss, John S., et al, eds. The Psychotherapy of Schizophrenia. 300p. 1980. 27.50 (ISBN 0-306-40497-4). Plenum Pub.
Strauss, Jose, ed. Pediatric Nephrology, Vol. 5. 1979. lib. bdg. 30.00 (ISBN 0-8240-7031-3). Garland Pub.
--Renal Failure. 1978. lib. bdg. 37.50 (ISBN 0-8240-7011-9). Garland Pub.
Strauss, K. Applied Science in the Casting of Metals. 1970. 50.00 (ISBN 0-08-015711-4). Pergamon.
Strauss, Lehman. Be Filled with the Spirit. 1976. pap. 1.95 o.p. (ISBN 0-310-33072-6). Zondervan.
--Eleven Commandments. 1946. pap. 3.50 (ISBN 0-87213-814-3). Loizeaux.
--Revelation. LC 64-8641. Orig. Title: Book of the Revelation. 6.75 (ISBN 0-87213-825-9). Loizeaux.
--Sense & Nonsense About Prayer. 1976. pap. 1.50 (ISBN 0-8024-7701-1). Moody.
Strauss, Leo. Political Philosophy: Six Essays. Gildin, Hilail, ed. LC 74-16290. (Traditions in Philosophy Ser). 1975. text ed. 17.95 (ISBN 0-672-63659-X). Pegasus.
--What Is Political Philosophy? LC 73-1408. 315p. 1973. Repr. of 1959 ed. lib. bdg. 22.50x (ISBN 0-8371-6802-3, STPP). Greenwood.
Strauss, Leo & Cropsey, Joseph. History of Political Philosophy. 2nd ed. LC 80-26907. xii, 850p. 1981. pap. text ed. 14.00x (ISBN 0-226-77690-5). U of Chicago Pr.
Strauss, Michel, ed. Impressionism & Modern Art: The Season at Sotheby Parke Bernet 1973-74. (Illus.). 288p. 1974. 40.00x (ISBN 0-85667-008-1, Pub. by Sotheby Parke Bernet England). Biblio Dist.
Strauss, Raymond, jt. auth. see Minnick, John.
Strauss, Richard & Von Hofmannsthal, Hugo. The Correspondence Between Richard Strauss & Hugo Von Hofmannsthal. Hammelmann, Hanns & Osers, Ewald, trs. LC 80-40072. 576p. 1981. 67.50 (ISBN 0-521-23476-X); pap. 17.95 (ISBN 0-521-29911-X). Cambridge U Pr.
Strauss, Richard & Zweig, Stefan. A Confidential Matter: The Letters of Richard Strauss & Stefan Zweig, 1931-1935. Knight, Max, tr. from Ger. 1977. 11.95 (ISBN 0-520-03036-2). U of Cal Pr.
Strauss, Robert, jt. ed. see Sbarra, Anthony J.
Strauss, Robert see Sbarra, Anthony J. & Strauss, Robert.
Strauss, Sheryl, ed. Security Problems in a Modern Society. (Illus.). 314p. 1980. text ed. 9.95 (ISBN 0-409-95079-3). Butterworths.
Strauss, Steven. The Pharmacist & the Law. 135p. 1980. softcover 9.95 (ISBN 0-683-08008-3). Williams & Wilkins.
Strauss, W. Patrick. American in Polynesia. (Illus.). vii, 187p. 1964. 5.00 (ISBN 0-87013-078-1). Mich St U Pr.
Strauss, Walter L. Hendrik Goltzius, Master Engraver: A Complete Pictorial Catalogue of His Engravings, Etchings, & Woodcuts. new ed. LC 76-22304. (Illus.). 768p. 1976. 120.00 (ISBN 0-913870-10-2). Abaris Bks.
Strauss, Walter L., ed. Tribute to Wolfgang Stechow. LC 75-44736. (Illus.). 29.50 (ISBN 0-87920-002-2). Abaris Bks.
Strauss, Werner. Industrial Gas Cleaning. 2nd, rev. ed. LC 74-8066. 632p. 1976. text ed. 82.00 (ISBN 0-08-017004-8); pap. 24.00 (ISBN 0-08-019933-X). Pergamon.
Strauss, Werner, ed. Air Pollution Control: Measuring & Monitoring Air Pollutants, Pt. III. LC 79-28773. (Environmental Science & Technology, a Wiley-Interscience Series of Texts & Monographs). 1978. 42.00 (ISBN 0-471-83323-1, Pub by Wiley-Interscience). Wiley.
Strauven, Francois. Renaat Braem Architect. (Archives d'Architecture Moderne). 150p. (Orig., Fr. & Eng.). 1980. write for info. (ISBN 0-8150-0922-4). Wittenborn.
Stravinsky, Igor. Petrushka. Hamm, Charles, ed. (Illus., Orig., Critical Score). 1967. pap. 5.95x (ISBN 0-393-09770-6, NortonC). Norton.
Stravinsky, Igor & Craft, Robert. Expositions & Developments. (Orig.). 1981. pap. 4.95 (ISBN 0-520-04403-7, CAL 503). U of Cal Pr.
--Memories & Commentaries. (Orig.). 1981. pap. 4.95 (ISBN 0-520-04402-9, CAL 502). U of Cal Pr.
Stravinsky, Theodore. Catherine & Igor Stravinsky. LC 72-95737. 1973. 15.00 (ISBN 0-85162-008-6). Boosey & Hawkes.
Straw Dog. The Art of Ragtime Guitar. LC 73-94403. (Green Note Musical Publications Ser.). (Illus.). 1975. Repr. of 1974 ed. 10.95 (ISBN 0-02-871300-1); pap. 6.95 (ISBN 0-02-870990-X). Schirmer Bks.
--Improvising Blues Guitar. LC 70-143775. (Green Note Musical Publications Ser.). (Illus.). 1975. 10.95 (ISBN 0-02-871290-0); pap. 6.95 (ISBN 0-02-870980-2). Schirmer Bks.
--Slide Guitar. LC 72-76529. (Green Note Musical Publications Ser.). (Illus.). 1975. 10.95 (ISBN 0-02-871310-9); pap. 6.95 (ISBN 0-02-871000-2). Schirmer Bks.
Straw Dog & Saslow, Richard. The Art of Ragtime Guitar. LC 73-94403. (Guitar Heritage Ser.). 96p. 1974. pap. 8.95 (ISBN 0-912910-04-6). Green Note Music.
Straw Dog, jt. auth. see Heinz, Cecilia.
Straw Dog, jt. auth. see Saslow, Richard.
Straw Dog, ed. see Green Note Music Publications Staff.
Strawn, L. B. Poems. 1981. 6.50 (ISBN 0-8062-1637-9). Carlton.
Strawn, Richard R. Topics, Terms, & Research Techniques: Self-Instruction in Using Library Catalogs. LC 80-12569. 98p. 1980. 10.00 (ISBN 0-8108-1308-4). Scarecrow.
Strawser, Robert H., jt. auth. see Francia, Arthur J.
Strawson, John. Battle for North Africa. LC 73-93216. (Illus.). 1970. 7.95 o.p. (ISBN 0-684-10582-9, ScribT). Scribner.
Strayer, D. R. & Gillespie, D. H. The Nature & Organization of Retroviral Genes in Animal Cells. (Virology Monographs: Vol. 17). (Illus.). 117p. 1980. 39.80 (ISBN 0-387-81563-5). Springer-Verlag.
Strayer, J. R., ed. see Lansing, John R.
Strayer, Joseph R. The Reign of Philip the Fair. LC 79-3232. 1980. 35.00 (ISBN 0-691-05302-2); pap. 13.50 (ISBN 0-691-10089-6). Princeton U Pr.
Strayer, Joseph R. & Gatzke, Hans W. The Mainstream of Civilization: One-Vol. Edition. 3rd ed. 840p. 1979. text ed. 18.95 (ISBN 0-15-551562-4, HC); test manual avail. (ISBN 0-15-551563-2). HarBraceJ.
Strayer, Judy & Ahlborn, Lois A. Self-Assessment of Current Knowledge in Neurology & Neurosurgical Nursing. 1976. spiral bdg. 8.00 o.p. (ISBN 0-87488-243-5). Med Exam.
Strayer, Robert, et al. Protest Movements in Colonial East Africa-Aspects of Early African Response to European Rule. LC 73-85549. (Foreign & Comparative Studies-Eastern African Ser.: No.12). 96p. 1973. pap. 4.50x (ISBN 0-915984-09-1). Syracuse U Foreign Comp.
Strayhorn, Lloyd. Numbers & You: A Numerology Guide for Everyday Living. 154p. 1980. 9.95 (ISBN 0-937290-02-5). Yama Pub.
Strazhesko, D. N., ed. Adsorption & Adsorbents, No. 1. Barouch, A., tr. from Rus. LC 73-17749. 237p. 1973. 39.95 (ISBN 0-470-83324-6). Halsted Pr.
Strean, Herbert S. Clinical Social Work: Theory & Practice. LC 77-90147. 1978. text ed. 14.95 (ISBN 0-02-932210-3). Free Pr.
--Crucial Issues in Psychotherapy. LC 76-14907. 1976. 13.50 (ISBN 0-8108-0968-0). Scarecrow.
--New Approaches in Child Guidance. LC 74-15008. 1970. 10.00 (ISBN 0-8108-0330-5). Scarecrow.
--Personality Theory & Social Work Practice. LC 75-1132. 190p. 1975. 10.00 (ISBN 0-8108-0797-1). Scarecrow.
--Social Casework: Theories in Action. LC 76-160282. 1971. 12.00 (ISBN 0-8108-0408-5). Scarecrow.
--The Social Worker As Psychotherapist. LC 74-5086. 1974. 10.00 (ISBN 0-8108-0721-1). Scarecrow.
Strean, Herbert S., jt. auth. see Ormont, Louis.
Strean, Herbert S., ed. see Dickerson, Martha U.
Strean, Herbet S. Psychoanalytic Theory & Social Work Practice. Turner, Francis J., ed. LC 78-65223. (Treatment Approaches in the Human Services Ser.). 1979. text ed. 15.95 (ISBN 0-02-932220-0). Free Pr.
Streatfeild, Noel. Ballet Shoes. (gr. 4-6). 1979. pap. 1.75 (ISBN 0-440-41508-X, YB). Dell.
--The Boy Pharaoh. (Illus.). (gr. 2-7). 1972. 7.95 (ISBN 0-7181-0986-4, Pub. by Michael Joseph). Merrimack Bk Serv.
--Dancing Shoes. (gr. k-6). 1980. pap. 1.75 (ISBN 0-440-42289-2, YB). Dell.
--First Book of England. (First Bks). (Illus.). (gr. 4-6). 1958. PLB 4.90 o.p. (ISBN 0-531-00524-0). Watts.
--First Book of the Opera. LC 65-10097. (First Bks). (Illus.). (gr. 4-6). 1967. PLB 4.90 o.p. (ISBN 0-531-00602-6). Watts.
Streatfield, Noel. Beyond the Vicarage. LC 77-169824. 214p. (gr. 9 up). 1972. PLB 5.90 (ISBN 0-531-02018-5). Watts.
Streefland, Pieter. The Sweepers of Slaughterhouse: A Study of Conflict & Survival in a Karachi Neighbourhood. (Studies of Developing Countries Ser.: No. 23). 1979. pap. text ed. 14.25x (ISBN 90-232-1665-2). Humanities.
Streep, Norbert, jt. auth. see St. Maur, Suzan.
Street, Brian V. Savage in Literature. (International Library of Anthropology). 1975. 21.00 (ISBN 0-7100-8110-3). Routledge & Kegan.
Street, David, et al. The Welfare Industry: Functionaries & Recipients in Public Aid. LC 79-1167. (The City & Society: Vol. 4). 199p. 1979. 18.00x (ISBN 0-8039-1227-7); pap. 8.95x (ISBN 0-8039-1228-5). Sage.
Street, Don. Reptiles of Northern & Central Europe. 1979. 38.00 (ISBN 0-7134-1374-3, Pub. by Batsford England). David & Charles.
Street, Donald M., jt. ed. see Rickey, Michael.
Street, Donald M., Jr. Street's Cruising Guide to the Eastern Caribbean, Vol. 1. 1981. pap. 27.95 spiral bdg. (ISBN 0-393-03250-7). Norton.
Street, G. S. Autobiography of a Boy. LC 76-19978. (The Decadent Consciousness Ser.: Vol. 23). 1977. Repr. of 1894 ed. lib. bdg. 38.00 (ISBN 0-8240-2772-8). Garland Pub.
Street, H. E. & Cockburn, W. Plant Metabolism. 2nd ed. LC 76-174629. 332p. 1972. 25.00 (ISBN 0-08-016752-7); pap. 13.25 (ISBN 0-08-016753-5). Pergamon.
Street, H. E. & Opik, H. Physiology of Flowering Plants. 2nd ed. (Contemporary Biology Ser.). 1976. 18.50 (ISBN 0-444-19505-X); pap. 18.50 (ISBN 0-686-67620-3). Univ Park.
Street, H. E., ed. Plant Tissue & Cell Culture. 2nd ed. (Botanical Monographs: Vol. 11). 1978. 60.00x (ISBN 0-520-03473-2). U of Cal Pr.
Street, Jack C. Travel in the Nick of Time. 1981. 4.50 (ISBN 0-8062-1707-3). Carlton.
Street, James. Good-Bye, My Lady. (gr. 7-9). 1954. 10.95 (ISBN 0-397-00049-9). Lippincott.
--Good-Bye My Lady. (gr. 7-9). 1977. pap. 1.75 (ISBN 0-671-24289-X). Archway.
--Goodbye My Lady. (YA) (gr. 7-9). 1978. pap. 1.25 (ISBN 0-671-29879-8). PB.
Street, James H. & James, Dilmus D., eds. Technological Progress in Latin America: The Prospects for Overcoming Dependency. (Special Studies on Latin America & the Caribbean). 1979. lib. bdg. 24.50x (ISBN 0-89158-255-X). Westview.
Street, Philip. Animal Migration & Navigation. LC 75-30276. (Illus.). 1976. 9.95 o.p. (ISBN 0-684-14516-2, ScribT). Scribner.
Street, Robert L., jt. auth. see Vennard, John K.
Street Sesame. Up & Down Book Starring Ernie & Bert. (A Tell-a-Tale Reader Ser.). (Illus.). (gr. k-3). PLB 4.77 (ISBN 0-307-68402-4, Golden Pr). Western Pub.
Streeten, David H., jt. ed. see Elias, Merrill F.
Streeten, Paul. Aid to Africa: A Policy Outline for the Nineteen Seventies. LC 74-180854. (Special Studies in International Economics & Development). 1972. 24.50x (ISBN 0-275-28263-5). Irvington.
--Development Perspectives. 35.00 (ISBN 0-312-19690-3). St Martin.
--The Limits of Development Research. 75p. 1975. pap. text ed. 5.75 (ISBN 0-08-019796-5). Pergamon.
--Recent Issues in World Developement: A Collection of Survey Articles. (Illus.). 450p. 1981. 115.00 (ISBN 0-08-026812-9). Pergamon.
Streeter, Carol. My Kingdom for a Horse: A Owner's Manual. LC 78-69643. (Illus.). 128p. 1980. 9.95 (ISBN 0-498-02226-9). A S Barnes.
Streeter, Donald. Professional Smithing. (Illus.). 144p. 1980. 19.95 (ISBN 0-684-16530-9, ScribT). Scribner.
Streeter, Edwin W. Great Diamonds of the World. Hatton, Joseph & Keane, A. H., eds. LC 76-78238. 1971. Repr. of 1882 ed. 18.00 (ISBN 0-8103-3624-3). Gale.
Streeter, Philip. Ireland's Hope. LC 73-75961. 190p. (Orig.). 1973. pap. 1.95 o.p. (ISBN 0-88270-027-8). Logos.
Streetman, B. Solid State Electronic Devices. 2nd ed. 1980. 26.95 (ISBN 0-13-822171-5). P-H.
Streib, Dan. Down Under & Dirty. (Hawk Ser.: No. 9). (Orig.). 1981. pap. 1.95 (ISBN 0-515-05874-2). Jove Pubns.
--Hawk: The Cargo Gods. (Hawk Ser.: No. 10). (Orig.). 1981. pap. 1.95 (ISBN 0-515-05875-0). Jove Pubns.
--Hawk: The Deadly Crusader. (The Hawk Ser.: No. 1). (Orig.). pap. 1.95 (ISBN 0-515-05234-5). Jove Pubns.
--Hawk: The Death Riders. (Hawk Ser.: No. 7). 208p. (Orig.). 1981. pap. 1.95 (ISBN 0-515-05872-6). Jove Pubns.
--Hawk: The Enemy Within. (Hawk Ser.: No. 8). 192p. (Orig.). 1981. pap. 1.95 (ISBN 0-515-05873-4). Jove Pubns.
--Hawk: The Mind Twisters. (The Hawk Ser.: No. 2). pap. 1.95 (ISBN 0-515-05235-3). Jove Pubns.
--Hawk: The Power Barons. (The Hawk Ser.: No. 3). (Orig.). pap. 1.95 (ISBN 0-515-05236-1). Jove Pubns.
--Hawk: The Predators. (The Hawk Ser.: No. 4). (Orig.). pap. 1.95 (ISBN 0-515-05299-X). Jove Pubns.
--Hawk: The Seeds of Evil. (Hawk Ser.: No. 6). 224p. (Orig.). 1981. pap. 1.95 (ISBN 0-515-05301-5). Jove Pubns.
Streib, Don. Hawk: California Shakedown. (Hawk Ser.: No. 5). 192p. (Orig.). 1981. pap. 1.95 (ISBN 0-515-05300-7). Jove Pubns.
Streib, Gordon F., ed. The Changing Family: Adaptation & Diversity. LC 72-11076. 1973. pap. text ed. 5.50 (ISBN 0-201-07320-X). A-W.
Streib, Victor L. Juvenile Justice in America. (National University Pubns. Multi-Disciplinary Studies in the Law). 1978. 12.50 (ISBN 0-8046-9212-2). Kennikat.
Streiff, E. B., ed. Advances in Ophthalmology, Vol. 41. (Illus.). xvii, 216p. 1980. 96.00 (ISBN 3-8055-0375-X). S Karger.
--Advances in Ophthalmology, Vol. 42. (Illus.). 200p. 1980. 60.00 (ISBN 3-8055-1025-X). S Karger.
Streight, Mary E., jt. auth. see Birchenall, Joan M.
Streiker, Lowell D. Promise of Buber. LC 69-16963. (Promise of Theology Ser). 1969. pap. 1.50 o.p. (ISBN 0-397-10089-2). Lippincott.
Streilein, Wayne J. & Hughes, John D. Immunology: A Programmed Text. 1977. pap. text ed. 11.95 (ISBN 0-316-81919-0, Little Med Div). Little.
Streit, Fred. Research Review Nineteen Sixty-Six to Nineteen Eighty: Adolescent Problems. 71p. 1980. pap. 15.00. Essence Pubns.
Streit, Fred, ed. Peer Counseling & Students Tutoring Students. 23p. 1977. pap. 8.00 o.p. (ISBN 0-686-00911-8, D-101). Essence Pubns.
Streit, Fred & Halsted, Donald L., eds. Athletes in the School: A Psychological & Sociological Perspective. 27p. 1977. pap. 8.50 o.p. (ISBN 0-686-00902-9, D-104). Essence Pubns.
--Discipline-Causes & Remedies of Problem Behaviors in School. 1977. pap. 10.00 o.p. (ISBN 0-686-00904-5, D-103). Essence Pubns.
Streit, L., ed. Quantum Fields-Algebras, Processes. (Illus.). 144p. 1981. 40.20 (ISBN 0-387-81607-0). Springer-Verlag.
Streitmatter & Fiore. Microprocessors: Theory & Application. (Illus.). 1979. text ed. 18.95 (ISBN 0-8359-4371-2); students manual avail. (ISBN 0-8359-4372-0). Reston.
Streitmatter, Gene. Microprocessor Software: Programming Concepts & Techniques. (Illus.). 400p. 1981. text ed. 17.95 (ISBN 0-8359-4375-5). Reston.
Strejc, Vladimir. State Space Theory of Discrete Linear Control. 1981. price not set (ISBN 0-471-27594-8, Pub. by Wiley-Interscience). Wiley.
Strelets, K. L. Electrolytic Production of Magnesium. 1977. 56.95 (ISBN 0-470-99320-0). Halsted Pr.
Strelzoff, Samuel. Technology & Manufacture of Ammonia. 220p. 1981. 22.00 (ISBN 0-471-02722-7, Pub. by Wiley-Interscience). Wiley.
Strem, George G. The Life & Teaching of Lucius Annaeus Seneca. LC 79-67526. 175p. 1981. 10.00 (ISBN 0-533-04463-4). Vantage.
Stremler, Ferrel G. Introduction to Communication Systems. LC 76-12803. (Electrical Engineering Ser.). 1977. text ed. 25.95 (ISBN 0-201-07244-0); sol. man. avail. (ISBN 0-201-07245-9). A-W.

Stremnel, Stephen H., jt. auth. see West, William R.

Stremooukhoff, D. Vladimir Soloviev & His Messianic Work. Meyendorff, Elizabeth, tr. from Fr. LC 78-78264. 375p. (Orig.). 1980. pap. 37.50 (ISBN 0-913124-37-0). Nordland Pub.

Stren, Richard E. Urban Inequality & Housing Policy in Tanzania: The Problem of Squatting. LC 75-620118. (Research Ser.: No. 24). (Illus.). 128p. 1975. pap. 2.95x (ISBN 0-87725-124-X). U of Cal Intl St.

Streng, Frederick J., et al. Ways of Being Religious: Readings for a New Approach to Religion. (Illus.). 608p. 1973. 17.95 (ISBN 0-13-946277-5). P-H.

Strenge, K., jt. auth. see Sonntag, H.

Strenski, Ellen & Manfred, Madge. The Research Paper Workbook. (English & Humanities Ser.). (Illus.). 283p. (Orig.). pap. text ed. 7.95x (ISBN 0-582-28203-9). Longman.

Stresau, Hermann. Thornton Wilder. Schutze, Frieda, tr. LC 71-149478. (Modern Literature Ser.). 1971. 10.95 (ISBN 0-8044-2844-1); pap. 3.45 (ISBN 0-8044-6884-2). Ungar.

Stresemann, Wolfgang. The Berlin Philharmonic from Bulow to Karajan: Home & History of a World-Famous Orchestra. (Illus., Orig.). pap. 15.00x (ISBN 3-8777-6518-1). Heinman.

Streshinsky, Shirley, jt. auth. see Elder, Lauren.

Strete, Craig. The Bleeding Man & Other Science Fiction Stories. LC 77-4505. (gr. 7 up). 1977. 8.25 (ISBN 0-688-80118-8); PLB 7.92 (ISBN 0-688-84118-X). Greenwillow.

--If All Else Fails... LC 79-7117. (Doubleday D Science Fiction Ser.). 192p. 1980. 8.95 (ISBN 0-385-15237-X). Doubleday.

Stretton, H. Capitalism, Socialism & the Environment. (Illus.). 368p. 1976. 34.50 (ISBN 0-521-21057-7); pap. 10.95x (ISBN 0-521-29025-2). Cambridge U Pr.

Strevens, Peter. Teaching English As an International Language: From Practice to Principle. 128p. 1980. pap. 9.95 (ISBN 0-08-025333-4). Pergamon.

Stribley, Keith M., jt. ed. see Bynner, John.

Strick, David, jt. auth. see Sandoval, Ruben.

Strickberger, M. W. Experiments in Genetics with Drosophila. LC 62-16158. 1962. pap. 12.95x (ISBN 0-471-83373-8). Wiley.

Stricker, George, jt. ed. see Goldman, George D.

Strickland, A. J., III, jt. auth. see Thompson, Arthur A., Jr.

Strickland, A. J., 3rd, jt. auth. see Thompson, Arthur A., Jr.

Strickland, A. W. Reference Guide to American Science Fiction Films: Vol. II, 1930-1950. 400p. 1980. pap. text ed. write for info. (ISBN 0-89917-269-5). TIS Inc.

--Reference Guide to American Science Fiction Films: 1951-1979, Vol. III. 400p. 1980. pap. write for info. (ISBN 0-89917-270-9). TIS Inc.

Strickland, Alonzo J., III, jt. auth. see Scott, Charles R., Jr.

Strickland, G. Stendhal: The Education of a Novelist. 276p. 1974. 47.50 (ISBN 0-521-20385-6); pap. 12.50x (ISBN 0-521-09837-8). Cambridge U Pr.

--Structuralism or Criticism? 200p. Date not set. 39.50 (ISBN 0-521-23184-1). Cambridge U Pr.

Strickland, Irina. The Voices of Children 1700-1914. 1973. 12.50x o.p. (ISBN 0-631-11780-6, Pub. by Basil Blackwell England). Biblio Dist.

Strickland, L. H., ed. Soviet & Western Perspectives in Social Psychology. LC 79-40311. 1979. 41.00 (ISBN 0-08-023389-9). Pergamon.

Strickland, Lloyd H., et al, eds. Social Psychology in Transition. LC 76-22439. 361p. 1976. 29.50 (ISBN 0-306-30918-1, Plenum Pr). Plenum Pub.

Strickland, Margaret. Child-Snatched. LC 79-91709. 112p. 1979. pap. 4.95 (ISBN 0-935834-00-1). Rainbow-Betty.

Strickland, Rennard. Avoiding Teacher Malpractice. 1976. 8.95 (ISBN 0-8015-7457-9, Hawthorn). Dutton.

--How to Get into Law School. rev. ed. LC 73-10885. 1977. pap. 4.95 (ISBN 0-8015-3767-3, Hawthorn). Dutton.

Strickland, Ruth G. Language Arts in the Elementary School. 3rd ed. 1969. text ed. 12.95x (ISBN 0-669-20222-3). Heath.

Strickland, Stephen P. Research & Health of Americans. LC 77-25779. (Illus.). 1978. 17.95x (ISBN 0-669-02165-2). Lexington Bks.

Strickland, Walter G. Dictionary of Irish Artists, 2 vols. (Illus.). 1358p. 1968. Repr. of 1913 ed. 90.00x set (ISBN 0-7165-0602-5, Pub. by Irish Academic Pr Ireland). Biblio Dist.

Strickland, Winifred G. Expert Obedience Class Training for Dogs: The Instructors Manual. LC 70-138028. (Illus.). 1971. 10.95 o.s.i. (ISBN 0-02-615040-9). Macmillan.

Strickland, Winifred G. & Moses, James A. The German Shepherd Today. LC 73-19044. (Illus.). 512p. 1974. 17.95 (ISBN 0-02-615030-1). Macmillan.

Strickler, Carol & Taggart, Barbara. Weaving in Miniature. Ligon, Linda, ed. LC 80-80935. (Illus.). 86p. 1980. 6.95 (ISBN 0-934026-02-5). Interweave.

Strieber, Whitley. The Hunger. LC 80-21355. 320p. 1981. write for info. (ISBN 0-688-03757-7). Morrow.

Strieder, Peter. The Hidden Durer. LC 78-50816. (Illus.). 1978. 19.95 o.p. (ISBN 0-528-81041-3). Rand.

Strigel, W. Business Cycle Analysis: Papers Presented at the Fourteenth CIRET Conference Proceedings - Lisbon 1979. 456p. 1980. text ed. 50.00x (ISBN 0-566-00368-6, Pub. by Gower Pub. Co England). Renouf.

Strike, Kenneth A. & Egan, Kieran, eds. Ethics & Educational Policy. (International Library of the Philosophy of Education). 1978. 18.50x (ISBN 0-7100-8423-4); pap. 7.95 (ISBN 0-7100-0483-4). Routledge & Kegan.

Striker, Fran. The Lone Ranger & the Gold Robbery. (Lone Ranger Ser.: No. 3). 1978. pap. 1.75 (ISBN 0-523-40876-5, Dist. by Independent News Co.). Pinnacle Bks.

Striker, Frank. The Lone Ranger. (Western Fiction Ser.). 1980. lib. bdg. 9.95 (ISBN 0-8398-2676-1). Gregg.

Striker, John. Superthreats. 1981. pap. 2.95 (ISBN 0-440-17828-2). Dell.

Striker, John M. & Shapiro, Andrew. Power Plays. 1981. pap. 2.95 (ISBN 0-440-17203-9). Dell.

Striker, Randy. The Deep Six. (Dusky MacMorgan Ser.: No. 2). (Orig.). 1981. pap. 1.95 (ISBN 0-451-09568-5, J9568, Sig). NAL.

--Key West Connection. (Dusky MacMorgan Ser.: No. 1). (Orig.). 1981. pap. 1.95 (ISBN 0-451-09567-7, J9567, Sig). NAL.

Striker, Susan. The Anti-Coloring Book of Red-Letter Daus. (Illus.). 64p. (Orig.). 1981. pap. 3.95 (ISBN 0-03-057873-6). HR&W.

--The Third Anti-Coloring Book. (Illus.). 96p. (Orig.). 1980. pap. 3.95 (ISBN 0-03-056814-5). HR&W.

Strindberg, August. Apologia & Two Folk Plays: The Great Highway, the Crownbride & Swanwhite. Johnson, Walter, tr. from Swedish. LC 80-51072. (Illus.). 244p. 1981. 19.50 (ISBN 0-295-95760-3). U of Wash Pr.

--The Chamber Plays. 2nd, rev. ed. Sprinchorn, Evert, et al, trs. from Swedish. 288p. 1981. 15.00 (ISBN 0-8166-1028-2); pap. 6.95 (ISBN 0-8166-1031-2). U of Minn Pr.

--Eight Expressionist Plays. Paulson, Arvid, tr. LC 65-11852. 512p. 1972. 15.00x (ISBN 0-8147-6556-4); pap. 8.00 (ISBN 0-8147-6558-0). NYU Pr.

--The Father. Anderson, Valborg, ed. & tr. Bd. with A Dream Play. LC 64-20118. (Crofts Classics Ser.). 1964. pap. text ed. 2.95x (ISBN 0-88295-096-7). AHM Pub.

--Miss Julie. 1965. pap. 1.75 (ISBN 0-380-01416-5, 77412, Bard). Avon.

--Plays of Confession & Therapy: To Damascus I, to Damascus II, & to Damascus III. Johnson, Walter, tr. from Swedish. LC 78-20962. (Illus.). 260p. 1979. 19.50 (ISBN 0-295-95567-8). U of Wash Pr.

--Son of a Servant: The Story of the Evolution of a Human Being, 1849-1867. Sprinchorn, Evert, tr. & intro. by. 8.50 (ISBN 0-8446-3027-6). Peter Smith.

Strindberg, August see Caputi, Anthony.

Strindberg, August see Watson, E. Bradlee & Pressey, Benfield.

Strine, Gerald. Montpelier: Reflections of Marion DuPont Scott. 1977. 50.00 o.p. (ISBN 0-684-14798-X, ScribT). Scribner.

Strine, Gerry & Isaacs, Neil. Covering the Spread: How to Bet Pro Football. 1978. 8.95 (ISBN 0-685-63568-6). Random.

Stringer, Arthur. The City of Peril. 1976. lib. bdg. 14.85x (ISBN 0-89968-118-2). Lightyear.

--The Gun-Runner. 1976. lib. bdg. 16.70x (ISBN 0-89968-119-0). Lightyear.

--Phantom Wires. 1976. lib. bdg. 14.35x (ISBN 0-89968-120-4). Lightyear.

--The Prairie Wife. 1976. lib. bdg. 14.85x (ISBN 0-89968-122-0). Lightyear.

--The Wire Tappers. 1976. lib. bdg. 15.30x (ISBN 0-89968-121-2). Lightyear.

Stringer, Bruce. Earlihee the Turtle. 4.95 (ISBN 0-932298-06-0). Green Hill.

Stringer, E. T. Foundations of Climatology. LC 72-81920. (Illus.). 1972. text ed. 36.95x (ISBN 0-7167-0242-8). W H Freeman.

--Techniques of Climatology. LC 74-128094. (Illus.). 1972. text ed. 36.95x (ISBN 0-7167-0250-9). W H Freeman.

Stringer, Gail G. see O'Neal, William B.

Stringer, Gary A., ed. New Essays on Donne. (Salzburg Studies in English Literature, Elizabethan & Renaissance Studies: No. 57). 1977. pap. text ed. 25.00x (ISBN 0-391-01538-9). Humanities.

Stringer, J. An Introduction to the Electron Theory of Solids. 1967. 23.00 (ISBN 0-08-012219-1); pap. 9.75 (ISBN 0-08-012220-5). Pergamon.

Stringer, L. Teach Yourself German Reader. (Teach Yourself Ser). 1964. pap. 2.95 o.p. (ISBN 0-679-10218-3). McKay.

Stringer, Leslea & Bowman, Lea. Crafts Handbook for Children's Church: Graded Activities for Ages 3-7. (Teaching Help Ser.). (Orig.). 1981. pap. 6.95 (ISBN 0-8010-8197-1). Baker Bk.

Stringer, Llewellyn W. Emergency Treatment of Acute Respiratory Diseases: A Manual for Ambulance & Emergency Room Personnel. rev. ed. LC 73-4419. (Illus.). 101p. 1972. pap. 8.95 (ISBN 0-87618-073-X). R J Brady.

Stringer, Peter & Wenzel, K., eds. Transportation Planning for a Better Environment. LC 76-46276. (NATO Conference Ser., Series II: Systems Science: Vol. 1). 439p. 1976. 37.50 (ISBN 0-306-32841-0, Plenum Pr). Plenum Pub.

Stringer, T. Plasma Transport Meeting & MHD Theory: Proceedings of a Workshop at Varenna, Italy, 12-16 Sept. 1977. Rozzoli, R., ed. LC 78-40822. 1979. pap. text ed. 66.00 (ISBN 0-08-023426-7). Pergamon.

Stringfellow, ed. Interferon & Interfaron Inducers: Clinical Applications. 336p. 1980. 39.50 (ISBN 0-8247-6931-7). Dekker.

Stringfellow, Bill. All in the Name of the Lord. 176p. 1981. pap. 2.95 (ISBN 0-939286-00-9). Concerned Pubns.

Stringfellow, William. Instead of Death: New & Expanded Edition. rev. ed. 1976. pap. 3.95 (ISBN 0-8164-2120-X). Crossroad NY.

Stringham, E. J., jt. auth. see Murphy, Howard A.

Stripling, Scott R. The Picture Theory of Meaning: An Interpretation of Wittgenstein's Tractatus Logico-Philosophicus. LC 78-62176. 1978. pap. text ed. 7.50 (ISBN 0-8191-0109-5). U Pr of Amer.

Strobe, Wolfgang, jt. ed. see Eiser, J. R.

Strobel, H. A. Chemical Instrumentation. 2nd ed. 1973. 26.95 (ISBN 0-201-07301-3). A-W.

Strobel, Heinrich. Stravinsky: Classic Humanist. LC 73-4338. 186p. 1974. Repr. of 1955 ed. lib. bdg. 18.50 (ISBN 0-306-70580-X). Da Capo.

Strobel, Lee P. Reckless Homicide: Ford's Pinto Trial. (Illus.). 220p. 1980. 4.95 (ISBN 0-89708-022-X). And Bks.

Stroblas, Laurie. Urban Institute Press. LC 79-20083. (A Fun-to-Read Bk). (Illus.). (gr. 1-3). 1980. 6.95 (ISBN 0-688-41936-4); PLB 6.67 (ISBN 0-688-51936-9). Lothrop.

Strode, Hudson. Now in Mexico. LC 47-11420. (Illus.). 5.00 o.p. (ISBN 0-15-167691-7). HarBraceJ.

Strode, William. The Complete Guide to Kentucky Horse Country. LC 80-67138. (Orig.). 1980. write for info. (ISBN 0-937222-00-3). Classic Pub.

Stroethoff, Pieter. Photography for the Scale Modeller. LC 78-55052. (Illus.). 1978. 8.95 (ISBN 0-8069-8558-5); PLB 7.49 (ISBN 0-8069-8559-3). Sterling.

Strogonov, B. P., et al. Structure & Function of Plant Cells in Saline Habitats. Gollak, B., ed. Mercado, A., tr. from Rus. LC 73-13609. (Illus.). 284p. 1973. 44.95 (ISBN 0-470-83406-4). Halsted Pr.

Stroh, C. M. Vigilance: The Problem of Sustained Attention. 1971. 22.00 (ISBN 0-08-016711-X). Pergamon.

Stroh, Thomas F., jt. auth. see Hersker, Barry J.

Strohecker, H. F., et al. The Grasshoppers of California (Orthoptera: Acridoidea) (Bulletin of the California Insect Survey: Vol. 10). 1968. pap. 9.00x (ISBN 0-520-09035-7). U of Cal Pr.

Strohmeier, W. Variable Stars. 287p. 1972. text ed. 42.00 (ISBN 0-08-016675-X). Pergamon.

Strohmenger. How to Complete Job Application Forms. (NVGA Bk.). 36p. 1975. pap. 5.00 pkg. of 5 o.p. (ISBN 0-686-11202-4). Am Personnel.

Strohmer, Arthur F., Jr. The Skills of Managing. LC 76-136128. (Business Ser). (Prog. Bk.). 1970. pap. 8.95 (ISBN 0-201-07325-0). A-W.

Stroll, Avrum, jt. auth. see Popkin, Richard H.

Strom, Axel, jt. auth. see Eitinger, Leo.

Strom, Frederic A. Land Use & Environment Law Review: Annual. Incl. 1975 (ISBN 0-87632-116-3); 1976 (ISBN 0-87632-117-1); 1977 (ISBN 0-87632-118-X); 1978 (ISBN 0-87632-119-8); 1979 (ISBN 0-87632-120-1). LC 70-127585. 45.00 ea. Boardman.

Strom, Kay M. Special Women of the Bible. 1980. pap. 2.95 (ISBN 0-570-03495-7, 56-1712). Concordia.

Strom, Maryalls G. Library Services to the Blind & Physically Handicapped. LC 77-24686. 1977. 14.50 (ISBN 0-8108-1068-9). Scarecrow.

Strom, Robert D. Growing Through Play: Readings for Parents & Teachers. LC 80-23729. 212p. (Orig.). 1980. pap. text ed. 9.95 (ISBN 0-8185-0423-4). Brooks-Cole.

Stroman, Duane F. The Medical Establishment & Social Responsibility. 1976. 15.00 (ISBN 0-8046-9136-3, Natl U). Kennikat.

--The Quick Knife: Unnecessary Surgery U.S.A. (National University Publications). 1979. 15.00 (ISBN 0-8046-9226-2). Kennikat.

Stroman, James H. Secretary's Manual. (Orig.). 1968. pap. 1.50 o.p. (ISBN 0-451-08976-6, W8976, Sig). NAL.

Stromberg, Gustaf. Man, Mind, & the Universe. 1966. pap. 4.00 (ISBN 0-911336-10-9). Sci of Mind.

--The Searchers. 1967. pap. 6.50 (ISBN 0-911336-16-8). Sci of Mind.

Stromberg, Karl. Introduction to Classical Real Analysis. (Wadsworth International Mathematics Ser.). 576p. 1981. text ed. 29.95x (ISBN 0-686-69568-2). Wadsworth Pub.

Stromberg, R. European Intellectual History Since Seventeen Eighty-Nine. 3nd ed. 1981. pap. 4.95 (ISBN 0-13-291955-9). P-H.

Stromberg, Roland N. After Everything: Western Intellectual History Since 1945. LC 74-24980. 250p. (Orig.). 1975. 14.95 (ISBN 0-312-01085-0); pap. text ed. 6.95 (ISBN 0-312-01120-2). St Martin.

--European Intellectual History Since 1789. 2nd ed. LC 74-23541. 384p. 1975. pap. text ed. 14.95x (ISBN 0-13-292003-4). P-H.

--An Intellectual History of Modern Europe. 2nd ed. LC 74-22388. 595p. 1975. text ed. 19.95 (ISBN 0-13-469106-7). P-H.

Stromberg, Roland N., jt. auth. see Conkin, Paul K.

Strommen, Ellen, jt. auth. see Fitzgerald, Hiram E.

Strommen, Ellen A., et al. Developmental Psychology: The School-Aged Child. 1977. pap. 8.95x (ISBN 0-256-01939-8). Dorsey.

Strommen, Merton P. Five Cries of Youth. LC 73-18690. 192p. 1974. 4.95 (ISBN 0-06-067748-1, RD224, HarpR). Har-Row.

Stronach, Allan, jt. auth. see Hines, Barry.

Stronach, David. Pasargadae: A Report on the Excavations Conducted by the British Institute of Persian Studies from 1961 to 1963. (Illus.). 1978. 79.00x (ISBN 0-19-813190-9). Oxford U Pr.

Strong. Industrial, Labor & Community Relations. LC 68-59238. 144p. 1974. pap. 5.40 (ISBN 0-8273-0371-8); instructor's guide 1.60 (ISBN 0-8273-0372-6). Delmar.

Strong, Anna L. I Change Worlds. LC 79-23128. (Illus.). 468p. 1979. pap. 7.95 (ISBN 0-931188-05-9). Seal Pr WA.

Strong, Bethany. First Love. 1978. pap. 1.95 o.s.i. (ISBN 0-515-04504-7). Jove Pubns.

Strong, Bryan, et al. Human Sexuality: Essentials. (Illus.). 1978. pap. text ed. 10.50 (ISBN 0-8299-0154-X); test manual avail. (ISBN 0-8299-0576-6). West Pub.

Strong, C. R., jt. auth. see Hilsum, S.

Strong, Clinton, jt. auth. see Cooper, John M.

Strong, Daniel, jt. auth. see Pray, Thomas.

Strong, Dexter K. Handbook for New Heads: An Introduction to Independent School Administration. 1977. pap. 6.50 (ISBN 0-934338-27-2). NAIS.

Strong, Donald S. Leonardo on the Eye: An English Translation & Critical Commentary of MS.D in the Bibliotheque Nationale, Paris, with Studies on Leonardo's Methodology & Theories on Optics. LC 78-74382. (Fine Arts Dissertations, Fourth Ser.). (Illus.). 1980. lib. bdg. 44.00 (ISBN 0-8240-3968-8). Garland Pub.

Strong, Edward C., jt. auth. see Larreche, Jean-Claude.

Strong, Eithne. Sarah, in Passing. 72p. (Orig.). 1974. pap. text ed. 4.50x (ISBN 0-85105-267-3, Dolmen Pr). Humanities.

Strong, F. Bryan, et al. The Marriage & Family Experience: A Text with Readings. (Illus.). 1979. pap. text ed. 16.50 (ISBN 0-8299-0278-3); instrs.' manual avail. (ISBN 0-8299-0577-4). West Pub.

Strong, F. M. & Koch, H. Gilbert. Biochemistry Laboratory Manual. 3rd ed. 260p. 1981. write for info. wire coil (ISBN 0-697-04705-9). Wm C Brown.

Strong, Foster. General Physics Workbook: Physics Problems & How to Solve Them. (Illus.). 1972. wkbk. 10.95x (ISBN 0-7167-0339-4). W H Freeman.

Strong, James, jt. auth. see McClintock, John.

Strong, Jaryl. Escape from Islam. 1981. pap. 3.95 (ISBN 0-8423-0712-5). Tyndale.

Strong, John. Concepts of Classical Optics. LC 57-6918. (Physics Ser.). (Illus.). 1958. 28.95x (ISBN 0-7167-0301-7). W H Freeman.

Strong, June. Mindy. LC 77-77429. 1977. 11.95 (ISBN 0-8127-0139-9). Southern Pub.

--Project Sunlight. LC 80-13011. (Orion Ser.). 1980. pap. 2.95 (ISBN 0-8127-0289-1). Southern Pub.

--Where Are We Running? LC 78-26271. (Orion Ser.). 1979. pap. 1.95 (ISBN 0-8127-0207-7). Southern Pub.

Strong, Margaret, jt. auth. see Libien, Lois.

Strong, Maurice, ed. Who Speaks for Earth? 160p. 1973. 6.95 (ISBN 0-393-06392-5); pap. 2.95x (ISBN 0-393-09341-7). Norton.

Strong, Michael. Danger Feeds My Fear. 192p. 1980. 9.95 o.s.i. (ISBN 0-686-60241-2) (ISBN 0-8027-5419-8). Walker & Co.

Strong, Michael, jt. auth. see Cathcart, Ruth.

Strong, Roy. Britannia Triumphans: Inigo Jones, Rubens & Whitehall Palace. (Lectures Ser.). (Illus.). 72p. 1981. 10.95 (ISBN 0-500-55012-3). Thames Hudson.

--Nicholas Hilliard. (Folio Miniature Ser.). 1975. 4.95 (ISBN 0-7181-1301-2, Pub. by Michael Joseph). Merrimack Bk Serv.

--Tudor & Jacobean Portraits, 2 vol. (Illus.). 700p. 1980. Set. 160.00x (ISBN 0-312-82220-0). St Martin.

Strong, S. J. & Corney, G. The Placenta in Twin Pregnancy. 1967. 50.00 (ISBN 0-08-012223-X). Pergamon.

Strong, Thomas N. Cathlamet on the Columbia. new ed. (Illus.). 1981. pap. 4.95 (ISBN 0-8323-0378-X). Binford.

Strong, Tracy B. Friedrich Nietzche & the Politics of Transfiguration. LC 74-81442. 380p. 1976. 23.75x (ISBN 0-520-02810-4). U of Cal Pr.

Strong, W. E. Trip to the Yellowstone National Park in July, August, & September, 1875. LC 68-15670. (Western Frontier Library: No. 39). (Illus.). 1968. 4.95 o.p. (ISBN 0-8061-0791-X). U of Okla Pr.

Strong, William. Sentence Combing & Paragraph Building. (Illus.). 320p. 1981. pap. text ed. 8.95 (ISBN 0-394-31264-3). Random.

Strong, William S. A Layman's Guide to Copyright. 192p. 1981. text ed. 12.50 (ISBN 0-262-19194-6). MIT Pr.

Strong-Boag, Veronica, ed. A Woman with a Purpose: The Diaries of Elizabeth Smith 1872-1884. (Social History of Canada Ser.). 320p. 1980. 25.00x (ISBN 0-8020-2360-6); pap. 10.00x (ISBN 0-8020-6397-7). U of Toronto Pr.

Stronge, William B., jt. auth. see McPheters, Lee R.

Strongin, Lynn. Bones & Kim. LC 80-5311. 100p. 1980. pap. 5.50 (ISBN 0-933216-02-5). Spinsters Ink.

Strongman, Harry, jt. auth. see Crosher, Judith.

Strongman, Harry, jt. auth. see Forman, Joan.

Strongman, Harry, jt. auth. see Gibson, Michael.

Strooker, J. R. Introduction to Categories, Homological Algebra & Sheaf Cohomology. LC 77-80849. 1978. 47.50 (ISBN 0-521-21699-0). Cambridge U Pr.

Stroschin, Jane. The Cloudy Day. LC 79-65792. (Illus.). 56p. (ps-2). 1979. 7.95 (ISBN 0-89526-099-9). Regnery-Gateway.

Strose, Susanne. Candle-Making. Kuttner, Paul, tr. LC 68-8759. (Little Craft Book Ser). (Illus.). (gr. 5-10). 1968. 5.95 (ISBN 0-8069-5100-1); PLB 6.69 (ISBN 0-8069-5101-X). Sterling.

--Making Paper Flowers. LC 69-19490. (Little Craft Book Ser). (Illus.). (gr. 6 up). 1969. 4.95 o.p. (ISBN 0-8069-5130-3); PLB 5.89 o.p. (ISBN 0-8069-5131-1). Sterling.

Strother, Edward, jt. auth. see Huckleberry, Alan W.

Strother, Edward S. & Huckleberry, Alan W. Effective Speaker. LC 68-7238. (Illus.). 1968. text ed. 15.50 (ISBN 0-395-05441-9). HM.

Strother, Elsie W. Follow Through to Love. (YA) 1977. 4.95 o.p. (ISBN 0-685-73816-7, Avalon). Bouregy.

--Island of Terror. (YA) 1976. 4.95 o.p. (ISBN 0-685-68913-1, Avalon). Bouregy.

Strother, G. K. & Weber, Robert L. Physics with Applications in Life Sciences. (Illus.). 1977. text ed. 20.95 (ISBN 0-395-21718-0); inst. manual 0.75 (ISBN 0-395-21719-9); ans. to selected probs. avail. (ISBN 0-685-79300-1). HM.

Strother, Horatio T. The Underground Railroad in Connecticut. LC 62-15122. 1962. 15.00x (ISBN 0-8195-3025-5, Pub. by Wesleyan U Pr); pap. 6.95 (ISBN 0-8195-6012-X). Columbia U Pr.

Strothman, F. W., jt. auth. see Lohnes, Walter.

Strothmann, F. W., jt. auth. see Lohnes, Walter F.

Strothmann, Werner. Johannes von Apamea. (Patristische Texte und Studien 11). 1972. 60.60x (ISBN 3-11-002457-8). De Gruyter.

Stroud, A. Approximate Calculation of Multiple Integrals. LC 77-159121. (Automatic Computation Ser). (Illus.). 1972. ref. ed. 26.95 (ISBN 0-13-043893-6). P-H.

Stroud, Barry. Hume. (Arguments of the Philosophers Ser.). 292p. 1981. pap. 10.00 (ISBN 0-7100-0667-5). Routledge & Kegan.

--Hume. (The Arguments of the Philosophers Ser.). 1977. 22.00x (ISBN 0-7100-8601-6). Routledge & Kegan.

Stroud, Dorothy. Capability Brown. 1975. 43.00 (ISBN 0-571-10267-0, Pub. by Faber & Faber). Merrimack Bk Serv.

--George Dance, Architect 1741-1825. 1971. 35.00 (ISBN 0-571-09007-9, Pub. by Faber & Faber). Merrimack Bk Serv.

Stroud, George M. Sketch of the Laws Relating to Slavery in the Several States of the United States of America. LC 68-55917. Repr. of 1956 ed. 11.50x (ISBN 0-8371-0673-7). Negro U Pr.

Stroud, James B., et al. Improving Reading Ability. 3rd ed. (Illus.). 1970. pap. text ed. 9.95 (ISBN 0-13-453605-3). P-H.

Stroud, John. Airports of the World. (Putnam Aeronautical Bks.). (Illus.). 576p. 1981. 55.00 (ISBN 0-370-30037-8, Pub. by Chatto Bodley Jonathan). Merrimack Bk Serv.

--European Transport Aircraft Since 1910. LC 66-28846. 1966. 15.95 o.p. (ISBN 0-370-00095-1). Aero.

Stroud, K. A. Laplace Transforms: Programmes & Problems. LC 73-6317. 273p. 1973. pap. text ed. 12.95 (ISBN 0-470-83415-3). Halsted Pr.

Stroud, Marion. I Love God - & My Husband. 96p. 1976. pap. 1.95 (ISBN 0-88207-734-1). Victor Bks.

Stroud, N., ed. see Babel, Isaak.

Stroud, Oxford S. Writing Prose That Makes a Difference, & the Grammar Minimum. LC 79-84651. 1979. pap. text ed. 5.00 (ISBN 0-8191-0740-9). U Pr of Amer.

Stroud, Parry. Stephen Vincent Benet. (U. S. Authors Ser.: No. 27). 1962. lib. bdg. 9.95 (ISBN 0-8057-0052-8). Twayne.

Stroud, Richard H. Marine Recreational Fisheries, Vol. 3. Clepper, Henry, ed. LC 76-22389. 1978. 15.00 (ISBN 0-686-65030-1). Sport Fishing.

--Marine Recreational Fisheries, Vol. 4. Clepper, Henry, ed. LC 76-22389. 1979. 15.00 (ISBN 0-686-65031-X). Sport Fishing.

Stroud, Ronald. The Axones & Kyrbeis of Drakon & Solon. LC 77-20329. (Publications in Classical Studies: Vol. 19). 1979. 8.00x (ISBN 0-520-09590-1). U of Cal Pr.

Stroud, T. Services for Children & Their Families. 1973. 32.00 (ISBN 0-08-016604-0); pap. 17.00 (ISBN 0-08-016605-9). Pergamon.

Stroumillo, Elisabeth De see De Stroumillo, Elisabeth.

Stroup, George W. The Promise of Narrative Theology: Recovering the Gospel in the Church. LC 80-84654. 216p. (Orig.). 1981. pap. 8.50 (ISBN 0-8042-0683-X). John Knox.

--The Promise of Narrative Theology: Recovering the Gospel in the Church. LC 80-84654. pap. 8.50 (ISBN 0-8042-0683-X). John Knox.

Stroup, Kala M., jt. auth. see Smith, Walter S.

Stroup, Richard, jt. auth. see Baden, John.

Stroup, Richard, jt. auth. see Gwartney, James D.

Stroup, Thomas B. Works of Nathaniel Lee, 2 vols. Cooke, Arthur L., ed. LC 54-14766. 1954. Set. 27.50 (ISBN 0-8108-0236-8). Scarecrow.

Stroup, Thomas B., ed. The University in the American Future. LC 66-16232. 128p. 1966. 6.00x (ISBN 0-8131-1116-1). U Pr of Ky.

Strouse, James C., et al, eds. Making Government Work: Essays in Honor of Conley H. Dillon. LC 80-8308. 478p. 1981. lib. bdg. 23.75 (ISBN 0-8191-1306-9); pap. text ed. 15.75 (ISBN 0-8191-1307-7). U Pr of Amer.

Strousse, Flora. John Milton. LC 62-13343. (gr. 7-11). 1960. 6.95 (ISBN 0-8149-0411-4). Vanguard.

Strout, Cushing. The Veracious Imagination: Essays on American History, Literature, & Biography. 328p. 1981. 17.50x (ISBN 0-8195-5048-5). Wesleyan U Pr.

Stroyer, Paul. Second Treasure Chest of Tales. (Illus.). 1960. 8.95 (ISBN 0-8392-3032-X). Astor-Honor.

--Treasure Chest of Tales. (Illus.). (gr. 3 up). 1959. 8.95 (ISBN 0-8392-3039-7). Astor-Honor.

Stroynowski, Julius, jt. auth. see Lewytzkyi, Borys.

Strub, A. S. & Ungemach, P., eds. Advances in European Geothermal Research. 1096p. 1980. lib. bdg. 63.00 (ISBN 90-277-1138-0, Pub. by D. Reidel). Kluwer Boston.

Strub, Richard L. & Black, F. William. Organic Brain Syndromes: An Introduction to Neurobehavioral Disorders. (Illus.). 500p. 1981. text ed. 25.00 (ISBN 0-8036-8209-3, 8209-3). Davis Co.

Strube, Gillian. A Woman's Health. 164p. 1980. 29.00x (ISBN 0-85664-940-6, Pub. by Croom Helm Ltd England). Biblio Dist.

Strubhar, Naomi. He Leadeth Me & Other Stories. Strubhar, Rosalyn B., ed. 1959. pap. 2.50x o.s.i. (ISBN 0-87813-202-3). Park View.

Strubhar, Rosalyn B., ed. see Strubhar, Naomi.

Struble, George. Business Information Processing with BASIC. LC 79-1423. 1980. text ed. 13.95 (ISBN 0-201-07640-3); wkbk. 4.50 (ISBN 0-201-07642-X). A-W.

Struble, George W. Assembler Language Programming: The IBM System 360. 2nd ed. 496p. 1975. text ed. 20.95 (ISBN 0-201-07322-6). A-W.

Struble, Mildred C. Critical Edition of Ford's "Perkin Warbeck". (Publications in Language & Literature: No. 3). (Illus.). 214p. 1926. pap. 5.00 (ISBN 0-295-73760-3). U of Wash Pr.

Struchen, Jeanette. Joan of Arc: Maid of Orleans. LC 67-12557. (Biography Ser). (gr. 7 up). 1967. PLB 5.90 o.p. (ISBN 0-531-00889-4). Watts.

--Pope John Twenty Third: The Good Shepherd. LC 73-79671. (Biography Ser). (gr. 7 up). 1969. PLB 6.90 (ISBN 0-531-00951-3). Watts.

Struening, Elmer L. & Guttentag, Marcia, eds. Handbook of Evaluation Research, 2 vols. LC 74-15764. 1975. 27.50x ea. (ISBN 0-8039-0428-2). Vol. 1. Vol. 2 (ISBN 0-8039-0429-0). Set. 55.00x (ISBN 0-8039-0429-0). Sage.

Strugatskii, Arkady & Strugatskii, Boris. Les. (Rus.). 1981. 10.00 (ISBN 0-88233-656-8); pap. 4.50 (ISBN 0-88233-657-6). Ardis Pubs.

Strugatskii, Boris, jt. auth. see Strugatskii, Arkady.

Strugatsky, Arkady & Strugatsky, Boris. Beetle in the Anthill. Bouis, Antonina W., tr. (Best of Soviet Science Fiction Ser.). 256p. 1980. 11.95 (ISBN 0-02-615120-0). Macmillan.

--Definitely Maybe. LC 77-16550. (Best of Soviet Science Fiction). 1978. 10.95 (ISBN 0-02-615180-4); pap. 1.95 (ISBN 0-02-025590-X). Macmillan.

--Roadside Picnic & Tale of the Troika. Bouis, Antonina W., tr. 1977. 10.95 (ISBN 0-02-615170-7, 61517). Macmillan.

--Space Apprentice. (Best of Soviet Science Fiction Ser.). 141p. 1981. 10.95 (ISBN 0-02-615220-7). Macmillan.

--The Ugly Swans. Nakhimovsky, Alexander, tr. 1979. 10.95 (ISBN 0-02-615190-1). Macmillan.

Strugatsky, Boris, jt. auth. see Strugatsky, Arkady.

Struggs, Callie F. Woman in Business. Ide, Arthur F., ed. LC 79-19011. (Woman in History Ser.: Vol. 56). (Illus.). 80p. (Orig.). 1981. 8.95 (ISBN 0-86663-020-1); pap. 6.95 (ISBN -086663-021-X). Ide Hse.

--Woman in Contemporary Education. Ide, Arthur F., ed. LC 79-19011. (Woman in History Ser.: Vol. 61). (Illus.). 82p. (Orig.). 1981. 12.95 (ISBN 0-86663-022-8); pap. 9.00 (ISBN 0-86663-023-6). Ide Hse.

Struglia, Erasmus J., ed. Standards & Specifications Information Sources. LC 65-24659. (Management Information Guide Ser.: No. 6). 1965. 30.00 (ISBN 0-8103-0806-1). Gale.

Strugnell, Ann, jt. auth. see Brown, Margaret W.

Strugnell, John, jt. auth. see Stone, Michael E.

Struhl, Paula R. & Karsten, J., eds. Philosophy Now: An Introductory Reader. 1972. pap. text ed. 8.95 o.p. (ISBN 0-394-31978-8). Random.

Struik, Dirk J. Concise History of Mathematics. 3rd rev. ed. (Illus.). (YA) (gr. 7-12). 1967. pap. text ed. 3.00 (ISBN 0-486-60255-9). Dover.

Struin, Leo. The Liver & Anasthesia. LC 72-97914. (Major Problem in Anaesthesia: Vol. 3). (Illus.). 1976. text ed. 26.00 (ISBN 0-7216-8625-7). Saunders.

Struk, D. S. A Study of Vasyl' Stefanyk: The Pain at the Heart of Existence. LC 72-89110. 225p. 1973. lib. bdg. 13.50x (ISBN 0-87287-056-1). Ukrainian Acad.

Struk, Danylo S., ed. Four Ukranian Poets. Bohachevska-Chomiak, Martha, tr. 1977. write for info. o.p. (ISBN 0-685-79417-2). Cataract Pr.

Strum, Robert D. & Ward, John R. Laplace Transform Solution of Differential Equations. (Orig., Prog. Bk.). 1968. pap. 16.95 ref. ed. (ISBN 0-13-522805-0). P-H.

Struminger, Laura S. Women & the Making of the Working Class: Lyon 1830-1870. LC 78-74841. 1979. 14.95 (ISBN 0-88831-027-7). EPWP.

Strung, Norman. Complete Hunter's Catalog. LC 77-23867. (Illus.). 1977. 14.95 o.p. (ISBN 0-397-01217-9); pap. 8.95 o.s.i. (ISBN 0-397-01242-X). Lippincott.

--The Encyclopedia of Knives. LC 76-10288. (Illus.). 1976. 12.50 o.s.i. (ISBN 0-397-01164-4). Lippincott.

--Misty Mornings & Moonless Nights: A Waterfowler's Guide. LC 74-8226. (Illus.). 256p. 1974. 9.95 o.s.i. (ISBN 0-02-615100-6). Macmillan.

Strung, Norman, jt. auth. see Morris, Dan.

Strung, Norman, et al. Whitewater! LC 75-26912. (Illus.). 256p. 1976. 14.95 o.s.i. (ISBN 0-02-615110-3, 61511). Macmillan.

Strunk, Oliver, ed. Source Readings in Music History, 5 vols. Incl. Vol. 1. Antiquity & the Middle Ages. pap. 4.95x (ISBN 0-393-09680-7); Vol. 2. The Renaissance Era. pap. 4.95x (ISBN 0-393-09681-5); Vol. 3. Baroque Era. pap. 4.95x (ISBN 0-393-09682-3); Vol. 4. Classic Era. pap. 4.95x (ISBN 0-393-09683-1); Vol. 5. Romantic Era. pap. 4.95x (ISBN 0-393-09684-X). 1950. one vol. ed 24.95x (ISBN 0-393-09742-0, NortonC). Norton.

Strutt, John W. & Rayleigh, Baron. The Theory of Sound, 2 vols. 2nd rev. & enl. ed. (Illus.). Set. 22.00 (ISBN 0-8446-3028-4). Peter Smith.

Strutt, Joseph. Sports & Pastimes of the People of England: Including Rural & Domestic Recreations. LC 67-23901. (Social History Reference Series). (Illus.). 1968. Repr. of 1903 ed. 18.00 (ISBN 0-8103-3260-4). Gale.

Strutt, Max J. Lame, Mathieu Funktionen. LC 66-23757. (Ger). 8.50 (ISBN 0-8284-0203-5). Chelsea Pub.

Strutt, Robert J. Life of John William Strutt, Third Baron Rayleigh, O.M., F.R.S. (Illus.). 1968. 35.00x (ISBN 0-299-04690-7). U of Wis Pr.

Strutt, Shelia. The Master of Craighill. (Harlequin Romance Ser.). (Orig.). 1980. pap. 1.25 o.p. (ISBN 0-373-02333-2, Pub. by Harlequin). PB.

Strutton, Bill. Commando Force, No. 133. 224p. 1981. pap. 2.50 (ISBN 0-553-13581-3). Bantam.

Strutynski, Udo, ed. see Dumezil, Georges.

Strutz. Five Hundred One German Verbs: Written in Japanese. Date not set. pap. 4.25 (ISBN 0-8120-2182-7). Barron. Postponed.

--Two Hundred One Englische Verben. Date not set. pap. 3.95 (ISBN 0-8120-0605-4). Barron. Postponed.

--Two Hundred One Franzoische Verben. Date not set. pap. 3.95 (ISBN 0-8120-0689-5). Barron. Postponed.

Strutz, Henry. One Thousand & One Pitfalls in German. (gr. 9-12). 1981. pap. 6.95 (ISBN 0-8120-0590-2). Barron.

Struve, G., tr. see Bunin, Ivan.

Struve, Gleb, jt. ed. see Riasanovsky, Nicholas V.

Struyk, Raymond, jt. auth. see Follain, James.

Struyk, Raymond J. A New System for Public Housing: Salvaging a National Resource. LC 80-53321. 254p. 1980. 20.00 (ISBN 0-87766-279-7). Urban Inst.

--Should Government Encourage Homeownership? (An Institute Paper). 85p. 1977. pap. 5.50 (ISBN 0-87766-192-8, 18700). Urban Inst.

Struyk, Raymond J., jt. auth. see Ozanne, Larry.

Struyk, Raymond J., et al. Housing Policies for the Urban Poor. 153p. 1978. pap. 7.50 (ISBN 0-87766-230-4, 23500). Urban Inst.

Stryer, Lubert. Biochemistry. 2nd ed. LC 80-24699. (Illus.). 1981. text ed. 29.95 (ISBN 0-7167-1226-1). W H Freeman.

Stryk, Lucien. Encounter with Zen: Writings on Poetry & Zen. 1981. 16.95 (ISBN 0-8040-0405-6); pap. 8.95 (ISBN 0-8040-0406-4). Swallow.

Stryk, Lucien, ed. Heartland II: Poets of the Midwest. LC 74-12817. 255p. 1975. o.p 10.00 (ISBN 0-87580-050-5); pap. 5.00 (ISBN 0-87580-517-5). N Ill U Pr.

--Prairie Voices: A Collection of Illinois Poets. 64p. 1980. pap. 4.00 (ISBN 0-933180-21-7). Spoon Riv Poetry.

--World of the Buddha: A Reader from the Three Baskets to Modern Zen. LC 68-11766. 1969. pap. 2.95 o.p. (ISBN 0-385-00407-9, A615, Anch). Doubleday.

Stryk, Lucien & Ikemoto, Takashi, eds. The Penguin Book of Zen Poetry. Stryk, Lucien & Ikemoto, Takashi, trs. from Japanese. 1981. pap. 4.95 (ISBN 0-14-042247-1). Penguin.

--The Penguin Book of Zen Poetry. LC 77-83237. 159p. 1978. 9.95 (ISBN 0-8040-0792-6). Swallow.

--Zen Poems of China & Japan: The Crane's Bill. LC 73-75168. pap. 1.95 o.p. (ISBN 0-385-04624-3, Anch). Doubleday.

Stryk, Lucien, tr. see Stryk, Lucien & Ikemoto, Takashi.

Stryk, Lucien, et al, trs. from Chinese Japanese. Zen Poems of China & Japan: The Crane's Bill. 208p. 1981. pap. 4.95 (ISBN 0-394-17912-9, BC). Grove.

Stryk, Raymond J. & Bendick, Mark, Jr., eds. Housing Vouchers for the Poor: Lessons from a National Experiment. 1981. 25.00 (ISBN 0-87766-280-0). Urban Inst.

Stryker, J. Dirck, jt. auth. see Pearson, Scott R.

Stryker, Jay, jt. auth. see Staley, James.

Stryker, John A. & Clement, John A. Therapeutic Radiology Continuing Education Review. 1977. spiral bdg. 12.00 o.p. (ISBN 0-87488-346-6). Med Exam.

Stryker, John A., et al. Radiation Therapy Technology Examination Review. LC 80-80369. 1980. pap. 14.00 (ISBN 0-87488-459-4). Med Exam.

Stryker, Lloyd P. The Art of Advocacy. 284p. 1979. pap. 5.95 (ISBN 0-89062-069-5, Pub. by Hughes Press). Pub Ctr Cult Res.

Stryker, S. Speech After Stroke. 2nd ed. (Illus.). 442p. 1980. pap. 22.75 (ISBN 0-398-04122-9). C C Thomas.

--Speech After Stroke. (Illus.). 440p. 1978. pap. 19.00 o.p. (ISBN 0-398-03234-3). C C Thomas.

Stryker, William N. The Stryker Family in America: A History of the Stryker & Striker Families, Vol 2. LC 78-75351. (Illus.). 500p. 1981. lib. bdg. 45.00 (ISBN 0-9602936-2-0). W N Stryker.

Stryker-Rodda, Harriet. How to Climb Your Family Tree: Genealogy for Beginners. LC 77-24667. (YA) 1977. 5.95 o.s.i. (ISBN 0-397-01159-8); pap. 3.95 (ISBN 0-397-01243-8). Lippincott.

Strzygowski, Josef. Altai-Iran und Voelkerwanderung. (Arbeiten des Kunsthistorischen Instituts der Universitat Wien: No. 5). (Illus., Ger.). 1981. Repr. of 1917 ed. lib. bdg. 100.00x (ISBN 0-89241-156-2). Caratzas Bros.

--Die Baukunst der Armenier und Europa, 2 vols. (Arbeiten des Kunsthistorischen Instituts der Universitat Wien: Nos. 9-10). (Illus.). xii, 888p. (Ger.). 1981. Repr. of 1918 ed. Set. lib. bdg. 200.00x (ISBN 0-89241-157-0). Caratzas Bros.

Stuard, Susan M., ed. Women in Medieval Society. LC 75-41617. (The Middle Ages Ser). 220p. 1976. 16.00x (ISBN 0-8122-7708-2); pap. 5.95x (ISBN 0-8122-1088-3). U of Pa Pr.

Stuart, A., jt. auth. see Kendall, M. G.

Stuart, A. & Kendall, M. G., eds. Statistical Papers of George Udny Yule. 1971. 27.25 (ISBN 0-02-853040-3). Hafner.

Stuart, A. E., et al, eds. Lymphomas Other Than Hodgkin's Disease. (Illus.). 75p. 1981. text ed. 30.00x (ISBN 0-19-261296-4). Oxford U Pr.

Stuart, Anne. Lord Satan's Bride. (Orig.). 1981. pap. 1.50 (ISBN 0-440-14787-5). Dell.

Stuart, Anthony. The London Affair. LC 80-66500. 1981. 9.95 (ISBN 0-87795-275-2). Arbor Hse.

--That Man Gull. 224p. 1981. pap. 1.95 (ISBN 0-445-04637-6). Popular Lib.

--Vicious Circles. 224p. 1981. pap. 1.95 (ISBN 0-445-04648-1). Popular Lib.

Stuart, Bruce, jt. auth. see Holahan, John.

Stuart, C. H., ed. see Williams, Basil.

Stuart, Darwin G. Systematic Urban Planning. LC 75-19825. (Special Studies). (Illus.). 1976. text ed. 24.50 o.p. (ISBN 0-275-56060-0). Praeger.

Stuart, Diane. Destiny's Bride. 1978. pap. 1.95 o.p. (ISBN 0-425-03996-X). Berkley Pub.

Stuart, Don G., ed. Linguistic Studies in Memory of Richard Slade Harrell. LC 67-31586. 1967. pap. 2.95 o.p. (ISBN 0-87840-156-3). Georgetown U Pr.

Stuart, Dorothy M. Boy Through the Ages. LC 77-89291. (Illus.). 1970. Repr. of 1926 ed. 15.00 (ISBN 0-8103-3578-6). Gale.

--The Girl Through the Ages. LC 70-89292. (Illus.). 264p. 1969. Repr. of 1933 ed. 15.00 (ISBN 0-8103-3581-6). Gale.

--Horace Walpole. 229p. 1980. Repr. of 1927 ed. lib. bdg. 30.00 (ISBN 0-8492-8119-9). R West.

Stuart, Douglas T. & Tow, William T., eds. China, the Soviet Union & the West: Strategic & Political Dimensions for the Nineteen Eighties. (Special Studies in International Relations). 320p. (Orig.). 1981. lib. bdg. 27.50x (ISBN 0-86531-091-2); pap. text ed. 12.50x (ISBN 0-86531-168-4). Westview.

Stuart, Duane R. Epochs of Greek & Roman Biography. LC 67-19532. 1928. 12.00x (ISBN 0-8196-0193-4). Biblo.

Stuart, Graham H. American Diplomatic & Consular Practice. 2nd ed. LC 52-13689. 1952. 34.50x (ISBN 0-89197-008-8). Irvington.

Stuart, Granville. Pioneering in Montana: The Making of a State 1864-1887. Phillips, Paul C., ed. LC 77-7651. Orig. Title: Forty Years on the Frontier. (Illus.). 1977. 12.50x (ISBN 0-8032-0933-9); pap. 5.25 (ISBN 0-8032-5870-4, BB 648, Bison). U of Nebr Pr.

--Prospecting for Gold: From Dogtown to Virginia City, 1852-1864. Phillips, Paul C., ed. LC 77-7244. Orig. Title: Forty Years on the Frontier. (Illus.). 1977. 12.50x (ISBN 0-8032-0932-0); pap. 5.25 (ISBN 0-8032-5869-0, BB 647, Bison). U of Nebr Pr.

Stuart, Jesse. Penny's Worth of Character. (Illus.). (gr. 3-5). 1964. PLB 7.95 o.p. (ISBN 0-07-062301-5, GB). McGraw.

--Thread That Runs So True. 1958. lib. rep. ed. 17.50x (ISBN 0-684-15160-X, ScribT); pap. 4.95 (ISBN 0-684-71904-5, SL44, ScribT). Scribner.

--Trees of Heaven. LC 80-51020. 344p. 1980. 17.50 (ISBN 0-8131-1446-2); pap. 6.50 (ISBN 0-8131-0150-6). U Pr of Ky.

Stuart, Jessica. The Moonsong Chronicles. 384p. (Orig.). 1981. pap. 2.75 (ISBN 0-523-41167-7). Pinnacle Bks.

Stuart, John. Ikons. 1975. 48.00 (ISBN 0-571-08846-5, Pub. by Faber & Faber). Merrimack Bk Serv.

--UFO Warning. 1976. pap. 7.95 (ISBN 0-685-81681-8). Saucerian.

Stuart, John M. & Stuart, Marjorie L. You Don't Have to Slay a Dragon. LC 75-14540. (Illus.). 313p. 1976. 8.95 (ISBN 0-915730-01-4). Marburger.

Stuart, Lea A. The Scary Bears. 1981. 4.95 (ISBN 0-8062-1714-6). Carlton.

Stuart, Marjorie L., jt. auth. see Stuart, John M.

Stuart, Mary. Both of Me. LC 79-8038. (Illus.). 480p. 1980. 13.95 (ISBN 0-385-14494-6). Doubleday.

Stuart, Matt. The Lonely Law. 1977. pap. 1.25 o.p. (ISBN 0-445-00434-7). Popular Lib.

Stuart, Monica & Soper, Gill. The Bazaar Stall. 1979. 11.95 o.p. (ISBN 0-571-11280-3, Pub. by Faber & Faber); pap. 5.95 (ISBN 0-571-11289-7). Merrimack Bk Serv.

--Come, Hear & See. 1976. 8.95 o.p. (ISBN 0-571-10935-7, Pub. by Faber & Faber). Merrimack Bk Serv.

--Ten Little Fingers. 1975. 8.95 (ISBN 0-571-10828-8, Pub. by Faber & Faber). Merrimack Bk Serv.

Stuart, Monroe, jt. auth. see Sperling, A. P.

Stuart, R., jt. auth. see Burgoyne, J.

Stuart, R., jt. ed. see Burgoyne, J.

Stuart, Reginald. Bailout: America's Billion Dollar Gamble on the "New" Chrysler Corporation. LC 80-70279. (Illus.). 210p. (Orig.). 1981. pap. write for info. (ISBN 0-89708-050-5). And Bks.

Stuart, Richard B. Helping Couples Change: A Social Learning Approach to Marital Therapy. (Guilford Family Therapy Ser.). 464p. 1980. 22.50 (ISBN 0-89862-604-8). Guilford Pr.

Stuart, Richard B. & Davis, Barbara. Slim Chance in a Fat World: Behavioral Control of Obesity. professional ed. (Illus., Orig.). 1972. pap. 10.95 incl. materials (ISBN 0-87822-060-7); (bk. alone) 8.95 (ISBN 0-87822-064-X); (materials alone) 2.95 (ISBN 0-87822-061-5). Res Press.

Stuart, Richard B., ed. Violent Behavior: Social Learning Approaches to Prediction, Management & Treatment. 400p. 1981. 20.00 (ISBN 0-87630-262-2). Brunner-Mazel.

Stuart, Robert, jt. auth. see Gregory, Paul.

Stuart, Robert C., jt. auth. see Gregory, Paul R.

Stuart, Rory, ed. The Strange World of Frank Edwards. 1979. pap. 1.95 o.p. (ISBN 0-425-03877-7). Berkley Pub.

Stuart, S. L., jt. auth. see Lerner, Lily.

Stuart, Sally E. The All-Occasion Game Book. (Illus.). 64p. (Orig.). 1981. pap. 2.95 (ISBN 0-87239-444-1, 2798). Standard Pub.

Stuart, Simon. New Phoenix Wings: Reparation in Literature. (Illus.). 1979. 25.00x (ISBN 0-7100-0179-7). Routledge & Kegan.

Stuart, V. A. The Cannons of Lucknow. (Alex Sheridan Ser., No. 4). 256p. (Orig.). 1974. pap. 1.25 o.p. (ISBN 0-523-00340-4). Pinnacle Bks.

Stuart, Vincent G. Changing Mind. LC 80-53447. 80p. 1981. 5.95 (ISBN 0-394-51791-1). Shambhala Pubns.

Stuart, Vincent G., ed. Maitreys Six: Order. 1977. pap. 4.50 o.p. (ISBN 0-394-73350-9). Random.

Stuart, Vivian. Darnley's Bride. 1976. pap. 1.25 o.s.i. (ISBN 0-515-04066-5). Jove Pubns.

Stuart-Kotze, Robin. Introduction to Organizational Behavior: A Situational Approach. (Illus.). 1980. text ed. 17.95 (ISBN 0-8359-3259-1). Reston.

Stub, Holger R. Sociology of Education: A Sourcebook. 3rd ed. (Anthropology & Sociology Ser.). 1975. pap. text ed. 11.50x (ISBN 0-256-01630-5). Dorsey.

Stubberud, Allen R. Analysis & Synthesis of Linear Time-Variable Systems. 1965. 18.00x (ISBN 0-520-01230-5). U of Cal Pr.

Stubbes, Philip. The Anatomie of Abuses, Part One. LC 71-170409. (The English Stage Ser.: Vol. 7). lib. bdg. 50.00 (ISBN 0-8240-0590-2). Garland Pub.

--The Second Part of the Anatomie of Abuses. LC 71-170409. (The English Stage Ser.: Vol. 8). lib. bdg. 50.00 (ISBN 0-8240-0591-0). Garland Pub.

Stubbings, F. H. Prehistoric Greece. 1979. 10.95x (ISBN 0-8464-0104-5). Beekman Pubs.

Stubblefield, Fern. Tim & His Lamb. 52p. pap. 0.40; pap. 1.00 3 copies. Faith Pub Hse.

Stubblefield, Phillip G., jt. ed. see Naftolin, Frederick.

Stubbs. U. F. O. Unidentified Flying Object. 7.95 (ISBN 0-233-97197-1). Andre Deutsch.

Stubbs, Ansel H. Wild Mushrooms Worth Knowing. LC 76-107330. Orig. Title: Wild Mushrooms of the Central Midwest. (Illus.). 160p. 1980. pap. 7.95 (ISBN 0-913504-58-0). Lowell Pr.

Stubbs, Bettie. Easy Bible Talks from Common Objects. Packard, Olga, ed. (Standard Ideas Ser.). (Illus.). 1978. pap. 1.75 (ISBN 0-87239-217-1, 2818). Standard Pub.

Stubbs, Jean. Love Is of the Valley. 378p. 1981. 12.95 (ISBN 0-312-49942-6). St Martin.

Stubbs, Joanna. Canary for King. (Illus.). (ps-5). 1970. 6.95 (ISBN 0-571-09374-4, Pub. by Faber & Faber). Merrimack Bk Serv.

--Happy Bear's Day. (Illus.). (ps-2). 1979. PLB 6.50 (ISBN 0-233-96999-3). Andre Deutsch.

Stubbs, Joanna, jt. auth. see Fitzpatrick, Eva.

Stubbs, Joyce. Home Book of Greek Cookery. 8.95 (ISBN 0-571-05477-3). Transatlantic.

Stubbs, Joyce M. Home Book of Greek Cookery. LC 64-35740. (Home Cookery Book Ser). 159p. 1967. 6.25x (ISBN 0-571-08187-8). Intl Pubns Serv.

--The Home Book of Greek Cookery. (Orig.). 1967. pap. 5.95 (ISBN 0-571-08187-8, Pub. by Faber & Faber). Merrimack Bk Serv.

Stubbs, Marcia & Barnet, Sylvan. The Little Brown Reader. 2nd ed. 1980. pap. text ed. 8.95 (ISBN 0-316-82002-4); instr's manual free (ISBN 0-316-82003-2). Little.

Stubbs, Marcia, jt. auth. see Barnet, Sylvan.

Stubbs, P. C., et al. Transport Economics. (Studies in Economics). (Illus.). 1980. text ed. 24.95x (ISBN 0-04-338088-3); pap. text ed. 12.50x (ISBN 0-04-338089-1). Allen Unwin.

Stubbs, Robert S., jt. auth. see McVay, Kipling L.

Stubbs, Thomas, jt. auth. see Richardson, Norman.

Stubbs, William. Seventeen Lectures on the Study of Medieval & Modern History. 1967. 15.00 (ISBN 0-86527-219-0). Fertig.

Stubel, Hans & Mitsuo, Shimizu. Le Stamme der Insel Hainan, 2 vols. (Asian Folklore & Social Life Monographs: Vols. 85-86). (Ger.). 1935. 15.00 (ISBN 0-89986-294-2). E Langstaff.

Stuber, Florian, jt. ed. see Mooney, Michael.

Stubis, Patricia. Sandwichery: Recipes, Riddles & Funny Facts About Food. LC 74-12294. (Illus.). 56p. (gr. k-3). 1975. 5.95 o.s.i. (ISBN 0-685-53688-2, Four Winds); PLB 5.41 o.s.i. (ISBN 0-8193-0780-7). Schol Bk Serv.

Stuckenbruck, Linn C., ed. Implementation of Project Management: The Professional's Handbook. LC 80-14898. 304p. 1981. text ed. price not set (ISBN 0-201-07260-2). A-W.

Stuckey. Sailing Pilots of the Bristol Channel. 1977. 14.95 (ISBN 0-7153-7373-0). David & Charles.

Stuckey, Gilbert B. Procedures in the Justice System. 2nd ed. (Public Service Technology Ser.). 280p. 1980. text ed. 16.95 (ISBN 0-675-08173-4); instructor's manual 3.95 (ISBN 0-686-63345-8). Merrill.

Stuckey, W. J. Caroline Gordon. (U. S. Authors Ser.: No. 200). lib. bdg. 10.95 (ISBN 0-8057-0332-2). Twayne.

Stucki, J. W. & Banwart, L., eds. Advanced Chemical Methods for Soil & Clay Minerals Reasearch. 488p. 1980. lib. bdg. 58.00 (Pub. by D. Reidel). Kluwer Boston.

Stucky, Steven. Lutoslawski & His Music. (Illus.). 300p. Date not set. price not set (ISBN 0-521-22799-2). Cambridge U Pr.

Studders, R. J., jt. auth. see Parker, Rollin J.

Studdert-Kennedy, Gerald. Evidence & Explanation in Social Science. 1975. 24.00x (ISBN 0-7100-8157-X). Routledge & Kegan.

Studdert-Kennedy, Gerald, jt. auth. see Moodle, Graeme C.

Studdert-Kennedy, M., jt. ed. see Bellugi, U.

Studer, Kenneth E. & Chubin, Daryl E. The Cancer Mission: Social Contexts of Biomedical Research. LC 80-10312. (Sage Library of Social Research: Vol. 103). (Illus.). 319p. 1980. 18.00x (ISBN 0-8039-1423-7); pap. 8.95x (ISBN 0-8039-1424-5). Sage.

Studer, Paul & Waters, E. G. Historical French Reader: Medieval Period. 1924. 22.50x (ISBN 0-19-815327-9). Oxford U Pr.

Studies in Medieval Culture, Ii, Kalamazoo. Proceedings. 1966. 5.00 o.p. (ISBN 0-686-14883-5). Medieval Inst.

Studies in Medieval Culture, IIII. Proceedings. Sommerfeldt, John R., ed. 1970. pap. 5.00 (ISBN 0-686-14884-3). Medieval Inst.

Studies in Medieval Culture I,Kalamazoo. Proceedings. Sommerfeldt, John R., ed. 1964. 5.00 o.p. (ISBN 0-686-14882-7). Medieval Inst.

Studies in Medieval Culture, IV 2, Kalamazoo. Proceedings, Vol. 2. Sommerfeldt, John R., et al, eds. 1974. pap. 5.00 (ISBN 0-686-14888-6). Medieval Inst.

Studies in Medieval Culture, V. Proceedings. Sommerfeldt, John R., et al, eds. 1975. pap. 5.00 (ISBN 0-686-14892-4). Medieval Inst.

Studva, K., jt. ed. see Pilapil, F.

Study Commission on Undergraduate Education & the Education of Teachers. Teacher Education in the United States: The Responsibility Gap. LC 75-34710. 1976. 10.00x (ISBN 0-8032-0875-8); pap. 2.95x (ISBN 0-8032-5839-9, BB 621, Bison). U of Nebr Pr.

Study Group Meeting, Haifa, Aug. 27-Sept. 4, 1973. Radiation Engineering in the Academic Curriculum: Proceedings. (Illus.). 362p. 1975. pap. 26.75 (ISBN 92-0-161075-0, IAEA). Unipub.

Study Project on Social Research & Development, National Research Council. Federal Investment in Knowledge of Social Problems. LC 78-7928. 1978. pap. text ed. 7.00 (ISBN 0-309-02747-0). Natl Acad Pr.

Stueart, Robert D. & Eastlick, John T. Library Management. LC 76-49568. (Library Science Text Ser.). 1977. lib. bdg. 15.00x (ISBN 0-87287-127-4). Libs Unl.

--Library Management. 2nd ed. LC 80-22895. (Library Science Text Ser.). 292p. 1980. text ed. 22.50x (ISBN 0-87287-241-6); pap. text ed. 14.50x (ISBN 0-87287-243-2). Libs Unl.

Stuebe, Isabel C. The Life & Works of William Hodges. LC 78-74383. (Outstanding Dissertations in the Fine Arts, Fourth Ser.). (Illus.). 1979. lib. bdg. 50.00 (ISBN 0-8240-3969-6). Garland Pub.

Stueck, William W., Jr. The Road to Confrontation: American Policy Toward China & Korea, 1947 - 1950. LC 80-11818. (Illus.). 337p. 1981. 22.00x (ISBN 0-8078-1445-8); pap. 10.00x (ISBN 0-8078-4080-7). U of NC Pr.

Stuempfle, Herman G., Jr. & Kearney, Peter J. Lent. LC 73-79350. (Proclmation 1: Aids for Interpreting the Lessons of the Church Year Ser. C). 64p. 1973. pap. 1.95 (ISBN 0-8006-4053-5, 1-4053). Fortress.

Stuenkel, Walter W. Books of the Old Testament. 1981. pap. 3.50 (ISBN 0-570-03749-2, 12-2653). Concordia.

Stuers, Cora Vreede de see Vreede-de Stuers, Cora.

Stugrin, Michael A., jt. ed. see Knapp, Peggy A.

Stuhler, Barbara & Kreuter, Gretchen, eds. Women of Minnesota: Selected Biographical Essays. LC 77-3361. (Illus.). 402p. 1977. 12.00 (ISBN 0-87351-112-3). Minn Hist.

Stuhlman, Beverly. The School Reading Teacher. (Teachers Education Ser.: No. 4). Date not set. pap. cancelled (ISBN 0-934402-08-6). BYLS Pr.

Stuhlman, Daniel D. How to Use the School Library. (Teacher Education Ser.: No. 3). (Orig.). Date not set. pap. 1.25 (ISBN 0-934402-06-X). BYLS Pr. Postponed.

--My Own Hanukah Story. (Illus., Orig.). (ps-1). 1980. pap. 3.95 (ISBN 0-934402-07-8); decorations 1.00 (ISBN 0-934402-08-6). BYLS Pr.

--My Own Pesach Story. (My Own Holiday Stories: No. 2). (Illus.). 1981. pap. 3.95 (ISBN 0-686-28904-8). BYLS Pr.

Stuhlman, Daniel D. & Brody, Arnold G. Teacher My Stomach Hurts! A Guide to Student Health Complaints. (Teachers Education Ser.: No. 2). 1980. pap. 1.25 (ISBN 0-934402-04-3). BYLS Pr.

Stuhlmueller, Carroll. Biblical Meditations for Advent & the Christmas Season. LC 80-82083. (Biblical Meditations Ser.: Vol. 3). 288p. (Orig.). 1980. pap. 3.95 (ISBN 0-8091-2318-5). Paulist Pr.

--Thirsting for the Lord: Essays in Biblical Spirituality. LC 76-51736. (Illus.). 1977. 7.95 o.p. (ISBN 0-8189-0341-4). Alba.

Stuhmueller, Carroll C. Biblical Meditations for the Easter Season. LC 80-81030. 1980. pap. 2.95 (ISBN 0-8091-2283-9). Paulist Pr.

Stuhr, David D., jt. auth. see Branham, Richard L.

Stukat, Karl-Gustaf. Current Trends in European Pre-School Research. (Council of Europe Trend Reports). (Orig.). 1976. pap. text ed. 10.50x (ISBN 0-85633-091-4, NFER). Humanities.

Stuke, J. & Brenig, W., eds. Amorphous & Liquid Semiconductors, 2 vols. LC 74-12437. 1441p. 1974. Set. 124.95 (ISBN 0-470-83485-4). Halsted Pr.

Stull, Daniel R., et al. Chemical Thermodynamics of Organic Compounds. LC 68-9250. 1969. 60.00 (ISBN 0-471-83490-4, Pub. by Wiley-Interscience). Wiley.

Stultz, Newell M. Afrikaner Politics in South Africa, 1934-1948. (Perspectives on Southern Africa: Vol. 13). 1974. 18.00x (ISBN 0-520-02452-4). U of Cal Pr.

Stumbo, C. R., et al. CRC Handbook of Tables of Commercial Thermal Processes for Low-Acid Canned Foods, 2 vols. Date not set. Vol. 1. 69.95 (ISBN 0-8493-2961-2); Vol. 2. 69.95 (ISBN 0-8493-2963-9). CRC Pr. Postponed.

Stumm, David A. Advanced Industrial Selling. 426p. 1981. 17.95 (ISBN 0-8144-5665-0). Am Mgmt.

Stumm, Werner & Morgan, James J. Aquatic Chemistry: An Introduction Emphasizing Chemical Equilibria in Natural Waters. 2nd ed. 806p. 1981. 38.00 (ISBN 0-471-04831-3, Pub. by Wiley-Interscience). Wiley.

Stumme, John R. Socialism in Theological Perspective: A Study of Paul Tillich, 1918-1933. LC 78-3675. (American Academy of Religion. Dissertation Ser.: No. 21). 1978. pap. 7.50 (ISBN 0-89130-232-8, 010121). Scholars Pr Ca.

Stummel, F. & Hainer, K. Introduction to Numerical Analysis. 276p. 1980. 15.00x (ISBN 0-7073-0130-0, Pub. by Scottish Academic Pr). Columbia U Pr.

Stumpf, P. K., jt. auth. see Conn, Eric E.

Stumpf, P. K. & Hatch, M. D., eds. The Biochemistry of Plants: A Comprehensive Treatise, Photosynthesis, Vol. 8. 1981. write for info. Acad Pr.

Stumphauzer, Jerome S. Progress in Behavior Therapy with Delinquents. (Illus.). 408p. 1979. 33.75 (ISBN 0-398-03733-7); pap. 25.50 (ISBN 0-398-03738-8). C C Thomas.

Stunard, E. Arthur, jt. auth. see Wagner, Betty J.

Stunkard, Albert J. I Almost Feel Thin. LC 77-70403. 1977. pap. 5.95 o.p. (ISBN 0-915950-11-1). Bull Pub.

Stunkel, Kenneth R. National Energy Profiles. (Praeger Special Studies Ser.). 1980. 32.95 (ISBN 0-03-050646-8). Praeger.

--Relations of Indian, Greek, & Christian Thought in Antiquity. LC 79-63750. 1979. pap. text ed. 9.00 (ISBN 0-8191-0737-9). U Pr of Amer.

Stuntz, Daniel, et al. How to Identify Mushrooms (to Genus IV) Keys to Families & Genera. (Illus.). 1977. pap. 5.50x (ISBN 0-916422-10-0). Mad River.

Stuntz, Daniel E., ed. see McKenny, Margaret.

Stupek, D., ed. see Anderson, George B.

Sturcken, H. Tracy. Don Juan Manuel. (World Authors Ser.: Spain: No. 303). 1974. lib. bdg. 10.95 (ISBN 0-8057-2590-3). Twayne.

Sturcken, H. Tracy, jt. auth. see Dalbor, John B.

Sturdivant, F. D. Ghetto Marketplace. LC 77-81932. 1969. 8.95 (ISBN 0-02-932290-1); pap. text ed. 5.95 o.p. (ISBN 0-02-932300-2). Free Pr.

Sturdivant, Frederick & Robinson, Larry M. The Corporate Social Challenge: Cases & Commentaries. rev. ed. 1981. pap. 12.50x (ISBN 0-256-02518-5). Irwin.

Sturdivant, Frederick A. Business & Society: A Managerial Approach. 1977. 18.95 (ISBN 0-256-01897-9). Irwin.

Sturdivant, Frederick D., jt. ed. see Andreasen, Alan R.

Sturdza, Ioana, et al, eds. Fairy Tales & Legends from Romania. (Illus.). 1972. 21.00x (ISBN 0-8057-5655-8). Irvington.

Sturgeon, S. & Rans, L. The Woman Offender: A Bibiliographic Sourcebook. vi, 63p. 1975. pap. 5.00 (ISBN 0-686-28749-5). Entropy Ltd.

Sturgeon, Theodore. Beyond. 1980. pap. 1.95 o.s.i. (ISBN 0-440-10740-7). Dell.

--More Than Human. 192p. 1981. pap. 2.25 (ISBN 0-345-28189-6, Del Rey). Ballantine.

--Some of Your Blood. 1977. pap. 1.50 o.p. (ISBN 0-345-25712-X). Ballantine.

--The Stars Are the Styx. 1981. pap. 2.75 (ISBN 0-440-18006-6). Dell.

--Starshine. 1977. pap. 1.50 o.s.i. (ISBN 0-515-04459-8). Jove Pubns.

--Sturgeon in Orbit. 1978. pap. 1.50 o.s.i. (ISBN 0-515-04477-6). Jove Pubns.

--Visions & Venturers. 1978. pap. 1.75 o.s.i. (ISBN 0-440-12648-7). Dell.

--A Way Home. 1978. pap. 1.50 o.p. (ISBN 0-515-04467-9). Jove Pubns.

Sturgeon, Wina. Depression. 256p. 1981. pap. 5.95 (ISBN 0-346-12514-6). Cornerstone.

Sturges, Hale, et al. Une Fois Pour Toutes: Revision Des Structures Essentielles De la Langue Francais. (Illus.). 1976. pap. text ed. 6.50x (ISBN 0-88334-079-8). Ind Sch Pr.

Sturges, Lena. Southern Country Cookbook. LC 72-83975. (Illus.). 1972. 12.95 (ISBN 0-8487-0234-4). Oxmoor Hse.

--Vegetables Cookbook. LC 74-18641. (Family Guidebooks Ser). (Illus.). 1975. pap. 1.95 (ISBN 0-8487-0365-0). Oxmoor Hse.

Sturgess, Rosemary. The Baby Book. LC 77-76097. 1977. 13.50 (ISBN 0-7153-7438-9). David & Charles.

Sturgis, Howard O. Belchamber. LC 76-15624. 1976. Repr. of 1905 ed. 14.50 (ISBN 0-86527-219-0). Fertig.

Sturgis, Russell. Dictionary of Architecture & Building, Biographical & Descriptive, 3 Vols. LC 66-26997. (Illus.). 1966. Repr. of 1902 ed. Set. 50.00 (ISBN 0-8103-3075-X). Gale.

Sturgis, William B. Fly-Tying. (Illus.). 1940. 8.95 o.p. (ISBN 0-684-10584-5, ScribT). Scribner.

Sturgul, jt. auth. see Merchant.

Sturgul, John R. & Merchant, M. J. Applied Fortran Four Programming. 2nd ed. 1977. pap. text ed. 15.95x (ISBN 0-534-00440-7). Wadsworth Pub.

Sturholm, Larry & Howard, John. All for Nothing. Shangle, Robert D., ed. (Illus.). 1976. 7.95 (ISBN 0-917630-01-7, Pub by Bls). Beautiful Am.

Sturkie, P. D., ed. Basic Physiology. (Illus.). 350p. 1981. 19.80 (ISBN 0-387-90485-9). Springer-Verlag.

Sturlaugson, Mary F. A Soul So Rebellious. 88p. 1980. 5.95 (ISBN 0-87747-841-4). Deseret Bk.

Sturluson, Snorri. Heims Kringla, History of the Kings of Norway. Hollander, Lee M., tr. from Old Norse. LC 64-10460. (Illus.). 1977. Repr. of 1964 ed. 27.50x (ISBN 0-89067-040-4). Am Scandinavian.

--The Prose Edda of Snorri Sturluson: Tales from Norse Mythology. Young, Jean I., tr. 1964. pap. 3.95x (ISBN 0-520-01232-1, CAMPUS55). U of Cal Pr.

Sturm, Harlan, jt. ed. see Walsh, Donald D.

Sturm, Mary M. & Grieser, E. H. Guide to Modern Clothing. (American Home & Family Ser.). (First ed. also avail. at same prices). (gr. 10-12). 1968. text ed. 13.20 (ISBN 0-07-062274-4, W); tchrs' manual 1.32 (ISBN 0-07-062226-4). McGraw.

Sturm, Sara. Lorenzo de' Medici. (World Authors Ser.: Italy: No. 288). 1974. lib. bdg. 12.50 (ISBN 0-8057-2609-8). Twayne.

Sturman, Julie & Schults, Dorothy. Breeding Cockatiels. (Illus.). 93p. 1980. 2.95 (ISBN 0-87666-889-9, KW-099). TFH Pubns.

Sturmberger, Ingeborg. The Comic Elements of Ben Jonson's Drama, 2 vols. (Salzburg Studies in English Literature, Jacobean Drama Studies Ser.: Nos. 54-55). 548p. 1975. Set. pap. text ed. 50.25x (ISBN 0-391-01540-0). Humanities.

Sturrock, David. Fruits for Southern Florida. 196p. 1980. pap. 7.95 (ISBN 0-9600046-2-9). Horticultural.

Sturt, B. A., et al. Geological Survey of Norway, No. 358, Bulletin 55. (Illus.). 60p. 1981. pap. 14.00x. Universitet.

Sturt, George. Journals, 2 Vols. Mackerness, E. D., ed. 1967. Set. 110.00 (ISBN 0-521-06569-0). Cambridge U Pr.

--A Small Boy in the Sixties. 1977. Repr. of 1952 ed. text ed. 13.00x (ISBN 0-85527-244-9). Humanities.

--Wheelwright's Shop. 32.50 (ISBN 0-521-06570-4); pap. 9.95 (ISBN 0-521-09195-0). Cambridge U Pr.

Sturtevant, E. H. Linguistic Change. 183p. 1980. Repr. of 1942 ed. lib. bdg. 30.00 (ISBN 0-89987-765-6). Darby Bks.

Sturtevant, Edgar H. & Hahn, E. A. Comparative Grammar of the Hittite Language. 1951. 45.00x (ISBN 0-686-51357-6). Elliots Bks.

Sturtevant, Simon. Metallica: Or, the Treatise of New Metallicall Inventions. LC 74-28887. (English Experience Ser.: No. 764). 1975. Repr. of 1612 ed. 9.50 (ISBN 90-221-0764-7). Walter J Johnson.

Sturtevant, William C., jt. ed. see Heizer, Robert F.

Sturtridge, G., jt. auth. see Geddes, M.

Sturzl, Erwin A., ed. Essays in Honour of Professor Tyrus Hillway. (Salzburg Studies in English Literature, Romantic Reassessment Ser.: No. 65). (Illus.). 1977. pap. text ed. 25.00x (ISBN 0-391-01539-7). Humanities.

Sturzo, Luigi. The International Community & the Right of War. LC 68-9649. 1971. Repr. of 1929 ed. 16.00 (ISBN 0-86527-104-6). Fertig.

Stutley, Margaret. Ancient Indian Magic & Folklore: An Introduction. LC 79-13211. (Illus.). 1980. 18.50 (ISBN 0-87773-712-6). Great Eastern.

Stutman, Fred A. & Africano, Lillian. The Doctor's Walking Book. (Orig.). 1980. pap. 6.95 (ISBN 0-345-28764-9). Ballantine.

Stutman, Osis, ed. Contemporary Topics in Immunobiology: Vol. 7, T Cells. (Illus.). 386p. 1977. 35.00 (ISBN 0-306-37807-8, Plenum Pr). Plenum Pub.

Stutts, Evelyn C. All That You Need to Know About Camp Counseling. (Illus.). 1981. 4.95 (ISBN 0-8062-1708-1). Carlton.

Stutz, Frederick P. Social Aspects of Interaction & Transportation. Natoli, Salvatore J., ed. LC 76-19932. (Resource Papers for College Geography Ser.). 1976. pap. text ed. 4.00 (ISBN 0-89291-117-4). Assn Am Geographers.

Stutz, Robert M., et al, eds. Exploring Behavior & Experience: Readings in General Psychology. LC 75-135022. (Illus.). 1971. pap. text ed. 10.95 (ISBN 0-13-296368-X). P-H.

Stutzman, Warren L. & Thiele, Gary A. Antenna Theory & Design. 672p. 1981. text ed. 26.95 (ISBN 0-471-04458-X). Wiley.

Stuvel, Pieke. Fancy Pants: Creative Patterns for Making Baby's First Wardrobe. (Illus.). 1979. pap. 4.95 (ISBN 0-8015-0484-8, Hawthorn). Dutton.

--A Touch of Style: Sewing Simple, Inventive Clothes. 96p. 1981. pap. 4.95 (ISBN 0-14-046482-4). Penguin.

Stuzin, Roz, jt. auth. see Edelman, Alice.

Stwertka, Albert, jt. auth. see Stwertka, Eve.

Stwertka, Eve & Stwertka, Albert. Marijuana. (First Bks.). (Illus.). (gr. 4 up). 1979. PLB 6.45 s&l (ISBN 0-531-02944-1). Watts.

--Steel Mill. LC 78-2319. (Industry at Work Ser.). (Illus.). (gr. 4-6). 1978. PLB 5.90 s&l (ISBN 0-531-02208-0). Watts.

Styan, J. L. Chekhov in Performance: A Commentary of the Major Plays. LC 73-134614. (Illus.). 1971. 42.00 (ISBN 0-521-07975-6); pap. 11.95 (ISBN 0-521-29345-6). Cambridge U Pr.

--Dark Comedy: The Development of Modern Comic Tragedy. 2nd ed. LC 68-23185. 42.00 (ISBN 0-521-06572-0); pap. 10.50x (ISBN 0-521-09529-8). Cambridge U Pr.

--Drama, Stage & Audience. LC 74-76948. 260p. 1975. 32.00 (ISBN 0-521-20504-2); pap. 8.50 (ISBN 0-521-09869-6). Cambridge U Pr.

--Dramatic Experience. 1965. 23.95 (ISBN 0-521-06573-9); pap. 8.95 (ISBN 0-521-09984-6). Cambridge U Pr.

--Elements of Drama. 1960. 36.00 (ISBN 0-521-06574-7); pap. text ed. 9.95x (ISBN 0-521-09201-9). Cambridge U Pr.

--Modern Drama in Theory & Practice, 3 vols. Incl. Vol. 1. Realism & Naturalism. Cloth (ISBN 0-521-22737-2); Vol. 2. Symbolism, Surrealism & the Absurd. Cloth (ISBN 0-521-22738-0); Vol. 3. Expressionism & Epic Theatre. Cloth (ISBN 0-521-22739-9). LC 79-15947. (Illus.). 250p. Date not set. 75.00 set; 29.50 ea. Cambridge U Pr. Postponed.

--The Shakespeare Revolution. LC 76-3043. (Illus.). 1977. 26.50 (ISBN 0-521-21193-X). Cambridge U Pr.

--Shakespeare's Stagecraft. (Illus.). 1967. 42.00 (ISBN 0-521-06902-5); pap. 8.95 (ISBN 0-521-09435-6). Cambridge U Pr.

Stych, F. S. How to Find Out About Italy. LC 70-123271. 1970. 21.00 (ISBN 0-08-015810-2). Pergamon.

Stycos, J. Mayone. Al Margen de la Vida: Poblacion y Pobreza en America Central. LC 72-90916. Orig. Title: The Margin of Life. (Illus., Span.). 1974. pap. text ed. 6.95x (ISBN 0-89197-653-1). Irvington.

Stycos, J. Mayone, ed. Clinics, Contraception & Communication: Evaluation Studies of Family Planning Programs in Four Latin American Countries. LC 79-184865. (Illus.). 1973. 20.00x (ISBN 0-89197-625-6); pap. text ed. 8.95x (ISBN 0-89197-700-7). Irvington.

Styles, B. T., jt. ed. see Burley, J.

Styles, E. Derek, ed. see Mendel Centennial Symposium - Fort Collins - 1965.

Styles, Showell. Backpacking: a Comprehensive Guide. 1977. 7.95 o.p. (ISBN 0-679-50722-1); pap. 4.95 o.p. (ISBN 0-679-50723-X). McKay.

--Mallory of Everest. LC 68-20610. (Illus.). (gr. 7 up). 1968. 4.95 o.s.i. (ISBN 0-02-788540-2). Macmillan.

Stylianopoulos, Theodore. Justin Martyr & the Mosaic Law. LC 75-22445. (Society of Biblical Literature. Dissertation Ser.). 1975. pap. 7.50 (ISBN 0-89130-018-X, 060120). Scholars Pr Ca.

Styring, John S., jt. auth. see Clegg, W. Paul.

Styron, William. Sophie's Choice. 640p. 1980. pap. 3.50 (ISBN 0-553-13545-7). Bantam.

Su, Kendall L. A Collection of Solved Problems in Circuits, Electronics, & Signal Analysis, Vol. 1. 96p. 1980. pap. text ed. 5.50 (ISBN 0-8403-2262-3). Kendall-Hunt.

--Fundamentals of Circuits, Electronics, & Signal Analysis. LC 77-74147. (Illus.). 1978. text ed. 26.95 (ISBN 0-395-25038-2); sol. manual 1.10 (ISBN 0-395-25039-0). HM.

Suami, Tetsuo, jt. ed. see Rinehart, Kenneth L.

Suares, Carlo. The Resurrection of the Word. LC 74-75098. 1975. 8.95 o.p. (ISBN 0-394-49520-9). Random.

Suares, J. C. The Literary Dog. 1978. pap. 7.95 o.p. (ISBN 0-425-03961-7). Berkley Pub.

Suares, J. C. & Chwast, Seymour. Literary Cat. LC 77-23583. (Illus.). (YA) 1977. 12.95 o.p. (ISBN 0-399-12034-3, Dist. by Putnam). Berkley Pub.

Suares, Jean C., ed. The Photographed Cat. LC 80-665. (Illus.). 128p. 1980. 15.95 (ISBN 0-385-17081-5). Doubleday.

--Photographed Cat. LC 80-665. (Illus.). 128p. 1980. pap. 8.95 (ISBN 0-385-17080-7, Dolp). Doubleday.

Suarez & Castroleal. Aprende En Espanol y En Ingles: Readiness Level. (gr. k-1). 1978. tchr's manual (a) 5.25 (ISBN 0-88345-364-9); tchr's manual (b) 5.25 (ISBN 0-88345-365-7); cassettes, teacher's manuals & spirit masters 100.00 (ISBN 0-685-78815-6). Regents Pub.

Suarez, Diamantina V., jt. auth. see Castroleal, Alicia.

Suarez-Caabro, Jose A. El Mar de Puerto Rico: Una Intoduccion a las Pesquerias de la Isla. (Illus., Sp.). 1979. 20.00 (ISBN 0-8477-2323-2). U of PR Pr.

Suarez-Kurtz, G., jt. ed. see Rocha e Silva, M.

Suarez-Torres, J. D. Perspectiva Humoristica En la Trilogia De Gironelia. 1975. 12.95 (ISBN 0-88303-021-7); pap. 10.95 (ISBN 0-685-73222-3). E Torres & Sons.

Suarez-Torrez, David. Contrastes Culturales. 336p. 1981. text ed. 11.95 case (ISBN 0-669-02662-X). Heath.

Subak-Sharpe, Gerald E., jt. auth. see Glaser, Arthur.

Subbarao, E. C., ed. Solid Electrolytes & Their Applications. (Illus.). 310p. 1980. 35.00 (ISBN 0-306-40389-7, Plenum Pr). Plenum Pub.

Subbarao, E. C. & Wallace, W. E., eds. Science & Technology of Rare Earth Materials. 1980. 29.00 (ISBN 0-12-675640-6). Acad Pr.

Subba Rao, N. S., ed. Recent Advences in Biological Nitrogen Fixation. 500p. 1980. text ed. 38.95x (ISBN 0-8419-5825-4). Holmes & Meier.

Subba Rao, T. V. Studies in Indian Music. 7.50x (ISBN 0-210-33960-8). Asia.

Subcommittee for Review of the KBS-II Plan, ed. see Committee on Radioactive Waste Management.

Subcommittee on Nuclear Reactors. Reactors for University Research. 1959. pap. 0.75 (ISBN 0-309-00075-0). Natl Acad Pr.

Subcommittee On Standards For Large Domestic Laboratory Animals. Swine. LC 75-169293. (Standards & Guidelines for the Breeding, Care, & Management of Laboratory Animals Ser). 1971. pap. text ed. 3.25 o.p. (ISBN 0-309-01923-0). Natl Acad Pr.

Subcommittee on Toxicity in Animals, Board on Agricultural & Renewable Resources. Mineral Tolerance of Domestic Animals. 1980. pap. text ed. 15.50 (ISBN 0-309-03022-6). Natl Acad Pr.

Subercaseaux, Benjamin. Chile, A Geographic Extravaganza. Flores, Angel, tr. from Span. 1971. Repr. of 1943 ed. 14.75 o.s.i. (ISBN 0-02-853090-X). Hafner.

Subin, Harry I. Criminal Justice in Metropolitan Court. LC 72-172177. (American Constitutional & Legal History Ser). 234p. 1973. Repr. of 1966 ed. lib. bdg. 22.50 (ISBN 0-306-70239-8). Da Capo.

Subiotto, A. V. Gunther Grass: The Literature of Politics. (German Literature & Society Ser.: Vol. 3). 1980. pap. text ed. write for info. (ISBN 0-85496-076-7). Humanities.

Subira, Jose. Historia De la Musica Teatral en Espana. LC 80-2304. 1981. Repr. of 1945 ed. 27.50 (ISBN 0-404-18871-0). AMS Pr.

Subitzky, Seymour & Gill, Harold E., eds. Geology of Selected Areas in New Jersey & Eastern Pennsylvania & Guidebook of Excursions. 1969. 25.00 (ISBN 0-8135-0606-9). Rutgers U Pr.

Subloff, Jeremy A., ed. see Smith, Ledyard.

Subotnick, Steven. The Running Foot Doctor. LC 77-73653. (Illus.). 144p. 1977. pap. 3.95 (ISBN 0-89037-117-2); handbk. 6.95 (ISBN 0-89037-116-4). Anderson World.

Subrahmanian, N. History of Tamilnadu to A. D. 1336. (Illus.). 428p. 1974. text ed. 10.00 (ISBN 0-88253-434-3). Ind-US Inc.

Subrahmanyam, Sarada & Kutty, K. Madhaven. A Concise Textbook of Physiology. 332p. 1979. 15.00 (ISBN 0-86131-026-8, Pub. by Orient Longman India). State Mutual Bk.

Subrahmanyam, Sarada & Kutty, K. Madhaven, eds. A Textbook of Physiology. 2nd ed. 818p. 1979. 30.00x (ISBN 0-86125-415-5, Pub. by Orient Longman India). State Mutual Bk.

Subramaniam, C. The New Strategy in Indian Agriculture. text ed. 12.50 (ISBN 0-7069-0921-6, Pub. by Vikas India). Advent Bk.

Subramaniam, K. Brahmin Priest of Tamil Nadu. LC 74-13072. 183p. 1974. 13.95 (ISBN 0-470-83535-4). Halsted Pr.

Subramaniam, V. Parched Earth: The Maharashtra Drought, 1970-73. LC 75-903997. 1975. 16.00x o.p. (ISBN 0-88386-656-0). South Asia Bks.

Subramanian, Sujatha B. The House in the Hills & Other Short Stories. (Indian Short Stories Ser.). 123p. 1974. 6.85 (ISBN 0-88253-464-5). Ind-US Inc.

Subramanyam, B. R., ed. Computer Applications in Large Scale Power Systems: Proceedings of the Symposium, New Delhi, India, 16-19 August 1979, 3 vols. (Illus.). 1100p. 1980. 205.00 (ISBN 0-08-024450-5). Pergamon.

Subramanyam, Ka N., tr. see Padmanabhan, Neela.

Subramanyam, Ka Naa, ed. Tamil Short Stories. 1981. text ed. 10.50x (ISBN 0-7069-1241-1, Pub by Vikas India). Advent Bk.

Subtelny, Joanne. Speech Assessment & Speech Improvement for the Hearing Impaired. 1980. 19.95 (ISBN 0-88200-138-8). Bell Assn Deaf.

Subtelny, Joanne D., ed. Speech Assessment & Speech Improvement for the Hearing Impaired. 420p. 1980. pap. text ed. 19.95 (ISBN 0-88200-138-8, A0138). Alexander Graham.

Subtelny, Orest, tr. see Wynar, Lubomyr R.

Such, Dennis T. Nickel & Chromium Plating. 1972. pap. text ed. 34.95 (ISBN 0-408-00086-4). Butterworths.

Sucher, Floyd, jt. auth. see Nielsen, Patricia H.

Sucher, Floyd, et al. The Principal's Role in Improving Instruction. (Illus.). 112p. 1980. 11.75 (ISBN 0-398-04123-7). C C Thomas.

Sucher, Harry V. Simplified Boatbuilding: Flat Bottom. (Illus.). 1973. 24.95 (ISBN 0-393-03173-X). Norton.

Suchet, J. P. Electrical Conduction in Solid Materials: Physico-Chemical Bases & Possible Applications. 204p. 1976. text ed. 27.00 (ISBN 0-08-018052-3). Pergamon.

Suchier, Hermann & Suchier, Walther, eds. Aucassin & Nicolette: Kritischer Text Mit Paradigmen & Glossar. LC 80-2239. 1981. Repr. of 1932 ed. 31.00 (ISBN 0-404-19035-9). AMS Pr.

Suchier, Walther, jt. ed. see Suchier, Hermann.

Suchlicki, Jaime. Cuba: From Columbus to Castro. LC 73-1325. 256p. 1974. 7.95 o.p. (ISBN 0-684-13715-1, ScribC); pap. text ed. 4.95x o.p. (ISBN 0-684-13762-3, ScribC). Scribner.

Suchman, Edward A. Sociology & the Field of Public Health. LC 63-21228. 1963. pap. 2.00 (ISBN 0-87154-864-X). Russell Sage.

Suchoff, Benjamin, ed. B'ela Bart'ok: Essays. LC 76-5202. (Illus.). 1976. 75.00 (ISBN 0-312-07350-X). St Martin.

Su-Chu, Wu, jt. auth. see Bodman, N. C.

Suckle, Abby, ed. By Their Own Design. (Illus.). 1980. 19.95 (ISBN 0-8230-7097-2, Whitney Lib). Watson-Guptill.

Suckling, C. J., et al. Chemistry Through Models. LC 77-71429. (Illus.). 1978. 47.50 (ISBN 0-521-21661-3). Cambridge U Pr.

Suckling, Colin J. & Suckling, Keith E. Biological Chemistry. LC 79-51830. (Cambridge Texts in Chemistry & Biochemistry Ser.). (Illus.). 350p. 1980. 59.50 (ISBN 0-521-22852-2); pap. 19.95 (ISBN 0-521-29678-1). Cambridge U Pr.

Suckling, Colin J., et al. Chemistry Through Models. LC 77-71429. (Illus.). 321p. 1980. pap. 13.95x (ISBN 0-521-29932-2). Cambridge U Pr.

Suckling, Keith E., jt. auth. see Suckling, Colin J.

Sucksdorff, Astrid B. Tooni, the Elephant Boy. LC 73-137762. (Illus.). 48p. (gr. 3 up). 1971. 5.95 o.p. (ISBN 0-15-289426-8, HJ). HarBraceJ.

Sucksmith, Harvey P., ed. see Dickens, Charles.

Suczek, Robert F. The Best Laid Plans: Student Development in an Experimental College Program. LC 72-5891. (Higher Education Ser.). 1972. 11.95x o.p. (ISBN 0-87589-149-7). Jossey-Bass.

Sud, K. N. Eternal Flame: Aspects of Ghalib's Life & Works. 1969. 5.50x o.p. (ISBN 0-8426-1558-X). Verry.

Suda, Zdenek L. Zealots & Rebels: A History of the Ruling Communist Party of Czechoslovakia. (Publication Ser.: No. 234). 265p. (Orig.). 1980. pap. 8.95 (ISBN 0-8179-7342-7). Hoover Inst Pr.

Suddarth, D., jt. auth. see Brunner, L.

Suddarth, Doris S., jt. auth. see Brunner, Lillian S.

Sudduth, Sanse, jt. auth. see Sudduth, Tom.

Sudduth, Tom & Sudduth, Sanse. Colorado Front Range Ski Tours. LC 75-27837. (Illus.). 1975. pap. 6.95 o.p. (ISBN 0-911518-34-7). Touchstone Pr Ore.

Sudhalter. The Management Option. LC 80-12992. 256p. 1980. 16.95 (ISBN 0-87705-084-8). Human Sci Pr.

Sudhalter, Richard M. & Evans, Philip R. Bix: Man & Legend. (Illus.). 1975. pap. 5.95 (ISBN 0-02-872500-X). Schirmer Bks.

Sudilovsky, A., et al, eds. Predictability in Psychopharmacology: Preclinical & Clinical Correlations. LC 74-14483. 350p. 1975. 39.50 (ISBN 0-89004-017-6). Raven.

Sudworth, George B. Forest Trees of the Pacific Slope. (Illus.). 11.00 (ISBN 0-8446-3031-4). Peter Smith.

--Forest Trees of the Pacific Slope. (Illus.). 1967. pap. 6.95 (ISBN 0-486-21752-3). Dover.

Sue, Derald W., jt. auth. see Schroth, Marvin L.

Sue Ann. Astrology for & About Young People. LC 80-65881. (Illus.). 177p. 1980. pap. 9.95 perfect bdg. (ISBN 0-9604172-0-6). Sue Ann.

Suelflow, August R. Religious Archives: An Introduction. LC 80-17159. (SAA Basic Archival Manual Ser.). 1980. pap. text ed. 7.00 (ISBN 0-931828-20-1). Soc Am Archivists.

Suen, James Y. & Myers, Eugene N., eds. Cancer of the Head & Neck. 900p. 1980. text ed. 89.00x (ISBN 0-443-08045-3). Churchill.

Suenaga, Masaki & Clark, Alan F., eds. Filamentary A-Fifteen Superconductors. (Cryogenic Materials Ser.). 385p. 1980. 45.00 (ISBN 0-306-40622-5). Plenum Pub.

Suenens, Leon J. A New Pentecost? 1975. 8.95 (ISBN 0-8164-0276-0). Crossroad NY.

--A New Pentecost? (Orig.). 1977. pap. 1.95 (ISBN 0-8164-2139-0). Crossroad NY.

--Ways of the Spirit. Hamilton, Elizabeth, ed. 1976. 5.95 (ISBN 0-8164-1218-9). Crossroad NY.

--Your God? 1978. pap. 4.95 (ISBN 0-8164-2192-7). Crossroad NY.

Suess, Hans E., jt. ed. see Berger, Rainer.

Suess, M. J. Examination of Water for Pollution Control: Handbook for Management & Analysts. (Illus.). 1700p. 1981. 300.00 (ISBN 0-08-025255-9). Pergamon.

Suess, Manfred E., jt. auth. see Kern, Roy F.

Suessmuth, Patrick. Ideas for Training Managers & Supervisors. LC 77-93408. 328p. 1978. pap. 17.50 (ISBN 0-88390-143-9). Univ Assocs.

Suetin, A. S. Modern Chess Opening Theory. Clarke, P. H., ed. Richards, D. J., tr. (Pergamon Chess Ser.). (Illus.). 1965. text ed. 18.00 (ISBN 0-08-011199-8); pap. text ed. 9.50 (ISBN 0-08-011198-X). Pergamon.

Suetin, Aleksei. A Contemporary Approach to the Middle Game. 1976. 18.95 (ISBN 0-7134-3123-7, Pub. by Batsford England). David & Charles.

Suetonius. Divus Julius Caesar. Butler, H. E. & Cary, M., eds. 1927. 13.95x (ISBN 0-19-814418-0). Oxford U Pr.

Sueur, Meridel Le see Le Sueur, Meridel.

Suffern, Arthur E. Coal Miners' Struggle for Industrial Status. (Brookings Institution Reprint Ser). lib. bdg. 28.50x (ISBN 0-697-00170-9); pap. 9.95x (ISBN 0-89197-703-1). Irvington.

Suffet, I. H. Fate of Pollutants in the Air & Water Environments, 2 pts. LC 76-58408. (Advances in Environmental Science & Technology). 1977. Pt. 1. 37.50 (ISBN 0-471-83539-0, Pub. by Wiley-Interscience); Pt. 2. 37.50 (ISBN 0-471-01803-1). Wiley.

Suffet, Stephen L. The Five Hundred Dollar Way to Start a U.S. Stamp Investment Program. LC 80-230. 1980. 3.50 (ISBN 0-87576-089-9). Pilot Bks.

Suffian, Tun M., et al, eds. The Constitution of Malaysia: Its Development, Nineteen Fifty-Seven to Nineteen Seventy-Seven. 1979. 29.00x (ISBN 0-19-580406-6). Oxford U Pr.

Suffling, Ernest. Church Festival Decorations. 2nd enl. ed. LC 74-6266. (Illus.). vi, 156p. 1974. Repr. of 1907 ed. 20.00 (ISBN 0-8103-4015-1). Gale.

Sufrin, Mark. Surfing: How to Improve Your Technique. LC 73-2942. (Career Concise Guides Ser.). (gr. 5 up). 1973. PLB 4.90 o.p. (ISBN 0-531-02628-0). Watts.

Sugar, A. T., tr. see Von Frisch, Karl.

Sugar, Andrew. The Complete Tent Book. 1979. 12.95 o.p. (ISBN 0-8092-7522-8); pap. 5.95 o.p. (ISBN 0-8092-7520-1). Contemp Bks.

Sugar, Bert & Grafton, John. Baseball Picture Quiz Book. (Illus.). 128p. (Orig.). 1980. pap. 5.00 (ISBN 0-486-23987-X). Dover.

Sugar, Bert, ed. Souvenir Programs of Five Great World Series. (Illus.). 1980. pap. 6.95 (ISBN 0-486-23858-X). Dover.

Sugar, Bert R. Collectibles: The Nostalgia Collectors Bible. 1981. pap. 8.95 (ISBN 0-8256-3149-1, Quick Fox). Music Sales.

--Hit the Sign & Win a Free Suit of Clothes from Harry Finklestein. 1978. 11.95 o.p. (ISBN 0-8092-7787-5). Contemp Bks.

Sugar, Burt R. The Baseball Trivia Book. LC 75-44566. Orig. Title: Who Was Harry Steinfeldt? & Other Baseball Trivia Questions. 176p. 1981. pap. 1.95 (ISBN 0-87216-824-7). Playboy Pbks.

Sugar, Max, ed. Female Adolescent Development. LC 78-31743. 1979. 22.50 (ISBN 0-87630-192-8). Brunner-Mazel.

Sugar, Peter F. Southeastern Europe Under Ottoman Rule, 1354-1804. LC 76-7799. (History of East Central Europe Ser.: Vol. 5). 384p. 1977. 18.95 (ISBN 0-295-95443-4). U of Wash Pr.

Sugar, Peter F., ed. Ethnic Diversity & Conflict in Eastern Europe. 500p. 1980. 22.50 (ISBN 0-87436-297-0). ABC-Clio.

Sugar, Robert. The Jews of Spain: Journey of Fifteen Centuries. 1973. 8.00 (ISBN 0-8074-0139-0, 561010); tchrs'. resource kit 10.00 (ISBN 0-8074-0140-4, 201010). UAHC.

Sugarman, Daniel, jt. auth. see Hopkins, Jerry.

Sugarman, Daniel A. Priceless Gifts: A Psychologist Guide to Loving & Caring. 1978. 9.95 (ISBN 0-02-615270-3). Macmillan.

Sugarman, Daniel A. & Hochstein, Rolaine. Seventeen Guide to Knowing Yourself. (gr. 7-12). 1968. 9.95 (ISBN 0-02-615300-9). Macmillan.

Sugarman, Joan G., jt. auth. see Freeman, Grace.

Sugarman, Leone K., jt. auth. see Cafferty, Kathryn W.

Sugarman, Stephen D., jt. auth. see Coons, John E.

Sugawa, Choichi & Schuman, Bernard M. Primer of Gastrointestinal Fiberoptic Endoscopy. 1981. text ed. write for info (ISBN 0-316-82150-0). Little.

Sugden, D. E. & John, B. S. Glaciers & Landscape: A Geomorphological Approach. LC 76-11014. 1976. 19.95x (ISBN 0-470-15113-7). Halsted Pr.

Sugden, Howard F. Storming the Gates of Hell. LC 76-50296. 1977. pap. 1.45 o.p. (ISBN 0-916406-63-6). Accent Bks.

Sugden, Robert & Williams, Alan. The Principles of Practical Cost-Analysis. (Illus.). 290p. 1978. text ed. 33.00x (ISBN 0-19-877040-5); pap. text ed. 14.50x (ISBN 0-19-877041-3). Oxford U Pr.

Sugerman, A. Arthur, jt. ed. see Tarter, Ralph E.

Sugerman, Danny, jt. auth. see Hopkins, Jerry.

Sugerman, Shirley, et al, eds. The Evolution of Consciousness: Studies in Polarity. LC 75-27592. (Illus.). 1976. lib. bdg. 17.50x (ISBN 0-8195-4094-3, Pub. by Wesleyan U Pr). Columbia U Pr.

Sugg, Redding S., Jr., ed. Walter Anderson's Illustrations of Epic & Voyage. LC 80-12239. (Illus.). 160p. 1980. 18.95 (ISBN 0-8093-0973-4). S Ill U Pr.

Sugg, Richard P. Appreciating Poetry. 1975. pap. text ed. 9.50 (ISBN 0-395-19375-3); instructor's manual pap. 1.50 (ISBN 0-395-19373-7). HM.

Suggitt, G., jt. auth. see McArdle, H.

Suggs, James C., ed. This We Believe. 1977. pap. 1.95 (ISBN 0-8272-3623-9). Bethany Pr.

Suggs, William W. Meet the Orchestra. (gr. 4-6). 1966. 4.95 o.s.i. (ISBN 0-02-788610-7). Macmillan.

Sugihara, Yoshie & Plath, David W. Sensei & His People: The Building of a Japanese Commune. LC 69-15427. 1969. 18.50x (ISBN 0-520-01449-9). U of Cal Pr.

Sugimura, et al. American & Japanese Coloring & Talking Books, Bk. 8. (gr. k-4). pap. 0.75 ea.; Bk. 6, Customs. o.s.i. (ISBN 0-8048-0012-X); Bk. 8, Riding. (ISBN 0-8048-0017-0); Bk. 9, Houses. o.s.i. (ISBN 0-8048-0016-2). Bk. 10, Story Book Heroes. o.s.i. (ISBN 0-8048-0019-7). C E Tuttle.

Sugimura, Takashi, ed. The Nitroquinolines. (Carcinogenesis, A Comprehensive Survey: Vol. 6). 166p. 1981. text ed. 22.00 (ISBN 0-89004-162-8). Raven.

Sugita, Hiroshi, jt. auth. see Goodenough, Ward H.

Sugita, Yutaka. The Mouse's Feast. (Illus.). (ps-6). 1980. 6.95 (ISBN 0-8120-5370-2). Barron.

Sugnet, Charles, jt. auth. see Burns, Alan.

Suh, C. H. & Radcliffe, C. W. Kinematics & Mechanisms Design. LC 77-7102. 1978. 30.95 (ISBN 0-471-01461-3). Wiley.

Suhl, Benjamin. Jean-Paul Sartre: The Philosopher As a Literary Critic. LC 71-116377. 311p. 1973. 20.00x (ISBN 0-231-03338-9); pap. 7.50x (ISBN 0-231-08319-X). Columbia U Pr.

Suhl, H., jt. ed. see Rado, George T.

Suhl, Yuri. An Album of the Jews in America. LC 72-5475. (Picture Albums Ser). (Illus.). 96p. (gr. 4 up). 1972. PLB 5.90 o.p. (ISBN 0-531-01513-0). Watts.

--On the Other Side of the Gate. LC 74-13452. 160p. (gr. 7 up). 1975. PLB 5.90 o.p. (ISBN 0-531-02792-9). Watts.

--The Purim Goat. LC 79-6551. (Illus.). 64p. (gr. 2-6). 1980. 7.95 (ISBN 0-590-07658-2, Four Winds). Schol Bk Serv.

--Simon Boom Gives a Wedding. LC 70-161015. (Illus.). 48p. (gr. k-3). 1972. 6.72 (ISBN 0-590-07209-9, Four Winds). Schol Bk Serv.

--Uncle Misha's Partisans. LC 73-76459. 224p. (gr. 5-10). 1973. 6.95 (ISBN 0-590-07295-1, Four Winds). Schol Bk Serv.

Suhr, Elmer G. The Ancient Mind & Its Heritage, 2 vols. Incl. Vol. 1. Exploring the Primitive, Egyptian & Mesopotamian Cultures. 1959. text ed. 5.00 o.p. (ISBN 0-682-40097-1); Vol. 2. Exploring the Hebrew, Hindu, Greek & Chinese Cultures. 1960. text ed. 5.00 o.p. (ISBN 0-682-40098-X). University). Exposition.

--The Mask, the Unicorn & the Messiah: A Study in Solar-Eclipse Symbolism. (Illus.). 1970. 7.95 (ISBN 0-87037-025-1). Helios.

Suhrke, Astri & Noble, Lela G. Ethnic Conflict in International Relations. LC 77-83444. (Praeger Special Studies). 1978. 24.95 (ISBN 0-03-040681-1). Praeger.

Suib, Leonard & Broadman, Muriel. Marionettes, Onstage! LC 75-6363. (Illus.). 256p. 1975. 16.95 o.s.i. (ISBN 0-06-014166-2, HarpT). Har-Row.

Suid, Murray. Demonic Mnemonics. LC 80-82982. 1981. pap. 5.50 (ISBN 0-8224-6464-0). Pitman Learning.

Suid, Murray & Morrow, James. Moviemaking Illustrated: The Comicbook Filmbook. (Illus.). (gr. 7-12). 1973. pap. text ed. 7.25 (ISBN 0-8104-5727-X). Hayden.

Suid, Murray, jt. auth. see Morrow, James.

Suinn, Richard M. Fundamentals of Behavior Pathology. 2nd ed. LC 74-30206. (Series in Psychology). 1975. text ed. 23.95x (ISBN 0-471-83547-1). Wiley.

Suiter, Patricia, jt. auth. see Mann, Philip H.

Suiter, Patricia A., jt. auth. see Mann, Philip H.

Suitor, Carol W. & Hunter, Merrily F. Nutrition: Principles & Application in Health Promotion. LC 79-22569. 468p. 1980. text ed. 18.25 (ISBN 0-397-54256-9). Lippincott.

Suits, Daniel B. The Theory & Application of Econometric Models. LC 65-6906. (Center of Economic Research Training Seminar Ser.: No. 3). (Illus.). 147p. 1963. pap. 7.50x (ISBN 0-8002-2421-3). Intl Pubns Serv.

Sujata. Beginning to See. rev., enl. ed. 1980. pap. 4.50 (ISBN 0-913300-06-3). Unity Pr.

Sukedo, Iris D. The Sociology of Racial Intergration in Guyana. 224p. 1981. 9.50 (ISBN 0-682-49686-3). Exposition.

Sukenick, Ronald. Out: A Novel. LC 72-96165. 295p. 1973. 10.95 (ISBN 0-8040-0630-X). Swallow.

--Out: A Novel. LC 72-96165. 1975. pap. 4.95 (ISBN 0-8040-0631-8). Swallow.

Sukhwal, Bheru L. South Asia: A Systematic Geographic Bibliography. LC 74-10852. 1974. 32.50 (ISBN 0-8108-0761-0). Scarecrow.

Sukus, Jan. My Toolbox Book. (Illus.). 24p. (ps-3). 1977. PLB 5.38 (ISBN 0-307-68853-4, Golden Pr). Western Pub.

--The Raggedy Ann & Andy Book. (Illus.). (ps-1). 1973. PLB 5.38 (ISBN 0-307-68942-5, Golden Pr). Western Pub.

Sukus, Jan & Dugan, William. The Shopping Book. (Illus.). (ps-1). 1972. PLB 5.38 (ISBN 0-307-68923-9, Golden Pr). Western Pub.

Sulavik, Stephen & Katz, Sol. Pleural Effusion: Some Infrequently Emphasized Causes. 104p. 1963. pap. 6.50 spiral (ISBN 0-398-01876-6). C C Thomas.

Suleiman, Ezra N., jt. ed. see Rose, Richard.

Suleiman, Ezra N., jt. ed. see Warnecke, Steven J.

Suleiman, Susan & Crosman, Inge, eds. The Reader in the Text: Essays on Audience & Interpretation. LC 79-27619. 1980. 30.00x (ISBN 0-691-06436-9); pap. 9.95 (ISBN 0-691-10096-9). Princeton U Pr.

Suleiman, Susan, tr. see Friedlander, Saul.

Sulik, Boleslaw, intro. by. Polanski: Three Films; Knife in the Water; Repulsion; Cul-De-Sac. LC 74-24656. (Icon Editions, Masterworks Film Ser). (Illus.). 216p. 1975. pap. 4.95x o.s.i. (ISBN 0-06-430062-5, IN-62, HarpT). Har-Row.

Sulimirski, T. Corded Ware & Globular Amphora North-East of the Carpathians. 1968. text ed. 41.00x (ISBN 0-485-11091-1, Athlone Pr). Humanities.

Sullivan, Alan. The Rapids. LC 74-163830. (Social History of Canada Ser.). 256p. 1972. pap. 4.50 (ISBN 0-8020-6148-6). U of Toronto Pr.

Sullivan, Arthur, jt. auth. see Gilbert, W. S.

Sullivan Assoc. Comprehension Readers, 84 bks. pap. text ed. 1.00 ea. (ISBN 0-8449-3800-9). Learning Line.

--I Can Read, 8 bks. pap. text ed. 1.75 ea. Learning Line.

--Instructional Objectives & Teacher's Guide, 1 bk. pap. text ed. 8.50 (ISBN 0-8449-2979-4). Learning Line.

--M. W. Sullivan Stories, 60 bks. pap. text ed. 1.50 ea. (ISBN 0-8449-1908-X). Learning Line.

--Reading Readiness Readers, 6 bks. pap. text ed. 1.50 ea. (ISBN 0-8449-3701-0). Learning Line.

--Reading Vocabulary, 5 bks. pap. text ed. 2.75 ea. (ISBN 0-8449-4105-0); tchr's guide for bks. 1-4 avail. Learning Line.

--Short Short Stories, 5 vols. pap. text ed. 3.75 ea. Learning Line.

--Sullivan Basal Mathematics Program, 37 bks. pap. text ed. 3.00 ea. (ISBN 0-8449-0304-3). Learning Line.

--Sullivan Fun Readers, 12 vols. 1972. pap. 3.50 ea. (ISBN 0-8449-4080-1). Learning Line.

--Sullivan Reading Plays, 1 bk. pap. text ed. 4.50 (ISBN 0-8449-4050-X). Learning Line.

--Sullivan Reading Program, 25 texts. 1980. pap. text ed. 2.50 ea. (ISBN 0-8449-1902-0); 6 tchr's manual, 6 tests avail. Learning Line.

--Sullivan Topic Readers, 20 vols. 1972. pap. 2.00 ea. (ISBN 0-8449-4201-4). Learning Line.

--Supervisor's Manual for Amanecer, 1 bk. text ed. 15.00 (ISBN 0-8449-4168-9). Learning Line.

--Teacher's Enrichment Activities Guide, 1 bk. pap. text ed. 5.00 (ISBN 0-8449-1980-2). Learning Line.

Sullivan Associates. Math Word Problems, 3 vols. (gr. 2-6). 1972. pap. text ed. 2.50 each ans. key 1, 2, 3 (ISBN 0-686-57755-8). Learning Line.

--Read & Think Storybook Series, 15 bks. Bks. 1-7. 6.56x (W); Bk. 8-15. 7.60x. tchrs. guide 9.20x (ISBN 0-686-60810-0). McGraw.

Sullivan, Barbara. A Page a Day for Lent Nineteen Eighty-One. 100p. 1981. pap. 2.50 (ISBN 0-8091-2340-1). Paulist Pr.

Sullivan, Barbara P., jt. ed. see Kellogg, Carolyn J.

Sullivan, C., jt. auth. see Perles, B.

Sullivan, Caroline. Making Soft Furnishings. LC 78-74080. (Penny Pincher Ser.). 1979. 2.95 (ISBN 0-7153-7752-3). David & Charles.

Sullivan, Charles A., et al. Federal Statutory Law of Employment Discrimination. 1000p. 1980. text ed. 45.00 (ISBN 0-672-83697-1). Bobbs.

Sullivan, Charles W., 3rd. As Tomorrow Becomes Today. 480p. 1974. pap. text ed. 8.95 (ISBN 0-13-050021-6). P-H.

Sullivan, Clara K. Tax on Value Added. LC 65-14322. 1965. 20.00x (ISBN 0-231-02807-5). Columbia U Pr.

Sullivan, Colin E., et al, eds. The Control of Breathing During Sleep. (Sleep Ser.: Vol. 3, No. 3-4). 256p. 1981. text ed. 30.00 (ISBN 0-89004-652-2). Raven.

Sullivan, Daniel J. Introduction to Philosophy. rev. ed. 1964. 7.95 (ISBN 0-02-829320-7). Macmillan.

Sullivan, David J. Practice Made Perfect: How to Design, Establish, & Maintain Your Medical Office or Diagnose & Prescribe for Your Ailing One. rev. ed. Russo, Robert, ed. LC 78-65989. (Illus.). 304p. 1979. 39.95 (ISBN 0-9605606-0-2). Medi-Pub.

Sullivan, David S. & Sattler, Martin J., eds. Change & the Future International System. 1972. 20.00 (ISBN 0-231-03565-9); pap. 5.00 (ISBN 0-231-08304-1). Columbia U Pr.

--Revolutionary War: Western Response. LC 73-171976. 1971. 20.00x (ISBN 0-231-03564-0); pap. 5.00x (ISBN 0-231-08664-4). Columbia U Pr.

Sullivan, Denis, et al. Explorations in Convention Decision Making: The Democratic Party in the 1970s. LC 76-4527. (Illus.). 1976. text ed. 14.95x (ISBN 0-7167-0488-9); pap. text ed. 7.95x (ISBN 0-7167-0487-0). W H Freeman.

Sullivan, Donald & Danforth, Brian. Bronx Art Deco Architecture: An Exposition. (Illus.). 32p. 1976. pap. 3.50 (ISBN 0-89062-024-5, Pub. by W Bronx Rest). Pub Ctr Cult Res.

Sullivan, Dorothy D. & Humphrey, James H. Teaching Reading Through Motor Learning. (Illus.). 160p. 1973. text ed. 11.75 (ISBN 0-398-02732-3). C C Thomas.

Sullivan, Dorothy D., jt. auth. see Humphrey, J. H.

Sullivan, Edith, jt. auth. see Wesley, Frank.

Sullivan, Edward D; see Mead, Robert G., Jr.

Sullivan, Eleanor, ed. Alfred Hitchcock's Tales to Fill You with Fear & Trembling. 350p. 1980. 9.95 (ISBN 0-8037-0392-9). Dial.

--Alfred Hitchcock's Tales to Make Your Hair Stand on End. 348p. 1981. 10.95 (ISBN 0-8037-0028-8). Davis Pubns.

--Alfred Hitchcock's Tales to Make Your Teeth Chatter. 348p. 1980. 9.95 (ISBN 0-8037-0173-X). Davis Pubns.

Sullivan, Eugene. Education in Social Change. 5.50x (ISBN 0-210-22206-9). Asia.

Sullivan, Eugene T. & Sullivan, Marilynn C., eds. Celebrate! No. V. LC 75-24148. 1978. 12.95 (ISBN 0-912696-14-1). Wilton.

--The Wilton Book of Classic Deserts. LC 78-140191. 1970. 10.95 (ISBN 0-912696-02-8). Wilton.

--The Wilton Book of Wedding Cakes. LC 75-175098. 1971. 10.95 (ISBN 0-912696-03-6). Wilton.

Sullivan, Eugene T., jt. ed. see Sullivan, Marilynn C.

Sullivan, F. R. Lower Tertiary Nannoplankton from the California Coast Ranges, Pt. 2: Eocene. (U. C. Publ. in Geological Sciences: Vol. 53). 1965. pap. 7.50x (ISBN 0-520-09153-1). U of Cal Pr.

Sullivan, F. Russell. Faith & Reason in Kierkegaard. LC 78-60695. 1978. pap. text ed. 7.50 (ISBN 0-8191-0559-7). U Pr of Amer.

Sullivan, George. Baseball Rules Illustrated. 96p. (Orig.). 1981. pap. 3.95 (ISBN 0-346-12524-3). Cornerstone.

--Better Baseball for Boys. rev. ed. LC 80-22022. (Better Sports Ser.). (Illus.). 64p. (gr. 5 up). 1981. PLB 6.95 (ISBN 0-396-07912-1). Dodd.

--Better Basketball for Boys. new ed. LC 80-1011. (Better Sports Ser.). (Illus.). 64p. (gr. 5 up). 1980. PLB 5.95 (ISBN 0-396-07857-5). Dodd.

--Better Basketball for Girls. LC 78-7732. (Better Sports Ser.). (Illus.). (gr. 5 up). 1978. PLB 5.95 (ISBN 0-396-07580-0). Dodd.

--Better Football for Boys. new ed. LC 80-12597. (Better Sports Ser.). (Illus.). 64p. (gr. 5 up). 1980. 5.95 (ISBN 0-396-07843-5). Dodd.

--Better Ice Skating for Boys & Girls. LC 76-12425. (Better Sports Ser.). (gr. 4-6). 1976. 5.95 (ISBN 0-396-07339-5). Dodd.

--Better Soccer for Boys & Girls. LC 77-16869. (Better Sports Ser.). (gr. 4 up). 1978. 5.95 (ISBN 0-396-07533-9). Dodd.

--Better Track for Girls. LC 80-21399. (Better Sports Ser.). (Illus.). 64p. (gr. 5 up). 1981. PLB 6.95 (ISBN 0-396-07911-3). Dodd.

--Complete Book of Autographing Collecting. LC 75-37650. (gr. 4-7). 1971. 5.95 (ISBN 0-396-06385-3). Dodd.

--Complete Guide to Softball. LC 65-14629. (Illus.). 1965. 6.95 (ISBN 0-8303-0002-3). Fleet.

--Dave Cowens: A Biography. LC 76-50795. (gr. 3-7). 1977. PLB 5.95 (ISBN 0-385-11524-5). Doubleday.

--Discover Archaelogy. LC 79-7223. (Illus.). 1980. 10.95 (ISBN 0-385-14522-5). Doubleday.

--Do-It-Yourself Moving. (Illus.). 192p. 1973. pap. 3.95 o.s.i. (ISBN 0-02-082090-9, Collier). Macmillan.

--Dollar Squeeze - & How to Beat It. LC 79-113937. 1970. 5.95 o.s.i. (ISBN 0-02-615340-8). Macmillan.

--Fell's Teen Age Guide to Skin & Scuba Diving. LC 65-18211. 1975. 8.95 (ISBN 0-8119-0261-7); pap. 4.95 (ISBN 0-8119-0370-2). Fell.

--Football. LC 72-2790. (All Star Sports Ser). (Illus.). 128p. (gr. 4 up). 1972. 5.95 o.p. (ISBN 0-695-80035-3); PLB 5.97 o.p. (ISBN 0-695-40035-5). Follett.

--The Gold Hunter's Handbook. LC 80-5718. 208p. 1981. 14.95 (ISBN 0-8128-2788-0). Stein & Day.

--Guide to Badminton. LC 67-31525. (Illus.). 1968. 6.95 (ISBN 0-8303-0003-1). Fleet.

--Home Run! LC 76-53582. (gr. 5 up). 1977. 5.95 (ISBN 0-396-07402-2). Dodd.

--Marathon: The Longest Race. LC 80-6776. (Illus.). (gr. 5-8). 1980. PLB 9.95 (ISBN 0-664-32671-4). Westminster.

--On the Run: Franco Harris. LC 76-10357. (Sports Profiles Ser.). (Illus.). 48p. (gr. 4-11). 1976. PLB 8.50 (ISBN 0-8172-0138-6). Raintree Pubs.

--The Picture History of the Boston Celtics. LC 80-689. 256p. 1981. 19.95 (ISBN 0-672-52654-9). Bobbs.

--Plants to Grow Indoors. (Beginning-to-Read Bks). (Illus.). (ps). pap. 1.50 o.p. (ISBN 0-695-37114-2). Follett.

--Pro Football A to Z. LC 75-43128. 1976. pap. 4.50 o.p. (ISBN 0-684-14641-X, SL652, ScribT). Scribner.

--Run, Run Fast. LC 78-22502. (Illus.). 64p. (gr. 4 up). 1980. 8.95 (ISBN 0-690-03969-7, TYC-J); PLB 8.79 (ISBN 0-690-03970-0). T Y Crowell.

--Supertanker. LC 77-16870. (gr. 7 up). 1978. 6.95 (ISBN 0-396-07527-4). Dodd.

--Tennis Rules Illustrated. 96p. (Orig.). 1981. pap. 3.95 (ISBN 0-346-12525-1). Cornerstone.

--This Is Pro Basketball. LC 77-6497. (Illus.). (gr. 5 up). 1977. 6.50 (ISBN 0-396-07455-3). Dodd.

--This Is Pro Hockey. LC 75-38369. (Illus.). 128p. 1976. 5.95 (ISBN 0-396-07318-2). Dodd.

--This Is Pro Soccer. LC 78-10729. (Illus.). 1979. 6.95 (ISBN 0-396-07643-2). Dodd.

--Winning Plays in Pro Football. LC 75-6821. (Illus.). 128p. (gr. 5 up). 1975. PLB 4.95 (ISBN 0-396-07148-1). Dodd.

Sullivan, George, jt. auth. see Player, Gary.

Sullivan, George, ed. Discover Archaeology. 288p. 1981. pap. 4.95 (ISBN 0-14-046491-3). Penguin.

--A Reason to Read. 120p. 1976. pap. 3.00 (ISBN 0-89492-000-6). Interbk Inc.

Sullivan, George E. & Cox, Warren. Building Basic Sentences. West, K., et al, eds. (Writing Skills for Daily Living Ser.). (Illus.). 40p. (gr. 7-12). 1979. pap. text ed. 3.95x (ISBN 0-87453-097-0, 82097). Denoyer.

--Combining Sentences. West, K. & Johnston, D., eds. (Writing Skills for Daily Living Ser.). (Illus.). 40p. (gr. 7-12). 1979. pap. text ed. 3.95x (ISBN 0-87453-098-9). Denoyer.

--Using Parts of Speech. West, K. & Johnston, D., eds. (Writing Skills for Daily Living Ser.). (Illus.). 32p. (gr. 7-12). 1979. pap. text ed. 3.95x (ISBN 0-87453-096-2, 82096). Denoyer.

--Writing on Your Own. West, K. & Johnston, D., eds. (Writing Skills for Daily Living Ser.). (Illus.). 32p. (gr. 7-12). 1979. pap. text ed. 3.95x (ISBN 0-87453-099-7, 82099). Denoyer.

Sullivan, Gertrude A. Teacher As Gift. 64p. 1979. wire coil bdg. 4.95 (ISBN 0-697-01729-X). Wm C Brown.

Sullivan, Harold W. Contempts by Publication: The Law of Trial by Newspaper. xiv, 230p. 1980. Repr. of 1941 ed. lib. bdg. 24.00x (ISBN 0-8377-1114-2). Rothman.

Sullivan, Harry R. Walter Bagehot. LC 74-32309. (English Authors Ser.: No. 182). 1975. lib. bdg. 12.50 (ISBN 0-8057-1018-3). Twayne.

Sullivan, Harry S. Conceptions of Modern Psychiatry. 1953. 8.50x (ISBN 0-393-01050-3, Norton Lib); pap. 4.95 (ISBN 0-393-00740-5, Norton Lib). Norton.

--Schizophrenia As a Human Process. 400p. 1974. pap. 6.95 (ISBN 0-393-00721-9, Norton Lib). Norton.

Sullivan, Henry W. Juan Del Encina. LC 76-16068. (World Authors Ser.: Spain: No. 399). 1976. lib. bdg. 12.50 (ISBN 0-8057-6166-7). Twayne.

--Tirso De Molina & the Drama of the Counter Reformation. 1976. pap. text ed. 25.75x (ISBN 90-6203-399-7). Humanities.

Sullivan, J. P. Propertius: A Critical Introduction. LC 75-10038. 224p. 1976. 23.95 (ISBN 0-521-20904-8). Cambridge U Pr.

Sullivan, Jack. Elegant Nightmares: The English Ghost Story from le Fanu to Blackwood. LC 77-92258. 155p. 1980. pap. 4.95 (ISBN 0-8214-0569-1, 0569E). Ohio U Pr.

Sullivan, James. Fluid Power: Theory & Applications. (Illus.). 480p. 1975. 18.95 (ISBN 0-87909-272-6); instrs'. manual avail. Reston.

Sullivan, James A. Fundamentals of Fluid Mechanics. (Illus.). 1978. ref. ed. 17.95 (ISBN 0-8359-2999-X); students manual avail. Reston.

--Plumbing: Installation & Design. (Illus.). 480p. 1980. text ed. 17.95 (ISBN 0-8359-5552-4); instr's manual avail. Reston.

Sullivan, Jeremiah J. & Heggelund, Per O. Foreign Investment in the U. S. Fishing Industry. LC 79-2074. (Pacific Rim Research Ser.: No. 3). 208p. 1979. 21.95 (ISBN 0-669-03066-X). Lexington Bks.

Sullivan, Jerry, jt. auth. see Daniel, Glenda.

Sullivan, John. Letters & Papers of Major-General John Sullivan, Continental Army, Vol.3,1779-1795. Hammond, Otis G., ed. LC 32-27568. (Illus.). 677p. 1939. 17.50x (ISBN 0-915916-01-0). U Pr of New Eng.

Sullivan, John, jt. auth. see Rajhans, Gyan S.

Sullivan, John, ed. Spiritual Direction. LC 80-26654. (Carmelite Studies: No. I). 240p. (Orig.). 1980. pap. 6.95x (ISBN 0-9600876-8-0). ICS Pubns.

Sullivan, John, et al. The Funny Side of Football. (Illus.). 92p. (Orig.). 1980. pap. 3.95 (ISBN 0-89260-141-8). Hwong Pub.

Sullivan, John E. Ideas of Religion: A Prolegomenon to the Philosophy of Religion. LC 79-66230. 1979. pap. text ed. 9.50 (ISBN 0-8191-0808-1). U Pr of Amer.

Sullivan, John J. The Monkey & the Pumpkin. 1978. 4.50 o.p. (ISBN 0-533-03077-3). Vantage.

Sullivan, John L. & Feldman, Stanley. Multiple Indicators: An Introduction. LC 79-67015. (Quantitative Applications in the Social Sciences (a Sage University Paper Ser.): No. 15). (Illus.). 1979. pap. 3.50x (ISBN 0-8039-1369-9). Sage.

Sullivan, John M., ed. see Special Learning Corporation.

Sullivan, Judith, et al. Community Health Nursing. (Illus.). 384p. 1981. text ed. 15.00 (ISBN 0-86542-004-1). Blackwell Sci.

Sullivan, Kathryn, tr. see Gheddo, Pierro.

Sullivan, Kevin. Oscar Wilde. LC 73-186638. (Columbia Essays on Modern Writers Ser.: No. 64). 1972. pap. 2.00 (ISBN 0-231-03068-1, MW64). Columbia U Pr.

Sullivan, L. M. see La Tempa, Susan.

Sullivan, Linda, ed. Encyclopedia of Governmental Advisory Organizations. 3rd ed. 800p. 1981. 175.00 (ISBN 0-8103-0253-5). Gale.

Sullivan, Linda E. & Kruzas, Anthony T. Encyclopedia of Governmental Advisory Organizations: A Reference Guide to Presidential Advisory Committees, Public Advisory Committees, Interagency Committees & Other Government-Related Boards, Panels, Task Forces, Commissions, Conferences, & Other Similar Bodies Serving in a Consultative, Coordinating, Advisory, Research, or Investigative Capacity. 2nd ed. LC 75-15619. 400p. 1975. 110.00 o.p. (ISBN 0-8103-0251-9); New Governmental Advisory Organizations: Periodical Supplement (inter-ed sub.) 95.00 o.p. (ISBN 0-8103-0252-7). Gale.

Sullivan, Louis. A System of Architectural Ornament. LC 67-17016. 1967. 10.95x o.s.i. (ISBN 0-87130-018-4). Eakins.

Sullivan, M. W. A Linguistic Grammar of English. (gr. 10-12). 1972. pap. text ed. 5.00 (ISBN 0-8449-2720-1). Learning Line.

--Modern Spanish A & B, 7 bks. (gr. 8-12). 1968. pap. text ed. 7.00 each (ISBN 0-686-57758-2). Learning Line.

--Modern Spanish C, 5 vols. (gr. 8-12). 1972. pap. text ed. 6.00 each (ISBN 0-686-57759-0). Learning Line.

--Modern Spanish D, 3 bks. (gr. 8-12). 1972. pap. text ed. 6.00 each (ISBN 0-686-57760-4). Learning Line.

--A Programmed Introduction to the Game of Chess. 1972. text ed. 12.50 (ISBN 0-8449-1800-8). Learning Line.

Sullivan, Margaret P., jt. ed. see Van Eys, Jan.

Sullivan, Marianna P. France's Vietnam Policy: A Study in French-American Relations. LC 77-94749. (Contributions in Political Science: No. 12). 1978. lib. bdg. 17.50 (ISBN 0-313-20317-2, SUV/). Greenwood.

Sullivan, Marilynn C. & Sullivan, Eugene T., eds. Celebrate! No. VI. LC 75-24148. 160p. 1980. 12.95 (ISBN 0-912696-17-6). Wilton.

Sullivan, Marilynn C., jt. ed. see Sullivan, Eugene T.

Sullivan, Mark. Our Times, 6 vols. LC 70-138308. 1926. Set. 115.00 o.s.i. (ISBN 0-684-13861-1, ScribR); 23.62 ea. o.s.i. Scribner.

Sullivan, Mary Beth & Bourke, Linda. A Show of Hands: Say It in Sign Language. LC 80-15997. (Illus.). 96p. (gr. 4-8). 1980. PLB 6.95 (ISBN 0-201-07456-7, 7456, A-W Childrens). A-W.

Sullivan, Mary W. Bluegrass Iggy. LC 75-15912. 150p. (YA) (gr. 5 up). 1975. 6.95 o.p. (ISBN 0-525-66475-0). Elsevier-Nelson.

--The VW Connection. 128p. (gr. 5 up). 1981. 8.95 (ISBN 0-525-66701-6). Elsevier-Nelson.

Sullivan, Matthew B. Thresholds of Peace: German Prisoners & the People of Britain: 1944-1948. (Illus.). 1979. 30.00 (ISBN 0-241-89862-5, Pub. by Hamish Hamilton England). David & Charles.

Sullivan, Maurice, ed. see Heckmann, Manfred.

Sullivan, Maurice T., ed. see Kaufman, William I.

Sullivan, Michael. The Arts of China. rev. ed. LC 76-44639. (Cal Ser.: No. 350). (Illus.). 1978. 20.00 o.p. (ISBN 0-520-03366-3); pap. 9.95 (ISBN 0-520-03367-1). U of Cal Pr.

--The Cave Temples of Maichishan. LC 69-15829. (Illus.). 1969. 46.50x (ISBN 0-520-01448-0). U of Cal Pr.

--Chinese Landscape Painting in the Sui & T'ang Dynasties. (Illus.). 1980. 38.50 (ISBN 0-520-03558-5). U of Cal Pr.

--The Three Perfections: Chinese Painting, Poetry & Calligraphy. LC 80-18189. (Illus.). 64p. 10.00 (ISBN 0-8076-0996-X); pap. 4.95 (ISBN 0-8076-0997-8). Braziller.

Sullivan, Michael, jt. auth. see Mizrahi, Abe.

Sullivan, Michael P. International Relations: Theories & Evidence. (Illus.). 400p. 1976. 18.95 (ISBN 0-13-473470-X). P-H.

Sullivan, Neil V. & Stewart, Evelyn S. Now is the Time: Integration in the Berkeley Schools. LC 73-85102. 224p. 1970. 10.00x (ISBN 0-253-15841-9). Ind U Pr.

Sullivan, Neil V., et al. Walk, Run, or Retreat: The Modern School Administrator. LC 71-135013. 192p. 1971. 8.95x (ISBN 0-253-36305-5). Ind U Pr.

Sullivan, Nelson G., jt. auth. see Copeland, Benny R.

Sullivan, Nora. Dinosaurs. (Easy-Read Fact Book Ser.). (Illus.). 48p. (gr. 2-4). 1976. PLB 6.45 (ISBN 0-531-00365-5). Watts.

Sullivan, Patricia, et al. Manual of Therapeutic Exercise. 1981. text ed. 15.95 (ISBN 0-8359-4245-7). Reston.

Sullivan, Patricia T. Five Little Angels. (Illus.). 50p. 1980. pap. 1.95 (ISBN 0-933402-16-3). Charisma Pr.

Sullivan, Richard F., ed. Upgrading Coal Liquids. (ACS Symposium Ser.: No. 156). 1981. price not set (ISBN 0-8412-0629-5). Am Chemical.

Sullivan, Robert J., jt. auth. see Wright, Marion I.

Sullivan, Roger. Handbook for Data Processing Educators. Kerr, Edwin F., ed. (Illus.). 191p. (Orig.). 1979. pap. 18.00 (ISBN 0-89435-038-2). QED Info Sci.

Sullivan, Roger J. Morality & the Good Life: A Commentary on Aristotle's "Nicomachean Ethics". LC 77-13485. 222p. 1980. pap. text ed. 5.95x (ISBN 0-87870-111-7). Memphis St Univ.

Sullivan, Shaun J. Killing in Defense of Private Property: The Development of a Roman Catholic Moral Teaching, Thirteenth to Eighteenth Centuries. LC 75-38843. (American Academy of Religion. Dissertation Ser.). (Illus.). 1976. pap. 7.50 (ISBN 0-89130-067-8, 010115). Scholars Pr Ca.

Sullivan, Sheila. The Calling of Bara. 304p. 1981. pap. 2.50 (ISBN 0-380-53785-0, 53785). Avon.

Sullivan, Teddy. Good Morning Please. 1981. 11.95 (ISBN 0-87460-354-4); pap. 5.95. Lion.

Sullivan, Teresa A. Marginal Workers, Marginal Jobs: The Underutilization of American Workers. (Illus.). 1978. 17.95x o.p. (ISBN 0-292-75038-2). U of Tex Pr.

Sullivan, Thomas F., ed. Resource Conservation & Recovery Act: A Compliance Analysis. LC 78-78342. 162p. 1978. pap. text ed. 22.50 (ISBN 0-86587-077-2). Gov Insts.

Sullivan, Thomas F. & Heavner, Martin L., eds. Energy Reference Handbook. 3rd ed. LC 80-84728. 400p. 1981. 28.50 (ISBN 0-86587-082-9). Gov Insts.

Sullivan, Tom & Gill, Derek. Adventures in Darkness. (Illus.). 160p. (RL 5). Date not set. pap. 1.95 o.p. (ISBN 0-686-68444-3, J9376-3, Sig). NAL.

Sullivan, Vincent see O'Sullivan, Vincent.

Sullivan, William F & Claycombe, W. Wayne. Fundamentals of Forecasting. (Illus.). 1977. ref. ed. 18.95 (ISBN 0-87909-300-5). Reston.

Sullivan, William G., jt. auth. see Claycombe, William W.

Sullivan, William M., jt. ed. see Rabinow, Paul.

Sullivan & Sullivan. Programmed Astronomy: The Night Sky. 1972. pap. text ed. 9.00 incl. tchrs' manual & test (ISBN 0-8449-0504-6). Learning Line.

--Programmed Astronomy: The Solar System. 1972. pap. text ed. 9.00 incl. tchrs' manual & test (ISBN 0-8449-0500-3). Learning Line.

Sulloway, Alison G. Gerard Manley Hopkins & the Victorian Temper. 300p. 1972. 17.50x (ISBN 0-231-03645-0). Columbia U Pr.

Sulloway, Frank J. Freud, Biologist of the Mind: Beyond the Psychoanalytic Legend. 20.00 (ISBN 0-686-68084-7). Basic.

Sullwold, Stephen W., ed. see Rex, Percy F.

Sully, F. K. Motor Vehicle Mechanics Textbook. 4th ed. (Illus.). 1979. text ed. 13.95 (ISBN 0-408-00428-2). Butterworths.

Sully, G. Barry. Aerial Photo Interpretation. 1971. pap. text ed. 10.95x (ISBN 0-435-34865-5). Heinemann Ed.

Sully, James. Studies in Childhood. (Contributions to the History of Psycholgy Ser.: Psychometrics & Educational Psychology). 1978. Repr. of 1978 ed. 30.00 (ISBN 0-89093-162-3). U Pubns Amer.

Sulnick, Robert H. Civil Litigation & the Police: A Method of Communication. 168p. 1976. 14.75 (ISBN 0-398-03494-X). C C Thomas.

Suls, Jerry & Miller, Richard L. Social Comparison Processes: Theoretical & Empirical Perspectives. LC 77-8572. (Illus.). 1977. text ed. 23.50 (ISBN 0-470-99174-7). Halsted Pr.

Sultan, Gary, jt. auth. see Vogt, Douglas.

Sultan, Stanley. Ulysses, The Waste Land, & Modernism. (Literary Criticism Ser). 1977. 8.95 (ISBN 0-8046-9144-4, Natl U). Kennikat.

--Yeats at His Last. (New Yeats Papers Ser.: No. 11). 48p. 1975. pap. text ed. 5.00x (ISBN 0-85105-271-1, Dolmen Pr). Humanities.

Sultan, William J. Modern Pastry Chef: Cakes, Pies & Other Baked Goods, Vol. 1. (Illus.). 1977. lib. bdg. 32.50 (ISBN 0-87055-225-2); pap. text ed. 21.50 (ISBN 0-87055-310-0). AVI.

--Modern Pastry Chef: French Pastries, Cookies, Molded and Frozen Desserts, Vol. 2. (Illus.). 1977. lib. bdg. 32.50 (ISBN 0-87055-226-0); pap. text ed. 21.50 (ISBN 0-87055-311-9). AVI.

--Practical Baking. 3rd ed. (Illus.). 1976. text ed. 19.50 (ISBN 0-87055-214-7). AVI.

--Practical Baking Manual. (Illus.). 1976. pap. text ed. 10.50 (ISBN 0-87055-213-9). AVI.

Sultan, William J., jt. auth. see Fabbricante, Thomas.

Sultan, William J., jt. auth. see Tressler, Donald K.

Sultana, Donald. Benjamin Disraeli in Spain & Malta. (Salzburg Studies in English Literature, Romantic Reassessment Ser.: No. 51). (Illus.). 102p. 1975. pap. text ed. 25.00x (ISBN 0-391-01541-9). Humanities.

Sultana, Donald, ed. New Approaches to Coleridge: Biographical & Critical Essays. (Critical Studies Ser.). 256p. 1981. 28.50x (ISBN 0-389-20060-3). B&N.

Sultana, Donald E. Seige of Malta Rediscovered. 1977. 17.50x (ISBN 0-7073-0131-9, Pub. by Scottish Academic Pr Scotland). Columbia U Pr.

Sultz, Harry A., et al. Nurse Practitioners: USA. LC 78-19728. 1979. 25.95 (ISBN 0-669-02727-8). Lexington Bks.

Sultzkin, A. E., ed. see Paushkin, Ya. M., et al.

Sulvetta, Margaret B. An Analyst's Guide to TRIM: The Transfer Income Model. (An Institute Paper). 104p. 1976. pap. 4.50 (ISBN 0-87766-182-0, 16500). Urban Inst.

--The Impact of Welfare Reform on Benefits for the Poor: A Comparison of Eligibility Requirements & Benefit Levels Under the Proposed "Program for Better Jobs & Income" & the Current System. (Welfare Reform Policy Analysis Ser.: No. 3). 52p. 1978. pap. 3.50 (ISBN 0-87766-218-5, 21700). Urban Inst.

Sulz, Harry. Grantwriting for Health Professionals. 1981. pap. price not set (ISBN 0-316-82196-9). Little.

Sulzberger, C. L. The American Heritage Picture History of World War II. McCullough, David G., ed. LC 66-24214. (Illus.). 640p. 1966. Set. 20.00 (ISBN 0-8281-0331-3, B011R). Am Heritage.

--The Coldest War: The Russian Game in China. LC 74-1466. 1974. 5.95 o.p. (ISBN 0-15-118979-X). HarBraceJ.

--Postscript with a Chinese Accent: Memoirs & Diaries, 1972-73. LC 74-10507. (Illus.). 400p. 1974. 10.00 o.s.i. (ISBN 0-02-615320-3, 61532). Macmillan.

Sulzberger, Jean. Search: Journey on the Inner Path. LC 78-4430. 1979. 10.00 o.p. (ISBN 0-685-66357-4, HarpR); pap. 5.95 (ISBN 0-06-067765-1, RD 271, HarpR). Har-Row.

Sumanpouw, Mathilde. Les Nouvelles Conventions De la Haye: Leur Application Par les Juges Nationaux, Vol. II. 260p. (Fr.). 1980. 45.00x (ISBN 90-286-0870-2). Sijthoff & Noordhoff.

Sumberg, Theodore A. Foreign Aid As a Moral Obligation? LC 73-86711. (The Washington Papers: No. 10). 1973. 3.50x (ISBN 0-8039-0283-2). Sage.

Sumer, Faruk, et al, trs. from Turkish. The Book of Dede Korkut: A Turkish Epic. LC 72-3214. (Illus.). 236p. 1972. 12.00 (ISBN 0-292-71501-3). U of Tex Pr.

Sumera, Annabelle. What Lily Goose Found. (Young Reader Ser.). (Illus.). (gr. k-3). 1979. PLB 5.00 (ISBN 0-307-60163-3, Golden Pr). Western Pub.

Sumich, James L. & Dudley, Gordon H. Laboratory & Field Investigations in Marine Biology. 1980. pap. write for info. (ISBN 0-697-04594-3). Wm C Brown.

Sumichrast, Michael & Shafer, Ronald G. The Complete Book of Home Buying: A Consumer's Guide to Housing in the 80's. rev. ed. LC 80-11100. 366p. 1980. 14.95 (ISBN 0-87128-589-4). Dow Jones-Irwin.

Sumler, David E. A History of Europe in the Twentieth Century. 1973. pap. text ed. 12.50x (ISBN 0-256-01421-3). Dorsey.

Summer, Charles E., Jr., et al. The Managerial Mind: Science & Theory in Policy Decisions. 4th ed. 1977. text ed. 20.50x (ISBN 0-256-01922-3). Irwin.

Summer, Rosemary. Thomas Hardy, Psychologist Novelist. 19.95 (ISBN 0-312-80161-0). St Martin.

Summer Workshop on Invariant Imbedding - University of Southern California - Jun-Aug, 1970. Proceedings. LC 79-170660. (Lecture Notes in Operations Research & Mathematical Systems: Vol. 52). (Illus.). 1971. pap. 10.70 o.p. (ISBN 0-387-05549-5). Springer-Verlag.

Summerall, C. P., 3rd, et al. Monitoring Heart Rhythm. 1976. 14.50 (ISBN 0-471-83556-0). Wiley.

Summerfield, Geoffrey, ed. see Clare, John.

Summerfield, Geoffrey, jt. ed. see Smith, Peter.

Summerfield, Harry L. Power & Process. LC 73-17614. 1974. 16.25x o.p. (ISBN 0-8211-1826-9); text ed. 12.40x o.p. (ISBN 0-685-42642-4). McCutchan.

Summerfield, Henry, ed. A. E. S. Contributions to the Irish Statesman. (Collected Edition of the Writings of G. W. Russell II). 1979. text ed. 52.00x (ISBN 0-391-01121-9). Humanities.

Summerfield, R. J. & Bunting, A. H., eds. Advances in Legume Science. (Illus.). xvi, 667p. 1980. pap. 38.50x (ISBN 0-85521-223-3, Pub by Brit Mus Nat Hist England). Sabbot-Natural Hist Bks.

Summerhays, R. S. The Problem Horse. (Illus.). pap. 6.10 (ISBN 0-85131-225-X, Dist. by Sporting Book Center). J A Allen.

Summerhays, R. S. & Walker, Stella A. The Controversial Horse. (Illus.). 8.75 (ISBN 0-85131-075-3, Dist. by Sporting Book Center). J A Allen.

Summerhays, Reginald S. Problem Horses - Tested Guide for Curing Most Common & Serious Horse Behavior Habits. pap. 3.00 (ISBN 0-87980-200-6). Wilshire.

Summerlin, Lee R. Chemistry for the Life Sciences. Incl. P. S. Associates. wkbk. 6.95 (ISBN 0-394-32457-9); Hendrickson, William & Healy, Juanita. lab manual 6.95 (ISBN 0-394-32520-6). 631p. 1981. text ed. 19.95 (ISBN 0-394-32215-0). Random.

Summerlin, Sam. Latin America. LC 72-4254. (Associated Press Bks). (Illus.). 192p. (gr. 7-12). 1972. PLB 5.95 o.p. (ISBN 0-531-02576-4). Watts.

Summers, Andrew, ed. Me the Flunkie. 1974. pap. 1.25 o.p. (ISBN 0-449-30649-6, P649, Prem). Fawcett.

Summers, Anthony. Conspiracy. (Illus.). 656p. 1981. pap. 8.95 (ISBN 0-07-062400-3). McGraw.

Summers, Anthony & Mangold, Tom. The File on the Tsar. 1978. pap. 2.50 (ISBN 0-515-04508-X). Jove Pubns.

Summers, Anthony J. Metamorphosis. 1979. 2.75 (ISBN 0-918476-06-2). Cornerstone Pr.

Summers, Bob. Jesus Christ University. 1973. pap. 1.95 o.p. (ISBN 0-88270-051-0). Logos.

Summers, Bob, jt. auth. see Evans, Mike.

Summers, Claude J. Christopher Isherwood. LC 80-5335. (Modern Literature Ser.). 192p. 1980. 10.95 (ISBN 0-8044-2846-8). Ungar.

--Christopher Marlowe & the Politics of Power. (Salzburg Studies in English Literature, Elizabethan & Renaissance Studies: No. 22). 208p. 1974. pap. text ed. 25.00x (ISBN 0-391-01542-7). Humanities.

Summers, Claude J. & Pebworth, Ted-Larry. Ben Jonson. (English Authors Ser.: No. 268). 1979. 12.50 (ISBN 0-8057-6764-9). Twayne.

Summers, Claude J. & Pebworth, Ted-Larry, eds. Too Rich to Clothe the Sunne: Essays on George Herbert. LC 80-5255. (Illus.). 0278p. 1980. 16.95x (ISBN 0-8229-3421-3). U of Pittsburgh Pr.

Summers, David. Johnnie: The Barefoot Dreamer. 1974. 1.50 (ISBN 0-88243-535-3, 02 0535). Gospel Pub.

--Michelangelo & the Language of Art. LC 80-7556. (Illus.). 532p. 1981. 47.50x (ISBN 0-691-03957-7); pap. 16.50 (ISBN 0-691-10097-7). Princeton U Pr.

--The Sculpture of Vincenzo Danti. LC 77-94718. (Outstanding Dissertations in the Fine Arts Ser.). (Illus.). 641p. 1980. lib. bdg. 60.50 (ISBN 0-8240-3252-7). Garland Pub.

Summers, David, jt. ed. see Rappoport, Leon.

Summers, Dorothy. East Coast Floods. LC 78-62498. (Illus.). 1978. 16.95 (ISBN 0-7153-7456-7). David & Charles.

Summers, Edward L. An Introduction to Accounting for Decision Making & Control. 1974. text ed. 16.50x o.p. (ISBN 0-256-01499-X). Irwin.

Summers, Festus P. & Ambler, C. H. West Virginia: The Mountain State. 2nd ed. 1958. text ed. 19.95 (ISBN 0-13-951699-9). P-H.

Summers, Francis M., jt. ed. see Calkins, Gary N.

Summers, Gene F. & Selvik, Arne, eds. Nonmetropolitan Industrial Growth & Community Change. LC 78-22652. (Illus.). 1979. 23.95 (ISBN 0-669-02820-7). Lexington Bks.

Summers, Gene F., et al, eds. Industrial Invasion of NonMetropolitan America: A Quarter Century of Experience. LC 75-25026. (Special Studies). 1976. text ed. 26.50 (ISBN 0-275-56080-5). Praeger.

Summers, George J. Mind Teasers: Logic Puzzles & Games of Deduction. LC 77-79511. (Illus.). (gr. 6 up). 1977. 6.95 (ISBN 0-8069-4566-4); PLB 6.69 (ISBN 0-8069-4567-2). Sterling.

Summers, George W. & Peters, William S. Basic Statistics: An Introduction. 1977. text ed. 18.95x (ISBN 0-534-00471-7); wkbk. 8.95x (ISBN 0-534-00498-9). Wadsworth Pub.

--Basic Statistics in Business & Economics. 2nd ed. 1977. 20.95x (ISBN 0-534-00479-2); wkbk 9.95x (ISBN 0-534-00512-8). Wadsworth Pub.

Summers, Georgianna. Star Visit: A Play for Christmas. 8p. (Orig.). 1980. pap. text ed. 2.30 (ISBN 0-89536-424-7). CSS Pub.

Summers, Ian. The Art of the Brothers Hildebrandt. (Illus.). 1979. 8.95 (ISBN 0-345-27396-6); pap. 15.00 (ISBN 0-345-27830-5). Ballantine.

Summers, Ian & Kagan, Dan. Cattle Mutilations. 288p. (Orig.). 1981. pap. 2.95. Bantam.

Summers, Ian, ed. Tomorrow & Beyond. LC 78-7119. (Illus.). 1978. 19.95 (ISBN 0-89480-062-0, 1996); pap. 10.95 (ISBN 0-89480-055-8, 1988). Workman Pub.

--The Yearbook Book. 160p. (Orig.). 1975. pap. 5.95 o.p. (ISBN 0-345-24732-9). Ballantine.

Summers, Jack L. & Chartrand, Rene. Military Uniforms in Canada. (Illus.). 220p. 1981. 35.00 (ISBN 0-660-10346-X, 56434-7, Pub. by Natl Mus Canada). U of Chicago Pr.

Summers, JoAn. Fruitbasket Friends. LC 75-7481. (gr. 4-8). 1975. pap. 3.50 o.p. (ISBN 0-88270-121-5). Logos.

Summers, Joseph H., ed. Lyric & Dramatic Milton: Selected Papers from the English Institute. LC 65-22231. 1965. 12.50x (ISBN 0-231-02863-6). Columbia U Pr.

Summers, June N. Good Morning, Tecate. (Illus.). 62p. (Orig.). 1972. pap. text ed. 4.00 (ISBN 0-686-28871-8). J N Summers.

Summers, Laura, tr. see Samphan, Khieu.

Summers, Max, et al, eds. Baculoviruses for Insect Pest Control: Safety Considerations. LC 75-36871. 1975. 9.00 (ISBN 0-914826-07-7). Am Soc Microbio.

Summers, Montague. History of Witchcraft & Demonology. (Illus.). 370p. 1973. 28.00 (ISBN 0-7100-4970-6); pap. 12.50 (ISBN 0-7100-7613-4). Routledge & Kegan.

--Witchcraft & Black Magic. LC 70-174114. (Illus.). 1971. Repr. of 1916 ed. 22.00 (ISBN 0-685-02995-6). Gale.

Summers, Rachel. Mommy's Gone. 1976. pap. 1.25 o.p. (ISBN 0-685-69144-6, LB359ZK, Leisure Bks). Nordon Pubns.

Summers, Robert. Seeds in the Passes: Special Issue 25 - The Smith. pap. 1.00 o.p. (ISBN 0-685-78411-8). The Smith.

Summers, Robert S. & Howard, C. Law, Its Nature, Functions & Limits. 2nd ed. (Illus.). 1024p. 1972. text ed. 21.95 (ISBN 0-13-526400-6). P-H.

Summers, Robert S., jt. auth. see White, James J.

Summers, Robert S., ed. Essays in Legal Philosophy. (Library Reprint Ser.). 1976. 18.50x (ISBN 0-520-03213-6). U of Cal Pr.

--More Essays in Legal Philosophy: General Assessment of Legal Philosophies. 1971. 14.50x (ISBN 0-520-01971-7). U of Cal Pr.

Summers, Thomas O. Joseph Brown: Or, the Young Tennessean Whose Life Was Saved by the Power of Prayer. an Indian Tale. Bd. with Narrative of a Captivity Among the Mohawk Indians, & a Description of New Netherland in 1642-3. Jogues, Isaac. LC 75-7091. (Indian Captivities Ser.: Vol. 67). Repr. of 1856 ed. lib. bdg. 44.00 (ISBN 0-8240-1691-2). Garland Pub.

Summerson, John. The Architecture of Victorian London. LC 75-16130. (Illus.). 1976. 10.95x (ISBN 0-8139-0592-3). U Pr of Va.

--The Life & Work of John Nash, Architect. (Illus.). 288p. 1980. text ed. 35.00x (ISBN 0-262-19190-3). MIT Pr.

--Victorian Architecture: Four Studies in Evaluation. LC 74-89565. (Bampton Lectures in America Ser.: No. 19). 1969. 20.00 (ISBN 0-231-03261-7). Columbia U Pr.

Summerton, Margaret. A Dark & Secret Place. 1978. pap. 1.75 (ISBN 0-380-41301-9, 41301). Avon.

Summitt, Robert & Sliker, Alan. Wood. (CRC Handbook of Materials Science: Vol. IV). 464p. 1980. 59.95 (ISBN 0-8493-0234-X). CRC Pr.

Summitt, Robert L., ed. see Birth Defects Annual Conference, 10th Memphis, Tenn., June, 1977.

Sumner, Austin J. The Physiology of Peripheral Nerve Disease. (Illus.). 544p. 1980. text ed. 35.00 (ISBN 0-7216-8639-7). Saunders.

Sumner, Graham N. Mathematics for Physical Geographers. LC 78-12156. 1979. 17.95x (ISBN 0-470-26557-4). Halsted Pr.

Sumner, L. E., ed. Business Who's Who of Australia, 1980. 14th ed. LC 64-56752. 805p. 1980. write for info (ISBN 0-8002-2741-7). Intl Pubns Serv.

Sumner, L. W. Abortion & Moral Theory. LC 80-8578. 264p. 1981. 16.50x (ISBN 0-691-07262-0); pap. 4.95x (ISBN 0-691-02017-5). Princeton U Pr.

Sumner, L. W., et al, eds. Pragmatism & Purpose: Essays Presented to T. A. Goudge. 376p. 1981. 25.00x (ISBN 0-8020-5481-1). U of Toronto Pr.

Sumner, Lowell, jt. ed. see Monson, Gale.

Sumner, Margaret. Thought for Food. (Illus.). 129p. 1981. text ed. 13.95x (ISBN 0-19-217690-0); pap. text ed. 6.95 (ISBN 0-19-286003-8). Oxford U Pr.

Sumner, Michael. The Dollars & Sense of Hospital Malpractice Insurance. LC 78-67846. 1979. text ed. 22.50 (ISBN 0-89011-517-6). Abt Assoc.

Sumner, Michael T., jt. ed. see Parkin, Michael.

Sumner, R. & Bradley, K. Assessment for Transition: A Study of New Procedure. (Illus.). 1977. pap. text ed. 9.75 (ISBN 0-85633-132-5, NFER). Humanities.

Sumner, R. & Robertson, T. S. Criterion-Referenced Measurement & Criterion-Referenced Tests: Some Published Work Reviewed. (General Ser.). 1977. pap. text ed. 15.75x (ISBN 0-85633-116-3, NFER). Humanities.

Sumner, R. & Warburton, F. W. Achievement in Secondary School: Attitudes, Personality & School Success. (General Ser.). 208p. (Orig.). 1972. pap. text ed. 17.50x (ISBN 0-901225-76-2, NFER). Humanities.

Sumner, R., jt. auth. see Kyles, I.

Sumner, Ray. Looking at School Achievement. (Exploring Education Ser). 95p. 1974. pap. text ed. 5.75x (ISBN 0-85633-038-8, NFER). Humanities.

--Tests of Attainment in Mathematics in Schools: Vol. 1, Monitoring Feasability Study. (NFER Occasional Reports: Second Ser.). 200p. (Orig.). 1975. pap. text ed. 15.25x (ISBN 0-85633-084-1, NFER). Humanities.

Sumner, Ray, ed. Monitoring National Standards of Attainment in Schools. (Council of Europe: European Trend Reports on Educational Research Ser.: No. 5). (Illus.). 1977. pap. text ed. 38.50x (ISBN 0-85633-144-9, NFER). Humanities.

Sumner, Richard. Mistress of the Boards. 1976. 8.95 o.p. (ISBN 0-394-40857-8). Random.

--Mistress of the Boards. 1978. pap. 1.95 o.s.i. (ISBN 0-515-04422-9). Jove Pubns.

--Mistress of the King. (Orig.). 1979. pap. 1.95 o.s.i. (ISBN 0-515-04836-4). Jove Pubns.

--Mistress of the Streets. 1978. pap. 1.95 o.s.i. (ISBN 0-515-04487-3). Jove Pubns.

Sumner, Robert L. After the Revival--What? 1980. pap. 3.95 (ISBN 0-87398-026-3). Bibl Evang Pr.

--Armstrongism: The Worldwide Church of God Examined in the Searching Light of Scripture. 424p. 1974. 7.95 (ISBN 0-87398-025-5, Pub. by Bibl Evang Pr). Sword of Lord.

--Evangelism: The Church on Fire! 220p. 1960. 4.75 (ISBN 0-87398-211-8, Pub. by Bibl Evang Pr). Sword of Lord.

--Menace of Narcotics. 72p. 1971. pap. 1.95 (ISBN 0-87398-558-3, Pub. by Bibl Evang Pr). Sword of Lord.

--Powerhouse. 1978. pap. 3.95 (ISBN 0-87398-662-8, Pub. by Bibl Evang Pr). Sword of Lord.

--Saved by Grace...for Service. 1979. 8.95 (ISBN 0-87398-797-7, Pub. by Bibl Evang Pr). Sword of Lord.

--Wonder of the Word of God. 1969. pap. 0.95 (ISBN 0-87398-933-3, Pub. by Bibl Evang Pr). Sword of Lord.

Sumner, William see Lieber, Francis.

Sumner, William G. Andrew Jackson. LC 80-18576. (American Statesmen Ser.). 405p. 1981. pap. 6.95 (ISBN 0-87754-176-0). Chelsea Hse.

Sumner, Wm. G. & Keller, A. G. Science of Society, 4 vols. 1927. 50.00x ea.; 200.00x set (ISBN 0-685-69873-4). Elliots Bks.

Sumner-Boyd, Hilary & Freely, John. Strolling Through Istanbul. (Illus.). 1972. 15.00x (ISBN 0-686-16866-6). Intl Learn Syst.

Sumners, Cecil L. Governors of Mississippi. (Governors of the State Ser.). (Illus.). 180p. 1980. 13.95 (ISBN 0-88289-237-1). Pelican.

Sumption, Jonathan. Pilgrimage: An Image of Mediaeval Religion. (Illus.). 390p. 1975. 17.50x (ISBN 0-87471-677-2). Rowman.

Sumrall, Lester. Hostility. 1981. pap. 3.95 (ISBN 0-8407-5765-4). Nelson.

--Miracles Don't Just Happen. 1979. pap. 3.95 o.p. (ISBN 0-88270-369-2). Logos.

--Sixty Things God Said About Sex. 144p. 1981. pap. 3.95 (ISBN 0-8407-5756-5). Nelson.
Sumrall, Velma & Germany, Lucille. Telling the Story of the Local Church: The Who, What, When, Where & Why of Communication. (Orig.). 1979. pap. 6.95 (ISBN 0-8164-2193-5); wkbk. avail. (ISBN 0-685-59466-1). Crossroad NY.
Sun, Ruth Q., ed. Land of Seagull & Fox. LC 67-23010. (Illus.). 1967. 5.50 o.p. (ISBN 0-8048-0356-0). C E Tuttle.
Sunagel, Lois A. The Amethyst Quest. (YA) 1975. 5.95 (ISBN 0-685-52991-6, Avalon). Bouregy.
--A Promise to Keep. (Orig.). 1980. pap. 1.95 (ISBN 0-532-23133-3). Manor Bks.
--The Shadow of the Needle. (YA) 1976. 5.95 (ISBN 0-685-69052-0, Avalon). Bouregy.
Sund, Horst, ed. Pyridine Nucleotide - Dependent Dehydrogenases. 513p. 1977. text ed. 97.00x (ISBN 3-11007-091-X). De Gruyter.
Sund, Robert, jt. auth. see Piltz, Albert.
Sund, Robert B. & Bybee, Rodger W. Becoming a Better Elementary Science Teacher: A Reader. LC 72-90162. 1973. pap. text ed. 15.95x (ISBN 0-675-09059-8). Merrill.
Sund, Robert B. & Trowbridge, Leslie W. Teaching Science by Inquiry in the Secondary School. 2nd ed. LC 72-86024. 640p. 1973. text ed. 17.95x (ISBN 0-675-09051-2). Merrill.
Sund, Robert B., jt. auth. see Carin, Arthur A.
Sundaralingham, M. & Rao, S. R., eds. Structure & Conformation of Nucleic Acids & Protein-Nuclein Acid Interactions. (Illus.). 1975. 49.50 (ISBN 0-8391-0764-1). Univ Park.
Sundaram, P. S. R.K. Narayan. (Indian Writers Ser.). 1973. 8.50 (ISBN 0-89253-510-5). Ind-US Inc.
Sundaram, R. Bombay. (Illus.). 1966. 4.10 (ISBN 0-88253-412-2). Ind-US Inc.
Sunday, Billy. Billy Sunday Speaks. Gullen, Karen, ed. LC 76-127017. (Illus.). 220p. 1981. pap. 6.95 (ISBN 0-87754-141-8). Chelsea Hse.
Sundberg, Norman D. The Assessment of Persons. (Illus.). 1977. 18.95 (ISBN 0-13-049585-9). P-H.
Sundberg, Norman D., et al. Clinical Psychology: Expanding Horizons. 2nd ed. (Century Psychology Ser.). (Illus.). 1973. 20.95x (ISBN 0-13-137877-5). P-H.
Sundburg, M. & Goldkuhl, G. Information Systems Developement: A Systematic Approach. 1981. 24.50 (ISBN 0-13-464677-0). P-H.
Sundeen, Sandra, et al. Nurse-Client Interaction: Implementing the Nursing Process. (Illus.). 260p. 1981. pap. text ed. 11.95 (ISBN 0-8016-4844-0). Mosby.
Sundel, Martin & Sundel, Sandra S. Behavior Modification in the Human Services: Introduction to Concepts & Applications. LC 74-23342. 283p. 1975. pap. text ed. 11.50x o.p. (ISBN 0-471-83567-6). Wiley.
Sundel, Martin, jt. auth. see Sundel, Sandra S.
Sundel, Sandra S. & Sundel, Martin. Be Assertive: A Practical Guide for Human Service Workers. LC 79-20431. (Sage Human Service Guides: Vol. 11). (Illus.). 1980. pap. 8.00x (ISBN 0-8039-1289-7). Sage.
Sundel, Sandra S., jt. auth. see Sundel, Martin.
Sundelius, Bengt. Managing Transnationalism in Northern Europe. LC 78-59862. (Westview Replica Edition). 1978. lib. bdg. 19.00x (ISBN 0-89158-282-7). Westview.
Sundell, Abner, jt. auth. see Myron, Robert.
Sundell, Michael G., ed. Twentieth Century Interpretations of Vanity Fair. LC 73-79446. 1969. 7.95 o.p. (ISBN 0-13-940395-7, Spec); pap. 1.25 o.p. (ISBN 0-13-940387-6, Spec). P-H.
Sundene Wood, Barbara. Messages Without Words. LC 77-27848. (Read About Sciences Ser.). (Illus.). (gr. k-3). 1978. PLB 9.95 (ISBN 0-8393-0084-0). Raintree Child.
Sunder, John E. Bill Sublette, Mountain Man. (Illus.). 1978. pap. 5.95 (ISBN 0-8061-1111-9). U of Okla Pr.
Sunderlan, Ronald, jt. ed. see Shelp, Earl E.
Sunderland, Eric. Elements of Human & Social Geography (Some Anthropological Perspectives) LC 73-10060. 120p. 1974. text ed. 15.00 (ISBN 0-08-017689-5); pap. text ed. 7.00 (ISBN 0-08-017690-9). Pergamon.
Sunderland, John. Painting in Britain 1525 to 1975. LC 76-6505. (Illus.). 256p. 1976. usa 35.00x (ISBN 0-8147-7773-2). NYU Pr.
Sunderland, N., jt. auth. see Davies, P. Spencer.
Sunderlin, Sylvia, ed. Children & TV: Television's Impact on the Child. (Illus.). 1967. pap. 1.25x o.p. (ISBN 0-87173-016-2). ACEI.
--Toward Better Kindergartens. (Illus.). 1968. pap. 1.25x o.p. (ISBN 0-87173-044-8). ACEI.
Sunderman, Lloyd F. New Dimensions in Music Education. LC 73-189289. 1972. 10.00 (ISBN 0-8108-0482-4). Scarecrow.
Sundharam, K. P. & Vaish, M. C. Principles of Economics. rev. 13th ed. 1980. text ed. 27.50x (ISBN 0-7069-0285-8, Pub. by Vikas India). Advent Bk.
Sundkler, Bengt. Zulu Zion & Some Swazi Zionists. (Oxford Studies in African Affairs Ser.). 1976. 37.50x (ISBN 0-19-822707-8). Oxford U Pr.
Sundquist, James L. Dispersing Population: What America Can Learn from Europe. 290p. 1975. 14.95 (ISBN 0-8157-8214-4); pap. 5.95 (ISBN 0-8157-8213-6). Brookings.
--Dynamics of the Party System: Alignment & Realignment of Political Parties in the United States. 1973. 14.95 (ISBN 0-8157-8216-0); pap. 7.95 (ISBN 0-8157-8215-2). Brookings.
--Making Federalism Work: A Study of Program Coordination at the Community Level. 1969. 14.95 (ISBN 0-8157-8218-7); pap. 5.95 (ISBN 0-8157-8217-9). Brookings.
--Politics & Policy: The Eisenhower, Kennedy, & Johnson Years. LC 68-31837. 1968. 16.95 (ISBN 0-8157-8222-5); pap. 6.95 (ISBN 0-8157-8221-7). Brookings.
Sundstrom, Donald W. & Klei, Herbert E. Wastewater Treatment. LC 78-13058. (Illus.). 1979. 27.95 (ISBN 0-13-945832-8). P-H.
Sundstrom, Stephan, jt. ed. see Konigsson, Lars-Konig.
Sundt, Eilert. On Marriage in Norway. Drake, M., tr. from Norwegian. LC 79-42648. 1980. 29.50 (ISBN 0-521-23199-X). Cambridge U Pr.
Sundt, Wilbur A. Naval Science, Vol. 1. LC 78-56425. (Illus.). 320p. 1980. 7.50x (ISBN 0-87021-489-6). Naval Inst Pr.
Sung, Betty L. An Album of Chinese Americans. LC 76-45185. (Picture Albums Ser.). (Illus.). (gr. 4-6). 1977. PLB 5.90 s&l o.p. (ISBN 0-531-00366-3). Watts.
--The Chinese in America. LC 78-188774. (Illus.). (gr. 4-7). 1972. 6.95 o.s.i. (ISBN 0-02-788670-0). Macmillan.
Sung, Betty Lee. A Survey of Chinese-American Manpower & Employment. LC 76-14435. (Special Studies). (Illus.). 1976. text ed. 28.95 (ISBN 0-275-23090-2). Praeger.
Sungolowsky, Joseph. Beaumarchais. LC 74-10580. (World Authors Ser.: France: No. 334). 1974. lib. bdg. 10.95 (ISBN 0-8057-2122-3). Twayne.
Sung-won Ko, see Ko, Won.
Sunier, A. Dealing with Problem People. 84p. 1980. pap. text ed. 8.50x (ISBN 90-232-1761-6). Humanities.
Sunier, John. Slide, Sound, & Film Strip Production. (Illus.). 220p. 1981. 15.95 (ISBN 0-240-51074-7). Focal Pr.
Sunners, William. How to Make & Sell Original Crosswords & Other Puzzles. LC 80-52333. (Illus.). 256p. 1981. 12.95 (ISBN 0-8069-4632-6); lib. bdg. 11.69 (ISBN 0-8069-4633-4). Sterling.
Sunoo, Harold H. America's Dilemma in Asia: The Case of South Korea. LC 78-24029. 1979. 15.95x (ISBN 0-88229-357-5). Nelson-Hall.
--Japanese Militarism: Past & Present. LC 74-23366. 170p. 1975. 13.95 (ISBN 0-88229-217-X). Nelson-Hall.
Sunrise Publishing Company Editors, ed. The Greatest of Expositions: St. Louis World's Fair, 1904. rev. ed. 1981. pap. 8.95 (ISBN 0-86629-029-X). Sunrise MO.
Sunseri, Alvin. Seeds of Discord: New Mexico in the Aftermath of the American Conquest, 1846-1861. LC 78-24315. 1979. 15.95 (ISBN 0-88229-141-6). Nelson-Hall.
Sunset Editors. Islands of the South Pacific: Travel Guide. 3rd ed. LC 79-88018. (Illus.). 128p. 1979. pap. 5.95 (ISBN 0-376-06385-8, Sunset Bks). Sunset-Lane.
Sunset Editors. African Violets. 5th ed. LC 76-46656. (Illus.). 80p. 1977. pap. 2.95 (ISBN 0-376-03056-9, Sunset Bks). Sunset-Lane.
--Alaska: Travel Guide. 3rd ed. LC 77-90724. (Illus.). 112p. 1978. pap. 5.95 (ISBN 0-376-06035-2, Sunset Bks). Sunset-Lane.
--Arizona: Travel Guide. 5th ed. LC 78-53677. (Illus.). 112p. 1978. pap. 4.95 (ISBN 0-376-06056-5, Sunset Bks). Sunset-Lane.
--Australia. 4th ed. LC 80-80853. (Illus.). 128p. 1980. pap. 5.95 (ISBN 0-376-06064-6, Sunset Bks). Sunset-Lane.
--Basic Carpentry Illustrated. LC 72-77140. (Illus.). 88p. 1972. pap. 4.95 (ISBN 0-376-01014-2, Sunset Bks). Sunset-Lane.
--Basic Gardening Illustrated. LC 74-20013. (Illus.). 128p. 1975. pap. 3.95 o.p. (ISBN 0-376-03074-7, Sunset Bks). Sunset-Lane.
--Basic Gardening: Introduction to. 3rd ed. LC 80-53478. (Illus.). 160p. 1981. pap. 5.95 (ISBN 0-376-03075-5, Sunset Bks). Sunset-Lane.
--Basic Home Repairs Illustrated. LC 73-115166. (Illus.). 96p. 1971. pap. 4.95 (ISBN 0-376-01025-8, Sunset Bks). Sunset-Lane.
--Basic Masonry Illustrated. LC 80-53484. (Illus.). 96p. (Orig.). 1981. pap. 4.95 (ISBN 0-376-01360-5, Sunset Bks.). Sunset-Lane.
--Bathrooms. LC 80-80856. (Illus.). 80p. 1980. pap. 3.95 (ISBN 0-376-01326-5, Sunset Bks). Sunset-Lane.
--Beautiful California. 3rd ed. LC 76-29190. (Illus.). 224p. 1977. pap. 8.95 (ISBN 0-376-05035-7, Sunset Bks). Sunset-Lane.
--Beautiful Hawaii. LC 77-72508. (Illus.). 208p. 1977. pap. 8.95 (ISBN 0-376-05373-9, Sunset Bks). Sunset-Lane.
--Beautiful Northwest. LC 77-78147. (Illus.). 224p. 1977. pap. 8.95 (ISBN 0-376-05053-5, Sunset Bks). Sunset-Lane.
--Bedrooms. LC 80-80857. (Illus.). 80p. (Orig.). 1980. pap. 3.95 (ISBN 0-376-01111-4, Sunset Bks). Sunset-Lane.
--Bonsai. rev. 2nd ed. LC 75-26495. (Illus.). 80p. 1976. pap. 3.95 (ISBN 0-376-03044-5, Sunset Bks). Sunset-Lane.
--Bookshelves & Cabinets. LC 74-76541. (Illus.). 96p. (Orig.). 1974. pap. 3.95 (ISBN 0-376-01083-5, Sunset Bks). Sunset-Lane.
--Breakfast & Brunch. LC 79-90335. (Illus.). 96p. 1980. pap. 4.95 (ISBN 0-376-02104-7, Sunset Bks). Sunset-Lane.
--Building Barbecues. 2nd ed. LC 76-140161. (Illus.). 80p. 1971. pap. 3.95 (ISBN 0-376-01034-7, Sunset Bks). Sunset-Lane.
--Cabins & Vacation Houses. 3rd ed. LC 74-20017. (Illus.). 96p. 1975. pap. 2.95 (ISBN 0-376-01064-9, Sunset Bks). Sunset-Lane.
--Cactus & Succulents. LC 77-82873. (Illus.). 80p. 1978. pap. 3.95 (ISBN 0-376-03753-9, Sunset Bks.). Sunset-Lane.
--California Missions. 2nd ed. LC 79-88016. (Illus.). 320p. 1979. pap. 8.95 (ISBN 0-376-05171-X, Sunset Bks). Sunset-Lane.
--Canning, Freezing & Drying. 2nd ed. LC 80-53480. (Illus.). 128p. 1981. pap. 4.95 (ISBN 0-376-02213-2, Sunset Books). Sunset-Lane.
--Casserole Cook Book. 3rd ed. LC 80-80854. (Illus.). 96p. 1980. pap. 3.95 (ISBN 0-376-02254-X, Sunset Bks). Sunset-Lane.
--Children's Rooms & Play Yards. LC 79-90336. (Illus.). 96p. 1980. pap. 3.95 (ISBN 0-376-01054-1, Sunset Bks). Sunset-Lane.
--Convection Oven Cook Book. LC 80-81283. (Illus.). 96p. (Orig.). 1980. pap. 3.95 (ISBN 0-376-02311-2, Sunset Bks.). Sunset-Lane.
--Curtains, Draperies & Shades. LC 78-70270. (Illus.). 104p. 1979. pap. 4.95 (ISBN 0-376-01733-3, Sunset Bks). Sunset-Lane.
--Decks: How to Build. LC 79-90331. (Illus.). 96p. 1980. pap. 4.95 (ISBN 0-376-01076-2, Sunset Bks). Sunset-Lane.
--Desert Gardening. LC 67-27445. (Illus.). 96p. 1967. pap. 2.95 (ISBN 0-376-03132-8, Sunset Bks). Sunset-Lane.
--Desserts. LC 69-14150. (Illus.). 96p. 1968. pap. 3.95 (ISBN 0-376-02344-9, Sunset Bks). Sunset-Lane.
--Energy-Saving Projects. LC 80-53485. (Illus.). 96p. (Orig.). 1981. pap. 3.95 (ISBN 0-376-01230-7, Sunset Bks.). Sunset-Lane.
--Europe: Discovery Trips. 3rd ed. LC 80-80855. (Illus.). 144p. 1980. pap. 5.95 (ISBN 0-376-06173-1, Sunset Bks). Sunset-Lane.
--Fences & Gates. 3rd ed. LC 70-140162. (Illus.). 96p. 1971. pap. 2.95 (ISBN 0-376-01104-1, Sunset Bks). Sunset-Lane.
--Fireplaces: How to Build. rev ed. LC 79-90337. (Illus.). 96p. 1980. pap. 3.95 o.p. (ISBN 0-376-01155-6, Sunset Bks). Sunset-Lane.
--French Cook Book. LC 76-7666. (Illus.). 96p. 1976. pap. 3.95 (ISBN 0-376-02423-2, Sunset Bks.). Sunset-Lane.
--Furniture Upholstery. 2nd ed. LC 80-80858. (Illus.). 112p. 1980. pap. 4.95 (ISBN 0-376-01183-1, Sunset Bks.). Sunset-Lane.
--Garden & Patio Building Book. LC 69-13278. (Illus.). 96p. 1969. pap. 3.95 (ISBN 0-376-01213-7, Sunset Bks.). Sunset-Lane.
--Garden Color: Annuals & Perennials. LC 80-53479. (Illus.). 96p. 1981. pap. 3.95 (ISBN 0-376-03154-9, Sunset Bks). Sunset-Lane.
--Ghost Towns of the West. 2nd ed. LC 77-72507. (Illus.). 224p. 1978. pap. 8.95 (ISBN 0-376-05313-5, Sunset Bks.). Sunset-Lane.
--Gold Rush Country. 4th ed. LC 75-180518. (Illus.). 128p. 1972. pap. 3.95 (ISBN 0-376-06255-X, Sunset Bks). Sunset-Lane.
--Ground Beef. 2nd ed. LC 73-75750. (Illus.). 80p. 1973. pap. 2.95 o.p. (ISBN 0-376-02453-4, Sunset Bks). Sunset-Lane.
--Herbs: How to Grow. LC 73-181520. (Illus.). 80p. (Orig.). 1972. pap. 2.95 (ISBN 0-376-03322-3, Sunset Bks.). Sunset-Lane.
--Home Canning. LC 74-20016. (Illus.). 96p. (Orig.). 1975. pap. 2.95 o.p. (ISBN 0-376-02212-4, Sunset Bks.). Sunset-Lane.
--Hot Tubs, Spas & Home Saunas. LC 78-70274. (Illus.). 80p. 1979. pap. 3.95 (ISBN 0-376-01242-0, Sunset Bks). Sunset-Lane.
--Hot Tubs, Spas & Home Saunas. LC 78-70274. (Illus.). 80p. 1979. pap. 3.95 o.p. (ISBN 0-376-01242-0). Sunset-Lane.
--House Plants: How to Grow. 3rd ed. LC 76-7660. (Illus.). 80p. 1976. pap. 3.95 (ISBN 0-376-03335-5, Sunset Bks). Sunset-Lane.
--Indoor Plants: Decorating with. LC 79-90333. (Illus.). 80p. 1980. pap. 3.95 (ISBN 0-376-03341-X, Sunset Bks). Sunset-Lane.
--Insulation & Weatherstripping. LC 77-90718. (Illus.). 80p. 1978. pap. 4.95 (ISBN 0-376-01263-3, Sunset Bks). Sunset-Lane.
--Knitting. LC 76-7659. (Illus.). 80p. 1976. pap. 2.95 (ISBN 0-376-04432-2, Sunset Bks). Sunset-Lane.
--Macrame. 2nd ed. LC 75-6225. (Illus.). 80p. 1975. pap. 3.95 (ISBN 0-376-04544-2, Sunset Bks.). Sunset-Lane.
--Mexico: Travel Guide. 6th ed. LC 76-46655. (Illus.). 144p. 1977. pap. 5.95 (ISBN 0-376-06457-9, Sunset Bks). Sunset-Lane.
--Microwave Cook Book. 2nd ed. LC 80-53481. (Illus.). 1981. pap. 3.95 (ISBN 0-376-02504-2, Sunset Books). Sunset-Lane.
--National Parks of the West. LC 79-90339. (Illus.). 256p. 1980. pap. 8.95 (ISBN 0-376-05583-9, Sunset Bks). Sunset-Lane.
--Needlepoint. 2nd ed. LC 76-46659. (Illus.). 80p. 1977. pap. 3.95 (ISBN 0-376-04584-1, Sunset Bks). Sunset-Lane.
--New Zealand. 3rd ed. LC 77-90726. (Illus.). 128p. 1978. pap. 5.95 (ISBN 0-376-06534-6, Sunset Bks). Sunset-Lane.
--Northern California: Travel Guide. LC 79-90341. (Illus.). 128p. 1980. pap. 4.95 (ISBN 0-376-06557-5, Sunset Bks). Sunset-Lane.
--Oregon: Travel Guide. 3rd ed. LC 80-53486. (Illus.). 128p. 1981. pap. 5.95 (ISBN 0-376-06615-6, Sunset Bks.). Sunset-Lane.
--Oregon: Travel Guide to. 4th ed. LC 80-53486. (Illus.). 128p. 1981. pap. 5.95 (ISBN 0-376-06615-6, Sunset Bks.). Sunset-Lane.
--Oriental Cook Book. LC 78-100903. (Illus.). 96p. 1970. pap. 4.95 (ISBN 0-376-02533-6, Sunset Bks.). Sunset-Lane.
--Pasta Cook Book. LC 79-90338. (Illus.). 96p. 1980. pap. 3.95 (ISBN 0-376-02521-2, Sunset Bks). Sunset-Lane.
--Patio Roofs: How to Build. 3rd ed. LC 73-89579. (Illus.). 80p. 1974. pap. 3.95 (ISBN 0-376-01455-5, Sunset Bks.). Sunset-Lane.
--Pillows: How to Make. LC 80-80859. (Illus.). 80p. 1980. pap. 3.95 (ISBN 0-376-01431-8, Sunset Bks). Sunset-Lane.
--Planning Your New Home. LC 67-15741. (Illus.). 128p. 1967. pap. 2.95 o.p. (ISBN 0-376-01283-8, Sunset Bks.). Sunset-Lane.
--Quilting & Patchwork. LC 72-92518. (Illus.). 80p. 1973. pap. 3.95 (ISBN 0-376-04663-5, Sunset Bks.). Sunset-Lane.
--Roofing & Siding. LC 80-53487. (Illus.). 112p. (Orig.). 1981. pap. 4.95 (ISBN 0-376-01490-3, Sunset Bks). Sunset-Lane.
--Roses: How to Grow. rev. ed. LC 79-90334. (Illus.). 96p. 1980. pap. 3.95 (ISBN 0-376-03655-9, Sunset Bks). Sunset-Lane.
--Seafood Cook Book. 3rd ed. LC 80-53482. (Illus.). 128p. 1981. pap. 4.95 (ISBN 0-376-02586-7, Sunset Bks). Sunset-Lane.
--Seafood Cook Book. 5th ed. LC 80-53482. (Illus.). 128p. 1981. pap. 4.95 (ISBN 0-376-02586-7, Sunset Books). Sunset-Lane.
--Slipcovers & Bedspreads. LC 79-88157. (Illus.). 120p. 1979. pap. 4.95 (ISBN 0-376-01512-8, Sunset Bks). Sunset-Lane.
--Soft Toys & Dolls. LC 76-46657. (Illus.). 80p. 1977. pap. 2.95 o.p. (ISBN 0-376-04692-9, Sunset Bks.). Sunset-Lane.
--Solar Heating & Cooling: Homeowner's Guide. LC 78-53673. (Illus.). 96p. 1978. pap. 4.95 (ISBN 0-376-01523-3, Sunset Bks.). Sunset-Lane.
--Southern California: Travel Guide. 5th ed. LC 78-70269. (Illus.). 128p. 1979. pap. 4.95 (ISBN 0-376-06757-8, Sunset Bks). Sunset-Lane.
--Storage. 3rd ed. LC 74-20021. (Illus.). 96p. 1975. pap. 3.95 (ISBN 0-376-01554-3, Sunset Bks.). Sunset-Lane.
--Swimming Pools. 5th ed. LC 80-53488. (Illus.). 128p. 1981. pap. 4.95 (ISBN 0-376-01607-8, Sunset Bks.). Sunset-Lane.
--Tables & Chairs: Easy to Make. LC 75-26492. (Illus.). 80p. 1976. pap. 3.95 (ISBN 0-376-01653-1, Sunset Bks). Sunset-Lane.
--Tile: Remodeling. LC 77-90719. (Illus.). 80p. 1978. pap. 3.95 (ISBN 0-376-01672-8, Sunset Bks). Sunset-Lane.
--Vegetable Cook Book. LC 72-92516. (Illus.). 96p. 1973. pap. 3.95 (ISBN 0-376-02903-X, Sunset Bks.). Sunset-Lane.
--Vegetarian Cooking. LC 80-53483. (Illus.). 96p. (Orig.). 1981. pap. 3.95 (ISBN 0-376-02910-2, Sunset Books). Sunset-Lane.
--Western Garden Book: Sunset New. 4th rev. ed. LC 78-70266. (Illus.). 512p. 1979. pap. 11.95 (ISBN 0-376-03889-6, Sunset Bks). Sunset-Lane.
--Wine Country. LC 79-88017. (Illus.). 128p. 1979. pap. 4.95 o.p. (ISBN 0-376-06943-0, Sunset Bks). Sunset-Lane.
--Wine Country: California. LC 79-88017. (Illus.). 128p. 1979. pap. 4.95 (Sunset Bks.). Sunset-Lane.
--Wood Stoves. LC 79-88160. (Illus.). 96p. 1979. pap. 4.95 (ISBN 0-376-01882-8, Sunset Bks). Sunset-Lane.

--Woodworking Projects. 2nd ed. LC 75-6222. (Illus.). 96p. 1975. pap. 3.95 (ISBN 0-376-04884-0, Sunset Bks.). Sunset-Lane.

Sunshine, Irving, ed. CRC Handbook of Spectrophotometric Data of Drugs. 432p. 1981. 62.95 (ISBN 0-8493-3571-X). CRC Pr.

Sun Tzu. The Art of War. Griffith, Samuel B., tr. & intro. by. 1971. pap. 4.95 (ISBN 0-19-501476-6, 361, GB). Oxford U Pr.

Suny, Roger G. Baku Commune, 1917-1918: Class & Nationality in the Russian Revolution. LC 76-155966. (Studies of the Russian Institute Ser.). (Illus.). 1972. 22.00x (ISBN 0-691-05193-3). Princeton U Pr.

Sunyaev, R., ed. Soviet Scientific Reviews: Section E, Astrophysics & Space Physics Reviews, Vol. 1, Section E. 250p. 1981. 50.00 (ISBN 3-7186-0021-8). Harwood Academic.

Sun Yat-sen. The International Development of China. rev. 2nd ed. LC 74-34490. (China in the 20th Century Ser). (Illus.). ix, 265p. 1975. Repr. of 1929 ed. lib. bdg. 29.50 (ISBN 0-306-70697-0). Da Capo.

--San Min Chu I: The Three Principles of the People. Chen, L. T., ed. Price, Frank W., tr. from Chinese. LC 75-1033. (China in the 20th Century Ser). xvii, 514p. 1975. Repr. of 1927 ed. lib. bdg. 45.00 (ISBN 0-306-70698-9). Da Capo.

Sun Yun Chiang, Cecilia & Carr, Allan. Mandarin Way. rev. & expanded ed. Silva, Sharon, ed. LC 80-66580. (Illus.). 288p. 1980. 11.95 (ISBN 0-89395-062-9); pap. 7.95 (ISBN 0-89395-059-9). Cal Living Bks.

Suojanen, Waino & Henderson, Richard I. The Operating Manager: An Integrative Approach. (Illus.). 480p. 1974. ref. ed. 16.95 (ISBN 0-13-637942-7). P-H.

Super, Donald E. Work Values Inventory: MRC Machine-Scorable Test Booklets. 41.24 (ISBN 0-395-09529-8); directions manual 2.51 (ISBN 0-395-09530-1); specimen set. pap. 2.16 (ISBN 0-395-09531-X). HM.

Super, Donald E. & Overstreet, Phoebe L. The Vocational Maturity of Ninth-Grade Boys. LC 60-12516. 1960. text ed. 7.25x (ISBN 0-8077-2236-7). Tchrs Coll.

Super, Donald E., et al. Career Development: Self-Concept Theory. (Research Monograph: No. 4). 1963. pap. 6.00 (ISBN 0-87447-010-2, 213815). College Bd.

--Computer-Assisted Counseling. LC 71-137460. (Illus.). 1970. pap. 5.75x (ISBN 0-8077-2231-6). Tchrs Coll.

--Vocational Development. LC 57-11370. 1957. text ed. 7.50x (ISBN 0-8077-2233-2). Tchrs Coll.

Super, Robert H. Trollope in the Post Office. 1981. text ed. 10.00 (ISBN 0-472-10013-0). U of Mich Pr.

Supervia, Guillermina M., et al. Actualidad Hispanica. (gr. 7-12). 1972. text ed. 14.80 (ISBN 0-205-03046-7, 4230469); tchrs'. guide 4.96 (ISBN 0-205-03047-5, 4230477). Allyn.

Supervielle. Le Voleur de'Enfants. (Easy Reader, A). pap. 2.90 (ISBN 0-88436-111-X, FRA110052). EMC.

Supino, David J., jt. ed. see Schrank, Barbara.

Suponev, Michael. Olga Korbut: A Biographical Portrait. LC 73-11636. 96p. 1975. 6.95 o.p. (ISBN 0-385-09498-1). Doubleday.

Suppe, Frederick, ed. see Philosophy of Science Biennial Meeting, 1976.

Suppe, John. Geology of the Leech Lake Mountain Region, California: A Cross-Section of the North-Eastern Franciscan Belt & Its Tectonic Implications. (Publications in Geology, Vol. 107). 1974. pap. 11.00x (ISBN 0-520-09488-3). U of Cal Pr.

Suppes, Patrick, jt. auth. see Hawley, Newton.

Supple, Barry, ed. Essays in British Business History. 1977. 29.95x (ISBN 0-19-877087-1); pap. 16.50x (ISBN 0-19-877088-X). Oxford U Pr.

Supple, J. H., jt. auth. see Weller, P. F.

Supraner, Lauren, jt. auth. see Supraner, Robyn.

Supraner, Robyn. Fun-to-Make Nature Crafts. LC 80-23399. (Illus.). 48p. (gr. 2-5). 1980. PLB 6.92 (ISBN 0-89375-440-4); pap. 1.75 (ISBN 0-89375-441-2). Troll Assocs.

--Fun with Paper. LC 80-19859. (Illus.). 48p. (gr. 2-5). 1980. PLB 6.92 (ISBN 0-89375-430-7); pap. 1.75 (ISBN 0-89375-431-5). Troll Assocs.

--Giggly-Wiggly, Snickety-Snick. LC 76-14406. (Illus.). 40p. (ps-3). 1978. 7.25 (ISBN 0-590-17709-5, Four Winds); lib. bdg. 7.95 (ISBN 0-590-07709-0). Schol Bk Serv.

--Great Masks to Make. LC 80-24077. (Illus.). 48p. (gr. 2-5). 1980. PLB 6.92 (ISBN 0-89375-436-6); pap. 1.75 (ISBN 0-89375-437-4). Troll Assocs.

--Happy Halloween: Things to Make & Do. LC 80-23889. (Illus.). 48p. (gr. 2-5). 1980. lib. bdg. 6.92 (ISBN 0-89375-420-X); pap. 1.75 (ISBN 0-89375-421-8). Troll Assocs.

--Magic Tricks You Can Do! LC 80-19780. (Illus.). 48p. (gr. 2-5). 1980. PLB 6.92 (ISBN 0-89375-418-8); pap. 1.75 (ISBN 0-89375-419-6). Troll Assocs.

--Merry Christmas: Things to Make & Do. LC 80-23884. (Illus.). 48p. (gr. 2-5). 1980. PLB 6.92 (ISBN 0-89375-422-6); pap. 1.75 (ISBN 0-89375-423-4). Troll Assocs.

--Quick & Easy Cookbook. LC 80-24021. (Illus.). 48p. (gr. 2-5). 1980. PLB 6.92 (ISBN 0-89375-438-2); pap. 1.75 (ISBN 0-89375-439-0). Troll Assocs.

--Rainy Day Surprises You Can Make. LC 80-19858. (Illus.). 48p. (gr. 2-5). 1980. PLB 6.92 (ISBN 0-89375-428-5); pap. 1.75 (ISBN 0-89375-429-3). Troll Assocs.

--Science Secrets. LC 80-23794. (Illus.). 48p. (gr. 2-5). 1980. PLB 6.92 (ISBN 0-89375-426-9); pap. 1.75 (ISBN 0-89375-427-7). Troll Assocs.

--Stop & Look! Illusions. LC 80-23799. (Illus.). 48p. (gr. 2-5). 1980. PLB 6.92 (ISBN 0-89375-434-X); pap. 1.75 (ISBN 0-89375-435-8). Troll Assocs.

--Valentine's Day: Things to Make & Do. LC 80-23780. (Illus.). 48p. (gr. 2-5). 1980. PLB 6.92 (ISBN 0-89375-424-2); pap. 1.75 (ISBN 0-89375-425-0). Troll Assocs.

Supraner, Robyn & Supraner, Lauren. Plenty of Puppets to Make. LC 80-23785. (Illus.). 48p. (gr. 2-5). 1980. PLB 6.92 (ISBN 0-89375-432-3); pap. 1.75 (ISBN 0-89375-433-1). Troll Assocs.

Supree, Burton, jt. auth. see Charlip, Remy.

Supreme Court of the United States & Kurland, Philip B. Landmark Briefs & Arguments of the Supreme Court of the United States: Constitutional Law, 80 vols. 1977. Set. 4640.00 (ISBN 0-89093-000-7). U Pubns Amer.

Suraiya, Jug. The Interview. 10.00 (ISBN 0-89253-635-7); flexible cloth 5.00 (ISBN 0-89253-636-5). Ind-US Inc.

Suran, Bernard G. Oddballs: The Social Maverick & the Dynamics of Individuality. LC 77-16660. 1978. 13.95 (ISBN 0-88229-366-4); pap. 6.95 (ISBN 0-88229-557-8). Nelson-Hall.

Suran, Bernard G. & Rizzo, Joseph V. Special Children: An Integrative Approach. 1979. text ed. 17.95x (ISBN 0-673-15068-2). Scott F.

Surber, Jere P., tr. see Hegel, G. W.

Suresh Singh, K. The Indian Famine, Nineteen Sixty-Seven: A Study in Crisis & Change. LC 75-903386. 1975. 11.00 o.p. (ISBN 0-88386-602-1). South Asia Bks.

Surette, Dick. Trout & Salmon Fly Index. LC 78-24196. (Illus.). 128p. 1979. pap. 9.95 (ISBN 0-8117-2093-4). Stackpole.

Surface, William. The Track. LC 75-43560. 325p. 1976. 9.95 o.s.i. (ISBN 0-02-615410-2, 61541). Macmillan.

Surgenor, Douglas N., ed. The Red Blood Cell, 2 vols. 2nd ed. Vol. 1, 1974. 64.50 (ISBN 0-12-677201-0); Vol. 2, 1975. 65.50 (ISBN 0-12-677202-9); Set. 106.00. Acad Pr.

Surgeon General, USAF. German Aviation Medicine, World War Two, 2 vols. Aero Medical Center Staff, tr. from Ger. LC 77-168949. (Illus.). 1302p. 1971. Repr. of 1950 ed. Set. lib. bdg. 75.00 (ISBN 0-87936-000-3). Scholium Intl.

Suri, Ram Lal. Acoustics, Design & Practice, Vol. 1. 1966. 25.00x (ISBN 0-210-27067-5). Asia.

Suri, Surindar. Political Change in India, Nineteen Seventy-Seven: Elections & the Emergency Aftermath. 1981. 11.00x (ISBN 0-8364-0017-8); pap. text ed. 7.00x (ISBN 0-8364-0019-4). South Asia Bks.

Surincik, Don. Songs of Sorrow & Hate. (Contemporary Poets of Dorrance Ser.). 104p. 1981. 5.00 (ISBN 0-8059-2778-6). Dorrance.

Surjaatmadja, J. B., jt. auth. see Fitch, E. C.

Surman, Phyl. Oak & Maple. 1981. 6.75 (ISBN 0-8062-1709-X). Carlton.

Surmanek, Jim. Media Planning: Quick & Easy Guide. LC 80-67810. 1980. pap. text ed. 8.95 (ISBN 0-87251-046-8). Crain Bks.

Surmelian, Leon. Daredevils of Sassoun: The Armenian National Epic. LC 64-66183. 1964. 8.95 o.p. (ISBN 0-8040-0061-1). Swallow.

--Techniques of Fiction Writing: Measure & Madness. LC 66-24323. 1969. pap. 2.95 (ISBN 0-385-06391-1, A549, Anch). Doubleday.

Surowiecki, Sandra L. Joshua's Day. 2nd ed. LC 77-20479. 27p. (ps-1). 1977. pap. 2.75 (ISBN 0-914996-18-5). Lollipop Power.

Surrey, A. John, jt. auth. see Cook, P. Lesley.

Surrey, M. J. The Analysis & Forecasting of the British Economy. LC 75-171683. (National Institute of Economic & Social Research, Occasional Papers: No. 25). (Illus.). 100p. 1972. 15.50x (ISBN 0-521-09675-8). Cambridge U Pr.

--An Introduction to Econometrics. (Illus.). 88p. 1974. text ed. 12.50x (ISBN 0-19-877048-0). Oxford U Pr.

Surrey, M. J. C., ed. Macroeconomic Themes: Edited Readings in Macroeconomics. (Illus.). 1976. text ed. 37.50x (ISBN 0-19-877059-6); pap. text ed. 14.50x (ISBN 0-19-877060-X). Oxford U Pr.

Surrey, Peter J. The Small Town Church. (Creative Leadership Ser.). 128p. (Orig.). 1981. pap. 4.95 (ISBN 0-687-38720-5). Abingdon.

Surrey, Walter S. & Wallace, Don, Jr., eds. A Lawyer's Guide to International Business Transactions, Pt. IV. 471p. 1980. 55.00 (ISBN 0-686-28717-7, B96B4). ALI-ABA.

Surtees, Virginia. The Paintings & Drawings of Dante Gabriel Rossetti (1828-1882) A Catalogue Raisonne, 2 vols. 294p. 1971. 98.00x (ISBN 0-19-817174-9). Oxford U Pr.

Suryadinata, Leo. Political Thinking of Indonesian Chinese: Nineteen Hundred to Nineteen Seventy-Seven. 270p. 1980. 18.00 (ISBN 0-8214-0548-9); pap. 11.00 (ISBN 0-8214-0549-7). Swallow.

Suryanarayana, C., compiled by. Rapidly Quenched Metals--a Bibliography: 1973-1979. 310p. 1980. 75.00 (ISBN 0-306-65194-7). IFI Plenum.

Susag, S. O. Personal Experiences of S. O. Susag. 191p. pap. 1.75. Faith Pub Hse.

Susann, Jacqueline. Valley of the Dolls. 1970. pap. 3.50 (ISBN 0-685-03305-8, 12772-1). Bantam.

Suschinskii, M. M. Raman Spectra of Molecules & Crystals. LC 72-4139. 576p. 1969. 44.95 (ISBN 0-470-83630-X, Pub by Halsted Pr). Halsted Pr.

Suseelan, M. A., ed. Resource Book on Aging. 112p. (Orig.). 1981. pap. 8.95 (ISBN 0-8298-0447-1). Pilgrim NY.

Sushka, M. E., jt. auth. see Slovin, M. B.

Sushka, Marie E., jt. auth. see Slovin, Myron B.

Susic, I., jt. auth. see Marovic, D.

Suskind, Richard. Battle of Belleau Wood: The Marines Stand Fast. LC 69-12747 (Battle Books Ser). (Illus.). (gr. 5-8). 1969. 4.50 o.s.i. (ISBN 0-685-14701-0). Macmillan.

--By Bullet, Bomb & Dagger: The Story of Anarchism. (Illus.). (gr. 7 up). 1971. 5.50 o.s.i. (ISBN 0-02-788730-8). Macmillan.

Suskind, Robert M., ed. Malnutrition & the Immune Response. LC 75-14589. 1977. 43.50 (ISBN 0-89004-060-5). Raven.

--Textbook of Pediatric Nutrition. 680p. 1980. text ed. 55.00 (ISBN 0-89004-253-5). Raven.

Suskind, Sigmund, ed. see Stahl, Franklin W.

Suslov, Mikhail A. Suslov: Selected Speeches & Writings. LC 79-41075. 368p. 1980. 46.00 (ISBN 0-08-023602-2). Pergamon.

Suslov, Vitaly. Treasures of the Hermitage. LC 80-81382. (Illus.). 1980. 19.95 (ISBN 0-88225-301-8). Newsweek.

Susman, Gerald I. Autonomy at Work: A Sociotechnical Analysis. LC 75-23997. (Praeger Special Studies Ser). 256p. 1976. text ed. 26.50 (ISBN 0-275-56140-2). Praeger.

Susman, Jackwell, ed. Crime & Justice, 2 vols. (An AMS Anthology). 1972-1974. Set. lib. bdg. 60.00 (ISBN 0-404-10200-X); Vol. 1. lib. bdg. 30.00 (ISBN 0-404-10201-8); Vol. 2. lib. bdg. 30.00 (ISBN 0-404-10202-6); Vol. 2. pap. 5.95 (ISBN 0-404-10252-2). AMS Pr.

Susman, Jackwell, jt. ed. see Kittrie, Nicholas N.

Suss, Elaine. Money Marriage: A Novel. LC 79-23995. 240p. 1980. 9.95 (ISBN 0-8008-5319-9). Taplinger.

Susser, Bernard. Existence & Utopia: The Social & Political Thought of Martin Buber. LC 78-75188. 260p. 1981. 15.00 (ISBN 0-8386-2292-5). Fairleigh Dickinson.

Susser, Mervyn W. & Watson, W. Sociology in Medicine. 2nd ed. (Illus.). 1977. pap. text ed. 25.00x (ISBN 0-19-264912-4). Oxford U Pr.

Sussex, Ian M., jt. auth. see Steeves, Taylor A.

Sussex, J. N., jt. auth. see Glasscote, R. M.

Sussex, James N., jt. ed. see Busse, Ewald.

Sussex, Margie & Stapleton, John F. The Complete Real Estate Math Book. 320p. 1976. 14.95 (ISBN 0-13-162354-0). P-H.

Susskind, Harriet, et al. Primavera, Vols. VI & VII. Heller, Janet R., et al, eds. LC 76-647540. (Illus.). 120p. (Orig.). 1981. pap. 5.00 (ISBN 0-916980-06-5). Primavera.

Sussman, Aaron. The Amateur Photographer's Handbook. 8th ed. LC 72-2558. (Illus.). 420p. 1973. 12.50 (ISBN 0-690-05782-2, TYC-T). T Y Crowell.

Sussman, Alan & Guggenheim, Martin. The Rights of Parents. 288p. (Orig.). 1980. pap. 2.50 (ISBN 0-380-76729-5, 76729). Avon.

Sussman, Albert, intro. by. Shopping Centers, Nineteen Eighty-Eight: Answers for the Next Decade. LC 79-84514. 1979. pap. text ed. 27.00 (ISBN 0-913598-07-0). Intl Coun Shop.

Sussman, Barth J. Shanghai. (Orig.). 1981. pap. 2.75 (ISBN 0-451-09563-4, E9563, Sig). NAL.

Sussman, Cornelia & Sussman, Irving. Thomas Merton. LC 80-924. 176p. 1980. pap. 3.95 (ISBN 0-385-17172-2, Im). Doubleday.

Sussman, Cornelia, jt. auth. see Sussman, Irving.

Sussman, Ellen. Smiling Sentences: Sight Word Activities to Cut & Paste. (Spirit Duplicating Masters Ser.). (Illus.). 24p. (gr. 2-3). 1980. 4.95 (ISBN 0-933606-08-7). Monkey Sisters.

--Sunny Sentences: Sight Word Activities to Cut & Paste. (Spirit Duplicating Masters Ser.). (Illus.). 24p. (gr. 1-2). 1980. 4.95 (ISBN 0-933606-07-9). Monkey Sisters.

Sussman, Ellen J. Art Projects for the Mentally Retarded Child. (Illus.). 108p. 1976. 10.75 (ISBN 0-398-03535-0); pap. 7.00 (ISBN 0-398-03534-2). C C Thomas.

Sussman, Irving & Sussman, Cornelia. Thomas Merton: The Daring Young Man on the Flying Belltower. LC 76-34236. 192p. (gr. 7 up). 1976. 7.95 (ISBN 0-02-788630-1, 78863). Macmillan.

Sussman, Irving, jt. auth. see Sussman, Cornelia.

Sussman, Leon N. Paternity Testing by Blood Grouping. 2nd ed. (Illus.). 208p. 1976. 22.50 (ISBN 0-398-03523-7). C C Thomas.

Sussman, Les & Bordwell, Sally. The Rape File. 1981. 12.50 (ISBN 0-87754-094-2). Chelsea Hse.

Sussman, Lyle & Krivonos, Paul. Communication for Supervisors & Managers. LC 78-22716. (Illus.). 1979. pap. text ed. 10.95x (ISBN 0-88284-077-0). Alfred Pub.

Sussman, M. V. Elementary General Thermodynamics. LC 74-133896. 1972. text ed. 22.95 (ISBN 0-201-07358-7). A-W.

Sussman, Marvin, jt. auth. see Rockstein, Morris.

Sussman, Marvin B., ed. Sourcebook in Marriage & the Family. 4th ed. 432p. 1974. pap. text ed. 11.50 (ISBN 0-395-17538-0). HM.

Sussman, Marvin B., jt. ed. see Shanas, Ethel.

Sussman, Vic. Never Kiss a Goat on the Lips: Tales of a Suburban Homesteader. Stoner, Carol, ed. (Illus.). 288p. 1981. 12.95 (ISBN 0-87857-346-1); pap. 8.95 (ISBN 0-87857-347-X). Rodale Pr Inc.

Sutch, R., jt. auth. see Ransom, R.

Sutcliff, Rosemary. Brother Dusty-Feet. (Illus.). 240p. (gr. 6 up). 1980. Repr. of 1952 ed. 10.95 (ISBN 0-19-271444-9). Oxford U Pr.

--Frontier Wolf. LC 80-39849. (gr. 6 up). 1981. 10.95 (ISBN 0-525-30260-3). Dutton.

--The Light Beyond the Forest. LC 79-23396. 144p. (gr. 4-7). 1980. 8.95 (ISBN 0-525-33665-6). Dutton.

--Outcast. (Alpha Books). 92p. (Orig.). 1979. pap. text ed. 2.25x (ISBN 0-19-424210-2). Oxford U Pr.

--Song for a Dark Queen. LC 78-19514. (gr. 7 up). 1979. 6.95 (ISBN 0-690-03911-5, TYC-J); PLB 6.89 (ISBN 0-690-03912-3). T Y Crowell.

Sutcliffe, Anthony. The History of Urban & Regional Planning. 300p. 1980. 35.00 (ISBN 0-87196-303-5). Facts on File.

Sutcliffe, B. T., jt. auth. see McWeeny, R.

Sutcliffe, Frank, jt. auth. see McCabe, Sarah.

Sutcliffe, H., jt. auth. see Pass, G.

Sutcliffe, L. H., jt. ed. see Emsley, J. W.

Sutcliffe, Matthew. A Treatise of Ecclesiasticall Dicipline. LC 73-7082. (English Experience Ser.: No. 626). 1973. Repr. of 1590 ed. 21.00 (ISBN 90-221-0626-8). Walter J Johnson.

Sutcliffe, R., jt. ed. see Owen, R.

Suter, David W. Tradition & Composition in the Parables of Enoch. LC 79-17441. (Society of Biblical Literature. Dissertation Ser.: No. 47). 1979. 12.00 (ISBN 0-89130-335-9, 060147); pap. 7.50 (ISBN 0-89130-336-7). Scholars Pr Ca.

Suter, Ronald. Six Answers to the Problem of Taste. LC 79-84279. 1979. pap. text ed. 6.25 (ISBN 0-8191-0726-3). U Pr of Amer.

Suters, Everett T. Succeed in Spite of Yourself. 1974. pap. 3.95 o.p. (ISBN 0-8015-7314-9). Dutton.

Sutherland, A. E., Jr. Civil Rights & the South: A Symposium. LC 78-151047. (Symposia on Law & Society Ser.). 1971. Repr. of 1963 ed. lib. bdg. 17.50 (ISBN 0-306-70116-2). Da Capo.

Sutherland, Anne. Gypsies: The Hidden Americans. LC 75-3762. 1975. Repr. 16.95 (ISBN 0-02-932200-6). Free Pr.

Sutherland, Arthur E. Church Shall Be Free: A Glance at Eight Centuries of Church & State. LC 65-24000. (Orig.). 1965. pap. 1.95x (ISBN 0-8139-0232-0). U Pr of Va.

--Government Under Law. LC 68-26003. (Law, Politics & History Ser). (Illus.). 1968. Repr. of 1956 ed. lib. bdg. 45.00 (ISBN 0-306-71146-X). Da Capo.

Sutherland, C. Bruce, jt. auth. see Jost, Lee F.

Sutherland, C. H. Anglo-Saxon Sceattas in England: Their Origin, Chronology & Distribution. (Numismatic Chronicle Reprint Ser.). pap. 2.50 (ISBN 0-915018-30-6). Attic Bks.

Sutherland, C. H. & Kraay, C. M. Catalogue of Coins of the Roman Empire in the Ashmolean Museum: Augustus (c. 31 B.C. - A.D. 14, Pt. 1. (Illus.). 60p. 1975. 65.00x (ISBN 0-19-813189-5). Oxford U Pr.

Sutherland, D. S. Igneous Rocks of the British Isles. 560p. 1981. 94.00 (ISBN 0-471-27810-6, Pub. by Wiley-Interscience). Wiley.

Sutherland, Donald. On, Romanticism. LC 78-145514. (Illus.). 1971. 15.00x (ISBN 0-8147-7753-8). NYU Pr.

Sutherland, Donald, tr. see Euripides.

Sutherland, Donald W. The Assize of Novel Disseisin. 1973. 29.95x (ISBN 0-19-822410-9). Oxford U Pr.

Sutherland, Douglas. The English Gentleman. 1980. pap. 2.95 (ISBN 0-14-005597-5). Penguin.

--The English Gentleman's Child. (Illus.). 1981. pap. 3.50 (ISBN 0-14-005782-X). Penguin.

--The English Gentleman's Wife. 96p. 1981. pap. 2.95 (ISBN 0-14-005734-X). Penguin.

Sutherland, Douglas, ed. Common Names of Insects & Related Organisms. 1978. pap. 4.00 o.p. (ISBN 0-686-26208-5). Entomol Soc.

Sutherland, E. Ann & Almit, Zalman. Stay Slim for Good: A Proven Seven Week Program for Lifelong Weight Control. LC 75-36538. (Illus.). 192p. 1976. 8.95 o.s.i. (ISBN 0-8027-0520-0). Walker & Co.

Sutherland, E. Ann & Zalman Amit. Phobia Free. (Orig.). pap. 1.95 (ISBN 0-515-04700-7). Jove Pubns.

Sutherland, Efua. Playtime in Africa. (Illus.). (gr. 2-6). 1962. PLB 6.95 o.p. (ISBN 0-689-20589-9). Atheneum.

Sutherland, I. W., jt. auth. see Dawes, I. W.

Sutherland, Ivan E. Sketchpad: A Man-Machine Graphical Communication System. LC 79-50557. (Outstanding Dissertations in the Computer Sciences Ser.: Vol. 21). 176p. 1980. lib. bdg. 20.00 (ISBN 0-8240-4411-8). Garland Pub.

Sutherland, J., ed. see Thackeray, William M.

Sutherland, J. A. Fiction & the Fiction Industry. 1978. text ed. 20.75x (ISBN 0-485-11177-2, Athlone Pr). Humanities.

Sutherland, James, ed. see Defoe, Daniel.

Sutherland, James R. English Satire. 1958. 26.50 (ISBN 0-521-06584-4). Cambridge U Pr.

Sutherland, John. Best Sellers: Popular Fiction of the 1970s. 272p. 1981. 18.95 (ISBN 0-7100-0750-7). Routledge & Kegan.

--Thackeray at Work. (Illus.). 160p. 1974. text ed. 18.75x (ISBN 0-485-11146-2, Athlone Pr). Humanities.

Sutherland, John M. Fundamentals of Neurology. 272p. (Orig.). 1980. pap. 23.50 (ISBN 0-909337-29-2). ADIS Pr.

Sutherland, John M. & Eadie, Mervyn. The Epilepsies. 3rd ed. (Illus.). 176p. 1980. pap. text ed. 10.00x (ISBN 0-443-02184-8). Churchill.

Sutherland, John W. A General Systems Philosphy for the Social & Behavioral Sciences. Laszlo, Ervin, ed. (International Library of Systems Theory & Philosophy Ser). 1973. 7.95 (ISBN 0-8076-0724-X); pap. 6.95 (ISBN 0-8076-0725-8). Braziller.

--Managing Social Service Systems. LC 77-21806. (Illus.). 1977. text ed. 17.50 (ISBN 0-89433-004-7). Petrocelli.

Sutherland, Kenton see Robson, Barbara.

Sutherland, L. S., ed. see Clarke, Maude V.

Sutherland, Lucy S. The East Indian Company in Eighteenth Century Politics. LC 79-1593. 1981. Repr. of 1952 ed. 29.50 (ISBN 0-88355-898-X). Hyperion Conn.

Sutherland, Margaret. Dark Places, Deep Regions & Other Stories. LC 80-17008. 1980. 9.95 (ISBN 0-916144-53-4). Stemmer Hse.

Sutherland, Margaret B. Sex Bias in Education. (Theory & Practice in Education Ser.: Vol. 2). 208p. 1981. 25.00x (ISBN 0-631-10851-3, Pub. by Basil Blackwell England); pap. 12.50x (ISBN 0-631-12617-1). Biblio Dist.

Sutherland, Millie. Brae Houe. 1980. 12.95 (ISBN 0-7145-3646-6). Riverrun NY.

--Brae House. 1981. 11.95 (ISBN 0-7145-3646-6). Riverrun NY.

Sutherland, N. S., ed. Tutorial Essays in Psychology: A Guide to Recent Advances, 2 vols. LC 78-31703. (Tutorial Essays in Psychology Ser.). Vol. 1, 1977. 10.95 (ISBN 0-470-99138-0); Vol. 2, 1979. 14.95 (ISBN 0-470-26652-X). Halsted Pr.

Sutherland, N. S., ed. see Royal Society Discussion, March 7 & 8, 1979.

Sutherland, Robert D. Sticklewort & Feverfew. LC 79-92898. (Illus.). 360p. 1980. 16.00 (ISBN 0-936044-00-4); pap. 9.00 (ISBN 0-936044-01-2). Pikestaff Pr.

Sutherland, Robert I. & EIMAC Division of Varian Laboratory Staff. Care & Feeding of Power Grid Tubes. (Illus.). 158p. 1967. 5.95 (ISBN 0-933616-06-6). Radio Pubns.

Sutherland, Ronald. The Romaunt of the Rose & Le Roman de la Rose. LC 68-14794. (Eng. & Fr.). 1968. 17.50x (ISBN 0-520-01243-7). U of Cal Pr.

Sutherland, Ronald G., jt. auth. see Que Hee, Shane S.

Sutherland, Stewart R. Atheism & the Rejection of God: Contemporary Philosophy & "The Brothers Karamazov". 1977. 24.50x (ISBN 0-631-17500-8, Pub. by Basil Blackwell). Biblio Dist.

Sutherland, Thomas R. Why Psychology Has Failed. (Illus.). 125p. 1980. deluxe ed. 32.50 (ISBN 0-89920-010-9). Am Inst Psych.

Sutherland, Wilson A. Introduction to Metric & Topological Spaces. (Illus.). 196p. 1975. 19.95x (ISBN 0-19-853155-9); pap. 12.50x (ISBN 0-19-853161-3). Oxford U Pr.

Sutherland, Zena. The Arbuthnot Anthology of Children's Literature. 4th ed. 1976. 18.95x (ISBN 0-673-15000-3). Scott F.

Sutherland, Zena & Arbuthnot, May H. Children & Books. 5th ed. 1977. 18.95x (ISBN 0-673-15037-2). Scott F.

Sutherland, Zena, ed. Children in Libraries: Patterns of Access to Materials & Services in Schools & Public Libraries. LC 80-53135. (Studies in Library Science). 128p. 1981. lib. bdg. 10.00x (ISBN 0-226-78063-5). U of Chicago Pr.

Sutherland, Zena, et al. Children & Books. 6th ed. 1981. text ed. 18.95x (ISBN 0-673-15377-0). Scott F.

Sutich, A. & Vich, M. Reading in Humanistic Psychology. LC 74-75206. 1969. 9.95 (ISBN 0-02-932280-4); pap. text ed. 8.95 (ISBN 0-02-932320-7). Free Pr.

Sutinen, J. G., jt. auth. see Liu, P. T.

Sutliff, Mary. Reanaway Country. new ed. LC 79-66697. (Illus., Orig.). 1980. pap. 4.95 (ISBN 0-913140-39-2). Signpost Bk Pub.

Sutlive, Vinson H., Jr. The Iban of Sarawak. Goldschmidt, Walter, ed. LC 77-86045. (Worlds of Man Ser.). (Illus.). 1978. text ed. 11.50x (ISBN 0-88295-616-7); pap. text ed. 5.75x (ISBN 0-88295-617-5). AHM Pub.

Sutor, Andrew P. Police Operations-Tactical Approaches to Crimes in Progress. LC 76-16911. (Criminal Justice Ser.). 1976. 12.50 (ISBN 0-685-71453-5); pap. text ed. write for info. (ISBN 0-8299-0609-6); instrs.' manual avail. (ISBN 0-8299-0611-8). West Pub.

Sutphen, Dick. How to Be a Better Past Life Regression Receiver. 1977. 2.50 o.p. (ISBN 0-911842-16-0). Valley Sun.

--Past Life Hypnotic Regression Course. 1977. 24.95 (ISBN 0-911842-13-6). Valley Sun.

--Sex, Liquor, Tobacco and Candy Are Bad for You. LC 73-186725. 96p. 1972. pap. 2.25 o.p. (ISBN 0-911842-10-1). Valley Sun.

--Spirit Mountain Speak to Me. 1977. 2.95 o.p. (ISBN 0-911842-15-2). Valley Sun.

Sutte, Donald T., Jr. Appraisal of Roadside Advertising Signs. 1972. 7.00 (ISBN 0-911780-28-9). Am Inst Real Estate Appraisers.

Sutter, Robert G. Chinese Foreign Policy After the Cultural Revolution: 1966-1977. LC 77-7018. (Special Studies on China & East Asia Ser.). 1978. lib. bdg. 22.50x (ISBN 0-89158-342-4). Westview.

Sutter, Vera, et al. Wadsworth Anaerobic Bacteriology Manual. LC 79-29670. (Illus.). 1980. pap. text ed. 9.50 (ISBN 0-8016-4848-3). Mosby.

Suttie, J. W., jt. ed. see DeLuca, H. F.

Suttie, Jane I., tr. see Ferenczi, Sandor.

Suttles, Wayne P. Coast Salish & Western Washington Indians, Vol. 1: The Economic Life of the Coast Salish of Haro & Rosario Straits. (American Indian Ethnohistory Ser.: Indians of the Northwest). (Illus.). lib. bdg. 42.00 (ISBN 0-8240-0783-2). Garland Pub.

Suttmeier, Richard P. Science, Technology & China's Drive for Modernization. LC 79-88587. (Publication: No. 223). 133p. 1980. pap. 6.95 (ISBN 0-8179-7232-3). Hoover Inst Pr.

Suttner, Bertha von see Von Suttner, Bertha.

Sutton, jt. auth. see Wilcox.

Sutton, et al. How to Prepare for the Registered Nurse Licensing Examination. 1981. pap. 4.95 (ISBN 0-8120-2301-3). Barron.

Sutton, A., jt. auth. see Sutton, M.

Sutton, Andrew, jt. auth. see McPherson, Ian.

Sutton, Ann & Holtom, Pat. Tablet Weaving. LC 74-18323. (Illus.). 104p. 1975. 11.50 (ISBN 0-8231-5045-3). Branford.

Sutton, Ann & Sutton, Myron. Guarding the Treasured Lands: The Story of the National Park Service. LC 65-13436. (Illus.). (gr. 7-9). 1965. 4.95 o.p. (ISBN 0-397-30805-1). Lippincott.

--The Pacific Crest Trail: Escape to the Wilderness. LC 75-15920. (Illus.). 240p. 1975. 8.95 o.s.i. (ISBN 0-397-01061-3). Lippincott.

--Wilderness Areas of North America. LC 74-8860. (Funk & W Bk.). (Illus.). 428p. 1974. 10.95 o.s.i. (ISBN 0-308-10124-3, TYC-T). T Y Crowell.

--Wilderness Areas of North America. LC 74-8860. (Funk & W Bk.). (Illus.). 1975. pap. 4.95 o.s.i. (ISBN 0-308-10125-1, F117, TYC-T). T Y Crowell.

Sutton, Anthony C. Energy: The Created Crisis. LC 78-73737. (Illus.). 1979. 12.95 (ISBN 0-916728-04-8). Bks in Focus.

Sutton, Antony C. National Suicide: Military Aid to the Soviet Union. 1973. 8.95 o.p. (ISBN 0-87000-207-4). Arlington Hse.

--Wall Street & FDR. 1975. 7.95 o.p. (ISBN 0-87000-328-3). Arlington Hse.

--Wall Street & the Bolshevik Revolution. 1974. 7.95 o.p. (ISBN 0-87000-276-7). Arlington Hse.

Sutton, Antony C. & Wood, Patrick M. Trilaterals Over Washington. 206p. 1979. pap. 5.95 (ISBN 0-933482-01-9). August Corp.

Sutton, Audrey L. Bedside Nursing Techniques in Medicine & Surgery. 2nd ed. LC 69-12891. 1969. pap. 11.95 (ISBN 0-7216-8666-4). Saunders.

Sutton, C. J. Economics & Corporate Strategy. LC 79-4198. (Illus.). 1980. 31.50 (ISBN 0-521-22669-4); pap. 8.95x (ISBN 0-521-29610-2). Cambridge U Pr.

Sutton, Cort. Advertising Your Way to Success: How to Create Best-Selling Advertisements in All Media. (Illus.). 208p. 1981. text ed. 18.95 (ISBN 0-686-68610-1, Spec); pap. text ed. 9.95 (ISBN 0-13-018135-8, Spec). P-H.

Sutton, Dana F. Self & Society in Aristophanes. LC 80-5235. 125p. 1980. lib. bdg. 15.50 (ISBN 0-8191-1067-1); pap. text ed. 7.50 (ISBN 0-8191-1068-X). U Pr of Amer.

Sutton, David. A Textbook of Radiology & Imaging. 3rd ed. (Illus.). 1392p. 1980. lib. bdg. 149.00 in 1 vol. (ISBN 0-443-01700-X); lib. bdg. 175.00 in 2 vols. (ISBN 0-686-28870-X). Churchill.

--Textbook of Radiology & Imaging, 2 vols. 3rd ed. 1981. Vol. 1. text ed. 149.00 (ISBN 0-686-28939-0); Vol. 2. text ed. 175.00 (ISBN 0-686-28940-4). Churchill.

Sutton, Deny. Fads & Fancies. LC 79-64887. (Illus.). 240p. 1980. 25.00 (ISBN 0-8390-0263-7). Allanheld & Schram.

Sutton, Donald S. Provincial Militarism & the Chinese Republic: The Yunnan Army, Nineteen Hundred & Five to Nineteen Twenty-Five. (Michigan Studies on China). (Illus.). 384p. 1980. 18.50x (ISBN 0-472-08813-0). U of Mich Pr.

Sutton, E. Free-Hand Sketching for Engineering & Technical Students. 64p. 1980. 4.05x (ISBN 0-85950-057-8, Pub. by Thornes England). State Mutual Bk.

Sutton, Elisabeth. Dead Fingers. 295p. 1980. Repr. lib. bdg. 15.25x (ISBN 0-89968-208-1). Lightyear.

Sutton, Eve. My Cat Likes to Hide in Boxes. LC 73-12854. 40p. (ps-2). 1974. 5.95 o.s.i. (ISBN 0-8193-0752-1, Four Winds); PLB 5.41 o.s.i. (ISBN 0-8193-0753-X). Schol Bk Serv.

Sutton, George A. & Ross, Donald M. Rocket Propulsion Elements: An Introduction to the Engineering of Rockets. 4th ed. LC 75-29197. 592p. 1976. 37.50 (ISBN 0-471-83836-5, Pub. by Wiley-Interscience). Wiley.

Sutton, George M. Fifty Common Birds of Oklahoma & the Southern Great Plains. LC 77-24336. (Illus.). 113p. 1981. pap. 6.95 (ISBN 0-8061-1704-4). U of Okla Pr.

--Portraits of Mexican Birds: Fifty Selected Paintings. (Illus.). 106p. 1980. pap. 14.95 (ISBN 0-8061-1685-4). U of Okla Pr.

--Portraits of Mexican Birds: Fifty Selected Paintings. LC 74-15911. (Illus.). 120p. 1975. 35.00 o.p. (ISBN 0-8061-1236-0). U of Okla Pr.

Sutton, Graham. The Weather. (Teach Yourself Ser.). 1975. pap. 3.95 o.p. (ISBN 0-679-10410-0). McKay.

Sutton, Harry T. Battle for Britain. 1979. pap. 3.50 o.p. (ISBN 0-7134-2119-3, Pub. by Batsford England). David & Charles.

--Ghost Hunters: The Inside Story of Haunted Places. 1978. pap. 3.50 (ISBN 0-7134-1729-3, Pub. by Batsford England). David & Charles.

Sutton, Horace. Travellers. LC 80-14931. (Illus.). 320p. 1980. 12.50 (ISBN 0-688-03694-5). Morrow.

Sutton, Irv. Gambling Know-How. 64p. (Orig.). 1980. pap. 2.95 (ISBN 0-89650-716-5). Gamblers.

Sutton, Jane. Me & the Weirdos. (gr. 2-5). 1981. 6.95 (ISBN 0-395-30447-4). HM.

Sutton, Joan L. & Watson de Barros, Leda. Novia Hoy-Esposa Manana: Guia Para Novias. S. D. de Lerin, Olivia, tr. Orig. Title: Manual das Noivas. 1980. pap. 1.70 (ISBN 0-311-46056-9, Edit Mundo). Casa Bautista.

Sutton, John. Understanding Politics in Modern Britain. 1977. pap. text ed. 11.00x (ISBN 0-245-52880-6). Intl Ideas.

Sutton, John L. The War of the Polish Sucession: The War of the Polish Succession. LC 80-51021. 256p. 1980. 19.50x (ISBN 0-8131-1417-9). U Pr of Ky.

Sutton, Larry. The Case of the Smiley Faces. (The Carolrhoda Mini-Mysteries Ser.). (Illus.). 32p. (gr. 1-4). 1981. PLB 4.95 (ISBN 0-87614-133-5). Carolrhoda Bks.

--The Case of the Trick Note. (The Carolrhoda Mini-Mysteries Ser.). (Illus.). 32p. (gr. 1-4). 1980. PLB 4.95 (ISBN 0-87614-134-3). Carolrhoda Bks.

--Ghost Plane Over Hartley Field. (A Carolrhoda Mini-Mysteries). (Illus.). 32p. (gr. 1-4). 1981. PLB 4.95 (ISBN 0-87614-135-1). Carolrhoda Bks.

--The Mystery of the Blue Champ. (The Carolrhoda Mini-Mysteries Ser.). (Illus.). 32p. (gr. 1-4). 1981. PLB 4.95 (ISBN 0-87614-137-8). Carolrhoda Bks.

--The Mystery of the Late News Report. (The Carolrhoda Mini-Mysteries Ser.). (Illus.). 32p. (gr. 1-4). 1981. PLB 4.95 (ISBN 0-87614-136-X). Carolrhoda Bks.

Sutton, M. & Sutton, A. Yellowstone: A Century of the Wilderness Idea. Friede, Eleanor, ed. LC 72-183207. (Illus.). 224p. 1972. 8.98 o.s.i. (ISBN 0-02-615480-3). Macmillan.

Sutton, Marilyn, jt. auth. see Wilcox, Sandra.

Sutton, Martin P., jt. auth. see Keighton, Robert L.

Sutton, Maurice L., et al. Now: Essays & Articles. LC 69-12305. 1969. pap. text ed. 6.95x (ISBN 0-02-478760-4, 47876). Macmillan.

Sutton, Max K. R. D. Blackmore. (English Authors Ser.: No. 265). 1979. lib. bdg. 13.50 (ISBN 0-8057-6756-8). Twayne.

--W. S. Gilbert. (English Authors Ser.: No. 178). 1975. lib. bdg. 10.95 (ISBN 0-8057-1217-8). Twayne.

Sutton, Michael, jt. auth. see Brough, Walter.

Sutton, Myron, jt. auth. see Sutton, Ann.

Sutton, Nancy. More Adventures in Cooking with Health Foods. LC 73-90512. 1974. 6.95 (ISBN 0-8119-0229-3); pap. 4.95 (ISBN 0-8119-0390-7). Fell.

Sutton, Peter C. Pieter De Hooch: Complete Edition with a Catalogue Raisonne. LC 80-7667. (Illus.). 312p. 1980. slipcased 95.00x (ISBN 0-8014-1339-7). Cornell U Pr.

Sutton, Richard, jt. ed. see Burbidge, Peter.

Sutton, Robert C., Jr. The Sutton-Taylor Feud. (Illus.). 82p. 1974. 6.95 (ISBN 0-89015-06[illegible]). Nortex Pr.

Sutton, Roberta B. Speech Index. 4th ed. LC 6[illegible]13749. 1966. 29.50 (ISBN 0-8108-0138-8). Scarecrow.

Sutton, Roberta B. & Mitchell, Charity. Speech Index: An Index to Collections of World Famous Orations & Speeches for Various Occasions; Supplement 1966 to 1970. 4th ed. LC 66-13749. 1972. 10.00 (ISBN 0-8108-0498-0). Scarecrow.

Sutton, S. Woodlice. (Illus.). 144p. 1980. 12.00 (ISBN 0-08-025942-1). Pergamon.

Sutton, S. B., ed. Civilizing American Cities: A Selection of Frederick Law Olmsted's Writings on City Landscapes. (Illus.). 1971. pap. 7.95 (ISBN 0-262-65012-6). MIT Pr.

Sutton, Valerie J. The American Manual Alphabet. (Illus.). 1976. pap. text ed. 3.00x (ISBN 0-914336-31-2). Move Short Soc.

--Dance Writing, Sutton Movement Shorthand, the Classical Ballet Key: Key One. (Illus.). 1979. text ed. 20.00 (ISBN 0-914336-04-5); 8 hr. audio cassettes 35.00 (ISBN 0-685-91352-X); book & cassette 50.00x (ISBN 0-914336-05-3). Move Short Soc.

--The Lilac Fairy: Prologue from the Sleeping Beauty. (Illus.). 1973. pap. text ed. 1.25x o.p. (ISBN 0-914336-11-8). Move Short Soc.

--The Prelude: After Baldina. (Illus.). 1974. pap. text ed. 2.00x o.p. (ISBN 0-914336-12-6). Move Short Soc.

Sutton, Valerie J. & Beekman, Betty. Goldilocks & the Three Bears: Notated in Sutton Movement Shorthand. (Illus.). 1978. pap. text ed. 3.00x (ISBN 0-914336-34-7). Move Short Soc.

Sutton, Vivian, jt. auth. see Sutton, Walter.

Sutton, Walter & Sutton, Vivian. Plato to Alexander Pope: Backgrounds of Modern Criticism. LC 66-12945. 1966. pap. text ed. 8.95x (ISBN 0-672-63084-2). Irvington.

Sutton, Walter & Foster, Richard, eds. Modern Criticism; Theory & Practice. 1963. 29.50x (ISBN 0-672-63185-7); pap. text ed. 16.95x (ISBN 0-89197-853-4). Irvington.

Sutton, William A. Carl Sandburg Remembered. LC 78-31298. 1979. 13.50 (ISBN 0-8108-1202-9). Scarecrow.

--The Road to Winesburg: A Mosaic of the Imaginative Life of Sherwood Anderson. LC 73-181997. (Illus.). 1972. 20.50 (ISBN 0-8108-0312-7). Scarecrow.

Sutton, Willie & Linn, Edward. Where the Money Was. 1977. pap. 1.95 (ISBN 0-345-28122-5). Ballantine.

Sutton-Scott, Francis & Shapland, D. G. Batsford Guide to Veteran Cars. 1979. 14.95 (ISBN 0-7134-1182-1, Pub. by Batsford England). David & Charles.

Sutton-Smith, Brian. Folkstories of Children. LC 80-5010. (American Folklore Society Ser.). 1980. 19.95x (ISBN 0-686-61087-3). U of Pa Pr.

--How to Play with Your Children: And When Not to. 1974. pap. 4.95 (ISB[illegible]-8015-3685-5, Hawthorn). Dutton.

Sutton-Smith, Brian, jt. ed. see Herron, Robin.

Sutulor, Alexander, ed. International Molybdenum Encyclopedia, 3 vols. Incl. Vol. 1. Resources & Production. 402p. 1978; Vol. 2. Metallurgy & Processing. 375p. 1979; Vol. 3. Products, Uses & Trade. 341p. 1980. (Illus.). Set. text ed. 330.00 (ISBN 0-87930-098-1). Miller Freeman.

Sutulov, Alexander. Mineral Resources & the Economy of the USSR. LC 73-10266. (Illus.). 1973. 10.00 o.p. (ISBN 0-87930-101-5). Miller Freeman.

Sutulov, Alexander, ed. International Molybdenum Encyclopedia 1778-1978, 3 vols. Incl. Vol. 1. Resources & Production. 402p; Vol. 2. Metallurgy & Processing. 375p; Vol. 3. Products, Uses & Trade. 1978-80. 330.00 (ISBN 0-87930-098-1). Miller Freeman.

Suvak, Daniel. Memoirs of American Prisons: An Annotated Bibliography. LC 78-11107. 1979. lib. bdg. 11.00 (ISBN 0-8108-1180-4). Scarecrow.

Suydam, Charles R. U. S. Cartridges & Their Handguns. (Illus.). 333p. 1976. 15.95 (ISBN 0-917714-04-0); pap. 9.95 (ISBN 0-917714-07-5). Beinfeld Pub.

Suydam, Charles R., ed. see Frasca, Albert J. & Hill, Robert H.

Suyeoka, George. Momotaro. Tabrah, Ruth, ed. LC 72-86744. (Illus.). (gr. 1-7). 1972. pap. 5.95 (ISBN 0-89610-009-X). Island Her.

Suyeoka, George, tr. see Tabrah, Ruth.

Suzman, Cedric L., et al. Southeast Export: Profiles, Typology & the Role of Technology in Selected U. S. Firms. (Research Monograph: No. 90). 1981. spiral bdg. 15.00 (ISBN 0-88406-146-9). GA St U Busn Pub.

Suzue, Kitasu. Experimental Induction of Some Collagen Diseases. (Illus.). 1974. pap. 7.50 o.p. (ISBN 0-89640-015-8). Igaku-Shoin.

Suzuki, D. T. The Awakening of Zen. Humphreys, Christmas, ed. LC 79-17444. 1980. pap. 5.95 (ISBN 0-87773-715-0, Prajna). Great Eastern.

--Shin Buddhism. 3.95 o.p. (ISBN 0-685-47281-7). Weiser.

--Zen Buddhism: Selected Writings of D. T. Suzuki. 1956. pap. 2.50 (ISBN 0-385-09300-4, A90, Anch). Doubleday.

Suzuki, Daisetz T. Introduction to Zen Buddhism. 1964. pap. 2.95 (ISBN 0-394-17474-7, B341, BC). Grove.

--Sengai, the Zen Master. LC 68-25738. (Illus.). 1971. 15.00 o.p. (ISBN 0-8212-0319-3). NYGS.

Suzuki, Daisetz T., tr. The Lankavatara Sutra: A Mahayana Text. (Illus.). 1972. Repr. of 1932 ed. 26.00 (ISBN 0-7100-2165-8). Routledge & Kegan.

Suzuki, David T. & Griffiths, A. J. An Introduction to Genetic Analysis. LC 75-29480. (Illus.). 1976. 20.95x (ISBN 0-7167-0574-5); answers to problems 0.75 (ISBN 0-7167-0362-9). W H Freeman.

Suzuki, David T. & Griffiths, Anthony J. F. Introduction to Genetic Analysis. 2nd ed. LC 80-24522. (Illus.). 1981. text ed. price not set (ISBN 0-7167-1263-6); instrs.' guide avail.; solutions manual avail. W H Freeman.

Suzuki, Kakichi. Early Buddhist Architecture in Japan. Shatzman, Nancy, tr. from Japanese. LC 79-7342. (Japanese Arts Library: Vol. 9). (Illus.). 1980. 16.95 (ISBN 0-87011-386-0). Kodansha.

Suzuki, M., et al. Training in Radiological Protection: Curricula & Programming. (Technical Reports: No. 31). 1964. pap. 5.00 (ISBN 92-0-125164-5, IAEA). Unipub.

Suzuki, Shunryu. Zen Mind, Beginner's Mind. Dixon, Trudy, ed. LC 70-123326. 132p. 1970. 5.95 (ISBN 0-8348-0052-7); pap. 4.50 (ISBN 0-8348-0079-9). Weatherhill.

Svanidze, G. G. Mathematical Modeling of Hydrologic Processes. LC 79-57578. 1980. 25.00 (ISBN 0-686-64298-8). WRP.

Svara, James H., jt. ed. see Hawley, Willis D.

Svaren, Jacqueline. Lojor's Letters: A Space-Age Story About a Boy & a Gnome & Learning Italic Handwriting. (Illus.). 72p. (Orig.). (gr. 1 up). 1980. pap. 12.50 (ISBN 0-931474-04-3). TBW Bks.

Svarovsky. Solid Liquid Separation. (Chemical Engineering Ser). 1977. 64.95 (ISBN 0-408-70795-X). Butterworths.

Svartholm, N. Elementary Particle Theory: Relativistic Groups & Analyticity. (Nobel Symposium Ser.). 1969. 43.95 (ISBN 0-470-83842-6). Halsted Pr.

Svartvik, Jan, jt. auth. see Leech, Geoffrey.

Svatos, Ladislav. Dandelion. LC 73-20911. 32p. (gr. 1-3). 1976. PLB 5.95 (ISBN 0-385-04629-4). Doubleday.

Svec, J. J. & Jeffers, P. E. Modern Masonry Panel Construction Systems. LC 72-83307. (Illus.). 1971. 16.95 (ISBN 0-8436-0114-0). CBI Pub.

Svec, J. J., et al, eds. Electronic & Newer Ceramics. 1959. 14.95 (ISBN 0-8436-0604-5). CBI Pub.

Svehla, G., jt. ed. see Vogel, A. I.

Svehla, Gyula. Automatic Potentiometric Titrations. 1977. text ed. 50.00 (ISBN 0-08-021590-4). Pergamon.

Sveinsson, Einar Ol. Njals Saga: A Literary Masterpiece. Schach, Paul, tr. Schach, Paul, ed. LC 70-128914. 1971. 12.50x o.p. (ISBN 0-8032-0789-1). U of Nebr Pr.

Svelto, Orazio. Principles of Lasers. (Illus.). 376p. 1976. 25.00 (ISBN 0-306-30860-6, Plenum Pr). Plenum Pub.

Svendsen, Louise A. The Evelyn Sharp Collection. LC 78-51870. (Illus.). 1978. soft cover 7.50 (ISBN 0-89207-012-9). S R Guggenheim.

Svendson, May. Numbers Workbook Three (with Daring Dog) (Funny Face Activity Bks.). (Illus.). 48p. (ps-1). 1981. pap. 1.95 saddle-stitched (ISBN 0-394-84458-0). Random.

Svendson, Roger & Griffin, Tom. The Student Assistance Program: How It Works. 1980. pap. 3.95 (ISBN 0-89486-110-7). Hazelden.

Svenkerud, A., jt. auth. see Berulfsen, B.

Svennas, Elsie. Advanced Quilting. (Illus.). 144p. 1980. 16.95 (ISBN 0-684-16612-7, ScribT). Scribner.

Svennerholm, Lars, et al, eds. Structure & Function of the Gangliosides. (Advances in Experimental Medicine & Biology Ser.: Vol. 125). 580p. 1980. 49.50 (ISBN 0-306-40332-3, Plenum Pr). Plenum Pub.

Svensson, Frances. The Ethnics in American Politics: American Indians. LC 72-88751. (Critical Issues in Political Science Ser.). 1973. pap. 2.95 o.p. (ISBN 0-8087-1972-6). Burgess.

Sverdrup, E. Norway's Delights Cookbook. rev. ed. (Tanum of Norway Tokens Ser). 1980. pap. 11.00x (ISBN 8-2518-0089-7, N429). Vanous.

Sverstiuk, Ievhen. Clandestine Essays. Luckyj, George S., tr. from Ukrainian. Orig. Title: Ivan Kotliarevsky Smietsia. 100p. 1976. PLB 10.00x (ISBN 0-87287-151-7); pap. 7.50 (ISBN 0-87287-158-4). Ukrainian Acad.

Svet, Don, jt. auth. see Wadman, Robert C.

Svetloff, V. Anna Pavlova. Grey, A., tr. from Fr. (Illus.). 224p. 1974. pap. 6.95 (ISBN 0-486-23047-3). Dover.

Svevo, Italo. Further Confessions of Zeno. Johnson, Ben & Furbank, P. N., trs. LC 69-19076. 1969. 17.50x (ISBN 0-520-01436-7); pap. 2.45 (ISBN 0-520-01753-6, CAL226). U of Cal Pr.

--Short Sentimental Journey & Other Stories. 1967. 17.50x (ISBN 0-520-01244-5). U of Cal Pr.

Sviatoslavsky, I. N., tr. see Kapitza, S. P. & Melekhin, V. N.

Svinicki, Eunice. Flowercraft. (Step-by-Step Crafts Ser.). (Illus.). 1977. PLB 9.15 o.p. (ISBN 0-307-62020-4, Golden Pr); pap. 1.95 (ISBN 0-307-42020-5). Western Pub.

Svirski, Grigory. A History of Post-War Soviet Writing. Dessaix & Ulman, trs. from Rus. (Illus.). 1981. 17.50 (ISBN 0-88233-449-2). Ardis Pubs.

Svirsky, Grigory. Hostages: The Personal Testimony of a Soviet Jew. Clough, Gordon, tr. 1976. 10.00 o.p. (ISBN 0-394-49368-0). Knopf.

Svitak, Ivan. Czechoslovak Experiment, 1968-1969. LC 74-141888. (Illus.). 1971. 22.50x (ISBN 0-231-03462-8). Columbia U Pr.

--The Dialectic of Common Sense: The Master Thinkers. LC 78-65849. 1979. pap. text ed. 9.75 (ISBN 0-8191-0675-5). U Pr of Amer.

Svoboda, Antonin & James, Hubert M. Computing Mechanisms & Linkages. (Illus.). 1948. pap. text ed. 4.00 (ISBN 0-486-61404-2). Dover.

Svoronos, J. N. L' Hellenisme Primitif de la Macedoine Prouve par la Numismatique et l'Or Du Pangee. (Illus.). 1979. text ed. 50.00 (ISBN 0-916710-48-3). Obol Intl.

Swabey, W. C. Ethical Theory from Hobbes to Kant. LC 60-53161. 1961. 4.75 (ISBN 0-8022-1680-3). Philos Lib.

Swad, Randy, jt. auth. see Bandy, Dale.

Swados, Elizabeth. Skydance. LC 80-7913. (Illus.). 32p. (ps-3). 1981. 8.95 (ISBN 0-06-026073-4, HarpJ); PLB 8.79g (ISBN 0-06-026074-2). Har-Row.

Swados, Harvey, ed. American Writer & the Great Depression. LC 65-23009. (Illus., Orig.). 1966. pap. 10.50 (ISBN 0-672-60098-6, AHS63). Bobbs.

Swaffar, Janet K., jt. auth. see Cates, G. Truett.

Swaggart, Jimmy & Lamb, Robert P. To Cross a River. 1977. pap. 2.95 (ISBN 0-88270-293-9). Logos.

Swagler, Roger M. Consumers & the Market: An Introductory Analysis. 1979. pap. 8.95x (ISBN 0-669-01692-6). Heath.

Swaim, C. Richard & Mulcahy, Kevin. Public Policy & the Arts. (Special Studies in Public Policy & Public System Management). 300p. 1981. lib. bdg. 25.00x (ISBN 0-86531-115-3). Westview.

Swaim, Joseph C. Answers to Your Questions About the Bible. 15.00 o.s.i. (ISBN 0-8149-0217-0). Vanguard.

Swaim, Steven F. Surgery of Traumatized Skin: Management & Reconstruction in the Dog & Cat. (Illus.). 585p. 1980. text ed. 42.50 (ISBN 0-7216-8688-5). Saunders.

Swaiman, Kenneth & Ashwal, Stephen. Pediatric Neurology Case Studies. 1978. spiral 19.50 (ISBN 0-87488-007-6). Med Exam.

Swaiman, Kenneth F. & Wright, Francis S. Neuromuscular Diseases of Infancy & Childhood. (Illus.). 272p. 1970. 18.00 o.p. (ISBN 0-398-01885-5). C C Thomas.

--Pediatric Neuromuscular Diseases. LC 79-20238. 1979. text ed. 42.50 (ISBN 0-8016-4846-7). Mosby.

Swain, Barbara. Cookery for One or Two. LC 78-60432. (Illus.). 1978. pap. 5.95 (ISBN 0-912656-95-6). H P Bks.

Swain, C., jt. auth. see Buckley, A.

Swain, Clark. A Tuneup for Partners in Love. LC 80-84568. 250p. 1981. 7.95 (ISBN 0-88290-171-0, 2015). Horizon Utah.

Swain, David, jt. auth. see Shipton, Nathaniel N.

Swain, Dwight. Scripting for Video & Audiovisual Media. 1981. 22.95 (ISBN 0-240-51075-5). Focal Pr.

Swain, Dwight V. Techniques of the Selling Writer. LC 73-7419. 330p. 1981. pap. 7.50 (ISBN 0-8061-1191-7). U of Okla Pr.

Swain, Frederick M. Non-Marine Organic Geochemistry. (Cambridge Earth Science Ser). (Illus.). 1970. 83.50 (ISBN 0-521-07757-5). Cambridge U Pr.

Swain, James J., jt. auth. see Biles, William E.

Swain, Joseph W., tr. see Durkheim, Emile.

Swain, Kathleen M., jt. ed. see Ingram, William.

Swain, Lionel. Ephesians. (New Testament Message Ser.). 9.95 (ISBN 0-89453-136-0); pap. 4.95 (ISBN 0-89453-201-4). M Glazier.

Swain, Roger. Earthly Pleasures. (Illus.). 192p. 1981. 10.00 (ISBN 0-684-16657-7, ScribT). Scribner.

Swain, T., ed. see Phytochemical Society.

Swainbank, Todd, ed. Taking Gamefish: From Dry Flies to Downrigger Freshwater Fishing. LC 79-20982. (Illus.). 1979. 15.95 (ISBN 0-89594-026-4); pap. 8.95 (ISBN 0-89594-025-6). Crossing Pr.

Swainson, Charles. A Handbook of Weather Folk-Lore: Being a Collection of Proverbial Sayings in Various Languages Relating to the Weather. LC 73-5513. xii, 275p. 1974. Repr. of 1873 ed. 18.00 (ISBN 0-8103-3980-3). Gale.

Swainson, Nicola. The Development of Corporate Capitalism in Kenya, Nineteen Eighteen to Nineteen Seventy-Seven. 1980. 20.00 (ISBN 0-686-65115-4, CAMPUS 258); pap. 8.50 (ISBN 0-520-04019-8). U of Cal Pr.

Swales, Martin. Thomas Mann: A Study. 117p. 1980. 11.50x (ISBN 0-8476-6270-5). Rowman.

Swales, Martin, ed. Arthur Schnitzler: Professor Bernhardi. LC 73-183731. 153p. 1972. 6.70 (ISBN 0-08-016801-9); pap. 5.15 (ISBN 0-08-016806-X). Pergamon.

Swalin, Benjamin. The Violin Concerto. LC 72-8292. (Music Ser). 186p. 1973. Repr. of 1941 ed. lib. bdg. 19.50 (ISBN 0-306-70537-0). Da Capo.

Swalin, Richard A. Thermodynamics of Solids. 2nd ed. LC 72-6334. (Science & Technology of Materials Ser.). 448p. 1972. 38.50 (ISBN 0-471-83854-3, Pub. by Wiley-Interscience). Wiley.

Swallow, Alan. Editor's Essays of Two Decades. LC 72-94406. 401p. 1962. 7.95 (ISBN 0-8040-0073-5). Swallow.

--Nameless Sight: Selected Poems 1937-1956. 74p. 1963. pap. 3.95 (ISBN 0-8040-0223-1, 50). Swallow.

Swallow, Alan, ed. Anchor in the Sea: An Anthology of Psychological Fiction. LC 77-94406. 243p. 1947. pap. 4.95x (ISBN 0-8040-0010-7). Swallow.

Swallow, Jay. Pony Care. (Illus.). 128p. 1976. 9.50 o.p. (ISBN 0-04-636009-3). Allen Unwin.

Swallow, Mary, ed. see Thompson, R. O.

Swalls, Fred. Legal Rights & Responsibilities of Indiana Teachers. 3rd ed. LC 75-36710. 1976. pap. text ed. 4.50x o.p. (ISBN 0-8134-1784-8, 1784). Interstate.

Swalls, Fred, et al, eds. Legal Rights & Responsibilities of Indiana Teachers. 4th ed. 1980. pap. text ed. 8.95x (ISBN 0-8134-2152-7, 2152). Interstate.

Swami Kuvalayananda. Popular Yoga Asanas. LC 76-130420. (Illus.). (gr. 9 up). 1972. Repr. of 1931 ed. 12.50 (ISBN 0-8048-0673-X). C E Tuttle.

Swami, Shri P., tr. The Geeta. (Orig.). 1965. pap. 4.95 (ISBN 0-571-06157-5, Pub. by Faber & Faber). Merrimack Bk Serv.

Swami Chidbhavananda. The Bhagavad Gita. 1979. 8.50 (ISBN 0-89744-968-1). Auromere.

Swami Gambhirananda, tr. from Sanskrit. Katha Upanishad. (Upanishads with Shankara's Commentary Ser.). 136p. pap. 2.95 (ISBN 0-87481-201-1). Vedanta Pr.

--Mandukya Upanishad. (Upanishads with Shankara's Commentary Ser.). 240p. 1980. pap. 3.50 (ISBN 0-87481-202-X). Vedanta Pr.

Swami Jagadananda, tr. see Saradananda, Swami.

Swami Jyotirmayanada. Meditate the Tantric Yoga Way. 1973. 5.50 o.p. (ISBN 0-04-149022-3). Allen Unwin.

Swami Muktananda. In the Company of a Siddha: Interviews & Conversations with Swami Muktananda. LC 78-65085. 1978. 4.50 (ISBN 0-685-94386-0). SYDA Found.

--Kundalini-the Secret of Life. (Illus., Orig.). 1979. pap. 3.25 (ISBN 0-914602-47-0). SYDA Found.

--Light on the Path. 1972. 2.95 (ISBN 0-914602-54-3). SYDA Found.

--Meditate. (Transpersonal & Humanistic Psychology Ser.). 9.95 (ISBN 0-87395-497-1). State U NY Pr.

--Mukteshwari, Vol. I. 1972. 2.95 (ISBN 0-914602-61-6). SYDA Found.

--Mukteshwari, Vol. II. 1973. 2.95 (ISBN 0-914602-62-4). SYDA Found.

--Reflections of the Self. LC 80-50391. (Illus., Orig.). 1980. pap. 5.95 (ISBN 0-914602-50-0). SYDA Found.

Swaminathan, K. Ramana Maharshi. (National Biography Ser.). 1979. pap. 2.25 o.p. (ISBN 0-89744-197-4). Auromere.

Swami Nikhilananda, compiled by. Vivekananda: The Yogas & Other Works. LC 53-7534. (Illus.). 1018p. includes biography 14.95 (ISBN 0-911206-04-3). Ramakrishna.

Swami Satchidananda, see Mandelkorn, Philip.

Swami Sivananda Radha. Mantras: Words of Power. LC 80-10293. (Illus.). 150p. 1980. pap. 5.95 (ISBN 0-931454-05-0). Timeless Bks.

--Radha: Diary of a Woman's Search. Gray, Margaret & Padmananda, Swami, eds. LC 80-26470. (Illus.). 230p. (Orig.). 1981. pap. 7.95 (ISBN 0-931454-06-9). Timeless Bks.

Swami Vishwashrayananda. Swami Vijnanananda: His Life & Sayings. Devavrata Basu Ray, tr. from Bongali. 72p. 1981. pap. 1.95 (ISBN 0-87481-502-9). Vedanta Pr.

Swami Vividishananda. Spiritual Ideals for Modern Man. 198p. 1980. o. p. o.p. (ISBN 0-87481-566-5). Vedanta Pr.

Swamy, N. V. & Samuel, Mark A. Group Theory Made Easy for Scientists & Engineers. LC 78-11733. 1979. 18.50 (ISBN 0-471-05128-4, Pub. by Wiley-Interscience). Wiley.

Swan, Abraham. British Architect. 2nd ed. LC 67-25995. (Architecture & Decorative Art Ser). (Illus.). 1967. Repr. of 1758 ed. lib. bdg. 75.00 (ISBN 0-306-70961-9). Da Capo.

Swan, Alfred J. Scriabin. LC 75-76423. (Music Ser). 1969. Repr. of 1928 ed. lib. bdg. 16.50 (ISBN 0-306-71322-5). Da Capo.

Swan, D. K., ed. New Method Supplementary Readers. (Illus.). write for info (ISBN 0-686-00592-9). Longman.

Swan, Donald A., tr. see Lundman, Bertil J.

Swan, Dorothy, jt. auth. see Burns, Julie.

Swan, Helena. Girls' Christian Names, Their History, Meaning & Association. LC 68-17935. 1968. Repr. of 1900 ed. 20.00 (ISBN 0-8103-3135-7). Gale.

Swan, Helena, ed. Who's Who in Fiction: A Dictionary of Noted Names in Novels, Tales, Romances, Poetry & Drama. LC 73-167218. 1975. Repr. of 1906 ed. 24.00 (ISBN 0-8103-4114-X). Gale.

Swan, Howard. Music in the Southwest, 1825-1950. LC 77-5421. (Music Reprint Ser.). 1977. Repr. of 1952 ed. lib. bdg. 29.50 (ISBN 0-306-77418-6). Da Capo.

Swan, K. G. The Cardiovascular System: Disease, Diagnosis, Treatment. (Clinical Monographs Ser.). (Illus.). 1973. pap. 7.95 (ISBN 0-87618-058-6). R J Brady.

Swan, L. Alex. Families of Black Prisoners: Survival & Progress. (University Book Ser.). 1981. 188.95 (ISBN 0-8161-8412-7). G K Hall.

--The Politics of Riot Behavior. LC 79-5510. 1980. pap. text ed. 10.25 (ISBN 0-8191-0905-3). U Pr of Amer.

--Survival & Progress: The Afro-American Experience. LC 80-1197. (Contributions in Afro-American & African Studies: No. 58). (Illus.). 280p. 1981. lib. bdg. 25.00 (ISBN 0-313-22480-3, SSU). Greenwood.

Swan, Lester A. & Papp, Charles S. The Common Insects of North America. LC 75-138765. (Illus.). 752p. 1972. 17.50 o.p. (ISBN 0-06-014181-6, HarpT); lib. bdg. 13.27 (ISBN 0-06-014179-4). Har-Row.

Swan, Michael. Henry James. Dobree, Bonamy, et al, eds. Bd. with D. H. Lawrence. Young, Kenneth; Joseph Conrad. Warner, Oliver. LC 63-63096. (British Writers & Their Work Ser: Vol. 10). 1967. pap. 2.65x (ISBN 0-8032-5660-4, BB 459, Bison). U of Nebr Pr.

Swan, Oscar. A Concise Grammer of Polish. LC 77-18467. 1978. pap. text ed. 5.75x (ISBN 0-8191-0319-5). U Pr of Amer.

Swan, Richard G. Theory of Sheaves. LC 64-24979. (Chicago Lectures in Mathematics Ser). (Orig.). 1964. 8.00x (ISBN 0-226-78329-4). U of Chicago Pr.

Swan, Susan B. Plain & Fancy: American Women & Their Needlework, 1700-1850. LC 77-1627. (Illus.). 1977. 14.95 o.p. (ISBN 0-03-015121-X). HR&W.

Swan, Susan B., jt. auth. see Landon, Mary T.

Swanberg, Annette, jt. auth. see Charlton, Leigh.

Swanberg, Nancie. Dolls Through the Ages. (Illus.). (gr. 1-12). 1979. pap. 3.50 (ISBN 0-89844-005-X). Troubador Pr.

--Great Ballet Paper Dolls. (Illus.). 32p. (Orig.). 1981. pap. 3.50 (ISBN 0-89844-027-0). Troubador Pr.

Swanberg, W. A. Citizen Hearst. (Illus.). 1961. lib. rep. ed. 25.00x (ISBN 0-684-14503-0, ScribT). Scribner.

--Dreiser. (Illus.). 1965. lib. rep. ed. 25.00x (ISBN 0-684-14552-9, ScribT). Scribner.

--Norman Thomas: The Last Idealist. encore ed. LC 76-15591. (Encore Edition). (Illus.). 1976. 6.95 o.p. (ISBN 0-684-15958-9, ScribT). Scribner.

Swanborough. Civil Aircraft of the World. 1980. 12.95 (ISBN 0-684-16616-X, ScribT). Scribner.

Swanborough, Gordon, jt. auth. see Green, William.

Swanborough, Gordon, jt. auth. see Taylor, John W.

Swanfeldt, Andrew. Crossword Puzzle Dictionary. 4th, rev, new ed. LC 76-57994. 1977. 12.50 (ISBN 0-690-00426-5, TYC-T); thumb-indexed 13.95 (ISBN 0-690-01198-9). T Y Crowell.

Swanholm, Marx. Alexander Ramsey & the Politics of Survival. LC 77-23371. (Minnesota Historic Sites Pamphlet Ser.: No. 13). (Illus.). 1977. pap. 2.00 (ISBN 0-87351-114-X). Minn Hist.

--Lumbering in the Last of the White-Pine States. LC 78-14221. (Minnesota Historic Sites Pamphlet Ser.: No. 17). (Illus.). 1978. 2.00 (ISBN 0-87351-131-X). Minn Hist.

--Shadows in the Stillness: Early Man on the Rainy River. LC 77-180501. (Minn Historic Sites Pamphlet Ser.: No. 16). 28p. 1978. pap. 1.50 (ISBN 0-87351-123-9). Minn Hist.

Swank, Roy L., M.D., Ph.D. & Pullen, Mary-Helen. The Multiple Sclerosis Diet Book: A Low-Fat Diet for the Treatment of M.S. Heartdisease & Stroke. LC 76-24215. 1977. 9.95 (ISBN 0-385-12092-3). Doubleday.

Swank, Scott T., jt. ed. see Quimby, Ian M.

Swann, Brian. A Book of Voices. 1980. write for info.; pap. write for info. Latitudes Pr.

--Unreal Estate. 48p. 1981. 25.00 (ISBN 0-915124-39-4, Bookslinger); pap. 6.00 (ISBN 0-915124-40-8). Toothpaste.

Swann, Brian, jt. ed. see Bonazzi, Robert.

Swann, Brian, tr. see Anday, Melih C.

Swann, Brian, tr. see Bodini, Vittorio.

Swann, Brian, tr. see Cattafi, Bartolo.

Swann, Brian, jt. tr. see Feldman, Ruth.

Swann, Dennis, jt. auth. see Smith, Peter.

Swann, Gloria H. Increasing Programmer's Production Through Logic Development. (Illus.). 1978. text ed. 12.50 (ISBN 0-89433-065-9). Petrocelli.

--Top Down Structured Design Techniques. LC 77-27092. (PBI Series for Computer & Data Processing Professionals). 1978. text ed. 13.50 (ISBN 0-89433-094-2); pap. 11.50 (ISBN 0-89433-019-5). Petrocelli.

Swann, Harry K. Dictionary of English & Folk-Names of British Birds. LC 68-30664. 1968. Repr. of 1913 ed. 15.00 (ISBN 0-8103-3340-6). Gale.

Swann, Ingo, ed. What Will Happen to You When the Soviets Take Over. LC 80-25438. 244p. (Orig.). 1980. write for info. (ISBN 0-9604946-6-9). Starform.

Swann, James P., Jr. NLRB Elections: A Guidebook for Employers. 150p. (Orig.). 1980. pap. 10.00 (ISBN 0-87179-322-9). BNA.

Swann, Thomas B. A. A. Milne. (English Authors Ser.: No. 113). lib. bdg. 10.95 (ISBN 0-8057-1396-4). Twayne.

Swanney, Pamela J., jt. auth. see Marsh, John S.

Swanson, jt. auth. see Cassel.

Swanson, jt. auth. see Johnson.

Swanson, Allen J. Taiwan: Mainline Versus Independent Church Growth. LC 74-126424. 300p. 1973. pap. 5.95 (ISBN 0-87808-404-5). William Carey Lib.

Swanson, Andrew P. The Determinative Team. 1979. pap. 6.00 o.p. (ISBN 0-682-49248-5). Exposition.

Swanson, Bert E., et al. Small Towns & Small Towners: A Framework for Survival & Growth. LC 78-17697. (Sage Library of Social Research: Vol. 79). 1979. 18.00x (ISBN 0-8039-1017-7); pap. 8.95x (ISBN 0-8039-1018-5). Sage.

Swanson, Bessie R. Music in the Education of Children. 3rd ed. 1969. 18.95x (ISBN 0-534-00673-6). Wadsworth Pub.

--Music in the Education of Children. 4th ed. 448p. 1980. text ed. 18.95x (ISBN 0-534-00880-1). Wadsworth Pub.

Swanson, C. R., et al. Criminal Investigation. 2nd ed. Territo, Leonard, tr. 1980. text ed. write for info. (ISBN 0-8302-2060-7). Goodyear.

Swanson, Carl A. Steps to Take to Save a Business Which Is on the Verge of Collaspe. (The International Council for Excellence in Management Library). (Illus.). 105p. 1980. plastic spiral bdg. 24.95 (ISBN 0-89266-243-3). Am Classical Coll Pr.

Swanson, Carl B., et al. Cytogenetics: The Chromosome in Division, Inheritance, & Evolution. 2nd ed. (Biology Ser.). (Illus.). 1980. text ed. 23.95 (ISBN 0-13-196618-9). P-H.

Swanson, Carl L., jt. auth. see Sethi, S. Prakash.

Swanson, Carl P. & Webster, Peter. The Cell. 4th ed. (Foundation of Modern Biology Ser). (Illus.). 1977. 15.95 (ISBN 0-13-121707-0); pap. text ed. 13.95 (ISBN 0-13-121699-6). P-H.

Swanson, Carl P., et al. Cytogenetics. (Illus., Orig.). 1967. pap. 10.95x ref. ed. (ISBN 0-13-196634-0). P-H.

Swanson, David W., et al, eds. The Paranoid. 525p. 1970. 19.95 (ISBN 0-316-82475-5). Little.

Swanson, Don R., ed. The Role of Libraries in the Growth of Knowledge. LC 79-5467. 1980. lib. bdg. 10.00x (ISBN 0-226-78468-1). U of Chicago Pr.

Swanson, Don R. & Bookstein, Abraham, eds. Operations Research: Implications for Libraries (35th Annual Conference of the Graduate Library School, August 2-4, 1971) LC 73-185760. (University of Chicago Studies in Library Science). (Illus.). 160p. 1972. lib. bdg. 10.00 (ISBN 0-226-78466-5). U of Chicago Pr.

Swanson, Donald C. Names in Roman Verse: A Lexicon & Reverse Index of All Proper Names of History, Mythology & Geography Found in the Classical Roman Poets. 1967. 30.00x (ISBN 0-299-04560-9). U of Wis Pr.

Swanson, Donna. Mind Song. 1978. pap. text ed. 2.95x (ISBN 0-8358-0364-3). Upper Room.

Swanson, E. Burton, jt. auth. see Lientz, Bennet P.

Swanson, E. Burton, jt. auth. see Mason, Richard H.

Swanson, Edward. A Manual of AACR 2 Examples for Manuscripts. 50p. 1980. pap. 6.00 (ISBN 0-936996-12-9). Soldier Creek.

Swanson, Edward & Jones, Marilyn H., eds. A Manual of AACR 2 Examples. 2nd ed. 87p. (Orig.). 1980. pap. 7.50 (ISBN 0-936996-01-3). Soldier Creek.

Swanson, Edward & McClaskey, Marilyn J., eds. A Manual of AACR 2 Advanced Examples. 50p. 1980. pap. 6.00 (ISBN 0-936996-02-1). Soldier Creek.

Swanson, Edward, ed. see Aichele, Jean & Olson, Nancy B.

Swanson, Edward, ed. see Hanley, Mary D.

Swanson, Edward, jt. ed. see McClaskey, Marilyn J.

Swanson, Edward, ed. see Marion, Phyllis.

Swanson, Edward, ed. see Moore, Barbara N.

Swanson, Edward, ed. see Schilling, Irene A.

Swanson, Edward, ed. see Simonton, Wesley & Mannie, Phillip.

Swanson, Frederick J. Music Teaching in the Junior High & the Middle School. LC 72-94283. (Illus.). 304p. 1973. 14.95 (ISBN 0-13-608240-8). P-H.

Swanson, G. L C to Dewey Conversion Tables. 1974. 32.00 o.s.i. (ISBN 0-02-469550-5). Macmillan Info.

Swanson, H. Lee & Reinert, Henry R. Teaching Strategies for Children in Conflict: Curriculum, Methods & Materials. LC 79-40. (Illus.). 1979. pap. text ed. 15.95 (ISBN 0-8016-4106-3). Mosby.

Swanson, Harold D. Human Reproduction: Biology & Social Change. (Illus.). 300p. 1974. text ed. 12.95x (ISBN 0-19-501772-2); pap. text ed. 9.95x (ISBN 0-19-501771-4). Oxford U Pr.

Swanson, Leonard W. Linear Programming: Basic Theory & Applications. LC 79-10092. (Quantitative Methods for Management Ser.). (Illus.). 1979. 22.00 (ISBN 0-07-062580-8, C); instructor's manual 4.95 (ISBN 0-07-062581-6). McGraw.

Swanson, Leslie C. Covered Bridges in Illinois, Iowa, & Wisconsin. rev. ed. (Illus., Orig.). 1970. pap. 5.95 (ISBN 0-911466-14-2). Swanson.

Swanson, M. General Semantics Monographs No. 4: Scientific Epistemologic Backgrounds of General Semantics. 1959. 5.00x (ISBN 0-910780-04-8). Inst Gen Semantics.

Swanson, Peter W., jt. auth. see Fetters, Thomas T.

Swanson, R. N. Universities, Academics & the Great Schism. LC 78-56764. (Cambridge Studies in Medieval Life & Thought: 3rd Ser., No. 12). 1979. 38.50 (ISBN 0-521-22127-7). Cambridge U Pr.

Swanson, Reuben J. Roots Out of Dry Ground. 1979. 8.50 (ISBN 0-915948-06-0); pap. 6.50 (ISBN 0-686-57420-6). Western NC Pr.

Swanson, Richard. For Your Information: A Guide to Writing Reports. (Illus.). 160p. 1974. pap. text ed. 6.50 (ISBN 0-13-324905-0). P-H.

Swanson, Richard W. & Marquardt, Charles E. On Communications: A Fundamental Approach to Reading, Writing, Speaking & Listening. LC 73-7370. (Illus.). 192p. 1974. pap. text ed. 5.95x (ISBN 0-02-478750-7). Macmillan.

Swanson, Robert S. Plastic Technology, Basic Materials & Processes: Basic Materials & Processes. (gr. 11-12). 1965. text ed. 14.64 (ISBN 0-87345-483-9). McKnight.

Swanson, Rodney B., jt. auth. see Marshall, Robert H.

Swanson, Roger M., ed. The Freshman Writes. LC 70-179365. 1973. pap. 9.60 o.p. (ISBN 0-672-63039-7). Odyssey Pr.

Swanson, Roy A., ed. Pindar's Odes. LC 72-90908. (Library of Liberal Arts Ser.). (Illus.). 1974. 10.35 o.p. (ISBN 0-672-51543-1, LLA178); pap. text ed. 7.50 (ISBN 0-672-61245-3). Bobbs.

Swanson, Roy A., tr. see Catullus.

Swanson, S. A. & Freeman, M. A., eds. The Scientific Basis of Joint Replacement. LC 76-51524. 1977. 26.95 (ISBN 0-471-03012-0, Pub. by Wiley Medical). Wiley.

Swanson, Vern. Alma-Tadema. encore ed. (Illus.). 1977. 5.95 o.p. (ISBN 0-684-16366-7, ScribT). Scribner.

Swanson, Walter S. Deepwood. 1981. 10.95 (ISBN 0-316-82476-3). Little.

Swanton, Ian, ed. Hambro Euromoney Directory, 1979. 8th ed. LC 75-644094. (Orig.). 1979. pap. 42.50x o.p. (ISBN 0-903121-05-0). Intl Pubns Serv.

Swanton, Michael, ed. Anglo-Saxon Prose. (Rowman & Littlefield University Library). 188p. 1975. 11.00x (ISBN 0-87471-545-8); pap. 5.00x (ISBN 0-87471-544-X). Rowman.

Swanwick, Helena M. War in Its Effect Upon Women. LC 74-147727. (Library of War & Peace; the Character & Causes of War). lib. bdg. 38.00 (ISBN 0-8240-0280-6). Garland Pub.

Swanwick, Keith. A Basis for Music Education. (Orig.). 1979. pap. text ed. 13.25x (ISBN 0-85633-180-5). Humanities.

Swanzey, Thomas B., jt. auth. see Lynch, Robert E.

Swarbrick, B. The Road Home: Sketches of Rural Canada. 1976. 19.95 o.p. (ISBN 0-13-781559-X). P-H.

Swarbrick, Brian. The Duffer's Guide to Bogey Golf. LC 72-6539. (Illus.). 160p. 1973. 5.95 o.p. (ISBN 0-13-220939-X); pap. 2.95 o.p. (ISBN 0-13-220897-0). P-H.

Swart, Dorothy M., ed. see National Conference on Social Welfare.

Swarthout, Glendon. The Shootist. LC 74-17772. 192p. 1975. 6.95 o.p. (ISBN 0-385-06099-8). Doubleday.

--Skeletons. 1981. pap. write for info. (ISBN 0-671-83586-6). PB.

Swartley, John C. Eastern Hemlock & Its Variations. LC 79-18983. 272p. 1980. lib. bdg. 25.00 (ISBN 0-686-63240-0). Garland Pub.

Swartz, Ava, ed. see Manning, Jack.

Swartz, Clifford & Goldfarb, Theodore. A Search for Order in the Physical Universe. LC 73-19743. (Illus.). 1974. text ed. 22.95x (ISBN 0-7167-0345-9). W H Freeman.

Swartz, Clifford E. Used Math for the First Two Years of College Science. (Illus.). 320p. 1973. pap. 10.95 ref. ed. (ISBN 0-13-939736-1). P-H.

Swartz, Edward M. Hazardous Products Litigation. LC 73-77826. 416p. 1973. 47.50 (ISBN 0-686-05457-1). Lawyers Co-Op.

Swartz, Fred. The Pentax Guide. (Illus.). 136p. 1980. 11.95 (ISBN 0-8174-2471-7); pap. 6.95 (ISBN 0-8174-2143-2). Amphoto.

Swartz, H., jt. auth. see Franks, R.

Swartz, Harold M., et al, eds. Biological Applications of Electron Spin Resonance. LC 72-39768. 1972. 57.95 (ISBN 0-471-83870-5, Pub. by Wiley-Interscience). Wiley.

Swartz, M. Evelyn, jt. auth. see Rueschhoff, Phil H.

Swartz, Marc J. & Jordan, David K. Culture: The Anthropological Perspective. LC 79-9211. 1980. pap. text ed. 15.95x (ISBN 0-471-03333-2). Wiley.

Swartz, Marc J., et al, eds. Political Anthropology. LC 66-15210. 1966. 23.95x (ISBN 0-202-01026-0). Aldine Pub.

Swartz, Mark H., ed. An Introduction to Physical Diagnosis. Date not set. text ed. price not set (ISBN 0-89004-562-3). Raven.

Swartz, Mary, jt. auth. see Tokayer, Marvin.

Swartz, Melvin J. Don't Die Broke! A Guide to Secure Retirement. 252p. 1975. 8.95 o.s.i. (ISBN 0-02-615560-5). Macmillan.

Swartz, Morton N., jt. auth. see Remington, Jack S.

Swartz, R. Starting Point: A Guide to Basic Writing Skills. 1980. pap. 9.50 (ISBN 0-13-843029-2). P-H.

Swartz, Ronald M., et al. Knowledge & Fallibilism: Essays on Improving Education. LC 79-3068. 1980. 17.00x (ISBN 0-8147-7808-9). NYU Pr.

Swartz, Thomas R., jt. ed. see Bonello, Frank J.

Swartzentruber, Mrs. James. God Made the Animals. (God Is Good Ser.). 1976. 2.25 (ISBN 0-686-18185-9). Rod & Staff.

--We Should Be Thankful. (God Is Good Ser.). 1976. 2.00 (ISBN 0-686-18188-3). Rod & Staff.

Swary, Itzhak. Capital Adequacy Requirements & Bank Holding Companies. Dufey, Gunter, ed. (Research for Business Decisions). 161p. 1980. 24.95 (ISBN 0-8357-1129-3, Pub. by UMI Res Pr). Univ Microfilms.

Swarz, Robert, jt. auth. see Siewiorek, Daniel.

Swarzenski, Hanns. Eighteenth Century Creche. (Illus.). 1966. 7.50 (ISBN 0-87846-046-2); pap. 2.00 (ISBN 0-87846-162-0). Mus Fine Arts Boston.

--An Eighteenth Century Creche. LC 66-25450. (Illus.). 1966. pap. 2.00 (ISBN 0-87846-142-6, Pub. by Mus Fine Arts Boston). C E Tuttle.

Swarzenski, Hanns, frwd. by. The Rathbone Years: Masterpieces Acquired for the Museum of Fine Arts, Boston, 1955-1972 & for the St. Louis Art Museum, 1940-1955. (Illus.). 1972. pap. 6.50 (ISBN 0-87846-067-5). Mus Fine Arts Boston.

Swash, Michael, jt. auth. see Mason, Stuart.

Swassing, Raymond H., jt. auth. see Barbe, Walter B.

Swaton, J. Norman. Personal Finance: Getting Along & Getting Ahead. 1980. text ed. 15.95 (ISBN 0-442-28116-1); instr's. manual 3.95 (ISBN 0-442-26236-1). D Van Nostrand.

Swatridge, Colin & Swatridge, Susan. The Biblio File: An Index of Prose Passages. 354p. 1980. 19.50x (ISBN 0-631-92640-2, Pub. by Basil Blackwell); pap. 10.50x (ISBN 0-631-92[illegible]). Biblio Dist.

Swatridge, Susan, jt. auth. see Swatridge[illegible]

Swauger, Craig G., jt. ed. see Cook, Dav[illegible]

Swaybill, Roger. Threads. 1980. 12.95 ([illegible] 440-08319-2). Delacorte.

Swayne, Sam & Swayne, Zoa. Great-Gr[illegible] in the Honey Tree. (Illus.). (gr. 4-6). [illegible] PLB 3.95 o.p. (ISBN 0-670-34932-1). [illegible] Pr.

Swayne, Zoa, jt. auth. see Swayne, Sam.

Swayze, John C. The Art of Living. LC 78-78054. 1979. pap. 2.25 o.p. (ISBN 0-87216-545-0). Playboy Pbks.

Swayze, Nathan L. Fifty One Colt Navies. LC 67-19544. (Illus., Indexed). 1967. 15.00 (ISBN 0-9600228-0-5). Gun Hill.

Swearengen, Thomas F. Tear Gas Munitions: An Analysis of Commercial Riot Gas Guns, Tear Gas Projectiles, Grenades, Small Arms Ammunition & Related Tear Gas Devices. (Illus.). 596p. 1966. 59.75 (ISBN 0-398-01888-X). C C Thomas.

Swearer, Donald K. Secrets of the Lotus: Studies in Buddhist Meditation. Alexandre, C., ed. 1971. 6.95 o.s.i. (ISBN 0-02-615590-7); pap. 1.95 o.s.i. (ISBN 0-02-089610-7). Macmillan.

--Wat Haripunjaya: A Study of the Royal Temple of the Buddha's Relic, Lamphun, Thailand. LC 75-33802. (American Academy of Religion. Studies in Religion). 1976. pap. 7.50 (ISBN 0-89130-052-X, 010010). Scholars Pr Ca.

Swearer, Donald K., ed. see Bush, Richard C.

Swearingen, Rodger. The Soviet Union & Postwar Japan: Escalating Challenge & Response. LC 78-59866. (Publications Ser.: No. 197). 1978. 14.95 (ISBN 0-8179-6971-3). Hoover Inst Pr.

Swearingen, Roger G. The Prose Writings of Robert Louis Stevenson: A Guide. xxiii, 217p. 1980. 29.50 (ISBN 0-208-01826-3, Archon). Shoe String.

Sweat, Clifford H., ed. Morals & Early Adolescent Education: From Apathy to Action. LC 80-80727. 1980. pap. text ed. 4.25 (ISBN 0-8134-2134-9, 2134). Interstate.

Sweazey, George E. Preaching the Good News. 368p. 1976. 15.95 (ISBN 0-13-694802-2). P-H.

Swedberg, Harriet & Swedberg, Robert. Victorian Furniture Styles & Prices: Rev. Ed. Nineteen Seventy-Nine Prices. (Illus.). pap. 7.95 o.p. (ISBN 0-87069-265-8). Wallace-Homestead.

Swedberg, Robert, jt. auth. see Swedberg, Harriet.

Swedenberg, H. T. see Dryden, John.

Swedenberg, H. T., Jr., ed. England in the Restoration & Early Eighteenth Century: Essays on Culture & Socicty. LC 72-149943. 272p. 1972. 20.00x (ISBN 0-520-01973-3). U of Cal Pr.

Swedenborg, Emanual. Heaven & Hell. 1976. pap. 1.95 (ISBN 0-89129-110-5). Jove Pubns.

--Spiritual Diary, 5 Vols. LC 77-93540. Complete Set. 30.00 (ISBN 0-87785-081-X); Vol. 1. 8.50 (ISBN 0-87785-079-8); Vols. 2-5. 25.00 (ISBN 0-87785-080-1). Swedenborg.

Swedish Handcraft Guild. Counted Cross Stitch Patterns & Designs. (Illus.). 72p. 1981. pap. 8.95 (ISBN 0-684-16950-9, ScsribT). Scribner.

Swedlin, Rosalie. A World of Salads. LC 80-18134. (Illus.). 256p. 1981. 17.95 (ISBN 0-03-053391-0); pap. 9.95 (ISBN 0-686-69291-8). HR&W.

Swedlow, Rita, jt. auth. see Lindberg, Lucile.

Swedlund, Charles. Photography. (Illus.). 384p. 1981. 25.00 (ISBN 0-686-69125-3). HR&W.
Swedner, Harold. School Segregation in Malmo, Sweden. LC 70-158358. 1971. 2.35 (ISBN 0-912008-08-3). Integrated Ed Assoc.
Swedrup, Ivan. Dogs of the World in Color. Oldfield, Rosamund, tr. LC 70-77364. (Illus.). 1969. 3.50 o.p. (ISBN 0-668-01940-9). Arco.
--Pocket Encyclopedia of Dogs. LC 75-23131. (Macmillan Color Series). (Illus.). 256p. 1976. 8.95 (ISBN 0-02-615610-5, 61561). Macmillan.
Sweeeney, Francis, ed. The Knowledge Explosion: Liberation & Limitations. 249p. 1969. 4.95 (ISBN 0-374-18204-3). FS&G.
Sween, Roger, ed. Encyclopedia Buyers' Guide. vi, 74p. 1981. pap. 4.50 (ISBN 0-914054-51-1). Index Co.
Sweeney. A Combat Reporter's Report. (gr. 6 up). 1980. PLB 7.90 (ISBN 0-531-04171-9, E20). Watts.
Sweeney, Amin. Authors & Audiences in Traditional Malay Literature. (Monograph: No. 20). 86p. 1981. pap. 7.00x (Pub by Northern Ill Univ Ctr S E Asian Stud). Cellar.
--Reputations Live on: An Early Malay Autobiography. 150p. 1980. 20.00x (ISBN 0-520-04073-2). U of Cal Pr.
Sweeney, Amin, jt. auth. see Malm, William P.
Sweeney, B. M. Rhythmic Phenomena in Plants. (Experimental Botany Monographs, Vol. 3). 1969. 24.50 (ISBN 0-12-679050-7). Acad Pr.
Sweeney, Eugene T. An Introduction & Literature Guide to Mixing. (BHRA Fluid Engineering Ser., Vol. 5). 1978. pap. 21.00 (ISBN 0-900983-77-9, Dist. by Air Science Co.). BHRA Fluid.
Sweeney, Francis. Morning Window, Evening Window. 1980. 8.95 o.p. (ISBN 0-89182-025-6). Charles River.
Sweeney, Gerard M. Melville's Use of Classical Mythology. (Melville Studies in American Culture: Vol. 5). 169p. (Orig.). 1976. pap. text ed. 11.50x (ISBN 90-6203-258-3). Humanities.
Sweeney, K. Illustrated Tennis Dictionary for Young People. 1979. pap. 2.50 (ISBN 0-13-451278-2). P-H.
Sweeney, Karen O. Entertaining. (Concise Guides Ser.). (Illus.). (gr. 5-8). 1978. PLB 6.45 s&l (ISBN 0-531-01415-0). Watts.
--How to Make Money. LC 77-2406. (Career Concise Guides Ser.). (gr. 5-8). 1977. PLB 6.45 (ISBN 0-531-01278-6). Watts.
--Nature Runs Wild: True Disaster Stories. (Illus.). (gr. 5-8). 1979. PLB 7.45 s&l (ISBN 0-531-02220-X). Watts.
Sweeney, Mary, jt. auth. see Farrell, Kathy.
Sweeney, Neil R. Art of Managing Managers. 120p. 1981. text ed. price not set (ISBN 0-201-07644-6). A-W.
Sweeney, Robert. Selected Readings in Movement Education. LC 78-116865. (Health & Physical Education Ser). 1970. pap. 9.50 (ISBN 0-201-07387-0). A-W.
Sweeney, Russell, et al, eds. see Dewey, Melvil.
Sweeny, Allen. Accounting Fundamentals for Non-Financial Executives. LC 78-173320. 1972. 11.95 (ISBN 0-8144-5286-8). Am Mgmt.
Sweeny, H. W. & Rachlin, Robert. Handbook of Budgeting: Systems & Controls for Financial Management. 700p. 1981. 34.50 (ISBN 0-471-05621-9). Ronald Pr.
Sweerts, Emmanuel. Early Floral Engravings. Bleiler, E. F., ed. LC 73-76963. (Illus.). 256p. 1976. pap. 6.95 (ISBN 0-486-23038-4). Dover.
Sweet, Charles F. see Mickelwait, Donald R., et al.
Sweet, David G. & Nash, Gary B., eds. Struggle & Survival in Colonial America. 1981. 25.00 (ISBN 0-520-04110-0). U of Cal Pr.
Sweet, Donald H. The Modern Employment Function. 330p. 1973. text ed. 13.95 (ISBN 0-201-07388-9). A-W.
Sweet, Henry. The Oldest English Text. 668p. 1980. Repr. of 1885 ed. lib. bdg. 85.00 (ISBN 0-8482-6221-2). Norwood Edns.
--A Second Anglo-Saxon Reader: Archaic & Dialectal. 2nd ed. 1978. text ed. 19.95x (ISBN 0-19-811170-3); pap. 14.50 (ISBN 0-19-811176-2). Oxford U Pr.
--Student's Dictionary of Anglo-Saxon. 1896. 22.00x (ISBN 0-19-863107-3). Oxford U Pr.
Sweet, John J. Iron Arm: The Mechanization of Mussolini's Army, 1920-1940. LC 79-6825. (Contributions in Military History: No. 23). (Illus.). xxi, 217p. 1980. lib. bdg. 25.00 (ISBN 0-313-22179-0, SWM/). Greenwood.
Sweet, Leonard I. Black Images of America, 1784-1870. (Essays in American History Ser). 1976. pap. text ed. 4.95x (ISBN 0-393-09195-3). Norton.
Sweet, Morris L. & Walters, S. George. Mandatory Housing Finance Programs: A Comparative International Analysis. LC 75-19826. (Special Studies). (Illus.). 276p. 1976. text ed. 19.50 o.p. (ISBN 0-275-09290-9). Praeger.
Sweet, William. History of the Baptists. Repr. 18.95 (ISBN 0-686-12350-6). Church History.
Sweet, William H., jt. auth. see White, James C.
Sweet, William W. American Culture & Religion. LC 72-78372. ix, 114p. 1972. Repr. of 1951 ed. lib. bdg. 12.50x (ISBN 0-8154-0421-2). Cooper Sq.
--Methodism in American History. rev. ed. 1954. 6.50 (ISBN 0-687-25081-1). Abingdon.
--Religion in Colonial America. LC 65-17183. 1965. Repr. of 1942 ed. 27.50x (ISBN 0-8154-0226-0). Cooper Sq.
Sweeting, George. Como Iniciar la Vida Cristiana. new ed. Clifford, Alec, tr. from Eng. (Editorial Moody - Spanish Publications Ser.). 1977. pap. 1.95 (ISBN 0-8024-1615-2). Moody.
--How to Begin the Christian Life. 128p. 1976. pap. 1.50 (ISBN 0-8024-3626-9). Moody.
--How to Begin the Christian Life: Leader's Guide. (Leader's Guide Ser.). (Illus.). 1977. pap. 3.25 (ISBN 0-8024-3629-3). Moody.
--Special Sermons on the Family. (Special Sermon Ser.). 144p. 1981. pap. 2.95 (ISBN 0-8024-8208-2). Moody.
Sweeting, Marjorie M. Karst Landforms. LC 72-172813. (Illus.). 380p. 1973. 30.00x (ISBN 0-231-03623-X). Columbia U Pr.
Sweetman, Luke D. Gotch: The Story of a Cowhorse. LC 78-116053. (Illus.). 1970. pap. 4.95 (ISBN 0-8032-5726-0, BB 527, Bison). U of Nebr Pr.
Sweetser, Albert G. Bank Loans Secured by Field-Warehouse Receipts. LC 57-7980. 112p. (Orig.). 1957. pap. 5.00 (ISBN 0-9605500-1-1). A G Sweetser.
Sweezy, Paul M., jt. auth. see Magdoff, Harry.
Sweezy, Paul M., jt. ed. see Huberman, Leo.
Sweitzer, Peggy, ed. see Douglas, Herman.
Swell, Lila. Success: You Can Make It Happen. 1978. pap. 1.75 (ISBN 0-515-04711-2). Jove Pubns.
Swellengrebel, J. L., jt. auth. see Reiling, J.
Swendson, Ole, jt. auth. see Swendson, Patsy.
Swendson, Patsy & Swendson, Ole. A Couple of Cooks. (Illus.). 1980. 5.95. Corona Pub.
Swensen, Philip R., jt. auth. see Randle, Paul A.
Swenson, Allan. Big Fun to Grow Book. 1980. pap. 3.50 (ISBN 0-679-20510-1). McKay.
--Inflation Fighters' Preserving Guide. 1977. pap. 1.75 o.p. (ISBN 0-345-25159-8). Ballantine.
Swenson, Allan A. Allan Swenson's Big Fun to Grow Book. (gr. 4-6). 1980. pap. 3.50 o.p. (ISBN 0-679-20510-1). McKay.
--The Inflation Fighter's Victory Garden. 288p. (Orig.). 1975. pap. 1.50 o.p. (ISBN 0-345-24288-2). Ballantine.
--Landscape You Can Eat. (Illus.). 1977. 10.95 o.p. (ISBN 0-679-50647-0); pap. 5.95 o.p. (ISBN 0-679-50669-1). McKay.
--My Own Herb Garden. (Children's Collection Ser.). (Illus.). 72p. 1976. 6.95 (ISBN 0-87857-129-9). Rodale Pr Inc.
--Your Biblical Garden: Plants of the Bible & How to Grow Them. LC 79-7703. (Illus.). 240p. 1981. 13.95 (ISBN 0-385-14898-4). Doubleday.
Swenson, Ana M., tr. see Valentine, Foy.
Swenson, Ana Maria, tr. see Dolphin, Lambert T.
Swenson, Charles A., jt. auth. see Montgomery, Rex.
Swenson, Christian N. & Holdsworth, Eugene I. Physics of Sound for Musicians. LC 80-80008. (Illus.). 208p. (Orig.). 1980. pap. 15.00x (ISBN 0-916030-05-9). Bethany Coll Ks.
Swenson, D. F., tr. see Kierkegaard, Soren.
Swenson, John. The Eagles. (Headliners Ser.). 192p. (Orig.). (gr. 4 up). 1981. pap. 2.25 (ISBN 0-448-17174-0, Tempo). G&D.
Swenson, Leland C. Theories of Learning: Traditional Perspectives - Contemporary Development. 1979. text ed. 19.95x (ISBN 0-534-00698-1). Wadsworth Pub.
Swerdloff, Peter. Men & Women. (Human Behavior Ser.). 176p. 1975. 9.95 (ISBN 0-8094-1924-6); lib. bdg. avail. (ISBN 0-685-53585-1). Time-Life.
--Men & Women. LC 75-10885. (Human Behavior). (Illus.). (gr. 5 up). 1975. PLB 9.99 o.p. (ISBN 0-8094-1925-4, Pub. by Time-Life). Silver.
Swerdlow, Amy, et al. Household & Kin: Families in Flux. (Women's Lives - Women's Work Ser.). (Illus.). 192p. (Orig.). (gr. 11-12). 1981. 14.95 (ISBN 0-912670-91-6); pap. 5.95 (ISBN 0-912670-68-1). Feminist Pr.
Swerdlow, Irving. The Public Administration of Economic Development. LC 74-9426. (Special Studies). (Illus.). 426p. 1975. text ed. 38.95 (ISBN 0-275-05730-5). Praeger.
Swern, Daniel. Bailey's Industrial Oil & Fat Products, Vol. II. 4th ed. 675p. 1981. 50.00 (ISBN 0-471-83958-2, Pub. by Wiley-Interscience). Wiley.
--Bailey's Industrial Oil & Fat Products, Vol. 1. 4th ed. LC 78-31275. 1979. 55.00 (ISBN 0-471-83957-4, Pub. by Wiley-Interscience). Wiley.
Swetnam, George. Andrew Carnegie. (United States Authors Ser.: No. 355). 1980. lib. bdg. 10.95 (ISBN 0-8057-7239-1). Twayne.
Swett, Ira. Cars of Pacific Electric, Vol. 2. Walker, Jim, ed. (Special Ser.: No. 36). (Illus.). 212p. 1976. pap. 10.00 o.p. (ISBN 0-916374-24-6). Interurban.
Swett, Ira & Walker, Jim. Lines of Pacific Electric, Western & Southern Districts. 2nd rev. ed. (Special Ser.: No. 60). 1975. pap. 10.00 o.p. (ISBN 0-916374-02-5). Interurban.
Swett, Ira, jt. auth. see Myers, William.
Swett, Ira L. Cars of Pacific Electric: City & Suburban Cars, Vol. 1. 2nd rev. ed. Sebree, Mac, ed. (Special Ser.: No. 28). (Illus.). 1975. pap. 10.00 (ISBN 0-916374-03-3). Interurban.
--Cars of Pacific Electric: Locomotives, Combination Cars, Etc, Vol. 3. Walker, Jim, ed. (Special Ser.: No. 37). (Illus.). 1978. pap. 12.00 (ISBN 0-916374-30-0). Interurban.
--I. N. L. Effle, Mark, ed. (Extra Three Ser.). 1978. pap. 13.00 (ISBN 0-916374-34-3). Interurban.
Swettenham, John A. The Tragedy of the Baltic States: A Report from Official Documents & Eyewitnesses' Stories. LC 79-2924. (Illus.). 216p. 1981. Repr. of 1952 ed. 19.75 (ISBN 0-8305-0093-6). Hyperion Conn.
Swetz, Frank. The Mathematics Laboratory in the Elementary School: What?, Why? & How. Valenza, S. W., Jr., ed. LC 80-81349. (Illus., Orig.). 1980. 6.95 (ISBN 0-936918-03-9); pap. text ed. 6.95 (ISBN 0-686-61581-6). Intergalactic NJ.
Swezey, Robert W. Individual Performance Assessment: An Approach to Criterion-Referenced Test Development. 1981. text ed. 16.95 (ISBN 0-8359-3066-1). Reston.
Swezy, Olive, jt. auth. see Kofoid, C. A.
Swiatecka, M. Jadwiga. The Idea of the Symbol: Some Nineteenth Century Comparisons with Coleridge. LC 70-19802. 220p. 1980. 26.95 (ISBN 0-521-22362-8). Cambridge U Pr.
Swiatek, Anthony & Breen, Walter. Encyclopedia of United States Silver & Gold Commemorative Coins: 1892-1954. LC 80-14074. (Illus.). 224p. 1980. 16.95 (ISBN 0-668-04765-8, 4765-8). Arco.
Swidler, Arleen. Woman in a Man's Church. LC 72-86596. 96p. (Orig.). 1972. pap. 1.95 (ISBN 0-8091-1740-1, Deus). Paulist Pr.
Swidler, Arlene, ed. Sistercelebrations: Nine Worship Experiences. LC 74-80414. 96p. (Orig.). 1974. pap. 0.50 (ISBN 0-8006-1084-9, 1-1084). Fortress.
Swidler, Gerald. Handbook of Drug Interactions. 1971. 27.50 o.p. (ISBN 0-471-83975-2, Pub. by Wiley-Interscience). Wiley.
Swidler, Leonard. Women in Judaism: The Status of Women in Formative Judaism. LC 75-46561. 248p. 1976. 11.50 (ISBN 0-8108-0904-4). Scarecrow.
Swidler, Leonard, tr. see Lapide, Pinchas & Moltmann, Jurgen.
Swidrowski, Jozef. Exchange & Trade Controls-Principles & Procedures of Regulating International Economic Transaction. 480p. 1975. 50.00 (ISBN 0-7161-0223-4). Herman Pub.
Swiercinsky, Dennis. Manual for the Adult Neuropsychological Evaluation. (Illus.). 208p. 1978. spiral vinyl 19.75 (ISBN 0-398-03751-5). C C Thomas.
Swierczkowski, S. Sets & Numbers. (Library of Mathematics). 1972. pap. 5.00 (ISBN 0-7100-7137-X). Routledge & Kegan.
Swieringa, Robert J., jt. auth. see Sprouse, Robert T.
Swierkos, et al. Industrial Arts for Elementary Classrooms. 1973. pap. text ed. 6.60 (ISBN 0-87002-116-8). Bennett IL.
Swieson, Eddy & Norton, Howard. Good News About Trouble. 1978. pap. 1.95 pocketsize o.p. (ISBN 0-88270-319-6). Logos.
--When the Angels Laughed. 1978. pap. 3.95 o.p. (ISBN 0-88270-264-5). Logos.
Swietlicki, Alain, tr. see Martinez Estrada, Ezequiel.
Swift, Benjamin. Play-Off. (Sportellers Ser.). (Illus.). 64p. (gr. 5 up). 1981. PLB 7.95 (ISBN 0-516-02265-2). Childrens.
Swift, D. F. Sociology of Education: Introductory Analytical Perspectives. (Students Library of Sociology Ser). 1970. pap. text ed. 2.75x (ISBN 0-7100-6362-8). Humanities.
Swift, Donald C. Politics & Society in America 1607-1877. 1976. pap. text ed. 2.95x o.p. (ISBN 0-88273-240-4). Forum Pr MO.
Swift, Edward. Splendora. 264p. 1981. pap. 3.50 (ISBN 0-14-005756-0). Penguin.
Swift, Eric. Managing Your Export Office. 150p. 1977. text ed. 22.00x (ISBN 0-220-66310-6, Pub. by Busn Bks England). Renouf.
Swift, Ernest H. & Butler, Eliot A. Quantitative Measurements & Chemical Equilibria. LC 78-161009. (Chemistry Ser.). (Illus.). 1972. text ed. 31.95x (ISBN 0-7167-0170-7); tchrs' manual avail. W H Freeman.
Swift, Ernest W., jt. auth. see Knotts, Ulysses S.
Swift, Gay. Machine Stitchery. LC 74-23867. (Illus.). 96p. 1975. 10.50 o.p. (ISBN 0-8231-5046-1). Branford.
Swift, J. Nathan, ed. Research in Science Education 1948 Through 1952. LC 69-12580. (Illus.). 1969. text ed. 12.75x (ISBN 0-8077-2238-3). Tchrs Coll.
Swift, Jeremy. The Sahara. (The World's Wild Places Ser.). (Illus.). 184p. 1975. 12.95 (ISBN 0-8094-2015-5). Time-Life.
Swift, Jonathan. The Correspondence of Jonathan Swift, Vols. 4-5. Williams, Harold, ed. Incl. Vol. 4. 1732-1736; Vol. 5. 1737-1745; Appendixes & Indexes. 1965. Set. 55.00x (ISBN 0-19-811443-5). Oxford U Pr.
--Gulliver's Travels. rev. ed. Greenberg, Robert A., ed. (Critical Editions). (Annotated). (gr. 9-12). 1970. pap. text ed. 5.95x (ISBN 0-393-09941-5, 9941, NortonC). Norton.
--Gulliver's Travels. (Literature Ser). (gr. 10-12). 1970. pap. text ed. 3.58 (ISBN 0-87720-727-5). AMSCO Sch.
--Gulliver's Travels. Price, Martin, ed. LC 62-21262. 1964. pap. 5.95 (ISBN 0-672-60968-1, LL3). Bobbs.
--Gulliver's Travels. (gr. 7-9). 1962. 5.25g o.s.i. (ISBN 0-02-788770-7). Macmillan.
--Gulliver's Travels. (World's Classics Ser: No. 20). 3.95 o.p. (ISBN 0-19-250020-1). Oxford U Pr.
--Gulliver's Travels. Dixon, Peter & Chalker, J., eds. (English Library Ser.). 1967. pap. 2.25 (ISBN 0-14-043022-9). Penguin.
--Gulliver's Travels. LC 78-3394. (Raintree's Illustrated Classics). (Illus.). (gr. 5-8). 1978. PLB 9.65 (ISBN 0-8393-6207-2). Raintree Child.
--Gulliver's Travels & Other Writings. pap. 1.75. Bantam.
--Gulliver's Travels, Annotated. Asimov, Isaac, ed. & intro. by. (Clarkson N. Potter Bks.: Clarkson N. Potter Book). (Illus.). 320p. 1980. 19.95 (ISBN 0-517-53949-7). Crown.
--Gulliver's Travels with the Illustrations of J. J. Grandville. LC 80-22845. (Illus.). 544p. 1981. 37.50x (ISBN 0-915556-06-5). Great Ocean.
--Jonathan Swift: Selected Poems. Sisson, C. H., ed. (Fyfield). 1979. pap. 3.95 (ISBN 0-85635-134-2, Pub. by Carcanet New Pr England). Persea Bks.
--Poems of Jonathan Swift. Colum, Padraic, ed. 1962. pap. 0.95 o.s.i. (ISBN 0-02-070810-6, Collier). Macmillan.
--Poetical Works. Davis, Herbert, ed. (Oxford Standard Authors Ser). 1967. 23.00 (ISBN 0-19-254161-7). Oxford U Pr.
--Tale of a Tub. LC 71-170512. (Foundations of the Novel Ser: Vol. 8). 322p. 1973. Repr. of 1704 ed. lib. bdg. 50.00 (ISBN 0-8240-0520-1). Garland Pub.
--Tale of a Tub, Battle of the Books, & Mechanical Operation of the Spirit. 2nd ed. Guthkelch, A. C. & Smith, D. N., eds. 1958. 37.50x (ISBN 0-19-811404-4). Oxford U Pr.
--Viajes de Gulliver. (Span.). 7.95 (ISBN 84-241-5631-5). E Torres & Sons.
Swift, Mary G. Belles & Beaux on Their Toes: Dancing Stars in Young America. LC 79-6661. 1980. text ed. 19.75 (ISBN 0-8191-0922-3); pap. text ed. 12.00 (ISBN 0-8191-0923-1). U Pr of Amer.
--A Loftier Flight: The Life & Accomplishments of Charles Louis Didelot, Balletmaster. LC 73-15007. (De la Torre Bueno Prize Book, 1973). (Illus.). 336p. 1974. 17.50x (ISBN 0-8195-4070-6, Pub. by Wesleyan U Pr). Columbia U Pr.
--With Bright Wings: A Book of the Spirit. LC 75-44806. 1976. pap. 5.95 (ISBN 0-8091-1936-6). Paulist Pr.
Swift, Mildred. More Looking at Cooking. (Illus.). 1976. pap. 6.95 (ISBN 0-88289-096-4). Pelican.
Swift, R. N. International Law: Current & Classic. LC 68-23928. 1969. 22.95 o.p. (ISBN 0-471-83980-9). Wiley.
Swift, Richard. Concerto for Piano with Chamber Ensemble. (U. C. Publ. in Contemporary Music: Vol. 3). (Illus., Orig.). 1968. pap. 9.50x (ISBN 0-520-01245-3). U of Cal Pr.
Swift, Terrence J. Principles of Chemistry: A Model Approach. 730p. 1975. text ed. 15.95x o.p. (ISBN 0-669-93021-0); instructor's manual free o.p. (ISBN 0-669-94540-4). Heath.
Swift, Walter L., et al, eds. Vortex Flows. 171p. 1980. 28.00 (G00181). ASME.
Swift, William & Wilson, D. Principles of Finite Mathematics. (Illus.). 1977. ref. ed. 18.95 (ISBN 0-13-701359-0). P-H.
Swiger, Elinor Porter. Careers in the Legal Profession. LC 77-811. (Career Concise Guides Ser.). (gr. 7 up). 1977. PLB 6.45 (ISBN 0-531-01294-8). Watts.
Swigert, Victoria & Farrell, Ronald A. Murder, Inequality, & the Law: Differential Treatment & the Legal Process. LC 76-22222. 1976. 15.95 (ISBN 0-669-00881-8). Lexington Bks.
Swigert, Victoria L. & Farrell, Ronald A. The Substance of Social Deviance. LC 78-23970. (Illus.). 1979. pap. text ed. 9.95x (ISBN 0-88284-059-2). Alfred Pub.

Swiggart, Peter. Art of Faulkner's Novels. 1962. 12.95x o.p. (ISBN 0-292-73166-3). U of Tex Pr.

Swihart, Phillip J. Reincarnation, Edgar Cayce & the Bible. LC 75-5186. 64p. 1975. pap. 1.95 o.p. (ISBN 0-87784-416-X). Inter-Varsity.

Swihart, Stanley J. & Hefley, Beryl F. Computer Systems in the Library: Handbook for Manager & Designer. LC 73-603. (Information Sciences Ser.). (Illus.). 336p. 1973. 29.95 (ISBN 0-471-83995-7, Pub. by Wiley-Interscience). Wiley.

Swihart, Stephen D. Logos International Bible Commentary, Vo. 1. 1981. write for info. (ISBN 0-88270-500-8). Logos.

Swihart, Thomas L. Astrophysics & Stellar Astronomy. LC 73-603. (Space Science Text Ser.). 1968. 20.95 (ISBN 0-471-83990-6, Pub. by Wiley-Interscience). Wiley.

--Journey Through the Universe: An Introduction to Astronomy. LC 77-76343. (Illus.). 1978. text ed. 19.95 (ISBN 0-395-25518-X); inst. manual 0.45 (ISBN 0-395-25519-8). HM.

Swimmer, G., jt. auth. see Maslove, A.

Swinbank, C. Packaging of Chemicals & Other Industrial Liquids & Solids. 1973. text ed. 15.95 (ISBN 0-408-00106-2). Butterworths.

Swinburne, Algernon C. Poems & Ballads & Atalanta in Calydon. Peckham, Morse, ed. LC 79-117333. (Library of Literature Ser). 1970. 9.50 (ISBN 0-672-51119-3); text ed. 3.55 o.p. (ISBN 0-672-61000-0). Bobbs.

--Selected Poems. LC 80-19421. 339p. 1980. Repr. of 1951 ed. lib. bdg. 29.75x (ISBN 0-313-22649-0, SWSP). Greenwood.

--Study of Ben Jonson. Norland, Howard B., ed. LC 69-12400. 1969. pap. 3.65x (ISBN 0-8032-5709-0, BB 326, Bison). U of Nebr Pr.

Swinburne, Algernon C. see Nye, Robert.

Swinburne, Algernon C., Jr. William Blake: A Critical Essay. Luke, Hugh J., ed. LC 70-81397. 1970. pap. 4.75x (ISBN 0-8032-5707-4, BB 504, Bison). U of Nebr Pr.

Swinburne, Algernon Charles. A Year's Letters. Sypher, Francis J., ed. LC 74-15290. (Illus.). 195p. 1974. 10.00x (ISBN 0-8147-7758-9); pap. 5.00x (ISBN 0-8147-7804-6). NYU Pr.

Swinburne, Bruce R., jt. auth. see Sloan, Blanche C.

Swinburne, Henry. A Brief Treatise of Testaments & Last Wills. Berkowitz, David S. & Thorne, Samuel E., eds. LC 77-89255. (Classics of English Legal History in the Modern Era Ser.: Vol. 80). 342p. 1979. lib. bdg. 40.00 (ISBN 0-8240-3179-2). Garland Pub.

--A Briefe Treatise of Testaments & Last Wils, Newly Corrected & Augmented. LC 79-84140. (English Experience Ser.: No. 957). 620p. 1979. Repr. of 1635 ed. lib. bdg. 58.00 (ISBN 90-221-0957-7). Walter J Johnson.

Swinburne, Henry, jt. auth. see Heale, William.

Swinburne, Irene, jt. auth. see Swinburne, Laurence.

Swinburne, Laurence. Robby on Ice. LC 72-75124. (Mystery & Adventure Ser.). (gr. 2-4). 1973. PLB 6.75 (ISBN 0-87191-099-3). Creative Ed.

Swinburne, Laurence & Swinburne, Irene. America's First Football Game. LC 78-14865. (Famous Firsts Ser.). (Illus.). 1978. lib. bdg. 7.35 (ISBN 0-686-51096-8). Silver.

--Ancient Myths: The First Science Fiction. LC 77-10915. (Myth, Magic & Superstition Ser.). (Illus.). (gr. 4-5). 1977. PLB 9.65 (ISBN 0-8172-1042-3). Raintree Pubs.

--The Deadly Diamonds. LC 77-10764. (Great Unsolved Mysteries Ser.). (Illus.). (gr. 4-5). 1977. PLB 9.65 (ISBN 0-8172-1064-4). Raintree Pubs.

Swinburne, Richard. The Existence of God. 1979. 39.00x (ISBN 0-19-824611-0). Oxford U Pr.

Swindells, Tony. One-Thousand One Ways of Saving Money. 7.50 o.p. (ISBN 0-7153-7540-7). David & Charles.

Swindle, Robert E. Business Math Basics. 1979. pap. text ed. 13.95x (ISBN 0-534-00578-0). Wadsworth Pub.

Swindler, W. F. Chronology & Documentary Handbook of the State of Hawaii. 1978. 8.50 (ISBN 0-379-16136-2). Oceana.

--Chronology & Documentary Handbook of the State of Virginia. 1978. 8.50 (ISBN 0-379-16157-5). Oceana.

Swindoll, Charles. Hand Me Another Brick. 176p. 1981. pap. 2.25 (ISBN 0-553-14524-X). Bantam.

Swindoll, Charles R. Make up Your Mind. (Illus.). 100p. 1981. pap. 8.95 (ISBN 0-930014-61-8). Multnomah.

--Three Steps Forward, Two Steps Back. 176p. 1980. 8.95 (ISBN 0-8407-5187-7); pap. 4.95 (ISBN 0-8407-5723-9). Nelson.

Swineford, A., ed. National Conference on Clays & Clay Minerals, 9th: Proceedings. (International Ser. on Earth Sciences: Vol. 11). 1962. 22.00 o.p. (ISBN 0-08-009664-6). Pergamon.

--National Conference on Clays & Minerals, 8th: Proceedings. 1961. 28.50 o.p. (ISBN 0-08-009351-5). Pergamon.

Swineford, Oscar, Jr. Asthma & Hay Fever. (Amer. Lec. Allergy & Immunology Ser.). (Illus.). 508p. 1971. 26.75 (ISBN 0-398-02390-5). C C Thomas.

--Asthma & Hay Fever & Other Allergic Diseases for Victims & Their Families. (Illus.). 186p. 1973. pap. 18.75 photocopy ed. (ISBN 0-398-02767-6). C C Thomas.

Swinehart, Haldon J., ed. Cutting Tool Material Selection. LC 68-27332. (Manufacturing Data Ser). (Illus., Orig.). 1968. pap. 8.25x (ISBN 0-87263-010-2). SME.

Swinehart, James. Organic Chemistry: An Experimental Approach. (Illus., Orig.). 1969. pap. 16.95 (ISBN 0-13-640649-1). P-H.

Swinfen, Averil. Donkeys Galore. LC 76-2883. 1976. 11.95 (ISBN 0-7153-7150-9). David & Charles.

Swinford, Betty. Mystery of the Missing Totem Pole. 128p. (Orig.). (gr. 6-8). 1981. pap. 1.95 (ISBN 0-8024-5676-6). Moody.

Swinger, Marlys, jt. ed. see Society of Brothers.

Swingewood, A. Myth of Mass Culture. LC 77-4699. 1977. text ed. 18.25x (ISBN 0-391-00699-1); pap. text ed. 7.75x (ISBN 0-391-00724-6). Humanities.

Swingle, Diane, jt. auth. see Shaughnessy, Patrick.

Swinnerton, Frank. Arnold Bennett: A Last Word. LC 78-8204. 1978. 7.95 o.p. (ISBN 0-385-14545-4). Doubleday.

--Background with Chorus. 236p. 1980. Repr. of 1956 ed. lib. bdg. 30.00 (ISBN 0-8492-8124-5). R West.

--The Bookman's London. (Illus.). 161p. 1980. Repr. of 1951 ed. lib. bdg. 30.00 (ISBN 0-8492-8129-6). R West.

--Reflections from a Village. 1979. 19.95 (ISBN 0-241-89998-2, Pub. by Hamish Hamilton England). David & Charles.

Swinney, H. L. & Gollup, J. P., eds. Hydrodynamic Instabilities & the Transition to Turbulence. (Topics in Applied Physics Ser.: Vol. 45). (Illus.). 320p. 1981. 56.60 (ISBN 0-387-10390-2). Springer-Verlag.

Swinyard, Chester A. Decision Making & the Defective Newborn. (Illus.). 672p. 1978. 32.75 (ISBN 0-398-03662-4). C C Thomas.

Swiridoff, P., photos by. Bonn. (Illus.). 1971. 20.00 (ISBN 0-911268-19-7). Rogers Bk.

Swischuk, Leonard E. Radiology of the Newborn & Young Infant. 2nd ed. (Illus.). 912p. 1980. 82.50 (ISBN 0-683-08053-9). Williams & Wilkins.

Swisher, jt. auth. see Petz.

Swisher, Carl B. The Supreme Court in Modern Role. rev. ed. LC 79-26664. (New York University, James Stokes Lectureship on Politics Ser.). ix, 221p. 1980. Repr. of 1965 ed. lib. bdg. 21.00x (ISBN 0-313-22279-7, SWSU). Greenwood.

Swisher, Carl B., ed. Selected Papers of Homer Cummings. LC 79-168392. (FDR & the Era of the New Deal Ser.). (Illus.). 1972. Repr. of 1939 ed. lib. bdg. 32.50 (ISBN 0-306-70329-7). Da Capo.

Swisher, Scott N., jt. auth. see Enelow, Allen J.

Swisher, Scott N., jt. ed. see Petz, Lawrence D.

Switzer, Ellen. Our Urban Planet. LC 80-12225. (Illus.). 288p. (gr. 7 up). 1980. 10.95 (ISBN 0-689-30788-8). Atheneum.

Switzer, Ellen, jt. auth. see Singer, Jerome L.

Switzer, George S., jt. auth. see Hurlbut, Cornelius S., Jr.

Switzer, Richard, ed. & tr. see Chateaubriand, Francois R.

Switzer, Robert L., jt. auth. see Clark, John M., Jr.

Switzerland. Constitution. Federal Constitution of Switzerland. Hughes, Christopher, tr. Repr. of 1954 ed. lib. bdg. 15.00x (ISBN 0-8371-4036-6, SWFC). Greenwood.

Swoboda, Alexander K., jt. ed. see Mundell, Robert A.

Swomley, John M., Jr. Liberation Ethics. 248p. 1972. 6.95 o.s.i. (ISBN 0-02-615800-0); pap. 1.95 o.s.i. (ISBN 0-02-089620-4). Macmillan.

--Religion, the State & the School. LC 68-21040. 1968. 6.60 o.p. (ISBN 0-672-53584-X); pap. 5.50 (ISBN 0-672-63584-4). Bobbs.

Sworder, Mary, tr. see Fulcanelli.

Swords, David, ed. see Costa, Louis, et al.

Swords, Peter D. & Walwer, Frank K. The Costs and Resources of Legal Education: A Study in the Management of Educational Resources. new ed. LC 74-22459. 345p. 1975. 17.50x (ISBN 0-915120-00-3). Columbia U Pr.

Swords-Isherwood, N. Microelectronics of the Engineering Industry. 300p. 1980. 32.50x (ISBN 0-89397-094-8). Nichols Pub.

Swyhart, B., ed. see Piediscalzi, N., et al.

Sy, Wilfrido M. Gamma Image in Benign & Metabolic Bone Diseases, 2 vols. 1980. 64.95 ea. Vol. 1, 272p (ISBN 0-8493-5361-0). Vol. 2, 272p (ISBN 0-8493-5362-9). CRC Pr.

Syatauw, J. Decisions of the International Court of Justice, a Digest. 1963. 12.00 (ISBN 0-379-00187-X). Oceana.

Sybers, Robert G., jt. auth. see Shuford, Wade H.

Syckle, Edwin Van see Van Syckle, Edwin.

SYDA Foundation, illus. Shree Rudram: Namakam & Chamakam. (Illus., Orig.). 1978. pap. 3.50 (ISBN 0-914602-64-0). SYDA Found.

Sydell, Alfred E. The Approaching Collapse of the International Banking System. (Illus.). 127p. 1981. 67.85 (ISBN 0-930008-75-8). Inst Econ Pol.

Sydenham, M. J. The First French Republic, 1792-1804. 1974. 23.75x (ISBN 0-520-02577-6). U of Cal Pr.

Sydenham, Peter H. Transducers in Measurement & Control. rev ed. 1980. pap. text ed. 17.50 (ISBN 0-87664-460-4). Instru Soc.

Sydney Owenson, Lady Morgan. Florence MacCarthy: An Irish Tale. Wolff, Robert L., ed. (Ireland Nineteenth Century Fiction, Ser. Two: Vol. 8). 1979. lib. bdg. 46.00 ea. Garland Pub.

Sydnor, Charles S. American Revolutionaries in the Making. Orig. Title: Gentlemen Freeholders. 1965. pap. text ed. 3.50 (ISBN 0-02-932390-8). Free Pr.

Sydnor, Wm. Sunday's Scriptures. rev. ed. 1979. pap. 5.25 o.p. (ISBN 0-8192-1215-6). Morehouse.

Sydow, H., jt. auth. see Petrak, F.

Syer, John C., jt. auth. see Culver, John H.

Syers, W. E. The Backroads of Texas. LC 79-50253. 1979. pap. 6.95 (ISBN 0-88415-053-4). Pacesetter Pr.

Syers, William. The Devil Gun. 1978. pap. 1.75 o.p. (ISBN 0-445-04163-3). Popular Lib.

Sygoda, David, jt. auth. see Haskel, Sebastian.

Sykes, A. G. Kinetics of Inorganic Reactions. 1966. 22.00 (ISBN 0-08-011441-5); pap. 10.75 (ISBN 0-08-011440-7). Pergamon.

Sykes, Carolyn, jt. auth. see Coghland, Richard.

Sykes, Christopher. Crossroads to Israel 1917-1948. LC 72-93912. (Midland Bks.: No. 165). 416p. 1973. pap. 3.95x (ISBN 0-253-20165-9). Ind U Pr.

Sykes, Claud W. Alias William Shakespeare? 221p. 1980. Repr. of 1947 ed. lib. bdg. 25.00 (ISBN 0-89987-764-8). Century Bookbindery.

Sykes, Cristopher. Orde Wingate. (Return to Zion Ser.). 575p. 1981. Repr. lib. bdg. 35.00x (ISBN 0-87991-146-8). Porcupine Pr.

Sykes, D. H. Sidelights on Elizabethan Drama. 1967. Repr. of 1924 ed. text ed. 10.00x (ISBN 0-391-02050-1). Humanities.

Sykes, Gary, jt. ed. see Schaffarzick, Jon.

Sykes, Godfrey. Colorado Delta. LC 79-113298. 1970. Repr. of 1937 ed. 15.00 (ISBN 0-8046-1329-X). Kennikat.

Sykes, J., tr. see Livanova.

Sykes, J. B., ed. The Concise Oxford Dictionary of Current English. 6th ed. 1976. 19.95 (ISBN 0-19-861121-8); thumb-indexed 22.50 (ISBN 0-19-861122-6). Oxford U Pr.

--The Pocket Oxford Dictionary of Current English. 6th ed. 1978. 11.95 (ISBN 0-19-861129-3). Oxford U Pr.

Sykes, John P. Slaves Uprooted & the Mau Mau Massacre. 1978. 4.50 o.p. (ISBN 0-682-49035-0). Exposition.

Sykes, Marjorie. Quakers in India. (Illus.). 176p. 1980. 12.95 (ISBN 0-04-275003-2, 2585). Allen Unwin.

Sykes, Pamela. Mirror of Danger. (gr. 5-7). 1976. pap. 1.95 (ISBN 0-671-42892-6). Archway.

--Mirror of Danger. (gr. 5-7). 1976. pap. 1.75 (ISBN 0-671-41134-9). PB.

Sykes, Paul. The Public Library in Perspective. 184p. 1979. 15.00 (ISBN 0-89664-401-4, Pub. by K G Saur). Shoe String.

Sykes, Peter. The Search for Organic Reaction Pathways. LC 72-4192. 247p. 1972. 13.95 (ISBN 0-470-84130-3). Halsted Pr.

Sykes, S. W. Karl Barth: Studies of His Theological Method. 214p. 1979. text ed. 29.00x (ISBN 0-19-826649-9). Oxford U Pr.

Sykes, S. W. & Clayton, J. P. Christ, Faith & History. LC 70-176257. (Cambridge Studies in Christology). (Illus.). 280p. 1972. 44.00 (ISBN 0-521-08451-2); pap. text ed. 10.95x (ISBN 0-521-29325-1). Cambridge U Pr.

Sykes, Stephen. Friedrich Schleiermacher. LC 75-158145. (Makers of Contemporary Theology Ser). (Orig.). 1971. pap. 3.45 (ISBN 0-8042-0556-6). John Knox.

--The Integrity of Anglicanism. 1978. 8.95 (ISBN 0-8164-0405-4). Crossroad NY.

Syllabus for CME Credits, 130th, Toronto, Canada, 1977. Proceedings. 1977. 7.00 o.p. (ISBN 0-685-83184-1, 153-7). Am Psychiatric.

Sylte, T. Rivers of Norway. (Illus.). 1966. 15.00x (ISBN 82-09-00841-2, N447). Vanous.

Sylvander, Carolyn W. James Baldwin. LC 80-5338. (Modern Literature Ser.). 160p. 1981. 10.95 (ISBN 0-8044-2848-4); pap. 4.95 (ISBN 0-8044-6891-5). Ungar.

--Jessie Redmon Fauset: Black American Writer. LC 80-51050. (Illus.). 285p. 1980. 18.50x (ISBN 0-87875-196-3). Whitston Pub.

Sylvanus, Erwin. Stuecke. 203p. 1980. pap. 11.70 quality paper (ISBN 3-518-04387-0, Pub. by Insel Verlag Stucke). Suhrkamp.

Sylvester, Alfred. Alchemy Connection. 1980. 6.75 (ISBN 0-8062-1459-7). Carlton.

Sylvester, D. W. Robert Lowe & Education. LC 73-82446. (Cambridge Texts & Studies in the History of Education: No. 15). 260p. 1974. 29.50 (ISBN 0-521-20310-4). Cambridge U Pr.

Sylvester, David. Interviews with Francis Bacon. rev., enl. ed. (Illus.). 176p. 1981. pap. 9.95 (ISBN 0-500-27196-8). Thames Hudson.

Sylvester, David, jt. auth. see Compton, Michael.

Sylvester, James J. Collected Mathematical Papers, 4 Vols. LC 76-250188. 1973. Repr. of 1904 ed. text ed. 125.00 (ISBN 0-8284-0253-1). Chelsea Pub.

Sylvester, Joshua, tr. see De Saluste, Guillaume & Du Bartas, Sieur.

Sylvester, Richard S., ed. English Seventeenth-Century Verse, 2 vols. (Illus.). 720p. 1974. Vol I. pap. 6.95 (ISBN 0-393-00675-1, Norton Lib); Vol. 2. pap. 7.95 (ISBN 0-393-00676-X). Norton.

Sylvester-Bradley, P. C. & Ford, T. D., eds. Geology of the East Midlands. 1968. text ed. 20.00x (ISBN 0-7185-1072-0, Leicester). Humanities.

Sylvia, J. Gerin. Cast Metals Technology. LC 74-153067. 1972. text ed. 18.95 (ISBN 0-201-07395-1). A-W.

Sylvia's Home Help Series. Artistic Homes; or, How to Furnish with Taste. Stansky, Peter & Shewan, Rodney, eds. LC 76-17759. (Aesthetic Movement & the Arts & Crafts Movement Ser.). 1978. Repr. of 1881 ed. lib. bdg. 44.00x (ISBN 0-8240-2464-8). Garland Pub.

Sylwester, Roland. Teaching Bible Stories More Effectively with Puppets. (Illus.). 64p. 1976. pap. 2.95 (ISBN 0-570-03731-X, 12-2633). Concordia.

Sym, Cecilia, tr. see Rensch, Bernhard.

Symbas, Panagiotis N. Traumatic Injuries of the Heart & Great Vessels. (Illus.). 204p. 1972. text ed. 19.75 (ISBN 0-398-02425-1). C C Thomas.

Symcox, Geoffrey, tr. see Soboul, Albert.

Syme, Daniel B., ed. see Bearman, Jane.

Syme, Daniel B., ed. see Bial, Morrison D.

Syme, Daniel B., ed. see Freehof, Soloman B.

Syme, Daniel B., ed. see Freehof, Solomon B.

Syme, Daniel B., ed. see Marcus, Audrey F. & Zwerin, Raymond A.

Syme, G. J. & Syme, L. A. Social Structure in Farm Animals. LC 78-26088. (Developments in Animal & Veterinary Sciences Ser.: Vol. 4). 1979. 39.00 (ISBN 0-444-41769-9). Elsevier.

Syme, L. A., jt. auth. see Syme, G. J.

Syme, Ronald. Ammianus & the Historia Augusta. 1968. 26.00x (ISBN 0-19-814344-3). Oxford U Pr.

--Benedict Arnold: Traitor of the Revolution. (Illus.). (gr. 5-9). 1970. PLB 6.24 (ISBN 0-688-31083-4). Morrow.

--Cartier: Finder of the St. Lawrence. (Illus.). (gr. 3-7). 1958. PLB 6.24 (ISBN 0-688-31146-6). Morrow.

--De Soto: Finder of the Mississippi. (Illus.). (gr. 3-7). 1957. PLB 6.96 (ISBN 0-688-31224-1). Morrow.

--Emperors & Biography: Studies in the Historia Augusta. 1971. 24.95x o.p. (ISBN 0-19-814357-5). Oxford U Pr.

--Frontenac of New France. (Illus.). (gr. 5-9). 1969. 6.95 (ISBN 0-688-21318-9). Morrow.

--Fur Trader of the North: The Story of Pierre de la Verendrye. LC 72-13603. (Illus.). 192p. (gr. 5-9). 1973. 6.95 (ISBN 0-688-20076-1). Morrow.

--Geronimo. LC 74-16337. (Illus.). 96p. (gr. 3-7). 1975. 7.25 (ISBN 0-688-22013-4); PLB 6.96 (ISBN 0-688-32013-9). Morrow.

--History in Ovid. 1979. 29.95x (ISBN 0-19-814825-9). Oxford U Pr.

--John Smith of Virginia. (Illus.). (gr. 5-9). 1954. 6.95 (ISBN 0-688-21597-1). Morrow.

--Osceola, Seminole Leader. LC 75-22373. (Illus.). 96p. (gr. 3-7). 1976. 6.75 (ISBN 0-688-22054-1); PLB 6.48 (ISBN 0-688-32054-6). Morrow.

--Roman Papers, 2 vols. Badian, E., ed. (Illus.). 948p. 1976. 95.00x (ISBN 0-19-814367-2). Oxford U Pr.

--Roman Revolution. (Oxford Paperbacks Ser). 1939. pap. 11.95x (ISBN 0-19-881001-6). Oxford U Pr.

--La Salle of the Mississippi. (Illus.). (gr. 7 up). 1953. PLB 6.50 o.p. (ISBN 0-688-21591-2). Morrow.

--Tacitus, 2 vols. 874p. 1980. 55.00 (ISBN 0-19-814327-3). Oxford U Pr.

--Vancouver, Explorer of the Pacific Coast. (Illus.). (gr. 3-7). 1970. 6.95 (ISBN 0-688-21807-5); PLB 5.71 o.p. (ISBN 0-686-66493-0). Morrow.

--Vasco Da Gama: Sailor Toward the Sunrise. (Illus.). (gr. 3-7). 1959. PLB 6.00 o.p. (ISBN 0-688-31588-7). Morrow.

--Verrazano, Explorer of the Atlantic Coast. LC 72-7130. (Illus.). 96p. (gr. 3-7). 1973. 6.75 o.p. (ISBN 0-688-21771-0); PLB 6.48 o.p. (ISBN 0-688-31771-5). Morrow.

--Zapata, Mexican Rebel. LC 79-128118. (Illus.). (gr. 3-7). 1971. 6.75 o.p. (ISBN 0-688-21604-8); PLB 6.96 (ISBN 0-688-31604-2). Morrow.

Symes, Kenneth M. Two Voices: Writing About Literature. LC 75-31015. (Illus.). 320p. 1976. pap. text ed. 7.95 (ISBN 0-395-20607-3). HM.

Symes, Lillian. Rebel America. LC 76-172100. (Civil Liberties in American History Ser.). 408p. 1972. Repr. of 1934 ed. lib. bdg. 37.50 (ISBN 0-306-70226-6). Da Capo.

Symes, Patrick, jt. auth. see Greenidge, Gordon.

Symington, T., et al, eds. see Tenth Pfizer Intl. Symposium.

Symm, G. T., jt. auth. see Jaswon, M. A.

Symmers, W. St. C. Systemic Pathology, Vol. 6. 2nd ed. LC 75-3574. 1980. 85.00x (ISBN 0-443-01831-6). Churchill.

Symmes, ed. Ewbank's Indiana Criminal Law, 2 vols. 1956. with 1980 suppl. 75.00 (ISBN 0-672-84086-3, Bobbs-Merrill Law); 1980 suppl. 37.50 (ISBN 0-672-84282-3). Michie.

Symmons, Sarah. Daumier. (Oresko-Jupiter Art Bks). (Illus.). 104p. 1980. 17.95 (ISBN 0-905368-42-8, Pub. by Oresko-Jupiter England). Hippocrene Bks.

--Goya. LC 77-77884. (Illus.). 1977. 15.95 (ISBN 0-8467-0354-8, Pub. by Two Continents); pap. 9.95 (ISBN 0-8467-0353-X). Hippocrene Bks.

Symon, Keith R. Mechanics. 3rd ed. LC 75-128910. (Physics & Physical Science Ser). 1971. text ed. 24.95 (ISBN 0-201-07392-7). A-W.

Symon, Lindsay. Neurosurgery. 3rd ed. Rob, Charles & Smith, Rodney, eds. (Operative Surgery Ser). (Illus.). 1979. text ed. 135.00 (ISBN 0-407-00625-7). Butterworths.

Symonds, jt. auth. see Henry.

Symonds, Craig L., ed. New Aspects of Naval History. 1981. text ed. 32.95 (ISBN 0-87021-495-0). Naval Inst Pr.

Symonds, Curtis W. Basic Financial Management. rev. ed. (Illus.). 1978. 13.95 (ISBN 0-8144-5481-X). Am Mgmt.

Symonds, John & Grant, Kenneth, eds. The Confessions of Aleister Crowley: An Autobiography. 1979. 37.00 (ISBN 0-7100-0175-4). Routledge & Kegan.

Symonds, John A. Sir Philip Sidney. LC 67-23878. 1968. Repr. of 1886 ed. 15.00 (ISBN 0-8103-3056-3). Gale.

Symonds, P. S., jt. ed. see Lee, E. H.

Symonds, Richard. The British & Their Successors. 1966. 7.95 o.p. (ISBN 0-571-06677-1, Pub. by Faber & Faber). Merrimack Bk Serv.

Symons, Arthur. Notes on Joseph Conrad, with Some Unpublished Letters. (Orig.). 1925. 8.00 (ISBN 0-685-13669-8). Kelly.

--Studies in Two Literatures. LC 76-20002. (The Decadent Consciousness Ser.: Vol. 25). 1977. Repr. of 1897 ed. lib. bdg. 38.00 (ISBN 0-8240-2774-4). Garland Pub.

Symons, Arthur see Horne, Herbert P., et al.

Symons, Donald. The Evolution of Human Sexuality. 368p. 1981. pap. 6.95 (ISBN 0-19-502907-0, GB 638, OPB). Oxford U Pr.

--Play & Aggression: A Study of Rhesus Monkeys. LC 77-24638. 1978. 22.50x (ISBN 0-231-04334-1). Columbia U Pr.

Symons, Julian. Sweet Adelaide. LC 80-7610. 288p. 1980. 11.95 (ISBN 0-06-014207-3, HarpT). Har-Row.

--The Tell-Tale Heart: The Life & Works of Edgar Allan Poe. 1981. pap. 3.95 (ISBN 0-14-005371-9). Penguin.

--Thirties: A Dream Revolved. 1975. 11.95 (ISBN 0-571-10715-X, Pub. by Faber & Faber). Merrimack Bk Serv.

Symons, Leslie. Agricultural Geography. (Advanced Economic Geography Ser.). 1979. lib. bdg. 28.50x (ISBN 0-89158-499-4). Westview.

Symons, M. C. Chemical & Biochemical Aspects of Electron Spin Resonance Spectroscopy. LC 78-2837. 1978. 24.95 (ISBN 0-470-26359-8). Halsted Pr.

Sympoisum on Cropping Systems Research & Development for the Asian Rice Farmer. Proceedings. 454p. 1977. pap. 18.50 (R004, IRRI). Unipub.

Symposia in Applied Mathematics-New York-1958. Combinatorial Analysis: Proceedings, Vol. 10. Bellman, R. & Hall, M., Jr., eds. LC 50-1183. 1979. Repr. of 1960 ed. 24.40 (ISBN 0-8218-1310-2, PSAPM-10). Am Math.

Symposia in Applied Mathematics-New York-1963. Stochastic Processes in Mathematical Physics & Engineering: Proceedings, Vol. 16. Bellman, R., ed. LC 64-18128. 1980. Repr. of 1964 ed. 25.60 (ISBN 0-8218-1316-1, PSAPM-16). Am Math.

Symposia in Applied Mathematics - New York - 1960. Structure of Language & Its Mathematical Aspects: Proceedings, Vol. 12. Jakobson, R., ed. LC 50-1183. 1980. Repr. of 1961 ed. 19.60 (ISBN 0-8218-1312-9, PSAPM-12). Am Math.

Symposia in Pure Mathematics - Berkeley, Calif. - 1971. Partial Differential Equations: Proceedings, Vol. 23. Spencer, D. C., ed. LC 72-4071. 1977. Repr. of 1973 ed. 26.80 (ISBN 0-8218-1423-0, PSPUM-23). Am Math.

Symposia in Pure Mathematics, Humboldt State University, Arcata, Calif., July 29-August 16, 1974. Algebraic Geometry-Arcata 1974: Proceedings, Vol. 29. Hartstone, Robin, ed. LC 75-9530. 1979. Repr. of 1979 ed. with corrections 32.40 (ISBN 0-8218-1429-X, PSPUM-29). Am Math.

Symposia in Pure Mathematics-Los Angeles-July, 1967. Axiomatic Set Theory, 2 Vols, Vol. 13. LC 78-125172. Vol. 1 Ed. By Dana Scott. 24.00 (ISBN 0-8218-0245-3, PSPUM-13.1); Vol. 2 Ed. By T. J. Jech. 26.80 (ISBN 0-8218-0246-1, PSPUM-13.2). Am Math.

Symposia in Pure Mathematics-New York-1961. Recursive Function Theory: Proceedings, Vol. 5. Dekker, J., ed. LC 50-1183. 1979. Repr. of 1962 ed. with corrections 20.80 (ISBN 0-8218-1405-2, PSPUM-5). Am Math.

Symposia in Pure Mathematics-Northern Illinois Univ., May 1974. Mathematical Developments Arising from the Hilbert Problems: Proceedings, 2 pts, Vol. 28. Browder, F. E., ed. LC 76-20437. 1976. softcover 16.60 (ISBN 0-8218-1428-1, PSPUM-28). Am Math.

Symposia in Pure Mathematics-Pasadena-1960. Institute on Finite Groups, 1960: Proceedings, Vol. 6. LC 50-1183. 1979. Repr. of 1961 ed. 14.80 (ISBN 0-8218-1406-0, PSPUM-6). Am Math.

Symposia in Pure Mathematics-Pasadena-1963. Theory of Numbers: Proceedings, Vol. 8. Whiteman, A. L., ed. LC 65-17382. 1979. Repr. of 1965 ed. with additions 19.20 (ISBN 0-8218-1408-7, PSPUM-8). Am Math.

Symposia in Pure Mathematics-Seattle-1961. Convexity: Proceedings, Vol. 7. Klee, V., ed. LC 63-10760. 1979. Repr. of 1963 ed. 31.60 (ISBN 0-8218-1407-9, PSPUM-7). Am Math.

Symposia in Pure Mathematics, University of Calif. Berkeley June 1971. Tarski Symposium: Proceedings, Vol. 25. Henkin, L., ed. LC 74-8666. 1979. Repr. of 1974 ed. with additions 32.00 (ISBN 0-8218-1425-7, PSPUM-25). Am Math.

Symposium. I Wish I Had Known. 0.95 o.p. (ISBN 0-310-33122-6). Zondervan.

--Isotope Ratios As Pollutant Source & Behavior Indicators: Proceedings. (Illus.). 489p. 1975. pap. 36.50 (ISBN 92-0-010375-8, IAEA). Unipub.

Symposium at Roswell Park Memorial Institute, Buffalo, May 1980. Cancer Among Black Populations: Proceedings. Mettlin, Curtis & Murphy, Gerald P., eds. (Progress in Clinical & Biological Research Ser.: No. 53). 275p. 1981. 24.00x (ISBN 0-8451-0053-X). A R Liss.

Symposium by the New York University Medical Center & the National Foundation-March of Dimes, New York City, Mar. 1975. Infections of the Fetus & the Newborn Infant: Proceedings. Krugman, Saul & Gershon, Anne A., eds. LC 75-13856. (Progress in Clinical & Biological Research: Vol. 3). 204p. 1975. 23.00x (ISBN 0-8451-0003-3). A R Liss.

Symposium Held at the Radcliffe Infirmary, Oxford, England, April, 1975 Sponsod by the National Foundation - March of Dimes. The Eye & Inborn Errors of Metabolism: Proceedings. Bergsma, Daniel, et al, eds. LC 76-12112. (Birth Defects-Original Article Ser: Vol. 12, No. 3). 620p. 1976. 69.00x (ISBN 0-8451-1003-9). A R Liss.

Symposium Held by European Group for Rapid Virus Diagnosis, London, Jan. 1978. Diagnostic Methods in Viral Hepatitis: Proceedings. Howard, Colin R. & Gardner, P. S., eds. LC 78-20364. (Laboratory & Research Methods in Biology & Medicine: Vol. 2). 1978. 14.00x (ISBN 0-8451-1651-7). A R Liss.

Symposium in Honor of the Jackson Laboratory's Fiftieth Anniversary, Bar Harbor, Maine, July 1979. Mammalian Genetics & Cancer: Proceedings. Russell, Elizabeth S., ed. 1981. 42.00x (ISBN 0-8451-0045-9). A R Liss.

Symposium, Knoxville, July 15-19, 1974. Dynamic Studies with Radioisotopes in Medicine 1974, Vol. II: Proceedings. (Illus.). 443p. 1975. pap. 38.75 (ISBN 92-0-010175-5, ISP376-2, IAEA). Unipub.

Symposium Milan, Italy, November 1978. Antibiotics & Hospitals: Proceedings. Grassi, Carlo & Ostino, Guiseppe, eds. LC 79-5390. (Progress in Clinical & Biological Research Ser.: Vol. 35). 238p. 1979. 28.00x (ISBN 0-8451-0035-1). A R Liss.

Symposium, New Delhi, October 1978. Recent Advances in Reproduction & Regulation of Fertility: Proceedings. Talwar, G. P., ed. 1979. 73.25 (ISBN 0-444-80123-5, North Holland). Elsevier.

Symposium of Commission V, ISP on the Biomedical & Bioengineering Applications of Photogrammetry, Washington, D.C., Sept. 1974. Proceedings. 5.00 o.p. (ISBN 0-686-21665-2); non-members o.p. 12.50 o.p. (ISBN 0-686-21666-0). ASP.

Symposium of the Institute of Microbiology, Rutgers University, 1967. Nucleic Acids in Immunology: Proceedings. Plescia, O. J. & Braun, W., eds. (Illus.). 1968. 62.10 o.p. (ISBN 0-387-04290-3). Springer-Verlag.

Symposium of the International Society of Psychoneuroendocrinology Visgrad, Hungary, Dec. 1975 & Endroczi, E. Cellular & Molecular Bases of Neuroendocrine Processes: Proceedings. 1977. 40.00x (ISBN 0-8002-0436-0). Intl Pubns Serv.

Symposium of the Parkinson's Disease Information & Research Center, 2nd, Columbia University, 1965. Biochemistry & Pharmacology of the Basal Ganglia: Proceedings. Costa, E., et al, eds. LC 66-21554. 1966. 13.50 o.p. (ISBN 0-911216-03-0). Raven.

Symposium on Advanced Ozone Technology, Toronto Canada, May 1978. Advanced Ozone Technology: Proceedings. Netzer, Aharon, ed. text ed. cancelled o.s.i. (ISBN 0-918650-11-9). Intl Ozone.

Symposium on Aerobic Gram-Negative Bronchopneumonias, Brussels, Sep. 22, 1978. Aerobic Gram-Negative Bronchopneumonias: Proceedings. Kalstersky, J., et al, eds. LC 79-42759. (Illus.). 120p. 1980. 29.00 (ISBN 0-08-025533-7). Pergamon.

Symposium on Biological Effects of Low-Level Ionizing Radiation. Biological & Environmental Effects of Low-Level Radiation: Proceedings, Vol. 1. (Illus.). 1976. pap. 36.50 (ISBN 92-0-010076-7, ISP409-1, IAEA). Unipub.

--Biological & Environmental Effects of Low-Level Radiation: Proceedings, Vol. 2. (Illus.). 1976. pap. 45.00 (ISBN 92-0-010176-3, ISP409-2, IAEA). Unipub.

Symposium on Climate & Rice. Proceedings. 565p. 1976. pap. 37.50 (R025, IRRI). Unipub.

Symposium on Computers in Aerodynamics at the Aerodynamics Laboratories Polytechnic Institute of New York, 1979. Computers in Aerodynamics. Rubin, S. G. & Bloom, M. H., eds. 130p. 1980. 38.50 (ISBN 0-08-025426-8). Pergamon.

Symposium on Corrosion Fundamentals. Proceedings. Brasunas, Anton & Stansbury, E. E., eds. LC 56-13073. (Illus.). 1956. 12.50x (ISBN 0-87049-016-8). U of Tenn Pr.

Symposium on Educational Research,14th. Humanistic Education: Visions & Realities; Proceedings. Weller, Richard H., ed. LC 77-71196. 1977. 12.25 (ISBN 0-8211-2256-8, Co-Pub with McCutchan); pap. 10.00 (ISBN 0-87367-704-8, Pub with McCutchan). Phi Delta Kappa.

Symposium on Finite Groups, Urbana, Illinois, Nov. 24, 1967. Proceedings. Repr. of 1969 ed. 4.00 (ISBN 0-8218-0045-0, FIN). Am Math.

Symposium on Game Theory & Related Topics, Hagen & Bonn, Sept. 1978. Game Theory & Related Topics: Proceedings. Moeschlin, O. & Pallaschke, D., eds. 1979. 53.75 (ISBN 0-444-85342-1, North Holland). Elsevier.

Symposium on Insulin Action, Toronto, 1971. Insulin Action: Proceedings. Fritz, Irving, ed. 1973. 48.50 (ISBN 0-12-268750-7). Acad Pr.

Symposium on Interrelationship Between Agricultural Input Industry & Agriculture. Impact of Fertilizer Storage: Focus on Asia. (APO Project SYP-I-74 Ser.). (Illus.). 1976. pap. 16.50 (ISBN 92-833-2001-8, APO31, APO). Unipub.

Symposium on Ionizing Radiation for Sterilization of Medical Products & Biological Tissues, Bombay, Dec 9-13, 1974. Radiosterilization of Medical Products, 1974: Proceedings. (Illus.). 539p. 1975. pap. 48.25 (ISBN 92-0-010475-4, ISP383, IAEA). Unipub.

Symposium on Jet Pumps & Ejectors, 1st. Proceedings. 1972. 28.00. BHRA Fluid.

Symposium on Load-Curve Coverage in Future Electrical Power Generating Systems, Rome, Oct. 1977. Electrical Load-Curve Coverage: Proceedings. United Nations Economic Commission for Europe, ed. LC 78-40342. (Illus.). 1979. text ed. 105.00 (ISBN 0-08-022422-9). Pergamon.

Symposium on Microdosimetry, Sixth, Brussels, Belgium, May 1978. Proceedings, Vols. 1 & 2. Booz, J. & Ebert, H. G., eds. (European Applied Research Reports Topics). 558p. 1978. lib. bdg. 48.75 ea. Vol. 1 (ISBN 0-906346-02-9). Vol. 2 (ISBN 0-906346-03-7). Harwood Academic.

Symposium on Modelling & Simulation Methodology, Israel, August 1978. Methodology in Systems Modelling & Simulation: Proceedings. Zeigler, B. P., et al, eds. 1979. 66.00 (ISBN 0-444-85340-5, North Holland). Elsevier.

Symposium on Naval Hydrodynamics, 12th, Naval Studies Board. Naval Hydrodynamics: Proceedings. 1979. 18.75 (ISBN 0-309-02896-5). Natl Acad Pr.

Symposium on Nucleic Acids, Chemistry, 4th, Kyoto, 1976. Proceedings. 156p. 16.00. Info Retrieval.

Symposium on Nucleic Acids Chemistry, 5th, Mishima, Japan, 1977. Proceedings. 190p. 12.00. Info Retrieval.

Symposium on Nucleic Acids Chemistry, 6th, Nagoya, Japan, 1978. Proceedings. 227p. 15.00. Info Retrieval.

Symposium on Nucleic Acids Chemistry, 7th, Okayama, Japan, 1979. Proceedings. 250p. 16.00. Info Retrieval.

Symposium on Ocular Therapy. Proceedings, Vol. 8. Leopold, Irving H. & Burns, Robert P., eds. LC 66-22972. 92p. 1976. 24.00 (ISBN 0-471-52771-8, Pub. by Wiley). Krieger.

Symposium on Photo-Electronic Image Devices - 1st see Marton, L.

Symposium on Photo-Electronic Image Devices - 2nd see Marton, L.

Symposium on Photo-Electronic Image Devices - 3rd see Marton. L.

Symposium on Photo-Electronic Image Devices - 4th see Marton. L.

Symposium on Photo-Electronic Image Devices - 5th see Marton. L.

Symposium on Planetary Cratering Mechanics, Flagstaff, Ariz., 1976. Impact & Explosion Cratering--Planetary & Terrestrial Implications: Proceedings. Roddy, D. J., et al, eds. LC 77-24753. 900p. 1978. 150.00 (ISBN 0-08-022050-9). Pergamon.

Symposium on Psychophysiological Aspects of Space Flight, Brooks Air Force Base, Texas, 1960. Proceedings. Flaherty, Bernard E., ed. LC 60-15809. 1961. 22.50x (ISBN 0-231-02456-8). Columbia U Pr.

Symposium on Radioecology, Oregon State University, May 12-14, 1975. Radioecology & Energy Resources: Proceedings. Cushing, C. E., Jr., ed. (Ecological Society of America Special Publications Ser.: No. 1). 1977. 42.00 (ISBN 0-12-786290-0). Acad Pr.

Symposium on Surface Mining Hydrology, Sedimentology, & Reclamataion, December 4-7, 1979. Proceedings. 1979. 33.50 (ISBN 0-89779-024-3). U of Ky OES Pubns.

Symposium on the Chemistry of Nucleic Acids Components, 3rd, Czechoslovakia, 1975. Proceedings. 183p. 15.00. Info Retrieval.

Symposium on the Chemistry of Nucleic Acids Components, 4th, Czechoslovakia, 1978. Proceedings. 250p. 14.00. Info Retrieval.

Symposium on the Granites of West Africa, Ivory Coast, Nigeria, Cameroon, 1965. Proceedings. 1968. 17.50 (ISBN 0-685-20791-9, U488, UNESCO). Unipub.

Symposium on the Life and Work of Christiaan Huygens, Amsterdam, 22-25 August 1979. Studies on Christiaan Huygens: Invited Papers. Bos, H. J., et al, eds. 1980. text ed. 34.25 (ISBN 90-265-0333-4, Pub. by Swets Pub Serv Holland). Swets North Am.

Symposium on the Mechanisms of Vasodilation. Abstracts. Vanhoutte, P. M., ed. (Journal: Blood Vessels: Vol. 17, No. 3). 56p. 1980. soft cover 22.25 (ISBN 3-8055-1252-X). S Karger.

Symposium on the Renaissance, University of Wisconsin, 1959. The Renaissance: A Reconsideration of the Theories & Interpretations of the Age. Helton, Tinsley, ed. LC 80-21869. xiii, 160p. 1980. Repr. of 1961 ed. lib. bdg. 19.50x (ISBN 0-313-22797-7, SYRE). Greenwood.

Symposium on the State of the Art in Communication, Point Mugu, California, October 1975. Proceedings. 15.00 (ISBN 0-87703-145-2). Soc Tech Comm.

Symposium on Theory of Argumentation, Groningen, October 11-13, 1978. Argumentation: Approaches to Theory Formation: Proceedings. Marten & Barth, eds. (Studies in Language Companion Ser.: No. 8). 250p. 1980. text ed. 31.50x (ISBN 90-272-3007-2). Humanities.

Symposium On Underwater Physiology - 2nd - Feb. 25-26 - Washington D.C. - 1963. Proceedings. Mine Advisory Committee, ed. 1963. pap. 5.00 (ISBN 0-309-01181-7). Natl Acad Pr.

Symposium on Wind Energy, 1st. Proceedings. 1977. 65.00. BHRA Fluid.

Symposium on Wind Energy, 3rd. Proceedings. 1980. pap. 99.00 (ISBN 0-906085-47-0). BHRA Fluid.

Symposium, Roswell Park Memorial Institute, Buffalo, Sept. 1974. Conflicts in Childhood Cancer: An Evaluation of Current Management Proceedings. Sinks, Lucius F. & Godden, John O., eds. LC 75-13857. (Progress in Clinical & Biological Research: Vol. 4). 452p. 1975. 30.00x (ISBN 0-8451-0004-1). A R Liss.

Symposium, Stockholm, Sweden, June 2-5, 1975. Combined Effects of Radioactive Chemical & Thermal Releases to the Environment: Proceedings. (Illus.). 358p. 1976. pap. 32.75 (ISBN 92-0-020275-6, ISP404, IAEA). Unipub.

Symposium, Vienna, 1974. Siting of Nuclear Facilities: Proceedings. (Illus.). 625p. 1975. pap. 55.25 (ISBN 92-0-020175-X, ISP 348, IAEA). Unipub.

Symposium, Vienna, 20-24 October, 1975. Safeguarding Nuclear Materials, Vol. II: Proceedings. (Illus., Orig.). 1976. pap. 64.75 (ISBN 92-0-070176-0, ISP408-2, IAEA). Unipub.

Symposium, Woods Hole, Mass., October, 1978. Biomedical Applications of the Horseshoe Crab (Limulidae) Cohen, Elias, ed. LC 79-1748. (Progress in Clinical & Biological Research Ser.: Vol. 29). 720p. 1978. 52.00x (ISBN 0-8451-0029-7). A R Liss.

Symposium - 3rd - Madison - 1970. Polarization Phenomena in Nuclear Reactions: Proceedings. Barschall, Henry H. & Haeberli, Willy, eds. LC 71-143762. 1971. text ed. 60.00 (ISBN 0-299-05890-5). U of Wis Pr.

Synan, J. A. The Trinity, or the Tri-Personal Being of God. pap. 2.95 (ISBN 0-911866-00-0). Advocate.

Synder, Susan, ed. see De Saluste, Guillaume & Du Bartas, Sieur.

Synek, Elmer, jt. auth. see Harwood, Bruce.

Synge & Schild. Tensor Calculus. 1978. pap. text ed. 5.00 (ISBN 0-486-63612-7). Dover.

Synge, J. M. In Wicklow, West Kerry & Connemara. (Illus.). 166p. 1980. 19.50x (ISBN 0-8476-6260-8). Rowman.

--My Wallet of Photographs: The Collected Photographs of J. M. Synge Arranged & Introduced by Lilo Stephens. (Illus.). 53p. 1971. text ed. 17.00x (ISBN 0-85105-189-8, Dolmen Pr). Humanities.

Synge, John M. Deidre of the Sorrows: And the Tinker's Wedding & the Shadow of the Glen. (Unwin Book). 1967. pap. 2.95 (ISBN 0-04-822033-7). Allen Unwin.

--Playboy of the Western World. Bd. with Riders to the Sea. 93p. 1968. pap. 3.50 (ISBN 0-06-463226-1, EH 226, EH). Har-Row.

--Playboy of the Western World & Riders to the Sea. (Unwin Paperbacks Ser). 1962. pap. 2.95 (ISBN 0-04-822041-8). Allen Unwin.

--Plays, Poems, & Prose. 1968. 6.00x (ISBN 0-460-00968-0, Evman); pap. 5.95 (ISBN 0-460-01968-6). Dutton.

--Riders to the Sea. 60p. 1970. 40.00x (ISBN 0-7165-1410-9, Pub. by Irish Academic Pr Ireland). Biblio Dist.

Synge, John M; see Salerno, Henry F.

Synge, John M; see Watson, E. Bradlee & Pressey, Benfield.

Synge, Lanto. Chairs in Color. (Illus.). 1979. 12.95 (ISBN 0-7137-0828-X, Pub. by Blandford Pr England). Sterling.

Synge, P. M., jt. ed. see Chittenden, F. J.

Synge, Ursula. The People & the Promise. LC 74-10661. 192p. (gr. 7-10). 1974. 9.95 (ISBN 0-87599-208-0). S G Phillips.

--Weland: Smith of the Gods. LC 73-5945. (Illus.). 94p. (gr. 7 up). 1973. 9.95 (ISBN 0-87599-200-5). S G Phillips.

Syniavskyi, Oleksa. Normy Ukrains'koi Literaturnoi Movy. LC 78-202939. (Ukra.). 1967. text ed. 20.00 (ISBN 0-918884-14-4). Slavia Lib.

Syniawska, Nina, ed. Scientific Russian Reader. LC 61-7717. 1961. 15.00x (ISBN 0-231-02453-3). Columbia U Pr.

Sypher, Eleanor, tr. see Nivardus, Magister.

Sypher, F. J., tr. see Nivardus, Magister.

Sypher, Francis J., ed. see Swinburne, Algernon Charles.

Sypher, Wylie, ed. Enlightened England. rev. ed. (Illus.). 1962. 14.95x o.p. (ISBN 0-393-09425-1, NortonC). Norton.

Syracuse University. Maxwell Graduate School of Citizenship & Public Affairs. The United Nations Secretariat. Sayre, W. S., ed. LC 78-2884. (Carnegie Endowment for International Peace, United Nations Studies: No. 4). 1978. Repr. of 1950 ed. lib. bdg. 14.50x (ISBN 0-313-20331-8, UNNS). Greenwood.

Syracuse, Victor R., jt. auth. see Dicker, Ralph L.

Syrkin, Marie. The State of the Jews. 1980. 15.95 o.p. (ISBN 0-915220-60-1). New Republic.

Syson, Leslie. The Watermills of Britain. LC 80-66088. (Illus.). 192p. 1980. 24.00 (ISBN 0-7153-7824-4). David & Charles.

Syson, Michael, jt. auth. see Bulla, Clyde R.

Systems Symposium - 4th - Case Western Reserve University, Institute of Technology. Theoretical Approaches to Non-Numerical Problem Solving: Proceedings. Banerji, R. B. & Mesarovic, M. D., eds. LC 79-121996. (Lecture Notes in Operations Research & Mathematical Systems: Vol. 28). 1970. pap. 21.90 o.p. (ISBN 0-387-04900-2). Springer-Verlag.

Syz, Hans C. Of Being & Meaning. 1981. 6.00 (ISBN 0-8022-2374-5). Philos Lib.

Szabo, Denis, jt. auth. see Crelinsten, Ronald D.

Szabo, Denis, jt. auth. see Parizeau, Alice.

Szabo, Denis & Katzenelson, Susan, eds. Offenders & Corrections. LC 78-8399. (Praeger Special Studies). 1978. 24.95 (ISBN 0-03-044236-2). Praeger.

Szabo, Zoltan. Creative Watercolor Techniques. (Illus.). 176p. 1974. 18.95 (ISBN 0-8230-1119-4). Watson-Guptill.

Szajkowski, Soza. Analytical Franco-Jewish Gazetteer, 1939-1945. 1966. 50.00 (ISBN 0-685-13733-3). Ktav.

Szalavary, Anne. Hungarian Folk Designs for Embroiderers & Craftsmen. (Illus.). 160p. (Orig.). 1980. pap. 4.00 (ISBN 0-486-23969-1). Dover.

Szanto, George H. Narrative Consciousness: Structure & Perception in the Fiction of Kafka, Beckett & Robbe-Grillet. 260p. 1972. 12.50x o.p. (ISBN 0-292-75500-7). U of Tex Pr.

Szanton, Jules G. Food Values & Calorie Charts. (gr. 9 up). 1965. 5.95 o.s.i. (ISBN 0-8119-0059-2). Fell.

Szanton, Peter. Not Well Advised. LC 80-69174. 175p. 1981. text ed. 11.95x (ISBN 0-87154-874-7). Russell Sage.

Szanton, Peter, ed. Federal Reorganization. 1981. pap. 12.95x (ISBN 0-934540-11-X). Chatham Hse Pubs.

--Federal Reorganization: What Have We Learned? (Chatham House Series on Change in American Politics). 184p. 1981. pap. text ed. 12.95x (ISBN 0-934540-11-X). Chatham Hse Pubs.

Szara, Stephen, jt. ed. see Braude, Monique C.

Szara, Stephen I., jt. auth. see Weil-Malherbe, Hans.

Szarkowski, John, ed. Callahan. (Illus.). 1979. pap. 19.50 o.p. (ISBN 0-912334-76-2). Aperture.

--From the Picture Press. LC 72-82886. (Illus.). 96p. 1973. pap. 4.95 (ISBN 0-87070-334-X). Museum Mod Art.

Szarkowski, John, intro. by. Callahan. LC 76-42104. (Illus.). 1976. 35.00 o.p. (ISBN 0-912334-75-4); ltd. ed. o.p 400.00 o.p. (ISBN 0-89381-010-X). Aperture.

Szarmach, Paul, jt. ed. see Levy, Bernard.

Szarmach, Paul E., ed. Vercelli Homilies Nine to Twenty-Three. (Toronto Old English Ser.). 192p. 1981. 25.00x (ISBN 0-8020-5528-1). U of Toronto Pr.

Szasz, Ferenc. Radicals of Rings. LC 79-40509. 1981. 34.50 (ISBN 0-471-27583-2, Pub. by Wiley-Interscience). Wiley.

Szasz, Margaret C. Education & the American Indian: The Road to Self-Determination Since 1928. 2nd ed. LC 77-11742. (Illus.). 252p. 1979. pap. 5.95x (ISBN 0-8263-0468-0). U of NM Pr.

Szasz, Thomas S., M.D. Ceremonial Chemistry: The Ritual Persecution of Drugs, Addicts, & Pushers. LC 74-2834. 240p. 1975. pap. 2.95 o.p. (ISBN 0-385-06636-8, 1004, Anch). Doubleday.

--Ideology & Insanity - Essays on the Psychiatric Dehumanization of Man. LC 72-84397. 1970. pap. 2.95 (ISBN 0-385-02033-3, A704, Anch). Doubleday.

Szathmary, Louis. Bakery Restaurant Cookbook. LC 80-36675. 1980. 12.95 (ISBN 0-8436-2195-8). CBI Pub.

Szczawinski, Adam F. & Turner, Nancy J. Edible Garden Weeds of Canada. (Illus.). 1978. pap. 9.95 (ISBN 0-660-00026-1, 56327-8, Pub. by Natl Mus Canada). U of Chicago Pr.

Szczawinski, Adam F., jt. auth. see Soper, James H.

Szczawinski, Adam F., jt. auth. see Turner, Nancy J.

Szczepanski, Jan. Systems of Higher Education: Poland. 1978. pap. 5.00 o.p. (ISBN 0-89192-208-3). Interbk Inc.

Szczepinski, W. Introduction to the Mechanics of Plastic Forming Metals. 378p. 1979. 60.00x (ISBN 90-286-0126-0). Sijthoff & Noordhoff.

Szczesniak, Lenny, tr. see Zanzucchi, Anne M.

Szczesny, Gerhard. The Future of Unbelief. LC 60-1665. 1961. 5.95 o.s.i. (ISBN 0-8076-0124-1); pap. 2.95 (ISBN 0-8076-0375-9). Braziller.

Sze Mai-Mai. Way to Chinese Painting. (Illus.). 1959. pap. 3.95 (ISBN 0-394-70166-6, Vin). Random.

Szechter, Szymon. Bridge on Ice. Carroll, Frances & Karsov, Nina, trs. from Polish. 1978. 8.95 (ISBN 0-7145-2596-0, Pub. by M Boyars). Merrimack Bk Serv.

Szechy, K. & Varga, L. Foundation Engineering: Soil Exploration & Spread Foundations. LC 79-318873. (Illus.). 1978. 50.00x (ISBN 963-05-1489-3). Intl Pubns Serv.

Szecsi, Katalin. Hide-&-Seek. (gr. k-6). 5.50 (ISBN 9-6313-0515-5). Newbury Bks Inc.

Szeftel, Marc. Russian Institutions & Culture up to Peter the Great. 374p. 1980. 60.00x (ISBN 0-902089-80-3, Pub. by Variorum England). State Mutual Bk.

Szego, Giorgio. New Quantitative Techniques for Economic Analysis: Economic Theory, Econometrics & Mathematical Economics. 1980. write for info. (ISBN 0-12-680760-4). Acad Pr.

Szegoe, G. P., ed. see International Summer School on Mathematical Systems Theory & Economics, Varenna, Italy, 1967.

Szekely, A. Latin America & the Law of the Sea, Release 1. 1980. 32.50 (ISBN 0-379-10180-7). Oceana.

Szekely, Gy., et al, eds. Neural Communication & Control: Satellite Symposium of the 28th International Congress of Physiological Sciences, Debrechen, Hungary, 1980. (Advances in Physiological Sciences: Vol. 30). (Illus.). 350p. 1981. 35.00 (ISBN 0-08-027351-3). Pergamon.

Szekely, Julian, jt. auth. see Ray, Willis H.

Szekely, M., jt. auth. see Szelenyi, Z.

Szekely, Paul & Snaith, Linton. Heart Disease & Pregnancy. (Illus.). 208p. 1974. text ed. 27.50x (ISBN 0-443-01135-4). Churchill.

Szekeres, L., ed. Pharmacology of Antiarrhymthmic Agents. (Intermnational Encyclopedia of Pharmacology & Therapeutics Ser.: Section 105). (Illus.). 328p. 1980. 70.00 (ISBN 0-08-025897-2). Pergamon.

Szelenyi, Ivan, jt. auth. see Konrad, George.

Szelenyi, Z & Szekely, M. Contributions to Thermal Physiology: Proceedings of a Satellite Symposium of the 28th International Congress of Physiological Sciences, Budapest, 1980. LC 80-41854. (Advances in Physiological Sciences Ser.: Vol. 32). (Illus.). 560p. 1981. 60.00 (ISBN 0-08-027354-8). Pergamon.

Szendrey, Thomas, tr. see Malyusz, Edith C.

Szentagothai, J., et al. Regulatory Functions of the Cns - Sybsystems: Proceedings of the 28th International Congress of Physiological Sciences, Budapest, 1980. LC 80-41884. (Advances in Physiological Sciences: Vol. 2). (Illus.). 293p. 1981. 35.00 (ISBN 0-08-027371-8). Pergamon.

--Regulatory Functions of the CNS- Motion & Organization Principles: Proceedings of the 28th International Congress of Physiological Sciences, Budapest, 1980. LC 80-41885. (Advances in Physiological Sciences: Vol. 1). (Illus.). 300p. 1981. 35.00 (ISBN 0-08-026814-5). Pergamon.

Szentirmai, George, ed. Computer-Aided Filter Design. LC 73-85482. (IEEE Press Selected Reprint Ser.). 437p. 1973. 21.95 o.p. (ISBN 0-471-84301-6, Pub. by Wiley-Interscience). Wiley.

Szigethi, Agnes. French Paintings of the Seventeenth & Eighteenth Centuries. rev. ed. Hoch, Elisabeth, tr. from Hungarian. Gaster, Bertha, ed. (Illus.). 1977. 25.00 (ISBN 0-8283-1726-7). Branden.

Szigethy, Marion. Maurice Falcolm Tauber: A Biobibliography 1934-1973. LC 74-7401. 1974. 10.00 (ISBN 0-8108-0725-4). Scarecrow.

Szigeti, G., ed. see International Conference on the Physics & Chemistry on Semiconductor Heterjunctions & Layer Structures, Budapest, 1970.

Szigeti, Joseph. With Strings Attached: Reminiscences & Reflections. (Music Reprint Ser.). 1979. Repr. of 1947 ed. lib. bdg. 29.50 (ISBN 0-306-79567-1). Da Capo.

Szilagyi, M., jt. auth. see Nagy, G. A.

Szilard, Gertrude W., jt. ed. see Weart, Spencer.

Szilard, Paula & Woo, Juliana J. The Electric Vegetarian: Natural Cooking the Food Processor Way. 1981. 12.95. Johnson VA.

--Electric Vegetarian: Natural Cooking the Food Processor Way. 1980. pap. 10.95 (ISBN 0-933472-50-1). Johnson Colo.

Szilvasy, Linda. The Jeweled Egg. (Illus.). 1976. pap. 9.95 o.p. (ISBN 0-8096-1916-4, Assn Pr). Follett.

Szinovacz, Maximiliane, jt. auth. see Scanzoni, John.

Szobor, A. Crises in Myasthenia Gravis. Fenyo, P., tr. 1970. 12.00 o.s.i. (ISBN 0-02-853150-7). Hafner.

Szogyi, Alex, jt. auth. see Mankin, Paul.

Szoke, Hanna, tr. see Baer, Gabriel.

Szokolay, S. V. Solar Energy & Building. 2nd ed. LC 77-21700. 1977. 21.95x (ISBN 0-470-99235-2). Halsted Pr.

Szold, Adele, tr. see Liber, Maurice.

Szollosi-Nagy, A., jt. ed. see Wood, E. F.

Szolovits, Peter, ed. Artificial Intelligence in Medicine. (AAAS Selected Symposium: No. 51). 130p. 1981. lib. bdg. 15.00x (ISBN 0-89158-900-7). Westview.

Szonyi, David M., ed. see Steinitz, Lucy Y.

Szostak, John M. & Leighton, Frances S. In the Footsteps of Pope John Paul II. LC 80-20258. 1980. 11.95 (ISBN 0-13-476002-6). P-H.

Szoverffy, Joseph. An Anthology of Medieval Latin Love Poetry: No. 8. 1976. 18.00 o.p. (ISBN 0-686-23384-0). Classical Folia.

Szperski, N. & Grochla, E., eds. Design & Implementation of Computer-Based Information Systems. 383p. 1979. 47.50x (ISBN 90-286-0519-3). Sijthoff & Noordhoff.

Szpiro, L. Lectures on Equations Defining Space Curves. (Tata Institute Lectures on Mathematics). (Illus.). 81p. 1980. pap. 8.00 (ISBN 0-387-09544-6). Springer-Verlag.

Szporluk, Roman, ed. The Influence of East Europe & the Soviet West on the USSR. LC 75-3752. (Special Studies). (Illus.). 272p. 1976. text ed. 25.95 (ISBN 0-275-07500-1). Praeger.

Szuladzinski, Gregory. Dynamics of Structures & Machinery: Problems & Solutions. 700p. 1981. 50.00 (ISBN 0-471-09027-1, Pub. by Wiley Interscience). Wiley.

Szulc, Tad. Czechoslovakia Since World War Two. LC 70-83248. 1971. 14.00 o.p. (ISBN 0-670-25332-4). Viking Pr.

--The Energy Crisis. LC 74-17335. 160p. 1974. PLB 7.45 (ISBN 0-531-02752-X). Watts.

--The Invasion of Czechoslovakia: August, 1968. LC 73-12072. (World Focus Bks). (Illus.). 72p. (gr. 7 up). 1974. PLB 4.47 o.p. (ISBN 0-531-02172-6). Watts.

Szuprowicz, Bohdan O. Strategic Materials Geopolitics: How to Avoid Shortages, Cartels, Embargoes, & Supply Disruptions. 336p. 1981. 18.95 (ISBN 0-471-07843-3, Pub. by Wiley-Interscience). Wiley.

Szwed, John F., jt. auth. see Whitten, Norman E., Jr.

Szwengrub, Lili-Marie, jt. ed. see Durand-Drouhin, Jean-Louis.

Szycher, Michael & Robinson, William J., eds. Synthetic Biomedical Polymers: Concepts & Applications. LC 80-52137. (Illus.). 235p. 1980. 39.00 (ISBN 0-87762-290-6). Technomic.

Szyk, Arthur. Megillah: Book of Esther. 1974. 14.95x (ISBN 0-685-84454-4). Bloch.

Szykitka, Walter, jt. auth. see Sarshik, Steve.

Szyliowicz, Joseph S. & O'Neill, Bard E., eds. The Energy Crisis & U. S. Foreign Policy. LC 74-3140. (Special Studies). (Illus.). 280p. 1975. text ed. 31.50 (ISBN 0-275-09040-X); pap. text ed. 11.95 (ISBN 0-275-88840-1). Praeger.

Szymanski, Herman A., ed. Biomedical Applications of Gas Chromatography, 2 vols. Incl. Vol. 1. 324p. 1964. 37.50 (ISBN 0-306-37581-8); Vol. 2. 198p. 1968. 32.50 (ISBN 0-306-37582-6). LC 64-13147 (Plenum Pr). Plenum Pub.

Szymborska, Wislawa. Sounds, Feelings, Thoughts: Seventy Poems by Wislawa Szymborska. Krynski, Magnus J. & Maguire, Robert A., trs. from Pol. LC 80-8579. (Lockert Library of Poetry in Translation). 261p. 1981. 17.50x (ISBN 0-691-06469-5); pap. 7.95x (ISBN 0-691-01380-2). Princeton U Pr.

Szypula, George, jt. auth. see Szypula, June.

Szypula, June & Szypula, George. Contemporary Gymnastics. 1979. 6.95 o.p. (ISBN 0-8092-7702-6); pap. 3.95 (ISBN 0-8092-7701-8). Contemp Bks.

T

Taaffe, Edward & Gauthier, Howard L. Geography of Transportation. (Foundations of Economic Geography Ser.). (Illus.). 224p. 1973. pap. 7.95 ref. ed. (ISBN 0-13-351387-4). P-H.

Taaffe, James G. & Lincks, John. Reading English Poetry. LC 75-136271. 1971. pap. text ed. 4.50 o.s.i. (ISBN 0-02-932460-2). Free Pr.

Tab Editorial Staff. Concrete & Masonry. LC 76-1553. 392p. 1976. pap. 5.95 (ISBN 0-8306-5902-1, 902). TAB Bks.

Tab Editorial Staff. CB Radio Schematic-Servicing Manual, Vol. 3. LC 75-41727. 200p. 1976. vinyl o.p. 8.95 (ISBN 0-8306-6858-6); pap. 5.95 (ISBN 0-8306-5858-0, 858). TAB Bks.

--Popular Tube-Transistor Substitution Guide. LC 74-105968. (Illus.). 1971. pap. 3.95 (ISBN 0-8306-0570-3, 570). TAB Bks.

--Practical Home Construction-Carpentry Handbook. LC 76-1552. 448p. 1976. pap. 5.95 (ISBN 0-8306-5900-5, 900). TAB Bks.

Taba, Hilda. The Dynamics of Education: A Methodology of Progressive Educational Thought. 278p. 1980. Repr. of 1932 ed. lib. bdg. 35.00 (ISBN 0-89760-880-1). Telegraph Bks.

Taba, Hilda, et al. Teacher's Handbook to Elementary Social Studies. 2nd ed. LC 78-147815. (Education Ser). 1971. pap. 9.95 (ISBN 0-201-07426-5). A-W.

Tabachnick, Norman, et al. Accident or Suicide: Destruction by Automobile. 288p. 1973. 16.75 (ISBN 0-398-02819-2). C C Thomas.

Tabachnick, Stephen E. T. E. Lawrence. (English Authors Ser.: No. 233). 1978. lib. bdg. 10.95 (ISBN 0-8057-6704-5). Twayne.

Tabak, Daniel & Kuo, Benjamin C. Optimal Control by Mathematical Programming. LC 75-137985. 1971. 24.00 (ISBN 0-13-638106-5). SRL Pub Co.

Tabares, Edward F. How to Be Employed & Make a Spectacular Success in an Extra Business of Your Own: Which You Conduct in Your Spare Time. (The International Council for Excellence in Management Library). (Illus.). 107p. 1980. plastic spiral bdg. 38.95 (ISBN 0-89266-245-X). Am Classical Coll Pr.

Tabart, Marielle & Monod-Fontaine, Isabelle, eds. Brancusi Photographer. Sichel, Kim, tr. from Fr. LC 79-23563. (Illus.). 124p. 1980. 30.00 (ISBN 0-9601068-4-7); pap. 17.50 (ISBN 0-9601068-2-0). Agrinde Bks.

Tabatch, Jack, jt. auth. see Dow, Bea.

Tabb, William K. The Long Default: New York City & the Urban Fiscal Crisis. LC 80-8933. 1981. 16.00 (ISBN 0-85345-571-6). Monthly Rev.

Tabbara, Lina M. Survival in Beirut. (Illus.). 186p. 1977. cased 16.00; pap. 7.00. Three Continents.

Tabbarah, A. The Spirit of Islam. 18.00x (ISBN 0-686-63565-5). Intl Bk Ctr.

Tabberner, Jeffrey, tr. see Delessert, Etienne.

Taber, Anthony. Cats' Eyes. (Illus.). 1978. 9.95 o.p. (ISBN 0-525-07814-2). Dutton.

--Cat's Eyes. (Illus.). 1980. pap. 6.95 (ISBN 0-525-03162-6, Thomas Congdon Book). Dutton.

Taber, C. R., jt. ed. see Nida, Eugene A.

Taber, Gladys. Another Path. LC 63-17678. 1963. 8.95 (ISBN 0-397-00260-2). Lippincott.

--Country Chronicle. LC 73-19684. (Illus.). 1974. 6.95 o.s.i. (ISBN 0-397-01023-0). Lippincott.

--My Own Cook Book: From Stillmeadow & Cape Cod. LC 72-747. (Illus.). 1972. 8.95 (ISBN 0-397-00877-5). Lippincott.

--Still Cove Journal. Colby, Constance T., intro. by. LC 80-8220. (Illus.). 192p. 1981. 10.95 (ISBN 0-06-014227-8, HarpT). Har-Row.

Taber, M. R., jt. auth. see Tedeschi, F. P.

Taber, Margaret R. & Silgalis, Eugene. Electric Circuit Analysis. LC 78-69525. (Illus.). 1979. text ed. 19.50 (ISBN 0-395-26706-4); inst. manual write for info. 0.95 (ISBN 0-395-26707-2). HM.

Taber, Merlin, et al. Handbook for Community Professionals: An Approach for Planning & Action. (Illus.). 228p. 1972. text ed. 18.50 (ISBN 0-398-02426-X). C C Thomas.

Taber, Robert, jt. auth. see Parnell, Wilma T.

Taber, Robert W. & Dubach, Harold W. One Thousand One Questions Answered About the Oceans & Oceanography. LC 73-184136. (Illus.). 352p. 1972. 7.95 o.p. (ISBN 0-396-06496-5). Dodd.

Taberner, Ferran V., jt. ed. see D'Abadal y Vinyals, Ramon.

Taberner, P. V., jt. ed. see Pycock, C. J.

Tabery, Julia J., et al. Communicating in Spanish for Medical Personnel. LC 73-17667. 600p. 1975. pap. text ed. 15.95 (ISBN 0-316-83101-8); tapes 25.00 (ISBN 0-316-83102-6); pap. text ed. 30.00 incl. text & tapes (ISBN 0-316-83103-4). Little.

Tabler, Dave. VW Bodywork. Jorgensen, Eric, ed. (Illus.). 1978. pap. 7.95 (ISBN 0-89287-228-4, A109). Clymer Pubns.

Tabler, Edward C., ed. Trade & Travel in Early Barotseland: The Diaries of George Westbeech, 1885-1888, & Captain Norman Macleod 1875-1876. (Illus.). 1963. 25.00x (ISBN 0-520-01248-8). U of Cal Pr.

Tabor, D. Gases, Liquids & Solids. 2nd ed. LC 78-26451. (Illus.). 1980. 57.50 (ISBN 0-521-22383-0); pap. 15.95 (ISBN 0-521-29466-5). Cambridge U Pr.

Tabor, D., jt. auth. see Bowden, Frank P.

Tabor, Margaret E. Saints in Art. LC 68-18031. (Illus.). 1969. Repr. of 1908 ed. 15.00 (ISBN 0-8103-3076-8). Gale.

Tabor, Pauline. Pauline's. 256p. 1973. pap. 1.25 o.p. (ISBN 0-449-21842-2, P1842, Crest). Fawcett.

Tabor, R. W. & Crowder, D. F. Routes & Rocks in the Mt. Challenger Quadrangle. LC 68-9291. (Illus.). 47p. (Orig.). pap. 2.95 o.p. (ISBN 0-916890-14-7). Mountaineers.

Tabors, Richard D., et al. Land Use & the Pipe: The Effect of Sewer Extension. 1976. 19.95x o.p. (ISBN 0-669-99275-5). Lexington Bks.

Taborski, Boleslaw. Byron & the Theatre. (Salzburg Studies in English Literature, Poetic Drama & Poetic Theory: No. 1). (Illus.). 395p. 1972. pap. text ed. 25.00x (ISBN 0-391-01543-5). Humanities.

Taborsky, Edward. President Edvard Benes, Between East & West: 1938-1948. LC 80-83829. (Publication Ser.: No. 246). (Illus.). 280p. 1981. 19.95 (ISBN 0-8179-7461-X). Hoover Inst Pr.

Tabory, Mala. Multilingualism in International Law & Institutions. LC 80-51742. 304p. 1980. 32.50x (ISBN 90-286-0210-0). Sijthoff & Noordhoff.

Tabouis, Genevieve. They Called Me Cassandra. LC 76-172178. (Europe 1815-1945 Ser.). (Illus.). 448p. 1973. Repr. of 1942 ed. lib. bdg. 39.50 (ISBN 0-306-70298-3). Da Capo.

Tabouret-Keller, Andree, ed. Regional Language in France. (International Journal of the Sociology of Language: No. 25). 1980. pap. text ed. 21.00x (ISBN 90-279-3068-6). Mouton.

Tabrah, Ruth. Hawaii. (States of the Nation Ser.). (Illus.). 1980. 12.95 (ISBN 0-393-05680-5). Norton.

--The Old Man & the Astronauts. Suyeoka, George, tr. LC 75-16524. (Illus.). (gr. 1-7). 1975. 5.95 (ISBN 0-89610-015-4). Island Her.

Tabrah, Ruth, ed. Issunboshi. LC 74-80514. (Illus.). (gr. 1-7). 1974. 5.95 (ISBN 0-89610-004-9). Island Her.

Tabrah, Ruth, ed. see Buffet, Guy & Buffet, Pam.

Tabrah, Ruth, ed. see Goodman, Robert B. & Spicer, Robert A.

Tabrah, Ruth, ed. see Springer, Philipo.

Tabrah, Ruth, ed. see Suyeoka, George.

Tacchi, Derek. Ovarian Gynaecology. LC 76-26778. (Illus.). 1976. text ed. 26.00 (ISBN 0-7216-8725-3). Saunders.

Tachdjian, M. Congenital Dislocation of the Hip. Date not set. text ed. price not set (ISBN 0-443-08069-0). Churchill.

Tacheron, Donald G. & Udall, Morris K., eds. Job of the Congressman: An Introduction to Service in the U. S. House of Representatives. 2nd ed. LC 77-140113. (Orig.). 1970. pap. 9.50 (ISBN 0-672-51416-8). Bobbs.

Tachibana, S. The Ethics of Buddhism. 1975. text ed. 11.75x (ISBN 0-7007-0077-3). Humanities.

Tachibana, Shundo, pref. by. The Ethics of Buddhism. LC 74-20477. 288p. 1975. Repr. of 1926 ed. text ed. 18.50x (ISBN 0-06-496720-4). B&N.

Tacitus. Agricola & the Germania. Mattingly, Hugh, tr. (Classics Ser). 1971. pap. 2.50 (ISBN 0-14-044241-3). Penguin.

--Annals of Imperial Rome. Grant, Michael, tr. (Classics Ser.). 1956. pap. 3.95 (ISBN 0-14-044060-7). Penguin.

--De Vita Agricolae. 2nd ed. Ogilvie, R. M., et al, eds. (Illus.). 1967. 17.50x (ISBN 0-19-814438-5). Oxford U Pr.

--Opera Minora. Ogilive, R. M. & Winterbottom, M., eds. (Oxford Classical Texts Ser.). 124p. 1975. text ed. 10.50x (ISBN 0-19-814658-2). Oxford U Pr.

Tack, Alfred. Sell Your Way to Success. 6th ed. 256p. 1978. pap. 13.50x (ISBN 0-220-66366-1, Pub. by Busn Bks England). Renouf.

Tacker, W. A. & Geddes, L. A. Electrical Defibrillation. 224p. 1980. 69.95 (ISBN 0-8493-5359-9). CRC Pr.

Tackett, Arnett. The Hearthside Scrapbook. 53p. 1979. pap. 2.95 o.p. (ISBN 0-8059-2681-X). Dorrance.

Tackett, Jo J. & Hunsberger, Mabel. Family-Centered Care of Children & Adolescents: Nursing Concepts in Child Health. 800p. 1981. text ed. price not set (ISBN 0-7216-8740-7). Saunders.

Tacoma Art Museum. Philip McCracken. LC 80-51071. (Illus.). 136p. 1980. 14.95 (ISBN 0-295-95771-9). U of Wash Pr.

Tadlock, Max, jt. auth. see Carvell, Fred.

Tadmor, S. Silent Warriors. Rothstein, Raphael, ed. (Illus.). 1969. 5.95 o.s.i. (ISBN 0-02-615910-4). Macmillan.

Tadmor, Zehev & Gogos, Costas G. Principles of Polymer Processing. LC 78-17859. (SPE Monographs). 1979. 42.50 (ISBN 0-471-84320-2, Pub. by Wiley-Interscience). Wiley.

Tadokoro, Hiroyuki. Structure of Crystalline Polymers. LC 78-5412. 1979. 39.50 (ISBN 0-471-02356-6, Pub. by Wiley-Interscience). Wiley.

Taebel, Delbert A. & Cornehls, James V. The Political Economy of Urban Transportation. LC 77-23150. (National University Publications Interdisciplinary Urban Ser). (Illus.). 1977. 15.00 (ISBN 0-8046-9178-9); pap. 8.95 (ISBN 0-8046-9200-9). Kennikat.

Taeni, Rainer. Rolf Hochhuth. (Modern German Authors: No. 5). 1977. text ed. 9.25x (ISBN 0-85496-057-0). Humanities.

Taetzsch, Lyn. Winning Methods of Bluffing & Betting in Poker. LC 75-36140. (Illus.). 138p. (Orig.). 1981. pap. 6.95. Sterling.

Taeuber, Conrad, jt. auth. see Lively, C. E.

Taeuber, Conrad & Lambert, Richard D., eds. America Enters the Eighties: Some Social Indicators. (The Annals of the American Academy of Political & Social Science Ser.: No. 453). (Illus.). 350p. 1981. 10.00 (ISBN 0-87761-258-7); pap. 8.00 (ISBN 0-87761-259-5). Am Acad Pol Soc.

Tafel, Edgar. Apprentice to Genius: Years with Frank Lloyd Wright. 1980. 19.95 (ISBN 0-07-062815-7). McGraw.

Taff, Charles A. Commercial Motor Transportation. 6th ed. LC 80-12947. (Illus.). 1980. 20.00x (ISBN 0-87033-266-X). Cornell Maritime.

--Management of Physical Distribution and Transportation. 6th ed. 1978. text ed. 19.50 (ISBN 0-256-02016-7). Irwin.

Taff, Laurence G. Computional Spherical Astronomy. LC 80-18834. 320p. 1981. 25.00 (ISBN 0-471-06257-X, Pub. by Wiley-Interscience). Wiley.

Taffel, Alexander. Physics: Its Methods & Meanings. new ed. (gr. 9-12). 1973. text ed. 17.88 (ISBN 0-205-03780-1, 7337809); tchrs' guide 7.20 (ISBN 0-205-03783-6, 7337833); tests 4.00 (ISBN 0-205-02350-9, 7323506); tchrs'. guide 7.20 (ISBN 0-205-02351-7, 7323514); lab manual 5.12 (ISBN 0-205-03781-X, 7337817). Allyn.

Taffler, Richard. Answers: Decision-Making Techniques for Managers. rev. ed. (Illus.). 256p. 1981. 13.95 (ISBN 0-13-037861-5, Spectrum); pap. text ed. 6.95 (ISBN 0-13-037853-4). P-H.

Taft, Charles, jt. auth. see Reswick, James.

Taft, David D., jt. ed. see Miller, Emery P.

Taft, Edna. Puritan in Voodoo-Land. LC 73-174115. (Tower Bks). (Illus.). 1971. Repr. of 1938 ed. 20.00 (ISBN 0-8103-3919-6). Gale.

Taft, Jessie. Dynamics of Therapy in a Controlled Relationship. 7.50 (ISBN 0-8446-3045-4). Peter Smith.

Taft, Philip. Organizing Dixie: Organizing Alabama Workers in the Industrial Era. LC 80-546. (Contributions in Labor History: No. 9). (Illus.). xxv, 288p. 1981. lib. bdg. 35.00 (ISBN 0-313-21447-6, TAL/). Greenwood.

Taft, Robert W., ed. Progress in Physical Organic Chemistry, Vol. 12. LC 63-19364. 1976. 47.50 (ISBN 0-471-01738-8, Pub. by Wiley-Interscience). Wiley.

Taft, William H. Newspapers As Tools for Historians. 1970. text ed. 3.75x spiral bldg. (ISBN 0-87543-064-3). Lucas.

--The Physical, Political & International Value of the Panama Canal. (Illus.). 1979. deluxe ed. 39.75 (ISBN 0-930008-29-4). Inst Econ Pol.

--The President & His Powers. LC 38-32819. Orig. Title: Our Chief Magistrate & His Powers. 1967. pap. 5.00x (ISBN 0-231-08574-5, 74). Columbia U Pr.

--United States & Peace. LC 78-147594. (Library of War & Peace; Int'l. Organization, Arbitration & Law). lib. bdg. 38.00 (ISBN 0-8240-0355-1). Garland Pub.

Tafuri, Manfredo & Dal Co, Francesco. Modern Architecture. (History of World Architecture Ser.). (Illus.). 1980. 45.00 (ISBN 0-8109-1006-3). Abrams.

Tagare, G. V., tr. see Shastri, J. L.

Tagatz, Glenn E. Child Development & Individually Guided Education. LC 75-12103. (Individually Guided Education-Leadership Ser.). (Illus.). 224p. 1976. pap. text ed. 7.95 (ISBN 0-201-19111-3); tchrs guide 2.95 (ISBN 0-201-19121-0). A-W.

Tager, Mark & Jennings, Charles. Whole Person Health Care. rev. ed. LC 78-10103. (Illus.). 1979. pap. 9.95 o.p. (ISBN 0-918480-08-6). Victoria Hse.

Taggart. Informations Systems: An Introduction to Computers in Organizations. 608p. 1980. text ed. 20.95 (ISBN 0-205-06908-8, 2069083). Allyn.

Taggart, Barbara, jt. auth. see Strickler, Carol.

Taggart, Dorothy T. A Guide to Sources in Educational Media & Technology. LC 74-26849. 1975. 10.00 (ISBN 0-8108-0781-5). Scarecrow.

--Management & Administration of the School Library Media Program. 261p. 1980. 17.50 (ISBN 0-208-01853-0, Lib Prof Pubns); text ed. 13.50x (ISBN 0-208-01848-4, Lib Prof Pubns). Shoe String.

Taggart, Jean E. Motorboat, Yacht or Canoe - You Name It. LC 73-14607. 1974. 10.00 (ISBN 0-8108-0661-4). Scarecrow.

--Pet Names. LC 62-19730. 1962. 10.00 (ISBN 0-8108-0111-6). Scarecrow.

Taggart, Leo J. Your Personal Financial I.Q. Test. (Essential Knowledge Library). 1979. spiral bdg. 8.00 (ISBN 0-89266-171-2). Am Classical Coll Pr.

Taggart, Robert, ed. Ship Design & Construction. 3rd ed. (Illus.). 748p. 1980. 60.00 (ISBN 0-9603048-0-0). Soc Naval Arch.

Tagliacozzo, Rhoda. Saving Graces. LC 79-16343. 1979. 10.95 (ISBN 0-312-69988-3). St Martin.

Tagliaferri, Louis E. Creative Cost Improvement for Managers. (Self-Teaching Guide Ser.). 208p. 1981. pap. text ed. 8.95 (ISBN 0-471-08708-4). Wiley.

Taglianti, Augusto V. The World of Mammals. Gilbert, John, tr. LC 80-69173. (Abbeville Press Encyclopedia of Natural Science). (Illus.). 256p. 1980. 13.95 (ISBN 0-89659-183-2); pap. 7.95 (ISBN 0-89659-184-0). Abbeville Pr.

Tagliavia, Sheila. An Arrangement for Life. LC 79-3418. 1980. 12.95 (ISBN 0-06-014214-6, HarpT). Har-Row.

Tagnon, H. J. & Staquet, M., eds. Recent Advances in Cancer Treatment. LC 77-5277. (European Organization for Research & Treatment of Cancer (EORTC): Vol. 3). 1977. 32.00 (ISBN 0-89004-192-X). Raven.

Tagnon, Henri J. & Staquet, Maurice J., eds. Controversies in Cancer: Design of Trials & Treatment. LC 79-84480. (Illus.). 246p. 1979. 39.75 (ISBN 0-89352-049-7). Masson Pub.

Tagore, Rabindranath. A Bunch of Tagore Poems. Varma, Monika, tr. (Translated from bengali). 8.00 (ISBN 0-89253-611-X); flexible cloth 4.00 (ISBN 0-89253-612-8). Ind-US Inc.

--Chaturanga. Mitra, Ashok, tr. from Bengali. 101p. 1974. Repr. bds. 4.95 (ISBN 0-88253-279-0). Ind-US Inc.

--Collected Poems & Plays. 1966. 10.95 o.s.i. (ISBN 0-02-615920-1). Macmillan.

--Fifteen Longer Poems of Rabindranath Tagore. Choudhury, Rabindra N., tr. from Bengali. 248p. 1975. lib. bdg. 15.00 (ISBN 0-88253-735-0). Ind-US Inc.

--Fireflies. (Illus.). 1928. 11.95 (ISBN 0-02-615980-5). Macmillan.

--The Later Poems of Rabindranath Tagore. Bose, Aurobindo, tr. from Bengali. LC 75-34824. (Funk & W Bk.). 142p. 1976. 7.95 o.s.i. (ISBN 0-308-10239-8, TYC-T); pap. 3.95 (ISBN 0-308-10245-2, TYC-T). T Y Crowell.

--Lipika. Dutt, Indu, tr. 127p. 1969. pap. 3.00 (ISBN 0-88253-094-1). Ind-US Inc.

--Love Poems of Tagore. Chowdhury, Rabindra N., tr. from Benjali. 189p. 1976. pap. 2.50 o.p. (ISBN 0-89253-062-6). InterCulture.

--Tagore's Last Poems. Lal, P & Devi, Shyamashree, trs. (Translated from bengali). 5.00 o.p. (ISBN 0-89253-607-1); flexible cloth 4.00 o.p. (ISBN 0-89253-608-X). InterCulture.

--Towards Universal Man. 1969. Repr. 10.00x (ISBN 0-210-33972-1). Asia.

Taherzadeh, Adib. The Revelation of Baha'u'llah: Adrianople, 1863-1868, Vol. II. (Illus.). 1977. 15.95 (ISBN 0-85398-070-5, 7-31-92, Pub. by George Ronald England); pap. 8.95 (7-31-93, Pub. by George Ronald England). Bahai.

--Revelation of Baha'u'llah: Baghdad 1853-1863, Vol. I. (Illus.). 1974. 14.95 (ISBN 0-85398-052-7, 7-31-90, Pub. by George Ronald England); pap. 7.95 (ISBN 0-85398-057-8, 7-31-91). Baha'i.

Taherzadeh, Habib, tr. see Baha'u'llah.

Tai, En-Sai. Treaty Ports in China: A Study in Diplomacy. (Studies in Chinese History & Civilization). 202p. 1977. 17.50 (ISBN 0-89093-083-X). U Pubns Amer.

Tai, Hung-chao. Land Reform & Politics: A Comparative Analysis. 1974. 38.50x (ISBN 0-520-02337-4). U of Cal Pr.

Tai-yi Lin, ed. & tr. see Li, Ju-chen.

Taiganides, E. Paul, ed. Animal Wastes. (Illus.). 1977. 86.90 (ISBN 0-85334-721-2, Pub. by Applied Science). Burgess-Intl Ideas.

Taillepied, Noel. A Treatise of Ghosts. LC 71-162520. 1971. Repr. of 1933 ed. 18.00 (ISBN 0-8103-3741-X). Gale.

Taimni, I. K. Glimpses into the Psychology of Yoga. 1973. 10.95 (ISBN 0-8356-7290-5). Theos Pub Hse.

Taine, Hippolyte A. The French Revolution, 3 vols. 8.00 ea. (ISBN 0-8446-1435-1). Peter Smith.

--On Intelligence. (Contributions to the History of Psychology Ser.). 1978. 30.00 (ISBN 0-89093-152-6). U Pubns Amer.

Tainsh, J. A. The Key to Accounting & Costing. 119p. 1959. 11.75x (ISBN 0-85264-062-5, Pub. by Griffin England). State Mutual Bk.

Taira, Koji. Economic Development & the Labor Market in Japan. LC 78-111459. (Studies of the East Asian Institute Ser). 1970. 17.50x (ISBN 0-231-03272-2). Columbia U Pr.

Tait, A. A. The Landscape Garden in Scotland. 300p. 1980. 25.00x (ISBN 0-85224-372-3, Pub. by Edinburgh U Pr Scotland). Columbia U Pr.

Tait, David, jt. ed. see Middleton, John.

Tait, Elaine. Best Restaurants Philadelphia & Environs. rev. ed. (Best Restaurants Ser.). (Illus.). 225p. 1981. pap. 3.95 (ISBN 0-89286-189-4). One Hurd One Prods.

Tait, J. W. Bridge Match. 1976. 12.95 (ISBN 0-571-10949-7, Pub. by Faber & Faber). Merrimack Bk Serv.

Tait, James A. & Anderson, F. Douglas. Descriptive Cataloguing: A Student's Introduction to the Anglo-American Cataloguins Rules, 1967. 2nd ed. 1971. 10.50 o.p. (ISBN 0-208-01077-7, Linnet). Shoe String.
Tait, R. V. Elements of Marine Ecology. 3rd ed. (Illus.). 304p. 1981. pap. write for info. (ISBN 0-408-71054-3). Butterworth.
Tait, Vera D. Take Command. LC 80-53217. 144p. 1981. 3.95 (ISBN 0-87159-150-2). Unity Bks.
Tait, W. H. Radiation Detection. LC 80-40240: 1980. text ed. 54.95 (ISBN 0-408-10645-X). Butterworths.
Tait, William J., jt. auth. see Corbin, H. Dan.
Taitt, Peter S. Incubus & Ideal: Ecclesiastical Figures in Chaucer & Langland. (Salzburg Studies in English Literature, Elizabethan & Renaissance Studies Ser.: No. 44). 228p. (Orig.). 1975. pap. text ed. 25.00x (ISBN 0-391-01544-3). Humanities.
Taittonen, Edith, jt. auth. see Sauber, Mignon.
Takacs, James A. Your Mind Can Drive You Crazy. 204p. 1980. pap. 4.95 (ISBN 0-930306-34-1). Delphi Info.
Takagi, Paul, jt. ed. see Platt, Tony.
Takahama, Toshie. Origami for Displays. (Illus.). 32p. (Orig.). 1979. pap. 3.50 (ISBN 0-8048-1350-7, Pub by Shufunotomo Co. Ltd. Japan). C E Tuttle.
--Origami for Fun: Thirty-One Basic Models. (Illus.). 32p. (Orig.). 1980. Repr. of 1973 ed. pap. 3.50 (ISBN 0-8048-1352-3, Shufuntomo Co Ltd Japan). C E Tuttle.
--Origami Toys: Fifteen Simple Models. (Illus.). 32p. (Orig.). 1979. pap. 3.50 (ISBN 0-8048-1351-5, Pub by Shufunotomo Co. Ltd. Japan). C E Tuttle.
Takahara, Y., jt. auth. see Mesarovic, M. D.
Takahashi, M., jt. auth. see Parsons, Timothy R.
Takahashi, Masayoshi. Color Atlas of Cancer Cytology. 2nd ed. LC 80-85297. (Illus.). 550p. 1981. 125.00 (ISBN 0-89640-050-6). Igaku-Shoin.
Takahashi, Shinkichi. Afterimages: Zen Poems of Shinkichi Takahashi. LC 77-132582. 127p. 1970. 8.95 (ISBN 0-8040-0512-5). Swallow.
Takahashi, Y. An Introduction to Field Quantization. 1969. 32.00 (ISBN 0-08-012824-6). Pergamon.
Takahashi, Y., et al. Control & Dynamic Systems. 1970. 27.95 (ISBN 0-201-07440-0). A-W.
Takai, Fuyuji, et al. Geology of Japan. 1964. 30.00x (ISBN 0-520-01249-6). U of Cal Pr.
Takakusu, J. Essentials of Buddhist Philosophy. 3rd ed. 1975. Repr. 7.50 (ISBN 0-8426-0826-5). Orient Bk Dist.
Takalashi, Y., ed. see Yashiro, Nobutaka.
Takane, Masalaki. Political Elites in Japan. (Japan Research Monographs: No.1). 180p. 1981. pap. price not set (ISBN 0-912966-33-5). IEAS Ctr Chinese Stud.
Takashima, Shizuye. A Child in Prison Camp. (Illus.). 64p. (gr. 5 up). 1974. 9.25 (ISBN 0-688-20113-X); PLB 8.88 (ISBN 0-688-30113-4). Morrow.
Takayama, Taigan see Stryk, Lucien & Ikemoto, Takashi.
Takayanagi, M., jt. ed. see Otsu, T.
Takeda, Hideo. Bonsai Your Pet. (Illus., Orig.). 1980. pap. 5.95 (ISBN 0-8037-0678-2). Dial.
Takeda, Tsuneo. Kano Eitoku. Horton, H. Mack & Kaputa, Catherine, trs. from Jap. LC 76-44155. (Japanese Arts Library: Vol. 3). 178p. 1977. 16.95 (ISBN 0-87011-295-3). Kodansha.
Takemoto, Tadayoshi. Endoscopic Retrograde Cholangiopancreatography. LC 78-78228. (Illus.). 1979. 69.75 (ISBN 0-89640-032-8). Igaku-Shoin.
Takemoto, Tadayushi, jt. auth. see Tsuneoka, Kenji.
Takemoto, Toru. Failure of Liberalism in Japan: Shedehara Kijuro's Encounter with Anti-Liberals. LC 78-68695. 1979. pap. text ed. 10.50 (ISBN 0-8191-0698-4). U Pr of Amer.
Takenouti, Y. & Hood, D. W., eds. Bering Sea Oceanography: An Update Nineteen Seventy-Two to Nineteen Seventy-Four. 12.00 (ISBN 0-914500-06-6). U. of AK Inst Marine.
Takeshita, Glen. Koi for Home & Garden. 1969. 2.95 (ISBN 0-87666-754-X, PS659). TFH Pubns.
Takeuchi, S., ed. see International Conference, 2nd, Tokyo, 1972.
Tal, M., et al. Montreal Nineteen Seventy-Nine: Tournament of Stars. Neat, K. P., tr. LC 80-40715. (Illus.). 200p. 1980. 19.00 (ISBN 0-08-024132-8); pap. 11.90 (ISBN 0-08-024131-X). Pergamon.
Talamantes, Florence W., ed. see Pereda, Jose M.
Talarico, Ross. Pits Exercises: A Manual-Anthology for Teachers & Students. (Poetry in the Schools Programs). 64p. (Orig.). (gr. 10-12). 1981. pap. 3.95 (ISBN 0-933362-05-6). Assoc Creative Writers.
Talarzyk, W. Wayne, jt. auth. see Blackwell, Roger D.
Talarzyk, Wayne. Cases for Analysis in Marketing. 2nd ed. LC 80-65809. 384p. 1981. pap. text ed. 8.95 (ISBN 0-03-058179-6). Dryden Pr.
Talbert, Bill & Sports Illustrated Editors. Sports Illustrated Tennis. rev. ed. LC 72-37609. (Illus.). (YA) 1972. 5.95 (ISBN 0-397-00863-5); pap. 2.95 (ISBN 0-397-00862-7, LP-61). Lippincott.
Talbert, Charles G. The University of Kentucky: The Maturing Years. LC 65-11827. (Illus.). 224p. 1965. 8.00 (ISBN 0-8131-1095-5). U Pr of Ky.
Talbert, Charles H. Literary Patterns, Theological Themes & the Genre of Luke-Acts. LC 74-78620. (Society of Biblical Literature. Monograph). 159p. 1974. 9.00 (ISBN 0-89130-059-7, 060020); pap. 7.50 (ISBN 0-89130-058-9). Scholars Pr Ca.
Talbert, Luther M., ed. see University of North Carolina at Chapel Hill, Dept. of OB-GYN.
Talbert, R J. Timoleon & the Revival of Greek Cicily, 344-317 BC. 248p. 1974. 19.95 (ISBN 0-521-20419-4). Cambridge U Pr.
Talbot, Charlene J. An Orphan for Nebraska. LC 78-12179. (gr. 4-6). 1979. 8.95 (ISBN 0-689-30698-9). Atheneum.
Talbot, Karen H., jt. auth. see Allen, Susan W.
Talbot, Katherine. Theodosia. (Orig.). 1980. pap. 1.75 (ISBN 0-446-94142-5). Warner Bks.
Talbot, Mabel E. Edouard Seguin: A Study of an Educational Approach to the Treatment of Mentally Defective Children. LC 64-23753. 1964. pap. text ed. 3.50x (ISBN 0-8077-2242-1). Tchrs Coll.
Talbot, Michael. Mysticism & the New Physics. 224p. (Orig.). 1981. pap. 3.50 (ISBN 0-553-11908-7). Bantam.
Talbot, Mundy. Om, the Secret of Ahbor Valley. 392p. 1980. pap. 7.25 (913004-39). Point Loma Pub.
Talbot Press. Irish-English, English-Irish Dictionary. 9.50x o.s.i. (ISBN 0-686-05263-3). Colton Bk.
Talbot, Richard P. The Perfect Wheel: An Illustrated Guide to Bicycle Wheelbuilding. (Illus.). Date not set. 17.95 (ISBN 0-9602418-2-5). Manet Guild. Postponed.
Talbot, Ross B., ed. World Food Problem & U. S. Food Politics & Policies: 1977. 1978. pap. text ed. 7.50 (ISBN 0-8138-0970-3). Iowa St U Pr.
Talbot, Russell. The Shipping Situation Between New York City & Philadelphia: A Survey of the Factors Causing the Growth of Motor Truck Transportation for the Purpose of Presenting Specifications to Be Met in Coordinating Rail & Motor Truck Transportation for Intercity Service. 1931. pap. 27.50x (ISBN 0-685-89782-6). Elliots Bks.
Talbot, Samuel A. & Gessner, Urs. Systems Physiology. LC 72-10536. (Biomedical Engineering Ser.). 528p. 1973. 43.00 o.p. (ISBN 0-471-84415-2, Pub. by Wiley-Interscience). Wiley.
Talbot, Shaun, jt. auth. see Keene, Raymond.
Talbot, Simon. Land Explorers. 1978. 16.95 (ISBN 0-7134-0990-8, Pub. by Batsford England). David & Charles.
Talbot, Steve. Roots of Oppression: The American Indian Question. (Orig.). 1981. 14.00 (ISBN 0-7178-0591-3); pap. 4.75 (ISBN 0-7178-0583-2). Intl Pub Co.
Talbot, Toby. A Book About My Mother. 192p. 1980. 10.95 (ISBN 0-374-11542-7). FS&G.
Talbot, Tony. Two by Two. (gr. 1-3). 1974. 4.95 o.p. (ISBN 0-695-80484-7); lib ed. 4.98 o.p. (ISBN 0-695-40484-9). Follett.
Talbot, William S. Jasper F. Cropsey, Eighteen Twenty-Three to Nineteen Hundred. LC 76-23652. (Outstanding Dissertations in the Fine Arts - American). (Illus.). 1977. Repr. of 1972 ed. lib. bdg. 84.00 (ISBN 0-8240-2731-0). Garland Pub.
Talbot, William S., jt. auth. see Weisberg, Gabriel P.
Talbot-Ponsonby, J. Harmony in Horsemanship. (Illus.). 10.50 (ISBN 0-85131-169-5, Dist. by Sporting Book Center). J A Allen.
Talbott. The Chronic Mentally Ill. 1980. pap. text ed. 29.95x (ISBN 0-87705-086-4). Human Sci Pr.
Talbott, George R. Philosophy & Unified Science. (Illus.). 1978. 40.00 (ISBN 0-89744-126-5, Pub. by Ganesh & Co. India). Auromere.
Talbott, John. State Mental Hospitals: Problems & Potentials. LC 79-21928. 1979. 19.95x (ISBN 0-87705-394-4). Human Sci Pr.
Talbott, John A., ed. Self-Assessment of Current Knowledge in Psychiatry. 4th ed. 1980. pap. price not set o.p. (ISBN 0-685-48747-4). Med Exam.
Talbott, John A., ed. see Report of a Conference Held in January 1979.
Talbott, Richard E. & Humphrey, Donald R., eds. Posture & Movement: Perspective for Integrating Sensory & Motor Research on the Mammalian Nervous System. LC 77-85515. 1979. text ed. 32.50 (ISBN 0-89004-259-4). Raven.
Talbott, Strobe. Endgame: The Inside Story of Salt II. 288p. 1980. pap. 4.95 (ISBN 0-06-090809-2, CN-809, CN). Har-Row.
Talburt, W. F. & Smith, Ora, eds. Potato Processing. 3rd ed. 1975. lib. bdg. 49.50 (ISBN 0-87055-180-9). AVI.
Talese, Gay. Fame & Obscurity. 1981. pap. 3.25 (ISBN 0-440-12620-7). Dell.
--Honor Thy Father. 1978. pap. 2.95 (ISBN 0-449-23630-7, Crest). Fawcett.
--Honor Thy Father. 1981. pap. 3.25 (ISBN 0-440-13668-7). Dell.
--The Kingdom & the Power. LC 78-7770. 1978. pap. 6.95 (ISBN 0-385-14404-0, Anch). Doubleday.
--The Kingdom & the Power. 1981. pap. 3.25 (ISBN 0-440-14397-7). Dell.
--Thy Neighbor's Wife. 1981. pap. 3.95 (ISBN 0-440-18689-7). Dell.
Talhami, Ghada H. Suakin & Massawa Under Egyptian Rule, Eighteen Sixty-Five to Eighteen Eighty-Five. LC 79-66418. 1979. pap. text ed. 11.50 (ISBN 0-8191-0828-6). U Pr of Amer.
Taliaferro, Margaret. The Real Reason for Christmas: Letters to Children for the Twelve Nights of Christmas. LC 76-55080. 1977. 6.95 (ISBN 0-385-12414-7). Doubleday.
Taliaferro, W. H. & Humphrey, J. H., eds. Advances in Immunology, Vols. 1-30. Incl. Vol. 1. 1961. (ISBN 0-12-022401-1); Vol. 2. 1963 (ISBN 0-12-022402-X); Vol. 3. Dixon, F. J., Jr. & Humphrey, J. H., eds. 1963 (ISBN 0-12-022403-8); Vol. 4. 1964 (ISBN 0-12-022404-6); Vol. 5. 1966 (ISBN 0-12-022405-4); Vol. 6. 1967. o.s.i. (ISBN 0-12-022406-2); Vol. 7. Dixon, F. J., Jr. & Kunkel, Henry G., eds. 1967. (ISBN 0-12-022407-0); Vol. 8. 1968 (ISBN 0-12-022408-9); Vol. 9. 1968 (ISBN 0-12-022409-7); Vol. 10. 1969 (ISBN 0-12-022410-0); Vol. 11. 1969. (ISBN 0-12-022411-9); Vol. 12. 1970 (ISBN 0-12-022412-7); Vol. 13. 1971 (ISBN 0-12-022413-5); Vol. 14. 1971 (ISBN 0-12-022414-3); Vol. 15. 1972 (ISBN 0-12-022415-1); Vol. 16. 1973 (ISBN 0-12-022416-X); Vol. 17. 1973 (ISBN 0-12-022417-8); Vol. 18. 1974 (ISBN 0-12-022418-6); Vol. 19. 1974 (ISBN 0-12-022419-4); Vol. 20. 1975 (ISBN 0-12-022420-8); Vol. 21. 1975 (ISBN 0-12-022421-6); Vol. 22. 1976 (ISBN 0-12-022422-4); Vol. 23. 1976 (ISBN 0-12-022423-2); Vol. 24. 1976 (ISBN 0-12-022424-0); **Vol. 25. 1978. 32.00 (ISBN 0-12-022425-9); Vol. 26. Kunkel, Henry G. & Dixon, E. J., eds. 1978. 35.00 (ISBN 0-12-022426-7); Vol. 27. 1979. 32.50 (ISBN 0-12-022427-5); Vol. 28. 1980. 37.50 (ISBN 0-12-022428-3); Vol. 29. 1980. 35.00 (ISBN 0-12-022429-1). LC 61-17057. Vol. 1-24. 43.50 (ISBN 0-686-66773-5). Acad Pr.**
Talkington. Undersea Work Systems. 240p. 1981. write for info. (ISBN 0-8247-1226-9). Dekker.
Tall, D. O. Functions of a Complex Variable, 2 vols. (Library of Mathematics). 1970. Vol. 1. pap. 2.95 (ISBN 0-7100-6567-1); Vol. 2. pap. 2.95 (ISBN 0-7100-6785-2); pap. 6.50 set (ISBN 0-685-25621-9). Routledge & Kegan.
Tall, D. O., jt. auth. see Stewart, I. N.
Tall, David, jt. auth. see Stewart, Ian.
Tallach, John. God Made Them Great. 1978. pap. 4.25 (ISBN 0-85151-190-2). Banner of Truth.
Tallack, John C. Introduction to Elementary Vector Analysis. 1966. text ed. 16.95x (ISBN 0-521-07999-3). Cambridge U Pr.
Tallantire, A. C., jt. auth. see Lind, E. M.
Tallarico, Tony. I Can Draw Animals. Taub, Channa, ed. (I Can Draw Ser.). 80p. (Orig.). (gr. 3-7). 1980. pap. 2.50 (ISBN 0-671-41375-9). Wanderer Bks.
--I Can Draw Cars, Trucks, & Other Wheels. Scheider, Meg, ed. (I Can Draw Ser.). 80p. (Orig.). (gr. 3-7). 1981. pap. 2.75 (ISBN 0-671-42535-8). Wanderer Bks.
--Search-a-Picture Puzzles. Schneider, Meg, ed. (Puzzlebacks Ser.). 64p. (gr. 3-7). 1981. pap. 1.25 (ISBN 0-671-42656-7, Wanderer). S&S.
--Spooky Haunted House Puzzles. Schneider, Meg, ed. (Puzzlebacks Ser.). 64p. (gr. 3-7). 1981. pap. 1.25 (ISBN 0-671-42655-9, Wanderer). S&S.
Tallberg, Martin. Don Bolles: An Investigation into His Murder. 1978. pap. 1.95 o.p. (ISBN 0-445-04122-6). Popular Lib.
Tallcott, Emogene. Glacier Tracks. LC 70-101479. (Illus.). (gr. 5 up). 1970. PLB 7.63 o.p. (ISBN 0-688-51118-X). Lothrop.
Tallent, Annie D. The Black Hills; or, the Last Hunting Ground of the Dakotahs. LC 74-76330. 594p. 1974. Repr. of 1899 ed. 14.95 (ISBN 0-88498-017-0); lim. leath. ed. 50.00 (ISBN 0-685-50457-3). Brevet Pr.
Tallent, Norman. Psychological Report Writing. LC 75-33309. (Illus.). 272p. 1976. 19.95 (ISBN 0-13-732503-7). P-H.
--Report Writing in Special Education. (Illus.). 1980. text ed. 17.95 (ISBN 0-13-773606-1). P-H.
Tallent, Norman & Spungin, Charlotte I. Psychology: Understanding Ourselves & Others. new ed. (Illus.). (gr. 11-12). 1977. text ed. 10.68 (ISBN 0-278-47332-6); tchr's guide 2.01 (ISBN 0-278-47334-2); tests 23.97 (ISBN 0-278-47336-9). ABC.
Talleur, Richard W. Fly Fishing for Trout: A Guide for Adult Beginners. 1974. 11.95 (ISBN 0-87691-133-5). Winchester Pr.
Talley, David. Basic Carrier Telephony. 3rd, rev. ed. (Illus.). (gr. 10 up). 1977. pap. 8.95 (ISBN 0-8104-5848-9); exam 0.50 (ISBN 0-8104-0727-2); final exam 0.50 (ISBN 0-8104-0728-0). Hayden.
--Basic Telephone Switching Systems. 2nd ed. 1979. pap. 9.60 (ISBN 0-8104-5687-7). Hayden.
Tallie, Jean De La see De La Taille, Jean.
Tallmadge, Thomas E. The Story of England's Architecture. 363p. 1980. Repr. of 1934 ed. lib. bdg. 40.00 (ISBN 0-8495-5160-9). Arden Lib.
Tallman, Irving. Passion, Action, & Politics: A Perspective on Social Problems & Social-Problem Solving. LC 75-37959. (Illus.). 1976. text ed. 20.95x (ISBN 0-7167-0540-0); pap. text ed. 10.95x (ISBN 0-7167-0539-7). W H Freeman.
Tallmer, Margot, et al, eds. Children, Dying, & Grief. (Thanatology Service Ser.). 200p. 1981. pap. 9.95 (ISBN 0-930194-26-8). Highly Specialized.
--Thanatologic Aspects of Aging. (Thantology Service Ser.). 190p. 1980. pap. 9.95 (ISBN 0-930194-25-X). Highly Specialized.
Tallon. Zoophabets. (ps-3). 1980. pap. 1.95 (ISBN 0-590-30047-4, Schol Pap). Schol Bk Serv.
Tallon, Robert. The Alligator's Song. (Illus.). 48p. (ps-3). 4.95 (ISBN 0-8193-1043-3); PLB 5.95 (ISBN 0-8193-1044-1). Parents.
Tallon, Robert. The Alligator's Song. (Illus.). 48p. (ps-3). 1981. PLB 5.95 (ISBN 0-8193-1044-1); pap. 4.95 (ISBN 0-8193-1043-3). Parents.
Tally, David. Basic Electronic Switching for Telephone Systems. 1975. pap. 8.35 (ISBN 0-8104-5808-X); exam set 0.80 (ISBN 0-8104-0591-1); final exam 0.30 (ISBN 0-8104-0594-6). Hayden.
Talmadge, Marian & Gilmore, Iris. Colorado Hi-Ways & By-Ways: A Comprehensive Guide to Picturesque Trails & Tours. LC 74-83023. 1975. pap. 4.95 o.p. (ISBN 0-87108-079-6). Pruett.
Talmage, Frank. Disputation & Dialogue: Readings in the Jewish Christian Encounter. pap. 9.95x (ISBN 0-685-56218-2). Ktav.
Talmage, Harriet. Statistics As a Tool for Educational Practitioners. new ed. LC 75-31312. (Illus.). 264p. 1976. 16.65x (ISBN 0-8211-1905-2); text ed. 15.00x (ISBN 0-685-61060-8). McCutchan.
Talmage, Harriet, ed. Systems of Individualized Education. LC 74-24478. 200p. 1975. 16.00x (ISBN 0-8211-1904-4); text ed. 14.50x (ISBN 0-685-51465-X). McCutchan.
Talmage, James E. Jesus the Christ. 804p. pap. 2.95 (ISBN 0-87747-456-7). Deseret Bk.
Talman, Wilfred B. How Things Began...in Rockland County & Places Nearby. (Illus.). 1977. 12.50 (ISBN 0-89062-052-0); pap. write for info. Rockland County Hist.
Talmey, Alene. Weegee. LC 77-80020. (Aperture History of Photography Ser.: No. 8). (Illus.). 1978. 8.95 (ISBN 0-89381-021-5). Aperture.
Talmon, J. L. Israel Among the Nations. Mandel, To, ed. 1971. 11.95 (ISBN 0-02-616250-4). Macmillan.
--Political Messianism: The Romantic Phase. LC 60-14071. 1960. 34.50x (ISBN 0-89197-892-5). Irvington.
--The Unique & the Universal. LC 65-19565. 1965. 6.50 o.s.i. (ISBN 0-8076-0319-8). Braziller.
Talmor, Ezra. Descartes & Hume. LC 79-41748. 188p. 1980. 19.75 (ISBN 0-08-024274-X). Pergamon.
--Mind & Political Concepts. 1979. text ed. 30.00 (ISBN 0-08-023737-1); pap. text ed. 14.00 (ISBN 0-08-024269-3). Pergamon.
Talon, Henri A. John Bunyan, The Man & His Works. 340p. 1980. Repr. of 1951 ed. lib. bdg. 35.00 (ISBN 0-89987-810-5). Darby Bks.
Taloumis, George. Winterize Your Yard & Garden. LC 76-18862. (Illus.). 1976. 9.95 o.p. (ISBN 0-397-01178-4). Lippincott.
Talpe, J. Theory of Experiments in Paramagnetic Resonance. LC 79-137411. 272p. 1971. 32.00 (ISBN 0-08-016157-X). Pergamon.
Talwalker, Gopinath. Some Indian Saints. 64p. (Orig.). (gr. 5 up). 1980. pap. 1.50 (ISBN 0-89744-208-3, Pub. by Natl Bk Trust India). Auromere.
Talwar, G. P., ed. see Symposium, New Delhi, October 1978.
Talwick, Maria. The Leaning Tower. 1977. pap. 1.95 o.p. (ISBN 0-345-25723-5). Ballantine.
Tam, Billy K. & Tam, Mariam S. Acupuncture: An International Bibliography. LC 73-5772. 1973. 10.00 (ISBN 0-8108-0625-8). Scarecrow.

Tam, Mariam S., jt. auth. see Tam, Billy K.

Tamalelagi, Jeanne, ed. see Tuala.

Tamane, Jackson S. Tidal Wave Bait. LC 79-66394. 1981. 10.95 (ISBN 0-533-04385-9). Vantage.

Tamarin. Principles of Genetics. 608p. 1981. text ed. 21.95 (ISBN 0-87872-281-5). Duxbury Pr.

Tamarin, Alfred. Japan & the United States: The Early Encounters, 1791-1860. LC 78-99126. (Illus.). (gr. 9 up). 1970. 6.95 o.s.i. (ISBN 0-02-788810-X). Macmillan.

--We Have Not Vanished: Eastern Indians of the United States. (Illus.). 128p. (gr. 3-6). 1974. lib. ed. 5.97 o.p. (ISBN 0-695-40332-X). Follett.

Tamarin, Alfred, ed. Benjamin Franklin: An Autobiographical Portrait. LC 78-78091. (Illus.). (gr. 7 up). 1969. 6.50g o.s.i. (ISBN 0-02-788790-1). Macmillan.

Tamarin, G. R. The Israeli Dilemma: Essays on a Warfare State. (Publications of Polemological Centre of the Free University of Brussels: Vol. 2). 202p. 1973. pap. text ed. 16.00 (ISBN 90-237-6220-7, Pub. by Swets Serv Holland). Swets North Am.

Tamaru, K. & Ichikawa, M. Catalysis by Electron Donor-Acceptor Complexes: Their General Behavior & Biological Roles. LC 75-28051. 1976. 30.95 (ISBN 0-470-84435-3). Halsted Pr.

Tamasi, Barbara. I'll Stop Tomorrow. 450p. (Orig.). 1980. pap. 5.95 (ISBN 0-932260-06-3). Rock Harbor.

Tambiah, Henry W., jt. auth. see Jennings, William I.

Tambiah, J. World Conqueror & World Renouncer. LC 76-8290. (Cambridge Studies in Social Anthropology: No. 15). 1976. 49.95 (ISBN 0-521-21140-9); pap. 14.95x (ISBN 0-521-29290-5). Cambridge U Pr.

Tambiah, S. J. Buddhism & the Spirit Cults in Northeast Thailand. LC 73-108112. (Cambridge Studies in Social Anthropology: No. 2). (Illus.). 1970. 36.00 (ISBN 0-521-07825-3); pap. 14.95x (ISBN 0-521-09958-7). Cambridge U Pr.

Tambiah, S. J., jt. auth. see Goody, J. R.

Tambs, Lewis A., jt. auth. see Birkos, Alexander S.

Tambs, Lewis A., jt. auth. see Kleinfeld, Gerald R.

Tamchina, Jurgen. Dominique & the Dragon. LC 68-59618. (Illus.). (gr. 3-6). 1969. 6.50 o.p. (ISBN 0-15-223972-3, HJ). HarBraceJ.

Tamelen, E. E. Van see Van Tamelen, E. E.

Tames, Richard. The Arab World Today. (Today Ser.). (Illus.). 96p. 1980. text ed. 15.00x (ISBN 0-7182-0461-1, SpS). Soccer.

--Cities. Yapp, Malcolm, et al, eds. (World History Ser.). (Illus.). 32p. (gr. 10). 1980. Repr. of 1977 ed. lib. bdg. 5.95 (ISBN 0-89908-140-1); pap. text ed. 1.95 (ISBN 0-89908-115-0). Greenhaven.

--The French Revolution. Killingray, Margaret, et al, eds. (Wolrd History Ser.). (Illus.). 32p. (gr. 10). 1980. Repr. lib. bdg. 5.95 (ISBN 0-89908-136-3); pap. text ed. 1.95 (ISBN 0-89908-111-8). Greenhaven.

--India & Pakistan in the Twentieth Century. (Twentieth Century World History Ser.). (Illus.). 96p. (gr. 6 up). 1981. 15.95 (ISBN 0-7134-3415-5, Pub. by Batsford England). David & Charles.

--Napoleon. Yapp, Malcolm & Killingray, Margaret, eds. (World History Ser.). (Illus.). (gr. 10). 1980. Repr. of 1977 ed. lib. bdg. 5.95 (ISBN 0-89908-044-8); pap. text ed. 1.95 (ISBN 0-89908-019-7). Greenhaven.

--Somme. (Jackdaw Ser: No. 111). 1972. 5.95 o.p. (ISBN 0-670-65714-X, Grossman). Viking Pr.

--The World of Islam. (Jackdaw Ser: No. 143). (gr. 7 up). 1976. 5.95 o.p. (ISBN 0-670-78671-3). Viking Pr.

Tamir, Lois M. Communication & the Aging Process: Interaction Throughout the Life Cycle. (Pergamon General Psychology Ser.). 1980. 24.50 (ISBN 0-08-024621-4). Pergamon.

Tamke, Susan S. Make a Joyful Noise Unto the Lord: Hymns As a Reflection of Victorian Social Attitudes. LC 76-51693. 209p. 1978. 12.00x (ISBN 0-8214-0371-0); pap. text ed. 5.00x (ISBN 0-8214-0382-6). Ohio U Pr.

Tamm, Goren, et al. Man in Focus: New Approaches to Commercial Communications. (Communication Arts Bks.). 160p. (gr. 11-12). 1980. 14.50 o.p. (ISBN 0-8038-4734-3); pap. cancelled o.p. (ISBN 0-8038-4735-1). Hastings.

Tamm, Igor, jt. auth. see Horsfall, Frank L.

Tammann, G. A., jt. auth. see Sandage, Allan.

Tammany, Jane E. Henrik Ibsen's Theatre Aesthetic & Dramatic Art. LC 79-92436. (Illus.). 380p. 1980. 22.50 (ISBN 0-8022-2365-6). Philos Lib.

Tammen, Ronald L. MIRV & the Arms Race: An Interpretation of Defense Strategy. LC 73-9065. (Special Studies in International Politics & Government). 1973. 28.50x (ISBN 0-275-28749-1). Irvington.

Tamminga, F. Bunk Among Dragons: Poems & Translinguistic Adaptations. 1973. pap. 2.95 o.p. (ISBN 0-686-11994-0). Wedge Pub.

Tammuz, Benjamin. Minotaur. 1981. price not set (H401). NAL.

Tampion, John. Dangerous Plants. LC 76-55116. (Illus.). 1977. 12.50x o.s.i. (ISBN 0-87663-280-0). Universe.

Tamuno, T. N. The Evolution of the Nigerian State: The Southern Phase, 1898-1914. (Ibadan History Ser.). (Illus.). 250p. 1972. text ed. 14.00x (ISBN 0-391-00232-5). Humanities.

Tamura, T. & Natowitz, J. B., eds. Continuum Spectra of Heavy-Ion Reactions. (Nuclear Science Research Conference Ser.: Vol. 2). 490p. 1980. 48.50 (ISBN 3-7186-0028-5). Harwood Academic.

Tamura, T., et al. Continuum Spectra of Heavy-Ion Reactions. 590p. 1980. 48.50 (ISBN 3-7186-0028-5). Harwood Academic.

Tamus, V. P., jt. auth. see Sih, G. C.

Tan, Lek, jt. auth. see Caldwell, Malcolm.

Tan, Mark. The All Star Turn-About Quiz Book. 1977. pap. 2.00 o.p. (ISBN 0-685-75811-7, 0416-3). Price Stern.

Tan, Paul L. Encyclopedia of Seven Thousand, Seven Hundred Illustrations. (Illus.). 2400p. 1979. 34.95 (ISBN 0-88469-096-2). BMH Bks.

Tan, S. H., jt. auth. see Toh, K. A.

Tana, Pradumna Tana & Tana, Roselba. Traditional Designs from India for Artists & Craftsmen. (Illus.). 112p. (Orig.). 1981. pap. price not set (ISBN 0-486-24129-7). Dover.

Tana, Roselba, jt. auth. see Tana, Pradumna Tana.

Tana, Tomoe, jt. tr. see Nixon, Lucille M.

Tanabe, Y., et al, eds. Biological Rhythms in Birds: Neural & Endocrine Aspects. 373p. 1980. 49.60 (ISBN 0-387-10311-2). Springer-Verlag.

Tanagho, E. A., jt. ed. see Stanton, S. L.

Tanagras, A. Psychophysical Elements in Parapsychological Traditions. LC 67-19168. (Parapsychological Monograph No. 7). 1967. pap. 4.00 (ISBN 0-912328-10-X). Parapsych Foun.

Tanaka, Ikko. Japan Style. Earle, Joe, tr. from Japanese. LC 79-66243. (Illus.). 151p. 1980. text ed. 14.95 (ISBN 0-87011-400-X). Kodansha.

Tanaka, Minoru. Brotherhood of Mt. Shasta. 88p. 1981. pap. 4.50 (ISBN 0-89540-009-X). Sun Pub.

Tancer, Jack. Our Reader. (Illus.). 1964. pap. 1.50x (ISBN 0-88323-060-7, 158). Richards Pub.

T'An Chung-Yo, jt. auth. see Huang Shou-Fu.

Tancock, Leonard, tr. see Diderot, Denis.

Tancredi, Laurence, ed. see Institute of Medicine.

Tancredi, Lawrence, jt. auth. see Slaby, Andrew.

Tandberg-Hanssen, Einar, jt. ed. see Dryer, Murray.

Tandon, B. G. The Imagery of Lord Byron's Plays. (Salzburg Studies in English Literature: Poetic Drama & Poetic Theory: No. 31). (Illus.). 298p. (Orig.). 1976. pap. text ed. 25.00x (ISBN 0-391-01545-1). Humanities.

Tandon, Prakash. Beyond Punjab: A Sequel to Punjabi Century. LC 73-123620. (Center for South & Southeast Asia Studies, Uc Berkeley). 1971. 18.50x (ISBN 0-520-01759-5). U of Cal Pr.

--Punjabi Century, 1857-1947. 1968. 18.50x (ISBN 0-520-01252-6); pap. 5.95 (ISBN 0-520-01253-4, CAL164). U of Cal Pr.

--Return to the Punjab. 300p. 1981. 18.50x (ISBN 0-520-01759-5). U of Cal Pr.

Tandon, Yash. Problems of a Displaced Minority: The New Position of East Africa's Asians. (Minority Rights Group: No. 16). 1973. pap. 2.50 (ISBN 0-89192-102-8). Interbk Inc.

Tandy, Clifford. The Landscape of Industry. LC 75-28033. 314p. 1975. 55.95 (ISBN 0-470-84440-X). Halsted Pr.

Taneda, Santoka. Mountain Tasting: The Zen Haiku of Santoka Taneda. Stevens, John, tr. from Japanese. 100p. 1980. pap. 7.95 (ISBN 0-8348-0151-5, Pub. by John Weatherhill Inc Japan). C E Tuttle.

--Mountain Tasting: Zen Haiku. Stevens, John, tr. 112p. 1980. pap. 7.95 (ISBN 0-8348-0151-5). Weatherhill.

Taneja, Nawal K. Airlines in Transition. LC 80-8735. 1981. 23.95 (ISBN 0-669-04345-1). Lexington Bks.

--Airlines Traffic Forecasting. LC 78-874. (Illus.). 1978. 22.95 (ISBN 0-669-02186-5). Lexington Bks.

--The Commercial Airline Industry: Managerial Practices & Policies. LC 76-18052. 1976. 22.95x (ISBN 0-669-00129-5). Lexington Bks.

--U. S. Airfreight Industry. LC 78-24840. 272p. 1979. 21.00 (ISBN 0-669-02853-3). Lexington Bks.

--U. S. International Aviation Policy. LC 79-3039. 176p. 1980. 21.95x (ISBN 0-669-03320-0). Lexington Bks.

Taneja, P. N., jt. auth. see Ghai, O. P.

Tanenbaum, A. Structured Computer Organization. 1976. 24.95 (ISBN 0-13-854505-7). P-H.

Tanenbaum, Andrew S. Computer Networks: Toward Distributed Processing Systems. (Illus.). 544p. 1981. text ed. 28.00 (ISBN 0-13-165183-8). P-H.

Tanenbaum, Barry, jt. auth. see LaRosa, Linda J.

Tanenhaus, Joseph, jt. auth. see Somit, Albert.

Tanford, Charles. The Hydrophobic Effect: Formation of Micelles & Biological Membranes. 200p. 1973. 18.50 o.p. (ISBN 0-471-84460-8). Wiley.

Tanford, J. Alexander, jt. auth. see Bocchino, Anthony J.

Tang, Anthony M., et al. Evolution, Welfare & Time in Economics. (Illus.). 1976. 17.95 (ISBN 0-669-00736-6). Lexington Bks.

Tang, Chi-Yu. An Economic Study of Chinese Agriculture. LC 78-74306. (The Modern Chinese Economy Ser.: Vol. 14). 514p. 1980. lib. bdg. 55.00 (ISBN 0-8240-4262-X). Garland Pub.

T'Ang, Leang-Li. Inner History of the Chinese Revolution. (Studies in Chinese Government & Law). 391p. 1977. Repr. of 1930 ed. 23.50 (ISBN 0-89093-066-X). U Pubns Amer.

--New Social Order in China. (Studies in Chinese History & Civilization). 1977. Repr. of 1936 ed. 22.00 (ISBN 0-89093-090-2). U Pubns Amer.

T'Ang, Leang-Ti. China in Revolt: How a Civilization Became a Nation. (Studies in Chinese History & Civilization). 176p. 1977. Repr. of 1927 ed. 18.00 (ISBN 0-89093-070-8). U Pubns Amer.

Tang, Peter P. The New Manual of Kung Fu. LC 75-13890. (Illus.). 1976. 7.95 o.p. (ISBN 0-668-03851-9). Arco.

Tang, Roger Y. Transfer Pricing Practices in the United States & Japan. LC 78-19780. (Praeger Special Studies). 1979. 20.95 (ISBN 0-03-046551-6). Praeger.

Tang, W. H., jt. auth. see Ang, A. H.

Tang, Xianzu. Peony Pavilion (Mudan Ting) Birch, Cyril, tr. LC 79-9631. (Chinese Literature in Translation Ser.). 352p. 1980. 22.50x (ISBN 0-253-35723-3). Ind U Pr.

Tangborn, Wendell V. Glaciers. LC 65-18702. (A Let's-Read-&-Find-Out Science Bk). (Illus.). (gr. k-3). 1965. bds. 7.95 (ISBN 0-690-33118-5, TYC-J); PLB 7.89 (ISBN 0-690-33119-3). T Y Crowell.

Tangerman, E. J. Carving Flora & Fables in Wood. LC 80-54336. (Illus.). 128p. 1981. pap. 5.95 (ISBN 0-8069-8982-3). Sterling.

Tangye, Derek. When the Winds Blow. (Illus.). 1981. write for info. (ISBN 0-7181-1932-0). Merrimack Bk Serv.

Tanigawa, M. Frank Lloyd Wright. 1978. 185.00 o.p. (ISBN 0-685-05019-X, 0-911156-28-8). Porter.

Tanikawa, Kyuichi. Ultrastructural Aspects of the Liver & Its Disorders. 2nd ed. LC 79-84646. (Illus.). 1979. 62.50 (ISBN 0-89640-034-4). Igaku-Shoin.

Tanikawa, Shuntaro. Billy the Kid. Wright, Harold, tr. from Japanese. lmtd. ed. 5.00 (ISBN 0-931460-21-2, Broadside). Bieler.

Tanimoto, S. & Klinger, A., eds. Structured Computer Vision: Machine Perception Through Hierarchical Computation Structures. LC 80-14878. 1980. 21.00 (ISBN 0-12-683280-3). Acad Pr.

Tanis, Norman, jt. auth. see Perkins, David.

Tanis, Norman E., ed. see Dargan, James F.

Tanis, Norman E., ed. see Mayhew, Jonathan.

Tanizaki, Junichiro. Diary of an Old Man. Hibbett, Howard, tr. from Jap. (Perigee Japanese Library). 320p. Date not set. pap. 5.95 (ISBN 0-399-50524-5, Perigee). Putnam.

--The Key. Hibbett, Howard, tr. from Jap. (Perigee Japanese Library). 190p. 1981. pap. 4.95 (ISBN 0-399-50522-9, Perigee). Putnam.

--The Makioka Sisters. Seidensticker, Edward T., tr. from Jap. (Perigee Japanese Library). 538p. 1981. pap. 6.95 (ISBN 0-399-50520-2, Perigee). Putnam.

--Seven Japanese Tales. Hibbett, Howard, tr. from Jap. (Perigee Japanese Library). 320p. 1981. pap. 5.95 (ISBN 0-399-50523-7, Perigee). Putnam.

--Some Prefer Nettles. Seidensticker, Edward G., tr. from Jap. (Perigee Japanese Library). 224p. 1981. pap. 4.95 (ISBN 0-399-50521-0, Perigee). Putnam.

Tank, Kurt L. Gunter Grass. Conway, John, tr. LC 68-31458. (Modern Literature Ser.). 1969. 10.95 (ISBN 0-8044-2863-8); pap. 3.45 (ISBN 0-8044-6892-3). Ungar.

Tankle, Micheal. The Rantings of a Madman. Date not set. 4.75 (ISBN 0-8062-1669-7). Carlton.

Tan Kok Seng. Son of Singapore. (Writing in Asia Ser.). 1972. pap. text ed. 3.25x (ISBN 0-686-65342-4, 00220). Heinemann Ed.

Tann, Jennifer. Children at Work. (History in Focus Ser.). (Illus.). 72p. (gr. 6 up). 1981. 14.95 (ISBN 0-7134-3553-4, Pub. by Batsford England). David & Charles.

Tannahill, R. Neal. The Communist Parties of Western Europe: A Comparative Study. LC 77-94750. (Contributions in Political Science). 1978. lib. bdg. 19.95 (ISBN 0-313-20318-0, TCP/). Greenwood.

Tannahill, Reay. Food in History. LC 75-160342. (Illus.). 448p. 1974. pap. 8.95 (ISBN 0-8128-1752-4). Stein & Day.

--Sex in History. LC 79-15053. 480p. 1981. pap. 8.95 (ISBN 0-8128-6115-9). Stein & Day.

Tannehill, Ivan R. Hurricane Hunters. LC 55-9480. (Illus.). (gr. 9 up). 1955. 4.50 (ISBN 0-396-03789-5). Dodd.

Tannehill, Robert C. The Sword of His Mouth. Beardslee, William A., ed. LC 75-18948. (Semeia Studies). 236p. 1976. pap. 4.95 (ISBN 0-8006-1501-8, 1-1501). Fortress.

Tannen. The Wizard Children of Finn. LC 80-20955. (Illus.). 256p. (gr. 3 up). 1981. 8.95 (ISBN 0-394-84744-X); PLB 8.99 (ISBN 0-394-94744-4). Knopf.

Tannen, Mary. The Twits. LC 80-18410. (Illus.). 96p. (ps-5). 1981. 7.95 (ISBN 0-394-84599-4); PLB 7.99 (ISBN 0-394-94599-9). Knopf.

Tannenbaum, Abraham J., ed. see American Association for Gifted Children.

Tannenbaum, Abraham J., ed. see Hagen, Elizabeth.

Tannenbaum, Abraham J., ed. see Roedell, Wendy C., et al.

Tannenbaum, D. Leb. Baby Talk. (Illus.). 32p. (gr. 1-3). 1981. pap. 1.95 (ISBN 0-380-76935-2, Camelot). Avon.

Tannenbaum, Frank. Peace by Revolution, Mexico After 1910. LC 33-35455. (Illus.). 1933. pap. 7.50x (ISBN 0-231-08568-0). Columbia U Pr.

Tannenbaum, Steven R., jt. ed. see Whitaker, John R.

Tanner, Annie C. A Biography of Ezra Thompson Clark. (Utah, the Mormons, & the West: No. 5). 1975. 8.50 (ISBN 0-87480-156-7, Tanner). U of Utah Pr.

--A Mormon Mother: An Autobiography. (Utah, the Mormons, & the West: No. 1). 1976. pap. 5.00 (ISBN 0-87480-157-5, Tanner). U of Utah Pr.

Tanner, B. K. X-Ray Diffraction Topography. LC 75-45196. 1976. text ed. 32.00 (ISBN 0-08-019692-6). Pergamon.

Tanner, C. Kenneth & Williams, Earl J. Educational Planning & Decision Making: A View Through the Organizational Process. LC 80-8631. 1981. write for info. (ISBN 0-669-04330-3). Lexington Bks.

Tanner, Christine, jt. auth. see Aspinall, Mary Jo.

Tanner, Clara L. Southwest Indian Painting: A Changing Art. rev. ed. LC 74-160812. (Illus.). 1980. 50.00 (ISBN 0-8165-0309-5). U of Ariz Pr.

Tanner, Don, jt. auth. see Johnson, George.

Tanner, Don, jt. auth. see Popoff, Peter.

Tanner, Don, ed. see Popoff, Peter.

Tanner, Donna M. The Lesbian Couple. LC 77-16720. 1978. 15.95x (ISBN 0-669-02078-8). Lexington Bks.

Tanner, E., ed. see International Congress of Life Insurance, 13th, Madrid 1979.

Tanner, Fran A. Basic Drama Projects. rev. ed. 1977. lib. bdg. 6.60 (ISBN 0-931054-00-1). Clark Pub.

--Creative Communication. 402p. 1979. lib. bdg. 7.85 (ISBN 0-931054-01-X). Clark Pub.

Tanner, George S. & Richards, J. Morris. The Colonization of the Little Colorado. LC 77-73890. 1977. 12.50 o.p. (ISBN 0-87358-163-6). Northland.

Tanner, Helen H. Caddoan Indians Four. Horr, David A., ed. (American Indian Ethnohistory Ser.). 1978. lib. bdg. 42.00 (ISBN 0-8240-0765-4). Garland Pub.

--Ojibwas: A Critical Bibliography. LC 76-12376. (Newberry Library Center for the History of the American Indian Bibliographical Ser.). 88p. 1976. pap. 3.95x (ISBN 0-253-34165-5). Ind U Pr.

Tanner, J. M. A History of Studies of Human Growth. (Illus.). 500p. Date not set. price not set (ISBN 0-521-22488-8, 40485). Cambridge U Pr.

Tanner, J. M., jt. auth. see Eveleth, P. B.

Tanner, James T. Guide to the Study of Animal Populations. LC 77-13630. 1978. 9.95x (ISBN 0-87049-235-7). U of Tenn Pr.

Tanner, Janet. The Hours of Light. 518p. 1981. 13.95. St Martin.

Tanner, Joseph R., ed. Constitutional Documents of the Reign of James 1, 1603-1625. 1930. pap. 14.50x (ISBN 0-521-09122-5). Cambridge U Pr.

Tanner, Nancy. On Becoming Human. LC 80-21526. (Illus.). 350p. Date not set. 29.95 (ISBN 0-521-23554-5); pap. 10.95 (ISBN 0-521-28028-1). Cambridge U Pr.

Tanner, Norman P., ed. Heresy Trials in the Diocese of Norwich: 1428-31. (Royal Historical Society: Camden Society Fourth Ser.: Vol. 20). 233p. 1977. 20.00x (ISBN 0-8476-3305-5). Rowman.

Tanner, Ogden. The Battle of the Bulge. (World War II Ser.). (Illus.). 1979. lib. bdg. 14.94 (ISBN 0-8094-2531-9); kivar bdg. 9.93 (ISBN 0-8094-2532-7). Silver.
--The Canadians. (Old West Ser.). (Illus.). (gr. 5 up). 1977. 12.96 (ISBN 0-8094-1543-7, Pub. by Time-Life). Silver.
--Garden Construction. Time-Life Books, ed. (The Time-Life Encyclopdia of Gardening). (Illus.). 1978. 11.95 (ISBN 0-8094-2583-1). Time-Life.
--Herbs. LC 76-51513. (Time-Life Encyclopedia for Gardening Ser.). (Illus.). (gr. 6 up). 1977. pap. text ed. 11.97 (ISBN 0-8094-2551-3, Pub. by Time-Life). Silver.
--The New England Wilds. (The American Wilderness Ser.). (Illus.). 184p. 1974. 12.95 (ISBN 0-8094-1229-2). Time-Life.
--The New England Wilds. LC 73-92887. (American Wilderness). (Illus.). (gr. 6 up). 1974. PLB 11.97 (ISBN 0-8094-1230-6, Pub. by Time-Life). Silver.
--The Ranchers. LC 77-85283. (The Old West Ser.). (Illus.). 1977. lib. bdg. 12.96 (ISBN 0-686-51080-1). Silver.
--Stress. LC 75-33607. (Human Behavior). (Illus.). (gr. 5 up). 1976. PLB 12.40 o.p. (ISBN 0-8094-1929-7, Pub. by Time-Life). Silver.
--Stress. (Human Behavior Ser.). 9.95 (ISBN 0-8094-1928-9). Time-Life.
--Urban Wilds. (The American Wilderness Ser.). (Illus.). 184p. 1975. 12.95 (ISBN 0-8094-1221-7). Time-Life.
--Urban Wilds. (American Wilderness). (Illus.). (gr. 6 up). 1975. PLB 11.97 (ISBN 0-8094-1335-3, Pub. by Time-Life). Silver.
Tanner, Ogden, jt. auth. see Crockett, James U.
Tanner, Ogden, ed. The Canadians. (The Old West Ser.). 1977. 12.95 (ISBN 0-8094-1541-0). Time-Life.
Tanner, Paul & Gerow, Maurice. A Study of Jazz. 4th ed. 225p. 1981. pap. text ed. write for info. (ISBN 0-697-03442-9); instr's manual avail. (ISBN 0-697-03443-7). Wm C Brown.
Tanner, Ruben. The Teddy Bears' Picnic: A Counting Book. LC 79-1867. (Illus.). (ps-k). 1979. 1.95 (ISBN 0-525-69000-X, Gingerbread Bks); PLB 5.95 (ISBN 0-525-69001-8, Gingerbread Bks.). Dutton.
--Too Many Wheels. LC 79-1909. (Illus.). (ps-2). 1979. 1.95 (ISBN 0-525-69014-X, Gingerbread Bks); PLB 5.95 o.p. (ISBN 0-525-69015-8). Dutton.
Tanner, T. The Reign of Wonder. LC 76-62589. 1977. pap. 11.50x (ISBN 0-521-29198-4). Cambridge U Pr.
Tanner, Tony, ed. see Austen, Jane.
Tanner, William, ed. Industrial Robots: Applications, Vol. II. LC 78-71001. (Manufacturing Update Ser). 1979. text ed. 29.00x (ISBN 0-87263-046-3). SME.
--Industrial Robots: Fundamentals, Vol. I. new ed. LC 78-71001. (Manufacturing Update Ser.). (Illus.). 1978. text ed. 29.00x (ISBN 0-87263-045-5). SME.
Tannock, P. D. Organization & Administration of Catholic Education in Australia. 1975. 14.50x (ISBN 0-7022-0954-6). U of Queensland Pr.
Tanous, Helen N. Designing Dress Patterns. rev. ed. (Illus.). (gr. 10-12). 1971. text ed. 13.28 (ISBN 0-87002-112-5). Bennett IL.
Tanous, Peter & Rubinstein, Paul. The Wheat Killing. LC 77-27682. 1979. 10.00 (ISBN 0-385-14233-1). Doubleday.
Tansey, Richard G., jt. auth. see De la Croix, Horst.
Tansik & Elliot. Managing Police Organizations. (Illus.). 250p. 1981. pap. text ed. 9.95 (ISBN 0-87872-275-0). Duxbury Pr.
Tansik, David A., et al. Management: A Life Cycle Approach. 1980. 18.95x (ISBN 0-256-02278-X). Irwin.
Tansill, Charles C., ed. see U. S. Library of Congress Legislative Reference Service.
Tansley, A. E. Reading & Remedial Reading. 1967. text ed. 9.25x (ISBN 0-7100-2169-0). Humanities.
Tansley, A. E. & Gulliford, R. Education of Slow Learning Children. 2nd ed. (Orig.). 1966. text ed. 15.00x (ISBN 0-7100-2170-4); pap. text ed. 3.50x (ISBN 0-7100-4650-2). Humanities.
Tansley, A. G. Britain's Green Mantle. 1968. text ed. 25.00x (ISBN 0-04-580004-9). Allen Unwin.
Tansley, Arthur G. British Islands & Their Vegetation, 2 Vols. 1949. Set. 125.00 (ISBN 0-521-06600-X). Cambridge U Pr.
Tansley, David V. Dimensions of Radionics. 224p. 1977. 18.95x (ISBN 0-8464-1005-2). Beekman Pubs.
--Radionics & the Subtle Anatomy of Man. 1980. 5.50 (ISBN 0-8464-1044-3). Beekman Pubs.
--Radionics Interface with the Ether Fields. 112p. 1979. pap. text ed. 10.95x (ISBN 0-8464-1045-1). Beekman Pubs.
Tantaquidgeon, Gladys. Folk Medicine of the Delaware & Related Algonkian Indians. LC 73-620801. (Pennsylvania Historical & Museum Commission Anthropological Ser.: No. 3). (Illus.). 145p. 1972. 7.00 (ISBN 0-911124-70-5); pap. 4.00 (ISBN 0-911124-69-1). Pa Hist & Mus.
Tanter, Raymond, jt. auth. see Stein, Janice G.
Tanur, J. M., et al, eds. Statistics: A Guide to Biological & Health Sciences. 1977. pap. text ed. 5.95x (ISBN 0-8162-8564-0). Holden-Day.
Tanur, Judilh M., et al, eds. Statistics: A Guide to Business & Economics. LC 76-5708. 120p. 1976. pap. text ed. 5.95x (ISBN 0-8162-8584-5). Holden-Day.
Tanur, Judith M., et al, eds. Statistics: A Guide to Political & Social Issues. LC 76-50852. 1977. pap. text ed. 5.95x (ISBN 0-8162-8574-8). Holden-Day.
--Statistics: A Guide to the Unknown. 2nd ed. 1978. pap. text ed. 11.50x (ISBN 0-8162-8605-1). Holden-Day.
Tanyzer, et al. Growing-with-Language Program, 10 readers. (gr. 2-4). text ed. 3.60 ea. o.p.; laboratory manual 1.92 ea. o.p. Pitman Learning.
Tanzer, Herbert & Lyons, Nick. Your Pet Isn't Sick: (He Just Wants You to Think So) 1978. pap. 1.75 (ISBN 0-515-04599-3). Jove Pubns.
--Your Pet Isn't Sick: He Justs Wants You to Think So. 1977. 6.95 o.p. (ISBN 0-525-24020-9). Dutton.
Tanzer, Radford C. & Edgerton, Milton T., eds. Symposium on Reconstruction of the Auricle, Vol. X. LC 79-7329. 1974. 49.50 (ISBN 0-8016-4852-1). Mosby.
Tao, D. C. Fundamentals of Applied Kinematics. (Illus.). 1967. 17.95 (ISBN 0-201-07451-6). sol. manual o.p. 1.50 (ISBN 0-686-66351-9). A-W.
Tao, Jing-shen. The Jurchen in Twelfth-Century China: A Study of Sinicization. LC 76-7800. (Publications on Asia of the School of International Studies: No. 29). (Illus.). 236p. 1977. 12.50 (ISBN 0-295-95514-7). U of Wash Pr.
T'Ao Ch'Ien. Poetry of T'ao Ch'ien. Hightower, James R., ed. (Illus.). 24.95x (ISBN 0-19-815440-2). Oxford U Pr.
Tapasyananda, Swami, tr. see Bhattatiri, M. N.
Tapasyananda, Swami, tr. see Puri, Vishnu.
Tapia, John R. The Indian in the Spanish-American Novel. LC 80-6182. 120p. (Orig.). 1981. lib. bdg. 16.25 (ISBN 0-8191-1428-6); pap. text ed. 7.75 (ISBN 0-8191-1438-3). U Pr of Amer.
--The Spanish Romantic Theater. LC 80-5565. 87p. 1980. lib. bdg. 13.75 (ISBN 0-8191-1276-3); pap. text ed. 6.50 (ISBN 0-8191-1277-1). U Pr of Amer.
Tapie, Victor L. France in the Age Louis Thirteenth & Richelieu. LC 74-8919. (Illus.). 664p. 17.50 o.p. (ISBN 0-275-52530-9). Praeger.
Tapio, Pat D. The Lady Who Saw the Good Side of Everything. LC 75-4610. (Illus.). 32p. (ps-3). 1975. 6.95 (ISBN 0-395-28826-6, Clarion). HM.
Tapley, J. G. & Parkman, N. Polymer Films in Electrical Applications. (Iee Electrical & Electronic Materials & Devices Ser.). (Illus.). 192p. Date not set. write for info. (Pub. by Peregrinus London). Inst Elect Eng. Postponed.
Tapley, Richard P., jt. ed. see De Vito, Robert A.
Taplin, ed. see Dance in Canada Annual Conference, 7th, Waterloo, Ontario, June 27-July 2, 1979.
Taplin, Oliver. Greek Tragedy in Action. 1979. 20.00x (ISBN 0-520-03704-9); pap. 4.95 (ISBN 0-520-03949-1). U of Cal Pr.
Tapp, Edwin. Policies of Survival. (Studies in Twentieth Century History). 1979. pap. text ed. 4.50 (ISBN 0-686-65413-7, 00549). Heinemann Ed.
Tapp, Hambleton & Klotter, James C., eds. The Union, the Civil War & John W. Tuttle: A Kentucky Captains Account. LC 79-89244. 1980. 20.00 (ISBN 0-916968-08-1). Kentucky Hist.
Tapp, John. The Path-Way to Knowledge: Containing the Whole Art of Arithmeticke. LC 68-54667. (English Experience Ser.: No. 66). 1968. Repr. of 1613 ed. 49.00 (ISBN 90-221-0066-9). Walter J Johnson.
Tapp, June L. & Krinsky, Fred. Ambivalent America: A Psycho-Political Dialogue. 1971. pap. text ed. 4.95x (ISBN 0-02-478870-8, 47887). Macmillan.
Tappan, Frances. Healing Massage Techniques: A Study of Eastern & Western Methods. (Illus.). 1978. ref. ed. 15.95 (ISBN 0-8359-2821-7); pap. 6.95 (ISBN 0-8359-2819-5). Reston.
Tappan, Helen. The Paleobiology of Plant Protists. LC 80-14675. (Geology Ser.). (Illus.). 1980. text ed. 95.00x (ISBN 0-7167-1109-5). W H Freeman.
Tappan, Melrose H., ed. & pref. by see Masters, Roy.
Tappan, William T. The Real Estate Acquisition Handbook: Money-Making Techniques for the Serious Investor. 1980. 16.95 (ISBN 0-13-762633-9, Spec); pap. 7.95 (ISBN 0-13-762625-8). P-H.
Tapper, Colin. Computer Law. (Business Data Processing Ser.). 1978. text ed. 19.95 (ISBN 0-582-45063-2). Longman.
Tapper, Mildred, ed. see Blake, Robert R. & Mouton, Jane S.
Tapper, Ted & Salter, Brian. Education & the Political Order. 1978. text ed. 26.00x (ISBN 0-333-22691-7); pap. text ed. 11.75x (ISBN 0-333-22692-5). Humanities.
Tappert, Theodore G. & Lehmann, Helmut T., eds. Luther's Works: Table Talk, Vol. 54. Tappert, Theodore G., tr. LC 55-9893. 1967. 12.95 (ISBN 0-8006-0354-0, 1-354). Fortress.
Tappert, Theodore G., ed. & tr. see Spener, Philip J.
Tappert, Theodore G., tr. Augsburg Confession: Anniversity Edition. 64p. 1980. pap. 1.25 (ISBN 0-8006-1385-6, 1-1385). Fortress.
Tappert, Theodore G., tr. see Tappert, Theodore G. & Lehmann, Helmut T.
Tapping, G. Craig. Austin Clarke: A Study of His Writing. 368p. 1980. lib. bdg. 29.00x (ISBN 0-389-20041-7). B&N.
Tapscott, Bangs L. Elementary Applied Symbolic Logic. (Illus.). 512p. 1976. text ed. 16.95 (ISBN 0-13-252940-8). P-H.
Tapscott, Betty. Inner Healing Through Healing of Memories. 1975. pap. 2.95 (ISBN 0-917726-29-4). Hunter Bks.
--Out of the Valley. 128p. 1981. pap. 3.95 (ISBN 0-8407-5761-1). Nelson.
--Set Free. 1978. pap. 3.50 (ISBN 0-917726-24-3). Hunter Bks.
Tapscott, Stephen. Mesopotamia. LC 75-11617. (Wesleyan Poetry Program: Vol. 78). 72p. (Orig.). 1975. pap. 4.95x (ISBN 0-8195-1078-5, Pub. by Wesleyan U Pr). Columbia U Pr.
Tar, Zolton. The Frankfurt School: The Critical Theories of Max Horkheimer & Theoder W. Adorno. LC 77-2353. 1977. 23.95 (ISBN 0-471-84536-1, Pub. by Wiley-Interscience). Wiley.
Taraboi, V. Organization, Functioning & Activities of National Documentary Information Systems in the Scientific, Technical & Economic Fields. LC 67-1784. 88p. 1973. pap. text ed. 35.00 (ISBN 0-08-017725-5). Pergamon.
Tarachow, Michael. Interlude. (Illus.). 1979. signed ltd. ed. 7.50 (ISBN 0-915316-68-4); pap. 3.50 (ISBN 0-915316-67-6). Pentagram.
Tarachow, Michael, ed. & intro. by. Toward a Further Definition. LC 76-21409. (Illus.). 1980. 18.50x (ISBN 0-915316-42-0); pap. 8.50 (ISBN 0-915316-41-2). Pentagram.
Taralon, Jean. Treasures of the Churches of France. LC 66-23097. (Illus.). 1966. 25.00 o.s.i. (ISBN 0-8076-0383-X). Braziller.
Taraman, Khalil S., ed. CAD-CAM, Meeting Today's Productivity Challenge. LC 80-69006. (Manufacturing Update Ser.). (Illus.). 281p. 1980. 29.00 (ISBN 0-87263-063-3). SME.
Taran, Leonardo, ed. see Apelt, Otto.
Taran, Leonardo, ed. see Billings, Grace H.
Taran, Leonardo, ed. see Billings, Thomas H.
Taran, Leonardo, ed. see Jones, Roger M.
Taran, Leonardo, ed. see Wilkins, Eliza G.
Tarazi, Fuad. Studies in Fundamentals of Arabic Language & Grammar. (Arabic.). 1969. 14.00x (ISBN 0-685-72060-8). Intl Bk Ctr.
Tarbell, Ida M. History of Standard Oil Company, 2 vols. in 1. (Illus.). 15.00 (ISBN 0-8446-1441-6). Peter Smith.
Tarbell, Roberta K., jt. auth. see Hills, Patricia.
Tarbert, Gary, jt. ed. see LaBeau, Dennis.
Tarbert, Gary C., ed. Book Review Index: Annual Cumulation Covering 1980. LC 65-9908. (Book Review Index Ser.). 1981. 78.00 (ISBN 0-8103-0571-2). Gale.
--Book Review Index Nineteen Sixty-Nine to Nineteen Seventy-Nine: A Master Cumulation, 6 vols. 3500p. 1981. Set. 375.00 (ISBN 0-8103-0570-4). Gale.
--Children's Book Review Index: Annual Clothbound Volumes. LC 75-27408. 42.00 ea.; Annual 1975. (ISBN 0-8103-0626-3); Annual 1976. (ISBN 0-8103-0627-1); Annual 1977. (ISBN 0-8103-0628-X); Annual 1978. (ISBN 0-8103-0629-8); Annual 1979. (ISBN 0-8103-0630-1). Gale.
--Children's Book Review Index: Nineteen-Eighty Annual. LC 75-27408. (Children's Book Review Index Ser.). 350p. 1981. 46.00 (ISBN 0-8103-0631-X). Gale.
Tarbox, Charles H. Five Ages of the Cinema. (Illus.). 128p. 1980. 20.00 (ISBN 0-682-49618-9). Exposition.
Tarbox, Gregory. Ideal Imperfection. 1979. 4.75 o.p. (ISBN 0-8062-1185-7). Carlton.
Tarbuck, E., jt. auth. see Lutgens, F.
Tarbuck, Edward & Lutgens, Fred. Earth Science. 2nd ed. 1979. text ed. 19.95 (ISBN 0-675-08303-6); instructor's manual 3.95 (ISBN 0-686-67288-7). Merrill.
Tarbuck, Kenneth J., ed. see Bukharin, Nikolai I.
Tarczan, Constance. An Educator's Guide to Psychological Tests: Descriptions & Classroom Implications. (Illus.). 128p. 1975. 12.75 (ISBN 0-398-02427-8); pap. 8.75 (ISBN 0-398-02491-X). C C Thomas.
Tardiff, Olive. They Paved the Way: A History of N. H. Women. vi, 98p. (gr. 9-12). 1980. pap. text ed. 3.95 (ISBN 0-917890-22-1). Heritage Bk.
Tardivel, Jules-Paul. For My Country. Fischman, Sheila, tr. LC 75-6862. (Social History of Canada Ser.). Orig. Title: Pour la Patrie. 1975. pap. 5.50 (ISBN 0-8020-6267-9). U of Toronto Pr.
Tardos,., et al, eds. Pharmacological Control of Heart & Circulation: Proceedings of the Third Congress of the Hungarian Pharmacological Society, Budapest, 1979. LC 80-41281. (Advances in Pharmacological Research & Practice Ser.: Vol. I). 445p. 1981. 84.00 (ISBN 0-08-026386-0). Pergamon.
Tardu, M. Human Rights: The International Petition System, Release 1. 1980. 35.00 (ISBN 0-379-20252-2). Oceana.
Tardy, Gene & Jackson, Al. Motorcycle: Cross-Country Racing. (Sports Action Ser.). (Illus.). (gr. 3-7). 1974. PLB 5.51 (ISBN 0-914844-00-8). J Alden.
--Motorcycle: Grand Prix Racing. (Sports Action Ser.). (Illus.). (gr. 3-7). 1974. PLB 5.51 (ISBN 0-914844-01-6). J Alden.
--Motorcycle: Moto-Cross Racing. (Sports Action Ser.). (Illus.). (gr. 3-7). 1974. PLB 5.51 (ISBN 0-914844-02-4). J Alden.
--Soccer: World's Most Popular Sport. bilingual ed. (Sports Action Ser.). (Illus.). 64p. (Span. - Eng.). (gr. 3-7). 1975. PLB 6.75 (ISBN 0-914844-11-3). J Alden.
Tardy, Gene, jt. auth. see Jackson, Al.
Tardy, Mary T., ed. The Living Female Writers of the South. LC 75-44070. 1979. Repr. of 1872 ed. 50.00 (ISBN 0-8103-4286-3). Gale.
Targ, Harry R., jt. ed. see Beres, Louis R.
Targ, Russell & Puthoff, Harold. Mind-Reach. 1976. 8.95 o.p. (ISBN 0-440-05688-8). Delacorte.
Targ, William. Indecent Pleasures. LC 75-15991. (Illus.). 448p. 1975. 14.95 o.s.i. (ISBN 0-02-619700-6, 61970). Macmillan.
Target, C. M. The Nun in the Concentration Camp. 1977. pap. 1.55 (ISBN 0-08-017611-9). Pergamon.
Tarharka. Black Manhood: The Building of Civilization by the Black Man of the Nile. rev. ed. LC 79-65009. 1979. pap. text ed. 11.25 (ISBN 0-8191-0780-8). U Pr of Amer.
Tari, Mel & Tari, Noni. Gentle Breeze of Jesus. LC 78-64960. 1978. pap. 2.50 (ISBN 0-89221-056-7, 056-7). New Leaf.
Tari, Noni, jt. auth. see Tari, Mel.
Tarikh. Tarikh: Egypt & the Nile Valley, Vol. 5, No. 2. Oroge, Adeniyij, ed. 65p. 1977. pap. text ed. 2.75x (ISBN 0-582-60874-0). Humanities.
--Tarikh: Protest Against Colonial Rule in West Africa, Vol. 5, No. 3. Asiwaju, A. I. & Crowder, M., eds. (Illus.). 1977. pap. text ed. 2.75x (ISBN 0-582-60957-7). Humanities.
Tarjan, Armen C. Check List of Plant & Soil Nematodes: A Nomenclatorial Compilation. LC 60-10226. xiii, 115p. 1960. 8.25 (ISBN 0-8130-0223-0); suppl. 1967 6.75 (ISBN 0-8130-0224-9). U Presses Fla.
--Supplement to Checklist of Plant & Soil Nematodes, 1961-1965: A Nomenclatorial Compilation. LC 60-10226. 1967. 6.75 (ISBN 0-8130-0224-9). U Presses Fla.
Tarjan, I. & Matrai, M. Laboratory Manual on Crystal Growth. (Illus.). 250p. 21.50 (ISBN 0-685-42284-4). Adler.
Tarjan, R. see Somogyi, J. C.
Tarling, R. J., jt. auth. see Cripps, T. F.
Tarlock, A. Dan, jt. auth. see Ellickson, Robert C.
Tarlock, A. Dan, ed. see Kitch, Edmund W.
Tarlow, David M. Student Guide to the Medical College Admission Test. 3rd ed. LC 78-53092. (Illus.). 1978. pap. 6.00 (ISBN 0-931572-00-2). Datar Pub.
--Student Guide to the Optometry College Admission Test. (Illus.). 1978. pap. 7.00 (ISBN 0-931572-04-5). Datar Pub.
--Student Guide to the Pharmacy College Admission Test. (Illus.). 1978. pap. 7.00 (ISBN 0-931572-05-3). Datar Pub.
Tarlow, David M. & Lichtenberg, Marc L. Student Guide to the Dental Aptitude Test. LC 78-53093. (Illus.). 1978. pap. 6.00 (ISBN 0-931572-01-0). Datar Pub.
Tarlow, David M., ed. see Glynn, Maryanne C.
Tarn, J. N. Five per Cent Philanthropy: An Account of Housing in Urban Areas, 1840-1914. LC 77-186253. (Illus.). 300p. 1973. 41.95 (ISBN 0-521-08506-3). Cambridge U Pr.
Tarn, W. W. Alexander the Great, 2 vols. LC 78-74533. (Illus.). 1979. Vol. 1. 23.50 (ISBN 0-521-22584-1); Vol. 1. pap. 6.95x (ISBN 0-521-29563-7); Vol. 2. 48.00 (ISBN 0-521-22585-X). Cambridge U Pr.

Tarn, William W. & Charlesworth, Martin P. Octavian, Antony & Cleopatra. rev. ed. (Orig.). 1965. pap. 6.95x (ISBN 0-521-09354-6). Cambridge U Pr.
Tarneja, Sukh R. Nature, Spirituality & Science. 240p. 1980. text ed. 27.50x (ISBN 0-7069-1203-9, Pub by Vikas India). Advent Bk.
Tarnopol, Lester. Learning Disabilities: Introduction to Educational & Medical Management. (Illus.). 412p. 1974. 18.75 (ISBN 0-398-01897-9); pap. 13.50 (ISBN 0-398-02894-X). C C Thomas.
Tarnower, Herman & Baker, Samm S. The Complete Scarsdale Medical Diet. 240p. 1981. pap. 2.95 (ISBN 0-553-14446-4). Bantam.
Tarnowski, Stanislaw, tr. see Siuchninski, Mateusz.
Tarpey, Lawrence X., et al. A Preface to Marketing Management. 1979. pap. 8.95x (ISBN 0-256-02207-0). Business Pubns.
Tarpley, Fred. One Thousand & One Texas Place Names. 256p. 1980. text ed. 14.95x (ISBN 0-292-76015-9); pap. 5.95 (ISBN 0-292-76016-7). U of Tex Pr.
Tarpy, Roger M. & Mayer, Richard E. Foundations of Learning & Memory. 1978. 15.95x (ISBN 0-673-15074-7). Scott F.
Tarr, Andrea, jt. auth. see Katz, William A.
Tarr, F. C. & Centeno, Augusto. A Graded Spanish Review: Grammar with Composition. 2nd ed. (gr. 9-12). 1973. text ed. 13.95 (ISBN 0-13-362160-X). P-H.
Tarr, Herbert. So Help Me God! 224p. 1980. pap. 2.75 (ISBN 0-553-14135-X). Bantam.
Tarr, Sr. Mary. Catholicism in Gothic Fiction. Bleiler, E. F., ed. LC 78-60815. (The Fiction of Popular Culture Ser.: Vol. 16). 148p. 1979. lib. bdg. 15.00 (ISBN 0-8240-9652-5). Garland Pub.
Tarr, W. A. Tables for Determination of Common Minerals & Rocks. 4th rev. ed. 1951. text ed. 0.95x spiral bdg. (ISBN 0-87543-045-7). Lucas.
Tarr, Yvonne Y. The Squash Cookbook. 1978. pap. 5.95 (ISBN 0-394-72473-9, Vin). Random.
--The Super-Easy Step-by-Step Book of Special Breads. (Orig.). 1975. pap. 2.95 o.p. (ISBN 0-394-72010-5, Vin). Random.
--The Super-Easy-Step-by-Step Sausagemaking. (Orig.). 1975. pap. 3.95 (ISBN 0-394-72011-3, Vin). Random.
--The Super Easy-Step-by-Step Winemaking. (Orig.). 1975. pap. 3.95 o.p. (ISBN 0-394-72012-1, Vin). Random.
Tarrach, R., jt. ed. see Alonso, J. L.
Tarrant, J. R., ed. Seneca: Agamemnon. LC 76-15668. (Cambridge Classical Texts & Commentaries Ser.: No. 18). (Illus.). 1977. 59.00 (ISBN 0-521-20807-6). Cambridge U Pr.
Tarrant, John. The Clauberg Trigger. (Orig.). 1980. pap. 1.95 (ISBN 0-505-51523-7). Tower Bks.
--The Rommel Plot. LC 77-5731. 1977. 8.95 o.p. (ISBN 0-397-01235-7). Lippincott.
Tarrant, John J. Drucker: The Man Who Invented the Corporate Society. LC 75-44263. 300p. 1976. 10.95 o.p. (ISBN 0-8436-0744-0). CBI Pub.
--Drucker: The Man Who Invented the Corporate Society. 1977. pap. 6.95 (ISBN 0-446-97702-0). Warner Bks.
--Tomorrow's Techniques for Today's Salesmen. 1969. 8.95 (ISBN 0-8015-7806-X, Hawthorn). Dutton.
Tarrant, John R. Agricultural Geography: Problems in Modern Geography. 1980. 28.00 (ISBN 0-7153-6286-0). David & Charles.
--Food Policies. LC 79-40740. (Wiley Series on Studies in Environmental Management & Resources Development). 338p. 1980. 44.50 (ISBN 0-471-27656-1, Pub. by Wiley-Interscience). Wiley.
Tarrasch, Siegbert. Best Games of Chess. Reinfeld, Fred, ed. 1947. pap. 6.00 (ISBN 0-486-20644-0). Dover.
Tarrow, Sidney, jt. ed. see Lange, Peter.
Tarrow, Sidney, et al. Territorial Politics in Industrial Nations. LC 77-83439. (Praeger Special Studies). 1978. 32.50 (ISBN 0-03-040961-6). Praeger.
Tarsaidze, Alexandre. Katia: Wife Before God. (Illus.). 1970. 12.95 (ISBN 0-02-616270-9). Macmillan.
Tarshis, Barry. The Average American Book. 1981. pap. 2.50 (ISBN 0-451-09486-7, E9486, Sig). NAL.
Tarshis, Maurice S. The L S D Controversy: An Overview. (Illus.). 96p. 1972. 9.75 (ISBN 0-398-02523-1). C C Thomas.
Tarski, Alfred. Logic, Semantics, Metamathematics. Corcoran, John, ed. Woodger, J. H., tr. from Polish. 1981. lib. bdg. 35.00 (ISBN 0-915144-75-1); pap. text ed. 17.50 (ISBN 0-915144-76-X). Hackett Pub. Postponed.
Tarsky, Sue. The Potted Plant Book. (Illus.). 48p. (gr. 5 up). 1981. 9.95 (ISBN 0-316-83206-5). Little.
--The Prickly Plant Book. (Illus.). 48p. (gr. 5 up). 1981. 9.95 (ISBN 0-316-83207-3). Little.
Tart, Charles T. The Application of Learning Theory to ESP Performance. LC 75-14709. (Parapsychological Monograph Ser.: No. 15). 1975. pap. 6.00 (ISBN 0-912328-25-8). Parapsych Foun.
Tart, Charles T., et al, eds. Mind at Large: Institute of Electrical & Electronic Engineers Symposia on the Nature of Extrasensory Perception. LC 79-9982. 288p. 1979. 25.95 (ISBN 0-03-050476-7). Praeger.
Tartak, Laura M. Cockatiels. (Illus.). 96p. 2.95 (ISBN 0-87666-885-6, KW-057). TFH Pubns.
Tartakovsky, V. K., jt. auth. see Sitenko, A. G.
Tartakow, I. Jackson & Vorperian, John H. Foodborne & Waterborne Diseases: Their Epidemiological Character. (Illus.). 1981. pap. 19.00 (ISBN 0-87055-368-2). AVI.
Tartan, Beth & Hayes, Rudy. Miss Lillian & Friends: The Plains, Georgia, Family Philosophy & Recipe Book. (Illus.). (RL 7). 1977. pap. 1.75 o.p. (ISBN 0-451-07852-7, E7852, Sig). NAL.
Tarter, Brent, jt. ed. see Scriber, Robert L.
Tarter, Brent, jt. ed. see Scribner, Robert L.
Tarter, Donald E. Turning Behavior Inside Out. LC 79-63749. 1979. pap. text ed. 11.00 (ISBN 0-8191-0736-0). U Pr of Amer.
Tarter, Ralph E. & Sugerman, A. Arthur, eds. Alcoholism: Interdisciplinary Approaches to an Enduring Problem. 880p. 1976. text ed. 33.50 (ISBN 0-201-08146-6, Adv Bk Prog); pap. text ed. 21.50 (ISBN 0-201-08145-8, Adv Bk Prog). A-W.
Tarthang Tulku. Hidden Mind of Freedom. Derman, Sylvia, ed. 1981. pap. 6.95. Dharma Pub.
Tarumoto, David H., ed. High-Performance Review: Audio Equipment & Recordings for the Perceptive Listener, Vol. 1. (Illus.). 480p. 1981. pap. 24.00x (ISBN 0-88232-068-8). Delbridge Pub Co.
Tarutis, Eleanor L., jt. auth. see De Leeuw, Frank.
Tarver, Sara G., jt. auth. see Kneedler, Rebecca D.
Tarwater, J. Dalton, et al. Men & Institutions in American Mathematics. (Graduate Studies: No. 13). (Orig.). 1976. pap. 6.00 (ISBN 0-89672-023-3). Tex Tech Pr.
Tarzian, Lucy, ed. Progressive Grocer's Marketing Guidebook. LC 68-126162. 1980. 149.00 (ISBN 0-911790-19-5). Prog Grocer.
--Progressive Grocer's Marketing Guidebook. LC 68-126162. 1981. 159.00 (ISBN 0-911790-20-9). Prog Grocer.
Tas, S. Indonesia: The Underdeveloped Freedom. LC 73-23034. 1974. 10.95 o.p. (ISBN 0-672-53655-2); pap. 8.95 (ISBN 0-672-63655-7). Pegasus.
Tasca, Diane, et al, eds. United States-Japanese Economic Relations: Cooperation, Competition & Confrontation. (Policy Studies). 1980. 18.25 (ISBN 0-08-025129-3). Pergamon.
Taschdjian, Claire. The Peking Man Is Missing. LC 77-3806. 1977. 10.00 o.p. (ISBN 0-06-014219-7, HarpT). Har-Row.
Taschdjian, Edgar, ed. see Von Bertalanffy, Ludwig.
Taseer, Salmaan. Bhutto: A Political Biography. 208p. text ed. cancelled o.s.i. (ISBN 0-7069-1085-0, Pub. by Vikas India). Advent Bk.
Tashakori, Maryam. Management Sucession: From Owner-Founder to Professional Resident. (Praeger Special Studies). 140p. 1980. 19.95 (ISBN 0-03-047076-5). Praeger.
Tashjian, Ann, jt. auth. see Tashjian, Dickran.
Tashjian, Dickran. William Carlos Williams & the American Scene, 1920-1940. LC 78-20657. (Cal. Ser.: No. 420). (Illus.). 1979. 34.50 (ISBN 0-520-03854-1); pap. 10.95 (ISBN 0-520-03878-9). U of Cal Pr.
Tashjian, Dickran & Tashjian, Ann. Memorials for Children of Change: The Art of Early New England Stonecarving. LC 73-6006. (Illus.). 336p. 1974. 27.95x (ISBN 0-8195-4061-7, Pub. by Wesleyan U Pr). Columbia U Pr.
Tashjian, Dickran L. Skyscraper Primitives: Dada & the American Avant-Garde, 1910-1925. LC 74-21925. (Illus.). 360p. 1975. 22.50x (ISBN 0-8195-4081-1, Pub. by Wesleyan U Pr). Columbia U Pr.
Tashjian, Virginia A. Juba This & Juba That. LC 69-10666. (Illus.). (gr. 1-3). 1969. 7.95 (ISBN 0-316-83230-8). Little.
Task Force on Alternatives in Print of the Social Responsibilities Round Table of the American Library Association. Alternatives in Print: An International Catalog of Books, Pamphlets, Periodicals & Audiovisual Materials. LC 76-54384. 1980. 39.95x (ISBN 0-918212-20-0). Neal-Schuman.
Task, Willard R., tr. see Corbin, Henri.
Tasker, R. V., ed. see Augustine, Saint.
Tasker, Randolph V. General Epistle of James. (Tyndale Bible Commentaries). 1957. pap. 2.95 (ISBN 0-8028-1415-8). Eerdmans.
--Gospel According to St. John. (Tyndale Bible Commentaries). 1960. pap. 3.95 (ISBN 0-8028-1403-4). Eerdmans.
Tasker, Ronald R., jt. auth. see Emmers, Raimond.
Tasker, Ronald R., et al. The Thalmus & the Midbrain of Man: A Physiological Atlas Using Electrical Stimulatiob. (American Lecture Neurosurgery Ser.). (Illus.). 464p. write for info. (ISBN 0-398-04475-9). C C Thomas.
Tasman, Nast, jt. auth. see Lea, Alice.
Tasman, Norma, jt. ed. see Lass, Abraham.
Tasman, Norma L., jt. ed. see Lass, Abraham H.
Tasnadi-Marik, K. Viennese Porcelain. (Illus.). 1975. 6.50 (ISBN 0-912728-05-1). Newbury Bks Inc.
Tasner, Paul, et al, eds. Industrial Fire Hazards. LC 79-66427. (Illus.). 1979. 30.00 (ISBN 0-87765-155-8, SPP-57). Natl Fire Prot.
Tassel, David D. Van see Van Tassel, David D.
Tassel, Dennie Van see Van Tassel, Dennie.
Tassel, Dennis Van see Van Tassel, Dennis.
Tassel, Katrina Van see Van Tassel, Katrina.
Tassi, Aldo. The Political Philosophy of the American Revolution. LC 78-59127. 1978. pap. text ed. 6.75 (ISBN 0-8191-0547-3). U Pr of Amer.
Tassi, Roberto. Sutherland: The Wartime Drawings. Andrews, Julian, ed. & tr. (Illus.). 172p. 1980. 40.00x (ISBN 0-85667-095-2, Pub. by Sotheby Parke Bernet England). Biblio Dist.
Tassin, Myron. The Bacchus. LC 74-20526. (Illus.). 96p. 1975. 15.00 (ISBN 0-88289-061-1). Pelican.
Tasso, Torquato. Discourses on the Heroic Poem. Cavalchini, Mariella & Samuel, Irene, eds. 1973. 29.95x (ISBN 0-19-815714-2). Oxford U Pr.
--The Householders Philosophie - the True Economia - of Housekeeping - Annexed a Dairie Booke for Huswives. Kyd, T., tr. LC 74-28888. (English Experience Ser.: No. 765). 1975. Repr. of 1588 ed. 8.00 (ISBN 90-221-0765-5). Walter J Johnson.
Tata, Robert J. Structural Changes in Puerto Rico's Economy 1947-1976. LC 80-19080. (Latin America Ser., Ohio University Papers in International Studies). (Illus.). 104p. (Orig.). 1981. pap. 11.95. Ohio U Ctr Intl.
Tatai, Kichinosuke. Biorhythm for Health Design. LC 76-29337. (Illus.). 152p. 1977. pap. 8.95 (ISBN 0-87040-393-1). Japan Pubns.
Tatalovich, Raymond, jt. auth. see Daynes, Byron W.
Tatar, Elayne S. Divorce-Texas Style. Date not set. price not set (ISBN 0-89896-060-6). Larksdale.
Tate, jt. auth. see Wright.
Tate, A., jt. auth. see Billington, E. W.
Tate, Allen. Fathers. LC 60-3394. 306p. 1960. pap. 5.95x (ISBN 0-8040-0108-1, 12). Swallow.
--Memoirs & Opinions: Nineteen-Twenty-Six to Nineteen-Seventy-Four. LC 75-10757. 225p. 1975. 10.95 (ISBN 0-8040-0662-8). Swallow.
--Stonewall Jackson: The Good Soldier. 1957. pap. 2.25 o.p. (ISBN 0-472-06009-0, 9, AA). U of Mich Pr.
Tate, Allen, ed. see Poe, Edgar A.
Tate, Charles, ed. Cable Television in the Cities: Community Control, Public Access & Minority Ownership. 3rd ed. 192p. 1971. pap. 3.95 o.p. (ISBN 0-87766-020-4). Urban Inst.
Tate, Curtis E., Jr., et al. Successful Small Business Management. rev. ed. 1978. 18.50x (ISBN 0-256-02074-4). Business Pubns.
Tate, D. J. The Making of South-East Asia: Vol. 2, The Western Impact--Economic & Social Change. (Illus.). 632p. 1979. text ed. 49.50x (ISBN 0-19-580332-9). Oxford U Pr.
Tate, Ernest C. Wordplay & Poetry. LC 80-52182. 1981. 5.95 (ISBN 0-533-04746-3). Vantage.
Tate Gallery. The Drawings of Henry Moore. Date not set. pap. 15.95 (ISBN 0-8120-2063-4). Barron.
Tate, Gary & Corbett, Edward P., eds. The Writing Teacher's Sourcebook. 400p. 1981. pap. text ed. 9.95x (ISBN 0-19-502878-3). Oxford U Pr.
Tate, James. Hottentot Ossuary. 1974. limited signed ed. o.p. 25.00 (ISBN 0-686-22817-0); pap. 2.95 (ISBN 0-686-22818-9). Temple Bar.
--Torches. 2nd rev. & enl. ed. 1971. 10.00 (ISBN 0-87775-003-3); pap. 5.00 (ISBN 0-87775-093-9). Unicorn Pr.
--Viper Jazz. LC 76-4943. (Wesleyan Poetry Program: Vol.82). 1976. lib. bdg. 10.00x (ISBN 0-8195-2082-9, Pub. by Wesleyan U Pr); pap. 4.95 (ISBN 0-8195-1082-3). Columbia U Pr.
Tate, Joan. Bill. (Joan Tate Ser.). pap. text ed. 1.95x o.p. (ISBN 0-435-11883-8). Heinemann Ed.
--Coal Hoppy. pap. text ed. 1.95x o.p. (ISBN 0-435-11872-2). Heinemann Ed.
--Crane. pap. text ed. 1.95x o.p. (ISBN 0-435-11873-0). Heinemann Ed.
--The Holiday. pap. text ed. 1.95x o.p. (ISBN 0-435-11882-X). Heinemann Ed.
--Jenny. pap. text ed. 1.95x o.p. (ISBN 0-435-11876-5). Heinemann Ed.
--Letters to Chris. pap. text ed. 1.95x o.p. (ISBN 0-435-11887-0). Heinemann Ed.
--Lucy. pap. text ed. 1.95x o.p. (ISBN 0-435-11875-7). Heinemann Ed.
--Luke's Garden. pap. text ed. 1.95x o.p. (ISBN 0-435-11889-7). Heinemann Ed.
--Mrs. Jenny. pap. text ed. 1.95x o.p. (ISBN 0-435-11884-6). Heinemann Ed.
--Not the Usual Kind of Girl. (gr. 7-12). 1975. pap. 1.25 o.p. (ISBN 0-590-09818-7, Schol Pap). Schol Bk Serv.
--Now That You Own a Puppy. (Illus.). 1976. pap. 3.95 (ISBN 0-8119-0394-X). Fell.
--Picture Charlie. pap. text ed. 1.95x o.p. (ISBN 0-435-11874-9). Heinemann Ed.
--The Rabbit Boy. pap. text ed. 1.95x o.p. (ISBN 0-435-11877-3). Heinemann Ed.
--Ring on My Finger. (gr. 7 up). 1977. pap. 1.25 (ISBN 0-590-10318-0, Schol Pap). Schol Bk Serv.
--Tad. pap. text ed. 1.95x o.p. (ISBN 0-435-11880-3). Heinemann Ed.
--Tina & David. (gr. 7-12). 1976. pap. 1.25 o.p. (ISBN 0-590-01656-3, Schol Pap). Schol Bk Serv.
--Tree. pap. text ed. 1.95x o.p. (ISBN 0-435-11879-X). Heinemann Ed.
--Wild Martin & the Crow. pap. text ed. 1.95x o.p. (ISBN 0-435-11888-9). Heinemann Ed.
Tate, Joan, jt. auth. see Hagerup, Inger.
Tate, Joan, tr. see Dahlin, Doris.
Tate, Joan, tr. see Lilius, Irmelin S.
Tate, Merze. The United States & the Hawaiian Kingdom: A Political History. LC 80-14045. (Illus.). ix, 374p. 1980. Repr. of 1965 ed. lib. bdg. 29.25x (ISBN 0-313-22441-2, TAUS). Greenwood.
Tate, Nahum. The History of King Lear. Black, James, ed. LC 74-82562. (Regents Restoration Drama Ser). xl, 111p. 1975. 8.95x (ISBN 0-8032-0382-9); pap. 2.65x (ISBN 0-8032-5382-6, BB 278, Bison). U of Nebr Pr.
Tate, Priscilla W. From Innocence Through Experience: Keats's Myth of the Poet. (Salzburg Studies in English Literature, Romantic Reassessment: No. 34). 147p. 1974. pap. text ed. 25.00x (ISBN 0-391-01546-X). Humanities.
Tate, R. B., ed. see Manuel, Don J.
Tate, Ro. Desert Animals. LC 79-185645. (Animal Life Ser.). (Illus.). 152p. 1972. pap. 2.95 o.p. (ISBN 0-06-014222-7, TD-121, HarpT). Har-Row.
Tate, Thad W., Jr. Negro in Eighteenth-Century Williamsburg. LC 73-153687. (Williamsburg Research Studies). 256p. (Orig.). 1965. 5.00x o.p. (ISBN 0-8139-0399-8); pap. 3.00x o.p. (ISBN 0-8139-0233-9). U Pr of Va.
Tate, Thaddeus W., Jr., ed. see Washington, George.
Tate, W. E. Parish Chest. 3rd ed. LC 67-28686. (Illus.). 1969. 41.00 (ISBN 0-521-06603-4). Cambridge U Pr.
Tate, William & Moorer, Thomas H. Great Issues 74: A Forum on Important Questions Facing the American Public, Vol. 6. 5.95. TSU Pr.
Tate-O'Brien, Judith. Love in Deed. rev. ed. (Illus.). 68p. 1980. pap. 2.95 (ISBN 0-936098-07-4). Natl Marriage.
--Welcome: Christian Parenting. 68p. (Orig.). 1980. pap. 4.00 (ISBN 0-936098-15-5); instrs.' guide 3.00 (ISBN 0-686-68853-8). Natl Marriage.
Tatford, Frederick. Daniel & His Prophecy. Date not set. 8.25 (ISBN 0-86524-045-0). Klock & Klock.
Tatham, David. John Henry Bufford: American Lithographer. 22p. 1976. pap. 3.00x o.p. (ISBN 0-912296-33-X, Dist. by U Pr of Va). Am Antiquarian.
Tatham, Eddison C., jt. auth. see Sandberg, Karl C.
Tatkon, D. Great Vitamin Hoax. 1967. 5.95 o.s.i. (ISBN 0-02-616300-4). Macmillan.
Tatlock, John S. & MacKaye, Percy. The Modern Reader's Chaucer. 1966. pap. text ed. 8.95 (ISBN 0-02-932410-6). Free Pr.
Tatlow, Peter, jt. auth. see Temple, Cliff.
Tatsch, J. H. Iron Deposits: Origin, Evolution, & Present Characteristics. LC 76-28095. (Illus.). Date not set. text ed. 180.00 (ISBN 0-912890-12-6). Tatsch.
Tattersall, C. E., jt. auth. see Kendrick, A. F.
Tattersall, Ian. Man's Ancestors: An Introduction to Primate & Human Evolution. (Illus.). 1971. pap. 7.50 (ISBN 0-7195-2188-2). Transatlantic.
Tattersall, Jill. Chanters Chase. LC 77-10910. 1978. 7.95 o.p. (ISBN 0-688-03262-1). Morrow.
--The Wild Hunt. 1977. pap. 1.75 o.p. (ISBN 0-449-23380-4, Crest). Fawcett.
--The Witches of All Saints. 240p. 1976. pap. 1.50 o.p. (ISBN 0-449-22776-6, Q2776, Crest). Fawcett.

Tattersall, Peter D. Conviction. LC 80-82368. (Illus.). 374p. 1980. 12.95 (ISBN 0-8119-0407-5, Pegasus Rex). Fell.

Tattersfield, D. Projects & Demonstrations in Astronomy. LC 79-84264. 1979. 29.95x (ISBN 0-470-26715-1). Halsted Pr.

Tatum, Billy Joe. Billy Joe Tatum's Wild Foods Cookbook & Field Guide. LC 75-8909. (Illus.). 256p. 1976. 8.95 (ISBN 0-911104-76-3); pap. 5.95 (ISBN 0-911104-77-1). Workman Pub.

Tatum, George B. Philadelphia Georgian: The City House of Samuel Powel & Some of Its 18th-Century Neighbors. LC 75-39905. (Illus.). 1976. 22.50x (ISBN 0-8195-4095-1, Pub. by Wesleyan U Pr); pap. 10.95 (ISBN 0-8195-6044-8). Columbia U Pr.

Tatum, Jack & Kushner, Bill. They Call Me Assassin. 1980. pap. 2.95 (ISBN 0-380-52480-5, 52480). Avon.

Tatum, James. Apuleius & the Golden Ass. LC 78-74220. (Illus.). 1979. 15.00x (ISBN 0-8014-1163-7). Cornell U Pr.

Taub, A. W., ed. see Von Neumann, John.

Taub, Channa, ed. see Tallarico, Tony.

Taub, Harald, jt. auth. see Shute, Wilfrid E.

Taub, Herbert. Digital Circuits & Microprocessors. (Electrical Engineering Ser.). (Illus.). 608p. 1981. text ed. 26.95x (ISBN 0-07-062945-5, C); solutions manual 12.95 (ISBN 0-07-062946-3). McGraw.

Taub, Howard, jt. auth. see Walker, Leila J.

Taube, E. Louis. Food Allergy & the Allergic Patient: A Simple Review of Problems Encountered by the Recently Diagnosed Patient. rev. ed. 96p. 1978. pap. 6.50 (ISBN 0-398-02733-1). C C Thomas.

Taube, Mortimer. Computers & Common Sense: The Myth of Thinking Machines. LC 61-17079. 1961. 15.50x (ISBN 0-231-02516-5). Columbia U Pr.

Taube, Ursula, tr. see Poirier, Jacques & Dumas, Jean-Louis R.

Taubenblat, Pierre W. Copper Base Powder Metallurgy. LC 80-81464. (New Perspectives in Powder Metallurgy Ser.: Vol. 7). (Illus.). 232p. 1980. 42.00 (ISBN 0-918404-47-9). Metal Powder.

Taubenfeld, H. Sex-Based Discrimination, Release 1. 1980. 35.00. Oceana.

Tauber, Catherine A. Taxonomy & Biology of the Lacewing Genus Meleoma (Neuroptera: Chrysopidae) (U. C. Publ. in Entomology: Vol. 58). 1969. pap. 8.00x (ISBN 0-520-09131-0). U of Cal Pr.

Tauber, M. J. Biology, Behavior & Emergence Rhythm of Two Species of Fannia (Diptera: Muscidae) (U. C. Publ. in Entomology: Vol. 50). 1968. pap. 8.00x (ISBN 0-520-09122-1). U of Cal Pr.

Tauber, Maurice F. Technical Services in Libraries. LC 54-10328. (Columbia Library Service Studies, No. 7). 1954. 25.00 (ISBN 0-231-02054-6). Columbia U Pr.

Tauber, Maurice F. & Stephens, Irlene R., eds. Library Surveys. LC 67-25304. (Columbia Library Service Studies: No. 16). 1967. 22.50x (ISBN 0-231-03056-8). Columbia U Pr.

Taubes, Hella. Bible Speaks, 3 vols. Bloch, Lolla, tr. (Illus.). (gr. 4-6). 1974. 7.50x ea.; Set. 20.00x. Bloch.

Taubes, Tonia, tr. see Cobler, Sebastian.

Taubman, Howard, ed. WOXR Guide to Listening Pleasure. (Illus.). 1968. 6.95 o.s.i. (ISBN 0-02-616400-0). Macmillan.

Taubman, Hyman H. Opera: Front & Back. LC 80-2306. 1981. Repr. of 1938 ed. 51.50 (ISBN 0-404-18872-9). AMS Pr.

Taubman, P., ed. see Carnegie Commission on Higher Education.

Taubman, Paul, jt. auth. see Fromm, Gary.

Tauc, J. Photo & Thermoelectric Effects in Semiconductors. 1962. 27.00 (ISBN 0-08-009611-5); pap. 15.00 (ISBN 0-08-013636-2). Pergamon.

Tauchert, Theodore R. Energy Principles in Structural Mechanics. 394p. 1981. Repr. of 1974 ed. lib. bdg. price not set (ISBN 0-89874-309-5). Krieger.

Taulbee, Earl S., et al. The Minnesota Multiphasic Personality Inventory: A Comprehensive, Annotated Bibliography 1966-1975. 1981. write for info. (ISBN 0-87875-161-0). Whitston Pub.

Ta'unga. Works of Ta'unga: Records of a Polynesian Traveller in the South Seas, 1833-1896. Crocombe, Ron, ed. (Pacific History Ser.: No. 2). (Illus.). 1968. 7.50x (ISBN 0-87022-165-5). U Pr of Hawaii.

Tauraso, Nicola M. & Batzler, L. Richard. How to Benefit from Stress. 1979. 10.95 (ISBN 0-935710-00-0). Hidden Valley.

Tauro, P., et al. Introductory Microbiology. 432p. Date not set. text ed. 27.50 (ISBN 0-7069-1181-4, Pub. by Vikas India). Advent Bk.

Taussig, Ellen. Your Host Peter Gust of the Park Lane Restaurant. LC 79-17799. (Illus.). 1979. 14.95 (ISBN 0-89047-033-2). Herman Pub.

Taussig, Michael. The Devil & Commodity Fetishism in South America. LC 79-17685. xiii, 264p. 1980. 19.50x (ISBN 0-8078-1412-1). U of NC Pr.

Taussig, Michael K., jt. auth. see Seneca, Joseph J.

Tausworthe, Robert C. Standardized Development of Computer Software: Part 1, Methods. 1977. Pt. 2, Standards. 24.95 (ISBN 0-13-842195-1); 24.95 (ISBN 0-13-842203-6); comb. set (pts 1&2) 43.93 (ISBN 0-13-842211-7). P-H.

Tavakolian, Susan, ed. Language Acquisition & Linguistic Theory. (Illus.). 336p. 1981. text ed. 19.95x (ISBN 0-262-20039-2). MIT Pr.

Tavard, George H. The Vision of the Trinity. LC 80-5845. 166p. (Orig.). 1981. lib. bdg. 17.75 (ISBN 0-8191-1412-X); pap. text ed. 8.75 (ISBN 0-8191-1413-8). U Pr of Amer.

--A Way of Love. LC 76-22542. 1977. 6.95x o.p. (ISBN 0-88344-700-2). Orbis Bks.

Tavares, Ildazio. Ditado. (Bi-Lingual Port. -Eng.). 1981. pap. 1.50. Ghost Dance.

Tavel, Charles. The Third Industrial Age: Strategy for Business Survival. LC 79-40199. (Illus.). 356p. 1980. 23.00 (ISBN 0-08-022506-3). Pergamon.

Tavel, Morton E., ed. see Baragan, Joseph, et al.

Taves, Donald R., jt. ed. see Johansen, Erling.

Taves, Isabella. True Ghost Stories. (Illus.). (gr. 5 up). 1978. PLB 6.90 s&l (ISBN 0-531-02225-0). Watts.

--The Widow's Guide. LC 80-6219. 256p. 1981. 9.95 (ISBN 0-8052-3769-0). Schocken.

Tavolga, William N., ed. Sound Production in Fishes. LC 76-28352. (Benchmark Papers in Animal Behavior: Vol. 9). 1977. 42.50, by subscription 33.00 (ISBN 0-12-787515-8). Acad Pr.

Tavris, Carol & Sadd, Susan. The Redbook Report on Female Sexuality. 1977. 8.95 o.p. (ISBN 0-440-07560-2). Delacorte.

Tawa, Nicholas. Sweet Music for Gentle Americans. LC 78-71394. 1980. 21.95 (ISBN 0-87972-130-8); pap. 10.95 (ISBN 0-87972-157-X). Bowling Green Univ.

Tawaststjerna, Erik. Sibelius, Vol. 1. LC 75-13147. 330p. 1976. 38.50x (ISBN 0-520-03014-1). U of Cal Pr.

Tawes, William I. Creative Bird Carving. LC 79-107781. (Illus.). 1969. 8.50 (ISBN 0-87033-141-8, Pub. by Tidewater). Cornell Maritime.

--Creative Sculpture. LC 76-10862. (Illus.). 1976. 10.00 (ISBN 0-87033-219-8, Pub. by Tidewater). Cornell Maritime.

--God, Man, Salt Water & the Eastern Shore. 2nd ed. LC 77-5735. (Illus.). 1977. 7.50 (ISBN 0-87033-231-7, Pub. by Tidewater). Cornell Maritime.

Tawney, James, et al. Programmed Environments Curriculum for the Handicapped. (Special Education Ser.). 1979. text ed. 21.95 (ISBN 0-675-08265-X); instructor's manual 3.95 (ISBN 0-686-67290-9). Merrill.

Tawney, R. H., ed. see Wilson, Thomas.

Tawney, R. H., tr. from Chinese. Agrarian China: Selected Source Materials from Chinese Authors. (Studies in Chinese History & Civilization). 257p. 1977. Repr. of 1938 ed. 18.75 (ISBN 0-89093-084-8). U Pubns Amer.

Tawstron, E. M., jt. auth. see Coats, B. E.

Tax, Herman R. Podopediatrics. (Illus.). 376p. 1980. lib. bdg. 40.00 (ISBN 0-683-08117-9). Williams & Wilkins.

Tax, Meredith. Families. (Illus.). 32p. (ps-3). 1981. 7.95 (ISBN 0-316-83240-5, Pub. by Atlantic). Little.

Tax, Sol & Freeman, Leslie G., eds. Horizons of Anthropology. 2nd ed. LC 76-46247. (Illus.). 1977. text ed. 19.95x (ISBN 0-202-01157-7); pap. text ed. 11.95x (ISBN 0-202-01158-5). Aldine Pub.

Tax, Sol, ed. see International Congress Of Americanists - 29th.

Tay, William, ed. China & the West: Comparative Literature Studies. (New Asia Economic Bulletin Ser.). 306p. 1980. 18.95 (ISBN 0-295-95694-1, Pub. by Chinese Univ Hong Kong). U of Wash Pr.

Taya, Teizo, jt. ed. see Bigman, David.

Tayler, Charles B. Mark Wilton: The Merchant's Clerk, Repr. Of 1848. Bd. with Eric; or, Little by Little, 1858. Farrar, Frederick W. (Victorian Fiction Ser.). 1975. lib. bdg. 66.00 (ISBN 0-8240-1566-5). Garland Pub.

Tayler, Edward W. Nature & Art in Renaissance Literature. LC 64-20484. (Illus.). 1964. 15.00x (ISBN 0-231-02718-4). Columbia U Pr.

Tayler, R. J. & Everest, A. S. The Origin of the Chemical Elements. (Wykeham Science Ser.: No. 23). 1972. 9.95x (ISBN 0-8448-1150-5). Crane Russak Co.

--The Stars: Their Structure & Evolution. (Wykeham Science Ser.: No. 10). 1970. 11.75x (ISBN 0-8448-1112-2). Crane Russak Co.

Taylerson, A. W., jt. auth. see Chamberlain, W. H.

Taylor. All the World's Aircraft Nineteen Eighty to Nineteen Eighty-One. 1980. 135.00 (ISBN 0-531-03953-6). Watts.

--All the World's Aircraft Nineteen Seventy-Nine to Nineteen Eighty. 1980. 99.50 (ISBN 0-531-03915-3). Watts.

--Digital Filter Design Handbook. Date not set. price not set (ISBN 0-8247-1357-5). Dekker.

--Emergency Squads. (gr. 5 up). 1980. PLB 7.90 (ISBN 0-531-04117-4, A48). Watts.

--Endosseous Dental Implants. (Illus.). 1970. 19.25 (ISBN 0-407-16770-6). Butterworths.

--English & Japanese in Contrast. 1979. 6.95 (ISBN 0-88345-356-8). Regents Pub.

Taylor, jt. auth. see Hewett.

Taylor, A. Speaking in Public. 1979. pap. 12.95 (ISBN 0-13-825844-9). P-H.

Taylor, A., tr. see Baernreither, Joseph M.

Taylor, A., et al. Early Cambridgestive. (Cambridge Town, Gown & Country Ser.: Vol. 28). 192p. 1977. 20.00 (ISBN 0-900891-08-4). Oleander Pr.

Taylor, A. D. Campstoves, Fireplaces & Chimneys. (Illus.). 112p. pap. 6.00 (ISBN 0-8466-6055-5, JJU-55). Shorey.

Taylor, A. H. & Shearing, H. Financial & Cost Accounting for Management. 7th ed. (Illus.). 384p. 1979. pap. text ed. 15.95x (ISBN 0-7121-0633-2, Pub. by Macdonald & Evans England). Intl Ideas.

Taylor, A. J. Politicians, Socialism & Historians. LC 80-6217. 252p. 1981. 15.95 (ISBN 0-8128-2796-1). Stein & Day.

--The War Lords. LC 77-13962. 1978. 10.00 o.p. (ISBN 0-689-10840-0). Atheneum.

Taylor, A. M. Imagination & the Growth of Science. LC 67-14963. 1970. 3.95x (ISBN 0-8052-3108-0); pap. 1.75 (ISBN 0-8052-0257-9). Schocken.

Taylor, A. R. The Study of the Child. 215p. 1980. Repr. of 1910 ed. lib. bdg. 35.00. Telegraph Bks.

Taylor, A. R., ed. see Gordon, Eric V.

Taylor, A. W. & Noakes, G. R. Superconductivity. (Wykeham Science Ser.: No. 11). 1970. 9.95x (ISBN 0-8448-1113-0). Crane Russak Co.

Taylor, Alan J. English History, Nineteen Nineteen to Nineteen Forty-Five. LC 65-27513. 1970. pap. 7.95 (ISBN 0-19-500304-7, GB311, GB). Oxford U Pr.

--English History, 1919-1945. (Oxford History of England Ser). 1965. 33.00x (ISBN 0-19-821715-3). Oxford U Pr.

--Origins of the Second World War. 1978. pap. 2.25 (ISBN 0-449-30797-2, Prem). Fawcett.

--Struggle for Mastery in Europe: 1848-1918. 1954. 45.00x (ISBN 0-19-822101-0). Oxford U Pr.

Taylor, Albert W., ed. The Application of Science & Medicine to Sport. (Illus.). 352p. 1975. 32.75 (ISBN 0-398-02961-X). C C Thomas.

--The Scientific Aspects of Sports Training. (Illus.). 344p. 1975. text ed. 28.50 (ISBN 0-398-03028-6). C C Thomas.

Taylor, Alexander, tr. see Thorup, Kirsten.

Taylor, Alice. How to Be a Minister's Wife & Love It. 1968. pap. 3.95 (ISBN 0-310-33131-5). Zondervan.

Taylor, Alison. Off Stage & On: An Introduction to Youth Drama. 1968. pap. text ed. 4.50 (ISBN 0-08-012968-4). Pergamon.

Taylor, Allen. Bordertown Blues. 1981. pap. 1.95 (ISBN 0-8439-0854-8, Leisure Bks). Nordon Pubns.

Taylor, Angela E. & Muller, Ralph, eds. The Relevance of Parasitology to Human Welfare Today. (Symposia of the British Society for Parasitology: Vol. 16). (Illus.). 1978. pap. 19.75 (ISBN 0-632-00422-3, Blackwell). Mosby.

Taylor, Angus E. & Mann, Robert W. Advanced Calculus. 2nd ed. (Illus.). 900p. 1972. text ed. 26.95x (ISBN 0-471-00587-8). Wiley.

Taylor, Anita & Taylor, Robert. Couples: The Art of Staying Together. rev. ed. 1980. 4.95 (ISBN 0-87491-403-5). Acropolis.

Taylor, Anita, et al. Communicating. 2nd ed. (Ser.in Speech Communication). (Illus.). 1980. text ed. 14.95 (ISBN 0-13-153080-1). P-H.

Taylor, Ann, jt. auth. see Taylor, Jane.

Taylor, Ann M. Short Model Essays. (Orig.). 1981. pap. text ed. 6.95 (ISBN 0-316-83358-4); tchrs'. manual free (ISBN 0-316-83359-2). Little.

Taylor, Anne R. Male Novelists & Their Female Voices: Literary Masquerades. LC 80-50841. 238p. 1981. 15.00x (ISBN 0-87875-195-5). Whitston Pub.

Taylor, Anya. Magic & English Romanticism. LC 78-5590. 288p. 1979. 16.00x (ISBN 0-8203-0453-0). U of Ga Pr.

Taylor, Ariel Y. Numerology Made Plain. LC 80-19322. 147p. 1980. Repr. of 1973 ed. lib. bdg. 9.95x (ISBN 0-89370-612-4). Borgo Pr.

Taylor, Arnold H. Travail & Triumph: Black Life & Culture in the South Since the Civil War. LC 76-5264. (Contributions in Afro-American & African Studies: No. 26). (Orig.). 1976. lib. bdg. 17.95x (ISBN 0-8371-8912-8, TTT/). Greenwood.

Taylor, Arthur J. Laissez-Faire & State Intervention in Nineteenth-Century Britain. (Studies in Economic & Social History). 64p. (Orig.). 1972. pap. text ed. 4.00x (ISBN 0-333-09925-7). Humanities.

Taylor, Arthur J., ed. The Study of History: A Collection of Inaugural Lectures in Two Volumes. Incl. Vol. 1. Beginnings to Nineteen Forty-Five; Vol. 2. Nineteen Forty-Five to Present. 1980. 30.00x set (ISBN 0-7146-3125-6, F Cass Co). Biblio Dist.

Taylor, Arthur R. Brass Bands. 1979. 29.95x (ISBN 0-8464-0057-X). Beekman Pubs.

Taylor, B. The Green Avenue: The Life & Writings of Forrest Reid, 1875-1947. LC 79-41418. 200p. 1980. 29.50 (ISBN 0-521-22801-8). Cambridge U Pr.

Taylor, B. C. The Greeks Had a Word for It. 1973. pap. text ed. 2.00x (ISBN 0-8077-8018-9). Tchrs Coll.

--Latin Is Alive & Well. 1973. pap. text ed. 2.25x (ISBN 0-8077-8017-0). Tchrs Coll.

Taylor, Barbara J. When I Do, I Learn: A Guide to Creative Planning for Teachers & Parents of Preschool Children. rev. ed. LC 74-2122. (Illus.). 250p. 1977. text ed. 12.95x o.p. (ISBN 0-8425-0954-2); pap. 7.95x (ISBN 0-8425-1023-0). Brigham.

Taylor, Barry. The Parents' Guide to Education. 1978. 13.50 (ISBN 0-7153-7526-1). David & Charles.

Taylor, Basil, ed. Investment Analysis & Portfolio Management. 1970. 39.95 o.p. (ISBN 0-236-17611-0, Pub. by Paul Elek). Merrimack Bk Serv.

Taylor, Benjamin J. & White, Thurman J., eds. Issues & Ideas in America. LC 76-18769. 1976. 19.95x (ISBN 0-8061-1327-8); pap. 8.95 (ISBN 0-8061-1386-3). U of Okla Pr.

Taylor, Bernard. Cruelly Murdered. 384p. 1980. 17.95 (ISBN 0-285-62387-7, Pub. by Souvenir Pr England). Intl Schol Bk Serv.

--The Reaping. 236p. 1981. 9.95 (ISBN 0-312-66528-8). St Martin.

--Sweetheart, Sweetheart. 1979. pap. 2.25 o.p. (ISBN 0-345-27846-1). Ballantine.

Taylor, Bernard & Hussey, David, eds. The Realities of Planning. (Illus.). 224p. 1981. 36.00 (ISBN 0-08-022226-9). Pergamon.

Taylor, Bernard, jt. ed. see Farmer, David.

Taylor, Bess. Witch in the Shrouds: A Voyage in Miniature. 148p. (gr. 4-6). 1980. 6.95 (ISBN 0-8059-2720-4). Dorrance.

Taylor, Betty B. Making Thoughts Become: A Handbook for Teachers & Adults. (Illus.). 1978. pap. 4.25x (ISBN 0-933198-00-0, Pub. by Childs Art Carnival). Pub Ctr Cult Res.

Taylor, Bill. A Tale of Two Cities: The Mormons-Catholics. 1981. pap. 4.00 (ISBN 0-933046-02-2). Little Red Hen.

Taylor, Brian. Perspectives in Paedophilia. 160p. 1981. 42.50 (ISBN 0-7134-3718-9, Pub. by Batsford England); pap. 16.95 (ISBN 0-7134-3719-7). David & Charles.

Taylor, C. Hegel. LC 74-25642. 700p. 1975. 57.50 (ISBN 0-521-20679-0); pap. 14.95 (ISBN 0-521-29199-2). Cambridge U Pr.

--Hegel & Modern Society. LC 78-54727. (Modern European Philosophy). 1979. 28.95 (ISBN 0-521-22083-1); pap. 6.95 (ISBN 0-521-29351-0). Cambridge U Pr.

Taylor, C. & Morgan, K., eds. Numerical Methods in Laminar & Turbulent Flow. LC 78-16077. 1978. 68.95x (ISBN 0-470-26462-4). Halsted Pr.

Taylor, C. Barr, jt. auth. see Ferguson, James M.

Taylor, C. C., tr. see Plato.

Taylor, C. T. & Silberston, Z. A. The Economic Impact of the Patent System: A Study of the British Experiment. LC 73-77173. (Department of Applied Economics Monographs, No. 23). (Illus.). 400p. 1973. 54.00 (ISBN 0-521-20255-8). Cambridge U Pr.

Taylor, C. W., ed. Climate for Creativity. 312p. 1972. text ed. 23.00 (ISBN 0-08-016329-7). Pergamon.

Taylor, Cecelia M., jt. auth. see Mereness, Dorothy A.

Taylor, Charlene M., ed. see Etherege, George.

Taylor, Charles. Explanation of Behaviour. 1964. text ed. 17.00x (ISBN 0-391-00099-3); pap. text ed. 9.75x (ISBN 0-7100-0491-5). Humanities.

--Snow Job: Canada, the United States & Vietnam (1954-1973) LC 74-77028. 209p. 1974. pap. 7.95 (ISBN 0-88784-619-X, Pub. by Hse Anansi Pr Canada). U of Toronto Pr.

--Sounds of Music. (Illus.). 1978. 15.95 (ISBN 0-684-15476-5, ScribT). Scribner.

Taylor, Charles A. Images: A Unified View of Diffraction & Image Formation with All Kinds of Radiation. LC 77-94101. (Wykeham Science Ser: No. 46). (Illus.). 1978. pap. 14.50x (ISBN 0-8448-1379-6). Crane-Russak Co.

Taylor, Charles D. Show of Force. 384p. 1981. pap. 2.95 (ISBN 0-441-76197-6). Charter Bks.

--Show of Force. 1980. 11.95 (ISBN 0-312-72314-8). St Martin.

Taylor, Charles G. & Kane, Jason. Yellowhair. (Custeriana Monograph: No. 6). 1979. Repr. of 1977 ed. limited ed. 10.00 (ISBN 0-686-27216-1). Monroe County Lib.

Taylor, Charles L. Gleanings. 1979. 2.00 (ISBN 0-686-28779-7). Forward Movement.

Taylor, Charles L. & Hudson, Michael C. World Handbook of Political & Social Indicators. 2nd ed. LC 70-179479. (Illus.). 464p. 1972. 28.00x o.p. (ISBN 0-300-01555-0); pap. 8.95x (ISBN 0-300-01871-1). Yale U Pr.

Taylor, Charles R. The Destiny of America. pap. cancelled o.s.i. (ISBN 0-89728-025-3, 532831). Omega Pubns OR.

Taylor, Christopher. Fieldwork in Medieval Archaeology. 1975. 30.00 (ISBN 0-7134-2850-3, Pub. by Batsford England); pap. 14.50 (ISBN 0-7134-2872-4). David & Charles.

--Looking at Cows-Field Archaeology in the Nineteen-Eighties. 1980. pap. 1.25x (ISBN 0-686-64696-7, Pub. by Coun Brit Arch England). Intl Schol Bk Serv.

Taylor, Clara M. & Riddle, Katharine P., eds. Annotated International Bibliography of Nutrition Education. LC 71-132937. 1971. pap. text ed. 5.75x (ISBN 0-8077-2255-3). Tchrs Coll.

Taylor, Clarence R. How to Be a Successful Inventor: Patenting, Protecting, Marketing & Selling Your Invention. 1972. 6.50 o.p. (ISBN 0-682-47473-8, Banner). Exposition.

Taylor, Clive R. Hodgkin's Disease & the Lymphomas, Vol. 1. 1977. 24.00 (ISBN 0-904406-48-2). Eden Med Res.

--Hodgkin's Disease & the Lymphomas, Vol. 2, 1977. LC 78-300154. 1978. 28.80 (ISBN 0-88831-015-3). Eden Med Res.

--Hodgkin's Disease & the Lymphomas, Vol. 3. Horrobin, D. F., ed. LC 78-300154. (Annual Research Reviews). 1979. 31.20 (ISBN 0-88831-043-9). Eden Med Res.

Taylor, Cliver R. Hodgkin's Disease & the Lymphomas. Horrobin, D. F., ed. LC 78-300154. (Annual Reviews Ser.: Vol. 4). 374p. 1980. 38.00 (ISBN 0-88831-089-7). Eden Med Res.

Taylor, Craig, jt. ed. see Ferguson, James.

Taylor, Curtis B., jt. auth. see Lowe, Jim.

Taylor, D. A. Merchant Ship Construction. (Illus.). 240p. 1980. text ed. 39.95 (ISBN 0-408-00408-8). Butterworths.

Taylor, D. Jane, jt. ed. see Bulbrook, R. D.

Taylor, D. R. The Computer in Contemporary Cartography, Vol. 1. LC 79-42727. (Progress in Contemporary Cartography Ser.). 256p. 1980. 41.25 (ISBN 0-471-27699-5). Wiley.

Taylor, D. R., jt. auth. see Stohr, Walter.

Taylor, D. R. & Obudho, R. A., eds. The Computer & Africa: Applications, Problems & Potential. LC 76-2910. (Special Studies). 1977. text ed. 37.95 (ISBN 0-275-56820-2). Praeger.

Taylor, Daniel. Declination: A Study of the Linguistic Theory of Marcus Terrentius Varro. (Studies in the History of Linguistics: No. 2). 1979. text ed. 25.75x (ISBN 0-391-01642-3). Humanities.

Taylor, Daniel M. Explanation & Meaning: An Introduction to Philosophy. LC 73-116837. (Illus.). 1970. 23.95 (ISBN 0-521-07910-1); pap. 6.95x (ISBN 0-521-09617-0). Cambridge U Pr.

Taylor, David. Acting & the Stage. (Greek & Roman Topics Ser.). (Illus.). 1978. pap. text ed. 3.95x (ISBN 0-04-930008-3). Allen Unwin.

--The Dog: An Owner's Maintenance Manual. (Illus.). 96p. (Orig.). 1980. pap. 3.50 (ISBN 0-04-636012-3, 2505). Allen Unwin.

--Elementary Blueprint Reading for Machinists. LC 80-65572. (Blueprint Reading Ser.). 160p. 1981. pap. text ed. 4.60 (ISBN 0-8273-1895-2); instr's. guide 1.50 (ISBN 0-8273-1892-8). Delmar.

--Going Wild: Adventures of a Zoo Vet. LC 80-18432. (Illus.). 242p. 1981. 12.95 (ISBN 0-8128-2756-2). Stein & Day.

--Is There a Doctor in the Zoo. LC 78-2595. (Illus.). 1978. 8.95 o.p. (ISBN 0-397-01284-5). Lippincott.

--Zoo Vet: Adventures of a Wild Animal Doctor. LC 76-56834. 1977. 8.95 o.p. (ISBN 0-397-01207-1). Lippincott.

Taylor, David & Yapp, Michael, eds. Political Identity in South Asia. (Collected Papers on South Asia Ser.: No. 2). 1979. text ed. 11.75x (ISBN 0-391-01005-0). Humanities.

Taylor, David, ed. see National Computing Centre.

Taylor, David, jt. ed. see Robb, Peter.

Taylor, David L. Drill Press Work. LC 79-50536. (Metalworking Ser.). (gr. 8). 1980. pap. text ed. 5.08 (ISBN 0-8273-1823-5); instr's manual 1.50 (ISBN 0-8273-1824-3). Delmar.

Taylor, Dawson. Mastering Bowling. (Mastering Ser.). (Illus.). 1981. 12.95 (ISBN 0-8092-7049-8); pap. 6.95 (ISBN 0-8092-7047-1). Contemp Bks.

Taylor, Dawson & Bradley, James. Aim for a Job in Automotive Service. LC 68-11891. (Aim High Vocational Guidance Ser.). (Illus.). (gr. 7 up). 1977. PLB 5.97 (ISBN 0-8239-0091-6); PLB 5.97 large type ed. o.p. (ISBN 0-8239-0165-3). Rosen Pr.

Taylor, Dawson & Smith, Horton. Master's Secrets of Putting. 2nd rev. ed. (Illus.). 200p. 1982. price not set (ISBN 0-498-02513-6). A S Barnes.

Taylor, Dawson, jt. auth. see Anthony, Earl.

Taylor, Day. Moss Rose. 1980. pap. 2.75 (ISBN 0-440-15969-5). Dell.

Taylor, Deems. Of Men & Music. LC 80-2305. 1981. Repr. of 1937 ed. 36.00 (ISBN 0-404-18873-7). AMS Pr.

Taylor, Demetria. Apple Kitchen Cookbook. 1978. pap. 3.95 (ISBN 0-445-08525-8). Popular Lib.

Taylor, Dennis. Hardy's Poetry, Eighteen Sixty to Nineteen Twenty-Eight. 256p. 1980. 20.00x (ISBN 0-231-05050-X). Columbia U Pr.

Taylor, Derek. How to Sell Banquets. rev. ed. 224p. 1981. 16.95 (ISBN 0-8436-2198-2). CBI Pub.

Taylor, Donald. After the First Death. LC 72-93479. 176p. 1973. 5.95 o.p. (ISBN 0-8076-0675-8). Braziller.

Taylor, Donald, jt. auth. see Staudt, Thomas A.

Taylor, Donald H. & Glezen, G. William. Auditing: Integrated Concepts & Procedures. LC 78-16264. 1979. text ed. 24.95 (ISBN 0-471-84654-6); solutions manual avail. (ISBN 0-471-04565-9); tchrs. manual (ISBN 0-471-05296-5). Wiley.

--Case Study in Auditing. LC 78-27496. 1979. pap. text ed. 13.50x (ISBN 0-471-04626-4); tchrs. manual avail. (ISBN 0-471-05297-3). Wiley.

Taylor, Dorice. Sun Valley. (Illus.). 264p. 1980. 20.00 (ISBN 0-9605212-0-8). Ex Libris Sun.

Taylor, Duane R. Home Rule in the District of Columbia: The First 500 Days. LC 78-58442. 1978. pap. text ed. 11.25 (ISBN 0-8191-0535-X). U Pr of Amer.

Taylor, Duncan N. The Celts. LC 74-17779. (Emergence of Man Ser.). (gr. 6 up). 1974. PLB 9.63 o.p. (ISBN 0-8094-1286-1, Pub. by Time-Life). Silver.

Taylor, E. O., jt. auth. see Say, M. G.

Taylor, Earl R., compiled by. A Checklist of the Robert A Feer Collection of World Fairs of North America. pap. 3.00. Boston Public Lib.

Taylor, Edward. The Poems of Edward Taylor. Stanford, Donald, ed. LC 60-6432. 1977. pap. 6.95x (ISBN 0-300-02134-8). Yale U Pr.

--Poetical Works of Edward Taylor. Johnson, Thomas H., ed. 1944. pap. 4.95 (ISBN 0-691-01275-X). Princeton U Pr.

Taylor, Edward S. Dimensional Analysis for Engineers. (Illus.). 174p. 1974. text ed. 29.95x (ISBN 0-19-856122-9). Oxford U Pr.

Taylor, Edwin, jt. auth. see Evans, Harold.

Taylor, Edwin F. & Wheeler, John A. Spacetime Physics. LC 65-13566. (Physics Ser.). (Illus.). 1966. pap. text ed. 9.95x (ISBN 0-7167-0336-X); answer book avail. W H Freeman.

Taylor, Elaine A., jt. auth. see Leonard, Jon N.

Taylor, Elizabeth W., tr. see Gernhardt, Robert.

Taylor, Eric. The House of Commons at Work. 9th ed. 1979. text ed. 18.25x (ISBN 0-333-23319-0). Humanities.

Taylor, Esther. Colorblind. Date not set. 12.95 (ISBN 0-87949-136-1). Ashley Bks.

Taylor, Evelyn, jt. auth. see Hausmann, Renee.

Taylor, F., jt. auth. see Kingsley, D.

Taylor, F., et al. Foundry Engineering. LC 59-11811. 1959. 27.95 (ISBN 0-471-84843-3). Wiley.

Taylor, F. A., ed. see Voltaire, Francois.

Taylor, F. E., jt. auth. see Down, P. J.

Taylor, F. J. The Right Way to a Good Job. 174p. 1979. pap. 9.75x (ISBN 0-220-66364-5, Pub. by Busn Bks England). Renouf.

Taylor, F. K. The Concepts of Illness, Disease & Morbus. LC 78-15123. 1979. 18.95 (ISBN 0-521-22433-0). Cambridge U Pr.

Taylor, F. R., jt. auth. see Hickson, D. C.

Taylor, Florence M. Hid in My Heart: The Word of God in Times of Need. 1974. 5.95 (ISBN 0-8164-1186-7). Crossroad NY.

--You Don't Have to Be Old When You Grow Old. 1979. pap. 3.95 o.p. (ISBN 0-88270-349-8). Logos.

Taylor, Francine. Race, School & Community: A Survey of Research & Literature. (General Ser.). 200p. 1974. pap. text ed. 12.00x (ISBN 0-85633-033-7, NFER). Humanities.

Taylor, Frank J., jt. auth. see Albright, Horace M.

Taylor, Frank S. A Survey of Greek Alchemy. LC 79-8627. Repr. of 1930 ed. 12.50 (ISBN 0-404-18493-6). AMS Pr.

Taylor, Fred I. & Smith, Steve L. Digital Signal Processing in Fortran. LC 75-28940. 192p. 1976. 27.95 (ISBN 0-669-00330-1). Lexington Bks.

Taylor, Fred M. Some Chapters on Money. LC 79-1594. 1981. Repr. of 1906 ed. 23.50 (ISBN 0-88355-899-8). Hyperion Conn.

Taylor, Frederick W. Principles of Scientific Management. 1967. pap. 4.95 (ISBN 0-393-00398-1, Norton Lib). Norton.

--The Principles of Scientific Management. 1923p. 1980. lib. bdg. 30.00 (ISBN 0-8495-5162-5). Arden Lib.

--Shop Management. 207p. 1980. Repr. of 1911 ed. lib. bdg. 30.00 (ISBN 0-8495-5200-1). Arden Lib.

Taylor, G. A. Organic Chemistry for Students of Biology & Medicine. 2nd ed. LC 77-2193. (Illus.). 1978. pap. text ed. 14.95x (ISBN 0-582-44041-6). Longman.

Taylor, G. J., jt. auth. see Fodor, R. V.

Taylor, G. R., jt. auth. see Jackson, S. E.

Taylor, G. Rattray. Sex in History. LC 76-139982. 1954. 12.50 (ISBN 0-8149-0220-0). Vanguard.

Taylor, G. Thomas, Jr., jt. auth. see Horan, James F.

Taylor, G. W., jt. auth. see Burfoot, J. C.

Taylor, Ganell. A Book of Rejects. 1980. 6.95 (ISBN 0-533-04796-X). Vantage.

Taylor, Gardner C., jt. auth. see Edwards, O. C., Jr.

Taylor, Geoffrey, jt. ed. see Betjeman, John.

Taylor, Geoffrey I. Scientific Papers, 4 vols. Batchelor, G. K., ed. Incl. Vol. 1. Mechanics of Solids. 90.00 (ISBN 0-521-06608-5); Vol. 2. Meteorology, Oceanography & Turbulent Flow. 1960. 90.00 (ISBN 0-521-06609-3); Vol. 3. Aerodynamics & the Mechanics of Projectiles & Explosions. 1963. 90.00 (ISBN 0-521-06610-7); Vol. 4. Mechanics of Fluids: Miscellaneous Topics. (Illus.). 1971. 90.00 (ISBN 0-521-07995-0). Cambridge U Pr.

Taylor, George. Japanese Sponsored Regime in North China. LC 78-4330. (The Modern Chinese Economy Ser.). 145p. 1980. lib. bdg. 16.50 (ISBN 0-8240-4287-5). Garland Pub.

Taylor, George & Ayres, N. Born & Bred Unequal. (Sociology of Education Ser). 1969. text ed. 6.00x (ISBN 0-582-32441-6); pap. text ed. 3.50x (ISBN 0-582-32442-4). Humanities.

Taylor, George, jt. ed. see Clarke, D. L.

Taylor, George see Jackson, B. D., et al.

Taylor, George A., jt. ed. see Palumbo, Dennis.

Taylor, George E. The Livestock of China. LC 78-74304. (The Modern Chinese Economy Ser.). 174p. 1980. lib. bdg. 22.00 (ISBN 0-8240-4286-7). Garland Pub.

Taylor, George R. & Jackson, Stanley E. Educational Strategies & Services for Exceptional Children. (Illus.). 276p. 1976. 19.75 (ISBN 0-398-03530-X). C C Thomas.

Taylor, George R., compiled by. American Economic History Before 1860. LC 70-79173. (Goldentree Bibliographies in American History Ser). (Orig.). 1969. pap. 6.95x (ISBN 0-88295-526-8). AHM Pub.

Taylor, Gerard W. & Wilkinson, John F. Clinical Surgery: Vascular Surgery & Reticulo-Endothelial System, Vol. 14. (Illus.). 1967. 22.00 o.p. (ISBN 0-397-58012-6). Lippincott.

Taylor, Glenn. Windsurfing: The Complete Guide. 288p. 1980. pap. 7.95 (ISBN 0-07-063154-9, GB). McGraw.

Taylor, H., ed. Edward J. Dent: Selected Essays. LC 78-62111. (Illus.). 1979. 34.50 (ISBN 0-521-22174-9). Cambridge U Pr.

Taylor, H. M. Anglo-Saxon Architecture. LC 65-3244. (Illus.). 1978. Vol. 1, 1965. 90.00 (ISBN 0-521-22481-0); Vol. 2. 85.00 (ISBN 0-521-22482-9); Vol. 3. 105.00 (ISBN 0-521-21692-3); Set. 235.00 (ISBN 0-521-21693-1). Cambridge U Pr.

Taylor, H. M. & Taylor, Joan. Anglo-Saxon Architecture, 2 vols. LC 65-3244. (Illus.). 868p. 1981. pap. 39.50 (ISBN 0-521-29914-4). Cambridge U Pr.

Taylor, Halsey P. & Taylor, Sheila F. Read to Write. 1980. pap. text ed. 7.95x (ISBN 0-673-15388-6). Scott F.

Taylor, Harold. On Education & Freedom. LC 53-13096. (Arcturus Books Paperbacks). 320p. 1967. pap. 2.65 (ISBN 0-8093-0246-2). S Ill U Pr.

Taylor, Helen L. Little Pilgrim's Progress. (gr. 2-6). pap. 2.50 (ISBN 0-8024-0003-5). Moody.

Taylor, Henry. Doctor to Basuto, Boer & Briton, 1877-1906: Memoirs of Dr. Henry Taylor. Hadley, Peter, ed. (Illus.). 213p. 1972. 10.50x (ISBN 0-8476-2394-7). Rowman.

Taylor, Henry O. English Mind. 1962. pap. 0.95 o.s.i. (ISBN 0-02-067750-2, Collier). Macmillan.

Taylor, Howard & Taylor, Mrs. Howard. J. Hudson Taylor: God's Man in China. 1977. pap. 6.95 (ISBN 0-8024-4225-0). Moody.

Taylor, Howard E., jt. auth. see Wade, Thomas L.

Taylor, Howard F. The I.Q. Game: A Methodological Inquiry into the Heredity-Environment Controversy. 300p. 1980. 19.50 (ISBN 0-8135-0902-5). Rutgers U Pr.

Taylor, Howard M., jt. auth. see Karlin, Samuel.

Taylor, Mrs. Howard. Behind the Ranges. 1980. pap. 3.95 (ISBN 0-85363-003-8). OMF Bks.

Taylor, Hudson. Union & Communion. 1971. pap. 1.95 (ISBN 0-87123-571-4, 200571). Bethany Fell.

Taylor, Hudson & Thompson, Phyllis. God's Adventurer. (Illus.). 1978. pap. 2.25 (ISBN 0-85363-094-1). OMF Bks.

Taylor, Hudson J. To China with Love. Orig. Title: A Retrospect, China Inland Mission Mid-1900s. 1972. pap. 1.95 (ISBN 0-87123-549-8, 200549). Bethany Fell.

Taylor, Iain W., tr. see Czech, Danuta, et al.

Taylor, Ian, et al. Critical Criminology. (International Library of Sociology). 1975. 22.50x (ISBN 0-7100-8023-9); pap. 10.95 (ISBN 0-7100-8024-7). Routledge & Kegan.

--New Criminology: For a Social Theory of Deviance. 1974. pap. 6.95x (ISBN 0-06-131812-4, TB1812, Torch). Har-Row.

--The New Criminology: For a Social Theory of Deviance. (International Library of Sociology). 342p. 1973. 19.95x o.p. (ISBN 0-7100-7472-7). Routledge & Kegan.

Taylor, Ida S. The Year Book of American Authors. 372p. 1980. lib. bdg. 30.00 (ISBN 0-89760-899-2). Telegraph Bks.

Taylor, Irving A. & Getzels, Jacob W., eds. Perspectives in Creativity. LC 74-22645. 392p. 1975. lib. bdg. 20.95x (ISBN 0-202-25121-7). Aldine Pub.

Taylor, Irwin. Public Schools: A Treatise on the Rights, Powers, Duties & Liabilities of School Boards, Officers & Teachers. 411p. 1980. Repr. of 1893 ed. lib. bdg. 30.00x (ISBN 0-8377-1204-1). Rothman.

Taylor, Isaac. Names & Their Histories. LC 68-17936. 1969. Repr. of 1898 ed. 22.00 (ISBN 0-8103-4217-0). Gale.

--Words & Places, or Etymological Illustrations of History, Ethnology, & Geography. 4th ed. 1968. Repr. of 1909 ed. 20.00 (ISBN 0-8103-3240-X). Gale.

Taylor, J. A. Climatic Resources & Economic Activity. LC 74-823. (Illus.). 264p. 1974. 21.95 (ISBN 0-470-84826-X). Halsted Pr.

Taylor, J. B. Plastering. 3rd ed. (Illus.). 257p. 1980. 27.50x (ISBN 0-7114-5588-0). Intl Ideas.

--Plastering: A Practical Handbook. 3rd ed. (Illus.). 1980. 27.50x. Intl Ideas.

Taylor, J. C. Gauge Theories of Weak Interactions. LC 75-9092. (Cambridge Monographs on Mathematical Physics). (Illus.). 200p. 1976. 47.95 (ISBN 0-521-20896-3); pap. 12.95x (ISBN 0-521-29518-1). Cambridge U Pr.

Taylor, J. F. Owen Roe O'Neill. 1981. Repr. 7.50 (ISBN 0-916620-27-1). Portals Pr.

Taylor, J. F., et al. Introduction to Literature & the Fine Arts. (Illus.). 418p. 1950. text ed. 10.00x (ISBN 0-87013-037-4). Mich St U Pr.

Taylor, J. G. Quantum Mechanics: An Introduction. (Unwin Studies in Physics & Applie Mathematics Ser.). 1970. text ed. 6.95x o.p. (ISBN 0-04-530014-3). Allen Unwin.

Taylor, J. Garth. Netsilik Eskimo Material Culture: The Roald Amundsen Collection from King William Island. (Illus.). 1974. pap. 17.00x (ISBN 8-200-08945-2, Dist. by Columbia U Pr). Universitet.

Taylor, J. Golden, ed. Literature of the American West. LC 71-132448. 1971. pap. text ed. 12.25 (ISBN 0-395-05458-3). HM.

Taylor, Jack R. & Hawkins, C. S. When Revival Comes. LC 80-66956. 1980. pap. 4.25 (ISBN 0-8054-6226-0). Broadman.

Taylor, James B. & Randolph, Jerry. Community Worker. LC 74-34067. 148p. 1975. 17.50x (ISBN 0-87668-191-7). Aronson.

Taylor, James C., jt. auth. see Bryson, Harold T.

Taylor, James R. The Intrinsic Inertia Universe. (Illus.). xii, 244p. 1971. 10.95 o.p. (ISBN 0-685-25833-5). Trend House.

Taylor, Jane & Taylor, Ann. Original Poems for Infant Minds, Repr. Of 1805 Ed. Bd. with Rhymes for the Nursery. Repr. of 1806 ed. LC 75-32151. (Classics of Children's Literature, 1621-1932: Vol. 17). 1977. PLB 38.00 (ISBN 0-8240-2265-3). Garland Pub.

Taylor, Jay. China & Southeast Asia: Peking's Relations with Revolutionary Movements. expanded & updated ed. LC 76-3679. (Praeger Special Studies Ser.). 416p. 1976. text ed. 27.95 (ISBN 0-275-56830-X); pap. text ed. 11.95 (ISBN 0-275-64490-1). Praeger.

Taylor, Jean, jt. auth. see Prichard, Allyn.

Taylor, Jennifer, jt. auth. see Andrews, John.

Taylor, Jenny & Ingleby, Terry. Seven Silly Stories. Incl. The Fox & Stork; Brer Rabbit & the Honey Pot; Noisy Neville; Mr. Stupid; The Foolish Tortoise; The Well Diggers; The Miller & His Donkey. (gr. k-4). 1976. pap. text ed. 15.60 set (ISBN 0-8372-2222-2). Bowmar-Noble.

Taylor, Jerome, tr. see Chenu, M. D.

Taylor, Jim, jt. auth. see Armstrong, Harvey.

Taylor, Joan. Asking for It. 258p. 1980. 9.95 (ISBN 0-312-92027-X). Congdon & Lattes.

--Asking for It. 258p. 1980. 10.95 (ISBN 0-312-92027-X). St Martin.

Taylor, Joan, jt. auth. see Taylor, H. M.

Taylor, Joan J. Bronze Age Goldwork of the British Isles. LC 75-12160. (Gulbenkian Archaeological Ser.). (Illus.). 188p. 1981. 95.00 (ISBN 0-521-20802-5). Cambridge U Pr.

Taylor, Joan P. Manual of Respiratory Therapy. 2nd ed. LC 77-22882. (Illus.). 1978. pap. text ed. 13.95 (ISBN 0-8016-0836-8). Mosby.

Taylor, Jody. A Child's Very Own First Book. (Gingerbread Bks.). (Illus.). (ps-2). 1980. 2.50 (ISBN 0-525-69035-2, Gingerbread); PLB 5.95 (ISBN 0-525-69036-0, Gingerbread). Dutton.

Taylor, Joe G. Louisiana: A Bicentennial History. (States & the Nation Ser.). (Illus.). 1976. 12.95 (ISBN 0-393-05602-3, Co-Pub by AASLH). Norton.

Taylor, John. Black Holes: The End of the Universe? 1975. pap. 2.25 (ISBN 0-380-00327-9, 46805). Avon.

--British Airports. pap. 3.00x (ISBN 0-392-07261-0, SpS). Soccer.

--Construction Construed & Constitutions Vindicated. LC 77-117311. (American Constitutional & Legal History Ser). 1970. Repr. of 1820 ed. lib. bdg. 35.00 (ISBN 0-306-71983-5). Da Capo.

--New Views of the Constitution of the United States. LC 75-124903. (American Constitutional & Legal History Ser). 1971. Repr. of 1823 ed. lib. bdg. 32.50 (ISBN 0-306-71996-7). Da Capo.

--Science & the Supernatural. 1980. 10.95 (ISBN 0-525-19790-7). Dutton.

--Superminds. 1977. pap. 1.95 o.s.i. (ISBN 0-446-89032-4). Warner Bks.

Taylor, John G. Special Relativity. (Oxford Physics Ser). (Illus.). 118p. 1975. 10.95x o.p. (ISBN 0-19-851823-4). Oxford U Pr.

Taylor, John H. The Half-Way Generation: A Study of Asian Youth in Newcastle-Upon-Tyne. 1976. pap. text ed. 17.00x (ISBN 0-85633-081-7, NFER). Humanities.

Taylor, John L. & Walford, Rex. Learning & the Simulation Game. LC 78-21338. (Illus.). 228p. 1979. 17.50 (ISBN 0-8039-1207-2). Sage.

--Learning & the Simulation Game. LC 78-21338. (Illus.). 228p. 1979. pap. 8.50 (ISBN 0-8039-1208-0). Sage.

--Learning & the Stimulation Game. LC 78-21338. (Illus.). 228p. 1979. 17.50 (ISBN 0-8039-1207-2). Sage.

Taylor, John R. How to Start & Succeed in a Business of Your Own. 1978. ref. ed. 15.95 (ISBN 0-8359-2927-2); instrs'. manual avail. Reston.

--Rise & Fall of the Well Made Play. LC 67-25684. 1967. pap. 1.95 o.p. (ISBN 0-8090-0546-8, Drama). Hill & Wang.

--Scattering Theory. LC 75-37938. 536p. 1972. 26.95 (ISBN 0-471-84900-6). Wiley.

Taylor, John R., ed. see Osborne, John.

Taylor, John R., intro. by. Masterworks of the British Cinema. Incl. Brief Encounter. Lean, David; The Third Man. Reed, Carol; Kind Hearts & Coronets. Hamer, Robert; Saturday Night & Sunday Morning. Reisz, Karel. LC 74-11709. (Icon Editions). (Illus.). 352p. 1975. pap. 4.95 o.s.i. (ISBN 0-06-430060-9, IN-60, HarpT). Har-Row.

Taylor, John V. The Go-Between God: The Holy Spirit & the Christian Mission. 1979. pap. 4.95x (ISBN 0-19-520125-6). Oxford U Pr.

Taylor, John W. Pictorial History of the R.A.F, 3 vols. Incl. Vol. 1. 1918-1939. 202p. 1969. 5.95 (ISBN 0-668-01857-7); Vol. 2. 1939-1945. Moyes, Philip J. 240p. 1968. o. p. 5.95 (ISBN 0-668-02137-3); Vol. 3. 1945-1969. Moyes, Philip J. 208p. 1970. 5.95 o.p. (ISBN 0-668-02421-6). LC 69-12569. (Illus.). Arco.

Taylor, John W. & Swanborough, Gordon. Civil Aircraft of the World. 3rd. ed. LC 77-74718. (Illus.). 1978. 9.95 (ISBN 0-684-15224-X, ScribT). Scribner.

Taylor, John W., ed. Jane's All the World's Aircraft 1976-77. 1976. 72.50 o.p. (ISBN 0-531-03260-4). Watts.

--Jane's Pocket Book of Helicopters. (Illus.). 260p. 1981. pap. 8.95 (ISBN 0-686-69548-8, Collier). Macmillan.

Taylor, John W., ed. see Jane's Pocket Books.

Taylor, Joseph H., jt. auth. see Manchester, Richard N.

Taylor, Joseph L. Measure Algebras. LC 73-5930. (CBMS Regional Conference Series in Mathematics: No. 16). 1979. pap. 7.20 (ISBN 0-8218-1666-7, CBMS-16). Am Math.

Taylor, Joshua C. The Fine Arts in America. LC 78-23643. (History of American Civilization Ser.: No. 27). xvi, 264p. 1981. pap. 7.95 (ISBN 0-226-79151-3). U of Chicago Pr.

--To See Is to Think: Looking at American Art. LC 74-26647. (Illus.). 117p. 1975. pap. 7.95 (ISBN 0-87474-177-7). Smithsonian.

Taylor, Joshua C., et al. Perceptions & Evocations: The Art of Elihu Vedder. LC 78-9915. (Illus.). 246p. 1979. 27.50 (ISBN 0-87474-902-6); pap. 15.50 (ISBN 0-87474-903-4). Smithsonian.

Taylor, Joy. The Foundations of Maths in the Infant School. (Unwin Education Books). 1976. text ed. 17.95x o.p. (ISBN 0-04-372014-5); pap. text ed. 7.50x o.p. (ISBN 0-04-372015-3). Allen Unwin.

Taylor, Joyce. Horses in Suburbia. (Illus.). 5.25 (ISBN 0-85131-085-0, Dist. by Sporting Book Center). J A Allen.

Taylor, Julie. Eva Peron: The Myths of a Woman. LC 79-19547. x, 176p. 1981. pap. write for info. (ISBN 0-226-79144-0). U of Chicago Pr.

--Eva Peron: The Myths of a Woman. LC 79-19547. (Illus.). 1980. 15.00 (ISBN 0-226-79143-2); pap. 5.95 (ISBN 0-226-79144-0). U of Chicago Pr.

Taylor, June & Yokell, Michael. Yellowcake: The International Uranium Cartel. (Pergamon Policy Studies). 1980. text ed. 33.00 (ISBN 0-08-022473-3). Pergamon.

Taylor, Katharine W. Parents & Children Learn Together. 2nd ed. LC 67-21500. 1968. pap. text ed. 8.95x (ISBN 0-8077-2257-X). Tchrs Coll.

--Parents & Children Learn Together: Parent Cooperative Nursery Schools. 3rd ed. 1981. pap. 6.95 (ISBN 0-8077-2638-9). Tchrs Coll.

Taylor, Kathryn S. & Hamblin, Stephen F. Handbook of Wild Flower Cultivation. (Illus.). 1962. 12.95 (ISBN 0-02-616760-3). Macmillan.

Taylor, Keith. The Political Ideas of the Utopian Socialists. 1981. 27.50x (ISBN 0-7146-3089-6, F Cass Co). Biblio Dist.

Taylor, Kenneth J. & Viscomi, Gregory N. Ultrasound in Emergency Medicine. (Clinics in Diagnostic Ultrasound). (Illus.). 225p. 1981. lib. bdg. 20.50 (ISBN 0-443-08156-5). Churchill.

Taylor, Kenneth N. Bible in Pictures for Little Eyes. (Illus.). (gr. 3-6). 1956. 7.95 (ISBN 0-8024-0595-9). Moody.

--Living Bibles International. 1979. pap. 6.20. Liv Bibles Intl.

Taylor, Kenneth N., tr. see Reid, J. Calvin.

Taylor, L. B., Jr. Chemistry Careers. (Career Concise Guides Ser.). (Illus.). (gr. 7 up). 1978. PLB 6.45 s&l (ISBN 0-531-01420-7). Watts.

--Rescue: True Stories of Heroism. (Illus.). (gr. 5 up). 1978. PLB 6.90 s&l (ISBN 0-531-02223-4). Watts.

--Shoplifting. (gr. 7 up). 1979. PLB 7.90 s&l (ISBN 0-531-02877-1). Watts.

Taylor, L. J., ed. A Librarian's Handbook, Vol. 1. 1977. pap. 33.00x (ISBN 0-85365-079-9, Pub. by Lib Assn England). Oryx Pr.

--A Librarian's Handbook, Vol. 2. 1980. pap. 49.50x (ISBN 0-85365-651-7, Pub. by Lib Assn England). Oryx Pr.

Taylor, L. O., et al. American Secondary School. LC 60-6321. 1960. text ed. 24.00x (ISBN 0-89197-021-5); pap. text ed. 10.95x (ISBN 0-89197-022-3). Irvington.

Taylor, L. R., jt. auth. see Lewis, Trevor.

Taylor, Lawrence. Trail of the Fox: The True Story of a Perfect Crime. 1980. 13.95 (ISBN 0-671-25227-5). S&S.

--A Trial of Generals: Homma, Yamashita, MacArthur. (Illus.). 260p. 1981. 13.95 (ISBN 0-89651-775-6). Icarus.

Taylor, Lawrence, jt. auth. see Purver, Jonathan.

Taylor, Lee. Idea People. LC 74-17805. 224p. 1975. 17.95 (ISBN 0-88229-149-1). Nelson-Hall.

Taylor, Lester. Telecommunications Demand: A Survey & Critique. 1980. 29.50 (ISBN 0-88410-496-6). Ballinger Pub.

Taylor, Lily R. Party Politics in the Age of Caesar. (Sather Classical Lectures: No. 22). 1949. pap. 5.95x (ISBN 0-520-01257-7, CAMPUS53). U. of Cal Pr.

--Roman Voting Assemblies: From the Hannibalic War to the Dictatorship of Caesar. LC 66-17025. (Jerome Lecture Ser). (Illus.). 1966. 7.50 o.p. (ISBN 0-472-04906-2). U of Mich Pr.

Taylor, Linda K. Not for Bread Alone: An Appreciation of Job Enrichment. 3rd ed. 202p. 1980. pap. 12.25x (ISBN 0-220-67019-6, Pub. by Busn Bks England). Renouf.

Taylor, Lisa, ed. Urban Open Spaces. (Illus.). 1981. pap. 9.95 (ISBN 0-8478-0304-X). Rizzoli Intl.

Taylor, Lloyd C., Jr. Margaret Ayer Barnes. (U. S. Authors Ser.: No. 231). 1974. lib. bdg. 10.95 (ISBN 0-8057-0037-4). Twayne.

Taylor, Louis. Ride American. LC 63-10624. (Illus.). 1963. 9.95 o.s.i. (ISBN 0-06-006720-9, HarpT). Har-Row.

--Ride Western: A Complete Guide to Western Horsemanship. LC 68-15998. (Illus.). 1968. 10.95 o.p. (ISBN 0-06-006696-2, HarpT). Har-Row.

Taylor, Lynda, jt. auth. see Worthington, Bonnie.

Taylor, Lynda K. A Fairer Slice of the Cake: The Task Ahead. 228p. 1976. text ed. 21.00x (ISBN 0-220-66284-3, Pub. by Busn Bks England). Renouf.

Taylor, Marcia W. A Computer Simulation of Innovative Decision-Making in Organizations. LC 78-56051. 1978. pap. text ed. 7.75 (ISBN 0-8191-0517-1). U Pr of Amer.

Taylor, Margaret. Basic Reference Sources: A Self-Study Manual. 2nd ed. LC 73-14500. 1981. 12.50 (ISBN 0-8108-0662-2). Scarecrow.

Taylor, Marion A. Bottom, Thou Art Translated: Political Allegory in a Midsummer Night's Dream & Related Literature. LC 72-83545. 253p. (Orig.). 1973. pap. text ed. 20.00x (ISBN 90-6203-038-6). Humanities.

Taylor, Mark. Young Melvin & Bulger. LC 79-7118. (Illus.). 48p. (gr. 4-6). 1981. 7.95a (ISBN 0-385-15190-X); PLB (ISBN 0-385-15191-8). Doubleday.

Taylor, Mark, jt. auth. see Arbuthnot, May H.

Taylor, Mark, ed. see Will, Paul J., et al.

Taylor, Mark C. Journeys to Selfhood: Hegel & Kierkegaard. 264p. 1981. 22.50x (ISBN 0-520-04167-4); pap. 7.95 (ISBN 0-520-04176-3, CAL 483). U. of Cal Pr.

Taylor, Mark C., et al. Religion & the Human Image. (Illus.). 1977. pap. text ed. 10.95x (ISBN 0-13-773424-7). P-H.

Taylor, Martin C., jt. auth. see Rudd, Margaret T.

Taylor, Marvin J. Introduction to Christian Education. 412p. 1975. pap. 8.50 (ISBN 0-687-19498-9). Abingdon.

Taylor, Mary & Dyk, Carol. Book of Rounds. 1977. pap. 14.95 (ISBN 0-87690-182-8). Dutton.

Taylor, Mary A. Romance in the Headlines. Bd. with Bon Voyage, My Darling. 1980. pap. 1.95 (ISBN 0-451-09175-2, J9175, Sig). NAL.

Taylor, Mary M., ed. School Library and Media Center Acquisitions Policies & Procedures. 1981. lib. bdg. 17.50 (ISBN 0-912700-70-X). Oryx Pr.

Taylor, Maurice. Island Hopping Through the Indonesian Archipelago. (Illus.). 1976. 19.95x o.p. (ISBN 0-905064-10-0). Intl Learn Syst.

--South American Survival: A Handbook for the Independent Traveller. (Illus.). 1977. 19.95x o.p. (ISBN 0-905064-12-7). Intl Learn Syst.

Taylor, Maxwell, et al. Operations Zapata: The "Ultrasensitive" Report & Testimony of the Board of Inquiry on the Bay of Pigs. 1980. 24.00 (ISBN 0-89093-185-2); pap. 8.00 (ISBN 0-89093-186-0). U Pubns Amer.

Taylor, Michael, jt. auth. see Hix, Charles.

Taylor, Michael A., ed. The Neuropsychiatric Mental Status Examination: A Phenomenologic Program Text. Date not set. text ed. price not set (ISBN 0-89335-130-X). Spectrum Pub.

Taylor, Michael E. Pseudodifferential Operators. LC 80-8580. (Princeton Mathematical Ser.: No. 34). 468p. 1981. 30.00x (ISBN 0-691-08282-0). Princeton U Pr.

Taylor, Michael J. Missles of the World. 3rd, rev. ed. 1980. 14.95 (ISBN 0-684-16593-7, ScribT). Scribner.

Taylor, Michael J., ed. The Sacraments: Readings in Contemporary Theology. LC 80-9534. 274p. (Orig.). 1981. pap. 7.95 (ISBN 0-8189-0406-2). Alba.

Taylor, Monica. Progress & Problems in Moral Education. (General Ser.). 239p. 1975. pap. text ed. 17.50x (ISBN 0-85633-069-8, NFER). Humanities.

Taylor, Monica, ed. see Close, John J., et al.

Taylor, O. R., ed. see De Voltaire, Framcois M.

Taylor, P. & Johnson, M., eds. Curriculum Development. (General Ser.). 200p. 1974. pap. text ed. 16.00x (ISBN 0-85633-035-3, NFER). Humanities.

Taylor, P. A. A Dictionary of Economic Terms. rev. ed. 1968. pap. 1.95 o.s.i. (ISBN 0-7100-6100-5). Routledge & Kegan.

Taylor, P. A., jt. auth. see Glass, D. V.

Taylor, P. H. & Richards, C. M. An Introduction to Curriculum Studies. (General Ser.). 1979. pap. text ed. 10.50x (ISBN 0-85633-164-3, NFER). Humanities.

Taylor, P. H., ed. Aims, Influences & Change in the Primary School Curriculum. (General Ser.). 143p. 1975. pap. text ed. 16.50x (ISBN 0-85633-072-8, NFER). Humanities.

Taylor, P. H. & Reid, W. A., eds. Curriculum, Culture & Classroom: Trends in Curriculum Studies. (General Ser.). 1980. pap. text ed. cancelled (ISBN 0-85633-163-5, NFER). Humanities.

Taylor, Paul B. & Auden, W. H., eds. The Elder Edda. 1975. pap. 2.95 o.p. (ISBN 0-571-10319-7, Pub. by Faber & Faber). Merrimack Bk Serv.

Taylor, Paul M., ed. Parent-Infant Relationship. (Monographs in Neonatology). 1980. 24.50 (ISBN 0-8089-1289-5). Grune.

Taylor, Paul W. Principles of Ethics: An Introduction. 1975. pap. 11.95x (ISBN 0-8221-0142-4). Dickenson.

--Problems of Moral Philosophy. 3rd ed. LC 75-167903. 1978. text ed. 17.95x (ISBN 0-534-00592-6). Wadsworth Pub.

Taylor, Paula. Basketball's Finest Center: Kareem Abdul-Jabbar. (The Allstars Ser.). (Illus.). (gr. 2-6). 1977. PLB 5.95 o.p. (ISBN 0-87191-584-7). Creative Ed.

--Bob Hope. LC 74-19116. (Illus.). 40p. (gr. 4-8). 1974. PLB 5.95 (ISBN 0-87191-408-5). Creative Ed.

--Cancer. (Sun Signs). (Illus.). (gr. 4-12). 1978. PLB 5.95 (ISBN 0-87191-644-4); pap. 2.95 (ISBN 0-89812-074-8). Creative Ed.

--Capricorn. (Sun Signs Ser.). (Illus.). (gr. 4-12). 1978. PLB 5.95 (ISBN 0-87191-650-9); pap. 2.95 (ISBN 0-89812-080-2). Creative Ed.

--Carole King. (Rock 'n Pop Stars Ser.). (Illus.). (gr. 4-12). 1976. PLB 5.95 (ISBN 0-87191-465-4); pap. 2.95 (ISBN 0-89812-111-6). Creative Ed.

--Coretta Scott King. LC 74-17360. (Illus.). (gr. 4-8). 1975. PLB 5.95 (ISBN 0-87191-410-7). Creative Ed.

--Elton John. (Rock 'n Pop Stars Ser.). (Illus.). (gr. 4-12). 1975. PLB 5.95 (ISBN 0-87191-457-3); pap. 2.95 (ISBN 0-685-82738-0). Creative Ed.

--Elvis Presley. LC 74-14546. (Rock'n Pop Stars Ser.). (Illus.). 32p. (gr. 3-6). 1974. PLB 5.95 (ISBN 0-87191-394-1); pap. 2.95 (ISBN 0-89812-103-5). Creative Ed.

--Frank Sinatra. (Rock 'n Pop Stars Ser.). (Illus.). (gr. 3-6). 1975. PLB 5.95 (ISBN 0-87191-460-3); pap. 2.95 (ISBN 0-89812-109-4). Creative Ed.

--Gemini. (Sun Signs Ser.). (Illus.). (gr. 4-12). 1978. PLB 5.95 (ISBN 0-685-86765-X); pap. 2.95 (ISBN 0-89812-073-X). Creative Ed.

--Henry Kissinger. LC 74-32470. (Creative Education Closeup Bk.). (Illus.). 32p. (gr. 3-6). 1975. PLB 5.95 (ISBN 0-87191-422-0). Creative Ed.

--Johnny Cash. LC 74-14549. (Rock'n Pop Stars Ser.). (Illus.). 32p. (gr. 3-6). 1974. PLB 5.95 (ISBN 0-87191-391-7); pap. 2.95 (ISBN 0-89812-102-7). Creative Ed.

--Leo. (Sun Signs Ser.). (Illus.). (gr. 4-12). 1978. PLB 5.95 (ISBN 0-87191-645-2); pap. 2.95 (ISBN 0-89812-075-6). Creative Ed.

--Pele' LC 76-5818. (Sports Superstars Ser.). (Illus.). (gr. 3-9). 1976. PLB 5.95 o.p. (ISBN 0-87191-513-8); pap. 2.75 o.p. (ISBN 0-89812-193-0). Creative Ed.

--Sagittarius. (Sun Signs Ser.). (Illus.). (gr. 4 up). 1978. PLB 5.95 (ISBN 0-87191-649-5); pap. 2.95 (ISBN 0-89812-079-9). Creative Ed.

Taylor, Paula, jt. auth. see Larson, Norita.

Taylor, Peter J. Quantitative Methods in Geography: An Introduction to Spatial Analysis. LC 75-26097. (Illus.). 384p. 1977. text ed. 19.95 (ISBN 0-395-18699-4). HM.

Taylor, Peter J., jt. auth. see Burnett, Alan D.

Taylor, Philip H. & Reid, W. A. The English Sixth Form: A Case Study in Curriculum Research. (International Library of Sociology). 1974. 14.00 (ISBN 0-7100-7832-3). Routledge & Kegan.

Taylor, Philip H., jt. auth. see Musgrove, Frank.

Taylor, Philip H. & Tye, Kenneth, eds. Curriculum, School & Society: An Introduction to Curriculum Studies. 1975. pap. text ed. 22.00x (ISBN 0-85633-065-5, NFER). Humanities.

Taylor, Phillip M. The Confessions of a Thug, 3vols.in 2. LC 80-2500. 1981. Repr. of 1839 ed. 104.00 (ISBN 0-404-19136-3). AMS Pr.

Taylor, Phoebe. How to Succeed in the Business of Finding a Job. LC 74-17812. 230p. 1975. 13.95 (ISBN 0-88229-162-9); pap. 7.95 (ISBN 0-88229-494-6). Nelson-Hall.

Taylor, Phoebe A. Banbury Bog. 1978. Repr. of 1938 ed. lib. bdg. 9.00x (ISBN 0-89966-247-1). Buccaneer Bks.

Taylor, Preston. Philippians: Joy in Jesus. 1976. pap. 1.75 (ISBN 0-8024-6507-2). Moody.

Taylor, R. Composite Reinforced Concrete. 104p. 1980. 50.00x (ISBN 0-7277-0077-4, Pub. by Telford England). State Mutual Bk.

--The Politics of the Soviet Cinema: Nineteen Seventeen to Nineteen Twenty-Nine. LC 78-67809. (International Studies). 1979. 27.50 (ISBN 0-521-22290-7). Cambridge U Pr.

Taylor, R. A., tr. see Opitz, H.

Taylor, R. D. Alleys: A Novel. LC 80-65066. 144p. 1980. 6.95 (ISBN 0-931604-06-0); pap. 3.95 (ISBN 0-931604-07-9). Curbstone Pub NY TX.

--The Book Where Michael Meets the Royal Street Elves & Learns About Whales & Whale Oil, the Electric Light, the Ostrich, & the Two-Headed Sea Serpent. Wray, Eje, ed. LC 78-55985. (Illus.). 80p. 1978. 6.95 o.p. (ISBN 0-931604-00-1); pap. 3.95 o.p. (ISBN 0-686-27762-7). Curbstone Pub NYTX.

Taylor, R. Gordon. The Hasselblad System. (Illus.). 64p. 1980. pap. 5.00 (ISBN 0-240-51087-9). Focal Pr.

Taylor, R. H. Magnetic Ions in Metals: A Review of Thier Study by Electron Spin Resonance. LC 76-53798. 1977. 19.95 (ISBN 0-470-99024-4). Halsted Pr.

Taylor, R. J. Food Additives. LC 79-42729. (The Institution of Environmental Sciences Ser.). 126p. 1980. 30.00 (ISBN 0-471-27684-7, Pub. by Wiley Interscience); pap. 13.75 (ISBN 0-471-27683-9). Wiley.
Taylor, R. W. Stored Data Description & Data Translation: A Model & Language. 1977. pap. text ed. 27.50 (ISBN 0-08-021624-2). Pergamon.
Taylor, Richard. The Drama of W. B. Yeats: Irish Myth & the Japanese No. LC 75-43336. 1976. 20.00x (ISBN 0-300-01904-1). Yale U Pr.
--Girty. LC 77-82790. (New World Writing Ser.). (Illus.). 1977. pap. 4.95 o.p. (ISBN 0-913666-18-1). Turtle Isl Foun.
--Good & Evil: A New Direction. 1970. 9.95 (ISBN 0-02-616690-9); pap. 1.95 (ISBN 0-02-089680-8). Macmillan.
--How to Raise Beautiful Comb Honey. LC 77-74619. (Illus.). 1977. 7.95 (ISBN 0-9603288-3-1); pap. 3.95 (ISBN 0-686-19087-4). Linden Bks.
--Introductory Readings in Metaphysics. 1979. pap. text ed. 10.95 (ISBN 0-13-502302-5). P-H.
--Metaphysics. 2nd ed. LC 73-5748. (Foundations of Philosophy Ser). 133p. 1974. pap. 7.95 ref. ed. (ISBN 0-13-578468-9). P-H.
Taylor, Richard & Pritchard, Colin. The Protest Makers: The British Nuclear Disarmament Movement 1958-1965, Twenty Years on. (Illus.). 180p. 1980. 24.00 (ISBN 0-08-025211-7). Pergamon.
Taylor, Richard, jt. auth. see Pritchard, Colin.
Taylor, Richard, ed. see Mill, John S.
Taylor, Richard, ed. see Schopenhauer, Arthur.
Taylor, Richard H. The Personal Notebooks of Thomas Hardy. 1979. 25.00x (ISBN 0-231-04696-0). Columbia U Pr.
Taylor, Richard L. Fair-Weather Flying. LC 73-20989. (Illus.). 224p. 1974. 12.95 (ISBN 0-02-616700-X). Macmillan.
--Instrument Flying. 1978. 12.95 (ISBN 0-02-616670-4). Macmillan.
Taylor, Richard S. The Disciplined Life. LC 62-7123. 110p. 1974. pap. 1.75 (ISBN 0-87123-098-4, 200098). Bethany Fell.
Taylor, Robert. Successful Building Primer. Case, Virginia, ed. LC 80-19490. (Successful Ser.). (Illus.). 176p. 1980. pap. 6.95 (ISBN 0-89999-010-X). Structures Pub.
Taylor, Robert, jt. auth. see Taylor, Anita.
Taylor, Robert, ed. The Computer in the School: Tutor, Tutee, Tool. 280p. (Orig.). 1980. pap. text ed. 14.95x (ISBN 0-8077-2611-7). Tchrs Coll.
Taylor, Robert B. Feeling Alive After 65: The Complete Medical Guide for Senior Citizens & Their Families. (Illus.). 224p. 1973. 8.95 o.p. (ISBN 0-87000-226-0). Arlington Hse.
--A Primer of Clinical Symptoms. (Illus.). 1973. 12.95x o.p. (ISBN 0-06-142542-7, Harper Medical). Har-Row.
Taylor, Robert B. & Dickinson. Cultural Ways: A Concise Edition of "Introduction to Cultural Anthropology". 2nd ed. 383p. 1976. pap. text ed. 6.95x o.p. (ISBN 0-205-04878-1); instr's manual free o.p. (ISBN 0-205-05495-1). Allyn.
Taylor, Robert E., ed. see Evans, Rupert & Herr, Edward.
Taylor, Robert H. Certain Small Works. LC 79-3891. (Illus.). 164p. 1980. 12.00 (ISBN 0-87811-023-2). Princeton Lib.
Taylor, Robert, Jr. Elder & His Work. 6.95 (ISBN 0-89315-041-X); pap. 6.95 (ISBN 0-89315-042-8). Lambert Bk.
Taylor, Robert R. The Word in Stone: The Role of Architecture in the Nationalist Socialist Ideology. (Illus.). 1974. 25.00x (ISBN 0-520-02193-2). U of Cal Pr.
Taylor, Robert R., Jr. The Bible Doctrine of Final Things. 1977. 7.50 (ISBN 0-89315-019-3). Lambert Bk.
--Studies in First & Second Thessalonians. 1977. pap. 1.95 (ISBN 0-89315-285-4). Lambert Bk.
Taylor, Robert S. Making of a Library: The Academic Library in Transition. LC 71-180245. (Information Sciences Ser). 1972. 22.95 o.p. (ISBN 0-471-84831-X, Pub. by Wiley-Interscience). Wiley.
Taylor, Ron & Taylor, Valerie, eds. Great Shark Stories. LC 76-27279. (Illus.). 1978. 12.95 o.s.i. (ISBN 0-06-014236-7, HarpT). Har-Row.
Taylor, Ronald. Literature & Society in Germany, 1918-1945. (Studies in Contemporary Literature & Culture). 363p. 1980. 28.50x (ISBN 0-389-20036-0). B&N.
Taylor, Ronald J. & Leviton, Alan E., eds. Mosses of North America. 170p. (Orig.). 1980. 11.95 (ISBN 0-934394-02-4). AAASPD.
Taylor, Ronald L., jt. ed. see Wilkinson, Doris Y.
Taylor, Ross, jt. auth. see Levinson, A. A.
Taylor, Rosser H. Ante-Bellum South Carolina: A Society & Cultural History. LC 79-98180. (American Scene Ser). 1970. Repr. of 1942 ed. lib. bdg. 25.00 (ISBN 0-306-71834-0). Da Capo.
Taylor, S. E. & Parmar, H. A. Aviation Law for Pilots. 3rd ed. 137p. 1978. text ed. 19.95x (ISBN 0-258-97114-2, Pub. by Granada England). Renouf.
--Ground Studies for Pilots. Incl. Vol. I. Radio Aids. 3rd ed. 200p. 1979. text ed. 26.50x (ISBN 0-246-11169-0); Vol. II. Plotting & Flight Planning. 130p. 1976. text ed. 19.95x (ISBN 0-246-11176-3); Vol. III. Navigation General. 232p. 1979. text ed. 26.50x (ISBN 0-246-11177-1). Pub. by Granada England). Renouf.
--Ground Studies for Pilots. 2nd ed. (Illus.). Date not set. 14.95 o.p. (ISBN 0-258-96983-0, ScribT). Scribner. Postponed.
Taylor, S. J. Introduction to Measure & Integration. LC 73-84325. 272p. 1975. pap. text ed. 15.50x (ISBN 0-521-09804-1). Cambridge U Pr.
Taylor, S. J., jt. auth. see Kingman, John F.
Taylor, Sally, jt. auth. see Emmery, Lena.
Taylor, Samuel G., 3rd, ed. Oncology. (Medical Examination Review Bk. Ser.: Vol. 29). 1973. spiral bdg. 16.50 (ISBN 0-87488-146-3). Med Exam.
Taylor, Sandra, jt. ed. see Orcutt, Georgia.
Taylor, Sandra, ed. see Orcutt, Georgia.
Taylor, Sedley. The Indebtedness of Handel to Works by Other Composers. (Music Reprint Ser.). 1979. Repr. of 1906 ed. lib. bdg. 22.50 (ISBN 0-306-79513-2). Da Capo.
Taylor, Selwyn, ed. Harlow's Modern Surgery for Nurses. 9th ed. (Illus.). 1973. text ed. 28.50x (ISBN 0-433-32205-5). Intl Ideas.
--Recent Advances in Surgery, No. 10. (Illus.). 352p. 1980. text ed. 27.50 (ISBN 0-443-01966-5). Churchill.
Taylor, Sheila F., jt. auth. see Taylor, Halsey P.
Taylor, Simon W., tr. see Jarry, Alfred.
Taylor, Steven J. & Biklen, Douglas. Understanding the Law: An Advocates Guide to the Law & Developmental Disabilities. 67p. 1980. pap. 3.25 (ISBN 0-937540-10-2, HPP-13). Human Policy Pr.
Taylor, Steven J., jt. auth. see Bogdan, Robert.
Taylor, Stuart R. Lunar Science - a Post-Apollo View. LC 74-17227. 372p. 1975. text ed. 31.00 (ISBN 0-08-018274-7); pap. text ed. 16.00 (ISBN 0-08-018273-9). Pergamon.
Taylor, Sydney. All-Of-A-Kind Family Downtown. (gr. 3-6). 1973. pap. 1.50 (ISBN 0-440-42032-6, YB). Dell.
--All-Of-A-Kind Family Uptown. (Illus.). (gr. 4-7). 1968. pap. 1.50 (ISBN 0-440-40091-0, YB). Dell.
--Danny Loves a Holiday. (Illus.). 80p. (gr. 1-3). 1980. 7.95g (ISBN 0-525-28510-5). Dutton.
--Dog Who Came to Dinner. (Beginning-to-Read Ser.). (Illus.). (gr. 1-3). 1966. 2.50 o.p. (ISBN 0-695-82086-9); lib. ed. 2.97 o.p. (ISBN 0-695-42086-0). Follett.
Taylor, Talbot J. Linguistic Theory & Structural Stylistics. (Language & Communication Library: Vol. 2). 140p. Date not set. 17.00 (ISBN 0-08-025821-2). Pergamon.
Taylor, Telford. Grand Inquest: The Story of Congressional Investigations. LC 73-19825. 358p. 1974. Repr. of 1955 ed. lib. bdg. 35.00 (ISBN 0-306-70620-2). Da Capo.
Taylor, Theodore. Air Raid Pearl Harbor: The Story of December 7, 1941. LC 76-132303. (Illus.). (gr. 5-8). 1971. 8.95 (ISBN 0-690-05373-8, TYC-J). T Y Crowell.
--Battle in the Arctic Seas: The Story of Convoy Pq 17. LC 75-33655. (Illus.). (gr. 5 up). 1976. 8.95 (ISBN 0-690-01084-2, TYC-J). T Y Crowell.
--The Cay. (gr. 3 up). 1977. pap. 1.75 (ISBN 0-380-00142-X, 51037, Camelot). Avon.
--The Odyssey of Ben O'Neal. LC 76-23800. (gr. 3-7). 1977. 5.95a o.p. (ISBN 0-385-00166-5); PLB (ISBN 0-385-00289-0). Doubleday.
--Rebellion Town: Williamsburg, 1776. LC 73-10187. (Illus.). (gr. 5-9). 1973. 8.95 (ISBN 0-690-00019-7, TYC-J). T Y Crowell.
--Teetoncey. LC 73-13097. 160p. (gr. 5 up). 1974. PLB 4.95 (ISBN 0-385-09587-2). Doubleday.
--Teetoncey. (Illus.). (gr. 3-7). 1975. pap. 1.95 (ISBN 0-380-00346-5, 52118, Camelot). Avon.
--Teetoncey & Ben O'Neal. LC 74-4875. 160p. (gr. 3-7). 1975. PLB 5.95 (ISBN 0-385-04504-2). Doubleday.
--Teetoncey & Ben O'neal. 1976. pap. 1.25 (ISBN 0-380-00764-9, 30536, Camelot). Avon.
Taylor, Theodore, jt. auth. see Irigaray, Louis.
Taylor, Thomas. Vindication of the Rights of Brutes. LC 66-10010. 1966. Repr. of 1792 ed. 20.00x (ISBN 0-8201-1045-0). Schol Facsimiles.
Taylor, Thomas C. The Fundamentals of Austrian Economics. (Study in Political Economy Ser.: No. 4). 76p. (Orig.). 1980. 2.00 (ISBN 0-932790-27-5). Cato Inst.
Taylor, Thomas N. Paleobotany: An Intro. to Plant Biology. (Illus.). 576p. 1981. text ed. 29.95 (ISBN 0-07-062954-4). McGraw.
--Paleobotany: An Introduction to Fossil Plant Biology. (Illus.). 576p. Date not set. text ed. 29.95 (ISBN 0-07-062954-4, C). McGraw. Postponed.
Taylor, Thomas T. Mechanics: Classical & Quantum. 1976. text ed. 42.00 (ISBN 0-08-018063-9); pap. text ed. 24.00 (ISBN 0-08-020522-4). Pergamon.
Taylor, Timothy D., tr. see Stahl, Friedrich J.
Taylor, Timothy D., tr. see Stahl, Friedrich Julius.
Taylor, Tom. Of Wrath & Praise. 224p. (Orig.). 1981. pap. 2.95 (ISBN 0-8024-9249-5). Moody.
Taylor, Tom, jt. auth. see Davis, Ken.
Taylor, Tom, tr. El Lazo Del Cazador. (Spanish Bks.). (Span.). 1978. 1.75 (ISBN 0-8297-0776-X). Life Pubs Intl.
Taylor, Una. Early Italina Love Stories Taken from the Originals. 144p. 1980. Repr. of 1899 ed. lib. bdg. 50.00 (ISBN 0-89760-882-8). Telegraph Bks.
Taylor, Valerie. Prism. 180p. (Orig.). 1981. pap. 5.95 (ISBN 0-930044-18-5). Naiad Pr.
Taylor, Valerie, jt. ed. see Taylor, Ron.
Taylor, Vernon L. Art of Argument. LC 71-150111. 1971. 10.00 (ISBN 0-8108-0376-3). Scarecrow.
Taylor, Victor H. Voici les Desmarets! 1958. pap. text ed. 1.95x o.p. (ISBN 0-435-37881-3). Heinemann Ed.
Taylor, Victor J. Constructing Modern Furniture. LC 79-91383. (Home Craftsman Bk.). (Illus.). 144p. 1980. pap. 5.95 (ISBN 0-8069-8888-6). Sterling.
Taylor, W., ed. The Hepatobiliary System: Fundamental & Pathological Mechanisms. LC 76-2486. (NATO Advanced Study Institutes Ser, Ser. A: Life Sciences: Vol. 7). 654p. 1976. 49.50 (ISBN 0-306-35607-4, Plenum Pr). Plenum Pub.
Taylor, W. D. Symbiosis Intelligentsia. 224p. 1981. 9.50 (ISBN 0-682-49675-8). Exposition.
Taylor, W. H. Fluid Therapy & Disorders of Electrolyte Balance. 2nd ed. (Illus.). 200p. 1970. 9.50 (ISBN 0-632-07430-2, Blackwell). Mosby.
Taylor, W. J. & Watling, T. F. The Basic Arts of Management. 207p. 1977. text ed. 22.00x (ISBN 0-220-66812-4, Pub. by Busn Bks England). Renouf.
--Successful Project Management. 269p. 1979. text ed. 29.50x (ISBN 0-220-67004-8, Pub. by Busn Bks England). Renouf.
Taylor, Walt, et al. Doughty's English. Commager, Steele, ed. Incl. Adjectives-from Proper Names; On the Diction of Tennyson; The Split Infinitive & a System of Clauses; Slang; The Growth of American English One; The Growth of American English Two; Completing the Record of English; Some Anomalies of Spelling; Index to Tracts XLI-LIX. (Society for Pure English Ser.: Vol. 6). 1979. lib. bdg. 42.00 (ISBN 0-8240-3670-0). Garland Pub.
Taylor, Walter S. & Vine, Richard P. Home Winemaker's Handbook. 1968. 10.95 o.p. (ISBN 0-06-115020-7, HarpT). Har-Row.
Taylor, Welford D. Amelie Rives (Princess Troubetzkoy) (U. S. Authors Ser.: No. 217). 1971. lib. bdg. 10.95 (ISBN 0-8057-0625-9). Twayne.
--Sherwood Anderson. LC 77-6948. (Modern Literature Ser.). 1977. 10.95 (ISBN 0-8044-2861-1). Ungar.
Taylor, Wendell H., jt. auth. see Barzun, Jacques.
Taylor, William. Athenian Odyssey. 4.95 (ISBN 0-89353-025-5). Green Hill.
--Heading for Change: The Management of Innovation in the Large Secondary School. (Orig.). 1973. 11.25x (ISBN 0-7100-7426-3); pap. 6.50 (ISBN 0-7100-7427-1). Routledge & Kegan.
--The Military Roads in Scotland. LC 76-9239. (Illus.). 1976. 14.95 (ISBN 0-7153-7067-7). David & Charles.
--Research & Reform in Teacher Education. (Council of Europe: European Trend Reports on Educational Research: No. 4). (Illus.). 1978. pap. text ed. 22.00x (ISBN 0-85633-140-6, NFER). Humanities.
Taylor, William & Braswell, Michael. Issues in Police & Criminal Psychology. LC 78-61915. 1978. pap. text ed. 10.25 (ISBN 0-8191-0624-0). U Pr of Amer.
Taylor, William, jt. auth. see Huxley, Anthony.
Taylor, William, jt. auth. see Orfield, Gary.
Taylor, William see Simon, Brian.
Taylor, William C. A History of Clay County. LC 73-87679. (Illus.). 200p. 1973. 12.50 (ISBN 0-8363-0118-8). Jenkins.
--Notes of a Tour in the Manufacturing Districts of Lancashire. LC 67-131562. Repr. of 1842 ed. 17.50x (ISBN 0-678-05088-0). Kelley.
Taylor, William J., Jr., et al, eds. Military Unions: U.S. Trends & Issues. LC 77-88632. (Sage Research Progress Series on War, Revolution, & Peacekeeping: Vol. 7). 1977. 20.00x (ISBN 0-8039-0934-9); pap. 9.95x (ISBN 0-8039-0935-7). Sage.
Taylor, William L. Productive Monopoly: The Effect of Railroad Control on New England Coastal Steamship Lines, 1870-1916. LC 70-111457. (Illus.). 323p. 1970. 15.00 (ISBN 0-87057-123-0, Pub. by Brown U Pr). Univ Pr of New England.
Taylor, William L., jt. auth. see Lang, Ewald.
Taylor, William M. Athenian Odyssey. 1977. 4.95 (ISBN 0-89353-025-5). W M Taylor.
--Miracles of Our Saviour. LC 74-79944. 1975. 10.95 (ISBN 0-8254-3806-3). Kregel.
--Parables of Our Saviour. LC 74-79943. 1975. 10.95 (ISBN 0-8254-3805-5). Kregel.
Taylor, William R. Cavalier & Yankee. LC 61-15493. 1961. 6.00 o.s.i. (ISBN 0-8076-0152-7). Braziller.
Taylor, Zack. Successful Waterfowling. 288p. (Orig.). 1981. pap. 13.95 (ISBN 0-8117-2147-7). Stackpole.
Taylor, Zack, jt. auth. see Angier, Bradford.
Taylor, Zack, ed. see MacQuarrie, Gordon.
Taylor-Gordon, Elaine, jt. auth. see Murphy, Patricia.
Taylor-Hyler, Ariel. Numerology Its Facts & Secrets. 1958. 6.95 (ISBN 0-910140-17-0). Anthony.
Taylor-Moore, Suzanne. How to by Suzanne. 64p. 1981. pap. 3.00 (ISBN 0-686-28091-1). MTM Pub Co.
--In Her Shadow. (Illus.). 1981. pap. 12.95 (ISBN 0-686-28089-X). MTM Pub Co.
--In Progress. 1978. 8.95 (ISBN 0-686-10295-9); pap. 4.95 (ISBN 0-686-10296-7). MTM Pub Co.
--Landlords Are People Too. 48p. 1980. pap. 2.50 (ISBN 0-686-28086-5). MTM Pub Co.
--Lucky. 1977. 6.95 (ISBN 0-686-10585-0). MTM Pub Co.
--Max of Skamania. 1980. pap. 14.95 (ISBN 0-686-28087-3). MTM Pub Co.
--Nail Biters Anonymous. 48p. 1981. pap. 3.00 (ISBN 0-686-28092-X). MTM Pub Co.
--Puppies Need Love Too. 48p. 1980. pap. 3.50 (ISBN 0-686-28088-1). MTM Pub Co.
--Taylor-Moore Lodge. 1981. pap. 2.50 (ISBN 0-686-28090-3). MTM Pub Co.
Taylor-Winniford, R. G. The Houston Downtown Flood. 75p. 1981. 6.95 (ISBN 0-87881-098-6). Mojave Bks.
Taynton, Mark. Shetland Sheepdogs. rev. ed. (Illus.). 128p. 1974. pap. 2.95 o.p. (ISBN 0-87666-387-0, HS1085). TFH Pubns.
Taynton, Mark, jt. auth. see Pisano, Beverly.
Tazewell, Charles. The Littlest Angel. 32p. (gr. k-6). 1980. pap. cancelled o.s.i. (ISBN 0-89542-922-5); pap. 2.25 o.s.i. (ISBN 0-89542-923-3). Ideals.
Tchaikovsky, Petr I. The Diaries of Tchaikovsky. Lakond, Wladimir, tr. LC 79-138104. (Illus.). 365p. 1973. Repr. of 1945 ed. lib. bdg. 28.50x (ISBN 0-8371-5680-7, CHDI). Greenwood.
Tchaikovsky, Piotr I. Letters to His Family: An Autobiography. Young, Percy M., ed. Von Meck, Galina, tr. LC 80-6162. 576p. 1981. 25.00 (ISBN 0-8128-2802-X). Stein & Day.
Tchemerzine, Avenir. Bibliographie d'edtions Originales & Rares d'auteurs Francais des XVe, XVIe, XVIIe, XVIIIe Siecles Contenant Environ 6,000 Fac-Similes de Titres & Gravures. LC 73-87061. (Illus.). 420p. (Fr., Originally published in 10 vols. & reprinted in reduced format in 1 vol.). 1973. Repr. of 1927 ed. 105.00x (ISBN 0-914146-03-3). Somerset Hse.
Tchernia, P. Descriptive Regional Oceanography. Densmore, D., tr. (Pergamon Marine Ser.: Vol. 3). (Illus.). 256p. 1980. 45.00 (ISBN 0-08-020925-4); pap. 19.50 (ISBN 0-08-020919-X). Pergamon.
Tchividjian, Gigi. Thank You, Lord, for My Home. 1980. Repr. of 1979 ed. 3.95 (ISBN 0-89066-023-9). World Wide Pubs.
--A Woman's Quest for Serenity. 1981. 7.95 (ISBN 0-8007-1183-1). Revell.
Tchobanoglous, George, jt. auth. see Metcalf & Eddy, Inc.
Tchobanoglous, George, et al, eds. Wastewater Management: A Guide to Information Sources. LC 74-11570. (Man & the Environment Information Guide Ser.: Vol. 2). 260p. 1976. 30.00 (ISBN 0-8103-1338-3). Gale.
Teacher, Lawrence, ed. Cat Notebook: Being an Illlustrated Book with Quotes. (Illus.). 96p. (Orig.). 1981. lib. bdg. 12.90 (ISBN 0-89471-131-8); pap. 4.95 (ISBN 0-89471-133-4). Running Pr.
Teacher, Lawrence, ed. see London, Jack.
Teacher, Lawrence, ed. see Twain, Mark.
Teachers College Library. Bibliographic Guide to Education: Nineteen Seventy-Eight. (Library Catalogs-Bibliographic Guides). 1979. lib. bdg. 75.00 (ISBN 0-8161-6852-0). G K Hall.

Tead, Ordway. College Teaching & College Learning. 1949. 16.50x (ISBN 0-685-69874-2). Elliots Bks.

Teague, Edward H. Henry Moore: Bibliography & Reproductions Index. LC 80-28048. (Illus.). 185p. 1981. lib. bdg. 21.00x (ISBN 0-89950-016-1). McFarland & Co.

Teague, Gerald V. & Heathington, Betty S. Process of Grant Proposal Development. LC 79-93120. (Fastback Ser.: No. 143). (Orig.). 1980. pap. 0.75 (ISBN 0-87367-143-0). Phi Delta Kappa.

Teague, Richard D. & Decker, Eugene, eds. Wildlife Conservation Principles & Practices. rev. ed. LC 79-2960. (Illus.). 280p. 1979. pap. 7.50 (ISBN 0-933564-06-6). Wildlife Soc.

Teague, Richard D., ed. see Wildlife Society, Inc.

Teal, Peter. Hand Woolcombing & Spinning: A Guide to Worsteds from the Spinning Wheel. (Illus.). 1979. 14.95 (ISBN 0-7137-0814-X, Pub. by Blandford Pr England). Sterling.

Teal, Thomas, tr. see Nilsson, Birgit.

Teale, Edwin W. The American Seasons. LC 76-11794. (Illus.). 1976. 17.50 (ISBN 0-396-07353-0). Dodd.

--Grassroot Jungles. rev. ed. LC 44-5481. (Illus.). (gr. 9 up). 1937. 6.95 (ISBN 0-396-01714-2). Dodd.

--A Naturalist Buys an Old Farm. LC 74-3779. (Illus.). 275p. 1974. 10.00 (ISBN 0-396-06974-6). Dodd.

--North with the Spring. LC 51-13966. (Illus.). (gr. 7 up). 1951. 10.00 (ISBN 0-396-03325-3). Dodd.

--A Walk Through the Year. LC 78-9786. (Illus.). 1978. 15.00 (ISBN 0-396-07621-1). Dodd.

Teale, Edwin W., ed. see Fabre, J. Henri.

Teale, Ruth, ed. Colonial Eve: Sources on Women in Australia, 1788-1914. 300p. 1978. 24.00x (ISBN 0-19-550545-X). Oxford U Pr.

Teare, B. R., jt. auth. see Ver Planck, Dennistown W.

Teasdale, A., jt. auth. see Hicks, E.

Teasdale, Graham, jt. auth. see Jennett, Bryan.

Teasdale, May S. Handbook of 20th Century Opera. LC 76-4920. (Music Reprint Ser.). 1976. Repr. of 1938 ed. lib. bdg. 22.50 (ISBN 0-306-70783-7). Da Capo.

Teasdale, Sara. Collected Poems of Sara Teasdale. Zaturenska, Marya, ed. 1967. 12.95 (ISBN 0-02-616890-1). Macmillan.

--Love Songs. LC 75-19068. (Illus.). 96p. 1975. 9.95 (ISBN 0-02-616880-4, 61688). Macmillan.

--Stars To-Night. (Illus.). (gr. 4-6). 1930. 3.95 o.s.i. (ISBN 0-02-789090-2). Macmillan.

Teasley, D. O. The Double Cure, or Redemption Twofold. 160p. pap. 1.50 large print. Faith Pub Hse.

--The Holy Spirit & Other Spirits. 192p. pap. 1.75. Faith Pub Hse.

--Rays of Hope. 95p. pap. 0.75. Faith Pub Hse.

Teason, James, jt. auth. see Whitehead, Robert.

Tebbel, John. The Battle of Fallen Timbers, August 20, 1794: President Washington Secures the Ohio Valley. LC 76-188480. (Focus Bks). (Illus.). 96p. (gr. 6-9). 1972. PLB 6.45 (ISBN 0-531-02457-1). Watts.

--The Media in America: A Social & Political History. LC 74-9891. 384p. 1975. 11.95 (ISBN 0-690-00500-8, TYC-T). T Y Crowell.

Tebbutt, T. H. Principles of Water Quality Control. 1971. 14.30 (ISBN 0-08-016128-6); pap. 7.70 (ISBN 0-08-016127-8). Pergamon.

Tebeau, Charlton W. A History of Florida. LC 80-53678. (Illus.). 1971. pap. 19.95x (ISBN 0-87024-303-9). U of Miami Pr.

Tebeaux, Elizabeth, jt. auth. see Lawrence, Nelda R.

Tebeaux, W. Gene, jt. auth. see Pierce, R. C.

Techmer, Fredrich, tr. see Kruszewski, Mikolaj.

Technical Committee, Vienna Jan. 20-24, 1975. Peaceful Nuclear Explosions - Four: Proceedings. (Illus.). 479p. 1975. pap. 36.50 (ISBN 92-0-061075-7, IAEA). Unipub.

Technical Staff of Barron's Educational Series, compiled by. Instant Metric Reference: A Pocket Book of Conversion Tables. Date not set. pap. cancelled (ISBN 0-8120-0825-1). Barron.

Technical Staff of the Machinability Data Center, ed. Machining Data Handbook, 2 vols. 3rd ed. LC 80-81480. (Illus.). 1980. Set. 150.00x (ISBN 0-936974-00-1). Metcut Res Assocs.

Technishe Universitaet, Dresden, ed. English-German Dictionary of Chemistry & Chemical Technology. 2nd ed. LC 76-455777. 1978. 47.50x (ISBN 0-8002-0401-8). Intl Pubns Serv.

Technocracy Inc., ed. Technocracy: Technological Social Design. (Illus.). 76p. (Orig.). 1975. pap. 1.00 (ISBN 0-686-28500-X). Technocracy.

Technology Assessment & Utilization Committee. A National Strategy for Improving Productivity in Building & Construction. LC 80-81951. xii, 209p. 1980. pap. text ed. 8.25 (ISBN 0-309-03080-3). Natl Acad Pr.

Techo, Robert. Data Communications: An Introduction to Concepts & Design. (Applications of Modern Technology in Business Ser.). 300p. 1980. 24.50 (ISBN 0-306-40398-6, Plenum Pr). Plenum Pub.

Teck, Alan. Mutual Savings Banks & Savings & Loan Associations: Aspects of Growth. LC 68-18999. (Charts). 1968. 20.00x (ISBN 0-231-03124-6). Columbia U Pr.

Teclaff, Ludwik A., jt. ed. see Utton, Albert E.

Teclaff, Ludwipk A. & Utton, Albert E., eds. International Environmental Law. LC 73-15198. (Special Studies). 262p. 1974. text ed. 25.00 (ISBN 0-275-08630-5). Praeger.

Tedder, J. M., jt. auth. see Nonhebel, D. C.

Teddlie, Tillit S. Great Christian Hymnal. 1965. 3.00 (ISBN 0-89137-600-3). Quality Pubns.

Tedesch, Philip, jt. ed. see Kimball, John P.

Tedeschi. Acetelyne Based Chemicals from Coal & Other Natural Sources. Date not set. price not set (ISBN 0-8247-1358-3). Dekker.

Tedeschi, Cesare G., et al, eds. Forensic Medicine, 3 vols. LC 74-4593. (Illus.). 1680p. 1977. Vol. 1. 50.00 (ISBN 0-7216-8772-5); Vol. 2. 35.00 (ISBN 0-7216-8773-3); Vol. 3. 40.00 (ISBN 0-7216-8774-1); 125.00 set (ISBN 0-7216-8771-7). Saunders.

Tedeschi, David H. & Tedeschi, Ralph E., eds. Importance of Fundamental Principles in Drug Evaluation. LC 68-56046. (Illus.). 1968. 31.50 (ISBN 0-911216-05-7). Raven.

Tedeschi, F. P. & Taber, M. R. Solid State Electronics. LC 75-27996. 1976. pap. 8.80 (ISBN 0-8273-1171-0); instructor's guide 1.60 (ISBN 0-8273-1172-9). Delmar.

Tedeschi, Frank P. & Scigiano, John A. Digital Computers & Logic Circuits. LC 78-11983. (Illus., Orig.). 1971. text ed. 6.95x (ISBN 0-02-478780-9, 47878); wkbk. 5.50x (ISBN 0-02-478830-9, 47883). Macmillan.

Tedeschi, G. Studies in Israel Law. (Hebrew University Legal Studies: No. 7). 1960. 10.00x (ISBN 0-8377-1200-9). Rothman.

Tedeschi, Henry. Cell Physiology: Molecular Dynamics. 1974. 23.50 (ISBN 0-12-685150-6). Acad Pr.

Tedeschi, James T. & Lindskold, Svern. Social Psychology, Interdependence, Interaction, & Influence. LC 75-38883. 1976. 24.50 (ISBN 0-471-85017-9, Pub. by Wiley-Interscience). Wiley.

Tedeschi, James T., ed. Impression Management Theory & Social Psychological Research. 1981. price not set (ISBN 0-12-685180-8). Acad Pr.

Tedeschi, Ralph E., jt. ed. see Tedeschi, David H.

Tedford, R. H. The Fossil Macropodidae from Lake Menindee, New South Wales. (U. C. Publ. in Geological Sciences: Vol. 64). 1967. pap. 8.50x (ISBN 0-520-09165-5). U of Cal Pr.

--A Review of the Macropodid Genus Sthenurus. (U. C. Publ. in Geological Sciences: Vol. 57). 1966. pap. 6.50x (ISBN 0-520-09158-2). U of Cal Pr.

Tedford, William. Hydrabyss Red. (Timequest Ser.: No. 2). 1981. pap. 2.25 (ISBN 0-8439-0887-4, Leisure Bks). Nordon Pubns.

--Rashanyn Dark. (Timequest Ser.: No. 1). 1981. pap. 2.25 (ISBN 0-8439-0869-6, Leisure Bks). Nordon Pubns.

Tedlock, Barbara. Time & the Highland Maya. (Illus.). 288p. 1981. 27.50 (ISBN 0-8263-0577-6). U of NM Pr.

Tedone, David. Complete Shellfisherman's Guide. (Illus.). 200p. 1981. pap. 7.95 (ISBN 0-933614-09-8). Peregrine Pr.

Tedrow, John C. Soils of the Polar Landscapes. 1977. 65.00 (ISBN 0-8135-0808-8). Rutgers U Pr.

Tee, Lim H. Malaysia. (World Bibliographical Ser.: No. 12). 1981. write for info. (ISBN 0-903450-23-2). Abc-Clio.

Teeguarden, Iona M. The Acupressure Way of Health: Jin Shin Do. (Illus., Orig.). 1978. pap. 9.95 (ISBN 0-87040-421-0). Japan Pubns.

Teele, James E. Mastering Stress in Child Rearing: Parental Coping Versus Spontaneous Remission. LC 79-48006. 1981. price not set (ISBN 0-669-03622-6). Lexington Bks.

Teeling, Charles H. History of the Irish Rebellion of Seventeen Ninety-Eight and Sequel. 1972. Repr. of 1876 ed. 14.00x o.p. (ISBN 0-7165-0014-0, Pub. by Irish Academic Pr Ireland). Biblio Dist.

Teen. The Bananas Yearbook 1979. pap. 2.25 o.p. (ISBN 0-590-12078-6, Schol Pap). Schol Bk Serv.

Teensma, E. Solipsism & Induction. 64p. 1974. pap. text ed. 6.50x (ISBN 90-232-1149-9). Humanities.

Teeple, Gary, ed. Capitalism & the National Question in Canada. LC 72-91690. 1972. pap. 6.50 (ISBN 0-8020-6171-0). U of Toronto Pr.

Teeple, Howard M. The Mosiac Eschatological Prophet. (Society of Biblical Literature, Monographs). 1957. pap. 7.50 (ISBN 0-89130-180-1, 060010). Scholars Pr Ca.

Teeples, Gary R., jt. auth. see Jackson, Ronald V.

Teer, F. & Spence, J. D. Political Opinion Polls. 1973. text ed. 10.50x (ISBN 0-09-115230-5, Hutchinson U Lib); pap. text ed. 6.00x (ISBN 0-09-115231-3). Humanities.

Teerink, H. Bibliography of the Writings of Jonathan Swift. 2nd ed. Scouten, Arthur H., ed. LC 62-11270. 1963. 25.00x o.p. (ISBN 0-8122-7373-7). U of Pa Pr.

Teeter, Don E. The Acoustic Guitar: Adjustment, Care, Maintenance, & Repair, Vol. I. LC 74-5962. (Illus.). 250p. 1975. 22.50 (ISBN 0-8061-1219-0). U of Okla Pr.

--The Acoustic Guitar: Adjustment, Care, Maintenance, & Repair, Vol. II. LC 79-5962. (Illus.). 208p. 1980. 20.00 (ISBN 0-8061-1607-2). U of Okla Pr.

Teff, Harvey. Drugs, Society & the Law. (Illus.). 219p. 1975. 23.95 (ISBN 0-347-01079-2, 97790-0, Pub. by Saxon Hse). Lexington Bks.

Teff, Harvey & Munro, Colin. Thalidomide-the Legal Aftermath. 1976. 21.95 (ISBN 0-566-00120-9, 00317-4, Pub. by Saxon Hse). Lexington Bks.

Teffault, Elizbeth M. One-More-Na-Bob Andd & Butt. 76p. 1979. 4.50 (ISBN 0-8059-2664-X). Dorrance.

Tefft, Stanton K., ed. Secrecy: A Cross-Cultural Perspective. LC 79-25454. 400p. 1980. text ed. 19.95x (ISBN 0-87705-442-8); pap. text ed. 9.95x (ISBN 0-87705-443-6). Human Sci Pr.

Tega, Vasile G., ed. Management & Economics Journals: An International Selection. LC 76-4578. (Management Information Guide Ser.: No. 33). 1977. 30.00 (ISBN 0-8103-0833-9). Gale.

Tegeler, Philip D., jt. auth. see Cole, Roland J.

Tegenfeldt, Herman. A Century of Growth: The Kachin Baptist Church of Burma. LC 74-4415. 540p. 1974. 10.95 (ISBN 0-87808-416-9). William Carey Lib.

Teger, Allan I., et al. Too Much Invested to Quit. (Illus.). 1980. 19.25 (ISBN 0-08-022995-6). Pergamon.

Tegg, William. Knot Tied: Marriage Ceremonies of All Nations. LC 75-99073. 1970. Repr. of 1877 ed. 26.00 (ISBN 0-8103-3585-9). Gale.

--The Last Act: Being the Funeral Rites of Nations & Individuals. LC 72-10592. (Illus.). 404p. 1973. Repr. of 1876 ed. 20.00 (ISBN 0-8103-3172-1). Gale.

Teggart, Frederick J. Theory & Processes of History. 1977. pap. 6.95x (ISBN 0-520-03176-8, CAMPUS162). U of Cal Pr.

Tegner & McGrath. Self-Defense & Assault Prevention for Girls & Women. 1980. pap. 2.95 (ISBN 0-87407-026-0). Thor.

Tegner, Bruce. Aikido & Jiu Jitsu Holds & Locks. LC 70-99026. (Orig.). 1969. pap. 2.95 o.p. (ISBN 0-87407-009-0). Thor.

--Black Belt Judo, Karate & Jujitsu: Advanced Techniques. 2nd, rev. ed. LC 80-11673. (Illus., Orig.). 1980. pap. 3.95 (ISBN 0-87407-033-3, T-33). Thor.

--Bruce Tegner's Complete Book of Jukado Self Defense: Jiu Jitsu Modernized. LC 67-21359. (Illus.). 1968. 6.95 o.s.i. (ISBN 0-87407-504-1). Thor.

--Defense Tactics for Law Enforcement: Weaponless Defense & Control & Baton Techniques. rev. ed. LC 77-28136. (Illus.). 1978. pap. 4.95 (ISBN 0-87407-028-7, T-28). Thor.

--Judo: Sport Techniques for Physical Fitness & Tournament. LC 76-18090. (Illus.). 144p. 1976. pap. 2.95 (ISBN 0-87407-025-2, T25). Thor.

--Karate: Self Defense & Traditional Sport Forms. LC 73-9742. (Illus.). 160p. (Orig.). 1973. pap. 2.95 (ISBN 0-87407-023-6). Thor.

--Kung Fu & Tai Chi: Chinese Karate & Classical Exercises. rev. ed. LC 73-4315. (Orig.). 1973. pap. 2.95 o.p. (ISBN 0-87407-015-5). Thor.

--Self-Defense: A Basic Course. LC 79-13556. (Illus.). 1979. 5.95 (ISBN 0-87407-517-3); kivar 3.95 (ISBN 0-87407-031-7). Thor.

--Self-Defense for Boys & Men: A Physical Education Course. rev. ed. LC 72-13186. (Illus., Orig.). (YA) (gr. 9 up). 1969. 4.95 o.p. (ISBN 0-87407-506-8). Thor.

--Self-Defense Nerve Centers & Pressure Points for Karate, Jujitsu & Atemi-Waza. rev. enlarged ed. LC 78-18169. (Illus.). 1978. 5.95 (ISBN 0-87407-519-X, T-29); pap. 2.95. Thor.

Teharanian, Majid, et al, eds. Communications Policy for National Development: A Comparative Perspective. 1977. 25.00x (ISBN 0-7100-8597-4). Routledge & Kegan.

Teicher, Handel. Blumenfeld: My 100 Best Photos. LC 80-51502. (Illus.). 139p. 1981. 30.00 (ISBN 0-8478-0340-6). Rizzoli Intl.

Teicher, Morton, intro. by. Values in Social Work: A Re-Examination. LC 65-15322. 107p. (Orig.). 1967. pap. text ed. 4.00x (ISBN 0-87101-345-2, CBO-345-I). Natl Assn Soc Wkrs.

Teicher, Morton I., et al, eds. Reaching the Aged: Social Services in Forty-Four Countries. LC 79-18525. (Social Service Delivery Systems: Vol. 4). 1979. 20.00x (ISBN 0-8039-1365-6); pap. 9.95x (ISBN 0-8039-1366-4). Sage.

Teichert, Curt, jt. ed. see Moore, Raymond C.

Teichert, Marilyn, tr. see Bouyer, Louis.

Teichler, Erich, et al. Higher Education & the Needs of Society. (NFER Ser.). 141p. 1980. pap. text ed. 11.00x (ISBN 0-85633-209-7, NFER). Humanities.

Teichler, Ulrich & Voss, Friederich. Bibliography of Japanese Education. 294p. 1974. pap. 19.50 (ISBN 3-598-03183-1, Pub. by K G Saur). Shoe String.

Teichman, Jenny, jt. ed. see Diamond, Cora.

Teichmann, Howard. Smart Aleck. new ed. (Illus.). 352p. 1976. 10.95 o.p. (ISBN 0-688-03034-3). Morrow.

Teichmann, Jenny. The Mind & the Soul: An Introduction to the Philosophy of the Mind. (Studies in Philosophical Psychology). 120p. 1973. text ed. 7.00x (ISBN 0-391-00338-0). Humanities.

Teichroew, Daniel, jt. auth. see Howell, James E.

Teigen, Ronald L. Readings in Money, National Income & Stabilization Policy. 4th ed. 1978. pap. text ed. 13.95 (ISBN 0-256-02031-0). Irwin.

Teigland, Martin W. Bruised Fight. 1981. 4.95 (ISBN 0-533-04386-7). Vantage.

Teilhard De Chardin, Pierre. Divine Milieu: An Essay on the Interior Life. pap. 3.95 (ISBN 0-06-090487-9, CN487, CN). Har-Row.

--Hymn of the Universe. LC 65-10375. 1969. pap. 3.95x (ISBN 0-06-131910-4, TB1910, Torch). Har-Row.

--Phenomenon of Man. pap. 4.95 (ISBN 0-06-090495-X, CN495, CN). Har-Row.

--Toward the Future. Hague, Rene, tr. from Fr. LC 74-23802. 224p. 1975. pap. 3.95 o.p. (ISBN 0-15-690780-1, HB310, Harv). HarBraceJ.

Teilmann, Katherine S., jt. ed. see Klein, Malcolm W.

Teissier, B., ed. see Zariski, Oscar.

Teitelbaum, M. J. & Johnson, D. Mangled Medicine. (Illus.). 1972. 6.95 (ISBN 0-87489-038-1). Med Economics.

Teitelbaum, Michael, ed. Sex Differences. LC 75-6172. 240p. 1976. pap. 2.95 (ISBN 0-385-00826-0, Anch). Doubleday.

Teitelbaum, Myron. Hypnosis Induction Techniques. 200p. 1980. 12.50 (ISBN 0-398-01907-X). C C Thomas.

Teitler, G. The Genesis of the Professional Officers' Corps. LC 77-23307. (Sage Series on Armed Forces & Society: Vol. 11). 1977. 18.00x (ISBN 0-8039-0841-5). Sage.

Teitler, Risa. Budgerigars, Taming & Training. (Illus.). 96p. 1979. 2.95 (ISBN 0-87666-887-2, KW-070). TFH Pubns.

--Cockatoos, Taming & Training. (Illus.). 96p. 1980. 2.95 (ISBN 0-87666-888-0, KW-071). TFH Pubns.

--Macaws: Taming & Training. (Illus.). 1979. 2.95 (ISBN 0-87666-884-8, KW-054). TFH Pubns.

Teja, A. S. Chemical Engineering & the Environment. (Critical Reports on Applied Chemistry). 115p. 1981. 27.95 (ISBN 0-470-27106-X). Halsted Pr.

--Chemical Engineering & the Environments. LC 80-26427. 115p. 1981. 27.95 (ISBN 0-470-27106-X). Halsted Pr.

Tejera, Gomez & Lopez, Cruz. La Escuela Puertorriquena. 1970. 16.95 (ISBN 0-87751-004-0, Pub by Troutman Press). E Torres & Sons.

Tekippe, Terry J. Christian Living Today: A Personal Credo. LC 77-14805. 1977. pap. 2.45 (ISBN 0-8091-2060-7). Paulist Pr.

Tekoah, Thomas. In the Face of the Nations. 1976. 10.00 (ISBN 0-8074-0087-4, 382600). UAHC.

Telang, K. T., tr. see Mueller, F. Max.

Teleki, Geza & Steffy, Karen. Goblin, a Wild Chimpanzee. (gr. 3-6). 1977. PLB 7.95 (ISBN 0-525-30747-8). Dutton.

Teleki, Geza P. see Harding, Robert S.

Teleki, Gloria A. Baskets of Rural America. (Illus.). 1975. pap. 7.50 (ISBN 0-525-47409-9). Dutton.

Telemaque, Eleanor W. Haiti Through Its Holidays. LC 79-52858. (Illus.). 64p. (gr. 4-6). 1980. 7.50 (ISBN 0-914110-12-8). Blyden Pr.

Telesio, Piero. Foreign Licensing Policy in Multinational Enterprises. (Praeger Special Studies). 21.95 (ISBN 0-03-047476-0). Praeger.

Television Research Committee. Second Progress Report & Recommendations. (Orig.). 1970. pap. text ed. 5.25x (ISBN 0-7185-1090-9, Leicester). Humanities.

Telfair, David. Duchess Polly. (Orig.). 1979. pap. text ed. 2.50 o.p. (ISBN 0-425-04152-2). Berkley Pub.

Telfair, Richard. Secret of Apache Canyon. 1978. pap. 1.25 o.p. (ISBN 0-449-13985-9, GM). Fawcett.

Telfer, Elizabeth. Happiness. LC 79-16373. 1980. cancelled (ISBN 0-312-36171-8). St Martin.

Telfer, Elizabeth, jt. auth. see Downie, R. S.

Telford, Charles W. & Sawrey, James. The Exceptional Individual. 3rd ed. LC 76-44470. (Illus.). 1977. ref. ed. 18.95x (ISBN 0-13-293837-5). P-H.

Telford, Charles W., jt. auth. see Sawrey, James M.

Telford, Lawrence. From Helgoland to Hollywood. 160p. 1981. 8.00 (ISBN 0-682-49738-X). Exposition.

Telford, Shirley. Economic & Political Peace, Vol. 2. LC 76-51755. 1977. 6.95 (ISBN 0-9600202-5-X). William & Rich.

Telford, W. M., et al. Applied Geophysics. LC 74-16992. (Illus.). 700p. 1975. 95.50 (ISBN 0-521-20670-7); pap. 29.95x (ISBN 0-521-29146-1). Cambridge U Pr.

Te Linde, Richard W. & Mattingly, Richard F. Operative Gynecology. 4th ed. LC 79-97124. (Span. & Portuguese eds. avail). 1970. 35.00 o.p. (ISBN 0-397-50266-4). Lippincott.

Tell, Sharon. Mini Value Plays. (gr. 2-3). 1977. pap. text ed. 3.25x (ISBN 0-933892-07-1). Child Focus Co.

Tellenbach, Gerd. Konigtum & Stamme in der Werdezeit Des Deutschen Reiches. LC 80-2002. 1981. Repr. of 1939 ed. 18.50 (ISBN 0-404-18600-9). AMS Pr.

Teller, Edward. Energy from Heaven & Earth. LC 79-4049. (Illus.). 1979. text ed. 17.95x (ISBN 0-7167-1063-3); pap. text ed. 9.95x (ISBN 0-7167-1064-1). W H Freeman.

Teller, Edward & Yoder, Paul V. Great Issues 72: Imortant Questions Facing the American Public. 1973. 5.95. TSU Pr.

Teller, Edward, ed. Fusion-Magnetic: Magnetic, Vol. 1. 1981. Pt.a. write for info. (ISBN 0-12-685201-4); Pt. B. write for info. (ISBN 0-12-685241-3). Acad Pr.

Teller, Edward, et al. Power & Security. LC 75-44722. (Critical Choices for Americans Ser.: Vol. 4). 1976. 15.95 (ISBN 0-669-00416-2). Lexington Bks.

Teller, Jane. Love Poem for a Bank Robber. (Illus., Orig.). 1981. pap. 2.50 (ISBN 0-914140-09-4). Carpenter Pr.

Teller, Lee S. Centennial Ball. (Historical Romance). 368p. (Orig.). 1981. pap. 2.75 (ISBN 0-515-05864-5). Jove Pubns.

Teller, Virginia & White, Sheila J., eds. Studies in Child Language & Multilingualism. LC 80-16810. 187p. 1980. 28.00x (ISBN 0-89766-078-1). NY Acad Sci.

Telleria, M. T. Contribucion Al Estudio De los Aphyllophorales Espanoles: With Key to Species in English. (Bibliotheca Mycologica: No. 74). (Illus.). 474p. (Span.). 1981. lib. bdg. 50.00x (ISBN 3-7682-1274-2, Pub. by Cramer Germany). Lubrecht & Cramer.

Teluk, John, jt. auth. see Katsaros, Thomas.

Teman, R. Navier-Stokes Equations. LC 79-15106. (Studies Inmathematics & Its Applications: Vol. 2). 520p. 1979. 68.50 (ISBN 0-444-85307-3, North Holland); pap. 24.50 (ISBN 0-444-85308-1, North-Holland). Elsevier.

Temes, Lloyd. Electronic Circuits for Technicians. (Illus.). 1970. text ed. 15.50 o.p. (ISBN 0-07-063485-8, G); answers 1.50 o.p. (ISBN 0-07-063486-6). McGraw.

Temkin, Samuel. Elements of Acoustics. 544p. 1981. text ed. 23.95 (ISBN 0-471-05990-0). Wiley.

Temkin, Sara, jt. auth. see Myers, Alpha.

Temko, Allan. Eero Saarinen. (Makers of Contemporary Architecture Ser). (Orig.). 1966. 6.95 o.s.i. (ISBN 0-8076-0199-3); pap. 3.95 o.s.i. (ISBN 0-8076-0391-0). Braziller.

Temko, Florence. Decoupage Crafts. LC 74-33666. 64p. (gr. 3-7). 1976. PLB 5.95 o.p. (ISBN 0-385-07791-2). Doubleday.

--Folk Crafts for World Friendship. LC 76-4215. (gr. 3-5). 1976. 9.95 (ISBN 0-385-11115-0). Doubleday.

--Paper Capers: All Kinds of Things to Make with Paper. (Illus.). (gr. 4-6). 1975. pap. 1.50 (ISBN 0-590-09938-8, Schol Pap). Schol Bk Serv.

Temme, Mark E. Searching for Truth. 96p. 1978. 3.95 (ISBN 0-8059-2601-1). Dorrance.

Tempa, Susan La see La Tempa, Susan.

Tempelton, Darlene. Woman in Yorkist England. Ide, Arthur F., ed. LC 79-19011. (Woman in History Ser.: Vol. 16). (Illus.). 80p. 12.95 (ISBN 0-86663-051-1); pap. 9.95. Ide Hse.

Temperley, Alan. Tales of Galloway. 319p. 1980. 12.50x (ISBN 0-7050-0076-1, Pub. by Skilton & Shaw England). State Mutual Bk.

Temperley, H. N. & Trevena, D. H. Liquids & Their Properties: A Molecular & Microscopic Treatise. LC 77-8177. 1978. 59.95 (ISBN 0-470-99203-4). Halsted Pr.

Temperley, H. W., ed. History of the Peace Conference of Paris, 6 vols. Incl. Vol. 1. 1920; Vol. 2. The Settlement with Germany; Vol. 3. Chronology, Notes & Documents; Vol. 4. 1921; Vol. 5. Economic Reconstruction & Protection of Minorities; Vol. 6. 1924. (Royal Institute of International Affairs Ser). 1924. 179.00x set (ISBN 0-19-821478-2). Oxford U Pr.

Temperley, Howard. The Price of Freedom. 1981. text ed. 16.50x (ISBN 0-391-01148-0). Humanities.

Temperley, Mary S., jt. auth. see Rivers, Wilga M.

Temperley, Nicholas. The Music of the English Parish Church, 2 vols. LC 77-84811. (Cambridge Studies in Music). (Illus.). 1980. Vol. 1. 79.50 (ISBN 0-521-22045-9); Vol. 2. 39.50 (ISBN 0-521-22046-7). Cambridge U Pr.

Tempest, D. W. see Rose, A. H., et al.

Tempest, N. R. Teaching Clever Children, 7-11. 1974. 10.00 (ISBN 0-7100-7805-6); pap. 4.75 (ISBN 0-7100-7806-4). Routledge & Kegan.

Tempest, W., ed. Infrasound & Low Frequency Vibration. 1977. 50.50 (ISBN 0-12-685450-5). Acad Pr.

Tempesta, Antonio. Metamorphoseon...Ovidianarum. LC 75-27861. (Renaissance & the Gods Ser.: Vol. 19). (Illus.). 1976. Repr. of 1606 ed. lib. bdg. 73.00 (ISBN 0-8240-2067-7). Garland Pub.

Temple, Carroll. Triazoles, One, Two, Four. (Monographs). 752p. 1980. 175.00 (ISBN 0-471-04656-6, Pub. by Wiley-Interscience). Wiley.

Temple, Cliff & Tatlow, Peter. Gymnastics for Girls. (Pelham Pictorial Sports Instruction Ser.). (Illus.). 1978. 12.50 (ISBN 0-7207-1013-8). Transatlantic.

Temple, Douglas M. Real Estate Investment for the Eighties: How to Build Financial Security in the Face of Inflation. (Illus.). 1981. 12.95 (ISBN 0-8092-7024-2). Contemp Bks.

Temple, Nigel. John Nash & the Village Picturesque. (Illus.). 172p. 1980. text ed. 33.00x (ISBN 0-904387-24-0). Humanities.

Temple, O. Notes on the Tribes, Provinces, Emirates & States of the Northern Province of Nigeria. 595p. 1965. 35.00x (ISBN 0-7146-1728-8, F Cass Co). Biblio Dist.

Temple, R. C., jt. ed. see Steel, Flora A.

Temple, Robert. The Sirius Mystery. LC 74-83583. (Orig.). 1978. pap. 6.95 (ISBN 0-312-72731-3). St Martin.

Temple, Sydney. The Carmel Mission, from Founding to Rebuilding. LC 79-57168. (Illus.). 176p. 1980. pap. 5.95 (ISBN 0-913548-71-5, Valley Calif). Western Tanager.

Temple, William. Christianity & Social Order. 1977. 5.95 (ISBN 0-8164-0348-1). Crossroad NY.

--What Christians Stand For in the Secular World. Sherman, Franklin, ed: LC 65-21081. (Facet Bks.). (Orig.). 1965. pap. 1.00 (ISBN 0-8006-3021-1, 1-3021). Fortress.

Templeman, Donald C. The Italian Economy. 400p. 1981. 26.95 (ISBN 0-03-057612-1). Praeger.

Templeman, Eleanor L. Virginia Heritage Address Book. 1975. pap. 2.95x o.p. (ISBN 0-685-83284-8). Templeman.

Templer, J. C. Further Listening Comprehension Tests. 1972. pap. text ed. 2.50x (ISBN 0-435-28728-1); tchr's ed. 3.50x (ISBN 0-435-28729-X). Heinemann Ed.

Templeton & Somorjai, eds. Low Energy Electron Diffraction. pap. 5.00 (ISBN 0-686-60375-3). Polycrystal Bk Serv.

Templeton, Darlene, et al. Woman & Medieval England. LC 79-19011. (Woman in History Ser.: Vol. 13). (Illus.). 80p. 1980. 15.95 (ISBN 0-86663-057-0); pap. 9.00 (ISBN 0-86663-058-9). Ide Hse.

Templeton, Janet. Lover's Knot. LC 80-2083. 192p. 1981. 9.95 (ISBN 0-385-17209-5). Doubleday.

Templin, Kevin. Finality Testament: Book of Life. 1981. 5.75 (ISBN 0-8062-1679-4). Carlton.

Templin, Mildred C. Certain Language Skills in Children: Their Development & Interrelationships. LC 57-8922. (Child Welfare Monograph Ser: No. 26). (Illus.). 1957. 10.95x (ISBN 0-8166-0152-6). U of Minn Pr.

Temporini, Hildegard. Die Frauen am Hofe Trajans. (Illus.). 1979. 66.80x (ISBN 3-11-007822-8). De Gruyter.

Ten, C. L. Mill on Liberty. 464p. 1981. 31.00 (ISBN 0-19-824643-9); pap. 14.95 (ISBN 0-19-824644-7). Oxford U Pr.

Tenaza, Richard. Penguins. (gr. 4 up). 1980. PLB 6.90 (ISBN 0-531-04104-2). Watts.

Ten Boom, Corrie. Cada Nuevo Dia. Clifford, Alejandro, tr. from Eng. 1980. pap. 3.60 (ISBN 0-311-40043-4, Edit Mundo). Casa Bautista.

Ten Boom, Corrie see Boom, Corrie T.

Ten Boom, Corrie, tr. Andarilha Para O Senhor. (Portugese Bks.). (Port.). 1979. 1.50 (ISBN 0-8297-0638-0). Life Pubs Intl.

--Cartas Da Prisao. (Portugese Bks.). (Port.). 1979. 1.20 (ISBN 0-8297-0734-4). Life Pubs Intl.

--En la Casa De Mi Padre. (Spanish Bks.). (Span.). 1978. 1.90 (ISBN 0-8297-0547-3). Life Pubs Intl.

--Mision Ineludible. (Spanish Bks.). (Span.). 1978. 1.95 (ISBN 0-8297-0586-4). Life Pubs Intl.

--Refugio Secreto. (Spanish Bks.). (Span.). 1978. 1.95 (ISBN 0-8297-0593-7). Life Pubs Intl.

TenBroek, Jacobus. Equal Under Law. rev. ed. Orig. Title: Anti Slavery Origins of the 14th Amendment. 1965. pap. 1.95 o.s.i. (ISBN 0-02-037810-6, Collier). Macmillan.

TenBroek, Jacobus, et al. Prejudice, War, & the Constitution: Causes & Consequences of the Evacuation of the Japanese Americans in World War II. 1954. pap. 6.95x (ISBN 0-520-01262-3). U of Cal Pr.

Ten Cate, A. Richard. Oral Histology: Development, Structure & Function. LC 79-18620. (Illus.). 500p. 1980. text ed. 29.95 (ISBN 0-8016-4886-6). Mosby.

Tencin, Claudine. The Siege of Calais. Shugrue, Michael F., ed. (The Flowering of the Novel, 1740-1775 Ser). 1974. Repr. of 1740 ed. lib. bdg. 50.00 (ISBN 0-8240-1101-5). Garland Pub.

Tendulkar, Vijay. The Vultures. Adarkar, Priya, tr. from Marathi. 140p. 1975. pap. 2.40 (ISBN 0-88253-682-6). Ind-US Inc.

Tenenbaum, Aaron, jt. auth. see Augenstein, Moshe.

Tenenbaum, Aaron M., jt. auth. see Augenstein, Moshe.

Tenenbaum, Frances. Gardening with Wildflowers. LC 73-1109. (Encore Editions). (Illus.). 1973. 3.95 o.p. (ISBN 0-684-15005-0, ScribT). Scribner.

Tenenti, Alberto. Piracy and the Decline of Venice, 1580-1615. Pullan, Janet & Pullan, Brian, trs. (Illus.). 1967. 20.00x (ISBN 0-520-01263-1). U of Cal Pr.

Tener, Robert L. The Phoenix Riddle: A Study of Irony in Comedy. (SSEL Poetic Drama Ser.: No. 44). (Orig.). 1979. pap. text ed. 25.00x (ISBN 0-391-01612-1). Humanities.

Teng, Wayne C. Foundation Design. (Illus.). 1962. ref. ed. 27.95x (ISBN 0-13-329805-1). P-H.

Tengbom, Mildred. Does Anyone Care How I Feel? 128p. (gr. 4 up). 1981. pap. 3.95 (ISBN 0-87123-142-5, 210142). Bethany Fell.

Ten Grotenhuis, Elizabeth, jt. auth. see Rosenfield, John M.

Tengstrom, Emin. A Study of Juvenal's Tenth Satire. 1981. pap. text ed. 14.00x (ISBN 91-7346-089-3). Humanities.

Tenhaeff, W. H. Telepathy & Clairvoyance: Views on Some Little Investigated Capabilities of Man. (Illus.). 176p. 1973. 16.75 (ISBN 0-398-02455-3). C C Thomas.

Tenhonen, Margita E. Gloomy Clouds Over the Danube. 169p. 1980. 7.95 (ISBN 0-533-04437-5). Vantage.

Tenison, Marika H. Book of Afternoon Tea. LC 79-56046. (Illus.). 96p. 1980. 11.95 (ISBN 0-7153-7929-1). David & Charles.

--Cooking with Vegetables. (Illus.). 284p. 1981. 16.95 (ISBN 0-224-01597-4, Pub. by Chatto-Bodley-Jonathan). Merrimack Bk Serv.

--New Fish Cookery. 1979. 14.95x (ISBN 0-8464-0060-X). Beekman Pubs.

--Recipes from a Country Kitchen. 1979. 14.95x (ISBN 0-8464-0063-4). Beekman Pubs.

Tenjack, Martha, tr. see Roy, Kristina.

Tenkte, Adriann & Wallace, Robert B. Protection & Development in Mexico. 1980. 35.00 (ISBN 0-312-65217-8). St Martin.

Tenn, William. Of Men & Monsters. 256p. (Orig.). 1981. pap. 2.50 (ISBN 0-345-29523-4, Del Rey). Ballantine.

--Of Men & Monsters. 256p. 1975. pap. 2.50 o.p. (ISBN 0-345-24884-8). Ballantine.

--The Square Root of Man. 224p. (Orig.). 1981. pap. 2.25 (ISBN 0-345-29230-8, Del Rey). Ballantine.

Tenn, William & Westlake, D. Once Against the Law. 1968. 6.95 o.s.i. (ISBN 0-02-616900-2). Macmillan.

Tennant, Alan. The Guadalupe Mountains of Texas, Vol 10. (Elma Dill Russell Spencer Foundation Ser: Vol. 10). (Illus.). 160p. Date not set. 29.95 (ISBN 0-292-72720-8). U of Tex Pr.

Tennant, Alan & Werler, John E. The Snakes of Texas: A Field Guide. (Illus.). 384p. 1981. text ed. 19.95 (ISBN 0-292-77559-8); pap. 9.95 (ISBN 0-292-77560-1). U of Tex Pr.

Tennant, Emma. The Last of the Country House Murders. LC 76-6976. 160p. (gr. 8 up). 1976. 7.95 o.p. (ISBN 0-525-66490-4). Elsevier-Nelson.

--Wild Nights. LC 79-3365. 132p. 1980. 9.95 (ISBN 0-15-196725-3). HarBraceJ.

Tennant, N. Natural Logic. 206p. 1979. 13.00x (ISBN 0-85224-347-2, Pub. by Edinburgh U Pr Scotland). Columbia U Pr.

Tennant, P. E. Theophile Gautier. (Athlone French Poets Ser). 150p. 1975. text ed. 20.00x (ISBN 0-485-14604-5, Athlone Pr); pap. text ed. 10.00x (ISBN 0-485-12204-9, Athlone Pr). Humanities.

Tennant, P. F. Ibsen's Dramatic Technique. 1965. Repr. of 1948 ed. text ed. 10.00x (ISBN 0-391-00471-9). Humanities.

Tennant, Roger. Joseph Conrad. LC 80-69393. 1981. 12.95 (ISBN 0-689-11152-5). Atheneum.

Tennant-Smith, J. Mathematics for the Manager. 1971. 17.95x (ISBN 0-17-761010-7). Intl Ideas.

Tennekes, J. Anthropology, Relativism & Method: An Inquiry into the Methodological Principles of a Science of Culture. (Studies of Developing Countries: No. 10). 1971. text ed. 22.25x (ISBN 90-232-0855-2). Humanities.

Tennenhouse, Dan J. Attorneys Medical Deskbook. LC 75-15123. 1975. 50.00 (ISBN 0-686-20645-2). Lawyers Co-Op.

Tennent, R. Principles of Programming Languages. 1981. 21.00 (ISBN 0-13-709873-1). P-H.

Tennessee Historical Commission, ed. see Sevier, John.

Tennessee Trails Association, jt. auth. see Means, Evan.

Tennessen, Herman. Problems of Knowledge. 88p. 1980. pap. text ed. 10.25x (ISBN 90-232-1762-4). Humanities.

Tenney, Frank F., Jr. The Enchanting Experience: Naples - Marco Island. Woolfolk, Doug, ed. (Illus.). 112p. 1981. 10.00 (ISBN 0-86518-016-4). Moran Pub Corp.

Tenney, Helen. Mark's Sketch Book of Christ. 1975. spiral bound 4.95 (ISBN 0-85151-075-2). Banner of Truth.

Tenney, Merill E., tr. Diccionario Biblico. (Spanish Bks.). (Span.). 1979. 3.50 (ISBN 0-8297-0540-6); pap. 2.50 (ISBN 0-686-28811-4). Life Pubs Intl.

Tenney, Merrill C. John: The Gospel of Belief. 1948. 8.95 (ISBN 0-8028-3252-0). Eerdmans.

--New Testament Survey. rev. ed. (Illus.). 1961. 13.95 (ISBN 0-8028-3251-2). Eerdmans.

Tenniel, Sir John, jt. auth. see Carroll, Lewis.

Tennis, Craig. Heeere's Johnny: A Behind the Scenes Closeup of Johnny Carson & the Tonight Show. (Orig.). 1980. pap. write for info. (ISBN 0-671-41451-8). PB.

--Here's Johnny: A Close-up of Johnny Carson & the Tonight Show. (Illus.). pap. 2.50 (ISBN 0-686-68808-2). PB.

Tennis Magazine, jt. ed. see Wiltse, David.

Tennis Magazine Editors. Instant Tennis Lessons. (Tennis Magazine Bks-Instant Lesson Ser.). (Illus.). 191p. 1978. pap. 4.95 (ISBN 0-914178-18-0). Golf Digest Bks.

--Instant Tennis Lessons. LC 77-92905. (Instant Lessons Ser.). (Illus.). 191p. 1978. pap. 4.95 (ISBN 0-914178-18-0, 24171, Pub. by Tennis Mag). Golf Digest.

--The Tennis Player's Handbook. LC 79-65033. (Tennis Magazine Bks). (Illus.). 318p. 1980. pap. 8.95 (ISBN 0-914178-32-6). Golf Digest Bks.

--Tennis Strokes & Strategies. LC 75-14065. (Illus.). 217p. 1975. 10.95 (ISBN 0-671-22073-X). Tennis Mag.

Tennis Magazine Editors, jt. auth. see Instruction Advisory Board.

Tennis Magazine Eds. & Instruction Advisory Board. Tennis: How to Play, How to Win. LC 77-92906. (Tennis Magazine Bks.). (Illus.). 222p. 1978. 11.95 (ISBN 0-914178-19-9). Golf Digest Bks.

Tennison, B. R. Sheaf Theory. LC 74-31791. (London Mathematical Society Lecture Note Ser: No. 20). 120p. 1976. pap. 16.95 (ISBN 0-521-20784-3). Cambridge U Pr.

Tennissen, A. C., jt. auth. see Eveland, H. E.

Tennissen, Anthony C. Colorful Mineral Identifier. LC 72-151706. (Illus.). (gr. 10 up). 1971. 6.95 (ISBN 0-8069-3040-3); PLB 6.69 (ISBN 0-8069-3041-1). Sterling.

Tennissen, Anthony T., ed. see Schumann, Walter.

Tennov, Dorothy. Psychotherapy: The Hazardous Cure. LC 75-40755. 320p. 1976. pap. 3.50 (ISBN 0-385-11657-8, Anch). Doubleday.

--Super Self: A Woman's Guide to Self-Management. LC 76-41721. (Funk & W Bk.). 1977. 8.95 o.s.i. (ISBN 0-308-10273-8, TYC-T). T Y Crowell.

--Super Self: A Woman's Guide to Self-Management. 1978. pap. 1.95 (ISBN 0-515-04510-1). Jove Pubns.

Tennyson, Alfred. Idylls of the King. (Classics Ser). (gr. 10 up). 1968. pap. 1.95 (ISBN 0-8049-0180-5, CL-180). Airmont.

--Idylls of the King & a Selection of Poems. pap. 1.95 (ISBN 0-451-51382-7, CJ1382, Sig Classics). NAL.

--Poems of Alfred, Lord Tennyson. Rausen, Ruth G., ed. LC 64-13910. (Poets Ser). (Illus.). (gr. 6 up). 1964. 8.95 (ISBN 0-690-64146-X, TYC-J). T Y Crowell.

Tennyson, Alfred L. A Choice of Tennyson's Verse. Cecil, David, ed. 1971. pap. 3.95 (ISBN 0-571-09184-9, Pub. by Faber & Faber). Merrimack Bk Serv.

--In Memoriam. Ross, Robert H., ed. LC 73-13041. (Critical Editions Ser.). 261p. 1974. 8.95 (ISBN 0-393-04365-7); pap. 3.95x (ISBN 0-393-09379-4). Norton.

Tennyson, Charles. Life's All a Fragment: Tennyson. 264p. 1980. Repr. of 1953 ed. lib. bdg. 30.00 (ISBN 0-89760-881-X). Telegraph Bks.

Tennyson, Elizabeth J., jt. ed. see Tennyson, G. B.

Tennyson, G. B. Victorian Devotional Poetry: The Tractarian Mode. LC 80-14416. 1980. text ed. 17.50x (ISBN 0-674-93586-1). Harvard U Pr.

Tennyson, G. B. & Tennyson, Elizabeth J., eds. Index to Nineteenth-Century Fiction: 1945-1975, Vols. 1-30. 1978. 17.50x (ISBN 0-520-03334-5). U of Cal Pr.

Tennyson, G. B., jt. ed. see Knoepflmacher, U. C.

Tennyson, Hallam, ed. Studies in Tennyson. LC 79-55520. 205p. 1981. text ed. 27.50x (ISBN 0-06-496807-3). B&N.

Tenore, Kenneth R. & Coull, Bruce C., eds. Marine Benthic Dynamics. LC 80-15941. (Belle Baruch Lib. in Marine Science: No. 11). 474p. 1980. text ed. 27.50 (ISBN 0-87249-401-2). U of SC Pr.

Ten Seldam, R. E. & Helwig, E. B. Histological Typing of Skin Tumours. (World Health Organization: International Histological Classification of Tumours Ser.). 1977. 70.00 (ISBN 92-4-176012-5, 70-1-012-20); incl. slides 158.50 (ISBN 92-4-176012-5, 70-1-012-00). Am Soc Clinical.

Tenth Pfizer Intl. Symposium. Cancer Assessment & Monitoring. Symington, T., et al, eds. (Illus.). 480p. 1980. text ed. 55.00 (ISBN 0-443-01955-X). Churchill.

Tentler, Leslie. Wage-Earning Women: Industrial Work & Family Life in the U. S., 1900-1930. 1979. 16.95x (ISBN 0-19-502627-6). Oxford U Pr.

Teodoro, Luis V., ed. Out of This Struggle: The Filipinos in Hawaii. (Illus.). 168p. 1981. 12.95 (ISBN 0-8248-0747-2). U Pr of Hawaii.

Teplick, J. George & Haskin, Marvin E. Sugical Radiology: A Complement in Radiology & Imaging to the Sabiston-Davis-Christopher Textbook of Surgery, 3 vols. (Illus.). 1152p. Date not set. text ed. 65.00 ea.; Vol. 1. (ISBN 0-7216-8781-4); Vol. 2. 65.00 (ISBN 0-7216-8782-2); Vol. 3. 65.00 (ISBN 0-7216-8791-1); Set. 250.00 (ISBN 0-7216-8783-0). Saunders. Postponed.

Teplitz, Jerry & Kellman, Shelly. How to Relax & Enjoy... LC 77-74655. (Illus.). 1977. pap. 6.95 o.p. (ISBN 0-87040-402-4). Japan Pubns.

Teplitz, Paul V., jt. auth. see Cambridge Research Institute.

Teplitz, Paul V., jt. auth. see Markham, Jesse W.

Teplitz, Saul, ed. Best Jewish Sermons 5733-34. LC 58-3698. (Best Jewish Sermons Ser: No. 12). 1974. 10.00x o.p. (ISBN 0-685-47974-9). Jonathan David.

Tepper, Bette & Godnick, Newton E. Mathematics for Retail Buying. 2nd ed. (Illus.). 224p. 1973. pap. 10.00 (ISBN 0-87005-215-2); answer manual 3.00 (ISBN 0-87005-216-0). Fairchild.

Tepper, I. Solid State Devices, 2 vols. 1974. Vol. 1, Theory. 14.95 (ISBN 0-201-07435-4); Vol. 2. 15.95 (ISBN 0-201-07436-2). A-W.

Tepper, Krysta, jt. auth. see Kohn, Rita.

Tepper, M. Advanced & Extra Class Amateur License Q & A Manual. 2nd ed. (gr. 10 up). 1978. pap. 7.25 (ISBN 0-8104-5814-4). Hayden.

--Novice & General Class Amateur License Q & A Manual. 2nd ed. (gr. 10 up). 1977. pap. 9.55 (ISBN 0-8104-5599-4). Hayden.

Tepper, Marvin. Basic Radio, Vols. 1-6. rev. 2nd ed. (Illus.). 888p. 1974. combined ed. o.p. 24.95 (ISBN 0-8104-5927-2); Vol. 1. pap. 6.50 (ISBN 0-8104-5921-3); Vol. 2. pap. 6.95 (ISBN 0-8104-5922-1); Vol. 3. pap. 6.20 (ISBN 0-8104-5923-X); Vol. 4. pap. 5.75 o.p. (ISBN 0-8104-5924-8); Vol. 5. pap. 5.75 o.p. (ISBN 0-8104-5925-6); Vol. 6. pap. 5.75 o.p. (ISBN 0-8104-5926-4); Set Of 6 Vols. pap. 29.55 o.p. (ISBN 0-8104-5920-5); transparencies. 106.20, 0.50 ea. exams for vols., 1, 2, or 3 (ISBN 0-8104-0576-8). Hayden.

--Electronic Ignition Systems. (gr. 10 up). 1977. pap. 5.95 (ISBN 0-8104-5746-6). Hayden.

--Quad Sound. (Illus.). 128p. 1976. pap. 4.95 o.p. (ISBN 0-8104-5987-6). Hayden.

Tepper, Nona D., jt. auth. see Tepper, Terri P.

Tepper, Terri P. & Tepper, Nona D. The New Entrepreneurs: Women Working from Home. LC 80-17578. (Illus.). 256p. 1980. 10.95 (ISBN 0-87663-342-4). Universe.

Tepperman, Barry, jt. auth. see Simosko, Vladimir.

Tepperman, Jay. Metabolic & Endocrine Physiology. 4th ed. (Illus.). 1980. write for info. (ISBN 0-8151-8755-6); pap. write for info. (ISBN 0-8151-8756-4). Year Bk Med.

Tepperman, Lorne, jt. auth. see Bell, David.

Teranishi, Roy. Agricultural & Food Chemistry: Past, Present, Future. (Illus.). 1978. lib. bdg. 36.50 (ISBN 0-87055-231-7). AVI.

Terasaki, Paul I. Histocompatibility Testing Nineteen Eighty, Vol. 1. LC 80-36737. (Illus.). 1980. 59.00 (ISBN 0-9604606-0-8). UCLA Tissue.

Terblanche, John, ed. see South African International Liver Conference, 1973.

Terdal, Leif see Nash, Eric.

Terence. The Comedies of Terence. Copley, Frank O., tr. Incl. The Brothers; The Eunuch; The Mother-in-Law; Phormio; The Self-Tormenter; The Woman of Andros. LC 67-20452. (Orig.). 1967. pap. 6.95 (ISBN 0-672-60279-2, LLA90). Bobbs.

--Comoediae. 2nd ed. Kauer, R. & Lindsay, W. M., eds. (Oxford Classical Texts Ser). 1926. 18.95x (ISBN 0-19-814636-1). Oxford U Pr.

Terenius, L. Y., jt. ed. see Kosterlitz, H. W.

Teresa, Vincent. Wiseguys. 1978. 7.95 o.p. (ISBN 0-525-23560-4). Dutton.

Teresa, Vincent & Renner, Thomas C. My Life in the Mafia. 368p. 1977. pap. 1.95 o.p. (ISBN 0-449-23246-8, Crest). Fawcett.

Teresa of Avila, St. Interior Castle. 1972. pap. 2.95 (ISBN 0-385-03643-4, Im). Doubleday.

--Way of Perfection. pap. 2.95 (ISBN 0-385-06539-6, D176, Im). Doubleday.

Teresi, Dick & Colligan, Doug. The Cyclist's Manual. LC 76-1344. (Illus.). 1981. 14.95 (ISBN 0-8069-5562-7); lib. bdg. 13.29 (ISBN 0-8069-5563-5). Sterling.

Tergie, Charles, ed. see Stendhal.

Ter Haar, D. Elements of Hamiltonian Mechanics. 2nd ed. 1971. 15.00 (ISBN 0-08-016726-8). Pergamon.

--L. D. Landau, Vol. 2. 1969. 16.50 (ISBN 0-08-006451-5); pap. 7.75 (ISBN 0-08-006450-7). Pergamon.

--The Old Quantum Theory. 1967. 26.00 (ISBN 0-08-012102-0); pap. 8.50 (ISBN 0-08-012101-2). Pergamon.

Ter-Haar, D. & Henin, F. Lectures on Selected Topics in Equilibrium & Non-Equilibrium Statistical Mechanics. LC 77-8300. 1977. text ed. 25.00 (ISBN 0-08-017937-1). Pergamon.

Ter Haar, D., ed. see Kapitza, P. L.

Ter Haar, D., ed. see Rogers, R. R., et al.

TerHorst, Jerald F. Gerald Ford & the Future of the Presidency. LC 74-82727. 1974. 11.95 (ISBN 0-89388-191-0). Okpaku Communications.

Ter Horst, Robert. Myth, Honor, and History in the Secular Drama of Don Pedro Calderon. LC 80-5183. (Studies in Romance Languages: No. 25). 1981. price not set (ISBN 0-8131-1440-3). U Pr of Ky.

TerHuen, Pat & Smith, Lynda. Being Fat (Has Nothing to Do with Food) A Handbook for the Yo-Yo-Dieter. LC 80-80247. (Illus.). 80p. 1981. pap. 3.95 (ISBN 0-89087-314-3). Celestial Arts.

Terhune, Mary V. Marion Harland's Autobiography. Baxter, Annette K., ed. LC 79-8816. (Signal Lives Ser.). 1980. Repr. of 1910 ed. lib. bdg. 45.00x (ISBN 0-405-12860-6). Arno.

Terkel, Studs. Giants of Jazz. rev. ed. LC 75-20024. (Illus.). 192p. (gr. 5 up). 1975. 10.95 (ISBN 0-690-00998-4, TYC-J). T Y Crowell.

Ter Kuile, jt. auth. see Gerson.

Terman, Douglas. First Strike. 1980. pap. 2.95 (ISBN 0-671-83466-5). PB.

Terman, Lewis M. & Miles, Catherine C. Sex & Personality. 600p. 1980. Repr. of 1936 ed. lib. bdg. 50.00 (ISBN 0-89987-811-3). Darby Bks.

Termini, B. & Lee, Y. Essentials of Echocardiography. (Illus.). 1976. 18.50 (ISBN 0-87489-094-2). Med Economics.

Termini, Maria. Silkscreening. LC 77-10719. (Creative Handcraft Ser.). (Illus.). 1978. 15.95 (ISBN 0-13-809996-0, Spec); pap. 6.95 (ISBN 0-13-809988-X, Spec). P-H.

Ternon, Yves. Armenians: History of a Genocide. LC 80-19499. 1980. write for info. (ISBN 0-88206-038-4). Caravan Bks.

Terpstra. International Marketing. 2nd ed. 1978. 21.95 (ISBN 0-03-039296-9). Dryden Pr.

Terra, Russel G. To See His Face: Homily Themes for Various Occasions. LC 77-24083. 1977. pap. 4.50 o.p. (ISBN 0-8189-0358-9). Alba.

Terrace, Herbert S. & Parker, Scott. Psychological Statistics, 7 vols. 1971. Set. 14.75 (ISBN 0-86589-014-5). Vol. 1, Units 1-3 (ISBN 0-86589-015-3). Vol. 2, Units 4,5 (ISBN 0-86589-016-1). Vol. 3, Units 6,7 (ISBN 0-86589-017-X). Vol. 4, Units 8,9 (ISBN 0-86589-018-8). Vol. 5, Units 10,11 (ISBN 0-86589-019-6). Vol. 6, Units 12,13 (ISBN 0-86589-020-X). Vol. 7, Units 14,15 (ISBN 0-86589-021-8). Individual Learn.

Terrace, Vincent. The Complete Encyclopedia of Television Programs, 2 vols. LC 74-10022. 1976. Set. 29.95 o.p. (ISBN 0-498-01561-0). A S Barnes.

--Complete Encyclopedia of Television Programs 1947-1979. 2nd rev. ed. LC 79-87791. (Illus.). 1200p. 1981. 29.95 (ISBN 0-498-02177-7); pap. 10.95 (ISBN 0-498-02488-1). A S Barnes.

--Radio's Golden Years: The Encyclopedia of Radio Programs 1930-1960. (Illus.). 288p. 1981. 15.00 (ISBN 0-498-02393-1). A S Barnes.

Terraine, John. The Road to Passchedndaele: The Flanders Offensive of 1917: a Study in Inevitability. (Illus.). xxiv, 365p. 1977. 27.50. Shoe String.

--To Win a War: Nineteen Eighteen, The Year of Victory. LC 79-7119. (Illus.). 288p. 1981. 14.95 (ISBN 0-385-15316-3). Doubleday.

Terras, Victor. Belinskii & Russian Literary Criticism: The Heritage of Organic Aesthetics. LC 73-2050. 384p. 1973. 32.50x (ISBN 0-299-06350-X). U of Wis Pr.

--A Karamazov Companion: Commentary on the Genesis, Language, & Style of Dostoevsky's Novel. 400p. 1981. 30.00 (ISBN 0-299-08310-1); pap. text ed. 9.95 (ISBN 0-299-08314-4). U of Wis Pr.

Terrass & Comfort. Teaching Occupational Home Economics. 1979. 9.24 (ISBN 0-87002-282-2). Bennett IL.

Terrell. Elementary Statistics for Business. 1979. 17.95 (ISBN 0-7216-8797-0). Dryden Pr.

Terrell, Carroll F. A Companion to The Cantos of Ezra Pound, Volume I, (Cantos 1-71) 800p. 1980. 28.50x (ISBN 0-520-03687-5). U of Cal Pr.

Terrell, David, jt. auth. see Cave, Frank.

Terrell, Donna M., jt. auth. see Terrell, John Upton.

Terrell, Elizabeth. Games They Paid Michael to Play. Ashton, Sylvia, ed. Date not set. 12.95 (ISBN 0-87949-149-3). Ashley Bks.

Terrell, James C., jt. auth. see Daniel, Wayne W.

Terrell, John, jt. auth. see Leonard, Anne.

Terrell, John U. The Plains Apache. LC 75-9601. 224p. (YA) 1975. 10.95 o.s.i. (ISBN 0-690-00969-0, TYC-T). T Y Crowell.

Terrell, John Upton & Terrell, Donna M. Indian Women of the Western Morning: Their Life in Early America. 200p. 1976. pap. 2.95 (ISBN 0-385-11038-3, Anch). Doubleday.

Terrell, M. E. Professional Food Preperation. 2nd ed. 741p. 1979. 24.50 (ISBN 0-471-85202-3). Wiley.

Terrell, Paul & Weisner, Stan. The Social Impact of Revenue Sharing: Planning, Participation, & the Purchase of Service. LC 76-12882. (Illus.). 1976. 22.95 (ISBN 0-275-23470-3). Praeger.

Terrell, Timothy P., jt. auth. see Freed, Daniel J.

Terrell, Timothy P., jt. auth. see Shanor, Charles A.

Terres, John, ed. see Rue, Leonard L., 3rd.

Terres, John K. The Audubon Society Encyclopedia of North American Birds. LC 80-7616. (Illus.). 1280p. 1980. 60.00 (ISBN 0-394-46651-9). Knopf.

--Songbirds in Your Garden. 3rd st ed. Conrad, Jeff, ed. (Illus.). 228p. 1980. pap. 6.95 (ISBN 0-8015-6945-1, Hawthorn). Dutton.

Terreur, Marc La see Halpenny, Francess.

Terrien, Samuel. Golden Bible Atlas. (Illus.). (gr. 9 up). 1957. 7.95 (ISBN 0-307-15749-0, Golden Pr); PLB 10.69 o.p. (ISBN 0-307-65749-3). Western Pub.

Terrien, Samuel, ed. New Testament in Shorter Form. LC 73-95182. Orig. Title: Reader's New Testament. 1970. 4.95 o.p. (ISBN 0-02-616980-0); pap. 2.95 (ISBN 0-02-089560-7). Macmillan.

Terrill, T. Starr. The Pot & the Kettle. LC 79-66885. 128p. 1980. pap. 8.95 o.p. (ISBN 0-935560-00-9). D Varden Pubns.

Terris, Susan. The Chicken Pox Papers. 1978. pap. 1.50 (ISBN 0-440-41402-4, YB). Dell.

--The Chicken Pox Papers. (Illus.). 128p. (gr. 4-6). 1976. PLB 5.90 o.p. (ISBN 0-531-00332-9). Watts.

--No Boys Allowed. LC 74-23348. 48p. (gr. 1-5). 1976. 5.95 o.p. (ISBN 0-385-04887-4); PLB write for info. o.p. (ISBN 0-385-05749-0). Doubleday.

--No Scarlet Ribbons. 176p. (gr. 5 up). 9.95 (ISBN 0-374-35322-0). FS&G.

--Stage Brat. LC 80-14065. 192p. (gr. 5-9). 1980. 8.95 (ISBN 0-590-07683-3, Four Winds). Schol Bk Serv.

--Two P's in a Pod. LC 77-8488. (gr. 5-9). 1977. 8.25 (ISBN 0-688-80107-2); PLB 7.92 (ISBN 0-688-84107-4). Greenwillow.

Terris, Virginia R., ed. Woman in America: A Guide to Information Sources. LC 73-17564. (American Studies Information Guide Ser.: Vol. 7). 1980. 30.00 (ISBN 0-8103-1268-9). Gale.

Territo, Leonard, tr. see Swanson, C. R., et al.

Territo, Leonard, et al. The Police Personnel Selection Process. LC 76-30889. (Illus.). 1977. pap. text ed. 10.95 (ISBN 0-672-61403-0). Bobbs.

Territorial Bureau of Immigration. The Resources of New Mexico. LC 73-80703. 76p. 1973. Repr. of 1881 ed. 9.50 (ISBN 0-88307-504-0); pap. 1.25 (ISBN 0-88307-503-2). Gannon.

Terry. Plaid for Principles of Management. 3rd ed. 1978. 5.50 (ISBN 0-256-02134-1, 11-0757-03). Learning Syst.

--Plaid for Supervision. 1975. pap. 5.50 (ISBN 0-256-01265-2, 08-0388-00). Learning Syst.

Terry, Bridget. The Popeye Story. 1980. pap. 2.75 (ISBN 0-440-06561-5). Dell.

Terry, Charles, tr. see Matsushita, Konosuke.

Terry, Charles S., tr. see Itoh, Teiji.

Terry, Charles S., tr. see Naito, Akira.

Terry, Dickson. There's a Town in Missouri. 136p. (Orig.). 1980. pap. 4.95 (ISBN 0-86629-016-8). Sunrise MO.

Terry, Garth M. East European Languages & Literatures: A Subject & Name Index to Articles in English-Language Journals, 1900-1977. 275p. 1978. 47.50. ABC-Clio.

Terry, George R. Principles of Management. 7th ed. 1977. text ed. 18.95 (ISBN 0-256-00562-1). Irwin.

--Supervision. rev. ed. 1978. pap. text ed. 12.50 (ISBN 0-256-02047-7). Irwin.

Terry, George R. & Stallard, John J. Office Management & Control. 8th ed. 1980. 17.95x (ISBN 0-256-02271-2). Irwin.

Terry, Gloria B., jt. auth. see Reber, Ralph W.

Terry, J. & Upton, D. Cicero: Speeches Against Antony, Philippics 4, 5, 6. (Modern School Classics Ser.). 1970. 5.95 (ISBN 0-312-13650-1). St Martin.

Terry, Patricia & Garronsky, Serge. Modern French Poetry: A Bilingual Anthology. Terry, Patricia & Garronsky, Serge, trs. from Fr. 192p. 1975. 15.00x (ISBN 0-231-03957-3); pap. 7.00x (ISBN 0-231-03958-1). Columbia U Pr.

Terry, Patricia, ed. Poems of the Vikings: The Elder Edda. LC 69-16528. (Library of Liberal Arts Ser). 1969. text ed. 8.95 (ISBN 0-672-60332-2, LLA128). Bobbs.

Terry, Patricia, jt. ed. see Caws, Mary Ann.

Terry, Patricia, tr. Song of Roland. LC 65-26528. (Orig.). 1965. pap. 5.50 (ISBN 0-672-60476-0, LLA221). Bobbs.

Terry, Patricia, tr. see Terry, Patricia & Garronsky, Serge.

Terry, Paul. Lyrics to a Lassie & Other Verse. 64p. (Orig.). 1980. pap. 4.95 (ISBN 0-937768-01-4). Expressions TX.

Terry, Robert A., jt. ed. see Kay, Robert S.

Terry, Robert M., jt. auth. see Steffensmeier, Darrell J.

Terry, W. Clinton, III. Teaching Religion: The Secularization of Religion Instruction in a West German School System. LC 80-5569. 208p. 1981. lib. bdg. 18.50 (ISBN 0-8191-1366-2); pap. text ed. 9.50 (ISBN 0-8191-1367-0). U Pr of Amer.

Terry, Walter. Alicia & Her Nacional Ballet De Cuba. LC 79-7879. (Illus.). 192p. 1981. pap. 10.95 (ISBN 0-385-14956-5, Anch). Doubleday.

--Ballet Guide. LC 75-20240. (Illus.). 400p. 1976. 15.00 (ISBN 0-396-07024-8). Dodd.

--Careers for the Seventies: Dance. (gr. 9 up). 1971. 4.95g o.s.i. (ISBN 0-02-789150-X, CCPr). Macmillan.

--The Dance in America. (Dance Ser.). (Illus.). xiv, 274p. 1981. Repr. of 1971 ed. lib. bdg. 25.00 (ISBN 0-306-76059-2). Da Capo.

--Frontiers of Dance: The Life of Martha Graham. LC 75-9871. (Women of America Ser.). (Illus.). 160p. (gr. 5-9). 1975. 10.95 (ISBN 0-690-00920-8, TYC-J). T Y Crowell.

--Great Male Dancers of the Ballet. 1978. pap. 10.00 (ISBN 0-385-04197-7, Anchor Pr). Doubleday.

--The King's Ballet Master: A Biography of Denmark's August Bournonville. LC 79-55736. (Illus.). 1979. 8.95 (ISBN 0-396-07722-6). Dodd.

Terry, William D. & Windhorst, Dorothy, eds. Immunotherapy of Cancer: Present Status of Trials in Man. LC 77-83696. (Progress in Cancer Research & Therapy Ser.: Vol. 6). 1978. 61.50 (ISBN 0-89004-182-2). Raven.

Tersine, Richard J. & Davidson, Fredrick. Problems & Models in Operations Management. 2nd ed. LC 79-21810. (Management Ser.). 1980. pap. text ed. 10.50 (ISBN 0-88244-207-4). Grid Pub.

Tertz, Abram, pseud. A Voice from the Chorus. LC 76-7526. 352p. 1976. pap. 10.00 (ISBN 0-374-28500-4). FS&G.

Terweil, Bareno J. Monks & Magic: An Analysis of Religious Ceremonies in Central Thailand. (Scandinavian Institute of Asian Studies Monographs: No. 24). (Orig.). 1976. pap. text ed. 13.75x (ISBN 0-7007-0091-9). Humanities.

Terwilliger, Robert E. & Holmes, Urban T. To Be a Priest: Perspectives on Vocation & Ordination. 192p. (Orig.). 1975. pap. 3.95 (ISBN 0-685-54447-8, 8164-2592-2). Crossroad NY.

Terzaghi, Karl & Peck, R. B. Soil Mechanics in Engineering Practice. 2nd ed. LC 67-17356. 1967. 34.95 (ISBN 0-471-85273-2, Pub. by Wiley-Interscience). Wiley.

Terzaghi, Karl, jt. auth. see Peck, R. B.

Terzibaschitsch, Stefan. Aircraft Carriers of the U. S. Navy. (Illus.). 336p. 1980. 35.00 (ISBN 0-8317-0109-9). Mayflower Bks.

Tesar, Delbert & Matthew, Gary K. The Dynamic Synthesis, Analysis, & Design of Modeled Cam Systems. LC 75-24655. 1976. 28.95 (ISBN 0-669-00226-7). Lexington Bks.

Teschner, Richard V., jt. auth. see Blansitt, Edward L., Jr.

Teschner, Richard V., jt. ed. see Stathatos, Constantine C.

Teschner, Richard V., et al, eds. The Spanish & English of United States Hispanos: A Critical, Annotated Linguistic Bibliography. LC 75-21564. 1975. pap. text ed. 8.95x (ISBN 0-87281-042-9). Ctr Appl Ling.

TeSelle, Sallie M. Literature & the Christian Life. (Publications in Religion Ser.: No. 12). 1966. 17.50x o.p. (ISBN 0-300-00989-5). Yale U Pr.

Teshigahara, Wafu. Japanese Flower Arrangement. LC 66-27558. (Illus.). 1966. 12.95 o.p. (ISBN 0-87011-036-5). Kodansha.

Tesio, Frederico. Breeding the Racehorse. Spinola, Edward, ed. & tr. (Illus.). 13.10 (ISBN 0-85131-028-1, Dist. by Sporting Book Center). J A Allen.

Tesitor, Irene A. & Sinks, Dwight B. Judicial Conduct Organization. 2nd ed. 96p. 1980. pap. 3.75 (8567). Am Judicature.

Teske, Edmund. Images from Within, the Photographs of Edmund Teske. Alinder, James, ed. LC 80-67614. (Untitled Ser.: No. 22). (Illus.). 88p. (Orig.). 1980. pap. 15.00 (ISBN 0-933286-18-X). Friends Photography.

Teskey, Benjamin J. & Shoemaker, James S. Tree Fruit Production. 3rd ed. (Illus.). 1978. text ed. 22.50 (ISBN 0-87055-265-1). AVI.

Tesla, Nikola. My Inventions: Moji Pronalasci. (Illus.). 112p. 1977. 35.00x (ISBN 0-686-63529-9). Heinman.

Tessai, Tomioka, illus. The Works of Tomioka Tessai. (Illus.). 152p. (Orig.). 1968. pap. 5.00 (ISBN 0-88397-015-5). Intl Exhibit Foun.

Tessier, Mitzi. Asheville: A Pictorial History. Fredman, Donna R., ed. (Illus.). 208p. 1981. pap. price not set (ISBN 0-89865-116-6). Donning Co.

Tessier, Paul A. Plastic Surgery of the Orbit & Eyelids. Wolfe, S. Anthony, tr. (Illus.). 320p. 1980. 40.00 (ISBN 0-89352-041-1). Masson Pub.

Tessier, Thomas. The Nightwalker. 1981. pap. 2.50 (ISBN 0-451-09720-3, E9720, Sig). NAL.

Tessina, Tina B., jt. auth. see Smith, Riley K.

Tessler, Diane J. Drugs, Kids & Schools: Practical Strategies for Educators & Other Concerned Adults. LC 80-17294. 1980. pap. 8.95 (ISBN 0-8302-2224-3). Goodyear.

Tessler, Mark A., ed. see Sherbiny, Naiem A.

Tessman, Lora Heims. Children of Parting Parents. LC 77-94094. 1978. 35.00x (ISBN 0-87668-307-3). Aronson.

Tesson, William, jt. auth. see Nadeau, Roland.

Testa, B., jt. auth. see Jenner, P.

Testa, Carlo. New Educational Facilities: An International Survey. LC 75-23359. (Illus.). 192p. 1976. 29.75 o.p. (ISBN 0-89158-505-2). Westview.

Testa, R. B., ed. Aerostructures, Selected Papers of Nicholas J. Hoff. LC 77-164024. 1971. 32.00 (ISBN 0-08-016834-5). Pergamon.

Testas, J., jt. auth. see Garcia-Pelayo, R.

Tester, Sylvia R. Billy's Basketball. LC 76-15632. (Kids in Sports Ser.). (Illus.). (gr. 1-3). 1976. PLB 4.95 (ISBN 0-913778-57-5); pap. 2.75 (ISBN 0-89565-124-6). Childs World.

--Chase! LC 80-14509. (Picture Word Bks.). (Illus.). 32p. (ps-1). 1980. PLB 5.50 (ISBN 0-89565-157-2). Childs World.

--A Day of Surprises. LC 78-23263. (Illus.). (ps-3). 1979. PLB 5.95 (ISBN 0-89565-022-3). Childs World.

--Family! LC 80-12373. (Picture Word Bks.). (Illus.). 32p. (ps-1). 1980. PLB 5.50 (ISBN 0-89565-156-4). Childs World.

--The Great Big Boat. LC 79-12176. (Bible Story Books). (Illus.). (ps-3). 1979. PLB 5.50 (ISBN 0-89565-087-8). Childs World.

--Jealous. (What Does It Mean Ser.). (Illus.). 1980. 7.35g (ISBN 0-516-06446-0). Childrens.

--The Loud-Noisy, Dirty-Grimy, Bad & Naughty Twins: A Book of Synonyms. LC 77-9483. (Using Words Ser.). (Illus.). (gr. k-3). 1977. PLB 5.50 (ISBN 0-913778-89-3). Childs World.

--Melinda. LC 76-30615. (Illus.). (ps-3). 1977. 5.50 (ISBN 0-913778-73-7). Childs World.

--Never Monkey with a Monkey: A Book of Homographic Homophones. LC 77-9503. (Using Words Ser.). (Illus.). (gr. k-3). 1977. PLB 5.50 (ISBN 0-913778-90-7). Childs World.

--Opposite Odelia: A Book of Antonyms. LC 78-5294. (Using Words Ser.). (Illus.). (gr. k-3). 1978. PLB 5.50 (ISBN 0-89565-036-3). Childs World.

--Sad. (What Does It Mean Ser.). (Illus.). 1980. 7.35g (ISBN 0-516-06448-7). Childrens.

--Sometimes I'm Afraid. LC 78-23262. (Illus.). (ps-3). 1979. PLB 5.95 (ISBN 0-89565-021-5). Childs World.

--Traffic Jam! abr. ed. LC 80-16303. (Picture Word Bks.). (Illus.). 32p. (ps-1). 1980. PLB 5.50 (ISBN 0-89565-158-0). Childs World.

--Using Words, 5 bks. Incl. The Loud-Noisy, Dirty-Grimy, Bad & Naughty Twins (ISBN 0-913778-91-5); Never Monkey with a Monkey (ISBN 0-89565-037-1); What Did You Say (77891-5); Opposite Opelia (65036-3); You Dance Like an Ostrich (65037-1). (Illus.). (gr. k-3). 1977. 27.50 set (ISBN 0-89565-002-9); 5.50 ea. Childs World.

--What Did You Say? A Book of Homophones. LC 77-9494. (Using Words Ser.). (Illus.). (gr. k-3). 1977. PLB 5.50 (ISBN 0-913778-91-5). Childs World.

--You Dance Like an Ostrich! A Book of Similes. LC 78-5833. (Using Words Ser.). (Illus.). (gr. k-3). 1978. PLB 5.50 (ISBN 0-89565-037-1). Childs World.

Tetel, Marcel. Montaigne. LC 74-2250. (World Authors Ser.: France: No. 317). 1974. lib. bdg. 12.50 (ISBN 0-8057-2623-3). Twayne.

Tether, John, jt. auth. see Smedley, Ronald.

Tetlow, Elizabeth N. Women & Ministry in the New Testament. LC 79-57398. 256p. (Orig.). 1980. pap. 6.95 (ISBN 0-8091-2249-9). Paulist Pr.

Tetrault, Jeanne. The Woman's Carpentry Book: Building Your Home from the Ground up. LC 78-22801. (Illus.). 400p. 1980. 19.95 (ISBN 0-385-17183-8, Anchor Pr); pap. 10.95 (ISBN 0-385-14269-2). Doubleday.

Tetrault, Jeanne & Thomas, Sherry. Country Women: A Handbook for the New Farmer. LC 75-32296. 8.95 (ISBN 0-385-03062-2, Anchor Pr). Doubleday.

Tetrazzini, Louisa, jt. auth. see Caruso, Enrico.

Tetreault, Wilfred F. Buying & Selling Business Opportunities: A Sales Transaction Handbook. LC 80-18771. 208p. 1981. text ed. 19.95 (ISBN 0-201-07711-6). A-W.

Tetreault, Wilfred F. & Clements, Robert W. How to Start & Succeed in Your Own Business. LC 80-66118. (Illus.). 210p. 1980. 16.95 (ISBN 0-937152-01-3). Am Busn Consult.

Tetreault, Wilfred F., et al. Business Opportunity Appraiser. (Illus.). 50p. 1980. text ed. 10.00 (ISBN 0-937152-03-X). Am Busn Consult.

--How to Buy & Sell Business Opportunities. LC 80-66117. (Illus.). 300p. 1980. text ed. 49.95 (ISBN 0-937152-00-5). Am Busn Consult.

Tetrick, N., jt. auth. see Rodolakis, A.

Tetsuzo Tanikawa & Shufunotomo Editorial Staff, eds. Gendai Chato Taikan: A General View of Contemporary Tea Ceremony & Ceramic Ware, 6 vols. (Illus., Japanese.). 1979. Set. 200.00 (ISBN 0-8048-1343-4, Pub. by Shufunotomo Co Ltd Japan). Vol. 1, 152p. Vol. 2, 164p. Vol. 3, 186p. Vol. 4, 186p. Vol. 5, 186p. Vol. 6, 200p. C E Tuttle.

Teubner, Christian, jt. auth. see Wolter, Annette.

Teune, Henry, jt. auth. see Przeworski, Adam.

Teuscher, Henry. Window-Box Gardening. (Illus.). 1956. 4.95 o.s.i. (ISBN 0-02-617000-0). Macmillan.

Teutsch, Gotthard M. & Von Loeper, Eisenhart, eds. Intensivhaltung von Nutztieren aus ethischer, rechtlicher und ethologischer Sicht: Rechtlicher und Ethologischer Sicht. (Tierhaltung-Animal Management: No. 8). (Ger.). 1979. pap. 18.00 (ISBN 3-7643-1119-3). Birkhauser.

Tevis, Lloyd P., Jr., jt. auth. see Linsdale, Jean M.

Tevis, Rose De see De Tevis, Rose, et al.

Tevis, Walter. Far from Home. LC 80-1073. (Double D Science Fiction Ser.). 192p. 1981. 9.95 (ISBN 0-385-17036-X). Doubleday.

--The Hustler. (Alpha Books). 94p. (Orig.). 1979. pap. text ed. 2.25x (ISBN 0-19-424209-9). Oxford U Pr.

--The Man Who Fell to Earth. 192p. (Orig.). 1981. pap. 2.25 (ISBN 0-553-14274-7). Bantam.

--The Man Who Fell to Earth. (Alpha Books). 94p. (Orig.). 1979. pap. 2.25x (ISBN 0-19-424231-5). Oxford U Pr.

--Mockingbird. 288p. 1980. pap. 2.95 (ISBN 0-553-14144-9). Bantam.

Tevoedjre, Albert. Poverty: Wealth of Mankind. 1979. text ed. 30.00 (ISBN 0-08-023367-8); pap. text ed. 14.00 (ISBN 0-08-023366-X). Pergamon.

Tew, Brian. The Evolution of the International Monetary System 1945-1977. 1979. pap. 10.95 (ISBN 0-470-26705-4). Halsted Pr.

Tewari, S. C. Indo-US Relations: 1947-1976. 1977. text ed. 12.50x (ISBN 0-391-01001-8). Humanities.

Tewary, V. K. Mechanics of Fibre Composites. LC 77-29117. 1978. 14.95x (ISBN 0-470-99240-9). Halsted Pr.

Tewfik Al, Hakim. Tree Climber: A Play in Two Acts. Johnson-Davies, D., tr. (Three Crown Bks.). 1966. pap. 1.95x o.p. (ISBN 0-19-911058-1). Oxford U Pr.

Tewinkel, Joseph M. Built Upon the Cornerstone. LC 80-65148. 178p. (Orig.). 1981. pap. 3.95 (ISBN 0-87509-280-2); pap. 1.50 leaders guide (ISBN 0-686-69527-5). Chr Pubns.

Texas A & M University Library. Energy Bibliography & Index, Vol. 3. 1400p. 1980. 295.00 (ISBN 0-87201-975-6). Gulf Pub.

--Energy Bibliography & Index, Vol. 4. 1400p. 1981. 295.00 (ISBN 0-87201-284-0). Gulf Pub.

Texas Instruments, Inc. Microprocessors-Microcomputers-System Design. (Texas Instruments Bk. Ser.). (Illus.). 1980. 24.50 (ISBN 0-07-063758-X, P&RB). McGraw.

Texas Instruments, Inc. Engineering Staff. The Line Driver & Line Receiver Data Book for Design Engineers Nineteen Eighty One. rev. ed. LC 80-54794. 296p. 1981. pap. write for info. (ISBN 0-89512-106-9, LCCJ290A). Tex Instr Inc.

--The Peripheral Driver Data Book for Design Engineers, Nineteen Eighty One. rev. ed. LC 80-54795. 144p. 1981. pap. write for info. (ISBN 0-89512-107-7, LCC4280A). Tex Instr Inc.

Texas Instruments Learning Center Staff. Sourcebook for Programmable Calculators. LC 78-57030. (Illus.). 1978. pap. text ed. 12.95 o.p. (ISBN 0-89512-025-9, LCB-3521). Tex Instr Inc.

Texas Symposium on Relativistic Astrophysics, 9th. Proceedings. Perry, Judith J., et al, eds. LC 80-11614. (N.Y. Academy of Sciences Annals: Vol. 336). 599p. 1980. 105.00x (ISBN 0-89766-045-5). NY Acad Sci.

Texas Tech University. Utilization of Solar Energy for Feedmill & Irrigation Operations. pap. cancelled (ISBN 0-930978-67-6). Solar Energy Info.

Texter. The Aging Gut & What to Do About It. 1981. write for info. Masson Pub.

Tey, Josephine. Brat Farrar. LC 79-19666. 1981. Repr. of 1949 ed. lib. bdg. 10.00x (ISBN 0-8376-0445-1). Bentley.

--Four, Five & Six by Tey. 1958. 8.95 o.s.i. (ISBN 0-02-617060-4). Macmillan.

--The Franchise Affair. LC 79-19129. 1981. Repr. of 1948 ed. lib. bdg. 10.00x (ISBN 0-8376-0446-X). Bentley.

--The Man in the Queue. LC 79-28589. 1981. Repr. of 1929 ed. lib. bdg. 10.00x (ISBN 0-8376-0450-8). Bentley.

--Miss Pym Disposes. LC 79-19665. 1981. Repr. of 1948 ed. lib. bdg. 10.00x (ISBN 0-8376-0447-8). Bentley.

Teyler, Timothy, ed. Behavioral Sciences: PreTest Self-Assessment & Review. LC 78-50594. (Basic Sciences: Pretest Self Assessment & Review Ser.). (Illus.). 1979. pap. 9.95 (ISBN 0-07-051606-5). McGraw-Pretest.

Teyler, Timothy J. A Primer of Psychobiology: Brain & Behavior. LC 74-20989. (Psychology Ser.). (Illus.). 1975. text ed. 13.95x (ISBN 0-7167-0749-7); pap. text ed. 6.95x (ISBN 0-7167-0748-9); tchr's manual avail. W H Freeman.

Teyler, Timothy J., intro. by. Altered States of Awareness: Readings from Scientific American. LC 76-190436. (Illus.). 1972. pap. text ed. 7.95x (ISBN 0-7167-0855-8). W H Freeman.

Tezak, Mark R., jt. auth. see Culbertson, Robert G.

TFH Publications Staff. Bulldogs. (Illus.). 125p. 1980. 2.95 (ISBN 0-87666-714-0, KW-101). TFH Pubns.

Thach, Charles C. Creation of the Presidency, Seventeen Seventy-Five to Seventeen Eighty-Nine. LC 74-87710. (American History, Politics & Law Ser). 1969. Repr. of 1922 ed. lib. bdg. 14.50 (ISBN 0-306-71680-1). Da Capo.

Thacher, Alida. Games for All Seasons. LC 77-19235. (Games & Activities Ser.). (Illus.). (gr. k-3). 1978. PLB 9.30 (ISBN 0-8172-1164-0). Raintree Pubs.

--In the Center: Kareem Abdul Jabbar. LC 76-11011. (Sports Profiles Ser.). (Illus.). 48p. (gr. 4-11). 1976. PLB 8.50 (ISBN 0-8172-0148-3). Raintree Pubs.

--Raising a Racket: Rosie Casals. LC 75-42036. (Sports Profiles Ser.). (gr. 4-11). 1976. PLB 8.50 (ISBN 0-8172-0132-7). Raintree Pubs.

Thacher, James. American Medical Biography, 2 Vols. 2nd ed. LC 67-25447. (American Medicine Ser). 1967. Repr. of 1828 ed. lib. bdg. 55.00 (ISBN 0-306-70944-9). Da Capo.

Thacker, Ron. Dowst Revisited. (Gambler's Book Shelf). 1976. pap. 2.95 (ISBN 0-89650-572-3). Gamblers.

Thacker, Ronald. Accounting Principles. 2nd ed. (Illus.). 1979. text ed. 19.95 (ISBN 0-13-002766-9). P-H.

Thacker, Ronald & Ellis, Loudell. Student Guide to Management Accounting: Concepts & Applications. 336p. 1980. pap. text ed. 8.95 (ISBN 0-8359-4196-5). Reston.

Thacker, Ronald J. Introduction to Modern Accounting. 3rd ed. (Illus.). 1977. pap. text ed. 19.95 (ISBN 0-13-487736-5); study guide 8.95 (ISBN 0-13-487710-1); working papers 9.95 (ISBN 0-13-488064-1). P-H.

Thacker, Ronald J. & Ellis, Loudell. Management Accounting: Concepts & Applications. (Illus.). 587p. 1980. text ed. 17.95 (ISBN 0-8359-4194-9); student guide 8.95 (ISBN 0-8359-4196-5); test bank free (ISBN 0-8359-4197-3); instr's. manual free (ISBN 0-8359-4195-7). Reston.

Thackeray, Helen, compiled by. Lion House Recipes. LC 80-19719. (Illus.). 122p. 1980. 8.95 (ISBN 0-87747-831-7). Deseret Bk.

Thackeray, Milton G., jt. auth. see Skidmore, R. A.

Thackeray, William M. The Book of Snobs. Sutherland, J., ed. LC 78-54067. 1978. 18.95x (ISBN 0-312-09011-0). St Martin.

--Rose & the Ring. (Illus.). 1947. 30.00 (ISBN 0-87598-006-6). Pierpont Morgan.

--Vanity Fair. 1957. 17.95x (ISBN 0-460-00298-8, Evman); pap. 4.95 (ISBN 0-460-01298-3). Dutton.

--Vanity Fair. (Literature Ser). (gr. 10-12). 1970. pap. text ed. 4.58 (ISBN 0-87720-741-0). AMSCO Sch.

Thackery, Geral, jt. auth. see Allen, Ray.

Thackrah, J. R. Europe Since the Second World War. 288p. 1979. pap. 9.95x (Pub. by Macdonald & Evans England). Intl Ideas.

Thackray, Patricia. Amazing Mumford Forgets the Magic Words. (A Young Reader Ser.). (Illus.). 24p. (gr. k-3). 1979. PLB 5.00 (ISBN 0-307-60178-1, Golden Pr). Western Pub.

--Raggedy Ann at the Carnival. (Look-Look Ser.). (Illus.). 1977. PLB 5.38 (ISBN 0-307-61830-7, Golden Pr); pap. 0.95 (ISBN 0-307-11830-4). Western Pub.

Thackston, Edward L. & Eckenfielder, W. W., eds. Process Design in Water Quality Engineering: New Concepts & Development. (Illus.). 15.00 (ISBN 0-8363-0079-3). Jenkins.

Thaden, E. C., ed. Russification in the Baltic Provinces & Finland, 1855-1914. LC 80-7557. 1980. 40.00 (ISBN 0-691-05314-6); pap. 17.50 (ISBN 0-691-10103-5). Princeton U Pr.

Thaden, Edward C. Russia Since 1801: The Making of a New Society. LC 71-144333. (Illus.). 1971. text ed. 23.95x (ISBN 0-471-85510-3). Wiley.

Thadepalli, Haragopal. Infectious Diseases: Focus on Clinical Diagnosis. pap. 24.50 (ISBN 0-87488-830-1). Med Exam.

Thaeler, C. S., Jr. An Analysis of the Distribution of Pocket Gopher Species in Northeastern California (Genus Thomomys). (U. C. Publ. in Zoology: Vol. 86). 1968. pap. 6.50x (ISBN 0-520-09343-7). U of Cal Pr.

Thain, William. Monitoring Toxic Gases in the Atmosphere. 1980. 25.00 (ISBN 0-08-023810-6). Pergamon.

Thaine, Marina & Griffin, Robert. Working in Hair-Dressing. 1980. 16.95 (ISBN 0-7134-3323-X). David & Charles.

Thakar, Vimala & Singh, Devendra, trs. Life As Yoga. 1977. 12.50 (ISBN 0-89684-241-X, Pub. by Motilal Banarsidass India); pap. 8.50 (ISBN 0-686-68508-3). Orient Bk Dist.

Thakur, Asaita. Vanio & Zanda Zulan. Richmond, Farley, tr. (Translated from Gujarati). 8.00 (ISBN 0-89253-658-6); flexible cloth 4.80 (ISBN 0-89253-659-4). Ind-US Inc.

Thakur, Shivesh C. Religion & Rational Choice. (Library of Philosophy & Religion Ser.). 176p. 1981. 32.50x (ISBN 0-389-20047-6). B&N.

Thakurdas, Frank. German Political Idealism. 368p. 1980. text ed. 22.50x (ISBN 0-391-01796-9). Humanities.

Thal, Helen M. Your Family & Its Money. (gr. 9-12). 1973. text ed. 13.28 (ISBN 0-395-14225-3). HM.

Thal, Herbert V., ed. see Bulwer-Lytton, Edward.

Thal, Herbert Van see Arlen, Michael.

Thal, Herbert Van see Broughton, Rhoda.

Thal, Herbert Van see Merriman, Henry S.

Thale, Jerome. Novels of George Eliot. LC 59-8377. 1959. 15.00x (ISBN 0-231-02328-6). Columbia U Pr.

Thale, Mary. The Autobiography of Francis Place 1771-1854. LC 78-174265. (Illus.). 344p. 1972. 42.00 (ISBN 0-521-08399-0). Cambridge U Pr.

Thaler, Alwin. Shakespeare & Our World. LC 66-11626. 1966. 12.50x (ISBN 0-87049-063-X). U of Tenn Pr.

Thaler, Mike. Chocolate Marshmelephant Sundae. 1980. pap. 1.50 (ISBN 0-380-49320-9, 49320, Camelot). Avon.

--Complete Cookie Book. 1980. pap. 1.95 (ISBN 0-380-76133-5, 76133, Camelot). Avon.

--Funny Bones. (Illus.). 96p. (gr. 4-6). 1976. PLB 4.90 o.p. (ISBN 0-531-00349-3). Watts.

--How Far Will a Rubber Band Stretch? LC 73-23052. (Illus.). 40p. (ps-3). 1974. 5.95 o.s.i. (ISBN 0-8193-0766-1, Four Winds); PLB 5.41 o.s.i. (ISBN 0-8193-0767-X). Schol Bk Serv.
--Madge's Magic Show. (Easy-Read Story Books Ser.). (Illus.). (gr. k-3). 1978. PLB 6.45 s&l (ISBN 0-531-01450-9). Watts.
--Mike Thaler's Complete Coptie Book. (Illus.). 96p. (gr. 1 up). 1980. pap. 1.95 (ISBN 0-380-76133-5, 76133, Camelot). Avon.
--Never Tickle a Turtle: Cartoons, Riddles & Funny Stories. (Illus.). (gr. 4-6). 1977. PLB 6.45 s&l (ISBN 0-531-00386-8). Watts.
--Oinker Away: Pig Riddles, Cartoons, Jokes and Other Amusing Things from the Creator of the Letterman. (Orig.). 1981. pap. 1.50 (ISBN 0-686-69579-8). Archway.
--Riddle Riot. (gr. 4-6). 1976. pap. 0.95 (ISBN 0-590-03594-0, Schol Pap). Schol Bk Serv.
--The Smiling Book. LC 79-116336. (Illus.). (gr. k-3). 1971. 7.25 o.p. (ISBN 0-688-41441-9); PLB 6.48 o.p. (ISBN 0-688-51435-9). Lothrop.
--Soup with Quackers: Funny Cartoon Riddles. LC 76-10308. (Illus.). 96p. (gr. 4 up). 1976. PLB 6.45 (ISBN 0-531-00344-2). Watts.
--There's a Hippopotamus Under My Bed. (Easy-Read Story Bks.). (Illus.). (gr. k-3). 1977. PLB 6.45 s&l (ISBN 0-531-01318-9). Watts.
--What Can a Hippopotamus Be? LC 74-30104. (Illus.). (gr. k-3). 1975. 5.95 o.s.i. (ISBN 0-8193-0809-9, Four Winds); PLB 5.41 o.s.i. (ISBN 0-8193-0810-2). Schol Bk Serv.
--What's up Duck. (Illus.). (gr. 4 up). 1978. PLB 6.90 s&l (ISBN 0-531-01479-7). Watts.
--Wuzzles. (gr. k-3). 1976. pap. 1.25 (ISBN 0-590-10164-1, Schol Pap). Schol Bk Serv.
--Yelllow Toad: Funny Frog Cartoons, Riddles, & Silly Stories. (gr. 3-6). 1980. pap. write for info (Bard). Avon.
--Yellow Brick Toad: Funny Frog Cartoons, Riddles & Silly Stories. (Illus.). (gr. 3-5). 1980. pap. 1.50 (ISBN 0-671-56035-2). Archway.
Thalmann, H. E., tr. see Goguel, Jean.
Thamer, Katie, illus. The Song of Songs. Orig. Title: Song of Solomon. (Illus.). 40p. (Orig.). 1981. pap. 9.95 (ISBN 0-914676-46-6). Green Tiger.
Thames Valley Group, ed. Student Project Work in Construction. 1971. pap. text ed. 11.95x (ISBN 0-7114-4903-1). Intl Ideas.
Thane, Elswyth. Dawn's Early Light. 1943. unabridged ed. 10.00 (ISBN 0-8015-1957-8, Hawthorn). Dutton.
--Dawn's Early Light. (Williamsburg Ser.: No. 1). 1981. lib. bdg. 16.95 (ISBN 0-8161-3167-8, Large Print Bks). G K Hall.
--Ever After. (Williamsburg Ser.: No. 3). 1981. lib. bdg. 17.95 (ISBN 0-8161-3165-1, Large Print Bks). G K Hall.
--Homing. (Williamsburg Ser.: No. 7). 1981. lib. bdg. 15.95 (ISBN 0-8161-3164-3, Large Print Bks). G K Hall.
--Kissing Kin. (Williamsburg Ser.: No. 5). 1981. lib. bdg. 16.95 (ISBN 0-686-69444-9, Large Print Bks). G K Hall.
--The Light Heart. (Williamsburg Ser.: No. 4). 1981. lib. bdg. 17.95 (ISBN 0-8161-3163-5, Large Print Bks). G K Hall.
--This Was Tomorrow. (Williamsburg Ser.: No. 6). 1981. lib. bdg. 14.95 (ISBN 0-8161-3161-9, Large Print Bks). G K Hall.
--Virginia Colony. LC 69-16488. (Forge of Freedom Ser). (Illus.). (gr. 5-8). 1969. 8.95 (ISBN 0-02-789180-1, CCPr). Macmillan.
--Williamsburg Novels, 7 vols. 1981. Set. lib. bdg. 105.00 (ISBN 0-8161-3177-5, Large Print Bks). G K Hall.
--Yankee Stranger. (Williamsburg Ser.: No. 2). 1981. lib. bdg. 16.95 (ISBN 0-8161-3166-X, Large Print Bks). G K Hall.
Thane, James L., Jr. A Governor's Wife on the Mining Frontier. (Utah, the Mormons, & the West: No. 7). 1976. 8.50 (ISBN 0-87480-161-3, Tanner). U of Utah Pr.
Thani Nayagam, S. X. Landscape & Poetry: A Study of Nature in Classical Tamil Poetry. 1967. 6.00x (ISBN 0-210-22734-6). Asia.
Thapar, Raj. Introducing India. 1966. pap. 2.50x (ISBN 0-210-22505-X). Asia.
Thapar, Romila. Ancient India. 2nd. ed. 1969. pap. 2.00 (ISBN 0-88253-275-8). Ind-US Inc.
--Medieval India. (Illus.). 1970. pap. 2.00 (ISBN 0-88253-276-6). Ind-US Inc.
Tharoor, Shashi. Reasons of State. 250p. 1981. text ed. 17.50x (ISBN 0-7069-1275-6, Pub by Vikas India). Advent Bk.
Tharp, C. Patrick, jt. auth. see Lecca, Pedro J.
Tharp, Constance. Total Thanks. 1978. pap. 3.95 o.p. (ISBN 0-88270-267-X). Logos.
Tharp, Roland & Wetzel, Ralph. Behavior Modification in the Natural Environment. LC 75-91418. 1969. 17.95 (ISBN 0-12-686050-5). Acad Pr.
Tharp, Roland G., jt. auth. see Watson, David L.
Tharp, Zeno C. Favorite Stories & Illustrations. 144p. 1956. 2.95 (ISBN 0-87148-327-0); pap. 2.25 (ISBN 0-87148-328-9). Pathway Pr.
--The Minister's Guide for Special Occasions. 1966. 5.25 (ISBN 0-87148-553-2). Pathway Pr.
Tharpe, Jac. John Barth: The Comic Sublimity of Paradox. LC 74-12263. (Arcturus Books Paperbacks). 146p. 1977. pap. 4.95 (ISBN 0-8093-0836-3). S Ill U Pr.
Tharpe, Jac L., ed. Elvis: Images & Fancies. LC 79-26044. 1980. 12.50 (ISBN 0-87805-113-9); pap. 6.00 (ISBN 0-87805-114-7). U Pr of Miss.
Thass-Thienemann, Theodore. The Interpretation of Language. rev. ed. Incl. Vol. 1. Understanding the Symbolic Meaning of Language. 512p. o.p. (ISBN 0-87668-087-2); Vol. 2. Understanding the Unconscious Meaning of Language. 448p (ISBN 0-87668-088-0). LC 73-79984. 1973. 17.50x ea. Aronson.
Thatcher, Alida. Elephant on Wheels. (Eager Readers Ser). (gr. k-3). 1975. PLB 5.00 (ISBN 0-307-60807-7, Golden Pr). Western Pub.
Thatcher, Floyd & Thatcher, Harriett. Long Term Marriage. 1980. 8.95 (ISBN 0-8499-0096-4). Word Bks.
Thatcher, Harriett, jt. auth. see Thatcher, Floyd.
Thatcher, J. B. The Continent of America: Its Discovery & Its Baptism. 1971. Repr. of 1896 ed. text ed. 42.50x (ISBN 90-6041-061-0). Humanities.
Thatcher, Julia. Inherit the Mirage. 1976. pap. 1.25 o.p. (ISBN 0-345-25209-8). Ballantine.
--Mask of Love. (Orig.). 1980. pap. 1.95 (ISBN 0-445-04553-1). Popular Lib.
--Nightgleams (Sagittarius) (Zodiac Gothics). 1976. pap. 1.25 o.p. (ISBN 0-345-25310-8). Ballantine.
Thatcher, N., ed. see International Cancer Congress, 12th, Buenos Aires 5-11 Oct. 1978.
Thatcher, Rebecca. Academic Skills: A Handbook for Working Adults Returning to School. 1976. pap. 1.50 (ISBN 0-87546-248-0). NY Sch Indus Rel.
Thaw, J. Program Innovation in Facilities for the Mentally Retarded. 1981. 12.50 (ISBN 0-685-32569-5). Univ Park.
Thaxton, Nolan A., jt. auth. see Bucher, Charles A.
Thayer, Ernest L. Casey at the Bat. (Illus.). (gr. 4 up). 1964. pap. 2.50 (ISBN 0-13-120402-5). P-H.
Thayer, H. S. see Dewey, John.
Thayer, H. Standish. Meaning & Action: A Critical History of Pragmatism. 592p. 1981. 25.00 (ISBN 0-915144-73-5); pap. text ed. 12.50 (ISBN 0-915144-74-3). Hackett Pub.
Thayer, J. H., ed. Greek-English Lexicon of the New Testament: Being Grimm's Wilke's Clavis Novi Testamenti, Transl. Revised & Enlarged. 4th ed. 746p. Repr. of 1901 ed. text ed. 25.00x (ISBN 0-567-01015-5). Attic Pr.
Thayer, James B. John Marshall. LC 76-155923. (American Constitutional & Legal History Ser.). 157p. 1974. Repr. of 1901 ed. lib. bdg. 19.50 (ISBN 0-306-70287-8). Da Capo.
Thayer, Jane. Andy & Mister Cunningham. (Illus.). (ps-3). 1969. PLB 6.48 o.p. (ISBN 0-688-31024-9). Morrow.
--Bunny in the Honeysuckle Patch. (Illus.). (ps-3). 1965. 7.75 (ISBN 0-688-21132-1); PLB 7.44 o.p. (ISBN 0-688-31132-6). Morrow.
--Clever Raccoon. LC 80-23119. (Junior Bks.). (Illus.). 32p. (gr. k-3). 1981. 7.95 (ISBN 0-688-00238-2); PLB 7.63 (ISBN 0-688-00239-0). Morrow.
--Gus & the Baby Ghost. LC 76-161874. (Illus.). 32p. (ps-3). 1972. PLB 7.44 (ISBN 0-688-31369-8). Morrow.
--Gus Was a Christmas Ghost. LC 77-101707. (Illus.). (ps-3). 1970. 7.25 o.p. (ISBN 0-688-21370-7); PLB 7.44 (ISBN 0-688-31370-1). Morrow.
--Gus Was a Friendly Ghost. (Illus.). (ps-3). 1962. PLB 7.44 (ISBN 0-688-31368-X). Morrow.
--Gus Was a Mexican Ghost. (Illus.). 32p. (ps-3). 1974. 7.75 (ISBN 0-688-20104-0); PLB 7.44 (ISBN 0-688-30104-5). Morrow.
--I Don't Believe in Elves. LC 74-32045. (Illus.). 32p. (ps-3). 1975. 7.25 o.p. (ISBN 0-688-22030-4); PLB 7.44 (ISBN 0-688-32030-9). Morrow.
--Mister Turtle's Magic Glasses. LC 74-118284. (Illus.). (ps-3). 1971. 7.25 (ISBN 0-688-21650-1). Morrow.
--The Mouse on the Fourteenth Floor. (Illus.). (ps-3). 1977. 7.75 (ISBN 0-688-22094-0); PLB 7.44 (ISBN 0-688-32094-5). Morrow.
--The Popcorn Dragon. (Illus.). (ps-3). 1953. PLB 6.48 (ISBN 0-688-31630-1). Morrow.
--Puppy Who Wanted a Boy. (Illus.). (ps-3). 1958. PLB 7.44 (ISBN 0-688-31631-X). Morrow.
--Quiet on Account of Dinosaur. (Illus.). (ps-3). 1964. PLB 7.44 (ISBN 0-688-31632-8). Morrow.
--Rockets Don't Go to Chicago, Andy. (Illus.). (ps-3). 1967. 6.95 (ISBN 0-688-21660-9). Morrow.
Thayer, John A. Italy & the Great War: Politics & Culture, 1870-1914. (Illus.). 1964. 37.50 (ISBN 0-299-03280-9). U of Wis Pr.
Thayer, Julie, jt. auth. see Outerbridge, David.
Thayer, Louis, ed. Fifty Strategies for Experiential Learning: Book One. LC 75-27735. Orig. Title: Affective Education. 230p. 1976. pap. 13.50 (ISBN 0-88390-108-0). Univ Assocs.
--Fifty Strategies for Experimental Learning: Book Two. 260p. (Orig.). 1981. pap. write for info. (ISBN 0-88390-164-1). Univ Assocs.
Thayer, Lynn W. Church Music Handbook. 9.95 (ISBN 0-310-36880-4). Zondervan.
Thayer, Marjorie & Emanuel, Elizabeth. Climbing Sun: The Story of a Hopi Indian Boy. LC 80-13743. (Illus.). 96p. (gr. 5 up). 1980. 6.95g (ISBN 0-396-07844-3). Dodd.
Thayer, Theodore. Pennsylvania Politics & the Growth of Democracy: 1740-1776. LC 54-9746. 1953. 8.00 (ISBN 0-911124-23-3). Pa Hist & Mus.
--Washington & Lee at Monmouth: The Making of a Scapegoat. 1976. 9.95 (ISBN 0-8046-9139-8, Natl U). Kennikat.
Thayer, William R. The Life & Times of Cavour, 2 Vols. LC 68-9634. (Illus.). 1971. Repr. of 1911 ed. Set. 38.50 (ISBN 0-86527-117-8). Fertig.
Thayne, Emma L. With Love, Mother. 31p. 1975. 0.75 o.p. (ISBN 0-87747-551-2). Deseret Bk.
The American Association for Gifted Children. The Gifted Child, the Family & the Community. LC 80-54030. 228p. 1981. 17.50 (ISBN 0-8027-0673-8). Walker & Co.
The American College Testing Program. College Planning - Search Book. 6th ed. LC 75-28517. (Illus., Orig.). (gr. 9-12). pap. text ed. 6.00 (ISBN 0-937734-00-4). Am Coll Testing.
The Arab Petroleum Research Center, Paris. Arab Oil & Gas Directory 1979-80. 5th ed. LC 75-646597. (Illus.). 415p. 1979. 150.00x (ISBN 0-8002-2231-8). Intl Pubns Serv.
The Beverly Hills Bar Association Barristers Committee. Actor's Manual. 1981. pap. 9.95 (ISBN 0-8015-0040-0, Hawthorn). Dutton.
The Cartographic Department of Oxford University Press, ed. The New Oxford Atlas. (Illus.). 204p. 1975. 24.00x o.p. (ISBN 0-19-891108-4). Oxford U Pr.
The Dudenredaktion, ed. see Pheby, John.
The Educational Research Council. The Age of Western Expansion. (The Human Adventure Concepts & Inquiry Ser). (gr. 6). 1975. pap. text ed. 7.20 (ISBN 0-205-04452-2, 804452X); tchrs'. guide 5.20 (ISBN 0-205-04453-0, 8044538). Allyn.
--Ancient Civilization. (The Human Adventure Concepts & Inquiry Ser). (gr. 5). 1975. pap. text ed. 6.30 (ISBN 0-205-04442-5, 8044422); tchrs'. guide 5.20 (ISBN 0-205-04443-3, 8044430). Allyn.
--The Challenge of Change. (The Human Adventure Concepts and Inquiry Ser). (gr. 6). 1975. pap. text ed. 7.20 (ISBN 0-205-04456-5, 8044562); tchrs'. guide 5.20 (ISBN 0-205-04457-3, 8044570). Allyn.
--Four World Views. (The Human Adventure, Concepts & Inquiry Ser). (gr. 5). 1975. pap. text ed. 6.20 (ISBN 0-205-04444-1, 8044449); tchrs'. guide 4.80 (ISBN 0-205-04445-X, 8044457). Allyn.
--Industry: People & the Machine. (Concepts & Inquiry Ser). (gr. 4). 1975. pap. text ed. 7.24 (ISBN 0-205-04438-7, 8044384); tchrs'. guide 7.24 (ISBN 0-205-04439-5, 8044392). Allyn.
--The Interaction of Cultures. (The Human Adventure Concepts & Inquiry). (gr. 6). 1975. pap. text ed. 7.20 (ISBN 0-205-04458-1, 8044589); tchrs'. guide 5.20 (ISBN 0-205-04459-X, 8044597). Allyn.
The Food Processors Institute. A Guide for Waste Management in the Food Processing Industry, Vol. II. Warrick, Louis F., ed. 555p. 1979. pap. text ed. 15.00 (ISBN 0-937774-01-4). Food Processors.
The G-Jo Institute. Pathways from Cancer: A Directory. 1980. pap. 3.00 (ISBN 0-916878-08-2). Falkynor Bks.
The Library of Congress & the University of Texas Library (Austin) Bibliographic Guide to Latin American Studies: 1980. (Library Catalogs Bib. Guides). 1981. lib. bdg. 275.00 (ISBN 0-686-69556-9). G K Hall.
The Minneapolis Institute of Arts. Sculptures from the David Daniels Collection. (Illus.). 1979. 15.00. Minneapolis Inst Arts.
The Pierpont Morgan Library. The Stavelot Triptych, Mosan Art, & the Legend of the True Cross. (Illus.). 48p. 1980. text ed. 24.95x (ISBN 0-19-520225-2). Oxford U Pr.
The Research Libraries of He New York Public Library & the Library of Congress. Bibliographic Guide to Law: 1980. (Library Catalogs Bib. Guides Ser.). 1981. lib. bdg. 125.00 (ISBN 0-8161-6889-X). G K Hall.
The Research Libraries of the New York Public Library & the Library of Congress. Bibliographic Guide to Art & Architecture: 1980. (Library Catalogs-Bib. Guides Ser.). 1981. lib. bdg. 135.00 (ISBN 0-8161-6881-4). G K Hall.
The Research Libraries of the New York Public Library & Columbia University, Teachers College Library. Bibliographic Guide to Education: 1980. (Library Catalog-Bib.Guides Ser.). 1981. lib. bdg. 85.00 (ISBN 0-8161-6880-6). G K Hall.
The Research Libraries of the New York Public Library & the Library of Congress. Bibliographic Guide to Technology: 1980. (Library Catalogs Bib. Guides). 1981. lib. bdg. 175.00 (ISBN 0-8161-6895-4). G K Hall.
The Research Libraries of the New York Pubic Library & the Library of Congress. Bibliographic Guide to Theatre Arts: 1980. (Library Catalogs-Bib. Guides Ser.). 1981 (ISBN 0-8161-6896-2). lib. bdg. 75.00 (ISBN 0-686-69557-7). G K Hall.
The Research Library of the New York Public Library & the Library of Congress. Bibliographic Guide to North American History: 1980. (Library Catalogs Bib.Guides Ser.). 1981. lib. bdg. 85.00 (ISBN 0-8161-6892-X). G K Hall.
The Royal Institute of International Affairs, ed. The Chatham House Annual Review: International Economic & Monetary Issues, Vol. 1. (PPS on International Politics). (Illus.). 200p. 1981. 20.00 (ISBN 0-08-027532-X). Pergamon.
The Throroughbred Owners & Breeders Association. A Supplement to the Blood-Horse: Stallion Register 1980. 1980. lib. bdg. 20.00 o.p. (ISBN 0-936032-28-6); pap. 10.00 o.p. (ISBN 0-686-10833-7). Thoroughbred Own and Breed.
The Training-Action Affinity Group. Building Social Change Communities. 112p. 1979. pap. 2.80 (ISBN 0-686-28496-8). Movement New Soc.
Theaker, Drachen. Eastern Rhythms. LC 79-89945. (Orig.). Date not set. pap. cancelled (ISBN 0-89793-017-7). Hunter Hse.
Theander & James. The Analysis of Dietary Fiber in Food. 288p. 1981. 35.00 (ISBN 0-8247-1192-0). Dekker.
Thear, Katie, jt. ed. see Fraser, Alistair.
Theatre Craft Editors, jt. ed. see Smith, C. Ray.
The Bab. Selections from the Writings of the Bab. LC 79-670141. 1976. 7.50 (ISBN 0-85398-066-7, 7-05-50). Bahai.
Thebaud, Jo, ed. Today & Other Days. (Illus.). 151p. (Orig.). 1971. pap. 3.25 (ISBN 0-88489-031-7). St Marys.
Theberge, James D. The Soviet Presence in Latin America. LC 74-82929. 1974. pap. 2.95x (ISBN 0-8448-0514-9). Crane-Russak Co.
Theberge, James D., jt. ed. see Salisbury, William T.
Theberge, James D., et al. Latin America: Struggle for Progress, Vol. 14. LC 75-74723. (Critical Choices for Americans Ser.). 1976. 16.95 (ISBN 0-669-00428-6). Lexington Bks.
Theberge, John. Kluane: Pinnacle of the Yukon. LC 80-1078. (Illus.). 224p. 1981. 35.00 (ISBN 0-385-17122-6). Doubleday.
Theberge, Leonard, ed. The Judiciary in a Democratic Society. LC 77-25740. 1979. 16.95 (ISBN 0-669-01508-3). Lexington Bks.
Theen, Rolf H., tr. see Valentinov, Nikolay.
Theibert, Richard, jt. auth. see Ezersky, Eugene.
Theil, Henri. Introduction to Econometrics. LC 77-14972. (Illus.). 1978. ref. 22.95 (ISBN 0-13-481028-7). P-H.
Theilheimer, W., ed. Yearbook Nineteen Eighty Mit deutschem Registerschluessel. (Synthetic Methods of Organic Chemistry Ser.: Vol. 34). 1980. 298.25 (ISBN 3-8055-0327-X). S Karger.
Thein, Aung. Oriental Cooking in a Yankee Kitchen. (Illus., Orig.). Date not set. pap. cancelled (ISBN 0-914016-54-7). Phoenix Pub.
Theis, Dan. The Education of Steven Bell. LC 76-54277. (Sports Fiction Ser.). (Illus.). (gr. 5-10). 1977. PLB 7.30 (ISBN 0-8172-0806-2). Raintree Pubs.
Theis, Dan, jt. auth. see Paulsen, Gary.
Theis, Daniel. The Crescent & the Cross: The Early Crusades. LC 78-2385. (gr. 6 up). 1978. 8.95 o.p. (ISBN 0-525-66596-X). Elsevier-Nelson.
Theiss, Herman C. Life with God. pap. 4.85 (ISBN 0-933350-05-8); tchrs. manual 1.65 (ISBN 0-933350-55-4). Morse Pr.
Thelen, David. New Citizenship: Origins of Progressivism in Wisconsin, 1885-1900. LC 79-158075. 1972. 15.00x (ISBN 0-8262-0111-3). U of Mo Pr.
Thelen, Marilyn. Sew Big...a Fashion Guide for the Fuller Figure. 1980. pap. 4.95 (ISBN 0-935278-04-4). Palmer-Pletsch.
Thelning, K. Steel & Its Heat Treatment: Bofors Handbook. 564p. 1975. 69.95 (ISBN 0-408-70651-1). Butterworths.
Theloall, Simon. Le Digest Des Briefes Originals, et Des Choses Concernant Eux. Berkowitz, David S. & Thorne, Samuel E., eds. LC 77-89257. (Classics of English Legal History in the Modern Era: Vol. 145). 1979. lib. bdg. 55.00 (ISBN 0-8240-3182-2). Garland Pub.

Thelwall, John. The Peripatetic, 3 vols. in 2. Reiman, Donald H., ed. LC 75-31262. (Romantic Context Ser.: Poetry 1789-1830). 1978. Set. lib. bdg. 47.00 (ISBN 0-8240-2208-4). Garland Pub.

--The Poetical Recreations of the Champion & His Literary Correspondents. Reiman, Donald H., ed. LC 75-31263. (Romantic Context Ser.: Poetry 1789-1830). 1978. Repr. of 1822 ed. lib. bdg. 47.00 (ISBN 0-8240-2209-2). Garland Pub.

Thelwell, Michael. The Harder They Come. 1980. pap. 7.95 (ISBN 0-394-17599-9, E749, Ever). Grove.

Thelwell, Norman. Brat Race. LC 78-9766. (Illus.). 1978. 6.95 o.p. (ISBN 0-684-15638-5, ScribT). Scribner.

--Leg at Each Corner: Thelwell's Complete Guide to Equitation. (Illus.). 1963. 4.50 o.p. (ISBN 0-525-14419-6). Dutton.

--Penelope. 1973. 4.95 o.p. (ISBN 0-525-17722-1). Dutton.

--A Plank Bridge by a Pool. (Encore Edition). (Illus.). 1979. 3.95 (ISBN 0-684-16695-X, ScribT). Scribner.

--Pony Birthday Book. (Illus.). 192p. 1979. 6.95 (ISBN 0-684-16235-0). Scribner.

--Thelwell Goes West. (Illus.). 1975. 4.95 o.p. (ISBN 0-87690-189-5). Dutton.

--Thelwell's Horse Box: Angel on Horseback, Leg at Each Corner, Riding Academy, & Thelwell Country. (Illus.). 1971. 8.95 o.p. (ISBN 0-525-21580-8). Dutton.

--Thelwell's Riding Academy. (Illus.). 1965. 4.95 o.p. (ISBN 0-525-21593-X). Dutton.

Themerson, Stefan. Professor MMAA's Lecture. LC 74-21585. 251p. 1975. 11.95 (ISBN 0-87951-029-3). Overlook Pr.

The Mother. Conversations. 1979. pap. 2.00 (ISBN 0-89744-935-5). Auromere.

--Prayers & Meditations. rev. ed. Aurobindo, Sri, tr. from Fr. 380p. (Orig.). 1979. pap. 10.00 (ISBN 0-89744-998-3, Sri Aurobindo Ashram Trust India). Auromere.

Thenebe, Carl. Touching Closeness. 2nd enl. ed. 1977. 7.00 o.p. (ISBN 0-682-48110-6). Exposition.

Theng, Benny K. The Chemistry of Clay-Organic Reactions. LC 74-12524. 343p. 1974. 67.95 o.p. (ISBN 0-470-85852-4). Halsted Pr.

Theobald, John. The Lost Wine: Seven Centuries of French into English Lyrical Poetry. (Illus.). 1981. 25.00 (ISBN 0-914676-36-9, Star & Elephants Bks). Green Tiger.

--Poems. 8.00 (ISBN 0-89253-741-8); flexible cloth 4.80 (ISBN 0-89253-742-6). Ind-US Inc.

Theobald, John & Theobald, Lillian. Wells Fargo in Arizona Territory. Fireman, Bert M., ed. LC 78-67555. 1978. 12.50 (ISBN 0-685-67972-1); pap. 10.00 (ISBN 0-685-67973-X). AZ Hist Foun.

Theobald, John, tr. see Morgenstern, Christian.

Theobald, Lewis. The History of the Loves of Antiochus & Stratonice, in Which Are Intersper'd Some Accounts Relating to Greece & Syria. LC 76-170540. (Foundations of the Novel Ser.: Vol. 29). lib. bdg. 50.00 (ISBN 0-8240-0541-4). Garland Pub.

Theobald, Lillian, jt. auth. see Theobald, John.

Theobald, Robert. Alternative Future for America Two: Essays & Speeches. rev.& enl. ed. LC 71-97027. Orig. Title: Alternative Future for America. 199p. 1970. 8.95x o.p. (ISBN 0-8040-0002-6); pap. 3.95x (ISBN 0-8040-0003-4). Swallow.

--An Alternative Future for America's Third Century. LC 76-3135. 266p. 1976. pap. 4.95x (ISBN 0-8040-0725-X). Swallow.

--Beyond Despair: Directions for America's Third Century. rev. ed. 208p. 1981. 11.95 (ISBN 0-932020-04-6); pap. 7.95 (ISBN 0-932020-05-4). Seven Locks Pr.

--The Economics of Abundance. 162p. 14.95x (ISBN 0-8290-0296-0); pap. text ed. 6.95x (ISBN 0-8290-0297-9). Irvington.

--Economizing Abundance: A Noninflationary Future. LC 79-125096. 151p. 1970. pap. 3.95x (ISBN 0-8040-0611-3). Swallow.

--Futures Conditional. LC 77-183105. 1972. pap. 7.95 (ISBN 0-672-61217-8). Bobbs.

Theobald, Robert & Scott, J. M. TEG's Nineteen Ninety-Four: An Anticipation of the Near Future. LC 70-150754. 210p. 1972. 7.95x (ISBN 0-8040-0509-5); pap. 3.95 o.s.i. (ISBN 0-8040-0510-9). Swallow.

Theobald, Robert, ed. Middle Class Support: A Route to Socioeconomic Security. LC 72-91921. 199p. 1972. pap. 4.95x (ISBN 0-8040-0612-1). Swallow.

Theobald, William F. Evaluation of Recreation & Park Programs. LC 78-24227. 1979. 19.95x (ISBN 0-471-01797-3). Wiley.

Theocaris, P. S. Moire Fringes in Strain Analysis. 1969. text ed. 32.00 (ISBN 0-08-012974-9); pap. text ed. 15.00 (ISBN 0-08-012973-0). Pergamon.

Theocharis, Reghinos D. Early Developments in Mathematical Economics. rev. ed. LC 80-16638. 1980. lib. bdg. 32.50x (ISBN 0-87991-808-X). Porcupine Pr.

Theocritus. Poems, 2 Vols. Gow, A. S., tr. 1952. Set. 130.00 (ISBN 0-521-06616-6). Cambridge U Pr.

Theodor, Oskar. Diptera: Asilidae Insecta II, Vol. 2. (Fauna Palaestina). (Illus.). 458p. 1981. text ed. 30.00x (ISBN 0-87474-910-7). Smithsonian.

--An Illustrated Catalogue of the Rothschild Collection of Nycteribiidae (Diptera) in the British Museum (Natural History) (Illus.). viii, 506p. 1967. 66.50x (ISBN 0-565-00655-X, Pub. by British Mus Nat Hist England). Sabbot-Natural Hist Bks.

--On the Structure of the Spermathecae & Aedeagus in the Asilidae & Their Importance in the Systematics of the Family. (Illus.). 175p. 1976. 25.00x (ISBN 0-87474-914-X, Pub. by Israel Academy of Sciences & Humanities). Smithsonian.

Theodore, Louis, jt. auth. see Buonicore, Anthony.

Theodore, Louis, et al. Energy & the Environment: Interactions, Vol. I, Pts. A & B. 1980. Pt. A, 208p. 57.95 (ISBN 0-8493-5562-1); Pt. B, 192p. 54.95 (ISBN 0-8493-5563-X). CRC Pr.

Theodorides, J., ed. Un Grand Medecin et Biologiste Cashmir - Joseph Davaine. 1969. pap. 42.00 (ISBN 0-08-012366-X). Pergamon.

Theodorson, Achilles G., jt. auth. see Theodorson, George A.

Theodorson, George A. & Theodorson, Achilles G. Modern Dictionary of Sociology. LC 69-18672. 1969. 12.95 o.s.i. (ISBN 0-690-55058-8, TYC-T). T Y Crowell.

--Modern Dictionary of Sociology. LC 69-18672. (Apollo Eds.). 1969. pap. 3.95 o.s.i. (ISBN 0-8152-0238-5, TYC-T). T Y Crowell.

Theofanis, Stavrou, jt. auth. see Alexeev, Wassilij.

Theophanpous, Andrew. Australian Democracy in Crisis: A New Theoretical Introduction to Australian Politics. 224p. 1980. 27.00 (ISBN 0-19-554200-2). Oxford U Pr.

Theophilus. On Divers Arts: The Foremost Medieval Treatise on Painting, Glassmaking, & Metalwork. Hawthorne, John G. & Smith, Cyril S., trs. from Latin. (Illus.). 1979. pap. text ed. 5.00 (ISBN 0-486-23784-2). Dover.

Theorell, Tores, jt. auth. see De Faire, Ulf.

Theory Conference, Phoenix, Arizona, February, 1980. Theoretical Developments in Marketing: Proceedings. Lamb, Charles W., Jr. & Dunne, Patrick M., eds. LC 80-12436. (Illus.). 269p. (Orig.). 1980. pap. text ed. 24.00 (ISBN 0-87757-138-4). Am Mktg.

Theosophy Company. Index to the Secret Doctrine. x, 172p. 1939. 6.00 (ISBN 0-938998-02-1). Theosophy.

Therborn, Goran. The Ideology of Power & the Power of Ideology: 144p. 1981. 12.50x (ISBN 0-8052-7095-7, Pub. by NLB England); pap. 5.50 (ISBN 0-8052-7094-9). Schocken.

--Science, Class & Society: On the Formation of Sociology & Historical Materialism. 461p. 1980. pap. 9.50 (ISBN 0-86091-724-X, Pub. by NLB). Schocken.

Therese of Lisieux, St. Autobiography of Saint Therese of Lisieux: The Story of a Soul. 1957. pap. 2.45 (ISBN 0-385-02903-9, D56, Im). Doubleday.

Theriault, Albert A., Jr. Guide to Writing Term Papers. (Orig.). (gr. 11-12). 1971. pap. text ed. 4.58 (ISBN 0-87720-350-4). AMSCO Sch.

Therman, E. Human Chromosomes. (Illus.). 235p. 1981. 19.80 (ISBN 0-387-90509-X). Springer-Verlag.

Thernstrom, Stephan, et al, eds. Harvard Encyclopedia of American Ethnic Groups. 1980. 60.00 (ISBN 0-674-37512-2). Harvard U Pr.

Theroux, Alexander. Darconville's Cat. LC 80-629. 624p. 1981. 15.95 (ISBN 0-385-15951-X). Doubleday.

--Master Snickup's Cloak. LC 79-1799. (Illus.). 1979. 7.95 o.p. (ISBN 0-06-014283-9, HarpT); lib. bdg. 7.89 o.p. (ISBN 0-06-014284-7). Harrow.

Theroux, Paul. The Great Railway Bazaar. 1976. pap. 2.50 (ISBN 0-345-25191-1). Ballantine.

Thetford, Eloise S., jt. auth. see Kraines, Samuel H.

Thetford, Owen. British Naval Aircraft Since Nineteen Hundred & Twelve. 4th ed. (Putnam Aeronautical Ser.). (Illus.). 1980. 23.95 (ISBN 0-370-30021-1, Pub. by Chatto Bodley Jonathan). Merrimack Bk Serv.

Thetford, William N., jt. ed. see Finegold, Julius J.

Theureau, S., jt. auth. see Fonteneau, M.

Theus, Will. How to Detect & Collect Antique Porcelain & Pottery. 1974. 8.95 o.s.i. (ISBN 0-394-49130-0). Knopf.

Thevenin. Animal Migration. 3.95 o.s.i. (ISBN 0-8027-0015-2). Walker & Co.

Thewlis, J., ed. Encyclopaedic Dictionary of Physics, 9 vols., 5 suppls. Incl. Vol. 1. Abbe Refractometer to Compensated Bars. 1961. 37.00 (ISBN 0-08-006540-6); Vol. 2. Compensator to Epecadmium Neutrons. 1961. 37.00 (ISBN 0-08-006541-4); Vol. 3. Epitaxy to Intermediate Image. 1961. 37.00 (ISBN 0-08-006542-2); Vol. 4. Intermediate Stage to Neutron Resonance Level. 1962. 37.00 (ISBN 0-08-006543-0); Vol. 5. Neutron Scattering to Radiation Constants. 1962. 37.00 (ISBN 0-08-006544-9); Vol. 6. Radiation, Continuous, to Stellar Luminosity. 1962. 37.00 (ISBN 0-08-006545-7); Vol. 7. Stellar Magnitude to Zwitter Ion. 1963. 37.00 (ISBN 0-08-006546-5); Vol. 8. Subject & Author Indexes. 1963. 37.00 (ISBN 0-08-006749-2); Vol. 9. Multilingual Glossary. 1964. 77.50 (ISBN 0-08-009928-9); Supplementary Volumes, 5 vols. 1966. Vol 1, 1966. 25.00 (ISBN 0-08-011835-6); Vol 2, 1967. 31.00 (ISBN 0-08-011889-5); Vol. 3, 1969. 31.00 (ISBN 0-08-012447-X); Vol. 4, 1971. 42.50 (ISBN 0-08-006359-4); Vol. 5, 1975. 50.00 **(ISBN 0-08-017056-0); Vol. 6, Date Not Set. price not set (ISBN 0-08-020642-5). 635.00 set (ISBN 0-08-018296-8). Pergamon.**

Thiam, Djibi. My Sister, the Panther. Cook, Mercer, tr. from Fr. LC 80-1016. 192p. (gr. 7 up). 1980. 6.95g (ISBN 0-396-07890-7). Dodd.

Thibault, John C. The Mystery of Ovid's Exile. 1964. 15.75x (ISBN 0-520-01265-8). U of Cal Pr.

Thibaut, tr. see Mueller, F. Max.

Thibaut, J. & Walker, L. Procedural Justice: A Psychological Analysis. LC 75-15944. 1975. text ed. 9.95x o.p. (ISBN 0-470-85868-0); pap. 4.95 (ISBN 0-470-85869-9). Halsted Pr.

Thibaut, John W., jt. auth. see Kelley, Harold H.

Thibodeau, Gary A., jt. auth. see Anthony, Catherine P.

Thibodeaux, Louis J. Chemodynamics: Environmental Movement of Chemicals in Air, Water, & Soil. LC 78-31637. 1979. 36.00 (ISBN 0-471-04720-1, Pub. by Wiley-Interscience). Wiley.

Thie, Paul R. An Introduction to Linear Programming & Game Theory. LC 78-15328. 1979. text ed. 20.95 (ISBN 0-471-04248-X); tchr's. manual avail. (ISBN 0-471-04267-6). Wiley.

Thiebaud, Twinka, ed. Henry Miller Dinner Chats. (Illus.). 128p. (Orig.). 1981. pap. 6.95 (ISBN 0-88496-166-4). Capra Pr.

Thiede, Carsten & Thiede, Peter. Ueber Reinhold Schneider. (Suhrkamp Taschenbuecher: No. 504). 368p. (Orig.). 1980. pap. text ed. 6.50 (ISBN 3-518-37004-9, Pub. by Insel Verlag Germany). Suhrkamp.

Thiede, Peter, jt. auth. see Thiede, Carsten.

Thiede, Walter. Water & Shore Birds. (Illus.). 144p. 1981. pap. 5.95 (ISBN 0-7011-2527-6, Pub. by Chatto-Bodley-Jonathan). Merrimack Bk Serv.

Thiel, Linda & Ledbetter, Marie. Tailoring: Traditional & Contemporary Techniques. (Illus.). 384p. 1980. text ed. 18.95 (ISBN 0-8359-7534-7); instrs' manual avail. Reston.

Thiel, Philip. Visual Awareness & Design: An Introductory Program in Perceptual Sensitivity, Conceptual Awareness, & Basic Design Skills. LC 80-51079. (Illus.). 272p. 1981. 35.00 (ISBN 0-295-95712-3); pap. 19.50 (ISBN 0-295-95786-7). U of Wash Pr.

Thielcke, Gerhard. Bird Sounds. Drury, John, tr. from Ger. LC 73-80579. (Ann Arbor Science Library). (Illus.). 176p. 1976. 6.95 o.p. (ISBN 0-472-00121-3). U of Mich Pr.

Thiele, Brian L., jt. auth. see Strandness, D. E.

Thiele, Edwin R. A Chronology of the Hebrew Kings. 1977. pap. 3.95 (ISBN 0-310-36001-3). Zondervan.

Thiele, Gary A., jt. auth. see Stutzman, Warren L.

Thiele, Margaret. Girl Alive. LC 80-11623. (Orion Ser.). 1980. pap. 1.95 (ISBN 0-8127-0268-9). Southern Pub.

Thiele, Victoria. Clinical Nutrition. 2nd ed. LC 80-13265. (Illus.). 300p. 1980. pap. text ed. 11.95 (ISBN 0-8016-4901-3). Mosby.

Thieliche, Helmut. Theological Ethics, 3 vols. Incl. Foundations. Vol. I. pap. 10.95 (ISBN 0-8028-1791-2); Politics. Vol. II. pap. 10.95 (ISBN 0-8028-1792-0); Vol. III. Sex. pap. 6.95 (ISBN 0-8028-1794-7). LC 78-31858. Set. 29.50 (ISBN 0-8028-1795-5). Eerdmans.

Thielicke, Helmot. The Waiting Father. LC 75-12284. (Jubilee Bks.). 192p. 1975. pap. 1.95 (ISBN 0-06-068011-3, HJ-3, HarpR). Harrow.

Thielicke, Helmut. The Doctor as Judge of Who Shall Live & Who Shall Die. Cooperrider, Edward A., tr. from Ger. LC 75-42836. 48p. (Orig.). 1976. pap. 1.00 (ISBN 0-8006-1228-0, 1-1228). Fortress.

--The Hidden Question of God. Bromiley, Geoffrey, tr. 1977. pap. 4.95 o.p. (ISBN 0-8028-1661-4). Eerdmans.

--How to Believe Again. Anderson, H. George, tr. from Ger. LC 72-75656. 224p. 1972. pap. 4.75 (ISBN 0-8006-0123-8, 1-123). Fortress.

--Our Heavenly Father. (Minister's Paperback Library Ser.). 1974. pap. 3.95 (ISBN 0-8010-8814-3). Baker Bk.

Thielsch, Helmut. Sense & Nonsense of Weld Defects. 2nd ed. (Monticello Bks). 56p. 1981. soft cover 5.00 (ISBN 0-686-28905-6). Jefferson Pubns.

Thienell, G. M. My Battle with Low Blood Sugar. 1971. 4.00 o.p. (ISBN 0-682-47198-4, Banner). Exposition.

Thier, tr. see Makhlis, F. A.

Thier, Herbert D. Teaching Elementary School Science: A Laboratory Approach. LC 78-113717. (Illus.). 1970. text ed. 10.95x o.p. (ISBN 0-669-51805-0). Heath.

Thier, Samuel O., jt. auth. see Smith, Lloyd H.

Thierauf, Robert J. An Introductory Approach to Operations Research. LC 77-23031. (Ser. on Management & Administration). 1978. text ed. 25.95 (ISBN 0-471-03125-9). Wiley.

--Systems Analysis & Design of Real-Time Management Information Systems. LC 74-28368. (Illus.). 624p. 1975. ref. ed. 21.95 (ISBN 0-13-881219-5). P-H.

Thierauf, Robert J. & Klekamp, Robert C. Decision Making Through Operations Research. 2nd ed. LC 74-19473. (Management & Administration Ser). 640p. 1975. 25.95 (ISBN 0-471-85861-7); instructors manual avail. (ISBN 0-471-85856-0); Wiley.

Thierauf, Robert J. & Niehaus, John F. An Introduction to Data Processing for Business. LC 79-20568. 1980. text ed. 21.95 (ISBN 0-471-03439-8); tchrs' manual avail. (ISBN 0-471-03440-1); study guide avail. (ISBN 0-471-07870-0). Wiley.

Thierauf, Robert J., et al. Management Principles & Practices: A Contingency & Questionnaire Approach. LC 77-23297. (Management & Administration Ser.). 1977. text ed. 23.95x (ISBN 0-471-29504-3); tchr's manual avail. (ISBN 0-471-03728-1). Wiley.

Thierens, A. E. Astrology & the Tarot. LC 80-53344. 159p. 1980. Repr. of 1975 ed. lib. bdg. 10.95x (ISBN 0-89370-631-0). Borgo Pr.

Thierry, James F. The Adventure of the Eleven Cuff-Buttons. 1979. pap. 6.50 (ISBN 0-915230-14-3). Rue Morgue.

Thiers, H., jt. auth. see Largent, David L.

Thiers, Louis A. Memoirs, 1870-1873. LC 79-80598. 834p. 1973. Repr. of 1915 ed. 19.50 (ISBN 0-86527-329-4). Fertig.

Thiery, P. & Goundry, J. H. Fireproofing: Chemistry, Technology, & Applications. (Illus.). 1970. 22.30x (ISBN 0-444-20062-2, Pub. by Applied Science). Burgess-Intl Ideas.

Thies, Dagmar. Cat Breeding. Ahrens, Christa, tr. from Ger. (Illus.). 128p. 1980. text ed. 2.95 (ISBN 0-87666-863-5, KW065). TFH Pubns.

--Cat Care. Madero, Thomas P., tr. from Ger. Orig. Title: Katzenhaltung, Katzenpflege. (Illus.). 96p. 1980. 2.95 (ISBN 0-87666-862-7, KW 064). TFH Pubns.

Thies, Wallace J. When Governments Collide: Coercion & Diplomacy in the Vietnam Conflict, 1964-1968. 500p. 1980. 20.00x (ISBN 0-520-03962-9). U of Cal Pr.

Thiesse, James L. Plumbing Fundamentals. (Contemporary Construction Ser.). (Illus.). 192p. (gr. 10-12). 1981. 16.95x (ISBN 0-07-064191-9, G). McGraw.

Thiessen, Delbert D., jt. ed. see Lindzey, Gardner.

Thiessen, Frank & Dales, D. N. Automotive Engines & Related Systems: Principles & Service. (Illus.). 1981. text ed. 18.95 (ISBN 0-8359-0280-3); pap. 14.95 (ISBN 0-8359-0279-X); instr's manual free. Reston.

Thiessen, Frank J. & Dales, Davis. Automotive Principles & Service. (Illus.). 1980. text ed. 19.95 (ISBN 0-8359-0287-0); free instrs'. manual (ISBN 0-8359-0288-9). Reston.

Thiessen, Henry C. Lectures in Systematic Theology. rev. ed. Doerksen, Vernon C., rev. by. 1981. 13.95 (ISBN 0-8028-1815-3). Eerdmans.

Thigpen, Corbett H. & Cleckley, Hervey M. The Three Faces of Eve. 1974. pap. 2.25 (ISBN 0-445-08137-6). Popular Lib.

Thiher, Allen. Celine: The Novel As Delirium. LC 77-185394. 1972. 18.50 (ISBN 0-8135-0717-0). Rutgers U Pr.

Thiman, Eric. Fugue for Beginners. (YA) (gr. 9 up). 1966. 3.90 (ISBN 0-19-321770-8). Oxford U Pr.

Thimann, I. C. Montmorillon: Portrait of a Provincial Town. 1970. 2.75 o.p. (ISBN 0-08-016005-0); pap. 1.85 o.p. (ISBN 0-08-015821-8). Pergamon.

--A Short History of French Literature. 1967. 15.00 (ISBN 0-08-012011-3); pap. 7.00 (ISBN 0-08-012010-5). Pergamon.

Thimann, Kenneth V. Senescence in Plants. 288p. 1980. 69.95 (ISBN 0-8493-5803-5). CRC Pr.

Thimann, Kenneth V., jt. ed. see Pincus, Gregory.

Thimm, Alfred L. The False Promise of Codetermination. LC 80-8422. 288p. 1980. 27.95x (ISBN 0-669-04108-4). Lexington Bks.

Thines, George. Phenomenology & the Science of Behaviour. 1977. text ed. 30.00x (ISBN 0-04-121018-2). Allen Unwin.

Thinley, Karma. The History of the Sixteen Karmapas of Tibet. Stott, David, ed. LC 80-179. (Illus.). 1980. pap. 6.95 (ISBN 0-87773-716-9, Prajna). Great Eastern.

Thio, Alex. Deviant Behavior. LC 77-90439. (Illus.). 1978. text ed. 18.50 (ISBN 0-395-25323-3); inst. manual 0.65 (ISBN 0-395-25324-1). HM.

Thiong'O, Ngugi Wa. Petals of Blood. 1978. 9.95 o.p. (ISBN 0-525-17828-7); pap. 4.95 (ISBN 0-525-04195-8). Dutton.

Third Annual Conference on Shock, Lake of the Ozarks, Missouri, June 1980. Advances in Shock Research, Vol. 5: Proceedings, Part One. Lefer, Allan M., ed. LC 79-63007. 150p. 1981. 26.00x (ISBN 0-8451-0604-X). A R Liss.

Third Annual Conference on Shock, Lake of the Ozarks, Missouri, June 1980, et al. Advances in Shock Research, Vol. 6: Proceedings, Part Two. Schumer, William & Spitzer, John J., eds. LC 79-63007. 150p. 1981. 26.00x (ISBN 0-8451-0605-8). A R Liss.

Third Colloquy for Directors of National Research Institutions in Education, Hamburg, 12-14 September 1978, Educational Research in Europe. Equality of Opportunity Reconsidered: Values in Education for Tomorrow, Proceedings. Carelli, M. Dino & Morris, John G., eds. 234p. 1979. pap. text ed. 19.50 (ISBN 90-265-0296-6, Pub. by Swets Pub Serv Holland). Swets North Am.

Third IFAC Symposium, Montreal, Canada, 18-20 August 1980. Automation in Mining, Mineral & Metal Processing: Proceedings. O'Shea, J. & Polis, M., eds. LC 80-40809. (Illus.). 712p. 1981. 145.00 (ISBN 0-08-026164-7); pap. 90.00 (ISBN 0-08-026143-4). Pergamon.

Third International Conference. Security Through Science & Engineering: Proceedings. De Vore, R. William & Jackson, J. S., eds. LC 80-83300. (Illus.). 1980. pap. 33.50 (ISBN 0-89779-042-1, UKYBU122); 4.50 (ISBN 0-89779-043-X). OES Pubns.

Third International Symposium on Dredging Technology. Proceedings. Stephens, H. S., ed. (Illus.). 446p. (Orig.). 1980. pap. write for info. (ISBN 0-906085-09-8). BHRA Fluid.

Thirion, Andre. Revolutionaries Without Revolution. LC 74-9859. (Illus.). 512p. 1975. 15.95 o.s.i. (ISBN 0-02-617400-6, 61740). Macmillan.

Thirkell, Angela. Wild Strawberries. LC 80-7834. (Barsetshire Ser.). 280p. 1980. pap. 2.25 (ISBN 0-06-080526-9, P526, PL). Har-Row.

Thirkettle, G. L. Advanced Economics. 2nd ed. 160p. (Orig.). 1976. pap. text ed. 10.00x (ISBN 0-7121-0164-0, Pub. by Macdonald & Evans England). Intl Ideas.

--Wheldon's Business Statistics. 8th ed. (Illus.). 256p. 1976. pap. text ed. 11.95x (ISBN 0-7121-2331-8, Pub. by Macdonald & Evans England). Intl Ideas.

Thirlby, G. F., jt. ed. see Buchanan, James M.

Thirlwall, A. P. The Balance of Payments Theory & the United Kingdom Experience. (Illus.). 323p. 1980. text ed. 35.00x (ISBN 0-8419-5077-6). Holmes & Meier.

--Growth & Development: With Special Reference to Developing Economics. 2nd ed. LC 77-8582. 1978. 24.95 (ISBN 0-470-99214-X); pap. 14.95 (ISBN 0-470-26988-X). Halsted Pr.

Thirlwall, A. P., jt. auth. see Dixon, R. J.

Thirlwall, A. P., jt. ed. see Crabtree, Derek.

Thiroux, Jacques P. Ethics: Theory and Practice. 1977. pap. text ed. 5.95 (ISBN 0-02-479230-6). Macmillan.

Thirring, Hans. Energy for Man. 1976. pap. 7.50x (ISBN 0-06-131861-2, TB 1861, Torch). Har-Row.

Thirsk, H. R., ed. Electrochemistry. 1977. text ed. 27.50 (ISBN 0-08-021676-5). Pergamon.

Thirsk, Joan. Economic Policy & Projects: The Development of a Consumer Society in Early Modern England. 1978. 24.95x (ISBN 0-19-828274-5). Oxford U Pr.

Thirsk, Joan & Cooper, J. P., eds. Seventeenth-Century Economic Documents. 1972. 33.00x (ISBN 0-19-828256-7). Oxford U Pr.

Thirty-Seventh Annual Scientific Meeting of the Committee on Problems of Drug Dependence Division of Medical Sciences, National Research Council. Problems of Drug Dependence 1975: Proceedings. LC 75-29630. vii, 1212p. 1975. pap. 22.50 (ISBN 0-309-02417-X). Natl Acad Pr.

This, Leslie E. A Guide to Effective Management: Practical Applications from Behavioral Science. (Illus.). 288p. 1974. pap. text ed. 8.95 (ISBN 0-201-07559-8). A-W.

Thiselton-Dyer, Thomas F. British Popular Customs, Present & Past. LC 67-23908. (Social History Reference Ser.). (Illus.). 1968. Repr. of 1876 ed. 18.00 (ISBN 0-8103-3261-2). Gale.

--English Folk-Lore. LC 75-150242. Repr. of 1878 ed. 20.00 (ISBN 0-8103-3680-4). Gale.

--Folk-Lore of Plants. LC 68-22054. 1968. Repr. of 1889 ed. 18.00 (ISBN 0-8103-3554-9). Gale.

--Folk-Lore of Women As Illustrated by Legendary & Traditionary Tales, Folk-Rhymes, Proverbial Sayings, Superstitions Etc. LC 68-24475. 1968. Repr. of 1906 ed. 15.00 (ISBN 0-8103-3555-7). Gale.

Thistlethwaite, F. The Great Experiment. (Illus.). 1977. pap. 11.95x (ISBN 0-521-29224-7). Cambridge U Pr.

Thistlethwaite, Mark. The Image of George Washington: Studies in Mid-Nineteenth-Century History Painting. LC 78-74384. (Fine Arts Dissertations, Fourth Ser.). (Illus.). 1980. lib. bdg. 38.00 (ISBN 0-8240-3970-X). Garland Pub.

Thivend, P., jt. auth. see Ruckebusch, Y.

Thivolet, J. & Schmitt, D. Cutaneous Immunopathology. (Illus.). 506p. 1978. pap. 19.50 (ISBN 2-85598-175-1). Masson Pub.

Thoburn, Tina, jt. auth. see Ogle, Lucille.

Thoday, J. M. see Demerec, M.

Thode, Jackson C., ed. William Henry Jackson's Rocky Mountain Railroad Album: Steel & Steam Across the Great Divide. (Illus.). 1977. 195.00 (ISBN 0-913582-14-X). Sundance.

Thode, Jackson C., et al, eds. see Sloan, Robert E. & Skowronski, Carl A.

Thodes, Sonya & Wilson, Josleen. Surviving Family Life: The Seven Crises of Living Together. 300p. 1981. 11.95 (ISBN 0-399-12507-8). Putnam.

Thody, Philip. Roland Barthes: A Conservative Estimate. LC 77-5918. 1977. text ed. 23.25x (ISBN 0-391-00730-0). Humanities.

Thoinan, E., jt. auth. see Nuitter, C.

Tholen, Gerald. Massism Vs. Natural Religion. 1980. pap. 3.00. Am Atheist.

Tholfsen, Trygve. Working Class Radicalism in Mid-Victorian England. LC 76-43323. 1977. 22.50x (ISBN 0-231-04234-5). Columbia U Pr.

Tholfsen, Trygve R. Sir James Kay-Shuttleworth on Popular Education. LC 73-15046. 1974. text ed. 8.75 (ISBN 0-8077-2402-5); pap. text ed. 4.00x (ISBN 0-8077-2411-4). Tchrs Coll.

Thollander, Earl. Back Roads of Washington. (Illus.). 208p. 1981. 15.95 (ISBN 0-517-54269-2); pap. 9.95 (ISBN 0-517-54270-6). Potter.

Thollander, Earl & Abbey, Edward. Back Roads of Arizona. LC 78-51122. (Illus.). 1978. 17.95 o.p. (ISBN 0-87358-170-9); pap. 12.50 o.p. (ISBN 0-87358-177-6). Northland.

Thom, A. Megalithic Remains in Britain & Brittany. (Illus.). 1979. 28.00x (ISBN 0-19-858156-4). Oxford U Pr.

Thom, Alexander. Megalithic Lunar Observatories. 1971. 21.00x (ISBN 0-19-858132-7). Oxford U Pr.

--Megalithic Sites in Britain. (Illus.). 1967. 28.00x (ISBN 0-19-813148-8). Oxford U Pr.

Thom, R. Structual Stability & Morphogenesis: An Outline of a General Theory of Models. Fowler, D. H., tr. from Fr. pap. 22.50 (ISBN 0-8053-9279-3). A-W.

Thom, Robert. Children of the Ladybug: A Drama in 2 Acts. 1956. 17.50x (ISBN 0-685-69875-0). Elliots Bks.

--New Wine Is Better. 1974. pap. 2.95 (ISBN 0-88368-036-X). Whitaker Hse.

Thom, William. The Struggle for Religious Freedom in Virginia: The Baptist. pap. 9.00 o.p. (ISBN 0-686-12395-6). Church History.

Thoma. Lausbubengeschichten. Dahlstrom, A. H., ed. 1932. text ed. 7.95x o.p. (ISBN 0-669-29884-0). Heath.

Thoma, Clemens. A Christian Theology of Judaism. Croner, Helga & Frizzell, Lawrence, trs. from Ger. LC 80-82252. (Studies in Judaism & Christianity). 212p. 1980. pap. 7.95 (ISBN 0-8091-2310-X). Paulist Pr.

Thoma, J. Bond Graphs: Introduction & Application. LC 75-9763. 192p. 1975. text ed. 27.00 (ISBN 0-08-018882-6); pap. text ed. 16.00 (ISBN 0-08-018881-8). Pergamon.

Thoma, Jean U. Modern Oil-Hydraulic Engineering. (Illus.). 1970. 52.00x (ISBN 0-85461-043-X). Intl Ideas.

Thomae, H. Beobachtung und Beurteilung von Kindern und Jugendlichen. 13th ed. (Psychologische Praxis: Band 15). (Illus.). vi, 90p. 1980. soft cover 7.25 (ISBN 3-8055-1526-X). S Karger.

Thomajah, Zareh. The Thief of State Street: 30 Years of Audacious Advertising with Zareh. LC 80-82894. (Illus.). 152p. (Orig.). 1980. pap. 15.00 (ISBN 0-686-28877-7). Garabed.

Thoman, G. Richard. Foreign Investment & Regional Development: The Theory & Practice of Investment Incentives, with a Case Study of Belgium. LC 72-85978. (Special Studies in International Economics & Development). 1973. 28.50x (ISBN 0-275-28681-9). Irvington.

Thoman, Richard S. The United States & Canada: Present & Future. (Geography Ser.). 1978. text ed. 19.95 (ISBN 0-675-08410-5); instructor's manual 3.95 (ISBN 0-686-66348-9). Merrill.

Thomann, Arthur E. Petroleum Drilling Equipment Terms & Phrases: English-Spanish, Spanish-English. 423p. 1980. lib. bdg. 50.00x (ISBN 0-930624-02-5). Marlin.

Thomas. A Manual of Time Study for Supervisors. 4.00 o.p. (ISBN 0-686-00164-8). Columbia Graphs.

Thomas, A., jt. auth. see Blackmore, D. R.

Thomas, A. F. & Abbey, F. Calculational Methods of Interacting Arrays of Fissile Material. LC 73-8604. 144p. 1973. text ed. 28.00 (ISBN 0-08-017660-7). Pergamon.

Thomas, A. R., jt. auth. see Jones, Morris.

Thomas, A. R. B. Chess Techniques. 1975. 15.00 (ISBN 0-7100-8098-0); pap. 6.50 (ISBN 0-7100-8099-9). Routledge & Kegan.

Thomas, A. V. Dictionnaire des difficultes de la langue francaise. (Fr). 23.50 (ISBN 0-685-13865-8, 3611). Larousse.

Thomas, Adin B. Stock Control in Manufacturing Industries. 2nd ed. 240p. 1980. text ed. 29.50 (ISBN 0-566-02140-4, Pub. by Gower Pub Co England). Renouf.

Thomas, Alan G., ed. see Durrell, Lawrence.

Thomas, Alexander, jt. ed. see Chess, Stella.

Thomas, Alexander, et al. Temperament & Behavior Disorders in Children. LC 68-13025. 309p. 1968. 15.00x (ISBN 0-8147-0415-8). NYU Pr.

Thomas, Alfred B., ed. Theodora De Croix & the Northern Frontier of New Spain 1776-1783. (American Exploration & Travel Ser.: No. 5). 1968. Repr. of 1941 ed. 13.95 (ISBN 0-8061-0093-1). U of Okla Pr.

Thomas, Alfred B., et al. Apache Indians VIII. Horr, David A., ed. (American Indian Ethnohistory Ser.). 1978. lib. bdg. 42.00 (ISBN 0-8240-0710-7). Garland Pub.

--Apache Indians XI. Horr, David A., ed. (American Indian Ethnohistory Ser.). 1978. lib. bdg. 42.00 (ISBN 0-8240-0712-3). Garland Pub.

Thomas, Allison. Benji. (Orig.). (gr. 5-9). 1975. pap. 1.75 (ISBN 0-515-05749-5). Jove Pubns.

Thomas, Andre & Autgaerden, S. Locomotion from Pre-to Post-natal Life. (Clinics in Developmental Medicine Ser. No. 24). 90p. 1966. 11.00 (ISBN 0-685-24723-6). Lippincott.

Thomas, Ann M., jt. auth. see Thomas, James W.

Thomas, Anne W. Colors from the Earth. 132p. 1980. 13.95 (ISBN 0-442-25786-4). Van Nos Reinhold.

Thomas, Anthony. Things We Cut. (Easy-Read Awareness Book Ser.). (Illus.). 32p. (gr. 1-3). 1976. PLB 4.47 o.p. (ISBN 0-531-01216-6). Watts.

--Things We Hear. (Easy-Read Awareness Book Ser.). (Illus.). 32p. (gr. 1-3). 1976. PLB 4.47 o.p. (ISBN 0-531-00363-9). Watts.

--Things We See. (Easy-Read Awareness Book Ser.). (Illus.). 32p. (gr. 1-3). 1976. PLB 4.47 o.p. (ISBN 0-531-01217-4). Watts.

--Things We Touch. (Easy-Read Awareness Book Ser.). (Illus.). 32p. (gr. 1-3). 1976. PLB 4.47 o.p. (ISBN 0-531-00364-7). Watts.

Thomas, Art. Archery Is for Me. LC 81-22. (Sports for Me Bks.). (Illus.). (gr. 2-5). 1981. PLB 5.95 (ISBN 0-8225-1091-X). Lerner Pubns.

--Backpacking Is for Me. LC 80-12847. (Sports for Me Books Ser.). (Illus.). 48p. (gr. 2-5). 1980. PLB 5.95g (ISBN 0-8225-1095-2). Lerner Pubns.

--Boxing Is for Me. LC 80-20086. (Sports for Me Bks.). (Illus.). (gr. 2-5). 1981. PLB 5.95 (ISBN 0-8225-1133-9). Lerner Pubns.

--Fishing Is for Me. LC 80-13442. (Sports for Me Books Ser.). (Illus.). 48p. (gr. 2-5). 1980. PLB 5.95g (ISBN 0-8225-1096-0). Lerner Pubns.

--Volleyball Is for Me. LC 80-12925. (Sports for Me Books). (Illus.). (gr. 2-5). 1980. PLB 5.95g (ISBN 0-8225-1094-4). Lerner Pubns.

Thomas, Art & Blackburn, Emily. Horseback Riding Is for Me. (Sports for Me Bks.). (Illus.). (gr. 2-5). 1981. PLB 5.95 (ISBN 0-8225-1092-8). Lerner Pubns.

Thomas, Arthur L., jt. ed. see Sterling, Robert R.

Thomas, B. E. Management of Shipboard Maintenance. (Illus.). 143p. 1981. 18.50x (ISBN 0-540-07354-7). Sheridan.

Thomas, Barry. Building the Herreshoff Dinghy: The Manufacturer's Method. (Illus.). 50p. 1977. pap. 4.00 (ISBN 0-913372-13-7). Mystic Seaport.

Thomas, Barry & Deaton, David. Labour Shortage & Economic Analysis: A Study of Occupational Labour Markets. (Warwick Studies in Industrial Relations Ser.). 1977. 36.00x (ISBN 0-631-18310-8, Pub by Basil Blackwell England). Biblio Dist.

Thomas, Benjamin E., et al. Africa. rev ed. LC 76-17679. (World Cultures Ser). (Illus.). (gr. 6 up). 1978. text ed. 9.95 ea. 1-4 copies o.p. (ISBN 0-88296-142-X); text ed. 7.96 ea. 5 or more copies o.p.; tchrs' guide 8.94 o.p. (ISBN 0-686-67612-2). Fideler.

Thomas, Benjamin P. Russo-American Relations, 1815-1867. LC 70-87709. (American History, Politics & Law Ser). 1969. Repr. of 1930 ed. lib. bdg. 22.50 (ISBN 0-306-71681-X). Da Capo.

Thomas, Benjamin P. & Hyman, Harold M. Stanton: The Life & Times of Lincoln's Secretary of War. LC 80-18970. (Illus.). xvii, 642p. 1980. Repr. of 1962 ed. lib. bdg. 49.50x (ISBN 0-313-22581-8, THSL). Greenwood.

Thomas, Benjamin P., ed. see Cadawallader, Sylvanus.

Thomas, Bertram. Alarms and Excursions in Arabia. LC 80-1911. 1981. Repr. of 1931 ed. 36.00 (ISBN 0-404-18986-5). AMS Pr.

Thomas, Bill. The Island: A Native History of America's Costal Islands. (Illus.). 1980. 29.95 (ISBN 0-393-01373-1). Norton.

--The Swamp. (Illus.). 1976. 29.95 (ISBN 0-393-08747-6). Norton.

Thomas, Bill & Stebel, S. L. The Shoe Leather Treatment. 1980. 10.00 o.p. (ISBN 0-312-90861-X). St Martin.

Thomas, Bill & Stebel, Sid. Shoe Leather Treatment... LC 79-56300. (Illus.). 1979. 11.95 (ISBN 0-312-90861-X). J P Tarcher.

Thomas, Bill, jt. auth. see Karsk, Roger.

Thomas, Bob. Bud and Lou: The Abbott & Costello Story. LC 76-54743. 1977. 10.00 o.p. (ISBN 0-397-01195-4). Lippincott.

Thomas, C., et al. Basic Blueprint Reading & Sketching. LC 76-56490. 1978. 6.60 (ISBN 0-8273-2050-7); instructor's guide 1.60 (ISBN 0-8273-2051-5). Delmar.

Thomas, C. K., jt. auth. see Sastry, N. S.

Thomas, Carol H. & Thomas, James L. Academic Library Services for Handicapped Students in the U. S. 350p. 1981. text ed. 45.00x (ISBN 0-912700-95-5). Oryx Pr.

Thomas, Carol H. & Thomas, James L., eds. Meeting the Needs of the Handicapped. 1980. lib. bdg. 18.50x (ISBN 0-912700-54-8). Oryx Pr.

Thomas, Charles. Britain & Ireland in Early Christian Times. LC 75-138860. (Illus., Orig.). 1971. pap. 3.95 o.p. (ISBN 0-07-064239-7, SP). McGraw.

--Make-Up: The Dramatic Student's Approach. 2nd ed. 1968. pap. 3.25 (ISBN 0-87830-560-2). Theatre Arts.

Thomas, Charles, jt. auth. see Hibbert, Christopher.

Thomas, Charles I. Cornea: Diseases. (Illus.). 1348p. 1956. 44.50 (ISBN 0-398-01914-2). C C Thomas.

--Ophthamology. 4th ed. (Medical Examination Review Book: Vol. 15). 1980. pap. 16.50 (ISBN 0-87488-115-3). Med Exam.

Thomas, Charles I., ed. Ophthalmology Review Book. 1972. spiral bdg. 13.00 (ISBN 0-87488-347-4). Med Exam.

Thomas, Charles K. An Introduction to the Phonetics of American English. 2nd ed. (Illus.). 1958. 15.50 (ISBN 0-8260-8630-6). Wiley.

Thomas, Charles W. Boys No More: A Black Psychologist's View of Community. 1971. pap. text ed. 4.95x (ISBN 0-02-478890-2, 47889). Macmillan.

Thomas, Charles W. & Petersen, David M. Prison Organization & Inmate Subcultures. 1977. pap. text ed. 4.00 (ISBN 0-672-61404-9). Bobbs.

Thomas, Charles W., jt. auth. see Petersen, David M.

Thomas, Charles W., jt. auth. see Peterson, David M.

Thomas, Claudewell S., jt. ed. see Bryce-Laporte, Roy S.

Thomas, Clayton L., ed. Taber's Cyclopedic Medical Dictionary. 14th ed. (Illus.). 1796p. 1981. text ed. write for info. (ISBN 0-8036-8307-3); Thumb-indexed Edition. text ed. write for info. (ISBN 0-8036-8306-5). Davis Co.

Thomas, Cleveland A., jt. auth. see Mooney, Frank V.

Thomas, Clive. Dependence & Transformation: The Economics of the Transition. LC 73-90081. 228p. 1974. 10.95 o.p. (ISBN 0-85345-317-9, CL3179). Monthly Rev.

Thomas, Craig. Snow Falcon. 416p. 1981. pap. 2.95 (ISBN 0-553-14625-4). Bantam.

Thomas, D. & Graham, D. Brain Tumors. LC 80-49930. 1980. 74.95 (ISBN 0-407-00157-3). Butterworths.

Thomas, D. Babatunde. Importing Technology into Africa: Foreign Investment and the Supply of Technological Innovations. LC 74-11606. (Praeger Special Studies Ser.). 224p. 1976. text ed. 22.95 o.p. (ISBN 0-275-05740-2). Praeger.

Thomas, D. Babatunde & Wionczek, Miguel S., eds. Integration of Science and Technology with Development: Caribbean and Latin American Problems in the Context of the United Nations Conference on Science and Technology for Development. (Pergamon Policy Studies). 1979. 33.00 (ISBN 0-08-023881-5). Pergamon.

Thomas, D. M. Love & Other Deaths. 1975. 10.95 (ISBN 0-236-31016-X, Pub. by Paul Elek). Merrimack Bk Serv.

--The White Hotel. LC 80-52004. 256p. 1981. 11.95 (ISBN 0-670-76292-X). Viking Pr.

Thomas, D. M., tr. see Akhmatova, Anna.

Thomas, D. T. Engineering Electromagnetics. 416p. 1972. text ed. 31.00 (ISBN 0-08-016778-0). Pergamon.

Thomas, D. Winton, ed. Archaeology & Old Testament Study. 1967. 33.50x (ISBN 0-19-813150-X). Oxford U Pr.

Thomas, Daniel H. & Case, Lynn M., eds. The New Guide to the Diplomatic Archives of Western Europe. LC 75-10127. 1975. 15.00x (ISBN 0-8122-7697-3). U of Pa Pr.

Thomas, David. Country Railway. LC 76-20128. 1976. 14.95 (ISBN 0-7153-7285-8). David & Charles.

--The Gospel of Matthew. LC 78-11502. (Kregel Bible Study Classics). Orig. Title: The Genius of the Gospel. 1980. 12.95 (ISBN 0-8254-3812-8). Kregel.

--Naturalism & Social Science. LC 79-14223. (Themes in Social Sciences Ser.). 1980. 38.50 (ISBN 0-521-22821-2); pap. 13.50 (ISBN 0-521-29660-9). Cambridge U Pr.

--A Regional History of the Railways of Great Britain: The West Country, Vol. 1. 4th ed. 15.95 o.p. (ISBN 0-7153-6208-9). David & Charles.

Thomas, David, ed. Wales: A New Study. 1977. 32.00 (ISBN 0-7153-7302-1). David & Charles.

Thomas, David N. Organising for Social Change: A Study in the Theory & Practice of Community Social Work. 2nd ed. (National Institute Social Services Library). 1977. pap. text ed. 7.50x o.p. (ISBN 0-04-361028-5). Allen Unwin.

Thomas, David N., jt. auth. see Henderson, Paul.

Thomas, David N. & Henderson, Paul, eds. Readings in Community Work. 196p. 1981. text ed. 29.50x (ISBN 0-04-361045-5, 2650-1); pap. text ed. 14.95x (ISBN 0-04-361046-3). Allen Unwin.

Thomas, David S. & Bermont, Hubert. Getting Published. 1974. pap. 3.95 (ISBN 0-06-090382-1, CN382, CN). Har-Row.

Thomas, David S. & Rocksborough Smith, Simon. Summer Saturdays in the West. (Illus.). 1973. 14.95 (ISBN 0-7153-5912-6). David & Charles.

Thomas, David St. John. The Great Way West: The History & Romance of the Great Western Railway's Route from Paddington to Penzanze. LC 75-10530. (Illus.). 1975. 14.95 (ISBN 0-7153-7063-4). David & Charles.

Thomas, David St John see St. John Thomas, David.

Thomas, Dian. Backyard Roughing It Easy. 1980. pap. 5.95 (ISBN 0-449-90018-5, Columbine). Fawcett.

--Roughing It Easy. (Illus.). 248p. 1976. pap. 2.75 (ISBN 0-446-95662-7). Warner Bks.

--Roughing It Easy, Two. (Illus.). 224p. (Orig.). 1978. pap. 2.75 (ISBN 0-446-95843-3). Warner Bks.

Thomas, Diana M., et al. The Effective Reference Librarian. (Library & Information Science). 1981. write for info. (ISBN 0-12-688720-9). Acad Pr.

Thomas, Donald. Captain Wunder. 300p. 1981. 12.95 (ISBN 0-670-20355-6). Viking Pr.

--The Philosophy of Divine Nutrition. 1977. 6.95 o.p. (ISBN 0-533-02744-6). Vantage.

--Swinburne: The Poet of His World. 1979. 14.95 (ISBN 0-19-520136-1). Oxford U Pr.

Thomas, Donald G. U.S. Silencer Patents, 2 vols. new ed. Brown, Robert K. & Lund, Peter C., eds. Incl. Vol. 1. 1888-1935. 329p. 15.95 o.p. (ISBN 0-87364-007-1). LC 74-180288. (Illus.). 1973. Set. 29.95 o.p. (ISBN 0-87364-006-3). Paladin Ent.

Thomas, Dorothy. Home Place. LC 36-16925. (Illus.). 1966. pap. 1.70 (ISBN 0-8032-5197-1, BB 346, Bison). U of Nebr Pr.

Thomas, Dorothy S. The Salvage. 1975. Repr. of 1952 ed. 24.75x (ISBN 0-520-02915-1). U of Cal Pr.

Thomas, Dorothy S. & Nishimoto, Richard. The Spoilage: Japanese-American Evacuation & Resettlement During World War Two. (California Library Reprint Ser.). 1974. Repr. 20.00x (ISBN 0-520-02637-3). U of Cal Pr.

Thomas, Duncan. Breakfast with Washington. 160p. 1978. 6.95 (ISBN 0-8059-2475-2). Dorrance.

Thomas, Dylan. Adventures in the Skin Trade & Other Stories. LC 55-7367. 1955. 4.50 (ISBN 0-8112-0779-X, NDP183); pap. 3.75 (ISBN 0-8112-0202-X, NDP183). New Directions.

--Child's Christmas in Wales. LC 59-13174. (Illus.). 1969. gift ed. 12.00 (ISBN 0-8112-0391-3). New Directions.

--Collected Poems. LC 53-7766. 1971. pap. 4.95 (ISBN 0-8112-0205-4, NDP316). New Directions.

--Quite Early One Morning. LC 54-12907. pap. 3.95 (ISBN 0-8112-0208-9, NDP90). New Directions.

Thomas, E., et al. From Single Cells to Plants. (Wykeham Science Ser.: No. 38). 1975. 9.95x (ISBN 0-8448-1165-3). Crane Russak Co.

Thomas, E. C., tr. see De Bury, Richard.

Thomas, E. J., jt. auth. see Biddle, B. J.

Thomas, Eben. Canoeing Maine, No. 1. rev. ed. LC 79-14500. (Illus.). 1979. lib. bdg. 9.50 o.p. (ISBN 0-89621-035-9); pap. 4.95 (ISBN 0-89621-034-0). Thorndike Pr.

--Canoeing Maine, No. 2. rev. ed. LC 79-14488. (Illus.). 1979. lib. bdg. 9.50 o.p. (ISBN 0-89621-037-5); pap. 4.95 (ISBN 0-89621-036-7). Thorndike Pr.

Thomas, Edith. Eve & the Others. Eirinberg, Estelle, tr. from Fr. LC 75-36694. Orig. Title: Eve et les Autres. 125p. 1976. case bound 6.95 (ISBN 0-916868-01-X); pap. 3.50 (ISBN 0-685-65847-3). Continent Edns.

Thomas, Edward. From Quarks to Quasars. 1977. pap. text ed. 11.25x (ISBN 0-485-12024-0, Athlone Pr). Humanities.

--Grail Yoga. 2nd ed. LC 74-84399. (A Grail Bk). (Illus.). 128p. 1975. pap. 2.95 (ISBN 0-914896-28-8). East Ridge Pr.

--A Literary Pilgrim in England. 318p. 1980. pap. 9.95 (ISBN 0-19-281291-2). Oxford U Pr.

--Richard Jefferies. Gant, Roland, ed. 1978. 12.95 (ISBN 0-571-11236-6, Pub. by Faber & Faber); pap. 7.95 (ISBN 0-571-11237-4). Merrimack Bk Serv.

Thomas, Edward J. The History of Buddhist Thought. 2nd ed. (History of Civilization Ser.). 1963. Repr. of 1957 ed. 24.00 (ISBN 0-7100-4971-4). Routledge & Kegan.

--Life of Buddha: As Legend & History. (History of Civilization Ser). 1969. Repr. of 1949 ed. 24.00 (ISBN 0-7100-4972-2). Routledge & Kegan.

--Life of Buddha: As Legend & History. (History of Civilization Ser). 1975. pap. 11.95 (ISBN 0-7100-8162-6). Routledge & Kegan.

Thomas, Edward J., ed. Song of the Lord, Bhagavadgita. (Wisdom of the East Ser). 3.00 o.p. (ISBN 0-7195-1407-X). Paragon.

Thomas, Edwin J., ed. Behavior Modification Procedure: A Sourcebook. LC 73-89513. 368p. 1974. text ed. 21.95x (ISBN 0-202-36018-0); pap. text ed. 10.95x (ISBN 0-202-36019-9). Aldine Pub.

Thomas, Ellen L. Reading Aids for Every Class: Four Hundred Activities for Instruction & Enrichment. 450p. 1980. text ed. 18.95 (ISBN 0-205-06955-X). Allyn.

Thomas, Ellen L. & Robinson, H. Alan. Improving Reading in Every Class: A Sourcebook for Teachers. 2nd ed. 480p. 1972. text ed. 21.95x (ISBN 0-205-05590-7, 2255901); pap. 8.95x abr. ed. (ISBN 0-205-05716-0, 2257165). Allyn.

Thomas, Emory M. American War & Peace, Eighteen Sixty to Eighteen Seventy-Seven. (Illus.). 240p. 1973. pap. 10.95 (ISBN 0-13-032391-8). P-H.

--The Confederate Nation Eighteen Sixty-One to Eighteen Sixty-Five. Morris, Richard B. & Commager, Henry S., eds. LC 76-26255. (New American Nation Ser.). (Illus.). 1979. pap. 6.95 (ISBN 0-06-090703-7, CN-703, CN). Har-Row.

--Confederate State of Richmond: A Biography of the Capital. 1971. 15.00 (ISBN 0-292-70085-7). U of Tex Pr.

Thomas, Eugene E. Brotherhood of Mr. Shasta. 307p. 1981. pap. 10.00 (ISBN 0-89540-067-7). Sun Pub.

Thomas, Eva. Behind That Door Lies Your Fortune. 4.50 o.p. (ISBN 0-685-33191-1). Vantage.

Thomas, Evan W. Brain-Injured Children: With Special Reference to Doman-Delacato Methods of Treatment. (Illus.). 196p. 1974. text ed. 19.75 photocopy ed. spiral (ISBN 0-398-01915-0). C C Thomas.

Thomas, F. W., ed. see Jaini, Jagmandar L.

Thomas, Frank. Sherlock Holmes & the Sacred Sword. 256p. (Orig.). 1980. pap. 2.50 o.p. (ISBN 0-523-41013-1). Pinnacle Bks.

Thomas, G. H. Metalwork Technology. (gr. 9 up). 1970. 10.95x (ISBN 0-7195-2654-X). Transatlantic.

Thomas, Gail E., ed. Black Students in Higher Education: Conditions & Experiences in the 1970's. LC 80-1702. (Contributions to the Study of Education: No. 1). 424p. 1981. lib. bdg. 29.95 (ISBN 0-313-22477-3, TBS/). Greenwood.

Thomas, Gareth & Goringe, Michael J. Transmission Electron Microscopy of Materials. LC 79-449. 1979. 27.95 (ISBN 0-471-12244-0, Pub. by Wiley-Interscience). Wiley.

Thomas, Gareth, et al, eds. Electron Microscopy & Structure of Materials: Proceedings of the Fifth Annual Symposium on the Structure & Properties of Materials, Berkeley, September, 1971. 1972. 50.00x (ISBN 0-520-02114-2). U of Cal Pr.

Thomas, George. Elements of Calculus & Analytic Geometry. 4th ed. Date not set. text ed. 20.80 (ISBN 0-201-07664-0, Sch Div); price not set tchrs. commentary (ISBN 0-201-07665-9); price not set solutions manual (ISBN 0-201-07666-7); price not set self study manual (ISBN 0-201-07667-5). A-W.

Thomas, George B., et al. Elementary Calculus from an Advanced Viewpoint. 1967. 17.95 (ISBN 0-201-07558-X). A-W.

Thomas, George B., Jr. Calculus. 3rd ed. 1969. text ed. 22.95 (ISBN 0-201-07503-2). A-W.

Thomas, George B., Jr. & Finney, Ross L. Calculus & Analytic Geometry. 5th ed. LC 78-55832. (Illus.). 1979. Combined Ed. text ed. 27.95 (ISBN 0-201-07540-7); Pt. 1. student suppl. & self-study manual avail. 20.95 (ISBN 0-201-07541-5); Pt. 2. 20.95 (ISBN 0-201-07542-3). A-W.

Thomas, George J., jt. auth. see Munster, Andrew M.

Thomas, George R., ed. The Collected Poems of Edward Thomas. 240p. 1981. pap. 9.95 (ISBN 0-19-281288-2). Oxford U Pr.

Thomas, Gilbert. Collected Poems. 1969. text ed. 6.50x o.p. (ISBN 0-04-821023-4). Allen Unwin.

Thomas, Gordon & Morgan-Witts, Max. The Day the Bubble Burst: A Social History of the Wall Street Crash of 1929. 1980. pap. 5.95 (ISBN 0-14-005640-8). Penguin.

Thomas, Gordon & Witts, Max M. Enola Gay. 400p. pap. 2.75 (ISBN 0-671-42116-6). PB.

--Enola Gay. LC 76-44343. 1977. 35.00x (ISBN 0-8128-2150-5). Stein & Day.

--Guernica. 1977. pap. 1.95 o.p. (ISBN 0-345-25454-6). Ballantine.

--The San Francisco Earthquake. pap. 2.95 (ISBN 0-8128-7028-X). Stein & Day.

Thomas, Gordon K. Wordsworth's Dirge & Promise: Napoleon, Wellington, & the Convention of Cintra. LC 77-125102. 190p. 1971. 7.95x o.p. (ISBN 0-8032-0777-8). U of Nebr Pr.

Thomas, Gough. Shotguns & Cartridges for Game & Clays. 3rd ed. (Illus.). 254p. 1976. 25.00 (ISBN 0-7136-1583-4). Transatlantic.

Thomas, Graham S. The Old Shrub Roses. (Illus.). 1965. 15.95x o.p. (ISBN 0-460-07792-9, Pub. by J. M. Dent England). Biblio Dist.

--Plants for Ground Cover. 1970. 12.50 o.p. (ISBN 0-8231-6037-8). Branford.

Thomas, Graham St. The Old Shrub Roses. rev. ed. (Illus.). 232p. 1979. 15.95x (ISBN 0-460-04345-5, Pub. by J M Dent England). Biblio Dist.

Thomas, Gregory S., et al. Exercise & Health: The Evidence & the Implications. LC 80-23376. 128p. 1981. lib. bdg. 17.50 (ISBN 0-89946-048-8). Oelgeschlager.

Thomas, Gwynne E. H. Political History of the Ancient World. 1981. 7.95 (ISBN 0-8062-1680-8). Carlton.

Thomas, Hadley A., et al. Oral English. (Reading Readiness). (Illus.). (gr. k-1). 1972. text ed. 2.28 (ISBN 0-87892-725-5); tchr's manual 2.28 (ISBN 0-87892-726-3). Economy Co.

Thomas, Harold. The World Power Foundation: Its Goals & Platform. 1980. pap. 6.95. Loompanics.

Thomas, Harry. Handbook of Information Display Devices. 1981. 24.95 (ISBN 0-8359-2743-1). Reston.

Thomas, Haywood. Apology of Actors. Bd. with A Refutation of the Apology for Actors. 20.00x (ISBN 0-8201-1198-8). Schol Facsimiles.

Thomas, Helen. As It Was & World Without End. (Orig.). 1972. pap. 7.95 (ISBN 0-571-10135-6, Pub. by Faber & Faber). Merrimack Bk Serv.

--Dateline: White House. (Illus.). 320p. 1975. 9.95 o.s.i. (ISBN 0-02-617620-3). Macmillan.

Thomas, Henry. Better English Made Easy. (YA) (gr. 7-12). 1975. pap. 1.95 (ISBN 0-445-08401-4). Popular Lib.

--Grail Yoga. 128p. 1978. pap. 3.95 (ISBN 0-8334-1715-0). Multimedia.

Thomas, Hilary. Complete Games of Mikhail Tal, 1936-59. LC 80-69576. 192p. 1981. 15.00 (ISBN 0-668-05187-6, 5187). Arco.

Thomas, Hubert. Words for Writing. (gr. 2-5). 1977. 1.75x (ISBN 0-933892-13-6). Child Focus Co.

Thomas, I. D., et al. Astrologia: Que Dice la Biblia? Martinez Diaz, Jose Luis, tr. from Eng. (Coleccion Doctrinas Modernas Ser.: No. 7). Orig. Title: Astrology & the Bible. 1980. pap. 0.55 (ISBN 0-311-05031-X, Edit Mundo). Casa Bautista.

Thomas, Ianthe. Willie Blows a Mean Horn. LC 74-2637. (Illus.). 24p. (gr. k-3). 1981. 7.95 (ISBN 0-06-026106-4, HarpJ); PLB 7.89 (ISBN 0-06-026107-2). Har-Row.

Thomas, Isaiah. Three Autobiographical Fragments. 1962. pap. 4.50x (ISBN 0-912296-32-1, Dist. by U Pr of Va). Am Antiquarian.

Thomas, J. A. An Introduction to Geological Maps. 2nd rev ed. (Illus.). 1977. pap. text ed. 4.95x (ISBN 0-04-550018-5). Allen Unwin.

Thomas, J. Alan. The Productive School: A Systems Analysis Approach to Educational Administration. LC 80-12531. 144p. 1980. Repr. of 1971 ed. lib. bdg. write for info. (ISBN 0-89874-164-5). Krieger.

Thomas, J. Alan, jt. ed. see Dreeben, Robert.

Thomas, J. B. Self Concept in Psychology & Education. (Bibliographies Ser). 28p. (Orig.). 1973. pap. text ed. 3.75x (ISBN 0-85633-019-1, NFER). Humanities.

Thomas, J. C. Chasin the Trane. LC 76-6560. 1976. pap. 6.95 (ISBN 0-306-80043-8). Da Capo.

Thomas, J. E. English Prison Officer Since Eighteen Fifty: A Study in Conflict. (International Library of Social Policy). 1972. 22.00x (ISBN 0-7100-7280-5). Routledge & Kegan.

Thomas, J. Heywood. Paul Tillich. Nineham, D. E. & Robertson, E. H., eds. LC 66-11072. (Makers of Contemporary Theology Ser). 1966. pap. 3.45 (ISBN 0-8042-0678-3). John Knox.

Thomas, J. Heywood, ed. see France, Anatole.

Thomas, J. M. & Lambert, R. M. Characterization of Catalysts. 1980. write for info. (ISBN 0-471-27874-2, Pub. by Wiley-Interscience). Wiley.

Thomas, J. Merlin, jt. ed. see Howarth, W. D.

Thomas, J. O. see Bull, Alan T., et al.

Thomas, J. R. The Self in Education. 114p. 1981. pap. text ed. 18.00x (ISBN 0-85633-212-7, NFER). Humanities.

Thomas, J. W. & Dussere, Carolyn, trs. from Ger. The Legend of Duke Ernst. LC 79-19843. x, 126p. 1980. 11.50x (ISBN 0-8032-4406-1). U of Nebr Pr.

Thomas, J. W., tr. see Hartmann, Von Aue.

Thomas, J. W., tr. see Wildonie, Herrandv.

Thomas, Jack R. & Patsouras, Louis. Varieties & Problems of Twentieth Century Socialism. LC 79-21450. 214p. 1981. text ed. 15.95 (ISBN 0-88229-444-X); pap. text ed. 8.95 (ISBN 0-88229-743-0). Nelson-Hall.

Thomas, James H. The Long Haul: Truckers, Truck Stops, & Trucking. (Illus.). 12.95 (ISBN 0-87870-055-2); pap. 6.95 (ISBN 0-87870-057-9). Memphis St Univ.

Thomas, James L. Turning Kids on to Print Using Nonprint. LC 78-9075. (Illus.). 1978. lib. bdg. 17.50x (ISBN 0-87287-184-3). Libs Unl.

Thomas, James L., jt. auth. see Thomas, Carol H.

Thomas, James L., jt. ed. see Thomas, Carol H.

Thomas, James W. & Thomas, Ann M. Finite Mathematics. 2nd ed. 1978. text ed. 17.80 (ISBN 0-205-05996-1); instr's man. avail. (ISBN 0-205-05997-X). Allyn.

Thomas, Jane R. The Comeback Dog. (Illus.). 64p. (gr. 2-5). 1981. 7.95 (ISBN 0-395-29432-0, Clarion). HM.

--Elizabeth Catches a Fish. LC 76-28318. (Illus.). (gr. 1-4). 1977. 6.95 (ISBN 0-395-28827-4, Clarion). HM.

Thomas, Jean. Devil's Ditties: Being Stories of the Kentucky Mountain People, Told by Jean Thomas, with the Songs They Sing. LC 75-16369. (Illus.). viii, 180p. 1976. Repr. of 1931 ed. 22.00 (ISBN 0-8103-3999-4). Gale.

Thomas, John. Dry Martini. (Lost American Fiction Ser.). 1975. pap. 1.50 o.p. (ISBN 0-445-03093-3). Popular Lib.

--Forgotten Railways: Scotland. (Forgotten Railways Ser.). (Illus.). 144p. 1976. 14.95 (ISBN 0-7153-6961-X). David & Charles.

--Leonardo Da Vinci. LC 57-6244. (Illus.). (gr. 6-10). 1957. 9.95 (ISBN 0-87599-112-2). S G Phillips.

--The North British Railway, 2 vols. LC 70-469296. (Illus.). 1975. Vol. 1. 17.95 (ISBN 0-7153-4697-0); Vol. 2. 17.95 (ISBN 0-7153-6699-8). David & Charles.

--A Regional History of the Railways of Great Britain: Scotland, the Lowland & the Borders, Vol. 6. (Illus.). 288p. 1971. 19.95 (ISBN 0-7153-5408-6). David & Charles.

--Scottish Railway Book. 1977. 9.95 o.p. (ISBN 0-685-74791-3). David & Charles.

--The Skye Railway. 1977. 8.95 (ISBN 0-7153-7383-8). David & Charles.

--Tay Bridge Disaster: New Light on the 1879 Tragedy. 1972. 11.95 (ISBN 0-7153-5198-2). David & Charles.

--The West Highland Railway. LC 76-26734. (Illus.). 1976. 10.50 (ISBN 0-7153-7281-5). David & Charles.

Thomas, John A. Textbook of Endocrine Pharmacology. Date not set. price not set (ISBN 0-8067-1901-X). Urban & S.

Thomas, John A., ed. Advances in Sex Hormone Research, Vol. 4. Singhal, Radhey L. LC 79-25717. (Illus.). 1980. text ed. 32.50 (ISBN 0-8067-1914-1). Urban & S.

Thomas, John B. An Introduction to Applied Probability & Random Processes. (Illus.). 1981. Repr. of 1971 ed. lib. bdg. write for info. (ISBN 0-89874-232-3). Krieger.
--Introduction to Statistical Communication Theory. LC 68-8108. 1969. 35.95 (ISBN 0-471-85893-5). Wiley.
Thomas, John I. Education for Communism: School & State in the People's Republic of Albania. LC 69-17329. (Studies: No. 22). 131p. 1969. 6.50 (ISBN 0-8179-3221-6); pap. 4.00 (ISBN 0-8179-3222-4). Hoover Inst Pr.
Thomas, John L. The American Catholic Family. LC 80-15221. (Illus.). xii, 471p. 1980. Repr. of 1956 ed. lib. bdg. 33.50x (ISBN 0-313-22473-0, THAC). Greenwood.
--Beginning Your Marriage, 2 vols. 1980. pap. 1.95 standard ed., LC 80-65486 (ISBN 0-915388-06-5); pap. 1.95 interfaith ed., LC 80-65487 (ISBN 0-915388-07-3). Buckley Pubns.
--The Law of Constructive Contempt: The Shepherd Case Reviewed. 270p. 1980. Repr. of 1904 ed. lib. bdg. 24.00x (ISBN 0-8377-1203-3). Rothman.
--Law of Lotteries, Frauds & Obscenity in the Mails. xviii, 358p. 1980. Repr. of 1903 ed. lib. bdg. 32.50x (ISBN 0-8377-1202-5). Rothman.
Thomas, John N., tr. see Barth, Karl.
Thomas, John W. Making Changes: A Guide to Future Oriented Education. (Education Futures: No. 6). (Illus.). (gr. 6-12). 1981. pap. text ed. 8.95 (ISBN 0-88280-081-7); tchrs' ed. 19.95 (ISBN 0-88280-082-5). ETC Pubns.
Thomas, Joseph. Universal Pronouncing Dictionary of Biography & Mythology, 2 vols. LC 79-167222. 1976. Repr. of 1870 ed. Set. 135.00 (ISBN 0-8103-4221-9). Gale.
Thomas, Joseph see Brehier, Emile.
Thomas, Judith A. Interethnic Sensitivity Materials for Educators Who Want to Know. 1978. pap. text ed. 10.00 (ISBN 0-8191-0387-X). U Pr of Amer.
Thomas, Kas. Personal Aircraft Maintenance. (Aviation Ser.). (Illus.). 256p. 1980. 19.50 (ISBN 0-07-064241-9, P&RB). McGraw.
Thomas, Kathleen. West Country Cookery. 1979. 24.00 (ISBN 0-7134-0041-2, Pub. by Batsford England). David & Charles.
Thomas, Kathleen M., ed. see Wheat Flour Institute.
Thomas, Keith. Religion & the Decline of Magic. LC 74-141707. 1971. pap. text ed. 13.95x (ISBN 0-684-14542-1, ScribC). Scribner.
Thomas, Keith, jt. ed. see Pennington, Donald.
Thomas, L. Color Angle. LC 79-64280. (Illus., Orig.). 1979. pap. 16.00 (ISBN 0-934190-00-3). Real Comp & Int.
Thomas, L. J. An Introduction to Mining: Exploration, Feasibility, Extraction, Rock Mechanics. LC 73-14857. 1977. pap. 19.95 (ISBN 0-470-99220-4). Halsted Pr.
Thomas, L. Joseph, jt. auth. see Dyckman, Thomas.
Thomas, L. Joseph, jt. auth. see Dyckman, Thomas R.
Thomas, L. M., jt. auth. see Gurdjian, E. S.
Thomas, L. R. Does the Bible Teach Millennialism. pap. 2.25 (ISBN 0-685-36796-7). Reiner.
Thomas, Leslie. Bare Nell. LC 78-3960. 1978. 8.95 o.p. (ISBN 0-312-06641-4). St Martin.
Thomas, Lewis. The Medusa & the Snail. 1980. pap. 7.95 (ISBN 0-8161-3102-3, Large Print Bks). G K Hall.
Thomas, Linda. Caring & Cooking for the Allergic Child. rev. ed. LC 79-91379. (Illus.). 144p. 1980. 12.95 (ISBN 0-8069-5552-X); lib. bdg. 11.69 (ISBN 0-8069-5553-8); pap. 5.95 (ISBN 0-8069-8906-8). Sterling.
--Meet the Goalies. (Meet the Players: Hockey). (Illus.). (gr. 2-4). 1976. PLB 5.95 o.p. (ISBN 0-87191-533-2). Creative Ed.
--Muhammad Ali. LC 75-28194. (Creative Superstars Ser.). 1975. PLB 5.95 (ISBN 0-87191-262-7); pap. 2.95 (ISBN 0-89812-188-4). Creative Ed.
Thomas, Lindon. Fundamentals of Heat Transfer. (Illus.). 1980. text ed. 27.95 (ISBN 0-13-339903-6). P-H.
Thomas, Lionel, ed. see Morike, Eduard.
Thomas, Lisa. So Narrow the Bridge & Deep the Water. LC 80-52865. 156p. 1980. pap. 4.95 (ISBN 0-686-28642-1). Seal Pr WA.
Thomas, Liz. Dust of Life. (Illus.). 1978. 8.95 o.p. (ISBN 0-525-09580-2). Dutton.
Thomas, Lowell. Good Evening Everybody: From Cripple Creek to Samarkand. (Illus.). 384p. 1976. 12.50 o.p. (ISBN 0-688-03068-8). Morrow.
--So Long Until Tomorrow. 1977. 10.95 o.p. (ISBN 0-688-03236-2). Morrow.
Thomas, Lynn. The Backpacking Woman. LC 79-6890. 288p. (Orig.). 1980. pap. 6.95 (ISBN 0-385-15303-1, Anch). Doubleday.
Thomas, M. Angele, ed. The Yet to Be Served: Special Issue of Exceptional Children. 96p. 1979. pap. 3.75 (ISBN 0-86586-095-5). Coun Exc Child.
Thomas, M. Donald. Parents Have Rights, Too! LC 78-63270. (Fastback Ser.: No. 120). 1978. pap. 0.75 (ISBN 0-87367-120-1). Phi Delta Kappa.
Thomas, Marcel, ed. The Grandes Heures of Jean, Duke of Berry. LC 75-167761. (Illus.). 192p. 1971. 70.00 (ISBN 0-8076-0613-8). Braziller.
Thomas, Mary. Mary Thomas's Book of Knitting Patterns. (Illus.). 340p. 1972. pap. 4.50 (ISBN 0-486-22818-5). Dover.
Thomas, Mary, ed. see American School of Needlework.
Thomas, Maurice J. Of Primary Importance. LC 63-22538. (Illus.). 1963. pap. text ed. 1.00x o.p. (ISBN 0-8134-0151-8, 151). Interstate.
Thomas, Mayor I., tr. Vida Salvadora De Cristo. (Spanish Bks.). (Span.). 1979. 1.90 (ISBN 0-8297-0455-8). Vida Pub.
Thomas, Merlin, ed. see Anouilh, Jean.
Thomas, Michael F. Tropical Geomorphology: A Study of Weathering & Land Form Development in Warm Climates. LC 73-13428. 1976. pap. 12.95 (ISBN 0-470-98939-4). Halsted Pr.
Thomas, Nicholas. Guide to Prehistoric England. 1977. 30.00 (ISBN 0-7134-3267-5, Pub. by Batsford England); pap. 14.50 (ISBN 0-7134-3268-3, Pub. by Batsford England). David & Charles.
Thomas, Norman. War: No Glory, No Profit, No Need. Johnpoll, Bernard K., ed. Bd. with Challenge of War: An Economic Interpretation. Thomas, Norman. LC 70-147530. (Library of War & Peace; Labor, Socialism & War). lib. bdg. 38.00 (ISBN 0-8240-0313-6). Garland Pub.
Thomas, Norman, jt. auth. see Laidler, Harry W.
Thomas, Norman C. & Stoerker, Fredrick C. Your American Government. LC 79-26788. 1980. text ed. 15.95 o.p. (ISBN 0-471-03031-7); write for info tchr's ed o.p. (ISBN 0-471-06330-4); study guide o.p. (ISBN 0-471-07907-3). Wiley.
Thomas, Norman C., jt. ed. see Altshuler, Alan A.
Thomas, Norman L. Modern Logic: An Introduction. (Illus., Orig.). 1966. pap. 3.95 (ISBN 0-06-460103-X, CO 103, COS). Har-Row.
Thomas, Owen, ed. see Thoreau, Henry D.
Thomas, P. D. British Politics & the Stamp Act Crisis: The First Phase of the American Revolution 1763-1767. 395p. 1975. 37.50x (ISBN 0-19-822431-1). Oxford U Pr.
Thomas, Pamela, ed. see Honig, Donald & Ritter, Lawrence S.
Thomas, Payne E. Guide for Authors: Manuscript, Proof & Illustration. 2nd ed. (Illus.). 96p. 1980. pap. 5.25 (ISBN 0-398-03443-5). C C Thomas.
Thomas, Payne E., jt. auth. see Cavanaugh, Tom R.
Thomas, Phil J. Songs of the Pacific Northwest. (Resource Ser). (Illus.). 1979. 14.95 (ISBN 0-87663-551-6). Hancock Hse.
Thomas, Piri. Stories from El Barrio. (YA) (gr. 9 up). 1980. pap. 1.75 (ISBN 0-380-50013-2, 50013). Avon.
Thomas, R. Resource Allocation & Cost Benefit Analysis. (Studies in the British Economy). Date not set. pap. text ed. write for info. (ISBN 0-435-84561-6). Heinemann Ed.
Thomas, R. E. Business Policy. 256p. 1977. 36.00x (ISBN 0-86003-502-6, Pub. by Allan Pubs England); pap. 18.00x (ISBN 0-86003-602-2). State Mutual Bk.
--The Government of Business. 224p. 1976. 30.00x (ISBN 0-86003-501-8, Pub. by Allan Pubs England); pap. 15.00x (ISBN 0-86003-601-4). State Mutual Bk.
Thomas, R. H. The Liverpool & Manchester Railway. LC 79-57313. (Illus.). 264p. 1980. 45.00 (ISBN 0-7134-0537-6, Pub. by Batsford England). David & Charles.
--London's First Railway. 1972. 27.00 (ISBN 0-7134-0468-X, Pub. by Batsford England). David & Charles.
Thomas, R. Murray. Comparing Theories of Child Development. 1978. text ed. 20.95x (ISBN 0-534-00591-8). Wadsworth Pub.
Thomas, R. P., jt. auth. see North, D. C.
Thomas, R. S., ed. A Choice of George Herbert's Verse. Herbert, George. 1967. pap. 4.95 (ISBN 0-571-08189-4, Pub. by Faber & Faber). Merrimack Bk Serv.
Thomas, R. S., ed. see Wordsworth, William.
Thomas, R. T. Britain & Vichy: The Dilemma of Anglo-French Relations, 1940-42. (The Making of the Twentieth Century Ser.). 1979. 19.95 (ISBN 0-312-09822-7). St Martin.
Thomas, Ralph. Handbook of Fictitious Names. LC 70-90248. 1969. Repr. of 1868 ed. 18.00 (ISBN 0-8103-3145-4). Gale.
Thomas, Ralph H. Ultrasonics in Packaging & Plastics Fabrication. LC 73-76443. 1974. 21.50 (ISBN 0-8436-1102-2). CBI Pub.
Thomas, Ralph H. & Perez-Mendez, Victor, eds. Advances in Radiation Protection & Dosimetry. (Ettore Najorana International Science Ser., Life Sciences: Vol. 2). 650p. 1980. 69.50 (ISBN 0-306-40468-0). Plenum Pub.
Thomas, Ralph L. Policies Underlying Corporate Giving. LC 65-25263. 1965. 17.50 (ISBN 0-686-10124-3). R L Thomas.
Thomas, Richard. Poems by Richard Thomas. 1975. pap. 2.95 (ISBN 0-380-01106-9, 45286). Avon.
Thomas, Robert C., jt. ed. see Kruzas, Anthony T.
Thomas, Robert D. The Man Who Would Be Perfect: John Humphrey Noyes & the Utopian Impulse. LC 76-53198. 1977. 13.95x (ISBN 0-8122-7724-4). U of Pa Pr.
Thomas, Roberta. Teacher's Dictation Library, 2 pts. (gr. 11-12). 1974. pap. text ed. 19.95 ea. Pt. 1 (ISBN 0-89420-064-X, 139555). Pt. 2 (ISBN 0-89420-065-8, 139666). pt. 1 cassette recordings 229.95 (ISBN 0-89420-212-X, 139000); pt. 2 cassette recordings 289.95 (ISBN 0-89420-213-8, 139300). Natl Book.
Thomas, Roger D., jt. auth. see Olson, Everett.
Thomas, Roger D. K. & Olson, Everett C., eds. A Cold Look at the Warm-Blooded Dinosaurs. (AAAS Selected Symposium: No. 28). (Illus.). 516p. 1980. lib. bdg. 28.50x (ISBN 0-89158-464-1). Westview.
Thomas, Roger W. A Shout in the Street. Root, Orrin, ed. LC 76-47988. 1977. pap. 1.95 o.p. (ISBN 0-87239-124-8, 40041). Standard Pub.
Thomas, Ronald B. Manhattanville Music Curriculum Synthesis: A Structure for Music Education. 165p. (Orig.). 1971. pap. 5.50 o.p. (ISBN 0-686-63975-8). Media Materials.
Thomas, Rosamund. The British Philosophy of Administration: A Comparison of British & American Ideas 1900-1939. LC 77-5938. (Illus.). 1978. text ed. 24.00x (ISBN-0-582-50124-5). Longman.
Thomas, Rosemary. Selected Poems of Rosemary Thomas. LC 67-25189. 161p. 1968. text ed. 17.95x (ISBN 0-8290-0204-9). Irvington.
Thomas, Ross. The Fools in Town Are on Our Side. 1975. pap. 1.75 (ISBN 0-380-00687-1, 28290). Avon.
--Yellow-Dog Contract. 1977. pap. 1.75 o.p. (ISBN 0-380-01828-4, 36186). Avon.
Thomas, Roy, ed. Insurance Information Sources. LC 75-137575. (Management Information Guide Ser.: No. 24). 1971. 30.00 (ISBN 0-8103-0824-X). Gale.
Thomas, S. E. Economics. (Teach Yourself Ser.). 1975. pap. 2.95 o.p. (ISBN 0-679-10381-3). McKay.
Thomas, Sherry. We Didn't Have Much but We Sure Had Plenty: Stories of Rural Women. LC 80-956. (Illus.). 208p. 1981. pap. 7.95 (ISBN 0-385-14951-4, Anch). Doubleday.
Thomas, Sherry, jt. auth. see Tetrault, Jeanne.
Thomas, Stephen. Practical Reasoning in Natural Language. (Illus.). 352p. 1981. pap. text ed. 9.95 (ISBN 0-13-692137-X). P-H.
Thomas, Sydney F., jt. auth. see Weigan, John F.
Thomas Telford Editorial Staff, Ltd. Arch Dams: A Review of British Research & Development. 168p. 1980. 60.00x (ISBN 0-901948-14-4, Pub. by Telford England). State Mutual Bk.
--A Century of Soil Mechanics. 490p. 1980. 35.00x (ISBN 0-901948-15-2, Pub. by Telfor England). State Mutual Bk.
Thomas Telford Editorial Staff, Ltd., ed. Clay Fills. 330p. 1980. 90.00x (ISBN 0-7277-0069-3, Pub. by Telford England). State Mutual Bk.
Thomas Telford Editorial Staff, Ltd, ed. Computer Methods in Tunnel Design. 284p. 1980. 70.00x (ISBN 0-7277-0061-8, Pub. by Telford England). State Mutual Bk.
Thomas Telford Editorial Staff, Ltd. Corrosion in Civil Engineering. 172p. 1980. 40.00x (ISBN 0-7277-0079-0, Pub. by Telford England). State Mutual Bk.
--Design & Construction of Offshore Structures. 184p. 1980. 60.00x (ISBN 0-7277-0041-3, Pub. by Telford England). State Mutual Bk.
Thomas Telford Editorial Staff, Ltd, ed. Ground Treatment by Deep Compaction. 166p. 1980. 30.00x (ISBN 0-7277-0024-3, Pub. by Telford England). State Mutual Bk.
Thomas Telford Ltd, Editorial Staff. Hazards in Tunnelling & on Falsework. 130p. 1980. 40.00x (ISBN 0-7277-0013-8, Pub. by Telford England). State Mutual Bk.
Thomas Telford Ltd. Editorial Staff. Informal Meeting, Steel Box Girder Bridges. 118p. 1980. pap. 25.00x (Pub. by Telford England). State Mutual Bk.
Thomas Telford Ltd. Editorial Staff. Maintenance of Maritime Structures. 252p. 1980. 40.00x (ISBN 0-7277-0050-2, Pub. by Telford England). State Mutual Bk.
Thomas Telford Ltd. Editorial Staff. The Marine Environment & Oil Facilities. 168p. 1980. 69.00x (ISBN 0-7277-0075-8, Pub. by Telford England). State Mutual Bk.
--Milestones in Soil Mechanics. 338p. 1980. 40.00x (ISBN 0-7277-0010-3, Pub. by Telford England). State Mutual Bk.
--Non-Destructive Testing of Concrete & Timber. 126p. 1980. 80.00x (ISBN 0-901948-27-6, Pub. by Telford England). State Mutual Bk.
--Offshore Structures. 208p. 1980. 75.00x (ISBN 0-7277-0008-1, Pub. by Thomas Telford England). State Mutual Bk.
--Prestressed Concrete Pressure Vessels. 762p. 1980. 79.00x (ISBN 0-901948-45-4, Pub. by Telford England). State Mutual England.
--Safety on Construction Sites. 122p. 1980. 75.00x (Pub. by Telford England). State Mutual Bk.
Thomas Telford Ltd, Editorial Staff. Steel Box Girder Bridges. 324p. 1980. 60.00x (Pub. by Telford England). State Mutual Bk.
Thomas Telford Ltd. Editorial Staff. Ultimate Load Design of Concrete Structures. 104p. 1980. 25.00 (Pub. by Telford England). State Mutual Bk.
Thomas, Terry. An Evaluation of Urban Public Transport Alternatives. Date not set. cancelled (ISBN 0-08-023734-7). Pergamon.
Thomas, Terry C. Adios, Amor Mio. Bautista, Sara, tr. from Eng. LC 77-79933. 202p. (Orig., Span.). 1977. pap. 2.50 (ISBN 0-89922-089-4). Edit Caribe.
Thomas, Tony. The Films of the Forties. 1977. pap. 6.95 (ISBN 0-8065-0571-0). Citadel Pr.
--The Great Adventure Films. pap. 7.95 (ISBN 0-8065-0747-0). Lyle Stuart.
--Song & Dance Man: The Films of Gene Kelly. LC 73-90949. (Illus.). 256p. 1974. 12.00 (ISBN 0-8065-0400-5). Citadel Pr.
Thomas, Vaughan. Better Physical Fitness. LC 76-501663. (Better Sports Ser.). (Illus.). 93p. 1979. 8.50x (ISBN 0-7182-1461-7). Intl Pubns Serv.
Thomas, Virginia, jt. auth. see Ng, David.
Thomas, Virginia C. My Secrets of Natural Beauty. LC 72-76464. 224p. 1972. 5.95 (ISBN 0-87983-019-0); pap. 2.25 (ISBN 0-87983-020-4). Keats.
Thomas, Virginia R. Flying with Broken Wings. Date not set. 6.95 (ISBN 0-533-04791-9). Vantage.
Thomas, W., jt. auth. see Mathies, Lorraine.
Thomas, W. A., jt. auth. see Morgan, E. Victor.
Thomas, W. Griffith. Christianity Is Christ. (Shepherd Illustrated Classics). (Illus.). 200p. Date not set. pap. 5.95 (ISBN 0-87983-238-X). Keats.
--Christianity Is Christ. (Shepherd Illustrated Classics Ser.). (Illus.). 200p. 1979. pap. 5.95 (ISBN 0-87983-238-X). Keats.
--How We Got Our Bible. 1926. pap. 1.50 (ISBN 0-8024-3796-6). Moody.
Thomas, W. I. Saving Life of Christ. 1961. pap. 2.50 (ISBN 0-310-33262-1). Zondervan.
Thomas, W. J., ed. & intro. by. The Demand for Food: An Exercise in Household Budget Analysis. (Illus.). 136p. 1972. text ed. 11.50x (ISBN 0-7190-0512-4). Humanities.
Thomas, W. L., jt. auth. see Spencer, J. E.
Thomas, W. O., jt. auth. see Evans, H. Meurig.
Thomas, Wayne. Bail Reform in America. 1977. 15.95 (ISBN 0-520-03131-8). U of Cal Pr.
Thomas, Wilbur. General George H. Thomas, the Indomitable Warrior. 1964. 25.00 o.p. (ISBN 0-682-42066-2, Lochinvar). Exposition.
Thomas, William. The Philosophical Radicals: Nine Studies in Theory & Practice, 1817 to 1841. (Illus.). 506p. 1979. text ed. 45.00x (ISBN 0-19-822490-7). Oxford U Pr.
Thomas, William E. Backstage Broadway: Careers in the Theater. LC 80-10393. (Career Bks.). (Illus.). 160p. (gr. 7 up). 1980. PLB 7.79 (ISBN 0-671-33002-0). Messner.
--The New Boy Is Blind. LC 80-349. (Illus.). 64p. (gr. 3-6). 1980. PLB 6.97 (ISBN 0-671-33094-2). Messner.
Thomas, William G., jt. auth. see Hallberg, Edmond C.
Thomas Acquinas. The Pocket Acquinas. pap. 2.95 (ISBN 0-671-42141-7, 48131-2). WSP.
Thomas a Kempis. The Imitation of Christ. Blaiklock, E. M., tr. 228p. 1981. pap. 4.95 (ISBN 0-8407-5760-3). Nelson.
Thomas Aquinas, Saint Basic Writings, Vol. 1. Pegis, Anton C., ed. 1945. 15.00 o.p. (ISBN 0-394-41617-1). Random.
--Political Ideas of St. Thomas Aquinas. Bigongiari, Dino, ed. (Library of Classics Ser.: No. 15). 1973. pap. text ed. 4.95 (ISBN 0-02-840380-0). Hafner.
Thomas Aquinas, St. Selected Writings of St. Thomas Aquinas. Goodwin, Robert P., tr. Incl. The Principles of Nature; On Being & Essence; On the Virtues in General; On Free Choice. LC 65-26529. (Orig.). 1965. pap. 2.95 (ISBN 0-672-60469-8, LLA217). Bobbs.
--Summa Theologiae. Gilby, Thomas, ed. Incl. Vol. 1. The Existence of God. LC 70-84399. pap. 3.95 (ISBN 0-385-02768-0, Im). Doubleday.
Thomasma, David C., jt. auth. see Pellegrino, Edmund D.

Thomason, James C. Common Sense About Your Family Dollars. 1979. pap. 3.95 (ISBN 0-88207-636-1). Victor Bks.

Thomason, Michael G., jt. auth. see Gonzalez, Rafael C.

Thomason, Michael V., jt. auth. see McLaurin, Melton A.

Thomison, Dennis, jt. auth. see Schlachter, Gail.

Thomison, Dennis, ed. Readings About Adolescent Literature. LC 79-9913. 1970. 10.00 (ISBN 0-8108-0282-1). Scarecrow.

Thomkins, Jasper. The Catalog. (Illus.). 60p. (Orig.). 1981. pap. 5.95 (ISBN 0-914676-54-7). Green Tiger.

Thomlinson, Ralph. Demographic Problems: Controversy Over Population Control. 2nd ed. (Contemporary Social Problems Ser.). 1975. pap. text ed. 7.95x (ISBN 0-8221-0166-1). Dickenson.

Thompson. Gamefish of New England. 426p. 1980. 14.95 (ISBN 0-89272-063-8). Down East.

--The Hitchikers. (Triumph Bks.). (gr. 6 up). 1980. PLB 6.90 (ISBN 0-531-04115-8, B17). Watts.

Thompson, A. Meilluer: Mobility of Employment International for Librarians in Europe. (Research Publication Ser.: No. 20). 1977. pap. 15.50x (ISBN 0-85365-660-6, Pub. by Lib Assn England). Oryx Pr.

Thompson, A. D., ed. see Pavese, C.

Thompson, A. E., jt. auth. see Gray, A.

Thompson, A. M. Bibliography of Nursing Literature: Eighteen Fifty-Nine to Nineteen Sixty. 1969. 27.95x (ISBN 0-85365-470-0, Pub. by Lib Assn England). Oryx Pr.

Thompson, A. M., ed. Bibliography of Nursing Literature: Nineteen Sixty-One to Nineteen Seventy. 1974. lib. bdg. 43.50x (ISBN 0-85365-316-X, Pub. by Lib Assn England). Oryx Pr.

Thompson, Alden. Responsibility for Evil in the Theodicy of IV Ezra. LC 76-40915. (Society of Biblical Literature. Dissertation Ser.). 1977. pap. 9.00 (ISBN 0-89130-091-0, 060129). Scholars Pr Ca.

Thompson, Alice Smith, compiled by. The Drake Family of New Hampshire: Robert, of Hampton, & Some of His Descendants, A Geneology. LC 63-62916. (Illus.). 1962. text ed. 15.00x (ISBN 0-915916-03-7). U Pr of New Eng.

Thompson, Allyn J. Making Your Own Telescope. rev. ed. (Illus.). 1980. Repr. of 1947 ed. 8.95 (ISBN 0-933346-12-3). Sky Pub.

Thompson, Ann M. & Wood, Marcia D. Management Strategies for Women: Or, Now That I'm Boss, How Do I Run This Place? 1981. 10.95 (ISBN 0-671-25476-6). S&S.

Thompson, Anne A. The Romanov Ransom. 1978. pap. 1.95 o.s.i. (ISBN 0-685-54632-2, 04723-6). Jove Pubns.

Thompson, Anthony. Russia - U. S. S. R. (World Bibliographical Ser.: No. 6). 287p. 1979. 34.75 (ISBN 0-903450-18-6). ABC-Clio.

Thompson, Arthur A., Jr. Economics of the Firm: Theory & Practice. 2nd ed. (Illus.). 1977. 19.95 (ISBN 0-13-231407-X); pap. 8.95 study guide & wkbk. (ISBN 0-13-227553-8). P-H.

Thompson, Arthur A., Jr. & Strickland, A. J., III. Strategy & Policy. 1978. text ed. 19.95 (ISBN 0-256-02083-3). Business Pubns.

Thompson, Arthur A., Jr. & Strickland, A. J., 3rd. Strategy Formulation & Implementation: Tasks of the General Manager. 1980. pap. 10.50x (ISBN 0-256-02277-1). Business Pubns.

Thompson, Arthur W., intro. by see Giddings, Joshua R.

Thompson, B. A., jt. auth. see Belson, W. A.

Thompson, B. J. All the Silver Pennies. (Illus.). (gr. 1-6). 1967. 7.95 o.s.i. (ISBN 0-02-789330-8). Macmillan.

Thompson, B. J., ed. see International Commission on Optics International Congress, 9th.

Thompson, B. W. Africa: The Climatic Background. (Studies in the Development of African Resources). (Illus.). 72p. 1975. pap. 5.25x o.p. (ISBN 0-19-575253-8). Oxford U Pr.

Thompson, Barbara, tr. see Duby, Georges.

Thompson, Bard. Renaissance & Reformation. (Texts & Studies in Religion, Vol. 11). (Orig.). 1981. soft cover 24.95x (ISBN 0-88946-915-6). E Mellen.

Thompson, Bard, ed. see Nevin, John W.

Thompson, Bard, ed. see Schaff, Philip.

Thompson, Bard, et al. Essays on the Heidelberg Catechism. LC 63-21522. 1963. pap. 5.95 (ISBN 0-8298-0325-4). Pilgrim NY.

Thompson, Ben. Ride to Hell. 1978. pap. 1.50 (ISBN 0-505-51287-4). Tower Bks.

Thompson, Bert. Theistic Evolution. pap. 5.50 (ISBN 0-89315-300-1). Lambert Bk.

Thompson, Bill. Constructing Cross-Country Obstacles. (Illus.). 17.35 (ISBN 0-85131-140-7, Dist. by Sporting Book Center). J A Allen.

Thompson, Bill, jt. auth. see Charlton, Jim.

Thompson, Bradbury, ed. The Washburn College Bible. 1808p. 1980. 65.00 (ISBN 0-19-502786-8). Oxford U Pr.

Thompson, Brenda. Learning to Read: A Guide for Teachers & Parents. 1970. 7.50x (ISBN 0-8464-0549-0). Beekman Pubs.

Thompson, Brian. Buddy Boy. LC 77-6109. 1978. 7.95 o.p. (ISBN 0-312-10684-X). St Martin.

Thompson, Bruce. Black Walnut for Profit. 285p. 1978. pap. 7.95x (ISBN 0-917304-40-3, Pub. by Timber Pr). Intl Schol Bk Serv.

--Black Walnut for Profit: A Guide to Risks & Rewards. (Illus.). 285p. Date not set. 9.95 o.p. (ISBN 0-686-69373-6); pap. 7.95 (ISBN 0-917304-40-3). Walnut AZ.

Thompson, C. J. Hand of Destiny: The Folk-Lore & Superstition of Everyday Life. LC 70-125600. 1970. Repr. of 1932 ed. 22.00 (ISBN 0-8103-3419-4). Gale.

--Love, Marriage & Romance in Old London. LC 70-76076. (Illus.). 1971. Repr. of 1936 ed. 18.50 (ISBN 0-8103-3211-6). Gale.

--The Lure & Romance of Alchemy. LC 76-167224. (Illus.). vi, 249p. 1975. Repr. of 1932 ed. 18.00 (ISBN 0-8103-4000-3). Gale.

--Magic & Healing. LC 73-2850. (Illus.). 176p. 1973. Repr. of 1947 ed. 18.00 (ISBN 0-8103-3275-2). Gale.

--Mysteries & Secrets of Magic. LC 78-174119. (Tower Bks). (Illus.). 1971. Repr. of 1928 ed. 24.00 (ISBN 0-8103-3213-2). Gale.

--Mysteries of History, with Accounts of Some Remarkable Characters & Charlatans. LC 76-164056. (Tower Bks). 1971. Repr. of 1928 ed. 18.00 (ISBN 0-8103-3908-0). Gale.

--Mystery & Art of the Apothecary. LC 78-89294. (Illus.). 1971. Repr. of 1929 ed. 20.00 (ISBN 0-8103-3210-8). Gale.

--The Mystery & Lore of Apparitions, with Some Account of Ghosts, Spectres, Phantoms & Boggarts in Early Times. LC 70-167225. (Illus.). 331p. 1975. Repr. of 1930 ed. 18.00 (ISBN 0-8103-3981-1). Gale.

--Mystery & Lure of Perfume. LC 74-75789. 1969. Repr. of 1927 ed. 15.00 (ISBN 0-8103-3842-4). Gale.

--Mystery & Romance of Astrology. LC 71-89295. 1969. Repr. of 1929 ed. 18.00 (ISBN 0-8103-3146-2). Gale.

--The Mystic Mandrake. LC 74-19199. (Illus.). 253p. 1975. Repr. of 1934 ed. 20.00 (ISBN 0-8103-4138-7). Gale.

--Quacks of Old London. LC 75-89296. (Tower Bks). (Illus.). 1971. Repr. of 1929 ed. 20.00 (ISBN 0-8103-3212-4). Gale.

Thompson, Carl. Controls of Eating. LC 79-17853. (Monographs in Pharmacology & Physiology: Bol. 4). 296p. 1979. text ed. 40.00 (ISBN 0-89335-100-8). Spectrum Pub.

Thompson, Carol L., et al, eds. The Current History Encyclopedia of Developing Nations. (Illus.). 384p. 1981. 34.95 (ISBN 0-07-064387-3, P&RB). McGraw.

Thompson, Charles H. Fundamentals of Pipe Drafting. LC 58-13471. 1958. pap. 10.00 (ISBN 0-471-85998-2, Pub. by Wiley-Interscience). Wiley.

Thompson, Colin J. Mathematical Statistical Mechanics. LC 78-70319. 1979. 15.00x (ISBN 0-691-08219-7); pap. 5.95 (ISBN 0-691-08220-0). Princeton U Pr.

Thompson, Colin P. The Poet & the Mystic: A Study of the Cantico Espiritual of San Juan de la Cruz. (Oxford Modern Languages & Literature Monographs). 1978. 33.00x (ISBN 0-19-815531-X). Oxford U Pr.

Thompson, Corrie. Beach Buddies of Bygone Days. (gr. 1-3). 4.95 o.p. (ISBN 0-685-48835-7). Nortex Pr.

--My Beach Buddies of by Gone Days. 1st ed. (Illus.). 91p. (gr. 4 up). 1974. 5.00 o.p. (ISBN 0-685-54129-0). Nortex Pr.

Thompson, Craig R., tr. see Erasmus, Desiderius.

Thompson, D. The Uses of Poetry. LC 77-82517. 1978. 36.00 (ISBN 0-521-21804-7); pap. 10.95x (ISBN 0-521-29287-5). Cambridge U Pr.

Thompson, D., ed. see Sampson, George.

Thompson, D. L. & Dalrymple, D. J. Retail Management Cases. LC 69-18525. 1969. pap. text ed. 7.95 (ISBN 0-02-932500-5). Free Pr.

Thompson, D. S., ed. Everywoman's Health: The Complete Guide to Body & Mind. LC 79-6095. (Illus.). 792p. 1980. 19.95 (ISBN 0-385-15567-0). Doubleday.

Thompson, D'Arcy W. On Growth & Form, 2 Vols. 1952. Set. 125.00 (ISBN 0-521-06622-0). Cambridge U Pr.

--On Growth & Form. abr. ed. Bonner, John T., ed. 49.50 (ISBN 0-521-06623-9); pap. 13.95x (ISBN 0-521-09390-2). Cambridge U Pr.

Thompson, Dave. Play Backgammon Tonight. (Gamblers Book Shelf). (Illus.). 61p. 1976. pap. 2.95 (ISBN 0-89650-558-8). Gamblers.

Thompson, David, ed. France: Empire & Republic, 1850-1940. LC 68-27380. (Documentary History of Western Civilization Ser). 1968. 15.00x o.s.i. (ISBN 0-8027-2009-9). Walker & Co.

Thompson, David A. Five Steps Toward a Better Marriage. 96p. (Orig.). 1980. pap. 3.95 (ISBN 0-87123-164-6, 210164). Bethany Fell.

--A Premarital Guide for Couples & Their Counselors. 1979. pap. 3.95 (ISBN 0-87123-465-3, 210465). Bethany Fell.

Thompson, David M. A History of Harmonic Theory in the United States. LC 80-82202. (Illus.). 211p. 1980. 14.50x (ISBN 0-87338-246-3). Kent St U Pr.

Thompson, David M., ed. Nonconformity in the Nineteenth Century. (The Birth of Modern Britain Ser.). 1972. 15.00 (ISBN 0-7100-7274-0); pap. 8.95 (ISBN 0-7100-7275-9). Routledge & Kegan.

Thompson, David T. Easy Woodstuff for Kids. LC 80-84599. (Illus.). 130p. 1981. pap. 7.95 (ISBN 0-87659-101-2). Gryphon Hse.

Thompson, David W. Managing People: Influencing Behavior. LC 77-15993. 1978. pap. text ed. 9.95 (ISBN 0-8016-4933-1). Mosby.

Thompson, Dennis F. John Stuart Mill & Representative Government. 236p. 1976. text ed. 16.50 (ISBN 0-691-07582-4); pap. 4.95 (ISBN 0-691-02187-2). Princeton U Pr.

Thompson, Dennis L. Taxation of American Railroads: A Policy Analysis. LC 79-6194. (Contributions in Economics & Economic History: No. 34). (Illus.). 248p. 1981. lib. bdg. 29.95 (ISBN 0-313-22248-7, TTR/). Greenwood.

Thompson, Denys. Change & Tradition in Rural England: An Anthology of Writings on Country Life. LC 79-41613. 288p. 1981. 27.50 (ISBN 0-521-22546-9). Cambridge U Pr.

Thompson, Denys, ed. Children As Poets. 1972. pap. text ed. 11.95x (ISBN 0-435-14893-1). Heinemann Ed.

--Matthew Arnold: Selected Poems & Prose. (The Poetry Bookshelf Ser.). 1971. pap. text ed. 5.95 (ISBN 0-435-15063-4). Heinemann Ed.

Thompson, Donald A. Cardiovascular Assessment: Guide for Nurses & Health Professionals. (Illus.). 185p. 1981. pap. text ed. 10.95 (ISBN 0-8016-4954-4). Mosby.

Thompson, Dorothy B. Ptolemaic Oinochoai & Portraits in Faience: Aspects of the Ruler-Cult. (Oxford Monographs on Classical Archeology). (Illus.). 252p. 1973. 79.00x (ISBN 0-19-813211-5). Oxford U Pr.

Thompson, Dr. Alex see Stearn, Jess.

Thompson, E. A. Human Evolutionary Trees. LC 75-2739. (Illus.). 160p. (Orig.). 1975. pap. 23.95x (ISBN 0-521-09945-5). Cambridge U Pr.

Thompson, E. Brad & Lippman, Marc E. Steroid Receptors & the Management of Cancer, 2 vols. 1979. Vol. 1, 272p. 64.95 (ISBN 0-8493-5477-3); Vol. 2, 176p. 44.95 (ISBN 0-8493-5478-1). CRC Pr.

Thompson, E. V. Ben Retallick. 406p. 1981. 12.95 (ISBN 0-312-07517-0). St Martin.

Thompson, Edward J., jt. auth. see Thompson, Mildred L.

Thompson, Edward M., ed. see Adam, of Usk.

Thompson, Edward P. Passions of Animals. (Contributions to the History of Psychology Ser.: Comparative Psychology). 1980. Repr. of 1851 ed. 30.00 (ISBN 0-89093-322-7). U Pubns Amer.

Thompson, Eleanor D. Pediatric Nursing: An Introductory Text. 400p. 1981. pap. text ed. price not set (ISBN 0-7216-8843-8). Saunders.

Thompson, Ella M. & Rosdahl, Caroline B. Textbook of Basic Nursing. 2nd ed. 875p. 1973. text ed. 15.75 o.s.i. (ISBN 0-397-54146-5). Lippincott.

Thompson, Emmanuel B. Drug Screening: Fundamentals of Drug Evaluation Techniques in Pharmacology. LC 80-83409. (Illus.). 325p. (Orig.). 1981. text ed. 23.00x (ISBN 0-932126-06-5); pap. text ed. 18.00x (ISBN 0-932126-07-3). Graceway.

Thompson, Era B. American Daughter. rev. ed. (Midway Reprint Ser). x, 302p. 1974. pap. 7.95x o.s.i. (ISBN 0-226-79784-8). U of Chicago Pr.

Thompson, Eric E. Motor Cycles in Color. (Color Ser.). (Illus.). 1974. 9.95 (ISBN 0-7137-0711-9, Pub. by Blandford Pr England). Sterling.

Thompson, Ernest. On Golden Pond. LC 79-12879. 1979. 7.95 (ISBN 0-396-07710-2). Dodd.

Thompson, Ernest T. Presbyterians in the South, 3 vols. Incl. Vol. 1. 1607-1861. 1963 (ISBN 0-8042-0996-0); Vol. 2. 1861-1890. 1973 (ISBN 0-8042-0997-9); Vol. 3. 1890-1972. 1973. 15.00 (ISBN 0-8042-0998-7). LC 63-19121. 15.00 ea.; Set. 39.95 (ISBN 0-8042-0999-5). John Knox.

Thompson, Estelle. To Catch a Rainbow. LC 80-24246. 278p. 1980. Repr. of 1979 ed. large print ed. 9.95 (ISBN 0-89621-251-3). Thorndike Pr.

--To Catch a Rainbow. 192p. 1980. 9.95 o.s.i. (ISBN 0-8027-0652-5). Walker & Co.

Thompson, Evelina, jt. auth. see Reid, G. A.

Thompson, Evelina, et al. Pitman Secretarial Shorthand for Colleges with Student's Transcript. LC 77-80300. 1978. pap. 15.00 (ISBN 0-8224-2121-6); instr's. handbk. & supplementary dictation 8.80 (ISBN 0-8224-2123-2). Pitman Learning.

Thompson, Ewa M. Witold Gombrowicz. (World Authors Ser.: No. 510). 1979. lib. bdg. 14.50 (ISBN 0-8057-6351-1). Twayne.

Thompson, F. M. Hampstead: Building a Borough 1650-1964. (Illus.). 470p. 1974. 37.00x (ISBN 0-7100-7747-5). Routledge & Kegan.

Thompson, Flora. Lark Rise to Candleford: A Trilogy. (Illus.). 576p. 1979. Repr. of 1945 ed. text ed. 17.95x (ISBN 0-19-211759-9). Oxford U Pr.

Thompson, Francis. The Uists & Barra. LC 74-81056. (Islands Ser). (Illus.). 192p. 1974. 16.95 (ISBN 0-7153-6676-9). David & Charles.

--Victorian & Edwardian Highlands. 1976. pap. 10.50 (ISBN 0-7134-3220-9, Pub. by Batsford England). David & Charles.

Thompson, Francis & Bond, D. Victorian & Edwardian Northumbria. 1976. 22.50 (ISBN 0-7134-3092-3, Pub. by Batsford England). David & Charles.

Thompson, Frank E., Jr. Diving, Cutting & Welding in Underwater Salvage Operations. LC 70-92687. (Illus.). 1944. pap. 4.00x (ISBN 0-87033-139-6). Cornell Maritime.

Thompson, Frank J. Personnel Policy in the City: The Politics of Jobs in Oakland. 1975. 18.50x (ISBN 0-520-02797-3); pap. 4.95x (ISBN 0-520-03509-7). U of Cal Pr.

--Policy, Bureaucracy, & the Public's Health. 288p. 1981. text ed. 19.95x (ISBN 0-262-20041-4). MIT Pr.

Thompson, Fred & Stanbury, W. T. The Political Economy of Interest Groups in the Legislative Process in Canada. 53p. 1979. pap. text ed. 3.00x (ISBN 0-920380-27-1, Pub. by Inst Res Pub Canada). Renouf.

Thompson, Fred, Jr. What the Bible Says About Heaven & Hell. (What the Bible Says Ser.). 400p. 1981. 13.50 (ISBN 0-89900-081-9). College Pr Pub.

Thompson, G. G., jt. auth. see Brackbill, Yvonne.

Thompson, G. L., jt. auth. see Morgenstern, Oskar.

Thompson, G. L., jt. auth. see Sethi, S. P.

Thompson, G. McKecknie & Rodin, S. Colliery Spoil Tips-After Aberfan. 98p. 1980. pap. 15.00x (ISBN 0-901948-59-4, Pub. by Telford England). State Mutual Bk.

Thompson, G. R. & Lokke, Virgil L., eds. Ruined Eden of the Present: Hawthorne, Melville, & Poe. LC 80-80816. (Illus.). 320p. (Critical essays in honor of darrel abel). 1981. 15.75 (ISBN 0-911198-60-1). Purdue.

Thompson, G. V. Artificial Satellites. (gr. 4 up). 1962. 4.25 o.p. (ISBN 0-298-78953-1). Dufour.

Thompson, Gene E. & Handelman, Ira. Health Data & Information Management. (Illus.). 1978. 29.95 (ISBN 0-409-95008-4). Butterworths.

Thompson, George C. & Brady, Gerald P. Shortened CPA Law Review. 4th ed. 1977. 19.95x (ISBN 0-534-00496-2). Wadsworth Pub.

--Shortened CPA Law Review. (Business Ser.). 560p. 1980. text ed. 17.95x (ISBN 0-686-69155-5). Kent Pub Co.

Thompson, George G., ed. Social Development & Personality. LC 77-146673. (Readings in Educational Research Ser.). 1971. 25.00 (ISBN 0-471-86005-0); text ed. 22.50 ten or more copies (ISBN 0-685-52962-2). McCutchan.

Thompson, George N. The God Gap, 2 vols. 192p. 1980. Set. 10.00 (ISBN 0-686-28944-7). Directions Pr.

Thompson, Gerald E. Management Science: Introduction to Modern Quantitative Analysis & Decision Making. 1976. text ed. 19.95 (ISBN 0-07-064360-1, C); instructor's manual 4.95 (ISBN 0-07-064361-X). McGraw.

Thompson, Gladys. Patterns for Guernseys, Jerseys & Arans: Fishermen's Sweaters from the British Isles. (Illus.). 1971. pap. 4.50 (ISBN 0-486-22703-0). Dover.

Thompson, Gordon B. Memo from Mercury: Information Technology Is Different. 62p. 1979. pap. text ed. 3.00x (ISBN 0-920380-29-8, Pub. by Inst Res Pub Canada). Renouf.

Thompson, H. C. & Bonnie, Fred. Growing Flowers. LC 74-18642. (Illus.). 1975. 7.95 o.p. (ISBN 0-8487-0391-X). Oxmoor Hse.

Thompson, H. Doyle & Stevenson, Warren H., eds. Laser Velocimetry & Particle Sizing: Proceedings. new ed. LC 79-59. (Illus.). 1979. text ed. 56.95 (ISBN 0-89116-150-3). Hemisphere Pub.

Thompson, H. E. & Bernstine, R. L. Diagnostic Ultrasound in Clinical Obstetrics & Gynecology. 192p. 1978. 34.95 (ISBN 0-471-86080-8, 1-322). Wiley.

Thompson, Harrison R. Seventh Sense. (Orig.). 1979. pap. 2.25 (ISBN 0-532-23275-5). Manor Bks.

Thompson, Harwood. Florida Real Estate. (Illus.). 672p. 1980. ref. ed. 19.95; text ed. 16.95 (ISBN 0-8359-2067-4). Reston.

Thompson, Harwood & Ellis. Florida Real Estate Resource Book. 1978. pap. 7.95 ref. ed. (ISBN 0-87909-739-6). Reston.

Thompson, Herbert M. The Theory of Wages: And Its Application to the Eight Hour Question & Other Labour Problems. LC 79-51868. 1981. Repr. of 1892 ed. 16.50 (ISBN 0-88355-960-9). Hyperion Conn.

Thompson, Holland see Johnson, Allen & Nevins, Allan.

Thompson, Homer A. The Athenian Agora, a Short Guide. rev. ed. (Excavations of the Athenian Agora Picture Bks.: No. 16). (Illus.). 1980. pap. 1.50x (ISBN 0-87661-622-8). Am Sch Athens.

Thompson, Howard E., jt. ed. see Krajewski, Lee J.

Thompson, Hunter. The Great Shark Hunt. 1980. pap. 3.50 (ISBN 0-445-04596-5). Popular Lib.

Thompson, Hunter S. Hell's Angels. 1975. pap. 2.75 (ISBN 0-345-29238-3). Ballantine.

Thompson, I. A. War & Government in Habsburg Spain 1560-1620. 1976. text ed. 36.50x (ISBN 0-485-11166-7, Athlone Pr). Humanities.

Thompson, Ian. Corsica. (Islands Ser.). 1974. 14.95 (ISBN 0-7153-5329-2). David & Charles.

Thompson, Ian, ed. see Pinder, David.

Thompson, J. Foundations of Vocational Education: Social & Philosophical Concepts. (Illus.). 1973. ref. ed. 17.95 (ISBN 0-13-330068-4). P-H.

Thompson, J. A. The Bible & Archaeology. wnd, rev. ed. 512p. 1981. 13.95 (ISBN 0-8028-3545-7). Eerdmans.

Thompson, J. A., jt. ed. see Bratcher, R. G.

Thompson, J. B. Critical Hermeneutics: A Study in the Thought of Paul Ricoeur & Jurgen Habermas. LC 80-41935. 238p. Date not set. price not set (ISBN 0-521-23932-X). Cambridge U Pr.

Thompson, J. C. Electrons in Liquid Ammonia. (Monographs on the Physics & Chemistry of Materials). (Illus.). 1976. 55.00x (ISBN 0-19-851343-7). Oxford U Pr.

Thompson, J. Dana, jt. ed. see Glantz, Micheal H.

Thompson, J. Eric. Maya Hieroglyphic Writing: An Introduction. (Civilization of the American Indian Ser.: No. 56). (Illus.). 1975. 29.95 o.p. (ISBN 0-8061-0447-3); pap. 17.95 (ISBN 0-8061-0958-0). U of Okla Pr.

Thompson, J. Eric, ed. see Gage, Thomas.

Thompson, J. G., Jr. The Miracle Makers. Date not set. 22.50 (ISBN 0-915926-11-3). Magic Ltd.

Thompson, J. M. Fish of the Ocean & Shore. 208p. 1980. 13.95x (ISBN 0-686-68861-9, Pub. by W Collins Australia). Intl Schol Bk Serv.

--The French Revolution. 2nd ed. (Illus.). 544p. 1980. pap. 10.95x (ISBN 0-631-11921-3, Pub. by Basil Blackwell). Biblio Dist.

--Leaders of the French Revolution. (Illus.). 272p. 1980. pap. 9.95x (ISBN 0-631-11931-0, Pub. by Basil Blackwell). Biblio Dist.

Thompson, J. W. A History of Historical Writing, 2 vols. 35.00 (ISBN 0-8446-1448-3). Peter Smith.

Thompson, Jack, jt. auth. see Miller, Albert.

Thompson, Jacquelin. Image Impact. (Illus.). 288p. 1981. 10.95 (ISBN 0-89479-072-2). A & W Pubs.

Thompson, Jacqueline. The Very Rich Book: America's Super-Millionaires & Their Money-Where They Got It, How They Spend It. LC 80-21618. (Illus.). 454p. 1981. 13.95 (ISBN 0-688-00072-X). Morrow.

Thompson, James. An Introduction to a University Library Administration. 3rd rev. ed. 256p. 1979. 18.75 (ISBN 0-89664-407-3, Pub. by K G Saur). Shoe String.

--The Letter to the Hebrews. Ferguson, Everett, ed. LC 70-163750. (Living Word New Testament Commentary Ser.: Vol. 15). 1971. 7.95 (ISBN 0-8344-0071-5). Sweet.

--Our Life Together. LC 77-79338. (Journey Bks.). 1977. pap. 2.35 (ISBN 0-8344-0095-2). Sweet.

--Second Letter of Paul to the Corinthians. Ferguson, Everett, ed. (Living Word New Testament Commentary Ser.: Vol. 9). 1970. 7.95 (ISBN 0-8344-0054-5). Sweet.

--Strategy for Survival. LC 79-67274. (Journey Bks). 144p. 1980. pap. 2.35 (ISBN 0-8344-0113-4). Sweet.

Thompson, James C. & Vidmer, Richard F. Political Administration in the Soviet Union & the United States. 240p. 1981. 22.95 (ISBN 0-89789-009-4). J F Bergin.

Thompson, James M. Robespierre & the French Revolution. 1962. pap. 1.95 o.s.i. (ISBN 0-02-037840-8, Collier). Macmillan.

Thompson, James M., jt. auth. see Dallas, Richard J.

Thompson, James R. Leigh Hunt. (English Authors Ser.: No. 210). 1977. lib. bdg. 10.95 (ISBN 0-8057-6679-0). Twayne.

Thompson, James S. & Thompson, Margaret W. Genetics in Medicine. 3rd ed. LC 78-64726. (Illus.). 396p. 1980. text ed. 16.00 (ISBN 0-7216-8857-8). Saunders.

Thompson, James W. Feudal Germany. LC 80-2001. 1981. Repr. of 1928 ed. 67.50 (ISBN 0-404-18601-7). AMS Pr.

Thompson, Jean. Brother of the Wolves. LC 78-18014. (gr. 4-6). 1978. 7.95 (ISBN 0-688-22168-8); PLB 7.63 (ISBN 0-688-32168-2). Morrow.

Thompson, Jesse J., jt. auth. see Scott, Louise B.

Thompson, Joan. Harbor of the Heart. 192p. 1981. pap. 2.25 (ISBN 0-345-28747-9). Ballantine.

--Interesting Times. 322p. 1981. 12.95 (ISBN 0-312-41914-7). St Martin.

Thompson, John. Country Bed & Breakfast Places in Canada. rev ed. 1981. pap. 7.95 (ISBN 0-88879-045-7). Berkshire Traveller.

--Country Bed & Breakfast Places in Canada. 1979. pap. 5.95 o.p. (ISBN 0-88879-014-7). Berkshire Traveller.

--Stilt Jack. (House of Anansi Poetry Ser.: No. 36). 48p. (Orig.). 1978. pap. 6.95 (ISBN 0-88784-055-8, Pub. by Hse Anansi Pr Canada). U of Toronto Pr.

Thompson, John, ed. Horse-Drawn Carriages: A Source Book. (Illus.). 100p. (Orig.). 1980. pap. 8.50x (ISBN 0-906922-00-3). Intl Pubns Serv.

--New Zealand Literature to Nineteen Seventy-Seven: A Guide to Information Sources. LC 74-11537. (American Literature, English Literature, & World Literature in English Information Guide Ser.: Vol. 30). 250p. 1980. 30.00 (ISBN 0-8103-1246-8). Gale.

Thompson, John A. Bible & Archaeology. (Illus.). 1962. 13.95 (ISBN 0-8028-3268-7). Eerdmans.

--The Book of Jeremiah. LC 79-16510. (New International Commentary on the Old Testament Ser.). 1980. 22.50 (ISBN 0-8028-2369-6). Eerdmans.

Thompson, John C. A Reader's Guide to Fifty British Plays: 1660-1900. (Reader's Guide Ser.). 448p. 1980. 16.50x (ISBN 0-389-20139-1). B&N.

Thompson, John D. Applied Health Services Research. LC 75-12482. (Illus.). 1977. 19.95 (ISBN 0-669-00028-0). Lexington Bks.

Thompson, John H., ed. Geography of New York State. LC 66-14602. (Illus.). 1977. pap. 25.00x (ISBN 0-8156-2182-5); supplement & 3 color maps o.p. 6.95x (ISBN 0-8156-2185-X); supplement only o.p. 2.95 (ISBN 0-8156-2190-6). Syracuse U Pr.

Thompson, John L. Giovanni Segantini: A Vision of His Art & of His Letters. (Illus.). 107p. 1981. 41.85 (ISBN 0-930582-94-2). Gloucester Art.

Thompson, John L., jt. auth. see Vane, Howard R.

Thompson, John S. The Mechanism of the Linotype. Bidwell, John, ed. Bd. with History of Composing Machines. LC 78-74413. (Nineteenth Century Book Arts & Printing History Ser.: Vol. 23). (Illus.). 1980. lib. bdg. 38.00 (ISBN 0-8240-3897-5). Garland Pub.

Thompson, John S., jt. auth. see Corry, Robert J.

Thompson, John T. Policy-Making in American Public Education: A Framework for Analysis. LC 75-5841. (Illus.). 304p. 1975. 16.95 (ISBN 0-13-685370-6). P-H.

Thompson, John W., jt. ed. see Slauson, Nedra.

Thompson, Joseph & Buchanan, William. Analyzing Psychological Variables. 1979. pap. text ed. 10.95x (ISBN 0-684-15981-3, ScribC). Scribner.

Thompson, Joseph R. & Hasso, Anton N. Correlative Sectional Anatomy of the Head & Neck: A Color Atlas, Vol. I. LC 79-19978. (Illus.). 1979. text ed. 175.00 (ISBN 0-8016-4934-X). Mosby.

Thompson, Joyce. Willie & Phil. 1980. pap. 1.95 (ISBN 0-686-69243-8, 75804). Avon.

Thompson, Judi. Healthy Pregnancy the Yoga Way. LC 76-23818. 160p. 1977. pap. 3.95 o.p. (ISBN 0-385-11631-4, Dolp). Doubleday.

Thompson, June M. & Bowers, Arden C. Clinical Manual of Health Assessment. (Illus.). 1980. pap. text ed. 17.95 (ISBN 0-8016-4935-8). Mosby.

Thompson, K., jt. auth. see Salaman, G.

Thompson, K. C. & Reynolds, R. J. Atomic Absorption Fluorescence & Flame Emission Spectroscopy: A Practical Approach. 2nd ed. 1979. 47.95 (ISBN 0-470-26478-0). Halsted Pr.

Thompson, Keith. Education & Philosophy: A Practical Approach. 1977. pap. 8.50x (ISBN 0-631-94440-0, Pub. by Basil Blackwell England). Biblio Dist.

Thompson, Kenneth. Auguste Comte: The Foundation of Sociology. LC 75-12566. 1975. 19.95 (ISBN 0-470-85988-1). Halsted Pr.

--The Films of Paul Newman. Castell, David, ed. (The Films of...Ser.). (Illus.). (gr. 7-12). 1978. Repr. of 1974 ed. PLB 5.95 (ISBN 0-912616-87-3). Greenhaven.

Thompson, Kenneth, jt. ed. see Salaman, Graeme.

Thompson, Kenneth R., jt. auth. see Luthans, Fred.

Thompson, Kenneth W. Interpreters & Critics of the Cold War. LC 78-57575. 1978. pap. text ed. 6.75 (ISBN 0-8191-0504-X). U Pr of Amer.

Thompson, Kenneth W. & Fogel, Barbara R. Higher Education & Social Change: Promising Experiments in Developing Countries, Vol. I. LC 76-14474. (Illus.). 1976. text ed. 17.50 o.p. (ISBN 0-275-23390-1). Praeger.

Thompson, Kenneth W., ed. Herbert Butterfield: The Ethics of History & Politics. LC 79-5375. 1979. text ed. 12.00 (ISBN 0-8191-0875-8); pap. text ed. 7.25 (ISBN 0-8191-0876-6). U Pr of Amer.

--The Moral Imperatives of Human Rights: A World Survey. LC 79-3736. 1980. text ed. 17.50 (ISBN 0-8191-0920-7); pap. text ed. 8.75 (ISBN 0-8191-0921-5). U Pr of Amer.

--The Virginia Papers of the Presidency, Vol. V: The White Burkett Miller Center Forums, 1981, Pt. 1. 91p. 1981. lib. bdg. 11.75 (ISBN 0-8191-1502-9); pap. text ed. 5.50 (ISBN 0-8191-1503-7). U Pr of Amer.

--The Virginia Papers on the Presidency, Vol. 3: The White Burkett Miller Center Forums, Pt. 1. LC 79-66241. 133p. 1980. lib. bdg. 13.25 o.p. (ISBN 0-8191-1120-1); pap. text ed. 6.25 o.p. (ISBN 0-8191-1121-X). U Pr of Amer.

Thompson, Kenneth W, et al, eds. Higher Education & Social Change: Promising Experiments in Developing Countries, Vol. 2: Case Studies. LC 76-14474. 1976. text ed. 32.50 o.p. (ISBN 0-275-23390-1). Praeger.

Thompson, Kenneth W., et al, eds. Higher Education & Social Change, Vol. 2. 1977. pap. 7.50 o.p. (ISBN 0-275-23390-1). Interbk Inc.

Thompson, L. The Later Years: 1938-1963. Frost, Robert, ed. pap. 17.95 o.p. (ISBN 0-686-67508-8). HR&W.

Thompson, L., ed. Robert Frost: The Early Years, 1894-1915. LC 66-20523. 1966. 12.50 o.p. (ISBN 0-03-059770-6). HR&W.

--Robert Frost: The Years of Triumph, 1915-1938. LC 66-20523. 1970. 15.00 o.p. (ISBN 0-03-084530-0). HR&W.

Thompson, Laurence G. The Chinese Way in Religion. (Religious Life of Man Ser.). 1973. pap. 7.95x (ISBN 0-8221-0109-2). Dickenson.

Thompson, Lawrance, ed. see Frost, Robert.

Thompson, Lawrence, jt. auth. see Winnick, R. H.

Thompson, Leonard. Survival in Two Worlds: Moshoeshoe of Lesotho, 1786-1870. (Illus.). 366p. 1976. text ed. 36.00x (ISBN 0-19-821693-9). Oxford U Pr.

--Survival in Two Worlds: Moshoeshoe of Lesotho 1786-1870. (Illus.). 1975. pap. 12.50x (ISBN 0-19-822702-7). Oxford U Pr.

Thompson, Lida F., et al. Sociology: Nurses & Their Patients in a Modern Society. 9th ed. LC 74-34417. 1975. text ed. 10.95 (ISBN 0-8016-4942-0). Mosby.

Thompson, Lloyd J. Reading Disability: Developmental Dyslexia. (Illus.). 228p. 1974. pap. text ed. 10.75 (ISBN 0-398-03123-1). C C Thomas.

Thompson, M., tr. see Belozerskaya-Bulgakova, L. E.

Thompson, M. W. Defects & Radiation Damage in Metals. LC 69-10434. (Cambridge Monographs on Physics). (Illus.). 1969. 60.50 (ISBN 0-521-07068-6); pap. 18.50x (ISBN 0-521-09865-3). Cambridge U Pr.

--General Pitt-Rivers. 1977. pap. text ed. 6.50x (ISBN 0-239-00162-1). Humanities.

Thompson, Malcolm H., jt. auth. see Jastrow, Robert.

Thompson, Margaret H., jt. auth. see Keithley, Erwin.

Thompson, Margaret W., jt. auth. see Thompson, James S.

Thompson, Marilou B. Abiding Appalachia: Where Mountain & Atom Meet. LC 78-12970. (Illus.). 1978. 8.95 (ISBN 0-918518-09-1); pap. 6.95 (ISBN 0-918518-15-6). St Luke TN.

Thompson, Marilou B., ed. Poets of the River City. LC 78-15274. 1978. pap. 1.00 (ISBN 0-918518-08-3). St Luke TN.

Thompson, Mark S. Benefit-Cost Analysis for Program Evaluation. LC 80-13110. (Illus.). 310p. 1980. 20.00 (ISBN 0-8039-1483-0); pap. 9.95 (ISBN 0-8039-1484-9). Sage.

Thompson, Martha. Shock Syndrome: Mechanisms & Manifestations; Nursing Assessment Intervention & Evaluation. (Illus.). 1978. 7.95 (ISBN 0-201-07660-8, M&N Div). A-W.

Thompson, Martin. Antitrust & the Health Care Provider. LC 79-9371. 1979. text ed. 30.00 (ISBN 0-89443-159-5). Aspen Systems.

Thompson, Mary M., jt. auth. see Dressel, Paul L.

Thompson, Mary P; see Bree, Germaine.

Thompson, Maynard, jt. auth. see Maki, Daniel.

Thompson, Merle O., jt. auth. see Boltz, Carol.

Thompson, Mildred L. & Thompson, Edward J. Begonias: The Complete Reference Guide. 352p. 1981. 35.00 (ISBN 0-8129-0932-1). Times Bks.

Thompson, Mindy. A History of the National Negro Labor Council. (Occasional Papers: No. 27). 1978. 2.25 (ISBN 0-89977-022-3). Am Inst Marxist.

Thompson, Morton. Not As a Stranger. 1971. pap. 2.25 o.p. (ISBN 0-451-07786-5, E7786, Sig). NAL.

Thompson, Mother. One Hundred Ways to Stretch Your Dollar. (Illus.). 1979. pap. 12.95 o.p. (ISBN 0-930490-16-9). Future Shop.

Thompson, Murray S. Grace & Forgiveness in Ministry. LC 80-23613. 176p. (Orig.). 1981. pap. 6.95 (ISBN 0-687-15680-7). Abingdon.

Thompson, Neil. A Closer Look at Horses. (Closer Look at Ser.). (Illus.). (gr. 4 up). 1978. PLB 6.90 (ISBN 0-531-01428-2); pap. 1.95 (ISBN 0-531-02486-5). Watts.

Thompson, Neville. Anti-Appeasers: Conservative Opposition to Appeasement in the 1930's. 1971. 28.50x (ISBN 0-19-821487-1). Oxford U Pr.

Thompson, Newton, ed. see Scanlon, Cora C. & Scanlon, Charles L.

Thompson, Oscar. Debussy: Man & Artist. (Illus.). 1937. pap. 6.00 (ISBN 0-486-21783-3). Dover.

--Debussy Man & Artist. 395p. 1980. Repr. of 1940 ed. lib. bdg. 30.00 (ISBN 0-89984-474-X). Century Bookbindery.

--How to Understand Music. 347p. 1980. Repr. of 1935 ed. lib. bdg. 30.00 (ISBN 0-89984-453-7). Century Bookbindery.

--International Encyclopedia of Music & Musicians. 10th, rev. ed. Bohle, Bruce, ed. LC 64-23285. (Illus.). 2600p. 1975. 49.95 (ISBN 0-396-07005-1). Dodd.

--Practical Musical Criticism. (Music Reprint Ser.: 1979). 1979. Repr. of 1934 ed. lib. bdg. 19.50 (ISBN 0-306-79514-0). Da Capo.

Thompson, P. M. The Shen Tzu Fragments. (London Oriental Ser.). (Illus.). 1979. 125.00x (ISBN 0-19-713579-X). Oxford U Pr.

Thompson, Paul. The Children's Crusade. 1975. pap. text ed. 2.95 (ISBN 0-435-23880-9). Heinemann Ed.

--Edwardians: The Remaking of British Society. LC 75-10897. (Illus.). 396p. 1975. 15.00x (ISBN 0-253-31941-2). Ind U Pr.

--The Hitchikers No. 2. (Hi Lo Ser.). 96p. (gr. 6 up). 1981. pap. 1.50 (ISBN 0-553-14619-X). Bantam.

Thompson, Paul J. Freedom-Love & Playing-Love & Other Special Kinds. LC 78-65331. 1977. 4.95 (ISBN 0-9601288-2-4); pap. 2.95 (ISBN 0-9601288-1-6). P J Thompson.

Thompson, Philip & Davenport, Peter, eds. Dictionary of Visual Language. (Illus.). 288p. 1981. 30.00x (ISBN 0-312-20108-7). St Martin.

Thompson, Philip D. & O'Brien, Robert. Weather. LC 65-14589. (Life Science Library). (Illus.). (gr. 5 up). 1968. PLB 8.97 o.p. (ISBN 0-8094-0467-2, Pub. by Time-Life). Silver.

Thompson, Phyllis. Count It All Joy! LC 78-64550. 1978. pap. 2.50 (ISBN 0-87788-103-0). Shaw Pubs.

Thompson, Phyllis, jt. auth. see Taylor, Hudson.

Thompson, R. A., ed. Recent Advances in Clinical Immunology, No. 2. (Recent Advances Ser.). (Illus.). 361p. 1980. text ed. 49.00x (ISBN 0-443-01963-0). Churchill.

Thompson, R. F., jt. auth. see Riesen, A. H.

Thompson, R. O. Progress in Oceanography, Vol. 7, Pt. 4: Observations of Rossby Waves Near Site D. Swallow, Mary, ed. LC 63-15353. 1977. pap. text ed. 8.75 (ISBN 0-685-86323-9). Pergamon.

Thompson, R. W. Churchill & the Montgomery Myth. LC 68-18714. 272p. 1968. 5.95 (ISBN 0-87131-001-5). M Evans.

--The History of Protective Tariff Laws. (The Neglected American Economists Ser.). 1974. lib. bdg. 50.00 (ISBN 0-8240-1022-1). Garland Pub.

Thompson, Ralph B., ed. Florida Statistical Abstract, Nineteen Eighty. LC 67-7393. 1980. 20.00x (ISBN 0-8130-0677-5); pap. 11.50 (ISBN 0-8130-0678-3). U Presses Fla.

--Florida Statistical Abstract, 1980. (Illus.). 695p. 1980. 20.00x (ISBN 0-8130-0677-5); pap. 11.50 (ISBN 0-8130-0678-3). U Presses Fla.

Thompson, Ralph S. The Sucker's Visit to the Mammoth Cave. Repr. of 1870 ed. 7.00 (ISBN 0-914264-33-8). Zephyrus Pr.

Thompson, Raymond & Daly, Treve. The Number to Call Is.... 288p. 1981. pap. 2.50 (ISBN 0-380-53769-9, 53769). Avon.

Thompson, Raymond H., jt. ed. see Spicer, Edward H.

Thompson, Richard. Toulouse-Lautrec. LC 77-21483. (The Oresko Art Book). (Illus.). 1977. 15.95 (ISBN 0-8467-0372-6, Pub. by Two Continents); pap. text ed. 9.95 (ISBN 0-8467-0382-3). Hippocrene Bks.

--World Coins & Their Values. 224p. (gr. 8 up). Date not set. 3.95 (ISBN 0-307-24408-3, Golden Pr). Western Pub.

Thompson, Richard A. & Stanford, Gene. Child Life in Hospitals. 1981. write for info (ISBN 0-398-04445-7). C C Thomas.

Thompson, Richard A. & Green, J. R., eds. Infectious Diseases of the Central Nervous System. LC 74-79192. (Advances in Neurology Ser: Vol. 6). 1974. 34.50 (ISBN 0-911216-82-0). Raven.

--Stroke. LC 75-25129. (Advances in Neurology Ser.: Vol. 16). 1977. 25.00 (ISBN 0-89004-098-2). Raven.

Thompson, Richard A. & Green, John R., eds. Complications of Nervous System Trauma. LC 78-52425. (Advances in Neurology Ser.: Vol. 22). 1979. text ed. 34.50 (ISBN 0-89004-295-0). Raven.

--Critical Care of Neurologic & Neurosurgical Emergencies. 1979. text ed. 22.50 (ISBN 0-89004-401-5). Raven.

--Neoplasia in the Central Nervous System. LC 75-25113. (Advances in Neurology Ser.: Vol. 15). 394p. 1976. 41.50 (ISBN 0-89004-058-3). Raven.

Thompson, Richard E. Helping Hospital Trustees Understand Physicians. LC 79-21428. 96p. (Orig.). 1979. pap. 11.25 (ISBN 0-87258-287-6, 1347). Am Hospital.

Thompson, Richard F. Introduccion a la Psicologia Fisliologica. (Span.). 1977. pap. text ed. 12.00 (ISBN 0-06-317100-7, IntlDept). Har-Row.

Thompson, Richard F. & Patterson, Michael, eds. Bioelectric Recording Techniques, 3 pts. Incl. Pt. A. Cellular Processes & Brain Potentials. 1973. 46.00 (ISBN 0-12-689401-9); Pt. B. 1974. 32.50 (ISBN 0-12-689402-7); Pt. C. Receptor & Effector Processes. 1974. 32.50 (ISBN 0-12-689403-5). 89.00 set (ISBN 0-686-66929-0). Acad Pr.

Thompson, Richard F. & Voss, James F., eds. Topics in Learning & Performance. 1972. 27.00 o.p. (ISBN 0-12-689450-7). Acad Pr.

Thompson, Richard F., intro. by. Progress in Psychobiology: Readings from Scientific American. LC 75-42362. (Illus.). 1976. text ed. 19.95x (ISBN 0-7167-0532-X); pap. text ed. 9.95x (ISBN 0-7167-0531-1). W H Freeman.

Thompson, Richard F., et al, eds. Neural Mechanisms of Goal-Directed Behavior & Learning. LC 79-6775. 1980. 49.50 (ISBN 0-12-688980-5). Acad Pr.

Thompson, Robert. The Feasts of the Lord. pap. 5.95 (ISBN 0-89728-029-6, 645571). Omega Pubns OR.

--The Land of Promise. pap. 3.95 (ISBN 0-89728-042-3, 670209). Omega Pubns OR.

Thompson, Robert E. Elements of Political Economy, with Special Reference to the Industrial History of Nations. (The Neglected American Economists Ser.). 1974. lib. bdg. 50.00 (ISBN 0-8240-1020-5). Garland Pub.

Thompson, Robert F. African Art in Motion: Icon & Act in the Collection of Katherine Coryton White. (Illus.). 1974. 35.00 (ISBN 0-520-03844-4); pap. 14.95 (ISBN 0-520-03843-6). U of Cal Pr.

Thompson, Robert G. BASIC: A First Course. (Data Processing Ser.). (Illus.). 352p. 1981. text ed. 13.95 (ISBN 0-675-08057-6); tchr's. manual avail. Merrill.

Thompson, Robert S., jt. auth. see Oakley, John B.

Thompson, Roger. Samuel Pepys' Penny Merriments. LC 76-50544. 1977. 18.00x (ISBN 0-231-04280-9); pap. 6.95 (ISBN 0-231-04281-7). Columbia U Pr.

--Women in Stuart England & America: A Comparative Study. 1978. pap. 8.95 (ISBN 0-7100-8900-7). Routledge & Kegan.

Thompson, Roger, jt. ed. see Allen, H. C.

Thompson, Ruth H., ed. see Hunt, Harrison J.

Thompson, S. & Kahn, J. H. The Group Process As a Helping Technique. LC 79-124667. 1970. 15.00 (ISBN 0-08-016220-7); pap. 7.00 (ISBN 0-08-016219-3). Pergamon.

Thompson, S. C. All-Time Rosters of Major League Baseball Clubs. LC 73-156. 800p. 1973. 12.00 o.p. (ISBN 0-498-01380-4). A S Barnes.

Thompson, S. J., jt. ed. see Lenihan, J. M.

Thompson, Samuel, et al. The Adrenal Medulla of Rats: Comparative Physiology, Histology, & Pathology. (Illus.). 112p. 1980. 18.75 (ISBN 0-398-04091-5). C C Thomas.

Thompson, Samuel C., Jr. Federal Income Taxation of Domestic & Foreign Business Transactions. (Contemporary Legal Education Ser.). 1200p. 1980. 40.00 (ISBN 0-672-84075-8); text ed. 25.00 (ISBN 0-686-68532-6). Bobbs.

Thompson, Samuel W. The Pathology of Parenteral Nutrition with Lipids. (Illus.). 952p. 1974. 55.75 (ISBN 0-398-02748-X). C C Thomas.

--Selected Histochemical & Histopathological Methods. (Illus.). 1680p. 1974. text ed. 90.50 (ISBN 0-398-03132-0). C C Thomas.

Thompson, Samuel W., 2nd & Luna, Lee G. An Atlas of Artifacts: Encountered in the Preparation of Microscopic Tissue Sections. (Illus.). 208p. 1978. 27.75 (ISBN 0-398-03624-1). C C Thomas.

Thompson, Sandra A., jt. auth. see Li, Charles N.

Thompson, Seymour D. Charging the Jury: A Monograph. 196p. 1980. Repr. lib. bdg. 20.00x (ISBN 0-8377-2628-X). Rothman.

Thompson, Silvanus P. Calculus Made Easy. 3rd ed. 1946. 4.95 (ISBN 0-312-11410-9, Papermac); pap. 5.95 (ISBN 0-686-66541-4). St Martin.

--Michael Faraday: His Life & Work. 2nd ed. Date not set. 12.95 (ISBN 0-8284-0311-2). Chelsea Pub.

Thompson, Stephanie. Clothes & Ornaments. LC 78-64657. (Fact Finders Ser.). (Illus.). 1979. lib. bdg. 3.96 (ISBN 0-686-51126-3). Silver.

--Shops & Markets. LC 78-64655. (Fact Finders Ser.). (Illus.). 1979. lib. bdg. 3.96 (ISBN 0-686-51131-X). Silver.

Thompson, Stith. The Folktale. 1977. 20.00x (ISBN 0-520-03359-0); pap. 8.95x (ISBN 0-520-03537-2). U of Cal Pr.

--Motif-Index of Folk-Literature, 6 Vols. rev. ed. Incl. Vol. 1. 560p. 32.50x (ISBN 0-253-33881-6); Vol. 2. 520p. 32.50x (ISBN 0-253-33882-4); Vol. 3. 520p. 32.50x (ISBN 0-253-33883-2); Vol. 4. 500p. 32.50x (ISBN 0-253-33884-0); Vol. 5. 568p. 32.50x (ISBN 0-253-33885-9); Vol. 6. 896p. 45.00x (ISBN 0-253-33886-7). LC 55-8055. 1955-58. Set. 160.00x (ISBN 0-253-33887-5). Ind U Pr.

Thompson, Susan L. One More Thing, Dad. Tucker, Kathleen, ed. LC 79-27887. (A Self-Starter Bk.). (Illus.). (ps-1). 1980. PLB 6.50g (ISBN 0-8075-6095-2). A Whitman.

Thompson, T. E. Biology of Ophisthobranch Molluscs, Vol. 1. (Illus.). 1976. 36.00x (ISBN 0-903874-04-0, Pub. by Brit Mus Nat Hist). Sabbot-Natural Hist Bks.

--Nudibranchs. (Illus., Orig.). 1976. pap. 5.95 (ISBN 0-87666-459-1, PS-696). TFH Pubns.

Thompson, T. J. Ten Red Rods. LC 80-83135. (Illus.). 16p. (Orig.). (ps-1). 1980. pap. text ed. 1.50 (ISBN 0-915676-02-8). Montessori Wkshps.

Thompson, T. Philips. The Politics of Labor. LC 75-9924. (Social History of Canada Ser.). 1975. pap. 5.95 (ISBN 0-8020-6270-9). U of Toronto Pr.

Thompson, Thea. Edwardian Childhoods. (Illus.). 256p. 1981. 27.50 (ISBN 0-7100-0676-4). Routledge & Kegan.

Thompson, Thomas. Blood & Money. 1981. pap. 3.25 (ISBN 0-440-10679-6). Dell.

--Range Drifter. 192p. 1981. pap. 1.95 (ISBN 0-553-14541-X). Bantam.

--Richie. 1981. pap. 2.50 (ISBN 0-440-17401-5). Dell.

--Serpentine. 1981. pap. 3.50 (ISBN 0-440-17611-5). Dell.

--Shadow of the Butte. 144p. (Orig.). 1981. pap. 1.75 (ISBN 0-553-14747-1). Bantam.

Thompson, Thomas T. Primer of Clinical Radiology. (Illus.). 1973. pap. 13.95 o.p. (ISBN 0-316-84169-2). Little.

--Primer of Clinical Radiology. 2nd ed. 1980. pap. text ed. 14.95 (ISBN 0-316-84184-6). Little.

Thompson, Todd, jt. auth. see Harvard, Andrew.

Thompson, Tom. Organizational TV News. LC 80-81874. (Illus.). 217p. (Orig.). 1980. pap. 16.95 (ISBN 0-935608-00-1); pap. text ed. 16.95 (ISBN 0-686-63501-9). Media Concepts.

Thompson, Tracy, jt. ed. see Morsberger, Robert.

Thompson, Travis & Dews, Peter B., eds. Advances in Behavioral Pharmacology, Vol. 2. LC 74-10187. 1979. 25.50 (ISBN 0-12-004702-0); library ed. 33.00 (ISBN 0-12-004772-1); microfiche 18.00 (ISBN 0-12-004773-X). Acad Pr.

Thompson, Travis & Grabowski, John G., eds. Reinforcement Schedules & Multioperant Analysis. LC 76-182306. (Illus.). 1972. 19.95 (ISBN 0-13-771709-1). P-H.

Thompson, Vincent B. Africa & Unity: The Evolution of Pan-Africanism. 412p. 1969. pap. text ed. 12.00x (ISBN 0-582-64522-0). Humanities.

Thompson, Virginia. Help Me Lord--I Hurt. LC 78-55505. (Illus., Orig.). 1978. pap. 2.25 (ISBN 0-89081-145-8, 1458). Harvest Hse.

--Speak to Me Lord--I'm Listening. LC 78-55479. 1981. pap. 2.25 (ISBN 0-89081-117-2, 1172). Harvest Hse.

Thompson, Virginia & Adloff, Richard. The French Pacific Islands: French Polynesia & New Caledonia. LC 71-138634. (Illus.). 1971. 32.50x (ISBN 0-520-01843-5). U of Cal Pr.

--Historical Dictionary of the People's Republic of the Congo (Congo-Brazzaville) LC 74-14975. (African Historical Dictionaries Ser.: No. 2). 1974. 10.00 (ISBN 0-8108-0762-9). Scarecrow.

--The Western Saharans: Background to Conflict. 348p. 1980. 27.50 (ISBN 0-389-20148-0). B&N.

Thompson, W. Scott. Ghana's Foreign Policy, Nineteen Fifty-Seven - Nineteen Sixty-Six: Diplomacy, Ideology, & the New State. LC 68-56322. 1969. 26.00x (ISBN 0-691-03076-6). Princeton U Pr.

Thompson, W. Scott & Frizzell, D. D., eds. The Lessons of Vietnam. LC 76-20821. 1977. 19.50x (ISBN 0-8448-0973-X). Crane-Russak Co.

Thompson, W. T. Agricultural Chemical Books, 4 bks. Incl. Bk. 1. Insecticides, Acaracides & Ovicides; Bk. 2. Herbicides; Vol. 3. Fumigants, Growth Regulators, Repellents, Rodenticides (ISBN 0-913702-08-0); Bk. 4. Fungicides. LC 64-24795. 1976. 13.50 ea. Thomson Pub CA.

Thompson, Waite & Gottleib, Richard M. The Santa Fe Guide. Hausman, Gerald, ed. LC 80-18575. (Illus.). 64p. (Orig.). 1980. pap. 4.50 (ISBN 0-913270-89-X). Sunstone Pr.

Thompson, Wayne N. Responsible & Effective Communication. LC 77-77006. (Illus.). 1978. text ed. 13.50 (ISBN 0-395-25075-7); inst. manual 0.55 (ISBN 0-395-25076-5). HM.

Thompson, William. Calculus with Applications in the Management & Social Sciences. (Illus.). 1977. text ed. 18.95 (ISBN 0-13-112151-0). P-H.

--Music for Listeners. (Illus.). 1978. text ed. 16.95 (ISBN 0-13-608026-X); records 16.95 (ISBN 0-13-608018-9). P-H.

Thompson, William B. Introduction to Plasma Physics. 2nd ed. 1964. text ed. 27.00 o.p. (ISBN 0-08-011180-7). Pergamon.

Thompson, William D. Preaching Biblically: Exegesis & Interpretation. (Abingdon Preacher's Library). (Orig.). 1981. pap. 4.95 (ISBN 0-687-33840-9). Abingdon.

Thompson, William I. At the Edge of History: Speculations on the Transformation of Culture. LC 70-138769. (Illus.). 1971. 9.95 o.s.i. (ISBN 0-06-014316-9, HarpT). Har-Row.

--Passages About Earth: An Exploration of the New Planetary Culture. LC 73-14298. 192p. 1981. pap. 3.95 (ISBN 0-06-090835-1, CN 835, CN). Har-Row.

Thompson, William M. Jesus, Lord & Savior. LC 80-80152. 288p. 1980. pap. 8.95 (ISBN 0-8091-2306-1). Paulist Pr.

Thompson, William R., jt. auth. see Fuller, John L.

Thomsen, Frieda. The Second Lady Cameron. 1977. pap. 1.50 (ISBN 0-505-51204-1). Tower Bks.

Thomsen, Robert. Bill W. LC 74-1861. (Illus.). 382p. 1975. 15.95 (ISBN 0-06-014267-7, HarpT). Har-Row.

Thomsett, Michael C. Builder's Office Manual. (Illus.). 1981. pap. 13.25 (ISBN 0-910460-73-6). Craftsman.

Thomsett, Rob. People & Project Management. LC 80-51921. (Illus., Orig.). 1980. pap. 10.50 (ISBN 0-917072-21-9). Yourdon.

Thomson, A. J. & Martinet, A. V. A Practical English Grammar. 3rd ed. 384p. 1980. pap. 7.95 (ISBN 0-19-431336-0). Oxford U Pr.

--A Practical English Grammar: Combined Exercises. 240p. 1979. pap. text ed. 3.95x o.p. (ISBN 0-19-432753-1). Oxford U Pr.

--A Practical English Grammar: Exercise One. 176p. 1980. 5.50x (ISBN 0-19-431337-9). Oxford U Pr.

--A Practical English Grammar: Exercises Two. 205p. 1980. 5.50x (ISBN 0-19-431338-7). Oxford U Pr.

Thomson, A. W. J. Introduction to Collective Bargining in Higher Education. (Key Issues Ser.: No. 16). 1974. pap. 2.00 (ISBN 0-87546-250-2). NY Sch Indus Rel.

Thomson, A. W. J. & Beaumont, P. B. Collective Bargaining in the British Public Sector. LC 78-71279. 1979. 25.95 (ISBN 0-03-050481-3). Praeger.

Thomson, Andrew H. The Feldman Method. rev. ed. LC 70-92025. 1977. 9.95 (ISBN 0-910580-01-4); pap. 5.95 (ISBN 0-910580-95-2). Farnswth Pub.

Thomson, Arthur. Handbook of Anatomy for Art Students. 5th ed. (Illus.). (YA) (gr. 9-12). 1929. pap. text ed. 5.00 (ISBN 0-486-21163-0). Dover.

Thomson, Bailey, ed. Historic Shreveport. LC 80-54715. (Illus.). 128p. (Orig.). 1980. pap. 6.95 (ISBN 0-939042-00-2). Shreveport Pub.

Thomson, C. Leslie, ed. see Thomson, James C.

Thomson, Charles M. & Marcus, Abraham. Electricity for Technicians. 2nd ed. (Illus.). 512p. 1975. ref. ed. 18.95 (ISBN 0-13-248658-X). P-H.

Thomson, Clarence, ed. The Resource Guide for Adult Religious Education. rev. 2nd ed. 208p. soft cover, perfect bdg. 9.95 (ISBN 0-934134-10-3). Natl Cath Reporter.

Thomson, D. F., tr. see Erasmus, Desiderius.

Thomson, Daisy. In Love, in Vienna. (Orig.). 1977. pap. 1.25 o.s.i. (ISBN 0-515-04417-2). Jove Pubns.

--Journey to Love. 1978. pap. 1.25 (ISBN 0-515-04479-2). Jove Pubns.

--Love at Leisure. (Orig.). 1978. pap. 1.50 o.s.i. (ISBN 0-515-04558-6). Jove Pubns.

--Myrtle for My Love. 1977. pap. 1.25 o.s.i. (ISBN 0-515-04242-0). Jove Pubns.

--A Nightingale for Love. 1978. pap. 1.50 o.s.i. (ISBN 0-515-04488-1). Jove Pubns.

--Prelude to Love. pap. 1.50 o.s.i. (ISBN 0-515-04445-8). Jove Pubns.

--Suddenly It Was Love. 1977. pap. 1.25 o.s.i. (ISBN 0-515-04447-4). Jove Pubns.

--A Time for Love. 1978. pap. 1.50 o.s.i. (ISBN 0-515-04430-X). Jove Pubns.

Thomson, David. The Biographical Dictionary of Film. 2nd, rev. ed. LC 80-20500. 700p. 1981. 15.95 (ISBN 0-688-00132-7); pap. 10.95 (ISBN 0-688-00131-9). Morrow.

--A Biographical Dictionary of Film. LC 75-20044. 1976. pap. 10.95 (ISBN 0-688-07974-1). Morrow.

--Democracy in France Since Eighteen Seventy. 5th ed. (Royal Institute of Int'l Affairs Ser.). (Orig.). 1969. pap. 7.95x (ISBN 0-19-285036-9). Oxford U Pr.

--Language. LC 75-24866. (Human Behavior). (Illus.). (gr. 5 up). 1975. lib. bdg. 9.99 o.p. (ISBN 0-685-72980-X, Pub. by Time-Life). Silver.

--Language. (Human Behavior Ser.). 9.95 (ISBN 0-8094-1966-1). Time-Life.

--The Seine Net: Its Origin, Evolution & Use. 1980. 12.00 (FN). Unipub.

Thomson, David & Evans, George E. The Leaping Hare. (Illus.). 1972. 9.95 (ISBN 0-571-09559-3, Pub. by Faber & Faber); pap. 4.95 (ISBN 0-571-10630-7). Merrimack Bk Serv.

Thomson, David, ed. see Smith, Elizabeth.

Thomson, E. W. Old Man Savarin Stories: Tales of Canada & Canadians. LC 73-91557. (Literature of Canada Ser.). 1974. pap. 4.50 (ISBN 0-8020-6207-5). U of Toronto Pr.

Thomson, Elizabeth, ed. see Professional Staff of Hewlett-Woodmere Public Library.

Thomson, F. J. Elsevier's Dictionary of Financial Terms. LC 79-11810. 496p. (Eng., Ger., Span., Fr., Ital., Dutch.). 1979. 122.00 (ISBN 0-686-62653-2). Elsevier.

Thomson, F. P. Money in the Computer Age. 1968. 23.00 (ISBN 0-08-012856-4); pap. 11.25 (ISBN 0-08-012855-6). Pergamon.

Thomson, G. T., ed. see Barth, Karl.

Thomson, George. The Butterflies of Scotland: A Natural History. (Illus.). 267p. 1980. 50.00x (ISBN 0-7099-0383-9, Pub. by Croom Helm Ltd England). Biblio Dist.

--The First Philosophers. 2nd ed. (Studies in Ancient Society). (Illus.). 1961-1977. pap. text ed. 6.50x (ISBN 0-85315-406-6). Humanities.

Thomson, George M. The Prime Ministers. LC 80-83530. (Illus.). 304p. 1981. 15.95 (ISBN 0-688-00432-6). Morrow.

--The Search for the Northwest Passage. LC 75-15814. (Illus.). 288p. 1975. 12.95 o.s.i. (ISBN 0-02-617750-1, 61775). Macmillan.

Thomson, George P., jt. auth. see Thomson, Joseph J.

Thomson, Harry C. China & the Powers: A Narrative of the Outbreak of 1900. LC 79-2840. (Illus.). 285p. 1981. Repr. of 1902 ed. 26.50 (ISBN 0-8305-0017-0). Hyperion Conn.

Thomson, J., et al. Frequency Conversion. (Wykeham Technology Ser.: No. 1). 1969. 9.95x (ISBN 0-8448-1172-6). Crane Russak Co.

Thomson, J. A. Popes & Princes Fourteen Seventeen to Fifteen Seventeen: Politics & Polity in Late Medieval Church. (Early Modern Europe Today Ser.). 256p. 1980. text ed. 19.50x (ISBN 0-04-901027-1, 2546). Allen Unwin.

Thomson, J. A., tr. see Tredennick, Hugh.

Thomson, J. M. A Field Guide to the Common Sea & Estuary Fishes of Ono-Tropical Australia. 144p. 1980. 17.95x (ISBN 0-00-219271-3, Pub. by W Collins Australia). Intl Schol Bk Serv.

Thomson, J. Oliver. History of Ancient Geography. LC 64-23024. 1948. 15.00x (ISBN 0-8196-0143-8). Biblo.

Thomson, J. R. An Introduction to Seed Technology. LC 79-4412. 252p. 1979. 49.95 (ISBN 0-470-26644-9). Halsted Pr.

Thomson, J. S. Personalities of the West & Midwest. 6th ed. 579p. 1980. 44.95x (ISBN 0-934544-07-7, Pub. by Intl Biog). Biblio Dist.

Thomson, J. S., ed. Community Leaders & Noteworthy Americans. 10th ed. 609p. 1980. 44.95x (ISBN 0-934544-02-6, Pub. by Intl Biog). Biblio Dist.

--Personalities of the South. 9th ed. 641p. 1980. 44.95x (ISBN 0-686-28826-2, Pub. by Intl Biog). Biblio Dist.

--Personalities of the South. 10th ed. 634p. 1981. 49.95x (ISBN 0-934544-03-4, Pub. by Intl Biog). Biblio Dist.

Thomson, James C. Your Heart. Thomson, C. Leslie, ed. 80p. 1974. pap. 3.50x (ISBN 0-8464-1058-3). Beekman Pubs.

Thomson, James W. An Introduction to the Fundamentals of Financial Analysis for Business Students. LC 79-8512. 1979. pap. text ed. 12.25 (ISBN 0-8191-0872-3). U Pr of Amer.

Thomson, Jessie. Natural & Healthy Childhood. 120p. 1976. pap. 6.00x (ISBN 0-8464-1034-6). Beekman Pubs.

Thomson, John, jt. auth. see Graham, Daniel.

Thomson, John A. Introduction to Clinical Endocrinology. 2nd ed. (Churchill Livingstone Medical Text Ser.). (Illus.). 220p. 1981. text ed. 10.75 (ISBN 0-443-02307-7). Churchill.

Thomson, Joseph J. & Thomson, George P. Conduction of Electricity Through Gases, 2 Vols. LC 68-8881. (Illus.). 1969. pap. text ed. 4.50 ea.; Vol. 1. pap. text ed. (ISBN 0-486-62007-7); Vol. 2. pap. text ed. (ISBN 0-486-62008-5). Dover.

Thomson, Katharine. The Masonic Thread in Mozart. (Illus.). 1977. text ed. 13.50x (ISBN 0-85315-381-7). Humanities.

Thomson, Malcolm M. The Beginning of the Long Dash: A History of Timekeeping in Canada. 1978. 17.50x (ISBN 0-8020-5383-1). U of Toronto Pr.

Thomson, Oliver. Mass Persuasion in History: An Historical Analysis of the Development of Propaganda Techniques. 1977. 14.50 (ISBN 0-8448-1076-2). Crane-Russak Co.

Thomson, Patricia. George Sand & the Victorians: Her Influence & Reputation in 19th Century England. 1976. 20.00x (ISBN 0-231-04262-0). Columbia U Pr.

Thomson, Patricia, ed. Wyatt: The Critical Heritage. (The Critical Heritage Ser.). 196p. 1974. 24.00 (ISBN 0-7100-7907-9). Routledge & Kegan.

Thomson, Paul Van K. Francis Thompson: A Critical Biography. LC 73-165666. 280p. 1973. Repr. of 1961 ed. text ed. 9.00 (ISBN 0-87752-155-7). Gordian.

Thomson, Robert G., jt. auth. see Abramoff, Peter.

Thomson, Robert W., ed. see Moses Of Chorene.

Thomson, Rosemary. The Price of Liberty. 1978. 3.95 (ISBN 0-88419-183-4, Pub by Mansions Pr). Creation Hse.

Thomson, Tom. Ideas from Chemistry. (Science Modules Ser.). (gr. 7-8). 1973. pap. text ed. 6.44 (ISBN 0-201-07578-4, Sch Div); tchr's manual 2.84 (ISBN 0-201-07579-2). A-W.

Thomson, W. T. Agricultural Chemicals, Book 1: Insecticides. rev. ed. 240p. 1981. pap. 13.50 (ISBN 0-913702-13-7). Thomson Pub Ca.

--Agricultural Chemicals, Book 2: Herbicides. rev. ed. 260p. 1981. pap. 13.50 (ISBN 0-913702-12-9). Thomson Pub Ca.

--Tree, Turf & Ornamental Pesticide Guide, 1976. rev. ed. 1979. pap. 10.00 (ISBN 0-913702-02-1). Thomson Pub Ca.

Thomson, W. T., jt. auth. see Page, B. G.

Thomson, William. Theory of Vibrations with Applications. 2nd ed. (Illus.). 608p. 1981. text ed. 26.95 (ISBN 0-13-914523-0). P-H.

Thomson, William, ed. see Gillett, Dorothy.

Thomson, William A. Herbs That Heal. LC 77-72361. (Encore Edition). (Illus.). 1977. pap. 1.95 (ISBN 0-684-16928-2, ScribT). Scribner.

Thomson, William E. Introduction to Music Reading: Concepts & Applications. 2nd ed. 320p. 1980. pap. text ed. 12.95x (ISBN 0-534-00817-8). Wadsworth Pub.

Thomson, William T. Theory of Vibration with Applications. (Illus.). 480p. 1973. 26.95 (ISBN 0-13-914549-4). P-H.

Thonet Co. Thonet Bentwood & Other Furniture: The 1904 Illustrated Catalogue & Supplements. (Illus.). 154p. 1980. pap. 8.95 (ISBN 0-486-24024-X). Dover.

Thonner, F. The Flowering Plants of Africa: An Analytical Key to the Genera of African Phanerogams. 1962. Repr. of 1916 ed. 90.00 (ISBN 3-7682-0118-X). Lubrecht & Cramer.

Thonssen, Lester, et al. Speech Criticism. 2nd ed. 1970. 18.50 o.p. (ISBN 0-8260-8645-4). Wiley.

Thorbjarnarson, Bjorn. Surgery of the Biliary Tract. LC 74-25482. (Mpcs Ser.: Vol. 16). (Illus.). 166p. 1975. text ed. 18.00 (ISBN 0-7216-8858-6). Saunders.

Thorburn, Anna H. & Turner, Phyllis. Living Salt Free and Easy! LC 74-16983. (Illus.). 210p. 1975. 8.95 (ISBN 0-913264-19-9). Douglas-West.

Thorburn, Hugh G. Politics in New Brunswick. 1961 ed. LC 63-25108. 17.50x o.p. (ISBN 0-8020-7057-4). U of Toronto Pr.

Thore, Sten. Programming the Network of Financial Intermediation. 224p. 1983. pap. text ed. 14.00x (ISBN 82-00-05379-2). Universitet.

Thoreau, David. The Santanic Condition. LC 80-66499. 1981. 10.95 (ISBN 0-87795-274-4). Arbor Hse.

Thoreau, Henry D. Cape Cod. (Apollo Eds.). (YA) (gr. 9-12). pap. 4.95 (ISBN 0-8152-0116-8, A116, TYC-T). T Y Crowell.

--Clear Sky, Pure Light: Encounters with Henry David Thoreau. Childs, Christopher, ed. LC 78-56627. 1978. 12.00 (ISBN 0-915778-27-0); deluxe ed. 50.00x (ISBN 0-915778-26-2). Penmaen Pr.

--Consciousness in Concord: The Text of Thoreau's Hitherto "Lost Journal," 1840-1841. LC 80-2519. 1981. Repr. of 1958 ed. 29.50 (ISBN 0-404-19067-7). AMS Pr.

--The First & Last Journeys of Thoreau, 2 vols. in 1. Sanborn, Franklin B., ed. LC 80-2520. 1981. Repr. of 1905 ed. 45.00 (ISBN 0-404-19068-5). AMS Pr.

--Henry David Thoreau: Essays, Journals & Poems. Flower, Dean, ed. 640p. (Orig.). 1975. pap. 2.50 o.p. (ISBN 0-449-22378-7, L2378, Crest). Fawcett.

--Maine Woods. (Apollo Eds.). (YA) (gr. 9-12). pap. 4.95 (ISBN 0-8152-0117-6, A117, TYC-T). T Y Crowell.

--The Moon. LC 80-2521. 1981. Repr. of 1927 ed. 17.50 (ISBN 0-404-19069-3). AMS Pr.

--Sir Walter Raleigh. Sanborn, Franklin B., ed. LC 80-2523. 1981. Repr. of 1905 ed. 24.50 (ISBN 0-686-28929-3). AMS Pr.

--Some Unpublished Letters of Henry D. & Sophia E. Thoreau: A Chapter in the History of a Still-Born Book. Jones, Samuel A., ed. LC 80-2684. 1981. Repr. of 1899 ed. 15.50 (ISBN 0-404-19078-2). AMS Pr.

--Thoreau: Selected Writings. Leary, Lewis, ed. LC 58-5337. (Crofts Classics Ser.). 1958. pap. text ed. 2.95 (ISBN 0-88295-099-1). AHM Pub.

--Thoreaus Minnesota Journey: Two Documents. Harding, Walter, ed. LC 80-2524. 1981. Repr. of 1962 ed. 18.50 (ISBN 0-404-19072-3). AMS Pr.

--Walden. (Literature Ser). (gr. 7-12). 1969. pap. text ed. 3.67 (ISBN 0-87720-719-4). AMSCO Sch.

--Walden, 2vols. Sanborn, F. B., ed. LC 80-2685. 1981. Repr. of 1909 ed. 58.50 (ISBN 0-404-19080-4). AMS Pr.

--Walden & Civil Disobedience. Thomas, Owen, ed. (Critical Editions). (Annotated). (gr. 9-12). 1966. pap. text ed. 4.95x (ISBN 0-393-09665-3, Nortonc). Norton.

--Walden & Civil Disobedience. 1973. pap. 1.75 (ISBN 0-451-51339-8, CE1339, Sig Classics). NAL.

--Walden & Other Writings. pap. 1.75. Bantam.

--Walden: Selected Essays. Whicher, George F., ed. 1973. pap. 3.45 (ISBN 0-87532-109-7). Hendricks House.

--Walden with Reader's Guide. (Literature Program Ser.). (Orig.). (gr. 7-12). 1973. pap. text ed. 4.33 (ISBN 0-87720-818-2); tchr's ed. s.p. 2.80 (ISBN 0-87720-918-9). AMSCO Sch.

Thoreau, Henry D. see Kaiser, Leo.

Thoreau, Henry D; see Lynd, Staughton.

Thoreau, Henry David. Walden. pap. 2.95 (ISBN 0-385-09503-1, C10, Anch). Doubleday.

Thorek, Philip. Surgical Diagnosis. 3rd ed. LC 77-8532. (Illus.). 1977. 24.75 o.p. (ISBN 0-397-50370-9). Lippincott.

Thorelli, Hans & Becker, Helmut, eds. International Marketing Strategy. rev. ed. LC 80-14689. (Pergamon Policy Studies on Business). 400p. 1980. 40.00 (ISBN 0-08-025542-6); pap. 12.95 (ISBN 0-08-025543-4). Pergamon.

Thorelli, Hans, et al. The Information Seekers: An International Study of Consumer Information & Advertising Image. LC 74-9635. 288p. 1975. text ed. 20.00 o.p. (ISBN 0-88410-265-3). Ballinger Pub.

Thorelli, Hans B. & Thorelli, Sarah V. Consumer Information Handbook: Europe & North America. LC 73-10953. (Special Studies). 526p. 1974. 24.95 (ISBN 0-275-07890-6). Praeger.

Thorelli, Hans B., et al. Player's Manual for International Operations Simulation. LC 63-13249. 1963. pap. text ed. 7.95 (ISBN 0-02-932530-7). Free Pr.

Thorelli, Sarah V., jt. auth. see Thorelli, Hans B.

Thorensen, Marilyn J., ed. see Shirley, James.

Thoresen, Carl E. The Behavior Therapist. LC 80-11725. 120p. (Orig.). 1980. pap. text ed. 5.95 (ISBN 0-8185-0408-0). Brooks-Cole.

Thorington, Richard, Jr., ed. see Institute for Laboratory Animal Resources.

Thorlin, Anders. Ideas for Woodturning. (Creative Handcrafts Ser.). (Illus.). 128p. 1980. 12.95 (ISBN 0-13-450361-9, Spec); pap. 5.95 (ISBN 0-13-450353-8). P-H.

Thorlin, Eldora & Brannen, Noah. Everyday Japanese. LC 69-19854. 180p. 1969. 3.95 (ISBN 0-8348-0037-3). Weatherhill.

Thorlin, Eldora & Henthorn, Taesoon. Everyday Korean. LC 71-183519. 180p. 1972. 3.95 (ISBN 0-8348-0069-1). Weatherhill.

Thorman, George. Family Therapy: A Handbook. LC 65-28619. 1965. pap. 6.50x o.p. (ISBN 0-87424-047-6). Western Psych.

--Family Violence. 196p. 1980. text ed. 16.50 (ISBN 0-398-03953-4). C C Thomas.

Thorman, Richard. Bachman's Law: A Novel. 1981. 12.95 (ISBN 0-393-01443-6). Norton.

Thorn, Caroline & Thorn, Frank, eds. Somerset: From a Draft Translation Prepared by Frank Thorn. (Domesday Book Ser.). (Illus.). 405p. 1980. 32.50x (ISBN 0-8476-3261-X). Rowman.

Thorn, Caroline, jt. ed. see Thorn, Frank.

Thorn, Frank, ed. Rutland. (Domesday Book Ser.). (Illus.). 52p. (From a draft translation prepared by Celia Parker). 1980. 15.00x (ISBN 0-8476-3260-1). Rowman.

Thorn, Frank & Thorn, Caroline, eds. Northamptonshire. (Domesday Bk.: Vol. 21). (Illus.). 231p. 1980. 20.00x (ISBN 0-8476-3142-7). Rowman.

Thorn, Frank, jt. ed. see Thorn, Caroline.

Thorn, John. Baseball's Ten Greatest Games. LC 80-66251. (Illus.). 208p. (gr. 5 up). 1981. 9.95 (ISBN 0-590-07665-5, Four Winds). Schol Bk Serv.

Thorn, John, et al. History of England: From Prehistoric Times to the End of World War Two. (Apollo Eds.). (YA) (gr. 9-12). pap. 4.50 o.s.i. (ISBN 0-8152-0070-6, A70, TYC-T). T Y Crowell.

Thorn, Richard S. Monetary Theory & Policy. LC 75-41865. 1976. pap. 9.95 o.p. (ISBN 0-275-64470-7). Praeger.

Thornberg, Newton. Valhalla. 372p. 1981. 10.95 (ISBN 0-316-84393-8). Little.

Thornberg, Samual T. The Complete Handbook of Electrical Principles & Applications. 1980. 24.95 o.p. (ISBN 0-932812-02-3). Bradley CPA.

Thornberg, Samual T., jt. auth. see Johnson, Phillip A.

Thornberry, Terence P. & Sagarin, Edward, eds. Images of Crime: Offenders & Victims. LC 73-21460. (Special Studies). (Illus.). 150p. 1974. text ed. 24.95 (ISBN 0-275-08640-2). Praeger.

Thornborough, Laura. Great Smoky Mountains. rev. ed. (Illus.). 1962. 7.50 (ISBN 0-87049-034-6). U of Tenn Pr.

Thorndike, ed. Minor Elizabethan Drama, Vol. 2. 1959. 5.00x o.p. (ISBN 0-460-00492-1, Evman). Dutton.

Thorndike, E. L. Animal Intelligence: Experimental Studies. 1965. Repr. of 1911 ed. 11.95 (ISBN 0-02-853470-0). Hafner.

--Human Nature & the Social Order. 1019p. 1980. Repr. of 1940 ed. lib. bdg. 100.00 (ISBN 0-89987-812-1). Darby Bks.

Thorndike, Edward. The Human Nature Club. 231p. 1980. Repr. of 1900 ed. lib. bdg. 25.00 (ISBN 0-8492-8410-4). R West.

Thorndike, Edward L. The Psychology of Arithmetic. 314p. 1980. Repr. of 1922 ed. lib. bdg. 30.00 (ISBN 0-89760-890-9). Telegraph Bks.

--A Teacher's Word Book of the Twenty Thousand Words Found Most Frequently & Widely in General Reading for Children & Young People. rev. ed. LC 73-5527. 182p. 1975. Repr. of 1932 ed. 22.00 (ISBN 0-8103-4108-5). Gale.

Thorndike, Jack. The Complete Trout & Salmon Fisherman. LC 78-60987. (Illus.). 1978. 17.95 (ISBN 0-7153-7717-5). David & Charles.

Thorndike, Joseph J., ed. see Laing, Alexander.

Thorndike, Joseph J., Jr. Discovery of Lost Worlds. LC 79-15881. (Illus.). 352p. 1980. 14.95 (ISBN 0-8281-0312-7, Dist by Scribner); pap. 9.95 (ISBN 0-686-65846-9). Scribner.

--The Magnificent Builders & Their Dream Houses. LC 78-18371. (Illus.). 352p. 1978. 12.95 (ISBN 0-8281-3064-7, Dist. by Scribner); deluxe ed. 39.95 slipcased (ISBN 0-8281-3072-8). Am Heritage.

--The Very Rich: A History of Wealth. LC 76-22578. (Illus.). 352p. 1976. deluxe ed. 345.00 (ISBN 0-8281-0334-8, Dist. by Scribner). Am Heritage.

Thorndike, Joseph J., Jr., ed. Discovery of Lost Worlds. LC 79-15881. (Illus.). 352p. 1979. 34.95 (ISBN 0-8281-0308-9, Dist. by Scribner); deluxe ed. 39.95 (ISBN 0-8281-0309-7, Dist. by Scribner). Am Heritage.

--Mysteries of the Deep. LC 80-7804. (Illus.). 352p. 1980. 34.95 (ISBN 0-8281-0407-7, Dist. by Scribner); deluxe ed. 39.95 (ISBN 0-8281-0408-5, Dist. by Scribner). Am Heritage.

Thorndike, Joseph J., Jr., ed. see Casson, Lionel, et al.

Thorndike, Lynn. A History of Magic & Experimental Science, 8 vols. Incl. Vols. 1 & 2. The First Thirteen Centuries. 1923. Vol. 1. (ISBN 0-231-08794-2); Vol. 2. (ISBN 0-231-08795-0); Vols. 3 & 4. Fourteenth & Fifteenth Centuries. Vol. 3. (ISBN 0-231-08796-9); Vol. 4. (ISBN 0-231-08797-7). Vols. 5 & 6. The Sixteenth Century. 1941. Vol. 5. (ISBN 0-231-08798-5); Vol. 6. (ISBN 0-231-08799-3); Vols. 7 & 8. The Eighteenth Century. 1958. Vol. 7. (ISBN 0-231-08800-0); Vol. 8. (ISBN 0-231-08801-9). LC 23-2984. 30.00x ea. Columbia U Pr.

Thorndike, Lynn, tr. University Records & Life in the Middle Ages. (Columbia University Records of Civilization Ser.). 476p. 1975. pap. text ed. 6.95x (ISBN 0-393-09216-X). Norton.

Thorndike Press, ed. Maine Animals. LC 78-9725. (Maine Nature Ser.). (Illus.). lib. bdg. 8.50 o.p. (ISBN 0-89621-013-8); pap. 2.95x (ISBN 0-89621-012-X). Thorndike Pr.

--Maine Birds. LC 78-9702. (Maine Nature Ser.). (Illus.). 1978. 8.50x o.p. (ISBN 0-89621-011-1); pap. 2.95x o.p. (ISBN 0-89621-010-3). Thorndike Pr.

--Maine Fish. LC 78-17234. (Maine Nature Ser.). (Illus.). 1978. 8.50x o.p. (ISBN 0-89621-015-4); pap. 2.95x o.p. (ISBN 0-89621-014-6). Thorndike Pr.

--Maine Rivers. LC 79-12996. (Maine Nature Ser.). (Illus., Orig.). 1979. lib. bdg. 8.50x o.p. (ISBN 0-89621-039-1); pap. 2.95x (ISBN 0-89621-038-3). Thorndike Pr.

Thorndike, R. M. Correlational Procedures for Research. LC 76-8462. 340p. 1978. 21.50 (ISBN 0-470-15090-4). Halsted Pr.

Thorndike, Rachel S., ed. Sherman Letters. 2nd ed. LC 68-8693. (American Scene Ser.). 1969. Repr. of 1894 ed. lib. bdg. 39.50 (ISBN 0-306-71175-3). Da Capo.

Thorndike, Robert M. Principles of Data Collection. (Gardner Press Ser. on Measurement & Statistics). 350p. 1981. text ed. 22.00 (ISBN 0-89876-022-4). Gardner Pr.

Thorndike, Susan. The Electric Radish & Other Jokes. LC 75-183615. 48p. (gr. 1-3). 1973. PLB 4.95 (ISBN 0-385-06401-2). Doubleday.

Thorne. Introductory Statistics for Psychology. LC 79-10613. 1980. text ed. 14.95 (ISBN 0-87872-222-X). Duxbury Pr.

Thorne, Christopher. Approach of War, 1938-1939. (gr. 11 up). 1969. 6.95 (ISBN 0-312-04655-3). St Martin.

Thorne, D. Wynne, jt. auth. see Thorne, Marlowe D.

Thorne, David, ed. see Kerry, John F., Jr. & Vietnamese Veterans Against the War.

Thorne, Evelyn. Of Bones & Stars. 24p. (Orig.). 1981. pap. 3.00 (ISBN 0-934996-12-1). Am Stud Pr.

Thorne, Guy, tr. see Gautier, Theophile.

Thorne, Ian. The Great Centers. (Stars of the NHL Ser.). (Illus.). (gr. 4-12). 1976. PLB 7.95 (ISBN 0-87191-492-1). Creative Ed.

--The Great Defensemen. (Stars of the NHL Ser.). (Illus.). (gr. 4-12). 1976. PLB 7.95 (ISBN 0-87191-493-X). Creative Ed.

--The Great Goalies. (Stars of the NHL Ser.). (Illus.). (gr. 4-12). 1976. PLB 7.95 (ISBN 0-87191-491-3). Creative Ed.

--The Great Wingmen. (Stars of the NHL Ser.). (Illus.). (gr. 4-12). 1976. PLB 7.95 (ISBN 0-87191-494-8). Creative Ed.

--Meet the Defensive Linemen. (Meet the Players: Football). (Illus.). (gr. 2-4). 1975. PLB 5.45 o.p. (ISBN 0-87191-467-0). Creative Ed.

--Meet the Linebackers. (Meet the Players: Football). (Illus.). (gr. 2-4). 1975. PLB 5.45 o.p. (ISBN 0-87191-471-9). Creative Ed.

--Meet the Quarterbacks. (Meet the Players: Football). (Illus.). (gr. 2-4). 1975. PLB 5.45 o.p. (ISBN 0-87191-469-7). Creative Ed.

--Meet the Receivers. (Meet the Players: Football). (Illus.). (gr. 2-4). 1975. PLB 5.45 o.p. (ISBN 0-87191-468-9). Creative Ed.

--Meet the Running Backs. (Meet the Players: Football). (Illus.). (gr. 2-4). 1977. PLB 5.45 o.p. (ISBN 0-87191-470-0). Creative Ed.

Thorne, J. O. & Collocott, T. C., eds. Chambers Biographical Dictionary. LC 75-56110. 1974. 25.00 (ISBN 0-8467-0510-9, Pub. by Two Continents). Hippocrene Bks.

Thorne, Marlowe D. & Thorne, D. Wynne. Soil, Water & Crop Production. 1979. text ed. 18.50 (ISBN 0-87055-281-3). AVI.

Thorne, Martha C. Handling Your Own Dog--for Show Obedience & Field Trials. LC 73-81451. (Illus.). 1979. 17.95 (ISBN 0-385-07391-7). Doubleday.

Thorne, Nicola. The Perfect Wife & Mother. 266p. 1981. 11.95 (ISBN 0-312-60077-1). St Martin.

--Sisters & Lovers. LC 80-509. 600p. 1981. 14.95 (ISBN 0-385-15857-2). Doubleday.

Thorne, Ramsay. Renagade No. Four: Death Hunter. (Orig.). 1980. pap. 1.95 (ISBN 0-446-90902-5). Warner Bks.

--Renagade No. Three: Fear Merchant. (Orig.). 1980. pap. 1.95 (ISBN 0-446-90761-8). Warner Bks.

--Renegade No. Eight: Over the Andes to Hell. 192p. (Orig.). 1981. pap. 1.95 (ISBN 0-446-90549-6). Warner Bks.

--Renegade No. Five: Macumba Killer. 224p. (Orig.). 1980. pap. 1.95 (ISBN 0-446-90234-9). Warner Bks.

--Renegade No. One. (Orig.). 1979. pap. 1.95 (ISBN 0-446-90976-9). Warner Bks.

--Renegade No. Seven: Death in High Places. 192p. (Orig.). 1981. pap. 1.95 (ISBN 0-446-90548-8). Warner Bks.

--Renegade No. Six: Panama Gunner. 256p. (Orig.). 1980. pap. 1.95 (ISBN 0-446-90235-7). Warner Bks.

--Renegade No. Two: Blood Runner. (Orig.). 1979. pap. 1.75 (ISBN 0-446-94231-6). Warner Bks.

Thorne, Robert, ed. Fugitive Facts. 2nd ed. LC 69-19882. 1969. Repr. of 1889 ed. 20.00 (ISBN 0-8103-3750-9). Gale.

Thorne, Sabina. Reruns. LC 80-52008. 228p. 1981. 11.95 (ISBN 0-670-59526-8). Viking Pr.

Thorne, Samuel, ed. see Bentham, Jeremy.

Thorne, Samuel, jt. ed. see Berkowitz, David.

Thorne, Samuel, ed. see Best, William M.

Thorne, Samuel, ed. see Brydall, John.

Thorne, Samuel, ed. see Chitty, Joseph.

Thorne, Samuel, ed. see De Lolme, Jean L.

Thorne, Samuel, ed. see Finch, Sir Henry.

Thorne, Samuel, ed. see Hale, Sir Matthew.

Thorne, Samuel, ed. see Hallam, Henry.

Thorne, Samuel, ed. see Holt, Francis L.

Thorne, Samuel, ed. see Kyd, Stewart.

Thorne, Samuel, ed. see Lodowick, Lloyd.

Thorne, Samuel, ed. see Manwood, John.

Thorne, Samuel, ed. see Nolan, Michael.

Thorne, Samuel, ed. see Palmer, Sir Francis B.

Thorne, Samuel, ed. see Petyt, George.

Thorne, Samuel, ed. see Powell, John J.

Thorne, Samuel, ed. see Sheppard, William.

Thorne, Samuel E. see Jones, Sir William.

Thorne, Samuel E., ed. see Acherley, Roger.

Thorne, Samuel E., ed. see Anstey, Thomas, et al.

Thorne, Samuel E., ed. see Bacon, Francis & Francis, Richard.

Thorne, Samuel E., ed. see Bacon, Sir Francis.

Thorne, Samuel E., jt. ed. see Berkowitz, David S.

Thorne, Samuel E., ed. see Best, William M. & Stephen, James F.

Thorne, Samuel E., ed. see Blackstone, Sir William.

Thorne, Samuel E., ed. see Blount, Charles, et al.

Thorne, Samuel E., ed. see Bott, Edmund.

Thorne, Samuel E., ed. see Bracton, Henry.

Thorne, Samuel E., ed. see Brydall, John & Highmore, Anthony.

Thorne, Samuel E., ed. see Buller, Francis.

Thorne, Samuel E., ed. see Chitty, Joseph.

Thorne, Samuel E., ed. see Chitty, Joseph, Jr.

Thorne, Samuel E., ed. see Coke, Edward & Highmore, Anthony, Jr.

Thorne, Samuel E., ed. see Davenport, Humphrey.

Thorne, Samuel E., ed. see De Lolme, Jea L.

Thorne, Samuel E., ed. see Filmer, Sir Robert.

Thorne, Samuel E., ed. see Gilbert, Sir Gefrey & Peake, Thomas.

Thorne, Samuel E., ed. see Hale, Matthew & Giles, Jacob.

Thorne, Samuel E., ed. see Hammond, Henry.

Thorne, Samuel E., ed. see Haslam, John.

Thorne, Samuel E., ed. see Hawkins, William.

Thorne, Samuel E., ed. see Heale, William & Swinburne, Henry.

Thorne, Samuel E., ed. see Jacob, Giles, et al.

Thorne, Samuel E., ed. see Jenkins, David, et al.

Thorne, Samuel E., ed. see Littlton, Thomas.

Thorne, Samuel E., ed. see Mantell, Walter, et al.

Thorne, Samuel E., ed. see Nelson, William.

Thorne, Samuel E., ed. see Perkins, John.

Thorne, Samuel E., ed. see Pettus, Sir John.

Thorne, Samuel E., ed. see Pratt, John T.

Thorne, Samuel E., ed. see Prynne, Wiliam, et al.

Thorne, Samuel E., ed. see Pulton, Ferdinand.

Thorne, Samuel E., ed. see Raleigh, Sir Walter, et al.

Thorne, Samuel E., ed. see Robinson, Henry, et al.

Thorne, Samuel E., ed. see Russell, Sir William O.

Thorne, Samuel E., ed. see Somers, John & Jacob, Giles.

Thorne, Samuel E., ed. see Staunford, William & Romilly, Samuel.

Thorne, Samuel E., ed. see Stephen, Henry J.

Thorne, Samuel E., ed. see Swinburne, Henry.

Thorne, Samuel E., ed. see Theloall, Simon.

Thorne, Samuel E., ed. see Toland, John, et al.

Thorne, Samuel E., ed. see Towers, Joseph & Maseres, Francis.

Thorne, Samuel E., ed. see Tyrrell, Sir James.

Thorne, Samuel E., ed. see Webb, Philip C. & Grove, Joseph.

Thorne, Samuel E., ed. see West, Richard, et al.

Thorne, Samuel E., ed. see West, William.

Thorne, Samuel E., ed. see White, George.

Thorne, Samuel E., ed. see Williams, Thomas & Somers, John.

Thorne, Samuel E., ed. see Wood, Thomas.

Thorne, William. The Low Carbohydrate Dieter's Cookbook. 1978. pap. 1.50 o.p. (ISBN 0-523-40194-9). Pinnacle Bks.

Thorner, Marvin E. Convenience & Fast Food Handbook. (Illus.). 1973. text ed. 24.50 (ISBN 0-87055-134-5). AVI.

Thorner, Marvin E. & Herzberg, R. J. Non-Alcoholic Food Service Beverage Handbook. 2nd ed. 1979. lib. bdg. 29.00 (ISBN 0-87055-279-1). AVI.

Thorner, Marvin E. & Manning, Peter B. Quality Control in Food Service. (Illus.). 1976. lib. bdg. 29.50 o.p. (ISBN 0-87055-195-7); pap. text ed. 17.50 (ISBN 0-87055-309-7). AVI.

Thorner, Michael O., et al. Bromocriptine: A Clinical & Pharmacologica Review. 189p. 1980. text ed. 24.00 (ISBN 0-89004-419-8). Raven.

Thornes, Barbara & Collard, Jean. Who Divorces? (Orig.). 1979. pap. 14.50 (ISBN 0-685-67323-5). Routledge & Kegan.

Thornes, John, jt. ed. see Embleton, Clifford.

Thorne-Thomsen, Kathleen & Brownridge, Linda. Why the Cake Won't Rise & the Jelly Won't Set: A Complete Guide to Avoiding Kitchen Failures. LC 78-6997. (Illus.). 1979. 10.95 (ISBN 0-89479-036-6). A & W Pubs.

Thornett, John. How to Play Rugby Union. (Illus.). 157p. 1976. pap. 5.25 (ISBN 0-909950-09-1). Reed.

Thornley, Jennifer, jt. auth. see Minns, Richard.

Thorns, David C. Quest for Community: Social Aspects of Residential Growth. LC 75-16914. 1976. 19.95 (ISBN 0-470-86494-X). Halsted Pr.

Thornton, A. P. Imperialism in the Twentieth Century. LC 77-81211. xii, 363p. 1980. pap. 10.95x (ISBN 0-8166-0993-4). U of Minn Pr.

--Imperialism in the Twentieth Century. LC 77-81211. 1978. 22.50x (ISBN 0-8166-0820-2). U of Minn Pr.

Thornton, Billy M. & Preston, Paul. An Introduction to Management Science: Quantitative Approach to Managerial Decisions. (Business Ser.). 1977. text ed. 18.95 (ISBN 0-675-08518-7); instructor's manual 3.95 (ISBN 0-686-67524-X); card deck 3.95 (ISBN 0-686-67525-8); transparencies 3.95 (ISBN 0-686-67526-6). Merrill.

Thornton, Carol A., jt. auth. see Bley, Nancy S.

Thornton, Carolyn. The Heart Never Forgets. 192p. (Orig.). 1980. pap. 1.50 (ISBN 0-671-57019-6). S&S.

Thornton, E. C. South Coast Pleasure Steamers. (Illus.). 1967. pap. 7.95 o.p. (ISBN 0-7153-4203-7). David & Charles.

Thornton, Henry D. The Metaphysics of the Womb. (Illus.). 141p. 1981. 49.85 (ISBN 0-89266-271-9). Am Classical Coll Pr.

Thornton, J. Quinn. Camp of Death: The Donner Party Mountain Camp, 1846-47. Jones, William R., ed. 1978. pap. 4.95 (ISBN 0-89646-037-1). Outbooks.

Thornton, John W., ed. Pulpit of the American Revolution: Political Sermons of the Period of 1776. LC 71-109611. (Era of the American Revolution Ser). 1970. Repr. of 1860 ed. lib. bdg. 45.00 (ISBN 0-306-71907-X). Da Capo.

Thornton, Judith, ed. Economic Analysis of the Soviet-Type System. LC 75-12468. 256p. 1976. 54.00 (ISBN 0-521-20718-5). Cambridge U Pr.

Thornton, Norman. Management Accounting. 1978. pap. text ed. 21.00x (ISBN 0-434-91960-8). Intl Ideas.

Thornton, Peter. Baroque & Rococo Silks. 1965. 33.00 o.p. (ISBN 0-571-06315-2, Pub. by Faber & Faber). Merrimack Bk Serv.

Thornton, R. H. British Shipping. 2nd ed. (English Institution Ser.). 1959. 29.95 (ISBN 0-521-06626-3). Cambridge U Pr.

Thornton, R. K., ed. see Hopkins, Gerard M.

Thornton, Richard C. China: A Political History. 500p. (Orig.). 1981. lib. bdg. 27.50x (ISBN 0-86531-197-8); pap. text ed. 12.00x (ISBN 0-86531-198-6). Westview.

--China, the Struggle for Power, 1917-1972. LC 73-77856. 416p. 1974. 15.00x (ISBN 0-253-31353-8). Ind U Pr.

Thornton, Robert. William Maxwell to Robert Burns. 269p. 1980. text ed. 26.00x (ISBN 0-85976-052-9). Humanities.

Thornton, W. T. Overpopulation, & Its Remedy. 446p. 1971. Repr. of 1846 ed. 25.00x (ISBN 0-686-28337-6, Pub. by Irish Academic Pr). Biblio Dist.

Thornton, Weldon. J. M. Synge & the Western Mind. (Irish Literary Studies: No. 4). 1979. text ed. 20.75x (ISBN 0-901072-89-3). Humanities.

Thornton, Wendy A., ed. Hydrotransport Bibliography. 1970. text ed. 25.00 (ISBN 0-900983-09-4, Dist. by Air Science Co.). BHRA Fluid.

Thornton, Wendy A. & Richardson, Christine A., eds. Jet Cutting Technology: A Bibliography. 1973. pap. 24.00 (ISBN 0-900983-22-1, Dist. by Air Science Co.). BHRA Fluid.

Thornton, William T. On Labour: Its Wrongful Claims & Rightful Dues: Its Actual Present & Possible Future. 2nd ed. (The Development of Industrial Society Ser.). 499p. 1980. Repr. 35.00x (ISBN 0-7165-1788-4, Pub. by Irish Academic Pr). Biblio Dist.

Thornton, Willis. Almanac for Americans. LC 70-175784. (Illus.). viii, 418p. 1973. Repr. of 1941 ed. 22.00 (ISBN 0-8103-3276-0). Gale.

Thorogood, Lucy Lopez de see Robson, Ernest.

Thorold, Algar, tr. from It. & see St. Catherine Of Siena.

Thorold, C. A. Diseases of Cocoa. (Illus.). 438p. 1975. text ed. 54.00x (ISBN 0-19-854507-X). Oxford U Pr.

Thorold, H. & Williams, T. B. Staffordshire: a Shell Guide. (Illus.). 1978. 14.95 (ISBN 0-571-10516-5, Pub. by Faber & Faber). Merrimack Bk Serv.

Thorold, Henry. County Durham: A Shell Guide. (Illus.). 192p. 1981. 14.95 (ISBN 0-571-11640-X, Pub. by Faber & Faber). Merrimack Bk Serv.

Thorold, Henry, jt. auth. see Yates, Jack.

Thorou, L., jt. auth. see Heilbroner, R.

Thoroughbread Owners & Breeders Association. Sires of Runners of 1978: Supplement. 1978. lib. bdg. 15.00 (ISBN 0-936032-17-0); pap. 10.00 (ISBN 0-936032-18-9). Thoroughbred Own and Breed.

--Stakes Winners of 1978: Supplement. 1978. lib. bdg. 15.00 (ISBN 0-936032-21-9); pap. 10.00 (ISBN 0-936032-22-7). Thoroughbred Own and Breed.

Thoroughbred Owners & Breeders Association. The Breeder's Guide for 1980. 1981. 57.50 (ISBN 0-936032-41-3). Thoroughbred O.

--Thoroughbred Broodmare Records, 1980. 1981. text ed. 66.75 (ISBN 0-936032-42-1); leather bdg. 77.75 (ISBN 0-936032-43-X). Thoroughbred O.

Thorp, Cary see Lee, Sang M.

Thorp, N. Howard & Clark, Neil M. Pardner of the Wind. LC 77-7243. (Illus.). 1977. 14.50x (ISBN 0-8032-0938-X); pap. 4.75 (ISBN 0-8032-5875-5, BB 638, Bison). U of Nebr Pr.

Thorp, R., jt. ed. see Urguidi, V. L.

Thorp, Willard. Songs from the Restoration Theatre. LC 76-102003. (Music Ser). 1970. Repr. of 1934 ed. lib. bdg. 17.50 (ISBN 0-306-71867-7). Da Capo.

Thorp, Willard & Drinker, Henry S. Two Addresses Delivered to Members of the Grolier Club: Trollope's America; the Lawyers of Anthony Trollope. 1950. 6.00x o.p. (ISBN 0-686-28528-X, Dist. by U Pr of Va). Grolier Club.

Thorp, William & Drinker, Henry S. Two Addresses Delivered to Members of The Grolier Club. (Incl. I. Trollope's (Willard Thorp) & II, The Lawyers of Anthony Trollope (Henry S. Drinker)). 1950. 6.00x o.p. (ISBN 0-8139-0463-2, Grolier Club). U Pr of Va.

Thorpe, Arthur L., jt. auth. see Barrett, Franklin A.

Thorpe, Azalea S. & Larson, J. L. Elements of Weaving. Lyon, Mary, ed. LC 67-11164. (Illus.). 10.95 o.p. (ISBN 0-385-03473-3). Doubleday.

Thorpe, Benjamin, rev. by. & t see Lappenberg, Johann M.

Thorpe, Clarence D., ed. see Keats, John.

Thorpe, D. H., et al. Out of Care: The Community Support of Juvenile Offenders. (Illus.). 224p. 1980. text ed. 27.50x (ISBN 0-04-364018-4, 2544); pap. text ed. 10.95x (ISBN 0-04-364019-2, 2545). Allen Unwin.

Thorpe, Denis & Dunn, Alan. The Shepherd's Year. LC 78-74075. 1979. 11.95 (ISBN 0-7153-7762-0). David & Charles.

Thorpe, Frances & Pronay, Nicholas. British Official Films in the Second World War: A Descriptive Catalog. 321p. 1980. 45.00 (ISBN 0-903450-27-5). ABC Clio.

Thorpe, Francis N. Constitutional History of the United States, 3 Vols. LC 76-124906. (American Constitutional & Legal History Ser). 1970. Repr. of 1901 ed. Set. lib. bdg. 175.00 (ISBN 0-306-71998-3). Da Capo.

Thorpe, Heather G. Handweaver's Workbook. (Illus.). 1966. 5.95 o.s.i. (ISBN 0-02-618500-8). Macmillan.

--Handweaver's Workbook. (Illus.). 1966. pap. 2.95 o.s.i. (ISBN 0-02-011970-4, Collier). Macmillan.

Thorpe, James. Gifts of Genius. LC 80-80077. (Illus.). 200p. 1980. 10.00 (ISBN 0-87328-110-1). Huntington Lib.

--Principles of Textual Criticism. LC 72-179135. 1972. 8.50 (ISBN 0-87328-054-7); pap. 4.00 (ISBN 0-87328-055-5). Huntington Lib.

Thorpe, James, ed. Aims & Methods of Scholarship in Modern Languages & Literatures. 2nd ed. 81p. (Orig.). 1970. pap. 3.75x o.p. (ISBN 0-87352-013-0). Modern Lang.

--Milton Criticism: Selections from Four Centuries. LC 66-19730. 1969. pap. text ed. 2.45 o.s.i. (ISBN 0-02-054730-7, Collier). Macmillan.

Thorpe, James, et al. Founding of the Henry E. Huntington Library & Art Gallery: Four Essays. (Illus.). 1969. 2.50 (ISBN 0-87328-105-5). Huntington Lib.

Thorpe, Kay. Chance Meeting. (Harlequin Romance Ser.). 192p. 1980. pap. 1.50 (ISBN 0-373-10378-6, Pub. by Harlequin). PB.

--Floodtide. (Harlequin Presents Ser.). 192p. 1981. pap. 1.50 (ISBN 0-373-10425-1, Pub. by Harlequin). PB.

Thorpe, Lewis, tr. & intro. by. see Einhard & Nofker The Stammerer.

Thorpe, Michael. Doris Lessing's Africa. LC 79-15676. 1979. text ed. 17.50x (ISBN 0-8419-6000-3); pap. text ed. 8.50x (ISBN 0-8419-6001-1). Holmes & Meier.

Thorpe, Michael, ed. Clough: The Critical Heritage. 1972. 34.00 (ISBN 0-7100-7156-6). Routledge & Kegan.

Thorpe, Michael, ed. see Clough, Arthur H.

Thorpe, Peter. Eighteenth-Century English Poetry. LC 74-17807. 14.95 (ISBN 0-88229-196-3); pap. 7.95x (ISBN 0-88229-581-0). Nelson-Hall.

Thorpe, Sylvia. Fair Shine the Day. 1977. pap. 1.75 o.p. (ISBN 0-449-23229-8, Crest). Fawcett.

--No More A-Roving. (A Regency Romance Ser.). 1979. pap. 1.75 o.p. (ISBN 0-449-24080-0, Crest). Fawcett.

--Rogues' Covenant. 1976. pap. 1.50 o.p. (ISBN 0-449-23041-4, Crest). Fawcett.

--The Silver Nightingale. 224p. 1977. pap. 1.50 o.p. (ISBN 0-449-23379-0, Crest). Fawcett.

--Spring Will Come Again. 1977. pap. 1.50 o.p. (ISBN 0-449-23346-4, Crest). Fawcett.

--Sword of Vengeance. 240p. 1977. pap. 1.50 o.p. (ISBN 0-449-23136-4, Crest). Fawcett.

Thorpe, Sylvia A., tr. see Ramon Y Cajal, Santiago.

Thorpe, W. A. History of English & Irish Glass to 1969. 75.00x (ISBN 0-87556-334-1). Saifer.

Thorpe, W. H. Bird Song: Biology of Vocal Communication & Expression Inbirds. (Cambridge Monographs in Experimental Biology Ser: No. 12). 25.95 (ISBN 0-521-00628-X). Cambridge U Pr.

--The Origins & Rise of Ethology. 21.95 (ISBN 0-03-053251-5). Praeger.

Thorpe, William. The Examinacions of Thorpe & Oldcastell. LC 74-28889. (English Experience Ser.: No. 766). 1975. Repr. of 1530 ed. 7.00 (ISBN 90-221-0766-3). Walter J Johnson.

Thorsen, Kristine A., jt. auth. see Reardon, Joan.

Thorson, J. A. & Cook, T. C., Jr. Spiritual Well-Being of the Elderly. 1980. 22.50 o.p. (ISBN 0-398-03998-4). C C Thomas.

Thorson, James A. & Cook, Thomas C., Jr. Spritual Well-Being of the Elderly. (Illus.). 260p. 1980. text ed. 22.50 (ISBN 0-398-03998-4). C C Thomas.

Thorson, John, jt. auth. see White, D. C.

Thorson, Victoria. Rodin Graphics: A Catalogue Raisonne of Drypoints & Book Illustrations. LC 75-16941. (Illus.). 1977. pap. 4.95 (ISBN 0-88401-007-4, Pub. by Fine Arts Mus). C E Tuttle.

Thorstenson, Clark T., jt. auth. see Heaton, Israel C.

Thorton, J. L. & Tully, R. I. Scientific Books, Libraries, & Collectors. 3rd ed. 1971. 31.00x (ISBN 0-85365-424-7, Pub. by Lib Assn England); suppl. 1978 15.50x (ISBN 0-85365-920-6). Oryx Pr.

Thorton, Wendy A., ed. The Pneumotransport Bibliography. 1972. text ed. 28.00 (ISBN 0-900983-17-5, Dist. by Air Science Co.). BHRA Fluid.

Thorum, Arden R. Language Assessment Instruments: Infancy Through Adulthood. (Illus.). 320p. 1980. write for info. o.p. (ISBN 0-398-04107-5). C C Thomas.

--Language Assessment Instruments: Infancy Through Adulthood. 320p. 1980. text ed. 19.75 (ISBN 0-398-04107-5). C C Thomas.

Thorum, Arden R., jt. auth. see Bell, T. H.

Thorup, Kirsten. Baby: A Novel. Christensen, Nadia, tr. from Danish. LC 80-17844. (Pegasus Prize for Literature Ser.). 208p. 1980. 9.95 (ISBN 0-8071-0772-7). La State U Pr.

--Love from Trieste. Christensen, Nadia & Taylor, Alexander, trs. 64p. (Orig.). 1980. pap. 5.00 (ISBN 0-915306-20-4). Curbstone.

Thorwald, Juergen. Defeat in the East. 304p. 1980. pap. 2.50 (ISBN 0-553-13469-8). Bantam.

Thorwald, Jurgen. Century of the Detective. LC 64-18296. (Helen & Kurt Wolff Bk). (Illus.). 1965. 12.50 o.p. (ISBN 0-15-116350-2). HarBraceJ.

Thosteson, George. The Everyday Medical Handbook. 304p. 1977. pap. 1.75 o.p. (ISBN 0-449-13761-9, 0-449-13761-9, GM). Fawcett.

Thouless, R. H. An Introduction to the Psychology of Religion. 3rd ed. LC 76-184142. 160p. 1972. pap. 29.50 (ISBN 0-521-08149-1); pap. 7.95x (ISBN 0-521-09665-0). Cambridge U Pr.

Thouless, Robert H. From Anecdote to Experiment in Psychical Research. 1972. 17.50 (ISBN 0-7100-7285-6). Routledge & Kegan.

--Map of Educational Research. 1969. text ed. 20.00x (ISBN 0-901225-06-1, NFER). Humanities.

Thrall, Debra. Demon Stalking. (Orig.). 1979. pap. 1.95 (ISBN 0-532-23116-3). Manor Bks.

Thrall, James H. Endocrinological Imaging. 280p. 1981. 25.00 (ISBN 0-87527-235-5). Green.

Thrall, Robert M., jt. ed. see Cobb, Loren.

Thrapp, Dan L. Conquest of Apacheria. (Illus.). 1967. 16.95 (ISBN 0-8061-0751-0); pap. 7.95 (ISBN 0-8061-1286-7). U of Okla Pr.

--Victorio & the Mimbres Apaches. (The Civilization of the American Indian Ser.: Vol. 125). (Illus.). 393p. 1980. pap. 9.95 (ISBN 0-8061-1645-5). U of Okla Pr.

--Victorio & the Mimbres Apaches. LC 72-9269. (Civilization of the American Indian Ser: No. 125). (Illus.). 400p. 1974. 16.95 o.p. (ISBN 0-8061-1076-7). U of Okla Pr.

Threadgold, L. T. The Ultrastructure of the Animal Cell. 2nd ed. Kerkut, G. A., ed. 472p. 1976. text ed. 55.00 (ISBN 0-08-018958-X); pap. text ed. 25.00 (ISBN 0-08-018957-1). Pergamon.

Threlfall, A. J. Design Charts for Water Retaining Structures: BS 5337. (Viewpoint Publication Ser). (Illus.). 1978. pap. text ed. 17.50 (ISBN 0-7210-1104-7). Scholium Intl.

Threlfall, W., jt. auth. see Seifert, Herbert.

Threlkeld, James L. Thermal Environmental Engineering. 2nd ed. 1970. ref. ed. 26.95 (ISBN 0-13-914721-7). P-H.

Threlkeld, John L., ed. see Helmer, M. Jane.

Thrift, Nigel, jt. auth. see Parkes, Don.

Thrift, Richard. The Hinderers. LC 78-51481. 1978. 10.95 (ISBN 0-9604520-0-1). R Thrift.

Thring, Meredith W., jt. auth. see Johnstone, Robert E.

Throckmorton, Burton H., Jr. Adopted in Love: Contemporary Studies in Romans. LC 77-22143. 1978. pap. 3.95 (ISBN 0-8164-1230-8). Crossroad NY.

Thron, W. J., jt. auth. see Jones, William B.

Throop, Sara & Wick, Barbara H. Mathematics Readiness Program. (gr. k). 1975. pap. text ed. 3.84 (ISBN 0-87895-024-9); tchrs' ed. 2.00 (ISBN 0-87895-025-7). Modern Curr.

Thrower, jt. auth. see Walker.

Thrower, James A. The Alternative Tradition: A Study of Unbelief in the Ancient World. (Religon & Society Ser.). 1979. 35.25x (ISBN 90-279-7997-9). Mouton.

Thrower, James R., jt. auth. see Marcus, Abraham.

Thrower, N. Maps & Man: An Examination of Cartography in Relation to Culture & Civilization. 1972. pap. 7.95 (ISBN 0-13-555953-7). P-H.

Thrower, Norman J., ed. The Compleat Plattmaker: Essays on Chart, Map, & Globe-Making in England in the 17th & 18th Centuries. LC 77-78415. 1979. 18.50x (ISBN 0-520-03522-4). U of Cal Pr.

Thrower, Rayner. Pirate Picture. (Illus.). 171p. 1980. 12.50x (ISBN 0-8476-6267-5). Rowman.

Thrupp, Sylvia L. Merchant Class of Medieval London. 1962. pap. 5.95 (ISBN 0-472-06072-4, 72, AA). U of Mich Pr.

Thubron, Colin. Istanbul. new ed. Time-Life Books, ed. (The Great Cities). (Illus.). 1979. 14.95 (ISBN 0-8094-2335-9). Time-Life.

--Istanbul. (The Great Cities Ser.). (Illus.). 1978. lib. bdg. 14.94 (ISBN 0-686-51004-6). Silver.

--Jerusalem. (Great Cities Ser.). (Illus.). 1976. 14.95 (ISBN 0-8094-2250-6). Time-Life.

--Jerusalem. (The Great Cities Ser.). (Illus.). (gr. 6 up). 1976. 14.94 (ISBN 0-8094-2251-4, Pub by Time-Life). Silver.

--The Venetians. Time-Life Books, ed. (Seafarers Ser.). (Illus.). 176p. 1980. 14.95 (ISBN 0-8094-2681-1). Time-Life.

Thucydides. Historiae, 2 vols. Jones, H. W., ed. (Oxford Classical Texts Ser). 1942. Vol. 1 Bks.1-4. 18.95x (ISBN 0-19-814550-0); Vol. 2 Bks. 5-8. 18.95x (ISBN 0-19-814551-9). Oxford U Pr.

--Thucydides, Bks. 6 & 7. Dover, K. J., ed. 1965. Bk.6. 14.95x (ISBN 0-19-831832-4); Bk. 7. 12.50x (ISBN 0-19-831829-4); pap. 12.95x (ISBN 0-19-872098-X). Oxford U Pr.

--Writings, Bk. 4. Wordsworth, J. C., ed. (Gr). text ed. 4.95x (ISBN 0-521-06634-4). Cambridge U Pr.

Thuente, Mary W. W. B. Yeats & Irish Folklore. 286p. 1981. 26.50x (ISBN 0-389-20161-8). B&N.

Thuesen, G. J., jt. auth. see Fabrycky, W. J.

Thuesen, G. J., jt. auth. see Fabrycky, Walter J.

Thulin, Richard L. The Lesser Festivals 1: Saints' Days & Special Occasions. Achtemeier, Elizabeth, et al, eds. LC 79-7377. (Proclamation 2: Aids for Interpreting the Lessons of the Church Year). 64p. (Orig.). 1980. pap. 2.50 (ISBN 0-8006-1393-7, 1-1393). Fortress.

Thulin, Richard L., jt. auth. see Furnish, Victor P.

Thum, Marcella. Abbey Court. LC 76-3136. 1976. 7.95 o.p. (ISBN 0-385-12040-0). Doubleday.

--Fernwood. 1978. pap. 1.75 o.p. (ISBN 0-449-23443-6, Crest). Fawcett.

Thumb, Albert & Marbe, Karl. Experimentelle Untersuchungen Uber Die Psychologischen Grundlagen der Sprachlichen Analogiebildung. (Classics in Psycho-Linguistics). 108p. 1980. text ed. 28.50x (ISBN 0-686-61364-3). Humanities.

Thumboo, Edwin. Gods Can Die. (Writing in Asia Ser.). 1977. pap. text ed. 3.25 o.p. (ISBN 0-686-60436-9, 00223). Heinemann Ed.

Thumm, W., jt. auth. see Ridgway, A.

Thumm, Walter, jt. auth. see Tilley, Donald E.

Thunberg, Lars. Microcosm & Mediator: The Theological Anthropology of Maximus the Confessor. Allchin, A. L., rev. by. LC 80-2368. 1981. Repr. of 1965 ed. 58.00 (ISBN 0-404-18917-2). AMS Pr.

Thundy, Zacharias, jt. ed. see Vasta, Edward.

Thunell, Lars H. Political Risks in International Business: Investment Behavior of Multinationals. LC 77-2940. (Special Studies). 1977. text ed. 16.95 o.p. (ISBN 0-275-24500-4). Praeger.

Thurau, K. Kidney & Urinary Tract Physiology, Vol. III. 1982. 39.50 (ISBN 0-685-32572-5). Univ Park. Postponed.

--Kidney & Urinary Tract Physiology, II. (International Review of Physiology: Vol. II). 1976. 29.50 (ISBN 0-8391-1060-X). Univ Park.

Thurber, Clarence E. & Graham, Lawrence S. Development Administration in Latin America. LC 72-96986. (Comparative Adminstration Group of the American Society for Public Administration Ser.). 550p. 1973. 19.75 (ISBN 0-8223-0292-6). Duke.

Thurber, James. Alarms & Diversions. LC 80-8401. 367p. 1981. pap. 4.95 (ISBN 0-06-090830-0, CN 830, CN). Har-Row.

--Last Flower. (Illus.). 1971. pap. 3.50 o.p. (ISBN 0-06-090232-9, CN232, CN). Har-Row.

--Thurber & Company. LC 64-18067. (Illus.). 1966. 10.95 o.p. (ISBN 0-06-014305-3, HarpT). Har-Row.

--The Years with Ross. 288p. 1975. pap. 1.95 o.p. (ISBN 0-345-24649-7). Ballantine.

Thurber, Kenneth J. & Masson, G. M. Distributed Processor Communication Architecture. LC 79-1563. (Illus.). 288p. 1979. 23.95 (ISBN 0-669-02914-9). Lexington Bks.

Thurber, Kenneth J. & Patton, Peter C. Data Structures & Computer Architecture. LC 76-12688. 1977. 19.95 (ISBN 0-669-00723-4). Lexington Bks.

Thurber, Packard. Evaluation of Industrial Disability. 2nd ed. California Medical Association & Industrial Accident Commission, eds. 1960. pap. 4.50x (ISBN 0-19-501143-0). Oxford U Pr.

Thurber, Walter A. & Kilburn, Robert E. Exploring Life Science. (gr. 7-9). 1975. text ed. 15.52 (ISBN 0-205-04555-3, 6945554); tchrs'. guide 4.40 (ISBN 0-205-04556-1, 6945562); record bk. 7.20 (ISBN 0-205-04562-6, 6945627); tchrs'. ed. 7.20 (ISBN 0-205-04563-4, 6945635); tests & dup. masters 44.00 (ISBN 0-205-04557-X, 6945570). Allyn.

Thurber, Walter A., et al. Astronomy. (Exploring Earth Science Program Ser.). (gr. 7-12). 1976. pap. text ed. 4.96 (ISBN 0-205-04743-2, 6947433). Allyn.

--Exploring Earth Science. (gr. 7-12). 1976. text ed. 15.52 (ISBN 0-205-04734-3, 6947344); tchrs'. guide 4.40 (ISBN 0-205-04737-8, 6947379); tests 44.00 (ISBN 0-205-04740-8, 6947409); tchrs'. guide 7.20 (ISBN 0-205-04739-4, 6947395); record bk. 7.20 (ISBN 0-205-04738-6, 6947387). Allyn.

--Geology. (Exploring Earth Science Program Ser.). (gr. 7-12). 1976. pap. text ed. 4.96 (ISBN 0-205-04741-6, 6947417). Allyn.

--Oceanography. (Exploring Earth Science Program Ser.). (gr. 7-12). 1976. pap. text ed. 4.60 (ISBN 0-205-04745-9, 694745X). Allyn.

Thurley, Geoffrey. The American Moment: American Poetry in the Mid-Century. LC 77-91071. 1978. 22.50 (ISBN 0-312-02884-9). St Martin.

Thurlow, Edward. Moonlight: The Doge's Daughter, Ariadne, Carmen Britanicum. Reiman, Donald H., ed. LC 75-31266. (Romantic Context Ser.: Poetry 1789-1830). 1978. Repr. of 1814 ed. lib. bdg. 47.00 (ISBN 0-8240-2212-2). Garland Pub.

Thurman, Harold V. Introductory Oceanography. 3rd ed. (Illus.). 596p. 1981. text ed. 19.95 (ISBN 0-675-08058-4); tchr's. ed. 3.95 (ISBN 0-686-69493-7). Merrill.

--Introductory Oceanography. 2nd ed. 1978. text ed. 19.95 (ISBN 0-675-08428-8); instructor's manual 3.95 (ISBN 0-686-67980-6). Merrill.

Thurman, Howard. The Centering Moment. LC 80-67469. 1980. pap. 3.95 (ISBN 0-913408-64-6). Friends United.

--Deep River. Bd. with The Negro Spiritual Speaks of Life & Death. LC 75-27041. 136p. 1975. pap. 2.95 (ISBN 0-913408-20-4). Friends United.

Thurman, Ronald, ed. Alcohol & Aldehyde Metabolizing Systems. (Advances in Experimental Medicine & Biology Ser.). 335p. 1980. 75.00 (ISBN 0-306-40476-1, Plenum Pr). Plenum Pub.

Thurman, Ronald G., et al, eds. Alcohol & Aldehyde Metabolizing Systems, 3 vols. (Johnson Foundation Colloquia Ser.). 1974-78. Vol. 1. 38.50 (ISBN 0-12-691450-8); Vol. 2. 41.00 (ISBN 0-12-691402-8); Vol. 3. 41.00 (ISBN 0-12-691403-6); Set. 98.00. Acad Pr.

Thurman, Wallace. Infants of the Spring: A Novel. LC 78-16906. (Lost American Fiction Ser.). 314p. 1979. Repr. of 1932 ed. 13.95 (ISBN 0-8093-0864-9). S Ill U Pr.

Thurman, Wayne L., jt. auth. see Hanley, Theodore O.

Thurmer, Tressa E., jt. auth. see Pisano, Beverly.

Thurmond, John T. & Jones, Douglas E. Fossil Vertebrates of Alabama. LC 80-13075. (Illus.). 256p. 1981. 22.50x. U of Ala Pr.

Thurner, Cass. Deep in Debt Valley. LC 78-74744. 1979. 6.00 (ISBN 0-915854-12-0); pap. 3.00 (ISBN 0-915854-16-3). Friend Freedom.

Thurneysen, R. Grammar of Old Irish. 1961. 30.00x (ISBN 0-686-00866-9). Colton Bk.

--Old Irish Reader. 1949. 7.50x (ISBN 0-686-00879-0). Colton Bk.

Thurow, Harold F. Real Estate Law of Texas. 7th, rev. ed. (Orig.). 1980. 12.95x (ISBN 0-914696-11-4); pap. 9.50x (ISBN 0-914696-12-2). Hemphill.

Thurow, Lester C. Poverty & Discrimination. (Studies in Social Economics). 1969. 10.95 (ISBN 0-8157-8444-9). Brookings.

--The Zero-Sum Society. 230p. 1981. pap. 4.95 (ISBN 0-14-005807-9). Penguin.

Thurow, Lester C., jt. auth. see Heilbroner, Robert L.

Thurow, Raymond C. Atlas of Orthodontic Principles. 2nd ed. LC 77-7096. (Illus.). 1977. text ed. 38.50 (ISBN 0-8016-4951-X). Mosby.

Thursland, Arthur. Work Measurement: A Guidebook to Word Processing Management. rev. ed. 1980. text ed. 45.00 (ISBN 0-935220-01-1). Intl Word Process.

Thurson, Hazel. The Balearic Islands: Majorca, Minorca, Ibiza & Formentera. 1977. 24.00 (ISBN 0-7134-0882-0). David & Charles.

Thurston, Attwater, ed. see Butler, A.

Thurston, David B. Home Built Aircraft. (McGraw-Hill Series in Aviation). (Illus.). 224p. 1981. 24.95 (ISBN 0-07-064552-3, P&RB). McGraw.

Thurston, Ellen. Management Assistance for the Arts: A Survey of Programs. Benedict, Stephen, ed. LC 80-440. 54p. (Orig.). 1980. pap. 4.00 (ISBN 0-89062-046-6, Pub. by Ctr for Arts Info). Pub Ctr Cult Res.

Thurston, Frederick. Clarinet Technique. 3rd ed. King, Thea, ed. (Technique Books). 1977. 7.75 (ISBN 0-19-318610-1). Oxford U Pr.

Thurston, Hazel. The Travellers' Guide to Tunisia. LC 73-174608. (Travellers' Guide Ser.). (Illus.). 1979. 9.95 (ISBN 0-224-00803-X, Pub. by Chatto Bodley Jonathan). Merrimack Bk Serv.

Thurston, Mark. How to Interpret Your Dreams. 1978. pap. 4.95 (ISBN 0-87604-107-1). ARE Pr.

Thurston, Mark, jt. auth. see Puryear, Herbert B.

Thurston, Mark A. Experiments in a Search for God: The Edgar Cayce Path of Application. 1976. pap. 3.95 (ISBN 0-87604-090-3). ARE Pr.

--Experiments in Practical Spirituality: Keyed to a Search for God, Book II. (Illus.). 147p. (Orig.). 1980. pap. 4.95 (ISBN 0-87604-122-5). ARE Pr.

Thurston, Robert, jt. auth. see Larson, Glen A.

Thurston, Robert N., jt. ed. see Mason, Warren P.

Thursz, Daniel & Vigilante, Joseph L., eds. Meeting Human Needs: An Overview of Nine Countries. LC 73-86705. (Social Service Delivery Systems: Vol. 1). 1975. 20.00x (ISBN 0-8039-0314-6); pap. 9.95x (ISBN 0-8039-0589-0). Sage.

--Meeting Human Needs Two: Additional Perspectives from Thirteen Countries. LC 76-6314. (Social Service Delivery Systems: Vol. 2). (Illus.). 286p. 1976. 20.00x (ISBN 0-8039-0590-4); pap. 9.95x (ISBN 0-8039-0591-2). Sage.

--Reaching People: The Structure of Neighborhood Services. LC 77-79869. (Social Service Delivery Systems: Vol. 3). (Illus.). 1978. 20.00 (ISBN 0-8039-0817-2); pap. 9.95 (ISBN 0-8039-0818-0). Sage.

Thusing, Wilhelm, jt. auth. see Rahner, Karl.

Thwaite, Ann. Chatterbox. (Illus.). (ps-3). 1979. PLB 7.95 (ISBN 0-233-96967-5). Andre Deutsch.

Thwaite, Anthony. Beyond the Inhabited World: Roman Britain. LC 76-17526. (Illus.). (gr. 6 up). 1977. 8.95 (ISBN 0-395-28926-2, Clarion). HM.

--A Portion for Foxes. 1977. pap. 6.95x (ISBN 0-19-211872-2). Oxford U Pr.

Thwaite, Mary F. From Primer to Pleasure in Reading. LC 72-82182. (Illus.). 312p. 1972. 14.00 (ISBN 0-87675-275-X). Horn Bk.

Thwaites, C. J. Soldering. (Engineering Design Guides Ser). (Illus.). 30p. 1975. pap. 9.95x (ISBN 0-19-859139-X). Oxford U Pr.

Thwing, Annie H. Crooked & Narrow Streets of the Town of Boston, 1630-1822. LC 74-129974. (Illus.). 1970. Repr. of 1920 ed. 18.00 (ISBN 0-8103-3538-7). Gale.

Thwing, Carrie F., jt. auth. see Thwing, Charles F.

Thwing, Charles F. & Thwing, Carrie F. The Family: An Historical & Social Study. 258p. 1980. Repr. of 1913 ed. lib. bdg. 40.00 (ISBN 0-8495-5157-9). Arden Lib.

Thybony, Scott. Guide to Inner Canyon Hiking: Grand Canyon National Park. rev. ed. (Illus.). pap. 1.75 (ISBN 0-938216-12-0). Grand Canyon.

Thygerson, A. L. Accidents & Disasters: Causes & Countermeasures. (Illus.). 1977. 16.95x (ISBN 0-13-000968-7). P-H.

Thygerson, Alton L. Safety: Concepts & Instruction. 2nd ed. (Illus.). 160p. 1976. pap. text ed. 7.95 (ISBN 0-13-785733-0). P-H.

Thyne, J. M. The Principles of Examining. LC 74-4381. 278p. 1974. text ed. 15.95 (ISBN 0-470-86700-0). Halsted Pr.

Tiao, George C., jt. auth. see Box, George E.

Tibbetts, A. M. & Tibbetts, Charlene. Strategies of Rhetoric. 3rd ed. 1979. pap. text ed. 10.95x (ISBN 0-673-15179-4). Scott F.

Tibbetts, A. M., jt. auth. see Tibbetts, Charlene.

Tibbetts, Alan C. Why Seek Ye the Dead Among the Living? A Guide for Widows. LC 80-68057. 108p. 1980. 5.95 (ISBN 0-8059-2754-9). Dorrance.

Tibbetts, Charlene & Tibbetts, A. M. Strategies: A Rhetoric & Reader. 1981. pap. text ed. 8.95x (ISBN 0-673-15461-0). Scott F.

Tibbetts, Charlene, jt. auth. see Tibbetts, A. M.

Tibbetts, Edith, jt. auth. see Goldfarb, Johanna.

Tibbetts, Orlando L. Sidewalk Prayers. LC 71-139501. 1971. pap. 1.95 o.p. (ISBN 0-8170-0489-0). Judson.

--The Work of the Church Trustee. 1979. pap. 4.50 (ISBN 0-8170-0825-X). Judson.

Tibbits, George see Carey, Mathew.

Tibbitts, T. & Kozlowski, T. K., eds. Controlled Environment Guidelines for Plant Research. LC 79-23521. 1980. 25.00 (ISBN 0-12-690950-4). Acad Pr.

Tibble, Anne. Story of English Literature: A Critical Survey. 1970. text ed. 10.50x (ISBN 0-7206-7604-5); pap. text ed. 6.75 (ISBN 0-7206-0244-0). Humanities.

Tibble, J. W., ed. The Future of Teacher Education. 1971. 11.00 (ISBN 0-7100-7189-2). Routledge & Kegan.

--Study of Education. (Students Library of Education). 1970. text ed. 6.25x (ISBN 0-7100-4205-1). Humanities.

Tibbles, Thomas H. Buckskin & Blanket Days: Memoirs of a Friend of the Indians. LC 57-7289. 1969. pap. 3.95 (ISBN 0-8032-5199-8, BB 503, Bison). U of Nebr Pr.

--The Ponca Chiefs: An Account of the Trial of Standing Bear. Graber, Kay, ed. LC 73-181595. xiv, 143p. 1972. 9.50x (ISBN 0-8032-0814-6); pap. 2.25 (ISBN 0-8032-5763-5, BB 547, Bison). U of Nebr Pr.

Tibbs, Ruth N., jt. auth. see McHose, Allen I.

Tibi, Bassam, ed. Arab Nationalism: A Critical Inquiry. 1980. 20.00 (ISBN 0-312-04716-9). St Martin.

Tice, George A. Urban Landscapes: A New Jersey Portrait. LC 75-30549. (Illus.). 112p. 1976. pap. 17.50 o.p. (ISBN 0-8135-0813-4). Rutgers U Pr.

Tice, Terrence N., tr. see Schleiermacher, Friedrich.

Tichelman, Fritjov. The Social Evolution of Indonesia: The Asiatic Mode of Production & Its Legacy. (Studies in Social History: No. 5). 314p. 1980. lib. bdg. 44.75 (ISBN 90-247-2389-2, Pub. by Martinus Nijhoff). Kluwer Boston.

Tichenor, Philip J., et al. Community Conflict & the Press. LC 79-24401. (People & Communication Ser.: Vol. 8). 240p. 1980. 20.00x (ISBN 0-8039-1425-3); pap. 9.95x (ISBN 0-8039-1426-1). Sage.

Tichenor, Tom. Neat-O, the Supermarket Mouse. LC 80-24770. 32p. (gr. k-3). 1981. 8.95g (ISBN 0-687-27690-X). Abingdon.

--Sir Patches & the Dragon. LC 78-128454. (Illus.). (gr. 1-7). 1971. 5.95 o.s.i. (ISBN 0-87695-108-6). Aurora Pubs.

Tichenor, Trebor J. Ragtime Rarities. LC 74-28941. (Illus.). 320p. (Orig.). 1975. pap. 7.95 (ISBN 0-486-23157-7). Dover.

Ticher, Kurt. Irish Silver in the Rococo Period. 142p. 1972. 20.00x (ISBN 0-7165-0039-6, Pub. by Irish Academic Pr Ireland). Biblio Dist.

Ticho, Suzy. Directory of Artists Slide Registries. 65p. (Orig.). 1980. pap. 6.95 (ISBN 0-915400-25-1). Am Council Arts.

Tichy, H. Effective Writing for Engineers-Managers-Scientists. LC 66-21062. 1966. 18.50 (ISBN 0-471-86778-0, Pub. by Wiley-Interscience). Wiley.

Tichy, M. & Rakosnik, J. Plastic Analysis of Concrete Frames: With Particular Reference to Limit States Des. Dagmar, et al, trs. from Czech. (Illus.). 320p. 1977. text ed. 35.00x (ISBN 0-569-08199-8, Pub. by Collets England). Scholium Intl.

Tichy, Milik & Vorlicek, M. Statistical Theory of Concrete Structures. 364p. 1972. 30.00x (ISBN 0-7165-2080-X, Pub. by Irish Academic Pr Ireland). Biblio Dist.

Tichy, Monique K. Behavioral Science Techniques: An Annotated Bibliography for Health Professionals. LC 75-3628. 132p. 1975. text ed. 16.50 o.p. (ISBN 0-275-05250-8). Praeger.

--Health Care Teams: An Annotated Bibliography. LC 74-14674. (Special Studies). 190p. 1974. text ed. 24.95 (ISBN 0-275-05750-X). Praeger.

Tichy, Noel M. Organization Design for Primary Health Care: The Case of the Dr. Martin Luther King Jr. Health Center. LC 75-44941. (Praeger Special Studies). 1977. 24.95 (ISBN 0-275-23030-9). Praeger.

Tichy, William. Poisons, Antidotes & Anectodes. LC 76-51188. (Illus.). (gr. 7 up). 1977. 8.95 (ISBN 0-8069-3738-6); PLB 8.29 (ISBN 0-8069-3739-4). Sterling.

Tickell, Chrispin. Climate Change & World Affairs. 1978. text ed. 13.25 (ISBN 0-08-022228-5). Pergamon.

Tickle, John. Discovering the Bible, Bk. 2. 96p. (Orig.). 1980. pap. 3.95 (ISBN 0-89243-133-4). Liguori Pubns.

--Discovering the Bible: 8 Simple Keys for Learning & Praying. 1978. pap. 3.95 (ISBN 0-89243-074-5). Liguori Pubns.

--Un Estudio de la Biblia. Diaz, Olimpia, Sr., tr. from Eng. 96p. 1980. pap. 1.95 (ISBN 0-89243-131-8). Liguori Pubns.

Tickle, Les & Hargreaves, Andy. Middle School. 1980. text ed. 21.00 (ISBN 0-06-318134-7, IntlDept); pap. text ed. 13.10 (ISBN 0-06-318135-5). Har-Row.

Tickle, Phyllis A. On Beyond Koch. (Illus.). 160p. 1981. pap. 2.95 (ISBN 0-918518-20-2). St Luke TN.

Ticktin, George B. How to Be One Hundred Years Young. LC 78-12702. 1979. 9.95 (ISBN 0-8119-0318-4). Fell.

Tidbury, Guy, tr. see Pawlowski, J.

Tiddens, Paul, ed. The Atlas of the Body & Mind. LC 75-41710. (Illus.). 208p. 1976. 19.95 (ISBN 0-528-83095-3). Rand.

--Family World Atlas. LC 73-3377. (Illus.). 1978. 14.95 (ISBN 0-528-83092-9); deluxe ed. 16.95 (ISBN 0-528-83115-1). Rand.

--The International Atlas. rev. 2nd ed. LC 77-78100. 558p. 1977. 45.00 o.p. (ISBN 0-528-83046-5); leather binding 100.00 o.p. (ISBN 0-528-83044-9). Rand.

Tidg, Michael & Leeming, Donald. History of Africa Eighteen-Forty to Nineteen-Fourteen, Vol. 1. (Illus.). 188p. 1981. pap. text ed. 14.24x (ISBN 0-686-69152-0, Africana). Holmes & Meier.

Tidrick, Kathryn. Heart-Beguiling Araby. (Illus.). 256p. Date not set. price not set (ISBN 0-521-23483-2). Cambridge U Pr.

Tidwell, Victor H. & Raby, William L. An Introduction to Federal Taxation: 1981 Edition. (Illus.). 480p. 1981. text ed. 21.00 (ISBN 0-13-483404-6); pap. 9.95 study guide (ISBN 0-13-483446-1). P-H.

Tiechert, Curt, jt. ed. see Robison, Richard A.

Tieck, Ludwig. Puss-in-Boots (der Gestiefelte Kater) Gillespie, Gerald, ed. & tr. from Ger. LC 73-20869. (Edinburgh Bilingual Library Ser.: No. 8). 138p. 1974. 9.50x o.p. (ISBN 0-292-72702-X); pap. 3.45x o.p. (ISBN 0-292-72703-8). U of Tex Pr.

Tieck, William A. Schools & School Days in Riverdale, Kingsbridge, Spuyten Duyvil: New York City. LC 77-149738. (Illus.). 1971. 19.50x (ISBN 0-9600398-1-3). W A Tieck.

Tiede, David L. The Charismatic Figure As Miracle Worker. LC 72-87359. (Society of Biblical Literature. Dissertations Ser.: No. 1). (Illus.). pap. 10.50 (ISBN 0-89130-158-5, 060101). Scholars Pr Ca.

--Prophecy & History in Luke-Acts. LC 79-8897. 180p. 1980. 9.95 (ISBN 0-8006-0632-9, 1-632). Fortress.

Tiede, David L. & Kavanagh, Aidan. Pentecost 1. Achtemeier, Elizabeth, et al, eds. LC 79-7377. (Proclamation 2: Aids for Interpreting the Lessons of the Church Year, Ser. A). 64p. (Orig.). 1981. pap. 2.50 (ISBN 0-8006-4096-9, 1-4096). Fortress.

Tiedeman, C. G. Treatise on the Limitations of Police Power in the United States. LC 73-150421. (American Constitutional & Legal History Ser). 1971. Repr. of 1886 ed. lib. bdg. 59.00 (ISBN 0-306-70104-9). Da Capo.

Tiedeman, Herman R. Fundamentals of Psychological & Educational Measurement. (Illus.). 144p. 1972. 15.75 (ISBN 0-398-02429-4). C C Thomas.

Tiedemann, Arthur E., ed. An Introduction to Japanese Civilization. 626p. 1974. 27.50x (ISBN 0-231-03651-5). Columbia U Pr.

Tiedman, Gary, jt. auth. see Hawkins, Richard.

Tiedt. Language Arts Activities for the Classroom. 1978. text ed. 16.95 (ISBN 0-205-05896-5); pap. text ed. 10.50 (ISBN 0-205-05912-0). Allyn.

Tiedt, I. & Tiedt, S. Contemporary English in the Elementary School. 2nd ed. 1975. 17.95 (ISBN 0-13-169961-X). P-H.

Tiedt, Iris M. Exploring Books with Children. LC 78-69530. (Illus.). 1978. text ed. 16.75 (ISBN 0-395-25498-1). HM.

Tiedt, Iris M., jt. auth. see Tiedt, Pamela.

Tiedt, Pamela & Tiedt, Iris M. Multicultural Teaching: A Handbook of Activities, Information, & Resources. new ed. 1979. text ed. 17.95 (ISBN 0-205-06445-0); pap. text ed. 9.95x (ISBN 0-205-06522-8, 2365227). Allyn.

Tiedt, S., jt. auth. see Tiedt, I.

Tiedt, Sidney W., ed. Teaching the Disadvantaged Child. 1968. 8.95x (ISBN 0-19-501086-8). Oxford U Pr.

Tiefenbrun. Signs of the Hidden. 1980. pap. text ed. 28.50x (ISBN 9-0040-3778-0). Humanities.

Tiefer, Leonore, jt. auth. see Fleming, Joyce D.

Tieghem, Philippe Van see Van Tieghem, Philippe.

Tiegs, Cheryl. The Way to Natural Beauty. (Illus.). 1980. 12.95 (ISBN 0-686-68753-1, 24894). S&S.

Tiek, Ludwig & Brentano. Der Blonde Eckbert & Geschichte Vom Braven Kasperl und Dem Schonen Annerl. 7th ed. Atkinson, Margaret E., ed. (Blackwell's German Text Ser.). 1972. pap. 5.50x (ISBN 0-631-01560-4, Pub. by Basil Blackwell). Biblio Dist.

Tiek, Ludwig, jt. auth. see Wackenroder, William H.

Tiemp-Torrevillas, Rowena. Upon the Willows & Other Stories. 192p. 1980. pap. 5.75x (ISBN 0-686-28650-2). Cellar.

Tien, Chang-Lim & Lienhard, John H. Statistical Thermodynamics. (McGraw-Hill Hemisphere Ser. in Thermal & Fluids Engineering). 1979. pap. 25.95 (ISBN 0-07-064570-1, C); solution manual 5.95 (ISBN 0-07-064571-X). McGraw.

Tierney, Brian & Linehan, Peter, eds. Authority & Power. 274p. 1981. 59.50. Cambridge U Pr.

Tierney, Brian, et al, eds. Martin Luther--Reformer or Revolutionary? 3rd ed. (Historical Pamphlets). 1977. pap. text ed. 1.50x (ISBN 0-394-32055-7). Random.

Tierney, Gene & Hershowitz, Mickey. Self-Portrait. 1980. pap. 2.75 (ISBN 0-425-04485-8). Berkley Pub.

Tierney, John A. Calculus & Analytic Geometry. 3rd ed. 725p. (gr. 12 up). 1975. text ed. 21.95x o.p. (ISBN 0-205-04645-2, 5646456); instr's manual free o.p. (ISBN 0-205-04646-0); student sol. manual 7.95 o.p. (ISBN 0-205-04712-2). Allyn.

--Calculus & Analytic Geometry. 4th ed. 1979. text ed. 27.25x (ISBN 0-205-06454-X); instr's man. avail. (ISBN 0-205-06455-8); solutions man. avail. (ISBN 0-205-06456-6); self-test supplement avail. (ISBN 0-205-06457-4). Allyn.

--Differential Equations. 1978. text ed. 20.95x (ISBN 0-205-06167-2). Allyn.

Tierney, John T. Postal Reorganization: Managing the Public's Business. 200p. 1981. 19.95 (ISBN 0-86569-061-8). Auburn Hse.

Tierney, Kevin. Courtroom Testimony: A Policeman's Guide. LC 75-98530. (Funk & W Bk.). 1970. 7.95 o.s.i. (ISBN 0-308-40087-9, TYC-T). T Y Crowell.

Tierney, Michael. Eoin Macneill: Scholar & Man of Action, 1867 - 1945. Martin, F. X., ed. (Illus.). 492p. 1981. 67.50x (ISBN 0-19-822440-0). Oxford U Pr.

Tierney, Tom. Pavlova & Nijinsky Paper Dolls in Full Color. (Illus.). 32p. (Orig.). 1981. pap. price not set (ISBN 0-486-24093-2). Dover.

Tierney, William F. Modern Upholstering Methods. (gr. 9 up). 1965. text ed. 14.00 (ISBN 0-87345-482-0). McKnight.

Tierra, Michael. The Way of Herbs. (Illus., Orig.). 1980. pap. 6.95 (ISBN 0-913300-43-8). Unity Pr.

Tiersky, Ronald. French Communism, 1920-1972. LC 74-921. 416p. 1974. 22.50x (ISBN 0-231-03754-6). Columbia U Pr.

Tietjen, Mary L. Summer Savory: A Family Resource Book. LC 77-78961. 1977. pap. 3.95 (ISBN 0-8091-2034-8). Paulist Pr.

Tietjen, Sari B. The Dog Judge's Handbook. LC 80-36820. (Illus.). 224p. 1980. 10.95 (ISBN 0-87605-512-9). Howell Bk.

Tietjens, O. G., jt. auth. see Prandtl, Ludwig.

Tietz, Harrison M. An Index to the Described Life Histories, Early Stages & Hosts of the Macrolepidoptera of the Continental United States & Canada, 2 vols. iv, 1041p. 1972. text ed. 25.00x (ISBN 0-913492-01-9). Entomological Repr.

Tietze, Andreas. The Koman Riddles & Turkic Folklore. (U. C. Publ. in Near Eastern Studies: Vol. 8). 1966. pap. 9.00x (ISBN 0-520-09301-1). U of Cal Pr.

Tietze, Andreas, jt. auth. see Basgoz, Ihlan.

Tieu, E. V., tr. see Homer.

Tifer, J. K., ed. see Brand, J. C. & Speakman, J. C.

Tiffany, Francis. Dorothea Lynde Dix. LC 70-145702. 1971. Repr. of 1918 ed. 24.00 (ISBN 0-8103-3655-3). Gale.

Tiffany, Lewis H. Algae: The Grass of Many Waters. 2nd ed. (Illus.). 216p. 1968. 11.75 (ISBN 0-398-01926-6). C C Thomas.

Tiffany, Robert, ed. Cancer Nursing: Surgical. (Cancer Nursing Ser.: Vol. 3). (Illus.). 272p. 1980. 39.00 (ISBN 0-571-11364-8, Pub. by Faber & Faber); pap. 12.95 (ISBN 0-571-11365-6, Pub. by Faber & Faber). Merrimack Bk Serv.

--Oncology for Nurses & Health Care Professionals, Vol. 1. (Illus.). 1978. text ed. 35.00x (ISBN 0-04-610009-1); pap. text ed. 18.95x (ISBN 0-04-610010-5). Allen Unwin.

--Oncology for Nurses & Health Care Professionals, Vol. 2. (Illus.). 1978. text ed. 25.00x (ISBN 0-04-610006-7); pap. text ed. 13.95x (ISBN 0-04-610007-5). Allen Unwin.

Tiffany, Sharon W., ed. Women & Society: An Anthropological Reader. 1979. 20.95 (ISBN 0-920792-01-4). EPWP.

Tiffany Studios Editors, ed. Antique Chinese Rugs. LC 69-16178. (Illus.). 1969. Repr. of 1908 ed. 11.00 (ISBN 0-8048-0025-1). C E Tuttle.

Tiffin, Joseph, jt. auth. see McCormick, Ernest J.

Tiffin, Robert, jt. auth. see Diamond, Dorothy.

Tiffney, John, jt. auth. see Aston, Graham.

Tiffon, Y., jt. ed. see Smith, D. C.

Tigar, Michael E. & Levy, Madeleine R. Law & the Rise of Capitalism. LC 77-70968. 1977. 16.00 o.p. (ISBN 0-85345-411-6, CL 411-6). Monthly Rev.

Tiger, Edith, ed. see Rabinowitz, Victor.

Tiger, Lionel, ed. Female Hierarchies. Fowler, Heather T. 1978. lib. bdg. 12.50 o.p. (ISBN 0-202-01161-5). Beresford Bk Serv.

Tiger, Peggy & Babcock, Molly. The Life & Art of Jerome Tiger: War to Peace, Death to Life. LC 80-5245. (Illus.). 300p. 1980. 39.95 (ISBN 0-8061-1656-0). U of Okla Pr.

Tiger, R. P., jt. auth. see Entelis, S. G.

Tigerman, Stanley. Chicago Tribune Tower Competition & Late Entries, 2 vols. LC 80-51371. (Orig.). 1980. Set. pap. 30.00 (ISBN 0-8478-0333-3). Vol. 1, 193p. Vol. 2, 113p. Rizzoli Intl.

Tighe, Donald J., jt. auth. see Casty, Alan.

Tighe, Kevin P., jt. auth. see Lindstrom, Talbot S.

Tighe, Mary. Psyche; or, the Legend of Love. Reiman, Donald H., ed. LC 75-31268. (Romantic Context Ser.: Poetry 1789-1830: Vol. 114). 1978. Repr. of 1805 ed. lib. bdg. 47.00 (ISBN 0-8240-2214-9). Garland Pub.

Tigner, Marcy. Little Marcy & Her Friends. LC 80-80092. (Orig.). 1980. pap. 1.25 (ISBN 0-89081-229-2). Harvest Hse.

--Little Marcy Loves Jesus. (Orig.). 1980. pap. 1.25 (ISBN 0-89081-227-6). Harvest Hse.

Tignor, Robert L. Modernization & British Colonial Rule in Egypt, 1882-1914. (Princeton Studies on the Near East). 1966. 21.00x (ISBN 0-691-03037-5). Princeton U Pr.

Tignor, Robert L. & Abdel-Khalek, Goudal, eds. Political Economy of Income Distribution in Egypt. LC 80-26932. (The Political Economy of Income Distribution in Developing Countries Ser.). 500p. 1981. text ed. 45.00x (ISBN 0-8419-0633-5). Holmes & Meier.

Tihany, Leslie C. The History of Middle Europe: From the Earliest Times to the Age of the World Wars. LC 75-25945. 1976. 21.00 (ISBN 0-8135-0814-2). Rutgers U Pr.

Tihista, Rene, jt. auth. see Dempcy, Mary.

Tikhonov, V. N. Analytical Chemistry of Aluminum. LC 72-4102. (Analytical Chemistry of the Elements Ser.). 250p. 1973. 41.95 (ISBN 0-470-86787-6). Halsted Pr.

Tikku, G. L. Persian Poetry in Kashmir, 1339-1846: An Introduction. (U. C. Publ. in Occasional Papers: No. 4). 1971. pap. 15.00x (ISBN 0-520-09312-7). U of Cal Pr.

Tiktin, Carl. The Hourglass Man. 1978. pap. 1.75 o.p. (ISBN 0-451-08083-1, E8083, Sig). NAL.

Til, Cornelius Van see Van Til, Cornelius.

Til, William Van see Van Til, William.

Til, William Van see Van Til, William, et al.

Tilak, Devarakunda B. Song of the Cosmos. (Translated from Telugu). 8.00 (ISBN 0-89253-613-6); flexible cloth 4.80 (ISBN 0-89253-614-4). Ind-US Inc.

Tilbury, Fred & Edward, Derek. Casework in Context: A Basis for Practice. 250p. 1977. text ed. 25.00 (ISBN 0-08-019744-2); pap. text ed. 14.00 (ISBN 0-08-019743-4). Pergamon.

Tilbury, R. H., ed. Developments in Food Preservatives, No. 1. x, 168p. 1981. 34.00x (ISBN 0-85334-918-5). Intl Ideas.

Tilden, Bill. How to Play Better Tennis. 144p. 1962. pap. 3.95 (ISBN 0-346-12349-6). Cornerstone.

Tiles, J. E. Things That Happen. Brennan, Andrew & Lyons, William E., eds. (Scots Philosophical Monograph: Vol. 1). (Illus.). 157p. 1980. 13.50 (ISBN 0-08-025724-0). Pergamon.

Tileston, Mary W. Great Souls at Prayer. 366p. Repr. of 1898 ed. text ed. 9.50 (ISBN 0-227-67474-X). Attic Pr.

Tilford, Tony, jt. auth. see Avon, Dennis.

Tilgner, Inez H. Instead of Champagne. 148p. 1979. 6.95 (ISBN 0-8059-2668-2). Dorrance.

Tilke, Max. Costume Patterns & Designs. (Illus.). 1974. 65.00 o.s.i. (ISBN 0-8038-1191-8). Hastings.

--National Costumes. (Illus.). 1978. 67.50 (ISBN 0-8038-5381-5). Hastings.

Tilkian, Sarko M., et al. Clinical Implications of Laboratory Tests, Nineteen Seventy-Nine. 2nd ed. LC 78-16221. (Illus.). 1979. pap. text ed. 12.95 (ISBN 0-8016-4962-5). Mosby.

Till, Roger. Statistical Methods for the Earth Scientist: An Introduction. LC 73-22704. 1978. pap. 16.95 (ISBN 0-470-26340-7). Halsted Pr.

Tilleard-Cole, R. R. & Marks, J. The Fundamentals of Psychological Medicine. LC 75-15862. 290p. 1975. 26.95 (ISBN 0-470-86791-4). Halsted Pr.

Tiller, David J., jt. auth. see McGovern, Vincent J.

Tillet, Dorothy S. The Man Who Killed Fortescue. LC 80-8413. 320p. 1981. pap. 2.25 (ISBN 0-06-080536-6, P 536, PL). Har-Row.

Tillett, Jeffrey, ed. see Dickens, Charles.

Tillett, Leslie. African Art in Needlework: Needlework Motifs Inspired by African Culture. LC 78-3320. (Illus.). 1979. 20.95 o.s.i. (ISBN 0-690-01404-X, TYC-T); pap. 9.95 o.s.i. (ISBN 0-690-01793-6, TYC-T). T Y Crowell.

--Zoophabet Needlework Book. LC 76-45763. (Illus.). 1977. 14.95 o.p. (ISBN 0-690-01211-X, TYC-T). T Y Crowell.

Tillett, Leslie, ed. Wind on the Buffalo Grass. LC 76-6098. (Illus.). 1976. 35.00 o.s.i. (ISBN 0-690-01155-5, TYC-T). T Y Crowell.

Tilley, D. R. & Tilley, J. Superfluidity & Superconductivity. LC 73-11584. 1975. 39.95 (ISBN 0-470-86788-4). Halsted Pr.

Tilley, David R. & Tilley, John. Superfluidity & Superconductivity. LC 74-7081. 262p. 1974. 29.95 (ISBN 0-470-86788-4, Pub. by Wiley). Krieger.

Tilley, Donald E. Contemporary College Physics. LC 78-57146. 1979. pap. text ed. 22.95 (ISBN 0-8053-9290-4); instr's guide 3.95 (ISBN 0-8053-9291-2). Benjamin-Cummings.

--University Physics for Science & Engineering. LC 75-14974. 1976. 21.95 (ISBN 0-8465-7536-1); instr's guide 3.75 (ISBN 0-8465-7537-X). Benjamin-Cummings.

Tilley, Donald E. & Thumm, Walter. Physics for College Students. alt. ed. 1976. 23.95 (ISBN 0-8465-7534-5); 3.95 o.p. instr's guide (ISBN 0-8465-7533-7). Benjamin-Cummings.

Tilley, J., jt. auth. see Tilley, D. R.

Tilley, John, jt. auth. see Tilley, David R.

Tilley, Lawrence P. Essentials of Canine & Feline Electrocardiography. LC 79-14374. (Illus.). 1979. 32.50 (ISBN 0-8016-4963-3). Mosby.

Tilley, M. R. Business Maths & Statistics. (Illus.). 1978. pap. text ed. 11.95x (ISBN 0-7131-0152-0). Intl Ideas.

Tilley, Pauline. Art in the Education of Subnormal Children. (Illus.). 128p. (Orig.). 1975. 10.00x o.s.i. (ISBN 0-8464-0151-7). Beekman Pubs.

Tillich, Paul. Eternal Now. LC 63-17938. 1963. pap. 3.95 (ISBN 0-684-71907-X, SL114, ScribT). Scribner.

--The Relation of Religion & Health. 150p. 1981. 15.00 (ISBN 0-913028-81-9); pap. 5.95 (ISBN 0-686-69475-9). North Atlantic.

--Shaking of the Foundations. 1948. pap. 3.95 (ISBN 0-684-71910-X, SL 684, ScribT). Scribner.

--Theology of Culture. Kimball, Robert C., ed. 1964. pap. 5.95 (ISBN 0-19-500711-5, GB). Oxford U Pr.

--What Is Religion. 1973. pap. 4.95x (ISBN 0-06-131732-2, TB1732, Torch). Har-Row.

Tillich, Paul J. Christianity & the Encounter of the World Religions. LC 63-7508. 1963. 12.50x (ISBN 0-231-02602-1); pap. 3.00 (ISBN 0-231-08555-9). Columbia U Pr.

Tilling, Laura, ed. see Newton, Isaac.

Tilling, Meriel. The Observer's Book of Sewing. (Illus.). 1977. 2.95 (ISBN 0-684-14939-7, ScribT). Scribner.

Tilling, Thomas, jt. auth. see Donoghue, William E.

Tillinghast, Richard. The Knife & Other Poems. (Wesleyan Poetry Program Ser.: No. 100). 26p. 1980. 8.00 (ISBN 0-8195-1100-5); pap. 3.95 (ISBN 0-8195-2100-0). Wesleyan U Pr.

Tillman. Optimization of Systems Reliability. 328p. 1980. 37.50 (ISBN 0-8247-6989-9). Dekker.

Tillman, Barrett. MIG Master: The Story of the F-8 Crusader. LC 80-83019. (Illus.). 260p. 1980. 17.95 (ISBN 0-933852-17-7). Nautical & Aviation.

Tillman, David A., jt. auth. see Anderson, Larry L.

Tillman, Frank A. & Cahn, Steven M., eds. Philosophy of Art & Aesthetics: From Plato to Wittgenstein. LC 69-12552. 1969. text ed. 24.50 scp o.p. (ISBN 0-06-046628-6, HarpC). Har-Row.

Tillman, Helene. Die Papstlichen Legaten in England Bis Zur Beendigung der Legation Gualas, 1218. LC 80-2208. 1981. Repr. of 1926 ed. 27.50 (ISBN 0-404-18795-1). AMS Pr.

Tillman, June, et al, eds. The Galliard Book of Carols. (Illus.). 248p. 1980. 30.00x (ISBN 0-389-20146-4). B&N.

Tillman, Kenneth G., jt. auth. see Camaione, David N.

Tillman, Robert. Green Fly Swamp: Environmental Assessment. 1975. pap. 5.80 o.p. (ISBN 0-89327-228-0). NY Botanical.

Tillman, Robert & Goodland, Robert. National Power Study Prefeasibility Investigation: Nicaragua, Environmental Impact Reconnaissance. LC 76-22812. (Illus.). 1976. pap. 5.00 o.p. (ISBN 0-89327-202-7). NY Botanical.

Tillman, Rollie & Kirkpatrick, C. A. Promotion: Persuasive Communication in Marketing. rev ed. 1972. text ed. 16.50x o.p. (ISBN 0-256-00563-X). Irwin.

Tillotson, Geoffrey. Pope & Human Nature. 1958. 19.50x (ISBN 0-19-811581-4). Oxford U Pr.

--A View of Victorian Literature. 1978. 19.95 (ISBN 0-19-812044-3). Oxford U Pr.

Tillotson, Kathleen. Novels of the Eighteen-Forties. 1954. pap. 3.95x o.p. (ISBN 0-19-881015-6, OPB). Oxford U Pr.

Tilly, Bertha, ed. see Vergil.

Tilly, Charles. From Mobilization to Revolution. LC 77-79468. (Illus.). 1978. pap. text ed. 8.95 (ISBN 0-201-07571-7). A-W.

--The Vendee: A Sociological Analysis of the Counter-Revolution of 1973. LC 64-21247. (Illus.). 1976. 17.50x (ISBN 0-674-93300-1); pap. 7.95 (ISBN 0-674-93302-8). Harvard U Pr.

Tilly, Charles, et al. The Rebellious Century: 1830-1930. LC 74-16802. 1975. 18.50 (ISBN 0-674-74955-3). Harvard U Pr.

Tilly, Richard. Financial Institutions & Industrialization in the Rhineland, 1815-1870. (Illus.). 1966. 20.00x (ISBN 0-299-03920-X). U of Wis Pr.

Tillyard, Angela. Land & People of Yugoslavia. (gr. 5-9). 1963. 3.95g o.s.i. (ISBN 0-02-789350-2). Macmillan.

Tilove, Robert. Public Employee Pension Funds: A Twentieth Century Fund Report. 384p. 1976. 22.50x (ISBN 0-231-04015-6). Columbia U Pr.

Tilstra, Albertine J. A Dutchman Bound for Paradise. Van Dolson, Bobbie J., ed. 128p. 1980. pap. write for info. (ISBN 0-8280-0021-2). Review & Herald.

Tilton, Doreen B., ed. Housing & Urban Affairs, Nineteen Sixty-Five to Nineteen Seventy-Six: A Bibliographic Guide to the Microform Collection. 342p. 1978. 50.00 (ISBN 0-667-00519-6). Microfilming Corp.

Tilton, Helga, ed. Deutsch Mit Emil. 1980. pap. text ed. 5.95x (ISBN 0-393-95111-1). Norton.

Tilton, John E. The Future of Nonfuel Minerals. 1977. 9.95 (ISBN 0-8157-8460-0). Brookings.

--International Diffusion of Technology: The Case of Semiconductors. LC 72-161593. (Studies in the Regulation of Economic Activity). 1971. 11.95 (ISBN 0-8157-8458-9). Brookings.

Tilton, John W. Cosmic Satire in the Contemporary Novel. LC 75-18240. 150p. Date not set. cancelled o.p. (ISBN 0-8387-1801-9). Bucknell U Pr.

Tilton, Richard C., ed. Microbiology. 2nd ed. LC 79-8372. (Basic Sciences PreTest Self-Assessment & Review Ser.). (Illus.). 1979. 9.95 (ISBN 0-07-050966-2). McGraw-Pretest.

Tilton, Timothy, jt. auth. see Furniss, Norman.

Timagenis. International Control of Marine Pollution, Vols. 1-2. 1980. 37.50 ea. Vol. 1 (ISBN 0-379-20685-4). Vol. 2 (ISBN 0-379-20686-2). Oceana.

Timber Research & Development Association. Structural Recommendations for Timber Frame Housing. (Illus.). 1981. 38.00 (ISBN 0-86095-890-6). Longman.

Timberg, Thomas A. The Federal Executive: The President & the Bureaucracy. LC 77-17490. (Orig.). 1978. pap. text ed. 7.95x (ISBN 0-89197-641-8). Irvington.

Timberlake, Charles E. Detente: A Documentary Record. LC 78-19465. 1978. 26.50 (ISBN 0-03-046666-0). Praeger.

Timberlake, P. H. A Contribution to the Systematics of North American Species of Synhalonia (Hymenoptera, Apoidea) (U. C. Publ. in Entomology: Vol. 57). 1969. pap. 7.00x (ISBN 0-520-09130-2). U of Cal Pr.

--The North American Species of Heterosarus Robertson (Hymenoptera, Apoidea) (Publicaions in Entomology: Vol. 77). 1975. pap. 9.50x (ISBN 0-520-09528-6). U of Cal Pr.

--Revision of the Genus Pseudopanurgus of North America (Hymenoptera: Apoidea) (U. C.Publications in Entomology: Vol. 72). 1973. pap. 7.50x (ISBN 0-520-09475-1). U of Cal Pr.

--A Revisional Study of the Bees of the Genus Perdita F. Smith, with Special Reference to the Fauna of the Pacific Coast (Hymenoptera, Apoidea) Incl. Pt. IV. (U. C. Publ. in Entomology: Vol. 17.1). 1960. pap. 7.00x (ISBN 0-520-09076-4); Pt. V. (U. C. Publ. in Entomology: Vol. 28.1). 1962. pap. 7.00x (ISBN 0-520-09094-2); Pt. VII (Including Index to Pts. I to VII) (U. C. Publ. in Entomology: Vol. 49). 1968. pap. 10.00x (ISBN 0-520-09121-3). U of Cal Pr.

--Supplementary Studies on the Systematics of the Genus Perdita (Hymenoptera: Andrenidae) (U. C. Publ. in Entomology: Vol. 66). 1971. pap. 6.00x (ISBN 0-520-09397-6). U of Cal Pr.

--Supplementary Studies on the Systematics of the Genus Perdita (Hymenoptera, Andrenidae, Part II. (U. C. Publications in Entomology Ser.: Vol. 85). 1980. pap. 9.00 (ISBN 0-520-09605-3). U of Cal Pr.

Timberlake, R. R., ed. see Euripides.

Timbie, William H. & Kusko, A. C. Elements of Electricity. 4th ed. LC 53-6444. 1953. text ed. 22.95x (ISBN 0-471-86955-4). Wiley.

Timbie, William H. & Pike, Arthur L. Essentials of Electricity. 3rd ed. LC 63-8053. 1963. text ed. 19.55x (ISBN 0-471-87036-6). Wiley.

Timbrook, Janice, ed. see Eaton, Margaret H. & Amey, Vera E.

Timbs, John. Clubs & Club Life in London with Anecodotes of Its Famous Coffee-Houses, Hostelries, & Taverns from the Seventeenth Century to the Present Time. LC 66-28045. 1967. Repr. of 1872 ed. 15.00 (ISBN 0-8103-3262-0). Gale.

--Curiosities of London. rev. ed. LC 68-22056. 1968. Repr. of 1867 ed. 26.00 (ISBN 0-8103-3497-6). Gale.

--English Eccentrics & Eccentricities. LC 69-18076. 1969. Repr. of 1875 ed. 20.00 (ISBN 0-8103-3556-5). Gale.

--Historic Ninepins. LC 68-22057. 1969. Repr. of 1869 ed. 18.00 (ISBN 0-8103-3539-5). Gale.

--Romance of London. LC 68-22058. 1968. Repr. of 1865 ed. 38.00 (ISBN 0-8103-3498-4). Gale.

--Things Not Generally Known. Wells, David A., ed. LC 68-30584. 1968. Repr. of 1857 ed. 24.00 (ISBN 0-8103-3101-2). Gale.

Time & Life Editors, ed. New Living Spaces. LC 72-72104. (Home Repair & Improvement). (Illus.). (gr. 7 up). 1977. PLB 11.97 (ISBN 0-8094-2375-8, Pub by Time-Life). Silver.

Time-Life Bks, ed. Pork. (The Good Cook Ser.). (Illus.). 176p. 1980. 12.95 (ISBN 0-8094-2875-X). Time-Life.

--Walls & Ceilings. (Home Repair & Improvement Ser.). (Illus.). 128p. 1980. 10.95 (ISBN 0-8094-3450-4). Time-Life.

Time-Life Bks, ed. see Hertzstein, Robert.

Time-Life Bks, ed. see Whipple, A. B.

Time Life Bks Editors. The Boat. LC 74-19438. (Time Life Library of Boating Ser.). (Illus.). (gr. 6 up). 1975. PLB 13.95 (ISBN 0-8094-2101-1). Silver.

--Boat Handling. LC 74-29194. (Time Life Library of Boating Ser.). (Illus.). (gr. 6 up). 1975. PLB 13.95 (ISBN 0-8094-2105-4). Silver.

--Classic Techniques. LC 73-85529. (Art of Sewing Ser.). (Illus.). 208p. (gr. 6 up). 1973. lib. bdg. 11.97 (ISBN 0-8094-1703-0). Silver.

--Creative Design. LC 74-29449. (Art of Sewing Ser.). (Illus.). 208p. (gr. 6 up). 1975. lib. bdg. 11.97 (ISBN 0-8094-1743-X). Silver.

--Delicate Wear. LC 74-21557. (Art of Sewing Ser.). (Illus.). 208p. (gr. 6 up). 1975. lib. bdg. 11.97 (ISBN 0-8094-1739-1). Silver.

--How Things Work in Your Home. LC 74-24853. 1975. lib. bdg. 16.95 o.p. (ISBN 0-8094-1640-9). Silver.

Time-Life Bks. Editors, ed. The Best of Life. (Illus.). 1973. kivar 19.92 o.p. (ISBN 0-685-72981-8, Pub. by Time-Life). Silver.

Time-Life Bks. Eds., ed. Pies & Pastries. (The Good Cook Ser.). (Illus.). 176p. 1981. 12.95 (ISBN 0-8094-2895-4). Time-Life.

Time-Life Bks. Eds., ed. see Fisher, Arthur.

Time-Life Bks. Eds., ed. see O'Neil, Paul.

Time-Life Bks. Eds., ed. see Walker, Bryce.

Time-Life Books. Breads. (The Good Cook Ser.). (Illus.). 176p. 1981. 12.95 (ISBN 0-8094-2900-4). Time Life.

--Doors & Windows. (Home Repair & Improvement). (Illus.). 1978. 10.95 (ISBN 0-8094-2406-1). Time-Life.

--Kitchens & Bathrooms. LC 77-83171. (Home Repairs & Improvement Ser.). (Illus.). 1977. lib. bdg. 11.97 (ISBN 0-685-80981-1). Silver.

Time Life Books, ed. Basic Tailoring. LC 74-80076. (Art of Sewing Ser.). (gr. 6 up). 1974. lib. bdg. 11.97 (ISBN 0-8094-1719-7, Pub. by Time-Life). Silver.

Time-Life Books, ed. The Classic Boat. (The Time-Life Library of Boating). 1977. 14.95 (ISBN 0-8094-2144-5). Time-Life.

Time Life Books, ed. The Classic Boat. LC 76-55862. (Illus.). (gr. 6 up). 1977. PLB 13.95 (ISBN 0-8094-2145-3, Pub. by Time-Life). Silver.

--Crime. LC 76-29184. (Human Behavior). (Illus.). (gr. 5 up). 1976. PLB 9.99 o.p. (ISBN 0-8094-1963-7, Pub. by Time-Life). Silver.

--Cruising. LC 75-27445. (Library of Boating Ser.). (gr. 6 up). 1975. PLB 13.95 (ISBN 0-8094-2121-6, Pub. by Time-Life). Silver.

--Cruising Grounds. LC 76-9629. (Library of Boating Ser.). (Illus.). (gr. 6 up). 1976. PLB 13.95 (ISBN 0-8094-2133-X, Pub. by Time-Life). Silver.

Time-Life Books, ed. Decorative Techniques. LC 75-29597. (The Art of Sewing). (Illus.). (gr. 6 up). 1976. PLB 11.97 (ISBN 0-8094-1763-4, Pub. by Time-Life). Silver.

--Greenhouse Gardening. (The Encyclopedia of Gardening). (Illus.). 1977. 11.95 (ISBN 0-8094-2562-9). Time-Life.

--The Handy Boatman. (The Library of Boating Ser.). (Illus.). 1976. 14.95 (ISBN 0-8094-2140-2). Time-Life.

--Heating & Cooling. LC 77-80200. (Home Repair & Improvement Ser.). (Illus.). (gr. 7 up). 1977. lib. bdg. 11.97 (ISBN 0-685-77684-0, Pub. by Time-Life). Silver.

--Heating & Cooling. (Home Repair & Improvement Ser.). 1977. 10.95 (ISBN 0-8094-2378-2). Time-Life.

--Herbs. (The Time-Life Encyclopedia of Gardening Ser.). 1977. 11.95 (ISBN 0-8094-2550-5). Time-Life.

--Island Life. (Wild, Wild World of Animals). (Illus.). 1978. 10.95 (ISBN 0-913948-19-5). Time-Life.

--Kitchens & Bathrooms. (Home Repair Ser.). (Illus.). 1977. 10.95 (ISBN 0-8094-2386-3). Time-Life.

Time Life Books, ed. Life Before Man. LC 72-86602. (Emergence of Man Ser). (Illus.). (gr. 6 up). 1972. lib. bdg. 9.63 o.p. (ISBN 0-8094-1252-7, Pub. by Time-Life). Silver.

--Maintenance. LC 75-18911. (Library of Boating Ser.). (Illus.). (gr. 6 up). 1975. PLB 13.95 (ISBN 0-8094-2117-8, Pub. by Time-Life). Silver.

--Masonry. LC 76-25711. (Home Repair & Improvement). (Illus.). (gr. 7 up). 1976. PLB 11.97 (ISBN 0-8094-2363-4, Pub. by Time-Life). Silver.

Time-Life Books, ed. Matthew Brady & His World. 1977. 29.95 (ISBN 0-8094-2575-0). Time-Life.

--New Living Spaces. (Home Repair & Improvement Ser.). 1977. 10.95 (ISBN 0-8094-2374-X). Time-Life.

Time Life Books, ed. Offshore-Cruising Navigation Racing. LC 76-417. (Library of Boating Ser.). (Illus.). (gr. 6 up). 1976. lib. bdg. 13.95 (ISBN 0-685-73295-9, Pub. by Time-Life). Silver.

--Paint & Wallpaper. LC 76-3377. (Home Repair & Improvement). (Illus.). (gr. 7 up). 1976. PLB 11.97 (ISBN 0-8094-2355-3, Pub. by Time-Life). Silver.

--Personal Touch. LC 74-77030. (Art of Sewing Ser.). (gr. 6 up). 1974. lib. bdg. 11.97 (ISBN 0-8094-1727-8, Pub. by Time-Life). Silver.

Time-Life Books, ed. Photography Year: 1979. (Illus.). 1979. 14.95 (ISBN 0-8094-1671-9). Time-Life.

Time Life Books, ed. Plumbing. LC 76-46139. (Home Repair & Improvement). (Illus.). (gr. 7 up). 1976. PLB 11.97 (ISBN 0-8094-2367-7, Pub. by Time-Life). Silver.

--Racing. LC 75-34791. (Library of Boating Ser.). (Illus.). (gr. 6 up). 1976. PLB 13.95 (ISBN 0-8094-2125-9, Pub. by Time-Life). Silver.

--Restyling Your Wardrobe. LC 76-37283. (The Art of Sewing). (Illus.). (gr. 6 up). 1976. 11.97 (ISBN 0-8094-1767-7, Pub. by Time-Life). Silver.

Time-Life Books, ed. Soups. (The Good Cook Ser.). 1980. 12.95 (ISBN 0-8094-2866-0). Time-Life.

Time Life Books, ed. Space & Storage. LC 75-34852. (Home Repair & Improvement). (Illus.). (gr. 7 up). 1976. PLB 11.97 (ISBN 0-8094-2351-0, Pub. by Time-Life). Silver.

--Weatherproofing. LC 76-55869. (Home Repair & Improvement Ser.). (Illus.). (gr. 7 up). 1977. lib. bdg. 11.97 (ISBN 0-685-77685-9, Pub. by Time-Life). Silver.

Time-Life Books, ed. Weatherproofing. (The Home Repair Ser.). (Illus.). 1977. 10.95 (ISBN 0-8094-2370-7). Time-Life.

--Wild-Flower Gardening. (The Time-Life Encyclopedia of Gardening Ser.). 1977. 11.95 (ISBN 0-8094-2554-8). Time-Life.

Time-Life Books & Time-Life Books, eds. The Ranchers. (Old West Ser.). (Illus.). 1978. 12.95 (ISBN 0-8094-1508-9). Time-Life.

Time-Life Books & Time Life Books Editors, eds. Decorating with Plants. (Encyclopedia of Gardening Ser.). (Illus.). 1978. 9.95 (ISBN 0-8094-2579-3). Time-Life.

--Gardening Under Lights. (The Encyclopedia of Gardening Ser.). (Illus.). 1978. 11.95 (ISBN 0-8094-2570-X). Time-Life.

Time-Life Books, ed. see Allen, Oliver.

Time-Life Books, ed. see Allen, Oliver E.

Time Life Books, ed. see Bailey, Ronald.

Time-Life Books, ed. see Bailey, Ronald H.

Time-Life Books, ed. see Bethell, Nicholas.

Time-Life Books, ed. see Bonavia, David.

Time-Life Books, ed. see Botting, D.

Time-Life Books, ed. see Botting, Douglas.

Time-Life Books, ed. see Bowen, Ezra.

Time-Life Books, ed. see Davenport, William.

Time-Life Books, ed. see Davis, Franklin M.

Time-Life Books, ed. see Elegant, Robert.

Time-Life Books, ed. see Gilmore, C. P.

Time-Life Books, ed. see Howarth, D.

Time-Life Books, ed. see Koning, Hans.

Time-Life Books, ed. see Lehane, B.

Time-Life Books, ed. see Maddocks, Melvin.

Time-Life Books, ed. see Miller, Russell.

Time-Life Books, ed. see Moorhouse, Geoffrey.

Time Life Books, ed. see Moser, Don.

Time-Life Books, ed. see Nevin, David.

Time-Life Books, ed. see Perl, Philip.

Time-Life Books, ed. see Pitt, Barrie.

Time-Life Books, ed. see Prendergast, Curtis.

Time-Life Books, ed. see Pryce-Jones, David.

Time-Life Books, ed. see Skelsey, Alice.

Time-Life Books, ed. see Tanner, Ogden.

Time-Life Books, ed. see Thubron, Colin.

Time-Life Books, ed. see Wallace, Robert.

Time-Life Books, ed. see Wernick, Robert.

Time-Life Books, ed. see Whipple, A. B.

Time-Life Books Editors. Advertising Giveaways to Baskets. LC 77-99201. (The Encyclopedia of Collectibles Ser.). (Illus.). 1978. lib. bdg. 10.98 (ISBN 0-686-50972-2). Silver.

--American Painting, Nineteen Hundred to Nineteen Seventy. (Library of Art). (Illus.). 1970. 15.95 (ISBN 0-8094-0258-0). Time-Life.

--Beads to Boxes. LC 78-50707. (The Encyclopedia of Collectibles Ser.). (Illus.). 1978. lib. bdg. 10.95 (ISBN 0-686-50973-0). Silver.

Time Life Books Editors. Beavers & Other Pond Dwellers. (Wild, Wild World of Animals). (Illus.). 1978. 10.95 (ISBN 0-913948-16-0). Time-Life.

Time-Life Books Editors. Buttons to Chess Sets. LC 78-54098. (The Encyclopedia of Collectibles Ser.). (Illus.). 1978. lib. bdg. 10.98 (ISBN 0-686-50974-9). Silver.

--Cabins & Cottages. (Home Repair & Improvement). (Illus.). 1979. 12.95 (ISBN 0-8094-2410-X). Time-Life.

--Children's Books to Comics. LC 77-99201. (The Encyclopedia of Collectibles Ser.). (Illus.). 1978. lib. bdg. 10.98 (ISBN 0-686-50975-7). Silver.

--Cookbooks to Detective Fiction. LC 77-99201. (The Encyclopedia of Collectibles Ser.). (Illus.). 1978. lib. bdg. 10.98 (ISBN 0-686-50976-5). Silver.

--Dogs to Fishing Tackle. (The Encyclopedia of Collectibles Ser.). (Illus.). 1978. lib. bdg. 10.98 (ISBN 0-686-50977-3). Silver.

Time Life Books Editors. Floors & Stairways. (Home Repair Ser.). (Illus.). 1978. 10.95 (ISBN 0-8094-2394-4). Time-Life.

Time-Life Books Editors. Folk Art to Horse-Drawn Carriages. (The Encyclopedia of Collectibles Ser.). (Illus.). 1979. lib. bdg. 10.98 (ISBN 0-686-50978-1). Silver.

--Guide to the Natural World & Index to the Life Nature Library. LC 65-22668. (Life Nature Library). 1965. lib. bdg. 8.97 o.p. (ISBN 0-8094-0932-1, Pub. by Time-Life). Silver.

--The Home Workshop. (Home Repair & Improvement Ser.). (Illus.). 128p. 1980. 10.95 (ISBN 0-8094-3454-7, Silver Burdett). Time-Life.

--Inkwells to Lace. (The Encyclopedia of Collectibles Ser.). (Illus.). 1979. lib. bdg. 10.98 (ISBN 0-686-50979-X). Silver.

Time Life Books Editors. Kangaroos & Other Creatures from Down Under. (Wild, Wild World of Animals). (Illus.). 1978. 10.95 (ISBN 0-913948-17-9). Time-Life.

Time-Life Books Editors. Lalique to Masks. (The Encyclopedia of Collectibles Ser.). (Illus.). 1979. lib. bdg. 10.98 (ISBN 0-686-50980-3). Silver.

Time Life Books Editors. Life in the Coral Reef. (Wild, Wild World of Animals Ser.). (Illus.). 1977. 10.95 (ISBN 0-913948-15-2). Time-Life.

Time-Life Books Editors. Matchsafes to Nursing Bottles. (The Encyclopedia of Collectibles Ser.). (Illus.). 1979. lib. bdg. 10.98 (ISBN 0-8094-2787-7); kivar bdg. 8.95 (ISBN 0-8094-2788-5). Silver.

--Modern American Painting: 1900 - 1970. (Library of Art Ser.). (Illus.). (gr. 6 up). 1970. kivar 12.96 (ISBN 0-8094-0287-4, Pub. by Time-Life). Silver.

--Oak Furniture to Pharmacist's Equipment. (The Encyclopedia of Collectibles Ser.). (Illus.). 1979. lib. bdg. 10.98 (ISBN 0-8094-2791-5); kivar bdg. 8.95 (ISBN 0-8094-2792-3). Silver.
--The Old House. (Home Repair & Improvement Ser.). (Illus.). 1980. 10.95 (ISBN 0-8094-2422-3). Time-Life.
--Pasta. (The Good Cook Ser.). (Illus.). 176p. 1981. 12.95 (ISBN 0-8094-2891-1). Time-Life.
--Pewter to Quilts. (The Encyclopedia of Collectibles Ser.). (Illus.). 1979. lib. bdg. 10.98 (ISBN 0-8094-2795-8); kivar bdg. 8.95 (ISBN 0-8094-2796-6). Silver.
--Porches & Patios. (Home Repair & Improvement Ser). (Illus.). 128p. 1981. 10.95 (ISBN 0-8094-3474-1). Time-Life.
--Salads. (Good Cook Ser.). (Illus.). 176p. 1980. 12.95 (ISBN 0-8094-2879-2). Time-Life.
--Seven Centuries of Art. (Library of Art). (Illus.). 200p. 1970. 15.95 (ISBN 0-8094-0259-9). Time-Life.
--Snacks & Sandwiches. (The Good Cook Ser.). (Illus.). 1980. 12.95 (ISBN 0-8094-2883-0). Time-Life.
--Special Purpose Rooms. (Home Repair & Improvement Ser.). (Illus.). 128p. 1981. 10.95 (ISBN 0-8094-3458-X). Time-Life.
--The Sporting Scene. LC 75-717. (The Art of Sewing). (Illus.). (gr. 6 up). 1975. PLB 11.97 (ISBN 0-8094-1747-2, Pub. by Time-Life). Silver.
--Sports Afloat. LC 76-17459. (Library of Boating Ser.). (gr. 6 up). 1976. 13.95 (ISBN 0-8094-2129-1, Pub. by Time-Life). Silver.
--This Fabulous Century, 8 vols. (gr. 6 up). kivar 9.93 ea. o.p. (Pub. by Time-Life). Silver.
Time Life Books Editors. The Time-Life Gardening Yearbook. (Encyclopedia of Gardening Ser.). (Illus.). 1978. 11.95 (ISBN 0-685-86572-X). Time-Life.
Time-Life Books Editors. The Time-Life Holiday Cookbook. 1976. 19.95 (ISBN 0-8094-1932-7). Time-Life.
Time-Life Books Editors & Bailey, George. Munich. (The Great Cities Ser.). (Illus.). 200p. 1981. 14.95 (ISBN 0-8094-3120-3). Time-Life.
Time-Life Books Editors & Botting, Douglas. The Giant Airships. (The Epic of Flight). (Illus.). 176p. 1981. 12.95 (ISBN 0-8094-3270-6). Time-Life.
Time-Life Books Editors & Halloran, Richard. The Home Front: Japan. (World War II Ser.). (Illus.). 208p. 1981. 13.95 (ISBN 0-8094-3415-6). Time-Life.
Time-Life Books Editors & Jackson, Donald D. The Aeronauts. (The Epic of Flight Ser.). (Illus.). 176p. 1980. 12.95 (ISBN 0-8094-3268-4). Time-Life.
Time-Life Books Editors & Moorehouse, Geoffrey. Prague. (The Great Cities Ser.). (Illus.). 200p. 1981. 14.95 (ISBN 0-8094-3116-5). Time-Life.
Time-Life Books Editors & Whipple, A. B. The Racing Yachts. (The Seafarers Ser.). (Illus.). 176p. 1981. 14.95 (ISBN 0-8094-2693-5). Time-Life.
Time-Life Books Editors & Ziemke, Earl. The Soviet Juggernaut. (World War II Ser.). (Illus.). 208p. 1981. 13.95 (ISBN 0-8094-3387-7). Time-Life.
Time-Life Books Editors, jt. auth. see Reiter, Joan.
Time-Life Books Editors, jt. auth. see Steinberg, Rafael.
Time-Life Books Editors, jt. auth. see Whipple, A. B.
Time-Life Books Editors, ed. Built-Ins. (Home Repairs & Improvement Ser.). (Illus.). 1980. 10.95 (ISBN 0-8094-2430-4). Time-Life.
--Pest & Diseases. (Encyclopedia of Gardening Ser.). (Illus.). 1978. 11.95 (ISBN 0-8094-2566-1). Time-Life.
--Photography Year: 1980. (Illus.). 1980. 14.95 (ISBN 0-8094-1685-9). Time-Life.
--Recreational Areas. (Home Repair & Improvement Ser.). (Illus.). 1980. 10.95 (ISBN 0-686-59879-2). Time-Life.
Time Life Books Editors, ed. Songbirds. (Wild, Wild World of Animals Ser.). (Illus.). 1978. 10.95 (ISBN 0-913948-18-7). Time-Life.
Time-Life Books Editors, ed. see Allen, Oliver.
Time-Life Books Editors, ed. see Porter, Peter.
Time Life Books Editors, jt. ed. see Time-Life Books.
Time-Life Books Editors, ed. see Wheeler, Keith.
Time-Life Editors. Birds of Field & Forest. new ed. (Wild, Wild World of Animals Ser.). (Illus.). 1977. 10.95 (ISBN 0-913948-13-6). Time-Life.
--Community. (Human Behavior Ser). 9.95 (ISBN 0-8094-1958-0). Time-Life.
--Foods of the World. 1980. 14.95 (ISBN 0-686-68054-5). Time-Life.
--The Handy Boatman. LC 76-26732. (Time-Life Library of Boating). 1976. lib. bdg. 13.95 (ISBN 0-8094-2141-0). Silver.
--Outdoor Structures. (Home Repair Ser.). (Illus.). 1978. 10.95 (ISBN 0-8094-2402-9). Time-Life.
--Roofs & Siding. (Home Repair & Improvement Ser.). 1977. 10.95 (ISBN 0-8094-2390-1). Time-Life.
--Time-Life Book of Needlecraft. LC 76-25399. 1976. lib. bdg. 17.70 o.p. (ISBN 0-8094-1938-6). Silver.
Time-Life Editors, jt. auth. see Grunfeld, Frederic V.
Time-Life Editors, jt. auth. see Wheeler, Keith.
Time-Life Television. Bears & Other Carnivores. (The Wild, Wild World of Animals Ser.). (Illus.). 1976. 10.95 (ISBN 0-913948-08-X). Time-Life.
--Birds of Field & Forest. LC 77-5596. (Wild World of Animals Ser.). (gr. 5 up). 1977. lib. bdg. 11.98 (ISBN 0-685-80980-3). Silver.
--Spider & Insects. (The Wild, Wild World of Animals Ser.). (Illus.). 1977. 10.95 (ISBN 0-913948-12-8). Time-Life.
--Wild Herds. (The Wild, Wild World of Animals Ser.). (Illus.). 1977. 10.95 (ISBN 0-913948-11-X). Time-Life.
Time-Life Television, ed. Whales & Other Sea Animals. (Wild Wild World of Animal Ser.). 1977. 10.95 (ISBN 0-913948-10-1). Time-Life.
Time-Life Television Editors. Animal Defenses. (The Wild, Wild World of Animals). (Illus.). 1979. 10.95 (ISBN 0-913948-23-3). Time-Life.
--Fishes of Lakes, Rivers & Oceans. new ed. (Wild, Wild World of Animals Ser). (Illus.). 1978. 10.95 (ISBN 0-913948-20-9). Time-Life.
--Life in Zoos & Preserves. new ed. (Wild, Wild World of Animals Ser.). (Illus.). 1978. 10.95 (ISBN 0-913948-21-7). Time-Life.
--Rabbits & Other Small Mammals. new ed. (The Wild, Wild World of Animals). (Illus.). 1979. 10.95 (ISBN 0-913948-22-5). Time-Life.
Time Periodicals Ltd., ed. Straits Times Dictionary of Singapore. 948p. 1980. 58.50x (ISBN 0-8002-2750-6). Intl Pubns Serv.
Timerlake, Richard H., Jr. & Selby, Edward B., Jr. Money & Banking. 1972. 16.95x (ISBN 0-534-00108-4). Wadsworth Pub.
Times Bks. & British Medical Association. The Book of Executive Health: A Guide for Men & Women Executives Who Want to Live Longer. (Illus.). 224p. 1981. 12.95 (ISBN 0-13-080010-4, Spec); pap. 5.95 (ISBN 0-13-080002-3). P-H.
Timiras, P. S. Developmental Physiology & Aging. (Illus.). 692p. 1972. text ed. 25.95 (ISBN 0-02-420840-X). Macmillan.
Timiras, Paola, jt. auth. see Sherwood, Nancy.
Timko, Michael. Innocent Victorian: The Satiric Poetry of Arthur Hugh Clough. LC 66-11301. xvi, 198p. 1966. 12.00x (ISBN 0-8214-0016-9). Ohio U Pr.
Timm, Neil H. Multivariate Analysis with Applications in Education & Psychology. LC 74-83250. (Statistics Ser.). (Illus.). 1975. text ed. 31.95 o.p. (ISBN 0-8185-0096-4). Brooks-Cole.
Timm, Paul R. Managerial Communication: A Finger on the Pulse. (Illus.). 1980. text ed. 15.95 (ISBN 0-13-549824-4). P-H.
Timm, Peter G. Attack of the Cat. LC 80-27359. (Prime Time Adventures Ser.). (Illus.). 64p. (gr. 4 up). 1981. PLB 7.95 (ISBN 0-516-02101-X). Childrens.
Timm, Simon, ed. Directory of Shipowners, Shipbuilders & Marine Engineers 1980. 78th ed. LC 25-4199. 1514p. 1980. 55.00x (ISBN 0-617-00301-7). Intl Pubns Serv.
Timman, R., jt. auth. see Kuipers, L.
Timmer, John. Acts, a Study Guide. (Revelation Ser. for Adults). 1981. pap. text ed. 1.45 (ISBN 0-933140-20-7). Bd of Pubns CRC.
Timmerhaus, Klaus D., ed. Energy Resources Recovery in Arid Lands. (Illus.). 200p. 1981. price not set (ISBN 0-8263-0582-2); pap. price not set (ISBN 0-8263-0583-0). U of NM Pr.
Timmermann, Tim. Growing up Alive: Humanistic Education for the Pre-Teen. LC 75-21159. (Mandala Series in Education). (Illus.). 232p. 1975. pap. text ed. 8.95x (ISBN 0-916250-01-6). Irvington.
Timmermann, Tim & Ballard, Jim. Strategies in Humanistic Education, 3 vols. LC 75-25394. (Mandala Series in Education). 592p. 1976. Vol. 1. pap. 6.95x (ISBN 0-916250-03-2); Vol. 2. pap. 7.95 (ISBN 0-916250-11-3); Vol. 3. pap. 7.95 (ISBN 0-916250-25-3). Irvington.
Timmermans, Felix. The Perfect Joy of St. Francis. 280p. 1974. pap. 2.50 (ISBN 0-385-02378-2, Im). Doubleday.
Timmers, J. J. A Handbook of Romanesque Art. (Icon Editions). (Illus.). 240p. 1976. pap. 5.95x o.s.i. (ISBN 0-06-430073-0, IN-73, HarpT). Har-Row.
Timmins, Alice. Making Fabric Wall Hangings. LC 71-119561. (Illus.). 1970. 9.25 (ISBN 0-8231-5024-0). Branford.
--Patchwork: Technique & Design. (Illus.). 144p. 1980. 24.00 (ISBN 0-7134-3296-9, Pub. by Batsford England). David & Charles.
Timmins, Lois. Understanding Through Communication: Structural Experiments in Self-Exploration. 336p. 1972. 17.75 (ISBN 0-398-02430-8). C C Thomas.
Timmins, Robert S., jt. ed. see Baddour, Raymond F.
Timmons, Christine & Gibney, Frank, eds. Britannica Book of English Usage. LC 79-7706. (Encyclopedia Britannica Ser.). (Illus.). 504p. 1980. 17.95 (ISBN 0-385-14193-9). Doubleday.
Timmons, Jeffry A., et al. New Venture Creation: A Guide to Small Business Development. 1977. pap. 18.50 (ISBN 0-256-01887-1). Irwin.
Timmons, Tim. Loneliness Is Not a Disease. LC 80-83845. 1981. pap. 4.95 (ISBN 0-89081-264-0). Harvest Hse.
Timms, Art. Finding Out About Trucks. LC 80-14559. (Finding-Out Books). (Illus.). 64p. (gr. 4-9). 1980. PLB 6.95 (ISBN 0-89490-037-4). Enslow Pubs.
Timms, Duncan. Urban Mosaic: Towards a Theory of Residential Differentiation. LC 70-123665. (Geographical Studies: No. 2). (Illus.). 1971. 39.50x (ISBN 0-521-07964-0); pap. 13.95x (ISBN 0-521-09988-9). Cambridge U Pr.
Timms, E. V. Pathway of the Sun. 1977. pap. 1.50 o.s.i. (ISBN 0-515-04398-2). Jove Pubns.
--Robina. 1977. pap. 1.50 o.s.i. (ISBN 0-515-04399-0). Jove Pubns.
--They Came from the Sea. 1977. pap. 1.50 o.s.i. (ISBN 0-515-04400-8). Jove Pubns.
Timms, Moira. Prophecies & Predictions: Everyone's Guide to the Coming Changes. rev. ed. (Illus.). 288p. 1980. pap. 7.95 (ISBN 0-913300-55-1). Unity Pr.
Timms, Noel. Language of Social Casework. (Library of Social Work). 1968. pap. text ed. 3.75x (ISBN 0-7100-6214-1). Humanities.
--Recording in Social Work. (Library of Social Work). 1972. 12.50 (ISBN 0-7100-7288-0); pap. 6.95 (ISBN 0-7100-7289-9). Routledge & Kegan.
Timms, Noel, jt. auth. see Mayer, John E.
Timms, Noel & Watson, David, eds. Philosophy in Social Work. (International Library of Welfare & Philosophy Ser.). 1978. 17.50 (ISBN 0-7100-8786-1); pap. 8.95 (ISBN 0-7100-8787-X). Routledge & Kegan.
Timoney, Francis. The Three Talking Trees. LC 74-18902. (Illus.). 32p. (gr. 4-7). 1974. 3.95 o.p. (ISBN 0-87973-788-3); pap. 1.95 (ISBN 0-87973-388-8). Our Sunday Visitor.
Timoney, John F., jt. auth. see Gillespie, James H.
Timpane, P. Michael, ed. see Pechman, Joseph A. K.
Timpane, P. Michael, jt. ed. see Rivlin, Alice M.
Tinao, D., et al, trs. see Brister, C. W.
Tinbergen, E. A. & Tinbergen, N. Early Childhood Autism: An Ethological Approach. (Advances in Ethology Ser.: Vol. 10). (Illus.). 53p. (Orig.). 1972. pap. text ed. 14.00 (ISBN 3-489-78036-1). Parey Sci Pubs.
Tinbergen, Jan. Dynamics of Business Cycles. Polak, J. J., tr. from Dutch. (Midway Reprint Ser). x, 366p. 1975. pap. 15.00x o.s.i. (ISBN 0-226-80418-6). U of Chicago Pr.
--The Rio Report: Reshaping the International Order: a Report to the Club of Rome Coordinator. 1977. pap. 2.50 (ISBN 0-451-07708-3, E7708, Sig). NAL.
--RIO: Reshaping the International Order. LC 76-6556. 1976. 10.00 (ISBN 0-525-19250-6); pap. 4.95 o.p. (ISBN 0-525-04340-3). Dutton.
Tinbergen, N., jt. auth. see Tinbergen, E. A.
Tinbergen, Niko. Animal Behavior. LC 65-13829. (Life Nature Library). (Illus.). (gr. 5 up). 1965. PLB 8.97 o.p. (ISBN 0-8094-0634-9, Pub. by Time-Life). Silver.
--Animal Behavior. (Young Readers Library). (Illus.). 1977. lib. bdg. 7.95 (ISBN 0-686-51084-4). Silver.
Tindal, Matthew. Christianity As Old Creation or the Gospel. Wellek, Rene, ed. LC 75-11256. (British Philosophers & Theologians of the 17th & 18th Centuries Ser.). 1978. lib. bdg. 42.00 (ISBN 0-8240-1806-0). Garland Pub.
Tindale, Norman B. Aboriginal Tribes of Australia: Their Terrain, Environmental Controls, Distribution, Limits, & Proper Names. (Illus.). 1975. 82.50x (ISBN 0-520-02005-7). U of Cal Pr.
Tindall, William. A Readers' Guide to James Joyce. 304p. 1959. pap. 5.95 (ISBN 0-374-50112-2). FS&G.
Tindall, William Y. Samuel Beckett. LC 64-22640. (Columbia Essays on Modern Writers Ser.: No. 4). (Orig.). 1964. pap. 2.00 (ISBN 0-231-02659-5, MW4). Columbia U Pr.
Tindell-Hopwood, A. & Hollyfield, J. P. Fossil Mammals of Africa, No. 8: An Annotated Bibliography of the Fossil Mammals of Africa 1742-1950. 194p. 1954. pap. 16.00x (ISBN 0-565-00179-5). Sabbot-Natural Hist Bks.
Tinelli, Henri. Creole Phonology. (Janua Linguarum, Ser. Practica: No. 117). 1980. pap. text ed. 40.00x (ISBN 90-279-3048-1). Mouton.
Tiner, John H. The Seven Day Mystery. (Voyager Ser.). 176p. (Orig.). (gr. 6-10). 1981. pap. 2.95 (ISBN 0-8010-8856-9). Baker Bk.
Ting, E. C., jt. ed. see Chen, W. F.
Ting, Irwin P. Plant Psysiology. LC 80-16448. (Illus.). 635p. 1981. text ed. 19.95 (ISBN 0-201-07406-0). A-W.
Tingay & Badcock. These Were the Romans. (Illus.). pap. 8.95 (ISBN 0-7175-0591-X). Dufour.
Tingley, Donald F., ed. Social History of the United States: A Guide to Information Sources. LC 78-13196. (American Government & History Information Guide Ser: Vol. 3). 1979. 30.00 (ISBN 0-8103-1366-9). Gale.
Tingley, Donald F., jt. ed. see Tingley, Elizabeth.
Tingley, Elizabeth & Tingley, Donald F., eds. Women & Feminism: A Guide to Information Sources. (American Government & History Information Guide Ser.: Vol. 12). 325p. 1981. 30.00 (ISBN 0-8103-1492-4). Gale.
Tingley, Katherine. Theosophy: The Path of the Mystic. 3rd rev ed. LC 77-82604. 1977. 6.00 (ISBN 0-911500-33-2); softcover 3.50 (ISBN 0-911500-34-0). Theos U Pr.
Tinic, Seha M. & West, Richard R. Investing in Securities: An Efficient Markets Approach. LC 78-55833. 1979. text ed. 20.95 (ISBN 0-201-07631-4); instr's manual avail. (ISBN 0-201-07632-2). A-W.
Tinkcom, Harry M. Republicans & Federalists in Pennsylvania: 1790-1801. LC 50-9356. (Orig.). 1950. pap. 5.00 (ISBN 0-911124-24-1). Pa Hist & Mus.
Tinker, Anthea. The Elderly in Modern Society. (Social Policy in Modern Britain Ser.). (Illus.). 320p. 1981. pap. text ed. 13.95x (ISBN 0-582-29513-0). Longman.
Tinker, C. B., ed. see Arnold, Matthew.
Tinker, Carol. The Pillow Book of Carol Tinker. Miller, Jeffrey, ed. LC 79-57557. 100p. 1980. signed ltd. 20.00 (ISBN 0-932274-09-9); pap. 5.00 (ISBN 0-932274-08-0). Cadmus Eds.
Tinker, Chauncey B. Translations of Beowulf: A Critical Biography. LC 67-21717. 1967. Repr. of 1903 ed. 6.00 (ISBN 0-87752-114-X). Gordian.
Tinker, Edward L. Centaurs of Many Lands. (Illus.). 5.25 (ISBN 0-85131-072-9, Dist. by Sporting Book Center). J A Allen.
--Horsemen of the Americas & the Literature They Inspired. (Illus.). 1966. 20.00 (ISBN 0-292-73657-6). U of Tex Pr.
--Lafcadio Hearn's American Days. LC 71-99064. (Library of Lives & Letters). (Illus.). 1970. Repr. of 1924 ed. 20.00 (ISBN 0-8103-3366-X). Gale.
Tinker, Hugh. A New System of Slavery: The Export of Indian Labor Overseas 1830-1920. (Illus.). 472p. 1974. 24.00x (ISBN 0-19-218410-5). Oxford U Pr.
--The Ordeal of Love: C. F. Andrews & India. (Illus.). 356p. 1979. text ed. 17.95x. Oxford U Pr.
Tinker, Irene & Bramsen, Michelle B., eds. Women & World Developmemt, 2 vols, Vol.1. Incl. Vol. 2. An Annotated Bibliography. Buvinic, Mayra. 416p. Set. pap. 6.95. Overseas Dev Council.
Tinker, Irene & Buvinic, Mayra, eds. The Many Facets of Human Settlement: Science & Society. LC 77-6307. 1977. text ed. 125.00 (ISBN 0-08-021994-2). Pergamon.
Tinker, Irene, et al, eds. Women & World Development. LC 76-20602. 1976. 29.95 (ISBN 0-275-56520-3). Praeger.
--Women & World Development with an Annotated Bibliography, 2 vols. 416p. 1976. pap. 6.95. Overseas Dev Council.
Tinker, Jack & Porter, Susan W. A Course in Intensive Therapy Nursing. 294p. 1980. 30.00x (ISBN 0-7131-4347-9, Pub. by Arnold Pubs England). State Mutual Bk.
Tinker, Miles A. & McCullough, Constance M. Teaching Elementary Reading. 4th ed. (Illus.). 640p. 1975. 18.95x (ISBN 0-13-892083-4). P-H.
Tinkham, Michael. Introduction to Superconductivity. (International Ser. in Pure & Applied Physics). (Illus.). 320p. 1975. text ed. 23.00 o.p. (ISBN 0-07-064877-8, C). McGraw.
Tinkle, Donald W. see Alexander, Richard D.
Tinkle, L. & Maxwell, A. Cowboy Reader. reissue ed. LC 76-16347. (gr. 7 up). 1976. 9.95 o.p. (ISBN 0-679-50677-2); pap. 4.95 o.p. (ISBN 0-679-50678-0). McKay.
Tinkle, Lon. Story of Oklahoma. (Landmark Ser, No. 100). (Illus.). (gr. 5-8). 1962. PLB 4.39 o.p. (ISBN 0-394-90400-1, BYR). Random.
--Texas. LC 73-5198. 1976. 17.95 (ISBN 0-684-13415-2, ScribT); pap. 12.50 (ISBN 0-684-14643-6, ScribT). Scribner.
--Valiant Few: Crisis at the Alamo. (gr. 5-9). 1964. 4.50g o.s.i. (ISBN 0-02-789380-4). Macmillan.
Tinnell, Richard W. Television Symptom Diagnosis. 1977. instructor's manual 6.67 (ISBN 0-672-97618-8). Bobbs.
Tinnell, Roger D. An Annotated Discography of Music in Spain Before 1650. 146p. 1980. 12.00. Hispanic Seminary.

Tinney, James S. & Rector, Justine J. Issues & Trends in Afro-American Journalism. LC 80-6074. 371p. 1980. lib. bdg. 20.75 (ISBN 0-8191-1352-2); pap. text ed. 12.50 (ISBN 0-8191-1353-0). U Pr of Amer.

Tinoco, Ignacio, Jr., et al. Physical Chemistry: Principles & Applications in Biological Sciences. LC 77-25417. 1978. text ed. 22.95 (ISBN 0-13-665901-2); solutions 4.95 (ISBN 0-13-665919-5). P-H.

Tinsley, Ian J. Chemical Concepts in Pollutant Behavior. LC 78-24301. (Environmental Science & Technology Ser.). 1979. 26.95 (ISBN 0-471-03825-3, Pub. by Wiley-Interscience). Wiley.

Tinsley, Jim B. Sailfish: Swashbuckler of the Open Seas. LC 64-7908. 1964. deluxe ed. 16.50 (ISBN 0-8130-0328-8). U Presses Fla.

Tinsley, Russell. Hunting the Whitetailed Deer. rev. ed. LC 65-14986. (Funk & W Bk.). (Illus.). 1977. 9.95 (ISBN 0-308-10326-2, TYC-T); pap. 4.50 (ISBN 0-308-10327-0, TYC-T). T Y Crowell.

Tinsley, Russell, ed. All About Small Game Hunting in America. 1976. 11.95 (ISBN 0-87691-222-6). Winchester Pr.

Tint, Herbert. France Since Nineteen Eighteen. 1970. 24.00 (ISBN 0-7134-1505-3, Pub. by Batsford England). David & Charles.

Tinterow, Maurice M. Foundations of Hypnosis: From Mesmer to Freud. (Illus.). 620p. 1970. 59.75 (ISBN 0-398-01928-2). C C Thomas.

Tintner, Gerhard & Sengupta, Jati K. Stochastic Economics: With Applications of Stochastic Processes, Control & Programming. 1972. 35.00 (ISBN 0-12-691650-0). Acad Pr.

Tipler, Frank J., ed. Essays in General Relativity. LC 80-517. 1980. 30.00 (ISBN 0-12-691380-3). Acad Pr.

Tipler, Paul A. Modern Physics. 2nd ed. LC 77-58725. 1977. text ed. 11.95x (ISBN 0-87901-088-6). Worth.

--Physics, 2 vols. LC 74-82693. 1976. Set. 26.95 (ISBN 0-87901-041-X); 15.95x ea. Vol. 1 (ISBN 0-87901-094-0). Vol. 2 (ISBN 0-87901-095-9). study guide 7.95x (ISBN 0-87901-055-X). Worth.

Tippett, Alan. Aspects of Pacific Ethnohistory. LC 73-8820. (Illus.). 216p. (Orig.). 1973. pap. 5.95 (ISBN 0-87808-132-1). William Carey Lib.

Tippett, Alan R. The Deep-Sea Canoe: The Story of Third World Missionaries in the South Pacific. LC 77-8660. (Illus.). 1977. pap. 3.95x (ISBN 0-87808-158-5). William Carey Lib.

Tippett, Harry M. The Power of Kindness. (Uplook Ser.). 32p. 1955. pap. 0.75 (ISBN 0-8163-0076-3, 16415-2). Pacific Pr Pub Assn.

Tippette, Giles. Saturday's Children: One Fighting Season with Texas College Football. 288p. 1973. 6.95 o.s.i. (ISBN 0-02-619060-5). Macmillan.

--The Survivalists. 1975. 7.95 o.s.i. (ISBN 0-02-619020-6). Macmillan.

--Wilson's Choice. (Orig.). 1981. pap. 1.95 (ISBN 0-440-19518-7). Dell.

Tipping, Marjorie, ed. Ludwig Becker: Artist & Naturalist with the Burke & Wills Expedition. LC 79-67093. 1979. text ed. 70.00x (ISBN 0-522-84189-9, Pub. by Melbourne U Pr). Intl Schol Bk Serv.

Tippit, Sammy. Reproduced by Permission of the Author. 144p. 1979. pap. 2.50 (ISBN 0-88207-579-9). Victor Bks.

Tippit, Sammy & Jenkins, Jerry. You Me He. 1978. pap. 2.50 (ISBN 0-88207-766-X). Victor Bks.

Tippo, Oswald & Stern, William L. Humanistic Botany. (Illus.). 1977. text ed. 14.95x (ISBN 0-393-09126-0); tchrs. manual gratis (ISBN 0-393-09130-9). Norton.

Tipsen, E., jt. auth. see Clausen, H.

Tipson, R. Stuart, jt. auth. see Horton, Dereck.

Tipson, R. Stuart & Horton, Derek, eds. Advances in Carbohydrate Chemistry & Biochemistry, Vol. 39. (Serial Publication Ser.). write for info. Acad Pr.

Tipson, R. Stuart see Pigman, Ward & Wolfrom, Melville L.

Tipson, Stuart R. see Pigman, Ward & Wolfrom, Melville L.

Tipton, I. C., ed. Locke on Human Understanding: Selected Essays. 1977. pap. text ed. 5.95x (ISBN 0-19-875039-0). Oxford U Pr.

Tipton, James see Hilberry, Conrad, et al.

Tiranti, John. Glass Fibre for Schools. (gr. 9-12). 1972. 8.95 (ISBN 0-85458-330-0); pap. 4.95 (ISBN 0-85458-340-8). Transatlantic.

Tirapegui, Enrique, jt. ed. see Antoine, Jaen-Pierre.

Tiritilli, Robert A., jt. auth. see Hellman, Charles S.

Tirner, Peter, tr. see Niedermayer, Franz.

Tirso De Molina. Venganza De Tamar. Paterson, A. K., ed. text ed. 27.00x (ISBN 0-521-07205-0). Cambridge U Pr.

Tirtha, Ranjit. Society & Development in Contemporary India. (Illus.). 368p. 1980. 13.50 (ISBN 0-8187-0040-8). Harlo Pr.

--Society & Development in Contemporary India: Geographical Perspectives. (Illus.). 368p. 1980. 13.50 (ISBN 0-686-27540-3). R Tirtha.

Tiryakian, Edward A., ed. Phenomenon of Sociology: A Reader in the Sociology of Sociology. LC 76-130794. 1981. 24.50x (ISBN 0-89197-882-8); pap. text ed. 12.95x (ISBN 0-89197-339-7). Irvington.

Tischer, Robert G., et al. Problem Solving in Medical Technology & Microbiology. LC 79-11337. (Illus.). 1979. pap. text ed. 25.00 (ISBN 0-89189-068-8, 45-7-010-00). Am Soc Clinical.

Tischler, Henry L., jt. auth. see Berry, Brewton.

Tischler, Morris. Experiments in General & Biomedical Instrumentation. Haas, Mark, ed. (Illus.). 176p. 1980. pap. text ed. 8.95x (ISBN 0-07-064781-X, G). McGraw.

--Experiments in Telecommunications. Haas, Mark, ed. (Linear Integrated Circuit Applications Ser.). (Illus.). 176p. (gr. 12 up). 1980. pap. text ed. 7.95x (ISBN 0-07-064782-8). McGraw.

Tischler, Nancy M. Dorothy L. Sayers: A Pilgrim Soul. LC 79-87739. 1980. 8.95 (ISBN 0-8042-0882-4). John Knox.

Tischler, Steven. Footballers & Businessmen: The Origin of Professional Soccer in England. 180p. 1981. text ed. 24.00x (ISBN 0-8419-0658-0). Holmes & Meier.

Tisdale, Joanna. Little Black Boy, I Saw Your Face. 1981. 7.95 (ISBN 0-533-04828-1). Vantage.

Tisdall, Caroline & Bozzola, Angelo. Futurism. LC 77-76819. (World of Art Ser.). (Illus.). 1978. 17.95 (ISBN 0-19-519983-9); pap. 9.95 (ISBN 0-19-519980-4). Oxford U Pr.

Tisdall, Caroline, tr. see Carra, Massimo, et al.

Tisdell, C. A. & McDonald, P. W. Economics of Fibre Markets: Interdependence Between Man-Made Fibres, Wool, & Cotton. 1979. text ed. 45.00 (ISBN 0-08-022468-7). Pergamon.

Tishler, Hace S. Self-Reliance & Social Security, 1870-1917. LC 79-139361. (National University Publications). 1971. 13.50 (ISBN 0-8046-9012-X). Kennikat.

Tisserand, R. B. The Art of Aromatherapy. 320p. 1977. 18.00x (ISBN 0-8464-0993-3). Beekman Pubs.

Tisserand, Robert. The Art of Aromatherapy. 1978. pap. 7.95 (ISBN 0-685-62088-3). Weiser.

Tisserand, Robert B. The Art of Aromatheraphy: The Beautifying & Healing Properties of the Essential Oils of Flowers & Herbs. (Illus.). 1978. pap. 7.95 (ISBN 0-89281-001-7). Inner Tradit.

Tissot, Jan D. The Hidden Seed. 8.00 (ISBN 0-89253-743-4); flexible cloth 4.80 (ISBN 0-89253-744-2). Ind-US Inc.

Titard, Pierre, jt. auth. see DeFatta, Joseph.

Titchmarsh, Edward C. Introduction to the Theory of Fourier Integrals. 2nd ed. 1948. 48.00x (ISBN 0-19-853320-9). Oxford U Pr.

--Theory of Functions. 2nd ed. 1939. 17.95x (ISBN 0-19-853349-7). Oxford U Pr.

Titcomb, Margaret. Native Use of Marine Invertebrates in Old Hawaii. 1979. pap. text ed. 6.95x (ISBN 0-8248-0715-4). U Pr of Hawaii.

--Voyage of the Flying Bird. LC 74-94023. (Illus.). (gr. 7-9). 1970. 3.95 o.s.i. (ISBN 0-8048-0723-X). C E Tuttle.

Tite, C. G. Impeachment & Parlimentary Judicature in Early Stuart England. (University of London Historical Studies: No. 37). 256p. 1974. text ed. 30.00x (ISBN 0-485-13137-4, Athlone Pr). Humanities.

Titelbaum, Olga A., tr. see Sivachev, Kolai V. & Yakovlev, Nikolai N.

Titiev, Estelle, tr. see Chaplina, Vera.

Title, Carol K., jt. ed. see Jaeger, Richard.

Title, Stanley H. & Klein, Charles M. Sensibly Thin. LC 78-27039. 1979. 11.95 (ISBN 0-88229-446-6); pap. 6.95 (ISBN 0-88229-665-5). Nelson-Hall.

Titler, Dale. Wings of Mystery: True Stories of Aviation History. rev. ed. (Illus.). 1981. 8.95 (ISBN 0-396-07826-5). Dodd.

Titley, Paul. The Ancient World. (Let's Make History Ser.). (Orig.). 1980. pap. 3.50 (ISBN 0-263-06335-6). Transatlantic.

--The Dark Ages. (Let's Make History Ser.). (Orig.). 1980. pap. 3.50 (ISBN 0-263-06337-2). Transatlantic.

--The Middle Ages. (Let's Make History). (Orig.). 1980. pap. 3.50 (ISBN 0-263-06338-0). Transatlantic.

--The Roman World. (Let's Make History Ser.). (Orig.). 1980. pap. 3.50 (ISBN 0-263-06336-4). Transatlantic.

Titli, A. & Singh, M. G. Large Scale Systems: Theories & Applications: Proceedings of the 2nd IFAC Symposium on Large Scale Systems Theory & Applications, Toulouse, France 25-27 June 1980. LC 80-49946. (IFAC Proceedings Ser.). 550p. 1981. 105.00 (ISBN 0-08-024484-X). Pergamon.

Titli, A., jt. auth. see Singh, M. G.

Titlow, Richard E. Americans Import Merit: Origins of the United States Civil Service System & the Influence of the British Model. LC 78-65352. 1978. pap. text ed. 12.50 (ISBN 0-8191-0655-0). U Pr of Amer.

Titmuss, Richard M. Commitment to Welfare. 1976. text ed. 22.50x (ISBN 0-04-361020-X); pap. text ed. 8.95x (ISBN 0-04-361021-8). Allen Unwin

Titova, L. K., jt. auth. see Vinnikov, Ya. A.

Titow, J. Z. Winchester Yields: A Study in Medieval Agricultural Productivity. LC 72-171685. (Cambridge Studies in Economic History). 1972. 89.50 (ISBN 0-521-08349-4). Cambridge U Pr.

Titow, W. V. & Lanham, B. J. Reinforced Thermoplastics. LC 75-16335. 295p. 1975. 39.95 (ISBN 0-470-87518-6). Halsted Pr.

Tittensor, Andrew. The Red Squirrel. (Mammal Society Ser.). (Illus.). 50p. 1980. 6.95 (ISBN 0-7137-0902-2, Pub. by Blandford Pr England). Sterling.

Tittle, Carol K. Student Teaching: Attitude & Research Bases for Change in School & University. LC 73-20477. 1974. 10.00 (ISBN 0-8108-0694-3). Scarecrow.

Tittle, Carol K. & Denker, Elenor R. Returning Women Students in Higher Education: Defining Policy Issues. LC 80-13993. 224p. 1980. 21.95 (ISBN 0-03-050656-5). Praeger.

Tittle, Carol K., jt. ed. see Jaeger, Richard M.

Tittle, Charles R. Sanctions & Social Deviance: The Question of Deterrence. LC 79-24397. 368p. 1980. 27.95 (ISBN 0-03-052156-4). Praeger.

Tittler, Robert & Loach, Jennifer, eds. The Mid-Tudor Polity, c. Fifteen Forty to Fifteen Sixty. 227p. 1980. 20.00x (ISBN 0-8476-6257-8). Rowman.

Titus, Charles W. & Jones, Thomas E. The Old Line State: Her Heritage. LC 79-180858. (Illus.). 1971. pap. 4.00 (ISBN 0-87033-159-0, Pub. by Tidewater). Cornell Maritime.

Titus, Christopher A. TEA: 8080-8085 Co-Resident Editor-Assembler. LC 79-65751. 1979. pap. 10.95 (ISBN 0-672-21628-0, 21628). Sams

Titus, Christopher A., et al. Eighty-Eighty - Eighty-Eighty-Five Software Design, Bk 2. LC 78-57207. 1979. pap. 10.95 (ISBN 0-672-21615-9, 21615). Sams.

Titus, David A. Palace & Politics in Pre-War Japan. (Studies of the East Asian Institute, Columbia University). 368p. 1974. 22.50x (ISBN 0-231-03622-1). Columbia U Pr.

Titus, Elizabeth A., jt. auth. see Singer, Philip.

Titus, Elizabeth A., ed. see Johnson, O.

Titus, Elizabeth M., jt. auth. see Singer, Philip.

Titus, Eve. Basil & the Lost Colony. (gr. 3-6). 1981. pap. 1.50 (ISBN 0-671-41602-2). Archway.

--Basil & the Pygmy Cats. (Illus.). 178p. (gr. 3-6). 1980. pap. 1.75 (ISBN 0-671-41478-X). Archway.

--Basil of Baker Street. (gr. 3-6). 1958. pap. 1.75 (ISBN 0-671-41729-0). Archway.

--Mr. Shaw's Shipshape Shoeshop. LC 76-77789. (Illus.). 48p. (gr. k-3). 5.95 o.s.i. (ISBN 0-8193-0366-6, Four Winds); PLB 5.41 o.s.i. (ISBN 0-8193-0367-4). Schol Bk Serv.

Titus, Jonathan A., et al. Microcomputer-Analog Converter Software & Hardware Interfacing. LC 78-57201. 1978. pap. 10.50 (ISBN 0-672-21540-3). Sams.

Titus, Parvin S. & Graham, Ben S., Jr. The Amazing Oversight: Total Participation for Productivity. LC 79-10070. 1979. 13.95 (ISBN 0-8144-5510-7). Am Mgmt.

Titus, S., tr. see Kaufman, William I.

Titus, William A. Wisconsin Writers. LC 77-145704. 1974. Repr. of 1930 ed. 24.00 (ISBN 0-8103-3658-8). Gale.

Tivy, Joy. Biogeography: A Study of Plants in the Ecosphere. (Illus.). 1977. pap. text ed. 8.00x (ISBN 0-05-003122-8). Longman.

Tivy, Louis, ed. Your Loving Anna: Letters from the Ontario Frontier. LC 72-86392. 1972. 10.00 o.p. (ISBN 0-8020-1927-7); pap. 3.50 o.p. (ISBN 0-8020-6166-4). U of Toronto Pr.

Tiwari, K. S., et al. A Textbook of Organic Chemistry. 1978. 35.00 (ISBN 0-7069-0442-7, Pub. by Vikas India). Advent Bk.

Tiwari, P. N. Fundamentals of Nuclear Science: With Applications in Agriculture & Biology. LC 74-1290. 1974. 12.95 (ISBN 0-470-87522-4). Halsted Pr

Tiwari, R. D. & Sharma, J. P. The Determination of Carboxylic Functional Groups. LC 73-104121. 1970. 21.00 (ISBN 0-08-015516-2). Pergamon.

Tiwari, S. C., jt. ed. see Singh, Indera P.

Tixier, P. Contribution a L'etude du Genre Colo-Lejeuna. Les Colclejeuniceas de Nouvelles Caledonie. (Illus.). 1979. pap. text ed. 15.00x (ISBN 3-7682-1230-0). Lubrecht & Cramer.

Tizard, Barbara. Early Childhood Education (a Report Sponsored by the Social Science Research Council) 160p. 1975. pap. text ed. 12.00x (ISBN 0-85633-076-0, NFER). Humanities.

Tjur, Tue. Probability Based on Radon Measures. LC 80-40503. (Wiley Series in Probability & Mathematical Statistics Ser.). 256p. 1980. 55.50 (ISBN 0-471-27824-6, Pub. by Wiley-Interscience). Wiley.

Tlali, Miriam. Muriel at Metropolitan. 190p. (Orig.). 1979. 9.00 (ISBN 0-89410-101-3); pap. 5.00 (ISBN 0-89410-100-5). Three Continents.

Tlusty, J., jt. auth. see Koenigsberger, F.

Toates, F. M. Control Theory in Biology & Experimental Psychology. 1980. text ed. 21.00x (ISBN 0-09-119660-4, Hutchinson U Lib). Humanities.

Toates, Frederick M. Animal Behaviour: A Systems Approach. LC 79-41405. 304p. 1980. 50.00 (ISBN 0-471-27724-X); pap. 19.00 (ISBN 0-471-27723-1). Wiley.

Tobach, Ethel & Rosoff, Betty, eds. Genetic Determinism & Children. (Genes & Gender Ser.: No. 3). 176p. (Orig.). 1980. pap. text ed. 7.95 (ISBN 0-87752-221-9). Gordian.

Toback, Charles. Pediatrician's Psychological Handbook. LC 79-92916. 1980. pap. 10.50 (ISBN 0-87488-687-2). Med Exam.

Tober, James. Who Owns the Wildlife? The Political Economy of Conservation in Nineteenth Century America. LC 80-23482. (Contributions in Economics & Economic History Ser.: No. 37). (Illus.). 300p. 1981. lib. bdg. 29.95 (ISBN 0-313-22597-4, TOW/). Greenwood.

Tobey, Jeremy L. The History of Ideas: A Bibliographical Introduction, 2 vols. 320p. 1975-76. Vol. 1 Classical Antiquity. text ed. 11.65 (ISBN 0-87436-143-5, LC 74-83160); Vol. 2 Medieval & Early Modern Europe. text ed. 28.75 o.p. (ISBN 0-87436-239-3, LC 76-8017). ABC-Clio.

Tobia, Andrew. The Only Investment Guide You'll Ever Need. 200p. 1981. pap. 2.75 (ISBN 0-553-14481-2). Bantam.

Tobias, A. Honor Grades on Fifteen Hours a Week. 1969. pap. 1.25 o.s.i. (ISBN 0-02-082100-X, Collier). Macmillan.

Tobias, Andrew. Fire & Ice. (Illus.). 1977. pap. 2.25 o.s.i. (ISBN 0-446-82409-7). Warner Bks.

--Fire & Ice: The Charles Revson-Revlon Story. LC 76-6124. 1976. 10.00 o.p. (ISBN 0-688-03023-8). Morrow.

--Getting by on One Hundred Thousand Dollars a Year & Other Sad Tales of the Seventies. 1980. 10.95 (ISBN 0-671-25518-5). S&S.

Tobias, Ann. Pot -- What It Is, What It Does. LC 78-10817. (Read-Alone Bk.). (Illus.). 48p. (gr. 1-3). 1981. pap. 2.95 (ISBN 0-688-00463-6). Greenwillow.

Tobias, Arthur & Hardesty, Jim, trs. The View from Cold Mountain: Translations of Han-Shan. 1976. 1.50 o.p. (ISBN 0-934834-16-4). White Pine.

Tobias, Charles W., jt. ed. see Gerischer, Heinz.

Tobias, Charles W., ed. see Gerischer, Heinz.

Tobias, Jerry V. & Schubert, Earl D., eds. Hearing & Research Theory, Vol. I. (Serial Publication). 1980. 18.50 (ISBN 0-12-312101-9). Acad Pr.

Tobias, Marc W. Locks, Safes, & Security: A Handbook for Law Enforcement Personnel. 352p. 1971. pap. 18.00 spiral (ISBN 0-398-02155-4). C C Thomas.

--Police Communications. (Illus.). 650p. 1974. text ed. 39.50 (ISBN 0-398-02970-9); pap. text ed. 27.75 (ISBN 0-398-02994-6). C C Thomas.

Tobias, Marc W. & Petersen, R. David. Pre-Trial Criminal Procedure: A Survey of Constitutional Rights. (Illus.). 448p. 1972. 23.75 (ISBN 0-398-02613-0). C C Thomas.

Tobias, Michael. Deva. 260p. (Orig.). 1981. pap. text ed. 6.95 (ISBN 0-932238-10-6). Word Shop.

Tobias, P. V., jt. ed. see Leakey, L. S.

Tobias, Phillip V. Brain in Hominid Evolution. LC 78-158458. (Illus.). 1971. 27.50x (ISBN 0-231-03518-7). Columbia U Pr.

Tobias, Richard. T. E. Brown. (English Authors Ser.: No. 213). 1978. 12.50 (ISBN 0-8057-6682-0). Twayne.

Tobias, Richard C. The Art of James Thurber. LC 68-20938. vi, 196p. 1969. 13.50x (ISBN 0-8214-0058-4). Ohio U Pr.

Tobias, Richard C. & Zolbrod, Paul G., eds. Shakespeare's Late Plays: Essays in Honor of Charles Crow. LC 74-27704. xiv, 235p. 1974. 14.00x (ISBN 0-8214-0178-5). Ohio U Pr.

Tobias, Ronald. They Shoot to Kill: A Psycho-Survey of Criminal Sniping. 240p. (Orig.). 1981. 14.95 (ISBN 0-87364-207-4). Paladin Ent.

Tobias, S. A. & Koenigsbergen, T. Proceedings of the Seventeenth International Machine, Tool, Design & Research Conference. 1978. 109.95 (ISBN 0-470-99076-7). Halsted Pr.

Tobias, S. A. & Koenigsberger, F., eds. Proceedings of the Thirteenth International Machine Tool Design & Research Conference. LC 73-2955. 1973. 89.95 (ISBN 0-470-87529-1). Halsted Pr.

Tobias, S. A., jt. ed. see Koenigsberger, T.

Tobias, S. A., ed. see Machine Tool & Design Research International Conference, 14th.

Tobias, S. A., ed. see Machine Tool Design & Research International Conference, 12th.

Tobias, S. A., ed. see Machine Tool Design & Research International Conference 15th.

Tobias, Sheila, et al, eds. Cornell Conference on Women. 93p. 1969. pap. 3.00x o.p. (ISBN 0-912786-13-2). Know Inc.

Tobias, Thomas J. Towards Analysis of Marmoset Motor Cortex. (Illus.). 50p. 1980. pap. text ed. 16.00 (ISBN 0-9604634-0-2). Learn Mich.

Tobias, Tobi. Arthur Mitchell. LC 74-13730. (Biography Ser.). (Illus.). (gr. 1-5). 1975. PLB 7.89 (ISBN 0-690-00662-4, TYC-J). T Y Crowell.

--How We Got Our First Cat. (gr. 1-3). 1980. 5.95 (ISBN 0-531-02870-4, G35); PLB 7.90 (ISBN 0-531-04173-5, F20). Watts.

--Isamu Noguchi: The Life of a Sculptor. LC 72-7560. (Illus.). 48p. (gr. 2-5). 1974. 7.89 (ISBN 0-690-45014-1, TYC-J). T Y Crowell.

--Liquid or Solid? That's a Good Question! LC 77-4845. (Illus.). 1977. PLB 7.95 o.p. (ISBN 0-516-03537-1). Childrens.

--Maria Tallchief. LC 77-87159. (Biography Ser). (Illus.). (gr. 2-5). 1970. PLB 7.89 (ISBN 0-690-51829-3, TYC-J). T Y Crowell.

--Marian Anderson. LC 79-139101. (Biograohy Ser.). (Illus.). (gr. 1-5). 1972. PLB 7.89 (ISBN 0-690-51847-1, TYC-J). T Y Crowell.

--Where Does It Come from? That's a Good Question. (Illus.). (gr. k-3). 1977. PLB 7.95 o.p. (ISBN 0-516-03667-X). Childrens.

Tobin, Charles E. Human Anatomy. LC 75-78589. (Allied Health Ser). 1975. pap. 7.65 (ISBN 0-672-61375-1). Bobbs.

Tobin, Charles E. & Jacobs, John J. Shearer's Manual of Human Dissection. 6th ed. (Illus.). 352p. 1981. pap. text ed. 16.95 (ISBN 0-07-064926-X). McGraw.

Tobin, Eugene M., jt. ed. see Ebner, Michael H.

Tobin, G., jt. auth. see Muller, H. G.

Tobin, Helen M. & Yoder, Pat S. The Process of Staff Development: Components for Change. 2nd ed. LC 78-31459. (Illus.). 1979. text ed. 17.95 (ISBN 0-8016-4996-X). Mosby.

Tobin, Joseph R. Mozart & the Sonata Form. LC 76-125063. (Music Ser). 1970. Repr. of 1916 ed. lib. bdg. 15.00 (ISBN 0-306-70027-1). Da Capo.

Tobin, McLean. The Black Female Ph.D. Education & Career Development. LC 80-5578. 133p. 1980. lib. bdg. 15.25 (ISBN 0-8191-1312-3); pap. text ed. 7.25 (ISBN 0-8191-1313-1). U Pr of Amer.

Tobin, Marvin C. Laser Raman Spectroscopy. LC 80-11511. 184p. 1981. Repr. of 1971 ed. lib. bdg. write for info. (ISBN 0-89874-159-9). Krieger.

Tobin, Mary L. Hope Is an Open Door. LC 80-21414. (Journeys in Faith Ser). 1981. 7.95 (ISBN 0-687-17410-4). Abingdon.

Tobin, Richard J. The Social Gamble. LC 78-19229. 1979. 18.95 (ISBN 0-669-02468-6). Lexington Bks.

Tobin, Wallace E. Mariner's Pocket Companion, Nineteen Eighty. LC 75-21689. 1979. pap. 5.95 o.p. (ISBN 0-87021-380-6). Naval Inst Pr.

Tobis, Jerome S., jt. auth. see Buerger, Alfred A.

Toboldt, Bill. Fix Your Chevrolet. (Illus.). 1978. 6.00 (ISBN 0-87006-255-7). Goodheart.

--Fix Your Ford. (Illus.). 1978. 6.00 (ISBN 0-87006-254-9). Goodheart.

Toboldt, William K. Automotrix: Manual De Reparaciones Automotrices. Loinaz, George, ed. & tr. from Span. LC 76-22993. (Illus.). (gr. 11 up). 1977. 35.00 o.p. (ISBN 0-916628-01-9). Lineal Cleworth.

--Automotrix Two: Manual De Reparaciones Automotrices. rev. ed. LC 80-81966. (Illus., Span.). 1980. 45.00 (ISBN 0-916628-02-7). Lineal Cleworth.

Toboldt, William K. & Johnson, Larry. Automotive Encyclopedia. LC 78-27798. (Illus.). 792p. 1981. text ed. 16.00 (ISBN 0-87006-314-6). Goodheart.

--Automotive Encyclopedia. rev. ed. (Illus.). 792p. 1981. text ed. 16.00 (ISBN 0-87006-314-6). Goodheart.

Tobriner, Marian L. Vives' Introduction to Wisdom: A Renaissance Textbook. LC 68-54677. 1968. text ed. 8.75 (ISBN 0-8077-2278-2); pap. text ed. 4.00x (ISBN 0-8077-2275-8). Tchrs Coll.

Tobriner, Stephen. The Genesis of Noto: An Eighteenth-Century Sicilian City. 1980. 40.00x (ISBN 0-520-03526-7). U of Cal Pr.

Toby, Jackson, jt. auth. see Bredemeier, Harry C.

Tocci, Ronald J. Digital Systems: Principles & Applications. rev. & enl. ed. (Illus.). 1980. text ed. 14.95 (ISBN 0-13-212290-1). P-H.

--Fundamentals of Electronic Devices. 2nd ed. Oppenheimer, Samuel L., ed. (Technology Ser). (Illus.). 496p. 1975. text ed. 20.95 (ISBN 0-675-08771-6); instructor's manual 3.95 (ISBN 0-686-67096-5). Merrill.

--Fundamentals of Pulse & Digital Circuits. 2nd ed. (Electronics Technology Ser.). 1977. text ed. 20.95 (ISBN 0-675-08492-X); instructor's manual 3.95 (ISBN 0-686-67521-5). Merrill.

--Introduction to Electric Circuit Analysis. 1973. text ed. 22.95x (ISBN 0-675-08985-9); instructor's manual 3.95 (ISBN 0-686-66873-1). Merrill.

Toch, Ernst. The Shaping Forces in Music: An Inquiry into the Nature of Harmony, Melody, Counterpoint, Form. 1977. pap. text ed. 3.50 (ISBN 0-486-23346-4). Dover.

Toch, Hans. Peacekeeping: Police, Prisons & Violence. LC 76-5622. 1976. 16.95 (ISBN 0-669-00652-1). Lexington Bks.

--Social Psychology of Social Movements. LC 64-66077. 1965. pap. 5.50 (ISBN 0-672-60847-2). Bobbs.

--Violent Men. 1981. text ed. 13.95x (ISBN 0-87073-888-7); pap. text ed. 7.95 (ISBN 0-685-99685-9). Schenkman.

Toch, Henry. Economics for Professional Studies. (Illus.). 240p. 1977. pap. 12.95 (ISBN 0-7121-0568-9, Pub. by Macdonald & Evans England). Intl Ideas.

Tocqueville, Alexis C. de see De Tocqueville, Alexis C.

Tocqueville, Alexis de. Democracy in America. Mayer, J. P. & Kerr, A. P., eds. 1969. pap. 7.95 (ISBN 0-385-08170-7, A05, Anch). Doubleday.

--Old Regime & the French Revolution. Mayer, J. P. & Kerr, A. P., eds. LC 55-10160. 1955. pap. 3.50 (ISBN 0-385-09260-1, A60, Anch). Doubleday.

Tocqueville, Alexis De see De Beaumont, Gustave & De Tocqueville, Alexis.

Tocqueville, Alexis De see De Tocqueville, Alexis.

Tod, M. N. Ancient Greek Numerical Systems. 128p. 1979. 20.00 (ISBN 0-89005-290-5). Ares.

Tod, Osma G. & Benson, Oscar H. Weaving with Reeds & Fibers. Orig. Title: Hand Weaving with Reeds & Fibers. (Illus.). 224p. 1975. pap. 3.00 (ISBN 0-486-23143-7). Dover.

Todaro, Michael P. Economic Development in the Third World. 2nd ed. (Illus.). 544p. 1981. text ed. 17.95 (ISBN 0-582-29532-7). Longman.

--Economic Development in the Third World. LC 76-49626. (Illus.). 1977. text ed. 17.95x (ISBN 0-582-44628-7). Longman.

Todaro, Michael P. & Stilkind, Jerry. City Bias & Rural Neglect: The Dilemma of Urban Development. LC 80-26071. (Public Issues Papers). (Illus.). xiv, 93p. (Orig.). 1981. pap. text ed. 2.50 (ISBN 0-87834-042-4). Population Coun.

Today's Transport International Staff. Today's Fleet Maintainance: A Reader for Fleet Executives. LC 75-21975. 1975. 12.95 o.p. (ISBN 0-917408-02-0). Intercontinental Pubns.

Todd, jt. auth. see Barnes.

Todd, A. C. & Laws, Peter. The Industrial Archaeology of Cornwall. (Industrial Archaeology of the British Isles Ser). (Illus.). 288p. 1973. 14.95 (ISBN 0-7153-5590-2). David & Charles.

Todd, Charles B. In Olde Connecticut. LC 68-26612. 1968. Repr. of 1906 ed. 15.00 (ISBN 0-8103-3540-9). Gale.

--In Olde Massachusetts: Sketches of Old Times & Places During the Early Days of the Commonwealth. LC 77-99060. 1971. Repr. of 1907 ed. 15.00 (ISBN 0-8103-3775-4). Gale.

--Life & Letters of Joel Barlow: Poet, Statesman, Philosopher. LC 70-106988. (American Public Figures Ser). 1970. Repr. of 1886 ed. lib. bdg. 32.50 (ISBN 0-306-71875-8). Da Capo.

Todd, David K., ed. Water Encyclopedia. LC 76-140311. 1970. 40.00 o.s.i. (ISBN 0-912394-01-3). Water Info.

Todd, Dorothy & Mortimer, Raymond. The New Interior Decoration. LC 77-4444. (Architecture & Decorative Art Ser.). (Illus.). 1977. Repr. of 1929 ed. lib. bdg. 45.00 (ISBN 0-306-70899-X). Da Capo.

Todd, Doug, ed. How to Talk Country. 64p. (Orig.). 1980. pap. 1.50 (ISBN 0-553-14346-8). Bantam.

Todd, H. Ralph, Jr., jt. auth. see Steinmetz, Lawrence L.

Todd, Harry F., Jr., jt. ed. see Nader, Laura.

Todd, Helen. Mary Musgrove: Georgia Indian Princess. LC 80-54424. 147p. (gr. 6-12). 1981. pap. 4.49 (ISBN 0-9605514-0-9). Seven Oaks.

Todd, I. P. Colon, Rectum & Anus. 3rd ed. (Operative Surgery Ser.). 1977. 95.00 (ISBN 0-407-00606-0). Butterworths.

Todd, Ian. The Prehistoric of Central Anatolia I: The Neolithic Period. (Studies in Mediterranean Archaeology: Vol. LX). 177p. 1981. pap. text ed. 42.00x (ISBN 91-85058-87-4, Pub. by Astroms, Sweden). Humanities.

Todd, Ian P., ed. Intestinal Stomas. 1979. 28.50x (ISBN 0-433-32501-1). Intl Ideas.

Todd, Janet, ed. Be Good, Sweet Maid: An Anthology of Women & Literature. 175p. 1981. text ed. 22.00x (ISBN 0-8419-0692-0). Holmes & Meier.

--Bibliography of Women & Literature. 150p. 1981. text ed. 22.00x (ISBN 0-8419-0693-9). Holmes & Meier.

--Gender & Literary Voice. (Women & Literature: Vol. 1). 250p. 1981. text ed. 24.50x (ISBN 0-8419-0656-4); pap. text ed. 12.50x (ISBN 0-8419-0657-2). Holmes & Meier.

Todd, Janet M., ed. Wollstonecraft Anthology. LC 77-72192. (Illus.). 288p. 1977. 16.50x (ISBN 0-253-36605-4). Ind U Pr.

Todd, Jerry D., jt. auth. see Hold, William T.

Todd, Joseph D. Structural Theory & Analysis. LC 75-327936. (Illus.). 1975. 28.50x (ISBN 0-333-18021-6); pap. 18.95x (ISBN 0-333-15693-5). Scholium Intl.

Todd, Loreto. Pidgins & Creoles. (Language & Society Ser.). 1974. 12.00x (ISBN 0-7100-7865-X); pap. 4.95 (ISBN 0-7100-7927-3). Routledge & Kegan.

--Some Day Been Dey: West African Pidgin Folktale. (Orig.). 1979. pap. 18.50 (ISBN 0-7100-0024-3). Routledge & Kegan.

Todd, Loreto, jt. auth. see O'Donnell, W. R.

Todd, Mabel E. Thinking Body: A Study of Balancing Forces of Dynamic Man. LC 68-28048. (Illus.). 1968. pap. 8.25 (ISBN 0-87127-014-5). Dance Horiz.

Todd, Mabel L., ed. see Dickinson, Emily.

Todd, Malcolm. The Barbarians. 1981. 27.00 (ISBN 0-7134-1669-6, Pub. by Batsford England). David & Charles.

--The Northern Barbarians: 100bc-300ad. (Illus., Orig.). 1975. text ed. 18.75x (ISBN 0-09-122220-6, Hutchinson U Lib). Humanities.

--Studies in the Romano - British Villa. 220p. 1977. pap. text ed. 19.00x (ISBN 0-7185-1149-2, Leicester). Humanities.

Todd, Nancy J., ed. Journal of the New Alchemists, No. 7. (Illus.). 184p. 1981. 15.95 (ISBN 0-8289-0405-7); pap. 9.95 (ISBN 0-8289-0406-5). Greene.

Todd, O. J., jt. auth. see Rupert, Milan.

Todd, Pamela & Fordham, David. Private Tucker's Boer War Diary. (Illus.). 192p. 1980. 27.00 (ISBN 0-241-10272-3, Pub. by Hamish Hamilton England). David & Charles.

Todd, Ralph, jt. auth. see Costley, Dan L.

Todd, Richard E., ed. Baptism. (Grace Bible Ser.). (Illus.). 16p. (Orig.). (gr. 1-6). 1980. pap. 0.50 (ISBN 0-9605324-0-4). R E Todd.

Todd, Sharon. Adventures in Nameless Valley Ranch. Van Dolson, Bobbie J., ed. 96p. 1981. pap. price not set (ISBN 0-8280-0032-8). Review & Herald.

Todd, W. E. Clyde. Birds of the Labrador Peninsula. LC 80-66715. (Illus.). 1980. 70.00x (ISBN 0-931130-06-9). Buteo.

Toddes, E. Mandelstamm I Tjutcev. (Pdr Press Publications on Osip Mandel'shtam Ser.: No. 1). (Orig.). 1974. pap. text ed. 3.50x (ISBN 90-3160-033-4). Humanities.

Toder, Eric J., et al. Trade Policy & the U. S. Automobile Industry. LC 77-16273. (Praeger Special Studies). 1978. 25.95 (ISBN 0-03-040956-X). Praeger.

Toder, Nancy. Choices. LC 80-20836. 320p. (Orig.). 1980. pap. 6.00 (ISBN 0-930436-05-9). Persephone.

Todes, Jay L., et al. Management & Motivation: An Introduction to Supervision. 1977. text ed. 16.95 scp (ISBN 0-06-046636-7, HarpC); instructor's manual avail. (ISBN 0-685-74059-5). Har-Row.

Todhunter, Hazel. Make It in Cheesecloth. 1979. 14.95 (ISBN 0-7134-1264-X, Pub. by Batsford England). David & Charles.

Todhunter, Isaac. History of the Calculus of Variations in the Nineteenth Century. LC 61-18586. 15.95 (ISBN 0-8284-0164-0). Chelsea Pub.

--History of the Mathematical Theory of Probability. LC 51-146. 1949. 15.95 (ISBN 0-8284-0057-1). Chelsea Pub.

Todorov, I. T. Analytic Properties of Feynman Diagrams in Quantum Field Theory. Risk, Clifford, tr. 168p. 1971. 27.00 (ISBN 0-08-016544-3). Pergamon.

Todorov, Tzvetan. Litterature et signification. (Fr). pap. 12.25 (ISBN 0-685-13971-9, 3636). Larousse.

Toelken, Barre. The Dynamics of Folklore. LC 78-69536. (Illus.). 1978. text ed. 14.50 (ISBN 0-395-27068-5); inst. manual 0.40 (ISBN 0-395-27069-3). HM.

Toen, Donna van see Van Toen, Donna.

Toender, O., jt. auth. see Aarli, J. A.

Toepfer, Thomas. American Beer Can Encyclopedia. (Illus.). 1979. pap. 7.95 (ISBN 0-89145-150-1). Collector Bks.

Toeplitz, Otto. Calculus: A Genetic Approach. Kothe, Gottfried, ed. Lange, Luise, tr. LC 63-9731. (Illus.). 1963. 8.75x o.s.i. (ISBN 0-226-80665-0). U of Chicago Pr.

Toeplitz, Otto, jt. auth. see Hellinger, Ernst.

Toepperwein, Emilia, jt. auth. see Toepperwein, Fritz.

Toepperwein, Emilie & Toepperwein, Fritz. Chinto, the Chaparral Cock. (gr. 4-7). 2.00 (ISBN 0-910722-04-8). Highland Pr.

Toepperwein, Emilie & Toepperwein, Fritz A. Jose & the Mexican Jumping Bean. (Illus.). (gr. 4-7). 1965. PLB 2.00 (ISBN 0-910722-05-6). Highland Pr.

Toepperwein, Emilie & Toepperwein, Fritz. The Missions of San Antonio. pap. text ed. 1.50 (ISBN 0-910722-12-9). Highland Pr.

--O. Henry Almanac. pap. 1.00 (ISBN 0-910722-07-2). Highland Pr.

Toepperwein, Emilie, jt. auth. see Toepperwein, Fritz.

Toepperwein, Fritz & Toepperwein, Emilia. Footnotes of the Buckhorn: Centennial Edition 1881-1981. pap. 3.50 (ISBN 0-910722-14-5). Highland Pr.

Toepperwein, Fritz & Toepperwein, Emilie. The San Antonio River. 1977. pap. 1.50 (ISBN 0-910722-11-0). Highland Pr.

Toepperwein, Fritz, jt. auth. see Toepperwein, Emilie.

Toepperwein, Fritz A., jt. auth. see Toepperwein, Emilie.

Toepperwein, Herman. Jim Bowie & Lost Mine. pap. text ed. 1.50 (ISBN 0-910722-08-0). Highland Pr.

--Sam Houston. pap. 1.50 (ISBN 0-910722-09-9). Highland Pr.

--Showdown: Western Gunfighters in Moments of Truth. LC 74-84581. (Illus.). 101p. 1974. 8.95 (ISBN 0-89052-013-5). Madrona Pr.

--The Texas Ranger. pap. 1.50 (ISBN 0-910722-10-2). Highland Pr.

Toews, John E. Hegelianism: The Path Toward Dialectic Humanism, 1805 to 1841. LC 80-16370. 512p. Date not set. 39.50 (ISBN 0-521-23048-9). Cambridge U Pr.

Tofani. Durer: Paintings. (The Jewel Ser.). Date not set. 4.95 (ISBN 0-8120-5346-X). Barron.

Toffler, Alvin. The Third Wave. LC 79-26690. 448p. 1980. 12.95 (ISBN 0-688-03597-3). Morrow.

--The Third Wave. 576p. (Orig.). 1981. pap. 3.95 (ISBN 0-553-14431-6). Bantam.

Toffler, Alvin, ed. Learning for Tomorrow: The Role of the Future in Education. 1974. 12.95 o.p. (ISBN 0-394-48313-8). Random.

Toghill, Jeff. Boat Owner's Fitting-Out Manual. 224p. 22.95 (ISBN 0-442-26199-3). Van Nos Reinhold.

--Boat Owner's Maintenance Manual. (Illus.). 308p. 1976. Repr. of 1970 ed. 16.95 (ISBN 0-589-07057-6, Pub. by Reed Books Australia). C E Tuttle.

--Boat Owner's Maintenance Manual. (Illus.). 308p. 1970. Repr. 16.95 (ISBN 0-589-07057-6, Dist. by C E Tuttle). Reed.

--Celestial Navigation for Beginners. (Illus.). 112p. (Orig.). 1978. pap. 6.75 (ISBN 0-589-50042-2, Pub. by Reed Books Australia). C E Tuttle.

--Celestial Navigation for Beginners. (Orig.). 1980. pap. 8.95 (ISBN 0-8464-0998-4). Beekman Pubs.

--Coastal Navigation for Beginners. 1980. pap. 7.95x (ISBN 0-8464-1001-X). Beekman Pubs.

--Coastal Navigation for Beginners. (Illus.). 1976. pap. 5.25 (ISBN 0-589-07191-2, Dist. by C. E. Tuttle). Reed.

--Knots & Splices. (Illus.). 64p. (Orig.). 1979. pap. 3.50 (ISBN 0-589-50079-1, Pub. by Reed Books Australia). C E Tuttle.

--Navigating with Chart & Compass. (Illus.). 96p. (Orig.). 1980. pap. 8.25 (ISBN 0-589-50183-6, Pub. by Reed Bks Australia). C E Tuttle.

Toglia, Joseph U. Electronystagmography: Technical Aspects & Atlas. (Illus.). 168p. 1976. 18.50 (ISBN 0-398-03537-7). C C Thomas.

Togliatti, Palmiro. On Gramsci & Other Writings. Sassoon, Donald, ed. 1980. text ed. 24.75x (ISBN 0-391-01679-2). Humanities.

Tognoni, Gianni, et al, eds. Frontiers in Therapeutic Drug Monitoring. (Monographs of the Mario Negri Institute for Pharmacological Research). 200p. 1980. text ed. 21.50 (ISBN 0-89004-508-9). Raven.

Toguchi, Masaru. Oriental Herbal Wisdom. (Orig.). 1973. pap. 1.50 o.s.i. (ISBN 0-515-02906-8, V2906). Jove Pubns.

Toh, K. A. & Tan, S. H. Objective Questions in Physics for Advanced Level. 1977. pap. text ed. 8.50x o.p. (ISBN 0-435-68826-X). Heinemann Ed.

Tohei, Koichi. The Book of "Ki". Co-Ordinating Body and Mind in Daily Life. LC 76-29340. (Illus.). 128p. 1976. pap. 7.95 (ISBN 0-87040-379-6). Japan Pubns.

Tohen, Z. Alfonso. Manual of Mechanical Orthopaedics. (Illus.). 340p. 1973. 18.75 (ISBN 0-398-02614-9). C C Thomas.

Toigo, Angela, Sr. God & a Mouse. LC 72-84198. (Illus.). 52p. 1980. 5.00 (ISBN 0-913180-01-7). Benedict Con Adoration.

Toigo, M. A. Caves & Canyons. LC 79-54772. (Illus.). 52p. 1979. 5.00 (ISBN 0-913180-02-5). Benedict Con Adoration.

Toit, Brian M. Du see Du Toit, Brian M.

Toit, Darcy du see Du Toit, Darcy.
Tokay, Elbert. Fundamentals of Physiology: The Human Body & How It Works. rev. ed. 1970. pap. 3.95 (ISBN 0-06-463221-0, EH 221, EH). Har-Row.
Tokayer, Marvin & Swartz, Mary. Desperate Voyagers. 1980. pap. 2.75 (ISBN 0-440-12223-6). Dell.
Tokes, Rudolf L., jt. auth. see Morton, Henry W.
Tokes, Rudolph L., ed. Eurocommunism & Detente. LC 77-92750. 1978. cobee 25.00x (ISBN 0-8147-8161-6); pap. 11.00x cobee (ISBN 0-8147-8162-4). NYU Pr.
Toklas, Alice B. Alice B. Toklas Cook Book. 1954. pap. 2.50 (ISBN 0-385-09439-6, A196, Anch). Doubleday.
Toklas, Alice B., jt. auth. see Stein, Gertrude.
Tokson, Elliot. Appointment in Calcutta. 1979. pap. 1.95 o.p. (ISBN 0-449-14131-4, GM). Fawcett.
--Cavender's Balkan Quest. 1977. pap. 1.75 o.p. (ISBN 0-449-13917-4, GM). Fawcett.
Tokson, Elliott. Desert Captive. 288p. 1977. pap. 1.75 o.p. (ISBN 0-449-13722-8, GM). Fawcett.
Toland, John. Adolf Hitler. 1056p. 1981. pap. 9.95 (ISBN 0-345-29470-X). Ballantine.
--Christianity Not Mysterious. Wellek, Rene, ed. LC 75-11257. (British Philosophers & Theologians of the 17th & 18th Centuries Ser.). 1978. lib. bdg. 42.00 (ISBN 0-8240-1807-9). Garland Pub.
--A Collection of Several Pieces, 2 vols. Wellek, Rene, ed. LC 75-11258. (British Philosophers & Theologians of the 17th & 18th Centuries: Vol. 57). 1977. Repr. of 1726 ed. Set. lib. bdg. 76.00 (ISBN 0-8240-1808-7); lib. bdg. 42.00 ea. Garland Pub.
--Flying Tigers. (Landmark Ser: No. 105). (Illus.). (gr. 7-8). 1963. PLB 5.99 (ISBN 0-394-90405-2). Random.
--The Flying Tigers. (YA) 1979. pap. 1.50 (ISBN 0-440-92621-1, LFL). Dell.
--The Great Dirigibles, Their Triumphs & Disasters. Orig. Title: Ships in the Sky: the Story of the Great Dirigibles. (Illus.). 8.50 (ISBN 0-8446-4612-1). Peter Smith.
--Letters to Serena. Wellek, Rene, ed. LC 75-11259. (British Philosophers & Theologians of the 17th & 18th Centuries: Vol. 58). 1977. Repr. of 1704 ed. lib. bdg. 42.00 (ISBN 0-8240-1809-5). Garland Pub.
--No Mans Land, Nineteen Eighteen: The Last Year of the Great War. LC 78-22761. (Illus.). 672p. 1980. 17.95 (ISBN 0-385-11291-2). Doubleday.
--Pantheisticon. Wellek, Rene, ed. LC 75-11260. (British Philosophers & Theologians of the 17th & 18th Centuries: Vol. 59). 1977. Repr. of 1751 ed. lib. bdg. 42.00 (ISBN 0-8240-1810-9). Garland Pub.
Toland, John, et al. Anglia Libera. Berkowitz, David S. & Thorne, Samuel E., eds. LC 77-89231. (Classics of English Legal History in the Modern Era Ser.: Vol. 71). 400p. 1979. lib. bdg. 40.00 (ISBN 0-8240-3171-7). Garland Pub.
Tolansky, S. Multiple-Beam Interferometry of Surfaces & Films. (Illus.). 1971. pap. text ed. 3.00 (ISBN 0-486-62215-0). Dover.
Tolbert, Audrey. Four Plays. 1981. 4.95 (ISBN 0-8062-1664-6). Carlton.
Tolbert, E. L. Counseling for Career Development. 2nd ed. LC 79-89452. (Illus.). 1980. text ed. 16.95 o.p. (ISBN 0-686-65937-6); inst. manual 0.65 o.p. (ISBN 0-686-65938-4). HM.
Tolbert, Emory J. UNIA & Black Los Angeles: Ideology & Community in the American Garvey Movement. Hill, Robert A., ed. LC 80-18054. (Afro-American Culture & Society Monograph: No. 3). (Illus.). 138p. 1980. 13.95 (ISBN 0-934934-04-5); pap. 8.95 (ISBN 0-934934-05-3). Ctr Afro-Am Stud.
Tolbert, Frank X. Day of San Jacinto. 2nd ed. (Texas Heritage Ser). (Illus.). 1969. 12.95 (ISBN 0-8363-0025-4). Jenkins.
Toledano, Ralph De see De Toledano, Ralph.
Toledano, Roulhac B. & Christovich, Mary Louise. New Orleans Architecture, Vol. 6: Faubourg Treme & the Bayou Road. (New Orleans Architecture Ser.). (Illus.). 224p. 1980. 34.95 (ISBN 0-88289-166-9). Pelican.
Toledo, Gaspar Gomez De see Gomez De Toledo, Gaspar.
Toledo Museum of Art Staff. American Paintings in the Toledo Museum of Art. (Illus.). 276p. 1980. lib. bdg. cancelled (ISBN 0-935172-00-9); pap. cancelled (ISBN 0-935172-01-7). Toledo Mus Art.
Toledo Museum Staff. Toledo Museum of Art, American Paintings. LC 79-66974. (Illus.). 228p. 1980. lib. bdg. 24.50 (ISBN 0-935172-00-9); pap. 14.50 (ISBN 0-935172-01-7). Toledo Mus Art.
Toledo, Romeo T. Fundamentals of Food Process Engineering. (Illus.). 1980. pap. text ed. 24.50 (ISBN 0-87055-338-0). AVI.
Tolegian, Aram, tr. Armenian Poetry Old & New: A Bilingual Anthology. LC 79-971. (Eng. & Armenian.). 1979. 18.95x (ISBN 0-8143-1608-5). Wayne St U Pr.
Toleman, Eric. Growing Vegetables. (Practical Gardening Ser.). (Illus.). 112p. (Orig.). 1979. pap. 10.50 (ISBN 0-589-01239-8, Pub. by Reed Bks Australia). C E Tuttle.
Tolentino, Felipe L., et al. Vitreoretinal Disorders: Diagnosis & Management. LC 73-81838. (Illus.). 1976. text ed. 65.00 o.p. (ISBN 0-7216-8870-5). Saunders.
Tolf, Robert W. The Russian Rockefellers: The Saga of the Nobel Family & the Russian Oil Industry. (Publications Ser.: No. 158). (Illus.). 1976. 14.95 (ISBN 0-8179-6581-5). Hoover Inst Pr.
Tolgyessy, J., et al. Isotope Dilution Analysis. 196p. 1972. 27.00 (ISBN 0-08-015856-0). Pergamon.
Tolis, George, et al, eds. Clinical Neuroendocrinology: A Pathophysiological Approach. LC 78-64844. 1979. text ed. 50.00 (ISBN 0-89004-355-8). Raven.
Toliver, Harold. The Past That Poets Make. LC 80-18825. 304p. 1981. text ed. 24.00 (ISBN 0-674-65676-8). Harvard U Pr.
Toliver, Raymond & Constable, Trevor. Fighter Aces of the U. S. A. LC 79-53300. (Illus.). 1979. 24.95 (ISBN 0-8168-5792-X). Aero.
Tolkien, Christopher, ed. see Tolkien, J. R.
Tolkien, J. R. Lord of the Rings: Anniversary Edition, 3 vols. 1981. Set. 50.00 (ISBN 0-686-69051-6). HM.
--The Old English Exodus. Turville-Petre, Joan, ed. 128p. 1981. 24.00 (ISBN 0-19-811177-0). Oxford U Pr.
--Unfinished Tales. Tolkien, Christopher, ed. (Illus.). 368p. 1980. 15.95 (ISBN 0-395-29917-9). HM.
Tolkien, J. R. & Gordon, E. V., eds. Sir Gawain & the Green Knight. 2nd ed. 1967. pap. 8.95x (ISBN 0-19-811486-9). Oxford U Pr.
Toll, Robert C. Blacking up: The Minstrel Show in Nineteenth-Century America. LC 74-83992. (Illus.). 1977. pap. 5.95 (ISBN 0-19-502172-X, 489, GB). Oxford U Pr.
Tollefson, Stephen & Davis, Kim. Reading & Writing About Language. 1979. pap. text ed. 7.95x (ISBN 0-534-00617-5). Wadsworth Pub.
Toller, Jane. Discovering Antiques. LC 75-24713. (Illus.). 176p. 1976. 7.95 o.p. (ISBN 0-498-01844-X). A S Barnes.
Tollers, Vincent, jt. ed. see Maier, John.
Tollerton, V. P., Jr. Exoterica: Poems & Drawings. (Illus.). 48p. 1980. 3.95 (ISBN 0-915102-01-3). Eastham Edns.
Tolles, Bryant F., Jr. & Tolles, Carolyn K. New Hampshire Architecture: An Illustrated Guide. LC 78-63586. (Illus.). 420p. 1979. text ed. 15.00 (ISBN 0-87451-165-8); pap. 7.50 (ISBN 0-87451-167-4). U Pr of New Eng.
Tolles, Bryant F., Jr., jt. auth. see Oliver, Andrew.
Tolles, Carolyn K., jt. auth. see Tolles, Bryant F., Jr.
Tollett, Susan M., jt. ed. see Levenson, Alvin J.
Tolley, B. Stuart. Advertising & Marketing Research: A New Methodology. LC 77-1120. 1977. 21.95x (ISBN 0-88229-179-3). Nelson-Hall.
Tolley, George, et al. Air Quality. (Environmental Policy Ser.: Vol. II). 1981. write for info. (ISBN 0-88410-626-8). Ballinger Pub.
--Elements of Environmental Analysis. (Environmental Policy Ser.: Vol. I). 1981. write for info. (ISBN 0-88410-625-X). Ballinger Pub.
Tolley, George S. & Vaughan, Roger J. Recreation & Aesthetics. (Environmental Policy Ser.: Vol. V). 1980. write for info. (ISBN 0-88410-628-4). Ballinger Pub.
Tolley, George S., et al. Environmental Policy: Water Quality, Vol. 3. 1981. write for info. (ISBN 0-88410-632-2). Ballinger Pub.
Tolley, H. & Orrell, K. Yorkshire & North Lincolnshire. 3rd ed. LC 77-87393. (Geography of the British Isles Ser.). (Illus.). 1978. limp bdg. 6.95x (ISBN 0-521-21918-3). Cambridge U Pr.
Tolley, Howard B., Jr. Children & War: Political Socialization to International Conflict. LC 72-90521. (Illus.). 274p. 1973. pap. text ed. 6.50x (ISBN 0-8077-2280-4). Tchrs Coll.
Tolley, Kemp. Cruise of the Lanikai. LC 73-82484. (Illus.). 356p. 1973. 13.50 o.p. (ISBN 0-87021-132-3). Naval Inst Pr.
Tollinchi, Esteban. Arte y Sensualidad: Cincuenta Imagenes Del Hombre y De la Tierra. LC 79-19403. (Illus.). 710p. 1980. write for info. (ISBN 0-8477-2111-6); pap. write for info. (ISBN 0-8477-2112-4). U of PR Pr.
Tollison, Robert D., ed. The Political Economy of Antitrust: Principal Paper by William Baxter. LC 80-7928. 1980. 16.95x (ISBN 0-669-03876-8). Lexington Bks.
Tolliver, Raymond F. Nazi Interrogator. 464p. 1980. pap. 2.95 (ISBN 0-89083-649-3). Zebra.
Tolliver, Ruby C. Decision at Sea. LC 80-65972. (gr. 9-12). 1980. pap. 4.95 (ISBN 0-8054-7314-9). Broadman.
Tolman, Edward C. Purposive Behavior in Animals & Men. LC 67-20666. (Century Psychology Ser.). (Illus.). 1967. text ed. 28.50x (ISBN 0-89197-544-6); pap. text ed. 9.95x (ISBN 0-89197-545-4). Irvington.
Tolman, Newton F. & Gilbert, Kay. Nelson Music Collection. 6.00x o.p. (ISBN 0-87233-014-1). Bauhan.
Tolman, Richard C. The Principles of Statistical Mechanics. LC 79-52649. 1980. pap. text ed. 8.95 (ISBN 0-486-63896-0). Dover.
Tolnay, Charles Q. De see De Tolnay, Charles Q.
Tolor, Alexander & Brannigan, Gary. Research & Clinical Applications of the Bender-Gesalt Test. (Illus.). 224p. 1980. 22.50 (ISBN 0-398-04088-5). C C Thomas.
Tolson, Melvin. Harlem Gallery. 1969. pap. 1.50 o.s.i. (ISBN 0-02-070910-2, Collier). Macmillan.
--Libretto for the Republic of Liberia. 1970. pap. 1.50 o.s.i. (ISBN 0-02-070900-5, Collier). Macmillan.
Tolstoi, D. M., ed. English-Russian Physics Dictionary. LC 78-40718. 1979. 75.00 (ISBN 0-08-023057-1). Pergamon.
Tolstoi, Leo. Sebastopol. 1961. pap. 4.50 (ISBN 0-472-06058-9, 58, AA). U of Mich Pr.
Tolstoy, Alexei. Aelita. Bouis, Antonina W., tr. from Rus. (Best of Soviet Science Fiction Ser.). 156p. 1981. 9.95 (ISBN 0-02-619200-4). Macmillan.
--Great Big Enormous Turnip. LC 69-10277. (Illus.). (gr. k-3). 1969. PLB 3.90 o.p. (ISBN 0-531-01684-6). Watts.
Tolstoy, Leo. Anna Karenin. rev. ed. Edmonds, Rosemary, tr. from Rus. (Classics Ser). 1978. pap. 3.95 (ISBN 0-14-044041-0). Penguin.
--The Death of Ivan Ilyich. pap. 1.95. Bantam.
--Master & Man. Aitken, Eleanor, ed. LC 70-77293. 1969. text ed. 14.50x (ISBN 0-521-07466-5). Cambridge U Pr.
--Recollections & Essays. Maude, Aylmer, tr. (World's Classics Ser). 10.95 (ISBN 0-19-250459-2). Oxford U Pr.
--War - Patriotism - Peace. LC 77-147488. (Library of War & Peace; the Character & Causes of War). lib. bdg. 38.00 (ISBN 0-8240-0281-4). Garland Pub.
--War & Peace. Garnett, Constance, tr. LC 76-6103. 1320p. 1976. 12.50 o.s.i. (ISBN 0-690-01108-3, TYC-T). T Y Crowell.
--What Is Art. Maude, Aylmer, tr. LC 60-9557. 1960. pap. 5.50 (ISBN 0-672-60221-0, LLA51). Bobbs.
Tolzmann, Don H. German-American Literature. LC 77-21596. 1977. 17.00 (ISBN 0-8108-1069-7). Scarecrow.
--German Americana: A Bibliography. LC 74-28085. 1975. 18.00 (ISBN 0-8108-0784-X). Scarecrow.
Tom, Katie. Ever Get Depressed. (Uplook Ser.). 1977. pap. 0.75 (ISBN 0-8163-0280-4). Pacific Pr Pub Assn.
Toma, Peter A. & Volgyes, Ivan. Politics in Hungary. LC 76-29613. (Illus.). 1977. text ed. 17.95x (ISBN 0-7167-0557-5). W H Freeman.
Tomalin, Ruth. Gone Away. LC 79-670253. (gr. 4 up). 1979. 10.95 (ISBN 0-571-11342-7, Pub. by Faber & Faber). Merrimack Bk Serv.
--The Sea Mice. (Illus.). 1962. 6.95 (ISBN 0-571-05213-4, Pub. by Faber & Faber). Merrimack Bk Serv.
--The Spring House. 1968. 6.50 (Pub. by Faber & Faber). Merrimack Bk Serv.
--A Stranger Thing. (Illus.). 1975. 8.95 (ISBN 0-571-10748-6, Pub. by Faber & Faber). Merrimack Bk Serv.
Toman, J., jt. auth. see Scindler, D.
Toman, W. An Introduction to Psychoanalytic Theory of Motivation. 1960. text ed. 18.75 (ISBN 0-08-009485-6). Pergamon.
Tomar, Russell H., jt. auth. see Peacock, Julia E.
Tomasevic, Nebojsa. Naive Painters of Yugoslavia. (Illus.). 1978. 22.50 o.p. (ISBN 0-8467-0467-6, Pub. by Two Continents). Hippocrene Bks.
--Yugoslav Naive Art: Eighty Self-Taught Artists Speak About Themselves & Their Work. (Illus.). 1976. 30.00x o.p. (ISBN 0-686-19996-0). Intl Learn Syst.
Tomasi, Lydio F., ed. The Italian in America: The Progressive View, 1891-1914. rev ed. LC 72-80258. (Illus.). 221p. 1978. pap. text ed. 9.95x (ISBN 0-913256-03-X, Dist. by Ozer). Ctr Migration.
Tomasi, Lydio F., ed. see Annual Legal Conference on the Representation of Aliens 1978.
Tomasi, S. M., ed. Perspectives in Italian Immigration & Ethnicity. LC 77-74178. 1977. pap. text ed. 9.95x (ISBN 0-913256-26-9, Dist. by Ozer). Ctr Migration.
Tomasi, Silvano M. Piety & Power: The Role of Italian Parishes in the New York Metropolitan Area (1880-1930) LC 74-79913. 201p. 1975. 14.95x (ISBN 0-913256-16-1, Dist. by Ozer). Ctr Migration.
Tomasi, Silvano M. & Engel, Madeline H. The Italian Experience in the United States. 1970. pap. 9.95x (ISBN 0-913256-01-3, Dist. by Ozer). Ctr Migration.
Tomasi, T. B. The Immune System of Secretion. (Foundation of Biology Ser.). (Illus.). 176p. 1976. ref. ed. 22.95x (ISBN 0-13-451609-5). P-H.
Tomasino, Joseph, jt. auth. see Vasi, Susanne.
Tomasson, Katherine & Buist, Francis. Battles of the Forty-Five. 1978. 27.00 (ISBN 0-7134-0769-7, Pub. by Batsford England). David & Charles.
Tomb, David A. Psychiatry for the House Officer. (House Officer Ser.). (Illus.). 231p. 1980. softcover 10.95 (ISBN 0-683-08336-8). Williams & Wilkins.
Tomback, Richard S. A Comparative Semitic Lexicon of the Phoenician & Punic Languages. LC 76-55377. (Society of Biblical Literature. Dissertation Ser.: No. 32). 1978. pap. 10.50 (ISBN 0-89130-126-7, 060132). Scholars Pr Ca.
Tombaugh, Clyde, jt. auth. see Moore, Patrick.
Tombs, David. Sound Recording: From Microphone to Master Tape. (Illus.). 192p. 1980. 24.00 (ISBN 0-7153-7954-2). David & Charles.
Tomcsanyi, Linda, illus. Color Me Greene. (Illus.). 1980. 3.00 (ISBN 0-686-26237-9). E S Cunningham.
Tomeh, George, ed. Israel & South Africa. 2nd ed. 1973. pap. 1.95 o.p. (ISBN 0-911026-02-9). New World Press NY.
Tomek, Ivan. Introduction to Computer Organization. (Illus.). 200p. 1981. text ed. 21.95 (ISBN 0-914894-08-0). Computer Sci.
--Introduction to Computer Organization Workbook. (Illus., Orig.). 1981. pap. text ed. price not set (ISBN 0-914894-70-6). Computer Sci.
Tomek, William G. & Robinson, Kenneth L. Agricultural Product Prices. (Illus.). 392p. 1972. 16.50x (ISBN 0-8014-0748-6). Cornell U Pr.
--Agricultural Product Prices. 2nd ed. LC 80-16085. 400p. 1981. 19.50x (ISBN 0-8014-1337-0). Cornell U Pr.
Tomescu, Ioan. Introduction to Combinatorics. Lloyd, E. Keith, ed. Rudeanu, S., tr. from Romanian. Orig. Title: Introducere in Combinatorica. (Illus.). 250p. 1975. text ed. 28.50x (ISBN 0-569-08057-6, Pub. by Collets England). Scholium Intl.
Tomeski, Edward A. Computer Revolution: The Executive & the New Information Technology. (Illus.). 1969. 6.95 o.s.i. (ISBN 0-02-619510-0). Macmillan.
--Fundamentals of Computers in Business: A Systems Approach. LC 78-54208. 1979. text ed. 18.95x (ISBN 0-8162-8733-3); instructor's manual 4.50 (ISBN 0-8162-8734-1); wkbk. 6.00 (ISBN 0-8162-8735-X). Holden-Day.
Tometsko, Andrew M. & Richard, Frederic M., eds. Applications of Photochemistry in Probing Biological Targets. LC 80-15368. (N.Y. Academy of Sciences Annals: Vol. 346). 1980. 88.00x (ISBN 0-89766-080-3); pap. write for info. (ISBN 0-89766-081-1). NY Acad Sci.
Tomevlin, John. The High Tower. 224p. (Orig.). 1980. pap. 2.25 (ISBN 0-553-02982-7). Bantam.
Tomie, Paola De see De Paola, Tomie.
Tomikel, John. Basic Earth Science. LC 80-66211. (Earth Science Ser.: No. 1). (Illus.). 166p. (Orig.). (gr. 9-12). 1981. pap. 6.00x (ISBN 0-910042-38-1). Allegheny.
--Taiwan Journal: Ten Historic Days. LC 79-53164. (Illus.). 1979. lib. bdg. 10.00 (ISBN 0-910042-37-3); pap. 4.00 (ISBN 0-910042-36-5). Allegheny.
Tomimas, Shutaro. The Open-Door Policy & the Territorial Integretiy of China. (Studies in Chinese History & Civilization). 1977. 17.00 (ISBN 0-89093-095-3). U Pubns Amer.
Tomimoto, Kenkichi, jt. auth. see Sanders, Herbert H.
Tominaga, Thomas T. & Schneidermeyer, Wilma. Iris Murdoch & Muriel Spark: A Bibliography. LC 76-909. (Author Bibliographies Ser.: No. 27). 253p. 1976. 12.00 (ISBN 0-8108-0907-9). Scarecrow.
Tominsky, John. Treasure from Hell. 1981. 5.75 (ISBN 0-8062-1695-6). Carlton.
Tomita, Kokei. Peasant Sage of Japan: The Life & Work of Sontoku Ninomiya. (Studies in Japanese History & Civilization). 1979. Repr. of 1912 ed. 24.00 (ISBN 0-89093-258-1). U Pubns Amer.
Tomkeieff, S. I., ed. see Vlasov, K. A., et al.
Tomkins, Calvin. The Bride & the Bachelors. (Illus.). 1976. pap. 4.95 (ISBN 0-14-004313-6). Penguin.

--Eric Hoffer, an American Odyssey. LC 68-28887. (Illus.). 1968. 5.50 o.p. (ISBN 0-525-09948-4). Dutton.
--Off the Wall: Robert Rauschenberg & the Art World of Our Time. 1981. pap. 5.95 (ISBN 0-14-005812-5). Penguin.
--World of Marcel Duchamp. (Library of Art). (Illus.). 1966. 15.95 (ISBN 0-8094-0236-X). Time-Life.
--World of Marcel Duchamp. LC 66-28544. (Library of Art Ser.). (Illus.). (gr. 6 up). 1966. 12.96 (ISBN 0-8094-0265-3, Pub. by Time-Life). Silver.
Tomkins, D. Michael. Trial & Error. LC 80-39757. 1981. 9.95 (ISBN 0-396-07944-X). Dodd.
Tomkins, Mary E. Ida M. Tarbell. LC 73-2293. (U. S. Authors Ser.: No. 247). 184p. 1974. lib. bdg. 10.95 (ISBN 0-8057-0714-X). Twayne.
Tomkins, Reginald, jt. auth. see Popovych, Orest.
Tomkins, Walter A. Santa Barbara County "California's Wonderful Corner". 1974. 4.50x (ISBN 0-686-17214-0). Sandollar Pr.
Tomkins, William. Indian Sign Language. Orig. Title: Universal Indian Sign Language of the Plains Indians of North America. (Illus.). 1969. pap. 2.00 (ISBN 0-486-22029-X). Dover.
Tomkinson, Michael. Kenya: A Vacation Guide. rev. ed. LC 77-70382. (Illus.). 1977. 5.95 o.p. (ISBN 0-684-14911-7, SL696, ScribT). Scribner.
Tomkys, W. H., jt. auth. see Plumpton, C.
Tomlin, E. W. Japan. (Nations & Peoples Library). 1973. 8.50x o.s.i. (ISBN 0-8027-2127-3). Walker & Co.
Tomlin, Maurice. English Furniture: An Illustrated Handbook. 1972. 26.00 o.p. (ISBN 0-571-08381-1, Pub. by Faber & Faber). Merrimack Bk Serv.
Tomlin, Pinky. The Object of My Affection: An Autobiography. LC 80-5938. (Illus.). 300p. 1981. 12.50 (ISBN 0-8061-1719-2). U of Okla Pr.
Tomlinson, A. Military Journals of Two Private Soldiers, 1758-1775. LC 75-146146. (Era of the American Revolution Ser). 1971. Repr. of 1855 ed. lib. bdg. 17.50 (ISBN 0-306-70134-0). Da Capo.
Tomlinson, Brian, jt. auth. see Bolitho, Red.
Tomlinson, Charles. Some Americans: A Personal Record. (A Quantum Bk.). 100p. 1981. 10.00 (ISBN 0-520-04037-6). U. of Cal Pr.
Tomlinson, Charles, ed. Marianne Moore: A Collection of Critical Essays. 1969. pap. 1.95 o.p. (ISBN 0-13-556035-7, Spec). P-H.
--The Oxford Book of Verse in English Translation. 750p. 1980. 37.50 (ISBN 0-19-214103-1). Oxford U Pr.
Tomlinson, F., jt. auth. see Walsh, J. H.
Tomlinson, H. The Divination of Disease. 1980. 9.50x (ISBN 0-8464-1006-0). Beekman Pubs.
--Medical Divination. 1980. 15.75x (ISBN 0-85032-133-6, Pub. by Daniel Co England). State Mutual Bk.
--Medical Divination. 88p. 1966. 5.50x (ISBN 0-8464-1031-1). Beekman Pubs.
Tomlinson, H. M., ed. Great Sea Stories of All Nations. 1108p. 1980. Repr. of 1930 ed. 40.00 (ISBN 0-89760-884-4). Telegraph Bks.
Tomlinson, Hilda. Hilda, the Hen Who Wouldn't Give up. LC 79-3764. (Illus.). 96p. (gr. 1-5). 1980. Repr. of 1967 ed. 5.95 (ISBN 0-15-234455-1, HJ). HarBraceJ.
Tomlinson, James & Dibden, Kenneth. Information Sources in Education & Work. LC 80-41801. (Butterworths Guides to Information Sources Ser.). 168p. 1980. text ed. 22.95 (ISBN 0-408-70923-5). Butterworths.
Tomlinson, Jill. The Bus That Went to Church. (Illus.). (ps-5). 1970. 4.95 o.p. (ISBN 0-571-06337-3, Pub. by Faber & Faber); pap. 2.50 (ISBN 0-571-09407-4). Merrimack Bk Serv.
--Lady Bee's Bonnets. 1971. pap. 2.95 (ISBN 0-571-11133-5, Pub. by Faber &Faber). Merrimack Bk Serv.
Tomlinson, M. An Introduction to the Chemistry of Benzenoid Components. 1971. 22.00 (ISBN 0-08-015659-2); pap. 9.75 (ISBN 0-08-016921-X). Pergamon.
Tomlinson, M. J. Pile Design & Construction Practice. (Viewpoint Ser.). (Illus.). 1978. 52.50x (ISBN 0-7210-1013-X). Scholium Intl.
Tomlinson, P. B. see Metcalfe, C. R.
Tomlinson, P. B. & Zimmermann, M. H., eds. Tropical Trees As Living Systems. LC 77-8579. (Illus.). 1978. 75.00 (ISBN 0-521-21686-9). Cambridge U Pr.
Tomlinson, Sally. Educational Subnormality. (International Library of Sociology Ser.). 300p. 1981. price not set (ISBN 0-7100-0697-7). Routledge & Kegan.
Tomlinson, Thomas B. Study of Elizabethan & Jacobean Tragedy. 1964. 48.00 (ISBN 0-521-06642-5). Cambridge U Pr.
Tompert, Ann. The Clever Princess. LC 77-72559. (Illus.). 39p. (gr. k-4). 1977. 6.75 (ISBN 0-914996-15-0); pap. 3.00 (ISBN 0-914996-13-4). Lollipop Power.
--Horse for Charlie. (A Tell-a-Tale Reader Ser.). (Illus.). (gr. k-3). 1979. PLB 4.77 (ISBN 0-307-68411-3, Whitman). Western Pub.
--It May Come in Handy Someday. LC 74-19487. (Illus.). 48p. (gr. 4-6). 1975. 5.95 o.p. (ISBN 0-685-50951-6, GB); PLB 5.72 o.p. (ISBN 0-07-064933-2). McGraw.
Tompkins, B. A. The Carpenter's Wife. 1977. pap. 1.00 o.p. (ISBN 0-931832-05-5). No Dead Lines.
Tompkins, Iverna. The Way to Happiness. 1978. pap. 1.95 pocketsize o.p. (ISBN 0-88270-292-0). Logos.
Tompkins, J. M. Ann Radcliffe & Her Influence on Later Writers. Varma, Devendra P., ed. LC 79-8485. (Gothic Studies & Dissertations Ser.). 1980. lib. bdg. 22.00x (ISBN 0-405-12681-6). Arno.
--The Art of Rudyard Kipling. LC 65-26135. 1965. pap. 3.95x (ISBN 0-8032-5200-5, BB 332, Bison). U of Nebr Pr.
--Popular Novel in England, 1770-1800. LC 32-24699. 1961. pap. 4.95x (ISBN 0-8032-5201-3, BB 121, Bison). U of Nebr Pr.
Tompkins, Jane P., ed. Reader-Response Criticism: From Formalism to Post-Structuralism. LC 80-7966. 320p. 1981. text ed. 20.00x (ISBN 0-8018-2400-1); pap. text ed. 6.95x (ISBN 0-8018-2401-X). Johns Hopkins.
Tompkins, John B. A Voyage of Pleasure: The Log of Bernard Gilboy's Transpacific Cruise in the Boat "Pacific" 1882-1883. LC 56-12045. (Illus.). 1956. pap. 6.00 (ISBN 0-87033-004-7). Cornell Maritime.
Tompkins, Peter. Mysteries of the Mexican Pyramids. LC 74-15857. (Illus.). 320p. (YA) 1976. 25.00 (ISBN 0-06-014324-X, HarpT). Har-Row.
Tompkins, Peter & Bird, Christopher. The Secret Life of Plants. LC 72-9160. (Illus.). 416p. 1973. 12.95 o.s.i. (ISBN 0-06-014326-6, HarpT). Har-Row.
Tompkins, R. P. T., jt. auth. see Janz, George J.
Tompkins, Sandra, jt. auth. see Miller, Gail.
Tompkins, Stuart R. The Triumph of Bolshevism: Revolution or Reaction? LC 66-22714. (Illus.). 331p. (Orig.). 1967. pap. 7.95x (ISBN 0-8061-1158-5). U of Okla Pr.
Tompkins, Virginia L. Life of a Sheriff. Date not set. 5.95 (ISBN 0-533-04768-4). Vantage.
Tompkins, Walker A. Lion of the Lavabeds. 144p. (Orig.). 1976. pap. 0.95 o.p. (ISBN 0-445-00706-0). Popular Lib.
Tompson, June. The Long Revenge. 160p. 1981. pap. 2.25 (ISBN 0-553-14723-4). Bantam.
Toms, Agnes. Eat, Drink & Be Healthy. 1968. pap. 1.50 (ISBN 0-515-04606-X). Jove Pubns.
Toms, Paul E. This Land Is Your Land. LC 75-23512. 1977. pap. 2.25 (ISBN 0-8307-0365-9, S312-1-07). Regal.
Tondeur, D., jt. ed. see Rodriques, A.
Toner, Jules J. A Commentary on Saint Ignatius' Rules for the Discernment of Spirits: A Guide to the Principles & Practice. LC 79-89606. 400p. Date not set. 14.00 (ISBN 0-912422-43-2); pap. 12.00 smyth sewn paper (ISBN 0-912422-42-4). Inst Jesuit. Postponed.
Toner, Raymond J. Gamble of the Marines. LC 62-19561. (Illus.). (gr. 5-7). 1963. 5.95g o.p. (ISBN 0-8075-2735-1). A Whitman.
Toney, Anthony. One Hundred Fifty Masterpieces of Drawing. (Illus., Orig.). 1963. pap. 5.00 (ISBN 0-486-21032-4). Dover.
Tong. Gary Tong's Crazy Cut-Outs. (ps-3). pap. 1.50 (ISBN 0-590-05738-3, Schol Pap). Schol Bk Serv.
Tong, Hollington K., jt. ed. see Chinese Ministry of Information.
Tong, T. K. & Tsung-Jen, Li, eds. The Memoirs of Li Tsung-Jen. 1979. lib. bdg. 33.00x (ISBN 0-89158-343-2). Westview.
Tong, Te-Kong. The Third Americans: A Selected Bibliography of Asians in America with Annotations. 1980. 4.50 (ISBN 0-937256-00-5). CHCUS Inc.
Tongue, Ruth L. The Chime Child: Or, Somerset Singers - Being an Account of Some of Their Songs Collected Over Sixty Years. LC 68-77292. x, 102p. Repr. of 1968 ed. 15.00 (ISBN 0-8103-5022-X). Gale.
--Forgotten Folk-Tales of the English Counties. 1970. 17.50 (ISBN 0-7100-6833-6). Routledge & Kegan.
Tonkin, Humphrey. The World in the Curriculum: Curricular Strategies for the 21st Century. LC 80-69765. 200p. (Orig.). 1980. pap. 6.95 (ISBN 0-915390-28-0). Change Mag.
Tonkin, John M. Church & the Secular Order in Reformation Thought. LC 73-143390. 236p. 1971. 17.50x (ISBN 0-231-03374-5). Columbia U Pr.
Tonkinson, Robert. The Jigalong Mob: Aboriginal Victors of the Desert Crusade. LC 73-85115. (Illus.). 166p. 1974. pap. 6.95 (ISBN 0-8465-7549-3). Benjamin-Cummings.
Tonn, Katie. I Ran Away from Home Last Week. (Uplook Ser.). 1975. pap. 0.75 (ISBN 0-8163-0174-3, 09107-4). Pacific Pr Pub Assn.
--Sometimes I Hate Myself. (Uplook Ser.). 1978. pap. 0.75 (ISBN 0-8163-0386-X, 19422-5). Pacific Pr Pub Assn.
--Try God, You'll Like Him. (Uplook Ser.). 1975. pap. 0.75 (ISBN 0-8163-0178-6, 20340-6). Pacific Pr Pub Assn.
Tonna, Benjamin, jt. auth. see Hall, Brian.
Tonna, Charlotte E. Falsehood & Truth. Wolff, Robert L., ed. Bd. with Conformity. LC 75-488. (Victorian Fiction Novels of Faith & Doubt Ser.). 1975. Repr. of 1841 ed. lib. bdg. 66.00 (ISBN 0-8240-1564-9). Garland Pub.
Tonne, Herbert. The Human Dilemma. LC 80-81391. (Library of Liberal Religion). 240p. 1980. 13.95 (ISBN 0-87975-135-5). Prometheus Bks.
Tonner, Leslie. The Five Towns. LC 80-52418. 416p. 1981. 12.95 (ISBN 0-87223-652-8). Seaview Bks.
--Fortunoff's Child. 1980. 10.95 (ISBN 0-8037-3354-2). Dial.
--Love Song. 1981. pap. 2.50 (ISBN 0-425-04832-2). Berkley Pub.
--Nothing but the Best. 160p. 1976. pap. 1.50 o.p. (ISBN 0-345-24966-6). Ballantine.
Tonnessen, Joh. N., jt. auth. see Johnsen, Arne Odd.
Tonnies, Ferdinand. Community & Society. Loomis, Charles P., tr. LC 57-8428. 1977. pap. text ed. 3.95x o.p. (ISBN 0-06-131116-2, TB1116, Torch). Har-Row.
--On Social Ideas & Ideologies. Jacoby, E. G., ed. & tr. 1974. pap. 5.95x o.p. (ISBN 0-06-139533-1, HR1810, Torch). Har-Row.
Tonnis, John & Rausch, Gerald. Chemical Investigations for the Nonscientist. 1980. coil binding 6.95 (ISBN 0-88252-109-8). Paladin Hse.
Tonry, Michael, jt. auth. see Morris, Norval.
Tonry, Michael, ed. see Morris, Norval.
Tonry, Michael, jt. ed. see Morris, Norval.
Toogood, Alan. Propagation. LC 80-6164. (Illus.). 336p. 1981. 13.95 (ISBN 0-8128-2772-4). Stein & Day.
Toogood, Alan & Stanley, John. The Modern Nurseryman. (Illus.). 432p. 1981. 45.00 (ISBN 0-571-11544-6, Pub. by Faber & Faber); pap. 22.00 (ISBN 0-571-11547-0). Merrimack Bk Serv.
Toogood, Alan R., tr. see Huxley, Anthony.
Toohey, Barbara, jt. auth. see Bierman, June.
Toohey, Barbara, jt. auth. see Biermann, June.
Toohey, William. Life After Birth: Spirituality for College Students. 112p. 1980. pap. 3.95 (ISBN 0-8164-2290-7). Seabury.
Tooke, Andrew. The Pantheon. LC 75-27880. (Renaissance & the Gods Ser.: Vol. 35). (Illus.). 1976. Repr. of 1713 ed. lib. bdg. 73.00 (ISBN 0-8240-2084-7). Garland Pub.
Tooke, Joan & Russell, Ken. Projects in Religious Education. 1974. 16.95 (ISBN 0-7134-2840-6, Pub. by Batsford England). David & Charles.
Tooke, Thomas R., jt. auth. see Gillard, William H.
Tooke, William. The Loves of Othniel & Achsah, Translated from the Chaldee, 1769, 2 vols. LC 74-14953. (Novel in England, 1700-1775 Ser). 1974. lib. bdg. 50.00 ea. (ISBN 0-8240-1188-0). Garland Pub.
Toolan, Suzanne. Keeping Festival. 1979. pap. 4.95 (ISBN 0-89390-011-7). Resource Pubns.
Toole, Darlene. Courageous Deaf Adults. 96p. 1980. 4.95 (ISBN 0-86575-132-3). Dormac.
--Successful Deaf Americans. 88p. 1979. 4.95 (ISBN 0-86575-118-8). Dormac.
Toole, John K. A Confederacy of Dunces. LC 80-8922. 416p. 1981. pap. 3.50 (ISBN 0-394-17800-9, BC). Grove.
Toole, K. Ross. Twentieth-Century Montana: A State of Extremes. LC 75-177348. 300p. 1979. Repr. of 1972 ed. 10.95 (ISBN 0-8061-0992-0). U of Okla Pr.
Tooley, M. J. Sea-Level Changes: North-West England During the Flandrian Stage. (Research Studies in Geography Ser.). (Illus.). 1979. 39.50x (ISBN 0-19-823228-4). Oxford U Pr.
Tooley, M. J., jt. auth. see Kidson, C.
Tooley, M. J. see Bowen, D. Q.
Tooley, Ronald V. Some English Books with Coloured Plates. LC 75-162521. 1971. Repr. of 1935 ed. 21.00 (ISBN 0-8103-3762-2). Gale.
Toomer, G. J., jt. ed. see Benjamin, Francis S., Jr.
Toomer, Jean see Harrison, Paul C.
Toomey, Beverly G., jt. ed. see Beran, Nancy J.
Toomey, Lee. Down & Out. LC 73-173720. (New Citizen Books). (Illus.). 80p. 1973. 7.50x (ISBN 0-85340-237-X). Intl Pubns Serv.
Toon, Peter. God's Church for Today. LC 80-65330. (Christian Faith for Today Ser.). 144p. (Orig.). 1980. pap. 3.95 (ISBN 0-89107-183-0). Good News.
--God's Kingdom for Today. LC 80-65331. (Christian Faith for Today Ser.). 128p. 1980. pap. 3.95 (ISBN 0-89107-188-1, Cornerstone Bks). Good News.
--God's Salvation for Today. (Christian Faith for Today Ser.). 144p. 1981. pap. 3.95 (ISBN 0-89107-194-6, Cornerstone Bks). Good News.
--God's Word for Today. (Christian Faith for Today Ser.). 144p. (Orig.). 1981. pap. 3.95 (ISBN 0-89107-193-8, Cornerstone Bks). Good News.
--One God in Trinity. LC 79-57395. 192p. 1980. 12.95 (ISBN 0-89107-187-3, Cornerstone Bks.). Good News.
Toon, Peter & Martin, Peter, eds. Evangelical Theology, Eighteen Thirty-Three to Eighteen Fifty-Six: A Response to Tractarianism. LC 79-16701. (New Foundations Theological Library Ser.). 254p. 18.50 (ISBN 0-8042-3703-4). John Knox.
Toon, Peter, ed. see Avis, Paul D.
Toon, Peter, ed. see Carson, D. A.
Toon, Peter, ed. see Martin, Ralph.
Toone, Betty L. Appalachia: The Mountains, the Place, & the People. LC 72-3119. (First Bks). (Illus.). 96p. (gr. 5-8). 1972. PLB 4.90 o.p. (ISBN 0-531-00769-3). Watts.
Toothman, John M. Conducting the Small Group Experience. LC 78-59854. 1978. pap. 7.50 (ISBN 0-8191-0554-6). U Pr of Amer.
Tooze, John, ed. DNA Tumor Viruses: Molecular Biology of Tumor Viruses, Vol. 10b. 2nd ed. LC 79-19882. (Cold Spring Harbor Monograph Series). 945p. 1980. 65.00 (ISBN 0-87969-126-3). Cold Spring Harbor.
Tooze, John, jt. ed. see Watson, James D.
Topalis, Mary & Aguilera, Donna. Psychiatric Nursing. 7th ed. LC 77-13051. (Illus.). 1978. pap. text ed. 16.95 (ISBN 0-8016-3148-3). Mosby.
Topazian, Richard G. & Goldberg, Morton H. Management of Infections of the Oral & Maxillofacial Regions. (Illus.). 500p. 1981. text ed. price not set (ISBN 0-7216-8879-9). Saunders.
Tope, D., et al. Social Sciences View School Administration. 1965. 9.95 o.p. (ISBN 0-13-818328-7). P-H.
Topilow, Arthur A. & Wilson, Merlin R. Hematology. (Medical Examination Review Book: Vol. 32). 1974. spiral bdg. 15.00 o.s.i. (ISBN 0-87488-148-X). Med Exam.
Toplin, Robert B. Freedom & Prejudice: The Legacy of Slavery in the United States & Brazil. LC 80-656. (Contributions in Afro-American & African Studies: No. 56). 1981. lib. bdg. 33.95 (ISBN 0-313-22008-5, TFP/). Greenwood.
--Unchallenged Violence: An American Ordeal. LC 75-72. 1975. lib. bdg. 17.95 (ISBN 0-8371-7748-0, TLV/). Greenwood.
Topliss, Eda. Provision for the Disabled. (Aspects of Social Policy Ser.). 1975. 14.00x o.p. (ISBN 0-631-16220-8, Pub. by Basil Blackwell England); pap. 6.50x o.p. (ISBN 0-631-16510-X). Biblio Dist.
Topliss, Eda & Gould, Bryan. Charter for the Disabled: The Chronically Sick & Disabled Persons Act 1970. (Aspects of Social Policy Ser.). 160p. 1981. 19.95x (ISBN 0-631-12833-6, Pub. by Basil Blackwell England). Biblio Dist.
Topliss, Patricia. Rhetoric of Pascal. 1966. text ed. 18.75x (ISBN 0-7185-1062-3, Leicester). Humanities.
Topliss, W. S. The Optical Dispensing & Workshop Practice. 1975. 39.95 (ISBN 0-407-00025-9). Butterworths.
Toplitsky, Tania S. The Russian Revolution in Nineteen Hundred Five. 164p. 1981. 13.50 (ISBN 0-682-49720-7). Exposition.
Topoff, Howard R., ed. see Schneirla, T. C.
Topor, Roland. Leonardo Was Right. Wright, Barbara, tr. 1980. pap. 3.95 (ISBN 0-7145-3671-7). Riverrun NY.
Toporek, Milton. Basic Chemistry of Life. LC 80-11980. (Illus.). 522p. 1980. pap. text ed. 16.95 (ISBN 0-8016-5002-X). Mosby.
Topp, William R., jt. auth. see Smith, Douglas B.
Toppen. From Caxton to Beckett. 1979. text ed. 42.75x (ISBN 90-6203-581-7). Humanities.
Topper, Michael A., jt. auth. see Ewen, Dale.
Topper, Suzanne. Astaire & Rogers. (Illus.). 1976. pap. 1.50 o.p. (ISBN 0-8439-0380-5, LB380DK, Leisure Bks). Nordon Pubns.
--Doesn't Everyone...? (Orig.). 1976. pap. 1.50 o.p. (ISBN 0-685-64270-4, LB338DK, Leisure Bks). Nordon Pubns.
--The Fruit Cookbook. 1973. pap. 2.95 o.p. (ISBN 0-380-01202-2, 14803). Avon.
Toppin, Edgar A. The Black American in United States History. new ed. (gr. 9-12). 1973. text ed. 12.20 (ISBN 0-205-03303-2, 7833032); tchrs.' guide 4.12 (ISBN 0-205-03304-0, 7833040). Allyn.
Toppin, Edgar A., jt. auth. see Dobler, Lavinia G.
Topping, A. Bonnes Vacances. (Illus., Fr.). (gr. 4-9). 1965. pap. text ed. 4.95 (ISBN 0-312-08785-3). St Martin.
Topping, Audrey. Splendors of Tibet. 1980. 25.00 (ISBN 0-86519-003-8). Caroline Hse.

Topping, Peter. Studies on Latin Greece A. D. 1205-1715. 400p. 1980. 60.00x (ISBN 0-86078-012-0, Pub. by Variorum England). State Mutual Bk.
Topsell, Edward. History of Four-Footed Beasts, & Serpents & Insects, 3 Vols. 2nd ed. LC 65-23391. 1967. Repr. of 1658 ed. Set. lib. bdg. 150.00 (ISBN 0-306-70923-6). Da Capo.
Topsell, Edward, tr. see Pliny.
Topsfield, L. T. Chretien de Troyes. 300p. Date not set. 49.50 (ISBN 0-521-23361-5). Cambridge U Pr.
--Troubadours & Love. LC 74-14440. (Illus.). 304p. 1975. 42.00 (ISBN 0-521-20596-4); pap. 11.95x (ISBN 0-521-09897-1). Cambridge U Pr.
Torack, Richard M. Your Brain Is Younger Than You Think: A Guide to Mental Aging. LC 80-21239. 164p. 1981. text ed. 14.95 (ISBN 0-88229-538-1); pap. 7.95 (ISBN 0-88229-761-9). Nelson-Hall.
Toraldo Di Francia, G. Investigation of the Physical World. LC 80-12791. (Illus.). 480p. Date not set. price not set (ISBN 0-521-29925-X); pap. price not set (ISBN 0-521-23338-0). Cambridge U Pr.
Torbe, Mike & Protherough, Robert. Classroom Encounters: Language & English Teaching. 214p. 1979. pap. text ed. 7.45x (ISBN 0-7062-3482-0, 6064-5, Pub. by Ward Lock Educational England). Hayden.
Torbert, Eugene C. Cervantes' Place-Names: A Lexicon. LC 78-6111. 1978. lib. bdg. 11.50 (ISBN 0-8108-1139-1). Scarecrow.
Torbert, Floyd J. Postmen the World Over. (Illus.). (gr. 4-6). 1966. 4.95g o.s.i. (ISBN 0-8038-5722-5). Hastings.
Torbet, Laura & Sternfield, Jonathan. The Complete Book of Mopeds. (Funk & W Bk.). (Illus.). 1977. 9.95 o.s.i. (ISBN 0-308-10307-6, TYC-T); pap. 5.95 o.s.i. (ISBN 0-308-10308-4, TYC-T). T Y Crowell.
Torbet, Laura, jt. auth. see Nicholson, Luree.
Torbett, Harvey. Coarse Fishing. 10.00x (ISBN 0-392-06501-0, SpS). Soccer.
--Sea Fishing. 10.00x (ISBN 0-392-06546-0, SpS). Soccer.
Torchia, Joseph. The Kryptonite Kid. LC 79-1078. 192p. 1980. pap. 2.95 (ISBN 0-03-057798-5). HR&W.
Torchinsky, Yu. M. Sulfur in Proteins. (Illus.). 304p. 1981. 96.00 (ISBN 0-08-023778-9); pap. cancelled. Pergamon.
Torcia, Charles E. Wharton's Criminal Evidence: 1972-73, 4 vols. 13th ed. LC 72-84859. 1972. 170.00 (ISBN 0-686-14501-1). Lawyers Co-Op.
--Wharton's Criminal Procedure, 4 vols. 12th ed. LC 74-84181. 1976. 170.00 (ISBN 0-686-14562-3). Lawyers Co-Op.
Torczyner, Harry. Magritte: Ideas & Images. LC 77-79323. (Contemporary Artists Ser.). (Illus.). 1977. 55.00 o.p. (ISBN 0-8109-1300-3). Abrams.
Tord, Bijou Le see Le Tord, Bijou.
Torda, C. Memory & Dreams: A Modern Physics Approach. (Illus.). 453p. 1980. 24.95. Walters.
Torda, Clara. Catecholamines of Developing Brain: Preconditioning of Behavior. 1977. 14.95 (ISBN 0-686-27726-0). W Torda.
Tordoff, William, ed. Government & Politics in Zambia. LC 73-86660. (Perspectives on Southern Africa Ser). 1975. 22.75x (ISBN 0-520-02593-8). U of Cal Pr.
Torgersen, Don A. The Wicked Witch of Troll Cave. LC 80-12043. (Troll Stories Ser.). (Illus.). 32p. (gr. k-4). 1980. PLB 7.95 (ISBN 0-516-03672-6). Childrens.
Torgerson, Paul E., jt. auth. see Weinstock, Irwin T.
Torgerson, Theodore L., jt. auth. see Schubert, Delwyn G.
Torgerson, Warren S. Theory & Method of Scaling. LC 58-10812. (Illus.). 1958. 26.95 (ISBN 0-471-87945-2). Wiley.
Torgeson, Dewayne C., ed. Fungicides: An Advanced Treatise, Vols. 1-2. 1967. Vol. 1. 68.50 (ISBN 0-12-695601-4). Vol. 2. 68.50 (ISBN 0-12-695602-2). Acad Pr.
Torgeson, Joseph see Hetherington, E. Mavis.
Torgeson, Roy. Chrysalis Eight. LC 80-649. (Double D Science Fiction Ser.). 192p. 1980. 9.95 (ISBN 0-385-17040-8). Doubleday.
Torgovnick, Marianna. Closure in the Novel. LC 80-8581. 272p. 1981. 16.50x (ISBN 0-691-06464-4). Princeton U Pr.
Toribara, T. Y., et al, eds. Polluted Rain. (Environmental Science Research Ser.: Vol. 17). 510p. 1980. 49.50 (ISBN 0-306-40353-6, Plenum Pr). Plenum Pub.
Torjesen, Hakon. It's a New Day: Reflections of a House Husband. 1981. 7.95 (ISBN 0-9602790-6-7). The Garden.
Torjesen, Hakon, et al. The Gift of the Refugees: Notes of a Volunteer Family of a Refugee Camp. 1981. 9.95 (ISBN 0-9602790-3-2). The Garden.
Torkelson, T. R. Doctor Upstairs. LC 70-103126. (Stories That Win Ser.). 64p. 1960. pap. 0.95 o.p. (ISBN 0-8163-0052-6, 04423-0). Pacific Pr Pub Assn.
Torkington, Rayner. Peter Calvay -- Hermit: A Personal Rediscovery of Prayer. LC 80-13188. 107p. (Orig.). 1980. pap. 3.95 (ISBN 0-8189-0404-6). Alba.
Torloni, H., jt. auth. see Scarff, R. W.
Tornatzky, Louis G. Innovation & Social Process: A National Experiment in Implementing Social Technology. LC 80-36809. (Pergamon Policy Studies on Politics, Policy & Modeling). 150p. 1980. 25.00 (ISBN 0-08-026303-8). Pergamon.
Tornborg, Pat. Spring Cleaning. (Sesame Street Early Bird Bks). (Illus.). (ps). 1981. 3.50 (ISBN 0-307-11601-8, Golden Pr). Western Pub.
Torneden, Roger L. Foreign Disinvestment by U. S. Multinational Corporations: With Eight Case Studies. LC 75-1136. (Special Studies). (Illus.). 174p. 1975. text ed. 24.95 (ISBN 0-275-05830-1). Praeger.
Torney, J., jt. auth. see Oppenheim, A. N.
Torney, John A., Jr. & Clayton, Robert D. Teaching Aquatics. (Sport Teaching Ser.). 239p. 1980. pap. text ed. 9.95 (ISBN 0-8087-3617-5). Burgess.
Torney, Judith, et al. Civic Education in Ten Countries: An Empirical Study. LC 75-42147. (International Studies in Evaluation: Vol. 6). 1976. pap. 28.95 (ISBN 0-470-14989-2). Halsted Pr.
Torng. Switching Circuits: Theory & Logic Design. 1976. 18.95 (ISBN 0-201-07576-8). A-W.
Tornoe. Columbus in the Arctic. 1965. text ed. 5.50x. Humanities.
Toro, M. De see De Toro, M. & Gisbert.
Toro, V. Del see Del Toro, V.
Torok, Lou. The Strange World of Prison. LC 72-88761. 1973. 6.50 o.p. (ISBN 0-672-51711-6). Bobbs.
Torok, T., jt. auth. see Mika, J.
Torp, Alf, jt. auth. see Falk, H. S.
Torpey, William G. Judicial Doctrines of Religious Rights in America. LC 78-132289. (Civil Liberties in American History Ser). 1970. Repr. of 1948 ed. lib. bdg. 39.50 (ISBN 0-306-70067-0). Da Capo.
Torrado, Ester. A Manual of English Grammar. Handbook Unit 2. pap. 3.75 o.p. (ISBN 0-8477-3308-4); Set. (ISBN 0-8477-3306-8). U of PR Pr.
Torrado, Ester & Adams, Rhenna L. Manual for the Basic Course in English: Structure. 6th ed. pap. 3.75 o.p. (ISBN 0-8477-3314-9). U of PR Pr.
Torrance, E. Paul & Myers, R. E. Creative Learning & Teaching. (Illus.). 1970. text ed. 11.95x scp (ISBN 0-06-046633-2, HarpC). Har-Row.
Torrance, G. F. see Barth, Karl.
Torrance, John. Estrangement, Alienation, & Exploitation: A Sociological Approach to Historical Materialism. LC 77-8246. 1977. 25.00x (ISBN 0-231-04448-8). Columbia U Pr.
Torrance, Robert M. The Comic Hero. LC 77-16316. 1978. 16.50x (ISBN 0-674-14431-7). Harvard U Pr.
Torrance, Thomas F., ed. Belief in Science & in Christian Life. 160p. 1981. pap. 11.00x (ISBN 0-905312-11-2, Pub. by Scttish Academic Pr Scotland). Columbia U Pr.
Torre, Betty L. The Complete Beginners Guide to Everyday Italian Cooking. LC 74-2527. (gr. 9 up). 1975. 5.95 o.p. (ISBN 0-385-08981-3). Doubleday.
--It's Easy to Cook - Favorite American Recipes. LC 76-2826. (gr. 3 up). 1977. 5.95 o.p. (ISBN 0-385-11091-X); PLB write for info. o.p. (ISBN 0-385-11092-8). Doubleday.
Torre Bueno, Laura de la see Graham, Munir & De La Torre Bueno, Laura.
Torregrosa de Torres, Doris. A Manual of English Grammar for Spanish Speakers: Workbooks, 4 units. pap. 12.50 set (ISBN 0-8477-3317-3); Unit 1-2. (ISBN 0-8477-3318-1). Unit 3-4. (ISBN 0-8477-3319-X). Set. (ISBN 0-8477-3317-3). U of PR Pr.
Torrence, Bruce. Those Fabulous Film Factories: The History of Motion Picture Studios in California. (Illus.). 240p. Date not set. price not set (ISBN 0-87905-086-1). Peregrine Smith. Postponed.
Torrence, Kathy. An Art Noveau Album. (Illus.). 80p. 1981. 19.95 (ISBN 0-525-06980-1); pap. 10.95 (ISBN 0-525-47635-0). Dutton.
Torrence, Rosemary. Mending Our Nets. 176p. 1980. wire coil bdg. 7.95 (ISBN 0-697-01757-5); pap. 7.95. Wm C Brown.
Torrence, Rosemary, jt. auth. see Diocese of Cleveland.
Torrens, Paul R. The American Health Care System: Issues & Problems. LC 78-4666. (Issues & Problems in Health Care Ser.). 1978. pap. text ed. 8.95 (ISBN 0-8016-5012-7). Mosby.
Torrens, Robert. On Wages & Combination. (The Development of Industrial Society Ser.). 133p. 1980. Repr. of 1834 ed. 10.00x (ISBN 0-7165-1595-4, Pub. by Irish Academic Pr Ireland). Biblio Dist.
Torres, Angelo, jt. auth. see DeBartolo, Dick.
Torres, Angelo, jt. auth. see Siegel, Larry.
Torres, Elias L. Twenty Episodes in the Life of Pancho Villa. Ohlendorf, Sheila, tr. from Spanish. 1973. 7.50 o.p. (ISBN 0-88426-017-8). Encino Pr.
Torres, Hazel O. & Mazzucchi, Lois E. A Review of Dental Assisting. (Illus.). 350p. 1980. write for info. (ISBN 0-7216-8883-7). Saunders.
Torres, Rafael A. Gonzalez see Gonzalez Torres, Rafael A.
Torres, Sergio & Eagleson, John, eds. The Challenge of Basic Christian Communities. Drury, John, tr. 192p. (Orig.). 1981. pap. 7.95 (ISBN 0-88344-503-4). Orbis Bks.
Torres, Victor & Wilkerson, Don. Son of Evil Street. LC 73-10828. 1977. pap. 1.95 (ISBN 0-87123-516-1, 200516). Bethany Fell.
Torres-Reilly, Marta, et al. Guide to Professional Organizations. LC 80-110700. 168p. (Orig.). 1979. pap. text ed. 3.50 (ISBN 0-89763-015-7). Natl Clearinghouse Bilingual Ed.
Torres-Rioseco, Arturo, ed. Antologia De la Literatura Hispano-Americana. (Span.). (gr. 11-12). 1979. text ed. 26.50x o.p. (ISBN 0-8290-0022-4); pap. text ed. 14.95x o.p. (ISBN 0-89197-546-2). Irvington.
Torrey Botanical Club, N.Y. Annual Index to Botanical Literature: 1979. 1980. lib. bdg. 130.00 (ISBN 0-8161-0369-0). G K Hall.
Torrey, Charles C. The Lives of the Prophets. (Society of Biblical Literature. Monographs: No. 1). 1946. pap. 6.00 (ISBN 0-89130-171-2, 060001). Scholars Pr Ca.
Torrey, Charles C., ed. History of the Conquest of Egypt & North Africa & Spain Known As the Futuh Misr of Ibn'Abd Alhakam. (Yale Oriental Researches Ser.: No. III). (Arabic.). 1922. 65.00x (ISBN 0-685-69878-5). Elliots Bks.
Torrey, James M. Pheasant Run Pubns. LC 77-4567. (Illus.). 1977. 15.95 (ISBN 0-669-01372-2). Pheasant Run.
Torrey, John & Gray, Asa. Flora of North America, 2 Vols. (Classica Botanica Americana Ser.: Vol. 4). 1968. Repr. Set. 71.50 o.s.i. (ISBN 0-02-853640-1). Hafner.
Torrey, Norman L., jt. auth. see Fellows, Otis E.
Torrey, Norman L; see Kellenberger, Hunter.
Torrey, R. A. The Baptism with the Holy Spirit. 96p. 1972. pap. 1.95 (ISBN 0-87123-029-1); pap. 0.95 (ISBN 0-87123-030-5). Bethany Fell.
--Como Obtener la Plenitud Del Poder. Rivas, Jose G., tr. from Eng. Orig. Title: How to Obtain Fullness of Power. 112p. (Span.). Date not set. pap. price not set (ISBN 0-311-46083-6). Casa Bautista.
--How to Bring Men to Christ. 128p. 1981. pap. 2.50 (ISBN 0-88368-098-X). Whitaker Hse.
--How to Bring Men to Christ. LC 76-57111. 1977. pap. 2.25 (ISBN 0-87123-230-8, 200230). Bethany Fell.
--How to Find Fullness of Power. Orig. Title: How to Obtain Fullness of Power. 1971. pap. 1.50 (ISBN 0-87123-219-7, 200219). Bethany Fell.
--Revival Addresses. 282p. 1974. Repr. of 1903 ed. 10.50 (ISBN 0-227-67808-7). Attic Pr.
Torrey, R. A., tr. Ce Que la Bible Enseigne. (French Bks.). (Fr.). 1979. 6.00 (ISBN 0-686-28818-1). Life Pubs Intl.
Torrey, Reuben A. How to Pray. pap. 1.50 (ISBN 0-8024-3709-5). Moody.
--How to Succeed in the Christian Life. pap. 3.25 (ISBN 0-8024-3659-5). Moody.
--Preguntas Practicas y Dificiles. Orig. Title: Practical & Perplexing Questions Answered. (Span). 1909. pap. 1.50 (ISBN 0-8024-6810-1). Moody.
Torrey, S., ed. Adhesive Technology: Developments Since 1977. LC 79-25936. (Chemical Technology Review Ser.: No. 148). (Illus.). 1980. 54.00 (ISBN 0-8155-0787-9). Noyes.
Torrey, Theodore W. & Feduccia, Alan. Morphogenesis of the Vertebrates. 4th ed. LC 78-17196. 1979. 24.95 (ISBN 0-471-03232-8). Wiley.
Torrey, Volta. Wind-Catchers: American Windmills of Yesterday & Tomorrow. (Illus.). 240p. (Orig.). 1981. pap. 9.95 (ISBN 0-8289-0438-3). Greene.
Torrie, Arthur. Illustrated Glossary of Environmental & Ecological Terms. (Illus.). 1977. pap. text ed. 6.50x o.p. (ISBN 0-435-59896-1). Heinemann Ed.
Torriente, Donna D. De La see De La Torriente, Donna D.
Torshavn, jt. auth. see Leikur.
Tortolano, William. Original Music for Men's Voices: A Selected Bibliography. 2nd ed. LC 80-25917. 206p. 1981. 12.50 (ISBN 0-8108-1386-6). Scarecrow.
--Samuel Coleridge-Taylor: Anglo-Black Composer, 1875-1912. LC 76-57172. (Illus.). 1977. 10.00 (ISBN 0-8108-1010-7). Scarecrow.
Tortora, Daniel. The Right Dog for You. 1980. 12.95 (ISBN 0-686-62850-0, 24221). S&S.
Tortora, Gerald & Anagnostakos, Nicholos. Anatomia y Fisiologica. (Span.). 1977. pap. text ed. 12.50 (ISBN 0-06-317150-3, IntlDept). Har-Row.
Torvik, P. J., ed. Damping Applications for Vibration Control. (AMD: Vol. 38). 160p. 1980. 24.00 (G00171). ASME.
Toscano, Eamon. Framing: Step-by-Step. (Step-by-Step Craft Ser). 1971. PLB 9.15 o.p. (ISBN 0-307-62007-7, Golden Pr); pap. 2.95 (ISBN 0-307-42007-8, Golden Pr). Western Pub.
Toscano, W. M., et al. Cryogenic Processes & Equipment in Energy Systems. 193p. 1980. 40.00 (H00164). ASME.
Tosco, Uberto. Mushrooms in the Wild. Tribe, Ian, ed. LC 77-82738. (Illus.). 1977. 7.95 o.p. (ISBN 0-8467-0371-8, Pub. by Two Continents). Hippocrene Bks.
Tosh & Ordway. Real Estate Math Made Easy. 1981. text ed. 15.95 (ISBN 0-8359-6556-2); instr's. manual free (ISBN 0-8359-6557-0). Reston.
Tosh, John. Clan Leaders & Colonial Chiefs in Lango: The Political History of an East African Stateless Society, 1800-1939. (Studies in African Affairs). (Illus.). 1979. 42.00x (ISBN 0-19-822711-6). Oxford U Pr.
Tosi, Henry L. Readings in Management: Contingencies, Structure & Process. LC 76-5292. (Illus.). 1976. pap. text ed. 9.25 (ISBN 0-914292-07-2). Wiley.
Tosi, Henry L. & Carroll, Stephen J. Management: Contingencies, Structure & Process. LC 75-43280. (Series in Critical Sociologies). (Illus.). 608p. 1976. text ed. 21.95 (ISBN 0-914292-04-8). Wiley.
Tosi, Henry L., jt. auth. see Carroll, Stephen J.
Tosi, Henry L. & Hamner, W. Clay, eds. Organizational Behavior & Management: A Contingency Approach. rev. ed. LC 77-77475. (Series in Critical Sociologies). 1977. pap. text ed. 15.95 (ISBN 0-914292-09-9). Wiley.
Tosi, M. P., jt. auth. see March, N. H.
Tosi, Pietro F. Observations on the Florid Song. 2nd ed. Repr. of 1743 ed. 25.00 (ISBN 0-384-60980-5). Johnson Repr.
Toskes, P. The Digestive System: Disease, Diagnosis, Treatment. (Clinical Monographs Ser.). (Illus.). 1975. pap. 7.95 (ISBN 0-87618-063-2). R J Brady.
Toskes, P. P. Antibiotic Therapy. (Clinical Monographs Ser.). (Illus.). 1974. pap. 7.95 (ISBN 0-87618-061-6). R J Brady.
Toski, Bob. Complete Guide to Better Golf. (Illus.). 1977. 12.95 o.p. (ISBN 0-689-10722-6). Atheneum.
Toski, Bob & Aultman, Dick. Bob Toski's Complete Guide to Better Golf. LC 75-39958. (Illus.). 1980. pap. 7.95 (ISBN 0-689-70592-1). Atheneum.
--The Touch System for Better Golf. Golf Digest Magazine, ed. LC 70-161626. (Illus.). 128p. 1980. pap. 6.95 (ISBN 0-914178-36-9). Golf Digest.
Toski, Bob, et al. How to Become a Complete Golfer. LC 77-92909. (Illus.). 288p. 1978. 14.95 (ISBN 0-914178-15-6, 24169). Golf Digest.
Tosteson, D. C. & Ovchinnikov, Yu. A., eds. Membrane Transport Processes, Vol. 2. LC 76-19934. 1977. 43.50 (ISBN 0-89004-174-1). Raven.
Toth, Charles W. American Revolution & the West Indies. 1975. 12.95 (ISBN 0-8046-9110-X, Natl U). Kennikat.
Toth, Max & Nielsen, Greg. Pyramid Power. (Warner Destiny Bk.). (Orig.). 1976. pap. 2.25 o.s.i. (ISBN 0-446-82569-7). Warner Bks.
Toth, Susan A. Blooming: A Small-Town Girlhood. 244p. 1981. 10.95 (ISBN 0-316-85076-4). Little.
Totman, Conrad. Japan Before Perry: A Short History. (Illus.). 275p. 1981. 20.00x (ISBN 0-520-04132-1). U of Cal Pr.
Toto, Patrick D., et al. Pathology of the Oral Cavity. (Atlases of the Pathology of the Head & Neck). 1976. text & slides 76.50 (ISBN 0-89189-030-0, 15-1-018-00). Am Soc Clinical.
Totten, George O., III, jt. ed. see Schmidhauser, John R.
Totten, Herman L., jt. ed. see Cassata, Mary B.
Totterdell, B. & Bird, J. The Effective Library. Redfern, M., ed. 1976. 31.00x (ISBN 0-85365-248-1, Pub. by Assn England). Oryx Pr.
Tottie, Malcolm, jt. ed. see Sjoqvist, Folke.
Tottle, C. R. Science of Engineering Materials. 1966. pap. text ed. 8.95x o.p. (ISBN 0-435-71785-5). Heinemann Ed.
Tou, J. T. & Gonzalez, R. C. Pattern Recognition Principles: Applied Mathematics & Computation Ser. 2nd ed. 1975. text ed. 28.50 (ISBN 0-201-07587-3); instr's man. 3.50 (ISBN 0-201-07588-1). A-W.

Tou, Julius. Software Engineering, Vols. 1-2. 1970. Vol. 1. 38.50 (ISBN 0-12-696201-4); Vol. 2. 38.50 (ISBN 0-12-696202-2). Acad Pr.

Tou, Julius T., ed. Applied Automata Theory. LC 68-26634. (Electrical Science Ser). 1969. 48.50 (ISBN 0-12-696230-8). Acad Pr.

Touche Ross & Co. The Standard Manual of Accounting for Shopping Centers. LC 73-163156. (Illus.). 40p. 1971. pap. 12.00 (ISBN 0-87420-908-0). Urban Land.

Touche Ross & Company, jt. auth. see Urban Land Institute Real Estate Financial Reporting & Steering Committees.

Touchstone, Joseph C. & Rogers, Dexter. Thin Layer Chromatography: Quantitative Environmental & Clinical Applications. LC 80-36871. 384p. 1980. 27.50 (ISBN 0-471-07958-8, Pub. by Wiley-Interscience). Wiley.

Touchton, Ken, jt. auth. see Knight, Walker.

Touchton, Ken, jt. auth. see Nicholas, Tim.

Tough, Joan. The Development of Meaning: A Study of Children's Use of Language. 1977. pap. text ed. 17.95 (ISBN 0-470-15178-1). Halsted Pr.

Toulmin, Stephen. Reason in Ethics. 1950-1960. 35.00 (ISBN 0-521-06643-3); pap. 8.95x (ISBN 0-521-09116-0, 116). Cambridge U Pr.

--Uses of Argument. 1958-1964. 32.95 (ISBN 0-521-06644-1); pap. 8.95x (ISBN 0-521-09230-2). Cambridge U Pr.

Touloukian, Robert J. & Krizek, Thomas J., eds. Diagnosis & Early Management of Trauma Emergencies: A Manual for the Emergency Service. (Illus.). 160p. 1974. text ed. 15.75 (ISBN 0-398-03133-9); pap. text ed. 9.75 (ISBN 0-398-03134-7). C C Thomas.

Touloukian, U. S. & Ho, C. Y. Physical Properties of Rocks & Minerals, Vol. II. (M-H-CINDAS Data Series on Material Properties). (Illus.). 576p. 1981. text ed. 44.50 (ISBN 0-07-065032-2). McGraw.

Touloukian, Y. S. & Ho, C. Y. Properties of Nonmetallic Fluid Elements, Vol. III. (M-H-CINDAS Data Series on Material Properties). 224p. 1981. text ed. 33.50 (ISBN 0-07-065033-0). McGraw.

--Properties of Selected Ferrous Alloying Elements, Vol. III. (M-H-CINDAS Data Series on Material Properties). 288p. 1981. text ed. 33.50 (ISBN 0-07-065034-9). McGraw.

--Thermal Accommodation & Adsorption Coefficients of Gases, Vol. Ii-1. 1st ed. (McGraw-Hill CINDAS Data Ser. on Material Properties). 448p. (Orig.). 1980. 42.50 (ISBN 0-07-065031-4). McGraw.

Toumazou, Michael, tr. see Lambros, Paul.

Touraine, Alain. May Movement: Revolt & Reform. Mayhew, Leonard F., tr. LC 76-103977. 1979. 24.50x (ISBN 0-394-46256-4); pap. text ed. 9.95x (ISBN 0-89197-626-4). Irvington.

--The Voice & the Eye: The/Analysis of Social Movements. Duff, Alan, tr. from Fr. Orig. Title: Le Voix et le Regard. Date not set. 37.59 (ISBN 0-521-23874-9); pap. 12.95 (ISBN 0-521-28271-3). Cambridge U Pr.

Touraine, Alain, ed. see Carnegie Commission on Higher Education.

Tourangeau, Kevin. Strategy Management: How to Plan, Execute & Control Strategic Plans for Your Business. 256p. 1980. 16.95 (ISBN 0-07-065043-8, P&RB). McGraw.

Tourbier, Joachim & Westmacott, Richard. Lakes & Ponds. LC 76-19607. (Technical Bulletin Ser.: No. 72). (Illus.). 70p. 1976. pap. 14.50 (ISBN 0-87420-072-5). Urban Land.

Tourgee, Albion W., jt. auth. see MacKaye, Steele.

Tourism Education Corporation. Wine Service Procedures. 1976. 13.95 (ISBN 0-8436-2088-9). CBI Pub.

Tourneau, Roger Le see Le Tourneau, Roger.

Tourneur, Cyril. Revenger's Tragedy. Ross, Lawrence J., ed. LC 66-12744. (Regents Renaissance Drama Ser). 1966. 8.95x (ISBN 0-8032-0283-0); pap. 2.75x (ISBN 0-8032-5284-6, BB 218, Bison). U of Nebr Pr.

Tourneur, Dina K. Buddy Paints a Picture. (Buddy Books Ser.). (ps). 1978. 1.95 o.p. (ISBN 0-89191-124-3). Cook.

--Buddy Plants a Seed. (Buddy Books Ser.). (ps). 1978. 1.95 o.p. (ISBN 0-89191-125-1). Cook.

Tourney, Leonard. The Player's Boy Is Dead. LC 80-7611. 208p. 1980. 10.95 (ISBN 0-06-014341-X, HarpT). Har-Row.

Tourney, Leonard D. Joseph Hall. (English Authors Ser.: No. 250). 1979. lib. bdg. 11.95 (ISBN 0-8057-6740-1). Twayne.

Tournier, Paul. The Adventure of Living. LC 65-20459. 256p. 1976. pap. 4.95 (ISBN 0-06-068294-9, RD 260, HarpR). Har-Row.

--Meaning of Gifts. LC 63-19172. 1963. 4.25 (ISBN 0-8042-2124-3). John Knox.

--The Meaning of Gifts. LC 63-19122. 1976. pap. 1.25 (ISBN 0-8042-3604-6). John Knox.

--Meaning of Persons. 1957. 7.95 (ISBN 0-06-068370-8, HarpR); pap. 1.95 (ISBN 0-685-11826-6, P-304, HarpR). Har-Row.

--Seasons of Life. Gilmour, John S., tr. LC 63-8709. 1963. 4.25 (ISBN 0-8042-2160-X). John Knox.

--Seasons of Life. Gilmour, John S., tr. LC 63-8709. 1976. pap. 1.25 (ISBN 0-8042-3651-8). John Knox.

--Seasons of Life. 1976. pap. 1.25 (ISBN 0-89129-170-9). Jove Pubns.

--Secrets. Embry, J., tr. LC 65-13442. 1965. 4.25 (ISBN 0-8042-2165-0). John Knox.

--Secrets. LC 65-13442. 1976. pap. 1.25 (ISBN 0-8042-3655-0). John Knox.

--Secrets. 1976. pap. 1.25 (ISBN 0-89129-169-5). Jove Pubns.

--To Resist or Surrender. LC 64-16248. 1977. pap. 1.25 (ISBN 0-8042-3663-1). John Knox.

--To Resist or To Surrender? Gilmour, John S., tr. LC 64-16248. 1964. Repr. 4.25 (ISBN 0-8042-2232-0). John Knox.

--To Understand Each Other. Gilmour, John S., tr. LC 67-15298. (Illus.). 1967. 4.25 (ISBN 0-8042-2235-5). John Knox.

--To Understand Each Other. 1976. pap. 1.25 o.p. (ISBN 0-8042-3673-9). John Knox.

Tournier, Paul, et al. Are You Nobody? LC 66-21649. (Orig.). 1966. pap. 2.45 (ISBN 0-8042-3356-X). John Knox.

Tourret. Performance & Testing of Gear Oils & Transmission Fluids. 1980. write for info. (ISBN 0-85501-326-5). Heyden.

Tourrette, Jacqueline La see La Tourrette, Jacqueline.

Tourtellot, Arthur B. Lexington & Concord. (Illus.). 1963. pap. 5.95 (ISBN 0-393-00194-6, Norton Lib). Norton.

Tousimis, A. J. see Marton, L.

Toussaint, G. C., tr. see Tsogyal, Yeshe.

Toussaint, J. P., jt. auth. see Duvillard, A.

Toussaint, W. D., jt. auth. see Bishop, Charles E.

Toussoun, T. A., et al, eds. Root Diseases & Soil-Borne Pathogens. LC 73-84531. (Illus.). 1970. 38.50x (ISBN 0-520-01582-7). U of Cal Pr.

Tout, Thomas F. The Empire & the Papacy, Nine Eighteen to Twelve Seventy-Three. 8th ed. LC 80-18865. (Periods of European History: Period II). (Illus.). vii, 526p. 1980. Repr. of 1965 ed. lib. bdg. 35.00x (ISBN 0-313-22372-6, TOEP). Greenwood.

Toutant, William H. Fundamental Concepts of Music. 336p. 1979. pap. text ed. 14.95x (ISBN 0-534-00743-0). Wadsworth Pub.

Touwen, Bert C. The Examination of the Child with Minor Neurological Dysfunction. 2nd ed. (Clinics in Developmental Medicine Ser.: No. 71). 150p. 1979. 25.00 (ISBN 0-685-24730-9). Lippincott.

Tov, Emanual. The Septuagint Translation of Jeremiah & Baruch: A Discussion of an Early Revision of the IXX of Jeremiah 29-52 & Baruch 1: 1-3: 8. LC 75-43872. (Harvard Semitic Monographs). 1976. 9.00 (ISBN 0-89130-070-8, 040008). Scholars Pr Ca.

Tov, Emanuel. The Book of Baruch. LC 75-30775. (Society of Biblical Literature. Texts & Translation-Pseudepigrapha Ser). 1975. pap. 4.50 (ISBN 0-89130-043-0, 060208). Scholars Pr Ca.

Tovell, Harold & Dank, Leonard. Operaciones Ginecologicas. (Span.). 1980. pap. text ed. write for info. (ISBN 0-06-319301-9, Pub. by HarLA Mexico). Har-Row.

Tovell, Rosemarie L. Reflections in a Quiet Pool: The Prints of David Milne. (National Gallery of Canada Ser.). (Illus.). 256p. 1981. lib. bdg. 45.00x (ISBN 0-88884-461-1, 56494-0, Pub. by Natl Mus Canada). U of Chicago Pr.

Tovey, Doreen. Cats in May. 1976. 9.95 (ISBN 0-236-40079-7, Pub. by Paul Elek). Merrimack Bk Serv.

--Cats in the Belfry. 1978. 9.95 (ISBN 0-236-30847-5, Pub. by Paul Elek). Merrimack Bk Serv.

--A Comfort of Cats. (Illus.). 181p. 1980. 9.95 (ISBN 0-312-15088-1). St Martin.

--Life with Grandma. 1964. 7.95 o.p. (ISBN 0-236-31146-8, Pub. by Paul Elek). Merrimack Bk Serv.

Tovey, John. The Technique of Kinetic Art. 1971. 19.95 (ISBN 0-7134-2518-0, Pub. by Batsford England). David & Charles.

Tow, Robert, ed. see Callahan, Harry.

Tow, William T., jt. ed. see Stuart, Douglas T.

Towbin, Richard B. Endocardial Cushion Defects: Embryology, Anatomy & Angiography. 280p. 1981. 32.50 (ISBN 0-87527-252-5). Green.

Towell, D. & Harries, C. Innovations in Patient Care. 224p. 1980. 30.00x (ISBN 0-85664-692-X, Pub. by Croom Helm England). State Mutual Bk.

Tower, Charlemagne. Marquis De Lafayette in the American Revolution with Some Account of the Attitude of France Toward the War of Independence, 2 Vols. LC 79-112310. (Era of the American Revolution Ser). 1970. Repr. of 1901 ed. lib. bdg. 75.00 (ISBN 0-306-71914-2). Da Capo.

Tower, D. B., ed. The Nervous System, 3 vols. Incl. Vol. 1. Basic Neurosciences. 20.00 (ISBN 0-89004-075-3); Vol. 2. Clinical Neurosciences. 20.00 (ISBN 0-89004-076-1); Vol. 3. Human Communication & Its Disorders. 20.00 (ISBN 0-89004-077-X). LC 75-33499. 1800p. 1975. Set. 59.50 (ISBN 0-685-61107-8). Raven.

Towers, Bernard. Teilhard De Chardin. Nineham, D. E. & Robertson, E. H., eds. LC 66-15515. (Makers of Contemporary Theology Ser). (Orig.). 1966. pap. 2.25 (ISBN 0-8042-0723-2). John Knox.

Towers, Bernard, jt. auth. see Lewis, John.

Towers, Brian, jt. auth. see Kniveton, Bromley.

Towers, J. Role Playing for Managers. 1975. text ed. 34.00 (ISBN 0-08-017827-8); pap. text ed. 20.00 (ISBN 0-08-018984-9). Pergamon.

Towers, John. Dictionary-Catalogue of Operas & Operettas, 2 Vols. LC 67-25996. (Music Ser). 1967. Repr. of 1910 ed. lib. bdg. 59.50 (ISBN 0-306-70962-7). Da Capo.

Towers, Joseph & Maseres, Francis. An Enquiry into the Question Whether Juries Are, or Are Not, Judges of the Law. Berkowitz, David S. & Thorne, Samuel E., eds. LC 77-86680. (Classics of English Legal History in the Modern Era Ser.: Vol. 51). 228p. 1979. lib. bdg. 40.00 (ISBN 0-8240-3150-4). Garland Pub.

Towers, T. D. & Libes, Sol. Semiconductor Circuit Elements. (Illus.). (gr. 10 up). 1977. pap. 8.35 (ISBN 0-8104-0859-7). Hayden.

Towill, Denis R. Coefficient Plane Models for Control System Analysis & Design. (Mechanical Engineering Research Studies: Vol. 1). 260p. 1981. 44.50 (ISBN 0-471-27955-2, Pub. by Wiley-Interscience). Wiley.

Towl, Andrew R., jt. auth. see Copeland, Melvin T.

Towle, Anne V., tr. see Sato, Masahiko.

Towle, Charlotte. Common Human Needs. rev. ed. LC 65-22393. 1965. pap. 4.00x (ISBN 0-87101-014-3, CBO-014-C). Natl Assn Soc Wkrs.

Towle, Laird C., ed. New England Annals: History & Genealogy, Vol. 1. 500p. 1980. 20.00 (ISBN 0-917890-19-1). Heritage Bk.

Towle, Laird C., ed. see Mayhew, Catherine M.

Towle, Tony. Autobiography & Other Poems. LC 77-3591. 1977. pap. 4.00 (ISBN 0-915342-18-9). SUN.

--North: "the Frank O'Hara Award Series". LC 70-125619. (A Full Court Rebound Bk.). 1978. 14.95 (ISBN 0-231-03471-7); pap. 6.00 (ISBN 0-231-03472-5). Full Court NY.

Towle, W. Wilder. The Oral History of James Nunn: A Unique North Carolinian. 230p. (Orig.). 1980. pap. 5.95 (ISBN 0-86629-001-X). Sunrise MO.

Towlson, Clifford W. Moravian & Methodist. 1957. 15.00x (ISBN 0-8401-2387-6, 8401-2387-6). Allenson.

Town, H. C. & Moore, H. Inspection Machines: Measuring Systems & Instruments. 1978. 22.50 (ISBN 0-7134-0795-6); pap. 13.50 (ISBN 0-7134-0796-4). David & Charles.

--Manufacturing Technology, Vol. 1. 1979. 27.00 (ISBN 0-7134-1094-9, Pub. by Batsford England); pap. 14.95 (ISBN 0-7134-1095-7). David & Charles.

--Manufacturing Technology: Advanced Machines & Processes. (Illus.). 352p. 1980. 39.00 (ISBN 0-7134-1096-5, Pub. by Batsford England); pap. 17.95 (ISBN 0-7134-1097-3). David & Charles.

Towne, Mary. Glass Room. (Illus.). (gr. 5-7). 1972. pap. 0.75 (ISBN 0-671-29544-6). PB.

Towne, Peter. George Washington Carver. LC 74-34296. (Biography Ser.). (Illus.). 40p. (gr. 1-4). 1975. PLB 7.84 (ISBN 0-690-00777-9, TYC-J). T Y Crowell.

Towne, Ruth. Senator William J. Stone & the Politics of Compromise. (National University Publications, Political Science Ser). 1979. 15.00 (ISBN 0-8046-9232-7). Kennikat.

Towne, Sumner A., Jr., ed. see Morris, Paul C. & Morin, Joseph F.

Townend, Peter. Triple Exposure. (Quest Ser.: No. 1). 1979. pap. 1.75 o.p. (ISBN 0-523-40163-9). Pinnacle Bks.

--Zoom! 208p. 1975. pap. 1.25 o.p. (ISBN 0-523-22586-5). Pinnacle Bks.

Towner, Donald. Creamware. LC 78-320727. (Illus.). 1978. 43.00 (ISBN 0-571-04964-8, Pub. by Faber & Faber). Merrimack Bk Serv.

Towner, George. The Architecture of Knowledge. LC 80-5127. 220p. 1980. text ed. 17.75 (ISBN 0-8191-1049-3); pap. text ed. 9.50 (ISBN 0-8191-1050-7). U Pr of Amer.

Towner, Wesley. The Elegant Auctioneers. (Illus.). 632p. 1970. 10.00 (ISBN 0-8090-4171-5). Hill & Wang.

Townes, Henry. The Genera of Ichneumonidae, Pt. 1, Ephialtinae To Agriotypinae. (Memoirs Ser: No. 11). (Illus.). 300p. 1969. 20.00 (ISBN 0-686-00418-3). Am Entom Inst.

--The Genera of Ichneumonidae, Pt. 2, Gelinae. (Memoirs Ser: No. 12). (Illus.). 537p. 1970. 35.00 (ISBN 0-686-00419-1). Am Entom Inst.

--The Genera of Ichneumonidae, Pt. 3, Lycorininae To Porizontinae. (Memoirs Ser: No. 13). (Illus.). 307p. 1970. 20.00 (ISBN 0-686-00420-5). Am Entom Inst.

--Genera of Ichneumonidae, Pt. 4, Cremastinae To Diplazontinae. (Memoirs Ser: No. 17). (Illus.). 372p. 1971. 28.00 (ISBN 0-686-01268-2). Am Entom Inst.

Townes, Henry & Chiu, Shui-Chen. The Indo-Australian Species of Xanthopimpla - Ichneumonidae. (Memoirs Ser: No. 14). (Illus.). 372p. 1970. 25.00 (ISBN 0-686-17147-0). Am Entom Inst.

Townes, Henry & Gupta, Virendra K. Ichneumonidae of America North of Mexico: Subfamily Gelinae, Tribe Hemigasterini. (Memoirs Ser: No. 2). (Illus.). 20.00 (ISBN 0-686-00421-3). Am Entom Inst.

Townes, Henry & Townes, Marjorie. Catalogue & Reclassification of the Neotropic Ichneumonidae. (Memoirs Ser: No. 8). 1966. 25.00 (ISBN 0-686-00416-7). Am Entom Inst.

Townes, Henry, et al. Catalogue & Reclassification of the Eastern Palearctic Ichneumonidae. (Memoirs Ser.: No. 5). 661p. 1965. 40.00 (ISBN 0-686-00414-0). Am Entom Inst.

--Catalogue & Reclassification of the Indo-Australian Ichneumonidae. (Memoirs Ser: No. 1). 522p. 1961. 33.00 (ISBN 0-686-00415-9). Am Entom Inst.

Townes, Marjorie, jt. auth. see Townes, Henry.

Townley, Helen M. & Gee, Ralph C. Thesaurus-Making: Grow Your Own Word-Stock. (Grafton Ser.). 208p. 1981. lib. bdg. 25.00x (ISBN 0-86531-107-2). Westview.

Townley, Mary. Another Look, 3 levels. (Townley Art Project Ser.). (gr. k-2). 1978. Level A. pap. text ed. 6.32 (ISBN 0-201-07646-2, Sch Div); Level B. pap. text ed. 6.32 (ISBN 0-201-07647-0); Level C. pap. text ed. 6.32 (ISBN 0-201-07648-9); 24.44 o.p. tchr's ed. (ISBN 0-201-07649-7). A-W.

Townley, Pamela. The Image. 360p. (Orig.). 1981. pap. 2.75 (ISBN 0-345-29115-8). Ballantine.

Townley, Rod. Sumner Street. 1976. 1.00 o.p. (ISBN 0-685-78417-7). The Smith.

Townroe, Peter. The Industrial Movement: Experience in the United States & the United Kingdom. 1979. text ed. 38.65x (ISBN 0-566-00279-5, Pub. by Gower Pub Co England). Renouf.

Towns, Elmer. The Successful Sunday School & Teachers Guidebook. new ed. LC 75-23009. (Illus.). 430p. 1976. pap. 10.95 (ISBN 0-88419-118-4). Creation Hse.

Towns, Payton. Educating Disturbed Adolescents: Theory & Practice. (Current Issues in Behavioral Psychology Ser.). 1981. 19.50 (ISBN 0-8089-1312-3). Grune.

Townsend, A. A. The Structure of Turbulent Shear Flow. 2nd ed. LC 79-8526. (Cambridge Monographs on Mechanics & Applied Mathematics). (Illus.). 441p. 1980. pap. 19.95x (ISBN 0-521-29819-9). Cambridge U Pr.

--The Structure of Turbulent Shear Flow. 2nd ed. LC 74-14441. (Monographs on Mechanics & Applied Mathematics). 300p. 1975. 74.50 (ISBN 0-521-20710-X). Cambridge U Pr.

Townsend, Anita. The Kangaroo. LC 78-68536. (First Look at Nature Ser.). (Illus.). (gr. 2-4). 1979. 2.50 (ISBN 0-531-09141-4); PLB 6.45 s&l (ISBN 0-531-09152-X). Watts.

Townsend, Carl. How to Get Started with CP-M: Control Programs for Microcomputers. 200p. 1981. pap. 9.95 (ISBN 0-918398-32-0). Dilithium Pr.

Townsend, Carl & Miller, Merl. How to Make Money with Your Micro-Computer. LC 79-53477. 1979. pap. 9.95 (ISBN 0-89661-001-2). Robotics Pr.

Townsend, Carolynn E. Nutrition & Diet Modifications. 3rd ed. LC 78-74166. (Health Occupations Ser.). (gr. 9). 1980. pap. text ed. 10.40 (ISBN 0-8273-1324-1); instructor's guide 1.50 (ISBN 0-686-59749-4). Delmar.

Townsend, Charles B. Merlin's Catalog of Magic. (Puzzler Ser.). 128p. (Orig.). (gr. 9 up). 1981. pap. 4.95 (ISBN 0-8437-2099-9). Hammond Inc.

Townsend, Doris M. Diet Without Hunger. LC 77-11603. 1978. pap. 2.95 (ISBN 0-87469-016-1, 8084). Larousse.

Townsend, Duane E., jt. auth. see Morrow, C. Paul.

Townsend, George A. The Entailed Hat. LC 55-14663. (Illus.). 1955. 10.00 (ISBN 0-87033-135-3, Pub. by Tidewater). Cornell Maritime.

--The Life, Crime, & Capture of John Wilkes Booth. LC 80-129018. (Illus.). 65p. pap. text ed. 10.00 (ISBN 0-686-28746-0). J L Barbour.

Townsend, Guy, et al. Rex Stout: A Primary & Secondary Bibliography. LC 80-8507. 210p. 1980. lib. bdg. 30.00. Garland Pub.

Townsend, H. E. Immigrant Pupils in England: The L. E. A. Response. (Research Reports). 1971. text ed. 13.75x (ISBN 0-901225-67-3, NFER). Humanities.

Townsend, James B., Jr. Extraterritorial Antitrust: The Sherman Act vs. the Market Entry Strategy of Selected Multinational Corporations. LC 79-18802. (Special Studies in International Economics & Business). 1980. lib. bdg. 28.50x (ISBN 0-89158-483-8). Westview.

Townsend, James R. Political Participation in Communist China. (Center for Chinese Studies, UC Berkeley). 1967. 19.50x (ISBN 0-520-01279-8); pap. 5.95x (ISBN 0-520-01416-2, CAMPUS83). U of Cal Pr.

Townsend, James R. & Bush, Richard C., eds. The People's Republic of China: A Basic Handbook. 2nd, rev. ed. (Illus., Orig.). 1980. pap. text ed. 4.50 (ISBN 0-936876-13-1). Learn Res Intl Stud.

Townsend, John M. Cultural Conceptions & Mental Illness: A Comparison of Germany & America. LC 77-22342. (Illus.). 1978. lib. bdg. 11.00x (ISBN 0-226-81098-4). U of Chicago Pr.

Townsend, John R. Good-Bye to the Jungle. LC 67-10335. (gr. 7-9). 1967. PLB 5.53 o.p. (ISBN 0-397-31426-4). Lippincott.

--Pirate's Island. LC 68-14619. (Illus.). (gr. 4-7). 1968. PLB 5.53 o.p. (ISBN 0-397-31425-6). Lippincott.

--The Runaways. Fickling, David, ed. (Australian Bibliographies Ser.). 96p. (Orig.). 1979. pap. text ed. 2.24x (ISBN 0-19-424211-0). Oxford U Pr.

--A Sense of Story: Essays on Contemporary Writers for Children. 216p. 1973. pap. 6.50 (ISBN 0-87675-276-8). Horn Bk.

--The Summer People. LC 72-3270. 224p. (gr. 9 up). 1972. 9.95 (ISBN 0-397-31421-3). Lippincott.

--Top of the World. LC 76-48219. 1977. 8.95 (ISBN 0-397-31728-X). Lippincott.

--Written for Children: An Outline of English-Language Children's Literature. (Illus.). 1976. pap. 6.50 (ISBN 0-87675-278-4). Horn Bk.

Townsend, Joseph. A Dissertation on the Poor Laws: By a Well-Wisher to Mankind. 1971. 15.75x (ISBN 0-520-01700-5). U of Cal Pr.

Townsend, Marvin. Laugh It up. McCarthy, Patricia, ed. (Pal Paperbacks Ser., Kit A). (Illus., Orig.). (gr. 7-12). 1974. pap. text ed. 1.25 (ISBN 0-8374-3472-6). Xerox Ed Pubns.

Townsend, Mary E. Origins of Modern German Colonialism, 1871-1885. LC 74-2493. (Columbia University Studies in History, Economics, & Public Law). 205p. 1975. Repr. of 1921 ed. 15.75 (ISBN 0-86527-144-5). Fertig.

Townsend, Neal R. & Wheatley, Grayson. Developing Skills in Statistics. 1978. text ed. 17.80 (ISBN 0-205-05994-5); instr's man. avail. (ISBN 0-205-05995-3). Allyn.

Townsend, P. D. & Kelley, J. C. Colour Centres & Imperfections in Insulators & Semiconductors. LC 73-76960. 250p. 1973. 24.00x (ISBN 0-8448-0209-3). Crane-Russak Co.

Townsend, Peter. Poverty in the United Kingdom: A Survey of Household Resoures & Standards of Living. 1980. 40.00x (ISBN 0-520-03871-1); pap. 16.95x (ISBN 0-520-03976-9, CAMPUS NO. 242). U of Cal Pr.

--The Smallest Pawns in the Game. 256p. 1980. 14.95 (ISBN 0-316-85129-9). Little.

Townsend, Richard F. State & Cosmos in the Art of Tenochtitlan. LC 79-63726. (Sutdies in Pe-Columbian Art & Archaeology: No. 20). (Illus.). 78p. 1979. pap. 5.00 (ISBN 0-88402-083-5, Ctr. Pre-Columbian). Dumbarton Oaks.

Townsend, Robert. Up the Organization. 240p. 1978. pap. 2.50 (ISBN 0-449-23368-5, Crest). Fawcett.

Townsend, Rochelle, tr. Russian Short Stories. 1979. 8.95x (ISBN 0-460-00758-0, Evman); pap. 3.75 o.p. (ISBN 0-460-01758-6). Dutton.

Townsend, Sallie & Ericson, Virginia. The Amateur Navigator's Handbook. LC 73-15985. (Illus.). 256p. 1974. 11.95 (ISBN 0-690-00192-4, TYC-T). T Y Crowell.

Townsend, William C. Lazaro Cardenas: Mexican Democrat. 2nd rev. enlarged ed. 1979. pap. 4.95 (ISBN 0-935340-00-9). Intl Friend.

Townshend, A., jt. auth. see Burns, D. T.

Townshend, George. Christ & Baha'u'llah. LC 68-168. 1966. 5.50 (ISBN 0-85398-016-0, 7-31-09, Pub. by G Ronald England); pap. 2.00 o.s.i. (ISBN 0-85398-005-5, 7-31-10). Baha'i.

--The Heart of the Gospel. 2nd rev. ed. 5.50 (ISBN 0-85398-025-X, 7-31-16); pap. 1.75 (ISBN 0-85398-020-9, 7-31-17, Pub. by G Ronald England). Baha'i.

--The Mission of Baha'u'llah and Other Literary Pieces. 1952. 6.50 (ISBN 0-85398-021-7, 7-31-18, Pub. by G Ronald England). Baha'i.

--The Promise of All Ages. rev., 3rd ed. 1972. 5.75 (ISBN 0-85398-044-6, 7-31-25, Pub. by G Ronald England); pap. 1.75 (ISBN 0-85398-006-3, 7-31-26, Pub. by George Ronald England). Baha'i.

Townshend, J. R., ed. Terrain Analysis & Remote Sensing. (Illus.). 240p. (Orig.). text ed. 45.00x (ISBN 0-04-551036-9, 2597); pap. text ed. 22.50x (ISBN 0-04-551037-7, 2598). Allen Unwin.

Townson, D. Muslim Spain. (Introduction to the History of Mankind Ser.). (Illus.). 48p. 1973. 3.95 (ISBN 0-521-20251-5). Cambridge U Pr.

Townson, Duncan. Alexander. Killingray, Margaret, et al, eds. (World History Ser.). (Illus.). 32p. (gr. 10). 1980. Repr. of 1977 ed. lib. bdg. 5.95 (ISBN 0-89908-039-1); pap. text ed. 1.95 (ISBN 0-89908-014-6). Greenhaven.

--Famous Generals. LC 78-70608. (Illus.). (gr. 4-6). 1979. PLB 6.90 s&l (ISBN 0-531-09120-1). Watts.

--Spices & Civilizations. Yapp, Malcolm, et al, eds. (World History Ser.). (Illus.). (gr. 10). 1980. Repr. of 1977 ed. lib. bdg. 5.95 (ISBN 0-89908-029-4); pap. text ed. 1.95 (ISBN 0-89908-004-9). Greenhaven.

Towse, G., ed. Myocardial Protection & Exercise Tolerance: The Role of Lidoflazine, a New Anti-Anginal Agent. (Royal Society of Medicine International Congress & Symposium Ser.: No. 29). 1980. 18.50 (ISBN 0-8089-1290-9). Grune.

Towsen, John. Clowns. LC 75-41793. (Illus.). 1978. pap. 6.95 (ISBN 0-8015-3963-3, Hawthorn). Dutton.

Toy, A. D. The Chemistry of Phosphorous. (Pergamon Texts in Inorganic Chemistry: Vol. 3). 158p. 1975. text ed. 27.00 (ISBN 0-08-018780-3); pap. text ed. 14.00 (ISBN 0-08-018779-X). Pergamon.

Toy, C. H. Proverbs. LC 99-5903. (International Critical Commentary Ser.). 592p. Repr. of 1899 ed. text ed. 23.00x. Attic Pr.

Toy, Wing N., jt. auth. see Kraft, George D.

Toye, Charles. Prayers & Meditations for Healing. LC 80-82813. 96p. (Orig.). 1981. pap. 3.95 (ISBN 0-8091-2342-8). Paulist Pr.

Toye, Clive. First Book of Soccer. LC 68-25725. (First Bks). (Illus.). (gr. 4-6). 1968. PLB 6.45 (ISBN 0-531-00633-6). Watts.

--Soccer. 2nd rev. ed. (First Bks.). (Illus.). (gr. 4-6). 1979. PLB 6.45 s&l (ISBN 0-531-02936-0). Watts.

Toye, F. J. Public Expenditure & Indian Development Policy Nineteen Sixty to Nineteen Seventy. LC 80-41011. 284p. Date not set. 39.50 (ISBN 0-521-23081-0). Cambridge U Pr.

Toye, Hugh. Subhash Chandra Bose: The Springing Tiger. 1970. pap. 2.80 (ISBN 0-88253-190-5). Ind-US Inc.

Toye, J. F., ed. Taxation & Economic Development: Twelve Critical Studies. (Twelve Critical Studies Ser.). 299p. 1978. 26.00x (ISBN 0-7146-3016-0, F Cass Co). Biblio Dist.

Toye, John, jt. ed. see Smith, Sheila.

Toye, Kenneth. Regional French Cookery. (Illus.). 1979. 13.50 (ISBN 0-7153-6327-1). David & Charles.

Toye, Randall & Gaffney, Judith H. The Agatha Christie Crossword Puzzle Book. 132p. (Orig.). 1981. pap. 6.95 (ISBN 0-686-69122-9). HR&W.

Toynbee, Arnold J. Acquaintances. 1967. 14.95 (ISBN 0-19-500189-3). Oxford U Pr.

--Constantine Porphyrogenitus & His World. (Illus.). 792p. 1973. 45.00x (ISBN 0-19-215253-X). Oxford U Pr.

--Hellenism: The History of a Civilization. LC 80-27772. xii, 272p. 1981. Repr. of 1959 ed. lib. bdg. 25.00x (ISBN 0-313-22742-X, TOHM). Greenwood.

--An Historian's Approach to Religion. 2nd ed. 1979. 19.95 (ISBN 0-19-215260-2). Oxford U Pr.

--A Study of History. (Royal Institute of International Affairs). 1954. Vols. 1-6. o.p. (ISBN 0-19-500198-2); Vols. 7-10. maroon cloth 60.00 (ISBN 0-19-519689-9); Vols. 11-12 (vol. 11 O.p.) maroon cloth 19.95 (ISBN 0-19-500197-4). Oxford U Pr.

--A Study of History: Introduction the Genesis of Civilization, & the Growth of Civilization, 3 vols. 2nd ed. (Royal Institute of International Affairs Ser.). 1935. Vol. 1. 26.50x (ISBN 0-19-215207-6); Vol. 2. 29.95x (ISBN 0-19-215208-4); Vol. 3. 29.00x (ISBN 0-19-215209-2). Oxford U Pr.

--A Study of History: Reconsideration. 1961. Vol. 12. 26.00x (ISBN 0-19-215225-4). Oxford U Pr.

--A Study of History: The Disintegrations of Civilization. (Royal Institute of International Affairs Ser.). 1939. Vol. 4. 29.00x (ISBN 0-19-215211-4); Vol. 5. 13.95x (ISBN 0-19-215212-2); Vol. 6. 29.95x (ISBN 0-19-215213-0). Oxford U Pr.

--The Western Question in Greece & Turkey: A Study in the Contrast of Civilizations. 2nd ed. LC 68-9598. (Illus., Maps). 1970. Repr. of 1922 ed. 18.00 (ISBN 0-86527-209-3). Fertig.

Toynbee, J. M. Death & Burial in the Roman World. Scullard, H. H., ed. LC 77-120603. (Aspects of Greek & Roman Life Ser). (Illus.). 336p. 1971. 19.50x (ISBN 0-8014-0593-9); pap. 4.95 o.p. (ISBN 0-8014-9165-7). Cornell U Pr.

Toynbee, Paget J. Dictionary of Proper Names & Notable Matters in the Works of Dante. 2nd ed. Singleton, Charles S., ed. 1968. 63.00x (ISBN 0-19-815356-2). Oxford U Pr.

Toyne, Peter. Organization, Location & Behavior: Decision Making in Economic Geography. LC 73-22708. 285p. 1974. text ed. 17.95 (ISBN 0-470-88100-3). Halsted Pr.

Toyoda, Takeshi, jt. ed. see Hall, John W.

Toyoda, Toshiyuka, jt. ed. see Epstein, William.

Toys 'n Things Training & Resource Center. Teachables from Trashables: Home-Made Toys That Teach. LC 79-64910. (Illus., Orig.). 1979. pap. 5.95 (ISBN 0-934140-00-6); spiral bound o.p. 6.95 (ISBN 0-934140-01-4). Toys N Things.

Tozer, A. W. The Best of A. W. Tozer. (Best Ser). 1978. pap. 2.50 (ISBN 0-8010-8845-3). Baker Bk.

--La Busqueda De Dios. Bruchez, Dardo, tr. 130p. (Orig.). 1979. pap. 2.00 (ISBN 0-87509-162-8); pap. 1.50 mass mkt. (ISBN 0-87509-159-8). Chr Pubns.

--Keys to the Deeper Life. 56p. 1973. pap. 1.25 (ISBN 0-310-33362-8). Zondervan.

--Renewed Day by Day: Three Hundred & Sixty Five Daily Devotions. 1981. 12.95 (ISBN 0-8010-8861-5). Baker Bk.

Tozer, Aiden W. Born After Midnight. 3.95 (ISBN 0-87509-258-6); pap. 2.75 (ISBN 0-87509-167-9); pap. 1.95 mass mkt (ISBN 0-87509-258-6). Chr Pubns.

--Renewed Day by Day. LC 80-69301. 380p. pap. 6.95 (ISBN 0-87509-292-6). Chr Pubns.

Tozer, Henry F. History of Ancient Geography. 2nd ed. LC 54-13396. 1897. 15.00x (ISBN 0-8196-0138-1). Biblo.

Tozer, Thomas N., jt. auth. see Rowland, Malcolm.

Tozer, Zibby. The Art of Flower Arranging. (Orig.). 1981. pap. 7.95 (ISBN 0-446-97760-8). Warner Bks.

Tozzer, Alfred M. Chichen Itza & Its Cenote of Sacrifice: A Comparative Study of Contemporaneous Maya & Toltec. LC 58-1778. (Peabody Museum Memoirs: Vols. 11-12). 1957. pap. 50.00 (ISBN 0-87365-684-9). Peabody Harvard.

Trabucchi, Marco, jt. ed. see Costa, E.

Trabucchi, Marco, jt. ed. see Costa, Erminio.

Trabucco, Peter D. Panning for Gold in a Single's Bar. (Illus.). 96p. (Orig.). 1980. pap. 6.95 (ISBN 0-9605106-0-5). PT Marketing.

Tracey, Edmund, tr. see Mannn, William.

Tracey, Margot. Red Rose. (Illus.). 1978. 17.95 (ISBN 0-7153-7440-0). David & Charles.

Tracht, Myron E. & Ali, Majid, eds. Pathology Specialty Board Review. 4th ed. 1976. spiral bdg. 16.50 (ISBN 0-87488-305-9). Med Exam.

Tracht, Myron E., et al, eds. Digestive System Basic Sciences. (Basic Science Review Bks.). 1973. spiral bdg. 8.00 o.p. (ISBN 0-87488-215-X). Med Exam.

--Urinary System Basic Sciences. 1973. spiral bdg. 10.00 o.p. (ISBN 0-87488-214-1). Med Exam.

Trachtenberg, Alan. Classic Essays on Photography. LC 78-61844. 1980. 12.95 (ISBN 0-918172-07-1); pap. 8.95 (ISBN 0-918172-08-X). Leetes Isl.

--Hart Crane: A Collection of Critical Essays. (Twentieth Century Views Ser.). 224p. 1981. 13.95 (ISBN 0-13-383935-4, Spec); pap. 5.95 (ISBN 0-13-383927-3). P-H.

Trachtenberg, Alan, jt. auth. see Coles, Robert.

Trachtenberg, Inge. An Arranged Marriage. 272p. 1975. 6.95 o.p. (ISBN 0-393-08705-0). Norton.

Trachtenberg, Leo. The Sponsor's Guide to Filmmaking. 1978. 6.95 o.p. (ISBN 0-911974-26-1); pap. write for info. o.p. (ISBN 0-911974-28-8). Hopkinson.

Trachtenberg, Marc. Reparation in World Politics: France & European Economic Diplomacy, 1916-1923. LC 79-26898. 1980. 25.00x (ISBN 0-231-04786-X). Columbia U Pr.

Trachtman, Paul. The Gunfighters. LC 74-80284. (Old West Ser.). (gr. 5 up). 1974. lib. bdg. 12.96 (ISBN 0-8094-1481-3, Pub. Time-Life). Silver.

--The Gunfighters. (The Old West Ser). (Illus.). 1974. 12.95 (ISBN 0-8094-1479-1). Time-Life.

Trachtman, Paula. Disturb Not the Dream. Aymar, Brandt, ed. 320p. 1981. 11.95 (ISBN 0-517-54322-2). Crown.

Traci, Philip, jt. auth. see Felheim, Marvin.

Tracton, Ken. Programmer's Guide to LISP. (Illus.). 1979. 10.95 (ISBN 0-8306-9761-6); pap. 6.95 (ISBN 0-8306-1045-6, 1045). TAB Bks.

Tracy, Ann B. Patterns of Fear in the Gothic Novel: 790-1830. Varma, Devendra P., ed. LC 79-8487. (Gothic Studies & Dissertations Ser.). 1980. lib. bdg. 35.00x (ISBN 0-405-12682-4). Arno.

Tracy, C., ed. see Savage, Richard.

Tracy, David. The Analogical Imagination: Christian Theology & the Culture of Pluralism. 288p. 1981. 17.50 (ISBN 0-8245-0122-5). Crossroad NY.

--Blessed Rage for Order: The New Pluralism in Theology. 1975. 14.95 (ISBN 0-8164-4707-1). Crossroad NY.

--Blessed Rage for Order: The New Pluralism in Theology. (Library of Contemporary Theology Ser.). 1979. pap. 8.95 (ISBN 0-8164-2202-8). Crossroad NY.

Tracy, David, jt. ed. see Eliade, Mircea.

Tracy, David, et al, eds. Towards Vatican III: The Work That Has to Be Done. 1978. 14.95 (ISBN 0-8164-0379-1); pap. 5.95 (ISBN 0-8164-2173-0). Crossroad NY.

Tracy, Dick, jt. auth. see Scannell, Dale.

Tracy, George M. How to Interpret the Warning Signals Which the Stock Market Emits Foretelling the Future Course of Security & Commodity Prices. (Illus.). 1980. 37.45 (ISBN 0-918968-49-6). Inst Econ Finan.

Tracy, Jack. The Encyclopaedia Sherlockiana. 1979. pap. 7.95 (ISBN 0-380-46490-X, 46490). Avon.

Tracy, James D., ed. True Ocean Found: Paludanus's Letters on Dutch Voyages to the Kara Sea, 1595-1596. LC 80-13962. (A Publication from the James Ford Bell Library at the University of Minnesota). (Illus.). 1980. 10.00x (ISBN 0-8166-0961-6). U of Minn Pr.

Tracy, John A. Fundamentals of Financial Accounting. 2nd ed. 1978. text ed. 22.95 (ISBN 0-471-88160-0); study guide 7.50 (ISBN 0-471-88161-9); tchrs. manual 14.95 (ISBN 0-471-02293-4); working papers 11.95 (ISBN 0-471-88162-7). Wiley.

--Fundamentals of Management Accounting. LC 75-26988. 565p. 1976. text ed. 21.95 (ISBN 0-471-88151-1, Pub. by Wiley-Hamilton). Wiley.

--How to Read a Financial Report: Wringing Cash Flow & Other Vital Signs Out of the Numbers. LC 79-18853. 1980. 14.95 (ISBN 0-471-05712-6, Pub. by Wiley-Interscience). Wiley.

Tracy, Joseph. The Great Awakening. 1976. 11.95 (ISBN 0-85151-233-X). Banner of Truth.

--Pilot's Sketchbook. LC 80-66116. 1981. pap. 8.95 (ISBN 0-8168-7408-5). Aero.

Tracy, Lane, jt. auth. see Peterson, Richard B.

Tracy, Marian. Real Food: Simple, Sensuous & Splendid. pap. 5.95 (ISBN 0-14-046468-9). Penguin.

Tracy, Patricia. Jonathan Edwards: Pastor. 288p. 1980. 14.95 (ISBN 0-8090-6195-3); pap. 5.95 (ISBN 0-8090-0149-7). Hill & Wang.

Tracy, Robert. Trollope's Later Novels. LC 76-55572. 1978. 17.50x (ISBN 0-520-03407-4). U of Cal Pr.

Tracy, Robert, ed. see Trollope, Anthony.

T.R.A.D.A. Timbers of the World, Vol. 2. (Illus.). 1980. text ed. 38.00 (ISBN 0-86095-837-X, Construction Pr). Longman.

Trade & Technical Press, ed. Industrial Fasteners Handbook. (Illus.). 115.00x (ISBN 0-85461-062-6). Intl Ideas.

Trade & Technical Press Editors. Pneumatic Data, Vol. 2. 130p. 1967. 20.00x (ISBN 0-85461-012-X, Pub by Trade & Tech England). Renouf.

--Pneumatic Data, Vol. 3. 100p. 1978. 21.00x (ISBN 0-85461-069-3, Pub by Trade & Tech England). Renouf.

--Pneumatic Engineering Calculations. 120p. 1969. 16.00x (ISBN 0-85461-038-3, Pub by Trade & Tech England). Renouf.

--Pneumatic Power Glossary. 80p. 1970. 17.00x o.p. (ISBN 0-686-65529-X, Pub by Trade & Tech England). Renouf.

Trade & Technical Press Ltd, ed. Handbook of Industrial Fire Protection & Security. 105.00x (ISBN 0-85461-059-6). Intl Ideas.

--Handbook of Instruments & Instrumentation. (Illus.). 105.00x (ISBN 0-85461-064-2). Intl Ideas.

--Handbook of Mechanical Power Drives. 2nd ed. (Illus.). 1978. 105.00x (ISBN 0-85461-067-7). Intl Ideas.

--Handbook of Noise & Vibration. 4th ed. (Illus.). 1978. 110.00x o.p. (ISBN 0-85461-073-1). Intl Ideas.

--Hydraulic Handbook. 7th ed. (Illus.). 110.00 o.p. (ISBN 0-85461-074-X). Intl Ideas.

--Hydraulic Technical Data, Vol. 4. 21.00x (ISBN 0-85461-066-9). Intl Ideas.

--Pneumatic Handbook. 5th ed. (Illus.). 1978. 115.00x (ISBN 0-85461-068-5). Intl Ideas.

--Pneumatic Technical Data, Vol. 3. 27.50x (ISBN 0-85461-069-3). Intl Ideas.

--Principles of Hydraulics. (Illus.). 24.00x (ISBN 0-685-90212-9). Intl Ideas.

--Principles of Pneumatics. (Illus.). 24.00x (ISBN 0-685-90213-7). Intl Ideas.

--Pump User's Handbook. 2nd ed. (Illus.). 1979. 32.95x o.p. (ISBN 0-685-66962-9). Intl Ideas.
--Pumping Data, Vol. 2. 22.50x (ISBN 0-685-90215-3). Intl Ideas.
--Pumping Data, Vol. 3. 1969. 22.50x (ISBN 0-685-90214-5). Intl Ideas.
--Pumping Manual. 6th ed. (Illus.). 1979. 115.00x (ISBN 0-85461-081-2). Intl Ideas.
Trafzer, Clifford, jt. auth. see Scheuerman, Richard.
Tragatsch, Erwin, ed. The Complete Illustrated Encyclopedia of the World's Motorcycles. LC 77-71370. (Illus.). 1977. 22.95 o.p. (ISBN 0-03-019296-X). HR&W.
Trager. School Survival Guide. (gr. 7-12). Date not set. pap. cancelled (ISBN 0-590-30915-3, Schol Pap). Schol Bk Serv.
Trager, Carolyn. Moving Time. LC 78-7722. (Illus.). (gr. 5-8). 1978. PLB 6.45 s&l (ISBN 0-531-02219-6). Watts.
Trager, Helen G., jt. auth. see Aung, Maung Htin.
Trager, Robert, jt. auth. see Stonecipher, Harry W.
Trahan, E. W. Gruppe 47: Ein Querschmitt. 1969. text ed. 7.95x o.p. (ISBN 0-471-00595-9). Wiley.
Trahan, Elizabeth, ed. Gogol's "Overcoat". An Anthology of Critical Essays. 1981. 15.00 (ISBN 0-88233-614-2). Ardis Pubs.
Trailer Life Editors, jt. auth. see Longsdorf, Bob.
Traill, Henry D. Coleridge. LC 67-23874. 1968. Repr. of 1884 ed. 18.00 (ISBN 0-8103-3052-0). Gale.
Traill, Robert. The Works of Robert Traill, 2 vols. 1975. Set. 27.95 (ISBN 0-686-12488-X). Vol. 1 (ISBN 0-85151-229-1). Vol. 2 (ISBN 0-85151-230-5). Banner of Truth.
Train, John. The Dance of the Money Bees: A Professional Speaks Frankly on Investing. LC 74-5796. 256p. 1974. 10.95 o.p. (ISBN 0-06-014349-5, HarpT). Har-Row.
--Remarkable Names of Real People. (Illus.). 1977. 5.95 (ISBN 0-517-53130-5). Potter.
--Remarkable Occurrences. (Illus.). 1978. 5.95 (ISBN 0-517-53505-X, Dist. by Crown). Potter.
--Remarkable Words: With Astonishing Origins, Remarkable Ser. (Clarkson N. Potter Bks.). 1980. 5.95 (ISBN 0-517-54185-8). Crown.
Trainer, Glynnis. The Metalworking Industry. 200p. 1981. cancelled (ISBN 0-86569-062-6). Auburn Hse.
Trainer, Luke. Origins of the First World War. 1974. pap. text ed. 3.95 (ISBN 0-435-31900-0). Heinemann Ed.
Trainer, Thomas D., jt. auth. see Howard, Phillip L.
Trainer, Thomas D., et al. Radioisotopes in the Clinical Laboratory. (Atlas Ser.). (Illus.). 1976. text & slides 70.00 (ISBN 0-89189-093-9, 15-8-01-00); microfiche ed. 22.00 (ISBN 0-89189-094-7, 17-8-001-00). Am Soc Clinical.
Training & Retraining Inc. Basic Electricity - Electronics. LC 63-23001. 1968. Bk 1. 12.10 o.p. (ISBN 0-672-20711-7); Bk 2. 12.10 o.p. (ISBN 0-672-20712-5); tchr's guide 6.67 o.p. (ISBN 0-672-20174-7). Bobbs.
Training & Retraining, Inc. Basic Electricity-Electronics, Vol. 1: Basic Principles. 2nd ed. LC 80-5004. 1980. pap. 6.95 o.p. (ISBN 0-672-21501-2). Bobbs.
Training & Retraining Inc. Basic Electricity Electronics, 5 vols. 2nd ed. Incl. Vol. 1. Basic Principles. LC 80-50045. 6.95 (ISBN 0-672-21501-2); Vol. 2. How AC & DC Circuits Work. LC 63-23002 (ISBN 0-672-20168-2, 20168); Vol. 3. Understanding Tube & Transistor Circuits. LC 64-14336 (ISBN 0-672-20169-0, 20169); Vol. 4. Understanding & Using Test Instruments. LC 64-14337 (ISBN 0-672-20170-4, 20170); Vol. 5. Motors & Generators - How They Work. LC 64-14338. pap. (ISBN 0-672-20171-2, 20171). (YA) 1966. pap. 5.50 ea.; pap. 26.95 set (ISBN 0-672-21740-6, 21740). Sams.
--Transistor Fundamentals, 3 vols. Incl. Vol. 1. Basic Semiconductor & Circuit Principles (ISBN 0-672-20641-2, 20641); Vol. 2. Basic Transistor Circuits (ISBN 0-672-20642-0, 20642); Vol. 3. Digital & Special Circuits (ISBN 0-672-20644-7, 20644). LC 68-21313. (Illus., Prog. Bk.). 1968. pap. 5.75 ea.; pap. 15.75 set (ISBN 0-672-21796-1). Sams.
Training & Retraining, Inc. Transistor Fundamentals. LC 68-21313. 1968. 10.35 o.p. (ISBN 0-672-20744-3); Bk 2. 10.35 o.p. (ISBN 0-672-20745-1); instructor's guide 5.00 o.p. (ISBN 0-672-20647-1). Bobbs.
Training Workshop on Water Management for Arid Regions, Ministry of Irrigation, Government of Egypt, in Cooperation with the United Nations Environment Programme, Cairo, Egypt. Water Management for Arid Lands: Proceedings. Samaha, M. A., et al, eds. LC 79-40504. (Water Development, Supply & Management: Vol. 13). (Illus.). 280p. 1980. 40.00 (ISBN 0-08-022431-8). Pergamon.
Trainor, Jim. The Complete Baseball Play Book. LC 77-165387. 352p. 1972. pap. 6.95 (ISBN 0-385-00075-8). Doubleday.
Trainor, Lynn & Wise, Mark B. From Physical Concept to Mathematical Structure: An Introduction to Theoretical Physics. LC 78-11616. (Mathematical Expositions Ser.). 1979. 25.00x (ISBN 0-8020-5432-3); pap. 10.00x (ISBN 0-8020-6432-9). U of Toronto Pr.
Traisman, Barbara. Handed Down: The Artisan Tradition. LC 80-67829. 1980. pap. 12.95 (ISBN 0-916860-07-8). Bean Pub.
Traisman, Howard S. Management of Juvenile Diabetes Mellitus. 3rd ed. LC 79-24675. (Illus.). 1980. text ed. 42.50 (ISBN 0-8016-5020-8). Mosby.
Traister, John. Clyde Baker's Modern Gunsmithing. (Illus.). 544p. 1981. 19.95 (ISBN 0-8117-0983-3). Stackpole.
--Electrical Blueprint Reading. LC 75-5415. (Illus.). 1975. pap. 5.95 o.p. (ISBN 0-672-21181-5, 21181). Sams.
--Learn Gunsmithing: The Troubleshooting Method. (Illus.). 288p. 1980. 12.95 (ISBN 0-87691-317-6). Winchester Pr.
Traister, John E. Construction Electrical Contracting. LC 78-13441. (Wiley Series on Practical Construction Guides). 299p. 1978. 29.95 (ISBN 0-471-02986-6). Wiley.
--Electrical Inspection Guidebook. (Illus.). 1979. text ed. 19.95 (ISBN 0-8359-1629-4). Reston.
--Electrical Specifications for Building Construction. (Illus.). 1978. text ed. 16.95 (ISBN 0-87909-214-9). Reston.
--Gun Digest of Gunsmithing Tools...& Their Uses. 1980. pap. 7.95 (ISBN 0-695-81452-4). DBI.
--Handbook of Electrical Systems Design Practices. (Illus.). 1978. ref. ed. 16.95 (ISBN 0-87909-348-X). Reston.
--Handbook of Modern Electrical Wiring. (Illus.). 1979. text ed. 16.95 (ISBN 0-8359-2754-7). Reston.
--How to Build Your Own Boat from Scratch. 1978. pap. 6.95 (ISBN 0-8306-7923-5, 923). TAB Bks.
Traister, John E. & Traister, Robert J. How to Build Metal-Treasurer Locators. LC 77-7510. (Illus.). 1977. 7.95 o.p. (ISBN 0-8306-7909-X); pap. 3.95 (ISBN 0-8306-6909-4, 909). TAB Bks.
Traister, Robert. Principles of Biomedical Instrumentation & Monitoring. 300p. 1981. text ed. 24.95 (ISBN 0-8359-5611-3). Reston.
Traister, Robert J. DC Power Supplies: Application & Theory. (Illus.). 1979. text ed. 16.95 (ISBN 0-8359-1275-2). Reston.
--The Giant Book of Amateur Radio Antennas. (Illus.). 1979. pap. 8.95 (ISBN 0-8306-8802-1); pap. 8.95 (ISBN 0-8306-8802-1, 802). TAB Bks.
Traister, Robert J., jt. auth. see Traister, John E.
Trakatellis, Demetrius C. The Pre-Existence of Christ in Justin Martyr. LC 76-44913. (Harvard Theological Review Ser.). 1976. pap. 7.50 (ISBN 0-89130-098-8, 020106). Scholars Pr Ca.
Trakimas, Winifred, et al. Blueprint of the Plant. 3rd rev. ed. 178p. 1980. pap. text ed. 10.95 (ISBN 0-8087-3614-0). Burgess.
Trambouze, P., jt. ed. see Villermaux, J.
Tramel, Mary E. & Reynolds, Helen. Executive Leadership: How to Get It - & Make It Work. (Illus.). 272p. 1981. 13.95 (ISBN 0-13-294132-5, Spec); pap. 6.95 (ISBN 0-686-69280-2). P-H.
Trams, Albert F. More Marginalia. 50p. 1980. Repr. of 1931 ed. lib. bdg. 12.50 (ISBN 0-8482-2740-9). Norwood Edns.
Tramutola, J., jt. auth. see Laudicina, R.
Tramutola, Joseph L., jt. ed. see Laudicina, Robert A.
Tranel, Bernard. Concreteness in Generative Phonology: Evidence from French. LC 80-51243. 400p. 1980. 29.50x (ISBN 0-520-04165-8). U of Cal Pr.
Trani, Eugene P. The Treaty of Portsmouth: An Adventure in American Diplomacy. LC 69-19767. (Illus.). 208p. 1969. 10.00x (ISBN 0-8131-1174-9). U Pr of Ky.
Tranquillus, Gaius S. The Twelve Caesars: An Illustrated Edition. Graves, Robert, tr. 1979. pap. 14.95 (ISBN 0-14-005416-2). Penguin.
Trans World Airlines. Legacy of Leadership: Pictorial History of Trans World Airlines. (Illus.). 1973. 15.00 o.p. (ISBN 0-911721-47-9). Aviation.
Transtromer, Tomas. Selected Poems. Fulton, Robin, tr. from Swed. 1981. 15.00x (ISBN 0-88233-462-X); pap. 5.00x (ISBN 0-88233-463-8). Ardis Pubs.
--Truth Barriers: Poems by Tomas Transtromer. Bly, Robert, tr. from Swedish. LC 80-13310. (Illus.). 64p. 1980. 9.95 (ISBN 0-87156-235-9); pap. 5.95 (ISBN 0-87156-239-1). Sierra.
Tranter, N. L., ed. Population & Industrialization: The Evolution of a Concept & Its Practical Application. (Documents in Economic History Ser.). 1973. text ed. 15.75x (ISBN 0-7136-1310-6). Humanities.
Tranter, Neil L. Population Since the Industrial Revolution: The Case of England & Wales. 1973. text ed. 10.50x (ISBN 0-85664-012-3). Humanities.
Tranter, Nigel. Scotland. LC 68-1791. (Pegasus Books: No. 2). 1964. 7.50x (ISBN 0-234-77793-1). Intl Pubns Serv.
Tranter, P., jt. auth. see Dunn, M.
Tranter, William, jt. auth. see Ziemer, Rodger E.
Trapnell, Coles. Teleplay: An Introduction to Television Writing. 256p. 1974. pap. text ed. 5.95 (ISBN 0-8015-7486-2, Hawthorn). Dutton.
Trapnell, D. H. Principles of X-Ray Diagnosis. 1967. 29.95 (ISBN 0-407-36560-5). Butterworths.
Trapnell, D. H. & Bowerman, J. E. Dental Manifestations of Systemic Disease. (Radiology in Clinical Diagnosis Ser.,). 1973. 24.95 (ISBN 0-407-14400-5). Butterworths.
Trapp, Frithjof. Kunst als Gesellschaftanalyse bei Heinrich Mann. (Quellen und Forschungen Zur Sprach und Kulturgeschichte der Germanischen Voelker NF 64-188). vi, 328p. 1975. text ed. 50.60x (ISBN 3-11-005968-1). De Gruyter.
Trapp, J. B., ed. Background to the English Renaissance: Introductory Lectures, (Dickens, Gombrich, Hale, Pattison, & Trapp) 1974. 13.00x o.p. (ISBN 0-85641-022-5, Pub. by Basil Blackwell England); pap. 5.00x o.p. (ISBN 0-85641-023-3). Biblio Dist.
Trapp, John. A Commentary on the New Testament. 864p. 1981. Repr. of 1865 ed. 19.95 (ISBN 0-8010-8855-0). Baker Bk.
Trappl, R., jt. ed. see Pichler, F.
Trappl, Robert, ed. Cybernetics: A Sourcebook. 1982. text ed. 39.50 (ISBN 0-89116-128-7). Hemisphere Pub. Postponed.
Trappl, Robert, et al, eds. Progress in Cybernetics & Systems Research, 5 vols. Incl. Vol. 1. General Systems, Engineering Systems, Biocybernetics & Neural Systems. 24.50 (ISBN 0-470-88475-4); Vol. 2. Socio-Economic Systems, Cognition & Learning, Systems Education, Organization & Management. 24.50 (ISBN 0-470-88476-2); Vol. 3. General Systems Methodology, Fuzzy Mathematics & Fuzzy Systems, Biocybernetics & Theoretical Neurobiology. 40.00 (ISBN 0-470-26371-7); Vol. 4. Cybernetics of Cognition & Learning, Structure & Dynamics of Socioeconomic Systems, Health Care Systems, Engineering Systems Methodology. 40.00 (ISBN 0-470-99380-4); Vol. 5. Organization & Management, Organic Problem-Solving in Management System Approach in Urban & Regional Planning, Computer Performance, Control & Evaluation of Computer Linguistics. 50.00 (ISBN 0-470-26553-1). LC 75-6641. 1975-79. Halsted Pr.
Traschen, Isadore, jt. auth. see Frakes, James R.
Trask, Anne E., jt. auth. see Gross, Neal.
Trask, David F. The War with the Spain in Eighteen Ninety-Eight. Morton, Louis, ed. LC 80-2314. (The Macmillan Wars of the United States Ser.). (Illus.). 775p. 1981. 29.95 (ISBN 0-02-932950-7). Macmillan.
Trask, David F., et al, eds. Bibliography of United States - Latin American Relations Since 1810: A Selected List of Eleven Thousand Published References. LC 67-14421. 1968. 19.75x (ISBN 0-8032-0185-0). U of Nebr Pr.
Trask, Jonathan. The Camp. 1977. pap. 1.50 (ISBN 0-505-51214-9). Tower Bks.
Trask, W. R. see Zuckerland, Victor.
Trask, Willard R., tr. see Casanova, Giacomo.
Trask, Willard R., tr. see Curtius, E. R.
Trask, Willard R., tr. see Eliade, Mircea.
Tratsart, M. Medical Correspondence Workbook. 1974. wire bound wkbk. 14.95x (ISBN 0-433-32645-X). Intl Ideas.
Trattner, Walter I. From Poor Law to Welfare State: A History of Social Welfare in America. 2nd ed. LC 78-58914. 1979. 14.95 (ISBN 0-02-932890-X); pap. text ed. 7.95 (ISBN 0-02-932900-0). Free Pr.
Traub, Hamilton P. The Call of Destiny: The Epic of the American Republic. LC 79-52732. (Illus.). 614p. 1980. 14.95x (ISBN 0-9605364-0-X); pap. 9.95x. Golden Hill.
Traub, Jack. Accounting & Reporting Practices of Private Foundations: A Critical Evaluation. LC 77-5344. (Special Studies). 1977. text ed. 26.50 (ISBN 0-275-24530-6). Praeger.
Traub, Stuart H. & Little, Craig B., eds. Theories of Deviance. 2nd ed. LC 79-91105. 400p. 1980. pap. text ed. 9.95 (ISBN 0-87581-247-3). Peacock Pubs.
Traudl. Kostas the Rooster. LC 68-14071. (Illus.). (gr. k-3). PLB 5.28 o.p. (ISBN 0-688-51171-6). Lothrop.
Traugott, Elizabeth, ed. see International Conference on Historical Linguistics, 4th.
Traum, Happy. Folk Guitar As a Profession. Milano, Dominic, ed. LC 76-57470. (Illus.). 70p. 1977. pap. 5.95 (ISBN 0-8256-9507-4). Guitar Player.
Traupman, John C. German English Dictionary. 764p. (Orig.). 1981. pap. 2.50 (ISBN 0-553-14155-4). Bantam.
--New College Latin & English Dictionary. (gr. 7-12). 1966. pap. text ed. 6.25 (ISBN 0-87720-560-4). AMSCO Sch.
Traupman, John C., ed. The Bantam New College German & English Dictionary. 768p. (Orig.). (gr. 7-12). 1981. pap. 2.50 (ISBN 0-553-14155-4). Bantam.
Trautlein, J., ed. Aerosols, Airways & Asthma. 121p. 1981. text ed. 20.00 (ISBN 0-89335-059-1). Spectrum Pub.
Trautmann, Frederic. The Voice of Terror: A Biography of Johann Most. LC 79-8279. (Contributions in Political Science: No. 42). (Illus.). xxv, 288p. 1980. lib. bdg. 25.00 (ISBN 0-313-22053-0, TVT/). Greenwood.
Trautmann, Joanne, ed. see Woolf.
Trautmann, Thomas R. Dravidian Kinship. LC 80-24214. (Cambridge Studies in Social Anthropology: No. 36). (Illus.). 704p. Date not set. price not set (ISBN 0-521-23703-3). Cambridge U Pr.
Trautschold. Gear Designs & Production. 6.50 o.p. (ISBN 0-686-00165-6). Columbia Graphs.
Traux, Carol. Gourmet Cooking on a Budget. 192p. (Orig.). 1976. pap. 1.95 o.p. (ISBN 0-345-25382-5). Ballantine.
Travelaid Staff. Travelaid Guide to Greece. (Travelaid Guides Ser.). (Illus., Orig.). 1978. pap. 5.95 (ISBN 0-8467-0435-8, Pub. by Two Continents). Hippocrene Bks.
Traven, B. El Tesoro De la Sierra Madre. Rodriguez, M., ed. (Span.). 1963. 8.95 (ISBN 0-13-273771-X). P-H.
Traver, Hope. Love Is for Tomorrow. 271p. 1978. pap. 4.95 (ISBN 0-930756-37-1, 4230-TR1). Women's Aglow.
Traver, Robert. Anatomy of a Murder. 2.95 (ISBN 0-89559-009-3). Green Hill.
Travers, Ben. Mischief. Incl. Rookery Nook; Cuckoo in the Nest. LC 78-4746. 1978. 13.95 o.s.i. (ISBN 0-06-014347-9, HarpT). Har-Row.
Travers, Henry J. Organizations: Size & Intensity. LC 78-52294. 1978. pap. text ed. 6.75x (ISBN 0-8191-0483-3). U Pr of Amer.
Travers, J. F. The Growing Child: Introduction to Child Development. 1977. 19.95x (ISBN 0-471-88500-2); study guide 6.95x. Wiley.
Travers, Pamela L. Friend Monkey. LC 70-161389. (gr. k-3). 1971. 6.95 o.p. (ISBN 0-15-229555-0, HJ). HarBraceJ.
Traversa, Vincenzo. Parola E Pensiero: Introduzione Alla Lingua Italiana Moderna. 3rd ed. (Illus.). 437p. 1980. text ed. 18.95 scp (ISBN 0-06-046653-7, HarpC); avail. instrs' manual; wkbk. scp 5.50 (ISBN 0-06-046654-5); tapes 229.00. Har-Row.
Traversi, Derek, intro. by. Renaissance Drama. 128p. 1981. pap. 5.95 (ISBN 0-312-67160-1). St Martin.
Traverso, E. Korea & the Limits of Limited War. Brown, Richard H. & Halsey, Van R., eds. (Amherst Ser.). (gr. 9-12). 1970. pap. text ed. 4.52 (ISBN 0-201-07582-2, Sch Div); tchrs' manual 1.92 (ISBN 0-201-07584-9). A-W.
Traverton, Gregory, ed. Crisis Management & the Super-Powers in the Middle East. LC 80-67837. (Adelphi Library: Vol. 5). 172p. 1981. text ed. 29.50 (ISBN 0-916672-73-5). Allanheld.
Travis, Anthony, jt. auth. see Mapes, Lynn G.
Travis, Charles, jt. auth. see Rosenberg, Jay F.
Travis, Gretchen. Two Spruce Lane. 224p. 1976. pap. 1.50 o.p. (ISBN 0-345-25164-4). Ballantine.
Travis, Jeffrey C. Clinical Radioimmunoassy: State of the Art. (Illus.). 1980. 39.00 (ISBN 0-930914-06-6). Sci Newsletters.
--Fundamentals of RIA & Other Ligand Assays: A Programmed Text. (Illus.). 1977. 22.50 (ISBN 0-930914-05-8). Sci Newsletters.
Travis, John W. A Guide to Restringing. LC 61-9870. (Illus.). 1972. 13.50x (ISBN 0-9600394-0-6); pap. 10.95x (ISBN 0-9600394-1-4). Travis.
--Let's Tune Up. Rathman, R. Annabel, ed. LC 68-14025. (Illus.). 1968. 20.00x (ISBN 0-9600394-2-2); pap. 17.50x (ISBN 0-9600394-3-0). Travis.
Travis, John W., jt. auth. see Ryan, Regina S.
Travis, Patricia Y. & Travis, Robert P. Vitalizing Intimacy in Marriage. LC 79-4374. 1979. 11.95 (ISBN 0-88229-398-2). Nelson-Hall.
Travis, Robert P., jt. auth. see Travis, Patricia Y.
Travis, Roy. Duo Concertante for Violin & Piano. (U.C. Publ. in Contemporary Music: Vol. 4). 1970. pap. 11.00x (ISBN 0-520-09055-1). U of Cal Pr.
Travis, Stephen, jt. auth. see Hughes, Gerald.
Travis, Stephen H. Christian Hope & the Future. Marshall, I. Howard, ed. LC 80-7471. (Issues in Contemporary Theology Ser.). 160p. (Orig.). 1980. pap. 4.95 (ISBN 0-87784-463-1). Inter-Varsity.

Travitsky, Betty, compiled by. The Paradise of Women: Writings by Englishwomen of the Renaissance. LC 80-1705. (Contributions in Women's Studies: No. 22). 312p. 1981. lib. bdg. 29.95 (ISBN 0-313-22177-4, TPW/). Greenwood.

Travitsky, Betty, ed. The Paradise of Women: Writings by Englishwomen of the Rennaissance. LC 80-1705. (Contributions in Women's Studies: No. 22). 312p. 1981. lib. bdg. 29.95 (ISBN 0-313-22177-4, TPW/). Greenwood.

Traweek, Eleanor. Of Such As These: A History of Motley Country. 15.00 o.p. (ISBN 0-685-48803-9). Nortex Pr.

Trawick, Buckner B. Bible As Literature: Old Testament & the Apocrypha. 2nd ed. 1970. pap. 4.50 (ISBN 0-06-460056-4, CO 56, COS). Har-Row.

--Bible As Literature: The New Testament. 2nd ed. (Orig.). 1968. pap. 2.95 (ISBN 0-06-460057-2, CO 57, COS). Har-Row.

Trawicki, D. J., jt. auth. see Beyer, R.

Trawicki, Donald J., jt. auth. see Beyer, Robert.

Traylor, Idris R., Jr., jt. ed. see King, Mary E.

Traynis, V. V. Parameters & Flow Regimes for Hydraulic Transport of Coal by Pipelines. Cooley, W. C. & Faddick, R. R., eds. Peabody, Albert, tr. from Rus. LC 77-77840. (Illus., Eng.). 1977. 45.00x o.p. (ISBN 0-918990-01-7). Terraspace.

Traynor, Mark. Mark Traynor's Guide to Professional Make-up Techniques. 5.71 (ISBN 0-685-92164-6, 1579-00). Keystone Pubns.

Traynor, Mark & Seide, Diane. Mark Traynor's Beauty Book. LC 79-7881. (Illus.). 256p. 1980. 11.95 (ISBN 0-385-14775-9). Doubleday.

Treacher, Andrew, jt. auth. see Baruch, Geoffrey.

Treacy, William & Levine, Raphael. Wild Branch on the Olive Tree. LC 74-24492. (Illus.). 200p. 1975. 6.95 o.p. (ISBN 0-8323-0240-6). Binford.

Treadgold, Donald W. A History of Christianity. LC 78-78118. 277p. (Orig.). 1979. 22.50 (ISBN 0-913124-35-4); pap. 7.95 (ISBN 0-913124-35-4). Nordland Pub.

Treadgold, W. T. The Nature of the Bibliotheca of Photius. (Dumbarton Oaks Studies: Vol. 18). 1980. write for info. (ISBN 0-88402-090-8, Ctr Byzantine). Dumbarton Oaks.

Treadgold, Warren T. The Nature of the Bibliotheca of Photius. (Dumbarton Oaks Studis: Vol. 18). (Illus.). 201p. 1980. write for info. (ISBN 0-88402-090-8, Ctr Byzantine). Dumbarton Oaks.

Treadway, F. H., Jr. Impact of Electric Power Transmission Line Easements on Real Estate Values. 1972. 7.00 (ISBN 0-911780-29-7). Am Inst Real Estate Appraisers.

Treadwell, Edward F. The Cattle King. (Illus.). xii, 375p. 1981. pap. 6.95 (ISBN 0-934136-10-6). Western Tanager.

Treadwell, Harry, ed. see Walsh, James P.

Treadwell, William C., Jr., jt. auth. see McSwain, Larry L.

Treager, Irwin. Aircraft Gas Turbine Engine Technology. 2nd ed. (Illus.). 1978. pap. text ed. 22.75 (ISBN 0-07-065158-2, G). McGraw.

Trease, Geoffrey. Concise History of London. LC 75-14077. (Encore Edition). (Illus.). 1975. 5.95 o.p. (ISBN 0-684-15466-8, ScribT). Scribner.

--Escape to King Alfred. LC 58-9224. (gr. 6 up). 1958. 6.95 (ISBN 0-8149-0428-9). Vanguard.

--Follow My Black Plume. LC 63-13784. (gr. 6-10). 6.95 (ISBN 0-8149-0426-2). Vanguard.

--Italian Story. LC 64-16262. (Illus.). 1964. 8.95 (ISBN 0-8149-0221-9). Vanguard.

--Popinjay Stairs: An Historical Adventure About Samuel Pepys. LC 74-30873. (gr. 3-6). Date not set. 5.95 (ISBN 0-8149-0758-X). Vanguard. Postponed.

--Red Towers of Granada. LC 67-18646. (Illus.). (gr. 6-10). 6.95 (ISBN 0-8149-0424-6). Vanguard.

--Seven Kings of England. LC 55-7892. (gr. 6 up). 1955. 7.95 (ISBN 0-8149-0431-9). Vanguard.

--Seven Queens of England. LC 53-6900. (gr. 6 up). 5.95 (ISBN 0-8149-0430-0). Vanguard.

--Seven Sovereign Queens. LC 71-89662. (Illus.). (gr. 7 up). 1969. 7.95 (ISBN 0-8149-0660-5). Vanguard.

--Seven Stages. LC 65-26138. (Illus.). (gr. 7-9). 1965. 7.95 (ISBN 0-8149-0425-4). Vanguard.

--Silken Secret. LC 54-11525. (gr. 6 up). 1954. 6.95 (ISBN 0-8149-0432-7). Vanguard.

--Victory at Valmy. LC 60-15072. (gr. 7-11). 1960. 7.95 (ISBN 0-8149-0427-0). Vanguard.

--Web of Traitors. LC 52-11124. (gr. 6 up). 6.95 (ISBN 0-8149-0433-5). Vanguard.

--A Whiff of Burnt Boats. (Autobiography). 1971. 7.95 o.p. (ISBN 0-312-86730-1). St Martin.

--White Nights of St. Petersburg. LC 67-29447. (gr. 7 up). 1968. 6.95 (ISBN 0-8149-0423-8). Vanguard.

Treat, jt. auth. see King.

Treat, Asher E. Mites of Moths & Butterflies. LC 75-7147. (Illus.). 368p. 1975. 45.00x (ISBN 0-8014-0878-4). Comstock.

Treat, Roger. The Encyclopedia of Football. 14th ed. Palmer, Pete, ed. LC 75-38433. (Illus.). 1976. 14.95 o.p. (ISBN 0-498-01906-3). A S Barnes.

Trebach, Arnold S., ed. Drugs, Crime, & Politics. LC 78-5735. (Praeger Special Studies). 1978. 23.95 (ISBN 0-03-042286-8). Praeger.

Trebbi, Diana, jt. auth. see Shaughnessy, Edward J.

Treble, Henry A. Classical & Biblical Reference Book. (YA) (gr. 9 up). 1959. 6.00 (ISBN 0-7195-1426-6). Transatlantic.

Treble, J. H. Urban Poverty in Britain, Eighteen Thirty to Nineteen Sixty. 1979. 45.00 (ISBN 0-7134-1906-7, Pub. by Batsford England). David & Charles.

Trebst, A., jt. ed. see Bothe, H.

Tredd, William E. Dice Games New & Old. (Oleander Games & Pastimes Ser.: Vol. 3). (Illus.). 64p. 1981. 9.95 (ISBN 0-906672-00-7); pap. 4.75 (ISBN 0-906672-01-5). Oleander Pr.

Treddenick, J. M., jt. auth. see Boadway, R. W.

Tredennick, Hugh, ed. The Ethics of Aristotle: The Nicomachean Ethics. rev ed. Thomson, J. A., tr. 1977. pap. 3.95 (ISBN 0-14-044055-0). Penguin.

Tredennick, Hugh, tr. see Plato.

Tree Communications. The Cold Weather Catalog: Learning to Love Winter. 1977. pap. 7.95 o.p. (ISBN 0-385-13494-0, Dolp). Doubleday.

--Marathons. (Illus.). 1979. pap. 7.95 o.p. (ISBN 0-385-15227-2, Dolp). Doubleday.

Tree, Ronald. A History of Barbados. 2nd ed. 1979. 14.95x (ISBN 0-8464-0105-3). Beekman Pubs.

Treece, Eleanor W. & Treece, James W., Jr. Elements of Research in Nursing. 2nd ed. LC 76-7521. (Illus.). 1977. pap. text ed. 12.95 (ISBN 0-8016-5104-2). Mosby.

Treece, Henry. Further Adventures of Robinson Crusoe. LC 58-9623. (Illus.). (gr. 7-11). 1958. 9.95 (ISBN 0-87599-116-5). S G Phillips.

--Know About the Crusades. (Illus.). (gr. 6-9). 1967. 7.50 (ISBN 0-8023-1112-1). Dufour.

--Men of the Hills. LC 58-5448. (Illus.). (gr. 6-9). 1958. 9.95 (ISBN 0-87599-115-7). S G Phillips.

--Ride into Danger. LC 59-12203. (Illus.). (gr. 7-10). 1959. 9.95 (ISBN 0-87599-113-0). S G Phillips.

--Road to Miklagard. LC 57-12280. (Illus.). (gr. 6-10). 1957. 9.95 (ISBN 0-87599-118-1). S G Phillips.

--Viking's Dawn. LC 56-9962. (Illus.). (gr. 7-9). 1956. 9.95 (ISBN 0-87599-117-3). S G Phillips.

--Westward to Vinland. LC 67-22812. (gr. 7-9). 1967. 9.95 (ISBN 0-87599-136-X). S. G. Phillips.

Treece, James W., Jr., jt. auth. see Treece, Eleanor W.

Treece, Malra. Communication for Business & the Professions. 1978. text ed. 19.95 (ISBN 0-205-05956-2); instr's man. avail. (ISBN 0-205-05957-0). Allyn.

Treen, Alfred & Treen, Esmeralda. The Dalmatian: Coach Dog-Firehouse Dog. LC 80-10650. (Complete Breed Bk.). (Illus.). 288p. 1980. 14.95 (ISBN 0-87605-109-3). Howell Bk.

Treen, Esmeralda, jt. auth. see Treen, Alfred.

Treet, Brenda. Rising Star. 192p. 1981. pap. 1.50 (ISBN 0-671-57056-0). S&S.

Trefethen, James B. An American Crusade for Wildlife. (Illus.). 384p. 1975. 13.95 (ISBN 0-87691-207-2). Winchester Pr.

Trefil, James & Rood, Robert. Are We Alone? (Illus.). 224p. 1981. 10.95 (ISBN 0-684-16826-X, ScribT). Scribner.

Trefil, James S. Introduction to the Physics of Fluids & Solids. 320p. 1976. text ed. 28.00 (ISBN 0-08-018104-X). Pergamon.

--Physics As a Liberal Art. LC 77-6729. 1978. text ed. 16.95 (ISBN 0-08-019863-5). Pergamon.

Trefousse, Hans, ed. see McPherson, Edward.

Trefousse, Hans L., ed. Germany & America: Essays on Problems of International Relations & Immigration. 270p. 1981. 23.00x (ISBN 0-930888-06-5). Brooklyn Coll Pr.

Trefren, Doris. From Headhunters to Hallelujahs. 190p. (Orig.). 1980. pap. 3.75 (ISBN 0-89957-047-X). AMG Pubs.

Trefzger, John D. Reading the Bible with Understanding: A Guide for Beginners. 1978. pap. 1.95 (ISBN 0-8272-3209-8). Bethany Pr.

Tregarthen, Enys. The Doll Who Came Alive. rev. ed. Yates, Elizabeth, ed. LC 70-179780. (Illus.). 80p. (gr. 1-4). 1972. Repr. of 1942 ed. 6.95 (ISBN 0-381-99683-2, A19760, JD-J). John Day.

Tregarthen, Timothy D. Food, Fuel, & Shelter: A Watershed Analysis of Land-Use Trade-Offs in a Semi-Arid Region. LC 77-19355. (Westview Special Studies in Natural Resources & Energy Management Ser.). 1978. lib. bdg. 20.00x (ISBN 0-89158-070-0). Westview.

Tregaskis, Richard. Woman & the Sea. (Illus.). 6.50 (ISBN 0-910550-17-4). Elysium.

Tregear, Mary. Catalogue of Chinese Greenware in the Ashmolean Museum-Oxford. (Illus.). 1977. 79.00x (ISBN 0-19-813167-4). Oxford U Pr.

Tregear, P., jt. auth. see Burley, T.

Tregear, Thomas R. China: A Geographical Survey. 372p. 1980. 42.50x (ISBN 0-470-26925-1); pap. text ed. 19.95x (ISBN 0-470-26926-X). Halsted Pr.

Treger, Harvey. The Police-Social Work Team. (Illus.). 308p. 1975. pap. 21.75 (ISBN 0-398-03317-X). C C Thomas.

Tregle, J. G., Jr., ed. see Hutchins, Thomas.

Treglown, Jeremy, ed. see Wilmot, John.

Tregoe, Benjamin B. & Zimmerman, John W. Top Management Strategy. 1980. 9.95 (ISBN 0-671-25401-4). S&S.

Treharne, R. E., ed. see Muir, Ramsey.

Treherne, J. E. Neurochemistry of Arthropods. (Cambridge Monographs in Experimental Biology). 1966. 28.95 (ISBN 0-521-06645-X). Cambridge U Pr.

Treib, Marc & Herman, Ron. A Guide to the Gardens of Kyoto. (Illus.). 200p. 1979. 9.95 o.p. (ISBN 0-8048-1345-0). C E Tuttle.

--A Guide to the Gardens of Kyoto. 216p. 1980. pap. text ed. 9.95 (ISBN 0-89955-312-5, Pub. by Shufunotomo Japan). Intl Schol Bk Serv.

Treiman, Sam B. & Jackiw, Roman. Lectures on Current Algebra & Its Applications. LC 70-181519. (Princeton Series in Physics). 280p. 1972. 19.50x (ISBN 0-691-08118-2); pap. 6.95 o.p. (ISBN 0-691-08107-7). Princeton U Pr.

Treitschke, Heinrich Von see Von Treitschke, Heinrich.

Trejo, Arnulfo D., ed. Bibliografia Chicana: A Guide to Information Sources. LC 74-11562. (Ethnic Studies Information Guide: Vol. 1). 240p. 1975. 30.00 (ISBN 0-8103-1311-1). Gale.

Trejo, Cesar. Funciones De Variable Compleja. Orig. Title: Variable Compleja. (Span.). 1974. 8.30 (ISBN 0-06-319300-0, IntlDept). Har-Row.

Trejo, Ernesto, tr. see Sabines, Jaime.

Trelease, Frank J. Cases & Materials on Water Law. 3rd ed. LC 79-22224. (American Casebook Ser.). 833p. 1979. text ed. 20.95 (ISBN 0-8299-2063-3). West Pub.

Treloar, L. R. & Archenhold, W. F. Introduction to Polymer Science. (Wykeham Science Ser.: No. 9). 1970. pap. 9.95x (ISBN 0-8448-1347-8). Crane-Russak Co.

Treloar, L. R. G. The Physics of Rubber Elasticity. 3rd ed. (Monographs on the Physics & Chemistry of Materials). (Illus.). 322p. 1975. 55.00x (ISBN 0-19-851355-0). Oxford U Pr.

Tremain, Ruthven. My Friends: A Self-Portrait Autograph Book. (Illus.). (gr. 4 up). 1971. 2.50 o.s.i. (ISBN 0-02-789590-4). Macmillan.

--Nineteen Seventy Five Calendar for Children. (Illus.). 14p. (gr. 1-6). 1974. pap. 2.50 o.s.i. (ISBN 0-02-789450-9). Macmillan.

--Summer Diary. (Illus.). (gr. 5 up). 1970. pap. 1.95 o.s.i. (ISBN 0-02-789410-X). Macmillan.

Tremaine, Jennie. Tilly. (Candlelight Romance Ser.). (Orig.). 1981. pap. 1.50 (ISBN 0-440-18637-4). Dell.

Tremayne, Nick, jt. auth. see Redford, Ken.

Tremayne, Peter. The Revenge of Dracula. 1981. pap. 2.50 (ISBN 0-440-17374-4). Dell.

Tremayne, Sydney. Tatlings. LC 79-56432. (Illus.). 64p. 1980. 8.95 (ISBN 0-7153-7908-9). David & Charles.

Tremblay, Jean P. & Bunt, Richard B. Structured Pascal. 448p. 1980. pap. text ed. 10.95 (ISBN 0-07-065159-0, C). McGraw.

--Structured PL-One (PL-C) Programming. 1979. pap. text ed. 11.95x (ISBN 0-07-065173-6). McGraw.

Tremblay, Jean-Paul & Bunt, Richard B. An Introduction to Computer Science: An Algorithmic Approach, Short Edition. Stewart, Charles E., ed. (Illus.). 432p. 1980. text ed. 16.95 (ISBN 0-07-065167-1, C). McGraw.

Trembly, Diane L. Petticoat Medic in Vietnam: Adventures of a Woman Doctor. 6.95 (ISBN 0-533-01937-0). Vantage.

Tremillon, B., jt. auth. see Charlot, G.

Treml, Vladimir G., ed. Studies in Soviet Input-Output Analysis. LC 77-2739. (Praeger Special Studies). 1977. text ed. 44.50 (ISBN 0-275-56550-5). Praeger.

Tremolieres, J., ed. Alcohols & Derivatives, 2 vols. 1970. Set. 82.00 (ISBN 0-08-006937-1). Pergamon.

Trench, R. C. Notes on the Parables of Our Lord. (Twin Brooks Ser). pap. 4.95 (ISBN 0-8010-8774-0). Baker Bk.

Trench, Richard C. Commentary on the Epistle to the Seven Churches. 1978. 8.50 (ISBN 0-686-12951-2). Klock & Klock.

Trench, William F. & Kolman, Bernard. Answers to Selected Problems in Multi-Variable Calculus with Linear Algebra & Series. 1972. 3.00 (ISBN 0-12-699056-5). Acad Pr.

--Multivariable Calculus with Linear Algebra & Series. 758p. 1972. text ed. 22.95 (ISBN 0-12-699050-6). Acad Pr.

Trend, M. G. Housing Allowances for the Poor: A Social Experiment. LC 78-52057. (A Westview Replica Edition Ser.). 1978. lib. bdg. 28.50 o.p. (ISBN 0-89158-057-3). Westview.

Trendall, A. D. & Cambitoglou, A. The Red-Figured Vases of Apulia, Vol. I. (Monographs on Classical Archaeology). (Illus.). 1978. 79.00 (ISBN 0-19-813218-2). Oxford U Pr.

Trengove, John. Mr. September. 192p. 1980. 10.95 (ISBN 0-8253-0018-5). Beaufort Bks NY.

Trenholm, Virginia C. Arapahoes, Our People. LC 76-108799. (Civilization of the American Indian Ser.: Vol. 105). (Illus.). 1970. 16.95 (ISBN 0-8061-0908-4). U of Okla Pr.

Trenholm, Virginia C. & Carley, Maurine. Shoshonis: Sentinels of the Rockies. (Civilization of the American Indian Ser: No. 74). (Illus.). 1964. pap. 8.95 (ISBN 0-8061-1055-4). U of Okla Pr.

Trenkle, Clare. You. 1966. text ed. 5.95x (ISBN 0-88323-086-0, 182); wkbk. 2.25x (ISBN 0-88323-087-9, 183). Richards Pub.

Trenn, T. J., ed. Radioactivity & Atomic Theory. LC 74-19168. 517p. 1975. 49.95 (ISBN 0-470-88520-3). Halsted Pr.

Trent, Darrel, jt. auth. see Kupperman, Robert.

Trent, E. M. Metal Cutting. 1977. 34.95 (ISBN 0-408-10603-4). Butterworths.

Trent, May W. Oriental Barbecues: Recipes & Menus from Six Asian Countries. (Illus.). 96p. 1974. pap. 2.95 o.s.i. (ISBN 0-02-010380-8, Collier). Macmillan.

Trentin, J. J. Cross-Reacting Antigens & Neoantigens. 138p. 1967. 10.25 o.p. (ISBN 0-685-54441-9). Krieger.

Trento, Salvatore M. The Search for Lost America: The Mysteries of the Stone Ruins. LC 77-91180. 1978. 10.95 o.p. (ISBN 0-8092-7852-9). Contemp Bks.

Trenton, Patricia. Picturesque Images from Taos & Santa Fe. (Illus.). 1974. pap. 12.95 (ISBN 0-914738-20-8). Denver Art Mus.

Trenton, Rudolph W. Basic Economics. 4th ed. 1978. pap. text ed. 14.95 (ISBN 0-13-059139-4). P-H.

Trepp, Leo. The Complete Book of Jewish Observance. LC 79-1352. (Behrman House Book). (Illus.). 370p. 1980. 14.95 (ISBN 0-671-41797-5). Summit Bks.

--The Complete Book of Jewish Observance. LC 79-1352. (Illus.). 1979. 14.95 (ISBN 0-87441-281-1). Behrman.

Trescott, Martha M. The Rise of the American Electrochemicals Industry, 1880-1910: Studies in the American Technological Environment. LC 80-23469. (Contributions in Economics & Economic History Ser.: No. 38). (Illus.). 424p. 1981. lib. bdg. 45.00 (ISBN 0-313-20766-6, TRI/). Greenwood.

Trescott, Martha M., ed. Dynamos & Virgins Revisited: Women & Technological Change in History: an Anthology. LC 79-21404. 235p. 1979. 15.00 (ISBN 0-8108-1263-0). Scarecrow.

Tresemer, David. The Scythe Book: Mowing Hay, Cutting Weeds, & Harvesting Small Grains with Hand Tools. LC 80-70277. (Illus.). 112p. (Orig.). 1981. pap. 5.95 (ISBN 0-938670-00-X). By Hand & Foot.

Tress, Arthur & Minahan, John. The Dream Collector. LC 72-88362. (Illus.). 1973. pap. 4.95 o.p. (ISBN 0-380-01149-2, 17392). Avon.

Tressel, George W., et al. The Future of Educational Telecommunications. LC 74-27645. 1975. 15.95x (ISBN 0-669-97691-1). Lexington Bks.

Tresselt, Alvin. The Dead Tree. LC 72-174601. (gr. k-4). 1972. PLB 5.41 o.s.i. (ISBN 0-8193-0564-2, Four Winds). Schol Bk Serv.

--Thousand Lights & Fireflies. LC 65-11652. (Illus.). (gr. k-3). 1965. 5.95 o.s.i. (ISBN 0-8193-0123-X, Four Winds); PLB 5.41 o.s.i. (ISBN 0-8193-0124-8). Schol Bk Serv.

Tresselt, Alvin, ed. Humpty Dumpty's Bedtime Stories. LC 79-136997. (Illus.). (gr. k-3). 1971. 5.95 o.s.i. (ISBN 0-8193-0502-2, Four Winds); PLB 5.41 o.s.i. (ISBN 0-8193-0503-0). Schol Bk Serv.

--Humpty Dumpty's Holiday Stories. LC 72-8116. (Illus.). 72p. (gr. k-3). 1973. 5.95 o.s.i. (ISBN 0-8193-0644-4, Four Winds); PLB 5.41 o.s.i. (ISBN 0-8193-0645-2). Schol Bk Serv.

Tresselt, Alvin, tr. see Baba, Noburo.

Tresselt, Alvin, tr. see Guggenmos, Josef.

Tresselt, Alvin, tr. see Hamada, Hirosuke.

Tresselt, Alvin, tr. see Kimishima, Hisako.

Tresselt, Alvin, tr. see Kishi, Nami.

Tresselt, Alvin, tr. see Matsutani, Miyoko.

Tresselt, Alvin, tr. see Niklewiczowa, Maria.

Tresselt, Alvin, tr. see Yamanushi, Toshiko.

Tresselt, Alvin R. Rain Drop Splash. (Illus.). (gr. k-3). 1946. PLB 8.16 (ISBN 0-688-51165-1). Lothrop.

Tressler, Donald K. & Joslyn, M. A. Fruit & Vegetable Juice Processing Technology. 2nd ed. (Illus.). 1971. 36.00 o.p. (ISBN 0-87055-098-5). AVI.

Tressler, Donald K. & Sultan, William J. Food Products Formulary, Vol. 2: Cereals, Baked Goods, Dairy & Egg Products. (Illus.). 1975. lib. bdg. 49.50 (ISBN 0-87055-170-1). AVI.

Tressler, Donald K. & Woodroof, Jasper G. Food Products Formulary, Vol. 3: Fruit, Vegetables & Nut Products. (Illus.). 1976. lib. bdg. 49.50 (ISBN 0-87055-202-3). AVI.

Tressler, Donald K., jt. auth. see Desrosier, Norman W.

Tressler, Donald K., jt. auth. see Nelson, Philip E.

Tressler, Donald K., et al. Freezing Preservation of Foods, 4 vols. 4th ed. Incl. Vol. 1. Principles of Refrigeration; Equipment for Freezing & Transporting Food. 32.00 (ISBN 0-87055-044-6); Vol. 2. Factors Affecting Quality in Frozen Foods. 35.00 (ISBN 0-87055-045-4); Vol. 3. Commercial Freezing Operations; Fresh Foods. 39.00 (ISBN 0-87055-046-2); Vol. 4. Freezing of Precooked & Prepared Foods. 39.00 (ISBN 0-87055-047-0). (Illus.). 1968. AVI.

Trester, Kenneth R. The Complete Option Player. (Illus.). 316p. 1977. 20.00 (ISBN 0-9604914-0-6). Investrek.

--The Option Players Advanced Guidebook: Turning the Tables on the Options Markets. LC 80-83175. (Illus.). 275p. 1980. 35.00 (ISBN 0-9604914-1-4). Investrek.

Tretkoff, M. see Siegel, C. L.

Tretten, Rudie, jt. auth. see Long, Cathryn.

Tretter, tr. see Bohler, Lorenz & Bohler, Jorg.

Tretter, Steven A. Introduction to Discrete-Time Signal Processing. LC 76-25943. 1976. text ed. 32.95 (ISBN 0-471-88760-9). Wiley.

Tret'yakov, A. K. & Filonidov, A. M. Ultrasound in the Production & Inspection of Concrete: Pt. 2, Inspection of Hydraulic Construction. 1965. 29.50 (ISBN 0-306-17036-1, Consultants). Plenum Pub.

Treusch, M., jt. auth. see Gaby, D.

Trevallion, B. A. Metropolitan Kano, 2 vols. 1967. Set. 75.00 (ISBN 0-08-012635-9). Pergamon.

Trevan, Michael D. Immobilized Enzymes: An Introduction & Applications in Biotechnology. LC 80-40502. 1980. write for info. (ISBN 0-471-27826-2, Pub. by Wiley-Interscience); pap. write for info. (ISBN 0-471-27825-4). Wiley.

Trevanian. The Eiger Sanction. 1973. pap. 2.25 (ISBN 0-380-00176-4, 42671). Avon.

--Shibumi. 448p. 1980. Repr. of 1979 ed. pap. 2.95 (ISBN 0-345-28585-9). Ballantine.

Trevelyan, G. M. Illustrated History of England. (Illus.). 824p. 1974. text ed. 31.00x (ISBN 0-582-48471-5). Longman.

Trevelyan, George M. English Revolution, Sixteen Eighty-Eight to Sixteen Eighty-Nine. (YA) (gr. 9 up). 1965. pap. 4.95 (ISBN 0-19-500263-6, GB). Oxford U Pr.

--Mahin & the Venetian Revolution of 1848. LC 75-80597. xvi, 284p. 1974. Repr. of 1923 ed. 16.00 (ISBN 0-86527-122-4). Fertig.

Trevelyan, George O. The Life & Letters of Lord Macaulay. 1978. pap. 14.95 (ISBN 0-19-822487-7). Oxford U Pr.

Trevelyan, Humphrey. Public & Private. 208p. 1980. 27.00 (ISBN 0-241-10357-6, Pub. by Hamish Hamilton England). David & Charles.

Trevelyan, Raleigh. The Shadow of Vesuvius-Pompeii A. D. Seventy-Nine. (Illus.). 1976. 9.95 o.p. (ISBN 0-7181-1557-0, Pub. by Michael Joseph). Merrimack Bk Serv.

Trevena, D. H. & Cooke, R. J. The Liquid Phase. LC 75-19034. (Wykeham Science Ser.: No. 37). 1975. 9.95x (ISBN 0-8448-1164-5). Crane-Russak Co.

Trevena, D. H., jt. auth. see Temperley, H. N.

Treverton, Gregory, ed. Energy & Security. LC 80-67838. (Adelphi Library: Vol. 1). 172p. 1980. text ed. 29.50 (ISBN 0-916672-71-9). Allanheld.

Treverton, Gregory F. The Dollar Drain & American Forces in Germany: Managing the Political Economics of Alliance. LC 76-51689. xvi, 226p. 1978. 14.00x (ISBN 0-8214-0368-0). Ohio U Pr.

Treves, J. F. Introduction to Pseudodifferential & Fourier Integral Operators. Incl. Vol. 1. Pseudodifferential Operators. 300p (ISBN 0-306-40403-6); Vol. 2. Fourier Integral Operators. 340p (ISBN 0-306-40404-4). (The Univeristy Ser. in Mathematics). 1980. 29.95 ea. (Plenum Pr). Plenum Pub.

Treves, Ralph. How to Make Your Own Recreation & Hobby Rooms. rev. ed. LC 68-31229. (Popular Science Skill Books Ser.). (Illus.). 164p. 1976. pap. 3.95 o.s.i. (ISBN 0-06-014364-9, TD-268, HarpT). Har-Row.

Treves, Ralph, jt. auth. see Habeeb, Virginia.

Trevethan, Thomas. Our Joyful Confidence: The Lordship of Jesus in Colossians. 220p. (Orig.). 1981. pap. 5.95 (ISBN 0-87784-749-5). Inter Varsity.

Trevifio, Alejandro, tr. see Harvey, H.

Trevino, Alejandro. El Predicador: Platicas a Mis Estudiantes. 155p. 1980. pap. 2.30 (ISBN 0-311-42016-8). Casa Bautista.

Trevino, E. B. My Heart Lies South: The Story of My Mexican Marriage. 2nd ed. LC 53-8429. (Illus.). 1972. 6.95 o.s.i. (ISBN 0-690-56905-X, TYC-T). T Y Crowell.

Trevino, Elizabeth B. De. Casilda of the Rising Moon. LC 67-10389. 224p. (gr. 7 up). 1967. 3.95 (ISBN 0-374-31188-9). FS&G.

--I, Juan De Pareja. LC 65-19330. 192p. (gr. 7 up). 1965. 8.95 (ISBN 0-374-33531-1). FS&G.

Trevino, Lee & Aultman, Dick. Groove Your Golf Swing My Way. LC 75-41853. 1976. 12.95 o.p. (ISBN 0-689-10723-4). Atheneum.

Trevino, S. N. Spoken Spanish. LC 75-15933. (Spoken Language Ser.). (Prog. Bk.). 1975. Book, Units 1-12. pap. 9.00x (ISBN 0-87950-220-7); records 40.00x (ISBN 0-87950-223-1); records 6 12-inch LPs 40.00x (ISBN 0-87950-224-X); cassettes 60.00x (ISBN 0-87950-225-8); cassettes with course-bk. 65.00x (ISBN 0-87950-226-6). Spoken Lang Serv.

Trevithick, J. A. & Mulvey, C. The Economics of Inflation. LC 75-256. 184p. 1975. 24.95 (ISBN 0-470-88775-3); pap. 12.95x (ISBN 0-470-26894-8). Halsted Pr.

Trevor, Elleston. The Theta Syndrome. LC 76-55904. 1977. 7.95 o.p. (ISBN 0-385-07463-8). Doubleday.

Trevor, Hugh. Multi-Channel Japan. 1980. pap. 1.00 (ISBN 0-85363-075-5). OMF Bks.

Trevor, Meriol. The Civil Prisoners. 1977. 7.95 o.p. (ISBN 0-525-08175-5). Dutton.

Trevor-Roper, Hugh R. European Witch Craze in the Sixteenth & Seventeenth Centuries & Other Essays. 1969. pap. 3.95x (ISBN 0-06-131416-1, TB1416, Torch). Har-Row.

Trew, Anthony. Kleber's Convoy. 224p. 1975. pap. 1.50 o.p. (ISBN 0-445-03070-4). Popular Lib.

--Sea Fever. 229p. 1981. 10.95 (ISBN 0-312-70813-0). St Martin.

Trew, Antony. Ultimatum. LC 76-5379. 1976. 8.95 o.p. (ISBN 0-312-82845-4). St Martin.

Trewatha, Robert L. & Newport, M. Gene. Management: Functions & Behavior. rev. ed. 1979. text ed. 17.50x (ISBN 0-256-02214-3). Business Pubns.

Trewin, Ion. Journalism. (Profession Ser.). 144p. 1976. 13.50 (ISBN 0-7153-6891-5). David & Charles.

Trewin, J. C. The House of Special Purpose: An Intimate Portrait of the Last Days of the Russian Imperial Family. LC 74-30457. 148p. 1981. pap. 8.95 (ISBN 0-8128-6119-1). Stein & Day.

Trewin, J. C., ed. Plays of the Year, Vol. 46. 1978. 15.95 (ISBN 0-8044-2924-3). Ungar.

--Plays of the Year, Vol. 47. 1979. 15.95 (ISBN 0-8044-2925-1). Ungar.

--Plays of the Year, Vol. 48. 1980. 15.95 (ISBN 0-8044-2926-X). Ungar.

Trewin, John C. Going to Shakespeare. 1978. text ed. 22.95x (ISBN 0-04-792010-6). Allen Unwin.

--Portrait of the Shakespeare Country. LC 75-503070. (Portrait Bks.). (Illus.). 1970. 10.50x (ISBN 0-7091-1342-0). Intl Pubns Serv.

Trewin, John C., ed. Plays of the Year Series: Selections from the London Theatre Season, 2 vols. a year, starting with vol. 42, 1972. 10.50 ea. (ISBN 0-686-66561-9). Ungar.

Trexler, Richard C. Public Life in Renaissance Florence. LC 80-979. (Studies in Discontinuity). 1980. 45.00 (ISBN 0-12-699550-8). Acad Pr.

Treybal, Robert E. Mass Transfer Operations. 2nd ed. (Chemical Engineering Ser.). 1968. text ed. 26.50 (ISBN 0-07-065176-0, C); solutions manual 9.95 (ISBN 0-07-065177-9). McGraw.

--Mass Transfer Operations. (Chemical Engineering Ser.). (Illus.). 1979. text ed. 29.00x (ISBN 0-07-065176-0, C). McGraw.

Trezel, Roger, jt. auth. see Reese, Terence.

Trezise, Philip H. The Atlantic Connection. 200p. 1975. pap. 3.95 (ISBN 0-8157-8527-5). Brookings.

--Rebuilding Grain Reserves: Toward an International System. 1976. pap. 3.95 (ISBN 0-8157-8529-1). Brookings.

Trezise, Philip H., ed. The European Monetary System: Its Promise & Prospects. LC 79-55581. 96p. 1979. pap. 4.50 (ISBN 0-8157-8531-3). Brookings.

Triandis & Draguns. Handbook of Cross-Cultural Psychology: Psychopathology, Vol. 6. 410p. 1981. text ed. 25.95 (ISBN 0-205-06502-3, 796502-8). Allyn.

Triandis, Harry C. Attitude & Attitude Change. LC 76-140555. (Foundations of Social Psychology Ser). (Illus.). 1971. pap. text ed. 9.50 (ISBN 0-471-88831-1). Wiley.

Triandis, Harry C. & Lambert, William W. Handbook of Cross-Cultural Psychology: Perspectives, 6 vols. 1979. Vols. I & II. text ed. 25.95x ea. Vol. I (ISBN 0-205-06497-3). Vol. II (ISBN 0-205-06498-1). Vols. III-VI. text ed. write for info. Vol. III (ISBN 0-205-06499-X). Vol. IV (ISBN 0-205-06500-7). Vol. V (ISBN 0-205-06501-5). Vol. VI (ISBN 0-205-06502-3). Allyn.

Triandis, Harry C., ed. Analysis of Subjective Culture. LC 74-178910. (Comparative Studies in Behavioral Science Ser). 1972. 34.50 (ISBN 0-471-88905-9, Pub. by Wiley-Interscience). Wiley.

Trias Monge, Jose. Historia Constitucional De Puerto Rico, Vol. I. LC 79-15893. vi, 748p. (Sp.). 1980. 20.00 (ISBN 0-8477-0861-6). U of PR Pr.

Tribble, Edwin, ed. A President in Love: The Courtship Letters of Woodrow Wilson & Edith Bolling Galt. (Illus.). 1981. 12.95 (ISBN 0-395-29482-7). HM.

Tribe, Ian, ed. see Tosco, Uberto.

Tribe, Keith. Land, Labour & Economic Discourse. 1978. 22.50 (ISBN 0-7100-0002-2); pap. 10.00 (ISBN 0-7100-0003-0). Routledge & Kegan.

Tribe, M. A. & Eraut, M. R. Hormones Book. LC 77-87396. (Basic Biology Course Ser.: No. 11). 1979. 35.50 (ISBN 0-521-21371-1); pap. 11.95x (ISBN 0-521-21370-3); film strip 19.95x (ISBN 0-521-22956-1). Cambridge U Pr.

--Nerves & Muscle, Bk. 10. LC 76-55511. (Basic Biology Course Ser.). (Illus.). 1977. 32.50 (ISBN 0-521-21369-X); pap. 11.95x (ISBN 0-521-21368-1). Cambridge U Pr.

Tribe, M. A. & Peacock, D. The Ecology Game. (Basic Biology Course Ser.). (Illus.). 1976. 44.50 (ISBN 0-521-21030-5). Cambridge U Pr.

Tribe, M. A., et al. Dynamic Aspects of Cells. LC 75-46198. (Basic Biology Course: Bk.3). (Illus.). 112p. 1976. 29.95 (ISBN 0-521-21175-1); pap. 9.75x (ISBN 0-521-21176-X). Cambridge U Pr.

--Enzymes. LC 75-14642. (Cambridge Biology Course Ser.: Bk. 7). (Illus.). 128p. 1975. 35.50 (ISBN 0-521-20870-X); limp bdg. 10.95x (ISBN 0-521-20960-9). Cambridge U Pr.

--Metabolism & Mitochondria. LC 75-25427. (Basic Biology Course Ser.: Bk. 8). (Illus.). 160p. 1976. 35.50 (ISBN 0-521-20952-8); pap. 11.95x (ISBN 0-521-20953-6). Cambridge U Pr.

--Photosynthesis, Bk. 6. LC 75-12162. (Basic Biology Course Ser). (Illus.). 88p. (Prog. Bk.). 1975. text ed. 23.95 (ISBN 0-521-20820-3); pap. text ed. 9.50x (ISBN 0-521-20821-1). Cambridge U Pr.

--Protein Synthesis. LC 76-2260. (Basic Biology Course Ser.: Bk. 9). (Illus.). 120p. 1976. 30.00 (ISBN 0-521-21092-5); pap. 10.95x (ISBN 0-521-21093-3). Cambridge U Pr.

--Ecological Principles, No. 4. LC 75-6285. (Basic Biology Course Ser). (Illus.). 160p. (Prog. Bk.). 1975. 35.95 (ISBN 0-521-20658-8); pap. 13.95x (ISBN 0-521-20638-3). Cambridge U Pr.

--Electron Microscopy & Cell Structure. LC 75-6284. (Basic Biology Course Ser.: No. 2). (Illus.). 120p. 1975. 24.95 (ISBN 0-521-20657-X); pap. 11.95x (ISBN 0-521-20557-3); film 15.95x (ISBN 0-521-20907-2); tape commentary for film 15.95x (ISBN 0-521-20965-X). Cambridge U Pr.

Tribe, Michael A., et al. Case Studies in Genetics. LC 77-75778. (Basic Biology Course Ser.: Bk. 12). (Illus.). 1977. 29.95 (ISBN 0-521-21373-8); pap. 11.95x (ISBN 0-521-21372-X). Cambridge U Pr.

Tribolet, J. Seismic Applications of Homomorphic Signal Processing. 1979. 29.00 (ISBN 0-13-779801-6). P-H.

Trice, Harrison M., jt. auth. see Beyer, Janice M.

Trice, Jim. Butter Molds, Identification & Value Guide. (Illus.). 1980. pap. 7.95 (ISBN 0-89145-131-5). Collector Bks.

Trick, Timothy N. An Introduction to Circuit Analysis. LC 77-10843. 1978. 26.95 (ISBN 0-471-88850-8); solutions manual 6.00 (ISBN 0-471-03041-4). Wiley.

Tricker, R. A. Contributions of Faraday & Maxwell to Electrical Science. 1966. 23.00 (ISBN 0-08-011977-8); pap. 11.25 (ISBN 0-08-011976-X). Pergamon.

--Early Electrodynamics. 1965. 15.00 (ISBN 0-08-010794-X); pap. 7.50 (ISBN 0-08-010793-1). Pergamon.

Tricker, R. A., jt. auth. see Vigoureux, P.

Tricker, R. I., ed. The Individual, the Enterprise & the State. LC 77-78350. 1977. 18.95 (ISBN 0-470-99211-5). Halsted Pr.

Trickett, Jill. The Prevention of Food Poisoning. 1980. 11.85x (ISBN 0-85950-084-5, Pub. by Thornes England). State Mutual Bk.

Trickey, David L. Self-Assessment of Current Knowledge in Anesthesiology. 2nd. ed. 1980. pap. 14.75 (ISBN 0-87488-245-1). Med Exam.

Tricomi, G, et al, eds. Xeroradiography of the Lung & Mediastinum. 223p. 1979. 122.00 (ISBN 0-686-63099-8, Excerpta Medica). Elsevier.

Triebel, Hans. Fourier Analysis. LC 77-555434. 1977. pap. 9.50x (ISBN 0-8002-0808-0). Intl Pubns Serv.

Triebel, Walter A. Integrated Digital Electronics. (Illus.). 1979. ref. 19.95 (ISBN 0-13-468900-3). P-H.

Trieger, Norman. Pain Control. (Illus.). 143p. 1974. 24.00. Quint Pub Co.

Trier, James R., jt. auth. see Beck, William C.

Trieschman, Albert E., jt. ed. see Whittaker, James K.

Trieschman, Albert E., et al. The Other Twenty Three Hours: Child Care Work with Emotionally Disturbed Children in a Therapeutic Milieu. (Modern Applications of Psychology Ser.). 1969. 12.95x o.p. (ISBN 0-202-26023-2). Beresford Bk Serv.

Trieste Symposium, 1968. Contemporary Physics, 2 Vols. (Illus., Orig.). 1969 (IAEA). Vol. 1. pap. 32.25 (ISBN 92-0-130069-7); Vol. 2. pap. 25.75 (ISBN 92-0-130169-3). Unipub.

Trifonov, Yury V. The Long Goodbye: A Trilogy. Burlingame, Helen & Proffer, Ellendea, trs. from Rus. LC 77-17658. (Ardis Bk.). 1978. 15.00 o.s.i. (ISBN 0-06-014371-1, HarpT). Har-Row.

Trigg, C. F., jt. auth. see Anderson, H. G.

Trigg, George L. Landmark Experiments in 20th Century Physics. LC 74-21664. 1975. 24.50x (ISBN 0-8448-0602-1); pap. 9.50x (ISBN 0-8448-0603-X). Crane-Russak Co.

Trigg, George L., ed. Crucial Experiments in Modern Physics. LC 75-21567. 1975. pap. 4.95x (ISBN 0-8448-0765-6). Crane-Russak Co.

Trigg, George L., jt. ed. see Lerner, Rita G.

Trigg, Harry D. & Trigg, Yolanda L. Compleat Motion Picture Quiz Book; or, Sixty Thousand Points About Motion Pictures. LC 74-27590. 384p. 1975. pap. 4.95 o.p. (ISBN 0-385-05185-9). Doubleday.

Trigg, R. Reason & Commitment. LC 72-89806. 192p. 1973. 23.95 (ISBN 0-521-20119-5); pap. 6.95x (ISBN 0-521-09784-3). Cambridge U Pr.

Trigg, Roger. Reality at Risk: A Defence of Realism in Philosophy & the Sciences. 216p. 1980. 26.50x (ISBN 0-389-20037-9). B&N.

Trigg, Yolanda L., jt. auth. see Trigg, Harry D.

Trigger, Bruce G. Gordon Childe: Revolutions in Archaeology. 224p. 1980. 22.50x (ISBN 0-231-05038-0). Columbia U Pr.

--Northeast, Vol. 15. LC 77-17162. (Handbook of North American Indians). (Illus.). 924p. 1979. text ed. 14.50 (ISBN 0-87474-195-5). Smithsonian.

--Time & Traditions. 1978. 15.00x (ISBN 0-231-04548-4). Columbia U Pr.

Triggs, Thomas & Pickett, Ronald. Human Factors in Health Care. LC 74-16935. 288p. 1975. 23.95 (ISBN 0-669-95885-9). Lexington Bks.

Trillin, Alice S., et al. Teaching Basic Skills in College: A Guide to Objectives, Skills Assessment, Course Content, Teaching Methods, Support Services, & Administration. LC 79-92469. (Higher Education Ser.). 1980. text ed. 15.95x (ISBN 0-87589-456-9). Jossey-Bass.

Trillin, Calvin. Floater. LC 80-17337. 1980. 9.95 (ISBN 0-89919-017-0). Ticknor & Fields.

Trilling, Diana, ed. see Trilling, Lionel.

Trilling, Lionel. The Liberal Imagination: Essays on Literature & Society. LC 76-13426. 320p. 1976. 10.00 o.p. (ISBN 0-684-14731-9, ScribT); pap. 3.95 o.p. (ISBN 0-684-14732-7, SL673, ScribT). Scribner.

--The Middle of the Journey. LC 76-626. 320p. 1976. 8.95 o.p. (ISBN 0-684-14619-3, ScribT). Scribner.

--Speaking of Literature & Society. Trilling, Diana, ed. LC 80-7944. 448p. 1980. 17.95 (ISBN 0-15-184710-X). HarBraceJ.

Trilling, Richard J. Party Image & Electoral Behavior. LC 76-24794. 1976. 20.95 (ISBN 0-471-88935-0, Pub. by Wiley-Interscience). Wiley.

Trim, J. L. Developing a Unit-Credit Scheme of Adult Language Learning. LC 80-40756. (Council of Europe Modern Languages Project). 96p. 1980. pap. 10.00 (ISBN 0-08-024596-X). Pergamon.

Trim, J. L., jt. ed. see Perren, G. E.

Trim, J. L., et al. Systems Development in Adult Language Learning. LC 79-42775. (Council of Europe Language Learning Series). (Illus.). 150p. 1980. pap. 9.50 (ISBN 0-08-024586-2). Pergamon.

Trim, Marj, jt. auth. see Childerhose, R. J.

Trimberger, George W. Dairy Cattle: Judging Techniques. 2nd ed. LC 76-2672. (Illus.). 1977. 18.95 (ISBN 0-13-197020-8). P-H.

Trimble, John R. Writing with Style: Conversations on the Art of Writing. (Illus.). 160p. 1975. pap. text ed. 6.50 (ISBN 0-13-970368-3). P-H.

Trimble, Michael R. Neuropsychiatry. 304p. 1981. 37.50 (ISBN 0-471-27827-0, Pub. by Wiley-Interscience). Wiley.

Trimby, Elisa. Mr. Plum's Oasis. LC 80-17662. (Illus.). 32p. (gr. 1-4). 1981. 7.95 (ISBN 0-688-41991-7); PLB 7.63 (ISBN 0-688-51991-1). Morrow.

Trimby, Robin. Your Book of Soccer. (Illus.). (gr. 7 up). 1968. 6.95 (ISBN 0-571-04752-1). Transatlantic.

Trimingham. Two Worlds Are Ours (Islamic Studies) 6.00 o.p. (ISBN 0-685-85424-8). Intl Bk Ctr.

Trimingham, J. Spencer. Christianity Among the Arabs in Pre-Islamic Times. (Arab Background Ser). (Illus.). 1979. text ed. 30.00x (ISBN 0-582-78081-0). Longman.

--Sufi Orders in Islam. 1971. 27.00x (ISBN 0-19-826524-7). Oxford U Pr.

--The Sufi Orders in Islam. 344p. 1973. pap. 4.95 (ISBN 0-19-501662-9, GB). Oxford U Pr.

Trimingham, John S. Islam in West Africa. 1959. 22.50x (ISBN 0-19-826511-5). Oxford U Pr.

Trimmer. Understanding & Servicing Alarms. 1981. text ed. price not set. Butterworth.

Trimmer, Eric. Basic Sexual Medicine. 1978. 24.00x (ISBN 0-433-32660-3). Intl Ideas.

Trimmer, Joseph & Hairston, Maxine. The Riverside Reader. LC 80-82759. 544p. 1981. pap. text ed. 7.95 (ISBN 0-395-28940-8); instr's manual 0.75. HM.

Trimmer, Joseph & Kettler, Robert. American Oblique: Writing About the American Experience. LC 75-31025. (Illus.). 416p. 1976. pap. text ed. 9.25 (ISBN 0-395-21917-5); inst. manual 1.45 (ISBN 0-395-21920-5). HM.

Trimmer, Sarah. Fabulous Histories, Designed for the Instruction of Children, Respecting Their Treatment of Animals, Repr. Of 1786 Ed. Bd. with The Dairyman's Daughter. Richmond, Legh. Repr. of 1810 ed. LC 75-32147. (Classics of Children's Literature, 1621-1932: Vol. 13). 1976. PLB 38.00 (ISBN 0-8240-2261-0). Garland Pub.

Trinci, A. P., jt. ed. see Burnett, J. H.

Trinder, Barrie, jt. auth. see Cossons, Neil.

Tringham, Ruth. Hunters, Fishers & Farmers of Eastern Europe, 6000-3000 B.C. 1971. text ed. 8.00x (ISBN 0-09-108790-2, Hutchinson U Lib). Humanities.

Trinkaus, J. P. Cells into Organs: The Forces That Shape the Embryo. 1969. pap. 11.95x ref. ed. (ISBN 0-13-121640-6). P-H.

Trinkle, J. Kent. Management of Thoracic Trauma Victims. (Illus.). 139p. 1980. pap. text ed. 11.75 (ISBN 0-397-50415-2). Lippincott.

Trinks, W. Industrial Furnaces, 2 vols. Incl. Vol. 1. Principals of Design & Operation. 5th ed. 1961 (ISBN 0-471-89034-0); Vol. 2. Fuels, Furnace Types & Furnace Equipment: Their Selection & Influence Upon Furnace Operation. 4th ed. 1967 (ISBN 0-471-89068-5). LC 61-11493. 39.95 ea. (Pub. by Wiley-Interscience). Wiley.

Triola, M. F. Elementary Statistics. 1980. 16.95 (ISBN 0-8053-9305-6); instrs manual 3.95 (ISBN 0-8053-9307-2). A-W.

Triola, Mario F. Elementary Statistics. 16.95 (ISBN 0-8053-9305-6); pap. text ed. 3.95 (ISBN 0-8053-9307-2). Benjamin-Cummings.

Trip, Maggie, ed. Woman in the Year Two Thousand. LC 74-80707. 1981. pap. 6.00 (ISBN 0-686-68893-7). Arbor Hse.

Tripartite report by fifteen experts from the European Community, Japan, & North America. Cooperative Approaches to World Energy Problems. 51p. 1974. pap. 2.00 (ISBN 0-8157-1555-2). Brookings.

--Economic Relations Between East & West: Prospects & Problems. 1978. pap. 2.00 (ISBN 0-8157-2091-2). Brookings.

Tripartite report by fourteen economists from Japan, Europe, & North America. Domestic Economic Policies in the Industrial Countries. 1978. pap. 2.00 (ISBN 0-8157-1893-4). Brookings.

Tripartite report by fourteen economists from Japan, the European Community & North America. World Trade & Domestic Adjustment. 19p. 1973. pap. 2.00 (ISBN 0-8157-9543-2). Brookings.

Tripartite report by fourteen experts from North America, the European Community, & Japan. Toward the Integration of World Agriculture. 29p. 1973. pap. 2.00 (ISBN 0-8157-8511-9). Brookings.

Tripartite report by Saxteen economists from the European Community, Japan & North America. Economic Prospects & Policies in the Industrial Countries. 1977. pap. 2.00 (ISBN 0-8157-2089-0). Brookings.

Tripathi, R. S. History of Ancient India. 1977. 11.50 (ISBN 0-89684-215-0); pap. 6.95 (ISBN 0-686-51747-4). Orient Bk Dist.

Tripathy, K. C. Lithic Industries in India: A Study of South Western Orissa. 190p. 1980. text ed. 12.50x (ISBN 0-391-02139-7). Humanities.

Triplett, Frank. The History of the Great American Crimes. (American Culture Library Bks.). (Illus.). 127p. 1981. 69.75 (ISBN 0-89901-031-8). Found Class Reprints.

--Life, Times & Treacherous Death of Jesse James. Snell, Joseph, ed. LC 70-75734. (Illus.). 344p. 1970. 16.95 (ISBN 0-8040-0187-1, SB); limited ed. 30.00 (ISBN 0-8040-0188-X). Swallow.

Tripodi, Tony. Uses & Abuses of Social Research in Social Work. 208p. 1974. 17.50x (ISBN 0-231-03662-0); pap. text ed. 6.00x (ISBN 0-231-03663-9). Columbia U Pr.

Tripodi, Tony, jt. auth. see Epstein, Irwin.

Tripodi, Tony, et al. Assessment of Social Research: Guidelines for the Use of Research in Social Work & Social Science. LC 69-20179. 1969. pap. text ed. 9.95 (ISBN 0-87581-033-0). Peacock Pubs.

--Differential Social Program Evaluation. LC 77-83401. 1978. pap. text ed. 6.50 (ISBN 0-87581-227-9). Peacock Pubs.

Tripodi, Tony, et al, eds. Social Workers at Work. 2nd ed. LC 76-41993. 1977. pap. text ed. 8.50 (ISBN 0-87581-216-3). Peacock Pubs.

Tripp, Edward. Crowell's Handbook of Classical Mythology. LC 74-127614. (Illus.). 1970. 17.50 o.s.i. (ISBN 0-690-22608-X, TYC-T). T Y Crowell.

Tripp, Eleanor B. To America. LC 69-11493. (Curriculum Related Bks). (Illus.). (gr. 8-11). 1969. 5.95 o.p. (ISBN 0-15-289040-8, HJ). HarBraceJ.

Tripp, Rhoda T., ed. International Thesaurus of Quotations. LC 73-106587. 1970. 11.95 (ISBN 0-690-44584-9, TYC-T); thumb-indexed 12.95 (ISBN 0-690-44585-7). T Y Crowell.

Tripp, Robert C., jt. ed. see Gortler, Leon B.

Tripp, Robert M., ed. see Computerist Inc.

Tripp, Robert M., ed. see Micro Ink, Inc.

Tripp, Robert M., et al, eds. see Computerist Inc.

Tripp, Wallace. A Great Big Ugly Man Came up & Tied His Horse to Me: A Book of Nonsense Verse. (Illus.). 48p. (gr. k-3). 1973. 6.95g (ISBN 0-316-85280-5); pap. 3.95 (ISBN 0-316-85281-3). Little.

Trippet, Frank. The First Horsemen. (Emergence of Man Ser.). (Illus.). 1974. 9.95 (ISBN 0-8094-1278-0); lib. bdg. avail. (ISBN 0-685-50286-4). Time-Life.

Trippett, Frank. The First Horsemen. (gr. 6 up). 1974. PLB 11.56 o.p. (ISBN 0-8094-1279-9, Pub. by Time-Life). Silver.

Triseliotis, John. In Search of Origins: The Experiences of Adopted People. 190p. 1973. 17.00x (ISBN 0-7100-7534-0). Routledge & Kegan.

Trishanku, K. M. Onion Peel. (Indian Novels Ser, Vol. 2). 175p. 1974. 7.50 (ISBN 0-88253-465-3). Ind-US Inc.

Triska, Jan F., jt. auth. see Slusser, Robert M.

Triska, Jan F., ed. Communist Party States: Comparative & International Studies. LC 69-15728. 1969. pap. 6.90 o.p. (ISBN 0-672-61254-2). Bobbs.

Triska, Jan G. & Cocks, Paul M., eds. Political Development in Eastern Europe. LC 76-19551. (Special Studies). 1977. text ed. 39.95 (ISBN 0-275-23600-5); pap. 8.95 (ISBN 0-275-89640-4). Praeger.

Tristan, Flora. Union Ouvrieve, Troisieme Edition. (Fr.). 1977. lib. bdg. 23.75x o.p. (ISBN 0-8287-0832-0); pap. 13.75x o.p. (ISBN 0-685-76998-4). Clearwater Pub.

Triston, H. U. Men in Cages. LC 70-174122. (Illus.). 1971. Repr. of 1938 ed. 20.00 (ISBN 0-8103-3801-7). Gale.

Trites, A. A. The New Testament Concept of Witness. LC 76-11067. (Society for New Testament Studies Monograph: No. 31). 1977. 48.00 (ISBN 0-521-21015-1). Cambridge U Pr.

Tri T. Ha. Solid-State Microwave Amplifier Design. 350p. 1981. 30.00 (ISBN 0-471-08971-0). Wiley.

Tritonio, Antonio M., jt. auth. see Conti, Natale.

Tritton, Arthur S. Islam: Belief & Practices. LC 79-2883. 200p. 1981. Repr. of 1954 ed. 18.00 (ISBN 0-8305-0051-0). Hyperion Conn.

--The Rise of the Imams of Sanaa. LC 79-2887. 144p. 1981. Repr. of 1925 ed. 15.00 (ISBN 0-8305-0053-7). Hyperion Conn.

Tritton, S. M. Amateur Wine Making. 4th ed. (Illus.). 1968. 7.95 o.p. (ISBN 0-571-04646-0, Pub. by Faber & Faber). Merrimack Bk Serv.

--Guide to Better Wine & Beer Making for Beginners. 157p. 1969. pap. 2.50 (ISBN 0-486-22528-3). Dover.

--Tritton's Guide to Better Wine & Beer Making for Beginners. (Illus., Orig.). 1969. pap. 4.50 (ISBN 0-571-09171-7, Pub. by Faber & Faber). Merrimack Bk Serv.

Trivedi, H. M. Indian Shipping in Perspective. 540p. 1981. 40.00x (ISBN 0-7069-1202-0, Pub. by Vikas India). Advent Bk.

Trivedi, P. S., jt. auth. see Pandey, S. N.

Trivedi, R. D. Compendious History of English Literature. 866p. 1976. 15.00x (ISBN 0-7069-0427-3). Intl Pubns Serv.

Trivelpiece, Laurel. During Water Peaches. LC 78-14393. 1979. 8.95 (ISBN 0-397-31831-6). Lippincott.

--In Love & in Trouble. (Orig.). 1981. pap. 1.95 (ISBN 0-671-41274-4). PB.

Trivers, James. Hamburger Heaven. (YA) 1979. pap. 1.75 (ISBN 0-380-48355-6, 48355). Avon.

Trivett, Daphne & Trivett, John. Time for Clocks. LC 78-4782. (Illus.). (gr. 2-5). 1979. PLB 7.89 (ISBN 0-690-03896-8, TYC-J). T Y Crowell.

Trivett, Daphne H. Shadow Geometry. LC 72-7561. (Young Math Ser.). (Illus.). (gr. 1-4). 1974. PLB 6.89 o.p. (ISBN 0-690-73057-8, TYC-J). T Y Crowell.

Trivett, John, jt. auth. see Trivett, Daphne.

Trivett, John V. Building Tables on Tables: A Book About Multiplication. LC 74-11263. (Young Math Ser.). (Illus.). 40p. (gr. k-3). 1975. 7.95 (ISBN 0-690-00593-8, TYC-J); PLB 7.89 (ISBN 0-690-00600-4). T Y Crowell.

Trivieri, Lawrence A. Fundamental Concepts of Elementary Mathematics. 1977. text ed. 19.50 scp o.p. (ISBN 0-06-046675-8, HarpC); ans. to selected even numbered exercises free o.p. (ISBN 0-06-366685-5). Har-Row.

Trivisone, Margaret, jt. auth. see Sentlowitz, Michael.

Trnka, Bohumil. Selected Papers in Structural Linguistics. (Janua Linguarum, Ser. Major: No. 88). 1980. text ed. 37.50x (ISBN 90-279-3148-8). Mouton.

Trobisch, Ingrid. The Joy of Being a Woman. LC 75-9324. (Jubilee Ser.). 144p. 1975. pap. 3.95 (ISBN 0-06-068453-4, RD 353, HarpR). Har-Row.

Trobisch, Ingrid & Roetzer, Elisabeth. An Experience of Love: Understanding Natural Family Planning. Date not set. 6.95 (ISBN 0-8007-1184-X). Revell. Postponed.

Trobisch, Walter. A Baby Just Now? 6th ed. LC 80-17213. 56p. 1980. pap. 2.25 (ISBN 0-87784-849-1). Inter-Varsity.

--I Loved a Girl. LC 75-12281. (Jubilee Bks.). 128p. 1975. pap. 3.95 (ISBN 0-06-068443-7, RD 352, HarpR). Har-Row.

--I Married You. LC 78-148437. (Jubilee Bks.). 144p. 1975. pap. 3.95 (ISBN 0-06-068452-6, RD 351, HarpR). Har-Row.

--Living with Unfulfilled Desires. LC 79-2718. (Orig.). 1979. pap. 3.50 (ISBN 0-87784-736-3). Inter-Varsity.

Trobisch, Walter, et al. His Essays on Love, Vol. 1. LC 68-57741. pap. 2.95 o.p. (ISBN 0-87784-669-3). Inter-Varsity.

Trobridge, George. Swedenborg: Life & Teaching. 1976. pap. 1.95 (ISBN 0-89129-058-3). Jove Pubns.

Trocchi, Alexander. Cain's Book. LC 79-56749. 256p. (Orig.). 1981. pap. 3.50 (ISBN 0-394-17403-8, B-432, BC). Grove.

--Man at Leisure. LC 74-195409. 1979. 9.95 (ISBN 0-7145-0357-6, Pub. by M Boyars); pap. 5.95 (ISBN 0-7145-0358-4). Merrimack Bk Serv.

Trocchi, Alexander, tr. see Douassot, Jean.

Trocchi, Alexander, et al. New Writers Three. 1980. pap. 6.00 (ISBN 0-7145-0401-7). Riverrun NY.

Trocchio, Julie. Home Care for the Elderly. LC 80-19713. 176p. 1980. pap. 8.95 (ISBN 0-8436-0770-X). CBI Pub.

Trocke, John K., jt. auth. see Downey, W. David.

Troebst, Cord Christian. The Art of Survival. LC 74-10030. 288p. 1975. pap. 3.50 o.p. (ISBN 0-385-01129-6, Dolp). Doubleday.

Troeh, Frederick R., et al. Soil & Water Conservation. Troeh, Miriam, ed. (Illus.). 1980. text ed. 25.95 (ISBN 0-13-822155-3). P-H.

Troeh, Miriam, ed. see Troeh, Frederick R., et al.

Troelstra, A. S. Choice Sequences: A Chapter of Intuitionistic Mathematics. (Oxford Logic Guides Ser.). 1977. 21.00x (ISBN 0-19-853163-X). Oxford U Pr.

Troen, Philip & Nankin, Howard, eds. The Testis in Normal & Infertile Men. LC 76-19852. 1977. 48.50 (ISBN 0-89004-129-6). Raven.

Troike, Rudolph D., jt. ed. see Abraham, Roger D.

Troise, Joe. Cherries & Lemons. 1980. pap. 1.95 (ISBN 0-446-90547-X). Warner Bks.

Trojan, Judith. American Family Life Films. LC 80-14748. 508p. 1981. 25.00 (ISBN 0-8108-1313-0). Scarecrow.

Trojan, Paul K., jt. auth. see Flinn, Richard.

Trojan, Paul K., jt. auth. see Flinn, Richard A.

Trojanowicz, John, jt. auth. see Trojanowicz, Robert C.

Trojanowicz, R. Environment of the First Line Supervisors. 1980. 13.95 (ISBN 0-13-282848-0). P-H.

Trojanowicz, Robert & Dixon, Samuel. Criminal Justice & the Community. (Illus.). 464p. 1974. ref. ed. 17.95x (ISBN 0-13-193557-7). P-H.

Trojanowicz, Robert C. & Trojanowicz, John. Police Supervision. (Illus.). 1980. text ed. 13.95 o.p. (ISBN 0-13-684043-4). P-H.

Troll, et al. Looking Ahead: A Woman's Guide to the Problems & Joys of Growing Older. 1977. 10.95 (ISBN 0-13-540310-3, Spec); pap. 4.95 (ISBN 0-13-540302-2). P-H.

Trollinger, Ira R., jt. auth. see Hounshell, Paul B.

Trollope, A. Australia & New Zealand. (Colonial History Ser.). 1968. Repr. of 1873 ed. 35.00 o.p. (ISBN 0-7129-0729-7, Dist by Shoe String). Dawson Pub.

Trollope, Anthony. Barchester Towers. 1956. 12.95x (ISBN 0-460-00030-6, Evman); pap. 4.50 (ISBN 0-460-01030-1). Dutton.

--Barchester Towers. pap. 2.95 (ISBN 0-451-51380-0, CE1380, Sig Classics). NAL.

--Barchester Towers. (The Zodiac Press Ser.). 1978. 9.95 (ISBN 0-7011-1250-6, Pub. by Chatto Bodley Jonathan). Merrimack Bk Serv.

--Castle Richmond. Wolff, Robert L., ed. (Ireland Nineteenth Century Fiction Ser. 2: Vol. 55). 912p. 1979. lib. bdg. 32.00 (ISBN 0-8240-3504-6). Garland Pub.

--Clergymen of the Church of England. (Victorian Library). 134p. 1974. Repr. of 1866 ed. text ed. 14.50x (ISBN 0-7185-5023-4, Leicester). Humanities.

--Dr. Thorne. 1953. 12.95x (ISBN 0-460-00360-7, Evman). Dutton.

--Dr. Thorne. (The Zodiac Press Ser.). 1978. 9.95 (ISBN 0-7011-1251-4, Pub. by Chatto Bodley Jonathan). Merrimack Bk Serv.

--The Eustace Diamonds. 1976. lib. bdg. 14.95x (ISBN 0-89968-140-9). Lightyear.

--An Eye for an Eye. Wolff, Robert L., ed. (Ireland Nineteenth Century Fiction - Ser. Two: Vol. 56). 440p. 1979. lib. bdg. 32.00 (ISBN 0-8240-3505-4). Garland Pub.

--The Kellys & the OKelleys. (World's Classics Ser: No. 341). 1975. 10.95 (ISBN 0-19-250341-3). Oxford U Pr.

--The Kellys & the O'Kellys. Wolff, Robert L., ed. (Ireland Nineteenth Century Fiction - Ser. Two: Vol. 54). 888p. 1979. lib. bdg. 32.00 (ISBN 0-8240-3503-8). Garland Pub.

--The Land-Leaguers. Wolff, Robert L., ed. (Ireland Nineteenth Century Fiction - Ser. Two: Vol. 57). 894p. 1979. lib. bdg. 32.00 (ISBN 0-8240-3506-2). Garland Pub.

--The Macdermots of Ballycloran. Wolff, Robert L., ed. (Ireland Nineteenth Century Fiction - Ser. Two: Vol. 53). 1372p. 1979. lib. bdg. 32.00 (ISBN 0-8240-3502-X). Garland Pub.

--Small House at Allington. 1963. 12.95x (ISBN 0-460-00361-5, Evman). Dutton.

--Small House at Allington. (World's Classics Ser.: No. 472). 15.95 (ISBN 0-19-250472-X). Oxford U Pr.

--Thackeray. LC 67-23880. 1968. Repr. of 1879 ed. 18.00 (ISBN 0-8103-3060-1). Gale.

--The Three Clerks. 497p. 1981. pap. price not set (ISBN 0-486-24099-1). Dover.

--The Warden. (The Zodiac Press Ser.). 1978. 9.95 (ISBN 0-7011-1255-7, Pub. by Chatto Bodley Jonathan). Merrimack Bk Serv.

--Warden. Clay, N. L., ed. (Guide Novel Ser.). pap. text ed. 3.95x o.p. (ISBN 0-435-16880-0). Heinemann Ed.

--Way We Live Now. Tracy, Robert, ed. LC 74-132935. (Library of Literature Ser.). 1974. pap. 13.95 (ISBN 0-672-61016-7, LL32). Bobbs.

Trollope, Christine, tr. see Zacharias, Gerhard.

Trollope, Frances M. Father Eustace: A Tale of the Jesuits. Wolff, Robert L., ed. LC 75-448. (Victorian Fiction Ser.). 1975. Repr. of 1847 ed. lib. bdg. 66.00 (ISBN 0-8240-1528-2). Garland Pub.

--The Vicar of Wrexhill. Wolff, Robert L., ed. LC 75-486. (Victorian Fiction Ser.). 1975. Repr. of 1837 ed. lib. bdg. 66.00 (ISBN 0-8240-1563-0). Garland Pub.

Trollope, Joanna. Eliza Stanhope. 1980. pap. 2.25 o.s.i. (ISBN 0-440-12356-9). Dell.

Tromba, Anthony J., jt. auth. see Marsden, Jerold E.

Tromba, Anthony J., jt. auth. see Marsden, Jerrold E.

Trombetta, Michael. Basic for Business Students. LC 80-15605. 320p. 1981. pap. text ed. 9.95 (ISBN 0-201-07611-X). A-W.

Trombley, Richard. The World's Greatest Airplanes: The Heinkel HE 111 to the Concorde. (Superwheels & Thrill Sports Ser.). (Illus.). (gr. 4 up). 1981. PLB 6.95 (ISBN 0-8225-0501-0). Lerner Pubns.

--The World's Greatest Airplanes: The Wright Flyer to the Piper Cub. (Superwheels & Thrill Sports Bks.). (Illus.). (gr. 4 up). 1981. PLB 6.95 (ISBN 0-8225-0500-2). Lerner Pubns.

Tromp, S. W. & Weihe, W. H., eds. Biometerology-2: Proceedings, International Bioclimatological Congress - 3rd, Pts. 1 & 2. 1967. 54.45 o.p. (ISBN 0-08-011045-2). Pergamon.

Tromp, Solco W. Progress in Human Biometeorology: The Effect of Weather & Climate on Man & His Living Environment, Period 1963 to 1970-75, Vol. 1. Incl. Pt. 1. The Micro & Macroenvironments in the Atmosphere & Their Effects on Basic Physiological Mechanisms of Man. 726p. 1974. pap. text ed. 144.00 (ISBN 90-265-0167-6); Pt. 2. Pathological Biometeorology. 444p. 1977. pap. text ed. 86.50 (ISBN 90-265-0245-1); Pt. 3. Biometeorological Aspects of Plants, Trees & Animals in Human Life. 158p. 1972. pap. text ed. 31.50 (ISBN 90-265-0156-0). (Progress in Biometeorology Ser., Pub. by Swets Pub Serv Holland). Swets North Am.

Trompf, G. W. The Idea of Historical Recurrence in Western Thought: From Antiquity to the Reformation. 1979. 22.75x (ISBN 0-520-03479-1). U of Cal Pr.

Tronick, E. The Development of the Human Communication & Joint Regulation of Behavior. 1981. 18.00 (ISBN 0-8391-1510-5). Univ Park.

Tronik, Ruth. Israeli Periodicals & Serials in English & Other European Languages: A Classified Bibliography. LC 73-14901. 1974. 10.00 (ISBN 0-8108-0682-7). Scarecrow.

Tronti, Mario, et al, eds. Working Class Autonomy & the Crisis. 1981. text ed. 33.75x (ISBN 0-391-01811-6); pap. text ed. write for info. (ISBN 0-391-01812-4). Humanities.

Troop, Elizabeth. Darling Daughters. 224p. 1981. 9.95 (ISBN 0-312-18281-3). St Martin.

Tropman, John E. & Lind, Roger M. New Strategic Perspectives on Social Policy. (Policy Studies). Date not set. 47.51 (ISBN 0-08-025554-X); pap. 14.51 (ISBN 0-08-025553-1). Pergamon.

Tropman, John E., et al, eds. Strategic Perspectives on Social Policy. LC 74-14737. 1976. text ed. 23.00 (ISBN 0-08-018227-5); pap. text ed. 12.75 (ISBN 0-08-018226-7). Pergamon.

Troppman, R. J., jt. auth. see Fuoss, D. E.

Trosclair. A Cajun Night Before Christmas. Jacobs, Howard, ed. (Illus.). 48p. (gr. 6-12). 1973. 7.95 (ISBN 0-88289-002-6). Pelican.

Trost, Barry M. & Hutchinson, C. R., eds. Organic Synthesis - Today & Tomorrow: Third IUPAC Symposium on Organic Synthesis, Madison, Wisconsin, U.S.A., 15-20 June 1980. (IUAC Symposium Ser,). (Illus.). 360p. 1981. 96.00 (ISBN 0-08-025268-0). Pergamon.

Trostyanskaya, E. B., ed. see Babaevsky, P. G., et al.

Trotman, R. E. Technological Aids to Microbiology. (Illus.). 1978. pap. text ed. 15.95x (ISBN 0-7131-4293-6). Intl Ideas.

Trotman-Dickenson, A. F. & Parfitt, G. D. Chemical Kinetics & Surface & Colloid Chemistry. (Illus.). 1966. 15.00 (ISBN 0-08-011257-9); pap. 7.00 (ISBN 0-08-011256-0). Pergamon.

Trotman-Dickenson, D. I. Economic Workbooks & Data. 1969. 16.50 (ISBN 0-08-012958-7); pap. 7.75 (ISBN 0-08-012957-9). Pergamon.

Trotsky, Leon. History of the Russian Revolution. 1980. pap. 14.95 (ISBN 0-913460-83-4). Monad Pr.

--Literature & Revolution. 1960. pap. 6.95 (ISBN 0-472-06043-0, 43, AA). U of Mich Pr.

--Russian Revolution: The Overthrow of Tzarism & the Triumph of the Soviets. abr. ed. LC 59-6990. 1959. pap. 3.50 (ISBN 0-385-09398-5, A170, Anch). Doubleday.

--The War Correspondence of Leon Trotsky: The Balkan Wars (1912-13, Pt. 1. 1981. lib. bdg. 30.00 (ISBN 0-913460-67-2); pap. 8.95 (ISBN 0-913460-68-0). Monad Pr.

Trott, jt. auth. see Bateman.

Trott, Lamarr B. Contributions to the Biology of Carapid Fishes (Paracanthopterygii, Gadiformes) (U. C. Publ. in Zoology: Vol. 89). 1970. pap. 6.00x (ISBN 0-520-09346-1). U of Cal Pr.

Trotter, Alexander. To the Greenland Whaling. 80p. 1980. pap. 9.95 (ISBN 0-906191-24-6, Pub. by Thule Pr England). Intl Schol Bk Serv.

Trotter, Ann. The Continuing Revolution: China Since 1894. 2nd, rev, enl. ed. (Illus.). 72p. 1975. pap. 4.50x o.p. (ISBN 0-8002-0677-0). Intl Pubns Serv.

Trotter, Ann, ed. Continuing Revolution: China Since 1894. 2nd rev. & enl. ed. (Illus.). 72p. 1975. pap. 4.50x (ISBN 0-686-65040-9). Intl Pubns Serv.

Trotter, Gwendolyn, jt. auth. see Kahan, Jane.

Trotter, Gwendolyn, jt. auth. see Kakn, Jane.

Trotter, Hale, jt. auth. see Williamson, Richard.

Trotter, Lionel J. Warren Hastings. (Rulers of India Ser). 1962. 3.50x o.p. (ISBN 0-8426-1572-5). Verry.

Trotter, W. F., tr. see Pascal, Blaise.

Trotter, Wilfred. Instincts of the Herd in Peace & War. 2nd ed. LC 74-19217. 264p. 1975. Repr. of 1923 ed. 18.00 (ISBN 0-8103-4090-9). Gale.

Trotter, William R., jt. auth. see Anderson, Thomas J.

Trotti, John B. The Lesser Festivals 2: Saints' Days & Special Occasions. Achtemeier, Elizabeth, et al, eds. (Proclamation 2: Aids for Interpreting Thee Lessons of the Church Year). 64p. (Orig.). 1980. pap. 2.50 (ISBN 0-8006-1394-5, 1-1394). Fortress.

Troubridge, Una V., tr. see Colette.

Trounce, J. R. Clinical Pharmacology for Nurses. 9th ed. (Illus.). 432p. 1981. pap. text ed. 10.00 (ISBN 0-443-02333-6). Churchill.

Trounce, J. R., ed. Clinical Pharmacology for Nurses. 9th ed. (Illus.). Date not set. text ed. price not set (ISBN 0-443-02333-6). Churchill.

Troup. Workboats. 1980. write for info. (ISBN 0-85501-212-9). Heyden.

Troupe, Quincy & Shulte, Rainer, eds. Giant Talk: An Anthology of Third World Writings. 1975. pap. 6.95 (ISBN 0-394-71443-1, V-443, Vin). Random.

Trout, Andrew. Jean-Baptiste-Colbert. (World Leaders Ser.: No. 64). 1978. lib. bdg. 13.95 (ISBN 0-8057-7715-6). Twayne.

Trout, Jack, jt. auth. see Ries, Al.

Trout, John M. The Voyage of Prudence: The World View of Alan of Lille. LC 79-66473. 1979. pap. text ed. 9.00 (ISBN 0-8191-0840-5). U Pr of Amer.

Troutman, Richard C. Microsurgery of the Anterior Segment of the Eye: The Cornea, Vol. 2. LC 74-12453. (Illus.). 1977. 56.50 (ISBN 0-8016-5106-9). Mosby.

Troutt, Margaret. The General Was a Lady. 325p. 1980. 9.95 (ISBN 0-87981-139-0); pap. 5.95 (ISBN 0-87981-141-2). Holman.

Trow, Martin, ed. see Carnegie Commission on Higher Education.

Trow, Nigel. Lancia: The Shield & the Flag. LC 79-56053. (Illus.). 272p. 1980. 38.00 (ISBN 0-7153-7882-1). David & Charles.

Trowbridge, Berta C., ed. Old Houses of Connecticut. (Illus.). 1923. 125.00x (ISBN 0-685-89768-0). Elliots Bks.

Trowbridge, Hoyt. From Dryden to Jane Austen: Essays on English Critics & Writers, 1660-1818. LC 76-21490. 1978. Repr. of 1977 ed. 15.00x (ISBN 0-8263-0430-3). U of NM Pr.

Trowbridge, L. W. Experiments in Meteorology: Investigations for the Amateur Scientist. LC 70-171324. 312p. 1973. 7.95 o.p. (ISBN 0-385-08238-X). Doubleday.

Trowbridge, Leslie, et al. Becoming a Secondary School Science Teacher. 3rd ed. 352p. 1981. pap. text ed. 15.95 (ISBN 0-675-08030-4). Merrill.

Trowbridge, Leslie W., jt. auth. see Sund, Robert B.

Trower, Peter, jt. auth. see Argyle, Michael.

Trower-Subira, George. Black Folks' Guide to Making Big Money in America. 184p. 1980. 11.00 (ISBN 0-9605304-0-1). VSBE.

Troxell, Mary D. & Stone, Elaine. Fashion Merchandising. 3rd ed. LC 80-25077. (Gregg McGraw-Hill Marketing Ser.). (Illus.). 480p. 16.50 (ISBN 0-07-065280-5). McGraw.

Troy, George. Native to the Grain. LC 61-6646. 1961. 3.95 o.p. (ISBN 0-15-164793-3). HarBraceJ.

Troy, June, ed. see Bonser, Wilfred.

Troy, Kathryn. Annual Survey of Corporate Contributions, 1977. LC 76-24946. (Report Ser.: No. 759). (Illus.). 1979. pap. 15.00 o.p. (ISBN 0-8237-0195-6). Conference Bd.

--Managing Corporate Contributions, Report No. 792. (Illus.). vii, 95p. (Orig.). 1980. pap. 30.00 (ISBN 0-8237-0228-6). Conference Bd.

Troy, Leo. Management & the Local Independent Union. 1966. pap. 2.50 (ISBN 0-87330-003-3). Indus Rel.

Troy, P. N., ed. Equity in the City. 192p. 1981. text ed. 22.50x (ISBN 0-86861-250-2, 2647). Allen Unwin.

--A Just Society? Essays on Equity in Australia. 192p. 1981. text ed. 22.50x (ISBN 0-86861-234-0, 2655). Allen Unwin.

Troyanovich, Helen I. The Newcomer. 160p. 1979. 6.95 (ISBN 0-8059-2658-5). Dorrance.

Troyat, Henri. La Tete Sur les Epaules. (Easy Readers, C). (Illus.). pap. text ed. 3.75 (ISBN 0-88436-285-X). EMC.

Troyen, Carol. The Boston Tradition: American Paintings from the Museum of Fine Arts, Boston. LC 80-69210. (Illus.). 216p. (Orig.). 1980. pap. 15.95 (ISBN 0-917418-66-2). Am Fed Arts.

Troyer, Henry. Principles & Techniques of Histochemistry. LC 80-80592. 1980. text ed. 22.95 (ISBN 0-316-85310-0). Little.

Troyer, Robert J., jt. auth. see Snapper, Ernst.

Troyka, Lynn Q. Structured Reading. (Illus.). 1978. pap. text ed. 10.50 (ISBN 0-13-854513-8). P-H.

Troyka, Lynn Q. & Nudelman, J. Steps in Composition. 2nd ed. 416p. 1976. 9.95 (ISBN 0-13-846501-0). P-H.

Troyka, Lynn Q. & Nudelman, Jerrold. Steps in Composition: Alternate. 2nd ed. (Illus.). 1979. pap. text ed. 9.95 (ISBN 0-13-846550-9). P-H.

--Taking Action: Writing, Reading, Speaking & Listening Through Simulation Games. (Illus.). 176p. 1975. pap. text ed. 7.95 (ISBN 0-13-882571-8). P-H.

Truax, Carol. All About Steam Cooking. LC 79-6878. (Illus.). 272p. 1981. 12.95 (ISBN 0-385-15548-4). Doubleday.

Trubetzkoy, N. S. Vorlesungen Ueberdie Altrussische Literatur (Mitteinem Nachwort Von R.O. Jakobson) 167p. 1973. pap. 10.95x o.p. (ISBN 0-685-47487-9). Schoenhof.

Trubitt, Allen R. & Hines, Robert S. Ear Training & Sight-Singing: An Integrated Approach, Book 1. LC 77-5214. 1979. pap. text ed. 12.95 (ISBN 0-02-870810-5); tapes 49.50 (ISBN 0-02-870770-2). Schirmer Bks.

--Ear Training & Sight-Singing: Book II, an Integrated Approach. LC 77-5214. 1980. pap. text ed. 14.95 (ISBN 0-02-870820-2); tapes 49.50 (ISBN 0-02-872670-7). Schirmer Bks.

Trubner, Henry, jt. auth. see Hayashiya, Seizo.

Trubner, Nikolaus. Trubner's Bibliographical Guide to American Literature. 1966. Repr. of 1859 ed. 32.00 (ISBN 0-8103-3315-5). Gale.

Trubo, Richard, jt. auth. see Behrstock, Barry.

Trubo, Richard, jt. auth. see Bresher, David.

Truby, J. David. Quiet Killers II: Silencer Update. (Illus.). 80p. (Orig.). 1979. pap. 6.00 (ISBN 0-87364-163-9). Paladin Ent.

Truby, J. David & Minnery, John. Improvised Modified Firearms, Vol. 1. Lund, Peder C., ed. (Illus.). 140p. 1975. 9.95 o.p. (ISBN 0-685-52026-9). Paladin Ent.

--Improvised Modified Firearms, Vol. 2. new ed. Lund, Peder C., ed. (Illus.). 140p. 1975. 9.95 o.p. (ISBN 0-87364-030-6). Paladin Ent.

Truch, Stephen. TM Technique & the Art of Learning. (Quality Paperback Ser: No. 329). 1977. pap. 4.95 (ISBN 0-8226-0329-2). Littlefield.

Truck, Fred. The Polyp (A Quetzalcoatl Production) Tych: Polyptych Striking Camp. 1.00 (ISBN 0-938236-01-6). Cookie Pr.

Truck, Fred, jt. auth. see Dzacab, Bolon.

Truck, Fred, ed. The Des Moines Festival of the Avant-Garde Invites You to a Show Without Really Being There. (Orig.). pap. text ed. 7.50 (ISBN 0-938236-02-4). Cookie Pr.

Truckenbrodt, Erich A., jt. auth. see Schlichting, Hermann T.

Trucksess, Fran. Creative Art, Elementary Grades. rev. ed. (Illus.). 1962. pap. 4.95x o.p. (ISBN 0-87108-169-5). Pruett.

Trudeau, G. B. He's Never Heard of You, Either. (Doonesbury Ser.). (Illus., Orig.). 1981. pap. 4.95 (ISBN 0-03-049196-7). HR&W.

--Just a French Major from the Bronx: Selected Cartoons from "Still a Few Bugs in the System". (Doonesbury Ser.). (Illus.). 128p. 1981. pap. 1.75 (ISBN 0-445-00623-4). Popular Lib.

--A Tad Overweight but Violet Eyes to Die for. 1981. pap. 1.75 (ISBN 0-553-14337-9). Bantam.

Trudeau, Gary. Don't Ever Change, Boopsie. (Doonesbury Ser). (Illus.). 1981. pap. 1.75 (ISBN 0-445-00608-0). Popular Lib.

--I Have No Son. (Doonesbury Ser.). (Illus.). 1975. pap. 1.75 (ISBN 0-445-08323-9). Popular Lib.

--Like Chocolate Chip Cookies. 1980. pap. 1.50 o.p. (ISBN 0-445-00622-6). Popular Lib.

Trudeau, Gary B. Even Revolutionaries Like Chocolate Chip Cookies: Selected Cartoons from "Still a Few Bugs in the System". (Doonesbury Ser.). (Illus.). 128p. 1974. pap. 1.75 (ISBN 0-445-00622-6). Popular Lib.

Trudel, Marcel see Halpenny, Francess.

Trudgill, P. The Social Differentiation of English in Norwich. LC 73-77178. (Studies in Linguistics). 208p. 1974. 32.50 (ISBN 0-521-20264-7); pap. text ed. 14.95 (ISBN 0-521-29745-1). Cambridge U Pr.

Trudgill, P., jt. auth. see Chambers, J. K.

Trudgill, Stephen A. Soil & Vegetation Systems. (Contemporary Problems in Geography Ser.). (Illus.). 1977. 29.95x (ISBN 0-19-874058-1); pap. 9.95x (ISBN 0-19-874059-X). Oxford U Pr.

Trudinger, P., jt. auth. see Roy, A. B.

Trudinger, P. A. Biogeochemistry of Ancient & Modern Environments. 723p. 1981. 52.00 (ISBN 0-387-10303-1). Springer-Verlag.

True, D. L., jt. ed. see Meighan, Clement.

True, D. L., et al. Archaeological Investigations at Molpa, San Diego County, California. (U. C. Publ. in Anthropology: Vol. 11). pap. 10.50x (ISBN 0-520-09490-5). U of Cal Pr.

True, Herb & Mang, Anna. Humor Power: How to Get It, Give It & Gain. LC 79-55370. 240p. 1980. 9.95 (ISBN 0-385-14618-3). Doubleday.

Trueba, Henry T., et al, eds. Culture & the Bilingual Classroom: Studies in Classroom Ethnography. (Bilingual Multicultural Education Ser.). 288p. (Orig.). 1981. pap. text ed. 15.95 (ISBN 0-88377-182-9). Newbury Hse.

Trueblood, Cecil R., jt. auth. see Heimer, Ralph T.

Trueblood, D. E. Trustworthiness of Religious Experience. LC 78-24656. 1979. pap. 2.45 (ISBN 0-913408-45-X). Friends United.

Trueblood, David E. Philosophy of Religion. LC 75-31446. 324p. 1976. Repr. of 1957 ed. lib. bdg. 25.25x (ISBN 0-8371-8514-9, TRPHR). Greenwood.

Trueblood, Elton. Company of the Committed. LC 61-12834. 1961. 3.95 (ISBN 0-06-068551-4, RD 317, HarpR). Har-Row.

--The Humor of Christ. LC 75-12280. 128p. 1975. pap. 4.95 (ISBN 0-06-068631-6, RD 298, HarpR). Har-Row.

--New Man for Our Time. LC 77-85059. 1970. 5.95 o.p. (ISBN 0-06-068532-8, HarpR). Har-Row.

Trueblood, Felicity M., jt. ed. see Cornelius, Wayne A.

Trueblood, Felicity M., jt. ed. see Rabinovitz, Francine J.

Trueblood, Kenneth N., jt. auth. see Glusker, Jenny P.

Trueblood, Paul G. Byron & Europe: The Interplay of Poetry & Politics. 1980. write for info. (ISBN 0-391-02164-8). Humanities.

--Lord Byron. 2nd ed. (English Authors Ser.: No. 78). 1977. lib. bdg. 10.95 (ISBN 0-8057-6694-4). Twayne.

Truell, George F. How to Manage for More Profitable Results. 1974. 55.50 o.p. (ISBN 0-85013-038-7). Dartnell Corp.

Trueman, E. R., jt. ed. see Elder, H. Y.

Trueman, R. Introduction Quant. Meth. Dec. Marketing. 2nd ed. 1977. 19.95 (ISBN 0-03-018391-X). Dryden Pr.

Trueman, Richard E. Quantitative Methods for Decision Making in Business. 3rd ed. LC 80-65810. 384p. 1981. text ed. 19.95 (ISBN 0-03-051356-1). Dryden Pr.

Truesdale, C. W. Cold Harbors. 1973. 4.50 (ISBN 0-686-27598-5) (ISBN 0-686-27599-3). Latitudes Pr.

Truesdell, C. & Bharatha, S. The Concept & Logic of Classical Thermodynamics As a Theory of Heat Engines. Rigorously Constructed Upon Foundations Laid by S. Carnot & F. Reech. LC 76-48115. (Texts & Monographs in Physics). (Illus.). 1978. 28.70 (ISBN 0-387-07971-8). Springer-Verlag.

Truesdell, C. A. Elements of Continuum Mechanics. 1966. pap. 14.70 o.p. (ISBN 0-387-03683-0). Springer-Verlag.

Truesdell, Clifford A. A First Course in Rational Continuum Mechanics: General Concepts, Vol. 1. (Pure & Applied Math Ser.). Vol. 1, 1977. 32.00 (ISBN 0-12-701301-6); Vol. 2, 1981. write for info. (ISBN 0-12-701302-4). Acad Pr.

Truett, Randle B. & Federal Writers' Project, eds. Washington, D.C. A Guide to the Nation's Capital. rev. ed. LC 67-25608. (American Guide Ser.). (Illus.). 1968. 12.95 (ISBN 0-8038-8010-3). Hastings.

Truex, Raymond C., jt. ed. see Buchheit, William.

Truitt, John O. & Brewer, Donald D. Dynamics of Corrections Administration. (Illus.). 125p. 1981. pap. text ed. price not set (ISBN 0-87084-854-2). Anderson Pub Co.

Truitt, Velma S. On the Hoof in Nevada. (Illus.). 1950. 50.00 (ISBN 0-913814-06-7). Nevada Pubns.

Truitt, Willis H. & Solomons, T. W. Science, Technology, & Freedom. 432p. 1974. pap. text ed. 9.75 (ISBN 0-395-17685-9). HM.

Trukhanovsky, V. Winston Churchill: A Political Biography. 1978. 9.00 (ISBN 0-8285-9151-2). Progress Pubs.

Trull, Joe E. Forty Object Sermons for Children. (Object Lesson Ser.). 96p. 1975. pap. 2.95 (ISBN 0-8010-8831-3). Baker Bk.

Truman, D. E. The Biochemistry of Cytodifferentiation. LC 73-21785. 122p. 1974. text ed. 13.95 (ISBN 0-470-89190-4). Halsted Pr.

Truman, Harry S. Truman Speaks: On the Presidency, the Constitution, and Statecraft. LC 60-8389. 160p. 1975. 12.50x (ISBN 0-231-02384-7); pap. 5.00 (ISBN 0-231-08339-4). Columbia U Pr.

Truman, Margaret. Harry S. Truman in Family. LC 80-70224. 256p. 1981. 12.95 (ISBN 0-87795-313-9). Arbor Hse.

--Murder in the White House. 1980. lib. bdg. 13.95 (ISBN 0-8161-3171-6, Large Print Bks). G K Hall.

--Murder on Capitol Hill. LC 80-70223. 256p. 1981. 11.95 (ISBN 0-87795-312-0). Arbor Hse.

Truman, Ruth. How to Be a Liberated Christian. LC 80-27302. 160p. 1981. 7.95 (ISBN 0-687-17710-3). Abingdon.

Trumble, Alfred. Representative Works of Contemporary American Artists. Weinberg, H. Barbara, ed. LC 75-28879. (Art Experience in Late 19th Century America Ser.: Vol. 13). (Illus.). 1976. Repr. of 1887 ed. lib. bdg. 72.50 (ISBN 0-8240-2237-8). Garland Pub.

Trumbler, Eberhard. Understanding Your Dog. (Illus.). 1973. 9.95 (ISBN 0-571-10373-1, Pub. by Faber & Faber). Merrimack Bk Serv.
Trumbo, Don A., jt. auth. see Landy, Frank J.
Trumbull, John. Autobiography of Colonel John Trumbull. Sizer, T., ed. LC 79-116912. (Library of American Art Ser). (Illus.). 1970. Repr. of 1953 ed. lib. bdg. 39.50 (ISBN 0-306-71242-3). Da Capo.
Trump, Benjamin F., jt. auth. see Cowley, R. Adams.
Trump, Benjamin F. & Arstila, A. U., eds. Pathobiology of Cell Membranes, 2 vols, Vol. 1. 1975. 52.75 (ISBN 0-12-701501-9). Acad Pr.
Trump, J. Lloyd & Miller, Delmas F. Secondary School Curriculum Improvement: Challenges, Humanism, Accountability. 2nd ed. 1973. text ed. 13.95x o.s.i. (ISBN 0-205-03733-X, 2237334). Allyn.
--Secondary School Curriculum Improvement: Meeting Challenges of the Times. 3rd ed. 1979. pap. text ed. 11.95 (ISBN 0-205-06600-3, 2366002). Allyn.
Trungpa, Chogyam. Born in Tibet. LC 76-53358. (The Clear Light Ser.). (Illus.). 1981. pap. 8.95 (ISBN 0-87773-718-5). Great Eastern.
--Glimpses of Abhidharma. 1978. pap. 5.95 (ISBN 0-87773-708-8, Prajna). Great Eastern.
--The Rain of Wisdom. Nalanda Translation Committee, tr. from Tibetan. LC 80-51130. Orig. Title: Bka'-Rgyud Mgur-Mtsho. 400p. 1980. 17.50 (ISBN 0-394-51412-2); pap. 9.95 (ISBN 0-394-73972-8). Shambhala Pubns.
Trungpa, Chogyam, ed. Empowerment. LC 76-17439. 1978. pap. 3.95 o.p. (ISBN 0-87773-705-3, Prajna). Great Eastern.
Trungpa, Chogyam, jt. tr. see Fremantle, Francesca.
Trunk, Isaih. Jewish Responses to Nazi Persecution. LC 78-6378. 384p. 1981. pap. 9.95 (ISBN 0-8128-6103-5). Stein & Day.
Trupin, James E., ed. In Prison. (Orig.). 1975. pap. 2.50 o.p. (ISBN 0-451-61437-2, ME1437, Ment). NAL.
Trupp, Beverly. Color It Home: A Builder's Guide to Interior Design & Merchandising. (Illus.). 240p. 1981. 34.95 (ISBN 0-8436-0136-1). CBI Pub.
Truscott, Alan. Contract Bridge. LC 80-70959. 112p. 1982. pap. 2.95 (ISBN 0-8119-0422-9). Fell. Postponed.
Truscott, Dorothy A. Bid Better, Play Better. 1976. pap. 1.95 o.p. (ISBN 0-523-00997-6). Pinnacle Bks.
Trusky, Tom, ed. see Ehrlich, Gretel.
Trusler, Ivan & Ehret, Walter. Functional Lessons in Singing. 2nd ed. LC 73-180598. (Illus.). 240p. 1972. pap. 14.95 ref. ed. (ISBN 0-13-331801-X). P-H.
Trusler, John see Outcast, Gabriel, pseud.
Trussell, John B., Jr. Birthplace of an Army: A Study of the Valley Forge Encampment. LC 77-621150. 1976. 6.50 (ISBN 0-911124-88-8); pap. 4.00 (ISBN 0-911124-87-X). Pa Hist & Mus.
--Pennsylvania Historical Bibliography: III. Additions Through 1976. 100p. (Orig.). 1980. pap. 4.00 (ISBN 0-89271-014-4). Pa Hist & Mus.
--Pennsylvania Historical Bibliography: III. Additions Through 1973. 87p. (Orig.). 1979. pap. 4.00 (ISBN 0-89271-004-7). Pa Hist & Mus.
--The Pennsylvania Line: Regimental Organization & Operations, 1775-1783. LC 78-621999. 1976. 12.00 (ISBN 0-911124-85-3). Pa Hist & Mus.
--William Penn, Architect of a Nation. (Illus.). 79p. (Orig.). 1980. pap. 2.25 (ISBN 0-89271-008-X). Pa Hist & Mus.
Trussell, John B., Jr., compiled by. Pennsylvania Historical Bibliography: I Additions Through 1970. 1979. 4.00 (ISBN 0-89271-003-9). Pa Hist & Mus.
Trussell, John R. Introduction to Furniture Making. LC 73-3299. (Illus.). 1973. pap. 5.95 (ISBN 0-8069-8448-1). Sterling.
Trussell, Patricia, et al. Finding, Reading & Interpreting Nursing Research. LC 80-84150. 225p. 1981. text ed. price not set (ISBN 0-913654-70-1). Nursing Res.
Trussler, Simon. John Arden. (Columbia Essays on Modern Writers Ser.: No. 65). 1973. pap. 2.00 (ISBN 0-231-03533-0, MW65). Columbia U Pr.
--Plays of John Osborne: An Assessment. 1969. pap. text ed. 4.00x (ISBN 0-575-00267-0). Humanities.
Trusted, Jennifer. Logic of Scientific Inference: An Introduction. (Modern Introductions to Philosophy Ser.). 144p. 1980. text ed. 20.00x (ISBN 0-333-26669-2); pap. text ed. 10.00x (ISBN 0-333-26670-6). Humanities.
Trustrum, Kathleen. Linear Programming. (Library of Mathematics). 1971. pap. 5.00 (ISBN 0-7100-6779-8). Routledge & Kegan.
Trusty, Francis M., ed. Administering Human Resources: A Behavioral Approach to Educational Administration. LC 71-146311. (Orig.). 1971. 19.75x (ISBN 0-8211-1903-6); text ed. 17.75x (ISBN 0-685-04200-6). McCutchan.
Trutko, John, et al. A Comparison of the Experimental Housing Allowance Program & Great Britain's Rent Allowance Program. (An Institute Paper). 52p. 1978. pap. 5.00 (ISBN 0-87766-222-3, 22500). Urban Inst.
Truzzi, Marcello. Sociology & Everyday Life. (Orig.). 1968. pap. text ed. 10.95 (ISBN 0-13-821215-5). P-H.
--Sociology for Pleasure. (Illus.). 416p. 1974. pap. text ed. 9.95 o.p. (ISBN 0-13-821256-2). P-H.
--Verstehen: Subjective Understanding in the Social Sciences. LC 73-1849. 1973. text ed. 5.95 (ISBN 0-201-07602-0). A-W.
Truzzi, Marcello & Petersen, David M., eds. Criminal Life: Views from the Inside. 240p. 1972. pap. text ed. 9.95 (ISBN 0-13-192955-0). P-H.
TRW - Energy Systems Planning Division. Energy Balances in the Production & End-Use of Alcohols Derived from Biomass. 125p. 1981. pap. 15.00 (ISBN 0-89934-116-0). Solar Energy Info.
Tryck, Keith. Yukon Passage: Rafting 2,000 Miles to the Bering Sea. 288p. 1981. 15.00 (ISBN 0-8129-0926-7). Times Bks.
Trygstad-Durland, Louise, jt. auth. see Jasmin, Sylvia.
Trylinski, W. Fine Mechanisms & Precision Instruments, Principles of Design. 1971. 75.00 (ISBN 0-08-006361-6). Pergamon.
Tryon, Clarence A. C. A. T. Tells Tales. 1979. pap. 4.95 (ISBN 0-910286-54-X). Boxwood.
Trypanis, C. A. The Glass Adonis. 1973. pap. 3.95 (ISBN 0-571-10170-4, Pub. by Faber & Faber). Merrimack Bk Serv.
Trythall, Anthony J. Boney Fuller: Soldier, Strategist & Writer, 1878-1966. 1977. 20.00 (ISBN 0-8135-0844-4). Rutgers U Pr.
Trzyna, Thaddeus C., ed. The California Handbook: A Comprehensive Guide to Sources of Current Information & Action. 4th ed. LC 75-171691. (California Information Guides). (Illus., Orig.). 1981. pap. 20.00x (ISBN 0-912102-44-6). Cal Inst Public.
Trzyna, Thomas N., et al, eds. Careers for Humanities - Liberal Arts Majors: A Guide to Programs & Resources. LC 80-50352. 188p. (Orig.). 1980. pap. 22.50x (ISBN 0-9604078-0-4). Weatherford.
Tsagarakis, Odysseus. Nature & Background of Major Concepts of Divine Power in Homer. 1977. pap. text ed. 34.25x (ISBN 90-6032-083-2). Humanities.
Tsagris, B. E. Modern Real Estate Principles in California. 2nd ed. 550p. 1980. pap. 21.95 o.p. (ISBN 0-695-81493-1). Real Estate Ed Co.
Tsai, N. T., ed. see Browne, A. L.
Tsai, Stephen W. & Hahn, H. Thomas. Introduction to Composite Materials. LC 80-51965. 475p. 1980. 35.00 (ISBN 0-87762-288-4). Technomic.
Tsai, Yamei. Chinese Cookbook. 1978. 9.95 o.p. (ISBN 0-214-20506-1, 8067, Dist. by Arco). Barrie & Jenkins.
Tsang, Chiu-Sam. Society, Schools & Progress in China. LC 68-21109. 1968. 22.00 (ISBN 0-08-012844-0); pap. 11.25 (ISBN 0-08-012843-2). Pergamon.
Tsang, Wing-Sum & Griffin, Gary W. Metabolic Activation of Polynuclear Aromatic Hydrocarbons. (Illus.). 1979. 37.00 (ISBN 0-08-023835-1). Pergamon.
Tsanoff, Radoslav A. Civilization & Progress. LC 74-160051. 384p. 1971. 17.00x (ISBN 0-8131-1255-9). U Pr of Ky.
Tsao, C. K. Bibliography of Mathematics Published in Communist China During the Period of Nineteen Forty-Nine to Nineteen Sixty. 1961. 1.00 o.p. (ISBN 0-686-67534-7, CCBIB). Am Math.
Tsao, C. K., compiled by. Contemporary Chinese Research Mathematics, Vol. 1: Bibliography of Mathematics Published in Communist China During the Period 1949-1960. 83p. 1961. 1.00 o.p. (ISBN 0-686-66979-7, CCBIB). Am Math.
Tsao, G. T., jt. ed. see Perlman, D.
Ts'ao Yu. Wilderness (Yuan-yeh) Rand, Christopher C. & Lau, Joseph S., trs. from Chinese. LC 78-65981. (Chinese Literature in Translation Ser.). 160p. 1980. 12.50x (ISBN 0-253-17297-7). Ind U Pr.
Tschesche, J., jt. ed. see Holzer, H.
Tschirhart, William, jt. auth. see Munem, Mustafa.
Tse, Francis S., et al. Mechanical Vibrations: Theory & Applications. 2nd ed. 1978. text ed. 27.95 (ISBN 0-205-05940-6, 3259404); sol. man. avail. (ISBN 0-205-05941-4, 3259412). Allyn.
Tselementes, Nicholas. Greek Cookery. 3rd ed. 1956. 5.00 (ISBN 0-685-09035-3). Divry.
Tseng, C. Howard, ed. Atlas of Ultrastructure: Ultrastructural Features in Pathology. 224p. 1980. 32.50x (ISBN 0-8385-0462-0). ACC.
Tseng, Henry P. Complete Guide to Legal Materials in Microforms: 1980 Supplement. 1980. perfect bdg. 25.00 (ISBN 0-686-68702-7). AMCO Intl.
Tseng, Rosy. Chinese Cooking Made Easy. LC 63-21064. (Illus.). 1964. bds. 4.95 (ISBN 0-8048-0097-9). C E Tuttle.
Tse Tung, Mao. A Critique of Soviet Economics. Roberts, Moss, tr. from Chinese. LC 77-70971. 1977. 10.00 o.p. (ISBN 0-85345-412-4, CL4124). Monthly Rev.
Tsichritzis, Dennis & Klug, Anthony, eds. The ANSI-X3-SPARC DBMS Framework Report of the Study Group on Database Management Systems. (Illus.). xii, 19p. 1978. saddle-stitch 7.00 (ISBN 0-88283-013-9). AFIPS Pr.
Tsichritzis, Dennis C. & Lochovsky, F. H. Data Base Management Systems. 1977. text ed. 20.95 (ISBN 0-12-701740-2). Acad Pr.
Tsien, Richard W., jt. ed. see Stevens, Charles F.
Tsirkas, Stratis. Drifting Cities. Cicellis, Kay, tr. 1974. 10.00 o.p. (ISBN 0-394-46971-2). Knopf.
Tsirpanlis, Constantine. Two Hundred One Modern Greek Verbs. LC 80-13900. 1980. pap. 8.95 (ISBN 0-8120-0475-2). Barron.
Ts'o. Basic Principles of Nucleic Chemistry. 1974. Vol. 1. 55.50, subscription 45.00 (ISBN 0-12-701901-4); Vol. 2, 1974. 52.50, subscription 42.50 (ISBN 0-12-701902-2). Acad Pr.
Tso, Lin. How to Make Money Trading Listed Puts. LC 78-9295. 1978. 10.95 (ISBN 0-8119-0295-1). Fell.
Tso, Shih K. The Labor Movement in China. LC 79-2842. 230p. 1981. Repr. of 1928 ed. 19.75 (ISBN 0-8305-0018-9). Hyperion Conn.
Tso, T. C., ed. see Phytochemical Society of North America.
Tsogyal, Yeshe. The Life & Liberation of Padmasambhava, 2 vols. Toussaint, G. C. & Douglas, Kenneth, trs. (Tibetan Translation Ser.). (Illus.). 1978. 55.00 set (ISBN 0-685-80849-1). Vol. I (ISBN 0-913546-18-6). Vol. II (ISBN 0-913546-20-8). Dharma Pub.
Tsokos, Chris P. Mainstreams of Finite Mathematics with Applications. (Mathematics Ser.). 1978. text ed. 18.95 (ISBN 0-675-08436-9); instructor's manual 3.95 (ISBN 0-685-86838-9). Merrill.
Tsoumis, G. Wood As a Raw Material. 1968. 19.00 o.p. (ISBN 0-08-012378-3). Pergamon.
Tsuan, T. H., tr. see Yeh Ch'ing.
Tsuang, Ming T. & VanderMey, Randall. Genes & the Mind: Inheritance of Mental Illness. (Illus.). 158p. 1980. text ed. 12.95x (ISBN 0-19-261268-9). Oxford U Pr.
Tsuchitani, Patricia J., jt. ed. see Kaplan, Henry S.
Tsuji, Masatugu. Potential Theory in Modern Function Theory. 2nd ed. LC 74-4297. 600p. 1975. text ed. 19.50 (ISBN 0-8284-0281-7). Chelsea Pub.
Tsuji, Shizuo. Japanese Cooking: A Simple Art. LC 79-66244. (Illus.). 517p. 1980. 14.95 (ISBN 0-87011-399-2). Kodansha.
Tsujita, Mariko & Ikeda, Kyoko. Chinese Cooking for Everyone. (Illus.). 96p. 1980. 4.50 (ISBN 0-86628-003-0). Ridgefield Pub.
Tsukamoto, Jack T., jt. ed. see Williams, Nyal Z.
Tsukimura, Reiko, tr. see Kawabata, Yasunari.
Tsuneishi, Warren, et al, eds. Issues in Library Administration. 140p. 1974. 12.50x (ISBN 0-231-03818-6). Columbia U Pr.
Tsuneoka, Kenji & Takemoto, Tadayushi. Fiberoscopy of Gastric Diseases. (Illus.). 250p. 1973. 95.50 (ISBN 0-89640-043-3). Igaku-Shoin.
Tsuneta Yano Memorial Society (Tokyo), ed. Nippon: A Chartered Survey of Japan, 1980-81. 25th ed. (Illus.). 347p. 1980. 37.50x (ISBN 0-8002-2748-4). Intl Pubns Serv.
Tsunetomo, Yamamoto. The Hagakure: A Code to the Way of the Samurai. Mukoh, Takao, tr. from Japanese. xii, 182p. 1980. pap. 13.50 (ISBN 0-89346-169-5, Pub. by Hokuseido Pr). Heian Intl.
Tsung-Jen, Li, jt. ed. see Tong, T. K.
Tsunoda, S., et al, eds. Brassica Crops & Wild Allies. 360p. 1980. 38.00x (ISBN 0-89955-211-0, Pub. by JSSP Japan). Intl Schol Bk Serv.
Tsunoyama, Yokihiro. Textiles of the Andes: Catalogue of the Amano Collection. Ray, Karl, ed. Ooka, D. T., tr. from Japanese. (Illus.). 248p. 1979. Repr. of 1977 ed. 85.00 (ISBN 0-89346-017-6, Pub. by Heian/Dohosha). Heian Intl.
Ts'Un-Yan, Liu, jt. auth. see Mao, Nathan K.
Tsurayuki, Kino. The Tosa Diary. Porter, William N., tr. from Japanese. LC 80-51194. 160p. 1981. Repr. of 1912 ed. 9.75 (ISBN 0-8048-1371-X). C E Tuttle.
Tsurumi, Y. Sogoshosha: Engines of Export-Based Growth. 91p. 1980. pap. text ed. 8.95x (ISBN 0-920380-58-1, Pub. by Inst Res Pub Canada). Renouf.
Tsurumi, Yoshi. Japanese Business: A Research Guide with Annotated Bibliography. LC 78-70324. (Praeger Special Studies). 1978. 22.95 (ISBN 0-03-044251-6). Praeger.
--Multinational Management: Business Strategy & Government Policy. 622p. 1976. write for info. (ISBN 0-88410-297-1). Ballinger Pub.
Tsuruta, T., ed. International Congress of Pure & Applied Chemistry, XXVI: Chemistry for the Welfare of Mankind, Vol. 1. (IUPAC Symposia Ser.). 1979. text ed. 115.00 (ISBN 0-08-022007-X). Pergamon.
Tsuzuki, C. Edward Carpenter: Eighteen Forty-Four to Nineteen Twenty Nine. LC 80-40152. 240p. 1980. 34.50 (ISBN 0-521-23371-2). Cambridge U Pr.
Tsuzuku, T. Finite Groups & Finite Geometrics. (Cambridge Tracts in Mathematics Ser.: No. 78). (Illus.). 250p. Date not set. price not set (ISBN 0-521-22242-7). Cambridge U Pr.
Tsvetaeva, Marina. Versty. (Rus.). 1972. pap. 3.50 (ISBN 0-88233-031-4). Ardis Pubs.
Tsvetkov, Alexei, tr. see Nabokov, Vladimir.
Tsytovich, V. N. An Introduction to the Theory of Plasma Turbulence. 142p. 1972. text ed. 30.00 (ISBN 0-08-016587-7). Pergamon.
Tsytovich, V. N., jt. auth. see Kaplan, S. A.
Tu, Anthony T. Venoms: Chemistry & Molecular Biology. LC 76-30751. 1977. 47.50 (ISBN 0-471-89229-7, Pub. by Wiley-Interscience). Wiley.
Tu, Wei-Ming. Neo-Confucian Thought in Action: Wang Yang-Ming's Youth. 1976. 17.50x (ISBN 0-520-02968-2). U of Cal Pr.
Tuala. Tuala Speaks. Tamalelagi, Jeanne, ed. LC 80-67870. 220p. (Orig.). 1980. pap. 8.95 (ISBN 0-87516-425-0). De Vorss.
Tuan, Yi-Fu. The Hydrologic Cycle & the Wisdom of God: A Theme in Geoteleology. 1980. Repr. of 1968 ed. 20.00x (ISBN 0-8020-7112-0). U of Toronto Pr.
--Landscapes of Fear. LC 79-1890. 272p. 1981. pap. 8.95 (ISBN 0-8166-1021-5). U of Minn Pr.
--Space & Place: The Perspective of Experience. (Illus., LC 77-072910). 1977. 8.95x (ISBN 0-8166-0808-3); pap. 6.95 (ISBN 0-8166-0884-9). U of Minn Pr.
Tuan Yi-Fu. Topophilia: A Study of Environmental Perception, Attitudes & Values. (Illus.). 272p. 1974. pap. text ed. 8.95 (ISBN 0-13-925230-4). P-H.
Tuazon, Redentor M. & Schaffer, Edy G. New Comprehensive A-Z Crossword Dictionary. 1974. pap. 3.95 (ISBN 0-380-00168-3, 50492). Avon.
Tubaki, K. Hyphomycetes: Their Perfect-Imperfect Connexions. 300p. 1981. lib. bdg. 20.00x (ISBN 3-7682-1267-X). Lubrecht & Cramer.
Tubb, E. C. Argentis. 112p. 1980. Repr. lib. bdg. 9.95x cancelled (ISBN 0-89370-097-5). Borgo Pr.
--Mayenne. Bd. with Jondelle. (Science Fiction Ser.). 1981. pap. 2.50 (ISBN 0-87997-614-4, UE1614). NAL.
--Prison of Night: Dumarest No. 7. (Science Fiction Ser). (Orig.). 1977. pap. 1.50 o.p. (ISBN 0-87997-346-3, UW1346). DAW Bks.
--World of Promise. 1980. pap. 1.75 (ISBN 0-87997-579-2, UE1579). DAW Bks.
Tubbs, D. B. Zeiss Ikon Cameras: Nineteen Twenty Six-Nineteen Thirty-Nine. 25.00 (ISBN 0-85242-604-6, Pub. by Fountain). Morgan.
Tubbs, D. B., tr. see Schrader, Halwart & Demand, Carlo.
Tubbs, E. C. Nectar of Heaven. 1981. pap. 1.95 (ISBN 0-87997-613-6, UJ1613). DAW Bks.
Tubbs, Stewart L. & Carter, Robert M. Shared Experiences in Human Communication. 1978. pap. text ed. 10.75x (ISBN 0-8104-6089-0). Hayden.
Tubbs, Stewart L. & Moss, Sylvia. Human Communication. 2nd ed. 1977. text ed. 11.95x o.p. (ISBN 0-685-86655-6). Random.
--Interpersonal Communication. 2nd ed. 299p. 1981. pap. text ed. 10.95 (ISBN 0-394-32684-9). Random.
Tubesing, Donald A. Kicking Your Stress Habits: A Do-It-Yourself Guide for Coping with Stress. LC 80-54046. (Orig.). 1981. pap. 10.00 (ISBN 0-938586-00-9). Whole Person.
--Wholistic Health: A Whole Person Approach to Primary Health Care. LC 78-3466. 1978. 19.95 (ISBN 0-87705-370-7). Human Sci Pr.
Tubis, Manuel & Wolf, Walter. Radiopharmacy. LC 75-28385. 911p. 1976. 68.50 (ISBN 0-471-89227-0, Pub. by Wiley-Interscience). Wiley.
Tucci, Giuseppe. Tibet: Land of Snows. 1973. 21.95 (ISBN 0-236-31094-1, Pub. by Paul Elek). Merrimack Bk Serv.
--To Lhasa & Beyond. Carelli, Mario, tr. from Ital. LC 78-56120. (Illus.). 1978. pap. 8.75 o.p. (ISBN 0-87773-703-7, Prajna). Great Eastern.
Tuccille, Jerome. Dynamic Investing: The System for Automatic Profits -- No Matter Which Way the Market Goes. 1981. pap. 9.95 (H398). NAL.

Tucek, S., et al, eds. see International Conference on the Synapse, Czechoslovakia, May, 1978.

Tuch, Barbara & Judy, Harriet. How to Teach Children to Draw, Paint and Use Color. 1975. 13.95 o.p. (ISBN 0-685-73737-3). P-H.

Tuch, R., jt. ed. see Straszak, A.

Tuchman, Barbara. A Distant Mirror. 1980. pap. 8.95 (ISBN 0-345-29542-0). Ballantine.

Tuchman, Barbara W. Guns of August. (Illus.). (gr. 9 up). 1962. 16.95 (ISBN 0-02-620310-3). Macmillan.

--Notes from China. LC 72-93468. 128p. 1972. pap. 2.95 (ISBN 0-02-074800-0, Collier). Macmillan.

--Proud Tower. 1966. 16.95 (ISBN 0-02-620300-6). Macmillan.

--Stilwell & the American Experience in China, 1911-45. LC 77-135647. (Illus.). 1971. 19.95 (ISBN 0-02-620290-5). Macmillan.

--Zimmermann Telegram. 1966. 11.95 (ISBN 0-02-620320-0). Macmillan.

Tuchman, Gaye. Making News: A Study in the Construction of Reality. LC 78-53075. (Illus.). 1980. pap. text ed. 8.95 (ISBN 0-02-932960-4). Free Pr.

Tuchman, Gaye, et al, eds. Hearth & Home: Images of Women in the Mass Media. 1978. text ed. 16.95x (ISBN 0-19-502351-X); pap. text ed. 5.95x (ISBN 0-19-502352-8). Oxford U Pr.

Tuchman, Maurice, jt. ed. see Barron, Stephanie.

Tuchmann-Depleiss, M. Drug Effects on the Fetus. (Illus.). 267p. 1975. text ed. 21.50 (ISBN 0-9599827-4-4). ADIS Pr.

Tuchmann-Duplessis, H., et al. Illustrated Human Embryology, 3 vols. Hurley, L. S., tr. Incl. Vol. 1. Embryogenesis. 1972. pap. 7.10 (ISBN 0-387-90018-7); Vol. 2. Organogenesis. 1972. pap. 11.20 (ISBN 0-387-90019-5); Vol. 3. Nervous System & Endocrine Glands. 1973. pap. 12.40 (ISBN 0-387-90020-9). LC 72-177236. Springer-Verlag.

Tuck, Curt, ed. The Fannie Mae Guide to Buying, Financing & Selling Your Home. rev. ed. LC 78-1017. 1978. pap. 5.95 (ISBN 0-385-14382-6, Dolp). Doubleday.

Tuck, Richard. Natural Rights Theories. LC 78-73819. 1980. 29.95 (ISBN 0-521-22512-4). Cambridge U Pr.

Tuck, William P. Knowing God: Religious Knowledge in the Theology of John Baillie. LC 78-52865. 1978. pap. text ed. 7.75x (ISBN 0-8191-0484-1). U Pr of Amer.

Tucker. Surgery for Phonatory Disorders. 1981. text ed. write for info. (ISBN 0-443-08058-5). Churchill.

Tucker, A. N. Eastern Sudanic Languages, Vol. 1. (African Language & Linguistics Series). (Illus.). 1967. 30.00x (ISBN 0-7129-0203-1). Intl Pubns Serv.

Tucker, Abraham. The Light of Nature Pursued, 7 vols. Wellek, Rene, ed. LC 75-11262. (British Philosophers & Theologians of the 17th & 18th Centuries: Vol. 60). 1977. Repr. of 1805 ed. Set. lib. bdg. 231.00 (ISBN 0-8240-1811-7); lib. bdg. 42.00 ea. Garland Pub.

Tucker, Alan, ed. McKay's Big Book of the Army. (gr. 4 up). 1980. cancelled (ISBN 0-679-20538-1). McKay.

Tucker, Betty. Curlers & Camping. (Illus.). 1971. 1.00 (ISBN 0-910856-42-7). La Siesta.

Tucker, Charles O., jt. auth. see Hess, Herbert J.

Tucker, D. G. & Gazey, B. K. Applied Underwater Acoustics. 1966. 27.00 (ISBN 0-08-011817-8); pap. 15.00 (ISBN 0-08-011816-X). Pergamon.

Tucker, Frank H. The Frontier Spirit & Progress. LC 79-19372. 368p. 1981. text ed. 23.95 (ISBN 0-88229-376-1); pap. text ed. 11.95 (ISBN 0-88229-757-0). Nelson-Hall.

Tucker, Gabe, jt. auth. see Crumbaker, Marge.

Tucker, Gene M., ed. see Lance, H. Darrell.

Tucker, Gina. Science of Housekeeping. 2nd ed. 1973. pap. 10.95 (ISBN 0-8436-0577-4). CBI Pub.

Tucker, Gina & Schneider, Madelin S. The Professional Housekeeper. LC 75-29010. (Illus.). 240p. 1976. 23.95 (ISBN 0-8436-0591-X). CBI Pub.

Tucker, H., ed. see IFIP Workshop on Methodology in Computer Graphics, France, May 1976.

Tucker, Helen. A Reason for Rivalry. (Regency Romance Ser). 1979. pap. 1.75 o.p. (ISBN 0-449-24139-4, Crest). Fawcett.

Tucker, Herbert F. Browning's Beginnings: The Art of Disclosure. 350p. 1980. 22.50x (ISBN 0-8166-0946-2). U of Minn Pr.

Tucker, Howard. Automatic Transmissions Workbook on Service & Repair. LC 80-67593. (Automotive Technology Ser.). (Illus.). 64p. (Orig.). 1981. pap. text ed. 6.00 (ISBN 0-8273-1894-4). Delmar.

Tucker, Howard F. Automatic Transmissions. LC 78-62623. (gr. 7-12). 1980. pap. text ed. 13.20 (ISBN 0-8273-1648-8); instructor's guide 1.25 (ISBN 0-8273-1649-6). Delmar.

Tucker, Howard G. Graduate Course in Probability. (Probability & Mathematical Statistics: Vol. 2). 1967. text ed. 21.95 (ISBN 0-12-702646-0). Acad Pr.

Tucker, I. Adjustment: Models & Mechanisms. 1970. text ed. 18.95 (ISBN 0-12-702850-1). Acad Pr.

Tucker, Irving. Psychology of Adjustment. 489p. 1970. text ed. 18.95 (ISBN 0-12-702850-1). Acad Pr.

Tucker, James. The Novels of Anthony Powell. LC 76-15201. 1976. 15.00x (ISBN 0-231-04150-0). Columbia U Pr.

Tucker, K. A. Concentration & Costs in Retailing. 188p. 1978. 21.95x (ISBN 0-566-00165-9, Pub. by Saxon Hse England). Lexington Bks.

Tucker, Kathleen, ed. see Brown, Fern.

Tucker, Kathleen, ed. see Bunting, Eve.

Tucker, Kathleen, ed. see Goldman, Susan.

Tucker, Kathleen, ed. see Haas, Dorothy.

Tucker, Kathleen, ed. see Heide, Florence P. & Heide, Roxanne.

Tucker, Kathleen, ed. see Knox-Wagner, Elaine.

Tucker, Kathleen, ed. see Lasker, Joe.

Tucker, Kathleen, ed. see Litchfield, Ada B.

Tucker, Kathleen, ed. see Nixon, Joan L.

Tucker, Kathleen, ed. see Quackenbush, Robert.

Tucker, Kathleen, ed. see Raynor, Dorka.

Tucker, Kathleen, ed. see Sharmat, Mitchell.

Tucker, Kathleen, ed. see Simon, Norma.

Tucker, Kathleen, ed. see Stanek, Muriel.

Tucker, Kathleen, ed. see Thompson, Susan L.

Tucker, Kenneth A., ed. Business History: Selected Readings. 442p. 1977. 32.50x (ISBN 0-7146-3030-6, F Cass Co). Biblio Dist.

Tucker, Martin. Joseph Conrad. LC 75-37265. (Modern Literature Ser.). 1980. 10.95 (ISBN 0-8044-2928-6). Ungar.

Tucker, Martin, jt. ed. see Ferres, John H.

Tucker, Maurice E., jt. ed. see Matter, Albert.

Tucker, N. The Child & the Book. 275p. Date not set. 29.95 (ISBN 0-521-23251-1). Cambridge U Pr.

Tucker, N. I., jt. auth. see Shaw, B. L.

Tucker, Nathaniel. The Complete Published Poems of Nathaniel Tucker, Together with Columbinus: A Mask (1783) LC 73-12391. 192p. 1973. lib. bdg. 25.00x (ISBN 0-8201-1121-X). Schol Facsimiles.

Tucker, Nicholas, ed. Mother Goose Abroad: Nursery Rhymes. LC 73-2831. (Illus.). (ps-3). 1975. 7.39 o.p. (ISBN 0-690-00093-6, TYC-J). T Y Crowell.

--Suitable for Children? Controversies in Children's Literature. 1976. 17.50x (ISBN 0-520-03236-5). U of Cal Pr.

Tucker, Raymond, et al. Research in Speech Communication. (Ser. in Speech Communication). (Illus.). 352p. 1981. text ed. 18.95 (ISBN 0-13-774273-8). P-H.

Tucker, Richard N. The Organisation & Management of Educational Technology. (New Patterns of Learning Ser.). 167p. (Orig.). 1979. 26.00x (ISBN 0-85664-941-4, Pub. by Croom Helm Ltd England). Biblio Dist.

Tucker, Robert C. Philosophy & Myth in Karl Marx. 2nd ed. LC 70-180022. 250p. 1972. 32.95 (ISBN 0-521-08455-5); pap. 8.95x (ISBN 0-521-09701-0). Cambridge U Pr.

Tucker, Robert C., ed. Stalinism: Essays in Historical Interpretation. 1977. 19.95 (ISBN 0-393-05608-2, N892, Norton Lib); pap. 7.95 (ISBN 0-393-00892-4). Norton.

Tucker, Spencer A. & Lennon, Thomas H. Production Standards in Profit Planning. 256p. 1981. 19.95 (ISBN 0-444-00456-4, Thomond). Elsevier.

Tucker, Susan M. & Bryant, Sandra. Fetal Monitoring & Fetal Assesment in High Risk Pregnancy. 1978. pap. text ed. 11.95 (ISBN 0-8016-5121-2). Mosby.

Tucker, Susan M., et al. Patient Care Standards. 2nd ed. LC 79-24410. (Illus.). 1980. pap. text ed. 17.95 (ISBN 0-8016-5122-0). Mosby.

Tucker, Susie I. Enthusiasm: A Study of a Word & Its Relatives. LC 79-161296. 1972. 29.50 (ISBN 0-521-08263-3). Cambridge U Pr.

Tucker, Tarvez. Birth Control. 1981. pap. 2.50 (ISBN 0-440-00566-3). Dell.

Tucker, Ted. Practical Projects for the Blacksmith. (Illus.). 1980. 11.95 (ISBN 0-87857-312-7); pap. 7.95 (ISBN 0-87857-294-5). Rodale Pr Inc.

Tucker, Valerie. Women's Soccer Guide. LC 79-64301. (Illus.). 140p. (Orig.). 1981. pap. 4.95 (ISBN 0-89037-221-7). Anderson World.

Tucker, W. E. & Castle, Molly. Sportsmen & Their Injuries: Fitness, First Aid, Treatment, & Rehabilitations. (Illus.). 1978. 12.95 o.p. (ISBN 0-7207-0957-1). Transatlantic.

Tucker, W. Leon. Studies in Revelation. LC 80-16206. (Kregel Bible Study Classics Ser.). 400p. 1980. Repr. of 1935 ed. 10.95 (ISBN 0-8254-3826-8). Kregel.

Tucker, Wayne C. Diver's Handbook of Underwater Calculations. (Illus.). 1980. pap. 10.00x (ISBN 0-87033-254-6, 2546). Cornell Maritime.

Tucker, William R. The Fascist Ego: A Political Biography of Robert Brasillach. 1975. 30.00x (ISBN 0-520-02710-8). U of Cal Pr.

Tucker, Wilson. Ice & Iron. 192p. 1975. pap. 1.50 o.p. (ISBN 0-345-24660-8). Ballantine.

Tuckerman, E. Collected Lichenological Papers, 2 vols. Culberson, W. L., ed. 1964. Vol. 1. 45.00 (ISBN 3-7682-0221-6); Vol. 2. 54.00 (ISBN 3-7682-0222-4); Set. 99.00 (ISBN 3-7682-0220-8). Lubrecht & Cramer.

Tuckerman, Henry T. The Life of John Pendleton Kennedy. 490p. 1980. lib. bdg. 65.00 (ISBN 0-89987-813-X). Darby Bks.

Tuckett, Guin R. Get Out There & Reap. 1976. pap. 1.00 (ISBN 0-8272-1229-1). Bethany Pr.

Tuckett, J. D. A History of the Past & Present State of the Labouring Population, 2 vols. 916p. 1971. Repr. of 1846 ed. 60.00x (ISBN 0-7165-1572-5, Pub. by Irish Academic Pr Ireland). Biblio Dist.

Tuckey, L., et al. Handicapped School Leavers: Their Further Education Training & Employment. 1973. pap. text ed. 4.50x (ISBN 0-85633-017-5, NFER). Humanities.

Tuckman, Bruce W. Evaluating Instructional Programs. new ed. 1979. text ed. 18.95 (ISBN 0-205-06172-9). Allyn.

Tuckman, Howard P. Publication, Teaching, & the Academic Reward Structure. 1976. 16.95x (ISBN 0-669-00650-5). Lexington Bks.

Tuckman, Howard P. & Whalen, Edward L., eds. Subsidies to Higher Education: The Issues. 320p. 1980. 27.95 (ISBN 0-03-055791-7). Praeger.

Tuckwell, James H. Religion & Reality. LC 77-118552. 1971. Repr. of 1915 ed. 13.00 (ISBN 0-8046-1177-7). Kennikat.

Tudeer, L. O. Die Tetradrachmenpragung Von Syrakus, in der Periode der Signierenden Kunstler. (Illus.). 1979. 40.00 (ISBN 0-916710-53-X). Obol Intl.

Tuden, Arthur & Plotnicov, Leonard. Social Stratification in Africa. LC 78-91223. 1970. 17.95 (ISBN 0-02-932780-6). Free Pr.

Tudjman, Franjo. Nationalism in Contemporary Europe. (East European Monographs: No. 76). 352p. 1981. text ed. 21.50x (ISBN 0-914710-70-2). East Eur Quarterly.

Tudor, Dean. Wine, Beer, and Spirits. LC 74-80964. (Spare Time Guides Ser.: No. 6). 200p. 1975. lib. bdg. 11.50x o.p. (ISBN 0-87287-081-2). Libs Unl.

Tudor, Dean & Armitage, Andrew. Popular Music Periodicals Index, 1974. LC 74-11578. 1975. 18.00 (ISBN 0-8108-0867-6). Scarecrow.

Tudor, Dean & Biesenthal, Linda. Annual Index to Popular Music Record Reviews 1977. LC 73-8909. 1979. 25.00 (ISBN 0-8108-1217-7). Scarecrow.

--Popular Music Periodicals Index, 1976. LC 74-11578. 1977. 12.00 (ISBN 0-8108-1079-4). Scarecrow.

Tudor, Dean & Tudor, Nancy. Black Music. LC 78-15563. (American Popular Music on Elpee Ser). 1979. lib. bdg. 22.50x (ISBN 0-87287-147-9). Libs Unl.

--Contemporary Popular Music. LC 78-32124. (American Popular Music on Elpee). 1979. lib. bdg. 22.50x (ISBN 0-87287-191-6). Libs Unl.

--Grass Roots Music. LC 78-31686. (American Popular Music on Elpee). 1979. lib. bdg. 25.00x (ISBN 0-87287-133-9). Libs Unl.

--Jazz. LC 78-11737. (American Popular Music on Elpee). 1979. lib. bdg. 22.50 (ISBN 0-87287-148-7). Libs Unl.

--Popular Music Periodicals Index: 1973. LC 74-11578. 1974. 14.50 (ISBN 0-8108-0763-7). Scarecrow.

Tudor, Dean, jt. auth. see Armitage, Andrew D.

Tudor, Dean & Armitage, Andrew D., eds. Popular Music Periodicals Index, 1975. LC 74-11578. 376p. 1976. 18.00 (ISBN 0-8108-0927-3). Scarecrow.

Tudor, Dean, et al. Annual Index to Popular Music Record Reviews 1976. LC 73-8909. 1977. 25.00 (ISBN 0-8108-1070-0). Scarecrow.

Tudor, Joan. The Golden Retriever: Its Care & Training. (Illus.). 100p. 1980. 3.95 (ISBN 0-903264-33-1, 4945-6, Pub. by K & R Bks England). Arco.

Tudor, Mary J. Child Development. 544p. 1981. text ed. 22.95 (ISBN 0-07-065412-3, HP). McGraw.

Tudor, Nancy, jt. auth. see Tudor, Dean.

Tudor, Tasha. Dolls' Christmas. LC 59-12744. (Illus.). (gr. k-3). 1950. 5.95g (ISBN 0-8098-1026-3); pap. 2.50 (ISBN 0-8098-2912-6). Walck.

--A Time to Keep: The Tasha Tudor Book of Holidays. LC 77-9067. (Illus.). (gr. 4-8). 1977. 6.95 (ISBN 0-528-82019-2); PLB 6.97 o.s.i. Rand.

Tudor, Tasha, ed. & illus. Wings from the Wind: An Anthology of Poetry. LC 64-19059. (gr. k-6). 1964. PLB 7.89 (ISBN 0-397-30789-6). Lippincott.

Tudor, William. Life of James Otis of Massachusetts. LC 70-118203. (Era of the American Revolution Ser). Repr. of 1823 ed. lib. bdg. 49.50 (ISBN 0-306-71936-3). Da Capo.

Tudor-Hart, Beatrice. Toys, Play & Discipline in Childhood. 1972. pap. 8.00 (ISBN 0-7100-6872-7). Routledge & Kegan.

Tuedoes, F., ed. see International Symposium on Macro Molecular Chemistry.

Tuer, Andrew W. Japanese Stencil Designs: One Hundred Outstanding Examples. Orig. Title: Book of Delightful & Strange Designs Being One Hundred Facsimile Illustrations of the Art of the Japanese Stencil-Cutter, Il. pap. 4.00 (ISBN 0-486-21811-2). Dover.

--Old London Street Cries. (Illus.). 137p. 1978. pap. 2.50 (ISBN 0-85967-402-9, Pub. by Scolar Pr England); pkg. of 10 24.95 (ISBN 0-686-28431-3). Biblio Dist.

--One Thousand Quaint Cuts from Books of Other Days. LC 68-31097. 1968. Repr. of 1886 ed. 18.00 (ISBN 0-8103-3494-1). Gale.

--Pages & Pictures from Forgotten Children's Books. LC 68-31096. (Illus.). 1969. Repr. of 1899 ed. 18.00 (ISBN 0-8103-3488-7). Gale.

--Stories from Old-Fashioned Children's Books, Brought Together & Introduced to the Reader. LC 68-31438. 1968. Repr. of 1899 ed. 18.00 (ISBN 0-8103-3489-5). Gale.

Tuerck, David G., jt. auth. see Yeager, Leland B.

Tuerck, David G., ed. The Political Economy of Advertising. 1978. 13.25 (ISBN 0-8447-2120-4); pap. 4.75 (ISBN 0-685-25906-4). Am Enterprise.

Tufte, Edward R. Data Analysis for Politics & Policy. (Illus.). 192p. 1974. pap. text ed. 7.95 (ISBN 0-13-197525-0). P-H.

Tufte, Edward R., ed. The Quantitative Analysis of Social Problems. (Probability & Statistics Ser). 1970. text ed. 13.95 (ISBN 0-201-07610-1). A-W.

Tufte, Virginia & Myerhoff, Barbara. Changing Images of the Family: Multidisciplinary Perspectives. LC 79-537. (Illus.). 413p. 1981. pap. 6.95 (ISBN 0-300-02671-4). Yale U Pr.

Tufte, Virginia & Myerhoff, Barbara, eds. Changing Images of the Family. LC 79-537. 1979. 25.00 (ISBN 0-300-02361-8). Yale U Pr.

Tugal, Dogan & Tugal, Osman. Data Transmission: Analysis; Design; Applications. (Illus.). 384p. 1982. 19.50 (ISBN 0-07-065427-1). McGraw.

Tugal, Osman, jt. auth. see Tugal, Dogan.

Tugarinov, A. I., ed. Recent Contributions to Geochemistry & Analytical Chemistry. Slutzkin, D., tr. from Rus. LC 74-8165. 694p. 1976. 79.95 (ISBN 0-470-89228-5). Halsted Pr.

Tuggle, Diane. Spencer's Toothbrush. LC 80-54611. (Illus.). 72p. (Orig.). (gr. k-6). 1981. text ed. 9.95 (ISBN 0-932238-09-2); pap. text ed. 6.95 (ISBN 0-932238-08-4). Word Shop.

Tuggle, Francis D. How to Program a Computer (Using Fortran IV) LC 74-31654. (Computer Science Ser.). 1975. pap. text ed. 10.95 o.p. (ISBN 0-88244-082-9). Grid Pub.

--Organizational Processes. Mackenzie, Kenneth D., ed. LC 77-86001. (Organizational Behavior Ser.). (Illus.). 1978. pap. text ed. 9.95x (ISBN 0-88295-455-5). AHM Pub.

Tuggle, Sharon. Assembler Language Programming: Systems-360 & 370. LC 74-84276. 400p. 1975. pap. text ed. 15.95 (ISBN 0-574-19160-7, 13-4015); instr's guide avail. (ISBN 0-574-19161-5, 13-4016). SRA.

Tugwell, Rexford G. Roosevelt's Revolution: The First Year-a Personal Perspective. 1977. 14.95 o.s.i. (ISBN 0-02-620370-7, 62037). Macmillan.

Tugwell, Rexford G., ed. see Patten, Simon.

Tuiteleleapaga, Napoleone A. Samoa: Yesterday, Today & Tommorow. 160p. 1980. 9.95 (ISBN 0-89962-018-3). Todd & Honeywell.

Tuke, Diana. Getting Your Horse Fit. (Illus.). pap. 5.10 (ISBN 0-85131-255-1, Dist. by Sporting Book Center). J A Allen.

--The Rider's Handbook. (Illus.). pap. 4.55 (ISBN 0-85131-258-6). J A Allen.

Tuke, Diana R. Bit by Bit. (Illus.). 13.85 (ISBN 0-85131-033-8). J A Allen.

--Horse by Horse. (Illus.). 19.25 (ISBN 0-85131-203-9, Dist. by Sporting Book Center); pap. 12.25 (ISBN 0-685-85287-3). J A Allen.

Tuke, Diane R. Feeding Your Horse. (Illus.). 104p. (Orig.). 1980. pap. 13.10 (ISBN 0-85131-334-5). J A Allen.

Tuke, Samuel, ed. Epistles of George Fox. LC 78-24657. 1979. pap. 2.95 (ISBN 0-913408-46-8). Friends United.

Tukey, Harold B. Dwarfed Fruit Trees. LC 77-12289. (Illus.). 576p. 1978. 32.50x (ISBN 0-8014-1126-2). Comstock.

Tukey, J. W., et al. Robust Estimates of Location: Survey & Advances. LC 72-39019. 376p. 1972. 12.50 o.p. (ISBN 0-691-08113-1); pap. 8.50x (ISBN 0-691-08116-6). Princeton U Pr.

Tulane University, New Orleans. Catalog of the Latin American Library of the Tulane University Library: Third Supplement, 2 vols. 1978. Set. lib. bdg. 260.00 (ISBN 0-8161-0005-5). G K Hall.

Tulcea, C. I. A Book on Casino Craps, Other Dice Games & Gambling Systems. 160p. 1980. 12.95 (ISBN 0-442-26713-4); pap. 8.95 (ISBN 0-442-25725-2). Van Nos Reinhold.

Tulchin, Joseph S., ed. Latin America in the Year Two-Thousand. LC 74-19702. 408p. 1975. text ed. 14.95 (ISBN 0-201-07603-9). A-W.

Tulchin, Joseph S., ed. see Hughes, Charles E.

Tulchinsky, Dan & Ryan, Kenneth J. Maternal-Fetal Endocrinology. LC 79-66046. (Illus.). 418p. 1980. text ed. 42.00 (ISBN 0-7216-8911-6). Saunders.

Tuleja, Tad, jt. auth. see Samtur, Susan J.

Tulisen. Narrative of the Chinese Embassy to the Khan of the Tourgouth Tartars, 1712-1715. Staunton, George L., tr. from Chinese. (Studies in Chinese History & Civilization). 330p. Date not set. Repr. of 1821 ed. 24.00 (ISBN 0-89093-073-2). U Pubns Amer.

Tulku, Tarthang. Gesture of Balance: A Guide to Awareness, Self-Healing & Meditation. LC 75-5255. (Illus.). 1976. 12.95 (ISBN 0-913546-17-8); pap. 6.50 (ISBN 0-913546-16-X). Dharma Pub.

--Reflections of Mind: Western Psychology Meets Tibetan Buddhism. LC 75-5254. (Illus.). 1975. 12.95 (ISBN 0-913546-15-1); pap. 5.95 o.p. (ISBN 0-913546-14-3). Dharma Pub.

Tulku, Tarthang, ed. Annals of the Nyingma Lineage, Vol. 11. (Illus.). 1977. pap. 15.00 (ISBN 0-913546-32-1). Dharma Pub.

Tull, James F. Geology & Structure of Vestvagoey, Lofoten, North Norway. (Geological Survey of Norway Ser: No. 333, Bulletin 42). 1978. pap. 12.00x (ISBN 82-00-31367-0, Dist. by Columbia U Pr). Universitet.

Tulleners, Tonny. Beginning Karate. Corcoran, John, ed. LC 74-78904. (Ser. 206s). (Illus.). 1974. pap. text ed. 6.95 (ISBN 0-89750-027-X). Ohara Pubns.

Tuller, Martin A. Acid-Base Homeostasis & Its Disorders. 98p. 1971. spiral bdg. 6.00 (ISBN 0-87488-601-5). Med Exam.

Tullio, Benigno Di see Di Tullio, Benigno.

Tullis, F. LaMond. Modernization in Brazil: Story of Political Dueling Among Politicians, Charismatic Leaders & Military Guardians. (Charles E. Merrill Monograph Series in the Humanities & Social Sciences: Vol. 3, No. 1). 1973. pap. 2.00 o.p. (ISBN 0-8425-0630-6). Brigham.

Tullis, James L. Clot. (Illus.). 592p. 1976. 54.50 (ISBN 0-398-03298-X). C C Thomas.

Tullius, John, jt. auth. see Burwash, Peter.

Tulloch, Alexander, tr. see Gogol, Nikolai.

Tulloch, Graham. The Language of Walter Scott. (Andre Deutsch Language Library). 384p. 1980. lib. bdg. 35.00x (ISBN 0-86531-061-0, Pub. by Andre Deutsch). Westview.

Tulloch, J. G., tr. A Home Is Not a Home: Life Within a Nursing Home. LC 75-28220. 142p. 1975. 6.95 (ISBN 0-8164-9269-7). Continuum.

Tulloch, P., jt. auth. see Morton, K.

Tulloch, Rodney W., jt. auth. see Binkley, Harold R.

Tullock, Gordon. Trials on Trial: The Pure Theory of Legal Procedure. LC 80-13113. 264p. 1980. 20.00x (ISBN 0-231-04952-8). Columbia U Pr.

Tullock, Gordon, jt. auth. see Buchanan, James M.

Tullock, Gordon, jt. auth. see McKenzie, Richard B.

Tullock, Gordon & Wagner, Richard, eds. Policy Analysis & Deductive Reasoning. LC 77-18380. (Policy Studies Organization Ser.). 1978. 19.95 (ISBN 0-669-02080-X). Lexington Bks.

Tulloh, Bruce see Milne, John.

Tulloss, Rod. December Nineteen Seventy-Five. (Xtras Ser.: No. 7). 20p. (Orig.). 1978. pap. 1.50 (ISBN 0-89120-037-1). From Here.

Tully, Alice, jt. auth. see Tully, Marianne.

Tully, Andrew. Inside the F.B.I. LC 80-14092. 240p. 1980. 12.95 (ISBN 0-07-065425-5, GB). McGraw.

Tully, Gordon F. Solar Heating Systems: Analysis & Design with the Sun-Pulse Method. (Energy Learning Systems Bks.). (Illus.). 232p. 1981. 23.95 (ISBN 0-07-065441-7). McGraw.

Tully, J. R., jt. auth. see Bollinger, L. L.

Tully, Marianne. Dread Diseases. (First Bks). (Illus.). (gr. 4-6). 1978. PLB 6.45 s&l (ISBN 0-531-01406-1). Watts.

Tully, Marianne & Tully, Alice. Heart Disease. (gr. 4 up). 1980. PLB 6.45 (ISBN 0-531-04163-8). Watts.

Tully, Marianne & Tully, Mary A. Facts About the Human Body. (First Bks.). (Illus.). (gr. 4-6). 1977. PLB 6.45 s&l (ISBN 0-531-00395-7). Watts.

Tully, Mary A., jt. auth. see Tully, Marianne.

Tully, Mary J. A Family Book of Praise: Or Would You Rather Be a Hippopotamus? (Illus.). 128p. (Orig.). 1980. 7.95 (ISBN 0-8215-6543-5); pap. 5.95 (ISBN 0-8215-6542-7). Sadlier.

Tully, Mary Jo & Hirstein, Sandra J. Focus on Believing. (Light of Faith Ser.). (Orig.). (gr. 3 up). 1981. pap. text ed. 3.00 (ISBN 0-697-01767-2); tchr's ed. 7.60 (ISBN 0-697-01768-0). Wm C Brown.

--Focus on Belonging. (Light of Faith Ser.). (Orig.). (gr. 2 up). 1981. pap. text ed. 2.65 (ISBN 0-697-01765-6); tchrs' ed. 7.60 (ISBN 0-697-01766-4). Wm C Brown.

--Focus on Celebrating. (Light of Faith Ser.). (Orig.). (gr. 5 up). 1981. pap. text ed. 3.00 (ISBN 0-697-01771-0); tchrs' ed. 7.60. Wm C Brown.

--Focus on Living. (Light of Faith Ser.). (Orig.). (gr. 4 up). 1981. pap. text ed. 3.00 (ISBN 0-697-01769-9); tchrs' ed. 7.60 (ISBN 0-697-01770-2). Wm C Brown.

--Focus on Loving. (Light of Faith Ser.). (Orig.). (gr. 1). 1981. pap. text ed. 2.65 (ISBN 0-697-01763-X); tchrs' ed. 7.60 (ISBN 0-697-01763-X). Wm C Brown.

--Focus on Relating. (Light of Faith Ser.). (Orig.). (gr. 6). 1981. pap. text ed. 3.00 (ISBN 0-697-01773-7); tchrs' ed. 7.60 (ISBN 0-697-01774-5). Wm C Brown.

Tully, R. I., jt. auth. see Thorton, J. L.

Tuma, Elias H. Twenty-Six Centuries of Agrarian Reform: A Comparative Analysis. (Near Eastern Center, UCLA). 1965. 20.00x (ISBN 0-520-01286-0). U of Cal Pr.

Tuma, Elias H., ed. Food & Population in the Middle East. LC 76-57917. 83p. 1976. pap. 5.00 (ISBN 0-934484-08-2). Inst Mid East & North Africa.

Tuma, George W. The Fourteenth Century English Mystics, Vol. 2. (Salzburg Studies in English Literature; Elizabethan & Renaissance Studies: No.62). 1977. pap. text ed. 25.00x (ISBN 0-391-01548-6). Humanities.

Tuma, J. & Abdel-Hady, M. Engineering Soil Mechanics. 1973. ref. ed. 24.95x (ISBN 0-13-279505-1). P-H.

Tuma, Jan J. & Reddy, M. N. Schaum's Outline of Space Structural Analysis. (Illus.). 272p. 1981. pap. 8.95 (ISBN 0-07-065432-8). McGraw.

Tumin, Melvin M. & Feldman, Arnold S. Social Class & Social Change in Puerto Rico. LC 70-145756. 1971. 28.50x (ISBN 0-672-61375-1); pap. text ed. 14.95x (ISBN 0-89197-939-5). Irvington.

Tumin, Melvin M. & Plotch, Walter, eds. Pluralism in a Democratic Society. LC 76-12877. 1977. text ed. 22.95 (ISBN 0-275-23310-3). Praeger.

Tumulty, Philip A. The Effective Clinician: His Methods & Approach to Diagnosis & Care. LC 73-77942. 379p. 1973. text ed. 15.00 (ISBN 0-7216-8915-9). Saunders.

Tunberg, Karl & Tunberg, Terence. Master of Rosewood. (Orig.). 1980. pap. 2.50 (ISBN 0-446-91134-8). Warner Bks.

Tunberg, Terence, jt. auth. see Tunberg, Karl.

Tung, Julia, compiled by. Bibliography of Chinese Government Serials: 1880-1949. LC 79-2456. 136p. (Orig.). 1979. pap. 5.00 (ISBN 0-8179-4242-4). Hoover Inst Pr.

Tung, Robert, ed. Proscribed Chinese Writing. 2nd ed. (Scandinavian Institute of Asian Studies Monographs: No. 21). (Illus.). 1979. pap. text ed. 13.00x (ISBN 0-7007-0090-0). Humanities.

Tung Yen Lin & Stotesbury, Sidney D. Structural Concepts & Systems for Architects & Engineers. 1981. text ed. 23.95 (ISBN 0-471-05186-1). Wiley.

Tunis, Edwin. Chipmunks on the Doorstep. LC 73-13205. (Illus.). (gr. 5-8). 1971. 7.95 o.p. (ISBN 0-690-19044-1, TYC-J); PLB 7.89 (ISBN 0-690-19045-X). T Y Crowell.

--Colonial Living. LC 75-29611. (Illus.). 160p. (gr. 7 up). 1976. 12.95 (ISBN 0-690-01063-X, TYC-J). T Y Crowell.

--Frontier Living. LC 75-29639. (Illus.). 168p. (gr. 7 up). 1976. 12.95 (ISBN 0-690-01064-8, TYC-J). T Y Crowell.

--Oars, Sails & Steam: A Picture Book of Ships. LC 76-25453. (Illus.). (gr. 6 up). 1977. 12.95 (ISBN 0-690-01284-5, TYC-J). T Y Crowell.

--Shaw's Fortune: The Picture Story of a Colonial Plantation. LC 75-29640. (Illus.). 64p. (gr. 2-6). 1976. 12.95 (ISBN 0-690-01066-4, TYC-J). T Y Crowell.

--Weapons: A Pictorial History. LC 76-29699. (Illus.). (gr. 6 up). 1977. 14.95 (ISBN 0-690-01340-X, TYC-J). T Y Crowell.

--Wheels: A Pictorial History. LC 76-25809. (Illus.). (gr. 6 up). 1977. 12.95 (ISBN 0-690-01341-8, TYC-J). T Y Crowell.

--The Young United States 1783 to 1830. LC 75-29613. (Illus.). 160p. (gr. 7 up). 1976. 12.95 (ISBN 0-690-01065-6, TYC-J). T Y Crowell.

Tunis, John R. City for Lincoln. LC 45-35202. (gr. 7 up). 4.95 o.p. (ISBN 0-15-218579-8, HJ). HarBraceJ.

--Go, Team, Go. (gr. 7 up). 1954. 7.75 (ISBN 0-688-21349-9). Morrow.

--Silence Over Dunkerque. (Illus.). (gr. 7 up). 1962. PLB 8.40 (ISBN 0-688-31760-X). Morrow.

Tunis, Roslyn, ed. Charles Eldred: Sculpture & Drawing. LC 80-80820. (Illus.). 1980. 10.00 (ISBN 0-89062-078-4, Pub. by Roberson Ctr). Pub Ctr Cult Res.

Tunley, David see Callaway, Frank.

Tunley, M. Library Structures & Staffing Systems. Wilson, A., ed. (Management Pamphlet Ser.). 1979. pap. 8.95x (ISBN 0-85365-771-8, Pub. by Lib Assn England). Oryx Pr.

Tun Li-Ch'En. Annual Customs & Festivals in Peking. Bodde, Derk, tr. from Chinese. (Illus.). 175p. 1981. 10.00 (ISBN 0-85656-029-4). Great Eastern.

Tunnard, Christopher & Pushkarev, Boris. Man-Made America: Chaos or Control. Bell, Harriet, ed. 1981. 12.95 (ISBN 0-517-54379-6, Harmony). Crown.

Tunney, Christopher. Aircraft. LC 79-64384. (Question & Answer Books). (Illus.). 36p. (gr. 3-6). 1980. PLB 5.95g (ISBN 0-8225-1176-2). Lerner Pubns.

--Aircraft Aerobatics. LC 79-64384. (Question & Answer Books). (Illus.). (gr. 3-6). 1980. PLB 5.95g o.p. (ISBN 0-8225-1176-2). Lerner Pubns.

--Biographical Dictionary of World War Two. LC 72-90763. 216p. 1973. 8.95 o.p. (ISBN 0-685-31230-5). St Martin.

Tunstall, Jeremy. The Media Are American. 1979. pap. 8.00x (ISBN 0-231-04293-0). Columbia U Pr.

--The Media Are American. LC 77-2581. 1977. 17.50x (ISBN 0-231-04292-2). Columbia U Pr.

Tunstall, Jeremy & Walker, David. Media Made in California: Hollywood, Politics, & the News. (Illus.). 224p. 1981. 15.95 (ISBN 0-19-502922-4). Oxford U Pr.

Tunyogi, Andrew C. Divine Struggle for Human Salvation: Biblical Convictions in Their Historical Settings. LC 78-65852. 1979. pap. text ed. 15.50 (ISBN 0-8191-0676-3). U Pr of Amer.

Tunzelman, G. N. Von see Von Tunzelman, G. N.

Tuohy, Frank. W. B. Yeats. (Illus.). 1976. 17.95 o.s.i. (ISBN 0-02-620450-9). Macmillan.

Tuohy, James, jt. auth. see McComas, Tom.

Tuomey, Michael & Holmes, Francis S. Pleiocene Fossils of South Carolina. (Illus.). 1974. Repr. of 1857 ed. 9.00 (ISBN 0-87710-365-8). Paleo Res.

Tuomikowski, A., jt. auth. see Riikon, E.

Tuplin, W. A. The Steam Locomotive. 1980. text ed. 20.75 (ISBN 0-239-00198-2). Humanities.

Tupper, E. C., jt. auth. see Rawson, K. J.

Tupper, Frederick. Types of Society in Medieval Literature. LC 67-29555. 1968. Repr. of 1926 ed. 7.00x (ISBN 0-8196-0212-4). Biblo.

Turanszky, Ilona. Azerbaijan: Mosques, Turrets, Palaces. Boros, Laszlo, tr. (Illus.). 184p. 1979. 22.50x (ISBN 963-13-0321-7). Intl Pubns Serv.

Turban, Efraim & Meredith, Jack. Fundamentals of Management Science. 1977. 19.95x (ISBN 0-256-01812-X). Business Pubns.

Turban, Efraim & Loomba, N. Paul, eds. Readings in Management Science. 1976. pap. 10.95x (ISBN 0-256-01705-0). Business Pubns.

Turban, Ephraim, et al. Cost Containment in Hospitals. LC 80-13272. 648p. 1980. text ed. 39.75 (ISBN 0-89443-279-6). Aspen Systems.

Turbayne, Colin M., ed. see Berkeley, George.

Turbayne, Colin M., tr. see Berkeley, George.

Turber, Walter A. & Kilburn, Robert E. The Earth's Surface. (Exploring Earth Science Program Ser.). (gr. 7-12). 1976. pap. text ed. 5.12 (ISBN 0-205-04742-4, 6947425). Allyn.

Turber, Walter A., et al. The Atmosphere. (Exploring Earth Science Program Ser.). (gr. 7-12). 1976. pap. text ed. 4.96 (ISBN 0-205-04744-0, 6947441). Allyn.

Turchaninov, S. P. The Life of Hydrotransport Pipelines. rev. ed. Cooley, W. C., ed. Peabody, Albert L., tr. from Rus. LC 79-66406. Orig. Title: Dolgovechnost' Gidrotransportnykh Truboprovodov. (Illus.). 50.00x o.p. (ISBN 0-918990-04-1). Terraspace.

Turchi, Peter J., ed. Megagauss Physics & Technology. 678p. 1980. 69.50 (ISBN 0-306-40461-3, Plenum Pr). Plenum Pub.

Turchin, Valentin. The Inertia of Fear. Daniels, Guy, tr. from Russian. LC 80-36818. 336p. 1981. 16.95 (ISBN 0-231-04622-7). Columbia U Pr.

Turchin, Valentin F. The Phenomenon of Science. Frentz, Brand, tr. from Russian. LC 77-4330. 1977. 20.00x (ISBN 0-231-03983-2). Columbia U Pr.

Turco, Lewis. A Cage of Creatures. (Illus.). 1979. pap. 2.50 (ISBN 0-686-52326-1); pap. 4.50 signed (ISBN 0-918092-08-6). Tamarack Edns.

--The Complete Melancholick. 1981. price not set (ISBN 0-931460-12-3); pap. price not set (ISBN 0-931460-15-8). Bieler.

Turco, Vincent J. Club Foot. (Illus.). 1981. text ed. price not set (ISBN 0-443-08033-X). Churchill.

Turcotte, L., tr. see Kierkegaard, Soren.

Ture, Norman B. Corporate Profits in Company Financial Reports, Tax Returns & the National Income & Product Accounts. LC 77-95350. 1978. 1.50 (ISBN 0-685-91791-6). Finan Exec.

Turekian, Karl K. Oceans. 2nd ed. (Illus.). 160p. 1976. pap. 6.95 (ISBN 0-13-630418-4); 11.95 (ISBN 0-13-630426-5). P-H.

Turen, Jerry, jt. auth. see LaRocca, Joseph.

Turetzky, Bertram. The Contemporary Contrabass. (The New Instrumentation Ser: Vol. 1). (Illus., Orig.). 1974. pap. 12.95x (ISBN 0-520-02291-2). U of Cal Pr.

Turgenev, Ivan. Fathers & Sons. Matlaw, Ralph E., ed. (Critical Editions). (Annotated). (gr. 9-12). 1966. pap. text ed. 5.95x (ISBN 0-393-09652-1, 9652, NortonC). Norton.

--Fathers & Sons. (Literature Ser). (gr. 10-12). 1970. pap. text ed. 3.42 (ISBN 0-87720-724-0). AMSCO Sch.

--Fathers & Sons. Edmonds, Rosemary, tr. (Classics Ser). 1965. pap. 2.95 (ISBN 0-14-044147-6). Penguin.

--First Love & Other Tales. Magarshack, David, tr. Orig. Title: Selected Tales of Ivan Turgenev. 1968. pap. 4.95 (ISBN 0-393-00444-9, Norton Lib). Norton.

Turgeon, A. J. & Giles, Floyd. Turfgrass Management. (Illus.). 1980. text ed. 16.95 (ISBN 0-8359-7885-0); instrs' manual avail. Reston.

Turgeon, Charles, jt. auth. see Turgeon, Charlotte.

Turgeon, Charlotte. Of Cabbages & Kings Cookbook. LC 77-85390. (Illus.). 1977. 8.95 (ISBN 0-89387-014-5). Sat Eve Post.

--The Saturday Evening Post Small-Batch Canning & Freezing Cookbook. LC 78-53040. (Illus.). 1978. 8.95 (ISBN 0-89387-020-X); pap. 4.95 (ISBN 0-89387-020-X). Sat Eve Post.

Turgeon, Charlotte & Birmingham, Frederic A. The Saturday Evening Post: All American Cookbook. LC 75-32275. (Illus.). 320p. 1976. 9.95 o.p. (ISBN 0-8407-4054-9). Nelson.

Turgeon, Charlotte & Turgeon, Charles. The Saturday Evening Post Time to Entertain Cookbook. LC 78-73386. 1978. 9.95 (ISBN 0-89387-025-0). Sat Eve Post.

Turgeon, Lynn. The Advanced Capitalist System: A Revisionist View. LC 80-51202. 192p. 1980. 15.00 (ISBN 0-87332-171-5); pap. 7.95 (ISBN 0-87332-172-3). M E Sharpe.

Turi, Johan O. Turi's Book of Lappland. (Illus.). 1966. pap. text ed. 8.75x (ISBN 0-391-02064-1). Humanities.

Turk, Frederick J., jt. auth. see Nelson, Charles A.

Turk, Gayle. Trial & Triumph. (Illus.). 60p. (Orig.). 1978. pap. 2.50 (ISBN 0-936564-11-3). Little London.

Turk, Jerry, jt. auth. see Mueller, Ralph.

Turk, Laurel H. & Espinosa, Aurelio M. Foundation Course in Spanish. 5th ed. (Illus.). 439p. 1981. text ed. 16.95 (ISBN 0-669-02637-9); wkbk. 5.95 (ISBN 0-669-02638-7); answer keys with tests avail. (ISBN 0-669-02639-5); tapescript avail. (ISBN 0-669-02640-9); reels set of 15 75.00 (ISBN 0-669-02641-7); cassettes set of 15 75.00 (ISBN 0-669-02643-3); demo tape avail. (ISBN 0-669-02644-1). Heath.

Turk, Laurel H., et al. Foundation Course in Spanish. 4th ed. 1978. text ed. 16.95x o.p. (ISBN 0-669-00491-X); inst. manual free o.p. (ISBN 0-669-00492-8); wkbk. 5.95 o.p. (ISBN 0-669-00493-6); indiv. prog. 4.95x o.p. (ISBN 0-669-00993-8); reels 85.00 o.p. (ISBN 0-669-00495-2); cassettes 85.00 o.p. (ISBN 0-669-00494-4). Heath.

Turk, Peter B., jt. auth. see Jugenheimer, Donald W.

Turk, Ruth. More Than Friends. 256p. (Orig.). 1980. pap. 2.50 (ISBN 0-553-13661-5). Bantam.

Turk, Vito, et al, eds. Intracellular Protein Catabolism, III. LC 77-72034. 368p. 1977. 35.00 (ISBN 0-306-31037-6, Plenum Pr). Plenum Pub.

Turkel, Judi K. & Peterson, Franklynn. Good Writing. (New Viewpoints Vision Bks.). 320p. Date not set. 9.95 (ISBN 0-531-06376-3). Watts.

Turleau, Catherine, jt. auth. see De Grouchy, Jean.

Turley, Katherine, tr. see Corbasson, Nadine & De Bruchard, Gisele.

Turn, Rein. Computers in the Nineteen Eighties. 224p. 1974. 17.50x (ISBN 0-231-03844-5); pap. 5.00x (ISBN 0-231-03845-3). Columbia U Pr.

Turn, Rein & Roth, Alexander D., eds. Supporting Documents: Transborder Data Flows: Concerns in Privacy Protection & Free Flow of Information, Vol. II. 300p. 1979. pap. 25.00 (ISBN 0-88283-024-4). AFIPS Pr.

Turn, Rein, ed. see Report of the AFIPS Panel on Transborder Data Flow.

Turnage. The Principal: Change-Agent in Desegregation. LC 72-87658. pap. 2.75 (ISBN 0-912008-07-5). Integrated Ed Assoc.

Turnage, Anne S., jt. auth. see Turnage, Mac N.

Turnage, Mac N. & Turnage, Anne S. People, Families, & God. 1976. pap. 3.95 (ISBN 0-8042-8077-0). John Knox.

Turnage, Thomas W., jt. auth. see Horton, David L.

Turnbull. Development & Implement Individualized Education Program. 1978. 12.95 (ISBN 0-675-08318-4). Merrill.

Turnbull, A. B. Government Budgeting & PPBS: A Programmed Introduction. 1970. pap. 12.95 (ISBN 0-201-07615-2). A-W.

Turnbull, Agnes S. The Richlands. 240p. 1976. pap. 1.50 o.p. (ISBN 0-449-22844-4, Q2844, Crest). Fawcett.

--Rolling Years. 1953. 12.95 (ISBN 0-02-620730-3). Macmillan.

--The Two Bishops. 1980. lib. bdg. 14.95 (ISBN 0-8161-3173-2, Large Print Bks). G K Hall.

Turnbull, Andrew. Scott Fitzgerald. LC 62-9315. 1975. 4.95 o.p. (ISBN 0-684-14661-4, ScribT). Scribner.

Turnbull, Ann. The Frightened Forest. LC 74-19358. (gr. 3-6). 1975. 7.95 (ISBN 0-395-28884-3, Clarion). HM.

--The Wolf King. LC 75-25513. (gr. 4-8). 1976. 5.95 (ISBN 0-395-28927-0, Clarion). HM.

Turnbull, Ann & Turnbull, H. R. Parents Speak Out: Views from the Other Side of the Two-Way Mirror. 1978. pap. 7.50 (ISBN 0-675-08385-0). Merrill.

Turnbull, Ann P. & Schulz, Jane B. Mainstreaming Handicapped Students: A Guide for the Classroom Teacher. 1979. text ed. 18.95 (ISBN 0-205-06107-9). Allyn.

Turnbull, Colin M. Man in Africa. LC 75-32015. 280p. 1977. pap. 2.95 o.p. (ISBN 0-385-05674-5, Anch). Doubleday.

--Mountain People. 1972. 8.95 (ISBN 0-671-21320-2); pap. 3.95 (ISBN 0-686-68504-0). S&S.

--Wayward Servants: The Two Worlds of the African Pygmies. LC 75-5002. (Illus.). 1976. Repr. of 1965 ed. lib. bdg. 37.00x (ISBN 0-8371-7927-0, TUWS). Greenwood.

Turnbull, H. R., jt. auth. see Turnbull, Ann.

Turnbull, H. W., ed. see Newton, Isaac.

Turnbull, Herbert Westren. The Great Mathematicians. LC 61-16934. (Illus.). 1961. usa 8.00x (ISBN 0-8147-0419-0). NYU Pr.

Turnbull, J. G., et al. Economic & Social Security. 4th ed. 728p. 1973. 21.95 (ISBN 0-471-06643-5). Wiley.

Turnbull, John G., et al. Economic & Social Security. 4th ed. LC 68-5498. 700p. 1973. 21.95x (ISBN 0-8260-8766-3). Ronald Pr.

Turnbull, Laura S. Woodrow Wilson: A Selected Bibliography. LC 70-159106. 1971. Repr. of 1948 ed. 11.50 (ISBN 0-8046-1650-7). Kennikat.

Turnbull, Patrick. Corsica. 1976. 24.00 (ISBN 0-7134-3134-2). David & Charles.

--Discovering Provence. 1973. 24.00 (ISBN 0-7134-2860-0, Pub. by Batsford England). David & Charles.

--Dordogne. (Illus.). 155p. 1980. 24.00 (ISBN 0-7134-1335-2, Pub. by Batsford England). David & Charles.

Turnbull, Stephen. The Samurai -- a Military History. LC 76-50595. 1977. 22.95 (ISBN 0-02-620540-8, 62054). Macmillan.

Turndorf, Herman & Chalon, Jack. Circulatory Control & Management, Vol. I. (Current Problems in Anesthesiology Ser.). (Illus.). 300p. 1980. lib. bdg. cancelled (ISBN 0-683-08473-9). Williams & Wilkins.

Turndorf, Herman, jt. auth. see Cottrell, James E.

Turner. Life Time Encyclopedia of Real Estate Classified Advertising. 1977. 24.95 o.p. (ISBN 0-13-536458-2). P-H.

Turner & McCreery. Chemistry of Fire & Hazardous Materials. 1980. text ed. 16.95 (ISBN 0-205-06912-6, 826912-2). Allyn.

Turner & Rogers. The Benedictines in Britain. Date not set. 12.95 (ISBN 0-8076-0992-7). Braziller.

Turner, A. Mason & Sears, Curtis T. Inquiries in Chemistry. (gr. 9-12). 1974. text ed. 15.36 (ISBN 0-205-03373-3, 683373X); tchrs'. guide 7.56 (ISBN 0-205-03374-1, 6833748); lab ex. 6.20 (ISBN 0-205-03375-X, 683375X); tests & dup. masters 40.00 (ISBN 0-205-05401-3, 685401X). Allyn.

Turner, A. N. & Lombard, G. F. Interpersonal Behavior and Administration. LC 69-11486. 1969. text ed. 16.95 (ISBN 0-02-932760-1). Free Pr.

Turner, Alberta, ed. Fifty Contemporary Poets: The Creative Process. LC 76-56750. 1977. text ed. 15.95x (ISBN 0-582-28024-9, Pub by McKay); pap. 9.95x (ISBN 0-582-28025-7). Longman.

--Poets Teaching: The Creative Process. (English & Humanities Ser.). 1980. pap. 9.95 (ISBN 0-582-28105-9). Longman.

Turner, Alford E., ed. The Earps Talk. LC 80-65456. (Illus.). 193p. 1979. 15.50 (ISBN 0-932702-05-8); collector's edition 75.00 (ISBN 0-932702-06-6). Creative Texas.

Turner, Alice K. Yoga for Beginners. LC 73-5712. (Career Concise Guides Ser.). (gr. 5 up). 1973. PLB 4.90 o.p. (ISBN 0-531-02643-4). Watts.

Turner, Alta R. Finger Weaving: Indian Braiding. (Little Craft Book Ser.). (Illus.). 48p. (gr. 3 up). 1973. 4.95 o.p. (ISBN 0-8069-5264-4); PLB 5.89 o.p. (ISBN 0-8069-5265-2). Sterling.

Turner, Amedee. The Law of the New European Patent. 1979. lib. bdg. 50.00 (ISBN 0-8240-7126-3). Garland Pub.

Turner, Anthony & Brown, Christopher. Burgundy. 1977. 24.00 (ISBN 0-7134-0889-8). David & Charles.

Turner, Arlin. Miss Ravenel's Conversion from Secession to Loyalty: (Standard Ed.) LC 75-100633. 1969. pap. text ed. 2.95x (ISBN 0-675-09390-2). Merrill.

Turner, B. C. A. Better Winemaking & Brewing for Beginners. 1972. 10.00 (ISBN 0-7207-0518-5). Transatlantic.

Turner, Barry. Industrialism. LC 73-94222. (Aspects of Modern Sociology Ser). 1975. text ed. 10.95x o.p. (ISBN 0-582-48058-2). Longman.

Turner, Barry T. Effective Technical Writing & Speaking. 2nd ed. 220p. 1978. text ed. 22.00x (ISBN 0-220-66344-0, Pub. by Busn Bks England). Renouf.

Turner, Ben. Winemaking & Brewing. (Illus.). 1976. 12.95 (ISBN 0-7207-0924-5, Pub. by Michael Joseph). Merrimack Bk Serv.

Turner, Bryan S. For Weber: Essays in the Sociology of Fate. 360p. 1981. price not set (ISBN 0-7100-0780-9). Routledge & Kegan.

--Weber & Islam. (International Library of Sociology). 1974. 22.00x (ISBN 0-7100-7848-X). Routledge & Kegan.

--Weber & Islam: A Critical Study. 1978. pap. 8.95 (ISBN 0-7100-8942-2). Routledge & Kegan.

Turner, C. M., jt. auth. see Rowley, J. E.

Turner, Christopher. Family & Kinship in Modern Britain. (Students Library of Sociology). 1969. text ed. 3.75x (ISBN 0-7100-6535-3); pap. text ed. 1.50x (ISBN 0-7100-6347-4). Humanities.

Turner, Clair E. Planning for Health Education in Schools. 1966. 6.50 (ISBN 92-3-100626-6, U452, UNESCO). Unipub.

Turner, Clive, jt. auth. see Turner, Edward.

Turner, D. R. Shadow Cabinet in British Politics. 1969. text ed. 6.00x (ISBN 0-7100-6489-6). Humanities.

Turner, Dan S., jt. auth. see Ball, Douglas.

Turner, Darwin T. Black American Literature: Essays, Poetry, Fiction, Drama. 1970. pap. text ed. 12.95x (ISBN 0-675-09278-7). Merrill.

Turner, David R. American College Testing Program Exams. 7th ed. LC 77-7519. (gr. 11-12). 1977. lib. bdg. 6.00 o.p. (ISBN 0-668-04355-5); pap. 5.00 o.p. (ISBN 0-668-04363-6). Arco.

--Complete Guide to U.S. Civil Service Jobs. 7th ed. LC 72-148867. (Illus.). 1971. pap. 4.00 (ISBN 0-668-00537-8). Arco.

--Graduate Management Admission Test. 1st ed. LC 77-7368. 1977. pap. 6.00 o.p. (ISBN 0-668-04360-1). Arco.

--Graph, Chart & Table: Interpretation for Test-Takers. LC 80-14351. 224p. 1980. pap. 8.00 (ISBN 0-668-04817-4, 4817-4). Arco.

--Life Insurance. 2nd ed. LC 70-92372. 1970. pap. 6.00 o.p. (ISBN 0-668-02343-0). Arco.

--Medical College Admission Test. 1977. pap. 6.00 o.p. (ISBN 0-668-04289-3). Arco.

--The New High School Equivalency Diploma Tests. LC 77-20196. 576p. 1978. lib. bdg. 10.00 (ISBN 0-668-04447-0); pap. 5.95 (ISBN 0-668-04451-9). Arco.

--New York State Regents Scholarship Exams. rev. ed. LC 66-27875. (Orig.). (YA) 1975. pap. 5.00 o.p. (ISBN 0-668-00400-2). Arco.

--Preliminary Practice for the High School Equivalency Diploma Test. 5th ed. LC 75-34848. (gr. 9-12). 1972. pap. 5.00 (ISBN 0-668-01441-5). Arco.

--Preliminary Scholastic Aptitude Test: National Merit Scholarship Qualifying Test (PSAT-NMSQT) rev. ed. LC 80-18207. 285p. (Orig.). 1981. pap. 6.00 (ISBN 0-668-04980-4, 4980-4). Arco.

--School Secretary. LC 66-20315. (Orig.). 1971. pap. 4.00 o.p. (ISBN 0-668-00117-8). Arco.

--Teacher of Home Economics: Junior High School, High School. LC 65-23062. (Orig.). 1970. pap. 6.00 o.p. (ISBN 0-668-01316-8). Arco.

--Teacher of Social Studies, Junior High School & High School. 6th ed. LC 63-21436. (Orig.). 1970. pap. 6.00 o.p. (ISBN 0-668-00815-6). Arco.

--Tractor Operator. LC 80-11822. 224p. 1980. pap. 5.00 (ISBN 0-668-04971-5, 4971-5). Arco.

--Vocabulary Builder & Guide to Verbal Tests. 5th ed. LC 73-77242. 1973. pap. 5.00 (ISBN 0-668-00535-1). Arco.

Turner, David R., ed. Miller Analogies Test: Fourteen Hundred Analogy Questions. 3rd ed. LC 72-50. 1973. lib. bdg. 8.00 (ISBN 0-668-01115-7); pap. 5.00 (ISBN 0-668-01114-9). Arco.

Turner, Dixie M. A Jungian Psychoanalytic Interpretation of William Faulkner's "As I Lay Dying". LC 80-5582. 107p. 1981. lib. bdg. 16.50 (ISBN 0-8191-1451-0); pap. text ed. 7.50 (ISBN 0-8191-1452-9). U Pr of Amer.

Turner, Donald F., jt. auth. see Areeda, Phillip E.

Turner, Dorothea. Jane Mander. (World Authors Ser.: New Zealand: No. 178). lib. bdg. 10.95 (ISBN 0-8057-2576-8). Twayne.

Turner, E. G., ed. see Dale, A. M.

Turner, E. G., tr. see Menander.

Turner, E. S. Boys Will Be Boys. 1979. 8.95 o.p. (ISBN 0-7181-1282-2, Pub. by Michael Joseph). Merrimack Bk Serv.

Turner, Edith, jt. auth. see Turner, Victor.

Turner, Edward & Turner, Clive. Frogs & Toads. Brenner, Barbara, ed. LC 76-13653. (Young Naturalist Ser.). (Illus.). 80p. (gr. 3-7). 1976. PLB 8.25 (ISBN 0-8172-0331-1). Raintree Pubs.

Turner, Elsa. Look High, Grow Tall. 4.50 o.p. (ISBN 0-685-48833-0). Nortex Pr.

Turner, Elsa M. Berta Hart Nance: A Brand of Innocence. 1st ed. (Illus.). 248p. 1974. 15.00 o.p. (ISBN 0-89015-059-1). Nortex Pr.

Turner, Ernest S. Boys Will Be Boys. LC 76-175338. (Illus.). 1977. Repr. of 1948 ed. 21.00 (ISBN 0-8103-4091-7). Gale.

Turner, F. H. Concrete & Cryogenics. (Viewpoint Publication Ser.). (Illus.). 125p. 1979. pap. text ed. 27.50x (ISBN 0-7210-1124-1, Pub by C&CA London). Scholium Intl.

--Concrete & Cryogenics. (Viewpoint Publications Ser.). 1979. text ed. 27.50x (ISBN 0-7210-1124-1). Scholium Intl.

Turner, F. H., tr. see Guyon, Y.

Turner, F. H., tr. see Petzold, A. & Rohrs, M.

Turner, F. H., tr. see Seiffert, Karl.

Turner, Francis J. Differential Diagnosis & Treatment in Social Work. 2nd ed. LC 75-26054. 1976. text ed. 18.95 (ISBN 0-02-932730-X). Free Pr.

--Metamorphic Petrology. 2nd ed. LC 79-27496. (International Earth & Planetary Sciences Ser.). (Illus.). 512p. 1980. text ed. 29.95 (ISBN 0-07-065501-4, C). McGraw.

Turner, Francis J., ed. Psychosocial Therapy: A Social Work Perspective. LC 77-90456. (Treatment Approaches in the Human Services Ser.). 1978. text ed. 14.95 (ISBN 0-02-932720-2). Free Pr.

Turner, Francis J., ed. see Dickerson, Martha U.

Turner, Francis J., ed. see Strean, Herbet S.

Turner, Frank M. Greek Heritage in Victorian Britain. LC 80-24013. (Illus.). 512p. 1981. text ed. 30.00x (ISBN 0-300-02480-0). Yale U Pr.

Turner, Freda, jt. auth. see Callahan, Thomas C.

Turner, Frederick. A Double Shadow. (YA) 1978. 7.95 o.p. (ISBN 0-399-12150-1). Berkley Pub.

--A Double Shadow. 1979. pap. 1.75 o.p. (ISBN 0-425-03951-X). Berkley Pub.

Turner, Frederick J., ed. Correspondence of the French Ministers to the United States, 1791-1797. LC 75-75268. (American History, Politics & Law Ser). 1969. Repr. of 1904 ed. lib. bdg. 95.00 (ISBN 0-306-71315-2). Da Capo.

Turner, G. P. Introduction to Paint Chemistry. 1967. pap. 7.50 o.p. (ISBN 0-470-89311-7). Halsted Pr.

Turner, Geoffrey. Indians of North America. (Illus.). 261p. 1980. pap. 6.95 (ISBN 0-7137-1122-1, Pub. by Blandford Pr England). Sterling.

Turner, George. Transit of Cassidy. 1979. 14.95 (ISBN 0-241-10093-3, Pub. by Hamish Hamilton England). David & Charles.

Turner, George A. The New & Living Way. LC 74-23104. 240p. 1974. pap. 4.95 (ISBN 0-87123-388-6, 210388); study guide 0.75 (ISBN 0-87123-522-6, 210522). Bethany Fell.

Turner, George E., jt. auth. see Price, Michael H.

Turner, George K. Hagar's Hoard. LC 75-104762. (The Novel As American Social History Ser.). 320p. 1970. 10.00x (ISBN 0-8131-1208-7); pap. 4.50 (ISBN 0-8131-0129-8). U Pr of Ky.

Turner, Gerard L. Collecting Microscopes. (The Christies International Collectors Ser.). (Illus.). 128p. 1980. 14.95 (ISBN 0-8317-5950-X). Mayflower Bks.

Turner, Gerry A. The Teen Model: Fact Book. LC 80-18228. (Illus.). 224p. (gr. 7 up). 1980. PLB 9.29 (ISBN 0-671-33022-5). Messner.

Turner, Glen O. Cardiovascular Care Unit: A Guide for Planning & Operation. LC 77-14215. 1978. 27.50 o.p. (ISBN 0-471-03022-8, Pub. by Wiley Medical). Wiley.

Turner, H. A. The Last Colony: But Whose?; a Study of the Labour Movement, Labour Market & Labour Relations in Hong Kong. LC 80-41112. (Department of Applied Economics Papers in Industrial Relations & Labour: No. 5). (Illus.). 1981. 24.95 (ISBN 0-521-23701-7). Cambridge U Pr.

Turner, H. A., et al. Management Characteristics & Labour. LC 77-76076. (DAE Papers in Industrial Relations Ser.: No. 3). (Illus.). 1977. 14.50 (ISBN 0-521-21734-2); pap. 7.95x (ISBN 0-521-29245-X). Cambridge U Pr.

Turner, Harry. Triad Optical Illusions & How to Design Them. LC 77-81212. (Illus.). 1977. pap. 1.95 (ISBN 0-486-23549-1). Dover.

Turner, Henry S. Original Journals of Henry Smith Turner: With Stephen Watts Kearny to New Mexico & California. Clarke, Dwight L., ed. (American Exploration & Discovery Ser.: No. 51). 1967. pap. 2.95 (ISBN 0-8061-1157-7). U of Okla Pr.

Turner, J. & Starnes, C. Inequality: Privilege & Poverty in America. 1976. 12.95 (ISBN 0-87620-419-1); pap. text ed. 9.95 (ISBN 0-685-93530-2). P-H.

Turner, J. E., jt. auth. see Hurst, G. S.

Turner, J. Howard. Care & Operation of Small Engines, 2 vols. 4th ed. Vol. 1. 7.95 (ISBN 0-914452-23-1); Vol. 2. 9.95 (ISBN 0-914452-24-X). Green Hill.

--Maintenance & Repair of Small Engines. 9.95 (ISBN 0-914452-45-2). Green Hill.

Turner, J. J. Church According to the Bible. pap. 1.95 (ISBN 0-89315-016-9). Lambert Bk.

--Leadership & Church Growth. pap. 2.50 (ISBN 0-89315-137-8). Lambert Bk.

--Life, Death & Beyond. pap. 1.95 (ISBN 0-89315-138-6). Lambert Bk.

--Practical Sermons That Motivate. pap. 2.95 (ISBN 0-89315-211-0). Lambert Bk.

--Snatching Men Out of the Fire & Other Ser. pap. 3.95 (ISBN 0-89315-257-9). Lambert Bk.

--Study of Bible Leaders. pap. 2.50 (ISBN 0-89315-290-0). Lambert Bk.

Turner, J. M., jt. auth. see Campkin, T. V.

Turner, J. S. Bouyancy Effects in Fluids. LC 72-76085. (Cambridge Monographs on Mechanics & Applied Mathematics). (Illus.). 350p. 1973. 47.95 (ISBN 0-521-08623-X). Cambridge U Pr.

--Buoyancy Effects in Fluids. LC 79-7656. (Monographs on Mechanics & Applied Mathematics). (Illus.). 1980. pap. 19.95x (ISBN 0-521-29726-5). Cambridge U Pr.

Turner, J. S., tr. see Fedorov, K. N.

Turner, James, jt. ed. see Prescott, David.

Turner, James F. Fundamental Electronics. LC 72-169985. 480p. 1972. text ed. 19.95 (ISBN 0-675-09175-6). Merrill.

Turner, John, ed. Encyclopedia of Social Work, 2 vols. 1977 ed. LC 30-30948. 40.00x (ISBN 0-87101-074-7, CHO-075-C). Natl Assn Soc Wkrs.

Turner, John A., tr. A Golden Treasury of Chinese Poetry: 121 Classical Poems. LC 75-42790. (Renditions). 352p. 1976. 12.50 (ISBN 0-295-95506-6). U of Wash Pr.

Turner, John D. Thomas the Contender: The Coptic Text of the Book of Thomas. LC 75-22446. (Society of Biblical Literature. Dissertation Ser.). 250p. 1975. pap. 7.50 (ISBN 0-89130-017-1, 060123). Scholars Pr Ca.

Turner, John E., jt. ed. see Holt, Robert T.

Turner, John H. Architectural Practice: Architecture-Professional & Technical. 1979. 33.00 (ISBN 0-7134-2799-X, Pub. by Batsford England). David & Charles.

--The London Brighton & South Coast Railway, Vol I: Origins & Formation. (Illus.). 1977. 12.95 o.s.i. (ISBN 0-7134-0275-X). Hippocrene Bks.

--London, Brighton & South Coast Railway, Vol. 1. 1977. 30.00 (ISBN 0-7134-0275-X, Pub. by Batsford England). David & Charles.

--London, Brighton & South Coast Railway, Vol. 2. 1978. 30.00 (ISBN 0-7134-1198-8, Pub. by Batsford England). David & Charles.

--London, Brighton & South Coast Railway, Vol. 3. 1979. 30.00 (ISBN 0-7134-1389-1, Pub. by Batsford England). David & Charles.

--Studies in Managerial Process & Organizational Behavior. 493p. 1972. pap. 7.95x o.p. (ISBN 0-673-07624-5). Scott F.

Turner, John K. Barbarous Mexico. new ed. (Texas Pan American Series). (Illus.). 1969. 12.95 (ISBN 0-292-78418-X). U of Tex Pr.

Turner, John P., Jr. & Orgel, Stephen, eds. St. Patrick for Ireland by James Shirley. LC 78-66857. (Renaissance Drama Ser.). 1979. lib. bdg. 28.00 (ISBN 0-8240-9729-7). Garland Pub.

Turner, Jonathan H. The Structure of Sociological Theory. rev. ed. 1978. text ed. 16.95x (ISBN 0-256-02061-2). Dorsey.

Turner, Jonathan H. & Maryanski, Alexandra. Functionalism. (Series in Social Theory). 1979. pap. 6.95 (ISBN 0-8053-9338-2). Benjamin-Cummings.

Turner, Katy. The Legacy of the Great Wheel. LC 80-83331. (Illus.). 128p. 1980. pap. 8.95 (ISBN 0-910458-15-4). Select Bks.

Turner, Keith. Darts. LC 79-56063. (Illus.). 128p. 1980. 14.95 (ISBN 0-7153-7943-7). David & Charles.

--The Leek & Manifold Railway. LC 79-56057. (Illus.). 96p. 1980. 13.50 (ISBN 0-7153-7950-X). David & Charles.

--North Wales Tramways. LC 79-74089. 1979. 17.95 (ISBN 0-7153-7769-8). David & Charles.

Turner, L. W. Electronic Engineer's Reference Book. 4th ed. 1976. text ed. 79.95x (ISBN 0-408-00168-2). Butterworths.

Turner, Lawrence. Pilot Reference Manual. Date not set. pap. 10.00x cancelled (ISBN 0-685-85020-X). Scientific Pr.

Turner, Louis. Oil Companies in the International System. 1978. text ed. 25.00x (ISBN 0-04-382020-4). Allen Unwin.

Turner, Louis & Bedore, James. Middle East Industrialisation: A Study of Saudi & Iranian Downstream Investment. LC 79-89599. (Praeger Special Studies). (Illus.). 230p. 1980. 29.95 (ISBN 0-03-053381-3). Praeger.

Turner, Mark. Hardy Boys. (T.V. & Movie Tie-Ins Ser.). (gr. 4-12). 1979. PLB 5.95 (ISBN 0-87191-703-3); pap. 2.95 (ISBN 0-89812-035-7). Creative Ed.

Turner, Martha A. Texas Epic: An American Story. 11.95 (ISBN 0-685-48782-2). Nortex Pr.

--The Yellow Rose of Texas: Her Saga & Her Song. (Illus.). 128p. 1976. 7.45 (ISBN 0-88319-025-7). Shoal Creek Pub.

Turner, Mary A., ed. see Bosco, James S.

Turner, Mary C., ed. Libros en Venta Supplement 1976-77. 1978. 59.00 o.p. (ISBN 0-8352-1027-8). Bowker.

--Libros En Venta Supplement 1978. 1980. 42.50 (ISBN 0-8352-1278-5). Bowker.

Turner, Merle B. Philosophy & the Science of Behavior. LC 66-25267. (Century Psychology Ser.). (Illus.). 1967. 28.50x (ISBN 0-89197-341-9); pap. text ed. 9.50x (ISBN 0-89197-342-7). Irvington.

--Psychology & the Philosophy of Science. (Century Psychology Ser.). pap. text ed. 9.50x (ISBN 0-8290-0363-0). Irvington.

--Realism & the Explanation of Behavior. (Century Psychology Ser.). 270p. 1980. text ed. 24.50x (ISBN 0-8290-0361-4); pap. text ed. 8.95x (ISBN 0-8290-0362-2). Irvington.

Turner, Michael & Vaisey, David. Art for Commerce. Date not set. cancelled o.p. (ISBN 0-8038-0382-6). Hastings.

Turner, Nancy J. & Szczawinski, Adam F. Edible Wild Fruits & Nuts of Canada. (Illus.). 1979. pap. 9.95 spiral bdg. (ISBN 0-660-00128-4, 56328-6, Pub. by Natl Mus Canada). U of Chicago Pr.

Turner, Nancy J., jt. auth. see Szczawinski, Adam F.

Turner, Nigel. Grammatical Insights into the New Testament. LC 66-71386. 208p. Repr. of 1965 ed. text ed. 15.95x (ISBN 0-567-01017-1). Attic Pr.

Turner, P. H. Business Economics: A Comprehensive Course, 2 vols. 1974. Set. pap. text ed. 19.95x (ISBN 0-685-83708-4) (ISBN 0-245-52375-8). Vol. 1. (ISBN 0-245-52376-6). Vol. 2. Intl Ideas.

Turner, P. S. Heinkel. LC 70-136294. (Aircraft Album Ser No. 1). (Illus.). 1970. pap. 3.95 o.p. (ISBN 0-668-02414-3). Arco.

Turner, P. W., jt. auth. see Haigh, R. H.

Turner, Paul. Tennyson. (Routledge Author Guides Ser.). 1980. pap. 6.95 (ISBN 0-7100-0475-3). Routledge & Kegan.

Turner, Paul & Volans, Glyn. The Drugs Handbook. 1978. text ed. 20.75x (ISBN 0-333-21612-1). Humanities.

Turner, Paul, jt. auth. see Silverstone, Trevor.

Turner, Paul, ed. Bilingualism in the Southwest. 2nd, rev. ed. 1982. pap. text ed. write for info. (ISBN 0-8165-0729-5). U of Ariz Pr.

Turner, Paul & Shand, David G., eds. Recent Advances in Clinical Pharmacology, No. 2. (Recent Advances Ser.). (Illus.). 178p. 1981. lib. bdg. 40.00 (ISBN 0-443-02183-X). Churchill.

Turner, Paul, ed. see Browning, Robert.

Turner, Paul V. The Education of le Corbusier. LC 76-23658. (Outstanding Dissertations in the Fine Arts - Twentieth Century). (Illus.). 1977. Repr. of 1971 ed. lib. bdg. 48.00 (ISBN 0-8240-2732-9). Garland Pub.

Turner, Pearl. The Collector's Index. (Useful Reference Ser. of Library Books: Vol. 115). 1980. 21.00 (ISBN 0-87305-119-X). Faxon.

Turner, Peter, jt. ed. see Osman, Colin.

Turner, Philip. Devil's Nob. LC 72-8918. 190p. (gr. 6-9). 1973. 6.95 o.p. (ISBN 0-525-66270-7). Elsevier-Nelson.

Turner, Philip M. Handbook for School Media Personnel. 2nd ed. LC 80-21152. (Illus.). 132p. 1980. pap. text ed. 9.50x (ISBN 0-87287-225-4). Libs Unl.

Turner, Phyllis, jt. auth. see Thorburn, Anna H.

Turner, Phyllis S. Self-Assessment of Current Knowledge in Intensive Care Nursing. 1980. pap. 9.75 (ISBN 0-87488-227-3). Med Exam.

Turner, Priscilla, jt. auth. see Geline, Robert.

Turner, R. Gerald, jt. ed. see Willerman, Lee.

Turner, R. J., jt. auth. see Manning, M. J.

Turner, Ralph & Killian, Lewis. Collective Behavior. 2nd ed. (Illus.). 480p. 1972. text ed. 18.95 (ISBN 0-13-140657-4). P-H.

Turner, Ralph H. Family Interaction. LC 71-118627. (Illus.). 505p. 1970. 21.95 (ISBN 0-471-89300-5). Wiley.

Turner, Ralph L. R. L. Turner: Collected Papers 1912-1973. 432p. 1975. 35.00x (ISBN 0-19-713582-X). Oxford U Pr.

Turner, Sir Ralph. A Comparative Dictionary of the Indo-Aryan Languages. 862p. 1966. text ed. 69.00x (ISBN 0-19-713550-1). Oxford U Pr.

Turner, Raymond, jt. auth. see Hastings, James R.

Turner, Richard A. The Vision of Landscape in Renaissance Italy. LC 66-11977. (Illus.). 336p. 1974. 26.50x (ISBN 0-691-03849-X, 319); pap. 7.95 (ISBN 0-691-00307-6, 319). Princeton U Pr.

Turner, Robert. Vancouver Island Railroads. LC 72-95484. (Illus.). 170p. 18.95 (ISBN 0-87095-046-0). Golden West.

Turner, Robert A. & Hebborn, Peter. Screening Methods in Pharmacology, Vol. 2. 1971. 43.00 o.p. (ISBN 0-12-704252-0). Acad Pr.

Turner, Robert K., Jr. & Williams, George W. Romeo & Juliet. 1970. pap. 4.95x (ISBN 0-673-07519-2). Scott F.

Turner, Robert K., Jr., ed. see Heywood, Thomas.

Turner, Robert P. Up to the Front of the Line: The Black Man in the American Political System. 1975. 12.95 (ISBN 0-8046-9097-9, Natl U). Kennikat.

Turner, Robert W. I'll Never Lie to You: Jimmy Carter in His Own Words. (Orig.). 1976. pap. 1.75 o.p. (ISBN 0-345-25702-2). Ballantine.

Turner, Roland & Goulden, Steven L., eds. Greag Engineers: From Antiquity Through the Industrial Revolution, Vol. I. (Illus.). 630p. 1981. 65.00x (ISBN 0-312-34574-7). St Martin.

Turner, Ronald C. Real-Time Programming with Microcomputers. new ed. LC 77-80773. 1978. 18.95x (ISBN 0-669-01666-7). Lexington Bks.

Turner, Roy, jt. auth. see Bragg, R. J.

Turner, Rufus. Mosfet Circuits Guidebook: With One Hundred Tested Projects. LC 75-27483. (Illus.). 196p. 1975. 7.95 (ISBN 0-8306-5796-7); pap. 6.95 (ISBN 0-8306-4796-1, 766). TAB Bks.

Turner, Rufus P. A B C's of Integrated Circuits. LC 70-143034. (Illus., Orig.). 1971. pap. 3.50 o.p. (ISBN 0-672-20823-7, 20823). Sams.

--ABC's of FETS. 2nd ed. LC 77-99108. 1978. pap. 3.95 o.p. (ISBN 0-672-21510-1). Sams.

--Simple IC Test Instruments You Can Build. LC 79-90832. 1979. pap. 4.95 (ISBN 0-672-21683-3). Sams.

--Solar Cells & Photocells. 2nd ed. LC 80-50048. (Illus.). 1980. pap. 4.95 (ISBN 0-672-21711-2). SAMS.

Turner, Sandra. The House of Time Travel. Date not set. 6.95 (ISBN 0-533-04100-7). Vantage.

Turner, Sharon. The History of the Anglo-Saxons from the Earliest Period to the Norman Conquest, 3 vols. 7th ed. LC 80-2207. 1981. Repr. of 1852 ed. 160.00 (ISBN 0-404-18790-0). AMS Pr.

Turner, Sue. Wheels & Grindstones. 1980. pap. 4.95 (ISBN 0-87397-180-9). Strode.

Turner, Susan. The Padarn & Penrhyn Railways. LC 74-76199. (Railway History Ser). (Illus.). 168p. 1975. 14.95 (ISBN 0-7153-6547-9). David & Charles.

Turner, Thomas. Creative Activities Resource Book for Elementary School Teachers. (Illus.). 1978. pap. text ed. 13.95 (ISBN 0-87909-205-X). Reston.

Turner, V. Dean & Prouse, Howard L. Introduction to Mathematics. 1972. 13.95x o.p. (ISBN 0-673-05960-X). Scott F.

Turner, Victor. Dramas, Fields, & Metaphors: Symbolic Action in Human Society. LC 73-16968. (Symbol, Myth & Ritual Ser.). (Illus.). 312p. 1975. pap. 5.95 o.p. (ISBN 0-8014-9151-7). Cornell U Pr.

--Process, Performance & Pilgrimage. 1979. text ed. 12.50x (ISBN 0-391-01929-5). Humanities.

Turner, Victor & Turner, Edith. Image & Pilgrimage in Christian Culture. (Lectures on the History of Religions Ser.). 1978. 17.50x (ISBN 0-231-04286-8). Columbia U Pr.

Turner, Virginia C. Cat Claws & Tree Bark. 111p. 1972. 2.00. Pikeville Coll.

Turner, Walter J. Mozart: The Man & His Works. LC 78-20497. (Encore Music Editions Ser.). 1981. Repr. of 1938 ed. 28.50 (ISBN 0-88355-873-4). Hyperion Conn.

Turner, Wesley B. Life in Upper Canada. (gr. 6-10). 1980. PLB 6.90 (ISBN 0-531-00447-3). Watts.

Turner, William. Book of Wines. LC 41-26942. 1980. Repr. of 1568 ed. 22.00x (ISBN 0-8201-1200-3). Schol Facsimiles.

Turner, William, jt. auth. see Hinckle, Warren.

Turner, William A. Epilepsy: A Study of the Idiopathic Disease. LC 73-82850. 289p. 1973. Repr. of 1907 ed. 11.00 (ISBN 0-911216-62-6). Raven.

Turner, William B. Theology - the Quintessence of Science. LC 80-82649. 1981. 14.95 (ISBN 0-8022-2375-3). Philos Lib.

Turner, William C. Thermal Insulation for Buildings: Economic Design for Comfort & Safety in Homes & Buildings. 1981. write for info. (ISBN 0-88275-985-X). Krieger.

Turner, William C. & Malloy, John F. Thermal Insulation Handbook. 624p. 1981. 62.50 (ISBN 0-07-039805-4). McGraw.

Turner, William O. Shortcut to Devil's Claw. (Orig.). 1977. pap. 1.25 o.p. (ISBN 0-425-03410-0). Berkley Pub.

Turner, Wilson G. Maya Design Coloring Book. (Illus.). 48p. (Orig.). (gr. 1-6). 1980. pap. 2.00 (ISBN 0-486-24047-9). Dover.

Turner Ettlinger, D. M., ed. Natural History Photography. 1975. 40.50 (ISBN 0-12-703950-3). Acad Pr.

Turney, Alan, tr. see Soseki, Natsume.

Turney, Alfred W. Disaster at Moscow: Von Bock's Campaigns, 1941-1942. LC 74-107098. 1970. 6.95 o.p. (ISBN 0-8263-0167-3). U of NM Pr.

Turney, C., ed. Pioneers of Australian Education, Vol. 3. (Pioneers of Australian Education Ser). (Illus.). 1981. write for info. (ISBN 0-686-16294-3, Pub. by Sydney U Pr). Intl Schol Bk Serv.

Turney, C., et al. Isolated Schools. 152p. 1980. pap. 8.50x (ISBN 0-424-00068-7, Pub. by Sydney U Pr Australia). Intl Schol Bk Serv.

Turney-High, Harry H. Man & System: Foundations for the Study of Human Relations. LC 68-16216. (Illus.). 1968. 28.50x (ISBN 0-89197-547-0). Irvington.

--The Military. 1981. pap. 12.00 (ISBN 0-8158-0403-2). Chris Mass.

Turnock, David. An Economic Geography of Romania. (Advanced Economic Geography Ser.). 1974. lib. bdg. 28.50x (ISBN 0-7135-1628-3). Westview.

--The New Scotland. LC 78-58561. 1979. 24.00 (ISBN 0-7153-7560-1). David & Charles.

Turnovsky, S. J. Macroeconomic Analysis & Stabilization Policy. LC 76-46862. (Illus.). 1977. 44.50 (ISBN 0-521-21520-X); pap. 15.95x (ISBN 0-521-29187-9). Cambridge U Pr.

Turoff, Murray, jt. auth. see Hiltz, Starr R.

Turoff, Murray, jt. ed. see Linstone, Harold A.

Turok, Ben. Revolutionary Thought in the Twentieth Century. 360p. (Orig.). 1980. 18.95 (ISBN 0-905762-42-8, Pub. by Zed Pr); pap. 8.95 (ISBN 0-905762-43-6). Lawrence Hill.

Turov, E. A. & Petrov, M. P. Nuclear Magnetic Resonance in Ferro & Antiferromagnetics. 206p. 1972. 49.95 (ISBN 0-470-89323-0). Halsted Pr.

Turow, Rita. Daddy Doesn't Live Here Anymore. LC 78-7771. 1978. pap. 3.50 (ISBN 0-385-14512-8, Anch). Doubleday.

Turpin, Lorna. The Sultan's Snakes. LC 80-10956. (Illus.). 48p. (gr. k-3). 1980. 7.95 (ISBN 0-688-80260-5); PLB 7.63 (ISBN 0-688-84260-7). Greenwillow.

Turpin, William N. Soviet Foreign Trade. LC 76-47337. 1977. 17.95x (ISBN 0-669-01143-6). Lexington Bks.

Turrell, G. Infrared & Raman Spectra of Crystals. 1972. 53.00 o.s.i. (ISBN 0-12-705050-7). Acad Pr.

Turretin, Francis. The Doctrine of Scripture: Locus 2 of Institutio Theologiae Elencticae. Beardslee, John W., III, ed. 200p. (Orig.). 1981. 12.95 (ISBN 0-8010-8858-5); pap. 7.95 (ISBN 0-8010-8857-7). Baker Bk.

Turro, Nicholas J., ed. see McLafferty, Fred W.

Tursi, Joseph A., jt. auth. see Cincinnato, Paul D.

Tursi, Joseph A., ed. FLs & the 'new' Student. 1970. pap. 7.95x (ISBN 0-915432-70-6). NE Conf Teach.

Turska, Krystyna. The Magician of Cracow. LC 75-8846. (Illus.). 32p. (gr. k-4). 1975. 9.25 (ISBN 0-688-80010-6). Greenwillow.

--Tamara & the Sea Witch. LC 70-164896. (gr. k-3). 1972. PLB 5.95 o.s.i. (ISBN 0-8193-0530-8, Four Winds); PLB 5.41 o.s.i. (ISBN 0-8193-0531-6). Schol Bk Serv.

--The Woodcutter's Duck. LC 72-85763. (Illus.). 32p. (gr. k-3). 1973. 5.95g o.s.i. (ISBN 0-02-789540-8). Macmillan.

Tursun, Beg. The History of Mehmed the Conqueror. LC 77-89803. 1978. 30.00x (ISBN 0-88297-018-6). Bibliotheca.

Turton, B. J., jt. ed. see Phillips, A. D.

Turvey, Alan, jt. auth. see Moore, James.

Turvey, David J., jt. auth. see Germain, Jocelyn P.

Turvey, Ralph. Demand & Supply. 2nd ed. (Illus.). 128p. 1980. text ed. 17.95x (ISBN 0-04-330302-1, 2479); pap. text ed. 4.95 (ISBN 0-04-330303-X, 2480). Allen Unwin.

Turville-Petre, Gabriel. Origins of Icelandic Literature. 1953. 35.00x (ISBN 0-19-811114-2). Oxford U Pr.

Turville-Petre, Joan, ed. see Tolkien, J. R.

Turyn, Alexander. Dated Greek Manuscripts of the Thirteenth & Fourteenth Centuries in the Libraries of Great Britian. LC 80-81547. (Dumbarton Oaks Studies: Vol. 17). (Illus.). 198p. 1980. 65.00 (ISBN 0-88402-077-0, Ctr Byzantine). Dumbarton Oaks.

Tuschling, Burkhard. Metaphysische und transzendentale Dynamik in Kant opus postumum. (Quellen und Studien Zur Philosophie, 3). 224p. 1971. 33.50x (ISBN 3-11-001889-6). De Gruyter.

Tushnet, Mark V. The American Law of Slavery, Eighteen Ten-Eighteen Sixty: Considerations of Humanity & Interest. LC 80-8582. 288p. 1981. 20.00x (ISBN 0-691-04681-6); pap. 9.50x (ISBN 0-691-10104-3). Princeton U Pr.

Tuska, Jon, et al, eds. Close-Up: The Contemporary Director. LC 80-23551. 437p. 1981. 22.50 (ISBN 0-8108-1366-1). Scarecrow.

--Close up: The Contract Director. LC 76-41345. 1976. 21.00 (ISBN 0-8108-0961-3). Scarecrow.

--Close-up: The Hollywood Director. LC 77-14114. 1978. 21.00 (ISBN 0-8108-1085-9). Scarecrow.

Tusler, Robert L. Style of J. S. Bach's Chorale Preludes. 2nd ed. LC 68-13275. (Music Ser). 1968. Repr. of 1956 ed. lib. bdg. 12.50 (ISBN 0-306-70942-2). Da Capo.

Tuso, Joseph F., ed. Beowulf: A Norton Critical Edition. new ed. Donaldson, E. Talbot, tr. 224p. 1976. 10.00 (ISBN 0-393-04413-0); pap. text ed. 3.95x (ISBN 0-393-09225-9). Norton.

Tussing, Arlon R. & Erickson, Gregg K. Mining & Public Policy in Alaska: Mineral Policy, the Public Lands, & Economic Development. LC 72-629327. (Joint Institute of Social & Economic Research Ser.: No. 21). 142p. 1969. pap. 5.00 (ISBN 0-295-95118-4). U of Wash Pr.

Tustin, Frances. Autism & Childhood Psychosis. LC 72-85216. 1973. 20.00x (ISBN 0-87668-055-4). Aronson.

Tute, Warren. The Cruiser. 1981. pap. 2.75 (ISBN 0-345-29573-0). Ballantine.

--D-Day. 1974. pap. 9.95 (ISBN 0-02-038090-9, Collier). Macmillan.

Tutela, Dawn. Jenny Moves. Newberger, Eli, ed. (The Jenny Ser.). (Illus.). (gr. 4-9). 1981. pap. 2.95 (ISBN 0-8326-2609-0, 7611). Delair.

--Jenny's First Friend. Newberger, Eli, ed. (Jenny Ser.). (Illus.). (gr. 4-9). 1981. pap. 2.95 (ISBN 0-8326-2608-2, 7610). Delair.

Tuten, Frederic. Monarch Notes on Dostoyevsky's Crime & Punishment. (Orig.). pap. 1.95 (ISBN 0-671-00517-0). Monarch Pr.

Tuteru, Franz B., jt. auth. see Stark, Henry.

Tuthill, Arthur H., et al. Corrosion Resistance of Alloys to Bleach Plant Environments. (TAPPI PRESS Reports). (Illus.). 99p. 1980. pap. 94.95 (ISBN 0-89852-384-2, 01-01-RO84). Tappi.

Tuthill, Lewis H., jt. auth. see McMillan, F. R.

Tuthill, Marge. In the Image of God: Art Projects with Eight Years-Old & up. LC 75-42050. (Illus.). 1976. pap. 2.95 (ISBN 0-8091-1926-9). Paulist Pr.

Tuthill, William B. Interiors & Interior Details. (Architecture & Decorative Arts Ser). (Illus.). 1975. Repr. of 1882 ed. lib. bdg. 35.00 (ISBN 0-306-70747-0). Da Capo.

Tutin, T. G., et al. Flora Europaea. Incl. Vol. 1. Lycopodiaceae to Plantanaceae. 1964. 90.00 (ISBN 0-521-06661-1); Vol. 2. Rosaceae to Umbelliferae. 1968. 90.00 (ISBN 0-521-06662-X); Vol. 3. Diapseniaceae to Myoporaceae. 90.00 (ISBN 0-521-08489-X); Vol. 4. Plantaginaceae to Compositae (& Rubiaceae) 1976. 90.00 (ISBN 0-521-08717-1). LC 64-24315. Cambridge U Pr.

--Flora Europaea: Alismataceae to Orchidaceae, Vol. 5. LC 64-24315. (Illus.). 1980. 105.00 (ISBN 0-521-20108-X). Cambridge U Pr.

Tutko, Thomas & Bruns, William. Winning Is Everything & Other American Myths. 224p. 1976. 8.95 o.s.i. (ISBN 0-02-620770-2). Macmillan.

Tutko, Thomas & Richards, Jack. Psychology of Coaching. 1971. text ed. 18.95 (ISBN 0-205-02904-3, 6229042). Allyn.

Tutko, Thomas A., jt. auth. see Neal, Patsy.

Tutorow, Norman E., ed. The American-Mexican War: An Annotated Bibliography. LC 80-1789. (Illus.). 456p. 1981. lib. bdg. 39.95 (ISBN 0-313-22181-2, TMA/). Greenwood.

Tutorow, Norman E., compiled by. The Mexican-American War: An Annotated Bibliography. LC 80-1789. (Illus.). 456p. 1981. lib. bdg. 39.95 (ISBN 0-313-22181-2, TMA/). Greenwood.

Tutt, Norman, ed. Alternative Strategies for Coping with Crime. (Aspects of Social Policy Ser.). 1978. 29.50x (ISBN 0-631-16240-2, Pub. by Basil Blackwell); pap. 12.50x (ISBN 0-631-16250-X). Biblio Dist.

Tutte, W. T., ed. Recent Progress in Combinatorics: Proceedings. 1969. 48.50 (ISBN 0-12-705150-3). Acad Pr.

Tutte, William T. Connectivity in Graphs. LC 67-5800. 1967. 12.50x o.p. (ISBN 0-8020-1425-9). U of Toronto Pr.

Tuttle, Anthony. The Catchers. LC 76-8456. (Stars of the Nl & Al Ser). (Illus.). (gr. 4-12). 1976. PLB 7.50 o.p. (ISBN 0-87191-519-7). Creative Ed.

Tuttle, Frederick B., Jr., jt. auth. see Collins, Sarah H.

Tuttle, Gary, ed. Biblical & Near Eastern Studies. 1978. 15.00 o.p. (ISBN 0-8028-3500-7). Eerdmans.

Tuttle, Gene. Rusty Colt of the Cross L. 192p. (YA) 1975. 5.95 (ISBN 0-685-51771-3, Avalon). Bouregy.

Tuttle, Goerge E., Jr., jt. auth. see Morlan, Don M.

Tuttle, James C., ed. International Human Rights: Law & Practice. LC 78-61659. (Professional Education Publications Ser.). 1978. pap. text ed. 15.00 (ISBN 0-89707-006-2). Amer Bar Assn.

Tuttle, Margaret W. The Crimson Cage. (Orig.). (gr. 8-12). 1978. pap. 4.50 (ISBN 0-932384-01-3). Tashmoo.

Tuttle, Robert. John Wesley: His Life & Theology. 1978. 11.95 (ISBN 0-310-36660-7). Zondervan.

Tuttle, Robert G. My Burden Is Light. 128p. (Orig.). 1980. pap. text ed. 5.00 (ISBN 0-89536-459-X). CSS Pub.

Tuttle, Russell H., ed. Paleoanthropology: Morphology & Paleoecology. (World Anthropology Ser.). (Illus.). 608p. 1975. 40.50x o.p. (ISBN 0-202-90012-6). Beresford Bk Serv.

Tuttle, Sherwood D. Landforms & Landscapes. 3rd ed. 1980. pap. text ed. 4.95x (ISBN 0-697-05020-3). Wm C Brown.

Tuttle, W. C. Mission River Justice. 256p. (YA) 1975. 5.95 (ISBN 0-685-50844-7, Avalon). Bouregy.

--Renegade Sheriff. (YA) 1972. 4.95 o.p. (ISBN 0-685-26711-3, Avalon). Bouregy.

--Thunderbird Range. 256p. (YA) 1974. 5.95 (ISBN 0-685-39470-0, Avalon). Bouregy.

Tuttle, Wilbur C. Hashknife of Stormy River. 252p. 1980. Repr. of 1936 ed. lib. bdg. 12.95x (ISBN 0-89968-132-8). Lightyear.

--Hashknife of the Double Bar Eight. 244p. 1980. Repr. of 1936 ed. lib. bdg. 12.95x (ISBN 0-89968-133-6). Lightyear.

--The Morgan Trail: A Story of Hashknife Hartley. 1976. lib. bdg. 14.75x (ISBN 0-89968-127-1). Lightyear.

--Sad Sontag Plays His Hunch. 1976. lib. bdg. 10.95x (ISBN 0-89968-129-8). Lightyear.

Tuttleton, James W. Thomas Wentworth Higginson. (United States Authors Ser.: No. 313). 1978. lib. bdg. 12.50 (ISBN 0-8057-7236-7). Twayne.

Tuttman, Saul. Object & Self: A Developmental Approach. 600p. 1981. text ed. 40.00x (ISBN 0-8236-3700-X, 00-3700). Intl Univs Pr.

Tutton, A. E. Crystallography & Practical Crystal Measurement, 2 vols. 2nd ed. Incl. Vol. 1. Form & Structure; Vol. 2. Physical & Chemical. 1964. Set. 25.00 (ISBN 0-934454-27-2). Lubrecht & Cramer.

Tuve, George L. Energy, Environment, Population & Food: Our Four Interdependent Crises. LC 76-40351. 1976. 29.95 (ISBN 0-471-02091-5, Pub. by Wiley-Interscience); pap. 13.50 (ISBN 0-471-02090-7). Wiley.

Tuveson, Ernest L. The Avatars of Thrice Great Hermes: An Approach to Romanticism. LC 78-75206. 280p. 1981. 17.50 (ISBN 0-8387-2264-4). Bucknell U Pr.

--Redeemer Nation: The Idea of America's Millenial Role. LC 68-14009. 1968. 10.00x o.s.i. (ISBN 0-226-81919-1). U of Chicago Pr.

Tuyl, Barbara Van see Van Tuyl, Barbara.

Tuyl, Tina Van see Van Tuyl, Tina.

Tuzin, Donald F. The Ilahita Arapesh: Dimensions of Unity. 1976. 26.75x (ISBN 0-520-02860-0). U of Cal Pr.

--The Voice of the Tambaran: Truth & Illusion in Ilahita Arapesh Religion. 350p. 1980. 20.00x (ISBN 0-520-03964-5). U of Cal Pr.

T.V. Guide. TV Guide Book of Crossword Puzzles. (Puzzle Ser.: No. 8). (Orig.). 1979. pap. 1.50 (ISBN 0-445-04479-9). Popular Lib.

TV Guide. TV Guide Book of Crossword Puzzles. (Puzzle Ser: No. 5). pap. 1.50 (ISBN 0-445-08342-5). Popular Lib.

Tvedtnes, John. The Church of the Old Testament. rev. ed. LC 80-18595. 111p. 1980. 5.95 (ISBN 0-87747-827-9). Deseret Bk.

Tver, David F. Dictionary of Industrial Pollution, Ecology & Environment. (Illus.). 1981. price not set (ISBN 0-8311-1060-0). Indus Pr.

Twaddell, W. F. The English Verb Auxiliaries. 2nd ed. LC 63-10462. 1978. pap. 1.50 (ISBN 0-87057-072-2, Pub. by Brown U Pr). Univ of Pr New England.

Twaddell, W. F., tr. see Meyer, Conrad F.

Twaddle, Andrew C. Sickness Behavior & the Sick Role. 1981. pap. text ed. 7.95 (ISBN 0-87073-886-0). Schenkman.

Twaddle, Andrew C. & Hessler, Richard M. A Sociology of Health. LC 76-41215. (Illus.). 1977. pap. text ed. 14.95 (ISBN 0-8016-5153-0). Mosby.

Twaddle, Michael. Expulsion of a Minority: Essays on Ugandan Asians. (Commonwealth Papers Ser: No. 18). 96p. 1975. pap. text ed. 21.25x (ISBN 0-485-17618-1, Athlone Pr). Humanities.

Twain, Mark. Adventures of Huckleberry Finn. (Literature Ser). (gr. 7-12). 1969. pap. text ed. 3.75 (ISBN 0-87720-701-1). AMSCO Sch.

--Adventures of Huckleberry Finn. Marx, Leo, ed. LC 66-30699. 1967. 6.50 o.p. (ISBN 0-672-51108-8, LL4); pap. 5.75 (ISBN 0-672-60969-X, LL4). Bobbs.

--Adventures of Huckleberry Finn. (gr. 7 up). 1962. 5.95g o.s.i. (ISBN 0-02-789550-5). Macmillan.

--The Adventures of Huckleberry Finn. rev. ed. Dixson, Robert J., ed. (American Classics Ser.: Bk. 9). (gr. 9-12). 1973. pap. 2.75 (ISBN 0-88345-205-7, 18128); cassettes 40.00 (ISBN 0-685-38990-1); tapes 40.00 (ISBN 0-685-38991-X). Regents Pub.

--Adventures of Huckleberry Finn with Reader's Guide. (Amsco Literature Program). (gr. 9-12). 1972. pap. text ed. 4.58 (ISBN 0-87720-816-6); with model ans. 2.95 (ISBN 0-87720-916-2). AMSCO Sch.

--Adventures of Tom Sawyer. (Literature Ser). (gr. 7-12). 1969. pap. text ed. 3.42 (ISBN 0-87720-702-X). AMSCO Sch.

--Adventures of Tom Sawyer. holiday ed. (Illus.). 10.00 o.p. (ISBN 0-06-014465-3, HarpT); PLB 7.87 o.p. (ISBN 0-06-014427-0). Har-Row.

--Adventures of Tom Sawyer. (Illus.). (gr. 5-8). 1962. 3.95g o.s.i. (ISBN 0-02-789630-7). Macmillan.

--The Adventures of Tom Sawyer. Gerber, John C., et al, eds. Incl. Tom Sawyer Abroad; Tom Sawyer Detective. (The Iowa-California Works of Mark Twain). 1980. 27.50 (ISBN 0-520-03353-1). U of Cal Pr.

--The Adventures of Tom Sawyer. LC 78-2796. (Raintree's Illustrated Classics). (Illus.). (gr. 5-8). 1978. PLB 9.65 (ISBN 0-8393-6205-6). Raintree Child.

--Autobiography of Mark Twain. Neider, Charles, ed. (Illus.). 1959. 20.00 o.s.i. (ISBN 0-06-014368-1, HarpT). Har-Row.

--Aventuras de Tom Sawyer. (Span.). 9.00 (ISBN 84-241-5630-7). E Torres & Sons.

--The Comic Mark Twain Reader: The Most Humorous Selections from His Stories, Sketches, Novels, Travel Books & Speeches. LC 76-23785. 1977. 10.95 (ISBN 0-385-11334-X). Doubleday.

--Complete Essays of Mark Twain. LC 63-7714. 1963. 10.95 (ISBN 0-385-06590-6). Doubleday.

--Complete Humorous Sketches & Tales of Mark Twain. LC 61-6503. 1961. 12.95 (ISBN 0-385-01094-X). Doubleday.

--Complete Short Stories of Mark Twain. LC 57-5536. 1957. 10.95 (ISBN 0-385-01502-X). Doubleday.

--A Connecticut Yankee in King Arthur's Court. pap. 1.50. Bantam.

--Connecticut Yankee in King Arthur's Court. (Literature Ser). (gr. 7-12). 1970. pap. text ed. 3.67 (ISBN 0-87720-723-2). AMSCO Sch.

--The Family Mark Twain, 2 vols. 1975. boxed set 20.00 o.s.i. (ISBN 0-06-010128-8, HarpT). Har-Row.

--Gilded Age: A Tale of to-Day. French, Bryant M., ed. LC 76-183110. 1972. 8.95 (ISBN 0-672-61028-0). Bobbs.

--Innocents Abroad. (Illus.). Repr. of 1869 ed. 12.95x o.s.i. (ISBN 0-06-014380-0, HarpT). Har-Row.

--Innocents Abroad. pap. 2.50 (ISBN 0-451-51142-5, CE1379, Sig Classics). NAL.

--Life on the Mississippi. (Literature Ser). (gr. 7-12). 1969. pap. text ed. 3.58 (ISBN 0-87720-707-0). AMSCO Sch.

--Life on the Mississippi. holiday ed. 10.95 o.s.i. (ISBN 0-06-014455-6, HarpT). Har-Row.

--Life on the Mississippi. (Illus., TV tie-in edition). 1980. pap. 1.75 (ISBN 0-451-51448-3, CE1448, Sig Classics). NAL.

Twain, Mark, pseud. Mark Twain in Hawaii. Jones, William R., ed. (Illus.). 96p. 1981. pap. 4.95 (ISBN 0-89646-070-3). Outbooks.

Twain, Mark. Mark Twain's Correspondence with Henry Huttleston Rogers, 1893-1909. Leary, Lewis, ed. LC 68-23900. (Mark Twain Papers). 1969. 32.50x (ISBN 0-520-01467-7). U of Cal Pr.

--Mark Twain's Hannibal, Huck & Tom. Blair, Walter, ed. LC 69-10575. (Mark Twain Papers). 1969. 24.50x (ISBN 0-520-01501-0). U of Cal Pr.

--Mark Twain's Letters to His Publishers, 1867-1894. Hill, Hamlin, ed. (Mark Twain Papers). 1967. 24.50x (ISBN 0-520-00560-0). U of Cal Pr.

--Mark Twain's Mysterious Stranger Manuscripts. Gibson, William M., ed. LC 69-10576. (Mark Twain Papers). 1969. 24.50 (ISBN 0-520-01473-1). U of Cal Pr.

--Mark Twain's Notebooks & Journals: Vol. 3, 1883-1891. Anderson, Frederick, et al, eds. (The Mark Twain Papers Ser.). 1980. 42.50x (ISBN 0-520-03383-3). U of Cal Pr.

--Mark Twain's Notebooks & Journals, 1855-1873, Vol. 1. Anderson, Frederick, et al, eds. 700p. 1976. 30.00x (ISBN 0-520-02326-9). U of Cal Pr.

--Mark Twain's Notebooks & Journals, 1877-1883, Vol. 2. Anderson, Frederick, et al, eds. 700p. 1976. 30.00x (ISBN 0-520-02542-3). U of Cal Pr.

--Pudd'nhead Wilson. (Classics Ser). (gr. 8 up). pap. 1.25 (ISBN 0-8049-0124-4, CL-124). Airmont.

--Tom Sawyer. LC 80-22095. (Raintree Short Classics). (Illus.). 48p. (gr. 4-8). 1981. PLB 9.95 (ISBN 0-8172-1665-0). Raintree Pubs.

--Twain Unabridged. Teacher, Lawrence, ed. LC 76-43094. (Illus.). 1250p. (Orig.). 1976. lib. bdg. 19.80 (ISBN 0-914294-53-9); pap. 9.95 (ISBN 0-914294-54-7). Running Pr.

--Twain Unabridged Two. Teacher, Lawrence, ed. LC 79-9576. 1979. 21.50 (ISBN 0-89471-071-0); lib. bdg. 19.80 (ISBN 0-89471-087-7); pap. 9.95 (ISBN 0-89471-086-9). Running Pr.

Twain, Mark & Howells, William D. Selected Mark Twain-Howells Letters. Anderson, Frederick, et al, eds. LC 67-13251. 1968. pap. 5.95 (ISBN 0-689-70004-0, 114). Atheneum.

Twain, Mark & Warner, Charles D. Gilded Age. pap. 2.75 (ISBN 0-451-51375-4, CE1375, Sig Classics). NAL.

Twaite, James A. & Monroe, Jane A. Introductory Statistics. 1979. text ed. 17.95x (ISBN 0-673-15097-6). Scott F.

Twarog, Leon I; see Bishop, G. Reginald, Jr.

Tweed, William C. Sequoia-Kings Canyon: The Story Behind the Scenery. DenDooven, Gweneth R., ed. LC 79-87571. (Illus.). 7.95 (ISBN 0-916122-66-2); pap. 3.50 (ISBN 0-916122-65-4). K C Pubns.

Tweeten, Luther. Foundations of Farm Policy. LC 71-83145. 1970. 12.50x o.p. (ISBN 0-8032-0721-2). U of Nebr Pr.

Twelvetrees, A. C. Community Associations & Centres: A Comparative Study. 146p. 1976. text ed. 23.00 (ISBN 0-08-019938-0); pap. text ed. 12.75 (ISBN 0-08-019937-2). Pergamon.

Tweney, Ryan D., et al, eds. On Scientific Thinking. 496p. 1981. 25.00x (ISBN 0-231-04814-9); pap. 12.50x (ISBN 0-231-04815-7). Columbia U Pr.

Twentieth Century Fund. Abuse on Wall Street: Conflicts of Interest in the Securities Markets. LC 79-8295. (Illus.). 1980. lib. bdg. 35.00 (ISBN 0-89930-001-4, TWC/, Quorum Bks). Greenwood.

--Confronting Youth Crime: Report of the Twentieth Century Fund Task Force on Sentencing Policy Toward Young Offenders. LC 78-3612. (Illus.). 1978. text ed. 14.95x (ISBN 0-8419-0381-6); pap. text ed. 5.75 o.p. (ISBN 0-8419-0382-4). Holmes & Meier.

Twentieth Century Fund, Inc. Building a Broader Market: Report of the Twentieth Century Fund Task Force on the Municipal Bond Market. LC 76-28368. 1976. 7.95 (ISBN 0-07-065629-0, P&RB); pap. 3.95 o.p. (ISBN 0-07-065630-4). McGraw.

--Funds for the Future: Report of the Twentieth Century Fund Task Force on College & University Endowment Policy. (Illus.). 1975. 7.95 o.p. (ISBN 0-07-065619-3, P&RB); pap. 4.50 o.p. (ISBN 0-07-065620-7). McGraw.

--Rights in Conflict: Report of the Twentieth Century Fund Task Force on Justice, Publicity & the First Amendment. LC 75-43831. 1976. text ed. 6.95 o.p. (ISBN 0-07-065625-8, P&RB); pap. text ed. 3.95 o.p. (ISBN 0-07-065626-6). McGraw.

Twerski, Abraham. Like Yourself: And Others Will Too. LC 78-16816. 1978. 10.95 (ISBN 0-13-536474-4, Spec); pap. 5.95 (ISBN 0-13-536466-3). P-H.

Twerski, Abraham J. Caution: Kindness Can Be Dangerous to the Alcholic. 1981. 10.95 (ISBN 0-13-121244-3); pap. 4.95 (ISBN 0-13-121236-2). P-H.

Twichell, Chase. Northern Spy. LC 80-54061. (Pitt Poetry Ser). 80p. 1981. 9.95 (ISBN 0-8229-3437-X); pap. 4.50 (ISBN 0-8229-5328-5). U of Pittsburgh Pr.

Twichell, Heath, Jr. Allen: The Biography of an Army Officer 1859-1930. 1974. 23.50 (ISBN 0-8135-0778-2). Rutgers U Pr.

Twigg, Bernard, jt. auth. see Kramer, Amihud.

Twigg, Bernard A., jt. auth. see Kramer, Amihud.

Twin, Stephanie. Out of the Bleachers. (Women's Lives-Women's Work Ser). (Illus.). 1979. pap. 5.50 (ISBN 0-912670-59-2, Co-Pub. by McGraw). Feminist Pr.

Twinem, F. P. You & Your Prostate. (Illus.). 120p. 1980. lexotone 7.75 (ISBN 0-398-04012-5); pap. 5.95 lexotone (ISBN 0-398-04014-1). C C Thomas.

Twining, James E., jt. auth. see Giroux, James A.

Twining, R. H. Science and Religion-Convergence or Collision. pap. 2.50 (ISBN 0-686-12939-3). Pyramid Iowa.

Twiss, B. C. Managing Technological Innovation. (Illus.). 272p. 1974. text ed. 18.95x o.p. (ISBN 0-582-45040-3). Longman.

Twiss, Benjamin. Lawyers & the Constitution. LC 73-10765. 271p. 1974. Repr. of 1942 ed. lib. bdg. 15.75x (ISBN 0-8371-7033-8, TWLC). Greenwood.

Twiss, Brian C. Managing Technological Innovation. 2nd. ed. 272p. 1980. text ed. 25.00 (ISBN 0-582-49708-6). Longman.

Twiss, T. Two Lectures on Machinery. 76p. 1971. Repr. of 1844 ed. 17.00x (ISBN 0-7165-0619-X, Pub. by Irish Academic Pr Ireland). Biblio Dist.

Twitchell, Hanford. Summer Pioneers: Memories of Old Field. 1977. 4.50 o.p. (ISBN 0-682-48979-4). Exposition.

Twitchell, James B. The Living Dead: A Study of the Vampire in Romantic Literature. LC 79-54290. 1981. 14.95 (ISBN 0-8223-0438-4). Duke.

Twitchett see Wright, Arthur F.

Twitchett, Carol C. A Framework for Development: The EEC & the ACP. 160p. 1981. text ed. 28.50x (ISBN 0-04-338094-8, 2592). Allen Unwin.

Twitchett, Carol C., ed. Harmonization in the EEC. 1980. write for info. (ISBN 0-312-36309-5). St Martin.

Twitchett, D. C. Financial Administration Under the T'ang Dynasty. 54.00 (ISBN 0-521-07823-7). Cambridge U Pr.

Twitchett, Denis. Printing & Publishing in Medieval China. (Illus.). 1981. pap. 14.50 (ISBN 0-913720-08-9). Sandstone.

Twitty, Victor C. Of Scientists & Salmanders. LC 66-24954. (Biology Ser.). (Illus.). 1966. 10.95x (ISBN 0-7167-0652-0). W H Freeman.

Two-Phase Flow & Heat Transfer Workshop, Ft. Lauderdale, Oct. 1976. Two-Phase Transport & Reactor Safety: Proceedings, 4 vols. Veziroglu, T. N. & Kakac, S., eds. LC 77-14094. 1978. Set. text ed. 225.00 (ISBN 0-89116-168-6). Hemisphere Pub.

Twohig, Dorothy, ed. Journal of the Proceedings of the President: 1793 to 1797. LC 80-17174. (Papers of George Washington). 1981. price not set (ISBN 0-8139-0874-4). U Pr of Va.

Twohig, Elizabeth S. The Megalithic Art of Western Europe. (Illus.). 432p. 1980. 89.00 (ISBN 0-19-813193-3). Oxford U Pr.

Twombly, Gerald H. Major Themes from the Minor Prophets. (Adult Study Guide). 144p. (Orig.). 1981. pap. 3.95 (ISBN 0-88469-132-2). BMH Bks.

Twombly, Neil J., jt. auth. see Price, Douglas B.

Twombly, Robert C. Frank Lloyd Wright: His Life & His Architecture. LC 78-9466. 1979. 22.50 (ISBN 0-471-03400-2, Pub. by Wiley-Interscience). Wiley.

Twomey, Gerald, ed. Thomas Merton: Prophet in the Belly of a Paradox. LC 78-61717. 1978. 9.95 (ISBN 0-8091-0268-4). Paulist Pr.

Twycross, R. G. & Ventafridda, V. The Continuing Care of Terminal Cancer Patients: Proceedings of an International Seminar on Continuing Care of Terminal Cancer Patients, 19-20 October 1979, Milan, Italy. 300p. 1980. 44.00 (ISBN 0-08-024943-4). Pergamon.

Twyford, John. Graphic Communication. (Illus.). 120p. (gr. 9-12). 1981. pap. 17.50 (ISBN 0-7134-3388-4, Pub. by Batsford England). David & Charles.

Twyman, Leo, tr. see Lindholm, Dan.

Twyman, Mary E. Letters to the Pope. 158p. 1981. 6.95 (ISBN 0-934400-15-6). Landmark Bks.

Twyman, Michael. Lithography Eighteen Hundred to Eighteen Fifty: The Techniques of Drawing on Stone in England & France & Their Application in Works of Topography. 1970. 26.00x (ISBN 0-19-215168-1). Oxford U Pr.

Twyne, Thomas, tr. see Petrarca, Francesco.

Tyabji, Badr-Ud-Din. Chaff & Grain. 10.00x (ISBN 0-210-26979-0). Asia.

Tyack, David B. The One Best System: A History of American Urban Education. LC 74-77184. (Illus.). 368p. 1974. text ed. 16.50x (ISBN 0-674-63780-1); pap. 3.95 (ISBN 0-674-63782-8). Harvard U Pr.

--Turning Points in American Educational History. 1967. pap. 16.50 (ISBN 0-471-00596-7). Wiley.

Tyagi, R. B. Recent Trends in the Cooperative Movement in India. 15.50x o.p. (ISBN 0-210-22596-3). Asia.

Tyagisananda, Swami, tr. Svetasvataropanisad. (Sanskrit & Eng.). pap. 2.00 (ISBN 0-87481-418-9). Vedanta Pr.

Tyalor, Dawson, ed. The Masters: Profiles of a Tournament. 3rd rev. ed. (Illus.). 192p. 1981. 19.95 (ISBN 0-498-01661-7). A S Barnes.

Tyau, Min-Chi'En T. China's New Constitution & International Problems. (Studies in Chinese Government & Law). 286p. 1977. Repr. of 1918 ed. 19.50 (ISBN 0-89093-064-3). U Pubns Amer.

Tychyna, Pavlo Hryhorovych. Zolotyi Homin. LC 68-52067. (Shkil'na Biblioteka Ser.). 1967. pap. text ed. 4.00 (ISBN 0-918884-25-X). Slavia Lib.

Tydeman, W. The Theatre in the Middle Ages. LC 77-85683. (Illus.). 1979. 42.00 (ISBN 0-521-21891-8); pap. 10.50x (ISBN 0-521-29304-9). Cambridge U Pr.

Tye, Kenneth, jt. ed. see Taylor, Philip H.

Tye, Kenneth A. & Novotney, Jerrold M. Schools in Transition. (I-D-E-A Reports on Schooling). 288p. 1975. 9.95 o.p. (ISBN 0-07-065690-8, P&RB). McGraw.

Tyers, G. Frank, ed. Self-Assessment of Current Knowledge in Cardiothoracic Surgery. 2nd. ed. LC 79-92911. 1980. pap. 18.00 (ISBN 0-87488-276-1). Med Exam.

Tyl, Noel. Teaching & Study Guide to the Principles & Practice of Astrology. 1976. 15.00 (ISBN 0-87542-812-6). Llewellyn Pubns.

Tyldesley, W. R. Oral Diagnosis. 172p. 1969. 19.25 (ISBN 0-08-013038-0). Pergamon.

--Oral Medicine. (Illus.). 225p. 1981. pap. text ed. 22.95x (ISBN 0-19-261275-1). Oxford U Pr.

Tylecote, Andrew. The Causes of the Present Inflation: An Interdisciplinary Explanation Centered on Britain, Germany & the United States. 180p. 1980. text ed. 24.95x (ISBN 0-470-26953-7). Halsted Pr.

Tyler, et al, trs. see Keene, Donald.

Tyler, Anne. Morgan's Passing. (Large Print Bks.). 1980. lib. bdg. 16.95 (ISBN 0-8161-3131-7). G K Hall.

Tyler, Benjamin & Witney, Fred. Labor Relations Law. 3rd ed. 1979. text ed. 23.95 (ISBN 0-13-519645-0). P-H.

Tyler, Bennet & Bonar, Andrew. The Life & Labours of Asahel Nettleton. 1975. 8.95 (ISBN 0-85151-208-9). Banner of Truth.

Tyler, Chaplin, jt. auth. see Gee, Edwin A.

Tyler, Christopher & Hirsch, Richard. Raku: Techniques for Contemporary Potters. (Illus.). 192p. 1975. 18.95 o.p. (ISBN 0-8230-4503-X). Watson-Guptill.

Tyler, Daniel. A Concise History of the Mormon Battalion in the Mexican War, 1846-1848. LC 64-15125. (Beautiful Rio Grande Classics Ser). Repr. of 1881 ed. lib. bdg. 12.00 (ISBN 0-87380-011-7). Rio Grande.

Tyler, E. J. Clock Types. 1980. pap. 10.95 (ISBN 0-85936-159-4, Pub. by Midas Bks England). Intl Schol Bk Serv.

Tyler, Gary R., jt. auth. see Coleman, Arthur.

Tyler, H. Richard & Dawson, David, eds. Current Neurology, Vol. 1. (Illus.). 1978. 29.00x o.p. (ISBN 0-89289-101-7). HM Prof Med Div.

--Current Neurology, Vol. 2. (Illus.). 1979. 34.00x (ISBN 0-89289-105-X). HM Prof Med Div.

Tyler, Hamilton. Owls of the Southwest & Mexico. (Illus.). 204p. 1979. 17.50 (ISBN 0-87358-219-5); pap. 9.95 (ISBN 0-87358-225-X). Northland.

Tyler, James. The Early Guitar: A History & Handbook. (Early Music Ser.). (Illus.). 176p. (Orig.). 1980. pap. text ed. 22.95x (ISBN 0-19-323182-4). Oxford U Pr.

Tyler, Jenny & Watts, Lisa. Children's Book of the Seas. LC 77-15549. (Children's Guides Ser.). (Illus.). (gr. 3 up). 1978. PLB 6.95 (ISBN 0-88436-464-X). EMC.

Tyler, Jenny, jt. auth. see Watts, Lisa.

Tyler, John E. Black Forest Clocks. (Illus.). 1977. 17.95x (ISBN 0-7198-0100-1). Intl Ideas.

Tyler, Leona, jt. auth. see Walsh, W. Bruce.

Tyler, Leona E. Work of the Counselor. 3rd ed. 1969. 17.95x (ISBN 0-13-965087-3). P-H.

Tyler, Lyon G. Letters & Times of the Tylers, 3 Vols. LC 71-75267. (American Public Figures Ser). 1970. Repr. of 1884 ed. lib. bdg. 125.00 (ISBN 0-306-71316-0). Da Capo.

Tyler, Margaret L. Homeopathic Drug Pictures. 885p. 1952. text ed. 29.95x (ISBN 0-8464-1020-6). Beekman Pubs.

Tyler, Martin W. Tidal Wave. (Orig.). 1975. pap. 1.50 o.p. (ISBN 0-685-52938-X, LB271ZK, Leisure Bks). Nordon Pubns.

Tyler, Moses C. History of American Literature, 1607-1765. Jones, Howard M., frwd. by. 584p. 1966. 25.00x (ISBN 0-8014-0433-9). Cornell U Pr.

--Patrick Henry. LC 80-18577. (American Statesmen Ser.). 460p. 1980. pap. 6.95 (ISBN 0-87754-190-6). Chelsea Hse.

Tyler, O. Z., Jr., ed. see Cohen, Myer M.

Tyler, Poyntz, ed. Airways of America. (Reference Shelf Ser.). 1958. 6.25 (ISBN 0-8242-0063-2). Wilson.

--Securities, Exchanges & the SEC. (Reference Shelf Ser: Vol. 37, No. 3). 1965. 6.25 (ISBN 0-8242-0086-1). Wilson.

Tyler, R. A. Bloody Provost: An Account of the Provost Service of the British Army & the Early Years of the Corps of Royal Military Police. (Illus.). 246p. 1980. 23.75x (ISBN 0-8476-3166-4). Rowman.

Tyler, Ralph, ed. From Youth to Constructive Adult Life: The Role of the Public School. LC 77-95249. (National Society for the Study of Education, Series on Contemp. Educ. Issues). 1978. 15.75 (ISBN 0-8211-1907-9); text ed. 14.25 ten copies (ISBN 0-685-04972-8). McCutchan.

Tyler, Ralph W. Prospects for Research & Development in Education. new ed. LC 75-36111. 190p. 1978. 15.50x (ISBN 0-8211-1906-0); text ed. 14.00x (ISBN 0-685-61058-6). McCutchan.

Tyler, Ralph W. & Wolf, Richard M. Crucial Issues in Testing. LC 73-20855. 1974. 15.25x (ISBN 0-8211-1714-9); text ed. 13.75x (ISBN 0-685-42643-2). McCutchan.

Tyler, Ronnie C. The Mexican War: A Lithographic Record. LC 93-88280. (Illus.). 108p. 1974. 10.00 (ISBN 0-87611-031-6); collector's ed. 45.00 (ISBN 0-87611-032-4); portfolio of 16 prints 7.50 (ISBN 0-87611-034-0). Tex St Hist Assn.

--Santiago Vidaurri & the Southern Confederacy. LC 73-186709. 1973. 8.00 (ISBN 0-87611-029-4). Tex St Hist Assn.

Tyler, Royall. Algerine Captive. LC 67-10272. 1967. Repr. of 1797 ed. 48.00x (ISBN 0-8201-1046-9). Schol Facsimiles.

--Verse of Royall Tyler. Peladeau, Marius B., ed. LC 68-14026. 1968. 10.95x (ISBN 0-8139-0235-5). U Pr of Va.

Tyler, Thomas G., compiled by. Statistical Abstract of Colorado, 1978-79. 2nd ed. (Illus., Orig.). Date not set. pap. cancelled (ISBN 0-918370-04-3). Transrep.

Tyler, W. T. The Ants of God. 288p. 1981. 10.95 (ISBN 0-8037-0270-1). Dial.

--The Man Who Lost the War. 384p. 1981. pap. 2.95 (ISBN 0-425-04852-7). Berkley Pub.

Tyler, William G. Advanced Developing Countries As Export Competitors in Third World Markets: The Brazilian Experience, Vol. II. LC 80-67710. (Significant Issues Ser.: No. 9). 88p. 1980. 5.95 (ISBN 0-89206-022-0). CSI Studies.

--The Brazilian Industrial Economy. LC 79-5440. 1981. price not set (ISBN 0-669-03448-7). Lexington Bks.

--Issues & Prospects for New International Economic Order. LC 77-78367. (Illus.). 1977. 19.95 (ISBN 0-669-01445-1). Lexington Bks.

Tyler, William G., jt. ed. see Rosenbaum, H. Jon.

Tyler, Zack. Foxx! (Orig.). 1981. pap. 1.95 (ISBN 0-440-12742-4). Dell.

--Foxx Hunting. (Orig.). 1981. pap. 2.25 (ISBN 0-440-12451-4). Dell.

--Foxx's Gold. (Orig.). 1981. pap. 1.95 (ISBN 0-440-13552-4). Dell.

--Foxx's Herd. (Orig.). Date not set. pap. 1.95 (ISBN 0-440-12730-0). Dell.

Tylman, Stanley D. & Malone, William F. Tylman's Theory & Practice of Crown & Fixed Partial Prosthodontics (Bridge) 7th ed. LC 78-17821. 1978. text ed. 37.50 (ISBN 0-8016-5166-2). Mosby.

Tylutki, Edmund E. Mushrooms of Idaho & the Pacific Northwest (Discomycetes) LC 79-64127. (GEM Books-Natural History). (Illus.). 166p. (Orig.). 1979. pap. 5.95 (ISBN 0-89301-062-6). U Pr of Idaho.

Tymchenko, Ievhen. Kurs Istorii Ukrains'koho Iazyka: Vstup Fonetyka. LC 75-571931. (Shkil'na Biblioteka). (Ukra.). 1972. text ed. 10.00 (ISBN 0-918884-17-9). Slavia Lib.

Tymchuk, Alexander J. Behavior Modification with Children: A Clinical Training Manual. (Illus.). 149p. 1974. pap. text ed. 8.00 o.p. (ISBN 0-398-03125-8). C C Thomas.

--The Mental Retardation Dictionary. LC 73-80058. 149p. 1980. pap. 7.00x (ISBN 0-87424-125-1). Western Psych.

Tymme, T., tr. see Adrichem, Christianus van.

Tymms, Jean. I Like to See: A Book About the Five Senses. (Tell-a-Tale Readers). (Illus.). (gr. k-2). 1973. pap. 4.77 (ISBN 0-307-68443-1, Whitman). Western Pub.

Tymn, Marshall. American Fantasy & Science Fiction. LC 80-19217. 224p. 1980. Repr. of 1979 ed. lib. bdg. 12.95x (ISBN 0-89370-029-0). Borgo Pr.

Tymn, Marshall B. Horror & Supernatural Literature. 320p. 1981. 22.50 (ISBN 0-8352-1341-2). Bowker.

Tymoczko, Maria, tr. Two Death Tales: from the Ulster Cycle: The Death of Cu Roi & the Death of Cu Chulainn. (Dolmen Texts: No. 2). 1980. text ed. 31.25x (ISBN 0-85105-342-4, Dolmen Pr). Humanities.

Tyms, James D. The Rise of Religious Education Among Negro Baptists. LC 79-66419. 1979. pap. text ed. 13.00 (ISBN 0-8191-0827-8). U Pr of Amer.

--Spiritual (Religious) Values in the Black Poet. 1977. 10.75 (ISBN 0-8191-0296-2). U Pr of Amer.

Tyna, Eugene J., jt. auth. see Cain, J. Allan.

Tynan, Eugene J. & Cain, J. Allen. Geology: A Synopsis Part 2 Historical Geology. LC 79-92086. 192p. 1981. pap. text ed. 7.95 (ISBN 0-8403-2306-9). Kendall-Hunt.

Tynan, Kathleen. Agatha. 1979. pap. 2.25 (ISBN 0-345-27586-1). Ballantine.

Tynan, Kenneth. Show People. 1981. pap. 2.95 (ISBN 0-425-04750-4). Berkley Pub.

Tyndale, William. A Compendious Introduccion Unto the Pistle off Paul to the Romayns. LC 74-28890. (English Experience Ser.: No. 767). 1975. Repr. 3.50 (ISBN 90-221-0767-1). Walter J Johnson.

Tyndall, John. The Art of Physical Investigation & the Scientific Use of Man's Imagination. (Illus.). 1979. Repr. of 1898 ed. 47.75 (ISBN 0-89901-001-6). Found Class Reprints.

--The Scientific Use of Man's Imagination. (Illus.). 181p. 1977. 43.15 (ISBN 0-89266-037-6). Am Classical Coll Pr.

Tyne, Claude H. Van see Van Tyne, Claude H.

Tyner, Wallace E., et al. Western Coal: Promise or Problem? LC 78-3005. (Illus.). 1978. 19.95 (ISBN 0-669-02320-5). Lexington Bks.

Tynyanov, Yury. The Problem of Verse Language. Sosa, Michael & Harvey, Brent, trs. from Rus. 1981. 15.00 (ISBN 0-88233-464-6); pap. 6.50x (ISBN 0-88233-465-4). Ardis Pubs.

Typony. Etctera: Graphic Devices. 176p. 1980. pap. 12.95 (ISBN 0-442-24456-8). Van Nos Reinhold.

Tyrack, Mildred & Van Eperen, Jeannine, eds. Five Generations of Obesity: A Compilation of Family Recipes Making Getting Fat Look Easy. (Illus.). 116p. (Orig.). 1981. pap. 4.95 (ISBN 0-937268-03-8). Alpha Printing.

Tyrell, Arthur. The Basics of Reprography. (Reprographic Library). Date not set. 12.50 o.p. (ISBN 0-8038-0733-3). Hastings.

Tyrell, R. Y., ed. see Cicero.

Tyrer, J. H., jt. auth. see Eadie, M. J.

Tyrer, John H., jt. auth. see Eadie, Mervyn J.

Tyrka, Hilary, jt. auth. see Shapiro, Stephen.

Tyrmand, Leopold, ed. Kultura Essays. LC 70-99732. 1970. 10.95 o.s.i. (ISBN 0-02-932820-9). Free Pr.

Tyror, J. G. & Vaughan, R. I. Introduction to Neutron Kinetics of Nuclear Power Reactors. LC 76-94936. 1970. 25.00 (ISBN 0-08-006667-4). Pergamon.

Tyrrell, Bernard. Christotherapy: Healing Through Enlightenment. 250p. 1975. 8.95 (ISBN 0-8164-0278-7). Crossroad NY.

Tyrrell, D. A., et al. More Technologies for Rural Health. (Proceedings of the Royal Society, Series B.: Vol. 209). 186p. 1980. text ed. 30.00x (ISBN 0-85403-148-0, Pub. by Royal Soc London). Scholium Intl.

Tyrrell, David A., ed. Aspects of Slow & Persistent Virus Infections. (New Perspectives in Clinical Microbiology Ser.: Vol. 2). 286p. 1980. lib. bdg. 42.10 (ISBN 90-247-2281-0, Pub. by Martinus Nijhoff). Kluwer Boston.

Tyrrell, G. N. Apparitions. 1962. pap. 0.95 o.s.i. (ISBN 0-02-078090-7, Collier). Macmillan.

Tyrrell, J. A. & Semple, J. G. Generalized Clifford Parallelism. LC 74-134625. (Tracts in Mathematics Ser.: No. 61). 1971. 23.95 (ISBN 0-521-08042-8). Cambridge U Pr.

Tyrrell, Sir James. Bibliotheca Politica, 2 vols. Berkowitz, David S. & Thorne, Samuel E., eds. (English Legal History Ser.: Vol. 80). 1094p. 1979. 55.00 ea. (ISBN 0-8240-3067-2). Garland Pub.

Tyrrell, Robert. Work of the Television Journalist. 2nd ed. LC 80-41970. 200p. 1981. 22.95 (ISBN 0-240-51051-8). Focal Pr.

Tyrrell, Ronald, et al. Growing Pains in the Classroom: A Guide for Teachers of Adolescents. (Illus.). 368p. 1977. text ed. 11.95 (ISBN 0-87909-312-9). Reston.

Tyrwhitt, Jaqueline, ed. see Institute of Child Health Athens International Symposium 2-8, July 1978 Athens, Greece.

Tyrwhitt, Thomas. An Essay on the Language & Versification of Chaucer. 76p. 1980. Repr. of 1775 ed. text ed. 15.00 (ISBN 0-8492-8409-0). R West.

--An Introductory Discourse to the Canterbury Tales. 52p. 1980. Repr. of 1778 ed. lib. bdg. 15.00 (ISBN 0-8495-5161-7). Arden Lib.

Tysen, Frank J. District Administration in Metropolitan Calcutta. 3.25x o.p. (ISBN 0-210-27116-7). Asia.

Tysinger, D. S., Jr. The Clinical Physics & Physiology of Chronic Lung Disease, Inhalation Therapy, & Pulmonary Function Testing. (Illus.). 264p. 1973. text ed. 17.50 (ISBN 0-398-02777-3). C C Thomas.

Tyson, Archie M. Every Woman in Her Humor: A Critical Edition. Orgel, Stephen, ed. LC 79-54327. 300p. 1980. lib. bdg. 33.00 (ISBN 0-8240-4479-7). Garland Pub.

Tyson, J., tr. see Vydra, F., et al.

Tyson, James L. Target America. 215p. 1981. 10.95 (ISBN 0-89526-669-5). Regnery-Gateway.

Tyson, John C. & Piele, Linda J. Materials & Methods for Business Research. LC 80-20332. (Bibliographic Instruction Ser.). 1980. lib. bdg. 14.95x (ISBN 0-918212-15-4); wkbk. 5 or more 4.95 (ISBN 0-918212-14-6). Neal-Schuman.

Tyson, Laura D. The Yugoslav Economic System & Its Performance in the Nineteen Seventies. LC 80-24650. (Research Ser.: No. 44). x, 115p. 1980. pap. 4.50x (ISBN 0-87725-144-4). U Cal LA Indus Rel.

Tyson, Laura D., jt. ed. see Neuberger, Egon.

Tyson, Mary C. & Tyson, Robert. Psychology of Successful Weight Control. LC 73-84207. 192p. 1974. 11.95 (ISBN 0-88229-103-3). Nelson-Hall.

Tyson, Robert, jt. auth. see Tyson, Mary C.

Tysse, Agnes M., ed. International Education: The American Experience, A Bibliography, 2 pts, Vol. 2, Periodical Articles. rev. ed. Incl. Part 1. General; Part 2. Area Studies, & Indexes. LC 73-16429. 1977. 45.00 (ISBN 0-8108-1009-3). Scarecrow.

Tysse, Agnes N. International Education: the American Experience a Bibliography: Vol. 1: Dissertations & Theses. 1974. 10.00 (ISBN 0-8108-0686-X). Scarecrow.

Tzannes, Basil, jt. auth. see Tzannes, Nicolaos.

Tzannes, N. S., jt. ed. see Lainiotis, D. G.

Tzannes, Nicolaos & Tzannes, Basil. Backgammon Games & Strategies. LC 74-9300. (Illus.). 256p. 1976. 9.95 o.p. (ISBN 0-498-01497-5). A S Barnes.

Tzara, Tristan. Seven Dada Manifestos. Wright, Barbara, tr. 1979. 8.95 (ISBN 0-7145-3557-5); pap. 4.95. Riverrun NY.

Tze-Chung Li. A Manual for Basic DIALOG Searching. LC 80-67847. 1980. 3.00 (ISBN 0-937256-01-3). CHCUS Inc.

Tzu-Kuang, Hsu, jt. auth. see Han, Li.

U

U. S.-Japan Seminar or Inelastic Light Scattering, Santa Monica, California. January 22-25, 1979. Inelastic Light Scattering: Proceedings. Burstein, E. & Kawamura, H., eds. 124p. 1980. 23.00 (ISBN 0-08-025425-X). Pergamon.

U. S. U. L. A. Lifesaving & Marine Safety. 1981. price not set (Assn Pr). Follett.

Ubamadu, H. Oziri. A Handbook for Prospective African Students to the U.S.A. LC 78-53791. 1978. pap. text ed. 5.50x (ISBN 0-8191-0514-7). U Pr of Amer.

Ubbelohde, A. R. The Molten State of Matter: Melting & Crystal Structure. LC 77-28300. 454p. 1979. 68.95 (ISBN 0-471-99626-2). Wiley.

Ubbelohde, Carl. Colorado Reader. 6.50 o.p. (ISBN 0-87108-028-1). Pruett.

Ubben, Gerald C., jt. auth. see Hughes, Larry W.

Ubelaker, Douglas H. Human Skeletal Remains: Excavation, Analysis, Interpretation. LC 77-95323. (Manuals on Archeology: No. 2). (Illus.). xi, 116p. 1980. Repr. of 1978 ed. 18.00x (ISBN 0-9602822-1-1). Taraxacum.

--Human Skeletal Remains: Excavation, Analysis, Interpretation. (Aldine Manuals on Archeology). (Illus.). 1978. 12.50 o.p. (ISBN 0-202-33037-0). Beresford Bk Serv.

Ubell, Al. Al Ubell's Energy-Saving Guide. (Orig.). 1980. pap. 4.95 (ISBN 0-446-97666-0). Warner Bks.

Uberall, Herbert. Electron Scattering from Complex Nuclei Pts. A & B. (Pure & Applied Physics Ser: Vol. 25). 1971. Pt. A. 51.00 (ISBN 0-12-705701-3); Pt. B. 48.50 (ISBN 0-12-705702-1); Set. 81.00 (ISBN 0-685-02415-6). Acad Pr.

UBS Committee, ed. Preliminary & Interim Report on the Hebrew Old Testament Text Project, Vol. 1. (Pentateuch Ser.). (Eng. & Fr.). 1973. pap. 2.60 (ISBN 0-8267-0008-X, 08520). United Bible.

--Preliminary & Interim Report on the Hebrew Old Testament Text Project, Vol. 2. (Historical Bks.). (Eng. & Fr.). 1976. pap. 4.35 (ISBN 0-8267-0009-8, 08521). United Bible.

Ucelay, M., jt. ed. see DaCal, E. G.

Uche, U. U. Contractual Obligations in Ghana & Nigeria. 300p. 1971. 29.50x (ISBN 0-7146-2611-2, F Cass Co). Biblio Dist.

Uchelen, Rod Van see Van Uchelen, Rod.

Uchida, Yoshiko. The Rooster Who Understood Japanese. LC 76-13450. (Illus.). 32p. (gr. 1-3). 1976. reinforced bdg. 6.95 (ISBN 0-684-14672-X, ScribJ). Scribner.

Uchill, Ida L. Pioneers, Peddlers, & Tsadikim: The Story of the Jews in Colorado. 2nd ed. LC 57-57817. 327p. 1979. pap. 10.00 (ISBN 0-9604468-0-X). Uchill.

Uchiyama, Kosho. Approach to Zen: The Reality of Zazen. LC 73-83957. (Illus.). 128p. 1973. pap. 4.75 o.p. (ISBN 0-87040-252-8). Japan Pubns.

Uchtmann, Donald L. & Looney, J. W. Agricultural Law: Principles & Cases. (Illus.). 624p. 1981. text ed. 24.95 (ISBN 0-07-065746-7). McGraw.

Ucko, David. Living Chemistry. 1977. text ed. 18.50 (ISBN 0-12-705950-4); lab manual 6.50 (ISBN 0-12-705956-3); transparency masters avail. (ISBN 0-12-705956-3). Acad Pr.

UCLA Law Review Staff. Computerization of Government Files: What Impact on the Individual? 124p. 1969. Repr. 3.00 o.p. (ISBN 0-685-22685-9). Am Bar Foun.

UCLA Moot Court Honors Program. Handbook of Appellate Advocacy. rev. ed. Dizenfeld, Bruce, et al, eds. LC 79-23768. 260p. 1980. pap. text ed. 6.95 (ISBN 0-8299-2068-4). West Pub.

Udall, Lee, ed. see Wilson, Joseph T.

Udall, Morris K. Education of a Congressman: The Newsletters of Morris K. Udall. LC 72-79739. 1972. pap. text ed. 7.50 (ISBN 0-672-61312-3). Bobbs.

Udall, Morris K., jt. ed. see Tacheron, Donald G.

Udall, Stewart. The National Parks. (Jackdaw Ser: No. A9). 1974. 5.95 o.s.i. (ISBN 0-670-50457-2, Grossman). Viking Pr.

Uddin, Jasim. Gipsy Wharf. LC 70-10225. (Unesco's Pakistan Ser). (Illus.). 1970. 9.95 (ISBN 0-672-53544-0). Pegasus.

Udell, Jon G. & Laczniak, Gene R. Marketing in an Age of Change. (Marketing Ser.). 650p. 1981. text ed. 19.95 (ISBN 0-471-08169-8); tchrs.' ed. avail. (ISBN 0-471-08184-1); test file avail. (ISBN 0-471-08187-6). Wiley.

Udell, Jonathan. Toward Conceptual Codification: In Race & Ethnic Relations. LC 79-84196. 1980. 7.95 (ISBN 0-87212-119-4). Libra.

Udell, Rochelle, jt. auth. see Stein, Frances P.

Udell, William L., jt. auth. see Franke, Lois.

Uden, A. van see Van Uden, A.

Uden, Grant, jt. auth. see Cooper, Richard.

Udenfriend, Sidney. Fluorescence Assay in Biology & Medicine, 2 Vols. (Molecular Biology: Vol. 3). (Illus.). Vol. 1, 1962. 46.00 (ISBN 0-12-705850-8); Vol. 2. 47.50 (ISBN 0-12-705802-8). Acad Pr.

Uderzo, jt. auth. see Goscinny.

Udet, Ernst. Ace of the Iron Cross. Ulanoff, Stanley M., ed. Riehn, Richard K., tr. from Ger. LC 80-26156. (Air Combat Classics). (Illus.). 256p. 1981. 9.95 (ISBN 0-668-05161-2); pap. 5.95 (ISBN 0-668-05163-9). Arco.

Udintsev, G. B., jt. ed. see Vinogradov, A. P.

Udo, Reuben K. Geographical Regions of Nigeria. LC 70-94980. (Illus.). 1970. 25.00x (ISBN 0-520-01588-6). U of Cal Pr.

Udolf, Roy. The College Instructor's Guide to Teaching & Academia. LC 76-7462. 172p. 1976. text ed. 13.95 (ISBN 0-88229-241-2). Nelson-Hall.

--Handbook of Hypnosis for Professionals. 384p. 1981. text ed. 24.50 (ISBN 0-442-28881-6). Van Nos Reinhold.

--Logic Design for Behavioral Scientists. LC 73-75522. 1973. 16.95 (ISBN 0-911012-54-0). Nelson-Hall.

Udovitch, A. L. The Middle East: Oil, Conflict & Hope, Vol. 10. LC 75-44728. (Critical Choices for Americans Ser.). 1976. 25.95 (ISBN 0-669-00424-3). Lexington Bks.

Udovitch, A. L., ed. Islamic Middle East 700-1900: Studies in Economic & Social History. LC 79-52703. (Illus.). 832p. 1981. 24.95x (ISBN 0-87850-030-8). Darwin Pr.

Udry, Janice M. Glenda. (Illus.). (gr. 3-5). 1976. pap. 0.95 (ISBN 0-671-29784-8). PB.

--How I Faded Away. Rubin, Caroline, ed. LC 75-30863. (Concept Bks). (Illus.). 32p. (gr. 2-4). 1975. 6.95g (ISBN 0-8075-3416-1). A Whitman.

--Mary Jo's Grandmother. LC 78-126433. (Mary Jo Stories Ser). (Illus.). 32p. (gr. k-3). 1970. 6.95g (ISBN 0-8075-4984-3). A Whitman.

--Sunflower Garden. LC 69-17738. (Illus.). (gr. 2-5). 1969. PLB 5.39 o.p. (ISBN 0-8178-4472-4). Harvey.

--What Mary Jo Shared. LC 66-16082. (Illus.). 40p. (gr. k-2). 1966. 6.95g (ISBN 0-8075-8842-3). A Whitman.

--What Mary Jo Wanted. LC 68-9123. (Illus.). 40p. (gr. k-3). 1968. 5.95g o.p. (ISBN 0-8075-8848-2). A Whitman.

Udupa, K. N. & Mishra, S. K. Thyroid Diseases in Tropics. 320p. Date not set. text ed. 25.00x (ISBN 0-7069-1173-3, Pub. by Vikas India). Advent Bk.

Udwadia, Farokh E. Diagnosis & Management of Acute Respiratory Failure. (Illus.). 1979. text ed. 29.95x (ISBN 0-19-561072-5). Oxford U Pr.

Ueberall, H., jt. auth. see Cannata, F.

Uecker, Bob & Herskowitz, Mickey. The Catcher in the Wry. 320p. 1981. 10.95 (ISBN 0-399-12586-8). Putnam.

Ueda, Makato, compiled by. Modern Japanese Haiku: An Anthology. LC 74-75035. 1976. pap. 7.50 (ISBN 0-8020-6245-8). U of Toronto Pr.

Uehara, Goro & Gillman, Gavin P. The Mineralogy, Chemistry, & Physics of Tropical Soils with Variable Charge Clays. (Tropical Agriculture Ser.). 1981. lib. bdg. 27.50x (ISBN 0-89158-484-6). Westview.

Uehling, Harold F. Correction of a Correctional Psychologist in Treatment of the Criminal Offender. (American Lectures in Behavioral Science & Law Ser.). 232p. 1973. 16.75 (ISBN 0-398-02615-7). C C Thomas.

Uekusa, Masu, jt. auth. see Caves, Richard E.

Uelsmann, Jerry N. Jerry N. Uelsmann Photographs from Nineteen Seventy-Five to Nineteen Seventy-Nine. Klindt, Steven, ed. (Illus.). 90p. (Orig.). 1980. pap. 7.95 (ISBN 0-932026-04-4). Chicago Contemp Photo.

Uffelman, Larry K. Charles Kingsley. (English Authors Ser.: No. 273). 1979. 13.50 (ISBN 0-8057-6752-5). Twayne.

Ugalda, Sharon K. Gabriel Celaya. (World Authors Ser.: No. 483 Spain). 1978. 12.50 (ISBN 0-8057-6324-4). Twayne.

Ugalde, Antonio, et al. The Urbanization Process of a Poor Mexican Neighborhood. LC 74-620102. 68p. 1974. pap. 3.95 (ISBN 0-292-78503-8). U of Tex Pr.

Ugarte, Francisco. Elementary Spanish: A Conversational Approach. LC 66-30529. 1967. 11.95 (ISBN 0-672-63163-6). Odyssey Pr.

--Espana y Su Civilizacion. 2nd ed. LC 64-23908. 1965. 9.95 (ISBN 0-672-63165-2). Odyssey Pr.

--Gramatica Espanola De Repaso. 2nd ed. Gordon, F. L., ed. LC 78-81805. 1969. 8.95 (ISBN 0-672-63173-3). Odyssey Pr.

Ugelstad, E., jt. auth. see Jorstad, J.

Ugolotti, Bruno. The Maturity. 1978. 6.95 o.p. (ISBN 0-533-02968-6). Vantage.

Ugural, Ansel C. Stresses in Plates & Shells. (Illus.). 352p. text ed. 29.95x (ISBN 0-07-065730-0, C); solutions manual 6.95 (ISBN 0-07-065731-9). McGraw.

Ugwuegbu, Denis, jt. auth. see Siann, Gerda.

Uhde, George I., ed. Self-Assessment of Current Knowledge in Otolaryngology. 2nd ed. 1976. spiral bdg. 14.50 (ISBN 0-87488-270-2). Med Exam.

Uhl, Kenneth P., jt. auth. see Schoner, Bertram.

Uhlan, Edward, jt. auth. see Peacock, A. D.

Uhley, Herman N. Vector Electrocardiography. (Illus.). 1962. 8.50 o.p. (ISBN 0-397-50086-6). Lippincott.

Uhlfelder, Myra, ed. & tr. see John The Scot.

Uhlfelder, Myra L., tr. see Gregory The Great.

Uhlich, Richard. Twenty Minutes to Live. Uhlich, Richard, ed. (Bluejeans Paperback Ser.). (Illus., Orig.). (gr. 7-12). 1978. pap. text ed. 1.25 (ISBN 0-8374-5004-7). Xerox Ed Pubns.

Uhlich, Richard, ed. see Carlson, Diane.

Uhlich, Richard, ed. see Carlson, Gordon.

Uhlich, Richard, ed. see Hogan, Elizabeth.

Uhlich, Richard, ed. see Otfinoski, Steven.

Uhlich, Richard, ed. see Sorensen, Robert.

Uhlig, Frank J., ed. Naval Review Nineteen Eighty. LC 62-21028. (Illus.). 264p. 1980. 11.00x (ISBN 0-87021-490-X). Naval Inst Pr.

Uhlig, H., ed. System & Theory of Geosciences, 2 pts. 103p. 1975. Vol. 1. pap. text ed. 24.00 (ISBN 0-08-019664-0); Vol. 7, Pt. 1. pap. text ed. 24.00 (ISBN 0-08-019670-5). Pergamon.

Uhlig, Herbert H. Corrosion & Corrosion Control: An Introduction to Corrosion Science & Engineering. 2nd ed. LC 71-162425. 419p. 1971. 32.50 (ISBN 0-471-89563-6, Pub. by Wiley-Interscience). Wiley.

--Corrosion Handbook. 1948. 52.50 (ISBN 0-471-89562-8, Pub. by Wiley-Interscience). Wiley.

Uhlig, Klaus. Pedestrian Malls. Date not set. 40.00 (ISBN 0-8038-0209-9). Hastings.

Uhlman, Thomas M. Racial Justice: Black Judges & Defendants in an Urban Trial Court. LC 78-19569. 144p. 1979. 15.50 (ISBN 0-669-02625-5). Lexington Bks.

Uhlmann, Dietrich. Hydrobiology: A Text for Engineers & Scientists. LC 77-24258. 1979. 51.95 (ISBN 0-471-99557-6, Pub. by Wiley-Interscience). Wiley.

Uhlmann, L., jt. auth. see Ray, G. F.

Uhr, Carl G. Economic Doctrines of Knut Wicksell. (Institute of Business & Economic Research UC Berkeley). 1960. 27.50x (ISBN 0-520-01290-9). U of Cal Pr.

Uhr, Leonard. Pattern Recognition, Learning & Thought: Computer-Programmed Models of Higher Mental Processes. (Illus.). 528p. 1973. ref. ed. 18.95 (ISBN 0-13-654095-3). P-H.

Uiker, John J., jt. auth. see Shigley, Joseph E.

Uinbook, ed. Houston: City of Destiny. 176p. 1980. 19.95 (ISBN 0-02-620900-4). Macmillan.

Uitti, Karl D. Linguistics & Literary Theory. new ed. 264p. 1974. pap. text ed. 5.95x (ISBN 0-393-09293-3). Norton.

Ukers, William H. All About Coffee. LC 71-178659. (Illus.). 1975. Repr. of 1935 ed. 50.00 (ISBN 0-8103-4092-5). Gale.

Ukoli, Neville M. Twins of the Rain Forest. (Orig.). 1968. pap. text ed. 2.25x (ISBN 0-582-64005-9). Humanities.

Ukrainka, Lesia. Boiarynia. 56p. 1970. pap. 2.00. Slavia Lib.

Ulam, Adam B. Bolsheviks. 1968. pap. 7.95 (ISBN 0-02-038100-X, Collier). Macmillan.

--Russia's Failed Revolutions: From the Decembrists to the Dissidents. LC 80-50534. 432p. 1981. 18.95 (ISBN 0-465-07152-X). Basic.

--The Unfinished Revolution. 1979. lib. bdg. 24.50x (ISBN 0-89158-485-4); pap. 9.50 (ISBN 0-89158-496-X). Westview.

Ulam, Stanislaw M. Stanislaw Ulam Sets, Numbers, & Universes: Selected Works. Beyer, William, et al, eds. LC 73-21686. 654p. 1974. 40.00x (ISBN 0-262-02108-0). MIT Pr.

Ulanoff, Stanley M., ed. see Udet, Ernst.

Ulanoff, Stanley M., ed. see Von Richthofen, Manfred.

Ulanov, Ann B. Receiving Woman: Studies Inthe; Psychology & Theology Jof the Feminine0. LC 80-26815. 1981. pap. 9.95 (ISBN 0-664-24360-6). Westminster.

Ulanov, Barry. A History of Jazz in America. LC 74-37324. 382p. 1972. Repr. of 1955 ed. lib. bdg. 25.00 (ISBN 0-306-70427-7). Da Capo.

Ular, Alexander. Russo-Chinese Empire. (Studies in Chinese History & Civilization). 334p. 1977. Repr. of 1904 ed. 24.00 (ISBN 0-89093-086-4). U Pubns Amer.

Ulasi, A. L. Many Thing Begin for Change. 1975. pap. 1.75 o.p. (ISBN 0-531-06064-0, Fontana Pap). Watts.

Ulbrich, Holley H. & Yandle, Bruce. Managing Personal Finance. 1979. 15.50x (ISBN 0-256-02208-9). Business Pubns.

Ulc, Otto. The Judge in a Communist State: A View from Within. LC 71-141382. xiv, 307p. 1972. 12.00x (ISBN 0-8214-0091-6). Ohio U Pr.

--Politics in Czechoslovakia. LC 74-11106. (Illus.). 1974. text ed. 17.95x (ISBN 0-7167-0779-9). W H Freeman.

Uldall, Robert. Renal Nursing. 2nd ed. (Blackwell Scientific Pubns.). 1977. 16.00 (ISBN 0-632-00086-4). Mosby.

Ulett, G. A., jt. ed. see Steinhilber, R. M.

Ulett, George A. & Smith, Kathleen. A Synopsis of Contemporary Psychiatry. 6th ed. LC 79-14554. (Illus.). 1979. pap. text ed. 18.95 (ISBN 0-8016-5176-X). Mosby.

ULI Commercial & Office Development Council. Shopping Center Development Handbook. Spink, Frank H., Jr., ed. LC 77-79326. (Community Builders' Handbook Ser.). 1976. 29.00 (ISBN 0-87420-576-X). Urban Land.

ULI Industrial Council. Industrial Development Handbook. Spink, Frank H., Jr., ed. LC 75-37218. (Community Builders Handbook Ser.). (Illus.). 256p. 1975. 29.00 (ISBN 0-87420-562-X). Urban Land.

ULI Research Division. Effects of Regulations on Housing Costs: Two Case Studies. LC 77-82249. (ULI Research Report Ser.: No. 27). (Illus.). 34p. 1977. pap. 11.75 (ISBN 0-87420-327-9). Urban Land.

--Large Scale Development: Benefits, Constraints, & State & Local Policy Incentives. LC 77-74659. (Management & Control of Growth Ser.). (Illus.). 135p. 1977. pap. 11.00 (ISBN 0-87420-573-5). Urban Land.

--New Opportunities, for Residential Development in Central Cities. (Research Report Ser.: No. 25). 1976. pap. 6.00 (ISBN 0-87420-325-2). Urban Land.

ULI Research Division & Gladstone Associates. Joint Development: Making the Real Estate-Transit Connection. LC 79-66189. (Illus.). 216p. 1979. pap. text ed. 25.75 (ISBN 0-87420-588-3). Urban Land.

Ulibarri, Sabine R. Tierra Amarilla: Stories of New Mexico, Cuentos De Nuevo Mexico. LC 75-153942. (Illus.). 167p. (Eng. & Span.). 1978. pap. 4.95 (ISBN 0-8263-0212-2). U of NM Pr.

Ulich, Robert. History of Religious Education: Documents & Interpretations from the Judaeo - Christian Tradition. LC 68-29433. 1968. 15.00x (ISBN 0-8147-0420-4). NYU Pr.

Ulin, Priscilla & Segall, Marshall, eds. Traditional Health Care Delivery in Contemporary Africa. LC 80-27442. (African Foreign & Comparative Studies Program: Vol. 35). vii, 98p. (Orig.). 1980. 8.00x (ISBN 0-915984-57-1). Syracuse U Foreign Comp.

Ulin, Priscilla, jt. ed. see Segall, Marshall.

Ulisse, Gael C. POMR: Application to Nursing Records. LC 78-60718. 1978. 7.95 (ISBN 0-201-07880-5, 07880, M&N Div). A-W.

Ullendorff, Edward, ed. & tr. see Haile Sellasie I.

Ullman, Agnes, jt. ed. see Lwoff, Andre.

Ullman, Berthold L. Ancient Writing & Its Influence. (Medieval Academy Reprints for Teaching Ser.). 260p. 1981. pap. 7.50x (ISBN 0-8020-6435-3). U of Toronto Pr.

Ullman, Edward L. Geography as Spatial Interaction. Boyce, Ronald R., ed. LC 79-6759. 252p. 1980. 16.50 (ISBN 0-295-95711-5). U of Wash Pr.

Ullman, Gerald H. Ocean Freight Forwarder, the Exporter & the Law. LC 67-25958. 1967. 6.00x (ISBN 0-87033-072-1). Cornell Maritime.

Ullman, James M. How to Hold a Garage Sale. LC 80-53812. (Illus.). 96p. (Orig.). 1981. pap. 3.95 (ISBN 0-528-88040-3). Rand.

Ullman, James R. Banner in the Sky. (gr. 7-9). 1980. pap. 1.75 (ISBN 0-671-56081-6). Archway.

Ullman, Jeffrey D. Programming Systems. LC 75-374. (Illus.). 336p. 1976. text ed. 19.95 (ISBN 0-201-07654-3). A-W.

Ullman, Jeffrey D., jt. auth. see Aho, Alfred V.

Ullman, Jeffrey D., jt. auth. see Hopcroft, John E.

Ullman, Joan C., tr. see Vicens Vives, Jaime.

Ullman, Michael. Jazz Lives. (Illus.). 1980. 9.95 o.p. (ISBN 0-915220-51-2). New Republic.

Ullman, Montague & Krippner, Stanley. Dream Studies & Telepathy. LC 71-113639. (Parapsychological Monograph No. 12). 1970. pap. 4.00 (ISBN 0-912328-16-9). Parapsych Foun.

Ullman, Montague, ed. see International Conference on Hypnosis, Drugs, Dreams, & Psi, France, 1967.

Ullman, Neil R. Elementary Statistics: An Applied Approach. LC 77-10828. 1978. text ed. 18.95 (ISBN 0-471-02105-9); tchrs'. manual avail.; wkbk & study guide 6.95x (ISBN 0-471-03209-3). Wiley.

Ullman, Pierre L. Mariano De Larra & Spanish Political Rhetoric. 1971. 35.00 (ISBN 0-299-05750-X). U of Wis Pr.

Ullman, Ralph, jt. auth. see Stratmann, William C.

Ullman, Richard, jt. auth. see Dunn, Robert.

Ullman, Victoria. Dewdrops. 1981. 5.50 (ISBN 0-8062-1683-2). Carlton.

Ullman, Walter. The Church & the Law in the Earlier Middle Ages. 406p. 1980. 60.00x (ISBN 0-902089-79-X, Pub. by Variorum England). State Mutual Bk.

--Medieval Foundations of Renaissance Humanism. LC 77-278. 1977. 19.50x (ISBN 0-8014-1110-6). Cornell U Pr.

--Medieval Papalism: The Political Theories of the Medieval Canonists. LC 79-1644. 1981. Repr. of 1949 ed. 19.50 (ISBN 0-88355-946-3). Hyperion Conn.

Ullmann, John E., ed. The Improvement of Productivity: Myths & Realities. 24.95 (ISBN 0-03-055301-6). Praeger.

--The Suburban Economic Network: Economic Activity, Resource Use, & the Great Sprawl. LC 76-12883. (Special Studies). 1977. text ed. 28.50 (ISBN 0-275-23560-2). Praeger.

Ullmann, L. P. Institution & Outcome. 1967. 27.00 (ISBN 0-08-012205-1). Pergamon.

Ullmann, Leonard & Krasner, Leonard. A Psychological Approach to Abnormal Behaviour. 2nd ed. LC 74-28271. 832p. 1975. text ed. 22.95 (ISBN 0-13-732545-2). P-H.

Ullmann, Leonard P. Research in Clinical Psychology: Effective Coping Through Data Collection. (Pergamon General Psychology Ser.). 325p. Date not set. write for info. (ISBN 0-08-025945-6); pap. write for info. (ISBN 0-08-025944-8). Pergamon.

Ullmann, Stephen. Style in the French Novel. 1964. 29.50x (ISBN 0-631-07960-2, Pub. by Basil Blackwell). Biblio Dist.

Ullmann, Walter. Jurisprudence in the Middle Ages. 390p. 1980. 75.00x (ISBN 0-86078-065-1, Pub. by Variorum England). State Mutual Bk.

--The Papacy & Political Ideas in the Middle Ages. 408p. 1980. 60.00x (ISBN 0-902089-87-0, Pub. by Variorum England). State Mutual Bk.

--The United States in Prague, 1945-1948. (East European Monographs: No. 36). 1978. text ed. 13.00x (ISBN 0-914710-29-X, Dist. by Columbia U Pr). East Eur Quarterly.

Ullom, Harry H., ed. see Houston, Samuel.

Ullrich, Heinz M., jt. auth. see Neuder, Gustav F.

Ullrich, Robert A., jt. auth. see Wieland, George F.

Ullrich, Volker, et al, eds. Microsomes & Drug Oxidations. 1977. text ed. 90.00 (ISBN 0-08-021523-8). Pergamon.

Ullyet, Kenneth. Ham Radio. LC 76-54072. 1977. 14.95 (ISBN 0-7153-7247-5). David & Charles.

Ullyot, Joan. Women's Running. LC 75-20962. (Illus.). 1976. pap. 4.95 (ISBN 0-89037-074-5); handbk. 5.95 (ISBN 0-89037-100-8). Anderson World.

Ulm, Otis M., jt. auth. see Gray, A. William.

Ulman, tr. see Svirski, Grigory.

Ulmer, Donald E. & Juergenson, E. M. Approved Practices in Raising & Handling Horses. LC 73-80303. 1974. 14.00 (ISBN 0-8134-1594-2, 1594); text ed. 10.50x (ISBN 0-685-42152-X). Interstate.

Ulmer, Louise. The Son Who Said He Wouldn't. (Arch Bks.: No. 18). 1981. pap. 0.79 (ISBN 0-570-06145-8, 59-1262). Concordia.

Ulmer, S. S., ed. Courts, Law & Judical Processes. LC 80-1856. (Illus.). 1981. pap. text ed. 11.95 (ISBN 0-02-932970-1). Free Pr.

Ulrey, Harry F. Carpentry & Building. LC 66-29074. 10.95 (ISBN 0-672-23142-5, 23142). Audel.

Ulrich, Albert, et al. Strawberry Deficiency Symptoms: A Visual & Plant Analysis Guide to Fertilization. LC 79-67379. (Illus.). 58p. pap. text ed. 8.00x (ISBN 0-931876-37-0). Ag Sci Pubns.

Ulrich, Eugene C., Jr. The Qumran Text of Samuel & Josephus. LC 78-15254. (Harvard Semitic Museum. Harvard Semitic Monographs: No. 19). 1978. 10.50 (ISBN 0-89130-256-5, 040019). Scholars Pr Ca.

Ulrich, Heinz & Conner, Robert. National Job Finding Guide. LC 79-6182. 336p. 1981. pap. 10.95 (ISBN 0-385-15782-7, Dolp). Doubleday.

Ulrich, Homer. Chamber Music. 2nd ed. LC 66-17909. 1966. 22.50x (ISBN 0-231-02763-X); pap. text ed. 10.00x (ISBN 0-231-08617-2). Columbia U Pr.

--Symphonic Music: Its Evolution Since the Renaissance. LC 52-12033. 1952. 20.00x (ISBN 0-231-01908-4). Columbia U Pr.

Ulsh, Wayne C. McDade. 1981. pap. 1.95 (ISBN 0-8439-0875-0, Leisure Bks). Nordon Pubns.

Ulutin, O. N., ed. Recent Progress in Cell Biology: Leukocytes & Platelets. (Bibliotheca Haematologica: No. 45). (Illus.). 1978. pap. 56.50 (ISBN 3-8055-2897-3). S Karger.

Uman, Myron F. Introduction to the Physics of Electronics. 1974. 25.95 (ISBN 0-13-492702-8). P-H.

Umbach, Arnold, jt. auth. see Peery, Rex.

Umbeck, John R. A Theory of Property Rights-with Special Applications to the California Gold Rush. (Illus.). 160p. 1981. text ed. 9.50 (ISBN 0-8138-1675-0). Iowa St U Pr.

--Theory of Property Rights: With Special Application to the 1948 California Gold Rush. 1981. write for info. (ISBN 0-8138-1675-0). Iowa St U Pr.

Umbreit, W. see Umbreit, Wayne W.

Umbreit, Wayne W., ed. Advances in Applied Microbiology. Incl. Vol. 1. 1959. 48.00 (ISBN 0-12-002601-5); Vol. 2. 1960. 48.00 (ISBN 0-12-002602-3); Vol. 3. 1961. o.s.i. (ISBN 0-12-002603-1); Vol. 4. 1962. 48.00 (ISBN 0-12-002604-X); Vol. 5. 1963. 48.00 (ISBN 0-12-002605-8); Vol. 6. 1964. o.s.i. (ISBN 0-12-002606-6); Vol. 7. 1965. 48.00 o.s.i. (ISBN 0-12-002607-4); Vol. 8. 1966. (ISBN 0-12-002608-2); Vol. 9. 1968, 48.00 (ISBN 0-12-002609-0); Vol. 10. Perlman, D. & Umbreit, W., eds. 1968. 48.00 (ISBN 0-12-002610-4); Vol. 11. Perlman, D., ed. 1969. 48.00 (ISBN 0-12-002611-2); Vol. 12. Perlman, D. & Umbreit, W., eds. 1970. 48.00 (ISBN 0-12-002612-0); Vol. 13. Perlman, D. & Umbreit, W., eds. 1970. 48.00 (ISBN 0-12-002613-9); Vol. 14. Perlman, D. & Umbreit, W., eds. 1971. 48.00 (ISBN 0-12-002614-7); Vol. 15. Perlman, D., ed. 1972. 48.00 (ISBN 0-12-002615-5); Vol. 16. Perlman, David, ed. 1973. 48.00 (ISBN 0-12-002616-3); Vol. 21. Perlman, David, ed. 1977. 39.00 (ISBN 0-12-002621-X); Vol. 22. Perlman, David, **ed. 1977. 37.50 (ISBN 0-12-002622-8); Vol. 23. Perlman, David, ed. 1978. 29.50 (ISBN 0-12-002623-6); Vol. 24. Perlman, David, ed. 1978. 31.50 (ISBN 0-12-002624-4); Vol. 25. 1979. 31.00 (ISBN 0-12-002625-2); Vol. 26. 1980. 29.50 (ISBN 0-12-002626-0). Acad Pr.**

Umezawa, Hamad, et al, eds. Bioactive Peptides Produced by Microorganisms. LC 78-11402. 1979. 49.95x (ISBN 0-470-26562-0). Halsted Pr.

Umhoefer, Jim. Guide to Wisconsin's State Parks, Forests, & Trails. (Illus.). 160p. (Orig.). 1981. pap. 7.95 (ISBN 0-915024-26-8). Tamarack Edns.

Umiker-Sebeok, D. J., jt. ed. see Sebeok, Thomas A.

Umiker-Sebeok, Jean, jt. auth. see Sebeok, Thomas A.

Umlauf, Hana & McDowell, Barbara, eds. Woman's Almanac. LC 77-75353. 1977. pap. 3.95x o.p. (ISBN 0-911818-07-3). World Almanac.

Umlauf, Hana, jt. ed. see McDowell, Barbara.

Umlauf Lane, Hana. The World Almanac & Book of Facts 1981. 1980. 8.95 o.p. (ISBN 0-911818-18-9); pap. 4.50 o.p. (ISBN 0-911818-17-0). Newspaper Ent.

Umlauf Lane, Hana, ed. World Almanac Book of Who. 352p. (Orig.). 1980. pap. 5.95 (ISBN 0-911818-11-1). World Almanac.

Umobuarie, David. Black Justice. (Three Crown Books Ser.). 204p. (Orig.). 1976. pap. 8.95 (ISBN 0-19-575232-5). Oxford U Pr.

Umphlett, Wiley L. Mythmakers of the American Dream: The Nostalgic Vision in Popular Culture. LC 78-75342. (Illus.). Date not set. cancelled o.p. (ISBN 0-498-02288-9). A S Barnes. Postponed.

Un. Causes of & Solutions to Coastal Erosion in Benin & Togo. Date not set. price not set. Gordon.

Unamuno, Miguel De. Selected Works: The Agony of Christianity & Essays on Faith, Vol. 5. Kerrigan, Anthony & Nozick, Martin, eds. Kerrigan, Anthony, tr. from Span. LC 67-22341. (Bollingen Ser.: Vol. 85). 300p. 1974. 16.00 (ISBN 0-691-09933-2). Princeton U Pr.

--Selected Works: Tragic Sense of Life, Vol. 4. Kerrigan, Anthony, ed. (Bollingen Ser.: Vol. 85). 1968. 25.00x (ISBN 0-691-09860-3); pap. 6.95 (ISBN 0-691-01820-0). Princeton U Pr.

Unamuno, Miguel De see De Unamuno, Miguel.

Unanue, Emil, jt. auth. see Benacerraf, Baruj.

Unanue, Emil R. & Rosenthal, Alan S., eds. Macrophage Regulation of Immunity. LC 79-24609. 1980. 27.50 (ISBN 0-12-708550-5). Acad Pr.

Unbegan, Boris O. Russian Surnames. 452p. 1972. 37.50x (ISBN 0-19-815635-9). Oxford U Pr.

Unbegaun, B. O., jt. ed. see Wheeler, Marcus.

Unbegaun, Boris O. Russian Grammar. 1957. 19.50x (ISBN 0-19-815611-1). Oxford U Pr.

Unbehauen, H., ed. Methods in Adaptive Control: Proceedings. (Lecture Notes in Control & Information Sciences: Vol. 24). (Illus.). 309p. 1980. pap. 21.60 (ISBN 0-387-10226-4). Springer-Verlag.

Unbehaun, Laraine, et al. Principles of Biology Laboratory Manual. 222p. (Orig.). 1980. pap. text ed. 10.95 (ISBN 0-8087-2115-1). Burgess.

Uncle Ben's Inc. Rice Cookery. LC 77-93278. 1977. pap. 5.95 (ISBN 0-912656-78-6). H P Bks.

Underal, Arild. The Politics of International Fisheries Management. 234p. 1981. pap. 20.00x. Universitet.

Underdown, David. Pride's Purge. 1971. 37.50x (ISBN 0-19-822342-0). Oxford U Pr.

Underhill, James C., et al. General Zoology Laboratory Guide. 3rd ed. (Et Al). 1978. pap. 6.95 spiral bdg. (ISBN 0-8087-2108-9). Burgess.

Underhill, Janet, jt. auth. see Faulhaber, Martha.

Underhill, Lonnie E. Genealogy Records of the First Arizona Volunteer Infantry Regiment. LC 80-24778. (Illus.). iv, 124p. 1980. pap. 18.50 (ISBN 0-933234-02-3). Roan Horse.

Underhill, Richard G., et al. Diagnosing Mathematical Difficulties. (Elementary Education Ser.: No. C22). 408p. 1980. text ed. 15.95 (ISBN 0-675-08195-5). Merrill.

Underhill, Robert G. Teaching Elementary School Mathematics. 2nd ed. (Elementary Education Ser.). 1977. text ed. 17.95 (ISBN 0-675-08541-1); instructor's manual 3.95 (ISBN 0-686-67644-0). Merrill.

--Teaching Elementary School Mathematics. 3rd ed. 1981. write for info; instr's. manual 3.95 (ISBN 0-686-69502-X). Merrill.

Underhill, Robert J. Methods of Teaching Elementary School Mathematics. new ed. (Elementary Education Ser). 224p. 1975. pap. text ed. 7.95x (ISBN 0-675-08780-5); media: audiocassettes & filmstrips 495.00 (ISBN 0-675-08781-3); 2-3 sets 395.00; 4 or more set 315.00. Merrill.

Underhill, Ruth. First Penthouse Dwellers of America. LC 75-23849. (Illus.). 1976. 15.00 (ISBN 0-88307-525-3); pap. 4.95 (ISBN 0-88307-526-1). Gannon.

Underhill, Ruth M. Navajos. rev. ed. (Civilization of the American Indian Ser: No. 43). (Illus.). 1978. Repr. of 1956 ed. 12.95 (ISBN 0-8061-0341-8). U of Okla Pr.

--Red Man's America: A History of Indians in the United States. rev. ed. LC 79-171345. 398p. 1971. pap. 7.95 (ISBN 0-226-84165-0, P437, Phoen). U of Chicago Pr.

--Singing for Power: The Song Magic of the Papago Indians of Southern Arizona. (Library Reprint Ser.). 1977. 15.75x (ISBN 0-520-03310-8); pap. 2.95 (ISBN 0-520-03280-2). U of Cal Pr.

Underhill, Terry. Heaths & Heathers. 1975. 14.00 o.p. (ISBN 0-7153-4970-8). David & Charles.

Underhill, Tim & Miller, Chuck, eds. Jack Vance. (Writers of the 21st Century Ser.). 1981. 12.95 (ISBN 0-8008-4294-4); pap. 5.95 (ISBN 0-8008-4295-2). Taplinger.

Underhill, William R. The Truman Persuasions. 1981. 19.95 (ISBN 0-8138-1640-8). Iowa St U Pr.

Underwood, Arthur L., jt. auth. see Day, R. A., Jr.

Underwood, Benton J. Experimental Psychology. 2nd ed. (Illus.). 1966. 19.95 (ISBN 0-13-295113-4); wkbk. - problems in experimental design & influence 6.95 (ISBN 0-13-295147-9). P-H.

--Psychological Research. 1957. 15.95 (ISBN 0-13-732529-0). P-H.

Underwood, C. H. Texas Six Man Football. (Illus.). 107p. 1974. 6.95 (ISBN 0-89015-078-8). Nortex Pr.

Underwood, E. E. Quantitative Stereology. 1970. 21.95 (ISBN 0-201-07650-0). A-W.

Underwood, G. Attention & Memory. LC 75-17614. 231p. 1975. text ed. 34.00 (ISBN 0-08-019615-2); pap. text ed. 14.00 (ISBN 0-08-018754-4). Pergamon.

Underwood, Gary & Underwood, Marylyn. First Principles: Topical Studies for New Converts. 1978. 3.45 (ISBN 0-89137-709-3). Quality Pubns.

Underwood, George W. Practical Fire Precautions. 1979. text ed. 50.50x (ISBN 0-566-02124-2, Pub. by Gower Pub Co England). Renouf.

Underwood, J. A., tr. see Parmelin, Helene.

Underwood, Jane H. Human Variation & Human Microevolution. (Illus.). 1979. pap. 10.95 (ISBN 0-13-447573-9). P-H.

Underwood, John C. Literature & Insurgency. 1914. 17.50x (ISBN 0-8196-0160-8). Biblo.

Underwood, John W. Lightplane Since Nineteen Hundred & Nine. 3rd ed. (Illus.). 1981. pap. 10.00 (ISBN 0-911721-56-8). Aviation.

Underwood, Leon. Bronzes of West Africa. (gr. 10 up). 1968. 6.50 o.p. (ISBN 0-85458-090-5). Transatlantic.

Underwood, Lorraine A. Women in Federal Employment Programs. (An Institute Paper). 53p. 1979. pap. 4.00 (ISBN 0-87766-242-8, 24400). Urban Inst.

Underwood, Louis E., jt. auth. see Ontjes, David A.

Underwood, Marylyn, jt. auth. see Underwood, Gary.

Underwood, Michael. Murder with Malice. LC 76-28064. Date not set. 7.95 (ISBN 0-312-55336-6). St Martin.

Underwood, Richard A. Shakespeare's "The Pheonix & Turtle". A Survey of Scholarship. (Salzburg Studies in English Literature, Elizabethan & Renaissance Studies: No. 15). 366p. 1974. pap. text ed. 25.00x (ISBN 0-391-01549-4). Humanities.

Underwood, T. L., ed. see Bunyan, John.

Underwood, Trevor, ed. Foreign Exchange Yearbook, 1979: A Listing of Daily Foreign Exchange & Euro-Currency Deposit Rates for Leading World Currencies. 1979. 31.95 (ISBN 0-470-26694-5). Halsted Pr.

--Foreign Exchange Yearbook 1981. 264p. 1980. 60.00x (Pub. by Woodhead-Faulkner England). State Mutual Bk.

Underwood, Virginia & Kett, Merriellyn. College Writing Skills. 2nd ed. 320p. 1981. pap. text ed. 10.95 (ISBN 0-675-08046-0); test bank 3.95 (ISBN 0-686-69487-2); instr's. manual 3.95 (ISBN 0-686-69488-0); write for info 9 audiocassettes (ISBN 0-675-08031-2). Merrill.

--Writing Skills. 1977. pap. text ed. 9.50 o.p. (ISBN 0-675-08484-9); audio cassettes 125.00 o.p. (ISBN 0-686-67619-X); 2-5 sets 75.00, 6 or more sets 50.00 o.p. (ISBN 0-675-08467-9). Merrill.

Underwood, Wes, jt. auth. see Sehlinger, Bob.

Undset, Sigrid. Four Stories. Walford, Naomi, tr. from Norwegian. LC 78-16903. 1978. Repr. of 1969 ed. lib. bdg. 19.75x (ISBN 0-313-20566-3, UNFS). Greenwood.

Unell, Barbara. Kansas City Catalog. 96p. (Orig.). (gr. 4 up). 1980. pap. 7.00 (ISBN 0-8309-0286-4). Independence Pr.

Unesco. Race, Science, & Society. 368p. 1975. 15.00x (ISBN 0-231-03908-5); pap. 7.00x (ISBN 0-231-03910-7). Columbia U Pr.

--Ten Years of Films on Ballet & Classical Dance, 1955-1965,Catalogue. 1968. pap. 4.25 (ISBN 92-3-100656-8, U674, UNESCO). Unipub.

--Urbanization in Latin America. Hauser, Philip M., ed. 1961. 20.00x (ISBN 0-231-03189-0). Columbia U Pr.

Ungar, Eric E., jt. ed. see Snowdon, John C.

Ungar, Frederick, ed. see Goethe, Johann W.

Ungaro, Peter C. Hematologic Diseases - New Directions in Therapy. 2nd ed. 1979. pap. 15.50 (ISBN 0-87488-682-1). Med Exam.

Ungaro, Susan. The H & R Block Family Budget Workbook. (H & R Block Ser.). 160p. 1980. pap. 4.95 (ISBN 0-02-007320-8, Collier). Macmillan.

Ungemach, P., jt. ed. see Strub, A. S.

Unger, jt. auth. see Maxwell, W.

Unger, Abraham. Glorious Obsession. 1978. pap. 1.75 (ISBN 0-505-51253-X). Tower Bks.

--Rx for Hilarity. 1980. pap. 1.50 (ISBN 0-505-51468-0). Tower Bks.

Unger, Carl. Trails of Thinking, Feeling & Willing. 1980. pap. 3.00 (ISBN 0-916786-47-1). St George Bk Serv.

Unger, E. A. & Ahmed, Nasir. Computer Science Fundamentals: An Algorithmic Approach Via Structured Programming. 1979. text ed. 17.95 (ISBN 0-675-08301-X); instructor's manual 3.95 (ISBN 0-686-67287-9). Merrill.

Unger, H. G. Introduction to Quantum Electronics. LC 76-86534. 1970. 19.50 (ISBN 0-08-006368-3). Pergamon.

Unger, Jim. And You Wonder, Herman, Why I Never Want to Go to Italian Restaurants? (Alligator Books Ser.). 1977. pap. 2.50 (ISBN 0-8362-0702-5). Andrews & McMeel.

--Apart from a Little Dampness, Herman, How's Everything Else? (Alligator Bks). (Illus.). 96p. 1975. pap. 2.50 (ISBN 0-8362-0622-3). Andrews & McMeel.

--Herman Hang-Ups. 20p. (gr. 4 up). 1980. pap. 4.95 (ISBN 0-8362-1954-6). Andrews & McMeel.

--Where's the Kids, Herman? 1978. pap. 2.50 (ISBN 0-8362-1105-7). Andrews & McMeel.

Unger, Leonard, ed. American Writers: A Collection of Literary Biographies, 6 vols. LC 73-1759. 1979. Set. lib. bdg. 275.00 (ISBN 0-684-16104-4). Scribner.

Unger, Max. Muzio Clementis Leben. LC 72-158959. (Music Ser). 1971. Repr. of 1914 ed. lib. bdg. 27.50 (ISBN 0-306-70192-8). Da Capo.

Unger, Merrill. Unger's Bible Dictionary (Thumb Indexed Edition) 1961. 22.95 (ISBN 0-8024-9036-0). Moody.

Unger, Merrill F. Archaeology & the New Testament. (Illus.). 1962. 12.95 (ISBN 0-310-33380-6). Zondervan.

--Mensaje De la Biblia: Unger's Bible Handbook. 960p. 1975. 9.95 (ISBN 0-8024-5244-2). Moody.

--New Testament Teaching on Tongues. LC 70-165057. 1971. pap. 2.95 (ISBN 0-8254-3900-0). Kregel.

--Unger's Bible Commentary: Genesis-Song of Solomon. (Commentary Series on the Entire Bible). 360p. 1981. text ed. 17.95 (ISBN 0-8024-9028-X). Moody.

--Zechariah. 12.95 (ISBN 0-310-33420-9). Zondervan.

Unger, Peter K., jt. ed. see Munitz, Milton K.

Unger, Roberto M. Knowledge & Politics. LC 74-15369. 1976. pap. text ed. 5.95 (ISBN 0-02-932870-5). Free Pr.

--Law in Modern Society. LC 74-27853. 1977. pap. text ed. 6.95 (ISBN 0-02-932880-2). Free Pr.

Unger, Roni. Poesia in Voz Alta in the Theater of Mexico. 184p. 1981. text ed. 15.00x (ISBN 0-8262-0333-7). U of Mo Pr.

Ungerer, Tomi. Allumette. LC 73-23055. (Illus.). 40p. (gr. k-3). 1974. 5.95 o.s.i. (ISBN 0-8193-0730-0, Four Winds); PLB 5.41 o.s.i. (ISBN 0-8193-0731-9). Schol Bk Serv.

--Hat. LC 78-999134. (Illus.). (gr. k-3). 1970. 5.95 o.s.i. (ISBN 0-8193-0378-X, Four Winds); PLB 5.41 o.s.i. (ISBN 0-8193-0379-8). Schol Bk Serv.

Ungerer, Tomi, compiled by. & illus. A Storybook: A Collection of Stories Old & New. LC 74-3504. (Illus.). 96p. (gr. k-6). 1974. 4.95 o.p. (ISBN 0-531-02742-2); PLB 5.88 o.p. (ISBN 0-531-02741-4). Watts.

Unger-Hamilton, Clive. The Entertainers. (Illus.). 320p. 1980. 29.95 (ISBN 0-312-25694-9). St Martin.

Ungerleider, J. Thomas, ed. The Problems & Prospects of LSD. (Illus.). 132p. 1972. 9.75 (ISBN 0-398-01952-5). C C Thomas.

Ungerman, Larry. Real Estate Professional's Design-a-Day: Nineteen Eighty Canadian Edition. 1979. text ed. 18.95 o.p. (ISBN 0-8359-6585-6). Reston.

Ungerson, Clare. Moving Home. 99p. 1971. pap. text ed. 5.00x (Pub. by Bedford England). Renouf.

Ungrue, Dawn & Gillespie, Laurel. Conferencing in California: A Guide to Affordable Retreats & Centers. LC 79-26005. 1980. pap. 6.95 (ISBN 0-915166-39-9). Impact Pubs Cal.

Ungs, Thomas, jt. auth. see Nimmo, Dan.

Ungurait, jt. auth. see Bohn, Hiebert.

Ungvary. Functional Morphology of Hepatic Vascular System. 1977. 17.00 (ISBN 0-9960006-7-4, Pub. by Kaido Hungary). Heyden.

Uniacke, Richard J. Nova Scotia Statutes: Statutes at Large, Vols. 1-4. LC 76-612783. 1970. Repr. Set. lib. bdg. 160.00x (ISBN 0-912004-06-1). W W Gaunt.

Unibook Staff. Mexico: The Macmillan Concise Illustrated Encyclopedia. Rubio, Pascal O., 3rd, ed. (Illus.). 416p. 1981. 21.95 (ISBN 0-02-620910-1). Macmillan.

Union for Radical Political Enconomics (URPE), ed. Crisis in the Public Sector: A Reader. LC 80-8936. 1981. pap. 7.50 (ISBN 0-85345-575-9). Monthly Rev.

United Fresh Fruit & Vegetable Association, jt. auth. see Celebrity Kitchen.

United Nations. Demographic Yearbook 1978. 30th ed. Incl. 1962. 25.00 (ISBN 0-685-60085-8). LC 50-641. 1980. 36.00x (ISBN 0-8002-1051-4). Intl Pubns Serv.

--Economic Survey of Latin America 1977. LC 50-3616. 462p. 1977. pap. 22.00x (ISBN 0-8002-1066-2). Intl Pubns Serv.

--Economic Survey of Latin America 1977. LC 50-3616. 536p. (Orig.). 1978. pap. 22.00x (ISBN 0-8002-1067-0). Intl Pubns Serv.

--The International Bill of Human Rights. 132p. 1981. 7.95 (ISBN 0-934558-06-X); pap. 2.95 (ISBN 0-934558-07-8). Entwhistle Bks.

--Statistical Yearbook for Asia & the Pacific, 1978: Annuaire Statistique pour l'asle et le Pacifique. 11th ed. LC 76-641968. (Illus.). 536p. (Orig.). 1979. pap. 28.00x (ISBN 0-8002-1083-2). Intl Pubns Serv.

--Statistical Yearbook for Latin America, 1978. 471p. 1979. pap. 32.00x (ISBN 0-8002-1087-5). Intl Pubns Serv.

--World Economic Survey, 1979-80. LC 48-1401. 116p. (Orig.). 1980. pap. 10.00x (ISBN 0-8002-1108-1). Intl Pubns Serv.

--Yearbook of Industrial Statistics, 1977, 2 vols. 11th ed. Incl. Vol. 1. General Industrial Statistics. 639p. 30.00x (ISBN 0-8002-2335-7); Vol. 2. Commodity Production Data, 1967 to 1977. 750p. 30.00x (ISBN 0-8002-2336-5). LC 76-646970. (Illus.). 1389p. 1979. write for info. Intl Pubns Serv.

United Nations Asian & Pacific Development Inst., ed. Local Level Planning & Rural Development: Alternative Strategies. 409p. 1980. text ed. 20.50x (ISBN 0-391-02171-0, Pub. by Concept India). Humanities.

United Nations Centre for Natural Resources, Energy & Transport. State Petroleum Enterprises in Developing Countries. LC 79-20681. (Pergamon Policy Studies). 185p. 1980. 28.00 (ISBN 0-08-025126-9). Pergamon.

United Nations Conference on Human Settlements. Aspects of Human Settlement Planning. LC 77-9877. (Habitat Ser.). 350p. 1978. 52.00 (ISBN 0-08-022011-8). Pergamon.

United Nations Economic Commission for Europe, Geneva, ed. see Seminar on Engineering Equipment for Foundries & Advanced Methods of Producing Such Equipment, Geneva, 1977.

United Nations Economic Commission for Europe, ed. see Symposium on Load-Curve Coverage in Future Electrical Power Generating Systems, Rome, Oct. 1977.

United Nations Economic Commission for Europe, Timber Committee. Behaviour of Wood Products in Fire: Proceedings, Oxford, 1977. 1977. pap. text ed. 30.00 (ISBN 0-08-021990-X). Pergamon.

United Nations Economic Commission for Europe. Coal: Nineteen Eighty-Five & Beyond - A Perspective Study. LC 77-30437. 1978. pap. text ed. 25.00 (ISBN 0-08-022409-1). Pergamon.

--Combined Production of Electric Power & Heat: Proceedings of a Seminar Organized by the Committee on Electric Power of the United Nations Economic Commission for Europe, Hamburg, FR Germany, 6-9 November 1978. LC 80-755. (Illus.). 150p. 32.00 (ISBN 0-08-025677-5). Pergamon.

United Nations Economic Commission for Europe, Geneva, Switzerland, ed. Energy Aspects of the Forest Industries: Proceedings of a Seminar Organized by the Timber Committee of the United Nations Economic Commission for Europe, Udine, Italy 13-17 Nov. 1978. LC 79-42869. (Illus.). 428p. 1979. 63.00 (ISBN 0-08-025661-9). Pergamon.

--Environment & Energy: Environmental Aspects of Energy Production & Use with Particular Reference to New Technologies. LC 79-40550. 1979. 21.00 (ISBN 0-08-024468-8). Pergamon.

United Nations Economic Commission for Europe. Factors of Growth & Investment Policies: An International Approach. 1978. pap. 23.00 (ISBN 0-08-021992-6). Pergamon.

--Fine Particulate Pollution. 1978. text ed. 30.00 (ISBN 0-08-023399-6). Pergamon.

United Nations Economic Commission for Europe & United Nations, Food & Agricultural Organization. Frozen & Quick-Frozen Food: New Agricultural Production & Marketing Aspects, Proceedings of a Joint Symposium, Budapest, 1977. LC 77-30194. 1977. pap. 35.00 (ISBN 0-08-022031-2). Pergamon.

United Nations Economic Commission for Europe, Commission on Gas, Minsk, USSR, 1977. The Gas Industry & the Environment: Proceedings. 1978. text ed. 51.00 (ISBN 0-08-022412-1). Pergamon.

United Nations Economic Commission for Europe. The Gas Situation in the ECC Region Around the Year 1990. (European Committee for Economic Perspectives: Vol. 18). 1979. 69.00 (ISBN 0-08-024465-3). Pergamon.

--Housing for Special Groups: Proceedings. 1977. pap. text ed. 34.00 (ISBN 0-08-021985-3). Pergamon.

United Nations Economic Commission for Europe, Geneva, Switzerland. Human Settlements in the Arctic: An Account of the ECE Symposium on Human Settlements Planning & Development in the Arctic, Godthab, Greenland, Aug. 18-25, 1978. LC 79-42797. (ECE Seminars & Symposia). (Illus.). 122p. 1980. 26.00 (ISBN 0-08-023448-8). Pergamon.

--Hydroelectricity Prospects in the New Energy Situation: Proceedings of a Symposium of the Committee on Electric Power of the United Nations Commission for Europe, Athens, Greece, 5-9 Nov. 1979. LC 80-40819. 530p. Date not set. price not set (ISBN 0-08-025702-X). Pergamon.

United Nations Economic Commission for Europe. Non-Waste Technology & Production: Proceedings of an International Seminar Held in Paris, Nov.-Dec. 1976. 1978. pap. 115.00 (ISBN 0-08-022028-2). Pergamon.

United Nations Economic Commission for Europe, Geneva, Switzerland. Oils & Gases from Coal: A Review of the State-of-the-Art in Europe & North America Based on the Work of the Symposium on the Gasification & Liquefaction of Coal Held Under the Auspices of the UNECE, Katowice, Poland. 23-27 April 1979. (ECE Seminars & Symposia Ser.). (Illus.). 316p. 1980. 59.00 (ISBN 0-08-025678-3). Pergamon.

United Nations Economic Commission for Europe. Problems of the Agricultural Development of Less-Favoured Areas. (European Committee for Economic Perspectives). 1979. 48.00 (ISBN 0-08-024456-4). Pergamon.

United Nations Economic Commission for Europe, Committee on Water Problems. Selected Water Problems in Islands & Coastal Waters: Proceedings, Malta, 1978. (ECE Seminars & Symposia). (Illus.). 92.00 (ISBN 0-08-024447-5). Pergamon.

United Nations Economic Commission for Western Asia, Natural Resources, Science & Technology Division. Technology Transfer & Change in the Arab World: Proceedings of a Seminar, Beirut, Oct. 1977. Zahlan, A. B., ed. 1978. text ed. 72.00 (ISBN 0-08-022435-0). Pergamon.

United Nations Economic Commission for Latin America. Water Management & Environment in Latin America: Analysis & Case Studies of Water Management, Including New Approaches Through Simulation Modelling & the Environmental Consequences of Past & Potential Trends in Water Use. (Environmental Sciences & Applications Ser.: Vol. 12). 1979. 68.00 (ISBN 0-08-023580-8); pap. 23.00 (ISBN 0-08-024457-2). Pergamon.

United Nations Environment Programme, Nairobi & Environment Training Programme, Dakar. Environment & Development in Africa. (UNEP Studies). (Illus.). 100p. Date not set. 15.71 (ISBN 0-08-025667-8). Pergamon.

United Nations, Food & Agricultural Organization, jt. auth. see United Nations Economic Commission for Europe.

United Nations Institute for Training & Research. International Conference on the Future Supply of Nature-Made Petroleum & Gas: Proceedings. 1977. text ed. 76.00 (ISBN 0-08-021734-6); pap. text ed. 51.00 (ISBN 0-08-021735-4). Pergamon.

United Nations, Secretariat. Conference on Desertification, Nairobi 1977. Desertification: Its Causes & Consequences. LC 77-81423. 1977. text ed. 82.00 (ISBN 0-08-022023-1); pap. text ed. 42.00 (ISBN 0-08-022395-8). Pergamon.

U. S. Armed Forces. Dictionary of Spoken Spanish Words, Phrases, Sentences. LC 30-900. pap. 5.95 (ISBN 0-385-00976-3). Doubleday.

U. S. Army. Basic Theory & Application of Transistors. (Illus.). 1962. pap. text ed. 3.50 (ISBN 0-486-20380-8). Dover.

--Concrete, Masonry & Brickwork: A Practical Handbook for the Homeowner & Small Builder. LC 75-12130. Orig. Title: Concrete & Masonry. (Illus.). 204p. 1975. pap. 5.00 (ISBN 0-486-23203-4). Dover.

U. S. Army Natick Laboratories. Glossary of Environmental Terms (Terrestrial) LC 73-2851. 149p. 1973. Repr. of 1968 ed. 18.00 (ISBN 0-8103-3277-9). Gale.

United States Atomic Energy Commission, ed. In the Matter of J. Robert Oppenheimer. 1971. 23.00x (ISBN 0-262-21003-7); pap. 5.95x (ISBN 0-262-71002-1). MIT Pr.

United States Bureau Of Labor Statistics. History of Wages in the United States from Colonial Times to 1928 with Supplement, 1929-1933. LC 67-13749. 1966. Repr. of 1934 ed. 25.00 (ISBN 0-8103-3363-5). Gale.

United States, Bureau of the Budget, Committee on Records of War Administration. The United States at War. LC 79-169909. (FDR & the Era of the New Deal Ser.). 553p. 1972. Repr. of 1946 ed. lib. bdg. 55.00 (ISBN 0-306-70330-0). Da Capo.

U. S. Children's Bureau. Handbook for Recreation. rev. 1959 ed. LC 74-174126. (Children's Bureau Publication Ser.: No. 231). (Illus.). x, 148p. 1975. Repr. of 1960 ed. 16.00 (ISBN 0-8103-4001-1). Gale.

United States Civil Service Commission. U.S. Government Jobs: Career Opportunities for College Students. LC 77-6827. (gr. 12). pap. text ed. cancelled o.s.i. (ISBN 0-8120-0866-9). Barron.

United States Coast Guard Auxiliary. Boating Skills & Seamanship. 8th ed. LC 74-164688. (Illus.). 1979. pap. text ed. 7.00 (ISBN 0-930028-00-7). US Coast Guard.

--Sailing & Seamanship. 3rd ed. LC 76-29794. (Illus.). 1980. pap. text ed. 7.50 (ISBN 0-930028-02-3). US Coast Guard.

United States, Commission on Government Security. Report of the Commission on Government Security. LC 79-152788. (Civil Liberties in American History Ser). 1971. Repr. of 1957 ed. lib. bdg. 75.00 (ISBN 0-306-70146-4). Da Capo.

U. S. Committee for the Global Atmospheric Research Program. Understanding Climatic Change: A Program for Action. 1975. pap. 9.00 (ISBN 0-309-02323-8). Natl Acad Pr.

U. S. Committee on Public Information. The Creel Report. LC 75-37319. (Civil Liberties in American History Ser). 290p. 1972. Repr. of 1920 ed. lib. bdg. 32.50 (ISBN 0-306-70241-X). Da Capo.

United States Congress. Investigation of the Administration of Louis F. Post, Assistant Secretary of Labor in the Matter of Deportation of Aliens. LC 72-124850. (Civil Liberties in American History Ser). Repr. of 1921 ed. lib. bdg. 29.50 (ISBN 0-306-71962-2). Da Capo.

U. S. Congress. U. S. Congress House: Report...Washington, 1813. Washburn, Wilcomb E., ed. LC 75-7057. (Narratives of North American Captivities Ser.). 1977. lib. bdg. 44.00 (ISBN 0-8240-1659-9). Garland Pub.

U. S. Congress, House Committee on Agriculture. Food Costs-Farm Prices: A Compilation or Information Relating to Agriculture. (Illus.). x, 114p. 1973. Repr. of 1970 ed. 15.00 (ISBN 0-8103-3278-7). Gale.

U. S. Congress, 92nd. Review-1970 Session of the Congress & Index of AEI, Publications. (Legislative Analysis Ser.: No. 1). 1971. pap. 2.00 o.p. (ISBN 0-8447-0125-4). Am Enterprise.

U. S. Department of Agriculture. Climate & Man: Nineteen Forty-One Yearbook of Agriculture, House Document No. 27, 77th Congress, 1st Session. LC 74-6297. 1248p. 1975. Repr. of 1941 ed. 60.00 (ISBN 0-8103-4016-X). Gale.

--Common Weeds of the United States. 1970. pap. 6.50 (ISBN 0-486-20504-5). Dover.

U. S. Department of Agriculture Forest Service. A Tree Hurts, Too. (Encore Edition). 32p. 1975. 1.79 o.p. (ISBN 0-684-15857-4, ScribT). Scribner.

United States Department of Agriculture. The World Food Situation: Problems & Prospects to 1985, Vol. 2. 1976. 37.50 (ISBN 0-379-00573-5). Oceana.

U. S. Department of Energy, jt. auth. see Inst. Real Estate.

U. S. Department of Energy. Distributed Energy Systems in California's Future. 359p. 1980. pap. 19.95 cancelled (ISBN 0-89934-011-3). Solar Energy Info.

--Proceeding of Second International Symposium on Alcohol Fuel Technology: Methanol & Ethanol U. S. Department of Energy. 1979. 49.95 (ISBN 0-89934-000-8); pap. 34.95 (ISBN 0-930978-86-2). Solar Energy Info.

--The Report of the Alcohol Fuels Policy Review. 119p. 1979. pap. 10.95 (ISBN 0-89934-024-5). Solar Energy Info.

U. S. Department of Health, Education & Welfare Library. Basic Readings in Social Security. LC 68-55120. (Illus.). 1968. Repr. of 1960 ed. lib. bdg. 15.00x (ISBN 0-8371-0705-9, RESS). Greenwood.

U. S. Department of Health, Education, & Welfare, Washington, D. C. Subject Catalog of the Department Library: First Supplement, 4 vols. 1973. Set. 315.00 (ISBN 0-8161-1109-X). G K Hall.

U. S. Department of Health, Education, & Welfare. Work in America: Report of a Special Task Force to the Secretary of Health, Education, & Welfare. 262p. 1973. pap. 4.95 (ISBN 0-262-58023-3). MIT Pr.

U. S. Department of Justice. Prejudice & Property, an Historic Brief Against Racial Convenants. Clark, Tom C. & Perlman, Philip B., eds. Repr. of 1948 ed. lib. bdg. 11.50x (ISBN 0-8371-2221-X, PRPR). Greenwood.

U. S. Department of Labor. Jobs, Jobs, Jobs for the College Graduate. LC 77-23041. 1977. pap. 3.75 o.p. (ISBN 0-8120-0671-2). Barron.

U. S. Dept. of Agriculture. Home Canning of Fruits & Vegetables. (Illus.). 31p. Repr. pap. 2.50. Shorey.

--Home Freezing of Fruits & Vegetables. (Illus.). 48p. pap. 2.50 (ISBN 0-8466-6056-3). Shorey.

--Small-Scale Fuel Alcohol Prod. 242p. 1980. 24.95 (ISBN 0-89934-047-4, B946-PP); pap. 14.95 (ISBN 0-89934-046-6, B046-PP). Solar Energy Info.

United States Dept. of Agriculture. Vacation Homes & Cabins: 16 Complete Plans. 8.00 (ISBN 0-8446-5674-7). Peter Smith.

U. S. Dept. of Energy. Domestic Policy Review of Solar Energy. 153p. 1980. 29.50 (ISBN 0-89934-061-X, V953-PP); pap. 14.50. Solar Energy Info.

--Solar, Geothermal, Electric & Storage Systems Program Summary Document. 475p. 1979. pap. 19.95 (ISBN 0-686-63324-5, H031-PP). Solar Energy Info.

U. S. Dept. of Forestry. Encyclopedia of Wood. LC 77-7728. (Illus.). 384p. 1980. pap. 12.95 (ISBN 0-8069-8890-8). Sterling.

U. S. Dept. of State. Consultation Among the American Republics with Respect to the Argentine Situation. LC 76-29632. (Latin America in the 20th Century Ser.). 1976. Repr. of 1946 ed. lib. bdg. 15.00 (ISBN 0-306-70838-8). Da Capo.

U. S. Emergency Council. Report on Economic Conditions of the South. LC 70-172009. 1972. Repr. lib. bdg. 12.50 (ISBN 0-306-70438-2). Da Capo.

U. S. Environmental Data Service. Weather Atlas of the United States. LC 74-11931. 1975. 40.00 (ISBN 0-8103-1048-1). Gale.

U. S. Federal Trade Commission. Memorandum on Unfair Competition at the Common Law. 305p. 1980. Repr. of 1916 ed. lib. bdg. 28.50x (ISBN 0-8377-1228-9). Rothman.

U. S. Federal Works Agency. Final Statistical Report of the Federal Emergency Relief Administration. LC 76-179755. (FDR & the Era of the New Deal Ser). 406p. 1972. Repr. of 1942 ed. lib. bdg. 42.50 (ISBN 0-306-70455-2). Da Capo.

United States Geographic Board. Sixth Report of the United States Geographic Board. LC 67-8571. 1967. Repr. of 1933 ed. 24.00 (ISBN 0-685-11676-X). Gale.

U. S. House of Representatives, 55th Congress, 2nd Session, Doc. No. 575, Pt. 3. Annual Report of the Board of Regents of the Smithsonian Institution Showing the Operation, Expenditures & Condition of the Institution for the Year Ending June 30, 1897: A Memorial of George Brown Goode Together with a Selection of His Papers on Museums & on the History of Science in America. Cohen, I. Bernard, ed. LC 79-7964. (Three Centuries of Science in America Ser.). (Illus.). 1980. Repr. of 1901 ed. lib. bdg. 55.00x (ISBN 0-405-12545-3). Arno.

United States Immigration Commission. Dictionary of Races or Peoples. LC 68-30665. 1969. Repr. of 1911 ed. 15.00 (ISBN 0-8103-3364-3). Gale.

U. S. Industrial Commission, Washington, D. C., 1900-1902. Reports, 19 vols. LC 73-103309. (Illus.). 1900-02. Repr. lib. bdg. 500.00x (ISBN 0-8371-9920-4, RIC). Greenwood.

U. S. Library of Congress, General Reference & Bibliography Division. Sixty American Poets, Eighteen Ninety-Six - Nineteen Fourty-Four. rev. ed. LC 73-5993. xii, 155p. Repr. of 1954 ed. 15.00 (ISBN 0-8103-3365-1). Gale.

U. S. Library of Congress Legislative Reference Service. Proposed Amendments to the Constitution of the United States Introduced in Congress from Dec. 4, 1889 to July 2, 1926. Tansill, Charles C., ed. LC 75-35363. (U.S. Government Documents Program Ser.). 148p. 1976. Repr. of 1926 ed. lib. bdg. 13.75x (ISBN 0-8371-8606-4, USPA). Greenwood.

--Provisions of Federal Law Held Unconstitutional by the Supreme Court of the United States. Gilbert, Wilfred C., ed. LC 75-35364. (U.S. Government Documents Program Ser.). 148p. 1976. Repr. of 1936 ed. lib. bdg. 13.75x (ISBN 0-8371-8605-6, USPF). Greenwood.

U. S. National Committee for the International Hydrological Decade. Advanced Concepts & Techniques in the Study of Snow & Ice Resources. Santeford, H. & Smith, J., eds. x, 789p. 1974. pap. 15.25 (ISBN 0-309-02235-5). Natl Acad Pr.

U. S. National Committee for Geochemistry. Geochemistry & the Environment: The Relation of Other Selected Trace Elements to Health & Disease, Vol. II. 1977. pap. 12.00 (ISBN 0-309-02548-6). Natl Acad Pr.

U. S. National Committee for the International Council for Building Research, Studies & Documentation, National Research Council. Modeling Techniques for Community Development. LC 75-37377. x, 86p. 1975. pap. 5.75 (ISBN 0-309-02420-X). Natl Acad Pr.

U. S. National Committee for the International Union of Pure & Applied Physics. Physics Fifty Years Later. (Illus.). 416p. 1973. 15.25 (ISBN 0-309-02138-3). Natl Acad Pr.

U. S. National Committee on Rock Mechanics, 15th, South Dakota School of Mines & Technology, Sept. 1973 & American Society of Civil Engineers. Application of Rock Mechanics: Proceedings. Haskins, Earl R., Jr., ed. 672p. 1976. text ed. 27.00 (ISBN 0-87262-154-5). Am Soc Civil Eng.

U. S. National Oceanic & Atmospheric Administration. The Complete Underwater Diving Manual. (Nautical Ser.). (Illus.). 1977. 14.95 o.p. (ISBN 0-679-50774-4); pap. 8.95 (ISBN 0-679-50826-0). McKay.

U. S. National Office of Vital Statistics. Vital Statistics of the United States, 1937-1956, 43 vols. Incl. 1937, 2 vols. Vol. 1. 23.50 (ISBN 0-8371-1670-8, VITA); Vol. 2. 23.50 (ISBN 0-8371-1671-6, VITB); 1938, 2 vols. Vol. 1. 23.50 (ISBN 0-8371-1672-4, VITC); Vol. 2. 23.50 (ISBN 0-8371-1673-2, VITD); 1939, 2 vols. Vol. 1. 23.50 (ISBN 0-8371-1674-0, VITE); Vol. 2. 23.50 (ISBN 0-8371-1675-9, VITF); 1940, 3 vols. Vol. 1. 26.50 (ISBN 0-8371-1676-7, VITG); Vol. 2. 26.50 (ISBN 0-8371-1677-5, VITH); Vol. 3. 26.50 (ISBN 0-8371-1678-3, VITI); 1941, 2 vols. Vol. 1. 19.50 (ISBN 0-8371-1679-1, VITJ); Vol. 2. 19.50 (ISBN 0-8371-1680-5, VITK); 1942, 2 vols. Vol. 1. 21.75 (ISBN 0-8371-1681-3, VITL); Vol. 2. 21.75 (ISBN 0-8371-1682-1, VITM); 1943, 2 vols. Vol. 1. 24.00 (ISBN 0-8371-1683-X, VITN); Vol. 2. 24.00 (ISBN 0-8371-1684-8, VITO); 1944, 2 vols. Vol. 1. 25.00 (ISBN 0-8371-1685-6, VITP); Vol. 2. 25.00 (ISBN 0-8371-1686-4, VITQ); 1945, 2 vols. Vol. 1. 24.00 (ISBN 0-8371-1687-2, VITR); Vol. 2. 24.00 (ISBN 0-8371-1688-0, VITS); **1946, 2 vols. Vol. 1. 25.75 (ISBN 0-8371-1689-9, VITT); Vol. 2. 25.75 (ISBN 0-8371-1690-2, VITU); 1947, 2 vols. Vol. 1. 25.75 (ISBN 0-8371-1691-0, VITW); Vol. 2. 25.75 (ISBN 0-8371-1692-9, VITX); 1948, 2 vols. Vol. 1. 25.50 (ISBN 0-8371-1693-7, VITY); Vol. 2. 25.50 (ISBN 0-8371-1694-5, VITZ); 1949, 2 vols. Vol. 1. 28.00 (ISBN 0-8371-1695-3, VIUA); Vol. 2. 28.00 (ISBN 0-8371-1696-1, VIUB); 1950, 3 vols. Vol. 1. 28.00 (ISBN 0-8371-1697-X, VIUC); Vol. 2. 28.00 (ISBN 0-8371-1698-8, VIUD); Vol. 3. 28.00 (ISBN 0-8371-1699-6, VIUE); 1951, 2 vols. Vol. 1. 27.00 (ISBN 0-8371-1700-3, VIUF); Vol. 2. 27.00 (ISBN 0-8371-1701-1, VIUG); 1952, 2 vols. Vol. 1. 26.00 (ISBN 0-8371-1702-X, VIUH); Vol. 2. 26.00 (ISBN 0-8371-1703-8, VIUI); 1953, 2 vols. Vol. 1. 27.00 (ISBN 0-8371-1704-6, VIUJ); Vol. 2. 27.00 (ISBN 0-8371-1705-4, VIUK); 1954, 2 vols. Vol. 1. 26.00 (ISBN 0-8371-1707-0, VIUL); Vol. 2. 26.00 (ISBN 0-686-66669-0, VIUM); 1955, 3 vols. Vol. 1. 26.00 (ISBN 0-8371-1708-9, VIUN); Vol. 2. 26.00 (ISBN 0-8371-1709-7, VIUO); Vol. 3. 26.00 (ISBN 0-8371-1710-0, VIUP); 1956, 2 vols. Vol. 1. 28.00 (ISBN 0-8371-1711-9, VIUQ); Vol. 2. 28.00 (ISBN 0-8371-1712-7, VIUR). (Illus.). 1968. Repr. of 1956 ed. Set. lib. bdg. 990.00x (ISBN 0-8371-2512-X, VISU); single years avail. (ISBN 0-685-24752-X). Greenwood.**

United States National Resources Committee. Consumer Incomes in the United States. LC 75-174476. (FDR & the Era of the New Deal Ser.). 104p. 1972. Repr. of 1938 ed. lib. bdg. 20.00 (ISBN 0-306-70386-6). Da Capo.

United States, National Resources Committee. Regional Factors in National Planning & Development. LC 72-174478. (FDR & the Era of the New Deal Ser.). 223p. 1975. Repr. of 1935 ed. lib. bdg. 25.00 (ISBN 0-306-70387-4). Da Capo.

U. S. National Resources Committee. Research: A National Resource, 3 vols. in 1. Cohen, I. Bernard, ed. LC 79-7985. (Three Centuries of Science in America Ser.). (Illus.). 1980. Repr. of 1941 ed. lib. bdg. 78.00x (ISBN 0-405-12567-4). Arno.

United States National Resources Committee. The Structure of the American Economy, 2 vols. in 1. LC 78-173418. (FDR & the Era of the New Deal Ser). 1972. Repr. of 1939 ed. lib. bdg. 45.00 (ISBN 0-306-70388-2). Da Capo.

United States National Resources Planning Board, Public Works Committee. The Economic Effects of the Public Works Expenditures, 1933-1938. Galbraith, J. K. & Johnson, G. G., eds. (FDR & the Era of the New Deal Ser). vii, 131p. 1975. Repr. of 1940 ed. lib. bdg. 20.00 (ISBN 0-306-70713-6). Da Capo.

United States National Resources Planning Board. Security Work & Relief Policies. LC 72-2385. (FDR & the Era of the New Deal Ser.). 640p. 1973. Repr. of 1942 ed. lib. bdg. 65.00 (ISBN 0-306-70520-6). Da Capo.

United States. Nautical Almanac Office & Gale Research Company. Sunrise & Sunset Tables for Key Cities & Weather Stations in the United States. LC 76-24796. 1977. 40.00 (ISBN 0-8103-0464-3). Gale.

U. S. Naval Institute. Space Atlas, No. 1447. (Illus.). 1979. pap. 2.95 (ISBN 0-8416-1447-4). Am Map.

U. S. Navy (Bureau of Naval Personnel) Basic Electricity. 1960. pap. 6.50 (ISBN 0-486-20973-3). Dover.

--Second-Level Basic Electronics. Orig. Title: Basic Electronics Vol. 2. (Illus.). 352p. 1971. pap. text ed. 4.50 (ISBN 0-486-22841-X). Dover.

U. S. News And World Report. U. S. on the Moon. 1970. 9.95 (ISBN 0-02-620990-X). Macmillan.

U. S. News & World Report. U. S. on the Moon. (gr. 7 up). 1969. pap. 2.95 o.s.i. (ISBN 0-02-074860-4, Collier). Macmillan.

U. S. Office of Education. Bibliography of Research Studies in Education, Nineteen Twenty-Six to Nineteen Forty, 4 vols. LC 74-1124. 4801p. 1974. Repr. of 1928 ed. Set. 195.00 (ISBN 0-8103-0975-0). Gale.

U. S. Pharmacopeial Convention. The Physicians' & Pharmacists' Guide to Your Medicines. 544p. (Orig.). 1981. pap. 9.95 (ISBN 0-345-29635-4). Ballantine.

U. S. Post Office Department. Street Directory of the Principal Cities of the United States: Embracing Letter-Carrier Offices Established to April 30, 1908. 5th ed. LC 76-179692. 904p. Repr. of 1908 ed. 42.00 (ISBN 0-8103-3072-5). Gale.

United States Senate Committee On The Judiciary - 89th Congress - 1st Session. Internal Security & Subversion: Principal State Laws & Cases. LC 70-167844. (Civil Liberties in American History Ser.). 1971. Repr. of 1965 ed. lib. bdg. 69.50 (ISBN 0-306-70121-9). Da Capo.

United States Senate, Committee on the Judiciary Ninety-First Congress, 2nd Session. A Judge on Trial: Hearings on the Nomination of George Harrold Carswell: Proceedings. LC 70-3962. (American Constitutional & Legal History Ser). 467p. 1974. Repr. of 1970 ed. lib. bdg. 27.50 (ISBN 0-306-70209-6). Da Capo.

United States Senate Committee on the Judiciary, 75th Congress, 1st Session. Reorganization of the Federal Judiciary, 6 vols. in 3. LC 73-124924. (American Constitutional & Legal History Ser.). 1970. Repr. of 1937 ed. lib. bdg. 175.00 (ISBN 0-306-71991-6). Da Capo.

United States Superintendent of Documents. Decennial Cumulative Index 1941-1950 to United States Government Publications Monthly Catalog, 2 Vols. LC 77-84611. 1972. Repr. of 1953 ed. 56.00 (ISBN 0-8103-3361-9). Gale.

U. S. War Department. Dictionary of Spoken Russian: Russian-English: English-Russian. 1959. pap. 7.50 (ISBN 0-486-20496-0). Dover.

--Dictionary of Spoken Spanish: Spanish-English, English-Spanish. pap. 4.95 (ISBN 0-486-20495-2). Dover.

United States Works Progress Administration. Research Monograph, 27 vols. (FDR & the Era of the New Deal Ser.). 1971. lib. bdg. 345.00 (ISBN 0-306-70359-9). Da Capo.

United States, 66th Congress, House of Representatives, 1st. Session. Case of Victor L. Berger of Wisconsin, 2 vols. LC 78-39129. (Civil Liberties in American History Ser). 1972. Repr. of 1920 ed. lib. bdg. 105.00. Vol. 1 (ISBN 0-306-70465-X). Vol. 2 (ISBN 0-306-70466-8). Set. lib. bdg. 85.00 (ISBN 0-686-57599-7). Da Capo.

United States, 79th Congress, 2nd Session. Report of the Joint Committee on the Investigation of the Pearl Harbor Attack. LC 74-166954. (FDR & the Era of the New Deal Ser.). (Illus.). 1972. Repr. of 1946 ed. lib. bdg. 49.50 (ISBN 0-306-70331-9). Da Capo.

United Tech. Pubs. Modern Applications of Linear IC's. LC 73-90737. 1974. 12.95 o.p. (ISBN 0-8306-4708-2); pap. 9.95 (ISBN 0-8306-3708-7, 708). TAB Bks.

Univ. of Sheffield 8-9 April 1976 Conference. Hydraulic Cement Pastes, Their Structure & Properties: Proceedings. (Illus.). 1976. pap. 27.50 (ISBN 0-7210-1047-4). Scholium Intl.

Universal House of Justice. The Baha'i World: An International Record 1954-1963, Vol. XIII. LC 27-5882. (Illus.). 1970. 17.50x o.s.i. (ISBN 0-87743-042-X, 7-33-13). Baha'i.

--The Baha'i World: An International Record 1963-1968, Vol. XIV. LC 27-5882. (Illus.). 1974. 16.00 (ISBN 0-87743-099-3, 7-33-14). Baha'i.

--The Baha'i World: An International Record 1968-1973, Vol. XV. (Illus.). 1976. 17.50x o.s.i. (ISBN 0-85398-059-4, 7-33-15). Baha'i.

--The Baha'i World: An International Record 1973-1976, Vol. XVI. (Illus.). 1979. 20.00 (ISBN 0-85398-075-6, 7-33-16). Baha'i.

--Messages from the Universal House of Justice: 1968-1973. LC 75-11795. 1976. 9.00 (ISBN 0-87743-076-4, 7-25-05); pap. 5.00 (ISBN 0-87743-096-9, 7-25-06). Baha'i.

--Wellspring of Guidance: Messages 1963-1968. rev. ed. LC 76-129996. 1976. 9.00 (ISBN 0-87743-032-2, 7-25-05); pap. 5.00 (ISBN 0-87743-033-0, 7-25-06). Baha'i.

Universal House of Justice Staff. Baha'i Holy Places at the World Centre. LC 78-15959. 1968. 2.00 (ISBN 0-87743-066-7, 7-15-02). Baha'i.

University of California. The Bancroft Library, University of California, Berkeley: Catalog of Printed Books, Third Supplement. (Library Catalogs-Bib. Guides). 1979. lib. bdg. 795.00 (ISBN 0-8161-1163-4). G K Hall.

University of California, Berkeley, Library. Guide to Special Collections. Phillips, Audrey E., ed. LC 73-9572. 1973. 10.00 (ISBN 0-8108-0657-6). Scarecrow.

University of California, Davis, ed. Biomass Alcohol for California: a Potential for the 1980's: Proceedings. 52p. 1980. Repr. pap. 11.95 (ISBN 0-89934-059-8, B002-PP). Solar Energy Info.

University Of California Philosophical Union - 1932. Causality: Lectures. (Publications in Philosophy Ser: Vol. 15). pap. 17.00 (ISBN 0-384-07040-X). Johnson Repr.

University Of California Philosophical Union - 1941. Civilization: Lectures. (Publications in Philosophy Ser: Vol. 23). 1941. pap. 17.00 (ISBN 0-384-07050-7). Johnson Repr.

University of Cambridge. Classification Scheme & List of Subject Headings for the Squire Library of the Library of Cambridge. 1974. 20.00 (ISBN 0-379-20060-0). Oceana.

University of Chicago Press. Manual of Style. rev. 12th ed. LC 68-40582. 1969. 17.50 (ISBN 0-226-77008-7). U of Chicago Pr.

University Of Colorado Department Of Philosophy. Readings on Fascism & National Socialism. 112p. (Orig.). 1952. pap. 3.95x (ISBN 0-8040-0259-2, 3). Swallow.

University of Florida. Catalog of the Latin American Collection, University of Florida Libraries, First Supplement. 1979. lib. bdg. 950.00 (ISBN 0-8161-1090-5). G K Hall.

University of Guelph. Biophysics Handbook I. 208p. 1980. pap. text ed. 8.95 (ISBN 0-8403-2280-1). Kendall-Hunt.

University of Hawaii Music Project & Burton, Leon. Comprehensive Musicianship Through Classroom Music: Zone 2, Hawaii. (gr. 2-3). 1972. Bk. A. text ed. 4.88 (ISBN 0-201-00785-1, Sch Div); Bk. B. text ed. 6.20 (ISBN 0-201-00856-4); tchr's bk. for bk. A 11.48 (ISBN 0-201-00788-6); tchr's bk. for bk. B 11.48 (ISBN 0-201-00857-2). A-W.

University of London, Institute of Education. Catalogue of the Comparative Education Library: Second Supplement. (Library Catalogs-Bib. Guides). 1979. lib. bdg. 350.00 (ISBN 0-8161-0285-6). G K Hall.

University of Maryland Mathematics Project. Unifying Concepts & Processes in Elementary Mathematics. 1978. pap. text ed. 20.95 (ISBN 0-205-05844-2, 5658446); instr's manual avail. (ISBN 0-205-05845-0). Allyn.

University of Minnesota, jt. auth. see James Ford Bell Library, University of Minnesota.

University of Missouri - Home Economics Resource Unit. Adult Homemaking. text ed. 2.00x spiral bdg. (ISBN 0-87543-021-X). Lucas.

--Child Development & Curriculum Materials. text ed. 1.75x spiral bdg. (ISBN 0-87543-022-8). Lucas.

--Family Living. text ed. 2.00x spiral bdg. (ISBN 0-87543-023-6). Lucas.

--Home Management. text ed. 2.75x spiral bdg. (ISBN 0-87543-024-4). Lucas.

--Housing & Home Furnishing. text ed. 2.75x spiral bdg. (ISBN 0-87543-025-2). Lucas.

--Meal Management. text ed. 2.50x spiral bdg. o.p. (ISBN 0-87543-026-0). Lucas.

University of Missouri - Home Economics Resource Units. Science Principles. text ed. 2.75x spiral bdg. (ISBN 0-87543-027-9). Lucas.

University of Montpellier Faculty of Medicine. Polyphonie Du XIIIe Siecle, 4 vols. LC 80-2191. (Illus.). 1981. Repr. of 1939 ed. 365.00 (ISBN 0-404-19040-5). AMS Pr.

University of North Carolina at Chapel Hill, Dept. of OB-GYN. Infertility, a Practical Guide for the Physician. Hammond, Mary G. & Talbert, Luther M., eds. LC 80-84920. (Illus.). 128p. (Orig.). 1981. 14.95x (ISBN 0-938938-00-2, 810-M*O-001). Health Sci Consort.

University of Oklahoma Science & Public Policy Program. Energy from the West: A Technology Assessment of Western Energy Resource Development. LC 80-5936. (Illus.). 500p. 1981. 25.00 (ISBN 0-8061-1750-8); pap. 9.95 (ISBN 0-8061-1751-6). U of Okla Pr.

University of Oregon. Didactics & Mathematics. 1978. 12.00 (ISBN 0-88488-088-5). Creative Pubns.

University of Southampton. World Shipping Law, Release 2. 1980. 80.00 (ISBN 0-379-10168-8). Oceana.

University of Southern California Center for Health Services Research. Health Technology: Issues & Activities. LC 77-12491. 1977. pap. 8.25 o.p. (ISBN 0-87258-220-5, 1755). Am Hospital.

University of Southern Main - Center for Real Estate Education. An Introduction to Real Estate Law. 250p. (Orig.). 1981. pap. 14.95 (ISBN 0-88462-428-5). Real Estate Ed Co.

University of Texas. Catalog of the Texas Collection in the Barker Texas History Center. (Library Catalogs-Bib. Guides). 1979. lib. bdg. 1200.00 (ISBN 0-8161-0273-2). G K Hall.

University of the West Indies - British Council. West Indian Science Curriculum, 3 wkbks. (gr. 7-10). 1974-75. pap. text ed. 1.95x ea. o.p.; Bk. 1. pap. (ISBN 0-435-57100-1); Bk. 2. pap. (ISBN 0-435-57101-X); Bk. 3. pap. (ISBN 0-435-57102-8); Bk. 1. tchr's guide 12.95x o.p. (ISBN 0-435-57103-6); Bk. 2. tchr's guide 14.75x o.p. (ISBN 0-435-57104-4); Bk. 3. tchr's guide 13.95x o.p. (ISBN 0-435-57105-2). Heinemann Ed.

University of Wisconsin, Division of Humanities. Twelfth-Century Europe & the Foundations of Modern Society. Clagett, Marshall, et al, eds. LC 80-21872. (Illus.). xvi, 219p. 1980. Repr. of 1966 ed. lib. bdg. 29.75x (ISBN 0-313-22798-5, WITC). Greenwood.

Unkelbach, Kurt. American Dog Book. 1976. 14.95 (ISBN 0-87690-201-8). Dutton.

--Both Ends of the Leash: Selecting & Training Your Dog. (Illus.). (gr. 3-7). 1968. PLB 4.95 (ISBN 0-13-080275-1); pap. 1.50 (ISBN 0-13-080903-9). P-H.

--How to Show Your Dog & Win. LC 75-40179. (Illus.). 144p. (gr. 6 up). 1976. PLB 6.90 o.p. (ISBN 0-531-02622-1). Watts.

--How to Teach an Old Dog New Tricks. LC 78-22430. (Illus.). 1979. 6.95 (ISBN 0-396-07669-6). Dodd.

Unknown Christian. The Kneeling Christian. 1979. pap. 2.50 (ISBN 0-310-33492-6); large print kivar 4.95 (ISBN 0-310-33497-7). Zondervan.

Unnerstad, Edith. Cats from Summer Island. (gr. 2-4). 1963. 3.95g o.s.i. (ISBN 0-02-789680-3). Macmillan.

--Peep-Larssons Go Sailing. (Illus.). (gr. 4-6). 1966. 4.50g o.s.i. (ISBN 0-02-789730-3). Macmillan.

Uno, Kuzo. Principles of Political Economy. (Marxist Theory & Contemporary Capitalism Ser.: No. 24). 1980. text ed. 50.00x (ISBN 0-391-01210-X). Humanities.

Unrau, William E. Emigrant Indians of Kansas: A Critical Bibliography. LC 79-2169. (Newberry Library Center for the History of the American Indian Bibliographical Ser.). 96p. (Orig.). 1980. pap. 3.95x (ISBN 0-253-36816-2). Ind U Pr.

Unrau, William E., ed. Tending the Talking Wire: A Buck Soldier's View of Indian Country, 1863-1866. LC 73-30154. (University of Utah Publications in the American West: Vol. 12). (Illus.). 1979. 20.00 (ISBN 0-87480-131-1). U of Utah Pr.

Unruh, Adolph & Willier, Robert A. Public Relations for Schools. LC 73-91798. 1974. pap. 5.95 (ISBN 0-8224-5750-4). Pitman Learning.

Unruh, Glenys G. Responsive Curriculum Development: Theory & Action. LC 74-24476. (Illus.). 250p. 1975. 17.50x (ISBN 0-8211-2002-6); text ed. 15.75x (ISBN 0-685-51462-5). McCutchan.

Unruh, John. Bright Eyes: The Life of a Baby Jack Rabbit. LC 80-18667. (Illus.). 112p. (Orig.). (gr. 4 up). 1980. pap. 4.95 (ISBN 0-914598-02-3). Padre Prods.

Unschuld, Paul. Medical Ethics in Imperial China: A Study in Historical Anthropology. LC 78-80479. (Comparative Studies of Health Systems & Medical Care). 1979. 15.75x (ISBN 0-520-03543-7). U of Cal Pr.

Unseld, Charles T., et al, eds. Sociopolitical Effects of Energy Use & Policy. LC 79-93181. (Study of Nuclear & Alternative Energy Systems Ser.). xxi, 511p. 1980. pap. text ed. 11.75 (ISBN 0-309-02948-1). Natl Acad Pr.

Unseld, D. W. German-English & English-German Medical Dictionary. 6th rev. & enl. ed. 1971. 25.00 o.p. (ISBN 3-8047-0567-7). Heinman.

Unsinger, Peter C. & Kuykendall, Jack L. Community Police Administration. LC 75-2119. (Nelson-Hall Law Enforcement Ser.). 475p. 1975. 19.95 (ISBN 0-88229-158-0). Nelson-Hall.

Unsoeld, A. New Cosmos. McCrea, W. H., tr. from Ger. LC 68-8301. (Heidelberg Science Library: Vols. 5 & 6). (Illus.). 1970. 15.50 (ISBN 0-387-90017-9); pap. 11.90 o.p. (ISBN 0-387-90007-1). Springer-Verlag.

Unstead, R. J. British Castles. LC 74-94224. (Illus.). (gr. 5-8). 1970. 9.95 (ISBN 0-690-16029-1, TYC-J). T Y Crowell.

--Dictionary of History. (Illus.). (gr. 4-8). 1977. 12.95 (ISBN 0-8467-0230-4, Pub. by Two Continents). Hippocrene Bks.

--History of the Modern World. Incl. World War One. LC 72-92427 (ISBN 0-382-06091-1); The Twenties. LC 72-92427 (ISBN 0-382-06094-6); The Thirties. LC 72-92430 (ISBN 0-382-06095-4); World War Two. LC 72-92428 (ISBN 0-382-06093-8); Turn of the Century. LC 74-26174 (ISBN 0-382-06096-2); The Forties & Fifties. LC 74-31819 (ISBN 0-382-06097-0); The Sixties. LC 75-18048 (ISBN 0-382-06098-9). (Illus.). (gr. 4 up). lib. bdg. 7.95 (ISBN 0-686-57850-3, Pub. by Macdonald Ed). Silver.

--Houses. (Junior Reference Ser.). (Illus.). 96p. (gr. 7 up). 7.95 (ISBN 0-7136-1301-7). Dufour.

--How They Lived in Cities Long Ago. (Illus.). 80p. (gr. 6 up). 1981. 9.95 (ISBN 0-668-05188-4, 5188). Arco.

--Living in a Medieval Village. LC 73-1667. (Living in Medieval Times Ser.). (Illus.). 44p. (gr. 4 up). 1973. PLB 5.95 o.p. (ISBN 0-201-08493-7, A-W Childrens). A-W.

--Looking at Ancient History. (Illus.). (gr. 4-6). 1960. 9.95 (ISBN 0-02-790650-7). Macmillan.

--A Pictorial History, 8 vols. Incl. Vol. 1. Invaded Island. LC 78-169914. 1972 (ISBN 0-382-06063-6); Vol. 2. Kings, Barons, & Serfs. LC 71-169915. 1972 (ISBN 0-382-06064-4); Vol. 3. Years of the Sword. LC 75-169916. 1972 (ISBN 0-382-06065-2); Vol. 4. Struggle for Power. LC 72-172430. 1972 (ISBN 0-382-06066-0); Vol. 5. Emerging Empire. LC 76-172431. 1972 (ISBN 0-382-06067-9); Vol. 6. Freedom & Revolution. LC 70-172432. 1972 (ISBN 0-382-06068-7); Vol. 7. Age of Machines. LC 73-172433. 1973 (ISBN 0-382-06069-5); Vol. 8. Incredible Century. LC 77-172434. 1975 (ISBN 0-382-06070-9). (Illus.). (gr. 4 up). lib. bdg. 7.95 (ISBN 0-685-36802-5). Silver.

--See Inside an Egyptian Town. LC 77-85159. (See Inside Bks.). (Illus.). (gr. 4-6). 1978. PLB 5.90 s&l o.p. (ISBN 0-531-09068-X). Watts.

Unsworth, Barry. The Idol Hunter. 1980. 10.95 (ISBN 0-671-25357-3). S&S.

Unsworth, Richard P., jt. auth. see Kenseth, Arnold.

Unterecker, John. Dance Sequence. (Illus.). 1975. pap. 2.00 o.p. (ISBN 0-87711-056-5). Kayak.

--Lawrence Durrell. LC 64-22642. (Columbia Essays on Modern Writers Ser.: No. 6). (Orig.). 1964. pap. 2.00 (ISBN 0-231-02655-2, MW6). Columbia U Pr.

--Yeats & Patrick McCartan. (Yeats Centenary Papers: No. 10). 1967. text ed. 3.75x (ISBN 0-85105-469-2, Dolmen Pr). Humanities.

Unterecker, John E., ed. Yeats: A Collection of Critical Essays. 1963. 8.95 o.p. (ISBN 0-13-971929-6, Spec); pap. 2.45 o.p. (ISBN 0-13-971911-3, Spec). P-H.

Unterman, Alan. Jews: Their Religious Beliefs & Practices. (Library of Religious Beliefs & Practices). 288p. 1980. write for info. (ISBN 0-7100-0743-4). Routledge & Kegan.

Unterman, Dr. Israel. Understanding the Balance Sheet & Profit & Loss Statement. rev. ed. LC 73-77431. 1976. 7.95 (ISBN 0-910580-14-6). Farnswth Pub.

Untermann, Richard. Principles & Practices of Grading, Drainage & Road Alignment: An Ecological Approach. (Illus.). 1978. ref. ed. 20.95 (ISBN 0-87909-641-1); instrs'. manual avail. Reston.

Untermeyer, Louis. Pour toi. (Illus., Fr.). 1968. 1.95 (ISBN 0-88332-128-9, 4420). Larousse.

Untermeyer, Louis, ed. Golden Book of Fun & Nonsense. (Illus.). (gr. 4-9). 1970. PLB 9.15 o.p. (ISBN 0-307-66507-0, Golden Pr). Western Pub.

--Paths of Poetry: Twenty-Five Poets & Their Poems. (Illus.). (gr. 7 up). 1966. PLB 4.17 o.s.i. (ISBN 0-440-06825-8). Delacorte.

Untermeyer, Louis, ed. see Frost, Robert.

Untersee, Philip A., jt. auth. see Curtiss, Ellen T.

Untersteiner, Mario. The Sophists. Freeman, Kathleen, tr. 1954. 24.50x (ISBN 0-631-04600-3, Pub. by Basil Blackwell). Biblio Dist.

Unthank, L. L. & Behrendt, Harry M. What You Should Know About Individual Retirement Accounts. LC 77-90480. 1978. 12.95 o.p. (ISBN 0-87094-156-9). Dow Jones-Irwin.

Untracht, Oppi. Metal Techniques for Craftsmen. LC 65-16397. 1968. 22.95 (ISBN 0-385-03027-4). Doubleday.

Unwin, Derick. Leyes De Movimiento De Newton. (Sp.). 1970. pap. 2.00 (ISBN 0-06-317011-6, IntlDept). Har-Row.

Unwin, J. C. The Hungry Forties: Life Under the Bread Tax. 288p. Date not set. Repr. of 1904 ed. 24.00x (ISBN 0-686-28338-4, Pub. by Irish Academic Pr). Biblio Dist.

Unwin, Kenneth. Langenscheidt's Standard French Dictionary: French-English, English-French. Orig. Title: Standard French Dictionary. 1216p. 1974. 11.95 (ISBN 0-88254-285-0). Hippocrene Bks.

Unwin, Noras, ed. see Barrie, James M.

Unwin, Philip. The Printing Unwins. (Illus.). 159p. 1976. 14.50 (ISBN 0-913720-14-3). Sandstone.

--The Stationers' Company 1918-1977: A Livery Company in the Modern World. 1978. lib. bdg. 16.50 o.p. (ISBN 0-510-00019-3). Westview.

Upadhyay, H. P. Monograpgh of Ceratocystis & Ceratocystiopsis. (Illus.). 288p. 1981. 27.50x (ISBN 0-8203-0539-1). U of Ga Pr.

Upadhyaya, R. B. Social Responsibility of Business & the Trusteeship Theory of Mahatma Gandhi. 1976. text ed. 22.50x o.p. (ISBN 0-8426-0927-X). Verry.

Upanisads. Isa & Kena Upanisads. Das, Deb K., tr. (Translated from Sanskrit). 8.00 (ISBN 0-89253-515-6); flexible cloth 4.80 (ISBN 0-89253-499-0). Ind-US Inc.

--Mahanarayana Upanisasd. Lal, P., tr. 1973. 11.00 (ISBN 0-88253-302-9); flexible cloth 6.75 (ISBN 0-89253-522-9). Ind-US Inc.

Upchurch, Michael. Jamboree. LC 80-18489. 192p. 1981. 9.95 (ISBN 0-394-51150-6). Knopf.

Updegraff, John C. The Christian Church (Disciples of Christ) in Florida: Its History & Development. 384p. 1981. write for info. (ISBN 0-89305-034-2). Anna Pub.

Updike, Daniel B. Printing Types: Their History, Forms & Use, 2 vols. 1980. pap. 8.95 ea. Vol. 1 (ISBN 0-486-23928-4). Vol. 2 (ISBN 0-486-23929-2). Dover.

Updike, John. Museums & Women. 256p. 1973. pap. 1.25 o.p. (ISBN 0-449-22007-9, P2007, Crest). Fawcett.

--The Music School. 1977. pap. 1.75 o.p. (ISBN 0-449-23279-4, Crest). Fawcett.

--Of the Farm. 128p. 1981. pap. 2.50 (ISBN 0-686-69195-4, Crest). Fawcett.

--Poorhouse Fair. 1977. pap. 1.50 o.p. (ISBN 0-449-23314-6, Crest). Fawcett.

--Problems. 288p. 1981. pap. 2.95 (ISBN 0-449-24360-5, Crest). Fawcett.

--Rabbit Run. 1978. pap. 2.50 (ISBN 0-449-24031-2, Crest). Fawcett.

--Too Far to Go. 1979. pap. 2.50 (ISBN 0-449-24002-9, Crest). Fawcett.

Upham, T. C. Life of Madam Guyon. 1961. 10.50 (ISBN 0-227-67521-5). Attic Pr.

Upham, Thomas. Abridgement of Mental Philosophy. LC 79-10925. (History of Psychology Ser.). 1979. Repr. of 1861 ed. lib. bdg. 57.00x (ISBN 0-8201-1331-X). Schol Facsimiles.

Uphaus, Robert W. The Impossible Observer: Reason & the Reader in Eighteenth-Century Prose. LC 79-4014. 176p. 1979. 14.50x (ISBN 0-8131-1389-X). U Pr of Ky.

Uphaus, Suzanne H. John Updike. LC 79-48076. (Modern Literature Ser.). 160p. 1980. 10.95 (ISBN 0-8044-2934-0); pap. 4.95 (ISBN 0-8044-6945-8). Ungar.

Uphoff, Norman T., jt. auth. see Altbach, Philip G.

Uphoff, Norman T., jt. auth. see Ilchman, Warren F.

Uphoff, Norman T. & Ilchman, Warren F., eds. The Political Economy of Development: Theoretical & Empirical Contributions. LC 77-161999. 1972. 24.50 o.p. (ISBN 0-520-02062-6); pap. 9.95x (ISBN 0-520-02314-5, CAMPUS84). U of Cal Pr.

Upjohn, Everard M. Richard Upjohn, Architect & Churchman. LC 68-26119. (Architecture & Decorative Art Ser.). (Illus.). 1968. Repr. of 1939 ed. lib. bdg. 25.00 (ISBN 0-306-71043-9). Da Capo.

Upjohn, Richard. Upjohn's Rural Architecture. LC 74-16022. (Architecture & Decorative Art Ser). (Illus.). 14p. 1975. Repr. of 1852 ed. lib. bdg. 39.50 (ISBN 0-306-70639-3). Da Capo.

Uppal, J. S. & Salkever, Louis K. Africa: Problems in Economic Development. LC 78-169240. 1972. 17.95 (ISBN 0-02-932910-8). Free Pr.

Uppal, J. S., jt. auth. see Pettengill, Robert B.

Upper, Dennis & Cautela, Joseph R., eds. Covert Conditioning. LC 79-61. (Pergamon General Psychology Ser.). (Illus.). 300p. 1980. 42.00 (ISBN 0-08-023347-3); pap. 12.95 (ISBN 0-08-023346-5). Pergamon.

Upper, Dennis & Ross, Steven M., eds. Behavioral Group Therapy 1980: An Annual Review. (Illus., Orig.). 1980. text ed. 24.95 (ISBN 0-87822-210-3). Res Press.

Upton & Upton. Photography. 2nd ed. 1981. pap. text ed. 15.95 (ISBN 0-316-88747-1). Little.

Upton, Anthony F. The Finnish Revolution. (Nordic Ser.: Vol. 3). 600p. 1981. 39.50x (ISBN 0-8166-0905-5). U of Minn Pr.

Upton, Anthony F., tr. see Paasivirt, Juhani.

Upton, Charles W., jt. auth. see Miller, Merton H.

Upton, D., jt. auth. see Terry, J.

Upton, G., ed. Physical & Creative Activities for the Mentally Handicapped. LC 77-82519. (Illus.). 1979. 13.95x (ISBN 0-521-21778-4). Cambridge U Pr.

Upton, George P., ed. Theodore Thomas: A Musical Autobiography. 2nd ed. LC 64-18990. (Music Reprint Ser). 1964. Repr. of 1905 ed. lib. bdg. 35.00 (ISBN 0-306-70904-X). Da Capo.

Upton, John. A Woodcarver's Primer. LC 73-4345. (Illus.). 210p. 1979. 9.95 o.p. (ISBN 0-8069-8786-3); pap. 6.95 (ISBN 0-8069-8788-X). Sterling.

Upton, M. Agricultural Production Economics & Resource-Use. (Illus.). 1976. 45.00x (ISBN 0-19-859452-6). Oxford U Pr.

Upton, Martin. Farm Management in Africa: The Principles of Production & Planning. 1973. 37.50x (ISBN 0-19-215646-2). Oxford U Pr.

Upton, Neil. An Illustrated History of Civil Engineering. LC 76-41092. 1976. 17.50x (ISBN 0-8448-1032-0). Crane-Russak Co.

Upton, Peter. Green Hill Far Away. 1978. pap. 2.25 o.p. (ISBN 0-345-27208-0). Ballantine.

Upton, William T. William Henry Fry. LC 73-20224. (Music Ser.). 346p. 1974. Repr. of 1954 ed. lib. bdg. 25.00 (ISBN 0-306-70625-3). Da Capo.

Uraguchi, Kenji & Yamazaki, Mikio, eds. Toxicology, Biochemistry & Pathology of Mycotoxins. LC 78-8992. 1978. 34.95 (ISBN 0-470-26423-3). Halsted Pr.

Ural, Oktay, ed. Energy Resources & Conservation Related to Built Environment: Proceedings of the International Conference, Dec. 7-12, 1980, Miami Beach, Florida, 2 vols. (Pergamon Policy Studies on International Development). 1290p. 1981. Set. 150.00 (ISBN 0-08-027170-7). Pergamon.

Ural, Oktay, ed. see International Conference on Housing, Planning, Financing, Construction, 2-7 December, 1979, Miami Beach, Florida.

Urang, Gunnar. Shadows of Heaven: Religion & Fantasy in the Writing of C. S. Lewis, Charles Williams & J. R. R. Tolkien. LC 73-153998. 208p. 1971. 7.95 (ISBN 0-8298-0197-9). Pilgrim NY.

Uranium Seminar, Fourth. Proceedings. LC 80-70454. (Uranium Seminars Ser.). 1980. pap. 20.00x (ISBN 0-89520-280-8). Soc Mining Eng.

Urban & Regional Planning Advisory Committee, ed. see Hart, Douglas.

Urban Design Group of the Department of City Planning, New York, jt. auth. see Ramati, Racquel.

Urban, Glen & Hauser, John R. Design & Marketing of New Products. (Illus.). 1980. 28.00 (ISBN 0-13-201269-3); text ed. 24.00 (ISBN 0-686-66020-X). P-H.

Urban, Hugh B., jt. auth. see Ford, Donald H.

Urban Innovations Group, Inc. The Arts in the Economic Life of the City. LC 79-29764. (Illus.). 150p. (Orig.). 1980. text ed. 14.95 (ISBN 0-915400-16-2); pap. text ed. 9.95 (ISBN 0-915400-17-0). Am Council Arts.

Urban Institute, ed. Struggle to Bring Technology to Cities. 1971. pap. 1.95 o.p. (ISBN 0-87766-013-1, 70001). Urban Inst.

Urban, John & Williams, Walley. AMC White Water Handbook for Canoe & Kayak. (Illus.). 200p. 1981. pap. 4.95 (ISBN 0-910146-28-4). Appalach Mtn.

Urban, John T. AMC White Water Handbook for Canoe & Kayak. LC 66-86174. (Illus.). 1976. pap. 3.95 o.p. (ISBN 0-910146-00-4). Appalach Mtn.

Urban Land Institute Editors, ed. Parking Requirements for Shopping Centers. LC 65-28845. (Technical Bulletin Ser.: No. 53). 1965. pap. 4.75 (ISBN 0-87420-053-9); pap. 3.00 uli members (ISBN 0-685-20873-7). Urban Land.

Urban Land Institute Real Estate Financial Reporting & Steering Committees & Touche Ross & Company. Real Estate Financial Reporting. LC 72-90085. (Special Report Ser.). 40p. 1972. pap. 4.75 (ISBN 0-87420-555-7). Urban Land.

Urban, M., jt. auth. see Carsky, P.

Urban, P., ed. Field Theory & Strong Interactions: Proceedings. (Acta Physica Austriaca Supplementum Ser.: No. 22). (Illus.). 815p. 1981. 98.00 (ISBN 0-387-81615-1). Springer-Verlag.

Urban, Thomas F., jt. auth. see Klatt, Lawrence A.

Urban, William. The Prussian Crusade. LC 80-5647. 469p. 1980. lib. bdg. 24.00 (ISBN 0-8191-1278-X); pap. text ed. 15.50 (ISBN 0-8191-1279-8). U Pr of Amer.

Urbanek, Mae. Ghost Trails of Wyoming. (Illus.). 236p. 1978. 16.95; pap. 8.95. Urbanek.

Urbaniak, James R., ed. see American Academy of Orthopaedic Surgeons.

Urbanski, E. Hispanoamerica y Sus Razas y Civilizaciones. 1973. 15.00 (ISBN 0-88303-014-4); pap. 10.95 (ISBN 0-685-73217-7). E Torres & Sons.

Urbantke, Carl. Texas Is the Place for Me. Cotner, Robert C., ed. (Illus.). 8.50 (ISBN 0-8363-0094-7). Jenkins.

Urbont, Rosalind, jt. auth. see Dinkin, Eleanor.

Urdang. Urdang Dictionary of Current Medical Terms. 464p. 1981. 12.95 (ISBN 0-471-05853-X, Pub. by Wiley Med). Wiley.

Urdang Assoc., ed. Biographical Encyclopedia of Scientists, 2 vols. 1981. lib. bdg. 80.00 (ISBN 0-87196-396-5). Vol. 1, 600p. Vol. 2, 600p. Facts on File.

Urdang, Constance. The Lone Woman & Others. LC 80-5261. (Pitt Poetry Ser.). 1980. 9.95 (ISBN 0-8229-3430-2); pap. 4.50 (ISBN 0-8229-5320-X). U of Pittsburgh Pr.

Urdang, Laurance, ed. Allusions: Cultural, Literary, Biblical, & Historical: A Thematic Dictionary. 1980. 45.00 (ISBN 0-8103-1124-0). Gale.

Urdang, Laurence. The Timetables of American History. 1981. 24.95 (ISBN 0-686-63196-X). S&S.

Urdang, Laurence, ed. Twentieth-Century American Nicknames. 1979. 18.00 (ISBN 0-8242-0642-8). Wilson.

Urdang, Laurence, jt. ed. see LaRoche, Nancy.

Urdang, Laurence, et al, eds. Nelson's Encyclopedia for Young Readers, 2 vols. 973p. 1980. Set. 29.95 (ISBN 0-8407-5184-2). Nelson.

Ure, A. M., jt. auth. see Ottaway, J. M.

Ure, Andrew. Philosophy of Manufactures. LC 66-21697. Repr. of 1835 ed. 30.00x (ISBN 0-678-05092-9). Kelley.

Ure, Peter. Yeats the Playwright: A Commentary on Character & Design in the Major Plays. 1963. cased 16.00x (ISBN 0-7100-2351-0); pap. 6.00 (ISBN 0-7100-6550-7). Routledge & Kegan.

Urguhant, Brian. Hammarskjold. 1972. 12.50 o.p. (ISBN 0-394-47960-2). Knopf.

Urguidi, V. L. & Thorp, R., eds. Latin America in the International Economy: Proceedings of a Conference Held by the International Economic Association at Mexico City. LC 72-13779. 1973. 26.50 o.p. (ISBN 0-470-89646-9). Halsted Pr.

Uri, Pierre. Development Without Dependence. LC 75-19829. (Praeger Special Studies). 160p. 1976. text ed. 18.95 o.p. (ISBN 0-275-55830-4); pap. text ed. 11.95 (ISBN 0-275-89470-3). Praeger.

Uri, Pierre, jt. ed. see Basagni, Fabio.

Urich, Mike. Forty-One Fifty Holley Carburetor Handbook. (Orig.). 1980. pap. 3.95 (ISBN 0-89586-047-3). H P Bks.

--Twenty-Three Hundred Holley Carburetor Handbook. (Orig.). 1981. pap. 3.95 (ISBN 0-89586-048-1). H P Bks.

Urich, Mike & Fisher, Bill. Holley Carburetors & Manifolds. rev. ed. LC 73-187040. (Illus.). 1976. pap. 7.95 (ISBN 0-912656-48-4). H P Bks.

Uricoechea, Fernando. The Patrimonial Foundations of the Brazilian Bureaucratic State. 248p. 1980. 18.50x (ISBN 0-520-03853-3). U of Cal Pr.

Uris, Auren. The Blue Book of Broadminded Business Behavior. LC 76-54769. 1977. 14.95 o.p. (ISBN 0-690-01422-8, TYC-T). T Y Crowell.

--The Dictation Book. rev. ed. 113p. pap. text ed. 8.95 (ISBN 0-935220-05-4). Intl Word Process.

--Executive Housekeeping. 1976. 7.95 o.p. (ISBN 0-688-03000-9). Morrow.

--Over Fifty: The Definitive Guide to the Best Years of Your Life. 624p. 1981. pap. 9.95 (ISBN 0-553-01297-5). Bantam.

Uris, Dorothy. Say It Again: Dorothy Uris's Personal Collection of Quotes & Anecdotes. 1979. 12.50 o.p. (ISBN 0-87690-308-1). Dutton.

--A Woman's Voice. 1978. pap. 2.95 (ISBN 0-06-463471-X, EH 471, EH). Har-Row.

Uris, Leon. Armageddon. pap. 3.50 (ISBN 0-440-10290-1). Dell.

--Exodus. 608p. 1981. pap. 3.50 (ISBN 0-553-14867-2). Bantam.

--Exodus. LC 62-16691. 1958. 14.95 (ISBN 0-385-05082-8). Doubleday.

--Trinity. LC 75-14844. 384p. 1976. 13.95 (ISBN 0-385-03458-X). Doubleday.

Uris, Norman B. Doodle Book. (Illus.). 1970. pap. 1.25 o.s.i. (ISBN 0-02-078120-2, Collier). Macmillan.

Urist, M. R., ed. see Association of Bone & Joint Surgeons.

Urist, Marshall, ed. see Association of Bone & Join Surgeons.

Urist, Marshall, ed. see Association of Bone & Joint Surgeons.

Urist, Marshall R., ed. Fundamental & Clinical Bone Physiology. (Illus.). 416p. 1980. text ed. 38.50 (ISBN 0-397-50470-5). Lippincott.
Urist, Marshall R., ed. see Association of Bone & Joint Surgeons.
Urkowitz, Steven. Shakespeare's Revision of King Lear. LC 79-3234. (Princeton Lectures in Literature Ser.). 1980. 13.50x (ISBN 0-691-06432-6). Princeton U Pr.
Urlin, Ethel L. Short History of Marriage: Marriage Rites, Customs, & Folklore in Many Countries in All Ages. LC 69-16071. 1969. Repr. of 1913 ed. 20.00 (ISBN 0-8103-3569-7). Gale.
Urmston, John. Birds & Fools Fly. 13.50x (ISBN 0-392-06708-0, SpS). Soccer.
Urness, Carol, jt. ed. see Parker, John.
Urofsky, Melvin. Louis B. Brandeis & the Progressive Tradition. 208p. 1981. 11.95 (ISBN 0-316-88787-0). Little.
Urofsky, Melvin, ed. Essays in American Zionism Nineteen-Seventeen to Nineteen Forty-Eight. 1979. 12.50 (ISBN 0-930832-56-6). Herzl Pr.
Urofsky, Melvin I. Lows D. Brandeis & the Progressive Tradition. (Library of American Biography). 1980. pap. text ed. 4.95 (ISBN 0-316-88788-9). Little.
--We Are One-American Jewry & Israel. LC 77-12878. 1978. 10.95 o.p. (ISBN 0-385-07580-4, Anchor Pr). Doubleday.
Urquhart, Colin. When the Spirit Comes. LC 75-21165. 128p. 1974. pap. 1.95 (ISBN 0-87123-645-1, 200645). Bethany Fell.
Urquhart, D. Wealth & Want. 116p. 1971. Repr. of 1845 ed. 21.00x (ISBN 0-7165-1787-6, Pub. by Irish Academic Pr Ireland). Biblio Dist.
Urquhart, Elizabeth. The Canadian Nonferrous Metals Industry: An Industrial Organization Study. 159p. (Orig.). 1978. pap. text ed. 8.00x (ISBN 0-88757-005-4, Pub. by Ctr Resource Stud Canada). Renouf.
Urquhart, Fred & Gordon, Giles, eds. Modern Scottish Short Stories. 1979. 19.95 (ISBN 0-241-10058-5, Pub by Hamish Hamilton). David & Charles.
Urquhart, Ian A., jt. auth. see Manaka, Yoshio.
Urquhart, Jane M., jt. auth. see Engeln, Oscar Dedrich Von.
Urquhart, John, ed. Controlled Release Pharmaceuticals. LC 80-70561. 160p. 1981. pap. 27.00 (ISBN 0-917330-34-X). Am Pharm Assn.
Urquhart, Judy. Food from the Wild. LC 77-85026. (Penny Pinchers Ser.). 1978. 2.95 (ISBN 0-7153-7545-8). David & Charles.
--Keeping Honey Bees. LC 77-85028. (Penny Pinchers Ser.). 1978. 2.95 (ISBN 0-7153-7548-2). David & Charles.
Urquhart, Kenneth T., jt. auth. see Foster, William L.
Urquidez, Benny. Training & Fighting Skills. Sobel, Stuart & Farkas, Emil, eds. (Illus.). 200p. (Orig.). 1981. pap. 10.95 (ISBN 0-86568-015-9). Unique Pubns.
Urquidi, Marjory, tr. see Mariategui, Jose C.
Urquidi, Marjory M., tr. see Cardoso, Fernando E. & Faletto, Enzo.
Urquidi, Victor L., ed. see International Symposium on Science & Technology for Development, Mexico City, 1979.
Urresti, Teodoro J., ed. Contestation in the Church. LC 71-168654. (Concilium Ser.: Religion in the Seventies: Vol. 68). 1971. pap. 4.95 (ISBN 0-8164-2524-8). Crossroad NY.
--Structures of the Church. (Concilium Ser.: Religion in the Seventies: Vol. 58). 1970. pap. 4.95 (ISBN 0-8164-2514-0). Crossroad NY.
Urrets-Zavalia, A. Diabetic Retinopathy. 125p. 1977. 24.75 (ISBN 0-89352-003-9). Masson Pub.
Urrutibeheity, H. N., jt. auth. see Politzer, R. L.
Urry, jt. auth. see Sherratt.
Urry, David & Urry, Katie. Flying Birds. LC 74-110974. 1969. 7.95 (ISBN 0-910294-20-8). Brown Bk.
Urry, J. & Wakeford, J. Power in Britain: Sociological Readings. 1973. text ed. 19.95 (ISBN 0-435-82900-9); pap. text ed. 15.95 (ISBN 0-435-82901-7). Heinemann Ed.
Urry, John. Reference Groups & the Theory of Revolution. (International Library of Sociology). 256p. 1973. 20.00x (ISBN 0-7100-7541-3). Routledge & Kegan.
Urry, John, jt. auth. see Keat, Russell.
Urry, Katie, jt. auth. see Urry, David.
Urry, W. Canterbury Under the Angevin Kings. (Univ. of London Historical Studies: No. 19). 1967. text ed. 67.75x (ISBN 0-485-13119-6, Athlone Pr). Humanities.
Ursell, H. D. & Young, L. C. Remarks on the Theory of Prime Ends. LC 52-42839. (Memoirs: No. 3). 1978. pap. 4.40 (ISBN 0-8218-1203-3, MEMO-3). Am Math.
Ursic, Henry S. & Pagano, LeRoy E. Security Management Systems. (Illus.). 384p. 1974. text ed. 29.75 photocopy ed. spiral (ISBN 0-398-02972-5). C C Thomas.
Ursin, Michael. Life in & Around the Salt Marshes. LC 72-78275. (Illus.). 1972. 6.95 o.s.i. (ISBN 0-690-48982-X, TYC-T). T Y Crowell.
Ursin, Michael J. Life in & Around the Salt Marshes. (Apollo Eds.). (Illus.). 144p. 1972. pap. 2.95 o.s.i. (ISBN 0-8152-0329-2, A329, TYC-T). T Y Crowell.
Urwick, E. J., ed. Study of Boy Life in Our Cities: London, 1904. LC 79-56942. (The English Working Class Ser.). 1980. lib. bdg. 28.00 (ISBN 0-8240-0125-7). Garland Pub.
Urwin, Derek W. From Ploughshare to Ballotbox. 356p. 1981. pap. 30.00x (ISBN 82-00-05394-6). Universitet.
Urwin, Kenneth, ed. A Short Old French Dictionary for Students. 108p. 1972. pap. 7.50x (ISBN 0-631-07970-X, Pub. by Basil Blackwell). Biblio Dist.
Ury, Zalman R. Musar Movement. 1970. pap. 3.00x o.p. (ISBN 0-685-00969-6). Bloch.
U.S. Army. Advisor Handbook for Counterinsurgency: Field Manual 31-73. (Illus.). 1977. pap. 5.00 o.p. (ISBN 0-87364-091-8). Paladin Ent.
--Basic Criminal Investigations. (Illus.). 1977. pap. 4.00 o.p. (ISBN 0-87364-086-1). Paladin Ent.
U.S. Army Infantry School, Ft. Benning, Ga. Ranger Handbook. (Illus.). 213p. 1977. pap. 8.00 (ISBN 0-87364-044-6). Paladin Ent.
U.S. Department of Agriculture. Handbook of the Nutritional Contents of Foods. LC 75-2616. (Illus.). 192p. 1975. pap. text ed. 4.00 (ISBN 0-486-21342-0). Dover.
U.S. Dept. of Energy. Anaerobic Fermentation of Agricultural Residue: Potential for Improvement & Implementation. 455p. 1981. pap. 39.50 (ISBN 0-89934-099-7). Solar Energy Info.
--Ocean Energy Systems Program Summary: Fiscal Year Nineteen Seventy Nine. 285p. 1981. pap. 30.00 (ISBN 0-89934-100-4). Solar Energy Info.
--Solar Energy Program Summary Document Nineteen Eighty One. 375p. 1981. pap. 34.50 (ISBN 0-89934-093-8). Solar Energy Info.
U.S. General Accounting Office. How the Internal Revenue Service Selects Individual Income Tax Returns for Audit. 1980. pap. 5.00 (ISBN 0-89499-007-1). Bks Business.
U.S. National Alcohol Fuels Commission. State Initiatives on Alcohol Fuels. 102p. 1981. pap. 15.00 (ISBN 0-89934-105-5). Solar Energy Info.
U.S. National Alcohols Fuels Commission. Fuel Alcohol on the Farm. 50p. 1981. pap. 4.95 (ISBN 0-89934-097-0). Solar Energy Info.
U.S. National Committee for Geochemistry, Div. of Earth Sciences. Orientations in Geochemistry. (Illus.). 152p. 1974. pap. 8.00 (ISBN 0-309-02147-2). Natl Acad Pr.
USA National Neutron Cross-Section Center & USSR Nuclear Data Centre. CINDA: 1976-1977 Index to the Literature on Microscopic Neutron Data, 2 vols. (Orig.). 1976. pap. 92.25 ea. (IAEA). Vol. 1 (ISBN 92-0-039076-5, Z52). Vol. 2 (Z53). Unipub.
Usami, T., jt. auth. see Lapwood, E. R.
Usdan, Michael D., et al. Education & State Politics: The Developing Relationship Between Elementary, Secondary & Higher Education. LC 69-17673. (Orig.). 1969. text ed. 9.25x (ISBN 0-8077-2291-X). Tchrs Coll.
Usdih, Earl & Bunney, William E. Neuroreceptors Basic & Clinical Aspects: Based on Symposia Held at the American College of Neuropsychology Annual Meeting December 1979. 280p. 1981. 60.50 (ISBN 0-686-69370-1, Pub. by Wiley-Interscience). Wiley.
Usdin, Earl & Efron, Daniel H. Psychotropic Drugs & Related Compounds. 2nd ed. LC 79-42886. 780p. 1979. 41.00 (ISBN 0-08-025510-8). Pergamon.
Usdin, Earl, ed. Neuropsychopharmacology of Monoamines & Their Regulatory Enzymes. LC 74-77231. (Advances in Biochemical Psychopharmacology Ser: Vol. 12). 530p. 1974. 41.50 (ISBN 0-911216-77-4). Raven.
Usdin, Earl & Snyder, Solomon, eds. Frontiers in Catecholamine Research: Proceedings, International Catecholamine Symposium, 3rd, Strasbourg, France, May, 1973. 1974. text ed. 95.00 (ISBN 0-08-017922-3). Pergamon.
Usdin, Earl, et al. Enzymes & Neurotransmitters in Mental Disease: Based on a Symposium Held at the Technion Faculty of Medicine, Haifa, Israel August 28-30 1979. LC 80-40130. 640p. 1980. 98.00 (ISBN 0-471-27791-6, Pub. by Wiley-Interscience). Wiley.
Usdin, Earl, et al, eds. Catecholamines: Basic & Clinical Frontiers: Proceedings of the Fourth International Catecholamine Symposium; Asilomar Conference Center, Pacific Grove, California; September 17-22, 1978, 2 vols. 1979. 220.00 (ISBN 0-08-022650-7). Pergamon.
Useem, Michael. Protest Movements in America. LC 74-34014. (Studies in Sociology Ser.). 68p. 1975. pap. text ed. 2.50 (ISBN 0-672-61356-5). Bobbs.
Usgaonkar, R. N. A Course on Reaction Mechanistics in Organic Chemistry. 320p. 1981. text ed. 18.95x (ISBN 0-7069-1236-5, Pub. by Vikas India). Advent Bk.
Usha, Brahmacharini, ed. Ramakrishna-Vedanta Wordbook: A Brief Dictionary of Hinduism. (Orig.). pap. 3.25 (ISBN 0-87481-017-5). Vedanta Pr.
Usher, Carolyn E., jt. auth. see McConnell, Stephen R.
Usher, Dan. The Economic Prerequisite to Democracy. 224p. 1981. 17.50x (ISBN 0-231-05280-4). Columbia U Pr.
Usher, George. A Dictionary of Plants Used by Man. LC 74-2707. 1974. 15.95 o.s.i. (ISBN 0-02-853800-5). Hafner.
Usher, John. European Community Law & National Law. (Studies on Contemporary Europe: No. 3). 96p. (Orig.). 1981. text ed. 15.95x (ISBN 0-04-341017-0, 2593); pap. text ed. 6.95x (ISBN 0-04-341018-9, 2594). Allen Unwin.
Usher, Michael & Bormuth, Robert. Experiencing Life Through Mathematics, Vol. 2. (Illus.). (gr. 9-12). 1980. pap. text ed. 4.92 (ISBN 0-913688-68-1); tchr's ed. 6.00x (ISBN 0-913688-69-X). Pawnee Pub.
Usher, Michael A. & Bormuth, Robert. Experiencing Life Through Mathematics, Vol. 1. rev. ed. (Illus.). 128p. (Orig.). (gr. 8-12). 1978. pap. text ed. 4.92x (ISBN 0-913688-66-5); tchrs. ed. 6.00x (ISBN 0-913688-67-3). Pawnee Pub.
Usherwood, P. N. Insect Muscle. 1975. 84.50 (ISBN 0-12-709450-4). Acad Pr.
Usherwood, P. N., jt. ed. see Newth, D. R.
Usigli, Rodolfo. Corona de Fuego: Primer Esquema Para una Tragedia Antihistorica Americana. Ballinger, Rex E., ed. LC 72-167893. (Span.). 1972. pap. text ed. 6.95x (ISBN 0-672-63025-7). Irvington.
Usinger, Robert L., jt. auth. see Storer, Tracy I.
Usinger, Robert L., ed. Aquatic Insects of California, with Keys to North American Genera & California Species. (Illus.). 1956. 22.75x (ISBN 0-520-01293-3). U of Cal Pr.
Uslander, Arlene & Weiss, Lee D. A Doctor Discusses Talking with Your Child About Sex. (Illus.). 1978. pap. 2.50 (ISBN 0-685-46343-5). Budlong.
Uslander, Arlene, et al. Their Universe: A Look into Children's Hearts & Minds. LC 72-6164. 1973. 6.95 o.p. (ISBN 0-440-08684-1). Delacorte.
Uslaner, Eric M. & Weber, Ronald E. Patterns of Decision Making in State Legislatures. LC 76-12884. (Special Studies). 1977. text ed. 23.95 (ISBN 0-275-23230-1). Praeger.
Uslenghi, Piergiorgio. Nonlinear Electromagnetics. 1980. 30.00 (ISBN 0-12-709660-4). Acad Pr.
Usoltseva, E. V. & Mashkara, K. I. Surgery of Diseases & Injuries of the Hand, 2 vols. LC 78-26990. (Illus.). 1979. Set. 39.50 (ISBN 0-8016-5198-0). Mosby.
Uspensky, Boris. The Poetics of Composition: Structure of the Artistic Text & the Typology of Compositional Forms. Zavarin, Valentina & Wittig, Susan, trs. LC 72-85517. 1974. 15.75x (ISBN 0-520-02309-9). U of Cal Pr.
Ussher, Arland. From a Dark Lantern: A Journal. Parisious, Roger N., et al, eds. 1978. text ed. 45.50x (ISBN 0-391-01594-X). Humanities.
--Journey Through Dread. LC 68-54234. 1955. 9.00x (ISBN 0-8196-0221-3). Biblo.
--The Juggler. 88p. 1980. text ed. write for info. (ISBN 0-85105-374-2, Dolmen Pr). Humanities.
--Sages & Schoolmen. 1965. 6.25 (ISBN 0-8023-1139-3). Dufour.
--Three Great Irishmen: Shaw, Yeats, Joyce. LC 68-54235. 1953. 9.00x (ISBN 0-8196-0222-1). Biblo.
--The Twenty-Two Keys of the Tarot. Weeney, L. Mac, tr. (Illus.). 1976. pap. text ed. 2.75x (ISBN 0-85105-297-5, Dolmen Pr). Humanities.
Ussher, Roland G., ed. see Aristophanes.
Ussing, H. H., et al, eds. see Alfred Benzon Symposium 5th.
USSR Nuclear Data Centre, jt. auth. see USA National Neutron Cross-Section Center.
USTA Facilities Committee. Tennis Courts. 1980. pap. text ed. 5.00 (ISBN 0-938822-09-8). USTA.
USTA Public Relations Office. Records of Selected Players, 1979. 1980. 6.00 (ISBN 0-938822-08-X). USTA.
Uston, Ken & Rapoport, Roger. The Big Player: How a Team of Blackjack Players Made a Million Dollars. LC 76-29919. 1977. 7.95 o.p. (ISBN 0-03-016921-6). HR&W.
Usui, Atsushi. Eel Culture. (Illus.). 190p. 19.50 (FN). Unipub.
Usui, Masao. Form & Function: Japanese Teapots. LC 78-71255. (Form & Function Ser.: Vol. 4). (Illus.). 1981. pap. 8.95 (ISBN 0-87011-392-5). Kodansha.
Utas, Bo. A Persian Sufi Poem: Vocabulary & Terminology. Concordance, Frequency Word-List, Statistical Survey, Arabic Loan-Words & Sufi-Religious Terminology in Tariq Ut-Tajqiq. (Scandinavian Institute of Asian Studies Monographs: No. 36). 1978. pap. text ed. 13.75x (ISBN 0-7007-0116-8). Humanities.
--Tariq Ut-Tahqiq. (Scandinavian Institute of Asian Studies Monograph: No. 13). 300p. (Orig.). 1975. pap. text ed. 12.50x (ISBN 0-7007-0062-5). Humanities.
Utete, C. Munhamu Botsio see Botsio Utete, C. Munhamu.
UTI. Materials & Building Research, Vol. 1. 1979. 50.00 (ISBN 0-86095-825-6). Longman.
Utian, Wulf H. Your Middle Years: A Doctor's Guide for Today's Woman. (Appleton Consumer Health Guides). 109p. 1980. 12.95 (ISBN 0-8385-9938-9); pap. 5.95 (ISBN 0-8385-9937-0). ACC.
Utlan. Your Middle Years: A Doctor's Guide for Today's Woman. 12.95 (ISBN 0-8385-9938-9). P-H.
Utley, B. G. IBM System-38: Technical Developments. (IBM Systems Design & Development Ser.). (Illus.). 109p. 1980. pap. 5.50 (ISBN 0-933186-03-7, G-580-0237-1). IBM Armonk.
Utley, Francis L., et al. Bear, Man & God: Eight Approaches to Faulkner's the Bear. 2nd ed. (Orig.). 1971. pap. text ed. 5.95x (ISBN 0-394-31546-4, RanC). Random.
Utley, Jon B. The Inflation Survival Book: A Jobs, Investment, Survival Guide. 300p. 1981. 12.95 (ISBN 0-89803-042-0). Caroline Hse.
Utley, Robert M. Frontiersmen in Blue: The United States Army & the Indian, 1848-1865. LC 80-27796. (Illus.). xvi, 384p. 1981. 23.50x (ISBN 0-8032-4550-5, BB 769, Bison); pap. 9.95 (ISBN 0-8032-9550-2). U of Nebr Pr.
Utley, Robert M. & Washburn, Wilcomb E. The American Heritage History of the Indian Wars. LC 77-23044. (Illus.). 352p. 1977. 12.95 (ISBN 0-8281-0202-3, Dist. by Scribner); deluxe ed. 39.95 slipcased (ISBN 0-8281-0203-1, Dist. by Scribner). Am Heritage.
Utrecht, jt. auth. see Caldwell.
Utt, Richard. New Frontiers in Good Health. (Uplook Ser.). 1979. pap. 0.75 (ISBN 0-8163-0325-8, 14400-6). Pacific Pr Pub Assn.
--Once You Start Climbing, Don't Look Down. LC 78-50438. (Redwood Ser.). 1978. pap. 3.95 (ISBN 0-8163-0092-5, 04441-2). Pacific Pr Pub Assn.
--Uncle Charlie. LC 77-85499. 1977. 6.95 (ISBN 0-8163-0288-X, 21070-8); pap. 4.95 (ISBN 0-8163-0289-8, 21069-0). Pacific Pr Pub Assn.
Utt, Walter. Home to Our Valleys. LC 75-30138. (Destiny Ser.). 1976. pap. 4.95 (ISBN 0-8163-0258-8, 08698-3). Pacific Pr Pub Assn.
Uttal, William R. A Taxonomy of Visual Processes. LC 80-18262. 802p. 1981. text ed. 45.00 (ISBN 0-89859-075-2). L Erlbaum Assocs.
Uttley, Alison. Adventures of Tim Rabbit. (Illus.). (ps-5). 1945. 6.95 (ISBN 0-571-05676-8, Pub. by Faber & Faber). Merrimack Bk Serv.
--Lavender Shoes: Eight Tales of Disenchantment. (Illus.). (ps-5). 1970. 6.95 (ISBN 0-571-09361-2, Pub. by Faber & Faber). Merrimack Bk Serv.
--Recipes from an Old Farmhouse. (Illus., Orig.). 1973. pap. 3.95 (ISBN 0-571-10178-X, Pub. by Faber & Faber). Merrimack Bk Serv.
--Secret Places & Other Essays. 1972. 8.50 (ISBN 0-571-09924-6, Pub. by Faber & Faber). Merrimack Bk Serv.
--Stories for Christmas. Lines, Kathleen, ed. (Illus.). 1977. 10.95 (ISBN 0-571-11074-6, Pub. by Faber & Faber). Merrimack Bk Serv.
--Tales of the Four Pigs & Brock the Badger. (Illus.). (ps-5). 1939. 5.95 (ISBN 0-571-06456-6, Pub. by Faber & Faber). Merrimack Bk Serv.
--A Traveller in Time. (Illus.). 331p. (gr. 3-7). 1981. 8.95 (ISBN 0-571-06182-6, Pub. by Faber & Faber). Merrimack Bk Serv.
Utton, Albert E. & Teclaff, Ludwik A., eds. Water in a Developing World: The Management of a Critical Resource. (Special Studies in Natural Resources & Energy Management). 1978. lib. bdg. 25.50x (ISBN 0-89158-050-6). Westview.
Utton, Albert E., jt. ed. see Teclaff, Ludwipk A.
Utton, Albert E., et al, eds. Natural Resources for a Democratic Society: Public Participation in Decision-Making. LC 76-15363. (Special Studies on Natural Resources Management Ser). 1976. pap. text ed. 10.50 (ISBN 0-89158-110-3). Westview.
Utton, M. A. Diversification & Competition. LC 79-11664. (NIESR, Occasional Papers Ser.: No. 31). 1979. 18.95 (ISBN 0-521-22725-9). Cambridge U Pr.

U Tun Wai. Economic Essays on Developing Countries. LC 80-83264. 512p. 1980. 70.00 (ISBN 90-286-0150-3). Sijthoff & Noordhoff.

Utz, Pamela J. Settling the Facts. LC 77-9119. 1978. 18.95x (ISBN 0-669-01673-X). Lexington Bks.

Utz, Peter. Video User's Handbook. rev. ed. LC 79-379. (Video Bookshelf Ser.). (Illus.). 410p. 1980. Repr. of 1980 ed. text ed. 19.95x (ISBN 0-914236-78-4). Knowledge Indus.

Uveges, Joseph A., Jr. The Dimensions of Public Administration. 3rd ed. 1978. pap. text ed. 13.95x (ISBN 0-205-06510-4). Allyn.

Uvezian, Sonia. Complete International Sandwich Cookbook. LC 80-5715. 288p. 1981. 14.95 (ISBN 0-8128-2787-2). Stein & Day.

Uviller, H. Richard. Processes of Criminal Justice: Adjudication. 2nd ed. (American Casebook Ser.). 768p. 1979. pap. text ed. 14.95 (ISBN 0-8299-2064-1). West Pub.

--The Processes of Criminal Justice: Investigation & Adjudication. 2nd ed. LC 79-16743. (American Casebook Ser.). 1384p. 1979. text ed. 24.95 (ISBN 0-8299-2057-9). West Pub.

--Processes of Criminal Justice: Investigation. 2nd ed. (American Casebook Ser.). 679p. 1979. pap. text ed. 13.95 (ISBN 0-8299-2065-X). West Pub.

Uxkull, Boris. Arms & Women. 1966. 5.95 o.s.i. (ISBN 0-02-621270-6). Macmillan.

Uyanga, Joseph T. A Geography of Rural Development in Nigeria. LC 79-9601. 188p. 1980. pap. text ed. 9.00 (ISBN 0-8191-0956-8). U Pr of Amer.

Uyeda, Akinari. Tales of Moonlight & Rain: Japanese Gothic Tales. Hamada, Kengi, tr. from Japanese. LC 79-175064. (Illus.). 1972. 15.00x (ISBN 0-231-03631-0). Columbia U Pr.

Uyeda, S., et al, eds. Geodynamics of the Western Pacific. (Advances in Earth & Planetary Sciences Ser.: Pt. 6). 592p. 1980. 49.50x (ISBN 0-89955-315-X, Pub. by JSSP Japan). Intl Schol Bk Serv.

Uyeda, Seiya. The New View of the Earth: Moving Continents & Moving Oceans. Ohnuki, Masako, tr. LC 77-9900. (Geology Ser.). (Illus.). 1978. text ed. 19.95x (ISBN 0-7167-0283-5); pap. text ed. 9.95x (ISBN 0-7167-0282-7). W H Freeman.

Uyehara, George E. The Political Development of Japan: 1867 to 1909. (Illus.). 296p. 1972. Repr. of 1910 ed. 31.00x (ISBN 0-686-28325-2, Pub. by Irish Academic Pr). Biblio Dist.

Uysal, Ahmet E., jt. auth. see Walker, Barbara K.

Uysal, Ahmet E., tr. see Walker, Barbara K. & Uysal, Ahmet E.

Uyterhoeven, Hugo E., et al. Strategy & Organization. rev ed. 1977. text ed. 19.50 (ISBN 0-256-01923-1). Irwin.

Uyttenbroeck, Frans. Gynecologic Surgery: Treatment of Complications & Prevention of Injuries. 288p. 1980. 29.50 (ISBN 0-89352-088-8). Masson Pub.

V

Vacalis, Terri D. Drug Use & Abuse. 1975. wire coil bdg. 2.95 o.p. (ISBN 0-88252-101-2). Paladin Hse.

Vacalopoulos, Apostolos. The Greek Nation, 1453-1669: The Cultural & Economic Background of Modern Greek Society. 472p. 1976. 32.50 (ISBN 0-8135-0810-X). Rutgers U Pr.

Vacalopoulos, Apostolos E. Origins of the Greek Nation: The Byzantine Period 1204-1461. Moles, Ian N., tr. (Byzantine Ser.). (Illus.). 1970. 27.50 (ISBN 0-8135-0659-X). Rutgers U Pr.

Vacation Work. Traveler's Survival Kit to the East. (Illus.). 130p. pap. 7.95 (ISBN 0-901205-65-6). Bradt Ent.

Vacca, Richard T. Content Area Reading. 1981. text ed. 14.95 (ISBN 0-316-89488-5). Little.

Vacca, Roberto. Modest Technologies for a Complicated World. 144p. Date not set. 26.00 (ISBN 0-08-024067-4); pap. cancelled (ISBN 0-08-024068-2). Pergamon.

Vaccara, Beatrice N., jt. auth. see Salant, Walter S.

Vaccaro, Michael A., illus. The Happy World of Strawberry Shortcake. LC 80-53104. (Board Bks.). (Illus.). 14p. (ps). 1981. boards 2.95 (ISBN 0-394-84734-2). Random.

Vacheron, Edith & Kahl, Virginia. Here Is Henri! LC 59-14326. (Illus.). 32p. (gr. k-3). 1959. 2.50 (ISBN 0-684-14661-4). Scribner.

Vachon, Andre see Halpenny, Francess.

Vachon, Nancy, ed. The Exchange Show: A Documentation. LC 79-124425. (Illus.). 79p. (Orig.). 1979. pap. 5.95 (ISBN 0-87870-084-6). Memphis St Univ.

Vachss, Andrew H. & Bakal, Yitzhak. The Life-Style Violent Juvenile. LC 77-2520. 1979. 25.95 (ISBN 0-669-01515-6). Lexington Bks.

Vactor, Lloyd Van see Washburn, Lindy & Van Vactor, Lloyd.

Vaden, Frank S., jt. auth. see Arnold, Tom.

Vadney, Thomas E. The Wayward Liberal: A Political Biography of Donald Richberg. LC 75-132832. 1970. 12.50x (ISBN 0-8131-1243-5). U Pr of Ky.

Vaenius, Otho. Horatii Emblemata. Orgel, Stephen, ed. LC 78-68200. (Philosophy of Images Ser.: Vol. 10). (Illus.). 1980. Repr. of 1612 ed. lib. bdg. 66.00 (ISBN 0-8240-3684-0). Garland Pub.

Vaenius, Otho V. Amorum Emblemata....Emblemes of Love. Orgel, Stephen, ed. LC 78-68196. (Philosophy of Images Ser.: Vol. 9). (Illus.). 1980. lib. bdg. 66.00 (ISBN 0-8240-3683-2). Garland Pub.

Vaeth, J. Gordon. Man Who Founded Georgia: The Story of James Edward Oglethorpe. LC 68-19026. (America in the Making Ser). (Illus.). (gr. 7 up). 1968. 3.50g o.s.i. (ISBN 0-02-791090-3, CCPr). Macmillan.

Vaeth, J. M., ed. Body Image, Self-Esteem, & Sexuality in Cancer Patients. (Frontiers of Radiation Therapy & Oncology: Vol. 14). (Illus.). x, 134p. 1980. 49.25 (ISBN 3-8055-0036-X). S Karger.

Vaganova, Agrippina. Basic Principles of Classical Ballet. rev. ed. Chujoy, Anatole, et al, trs. LC 68-17402. (Illus.). 1969. pap. 2.50 (ISBN 0-486-22036-2). Dover.

--Basic Principles of Classical Ballet: Russian Ballet Technique. (Illus.). 7.50 (ISBN 0-8446-0949-8). Peter Smith.

Vagg, Peter R., jt. ed. see Spielberger, Charles D.

Vaghefi, M. Reza, et al. Systems of Higher Education: Iran. 43p. 1978. pap. 3.50 (ISBN 0-89192-207-5). Interbk Inc.

Vago, Bela. Jewish Assimilation in Modern Times. 300p. 1981. lib. bdg. 24.50x (ISBN 0-86531-030-0). Westview.

Vago, Steven. Law & Society. (Ser. in Sociology). (Illus.). 352p. 1981. text ed. 16.95 (ISBN 0-13-526483-9). P-H.

Vagtborg, Harold. Research & American Industrial Development. LC 75-14439. 1976. text ed. 57.00 (ISBN 0-08-019791-4). Pergamon.

Vagts, Alfred. History of Militarism. rev. ed. LC 59-7194. 1967. pap. text ed. 8.95 (ISBN 0-02-933050-5). Free Pr.

Vahanian, Gabriel. The Death of God. LC 61-9962. 1961. 6.95 (ISBN 0-8076-0144-6); pap. 2.95 o.p. (ISBN 0-8076-0360-0). Braziller.

--God & Utopia. LC 77-24029. 1977. 8.95 (ISBN 0-8164-0358-9). Crossroad NY.

--No Other God. LC 66-28591. (Orig.). 1966. pap. 2.50 o.s.i. (ISBN 0-8076-0389-9). Braziller.

--Wait Without Idols. LC 64-11429. 1964. 6.95 o.s.i. (ISBN 0-8076-0255-8); pap. 2.95 o.s.i. (ISBN 0-8076-0374-0). Braziller.

Vahlen, J., ed. see Lachmann, Karl.

Vahtola, Olli, jt. auth. see Wildt, Albert R.

Vaid, Baldev K. Bimal in Bog, 2 vols. 1972. Set. 28.00 (ISBN 0-88253-818-7); Set. pap. text ed. 9.60 (ISBN 0-88253-819-5). Ind-US Inc.

Vaid, K. B., tr. see Varma, Shrikant.

Vaid, K. N. New Worker. 6.25x o.p. (ISBN 0-210-22205-0). Asia.

--Papers on Absenteeism. 1968. 7.00 o.p. (ISBN 0-210-22512-2). Asia.

--State & Labour in India. 7.50x (ISBN 0-210-26949-9). Asia.

Vaid, Krishna B. Silence & Other Stories. (Writers Workshop Greenbird Ser.). 94p. 1975. 14.00 (ISBN 0-88253-634-6); pap. text ed. 4.80 (ISBN 0-88253-633-8). Ind-US Inc.

--Steps in Darkness. 151p. 1972. pap. 2.45 (ISBN 0-88253-120-4). Ind-US Inc.

Vaid, Sudesh. The Divided Mind: Studies in Defoe & Richardson. 1979. text ed. 17.50x (ISBN 0-210-40619-4). Asia.

Vaidon, Lawdom. Tangier: A Different Way. LC 77-8601. (Illus.). 1977. 21.00 (ISBN 0-8108-1072-7). Scarecrow.

Vaidya, S. Figures of Cricket. 4.00x o.p. (ISBN 0-210-33858-X). Asia.

Vaidyanathaswamy, R. Set Topology. 2nd ed. LC 60-8968. 12.95 (ISBN 0-8284-0139-X). Chelsea Pub.

Vaihinger, Hans. Commentar Zu Kants Kritik der Reinen Vernunft, 2 vols. Beck, Lewis W., ed. Incl. Vol. 1. Stuttgart 1881; Vol. 2. Stuttgart & Berlin 1892. LC 75-32048. (Philosophy of Immanual Kant Ser.: Vol. 8). 1976. Repr. of 1892 ed. Set. lib. bdg. 66.00 (ISBN 0-8240-2332-3). Garland Pub.

Vail, David J. Technology for Ujamaa Village Developement in Tanzania. LC 74-25876. (Foreign & Comparative Studies-Eastern African Ser.: No. 18). 64p. 1975. pap. 3.50x (ISBN 0-915984-15-6). Syracuse U Foreign Comp.

Vail, Dennis. Robert Frost's Imagery & the Poetic Consciousness. (Graduate Studies: No. 12). (Orig.). 1976. pap. 4.00 (ISBN 0-89672-022-5). Tex Tech Pr.

Vail, Gladys E., et al. Foods. 7th ed. LC 77-74376. (Illus.). 1978. text ed. 18.50 (ISBN 0-395-25521-X); inst. guide 0.90 (ISBN 0-395-25522-8); lab. manual 8.25 (ISBN 0-395-25523-6). HM.

Vail, Leroy & White, Landeg. Capitalism & Colonialism in Mozambique: A Study of the Quelimane District. LC 80-22702. (Illus.). 424p. 1981. 45.00x (ISBN 0-8166-1039-8). U of Minn Pr.

Vail, Priscilla. One Thousand One Games for Better Writing: Writing Easily, Clearly & Enthusiastically. LC 80-54818. (Illus.). 288p. 1981. 16.95 (ISBN 0-8027-0682-7). Walker & Co.

Vail, Priscilla L., jt. auth. see Migdail, Sherry R.

Vaillancourt, Jean-Guy. Papal Power: A Study of Vatican Control Over Lay Catholic Elites. 375p. 1980. 16.95 (ISBN 0-520-03733-2). U of Cal Pr.

Vaillancourt, Sarah. Perspectives Francaises One. LC 80-12737. (Illus.). 1980. text ed. 8.95 (ISBN 0-88436-754-1); pap. text ed. 5.95 (ISBN 0-88436-755-X). EMC.

Vainio, Harri, et al, eds. Occupational Cancer & Carcinogenesis. (Illus.). 600p. 1980. text ed. 49.50 (ISBN 0-89116-193-7). Hemisphere Pub.

Vainshtain, B. K. Modern Crystallography I. (Springer Series in Solid-State Sciences: Vol. 15). (Illus.). 420p. 1981. 54.50 (ISBN 0-387-10052-0). Springer-Verlag.

Vainshtein, B. K. Structure Analysis by Electron Diffraction. 1964. 33.00 o.p. (ISBN 0-08-010241-7). Pergamon.

Vainshtein, Sevyan. Nomads of South Siberia: The Pastoral Economies of Tuva. Humphrey, Caroline, ed. Colenso, M., tr. from Russian. LC 78-504728. (Studies in Social Anthropology: No. 25). 1981. 39.50 (ISBN 0-521-22089-0). Cambridge U Pr.

Vainshtein, V. Introduction to Chess Openings. (Chess Player Ser.). 1977. pap. 3.95 o.p. (ISBN 0-906042-01-1, H-1276). Hippocrene Bks.

Vairo, Philip D., jt. auth. see Marcus, Sheldon.

Vaisey, David, jt. auth. see Betjeman, John.

Vaisey, David, jt. auth. see Turner, Michael.

Vaish, M. C., jt. auth. see Sundharam, K. P.

Vaisman. Foundations of Three Dimensional Euclidean Geometry. Date not set. 35.00 (ISBN 0-8247-6901-5). Dekker.

Vaisrub, S. Medicine's Metaphors: Messages & Menaces. 1977. 9.95 (ISBN 0-87489-011-X). Med Economics.

Vaitses, Allan. Lofting. LC 78-75110. 1980. pap. 15.00 (ISBN 0-87742-113-7). Intl Marine.

Vaitsos, Constantine V. Intercountry Income Distribution & Transnational Enterprises. 192p. 1974. 24.00x (ISBN 0-19-828195-1). Oxford U Pr.

Vaizey, John. Education: the State of Debate: Problems Facing Education in the United States, Britain, & Canada. 1976. text ed. 17.95x (ISBN 0-7156-0986-6). Intl Ideas.

Vaizey, John, ed. Economic Soverignty & Regional Policy. LC 74-22003. 1975. 32.95 (ISBN 0-470-89777-5). Halsted Pr.

Vaizey, John, et al. The Political Economy of Education: A Symposium on Regional Problems in Britain & Ireland. LC 72-10688. 297p. 1973. 21.95 (ISBN 0-470-89780-5). Halsted Pr.

Vajda, Albert. Lend Me an Eye. 1974. 11.95 (ISBN 0-236-31058-5, Pub. by Paul Elek). Merrimack Bk Serv.

Vajda, Imre & Simai, M., eds. Foreign Trade in a Planned Economy. LC 74-149433. 1971. 38.50 (ISBN 0-521-08153-X). Cambridge U Pr.

Vajda, Mihaly. The State & Socialism. (Allison & Busby Motive Ser.). 160p. 1981. pap. 7.95 (Pub. by Alison & Busby, England). Schocken.

Vajda, Miklos, ed. & intro. by. Modern Hungarian Poetry. LC 76-2453. (Illus.). 1977. 15.00x (ISBN 0-231-04022-9). Columbia U Pr.

Vajda, Miklos, ed. Modern Hungarian Poetry. 1979. pap. 7.95 (ISBN 0-231-08370-X). Columbia U Pr.

Vajda, S. Introduction to Linear Programming & the Theory of Games. 76p. 1963. pap. text ed. 4.95x o.p. (ISBN 0-412-20310-3, Pub. by Chapman & Hall). Methuen Inc.

--Introduction to Linear Programming & the Theory of Games. 1963. pap. 4.95 o.p. (ISBN 0-470-89782-1). Halsted Pr.

--Probabilistic Programming. (Probability & Mathematical Statistics Ser.). 1972. 18.00 (ISBN 0-12-710150-0). Acad Pr.

--Theory of Games & Linear Programming. 1967. pap. 4.95 o.p. (ISBN 0-470-89779-1). Halsted Pr.

Vajpeyi, Dhirendra, jt. auth. see Singh, Baljit.

Vajpeyi, Kailash. The Science of Mantras: A Manual of Happiness & Prosperity. 128p. 1980. 13.50 (ISBN 0-391-02213-X). Humanities.

Vakil, Rustom J. Romance of Healing. 6.95x o.p. (ISBN 0-210-33941-1). Asia.

Vala, Eduard. A Time, Place & Season. pap. 4.95 (ISBN 0-933350-15-5). Morse Pr.

Valdes, Alberto, ed. Food Security for Developing Countries. 350p. 1981. lib. bdg. 25.00x (ISBN 0-86531-071-8). Westview.

Valdes, Alberto, et al, eds. Economics & the Design of Small Farmer Technology. 1978. text ed. 16.00 (ISBN 0-8138-1910-5). Iowa St U Pr.

Valdes, Armando P. Jose. Cano, J. & Cameron, E., eds. 1932. 5.50 (ISBN 0-672-73223-8). Odyssey Pr.

Valdes, Mario J. & Miller, Owen J., eds. Interpretation of Narrative. LC 78-23683. 1978. 15.00x o.p. (ISBN 0-8020-5443-9). U of Toronto Pr.

Valdes-Fallis, Guadalupe. Code Switching & the Classroom Teacher. (Language in Education Ser.: No. 4). 1978. pap. 2.95 (ISBN 0-87281-080-1). Ctr Appl Ling.

Valdes-Fallis, Guadalupe, et al. Teaching Spanish to the Hispanic Bilingual: Issues, Aims, & Methods. 272p. 1981. text ed. 18.95 (ISBN 0-8077-2629-X). Tchrs Coll.

Valdez, Luis, jt. ed. see Steiner, Stan.

Valdiosera, R. Mexican Native Costumes: Oaxaca, Nayarit, San Luis Potosi. 12.50 (ISBN 0-911268-17-0). Rogers Bk.

Valdman, Albert & Highfield, Arnold, eds. Theoretical Orientations in Creole Studies. LC 80-26273. 1980. lib ed 29.50 (ISBN 0-12-710160-8). Acad Pr.

Valdman, Albert, jt. ed. see Highfield, Arnold R.

Valdoni, Pietro. Abdominal Surgery: An Atlas of Operative Techniques. Nardi, George, tr. LC 75-40641. (Illus.). 1976. text ed. 70.00 (ISBN 0-7216-8950-7). Saunders.

Vale, Adrian. Radio Controlled Model Aircraft. (Illus.). 181p. (Orig.). 1979. pap. 10.50x (ISBN 0-905418-04-2). Intl Pubns Serv.

Vale, Brenda & Vale, Robert. The Autonomous House: Design & Planning for Self-Sufficiency. LC 75-15354. (Illus.). 1977. pap. 5.95 (ISBN 0-87663-979-1). Universe.

Vale, J. & Cox, B. Drugs & the Eye. 1978. 19.95 (ISBN 0-407-00128-X). Butterworths.

Vale, J. A. & Meredith, T. J., eds. Poisoning: Diagnosis & Treatment. (Illus.). 1981. PLB 37.75 (ISBN 0-906141-81-8, Pub. by Update Books Ltd); pap. 30.75 (ISBN 0-906141-82-6). Kluwer Boston.

Vale, Jack R. Genes, Environment & Behavior: An Interactionist Approach. (Illus.). 470p. 1980. text ed. 21.50 scp (ISBN 0-06-046758-4, HarpC). Har-Row.

Vale, Michel, tr. see Fernandes, Florestan.

Vale, Michel, tr. see Komarov, Boris.

Vale, Michel, tr. see Wolter, Ulf.

Vale, Michel, et al, trs. see Cole, Michel.

Vale, Nancy. Knitting Nineteen Twenties & Nineteen Thirties Originals. (Illus.). 104p. 1980. pap. 8.95 (ISBN 0-686-61417-8, Pub. by Mills & Boon England). Hippocrene Bks.

Vale, Robert, jt. auth. see Vale, Brenda.

Valencak, Hannelore. A Tangled Web. Crampton, Patricia, tr. from Ger. (gr. 7-9). 1978. 7.95 (ISBN 0-688-22169-6); PLB 7.63 (ISBN 0-688-32169-0). Morrow.

Valencia, B. Michael, jt. auth. see Jackson, Michael P.

Valencia, Eugene, ed. Knights of the Sky. 216p. 1980. 21.95 (ISBN 0-9604784-0-X); special numbered ed 100.00. Valencia.

Valencia, Pablo & Merlonghi, Franca. En Contacto: A First Course in Spanish. 1980. pap. text ed. 16.75 (ISBN 0-395-27846-5); tchrs' ed. 18.70 (ISBN 0-395-27847-3); wkbk. 5.50 (ISBN 0-395-27848-1); recordings 154.36 (ISBN 0-395-27849-X). HM.

Valency, Maurice. The End of the World: An Introduction to Contemporary Drama. 1980. 19.95x (ISBN 0-19-502639-X). Oxford U Pr.

Valens, E. G. The Other Side of the Mountain. (Illus.). 1975. pap. 2.50 (ISBN 0-446-91320-0). Warner Bks.

Valens, Evans G., jt. auth. see Beier, Ernst G.

Valenstein, Elliot S. Brain Control: A Critical Examination of Brain Stimulation & Psychosurgery. LC 73-13687. (Illus.). 407p. 1973. 20.95 (ISBN 0-471-89784-1, Pub. by Wiley-Interscience); pap. 13.50x (ISBN 0-471-03328-6). Wiley.

Valenstein, Elliot S., ed. The Psychosurgery Debate: Scientific, Legal, & Ethical Perspectives. LC 80-11187. (Psychology Ser.). (Illus.). 1980. text ed. 26.95x (ISBN 0-7167-1156-7); pap. text ed. 13.95x (ISBN 0-7167-1157-5). W H Freeman.

Valente, William D. Law in the Schools. (Educational Administration Ser.: No. C21). 580p. 1980. text ed. 20.95 (ISBN 0-675-08165-3). Merrill.

--Local Government Law, Cases & Materials. 2nd ed. LC 80-10272. (American Casebook Ser.). 1048p. 1980. text ed. 21.95 (ISBN 0-8299-2087-0). West Pub.

Valenti, Helena. Vamos a Ver. 1972. pap. 3.50 (ISBN 0-912022-31-0). EMC.

Valenti, Justine. Love Island. (Orig.). 1981. pap. 1.50 (ISBN 0-440-14709-3). Dell.

Valenti, Tony & Yonan, Grazia P. The Tony Valenti Story. 160p. (Orig.). 1981. write for info. (ISBN 0-88243-752-6, 02-0752). Gospel Pub.

Valentin, Louis Di see Di Valentin, Maria & Di Valentin, Louis.

Valentin, Maria Di see Di Valentin, Maria & Di Valentin, Louis.

Valentine, Alan. Lord North, 2 Vols. (Illus.). 1967. Set. 27.50 (ISBN 0-8061-0752-9); Set. pap. 12.50x (ISBN 0-8061-1344-8). U of Okla Pr.

Valentine, Alan & Valentine, Lucia. The American Academy in Rome, 1894-1969. LC 72-92663. 200p. 1973. 10.95x (ISBN 0-8139-0444-7). U Pr of Va.

Valentine, Daniel W. United States Half Dimes. LC 74-80917. (Illus.). 384p. 1975. Repr. 35.00x (ISBN 0-88000-049-X). Quarterman.

Valentine, Foy. Layman's Bible Book Commentary: Hebrews, James, 1 & 2 Peter, Vol.23. 1981. 4.75 (ISBN 0-8054-1193-3). Broadman.

--Problemas De Actualidad. Swenson, Ana M., tr. 1978. Repr. of 1975 ed. 0.95 (ISBN 0-311-46039-9). Casa Bautista.

Valentine, Herman, jt. ed. see Leonard, Dick.

Valentine, James & Hanie, Robert. Guale: The Golden Coast of Georgia. LC 74-17220. (Earth's Wild Places Ser). (Illus.). 143p. 1974. 25.00 o.s.i. (ISBN 0-913890-02-2). Friends Earth.

Valentine, James W. Evolutionary Paleoecology of the Marine Biosphere. (Illus.). 512p. 1973. ref. ed. 26.95 (ISBN 0-13-293720-4). P-H.

Valentine, James W., jt. auth. see Ayala, Francisco J.

Valentine, Lucia, jt. auth. see Valentine, Alan.

Valentine, Orpha. Lafayette: A Historical Perspective. Woolfolk, Doug, ed. (Illus.). 120p. 1980. 12.50 (ISBN 0-86518-014-8). Moran Pub Corp.

Valentine, Tom. The Great Pyramid: Man's Monument to Man. (Illus.). 192p. 1980. pap. 2.25 o.p. (ISBN 0-523-40453-0). Pinnacle Bks.

--The Life & Death of Planet Earth. (Illus.). 176p. 1980. pap. 1.95 o.p. (ISBN 0-523-40960-5). Pinnacle Bks.

Valentine, William. What Can We Do? A Food, Land, Hunger Action Guide. (Illus., Orig.). 1980. pap. 2.45 (ISBN 0-935028-06-4). Inst Food & Develp.

Valentinov, Nikolay. The Early Years of Lenin. Theen, Rolf H., tr. from Rus. 1980. cancelled (ISBN 0-915042-05-3). Lib Soc Sci.

--Encounters with Lenin. Rosta, Paul & Pearce, Brian, trs. from Rus. 1980. cancelled (ISBN 0-915042-04-5). Lib Soc Sci.

Valentinuzzi, M., ed. The Organs of Equilibrium & Orientation As a Control System. (Biomedical Engineering & Computation Ser.: Vol. 2). 194p. 1980. text ed. 45.00 (ISBN 3-7186-0014-5). Harwood Academic.

Valenza, Joseph J. Program Housing Standards in the Experimental Housing Allowance Program: Analyzing Differences in the Demand & Supply Experiments. (An Institute Paper). pap. 4.00 (ISBN 0-87766-199-5, 19300). Urban Inst.

Valenza, S. W., Jr., jt. ed. see Gagliardi, R.

Valenza, S. W., Jr., ed. see Swetz, Frank.

Valenza, Samuel W., Jr. The Professor Googol Flying Time Machine & Atomic Space Capsule Math Primer. 3rd ed. (Illus.). 196p. (gr. 7-12). 1974. 9.50 (ISBN 0-936918-00-4). Intergalactic NJ.

Valenzuela, Rafael & Deodhar, Sharad D. Interpretation of Immunofluorescent Patterns in Renal Diseases. (Illus.). 144p. 1981. text ed. 45.00 (ISBN 0-89189-079-3, 16-A-003-00); atlas & slides 140.00 (ISBN 0-89189-098-X, 15-A-003-00). Am Soc Clinical.

Valera, Juan. Dona Luz. Serrano, M. J., tr. from Span. LC 75-1185. 284p. 1975. Repr. of 1891 ed. 16.50 (ISBN 0-86527-239-5). Fertig.

Valeri, C. Robert & Altschule, Mark D. Hypovalemic Anemia of Trauma: The Missing Blood Syndrome. 224p. 1981. 64.95 (ISBN 0-8493-5389-0). CRC Pr.

Valeriani, Richard. Travels with Henry. 1980. pap. 2.95 (ISBN 0-425-04649-4). Berkley Pub.

Valeriano Bolzani, Giovanni P. Hieroglyphica. LC 75-27864. (Renaissance & the Gods Ser.: Vol. 17). (Illus.). 1977. Repr. of 1602 ed. lib. bdg. 73.00 (ISBN 0-8240-2069-3). Garland Pub.

--Les Hieroglyphiques. Montlyard, I. de, tr. LC 75-27867. (Renaissance & the Gods Ser.: Vol. 23). (Illus., Fr.). 1977. Repr. of 1615 ed. lib. bdg. 73.00 (ISBN 0-8240-2072-3). Garland Pub.

Valerio, D. A., et al. Macaca Mulatta: Management of a Laboratory Breeding Colony. 21.50 o.p. (ISBN 0-12-710050-4); pap. 15.50 o.p. (ISBN 0-12-710056-3). Acad Pr.

Valery, Ann. Baron Von Kodak, Shirley Temple & Me. 14.95x (ISBN 0-8464-0168-1). Beekman Pubs.

Valery, Paul. Charmes ou Poemes. Whiting, Charles G., ed. (French Poets Ser.). 146p. 1973. text ed. 16.25x (ISBN 0-485-14701-7, Athlone Pr); pap. text ed. 8.75x (ISBN 0-485-12701-6, Athlone Pr). Humanities.

--Collected Works of Paul Valery, Vol. 14. Analects. Gilbert, Stuart, tr. LC 56-9337. (Bollingen Ser.: Vol. 45). 1969. 21.50x o.p. (ISBN 0-691-09837-9). Princeton U Pr.

--Descartes. 133p. 1980. Repr. lib. bdg. 10.00 (ISBN 0-89984-477-4). Century Bookbindery.

Vales, Pedro A., jt. ed. see Riedel, Marc.

Valesio, Paolo. Novantiqua: Rhetorics as a Contemporary Theory. LC 79-9632. (Advances in Semiotics Ser.). 384p. 1980. 22.50x (ISBN 0-253-11055-6). Ind U Pr.

Valeton, E. M. Dutch Costumes. (Illus.). 15.00 (ISBN 0-685-47296-5). Heinman.

Valett, Robert E. Modifying Children's Behavior: A Guide for Parents & Professionals. LC 70-79239. (Orig.). 1969. pap. text ed. 3.40 o.p. (ISBN 0-8224-4495-X). Pitman Learning.

--Programming Learning Disabilities. 1969. text ed. 12.60 o.p. (ISBN 0-8224-5620-6). Pitman Learning.

--Psychoeducational Treatment of Hyperactive Children. 1974. text ed. 8.00 (ISBN 0-8224-5651-6); pap. 5.00 (ISBN 0-8224-5650-8). Pitman Learning.

--Remediation of Learning Disabilities: A Handbook of Psychoeducational Resource Programs. 2nd ed. LC 67-26847. 1974. 3-ring bdg. 19.50 (ISBN 0-8224-5850-0). Pitman Learning.

Valette, Jean P. & Valette, Rebecca M. Learning Concepts, Inc. 1978. pap. text ed. 7.95x (ISBN 0-669-01162-2). Heath.

Valette, Jean-Paul & Valette, Rebecca. Contacts: Langue et Culture Francaises. LC 75-32873. 1976. text ed. 17.35 (ISBN 0-395-20690-1); tchrs. ed. 18.40 (ISBN 0-395-20689-8); wkbk. cahier d'exercices 5.55 (ISBN 0-395-20692-8). HM.

--Contacts: Langue et Culture Francaises. 2nd ed. (Illus.). 528p. 1981. text ed. 18.00 (ISBN 0-395-29328-6); tchrs. ed. 19.00 (ISBN 0-395-29329-4); wkbk 5.55 (ISBN 0-395-29330-8); reel-to-reel 250.00 (ISBN 0-395-29331-6); write for info. sample cassette (ISBN 0-395-29332-4). HM.

Valette, Rebecca, jt. auth. see Valette, Jean-Paul.

Valette, Rebecca M., jt. auth. see Valette, Jean P.

Vali, Ferenc. The Turkish Straits & NATO. LC 70-170205. (Studies Ser.: No. 32). (Illus.). 200p. 1972. pap. 6.95 (ISBN 0-8179-3322-0). Hoover Inst Pr.

Valin, Jonathan. Final Notice. LC 80-16654. 256p. 1980. 8.95 (ISBN 0-396-07898-2). Dodd.

--Lime Pit. LC 79-28205. 256p. 1980. 8.95 (ISBN 0-396-07818-4). Dodd.

Valiron, Georges. Theory of Integral Functions. LC 51-7375. 9.95 (ISBN 0-8284-0056-3). Chelsea Pub.

Valk, Barbara G., ed. Hispanic American Periodicals Index 1978. LC 75-642408. 1981. lib. bdg. price not set (ISBN 0-87903-404-1). UCLA Lat Am Ctr.

Valk, Henry, jt. auth. see Alonso, Marcelo.

Valk, J. Computed Tomography & Cerebral Infarctions. 190p. 1980. 29.50 (ISBN 0-89004-646-8). Raven.

Valkenburg, M. E. Van see Cruz, Jose B. & Van Valkenburg, M. E.

Valkenburg, M. E. Van see Van Valkenburg, M. E.

Valkenburgh, Van see Van Valkenburgh, et al.

Vall, Mark Van De see Van De Vall, Mark.

Vall, Stephen Du see Du Vall, Stephen.

Vallacher, Robin R., jt. auth. see Wegner, Daniel M.

Vallance, A., jt. auth. see Doughtie, Venton L.

Vallance, Elizabeth. Woman in the House: A Study of Women Members of Parliament. 1979. text ed. 23.75x (ISBN 0-485-11186-1, Athlone Pr). Humanities.

Vallance, Elizabeth, jt. auth. see Eisner, Elliot W.

Vallance, Elizabeth, ed. The State, Society & Self-Destruction. (Acton Society Studies Ser.). 1975. text ed. 27.50x (ISBN 0-04-350049-8). Allen Unwin.

Vallarino, L., jt. auth. see Quagliano, James.

Vallario, Edward J. Evaluation of Radiation Emergencies & Accidents: Selected Criteria & Data. (Technical Reports Ser.: No. 152). (Illus.). 135p. (Orig.). 1974. pap. 12.50 (ISBN 92-0-125074-6, IAEA). Unipub.

Vallat, Jean M., jt. auth. see Vital, Claude.

Valle, Gonzalez del see Shaw, Bradley & Del-Valle, Gonzalez.

Valle, Inclan Del see Del Valle, Inclan.

Valle, James E. Rocks & Shoals: Order & Discipline in the Old Navy, 1800-1861. LC 79-91914. (Illus.). 408p. 1980. 18.95 (ISBN 0-87021-538-8). Naval Inst Pr.

Valle, Ronald S. & Eckartsberg, Rolf Von, eds. The Metaphors of Consciousness. 500p. 1981. 25.00 (ISBN 0-306-40520-2, Plenum Pr). Plenum Pub.

Valle, Stephen K. Alcoholism Counseling: Issues for an Emerging Profession. (Illus.). 184p. 1979. 15.75 (ISBN 0-398-03877-5). C C Thomas.

Valle, Teresa La see Ralph, Margaret.

Vallee, Jacques & Vallee, Janine. Challenge to Science: The UFO Enigma. (Illus.). 352p. (Orig.). 1974. pap. 2.25 (ISBN 0-345-27086-X). Ballantine.

Vallee, Jacques, jt. auth. see Hynek, J. Allen.

Vallee, Janine, jt. auth. see Vallee, Jacques.

Vallee, Lillian, tr. see Milosz, Czeslaw.

Valle-Inclan, Ramon. The Pleasant Memoirs of the Marquis De Bradomin. Heywood Broun, May & Walsh, Thomas, trs. from Span. LC 76-28508. 1980. Repr. of 1924 ed. 20.00 (ISBN 0-86527-294-8). Fertig.

Vallejo, Antonio Buero see Buero Vallejo, Antonio.

Vallejo, Cesar. Cesar Vallejo: The Complete Posthumous Poetry. Eshleman, Clayton & Barcia, Jose R., trs. from Span. LC 77-93472. 1978. 20.00 (ISBN 0-520-03648-4); pap. 6.95. U of Cal Pr.

--Selected Poems of Cesar Vallejo. Hays, H. R., tr. from Sp. 122p. 1981. 13.50 (ISBN 0-937584-01-0); pap. 6.95 (ISBN 0-937584-02-9). Sachem Pr.

Vallejo, Doris. The Boy Who Saved the Stars. Snelson, Robin, ed. (Illus.). (gr. 3 up). 1978. 5.95 (ISBN 0-931064-05-8). Starlog.

--Windsound. (Orig.). 1981. pap. 2.25 (ISBN 0-425-04803-9). Berkley Pub.

Vallen, J., et al. The Art & Science of Managing Hotels-Restaurants-Institutions. Orig. Title: The Art & Science of Modern Innkeeping. 1978. 14.25x (ISBN 0-8104-9470-1). Hayden.

Vallen, Jerome J. Check in-Check Out: Principles of Effective Front Office Management. 2nd ed. 370p. 1980. pap. text ed. write for info. (ISBN 0-697-08412-4); instrs' manual avail. Wm C Brown.

Vallentine, John F. & Sims, Phillip L., eds. Range Science: A Guide to Information Sources. (Natural World Information Guide Ser.: Vol. 2). 250p. 1980. 30.00 (ISBN 0-8103-1420-7). Gale.

Valle-Spinka, Ramona F. La Conciencia Social De Miguel Delibes. 1975. 12.95 (ISBN 0-88303-022-5); pap. 9.50 (ISBN 0-685-73223-1). E Torres & Sons.

Valletuhi, Peter J., jt. auth. see Bender, Michael.

Valletutti, Peter J., jt. auth. see Greenberg, Sheldon F.

Vallier, Ivan, ed. Comparative Methods in Sociology: Essays on Trends & Applications. LC 76-121194. (Institute of International Studies, UC Berkeley). 1971. 22.75x (ISBN 0-520-01743-9); pap. 6.95x (ISBN 0-520-02488-5). U of Cal Pr.

Vallin, Jean. Plant World. (Basic Biology in Color Ser.). (gr. 7-12). 10.95 o.p. (ISBN 0-8069-3552-9); PLB 10.79 o.p. (ISBN 0-8069-3553-7). Sterling.

Vallings, H. G. Mechanisation in Building. 2nd ed. (Illus.). 1976. text ed. 33.60x (ISBN 0-85334-651-8). Intl Ideas.

Vallins, G. H. Better English. (Andre Deutsch Language Library). 1977. lib. bdg. 11.50x (ISBN 0-233-95526-7). Westview.

Vallintine, Reginald. Divers & Diving. (Illus.). 176p. 1981. 12.95 (ISBN 0-7137-0855-7, Pub. by Blandford Pr England); pap. 6.95 (ISBN 0-7137-1128-0). Sterling.

Vallis, Charles P. Hair Transplantation for the Treatment of Male Pattern Baldness. (Illus.). 608p. 46.75 (ISBN 0-398-04165-2). C C Thomas.

Valmiki. Ramayana: The Story of Rama. LC 74-77601. (Illus.). 72p. (gr. 5-12). 1975. 8.50 (ISBN 0-88253-292-8); pap. 3.50 (ISBN 0-88253-291-X). Ind-US Inc.

Valmy, Christine. Esthetics: The Keystone Guide to Skin Care. 1979. pap. 16.00 (ISBN 0-912126-36-1, 1257-00). Keystone Pubns.

Valonet, Jean. The Practice of Aromatherapy. (Illus.). 1981. pap. 8.95 (ISBN 0-89281-026-2). Inner Tradit.

Valtin, Eva W., tr. see Bischoff, Ernst P.

Valverde-Rodriguez, C. & Arechiga, H., eds. Comparative Aspects of Neuroendocrine Control of Behavior. (Frontiers of Hormone Research: Vol. 6). (Illus.). 1980. 58.75 (ISBN 3-8055-0571-X). S Karger.

Valzelli, L., jt. ed. see Essman, W.

Valzelli, Luigi. Psychobiology of Aggression & Violence. 265p. 1981. text ed. 24.00 (ISBN 0-89004-403-1). Raven.

Valzey, John, jt. auth. see Norris, Keith.

Valzey, John, jt. auth. see Sheehan, John.

Vamos, P., jt. auth. see Sharpe, D. W.

Vamos, T. see Frey, T.

Vamos, T., jt. ed. see Frey, T.

Van Valkenburgh, Nooger & Neville, Inc. Basic Electricity, Vol. 4. rev. ed. (Illus.). 1978. pap. 5.85 (ISBN 0-8104-0879-1). Hayden.

Van World Editors. Do-It-Yourselfer's Guide to Van Conversion. (Illus.). 1977. 8.95 o.p. (ISBN 0-8306-7992-8); pap. 6.95 (ISBN 0-8306-6992-2, 992). TAB Bks.

Van Aaken, Ernst. The Van Aaken Method. Beinhorn, George, tr. from Ger. LC 75-20964. (Illus.). 135p. 1976. pap. 4.95 (ISBN 0-89037-070-2); handbk. 5.95 (ISBN 0-89037-071-0). Anderson World.

Van Aarle, Thomas see Aarle, Thomas Van.

Van Adrichem, Christianus see Adrichem, Christianus van.

Vanags, Patricia. Imperial Rome. (Civilization Library). (Illus.). (gr. 5-8). 1979. PLB 6.90 s&l (ISBN 0-531-01445-2). Watts.

Vanags, Patricia, jt. auth. see Powell, Anton.

VanAllen, Leroy C. & Mallis, A. George. The Comprehensive Catalog & Encyclopedia of U.S. Morgan & Peace Silver Dollars. LC 76-18299. (Illus.). 1976. 25.00 (ISBN 0-668-04021-1). Arco.

Van Allsburg, Chris. Jumanji. 1981. 9.95 (ISBN 0-395-30448-2). HM.

Van Alstyne, Carol & Coldren, Sharon L. Cost of Implementing Federally Mandated Social Programs. 1976. pap. 3.50 o.p. (ISBN 0-685-83998-2). ACE.

Van Alstyne, Richard W. The United States & East Asia. (Library of World Civilization Ser). 1973. pap. 5.95x (ISBN 0-393-09368-9). Norton.

Van Amelsvoort, Vincent. Medical Anthropology in African Newspapers: An Annotated Facsimile Edition from the Third World. 116p. 1976. pap. text ed. 9.25x (ISBN 90-6234-105-5). Humanities.

Van Amerongen, Charles, tr. see Gunter, Altner.

Van Antwerp, Emily S. Iron Ore to Iron Lace. (Illus.). 150p. 1980. 10.00 (ISBN 0-914334-07-7). Museum Mobile.

Van Arman, C. Gordon, ed. White Cells in Inflammation. (Illus.). 160p. 1974. text ed. 19.00 (ISBN 0-398-03120-7). C C Thomas.

Van Arsdel, Wallace B., et al. Food Dehydration, 2 vols. 2nd ed. Incl. Vol. 1. Drying Methods & Phenomena. 34.50 (ISBN 0-87055-137-X); Vol. 2. Practices & Applications. 42.50 (ISBN 0-87055-138-8). (Illus.). 1973. AVI.

Van Arsdell, P. M. Corporation Finance: Policy, Planning, Administration. 1739p. 1968. 39.95. Wiley.

Van Arsdell, Paul M. Corporation Finance: Policy, Planning, Administration. LC 68-13475. 1739p. 1968. 39.95 (ISBN 0-8260-8840-6, 90991). Ronald Pr.

Vanasse, George A., ed. Spectrometric Techniques, Vol. II. 1981. write for info. (ISBN 0-12-710402-X). Acad Pr.

Van Atta, Dale, jt. auth. see Bradlee, Ben, Jr.

Van Atta, Frieda. Eighth Grade. 1.00 ea. Gr. 6 (ISBN 0-394-40976-0). Gr. 7 (ISBN 0-394-40977-9). Gr. 8 (ISBN 0-394-40978-7). Random.

Van Atta, Winfred. The Adam Sleep. 192p. 1981. pap. 2.25 (ISBN 0-380-53744-3, 53744). Avon.

Vanauken, Sheldon. Gateway to Heaven. 336p. 1981. pap. 2.95 (ISBN 0-553-14648-3). Bantam.

--A Severe Mercy. LC 77-6161. 1977. 12.95 (ISBN 0-06-068821-1, HarpR). Har-Row.

Van Baal, J. Reciprocity & the Position of Women: Anthropological Papers. 128p. 1976. pap. text ed. 9.25x (ISBN 90-232-1320-3). Humanities.

--Symbols for Communication. (Studies of Developing Countries). 354p. 1971. pap. text ed. 38.50x (ISBN 9-0232-0896-X). Humanities.

Van Baalen, Jan K. Gist of the Cults. 1944. pap. 1.25 o.p. (ISBN 0-8028-1205-8). Eerdmans.

--If Thou Shalt Confess. rev. ed. 1962. 2.95 o.p. (ISBN 0-8028-3279-2). Eerdmans.

Van Beethoven, Ludwig see Beethoven, Ludwig Van.

VanBekkum, D. W., ed. The Biological Activity of Thymic Hormones. LC 75-17617. 1975. 39.95 (ISBN 0-470-89835-6). Halsted Pr.

Van Bergen, William S. Obstetric Ultrasound for the Practitioner: Applications & Principals. LC 80-14969. 1980. 19.95 (ISBN 0-201-08001-X). A-W.

Vanbiervliet, Alan & Sheldon-Wildgen, Jan. Liability Issues in Community-Based Programs: Legal Principles, Problem Areas, & Recommendations. 136p. 1981. pap. text ed. 10.95 (ISBN 0-933716-08-7). P H Brookes.

Van Bieryliet, Alan & Sheldon-Wildgen, Jan. Liability Issues in Community-Based Programs: Legal Principles, Problem Areas & Rdcommendations. 136p. 1980. pap. 10.95 (ISBN 0-933716-08-7). P H Brookes.

Van Binsbergen, Wim M. J. Religious Change in Zambia: Exploratory Studies. (Monographs from the African Studies Centre, Leiden). (Illus.). 416p. 1981. price not set (ISBN 0-7103-0000-X). Routledge & Kegan.

Van Blank, Mark. Development of the Infant: The First Year of Life in Photographs. (Illus.). 1975. pap. 11.95x (ISBN 0-433-03235-9). Intl Ideas.

Van Bommel, W. J. & DeBoer, J. B. Road Lighting. (Philips Technical Library). (Illus.). 363p. 1980. text ed. 69.50x (ISBN 0-333-30679-1). Scholium Intl.

Van Brabant, Jozef M. East European Cooperation: The Role of Money & Finance. LC 76-2911. (Illus.). 1976. text ed. 34.50 (ISBN 0-275-56650-1). Praeger.

Van Breda, A. Adventures with Paper. 1955. 6.50 (ISBN 0-571-06982-7, Pub. by Faber & Faber). Merrimack Bk Serv.

--Paper Folding & Modelling. 1964. 6.50 (ISBN 0-571-06178-8, Pub. by Faber & Faber). Merrimack Bk Serv.

--Pleasure with Paper. 1954. 6.50 (ISBN 0-571-05172-3, Pub. by Faber & Faber). Merrimack Bk Serv.

Vanbreuseghem, R., et al. Practical Guide to Medical & Veterinary Mycology. LC 77-94829. (Illus.). 288p. 1978. text ed. 47.75 (ISBN 0-89352-018-7). Masson Pub.

Van Brink, J. M. & Vorontsov, N. N., eds. Animal Genetics & Evolution: Selected Papers. (Illus.). 393p. 1980. lib. bdg. 99.00 (ISBN 90-6193-602-0). Kluwer Boston.

Vanbrugh, John. Provoked Wife. Zimansky, Curt A., ed. LC 69-12337. (Regents Restoration Drama Ser). 1970. 9.50x (ISBN 0-8032-0374-8); pap. 2.65x (ISBN 0-8032-5373-7, BB 272, Bison). U of Nebr Pr.

--Relapse. Zimansky, Curt A., ed. LC 70-107279. (Regents Restoration Drama Ser). 1970. 9.95x (ISBN 0-8032-0376-4); pap. 2.75x (ISBN 0-8032-5375-3, BB 274, Bison). U of Nebr Pr.

Vanbrugh, Sir John. A Short Vindication of the Relapse & the Provok'd Wife. LC 75-170442. (The English Stage Ser.: Vol. 28). lib. bdg. 50.00 (ISBN 0-8240-0611-9). Garland Pub.

VanBrunt, H. L. And the Man Who Was Travelling Never Got Home. LC 80-65698. (Poetry Ser.). 1980. 9.95 (ISBN 0-915604-35-3); pap. 4.95 (ISBN 0-915604-36-1). Carnegie-Mellon.

Van Brunt, H. L. Uncertainties: The Smith - 9. 4.50 (ISBN 0-685-78418-5); pap. 2.25 (ISBN 0-912292-01-6). The Smith.

Van Buitenen, J. A., jt. auth. see Deutsch, Eliot.

Van Buitenen, J. A., ed. The Bhagavadgita in the Mahabharata: A Bilingual Edition. LC 79-13021. 1981. lib. bdg. price not set (ISBN 0-226-84660-1, P880, Phoen); pap. price not set (ISBN 0-226-84662-8). U of Chicago Pr.

Van Buitenen, J. A., tr. Two Plays of Ancient India. Incl. The Little Clay Cart; The Minister's Seal. LC 67-25441. viii, 278p. 1968. 17.00x (ISBN 0-231-03046-0). Columbia U Pr.

Van Buren, E. Ariane, jt. auth. see Foley, Gerald.

Van Buren, James & Dewett, Don. What the Bible Says About Praise & Promise. LC 80-66127. (What the Bible Says Ser.). 450p. 1980. 13.50 (ISBN 0-89900-078-9). College Pr Pub.

Van Buren, Martin. The Autobiography of Martin Van Buren, 2 vols. Fitzpatrick, John, ed. LC 72-75314. 820p. 1973. Repr. of 1920 ed. Set. lib. bdg. 69.50 (ISBN 0-306-71275-X). Da Capo.

Van Buren, Paul, jt. ed. see Allen, J. P.

Van Buren, Paul, ed. see Chomsky, Noam.

Van Buren, Paul M. The Burden of Freedom: Americans and the God of Israel. 1976. 6.95 (ISBN 0-8164-0318-X). Crossroad NY.

--Discerning the Way: A Theology of the Jewish-Christian Reality. 192p. 1980. 12.95 (ISBN 0-8164-0124-1). Crossroad NY.

Van Buskirk, William R., jt. auth. see Fruchiger, Fritz.

Van Caenegem, R. C. The Birth of the English Common Law. LC 72-89812. 150p. 1973. 26.95 (ISBN 0-521-20097-0). Cambridge U Pr.

Van Campen, Joseph A., jt. auth. see Sholiton, Robert D.

VanCaspel, Venita. Avoid the One-Way Trip to Washington. 1980. pap. 1.50 (ISBN 0-8359-0297-8). Reston.

--Energizing Your Investments. 1980. pap. 1.50 (ISBN 0-8359-1678-2). Reston.

--Life Insurance: The Great National Consumer Dilemma. 1980. pap. 1.50 (ISBN 0-8359-4022-5). Reston.

Van Caspel, Venita. The New Money Dynamics. (Illus.). 1978. 13.95 o.p. (ISBN 0-87909-518-0); instrs'. manual avail. o.p. Reston.

VanCaspel, Venita. The Real Rewards of Real Estate. 1980. pap. 1.50 (ISBN 0-8359-6605-4). Reston.

--To Win the Money Game. 1980. pap. 1.50 (ISBN 0-8359-8692-6). Reston.

Van Cauwenberge, H. & Franchimont, P. Assay of Protein & Polypeptide Hormones. LC 76-108930. 1970. 34.00 (ISBN 0-08-015685-1). Pergamon.

Vance Bibliographies. Index to Architecture Series Bibliography: No. a-155 to A-396, Jan. 1980 to Dec. 1980, No. A-155 To A-396, Jan. 1980 To Dec. 1980. (Architecture Ser.: Bibliography: A-397). 50p. 1981. pap. 7.50. Vance Biblios.

--Index to Public Administration Series Bibliography: No. P-394 to P-636, Jan. 1980 to Dec. 1980, No. P-394 To P-636, Jan. 1980 To Dec. 1980. (Public Administration Ser.: Bibliography: P-637). 81p. 1981. pap. 7.50. Vance Biblios.

Vance, Clarence H., ed. see Seabury, Samuel.

Vance, Edward F. Coupling to Shielded Cables. LC 78-16186. 1978. 22.00 (ISBN 0-471-04107-6, Pub. by Wiley-Interscience). Wiley.

Vance, Elbridge P. Introduction to Modern Mathematics. 2nd ed. 1968. text ed. 17.95 (ISBN 0-201-08015-X). A-W.

--Modern Algebra & Trigonometry. 3rd ed. LC 72-11471. 1973. text ed. 16.95 (ISBN 0-201-08036-2). A-W.

--Modern College Algebra. 3rd ed. LC 75-370. (Illus.). 320p. 1975. text ed. 15.95 (ISBN 0-201-08159-8). A-W.

--Trigonometry. 2nd ed. 1969. 9.95 (ISBN 0-201-08053-2); pap. 7.95 (ISBN 0-686-68494-X). A-W.

Vance, Eleanor G. The Tall Book of Fairy Tales. (Tall Bks). (Illus.). 124p. (gr. k-3). 1980. 5.95 (ISBN 0-06-025545-5, HarpJ); PLB 6.89 (ISBN 0-06-025546-3). Har-Row.

Vance, Eleanor G., ed. see Sewell, Anna.

Vance, Irvin, jt. auth. see Brumfiel, Charles.

Vance, Jack. The Book of Dreams. (Science Fiction Ser). 1981. pap. 1.95 (ISBN 0-87997-587-3, UJ1587). Daw Bks.

--Dust of Far Suns. (Science Fiction Ser.). 1981. pap. 1.75 (ISBN 0-87997-588-1, UE1588). Daw Bks.

--Marune: Alastor Nine Hundred Thirty-Three. 1981. pap. 2.25 (ISBN 0-87997-591-1, UE1591). Daw Bks.

--Marune: Alastor 933. 160p. (Orig.). 1975. pap. 1.50 o.p. (ISBN 0-345-24518-0). Ballantine.

--Maske: Thaery. 1976. 7.95 o.p. (ISBN 0-399-11797-0). Berkley Pub.

--Nopalgarth. (Science Fiction Ser.). 1980. pap. 2.25 (ISBN 0-87997-563-6, UE1563). Daw Bks.

--To Live Forever. 1976. pap. 1.50 o.p. (ISBN 0-345-25198-9). Ballantine.

--Trullion: Alastor Two Thousand, Two Hundred & Sixty-Two. 1981. pap. 2.25 (ISBN 0-87997-590-3, UE1590). Daw Bks.

Vance, James E., Jr. This Scene of Man: The Role & Structure of the City in the Geography of Western Civilization. (Ser. in Geography). 1977. text ed. 22.95 scp o.p. (ISBN 0-06-167407-9, HarpC). Har-Row.

Vance, Joel. Fats Waller: His Life & Times. 1979. pap. 2.25 o.p. (ISBN 0-425-04065-8). Berkley Pub.

--Grandma & the Buck Deer. (Illus.). 176p. 1980. 12.50 (ISBN 0-87691-322-2). Winchester Pr.

Vance, Malcolm. The Complete Movie Quizbook. LC 76-16395. (Illus.). 1976. pap. 4.95 o.p. (ISBN 0-8473-1335-2). Sterling.

Vance, Mary. City Planning: A Selected List of Books, 1970-1978. (Architecture Ser.: Bibliography A-224). 99p. 1980. pap. 10.50. Vance Biblios.

--Historical Society Architectural Publications: Vermont, Virginia, Washington, West Virginia, Wisconsin, Wyoming. (Architecture Ser.: Bibliography A-178). 51p. 1980. pap. 5.50. Vance Biblios.

--Interior Design & Decoration: A Bibliography of Books. (Architecture Ser.: Bibliography A-257). 75p. 1980. pap. 8.00. Vance Biblios.

--Landscape, Landscape Architecture & Landscape Gardening: A Selective List of Books. (Architecture Ser.: Bibliography A-197). 61p. 1980. pap. 6.50. Vance Biblios.

--New Publications for Architectural Libraries, March Nineteen Eighty. (Architecture Ser.: Bibliography A-196). 64p. 1980. pap. 7.00. Vance Biblios.

--New Publications for Architecture Libraries, April Nineteen Eighty. (Architecture Ser.: Bibliography A-218). 63p. 1980. pap. 7.00. Vance Biblios.

--New Publications for Architecture Libraries: February 1980. (Architecture Ser. Bibliography a-176). 56p. 1980. pap. 6.00. Vance Biblios.

--New Publications for Architecture Libraries, May Nineteen Eighty. (Architecture Ser.: Bibliography A-236). 55p. 1980. pap. 6.00. Vance Biblios.

--New Publications for Architecture Libraries, November Nineteen Eighty. (Architecture Ser.: Bibliography A-357). 50p. 1980. pap. 7.50. Vance Biblios.

--New Publications for Architecture Libraries, September Nineteen Eighty. (Architecture Ser.: Bibliography A-317). 55p. Date not set. pap. price not set. Vance Biblios.

--Remodeling: A Bibliography of Periodical Articles. (Architecture Ser.: Bibliography A-295). 68p. 1980. pap. 7.50. Vance Biblios.

Vance, R. & Hall, Marilyn C. How to Select Reinforcers. 1980. pap. 3.25 (ISBN 0-89079-052-3). H & H Ent.

Van Chi-Bonnardel, Regine, ed. The Atlas of Africa. LC 73-17932. 1974. 100.00 (ISBN 0-02-901070-5). Free Pr.

Vancil, Richard F., jt. auth. see Lorange, Peter.

Van Cise, Jerrold G. Understanding the Antitrust Laws. 7th ed. 1976. text ed. 30.00 o.p. (ISBN 0-685-85358-6, B1-1237). PLI.

Van Cise, Jerrold G. & Lifland, William T. Understanding the Antitrust Laws. 8th ed. LC 80-83813. 400p. 1980. text ed. 45.00 (ISBN 0-686-69172-5, B1-1276). PLI.

Van Cleave, W. R. & Cohen, S. T. Tactical Nuclear Weapons: An Examination of the Issues. LC 77-83272. 1978. 14.50x (ISBN 0-8448-1260-9). Crane-Russak Co.

Van Cleave Alexander, Michael. The First of the Tudors: A Study of Henry VII & His Reign. 280p. 1980. 22.50x (ISBN 0-8476-6259-4). Rowman.

Van Cleef, E. Cities in Action. LC 79-84197. 1971. 21.00 (ISBN 0-08-015622-3); pap. 12.75 (ISBN 0-08-016417-X). Pergamon.

Van Cleve, Thomas C. The Emperor Frederick Second of Hohenstaufen, Immutator Mundi. (Illus.). 618p. 1972. 45.00x (ISBN 0-19-822513-X). Oxford U Pr.

Van Clief, Sylvia, jt. auth. see Heide, Florence P.

Van Creveld, Martin L. Supplying War. LC 77-5550. 1979. pap. 9.95 (ISBN 0-521-29793-1). Cambridge U Pr.

--Supplying War: Logistics from Wallenstein to Patton. LC 77-5550. (Illus.). 1977. 27.50 (ISBN 0-521-21730-X). Cambridge U Pr.

Van Daele, A. Continuous Crossed Products & Type 111 von Neumann Algebras. LC 77-91096. (London Mathematical Society Lecture Note Ser.: No. 31). 1978. limp bdg. 11.95x (ISBN 0-521-21975-2). Cambridge U Pr.

Van Dalen, Deobold B. & Bennett, Bruce. World History of Physical Education: Cultural, Philosophical & Comparative. 2nd ed. 1971. ref. ed. 20.95x (ISBN 0-13-967919-7). P-H.

Van Dalen, Linda. My Life & Loves, Part II. 1976. pap. 1.50 o.p. (ISBN 0-685-72356-9, LB382DK, Leisure Bks). Nordon Pubns.

Vandall, Frank J. Police Training for Tough Calls. LC 75-33489. 1976. pap. 5.00 (ISBN 0-89937-009-8). Ctr Res Soc Chg.

Van Dallen, H. & Zeigler, L. Introduction to Political Science: People, Politics, & Perception. 1977. pap. 10.95 (ISBN 0-13-493205-6). P-H.

Vandam, Leroy. To Make the Patient Ready for Anesthesia: Medical Care of the Surgical Patient. LC 80-11190. (Clinical Practice Ser.). 1980. 24.95 (ISBN 0-201-07999-2). A-W.

Van Daniker, Relmond P., jt. auth. see McCullers, Levis D.

Van De Bogart, Doris. Introduction to the Humanities: Painting, Sculpture, Architecture, Music & Literature. LC 67-29656. (Orig.). 1968. pap. 4.95 (ISBN 0-06-463277-6, EH 277, EH). Har-Row.

Van De Gohm, Richard. Antique Maps for the Collector. LC 72-91999. 160p. 1973. 7.95 o.s.i. (ISBN 0-02-621540-3). Macmillan.

Van De Graaff, John H., et al. Academic Power: Patterns of Authority in Seven National Systems of Higher Education. LC 78-17172. (Praeger Special Studies). 1978. 23.95 (ISBN 0-03-045531-6). Praeger.

Van de Graaff, Kent. Human Anatomy Laboratory Textbook. 300p. 1981. pap. text ed. write for info. (ISBN 0-697-04598-6). Wm C Brown.

Van De Hulst, H. C. Multiple Light Scattering: Tables, Formulas & Applications, Vol.1. LC 79-51687. 1980. 33.50 (ISBN 0-12-710701-0). Acad Pr.

Van De Kamp, Peter. Principles of Astrometry: With Special Emphasis on Long-Focus Photographic Astrometry. LC 66-22077. (Illus.). 1967. 21.95x (ISBN 0-7167-0318-1). W H Freeman.

Vande Kieft, Ruth M. Eudora Welty. (U. S. Authors Ser.: No. 15). 1962. lib. bdg. 9.95 (ISBN 0-8057-0776-X). Twayne.

Vandel, A. Biospeology, the Biology of Cavernicolous Animals. 1965. 56.00 (ISBN 0-08-010242-5). Pergamon.

Van D'Elden, Karl H. West German Poets on Society & Politics. LC 78-20793. 1979. 14.95x (ISBN 0-8143-1628-X). Wayne St U Pr.

Van De Leuv, John H., ed. see American College of Emergency Physicians.

Vandell, Frank J. Police Training for Tough Calls: Discretionary Situations. 140p. 1980. pap. 9.95 o.p. (ISBN 0-686-64815-3). Carrollton Pr.

Vandeman, G. E. Look! No Doomsday. LC 71-141942. 1972. pap. 0.95 o.p. (ISBN 0-8163-0099-2, 12558-3). Pacific Pr Pub Assn.

--Psychic Roulette. 1973. pap. 3.95 (ISBN 0-8163-0136-0, 16693-4). Pacific Pr Pub Assn.

Van Demark, Paul J., jt. auth. see Seeley, Harry W., Jr.

VanDemark, Paul J., jt. auth. see Seeley, Harry W., Jr.

Van Den Berg, C. J., jt. ed. see Hommes, E. A.

Vandenberg, Donna, jt. ed. see Berkson, Larry C.

Van Den Berg, Leo, et al. Elements of Growth & Decline of Urban Development & Policy. Date not set. 48.01 (ISBN 0-08-023156-X). Pergamon.

Vandenberg, M., jt. auth. see Gage, Michael.

Vandenberg, Philipp. The Curse of the Pharaohs. Weyr, Tom, tr. LC 75-830. (Illus.). 1975. 9.95 (ISBN 0-397-01035-4). Lippincott.

--The Golden Pharaoh. (Illus.). 288p. 1981. 13.95 (ISBN 0-02-621580-2). Macmillan.

--Nefertiti: An Archaeological Biography. Hein, Ruth, tr. LC 77-28107. (Illus.). 1978. 10.00 o.s.i. (ISBN 0-397-01256-X). Lippincott.

Vandenberg, Steven G., ed. Methods & Goals in Human Behavior Genetics. 1965. 38.00 o.p. (ISBN 0-12-710650-2). Acad Pr.

Van Den Bergh, T. Trade Unions, What Are They? LC 79-97952. 1970. 19.50 (ISBN 0-08-006517-1); pap. 9.75 (ISBN 0-08-006516-3). Pergamon.

Van den Berghe, Pierre. Age & Sex in Human Societies: A Biosocial Perspective. 7.95x (ISBN 0-534-00311-7). Wadsworth Pub.

--South Africa: A Study in Conflict. 1975. pap. 6.95x (ISBN 0-520-01294-1, CAMPUS 159). U of Cal Pr.

Van Den Berghe, Pierre L. see Berghe, Pierre L. Van Den.

Van Den Berghe, Pierre L., jt. auth. see Colby, Benjamin N.

Vandenbosch, Amry. Dutch Foreign Policy Since Eighteen Fifteen: A Study in Small Power Politics. LC 79-2292. 1981. Repr. of 1959 ed. 23.50 (ISBN 0-88355-968-4). Hyperion Conn.

--South Africa & the World: The Foreign Policy of Apartheid. LC 76-111516. (Illus.). 312p. 1970. 13.00x (ISBN 0-8131-1223-0). U Pr of Ky.

Vandenbosch, Amry & Butwell, Richard. The Changing Face of Southeast Asia. LC 66-16234. (Illus.). 448p. 1966. 15.00x (ISBN 0-8131-1124-2); pap. 6.50 (ISBN 0-8131-0112-3). U Pr of Ky.

Vandenbosch, Amry, jt. auth. see Brookes, Edgar H.

Van Den Bosch, Robert see Nouwen, Henri J. M. & Gaffney, Walter J.

Van den Brink, G., ed. see International Symposium on Hearing, Fifth, Noordwijkerhout, the Netherlands, April 8-12, 1980.

Vandenbroeck, A., tr. see Schwaller De Lubicz, R. A.

Vandenbroeck, G., tr. see Schwaller De Lubicz, R. A.

Van Den Broecke, M. P. Hierarchies & Rank Orders in Distinctive Features. (Illus., Orig.). 1976. pap. text ed. 19.00x (ISBN 90-232-1369-6). Humanities.

Van Den Bruck, Arthur Moeller see Moeller Van Den Bruck, Arthur.

Vandenburgh, Jane, ed. see Botto, Ken.

Vandenburgh, Jane, ed. see Hamamura, John & Hamamura, Susan.

Vandenburgh, Jane, ed. see Hanauer, Gary.

Vandenburgh, Jane, ed. see Milligan, Charles & Higgs, Jim.

Vandenburgh, Jane, ed. see Pashdag, John & Woller, Jim.

Vanden Burgt, Robert J. The Religious Philosophy of William James. LC 80-22936. 176p. 1981. text ed. 16.95 (ISBN 0-88229-594-2); pap. text ed. 8.95 (ISBN 0-88229-767-8). Nelson-Hall.

Vandenbusche, Duane, jt. auth. see Smith, Duane.

Van Den Doel, H. Democracy & Welfare Economics. LC 78-21160. 1979. 29.50 (ISBN 0-521-22568-X); pap. 9.95x (ISBN 0-521-29555-6). Cambridge U Pr.

Vanden Eynden, Charles, jt. auth. see Eggan, Lawrence C.

Van Den Tak, Richard. The Scientific Proof of the Existence of Reincarnation & Transmigration. (Illus.). 1980. 16.50 (ISBN 0-89962-015-9). Todd & Honeywell.

Van den Wijngaert, Christine. The Political Offence Exception to Extradition. 260p. 1980. lib. bdg. 53.00 (ISBN 90-268-1185-3, Pub. by Kluwer Law & Taxation). Kluwer Boston.

Van de Pusse, Crispin. Metamorphoseon Ovidianarum. LC 78-68195. (The Philosophy of Images Ser.). (Illus.). 1980. lib. bdg. 66.00 (ISBN 0-8240-3682-4). Garland Pub.

Vander, Arthur, et al. Human Physiology. 3rd ed. (Illus.). 736p. 1980. text ed. 20.95 (ISBN 0-07-066961-9, C); instructor's manual 4.95 (ISBN 0-07-066955-4); wkbk. study guide 7.95 (ISBN 0-07-066963-5). McGraw.

Vander, Arthur J. Nutrition, Stress & Toxic Chemicals: An Approach to Environmental Health Controversies. 360p. 1981. text ed. 18.00 (ISBN 0-472-09329-0); pap. 9.95 (ISBN 0-472-06329-4). U of Mich Pr.

--Renal Physiology. (Illus.). 192p. (Orig.). 1975. pap. text ed. 7.95 o.p. (ISBN 0-07-066957-0, C). McGraw.

Vander, Arthur J., intro. by. Human Physiology & the Environment in Health & Disease: Readings from Scientific American. LC 76-1923. (Illus.). 1976. 19.95x (ISBN 0-7167-0527-3); pap. text ed. 9.95x (ISBN 0-7167-0526-5). W H Freeman.

Vander, Karen D. Ven see Vander Ven, Karen D.

Vander Ark, Nelle. Inspirations from Isaiah. (Good Morning Lord Ser.). 96p. 1980. 2.95 (ISBN 0-8010-9281-7). Baker Bk.

Vanderbeets, Richard see Bowen, James K.

VanDerBeets, Richard, ed. Held Captive by Indians: Selected Narratives, 1642-1836. LC 73-3448. (Illus.). 1973. 16.50x (ISBN 0-87049-145-8). U of Tenn Pr.

VanDerBeets, Richard, jt. ed. see Bowen, James K.

Vanderbilt, Amy. The Amy Vanderbilt Complete Book of Etiquette: A Guide to Contemporary Living. Balderige, Letitia, rev. by. 272p. 1981. pap. 3.50 (ISBN 0-553-14582-7). Bantam.

Vanderbilt, Amy see Baldridge, Letitia.

Vanderbilt, Arthur T. The Challenge of Law Reform. LC 76-3784. 194p. 1976. Repr. of 1955 ed. lib. bdg. 18.75x (ISBN 0-8371-8809-1, VALR). Greenwood.

Vanderburgh, Rosamund, jt. auth. see Salerno, Nan.

Vanderdecken. Yachts & Yachting. (Scolar Maritime Library). (Illus.). 485p. 1979. Repr. of 1873 ed. 60.00x (ISBN 0-85967-568-8, Pub. by Scolar Pr England). Biblio Dist.

Van Der Embse, Thomas J., jt. auth. see Murray, John V.

Van Der Eyken, W., ed. Learning & Earning: Aspects of Day - Release in Further Education. Barry, S. M. (General Ser.). (Illus.). 111p. 1975. pap. text ed. 9.50x (ISBN 0-85633-079-5, NFER). Humanities.

Van Der Geest, A. J. Some Aspects of Communicative Competence & Their Implications. 272p. 1975. pap. text ed. 20.75x (ISBN 90-232-1261-4). Humanities.

Vandergriff, Aola. The Bell Tower of Wyndspelle. (Orig.). 1975. pap. 1.95 o.s.i. (ISBN 0-446-89716-7). Warner Bks.

--Daughters of the Far Islands. (Orig.). 1979. pap. 2.95 (ISBN 0-446-93910-2). Warner Bks.

--Daughters of the Opal Skies. (Orig.). 1980. pap. 2.50 (ISBN 0-446-81930-1). Warner Bks.

--Daughters of the Southwind. (Orig.). 1977. pap. 2.95 (ISBN 0-446-93909-9). Warner Bks.

--Daughters of the Wild Country. (Orig.). 1978. pap. 2.95 (ISBN 0-446-93908-0). Warner Bks.

--Silk & Saber. 512p. (Orig.). 1981. pap. 2.75 (ISBN 0-446-85584-7). Warner Bks.

--Sisters of Sorrow. 1978. pap. 1.95 o.s.i. (ISBN 0-446-89999-2). Warner Bks.

Vandergrift, Kay E. Child & Story: The Literary Connection. Hannigan, Jane Anne, ed. (Diversity & Directions in Children's Literature Ser.). 349p. 1980. 14.95x (ISBN 0-918212-42-1). Neal-Schuman.

Van Der Groot, Georg, ed. Frans Hals, His Life, His Paintings: A Critique of His Art. 1979. deluxe ed. 22.45 (ISBN 0-930582-27-6). Gloucester Art.

Van Der Hammen, L. A Berlese, Acari Myriopoda et Scorpiones Eighteen Hundred Eighty-Two - Nineteen Hundred Three, 12 vols. 4616p. 1980. Set. 315.00 (ISBN 90-6193-603-9). Kluwer Boston.

Van Der Helm, F. G. Hydrophthalmia & Its Treatment: A General Study Based on 630 Cases in the Netherlands. 1963. 4.75 o.s.i. (ISBN 0-02-854100-6). Hafner.

Vanderhoef, Lois. Pets. (Illus.). (ps-2). PLB 5.38 (ISBN 0-307-68995-6, Golden Pr). Western Pub.

Van Der Hoeven, Johan. Karl Marx: The Roots of His Thought. 1976. 6.95x (ISBN 0-88906-001-0). Wedge Pub.

Van Der Hoeven, Johan see Hoeven, Johan Van Der.

Vanderhofen, Martinius. The Insuperable Opposition Between Catholicism & Liberalism. (Illus.). 107p. 1980. 39.75 (ISBN 0-930582-78-0). Gloucester Art.

Van Der Hoop, J. H. Conscious Orientation. Hutton, Luara, tr. 352p. 1980. Repr. of 1930 ed. lib. bdg. 50.00 (ISBN 0-89987-875-X). Darby Bks.

Vander Horck, Karl J. A Dutch Uncle's Guidebook to School Law. 194p. (Orig.). 1980. pap. 6.95 (ISBN 0-87839-035-9). North Star.

Van Der Horst, Brian. Rock Music. LC 73-4959. (First Bks.). (gr. 5 up). 1973. PLB 4.90 o.p. (ISBN 0-531-00789-8). Watts.

Vander Kam, James. Textual & Historical Studies in the Book of Jubilees. LC 76-45388. (Harvard Semitic Monograph). 1977. text ed. 9.00 (ISBN 0-89130-118-6, 040014). Scholars Pr Ca.

Van Der Kamp, Garth S. Periodic Flow of Groundwater: A Systematic Study of Wave Propagation Under Confined, Semiconfined & Unconfined Flow Conditions. LC 73-90103. (Illus.). 121p. (Orig.). 1976. pap. text ed. 14.25x (ISBN 90-6203-387-3). Humanities.

Van Der Klip, Rita. Crochet. (Illus.). 1977. 6.95 (ISBN 0-8467-0240-1, Pub. by Two Continents). Hippocrene Bks.

Van Der Knaap, G. A. Population Growth & Urban Systems Development. (Studies in Applied Regional Science: Vol. 18). 245p. 1980. lib. bdg. 16.00 (ISBN 0-89838-024-3, Martinus Nijhoff Pubs). Kluwer Boston.

Van Der Knapp, Bert, jt. auth. see Odell, P. R.

Van Der Kulk, W., jt. auth. see Schouten, Jan A.

Van Der Linden, Frank. Ronald Reagan. 288p. 1981. 10.95 (ISBN 0-686-69236-5). Morrow.

Vanderlint, Jacob. Money Answers All Things. LC 72-114079. 1978. 35.00x o.p. (ISBN 0-85409-233-1). Charles River Bks.

Van Der Loef, A. Rutgers. Avalanche. (Illus.). (gr. 7 up). 1958. 7.75 (ISBN 0-688-21055-4). Morrow.

Van Der Looy, H. Rule for a New Brother. 1976. pap. 1.95 (ISBN 0-87243-065-0). Templegate.

Van Der Lyn, Edita. Dachshunds. (Illus.). 128p. 1980. 2.95 (ISBN 0-87666-704-3, KW-085). TFH Pubns.

Vanderman, Timothy D. The Intelligent Anticipation of Stock Market Reversals for the Maximization of Speculative Profits. (The New Stock Market Reference Library). (Illus.). 116p. 1981. 41.75 (ISBN 0-918968-94-1). Inst Econ Fina.

Van Der Meer, Atie, jt. auth. see Van Der Meer, Ron.

Vandermeer, John. Elementary Mathematical Ecology. LC 80-15664. 320p. 1981. 25.00 (ISBN 0-471-08131-0, Pub. by Wiley-Interscience). Wiley.

Van Der Meer, Ron & Van Der Meer, Atie. Basil & Boris in London. 1979. pap. 1.45 available in 5 pk. (ISBN 0-85122-169-6, Pub. by Dinosaur Pubns). Merrimack Bk Serv.

--Naughty Sammy. (Illus.). 32p. 1980. 8.95 (ISBN 0-241-10140-9, Pub. by Hamish Hamilton England). David & Charles.

--Sammy & the Cat Party. (Illus.). 32p. 1980. 8.95 (ISBN 0-241-10141-7, Pub. by Hamish Hamilton England). David & Charles.

Van Der Meer, Wybe J. The Miracle Pond. 2nd ed. (Illus.). 48p. (gr. 1-4). 1980. PLB 8.49x (ISBN 0-934744-01-7). Vermeer Arts.

Van Der Meer, Wybe J., et al. The Old & the Beautiful: Living Historic Buildings; Durango Colorado. (Illus.). 110p. (Orig.). 1980. 15.00 (ISBN 0-934744-02-5). Vermeer Arts.

Van Der Meid, Louise B. Cats. (Orig.). pap. 2.00 (ISBN 0-87666-173-8, M503). TFH Pubns.

--Siamese Cats. (Orig.). pap. 2.00 (ISBN 0-87666-183-5, M509). TFH Pubns.

Van der Merwe, Hendrik & Schrire, Robert A., eds. Race & Ethnicity: South African & International Perspectives. 240p. 1981. pap. 12.95x (ISBN 0-8476-3651-8). Rowman.

Van Der Merwe, Hendrik W. & Charton, Nancy C. J., eds. African Perspectives on South Africa: Collection of Speeches, Articles & Doucuments, Vol. I. LC 78-20359. (Publications Ser.: No. 176). 1978. pap. 9.95 (ISBN 0-8179-6762-1). Hoover Inst Pr.

Van Der Merwe, Hendrik W., et al, eds. Towards an Open Society in South Africa: The Role of Voluntary Organisations. 140p. 1980. pap. 10.00x (ISBN 0-8476-3283-0). Rowman.

Van der Merwe, Henrik. South Africa: Morality & Action. (Studies in Quakerism). 60p. (Orig.). 1981. pap. 3.00 (ISBN 0-89670-007-0). Progresiv Pub.

Vandermeulen, Carl. Photography for Student Publications. LC 79-89332. 1979. pap. 12.95 (ISBN 0-931940-01-X). Middleburg Pr.

--Photography for Student Publications. LC 79-89332. 1980. 16.95 (ISBN 0-931940-02-8). Middleburg Pr.

Van der Meulen, Jan & Price, Nancy W. The West Portals of Chartres Cathedral, I: The Iconology of the Creation. LC 80-5586. 1981. lib. bdg. 19.75 (ISBN 0-8191-1402-2); pap. text ed. 10.50 (ISBN 0-8191-1403-0). U Pr of Amer.

VanderMey, Randall, jt. auth. see Tsuang, Ming T.

Vander Nieuwenhuizen, de Grass. Marine Aquarium Guide. 240p. 1974. 6.98 o.p. (ISBN 0-385-03518-7). Doubleday.

Van Der Plaat, G. N., jt. ed. see Boogman, J. C.

Van Der Plaats, G. J. Medical X-Ray Techniques in Diagnostic Radiology. 1979. lib. bdg. 79.50 (ISBN 90-247-2155-5, Martinus Nijhoff Pubs). Kluwer Boston.

Van Der Plank, J. E. Plant Diseases: Epidemics & Control. 1964. 37.50 (ISBN 0-12-711450-5). Acad Pr.

Van Der Poel, Jean, ed. see Smuts, J. C.

Vanderpool, James A. People in Pain: A Guide to Pastoral Care. 208p. 1979. 16.50 (ISBN 0-398-03846-5). C C Thomas.

Van Der Post, Laurens. African Cooking. (Foods of the World Ser). (Illus.). 1970. 14.95 (ISBN 0-8094-0046-4). Time-Life.

--African Cooking. LC 77-119620. (Foods of the World Ser.). (Illus.). (gr. 6 up). 1970. PLB 14.94 (ISBN 0-8094-0073-1, Pub. by Time-Life). Silver.

--The Heart of the Hunter. LC 80-15539. 1980. pap. 4.95 (ISBN 0-15-640003-0, Harv). HarBraceJ.

Van Der Put, M., jt. auth. see Gerritzen, L.

Van der Reis, L., ed. The Stomach. (Frontiers of Gastrointestinal Research: Vol. 6). (Illus.). xii, 188p. 1980. 55.25 (ISBN 3-8055-3071-4). S Karger.

Van Der Rhoer, Edward. Deadly Magic. LC 78-17120. (Illus.). 1978. 9.95 o.p. (ISBN 0-684-15873-6, ScribT). Scribner.

Van Der Rhoer, Edward see Rhoer, Edward Van Der.

Vander Salm, Thomas J., et al. Atlas of Bedside Procedures. LC 79-65313. 1979. pap. text ed. 18.95 (ISBN 0-316-89605-5). Little.

Van der Spoel, S. & Pierrot-Bults, A. C., eds. Zoogeography & Diversity in Plankton. LC 79-9494. 410p. 1979. 74.95x (ISBN 0-470-26798-4). Halsted Pr.

Van Der Sprenkel, Sybille. Legal Institutions in Manchu China: A Socialogical Analysis. (Monographs on Social Anthropology: No. 24). 1962. pap. text ed. 6.25x (ISBN 0-391-00755-6, Athlone Pr). Humanities.

Van Der Spuy, H. I., ed. The Psychology of Apartheid: A Psychosocial Perspective on South Africa. LC 78-63064. 1978. pap. text ed. 7.50 (ISBN 0-8191-0610-0). U Pr of Amer.

Van der Tak, Herman G., jt. auth. see Squire, Lyn.

Van Der Veen, K. W. I Give Thee My Daughter: A Study on Marriage & Hierarchy Among the Anvil Brahmans of South Gujarat. (Studies in Developing Countries: No. 13). 336p. 1972. text ed. 24.50x (ISBN 0-685-23725-7). Humanities.

Van Der Veer, Andrew. Bible Lessons for Juniors, 4 bks. Incl. Bk. 1. Creation Through Moses. 1.95 (ISBN 0-8010-9253-1); Bk. 2. Kings & Prophets. 1.95 (ISBN 0-8010-9251-5); Bk. 3. The Life of Christ. 1.95 (ISBN 0-8010-9257-4); Bk. 4. The Early Church. 1.50 (ISBN 0-8010-9255-8). Baker Bk.

Van Derveer, Paul D. & Haas, Leonard E., eds. International Glossary of Technical Terms for the Pulp & Paper Industry. LC 74-20168. (A Pulp & Paper Book). 238p. 1976. 35.00 (ISBN 0-87930-037-X). Miller Freeman.

Vander Velde, Frances. She Shall Be Called Woman. rev. ed. LC 57-13178. (Illus.). 1971. pap. 4.95 (ISBN 0-8254-3950-7). Kregel.

Vander Ven, Karen D. Home & Community Influences on Young Children. LC 76-14092. 1977. pap. text ed. 7.80 (ISBN 0-8273-0569-9); instructor's guide 1.60 (ISBN 0-8273-0570-2). Delmar.

Vander Vender, Mary Lou, ed. see Friends of the Earth Staff.

Vandervoort, Tom. Sailing Is for Me. (Sports for Me Bks.). (Illus.). (gr. 2-5). 1981. PLB 5.95 (ISBN 0-8225-1128-2). Lerner Pubns.

Van Der Waerden, B. L. Group Theory & Quantum Mechanics. (Grundlehren der Mathematischen Wissenschaften Ser.: Vol. 214). (Illus.). 211p. 1981. 39.00 (ISBN 0-387-06740-X). Springer-Verlag.

Van Der Waerden, B. L., ed. Sources of Quantum Mechanics. pap. text ed. 6.00 (ISBN 0-486-61881-1). Dover.

Van Der Wal, John, jt. auth. see Croom, George E., Jr.

Vanderwalker, F. N. Wood Finishing. rev. ed. LC 76-21190. (Illus.). 408p. 1980. pap. 6.95 (ISBN 0-8069-8798-7). Sterling.

--Wood Finishing-Plain & Decorative. LC 76-21190. (Illus.). 1970. 9.95 o.p. (ISBN 0-87749-024-4); pap. 6.95 o.p. (ISBN 0-8069-8798-7). Sterling.

Van der Walt, B., ed. Social Theory & Practice: Philosophical Essays in Honour of Prof. J. A. L. Taljaard. 1977. pap. 5.95x (ISBN 0-686-00490-6). Wedge Pub.

Van der Weele, Steven. The Critical Reputation of Restoration Comedy in Modern Times up to 1950, 2 vols, Vols. 1 & 2. (Salzburg Studies in English Literature, Poetic Drama & Poetic Theory: No. 36). 1978. pap. text ed. 25.00x ea. Vol. 1 (ISBN 0-391-01560-5). Vol. 2 (ISBN 0-391-01561-3). Humanities.

Vanderweide, Harry. The Book of Maine Fishing Maps. (Illus.). 96p. (Orig.). 1980. pap. 6.95 (ISBN 0-89933-007-X). DeLorme Pub.

--Grouse Foolish & Other Stories. (Illus.). 144p. 1979. 7.95 (ISBN 0-89933-006-1). DeLorme Pub.

Vanderweide, Harry, ed. see Godin, Alfred J.

Van der Werf, Tjeerd. Cardiovascular Pathophysiology. (Illus.). 320p. 1980. 19.95 (ISBN 0-19-261153-4); pap. text ed. 10.95x (ISBN 0-19-261229-8). Oxford U Pr.

Van Der Werff, T. J., jt. auth. see Collins, R.

Vanderwood, Paul J. Disorder & Progress: Bandits, Police, & Mexican Development. LC 80-22345. (Illus.). xx, 269p. 1981. 19.95x (ISBN 0-8032-4651-X, Bison); pap. 7.95 (ISBN 0-8032-9600-2, BB 767). U of Nebr Pr.

--Night Riders of Reelfoot Lake. LC 79-91959. (Illus.). 1980. pap. 6.95 (ISBN 0-87870-196-6). Memphis St Univ.

Vander Zanden, James W. American Minority Relations. 3rd ed. 1972. 17.95x (ISBN 0-8260-8870-8). Wiley.

--Social Psychology. 2nd ed. 524p. 1981. text ed. 17.95 (ISBN 0-394-32427-7). Random.

--Sociology. 4th ed. LC 78-14447. 1979. text ed. 17.95 (ISBN 0-471-04341-9); tchrs manual (ISBN 0-471-04846-1); study guide 6.50 (ISBN 0-471-04845-3); tchr's. manual journal entries avail. (ISBN 0-471-05813-0). Wiley.

Van Der Zee, J., jt. auth. see Wilkerson, M.

Van Der Zee, John. Stateline. LC 75-33627. 216p. 1976. 7.95 o.p. (ISBN 0-15-184905-6). HarBraceJ.

Van Der Zee, John & Jacobson, Boyd. Imagined City: San Francisco in the Minds of Its Writers. Larrick, Gail, ed. LC 80-65977. (Illus.). 96p. (Orig.). 1980. pap. 4.95 (ISBN 0-89395-043-2). Cal Living Bks.

Van Der Zee, Karen. Love Beyond Reason. (Harlequin Romances Ser.). 192p. 1981. pap. 1.25 (ISBN 0-373-02406-1, Pub. by Harlequin). PB.

--Sweet Not Always. (Harlequin Romance Ser.). (Orig.). 1980. pap. 1.25 o.p. (ISBN 0-373-02334-0, Pub. by Harlequin). PB.

Van Der Ziel, Albert. Noise: Sources, Characterization, Measurement. LC 71-112911. (Electrical Engineering Ser). 1970. ref. ed. 17.95 o.p. (ISBN 0-13-623165-9). P-H.

Van Der Ziel, Aldert. Introductory Electronics. (Illus.). 416p. 1974. ref. ed. 25.95 (ISBN 0-13-501700-9). P-H.

--Noise in Measurements. LC 76-12108. 228p. 1976. 21.50 (ISBN 0-471-89895-3, Pub. by Wiley-Interscience). Wiley.

--Nonlinear Electronic Circuits. LC 76-48145. 1977. 22.50 (ISBN 0-471-02227-6, Pub. by Wiley-Interscience). Wiley.

Vanderzwagg, Harold J. Toward a Philosophy of Sport. LC 71-174337. 1972. text ed. 15.95 (ISBN 0-201-08158-X). A-W.

Van Dessel, Sabine. How to Survive Without Meat. 1981. 6.95 (ISBN 0-533-04833-8). Vantage.

Van Deursen, A. Illustrated Dictionary of Bible Manners & Customs. (Illus.). 1967. pap. 4.75 (ISBN 0-8022-1762-1). Philos Lib.

Van Deusen, Glyndon G. Jacksonian Era: Eighteen Twenty-Eight to Eighteen Forty-Eight. (New American Nation Ser). 1959. 15.00x o.p. (ISBN 0-06-014485-8, HarpT). Har-Row.

--Thurlow Weed. LC 73-87698. (American Scene Ser.). 1969. Repr. of 1947 ed. lib. bdg. 39.50 (ISBN 0-306-71693-3). Da Capo.

Van De Vall, Mark. Labor Organizations: A Macro & Micro Sociological Comparison. 1970. 32.50 (ISBN 0-521-07637-4). Cambridge U Pr.

Van de Ven, Andrew H. & Ferry, Diane L. Measuring & Assessing Organizations. LC 79-20003. (Organizational Assessment & Change Ser.). 1980. 34.95 (ISBN 0-471-04832-1, Pub. by Wiley-Interscience). Wiley.

Vande Vere, E. K. Rugged Heart. LC 79-9291. (Horizon Ser.). 1979. pap. 4.50 (ISBN 0-8127-0241-7). Southern Pub.

Van de Warsenburg, Hans, compiled by. Cross-Cultural Review: Five Contemporary Flemish Poets, No. 3. Holmes, James S., et al, trs. Barkan, Stanley H., ed. 48p. 10.00 (ISBN 0-89304-604-3); pap. 4.00 (ISBN 0-89304-605-1). Cross Cult.

Van De Water, Frederic F. Glory Hunter: A Life of General Custer. LC 63-20840. (Illus.). 1964. Repr. of 1934 ed. 15.00. Argosy.

Van De Water, J. W. Chichee's Trunk: A Story of Roots & Branches. (Illus.). 130p. (Orig.). pap. 5.00x (ISBN 0-686-27489-X). Jonsalvania.

Van de Wetering, Jan. The Maine Massacre. (Orig.). 1980. pap. write for info. (ISBN 0-671-82865-7). PB.

Van de Wetering, Janwillem. The Mind-Murders. 1981. 9.95 (ISBN 0-686-69054-0). HM.

Vandezande, G., jt. auth. see Olthuis, J. H.

Vandi, Abdulai. A Model of Mass Communications & National Development: A Liberian Perspective. LC 79-89253. 1979. pap. text ed. 9.00 (ISBN 0-8191-0812-X). U Pr of Amer.

Vandi, Abdulai S., jt. ed. see Asante, Molefi K.

Van Dihn, jt. ed. see Sigham.

Van Dijen, F. S. Pneumatic Mechanisation. 296p. 1980. 20.25x (ISBN 0-686-64954-0, Pub. by Thornes England). State Mutual Bk.

Van Dijk, P. Judicial Review of Governmental Action & the Requirement of an Interest to Sue. LC 80-51740. 618p. 1980. 100.00x (ISBN 90-286-0120-1). Sijthoff & Noordhoff.

Van Dijk, Teun A. Macrostructures: An Interdisciplinary Study of Global Structures in Discourse, Interaction & Cognition. LC 79-27844. 336p. 1980. text ed. 24.95 (ISBN 0-89859-039-6). L Erlbaum Assocs.

--Text & Context: Some Explorations in the Semantics & Pragmatics of Discourse. (Longman Linguistics Library). (Illus.). 1977. text ed. 19.95x (ISBN 0-582-55085-8). Longman.

Van Dijkhuizen, N. From Stressors to Strains: Research into Their Interrelationships. xii, 292p. 1980. pap. text ed. 27.75 (ISBN 90-265-0351-2). Swets North Am.

VanDine, Stephen, et al. Restaining the Wicked: The Incapacitation of the Dangerous Criminal. (Illus.). 1979. 15.95 (ISBN 0-669-01774-4). Lexington Bks.

Van Diver, Bradford B. Upstate New York. (Geology Field Guide Ser.). (Illus.). 288p. 1980. pap. text ed. 10.95 (ISBN 0-8403-2214-3). Kendall-Hunt.

Vandiver, Frank E., jt. auth. see Sommers, Richard J.

Vandiver, Frank E., ed. see Wakelyn, Jon L.

Van Dixhoorn, J. J. & Evans, F. J., eds. Physical Structure in Systems Theory: Network Approaches Engineering & Economics. 1975. 46.00 (ISBN 0-12-712450-0). Acad Pr.

Van Dolson, Bobbie J., jt. auth. see Osman, Jack.

Van Dolson, Bobbie J., ed. see Aaen, Bernhard.

Van Dolson, Bobbie J., ed. see Degering, Etta B.

Van Dolson, Bobbie J., ed. see Dodd, Marjorie L.

Van Dolson, Bobbie J., ed. see Hills, Desmond B.

Van Dolson, Bobbie J., ed. see Johnston, Madeline.

Van Dolson, Bobbie J., ed. see Jones, Lucile.

Van Dolson, Bobbie J., ed. see Loller, Sherry G.

Van Dolson, Bobbie J., ed. see Parker, Lois M.

Van Dolson, Bobbie J., ed. see Tilstra, Albertine J.

Van Dolson, Bobbie J., ed. see Todd, Sharon.

Van Dolson, Bobbie J., ed. see Willis, Mary.

Van Dolson, Leo. God's Footprint on My Floor. LC 76-56996. (Horizon Ser.). 1977. pap. 4.95 (ISBN 0-8127-0132-1). Southern Pub.

Van Doorn, J. Disequilibrium Economics. LC 75-19139. 96p. 1976. pap. text ed. 8.95x (ISBN 0-470-89902-6). Halsted Pr.

Van Doorn, Jacques. The Soldier & Social Change: Comparative Studies in the History & Sociology of the Military. LC 74-31573. (Sage Ser. on Armed Forces & Society: Vol. 7). (Illus.). 189p. 1975. 20.00 (ISBN 0-8039-9948-8). Sage.

Van Doren, Carl. Benjamin Franklin & Jonathan Edwards. 1979. Repr. of 1920 ed. lib. bdg. 20.00 (ISBN 0-8495-5525-6). Arden Lib.

--James Branch Cabell. 87p. 1980. Repr. of 1928 ed. lib. bdg. 10.00 (ISBN 0-89984-475-8). Century Bookbindery.

Van Doren, Carl C. Benjamin Franklin. LC 73-8566. (Illus.). 845p. 1973. Repr. of 1938 ed. lib. bdg. 47.25x (ISBN 0-8371-6964-X, VABF). Greenwood.

Van Doren, Mark. The Essays of Mark Van Doren: Nineteen Twenty-Four to Nineteen Seventy-Two. Claire, William, ed. LC 79-8411. (Contributions in American Studies: No. 47). (Illus.). xxv, 270p. 1980. lib. bdg. 25.00 (ISBN 0-313-22098-0, CEV/). Greenwood.

--Good Morning: Last Poems by Mark Van Doren. 1973. 6.95 o.p. (ISBN 0-8090-5064-1). Hill & Wang.

Van Doren, Mark, ed. see Bartram, William.

Van Doren, W. H. Gospel of John, 2 vols. in 1. rev. ed. LC 80-8080. (Kregal Bible Study Classics Ser.). 1100p. 1981. Repr. of 1878 ed. text ed. 22.95 (ISBN 0-8254-3952-3). Kregel.

--Gospel of Luke, 2 vols. in 1. LC 80-8079. (Kregal Bible Study Classics Ser.). 1981. Repr. of 1878 ed. 22.95 (ISBN 0-8254-3953-1). Kregel.

Van Dorn, Charles H. Six Things Everyone Should Know. 201p. 1980. 7.95 (ISBN 0-533-03707-7). Vantage.

Van Dorn, William G. Oceanography & Seamanship: A Guide for Ocean Cruising. LC 73-15377. (Illus.). 550p. 1974. 22.50 (ISBN 0-396-06888-X). Dodd.

Van Driel, G. Cult of Assur. (Studia Semitica Neerlandica: No. 13). 1969. text ed. 24.50x (ISBN 0-685-12390-1). Humanities.

Van Duesen, Nancy. Music at Nevers Cathedral: Principal Sources of Mediaeval Chant. (Musicological Studies). 430p. 1980. lib. bdg. 55.00 pt. 1 (ISBN 0-912024-34-8); lib. bdg. 55.00 pt. 2 (ISBN 0-912024-33-X). Inst Mediaeval.

Van Duong, Quyen & Coburn, Jewell R. Beyond the EAST Wind: Legends & Folktales of Vietnam. LC 76-50345. (Illus.). 100p. 1976. 8.95 (ISBN 0-918060-01-X). Burn-Hart.

Van Dusen, C. R., jt. auth. see Cromwell, Harvey.

VanDusen, Gerald C. William Starbuck Mayo. (United States Authors Ser.: No. 345). 1979. lib. bdg. 13.50 (ISBN 0-8057-7278-2). Twayne.

Van Dusen Pysh, Margaret & Chalfant, James C. The Learning Disabilities Manual: Recommended Procedures & Practices. rev. ed. LC 79-90979. (Illus.). 100p. 1980. pap. 5.95 (ISBN 0-933922-00-0, P500). PEM Pr.

Van Duyn, A. V., tr. see DeJong, Dola.

Vanduyn, J. Practical Systems & Procedures Manual. LC 74-31160. (Illus.). 240p. 1975. 16.95 (ISBN 0-87909-634-9). Reston.

Van Duyn, John & Southworth. War at Sea, 4 vols. Incl. Bk. 1. The Ancient Fleets: The Story of Naval Warfare Under Oars, 2600 B.C. - 1597 A.D. LC 67-16200. 370p. o.p. (ISBN 0-685-59135-2, H-588); Bk. 2. The Age of Sails: The Story of Naval Warfare Under Sail, 1213 A.D. - 1853 A.D. LC 68-17224. 468p (H-589); Bk. 3. The Age of Steam, Pt. 1: 1783-1936 (H-590); Bk. 4. The Age of Steam, Pt. 2: The Story of Engine-Powered Naval Warfare, 1936-1972. LC 67-16200. 443p (H-591). (Illus.). 7.50 ea. Hippocrene Bks.

Van Duyne, Carl. Modsim: A Computer Program for Simulating Macroeconomic Models. Hepler, Molly L., ed. (Orig., User's man., 89 p.; instr's. man., 67 p.). 1980. User's Manual. pap. text ed. 5.00 (ISBN 0-686-27411-3); Instructor's Manual. 5.00 (ISBN 0-686-27412-1). Conduit.

Van Dyke, jt. auth. see Powell.

Van Dyke, Dick & Parker, Ray. Those Funny Kids! 1976. pap. 1.50 o.s.i. (ISBN 0-446-88274-7). Warner Bks.

Van Dyke, Henry. Dead Piano. 182p. 1971. 5.95 o.p. (ISBN 0-374-13550-9). FS&G.

Van Dyke, John C., ed. Modern French Masters. LC 75-28885. (Art Experience in Late 19th Century America Ser.: Vol. 19). (Illus.). 1976. Repr. of 1896 ed. lib. bdg. 52.00 (ISBN 0-8240-2243-2). Garland Pub.

Van Dyke, M., et al, eds. Annual Review of Fluid Mechanics, Vol. 13. LC 74-80866. (Illus.). 1981. text ed. 20.00 (ISBN 0-8243-0713-5). Annual Reviews.

Van Dyken, A. R., jt. ed. see Silverman, Joseph.

Van Dyke Platt, Nancy. Pastoral Care to the Cancer Patient. 84p. 1980. write for info. o.p. (ISBN 0-398-04051-6). C C Thomas.

Van Dyne, Frederick. Citizenship of the United States. xxvii, 385p. 1980. Repr. of 1904 ed. lib. bdg. 28.50x (ISBN 0-8377-1229-7). Rothman.

Vane, Howard R. & Thompson, John L. Monetarism: Theory, Evidence & Policy. 1979. pap. text ed. 10.95 (ISBN 0-470-26569-8). Halsted Pr.

Vane, J. R., jt. ed. see Robinson, H. J.

Vane, John R. & Bergstrom, Sune, eds. Prostacyclin. LC 78-601200. 1979. text ed. 46.50 (ISBN 0-89004-330-2). Raven.

Van Eeden, Frederik. Bride of Dreams. 2nd ed. LC 79-89934. 1980. cancelled (ISBN 0-89793-011-8). Hunter Hse.

--Paul's Awakening. Lake, H. S., tr. from Dutch. LC 78-70615. 1980. pap. cancelled (ISBN 0-89793-000-2). Hunter Hse.

Van Egmond, Dorothy. School Foodservice. 1974. text ed. 34.00 o.p. (ISBN 0-87055-160-4). AVI.

Van Egmond-Pannell, Dorothy. School Foodservice. (Illus.). 1981. pap. text ed. 17.00 (ISBN 0-87055-378-X). AVI.

Van Eijndhoven, J., ed. Religious Education of the Deaf. (Modern Approaches to the Diagnosis & Instruction of Multi-Handicapped Children Ser.: Vol. 11). 168p. 1973. text ed. 20.25 (ISBN 90-237-4111-0, Pub. by Swets Pub. Ser Holland). Swets North Am.

Van Ek, J. Threshold Level English. LC 79-42720. (Council of Europe Language Learning Ser.). 253p. 1980. pap. 7.95 (ISBN 0-08-024588-9). Pergamon.

--Waystage English. (Council of Europe Language Learning Ser.). 1980. pap. 5.95 (ISBN 0-08-024590-0). Pergamon.

Van Ek, J. A. The Threshold Level for Modern Language Learning in Schools. 1978. pap. text ed. 9.00x (ISBN 0-582-55700-3). Longman.

Vanek, Jaroslav. Participatory Economy: An Evolutionary Hypothesis & a Strategy for Development. LC 77-148024. (Illus.). 1971. 20.00x (ISBN 0-8014-0639-0); pap. 4.95 1974 ed. (ISBN 0-8014-9148-7). Cornell U Pr.

--The Participatory Economy: An Evolutionary Hyposthesis & a Strategy for Development. LC 77-148024. 181p. 1974. pap. 4.95 o.p. (ISBN 0-8014-9148-7, CP148). Cornell U Pr.

Van Els, T. J. Kassel Manuscript of Bede's Historia Ecclesiastica Gentis Anglorum & Its Old English Material. (Illus.). 280p. 1972. text ed. 30.25x (ISBN 0-685-27425-X, 90-232-0962-1). Humanities.

Van Eperen, Jeannine, jt. ed. see Tyrack, Mildred.

Van Eperen, Jeannine D. Albuquerque. 386p. 1980. 15.95 (ISBN 0-937268-02-X); pap. 8.95 (ISBN 0-937268-01-1). Alpha Printing.

--French Physician, Jeannine D. Van Eperen, Eperen/jeannine D. Van. 128p. (Orig.). 1980. pap. 4.95 (ISBN 0-937268-00-3). Alpha Printing.

Van Ess, Donald H. Heritage of Musical Style. LC 73-101138. (Illus.). text ed. 16.95x (ISBN 0-03-081241-0); listener's guide 3.95x (ISBN 0-03-081242-9). Irvington.

Van Essen, A. J. & Menting, J. P., eds. The Context of Foreign Language Learning. 200p. 1975. pap. text ed. 20.50x (ISBN 90-232-1250-9). Humanities.

Van Etten, G. M. Rural Health Development in Tanzania: A Case-Study of Medical Sociology in a Developing Country. (Studies of Developing Countries: No. 18). (Illus.). 1976. pap. text ed. 17.00x (ISBN 90-232-1378-5). Humanities.

Van Etten, Glen & Arkell, Claudia. The Severely & Profoundly Handicapped: Programs, Methods & Materials. LC 79-28841. 1980. pap. text ed. 19.95 (ISBN 0-8016-5215-4). Mosby.

Vaneven, Maxine T. How to Be Your Own Thin Self. 1981. pap. price not set (ISBN 0-916774-03-1). Tolvan Co.

--Luscious Low Calorie with Poundation Conversation by Maxine. LC 75-34770. (Illus.). 1975. pap. 3.95 (ISBN 0-916774-01-5). Tolvan Co.

Van Every, Dale. Disinherited: The Lost Birthright of the American Indian. 1967. pap. 2.95 (ISBN 0-380-01141-7, 51326, Discus). Avon.

Van Every, Edward. Sins of New York As "Exposed" by the Police Gazette. LC 70-174130. (Illus.). 299p. 1976. Repr. of 1930 ed. 20.00 (ISBN 0-8103-4038-0). Gale.

Van Eys, Jan. Humanity & Personhood: Personal Reaction to a World in Which Children Can Die. write for info. (ISBN 0-398-04467-8). C C Thomas.

Van Eys, Jan & Sullivan, Margaret P., eds. Status of the Curability of Childhood Cancers. (M. D. Anderson Clinical Conferences on Cancer: 24th). 350p. 1980. text ed. 34.00 (ISBN 0-89004-478-3). Raven.

Vanezis, P. N. Makarios: Pragmatism V. Idealism. (Illus.). 203p. 1975. 9.95 (ISBN 0-200-72207-7). Transatlantic.

Van Fossen, Richard W., ed. see Marlowe, Christopher.

VanFrassen, B. C. The Scientific Image. (Clarendon Library of Logic & Philosophy Ser.). 248p. 1980. text ed. 45.00x (ISBN 0-19-824424-X). Oxford U Pr.

Van Gelder, Patricia. Careers in the Insurance Industry. (Career Concise Guides Ser.). (Illus.). (gr. 7 up). 1978. PLB 6.45 s&l (ISBN 0-531-01421-5). Watts.

Van Gelder, R. G., jt. ed. see Mayer, William V.

Van Gelder, Richard G., jt. auth. see Bancroft, Henrietta.

Van Gemert, Lee, jt. auth. see La Dage, John H.

Vanger, Milton I. The Model Country: Jose Batlle y Ordonez of Uruguay, 1907-1915. LC 80-50489. (Illus.). 448p. (Orig.). 1980. text ed. 25.00x (ISBN 0-87451-184-4). U Pr of New Eng.

Vangermeersch, Richard. Financial Reporting Techniques in Twenty Industrial Companies Since 1861. LC 79-1238. (U of Fla. Accounting Ser.: No. 9). write for info. (ISBN 0-8130-0624-4). U Presses Fla.

Van Ghent, Dorothy. The English Novel: Form & Function. pap. 5.95x (ISBN 0-06-131050-6, TB1050, Torch). Har-Row.

Van Ghent, Dorothy & Maas, Willard, eds. The Essential Prose. LC 10-527. 1965. pap. 10.55 o.p. (ISBN 0-672-61329-8). Bobbs.

Van Gieson, Susan, jt. auth. see Kurtz, Regina.

Van Goetham, Larry. The Fifth Horseman Is Riding. LC 73-10786. 160p. 1974. 4.95 o.s.i. (ISBN 0-02-621600-0). Macmillan.

Van Gogh, Vincent. The Complete Letters of Vincent Van Gogh. LC 78-7073. (Illus.). 1978. Repr. of 1958 ed. 75.00 (ISBN 0-8212-0735-0, 152846). NYGS.

Van Gulik, Robert. The Chinese Bell Murders. LC 77-80378. 1977. pap. 3.25 (ISBN 0-226-84862-0). U of Chicago Pr.

--The Chinese Nail Murders. LC 77-80379. 1977. pap. 3.25 (ISBN 0-226-84863-9). U of Chicago Pr.

Van Gulik, Robert H. Sexual Life in Ancient China. 1974. Repr. of 1961 ed. text ed. 54.75x (ISBN 0-685-12486-X). Humanities.

Van Gundy, Arthur B. Techniques of Structured Problem Solving. 320p. 1981. text ed. 18.95 (ISBN 0-442-21223-2). Van Nos Reinhold.

Van Gytenbeek, G. P. The Way of a Trout. (Illus.). 1972. 8.95 o.p. (ISBN 0-397-00872-4). Lippincott.

Van Haaften, Julia, ed. see Frith, Francis.

Van Hall, H. Portraits of Dutch Painters & Other Artists of the Low Countries: Specime of an Iconography, Reportorium. 432p. 1963. text ed. 92.00 (ISBN 90-265-0027-0, Pub. by Swets Pub Serv Holland). Swets North Am.

Van Halsema, Thea B. This Was John Calvin. (Christian Biography Ser.). 184p. 1981. pap. 3.95 (ISBN 0-8010-9283-3). Baker Bk.

Van Harn, Roger E. Searchlight. rev. ed. 84p. 1980. pap. 1.95 (ISBN 0-933140-16-9). Bd of Pubns CRC.

Van Hasselt, Carlos, jt. auth. see Schatborn, Peter.

Van Hattum, Rolland J. Developmental Language Programming for the Retarded. new ed. 1978. text ed. 18.95 (ISBN 0-205-06452-3). Allyn.

Van Hazinga, Cynthia. Louisiana Lady. 320p. (Orig.). 1981. pap. 2.75 (ISBN 0-515-05152-7). Jove Pubns.

--White Columns. (Orig.). 1980. pap. 2.75 (ISBN 0-440-19419-9). Dell.

Van Heurck, Jan, tr. see Stieber, Wilhelm J.

Van Heurck, Jan, tr. see Von Der Grun, Max.

Van Heyningen, C., ed. see Manson, H. W.

Van Hoesen, Karl. Handbook of Conducting. rev. ed. (Eastman School of Music Ser.). (Illus.). 1950. 22.50x (ISBN 0-89197-205-6); pap. text ed. 8.95x (ISBN 0-89197-206-4). Irvington.

Van Holde, Kensal E., jt. ed. see Halvorson, Harlyn O.

Van Hook, Jay M., ed. see Ellul, Jacques, et al.

Van Hoosen, Bertha. Petticoat Surgeon. Baxter, Annette K., ed. LC 79-8820. (Signal Lives Ser.). 1980. Repr. of 1947 ed. lib. bdg. 30.00x (ISBN 0-405-12864-9). Arno.

Van Horn, Carl E. Policy Implementation in the Federal System: National Goals & Local Implementors. LC 78-19929. (Illus.). 1979. 19.95 (ISBN 0-669-02435-X). Lexington Bks.

Van Horn, Gene S. The Taxonomic Status of Pentachaeta. (U. C. Publ. in Botany: Vol. 65). 1973. pap. 7.50x (ISBN 0-520-09468-9). U of Cal Pr.

Van Horne, James C. Financial Management & Policy. 5th ed. (Illus.). 1980. text ed. 21.00 (ISBN 0-13-315820-9). P-H.

--Financial Market Rates & Flows. (Illus.). 1978. pap. text ed. 10.95 (ISBN 0-13-316190-0). P-H.

--Function & Analysis of Capital Market Rates. LC 73-99453. 1970. pap. 10.95 ref. ed. (ISBN 0-13-331934-2). P-H.

--Fundamentals of Financial Management. 4th ed. (Illus.). 1980. text ed. 21.00 (ISBN 0-13-339408-5); study guide 8.95 (ISBN 0-13-339424-7). P-H.

Van House, Charles & Hammond, Rogers. Accounting for Life Insurance Companies. 1969. text ed. 10.50 (ISBN 0-256-00570-2). Irwin.

Van Houten, Ron. How to Motivate Others Through Feedback. 1980. 3.25 (ISBN 0-89079-048-5). H & H Ent.

--How to Use Reprimands. 1980. pap. 3.25 (ISBN 0-89079-051-5). H & H Ent.

--Learning Through Feedback: A Systematic Approach for Improving Academic Performance. LC 79-19379. 182p. (Orig.). 1980. text ed. 14.95x (ISBN 0-87705-424-X); pap. text ed. 5.95x (ISBN 0-87705-440-1). Human Sci Pr.

Vanhoutte, P. M., jt. ed. see Shepherd, J. T.

Vanhoutte, P. M., ed. see Symposium on the Mechanisms of Vasodilation.

Vanhoutte, Paul M., jt. auth. see Shepherd, John T.

Vanhoutte, Paul M. & Leusen, Isadore, eds. Vasodilatation. 475p. 1981. 46.00 (ISBN 0-89004-602-6). Raven.

Vanhove, Norbert & Klaassen, Leo H. Regional Policy: A European Approach. LC 79-55648. 540p. 1980. text ed. 39.95 (ISBN 0-916672-49-2). Allanheld.

Vanier, Vean. Community & Growth. Shearer, Ann, tr. from Fr. LC 79-91602. 214p. 1979. pap. 6.95 (ISBN 0-8091-2294-4). Paulist Pr.

Van Iersel, B., jt. ed. see Murphy, R.

Van Iersel, B., jt. ed. see Schillebeeck, Edward.

Van Iersel, B., jt. ed. see Schillebeeckx, E.

Van Iersel, B., jt. ed. see Schillebeeckx, Edward.

Van Iersel, B., jt. ed. see Schillebeecky, E.

Van Iherbeek, A., ed. see International Institute of Refrigeration.

Van Impe, Jack & Campbell, Roger F. Alcohol: The Beloved Enemy. 1980. 7.95 (ISBN 0-8407-5192-3). Nelson.

Van Ingen, J. Aquarelle & Watercolor Complete. LC 78-180461. (Illus.). 80p. (YA) 1972. 12.95 o.p. (ISBN 0-8069-5210-5); PLB 11.69 o.p. (ISBN 0-8069-5211-3). Sterling.

Van Ishoven, Andre. Messerschmitt BF 109 at War. encore ed. (Illus.). 1978. 4.95 o.p. (ISBN 0-684-16367-5). Scribner.

Van Itallie, Jean-Claude. Bag Lady. 1980. pap. 1.25 (ISBN 0-686-68847-3). Dramatists Play.

Van Iterson, S. R. In the Spell of the Past. LC 74-31022. 192p. (gr. 7 up). 1975. PLB 6.96 (ISBN 0-688-32023-6). Morrow.

--The Smugglers of Buenaventura. 192p. (gr. 7 up). 1974. 6.75 o.p. (ISBN 0-688-20116-4); PLB 6.48 (ISBN 0-688-30116-9). Morrow.

--The Spirits of Chocamata. (gr. 7 up). 1977. 7.25 (ISBN 0-688-22108-4); lib. bdg. 6.96 (ISBN 0-688-32108-9). Morrow.

--Village of Outcasts. LC 74-168478. 240p. (gr. 7 up). 1972. PLB 6.96 (ISBN 0-688-31988-2). Morrow.

Vankat, John L. The Natural Vegetation of North America. LC 78-31264. 1979. pap. text ed. 13.50 (ISBN 0-471-01770-1). Wiley.

Van Katwijk, A. Accentuation in Dutch: An Experimental Linguistic Study. 188p. 1974. pap. text ed. 13.00x (ISBN 90-232-1209-6). Humanities.

Van Keuren, Dolores, jt. auth. see Siegel, Murray J.

Van Kleek, Peter E. Beverage Management & Bartending. 144p. 1981. pap. text ed. 7.95 (ISBN 0-8436-2209-1). CBI Pub.

Van Kreveld, D. Structure & Outcomes of Study Groups: A Method of Determining Several Properties of Group Structure & Some Relationships Observed with Group Outcome. (Orig.). 1970. pap. text ed. 4.75x (ISBN 90-232-0700-9). Humanities.

Van Krevelen, Alice. Summer Camp: A Guidebook for Parents. LC 80-26726. (Illus.). 168p. 1981. 11.95 (ISBN 0-88229-296-X). Nelson-Hall.

Van Kueren, Dolores, jt. auth. see Siegel, Murray J.

Vanlandingham, K. E., et al. Problems in Constitutional Law: A Symposium. LC 70-152835. (Symposia on Law & Society Ser). 1971. Repr. of 1968 ed. lib. bdg. 22.50 (ISBN 0-306-70148-0). Da Capo.

Van Landingham, S. L. Catalogue of the Fossil & Recent Genera & Species of Diatoms & Their Synonyms. Incl. Pt. 1. Acanthoceras - Bacillaria. 1967 (ISBN 3-7682-0471-5); Pt. 2. Bacteriastrum - Coscinodiscus. 1968 (ISBN 3-7682-0472-3); Pt. 3. Coscinophaena - Fibula. 1969 (ISBN 3-7682-0473-1); Pt. 4. Fragilaria - Maunema. 1971 (ISBN 3-7682-0474-X). pap. 50.00 ea. (ISBN 0-686-22227-X). Lubrecht & Cramer.

Van Langeren, Jacob see Langeren, Jacob Van.

Van Lear, Denise, ed. The Best About Backpacking. LC 74-76312. (Totebook). (Illus.). 382p. 1974. pap. 7.95 (ISBN 0-87156-099-2). Sierra.

Van Leeuwen, Jean. More Tales of Oliver Pig. LC 80-23289. (Easy-to-Read Ser.). (Illus.). 64p. (ps-3). 1981. PLB 5.99 (ISBN 0-8037-8714-6); pap. 2.50 (ISBN 0-8037-8713-8). Dial.

Van Leeuwen, Louis T., ed. see Howard, Ronald L., et al.

Van Leeuwen, Louis Th., ed. see Howard, Ronald L.

Van Leeuwenhoek, Antoni. The Collected Letters of Antoni van Leeuwenhoek, 10 vols. Incl. Vol. 1. 454p. 1939; Vol. 2. 506p. 1941 (ISBN 90-265-0041-6); Vol. 3. 560p. 1948; Vol. 4. 383p. 1952 (ISBN 90-265-0043-2); Vol. 5. 457p. 1958 (ISBN 90-265-0044-0); Vol. 6. 425p. 1961 (ISBN 90-265-0045-9); Vol. 7. 427p. 1965 (ISBN 90-265-0046-7); Vol. 8. 383p. 1967 (ISBN 90-265-0047-5); Vol. 9. 482p. 1976 (ISBN 90-265-0220-6); Vol. 10. 362p. 1979 (ISBN 90-265-0285-0). (Illus., Dutch & Eng.). text ed. 105.00 ea. (Pub. by Swets Serv Holland). Swets North Am.

Van Leuv, De John see American College of Emergency Physicians.

Van Lint, J. H. Coding Theory. 2nd rev. ed. (Lecture Notes in Mathematics: Vol. 201). viii, 136p. 1973. pap. 9.20 o.p. (ISBN 0-387-06363-3). Springer-Verlag.

Van Lint, J. H., jt. auth. see Cameron, P. J.

Vanlonkhuyzen, John H., jt. auth. see Nielsen, Kaj L.

Van-Loon, Antonia. Katherine. 320p. 1981. pap. 2.50 (ISBN 0-449-24381-8, Crest). Fawcett.

Van Loon, Bron, tr. see Lekachman, Robert.

Van Loon, Hendrik W. The Story of Mankind. rev. ed. LC 72-167290. 642p. (gr. 7 up). 1972. 11.95 (ISBN 0-87140-547-4). Liveright.

Van Loon, J. C., jt. auth. see Beamish, F. E.

Van Loon, Jon C., ed. Analytical Atomic Absorption Spectroscopy: Selected Methods. LC 79-25448. 1980. 35.00 (ISBN 0-12-714050-6). Acad Pr.

Van Luchene, Stephen R. Essays in Gothic Fiction: From Horace Walpole to Mary Shelley. Varma, Devendra P., ed. LC 79-8488. (Gothic Studies & Dissertations Ser.). 1980. lib. bdg. 25.00x (ISBN 0-405-12649-2). Arno.

Van Lustbader, Eric. Dai-San. 272p. 1981. pap. 2.50 (ISBN 0-425-04454-8). Berkley Pub.
--The Ninja. 512p. 1981. pap. 3.50 (ISBN 0-449-24367-2, Crest). Fawcett.
--Shallows of Night. 1980. pap. 2.50 (ISBN 0-425-04453-X). Berkley Pub.
--Shallows of Night. LC 77-12884. 1978. 7.95 o.p. (ISBN 0-385-12968-8). Doubleday.
--Sirens. Katz, Herbert M., ed. 504p. 1981. 12.95 (ISBN 0-87131-346-4). M Evans.
--The Sunset Warrior. 1978. pap. 1.50 (ISBN 0-515-04714-7). Jove Pubns.
--The Sunset Warrior. 1980. pap. 2.50 (ISBN 0-425-04452-1). Berkley Pub.

Van Lysebeth, Andre. Yoga Self-Taught. LC 74-181650. (Illus.). 262p. 1972. 10.95 o.p. (ISBN 0-06-014498-X, HarpT). Har-Row.

Van Maren, Jacobus W. Marquard Von Lindau: Die Zehe Gebot. (Dutch.). 1980. pap. 52.50 (ISBN 90-6203-771-2). Humanities.

Van Matre, Joseph G. & Gilbreath, Glenn H. Statistics for Business & Economics. 1980. text ed. 19.50x (ISBN 0-256-02276-3). Business Pubns.

VanMeer, Leo, ed. see VanMeer, Mary.

VanMeer, Mary. Executive's Guide to Coping with Stress, Tension & Anxiety-Producing Situations: (or, How to Take Control of Your Life) 200p. (Orig.). 1981. write for info. o.s.i. (ISBN 0-937826-01-4). VanMeer Pubns.
--See America Free. VanMeer, Leo, ed. LC 80-53384. (Illus.). 725p. (Orig.). 1981. pap. 6.95 (ISBN 0-937826-00-6). VanMeer Pubns.

Van Meerhaeghe, M. A. Economics: A Critical Approach. 516p. 1971. 19.50x (ISBN 0-8448-0042-2). Crane-Russak Co.
--International Economics. LC 72-90766. 259p. 1973. 19.50x (ISBN 0-8448-0150-X). Crane-Russak Co.
--Price Theory & Price Policy. 1969. text ed. 7.00x (ISBN 0-582-50005-2). Humanities.

Van Meerhaeghe, Marcel A. A Handbook of International Economic Institutions. 472p. 1980. lib. bdg. 76.50 (ISBN 90-247-2357-4, Pub. by Martinus Nijhoff). Kluwer Boston.

Van Meter, C. H. Principles of Police Interrogation. (Illus.). 148p. 1973. 11.75 (ISBN 0-398-02634-3). C C Thomas.

Van Meter, Marjie. Neurologic Care: A Guide for Patient Education. (Patient Education Series). 288p. pap. 9.50 (ISBN 0-8385-6706-1). ACC.

Van Mieghen, J. see Landsberg, H. E.

Van Mueller, Karl. Gold Panner's Handbook. 1981. pap. 4.00 (ISBN 0-89316-621-9); plastic bdg 6.00 (ISBN 0-686-69464-3). Exanimo Pr.

Vann, Barbara, jt. ed. see Laurie, Rona.

Vann, Sarah K. Melvil Dewey: His Enduring Presence in Librarianship. LC 77-21852. (Heritage of Librarianship Ser.: No. 4). 1978. lib. bdg. 20.00x (ISBN 0-87287-134-7). Libs Unl.
--Williamson Reports: A Study. LC 75-149992. 1971. 10.00 (ISBN 0-8108-0375-5). Scarecrow.

Van Nagell, John R., Jr. & Barber, Hugh R., eds. Modern Concepts of Gynecological Oncology. 350p. 1981. text ed. 30.00 (ISBN 0-88416-268-0). PSG Pub.

Van Name, Frederick W. & Flory, David. Elementary Physics. 2nd ed. (Illus.). 352p. 1974. ref. ed. 16.95 (ISBN 0-13-259515-X); pap. 4.95 study guide & wkbk. (ISBN 0-13-259523-0). P-H.

Van Ness, Bethann. The Bible Story Book. LC 63-9758. 1963. 11.95 (ISBN 0-8054-4402-5). Broadman.

Van Ness, John R., jt. auth. see Kutsche, Paul.

Van Ness, Peter. Revolution & Chinese Foreign Policy: Peking's Support for Wars of National Liberation. (Center for Chinese Studies UC Berkeley). 1970. 20.00x (ISBN 0-520-01583-5); pap. 6.95x (ISBN 0-520-02055-3, CAMPUS63). U of Cal Pr.

Vann Hunter, Mary. Sassafras. 288p. Date not set. pap. 2.50 (ISBN 0-523-41476-5). Pinnacle Bks.

Van Nice, Robert L. Saint Sophia in Istanbul: An Architectural Survey, Installment I. LC 65-29029. (Illus.). 1966. 80.00 o.p. (ISBN 0-88402-015-0, Ctr Byzantine). Dumbarton Oaks.

Vannicelli, Maurizio, jt. ed. see Lange, Peter.

Van Nieuwenhuijze, C., ed. Sociology of the Middle East: A Stocktaking & Interpretation. (Social, Economic & Political Studies of the Middle East: Vol. 1). (Illus.). 819p. 1971. text ed. 128.25x (ISBN 90-040-2564-2). Humanities.

Van Noord, Glenn see Hendricks, William & Noord, Glenn Van.

Van Nooten, Barend A. Mahabharata. (World Authors Ser.: India: No. 131). lib. bdg. 10.95 (ISBN 0-8057-2564-4). Twayne.

Van Norman, Richard W. Experimental Biology. 2nd ed. LC 74-105444. 1970. ref. ed. 19.95 (ISBN 0-13-294710-2). P-H.

Van Nostrand, A. D., et al. Functional Writing. LC 77-74098. (Illus.). 1977. pap. text ed. 10.95 (ISBN 0-395-25294-6); inst. guide 0.25 (ISBN 0-395-25293-8). HM.

Van Note, Gene. Catch an Angel's Wing. 76p. 1979. pap. 1.95 (ISBN 0-8341-0559-4, Beacon). Nazarene.

Vannoy, Russell. Sex Without Love: A Philosophical Exploration. LC 79-57534. 226p. 1980. text ed. 14.95 (ISBN 0-87975-128-2); pap. text ed. 7.95 (ISBN 0-87975-129-0). Prometheus Bks.

Van Nuys, Kelvin. A Holist Pilgrimage. LC 80-84738. 1981. 19.95 (ISBN 0-8022-2383-4). Philos Lib.

Vanocur, Edith. A Chicken in Every Pot. LC 75-46581. (Illus.). 176p. 1976. 6.95 o.s.i. (ISBN 0-690-00391-9, TYC-T). T Y Crowell.

Van Olphen, H. An Introduction to Clay Colloid Chemistry. 2nd ed. LC 77-400. 1977. 32.95 (ISBN 0-471-01463-X, Pub. by Wiley-Interscience). Wiley.

Van Olphen, H. & Fripiat, J. J., eds. Data Handbook for Clay Materials & Other Non-Metallic Minerals. (Illus.). 1979. text ed. 76.00 (ISBN 0-08-022850-X). Pergamon.

Van Orden, Phyllis & Phillips, Edith B., eds. Background Readings in Building Library Collections. 2nd ed. LC 78-31263. 1979. 13.50 (ISBN 0-8108-1200-2). Scarecrow.

Van Orman, H. A. Estimating for Residential Construction. LC 76-14083. 1978. pap. text ed. 12.00 (ISBN 0-8273-1605-4); instructor's guide 1.60 (ISBN 0-8273-1606-2). Delmar.

Van Oudenhoven, Nico J. Common Afghan Street Games. 78p. 1980. pap. 16.50 (ISBN 90-265-0293-1, Pub. by Swets Pub Serv Holland). Swets North Am.

Van Over, Raymond & Oteri, Laura, eds. William McDougall, Explorer of the Mind: Studies in Psychical Research. LC 67-23366. 1967. 8.50 o.p. (ISBN 0-912326-20-4). Garrett-Helix.

Van Oystaeyen, F., ed. Ring Theory, Antwerp Nineteen-Eighty: Prooceedings. (Lecture Notes in Mathematics Ser.: Vol. 825). 209p. 1981. pap. 14.00 (ISBN 0-387-10246-9). Springer-Verlag.

Van Parijs, Philippe. Evolutionary Explanation in the Social Sciences: An Emerging Paradigm. (Philosophy & Society Ser.). 1981. 25.00x (ISBN 0-8476-6288-8). Rowman.

Van Patter, Douglas M., jt. ed. see Marion, Jerry B.

Van Peebles, Melvin. Just an Old Sweet Song. 1976. pap. 1.50 (ISBN 0-345-28114-4). Ballantine.

Van Pelt, Ethel. Nest of the Kildeer. (YA) 1976. 5.95 (ISBN 0-685-68911-5, Avalon). Bouregy.
--Silver Threads to Love. 192p. (YA) 1976. 5.95 (ISBN 0-685-62628-8, Avalon). Bouregy.

Van Pelt, Nancy. The Compleat Parent. LC 79-9946. (Orion Ser.). 160p. 1976. pap. 2.95 (ISBN 0-8127-0229-8). Southern Pub.
--The Complete Marriage. LC 78-20770. (Orion Ser). 1979. pap. 2.95 (ISBN 0-8127-0218-2). Southern Pub.

Van Pelt Wilson, Helen see Wilson, Helen Van Pelt.

Van Peski, Adrian M. Outreach of Diakonia. (Orig.). 1968. pap. text ed. 11.50x (ISBN 0-685-12466-5). Humanities.

Van Poolen, H. K., et al. Fundamentals of Enhanced Oil Recovery. 176p. 1980. 30.00 (ISBN 0-87814-144-8). Pennwell Pub.

Van Praag. Handbook of Biological Psychiatry, Vol. 3. 400p. 1980. 29.50 (ISBN 0-8247-6965-1). Dekker.

Van Praag, et al. Handbook of Biological Psychiatry, Pt. 2. (Experimental & Clinical Psychology Ser.: Vol. 1). 544p. 1980. 46.50 (ISBN 0-8247-6892-2). Dekker.

Van Praagh, G. Chemistry by Discovery. (gr. 8-12). 5.95 (ISBN 0-7195-1439-8). Transatlantic.

Van Rensselaer, Alexander. Fun with Magic. LC 57-9854. (gr. 3-9). 1956. 4.95 o.p. (ISBN 0-385-02428-2). Doubleday.

Van Rensselaer, Mrs. John K. Prophetical, Educational & Playing Cards. LC 77-78249. (Illus.). 1971. Repr. of 1912 ed. 20.00 (ISBN 0-8103-3867-X). Gale.

Van Rensselaer, Mariana G. Book of American Figure Painters. Weinberg, H. Barbara, ed. LC 75-28875. (Art Experience in Late 19th Century America Ser.: Vol. 11). (Illus.). 1976. Repr. of 1886 ed. lib. bdg. 72.50 (ISBN 0-8240-2235-1). Garland Pub.

Van Rensselaer, Phillip. That Vanderbilt Woman. LC 80-83007. 320p. 1980. pap. 2.75 (ISBN 0-87216-787-9). Playboy Pbks.

Van Rijn, Rembrandt. Rembrandt: The Etchings. LC 77-87012. (Illus.). 1977. 29.95 (ISBN 0-8467-0411-0, Pub. by Two Continents); pap. 13.95 (ISBN 0-8467-0414-5). Hippocrene Bks.

Van Riper, Charles. A Career in Speech Pathology. LC 78-9678. 1979. pap. 7.95 ref. (ISBN 0-13-114769-2). P-H.
--Speech Corrections: Principles & Methods. 6th ed. (Illus.). 1978. ref. 19.95 (ISBN 0-13-829523-9). P-H.

Van Rjndt, Phillipe. Blueprint. 1979. Repr. of 1977 ed. pap. 2.25 o.p. (ISBN 0-425-03876-9). Berkley Pub.

Van Roden, Albert. You're Hired! (Illus.). 64p. 1981. pap. 2.95 (ISBN 0-89709-025-X). Liberty Pub.

VanRoekel, Byron, jt. auth. see Evertts, Eldonna.

VanRoekel, Byron, jt. auth. see Greenlaw, Jean.

Van Roosenbeek, Earl & Delclos, Luis. The Radioactive Patient. 1975. spiral bdg. 12.00 o.p. (ISBN 0-87488-966-9). Med Exam.

Van Rooten, Luis. Mots D'Heures: Gousses, Rames. LC 67-21230. 1967. 8.95 (ISBN 0-670-49064-4, Grossman). Viking Pr.

Van Royan, P. Alpine Flora of New Giunea, 4 vols. Incl. Vol. 1. General Part. 1980. lib. bdg. 50.00; Vol. 2. Taxonomic Part II: Cupressaceae to Poaceae. 1980. lib. bdg. 150.00 (ISBN 3-7682-1244-0); Vol. 3. Taxonomic Part 2: Winteraceae to Polygonaceae. 1981. lib. bdg. 100.00 (ISBN 3-7682-1245-9); Vol. 4. Taxonomic Part 3: Fagaceae to Asteraceae. 1981. lib. bdg. 100.00 (ISBN 3-7682-1246-7). 400.00 set (ISBN 3-7682-1247-5). Lubrecht & Cramer.

Van Ryn, August. John: Meditations. 1949. 3.00 (ISBN 0-87213-887-9). Loizeaux.
--Mark: Meditations. 1957. pap. 2.25 (ISBN 0-87213-892-5). Loizeaux.

Van Ryzin, Lani. Cutting a Record in Nashville, No. 3. (Hi Lo Ser.). 96p. (YA) (gr. 6 up). 1981. pap. 1.50 (ISBN 0-553-14620-3). Bantam.
--Disco. (Concise Guides). (Illus.). (gr. 6 up). 1979. PLB 6.45 s&l (ISBN 0-531-02891-7). Watts.
--A Patch of Earth. (Illus.). 64p. (gr. 3-5). 1981. PLB 6.97 (ISBN 0-686-69298-5). Messner.
--Sidewalk Games. LC 77-28327. (Games & Activities Ser.). (Illus.). (gr. k-3). 1978. PLB 9.30 (ISBN 0-8172-1166-7). Raintree Pubs.
--Starting Your Own Band: Rock, Disco, Folk, Jazz, Country & Western. (Illus.). 64p. (gr. 7 up). 1980. 6.95 (ISBN 0-8027-6391-X); PLB 7.85 (ISBN 0-8027-6392-8). Walker & Co.

Vansant, Carl. Strategic Energy Supply & National Security. LC 78-139882. (Special Studies in International Politics & Government). 1971. 28.00x (ISBN 0-89197-951-4); pap. text ed. 12.95x (ISBN 0-89197-952-2). Irvington.

Van Santvoord, George, ed. see Harris, Joel C.

Van Schaack, M. Without Words: An Introduction to Nonverbal Communication. 1977. 550.00 (ISBN 0-13-961417-6). P-H.

Van Schendelen, M. P., jt. auth. see Herman, V.

Van Schooneveld, C. H., ed. see Armstrong, D., et al.

Van Scott, Timothy & Weiss, Sidney J. Self-Assessment of Current Knowledge in Ophthalmology. 1977. spiral bdg. 16.50 (ISBN 0-87488-255-9). Med Exam.

Van Scotter, Richard D., et al. Foundations of Education: Social Perspective. (Illus.). 1979. text ed. 16.95 (ISBN 0-13-329268-1). P-H.

Van Scyoc, Sydney J. Cloudcry. LC 76-49828. 1977. 7.95 o.p. (ISBN 0-399-11947-7, Pub. by Berkley). Berkley Pub.

Van Sickle, John V. Freedom in Jeopardy: The Tyranny of Idealism. LC 68-54126. (Principles of Freedom Ser.). 204p. 1969. 9.95 (ISBN 0-89617-045-4). Inst Humane.

Van Sickle, Sylvia. First Reference Library, 50 bks, Bks. 1-25. Incl. Rivers & River Life (ISBN 0-356-03790-8); Snakes & Lizards. o.p. (ISBN 0-356-03791-6); Roads & Highways (ISBN 0-356-03792-4); Ports & Harbors (ISBN 0-356-04027-5); Bridges & Tunnels (ISBN 0-356-04028-3); Towns & Cities (ISBN 0-356-04029-1); Horses & Ponies (ISBN 0-356-04030-5); Airplanes & Balloons (ISBN 0-356-04031-3); The Story of Cars. o.p. (ISBN 0-356-04032-1); Mountains (ISBN 0-356-04099-2); Electricity (ISBN 0-356-04100-X); Television (ISBN 0-356-04101-8); Photography (ISBN 0-356-04102-6); The Jungle (ISBN 0-356-04275-8); The Dog Family (ISBN 0-356-04276-6); Gypsies & Nomads. o.p. (ISBN 0-356-04277-4); Ballet & Dance (ISBN 0-356-04278-2); Paper & Printing. o.p. (ISBN 0-356-04279-0); Food & Drink (ISBN 0-356-04280-4); Cloth & Weaving (ISBN 0-356-04281-2); Lakes & Dams (ISBN 0-356-04282-0); Building (ISBN 0-356-04283-9); Butterflies & Moths (ISBN 0-356-04284-7); Vanishing Animals (ISBN 0-356-04614-1); Animals That Burrow **(ISBN 0-356-04615-X). (Illus., Minimum order: 20 books). (gr. 1-4). 1976. PLB 7.30 ea. Raintree Child.**
--First Reference Library, Bks. 26-50. Incl. Spiders (ISBN 0-356-03669-3); Pirates & Buccaneers (ISBN 0-356-03670-7); Size (ISBN 0-356-03671-5); Fire (ISBN 0-356-03672-3); Weather (ISBN 0-356-03673-1); Deserts (ISBN 0-356-03674-X); Skyscrapers (ISBN 0-356-03675-8); Monkeys & Apes (ISBN 0-356-03676-6); Trains & Railroads (ISBN 0-356-03677-4); Trees & Woods (ISBN 0-356-03678-2); Cowboys (ISBN 0-356-03783-5); Time & Clocks (ISBN 0-356-03784-3); Light & Color (ISBN 0-356-03785-1); Birds & Migration (ISBN 0-356-03786-X); The Universe (ISBN 0-356-03787-8); Farms & Farmers. o.p. (ISBN 0-356-03788-6); Rocks & Mining. o.p. (ISBN 0-356-03789-4); Fuel & Energy (ISBN 0-356-04616-8); Animals with Shells (ISBN 0-356-04617-6); The Theater (ISBN 0-356-04618-4); Health & Disease (ISBN 0-356-04619-2); Pollution (ISBN 0-356-04620-6); The Movies. o.p.; Signals & Messages (ISBN 0-356-04622-2); Fishing. o.p. (ISBN 0-356-04623-0). (Illus., Minimum order: 20 bks.). (gr. 1-4). 1976. PLB 7.30 ea. Raintree Child.

Van Siclen, Charles C., III, ed. see Habachi, Labib.

Vansina, Jan. The Children of Woot: A History of the Kuba Peoples. LC 77-91061. (Illus.). 1978. 30.00 (ISBN 0-299-07490-0). U of Wis Pr.

--Kingdoms of the Savanna. (Illus.). 1966. pap. 8.95x (ISBN 0-299-03664-2). U of Wis Pr.

Vanski, Jean & Ozanne, Larry. Simulating the Housing Allowance Program in Green Bay & South Bend: A Comparison of the Urban Institute Housing Model with the Supply Experiment. (An Institute Paper). 93p. 1978. pap. 6.50 (ISBN 0-87766-236-3, 23800). Urban Inst.

Van Slyke, Helen. The Heart Listens. 576p. 1975. pap. 2.75 (ISBN 0-445-08520-7). Popular Lib.

--No Love Lost. 416p. 1981. pap. 2.95 (ISBN 0-553-14512-6). Bantam.

Van Slyke, L. L. & Price, W. V. Cheese. (Illus.). 522p. 1980. 35.00 (ISBN 0-917930-21-5); lib. bdg. 28.00 (ISBN 0-917930-31-2); pap. 18.00 (ISBN 0-917930-51-7); pap. text ed. 14.00x (ISBN 0-917930-11-8). Ridgeview.

Van Soelen, Philip. A Cricket in the Grass. LC 79-4108. (Sierra Club-Scribner's Juvenile Ser.). (Illus.). 128p. 1979. 9.95 (ISBN 0-684-16110-9). Scribner.

Van Son, Allene. Diabetes: A Guide for Patient Education. 288p. 1981. pap. 9.50 (ISBN 0-8385-1596-7). ACC.

Van Spiva, Ulysses. How to Get a Grant for Your Own Special Project. 1980. 7.75. TIS Inc.

Van Steenwyk, C. Illustrated Skating Dictionary for Young People. (Illus.). 1979. pap. 2.50 (ISBN 0-13-451260-X). P-H.

Vansteenwyk, E. Illustrated Horseback Riding Dictionary for Young People. 1980. pap. 2.50 (ISBN 0-13-450908-0). P-H.

Van Steenwyk, Elizabeth. Illustrated Riding Dictionary for Young People. LC 80-81789. (Illustrated Dictionaries). (Illus.). 128p. (gr. 5 up). 1981. PLB 6.89 (ISBN 0-8178-0015-8). Harvey.

--Illustrated Skating for Young People. LC 79-53149. (Illustrated Dictionaries Ser.). (Illus.). 128p. (gr. 4 up). 1969. PLB 6.79 (ISBN 0-8178-6285-4). Harvey.

--Quarter Horse Winner. Fay, Ann, ed. LC 79-28490. (A Springboard Bk.). (Illus.). 64p. (gr. 3-7). 1980. 5.75g (ISBN 0-8075-6707-8). A Whitman.

--Rivals on Ice. Pacini, Kathy, ed. LC 78-31102. (Springboard Bk.). (Illus.). 64p. (gr. 3-7). 1979. 5.75g (ISBN 0-8075-7071-0). A Whitman.

--Stars on Ice. LC 80-1012. (Illus.). (gr. 5 up). 1980. 6.95 (ISBN 0-396-07887-7). Dodd.

Van Stockum, Hilda, tr. see Broger, Achim.

Van Stone, James W. Athapaskan Adaptations: Hunters & Fishermen of the Subarctic Forests. LC 73-89518. (Worlds of Man Ser.). 176p. 1974. text ed. 11.00x (ISBN 0-88295-610-8); pap. text ed. 5.75x (ISBN 0-88295-611-6). AHM Pub.

Vanstone, W. H. The Risk of Love. 1978. 8.95 (ISBN 0-19-520053-5). Oxford U Pr.

Vanstory, Burnette. Georgia's Land of the Golden Isles. LC 80-28565. (Illus.). 225p. 1981. 15.00 (ISBN 0-8203-0557-X); pap. 8.95 (ISBN 0-8203-0558-8). U of Ga Pr.

Van Straaten, J. F. Thermal Performance of Buildings. (Illus.). 1967. text ed. 48.50x (ISBN 0-444-20011-8, Pub. by Applied Science). Burgess-Intl Ideas.

Van Syckle, Edwin. They Tried to Cut It All; Grays Harbor: Turbulent Years of Greed & Greatness. LC 80-16469. (Illus.). 308p. 1980. 17.95 (ISBN 0-9605152-0-8); pap. 9.95 (ISBN 0-9605152-1-6). Friends Aberdeen.

Van Tamelen, E. E., ed. Bioorganic Chemistry, 2 vols. Incl. Vol. 1. Enzyme Action. 1977. 49.75 (ISBN 0-12-714301-7); Vol. 2. 1978. 52.50, by subscription 83.00 (ISBN 0-12-714302-5). Acad Pr.

Van Tassel, David D., ed. Aging, Death, & the Completion of Being. LC 78-65111. (Illus.). 1979. 22.00 (ISBN 0-8122-7757-0); pap. 11.95x (ISBN 0-8122-1102-2). U of Pa Pr.

Van Tassel, Dennie. Basic-Pack Statistics Programs. (Ser. in Personal Computing). (Illus.). 240p. 1981. pap. text ed. 16.95 (ISBN 0-13-066381-6). P-H.

VanTassel, Dennie L. Introductory Cobol. 1979. pap. text ed. 14.95 (ISBN 0-8162-9133-0). Holden-Day.

Van Tassel, Dennis. The Compleat Computer. LC 75-31760. (Illus.). 250p. 1976. pap. text ed. 8.95 (ISBN 0-574-21060-1, 13-4060). SRA.

--Program Style, Design, Efficiency, Debugging & Testing. 2nd ed. (Illus.). 1978. ref. ed. 18.95 (ISBN 0-13-729947-8). P-H.

Van Tassel, Katrina. Trundlewheel. (Lamont Hall Chapbook Ser. for Poetry). 16p. (Orig.). 1981. 1.25 (ISBN 0-9603840-1-4). Andrew Mtn Pr.

Van Thal, Herbert, ed. see Arlen, Michael.

Van Thal, Herbert, ed. see Broughton, Rhoda.

Van Thal, Herbert, ed. see Merriman, Henry S.

Van Tieghem, Philippe. Dictionnaire de Victor Hugo. (Dictionnaires de l'homme du vingtieme siecle). (Orig., Fr). 1970. pap. 8.50 (ISBN 0-685-13864-X, 3722). Larousse.

Van Til, Cornelius. Christian Theistic Ethics. syllabus 4.50 (ISBN 0-87552-478-8). Presby & Reformed.

Van Til, William. Curriculum: Quest for Relevance. 2nd ed. LC 79-144319. 400p. 1974. pap. text ed. 12.95 (ISBN 0-395-17787-1, 3-57530). HM.

--Education: A Beginning. 2nd ed. 624p. 1974. text ed. 18.50 (ISBN 0-395-17576-3); instructors' manual 1.50 (ISBN 0-395-17850-9). HM.

--Secondary Education: School & Community. LC 77-76861. (Illus.). 1978. text ed. 16.75 (ISBN 0-395-25751-4); inst. manual 0.50 (ISBN 0-395-25764-6). HM.

Van Til, William, et al. Modern Education for the Junior High School Years. rev. ed. LC 66-26209. 1967. text ed. 13.50 (ISBN 0-672-60640-2). Bobbs.

Van Toen, Donna. Astrologer's Note Book. 128p. 1981. pap. 6.95 (ISBN 0-87728-521-7). Weiser.

Van Trees, H. L., ed. Satellite Communications. LC 78-65704. 1979. 42.95 (ISBN 0-87942-121-5). Inst Electrical.

Van Tuyl, Barbara. Sunbonnet: Filly of the Year. (RL 5). 1973. pap. 1.25 (ISBN 0-451-08152-8, Y8152, Sig). NAL.

Van Tuyl, Tina. Makers of British Canada. 1978. 1.95 (ISBN 0-87463-338-9). Chr Sch Intl.

Van Tyne, Claude H. Causes of the War of Independence. 8.50 (ISBN 0-8446-1459-9). Peter Smith.

Van Uchelen, Rod. Word Processing: A Guide to Typography, Taste & in-House Graphics. 128p. 1980. 14.95 (ISBN 0-442-28647-3); pap. 7.95 (ISBN 0-442-28646-5). Van Nos Reinhold.

Van Uden, A. A World of Language for Deaf Children: Basic Principles, a Maternal Reflective Method, Pt. 1. 3rd ed. (Modern Approaches to the Diagnosis & Instruction of Multi-Handicapped Children: Vol. 4). 348p. 1977. text ed. 36.00 (ISBN 90-265-0253-2, Pub. by Swets Pub Serv Holland). Swets North Am.

Van Vactor, Lloyd, jt. auth. see Washburn, Lindy.

Van Valkenburg, M. E. Introduction to Modern Network Synthesis. LC 60-10328. 1960. 30.95 (ISBN 0-471-89991-7). Wiley.

--Network Analysis. 3rd ed. (Illus.). 699p. 1974. 27.95 (ISBN 0-13-611095-9). P-H.

Van Valkenburg, M. E., jt. auth. see Cruz, Jose B.

Van Valkenburgh, et al. Basic Electricity, 5 Vols. rev. ed. (Illus.). 1978. combined ed. 25.15 (ISBN 0-8104-0881-3); Set. pap. 29.25 (ISBN 0-8104-0875-9); pap. 5.85 ea.; Vol. 1, Rev. Ed. pap. (ISBN 0-8104-0876-7); Vol. 2, Rev. Ed. pap. (ISBN 0-8104-0877-5); Vol. 3, Rev. Ed. pap. (ISBN 0-8104-0878-3). Vol. 5, rev. pap. (ISBN 0-8104-0880-5). Hayden.

Van Veen, J. H. Eppens see Eppens-Van Veen, J. H.

Van Veen, Ted. Rhododendrons in America. 2nd ed. LC 77-104390. (Illus.). 1980. pap. 25.00 (ISBN 0-8323-0374-7). Binford.

Van Velsen, J. The Politics of Kinship: A Study in Social Manipulation Among the Lakeside Tonga of Malawi. (Institute for African Studies). (Illus.). 338p. 1964. pap. text ed. 13.75x (ISBN 0-7190-1036-5). Humanities.

Van Vlack, Lawrence H. Materials Science for Engineers. LC 74-91151. (Metallurgy & Materials Ser). 1970. text ed. 24.95 (ISBN 0-201-08074-5). A-W.

--Physical Ceramics for Engineers. (Illus.). 1964. 22.95 (ISBN 0-201-08068-0). A-W.

--A Textbook of Materials Technology. LC 70-190614. 1973. text ed. 20.95 (ISBN 0-201-08066-4); instructor's manual 3.95 (ISBN 0-201-08067-2). A-W.

Van Vleck, John H. Theory of Electric & Magnetic Susceptibilities. (International Series of Monographs on Physics). (Illus.). 1932. pap. 29.95x (ISBN 0-19-851243-0). Oxford U Pr.

Van Vleck, L. Dale, jt. auth. see Schmidt, Glen H.

Van Vleck, William C. The Administrative Control of Aliens. LC 70-148084. (Civil Liberties in American History Ser.). Repr. of 1932 ed. lib. bdg. 29.50 (ISBN 0-306-70126-X). Da Capo.

Van Vogt, A. E. Away & Beyond. 1977. pap. 1.75 o.s.i. (ISBN 0-515-04426-1). Jove Pubns.

--The House That Stood Still. 1980. pap. write for info. (ISBN 0-671-80546-0). PB.

--The Mind Cage. 1981. pap. 2.25 (ISBN 0-671-42424-6). PB.

--Mission to the Stars. 1980. pap. write for info. (ISBN 0-671-83661-7). PB.

Van Voorhees, F. L. The Michigan Property Tax: A Crumbling Cornerstone. 35p. 1972. 2.00 (ISBN 0-932826-07-5). New Issues MI.

--Taxes 1985: Prospects for Tax Reform in the United States. 1976. 5.00 (ISBN 0-932826-12-1). New Issues MI.

Van Voorhis, Stanley N., ed. Microwave Receivers. (Illus.). 1948. pap. text ed. 5.00 (ISBN 0-486-61561-8). Dover.

Van Voorst, Dick. Corrugated Carton Crafting. LC 71-90803. (Little Craft Book Ser). (Illus.). (gr. 5 up). 1969. 5.95 (ISBN 0-8069-5138-9); PLB 6.69 (ISBN 0-8069-5139-7). Sterling.

Van Voorthuijsen, A. M. World Collectors Annuary, 31 vols. write for info. vols. 1-30, 1943-78; Vol. 30. vol. 31, 1979 100.00 (ISBN 0-685-52513-9). Heinman.

Van Voorthuisen, A. E., ed. Textbook of Radiodiagnosis. (Illus.). 486p. 1980. text ed. 67.50x (ISBN 0-19-261144-5). Oxford U Pr.

Van Voris, Jacqueline. Constance de Markievicz: In the Cause of Ireland. LC 67-11245. (Illus.). 1967. 15.00x (ISBN 0-87023-025-5); pap. 6.00 (ISBN 0-87023-058-1). U of Mass Pr.

Van Wade, David & Van Wade, Sarah. Second Chance. LC 75-20899. 1975. 5.95 (ISBN 0-88270-137-1); pap. 4.95 (ISBN 0-88270-138-X). Logos.

Van Wade, Sarah, jt. auth. see Van Wade, David.

Van Wagoner, Merrill Y. Spoken Arabic (Iraqi) LC 75-11338. (Spoken Language Ser.). (Prog. Bk.). 1975. pap. 10.00x (ISBN 0-87950-010-7); records 6 12-inch lP 50.00x (ISBN 0-87950-014-X); records with course-bk. 55.00x (ISBN 0-87950-015-8); cassettes 60.00x (ISBN 0-87950-016-6); cassettes with course-bk. 65.00x (ISBN 0-87950-017-4). Spoken Lang Serv.

Van Wagoner, Merrill Y., et al. English-Arabic Vocabulary: Students Pronouncing Dictionary. LC 80-81198. 452p. (Orig.). 1980. pap. text ed. 10.00x (ISBN 0-87950-028-X). Spoken Lang Serv.

--Spoken Arabic (Saudi) LC 76-17389. (Spoken Language Ser.). (Prog. Bk.). 1979. pap. 8.00x (ISBN 0-87950-410-2); cassettes 5 dual track 60.00 (ISBN 0-87950-411-0); cassettes with course-bk 65.00x (ISBN 0-87950-412-9). Spoken Lang Serv.

Van Walleghen, Michael see Walleghen, Michael Van.

Van Way, Charles W. & Buerk, Charles A. Surgical Skills in Patient Care. LC 78-4198. 1978. pap. text ed. 15.95 (ISBN 0-8016-5214-6). Mosby.

Van Welzen, J. Two Hundred Darkroom Tips: Color. 1978. pap. 5.00 o.p. (ISBN 0-85242-574-0, Pub. by Fountain). Morgan.

Van Wert, William. The Film Career of Alain Robbe-Grillet. Gottesman, Ronald, ed. (Three Directors Set). 1979. pap. 7.80 (ISBN 0-913178-58-6). Redgrave Pub Co.

Van Wert, William F. The Film Career of Alain Robbe-Grillet. (Orig.). 1979. pap. 7.80 (ISBN 0-913178-59-4, Pub. by Two Continents). Hippocrene Bks.

Van Wezel, A. L., jt. ed. see Hennessen, W.

Van Willigen, John. Anthropology in Use: The Bibliographic Chronology of the Development of Applied Anthropology. (Orig.). 1980. pap. 8.90 (ISBN 0-913178-66-7). Redgrave Pub Co.

Van Willigen, John, jt. ed. see Abbott, Susan.

Van Wimersma Greidanus, T. B. & Rees, L. H., eds. ACTH & LPH in Health & Disease. (Frontiers of Hormone Research Ser.: Vol. 8). (Illus.). 200p. 1981. 60.00 (ISBN 3-8055-1977-X). S Karger.

Van Winkle, jt. auth. see Heyne.

Van Winkle, Ted. Fred Boynton: Lobsterman, New Harbor Maine. LC 74-29368. (Illus.). 80p. 1975. 12.50 (ISBN 0-87742-050-5). Intl Marine.

Van Witsen, Betty. Perceptual Training Activities. rev ed. LC 79-17371. 1979. pap. 7.95x (ISBN 0-8077-2568-4). Tchrs Coll.

Van Woerden, Hugo, et al, eds. Oort & the Universe. 210p. 1980. PLB 29.00 (ISBN 0-686-28847-5, Pub. by D. Reidel); pap. 12.95 (ISBN 90-277-1209-3). Kluwer Boston.

Van Woerkom, Dorothy O. Abu Ali: Three Tales of the Middle East. LC 76-8401. (Ready to Read Ser.). (Illus.). (gr. 1-4). 1976. 7.95 (ISBN 0-02-791310-4, 79131). Macmillan.

--Donkey Ysabel. LC 78-5140. (Ready-to-Read Ser.). (Illus.). (gr. 1-4). 1978. 7.95 (ISBN 0-02-791280-9, 79128). Macmillan.

--The Friends of ABU ALI: Three More Tales of the Middle East. LC 77-12624. (Ready-to-Read Ser.). (Illus.). (gr. 1-4). 1978. 8.95 (ISBN 0-02-791320-1, 79132). Macmillan.

--Harry & Shellburt. LC 77-5352. (Ready-to-Read Ser.). (Illus.). (gr. 1-4). 1977. 7.95 (ISBN 0-02-791290-6, 79129). Macmillan.

--Sea Frog, City Frog. (Illus.). 48p. (gr. 1-4). 1975. 7.95 (ISBN 0-02-791300-7, 79130). Macmillan.

Van Wormer, Joe. World of the American Elk. LC 77-86080. (Illus.). 1969. 8.95 (ISBN 0-397-00621-7). Lippincott.

Van Wyck Mason, F. Blue Hurricane. pap. 1.95 o.p. (ISBN 0-425-03182-9). Berkley Pub.

--Rivers of Glory. pap. 1.95 o.p. (ISBN 0-425-03177-2). Berkley Pub.

--Trumpets Sound No More. pap. 1.95 o.p. (ISBN 0-425-03171-3). Berkley Pub.

Van Wylen, G. J. Fundamentals of Classical Thermodynamics: SI Version. (Series in Thermal & Transport Sciences). 1980. 13.95 (ISBN 0-471-04505-5). Wiley.

Van Wylen, G. J., jt. auth. see Sonntag, R. E.

Van Wylen, Gordon. Thermodynamics. LC 59-9356. (Illus.). 1959. text ed. 25.95x (ISBN 0-471-90222-5). Wiley.

Van Wylen, Gordon J. & Sonntag, Richard E. Fundamentals of Classical Thermodynamics: SI Version. 2nd rev. ed. LC 76-2405. 1976. text ed. 23.95 (ISBN 0-471-04188-2); solutions manual 9.00 (ISBN 0-471-04519-5); Arabic Translation avail. (ISBN 0-471-04505-5). Wiley.

Vany, Arthur S. de see De Vany, Arthur S., et al.

Van Zandt, Harold. International Business Prospects: Nineteen Seventy-Seven to Nineteen Ninety-Nine. LC 78-15745. (Key Issues Lecture Ser). 1978. 8.50 (ISBN 0-672-97221-2); pap. 5.50 (ISBN 0-672-97220-4). Bobbs.

Van Zandt, Joseph H., jt. auth. see Williams, W. P.

Van Zandt, Townes. For the Sake of the Song. 7.50 (ISBN 0-930324-04-8). Green Hill.

--For the Sake of the Song. LC 77-20732. (Illus.). 1977. 7.50 (ISBN 0-930324-04-8); pap. 5.00 (ISBN 0-930324-05-6). Wings Pr.

Van Zant, Nancy, ed. Personnel Policies in Libraries. LC 80-11734. 350p. 1980. 19.95 (ISBN 0-918212-26-X). Neal-Schuman.

Van Zant, William. Seven Epistles of Love. 1981. 5.95 (ISBN 0-8062-1719-7). Carlton.

Van Zanten, David. Architectural Polychromy of the Eighteen Thirty's. LC 76-23648. (Outstanding Dissertations in the Fine Arts - 2nd Ser. - Nineteenth Century). (Illus.). 1977. Repr. of 1970 ed. lib. bdg. 63.00 (ISBN 0-8240-2733-7). Garland Pub.

Van Zanten, David, ed. see Egbert, Donald D.

Van Zeggeren, F. & Storey, S. H. Computation of Chemical Equilibria. LC 78-92255. (Illus.). 1970. 35.50 (ISBN 0-521-07630-7). Cambridge U Pr.

Van Zeller, Hubert. Book of Private Prayer. 1973. pap. 3.95 (ISBN 0-87243-045-6). Templegate.

--Choice of God. 1973. pap. 3.95 (ISBN 0-87243-047-2). Templegate.

--Current of Spirituality. pap. 3.95 (ISBN 0-87243-048-0). Templegate.

--Ideas for Prayer. 1973. pap. 3.95 (ISBN 0-87243-046-4). Templegate.

Van Zijl, J. B. A Concordance to the Targum of Isaiah. LC 78-25832. (Society of Biblical Literature. Aramaic Studies: No. 3). 1979. pap. 9.00 (ISBN 0-89130-273-5, 061303). Scholars Pr Ca.

Van Zile, Judy A. Dance in India: An Annotated Guide to Source Materials. rev. ed. LC 73-90410. (A (Bibliographies), No. 3). xi, 129p. 1973. pap. text ed. 7.50x (ISBN 0-913360-06-6). Asian Music Pub.

Van Zoost, Brenda L., ed. Psychological Readings for the Dental Profession. LC 75-15892. 180p. 1975. 17.95 (ISBN 0-88229-244-7). Nelson-Hall.

Van Zuylen, Guirne. Eating with Wine. (Illus.). 1972. 8.95 (ISBN 0-571-09958-0). Transatlantic.

Van Zweden, J. God's Sovereignty in the Lives of Twin Brothers. pap. 1.95. Reiner.

Van Zwienen, John. Pivot. 1980. 2.25 (ISBN 0-515-05639-1). Jove Pubns.

Vaporis, Nomikos M., ed. see Poulos, George.

Vapp, Malcolm. The Enlightenment. Killingray, Margaret, et al, eds. (Greenhaven World History Ser.). (Illus.). 32p. (gr. 10). 1980. lib. bdg. 5.95 (ISBN 0-89908-225-4); pap. text ed. 1.95 (ISBN 0-89908-200-9). Greenhaven.

Vaquez, H. & Bordet, E. The Heart & the Aorta. 1920. 49.50x (ISBN 0-685-69879-3). Elliots Bks.

Vara, Albert C. Food & Beverage Industries: A Bibliography & Guidebook. LC 70-102058. (Management Information Guide Ser.: No. 16). 1970. 30.00 (ISBN 0-8103-0816-9). Gale.

Varadachari, V. K. Governor in the Indian Constitution. 1980. 13.00x (ISBN 0-8364-0658-3, Pub. by Heritage India). South Asia Bks.

Varadan, V. K., ed. see International Symposium on Recent Developments in Classical Wave Scattering, Ohio State Univ., Columbus, 1979.

Varadan, V. V., ed. see International Symposium on Recent Developments in Classical Wave Scattering, Ohio State Univ., Columbus, 1979.

Varadarajian, V. S. Lie Groups, Lie Algebras, & Their Representations. (Modern Analysis Ser.). 496p. 1974. ref. ed. 26.95 (ISBN 0-13-535732-2). P-H.

Varadhan, S. R. S. Diffusion Problems & Partial Differential Equations. (Tate Institute Lectures on Mathematics Ser.). 315p. 1981. pap. 10.70 (ISBN 0-387-08773-7). Springer-Verlag.

Varadharajan, B., jt. auth. see Amarchand, D.

Varady, Tibor. Secret of the Mouse Gray Room. Duff, Alan, tr. 1981. pap. 4.95 (ISBN 0-7145-3843-4). Riverrun NY.
Varady, Tibor, et al. New Writing & Writers Eighteen. 1980. pap. 6.00 (ISBN 0-7145-3815-9). Riverrun NY.
Varberg, Dale, jt. auth. see Fleming, Walter.
Varberg, Dale E., jt. auth. see Fleming, Walter.
Varble, Dale. Cases in Marketing Management. (Business Ser.). 272p. 1976. pap. text ed. 12.50 (ISBN 0-675-08638-8); instructor's manual 3.95 (ISBN 0-686-67246-1). Merrill.
Varcop, L., jt. auth. see Dolezal, R.
Vardaman, G. T. & Vardaman, P. B. Successful Writing: A Short Course for Professionals. 1977. 39.95 (ISBN 0-471-02428-7). Wiley.
Vardaman, George T. & Vardaman, Patricia B. Communication in Modern Organizations. LC 72-7391. (Management & Administration Ser.). 516p. 1973. text ed. 21.95x (ISBN 0-471-90300-0); instr's manual o.p. (ISBN 0-471-90301-9); (ISBN 0-685-27917-0). Wiley.
Vardaman, James. Call Collect, Ask for Birdman. (Illus.). 256p. 1980. 10.95 (ISBN 0-312-11425-7). St Martin.
Vardaman, P. B., jt. auth. see Vardaman, G. T.
Vardaman, Patricia B., jt. auth. see Vardaman, George T.
Vardi, Joseph & Avi-Itzhak, Benjamin. Electrical Energy Generation: Economics, Reliability & Rates. 192p. 1981. text ed. 24.95x (ISBN 0-262-22024-5). MIT Pr.
Vardin, Patricia & Brody, Ilene, eds. Children's Rights: Contemporary Perspectives. LC 78-12584. (Orig.). 1978. pap. 8.95x (ISBN 0-8077-2550-1). Tchrs Coll.
Vardy, Steven B. Modern Hungarian Historiography. (East European Monographs: No. 16). 268p. 1976. 18.00x (ISBN 0-914710-08-7, Dist. by Columbia U Pr). East Eur Quarterly.
Varecha, Vladimir, tr. see Wunderlich, Klaus & Gloede, Wolfgang.
Varecha, Vladimir, tr. see Wunderluch, Klaus & Gloede, Wolfgang.
Varela, Beatriz. Lo Chino en el Habla Cubana. LC 79-54025. (Coleccion Polymita). (Illus.). 64p. (Orig., Span.). 1980. pap. 6.95 (ISBN 0-89729-233-2). Ediciones.
Varela, G., jt. ed. see Somogyi, J. C.
Varenne, Herve. Americans Together: Structured Diversity in a Midwestern Town. LC 77-10109. 1977. pap. text ed. 10.25x (ISBN 0-8077-2519-6). Tchrs Coll.
Varese, L., et al, trs. see Proust, Marcel.
Varese, Louise, tr. see Baudelaire, Charles.
Varese, Louise, tr. see Rimbaud, Arthur.
Varga. The Monster Behind Black Rock. (Illus.). (gr. 3). 1980. pap. 3.50 incl. record (ISBN 0-590-24005-6, Schol Pap). Schol Bk Serv.
Varga, Andrew C. Main Issues in Bioethics: The Main Issues. 208p. (Orig.). 1980. pap. 8.95 (ISBN 0-8091-2327-4). Paulist Pr.
Varga, E. The Great Crisis & Its Political Consequences. 14.50 (ISBN 0-86527-089-9). Fertig.
Varga, E., et al, eds. Molecular & Cellular Aspects of Muscle Function: Proceedings of the 28th International Congress of Physiological Sciences, Budapest 1980 (Including Proceedings of the Satellite Symposium on Membrane Control of Skeletal Muscle Function) LC 80-42101. (Advances in Physiological Sciences: Vol. 5). (Illus.). 320p. 1981. 40.00 (ISBN 0-08-026817-X). Pergamon.
Varga, Judy. Circus Cannonball. LC 74-26796. (Illus.). 32p. (gr. k-3). 1975. 7.75 (ISBN 0-688-22026-6); PLB 7.44 (ISBN 0-688-32026-0). Morrow.
--The Crow Who Came to Stay. (Illus.). (ps-3). 1967. 8.25 (ISBN 0-688-21203-4); PLB 7.92 (ISBN 0-688-31203-9). Morrow.
--Once-a-Year Witch. (Illus.). 32p. (ps-3). 1973. PLB 7.92 (ISBN 0-688-31777-4). Morrow.
Varga, L., jt. auth. see Szechy, K.
Varga, William. The Number One Nazi Jew Baiter. 1981. 9.95 (ISBN 0-8062-1623-9). Carlton.
Vargaftik, N. B. Tables on the Thermophysical Properties of Liquids & Gases: In Normal & Dissociated States. 2nd ed. LC 75-14260. (Advances in Thermal Engineering Ser.). 758p. 1975. 49.50 (ISBN 0-470-90310-4). Halsted Pr.
Vargas, Alberto & Austin, Reid. Vargas. 1981. pap. 8.95 (ISBN 0-517-53048-1, Harmony). Crown.
Vargas, Carlos A., tr. see Cramer, Raymond L.
Vargas, Carlos A., tr. see Keller, Phillip.
Vargas, Glenn & Vargas, Martha. Diagrams for Faceting. LC 75-21404. (Illus.). 190p. 1975. 12.00 (ISBN 0-917646-02-9). Glenn Vargas.
Vargas, Joseph M., Jr. Management of Turfgrass Disease. (Orig.). 1981. write for info. (ISBN 0-8087-2214-X). Burgess.
Vargas, Martha, jt. auth. see Vargas, Glenn.
Vargo, Richard J., ed. Author's Guide to Journals in Administration, Business & Management. LC 80-16956. (Author's Guide to Journals Ser.). 432p. 1981. 24.95 (ISBN 0-917724-12-7). Haworth Pr.
Vargoshe, Richard & Steinberg, Peter. The Household Book of Animal Medicine. 208p. 1980. 12.95 (ISBN 0-13-395871-X, Spec); pap. 6.95 (ISBN 0-13-395863-9). P-H.
Varis, Tapio, jt. auth. see Nordenstreng, Kaarle.
Varkom Muhammed Basheer. Me Grandad Had an Elephant & Other Stories. Asher, R. E., tr. from Malayam. 150p. 1980. 12.00x (ISBN 0-85224-386-3, Pub. by Edinburgh U Pr Scotland); pap. 6.00x (ISBN 0-85224-387-1, Pub. by Edinburgh U Pr Scotland). Columbia U Pr.
Varlejs, Jana, ed. Young Adult Literature in the Seventies: A Selection of Readings. LC 78-6562. 1978. lib. bdg. 13.50 (ISBN 0-8108-1134-0). Scarecrow.
Varlejs, Jana, jt. auth. see Curley, Arthur.
Varlet, Jean-Francois. Declaration Solennelle des Droits De l'Homme Dans l'Etat Social. (Fr.). 1977. lib. bdg. 13.75x o.p. (ISBN 0-8287-0854-1); pap. text ed. 3.75x o.p. (ISBN 0-685-75742-0). Clearwater Pub.
Varley, H. Paul. Imperial Restoration in Medieval Japan. LC 73-124573. (Studies of the East Asian Institute of Col. Univ.). 1971. text ed. 17.50x (ISBN 0-231-03502-0). Columbia U Pr.
--Onin War: History of Its Origins & Background with a Selective Translation of the Chronicle of Onin. LC 66-14595. (Studies in Oriental Culture Ser.: No. 1). (Illus.). 1966. 17.50x (ISBN 0-231-02943-8). Columbia U Pr.
--A Syllabus of Japanese Civilization. rev. 2nd ed. LC 68-55815. (Companions to Asian Studies). 120p. 1972. pap. 5.00x (ISBN 0-231-03677-9). Columbia U Pr.
Varley, H. Paul, tr. from Japanese. A Chronicle of Gods & Sovereigns: Jinno Shotoki of Kitabatake Chikafusa. (Translations from Oriental Classics Ser.). 1980. 22.50x (ISBN 0-231-04940-4). Columbia U Pr.
Varley, John. Titan. 1979. 9.95 o.p. (ISBN 0-425-04468-8). Berkley Pub.
--Wizard. 1980. pap. 2.50. Berkley Pub.
Varley, Margaret. British Freshwater Fishes: Factors Affecting Their Distribution. (Illus.). 148p. 15.00 (ISBN 0-85238-107-7, FN). Unipub.
Varley, Mike, jt. auth. see Hughes, Paul.
Varma, Arvind, jt. ed. see Aris, Rutherford.
Varma, Baidya N., ed. New Survey of Social Sciences. 1963. 8.00x o.p. (ISBN 0-210-26861-1). Asia.
Varma, Devendra P., ed. see Coleman, William E.
Varma, Devendra P., ed. see Conger, Syndy M.
Varma, Devendra P., ed. see Durant, David S.
Varma, Devendra P., ed. see Fry, Carroll L.
Varma, Devendra P., ed. see Garrett, John.
Varma, Devendra P., ed. see Harfst, Betsy P.
Varma, Devendra P., ed. see Harris, John B.
Varma, Devendra P., ed. see Heller, Lynne E.
Varma, Devendra P., ed. see Henderson, Peter M.
Varma, Devendra P., ed. see Hinck, Henry W.
Varma, Devendra P., ed. see Lea, Sydney L.
Varma, Devendra P., ed. see May, Leland C.
Varma, Devendra P., ed. see Mise, Raymond W.
Varma, Devendra P., ed. see Platzner, Robert L.
Varma, Devendra P., ed. see Powers, Katherine R.
Varma, Devendra P., ed. see Reddin, Chitra P.
Varma, Devendra P., ed. see Roberts, Bette B.
Varma, Devendra P., ed. see Ronald, Ann.
Varma, Devendra P., ed. see Sandy, Stephen.
Varma, Devendra P., ed. see Scheuermann, Mona.
Varma, Devendra P., ed. see Scott, Shirley C.
Varma, Devendra P., ed. see Sedgwick, Eve K.
Varma, Devendra P., ed. see Sherman, Leona F.
Varma, Devendra P., ed. see Smith, Nelson C.
Varma, Devendra P., ed. see Soldati, Joseph A.
Varma, Devendra P., ed. see Tompkins, J. M.
Varma, Devendra P., ed. see Tracy, Ann B.
Varma, Devendra P., ed. see Van Luchene, Stephen R.
Varma, Devendra P., ed. see Weiss, Fredric.
Varma, Monika. Alakananda. 1976. 8.00 (ISBN 0-89253-823-6); flexible cloth 4.80 (ISBN 0-89253-824-4). Ind-US Inc.
--Dragonflies Draw Flame. 4.80 (ISBN 0-89253-745-0); flexible cloth 4.00 (ISBN 0-89253-746-9). Ind-US Inc.
--Facing Four. (Greybird Book). 47p. 1975. 8.00 (ISBN 0-88253-758-X); pap. 4.80 (ISBN 0-88253-849-7). Ind-US Inc.
--Gita Govinda & Other Poems. 4.80 (ISBN 0-89253-764-7); flexible cloth 4.00 (ISBN 0-89253-765-5). Ind-US Inc.
--Green Leaves & Gold. (Writers Workshop Redbird Book Ser.). 38p. 1975. 4.80 (ISBN 0-88253-552-8); pap. text ed. 4.00 (ISBN 0-88253-551-X). Ind-US Inc.
--Past Imperative: A Collection of Poems 1953-1964. 47p. 1974. 10.00 (ISBN 0-88253-423-8); pap. text ed. 4.80 (ISBN 0-88253-422-X). Ind-US Inc.
--Quartered Questions & Queries. 9.00 (ISBN 0-89253-747-7); flexible cloth 4.00 (ISBN 0-89253-748-5). Ind-US Inc.
Varma, Monika, tr. see Bandhopadyaya, Vibhuti Bhushan.
Varma, Monika, tr. see Tagore, Rabindranath.
Varma, Nirmal. The Hill Station & Other Stories. (Writers Workshop Greenbird Book Ser.). 115p. 1975. 14.00 (ISBN 0-88253-560-9); pap. text ed. 4.80 (ISBN 0-88253-559-5). Ind-US Inc.
Varma, Ravi & Hrubesh, Lawrence W. Chemical Analysis by Microwave Rotational Spectroscopy. LC 78-17415. (Chemical Analysis Series of Monographs on Analytical Chemistry & Its Application). 1979. 27.50 (ISBN 0-471-03916-0, Pub. by Wiley-Interscience). Wiley.
Varma, S. P. Modern Political Theory. 1976. 15.95 (ISBN 0-7069-0369-2, Pub. by Vikas India). Advent Bk.
Varma, Shrikant. Otherwise & Other Poems. (Translated from Hindi). 12.00 (ISBN 0-89253-615-2); flexible cloth 4.80 (ISBN 0-89253-616-0). Ind-US Inc.
--A Winter Evening. Ratan, Jai & Vaid, K. B., trs. from Hindi. 100p, (Eng.). 1975. 14.00 (ISBN 0-88253-674-5); pap. 4.80 (ISBN 0-88253-673-7). Ind-US Inc.
Varmavuori, A., ed. see International Congress of Pure & Applied Chemistry, 27th, Helsinki, Finland, Aug. 27-31, 1979.
Varmer, Devendra P., ed. see Stoler, John A.
Varmuza, K. Pattern Recognition in Chemistry. (Lecture Notes in Chemistry Ser.: Vol. 21). (Illus.). 217p. 1981. pap. 21.00 (ISBN 0-387-10273-6). Springer-Verlag.
Varney, Glenn. Management by Objectives. 1979. 59.50 (ISBN 0-85013-106-5). Dartnell Corp.
Varney, Glenn H. Management by Objectives Workbook. rev. ed. 1972. 4.95 (ISBN 0-686-05624-8). Mgmt Advisory.
--Organization Development Approach to Management Development. LC 75-9007. (Illus.). 192p. 1976. text ed. 10.94 (ISBN 0-201-07982-8). A-W.
--Organization Development for Managers. LC 77-73948. 1977. pap. text ed. 10.95 (ISBN 0-201-07983-6). A-W.
--Planning & Reviewing Employee Performance. rev. ed. 46p. 1974. pap. 4.95 (ISBN 0-686-05625-6). Mgmt Advisory.
Varney, Rosemary. Wispy, the Littlest Witch. LC 76-48097. (Illus.). (ps-3). 1977. 5.50 (ISBN 0-913778-70-2). Childs World.
Varnum, Brooke M. Play & Sing..It's Christmas! A Piano Book of Easy-to-Play Carols. LC 80-15967. (Illus.). 48p. 1980. PLB 10.95 (ISBN 0-02-791400-3); pap. 5.95 (ISBN 0-02-045420-1). Macmillan.
Varola, Franco. Typology of the Racehorse. (Illus.). 29.75 (ISBN 0-85131-196-2, Dist. by Sporting Book Center). J A Allen.
Varon, Benison, ed. see Carman, John S.
Varsanyi, G. Assignments for Vibrational Spectra of 700 Benzene Derivatives, 2 vols. LC 74-8113. 1974. Set. 79.95 (ISBN 0-470-90330-9). Halsted Pr.
--Vibrational Spectra of Benzene Derivatives. 1970. 59.50 (ISBN 0-12-714950-3). Acad Pr.
Vartanian, Michael M. The Computational Tools of Engineering. (Advances in Modern Engineering Ser.). (Illus.). 125p. 1974. pap. text ed. 9.95 (ISBN 0-201-07985-2). A-W.
Vartanian, Vartan, jt. auth. see Sifferlen, Thomas P.
Varty, Kenneth. Reynard the Fox: A Study of the Fox in Medieval Enlish Art. 1967. text ed. 25.00x (ISBN 0-391-01055-7, Leicester). Humanities.
Varute, A. T. & Bhatia, K. S. Cell Structure & Function. 1976. 15.00 (ISBN 0-7069-0461-3, Pub. by Vikas India). Advent Bk.
Varvaro, Alberto, ed. Congresso Internazionale Di Linguistica E Filologia Romanza XIV: Atti Volume II: Comunicazione. 1979. pap. text ed. 72.00x (ISBN 90-272-0943-X). Humanities.
--Congresso Internazionale di Linguistica e Filologia Romanza, XIV, Napoli 15-20 Aprile 1974: Atti 1. (Orig.). 1979. pap. text ed. 72.00x (ISBN 0-686-59701-X). Humanities.
Varwell, D. W. Police & the Public. 128p. 1978. 13.95x (ISBN 0-7121-1683-4, Pub. by Macdonald & Evans England). Intl Ideas.
Vary, Colin. The Victims. (Illus.). 52p. (Orig.). 1976. pap. 5.00x (ISBN 0-911038-70-1, Inst Hist Rev). Noontide.
Vary, James C., jt. ed. see Chambliss, Glenn.
Vasarely, Victor. Vasarely. (Alpine Fine Arts Collection). (Illus.). 152p. 1980. 50.00 (ISBN 0-933516-01-0, Pub by Alpine Fine Arts). Hippocrene Bks.
Vasari, Giorgio. Vitede 'piu Eccellenti Architetti, Pittori,et Scultori, 2 vols. (Documents of Art & Architectural History, Ser. 1: Vol. 1). (Ital.). 1980. Repr. of 1550 ed. Set. 85.00x (ISBN 0-89371-101-2). Broude Intl Edns.
Vasconez, Luis, jt. auth. see Gant, Thomas.
Vas Dias, Robert. Speech Acts & Happenings. LC 71-173226. 1972. pap. 2.45 o.p. (ISBN 0-672-51690-X). Bobbs.
Vasel, Major J., jt. auth. see Krell, Edwin D.
Vasey, Wayne, jt. ed. see O'Rand, Angela.
Vash, Carolyn, ed. see Institute for Information Studies, et al.
Vash, Carolyn, et al, eds. see Institute for Information Studies.
Vasi, Susanne & Tomasino, Joseph. Auditory, Reading & Dialogue Comprehension Exercises in Spanish. (gr. 9-12). 1973. pap. text ed. 2.95 cancelled (ISBN 0-88345-025-9, 18113); tchr's manual 3.50 (ISBN 0-88345-026-7, 18135); cassettes 40.00 (ISBN 0-685-48110-7). Regents Pub.
--Exercises in Spanish. 229p. 1981. pap. text ed. 3.25 (ISBN 0-88345-421-1, 18638). Regents Pub.
--Exercises in Spanish. new ed. 200p. 1980. pap. 3.25 (ISBN 0-88345-446-7, 18638); cassettes 25.00. Regents Pub.
Vasil, Indra K., ed. International Review of Cytology: Supplement 11, Part A: Perspectives in Plant Cell & Tissue Culture. (Serial Pub.). 1980. 29.50 (ISBN 0-12-364371-6). Acad Pr.
Vasil, Raj K. Ethnic Politics in Malaysia. (Illus.). 234p. 1980. text ed. 16.00x (ISBN 0-391-01770-5). Humanities.
Vasil'Ev, Aleksiei T. The Ochrana: The Russian Secret Police. LC 79-2925. (Illus.). 305p. 1981. Repr. of 1930 ed. 26.50 (ISBN 0-8305-0094-4). Hyperion Conn.
Vasil'Ev, L. A. Schlieren Methods. 1968. 36.95 (ISBN 0-470-90335-X). Halsted Pr.
Vasiliev, Alexander A. History of the Byzantine Empire, 324-1453, 2 Vols. (Illus., Orig.). 1968. pap. 7.50x ea.; Vol. 1. (ISBN 0-299-80925-0); Vol. 2. (ISBN 0-299-80926-9). U of Wis Pr.
Vasiliev, J. M. & Gelfand, I. M. Neoplastic & Normal Cells in Culture. LC 80-40075. (Development & Cell Biology: No. 8). (Illus.). 300p. Date not set. price not set (ISBN 0-521-23149-3). Cambridge U Pr.
Vasiliu, Mircea. A Day at the Beach. LC 76-24169. (Picturebacks Ser). (Illus.). (ps-1). 1977. pap. 1.25 (ISBN 0-394-83475-5, BYR). Random.
--Good Night, Sleep Tight Book. (Illus.). (ps-3). 1973. PLB 7.15 o.p. (ISBN 0-307-62504-4, Golden Pr). Western Pub.
Vasistha, K. K. Teacher Education in India: A Study in New Dimensions. 1979. text ed. 13.50x (ISBN 0-391-01841-8). Humanities.
Vasko, Donna. I'd Rather Be Flying. (Illus.). 100p. 1980. spiral bdg. 6.00. Aviation.
Vasko, Donna M. I'd Rather Be Flying. 100p. (Orig.). 1980. pap. 5.95 (ISBN 0-9604308-0-6). Calligraphy Donna.
Vasquez, Guillermo H. Lo Que los Padres y Maestros Deben Saber Acerca De las Drogas. 1978. pap. 0.95 (ISBN 0-311-46080-1). Casa Bautista.
Vasquez, Librado K. & Vasquez, Maria E. Regional Dictionary of Chicano Slang. 111p. 1975. 13.50 (ISBN 0-8363-0083-1). Jenkins.
Vasquez, Maria E., jt. auth. see Vasquez, Librado K.
Vass, I. Fencing. (Illus.). 1977. 13.00 (ISBN 0-912728-95-7). Newbury Bks Inc.
Vasse, William W., jt. auth. see Edwards, John H.
Vasseur, J. P. Properties & Applications of Transistors. 1964. 32.00 (ISBN 0-08-010244-1); pap. 17.25 (ISBN 0-08-013647-8). Pergamon.
Vassi, Marco. Metasex, Mirth & Madness. LC 75-165. 1975. 7.95 o.p. (ISBN 0-89110-002-4). Penthouse Pr.
Vassilakos, Aristarchus. The Trial of Jesus Christ. Orthodox Christian Educational Society, ed. 64p. (Orig.). 1950. pap. 2.00x (ISBN 0-938366-47-5). Orthodox Chr.
Vassilyeva, Larissa. Lara in London. Franklin, Olga, tr. 1978. text ed. 15.00 (ISBN 0-08-023718-5); pap. text ed. 7.65 (ISBN 0-08-023717-7). Pergamon.
Vassos, John H. Manna: True Stories of U. S. A. Life, 1900 to 1940 & the Utopia of Manna. 64p. 1981. 8.00x (ISBN 0-682-49655-3). Exposition.
Vasta, Edward & Thundy, Zacharias, eds. Chaucerian Problems & Perspectives. LC 78-62971. 1979. text ed. 19.95 (ISBN 0-268-00728-4). U of Notre Dame Pr.
Vasta, Ross. Studying Children: An Introduction to Research Methods. LC 78-25941. (Psychology Ser.). (Illus.). 1979. text ed. 15.95x (ISBN 0-7167-1067-6); pap. text ed. 7.95x (ISBN 0-7167-1068-4). W H Freeman.
Vasta, Ross F., jt. auth. see Whitehurst, Grover J.

Vastano, Joseph F. Elements of Food Production & Baking. 2nd ed. LC 77-26070. 1978. text ed. 14.95 (ISBN 0-672-97096-1); tchr's manual 6.67 (ISBN 0-672-97095-3); wkbk. 6.50 (ISBN 0-672-97094-5). Bobbs.

Vasto, Lanza Del see Del Vasto, Lanza.

Vastyan, James E., ed. see Kay, Ronald D.

Vasu, Srisa. An Introduction to the Yoga Philosophy. 1976. Repr. 6.50x o.p. (ISBN 0-685-71772-0). South Asia Bks.

Vasudev, P. S. Lord Ravan of Lanka. (Bluebird Bk.). 118p. 1975. 14.00 (ISBN 0-88253-829-2); pap. 8.00 (ISBN 0-88253-830-6). Ind-US Inc.

--The Sunflower. 15.00 (ISBN 0-89253-776-0); flexible cloth 6.75 (ISBN 0-89253-777-9). Ind-US Inc.

Vasudev, Uma. Two Faces of Indira Gandhi. 208p. 1977. 8.50x (ISBN 0-686-63736-4). Intl Pubns Serv.

Vasudevamoorthy, M. Social Action. 1966. pap. 3.50x (ISBN 0-210-22644-7). Asia.

Vatikiotis, P. J. Conflict in the Middle East. (Illus.). 1971. text ed. 27.50x (ISBN 0-04-327036-0). Allen Unwin.

Vatikiotis, Panayiotis J. The Egyptian Army in Politics: Pattern for New Nations. LC 72-6216. 300p. 1975. Repr. of 1961 ed. lib. bdg. 25.50x (ISBN 0-8371-6473-7, VAEA). Greenwood.

Vatter, Paul A., et al. Quantitative Methods in Management: Text & Cases. 1978. text ed. 20.95 (ISBN 0-256-02006-X). Irwin.

Vatter, William J. Accounting Measurements for Financial Reports. 1971. text ed. 13.95x o.p. (ISBN 0-256-00628-8). Irwin.

Vatuk, Sylvia. Kinship & Urbanization: White Collar Migrants in North India. LC 75-161993. 1973. 20.00x (ISBN 0-520-02064-2). U of Cal Pr.

VauDell, W. W. The Power of God Within You. 1980. 5.50 o.p. (ISBN 0-682-49157-8). Exposition.

Vauderheiden, G. Non-Vocal Communication Resource Book. 1978. 15.95 (ISBN 0-8391-1252-1). Univ Park.

Vaudrin, Bill. Tanaina Tales from Alaska. (Civilization of the American Indians Ser.: Vol. 96). 133p. 1980. pap. 3.95 (ISBN 0-8061-1414-2). U of Okla Pr.

Vaugham, Thomas, jt. auth. see O'Donnell, Terence.

Vaughan, Alden T. & Richter, Daniel K. Crossing the Cultural Divide: Indians & New Englanders, 1605-1763. 76p. 1980. pap. write for info. (ISBN 0-912296-48-8). Am Antiquarian.

Vaughan, Alden T., compiled by. The American Colonies in the Seventeenth Century. LC 78-151118. (Goldentree Bibliographies in American History Ser.). (Orig.). 1971. 10.95x (ISBN 0-88295-529-2); pap. 6.95x (ISBN 0-88295-528-4). AHM Pub.

Vaughan, Alden T. & Clark, Edward W., eds. Puritans Among the Indians: Accounts of Captivity & Redemption 1676-1724. (John Harvard Library Ser.). (Illus.). 352p. 1981. text ed. 20.00 (ISBN 0-674-73901-9). Harvard U Pr.

Vaughan, B. N. Expectation of the Poor. 192p. 1972. pap. 3.50 o.p. (ISBN 0-8170-0571-4). Judson.

Vaughan, B. W. Planning in Education. LC 77-82520. (Illus.). 1979. 26.50 (ISBN 0-521-21817-9); pap. 10.95x (ISBN 0-521-29285-9). Cambridge U Pr.

Vaughan, Betty A. Folk Art Painting: A Bit of the Past & Present. (Illus.). 52p. (Orig.). 1981. pap. 7.95 (ISBN 0-9605172-0-0). BETOM Pubns.

Vaughan, C. R. The Gifts of the Holy Spirit. 1975. 11.95 (ISBN 0-85151-222-4). Banner of Truth.

Vaughan, Carter. The River Devils. large print ed. LC 80-28166. 1981. Repr. of 1969 ed. 10.95 (ISBN 0-89621-266-1). Thorndike Pr.

Vaughan, Carter A. Fortress Fury. 1977. pap. 1.50 o.p. (ISBN 0-445-03189-1). Popular Lib.

Vaughan, Clark A. La Gramatica Funcional. (gr. 9-10). 1969. pap. text ed. 5.95 (ISBN 0-88334-014-3) (ISBN 0-685-39245-7). Ind Sch Pr.

Vaughan, Curry & Slosser, Bob. Battleground. pap. 3.95 o.p. (ISBN 0-88270-301-3, P301-2). Logos.

Vaughan, Curtis. Colossians - a Study Guide Commentary. 128p. 1973. pap. text ed. 3.50 (ISBN 0-310-33523-X). Zondervan.

--Colossians & Philemon: A Study Guide Commentary. (Study Guide Commentary Ser.). 144p. (Orig.). 1981. pap. 3.50 (ISBN 0-310-33583-3). Zondervan.

--Galatians. 128p. 1972. pap. 2.50 (ISBN 0-310-33543-4). Zondervan.

--James. pap. 3.50 (ISBN 0-310-33553-1). Zondervan.

--One, Two, Three, John. (Study Guide Ser). 1970. pap. 3.50 (ISBN 0-310-33563-9). Zondervan.

Vaughan, David J. & Craig, James R. Mineral Chemistry of the Metal Sulfides. LC 76-62585. (Earth Science Ser.). (Illus.). 1978. 59.50 (ISBN 0-521-21489-0). Cambridge U Pr.

Vaughan, David J., jt. auth. see Craig, James R.

Vaughan, Eleanor K., jt. auth. see Branley, Franklyn M.

Vaughan, Emmett J. & Elliot, Curtis M. Fundamentals of Risk & Insurance. 2nd ed. LC 77-18769. (Wiley-Hamilton Series in Risk & Insurance). 1978. text ed. 24.50 (ISBN 0-471-90353-1); tchrs'. manual avail. (ISBN 0-471-02164-4). Wiley.

Vaughan, Frances E. Awakening Intuition. LC 77-27685. 1979. pap. 3.95 (ISBN 0-385-13371-5, Anch). Doubleday.

Vaughan, G. Douglas. Introduction to Applied Economics. 1974. 19.95x (ISBN 0-434-92190-4); pap. 12.95x (ISBN 0-434-92191-2). Intl Ideas.

Vaughan, Harold. The Monroe Doctrine, 1823: A Landmark in American Foreign Policy. LC 72-8853. (Focus Bks.). (Illus.). 72p. (gr. 7 up). 1973. PLB 4.90 o.p. (ISBN 0-531-02461-X). Watts.

Vaughan, Harold C. Citizen Genet Affair: A Chapter in the Formation of American Foreign Policy. LC 76-114928. (Focus Bks). (Illus.). (gr. 7 up). 1970. PLB 4.90 o.p. (ISBN 0-531-01014-7). Watts.

--The Colony of Georgia. LC 74-8790. (First Bks). (Illus.). 96p. (gr. 5-8). 1975. PLB 4.90 o.p. (ISBN 0-531-02774-0). Watts.

--The Constitutional Convention. LC 75-25726. (Focus Bks Ser). (Illus.). 96p. (gr. 7 up). 1976. PLB 4.90 o.p. (ISBN 0-531-01104-6). Watts.

--The Hayes-Tilden Election of 1876: A Disputed Election in the Gilded Age. (Focus Books). (Illus.). 72p. (gr. 7 up). 1972. PLB 4.90 o.p. (ISBN 0-531-02452-0). Watts.

--The Versailles Treaty. LC 74-8865. (World Focus Bks). (Illus.). 72p. (gr. 6-9). 1975. PLB 4.47 o.p. (ISBN 0-531-02783-X). Watts.

--The XYZ Affair, 1797-98: The Diplomacy of the Adams Administration & an Undeclared War with France. LC 72-189759. (Focus Bks). (Illus.). 96p. (gr. 7 up). 1972. PLB 4.47 o.p. (ISBN 0-531-02459-8). Watts.

Vaughan, Henry. Henry Vaughan: Selected Poems. Shaw, Robert B., ed. (Fyfield Ser.). 1979. pap. 3.95 o.s.i. (ISBN 0-85635-138-5, Pub. by Carcanet New Pr England); pap. 3.95 (ISBN 0-85635-139-3). Persea Bks.

Vaughan, Henry H. Welsh Proverbs with English Translations. LC 68-17945. (Eng. & Welsh.). 1969. Repr. of 1889 ed. 20.00 (ISBN 0-8103-3205-1). Gale.

Vaughan, Herbert C., tr. see Mary da Bergamo, Cajetan.

Vaughan, J., et al, eds. Maintenance of Factory Services: Part Two, 2 vols. (Engineering Craftsmen: No. J23). (Illus.). 1969. Set. spiral bdg. 33.95x (ISBN 0-685-90156-4). Intl Ideas.

--Maintenance of Factory Services: Part One. (Engineering Craftsmen: No. J3). (Illus.). 1968. spiral bdg. 24.00x (ISBN 0-85083-028-1). Intl Ideas.

--Mechanical Maintenance (and Installation) II, 2 vols. (Engineering Craftsmen Ser.: No. J21). (Illus.). 342p. 1970. Set. 28.95x (ISBN 0-85083-080-X). Intl Ideas.

Vaughan, Jenny. The Easter Book. LC 80-83362. (Illus.). 48p. (gr. 1-6). 1981. 4.95 (ISBN 0-448-11541-7); lib. bdg. 10.15 (ISBN 0-448-13492-6). G&D.

Vaughan, Joseph L., Jr., jt. auth. see Estes, Thomas H.

Vaughan, Louise. Lovequest. 1979. pap. 2.25 o.s.i. (ISBN 0-515-04696-5). Jove Pubns.

Vaughan, Matthew. Major Stepton's War. LC 77-11369. 1978. 7.95 o.p. (ISBN 0-385-13607-2). Doubleday.

Vaughan, P. H. Meaning of Bama in the Old Testament. LC 73-89004. (Society for Old Testament Study Monographs: No. 3). (Illus.). 96p. 1974. 23.95 (ISBN 0-521-20425-9). Cambridge U Pr.

Vaughan, R. The Age of Great Cities. 384p. 1971. Repr. of 1843 ed. 25.00x (ISBN 0-7165-1597-0, Pub. by Irish Academic Pr Ireland). Biblio Dist.

Vaughan, R. C. The Hardy-Littlewood Method. (Cambridge Tracts in Mathematics: No. 80). 160p. Date not set. price not set (ISBN 0-521-23439-5). Cambridge U Pr.

Vaughan, R. I., jt. auth. see Tyror, J. G.

Vaughan, Richard. Arctic Summer: Birds in North Norway. (Illus.). 152p. 1980. 17.50 (ISBN 0-904614-01-8, Pub. by Anthony Nelson Ltd England). Buteo.

--Plovers. 160p. 1980. 25.00x (ISBN 0-900963-36-0, Pub. by Terence Dalton England). State Mutual Bk.

Vaughan, Roger J., jt. auth. see Tolley, George S.

Vaughan, Thomas & McMath, George A. A Century of Portland Architecture. (Illus.). 250p. 1981. pap. write for info. (ISBN 0-87595-005-1). Oreg Hist Soc.

Vaughan, Thomas, ed. see Seufert, Francis A.

Vaughan, Thomas, et al. Voyages of Enlightenment: Malaspina on the Northwest Coast, 1791-1792. LC 77-88147. (North Pacific Studies Ser.: No. 3). (Illus.). 72p. 1977. pap. 3.95 (ISBN 0-87595-058-2). Oreg Hist Soc.

Vaughan, William. Caspar David Friedrich Seventeen Seventy-Four to Eighteen Forty. (Tate Gallery Art Ser.). (Illus.). 1977. 11.95 o.p. (ISBN 0-8120-5145-9). Barron.

--German Romantic Painting. LC 80-13170. (Illus.). 288p. 1980. 45.00x (ISBN 0-300-02387-1). Yale U Pr.

--Romantic Art. LC 77-76818. (World of Art Ser.). 1978. 17.95 (ISBN 0-19-519984-7); pap. 9.95 (ISBN 0-19-519981-2). Oxford U Pr.

Vaughan Williams, Ralph. The Pilgrim's Progress. 36p. (Libretto only). 1961. 2.25 (ISBN 0-19-339227-5). Oxford U Pr.

Vaughan Williams, Ursula. R. V. W. A Biography of Ralph Vaughan Williams. (Illus.). 1964. 24.00x (ISBN 0-19-315411-0). Oxford U Pr.

Vaughan-Wrobel, Beth C. & Henderson, Betty. The Problem-Oriented System in Nursing: A Workbook. (Illus.). 184p. 1976. pap. 9.00 (ISBN 0-8016-5221-9). Mosby.

Vaughn, jt. auth. see Pattou.

Vaughn, Alan. Incredible Coincidence: The Baffling World of Synchronicity. 256p. 1980. pap. 2.25 (ISBN 0-451-09349-6, E9349, Sig). NAL.

Vaughn, Charles E. The Romantic Revolt. 507p. 1980. Repr. of 1907 ed. lib. bdg. 40.00 (ISBN 0-8495-5527-2). Arden Lib.

Vaughn, Charles L. Franchising. 2nd & rev. ed. LC 78-24841. (Illus.). 304p. 1979. 22.95 (ISBN 0-669-02852-5). Lexington Bks.

Vaughn, Frances, jt. auth. see Walsh, Roger.

Vaughn, George A., Jr. War Flying in France. 1980. pap. 23.00 (ISBN 0-89126-082-X). Military Aff Aero.

Vaughn, Gwenyth R. & Clark, Ruth M. Speech Facilitation: Extraoral & Intraoral Stimulation Technique for Improvement of Articulation Skills. (Illus.). 304p. 1979. text ed. 17.75 (ISBN 0-398-03828-7). C C Thomas.

Vaughn, Jack A. Early American Dramatists: From the Beginnings to 1900. LC 80-53703. (World Dramatists Ser.). (Illus.). 224p. 1981. 13.95 (ISBN 0-8044-2940-5). Ungar.

--Shakespeare's Comedies. LC 79-48080. (World Dramatists Ser.). (Illus.). 190p. 1980. 10.95 (ISBN 0-8044-2938-3). Ungar.

Vaughn, James A. & Deep, Samuel D. Program of Exercises for Management & Organizational Behavior. 1975. pap. text ed. 6.95x (ISBN 0-02-479440-6); tchrs' manual free (ISBN 0-02-479450-3). Macmillan.

Vaughn, Jesse W. The Reynolds Campaign on Powder River. (Illus.). 239p. 1961. 12.50 o.p. (ISBN 0-8061-0511-9). U of Okla Pr.

Vaughn, Ray, jt. auth. see Wallace, G. K.

Vaughn, Robert G. Conflict-of-Interest Regulation in the Federal Executive Branch. (Illus.). 1979. 21.00 (ISBN 0-669-02776-6). Lexington Bks.

Vaughn, Roberta. Golden Goddess of El Dorado. (Orig.). 1980. pap. write for info. (ISBN 0-671-41266-3). PB.

Vaughn, Ruth. Choice Readings. LC 63-7338. (Orig.). 1962. pap. 0.80 (ISBN 0-8054-9912-1). Broadman.

--Curtain Raisers for Evangelism. LC 76-11486. 1976. pap. 2.25 (ISBN 0-87239-110-8, 2768). Standard Pub.

--Does He Really Care: In Search of an Intimate God. (Orig.). 1981. pap. 3.95 (ISBN 0-88449-011-4). Vision Hse.

--Playlets & Skits. (Orig.). 1973. pap. 2.25 (ISBN 0-87239-374-7, 3093). Standard Pub.

Vaunauken, Sheldon. Gateway to Heaven: A Novel. LC 79-3600. (Illus.). 304p. 1980. 9.95 (ISBN 0-06-068822-X). Har-Row.

Vaux, Bernard Carra de see Carra de Vaux, Bernard.

Vaux, Calvert. Villas & Cottages. 2nd ed. LC 68-29858. (Architecture & Decorative Art Ser). (Illus.). 1968. Repr. of 1857 ed. lib. bdg. 29.50 (ISBN 0-306-71044-7). Da Capo.

Vavra, Robert. Felipe the Bullfighter. LC 68-10006. (Illus.). (gr. 4-6). 4.95 o.p. (ISBN 0-15-227510-X, HJ); PLB 3.99 o.p. (ISBN 0-15-227511-8). HarBraceJ.

Vawter, Bruce. On Genesis. LC 76-26354. 1977. 12.95 (ISBN 0-385-06104-8). Doubleday.

Vawter, Bruce & Carl, William J., III. Easter. LC 79-7377. (Proclamation 2: Aids for Interpreting the Lessons of the Church Year, Ser. A). 64p. (Orig.). 1981. pap. 6.95 (ISBN 0-8006-4095-0, 1-4095). Fortress.

Vawter, Bruce & Elliott, John H. Pentecost 3. LC 74-76929. (Proclamation 1: Aids for Interpreting the Lessons of the Church Year, Ser. A). 64p. 1975. pap. 1.95 (ISBN 0-8006-4068-3, 1-4068). Fortress.

Vawter, Bruce, C.M. Four Gospels: An Introduction, 2 Vols. LC 67-10408. 1969. pap. 3.50 vol. I (ISBN 0-385-01479-1, Im); Vol. 1. Volume II 3.50 (ISBN 0-385-06557-4, 255A). Vol. 2 (255B). Doubleday.

--This Man Jesus: An Essay Toward a New Testament Christology. LC 73-78174. 240p. 1975. pap. 2.45 (ISBN 0-385-02797-4, Im). Doubleday.

Vayhinger, John M. Before Divorce. Hulme, William E., ed. LC 72-171512. (Pocket Counsel Bks). 56p. 1972. pap. 1.75 (ISBN 0-8006-1106-3, 1-1106). Fortress.

Vaz, E. Aspects of Deviance. 1976. pap. 7.95 (ISBN 0-13-049304-X). P-H.

Vazakas, Byron. Nostalgias for a House of Cards: Poems. Orig. Title: Poems of Byron Vazakas. 1970. 4.95 (ISBN 0-8079-0159-8); pap. 1.95 (ISBN 0-8079-0160-1). October.

Vazquez, Adolfo S. Art & Society: Essays in Marxist Aesthetics. Riofrancos, Maro, tr. LC 72-92025. 288p. 1974. 13.50 o.p. (ISBN 0-85345-269-5, CL2695). Monthly Rev.

--The Philosophy of Praxis. Gonzalez, Mike, tr. LC 76-23235. (International Library of Social & Political Thought). 1977. text ed. 19.50x (ISBN 0-391-00650-9). Humanities.

Vazquez, Alberto M. Antologia De Cuentos Hispanoamericanos. (gr. 12). 1976. pap. text ed. 6.95 (ISBN 0-88345-264-2). Regents Pub.

Vazquez, Margot Arce De see Pales Matos, Luis.

Vazsonyi, Andrew. Introduction to Data Processing. 3rd ed. 1980. 18.95x (ISBN 0-256-02343-3). Irwin.

--Introduction to Electronic Data Processing. rev ed. 1977. text ed. 16.95x o.p. (ISBN 0-256-01834-0); study guide 5.95 o.p. (ISBN 0-256-01844-8). Irwin.

Vazsonyi, Andrew & Brunell, Richard. Business Mathematics for Colleges. rev ed. 1979. pap. text ed. 12.50 (ISBN 0-256-02116-3). Irwin.

Vdovenko, V. M. & Dubasov, Yu V. Analytical Chemistry of Radium. Mandel, N., tr. from Rus. LC 74-30131. (Analytical Chemistry of Elements Ser.). 198p. 1925. 45.95 (ISBN 0-470-90488-7). Halsted Pr.

Veall, Donald. Popular Movement for Law Reform 1640-1660. 1970. 12.50x o.p. (ISBN 0-19-825191-2). Oxford U Pr.

Vear, K. C., jt. auth. see Gill, N. T.

Vears. Microelectronics Systems One: Checkbook. 1981. text ed. price not set (ISBN 0-408-00552-1). Butterworth.

Veatch, et al. Key Words to Reading: The Language Experience Approach. 2nd ed. (Elementary Reading Ser.). 1979. pap. text ed. 8.95 (ISBN 0-675-08363-X). Merrill.

Veatch, Jeannette. Reading in the Elementary Schools. 2nd ed. LC 78-14722. 628p. 1978. text ed. 19.95x (ISBN 0-471-06884-5). Wiley.

Veatch, Robert M. Death, Dying, & the Biological Revolution: Our Last Quest for Responsibility. LC 75-43337. 1976. 17.50x (ISBN 0-300-01949-1); pap. 6.95x (ISBN 0-300-02290-5). Yale U Pr.

--Value-Freedom in Science & Technology: A Study of the Importance of Religious, Ethical, & Other Socio-Cultural Factors in Selected Medical Decisions Regarding Birth Control. LC 76-28192. (Harvard Dissertations in Religion). 1976. pap. 9.00 (ISBN 0-89130-080-5, 020108). Scholars Pr Ca.

Veblen, Eric P. The Manchester "Union Leader" in New Hampshire Elections. LC 74-15446. (Illus.). 218p. 1975. 12.50 (ISBN 0-87451-106-2). U Pr of New Eng.

Veblen, Thorstein. Imperial Germany & the Industrial Revolution. 1966. pap. 2.65 o.p. (ISBN 0-472-06114-3, 114, AA). U of Mich Pr.

Vecellio, Cesare. Vecellio's Renaissance Costume Book. LC 76-55952. (Pictorialarchive Ser.). (Illus.). 1977. pap. 5.00 (ISBN 0-486-23441-X). Dover.

Vecht, A., jt. auth. see Waite, M. S.

Vecsei, Paul, jt. auth. see Glaz, Edith.

Vecsey, Christopher & Venables, Robert W., eds. American Indian Environments: Ecological Issues in Native American History. LC 80-26458. (Illus.). 236p. 1980. text ed. 18.00x (ISBN 0-8156-2226-0); pap. text ed. 9.95x (ISBN 0-8156-2227-9). Syracuse U Pr.

Vecsey, George. Baseball's Most Valuable Players. (Major League Baseball Library: No. 5). (Illus.). (gr. 5-9). 1966. 2.50 o.p. (ISBN 0-394-80185-7, BYR); PLB 3.69 (ISBN 0-394-90185-1). Random.

Vecsey, George, jt. auth. see Lynn, Loretta.

Vedder, Clyde B. Gerontology: A Book of Readings. (Illus.). 448p. 1971. 14.75 (ISBN 0-398-01972-X). C C Thomas.

--Juvenile Offenders. rev., 6th ed. (Illus.). 368p. 1979. text ed. 14.25 (ISBN 0-398-03844-9). C C Thomas.

Vedder, Clyde B. & Kay, Barbara A. Penology: A Realistic Approach. (Illus.). 360p. 1973. 15.50 (ISBN 0-398-01975-4). C C Thomas.

Vedder, Clyde B., jt. auth. see Kay, Barbara A.

Vedder, Clyde B., ed. Problems of the Middle-Aged. 216p. 1965. photocopy ed. spiral 15.75 (ISBN 0-398-01974-6). C C Thomas.

Vedder, Richard. The American Economy in a Historical Perspective. 1976. text ed. 18.95x (ISBN 0-534-00465-2). Wadsworth Pub.

Vedder, Richard, jt. ed. see Klingaman, David.

Veder, Bob. Playing with Fire. 1980. 10.95 (ISBN 0-671-25354-9, Linden). S&S.
Vedlik, Csaba, jt. auth. see Dornan, Robert K.
Vedral, Joyce. A Literary Survey of the Bible. LC 72-94184. 280p. (gr. 10-12). 1973. text ed. 5.95 o.p. (ISBN 0-88270-024-3); pap. text ed. 3.50 o.p. (ISBN 0-88270-025-1); tchrs. manual 2.50 o.p. (ISBN 0-88270-026-X). Logos.
Vedres, V. see Otten, Anna.
Veen, J. J. De see De Veen, J. J.
Veen, Ted Va N see Van Veen, Ted.
Veenendaal, Cornelia. Green Shaded Lamps. LC 76-55615. 64p. 1977. pap. 4.95 (ISBN 0-914086-16-2). Alicejamesbooks.
--The Trans-Siberian Railway. LC 73-86246. 64p. 1973. pap. 4.95 (ISBN 0-914086-01-4). Alicejamesbooks.
Veer, Yajan. The Language of the Atharva-Veda. 1979. text ed. 16.50x (ISBN 0-391-01853-1). Humanities.
Veerasawmy, E. P. Indian Cookery. 1970. pap. 2.75 (ISBN 0-88253-197-2). Ind-US Inc.
Vega, Garcilasco De La see De La Vega, Garcilasco.
Vega, Jose L. Cesar Vallejo En Trilce. LC 79-26380. (Coleccion UPREX, 60 Ser.: Estudios Literarios). ix, 132p. Date not set. pap. write for info. (ISBN 0-8477-0060-7). U of PR Pr.
Vega, Lope De see De Vega, Lope.
Vega, Pedro, tr. see Alexander, David.
Vega, Pedro, tr. see Bordeaux, Michael.
Vega, Pedro, et al, trs. see Alexander, David.
Vega, S., jt. auth. see De las Heras, F. G.
Vega, Sara L. De La see De La Vega, Sara L. & Parr, Carmen S.
Vega Capiro, Lope F. El Primero Benavides. Reichenberger, Arnold G. & Foley, Augusta E., eds. LC 74-103336. (Haney Foundation Ser.). (Illus.). 406p. 1973. text ed. 27.50x (ISBN 0-8122-7637-X). U of Pa Pr.
--Ven Francia. LC 61-6615. 1963. 12.50x (ISBN 0-8122-7363-X). U of Pa Pr.
Veges, Istvan, tr. see Matyas, Antal.
Vegetarian Times Magazine. The Vegetarian Times Guide to Dining in the U. S. A. 1980. pap. 8.95 (ISBN 0-689-10966-0). Atheneum.
Veglahn, Nancy. Spider of Brooklyn Heights. LC 67-15493. (Encore Edition). (Illus.). (gr. 7-9). 1967. 1.99 o.p. (ISBN 0-684-15858-2, ScribT). Scribner.
Vehrenberg, Hans. Atlas of Deep Sky Splendors. 4th ed. (Illus.). 1978. 39.95 (ISBN 0-933346-03-4). Sky Pub.
Veiga, John F. & Yanouzas, John N. The Dynamics of Organization Theory: Gaining a Macro Perspective. (Illus.). 1979. text ed. 14.95 (ISBN 0-8299-0182-5); insts.' manual avail. (ISBN 0-8299-0578-2). West Pub.
Veilleux, Armand, tr. Pachomian Koinonia I: The Life of St. Pachomius. (Cistercian Studies: No. 45). 524p. (Coptic Greek.). 1981. write for info.; pap. price not set (ISBN 0-87907-945-2). Cistercian Pubns.
Veim, Joanc. An Introduction to Information, Data & File Structuring. 200p. 1981. pap. 13.00x (ISBN 82-00-05322-9). Universitet.
Veinott, Cyril G. Computer-Aided Design of Electric Machinery. Kusko, Alexander, ed. (Monographs in Electric Technology). 182p. 1973. 16.50x o.p. (ISBN 0-262-22016-4). MIT Pr.
Veinus, Abraham. Concerto. pap. 5.00 (ISBN 0-486-21178-9). Dover.
Veit, Lawrence A. Economic Adjustment to an Energy-Short World. (Atlantic Papers Ser.: No. 38). 78p. 1980. write for info. 0.00 (ISBN 0-916672-78-6). Allanheld.
Veitch, B. & Harms, T. A Child's Cookbook. (ps-4). 1981. 8.95 (ISBN 0-201-09430-4, 09426, Sch Div); tchr's guide free; recipe step book 15.00 (ISBN 0-686-69466-X). A-W.
Veitch, Helen, jt. auth. see Lawrie, Norman.
Veitch, Tom. The Luis Armed Story. LC 78-9676. 1978. 14.95 (ISBN 0-916190-06-4); pap. 6.00 (ISBN 0-916190-07-2). Full Court NY.
Veith, Ilza, tr. The Yellow Emperor's Classic of Internal Medicine. 1966. 17.50x (ISBN 0-520-01296-8); pap. 4.95 (ISBN 0-520-02158-4, CAL238). U of Cal Pr.
Veith, Richard H. Multinational Computer Nets: The Case of International Banking. 160p. 1981. 18.95x (ISBN 0-669-04092-4). Lexington Bks.
Veith, W. H. Intersystemare Phonologie: Exemplarisch an diastratisch-Diatopischen Differenzierungen im Deutschen. x, 310p. 1972. 53.00x (ISBN 3-11-004350-5). De Gruyter.
Vekerdi, Laszlo. Letters on Probability. Renyi, Alfred, tr. from Hung. LC 74-179559. (Waynebooks Ser: No. 33). 112p. (Eng.). 1973. pap. 3.95x (ISBN 0-8143-1465-1). Wayne St U Pr.
Vela, Irma. Bailes a Colores, 3 units. (Illus.). 1972-74. Unit I. basic dance kit o.p. 10.50 (ISBN 0-913632-04-X); Unit II. pap. 20.50 teacher's kit (ISBN 0-913632-10-4); Unit III. social studies system o.p. 83.50 (ISBN 0-913632-11-2). Am Univ Artforms.
Velazquez, et al, eds. A New Pronouncing Dictionary of the Spanish & English Languages. rev. ed. LC 72-94281. 1973. thumb-indexed 17.95 (ISBN 0-13-615534-0). P-H.
Velazquez, Clara, et al. English As a Second Language: An Interdisciplinary Approach, Vol. 4. 208p. 1980. pap. 9.95 (ISBN 0-8403-2279-8). Kendall-Hunt.
Velde, Frances Vander see Vander Velde, Frances.
Veley, Charles. Night Whispers. 320p. 1981. pap. 2.75 (ISBN 0-345-29150-6). Ballantine.
Veley, Victor F., jt. auth. see Smith, Richard J.
Velez, Jose R., tr. see Kunz, Marilyn & Schell, Catherine.
Velie, Alan R., jt. auth. see Marshburn, Joseph H.
Velikhov, E. P., et al, eds. Science, Technology & the Future: Soviet Scientists Analysis of the Problems of & Prospects for the Development of Science & Technology & Their Role in Society. LC 79-40113. (Illus.). 1980. 36.00 (ISBN 0-08-024743-1). Pergamon.
Velikovsky, et al. Scientists Confront Scientists Who Confront Velikovsky. 2nd ed. Greenberg, Lewis M., et al, eds. (Illus., Orig.). pap. 5.00 (ISBN 0-917994-06-X). Kronos Pr.
--Velikovsky & Establishment Science. Greenberg, L. M., et al, eds. LC 77-93288. (Illus.). 1977. 12.95 (ISBN 0-917994-03-5); pap. 6.00 (ISBN 0-917994-04-3). Kronos Pr.
Velikovsky, Immanuel. Oedipus & Ahknaton. 1980. pap. write for info. (ISBN 0-671-83193-3). PB.
Velimsky, V., jt. auth. see Krejci, Jaroslav.
Veljkovic, Vello. Theoretical Approach to Preselection of Carcinogens & Chemical Carcinogenesis. 150p. 1981. 25.00 (ISBN 0-677-05490-4). Gordon.
Vellaccio, Frank, jt. auth. see Kemp, Daniel S.
Vellacott, P. Ironic Drama. LC 74-19522. 276p. 1975. 36.00 (ISBN 0-521-20590-5); pap. 10.50 (ISBN 0-521-09896-3). Cambridge U Pr.
Vellacott, Philip, tr. see Aeschylus.
Velleman & Hogalin. Applications, Basics & Computing of Exploratory Data Analysis. (Illus.). 228p. 1981. pap. text ed. 10.95 (ISBN 0-87872-273-4). Duxbury Pr.
Velleman, Ruth A. Serving Physically Disabled People: An Information Handbook for All Libraries. LC 79-17082. 382p. 1979. 17.50 (ISBN 0-8352-1167-3). Bowker.
Vellinga, Menno. Economic Development & the Dynamics of Class: Industrialization, Power & Control in Monterrey, Mexico. 1979. pap. text ed. 21.50x (ISBN 90-232-1636-9). Humanities.
Vellios, Frank & Christopherson, W. M. Obstetric & Gynecologic Pathology. LC 79-10733. (Anatomic Pathology Slide Seminar Ser.). (Illus.). 1979. pap. text ed. 15.00 o.p. (ISBN 0-89189-070-X, 50-1-044-00); slides 85.00 o.p. (ISBN 0-686-67536-3, 01-1-078-01). Am Soc Clinical.
Vellucci, Augusto, jt. auth. see Nuzzolo, Luccio.
Velsen, Dorothee Von see Von Velsen, Dorothee.
Velsen, J. Van see Van Velsen, J.
Velson, Ruth Fraenkel Von see Ehrenberg, Victor.
Velten, Emmett C., Jr. & Sampson, Carlene. Rx for Learning Disability. LC 77-8595. 1978. 13.95 (ISBN 0-88229-330-3); pap. 7.95 (ISBN 0-88229-559-4). Nelson-Hall.
Veltrusky, Jiri. Drama As Literature. (Pdr Press Publications in Semiotics of Literature: No. 2). (Orig.). 1977. pap. text ed. 8.00x (ISBN 90-316-0127-6). Humanities.
Velz, Clarence J. Applied Stream Sanitation. LC 71-120710. (Environmental Science & Technology Ser). 1970. 55.00 (ISBN 0-471-90525-9, Pub. by Wiley-Interscience). Wiley.
Vemuri, V. Modeling of Complex Systems. (Operation Research & Industrial Engineering). 1978. text ed. 22.00 (ISBN 0-12-716550-9). Acad Pr.
Vemuri, V. & Karplus, Walter. Digital Computer Treatment of Partial Differential Equations. (Illus.). 480p. 1981. text ed. 26.50 (ISBN 0-13-212407-6). P-H.
Ven, Andrew H. Van de see Van de Ven, Andrew H. & Ferry, Diane L.
Venable, Alan. The Checker Players. LC 73-2883. (Illus.). 48p. (gr. k-3). 1973. 6.50 o.p. (ISBN 0-397-31479-5). Lippincott.
Venable, Emerson. The Hamlet Problem & Its Solution. 107p. 1980. Repr. of 1912 ed. lib. bdg. 20.00 (ISBN 0-8492-2835-2). R West.
--Poets of Ohio. LC 73-18459. 1974. Repr. of 1909 ed. 26.00 (ISBN 0-8103-3622-7). Gale.
Venable, Wallace, jt. auth. see Plants, Helen.
Venables, E. Leaving School & Starting Work. 1968. 6.05 o.p. (ISBN 0-08-012954-4); pap. 3.30 o.p. (ISBN 0-08-012953-6). Pergamon.
Venables, Ethel. The Young Worker at College. (Society Today & Tomorrow Ser.). (Illus., Orig.). 1967. 9.95 (ISBN 0-571-08070-7, Pub. by Faber & Faber). Merrimack Bk Serv.
Venables, Ethel C. Intelligence & Motivation Among Day Release Students. (General Ser.). 168p. 1974. pap. text ed. 15.00x (ISBN 0-85633-047-7, NFER). Humanities.
Venables, Robert W., jt. ed. see Vecsey, Christopher.
Venden, Morris. From Exodus to Advent. LC 79-22389. (Orion Ser.). 1979. pap. 2.95 (ISBN 0-8127-0255-7). Southern Pub.
Venden, Morris L. Salvation by Faith & Your Will. LC 78-7597. (Horizon Ser.). 1978. pap. 4.50 (ISBN 0-8127-0190-9). Southern Pub.
Venema, Jack E. & Waldman, John. English Made Simple Jr. Series. pap. 3.50 (ISBN 0-385-00986-0, Made). Doubleday.
Veney, James E., jt. auth. see Kaluzny, Arnold D.
Vengris, Jonas. Lawns -- Basic Factors, Construction & Maintenance of Fine Turf Areas. rev. ed. 10.00 (ISBN 0-913702-05-6). Thomson Pub CA.
Veniard, John. Fly Dressing Materials. 1978. 13.95 (ISBN 0-87691-267-6). Winchester Pr.
Venieris, Y. P. & Sebold, F. D. Macroeconomic, Models & Policy. 1977. 23.95 (ISBN 0-471-90560-7). Wiley.
Veninga, Robert L. & Spradley, James P. The Work-Stress Connection: How to Cope with Job Burnout. 348p. 1981. 12.95 (ISBN 0-316-80747-8). Little.
Venkatacharya, T. Sahityakantakodhara. 96p. 1980. text ed. 10.50 (ISBN 0-8426-1650-0). Verry.
Venkataraman, K. The Analytical Chemistry of Synthetic Dyes. LC 76-39881. 1977. 63.00 (ISBN 0-471-90575-5, Pub. by Wiley-Interscience). Wiley.
--Local Finance in Perspective. 4.50x o.p. (ISBN 0-210-27146-9). Asia.
--Power Development in India. LC 72-10341. 178p. 1972. 12.95 (ISBN 0-470-90578-6). Halsted Pr.
Venkataraman, Krishnasami, ed. The Chemistry of Synthethic Dyes, 8 vols. Incl. Vol. 1. 1952. 62.50 (ISBN 0-12-717001-4); Vol. 2. 1952. 62.50 (ISBN 0-12-717001-4); Vol. 3. 1970. 62.50 (ISBN 0-12-717003-0); Vol. 4. 1971. 62.50 (ISBN 0-12-717004-9); Vol. 5. 1972. 68.00 (ISBN 0-12-717005-7); Vol. 6. 1973. 62.50 (ISBN 0-12-717006-5); Vol. 7. 1974. 62.50 (ISBN 0-12-717007-3); Vol. 8. 1978. 62.50 (ISBN 0-12-717008-1). (Organic & Biological Chemistry Ser.). Set. 412.00 (ISBN 0-12-717002-2). Acad Pr.
Venkataramani, M. S. & Shrivastava, B. K. Quit India: The American Response in the Nineteen Forty-Two Struggle. 1979. 20.00x (ISBN 0-7069-0693-4, Pub. by Croom Helm Ltd. England). Biblio Dist.
--Roosevelt, Gandhi, Churchill. 300p. 1980. text ed. 18.50 (ISBN 0-391-01971-6). Humanities.
Venkatarmani, M. S. Facets of U.S. Interventionism. 300p. 1980. 18.50x (ISBN 0-391-01958-9). Humanities.
Venkatesananda, Swami. Yoga. (Illus., Orig.). 1981. pap. 7.95 (ISBN 0-89407-021-5). Strawberry Hill.
Venkateswaran, Lalitha. Declarations. 4.80 (ISBN 0-89253-760-4); flexible cloth 4.00 (ISBN 0-89253-761-2). Ind-US Inc.
--Rocking Horse. (Redbird Ser). 1975. 8.00 (ISBN 0-88253-618-4); pap. text ed. 4.80 (ISBN 0-88253-617-6). Ind-US Inc.
--Tree-Bird. 8.00 (ISBN 0-89253-749-3); flexible cloth 4.80 (ISBN 0-89253-750-7). Ind-US Inc.
Venn, John. Logic of Chance. 4th ed. LC 62-11698. (YA) (gr. 7-12). 12.95 (ISBN 0-8284-0173-X); pap. 4.95 o.p. (ISBN 0-8284-0169-1). Chelsea Pub.
--The Principles of Inductive Logic. 2nd ed. LC 72-119162. Orig. Title: The Principles of Empirical, or Inductive Logic. 624p. 1973. 18.50 (ISBN 0-8284-0265-5). Chelsea Pub.
--Symbolic Logic. 2nd ed. LC 79-119161. 1971. text ed. 15.95 (ISBN 0-8284-0251-5). Chelsea Pub.
Vennard, John K. & Street, Robert L. Elementary Fluid Mechanics. 5th ed. LC 74-31232. 740p. 1975. text ed. 26.95 (ISBN 0-471-90587-9). Wiley.
--Elementary Fluid Mechanics: SI Edition. 5th ed. LC 76-4885. 1976. 26.95 (ISBN 0-471-90589-5) (ISBN 0-685-68753-8). Wiley.
Vennewitz, Leila, tr. see Boll, Heinrich.
Venning, Ralph. The Plague of Plagues. 1965. pap. 2.45. Banner of Truth.
Venolia, Jan. Better Letters: A Handbook of Business & Personal Correspondence for Secretaries & Their Bosses. LC 80-82634. (Illus.). 175p. (Orig.). Date not set. write for info. (ISBN 0-9602584-3-4); pap. write for info. (ISBN 0-9602584-4-2); plastic spiral avail. Periwinkle Pr. Postponed.
Ventafridda, V., jt. auth. see Twycross, R. G.
Ventafridda, Vittorio, jt. ed. see Bonica, John J.
Ventakataramani, M. S. Undercurrents in American Foreign Relations. 7.50x (ISBN 0-210-22635-8). Asia.
Vento, Carla. Of Time & Value. (Illus.). 96p. (Orig.). 1980. tchr's ed 4.95 (ISBN 0-914634-76-3, 8002). DOK Pubs.
Ventolo & Williams. Fundamentals of Real Estate Appraisal. 2nd ed. 320p. (Orig.). 1979. pap. 22.95 (ISBN 0-88462-285-1). Real Estate Ed Co.
Ventolo, William L., Jr. Principles of Accounting. Davidson, Sidney, ed. (Illus.). 350p. (gr. 12). 1980. text ed. 15.95 (ISBN 0-686-28726-6); pap. text ed. 11.95 (ISBN 0-686-28727-4). Performance Pub.
Ventris, M. & Chadwick, J. Documents in Mycenaen Greek. 2nd ed. (Illus.). 600p. 1973. 110.00 (ISBN 0-521-08558-6). Cambridge U Pr.
Ventura, Paul, jt. ed. see Hoopes, David S.
Venturi, Ken & Barkow, Al. The Venturi Analysis: Learning Better Golf from the Champions. LC 80-69389. 1981. 14.95 (ISBN 0-689-11145-2). Atheneum.
Venturi, Lionello. History of Art Criticism. 1964. pap. 4.25 o.p. (ISBN 0-525-47123-5). Dutton.
Venturini, Joseph L., jt. auth. see Williams, Robert B.
Venugopal, B., jt. auth. see Luckey, T. D.
Venugopalan, M., jt. ed. see Veprek, S.
Venuti, Lawrence, tr. see Alberti, Barbara.
Veomett, Marilyn J., jt. auth. see Ham, Richard G.
Vepa, R. K. How to Set up a Small Scale Industry. 250p. 1980. text ed. 25.00 (ISBN 0-7069-1276-4, Pub by Vikas India). Advent Bk.
Veprek, S. & Venugopalan, M., eds. Plasma Chemistry: Volume III. (Topics in Current Chemistry: Vol. 94). (Illus.). 160p. 1980. 42.50 (ISBN 0-387-10166-7). Springer-Verlag.
Veraldi, Attilio. The Payoff. Quigley, Isabel, tr. from Italian. LC 77-11775. 1978. 8.95 o.s.i. (ISBN 0-06-014493-9, HarpT). Har-Row.
Verandakis, A. Hormones in Development & Aging. Date not set. text ed. price not set (ISBN 0-89335-140-7). Spectrum Pub.
Verba, S., et al. Participation & Political Equality. LC 77-88629. (Illus.). 1978. 32.50 (ISBN 0-521-21905-1); pap. 10.95x (ISBN 0-521-29721-4). Cambridge U Pr.
Verba, Sidney. Small Groups & Political Behavior: A Study of Leadership. (Center of International Studies Ser.). 1961. 14.50 (ISBN 0-691-09333-4); pap. 4.45 o.p. (ISBN 0-691-02815-X). Princeton U Pr.
VerBerg, Kenneth, jt. auth. see Press, Charles.
Verbit, Gilbert P. International Monetary Reform & the Developing Countries: The Rule of Law Problem. LC 74-22362. (International Legal Research Program Ser). 336p. 1975. 22.50x (ISBN 0-231-03832-1). Columbia U Pr.
Verbsky, Ray & Williams, Don. The Gay Print & Coloring Book. 1980. 7.95. Green Hill.
Verby, John E. Family Practice Specialty Board Recertification Review. 3rd ed. 1978. spiral bdg. 16.50 (ISBN 0-87488-309-1). Med Exam.
Vercoe, Bernice & Evans, Dorothy. Australian Book of Cake Decorating. 1973. 8.95x o.p. (ISBN 0-600-07190-1). Exposition.
--Discovering Cake Decorating. 1974. 4.75 o.p. (ISBN 0-600-07243-6). Exposition.
Verderber, Kathleen S., jt. auth. see Verderber, Rudolph F.
Verderber, Rudolph F. Challenge of Effective Speaking. 4th ed. 1979. pap. text ed. 10.95x (ISBN 0-534-00611-6). Wadsworth Pub.
--Communicate! 2nd ed. 1978. pap. text ed. 9.95x o.p. (ISBN 0-534-00559-4). Wadsworth Pub.
--Communicate. 3rd ed. 384p. 1980. pap. text ed. 10.95x (ISBN 0-534-00885-2). Wadsworth Pub.
Verderber, Rudolph F. & Verderber, Kathleen S. Inter-Act: Using Interpersonal Communication Skills. 2nd ed. 368p. 1980. pap. text ed. 9.95x (ISBN 0-534-00785-6). Wadsworth Pub.
Verdery, John D. It's Better to Believe. LC 64-20780. 224p. 1964. 7.95 (ISBN 0-87131-009-0). M Evans.
Verdeyen, Joseph T. Laser Electronics. (Illus.). 480p. 1981. 32.50 (ISBN 0-13-485201-X). P-H.
Verdi, Giuseppe. Falstaff. 480p. 1980. pap. 10.95 (ISBN 0-486-24017-7). Dover.
Verdick, Mary. A Dream Come True. Mooney, Thomas J., ed. (Beginning Pal Paperbacks Ser.). (Illus., Orig.). (gr. 7-12). 1977. pap. text ed. 1.25 (ISBN 0-8374-3451-3). Xerox Ed Pubns.
--Eight Exciting Adventures. Rich, Harry & Smolinski, Richard, eds. (Pal Paperbacks Ser., Kit A). (Illus., Orig.). (gr. 7-12). 1976. pap. text ed. 1.25 (ISBN 0-8374-3489-0). Xerox Ed Pubns.
--Good Times, Bad Times. Mooney, Thomas J., ed. (Beginning Pal Paperbacks Ser.). (Illus., Orig.). (gr. 7-12). 1977. pap. text ed. 1.25 (ISBN 0-8374-3453-X). Xerox Ed Pubns.
--His Chute Didn't Open. Mooney, Thomas, ed. (Pal Paperbacks, Pal Skills Ser.). (Illus., Orig.). (gr. 7-12). 1978. pap. text ed. 1.25 (ISBN 0-8374-6710-1). Xerox Ed Pubns.

--It's a Funny World. Mooney, Thomas J., ed. (Beginning Pal Paperbacks Ser.). (Illus., Orig.). (gr. 7-12). 1977. pap. text ed. 1.25 (ISBN 0-8374-3458-0). Xerox Ed Pubns.

--Sky Dive. Mooney, Thomas J., ed. (Pal Paperbacks Kit A Ser.). (Illus., Orig.). (gr. 7-12). 1976. pap. text ed. 1.25 (ISBN 0-8374-3498-X). Xerox Ed Pubns.

--The World of Animals. Mooney, Thomas J., ed. (Beginning Pal Paperbacks Ser.). (Illus., Orig.). (gr. 7-12). 1977. pap. text ed. 1.25 (ISBN 0-8374-3457-2). Xerox Ed Pubns.

Verdick, Mary, ed. Amazing Adventures. (Pal Paperbacks Ser., Kit A). (Illus., Orig.). (gr. 7-12). 1972. pap. text ed. 1.25 (ISBN 0-8374-3482-3). Xerox Ed Pubns.

--The Blood Suckers. (Pal Paperbacks Ser., Kit A). (Illus., Orig.). (gr. 7-12). 1976. pap. text ed. 1.25 (ISBN 0-8374-3500-5). Xerox Ed Pubns.

--Buried Alive. (Pal Paperbacks, Pal Skills Ser.). (Illus., Orig.). (gr. 7-12). 1978. pap. text ed. 1.25 (ISBN 0-8374-6705-5). Xerox Ed Pubns.

--Just for Kicks. (Pal Paperbacks Ser., Kit B). (Illus., Orig.). (gr. 7-12). 1973. pap. text ed. 1.25 (ISBN 0-8374-3516-1). Xerox Ed Pubns.

--The Magic Bottle. (Pal Paperbacks - Pal Skills Ser.). (Illus., Orig.). (gr. 7-12). 1978. pap. text ed. 1.25 (ISBN 0-8374-6712-8). Xerox Ed Pubns.

--Nine Daring Adventures. (Pal Paperbacks Kit B Ser.). (Illus., Orig.). (gr. 7-12). 1973. pap. text ed. 1.25 (ISBN 0-8374-3520-X). Xerox Ed Pubns.

--On the Ledge. (Pal Paperbacks Kit A Ser.). (Illus., Orig.). (gr. 7-12). 1976. pap. text ed. 1.25 (ISBN 0-8374-3495-5). Xerox Ed Pubns.

--Pal Paperbacks Ser., Kit A. (Pal Paperbacks, Ser., Kit A). (Illus., Orig.). (gr. 7-12). 1976. pap. text ed. 1.25 (ISBN 0-8374-3487-4). Xerox Ed Pubns.

--Real-Life Adventures. (Pal Paperbacks Kit B Ser.). (Illus., Orig.). (gr. 7-12). 1973. pap. text ed. 1.25 (ISBN 0-8374-3507-2). Xerox Ed Pubns.

--Remember Me? (Pal Paperbacks - Pal Skills Ser.). (Illus., Orig.). (gr. 7-12). 1978. pap. text ed. 1.25 (ISBN 0-8374-6709-8). Xerox Ed Pubns.

--Runaway. (Pal Paperbacks Kit A Ser.). (Illus., Orig.). (gr. 7-12). 1976. pap. text ed. 1.25 (ISBN 0-8374-3486-6). Xerox Ed Pubns.

--Summertime Blues. (Pal Paperbacks - Pal Skills Ser.). (Illus., Orig.). (gr. 7-12). 1978. pap. text ed. 1.25 (ISBN 0-8374-6702-0). Xerox Ed Pubns.

--The Switch. (Pal Paperbacks Kit A Ser.). (Illus., Orig.). (gr. 7-12). 1976. pap. text ed. 1.25 (ISBN 0-8374-3491-2). Xerox Ed Pubns.

--What Are Friends for? (Pal Paperbacks - Pal Skills Ser.). (Illus., Orig.). (gr. 7-12). 1978. pap. text ed. 1.25 (ISBN 0-8374-6703-9). Xerox Ed Pubns.

Verdick, Mary, ed. see Andrews, Freida.

Verdick, Mary, ed. see Carlson, Diane.

Verdick, Mary, ed. see Carlson, Gordon.

Verdick, Mary, ed. see Mooney, Thomas J.

Verdick, Mary, ed. see Otfinoski, Steve.

Verdick, Mary, ed. see Otfinoski, Steven.

Verdick, Mary, ed. see Senn, J. A.

Verdiere, Eugene La see LaVerdiere, Eugene.

Verdina, Joseph. Geometry. new ed. (Mathematics Ser). (Illus.). 400p. 1975. text ed. 17.95x (ISBN 0-675-08738-4); instructor's manual 3.95 (ISBN 0-685-50986-9). Merrill.

Verdon, Timothy. The Art of Guido Mazzoni. LC 77-94719. (Outstanding Dissertations in the Fine Arts Ser.). 1978. lib. bdg. 43.00x (ISBN 0-8240-3253-5). Garland Pub.

Verdu, Alfonso. Early Buddhist Philosophy in Light of the Four Noble Truths. LC 79-66172. 1979. pap. text ed. 9.50 (ISBN 0-8191-0189-3). U Pr of Amer.

Verducci, Frank M. Measurement Concepts in Physical Education: An Introduction. LC 79-27528. (Illus.). 374p. 1980. pap. 15.95 (ISBN 0-8016-5225-1). Mosby.

Verduin, J. Field Guide to Lakes. (Earth Science Curriculum Project Pamphlet Ser). 288p. 1971. pap. 3.20 (ISBN 0-395-02622-9, 2-14608). HM.

Verduin, John R., Jr. Curriculum Building for Adult Learning. LC 79-23111. 192p. 1980. 11.95x (ISBN 0-8093-0960-2). S Ill U Pr.

Verduin, John R., Jr., et al. Adults Teaching Adults: Principles & Strategies. 1977. 16.95 (ISBN 0-89384-015-7). Learning Concepts.

Verduin, Leonard. The Anatomy of a Hybrid. 184p. 1976. pap. 4.95 o.p. (ISBN 0-8028-1615-0). Eerdmans.

Vere, E. K. Vande see Vande Vere, E. K.

Verene, Donald P., ed. see Hegel Society of America Conference, 1976.

Verey, David, ed. see Witts, F. E.

Verey, Rosemary. The Herb Growing Book. (Illus.). 48p. (gr. 5 up). 1981. 9.95 (ISBN 0-316-89974-7). Little.

Verga, Giovanni. Mastro-Don Gesualdo. 1979. 15.75x (ISBN 0-520-03598-4). U of Cal Pr.

Vergara, William C. Mathematics in Everyday Things. (Illus.). 1959. 10.95 o.s.i. (ISBN 0-06-006990-2, HarpT). Har-Row.

--Science in the World Around Us. LC 72-79699. (Illus.). 288p. 1973. 10.95 o.s.i. (ISBN 0-06-014766-0, HarpT). Har-Row.

Verge, Roger. Roger Verge's Cuisine of the South of France. (Illus.). 1980. 14.95 (ISBN 0-688-03684-8). Morrow.

Verghese, C. P. Nirad C. Chaudhuri. (Indian Writers Ser.). 1973. 8.50 (ISBN 0-89253-509-1). Ind-US Inc.

Verghese, C. Paul. Nirad C. Chaudhuri. (Indian Writers Ser: No. 2). 118p. (Orig.). 1973. pap. text ed. 3.50x (ISBN 0-391-00430-1). Humanities.

Verghese, Habel. Search for Inner Peace. pap. 1.95 (ISBN 0-89728-055-5, 665278). Omega Pubns OR.

Vergil. Aeneid. 2nd ed. Copley, Frank O., ed. & tr. from Latin. LC 74-28088. (LLA Ser). 350p. 1975. pap. text ed. 6.95 (ISBN 0-672-61370-0). Bobbs.

--Story of Camilla. Tilly, Bertha, ed. text ed. 5.25x (ISBN 0-521-06701-4). Cambridge U Pr.

--Story of Pallas. Tilly, Bertha, ed. 1961. text ed. 5.25x- (ISBN 0-521-06703-0). Cambridge U Pr.

--Story of Trojan Aeneas. Kennedy, E. C. & Tilly, Bertha, eds. text ed. 4.25x (ISBN 0-521-06704-9). Cambridge U Pr.

Vergun, Dimitry, jt. auth. see Ambrose, James.

Verhelst, Wilbert. Sculpture: Tools, Materials, & Techniques. (Illus.). 304p. 1973. ref. ed. 20.95 (ISBN 0-13-796615-6). P-H.

Verheyden, Jack C., ed. see Schleiermacher, Friedrich.

Verheylezoon, Louis. Devotion to the Sacred Heart: Objects, Ends, Practice, Motives. LC 78-74569. 1979. pap. 6.00 (ISBN 0-89555-083-0, 129). TAN Bks Pubs.

Verhoeven, John D. Fundamentals of Physical Metallurgy. LC 75-4600. 567p. 1975. text ed. 30.95 (ISBN 0-471-90616-6). Wiley.

Verhonick, Phyllis. Nursing Research II. 1977. 13.50 (ISBN 0-316-90011-7). Little.

Verhonick, Phyllis J., ed. Nursing Research I. 1975. 13.50 (ISBN 0-316-90010-9). Little.

Verhulst, A. E., jt. auth. see Lyon, Bryce.

Verite, Marcelle. Animals Around the Year. (gr. 4-8). 1972. PLB 10.69 o.p. (ISBN 0-307-67848-2, Golden Pr). Western Pub.

Verity, A. W., ed. Milton's Paradise Lost, 3 vols. 750p. 1980. Repr. of 1921 ed. Set. lib. bdg. 85.00 (ISBN 0-8414-9349-9). Folcroft.

Verity, Arthur, tr. see Horne, Herbert P., et al.

Verity, Enid. Color Observed. 184p. 1980. 18.95 (ISBN 0-442-21906-7). Van Nos Reinhold.

Verkenburg, M. E. Van see Van Valkenburg, M. E.

Verkest, Susan. Crocheting Storybook Hand Puppets. 1980. pap. 1.50 (ISBN 0-486-23887-3). Dover.

Verkler, Linda A. & Zempel, Edward N. Convection Oven Cooking. LC 79-63184. (Illus.). 1979. 10.95 o.p. (ISBN 0-930358-04-X); pap. 6.95 (ISBN 0-930358-03-1). Spoon River.

Verkler, Linda A., jt. ed. see Zempel, Edward N.

Verkler, R. C., jt. auth. see Pegels, C. Carl.

Verlaine. Romances Sans Paroles. Hillery, D., ed. (French Poets Ser.). 110p. 1976. text ed. 11.25x (ISBN 0-485-14712-2, Athlone Pr); pap. text ed. 8.75x (ISBN 0-485-12712-1, Athlone Pr). Humanities.

Verlaine, Paul. Confessions of a Poet. Wolf, Ruth S. & Richardson, Joanna, trs. from Fr. 192p. 1981. Repr. of 1950 ed. lib. bdg. 30.00 (ISBN 0-89987-876-8). Darby Bks.

--Sagesse. Chadwick, Charles, ed. (Athlone French Poets Ser.). 1973. text ed. 16.25x (ISBN 0-485-14704-1, Athlone Pr); pap. text ed. 4.50x (ISBN 0-485-12704-0, Athlone Pr). Humanities.

Verma, Bhawati C. Chitralekha. Karki, Chandra B., tr. 1966. pap. 2.50 (ISBN 0-88253-198-0). Ind-US Inc.

Verma, G. K., et al. Illusion & Reality in Indian Secondary Education. 1979. text ed. 21.50x (ISBN 0-566-00292-2, Pub. by Gower Pub Co England). Renouf.

Verma, Gajendra K., jt. auth. see Bagley, Christopher.

Verma, Harish L. & Gross, Charles W. Introduction to Quantitative Methods: A Managerial Emphasis. LC 77-21089. 1978. text ed. 24.95 (ISBN 0-471-02610-7); tchrs. manual avail. (ISBN 0-471-02495-3, Pub. by Wiley-Hamilton). Wiley.

Verma, M. K. & Sharma, T. N. Intermediate Nepali Reader, 2 vols. 1980. Vol.1. write for info. (ISBN 0-8364-0652-4, Pub. by Manohar India); Vol. 2. write for info. (ISBN 0-8364-0653-2); Set. 32.50 (ISBN 0-686-69016-8). South Asia Bks.

Verma, R. N. Spectroscopic References to Polyatomic Molecules. 125p. 1980. 75.00 (ISBN 0-306-65190-4). IFI Plenum.

Verma, Rajni K. Master Tables for Electromagnetic Depth Sounding Interpretation. (IFI Data Base Library Ser.). 480p. 1980. 75.00 (ISBN 0-306-65188-2, IFI). Plenum Pub.

Verman, Lal C. Standardization, a New Discipline. 1973. 22.50 o.p. (ISBN 0-208-01285-0, Archon). Shoe String.

Vermeil, Edmond. Germany's Three Reichs. LC 68-9638. 1969. Repr. of 1944 ed. 19.00 (ISBN 0-86527-086-4). Fertig.

Vermes, Geza. Dead Sea Scrolls in English. (Orig.). 1962. pap. 3.50 (ISBN 0-14-020551-9, Pelican). Penguin.

--The Dead Sea Scrolls: Qumran in Perspective. LC 80-2382. 240p. 1981. pap. 8.50 (ISBN 0-8006-1435-6, 1-1435). Fortress.

--Jesus the Jew: A Historian's Reading of the Gospels. LC 73-18516. 286p. 1974. 6.95 o.s.i. (ISBN 0-685-39615-0). Macmillan.

--Jesus the Jew: A Historian's Reading of the Gospels. LC 80-2381. 288p. 1981. pap. 6.95 (ISBN 0-8006-1443-7, 1-1443). Fortress.

Vermes, Geza, et al, eds. see Schurer, Emil.

Vermes, H. Precision Bowling for Higher Scores. (Quick & Easy Ser). 1968. pap. 3.95 o.s.i. (ISBN 0-02-082160-3, Collier). Macmillan.

Vermes, Pamela. Buber on God & the Perfect Man. Neusner, J., et al, eds. LC 80-23406. (Brown Judaic Studies). 1981. 15.00 (ISBN 0-89130-426-6); pap. 10.50 (ISBN 0-89130-427-4). Scholars Pr CA.

Vermeule, Cornelius, jt. auth. see Comstock, Mary.

Vermeule, Cornelius C., jt. auth. see Comstock, Mary B.

Vermeule, Emily. Aspects of Death in Early Greek Art & Poetry. LC 76-55573. (Sather Classical Lectures: Vol. 46). 1979. 24.95x (ISBN 0-520-03405-8). U of Cal Pr.

--Aspects of Death in Early Greek Art & Poetry. (Sather Classical Lectures Ser.: No. 46). 1981. pap. 7.95 (ISBN 0-520-04404-5, CAL 504). U of Cal Pr.

--Greece in the Bronze Age. LC 64-23427. 406p. 1972. pap. 12.00 (ISBN 0-226-85354-3, P490, Phoen). U of Chicago Pr.

Vermeule, Emily T. Greece in the Bronze Age. LC 64-23427. (Illus.). 1964. 24.00x (ISBN 0-226-85353-5). U of Chicago Pr.

Vermeule, Emily T. see Euripides.

Vermilye, Dyckman W., ed. The Expanded Campus: Current Issues in Higher Education 1972. LC 72-6043. (Higher Education Ser.). 1972. 12.95x o.p. (ISBN 0-87589-143-8). Jossey-Bass.

--The Future in the Making: Current Issues in Higher Education 1973. LC 73-10935. (Higher Education Ser). 224p. 1973. 11.95x o.p. (ISBN 0-87589-202-7). Jossey-Bass.

--Individualizing the System: Current Issues in Higher Education 1976. LC 76-11947. (Higher Education Ser.). 1976. 12.95x o.p. (ISBN 0-87589-288-4). Jossey-Bass.

--Learner-Centered Reform: Current Issues in Higher Education 1975. LC 75-24001. (Higher Education Ser.). 252p. 1975. 12.95x o.p. (ISBN 0-87589-263-9). Jossey-Bass.

--Lifelong Learners-A New Clientele for Higher Education: Current Issues in Higher Education 1974. LC 74-6738. (Higher Education Ser.). 195p. 1974. 12.95x o.p. (ISBN 0-87589-240-X). Jossey-Bass.

Vermont-Salas, Refugio, jt. auth. see Blair, Robert W.

Vernadakis, Antonia, jt. ed. see Prasad, Kedar N.

Vernadakis, Nikos. Econometric Models for the Developing Economies: A Case Study of Greece. LC 78-61886. (Praeger Special Studies). 1979. 21.95 (ISBN 0-03-047231-8). Praeger.

Vernam, Glen R. & Rice, Lee M. They Saddled the West. LC 75-5734. (Illus.). 1975. 10.00 (ISBN 0-87033-199-X). Cornell Maritime.

Vernam, Glenn R. Incident at Bloody Axe. 1979. pap. 1.50 (ISBN 0-505-51451-6). Tower Bks.

--Man on Horseback: The Story of the Mounted Man from the Scythians to the American Cowboy. LC 64-20544. (Illus.). xii, 436p. 1972. pap. 4.95 (ISBN 0-8032-5770-8, BB 561, Bison). U of Nebr Pr.

Vernant, Jacques. Refugee in the Postwar World. 1953. 42.50x o.p. (ISBN 0-685-69880-7). Elliots Bks.

Vernant, Jean-Pierre & Vidal-Naquet, Pierre. Tragedy & Myth in Ancient Greece. Lloyd, Janet, tr. from Fr. (European Philosophy & the Human Sciences: No. 7). 1981. text ed. 50.00x (ISBN 0-391-01978-3). Humanities.

Vernant, Jean-Pierre, jt. auth. see Detienne, Marcel.

Vernazza, Marcelle, et al. Basic Materials for the Piano Student. 2nd. ed. 1972. plastic comb 7.95x o.p. (ISBN 0-697-03628-6). Wm C Brown.

Vernberg, F. J. & Vernberg, W. B., eds. Functional Adaptations of Marine Organisms. (Physiological Ecology Ser.). 1981. price not set (ISBN 0-12-718280-2). Acad Pr.

Vernberg, W. B., jt. ed. see Vernberg, F. J.

Verne. Captain Nemo's Fantastic Voyage. abr. ed. (gr. 3-5). pap. 1.25 (ISBN 0-590-05811-8, Schol Pap). Schol Bk Serv.

--De la Terre a la Lune. (Easy Reader, C). pap. 3.75 (ISBN 0-88436-048-2, FRA201053). EMC.

Verne, Donald P., ed. see Cassirer, Ernst.

Verne, Jules. The Annotated Jules Verne: From the Earth to the Moon. Miller, Walter J., tr. from Fr. LC 78-3327. (Illus.). 1978. 16.95 o.p. (ISBN 0-690-01701-4, TYC-T). T Y Crowell.

--The Annotated Jules Verne: Twenty Thousand Leagues Under the Sea. Miller, Walter J., ed. LC 76-10968. (Illus.). 1978. 16.95 o.s.i. (ISBN 0-690-01151-2, TYC-T). T Y Crowell.

--Around the Moon. (Childrens Illustrated Classics Ser). (Illus.). 1970. 9.00x o.p. (ISBN 0-460-05087-7, Pub. by J. M. Dent England). Biblio Dist.

--Captain at Fifteen. 1977. 5.50 (ISBN 0-200-72360-X); pap. 1.95 o.p. (ISBN 0-200-72361-8). Transatlantic.

--Doctor Ox's Experiment. 1963. 8.95 (ISBN 0-02-621810-0). Macmillan.

--Journey to the Center of the Earth. (Classics Ser). (gr. 6 up). pap. 1.50 (ISBN 0-8049-0060-4, CL-60). Airmont.

--Michael Strogoff. (Illustrated Classic). (Illus.). (gr. 7-11). 1927. 10.00 o.p. (ISBN 0-684-20972-1, ScribT). Scribner.

--Propeller Island. 1977. 7.95x o.s.i. (ISBN 0-8464-0769-8). Beekman Pubs.

--The Steam House, 2 pts. Incl. Pt. 1. The Demon of Cawnpore. 12.85 ea. (ISBN 0-88411-908-4); Pt. 2. Tigers & Traitors (ISBN 0-88411-909-2). (Illus.). Repr. of 1886 ed. lib. bdg. 12.00 (ISBN 0-686-67026-4). Amereon Ltd.

--Twenty Thousand Leagues Under the Sea. (Literature Ser). (gr. 7-12). 1970. pap. text ed. 3.67 (ISBN 0-87720-740-2). AMSCO Sch.

--Twenty Thousand Leagues Under the Sea. (Illus.). (gr. 7 up). 1962. 5.95 (ISBN 0-02-791640-5). Macmillan.

Verne, Julio. Viaje a la Luna. (Span.). 7.95 (ISBN 84-241-5635-8). E Torres & Sons.

Verner, Coolie, ed. see Pole, Thomas.

Verner, Elizabeth O. Mellowed by Time. 3rd ed. LC 70-127297. 1978. 12.00 (ISBN 0-937684-03-1). Tradd St Pr.

--The Stonewall Ladies. 1963. 6.00 (ISBN 0-937684-07-4). Tradd St Pr.

Verner, Lawrence. Mathematics for Health Practitioners: Basic Concepts & Clinical Applications. LC 78-12176. 1978. pap. 8.75 (ISBN 0-397-54223-2). Lippincott.

Verneuil, Alexander. Humanity's Three Major Contemporary False Prophets & Their Influence Upon the Decline & Chaos of Western Civilization. (Illus.). 1976. 47.80 (ISBN 0-89266-014-7). Am Classical Coll Pr.

Verneuil, M. P. & Grafton, Carol B. One Hundred & Five Art Nouveau Designs in Full Color. (Pictorial Archive Ser.). (Illus.). 48p. (Orig.). 1981. pap. price not set (ISBN 0-486-24112-2). Dover.

Verney, Frances P. Memoirs of the Verney Family, 1465-1696, 4 vols. Incl. Vol. I. During the Civil War. 362p; Vol. II. During the Civil War. 454p; Vol. III. During the Commonwealth, 1650-1660. 494p; Vol. IV. From the Restoration to the Revolution, 1660-1692. 510p. (Illus.). 1971. Repr. of 1892 ed. Set. 145.00x (ISBN 0-7130-0021-X, Pub. by Woburn Pr England). Biblio Dist.

Verney, Michael. Boat Repairs & Conversions. 2nd ed. LC 72-97994. 304p. 1977. 9.95 o.p. (ISBN 0-87742-031-9). Intl Marine.

Verney, Peter. Animals in Peril: Man's War against Wildlife. LC 79-2786. 190p. 1980. 12.95 (ISBN 0-8425-1714-6). Brigham.

--Anzio, Nineteen Forty-Four: An Unexpected Fury. (Illus.). 265p. 1980. 25.00 (ISBN 0-7134-1323-9, Pub. by Batsford England). David & Charles.

Verney, Peter, ed. The Batsford Book of Sporting Verse. (Illus.). 131p. 1980. 17.95 (ISBN 0-7134-2009-X, Pub. by Batsford England). David & Charles.

Verney, Stephen. People & Cities. 1971. pap. 2.45 o.p. (ISBN 0-8007-0437-1). Revell.

Vernier, Patricia. The California Factor. (Orig.). 1980. pap. 2.75 (ISBN 0-440-10989-2). Dell.

Vernon, Arthur. The History & Romance of the Horse. LC 70-185379. (Illus.). xviii, 525p. 1975. Repr. of 1939 ed. 22.00 (ISBN 0-8103-3982-X). Gale.

Vernon, Dorothy. Awaken the Heart. 192p. (Orig.). 1980. pap. 1.50 (ISBN 0-671-57011-0). S&S.

--Kissed by Moonlight. 192p. 1981. pap. 1.50 (ISBN 0-671-57059-5). S&S.

Vernon, Edward. Practice Makes Perfect. LC 77-10174. 1978. 8.95 o.p. (ISBN 0-312-63535-4). St Martin.

Vernon, Frank. The Twentieth-Century Theatre. 159p. 1980. Repr. of 1924 ed. lib. bdg. 30.00 (ISBN 0-89760-927-1). Telegraph Bks.

Vernon, Glenn M. Symbolic Aspects of Interaction. LC 78-69837. 1978. pap. text ed. 10.25 (ISBN 0-8191-0581-3). U Pr of Amer.
--A Time to Die. 1977. 7.50 (ISBN 0-8191-0126-5). U Pr of Amer.
Vernon, Grenville. Yankee Doodle-Doo: A Collection of Songs of the Early American Stage. LC 73-78662. 1972. Repr. of 1927 ed. 20.00 (ISBN 0-8103-3872-6). Gale.
Vernon, Hope J., ed. see Lowell, Maria.
Vernon, Ivan, Jr. & Lamb, Charles, eds. The Pricing Function: A Pragmatic Approach. LC 75-34945. 320p. 1976. 22.95 (ISBN 0-669-00440-5). Lexington Bks.
Vernon, J. A., jt. ed. see Smith, C. A.
Vernon, Jack. Macroeconomics. 464p. 1980. text ed. 19.95 (ISBN 0-03-042336-8). Dryden Pr.
Vernon, John. The First Explorers. 1978. 14.95 (ISBN 0-7134-0986-X, Pub. by Batsford England). David & Charles.
Vernon, M. D. Reading & Its Difficulties: A Psychological Study. LC 73-153013. 1971. 24.50 (ISBN 0-521-08217-X). Cambridge U Pr.
Vernon, Magdalen D. Human Motivation. LC 69-14396. 1969. 27.50 (ISBN 0-521-07419-3); pap. 8.95x (ISBN 0-521-09580-8, 580). Cambridge U Pr.
Vernon, Marjorie. Roses Out of Reach. (Aston Hall Romances Ser.). 192p. (Orig.). 1981. pap. 1.75 (ISBN 0-523-41127-8). Pinnacle Bks.
Vernon, P. F., ed. see Lee, Nathaniel.
Vernon, Philip E. Intelligence: Heredity & Environment. LC 78-11975. (Psychology Ser.). (Illus.). 1979. text ed. 17.50x o.p. (ISBN 0-7167-0738-1); pap. text ed. 10.95x (ISBN 0-7167-0737-3). W H Freeman.
Vernon, R. & Wells, L. T. The Economic Environment of International Business. 2nd ed. 272p. 1976. pap. text ed. 12.95x (ISBN 0-13-224311-3). P-H.
Vernon, R. H. Metamorphic Processes: Reactions & Microstructure Development. LC 75-9139. 1976. 24.95 (ISBN 0-470-90655-3). Halsted Pr.
Vernon, Raymond, jt. auth. see Wells, Louis T.
Vernon, Raymond, jt. auth. see Wells, Louis T., Jr.
Vernon, Raymond, ed. The Oil Crisis. 1976. pap. 6.95 (ISBN 0-393-09186-4). Norton.
Vernon, Thomas S. A Philosophy of Language Primer. LC 80-489. 136p. 1980. text ed. 15.75 (ISBN 0-8191-1023-X); pap. text ed. 7.50 (ISBN 0-8191-1024-8). U Pr of Amer.
Vernon-Jackson, Hugh O. Language, Schools, & Government in Cameroon. LC 67-21502. (Orig.). 1967. pap. text ed. 4.25x (ISBN 0-8077-2299-5). Tchrs Coll.
Verny, Thomas & Kelly, John. The Secret Life of the Unborn Child. 256p. 1981. 12.95 (ISBN 0-671-25312-3). Summit Bks.
Veroff, Joseph, et al. The Inner American: Life, Work, & Mental Health from 1957-1976. LC 80-68187. 492p. 1981. 30.00 (ISBN 0-465-03293-1). Basic.
--Mental Health in America, 1957-1976. LC 80-68959. 1981. 37.50x (ISBN 0-465-04479-4). Basic.
Veron, Enid L., jt. auth. see Redden, Kenneth R.
Verona, O. & Gambogi, P. Genera of Soil Microfungi. Byford, W. J., tr. 320p. 1981. pap. text ed. 25.00x (ISBN 3-7682-1259-9). Lubrecht & Cramer.
Veronesi, Giulia. Style & Design, Nineteen Hundred Nine to Nineteen Twenty-Three. LC 68-20093. (Illus.). 1968. 15.00 o.s.i. (ISBN 0-8076-0448-8). Braziller.
Veronesi, U., et al, eds. see International Union Against Cancer - Committee on Professional Education - Geneva.
Veronneau-Troutman, Suzanne, tr. see Hugonnier, Rene & Clayette-Hugonnier, Suzanne.
Ver Planck, Dennistown W. & Teare, B. R. Engineering Analysis. LC 54-8420. 1954. 23.95x (ISBN 0-471-90618-2). Wiley.
Verplanck, William. Dictionary of Psychology: With Thesaurus. Date not set. postponed 35.00x (ISBN 0-89197-729-5). Irvington. Postponed.
Verrall, Charles, jt. auth. see Scher, Anna.
Verralls, S. Anatomy & Physiology Applied to Obstetrics. (Illus.). 128p. 1969. pap. text ed. 5.00x o.p. (ISBN 0-8464-0132-0). Beekman Pubs.
Verrett, Jacqueline & Carper, Jean. Eating May Be Hazardous to Your Health. 240p. 1975. pap. 2.95 (ISBN 0-385-11193-2, Anchor Pr). Doubleday.
Verrier-Jones, John. Immunological Aspects of Kidney Disease. (Illus.). Date not set. text ed. write for info. (ISBN 0-443-08023-2). Churchill. Postponed.
Versailles, Elizabeth S. Hathaways Twelve Hundred to Nineteen-Eighty. 621p. (YA) 1980. lib. bdg. write for info. Versailles.
Verseau, Dominique. Yolanda. pap. 1.50 o.s.i. (ISBN 0-440-19452-0). Dell.
--Yolanda: Slaves of Space. 1978. pap. 1.95 o.p. (ISBN 0-8021-4018-1, GP4081). Grove.
--Yolanda: The Girl from Erosphere. 1975. pap. 1.50 o.p. (ISBN 0-685-56549-1, D9452, Dist. by Dell). Grove.
Versfeld, Marthinus. An Essays on the Metaphysics of Descartes. LC 68-26210. 1968. Repr. of 1940 ed. 10.00 (ISBN 0-8046-0481-9). Kennikat.
--Our Selves. 175p. 1979. pap. 7.95x (ISBN 0-8476-6223-3). Rowman.
Vershel, Allen. Your Future in Dentistry. LC 77-114127. (Career Guidance Ser). 1971. pap. 3.50 (ISBN 0-668-02239-6). Arco.
Vershueren, Jef. On Speech Act Verbs. (Pragmatics & Beyond: No.4). 91p. 1980. pap. text ed. 17.25x (ISBN 90-272-2508-7). Humanities.
Verstappen, Peter, jt. auth. see Jenkinson, Denis.
Verstappen, Peter, ed. Rand McNally Economy Guide to Europe. LC 78-70555. 1981. pap. 7.95 (ISBN 0-528-84537-3). Rand.
--Rand McNally Guide to France. LC 78-70557. 1981. pap. 6.95 (ISBN 0-528-84536-5). Rand.
--Rand McNally Guide to Great Britain & Ireland. LC 78-70556. (Illus.). 1981. pap. 7.95 (ISBN 0-528-84535-7). Rand.
Ver Steeg & Hofstadster. A People & a Nation. 2nd ed. 1977. 18.44 (ISBN 0-06-552070-X, SchDept); tchr's ed. 15.72 (ISBN 0-06-552252-4); wkbk. 4.08 (ISBN 0-06-552301-6); tchr's wkbk. 7.92 (ISBN 0-06-552452-7); test sets 4.52 ea. Har-Row.
Ver Steeg, Clarence L. Formative Years: 1607-1763. (Making of America Ser). 1964. 8.95 (ISBN 0-8090-4610-5); pap. 5.95 (ISBN 0-8090-0137-3). Hill & Wang.
Verstuyft, Allen W., jt. ed. see Dollberg, Donald D.
Vertuno, jt. auth. see Pecherer.
Vertuno, S., jt. auth. see Pecherer, A.
Vervalin, Charles H., ed. Fire Protection Manual for Hydrocarbon Processing Plants, Vol. 2. (Illus.). 300p. 1981. text ed. 49.95 (ISBN 0-87201-288-3). Gulf Pub.
--Management Handbook for the Hydrocarbon Processing Industries. 242p. 1981. pap. text ed. 16.95 (ISBN 0-87201-480-0). Gulf Pub.
Vervalin, Charlie, ed. Communication Guidelines for Technical Professionals. 220p. (Orig.). 1981. pap. 15.95 (ISBN 0-87201-127-5). Gulf Pub.
Vervliet, H. D., ed. Resource Sharing of Libraries in Developing Countries. (IFLA Publications: No. 14). 286p. 1979. 19.00 (ISBN 0-89664-114-7, Pub. by K G Saur). Shoe String.
Vervoren, Thora & Oppeneer, Joan. Workbook of Solutions & Dosage of Drugs, Including Arithmetic. 11th ed. (Illus.). 1980. pap. text ed. 9.50 (ISBN 0-8016-0236-X). Mosby.
Vervoren, Thora M., jt. auth. see Anderson, Ellen M.
Verwey, Gerlof. Economist's Handbook: A Manual of Statistical Sources. LC 74-157492. 1971. Repr. of 1934 ed. 32.00 (ISBN 0-8103-3728-2). Gale.
Verwey, Wil D. Economic Development, Peace, & International Law. 1972. text ed. 36.50x (ISBN 90-232-0992-3). Humanities.
Verwoerdt, Adriaan. Communication with the Fatally Ill. 196p. 1966. pap. 9.75 spiral (ISBN 0-398-01981-9). C C Thomas.
Veryan, Patricia. Nanette. 288p. 1981. 11.95 (ISBN 0-8027-0664-9). Walker & Co.
Verzar, F. & McDougall, E. J. Absorption from the Intestine. 1968. Repr. of 1936 ed. 18.00 o.s.i. (ISBN 0-02-854200-2). Hafner.
Verzella, Franco, et al. Phacoemulsification. write for info. (ISBN 0-8067-2051-4). Urban & S.
Verzijl, J. J. Production Planning & Information Systems. LC 76-7906. 1976. 29.95 (ISBN 0-470-90620-0). Halsted Pr.
Vesalius, Andreas. The Illustrations from the Works of Andreas Vesalius of Brussels. Saunders, J. B. & O'Malley, Charles D., eds. 13.50 (ISBN 0-8446-4830-2). Peter Smith.
Vesco, Renato. Intercept but Don't Shoot. 336p. 1981. pap. 2.50 (ISBN 0-553-13205-9). Bantam.
Vesely, Anton. Kawasaki Nine Hundred & 1000cc Four, 1973-1979: Includes Shaft Drive Service Repair Performance. Jorgensen, Eric, ed. (Illus.). 324p. (Orig.). 1980. pap. text ed. 9.95 (ISBN 0-89287-321-3, M359). Clymer Pubns.
Vesely, J., et al. Analysis with Ion-Selective Electrodes. 1978. 67.95 (ISBN 0-470-26296-6). Halsted Pr.
Veseth, Michael. Introductory Macroeconomics. 432p. 1980. 12.95 (ISBN 0-12-719550-5); instrs' manual 3.00 (ISBN 0-12-719555-6). Acad Pr.
Vesey, G. N., ed. Body & Mind: Readings in Philosophy. 1964. text ed. 27.50x o.p. (ISBN 0-04-130010-6); pap. text ed. 11.50x o.p. (ISBN 0-04-130014-9). Allen Unwin.
Vesey, Mollie. An Unnecessary Woman. (Orig.). 1980. pap. 2.25 (ISBN 0-505-51503-2). Tower Bks.
Vesey-Fitzgerald, Brian. Portrait of the New Forest. LC 67-70400. (Portrait Bks.). (Illus.). 1966. 10.50x (ISBN 0-7091-6400-9). Intl Pubns Serv.
Vesiland, P., et al. Unit Operations in Resource Recovery Engineering. (Illus.). 1980. text ed. 28.95 (ISBN 0-13-937953-3). P-H.
Vesilind, P. Aarne, jt. auth. see Harrison, Brenda.
Vesilind, P. Aarne, ed. see Klee, Albert J.
Vesper, Carl H. Engineers at Work: A Casebook. 1975. pap. text ed. 10.50 (ISBN 0-395-18407-X). HM.
Vesper, K. New Venture Strategies. 1980. 16.95 (ISBN 0-13-615948-6); pap. 10.95 (ISBN 0-13-615930-3). P-H.
Vessel, Matthew F., jt. auth. see Wong, Herbert H.
Vessey, D. W. Statius & the Thebaid. LC 72-83578. 300p. 1973. 49.50 (ISBN 0-521-20052-0). Cambridge U Pr.
Vest, Lamar. The Church & Its Youth. (CTC Ser.). 1980. 4.50 (ISBN 0-87148-170-7); pap. 3.50 (ISBN 0-87148-171-5); instr's guide 7.95 (ISBN 0-87148-172-3). Pathway Pr.
--What a Life. 1974. pap. 1.75 (ISBN 0-87148-904-X). Pathway Pr.
Vestal, Katherine W. Pediatric Critical Care Nursing. 464p. 1981. 17.95 (ISBN 0-471-05674-X, Pub. by Wiley Med). Wiley.
Vestal, Stanley. Happy Hunting Grounds. 219p. 1980. pap. 4.95 (ISBN 0-8061-1543-2). U of Okla Pr.
--Jim Bridger, Mountain Man. LC 73-108790. (Illus.). 1970. pap. 3.95 (ISBN 0-8032-5720-1, BB 519, Bison). U of Nebr Pr.
--Joe Meek, the Merry Mountain Man. LC 52-5211. (Illus.). 1963. pap. 3.95 (ISBN 0-8032-5206-4, BB 154, Bison). U of Nebr Pr.
--Missouri. LC 44-5196. (Illus.). 1964. pap. 4.50 (ISBN 0-8032-5207-2, BB 186, Bison). U of Nebr Pr.
--Queen of Cowtowns: Dodge City. LC 51-11962. (Illus.). 1972. pap. 3.45 (ISBN 0-8032-5758-9, BB 551, Bison). U of Nebr Pr.
--Sitting Bull, Champion of the Sioux: A Biography. rev.ed ed. (Civilization of the American Indian Ser: No. 46). (Illus.). 1980. Repr. of 1957 ed. 15.95 (ISBN 0-8061-0363-9). U of Okla Pr.
Vestal, Stanley, ed. see Seger, John H.
Vestdijk, Simon, et al. New Writers Two. 1980. pap. 6.00 (ISBN 0-7145-0399-1). Riverrun NY.
Vestermark, Mary, jt. auth. see Channels, Vera.
Vestermark, Mary J., jt. auth. see Johnson, Dorothy E.
Vestly, Anne-Catherine. Hello, Aurora. Amos, Eileen, tr. from Norwegian. LC 74-5008. (Illus.). 96p. (gr. 3-6). 1974. 7.95 o.p. (ISBN 0-690-00513-X, TYC-J). T Y Crowell.
Vet, Charles De see De Vet, Charles & MacLean, Katherine.
Vetter, Carole. Wishing Night. (Illus.). (gr. k-3). 1966. 4.50g o.s.i. (ISBN 0-02-791700-2). Macmillan.
Vetter, George B. Magic & Religion: Their Origins & Consequences. LC 73-82103. 1958. 6.00 (ISBN 0-8022-1776-1). Philos Lib.
Vetter, Harold J. & Rieber, Robert W., eds. Psychological Foundations of Criminal Justice: Contemporary Perpectives on Forensic Psychiartry & Psychology, Vol. 2. LC 78-18781. (Illus.). 416p. 1980. 20.00x (ISBN 0-89444-025-X). John Jay Pr.
Vetter, M. & Maddison, R. Data Base Design Methodology. 1980. 28.00 (ISBN 0-13-196535-2). P-H.
Vetter, Marjorie & Vitray, Laura. Questions Girls Ask. (gr. 7 up). 1959. PLB 5.50 o.p. (ISBN 0-525-37996-7). Dutton.
Vetterling-Braggin & Mary, eds. Sexist Language: A Modern Philosophical Analysis. (Littlefield, Adams Quality Paperbacks Ser.: No. 353). 1981. pap. 7.95 (ISBN 0-8226-0353-5). Littlefield.
Vetterling-Braggin, Mary, ed. Sexist Language: A Modern Philosophical Analysis. 1981. 22.50x (ISBN 0-8476-6293-4). Rowman.
Vettorazzi, Gaston. Hand Book of International Food Regulatory Toxicology, 2 vols. Incl. Vol. 1. Evaluations. 176p. 1980 (ISBN 0-89335-086-9); Vol. 2. Profiles. 256p. 1981. text ed. 30.00 ea. Spectrum Pub.
Veubeke, B. F. De see De Veubeke, B. F.
Vevers, Gwynne. London's Zoo. LC 76-363958. (Illus.). 1979. 12.50 (ISBN 0-370-10440-4, Pub. by Chatto Bodley Jonathan). Merrimack Bk Serv.
--Seashore Life in Color. (European Ecology Ser.). (Illus.). 1969. 9.95 (ISBN 0-7137-0012-2, Pub by Blandford Pr England). Sterling.
Vevers, Gwynne, tr. see Jocher, Willy.
Vevers, Gwynne, tr. see Schiotz, Arne.
Vevers, Gwynne, tr. see Wachtel, Hellmuth.
Vexler, R. I. Idaho Chronology & Factbook, Vol. 12. 1978. 8.50 (ISBN 0-379-16137-0). Oceana.
--Illinois Chronology & Factbook, Vol. 13. 1978. 8.50 (ISBN 0-379-16138-9). Oceana.
--Indiana Chronology & Factbook, Vol. 14. 1978. 8.50 (ISBN 0-379-16139-7). Oceana.
--Iowa Chronology & Factbook, Vol. 15. 1978. 8.50 (ISBN 0-379-16140-0). Oceana.
--Kansas Chronology & Factbook, Vol. 16. 1978. 8.50 (ISBN 0-379-16141-9). Oceana.
--Kentucky Chronology & Factbook, Vol. 17. 1978. 8.50 (ISBN 0-379-16142-7). Oceana.
--Louisiana Chronology & Factbook, Vol. 18. 1978. 8.50 (ISBN 0-379-16143-5). Oceana.
--Maine Chronology & Factbook. 1978. 8.50 (ISBN 0-379-16144-3). Oceana.
--Maryland Chronology & Factbook, Vol. 20. 1978. 8.50 (ISBN 0-379-16145-1). Oceana.
--New Mexico Chronology & Factbook, Vol. 31. 1978. 8.50 (ISBN 0-379-16156-7). Oceana.
--North Carolina Chronology & Factbook, Vol. 33. 1978. 8.50 (ISBN 0-379-16158-3). Oceana.
--North Dakota Chronology & Factbook, Vol. 34. 1978. 8.50 (ISBN 0-379-16159-1). Oceana.
--Ohio Chronology & Factbook, Vol. 35. 1978. 8.50 (ISBN 0-379-16160-5). Oceana.
--Oklahoma Chronology & Factbook, Vol. 36. 1978. 8.50 (ISBN 0-379-16161-3). Oceana.
--Oregon Chronology & Factbook, Vol. 37. 1978. 8.50 (ISBN 0-379-16162-1). Oceana.
--Pennsylvania Chronology & Factbook, Vol. 38. 1978. 8.50 (ISBN 0-379-16163-X). Oceana.
--Rhode Island Chronology & Factbook, Vol. 39. 1978. 8.50 (ISBN 0-379-16164-8). Oceana.
--South Carolina Chronology & Factbook, Vol. 40. 1978. 8.50 (ISBN 0-379-16165-6). Oceana.
--South Dakota Chronology & Factbook, Vol. 41. 1978. 8.50 (ISBN 0-379-16166-4). Oceana.
--Tennessee Chronology & Factbook, Vol. 42. 1978. 8.50 (ISBN 0-379-16167-2). Oceana.
--Texas Chronology & Factbook, Vol. 43. 1978. 8.50 (ISBN 0-379-16168-0). Oceana.
--Utah Chronology & Factbook, Vol. 44. 1978. 8.50 (ISBN 0-379-16169-9). Oceana.
--Vermont Chronology & Factbook. 1978. 8.50 (ISBN 0-379-16170-2). Oceana.
--Vice Presidents & Cabinet Members: Biographies Arranged Chronologically by Administration, Vols. 1-2. 1975. 35.00 ea. Vol. 1 (ISBN 0-379-12089-5). Vol. 2 (ISBN 0-379-12090-9). Oceana.
--Washington Chronology & Factbook, Vol. 47. 1978. 8.50 (ISBN 0-379-16172-9). Oceana.
--West Virginia Chronology & Factbook, Vol. 48. 1978. 8.50 (ISBN 0-379-16173-7). Oceana.
--Wisconsin Chronology & Factbook, Vol. 49. 1978. 8.50 (ISBN 0-379-16174-5). Oceana.
--Wyoming Chronology & Factbook, Vol. 50. 1978. 8.50 (ISBN 0-379-16189-3). Oceana.
Vey, jt. auth. see Von Der Osten.
Vezins, Elie De see De Vezins, Elie.
Veziroglu, T. N., ed. see Solar Cooling & Heating Forum, Dec. 13-15, 1976, Miami Beach.
Veziroglu, T. N., ed. see Two-Phase Flow & Heat Transfer Workshop, Ft. Lauderdale, Oct. 1976.
Veziroglu, T. N., ed. see World Hydrogen Energy Conference, 2nd, Zurich, Aug. 1978.
Veziroglu, T. N., et al, eds. see World Hydrogen Energy Conference, 3rd, Tokyo, Japan 23-26 June 1980, et al.
Veziroglu, T. Nejat, ed. Energy Conservation: Proceedings of the Energy Research & Development Administration Conference Held at the University of Miami, Dec. 1975. 1977. pap. text ed. 110.00 (ISBN 0-08-022134-3). Pergamon.
--Proceedings of the Clean Energy Research Institute, 1st, Miami Beach, 1976. 1976. pap. text ed. 225.00 (ISBN 0-08-021561-0). Pergamon.
Veziroglu, T. Nejat, ed. see Miami International Conference on Alternative Energy Sources, 2nd.
Veziroglu, T. Nejat, ed. see Solar Energy & Conservation Symposium-Workshop, Miami Beach, Florida, 1978.
Vezirogly, T. Nejat, ed. Solar Energy--International Progress: Proceedings of the International Symposium-Workshop on Solar Energy, 16-22 June 1978, Cairo, Egypt. 330.00 (ISBN 0-08-025077-7); pap. 200.00 (ISBN 0-08-025078-5). Pergamon.
Via, Dan O., Jr. The Parables: Their Literary & Existential Dimension. LC 67-11910. 232p. 1974. pap. 4.95 (ISBN 0-8006-1392-9, 1-1392). Fortress.
Via, Dan O., Jr., ed. see Beardslee, William A.
Via, Dan O., Jr., ed. see Doty, William G.
Via, Dan O., Jr., ed. see Perrin, Norman.
Viallet, Pierre. Juliette. LC 76-56393. 1977. pap. 1.75 o.p. (ISBN 0-345-25250-0). Ballantine.
Vialls, Christine. Coalbrookdale & the Iron Revolution: Introduction to the History of Mankind. LC 77-94224. (Illus.). 3.95 (ISBN 0-521-21672-9). Cambridge U Pr.
--Your Book of Industrial Archaeology. (Illus.). 80p. (gr. 4-12). 1981. 9.95 (ISBN 0-571-11633-7, Pub. by Faber & Faber). Merrimack Bk Serv.
Viano, Emilio & Cohn, Alvin W. Social Problems & Criminal Justice. LC 73-92238. (Nelson-Hall Law Enforcement Ser.). 288p. 1975. 18.95 (ISBN 0-88229-115-7). Nelson-Hall.
Viano, Emilio C., ed. Victims & Society. 2nd ed. LC 76-11949. 1980. text ed. 16.50x (ISBN 0-916818-03-9); pap. text ed. 9.95x (ISBN 0-685-96546-5). Visage Pr.

Viard, Jacques. Proust et Peguy: Des Affinites Meconnues. 64p. 1972. pap. text ed. 5.00x (ISBN 0-485-16106-0, Athlone Pr). Humanities.
Vicary, Richard. Manual of Advanced Lithography. LC 76-56890. (Illus.). 1977. 12.50 o.p. (ISBN 0-684-14937-0, ScribT). Scribner.
Vice, Fred H. The Armchair Millionaire. 120p. (Orig.). pap. 7.95 (ISBN 0-87364-204-X). Paladin Ent.
Vicens Vives, Jaime. Approaches to the History of Spain. rev. ed. Ullman, Joan C., tr. 1970. 14.50x (ISBN 0-520-01784-6); pap. 6.95x (ISBN 0-520-01422-7, CAMPUS22). U of Cal Pr.
Vicente, Jesus, et al, eds. Clinical Oncology: The Foundations of Current Patient Management, Vol. 4. LC 80-80729. (Cancer Management Series). (Illus.). 224p. 1980. 43.50 (ISBN 0-89352-083-7). Masson Pub.
Vich, M., jt. auth. see Sutich, A.
Vichenevetsky, Robert. Computer Methods for Partial Differential Equations: Elliptical Equations & the Finite Element Method, Vol. 1. (Illus.). 400p. 1981. text ed. 28.00 (ISBN 0-686-69327-2). P-H.
Vick, Edward. Speaking Well of God. LC 79-9336. (Anvil Ser.). 1979. pap. 6.95 (ISBN 0-8127-0245-X). Southern Pub.
Vick, Edward W. H. Jesus. LC 78-10253. (Anvil Ser.). 1979. pap. 4.95 (ISBN 0-8127-0220-4). Southern Pub.
Vick, James W. Homology Theory: An Introduction to Algebraic Topology. (Pure & Applied Mathematics Ser., Vol. 54). 1973. text ed. 22.95 (ISBN 0-12-721250-7). Acad Pr.
Vick, Nicholas A. Grinker's Neurology. 7th ed. (Illus.). 1104p. 1976. 49.75 (ISBN 0-398-03470-2). C C Thomas.
Vick, R. W. & Schoolbred, C. F. The Administration of Civil Justice in England & Wales. LC 67-31508. 1968. 23.00 (ISBN 0-08-013299-5); pap. 8.75 (ISBN 0-08-013285-5). Pergamon.
Vicker, Denise. God Let Me Out of This Marriage. Boneck, John, ed. LC 80-83459. 160p. 1981. pap. 3.50 (ISBN 0-89221-080-X). New Leaf.
Vickerman, R. W. The Economics of Leisure & Recreation. (Studies in Planning & Control). 1975. text ed. 25.00x o.p. (ISBN 0-333-18300-2). Verry.
Vickers, Brian. Francis Bacon & Renaissance Prose. LC 68-22664. (Illus.). 1968. 56.00 (ISBN 0-521-06709-X, X). Cambridge U Pr.
--Shakespeare: the Critical Heritage. Incl. Vol. 1. 1623-1692. 38.00x (ISBN 0-7100-7716-5); Vol. 2. 1693-1733. 40.00x (ISBN 0-7100-7807-2); Vol. 3. 1733-1752. 38.50x (ISBN 0-7100-7990-7); Vol. 4. 1753-1765. 1976. 41.00x (ISBN 0-7100-8297-5). (Critical Heritage Ser). 1974. Routledge & Kegan.
Vickers, Brian, ed. Shakespeare: The Critical Heritage, 1765-1774, Vol. 5. (Critical Heritage Ser). 1979. 38.50 (ISBN 0-7100-8788-8). Routledge & Kegan.
Vickers, Douglas. Financial Markets in the Capitalist Process. LC 77-20308. (Illus.). 1978. 16.00x (ISBN 0-8122-7739-2). U of Pa Pr.
Vickers, Geoffrey. Making Institutions Work. LC 73-11543. 1973. 19.95 (ISBN 0-470-90689-8). Halsted Pr.
Vickers, John. John Wesley. (Ladybird Ser.). 1977. 1.49 (ISBN 0-87508-841-4). Chr Lit.
--Making & Printing Color Negatives. 1974. 15.95 o.p. (ISBN 0-85242-280-6, Pub. by Fountain). Morgan.
Vickers, John A. Thomas Coke: Apostle of Methodism. 1969. 14.50 (ISBN 0-687-41856-9). Abingdon.
Vickers, M. D. & Wood-Smith, F. G. Drugs in Anesthetic Practice. 5th ed. (Illus.). 1978. text ed. 39.95 (ISBN 0-407-15503-1). Butterworths.
Vickers, Michael, jt. auth. see Post, Kenneth.
Vickery, A., jt. auth. see Vickery, B. C.
Vickery, B. C. Classification & Indexing in Science. 3rd ed. 228p. 1975. 27.95 (ISBN 0-408-70662-7). Butterworths.
Vickery, B. C. & Vickery, A. Information Science: Theory & Practice. 1981. text ed. price not set. Butterworth.
Vickery, D. M. Triage: Problem Oriented Sorting of Patients. (Illus.). 1976. pap. 13.95 (ISBN 0-87618-133-7). R J Brady.
Vickery, John B., ed. Myth & Literature: Contemporary Theory & Practice. LC 65-11563. 1969. pap. 4.50x (ISBN 0-8032-5208-0, BB 500, Bison). U of Nebr Pr.
Vickery, John B. & Sellery, J'nan M, eds. Scapegoat: Ritual & Literature. LC 70-166472. (Myth & Dramatic Form Ser). (Orig.). 1972. pap. text ed. 8.50 (ISBN 0-395-11256-7, 3-57680). HM.
Vickery, Oliver. Harbor Heritage. new ed. 1979. 15.00 (ISBN 0-89430-036-9). Morgan-Pacific.
Vickery, Robert L., Jr. Anthrophysical Form: Two Families & Their Neighborhood Environments. LC 73-183896. 1973. 9.95x (ISBN 0-8139-0393-9). U Pr of Va.
Vickery, Walter N. Alexander Pushkin. (World Authors Ser.: Russia: No. 82). lib. bdg. 9.95 (ISBN 0-8057-2726-4). Twayne.
Victor, Edward. Electricity. (Beginning Science Books). (Illus.). (gr. 2-4). 1967. 2.50 o.p. (ISBN 0-695-82166-0); PLB 3.39 o.p. (ISBN 0-695-42166-2). Follett.
--Friction. (Illus.). (gr. 2-4). 1961. 2.50 o.p. (ISBN 0-695-83205-0); lib. ed. 2.97 o.p. (ISBN 0-695-43205-2). Follett.
Victor, Joan B. Shells Are Skeletons. LC 75-23258. (Let's Read & Find Out Science Book Ser.). (Illus.). (gr. k-3). 1977. 7.89 (ISBN 0-690-01038-9, TYC-J). T Y Crowell.
Victoreen, John A. Basic Principles of Otometry. (Illus.). 232p. 1973. 16.75 (ISBN 0-398-02616-5). C C Thomas.
Victoria, Daizen, jt. auth. see Yokoi, Yuho.
Vida, Ginny, ed. Our Right to Love: A Lesbian Resource Book. LC 77-20184. 1978. 12.95 (ISBN 0-13-644401-6); pap. 9.95 (ISBN 0-13-644393-1). P-H.
Vidal, Gonzalo. Late Precambrian Microfossils from the Visingso Beds in Southern Sweden. (Fossils & Strata: No.9). 1976. pap. text ed. 18.00x (ISBN 8-200-09418-9, Dist. by Columbia U Pr). Universitet.
Vidal, Gore. Washington, D. C. Date not set. pap. 2.50 (ISBN 0-345-27946-8). Ballantine.
Vidal, Gore, jt. ed. see Stanton, Robert J.
Vidal-Naquet, P., jt. auth. see Austin, M. M.
Vidal-Naquet, Pierre, jt. auth. see Vernant, Jean-Pierre.
Vidaver, Doris & Sherry, Pearl A. Arch of a Circle. (Illus.). 144p. 1981. 7.95 (ISBN 0-8040-0807-8); pap. 3.95 (ISBN 0-8040-0808-6). Swallow.
Vide, V. V. American Tableaux, No. 1: Sketches of Aboriginal Life. LC 75-7085. (Indian Captivities Ser.: Vol. 62). 1976. Repr. of 1846 ed. lib. bdg. 44.00 (ISBN 0-8240-1686-6). Garland Pub.
Vidich, Arthur J. & Glasman, Ronald M., eds. Conflict & Control: Challenge to Legitimacy of Modern Governments. rev. ed. LC 78-19653. (Saga Focus Editions: Vol. 7). (Illus.). 304p. 1979. 18.95 (ISBN 0-8039-0974-8). Sage.
Vidigal, B., ed. Oxford Book of Portuguese Verse: 12th Century to 20th Century. 2nd ed. 1953. 11.25x o.p. (ISBN 0-19-812122-9). Oxford U Pr.
Vidler, A. R. Soundings: Essays Concerning Christian Understanding. 1962. 36.00 (ISBN 0-521-06710-3); pap. 10.95x (ISBN 0-521-09373-2). Cambridge U Pr.
--Variety of Catholic Modernists. (Sarum Lectures in the University of Oxford for the Year 1968-69). 1970. 36.00 (ISBN 0-521-07649-8). Cambridge U Pr.
Vidler, Virginia. American Indian Antiques. LC 74-9302. (Illus.). 1976. 20.00 o.p. (ISBN 0-498-01495-9). A S Barnes.
Vidmer, Richard F., jt. auth. see Thompson, James C.
Vidyarthi. The Tribal Culture of India. 1980. text ed. write for info. (ISBN 0-391-01167-7). Humanities.
Vidyarthi, L. P. Rise of World Anthropology. 180p. 1979. text ed. 9.00x (ISBN 0-391-01784-5). Humanities.
--The Sacred Complex in Hindu Gaya. 2nd ed. 264p. 1980. pap. text ed. 11.25x (ISBN 0-391-02214-8). Humanities.
--The Sacred Complex of Kashi. 1979. text ed. 17.50x (ISBN 0-391-01856-6). Humanities.
--South Asian Culture: An Anthropological Perspective. 1976. 11.00x o.p. (ISBN 0-88386-851-2). South Asia Bks.
--Trends in World Anthropology. 112p. 1979. text ed. 8.00x (ISBN 0-391-01783-7). Humanities.
Vidyarthi, L. P., et al. Changing Dietary Patterns & Habits. 1979. text ed. 15.00x (ISBN 0-391-01928-7). Humanities.
Vidyasagar, M. Input-Output Analysis of Large-Scale Interconnected Systems. (Lecture Notes in Control & Information Sciences Ser.: Vol. 29). 225p. 1981. pap. 16.50 (ISBN 0-387-10501-8). Springer-Verlag.
--Non Linear Systems Analysis. LC 77-24379. (Illus.). 1978. ref ed. 27.95x (ISBN 0-13-623280-9). P-H.
Vidyasagar, M., jt. auth. see Desoer, C. A.
Viehe, H. G., jt. auth. see Bohme, H.
Viehe, H. G., jt. ed. see Bohme, H.
Viel, Lyndon. Clay Giants II. (Illus.). 12.95 (ISBN 0-87069-314-X); pap. 1.50 Price Guide (ISBN 0-87069-315-8). Wallace-Homestead.
Vienna, Elizabeth. Nukey Poo. (Illus.). 1980. pap. 4.95 o.p. (ISBN 0-930490-30-4). Future Shop.
Vienna Institute for Comparative Economic Studies. Comecon Data Nineteen Seventy-Nine. LC 80-17577. 436p. 1980. text ed. 45.50x (ISBN 0-8419-0607-6). Holmes & Meier.
Vienna Institute for Comparative Economic Studies, ed. COMECON Foreign Trade Data Nineteen Eighty. LC 80-28569. (Illus.). 509p. 1981. lib. bdg. 40.00 (ISBN 0-313-22988-0, VIC/). Greenwood.
Vierck, Charles J., jt. auth. see French, Thomas E.
Viereck. The Summer I Was Lost. (gr. 3-5). 1980. pap. 1.25 (ISBN 0-590-30060-1, Schol Pap). Schol Bk Serv.
Viereck, Peter R. Terror & Decorum: Poems, 1940-1948. LC 78-178796. 110p. 1948. Repr. lib. bdg. 13.75x (ISBN 0-8371-6296-3, VTDE). Greenwood.
--The Unadjusted Man: A New Hero for Americans. LC 74-178795. 339p. 1973. Repr. of 1956 ed. lib. bdg. 25.00x (ISBN 0-8371-6285-8, VUMA). Greenwood.
Viereck, Phillip. Summer I Was Lost. LC 65-13735. (Illus.). (gr. 6-9). 1965. 8.95 (ISBN 0-381-99659-X, A75800, JD-J). John Day.
Viertel, Weldon. La Biblia Y Su Interpretation. Orig. Title: The Bible & Its Interpretation. 208p. Date not set. pap. write for info. (ISBN 0-311-03670-8). Casa Bautista.
Viertel, Weldon E. El Evangelio y Epistolas De Juan: Texto Programado. 304p. (Span.). 1981. pap. write for info. (ISBN 0-311-04347-X). Casa Bautista.
--Los Hechos De los Apostoles: Texto Programado. 208p. (Span.). 1981. pap. write for info. (ISBN 0-311-04348-8). Casa Bautista.
Vieth, David, ed. see Dryden, John.
Vietnamese Veterans Against the War, jt. auth. see Kerry, John F., Jr.
Vietor, Richard H. Environmental Politics & the Coal Coalition. LC 79-5277. (Environmental History Ser.: No. 2). 304p. 1980. 18.50 (ISBN 0-89096-094-1). Tex A&M Univ Pr.
Vieux, Jacques. The One Night Girl. 65p. (Orig.). 1980. pap. 2.95 (ISBN 0-89260-184-1). Hwong Pub.
Vigar, Penelope. The Novels of Thomas Hardy: Illusion & Reality. 236p. 1974. text ed. 17.50x (ISBN 0-391-00932-X). Humanities.
Vigdorchik, Michael. Submarine Permafrost on the Alaskan Continental Shelf. (Westview Special Studies in Earth Science). 1979. lib. bdg. 24.50x (ISBN 0-89158-659-8). Westview.
Vigenere, Blaise De see Philostratus.
Vigersky, Robert A. Anorexia Nervosa. LC 76-57005. 1977. 31.50 (ISBN 0-89004-185-7). Raven.
Vigeveno, H. S. Thirteen Men Who Changed the World. pap. 2.25 o.p. (ISBN 0-8307-0487-6, 5016207). Regal.
Vigfusson, Gudbrand, jt. ed. see Cleasby, Richard.
Vigil, Alberta G. The Complete Camper's Cookbook: Nearly 200 Easy Recipes for Family Outdoor Cooking. (Illus.). 104p. (Orig.). 1981. pap. 5.95 (ISBN 0-932906-09-5). Pan-Am Publishing Co.
--The Complete Campers Cookbook: Nearly 200 Easy Recipes for Family Outdoor Cooking. LC 80-83880. (Illus.). 104p. 1981. pap. 5.95 (ISBN 0-932906-09-5). Pan-Am Publishing Co.
Vigil, James D. From Indians to Chicanos: A Sociocultural History. LC 80-18539. (Illus.). 180p. pap. text ed. 10.95 (ISBN 0-8016-5230-8). Mosby.
Vigil, Maurilio. Chicano Politics. 1977. pap. text ed. 10.75x (ISBN 0-8191-0110-9). U Pr of Amer.
--Los Patrones: Profiles of Hispanic Political Leaders in New Mexico History. LC 79-6813. 179p. 1980. 17.75 (ISBN 0-8191-0962-2); pap. 8.75 (ISBN 0-8191-0963-0). U Pr of Amer.
Vigilante, Joseph L., jt. ed. see Thursz, Daniel.
Vigliani, E., ed. see International Workshop on Ergonomic Aspects of Visual Display Terminals, Milan, March 1980.
Vigliante, Mary. Source of Evil. (Orig.). 1979. pap. 1.95 (ISBN 0-532-23104-X). Manor Bks.
Viglini, Janelle. A. D. 1975. 12.50 o.p. (ISBN 0-685-54022-7, 0-911156-15-6). Porter.
--P. J. 1975. 12.50 o.p. (ISBN 0-685-54023-5, 0-911156-15-5). Porter.
--The Salvation Merchants. 1975. 7.50 o.p. (ISBN 0-685-53334-4, 0-911156-13-8). Porter.
--Saxon Garters. 1975. 7.50 o.p. (ISBN 0-685-52659-3, 0-911156-14-5). Porter.
--Viglini Letters, Vol. 2. 1976. 12.50 o.p. (ISBN 0-685-67144-5). Porter.
Vigna, Judith. Anyhow, I'm Glad I Tried. Rubin, Caroline, ed. LC 78-12883. (Concept Bks). (Illus.). 32p. (gr. k-2). 1978. 6.95g (ISBN 0-8075-0378-9). A Whitman.
--Couldn't We Have a Turtle Instead. LC 75-8848. (Self Starter Ser). 32p. (gr. k-2). 1975. 6.50g (ISBN 0-8075-1312-1). A Whitman.
--Everyone Goes As a Pumpkin. Rubin, Caroline, ed. LC 77-14254. (Self-Starter Books Ser.). (Illus.). 32p. (ps-1). 1977. 6.50g (ISBN 0-8075-2186-8). A Whitman.
--Gregorio y Sus Puntos. Rubin, Caroline, ed. Ada, Alma F., tr. from Eng. LC 76-47528. (Self-Starter Books Ser.). (Illus.). 32p. (Span.). (gr. k-3). 1976. 6.50g (ISBN 0-8075-3044-1). A Whitman.
--Gregory's Stitches. LC 73-22400. (Self Starter Bks.). (Illus.). 32p. (gr. k-2). 1974. 6.50g (ISBN 0-8075-3046-8). A Whitman.
--The Hiding House. Fay, Ann, ed. LC 79-17251. (Concept Bk.: Level I). (Illus.). 32p. (gr. 1-3). 1979. 6.95g (ISBN 0-8075-3275-4). A Whitman.
--The Little Boy Who Loved Dirt & Almost Became a Superslob. LC 74-14519. (Illus.). 32p. (ps-1). 1975. 6.95g (ISBN 0-8075-0865-9). A Whitman.
--She's Not My Real Mother. Fay, Ann, ed. LC 80-19073. (Concept Bks.). (Illus.). 32p. (gr. k-3). 1980. 6.95g (ISBN 0-8075-7340-X). A Whitman.
Vignaux, Paul. Philosophy in the Middle Ages. Hall, E. C., tr. LC 72-8244. 223p. 1973. Repr. of 1959 ed. lib. bdg. 13.00x o.p. (ISBN 0-8371-6546-6, VIPM). Greenwood.
Vigneron, Jeanette, tr. see Jousseaume, Andre.
Vignone, Joseph A. Collective Bargaining Procedures for Public Library Employees. LC 79-160579. 1971. 10.00 (ISBN 0-8108-0412-3). Scarecrow.
Vigor, P. H. The Soviet View of War, Peace & Neutrality. 1975. 22.00 (ISBN 0-7100-8143-X). Routledge & Kegan.
Vigor, Peter H. Guide to Marxism & Its Effects on Soviet Development. 1966. text ed. 8.00x (ISBN 0-391-00500-6). Humanities.
Vigoureux, P. & Tricker, R. A. Units & Standards of Electromagnetism. LC 77-153869. (Wykeham Science Ser.: No. 15). 1971. 9.95x (ISBN 0-8448-1117-3). Crane Russak Co.
Vigram, George V. The Englishman's Greek Concordance of the New Testament. rev. ed. 1980. pap. 23.95 (ISBN 0-8054-1388-X). Broadman.
Vikari, L. X-Out Cigarettes. 4.00 o.p. (ISBN 0-8062-1077-X). Carlton.
Vikhert, Anatolii M. & Zhdanov, Valentin S. The Effects of Various Diseases on the Development of Atherosclerosis. Muller, James E., ed. LC 80-13069. 220p. 1981. 9.50 (ISBN 0-08-025555-8). Pergamon.
Viking Press Eds., jt. auth. see Stout, Rex.
Vikmyhr, Ronald, jt. auth. see Hall, Keith.
Viksnins, George J. Financial Deepening in the Asian Countries. 96p. (Orig.). 1980. pap. 6.50x (ISBN 0-8248-0745-6). U Pr of Hawaii.
Vila. To the Fountain of Christianity. pap. 2.95 (ISBN 0-686-12322-0). Christs Mission.
Vila, Bob & Davison, Jane. This Old House: Restoring, Rehabilitating & Renovating. (Illus.). 336p. 1980. 22.50 (ISBN 0-316-17704-0); pap. 12.95 (ISBN 0-316-17702-4). Little.
Vila, Maria Arsuaga De see Arsuaga De Vila, Maria.
Vila, Robert & Stephen, George. Bob Vila's This Old House. 1981. 20.00 (ISBN 0-525-93192-9); pap. 13.95 (ISBN 0-525-47670-9). Dutton.
Vilain, Raymond & Michon, Jacques. Plastic Surgery of the Hand & Pulp. LC 78-61477. (Illus.). 184p. 1979. 31.25 (ISBN 0-89352-037-3). Masson Pub.
Vilakazi, Absolom L., et al. Africa's Rough Road: Problems of Change & Development. 1977. pap. text ed. 9.50x (ISBN 0-8191-0113-3). U Pr of Amer.
Vilar, Pierre. Spain: A Brief History. 2nd ed. 1977. text ed. 16.50 (ISBN 0-08-021462-2); pap. text ed. 6.25 (ISBN 0-08-021461-4). Pergamon.
Vilarino De Olivieri, Matilde. La Novelistica de Ciro Alegria. 2nd enlarged ed. LC 79-22294. (Coleccion Mente y Palabra). Orig. Title: Las Novelas de Ciro Alegria. 283p. (Sp.). 1980. 6.25 (ISBN 0-8477-0566-8); pap. 5.00 (ISBN 0-686-61425-9). U of PR Pr.
Vilcek, Jan, et al, eds. Regulatory Functions of Interferons. new ed. LC 80-25207. (Vol. 350). 641p. 1980. 124.00 (ISBN 0-89766-089-7). NY Acad Sci.
--Regulatory Functions of Interferons, Vol. 350. LC 80-25207. 641p. 1980. 124.00x (ISBN 0-89766-089-7); pap. write for info. (ISBN 0-89766-090-0). NY Acad Sci.
Vilela, Ernesto S., tr. see Green, Michael.
Vilela, Ernesto S., tr. see Jewett, Paul K.
Vilela, Ernesto S., tr. see Lewis, C. S.
Vilenkin, N. Ja. Special Functions & the Theory of Group Representations. LC 68-19438. (Translations of Mathematical Monographs: Vol. 22). 1978. Repr. of 1968 ed. 26.00 (ISBN 0-8218-1572-5, MMONO-22). Am Math.
Vilim, E., tr. see Pivovarov, A. A.
Villa, Paola. Corpus of Cypriote Antiquities No. One: Early & Middle Bronze Age Pottery of the Cesnola Collection in the Stanford University Museum. (Studies in Mediterranean Archaeology Ser.: No. XX, Pt. I). 1969. pap. text ed. 11.25x (ISBN 91-85058-21-1). Humanities.
Villadsen, John & Michelson, Michael. Solution of Differential Equation Models for Polynomial Approximation. LC 77-4331. (Illus.). 1977. 29.95 (ISBN 0-13-822205-3). P-H.

Villagran, M. C. Vegetationsgeschichtliche und Pflanzensoziologische Untersuchungen Im Vicente Perez Nationalpark: Chile. (Dissertationes Botanicae: No. 54). (Illus.). 166p. (Ger.). 1981. pap. text ed. 25.00x (ISBN 3-7682-1265-3). Lubrecht & Cramer.
Villalobos, Fernando, tr. see Bergey, Alyce.
Villalobos, Fernando, tr. see Bremm, M. M.
Villalobos, Fernando, tr. see Forell, Betty.
Villalobos, Fernando, tr. see Hill, Dave.
Villalobos, Fernando, tr. see Kramer, Janice.
Villalobos, Fernando, tr. see Latourette, Jane.
Villalobos, Fernando, tr. see Mueller, Virginia:
Villalobos, Fernando, tr. see Warren, Mary.
Villalobos, Fernando P., tr. see Benson, C. H.
Villalobos, Fernando P., tr. see Schultz, Samuel.
Villani, Jim, ed. Literary & Art Anthology, Vol. 2. 88p. 1976. pap. 4.95 (ISBN 0-917530-02-0). Pig Iron Pr.
--Literary & Art Anthology, Vol. 3. 104p. 1977. pap. 4.95 (ISBN 0-917530-06-3). Pig Iron Pr.
--Literary & Art Anthology, Vol. 4. 104p. 1978. pap. 4.95 (ISBN 0-917530-09-8). Pig Iron Pr.
--Literary & Art Anthology, Vol. 5. 96p. 1979. pap. 4.95 (ISBN 0-917530-10-1). Pig Iron Pr.
--Literary & Art Anthology, Vol. 6. 96p. 1979. pap. 4.95 (ISBN 0-917530-11-X). Pig Iron Pr.
Villani, Jim & Sayre, Rose, eds. Pig Iron, Number 8: The New Beats. (Literary & Art Anthology Ser.). 96p. 1980. pap. 4.95 (ISBN 0-917530-16-0). Pig Iron Pr.
Villanucci, R., et al. Electronic Techniques: Shop Practices & Construction. 2nd ed. 1981. 21.00 (ISBN 0-13-252486-4). P-H.
Villanucci, Robert S., et al. Electronic Techniques: Shop Practices & Construction. (Illus.). 1974. ref. ed. 20.95 (ISBN 0-13-252494-5). P-H.
Villanueva, Alma. Bastard Roses. 1981. pap. 4.00 (ISBN 0-915016-31-1). Second Coming.
Villanveva, D. Chicano Sports Heroes: Athletes & Athletics in the Spanish Speaking Community. 1975. 8.95 o.p. (ISBN 0-13-129809-7). P-H.
Villanveva, J. R., et al, eds. Yeast, Mould & Plant Protoplasts. 1974. 52.00 (ISBN 0-12-722160-3). Acad Pr.
Villard, Fanny G., ed. see Villard, Henry.
Villard, Henry. Memoirs of Henry Villard, 2 Vols. Villard, Fanny G., ed. LC 72-87695. (American Public Figures Ser). 1969. Repr. of 1904 ed. lib. bdg. 75.00 (ISBN 0-306-71696-8). Da Capo.
--The Past & the Present of the Pike's Peak Gold Regions. LC 76-87629. (The American Scene Ser). (Illus.). 186p. 1972. Repr. of 1932 ed. lib. bdg. 22.50 (ISBN 0-306-71804-9). Da Capo.
Villard, Kenneth L. & Whipple, Leland. Beginnings in Relational Communication. LC 75-33845. 275p. 1976. pap. text ed. 14.95x (ISBN 0-471-90812-6); instructor's manual avail. (ISBN 0-471-01479-6). Wiley.
Villareal, Ruben L. Tomatoes in the Tropics. (IADS Development-Oriented Ser.). 200p. 1980. lib. bdg. 22.00x (ISBN 0-89158-989-9). Westview.
Villarello, Ildefonso, tr. see Dana, H. E.
Villari, Jack & Villari, Kathleen S. The Official Guide to Disco Dance Steps. Hargrove, Jim, ed. LC 78-9849. (Illus.). 1978. 4.95 o.p. (ISBN 0-89009-259-1, Domus Bks); PLB 4.95 o.p. (ISBN 0-89196-025-2). Quality Bks IL.
Villari, Kathleen S., jt. auth. see Villari, Jack.
Villarreal, Herman. Hypertension. (Becker-Perspectives in Nephrology & Hypertension Ser.). 448p. 1981. 35.00 (ISBN 0-471-07900-6, Pub. by Wiley Med). Wiley.
Villarreeal, Jose Antonio. Pocho. LC 71-11196. 1970. pap. 1.95 (ISBN 0-385-06118-8, Anch). Doubleday.
Villars, Elizabeth. One Night in Newport. LC 80-718. (Illus.). 360p. 1981. 12.95 (ISBN 0-385-15328-7). Doubleday.
Villasenor, Emma Z., tr. see Eudaly, Maria S. De.
Villchur, Edgar. Reproduction of Sound in High Fidelity & Stereo Phonographs. (Illus.). 1966. pap. text ed. 2.00 (ISBN 0-486-21515-6). Dover.
Villee, C. A., ed. Control of Ovulation. 1961. pap. 16.00 (ISBN 0-08-013650-8). Pergamon.
Villee, Dorothy B. Human Endocrinology: A Developmental Approach. LC 73-91280. (Illus.). 479p. 1975. 20.00 (ISBN 0-7216-9041-6). Saunders.
Villegas, Daniel Cosio see Cosio Villegas, Daniel.
Villehardouin, Geoffrey De see De Villehardouin, Geoffrey & De Joinville, Jean.
Villermaux, J. & Trambouze, P., eds. Chemical Reaction Engineering: International Symposium on Chemical Reaction Engineering, Nice, France, March 25-27, 1980, Vol. 1, Contributed Papers. LC 79-41749. 540p. 1980. 77.00 (ISBN 0-08-024018-6). Pergamon.
--Chemical Reaction Engineering: Sixth International Symposium on Chemical Reaction Engineering--Plenary Lectures, Vol. 2. LC 79-41749. (Illus.). 259p. 1980. pap. 40.00 (ISBN 0-08-026234-1). Pergamon.
Villiard, Paul. Birds As Pets. LC 73-20722. 224p. (gr. 5-9). 1974. PLB 6.95 o.p. (ISBN 0-385-04337-6). Doubleday.
--Collecting Stamps. LC 73-10950. 208p. (gr. 5-7). 1974. PLB 7.95 (ISBN 0-385-08677-6). Doubleday.
--Gemstones & Minerals: A Guide for the Amateur Collector & Cutter. (Illus.). 1979. pap. 6.95 (ISBN 0-87691-282-X). Winchester Pr.
--Moths & How to Rear Them. 2nd, rev. ed. (Illus.). 9.50 (ISBN 0-8446-5254-7). Peter Smith.
--Raising Small Animals for Fun & Profit. LC 72-79368. (Illus.). 1975. pap. 3.95 o.p. (ISBN 0-684-14366-6, SL602, ScribT). Scribner.
--Wild Animals Around Your Home. (Illus.). 192p. 1975. 9.95 (ISBN 0-87691-170-X). Winchester Pr.
--Wild Animals Around Your Home. LC 74-16877. (Encore Edition). (Illus.). (gr. 2-7). 1975. pap. 0.95 (ISBN 0-684-15776-4, SL615, ScribT). Scribner.
Villiers, Alan. Battle of Trafalgar. (gr. 5-9). 1965. 4.50g o.s.i. (ISBN 0-02-791830-0). Macmillan.
--Captain James Cook. lib. rep. ed. 1970. Repr. 20.00x (ISBN 0-684-15553-2, ScribT). Scribner.
Villiers, DeL'Isle A. Axel. 1970. 10.95 (ISBN 0-19-647518-X). Dufour.
Villiers, Gerard De see De Villiers, Gerard.
Villiod, Eugene. Stealing Machine. Barnhart, Russell T., tr. LC 76-1271. 225p. 1975. 9.50 (ISBN 0-911996-99-0); pap. 4.50 (ISBN 0-686-67194-5). Gamblers.
Villoldo, Alberto & Dychtwald, Kenneth, eds. Millenium: Glimpses into the Twenty-First Century. (Illus.). 348p. 1981. 15.00 (ISBN 0-87477-145-5); pap. 8.95 (ISBN 0-87477-166-8). J P Tarcher.
Villoria, R., jt. auth. see Archibald, Russell D.
Vilman, James R. Banner in the Sky. (YA) (gr. 7-9). 1980. pap. 1.75 (ISBN 0-671-56081-6). PB.
Vilmorin-Andrieux, M. M. The Vegetable Garden. 620p. 1981. pap. 11.95 (ISBN 0-89815-041-8). Ten Speed Pr.
Vilnay, Zev. The Guide to Israel 1980. 21st ed. LC 66-33490. (Illus.). 662p. 1979. 10.00x (ISBN 0-8002-2713-1). Intl Pubns Serv.
Vinacke, Harold M. Far Eastern Politics in the Postwar Period. LC 55-10400. 1956. 20.00x (ISBN 0-89197-548-9); pap. text ed. 8.95x (ISBN 0-89197-756-2). Irvington.
Vinal, George W. Storage Batteries. 4th ed. LC 54-12826. 1955. 33.00 (ISBN 0-471-90816-9, Pub. by Wiley-Interscience). Wiley.
Vinaver, Eugene. Rise of Romance. 1971. 12.95 (ISBN 0-19-501446-4). Oxford U Pr.
Vinaver, Eugene, ed. see Malory, Thomas.
Vinayshil, Gautam, jt. ed. see Yadava, J. S.
Vincent, Benjamin. A Dictionary of Biography: Past & Present, Containing the Chief Events in the Lives of Eminent Persons of All Ages & Nations. LC 77-174132. 641p. 1974. Repr. of 1877 ed. 42.00 (ISBN 0-8103-3983-8). Gale.
Vincent, Clark E. Unmarried Mothers. LC 80-16580. x, 308p. 1980. Repr. of 1961 ed. lib. bdg. 25.00x (ISBN 0-313-22474-9, VIMO). Greenwood.
Vincent, Denis & Cresswell, Michael. Reading Tests in the Classroom. (General Ser.). 1976. pap. text ed. 15.25x (ISBN 0-85633-101-5, NFER). Humanities.
Vincent, Denis & Dean, Judy. One-Year Courses in Colleges & Sixth Forms: A Report from the Sixteen Plus Education Unit. 1977. pap. text ed. 8.75x (ISBN 0-85633-134-1, NFER). Humanities.
Vincent, E. R., tr. see Abba, Giuseppe C.
Vincent, Harold. Sonship Training. 64p. (Orig.). 1980. pap. 1.50 (ISBN 0-89841-009-6). Zoe Pubns.
Vincent, Howard P. The Trying-Out of Moby Dick. LC 80-16962. (Illus.). 417p. 1980. pap. 8.50x (ISBN 0-87338-247-1). Kent St U Pr.
Vincent, J. F. & Currey, J. D., eds. The Mechanical Properties of Biological Materials. LC 80-40111. (Society of Experimental Biology Symposia Ser.: No. 34). (Illus.). 400p. 1981. 69.50 (ISBN 0-521-23478-6). Cambridge U Pr.
Vincent, J. R., jt. auth. see Henning, D. R.
Vincent, Jack E. Project Theory: Interpretations & Policy Relevance. LC 78-59172. 1978. pap. text ed. 11.25 (ISBN 0-8191-0551-1). U Pr of Amer.
Vincent, James. A Season of Birds: A Norfolk Diary, Nineteen Eleven. (Illus.). 160p. 1980. 14.95 (ISBN 0-89479-068-4). A & W Pubs.
Vincent, Jean A. History of Art. 2nd ed. (Orig.). 1967. pap. 3.95 o.p. (ISBN 0-06-460095-5, 95, COS). Har-Row.
Vincent, Joan. African Elite: The Big Men of a Small Town. LC 79-132691. (Illus.). 1971. 22.50x (ISBN 0-231-03353-2); pap. text ed. 10.00x (ISBN 0-231-08332-7). Columbia U Pr.
--The Curious Rogue. (Orig.). 1981. pap. 1.50 (ISBN 0-440-11186-2). Dell.
--Rescued by Love. (Orig.). 1981. pap. 1.50 (ISBN 0-440-17433-3). Dell.
Vincent, Jon S. Joao Guimaraes Rosa. (World Authors Ser.: No. 506 (Brazil)). 1978. 13.50 (ISBN 0-8057-6347-3). Twayne.
Vincent, Keith. Nailsea Glass. (Illus.). 1975. 7.50 (ISBN 0-7153-6807-9). David & Charles.
Vincent, L. M. Competing with the Sylph: Dancers & the Pursuit of the Ideal Body Form. 143p. 1980. pap. 5.95 (ISBN 0-8362-2407-8). Andrews & McMeel.
Vincent, M. O. God, Sex & You. 1976. pap. 1.75 (ISBN 0-89129-191-1). Jove Pubns.
Vincent, M. R. Philippians & Philemon. LC 4-1629. (International Critical Commentary Ser.). 248p. Repr. of 1904 ed. text ed. 17.50x (ISBN 0-567-05031-9). Attic Pr.
Vincent, Marvin. Word Studies in the New Testament, 4 Vols. 1957. 42.50 (ISBN 0-8028-8083-5). Eerdmans.
Vincent, Stephen, ed. & intro. by. Five on the Western Edge. (Illus.). 1977. o.p. (ISBN 0-917672-01-1); pap. 4.95x (ISBN 0-917672-00-3). Momos.
Vincent, Stephen, ed. Omens from the Flight of Birds: The First 101 Days of Jimmy Carter. (Illus.). 1978. lib. bdg. o.p. (ISBN 0-917672-06-2); pap. 4.95x (ISBN 0-917672-05-4). Momos.
Vincent, Stephen & Zweig, Ellen, eds. The Poetry Reading. 1981. lib. bdg. 20.00 (ISBN 0-917672-36-4); pap. 7.95 (ISBN 0-917672-35-6). Momos.
Vincent, Ted. Mudville's Revenge. LC 80-52410. 384p. 1981. 12.95 (ISBN 0-87223-661-7). Seaview Bks.
Vincent, Thomas. The Shorter Catechism Explained from Scripture. (Puritan Paperbacks). 282p. (Orig.). 1980. pap. 3.95 (ISBN 0-85151-314-X). Banner of Truth.
Vincent, Thomas L. & Grantham, Walter J. Optimality in Parametric Systems. 250p. 1981. 30.00 (ISBN 0-471-08307-0, Pub. by Wiley-Interscience). Wiley.
Vincent, William F., jt. auth. see Spackman, Robert R., Jr.
Vincentius, Bellovacensis. Hier Begynneth the Table of the Rubrices of This Presente Volume Namde the Myrrour of the Worlde or Thymage of the Same. Caxton, William, tr. from Fr. LC 79-84143. (English Experience Ser.: No. 960). 204p. (Eng.). 1979. Repr. of 1481 ed. lib. bdg. 30.00 (ISBN 90-221-0960-7). Walter J Johnson.
Vinci, Leonardo. Li Zite 'ngalera. Brown, Howard M., ed. LC 76-21072. (Italian Opera Ser.: Vol. 25). 1979. lib. bdg. 75.00 (ISBN 0-8240-2624-1). Garland Pub.
Vinci, Leonardo Da see Da Vinci, Leonardo.
Vinciguerra, Matthew M., jt. auth. see Bay, Kenneth E.
Vinck, Jose De see Raya, Joseph & De Vinck, Jose.
Vine, Ian, jt. ed. see Von Cranach, Mario.
Vine, Louis D. Your Dog, His Health & Happiness: The Breeder's & Pet Owners Guide to Better Dog Care. LC 72-88607. 446p. 1973. pap. 4.95 (ISBN 0-668-02876-9). Arco.
Vine, P. A. London's Lost Route to the Sea: An Historical Account of the Inland Navigations Which Linked the Thames to the English Channel. 3rd ed. (Inland Waterways Histories Ser.). 1973. 14.95 (ISBN 0-7153-6203-8). David & Charles.
Vine, Richard A. John Barth: An Annotated Bibliography. LC 76-55322. (Author Bibliographies Ser.: No. 31). 1977. 10.00 (ISBN 0-8108-1003-4). Scarecrow.
Vine, Richard P. Commercial Winemaking: Processing & Controls. (Illus.). 1981. text ed. 19.50 (ISBN 0-87055-376-3). AVI.
Vine, Richard P., jt. auth. see Taylor, Walter S.
Vine, W. E. An Expository Dictionary of New Testament Words. 1978. 13.95 (ISBN 0-8407-5138-9). Nelson.
Vine, W. E., jt. auth. see Hogg, C. F.
Vineberg, Arthur M. Myocardial Revascularization by Arterial Ventricular Implants. LC 80-10654. (Illus.). 624p. 1981. text ed. 49.50 (ISBN 0-88416-191-9). PSG Pub.
Viner, Jim & Sagstetter, Brad. Officer in Trouble. 200p. (Orig.). 1981. price not set (ISBN 0-89896-001-0). Larksdale.
Vines, Alice G. Neither Fire nor Steel: Sir Christopher Hatton. LC 77-21424. 1978. 15.95 (ISBN 0-88229-372-9). Nelson-Hall.
Vines, Jerry. Great Events in the Life of Christ. 1979. pap. 1.95 (ISBN 0-88207-776-7). Victor Bks.
--I Shall Return: Jesus. 1977. pap. 2.50 (ISBN 0-88207-702-3). Victor Bks.
--Interviews with Jesus. 1981. 3.25 (ISBN 0-8054-5180-3). Broadman.
Vines, K. N; see Reisman, L., et al.
Vines, Lois. Guide to Language Camps in the United States. (Language in Education Ser.: No. 26). 1980. pap. text ed. 3.95 (ISBN 0-87281-114-X). Ctr Appl Ling.
Vines, Robert A. Trees of East Texas. (Illus.). 640p. 1977. text ed. 24.95x (ISBN 0-292-78016-8); pap. 9.95 (ISBN 0-292-78017-6). U of Tex Pr.
Vines, Sherard. Georgian Satirists: Edward Young, Christopher Smart, Charles Churchill. 217p. 1980. Repr. of 1934 ed. lib. bdg. 25.00 (ISBN 0-8495-5528-0). Arden Lib.
Vines, Steve see Kaldor, Mary, et al.
Viney, Wayne, et al, eds. The History of Psychology: A Guide to Information Sources. LC 79-9044. (Psychology Information Guide Ser.: Vol. 1). 1979. 30.00 (ISBN 0-8103-1442-8). Gale.
Vineyard, Ben S., jt. auth. see Kimbrell, Grady.
Vinge, Joan. The Snow Queen. 1981. pap. 3.25 (ISBN 0-440-17749-9). Dell.
Vinge, Joan D. Fireship. 1978. pap. 1.75 o.s.i. (ISBN 0-440-15794-3). Dell.
Vinge, Vernor see Martin, George R.
Vinger, Paul F. & Hoerner, Earl F., eds. Sports Injuries: The Unthwarted Epidemic. LC 79-22195. (Illus.). 450p. 1981. text ed. 49.50 (ISBN 0-88416-260-5). PSG Pub.
Vingoe, Frank J. Clinical Psychology & Medicine: An Interdisciplnary Approach. (Illus.). 480p. 1981. text ed. 35.00x. Oxford U Pr.
Vinh, Nguyen X., et al. Hypersonic & Planetary Entry Flight Mechanics. 376p. 1980. 29.95x (ISBN 0-472-10004-1). U of Mich Pr.
Vinh Quang Tran. Foreign Exchange Management in Multinational Firms. Dufey, Gunter, ed. (Research for Business Decisions). 246p. 1980. 27.95 (ISBN 0-8357-1133-1, Pub. by UMI Res Pr). Univ Microfilms.
Vining, Elizabeth G. I, Roberta. LC 67-26611. 1967. 4.95 o.s.i. (ISBN 0-397-00468-0). Lippincott.
--Windows for the Crown Prince: An American Woman's Four Years As Private Tutor to the Crown Prince of Japan. (Illus.). (gr. 7-9). 1952. 9.95 (ISBN 0-397-00037-5). Lippincott.
Vinitskii, I. M., jt. auth. see Samsonov, Gregory.
Vinje, Helge. Defensive Play in Bridge: Featuring the Distribution Signal. Reese, Terence, ed. LC 79-57451. (Illus.). 192p. 1980. 7.95 o.p. (ISBN 0-8069-4938-4); lib. bdg. 7.49 o.p. (ISBN 0-8069-4939-2). Sterling.
Vinne, Theodore L. De see De Vinne, Theodore L.
Vinnichenko, N. K. & Gorelik, A. G., eds. Advances in Satellite Meteorology, Vol. 2. Levi, M., tr. from Rus. 1974. text ed. 26.95 (ISBN 0-470-90836-X). Halsted Pr.
Vinnikov, Ya. A & Titova, L. K. The Organ of Corti: Its Histophysiology & Histochemistry. LC 62-21544. 253p. 1964. 32.50 (ISBN 0-306-10669-8, Consultants). Plenum Pub.
Vinogradov, A. P. & Udintsev, G. B., eds. The Rift Zones of the World Oceans. Kaner, N., tr. from Rus. LC 75-16178. 503p. 1975. 69.95 (ISBN 0-470-90838-6). Halsted Pr.
Vinogradov, G. V. & Malkin, A. Y. Rheology of Polymers. (Illus.). 468p. 1981. 58.00 (ISBN 0-387-09778-3). Springer-Verlag.
Vinogradova, O. S., jt. ed. see Sokolov, E. N.
Vinoi, Lawrence. God & Man: The Essential Knowledge Which Everyone, but Absolutely Everyone Ought to Possess About Human Nature & the Nature of God & How the Two Are Related. (Essential Knowledge Ser. Books). (Illus.). 1978. plastic spiral bdg. 24.75 (ISBN 0-89266-118-6). Am Classical Coll Pr.
Vinokur, G. O. Russian Language: A Brief History. Forsyth, J., ed. LC 70-127238. (Illus.). 1971. 28.50 (ISBN 0-521-07944-6). Cambridge U Pr.
Vinokur, Grigory. A Grain of Salt. LC 80-17406. 208p. 1981. 9.95 (ISBN 0-8119-0330-3). Fell.
Vinovskis, M. A., jt. auth. see Kaestle, C. F.
Vinovskis, Maris A., jt. ed. see Schneider, Carl.
Vins, Georgi. Georgi Vins Prisoner of Conscience. Bourdeaux, Michael, ed. Ellis, Jane, tr. from Rus. LC 75-18986. 288p. (Orig.). 1975. pap. 2.95 o.s.i. (ISBN 0-912692-84-7). Cook.
Vinsant, Marielle & Spence, Martha I. Commonsense Approach to Coronary Care: A Program. 3rd ed. LC 80-36795. 350p. 1980. pap. text ed. 13.95 (ISBN 0-8016-5235-9). Mosby.
Vinson, Donald E. & Sciglimpaglia, Donald. The Environment of Industrial Marketing. LC 74-20124. (Marketing Ser.). 1975. pap. text ed. 12.95 (ISBN 0-88244-074-8). Grid Pub.
Vinson, J. R., ed. Emerging Technologies in Aerospace Structures, Design, Structural Dynamics & Materials. 326p. 1980. 40.00 (H00157). ASME.
Vinson, Jack R. Structural Mechanics: The Behavior of Plates & Shells. LC 73-19881. 288p. 1974. 21.95 o.p. (ISBN 0-471-90837-1, Pub. by Wiley-Interscience). Wiley.
Vinson, James & Kirkpatrick, Daniel, eds. Great Dramatists. (Great Writers of the English Language Ser.). 700p. 1979. 45.00 (ISBN 0-312-34570-4). St Martin.
--Great Novelists & Prose Writers. (Great Writers of the English Language Ser.). 1400p. 1979. 45.00x (ISBN 0-312-34624-7). St Martin.

--Great Poets. (Great Writers of the English Language Ser.). 1200p. 1979. 45.00x (ISBN 0-312-34640-9). St Martin.

Vinson, Jim & Kirkpatrick, Daniel, eds. Contemporary Poets. 3rd ed. (Contemporary Writers Ser.). 1900p. 1980. lib. bdg. 60.00x (ISBN 0-312-16765-2). St Martin.

Vinson, Kathryn. Run with the Ring. LC 65-22747. (gr. 7 up). 1965. 5.50 o.p. (ISBN 0-15-269793-4, HJ). HarBraceJ.

Vinterberg, H. & Axelsen, J., eds. Danish-English, English-Danish Dictionary, 2 vols. 8th & 10th ed. 1979. Set. 50.00 (ISBN 0-685-36173-X). Vol. 1, Danish-English (ISBN 8-7001-1282-8). Vol. 2, English-Danish (ISBN 8-7013-3451-4). Heinman.

Vinton, Dearing see Dryden, John.

Vinton, Dearing A. see Dryden, John.

Vinton, John, ed. The Dictionary of Contemporary Music. 1974. 25.00 o.p. (ISBN 0-525-09125-4). Dutton.

Vinyard, Dale. Congress. (Orig.). 1968. pap. 2.45 o.p. (ISBN 0-684-12659-1, SL318, ScribT). Scribner.

--Presidency. pap. 2.65 o.p. (ISBN 0-684-12534-X, SL292, ScribT). Scribner.

Vinyard, William C. Diatoms of North America. 2nd ed. (Illus.). 1979. pap. 5.95x (ISBN 0-916422-15-1). Mad River.

Vinycomb, John. Fictitious & Symbolic Creatures in Art with Special Reference to Their Use in British Heraldry. LC 76-89300. (Illus.). 1969. Repr. of 1906 ed. 18.00 (ISBN 0-8103-3147-0). Gale.

Viola, Herman J. Diplomats in Buckskins: A History of Indian Delegations in Washington City. LC 80-607804. (Illus.). 1981. 17.50 (ISBN 0-87474-944-1). Smithsonian.

--Thomas L. McKenney, Architect of America's Early Indian Policy: 1816-1830. LC 74-18075. (Illus.). xii, 365p. (Orig.). 1981. pap. 8.95x (ISBN 0-8040-0669-5, SB). Swallow.

Viola, Herman J., jt. ed. see Kvasnicka, Robert M.

Violi, Paul. Harmatan: A Poem. LC 77-3648. 1977. pap. 4.00 (ISBN 0-915342-24-3). Sun.

Violi, Unicio J. Monarch Notes on Shakespeare's Measure for Measure. (Orig.). pap. 1.95 (ISBN 0-671-00636-3). Monarch Pr.

--Monarch Notes on the New Testament. (Orig.). pap. 2.50 (ISBN 0-671-00625-8). Monarch Pr.

Viollet-Le-Duc, Eugene E. Habitations of Man in All Ages. Bucknall, Benjamin, tr. LC 74-146922. 1971. Repr. of 1876 ed. 32.00 (ISBN 0-8103-3787-8). Gale.

Viorst, Judith. Alexander, Who Used to Be Rich, Last Sunday. 1980. pap. 1.95 (ISBN 0-689-70476-3, Aladdin). Atheneum.

--It's Hard to Be Hip Over Thirty & Other Tragedies of Married Life. 1980. 4.95 (ISBN 0-453-00276-5, H276). NAL.

--The Tenth Good Thing About Barney. (Illus.). (gr. k-4). 1975. pap. 2.95 (ISBN 0-689-70416-X, Aladdin). Atheneum.

Viorst, Milton. Fire in the Streets. 1981. 8.95 (ISBN 0-671-42814-4, Touchstone). S&S.

Viotti, Andrea. Garibaldi: The Revolutionary & His Men. (Illus.). 224p. 1980. 22.50 (ISBN 0-7137-0942-1, Pub. by Blandford Pr England). Sterling.

Viotti, Staffan, jt. auth. see Eidem, Rolf.

Vipond, Stanley, jt. auth. see Withers, Bruce.

Vira, Soma. Little Bit India-Little Bit U. S. A. Poems from East & West. 1981. 7.95 (ISBN 0-533-04911-3). Vantage.

Virdell, Paul. The Initiates. LC 80-70225. 288p. 1981. 11.95 (ISBN 0-87795-314-7). Arbor Hse.

Vireswarananda, Swami, tr. Srimad Bhagavad Gita. (Sanskrit & Eng.). 5.25 (ISBN 0-87481-421-9). Vedanta Pr.

Virga, Vincent. Gaywyck. 384p. 1980. 2.95 (ISBN 0-380-75820-2, 75820). Avon.

Virgil. Aeneid. 1957. 5.00x o.p. (ISBN 0-460-00161-2, Evman). Dutton.

--Aeneid. Knight, William F., tr. (Classics Ser.). (Orig.). 1956. pap. 2.95 (ISBN 0-14-044051-8). Penguin.

--Aeneid of Virgil. 1953. pap. 2.95 (ISBN 0-385-09318-7, A20, Anch). Doubleday.

--Aeneidos: Liber Quartus. Austin, R. G., ed. 1955. 14.50x (ISBN 0-19-872020-3). Oxford U Pr.

--Aeneidos: Liber Secundus. Austin, R. G., ed. 1964. 18.95x (ISBN 0-19-872018-1); pap. 13.95x (ISBN 0-19-872106-4). Oxford U Pr.

--Aeneidos: Libri VII & VIII. Christie, John D., ed. (Lat.). 1978. text ed. 36.00x (ISBN 0-19-713309-6). Oxford U Pr.

--Bucolics. Page, T. E., ed. Incl. Georgics. (Classic Ser). 396p. (Lat.). 1898. 9.95 o.p. (ISBN 0-312-84910-9). St Martin.

--Georgics. Bovie, Smith P., tr. LC 56-11264. 1966. pap. 4.00x o.s.i. (ISBN 0-226-06778-5); pap. 4.00x (ISBN 0-226-85740-9). U of Chicago Pr.

--Opera. Mynors, R. A., ed. (Oxford Classical Texts Ser). 1969. 14.95x (ISBN 0-19-814653-1). Oxford U Pr.

--Opera, 2 vols. LC 75-27849. (Renaissance & the Gods Ser.: Vol. 7). (Illus.). 1977. Repr. of 1544 ed. Set. lib. bdg. 146.00 (ISBN 0-8240-2056-1); lib. bdg. 73.00 ea. Garland Pub.

Virgines, George. Saga of the Colt Six Shooter: And the Famous Men Who Used It. LC 69-10772. (gr. 9 up). 1969. 7.95 (ISBN 0-8119-0148-3). Fell.

Virginia Council of Teachers of Mathematics. Practical Ways to Teach the Basic Mathematical Skills. 1979. pap. 7.50 (ISBN 0-686-65437-4). NCTM.

Virginia Historic Landmarks Commission. Historic American Buildings Survey, Virginia Catalog: A List of Measured Drawings, Photographs, & Written Documentation in the Survey. LC 74-7402. (Illus.). 350p. 1975. 20.00x (ISBN 0-8139-0518-4); pap. 7.95x (ISBN 0-8139-0708-X). U Pr of Va.

Virion, Charles. Charles Virion's French Country Cookbook. Backman, Beth, ed. (Illus.). 416p. 1980. pap. 7.95 (ISBN 0-8015-1198-4, Hawthorn). Dutton.

Virkler, Henry A. Hermeneutics: Principles & Processes of Biblical Interpretation. 200p. 1981. 12.95 (ISBN 0-8010-9282-5). Baker Bk.

Virtanen, John O. Molotov Cocktail. (Orig.). 1980. pap. 2.25 (ISBN 0-505-51517-2). Tower Bks.

Vis, Johan W. Scherzo. Date not set. 8.95 (ISBN 0-533-04811-7). Vantage.

Visak, Edward H. Milton Agonistes: A Metaphysical Criticism. 104p. 1980. Repr. of 1923 ed. lib. bdg. 17.50 (ISBN 0-8492-2834-4). R West.

Vischer, Lukas, jt. ed. see Feiner, Johannes.

Vischer, Peter, ed. Horse & Horseman. (Illus.). 15.75 o.p. (ISBN 0-85131-130-X, Dist. by Sporting Book Center). J A Allen.

Viscione, Jerry. Financial Analysis: Principles & Procedures. LC 76-13794. (Illus.). 1977. pap. text ed. 9.50 (ISBN 0-395-24455-2); inst. manual with solutions 1.50 (ISBN 0-395-24454-4). HM.

Viscione, Jerry & Aragon, George. Cases in Financial Management. LC 79-87854. 1979. text ed. 18.50 (ISBN 0-395-26715-3); instructor's manual 3.00 (ISBN 0-395-26716-1). HM.

Visco, Louis J. The Manager As an Editor: Reviewing Memos, Letters & Reports. 172p. 1981. pap. 8.95 (ISBN 0-8436-0852-8). CBI Pub.

Viscomi, Gregory N., jt. auth. see Taylor, Kenneth J.

Visconti, A. Quantum Field Theory, Vol. 1. LC 66-18237. 1969. 37.00 (ISBN 0-08-011821-6). Pergamon.

Viscusi, Margo. Literacy for Working: Functional Literacy in Rural Tanzania. (Educational Studies & Documents, No. 5). (Illus.). 57p. (Orig.). 1972. pap. 2.50 (ISBN 92-3-100905-2, U360, UNESCO). Unipub.

Visentin, Charles. A Message to an Aborted Baby Killed by the Cowardice of His Mother & the Venal Complicity of the Attending Physician. (Illus.). 1976. 29.50 (ISBN 0-89266-015-5). Am Classical Coll Pr.

Visher, Emily B. & Visher, John S. A Manual for Stepfamilies. 150p. 1981. 10.00 (ISBN 0-87630-268-1). Brunner-Mazel.

--Stepfamilies: Myths & Realities. 1980. pap. 6.95 (ISBN 0-8065-0743-8). Lyle Stuart.

Visher, John S., jt. auth. see Visher, Emily B.

Vishwanathan, C. G. Public Library Operations & Services. 2nd rev. ed. 5.50x (ISBN 0-210-33927-6). Asia.

Vishwanathan, K. S. Many Electron Problem. 10.00x (ISBN 0-310-26904-0). Asia.

Visiak, E. H. Life's Morning Hour. 1969. text ed. 6.25x (ISBN 0-212-99826-9). Humanities.

--Portent of Milton: Some Aspects of His Genius. 1969. Repr. of 1958 ed. text ed. 8.00x (ISBN 0-391-00473-5). Humanities.

Visick, Jacquey. Planning a Town Garden. (Design Centre Bks.). 1978. pap. 6.95 o.p. (ISBN 0-8256-3096-7). Music Sales.

Visigli, R. El Gesticulador: Pieza Para Demagogos En Tres Actos. Ballinger, R., ed. (Span.). 1963. 8.95 (ISBN 0-13-273771-X). P-H.

Visnapuu & Gaede, Inc. Fisher Hall, Miami University, Oxford, Ohio: Its Preservation Potential. (Consultant Service Grant Report). (Illus.). 25p. 1973. pap. 3.00 (ISBN 0-89133-012-7). Preservation Pr.

Visocchi, Mark, jt. auth. see Jenkins, David.

Visscher, Maurice B. Ethical Constraints & Imperatives in Medical Research. (American Lectures in Behavioral Science & Law Ser.). 128p. 1975. 12.50 (ISBN 0-398-03404-4). C C Thomas.

Visscher, Michel De see De Visscher, Michel.

Visser, H. The Quantity of Money. LC 75-4762. 294p. 1975. text ed. 18.95 (ISBN 0-470-90845-9). Halsted Pr.

Visser, John & Chapman, David. Snakes & Snakebite. 1980. 30.00x (Pub. by Bailey & Swinton South Africa). State Mutual Bk.

Visser, Pat. Feelings from A to Z. (A Young Reader Ser.). (Illus.). (gr. k-3). PLB 5.00 (ISBN 0-307-60200-1, Golden Pr). Western Pub.

Visser, W. A., ed. Geological Nomenclature. 568p. 1980. lib. bdg. 95.00 (ISBN 90-247-2403-1). Kluwer Boston.

Vistnes, Lars M., et al. Plastic & Reconstructive Surgery. 2nd ed. Laub, Donald R. & Ott, Richard F., eds. (Medical Examination Review Ser.: Vol. 27). 1977. spiral bdg. 19.50 (ISBN 0-87488-129-3). Med Exam.

Viswanathan, M., jt. ed. see Podolsky, Stephen.

Viswanathan, Raman. Diseases of the Chest. 1968. 15.95x o.p. (ISBN 0-210-31243-2). Asia.

Viswanathan, S. The Shakespeare Play As Poem. LC 79-41618. 250p. 1980. 29.50 (ISBN 0-521-22547-7). Cambridge U Pr.

Vita-Finzi, Claudio. Mediterranean Valleys: Geological Change in Historical Times. LC 69-10341. (Illus.). 1969. 32.50 (ISBN 0-521-07355-3). Cambridge U Pr.

Vital, Claude & Vallat, Jean M. Ultrastructural Study of the Human Diseased Peripheral Nerve. (Illus.). 200p. 1980. 35.00 (ISBN 0-89352-096-9). Masson Pub.

Vital, David. The Origins of Zionism. (Illus.). 412p. 1975. 12.95x (ISBN 0-19-827439-4); pap. 12.95x (ISBN 0-19-827439-4). Oxford U Pr.

Vitale, A., et al. Fathers & Mothers. 140p. 1973. pap. 7.00 (ISBN 0-88214-306-9). Spring Pubns.

Vitale, Barbara A., et al. A Problem Solving Approach to Nursing Care Plans: A Program. LC 77-14222. (Illus.). 1978. pap. text ed. 9.50 (ISBN 0-8016-5243-X). Mosby.

Vitale, Joseph J., ed. Advances in Human Clinical Nutrition. (Illus.). 236p. 1981. text ed. 24.50 (ISBN 0-88416-219-2). PSG Pub.

Vitale, Philip. Basic Tools of Research. 3rd ed. LC 74-8827. (gr. 9-12). 1975. pap. text ed. 3.50 (ISBN 0-8120-0627-5). Barron.

Vitanyi, B. The International Regime of River Navigation. 406p. 1980. 57.50x (ISBN 90-286-0529-0). Sijthoff & Noordhoff.

Vitarelli, Robert, ed. Eight Haunted Stories. (Pal Paperbacks Ser., Kit B). (Illus., Orig.). (gr. 7-12). 1973. pap. text ed. 1.25 (ISBN 0-8374-3519-6). Xerox Ed Pubns.

--The Honda Kid. (Pal Paperbacks Ser., Kit B). (Illus., Orig.). (gr. 7-12). 1973. pap. text ed. 1.25 (ISBN 0-8374-3512-9). Xerox Ed Pubns.

--Payoff in the Park. (Pal Paperbacks Kit A Ser.). (Illus., Orig.). (gr. 7-12). 1972. pap. text ed. 1.25 (ISBN 0-8374-3481-5). Xerox Ed Pubns.

--The Sacrifice. (Pal Paperbacks Kit A Ser.). (Illus., Orig.). (gr. 7-12). 1973. pap. text ed. 1.25 (ISBN 0-8374-3485-8). Xerox Ed Pubns.

--Sports Action. (Pal Paperbacks Kit A Ser.). (Illus., Orig.). (gr. 7-12). 1973. pap. text ed. 1.25 (ISBN 0-8374-3484-X). Xerox Ed Pubns.

--Strange Happenings. (Pal Paperbacks Kit B Ser.). (Illus., Orig.). (gr. 7-12). 1973. pap. text ed. 1.25 (ISBN 0-8374-3508-0). Xerox Ed Pubns.

--Ten Top Favorites. (Pal Paperbacks Kit B Ser.). (Illus., Orig.). (gr. 7-12). 1972. pap. text ed. 1.25 (ISBN 0-8374-3511-0). Xerox Ed Pubns.

--The Weird Witch's Spell. (Pal Paperbacks Kit A Ser.). (Illus., Orig.). (gr. 7-12). 1972. pap. text ed. 1.25 (ISBN 0-8374-3480-7). Xerox Ed Pubns.

Vitek, Donna. A Different Dream. 192p. (Orig.). 1980. pap. 1.50 (ISBN 0-671-57033-1). S&S.

--Promises from the Past. 192p. 1981. pap. 1.50 (ISBN 0-671-57066-8). S&S.

--Showers of Sunlight. 192p. (Orig.). 1980. pap. 1.50 (ISBN 0-671-57047-1). S&S.

Vitek, John D., jt. ed. see Coates, Donald R.

Viteles, Harry. A History of the Co-Operative Movement in Israel: A Source Book in Seven Volumes. Incl. Bk. 1. The Evolution of the Co-Operative Movement. 252p. 1966. (ISBN 0-85303-052-9); Bk. 2. The Evolution of the Kibbutz Movement. 749p. 1967. (ISBN 0-85303-053-7); Bk. 3. An Analysis of the Four Sectors of the Kibbutz Movement. 751p. 1968. (ISBN 0-85303-010-3); Bk. 4. Co-Operative Smallholders Settlements: The Moshav Movement. 405p. 1968. (ISBN 0-85303-012-X); Bk. 5. Workers Producers Transportation & Service Co-Operatives. 414p. 1968. (ISBN 0-85303-013-8); Bk. 6. Central Agricultural Co-Operatives. 750p. 1970. (ISBN 0-85303-031-6); Bk. 7. Consumers Co-Operative. 348p. 1970. 140.00x set (ISBN 0-686-23409-X). 100.00x set (ISBN 0-686-23407-3, Pub. by Vallentine Mitchell England); 20.00x ea. Biblio Dist.

Vitelli, James R. Randolph Bourne. (United States Authors Ser.: No. 408). 1981. lib. bdg. 12.95 (ISBN 0-8057-7337-1). Twayne.

--Van Wyck Brooks. (U. S. Authors Ser.: No. 134). 1969. lib. bdg. 10.95 (ISBN 0-8057-0096-X). Twayne.

Viterbi, Andrew J. & Omura, James K. Principles of Digital Communication & Coding. (Electrical Engineering Ser.). (Illus.). 1979. text ed. 31.95 (ISBN 0-07-067516-3, C); solution manual avail. (ISBN 0-07-067517-1). McGraw.

Vithoulkas, George. The Science of Homeopathy. 1980. 9.50 (ISBN 0-394-17560-3, E746, Ever). Grove.

Vitiello, Justin, ed. see Dolci, Danilo.

Vito, Joseph A. De see De Vito, Joseph A.

Vito, Joseph De see De Vito, Joseph A.

Vito, R. A. De see De Vito, Robert A. & Tapley, Richard P.

Vitousek, Paige, jt. auth. see Reilly, John.

Vitray, Laura, jt. auth. see Vetter, Marjorie.

Vitriano, Dorothy B. Legends of the Earth. 1976. pap. 4.95 (ISBN 0-8065-0534-6). Citadel Pr.

Vitrikas, Robert P. MGA: A History, & Restoration Guide. (Illus.). 208p. 1980. pap. 19.95 (ISBN 0-89404-031-6). Aztex.

Vitruvius. Ten Books on Architecture. Morgan, Morris H., tr. (Illus.). pap. text ed. 4.00 (ISBN 0-486-20645-9). Dover.

Vitsaxis, Vassilis G. Hindu Epics, Myths & Legends in Popular Illustrations. (Illus.). 1978. 10.95x (ISBN 0-19-560971-9). Oxford U Pr.

Vittitow, Mary L., jt. auth. see Liu, Sarah.

Vitzthum, Richard C. The American Compromise. 1978. pap. 5.95 (ISBN 0-8061-1477-0). U of Okla Pr.

--The American Compromise: Theme & Method in the Histories of Bancroft, Parkman, & Adams. LC 73-7429. 300p. 1974. 12.95x (ISBN 0-8061-1142-9). U of Okla Pr.

Vivante, Arturo. English Stories. LC 75-19938. (Illus.). 64p. (Orig.). 1975. pap. 4.95 o.p. (ISBN 0-914908-27-8). Street Fiction.

--Writing Fiction. 1980. 10.95 (ISBN 0-87116-122-2). Writer.

Vivante, Arturo, tr. see Vivante, Leone.

Vivante, Leone. Essays on Art & Ontology. Vivante, Arturo, tr. from It. 1980. 15.00x (ISBN 0-87480-100-1). U of Utah Pr.

Vivas, Eliseo. Two Roads to Ignorance: A QuasiBiography. LC 79-757. 318p. 1979. 18.95 (ISBN 0-8093-0916-5). S Ill U Pr.

Vivekananda, Swami. Inspired Talks, My Master & Other Writings. LC 58-13132. 280p. pocket ed. soft cover 3.50 (ISBN 0-911206-19-1). Ramakrishna.

--Letters of Swami Vivekananda. 2nd ed. 7.50 o.s.i. (ISBN 0-87481-093-0); pap. 6.95 o.s.i. (ISBN 0-87481-192-9). Vedanta Pr.

--Religion of Love. 114p. pap. 1.95 (ISBN 0-87481-129-5). Vedanta Pr.

Viveros-Long, Anamaria, jt. auth. see Bohen, Halcyone H.

Vivian, Charles. Science Experiments & Amusements for Children. LC 67-28142. Orig. Title: Science Games for Children, Il. (ps-6). 1967. pap. 2.50 (ISBN 0-486-21856-2). Dover.

Vivian, Charles H. & Jackson, Bernetta M. English Composition. (Orig.). 1961. pap. 4.50 (ISBN 0-06-460102-1, CO 102, COS). Har-Row.

Vivian, Gordon & Reiter, Paul. The Great Kivas of Chaco Canyon & Their Relationships. (School of American Research Monograph: No. 22). (Illus.). 112p. 1980. pap. 7.50 (ISBN 0-8263-0297-1). U of NM Pr.

Vividishananda, Swami, tr. see Shivananda, Swami.

Vivis, Antony, tr. see Vogt, Paul.

Vixman, Rachel, ed. see Robert, Henry M.

Vizard, David. How to Rebuild Small-Block Chevys. LC 78-52275. (Illus.). 1978. pap. 7.95 (ISBN 0-912656-66-2). H P Bks.

Vizenor, Gerald. Earthdivers: Tribal Narratives on Mixed Descent. (Illus.). 195p. 1981. 14.95 (ISBN 0-8166-1048-7). U of Minn Pr.

--The Everlasting Sky: New Voices from the People Named the Chippewa. LC 70-189729. (Illus.). (gr. 7 up). 1972. 7.95 (ISBN 0-02-792250-2, CCPr). Macmillan.

--Wordarrows: Indians & Whites in the New Fur Trade. LC 78-3202. xiv, 164p. 1981. pap. 6.95 (ISBN 0-8166-0862-8). U of Minn Pr.

Vizetelly, E., tr. see Zola, Emile.

Vizetelly, Frank H. Desk-Book of Errors in English. LC 74-3021. 1974. Repr. of 1920 ed. 18.00 (ISBN 0-8103-3637-5). Gale.

Vizetelly, Frank H. & De Bekker, Leander J. Desk-Book of Idioms & Idiomatic Phrases in English Speech & Literature. LC 73-121208. 1970. Repr. of 1923 ed. 24.00 (ISBN 0-8103-3291-4). Gale.

Vizi, E. S. & Wollemann, Marie, eds. Aminergic & Peptidergic Receptors: Satellite Symposium of the Third Congress of the Hungarian Pharmacological Society, Szeged, 1979. LC 80-41281. (Advances in Pharmacological Research & Practice Ser.: Vol. VII). 220p. 1981. 41.00 (ISBN 0-08-026839-0). Pergamon.

Vizi, E. S., ed. see Hungarian Pharmacological Society, 3rd Congress, Budapest, 1979.

Vizmathy-Susits, Gisela, tr. see Donath, Ferenc.

Vlach, John M. The Afro-American Tradition in Decorative Arts. LC 77-19326. (Illus.). 184p. 1978. pap. 12.00x (ISBN 0-910386-39-0, Pub. by Cleveland Mus Art). Ind U Pr.
Vlack, Don. Art Deco Architecture in New York, 1920-1940. LC 74-6577. (Icon Editions). (Illus.). 190p. 1975. 17.50x o.s.i. (ISBN 0-06-438850-6, HarpT). Har-Row.
Vlack, Lawrence H. Van see Van Vlack, Lawrence H.
Vlahos, Charles J. Fell's Guide to Operating Shortwave Radio. (gr. 9 up). 1969. 8.95 o.s.i. (ISBN 0-8119-0047-9). Fell.
Vlahov, R., ed. Chemistry of Natural Products, Eleven: International Symposium on Chemistry of Natural Products, 11th, Golden Sands, Bulgaria, 17-23 September, 1978. 1979. 41.00 (ISBN 0-08-022366-4). Pergamon.
Vlasic, Bob. One Hundred & One Pickle Jokes. 1974. pap. 1.25 o.s.i. (ISBN 0-515-03553-X, N3553). Jove Pubns.
Vlasov, K. A., et al. Lovozero Alkali Massif. Tomkeieff, S. I. & Battey, M. H., eds. (Illus.). 1966. 49.25 o.s.i. (ISBN 0-02-854230-4). Hafner.
Vlasto, A. P. Entry of the Slavs into Christendom: An Introduction to the Medieval History of the Slav. LC 70-98699. 1970. 44.50 (ISBN 0-521-07459-2). Cambridge U Pr.
Vlastos, Gregory. Platonic Studies. 2nd ed. LC 80-8732. 520p. 1981. 35.00x; pap. 12.50. Princeton U Pr.
Vlastos, Gregory, ed. see Plato.
Vleck, John H. Van see Van Vleck, John H.
Vleck, L. Dale Van see Schmidt, Glen H. & Van Vleck, L. Dale.
Vleck, William C. Van see Van Vleck, William C.
Vlesmas, Jerry, tr. see Makris, Kallistos.
Vliegenthart, A. W., jt. auth. see Ryskamp, Charles.
Vlieger, M. de see De Vlieger, M.
Voak, Sally A. Natural & Herbal Beauty. LC 77-85030. (Penny Pinchers Ser.). 1978. 2.95 (ISBN 0-7153-7550-4). David & Charles.
Vobis, G. Bau und Entwicklung der Flechtenpycnidien und Ihrer Goniedien. (Bibliotheca Lichenologica: No. 14). 200p. (Ger.). 1981. pap. text ed. 25.00x (ISBN 3-7682-1270-X, Pub. by Cramer Germany). Lubrecht & Cramer.
Vocke, William C. American Foreign Policy: An Analytical Approach. LC 74-19681. (Illus.). 1976. pap. text ed. 9.95 (ISBN 0-02-933420-9). Free Pr.
Vocolo, Joseph M., et al. Voces de juventud. (gr. 9-12). 1978. pap. text ed. 4.80 (ISBN 0-205-05816-7, 4258169). Allyn.
Vodar, B., ed. see International AIRAPT Conference, Le Creuset, France, July 30-Aug. 3, 1979.
Vodar, Boris & Romand, J. Some Aspects of Vacuum Ultraviolet Radiation Physics. LC 73-20163. 1974. text ed. 46.00 (ISBN 0-08-016984-8). Pergamon.
Vo-Dinh, jt. auth. see Hanh, Nhat.
Vodorsky-Shiraeff, Alexandria, ed. Russian Composers & Musicians: A Biographical Dictionary. LC 71-76422. (Music Ser.). 1969. Repr. of 1940 ed. lib. bdg. 19.50 (ISBN 0-306-71321-7). Da Capo.
Voe, Thomas F De see De Voe, Thomas F.
Voegele, Walter O., jt. auth. see Pfeiffer, William B.
Voegelin, Eric. Plato. LC 57-11670. 1966. pap. text ed. 6.95 (ISBN 0-8071-0102-8). La State U Pr.
Voehl, Dick, jt. auth. see Bellak, Rhoda.
Voelke, William. The Stavelot Triptych: Mosan Art & the Legand of the True Cross. LC 80-8970. (Illus.). 80p. 1980. pap. 3.70 (ISBN 0-87598-071-6). Pierpont Morgan.
Voelkle, William. The Spanish Forger. LC 78-60193. (Illus.). 77p. 1978. 35.00 (ISBN 0-87598-065-1); pap. 19.50 (ISBN 0-87598-054-6). Pierpont Morgan.
Voelter, W. & Weitzel, G., eds. Structure & Activity of Natural Peptides: Selected Topics. 480p. 1980. 91.00x (ISBN 3-11-008264-0). De Gruyter.
Voelter, Wolfgang, jt. auth. see Gupta, Derek.
Voet-Griselle, Jenny, jt. auth. see Vost, Leon.
Vogan, Sara. In Shelly's Leg. LC 80-20390. 256p. 1981. 10.95 (ISBN 0-394-51451-3). Knopf.
Voge, J., jt. auth. see David, P.
Voge, Marietta, jt. auth. see Markell, Edward K.
Vogel. Progress in Earthquake Prediction Research, Vol. 2. 1980. write for info. (ISBN 0-9940013-4-7, Pub. by Vieweg & Sohn Germany). Heyden.
Vogel, A. I. Elementary Practical Organic Chemistry: Pt. 2, Qualitative Organic Analysis. 2nd ed. 1966. 16.95 (ISBN 0-471-90963-7). Halsted Pr.
--Vogel's Elementary Practical Organic Chemistry: Small Scale Preparations, Pt. 1. 3rd ed. Smith & Waldron, eds. 1979. text ed. 24.00 (ISBN 0-582-47009-9). Longman.
--Vogel's Textbook of Quantitative Inorganic Analysis. 4th ed. Bassett, J., et al, eds. LC 77-5545. (Illus.). 1978. text ed. 42.00x (ISBN 0-582-46321-1). Longman.
Vogel, A. I. & Svehla, G., eds. Vogel's Textbook of Macro & Semimicro Qualitative Inorganic Analysis. 5th ed. LC 77-8290. 1979. 40.00x (ISBN 0-582-44367-9). Longman.
Vogel, Arthur A. The Gift of Grace. 1980. 1.50 (ISBN 0-686-28778-9). Forward Movement.
--The Power of His Resurrection: The Mystical Life of Christians. 150p. 1976. 6.95 (ISBN 0-8164-0298-1). Crossroad NY.
Vogel, Arthur A., jt. auth. see Krentz, Edgar.
Vogel, C. J. De see De Vogel, C. J.
Vogel, David, jt. auth. see Bradshaw, Thornton.
Vogel, David, jt. auth. see Powers, Charles W.
Vogel, David J., jt. auth. see Powers, Mark J.
Vogel, Ezra F. Japan As Number One: Lessons for America. LC 79-24059. 1980. pap. 4.95 (ISBN 0-06-090791-6, CN 791, CN). Har-Row.
--Japan's New Middle Class: The Salary Man & His Family in a Tokyo Suburb. new enl. ed. 1971. 19.50x (ISBN 0-520-02092-8); pap. 5.75x (ISBN 0-520-02100-2, CAMPUS72). U of Cal Pr.
Vogel, Ezra F., ed. Modern Japanese Organization & Decision-Making. 1975. 24.95x (ISBN 0-520-02857-0); pap. 5.95 o.p. (ISBN 0-520-03038-9). U of Cal Pr.
Vogel, Ezra F., jt. ed. see Bell, Norman W.
Vogel, F. Stephen, jt. auth. see Burger, Peter C.
Vogel, Henry J., jt. ed. see Jagiello, Georgiana.
Vogel, Henry J., jt. ed. see Pernis, Benvenuto.
Vogel, Ilse-Margaret. My Summer Brother. LC 80-7911. (Illus.). 96p. (gr. 2-5). 1981. 8.95 (ISBN 0-06-026324-5, HarpJ); PLB 8.79g (ISBN 0-06-026325-3). Har-Row.
Vogel, Ilse-Margret. Bear in the Boat. (Little Golden Reader). (Illus.). (gr. k-3). 1979. PLB 5.38 (ISBN 0-307-60397-0, Golden Pr). Western Pub.
--Daisy Dog's Wake-Up Book. (A Young Reader Ser.). (Illus.). 24p. (gr. k-3). 1979. PLB 5.00 (ISBN 0-307-60102-1, Golden Pr). Western Pub.
--My Little Dinosaur. (Illus.). 24p. (ps-2). 1971. PLB 5.00 (ISBN 0-307-60571-X, Golden Pr). Western Pub.
Vogel, Isle-Margret. Don't Be Scared Book. (Illus.). (ps-1). 1974. pap. 2.95 (ISBN 0-689-70307-4, Aladdin). Atheneum.
--Juggle with Me! (Illus.). (ps-1). 1970. PLB 5.00 (ISBN 0-307-60594-9, Golden Pr). Western Pub.
Vogel, J. H., ed. Current Concepts in Clinical Cardiology. (Advances in Cardiology Ser.: Vol. 27). (Illus.). viii, 360p. 1980. 118.75 (ISBN 3-8055-0098-X). S Karger.
Vogel, James M., et al. How to Live with Hemophilia. (Illus.). 140p. (Orig.). 1972. pap. 2.75 o.p. (ISBN 0-913456-66-7). Interbk Inc.
Vogel, Joseph F. Dante Gabriel Rossetti's Versecraft. LC 76-150655. (U of Fla. Humanities Monographs: No. 34). 1971. pap. 3.50 (ISBN 0-8130-0324-5). U Presses Fla.
Vogel, Linda J. Helping a Child Understand Death. LC 74-26325. 96p. 1975. pap. 2.50 (ISBN 0-8006-1203-5, 1-1203). Fortress.
Vogel, Lucy, ed. Alexander Blok: An Anthology of Essays & Memoirs. 1981. 17.50 (ISBN 0-88233-487-5). Ardis Pubs.
Vogel, Otto, jt. auth. see Siebert, Dick.
Vogel, R. A. & Krabbe, M. Mass Communications. LC 76-44136. (Ser. in Speech Communication). 1977. pap. text ed. 5.95 (ISBN 0-8465-7601-5); instr's. guide 3.95 (ISBN 0-8465-7607-4). Benjamin-Cummings.
Vogel, R. A., jt. ed. see Brooks, W. D.
Vogel, R. A., ed. see Kelley, Robert.
Vogel, R. A., ed. see Leth, Pamela C. & Leth, Steven A.
Vogel, Ronald J., jt. auth. see Blair, Roger D.
Vogel, Rosemarie, et al. Natural Proteinase Inhibitors. 1969. 24.00 (ISBN 0-12-722850-0). Acad Pr.
Vogel, Steven & Ewel, Katherine C. A Model Managerie: Laboratory Studies About Living Systems. 1972. pap. text ed. 7.95 (ISBN 0-201-08149-0). A-W.
Vogel, Steven & Wainwright, Stephen. A Functional Bestiary: Laboratory Studies About Living Systems. (Illus., Orig.). 1969. 7.95 (ISBN 0-201-08148-2). A-W.
Vogel, Susan M; see Ravenhill, Philip L.
Vogel, Victor H., jt. auth. see Maurer, David W.
Vogel, Virgil J. American Indian Medicine. LC 69-10626. (Civilization of the American Indian Ser.: Vol. 95). (Illus.). 1970. 19.95 (ISBN 0-8061-0863-0). U of Okla Pr.
Vogel, Virgil V. Indian in American History. 1968. pap. 1.25 (ISBN 0-685-38480-2). Integrated Ed Assoc.
Vogel, W. Structure & Crystallization of Glasses. 1971. 46.00 (ISBN 0-08-006998-3). Pergamon.
Vogel, Walther. Geschichte der deutschen Seeschiffart, Band I: Von der Urzeit Bis Zum Ende Des 15th Jahrhunderts. 560p. 1973. Repr. of 1915 ed. 111.75x (ISBN 3-11-002304-0). De Gruyter.
Vogeler, Ingolf. The Myth of the Farm Family: Agribusiness Dominance of U.S. Agriculture. (Westview Special Study Ser.). 300p. 1981. lib. bdg. 22.00x (ISBN 0-89158-910-4). Westview.
Vogeler, Ingolf & De Souza, Anthony, eds. Dialectics of Third World Development. LC 79-53704. (Illus.). 366p. 1980. text ed. 20.50 (ISBN 0-916672-33-6); pap. text ed. 9.50 (ISBN 0-916672-35-2). Allanheld.
Vogelman, Joyce. Getting It Right. 208p. 1981. pap. 2.25 (ISBN 0-380-77685-5). Avon.
Vogelpoel, D. A. Biosystematic Monograph of the Genus Lophocolea (Dum.) Dum. (Hepaticopsida) in Europe. (Bryophytorum Bibliotheca Ser.: No. 15). (Illus.). 1981. pap. text ed. 30.00 (ISBN 3-7682-1177-0). Lubrecht & Cramer. Postponed.
Vogelsinger, Hubert. How to Star in Soccer. LC 67-23549. (Illus.). 64p. (gr. 5-10). 1967. 4.95 (ISBN 0-590-07052-5, Four Winds). Schol Bk Serv.
--New Challenge of Soccer. rev. ed. (Illus.). 380p. 1981. 12.95 (ISBN 0-89037-179-2). Anderson World.
Vogelweide, Walther Von Der see Walther Von Der Vogelweide.
Vogely, Maxine A. A Proust Dictionary. 765p. 1981. 50.00x (ISBN 0-87875-205-6). Whitston Pub.
Voget, Fred W. Osage Indians, Vol. One: Osage Research Project. (American Indian Ethnohistory Ser: Plains Indians). (Illus.). lib. bdg. 42.00 (ISBN 0-8240-0747-6). Garland Pub.
Vogh, James. The Cosmic Factor: Bioastrology & You. LC 79-10628. 1979. 7.95 (ISBN 0-396-07685-8). Dodd.
Vogl, Frank. German Business After the Economic Miracle. LC 73-15142. 1973. 29.95 (ISBN 0-470-90970-6). Halsted Pr.
Vogl, O. & Simionescu, C. I. Unsolved Problems of Co- & Graft Polymerization. (Journal of Polymer Science Ser.: Polymer Symposium No. 64). 373p. 1979. 29.95 (ISBN 0-471-05696-0). Wiley.
Vogl, Otto, jt. ed. see Donaruma, L. Guy.
Vogler. The Politics of Congress. 3rd ed. 364p. 1980. pap. 8.95 (ISBN 0-205-06975-4, 7669755). Allyn.
Vogler, Thomas A. Preludes to Vision: The Epic Venture in Blake, Keats, Wordsworth, & Hart Crane. LC 70-107662. (No. 22). 1971. 15.75x (ISBN 0-520-01687-4). U of Cal Pr.
Vogt, A. E. Van see Van Vogt, A. E.
Vogt, A. E. van see Van Vogt, A. E.
Vogt, A. E. Van see Van Vogt, A. E.
Vogt, Andrew, jt. auth. see Carter, David S.
Vogt, Bill. How to Build a Better Outdoors: The Action Manual for Fisherman, Hunters, Backpackers, Hikers, Canoeists, Birders, & All Nature Lovers. (Illus.). 1978. 9.95 o.p. (ISBN 0-679-50857-0); pap. 4.95 o.p. (ISBN 0-679-50867-8). McKay.
Vogt, Christian. Christian Vogt: Photographs. (Living Photographers Ser.). (Illus.). 1981. 35.00 (ISBN 0-686-69478-3, Pub. by Roto-Vision). Norton.
--Photographs. 1980. 35.00. Norton.
Vogt, Douglas & Sultan, Gary. Reality Revealed: The Theory of Multidimensional Reality. LC 77-88915. 460p. 1979. 12.95 (ISBN 0-930808-01-0). Ross-Erikson.
Vogt, Esther L. Turkey Red. LC 75-4455. (Illus.). 128p. (Orig.). (gr. 6-7). 1975. pap. 1.95 (ISBN 0-912692-68-5). Cook.
Vogt, Evon. Bibliography of the Harvard Chiapas Project: the First Twenty Years, Nineteen Fifty-Seven to Nineteen Seventy-Seven: The First Twenty Years, 1957 to 1977. Condon, Lorna, ed. LC 78-51959. 1978. pap. text ed. 3.00 (ISBN 0-87365-794-2). Peabody Harvard.
Vogt, Evon Z. & Albert, Ethel M., eds. People of Rimrock: A Study of Values in Five Cultures. LC 66-23469. (Illus.). 1966. 17.50x (ISBN 0-674-66150-8). Harvard U Pr.
Vogt, Frederick, ed. Energy Conservation & Use of Renewable Energies in the Bio-Industries: Proceedings of the International Seminar on Energy Conservation & the Use of Solar & Other Renewable Energies in Agriculture, Horticulture & Fishculture, 15-19 September, 1980, Polytechnic of Central London. LC 80-49739. (Illus.). 580p. 1981. 100.00 (ISBN 0-08-026866-8). Pergamon.
--Energy Conservation & Use of Solar & Other Renewable Energy: Proceedings. (Illus.). 580p. 1981. 100.00 (ISBN 0-08-026866-8). Pergamon.
Vogt, George, jt. auth. see Bruns, Roger.
Vogt, Hannah. Burden of Guilt: A Short History of Germany, 1914-1945. Strauss, H., tr. (Illus.). (gr. 9-12). 1964. pap. 5.95x (ISBN 0-19-501093-0). Oxford U Pr.
Vogt, Hans. Grammaire de la Langue Georgienne. (Institutt for Sammenlignende Kulturforskning Serie B.: No. 58). 278p. 1971. 27.00x (ISBN 8-200-08720-4, Dist. by Columbia U Pr). Universitet.
Vogt, Helen E. Westward of Ye Laurall Hills, 1750-1850: 1750-1850. LC 75-21087. (Illus.). 1976. 15.00 (ISBN 0-87012-226-6). H Vogt.
Vogt, John. Portuguese Rule on the Gold Coast, 1469-1682. LC 77-18831. 288p. 1978. 19.50x (ISBN 0-8203-0443-3). U of Ga Pr.
Vogt, Lawrence J. & Conner, David A. Electrical Energy Management. LC 77-156. 1977. 14.95 (ISBN 0-669-01457-5). Lexington Bks.
Vogt, Paul. The Blue Rider. (Illus.). 1980. pap. 2.95 (ISBN 0-8120-2100-2). Barron.
--Expressionism: German Painting 1905-1920. Vivis, Antony & Wolf, Robert E., trs. from Ger. (Illus.). 1980. 35.00 (ISBN 0-8109-0852-2). Abrams.
Vogt, Paul, et al. Expressionism--German Institution, 1905-1920. Neugroschel, Joachim, tr. LC 80-67038. (Illus.). 336p. (Orig., Eng. & Ger.). 1980. pap. 17.95 (ISBN 0-89207-024-2). S R Guggenheim.
Vogt, Richard J. Altering Course. 1979. 10.95 (ISBN 0-393-03230-2). Norton.
Vogt, Rochus E., jt. auth. see Leighton, Robert B.
Vogt, Von O. Art & Religion. 1921. 37.50x o.p. (ISBN 0-685-69881-5). Elliots Bks.
Vohr, John H., ed. see Gross, William & Matsch, Lee A.
Vohra, Dewan C. India's Aid Diplomacy in the Third World. 256p. 1980. text ed. 22.50 (ISBN 0-7069-1058-3, Pub. by Vikas India). Advent Bk.
Vohra, Gautam. Poems. (Writers Workshop Redbird Ser.). 1975. 9.00 (ISBN 0-88253-612-5); pap. text ed. 4.80 (ISBN 0-88253-611-7). Ind-US Inc.
Voich, Dan, Jr., jt. auth. see Wren, Daniel A.
Voight. Black Bear. Orig. Title: Red Blade & the Black Bear. (gr. 5-6). 1979. pap. 1.25 (ISBN 0-590-31259-6, Schol Pap). Schol Bk Serv.
Voight, Melvin J., jt. ed. see Harris, Michael J.
Voight, Randall L. Airport Guide. 2nd ed. 1981. pap. 7.95 (ISBN 0-930318-01-3). Intl Res Eval.
--Waste Management & Resources Recovery Information Database. 1979. 400.00 (ISBN 0-930318-07-2); quarterly updates 125.00. Intl Res Eval.
Voight, Virginia F. Bobcat. LC 77-16876. (gr. 3-5). 1978. 5.95 (ISBN 0-396-07538-X). Dodd.
Voigt, Cynthia. Homecoming. LC 80-36723. 320p. (gr. 5 up). 1981. PLB 12.95 (ISBN 0-689-30833-7). Atheneum.
Voigt, David Q. America Through Baseball. LC 75-20434. 232p. 1976. 13.95 (ISBN 0-88229-272-2). Nelson-Hall.
--American Baseball. Incl. Vol. 1. From Gentlemen's Sport to Commissioner System. 336p. 1966. 15.95 (ISBN 0-8061-0702-2); Vol. 2. From Comissioners to Continental Expansion. 350p. 1970. 15.95 (ISBN 0-8061-0904-1). (Illus.). Set. o.p. 24.95 set (ISBN 0-8061-0941-6). U of Okla Pr.
Voigt, Ellen B. Claiming Kin. LC 76-5944. (Wesleyan Poetry Program: Vol.83). 1976. lib. bdg. 10.00x (ISBN 0-8195-2083-7, Pub. by Wesleyan U Pr); pap. 4.95 (ISBN 0-8195-1083-1). Columbia U Pr.
Voigt, John W. & Mohlenbrock, Robert H. Flora of Southern Illinois. LC 59-5094. (Illus.). 399p. 1959. 8.95x (ISBN 0-8093-0026-5). S Ill U Pr.
--Flora of Southern Illinois. LC 73-12984. (Arcturus Books Paperbacks). 399p. 1974. pap. 3.95 (ISBN 0-8093-0662-X). S Ill U Pr.
Voigt, Melvin J. & Dervin, Brenda, eds. Progress in Communication Sciences, Vol. 2. 400p. 1980. text ed. 32.50 (ISBN 0-89391-060-0). Ablex Pub.
Voigt, William, Jr. Public Grazing Lands: Use & Misuse by Industry & Government. LC 75-42250. (Illus.). 365p. 1976. 25.00 (ISBN 0-8135-0819-3). Rutgers U Pr.
--The Susquehanna Compact: Guardian of the River's Future. (Illus.). 352p. 1972. 23.00 (ISBN 0-8135-0722-7). Rutgers U Pr.
Voilante, Cinzio. La Societa Milanese Nell'eta Precomunale. LC 80-2000. 1981. Repr. of 1953 ed. 35.00 (ISBN 0-404-18602-5). AMS Pr.
Vois, Camille Le see Dondo, Muthurin & Le Vois, Camille.
Vojir, Dan. The Sunny Side of Castro Street. (Illus., Orig.). 1981. pap. 6.95 (ISBN 0-89407-034-7). Strawberry Hill.
Vokaer, R. & De Bock, G., eds. Sexual Endocrinology: Proceedings of the Fondation pour la recherche en endocrinologie sexuelle et la reproduction humaine. 252p. 1975. text ed. 44.00 (ISBN 0-08-018170-8). Pergamon.
Volans, Glyn, jt. auth. see Turner, Paul.
Volavkova, Hana. Synagogue Treasures of Bohemia & Monravia. (Illus.). 10.00x o.p. (ISBN 0-87556-525-5). Saifer.

Volbach, Walther R. Adolphe Appia: Prophet of the Modern Theatre; a Profile. LC 68-27547. (Illus.). 1968. 20.00x (ISBN 0-8195-3094-8, Pub. by Wesleyan U Pr). Columbia U Pr.
Volborth, Carl A. Von see Von Volborth, Carl A.
Volcker, Paul A. The Rediscovery of the Business Cycle. LC 78-19850. 1978. 12.95 (ISBN 0-02-933430-6). Free Pr.
Vold, George B. Theoretical Criminology. 2nd ed. 1979. 16.95x (ISBN 0-19-502530-X). Oxford U Pr.
Vold, Linda. Once Upon a Star. 0.95 (ISBN 0-8024-6062-3). Moody.
Volguine, Alexander. Ruler of the Nativity. LC 74-90427. (French Astrology Ser.). 1973. 6.95 (ISBN 0-88231-076-3). ASI Pubs Inc.
Volgyes, Ivan. Hungary: A Profile. (Nations of Contemporary Eastern Europe). (Illus.). 128p. 1981. lib. bdg. 16.50x (ISBN 0-89158-929-5). Westview.
--The Peasantry of Eastern Europe: Twentieth Century Developments. LC 78-18483. 240p. 1979. 28.00 (ISBN 0-08-023125-X). Pergamon.
Volgyes, Ivan & Volgyes, Nancy. The Liberated Female: Life, Work & Sex in Socialist Hungary. LC 77-82813. (Special Studies on the Soviet Union & Eastern Europe). 1977. lib. bdg. 18.50x (ISBN 0-89158-815-9). Westview.
Volgyes, Ivan, jt. auth. see Toma, Peter A.
Volgyes, Ivan, ed. The Peasantry of Eastern Europe: Roots of Rural Transformation, Vol. I. LC 78-18483. 200p. 1979 22.50 (ISBN 0-08-023124-1). Pergamon.
--Political Socialization in Eastern Europe: A Comparative Framework. LC 72-83575. (Special Studies). 202p. 1975. text ed. 24.95 (ISBN 0-275-09550-9). Praeger.
--Social Deviance in Eastern Europe. LC 78-58836. 1978. lib. bdg. 24.50x (ISBN 0-89158-068-9). Westview.
Volgyes, Ivan & Lonsdale, Richard E., eds. The Process of Rural Transformation: Eastern Europe, Latin America & Australia. LC 79-10190. (Pergamon Policy Studies). 1979. 39.50 (ISBN 0-08-023110-1). Pergamon.
Volgyes, Ivan, jt. ed. see Enyedi, Gyorgy.
Volgyes, Ivan, jt. ed. see Herspring, Dale R.
Volgyes, Nancy, jt. auth. see Volgyes, Ivan.
Volk & Huxley. Mergenthaler VIP Typeface Catalogs, 2 vols. 1152p. 1980. Set. pap. 40.00 (ISBN 0-442-23999-8); pap. 24.95 ea. Vol. 1 (ISBN 0-442-24001-5). Vol. 2 (ISBN 0-442-24000-7). Van Nos Reinhold.
Volk, B. W., jt. ed. see Aronson, S. M.
Volk, Craig. Mato, Come Heal Me. (Outlaws Ser.: Vol. 4). 1980. 8.95x (ISBN 0-917624-17-3); pap. 5.95x (ISBN 0-917624-15-7). Lame Johnny.
Volk, Mary C. Vicencio Carducho & Seventeenth Century Castilian Painting. (Outstanding Dissertations in the Fine Arts Ser.). 1977. lib. bdg. 63.00x (ISBN 0-8240-2734-5). Garland Pub.
Volk, Vic. Aunty. LC 75-30964. (Illus.). (ps-3). 1975. 3.95 (ISBN 0-916144-01-1). Stemmer Hse.
Volk, Wesley A. & Wheeler, Margaret F. Basic Microbiology. 4th ed. LC 79-25907. 611p. 1980. text ed. 19.50x (ISBN 0-397-54313-1). Lippincott.
Volk, William. Engineering Statistics with a Programmable Calculator. Davidson, Robert L., ed. (Illus.). 320p. 1981. text ed. 17.50 (ISBN 0-07-067552-X, P&RB). McGraw.
Volkell, R. Z. LSAT Law School Admission Test: A Practical Guide. 1977. 6.95 (ISBN 0-471-02138-5). Wiley.
Volkell, Randolph Z. GMAT Graduate Management Admission Test: A Test Preparation Guide. LC 80-21793. (Wiley Self-Teaching Guide Ser.). 185p. 1980. pap. text ed. 7.95 (ISBN 0-471-05286-8). Wiley.
Volken, Vamik D. Linking Objects and Linking Phenomena. 330p. 1981. text ed. 20.00 (ISBN 0-8236-3030-7, 00-3030). Intl Univs Pr.
Volkmor, Cara B., jt. auth. see Pasanella, Anne L.
Volkmor, Cora B., jt. auth. see Langstaff, Anne L.
Volkoff, Vladimir. Tchaikovsky: A Self-Portrait. LC 73-84133. 1975. 15.00 (ISBN 0-8008-7552-4, Crescendo). Taplinger.
Volkomer, Walter E. American Government. 2nd ed. LC 78-13663. (Illus.). 1979. pap. text ed. 12.50 (ISBN 0-13-027300-7). P-H.
Volkswagen of America Inc. Volkswagen Official Service Manual Type 1. Beetle, Super Beetle, & Karmann Ghia, 1970-1979. LC 78-75039. (Illus.). 448p. 1979. pap. 18.50 (ISBN 0-8376-0096-0). Bentley.
--Volkswagen Official Service Manual Type 2, Station Wagon-Bus, 1968-1979. 4th rev. ed. LC 78-75038. (Illus.). 464p. 1979. pap. 18.50 (ISBN 0-8376-0094-4). Bentley.
Voll, John. Historical Dictionary of the Sudan. LC 77-28798. (African Historical Dictionaries Ser.: No. 17). 1978. 10.00 (ISBN 0-8108-1115-4). Scarecrow.
Volle, Frank O. Mental Evaluation of the Disability Claimant. 132p. 1975. 14.75 (ISBN 0-398-03338-2). C C Thomas.
Vollenweider, Marie-Louise, jt. auth. see Boardman, John.
Vollmer, Howard M. Adaptations of Scientists & Organizations. LC 75-18091. (Science & Technology Management Ser., No. 2). Date not set. price not set (ISBN 0-685-52882-0). Pacific Bks.
--Going Through Divorce: Facing the Problems of Adjustment. 1980. 8.95 (ISBN 0-87015-198-3). Pacific Bks.
Vollrath, L. E. The Pineal Organ. (Hanbuch der Mikroskopischen Anatomie: Vol. VI-7). (Illus.). 600p. 1981. 259.60 (ISBN 0-387-10313-9). Springer-Verlag.
Volney, C. F. A New Translation of Volney's Ruins, 2 vols. Feldman, Burton & Richardson, Robert D., eds. LC 78-60900. (Myth & Romanticism Ser.: Vol. 25). (Illus.). 1979. Set. lib. bdg. 132.00 (ISBN 0-8240-3574-7); lib. bdg. 66.00 ea. Garland Pub.
Volpe, E. P., ed. The Amphibian in Transplantation Immunity. (Monographs in Developmental Biology: Vol. 14). (Illus.). x, 150p. 1980. pap. 74.25 (ISBN 3-8055-1087-X). S Karger.
Volpe, E. Peter. Human Heredity & Birth Defects. LC 75-124674. (Science & Society Ser). (Illus.). 1971. pap. 4.95 (ISBN 0-672-63549-6). Pegasus.
Volpe, Galvano D. Logic As a Positive Science. 288p. 1981. 19.95 (ISBN 0-8052-7096-5, Pub. by NLB England). Schocken.
Volpe, Peter E. Understanding Evolution. 4th ed. 240p. 1981. pap. text ed. write for info. (ISBN 0-697-04646-X). Wm C Brown.
Volpe, Richard, et al, eds. Maltreatment of the School-Aged Child. LC 79-3581. 224p. 1980. 18.95x (ISBN 0-669-03463-0). Lexington Bks.
Volpe, S. P. Construction Management Practices. 181p. 1972. 18.50 (ISBN 0-471-91010-4). Wiley.
Volpi, A. De see De Volpi, A., et al.
Volpi, Alexander De see De Volpi, Alexander.
Vol'Pin, M., ed. Soviet Scientific Reviews 011section B: Chemistry Reviews, Vol.2. (Soviet Scientific Reviews). 480p. 1980. 90.00 (ISBN 3-7186-0018-8). Harwood Academic.
Vol'Pin, M. E., ed. Soviet Scientific Review: Chemistry Review, Vol. 3, Section B. 1981. write for info. (ISBN 3-7186-0057-9). Harwood Academic.
--Soviet Scientific Reviews: Chemistry Reviews, Vol. 3, Section B. 1981. price not set (ISBN 3-7186-0057-9). Harwood Academic.
Voltaire. Voltaire: The Age of Louis XIV & Other Selected Writings. Brumfit, J. H., ed. & intro. by. 1963. text ed. 20.00x (ISBN 0-8290-0219-7). Irvington.
Voltaire, F. M. Candide: Bilingual Edition. Gay, P., ed. 300p. (Fr.). 1963. pap. 5.95 o.p. (ISBN 0-312-85190-1). St Martin.
Voltaire, Francois. Lettres Philosophiques. rev. ed. Taylor, F. A., ed. (French Texts Ser.). 1976. pap. text ed. 9.95x (ISBN 0-631-00450-5, Pub. by Basil Blackwell). Biblio Dist.
--Zadig; or, the Book of Fate, 1749. Shugrue, Michael F., ed. Incl. The Amours of Zeokinizul King of the Kofiranis, 1749. Crebillon, Claude. (The Flowering of the Novel, 1740-1775 Ser: Vol. 25). 1974. lib. bdg. 50.00 (ISBN 0-8240-1124-4). Garland Pub.
Voltaire, Francois M; see Johnson, Samuel.
Voltaire, Francois M. De. Age of Louis the Fourteenth. 1958. 6.00x (ISBN 0-460-00780-7, Evman); pap. 2.95 o.p. (ISBN 0-460-01780-2). Dutton.
Voltaire, Francois M. De see De Voltaire, Framcois M.
Voltaire, Francois M. De see De Voltaire, Francois M.
Voltaire, Francois M. De see Voltaire, Francois M. De.
Volterra, Enrico & Gaines, J. H. Advanced Strength of Materials. 1971. ref. ed. 27.95 (ISBN 0-13-013854-1). P-H.
Volti, Rudi. Science & Technology in China. (Special Studies on China & East Asia). 350p. 1981. lib. bdg. 25.00x (ISBN 0-89158-951-1). Westview.
Volwahsen, Andreas. Living Architecture: Indian. (Illus.). 1969. 15.00 (ISBN 0-912158-36-0). Hennessey.
Von, Rudolf Albertini see Von Albertini, Rudolf.
Von Albertini, Rudolf. Decolonization: The Administration & Future of the Colonies, Nineteen Nineteen to Nineteen Sixty. Gravie, Francisca, tr. from Ger. 680p. 1981. text ed. 29.50x (ISBN 0-8419-0603-3); pap. 11.50x (ISBN 0-8419-0654-8). Holmes & Meier.
Von Allman, Marie, jt. auth. see Nemiro, Beverly.
Von Allmen, et al. Roles in the Liturgical Assembly. O'Connell, Matthew J., tr. from Fr. (Orig.). 1981. pap. 12.50 (ISBN 0-916134-44-X). Pueblo Pub Co.
Von Arb, Sondra. Body Structure & Function: An Individualized Course Guide & Work Book for Nursing & Health Related Occupations. LC 79-83909. 1979. pap. text ed. 8.95 (ISBN 0-933474-06-7). Minn Scholarly.
Von Arnim, Achim see Scher, Helene, et al.
Von Arnim, J. see Arnim, J. Von.
Von Arx, J. A. see Arx, J. A. Von.
Von Arx, William S. An Introduction to Physical Oceanography. (Illus.). 1962. 26.50 (ISBN 0-201-08174-1, Adv Bk Prog). A-W.
Von Aue, Hartmann see Hartmann Von Aue.
Von Aulock, W. H. see Marton, L.
Von Balthasar, Hans Urs. The Heart of the World. Leiva, Erasmo, tr. from Ger. LC 79-84879. Orig. Title: Das Herz der Welt. 219p. (Orig.). 1980. pap. 5.95 (ISBN 0-89870-001-9). Ignatius Pr.
Von Balthasar, Hans Urs see Balthasar, Hans Urs Von.
Von Bekesy, Georg. Experiments in Hearing. LC 77-4715. 756p. 1980. Repr. of 1960 ed. lib. bdg. 32.50 (ISBN 0-88275-552-8). Krieger.
Von Bergen, Werner, ed. Wool Handbook. 3rd ed. LC 63-11600. (Illus.). 1963-70. 77.50 ea. Vol. 2, Pt. 1 (ISBN 0-471-91015-5). Vol. 2, Pt. 2 (ISBN 0-471-91016-3, Pub. by Wiley-Interscience). Wiley.
Von Bernus, Alexander, ed. Alt-Kraeuterbuchlein. (Insel-Taschenbuecher: It 456). (Illus.). 153p. (Ger.). 1980. pap. text ed. 4.55 (ISBN 3-458-32156-X, Pub. by Insel Verlag Germany). Suhrkamp.
Von Bertalanffy, Ludwig. General System Theory: Essays on Its Foundation & Development. rev. ed. LC 68-25176. 1969. 9.95 o.s.i. (ISBN 0-8076-0452-6); pap. 5.95 (ISBN 0-8076-0453-4). Braziller.
--Perspectives on General System Theory. Taschdjian, Edgar & Von Bertalanffy, Maria, eds. LC 75-10993. 220p. 1976. 8.95 (ISBN 0-8076-0797-5); pap. 3.95 o.s.i. (ISBN 0-8076-0798-3). Braziller.
--Robots, Men & Minds. LC 67-27524. 1969. pap. 4.95 o.p. (ISBN 0-8076-0428-3). Braziller.
--A Systems View of Man: Collected Essays by Ludwig Von Bertalanffy. LaViolette, Paul, ed. 190p. 1981. lib. bdg. 16.00 (ISBN 0-86531-084-X); pap. 7.95 (ISBN 0-86531-094-7). Westview.
Von Bertalanffy, Maria, ed. see Von Bertalanffy, Ludwig.
Von Beyme, Klaus, ed. German Political Studies, Vol. 1. LC 74-82535. 1974. 20.00x (ISBN 0-8039-9927-5). Sage.
--German Political Systems: Theory & Practice in the Two Germanies. LC 74-82535. (German Political Studies: Vol. 2). 1976. 20.00x (ISBN 0-8039-9963-1). Sage.
Von Beyme, Klaus, jt. ed. see Kaase, Max.
Von Bock, Maria P. Reminiscences of My Father, Peter A. Stolypin: An Annotated Translation from the Russian. Patoski, Margaret, tr. from Rus. LC 75-16442. 1970. 10.00 (ISBN 0-8108-0331-3). Scarecrow.
Von Boehn, Max. Dolls & Puppets. Nicoll, Josephine, tr. (Illus.). 1966. Repr. of 1932 ed. 25.00x (ISBN 0-8154-0026-8). Cooper Sq.
Von Bornstedt, Marianne & Prytz, Ulla. Folding Table Napkins. LC 72-81040. (Illus.). 48p. 1981. pap. 4.95 (ISBN 0-8069-8974-2). Sterling.
--Folding Table Napkins. LC 72-81040. (Little Craft Book Ser.). (Illus.). 48p. (gr. 6 up). 1972. 5.95 (ISBN 0-8069-5218-0); PLB 6.69 (ISBN 0-8069-5219-9). Sterling.
Von Brandt, Andres see Brandt, Andres von.
Von Campenhausen, Hans. Ecclesiastical Authority & Spiritual Power in the Church of the First Three Centuries. Baker, J. A., tr. 1969. 12.95x (ISBN 0-8047-0665-4). Stanford U Pr.
--The Formation of the Christian Bible. Baker, J. A., tr. from Ger. LC 73-171495. 360p. 1977. pap. 7.50 (ISBN 0-8006-1263-9, 1-1263). Fortress.
Von Chamisso, Adelbert. Peter Schlemihl. Loewenberg-Wertheim, tr. 1980. pap. 3.95 (ISBN 0-7145-0440-8). Riverrun NY.
Von Clausewitz, Carl. On War. Howard, Michael & Paret, Peter, eds. LC 75-30190. 1976. 23.50 (ISBN 0-691-05657-9). Princeton U Pr.
Von Clausewitz, Karl. On War. Rapoport, Anatol, ed. (Classics Ser.). 1968. pap. 3.95 (ISBN 0-14-040004-4, Pelican). Penguin.
Von Clausewitz, Karl see Clausewitz, Karl Von.
Von Closen, Ludwig. Revolutionary Journal of Baron Ludwig Von Closen, 1780-1783. Acomb, Evelyn M., ed. (Institute of Early American History & Culture Ser.). 1958. 19.50x (ISBN 0-8078-0745-1). U of NC Pr.
Von Cranach, Mario & Vine, Ian, eds. Social Communication & Movement: Studies of Interaction & Expression in Man & Chimpanzee. (European Monographs in Social Psychology Ser.). 1974. 66.00 (ISBN 0-12-724750-5). Acad Pr.
Von Cube, Hans L. & Staimle, Fritz. Heat Pump Technology. Goodall, E. G., tr. 1981. text ed. price not set (ISBN 0-408-00497-5, Newnes-Butterworth). Butterworth.
Von Daniken, Erich. Miracle of the Gods. 336p. 1976. 8.95 o.p. (ISBN 0-440-05595-4). Delacorte.
Von den Driesch, Angela. A Guide to the Measurement of Animal Bones from Archaeological Sites. LC 76-49773. (Peabody Museum Bulletins Ser.: No. 1). (Illus.). 1976. pap. text ed. 8.00x (ISBN 0-87365-950-3). Peabody Harvard.
Von Denffer, Dietrich, et al. Strasburger's Textbook of Botany. 30th ed. Bell, P., tr. from Ger. Bell, P. & Coombe, D. E., trs. from Ger. LC 75-11731. (Illus.). 879p. 1976. text ed. 35.00x (ISBN 0-582-44169-2). Longman.
Von Der Grun, Max. Howl Like the Wolves: Growing up in Nazi Germany. Van Heurck, Jan, tr. from Ger. LC 80-19144. Orig. Title: Wie War das Eigentlich? (Illus.). 288p. (gr. 7-9). 1980. 9.95 (ISBN 0-688-22252-8); PLB 9.55 (ISBN 0-688-32252-2). Morrow.
Von Der Mehden, Fred R. Religion & Nationalism in Southeast Asia: Burma, Indonesia, & the Philippines. (Illus.). 1963. pap. 6.95 (ISBN 0-299-02944-1). U of Wis Pr.
Von Der Mehden, Fred R., pseud. South East Asia 1930-1970: The Legacy of Colonialism & Nationalism. (Library of World Civilization Ser). (Illus.). 144p. 1974. 7.95x (ISBN 0-393-05513-2); pap. 5.95x (ISBN 0-393-09320-4). Norton.
Von Der Osten & Vey. Painting & Sculpture in Germany & the Netherlands: 1500 to 1600. (Pelican History of Art Ser.: No. 31). 1969. 40.00 (ISBN 0-670-53591-5). Viking Pr.
Von Der Porten, Ronald P. Introduction to Defensive Bidding. LC 67-25630. (Illus.). 1968. 5.95 o.p.; pap. 3.95 (ISBN 0-13-479808-2). P-H.
Von Der Vring, Georg see Otten, Anna.
Von Dittersdorf, Karl D. Autobiography of Karl Von Dittersdorf. Coleridge, A. D., tr. LC 77-100655. (Music Ser). (Ger). 1970. Repr. of 1896 ed. lib. bdg. 22.50 (ISBN 0-306-71864-2). Da Capo.
Von Dobschutz, E. The Influence of the Bible on Civilization. 200p. Repr. of 1914 ed. text ed. 2.95 (ISBN 0-567-02093-2). Attic Pr.
Von Dollinger, Johann J. Letters from Rome on the Council, by Quirinus, 2 vols in 1. LC 78-127193. (Europe 1815-1945 Ser.). 856p. 1973. Repr. of 1870 ed. lib. bdg. 75.00 (ISBN 0-306-70040-9). Da Capo.
Von Dorp, Rolf, tr. see Myrdal, Jan.
Vondra, Benedict L., Jr., jt. ed. see Wymer, Raymond G.
Von Eckardt, Wolf. Back to the Drawing Board: Planning for Livable Cities. LC 78-12257. (Illus.). 1978. 10.00 o.p. (ISBN 0-915220-45-8). New Republic.
--To Live the Good Life: Planning for the Arts. 1981. 9.95 (ISBN 0-915400-24-3). Am Council Arts.
Von Eckardt, Wolf & Gilman, Sander. Bertolt Brecht's Berlin: A Scrapbook of the Twenties. LC 73-9153. 1977. pap. 5.95 (ISBN 0-385-12363-9, Anch). Doubleday.
Von Eckartsberg, Rolf see Valle, Ronald S. & Eckartsberg, Rolf Von.
Von Emmichoven, J. E. A New Novalis? Short Brilliant Thought-Flashes & Great Unity. Spaey, Elizabeth, tr. 1976. pap. 2.00 o.p. (ISBN 0-916786-17-X, Pub by Elizabeth Spaey). St George Bk Serv.
Von Ende, Richard C. Church Music: An International Bibliography. LC 79-23697. 473p. 1980. lib. bdg. 22.00 (ISBN 0-8108-1271-1). Scarecrow.
Von Engeln, Oscar Dedrich see Engeln, Oscar Dedrich Von & Urquhart, Jane M.
Von Euler, C. & Lagercrantz, H., eds. Central Nervous Control Mechanisms in Breathing--Physiological & Clinical Aspects of Regular, Periodic & Irregualar Breathing in Adults & in the Perinatal Period: Proceedings of the International Symposium Held at the Wenner-Gren Center, Stockholm, Sweden, Sept. 4-6, 1978. (Wenne-Gren International Symposium Ser.: Vol. 32). (Illus.). 1979. 82.00 (ISBN 0-08-024942-6). Pergamon.
Von Euler, U. S. & Heller, H., eds. Comparative Endocrinology, 2 vols. Incl. Vol. 1. Glandular Hormones. 52.00 o.p. (ISBN 0-12-724901-X); Vol. 2. Invertebrate Hormones, Tissue Hormones. 36.00 o.s.i. (ISBN 0-12-724902-8). 1963. Acad Pr.
Von Euler, U. S., et al, eds. Mechanisms of Release of Biogenic Amines. 1966. 60.00 (ISBN 0-08-011698-1). Pergamon.
--Structure & Function of Inhibitory Neuronal Mechanisms. 1968. 79.00 (ISBN 0-08-012414-3). Pergamon.
Von Euler, Ulf S. & Pernow, Bengt, eds. Substance P. LC 76-52600. (Nobel Symposium Ser: No. 37). 1977. 31.50 (ISBN 0-89004-100-8). Raven.

Von Euw, Eric. Corpus of Maya Hieroglypic Inscriptions: Xultun, Vol. 5, Pt. 1. Condon, Lorna, ed. LC 78-50627. 1978. pap. text ed. 10.00 (ISBN 0-87365-184-7). Peabody Harvard.
Von Filek, Werner. Frogs in the Aquarium. new ed. Orig. Title: Frosche im Aquarium. (Illus.). 96p. (Orig.). 1973. pap. 5.95 (ISBN 0-87666-191-6, PS690). TFH Pubns.
Von Franz, M-L. Shadow & Evil in Fairytales. Hillman, James, ed. (Seminar Ser., No. 9). 250p. 1973. pap. 12.50 (ISBN 0-88214-109-0). Spring Pubns.
Von Franz, Marie-Louise. Alchemical Active Imagination. (Seminar Ser.). (Orig.). 1979. pap. text ed. 8.50 (ISBN 0-88214-114-7). Spring Pubns.
--Individuation in Fairytales. 1976. pap. 9.00 (ISBN 0-88214-112-0). Spring Pubns.
--An Introduction to the Interpretation of Fairy Tales. Hillman, James, ed. (Seminar Ser.). 159p. 1970. pap. text ed. 7.50 (ISBN 0-88214-101-5). Spring Pubns.
--The Passion of Perpetua. Welsh, Elizabeth, tr. (Seminar Ser.). 81p. (Orig.). 1979. pap. 6.50 (ISBN 0-88214-502-9). Spring Pubns.
--Patterns of Creativity Mirrored in Creation Myths. Hillman, James, ed. (Seminar Ser). 1972. pap. text ed. 11.50 (ISBN 0-88214-106-6). Spring Pubns.
--A Psychological Interpretation of 'the Golden Ass of Apuleius' Hillman, James, ed. (Seminar Ser.). 188p. 1970. pap. text ed. 9.50 (ISBN 0-88214-103-1). Spring Pubns.
Von Franz, Marie-Louise & Hillman, James. Lecture on Jung's Typology. 150p. 1971. pap. text ed. 7.50 (ISBN 0-88214-104-X). Spring Pubns.
Von Franz, Mary-Louise. Problems of the Feminine in Fairytales. Hillman, James, ed. (Seminar Ser.). 1972. pap. text ed. 8.50 (ISBN 0-88214-105-8). Spring Pubns.
Von Fraunhofer, J. A. Scientific Aspects of Dental Materials. 1975. 49.95 (ISBN 0-407-00001-1). Butterworths.
Von Frisch, Karl. Twelve Little Housemates. Sugar, A. T., tr. LC 78-40341. 1978. text ed. 15.75 (ISBN 0-08-021959-4); pap. text ed. 7.75 (ISBN 0-08-021958-6). Pergamon.
Von Furerhaimendorf, Christoph. The Gonds of Andhra Pradesh: Tradition & Change in an Indian Tribe. (Illus.). 569p. 1981. 40.00x (ISBN 0-7069-0718-3). Advent Bk.
Von Furstenberg, Ira. Young at Any Age. (Illus.). 208p. 1981. 12.95 (ISBN 0-02-622100-4). Macmillan.
Von Gentz, Friedrich see Gentz, Friedrich Von.
Von Goethe, Johann W. Faust, Parts 1 & 2. Passage, Charles E., tr. (Orig.). 1965. pap. 8.95 (ISBN 0-672-60414-0). Bobbs.
--Faust-the Tragedy: Part One. Prudhoe, John, tr. from Ger. 157p. 1974. pap. 7.00x (ISBN 0-06-492465-3). B&N.
--Kindred by Choice. Waidson, H. M., tr. 1980. pap. 4.95 (ISBN 0-7145-0324-X). Riverrun NY.
--Sufferings of Young Werther. Morgan, J. Q., tr. 1980. pap. 4.50 (ISBN 0-7145-0542-0). Riverrun NY.
--The Sufferings of Young Werther. Steinhauer, Harry, tr. 1970. 6.00x (ISBN 0-393-04314-2); pap. 4.45x (ISBN 0-393-09880-X). Norton.
--Wilhelm Meister: The Years of Apprenticeship. Waidson, H. M., tr. 1980. 11.95 ea.; Vol. I. (ISBN 0-7145-3675-X); Vol. II. (ISBN 0-7145-3699-7); Vol. 3. (ISBN 0-7145-3702-0). Riverrun NY.
Von Goethe, Johann W. see Goethe, Johann W. Von.
Von Gremp, Zella & Broadwell, Lucile. Practical Nursing Study Guide & Review. 3rd ed. 1971. pap. text ed. 8.95 o.p. (ISBN 0-397-54117-1). Lippincott.
Von Grimmelshausen, H. J. see Grimmelshausen, H. J. Von.
Von Gronicka, Andre & Bates-Yakobson, Helen. Essentials of Russian. 4th ed. 1964. text ed. 16.95 (ISBN 0-13-287706-6). P-H.
Von Grunebaum, Gustave E. & Caillois, Roger, eds. The Dream & Human Societies. (Near Eastern Center, UCLA). 1966. 29.75x (ISBN 0-520-01305-0). U of Cal Pr.
Von Haag, Michael. Egypt. LC 77-70186. (Countries Ser.). (Illus.). 1977. lib. bdg. 7.95 (ISBN 0-686-51151-4). Silver.
Von Haag, Michael & Crew, Anna. A Moneywise Guide to North America Canada, USA, Mexico. rev. ed. (Travelaid Travel Bks.). (Illus., Orig.). 1978. pap. 5.95 (ISBN 0-8467-0438-2, Pub. by Two Continents). Hippocrene Bks.
Von Haam, Emmerich. Cytology Examination Review Book, Essay Questions & Answers, Vol. 2. 1975. spiral bdg. 9.50 (ISBN 0-87488-367-9). Med Exam.
Von Hagen, Victor W. The Jicaque (Torrupan) Indians of Honduras. LC 76-44796. (Illus.). 128p. 1980. Repr. of 1943 ed. 18.25 (ISBN 0-404-15743-2). AMS Pr.
--The Royal Road of the Inca! 1976. 29.95 o.p. (ISBN 0-86033-009-5). Gordon-Cremonesi.
--Search for the Maya. 1978. pap. 8.50 (ISBN 0-86033-064-8). Gordon-Cremonesi.
Von Hagen, Victor W., ed. see Stephens, John L.
Von Hahn, H. P., jt. ed. see Andrews, J.
Von Harrison, Grant. BEST: Building Essential Skills Together. 1976. complete set 38.85 (ISBN 0-87892-261-X). Economy Co.
Von Hartmann, Frank. The Techniques of Astrological Geomancy. (Illus.). 137p. 1981. 47.85 (ISBN 0-89920-019-2). Am Inst Psych.
Von Hartz, John, jt. auth. see Groder, Martin G.
Von Hassler, Gerd. The Lost Survivors of the Deluge. Ebon, Martin, ed. (Illus., Orig.). 1978. pap. 1.75 o.p. (ISBN 0-451-08365-2, E8365, Sig). NAL.
Von Haxthausen, Baron. The Russian Empire: Its People, Institutions & Resources, 2 vols. (Russia Through European Eyes Ser.). 1968. Repr. of 1856 ed. Set. lib. bdg. 85.00 (ISBN 0-306-77024-5). Da Capo.
Von Heider, W. M. Come Unto These Yellow Sands. LC 79-55739. 1981. tchers & parents ed. 14.95 (ISBN 0-89742-031-4). Dawne-Leigh. Postponed.
Von Heider, W. M., compiled by. And Then Take Hands. LC 79-55738. 1981. tchers & parents ed. 14.95 (ISBN 0-89742-012-8). Dawne-Leigh.
Von Hildebrand, D. Man & Woman. 1981. pap. 3.95 (ISBN 0-89526-883-3). Regnery-Gateway.
Von Hippel, Arndt. A Manual of Thoracic Surgery. (Illus.). 264p. 1978. 18.75 (ISBN 0-398-03689-6); pap. 11.50 (ISBN 0-398-03690-X). C C Thomas.
Von Hirsch, Andrew, ed. Essays on Penal Desert. 1980. cancelled (ISBN 0-88410-796-5). Ballinger Pub.
Von Hirsch, Andrew, jt. ed. see Gross, Hyman.
Von Hoerschelmann, Fred see Otten, Anna.
Von Hofmannsthal, Hugo. Arabella, Lyrische Komodie in Drei Aufzugen. Schmidt, Hugo, ed. (Ger). 1963. pap. 2.95x (ISBN 0-393-09605-X, NortonC). Norton.
Von Hofmannsthal, Hugo see Hofmannsthal, Hugo Von.
Von Hofmannsthal, Hugo, jt. auth. see Strauss, Richard.
Von Holst, Hermann E. John C. Calhoun. LC 80-18653. (American Statesmen Ser.). 375p. 1980. pap. 5.95 (ISBN 0-87754-185-X). Chelsea Hse.
Vonier, Dick & Sanders, Peter. Split Decision. LC 75-20485. (The Venture Ser, a Reading Incentive Program). (Illus.). 76p. (gr. 7-12,RL 4.5-6.5). 1975. text ed. 23.25 ea. pack of 5 (ISBN 0-8172-0239-0). Follett.
Von Ignatowsky, W. Physikalisch-Mathematische Monographien, 3 vols. in 1. (Ger). 9.95 (ISBN 0-8284-0201-9). Chelsea Pub.
Von Kaas, H. K. Making Wage Incentives Work. LC 75-138572. 1971. 17.50 o.p. (ISBN 0-8144-5251-5). Am Mgmt.
Von Kardoff & Sittl. Seeing the Real Paris. 1981. pap. 7.95 (ISBN 0-8120-2179-7). Barron.
Von Karman, Theodore. Aerodynamics. (Illus.). 1964. pap. 3.95 o.p. (ISBN 0-07-067602-X, SP). McGraw.
Von Karman, Theodore, jt. ed. see Von Mises, Richard.
Von Kaulla, K. N. & Davidson, J. F., eds. Synthetic Fibrinolytic Thrombolytic Agents: Chemical, Biochemical, Pharmacological & Clinical Aspects. (Illus.). 528p. 1975. text ed. 46.75 (ISBN 0-398-02927-X). C C Thomas.
Von Kleist, Henrich see Kleist, Heinrich von.
Von Kleist, Sabine & Breuer, H., eds. Critical Evaluation of Tumor Markers. (Beitraege zur Onkologie (Contributions to Oncology): Vol. 7). (Illus.). x, 144p. 1981. pap. 28.75 (ISBN 3-8055-2353-X). S Karger.
Von Klemperer, Lily, jt. auth. see Garraty, John A.
Von Klenze, Camillo see Klenze, Camillo Von.
Von Knorring, L., jt. ed. see Perris, C.
Von Koerber, Hildegard, tr. see Lorber, Jakob.
Von Koerber, Nordewin, tr. see Lorber, Jakob.
Von Kuehneli, Erik M., jt. auth. see Faulk, Odie B.
Von Laue, Theodore H. Why Lenin? Why Stalin? a Reappraisal of the Russian Revolution, 1900-1930. 2nd ed. LC 79-152063. 1971. pap. text ed. 6.50 scp (ISBN 0-397-47200-5, HarpC). Har-Row.
Von Lenz, Wilhelm. The Great Piano Virtuosos of Our Time. LC 72-8049. (Music Ser). 184p. 1973. Repr. of 1899 ed. lib. bdg. 12.50 (ISBN 0-306-70528-1). Da Capo.
Von Linnaeus, Carl see Linnaeus, Carl von.
Von Loeper, Eisenhart, jt. ed. see Teutsch, Gotthard M.
Von Lutze, Lotha. John Websters Tragodienstil Als Ausdruck der Leidenschaftlichkeit. (Jacobean Drama Studies: No.84). 189p. (Orig.). 1980. 25.00 (ISBN 0-391-02196-6). Humanities.
Von Maltitz, Horst. The Evolution of Hitler's Germany. 480p. 1973. 12.95 o.p. (ISBN 0-07-067608-9, P&RB). McGraw.
Von Manstein, Christof H. Contemporary Memoirs of Russia from the Year 1727 to 1744. (Russia Through European Eyes Ser). Repr. of 1856 ed. lib. bdg. 42.50 (ISBN 0-306-77027-X). Da Capo.
Von Mauntz, Alfred. Heraldik im Diensten der Shakespeare-Forschung. LC 68-57296. 1969. Repr. of 1903 ed. 18.00 (ISBN 0-8103-3886-6). Gale.
Von Meck, Barbara, jt. auth. see Bowen, Catherine.
Von Meck, Galina, tr. see Tchaikovsky, Piotr I.
Von Mises, Ludwig. The Anti-Capitalistic Mentality. LC 56-12097. 140p. 1978. pap. 5.00 (ISBN 0-910884-06-4). Libertarian.
--Epistemological Problems of Economics. (The Institue for Humane Studies Ser. in Economic Theory). 264p. 1981. 20.00x (ISBN 0-8147-8757-6); pap. 7.00x (ISBN 0-8147-8758-4). NYU Pr.
--Liberalism, a Socio-Economic Exposition. Raico, Ralph, tr. from Ger. LC 78-8457. (Studies in Economic Theory). 207p. 1979. 15.00; pap. 4.95. NYU Pr.
--The Theory of Money & Credit. Batson, H. E., tr. from Ger. LC 79-25752. (Liberty Classics Ser.). 544p. 1981. 11.00 (ISBN 0-913966-70-3); pap. 5.00 (ISBN 0-913966-71-1). Liberty Fund.
Von Mises, Ludwig see Mises, Ludwig Von.
Von Mises, Ludwig see Mises, Ludwig von.
Von Mises, Margit. My Years with Ludwig Von Mises. 1977. 9.95 o.p. (ISBN 0-87000-368-2). Arlington Hse.
Von Mises, Richard & Von Karman, Theodore, eds. Advances in Applied Mechanics. Incl. Vol. 1. 1948. 44.00 (ISBN 0-12-002001-7); Vol. 2. 1951. 44.00 (ISBN 0-12-002002-5); Vol. 3. 1953. 44.00 (ISBN 0-12-002003-3); Vol. 4. Dryden, H. L., et al, eds. 1956. 44.00 (ISBN 0-12-002004-1); Vol. 5. 1958. 44.00 (ISBN 0-12-002005-X); Vol. 6. 1960. 44.00 (ISBN 0-12-002006-8); Vol. 7. 1962. 44.00 (ISBN 0-12-002007-6); Vol. 8. 1964. 44.00 (ISBN 0-12-002008-4); Vol. 9. Kuerti, G., ed. 1966. 44.00 (ISBN 0-12-002009-2); Vol. 10. Fascicle 1. 1967. o.s.i. (ISBN 0-12-002091-2); Vol. 11. Chia-Sun Yih, ed. 1971. 44.00 (ISBN 0-12-002011-4); Vol. 12. 1972. 44.00 (ISBN 0-12-002012-2); Vol. 13. 1973. 48.00 (ISBN 0-12-002013-0); Vol. 16. Yih, Chia-Shun, ed. 1976. 51.75 (ISBN 0-12-002016-5); lib ed 66.50 (ISBN 0-12-002043-2); microfiche 337.25 (ISBN 0-686-66621-6); Vol. 17. Yih, Chia-Shun, ed. 1977. 51.75 (ISBN 0-12-002017-3); lib. ed 66.50 (ISBN 0-12-002045-9); microfiche 37.25 (ISBN 0-686-66622-4); Vol. 18. Yih, Chia-Shun, ed. 1979. 43.50 **(ISBN 0-12-002018-1); lib. ed. 56.50 (ISBN 0-12-002047-5); microfiche 31.50 (ISBN 0-12-002048-3). LC 48-8503. Acad Pr.**
Von Misis, Ludwig. Socialism. LC 79-21701. Orig. Title: Die Gemeinwirtschaft. 1981. 11.00 (ISBN 0-913966-62-2, Liberty Classics); pap. 5.00 (ISBN 0-913966-63-0). Liberty Fund.
Von Misses, Ludwig. Planning for Freedom. 4th, enl. ed. LC 80-10765. 296p. 1980. pap. 6.00 (ISBN 0-910884-13-7). Libertarian.
Von Moltke, Konrad, ed. see Von Ranke, Leopold.
Von Moos, Stanislaus, jt. auth. see Bachmann, Jul.
Von Moschzisker, R. Judicial Review of Legislation. LC 78-153372. (American Constitutional & Legal History Ser.). 1971. Repr. of 1923 ed. lib. bdg. 19.50 (ISBN 0-306-70151-0). Da Capo.
Von Mueller, Ferdinand see Mueller, Ferdinand Von.
Von Mueller, Karl. Gold Dredger's Handbook. 2nd ed. 1980. pap. 4.00 (ISBN 0-89316-609-X); plastic bdg. 6.00 (ISBN 0-89316-610-3). Exanimo Pr.
--Placer Miner's Manual, Vol. 1. 1980. pap. 5.00 (ISBN 0-89316-611-1); plastic bdg. 7.50 (ISBN 0-89316-612-X). Exanimo Pr.
--Placer Miner's Manual, Vol. 2. 1980. pap. 5.00 (ISBN 0-89316-613-8); plastic bdg 7.50 (ISBN 0-89316-614-6). Exanimo Pr.
--Placer Miner's Manual, Vol. 3. 1980. pap. 5.00 (ISBN 0-89316-615-4); plastic bdg. 7.50 (ISBN 0-89316-616-2). Exanimo Pr.
--The Treasure Hunter's Manual. 1976. pap. 6.50 o.p. (ISBN 0-915920-09-3, SL625, ScribT). Scribner.
--Vibrating Gold Concentrators. 1980. pap. 4.00 (ISBN 0-89316-617-0); plastic bdg. 6.00 (ISBN 0-89316-618-9). Exanimo Pr.
Vonnegut, Kurt. Jailbird. 1980. pap. 8.95 (ISBN 0-8161-3022-1, Large Print Bks). G K Hall.
--Jailbird. 1980. pap. 3.25 (ISBN 0-440-15447-2). Dell.
--Palm Sunday. 1981. 13.95 (ISBN 0-440-06593-3). Delacorte.
Vonnegut, Kurt, Jr. Breakfast of Champions. 320p. pap. 2.75 (ISBN 0-440-13148-0). Dell.
--Cat's Cradle. pap. 2.50 (ISBN 0-440-11149-8). Dell.
--Five. pap. 8.40 boxed set o.s.i. (ISBN 0-685-45986-1). Dell.
--God Bless You, Mr. Rosewater. pap. 2.50 (ISBN 0-440-12929-X). Dell.
--Player Piano. 320p. pap. 2.75 (ISBN 0-440-17037-0). Dell.
--Sirens of Titan. pap. 2.75 (ISBN 0-440-17948-3). Dell.
--Slaughterhouse-Five. pap. 2.50 (ISBN 0-440-18029-5). Dell.
--Welcome to the Monkey House. pap. 2.75 (ISBN 0-440-19478-4). Dell.
Von Neumann, John. Collected Works, 6 vols. Taub, A. W., ed. Incl. Vol. 1. Logic, Theory of Sets & Quantum Mechanics. 1961. 110.00 (ISBN 0-08-009567-4); Vol. 2. Operators, Ergodic Theory & Almost Periodic Functions in a Group. 1962. 110.00 (ISBN 0-08-009568-2); Vol. 3. Rings of Operators. 1962. 110.00 (ISBN 0-08-009569-0); Vol. 4. 1963. 110.00 (ISBN 0-08-009570-4); Vol. 5. 1963. 110.00 (ISBN 0-08-009571-2); Vol. 6. Theory of Games, Astrophysics, Hydrodynamics & Meteorology. 1963. 110.00 (ISBN 0-08-009572-0). 1963. Set. 660.00 (ISBN 0-08-009566-6). Pergamon.
Von Noorden. Burian-Von Noordens Binocular Vision & Ocular Mortility Theory: Management of Strabismas. 2nd ed. LC 79-19275. 1979. 62.50 (ISBN 0-8016-0898-8). Mosby.
Von Ostermann, Georg F. Manual of Foreign Languages. 4th ed. 1952. Repr. of 1970 ed. 30.00 (ISBN 0-87632-165-1). Boardman.
Von Prince, K. & Yeakel, M. H. The Splinting of Burn Patients. (Illus.). 136p. 1974. 17.75 (ISBN 0-398-03198-3). C C Thomas.
Von Rad, Gerhard. Wisdom in Israel. Martin, James D., tr. from Ger. Orig. Title: Weisheit in Israel. 336p. 1973. 15.95 o.p. (ISBN 0-687-45756-4). Abingdon.
Von Raffler-Engel, Walburga & Hutcheson, Robert H. Language Intervention Programs in the United States, 1960-1974: Theoretical Issues, Experimental Research & Practical Application. 92p. (Orig.). 1975. pap. text ed. 12.00x (ISBN 90-232-1284-3). Humanities.
Von Raffler-Engel, Walburga & Lebrun, Yvan, eds. Baby Talk & Infant Speech. (Neurolinguistics Ser.: Vol. 5). 362p. 1976. text ed. 46.00 (ISBN 90-265-0229-X, Pub. by Swets Pub Serv Holland). Swets North Am.
Von Ranke, Leopold. A History of Servia & the Servian Revolution. LC 78-126598. (Europe 1815-1945 Ser). 506p. 1973. Repr. of 1848 ed. lib. bdg. 45.00 (ISBN 0-306-70051-4). Da Capo.
--The Theory & Practice of History. Iggers, Georg G. & Von Moltke, Konrad, eds. Iggers, Wilma, tr. from Ger. LC 79-167691. 1973. pap. text ed. 14.95x (ISBN 0-672-60920-7). Irvington.
Von Rauch, Georg see Rauch, Georg von.
Von Rauch, George. The Baltic States: Estonia, Latvia, Lithuania the Years of Independence, 1917-1940. 1974. 20.00x (ISBN 0-520-02600-4). U of Cal Pr.
Von Raumer, Frederick. England in Eighteen Thirty Five, 3 vols. 908p. 1971. Repr. of 1836 ed. 84.00x (ISBN 0-686-28334-1, Pub. by Irish Academic Pr). Biblio Dist.
Von Regel, C., jt. auth. see Von Wiesner, J.
Von Rezzori, Gregor. Memoirs of an Anti-Semite. 1981. 13.95 (ISBN 0-670-46783-9). Viking Pr.
Von Richthofen, Manfred. The Red Baron. Ulanoff, Stanley M., ed. Kilduff, Peter, tr. from Ger. LC 80-68107. (Illus.). 241p. 1980. Repr. 12.95 (ISBN 0-8168-7925-7). Aero.
Von Rosenstiel, Helene. American Rugs & Carpets: From the Seventeenth Century to Modern Times. LC 78-50700. (Illus.). 1978. 25.00 o.p. (ISBN 0-688-03325-3). Morrow.
Von Saldern, Axel. Ancient Glass in the Museum of Fine Arts, Boston. LC 67-31751. (Illus.). 1968. 8.50 o.p. (ISBN 0-87846-007-1); pap. 2.95 (ISBN 0-87846-157-4). Mus Fine Arts Boston.
Von Schiller, Friedrich. Wilhelm Tell. Jordan, Gilbert, tr. LC 63-12200. (Orig.). 1964. pap. 4.90 o.p. (ISBN 0-672-60416-7). Bobbs.
Von Simson, Otto. The Gothic Cathedral: Origins of Gothic Architecture & the Medieval Concept of Order. LC 72-11946. (Illus.). 300p. 1973. pap. text ed. 5.95 (ISBN 0-691-01789-1). Princeton U Pr.
Von Soden, Michael, ed. Richard Wagner: Lohengrin. (Insel Taschenbuecher: No. 445). (Illus.). 257p. 1980. pap. text ed. 5.85 (ISBN 3-458-32145-4, Pub. by Insel Verlag Germany). Suhrkamp.
Vonsovskii, S. V. Magnetism, 2 vols. Hardin, R., tr. from Rus. LC 73-16426. 1974. Set. 134.95 (ISBN 0-470-91193-X). Halsted Pr.
Vonsovskii, S. V., ed. Ferromagnetic Resonance. 1966. 34.00 (ISBN 0-08-011027-4); pap. 21.00 (ISBN 0-08-013670-2). Pergamon.
Von Staden, Wendelgard. Darkness Over the Valley. Peters, Mollie C., tr. from Ger. LC 80-15579. Orig. Title: Nacht Uber dem Tal. 1981. 9.95 (ISBN 0-89919-009-X). Ticknor & Fields.

Von Steinaecker, Michael. Domestic Taxation & Foreign Trade: The United States-European Border Tax Dispute. LC 72-83010. (Special Studies in International Economics & Development). 1973. 28.00x (ISBN 0-275-28652-5). Irvington.

Von Steppat, Michael. The Critical Reception of Shakespeare's "Antony & Cleopatra" from 1607 to 1905. (Bochum Studies in English: No. 9). 619p. 1980. text ed. 45.75x (ISBN 90-6032-188-X). Humanities.

Von Sternberg, Josef. Fun in a Chinese Laundry: An Autobiography. 352p. 1973. pap. 2.95 o.s.i. (ISBN 0-02-012870-3, Collier). Macmillan.

Von Strassburg, Gottfried. Tristan. (Classics Ser). 1960. pap. 3.95 (ISBN 0-14-044098-4). Penguin.

--Tristan und Isolt. Closs, A., ed. (Blackwell's German Text Ser.). 1974. pap. 9.95x (ISBN 0-631-01750-X, Pub. by Basil Blackwell). Biblio Dist.

Von Suttner, Bertha. Lay Down Your Arms: The Autobiography of Martha von Trilling. LC 79-147459. (Library of War & Peace; Peace Leaders: Biographies & Memoirs). lib. bdg. 38.00 (ISBN 0-8240-0318-7). Garland Pub.

Von Treitschke, Heinrich. Origins of Prussianism. 1942. 14.25 (ISBN 0-86527-145-3). Fertig.

Von Tunzelman, G. N. Steam Power & British Industrialization to 1860. (Illus.). 1978. 45.00x (ISBN 0-19-828273-7). Oxford U Pr.

Von Uexkull, J. D. German Laws Relating to Patents, Utility Models & Trade Marks & to Inventions of Employees. 157p. 1978. pap. 23.50x (ISBN 3-452-18469-2, Pub by C Heymanns Verlag KG West Germany). Rothman.

Von Velsen, Dorothee. Gegenreformation in den Furstentumern Liegnitz-Brirg-Wohlau, Ihre Vorgeschichte und Ihre Staatsrechtlichen Grundlagen. (Ger). Repr. of 1931 ed. 29.00 (ISBN 0-384-64224-1); pap. 23.00 (ISBN 0-685-02156-4). Johnson Repr.

Von Velson, Ruth Fraenkel see Ehrenberg, Victor.

Von Volborth, Carl A. Heraldry of the World. (Illus.). 251p. 1980. 12.95 (ISBN 0-7137-0647-3, Pub. by Blandford Pr England). Sterling.

Von Wartburg, Walter. Evolution et Structure De la Langue Francaise. 22.50 (ISBN 3-7720-0013-4). Adler.

Von Wellnitz, Marcus. Christ & the Patriarchs. LC 80-83035. 400p. 1981. 6.95 (ISBN 0-88290-164-8, 2045). Horizon Utah.

Von Westernhagen, C. The Forging of the "Ring". Whittall, Arnold & Whittall, Mary, trs. LC 76-7140. (Illus.). 1976. 27.50 (ISBN 0-521-21293-6). Cambridge U Pr.

--Wagner: A Bibliography, 2 vols. LC 77-88680. (Illus.). 1979. Vol. 1 (1813-64) 27.50 (ISBN 0-521-21930-2); Vol. 2 (1864-83) 27.50 (ISBN 0-521-21932-9); 49.50 set (ISBN 0-521-08774-0). Cambridge U Pr.

Von Wichert, P., ed. Clinical Importance of Surfactant Defects. (Progress in Respiration Research: Vol. 15). (Illus.). 210p. 1980. 48.00 (ISBN 3-8055-1011-X). S Karger.

Von Wiese, B., ed. Deutsche Gedichte: Von Den Anfaengen Bis Zur Gegenwart. (Ger). 1972. 10.95 (ISBN 0-685-20235-6). Schoenhof.

Von Wiesner, J. & Von Regel, C. Die Rohstoffe Des Pflanzenreichs, 7 pts. 5th ed. Incl. Pt. 1. Tanning Materials (Gerbstoffe) Endres, H., et al. (Eng. & Ger.). 1962. 40.00 (ISBN 3-7682-0111-2); Pt. 2. Antibiotiques (Antibiotica) Hagemann, G. (Fr.). 1964. 48.00 (ISBN 3-7682-0170-8); Pt. 3. Organic Acids. Whitting, G. C. 1964. 34.00 (ISBN 3-7682-0244-5); Pt. 4. Insecticides. Fuell, A. J. 1965. 40.00 (ISBN 3-7682-0259-3); Pt. 5. Glykoside. Zechner, L. 1966. 40.00 (ISBN 3-7682-0298-4); Pt. 6. Staerke. Samecl, E. & Bling, M. (Illus.). 1966. 40.00 (ISBN 3-7682-0186-4); Pt. 7. Aetherische Oele. Bournct, K. & Weber, M. (Illus.). 1968. 40.00 (ISBN 3-7682-0562-2). Lubrecht & Cramer.

Von Wilckens, Leonie. Mansions in Miniature: Four Centuries of Dolls' Houses. Orig. Title: Das Puppenhaus. (Illus.). 252p. 1980. 50.00 (ISBN 0-670-45410-9, Studio). Viking Pr.

Von Wright, G. H., ed. Ludwig Wittgenstein: Letters to Russell, Keynes, & Moore. LC 73-18518. 194p. 1974. 16.50x o.p. (ISBN 0-8014-0822-9). Cornell U Pr.

Von Wright, G. H., ed. see Wittgenstein, Ludwig.

Von Wright, Georg H. Causality & Determinism. 128p. 1974. 15.00x (ISBN 0-231-03758-9). Columbia U Pr.

Von Zittel, K. A. Text-Book of Palaeontology, 2 vols. Eastmann, C. R. & Woodward, A. Smith, eds. Incl. Vol. 2. Vertebrates I: Pisces, Amphibia, Reptile, Aves. 25.00 (ISBN 3-7682-7102-1); Vol. 3. Mammalia. 20.00. 1964. Set. 85.00 (ISBN 3-7682-7101-3). Lubrecht & Cramer.

Voogd, Henry. Seedtime & Harvest: A Popular Study of the Period Between the Testaments. 1977. pap. text ed. 9.50x (ISBN 0-8191-0169-9). U Pr of Amer.

Voogel, E. & Keyzer, P. Two Hundred Darkroom Tips: Black & White. 1978. pap. 5.00 o.p. (ISBN 0-85242-573-2, Pub. by Fountain). Morgan.

Voorhees, F. L. Van see Van Voorhees, F. L.

Voorhies, Barbara, jt. auth. see Martin, M. Kay.

Voorhis, Harold V. Story of the Scottish Rite. 1980. Repr. soft cover 5.00 (ISBN 0-686-68271-8). Macoy Pub.

Voorhis, Stanley N. Van see Van Voorhis, Stanley N.

Voorhoeve, P., jt. auth. see Ricklefs, M. C.

Voorst, Dick Van see Van Voorst, Dick.

Voorthuijsen, A. M. Van see Van Voorthuijsen, A. M.

Voorthuisen, A. E. Van see Van Voorthuisen, A. E.

Vopa, Anthony J. La see La Vopa, Anthony J.

Vorderwinkler, W., jt. auth. see Axelrod, Herbert.

Vorderwinkler, William, jt. auth. see Axelrod, Herbert R.

Vore, Irven De see Lee, Richard B. & De Vore, Irven.

Vore, R. W. De see Rose, J. G. & De Vore, R. W.

Vore, R. William de see Reucroft, P. J., et al.

Vore, R. William De see Third International Conference.

Vore, R. William De see De Vore, R. William.

Vore, R. William de see De Vore, R. William.

Vore, R. William de see De Vore, R. William & Carpenter, Stanley B.

Vore, R. William De see De Vore, R. William & Graves, Donald H.

Vore, R. William De see De Vore, R. William & Haan, Charles T.

Vore, R. William De see De Vore, R. William & Huffsey, R. R.

Vore, R. William de see De Vore, R. William & Jackson, J. S.

Vore, R. William De see De Vore, R. William & Jackson, John S.

Vore, R. William De see De Vore, R. William, et al.

Vorgrimler, Herbert. Karl Rahner: His Life, Thought & Work. Quinn, Edward, tr. 1966. pap. 1.95 (ISBN 0-8091-1609-X, Deus). Paulist Pr.

Vorgrimler, Herbert, jt. auth. see Rahner, Karl.

Voris, Harold C. & Whisler, Walter W. Treatment of Pain. (Illus.). 176p. 1975. 19.50 (ISBN 0-398-03353-6). C C Thomas.

Voris, Jacqueline Van see Van Voris, Jacqueline.

Vorlicek, M., jt. auth. see Tichy, Milik.

Vorndran, Richard A., ed. see Los Angeles Unified School District.

Vorndran, Richard A., ed. see Wallach, Paul.

Voroba, Barry. Experimenting in the Hearing & Speech Sciences: 1978. LC 78-63106. (Illus.). 204p. 1978. 21.95 (ISBN 0-9601970-2-8); pap. 14.95 (ISBN 0-9601970-1-X); ring binder 29.95 (ISBN 0-9601970-0-1). Starkey Labs.

Voroknov, M. G., jt. auth. see Biryukov, I. P.

Voronsky, A. Stat'i. (Rus.). 1981. 15.00 (ISBN 0-88233-512-X); pap. 6.00 (ISBN 0-88233-513-8). Ardis Pubs.

Vorontsov, N. N., jt. ed. see Van Brink, J. M.

Voros, Gerald J. & Alvarez, Paul, eds. What Happens in Public Relations. 275p. 1981. 17.95 (ISBN 0-8144-5652-9). Am Mgmt.

Vorperian, John H., jt. auth. see Tartakow, I. Jackson.

Vorrath, Harry H. & Brendtro, Larry K. Positive Peer Culture. LC 73-89515. 288p. 1974. 14.95x (ISBN 0-202-36020-2). Aldine Pub.

Vorspan, Albert. Great Jewish Debates & Dilemmas: Perspectives on Moral Issues in Conflict in the 80's. LC 80-21057. 240p. (gr. 10-12). 1980. pap. text ed. 5.95 (ISBN 0-8074-0049-1). UAHC.

--To Do Justly: A Junior Casebook for Social Action. rev. ed. (gr. 6 up). 1977. pap. text ed. 3.25 (ISBN 0-8074-0078-5); tchrs'. guide 1.25 (ISBN 0-8074-0079-3, 207272). UAHC.

Vorster, D. J., ed. Human Biology of Environmental Change. 1972. pap. text ed. 14.95x (ISBN 0-685-83590-1). Intl Ideas.

Vos, Geerhardus. Notes on Biblical Theology. 1948. pap. 6.95 (ISBN 0-8028-1209-0). Eerdmans.

--Redemptive History & Biblical Interpretation. Gaffin, Richard B., Jr., ed. 584p. 1981. 17.50 (ISBN 0-8010-9286-8). Baker Bk.

Vos, Howard. Archaelogy in Bible Lands. (Illus.). 1977. 12.95 (ISBN 0-8024-0293-3). Moody.

Vos, Howard F. Beginnings in the Old Testament. pap. 3.50 (ISBN 0-8024-0610-6). Moody.

--Philippians: A Study Commentary. (Study Guide Commentary Ser.). 96p. (Orig.). 1980. pap. 2.95 (ISBN 0-310-33863-8). Zondervan.

Vos, Howard F., jt. auth. see Pfeiffer, Charles F.

Vos, Nelvin. The Great Pendulum of Becoming. (Orig.). 1980. pap. 8.95 (ISBN 0-8028-1828-5). Eerdmans.

Vose, Allen D., jt. auth. see Kane, Robert M.

Vose, Clement E. Caucasians Only: The Supreme Court, the NAACP, & the Restrictive Covenant Cases. LC 59-8758. 1959. 19.50x (ISBN 0-520-01308-5); pap. 4.95x (ISBN 0-520-01309-3, CAMPUS1). U of Cal Pr.

Vose, Kenneth & DuKore, Lawrence. Greased Lightning. (Orig.). 1977. pap. 1.50 o.s.i. (ISBN 0-446-88399-9). Warner Bks.

Vose, P. B. Introduction to Nuclear Techniques in Agronomy & Plant Biology. (Illus.). 1980. 53.00 (ISBN 0-08-024924-8); pap. 29.00 (ISBN 0-08-024923-X). Pergamon.

Vose, Virginia. Buying Quality: A Handbook for the Discriminating Shopper & Those Who Sell Fine Merchandise. new ed. LC 80-65319. (Illus.). 175p. Date not set. pap. price not set (ISBN 0-9602050-2-0). Freelance Pubns. Postponed.

Vosko, Richard S. Through the Eye of a Rose Window: A Perspective on the Environment for Worship. 1981. pap. text ed. 8.95 (ISBN 0-89390-028-1). Resource Pubns.

Vosnjak, Mitja. Miracle of Propolis. 1978. pap. 3.95 o.s.i. (ISBN 0-7225-0408-X). Newcastle Pub.

Voss, Arthur. The American Short Story. LC 72-9264. 300p. 1973. 12.95 o.p. (ISBN 0-8061-1070-8). U of Okla Pr.

Voss, Fred E., ed. Directory of Management Education Programs. LC 77-82267. (Annual). 1977. 125.00 (ISBN 0-8144-5525-5). Am Mgmt.

Voss, Friederich, jt. auth. see Teichler, Ulrich.

Voss, J. Color Patterns of African Cichlids. Orig. Title: Les Livrees Ou Patrons De Coloration Chezles Poissons Chichlides Africains. (Illus.). 128p. 1980. 7.95 (ISBN 0-87666-503-2, PS-755). TFH Pubns.

Voss, James F., jt. ed. see Thompson, Richard F.

Voss, Ronald E. Onion Production in California. (Illus.). 1979. pap. 5.00x (ISBN 0-931876-35-4, 4097). Ag Sci Pubns.

Voss, Thomas G., jt. ed. see Bryant, William C., II.

Voss-Clesly, Patricia. Tendencies of Character Detection in the Domestic Novels of Burney, Edgeworth & Austen: A Consideration of Subjective & Objective World, Vols. 1-3. (Salzburg Romantic Reassessment Ser.: No. 95). (Orig.). 1979. pap. text ed. 25.00x ea.; Vol. 1. pap. text ed. (ISBN 0-391-01619-9); Vol. 2. pap. text ed. (ISBN 0-391-01622-9); Vol. 3. pap. text ed. (ISBN 0-391-01625-3). Humanities.

Vossius, Gerardus. De Theologia Gentili, 3 vols. LC 75-27872. (Renaissance & the Gods Ser.: Vol. 28). (Illus.). 1977. Repr. of 1641 ed. Set. lib. bdg. 219.00 (ISBN 0-8240-2077-4). Garland Pub.

Vossler, Otto. Jefferson & the American Revolutionary Ideal. Philippon, Catherine & Wishy, Bernard, trs. LC 79-6726. 1980. pap. text ed. 10.50 (ISBN 0-8191-0941-X); lib. bdg. 18.50 (ISBN 0-8191-0938-X). U Pr of Amer.

Vost, Leon & Voet-Griselle, Jenny. The Plantin Press at Antwerp: 1555-1589. 500p. (Dutch.). 1981. 250.00 ea.; Vol. 1. (ISBN 0-8390-0264-5); Vol. 2. (ISBN 0-8390-0265-3). Allanheld & Schram.

Votaw, Clyde W. Gospels & Contemporary Biographies in the Greco-Roman World. LC 79-135748. (Facet Bks.). 72p. 1970. pap. 1.00 (ISBN 0-8006-3061-0, 1-3061). Fortress.

Votaw, Dow. Legal Aspects of Business Administration. 3rd ed. 1969. text ed. 21.00 (ISBN 0-13-527531-8). P-H.

Votaw, Dow & Sethi, Prakash. The Corporate Dilemma: Traditional Values Versus Contemporary Problems. (Illus.). 288p. 1973. pap. text ed. 9.95 (ISBN 0-13-174185-3). P-H.

Voth, Alden H. Moscow Abandons Israel for the Arabs: Ten Crucial Years in the Middle East. LC 80-5478. 275p. 1980. lib. bdg. 18.25 o.p. (ISBN 0-8191-1111-2); pap. text ed. 10.25 o.p. (ISBN 0-8191-1112-0). U Pr of Amer.

Voth, Harold & Orth, Marjorie. Psychotherapy & the Role of the Environment. LC 72-13818. 368p. 1973. text ed. 24.95 (ISBN 0-87705-102-X). Human Sci Pr.

Voth, Norma J. Festive Cakes of Christmas. 80p. 1981. pap. 2.95 (ISBN 0-8361-1956-8). Herald Pr.

Vowels, R. A. ALGOL Sixty & FORTRAN IV. 1974. pap. 9.95 o.p. (ISBN 0-471-91192-5). Wiley.

Vowles, P. D. & Connell, D. W. Experiments in Environmental Chemistry: A Laboratory Manual. LC 80-40270. (Pergamon Ser. on Environmental Science: Vol. 4). (Illus.). 108p. 1980. 23.00 (ISBN 0-686-61744-4); pap. 9.95 (ISBN 0-08-024009-7). Pergamon.

Voxman, et al, eds. Advanced Calculus: An Introduction to Modern Analysis. 1981. 55.00 (ISBN 0-8247-6949-X). Dekker.

Voxman, Himie & Merriman, Lyle. Woodwind Ensemble. 18.00 (ISBN 0-686-15887-3). Instrumentalist Co.

--Woodwind Solo. 18.00 (ISBN 0-686-15888-1). Instrumentalist Co.

Voyat, Gilbert. Piaget Systematized. (Illus.). 300p. 1981. text ed. 24.95 (ISBN 0-89859-026-4). L Erlbaum Assocs.

Voyat, Gilbert, ed. see Wallon, Henri.

Voyce, Arthur. Art & Architecture of Medieval Russia. (Illus.). 1967. pap. 9.95 (ISBN 0-8061-1096-1). U of Okla Pr.

--Moscow & the Roots of Russian Culture. (Centers of Civilization Ser.: Vol. 14). 194p. 1980. pap. 3.95 (ISBN 0-8061-1701-X). U of Okla Pr.

Voydanoff, Patricia. Productivity Implications of Work & the Family. Date not set. price not set. Work in Amer.

Voyles, jt. auth. see Parker.

Voyles, Jean, jt. auth. see Bonner, William H.

Voznesensky, Andrei. Nostalgia for the Present. LC 72-76218. 1978. pap. 4.95 o.p. (ISBN 0-385-08368-8); pap. 4.95 Softbound o.p. (ISBN 0-385-08373-4). Doubleday.

Voznesensky, N. A. Economy of the USSR During World War II. 8.00 (ISBN 0-8183-0233-X). Pub Aff Pr.

Vraciu, Robert A., jt. ed. see Bisbee, Gerald E., Jr.

Vredenbregt, J. & Wartenweiler, J., eds. Biomechanics II. (Medicine & Sport Ser.: Vol. 6). (Illus.). 1971. 29.50 (ISBN 0-8391-0530-4, Pub by Karger). Univ Park.

Vredeveld, George, jt. auth. see Kamerschen, David R.

Vredevoe, Donna L., et al. Concepts of Oncology Nursing. (Illus.). 400p. 1981. text ed. 18.95 (ISBN 0-13-166587-1). P-H.

Vree, Dale. On Synthesizing Marxism & Christianity. LC 76-27706. 1976. 21.95 (ISBN 0-471-01603-9, Pub. by Wiley-Interscience). Wiley.

Vreede-de Stuers, Cora. Parda: A Study of Muslim Women's Life in Northern India. LC 70-1402. (Samenlevingen Buiten Europa--Non-European Societies Ser.: No. 8). (Illus.). xii, 128p. 1981. Repr. of 1968 ed. lib. bdg. 19.75x (ISBN 0-313-22915-5, VRPA). Greenwood.

Vreeken, Elizabeth. Boy Who Would Not Say His Name. (Beginning-to-Read Bks). (gr. 2-4). 2.50 o.p. (ISBN 0-695-80814-1); PLB 2.97 o.p. (ISBN 0-695-40814-3); pap. 1.50 o.p. (ISBN 0-695-30814-9). Follett.

--One Day Everything Went Wrong. (Beginning-to-Read Bks). (Illus.). (ps). pap. 1.50 o.p. (ISBN 0-695-36550-9). Follett.

Vreeland, Helen K., ed. see Austin, Mary S.

Vriends, Matthew M. Encyclopedia of Softbilled Birds. (Illus.). 221p. 1980. 12.95 (ISBN 0-87666-891-0, H-1026). TFH Pubns.

--Handbook of Canaries. (Illus.). 351p. 1980. 9.95 (ISBN 0-87666-876-7, H-994). TFH Pubns.

Vriends, Matthew M., jt. auth. see Harman, Ian.

Vries, J. de. The Netherlands Economy in the Twentieth Century: An Examination of the Most Characteristic Feature in the Period 1900-1970. (Aspects of Economic History, the Low Countries Ser.: No. 3). 1978. pap. text ed. 13.50x (ISBN 90-232-1594-X). Humanities.

Vries, J. De see De Vries, J.

Vries, J. J. De. Aqua-Vu: Groundwater Hydraulics. (Communications of the Inst. of Earth Sciences, Ser. A.: No. 6). 45p. 1975. pap. text ed. 8.75x (ISBN 0-685-66840-1). Humanities.

Vries, Leonard De see De Vries, Leonard.

Vries, Peter De see De Vries, Peter.

Vrieze, K., jt. auth. see Kepert, D. L.

Vrieze, M. The Community Idea in Canada. 1966. pap. 1.25 o.p. (ISBN 0-686-11995-9). Wedge Pub.

Vrijhoef, M., et al. Dental Amalgam. (Illus.). 114p. 1980. 46.00 (ISBN 0-931386-16-0). Quint Pub Co.

Vring, George Von De see Otten, Anna.

Vroman, H. William, jt. auth. see White, Donald.

Vroman, H. William, jt. auth. see White, Donald D.

Vroman, Mary E. Harlem Summer. (gr. 4-6). 1968. pap. 1.25 o.p. (ISBN 0-425-03778-9, Highland). Berkley Pub.

Vroom, Victor H. Work & Motivation. LC 64-17155. 1964. 24.95 (ISBN 0-471-91205-0). Wiley.

Vt. Life Mag. Editors, ed. Vermont for Every Season. (Illus.). 160p. 1980. 30.00. Greene.

Vuchic, Vukan. Urban Public Transportation. (Illus.). 672p. 1981. text ed. 38.95 (ISBN 0-13-939496-6). P-H.

Vucinish, jt. auth. see Arnakis, George.

Vugrinovich, R. G. Precambrian Geochronology of North America: An Annotated Bibliography,1951-1977. LC 80-68063. (Special Paper Ser.: No. 11). 1980. 4.00x (ISBN 0-8137-6011-9). Geol Soc.

Vuillaume, Maxime. Hommes et Choses du Temps de la Commune: Recits et Portraits Pour Servir a l'Histoire de la Premiere Revolution Sociale. (Commune de Paris en 1871 Ser.) (Fr.). 1977. lib. bdg. 17.50x o.p. (ISBN 0-8287-0877-0); pap. text ed. 7.50x o.p. (ISBN 0-685-75750-1). Clearwater Pub.

Vujnovich, Milos M. Yugoslavs in Louisiana. 1974. 12.50 (ISBN 0-686-61039-3). Ragusan Pr.

Vukcevich, Jovan V. Wedding Troika. 1980. pap. 4.95 (ISBN 0-910286-76-0). Boxwood.

Vukovic, V. The Art of Attack in Chess. 1965. 24.00 (ISBN 0-08-011197-1); pap. text ed. 11.90 (ISBN 0-08-011196-3). Pergamon.

Vukovich, Virginia C. & Grubb, Reba G. Care of the Ostomy Patient. 2nd ed. LC 76-58498. (Illus.). 1977. pap. text ed. 9.50 (ISBN 0-8016-5276-6). Mosby.

Vulliamy, Graham & Lee, Ed, eds. Pop Music in School. 2nd ed. LC 79-7708. (The Resources of Music Ser.: No. 13). (Illus.). 1980. 22.95 (ISBN 0-521-22930-8); pap. 8.95x (ISBN 0-521-29727-3). Cambridge U Pr.

Vvendenskii, Aleksandr. Polnoe Sobranie Sochinenii, Vol. I. Meilakh, M., ed. (Rus.). 1980. 15.00 (ISBN 0-88233-321-6); pap. 7.50 (ISBN 0-88233-322-4). Ardis Pubs.

Vyas, Girish N., et al, eds. Viral Hepatitis: Etiology, Epidemiology, Pathogenesis & Prevention. LC 78-882. (Clinical Ser). (Illus., Orig.). 1978. 64.50 (ISBN 0-89168-013-6). Franklin Inst Pr.

Vyas, R. N., jt. auth. see Bhattacharya, A. N.

Vydra, F., et al. Electrochemical Stripping Analysis. Tyson, J., tr. LC 76-10946. (Series on Analytical Chemistry). 1977. 60.95 (ISBN 0-470-15131-5). Halsted Pr.

Vye, George & Grossman, Stewart. Cooking with Grass. LC 75-39089. (Illus.). 128p. (Orig.). 1976. pap. 3.95 (ISBN 0-8467-0151-0, Pub. by Two Continents). Hippocrene Bks.

Vyn, Kathleen. Spring in the High Sierras. LC 79-25450. (Illus.). 64p. (gr. 3-5). 1980. PLB 6.97 (ISBN 0-671-33084-5). Messner.

Vysny, P. Neo-Slavism & the Czechs, 1898-1914. LC 76-4239. (Soviet & East European Studies). (Illus.). 1977. 41.00 (ISBN 0-521-21230-8). Cambridge U Pr.

Vysotsky, V. West Berlin: History of the Nineteen Seventy-One Agreement. (Illus.). 355p. 1975. 12.50x (ISBN 0-8464-0964-X). Beekman Pubs.

W

W., tr. Metabolic Disorders, Methods of Examination. (Developments in Ophthalmology: Vol. 4). (Illus.). 1981. 78.00 (ISBN 3-8055-2014-X). S Karger.

Waack, William L., ed. Careers & Career Education in the Performing Arts: An Annotated Bibliography. 57p. 3.50. Am Theatre Assoc.

Waag, Robert C., jt. auth. see Gramiak, Raymond.

Waage, Karl M., jt. auth. see Dunbar, Carl O.

Waal, M. de see De Waal, M.

Waal, Victor De see De Waal, Victor.

Waar, Bob, jt. auth. see Fisher, Bill.

Waard, J. De see De Waard, J. & Nida, E. A.

Waard, J. de see De Waard, J. & Smalley, W. A.

Wabash Center for the Mentally Retarded. Guide for Early Developmental Training. 1977. pap. text ed. 18.95 (ISBN 0-205-05810-8). Allyn.

--Guide to Early Developmental Training. new ed. 1977. 25.95 o.p. (ISBN 0-205-05811-6). Allyn.

Waber, Bernard. Anteater Named Arthur. LC 67-20374. (Illus.). (gr. k-3). 1967. reinforced bdg. 9.95 (ISBN 0-395-20336-8). HM.

--An Anteater Named Arthur. (gr. k-3). 1977. pap. 3.95 (ISBN 0-395-25936-3). HM.

--Dear Hildegarde. (gr. 3 up). 1980. 4.95 (ISBN 0-395-29745-1). HM.

--Lyle, Lyle, Crocodile. LC 65-19305. (Illus.). 48p. (gr. k-3). 1973. pap. 2.95 (ISBN 0-395-13720-9, Sandpiper). HM.

--You're a Little Kid with a Big Heart. (Illus.). (gr. k-3). 1980. 8.95 (ISBN 0-395-29163-1). HM.

Wace, Alan J. B. Nomads of the Balkans. 1973. Repr. 19.50x (ISBN 0-685-30613-5). Biblo.

Wach, Joachim & Kitagawa, Joseph M. The Comparative Study of Religions. LC 58-9237. (Lectures on the History of Religions: No. 4). 1958. pap. 6.00 (ISBN 0-231-08528-1). Columbia U Pr.

Wacher, John. The Towns of Roman Britain. LC 73-91663. (Illus.). 1975. 34.50x (ISBN 0-520-02669-1). U of Cal Pr.

Wachhorst, Wyn. Thomas Alva Edison: The Biography of a Myth. 288p. 1981. 15.00 (ISBN 0-262-23108-5). MIT Pr.

Wachs, Martin. Transportation for the Elderly: Changing Lifestyles, Changing Needs. 1979. 19.50x (ISBN 0-520-03691-3). U of Cal Pr.

Wachs, Saul P., jt. auth. see Lachs, Samuel T.

Wachsman, Harvey, jt. auth. see Pegalis, Steven.

Wachspress, Eugene L., jt. ed. see McLeod, Robin J.

Wacht, Richard F. A New Approach to Capital Budgeting for City & County Governments. LC 80-13336. (Research Monograph: No. 87). 170p. 1980. spiral bdg. 29.00 (ISBN 0-88406-140-X). Ga St U Busn Pub.

Wacht, Walter F. The Domestic Air Transportation Network of the United States. LC 73-92651. (Research Papers Ser.: No. 154). (Illus.). 98p. 1974. pap. 8.00 (ISBN 0-89065-061-6). U Chicago Dept Geog.

Wachtel, Betsy & Powers, Brian. Rising Above Decline. Seymour, Nancy, ed. 198p. (Orig.). 1979. pap. 4.50 (ISBN 0-917754-14-X). Inst Responsive.

Wachtel, Erna & Loken, Newton C. Girls' Gymnastics. rev ed. LC 63-19163. (gr. 6 up). 1967. 6.95 (ISBN 0-8069-4310-6); PLB 7.49 (ISBN 0-8069-4311-4). Sterling.

Wachtel, Hellmuth. Aquarium Ecology. Vevers, Gwynne, tr. from Ger. (Illus.). 128p. 1973. pap. 4.95 (ISBN 0-87666-024-3, PS-964). TFH Pubns.

Wachtel, Howard. The New Gnomes: Multinational Banks in the Third World. LC 77-81604. 1977. pap. 3.95 o.p. (ISBN 0-89758-006-0). Inst Policy Stud.

Wachtel, Thomas, jt. auth. see Fisher, Jack C.

Wachter, Heinz. Meteorology: Forecasting the Weather. LC 73-3786. (International Library). (gr. 7 up). 1973. PLB 6.90 o.p. (ISBN 0-531-02115-7). Watts.

Wachter, Susan. Latin American Inflation. LC 75-3829. 1976. 17.95 (ISBN 0-669-99622-X). Lexington Bks.

Wackenheim, A., et al. Cheirolumbar Dysostosis. (Illus.). 102p. 1981. pap. 34.30 (ISBN 0-387-10371-6). Springer-Verlag.

Wackenheim, A., et al, eds. Atlas of Pathological Computer Tomography, Vol. 1: Cranio-Cerebral Computed Tomography. (Illus.). 150p. 1980. Set. 116.90 (ISBN 0-387-09879-8). Springer-Verlag.

Wackenroder, William H. & Tiek, Ludwig. Herzensergieszungen Eines Kunstliebenden Klosterbruders. 2nd ed. Gillies, A., ed. (Blackwell's German Text Ser.). 1966. pap. 4.50x o.p. (ISBN 0-631-01720-8, Pub. by Basil Blackwell). Biblio Dist.

Wacker, Peter O. Land & People: A Cultural Geography of Preindustrial New Jersey--Origins & Settlement Patterns, Vol. 1. 520p. 1975. 35.00 (ISBN 0-8135-0742-1). Rutgers U Pr.

--The Musconetcong Valley of New Jersey: A Historical Geography. LC 68-18694. (Illus.). 1968. 15.00 (ISBN 0-8135-0575-5). Rutgers U Pr.

Wackerbarth, Marjorie & Graham, Lillian S. Games for All Ages. (Direction Bks). (Orig.). 1973. pap. 3.45 (ISBN 0-8010-9536-0). Baker Bk.

Wackernagel, Martin. The World of the Florentine Renaissance Artist: Projects & Patrons, Workshop & Art Market. Luchs, Alison, tr. from Ger. LC 80-8583. 496p. 1981. 32.50x (ISBN 0-691-03966-6); pap. 12.50x (ISBN 0-691-10117-5). Princeton U Pr.

Wackers, Frans J., ed. Thallium-201 & Technettium-99m-Pyrophosphate Nyocardial Imaging in the Coronary Care Unit. (Developments in Cardiovascular Medicine Ser.: No. 9). (Illus.). 255p. 1981. PLB 42.00 (ISBN 90-247-2396-5, Pub. by Martinus Nijhoff). Kluwer Boston.

Wada, John A., ed. Kindling. LC 76-5662. 1976. 20.50 (ISBN 0-89004-124-5). Raven.

--Kindling Two. 300p. 1981. 30.00 (ISBN 0-89004-630-1). Raven.

Waddams, A. L. Chemicals from Petroleum. 4th ed. (Illus.). 375p. 1980. 12.95 (ISBN 0-87201-104-6). Gulf Pub.

--Chemicals from Petroleum. 3rd ed. LC 73-3397. 1973. pap. 14.95 (ISBN 0-470-91303-7). Halsted Pr.

Waddams, Frank C. The Libyan Oil Industry. LC 80-13939. (Illus.). 352p. 1980. text ed. 30.00x (ISBN 0-8018-2431-1). Johns Hopkins.

Waddams, Herbert. The Church & Man's Struggle for Unity. 1973. pap. 5.95 (ISBN 0-7137-0480-2). Transatlantic.

Waddell, Elizabeth G. Edge of a Kingdom. LC 79-66934. 1981. 5.95 (ISBN 0-533-04419-7). Vantage.

Waddell, Helen, ed. Book of Medieval Latin for Schools. 3rd ed. 1979. pap. 7.50x (ISBN 0-06-497276-3). B&N.

Waddell, Joseph J. Precast Concrete: Handling & Erection. (Monograph: No. 8). 1974. 15.75 (ISBN 0-685-85142-7, M-8) (ISBN 0-685-85143-5). ACI.

Waddell, Louis M. Unity from Diversity: Extracts from Selected Pennsylvania Colonial Documents, 1681 to 1780, in Commeration of the Tercentenary of the Commonwealth. (Illus.). 89p. 1980. pap. 4.00 (ISBN 0-89271-009-8). Pa Hist & Mus.

Waddell, Marie L., et al. Art of Styling Sentences: Twenty Patterns to Success. LC 70-184892. (gr. 9-12). 1972. pap. text ed. 2.95 (ISBN 0-8120-0440-X). Barron.

Waddell, William C. Overcoming Murphy's Law. 618p. 1981. 14.95 (ISBN 0-8144-5628-6). Am Mgmt.

Wadden, Richard A. Energy Utilization & Enviromental Health: Methods for Prediction & Evaluation of Impact on Human Health. LC 78-9688. (Environmental Science & Technology.: Texts & Monographs). 200p. 1978. 31.95 (ISBN 0-471-04185-8, Pub. by Wiley-Interscience). Wiley.

Waddington, C. H. Operation Research in World War Two. 1973. 22.95 (ISBN 0-236-15463-X, Pub. by Paul Elek). Merrimack Bk Serv.

Waddington, Conrad H. New Patterns in Genetics & Development. LC 62-12875. (Illus.). 1962. 20.00x (ISBN 0-231-02509-2); pap. 6.00x (ISBN 0-231-08570-2). Columbia U Pr.

Waddington, Conrad H., jt. ed. see Jantsch, Erich.

Waddington, Lawrence C. Arrest, Search & Seizure. LC 73-7366. (Criminal Justice Ser). 320p. 1974. text ed. 12.95x (ISBN 0-02-478940-2). Macmillan.

--Criminal Evidence. 1978. text ed. 13.95x (ISBN 0-02-479510-0). Macmillan.

Waddington, Margaret. The Little C. Lions. (Illus.). 65p. 1980. pap. 3.95 (ISBN 0-914960-29-6). Academy Bks.

Waddington, P., ed. I. S. Turgenev: Dvoryanskoye Gnezdo. 1969. 22.00 (ISBN 0-08-012923-4); pap. 10.75 (ISBN 0-08-012922-6). Pergamon.

Waddington, Patrick. Turgenev & George Sand: An Improbable Entente. (Illus.). 146p. 1981. text ed. 28.50x (ISBN 0-389-20152-9). B&N.

Waddington, Raymond B. see Patrides, C. A.

Waddington, Raymond B., jt. ed. see Sloan, Thomas O.

Waddington, Richard. Catching Salmon. LC 77-85034. (Illus.). 1978. 17.95 (ISBN 0-7153-7533-4). David & Charles.

Waddy, Charis. Baalbeck Caravans. (Arab Background Ser.). 1967. 8.95x (ISBN 0-685-77106-7). Intl Bk Ctr.

--The Muslim Mind. LC 76-6522. (Illus.). 216p. 1976. text ed. 20.00x (ISBN 0-582-78061-6). Longman.

--Women in Muslim History. (Illus.). 1980. lib. bdg. 23.00 (ISBN 0-582-78084-5). Longman.

Waddy, Lawrence. Drama in Worship. LC 78-58952. 1978. pap. 8.95 (ISBN 0-8091-2107-7). Paulist Pr.

Waddy, Lawrence H. Faith of Our Fathers. 1975. pap. 3.95x (ISBN 0-8192-4063-X). Morehouse.

Wade. Miracle Protein. 10.95 (ISBN 0-13-585653-1). P-H.

Wade, Allen. Soccer: Guide to Training & Coaching. (Funk & W Bk.). (Illus.). 1977. 8.95 (ISBN 0-308-70339-1, TYC-T); pap. 4.95 o.s.i. (ISBN 0-308-10318-1, TYC-T). T Y Crowell.

Wade, Bonnie. Music in India: The Classical Traditions. 1979. 14.95 (ISBN 0-13-607036-1); pap. 10.95 (ISBN 0-13-607028-0). P-H.

Wade, C. ARA University Calculus & Subjects of the Plane: Arabic Edition. 1981. pap. price not set (ISBN 0-471-06324-X). Wiley.

Wade, Carlson. Book of Bran. (Orig.). 1976. pap. 2.25 o.p. (ISBN 0-515-05687-1, Jove). BJ Pub Group.

--The Bread Book. 170p. 1974. pap. 1.95 (ISBN 0-06-463383-7, EH 383, EH). Har-Row.

--Carlson Wade's Lecithin Book. LC 80-82319. 128p. (Orig.). 1980. pap. 2.25 (ISBN 0-87983-226-6). Keats.

--Fact-Book on Hypertension, High Blood Pressure & Your Diet. LC 74-31668. (Pivot Original Health Book Ser). (Illus.). 128p. (Orig.). 1975. pap. 1.95 (ISBN 0-87983-095-6). Keats.

--Fact-Book on Vitamins & Other Food Supplements. LC 72-86040. (Pivot Original Health Book). 128p. 1972. pap. 1.50 (ISBN 0-87983-028-X). Keats.

--Parties for All Occasions. large type ed. LC 76-37819. 128p. 1976. 7.95 o.p. (ISBN 0-498-01882-2). A S Barnes.

--Vitamin E: The Rejuvenation Vitamin. 1979. pap. 1.95 (ISBN 0-441-71231-2). Charter Bks.

--What's in It for You? The Shoppers' Complete Guide to Health Store Products. rev. ed. LC 80-84443. (Pivet Original Health Bk.). 144p. (Orig.). 1981. pap. 1.95 (ISBN 0-87983-244-4). Keats.

--The Yeast Flakes Cookbook. 1973. pap. 1.25 (ISBN 0-515-02904-1). Jove Pubns.

Wade, David. Pattern in Islamic Art. LC 75-33464. (Illus.). 144p. 1976. 27.95 (ISBN 0-87951-042-0). Overlook Pr.

Wade, David Van see Van Wade, David & Van Wade, Sarah.

Wade, E. C. S., jt. ed. see Bradley, A. W.

Wade, G. E., ed. see Alegria, Ciro.

Wade, Graham. Traditions of the Classical Guitar. 1981. 25.00 (ISBN 0-7145-3794-2). Riverrun NY.

--Your Book of the Guitar. (Your Book Ser.). (Illus.). 64p. (gr. 3-8). 1980. 8.95 (ISBN 0-571-11553-5, Pub. by Faber & Faber). Merrimack Bk Serv.

Wade, H. W., jt. auth. see Schwartz, Bernard.

Wade, Harlan. El Aceite. Contreras, Mamie M., tr. from Eng. LC 78-26613. (A Book About Ser.). (Illus., Sp.). (gr. k-3). 1979. PLB 7.30 (ISBN 0-8172-1485-2). Raintree Pubs.

--El Agua. Contreras, Mamie M., tr. from Eng. LC 78-26818. (A Book About Ser.). Orig. Title: Water. (Illus., Sp.). (gr. k-3). 1979. PLB 7.30 (ISBN 0-8172-1490-9). Raintree Pubs.

--La Arena. Contreras, Mamie M., tr. from Eng. LC 78-26821. (A Book About Ser.). Orig. Title: Sand. (Illus., Sp.). (gr. k-3). 1979. PLB 7.30 (ISBN 0-8172-1476-3). Raintree Pubs.

--Le Bois. Potvin, Claude & Potvin, Rose-Ella, trs. from Eng. (A Book About Ser.). Orig. Title: Wood. (Illus., Fr.). (gr. k-3). 1979. PLB 7.30 (ISBN 0-8172-1458-5). Raintree Pubs.

--El Calor. Contreras, Mamie M., tr. from Eng. LC 78-26916. (A Book About Ser.). Orig. Title: Heat. (Illus., Sp.). (gr. k-3). 1979. PLB 7.30 (ISBN 0-8172-1487-9). Raintree Pubs.

--La Chaleur. Potvin, Claude & Potvin, Rose-Ella, trs. from Eng. (A Book About Ser.). Orig. Title: Heat. (Illus., Fr.). (gr. k-3). 1979. PLB 7.30 (ISBN 0-8172-1462-3). Raintree Pubs.

--L' Eau. Potvin, Claude & Potvin, Rose-Ella, trs. from Eng. (A Book About Ser.). Orig. Title: Water. (Illus., Fr.). (gr. k-3). 1979. PLB 7.30 (ISBN 0-8172-1465-8). Raintree Pubs.

--La Electricidad. Contreras, Mamie M., tr. from Eng. LC 78-26829. (A Book About Ser.). (Illus., Sp.). (gr. k-3). 1979. PLB 7.30 (ISBN 0-8172-1488-7). Raintree Pubs.

--L' Electricite. Potvin, Claude & Potvin, Rose-Ella, trs. from Eng. (A Book About Ser.). (Illus., Fr.). (gr. k-3). 1979. PLB 7.30 (ISBN 0-8172-1463-1). Raintree Pubs.

--Electricity. rev. ed. LC 78-26825. (A Book About Ser.). (Illus.). (gr. k-3). 1979. PLB 7.30 (ISBN 0-8172-1537-9). Raintree Pubs.

--Los Engranes. Contreras, Mamie M., tr. from Eng. LC 78-26614. (A Book About Ser.). Orig. Title: Gears. (Illus., Sp.). (gr. k-3). 1979. PLB 7.30 (ISBN 0-8172-1486-0). Raintree Pubs.

--Les Engrenages. Potvin, Claude & Potvin, Rose-Ella, trs. from Eng. (A Book About Ser.). Orig. Title: Gears. (Illus., Fr.). (gr. k-3). 1979. PLB 7.30 (ISBN 0-8172-1461-5). Raintree Pubs.

--La Force. Potvin, Claude & Potvin, Rose-Ella, trs. from Eng. (A Book About Ser.). Orig. Title: Strength. (Illus., Fr.). (gr. k-3). 1979. PLB 7.30 (ISBN 0-8172-1453-4). Raintree Pubs.

--La Fuerza. Contreras, Mamie M., tr. from Eng. LC 78-26850. (A Book About Ser.). Orig. Title: Strength. (Illus., Sp.). (gr. k-3). 1979. PLB 7.30 (ISBN 0-8172-1478-X). Raintree Pubs.

--Gears. rev. ed. LC 78-21312. (A Book About Ser.). (Illus.). (gr. k-3). 1979. PLB 7.30 (ISBN 0-8172-1535-2). Raintree Pubs.

--Heat. rev. ed. LC 78-20959. (A Book About Ser.). (Illus.). (gr. k-3). 1979. PLB 7.30 (ISBN 0-8172-1536-0). Raintree Pubs.

--L' Huile. Potvin, Claude & Potvin, Rose-Ella, trs. from Eng. (A Book About Ser.). Orig. Title: Oil. (Illus., Fr.). (gr. k-3). 1979. PLB 7.30 (ISBN 0-8172-1460-7). Raintree Pubs.

--Ideas. rev. ed. LC 78-26632. (A Book About Ser.). (Illus.). (gr. k-3). 1979. PLB 7.30 (ISBN 0-8172-1530-1). Raintree Pubs.

--Las Ideas. Contreras, Mamie M., tr. from Eng. LC 78-26714. (A Book About Ser.). (Illus., Sp.). (gr. k-3). 1979. PLB 7.30 (ISBN 0-8172-1481-X). Raintree Pubs.

--Les Idees. Potvin, Claude & Potvin, Rose-Ella, trs. from Eng. (A Book About Ser.). Orig. Title: Ideas. (Illus., Fr.). (gr. k-3). 1979. PLB 7.30 (ISBN 0-8172-1456-9). Raintree Pubs.

--The Lever. rev. ed. LC 78-21175. (A Book About Ser.). (Illus.). (gr. k-3). 1979. PLB 6.60 o.p. (ISBN 0-8172-1538-7). Raintree Pubs.

--Le Levier. Potvin, Claude & Potvin, Rose-Ella, trs. from Eng. (A Book About Ser.). Orig. Title: The Lever. (Illus., Fr.). (gr. k-3). 1979. PLB 7.30 (ISBN 0-8172-1464-X). Raintree Pubs.

--La Madera. Contreras, Mamie M., tr. from Eng. LC 78-26849. (A Book About Ser.). Orig. Title: Wood. (Illus., Sp.). (gr. k-3). 1979. PLB 7.30 (ISBN 0-8172-1483-6). Raintree Pubs.

--Oil. rev. ed. LC 78-27069. (A Book About Ser.). (Illus.). (gr. k-3). 1979. PLB 7.30 (ISBN 0-8172-1534-4). Raintree Pubs.

--La Palanca. Contreras, Mamie M., tr. from Eng. LC 78-26992. (A Book About Ser.). Orig. Title: The Lever. (Illus., Sp.). (gr. k-3). 1979. PLB 7.30 (ISBN 0-8172-1489-5). Raintree Pubs.

--Los Resortes. Contreras, Mamie M., tr. from Eng. LC 78-26852. (A Book About Ser.). Orig. Title: Springs. (Illus., Sp.). (gr. k-3). 1979. PLB 7.30 (ISBN 0-8172-1480-1). Raintree Pubs.

--Resorts. Potvin, Claude & Potvin, Rose-Ella, trs. from Eng. (A Book About Ser.). Orig. Title: Springs. (Illus., Fr.). (gr. k-3). 1979. PLB 7.30 (ISBN 0-8172-1455-0). Raintree Pubs.
--La Roue. Potvin, Claude & Potvin, Rose-Ella, trs. from Eng. (A Book About Ser.). Orig. Title: The Wheel. (Illus., Fr.). (gr. k-3). 1979. PLB 7.30 (ISBN 0-8172-1457-7). Raintree Pubs.
--La Rueda. Contreras, Mamie M., tr. from Eng. LC 78-26747. (A Book About Ser.). Orig. Title: The Wheel. (Illus., Sp.). (gr. k-3). 1979. PLB 7.30 (ISBN 0-8172-1482-8). Raintree Pubs.
--Le Sable. Potvin, Claude & Potvin, Rose-Ella, trs. from Eng. (A Book About Ser.). Orig. Title: Sand. (Illus., Fr.). (gr. k-3). 1979. PLB 7.30 (ISBN 0-8172-1451-8). Raintree Pubs.
--Sand. rev. ed. LC 78-20971. (A Book About Ser.). (Illus.). (gr. k-3). 1979. PLB 7.30 (ISBN 0-8172-1526-3). Raintree Pubs.
--Size. rev. ed. LC 78-26785. (A Book About Ser.). (Illus.). (gr. k-3). 1979. PLB 7.30 (ISBN 0-8172-1533-6). Raintree Pubs.
--Le Son. Potvin, Claude & Potvin, Rose-Ella, trs. from Eng. (A Book About Ser.). Orig. Title: Sound. (Illus., Fr.). (gr. k-3). 1979. PLB 7.30 (ISBN 0-8172-1450-X). Raintree Pubs.
--El Sonido. Contreras, Mamie M., tr. from Eng. LC 78-26830. (A Book About Ser.). Orig. Title: Sound. (Illus., Sp.). (gr. k-3). 1979. PLB 7.30 (ISBN 0-8172-1475-5). Raintree Pubs.
--Sound. rev. ed. LC 78-20961. (A Book About Ser.). (Illus.). (gr. k-3). 1979. PLB 7.30 (ISBN 0-8172-1525-5). Raintree Pubs.
--Speed. rev. ed. LC 78-21033. (A Book About Ser.). (Illus.). (gr. k-3). 1979. PLB 7.30 (ISBN 0-8172-1540-9). Raintree Pubs.
--Springs. rev. ed. LC 78-21066. (A Book About Ser.). (Illus.). (gr. k-3). 1979. PLB 7.30 (ISBN 0-8172-1529-8). Raintree Pubs.
--Strength. rev. ed. LC 78-26848. (A Book About Ser.). (Illus.). (gr. k-3). 1979. PLB 7.30 (ISBN 0-8172-1528-X). Raintree Pubs.
--La Taille. Potvin, Claude & Potvin, Rose-Ella, trs. from Eng. (A Book About Ser.). Orig. Title: Size. (Illus., Fr.). (gr. k-3). 1979. PLB 7.30 (ISBN 0-8172-1459-3). Raintree Pubs.
--El Tamano. Contreras, Mamie M., tr. from Eng. LC 78-26786. (A Book About Ser.). Orig. Title: Size. (Illus., Sp.). (gr. k-3). 1979. PLB 7.30 (ISBN 0-8172-1484-4). Raintree Pubs.
--Le Temps. Potvin, Claude & Potvin, Rose-Ella, trs. from Eng. (A Book About Ser.). Orig. Title: Time. (Illus., Fr.). (gr. k-3). 1979. PLB 7.30 (ISBN 0-8172-1452-6). Raintree Pubs.
--El Tiempo. Contreras, Mamie M., tr. from Eng. LC 78-26772. (A Book About Ser.). Orig. Title: Time. (Illus., Sp.). (gr. k-3). 1979. PLB 7.30 (ISBN 0-8172-1477-1). Raintree Pubs.
--Time. rev. ed. LC 78-26771. (A Book About Ser.). (Illus.). (gr. k-3). 1979. PLB 7.30 (ISBN 0-8172-1527-1). Raintree Pubs.
--La Velocidad. Contreras, Mamie M., tr. from Eng. LC 78-26627. (A Book About Ser.). Orig. Title: Speed. (Illus., Sp.). (gr. k-3). 1979. PLB 7.30 (ISBN 0-8172-1479-8). Raintree Pubs.
--La Vitesse. Potvin, Claude & Potvin, Rose-Ella, trs. from Eng. (A Book About Ser.). Orig. Title: Speed. (Illus., Fr.). (gr. k-3). 1979. PLB 7.30 (ISBN 0-8172-1454-2). Raintree Pubs.
--Water. rev. ed. LC 78-21290. (A Book About Ser.). (Illus.). (gr. k-3). 1979. PLB 7.30 (ISBN 0-8172-1539-5). Raintree Pubs.
--The Wheel. rev. ed. LC 78-21128. (A Book About Ser.). (Illus.). (gr. k-3). 1979. PLB 7.30 (ISBN 0-8172-1531-X). Raintree Pubs.
Wade, Ira see Bishop, G. Reginald, Jr.
Wade, Jewel M. Jerry Works in a Service Station. (Illus., Special education ser. for slow learners). (gr. 7-12, RL 2.2). 1967. pap. 2.56 (ISBN 0-8224-4025-3); tchrs'. manual free (ISBN 0-8224-4024-5). Pitman Learning.
Wade, John. The Extraordinary Black Book. 2nd ed. (The Development of Industrial Society Ser.). 576p. 1980. Repr. 35.00x (ISBN 0-7165-1588-1, Pub. by Irish Academic Pr). Biblio Dist.
--A Short History of the Camera. 1978. pap. 13.95 o.p. (ISBN 0-85242-632-1, Pub. by Fountain). Morgan.
--A Short History of the Camera. LC 79-670346. (Illus., Orig.). 1979. pap. text ed. 12.50x (ISBN 0-85242-640-2). Intl Pubns Serv.
Wade, John S. Some of My Best Friends Are Trees. (Sparrow Poverty Pamphlets: No. 35). (Orig.). pap. 1.50 o.p. (ISBN 0-686-20776-9). Sparrow Pr.
Wade, Juhn, ed. see Epilepsy International Symposium, 10th.
Wade, L. G., Jr. & O'Donnell, Martin J., eds. Annual Reports in Organic Synthesis, 1979, Vol. 10. 1980. 23.50 (ISBN 0-12-040810-4). Acad Pr.
Wade, L. G., Jr., jt. ed. see Milller, R. Bryan.
Wade, L. L. & Kim, B. S. The Economic Development of South Korea: The Political Economy of Success. LC 78-2665. (Praeger Special Studies). 1978. 25.95 (ISBN 0-03-043591-9). Praeger.
Wade, Larry, jt. ed. see Samuels, Warren.
Wade, Larry L., jt. ed. see Samuels, Warren J.
Wade, Lord. Europe & the British Health Service. 94p. 1974. pap. text ed. 2.50x (ISBN 0-7199-0890-6, Pub. by Bedford England). Renouf.
Wade, R. G. & Harding, T. D. The Marshall Attack. (Batsford Chess Ser.). (Illus.). 1976. 13.95 o.p. (ISBN 0-7134-2847-3). Hippocrene Bks.
Wade, R. G., ed. Soviet Chess. 1976. pap. 3.00 (ISBN 0-87980-311-8). Wilshire.
Wade, Richard C., jt. auth. see Mayer, Harold M.
Wade, Robert & Harding, T. D. Marshall Attack. 1974. 21.50 (ISBN 0-7134-2847-3). David & Charles.
Wade, Robert & O'Connell, K. J. Games of Robert J. Fischer. 1973. pap. 29.95 (ISBN 0-7134-0370-5). David & Charles.
Wade, Robert, et al. Sicilian: Lasker-Pelikan. 1978. 15.95 (ISBN 0-7134-1634-3, Pub. by Batsford England). David & Charles.
Wade, Sarah Van see Van Wade, David & Van Wade, Sarah.
Wade, T. E., et al, eds. With Joy: Poems for Children. rev. ed. (Illus.). 48p. (gr. 1-6). 1980. pap. 0.95 (ISBN 0-930192-08-7). Gazelle Pubns.
Wade, Theodore E., Jr., et al. School at Home. 186p. 1980. pap. 5.95 (ISBN 0-930192-09-5). Gazelle Pubns.
Wade, Thomas L. & Taylor, Howard E. Contemporary Analytic Geometry. LC 79-22955. 338p. 1980. Repr. of 1969 ed. write for info (ISBN 0-89874-034-7). Krieger.
Wadekin, Karl-Eugen. The Private Sector in Soviet Agriculture. 2nd enl. & rev ed. Karcz, George, ed. Bush, Keith, tr. from Ger. LC 76-95322. Orig. Title: Privatproduzenten in der Sowjetischen Landwirtschaft. 350p. 1973. 29.50x (ISBN 0-520-01558-4). U of Cal Pr.
Wadekin, Karl-Eugen, ed. Agrarian Policies in Communist Europe: A Critical Introduction. LC 79-55000. (Studies in East European & Soviet Russian Agrarian Policy: Vol. 1). 250p. 1981. text ed. 22.50 (ISBN 0-916672-40-9). Allanheld.
--Agriculture in Eastern Europe & the Soviet Union: Comparative Studies. LC 80-636. (Studies in East European & Soviet Russian Agrarian Policy: Vol. 3). 450p. 1980. text ed. 45.00 (ISBN 0-916672-42-5). Allanheld.
Wademan, Victor. Money-Making Advertising: Guide to Advertising That Sells. LC 80-19059. 128p. 1980. 16.95 (ISBN 0-471-06276-6, Pub. by Ronald Pr). Wiley.
Wadey, Rosemary. Baking Breads. LC 77-85021. (Penny Pinchers Ser.). (Illus.). 1978. 2.95 (ISBN 0-7153-7535-0). David & Charles.
--Preserving & Pickling. LC 77-85031. (Penny Pinchers Ser.). 1978. 2.95 (ISBN 0-7153-7551-2). David & Charles.
Wadey, Rosemary, et al. The Pennypincher Householder Handbook. LC 79-52368. (Illus.). 1979. 17.95 (ISBN 0-7153-7844-9). David & Charles.
Wadhva, Charan D. Rural Banks for Rural Development. 1980. 16.00x (ISBN 0-8364-0642-7, Pub. by Macmillan India). South Asia Bks.
Wadler, Joyce. Phil Donahue: A Man for All Women. (Illus., Orig.). 1980. pap. 2.50 (ISBN 0-515-05434-8). Jove Pubns.
Wadley, D. A. Corporations in Recession: The Australian Agricultural Machinery Industry. (Department of Human Geography Monograph: No. 13). 109p. (Orig.). 1980. pap. 5.95 (ISBN 0-908160-26-7, 0455). Bks Australia.
Wadley, J. B., ed. see Durry, Jean.
Wadley, Susan, jt. auth. see Jacobson, Doranne.
Wadley, Susan S., ed. The Powers of Tamil Women. LC 80-25410. (South Asian Foreign & Comparative Studies Program: No. 6). xix, 170p. (Orig.). 1980. pap. 8.00x (ISBN 0-915984-82-2). Syracuse U Foreign Comp.
Wadlin, Horace G. The Boston Public Library of the City of Boston: A History. (Published by the Trustees of the Boston Public Library). 1911. 35.00. Boston Public Lib.
Wadlington, Walter J., et al. Cases & Materials on Law & Medicine. LC 80-23725. (University Casebook Ser.). 1077p. 1980. text ed. write for info. (ISBN 0-88277-015-2). Foundation Pr.
Wadman, Robert C. & Svet, Don. Rules & Regulations for State and Local Law Enforcement Agencies. 108p. 1975. pap. 7.75 (ISBN 0-398-03366-8). C C Thomas.
Wadman, Robert C., et al. Law Enforcement Supervision: A Case Study Approach. (Criminal Justice Ser.). 1975. pap. text ed. 9.50 (ISBN 0-8299-0631-2). West Pub.
Wadstrom, T., jt. ed. see Baker, D.
Wadsworth, Barry J. Piaget's Theory of Cognitive Development: An Introduction for Students of Psychology & Education. LC 73-151157. 1979. pap. 7.95 (ISBN 0-679-30314-6). Longman.
--Piaget's Theory of Cognitive Development. 2nd ed. LC 79-12347. 1979. pap. 7.95 (ISBN 0-582-28124-5). Longman.
Wadsworth, Bruce. An Adirondack Sampler, II: Backpacking Trips in the Adirondacks. (Orig.). 1981. pap. 6.95 (ISBN 0-935272-15-1). Adk Mtn Club.
Wadsworth, Charles E. & Wadsworth, Jean G., eds. Roots & Sky: Poetry from the Plays of Christopher Fry. (Illus., Ltd. ed. 220 copies). special bdg. 250.00 (ISBN 0-930954-17-3); limited ed. 200 copies avail. (ISBN 0-930954-17-3). Tidal Pr.
Wadsworth, Frank W. The Poacher from Stratford: A Partial Account of the Controversy Over the Authorship of Shakespeare's Plays. (California Library Reprint Series: No. 13). 1969. Repr. of 1958 ed. 18.50x (ISBN 0-520-01311-5). U of Cal Pr.
Wadsworth, George P., jt. auth. see Pease, Edward M.
Wadsworth, Jean G., jt. ed. see Wadsworth, Charles E.
Wadsworth, Michael, ed. Ways of Reading the Bible. 225p. 1981. 27.50x (ISBN 0-389-20162-6). B&N.
Wadsworth, Michael & Robinson, David, eds. Studies in Everyday Medical Life. 232p. 1981. 23.50x (ISBN 0-85520-147-9, Pub. by Martin Robertson England). Biblio Dist.
Wadsworth, Nelson B. Through Camera Eyes. LC 75-8657. (Illus.). 180p. 1975. 10.95 o.p. (ISBN 0-8425-0435-4). Brigham.
Wadsworth, Olive A. Over in the Meadow. (gr. k-3). 1971. pap. 1.95 (ISBN 0-590-09195-6, Schol Pap). Schol Bk Serv.
Wadsworth, Thomas G. The Elbow. (Illus.). 272p. 1981. text ed. price not set (ISBN 0-443-01931-2). Churchill.
Waechter, Friedrich K. Three Is Company. Allard, Harry, tr. LC 79-7790. (Illus.). (gr. k-3). 1980. 8.95a (ISBN 0-385-14632-9); PLB (ISBN 0-385-14633-7). Doubleday.
Waelti, Fred. Take Five. 7.75 (ISBN 0-8062-1627-1). Carlton.
Waelti-Walters, Jennifer. Fairy Tales & the Female Imagination. 225p. 1981. price not set (ISBN 0-920792-07-3). Eden Women.
Waelti-Walters, Jennifer R. J. M. G. Leclezio. (World Author Ser.: No. 426). 1977. lib. bdg. 12.50 (ISBN 0-8057-6266-3). Twayne.
Waerden, B. L. Van Der see Van Der Waerden, B. L.
Waesche, James F. Beautiful Maryland. Shangle, Robert D., ed. LC 79-22530. (Illus.). 72p. 1980. 14.95 (ISBN 0-915796-65-1); pap. 7.95 (ISBN 0-915796-64-3). Beautiful Am.
Wagar, W. Warren. World Views: A Study in Comparative History. LC 76-55505. 1977. pap. text ed. 9.95 o.p. (ISBN 0-03-088043-2). HR&W.
Wagar, W. Warren, ed. Idea of Progress Since the Renaissance. LC 76-81337. (Major Issues in History Ser.). 1969. pap. text ed. 6.95x o.p. (ISBN 0-471-91351-0). Wiley.
--Science, Faith & Man. LC 68-27382. (Documentary History of Western Civilization Ser). 1968. 15.00x o.s.i. (ISBN 0-8027-2020-X). Walker & Co.
Wagel, Srinvas. Finance in China. LC 78-74334. (The Modern Chinese Economy Ser.). 447p. 1980. lib. bdg. 55.00 (ISBN 0-8240-4268-9). Garland Pub.
Wagenaar, Theodore C. Readings for Social Research. 336p. 1980. pap. text ed. 10.95x (ISBN 0-534-00740-6). Wadsworth Pub.
Wagenblast, Ruth. A Journey into Love's Past. 1981. 5.95 (ISBN 0-533-04439-1). Vantage.
Wagener, Hans. The German Baroque Novel. (World Authors Ser.: Germany: No. 229). lib. bdg. 10.95 (ISBN 0-8057-2356-0). Twayne.
Wagener, Hans, jt. ed. see Sobel, Eli.
Wagener, Jerrold L. Principles of Fortran Seventy-Seven Programming. LC 79-17421. 1980. pap. text ed. 14.95 (ISBN 0-471-04474-1); tchr's manual (ISBN 0-471-07831-X). Wiley.
Wagenhaeuser, F. J., jt. ed. see Mueller, W.
Wagenheim, Kal. Clemente! 1974. pap. 1.45 o.s.i. (ISBN 0-671-48355-2). WSP.
Wagenheim, Kal & Wagenheim, Olga Jimenez de, eds. The Puerto Ricans: A Documentary History. 400p. 1975. pap. 3.50 o.p. (ISBN 0-385-08833-7, Anch). Doubleday.
Wagenheim, Olga Jimenez de, jt. ed. see Wagenheim, Kal.
Wagenknecht, Edward. Eve & Henry James: Portraits of Women & Girls in His Fiction. LC 77-18613. 1978. 12.50 o.p. (ISBN 0-8061-1422-3). U of Okla Pr.
--Henry David Thoreau: What Manner of Man? LC 80-23542. (New England Writers Ser.). 224p. 1981. lib. bdg. 12.50x (ISBN 0-87023-136-7); pap. 5.95 (ISBN 0-87023-137-5). U of Mass Pr.
--Movies in the Age of Innocence. (Illus.). 1962. 13.50x (ISBN 0-8061-0539-9); pap. 5.95 (ISBN 0-8061-1297-2). U of Okla Pr.
--A Trilogy of Personalities: Chaucer, Milton, Shakespeare, 3 vols. 22.50x o.p. (ISBN 0-8061-1268-9). U of Okla Pr.
Wagenknecht, Edward, jt. auth. see Slide, Anthony.
Wagenknecht, Edward, ed. Chaucer: Modern Essays in Criticism. (Orig.). 1959. pap. 6.95 (ISBN 0-19-500683-6, GB). Oxford U Pr.
Wagenknecht, Edward, ed. see Bierce, Ambrose.
Wagenknecht, Edward, ed. see Irving, Washington.
Wagenknecht, Edward C. Mark Twain: The Man & His Work. 3rd ed. 1967. 14.95 (ISBN 0-8061-0737-5). U of Okla Pr.
Wagenvoord, James. Bikes & Riders. pap. 3.95 Special Format o.s.i. (ISBN 0-380-01060-7, 13128). Avon.
--Cashing in on the Auction Boom: How to Buy Today's Goods at Yesterday's Prices. 1980. 13.95 (ISBN 0-89256-149-1); pap. 6.95 (ISBN 0-89256-151-3). Rawson Wade.
--Diet & Exercise Diary. (Illus.). 160p. 1981. 6.95 (ISBN 0-312-20996-7). St Martin.
--Golf Diary. (Illus.). 160p. 1981. 6.95 (ISBN 0-312-33806-6). St Martin.
--Oak Alley, 4 vols. (Illus.). 160p. 1981. 166.80 (ISBN 0-312-58050-9). St Martin.
--Photography Notes. (Illus.). 160p. 1981. 6.95 (ISBN 0-312-60840-3). St Martin.
--Tennis Notes, Vol. 3 Of 4 Vols. (Illus.). 160p. 1981. 6.95 (ISBN 0-312-79104-6). St Martin.
Wagenvoord, James, jt. auth. see Irwin, Yukiko.
Wagenvoord, James, ed. Men: A Book for Women. 1978. pap. 7.95 (ISBN 0-380-40212-2, 45708). Avon.
Wagenvoort, C. A. & Wagenvoort, Noeke. Pathology of Pulmonary Hypertension. LC 76-39782. (Wiley Ser. in Clinical Cardiology). 345p. 1977. text ed. 41.95 (ISBN 0-471-91355-3, Pub. by Wiley Medical). Wiley.
Wagenvoort, Hendrik. Studies in Roman Literature, Culture & Religion. Commager, Steele, ed. LC 77-70817. (Latin Poetry Ser.: Vol. 31). 1978. lib. bdg. 33.00 (ISBN 0-8240-2981-X). Garland Pub.
Wagenvoort, Noeke, jt. auth. see Wagenvoort, C. A.
Wager, L. R. & Brown, G. M. Layered Igneous Rocks. (Illus.). 1967. text ed. 41.95x (ISBN 0-7167-0236-3). W H Freeman.
Wager, W. The Longer Thou Livest. Benbow, R. Mark, ed. Bd. with Enough Is As Good As a Feast. LC 67-15815. (Regents Renaissance Drama Ser). 1967. 9.75x (ISBN 0-8032-0284-9); pap. 1.65x (ISBN 0-8032-5285-4, BB 225, Bison). U of Nebr Pr.
--Telefon. 1975. 7.95 o.s.i. (ISBN 0-02-622430-5). Macmillan.
Wager, Walter. Blue Leader. 336p. 1981. pap. 2.25 (ISBN 0-425-04628-1). Berkley Pub.
--Blue Moon. 1981. pap. 2.50 (ISBN 0-425-04929-9). Berkley Pub.
--Blue Murder. LC 80-67622. 1981. 10.95 (ISBN 0-87795-286-8). Arbor Hse.
--My Side, by King Kong. LC 76-49829. 1976. 7.95 o.s.i. (ISBN 0-02-622420-8). Macmillan.
--My Side, by King Kong. 1976. pap. 4.95 o.s.i. (ISBN 0-02-040750-5, Collier). Macmillan.
--Time of Reckoning. LC 77-22548. 288p. 1981. pap. 2.75 (ISBN 0-87216-857-3). Playboy Pbks.
Wager, Walter W., jt. auth. see Briggs, Leslie J.
Waggoner, E. J. The Glad Tidings. LC 72-81729. (Dimension Ser.). 1977. pap. 5.95 (ISBN 0-8163-0281-2). Pacific Pr Pub Assn.
Waggoner, Lawrence W. Future Interests in a Nutshell. LC 80-20195. (Nutshell Ser.). 338p. 1980. pap. 6.95 (ISBN 0-8299-2105-2). West Pub.
Waggoner, Lawrence W., jt. auth. see Kahn, Douglas A.
Waggoner, Leland T. You Can See the World in Forty Days. LC 76-14774. (Illus.). 1978. pap. 2.45 o.p. (ISBN 0-668-04608-2, 4609). Arco.
--You Can See the World in Forty Days. LC 76-14774. (Illus.). 1976. 8.95 o.p. (ISBN 0-668-04040-8). Arco.
Waggoner, Merrill Van Y. see Van Wagoner, Merrill Y., et al.
Wa-Githumo, Mwangi. Land & Nationalism: The Impact of Land Expropriation & Land Grievances Upon the Rise & Development of Nationalist Movements in Kenya, 1885-1939. LC 80-5589. 502p. 1981. lib. bdg. 24.50 (ISBN 0-8191-1491-X); pap. text ed. 15.50 (ISBN 0-8191-1492-8). U Pr of Amer.
Wagle, N. K., ed. Images of Maharashhtra: A Regional Profile in India. 160p. 1980. pap. text ed. 10.50 (ISBN 0-7007-0144-3). Humanities.

Wagley, Charles. Amazon Town: A Study of Man in the Tropics. (Illus.). 363p. 1976. pap. 6.95 (ISBN 0-19-519839-5, GB458, GB). Oxford U Pr.
--Introduction to Brazil. rev ed. (Illus.). 1971. 20.00x (ISBN 0-231-03542-X); pap. 7.50x (ISBN 0-231-03543-8). Columbia U Pr.
--Latin American Tradition: Essays on the Unity & the Diversity of Latin American Culture. LC 67-30968. 1968. 17.50x (ISBN 0-231-03006-1); pap. 6.00x (ISBN 0-231-08333-5). Columbia U Pr.
--Welcome of Tears: The Tapirape Indians of Central Brazil. LC 76-42665. (Illus.). 1978. pap. 7.95x (ISBN 0-19-502208-4). Oxford U Pr.
Wagley, Charles & Harris, Marvin. Minorities in the New World: Six Case Studies. LC 58-12214. 1958. 20.00x (ISBN 0-231-02280-8); pap. 6.00x (ISBN 0-231-08557-5). Columbia U Pr.
Wagley, Charles, jt. auth. see Linton, Adelin.
Wagley, Charles, ed. Social Science Research in Latin America. LC 65-11971. 1965. 22.50x (ISBN 0-231-02772-9). Columbia U Pr.
Wagman, John, jt. auth. see Pollock, Bruce.
Wagman, Michael. The Far Horizons. 1980. 12.95 (ISBN 0-440-02815-9). Delacorte.
Wagman, Robert J., jt. auth. see Engelmayer, Sheldon D.
Wagner, jt. auth. see Scheingold.
Wagner, Abe. The Transactional Manager: How to Solve People Problems with Transactional Analysis. (Illus.). 208p. 1981. 11.95 (ISBN 0-13-928192-4, Spec); pap. 5.95 (ISBN 0-13-928184-3). P-H.
Wagner, Anthony. Drake in England. rev. ed. (Illus.). 119p. 1970. text ed. 10.00x (ISBN 0-915916-04-5). U Pr of New Eng.
--Pedigree & Progress: Essays in the Genealogical Interpretation of History. 333p. 1975. 35.00x (ISBN 0-87471-782-5). Rowman.
Wagner, Anthony R. English Genealogy. 2nd ed. (Illus.). 1972. 45.00x (ISBN 0-19-822334-X). Oxford U Pr.
Wagner, Augusta. Labor Legislation in China. LC 78-22780. (The Modern Chinese Economy Ser.). 301p. 1980. lib. bdg. 33.00 (ISBN 0-8240-4283-2). Garland Pub.
Wagner, Betty J. & Stunard, E. Arthur. Making & Using Inexpensive Classroom Media. LC 76-29236. (Learning Handbooks Ser.). 1976. pap. 3.95 (ISBN 0-8224-1907-6). Pitman Learning.
Wagner, Betty J., jt. auth. see Moffett, James.
Wagner, C. Peter. Defeat of the Bird God. LC 67-11615. (Illus.). 256p. 1975. Repr. of 1967 ed. 5.95 (ISBN 0-87808-721-4). William Carey Lib.
--Your Church Can Grow. LC 75-39410. (Orig.). 1976. pap. 4.95 (ISBN 0-8307-0414-0, 54-033-08). Regal.
Wagner, C. Peter & Dayton, Edward R. Unreached Peoples, Eighty-One. (Orig.). 1981. pap. 8.95 (ISBN 0-89191-331-9). Cook.
Wagner, Charles R. The CPA & the Computer Fraud. LC 77-90861. (Illus.). 1979. 16.95 (ISBN 0-669-02079-6). Lexington Bks.
Wagner, D. Introduction to the Theory of Magnetism. 290p. 1972. text ed. 28.00 (ISBN 0-08-016595-8). Pergamon.
Wagner, Eileen N. For the Sake of Argument: Writing Editorials & Position Papers. LC 79-64515. 1979. pap. text ed. 9.25 (ISBN 0-8191-0763-8). U Pr of Amer.
Wagner, Eliot. My America. 1980. 13.95 (ISBN 0-671-25332-8, Kenan Pr). S&S.
Wagner, F. J. J. H. Shorthouse. (English Authors Ser.). 1979. 14.50 (ISBN 0-8057-6729-0). Twayne.
Wagner, G., et al, eds. Technology & Health: Man & World Proceedings. (Lecture Notes in Medical Informatics Ser.: Vol. 7). 243p. 1981. pap. 20.70 (ISBN 0-387-10230-2). Springer Verlag.
Wagner, Gary, jt. auth. see Adler, Bill.
Wagner, Geoffrey. Season of Assasins. 1980. pap. 1.75 (ISBN 0-505-51457-5). Tower Bks.
Wagner, H. P., ed. Entwicklung der paediatrischen Haematologie und Onkologie. (Paediatrische Fortbildungskurse fuer die Praxis: Vol. 50). (Illus.). 1980. soft cover 24.00 (ISBN 3-8055-0229-X). S Karger.
Wagner, Harvey M. Principles of Management Science: With Applications to Executive Decisions. 2nd ed. (Illus.). 576p. 1975. 21.95 (ISBN 0-13-709535-X). P-H.
--Principles of Operations Research: With Applications to Managerial Decisions. 2nd ed. (Illus.). 1088p. 1975. 29.95 (ISBN 0-13-709592-9). P-H.
Wagner, Henry, tr. see Hartfeld, Hermann.
Wagner, Hilmar. The Wagner Report: Readings for Teachers & Parents. 1976. pap. text ed. 7.00x (ISBN 0-8191-0032-3). U Pr of Amer.
Wagner, James K. Blessed to Be a Blessing. LC 80-52615. 144p. (Orig.). 1980. pap. 4.50 (ISBN 0-8358-0410-0). Upper Room.
Wagner, Jenny. Aranea. LC 78-55212. (Illus.). (gr. k-2). 1978. 7.95 (ISBN 0-87888-138-7). Bradbury Pr.
--John Brown, Rose & the Midnight Cat. LC 77-76836. (Illus.). (ps-2). 1978. 9.95 (ISBN 0-87888-120-4). Bradbury Pr.
Wagner, John C., jt. auth. see Sherwood, John R.
Wagner, John G. Biopharmaceutics & Relevant Pharmacokinetics. LC 75-160736. (Illus.). 375p. 1971. 16.50 (ISBN 0-914768-18-2). Drug Intl Pubns.
Wagner, Jon, ed. Images of Information: Still Photography in the Social Sciences. LC 79-16894. (Sage Focus Editions: Vol. 13). (Illus.). 1979. 18.95x (ISBN 0-8039-1088-6); pap. 9.95x (ISBN 0-8039-1089-4). Sage.
Wagner, K. A., jt. auth. see Bailey, Paul C.
Wagner, Ken. One Word Storybook. (Illus.). (ps-3). 1968. PLB 7.62 (ISBN 0-307-60867-0, Golden Pr). Western Pub.
Wagner, Lee. How to Have Fun Making Easter Decorations. LC 74-10595. (Creative Craft Bks.). (Illus.). 32p. (gr. 2-6). 1974. PLB 5.95 (ISBN 0-87191-361-5). Creative Ed.
--How to Have Fun Making Holiday Decorations. LC 74-112308. (Creative Craft Bks.). (Illus.). 32p. (gr. 2-6). 1974. PLB 5.95 (ISBN 0-87191-362-3). Creative Ed.
--How to Have Fun Pressing Flowers. LC 74-8926. (Creative Craft Bks.). (Illus.). 32p. (gr. 2-6). 1974. PLB 5.75 o.p. (ISBN 0-87191-365-8). Creative Ed.
--How to Have Fun with Decoupage. LC 74-9829. (Creative Craft Bks.). (Illus.). 32p. (gr. 2-6). 1974. PLB 5.95 (ISBN 0-87191-366-6). Creative Ed.
Wagner, Leopold. Manners, Customs & Observances. LC 68-22059. 1968. Repr. of 1894 ed. 15.00 (ISBN 0-8103-3097-0). Gale.
--More About Names. LC 68-17937. 1968. Repr. of 1893 ed. 20.00 (ISBN 0-8103-3099-7). Gale.
--Names & Their Meanings, a Book for the Curious. LC 68-22060. 1968. Repr. of 1893 ed. 20.00 (ISBN 0-8103-3098-9). Gale.
Wagner, Lilya. To Linger Is to Die. LC 75-18349. (Crown Ser.). 128p. 1975. pap. 4.50 (ISBN 0-8127-0102-X). Southern Pub.
Wagner, Linda W. Hemingway & Faulkner: Inventors-Masters. LC 75-23367. 1975. 13.50 (ISBN 0-8108-0862-5). Scarecrow.
Wagner, Marsden & Wagner, Mary. The Danish National Child Care System: A Successful System As Model for the Reconstruction of American Child Care. LC 75-33183. 200p. 1976. 19.00x (ISBN 0-89158-008-5). Westview.
Wagner, Marsha & Miller, James W., eds. Comparative Essays in Chinese Literature. 1981. text ed. 20.00 (ISBN 0-89581-453-6, Asian Humanities). Lancaster-Miller.
Wagner, Mary, jt. auth. see Wagner, Marsden.
Wagner, Mary M., ed. Care of the Burn-Injured Patient: A Multidisciplinary Involvement. 320p. 1981. 24.00 (ISBN 0-88416-249-4). PSG Pub.
Wagner, Maurice. La Sensacion de Ser Alguien. Cook, David A., tr. from Eng. LC 77-16714. 300p. (Orig., Span.). 1977. pap. 4.95 (ISBN 0-89922-104-1). Edit Caribe.
--The Sensation of Being Somebody. 256p. 1975. 9.95 (ISBN 0-310-33970-7). Zondervan.
Wagner, Michael. Introductory Musical Acoustics. (Illus.). 1978. pap. text ed. 10.00 (ISBN 0-89892-025-6). Contemp Pub Co of Raleigh.
Wagner, Michael P. Minnesota Legal Forms: Bankruptcy. Mason Publishing Staff, ed. 150p. 1981. ring binder 15.00 (ISBN 0-917126-92-0). Mason Pub.
Wagner, Norman E., ed. see Westermann, Claus.
Wagner, Pat. Bones. 1976. pap. 2.00 (ISBN 0-935060-00-6). Eggplant Pr.
Wagner, Pete. Buy This Book. LC 80-82890. (Illus.). 216p. (Orig.). 1980. pap. 6.95 (ISBN 0-937706-00-0). ME Pubns.
Wagner, Philip L. Human Use of the Earth. LC 60-7092. 1964. 7.95 o.s.i. (ISBN 0-02-933560-4); pap. text ed. 3.00 (ISBN 0-02-933570-1). Free Pr.
Wagner, R. R., jt. ed. see Fraenkel-Conrat, H.
Wagner, Richard. The Flying Dutchman: The Complete Text in German & English. Large, Brian & Butler, Peter, eds. (Illus.). 1975. text ed. 13.95x (ISBN 0-7156-0938-6). Intl Ideas.
--The Ring of the Nibelung. Porter, Andrew, tr. 1976. 26.95 (ISBN 0-393-02192-0, N867, Norton Lib); pap. 5.95 (ISBN 0-393-00867-3). Norton.
--The Space Shuttle Coloring Book. (Coloring Experience Ser). (Illus., Orig.). (gr. k-6). 1979. pap. 2.95 o.p. (ISBN 0-8431-0651-4). Price Stern.
Wagner, Richard, jt. ed. see Tullock, Gordon.
Wagner, Richard M. & Wright, Roy J. Progress & Prosperity. (Cincinnati Streetcars: No. 7). 1976. pap. 6.95 o.s.i. (ISBN 0-914196-16-2). Trolley Talk.
Wagner, Richard M., jt. auth. see Wright, Roy J.
Wagner, Robert, jt. ed. see Conrat, Heinz F.
Wagner, Robert, jt. ed. see Fraenkel-Conrat, Heinz.
Wagner, Robin S. Mork & Mindy: The Incredible Shrinking Mork. (Orig.). 1980. pap. write for info. (ISBN 0-671-83677-3). PB.
Wagner, Roger C., jt. auth. see Jain, Mahendra K.
Wagner, Roy W. The Invention of Culture. rev., exp. ed. 1981. lib. bdg. 21.00x (ISBN 0-226-86933-4); pap. 5.95 (ISBN 0-226-86934-2). U of Chicago Pr.
Wagner, Sharon. Embraces. (Orig.). 1980. pap. 2.50 (ISBN 0-89083-666-3, Kable News Co). Zebra.
--Gypsy, 3 bks. (gr. 9 up). Date not set. pap. 3.75 boxed set (ISBN 0-307-13619-1, Golden Pr). Western Pub.
--Gypsy & Nimblefoot. (Gypsy Bks.). (gr. 4 up). 1978. pap. 1.25 (ISBN 0-307-21545-8, Golden Pr). Western Pub.
--Gypsy from Nowhere. (Gypsy Bks.). (gr. 4 up). 1978. pap. 1.25 (ISBN 0-307-21509-1, Golden Pr). Western Pub.
Wagner, Susan E., ed. A Guide to Corporate Giving in the Arts. LC 78-55696. 402p. (Orig.). 1978. pap. 7.50 (ISBN 0-915400-12-X). Am Council Arts.
Wagner, Thomas, ed. see International Association for the Advancement of Appropriate Technology for Developing Countries, 1979 Symposium.
Wagner, Thomas, tr. see International Association for the Advancement of Appropriate Technology for Developing Countries, 1979 Symposium.
Wagner, Thomas J., et al. Basic Security Training Manual. 136p. 1979. text ed. 10.75 (ISBN 0-398-03949-6). C C Thomas.
Wagner, Walter, jt. auth. see Hoekstra, Ray.
Wagner, Walter F., Jr., ed. see Architectural Record Magazine.
Wagner, Warren H., Jr., jt. auth. see Barnes, Burton V.
Wagner, Wilhelm. Die Chinesische Landwirtschaft. LC 78-74338. (The Modern Chinese Economy Ser.: Vol. 15). 659p. 1980. lib. bdg. 72.00 (ISBN 0-8240-4263-8). Garland Pub.
Wagner, Wilhelm, ed. Medieval Greek Texts: Being a Collection of the Earliest Composition in Vulgar Greek, Prior to the Year 1500. 190p. 1970. Repr. of 1870 ed. text ed. 28.50x (ISBN 90-6032-432-3). Humanities.
Wagner, Willis H. Modern Carpentry. LC 79-11956. 1979. text ed. 14.00 (ISBN 0-87006-274-3); wkbk. 3.20 (ISBN 0-87006-282-4). Goodheart.
--Modern Woodworking. LC 80-18994. (Illus.). 1980. text ed. 13.28 (ISBN 0-87006-301-4); wkbk. 3.20 (ISBN 0-87006-300-6). Goodheart.
--Woodworking. LC 77-89985. (Illus.). 1978. text ed. 4.80 (ISBN 0-87006-257-3). Goodheart.
Wagoner, David. Collected Poems, 1956-1976. LC 75-28915. (Midland Bks.: No. 216). 320p. 1978. 12.50x (ISBN 0-253-11245-1); pap. 7.95x (ISBN 0-253-20216-7). Ind U Pr.
--Landfall. 1981. 9.95 (ISBN 0-316-91706-0, Pub. by Atlantic Monthly Pr); pap. 5.95 (ISBN 0-316-91707-9). Little.
--Who Shall Be the Sun?: Poems Based on the Lore, Legends, & Myths of Northwest Coast & Plateau Indians. LC 78-1836. (Illus.). 144p. 1978. 9.95x (ISBN 0-253-36527-9). Ind U Pr.
Wagoner, Jay. Arizona's Heritage. LC 77-10778. (Illus.). (gr. 8-12). 1977. text ed. 15.00x (ISBN 0-87905-028-4). Peregrine Smith.
Wagoner, Jay J. Arizona! (Illus.). (gr. 4). 1979. text ed. 11.95x (ISBN 0-87905-105-1). Peregrine Smith.
--Arizona Territory 1863-1912: A Political History. LC 69-16331. (Illus.). 512p. 1970. pap. 12.95x (ISBN 0-8165-0176-9). U of Ariz Pr.
Wagoner, Jennings L., Jr., jt. ed. see Mosher, Edith K.
Wagoner, Merrill Y. Van see Van Wagoner, Merrill Y.
Wagoner, Merrill Y. Van see Van Wagoner, Merrill Y., et al.
Wagoner, Walter D. Mortgages on Paradise: Life-Centered Sermons. LC 80-20138. 128p. (Orig.). 1981. pap. 4.95 (ISBN 0-687-27220-3). Abingdon.
Wagschal, Peter H., ed. Learning Tomorrows: Commentaries on the Future of Education. LC 78-19783. (Praeger Special Studies). 1979. 22.95 (ISBN 0-03-046716-0). Praeger.
Wahab, Ibrahim. Law Dictionary (English-Arabic) 1972. 20.00x (ISBN 0-685-72048-9). Intl Bk Ctr.
Wahba. English-French-Arabic Dictionary of Political Idioms. 30.00x (ISBN 0-686-65473-0). Intl Bk Ctr.
Wahba, Magdi. Dictionary of Literary & Linguistic Terms: Arabic-Arabic. 25.00x. Intl Bk Ctr.
--A Dictionary of Literary Terms (English-French-Arabic) 1974. 30.00 (ISBN 0-685-72035-7). Intl Bk Ctr.
Wah-Be-Gwo-Nese, pseud. Ojibwa Indian Legends. (Illus.). 1972. 2.95 (ISBN 0-918616-05-0). Northern Mich.
Wahl, Eberhard W. & Lahey, James F. Seven Hundred MB Atlas for the Northern Hemisphere: Five-Day Mean Heights, Standard Deviations, & Changes. LC 69-5. 1969. plastic comb. bdg. 50.00x (ISBN 0-299-05383-0). U of Wis Pr.
Wahl, Edward C. Geothermal Energy Utilization. LC 77-546. 1977. 33.00 (ISBN 0-471-02304-3, Pub. by Wiley-Interscience). Wiley.
Wahl, J. R., ed. see Rossetti, Dante G.
Wahl, Jan. Abe Lincoln's Beard. LC 75-156045. (Illus.). (ps-3). 1971. PLB 4.58 o.s.i. (ISBN 0-440-00413-6, Sey Lawr). Delacorte.
--Button Eye's Orange. LC 80-14429. (Illus.). 48p. (gr. k-3). 1980. 8.95g (ISBN 0-7232-6188-1). Warne.
--Christmas in the Forest. (Illus.). (gr. k-2). 1967. 4.95g o.s.i. (ISBN 0-02-792370-3). Macmillan.
--The Clumpets Go Sailing. LC 73-23083. (Illus.). (ps-3). 1975. 5.95 o.s.i. (ISBN 0-8193-0770-X, Four Winds); PLB 5.41 o.s.i. (ISBN 0-8193-0771-8). Schol Bk Serv.
--The Cucumber Princess. (Illus.). 40p. (gr. 2 up). 1981. 9.95 (ISBN 0-916144-76-3); pap. 5.95 (ISBN 0-916144-77-1). Stemmer Hse.
--Dracula's Cat. LC 77-27051. (Illus.). (gr. 1-3). 1978. 6.95 (ISBN 0-13-218933-X). P-H.
--Five in the Forest. (Picture Bk). (Illus.). 48p. (gr. k-3). 1974. 4.95 o.p. (ISBN 0-695-80446-4); lib. ed. 4.98 o.p. (ISBN 0-695-40446-6). Follett.
--Great-Grandmother Cat Tales. LC 76-5484. (Illus.). (gr. k-4). 1976. 3.95 o.p. (ISBN 0-394-83278-7); PLB 5.99 (ISBN 0-394-93278-1). Pantheon.
--The Muffletump Storybook. (Picture Bk.). (Illus.). 1975. 5.95 o.p. (ISBN 0-695-80477-4); lib. ed. 5.97 o.p. (ISBN 0-695-40477-6). Follett.
--The Muffletumps Christmas Party. (Picture Bk). (Illus.). 32p. (gr. k-3). 1975. 5.95 o.p. (ISBN 0-695-80617-3); PLB 5.97 o.p. (ISBN 0-695-40617-5). Follett.
--The Muffletumps' Halloween Scare. (Illus.). (ps-3). 6.95 o.p. (ISBN 0-695-80754-4); lib. bdg. 6.99 o.p. (ISBN 0-695-40754-6). Follett.
--The Muffletumps: The Story of Four Dolls. (gr. k-6). 1980. pap. 0.95 (ISBN 0-440-46079-4, YB). Dell.
--Runaway Jonah & Other Tales. LC 68-12084. (ps-3). 1968. 3.95g o.s.i. (ISBN 0-02-792340-1). Macmillan.
--Wolf of My Own. LC 69-10501. (Illus.). (gr. k-2). 1969. 5.95g o.s.i. (ISBN 0-02-792330-4). Macmillan.
Wahl, Jon. Youth's Magic Horn: Seven Stories. LC 77-29127. 1978. 6.95 o.p. (ISBN 0-525-66582-X). Elsevier-Nelson.
Wahl, P. N. Histological Typing of Oral & Oropharyngeal Tumours. (World Health Organization: International Histological Classification of Tumours Ser.). 1971. incl. slides 37.00 (ISBN 0-685-77232-2, 70-1-004-00). Am Soc Clinical.
Wahl, Ralph, jt. auth. see Haig-Brown, Roderick.
Wahl, William B. A Lone Wolf Howling: The Thematic Content of Ronald Duncan's Plays. (Salzburg Studies in English Literature, Poetic Drama, & Poetic Theory: No. 19). 320p. 1973. pap. text ed. 25.00x (ISBN 0-391-01552-4). Humanities.
--Poetic Drama Interviews: Robert Speaight, E Martin Browne & W. H. Auden. (Salzburg Studies in English Literature, Poetic Drama & Poetic Theory: No. 24). (Illus., Orig.). 1976. pap. text ed. 25.00x (ISBN 0-391-01553-2). Humanities.
--Ronald Duncan: Verse Dramatist & Poet Interviewed. (Salzburg Studies in English Literature, Poetic Drama, & Poetic Theory: No. 20). 171p. 1973. pap. text ed. 25.00x (ISBN 0-391-01551-6). Humanities.
Wahlberg, Rachel C., jt. auth. see Cooper, John C.
Wahle, Kent O. W. Don't Forget, Don't Forgive, Don't Hate. 1981. 6.95 (ISBN 0-533-04495-2). Vantage.
Wahler, Robert G., et al. Ecological Assessment of Child Problem Behavior. 1976. pap. text ed. 7.25 (ISBN 0-08-019586-5). Pergamon.
Wahlke, John C., et al, eds. Government & Politics: An Introduction to Political Science. 2nd ed. 1971. 13.95 (ISBN 0-394-31031-4); tchrs. manual free (ISBN 0-394-31605-3). Random.
Wahlman, Maude. Contemporary African Arts. LC 74-77117. (Illus.). 124p. 1974. pap. 5.00 (ISBN 0-914868-00-4, 25520-4). Field Mus.
Wahloo, Per, jt. auth. see Sjowall, Maj.
Wahlquist, Wayne L., et al, eds. Atlas of Utah. (Illus.). 298p. 1981. lib. bdg. 29.95 (ISBN 0-8425-1831-2). Brigham.
Wahlroos, Sven. Excuses: How to Spot Them, Deal with Them, & Stop Using Them. (Illus.). 1981. 11.95 (ISBN 0-02-623300-2). Macmillan.

--Family Communication. LC 73-11831. 300p. 1974. 8.95 o.s.i. (ISBN 0-02-622400-3). Macmillan.
Wahlstrom, Eric H., tr. see Aulen, Gustaf.
Wahlstrom, Ernest E. Optical Crystallography. 5th ed. LC 78-13695. 488p. 1979. text ed. 26.95 (ISBN 0-471-04791-0). Wiley.
Wahr, Frederick B. Emerson & Goethe. 197p. 1980. Repr. of 1915 ed. lib. bdg. 25.00 (ISBN 0-8492-2979-0). R West.
Wahrman, J. & Lewis, K. R., eds. Chromosomes Today, Vol. 4. LC 74-831. 441p. 1973. 59.95 (ISBN 0-470-91630-3). Halsted Pr.
Wahrmud. New German-Arabic Dictionary, 3 vols. 1974. 50.00x (ISBN 0-685-77129-6). Intl Bk Ctr.
Wai, Dunstan M. The African-Arab Conflict in the Sudan. LC 80-15410. 240p. 1981. text ed. 20.00x (ISBN 0-8419-0631-9, Africana). Holmes & Meier.
Waid, Robert L. Cavitation & Polyphase Flow Forum - 1979: Book No. 600143. 1979. pap. text ed. 4.00 (ISBN 0-685-81925-6). ASME.
Waidson, H. M. German Short Stories, Vol. 1. 1900-1945, Vol. 2. 1945-1955, Vol. 3. 1955-1965. Vol. 1. text ed. 4.75x (ISBN 0-521-06717-0); Vol. 2. text ed. 5.25x (ISBN 0-521-06718-9); Vol. 3. text ed. 5.75x (ISBN 0-521-07180-1). Cambridge U Pr.
--The Modern German Novel, 1945-1965. 2nd ed. 176p. 1971. pap. 10.95x o.p. (ISBN 0-19-713414-9). Oxford U Pr.
Waidson, H. M., rev. by see Bennett, E. K.
Waidson, H. M., ed. see Goethe, Johann W.
Waidson, H. M., ed. see Gotthelf, Jeremias.
Waidson, H. M., tr. see Gotthelf, Jeremias.
Waidson, H. M., tr. see Von Goethe, Johann W.
Wain, Barry, ed. see Allen, Thomas W.
Wain, E. L., ed. Misused Words. 1981. 28.50 o.p. (ISBN 0-686-68306-4). Porter.
Wain, Harry. A History of Preventive Medicine. 420p. 1970. text ed. 42.50 (ISBN 0-398-02000-0). C C Thomas.
Wain, John. Arnold Bennett. LC 67-16889. (Columbia Essays on Modern Writers Ser.: No. 23). (Orig.). 1967. pap. 2.00 (ISBN 0-231-02724-9, MW23). Columbia U Pr.
Wain, John, ed. Interpretations: Essays on Twelve English Poems. 2nd ed. 256p. 1972. 18.00x (ISBN 0-7100-7385-2); pap. 7.95 (ISBN 0-7100-7386-0). Routledge & Kegan.
Wain, John, ed. see Shakespeare, William.
Waine, Anthony, jt. ed. see Bartram, Graham.
Wainer, S. S, ed. see Logic Colloquim '79 Leeds, August 1979, et al.
Wainerdi, R. E. Analytical Chemistry in Space. 1970. text ed. 10.00 (ISBN 0-08-006887-1). Pergamon.
Wainger, Steve, jt. ed. see Weiss, Guido.
Wainhouse, Austryn, ed. see Sade, Marquis De.
Wainio, E. A. Monographia Cladoniarum Universalis, 3 vols. 1278p. (Lat. & Fr.). 1978. Set. lib. bdg. 200.00x (ISBN 3-87429-135-9). Lubrecht & Cramer.
Wainright, John. Death of a Big Man. 1979. pap. 1.95 o.p. (ISBN 0-425-04131-X). Berkley Pub.
Waintraub, Jack L., jt. auth. see Seidman, Arthur H.
Wainwright, Charles A. Television Commericals: How to Create Successful TV Advertising. rev. ed. (Communication Arts Bks.). (Illus.). 1970. 8.95 o.s.i. (ISBN 0-8038-7101-5); pap. text ed. 5.95x (ISBN 0-8038-7102-3). Hastings.
Wainwright, David. Piano Makers. (Illus.). 1975. text ed. 16.00x (ISBN 0-09-122950-2). Humanities.
Wainwright, Frederick T. Scandinavian England: Collected Papers. Finberg, H. P., ed. 387p. 1975. 27.50x (ISBN 0-87471-783-3). Rowman.
Wainwright, Geoffrey, jt. ed. see Jones, Cheslyn.
Wainwright, Gordon R. How to Read for Speed & Comprehension. (Illus.). 1978. 12.95 (ISBN 0-13-430769-0); pap. 4.95 (ISBN 0-13-430751-8). P-H.
Wainwright, John. Acquittal. 1980. pap. 1.95 (ISBN 0-425-04578-1). Berkley Pub.
--The Bastard. 1976. 7.95 o.p. (ISBN 0-312-06930-8). St Martin.
--Discovering Lapidary Work. (Illus.). 216p. 1973. 12.75 o.p. (ISBN 0-263-51531-1). Transatlantic.
--The Hard Hit. 1979. pap. 1.95 o.p. (ISBN 0-425-04136-0). Berkley Pub.
--Landscape with Violence. 1980. pap. 1.95 o.p. (ISBN 0-425-04464-5). Berkley Pub.
--Man of Law. 224p. 1981. 9.95 (ISBN 0-312-51088-8). St Martin.
--Pool of Tears. 1977. 7.95 o.p. (ISBN 0-312-63008-5). St Martin.
--Square Dance. 1979. pap. text ed. 1.95 o.p. (ISBN 0-425-04160-3). Berkley Pub.
--Take Murder. 176p. 1981. 9.95 (ISBN 0-312-78357-4). St Martin.
--Thief of Time. LC 77-94461. 1978. 8.95 o.p. (ISBN 0-312-79989-6). St Martin.
Wainwright, M. Doreen, jt. auth. see Matthews, Noel.
Wainwright, S. A., et al. Mechanical Design in Organisms. LC 75-11890. 433p. 1976. 24.95 (ISBN 0-470-91660-5). Halsted Pr.
Wainwright, S. D. Control Mechanisms & Protein Synthesis. LC 72-2348. (Molecular Biology Ser). 528p. 1972. 30.00x (ISBN 0-231-03432-6). Columbia U Pr.
Wainwright, Stephen, jt. auth. see Vogel, Steven.
Wainwrights, Doreen M., jt. ed. see Matthews, Noel.
Waisbren, Burton A. Critical Care Manual: A Systems Approach Method. 2nd ed. 1977. pap. 16.00 (ISBN 0-87488-983-9). Med Exam.
--Emergency Care Manual: A Systems Approach. 2nd. ed. 1980. pap. 9.50 (ISBN 0-87488-984-7). Med Exam.
Wait, James R. Wave Propagation Theory. LC 80-23286. 400p. 1981. 40.01 (ISBN 0-08-026345-3); pap. 20.01 (ISBN 0-08-026344-5). Pergamon.
Wait, John V., jt. auth. see Korn, Granino A.
Wait, R., jt. ed. see Gladwell, I.
Waite, Arthur E. The Quest of the Golden Stairs: A Mystery of Kinghood in Faerie. LC 80-19659. 176p. 1980. Repr. of 1974 ed. lib. bdg. 9.95x (ISBN 0-89370-628-0). Borgo Pr.
--Real History of the Rosicrucians. (Illus.). 454p. 1975. pap. 7.95 o.s.i. (ISBN 0-8334-1738-X). Steinerbks.
--Rider Tarot Deck. 8.00 (ISBN 0-685-47282-5). Weiser.
Waite, Arthur E., ed. see Paracelsus.
Waite, Arthur E., ed. & tr. see Paracelsus.
Waite, Frederick C. First Medical College in Vermont, Castleton, 1818-1862. (Illus.). 280p. 1949. 2.00x o.p. (ISBN 0-934720-14-2). VT Hist Soc.
Waite, Kathleen B. Educable Mentally Retarded Child: Guidance & Curriculum. (Illus.). 592p. 1971. text ed. 54.75.(ISBN 0-398-02002-7). C C Thomas.
Waite, M. O. & Ernst, Bernard D. Trapdoor Springfield. (Illus.). 300p. 1980. 29.95 (ISBN 0-917714-20-2). Beinfeld Pub.
Waite, M. S. & Vecht, A. Phosphors. (Illus.). 320p. 1981. write for info. (Pub. by Peregrinus London). Inst Elect Eng. Postponed.
Waite, Mitchell & Pardee, Michael. BASIC Programming Primer. LC 78-64987. 1979. pap. 10.95 (ISBN 0-672-21586-1). Sams.
Waite, Peter B. Life & Times of Confederation, 1864-1867: Politics, Newspapers, & the Union of British North America. LC 63-796. 1962. pap. 8.50 (ISBN 0-8020-6014-5). U of Toronto Pr.
Waite, Thomas D. & Freeman, Neil J. Mathematics of Environmental Processes. LC 76-25770. 1977. 21.00x (ISBN 0-669-00979-2). Lexington Bks.
Waite, Vincent. Portrait of the Quantocks. LC 66-4372. (Portrait Bks.). (Illus.). 1965. 10.50x (ISBN 0-7091-1158-4). Intl Pubns Serv.
Waite, Virginia. Austria. (Batsford Countries of Europe Ser.). 1970. 8.95 o.p. (ISBN 0-8038-0343-5). Hastings.
--Sardinia. 1977. 22.50 (ISBN 0-7134-0039-0, Pub. by Batsford England). David & Charles.
Waite, William M. Implementing Software for Non-Numeric Applications. (Automatic Computation Ser). (Illus.). 400p. 1973. ref. ed. 24.95x (ISBN 0-13-451898-5). P-H.
Waites, B. A., jt. auth. see Evans, B. H.
Waith, Eugene M., ed. Shakespeare: The Histories: A Collection of Critical Essays. 1965. pap. 2.95 (ISBN 0-13-807701-0, Spec). P-H.
Waitley, Douglas. The Age of the Mad Dragons: Steam Locomotives in North America. LC 80-27242. (Illus.). 192p. (gr. 6 up). 1981. 10.95 (ISBN 0-8253-0029-0). Beaufort Bks NY.
Waitly, Denis. The Winner's Edge: How to Develop the Critical Attitude of Success. 256p. 1980. 9.95 (ISBN 0-8129-0897-X). Times Bks.
Waits, Bert K., jt. auth. see Hart, William L.
Waitzkin, Howard & Waterman, Barbara. Exploitation of Illness in Capitalist Society. LC 73-19706. (Studies in Sociology Ser). 1974. pap. text ed. 3.95 (ISBN 0-672-61327-1). Bobbs.
Wakabayashi, J. F., tr. see Ozima, Minoru.
Wakabayashi, Mitsuru. Management Career Progress in a Japanese Organization. Dufey, Gunter, ed. (Research for Business Decisions). 550p. 1980. 29.95 (ISBN 0-8357-1108-0, Pub. by UMI Res Pr). Univ Microfilms.
Wake, Clive, tr. see Sassine, Williams.
Wakefield. An Introduction to Photography. 8.95 o.p. (ISBN 0-85242-050-1, Pub. by Fountain). Morgan.
Wakefield, B. J. The Chemistry of Organolithium Compounds. LC 73-10091. 336p. 1974. text ed. 49.00 (ISBN 0-08-017640-2). Pergamon.
Wakefield, Christa. A Measure of Days. (Orig.). 1979. pap. 1.95 (ISBN 0-686-68908-9). Manor Bks.
Wakefield, Connie L., jt. auth. see Jones, Harold K.
Wakefield, Dan. Going All the Way. 1970. 6.95 o.p. (ISBN 0-440-02955-4, Sey Lawr). Delacorte.
--Starting Over. 304p. 1973. 7.95 o.p. (ISBN 0-440-08256-0, Sey Lawr). Delacorte.
Wakefield, David. Fragonard. (Illus.). 1977. 15.95 (ISBN 0-8467-0246-0, Pub. by Two Continents); pap. 9.95 (ISBN 0-8467-0245-2). Hippocrene Bks.
Wakefield, Frances & Harkins, Dorothy. Track & Field. 4th ed. LC 77-170. (Fundamentals for Girls & Women). 1977. 9.95 (ISBN 0-8016-5328-2). Mosby.
Wakefield, G. L., jt. auth. see Dunn, J. F.
Wakefield, George. Practical Sensitometry. 1970. 11.95 o.p. (ISBN 0-85242-310-1, Pub. by Fountain). Morgan.
Wakefield, George L. Exposure Control in Enlarging. 1972. 9.95 o.p. (ISBN 0-85242-005-6, Pub. by Fountain). Morgan.
Wakefield, Joyce. Wide-Awake Timothy. LC 80-21843. (Illus.). 32p. (gr. k-4). 1981. PLB 7.95 (ISBN 0-516-03658-0). Childrens.
Wakefield, Norman. Listening. 1981. pap. 4.95 (ISBN 0-8499-2920-2). Word Bks.
Wakefield, Priscilla. Reflections on the Present Condition of the Female Sex: With Suggestions for Its Improvement. Luria, Gina, ed. (The Feminist Controversy in England, 1788-1810 Ser.). 1974. lib. bdg. 50.00 (ISBN 0-8240-0882-0). Garland Pub.
Wakefield, Ron, tr. see Schrader, Halwart.
Wakefield, Ruth G. Toll House Tried & True Recipes. 8.50 (ISBN 0-8446-5684-4). Peter Smith.
Wakefield, Sarah. Six Weeks in the Sioux Tepees: A Narrative of Indian Captivity, Repr. Of 1863 Ed. Bd. with Miss Coleson's Narrative of Her Capitivity Among the Sioux Indians. Coleson, Ann. Repr. of 1864 ed; Reminiscences of Col. John Ketcham, of Monroe County, Indiana, by His Pastor. Hopkins, Thomas M. Repr. of 1866 ed; Gertrude Moran: Or, Life & Adventures Among the Indians of the Far West. Repr. of 1866 ed. LC 75-7104. (Indian Captivities Ser.: Vol. 79). 1977. lib. bdg. 44.00 (ISBN 0-8240-1703-X). Garland Pub.
Wakefield, Tom. Special School. (Orig.). 1977. pap. 7.50 (ISBN 0-7100-8750-0). Routledge & Kegan.
Wakefield, Walter L. Heresy, Crusade, & Inquisition in Southern France, 1100-1250. 1974. 24.50x (ISBN 0-520-02380-3). U of Cal Pr.
Wakefield Washington Associates, Inc. Family Research: A Source Book, Analysis & Guide to Federal Funding, 2 vols. LC 79-7732. (Illus.). 1979. Set. lib. bdg. 95.00 (ISBN 0-313-21139-6, WFR/). Greenwood.
Wakeford, J., jt. auth. see Urry, J.
Wakeford, Jacqueline. Flytying Techniques. LC 80-1274. (Illus.). 176p. 1980. 29.95 (ISBN 0-385-17306-7, NLB). Doubleday.
Wakehurst, John D. The Truth About Mesopotamia, Palestine & Syria. LC 79-2887. 221p. 1981. Repr. of 1923 ed. 19.50 (ISBN 0-8305-0054-5). Hyperion Conn.
Wakelin, Martyn F. English Dialects: An Introduction. 1972. pap. text ed. 13.00x (ISBN 0-485-12020-8, Athlone). Humanities.
--Language & History in Cornwall. (Illus.). 1975. text ed. 20.00x (ISBN 0-7185-1124-7, Leicester). Humanities.
Wakely, Neal. Legend of the Silver Bars. 112p. 1979. 5.95 (ISBN 0-8059-2592-9). Dorrance.
Wakelyn, Jon L. Biographical Dictionary of the Confederacy. Vandiver, Frank E., ed. LC 72-13870. 1976. lib. bdg. 32.50x (ISBN 0-8371-6124-X, WCL). Greenwood.
Wakeman, Frederic. History & Will: Philosophical Perspectives of Mao Tse-Tung's Thought. 408p. 1976. pap. 7.95x (ISBN 0-520-02907-0). U of Cal Pr.
Wakeman, Frederic & Grant, Carolyn. Conflict & Control in Late Imperial China. LC 73-87247. 400p. 1976. 23.75x (ISBN 0-520-02597-0). U of Cal Pr.
Wakeman, Frederic E., Jr. Strangers at the Gate: Social Disorder in South China, 1839-1861. (Center for Chinese Studies, UC Berkeley). 1966. 18.50x o.p. (ISBN 0-520-01312-3); pap. 3.95x o. p. o.p. (ISBN 0-520-02634-9). U of Cal Pr.
Wakeman, Frederic, Jr. The Fall of Imperial China. LC 74-27854. (Transformation of Modern China Ser.). 1975. 10.95 (ISBN 0-02-933690-2); pap. text ed. 7.95 (ISBN 0-02-933680-5). Free Pr.
Wakeman, Fredric, Jr., ed. Ming & Qing: Historical Studies in the People's Republic of China. (China Research Monographs: No. 17). 1981. pap. 8.00 (ISBN 0-912966-27-0). IEAS Ctr Chinese Stud.
Wakeman, John, ed. World Authors: Nineteen Seventy to Nineteen Seventy-Five. 1979. 40.00 (ISBN 0-8242-0641-X). Wilson.
Wakeman, T. J. Modern Agricultural Mechanics. LC 76-28839. 1977. 19.65 (ISBN 0-8134-1851-8); text ed. 14.75x (ISBN 0-685-81722-9). Interstate.
Wakerly, John F. Microcomputer Architecture & Programming. 600p. 1981. text ed. 23.95 (ISBN 0-471-05232-9). Wiley.
Wakin & Scheuer. De-Romanization of the American Catholic Church. 3.95 o.p. (ISBN 0-452-25009-9, Z5009, Plume). NAL.
Wakin, E. E. How to Turn Down into up. (gr. 9). 1980. pap. 1.25 (ISBN 0-590-31263-4, Schol Pap). Schol Bk Serv.
Wakin, Edward. Jobs in Communications. LC 73-17470. (Exploring Careers Ser.). (Illus.). 96p. (gr. 5 up). 1974. 7.25 (ISBN 0-688-75006-0). Lothrop.
--Monday Morality: Right & Wrong in Daily Life. LC 80-80871. 96p. (Orig.). 1980. pap. 3.95 (ISBN 0-8091-2317-7). Paulist Pr.
Wakley, Jack, jt. auth. see Scheele, Ronald V.
Wakoski, Diane. Cap of Darkness. 117p. 1980. 14.00 (ISBN 0-87685-454-4); pap. 5.00 (ISBN 0-87685-453-6); signed ed. 20.00 (ISBN 0-87685-455-2). Black Sparrow.
--Fable of the Lion & the Scorpion. 1975. pap. 2.50x (ISBN 0-915316-19-6). Pentagram.
--Greed, Pts. 5-7. (Orig.). 1976. pap. 10.00 (ISBN 0-87685-095-6). Black Sparrow.
--Inside the Blood Factory. LC 68-27104. 1968. Softbound 4.95 o.p. (ISBN 0-385-05299-5). Doubleday.
--The Magellanic Clouds. 154p. (Orig.). 1978. 10.00 (ISBN 0-87685-078-6); pap. 5.00 (ISBN 0-87685-077-8). Black Sparrow.
--The Man Who Shook Hands. 118p. 1978. 5.50 (ISBN 0-87685-467-6). Black Sparrow.
--The Man Who Shook Hands. LC 77-80917. 1978. 6.95 o.p. (ISBN 0-385-13407-X); pap. 4.95 o.p. (ISBN 0-385-13408-8). Doubleday.
--Smudging. 150p. (Orig.). 1974. 10.00 (ISBN 0-87685-131-6); pap. 5.00 (ISBN 0-87685-130-8). Black Sparrow.
--Towards a New Poetry. (Poets on Poetry Ser.). 1979. pap. 5.95 (ISBN 0-472-06307-3). U of Mich Pr.
Waksler, jt. auth. see Douglas.
Waksman, B. H., jt. ed. see Byron, H.
Wala, Mario, jt. auth. see Rogowski, Piotr.
Walbank, F. W. A Historical Commentary on Polybius: Commentary on Books XIX-XL, Vol. 3. 872p. 1979. text ed. 65.00x (ISBN 0-19-814011-8). Oxford U Pr.
--A Historical Commentary on Polybius: Vol. 1, Commentary Books I-IV, Vol. 1. (Illus.). 804p. 1957. text ed. 49.00x (ISBN 0-19-814152-1). Oxford U Pr.
--Polybius. LC 72-189219. (Sather Classical Lectures, No. 42). 1973. 18.50x (ISBN 0-520-02190-8). U of Cal Pr.
Walberg, Herbert, jt. auth. see Kopan, Andrew.
Walberg, Herbert, jt. ed. see Amick, Daniel J.
Walberg, Herbert J. Evaluating Educational Performance. LC 73-17613. 1974. 19.50x (ISBN 0-685-42644-0); text ed. 17.50x (ISBN 0-685-42645-9). McCutchan.
Walberg, Herbert J., ed. Educational Environments & Effects: Evaluation, Policy, & Productivity. LC 78-62101. (Education Ser). 1979. 17.00 (ISBN 0-8211-2259-2); text ed. 15.20 in ten or more copies (ISBN 0-685-65115-0). McCutchan.
--Rethinking Urban Education: A Sourcebook of Contemporary Issues. Kopan, Andrew T. LC 72-83962. (Higher Education Ser.). 1972. 15.95x o.p. (ISBN 0-87589-140-3). Jossey-Bass.
Walberg, Herbert J., jt. ed. see Peterson, Penelope L.
Walberg, Herbert J., jt. ed. see Spodek, Bernard.
Walbruck, Rita M. Die Falsche Agentin: Reader 4. LC 80-22162. (Auf Heisser Spur Ser.). (gr. 9-12). 1981. pap. 1.95 (ISBN 0-88436-853-X). EMC.
--Im Anderen Deutschland: Reader 3. LC 80-22199. (Auf Heisser Spur Ser.). (gr. 9-12). 1981. pap. 1.95 (ISBN 0-88436-852-1). EMC.
--Das Ratsel Vom Waldsee: Reader 2. LC 80-22126. (Auf Heisser Spur Ser.). (gr. 9-12). 1981. pap. 1.95 (ISBN 0-88436-851-3). EMC.
--Der Verlorene Koffer: Reader 1. LC 80-22198. (Auf Heisser Spur Ser.). (gr. 9-12). 1981. pap. 1.95 (ISBN 0-88436-850-5). EMC.
Walch, Timothy & Sedlak, Michael W., eds. American Educational History: A Guide to Informational History. LC 80-19646. (American Government & History Information Guide Ser.: Vol. 10). 350p. 1981. 30.00 (ISBN 0-8103-1478-9). Gale.
Walchars, John. The Unfinished Mystery. (Orig.). 1978. pap. 4.95 (ISBN 0-8164-2184-6). Crossroad NY.
Walchenbach, John, jt. auth. see Battles, Ford L.
Walcher, Dwain N., et al, eds. Mutations: Biology & Society. Barnett, Henry L. & Kretchmer, Norman. LC 78-63411. (Illus.). 432p. 1978. 31.50 (ISBN 0-89352-020-9). Masson Pub.
Walcot, James. The New Pilgrim's Progress; or, the Pious Indian Convert, 1748. LC 74-16309. (Novel in England, 1700-1775 Ser). 1974. lib. bdg. 50.00 (ISBN 0-8240-1122-8). Garland Pub.
Walcot, Peter. Greek Drama in Its Theatrical & Social Context. 1976. pap. text ed. 8.25x o.p. (ISBN 0-7083-0602-0). Verry.

Walcott, Cynthia. The Gift. LC 76-5476. (Illus.). (gr. 1-5). 1976. 7.00 (ISBN 0-87743-105-1, 7-52-51); with cassette narration 12.00 (ISBN 0-87743-108-6, 7-52-52). Baha'i.
--El Regalo. Baha'i Publishing Committee, tr. from Span. LC 76-5502. (Illus.). (gr. 1-5). 1976. 7.00 (ISBN 0-87743-106-X, 7-93-68); with cassette narration 12.00 (ISBN 0-87743-109-4, 7-93-67). Baha'i.
Walcott, Derek. Dream on Monkey Mountain & Other Plays. 326p. 1970. pap. 5.95 (ISBN 0-374-50860-7, N390). FS&G.
--Dream on Monkey Mountain & Other Plays. 1970. 15.00 (ISBN 0-685-77062-1). Univ Place.
--The Fortunate Traveller. 1981. 10.95 (ISBN 0-374-15765-0). FS&G.
--Remembrance & Pantomime. 176p. 1980. 15.00 (ISBN 0-374-24912-1); pap. 6.95 (ISBN 0-374-51569-7). FS&G.
--The Star-Apple Kingdom. LC 78-11323. 98p. 1979. 10.00 (ISBN 0-374-26974-2); pap. 6.95 (ISBN 0-374-26974-2). FS&G.
Wald, Abraham. Sequential Analysis. LC 73-85900. 1973. pap. text ed. 4.00 (ISBN 0-486-61579-0). Dover.
Wald, Alan M. James T. Farrell: The Revolutionary Socialist Years. LC 77-84156. 1978. 15.00x (ISBN 0-8147-9179-4); pap. 5.00x (ISBN 0-8147-9180-8). NYU Pr.
Wald, G., et al. Twenty-Six Afternoons of Biology: An Introductory Laboratory Manual. 2nd ed. (gr. 9-12). 1966. pap. text ed. 11.95 (ISBN 0-201-08461-9); individual experiments 1.00 ea. A-W.
Wald, Heywood. Lo Paso Bien En los Estados Inidos. (gr. 9-12). 1981. pap. 0.95 (ISBN 0-8120-2318-8). Barron.
Wald, J. Bigg's Cost Accounts. (Illus.). 400p. (Orig.). 1978. pap. text ed. 15.95x (ISBN 0-7121-0263-9, Pub. by Macdonald & Evans England). Intl Ideas.
Wald, Michael, jt. auth. see Burt, Robert A.
Wald, Robert, illus. Introduction to Jewelry Casting. 1974. pap. 7.95 o.p. (ISBN 0-8096-1885-0, Assn Pr). Follett.
Wald, Robert M. Space, Time, & Gravity. LC 77-4038. viii, 132p. 1981. pap. 3.95 (ISBN 0-226-87031-6). U of Chicago Pr.
--Space, Time & Gravity: The Theory of the Big Bang & Black Holes. LC 77-4038. (Illus.). 1977. 10.95 (ISBN 0-226-87030-8); pap. 3.95 (ISBN 0-226-87031-6). U of Chicago Pr.
Waldberg, Patrick. Surrealism. (World of Art Ser.). (Illus.). 1978. pap. 9.95 (ISBN 0-19-520070-5). Oxford U Pr.
Waldbott, George L. Health Effects of Environmental Pollutants. 2nd ed. LC 77-26880. (Illus.). 1978. pap. text ed. 16.95 (ISBN 0-8016-5331-2). Mosby.
Waldcock, H. see Royal Institute of International Affairs.
Waldee, Lynne M. Cooking the French Way. (Easy Menu Ethnic Cookbooks). (Illus.). (YA) (gr. 5 up). 1981. PLB 4.95g (ISBN 0-8225-0904-0). Lerner Pubns.
Waldegrove, William. The Binding of Leviathan: Conservatism & the Future. 1979. 17.95 (ISBN 0-241-89866-8, Pub. by Hamish Hamilton England). David & Charles.
Waldeland, Lynne. John Cheever. (United States Authors Series: No. 335). 1979. lib. bdg. 10.95 (ISBN 0-8057-7251-0). Twayne.
Walden, Amelia. Where Was Everyone When Sabrina Screamed? (gr. 7-12). 1975. pap. 1.25 (ISBN 0-590-00091-8, Schol Pap). Schol Bk Serv.
Walden, Barbara & Lindner, Vicki. Easy Glamour. (Illus.). 224p. 1981. 9.95 (ISBN 0-688-00416-4). Morrow.
Walden, Daniel, ed. On Being Jewish. 480p. 1974. pap. 1.75 o.p. (ISBN 0-449-30696-8, X638, Prem). Fawcett.
Walden, David B., ed. Maize Breeding & Genetics. LC 78-6779. 1978. 62.50 (ISBN 0-471-91805-9, Pub. by Wiley-Interscience). Wiley.
Walden, Karen M. Now I Can Smile. 1981. 4.95 (ISBN 0-533-04493-6). Vantage.
Waldenfels, Bernhard. Der Spielraum Des Verhaltens. (Suhrkamp Taschenbuecher Wissenschaft: 311). 344p. (Ger.). pap. text ed. 9.10 (ISBN 3-518-07911-5, Pub. by Insel Verlag Germany). Suhrkamp.
Waldenfels, Hans. Absolute Nothingness: Foundations for a Buddhist-Christian Dialogue. Heisig, James W., tr. from Ger. Orig. Title: Absolutes Nichts. 214p. 1980. pap. 7.95 (ISBN 0-8091-2316-9). Paulist Pr.
Waldenstrom, Jan G. Paraneoplasia: Biological Signals in the Diagnosis of Cancer. LC 78-18494. 1978. text ed. 29.50 (ISBN 0-471-03490-8, Pub. by Wiley Medical). Wiley.
Walder, Barbara, jt. auth. see Schmidt, Mike.
Walders, Joe. World's Most Challenging TV Quiz. LC 77-11248. 1978. pap. 4.95 (ISBN 0-385-13054-6, Dolp). Doubleday.
Waldheim, Kurt. Austrian Example. 224p. 1973. 6.95 o.s.i. (ISBN 0-02-622490-9). Macmillan.
Waldhorn, Arthur & Zeiger, Arthur. English Made Simple. rev. ed. 1954. pap. 3.50 (ISBN 0-385-01208-X, Made). Doubleday.
--Word Mastery Made Simple. pap. 3.50 (ISBN 0-385-01213-6, Made). Doubleday.
Waldinger, Renee & Corbiere-Gille, Gisele. Promenades. Litteraires & Grammaticales. 1966. text ed. 11.95x (ISBN 0-669-28662-1); tapes. 6 reels o. p. 30.00 (ISBN 0-669-33977-6). Heath.
Waldman, Bess. The Book of Tziril: A Family Chronicle. 270p. 1981. pap. 6.00x (ISBN 0-916288-09-9). Micah Pubns.
Waldman, Charles. Strategies of International Mass Retailers. LC 78-19467. (Praeger Special Studies). 1978. 25.95 (ISBN 0-03-045626-6). Praeger.
Waldman, Diane. Kenneth Noland: A Retrospective. (Illus.). 1977. pap. 9.95 (ISBN 0-89207-009-9). S R Guggenheim.
--Mark Rothko, Nineteen Three-Nineteen Seventy: A Retrospective. new ed. LC 78-58411. (Illus.). 30.00 (ISBN 0-89207-014-5); softcover 14.85 (ISBN 0-89207-014-5). S R Guggenheim.
Waldman, Don E. Antitrust Action & Market Structure. LC 78-8813. (Illus.). 1978. 19.95 (ISBN 0-669-02401-5). Lexington Bks.
Waldman, Eric. Goose Step Is Verboten. LC 64-23077. 1964. 8.50 o.s.i. (ISBN 0-02-933650-3). Free Pr.
Waldman, Frank. Return of the Pink Panther. (Orig.). 1977. pap. 1.50 o.p. (ISBN 0-685-75032-9, 345-25123-1-150). Ballantine.
Waldman, Guido, tr. see Ariosto, Ludovico.
Waldman, Harry, ed. Encyclopedia of Indians of the Americas, Vols. 1-8. LC 74-5088. 1974-81. lib. bdg. 59.00 ea. Scholarly.
--World Encyclopedia of Black Peoples, Vols. 1 & 2. LC 74-28076. 1974-81. lib. bdg. 59.00 ea. Scholarly.
Waldman, John. Rapid Reading Made Simple. 1958. pap. 3.50 (ISBN 0-385-01226-8, Made). Doubleday.
Waldman, John, jt. auth. see Venema, Jack E.
Waldman, M., tr. see La Capria, Raffaele.
Waldman, Roy D. Humanistic Psychiatry: From Oppression to Choice. 1971. 12.00 (ISBN 0-8135-0681-6). Rutgers U Pr.
Waldmann, Hermann, jt. auth. see Lefkovitz, Ivan.
Waldmann, Raymond J. Direct Investment & Development in the U.S. A Guide to Incentive Programs, Laws & Restrictions, 1980-81. rev. ed. LC 80-51673. 453p. 1980. pap. text ed. 75.00 (ISBN 0-933678-01-0). Transnatl Invest.
Waldmann, Raymond J., ed. U S Foreign Trade Zones. (Orig.). 1981. pap. 45.00 (ISBN 0-933678-02-9). Transnatl Invest.
Waldner, George K. & Mitterhauser, Klaus. Professional Chef's Book of Buffets. 1968. 22.95 (ISBN 0-8436-0505-7). CBI Pub.
Waldo, C. Dwight. The Enterprise of Public Administration. Jones, Victor, ed. LC 80-13764. (Chandler & Sharp Publications in Poltical Science). 224p. (Orig.). 1980. pap. text ed. 6.95 (ISBN 0-88316-537-6). Chandler & Sharp.
Waldo, Dwight, ed. Public Administration in a Time of Turbulence. 1971. pap. text ed. 8.95 scp o.p. (ISBN 0-685-02949-2, HarpC). Har-Row.
Waldo, Kay C., jt. auth. see MacKenzie, Alec.
Waldo, Myra. Cooking for the Freezer. 240p. 1975. pap. 1.95 (ISBN 0-385-06295-8, Dolp). Doubleday.
--Flavor of Spain. 1970. pap. 1.50 o.s.i. (ISBN 0-02-010400-6, Collier). Macmillan.
--The Great International Barbeque Book. 216p. 1981. pap. 4.95 (ISBN 0-07-067778-6). McGraw.
--Hamburger Cookbook. (Orig.). 1962. pap. 0.95 o.s.i. (ISBN 0-02-010710-2, Collier). Macmillan.
--Myra Waldo's Restaurant Guide to New York City & Vicinity, 1981. 434p. 1981. pap. 6.95 (ISBN 0-02-098900-8, Collier). Macmillan.
--Myra Waldo's Travel Guide to Northern Europe, 1981. (Illus.). 730p. 1981. pap. 9.95 (ISBN 0-02-098910-5, Collier). Macmillan.
--Myra Waldo's Travel Guide to Southern Europe, 1981. (Illus.). 770p. 1981. pap. 9.95 (ISBN 0-02-098930-X, Collier). Macmillan.
--Myra Waldo's Travel Guide to the Orient & Asia, 1981. (Illus.). 505p. 1981. pap. 9.95 (ISBN 0-02-098890-7, Collier). Macmillan.
--Myra Waldo's Travel Guide to the South Pacific, 1981. (Illus.). 360p. 1981. pap. 8.95 (ISBN 0-02-098920-2, Collier). Macmillan.
Waldo, Myra, jt. auth. see Berg, Gertrude.
Waldo, Terry. This Is Ragtime. 1976. 10.95 (ISBN 0-8015-7618-0, Hawthorn). Dutton.
Waldo, Wayne M., jt. auth. see Carpenter, Max H.
Waldock, A. J. Paradise Lost & Its Critics. 1959. 6.50 (ISBN 0-8446-1463-7). Peter Smith.
Waldock, Arthur J. Sophocles the Dramatist. pap. 8.50x (ISBN 0-521-09374-0). Cambridge U Pr.
Waldock, H. see Royal Institute of International Affairs.
Waldowski, Therese F., jt. auth. see Gregorich, Barbara.
Waldren, Richard P. & Ehler, Stanley W. Crop Science: Laboratory Manual. 2nd ed. 1981. write for info. (ISBN 0-8087-3717-1). Burgess.
Waldron, ed. see Vogel, A. I.
Waldron, Ann. The Bluebury Collection. LC 80-21846. (gr. 4-7). 1981. PLB 9.95 (ISBN 0-525-26739-5). Dutton.
--The House on Pendleton Block. (Illus.). 160p. (gr. 4-7). 1975. PLB 6.95 (ISBN 0-8038-3033-5). Hastings.
--The Luckie Star. (gr. 4-7). 1977. PLB 7.50 o.p. (ISBN 0-525-34270-2). Dutton.
Waldron, Ellis & Wilson, Paul. Atlas of Montana Elections: Eighteen Eighty-Nine to Nineteen Seventy-Six. 1979. 33.00 (ISBN 0-686-23488-X); pap. 19.95. U of MT Pubns Hist.
Waldron, R. A. Sense & Sense Development. rev. ed. (Andre Deutsch Language Library). 1979. 35.50x (ISBN 0-233-95948-3). Westview.
Waldron, R. A., ed. Sir Gawain & the Green Knight. LC 75-129568. (York Medieval Texts Ser). 1970. text ed. 8.95 (ISBN 0-8101-0327-3); pap. text ed. 2.95 o.s.i. (ISBN 0-8101-0328-1). Northwestern U Pr.
Waldron, Randall H., ed. Mattie: The Letters of Martha Mitchell Whitman. LC 77-81906. (Illus.). 1978. 12.00x (ISBN 0-8147-9178-6). NYU Pr.
Waldron, Ronald, jt. ed. see Andrew, Malcolm.
Waldron, Ronald J., et al. The Criminal Justice System: An Introduction. 2nd ed. LC 79-65288. (Illus.). 1980. text ed. 17.95 (ISBN 0-395-28669-7); inst. manual 0.65 (ISBN 0-395-28668-9); study guide 4.95 (ISBN 0-395-29304-9). HM.
--The Criminal Justice System: An Introduction. LC 75-26098. (Illus.). 480p. 1976. pap. text ed. 15.75 o.p. (ISBN 0-395-18592-0); instr. manual o.p. 1.25 o.p. (ISBN 0-395-18785-0). HM.
Waldron, Sidney R., jt. auth. see Koehn, Peter.
Waldrop, John. Roller Coaster Fever. LC 79-63380. 1979. pap. 6.95 (ISBN 0-931064-08-2). Starlog.
Waldrop, Rosmarie, tr. see Jabes, Edmond.
Waldrop, Stanley. Boy, Girl, & Garden. LC 76-20983. 1976. 7.95 (ISBN 0-9603364-1-9). Waldrop Pubns.
--Closeness & Creativity. LC 77-84984. 1977. 6.95 (ISBN 0-9603364-0-0). Waldrop Pubns.
Waldrop, Sybil, jt. auth. see Rouse, Doris.
Waldschmidt, Ernest & Waldschmidt, Rose L. Nepal Art Treasures of the Himalayas. 1969. 19.95 (ISBN 0-236-17724-9, Pub. by Paul Elek). Merrimack Bk Serv.
Waldschmidt, Rose L., jt. auth. see Waldschmidt, Ernest.
Waldvogel, Francis A., et al. Osteomyelitis: Clinical Features, Therapeutic Considerations, & Unusual Aspects. (Illus.). 128p. 1971. 12.75 (ISBN 0-398-02156-2). C C Thomas.
Wale, Michael, jt. auth. see Paton, Tam.
Wale, William, ed. What Great Men Have Said About Great Men. LC 68-17944. 1968. Repr. of 1902 ed. 18.00 (ISBN 0-8103-3195-0). Gale.
Wales, Charles E., et al. Guided Engineering Design: An Introduction to Engineering Calculations. 432p. 1974. pap. text ed. 12.95 (ISBN 0-8299-0001-2); instrs.' manual avail. (ISBN 0-8299-0005-5). West Pub.
--Guided Engineering Design: An Introduction to Engineering Calculations. 2nd ed. (Illus.). 330p. 1980. pap. text ed. 13.95 (ISBN 0-8299-0353-4); Project Bk. 10.95 (ISBN 0-8299-0378-X). West Pub.
Wales, John N. Prologue to Education. 1979. 12.95 (ISBN 0-7100-0117-7). Routledge & Kegan.
Wales, Katie, compiled by. The Book of Elephants. LC 76-23139. (Illus.). 64p. (ps-5). 1977. 6.95 (ISBN 0-590-07723-6, Four Winds); PLB 5.41 o.p. (ISBN 0-8193-0892-7). Schol Bk Serv.
Wales, Ny see Snow, Helen, pseud.
Wales, T., ed. see Carnegie Commission on Higher Education.
Wales Tourist Board. Castles & Historic Places in Wales. rev. ed. (Illus.). 104p. 1981. pap. write for info. (ISBN 0-900784-77-6, Pub. by Auto Assn-British Tourist Authority England). Merrimack Bk Serv.
--Mid Wales: A Tourist Guide. (Illus.). 84p. Date not set. pap. price not set (ISBN 0-900784-72-5, Pub. by Auto Assn-British Tourist Authority England). Merrimack Bk Serv.
--North Wales: A Tourist Guide. rev. ed. (Illus.). 84p. Date not set. pap. price not set (ISBN 0-900784-71-7, Pub. by Auto Assn-British Tourist Authority England). Merrimack Bk Serv.
--South Wales: A Tourist Guide. rev. ed. (Illus.). 84p. 1981. pap. write for info. (ISBN 0-900784-73-3, Pub. by Auto Assn-British Tourist Authority England). Merrimack Bk Serv.
--Wales: Going Places. (Illus.). 72p. 1980. pap. write for info. (ISBN 0-900784-76-8, Pub. by Auto Assn-British Tourist Authority England). Merrimack Bk Serv.
--Wales: Where to Stay. rev. ed. (Illus.). 380p. 1981. pap. price not set (ISBN 0-900784-79-2, Pub. by Auto Assn-British Tourist Authority England). Merrimack Bk Serv.
Wales University. Dictionary of the Welsh Language, Vol. 1. A-ffysvr. 1950. Pts. 1-21. 90.00 (ISBN 0-7083-0504-0); Pts. 22-29. pap. 8.00x ea. Verry.
Walett, Francis G., ed. The Diary of Ebenezer Parkman 1703-1782: 1719-1755, Pt. 1. LC 68-30686. 316p. 1974. 22.50x (ISBN 0-912296-04-6, Dist. by U. Pr. of Va.). Am Antiquarian.
Waley, Arthur. The No Play of Japan. LC 75-28969. 1976. pap. 5.95 (ISBN 0-8048-1198-9). C E Tuttle.
--The Poetry & Career of Li Po. (Ethical & Religious Classics of East & West Ser.). 1951. 13.50 (ISBN 0-04-895012-2). Allen Unwin.
--Three Ways of Thought in Ancient China. LC 56-5973. 1956. pap. 2.50 (ISBN 0-385-09280-6, A75, Anch). Doubleday.
Waley, Arthur D. Analects of Confucius. 1938. 13.50 o.p. (ISBN 0-04-181002-3). Allen Unwin.
--The Life & Times of Po Chu-I. 1949. 9.50 o.p. (ISBN 0-04-951011-8). Allen Unwin.
--The Opium War Through Chinese Eyes. 1958. text ed. 12.50x (ISBN 0-04-951012-6). Allen Unwin.
Waley, Daniel P., jt. auth. see Hearder, H.
Waleys, Thomas. Metamorphosis Ovidiana Moraliter... Explanata Libellus. Orgel, Stephen, ed. LC 78-68208. (Philosophy of Images: Vol. 1). 1979. lib. bdg. 66.00 (ISBN 0-8240-3675-1). Garland Pub.
Walf, Knut, jt. ed. see Huizing, Peter.
Walfman, Walt & Fasold, Ralph W. The Study of Social Dialects in American English. 272p. 1974. ref. ed. 12.95 (ISBN 0-13-858787-6). P-H.
Walford, Alberto J. & Screen, J. E., eds. A Guide to Foreign Language Courses & Dictionaries. LC 77-26283. 1978. lib. bdg. 22.50 (ISBN 0-313-20100-5, WGL/). Greenwood.
Walford, J., ed. Developments in Food Colour - One. (Illus.). ix, 259p. 1980. 45.00x (ISBN 0-85334-881-2, Pub. by Applied Science). Burgess-Intl Ideas.
Walford, Lionel A. Marine Fishes of the Pacific Coast from Alaska to the Equator. LC 74-80976. 205p. 1975. Repr. of 1937 ed. 15.00x (ISBN 0-87474-153-X). Smithsonian.
Walford, Naomi, tr. see Undset, Sigrid.
Walford, Rex, jt. auth. see Taylor, John L.
Walford, Rex, ed. New Directions in Geography Teaching. (Illus.). 197p. 1973. pap. text ed. 5.00x o.p. (ISBN 0-582-31240-X). Longman.
Walgenbach, Paul H., et al. Principles of Accounting. 2nd ed. 1065p. 1980. text ed. 19.95 (ISBN 0-686-64997-4, HC); study guide 7.50 (ISBN 0-686-64998-2); solutions manual avail.; practice set A, practice set A with business papers, practice sets B&C & solutions manual avail.; working papers. set 1 8.95 (ISBN 0-686-64999-0); write for info. working papers set 2; test item file, achievement tests & ans. key avail.; transparencies avail. HarBraceJ.
Walheim, Lance, jt. auth. see Ray, Richard.
Walhout, Donald. Send My Roots Rain: A Study of Religious Experience in the Poetry of Gerard Manley Hopkins. LC 80-23549. 210p. 1981. 14.95x (ISBN 0-8214-0565-9). Ohio U Pr.
Wali, Mohan K., ed. see International Congress for Energy & the Ecosystem, University of North Dakota, 12-16 June 1978.
Walicki, Andrzei. The Slavophile Controversy: History of a Conservative Utopia in Nineteenth Century Russian Thought. Andrews, Hilda, tr. from Polish. 600p. 1975. 59.00x (ISBN 0-19-822507-5). Oxford U Pr.
Walii, Parve, jt. auth. see Monsted, Mette.
Walimbe, Y. S. Abhinavagupta on Indian Aesthetics. 1980. 9.50x (ISBN 0-8364-0624-9, Pub. by Ajanta). South Asia Bks.
Walitza, Eckehard, jt. auth. see Chmiel, Horst.
Walkden, Brian & Walkden, Mary. Growing & Storing Herbs. 1979. pap. 3.95 o.s.i. (ISBN 0-7225-0508-6). Newcastle Pub.
Walkden, Mary, jt. auth. see Walkden, Brian.
Walker & Smith. Practical Approach to Gastroenterology & Procedures in Childhood. (Postgraduate Pediatric Ser.). 1981. text ed. price not set. Butterworth.
Walker & Thrower. Chemistry & Physics of Carbon, Vol. 16. 376p. 1981. 42.50 (ISBN 0-8247-6991-0). Dekker.
Walker, et al. Clinical Methods. 2nd ed. 1980. 39.95 (ISBN 0-409-95190-0). Butterworths.
Walker, A., ed. see Puttenham, G.
Walker, A. C., ed. Design & Analysis of Cold Formed Sections. LC 75-1315. 190p. 1975. 18.95 o.p. (ISBN 0-470-91809-8). Halsted Pr.
Walker, A. C., jt. ed. see Rhodes, J.

Walker, A. Earl. Cerebral Death. 2nd ed. LC 80-26410. (Illus.). 1981. text ed. 32.50 (ISBN 0-8067-2142-1). Urban & S.

Walker, A. Earl, et al. The Late Effects of Head Injury. 580p. 1969. pap. 31.50 spiral (ISBN 0-398-02005-1). C C Thomas.

Walker, A. M. A New Look at the Commonwealth. 1978. text ed. 23.00 (ISBN 0-08-021823-7); pap. text ed. 11.25 (ISBN 0-08-021824-5). Pergamon.

Walker, A. N., jt. auth. see Brailsford, D. F.

Walker, Alan. Schumann. (Great Composers Ser.). (Illus.). 1976. 9.95 (ISBN 0-571-10269-7, Pub. by Faber & Faber). Merrimack Bk Serv.

Walker, Alan, ed. Franz Liszt: The Man & His Music. 1978. pap. 11.95 o.p. (ISBN 0-214-20345-X, 8021, Dist. by Arco). Barrie & Jenkins.

--Robert Schumann: The Man & His Music. 1978. pap. 11.95 o.p. (ISBN 0-214-20340-9, 8027, Dist. by Arco). Barrie & Jenkins.

Walker, Albert H. History of the Sherman Law of the United States of America. LC 80-12873. xiii, 320p. 1980. Repr. of 1910 ed. lib. bdg. 25.00x (ISBN 0-313-22475-7, WAHS). Greenwood.

Walker, Alexander. Double Takes: Notes & Afterthoughts on the Movies, 1956-1976. 1978. 17.95 (ISBN 0-241-89395-X, Pub. by Hamish Hamilton England). David & Charles.

--Garbo. LC 80-12717. (Illus.). 192p. 1980. 19.95 (ISBN 0-02-622950-1). Macmillan.

Walker, Alice. Langston Hughes, American Poet. LC 73-9565. (Biography Ser). (Illus.). 40p. (gr. 2-5). 1974. PLB 7.89 (ISBN 0-690-00219-X, TYC-J). T Y Crowell.

--The Third Life of Grange Copeland. LC 77-3427. 1977. pap. 3.95 (ISBN 0-15-689960-4, Harv). HarBraceJ.

--You Can't Keep a Good Woman Down: Stories by Alice Walker. LC 80-8761. 180p. 1981. 10.95 (ISBN 0-15-199754-3). HarBraceJ.

Walker, Angus. Marx: His Theory & Its Context. (Illus.). 1978. pap. text ed. 9.95x (ISBN 0-582-44196-X). Longman.

Walker, Ardis. The Rough & the Righteous. (Illus.). 1971. 14.00 (ISBN 0-685-59752-0). Acoma Bks.

Walker Art Center & Minneapolis Institute of Arts. American Indian Art: Form & Tradition. Ryan, ed. (Illus.). 1973. pap. 8.00 o.p. (ISBN 0-525-47347-5). Dutton.

Walker, Arthur L., Jr. Educating for Christian Missions. (Orig.). 1981. pap. 5.95 (ISBN 0-8054-6934-6). Broadman.

Walker, Ashley, jt. auth. see Walker, Taiko.

Walker, B. S., et al. Interactive Computer Graphics. LC 74-24985. (Computer Systems Engineering Ser.). 1976. 19.50x (ISBN 0-8448-0650-1). Crane-Russak Co.

Walker, Barbara. Barbara Walker's Learn to Knit Afghan Book. LC 73-10906. (Encore Edition). (Illus.). 1976. pap. 1.95 (ISBN 0-684-16929-0, SL666, ScribT). Scribner.

Walker, Barbara, ed. Ghost Stories. new ed. 128p. (gr. 7-12). 1975. PLB 6.95 o.p. (ISBN 0-07-067812-X, GB). McGraw.

Walker, Barbara K. Dancing Palm Tree & Other Nigerian Folktales. LC 68-21085. (Illus.). (gr. 3-7). 1968. 5.95 o.s.i. (ISBN 0-8193-0329-1, Four Winds); PLB 5.41 o.s.i. (ISBN 0-8193-0330-5). Schol Bk Serv.

--How the Hare Told the Truth About His Horse. LC 73-174604. (Illus.). 40p. (gr. k-3). 1972. 5.95 o.s.i. (ISBN 0-8193-0561-8, Four Winds); PLB 5.41 o.s.i. (ISBN 0-8193-0562-6). Schol Bk Serv.

--Round Sultan & the Straight Answer. LC 71-117559. (Illus.). (gr. k-3). 1970. 5.95 o.s.i. (ISBN 0-8193-0400-X, Four Winds). Schol Bk Serv.

Walker, Barbara K. & Uysal, Ahmet E. New Patches for Old: A Turkish Folktale Retold. Uysal, Ahmet E., tr. from Turk. LC 73-12951. (Illus.). 48p. (ps-3). 1974. 5.95 o.s.i. (ISBN 0-8193-0713-0, Four Winds); PLB 5.41 o.s.i. (ISBN 0-8193-0714-9). Schol Bk Serv.

Walker, Barbara K., compiled by. Laughing Together: Giggles & Grins from Around the World. LC 77-7789. (Illus., Paperback edition available only through the United Nations). (gr. 1 up). 1977. 8.95 (ISBN 0-590-07486-5, Four Winds). Schol Bk Serv.

Walker, Barbara K. & Walker, Warren S., eds. Erie Canal. (Selected Source Materials for College Research Papers). 1963. pap. text ed. 2.95x o.p. (ISBN 0-669-21600-3). Heath.

Walker, Barbara K., et al. To Set Them Free. 1981. 14.95; pap. 9.95. Tompson & Rutter.

--To Set Them Free: The Early Years of Mustafa Kemal Ataturk. LC 80-21127. (Illus.). 96p. 1981. 14.95 (ISBN 0-936988-00-2); pap. 9.95 (ISBN 0-936988-02-9). Tompson & Rutter.

Walker, Benjamin. Sex & the Supernatural. 128p. 1973. pap. 1.25 o.p. (ISBN 0-06-087043-5, HW). Har-Row.

Walker, Beth. Checklists: A Personal Organizer. 192p. (Orig.). Date not set. leatherette spiral binding 9.95 (ISBN 0-8027-7164-5). Walker & Co.

Walker, Braz. All About Cichlids. (Illus., Orig.). 1978. pap. 4.95 (ISBN 0-87666-472-9, PS-751). TFH Pubns.

--Angelfish. (Illus.). 1974. 4.95 (ISBN 0-87666-755-8, PS-711). TFH Pubns.

--Oddball Fishes & Other Strange Creatures of the Deep. LC 75-14510. (Illus.). 192p. 1975. 7.95 o.p. (ISBN 0-8069-3726-2); lib. bdg. 7.49 o.p. (ISBN 0-8069-3727-0). Sterling.

--Tropical Fish Identifier. LC 76-126851. (Illus.). 256p. 1981. pap. 6.95 (ISBN 0-8069-8968-8). Sterling.

Walker, Bruce, jt. auth. see Fenton, Alexander.

Walker, Bruce J. & Haynes, Joel B. Marketing Channels & Institutions: Selected Reading. 2nd ed. LC 76-50175. (Marketing Ser.). 1978. pap. text ed. 10.50 (ISBN 0-88244-149-3). Grid Pub.

Walker, Bryce. The Armada. Time-Life Bks. Eds., ed. (The Seafarers Ser.). (Illus.). 176p. 1981. 14.95 (ISBN 0-8094-2697-8). Time-Life.

--The Great Divide. LC 73-81327. (American Wilderness Ser). (Illus.). (gr. 6 up). 1973. lib. bdg. 11.97 (ISBN 0-8094-1185-7, Pub. by Time-Life). Silver.

--The Great Divide. (The American Wilderness Ser.). 1973. 12.95 (ISBN 0-8094-1184-9). Time-Life.

Walker, Byrd W, Jr. Federal Personnel Procedures Reference Manual. rev. ed. 1246p. 1976. pap. text ed. 20.00 (ISBN 0-87771-009-0). Grad School.

Walker, C. Eugene. Learn to Relax: 13 Ways to Reduce Tension. 1975. 12.95 (ISBN 0-13-527564-4, Spec); pap. 3.45 (ISBN 0-13-527556-3, Spec). P-H.

Walker, C. Eugene, ed. Clinical Practice of Psychology: A Practical Guide for Mental Health Professionals. (Pergamon General Psychology Ser.). Date not set. 27.51 (ISBN 0-08-025591-4); pap. 15.91 (ISBN 0-08-025590-6). Pergamon.

Walker, C. Eugene, et al. Clinical Procedures for Behavior Therapy. (Illus.). 464p. 1981. text ed. 18.95 (ISBN 0-13-137794-9). P-H.

Walker, Carol. Concise Course in Embroidery. (Illus.). 1979. pap. write for info. (ISBN 0-671-18391-5). Sovereign Bks.

Walker, Carroll. Norfolk: A Pictorial History. 2nd ed. Friedman, Donna R., ed. (Illus.). 208p. 1981. pap. write for info. (ISBN 0-89865-129-8). Donning Co.

Walker, Catherine B. Bible Workbook: New Testament. 1951. pap. 2.95 (ISBN 0-8024-0752-8). Moody.

--Bible Workbook: Old Testament. 1943. pap. 2.95 (ISBN 0-8024-0751-X). Moody.

Walker, Charles. Authentick Memoirs of...Sally Salisbury, Vol. 41. Shugrve, Michael, ed. Incl. The Agreeable Caledonian. Haywood, Eliza. LC 79-170557. (Foundations of the Novel Ser.). 1973. Repr. of 1723 ed. lib. bdg. 50.00 (ISBN 0-8240-0553-8). Garland Pub.

Walker, Charles R., ed. see Putnam, H. Phelps.

Walker, Christopher, jt. auth. see Lang, David M.

Walker, Christopher J. Armenia: The Survival of a Nation. LC 80-10461. 1980. 30.00 (ISBN 0-312-04944-7). St Martin.

Walker, Colin. Environmental Pollution by Chemicals. 1980. pap. text ed. 7.75x (ISBN 0-09-123891-9, Hutchinson U Lib). Humanities.

Walker, D., jt. auth. see McRae, R.

Walker, D. & West, R. G., eds. Studies in the Vegetation History of the British Isles. 79.00 (ISBN 0-521-07565-3). Cambridge U Pr.

Walker, Dale L. Jack London & Conan Doyle: A Literary Kinship. LC 80-67698. (Sherlock Holmes Monograph). (Illus.). 70p. 1981. 8.95x (ISBN 0-934468-03-6). Gaslight.

--Only the Clounds Remain: Ted Parsons of the Lafayette Escadrille. LC 80-68357. (Illus.). 72p. 1980. pap. 6.95 (ISBN 0-937748-00-5). Alandale Pr.

Walker, David. The Norman Conquerors. (A New History of Wales). (Illus.). 1977. text ed. 10.50x (ISBN 0-7154-0302-8). Humanities.

Walker, David, jt. auth. see Tunstall, Jeremy.

Walker, David, tr. & illus. see Perrault, Charles.

Walker, David F. Canadian Industrial Space-Economy. 261p. 1980. 27.95 (ISBN 0-470-27061-6). Halsted Pr.

Walker, David M. Principles of Scottish Private Law, 2 vols. 2nd ed. 2000p. 1975. 78.00x o.p. (ISBN 0-19-825336-2). Oxford U Pr.

Walker, Decker F., jt. ed. see Reid, William A.

Walker, Deward E., Jr. Myths of Idaho Indians. rev. ed. LC 79-57484. (Gem Bk. & Anthropological Monograph). (Illus.). 188p. (Orig.). 1980. pap. 7.50 (ISBN 0-89301-066-9). U Pr of Idaho.

Walker, Diana. Making Dolls' Clothes. LC 79-56449. (Illus.). 72p. 1980. 14.95 (ISBN 0-7134-3319-1, Pub. by Batsford England). David & Charles.

Walker, Donald B., jt. auth. see Kratcoski, Peter C.

Walker, Edmund M. The Odonata of Canada & Alaska, Vol. 1. LC 54-4344. (Illus.). 1953. 35.00x o.p. (ISBN 0-8020-7074-4). U of Toronto Pr.

--The Odonata of Canada & Alaska, Vol.2. LC 54-4344. 1958. 35.00x o.p. (ISBN 0-8020-7076-0). U of Toronto Pr.

Walker, Edward, ed. see Chomsky, Noam, et al.

Walker, Edward L. Psychological Complexity & Preference: A Hedgehog Theory of Behavior. LC 79-20291. 1980. text ed. 19.95 (ISBN 0-8185-0379-3). Brooks-Cole.

Walker, Edward L., jt. auth. see Weintraub, Daniel J.

Walker, Ernest. A History of Music in England. 3rd ed. Westrup, J. A., ed. LC 78-4596. (Music Reprint 1978 Ser.). 1978. Repr. of 1952 ed. lib. bdg. 35.00 (ISBN 0-306-77570-0). Da Capo.

Walker, Ernest P. & Animal Welfare Institute, eds. First Aid & Care of Small Animals. rev. ed. (Illus.). 54p. 1980. pap. text ed. 2.00 (ISBN 0-938414-04-6). Animal Welfare.

Walker, Ernest W. & Petty, J. William, II. Financial Management of the Small Firm. LC 78-873. (Illus.). 1978. ref. 18.95 (ISBN 0-13-316091-2). P-H.

Walker, Forrest A. The Civil Works Administration. Freidel, Frank, ed. LC 78-62516. (Modern American History Ser.: Vol. 18). 1979. lib. bdg. 23.00 (ISBN 0-8240-3641-7). Garland Pub.

Walker, Francis A. Land & Its Rent. LC 79-1595. 1981. Repr. of 1883 ed. 18.50 (ISBN 0-88355-900-5). Hyperion Conn.

Walker, Frank. The Lurcher. 1978. 8.95 o.s.i. (ISBN 0-440-05083-9). Delacorte.

Walker, Freda, jt. auth. see Reed, Brenda.

Walker, G. Soviet Book Publishing Policy. LC 77-12543. (Soviet & East European Studies). (Illus.). 1978. 23.95 (ISBN 0-521-21843-8). Cambridge U Pr.

Walker, G. S., ed. see National Computing Centre.

Walker, Gail. Spirits in His Parlor. LC 79-87733. (Destiny Ser.). 1980. pap. 4.95 (ISBN 0-8163-0387-8, 19499-3). Pacific Pr Pub Assn.

Walker, Geoffrey. Symposium on Advanced Medicine, 9th. 452p. 1973. 12.00 o.p. (ISBN 0-685-56381-2, Pub. by Williams & Wilkins). Krieger.

Walker, Geoffrey J. Spanish Politics & Imperial Trade, 1700-1789. LC 78-63107. 320p. 1979. 17.50x (ISBN 0-253-12150-7). Ind U Pr.

Walker, Granville T. Go Placidly Amid the Noise & Haste: Meditations on the "Desiderata". 2nd ed. 112p. 1976. pap. 1.25 (ISBN 0-8272-1217-8). Bethany Pr.

Walker, Greta. Living on Your Own. 1977. s&l 6.90 o.p. (ISBN 0-531-00126-1). Watts.

--Modeling Careers. LC 76-9811. (Career Concise Guides Ser.). (Illus.). 72p. (gr. 6 up). 1976. PLB 6.45 (ISBN 0-531-01206-9). Watts.

Walker, H. K., et al. Clinical Methods: The History, Physical, & Laboratory Examinations, 2 vols. LC 76-44215. 1977. 39.95 o.p. (ISBN 0-409-95006-8). Butterworths.

Walker, H. Thomas & Montgomery, Paula K. Teaching Media Skills: An Instructional Program for Elementary & Middle School Students. LC 76-30605. 1977. lib. bdg. 17.50x (ISBN 0-87287-135-5). Libs Unl.

Walker, Hallam. Moliere. (World Authors Ser.: France: No. 176). lib. bdg. 12.50 (ISBN 0-8057-2620-9). Twayne.

Walker, Henry. Illustrated Baseball Dictionary for Young People. (Illus.). 1978. pap. 2.50 (ISBN 0-13-450924-2). P-H.

--Illustrated Hockey Dictionary for Young People. (Treehouse Illustrated Sports Dictionaries Ser.). (Illus.). 1978. pap. 2.50 (ISBN 0-13-451138-7). P-H.

Walker, Henry P. & Bufkin, Don. Historical Atlas of Arizona. LC 78-58086. (Illus.). 1979. 14.95 (ISBN 0-8061-1489-4); pap. 7.95 (ISBN 0-8061-1490-8). U of Okla Pr.

Walker, Hill M. The Acting-Out Child: Coping with Classroom Disruption. 1979. pap. text ed. 10.95 (ISBN 0-205-06576-7); pap. text ed. 9.95 (ISBN 0-205-06569-4). Allyn.

Walker, Howard E. Teaching Yourself to Teach. 1974. kit 13.95 (ISBN 0-687-41137-8); wkbk. 0.85 (ISBN 0-687-41138-6). Abingdon.

Walker, Hugh. The Age of Tennyson. 309p. 1980. Repr. of 1932 ed. lib. bdg. 25.00 (ISBN 0-89760-914-X). Telegraph Bks.

Walker, Irma. The Lucifer Wine. 1979. pap. 1.95 o.p. (ISBN 0-345-27324-9). Ballantine.

Walker, J. Art Since Pop. LC 77-76780. (Modern Movements in Art Ser.). 1978. pap. 1.95 (ISBN 0-8120-0876-6). Barron.

--British Economic & Social History. 2nd ed. 448p. (Orig.). 1979. pap. text ed. 18.95x (ISBN 0-7121-0266-3, Pub. by Macdonald & Evans England). Intl Ideas.

Walker, J. A. Dynamical Systems & Evolution Equations - Theory & Applications. (Mathematical Concepts & Methods in Science & Engineering Ser.: Vol. 20). 240p. 1980. 29.50 (ISBN 0-306-40362-5, Plenum Pr). Plenum Pub.

Walker, J. H. Large Synchronous Machines: Design, Manufacture & Operation. (Monographs in Electrical & Electronic Engineering). (Illus.). 250p. 1981. 59.00 (ISBN 0-19-859364-3). Oxford U Pr.

Walker, J. M., jt. auth. see Perry, A. H.

Walker, J. N. First Steps in Chess. (Chess Bks). (Illus.). 1979. 9.95 (ISBN 0-19-217580-7); pap. 6.95 (ISBN 0-19-217580-7). Oxford U Pr.

--Test Your Chess: Piece Power. 160p. 1980. pap. cancelled o.p. (ISBN 0-19-217597-1). Oxford U Pr.

Walker, J. Samuel, jt. ed. see Haines, Gerald K.

Walker, James A., jt. auth. see Magoun, Francis P., Jr.

Walker, James E. Behavior Modification: A Practical Approach for Educators. 2nd ed. LC 79-21107. 1980. pap. text ed. 12.95 (ISBN 0-8016-5338-X). Mosby.

Walker, James P., jt. auth. see McQuitty, Robert A.

Walker, James R. Lakota Belief & Ritual. DeMallie, Raymond J. & Jahner, Elaine A., eds. LC 79-19816. (Illus.). xxx, 329p. 1980. 21.50 (ISBN 0-8032-2551-2). U of Nebr Pr.

Walker, James W., jt. auth. see Price, Karl F.

Walker, Jay. Physics Investigations. (gr. 11-12). 1973. pap. text ed. 6.42 (ISBN 0-87720-180-3). AMSCO Sch.

Walker, Jeanne M. Nailing up the Home Sweet Home. (CSU Poetry Ser.: No. 9). (Orig.). 1980. pap. 4.00 (ISBN 0-914946-24-2). Cleveland St Univ Poetry Ctr.

Walker, Jearl. The Flying Circus of Physics. LC 75-5670. 224p. 1975. 11.95 (ISBN 0-471-91808-3). Wiley.

Walker, Jearl, intro. by. Light & Its Uses: Making & Using Lasers, Holograms, Interferometers, & Spectroscopes-C. L. Stong's: "the Amateur Scientist" Readings from Scientific American. LC 79-27551. (Illus.). 1980. text ed. 17.95x (ISBN 0-7167-1184-2); pap. text ed. 8.95x (ISBN 0-7167-1185-0). W H Freeman.

--The Physics of Everyday Phenomena: Readings from Scientific American. LC 79-9287. (Illus.). 1979. text ed. 10.00x o.p. (ISBN 0-7167-1125-7); pap. text ed. 5.95x o.p. (ISBN 0-7167-1126-5). W H Freeman.

Walker, Jim. Key System Album. LC 78-55027. (Special Ser.: No. 68). (Illus.). 1978. 17.95 (ISBN 0-916374-31-9). Interurban.

--The Yellow Cars of Los Angeles. LC 77-71538. (Special Ser.: No. 43). 1977. 27.50 (ISBN 0-916374-25-4). Interurban.

Walker, Jim, jt. auth. see Roy, Willy.

Walker, Jim, jt. auth. see Swett, Ira.

Walker, Jim, ed. Lines of Pacific Electric, Northern & Eastern Districts. (Illus.). 112p. 1976. pap. 7.00 (ISBN 0-916374-21-1). Interurban.

Walker, Jim, ed. see Bradley, Bill.

Walker, Jim, ed. see McCaleb, Charles S.

Walker, Jim, ed. see Perles, Anthony.

Walker, Jim, ed. see Smallwood, Charles A.

Walker, Jim, ed. see Swett, Ira.

Walker, Jim, ed. see Swett, Ira L.

Walker, Joan & Walker, Morton. Help Your Mate Lose Weight. 1978. pap. 1.50 o.s.i. (ISBN 0-515-03872-5). Jove Pubns.

Walker, John. The Air Gun. (Illus.). 144p. 1981. 19.95 (ISBN 0-8117-0046-1). Stackpole.

--Constable. (Library of Great Painters). (Illus.). 1979. 35.00 (ISBN 0-8109-0752-6). Abrams.

--The Scottish Sketches of R. B. Cunningham Graham. (Illus.). 232p. 1981. 13.50x (ISBN 0-7073-0288-9, Pub. by Scottish Academic Pr Scotland). Columbia U Pr.

--Turner. LC 76-4090. (Library of Great Painters). (Illus.). 1976. 35.00 (ISBN 0-8109-0513-2). Abrams.

Walker, John & Walker, Katharine. The Walker Washington Guide. rev. ed. LC 75-4256. Orig. Title: The Washington Guidebook. (Illus.). 288p. (Orig.). 1981. pap. 4.95 (ISBN 0-915472-02-3). Guide Pr.

Walker, John, jt. auth. see Mee, Charles L., Jr.

Walker, John, ed. The Armand Hammer Collection: Five Centuries of Masterpieces. (Illus.). 296p. 1980. 85.00 o.p. (ISBN 0-686-62685-0, 1069-1). Abrams.

Walker, John R. Exploring Drafting. LC 78-15883. (Illus.). 320p. 1978. text ed. 10.96 (ISBN 0-87006-262-X); wkbk. 4.40 (ISBN 0-87006-295-6); metric wkbk 4.40 (ISBN 0-87006-242-5). Goodheart.

--Exploring Metalworking. LC 75-31808. 1976. text ed. 9.98 (ISBN 0-87006-199-2); wkbk. 3.20 (ISBN 0-87006-169-0). Goodheart.

--Exploring Metric Drafting. LC 79-24019. (Illus.). 320p. 1980. text ed. 10.96 (ISBN 0-87006-289-1). Good Heart.

--Exploring Power Technology. LC 76-2567. (Illus.). 1976. text ed. 9.96 (ISBN 0-87006-207-7); wkbk. 3.20 (ISBN 0-87006-216-6). Goodheart.
--Modern Metalworking. LC 76-22559. 1976. text ed. 13.92 (ISBN 0-87006-212-3); wkbk. 3.20 (ISBN 0-87006-223-9). Goodheart.
Walker, Joseph E., ed. Pleasure & Business in Western Pennsylvania: The Journal of Joshua Gilpin, 1809. (Illus.). 156p. 1975. 7.50 (ISBN 0-911124-78-0). Pa Hist & Mus.
Walker, Judith. Education in Two Languages: A Guide for Bilingual Teachers. LC 78-65847. 1979. pap. text ed. 7.00 (ISBN 0-8191-0674-7). U Pr of Amer.
Walker, Katharine, jt. auth. see Walker, John.
Walker, L., jt. auth. see Thibaut, J.
Walker, Leila J. & Taub, Howard. Fundamental Skills in Serology: Agglutination Tests, Syphilis Serology, Flourescent Staining. (Illus.). 486p. 1976. pap. 21.75 (ISBN 0-398-03510-5). C C Thomas.
Walker, Les. Housebuilding for Children. LC 76-47220. (Illus.). 176p. 1977. 10.95 (ISBN 0-87951-059-5). Overlook Pr.
Walker, Les & Milstein, Jeffrey. Designing Houses: An Illustrated Guide. LC 75-7684. (Illus.). 1979. pap. 5.95 (ISBN 0-87951-096-X). Overlook Pr.
Walker, Leslie J., tr. see Machiavelli, Niccolo.
Walker, Lorrin, jt. auth. see IFSTA Committee.
Walker, Louise J. Beneath the Singing Pines. (Illus.). (gr. 6-10). 1967. 7.95 (ISBN 0-910726-80-9). Hillsdale Educ.
Walker, Luci. Ribbons in Her Hair. Date not set. pap. 1.75 (ISBN 0-345-29278-2). Ballantine.
Walker, Lucille. What to Do When You Pray. 1978. 3.95 o.p. (ISBN 0-88270-279-3). Logos.
Walker, Lucy. Come Home, Dear. 192p. 1975. pap. 1.25 (ISBN 0-345-29556-0). Ballantine.
--Follow Your Star. 1976. pap. 1.75 (ISBN 0-345-29279-0). Ballantine.
--Home at Sundown. 1976. pap. 1.25 o.p. (ISBN 0-345-25235-7). Ballantine.
--Joyday for Jodi. 1976. pap. 1.25 o.p. (ISBN 0-345-25478-3). Ballantine.
--Kingdom of the Heart. 1971. pap. 1.75 (ISBN 0-345-29276-6). Ballantine.
--Man Called Masters. 1976. pap. 1.25 o.p. (ISBN 0-345-25232-2). Ballantine.
--Man from Out Back, No. 8. 192p. (Orig.). Date not set. pap. 1.75 (ISBN 0-345-29500-5). Ballantine.
--The Man from Outback. 1974. pap. 1.75 (ISBN 0-345-29500-5). Ballantine.
--The Moonshiner. 1976. pap. 1.25 o.p. (ISBN 0-345-25236-5). Ballantine.
--The Other Girl, No. 7. 192p. 1981. pap. 1.75 (ISBN 0-345-29422-X). Ballantine.
--Pool of Dreams. 1973. pap. 0.95 o.p. (ISBN 0-345-26518-1). Ballantine.
--So Much Love. 1977. pap. 1.50 o.p. (ISBN 0-345-25858-4). Ballantine.
--Wife to Order. Date not set. pap. 1.75 (ISBN 0-345-29275-8). Ballantine.
Walker, Luisa. Metodos De Ensenanza. (Spanish Bks.). 1979. 1.50 (ISBN 0-8297-0583-X). Life Pubs Intl.
Walker, Luisa, jt. tr. see Blattner, Elsie.
Walker, M., jt. auth. see Mellgren, L.
Walker, M., jt. auth. see Weinstein, S.
Walker, Mack. Johann Jakob Moser & the Holy Roman Empire of the German Nation. LC 79-27720. 352p. 1980. 26.00x (ISBN 0-8078-1441-5). U of NC Pr.
Walker, Mack, ed. Metternich's Europe. LC 68-27383. (Documentary History of Western Civilization Ser). 15.00x o.s.i. (ISBN 0-8027-2014-5). Walker & Co.
--Plombieres: Secret Diplomacy & the Rebirth of Italy. (Problems in European History Series). (Orig.). 1968. pap. 4.95x (ISBN 0-19-501096-5). Oxford U Pr.
Walker, Malcolm T. Politics & the Power Structure: A Rural Community in the Dominican Republic. LC 72-89624. 1972. text ed. 11.50x (ISBN 0-8077-2302-9). Tchrs Coll.
Walker, Marcia J. & Brodsky, Stanley L. Sexual Assault: The Victim & the Rapist. LC 75-24560. (Illus.). 208p. 1976. 18.95 (ISBN 0-669-00196-1). Lexington Bks.
Walker, Marcia J. & Brodsky, Stanley L., eds. Sexual Assault. 1978. pap. text ed. 6.95x o.p. (ISBN 0-669-01645-4). Heath.
Walker, Mark. Cassis. 1979. 8.95 o.s.i. (ISBN 0-8027-5405-8). Walker & Co.
Walker, Mary, jt. auth. see Otis, George.
Walker, Mary A. Maggot. LC 80-12238. 156p. (gr. 5-9). 1980. 8.95 (ISBN 0-689-30789-6). Atheneum.
Walker, Matthew. Down Below: Aboard the World's Classic Yachts. LC 80-12327. (Illus.). 136p. 1980. 16.95 (ISBN 0-87701-137-0). Chronicle Bks.
Walker, Michael. The Cocktail Book. (Orig.). 1980. pap. 4.95 (ISBN 0-89586-069-4). H P Bks.
Walker, Michael J. Wild Animals That Help People. (gr. 4-7). 1977. 7.95 o.p. (ISBN 0-679-20396-6). McKay.
Walker, Mitch. Visionary Love: A Spirit Book of Gay Mythology & Transmutational Faerie. LC 80-51514. (Illus.). 120p. (Orig.). 1980. pap. 4.95 (ISBN 0-9604450-0-5). Treeroots.
Walker, Mitchell. Men Loving Men: A Gay Sex Guide & Consciousness Book. 1977. pap. 8.95 o.p. (ISBN 0-917342-52-6, Pub. by Gay Sunshine). Bookpeople.
Walker, Mort. Beetle Bailey: On Parade. (Beetle Bailey Ser.: No. 6). 128p. (gr. 5 up). pap. 1.50 (ISBN 0-448-12258-8, Tempo). G&D.
--Beetle Bailey We're All in the Same Boat, No.7. 128p. (gr. 8-12). 1981. pap. 1.50 (ISBN 0-448-12259-6, Tempo). G&D.
--I'll Throw the Book at You. Wallace, Wendy, ed. (Beetle Bailey Ser.: No. 8). 128p. (gr. 2 up). pap. 1.50 (ISBN 0-448-12635-4, Tempo). G&D.
Walker, Mort & Brown, Dik. Hi & Lois: Beware Children at Play. (Hi and Lois Ser.). 128p. (gr. 5 up). pap. 1.50 (ISBN 0-448-14051-9). G&D.
Walker, Mort, jt. auth. see Fogel, Marvin.
Walker, Morton. How Not to Have a Heart Attack. 1980. 9.95 o.p. (ISBN 0-531-09927-X); pap. 7.95 (ISBN 0-531-09919-9). Watts.
--Rebounding Aerobics. Angelo, Frank, ed. LC 80-83600. (Illus.). 240p. (Orig.). 1980. pap. 6.95 (ISBN 0-938302-19-1). NIRH.
--Sport Diving: The Instructional Guide to Skin & Scuba. LC 76-6289. 1977. 14.95 o.p. (ISBN 0-8092-8176-7); pap. 6.95 (ISBN 0-8092-7855-3). Contemp Bks.
--Total Health. 276p. Date not set. pap. 3.95 (ISBN 0-346-12444-1). Cornerstone. Postponed.
Walker, Morton, jt. auth. see Hoffer, Abram.
Walker, Morton, jt. auth. see Walker, Joan.
Walker, N. A., jt. auth. see Hope, A. B.
Walker, N. W. Discover Your Fountain of Health. 60p. 1979. pap. 0.95 (ISBN 0-89019-070-4). O'Sullivan Woodside.
--Raw Vegetable Juices. 1971. pap. 1.75 (ISBN 0-515-05330-9, V2570). Jove Pubns.
Walker, Nicolette M. Introduction to Dinghy Sailing. (Illus.). 104p. 1981. 14.95 (ISBN 0-7153-8022-2). David & Charles.
Walker, Nigel. Punishment, Danger & Stigma: The Morality of Criminal Justice. 206p. 1980. 22.50x (ISBN 0-389-20129-4). B&N.
Walker, Nora S., jt. auth. see Ambrose, Mike.
Walker, P. L. An Introduction to Complex Analysis. LC 74-24686. 141p. 1974. 18.95 (ISBN 0-470-91807-1). Halsted Pr.
Walker, Pamela. Twyla. pap. 0.95 o.p. (ISBN 0-425-03076-8). Berkley Pub.
Walker, Patrick G. The Cabinet. 1972. text ed. 4.95 o.p. (ISBN 0-435-83915-2). Heinemann Ed.
Walker, Percy. Lancelot. 1978. pap. 2.95 (ISBN 0-380-01861-6, 51920, Bard). Avon.
Walker, Peter. Direct Current Motors: Characteristics & Applications. (Illus.). 1978. 15.95 (ISBN 0-8306-8931-1, 931). TAB Bks.
Walker, Peter S. Human Joints & Their Artificial Replacements. (Illus.). 528p. 1978. 64.75 (ISBN 0-398-03615-2). C C Thomas.
Walker, R. B. Yesterday's News. 256p. 1980. 30.00x (ISBN -0424-00079-2, Pub. by Sydney U Pr Australia). Intl Schol Bk Serv.
Walker, R. J. Old Westminster Bridge. LC 79-52379. (Illus.). 1980. 38.00 (ISBN 0-7153-7837-6). David & Charles.
Walker, R. O., jt. auth. see Kimmel, K.
Walker, Ralph C. Kant. (The Arguments of the Philosophers Ser.). 1978. 22.00x (ISBN 0-7100-8994-5). Routledge & Kegan.
Walker, Richard. Dick Walker's Angling: Theory & Practice, Past, Present & to Come. LC 79-51097. (Illus.). 1979. 19.95 (ISBN 0-7153-7814-7). David & Charles.
--Still Water Angling. new ed. (Illus.). 256p. 1975. 19.95 (ISBN 0-7153-7074-X). David & Charles.
Walker, Richard H; see Kellenberger, Hunter.
Walker, Richard L. Ancient Japan: And Its Influence in the Modern World. LC 74-28238. (First Bks). (Illus.). 96p. (gr. 5 up). 1975. PLB 4.90 o.p. (ISBN 0-531-00827-4). Watts.
--First Book of Ancient China. LC 72-83645. (First Bks). (Illus.). (gr. 7 up). 1969. PLB 4.90 o.p. (ISBN 0-531-00699-9). Watts.
Walker, Robert H., ed. American Studies: Topics & Sources. LC 75-35675. (Illus.). 320p. (Orig.). 1976. lib. bdg. 22.50 (ISBN 0-8371-8559-9, WBE/). Greenwood.
Walker, Robert J., jt. auth. see Leake, Lucy D.
Walker, Robert L., jt. auth. see Mathews, Jon.
Walker, Robert N. Psychology of the Youthful Offender. 2nd ed. 164p. 1973. 14.75 (ISBN 0-398-02859-1). C C Thomas.
Walker, Ronald & Institute for Responsive Action Staff. Education for All People: A Grassroots Primer. 155p. (Orig.). 1979. pap. text ed. 6.00 (ISBN 0-917754-09-3). Inst Responsive.
Walker, Ronald G. Infernal Paradise: Mexico & the Modern English Novel. LC 75-46046. 1978. 20.00x (ISBN 0-520-03197-0). U of Cal Pr.
Walker, S., jt. ed. see Straughan, B. P.
Walker, Samuel. A Critical History of Police Reform. LC 76-53866. 1977. 21.95x (ISBN 0-669-01292-0). Lexington Bks.
Walker, Sheila S. Ceremonial Spirit Possession in Africa & Afro-America: Forms, Meanings & Functional Significance for Individuals & Social Groups. 179p. 1972. text ed. 31.00x (ISBN 90-040-3584-2). Humanities.
Walker, Sloan. The Crazy Car Book. LC 72-95805. (Illus.). 48p. (gr. 1 up). 1973. 4.95 o.s.i. (ISBN 0-8027-6147-X); PLB 8.85 (ISBN 0-8027-6148-8). Walker & Co.
Walker, Stella A., jt. auth. see Summerhays, R. S.
Walker, Sydney, 3rd. Psychiatric Signs & Symptoms Due to Medical Problems. 1967. 13.25 o.p. (ISBN 0-398-02008-6). C C Thomas.
Walker, T. A Guide for Using the Foreign Exchange & Market. LC 80-21975. 280p. 1981. 20.95 (ISBN 0-471-06254-5, Ronald Pr). Wiley.
Walker, Taiko & Walker, Ashley. The Man in the Black Square. Bd. with Hotels Aren't for Sleeping. 1980. 7.95 (ISBN 0-533-04549-5). Vantage.
Walker, Ted. The Solitaries. LC 67-20026. 3.95 o.p. (ISBN 0-8076-0415-1). Braziller.
Walker, Ted, jt. auth. see Aldridge, Alan.
Walker, Terry. Introduction to Computer Science: An Interdisciplinary Approach. 840p. 1972. text ed. 18.95x o.p. (ISBN 0-205-03451-9, 2034514). Allyn.
Walker, Terry M. Fundamentals of Computer Science. 425p. 1975. text ed. 23.95x (ISBN 0-205-04715-7). Allyn.
--Fundamentals of FORTRAN Programming: With Watfor-Watfiv. 1975. 11.95x o.p. (ISBN 0-205-04885-4, 204885X). Allyn.
--Fundamentals of PL-1 Programming: A Structured Approach with PL-C. 1977. pap. text ed. 13.95 (ISBN 0-205-04892-7). Allyn.
--Introduction to Computer Science. Incl. BASIC Language Programming. o.p. (ISBN 0-205-03590-6, 2035901); COBOL Language Programming. o.p. (ISBN 0-205-03998-7, 2039982); FORTRAN Language Programming (ISBN 0-205-03578-7, 2035782). 6.95x ea. o.p. Allyn.
Walker, Thomas G., jt. auth. see Ippolito, Dennis S.
Walker, Thomas W. Nicaragua: A Profile. (Nations of Contemporary Latin America). 128p. 1981. lib. bdg. 16.50x (ISBN 0-89158-947-3). Westview.
Walker, Timothy. Introduction to American Law. LC 79-172176. (American Constitutional & Legal History Ser). 672p. 1972. Repr. of 1837 ed. lib. bdg. 59.50 (ISBN 0-306-70224-X). Da Capo.
Walker, Townsend. A Guide for Using the Foreign Exchange Market. 360p. 1981. 20.95 (ISBN 0-471-06254-5). Ronald Pr.
Walker, W. C. Print Quality Factor Classification. new ed. Walker, W. O., ed. (TAPPI PRESS Reports). (Illus.). 1979. pap. 14.95 (ISBN 0-89852-379-6, 01-01-R079). TAPPI.
Walker, W. C., et al. Print Quality Evaluation: A Bibliography. Ray, C. T. & Fetsko, J. M., eds. (TAPPI PRESS Reports). 1973. pap. 37.95 (ISBN 0-89852-350-8, 01-01-R050). TAPPI.
Walker, W. O., ed. see Walker, W. C.
Walker, Warren F., Jr. Dissection of the Fetal Pig. 2nd ed. (Illus.). 1974. pap. text ed. 3.25x o.p. (ISBN 0-7167-0587-7); tchr's guide avail. o.p.; individual exercises 0.50 ea. o.p. W H Freeman.
Walker, Warren S. Twentieth-Century Short Story Explication: Supplement 1 to Third Edition. (Short Story Explication Ser.). v, 257p. 1980. 27.50 (ISBN 0-208-01813-1, SSP). Shoe String.
Walker, Warren S., jt. ed. see Walker, Barbara K.
Walker, Willard. The Proto Algonquians. (Pdr Publications on North American Linguistic Prehistory Ser.: No.1). 18p. 1975. pap. text ed. 1.00x o.p. (ISBN 90-316-0058-X). Humanities.
Walker, Willard C., jt. auth. see Johnson, Kenneth W.
Walker, William. Peter Buchan, & Other Papers on Scottish & English Ballads & Songs. 1980. Repr. of 1915 ed. lib. bdg. 15.00 (ISBN 0-8414-2838-7). Folcroft.
Walker, William F. & Johnston, Ivan A. Metabolic Basis of Surgical Care. (Illus.). 1971. 17.95x (ISBN 0-433-34580-2). Intl Ideas.
Walker, William M. Juteopolis. 570p. 1979. 20.00x o.p. (ISBN 0-7073-0252-8, Pub. by Scottish Academic Pr Scotland). Columbia U Pr.
Walker, William O., III. Drug Control in the Americas. (Illus.). 328p. 1981. price not set (ISBN 0-8263-0579-2). U of NM Pr.
Walker, William S. William Sidney Walker (Seventeen Ninety-Five to Eighteen Forty-Six) Reiman, Donald H., ed. LC 75-31269. (Romantic Context Ser.: Poetry 1789-1830). 1977. lib. bdg. 47.00 (ISBN 0-8240-2215-7). Garland Pub.
Walker, Williston. History of the Christian Church. Repr. 17.95 (ISBN 0-686-12356-5). Church History.
Walker, Williston, ed. Creeds & Platforms of Congregationalism. LC 60-14698. 1960. 10.95 (ISBN 0-8298-0034-4). Pilgrim NY.
Walker, Winifred. Valley of Vision: Discovering God Around the World. 64p. (Orig.). 1981. pap. write for info. Upper Room.
Walkerly. The Motor Industry As a Career. 10.00x (ISBN 0-392-05929-0, SpS). Soccer.
Walker's Manual Inc. Walker's Manual of Western Corporations: 72nd Annual Edition, 2 vols. LC 10-19951. 1650p. 1981. Set. 182.00 (ISBN 0-916234-05-3). Walkers Manual.
Walkin, Carol. Using Letters in Art & Craft. 1975. 16.95 (ISBN 0-7134-2867-8, Pub. by Batsford England). David & Charles.
Walkington, Ethlyn. Gently Down the Stream. 1981. 5.95 (ISBN 0-8062-1606-9). Carlton.
Walkland, S. A., ed. The House of Commons in the Twentieth Century. 1979. 59.00x (ISBN 0-19-827193-X). Oxford U Pr.
Walkland, S. A. & Ryle, Michael, eds. The Commons in the Seventies. 285p. 1977. 25.50x (ISBN 0-85520-189-4, Pub. by Martin Robertson England). Biblio Dist.
Walkley, Christina & Foster, V. Crinolines & Crimping Irons: Victorian Clothes, How They Were Cleaned & Cared for. (Illus.). 1978. text ed. 22.50x (ISBN 0-7206-0500-8). Humanities.
Walklin, Carol, jt. auth. see Newland, Mary.
Walkowitz, Judith R. Prostitution & Victorian Society. LC 79-21050. 368p. 1980. 22.00 (ISBN 0-521-22334-2). Cambridge U Pr.
Wall, Barbara E. Love & Death in the Philosophy of Gabriel Marcel. 1977. pap. text ed. 6.50x o.p. (ISBN 0-8191-0190-7). U Pr of Amer.
Wall, Bernard. Alesandro Manzoni. 1954. 24.50 (ISBN 0-686-51343-6). Elliots Bks.
Wall, C. Edward. Media Review Digest, Vol. 6. 1975-76. 120.00 set (ISBN 0-685-70577-3). Vol. 1 (ISBN 0-87650-076-9). Vol. 2 (ISBN 0-87650-079-3). Pierian.
Wall, C. Edward & Przebienda, Edward. Words & Phrases Index, Vols. 1 & 3. LC 68-58894. 1969. 25.00 ea. Pierian.
Wall, C. Edward, et al, eds. Media Review Digest, Vol. 9. 1979. 1980. 120.00 (ISBN 0-87650-101-3). Pierian.
--Media Review Digest, Vol. 10, 1980. 1980. 120.00 (ISBN 0-87650-129-3). Pierian.
--Media Review Digest, Vol. 5. 1974-75. 120.00 set (ISBN 0-685-57150-5). Vol. 1 (ISBN 0-87650-065-3). Vol. 2 (ISBN 0-87650-066-1). Pierian.
Wall, C. T. A Geometric Introduction to Topology. LC 70-168765. 1972. text ed. 15.95 (ISBN 0-201-08432-5). A-W.
Wall, C. T., ed. Homological Groups Theory. LC 78-74013. (London Mathematical Society Lecture Note: No. 36). 1980. pap. 42.95x (ISBN 0-521-22729-1). Cambridge U Pr.
Wall, Carol. Bibliography of Pennsylvania History: A Supplement. 1977. 8.50 (ISBN 0-911124-90-X). Pa Hist & Mus.
Wall, Charles C. George Washington, Citizen-Soldier. LC 79-21241. 1980. 12.50x (ISBN 0-8139-0851-5); pap. 6.95 (ISBN 0-8139-0852-3). U Pr of Va.
Wall, E. J. Wall's History of Three Color Photography. Date not set. 46.95 o.p. (ISBN 0-8038-8954-2). Hastings.
Wall, Edward C., et al, eds. Media Review Digest, Vol. 9. 1979. 120.00 (ISBN 0-87650-101-3). Pierian.
Wall, Florence E. Aid to State Board Examinations in Cosmetology. 1975. pap. 5.00 (ISBN 0-912126-08-6, 1268-00). Keystone Pubns.
Wall, Frederick T. Chemical Thermodynamics: A Course of Study. 3rd ed. LC 73-13808. (Chemistry Ser.). (Illus.). 1974. text ed. 27.95x (ISBN 0-7167-0173-1); answers to problems avail. (ISBN 0-685-39026-8). W H Freeman.
Wall, Geoffrey, tr. see Macherey, Pierre.
Wall, H. S. Analytic Theory of Continued Fractions. LC 66-24296. 14.95 (ISBN 0-8284-0207-8). Chelsea Pub.
Wall, Hershel P. Pediatrics. 5th ed. LC 61-66847. (Medical Examination Review Book: Vol. 11). 1980. pap. 8.50 (ISBN 0-87488-111-0). Med Exam.
Wall, J. Charles. Devils. LC 69-16798. 1969. Repr. of 1904 ed. 18.00 (ISBN 0-8103-3541-7). Gale.
Wall, J. S. & Ross, W. M. Sorghum Production & Utilization. (Illus.). 1970. 39.50 o.p. (ISBN 0-87055-069-1). AVI.
Wall, James D., ed. Environmental Management Handbook for Hydrocarbon Processing Plants. (Illus.). 224p. (Orig.). 1980. pap. 16.95 (ISBN 0-87201-265-4). Gulf Pub.

Wall, James T. From the Law of Moses to the Magna Carta: Essays in Ancient & Medieval History. LC 79-66236. 1979. pap. text ed. 7.50 (ISBN 0-8191-0801-4). U Pr of Amer.

Wall, James T., ed. The Landscape of American History: Essays in Memorium to Richard W. Griffin. LC 79-89255. 1979. pap. text ed. 9.00 (ISBN 0-8191-0811-1). U Pr of Amer.

Wall, James W. Davie County: A Brief History. (Illus.). 1976. pap. 2.00 (ISBN 0-86526-126-1). NC Archives.

Wall, Jerry A., jt. auth. see Glueck, William F.

Wall, Jesse D. Introductory Physics: A Problem-Solving Approach. 1977. text ed. 15.95x (ISBN 0-669-00188-0). Heath.

Wall, Joan & Weatherspoon, Ricky. Anyone Can Sing: How to Become the Singer You Always Wanted to Be. LC 77-12892. 1978. pap. 5.95 (ISBN 0-385-13185-2, Dolp). Doubleday.

Wall, Joseph F. Iowa. (States & the Nation Ser.). (Illus.). 1978. 12.95 (ISBN 0-393-05671-6, Co-Pub by AASLH). Norton.

Wall, Louise. Sandstone of Time. LC 79-93208. (Illus.). 104p. (Orig.). 1980. 8.95x (ISBN 0-935834-01-X). Rainbow-Betty.

Wall, Patrick M. Eye-Witness Identification in Criminal Cases. 248p. 1975. 14.75 (ISBN 0-398-02009-4). C C Thomas.

Wall, R., jt. ed. see Laslett, P.

Wall, Robert E., Jr. Massachusetts Bay: The Crucial Decade, 1640-1650. LC 72-75210. 296p. 1972. 20.00x o.p. (ISBN 0-300-01484-8). Yale U Pr.

Wall, Steve, jt. auth. see Knight, Walker.

Wall Street Journal Editors. American Dynasties Today. LC 80-68102. (Illus.). 330p. 1980. 12.95 (ISBN 0-87094-228-X). Dow Jones-Irwin.

Wall, W. D., ed. Psychological Services for Schools. 1956. 7.00 (ISBN 0-685-36751-7, U501, UNESCO). Unipub.

Wall, Wendell. Laboratory Manual for Introductory Biology. coil binding 10.95 (ISBN 0-88252-101-2). Paladin Hse.

Walla, Feroze R. Satyajit Ray's Art. 132p. 1980. 15.00 (ISBN 0-89684-260-6, Pub. by Clarion India). Orient Bk Dist.

Wallaca, Sylvia. Empress. 336p. 1981. pap. 2.95 (ISBN 0-553-14589-4). Bantam.

Wallace & Pitz. Mathematics for Business with Machine Applications. 448p. 1977. text ed. 17.27 (ISBN 0-7715-0901-4); tchr's. manual with text solutions 11.93 (ISBN 0-7715-0902-2); tchr's. ed., wkbk. 1 9.27 (ISBN 0-7715-0904-9); tchr's. ed., wkbk. 2 9.93 (ISBN 0-7715-0906-5); wkbk. 1, units 1-9 4.60 (ISBN 0-7715-0903-0); wkbk. 2, units 10-22 5.27 (ISBN 0-7715-0905-7). Forkner.

Wallace, A. R. The Malay Archipelago. Date not set. 12.50 (ISBN 0-8446-3129-9). Peter Smith.

Wallace, Adam. The Parson of the Islands. LC 61-17566. 1961. 7.00 (ISBN 0-87033-077-2, Pub. by Tidewater). Cornell Maritime.

Wallace, Albert H. Guy de Maupassant. (World Authors Ser.: France: No. 265). 1973. lib. bdg. 9.95 (ISBN 0-8057-2602-0). Twayne.

Wallace, Anthony F. Religion: An Anthropological View. 1966. text ed. 10.95x (ISBN 0-394-30543-4). Random.

Wallace, Arthur. Can Mormonism Be Proved Experimentally? 2nd rev. ed. 170p. 1973. 4.00 (ISBN 0-937892-00-9); pap. 3.00 (ISBN 0-937892-01-7). LL Co.

Wallace, Arthur & Bousfield, Shirley. Successful Family Organizations, Record Keeping, & Genealogy in Family Activities. 3rd ed. (Illus.). 189p. 1978. pap. 3.95 (ISBN 0-937892-02-5). LL Co.

Wallace, Arthur, compiled by. America's Witness for Jesus Christ. 70p. 1978. pap. 1.95 (ISBN 0-937892-04-1). LL Co.

--L. D. S. Children's Comments, Vol. 1. 60p. 1978. pap. 1.95 (ISBN 0-937892-03-3). LL Co.

Wallace, B., jt. auth. see Harding, T.

Wallace, Barbara B. Hawkins & the Soccer Solution. LC 80-23016. 128p. (gr. 4-6). 1981. 7.95g (ISBN 0-687-16672-1). Abingdon.

--Julia & the Third Bad Thing. LC 75-2965. (Illus.). 64p. (gr. 2-4). 1975. 5.95 o.p. (ISBN 0-695-80590-8); PLB 5.97 o.p. (ISBN 0-695-40590-X). Follett.

--Palmer Patch. LC 76-2185. (Illus.). 128p. (gr. 3-6). 1976. 5.95 o.p. (ISBN 0-695-80668-8); lib. ed. 5.97 o.p. (ISBN 0-695-40668-X). Follett.

--Peppermints in the Parlor. LC 80-12326. 216p. (gr. 4-6). 1980. 8.95 (ISBN 0-689-30790-X). Atheneum.

--The Secret Summer of L. E. B. LC 73-93557. (Illus.). 192p. (gr. 3-6). 1974. 5.95 o.p. (ISBN 0-695-80481-2); lib. bdg. 5.97 o.p. (ISBN 0-695-40481-4). Follett.

--Victoria. (gr. 5 up). 1972. PLB 5.97 o.p. (ISBN 0-695-40322-2). Follett.

Wallace, Bruce. Basic Popultaion Genetics. LC 80-39504. (Illus.). 736p. 1981. 25.00x (ISBN 0-231-05042-9). Columbia U Pr.

--Chromosomes, Giant Molecules, & Evolution. (Illus.). 1966. 5.00x (ISBN 0-393-06343-7); pap. 3.95x (ISBN 0-393-09677-7, NortonC). Norton.

Wallace, Bruce, ed. Genetics, Evolution, Race, Radiation, Biology: Essays in Social Biology, Vol. 2. LC 79-167789. 1972. pap. text ed. 10.95x (ISBN 0-13-351155-3). P-H.

--People, Their Needs, Environment, Ecology: Vol. 1, Essays in Social Biology. LC 79-167789. 1972. pap. 10.95 (ISBN 0-13-656827-0). P-H.

Wallace, Dan, jt. auth. see Marier, Donald.

Wallace, David R. Idle Weeds: The Life of a Sandstone Ridge. LC 79-21447. (Illus.). 192p. 1980. 12.95 (ISBN 0-87156-271-5). Sierra.

Wallace, Diane S., jt. auth. see Baumann, Roland.

Wallace, Don, Jr. International Regulation of Multinational Corporations. LC 75-8411. (Special Studies). (Illus.). 1976. text ed. 24.95 (ISBN 0-275-05880-8). Praeger.

Wallace, Don, Jr. & Escobar, Helga, eds. The Future of International Economic Organizations. LC 75-44942. (Special Studies). 1977. text ed. 23.95 (ISBN 0-275-22990-4). Praeger.

Wallace, Don, Jr., jt. ed. see Surrey, Walter S.

Wallace, Edgar. The Four Just Men. 1976. lib. bdg. 14.95x (ISBN 0-89968-155-7). Lightyear.

Wallace, Emily M. A Bibliography of William Carlos Williams. LC 68-27541. (Illus.). 1968. 27.50x (ISBN 0-8195-3091-3, Pub. by Wesleyan U Pr). Columbia U Pr.

Wallace, Evelyn. Cake Decorating & Sugarcraft. LC 74-27499. (Illus.). 1975. 12.95 (ISBN 0-668-03766-0). Arco.

Wallace, Frank R. A B C's of Poker. 1980. pap. cancelled (ISBN 0-911752-31-5). I & O Pub.

--Consciousness: The End of Authority. 1980. pap. 2.00 (ISBN 0-911752-32-3). I & O Pub.

--Poker: A Guaranteed Income for Life. 1978. pap. 7.95 (ISBN 0-446-97455-2). Warner Bks.

--Poker Power. Date not set. cancelled (ISBN 0-911752-28-5). I & O Pub.

Wallace, Frank R. & Savage, Eric. Poker Troubleshooting Guide & Answer Book. Date not set. 100.00 (ISBN 0-911752-26-9). I & O Pub. Postponed.

Wallace, G. K. & Vaughn, Ray. Wallace-Vaughn Debate. 4.95 (ISBN 0-89315-350-8). Lambert Bk.

Wallace, George, jt. auth. see Capp, Al.

Wallace, George J. My World of Birds: Memoirs of an Ornithologist. 345p. 1979. 12.50 (ISBN 0-8059-2586-4). Dorrance.

Wallace, George J. & Mahan, Harold D. An Introduction to Ornithology. 3rd ed. (Illus.). 1974. text ed. 18.95 (ISBN 0-02-423980-1). Macmillan.

Wallace, Gerald & Larsen, Stephen C. Educational Assessment of Learning Problems: Testing for Teaching. new ed. 1978. text ed. 20.95 (ISBN 0-205-06090-0). Allyn.

--Educational Assessment of Learning Problems: Testing for Teaching. 1978. pap. text ed. 12.95 (ISBN 0-205-06089-7). Allyn.

Wallace, Gerald M. & Kauffman, James M. Teaching Children with Learning Problems. 2nd ed. (Special Education Ser.). 1978. text ed. 17.50 (ISBN 0-675-08425-3). Merrill.

Wallace, H. Vertebrate Limb Regeneration. 320p. 1981. price not set (ISBN 0-471-27877-7, Pub. by Wiley-Interscience). Wiley.

Wallace, H. R. Nematode Ecology & Plant Disease. LC 73-90720. 1973. 32.50x (ISBN 0-8448-0271-9). Crane Russak Co.

Wallace, Helen. Budgetary Politics: The Finances of the European Community. (Studies on Contemporary Europe Ser.: No. 1). (Illus.). 128p. (Orig.). 1980. text ed. 15.95x (ISBN 0-04-382023-9); pap. text ed. 6.95x (ISBN 0-04-382024-7). Allen Unwin.

Wallace, Helen M., et al, eds. Maternal & Child Health Practices: Problems, Resources & Methods of Delivery. (Illus.). 1400p. 1973. 52.75 (ISBN 0-398-02617-3). C C Thomas.

Wallace, Henry A. Democracy Reborn. Lord, Russell, ed. LC 72-2387. (FDR & the Era of the New Deal Ser.). 280p. Repr. of 1944 ed. lib. bdg. 27.50 (ISBN 0-306-70487-0). Da Capo.

Wallace, Hugh N. The Navy, the Company, & Richard King: British Exploration in the Canadian Arctic, 1829-1860. (Illus.). 265p. 1980. 21.95x (ISBN 0-7735-0338-2). McGill-Queens U Pr.

Wallace, Iain. The Transportation Impact of the Canadian Mining Industry. 155p. (Orig.). 1977. pap. text ed. 8.00x (ISBN 0-88757-002-X, Pub. by Ctr Resource Stud Canada). Renouf.

Wallace, Ian. The Lucifer Comet. (Science Fiction Ser.). 1980. pap. 2.25 (ISBN 0-87997-581-4, UE1584). DAW Bks.

--Promise Me You'll Sing Mud. 1980. 13.95 (ISBN 0-7145-3500-1). Riverrun NY.

Wallace, Irving. Special People, Special Times. 192p. (Orig.). 1981. pap. 2.25 (ISBN 0-523-41480-3). Pinnacle Bks.

Wallace, Irving, jt. auth. see Wallechinsky, David.

Wallace, Irving, et al. The Book of Lists Number Two. LC 79-3732. (Illus.). 1980. 12.95 (ISBN 0-688-03574-4). Morrow.

--The Book of Lists Two. 1981. pap. 3.50 (ISBN 0-553-13101-X). Bantam.

--The People's Almanac Presents the Book of Lists, No. 2. 576p. 1981. pap. 2.95 (ISBN 0-553-13101-X). Bantam.

Wallace, J. G. Stages & Transition in Conceptual Development: An Experimental Study. (General Ser.). (Illus.). 247p. (Orig.). 1972. pap. text ed. 18.50x (ISBN 0-901225-60-6, NFER). Humanities.

Wallace, Jane, ed. The American Quantity Cookbook: Tracing Our Food Traditions. LC 76-3419. 1976. 24.95 (ISBN 0-8436-2096-X). CBI Pub.

Wallace, Jim, jt. auth. see Wallace, Maureen.

Wallace, John M. Destiny His Choice: The Loyalism of Andrew Marvell. LC 68-10334. 1968. 44.00 (ISBN 0-521-06725-1). Cambridge U Pr.

--Destiny His Choice: The Loyalism of Andrew Marvell. 266p. 1981. pap. 13.50 (ISBN 0-521-28042-7). Cambridge U Pr.

Wallace, John M. & Hobbs, Peter. Atmospheric Sciences: An Introductory Survey. 467p. 1977. 22.95 (ISBN 0-12-732950-1). Acad Pr.

Wallace, Karl R., jt. auth. see Bryant, Donald C.

Wallace, Katherine. California: People, Politics, & Government. (Orig.). (gr. 11-12). 1976. pap. text ed. 6.25 (ISBN 0-87720-612-0). AMSCO Sch.

--California Through Five Centuries. (gr. 7-12). 1974. pap. text ed. 7.17 (ISBN 0-87720-607-4). AMSCO Sch.

Wallace, Lee A., Jr. A Guide to Virginia Military Organizations, 1861-1865. (Illus.). 348p. 1964. 35.00x o.p. (ISBN 0-685-65088-X). Va Bk.

Wallace, Lew. Ben Hur. (Classics Ser). (YA) (gr. 9 up). pap. 1.95 (ISBN 0-8049-0074-4, CL-74). Airmont.

--Ben Hur. De Reedy, Ginette D., tr. (Biblioteca de Libros Condensados). Date not set. pap. 1.50 (ISBN 0-311-37012-8). Casa Bautista.

Wallace, M. J. Handbook of Child Nursing Care. LC 75-134041. (Wiley Paperback Nursing Ser.). 138p. 1971. pap. 11.95 (ISBN 0-471-91850-4). Wiley.

Wallace, Margaret E. Learning Genetics with Mice. (Investigations in Biology Ser.). 1971. pap. text ed. 3.95x o.p. (ISBN 0-435-60284-5). Heinemann Ed.

Wallace, Martin. The Irish: How They Live & Work. (How They Live & Work Ser.). (Illus.). 1974. 11.95 (ISBN 0-7153-5492-2). David & Charles.

--A Short History of Ireland. 1974. 10.95 (ISBN 0-7153-6306-9). David & Charles.

Wallace, Mary E. & Wallace, Robert. Opera Scenes for Class & Stage. LC 78-11095. 314p. 1979. 18.95x (ISBN 0-8093-0903-3). S Ill U Pr.

Wallace, Mary L. Spelling. Raygor, Alton, ed. (Communication Skills Ser.). 288p. 1981. pap. text ed. 7.95 (ISBN 0-07-067901-0, C). McGraw.

Wallace, Maureen & Wallace, Jim. Snackers: Kick the Junk Food Habit. LC 78-638. 1978. pap. 4.95 (ISBN 0-914842-26-9). Madrona Pubs.

Wallace, Melvin. Partners in Business. 200p. 1981. 14.95 (ISBN 0-913864-66-8); pap. 7.95 (ISBN 0-913864-67-6). Enterprise Del.

Wallace, Michael, jt. ed. see Hofstadter, Richard.

Wallace, Michael D., jt. ed. see Singer, J. David.

Wallace, Neil, jt. ed. see Kareken, John H.

Wallace, P., jt. auth. see Grover, F.

Wallace, Pamela. Caresse. 1979. pap. 2.50 o.p. (ISBN 0-523-40516-2). Pinnacle Bks.

--Falling in Love Again. 288p. (Orig.). 1981. pap. 2.75 (ISBN 0-523-41055-7). Pinnacle Bks.

Wallace, Patricia, jt. auth. see Brown, Thomas S.

Wallace, Paul A. Indians in Pennsylvania. LC 61-63955. (Illus., Orig.). 1970. 7.00 (ISBN 0-911124-41-1); pap. 4.00 (ISBN 0-911124-40-3). Pa Hist & Mus.

Wallace, Paul A. W. Indian Paths of Pennsylvania. LC 66-4482. 1971. 9.00 (ISBN 0-685-19109-5). Pa Hist & Mus.

Wallace, Phyllis A. & LaMond, Annette M., eds. Women, Minorities, & Discrimination. LC 76-53903. (Illus.). 1977. 21.50 (ISBN 0-669-01282-3). Lexington Bks.

Wallace, R. H. Understanding & Measuring Vibrations. LC 78-135386. (Wykeham Technology Ser.: No. 4). 1970. 9.95x (ISBN 0-8448-1125-4). Crane Russak Co.

Wallace, Robert. The Gamblers. Time-Life Books, ed. (The Old West). (Illus.). 1979. 12.95 (ISBN 0-8094-2308-1). Time-Life.

--The Gamblers. LC 78-12281. (The Old West Ser.). (Illus.). 1978. lib. bdg. 12.96 (ISBN 0-686-51078-X). Silver.

--The Grand Canyon. (The American Wilderness Ser). (Illus.). 1972. 12.95 (ISBN 0-8094-1144-X). Time-Life.

--The Grand Canyon. LC 71-179463. (American Wilderness Ser). (Illus.). (gr. 6 up). 1972. lib. bdg. 11.97 (ISBN 0-8094-1145-8, Pub. by Time-Life). Silver.

--Hawaii. LC 73-179462. (American Wilderness Ser). (Illus.). (gr. 6 up). 1973. lib. bdg. 11.97 (ISBN 0-8094-1177-6, Pub. by Time-Life). Silver.

--Hawaii. (The American Wilderness Ser.). (Illus.). 1973. 12.95 (ISBN 0-8094-1176-8). Time-Life.

--How They Do It. (Illus.). 1980. pap. 4.95 (ISBN 0-688-08718-3, Quill). Morrow.

--The Italian Campaign. Time-Life Books, ed. (World War II). (Illus.). 1978. 12.95 (ISBN 0-8094-2502-5). Time-Life.

--The Italian Campaign. LC 78-52857. (World War II Ser.). (Illus.). 1978. lib. bdg. 14.94 (ISBN 0-686-51048-8). Silver.

--The Miners. LC 73-94242. (The Old West). (Illus.). (gr. 5 up). 1976. kivar 12.96 (ISBN 0-8094-1539-9, Pub. by Time-Life). Silver.

--Rise of Russia. (Great Ages of Man Ser). (Illus.). 1967. 12.95 (ISBN 0-8094-0353-6); lib. bdg. avail. (ISBN 0-685-04843-8). Time-Life.

--The World of Bernini. (Library of Art). (Illus.). 1970. 15.95 (ISBN 0-8094-0257-2). Time-Life.

--World of Bernini. LC 70-122329. (Library of Art Ser.). (Illus.). (gr. 6 up). 1970. 12.96 (ISBN 0-8094-0286-6, Pub. by Time-Life). Silver.

--World of Leonardo. (Library of Art). (Illus.). 1966. 15.95 (ISBN 0-8094-0234-3). Time-Life.

--World of Leonardo. LC 66-24104. (Library of Art Ser.). (Illus.). (gr. 6 up). 1966. 12.96 (ISBN 0-8094-0263-7, Pub. by Time-Life). Silver.

--World of Rembrandt. (Library of Art). (Illus.). 1968. 15.95 (ISBN 0-8094-0244-0). Time-Life.

--World of Rembrandt. LC 68-22321. (Library of Art Ser.). (Illus.). (gr. 6 up). 1968. 12.96 (ISBN 0-8094-0273-4, Pub. by Time-Life). Silver.

--World of Van Gogh. (Library of Art). (Illus.). 1969. 15.95 (ISBN 0-8094-0251-3). Time-Life.

--World of Van Gogh. LC 70-78988. (Library of Art Ser.). (Illus.). (gr. 6 up). 1969. 12.96 (ISBN 0-8094-0280-7, Pub. by Time-Life). Silver.

Wallace, Robert, jt. auth. see Wallace, Mary E.

Wallace, Robert, ed. The Miners. (Old West Ser.). (Illus.). 1976. 12.95 (ISBN 0-8094-1537-2). Time-Life.

Wallace, Robert B., jt. auth. see Tenkte, Adriann.

Wallace, Robert J., jt. auth. see Levin, Harold L.

Wallace, Robert K. A Century of Music-Making: The Lives of Josef & Rosina Lhevinne. LC 75-28908. (Illus.). 384p. 1976. 17.50x o.p. (ISBN 0-253-31330-9). Ind U Pr.

Wallace, Robert N. There Shall Be a General Convention of This Church. 1976. pap. 3.95x (ISBN 0-8164-1212-X). Crossroad NY.

Wallace, Roberta, et al. Staff Manual for Teaching Patients About Rheumatoid Arthritis. LC 78-20816. (Illus.). 472p. 1979. pap. 39.75 (ISBN 0-87258-252-3, 1320). Am Hospital.

Wallace, Roger, jt. auth. see Maid, Amy.

Wallace, Ronald. Plums, Stones, Kisses & Hooks: Poems by Ronald Wallace. LC 80-15907. 80p. 1981. text ed. 10.00x (ISBN 0-8262-0314-0). U of Mo Pr.

Wallace, Ruth A. & Wolf, Alison. Contemporary Sociological Theory. LC 79-13971. (Sociology Ser.). (Illus.). 1980. text ed. 17.95 (ISBN 0-13-170506-7). P-H.

Wallace, S. Concomitant Learnings: Hidden Influences in the Classroom. LC 78-68027. 1978. pap. 3.00 (ISBN 0-686-26202-6, 261-08432). Home Econ Educ.

Wallace, Sally F. Practically Painless English. (English Composition Ser.). 1979. pap. text ed. 7.50 (ISBN 0-13-692194-9). P-H.

Wallace, Samuel E. After Suicide. LC 73-9793. 269p. 1973. 21.95 (ISBN 0-471-91865-2, Pub. by Wiley-Interscience). Wiley.

--The Urban Environment. 1980. pap. 9.95 (ISBN 0-256-02218-6). Dorsey.

Wallace, Samuel E. & Eser, Albin, eds. Suicide & Euthanasia: The Rights of Personhood. LC 80-28799. 176p. 1981. 12.50x (ISBN 0-87049-299-3). U of Tenn Pr.

Wallace, Sylvia. The Fountains. 384p. 1976. 8.95 o.p. (ISBN 0-688-03040-8). Morrow.

Wallace, Tim, jt. auth. see Snodgrass, Milton M.

Wallace, Tina, jt. auth. see Moore, Robert.

Wallace, W. E., jt. ed. see Subbarao, E. C.

Wallace, W. V. Czechoslovakia. LC 76-4494. (Nations of the Modern World Ser). 1977. 32.50x (ISBN 0-89158-027-1). Westview.

Wallace, Walter L. Logic of Science in Sociology. LC 71-149845. 1971. 15.95x (ISBN 0-202-30193-1); pap. 6.95x (ISBN 0-202-30194-X). Aldine Pub.

Wallace, Wendy, ed. see Browne, Dik.

Wallace, Wendy, ed. see Burroughs, Edgar R.

Wallace, Wendy, ed. see Walker, Mort.

Wallace, William & Paterson, W. E., eds. Foreign Policy Making in Western Europe: A Comparative Approach. LC 78-58844. 1978. 23.95 (ISBN 0-03-046271-1). Praeger.

Wallace, William A. Causality & Scientific Explanation: Classical & Contemporary Science, Vol. 2. 432p. 1981. lib. bdg. 22.75 (ISBN 0-8191-1480-4); pap. text ed. 13.75 (ISBN 0-8191-1481-2). U Pr of Amer.

--Causality & Scientific Explanation: Medieval & Early Classical Science, Vol. 1. 298p. 1981. lib. bdg. 19.25 (ISBN 0-8191-1478-2); pap. text ed. 10.50 (ISBN 0-8191-1479-0). U Pr of Amer.

Wallace, William A., jt. auth. see Heroux, Richard L.

Wallace, William I., ed. see Gascoigne, George.

Wallace, William J., jt. auth. see Ingmanson, Dale E.

Wallace, William S. Dictionary of North American Authors Deceased Before 1950. LC 68-19955. 1968. Repr. of 1951 ed. 22.00 (ISBN 0-8103-3153-5). Gale.

Wallace-Brodeur, Ruth. The Kenton Year. LC 80-13448. 104p. (gr. 4-7). 1980. 7.95 (ISBN 0-689-50186-2, McElderry Bk). Atheneum.

Wallace-Hadrill, J. M. Early Germanic Kingship in England & on the Continent. (Oxford Lectures Ser). 1971. 22.50x (ISBN 0-19-821491-X). Oxford U Pr.

Wallace-Hadrill, J. M., tr. The Fourth Book of the Chronicle of Fredegar with Its Continuations. LC 80-28086. (Medieval Classics Ser.). (Illus.). lxvii, 137p. 1981. Repr. of 1960 ed. lib. bdg. 27.50x (ISBN 0-313-22741-1, WAFRE). Greenwood.

Wallach, Carla. Interior Decorating with Plants. (Illus.). 224p. 1976. pap. 8.95 o.s.i. (ISBN 0-02-012000-1, Collier). Macmillan.

Wallach, Carlo. The Reluctant Weekend Gardener. (Illus.). 200p. 1974. 7.95 o.s.i. (ISBN 0-02-623150-6). Macmillan.

Wallach, Donald F., ed. see Instrumentation Laboratory Spring Symposium, Boston, Ma, April 1980.

Wallach, Harold C. Making of Child & Family Policy. Chambers, Lyn, ed. (AAAS Selected Symposium Ser.: No. 56). 160p. 1980. lib. bdg. 20.00x (ISBN 0-89158-956-2). Westview.

Wallach, Janet. Working Wardrobe: An Easy, Affordable Approach to Successful Dressing. 1981. 14.95 (ISBN 0-87491-072-2). Acropolis.

Wallach, Joel. Ornaments & Mirrors in Stained Glass 1. (Illus.). 1979. pap. 4.95 o.p. (ISBN 0-934280-03-7). Glass Works.

Wallach, Joel L. Beginning Stained Glass Patterns, Bk. 1. (Illus.). 48p. (Orig.). 1980. pap. 4.95x (ISBN 0-934280-04-5). Glass Works.

--Beginning Stained Glass Patterns, Bk. 2. (Illus.). 48p. (Orig.). 1980. pap. 4.95x (ISBN 0-934280-05-3). Glass Works.

Wallach, Mark I. & Bracker, Jon. Christopher Morley. LC 76-17922. (U.S. Authors Ser.: No. 278). 1976. lib. bdg. 10.95 (ISBN 0-8057-7178-6). Twayne.

Wallach, Paul. Metric Drafting. Vorndran, Richard A., ed. 1979. text ed. 18.95 (ISBN 0-02-829690-7); instrs'. manual 6.20 (ISBN 0-02-829700-8); problems book 6.95 (ISBN 0-02-829710-5). Glencoe.

Wallach, Paul & Hepler, Don. Reading Construction Drawings: Trade Edition. (Illus.). 320p. 1980. 18.95 (ISBN 0-07-067940-1, P&RB). McGraw.

Wallach, Paul I. Basic Book of Drafting. (Illus.). 1979. 5.95 (ISBN 0-8269-1170-6). Am Technical.

Wallach, Theresa. Easy Motorcycle Riding. rev. enlarged ed. LC 78-57787. (Illus.). 1978. 7.95 (ISBN 0-8069-4134-0); lib. bdg. 7.49 (ISBN 0-8069-4135-9). Sterling.

Wallack, L. R. American Pistol & Revolver Design & Performance. 1978. 14.95 (ISBN 0-87691-255-2). Winchester Pr.

--American Shotgun Design & Performance. 1977. 14.95 (ISBN 0-87691-236-6). Winchester Pr.

--The Deer Rifle. (Illus.). 1978. 12.95 (ISBN 0-87691-269-2). Winchester Pr.

Wallack, Stanley S., jt. ed. see Callahan, James J., Jr.

Wallacker, Benjamin E. The Huai-nan-tzu, Book Eleven: Behavior, Culture, & the Cosmos. (American Oriental Ser.: Vol. 48). 1962. pap. 4.00x (ISBN 0-686-00028-5). Am Orient Soc.

Wallacker, Benjamin F., et al, eds. Chinese Walled Cities: A Collection of Maps from Shina Jokaku No Gaiyo. (Illus.). 266p. 1979. Repr. of 1940 ed. 50.00 (ISBN 0-295-95698-4, Pub. by Chinese Univ Press Hong Kong). U of Wash Pr.

Wallant, Edward L. The Tenants of Moonbloom. LC 63-13501. 245p. 1973. pap. 3.50 (ISBN 0-15-688535-2, HPL59, HPL). HarBraceJ.

Wallas, James & Whitaker, Pamela. Kwakiutl Legends. 150p. 1981. text ed. price not set (ISBN 0-88839-094-7). Hancock Hse.

Wallat, Cynthia & Goldman, Richard. Home-School-Community Interaction: What We Know & Why We Don't Know More. 1979. text ed. 14.95 (ISBN 0-675-08281-1). Merrill.

Wallat, Cynthia, jt. ed. see Green, Judith.

Wallbank, T. Walter, et al. Civilization Past & Present. 7th ed. 1976. pap. 9.95x ea.; Bk. 1. o.p. (ISBN 0-673-15078-X); Bk. 2. (ISBN 0-673-15079-8); Bk. 3. (ISBN 0-673-15080-1). Scott F.

--Civilization Past & Present: Prehistory to 1650. 5th ed. 1979. Vol. 1. pap. text ed. 12.95x (ISBN 0-673-15246-4). Scott F.

--Civilization Past & Present: Prehistory to Sixteen Fifty, Vol. 1. 1981. pap. text ed. 13.95x (ISBN 0-673-15235-9). Scott F.

--Civilization Past & Present: 1650 to the Present. 5th ed. 1979. Vol. 2. pap. text ed. 12.95x (ISBN 0-673-15247-2). Scott F.

--Western Civilization: People & Progress, 2 vols. Incl. Vol. 1. Ancient World to 1750 (ISBN 0-673-15082-8); Vol. 2. 1650 to the Present (ISBN 0-673-15083-6). 1977. pap. 8.95x ea. Scott F.

--Western Civilization: People & Progress. 1977. pap. 13.95x (ISBN 0-673-15081-X). Scott F.

--Civilization Past & Present. 5th ed. 1978. 19.95x (ISBN 0-673-07951-1). Scott F.

--Studying Civilization. 5th ed. 1978. pap. 5.95x (ISBN 0-673-15125-5). Scott F.

Wallbridge, David, jt. auth. see Davis, Madeleine.

Wallechinsky, David & Wallace, Irving. The Book of Lists. LC 77-1521. (Illus.). 1977. 12.95 (ISBN 0-688-03183-8). Morrow.

--The People's Almanac. LC 75-2856. 1536p. 1975. 15.95 (ISBN 0-385-04186-1); pap. 10.95 (ISBN 0-385-04060-1). Doubleday.

Wallechinsky, David, et al. The Book of Predictions. (Illus.). 576p. 1980. 12.95 (ISBN 0-688-00024-X). Morrow.

Walleghen, Michael Van. More Trouble with the Obvious. LC 80-24215. 76p. 1981. 10.00 (ISBN 0-252-00864-2); pap. 3.95 (ISBN 0-252-00865-0). U of Ill Pr.

Wallen, Carl J. Competency in Teaching Reading. LC 72-190104. 1972. pap. text ed. 12.95 (ISBN 0-574-18500-3, 13-1500); instr's guide avail. (ISBN 0-574-18508-9, 13-1508). SRA.

Wallen, Carl J. & Wallen, LaDonna. Effective Classroom Management. abr. ed. 1978. pap. text ed. 10.95 (ISBN 0-205-05985-6); text ed. 18.95 (ISBN 0-205-05893-0). Allyn.

Wallen, LaDonna, jt. auth. see Wallen, Carl J.

Wallender, Harvey W., jt. auth. see Behrman, Jack H.

Wallendorf, M., jt. auth. see Zaltman, G.

Wallendorf, Melanie & Zaltman, Gerald. Readings in Consumer Behavior: Individuals, Groups & Organizations. LC 78-13228. (Marketing Ser.). 1979. pap. text ed. 15.95x (ISBN 0-471-03021-X). Wiley.

Wallenkampf, Arnold V. New by the Spirit. LC 77-91485. (Dimension Ser.). 1978. pap. 5.95 (ISBN 0-8163-0091-7, 14390-9). Pacific Pr Pub Assn.

Wallenstein, Barry. Monarch Notes on Plath's Bell Jar. 1975. pap. 2.25 (ISBN 0-671-00965-6). Monarch Pr.

Wallenstein, Barry, jt. ed. see Salzman, Jack.

Waller, Bruce. Bismarck at the Crossroads: The Reorientation of German Foreign Policy After the Congress of Berlin 1878-1880. (University of London Historical Studies: No. 35). 273p. 1974. text ed. 32.50x (ISBN 0-485-13135-8, Athlone Pr). Humanities.

Waller County Historical Survey Committee. One Hundred One Heritage Homes. (Illus.). 224p. 1975. 14.95 (ISBN 0-89015-103-2). Nortex Pr.

Waller, D. J. Government & Politics of Communist China. 1973. text ed. 7.75x (ISBN 0-09-102870-1, Hutchinson U Lib). Humanities.

Waller, E. Nolan. Net Migration for Mississippi's Counties, 1960-1970. 1975. pap. 3.00 (ISBN 0-938004-05-0). U MS Bus Econ.

Waller, E. Nolan, jt. auth. see Lewis, Harvey S.

Waller, G. F. Mary Sidney, Countess of Pembroke: A Critical Study of Her Writings & Literary Milieu. (Elizabethan Studies: No. 87). 1980. pap. text ed. 25.00x (ISBN 0-391-02161-3). Humanities.

--The Triumph of Death & Other Unpublished & Uncollected Poems by Mary Sidney, Countess of Pembroke (1561-1621) (Salzburg Studies in English Literature: Elizabethan & Renaissance Studies Ser.: No. 65). 1977. pap. text ed. 25.00x (ISBN 0-391-01554-0). Humanities.

Waller, George M. American Revolution in the West. LC 75-44471. (Illus.). 155p. 1976. 18.95 (ISBN 0-88229-279-X). Nelson-Hall.

Waller, Irene. Fine-Art Weaving. (Illus.). 144p. 1980. 24.00 (ISBN 0-7134-0412-4, Pub. by Batsford England). David & Charles.

Waller, J. Irvin. Men Released from Prison. LC 73-85690. 1974. pap. 7.50 (ISBN 0-8020-6372-1). U of Toronto Pr.

Waller, John A. Press Tools & Presswork. (Illus.). 1980. 39.95 (ISBN 0-86108-005-X). Herman Pub.

Waller, John D., et al. Monitoring for Government Agencies. (An Institute Paper). 170p. 1976. pap. 5.00 (ISBN 0-87766-142-1, 11600). Urban Inst.

Waller, Julian A. Medical Impairment to Driving. (Illus.). 104p. 1974. 10.75 (ISBN 0-398-02891-5); pap. 7.50 (ISBN 0-398-02895-8). C C Thomas.

Waller, Kal. How to Recover Your Medical Expenses. 96p. 1981. pap. 5.95 (ISBN 0-02-098940-7, Collier). Macmillan.

Waller, Leslie. Blood & Dreams. 1980. 12.95 (ISBN 0-686-68359-5). Putnam.

--The Mob: The Story of Organized Crime in America. LC 73-6242. 160p. (gr. 7 up). 1973. 5.95 o.p. (ISBN 0-440-05720-5). Delacorte.

Waller, Marguerite R. Petrarch's Poetics & Literary History. LC 80-12893. 176p. 1980. lib. bdg. 13.50x (ISBN 0-87023-305-X). U of Mass Pr.

Waller, R. A. Building on Springs. 1969. 17.25 (ISBN 0-08-006399-3). Pergamon.

Waller, T. G. & Mackinnon, G. E., eds. Reading Research: Advances in Theory & Practice, Vol. 2. (Serial Publication). 1981. price not set (ISBN 0-12-572302-4). Acad Pr.

Waller, W. Sociology of Teaching. 1965. pap. text ed. 14.50 (ISBN 0-471-91890-3). Wiley.

Wallerstein, I. The Capitalist World Economy. LC 78-1161. (Studies in Modern Capitalism). 1979. 49.00 (ISBN 0-521-22085-8); pap. 11.95x (ISBN 0-521-29358-8). Cambridge U Pr.

Wallerstein, Immanual, ed. On the European Workers' Movements and Eurocommunism. 100p. 1980. pap. 5.001311. Synthesis Pubns.

Wallerstein, Immanuel. The Modern World-System I. 1980. pap. 9.50 lib ed (ISBN 0-12-785919-5). Acad Pr.

--The Modern World-System II: Mercantilism & the Consolidation of the European World-Economy, 1600-1750. LC 73-5318. (Studies in Social Discontinuity). 1980. 22.00 (ISBN 0-12-785923-3); pap. 9.50 o.s.i. (ISBN 0-12-785924-1). Acad Pr.

Wallerstein, Immanuel, jt. ed. see Hopkins, Terence K.

Wallerstein, Mitchell B. Food for War - Food for Peace: U. S. Food Aid in a Global Context. 378p. 1980. text ed. 30.00x (ISBN 0-262-23106-9). MIT Pr.

Walles, M., jt. auth. see Hanson, A.

Walleschek, Richard. Primitive Music. LC 72-125062. (Music Ser). 1970. Repr. of 1893 ed. lib. bdg. 25.00 (ISBN 0-306-70028-X). Da Capo.

Wallett, Tim. Shark Attack & Treatment of Victims in Southern African Waters. 1980. 25.00x (Pub. by Bailey & Swinton South Africa). State Mutual Bk.

Walley, B. H. Office Administration Handbook. 470p. 1975. text ed. 25.75x (ISBN 0-220-66281-9, Pub. by Busn Bks England). Renouf.

--Profit Planning Handbook. 325p. 1978. text ed. 29.50x (ISBN 0-220-66342-4, Pub. by Busn Bks England). Renouf.

Walley, David. No Commercial Potential: The Saga of Frank Zappa Then & Now. (Illus.). 192p. 1980. 6.95 (ISBN 0-525-93153-8). Dutton.

Wallick, Clair H. Looking for Ideas: A Display Manual for Libraries & Bookstores. LC 74-13003. (Illus.). 1970. 10.00 (ISBN 0-8108-0342-9). Scarecrow.

Wallig, Gaird. A Red-Tailed Hawk Named Bucket. LC 76-57546. (Illus.). 224p. 1980. 9.95 (ISBN 0-89087-276-7). Celestial Arts.

Wallimann, Isidor. Estrangement: Marx's Conception of Human Nature & the Division of Labor. LC 80-929. (Contributions in Philosophy: No. 16). 240p. 1981. lib. bdg. 29.95 (ISBN 0-313-22096-4, WAE/). Greenwood.

Wallin, Douglas, jt. auth. see Heller, Susan.

Wallin, Luke. The Redneck Poacher's Son. 224p. (gr. 7 up). 1981. 8.95 (ISBN 0-87888-174-3). Bradbury Pr.

Wallin, Marie-Louise. Tangles. Bothmer, Gerry, tr. from Swedish. LC 77-72619. (gr. 7up). 1977. 7.95 o.s.i. (ISBN 0-440-08502-0, Sey Lawr). Delacorte.

Walling, D. E., jt. auth. see Gregory, K. J.

Walling, D. E., jt. ed. see Gregory, K. J.

Walling, Ruth, jt. auth. see Farber, Evan I.

Walling, William A. Mary Shelley. (English Authors Ser.: No. 128). lib. bdg. 10.95 (ISBN 0-8057-1484-7). Twayne.

Wallington, C. E. Meteorology for Glider Pilots. 3rd ed. (Illus.). 331p. 1980. 24.00 (ISBN 0-7195-3303-1). Transatlantic.

Wallington, E. A., ed. see Carleton, H. M.

Wallington, Neil. Fireman: A Personal Account. LC 78-65762. 1979. 17.95 (ISBN 0-7153-7723-X). David & Charles.

--Firemen at War: The Work of London's Firefighters in the Second World War. LC 80-68692. (Illus.). 160p. 1981. 19.95 (ISBN 0-7153-7964-X). David & Charles.

Wallis, Booker. Marriage Counselling. 17.95x (ISBN 0-392-08121-0, SpS). Soccer.

Wallis, C. J. Practical Zoology. 6th ed. 1974. 19.95x (ISBN 0-433-34704-X). Intl Ideas.

Wallis, Celestina, et al. Anuska's Complete Body Makeover Book. (Illus.). 224p. 1981. 11.95 (ISBN 0-399-12579-5). Putnam.

Wallis, Charles G., et al, trs. see Pico Della Mirandola, Giovanni.

Wallis, Charles L. American Epitaphs Grave & Humorous. (Illus.). 7.50 (ISBN 0-8446-4832-9). Peter Smith.

--The Minister's Manual: Doran's Ninteen Eighty Edition. LC 25-21658. 1979. 8.95 o.p. (ISBN 0-06-069025-9, HarpR). Har-Row.

Wallis, Charles L., ed. Funeral Encyclopedia. (Source Bks for Ministers Ser.). 1973. pap. 5.95 (ISBN 0-8010-9539-5). Baker Bk.

Wallis, Charles L., compiled by. Treasure Chest. LC 65-15395. (Illus.). 1965. 17.95 (ISBN 0-06-069010-0, HarpR); deluxe ed. 16.95 (ISBN 0-06-069011-9); deluxe ed. 17.95 (white) (ISBN 0-06-069051-8). Har-Row.

Wallis, H., ed. Map Librarian in Modern World. Zogner, L. 295p. (Orig.). 1979. pap. text ed. 32.00 (ISBN 0-89664-131-7, Pub. by K G Saur). Gale.

Wallis, Hal & Higham, Charles. Starmaker: The Autobiography of Hal Wallis. (Illus.). 256p. 1980. 13.95 (ISBN 0-02-623170-0). Macmillan.

Wallis, J. H. Personal Counseling. 1973. text ed. 10.95x o.p. (ISBN 0-04-361015-3); pap. text ed. 5.95x o.p. (ISBN 0-04-361016-1). Allen Unwin.

Wallis, J. P., ed. see Blake, William.

Wallis, John. Thinking About Retirement. LC 72-652. 120p. 1976. text ed. 19.50 (ISBN 0-08-018269-0); pap. text ed. 8.25 (ISBN 0-08-018268-2). Pergamon.

Wallis, Kathleen. Let's Look at Korea. 1977. pap. 1.25 (ISBN 0-85363-118-2). OMF Bks.

Wallis, Kenneth F. Topics in Applied Econometrics. rev. 2nd ed. 176p. 1980. 19.50x (ISBN 0-8166-1014-2); pap. 6.95x (ISBN 0-8166-1017-7). U of Minn Pr.

--Topics in Applied Econometrics. 1973. pap. 36.00x (ISBN 0-85641-011-X, Pub. by Basil Blackwell England). Biblio Dist.

Wallis, Lila A. Cornell Medical Update - 1. LC 78-51071. (Illus.). 1978. pap. 32.00 (ISBN 0-914316-14-1). Yorke Med.

Wallis, Lila A., ed. Cornell Medical Update - 2. LC 79-65407. (Illus.). 1979. pap. text ed. 38.00 (ISBN 0-914316-19-2). Yorke Med.

Wallis, M. Industrial Relations & the Library Manager. Wilson, A., ed. (A Library Association Management Pamplet Ser.). 1980. pap. 8.95x (ISBN 0-85365-542-1, Pub. by Lib Assn Ehgland). Oryx Pr.

Wallis, Reginald. New Life. (gr. 3-7). Date not set. pap. 1.00 (ISBN 0-87213-912-3). Loizeaux.

--New Man. Date not set. pap. 0.80 (ISBN 0-87213-913-1). Loizeaux.

--The New Sovereignty. 1974. pap. 1.25 (ISBN 0-87123-391-6, 200391). Bethany Fell.

Wallis, Roy. The Road to Total Freedom. LC 76-27273. 1977. 15.00x (ISBN 0-231-04200-0). Columbia U Pr.

Wallis, Roy, ed. On the Margins of Science: The Social Construction of Rejected Knowledge. (Sociological Review Monograph: No. 27). 337p. 1979. pap. 28.00x (ISBN 0-8476-2300-9). Rowman.

--Sectarianism: Analyses of Religious & Non-Religious Sects. LC 75-9715. 1975. 18.95 (ISBN 0-470-91910-8). Halsted Pr.

Wallis, W. Allen & Roberts, Harry V. Nature of Statistics. LC 62-11024. 1965. pap. text ed. 3.95 (ISBN 0-02-933730-5). Free Pr.

--Statistics: A New Approach. 1956. text ed. 12.95 (ISBN 0-02-933720-8). Free Pr.

Wallis-Budge, A. E., tr. from Syriac. The Paradise of the Fathers, 2 vols. 1979. Repr. of 1907 ed. 20.00x set (ISBN 0-913026-21-2). St Nectarios.

Wallis Budge, Ernest A., tr. see Anan Isho.

Wallman, Jefferey M. Blood & Passion. (Orig.). 1980. pap. 2.25 (ISBN 0-505-51514-8). Tower Bks.

Wallman, Jeffery M. Deathtrek. (Orig.). 1980. pap. 1.75 (ISBN 0-505-51528-8). Tower Bks.

Wallman, Jeffrey M. Judas Cross. 1977. pap. 1.50 (ISBN 0-380-01846-2, 36426). Avon.

Wallman, Sandra. Take Out Hunger: Two Case Studies of Rural Development in Basutoland. (Monographs in Social Anthropology Ser). 1969. text ed. 16.25x (ISBN 0-485-19539-9, Athlone Pr). Humanities.

Wallman, Sandra, ed. Ethnicity at Work. 1979. text ed. 26.75 o.p. (ISBN 0-8419-5056-3); pap. text ed. 14.50x (ISBN 0-8419-5057-1). Holmes & Meier.

Wallmo, Olof C., ed. Mule & Black-Tailed Deer of North America. LC 80-20128. (Illus.). xvii, 650p. 1981. 29.95 (ISBN 0-8032-4715-X). U of Nebr Pr.

Wallon, Henri. Development of the Child. Voyat, Gilbert, ed. LC 80-69666. 260p. 1981. 30.00 (ISBN 0-87668-434-7). Aronson.

Wallop, Douglas. Regatta. 1981. 12.95 (ISBN 0-393-01364-2). Norton.

Wallop, Douglass. Mixed Singles. 1978. pap. 1.75 o.s.i. (ISBN 0-515-04521-7). Jove Pubns.

Wallower, Lucille. All About Pennsylvania. Wholey, Ellen J., ed. (Illus.). (gr. 3-4). 1961. pap. 3.15 (ISBN 0-931992-05-2). Penns Valley.

--Indians of Pennsylvania Workshop. LC 76-12651. (gr. 3-4). 1976. pap. 3.50 (ISBN 0-931992-01-X). Penns Valley.

--My Book About Abraham Lincoln. Gump, Patricia L., ed. (gr. 2-4). 1967. pap. 1.85 o.p. (ISBN 0-931992-10-9). Penns Valley.

--Pennsylvania: A Bicentennial Workshop. Brookshire, Annette, ed. LC 74-26216. (gr. 3-4). 1975. pap. 3.30 o.p. (ISBN 0-931992-03-6). Penns Valley.

--Pennsylvania ABC. Gump, Patricia L., ed. (Illus.). (gr. 2-5). 1964. pap. 3.50 (ISBN 0-931992-08-7). Penns Valley.

--Your State: Pennsylvania. Gump, Patricia L., ed. (gr. 3-4). 1963. pap. 3.50 (ISBN 0-931992-09-5). Penns Valley.

Wallower, Lucille & Porter, Marilyn M. African American Workshop. LC 76-52052. (gr. 3-4). 1977. pap. 4.60 (ISBN 0-931992-00-1); answerbook 0.40 (ISBN 0-931992-19-2). Penns Valley.

Wallower, Lucille & Wholey, Ellen J. They Came to Pennsylvania Workshop. LC 76-14140. (gr. 4-5). 1976. pap. 3.50 (ISBN 0-931992-02-8). Penns Valley.

Wallower, Lucille & Wier, Bernice. The New Pennsylvania Primer. (gr. 3-4). 1970. 6.25 (ISBN 0-931992-04-4). Penns Valley.

Walls, David S. & Stephenson, John B., eds. Appalachia in the Sixties: Decade of Reawakening. LC 78-160052. (Illus.). 1979. pap. 6.50x (ISBN 0-8131-0135-2). U Pr of Ky.

Walls, Francine E. The Church Library Workbook. 152p. 1980. pap. 4.95 (ISBN 0-89367-048-0). Light & Life.

Walls, Fred. First Book of Puzzles & Brain Twisters. LC 70-100096. (First Bks). (gr. 4-6). 1970. PLB 4.90 o.p. (ISBN 0-531-00693-X). Watts.

Walls, Gordon L., jt. auth. see Rubin, Melvin L.

Walls, Ian G. Tomato Growing Today. 1973. 14.95 (ISBN 0-7153-5435-3). David & Charles.

Walls, Jerry G. Conchs, Tibias, & Harps. (Illus.). 192p. 1980. 9.95 (ISBN 0-87666-629-2, S-103). TFH Pubns.

Wallsten, Thomas S., ed. Cognitive Processes in Choice & Decision Behavior. LC 79-27553. (Illus.). 304p. 1980. text ed. 24.95 (ISBN 0-89859-054-X). L Erlbaum Assocs.

Wallwille, Maria. Merkwuerdige und Interessante Lebensgeschichte der Frau Von Wallwille, Welche Vier Jahre Lang an Eien Irokesen Verheyrathet War. LC 75-7054. (Indian Captivities Ser.: Vol. 32). 1976. Repr. of 1809 ed. lib. bdg. 44.00 (ISBN 0-8240-1656-4). Garland Pub.

Wallwork, J. F. Language & Linguistics. 1969. pap. text ed. 6.95x (ISBN 0-435-10916-2); wkbk. 3.50x (ISBN 0-435-10917-0). Heinemann Ed.

Wallwork, S. C. & Grant, D. J. Physical Chemistry. 3rd ed. (Longman Text Series). (Illus.). 1977. pap. text ed. 23.00x (ISBN 0-582-44254-0). Longman.

Wally, Herbert. Eskimos. (International Library Ser.). (Illus.). 128p. (gr. 7 up). 1976. PLB 6.90 o.p. (ISBN 0-531-02124-6). Watts.

Walmsley, Anne, ed. The Sun's Eye: West Indian Writing for Young Readers. (Illus.). 1977. pap. text ed. 4.00x (ISBN 0-582-76702-4). Longman.

Walmsley, Frank & Walmsley, Judith A. Between Alchemy & Technology: The Chemical Laboratory. (Illus.). 272p. 1975. pap. text ed. 11.95 (ISBN 0-13-075945-7). P-H.

Walmsley, Judith A., jt. auth. see Walmsley, Frank.

Walmsley, Keith, jt. auth. see Edge, Graham.

Walne, Peter R. Culture of Bivalve Molluscs: Fifty Years' Experience at Conwy. (Illus.). 190p. 16.25 (ISBN 0-85238-063-1, FN). Unipub.

Waloff, N., ed. see Royal Entomological Society of London, Ninth.

Walpole, Horace. Castle of Otranto. 1963. pap. 1.95 (ISBN 0-02-055200-9, Collier). Macmillan.

Walpole, Ronald E., jt. auth. see Freund, John E.

Walpole, Ronald N. The Old French Johannis Translation of the Pseudo-Turpin Chronicle: A Critical Edition. 1976. 26.75x (ISBN 0-520-02707-8); suppl. 39.50x (ISBN 0-520-02840-6). U of Cal Pr.

Walrath, Jane. Toby, the Rock Hound. (A Tell-a-Tale Reader Ser.). (Illus.). (gr. k-3). 1979. PLB 4.77 (ISBN 0-307-68408-3, Golden Pr). Western Pub.

Walrath, Jane D. My Little Book of Horses. (Tell-a-Tale Reader). 32p. (ps-3). PLB 4.77 (ISBN 0-307-68410-5, Golden Pr). Western Pub.

Walraven, Gail. Basic Arrythmias. new ed. (Illus.). 510p. (Orig.). 1980. pap. text ed. 14.95 (ISBN 0-87619-627-X). R J Brady.

--Handbook of Emergency Drugs. 100p. 1978. pap. text ed. 7.95 (ISBN 0-87618-949-4). R J Brady.

Walrond, Eric. Tropic Death. 192p. 1972. pap. 1.95 o.s.i. (ISBN 0-02-055250-5, Collier). Macmillan.

Walrond, Sallie. A Guide to Driving Horses: Pelham Horsemaster Ser. (Illus.). 1978. 14.00 (ISBN 0-7207-1009-X). Transatlantic.

Walrond-Skinner, Sue. Family Therapy: The Treatment of Natural Systems. (Library of Social Work). 1976. 19.00 (ISBN 0-7100-8325-4); pap. 8.95 (ISBN 0-7100-8326-2). Routledge & Kegan.

Walsberg, Glenn E. The Ecology & Energetics of Contrasting Social Systems in the Phainopepla. (Publications in Zoology: Vol. 108). 1977. 8.50x (ISBN 0-520-09562-6). U of Cal Pr.

Walschap, Gerald. Marriage: Bibliotheca Neerlandica Ser. Incl. Ordeal. 1963. 10.00 (ISBN 0-8277-0261-2). British Bk Ctr.

Walser, David, tr. see Jacobs, Joseph.

Walser, Martin. Ein Fliehendes Pferd. (Suhrkamp Taschenbuecher: St 600). 176p. (Ger.). 1980. pap. text ed. 3.90 (ISBN 3-518-37100-2, Pub. by Insel Verlag Germany). Suhrkamp.

Walser, Richard. Literary North Carolina: A Brief Historical Survey. (Illus.). 1970. 5.00; pap. 2.00 (ISBN 0-86526-048-6). NC Archives.

--North Carolina Legends. (Illus.). viii, 86p. (Orig.). 1980. 6.00 (ISBN 0-86526-145-8); pap. 2.50 (ISBN 0-86526-139-3). NC Archives.

Walsh, Annmarie H. The Public's Business: The Politics & Practices of Government Corporations. LC 77-15595. 456p. 1978. 23.00x (ISBN 0-262-23086-0); pap. 9.95 (ISBN 0-262-73055-3). MIT Pr.

Walsh, Audley V., jt. auth. see Scarne, John.

Walsh, Barry & Douglas, Peter. Fitness the Footballer's Way. (Illus., Orig.). 1978. pap. 2.95 (ISBN 0-8467-0428-5, Pub. by Two Continents). Hippocrene Bks.

--Getting Fit the Hard Way. (Illus.). 1981. 12.50 (ISBN 0-7137-1086-1, Pub. by Blandford Pr England). Sterling.

Walsh, Chad. Doors into Poetry. 2nd ed. 1970. pap. text ed. 9.50 (ISBN 0-13-218727-2). P-H.

--From Utopia to Nightmare. LC 71-38130. 190p. 1972. Repr. of 1962 ed. lib. bdg. 13.75x (ISBN 0-8371-6325-0, WAFU); pap. 4.95 (ISBN 0-8371-8959-4, WAF). Greenwood.

--Hang Me Up My Begging Bowl. LC 80-26136. 96p. 1981. 8.95 (ISBN 0-8040-0351-3); pap. 4.95 (ISBN 0-8040-0358-0). Swallow.

--The Literary Legacy of C. S. Lewis. 1979. 10.95 o.p. (ISBN 0-15-152725-3). HarBraceJ.

--A Rich Feast: Encountering the Bible from Genesis to Revelation. LC 80-8356. 192p. 1981. 9.95 (ISBN 0-06-069249-9, HarpR, HarpR). Har-Row.

Walsh, Christopher. Enzymatic Reaction Mechanisms. LC 78-18266. (Illus.). 1979. text ed. 34.95x (ISBN 0-7167-0070-0). W H Freeman.

Walsh, Colin, jt. auth. see Levanthal, Lance A.

Walsh, D., jt. auth. see Solymar, L.

Walsh, D. C. & Egdahl, R. H., eds. Women, Work, & Health: Challenge to Corporate Policy. (Springer Ser. on Industry & Health: Vol. 8). 259p. 1980. pap. 12.00 (ISBN 0-387-90478-6). Springer-Verlag.

Walsh, Don, ed. The Law of the Sea: Issues in Ocean Resource Management. LC 77-7823. (Praeger Special Studies). 1977. 29.95 (ISBN 0-03-022666-X). Praeger.

Walsh, Don, jt. ed. see Yen, Teh Fu.

Walsh, Donald & Kiddle, L. B., eds. Cuentos Americanos. 3rd ed. (Illus., Span.). 1970. pap. 5.95x (ISBN 0-393-09907-5, NortonC). Norton.

Walsh, Donald, tr. see Cardenal, Ernesto.

Walsh, Donald D. Introductory Spanish. 1946. 5.95x (ISBN 0-393-09454-5, NortonC). Norton.

Walsh, Donald D; see Levy, Harold L.

Walsh, Donald D. & Sturm, Harlan, eds. Repaso. rev. ed. (Sp) 1971. text ed. 9.95x (ISBN 0-393-09955-5, NortonC). Norton.

Walsh, Donald D., ed. see Cardenal, Ernesto.

Walsh, Donald D., ed. see Goytortua, Jesus.

Walsh, Donald D., tr. see Cabestrero, Teofilo.

Walsh, Edward M. Energy Conversion: Electromechanical, Direct, Nuclear. (Illus.). 1967. 21.95 (ISBN 0-8260-9125-3). Wiley.

Walsh, Frank E. & Center, Allen H. Public Relations Practices: Case Studies. 2nd ed. (Illus.). 352p. 1981. pap. text ed. 12.95 (ISBN 0-13-738716-4). P-H.

Walsh, Gene, ed. Werner Herzog: Images at the Horizon. Eberto, Roger. (Facets Multimedia Ser.). (Illus., Orig.). 1980. pap. 4.00 (ISBN 0-918432-26-X). NY Zoetrope.

Walsh, Harry H., ed. Phonology & Speech Remediation: A Book of Readings. LC 78-32109. (Illus.). 268p. text ed. 18.95 (ISBN 0-933014-52-X). College-Hill.

Walsh, Harry M. The Outlaw Gunner. LC 71-180856. (Illus.). 1971. 12.50 (ISBN 0-87033-162-0, Pub. by Tidewater). Cornell Maritime.

Walsh, J., jt. ed. see Delves, L. M.

Walsh, J. H. & Tomlinson, F. Fields of Experience. 1968. pap. text ed. 2.50x o.p. (ISBN 0-435-10921-9). Heinemann Ed.

Walsh, James & Walsh, Phyllis A. Golden Retrievers. (Illus.). 128p. 1980. 2.95 (ISBN 0-87666-678-0, KW 067). TFH Pubns.

Walsh, James, ed. The Cloud of Unknowing. (Classics of Western Spirituality Ser.). 1981. 11.95 (ISBN 0-8091-0314-1); pap. 7.95 (ISBN 0-8091-2332-0). Paulist Pr.

Walsh, James, tr. see Guigo II.

Walsh, James J. Cures: The Story of Cures That Failed. LC 70-137343. 1971. Repr. of 1923 ed. 20.00 (ISBN 0-8103-3773-8). Gale.

Walsh, James P. The First Rotarian. (Illus.). 351p. 1980. 14.95 (ISBN 0-906360-02-1). Scan Pub.

--The First Rotarian: The Life & Times of Percy Paul Harris, Founder of Rotary. Treadwell, Harry, ed. (Illus.). 351p. 1979. 40.00 (ISBN 0-906360-02-1). Heinman.

Walsh, Jill P. The Island Sunrise: Prehistoric Culture in the British Isles. LC 75-4666. (Illus.). 128p. (gr. 6-12). 1976. 8.95 (ISBN 0-395-28928-9, Clarion). HM.

--Toolmaker. LC 73-7126. (Illus.). (gr. 3-6). 1974. 4.95 o.p. (ISBN 0-8164-3109-4, Clarion). HM.

Walsh, Jill Paton. A Chance Child. 144p. (YA) 1980. pap. 1.95 (ISBN 0-380-48561-3, 48561). Avon.

Walsh, Jim, jt. auth. see Yorkis, Paul G.

Walsh, Joan, jt. auth. see Anglund, Joan W.

Walsh, John. First Book of Physical Fitness. (First Bks). (Illus.). (gr. 4-6). 1961. PLB 4.90 o.p. (ISBN 0-531-00610-7). Watts.

--First Book of the Olympic Games. rev. ed. LC 63-10379. (First Bks). (Illus.). (gr. 4-6). 1971. PLB 4.90 o.p. (ISBN 0-531-00601-8). Watts.

Walsh, John E. Mayflower Compact November Eleventh, Sixteen Twenty: The First Democratic Document in America. LC 73-134369. (Focus Bks). (Illus.). (gr. 7 up). 1971. PLB 4.47 o.p. (ISBN 0-531-01019-8); pap. 1.25 o.p. (ISBN 0-531-02327-3). Watts.

--The Philippine Insurrection, 1899-1902: America's Only Try for an Overseas Empire. LC 72-8817. (Focus Bks.). (Illus.). 72p. (gr. 7 up). 1973. PLB 6.45 (ISBN 0-531-02462-8). Watts.

--Plumes in the Dust: The Love Affair of Edgar Allen Poe & Fanny Osgood. LC 79-27534. (Illus.). 1980. 14.95 (ISBN 0-88229-683-3). Nelson-Hall.

--Rakes & Ruffians: The Underworld of Georgian Dublin. 3rd, rev. ed. 1979. Repr. of 1851 ed. 10.00x (ISBN 0-8476-6233-0). Rowman.

Walsh, John E., Jr. Guidelines for Management Consultants in Asia. LC 73-83083. 205p. 1973. 15.00 (ISBN 92-833-1028-4, APO29, APO). Unipub.

--Preparing Feasibility Studies in Asia. LC 72-323074. 168p. 1971. 15.00 (ISBN 92-833-1001-2, APO55, APO). Unipub.

Walsh, John E., Jr., jt. auth. see Smith, Shea.

Walsh, Ken. Sometimes I Weep. LC 73-12523. 128p. (Orig.). 1974. tanalin 1.95 o.p. (ISBN 0-8170-0623-0). Judson.

Walsh, Kilian, tr. Bernard of Clairvaux on the Song of Songs, Vol. I. (Cistercian Fathers Er.: No. 4). pap. 4.00 (ISBN 0-87907-104-4). Cistercian Pubns.

Walsh, Kilian & Edmonds, Irene, trs. Bernard of Clairvaux: Sermons on the Song of Songs, Vol. III. (Cistercian Fathers Ser.: No. 31). 1979. 15.95; pap. 5.00 (ISBN 0-87907-931-2). Cistercian Pubns.

Walsh, L. A., jt. auth. see Winn, Charles S.

Walsh, L. S. International Marketing. 272p. 1978. pap. text ed. 11.95x (ISBN 0-7121-0943-9, Pub. by Macdonald & Evans England). Intl Ideas.

Walsh, M. M. Dolly Purdo. 1977. pap. 1.50 o.p. (ISBN 0-425-03299-X). Berkley Pub.

Walsh, Marcus, ed. see Smart, Christopher.

Walsh, Marilyn, jt. auth. see Edelhertz, Herbert.

Walsh, Marilyn E. The Fence: A New Look at the World of Property Theft. LC 76-5266. (Contributions in Sociology Ser.: No. 21). (Illus., Orig.). 1976. lib. bdg. 15.00 (ISBN 0-8371-8910-1, WTF/). Greenwood.

Walsh, Michael J. Chemistry. Kaplan, Stanley H., ed. LC 57-58729. (High School Regents Exams & Answer Ser.). (gr. 9-12). 1977. pap. 3.95 (ISBN 0-8120-0109-5). Barron.

Walsh, Michael J., et al. Religious Bibliographies in Serial Literature: A Guide. LC 81-312. 224p. 1981. lib. bdg. 35.00 (ISBN 0-313-22987-2, WRB/). Greenwood.

Walsh, Myles E. Understanding Computers: All the Basics for Managers & Users. LC 80-20547. 296p. 1981. 20.95 (ISBN 0-471-08191-4, Pub. by Wiley-Interscience). Wiley.

Walsh, P. G. Livy: His Historical Aims & Methods. 1961. 39.00 (ISBN 0-521-06729-4). Cambridge U Pr.

--Roman Novel. LC 78-98700. 1970. 34.00 (ISBN 0-521-07658-7). Cambridge U Pr.

Walsh, Peter, ed. see Cohn, Marjorie B. & Siegfried, Susan L.

Walsh, Peter, ed. see Mochon, Anne.

Walsh, Peter, ed. see Simpson, Marianna S.

Walsh, Phyllis A., jt. auth. see Walsh, James.

Walsh, R. Toward an Ecology of the Brain. (Illus.). 285p. 1981. text ed. 35.00 (ISBN 0-89335-087-7). Spectrum Pub.

Walsh, Raoul. Each Man in His Time. 1974. 10.00 o.p. (ISBN 0-374-14553-9). FS&G.

Walsh, Richard & Fox, William L. Maryland: A History, 1632-1974. LC 74-11875. (Illus.). 1974. 12.50 (ISBN 0-938420-09-7). Md Hist.

Walsh, Robb. Kingdom of the Dwarfs. (Illus.). 144p. 1981. 14.95 (ISBN 0-87818-018-4); ltd. signed ed. 25.00 (ISBN 0-87818-019-2). Centaur.

Walsh, Robb see Wenzel, David.

Walsh, Roger & Vaughn, Frances. Beyond Ego. 272p. 1981. pap. 6.95 (ISBN 0-87477-175-7). J P Tarcher.

Walsh, Roger N. & Greenough, William T., eds. Environments As Therapy for Brain Dysfunction. LC 76-1116. (Advances in Behavioral Biology Ser.: Vol. 17). 376p. 1976. 35.00 (ISBN 0-306-37917-1, Plenum Pr). Plenum Pub.

Walsh, S. Zoe, et al. The Human Fetal & Neonatal Circulation: Function & Structure. (American Lectures in Cerebral Palsy Ser.). (Illus.). 368p. 1974. 21.75 (ISBN 0-398-02662-9). C C Thomas.

Walsh, T. J. Second Empire Opera. 1981. 35.00 (ISBN 0-7145-3659-8). Riverrun NY.

Walsh, T. J. & Healy, R. J. The Protection of Assets Manual. 1981. 212.00 (ISBN 0-930868-04-8). Merritt Co.

Walsh, Thomas, tr. see Valle-Inclan, Ramon.

Walsh, W. Bruce & Tyler, Leona. Tests & Measurements. 3rd ed. (Foundations of Modern Psychology Ser.). (Illus.). 1979. ref. 12.95 (ISBN 0-13-911859-4); pap. 7.95 ref. (ISBN 0-13-911842-X). P-H.

Walsh, W. H. An Introduction to Philosophy of History. 1981. pap. text ed. 9.75x (ISBN 0-391-02163-X, Hutchinson U Lib). Humanities.

Walsh, W. M. A Primer in Family Therapy. (Illus.). 152p. 1980. 13.50 (ISBN 0-398-03992-5). C C Thomas.

Walsh, William. D. J. Enright: Poet of Humanism. LC 73-90814. 120p. 1974. 18.95 (ISBN 0-521-20383-X). Cambridge U Pr.

Walsh, William H. Introduction to Philosophy of History. 3rd rev. ed. 1967. text ed. 7.50x (ISBN 0-391-00672-X); pap. text ed. 7.50x (ISBN 0-391-02163-X). Humanities.

Walsh, William M. Counseling Children & Adolescents. new ed. LC 75-5097. 424p. 1976. 20.00x (ISBN 0-8211-2253-3); text ed. 18.00x (ISBN 0-685-61056-X). McCutchan.

Walsh, William S. Curiosities of Popular Customs. LC 66-23951. 1966. Repr. of 1898 ed. 40.00 (ISBN 0-8103-3008-3). Gale.

--Handy Book of Curious Information, Comprising Strange Happenings in the Life of Men & Animals, Odd Statistics, Extraordinary Phenomena & Out of the Way Facts Concerning the Wonderlands of the Earth. LC 68-30583. 1970. Repr. of 1913 ed. 38.00 (ISBN 0-8103-3100-4). Gale.

--Handy-Book of Literary Curiosities. LC 68-24370. 1966. Repr. of 1892 ed. 44.00 (ISBN 0-8103-0162-8). Gale.

--Heroes & Heroines of Fiction, 2 vols. LC 66-29782. 1966. Repr. of 1915 ed. 22.00 ea.; Vol. 1, Classical. 18.00 (ISBN 0-8103-0167-9); Vol. 2, Modern. 14.00 (ISBN 0-8103-0163-6). Gale.

--Story of Santa Klaus: Told for Children of All Ages, from Six to Sixty. LC 68-58166. (Holiday Ser). (Illus.). 1970. Repr. of 1909 ed. 20.00 (ISBN 0-8103-3370-8). Gale.

Walsh, William Thomas. Our Lady of Fatima. pap. 3.50 (ISBN 0-385-02869-5, D1, Im). Doubleday.

Walshaw & Jobson. Mechanics of Fluids. 3rd. ed. 1979. pap. 22.00 (ISBN 0-582-44495-0). Longman.

Walshe, G. Recent Trends in Monopoly in Great Britain. (Illus.). 132p. 1974. 16.95x (ISBN 0-521-09863-7). Cambridge U Pr.

Walshe, M. O. A Middle High German Reader: With Grammar, Notes & Glossary. 232p. 1974. pap. text ed. 11.95x (ISBN 0-19-872082-3); pap. text ed. 8.95x (ISBN 0-19-872082-3). Oxford U Pr.

Walshe, Peter. The Rise of African Nationalism in South Africa: The African National Congress, 1912-1952. (Perspectives on Southern Africa: No. 3). 1971. 29.50x (ISBN 0-520-01810-9). U of Cal Pr.

Walshe, Shan. Plants of Quetico & the Ontario Shiels. (Illus.). 216p. 1980. 25.00 (ISBN 0-8020-3370-9); pap. 7.95 (ISBN 0-8020-3371-7). U of Toronto Pr.

Walstedt, Bertil. State Manufacturing Enterprise in a Mixed Economy: The Turkish Case. LC 78-21398. (World Bank Ser.). 192p. 1980. text ed. 25.00x (ISBN 0-8018-2226-2); pap. text ed. 9.95x (ISBN 0-8018-2227-0). Johns Hopkins.

--The Turkish Case: The Turkishcase. LC 78-21398. 1979. 14.00x o.p. (ISBN 0-8018-2226-2); pap. 5.95 o.p. (ISBN 0-8018-2227-0). Johns Hopkins.

Walster, et al. Equity: Theory & Research. 1978. pap. text ed. 11.95 (ISBN 0-205-05929-5). Allyn.

Walster, Elaine H., jt. auth. see Berscheid, Ellen.

Walston, jt. auth. see Walston, Betty J.

Walston, Betty J. & Walston. The Nurse Assistant in Long Term Care: A New Era. LC 80-12308. (Illus.). 1980. pap. text ed. 8.95 (ISBN 0-8016-5355-X). Mosby.

Walstrom, Gordon J. Revelation of Israel's Messiah: The Seven Churches, Vol. 1. 1980. 11.95 (ISBN 0-533-04581-9). Vantage.

Walt, B. Van der see Van der Walt, B.

Walt Disley Studio, illus. Walt Disney's Nursery Tales. 1971. 4.95 (ISBN 0-307-12068-6, Golden Pr); PLB 9.15 o.p. (ISBN 0-307-62068-9). Western Pub.

Walt Disney. Donald Duck: Instant Millionaire. (Young Reader Ser.). (Illus.). (gr. k-3). 1979. PLB 5.00 (ISBN 0-307-60140-4, Golden Pr). Western Pub.

--Mickey Mouse & Goofy: The Big Bear Scare. (Young Reader Ser.). (gr. k-3). 1979. PLB 5.00 (ISBN 0-307-60318-0, Golden Pr). Western Pub.

Walt Disney Productions. ABC. (ps-1). 1979. PLB 6.08 (ISBN 0-307-61080-2, Golden Pr); pap. 1.95 o.p. (ISBN 0-307-11080-X). Western Pub.

--The Aristocats. LC 73-15626. (Illus.). 48p. 1974. 3.95 o.p. (ISBN 0-394-82553-5, BYR); PLB 4.99 o.p. (ISBN 0-394-92553-X). Random.

--The Black Hole. Davis, Edith, ed. (Illus.). 48p. (gr. 1-7). 1979. pap. 2.50 o.p. (ISBN 0-307-13505-5, Golden Pr). Western Pub.

--Black Hole. (Young Reader). 24p. (ps-3). 1980. PLB 5.00 (ISBN 0-307-60105-6, Golden Pr). Western Pub.

--Black Hole. (Illus.). (gr. 6-12). 1979. PLB 9.15 o.p. (ISBN 0-307-65305-6, Golden Pr). Western Pub.

--Black Hole. (gr. 4-8). 1979. PLB 7.62 (ISBN 0-307-65306-4, Golden Pr). Western Pub.

--The Black Hole. Davis, Edith, ed. (Illus.). 24p. (ps-3). 1979. 2.50 o.p. (ISBN 0-307-13506-3, Golden Pr). Western Pub.

--The Book of Tall Tales: Featuring "The Shaggy Dog". LC 77-74466. (Disney's World of Adventure). (Illus.). (gr. 2-6). 1978. 3.95 (ISBN 0-394-83596-4, BYR); PLB 4.99 (ISBN 0-394-93596-9). Random.

--Cars! Cars! Cars! Featuring "The Love Bug" & Other Fun on Wheels. LC 77-74465. (Disney's World of Adventure). (Illus.). (gr. 2-6). 1977. 3.95 (ISBN 0-394-83598-0, BYR); PLB 4.99 (ISBN 0-394-93598-5). Random.

--The Circus Book Featuring "Toby Tyler". LC 77-74462. (Disney's World of Adventure). (Illus.). (gr. 2-6). 1978. 3.95 (ISBN 0-394-83597-2, BYR); PLB 4.99 (ISBN 0-394-93597-7). Random.

--Counting. 32p. (ps-1). 1979. PLB 6.08 (ISBN 0-307-61076-4, Golden Pr); pap. 1.95 o.p. (ISBN 0-307-11076-1, Golden Pr). Western Pub.

--Donald Duck & the Super-Sticky Secret. (Tell-a-Tale Reader). 32p. (ps-3). 1980. PLB 4.77 (ISBN 0-307-68425-3, Golden Pr). Western Pub.

--Donald Duck Goes Camping. (Tell-a-Tale Readers). (Illus.). (gr. k-3). 1979. PLB 4.77 (ISBN 0-307-68609-4, Whitman). Western Pub.

--The Fox Finds a Friend. (Sturdy Shape Bks). 14p. (ps). 1981. 2.95 (ISBN 0-307-12261-1, Golden Pr). Western Pub.

--Friends to Find. (Winnie-the-Pooh Hunny Pot Bks.). 24p. (ps-3). 1980. PLB 5.38 (ISBN 0-307-68874-7, Golden Pr). Western Pub.

--Goofy Keeps Fit. (ps-1). 1979. PLB 6.08 (ISBN 0-307-61079-9, Golden Pr); pap. 1.95 o.p. (ISBN 0-307-11079-6). Western Pub.

--Goofy Presents the Olympics: A Fun & Exciting History of the Olympics from the Ancient Games to Today. LC 79-18177. (Illus.). 128p. (gr. 2-6). 1980. 6.95 (ISBN 0-394-84224-3, BYR); PLB 6.99 (ISBN 0-394-94224-8). Random.

--Hidden Pictures. (Winnie-the-Pooh Hunny Pot Bks.). 24p. (ps-3). 1980. PLB 5.38 (ISBN 0-307-68873-9, Golden Pr). Western Pub.

--The Hound Finds a Friend. (Sturdy Shape Bks). 14p. (ps). 1981. 2.95 (ISBN 0-307-12264-6, Golden Pr). Western Pub.

--How It Happens. (ps-1). 1979. PLB 6.08 (ISBN 0-307-61078-0, Golden Pr). Western Pub.

--Jokes & Riddles. (Winnie-the-Pooh Hunny Pot Bk.). 24p. (ps-3). 1980. PLB 5.38 (ISBN 0-307-68869-0, Golden Pr). Western Pub.

--The Love Bug. LC 78-13896. (Walt Disney's Wonderful World of Reading Ser.). (Illus.). (gr. k-3). 1979. 3.95 o.p. (ISBN 0-394-84139-5, BYR); PLB 4.39 o.p. (ISBN 0-394-94139-X). Random.

--Magic Tricks. (Winnie-the-Pooh Hunny Pot Bk.). 24p. (ps-3). 1980. PLB 5.38 (ISBN 0-307-68870-4, Golden Pr). Western Pub.

--The Outdoor Adventure Book. LC 77-74468. (Disney's World of Adventure). (Illus.). (gr. 2-6). 1977. 3.95 (ISBN 0-394-83601-4, BYR); PLB 4.99 (ISBN 0-394-93601-9). Random.

--Puzzles. (Winnie-the-Pooh Hunny Pot Bk.). 24p. (ps-3). 1980. PLB 5.38 (ISBN 0-307-68872-0, Golden Pr). Western Pub.

--That's What Friends Are for. (Look Look Bks.). (Illus.). 24p. (ps-k). 1981. pap. 1.25 (ISBN 0-307-11859-2, Golden Pr). Western Pub.

--The Underwater Adventure Book Featuring "20,000 Leagues Under the Sea". LC 77-90198. (Disney's World of Adventure Ser). (gr. 3-7). 1978. 3.95 (ISBN 0-394-83602-2, BYR); PLB 4.99 (ISBN 0-394-93602-7). Random.

--Walt Disney Productions Presents Goofy's Gags. LC 74-2043. (Disney's Wonderful World of Reading Ser: No. 19). (Illus.). 48p. (ps-3). 1974. 3.95 (ISBN 0-394-82558-6, BYR); PLB 4.99 (ISBN 0-394-92558-0). Random.

--Walt Disney Productions Presents "the Rescuers". LC 76-54412. (Disney's Wonderful World of Reading: No. 37). (Illus.). (ps-2). 1977. 3.95 (ISBN 0-394-83456-9, BYR); PLB 4.99 (ISBN 0-394-93456-3). Random.

--Walt Disney Productions Presents The Haunted House. LC 75-16430. (Disney's Wonderful World of Reading Ser.: No. 33). (Illus.). 48p. (ps-3). 1976. 3.95 (ISBN 0-394-82570-5, BYR); PLB 4.99 (ISBN 0-394-92570-X). Random.

--Walt Disney Productions Presents The Mystery of the Missing Peanuts. LC 75-1088. (Disney's Wonderful World of Reading Ser: No. 30). (Illus.). 48p. (gr. 1-2). 1975. 3.95 (ISBN 0-394-82572-1, BYR); PLB 4.99 (ISBN 0-394-92572-6). Random.

--Walt Disney's Cinderella. LC 74-22325. (Disney's Wonderful World of Reading Ser.: No. 16). (Illus.). 48p. (ps-3). 1974. 3.95 (ISBN 0-394-82552-7, BYR); PLB 4.99 (ISBN 0-394-92552-1). Random.

--Walt Disney's Mickey Mouse & Donald Duck at the Circus. (Colorforms Bks.). (Illus.). (ps-2). 1973. 2.95 o.p. (ISBN 0-394-82656-6, BYR). Random.

--Walt Disney's One Hundred One Dalmations. LC 74-10829. (Disney's Wonderful World of Reading: No. 23). (Illus.). 48p. (ps-3). 1975. 3.95 (ISBN 0-394-82571-3, BYR); PLB 4.99 (ISBN 0-394-92571-8). Random.

--Walt Disney's Peter & the Wolf. LC 74-6423. (Disney's Wonderful World of Reading Ser.: No. 20). (Illus.). 48p. (ps-3). 1974. 3.95 (ISBN 0-394-82563-2, BYR); PLB 4.99 (ISBN 0-394-92563-7). Random.

--Walt Disney's Snow White & the Seven Dwarfs. (Disney's Wonderful World of Reading Ser: No. 8). (Illus.). (ps-3). 1973. 3.95 (ISBN 0-394-82625-6, BYR); PLB 4.99 (ISBN 0-394-92625-0). Random.

--Walt Disney's the Brave Little Tailor. LC 74-1253. (Disney's Wonderful World of Reading Ser.: No. 18). (Illus.). 48p. (ps-3). 1974. 3.95 (ISBN 0-394-82559-4, BYR); PLB 4.99 (ISBN 0-394-92559-9). Random.

--Walt Disney's Winnie the Pooh & Tigger Too. LC 75-20349. (Disney's Wonderful World of Reading Ser: No. 35). (Illus.). 48p. (ps-3). 1976. 3.95 (ISBN 0-394-82569-1, BYR); PLB 4.99 (ISBN 0-394-92569-6). Random.

Walt Disney Productions, illus. Walt Disney Character Tubby Book. (Tubby Bks.). (Illus.). 10p. (ps). 1980. vinyl book 2.95 (ISBN 0-671-41334-1, Pub. by Windmill). S&S.

Walt Disney Studio. Bambi, Friends of the Forest. (Illus.). (gr. k-3). 1976. PLB 5.00 (ISBN 0-307-60132-3, Golden Pr). Western Pub.

--Donald Duck & the Witch Next Door. (Illus.). (ps-3). 1976. PLB 5.00 (ISBN 0-307-60217-6, Golden Pr). Western Pub.

--Mickey Mouse & the Marvelous Smell Machine. (A Golden Fragrance Book Ser.). (Illus.). (gr. k-3). 1979. PLB 9.92 (ISBN 0-307-64544-4, Golden Pr); pap. 4.95 (ISBN 0-307-13544-6). Western Pub.

--Pooh & Piglet's Book of Big & Little. (A Golden Story Book Ser.). (Illus.). (gr. k-3). 1979. PLB 9.15 (ISBN 0-307-62368-8, Golden Pr); pap. 1.95 (ISBN 0-307-12368-5). Western Pub.

--Pooh Sleepytime Stories. (A Golden Story Book Ser.). (Illus.). (gr. k-3). 1979. PLB 9.15 (ISBN 0-307-63735-2, Golden Pr); pap. 3.95 (ISBN 0-307-13735-X). Western Pub.

--Tigger & Winnie-the-Pooh. (Illus.). (ps-1). 1968. PLB 5.38 (ISBN 0-307-68948-4, Golden Pr). Western Pub.

--Walt Disney's Alice in Wonderland. (Illus.). 1951. 1.95 (ISBN 0-307-10426-5, Golden Pr); PLB 7.62 (ISBN 0-307-60426-8). Western Pub.

--Walt Disney's Bambi. (Illus.). (gr. k-3). 1941. 1.95 (ISBN 0-307-10450-8, Golden Pr); PLB 7.62 (ISBN 0-307-60450-0). Western Pub.

--Walt Disney's Cinderella. (Illus.). (ps-2). 1950. PLB 5.00 (ISBN 0-307-60114-5, Golden Pr). Western Pub.

--Walt Disney's Peter & the Wolf. (Illus.). (gr. k-3). 1976. PLB 5.00 (ISBN 0-307-60056-4, Golden Pr). Western Pub.

--Walt Disney's Pinocchio. (Illus.). (gr. k-3). 1953. 1.95 (ISBN 0-307-10580-6, Golden Pr); PLB 7.62 (ISBN 0-307-60580-9). Western Pub.

--Walt Disney's Snow White & the Seven Dwarfs. (Illus.). (gr. 1-4). 1952. 1.95 (ISBN 0-307-10451-6, Golden Pr); PLB 7.62 (ISBN 0-307-60451-9). Western Pub.

--Walt Disney's Story Land. (Illus.). (gr. 1-5). 1962. 6.95 (ISBN 0-307-16547-7, Golden Pr); PLB 13.77 (ISBN 0-307-66547-X). Western Pub.

Walt Disney Studio, illus. Walt Disney's Mother Goose. (Illus.). (gr. k-2). 1970. 1.95 (ISBN 0-307-10878-3, Golden Pr); PLB 7.62 (ISBN 0-307-60878-6). Western Pub.

Walt Disney Studios. Donald Duck & the Magic Mailbox. (Golden Look-Look Bks.). (ps-3). 1978. PLB 5.38 (ISBN 0-307-61851-X, Golden Pr); pap. 0.95 (ISBN 0-307-11851-7). Western Pub.

--Donald Duck, It's Play Time! (A Big Picture Bks.). 24p. (gr. k-3). PLB 7.62 (ISBN 0-307-60828-X, Golden Pr); pap. 1.95 (ISBN 0-307-10828-7). Western Pub.

--Hello, Winnie-the-Pooh! (Boxed Golden Bks. Ser.). (Contains 2 Little Golden Books, 2 Tell-A-Tale Books, 1 Shape Book & an activity book.). (ps-2). 1977. 3.95 set (ISBN 0-307-13692-2, Golden Pr). Western Pub.

--Mickey Mouse & the Great Lot Plot. (Illus.). 24p. (gr. k-3). 1976. PLB 5.00 (ISBN 0-307-60129-3, Golden Pr). Western Pub.

--Mickey Mouse, Hideaway Island. (A Big Picture Bks.). 24p. (gr. k-3). 1979. PLB 7.62 (ISBN 0-307-60829-8, Golden Pr); pap. 1.95 (ISBN 0-307-10829-5). Western Pub.

--Snow White & the Seven Dwarfs. (Young Reader Ser.). (Illus.). 24p. (gr. k-3). 1976. PLB 5.00 (ISBN 0-307-60066-1, Golden Pr); pap. 1.95 (ISBN 0-307-10451-6). Western Pub.

--Walt Disney's Christmas Parade. 1977. pap. 1.95 o.p. (ISBN 0-307-11191-1, Golden Pr). Western Pub.

--Walt Disney's Winnie-the-Pooh Meets Tigger. (Illus.). 1973. 1.95 (ISBN 0-307-10869-4, Golden Pr); PLB 7.62 (ISBN 0-307-60869-7). Western Pub.

Walt Disney Studios, illus. Walt Disney's Mickey & His Friends. (Kids Paperbacks). (Illus.). (ps-4). 1977. PLB 7.62 (ISBN 0-307-62364-5, Golden Pr); pap. 1.95 (ISBN 0-307-12364-2). Western Pub.

Waltar & Reynolds. Fast Breeder Reactors. 550p. Date not set. text ed. 35.00 (ISBN 0-08-025983-9); pap. text ed. 20.00 (ISBN 0-08-025982-0). Pergamon.

Walt Disney Productions. Walt Disney's Gulliver Mickey. LC 74-23399. (Disney's Wonderful World of Reading Ser: No. 27). (Illus.). 48p. (gr. 1-2). 1975. 3.95 (ISBN 0-394-82561-6, BYR); PLB 4.99 (ISBN 0-394-92561-0). Random.

Walter, Bruno. Gustav Mahler. Galston, James, tr. LC 78-87691. (Music Ser). 1970. Repr. of 1941 ed. lib. bdg. 19.50 (ISBN 0-306-71701-8). Da Capo.

--Theme & Variations: An Autobiography. Galston, James A., tr. from Ger. LC 80-25558. (Illus.). xi, 344p. 1981. Repr. of 1946 ed. lib. bdg. 35.00x (ISBN 0-313-22635-0, WATV). Greenwood.

Walter, C. Illustrated Skiing Dictionary for Young People. 1980. pap. 2.50 (ISBN 0-13-450858-0). P-H.

Walter, Carlton H. Traveling Wave Antennas. 1970. pap. text ed. 5.00 o.p. (ISBN 0-486-62669-5). Dover.

Walter, Claire. Illustrated Skiing Dictionary for Young People. LC 80-81790. (Illustrated Dictionaries). (Illus.). 128p. (gr. 4 up). 1981. PLB 6.89 (ISBN 0-8178-0017-4). Harvey.

Walter, D. Men & Music in Western Culture. 1969. pap. 8.95 o.p. (ISBN 0-13-574871-2). P-H.

Walter, Daniel. A Little Beard Book. (Illus.). 1975. pap. 2.00 (ISBN 0-686-22349-7). Oll Korrect.

--Spasmic Vistas. (Illus.). 1974. pap. 2.50 (ISBN 0-686-22348-9). Oll Korrect.

Walter, Ernest, ed. The Technique of the Film Cutting Room. 2nd ed. (Library of Communication Techniques). Date not set. 15.50 o.p. (ISBN 0-8038-7132-5). Hastings.

Walter, Eugene. American Cooking: Southern Style. (Foods of the World Ser). (Illus.). 1971. 14.95 (ISBN 0-8094-0051-0). Time-Life.

--American Cooking: Southern Style. LC 76-173191. (Foods of the World Ser.). (Illus.). (gr. 6 up). 1971. lib. bdg. 14.94 (ISBN 0-8094-0078-2, Pub. by Time-Life). Silver.

Walter, Eugene J., Jr. Why Animals Behave the Way They Do. (Illus.). 64p. (gr. 5 up). 1981. 9.95 (ISBN 0-684-16879-0). Scribner.

Walter, Gordon A. The Handbook of Experiential Learning & Change. 600p. 1981. 29.95 (ISBN 0-471-08355-0, Pub. by Wiley-Interscience). Wiley.

Walter, H. Horse Keepers Encyclopedia. LC 78-9000. 1979. pap. 2.95 o.p. (ISBN 0-668-04601-5). Arc Bks.

Walter, Ingo. International Economics. 2nd ed. 1975. 23.95 (ISBN 0-471-06644-3). Wiley.

--International Economics. 3rd ed. LC 80-21541. 528p. 1981. text ed. 19.95 (ISBN 0-471-04957-3). Wiley.

Walter, Ingo, jt. auth. see Gladwin, Thomas N.

Walter, Ingo, ed. Studies in International Environmental Economics. LC 75-38614. 364p. 1976. 40.95 (ISBN 0-471-91927-6, Pub. by Wiley-Interscience). Wiley.

Walter, Ingo I. see Altman, Edward I.

Walter, J. A. Sacred Cows. 224p. 1980. pap. 5.95 (ISBN 0-310-42421-6). Zondervan.

Walter, James. The Leader: A Political Biography of Gough Whitlam. (Illus.). 295p. 1981. text ed. 18.00x (ISBN 0-7022-1557-0). U of Queensland Pr.

Walter, John B. An Introduction to the Principles of Disease. LC 76-27063. (Illus.). 1977. text ed. 18.95 (ISBN 0-7216-9114-5). Saunders.

Walter, Mildred P. Ty's One-Man Band. LC 80-11224. (Illus.). 40p. (gr. k-3). 1980. 9.95 (ISBN 0-590-07580-2, Four Winds). Schol Bk Serv.

Walter, Ralph. Unmet Needs in Secondary Education. 144p. 1981. 5.00 (ISBN 0-8059-2773-5). Dorrance.

Walter, Richard J. Socialist Party of Argentina 1890-1930. LC 77-620003. (Latin American Monographs: No. 42). 1977. text ed. 14.95x (ISBN 0-292-77539-3); pap. text ed. 7.95 (ISBN 0-292-77540-7). U of Tex Pr.

Walters, A. A. Introduction to Econometrics. 1970. text ed. 12.95x (ISBN 0-393-09931-8, NortonC). Norton.

--Noise & Prices. (Illus.). 160p. 1975. 24.00x (ISBN 0-19-828197-8). Oxford U Pr.

Walters, Alan A., jt. auth. see Bennathan, Esra.

Walters, Alphonse J. Stanleys Emin Pasha Expedition. LC 80-1910. (Illus.). 1981. Repr. of 1890 ed. 43.00 (ISBN 0-404-18988-1). AMS Pr.

Walters, Sr. Annette & O'Hara, Sr. Kevin. Persons & Personality: An Introduction to Psychology. LC 52-13695. (Century Psychology Ser). 1953. 24.00x (ISBN 0-89197-550-0). Irvington.

Walters Art Gallery. Jewelry: Ancient to Modern. 1980. 35.00 (ISBN 0-670-40697-X, Studio). Viking Pr.

Walters, C. Etta. Mother-Infant Interaction. LC 74-12621. 1976. text ed. 22.95 (ISBN 0-87705-240-9); pap. text ed. 9.95 (ISBN 0-87705-284-0). Human Sci Pr.

Walters, C. Glenn. Consumer Behavior, Theory & Practice. 3rd ed. 1978. text ed. 18.95 (ISBN 0-256-01999-1). Irwin.

Walters, David W. The Intelligent Investor's Guide to Real Estate. LC 80-17718. (Professional Practitioners Ser.). 352p. 1980. 17.95 (ISBN 0-471-07874-3, Pub. by Ronald). Wiley.

Walters, Donald N. Reader: An Introduction to Oral Interpretation. LC 66-12939. (Orig.). 1966. pap. 2.65 o.p. (ISBN 0-672-63096-6). Odyssey Pr.

Walters, Dorothy. Flannery O'Connor. (U. S. Authors Ser.: No. 216). 1971. lib. bdg. 9.95 (ISBN 0-8057-0556-2). Twayne.

Walters, Dottie. Never Underestimate the Selling Power of a Woman. 1978. pap. 4.95 (ISBN 0-8119-0392-3). Fell.

Walters, Dottie, ed. Here Is Genius. (Illus.). 402p. 1980. 11.95 (ISBN 0-8119-0351-6). Fell.

--The Pearl of Potentiality. LC 79-91548. 296p. 1980. 11.95 (ISBN 0-8119-0338-9, Pub. by Royal CBC). Fell.

--Success Secrets of Successful Women. LC 78-68596. (Illus.). 276p. 1978. 11.95 (ISBN 0-8119-0339-7, Pub. by Royal CBC). Fell.

Walters, Douglas B., ed. Safe Handling of Chemical Carcinogens, Mutagens Teratogens & Highly Toxic Substances. LC 79-88922. 1980. Vol. 1. 33.95 (ISBN 0-250-40303-X); Vol. 2. 33.95 (ISBN 0-250-40354-4). Ann Arbor Science.

Walters, Elsa H. & Castle, E. B. Principles of Education. 1967. pap. text ed. 8.95x (ISBN 0-04-370018-7). Allen Unwin.

Walters, Gary C. & Grusec, Joan E. Punishment. LC 76-30920. (Psychology Ser.). (Illus.). 1977. text ed. 19.95x (ISBN 0-7167-0366-1); pap. text ed. 10.95x (ISBN 0-7167-0365-3). W H Freeman.

Walters, Gary H., jt. ed. see Feldman, Lawrence H.

Walters, Hugh. The Caves of Drach. LC 79-670249. (gr. 8-11). 1979. 9.95 (ISBN 0-571-11037-1, Pub. by Faber & Faber). Merrimack Bk Serv.

--The Dark Triangle. 128p. (gr. 5-12). 1981. 13.95 (ISBN 0-571-11584-5, Pub. by Faber & Faber). Merrimack Bk Serv.

--Murder on Mars. 1978. 6.95 o.p. (ISBN 0-571-10717-6, Pub. by Faber & Faber). Merrimack Bk Serv.

--Terror by Satellite. (Fanfares Ser.). (gr. 4 up). 1980. pap. 3.25 (ISBN 0-571-11492-X, Pub. by Faber & Faber). Merrimack Bk Serv.

Walters, J. Cummings. Tennyson, Poet, Philosopher, Idealist. 370p. 1980. Repr. of 1893 ed. lib. bdg. 40.00 (ISBN 0-89984-505-3). Century Bookbindery.

Walters, Janet L., jt. auth. see Bernace, Salvatore.

Walters, Jerry. Walt Disney's Dumbo: On Land, on Sea, in the Air. (Disney's Wonderful World of Reading Ser.: No. 1). (Illus.). (ps-3). 1973. 3.95 (ISBN 0-394-82518-7, BYR); PLB 4.99 (ISBN 0-394-92518-1). Random.

Walters, John & Parker, Michael. Keeping Chickens. (Illus.). 1979. 8.95 (ISBN 0-7207-0882-6, Pub. by Michael Joseph). Merrimack Bk Serv.

--Keeping Ducks, Geese & Turkeys. (Gardening Farming Ser.). 1976. 8.95 (ISBN 0-7207-0932-6, Pub. by Michael Joseph). Merrimack Bk Serv.

Walters, Julie. This Little Light of Mine: A Pre-School Religion Program. 1974. pap. tchrs. manual 1.95 o.p. (ISBN 0-87793-069-4); pap. parents manual 0.95 o.p. (ISBN 0-87793-070-8). Ave Maria.

Walters, Kenneth. Rheometry: Industrial Applications. 432p. 1981. write for info. (ISBN 0-471-27878-5, Pub. by Wiley-Interscience). Wiley.

Walters, LeRoy, jt. auth. see Beauchamp, Tom L.

Walters, Margaret. The Nude Male: A New Perspective. (Illus.). 1979. pap. 8.95 o.p. (ISBN 0-14-005188-0). Penguin.

Walters, Michael. The Complete Birds of the World. LC 79-56434. 256p. 1980. 38.00 (ISBN 0-7153-7666-7). David & Charles.

Walters, Patricia, et al. Women in Top Jobs: Four Studies in Achievement. (Political & Economic Planning Ser.). 1971. text ed. 35.00x (ISBN 0-04-331046-X). Allen Unwin.

Walters, Peter. The Text of the Septuagint: Its Corruption & Their Emendations. Gooding, D. W., ed. LC 74-161292. (Illus.). 440p. 1972. 77.00 (ISBN 0-521-07977-2). Cambridge U Pr.

Walters, R., jt. auth. see Blake, O.

Walters, Raymond. Alexander James Dallas, Lawyer-Politician-Financier. LC 75-86582. (American Scene Ser.). 1969. Repr. of 1943 ed. lib. bdg. 27.50 (ISBN 0-306-71814-6). Da Capo.

Walters, Ronald. Black America & International Issues. 1981. 12.95 (ISBN 0-933184-04-2); pap. 6.95 (ISBN 0-933184-05-0). Flame Intl.

Walters, S. George, jt. auth. see Sweet, Morris L.

Walters, S. M. Shaping of Cambridge Botany. (Illus.). 128p. Date not set. price not set (ISBN 0-521-23795-5). Cambridge U Pr.

Walters, Sally, jt. ed. see Wright, Michael.

Walters, Susan, ed. Canadian Almanac & Directory 1980. (Illus.). 1980. text ed. 59.95x (ISBN 0-8464-0232-7). Beekman Pubs.

Walters, Thomas N., jt. auth. see Stein, Allen F.

Walters, Thomas R. & Desposito, Franklin. Pediatric Hematology & Oncology Continuing Educaion Review. 1975. spiral bdg. 12.00 o.p. (ISBN 0-87488-360-1). Med Exam.

Walters, Vivienne. Class Inequality & Health Care: The Origins & Impact of the National Health Service. 175p. 1980. 26.00x (ISBN 0-85664-685-7, Pub. by Croom Helm Ltd England). Biblio Dist.

Walters, William, Jr. The Practice of Real Estate Management: For the Experienced Property Manager. Kirk, Nancye J., ed. LC 79-84053. 1979. 21.95 (ISBN 0-912104-37-6). Inst Real Estate.

Walthall, Joe E. & Love, Harold D. Habilitation of the Mentally Retarded Individual. (Illus.). 224p. 1974. 13.75 (ISBN 0-398-02908-3). C C Thomas.

Walthall, Joe E., jt. auth. see Love, Harold D.

Walthall, Melvin. Lightning Forward: A History of the 25th Infantry Division (Tropic Lightning) 1941-1978. 1979. 10.00 o.p. (ISBN 0-686-67704-8). Exposition.

Waltham, A. C., ed. Limestones & Caves of North-West England. (Illus.). 1974. 22.50 (ISBN 0-7153-6181-3). David & Charles.

Waltham, J. E. & Holmes, W. D. North East England. 2nd ed. LC 78-68119. (Geography of the British Isles). (Illus.). (YA) 1979. pap. 6.95x (ISBN 0-521-22473-X). Cambridge U Pr.

Walther, Elizabeth K., jt. auth. see Bluske, Margaret K.

Walther, James A. New Testament Greek Workbook: An Inductive Study of the Complete Text of the Gospel of John. LC 80-23762. (Illus.). 1981. lib. bdg. 12.00x (ISBN 0-226-87239-4). U of Chicago Pr.

--New Testament Greek Workbook: Inductive Study of the Complete Text of the Gospel of John. (Illus.). 1966. 11.00x o.s.i. (ISBN 0-226-87238-6). U of Chicago Pr.

Walther, Rudolph. Technical Dictionary of Production Engineering (English-German) 1973. text ed. 46.00 (ISBN 0-08-016959-7). Pergamon.

Walther, Tom. Make Mine Music: How to Make & Play Instruments & Why They Work. (Brown Paper School Ser.). (Illus.). 128p. (Orig.). (gr. 3-up). 1981. 9.95 (ISBN 0-316-92111-4); pap. 5.95 (ISBN 0-316-92112-2). Little.

Walther Von Der Vogelweide. Walther Von der Vogelweide: Gedichte (Mittelhochdeutscher Text und Uebertragung) 291p. 1965. pap. 2.60x o.p. (ISBN 0-685-47486-0). Schoenhof.

Waltman, Jerold. Copying Other Nations' Policies: Two American Case Studies. LC 80-12083. 110p. 1981. text ed. 11.25x (ISBN 0-87073-832-1). Schenkman.

Waltman, Stephen R. & Krupin, Theodore. Complications in Opthalmic Surgery. (Illus.). 333p. 1980. text ed. 37.00 (ISBN 0-397-50441-1). Lippincott.

Waltner, Elma & Waltner, Willard. Heritage Hobbycraft. LC 77-19087. 1978. lib. bdg. 7.95 (ISBN 0-8313-0105-8); pap. 7.95. Lantern.

Waltner, Elma, jt. auth. see Waltner, Willard.

Waltner, Willard & Waltner, Elma. Holiday Hobbycraft. (gr. 6 up). 1964. 6.70 o.p. (ISBN 0-8313-0093-0). Lantern.

Waltner, Willard, jt. auth. see Waltner, Elma.

Walton, A. W. & Henry, C. D., eds. Cenzoic Geology of the Trans-Pecos Volcanic Field of Texas. 202p. 1979. write for info. (GB 19). Bur Econ Geology.

Walton, Anne. Molecular & Crystal Structure Models. LC 78-40227. 1978. 27.95 (ISBN 0-470-26356-3). Halsted Pr.

Walton, Charles. Music Literature for Analysis & Study. 1972. pap. 13.95x (ISBN 0-534-00163-7). Wadsworth Pub.

Walton, Charles W. Basic Forms in Music. LC 73-81046. 1974. text ed. 9.95x (ISBN 0-88284-010-X). Alfred Pub.

Walton, Clarence, jt. auth. see Eells, Richard.

Walton, Clarence, ed. The Ethics of Corporate Conduct. (American Assembly Ser.). (Illus.). 1977. pap. 4.95 (ISBN 0-13-290536-1, Spec). P-H.

Walton, Clyde C., ed. see Ware, Eugene F.

Walton, Ed. The Rookies. LC 80-5892. 288p. 1981. 14.95 (ISBN 0-8128-2778-3). Stein & Day.

Walton, G., jt. auth. see Shepherd, J. F.

Walton, G. M. & Shepherd, J. F. The Economic Rise of Early America. LC 78-13438. (Illus.). 1979. 26.95 (ISBN 0-521-22282-6); pap. 6.50x (ISBN 0-521-29433-9). Cambridge U Pr.

Walton, Hanes, Jr. Black Political Parties: An Historical & Political Analysis. LC 76-143514. 1972. 10.95 (ISBN 0-02-933870-0). Free Pr.

--Black Republicans: The Politics of the Black & Tans. LC 75-6718. 217p. 1975. 10.00 (ISBN 0-8108-0811-0). Scarecrow.

--Political Philosophy of Martin Luther King Jr. LC 76-111260. (Contributions in Afro-American & African Studies: No. 10). 1971. text ed. 13.95 (ISBN 0-8371-4661-5); pap. 4.95 (ISBN 0-8371-8931-4). Negro U Pr.

--The Study & Analysis of Black Politics: A Bibliography. LC 73-12985. 1973. 10.00 (ISBN 0-8108-0665-7). Scarecrow.

Walton, Harry. Home & Workshop Guide to Sharpening. (Everday Handbook Ser.). (Illus.). 160p. 1974. pap. 2.95 o.p. (ISBN 0-06-463418-3, 418, EH). Har-Row.

Walton, Izaak. Compleat Angler. 1953. 6.00x (ISBN 0-460-00070-5, Evman); pap. 3.95 (ISBN 0-460-01070-0). Dutton.

--The Compleat Angler. facsimile ed. 1976. Repr. 11.95x o.p. (ISBN 0-85417-459-1, Pub. by Scolar Pr England). Biblio Dist.

Walton, Izaak & Cotton, Charles. Compleat Angler. (World's Classics Ser: No. 430). 7.95 o.p. (ISBN 0-19-250430-4). Oxford U Pr.

Walton, J. C., jt. auth. see Nonhebel, D. C.

Walton, J. Michael. Greek Theatre Practice. LC 79-8580. (Contributions in Drama & Theatre Studies: No. 3). (Illus.). viii, 237p. 1980. lib. bdg. 23.95 (ISBN 0-313-22043-3, WGT/). Greenwood.

Walton, John. Elites & Economic Development: Comparative Studies on the Political Economy of Latin American Cities. LC 75-620108. (Latin American Monographs: No. 41). 272p. 1977. 14.95x (ISBN 0-292-72017-3); pap. 6.95 (ISBN 0-292-72018-1). U of Tex Pr.

Walton, John & Carns, Donald. Cities in Change: Studies on the Urban Condition. 2nd ed. 1977. pap. text ed. 13.60x (ISBN 0-205-05579-6). Allyn.

Walton, John, jt. auth. see Portes, Alejandro.

Walton, John N., ed. see Brain.

Walton, Kathy, ed. AWP Catalogue of Writing Programs. 3rd. ed. LC 80-67017. 120p. 1980. pap. 5.00 (ISBN 0-936266-01-5). Assoc Writing.

Walton, Lewis. Thoughts in Springtime. 1979. pap. 1.25 (ISBN 0-8163-0247-2). Pacific Pr Pub Assn.

Walton, Lewis, et al. Six Extra Years: Health & Longevity Secrets of the Seventh-Day Adventists. (Illus.). 160p. 1981. pap. 4.95 (ISBN 0-912800-84-4). Woodbridge Pr.

Walton, Richard. The Power of Oil: Economic, Social, Political. LC 76-43985. (gr. 6 up). 1977. 7.95 (ISBN 0-395-28929-7, Clarion). HM.

Walton, Richard E. Interpersonal Peacemaking: Confrontations & Third Party Consultation. (Organization Development Ser). (Orig.). 1969. pap. text ed. 6.50 (ISBN 0-201-08435-X). A-W.

Walton, Richard J. The United States & Latin America. LC 76-171860. 192p. (gr. 7 up). 1972. 5.95 (ISBN 0-395-28930-0, Clarion). HM.

--The United States & the Far East. LC 73-14859. 192p. (gr. 6 up). 1974. 6.95 (ISBN 0-395-28931-9, Clarion). HM.

Walton, Robert C., ed. Bible Study Source Book: New Testament. LC 80-82195. 240p. 1981. pap. 9.95 (ISBN 0-8042-0009-2). John Knox.

--Bible Study Source Book: Old Testament. LC 80-82194. 216p. 1981. pap. 9.95 (ISBN 0-8042-0008-4). John Knox.

Walton, Robert M. Joel in Tananar. (Illus.). 1981. 7.95 (ISBN 0-914598-05-8). Padre Prods.

Walton, Ronald G. Women in Social Work. 1975. 25.00x (ISBN 0-7100-8041-7). Routledge & Kegan.

Walton, Sally & Wilkinson, Faye. We're Number One: State--Ole Miss Jokes. rev. ed. (Illus.). 72p. 1980. pap. 3.95 (ISBN 0-937552-04-6). Quail Ridge.

Walton, Stephen. No Transfer. LC 66-28880. 7.95 (ISBN 0-8149-0229-4). Vanguard.

Walton, T. Know Your Own Ship. Baxter, B., ed. 373p. 1970. 28.00x (ISBN 0-85264-151-6, Pub. by Griffin England). State Mutual Bk.

Walton, Thomas F. Communications & Data Management. Buckley, John W., ed. LC 76-10264. 1976. 33.50 (ISBN 0-471-91935-7, Pub. by Wiley-Interscience). Wiley.

Walton, Todd. Forgotten Impulses. 1981. pap. 2.50 (ISBN 0-451-09802-1, E9802, Signet Bks). NAL.

--Inside Moves. (RL 5). 1979. pap. 2.25 o.p. (ISBN 0-451-08596-5, E8596, Sig). NAL.

Walton, W. H., ed. Carbon Monoxide, Industry & Performance. 1976. pap. text ed. 27.50 (ISBN 0-08-019966-6). Pergamon.

Walton, William. A Narrative of the Captivity & Sufferings of Benjamin Gilbert & His Family. Washburn, Wilcomb E., ed. LC 75-7036. (Narratives of North American Indian Captivities: Vol. 15). 1975. lib. bdg. 44.00 (ISBN 0-8240-1639-4). Garland Pub.

Waltz, Carolyn & Bausell, Baker. Nursing Research: Design Statistics & Computer Analysis. (Illus.). 350p. 1981. pap. text ed. 13.95 (ISBN 0-8036-9040-1). Davis Co.

Waltz, Carolyn F. & Bausell, R. Barker. Research in Nursing. LC 80-18669. (Illus.). 350p. 1981. 13.95 (ISBN 0-686-65103-0). Davis Co.

Waltz, Jon R. Criminal Evidence. LC 74-12398. (Law Enforcement Ser). 448p. 1975. 21.95 (ISBN 0-88229-130-0); pap. text ed. 13.95 (ISBN 0-88229-586-1). Nelson Hall.

Waltz, Kenneth N. Man, the State & War: A Theoretical Analysis. LC 59-11482. (Institute of War & Peace Studies Ser). 1959. 17.50x (ISBN 0-231-02292-1); pap. 6.00x (ISBN 0-231-08564-8). Columbia U Pr.

Waltz, Kenneth N., jt. ed. see Art, Robert J.

Walvin, J., jt. auth. see Craton, M.

Walvoord, John F. Jesus Christ Our Lord. 318p. 1974. pap. text ed. 4.95 (ISBN 0-8024-4326-5). Moody.

--Millennial Kingdom. 1959. 10.95 (ISBN 0-310-34090-X). Zondervan.

--Philippians: Joy & Peace. (Everyman's Bible Commentary). 1971. pap. 2.95 (ISBN 0-8024-2050-8). Moody.

Walvoord, John F., jt. auth. see Chafer, Lewis S.

Walwer, Frank K., jt. auth. see Swords, Peter D.

Walwoord, John E., jt. tr. see Walwoord, John F.

Walwoord, John F. & Walwoord, John E., trs. Armagedom. (Portuguese Bks.). 1979. 1.40 (ISBN 0-8297-0639-9). Life Pubs Intl.

--Armagedon. (Spanish Bks.). (Span.). 1979. 1.90 (ISBN 0-8297-0495-7). Life Pubs Intl.

Walworth, Arthur. Woodrow Wilson. 3rd ed. 1978. 19.95x (ISBN 0-393-07533-8); pap. 10.95x (ISBN 0-393-09012-4). Norton.

Walworth, Ralph. Subdue the Earth. 1977. 9.95 o.s.i. (ISBN 0-440-08434-2). Delacorte.

Walz, Garry R. & Benjamin, Libby. Transcultural Counseling: Needs, Programs & Techniques. LC 77-26253. (New Vistas in Counseling Ser.: Vol. 7). 1978. text ed. 16.95 (ISBN 0-87705-320-0). Human Sci Pr.

Walz, Garry R., ed. see Jones, Brian, et al.

Walz, Garry R., ed. see Lamb, Jackie & Lamb, Wesley.

Walz, Garry R., ed. see Sinick, Daniel.

Walz, Rosemarie. How to Prepare for College Board Achievement Tests -- German. LC 79-21101. (gr. 11-12). 1980. pap. 4.50 (ISBN 0-8120-0977-0). Barron.

Walz, Rosemary, jt. auth. see Newmark, Maxim.

Walzer, Michael. Radical Principles: Reflections of an Unreconstructed Democrat. LC 79-56371. 310p. 1980. 15.00 (ISBN 0-465-06824-3). Basic.

Walzer, Richard, ed. Al-Farabi on the Perfect State: Abu Nast al-Farabi's "the Principles of the Views of the Citizens of the Best State". 1981. 45.00x (ISBN 0-19-824505-X). Oxford U Pr.

Walzer, Richard A. Skintelligence: How to Be Smart About Skin. (Appleton Consumer Health Guides). 256p. 1981. 12.95 (ISBN 0-8385-8569-8); pap. 6.95 (ISBN 0-8385-8568-X). ACC.

Wambaugh, Joseph. Black Marble. 1978. 9.95 o.s.i. (ISBN 0-440-00523-X). Delacorte.

--The Choirboys. pap. 2.95 (ISBN 0-440-11188-9). Dell.

--The Onion Field: A True Story. 488p. 1973. 8.95 o.s.i. (ISBN 0-440-06692-1). Delacorte.

Wampler, Joseph. El Barranca Del Cobre De Mexico. Neblett, Lucy Ann, tr. from Eng. LC 78-657149. (Illus., Span.). 1978. pap. 6.00 (ISBN 0-935080-007-7). J Wampler.

Wampler, Joseph & Heald, Weldon F. High Sierra: Mountain Wonderland. (Illus.). 125p. 1967. 5.50 (ISBN 0-686-11221-0). J Wampler.

Wampler, Joseph, et al. Havasu Canyon: Gem of the Grand Canyon. 3rd ed. (Illus.). 125p. 1978. 6.00 (ISBN 0-686-11222-9). J Wampler.

Wampler, Louis. Underground Homes. rev ed. LC 80-18701. (Illus.). 120p. 1980. pap. 5.95 (ISBN 0-88289-273-8). Pelican.

Wamser, Carl C., jt. auth. see Harris, J. Milton.

Wamsley, James. Virginia. (Illus.). 128p. 1981. 27.50 (ISBN 0-912856-66-1). Graphic Arts Ctr.

Wanamaker, Melissa C. Discordia Concors: The Wit of Metaphysical Poetry. 239p. 1975. 12.00 (ISBN 0-8046-9089-8, Natl U). Kennikat.

Wanat, John A. Hospital Security Guard Training Manual. (Illus.). 192p. 1977. 21.75 (ISBN 0-398-03656-X). C C Thomas.

Wanat, Stanley F., ed. Language & Reading Comprehension. LC 77-80380. (Linguistics & Reading Ser.: No. 2). 1977. pap. text ed. 5.50x (ISBN 0-87281-061-5). Ctr Appl Ling.

Wandel, Joseph. German Dimension of American History. LC 78-26050. 1979. 14.95 (ISBN 0-88229-147-5); pap. 7.95 (ISBN 0-88229-668-X). Nelson-Hall.

Wandelt. Quality Patient Care Scale. (Illus.). 1974. pap. 7.95 (ISBN 0-685-78465-7). ACC.

Wandersman, Abraham, et al. Humanism & Behaviorism: Dialogue & Growth. 400p. 1976. text ed. 42.00 (ISBN 0-08-019589-X); pap. text ed. 12.75 (ISBN 0-08-019588-1). Pergamon.

Wang, C. H. The Bell & the Drum: A Study of Shih Ching As Formulaic Poetry. (Illus.). 1975. 17.50x (ISBN 0-520-02441-9). U of Cal Pr.

Wang, C. K. Matrix Methods of Structural Analysis. (Illus.). 1977. Repr. of 1966 ed. text ed. 18.50x (ISBN 0-89534-000-3). Am Pub Co WI.

Wang, Chih H. & Willis, David L. Radiotracer Methodology in the Biological Environmental & Physical Sciences. (Illus.). 512p. 1975. 25.95 (ISBN 0-13-752212-6). P-H.

Wang, Hao. From Mathematics to Philosophy. (International Library of Philosophy & Scientific Method). 420p. 1973. text ed. 29.25x (ISBN 0-391-00335-6). Humanities.

--Logic, Computers & Sets. LC 70-113155. Orig. Title: Survey of Mathematical Logic. 1970. Repr. of 1962 ed. text ed. 19.95 (ISBN 0-8284-0245-0). Chelsea Pub.

Wang, J. Y., et al. Exploring Man's Environment. 1973. pap. text ed. 10.95 (ISBN 0-8465-3051-1). Benjamin-Cummings.

Wang, James C. Contemporary Chinese Politics. (Illus.). 1980. pap. text ed. 10.50 (ISBN 0-13-169987-3). P-H.

Wang, Jaw-Kai & Hagan, Ross E. Irrigated Rice Production Systems. (Tropical Agriculture Ser.). 1980. lib. bdg. 35.00x (ISBN 0-89158-486-2). Westview.

Wang, Joseph E., ed. Selected Legal Documents of the People's Republic of China. LC 76-5167. (Studies in Chinese Government & Law). 564p. 1979. 32.50 (ISBN 0-89093-067-8). U Pubns Amer.

--Selected Legal Documents of the People's Republic of China: Volume II. LC 76-5167. (Studies in Chinese Government & Law). 564p. 1979. 32.50 (ISBN 0-89093-241-7). U Pubns Amer.

Wang, Kuo-Wei. Wang Kuo-wei's "Jen-Chien Tz'u-Hua". A Study in Chinese Literary Criticism. Rickett, Adele A., tr. from Chinese. LC 78-21212. 150p. 1979. 10.00 (ISBN 0-295-95657-7). U of Wash Pr.

Wang, Lawrence K. & Pereira, Norman C., eds. Handbook of Environmental Engineering: Vol. 2, Solid Waste Processing & Resource Recovery. LC 79-91087. 1980. 49.50 (ISBN 0-89603-008-3). Humana.

Wang, Lucy Y. Modern Chinese for the Elementary School, First Year. 2nd ed. LC 66-24847. (Illus.). 242p. (gr. 4-6). 1972. perfect bdg. 8.00 (ISBN 0-9600176-0-7); classroom lab tape set 30.00 (ISBN 0-685-22813-4); student's cassette tape 10.00 (ISBN 0-685-22814-2). Ascension.

--Modern Chinese for the Elementary School, Second Year. 2nd ed. LC 66-24847. (Illus.). 276p. (gr. 5-7). 1979. spiral bdg. 8.00 (ISBN 0-9600176-1-5); classroom lab tape set 30.00 (ISBN 0-685-22815-0); students' record set 10.00 (ISBN 0-685-22816-9). Ascension.

--Modern Chinese for the Elementary School, Third Year. 2nd ed. LC 66-24847. (Illus.). 315p. (gr. 6-8). 1979. perfect bdg. 8.00 (ISBN 0-9600176-6-6). Ascension.

Wang, M., jt. auth. see De Rachwiltz, I.

Wang, Mary. With God in Red China. LC 77-78610. 1977. pap. 1.95 (ISBN 0-87123-186-7, 200186). Bethany Fell.

Wang, N. T., ed. Taxation & Development. LC 75-27023. (Special Studies). 1976. text ed. 29.95 (ISBN 0-275-56010-4). Praeger.

Wang, Ping'Chun. Numerical & Matrix Methods in Structural Mechanics, with Applications to Computers. LC 66-11529. 1966. 35.95 (ISBN 0-471-91950-0, Pub. by Wiley-Interscience). Wiley.

Wang, Robert. The Qabalistic Tarot. (Illus.). 320p. 1981. pap. 8.95 (ISBN 0-87728-520-9). Weiser.

--The Secret Temple. 1980. 15.00 (ISBN 0-87728-490-3); pap. 7.95 (ISBN 0-87728-518-7). Weiser.

Wang, Rosemary Y. & Kelley, Ann M. Self-Assessment of Current Knowledge in Oncology Nursing. 1979. spiral bdg. 10.50 (ISBN 0-87488-236-2). Med Exam.

Wang, Shen-Tsu. The Margary Affair & the Chefoo Agreement. LC 79-2844. (Illus.). 138p. 1981. Repr. of 1940 ed. 14.50 (ISBN 0-8305-0020-0). Hyperion Conn.

Wang, Tong-Eng. Economic Policies & Price Stability in China. LC 80-620008. (China Research Monographs: No. 16). (Illus.). 1980. pap. write for info. (ISBN 0-912966-24-6). IEAS Ctr Chinese Stud.

Wang, William S-Y & Lyovin, Anatole, eds. CLIBOC: Chinese Linguistics Bibliography on Computer. LC 74-85740. (Princeton-Cambridge Studies in Chinese Linguistic Ser). 1970. 90.00 (ISBN 0-521-07455-X). Cambridge U Pr.

Wang Chu-Kia & Eckel. Elementary Theory of Structures. (Civil Engineering Ser.). (Illus.). 1957. text ed. 23.50 o.p. (ISBN 0-07-068134-1, C). McGraw.

Wang Fang-Yu, et al. Walking to Where the River Ends. (Illus.). 96p. 1980. pap. 12.50x (ISBN 0-208-01882-4, Archon). Shoe String.

Wang Fan-Hsi. Chinese Revolutionary, Memoirs 1919-49. Benton, Gregor, tr. 256p. 1980. 45.00 (ISBN 0-19-211746-7). Oxford U Pr.

Wang Jen-Yu & Barger, Gerald L., eds. Bibliography of Agricultural Meteorology. 1962. 45.00x (ISBN 0-299-02510-1). U of Wis Pr.

Wangsness, Ronald K. Electromagnetic Fields. LC 78-15027. 1979. text ed. 25.95 (ISBN 0-471-04103-3); solutions manual avail. (ISBN 0-471-05936-6). Wiley.

Wangyal, T., jt. auth. see Olschak, B.

Wank, Solomon, ed. Doves & Diplomats: Foreign Offices & Peace Movements in Europe & America in the 20th Century. LC 77-20278. (Contributions in Political Science: No. 4). (Illus.). 1978. lib. bdg. 19.95 (ISBN 0-313-20027-0, WDD/). Greenwood.

Wanke, Marshall C., jt. auth. see Skidmore, Max J.

Wann, Kenneth D., et al. Fostering Intellectual Development in Young Children. LC 62-18037. (Orig.). 1962. pap. 6.50x (ISBN 0-8077-2305-3). Tchrs Coll.

Wannamaker, Olin D., tr. see Steiner, Rudolf.

Wanninen, Erkki, ed. Essays on Analytical Chemistry: In Memory of Professor Anders Ringbom. LC 77-4103. 1977. text ed. 82.00 (ISBN 0-08-021596-3). Pergamon.

Wanous, John P. Organizational Entry: Recruitment, Selection, & Socialization of Newcomers. 1980. pap. text ed. 6.95 (ISBN 0-201-08456-2). A-W.

Wansbrough, J. Quranic Studies: Sources & Methods of Scriptural Interpretations, Vol. 31. (London Oriential Ser). 1977. 55.00x (ISBN 0-19-713588-9). Oxford U Pr.

Want, E. Cleve, jt. auth. see Burt, Forest D.

Wantz, Molly, jt. auth. see Engs, Ruth.

Wantz, Molly S. & Gay, John E. The Aging Process: A Health Perspective. (Sociology Ser.). (Illus.). 320p. 1981. pap. text ed. 10.95 (ISBN 0-87626-008-3). Winthrop.

Wan-Z-Xian. Lie Algebras. LC 74-13832. 244p. 1976. text ed. 37.00 (ISBN 0-08-017952-5). Pergamon.

Wapner, Eleanor B. Recreation for the Elderly: A Leadership Theory & Source Book. (Illus.). 192p. 1981. 16.50 (ISBN 0-89962-052-3). Todd & Honeywell.

Warberg, Willetta. Cooking from Scratch: The Single Man's Guide to Making Out in the Kitchen. 320p. (Orig.). 1976. pap. 1.95 o.p. (ISBN 0-345-25383-3). Ballantine.

Warburg, Gabriel. The Sudan Under Wingate: Administration in the Anglo-Egyptian Sudan, 1899 to 1916. (Illus.). 245p. 1971. 26.00x (ISBN 0-7146-2612-0, F Cass Co). Biblio Dist.

Warburton, F. W., jt. auth. see Sumner, R.

Warburton, Frederick. Forty Years in Nuts & Bolts: The Wholesale Electrical Game. 280p. 1980. pap. text ed. 6.95 o.p. (ISBN 0-934616-05-1). Valkyrie Pr.

Warburton, Geoffrey B., ed. Dynamical Behaviour of Structures. 2nd ed. 1977. text ed. 50.00 (ISBN 0-08-020364-7); pap. text ed. 22.00 (ISBN 0-08-020363-9). Pergamon.

Warburton, Robert. Eighteen Years in the Khyber, 1879-1898. (Illus.). 15.50x o.p. (ISBN 0-19-636057-9). Oxford U Pr.

Warburton, William. A View of Lord Bolingbroke's Philosophy. Wellek, Rene, ed. LC 75-11263. (British Philosophers & Theologians of the 17th & 18th Centuries Ser.). 1978. lib. bdg. 42.00 (ISBN 0-8240-1812-5). Garland Pub.

Warburton-Brown, D. Investing in Value. 164p. 1975. 13.00 (ISBN 92-833-1031-4, APO35, APO). Unipub.

Warch, Constance. Sewing Fundamentals. 2nd ed. LC 79-88755. (Illus.). 1979. pap. 14.95x spiral bdg. (ISBN 0-916434-32-X). Plycon Pr.

Warch, Willard F., jt. auth. see Melcher, Robert A.

Ward, A. C. American Literature, Eighteen Hundred Eighty to Nineteen Thirty. LC 74-14490. 273p. 1975. Repr. of 1932 ed. lib. bdg. 11.50x (ISBN 0-8154-0506-5). Cooper Sq.

Ward, Alan. Science Tricks & Puzzles. 1977. 14.95 (ISBN 0-7134-0285-7, Pub. by Batsford England). David & Charles.

Ward, Alan J. The Easter Rising: Revolution & Irish Nationalism. LC 79-55729. (AHM Europe Since 1500 Ser.). (Illus., Orig.). 1980. pap. text ed. 5.95x (ISBN 0-88295-803-8). AHM Pub.

Ward, Albert. Book Production, Fiction, & the German Reading Public. 215p. (Eng. & Ger.). 1974. text ed. 26.00x (ISBN 0-19-818157-4). Oxford U Pr.

Ward, Allan L. Two Hundred & Thirty-Nine Days: Abdu'l-Baha's Journey in America. LC 79-14713. (Illus.). 1979. 10.00 (ISBN 0-87743-129-9, 7-32-05). Baha'i.

Ward, Annie, jt. ed. see Peterson, Donovan.

Ward, Arthur A., Jr., jt. ed. see Lockard, Joan S.

Ward, Audrey, jt. ed. see Silverstone, Rosalie.

Ward, Barbara. Lopsided World. 1968. 3.95 (ISBN 0-393-05360-1, NortonC); pap. 2.95x (ISBN 0-393-09805-2). Norton.

--Rich Nations & the Poor Nations. 1962. pap. 4.95 (ISBN 0-393-00746-4, Norton Lib). Norton.

--Spaceship Earth. LC 66-18062. (George B Pegram Ser). 1966. 15.00x (ISBN 0-231-02951-9); pap. 5.00x (ISBN 0-231-08586-9). Columbia U Pr.

Ward, Barbara, et al, eds. Widening Gap: Development in the 1970's. LC 75-151617. 1971. 30.00x (ISBN 0-231-03538-1). Columbia U Pr.

Ward, Benedicta, tr. Sayings of the Desert Fathers. (Cistercian Studies Ser.: No. 59). 1975. pap. 4.00 o.p. (ISBN 0-87907-959-2). Cistercian Pubns.

Ward, Benedicta & Russell, Norman, trs. from Gr. The Lives of the Desert Fathers: The Historia Monachorum in Aegypto. (Cistercian Studies: No. 34). 1981. price not set (ISBN 0-87907-834-0); pap. price not set (ISBN 0-87907-934-7). Cistercian Pubns.

Ward, Benjamin. Elementary Price Theory. LC 67-15673. (Orig.). 1967. pap. text ed. 3.00 o.s.i. (ISBN 0-02-933950-2). Free Pr.

Ward, Benjamin, jt. ed. see Cohn, Alvin W.

Ward, Bryan. Hospital. LC 78-61228. (Careers Ser.). (Illus.). 1978. lib. bdg. 7.95 (ISBN 0-686-51120-4). Silver.

Ward, C. H., et al, eds. Offshore Ecology Investigation. (Rice University Studies: Vol. 65, Nos. 4 & 5). (Illus.). 600p. (Orig.). 1980. pap. 11.00x (ISBN 0-89263-243-7). Rice Univ.

Ward, C. M. Clash: The Conflict of Modern Youth. 1955. pap. 0.50 o.p. (ISBN 0-88243-701-1, 02-0701). Gospel Pub.

--What You Should Know About Prophecy. (Radiant Life Ser.). 1976. pap. 1.95 (ISBN 0-88243-890-5, 02-0890, Radiant Books); teacher's ed. 2.50 (ISBN 0-88243-164-1, 32-0164). Gospel Pub.

Ward, Catherine C., jt. auth. see Ward, Robert E.

Ward, Clint, jt. auth. see Athans, George, Jr.

Ward, Colin. Anarchism for Beginners. (Pantheon Documentary Comic Books). (Illus.). 1981. 8.95 (ISBN 0-394-50923-4); pap. 2.95 (ISBN 0-394-74822-0). Pantheon.

Ward, Colin & Fyson, Anthony. Streetwork: The Exploding School. 150p. 1974. 14.00 (ISBN 0-7100-7683-5); pap. 7.95 (ISBN 0-7100-7702-5). Routledge & Kegan.

Ward, Colin, ed. see Kropotkin, Peter.

Ward, Daniel B. & Pritchard, Peter C., eds. Plants. LC 78-12121. (Rare & Endangered Biota of Florida Ser.: Vol. 5). 1979. pap. 10.50 o.p. (ISBN 0-8130-0638-4). U Presses Fla.

Ward, David. Sing a Rainbow: Musical Activities with Mentally Handicapped Children. (Illus.). 64p. (Orig.). 1979. pap. text ed. 8.95x (ISBN 0-19-317416-2). Oxford U Pr.

Ward, David A. & Schoen, Kenneth F. Confinement in Maximum Custody: New Last-Resort Prisons in the United States & Western Europe. LC 78-24630. 1981. write for info. (ISBN 0-669-02799-5). Lexington Bks.

Ward, David A., jt. ed. see Cressey, Donald R.

Ward, David J. & Niendorf, Robert M. Consumer Finance: The Consumer Experience. 1978. text ed. 17.95 (ISBN 0-256-02035-3). Irwin.

Ward, Dennis & Him, G. Russian Pronunciation Illustrated. 1966. text ed. 9.95x (ISBN 0-521-06738-3). Cambridge U Pr.

Ward, Dennis, jt. auth. see Jones, D.

Ward, Don & Dykes, J. C. Cowboys & Cattle Country. LC 61-18251. (American Heritage Junior Library). (Illus.). 153p. (gr. 5 up). 1961. 9.95 (ISBN 0-8281-0389-5, J008-0). Am Heritage.

Ward, Donald, ed. & tr. from Ger. The German Legends of the Brothers Grimm, 2 vols. LC 80-24596. (Translations in Folklore Studies Ser.). (Illus.). 1981. Set. 42.00 (ISBN 0-915980-79-7). Inst Study Human.

Ward, E. P. The Dynamics of Planning. 1970. 25.00 (ISBN 0-08-015512-X); pap. 12.75 (ISBN 0-08-015513-8). Pergamon.

Ward, Fay E. The Cowboy at Work. Date not set. 14.95 (ISBN 0-8038-1204-3). Hastings.

--Cowboy at Work: All About His Job & How He Does It. (Illus.). 1976. Repr. 12.95 o.p. (ISBN 0-8038-1116-0). Hastings.

Ward, George A., ed. see Curwen, Samuel.

Ward, H., ed. New Library Buildings: Nineteen Seventy-Four. 1974. pap. 22.50x (ISBN 0-85365-397-6, Pub. by Lib Assn England). Oryx Pr.

--New Library Buildings: Nineteen Seventy-Six. 1976. pap. 31.00x (ISBN 0-85365-089-6, Pub. by Lib Assn England). Oryx Pr.

Ward, H. Snowden, ed. see Berry, James.

Ward, Harry M. The Department of War, Seventeen Eighty-One to Seventeen Ninety-Five. LC 80-28410. xi, 287p. 1981. Repr. of 1962 ed. lib. bdg. 29.75x (ISBN 0-313-22895-7, WADW). Greenwood.

Ward, Howard L. A Periodontal Point of View: A Practical Expression of Current Problems, Integrating Basic Science with Clinical Data. (American Lectures in Dentistry Ser.). (Illus.). 496p. 1973. 27.75 (ISBN 0-398-02815-X). C C Thomas.

--A Preventive Point of View. (Amer. Lec in Dentistry Ser.). (Illus.). 600p. 1978. 43.75 (ISBN 0-398-03616-0). C C Thomas.

Ward, Howard L. & Simring, Marvin R. Manual of Clinical Periodontics. 2nd ed. LC 77-26934. 1978. text ed. 16.95 (ISBN 0-8016-5343-6). Mosby.

Ward, Mrs. Humphrey. Robert Elsmere. Ryals, Clyde De L., ed. LC 67-12116. 1967. pap. 2.85x (ISBN 0-8032-5210-2, BB 348, Bison). U of Nebr Pr.

Ward, I. M., ed. Structure & Properties of Oriented Polymers. LC 74-26599. 500p. 1975. 69.95 (ISBN 0-470-91996-5). Halsted Pr.

Ward, Ian & Watts, Denis. Athletics for Student & Coach. (Illus.). 180p. 1976. 14.00 (ISBN 0-7207-0881-8). Transatlantic.

Ward, J., Jr. & Jennings, E. Introduction to Linear Models. 1973. ref. ed. 21.95x (ISBN 0-13-486175-2). P-H.

Ward, J. Neville. The Use of Praying. 1977. 9.95 (ISBN 0-19-520106-X); pap. 4.95 (ISBN 0-19-519959-6). Oxford U Pr.

Ward, J. Neville, ed. Five for Sorrow Ten for Joy: A Consideration of the Rosary. LC 72-96263. 200p. 1974. pap. 1.45 o.p. (ISBN 0-385-09544-9, Im). Doubleday.

Ward, J. P. Poetry & the Sociological Idea. 256p. 1981. 23.50x (ISBN 0-389-20188-X). B&N.

Ward, J. T. & Fraser, Hamish. Workers & Employers: Documents on Trade Union & Industrial Relations in Britain Since the Eighteenth Century. 384p. 1980. 35.00 (ISBN 0-208-01878-6, Archon). Shoe String.

Ward, Jack A. & Hetzel, Howard R. Biology: Today & Tomorrow. (Illus.). 1980. text ed. 18.95 (ISBN 0-8299-0310-0); study guide 7.95 (ISBN 0-8299-0335-6); instrs.' manual avail. (ISBN 0-8299-0579-0). West Pub.

Ward, Jack A., jt. auth. see Crang, Richard E.

Ward, James. Psychology & Psychological Principles. (Contributions to the History of Psychology Ser.: Vol. 8, Pt. a, Orientations). 1978. 30.00 (ISBN 0-89093-157-7). U Pubns Amer.

--A Study of Kant. Beck, Lewis W., ed. Bd. with Immanual Kant (Seventeen Twenty-Four to Eighteen Hundred Four) The British Academy Annual Philosophical Lecture. LC 75-32045. (Philosophy of Immanuel Kant Ser.: Vol. 9). 1977. Repr. of 1922 ed. lib. bdg. 24.00 (ISBN 0-8240-2333-1). Garland Pub.

Ward, James A. J. Edgar Thomson, Master of the Pennsylvania. LC 79-6569. (Contributions in Economics & Economic History: No. 33). (Illus.). xviii, 265p. 1980. lib. bdg. 25.00 (ISBN 0-313-22095-6, WJE/). Greenwood.

Ward, Jane, jt. auth. see Scates, Allen.

Ward, Janet, jt. auth. see Saoben, Marten.

Ward, Janet, jt. auth. see Shoben, Martin.

Ward, Janet, jt. auth. see Ward, Shoben.

Ward, Jay A. The Critical Reputation of Byron's Don Juan. (Salzburg Institute for English Literature Jacobean Drama Studies). (Orig.). 1979. pap. text ed. 25.00x (ISBN 0-391-01722-5). Humanities.

Ward, John. The Social & Religious Plays of Strindberg. 1980. text ed. 32.25x (ISBN 0-485-11183-7, Athlone Pr). Humanities.

Ward, John R., jt. auth. see Strum, Robert D.

Ward, John W. Andrew Jackson: Symbol for an Age. (YA) (gr. 9 up). 1962. pap. 4.95 (ISBN 0-19-500699-2, GB). Oxford U Pr.

Ward, Jonas. Buchanan's Texas Treasure. (Buchanan Ser.). 1978. pap. 1.75 (ISBN 0-449-14175-6, GM). Fawcett.

Ward, Leila. I Am Eyes. Ni Macho. LC 78-1314. (Illus.). (gr. k-3). 1978. 8.95 (ISBN 0-688-80161-7); PLB 8.59 (ISBN 0-688-84161-9). Greenwillow.

Ward, Leo L., ed. see Newman, John H.

Ward, Leslie. Forty Years of Spy. LC 70-81512. 1969. Repr. of 1915 ed. 22.00 (ISBN 0-8103-3575-1). Gale.

Ward, Lynd. Biggest Bear. (Illus.). (gr. k-3). 1952. reinforced bdg. 8.95 (ISBN 0-395-14806-5). HM.

--The Biggest Bear. LC 52-8730. (Illus.). 80p. (gr. k-3). 1973. pap. 2.50 (ISBN 0-395-15024-8, Sandpiper). HM.

Ward, M. L. Readers & Library Users. 1977. 8.25x (ISBN 0-85365-479-4, Pub. by Lib Assn England). Oryx Pr.

Ward, Maisie. The Tragi-Comedy of Pen Browning. LC 72-1865. (Illus.). 1972. 10.00x (ISBN 0-8362-0494-8, Pub by Browning Inst). Pub Ctr Cult Res.

Ward, Margaret E. Rolf Hochhuth. (World Authors Ser.: No. 463). 1977. lib. bdg. 11.95 (ISBN 0-8057-6300-7). Twayne.

Ward, Margery W., ed. A Fragment: The Autobiography of Mary Jane Mount Tanner. (Utah, the Mormons, & the West: No. 9). 1980. 15.00 (ISBN 0-87480-183-4, Tanner). U of Utah Pr.

Ward, Martha C. Them Children: A Study in Language Learning. Spindler, George & Spindler, Louise, eds. (Case Studies in Education & Culture). 112p. pap. text ed. 6.95x (ISBN 0-8290-0323-1). Irvington.

Ward, Martha E. & Marquardt, Dorothy A. Authors of Books for Young People. 2nd ed. LC 70-157057. 1971. 20.50 (ISBN 0-8108-0404-2). Scarecrow.

--Authors of Books for Young People: Supplement to the 2nd Edition. LC 78-16001. 1979. lib. bdg. 13.00 (ISBN 0-8108-1159-6). Scarecrow.

--Illustrators of Books for Young People. 2nd ed. LC 75-9880. 223p. 1975. 10.00 (ISBN 0-8108-0819-6). Scarecrow.

Ward, Mary A. Helbeck of Bannisdale, 1898. Wolff, Robert L., ed. LC 75-465. (Victorian Fiction Ser.). 1975. lib. bdg. 66.00 (ISBN 0-8240-1543-6). Garland Pub.

--Robert Elsmere. Wolff, Robert L., ed. LC 75-1534. (Victorian Fiction Ser.). 1975. Repr. of 1888 ed. lib. bdg. 66.00 (ISBN 0-8240-1606-8). Garland Pub.

Ward, Mary A. & Barbaresi, Sara M. How to Raise & Train a Beagle. 1966. pap. 2.00 (ISBN 0-87666-242-4, DS1004). TFH Pubns.

Ward, Melanie & Curtis, Richard. Dreams to Come. 1978. pap. 2.25 o.s.i. (ISBN 0-515-04474-1). Jove Pubns.

Ward, Michael P., jt. auth. see Maloney, Michael P.

Ward, Nanda. Hi Tom. Date not set. 3.84 (ISBN 0-8038-2991-4). Hastings.

Ward, Norman. Public Purse: A Study in Canadian Democracy. LC 62-5636. 1962. 22.50x o.p. (ISBN 0-8020-7058-2). U of Toronto Pr.

Ward, P. L. & Burkett, J., eds. Introductory Guide to Research in Librarianship & Information Studies in the U. K. (Pamphlet Ser.: No. 37). 1975. pap. 7.95x (ISBN 0-85365-058-6, Pub. by Lib Assn England). Oryx Pr.

Ward, Patricia A. Farm Journal's Best-Ever Cookies. LC 80-948. (Illus.). 1980. 12.95 (ISBN 0-385-17146-3). Doubleday.

--Farm Journal's Speedy Skillet Meals. (Illus.). 232p. 1980. 8.95 (ISBN 0-89795-009-7). Farm Journal.

Ward, Philip. A Dictionary of Common Fallacies. (Oleander Reference Books Ser.). 1978. 16.50 o.p. (ISBN 0-900891-14-9). Oleander Pr.

--Garrity & Other Plays. (Dramascripts Ser.). 2.50 (ISBN 0-902675-01-X). Oleander Pr.

--Impostors & Their Imitators. (Oleander Modern Poets Ser.: Vol. 7). 1977. pap. 4.95 (ISBN 0-900891-22-X). Oleander Pr.

--A Lizard & Other Distractions: Stories. 1970. 4.00 (ISBN 0-902675-52-4). Oleander Pr.

--Lost Songs: Political & Other Poems. (Oleander Modern Poets Ser.: Vol. II). (Illus.). 48p. 1981. pap. 4.95 (ISBN 0-902675-51-6). Oleander Pr.

--Touring Cyprus. (Illus.). 6.50 (ISBN 0-902675-13-3). Oleander Pr.

--Touring Lebanon. (Illus.). 1971. 9.50 (ISBN 0-571-09433-3). Transatlantic.

Ward, R. Gerard & Proctor, Andrew, eds. South Pacific Agriculture: Choices & Constraints. LC 79-56229. (South Pacific Agricultural Survey 1979). 525p. 1980. text ed. 24.95 (ISBN 0-7081-1944-1, 0532). Bks Australia.

Ward, Rhode, tr. see Colson, Charles.

Ward, Rhode, tr. see Graham, Billy.

Ward, Rhode, tr. see Morison, Frank.

Ward, Rhode, tr. see Narramore, Clyde & Narramore, Ruth.

Ward, Richard, jt. auth. see Shores, Christopher F.

Ward, Richard, ed. & illus. see McDowell, Ernest R.

Ward, Richard A. Economics of Health Resources. LC 74-12804. 160p. 1975. text ed. 11.95 (ISBN 0-201-08522-4). A-W.

--The Economics of Health Resources. 150p. 1975. 10.25 (ISBN 0-686-68580-6, 14914). Hospital Finan.

--Introduction to Criminal Investigation. LC 74-19703. 368p. 1975. text ed. 13.95 (ISBN 0-201-08523-2). A-W.

Ward, Richard J., et al. A Palestine State: A Rational Approach. 1977. 12.95 (ISBN 0-8046-9159-2). Kennikat.

Ward, Robert E. Prince of Dublin Printers: The Letters of George Faulkner. LC 71-160053. 160p. 1972. 10.00x (ISBN 0-8131-1258-3). U Pr of Ky.

Ward, Robert E. & Ward, Catherine C. The Letters of Charles O'connor of Belanagare, Seventeen Seventy-Two to Seventeen Ninety, Vol. II. LC 80-11602. (Sponsor Ser.). 341p. 1980. 24.75 (ISBN 0-8357-0535-8, SS-00145, Pub. by Monograph). Univ Microfilms.

Ward, Robert E., ed. Political Development in Modern Japan. (Studies in the Modernization of Japan). 1968. 25.00 (ISBN 0-691-03045-6); pap. 9.95 (ISBN 0-691-00017-4). Princeton U Pr.

Ward, Roy C. Floods: A Geographical Perspective. (Focal Problems in Geography Ser.). 1978. 24.95 o.p. (ISBN 0-470-99383-9). Halsted Pr.

--Floods: A Geographical Perspective Paper. (Focal Problems in Geography Ser.). 244p. 1980. pap. text ed. 12.95x (ISBN 0-470-26965-0). Halsted Pr.

Ward, Russel, tr. see La Meslee, Edmond M.

Ward, S. & De Bruicker, S. Cases in Consumer Behavior. 1980. pap. 13.95 (ISBN 0-13-118356-7). P-H.

Ward, Scott & Robertson, Thomas, eds. Consumer Behavior: Theoretical Sources. (International Management Ser). (Illus.). 560p. 1973. ref. ed. 20.95 (ISBN 0-13-169391-3). P-H.

Ward, Scott, jt. ed. see Ray, Michael L.

Ward, Shoben & Ward, Janet. Pattern Cutting & Making up: Volume I, Basic Techniques & Sample Development. 1980. 35.50 (ISBN 0-7134-3338-8, Pub. by Batsford England); pap. 22.50 (ISBN 0-7134-3339-6). David & Charles.

Ward, Stanley H. From the Heat of the Earth. (University of Utah Frederick William Reynolds Lecture Ser.: No. 40). 1977. pap. 1.00 (ISBN 0-87480-127-3). U of Utah Pr.

Ward, T. M. Serum Proteins in Clinical Medicine. 1981. text ed. price not set (ISBN 0-407-00161-1). Butterworth.

Ward, T. S. The Distribution of Consumer Goods. LC 73-84321. (Dept. of Applied Economics, Occasional Papers: No. 38). (Illus.). 250p. 1973. 32.95 (ISBN 0-521-20145-4); pap. 14.95 (ISBN 0-521-09791-6). Cambridge U Pr.

Ward, Ted. Values Begin at Home. 1979. pap. 3.95 (ISBN 0-88207-637-X). Victor Bks.

Ward, Vernon. Resources for Educational Research & Development. (Research Reports). 160p. 1973. pap. text ed. 14.50x (ISBN 0-85633-026-4, NFER). Humanities.

Ward, W. Egypt & East Mediterranean World 2200-1900 B.C. (Arab Background Ser.). 1971. 18.00x (ISBN 0-685-72041-1). Intl Bk Ctr.

Ward, W. E. A History of Ghana. 1967. text ed. 18.95x o.p. (ISBN 0-04-966007-1). Allen Unwin.

Ward, William. Reporting Agriculture Through Newspapers, Magazines, Radio, Television. 2nd ed. 402p. 1959. 15.00 (ISBN 0-8014-0441-X). Cornell U Pr.

Ward, William B. Divine Physician. rev. ed. LC 53-11762. (Orig.). 1957. pap. 2.95 (ISBN 0-8042-2316-5). John Knox.

--Toward Responsible Discipleship. LC 61-7078. (Orig.). 1961. pap. 2.95 (ISBN 0-8042-4049-3); leader's guide o.p. 1.00 (ISBN 0-8042-4050-7). John Knox.

--When You're Married. (Orig.). 1947. pap. 1.50 (ISBN 0-8042-2604-0). John Knox.

Ward, William S. see Reiman, Donald H.

Ward, Winifred. Playmaking with Children from Kindergarten Through Junior High School. 2nd ed. (Illus.). 1957. text ed. 14.95 (ISBN 0-13-683888-X). P-H.

Warde, W., tr. see Alessio.

Wardell, Allen. Gold of Ancient America. Orig. Title: Pre-Columbian Gold in the Museum of Fine Arts, Boston. (Illus.). 1968. 12.00 o.p. (ISBN 0-87846-153-1). Mus Fine Arts Boston.

Wardell, Morris L. A Political History of the Cherokee Nation, 1838-1907. (Civilization of the American Indian Ser.: Vol. 17). (Illus.). 1938. 15.95 (ISBN 0-8061-1411-8). U of Okla Pr.

Wardell, Sandra. Pharmacology: A Comprehensive Guide to Drug Therapy. 1979. text ed. 12.95 (ISBN 0-8359-5542-7). Reston.

Warden, Ian. Do Polar Bears Experience Religious Ecstasy? (Illus.). 217p. (Orig.). 1981. pap. 7.25x (ISBN 0-7022-1519-8). U of Queensland Pr.

Warden, John. Fallax opus: Poet & Reader in the Elegies of Propertius. (Phoenix Supplementary Volumes Ser.). 1980. 15.00x (ISBN 0-8020-5470-6). U of Toronto Pr.

Warden, John, ed. Annual of Industrial Property Law, 1975. 1975. text ed. 36.00x (ISBN 0-8377-0206-2). Rothman.

Warden, Lewis C. Running Against the Wind. 1981. 9.75 (ISBN 0-8158-0401-6). Chris Mass.

Warden, Rob & Groves, Martha, eds. Murder Most Foul: And Other Great Crime Stories from the World Press. LC 78-51586. (Illus.). x, 348p. 1980. 15.00 (ISBN 0-8040-0796-9). Swallow.

Wardhaugh, Ronald & Brown, H. Douglas, eds. A Survey of Applied Linguistics. LC 75-31053. 1976. text ed. 14.00 o.p. (ISBN 0-472-08958-7); pap. 7.95x (ISBN 0-472-08959-5). U of Mich Pr.

Wardian, Jeanne, jt. auth. see Andrews, J. Austin.

Ward-Jackson, Annis. One Thousand One Glenwood. Duncan, Thomas, ed. (Illus.). 117p. (gr. 6 up). 1979. PLB 6.95. Era Pr NC.

Wardlaw, Ralph. Book of Proverbs. Date not set. 27.50 (ISBN 0-86524-042-6). Klock & Klock.

Wardle, D. English Popular Education: Seventeen Eighty to Nineteen Seventy. 2nd ed. LC 75-41713. 208p. 1976. 22.50 (ISBN 0-521-21202-2); pap. 7.95x (ISBN 0-521-29073-2). Cambridge U Pr.

Wardle, David. Education & Society in Nineteenth Century Nottingham. LC 71-154512. (Texts & Studies in the History of Education). (Illus.). 1971. 24.50 (ISBN 0-521-08206-4). Cambridge U Pr.

Wardle, John P., tr. see Los, F. J.

Wardle, M. E., jt. auth. see Bolt, Albert B.

Wardle, M. E., ed. From Problem to Program. (School Mathematics Project Computing Ser). (Illus.). (gr. 8-12). 1971. 16.95 (ISBN 0-521-08301-X); pap. 6.95 (ISBN 0-521-09684-7). Cambridge U Pr.

Wardle, Ralph M. Mary Wollstonecraft: A Critical Biography. LC 51-12250. 1966. pap. 3.75x (ISBN 0-8032-5211-0, BB 340, Bison). U of Nebr Pr.

Wardle, Ralph M., ed. Godwin & Mary: Letters of William Godwin & Mary Wollstonecraft. LC 76-13032. (Illus.). 1977. 7.95x (ISBN 0-8032-0901-0); pap. 2.65 (ISBN 0-8032-5852-6, BB 631, Bison). U of Nebr Pr.

Wardley-Smith, J. The Prevention of Oil Pollution. LC 79-63534. 1979. 49.95x (ISBN 0-470-26718-6). Halsted Pr.

Wardley-Smith, J., ed. Control of Oil Pollution on the Sea & Inland Waters. 1976. 37.50x (ISBN 0-86010-021-9). Intl Pubns Serv.

--Control of Oil Pollution on the Sea & Inland Waters. 251p. 1976. 26.00x (ISBN 0-686-64023-3, Pub. by Graham & Trotman England). State Mutual Bk.

Wardman, Alan. Plutarch's Lives. 1979. 19.95 o.p. (ISBN 0-236-17622-6, Pub. by Paul Elek). Merrimack Bk Serv.

Ward-Perkins, J. B. Roman Architecture. LC 75-29475. (Illus.). 1977. 45.00 (ISBN 0-8109-1022-5). Abrams.

Wardrip, E. K., jt. auth. see Hood, Lamartine F.

Wardropper, Bruce W., ed. Spanish Poetry of the Golden Age. LC 78-132806. (Illus.). 1977. 29.50x (ISBN 0-89197-981-6); pap. text ed. 16.95x (ISBN 0-89197-982-4). Irvington.

Wards, Ian. Shadow of the Land - a Study of British Policy & Racial Conflict in New Zealand 1832-1852. (Illus.). 1968. 10.50x o.p. (ISBN 0-8426-1586-5). Verry.

Ward - Steinman, David & Ward - Steinman, Susan L. Comparative Anthology of Musical Forms, 2 vols. 1976. pap. text ed. 15.95x ea. (ISBN 0-685-69709-6); Vol. 1. (ISBN 0-534-00439-3); Vol. 2. (ISBN 0-534-00459-8). Wadsworth Pub.

Ward - Steinman, Susan L., jt. auth. see Ward - Steinman, David.

Ward-Thomas, F. The Royal & Ancient. (Illus.). 200p. 1980. 14.95x (ISBN 0-7073-0260-9, Pub. by Scottish Academic Pr Scotland). Columbia U Pr.

Ward-Thomas, Pat, et al. The World Atlas of Golf. 1976. 25.00 o.p. (ISBN 0-394-40814-4). Random.

Wardwell, John M., jt. ed. see Brown, David L.

Ware. Producing Vegetable Crops. 2nd ed. 1975. 18.00 (ISBN 0-8134-2083-0). Thomson Pub CA.

Ware, Edith E. Business & Politics in the Far East. 1932. 27.50x o.p. (ISBN 0-685-89736-2). Elliots Bks.

Ware, Eugene F. Indian War of 1864. Walton, Clyde C., ed. LC 60-13875. (Illus.). 1963. pap. 4.95 (ISBN 0-8032-5212-9, BB 173, Bison). U of Nebr Pr.

Ware, George W. Complete Guide to Pest Control: With & Without Chemicals. LC 80-52306. 1980. 18.50 (ISBN 0-913702-09-9). Thomson Pub CA.

--The Pesticide Book. LC 78-16220. (Illus.). 1978. pap. text ed. 11.95x (ISBN 0-7167-0198-7). W H Freeman.

Ware, George W. & McCollum, J. P. Producing Vegetable Crops. 3rd ed. (Illus.). (gr. 9-12). 1980. 18.00 (ISBN 0-8134-2083-0); text ed. 13.50x (ISBN 0-686-60699-X). Interstate.

Ware, Harlan, jt. auth. see Hornaday, William H.

Ware, Isaac, ed. see Palladio, Andrea.

Ware, James R., tr. from Chinese. Alchemy, Medicine, & Religion in the China of A. D. 320: The Nei P'ien of Ko Hung (Pao-p'u tzu) 416p. 1981. pap. price not set (ISBN 0-486-24088-6). Dover.

Ware, James R., tr. see Confucius.

Ware, John P., jt. auth. see Duncan, Roger F.

Ware, Joseph E. The Emigrants' Guide to California. LC 79-87627. (The American Scene Ser). (Illus.). 64p. 1972. Repr. of 1932 ed. lib. bdg. 12.50 (ISBN 0-306-71806-5). Da Capo.

Ware, K. Communion & Intercommunion. 1980. pap. 1.95 (ISBN 0-937032-20-4). Light&Life Pub Co MN.

Ware, M. J., jt. auth. see Salthouse, J. A.

Ware, Michael. Narrow Boats at Work. 144p. 1980. 23.85x (ISBN 0-86190-006-5, Pub. by Allan Pubs England). State Mutual Bk.

Ware, Michael E. A Canalside Camera: Eighteen Forty-Five to Nineteen Thirty. LC 75-2916. (Camera Ser.). (Illus.). 95p. 1975. 8.95 (ISBN 0-7153-7001-4). David & Charles.

Ware, Mitchell. Operational Handbook for Narcotic Law Enforcement Officers. 128p. 1975. 16.75 (ISBN 0-398-03349-8). C C Thomas.

Ware, Susan. Beyond Suffrage: Women in the New Deal. (Illus.). 224p. 1981. text ed. 18.50 (ISBN 0-674-06921-8). Harvard U Pr.

Ware, Tim, jt. auth. see Ratner, Elaine.

Wareham, John. Secrets of a Corporate Headhunter. LC 79-55603. 1980. 10.95 (ISBN 0-689-11059-6). Atheneum.

Wareing, P. F. & Phillips, I. D. The Control of Growth & Differentiation in Plants. 2nd ed. LC 78-30561. 1979. text ed. 45.00 (ISBN 0-08-021526-2); pap. text ed. 18.50 (ISBN 0-686-68007-3). Pergamon.

--Growth & Diffentiation in Plants. 3rd ed. Orig. Title: The Control of Growth & Differentiation in Plants. (Illus.). 176p. 1981. 38.00 (ISBN 0-08-026351-8); pap. 19.00 (ISBN 0-08-026350-X). Pergamon.

Wareing, P. F., ed. see Mayer, A. M., et al.

Warenski, Marilyn. Patriarchs & Politics. (McGraw-Hill Paperbacks Ser.). 352p. 1980. pap. 6.95 (ISBN 0-07-068271-2). McGraw.

Wares, William A. The Theory of Dumping & American Commercial Policy. LC 76-54611. (Illus.). 1977. 16.95x (ISBN 0-669-01308-0). Lexington Bks.

Warfel, George H. Identification Technologies: Computer, Optical, & Chemical Aids to Personal ID. (Illus.). 200p. 1979. text ed. 19.50 (ISBN 0-398-03889-9). C C Thomas.

Warfel, Harry R. Language: A Science of Human Behavior. LC 62-9619. 1962. 19.00x (ISBN 0-8201-1047-7). Schol Facsimiles.

Warfel, Harry R., ed. see Percival, James G.

Warfel, John H. & Schlagenhauff, Reinhold E. Understanding Neurological Disease: A Textbook for Therapists. LC 79-28455. (Illus.). 147p. 1980. 9.75 (ISBN 0-8067-2131-6). Urban & S.

Warfield, B. B. Counterfeit Miracles. 1976. pap. 5.45 (ISBN 0-85151-166-X). Banner of Truth.

--Faith & Life. 1974. pap. 5.45 (ISBN 0-85151-188-0). Banner of Truth.

Warfield, Benjamin B. Calvin & Augustine. 1954. 7.95 (ISBN 0-87552-526-1). Presby & Reformed.

--Inspiration & Authority of the Bible. 2nd ed. 1948. 7.95 (ISBN 0-87552-527-X). Presby & Reformed.

--Perfectionism. 7.95 (ISBN 0-87552-528-8). Presby & Reformed.

--Studies in Tertullian & Augustine. Repr. of 1930 ed. lib. bdg. 29.00x (ISBN 0-8371-4490-6, WATT). Greenwood.

--The Works of Benjamin B. Warfield, 10 vols. 1981. Repr. of 1932 ed. 149.50 (ISBN 0-8010-9645-6). Baker Bk.

Warfield, Gerald. How to Write Music Manuscript (in Pencil) A Workbook in the Basics of Music Notation. LC 76-58400. (Music Ser.). 1977. pap. text ed. 9.95 (ISBN 0-679-30332-4, Pub. by MacKay). Longman.

--Layer Analysis: A Primer of Elementary Tonal Structures. (Music Ser.). 1978. pap. text ed. 11.95x (ISBN 0-582-28069-9). Longman.

Warfield, Gerald, jt. auth. see Brooks, Richard.

Warford, Jeremy J. Public Policy Toward General Aviation. LC 70-161598. (Studies in the Regulation of Economic Activity). 1971. 10.95 (ISBN 0-8157-9226-3). Brookings.

Warga, Richard G. Personal Awareness: A Psychology of Adjustment. 2nd ed. LC 78-69531. (Illus.). 1979. pap. text ed. 12.95 (ISBN 0-395-26795-1); inst. manual 1.10 (ISBN 0-395-26796-X). HM.

Wargo, Louis G., Jr., jt. auth. see Jaberg, Gene.

Warhaft, Sidney, ed. see Bacon, Francis.

Warham, Joyce. Introduction to Administration for Social Workers. (Orig.). 1967. pap. text ed. 6.50x (ISBN 0-391-00394-1). Humanities.

--An Open Case: The Organisational Context of Social Work. (Library of Social Work). 1977. 16.00 (ISBN 0-7100-8608-3); pap. 7.95 (ISBN 0-7100-8609-1). Routledge & Kegan.

Warin, Robert P. & Champion, Robert H. Urticaria. LC 73-89192. (Major Problems in Dermatology Ser.: Vol. 1). (Illus.). 185p. 1974. text ed. 16.00 (ISBN 0-7216-9111-0). Saunders.

Waring, A. G. Russian Science Grammar. 1967. 16.50 (ISBN 0-08-011342-7); pap. 7.75 (ISBN 0-08-011341-9). Pergamon.

Waring, H. Color-Change Mechanisms of Coldblooded Vertebrates. 1963. 31.50 (ISBN 0-12-735450-6). Acad Pr.

Waring, Janet. Early American Stencils on Walls & Furniture. (Illus.). 12.50 (ISBN 0-685-22719-7). Peter Smith.

Waring, L. P. Planning for Standby. 112p. 1977. pap. 12.95 (ISBN 0-85012-183-3, 5465-3, Pub. by Natl Computing Centre England). Hayden.

Waring, L. P., ed. see National Computing Centre.

Waring, Richard H., ed. see Oregon State University Biology Colloquium, 40th.

Waring, Walter. Thomas Carlyle. (English Author Ser.: No.238). 1978. 12.50 (ISBN 0-8057-6710-X). Twayne.

Warinner, Emily V. A Royal Journey to London. LC 75-28654. 1975. pap. 2.95 (ISBN 0-914916-11-4). Topgallant.

Wark, Edna. Drawin Fabric Embroidery. 1979. 24.00 (ISBN 0-7134-1476-6). David & Charles.

Wark, Robert R. British Landscape Drawings & Watercolors, Nineteen-Fifty to Nineteen-Fifty: Twenty-Four Examples from the Huntington Collection. (Illus.). 64p. write for info. (ISBN 0-87328-116-0). Huntington Lib.

Wark, Robert R., ed. Sir Joshua Reynolds: Discourses on Art. LC 74-17647. 408p. 1975. 35.00x (ISBN 0-300-01823-1). Yale U Pr.

Warken, Philip W. A History of the National Resources Planning Board, 1933-1943. Freidel, Frank, ed. LC 78-66882. (Modern American History Ser.: Vol. 19). 1979. lib. bdg. 24.00 (ISBN 0-8240-3642-5). Garland Pub.

Warkentin, John, jt. auth. see Harris, R. Cole.

Warkov, Seymour. Energy Policy in the United States: Social & Behavioral Dimensions. LC 78-8454. (Praeger Special Studies). 1978. 26.50 (ISBN 0-03-043486-6). Praeger.
Warman, Edwin G. American Cut Glass. (Illus.). 5.95 o.p. (ISBN 0-685-21838-4). Warman.
--Antiques Oddities & Curiosities. rev. ed. (Illus.). 1980. pap. cancelled o.p. (ISBN 0-685-21839-2). Warman.
--Cash from Trash. (Illus.). 3.95 o.p. (ISBN 0-685-21844-9). Warman.
--Fifty Ways for Antique Dealers to Beat Inflation. (Illus.). 1975. 5.95 o.p. (ISBN 0-685-55900-9). Warman.
--Fourth Print Price Guide. Repr. of 1976 ed. 7.95 o.p. (ISBN 0-685-73594-X). Warman.
Warmbrand, Max. Add Years to Your Heart. 1969. pap. 2.50 (ISBN 0-515-05720-7, N2046). Jove Pubns.
--Eat Well to Keep Well. 1970. pap. 1.25 o.s.i. (ISBN 0-515-02173-3, V2173). Jove Pubns.
--Encyclopedia of Health & Nutrition. 1974. pap. 1.95 o.s.i. (ISBN 0-515-03413-4, Y3413). Jove Pubns.
Warming, Wanda, jt. auth. see Gaworski, Michael E.
Warmsun, Carolyn H., et al. Womanist Therapy. (Pergamon General Psychology Ser.). 30.01 o.p. (ISBN 0-08-022274-9). Pergamon.
Warnant, Leon. Dictionnaire des rimes orales et ecrites. new ed. 553p. (Fr.). 1972. 23.50 (ISBN 2-03-020271-1, 3546). Larousse.
Warnath, Charles F. New Myths & Old Realities: College Counseling in Transition. LC 77-172879. (Higher Education Ser.). 1971. 11.95x o.p. (ISBN 0-87589-114-4). Jossey-Bass.
Warne, E. J. Russian Scientific Reader. (Rus). 1967. pap. 2.95x (ISBN 0-393-09712-9, NortonC). Norton.
Warnecke, Steven J. Uranium, Nonproliferation & Energy Security. (Atlantic Papers Ser.: No. 37). 121p. 1980. write for info. 0.00 (ISBN 0-916672-77-8). Allanheld.
Warnecke, Steven J., ed. European Community in the Nineteen Seventies. LC 79-170277. (Special Studies in International Politics & Government). 1972. 29.50x (ISBN 0-275-28224-4); pap. text ed. 16.50x (ISBN 0-89197-753-8). Irvington.
Warnecke, Steven J. & Suleiman, Ezra N., eds. Industrial Policies in Western Europe. LC 75-23998. 266p. 1975. text ed. 32.50 (ISBN 0-275-01670-6). Praeger.
Warner. Love Comes to Anne. (gr. 7-12). 1980. pap. 1.50 (ISBN 0-590-30027-X, Schol Pap). Schol Bk Serv.
Warner, Aaron W., ed. Environment of Change. LC 79-79572. (Seminar on Technology & Social Change Ser). 1969. 20.00x (ISBN 0-231-03151-3). Columbia U Pr.
--Impact of Science on Technology. LC 65-19445. (Seminar on Technology & Social Change Ser). 1965. 20.00x (ISBN 0-231-02823-7). Columbia U Pr.
Warner, Aaron W., jt. ed. see Morse, Dean.
Warner, Alan. Clay Is the Word: Patrick Kavanagh 1904-1967. 1974. text ed. 11.00x (ISBN 0-85105-210-X, Dolmen Pr); pap. text ed. 4.50x (ISBN 0-85105-206-1). Humanities.
Warner, Anne R., ed. Innovations in Community Health Nursing: Health Care Delivery in Shortage Areas. LC 77-20114. 1978. pap. text ed. 9.50 (ISBN 0-8016-5350-9). Mosby.
Warner, Carmen G. Conflict Intervention in Social-Domestic Violence. (Illus.). 256p. 1981. text ed. 14.95 (ISBN 0-87619-855-8); pap. text ed. 11.95 (ISBN 0-87619-854-X). R J Brady.
Warner, Carmen G., et al, eds. Emergency Care: Assessment & Intervention. 2nd ed. LC 77-18285. (Illus.). 1978. 19.95 (ISBN 0-8016-4744-4). Mosby.
Warner, Charles D. Washington Irving. LC 80-23548. (American Men & Women of Letters Ser.). 310p. 1981. pap. 4.95 (ISBN 0-87754-153-1). Chelsea Hse.
Warner, Charles D., jt. auth. see Twain, Mark.
Warner, Charles D., et al, eds. Biographical Dictionary & Synopsis of Books, Ancient & Modern. LC 66-4326. Repr. of 1902 ed. 26.00 (ISBN 0-8103-3023-7). Gale.
Warner, D. S. Salvation, Present, Perfect, Now or Never. 63p. pap. 0.40; pap. 1.00 3 copies. Faith Pub Hse.
Warner, D. S. & Riggle, H. M. The Cleansing of the Sanctuary. 541p. Repr. 5.50. Faith Pub Hse.
Warner, Edward L., III. The Military in Contemporary Soviet Politics: An Institutional Analysis. LC 77-83476. (Praeger Special Studies). 1978. 26.95 (ISBN 0-03-040346-4). Praeger.
Warner, Francis. Killing Time: A Play by Francis Warner. (Oxford Theatre Texts Ser.: No. 3). (Illus.). 1976. text ed. 7.25x (ISBN 0-85635-198-9). Humanities.
--Light Shadows. (Oxford Theatre Texts: No. 6). 1980. text ed. 8.50x (ISBN 0-86140-040-2). Humanities.
--Meeting Ends: A Play by Francis Warner. (Oxford Theatre Texts Ser.: No. 4). (Illus.). 1974. text ed. 5.25x (ISBN 0-85635-105-9). Humanities.
Warner, Gerald. Being of Sound Mind: A Book of Eccentric Wills. (Illus.). 112p. 1981. 14.50 (ISBN 0-241-10471-8, Pub. by Hamish Hamilton England). David & Charles.
Warner, Gertrude. Boxcar Children. LC 42-1418. (Boxcar Children Mysteries Ser.). (gr. 3-7). 6.95g (ISBN 0-8075-0851-9, Pilot Bks). A Whitman.
Warner, Gertrude C. Benny Uncovers a Mystery. Rubin, Caroline, ed. LC 76-15222. (Boxcar Children Mysteries-Pilot Bk.). (Illus.). 128p. (gr. 3-8). 1976. PLB 6.95 (ISBN 0-8075-0644-3). A Whitman.
--Bicycle Mystery. LC 79-126428. (Boxcar Children Mysteries-Pilot Bk.). (Illus.). 128p. (gr. 3-7). 1970. 6.95g (ISBN 0-8075-0708-3). A Whitman.
--Blue Bay Mystery. LC 61-15230. (Boxcar Children Mysteries-Pilot Bk.). (Illus.). (gr. 3-7). 6.95g (ISBN 0-8075-0793-8). A Whitman.
--Bus Station Mystery. LC 74-8293. (Boxcar Children Mysteries-Pilot Bk.). (Illus.). 128p. (gr. 3-7). 1974. 6.95g (ISBN 0-8075-0975-2). A Whitman.
--Caboose Mystery. LC 66-10791. (Boxcar Children Mysteries-Pilot Bk.). (Illus.). 128p. (gr. 3-7). 1966. 6.95g (ISBN 0-8075-1008-4). A Whitman.
--Houseboat Mystery. LC 67-26521. (Boxcar Children Mysteries-Pilot Bk.). (Illus.). 128p. (gr. 3-7). 1967. 6.95g (ISBN 0-8075-3412-9). A Whitman.
--Lighthouse Mystery. LC 63-20354. (Boxcar Children Mysteries-Pilot Bk.). (Illus.). 128p. (gr. 3-7). 1963. 6.95g (ISBN 0-8075-4545-7). A Whitman.
--Mike's Mystery. LC 60-8428. (Boxcar Children Mysteries-Pilot Bk.). (Illus.). 128p. (gr. 3-7). 1960. 6.95g (ISBN 0-8075-5140-6). A Whitman.
--Mountain Top Mystery. LC 64-7722. (Boxcar Children Mysteries-Pilot Bk.). (Illus.). 128p. (gr. 3-7). 1964. 6.95g (ISBN 0-8075-5292-5). A Whitman.
--Mystery Behind the Wall. LC 72-13356. (Boxcar Children Mysteries-Pilot Bk.). (Illus.). 128p. (gr. 3-7). 1973. 6.95g (ISBN 0-8075-5364-6). A Whitman.
--Mystery in the Sand. LC 70-165823. (Boxcar Children Mysteries-Pilot Bk.). (Illus.). 128p. (gr. 3-7). 1971. 6.95g (ISBN 0-8075-5373-5). A Whitman.
--Mystery Ranch. LC 58-9953. (Boxcar Children Mysteries-Pilot Bk.). (Illus.). 128p. (gr. 3-7). 1958. 6.95g (ISBN 0-8075-5390-5). A Whitman.
--Schoolhouse Mystery. LC 65-23889. (Boxcar Children Mysteries-Pilot Bk.). (Illus.). 128p. (gr. 3-7). 1965. 6.95g (ISBN 0-8075-7262-4). A Whitman.
--Snowbound Mystery. LC 68-9124. (Boxcar Children Mysteries-Pilot Bk.). (Illus.). (gr. 3-7). 1968. 6.95g (ISBN 0-8075-7517-8). A Whitman.
--Surprise Island. LC 49-49618. (Boxcar Children Mysteries-Pilot Bk.). (Illus.). (gr. 3-7). 6.95g (ISBN 0-8075-7673-5). A Whitman.
--Tree House Mystery. LC 77-91744. (Boxcar Children Mysteries-Pilot Bk.). (Illus.). 128p. (gr. 3-7). 1969. 6.95g (ISBN 0-8075-8086-4). A Whitman.
--Woodshed Mystery. LC 62-19726. (Boxcar Children Mysteries-Pilot Bk.). (Illus.). 128p. (gr. 3-7). 6.95g (ISBN 0-8075-9206-4). A Whitman.
--Yellow House Mystery. LC 53-13243. (Boxcar Children Mysteries-Pilot Bk.). (Illus.). 128p. (gr. 3-7). 6.95g (ISBN 0-8075-9365-6). A Whitman.
Warner, Gloria, jt. auth. see Bernstein, Anne E.
Warner, Gordon & Sasamori, Junzo. This Is Kendo: The Art of Japanese Fencing. LC 64-22900. 1964. 16.50 (ISBN 0-8048-0574-1). C E Tuttle.
Warner, Gordon, jt. auth. see Draeger, Donn F.
Warner, Jack, Jr. Bijou Dream. Baron, Carole, ed. 1981. 12.95 (ISBN 0-517-54333-8). Crown.
Warner, James. Taxation. 8th ed. LC 78-65093. 9.00 (ISBN 0-932788-04-1). Bradley CPA.
Warner, James A. & White, Margaret J. Best Friends. (Illus.). 176p. 1980. 27.50 (ISBN 0-89479-045-5). A & W Pubs.
Warner, James C. Bradley CPA Review Taxation. 8th ed. LC 78-65093. 1978. pap. 8.95 o.p. (ISBN 0-932788-04-1). Bradley CPA.
Warner, James C. & Weinberg, Frank F. Bradley CPA Review - A Practice. LC 79-83860. 1979. pap. 16.00 (ISBN 0-932788-06-8). Bradley CPA.
Warner, James C., ed. Bradley CPA Review Taxation. rev ed. LC 78-65093. 1980. pap. 9.00 (ISBN 0-932788-04-1). Bradley CPA.
Warner, Joan. Business English Handbook. 1981. text ed. 14.95 (ISBN 0-8359-0574-8). Reston.
Warner, Joan Elizabeth. Business Calculator Operations. (Illus.). 1978. pap. text ed. 13.50 (ISBN 0-87909-097-9); student manual avail. Reston.
Warner, Joan M. Learning Disabilities: Activities for Remediation. 2nd ed. 84p. 1980. pap. text ed. 3.95x (ISBN 0-8134-2118-7). Interstate.
Warner, June, jt. ed. see Mettler, Barbara.
Warner, Ken. Handloader's Digest Bullet & Powder Update. 96p. 1980. pap. 4.95 (ISBN 0-695-81418-4). Follett.
--The Practical Book of Guns. (Illus.). 1978. 13.95 (ISBN 0-87691-274-9). Winchester Pr.
--The Practical Book of Knives. 1976. 12.95 (ISBN 0-87691-218-8). Winchester Pr.
Warner, Ken, ed. Gun Digest Nineteen Eighty. 34th ed. (Illus.). 448p. 1979. pap. 9.95 o.p. (ISBN 0-695-81309-9). Follett.
--Gun Digest Review of Custom Guns. 256p. 1980. pap. 8.95 (ISBN 0-910676-10-0). DBI.
--Gun Digest 1981. 35th ed. 448p. 1980. pap. 10.95 (ISBN 0-910676-09-7). DBI.
--Knives Eighty One. 192p. 1980. pap. 5.95 (ISBN 0-910676-15-1). DBI.
Warner, Lloyd W. & Low, V. O. Yankee City. abr. ed. LC 63-7588. (Illus.). 448p. 1963. 27.50x o.p. (ISBN 0-300-01026-5). Yale U Pr.
Warner, Malcolm. Organizational Choice & Constraint. (Illus.). 1978. 24.95 (ISBN 0-566-00180-2, 01619-5, Pub. by Saxon Hse England). Lexington Bks.
Warner, Malcolm, ed. Sociology of the Workplace. LC 73-15572. 291p. 1973. 15.95 (ISBN 0-470-92113-7). Halsted Pr.
Warner, Marie P. & Gilbert, Miriam. Doctor Discusses Breast Feeding. (Illus.). 1980. pap. 2.50 (ISBN 0-685-03351-1). Budlong.
Warner, Marina. Joan of Arc: The Image of Female Heroism. LC 80-2720. (Illus.). 1981. 17.95 (ISBN 0-394-41145-5). Knopf.
Warner, Mickey. Industrial Foodservice & Cafeteria Management. LC 72-92378. 1973. 16.95 (ISBN 0-8436-0563-4). CBI Pub.
Warner, Mignon. The Tarot Murders. 1981. pap. 2.25 (ISBN 0-440-16162-2). Dell.
Warner, Noel L., ed. Contemporary Topics in Immunobiology, Vol. 11. (Illus.). 390p. 1980. 32.50 (ISBN 0-306-40419-2, Plenum Pr). Plenum Pub.
Warner, Oliver. A Portrait of Lord Nelson. (Illus.). 1979. 8.95 (ISBN 0-7011-1809-1, Pub. by Chatto Bodley Jonathan). Merrimack Bk Serv.
Warner, Oliver see Swan, Michael.
Warner, Oliver, ed. Nelson's Last Diary, a Facsimile. LC 70-165752. 1972. 9.00x (ISBN 0-87338-121-1). Kent St U Pr.
Warner, Pearl. How to Prepare for College Board Achievement Test -- French. rev. ed. LC 75-151972. (gr. 11-12). 1981. pap. text ed. 3.25 (ISBN 0-8120-0941-X). Barron.
Warner, Peter O. Analysis of Air Pollutants. LC 75-26685. (Environmental Science & Technology Ser.). 329p. 1976. 33.00 (ISBN 0-471-92107-6, Pub. by Wiley-Interscience). Wiley.
Warner, R. W., jt. auth. see Wasley, G. D.
Warner, Raleigh, Jr., jt. auth. see Silk, Leonard.
Warner, Ralph & Honigsberg, Peter. California Debtor's Handbook. 3rd ed. 1979. pap. 5.95 (ISBN 0-917316-14-2). Nolo Pr.
--California Debtor's Handbook. 4th ed. 1981. pap. 6.95 (ISBN 0-917316-34-7). Nolo Pr.
Warner, Ralph & Ihara, Toni. California Marriage & Divorce Law. 4th ed. 1981. pap. 7.95 (ISBN 0-917316-16-9). Nolo Pr.
Warner, Ralph E. Protect Your Home with a Declaration of Homestead. 3rd ed. (Illus.). 80p. 1978. pap. 4.95 (ISBN 0-917316-02-9). Nolo Pr.
Warner, Ralph E., et al. Protect Your Home with a Declaration of Homestead. 5th ed. (Illus.). 80p. 1980. pap. 5.95 (ISBN 0-917316-31-2). Nolo Pr.
Warner, Rex see Blackstone, Bernard.
Warner, Richard. Morality in Medicine: An Introduction to Medical Ethics. LC 79-23049. 1980. pap. 8.95 (ISBN 0-88284-103-3). Alfred Pub.
Warner, Richard & Segal, Herman. Ethical Issues of Imformed Consent in Dentistry. 112p. 1980. pap. 12.00 (ISBN 0-931386-33-0). Quint Pub Co.
Warner, Rita. Wonderful World of Horses Coloring Album. (Illus.). 32p. (Orig.). (gr. 3 up). 1976. pap. 3.50 (ISBN 0-912300-69-8, 69-8). Troubador Pr.
Warner, Rita, illus. Dogs & Puppies Coloring Album. (Illus.). 1977. pap. 3.50 (ISBN 0-912300-81-7, 87-7). Troubador Pr.
--North American Indians Coloring Album. (Illus.). 32p. (Orig.). 1978. pap. 3.50 (ISBN 0-912300-95-7, 95-7). Troubador Pr.
Warner, Robert. Don't Blame the Fish. (Illus.). 1974. 8.95 o.p. (ISBN 0-87691-127-0). Winchester Pr.
Warner, Ruth, tr. see Erdozain, Placido.
Warner, Sam B., Jr. Private City: Philadelphia in Three Periods of Its Growth. LC 68-21557. (Illus.). 1968. 10.00x (ISBN 0-8122-7575-6); pap. 4.95x (ISBN 0-8122-1003-4, Pa Paperbks). U of Pa Pr.
Warner, Steven D. & Schweer, Kathryn D. Author's Guide to Journals in Nursing & Related Fields. (Author's Guide to Journals Ser.). 1981. 19.95 (ISBN 0-917724-11-9). Haworth Pr.
Warner, W. Lloyd. Black Civilization: A Social Study of an Australian Tribe. rev. ed. (Illus.). 8.75 (ISBN 0-8446-0954-4). Peter Smith.
Warner, Wayne, ed. Touched by the Fire. 1978. pap. 2.95 o.p. (ISBN 0-88270-270-X). Logos.
Warner, William W. Beautiful Swimmers: Watermen, Crabs & the Chesapeake Bay. 1977. pap. 3.50 (ISBN 0-14-004405-1). Penguin.
Warner Hill, Frank. Labradors. LC 76-11026. (Illus.). 1976. bds. 2.25 o.p. (ISBN 0-668-03993-0). Arco.
Warnke, Harold. Abortion: A/Biblical Approach. 1980. 2.75 (ISBN 0-8100-0116-0). Northwest Pub.
Warnken, Kelly, ed. The Directory of Fee-Based Information Services 1980-81. LC 76-55469. 1980. pap. 6.95 (ISBN 0-936288-00-0). Info Alternative.
Warnock, C. Gayle. The Edsel Affair. LC 80-81129. (Illus.). 278p. 1980. 16.95 (ISBN 0-686-28039-3). Pro West.
Warnock, Mary. Education: A Way Ahead. 1979. 20.00x (ISBN 0-631-11281-2, Pub. by Basil Blackwell England); pap. 8.50x (ISBN 0-631-12902-2). Biblio Dist.
--Imagination. LC 75-22663. 1976. 20.00x (ISBN 0-520-03115-6); pap. 3.95 (ISBN 0-520-03115-6). U of Cal Pr.
--The Philosophy of Sartre. 1972. pap. text ed. 8.00x (ISBN 0-09-073752-0, Hutchinson U Lib). Humanities.
--Schools of Thought. 1977. 13.95 o.p. (ISBN 0-571-10963-2, Pub. by Faber & Faber); pap. 7.95 (ISBN 0-571-11161-0). Merrimack Bk Serv.
Warns, Johannes. Baptism. Date not set. 11.50 (ISBN 0-86524-063-9). Klock & Klock.
Warntz, William. Toward a Geography of Price. LC 57-7220. 1959. 5.00x o.p. (ISBN 0-8122-7124-6). U of Pa Pr.
Warntz, William & Wolff, Peter. Breakthroughs in Geography. 3.95 o.p. (ISBN 0-452-25040-4, Z5040, Plume). NAL.
Warr, Peter, et al. Developing Employee Relations. 216p. 1978. text ed. 21.75x (ISBN 0-566-00209-4, Pub. by Gower Pub Co England). Renouf.
Warrack, Alexander. Chambers Scots Dictionary. Repr. of 1911 ed. 14.95 (ISBN 0-550-11801-2, Pub. by Two Continents). Hippocrene Bks.
Warrack, B. D., jt. auth. see Naimpally, S. A.
Warrack, J. Carl Maria Von Weber. 2nd ed. LC 76-12915. (Illus.). 1976. 39.50 (ISBN 0-521-21354-1); pap. 13.95 (ISBN 0-521-29121-6). Cambridge U Pr.
Warrack, John. Tchaikovsky Ballet Music. LC 79-52144. (BBC Music Guides Ser.: No. 41). (Illus.). 72p. (Orig.). 1980. pap. 2.95 (ISBN 0-295-95697-6). U of Wash Pr.
Warrack, John, jt. ed. see Rosenthal, Harold.
Warrell, Susan E. Helping Young Children Grow: A Humanistic Approach to Parenting & Teaching. 240p. 1980. 12.95 (Spec); pap. 5.95. P-H.
Warren, Alister. Paper. (Illus.). pap. 8.95 (ISBN 0-584-62051-9). Dufour.
Warren, B. E. X-Ray Diffraction. (Metallurgy & Materials Ser). (Illus.). 1969. 20.95 (ISBN 0-201-08524-0). A-W.
Warren, Barbara. The Feminine Image in Literature. (Humanities Ser). 280p. (gr. 9-12). 1974. pap. text ed. 7.10x (ISBN 0-8104-5068-2). Hayden.
Warren, Bill. Imperialism: Pioneer of Capitalism. 296p. 1981. 19.50x (ISBN 0-8052-7089-2, Pub. by NLB England); pap. 8.50 (ISBN 0-8052-7088-4). Schocken.
Warren, Bruce, jt. ed. see Sears, M.
Warren, Bruce A. & Wunsch, Carol, eds. Evolution of Physical Oceanography: Essays in Honor of Henry Stommel. 768p. 1980. 37.50x (ISBN 0-262-23104-2). MIT Pr.
Warren, Cameron A., jt. auth. see Crow, James T.
Warren, Carl & Miller, Merl. From the Counter to the Bottom Line. LC 79-52263. 225p. 1979. pap. 13.95 (ISBN 0-918398-11-8). Dilithium Pr.
Warren, Carl, ed. Software. LC 79-67462. (Best of Interface Age Ser.: Vol. 2). 150p. 1980. pap. 9.95 (ISBN 0-918398-37-1). Dilithium Pr.
--Software in BASIC. LC 79-67462. (The Best of Interface Age Ser.: Vol. 1). 400p. 1979. pap. 14.95 (ISBN 0-918398-36-3). Dilithium Pr.
Warren, Carol A. Sociology: Change & Continuity. 1977. 17.95x (ISBN 0-256-01944-4). Dorsey.
Warren, Carol A., jt. auth. see DeLora, Joann S.

Warren, Charles. Bankruptcy in United States History. LC 75-172175. (American Constitutional & Legal History Ser). 196p. 1972. Repr. of 1935 ed. lib. bdg. 19.50 (ISBN 0-306-70214-2). Da Capo.
--History of the Harvard Law School & of Early Legal Conditions in America. LC 72-112311. (American Constitutional & Legal History Ser). 1970. Repr. of 1908 ed. lib. bdg. 75.00 (ISBN 0-306-71913-4). Da Capo.
--The Supreme Court & Sovereign States. LC 75-87626. (American Scene Ser). 160p. 1972. Repr. of 1924 ed. lib. bdg. 19.50 (ISBN 0-306-71807-3). Da Capo.
Warren, Christopher. The Allah Conspiracy. LC 80-27097. 224p. 1981. 10.95 (ISBN 0-8253-0052-5). Beaufort Bks NY.
Warren, Craig, jt. ed. see Moskowitz, H. R.
Warren, David. The Great Escaper. LC 78-26629. (Raintree Great Adventures). (Illus.). (gr. 3-6). 1979. PLB 8.95 (ISBN 0-8393-0152-9). Raintree Child.
Warren, David, ed. see Gresham, Stephen, et al.
Warren, David G. Problems in Hospital Law. 3rd. ed. LC 78-15865. 1978. text ed. 21.50 (ISBN 0-89443-045-9). Aspen Systems.
Warren, Dennis M., jt. auth. see Grindal, Bruce T.
Warren, Donald R., ed. History, Education, & Public Policy: Recovering the American Educational Past. LC 77-95251. (National Society for the Study of Education, Series on Contemp. Educ. Issues). 1978. 17.90 (ISBN 0-8211-2258-4); text ed. 16.20 ten copies (ISBN 0-685-04973-6). McCutchan.
Warren, Doug. A Case of Rape. (Orig.). 1975. pap. 1.75 o.s.i. (ISBN 0-515-03617-X, A3617). Jove Pubns.
Warren, E. Kirby. Long Range Planning: Executive Viewpoint. 1966. ref. ed. 15.95 (ISBN 0-13-540187-9). P-H.
Warren, Eugene. Geometries of Light. (The Wheaton Literary Ser.). 80p. (Orig.). 1981. pap. 3.95 (ISBN 0-87788-300-9). Shaw Pubs.
Warren, Frank A. Alternative Vision: The Socialist Party in the 1930's. LC 74-181. 288p. 1974. 12.50x (ISBN 0-253-30520-9). Ind U Pr.
Warren, Frank A. & Wreszin, Michael, eds. New Deal: An Anthology. LC 68-9745. (Orig.). 1969. pap. 4.95x o.p. (ISBN 0-88295-769-4). AHM Pub.
Warren, Frank Z. Freedom from Pain Through Acupressure. LC 75-16632. 1976. 9.95 (ISBN 0-8119-0256-0). Fell.
Warren, Frank Z. & Fischman, Walter I. Sexual Acupuncture. 1978. 14.95 o.p. (ISBN 0-525-20118-1); pap. 7.95 o.p. (ISBN 0-525-04435-3). Dutton.
Warren, G. Garry. The Handicapped Librarian: A Study in Barriers. LC 79-21811. 155p. 1979. 10.00 (ISBN 0-8108-1259-2). Scarecrow.
Warren, Geoffrey. Vanishing Street Furniture. 1978. 22.50 (ISBN 0-7153-7482-6). David & Charles.
Warren, George. Traffic Courts. Repr. of 1942 ed. lib. bdg. 15.75x (ISBN 0-8371-2568-5, WATC). Greenwood.
Warren, Gloria K., jt. auth. see Stead, Evelyn S.
Warren, Gordon H. Fountain of Discontent: The Trent Affair & Freedom of the Seas. LC 80-24499. (Illus.). 366p. 1981. price not set. NE U Pr.
Warren, Harris G. Herbert Hoover & the Great Depression. 1967. pap. 5.95 o.p. (ISBN 0-393-00394-9, Norton Lib). Norton.
--Herbert Hoover & the Great Depression. LC 80-19603. x, 372p. 1980. Repr. of 1970 ed. lib. bdg. 28.75x (ISBN 0-313-22659-8, WAHO). Greenwood.
--Paraguay & the Triple Alliance: The Post-War Decade, 1869 to 1878. (Latin-American Monographs: No. 44). 1978. 17.95x (ISBN 0-292-76445-6); pap. 9.95 (ISBN 0-292-76444-8). U of Tex Pr.
Warren, Henry. Artistic Anatomy of a Human Figure. (Art Appreciation Books Ser.). (Illus.). 1978. Repr. of 1868 ed. deluxe ed. 39.50 (ISBN 0-930582-12-8). Gloucester Art.
Warren, Jim, ed. Dr. Dobb's Journal of Computer Calisthenics & Orthodontia, Vol. 1. 1977. pap. 18.95 (ISBN 0-8104-5475-0). Peoples Computer.
Warren, Jim C., Jr., ed. National Computer Conference '78 Personal Computing Digest. (Illus.). iv, 425p. 1978. pap. 12.00 (ISBN 0-88283-011-2). AFIPS Pr.
Warren, Joanna. The Destined. (Belle Meade Ser.: No. 3). 432p. (Orig.). 1980. pap. 2.50 (ISBN 0-89083-693-0). Zebra.
Warren, John, ed. Highest State of Consciousness. LC 70-171340. 1972. pap. 3.50 (ISBN 0-385-04532-8, Anch). Doubleday.
Warren, Joyce W. A Mouse to Be Free. (Illus.). (gr. 1-4). 1975. pap. 1.25 (ISBN 0-380-00349-X, 31765, Camelot). Avon.
Warren, K. B., ed. see International Society For Cell Biology.
Warren, Katherine B., ed. see International Society For Cell Biology.
Warren, Katherine B., ed. see International Society for Cell Biology.
Warren, Kenneth. American Steel Industry Eighteen Fifty to Nineteen Seventy: A Geographical Interpretation. (Oxford Research Studies in Geography). (Illus.). 354p. 1973. 36.00x (ISBN 0-19-823214-4). Oxford U Pr.
--Chemical Foundations: The Alkali Industry in Britain to Nineteen Twenty-Six. (Oxford Research Studies in Geography). (Illus.). 220p. 1980. text ed. 46.00x (ISBN 0-19-823231-4). Oxford U Pr.
--World Steel: An Economic Geography. LC 74-24996. 1975. 19.50x (ISBN 0-8448-0651-X). Crane-Russak Co.
Warren, Kenneth, jt. auth. see Goffman, William.
Warren, Larkin, jt. auth. see Schneberg, Willa.
Warren, Lindsey D., ed. Headed in the Direction of Heaven. 1980. 2.25 (ISBN 0-934916-28-4). Natl Christian Pr.
Warren, M. L. Prairie Vengeance. (Orig.). 1980. pap. 1.75 (ISBN 0-505-51532-6). Tower Bks.
Warren, Malcom W. Training for Results: A Systems Approach to the Development of Human Resources in Industry. 2nd ed. 1979. pap. text ed. 8.95 (ISBN 0-201-08504-6). A-W.
Warren, Mary. La Barquilla que Casi Se Hundio. Villalobos, Fernando, tr. from Eng. (Libros Arco Ser.). (Illus.). 32p. (Orig., Span.). (gr. 1-3). 1978. pap. 0.95 (ISBN 0-89922-125-4). Edit Caribe.
--El Cojo que Camino de Nuevo. Lockward, J. Alfonso, tr. from Eng. (Libros Arco). (Illus.). 32p. (Orig., Span.). (gr. 1-3). 1975. pap. 0.95 o.s.i. (ISBN 0-89922-037-1). Edit Caribe.
--El Nino y el Gigante. Villalobos, Fernando, tr. from Eng. (Libros Arco). (Illus.). 32p. (Orig., Span.). (gr. 1-3). 1975. pap. 0.95 o.s.i. (ISBN 0-89922-044-4). Edit Caribe.
Warren, Mary A. The Nature of Woman: An Encyclopedia. LC 79-55299. 736p. 1980. 20.00 (ISBN 0-918528-07-0); pap. 16.00 (ISBN 0-918528-06-2). Edgepress.
Warren, Mary P. On Our Way to Christmas: A Family Activity Book for Advent. 32p. (Orig.). 1980. pap. 3.50 (ISBN 0-8066-1784-5, 10-4768). Augsburg.
Warren, Mashuri L. Introductory Physics. LC 78-22089. (Illus.). 1979. text ed. 21.95x (ISBN 0-7167-1008-0); tchr's manual avail. W H Freeman.
Warren, Max. Creo en la Gran Comision. Sipowicz, Edwin, tr. from Eng. LC 78-54272. (Serie Creo). 205p. (Orig., Span.). 1978. pap. 3.95 (ISBN 0-89922-112-2). Edit Caribe.
Warren, Meg. The New Book of Gymnastics. 8rev. ed. (Illus.). 120p. 1980. 13.50x (ISBN 0-213-16772-7, Pub. by Weidenfeld & Nicolson England). Biblio Dist.
--The New Book of Gymnastics. (Illus.). 120p. 1980. 13.50x (ISBN 0-213-16772-7). Biblio Dist.
Warren, Mercy Otis. Plays & Poems of Mercy Otis Warren. LC 80-16625. 1980. 40.00x (ISBN 0-8201-1344-1). Schol Facsimiles.
Warren, Mervyn A. Black Preaching: Truth & Soul. 1977. pap. text ed. 7.75x (ISBN 0-8191-0173-7). U Pr of Amer.
Warren, Michael, ed. Youth Ministry: A Book of Reading. LC 77-70639. 1977. pap. 2.95 (ISBN 0-8091-2018-6). Paulist Pr.
Warren, Nigel. Marine Conversions: Car Engine Conversions for Boats. 1979. 14.95x (ISBN 0-8464-0074-X). Beekman Pubs.
--Small Motor Cruises. 1979. 19.95x (ISBN 0-8464-0064-2). Beekman Pubs.
Warren, Paulette. Search in the Shadows. (Caliban Ser.). pap. 1.25 o.p. (ISBN 0-425-03113-6). Berkley Pub.
Warren, Peter. Minoan Stone Vases. LC 69-13794. (Cambridge Classical Studies). (Illus.). 1970. 49.50 (ISBN 0-521-07371-5). Cambridge U Pr.
Warren, Richard L. Education in Rebhausen: A German Village. Spindler, George & Spindler, Louise, eds. (Case Studies in Education & Culture). 123p. pap. text ed. 6.95x (ISBN 0-8290-0321-5). Irvington.
Warren, Richard M. Aspects of Auditory Perception: Non-Verbal Sounds & Speech. (Pergamon General Psychology Ser.). 225p. 1981. price not set (ISBN 0-08-025957-X). Pergamon.
Warren, Rita & Schneider, Dick. Mom, They Won't Let Us Pray. 1975. pap. 2.50 o.p. (ISBN 0-8499-4110-5, 4110-5, Dist. by Word Bks.); 1975 5.95 o.p. (ISBN 0-912376-10-4). Chosen Bks Pub.
Warren, Robert P. Being Here: Poetry Nineteen Seventy-Seven to Nineteen Eighty. 108p. 1980. 8.95 (ISBN 0-394-51304-5). Random.
--Brother to Dragons. 1953. 10.95 o.p. (ISBN 0-394-40312-6). Random.
--Democracy & Poetry. LC 74-31993. 102p. 1975. 6.95 (ISBN 0-674-19625-2); pap. 2.95 (ISBN 0-674-19626-0). Harvard U Pr.
--Incarnations: Poems 1966-1968. LC 68-28529. 1968. 7.95 (ISBN 0-394-40368-1); pap. 4.95 (ISBN 0-394-73935-3); lmtd. ed. 15.00 (ISBN 0-394-51305-3). Random.
--Jefferson Davis Gets His Citizenship Back. LC 80-51023. 120p. 1980. Repr. of 1980 ed. 8.75 (ISBN 0-8131-1445-4). U Pr of Ky.
--Now & Then: Poems, 1976-1978. 1978. 8.95 (ISBN 0-394-50164-0); pap. 4.95 (ISBN 0-394-73515-3); lmtd. ed. 15.00 (ISBN 0-394-50220-5). Random.
Warren, Robert P. & Brooks, Cleanth. Understanding Fiction. 3rd ed. 1979. pap. text ed. 9.50 (ISBN 0-13-936690-3). P-H.
Warren, Robert P., jt. auth. see Brooks, Cleanth.
Warren, Roger M., jt. auth. see Sternloff, Robert E.
Warren, Ronald L., et al. The Structure of Urban Reform. (Illus.). 256p. 1974. 18.95 (ISBN 0-669-92809-7); pap. 9.95 (ISBN 0-669-92817-8). Lexington Bks.
Warren, Ruth. The First Book of Modern Greece. LC 66-10130. (First Bks). (Illus.). 88p. (gr. 4-6). 1972. PLB 6.45 (ISBN 0-531-00544-5). Watts.
--First Book of the Arab World. (First Bks). (Illus.). (gr. 4-6). 1963. PLB 4.90 o.p. (ISBN 0-531-00469-4). Watts.
--Modern Greece. rev. ed. (First Bks.). (Illus.). (gr. 4 up). 1979. PLB 5.90 s&l o.p. (ISBN 0-531-02934-4). Watts.
Warren, Sue A., jt. auth. see Gardner, David C.
Warren, Thomas B. Charts You Can Use in Preaching, Teaching & Studying on Divorce & Remarriage. 1978. pap. 9.95 (ISBN 0-934916-29-2). Natl Christian Pr.
--Divorce & Remarriage: Are Non-Christians Amenable to the Law of Christ? 1977. pap. 3.95 (ISBN 0-934916-30-6). Natl Christian Pr.
--Have Atheists Proved There Is No God? 1974. 5.95 (ISBN 0-934916-33-0). Natl Christian Pr.
--Keeping the Lock in Wedlock. 1980. pap. 10.95 (ISBN 0-934916-26-8). Natl Christian Pr.
--Marriage Is for Those Who Love God & One Another. 1976. 4.95 (ISBN 0-934916-37-3). Natl Christian Pr.
--Our God: A "Sun & Shield" for Troubled Hearts. 1963. 4.95 (ISBN 0-934916-38-1). Natl Christian Pr.
--When Is an Example Binding? Biblical Hermeneutics. 1975. pap. 4.95 (ISBN 0-934916-43-8). Natl Christian Pr.
Warren, Thomas B. & Ballard, L. S. Warren-Ballard Debate. 1979. 7.95 (ISBN 0-934916-39-X). Natl Christian Pr.
Warren, Thomas B. & Matson, Wallace I. Warren-Matson Debate on the Existence of God. LC 78-64546. 1979. 12.95 (ISBN 0-934916-41-1); pap. 9.95 (ISBN 0-934916-45-4). Natl Christian Pr.
Warren, Thomas B., ed. Your Marriage Can Be Great. 1978. pap. 13.95 (ISBN 0-934916-44-6). Natl Christian Pr.
Warren, Thomas B. & Elkins, Garland, eds. The Church, the Beautiful Bride of Christ. 1980. pap. 16.95. Natl Christian Pr.
--God Demands Doctrinal Preaching. 1978. 10.95 (ISBN 0-934916-32-2); pap. 7.95 (ISBN 0-686-23947-4). Natl Christian Pr.
--The Home As God Would Have It & Contemporary Attacks Against It. 1979. 19.95 (ISBN 0-934916-34-9). Natl Christian Pr.
--The Living Messages of the Books of the New Testament. 1976. 10.95 (ISBN 0-934916-35-7). Natl Christian Pr.
Warren, Thomas B. & Noflew, A. G., eds. Warren-Flew Debate on the Existence of God. 1977. 12.95 (ISBN 0-934916-40-3). Natl Christian Pr.
Warren, W. C., et al. Criminal Law & Its Administration: The Ditchley Papers. LC 70-152650. (Symposia on Law & Society Ser). 1971. Repr. of 1966 ed. lib. bdg. 15.00 (ISBN 0-306-70130-8). Da Capo.
Warren, W. L. Henry Second. (English Monarchs Ser.). 1973. 31.50x (ISBN 0-520-02282-3); pap. 8.95 (ISBN 0-520-03494-5). U of Cal Pr.
--King John. rev. ed. (Campus Ser.: No. 209). 1978. o. p. 15.00x (ISBN 0-520-03610-7); pap. 6.50x (ISBN 0-520-03643-3). U of Cal Pr.
Warren, W. Preston. Roy Wood Sellars. LC 74-30132. (World Leaders Ser: No. 45). 1975. lib. bdg. 9.95 (ISBN 0-8057-3719-7). Twayne.
Warren, William M., jt. ed. see Rubin, Neville.
Warren-Davis, Ann, jt. auth. see Rutherford, Meg.
Warrick, Clyde E. Mastering the Twenty Basic Coefficients for Success in Commodity Futures Trading. (Illus.). 1980. deluxe ed. 37.45 (ISBN 0-918968-54-2). Inst Econ Pol.
Warrick, Louis F., ed. see The Food Processors Institute.
Warrick, Ruth & Preston, Don. The Confessions of Phoebe Tyler. LC 80-18272. 1980. 9.95 (ISBN 0-13-167403-X). P-H.
Warrin, George E., jt. auth. see Lopez, Ulises M.
Warriner, Doreen. Land & Poverty in the Middle East. LC 79-1596. 1981. Repr. of 1948 ed. 16.00 (ISBN 0-88355-901-3). Hyperion Conn.
Warring, R. H. Aeromodelling. 9.75x (ISBN 0-392-07177-0, LTB). Soccer.
--A Beginner's Guide to Making Electronic Gadgets. 1977. 9.95 o.p. (ISBN 0-8306-7958-8); pap. 5.95 (ISBN 0-8306-6958-2, 958). TAB Bks.
--Chemical Experiments. (Pegasus Books: No. 33). (Illus.). 152p. 1974. 10.50x (ISBN 0-234-77684-6). Intl Pubns Serv.
--Filters & Filtration. (Illus.). 1969. 35.00x (ISBN 0-85461-025-1). Intl Ideas.
--Fluids for Power Sysytems. (Illus.). 1970. 39.95x (ISBN 0-85461-040-5). Intl Ideas.
--Know Your Model Aero Engine. (Illus., Orig.). 1979. pap. 8.50x (ISBN 0-85242-607-0). Intl Pubns Serv.
--Pneumatic Engineering Calculations. 1969. 24.95x (ISBN 0-85461-038-3). Intl Ideas.
--Pumps Selection, Systems & Applications. (Illus.). 1969. 32.50x o.p. (ISBN 0-85461-039-1). Intl Ideas.
Warrington, Brian. Discover Data Communications. (Illus.). 128p. 1980. 14.95x (ISBN 0-7198-2581-4). Intl Ideas.
Warrington, John, tr. see Aristotle.
Warrior, Betsy, et al. Battered Women's Directory. 8th ed. 1981. pap. 5.00 (ISBN 0-9601544-5-0). B Warrior.
Warsaw, Jacqueline, jt. auth. see Gignac, Louis.
Warschaw, Tessa A. Negotiating to Win. 1980. 9.95 (ISBN 0-07-000780-2). McGraw.
--Winning by Negotiation. LC 80-14535. 264p. 1980. 10.95 (ISBN 0-07-000780-2, GB). McGraw.
Warsenburg, Hans van De see Van de Warsenburg, Hans.
Warshall, Peter. Septic Tank Practices. LC 77-76288. 1979. pap. 3.95 (ISBN 0-385-12764-2, Anch). Doubleday.
Warshauer, William, Jr., jt. auth. see Gross, Malvern J., Jr.
Warshaw, Jerry. The Funny Drawing Book. Rubin, Caroline, ed. LC 77-14389. (Activity Books Ser.). (Illus.). 48p. (gr. 2 up). 1978. 6.50g (ISBN 0-8075-2681-9). A Whitman.
--I-Can't-Draw Book. LC 73-165824. (Activity Bks.). (Illus.). 32p. (gr. 2 up). 1971. 6.50g (ISBN 0-8075-3502-8). A Whitman.
Warshaw, Thayer S. A Compact Guide to Bible Based Beliefs. LC 80-19820. 149p. (Orig.). 1981. pap. 1.50 (ISBN 0-687-09254-X). Abingdon.
Warshawsky, Abel G. The Memories of an American Impressionist. Bassham, Ben L., ed. LC 80-82203. (Illus.). 259p. 1980. 17.50 (ISBN 0-87338-249-8). Kent St U Pr.
Warshofsky, Fred & Stevens, S. Smith. Sound & Hearing. rev. ed. LC 65-28353. (Life Science Library). (Illus.). (gr. 5 up). 1969. PLB 8.97 o.p. (ISBN 0-8094-0471-0, Pub. by Time-Life). Silver.
Wartburg, Walter Von see Von Wartburg, Walter.
Wartenweiler, J., jt. ed. see Vredenbregt, J.
Warth, Jeanne, jt. auth. see Gorham, Georgia.
Warth, Robert D. Joseph Stalin. (World Leaders Ser: No. 10). 1969. lib. bdg. 9.95 (ISBN 0-8057-3080-X). Twayne.
--Leon Trotsky. (World Leaders Ser.: No. 72). 1977. lib. bdg. 12.50 (ISBN 0-8057-7720-2). Twayne.
Wartick, Wallace. Lessons on New Testament Evidences. 250p. 1980. pap. 4.95 (ISBN 0-89900-141-6). College Pr Pub.
--New Testament Evidences. rev. ed. LC 75-328412. (The Bible Study Textbook Ser.). (Illus.). 1975. 10.00 o.p. (ISBN 0-89900-052-5). College Pr Pub.
--Twenty-Six Lessons on the First Corinthians. (Bible Study Guide Ser.). 210p. (Orig.). 1980. pap. 3.95 (ISBN 0-89900-168-8). College Pr Pub.
Wartofsky, L. The Endocrine System: Disease, Diagnosis, Treatment. (Clinical Monographs Ser.). (Illus.). 1973. pap. 7.95 (ISBN 0-87618-060-8). R J Brady.
Wartofsky, Marx W. Feuerbach. LC 76-9180. 1977. 47.50 (ISBN 0-521-21257-X). Cambridge U Pr.
Wartofsky, Victor. The Passage. (Orig.). 1980. pap. 1.95 (ISBN 0-505-51506-7). Tower Bks.
Warton, Joseph. Odes on Various Subjects. LC 77-8452. 1977. Repr. of 1746 ed. 20.00x (ISBN 0-8201-1291-7). Schol Facsimiles.
Wartshi, Maureen C. A Boat to Nowhere. 1981. pap. 1.50 (ISBN 0-686-68722-1, W9678, Sig). NAL.
Wartski, Maureen C. A Long Way from Home. LC 80-19247. (gr. 6 up). 1980. PLB 9.95 (ISBN 0-664-32674-9). Westminster.
--My Brother Is Special. (YA) 1981. pap. 1.50 (ISBN 0-451-09578-2, W9578, Sig). NAL.
Warvelle, Geo W. Essays in Legal Ethics. xiii, 234p. 1980. Repr. of 1902 ed. lib. bdg. 22.50x (ISBN 0-8377-1305-6). Rothman.
Warwick, Alan R. Let's Look at Castles. LC 67-17416. (Let's Look Ser). (Illus.). (gr. 4-8). 1965. 4.95g o.p. (ISBN 0-8075-4464-7). A Whitman.

--Let's Look at Prehistoric Animals. LC 67-26522. (Let's Look Ser). (Illus.). (gr. 4-8). 1966. 4.95g o.p. (ISBN 0-8075-4489-2). A Whitman.
Warwick, Christopher. Two Centuries of Royal Weddings. LC 79-49276. (Illus.). 145p. 1980. 14.95 (ISBN 0-396-07838-9). Dodd.
Warwick, David. Team Teaching. 125p. 1971. 9.50x o.p. (ISBN 0-8448-0538-6). Crane-Russak Co.
Warwick, Donald P. The Teaching of Ethics in the Social Sciences. LC 80-10154. (The Teaching of Ethics Ser.). 69p. 1980. pap. 4.00 (ISBN 0-916558-11-8). Hastings Ctr Inst Soc.
Wasan, M. T. Stochastic Approximation. LC 69-11150. (Cambridge Tracts in Mathematics & Mathematical Physics). (Illus.). 1969. 35.50 (ISBN 0-521-07368-5). Cambridge U Pr.
Wasbauer, M. S. Revision of the Male Wasps of the Genus Brachycistis in America North of Mexico (Hymenoptera: Tiphiidae) (U. C. Publ. in Entomology: Vol. 43). 1966. pap. 7.50x (ISBN 0-520-09115-9). U of Cal Pr.
Wasby, Stephen, jt. ed. see Grumm, John.
Wasby, Stephen L. Small Town Police & the Supreme Court: Hearing the Word. LC 76-5621. 1976. 21.50 (ISBN 0-669-00654-8). Lexington Bks.
Wasby, Stephen L., ed. Civil Liberties: Policy & Policy Making. LC 76-43318. 256p. 1977. pap. 7.95 (ISBN 0-8093-0817-7). S Ill U Pr.
Wasby, Stephen L., jt. ed. see Grumm, John G.
Waschek, Brownlee, jt. auth. see Waschek, Carmen.
Waschek, Carmen & Waschek, Brownlee. Inflation Fighter's Big Book: Beat the High Cost of Operating Your Home. (Illus.). 1979. 13.95 (ISBN 0-8359-3068-8). Reston.
Wasco, James E. Not for Doctors Only: Breakthrough Reports from the Medical Front. 12.95 (ISBN 0-201-08297-7); pap. 7.95 (ISBN 0-201-08298-5). A-W.
Waseda, Yoshio. The Structure of Non-Crystalline Materials. (Illus.). 304p. 1980. text ed. 44.50 (ISBN 0-07-068426-X, C). McGraw.
Waser, P., ed. Cholinergic Mechanisms. LC 74-14485. 1975. 45.00 (ISBN 0-89004-009-5). Raven.
Washam, Veronica. The One-Hander's Book: Helpful Hints for Activities of Daily Living. LC 77-155019. (John Day Bk.). (Illus.). 160p. 1973. 10.00 o.s.i. (ISBN 0-381-97096-5, TYC-T). T Y Crowell.
Washbrook, D. A., jt. auth. see Baker, C. J.
Washbrook, H. The Board & Management Audit. 262p. 1978. text ed. 30.75x (ISBN 0-220-66334-3, Pub. by Busn Bks England). Renouf.
Washburn, Bradford. Tourist Guide to Mount McKinley. rev. ed. LC 76-28403. (Illus.). 1976. pap. 4.95 o.p. (ISBN 0-88240-089-4). Alaska Northwest.
Washburn, Bradford, jt. auth. see Shipton, Eric.
Washburn, Del, jt. auth. see Lucas, Jerry.
Washburn, Deric see Corrigan, Robert W.
Washburn, Dorothy, ed. Hopi Kachina: Spirit of Life. California Academy of Sciences. (Illus.). 160p. (Orig.). 1980. pap. 14.95 (ISBN 0-295-95751-4, Pub. by Calif Acad Sci). U of Wash Pr.
Washburn, Dorothy K. A Symmetry Analysis of Upper Gila Area Ceramic Design. LC 76-53125. (Papers of the Peabody Museum Ser.: Vol. 68). (Illus.). 1977. lib. bdg. cancelled (ISBN 0-685-84633-4); pap. 20.00 (ISBN 0-87365-193-6). Peabody Harvard.
Washburn, Emory. Sketches of the Judicial History of Massachusetts from 1630 to the Revolution in 1775. LC 74-6427. (American Constitutional & Legal History Ser.). 407p. 1974. Repr. of 1840 ed. lib. bdg. 42.50 (ISBN 0-306-70616-4). Da Capo.
Washburn, J. Nile. Book of Mormon Lands & Times. LC 73-75395. 1975. 6.50 (ISBN 0-88290-020-X). Horizon Utah.
Washburn, Lindy & Van Vactor, Lloyd. Twenty Longest Days. 197p. (Orig.). 1981. pap. 7.95 (ISBN 0-8298-0450-1). Pilgrim NY.
Washburn, Michael, jt. auth. see Wehr, Paul.
Washburn, S. L. & Moore, Ruth. Ape into Human: A Study of Human Evolution. 2nd ed. (Illus.). 194p. 1980. pap. text ed. 5.95 (ISBN 0-316-92374-5). Little.
Washburn, Sherwood L. & McCown, Elizabeth. Human Evolution: Biosocial Perspectives. LC 76-27931. (Perspectives on Human Evolution). 1978. text ed. 22.95 (ISBN 0-8053-9517-2). Benjamin-Cummings.
Washburn, Susan. Partners. LC 80-65985. 1981. 11.95 (ISBN 0-689-11103-7). Atheneum.
Washburn, W-Ilcomb E. & Aubrey, John. The North American Indian Captivity. LC 76-7664. (Reference Library of the Humanities Ser.: Vol. 70). (Illus.). 1977. lib. bdg. 24.00 o.p. (ISBN 0-8240-1736-6). Garland Pub.
Washburn, Wilcomb E. The Assault of Indian Tribalism: The General Allotment Law (Dawes Act) of 1887. LC 74-23141. (America's Alternatives Ser.). 79p. 1975. pap. 2.75 o.p. (ISBN 0-397-47337-0). Lippincott.
--The Governor & the Rebel: A History of Bacon's Rebellion in Virginia. (Illus.). 272p. 1972. pap. 5.95 (ISBN 0-393-00645-X, Norton Lib). Norton.
Washburn, Wilcomb E., jt. auth. see Utley, Robert M.
Washburn, Wilcomb E., ed. A Narrative of the Capture & Treatment of John Dodge, by the English at Detroit, Repr. Of 1779. Incl. An Entertaining Narrative of the Cruel & Barbarous Treatment & Extreme Sufferings of Mr. John Dodge During His Captivity. Repr. of 1780 ed; Narratives of a Late Expedition Against the Indians...& the Wonderful Escape of Dr. Knight & John Slover from Captivity. Brackenridge, Hugh H., ed. Repr. of 1783 ed; Indian Atrocities. Repr. of 1843 ed. (Narratives of North American Indian Captivities Ser.: Vol. 12). 1978. lib. bdg. 44.00 (ISBN 0-8240-1636-X). Garland Pub.
--A Narrative of the Lord's Wonderful Dealings with John Marrant, a Black, Repr. Of 1785. Bd. with A Very Remarkable Narrative of Luke Swetland, Who Was Taken Captive Four Times in the Space of Fifteen Months. Repr. of 1785 ed. 1875 ed. with additions incl. (ISBN 0-685-63632-1); Edward Merrifield: The Story of the Captivity & Rescue from the Indians of Luke Swetland. Merrifield, Edward. Repr. of 1915 ed; A Surprising Account of the Captivity & Escape of Philip M'Donald & Alexander M'Leod of Virginia from the Chickkemogga Indians. Repr. of 1786 ed. 1794 ed. incl. (ISBN 0-685-63633-X); A Surprising Account of the Discovery of a Lady Who Was Taken by the Indians in the Year 1777, & After Making Her Escape, She Retired to a Lonely Cave, Where She Lived Nine Years. in: Bickerstaff's Almanack for the Year...1788. Repr. of 1787 ed. 1794 ed. incl. (ISBN 0-685-63634-8). (Narratives of North American Indian Captivities Ser.). 1979. lib. bdg. 44.00 (ISBN 0-8240-1641-6). Garland Pub.
--Savage Barbarism. Translated from the Spanish Publication of March 1790. in: "Connecticut Centinel," Vol. XXXII, Tues., Nov. 12, 1805, P. 4, Repr. Of 1805. Bd. with A Narrative of the Captivity of Joseph Bartlett Among the French & Indians. Repr. of 1807 ed; Horrid Murder. By the Indians. Extract of a Letter from a Gentleman in Augustine to His Friend in Virginia. in: "The New-Jersey & Pennsylvania Almanac for the Year 1808". Repr. of 1808 ed; A Narrative of the Captivity of Isaac Webster. Repr. of 1808 ed; A Narrative of the Life, Occurences, Vicissitudes & Present Situation of K. White. Repr. of 1809 ed. (Narratives of North American Indian Captivities Ser.). 1979. lib. bdg. 44.00 (ISBN 0-8240-1651-3). Garland Pub.
--A Short Sketch of the Life of Mr. Lent Munson: Alexander Viets Criswold. Incl. A Narrative of the Captivity & Sufferings of Mr. Ebenezer Fletcher of Newipswich. (Repr. of 1798; 2nd ed., repr. of 1813; 4th ed., enl., repr. of 1827); Surprizing Account of the Captivity of Miss Hannah Willis... to Which Is Added an Affecting History, of the Dreadful Distresses of Frederic Manheim's Family. Repr. of 1799 ed; Narrative of the Singular Adventures & Captivity of Mr. Thomas Barry, Among the Monsipi Indians, in the Unexplored Regions of North America. Repr. of 1800 ed. (Narratives of North American Indian Captivities Ser.: Vol. 24). 1980. lib. bdg. 44.00 (ISBN 0-8240-1648-3). Garland Pub.
Washburn, Wilcomb E., ed. see Bishop, Harriet E.
Washburn, Wilcomb E., ed. see Cutler, Jervis.
Washburn, Wilcomb E., ed. see Kellet, Alexander.
Washburn, Wilcomb E., ed. see Kimber, Edward.
Washburn, Wilcomb E., ed. see U. S. Congress.
Washburn, Wilcomb E., ed. see Walton, William.
Washburne, Carolyn K., jt. auth. see Fleming, Jennifer B.
Washington, jt. auth. see Cerami.
Washington, Allyn J. Basic Technical Mathematics. 3rd ed. LC 77-71469. 1978. pap. text ed. 21.95 (ISBN 0-8053-9520-2); instr's guide 8.95 (ISBN 0-8053-9522-9). Benjamin-Cummings.
--Basic Technical Mathematics with Calculus. 3rd ed. LC 77-71470. 1978. pap. text ed. 22.95 (ISBN 0-8053-9521-0); instr's guide 8.95 (ISBN 0-8053-9522-9). Benjamin-Cummings.
--Basic Technical Mathematics with Calculus: Metric Version. 3rd ed. LC 77-71471. 1978. pap. text ed. 22.95 (ISBN 0-8053-9523-7); instr's guide 8.95 (ISBN 0-8053-9524-5). Benjamin-Cummings.
--Introduction to Technical Mathematics. 2nd ed. LC 77-85502. 1978. 19.95 (ISBN 0-8053-9525-3). Benjamin-Cummings.
--Technical Calculus with Analytical Geometry. 2nd ed. 1979. 18.95 (ISBN 0-8053-9519-9); instr's guide 3.95 (ISBN 0-8053-9533-4). Benjamin-Cummings.
Washington, Allyn J. & Edmond, Carolyn E. Plane Trigonometry. LC 76-7883. 1977. 17.95 (ISBN 0-8465-8622-3); instr's guide 7.95 (ISBN 0-8465-8623-1). Benjamin-Cummings.
Washington, Allyn J., et al. Essentials of Basic Mathematics. 2nd ed. LC 72-92390. (gr. 9-12). 1973. text ed. 14.95 o.p. (ISBN 0-8465-8544-8). Benjamin-Cummings.
Washington, Booker T. Up from Slavery. LC 13-41242. 1933. 7.95 (ISBN 0-385-00003-0). Doubleday.
Washington Consulting Group. Uplift: What People Themselves Can Do. LC 74-81131. (Illus.). 484p. 1974. pap. 7.95 o.p. (ISBN 0-913420-38-7). Olympus Pub Co.
Washington, E. S., jt. auth. see Lindsay, Donald.
Washington, George. Diaries of George Washington: January 1790 to December1799, Vol. 6. Jackson, Donald, ed. 1980. 30.00x (ISBN 0-8139-0807-8). U Pr of Va.
--George Washington: A Biography in His Own Words. Andrist, Ralph, ed. LC 72-76000. (The Founding Father Ser). (Illus.). 416p. (YA) 1973. 15.00 o.s.i. (ISBN 0-06-010127-X, HarpT). Har-Row.
--Journal of Major George Washington. Short, James R. & Tate, Thaddeus W., Jr., eds. 1963. 2.50x o.p. (ISBN 0-8139-0402-1). U Pr of Va.
Washington, George, jt. auth. see Britton, Jack.
Washington International Arts Letter Editors, jt. auth. see Millsaps, Daniel.
Washington, James. Uncle Juan. 1981. 4.50 (ISBN 0-8062-1661-1). Carlton.
Washington, Joseph R., Jr. Black Sects & Cults. LC 72-86649. 192p. 1972. pap. 2.95 o.p. (ISBN 0-385-00252-1, Anchor Pr). Doubleday.
Washington, Mary Helen, ed. Black-Eyed Susans: Classic Stories by & About Black Women. LC 75-6169. 200p. 1975. pap. 2.95 (ISBN 0-385-09043-9, Anch). Doubleday.
Washington Post Staff. The Fall of the President. 232p. 1974. 8.95 o.p. (ISBN 0-440-04550-9). Delacorte.
Washington Post Staff Members. The Pursuit of the Presidency. Harwood, Richard, ed. Date not set. pap. 5.95 (ISBN 0-686-28876-9). Berkley Pub.
Washington Post Writers Group. The Editorial Page. 1977. pap. text ed. 8.75 (ISBN 0-395-24015-8). HM.
--Of the Press, by the Press, for the Press (& Others, Too) 2nd ed. 1976. pap. text ed. 8.75 (ISBN 0-395-24016-6). HM.
--Writing in Style. 1975. pap. text ed. 8.75 (ISBN 0-395-24018-2). HM.
Washington, Robert O., jt. auth. see Meenaghan, Thomas M.
Washington, Rosemary G. Karting: Racing's Fast Little Cars. LC 80-12385. (Superwheels & Thrill Sports Bks.). (Illus.). (YA) (gr. 4 up). 1980. PLB 6.95g (ISBN 0-8225-0435-9). Lerner Pubns.
Washington State Women's Council. Women & the Law in Washington State. LC 77-6374. 1977. pap. 2.95 (ISBN 0-914842-19-6). Madrona Pubs.
Washington University Dept. of Medicine. Manual of Medical Therapeutics. 23rd ed. Freitag, Jeffrey J. & Miller, Leslie W., eds. (Little Brown Spiral Manual Ser.). 1980. 12.95 (ISBN 0-316-92403-2). Little.
Washington, Wilcomb E., ed. see Brown, O. Z.
Washizu, Kyuichiro. Variational Methods in Elasticity & Plasticity. 2nd ed. 1974. text ed. 64.00 (ISBN 0-08-017653-4). Pergamon.
Washnis, George J. Citizen Involvement in Crime Prevention. LC 75-5238. 160p. 1976. 16.95x (ISBN 0-669-99812-5). Lexington Bks.
--Municipal Decentralization & Neighborhood Resources: Case Studies of Twelve Cities. LC 72-80467. (Special Studies in U.S. Economic, Social & Political Issues). 1972. 29.50x (ISBN 0-685-70540-4); pap. text ed. 14.50x (ISBN 0-89197-860-7). Irvington.
Washton, Andrew D. What Happens Next? Stories to Finish for Intermediate Writers. 1978. pap. text ed. 5.95x (ISBN 0-8077-2454-8). Tchrs Coll.
Wasi, Muriel. Legends of India. 2nd. ed. (Illus.). 1973. pap. 2.25 (ISBN 0-88253-326-6). Ind-US Inc.
Waskey, Leah. Monster Gallery. (Fantasy Ser.). (Illus.). 32p. 1973. pap. 3.50 (ISBN 0-912300-32-9, 32-9). Troubador Pr.
Waskow, A. Bush Is Burning. 1971. pap. 1.95 o.s.i. (ISBN 0-02-089710-3, Collier). Macmillan.
Waskow, Arthur L. Freedom Seder: A New Haggadah for Passover. 1970. 3.95 o.p. (ISBN 0-03-084532-7); pap. 1.50 (ISBN 0-03-084681-1). HR&W.
Wasley, G. D. & Warner, R. W. Microbiology. (Teach Yourself Ser.). 1974. pap. 3.95 o.p. (ISBN 0-679-10404-6). McKay.
Wasley, John. Beginner's Guide to Photography. 1974. 20.00 (ISBN 0-7207-0696-3). Transatlantic.
Wasley, John & Hill, Ron. A Guide to Hi-Fi. 1977. 15.00 (ISBN 0-7207-0906-7). Transatlantic.
Wasley, Robert S., jt. auth. see Elliot, C. Orville.
Wason, Betty. Art of German Cooking. LC 67-11151. 1967. 8.95 (ISBN 0-385-06362-8). Doubleday.
--Art of Spanish Cooking. LC 62-15903. 1963. 7.95 o.p. (ISBN 0-385-03191-2). Doubleday.
Wason, Margaret O. Class Struggles in Ancient Greece. LC 72-80600. 262p. 1973. Repr. of 1947 ed. 13.50 o.p. (ISBN 0-86527-029-5). Fertig.
Wason, P. C. & Johnson-Laird, P. N. Psychology of Reasoning: Structure & Content. LC 78-189160. 1972. 12.50 (ISBN 0-674-72126-8); pap. 3.95 (ISBN 0-674-72127-6). Harvard U Pr.
Wason, P. C., jt. ed. see Johnson-Laird, P. N.
Wasow, T. Anaphora in Generative Grammar. (Studies in Generative Linguistic Analysis: No. 2). 1980. text ed. 44.25x (ISBN 90-6439-162-9). Humanities.
Wass, Alonzo. Data Book for Residential Contractors & Estimators. (Illus.). 1979. 19.95 (ISBN 0-87909-177-0). Reston.
--Estimating Residential Construction. (Illus.). 1980. text ed. 21.95 (ISBN 0-13-289942-6). P-H.
Wass, Alonzo & Sanders, Gordon. Materials & Procedures for Residential Construction. (Illus.). text ed. 19.95 (ISBN 0-8359-4284-8). Reston.
Wass, Alonzo & Saunders. Residential Roof Framing. (Illus.). 268p. 1980. text ed. 16.95 (ISBN 0-8359-6655-0). Reston.
Wass, C. A. & Garner, K. C. Introduction to Electronic Analogue Computers. 2nd ed. 1965. 22.00 (ISBN 0-08-011071-1); pap. 10.75 (ISBN 0-08-013655-9). Pergamon.
Wassell, Richard. A Textbook of Reinsurance. 224p. 1980. 27.00x (ISBN 0-85941-166-4, Pub. by Woodhead-Faulkner England). State Mutual Bk.
Wassenbergh, H. A. Aspects of Air Law & Civil Air Policy in the Seventies. LC 79-538221. 1970. 30.00x (ISBN 90-247-5003-2). Intl Pubns Serv.
Wasser, Clinton H., jt. auth. see Scott, Thomas G.
Wasser, Lyneil L., ed. see Crane, Barbara J.
Wasserberger, Jonathan & Eubanks, David. Paramedic Procedures. 2nd ed. (Illus.). 284p. 1981. pap. text ed. 12.95 (ISBN 0-8016-5353-3). Mosby.
Wasserman, Aaron O. Biology. 2nd ed. 832p. 1975. text ed. 19.95 (ISBN 0-201-08431-7); instr's manual 6.95 (ISBN 0-201-08434-1); study guide & wkbk. 4.95 (ISBN 0-686-67101-5); lab. manual 5.95 (ISBN 0-201-08403-1). A-W.
Wasserman, Carol, jt. auth. see Wasserman, Marvin.
Wasserman, Dan, ed. see Reese, Bob.
Wasserman, Dan, ed. see Reese, Bob, et al.
Wasserman, Dan, ed. see Reese, Bob.
Wasserman, Dan, ed. see Reese, Bob, et al.
Wasserman, Dan, ed. see Scoder, Judy.
Wasserman, Dan, ed. see Shebar, Sharon.
Wasserman, Dan, ed. see Willoughby, Alana.
Wasserman, Edward & Gromisch, Donald S. Survey of Clinical Pediatrics. 7th ed. (Illus.). 560p. 1981. text ed. 27.95 (ISBN 0-07-068431-6, HP). McGraw.
Wasserman, Edward D. & Gromisch, Donald S. Pediatrics - A Problem-Oriented Approach. 1980. spiral bdg. 9.75 (ISBN 0-87488-050-5). Med Exam.
Wasserman, Elga, et al, eds. Women in Academia: Evolving Policies Toward Equal Opportunities. LC 74-1734. (Special Studies). (Illus.). 188p. 1975. text ed. 22.95 (ISBN 0-275-09530-4). Praeger.
Wasserman, Emily. The American Scene-Early Twentieth Century. (Illus.). 1975. Repr. 5.95 o.p. (ISBN 0-88308-006-0). Lamplight Pub.
Wasserman, Fred W. & Miller, Michael C. Building a Group Practice. 188p. 1973. text ed. 11.75 (ISBN 0-398-02774-9); pap. text ed. 8.50 (ISBN 0-398-02793-5). C C Thomas.
Wasserman, G. Stability of Unfoldings. (Lecture Notes in Mathematics: Vol. 393). xxix, 164p. 1974. pap. 10.40 o.p. (ISBN 0-387-06794-9). Springer-Verlag.
Wasserman, George R. John Dryden. (English Authors Ser.: No. 14). 1964. lib. bdg. 10.95 (ISBN 0-8057-1176-7). Twayne.
--Samuel Butler. (English Author Ser.: No. 193). 1976. lib. bdg. 10.95 (ISBN 0-8057-6667-7). Twayne.
Wasserman, Gerald S. Color Vision: An Historical Introduction. LC 78-5346. (Wiley Ser. in Behavior). 1978. 25.95 (ISBN 0-471-92128-9, Pub. by Wiley-Interscience). Wiley.
Wasserman, Harvey. Energy War: Reports from the Front. 270p. 1979. 12.95 (ISBN 0-88208-105-5); pap. 5.95 (ISBN 0-88208-106-3). Lawrence Hill.
Wasserman, Jack. Leonardo. LC 80-645. (Illus.). 160p. 1980. 14.95 (ISBN 0-385-17167-6). Doubleday.

--Leonardo Da Vinci. LC 74-13112. (Library of Great Painters). (Illus.). 160p. 1975. 35.00 (ISBN 0-8109-0262-1). Abrams.

Wasserman, Lou. Raise & Show Guppies. (Illus.). 1977. pap. 4.95 (ISBN 0-87666-453-2, PS-738). TFH Pubns.

Wasserman, Mark, jt. auth. see Keen, Benjamin.

Wasserman, Marvin & Wasserman, Carol. Curso Primero. (gr. 8-10). 1979. 5.42 (ISBN 0-87720-521-3). AMSCO Sch.

--Prosa De la Espana Moderna. (gr. 11). 1972. pap. text ed. 5.17 (ISBN 0-87720-517-5). AMSCO Sch.

--Susana y Javier En Espana. (Orig.). (gr. 7-12). 1975. pap. text ed. 4.58 (ISBN 0-87720-502-7). AMSCO Sch.

Wasserman, Paul & Bossart, Jane. Health Organizations of the U.S., Canada & Internationally: A Directory of Voluntary Associations, Professional Societies & Other Groups Concerned with Health & Related Fields. 5th ed. 500p. 1977. 42.00 (ISBN 0-686-64907-9). Gale.

Wasserman, Paul, ed. Awards, Honors & Prizes: United States & Canada, Vol. 1. 4th ed. LC 78-16691. 1978. 62.00 (ISBN 0-8103-0378-7). Gale.

--Catalog of Museum Publications & Media. 2nd ed. LC 79-22633. 1980. 120.00 (ISBN 0-8103-0388-4). Gale.

--Health Organizations of the United States & Canada: A Directory of Voluntary Associations, Professional Societies & Other Groups Concerned with Health & Related Fields. 5th ed. 500p. 1981. 36.00 (ISBN 0-8103-0466-X). Gale.

--Learning Independently. 1st ed. LC 79-21025. 1979. 76.00 (ISBN 0-8103-0317-5). Gale.

--New Training & Development Organizations: Supplement to Training & Development Organizations Directory, 2nd Edition. 1981. Set. pap. 48.00 (ISBN 0-686-69180-6). Gale.

--Reader in Library Administration. Bundy, Mary Lee. LC 68-28324. (Reader Ser. in Library & Information Science: Vol. 1). 1969. 17.00 (ISBN 0-910972-16-8). IHS-PDS.

--Speakers & Lecturers: How to Find Them. 2nd ed. 350p. 1981. 68.00 (ISBN 0-8103-0393-0). Gale.

--Training & Development Organizations Directory. 2nd ed. 1980. 125.00 (ISBN 0-8103-0314-0). Gale.

Wasserman, Paul & Bernero, Jacqueline R., eds. Speakers & Lecturers: How to Find Them. LC 78-26025. 464p. 1979. 62.00 o.p. (ISBN 0-8103-0392-2). Gale.

Wasserman, Paul & Bossart, Jane, eds. Health Organizations of the U.S., Canada, & Internationally: A Directory of Voluntary Associations, Professional Societies & Other Groups Concerned with Health & Related Fields. 4th ed. LC 77-79000. 500p. 1977. 36.00 (ISBN 0-686-27874-7). Kruzas Assoc.

Wasserman, Paul & Herman, Esther, eds. Festivals Sourcebook: A Reference Guide to Fairs, Festivals, & Celebrations. 1st ed. LC 76-48852. 1977. 68.00 (ISBN 0-8103-0311-6). Gale.

Wasserman, Paul & Kaszubski, Marek, eds. Law & Legal Information Directory: A Guide to National & International Organizations, Bar Associations, Federal Court System, Federal Regulatory Agencies, Law Schools, Continuing Legal Education, Scholarships & Grants, Awards & Prizes, Special Libraries, Information Systems & Services, Research Centers, Etc. 800p. 1980. 110.00 (ISBN 0-8103-0169-5). Gale.

Wasserman, Paul & McLean, Janice, eds. New Consultants, Periodical Supplement for Consultants & Consulting Organizations Directory: Four Issues Covering the Period Between Editions, Issue 1. 4th ed. 1979. 130.00 (ISBN 0-8103-0354-X). Gale.

--Who's Who in Consulting: A Reference Guide to Professional Personnel Engaged in Consultation for Business, Industry & Government. 2nd ed. LC 73-16373. 1973. 90.00 (ISBN 0-8103-0360-4). Gale.

Wasserman, Paul & Morgan, Jean, eds. Consumer Sourcebook, 2 vols. 3rd ed. 1800p. 1981. Set. 78.00 (ISBN 0-8103-0383-3). Gale.

--Consumer Sourcebook: A Directory & Guide, 2 vols. 2nd ed. LC 77-279. 1978. 68.00 set o.p. (ISBN 0-8103-0382-5). Gale.

--Ethnic Information Sources of the United States: A Guide to Organizations, Agencies, Foundations, Institutions, Media, Commercial & Trade Bodies, Government Programs, Research Institutes, Libraries & Museums, Etc. LC 76-4642. 350p. 1976. 70.00 (ISBN 0-8103-0373-6). Gale.

Wasserman, Paul & Wasserman, Steven R., eds. Recreation & Outdoor Life Directory. LC 79-4594. 500p. 1979. 68.00 (ISBN 0-8103-0315-9). Gale.

Wasserman, Paul, et al, eds. Encyclopedia of Business Information Sources. 4th, rev. ed. LC 79-24771. 1980. 85.00 (ISBN 0-8103-0368-X). Gale.

--Encyclopedia of Geographic Information Sources. 3rd ed. LC 78-55032. 1978. 45.00 (ISBN 0-8103-0374-4). Gale.

Wasserman, Pauline & Wasserman, Sheldon. Guide to Fortified Wines. Larsen, Madelyn, ed. 128p. (Orig.). Date not set. pap. cancelled (ISBN 0-346-12446-8). Cornerstone.

Wasserman, Pauline, et al. Guide to Champagne & Sparkling Wines. 128p. Date not set. pap. cancelled (ISBN 0-346-12502-2). Cornerstone.

Wasserman, Rosanne, ed. see Pekarik, Andrew J.

Wasserman, Sheldon, jt. auth. see Wasserman, Pauline.

Wasserman, Steven R., jt. ed. see Wasserman, Paul.

Wasserman, Tamara E. & Hill, Jonathan S. Bolivian Indian Textiles: Traditional Designs & Costumes. (Pictorial Archive Ser.). (Illus.). 64p. (Orig.). 1981. pap. price not set (ISBN 0-486-24118-1). Dover.

Wasserman, William, jt. auth. see Neter, John.

Wassermann, G., ed. see International Symposium Clausthal - Zellerfeld, 1968.

Wasserstein, Bernard. Britain & the Jews of Europe 1939-1945. 1979. 19.95 (ISBN 0-19-822600-4). Oxford U Pr.

Wasserstrom, Richard. Philosophy & Social Issues: Five Studies. LC 79-9486. 224p. 1980. pap. text ed. 6.95 (ISBN 0-268-01536-8). U of Notre Dame Pr.

--War & Morality. 1970. pap. 7.95x (ISBN 0-534-00681-7). Wadsworth Pub.

Wasserstrom, Richard A. Morality & the Law. 1970. pap. 7.95x (ISBN 0-534-00167-X). Wadsworth Pub.

Wassersug, Joseph D. Jarm-How to Jog with Your Arms to Live Longer. 1981. 11.95 (ISBN 0-87949-197-3). Ashley Bks.

Wasson, Chester R. Strategy of Marketing Research. LC 64-15387. (Illus.). 1964. 24.50x (ISBN 0-89197-426-1); pap. text ed. 14.95x (ISBN 0-89197-953-0). Irvington.

Wasson, John M. Subject & Structure: An Anthology for Writers. 7th ed. 1981. pap. text ed. 7.95 (ISBN 0-316-92423-7); tchrs'. manual free (ISBN 0-316-92424-5). Little.

Wasson, R. Gordon. The Wonderous Mushroom: Mycolatry in Mesoamerica. LC 79-26895. (Illus.). 178p. 1980. 14.95 (ISBN 0-07-068441-3); deluxe ed. 435.00 (ISBN 0-07-068442-1); pap. 10.95 (ISBN 0-07-068443-X). McGraw.

Waswo, Ann. Japanese Landlords: The Decline of a Rural Elite. 1977. 15.75x (ISBN 0-520-03217-9). U of Cal Pr.

Waswo, Richard. The Fatal Mirror: Themes & Techniques in the Poetry of Fulke Greville. LC 75-188603. 1972. 10.95x (ISBN 0-8139-0392-0). U Pr of Va.

Wasz-Hoeckert, O., et al. The Infant Cry: A Spectographic & Auditory Analysis. (Clinics in Developmental Medicine Ser. No. 29). 42p. 1968. 12.00 (ISBN 0-685-24737-6). Lippincott.

Watanabe, M. S. Knowing & Guessing: A Quantitative Study of Inference & Information. 1969. 39.95 (ISBN 0-471-92130-0, Pub. by Wiley-Interscience). Wiley.

Watanabe, Masahiro & Nagashima, Kei. Instant Japanese. (Illus.). 188p. 1981. pap. 3.95 (ISBN 0-89346-182-2). Heian Intl.

Watanabe, Masahiro & Rogers, Bruce. Instant Japan. (Illus.). 202p. 1981. pap. 3.95 (ISBN 0-89346-181-4). Heian Intl.

Watanabe, Shigeo. Get Set! Go! (Illus.). 32p. (gr. 2-5). 1981. 6.95 (ISBN 0-399-20780-5); lib. bdg. 6.99 (ISBN 0-399-61175-4). Philomel.

Watanabe, Yuichi. Wally the Whale Who Loved Balloons. Ooka, Diane, tr. from Japanese. (Illus.). Date not set. 8.95 (ISBN 0-89346-150-4). Heian Intl. Postponed.

Water, Frederic F. Van De see Van De Water, Frederic F.

Water, John W. Van De see Van De Water, J. W.

Water Resources Center, University at Berkeley, Calif. Dictionary Catalog of the Water Resources Center: Sixth Supplement, 2 vols. 1978. Set. lib. bdg. 250.00 (ISBN 0-8161-0244-9). G K Hall.

Waterbury, John. Egypt: Burdens of the Past, Options for the Future. LC 78-3248. (Illus.). 336p. 1978. pap. 9.95x (ISBN 0-253-28092-3). Ind U Pr.

--North for the Trade: The Life & Times of a Berber Merchant. LC 70-174453. (Illus.). 200p. 1972. 20.00x (ISBN 0-520-02134-7). U of Cal Pr.

Waterbury, Larry. Hematology for the House Officer. (House Officer Ser.). (Illus.). 152p. 1981. softcover 10.95 (ISBN 0-683-08851-3). Williams & Wilkins.

Waterer, John W. Spanish Leather. (Illus.). 1971. 48.00 (ISBN 0-571-09043-5, Pub. by Faber & Faber). Merrimack Bk Serv.

Waterfield, Hermoine & Forbes, Christopher. Faberge Imperial Eggs & Other Fantasies. (Illus.). 1978. 19.95 o.p. (ISBN 0-684-15966-X, ScribT). Scribner.

Waterhouse, R. B. Fretting Corrosion. 1973. text ed. 37.00 (ISBN 0-08-016902-3). Pergamon.

Waterlow, S., tr. see Romains, Jules.

Waterman, Barbara, jt. auth. see Waitzkin, Howard.

Waterman, Cary. The Salamander Migration & Other Poems. LC 79-24291. (Pitt Poetry Ser.). 1980. 9.95 (ISBN 0-8229-3415-9); pap. 4.50 (ISBN 0-8229-5315-3). U of Pittsburgh Pr.

Waterman, John T. Leibniz & Ludolf on Things Linguistic: Excerpts from Their Correspondence, (1688-1703) (Publications in Linguistics: No. 88). 1978. pap. 9.50x (ISBN 0-520-09586-3). U of Cal Pr.

Waterman, Kenneth O. No Tears for Mao. 1981. 4.95 (ISBN 0-8062-1698-0). Carlton.

Waterman, Marvin, et al. Essays on Business Finance. 4th ed. LC 57-1744. 1952. 10.00 (ISBN 0-685-73275-4). Masterco Pr.

Waterman, Paul. Great Adventures of the Old Testament. LC 22-769. (Activity Book Ser.). (ps-2). Vol. 1. pap. 0.79 (ISBN 0-87123-751-2, 220751); Vol. 2. pap. 0.79 (ISBN 0-87123-769-5). Bethany Fell.

Waterman, T. H., ed. The Physiology of Crustacea, 2 vols. Incl. Vol. 1. Metabolism & Growth. 1960. 48.00 (ISBN 0-12-737601-1); Vol. 2. Sense Organs, Integration & Behavior. 1961. 48.00 (ISBN 0-12-737602-X). Set. 90.00 (ISBN 0-685-23209-3). Acad Pr.

Watermulder, David B. & Krodel, Gerhard. Advent-Christmas. LC 73-79329. (Proclamation 1: Aids for Interpreting the Lessons of the Church Year, Ser. C). 64p. 1973. pap. 1.95 (ISBN 0-8006-4051-9, 1-4051). Fortress.

Waters, Brent G. & Jurek, Mary B., eds. Self-Assessment of Current Knowledge in Psychosis. LC 80-18729. 1980. pap. 18.00 (ISBN 0-87488-233-8). Med Exam.

Waters, Chocolate. Take Me Like a Photograph. (Illus.). 1977. pap. 4.00 (ISBN 0-935060-02-2). Eggplant Pr.

--Take Me Like a Photograph. 2nd ed. 1980. 4.75 (ISBN 0-935060-02-2). Eggplant Pr.

--To the Man Reporter from the Denver Post. rev. ed. 1980. 3.75 (ISBN 0-935060-05-7). Eggplant Pr.

Waters, D. D., jt. auth. see Methold, K.

Waters, E. G., jt. auth. see Studer, Paul.

Waters, E. K. Human Relations for the Educational Environment. LC 78-54601. 1978. pap. text ed. 6.75x (ISBN 0-8191-0510-4). U Pr of Amer.

Waters, Edward N. Victor Herbert: A Life in Music. LC 78-9597. (Music Reprint, 1978 Ser.). 1978. Repr. of 1955 ed. lib. bdg. 45.00 (ISBN 0-306-79502-7). Da Capo.

Waters, Ethel & Michel, Charles. His Eye Is on the Sparrow. 1972. pap. 2.25 (ISBN 0-515-05287-6). Jove Pubns.

Waters, Frank. Book of the Hopi. (Illus.). 1974. pap. 2.50 (ISBN 0-345-27573-X). Ballantine.

--The Earp Brothers of Tombstone: The Story of Mrs. Virgil Earp. LC 75-38611. (Illus.). viii, 247p. 1976. 14.95x (ISBN 0-8032-0873-1); pap. 3.75 (ISBN 0-8032-5838-0, BB 618, Bison). U of Nebr Pr.

--Man Who Killed the Deer. LC 73-149327. 266p. 1942. 9.95 o.p. (ISBN 0-8040-0193-6, SB); pap. 5.95 (ISBN 0-8040-0194-4, 12). Swallow.

--The Man Who Killed the Deer. pap. 2.50 (ISBN 0-671-43295-8). PB.

--Masked Gods: Navaho & Pueblo Ceremonialism. LC 73-1799. 438p. 1950. 15.00 (ISBN 0-8040-0196-0, SB); pap. 7.95 (ISBN 0-8040-0641-5, SB). Swallow.

--Midas of the Rockies: The Story of Stratton & Cripple Creek. LC 73-163716. 347p. 1972. pap. 5.95 (ISBN 0-8040-0591-5). Swallow.

--People of the Valley. LC 78-137435. 201p. 1941. 10.95 (ISBN 0-8040-0242-8, SB); pap. 5.95 (ISBN 0-8040-0243-6). Swallow.

--Pumpkin Seed Point: Being Within the Hopi. LC 76-75741. 175p. 1969. 8.50 (ISBN 0-8040-0255-X, SB); pap. 4.95 (ISBN 0-8040-0635-0). Swallow.

--The Woman at Otowi Crossing: A Novel. LC 66-25961. 300p. 1981. pap. 6.95 (ISBN 0-8040-0415-3, SB). Swallow.

--The Yogi of Cockroach Court. LC 72-91922. 277p. 1947. pap. 5.95 (ISBN 0-8040-0613-X, SB). Swallow.

Waters, Harold. Cancer Immunology: Vol. 7, Immune Function & Dysfunction in Relation to Cancer, Vol. 7. LC 80-774. 384p. 1980. lib. bdg. 57.50 (ISBN 0-8240-7111-5). Garland Pub.

--Smugglers of Spirits: Prohibition & the Coast Guard Patrol. 1971. 7.95 (ISBN 0-8038-6705-0). Hastings.

Waters, J. Erwin, jt. auth. see Porter, W. Curtis.

Waters, John F. Camels: Ships of the Desert. LC 73-14514. (A Let's Read-&-Find-Out Science Bk). (Illus.). (ps-3). 1974. 7.95 (ISBN 0-690-00394-3, TYC-J); PLB 7.89 (ISBN 0-690-00395-1). T Y Crowell.

--Carnivorous Plants. LC 73-21976. (First Bks). (Illus.). 72p. (gr. 4-6). 1974. PLB 4.90 o.p. (ISBN 0-531-02700-7). Watts.

--Crab from Yesterday: The Life Cycle of a Horseshoe Crab. LC 74-161067. (gr. 2-5). 1970. PLB 4.95 o.p. (ISBN 0-7232-6085-0). Warne.

--Creatures of Darkness. LC 74-78113. (Illus.). 128p. (gr. 3-7). 1975. 5.95 o.p. (ISBN 0-8027-6199-2); PLB 5.83 (ISBN 0-8027-6200-X). Walker & Co.

--Crime Labs: The Science of Forensic Medicine. (Impact Ser.). (Illus.). (gr. 7 up). 1979. PLB 6.90 s&l (ISBN 0-531-02286-2). Watts.

--Fishing. (First Bks.). (Illus.). (gr. 4-6). 1978. PLB 6.45 s&l (ISBN 0-531-01407-X). Watts.

--Giant Sea Creatures, Real & Fantastic. LC 72-85584. (Illus.). 160p. (gr. 4-6). 1973. 4.95 o.p. (ISBN 0-695-80371-9); lib. ed. 4.98 o.p. (ISBN 0-695-40371-0). Follett.

--Green Turtle Mysteries. LC 70-158701. (A Let's-Read-&-Find-Out Science Bk). (Illus.). (gr. k-3). 1972. 7.95 (ISBN 0-690-35994-2, TYC-J); PLB 7.89 (ISBN 0-690-35995-0). T Y Crowell.

--Hungry Sharks. LC 72-7563. (A Let's-Read-&-Find-Out Science Bk). (Illus.). 40p. (ps-3). 1974. PLB 7.89 (ISBN 0-690-01121-0, TYC-J). T Y Crowell.

--Maritime Careers. (Career Concise Guides Ser.). (Illus.). 1977. 6.45 (ISBN 0-531-01283-2). Watts.

Waters, Kathleen & Murphy, Gretchen. Medical Records in Health Information. LC 79-18793. 1979. text ed. 32.95 (ISBN 0-89443-157-9). Aspen Systems.

Waters, Kenneth H. Reflection Seismology. 2nd ed. 350p. 1981. 34.95 (ISBN 0-471-08224-4, Pub. by Wiley-Interscience). Wiley.

Waters, T. A. Psychologistics. 1972. 8.95 o.p. (ISBN 0-394-46922-4). Random.

Waters, Udell. Mother O'Possum's Problem. 1980. 4.95 (ISBN 0-8062-1494-5). Carlton.

Waters, William R. Employer Pension Plan Membership & Household Wealth. LC 79-92473. (S. S. Huebner Foundation Monograph: No. 10). (Illus.). 1981. pap. price not set (ISBN 0-918930-10-3). Huebner Foun Insur.

Waterson, A. P. & Wilkinson, L. An Introduction to the History of Virology. LC 77-17892. (Illus.). 1978. 38.50 (ISBN 0-521-21917-5). Cambridge U Pr.

Waterson, A. P., ed. Recent Advances in Clinical Virology, No. 2. (Illus.). 178p. 1980. text ed. 40.00 (ISBN 0-443-02094-9). Churchill.

Waterson, Natalie. Uzbeck-English Dictionary. 240p. 1980. 55.00x (ISBN 0-19-713597-8). Oxford U Pr.

Waterston, Elizabeth. Brush up Your Basics: Clear Thinking, Clear Writing. 112p. 1981. pap. text ed. 5.95 (ISBN 0-8403-2387-5). Kendall-Hunt.

Waterton, Betty. Pettranella. (Illus.). 32p. (gr. 1-4). 1981. 8.95 (ISBN 0-8149-0844-6). Vanguard.

Waterton, Charles. Wanderings in South America. Phelps, Gilbert, intro. by. (Illus.). 257p. 1974. 15.00x (ISBN 0-85314-155-X). Transatlantic.

Wathen, James F. The Great Sacrilege. LC 76-183571. 1971. 5.00 o.p. (ISBN 0-89555-016-4, 120); pap. text ed. 3.50 (ISBN 0-89555-014-8). TAN Bks Pubs.

Wathen, Richard B. Wathen's Law. LC 80-51730. 306p. (Orig.). 1980. pap. 5.95 (ISBN 0-89526-891-4). Regnery-Gateway.

Wathen, Thomas W. Security Subjects: An Officer's Guide to Plant Protection. (Illus.). 1972. pap. 6.50 o.p. (ISBN 0-398-02492-8). C C Thomas.

Watjen, Richard L. Dressage Riding. (Illus.). 1978. Repr. 10.35 (ISBN 0-85131-275-6, Dist. by Sporting Book Center). J A Allen.

Watkin, Brian. The National Health Service: The First Phase 1948-1974 & After. 1978. text ed. 25.00x (ISBN 0-04-362025-6); pap. text ed. 8.95x (ISBN 0-04-362026-4). Allen Unwin.

Watkin, Bruce. Surrey: A Shell Guide. 1977. 13.95 (ISBN 0-571-09609-3, Pub. by Faber & Faber). Merrimack Bk Serv.

Watkin, D. The Triumph of the Classical. LC 77-12164. (Illus.). 1977. 16.00 (ISBN 0-521-21854-3); pap. 8.95 (ISBN 0-521-29292-1). Cambridge U Pr.

Watkin, David. English Architecture: A Concise History. (World of Art Ser.). (Illus.). 1979. 17.95 (ISBN 0-19-520147-7); pap. 9.95 (ISBN 0-19-520148-5). Oxford U Pr.

--The Life & Work of C. R. Cockerell. (Studies in Architecture). (Illus.). 1975. 37.50 o.p. (ISBN 0-8390-0152-5). Allanheld & Schram.

Watkin, David, jt. auth. see Middleton, Robin.

Watkin, Virginia G. Taxes & Tax Harmonization in Central America. LC 67-26564. (Illus.). 534p. (Orig.). 1967. pap. 15.00x (ISBN 0-915506-07-6). Harvard Law Intl Tax.

Watkins, A. J. Electrical Installation Calculations, Vol. 1. 3rd ed. 100p. 1980. 13.00x (ISBN 0-7131-3422-4, Pub. by Arnold Pubs England). State Mutual Bk.

--Electrical Installation Calculations: SJ Units, Vol. 2. 2nd ed. 106p. 1980. 13.00x (Pub. by Arnold Pubs England). State Mutual Bk.

--Electrical Installation Calculations: SI Units, Vol. 3. 154p. 1980. 13.00x (ISBN 0-7131-3224-8, Pub. by Arnold Pubs England). State Mutual Bk.

Watkins, A. M. How to Judge a House. 1972. pap. 3.50 (ISBN 0-8015-3732-0, Hawthorn). Dutton.

Watkins, A. T., jt. auth. see Reese, Terence.

Watkins, Alfred J. The Practice of Urban Economics. LC 80-13809. (Sage Library of Social Research: Vol. 107). (Illus.). 248p. 1980. 18.00 (ISBN 0-8039-1380-X); pap. 8.95 (ISBN 0-8039-1381-8). Sage.

Watkins, Art. How to Avoid the Ten Biggest Home Buying Traps. 1979. pap. 4.50 (ISBN 0-8015-3895-5, Hawthorn). Dutton.

Watkins, Arthur M. The New Complete Book of Home Remodeling, Improvement, & Repair. (Encore Edition). (Illus.). 1979. 7.95 (ISBN 0-684-16731-X, ScribT). Scribner.

Watkins, Arthur R., jt. auth. see Rogers, R. M.

Watkins, B. Radiation Therapy Mold Technology: Principles. Design & Applications. (Illus.). 224p. 1981. 30.00 (ISBN 0-08-025373-3). Pergamon.

Watkins, Bruce O., jt. auth. see Jensen, Randall W.

Watkins, C. Ken. Social Control. (Aspects of Modern Sociology Ser). 176p. 1975. pap. text ed. 8.95x (ISBN 0-582-48714-5). Longman.

Watkins, Carleton E. Photographs of the Columbia River & Oregon. Alinder, James, ed. LC 79-54978. (Illus.). 1979. 29.50 o.p. (ISBN 0-933286-13-9); pap. 16.50 (ISBN 0-933286-14-7). Friends Photography.

Watkins, David. Thomas Hope & the Neo-Classical Idea. 1970. 24.00 (ISBN 0-7195-1819-9). Transatlantic.

Watkins, Derek. Good Photography Made Easy. LC 76-8616. (Leisure and Travel Ser). (Illus.). 128p. 1976. 8.95 (ISBN 0-7153-7212-2). David & Charles.

--Practical Photographic Enlarging. 224p. 1974. 9.95 o.p. (ISBN 0-13-692269-4, Spec); pap. 4.95 (ISBN 0-13-692251-1, Spec). P-H.

--SLR Photography. LC 76-54090. 1977. 14.95 (ISBN 0-7153-7301-3). David & Charles.

Watkins, Don. Newspaper Advertising Handbook. LC 80-10996. (Illus.). 112p. 1980. 12.95 (ISBN 0-936294-01-9); pap. 7.95 (ISBN 0-936294-00-0). Newspaper Bk.

Watkins, Fincham. Construction Science & Materials for Technicians 2. 1981. text ed. price not set (ISBN 0-408-00488-6). Butterworth.

Watkins, Floyd C. & Dillingham, William B. Practical English Handbook. 5th ed. LC 77-75888. (Illus.). 1977. pap. text ed. 7.50 (ISBN 0-395-25825-1); inst. annot. ed. 8.75 (ISBN 0-395-25824-3); wkbk. 6.75 (ISBN 0-395-25830-8); inst. manual 0.40 (ISBN 0-395-25831-6); diagnostic test 1.50 (ISBN 0-395-29305-7). HM.

Watkins, Frederick, jt. auth. see Kramnick, Isaac.

Watkins, George. The Steam Engine in Industry-One. 128p. 1980. 25.00x (ISBN 0-686-64742-4, Pub. by Moorland England). State Mutual Bk.

Watkins, George T. Bibliography of Printing in America. Lew, Irving, ed. (Bibliographical Reprint Ser.). 1962. pap. 15.00 ltd. ed. (ISBN 0-89782-002-9). Battery Pk.

Watkins, Gwen, ed. see Watkins, Vernon.

Watkins, Helen H., jt. auth. see Watkins, John G.

Watkins, Janet. Savoring the Sabbath. LC 80-83865. 80p. (Orig.). 1980. pap. 4.95 (ISBN 0-88290-165-6, 1058). Horizon Utah.

Watkins, John G. & Watkins, Helen H. Ego-States & Hidden Observers & the Women in Black & the Lady in White. (Sound Seminars Ser.). 1980. transcript & tapes 29.50x (ISBN 0-88432-066-9, 29400-29401). J Norton Pubs.

Watkins, K. W. Practice of Politics. 1975. 15.95x (ISBN 0-17-711127-5). Intl Ideas.

Watkins, Keith. Faithful & Fair: Transcending Sexist Language in Worship. LC 80-39698. 128p. 1981. pap. 4.95 (ISBN 0-687-12707-6). Abingdon.

--The Feast of Joy: Ministering the Lord's Supper in the Free Tradition. 1977. pap. 2.50 (ISBN 0-8272-1006-X). Bethany Pr.

Watkins, Larry C., et al. Bats of Jalisco, Mexico. (Special Publications: No. 1). (Illus., Orig.). 1972. pap. 2.00 (ISBN 0-89672-026-8). Tex Tech Pr.

Watkins, Leroy. Evangelismo En Accion. 1979. 4.95 (ISBN 0-311-13831-4). Casa Bautista.

Watkins, Lillian, jt. ed. see Loban, Walter.

Watkins, Mary L., jt. auth. see Jensen, Ann.

Watkins, Miles A., et al. Alternative Three. 1979. pap. 2.25 (ISBN 0-380-44677-4). Avon.

Watkins, Morris. Literacy, Bible Reading & Church Growth Through the Ages. LC 78-15315. (Illus.). 1978. pap. 5.95 (ISBN 0-87808-325-1). William Carey Lib.

Watkins, Nina, ed. International Who's Who in Community Service. 851p. 1974. 32.50x (ISBN 0-85649-012-1, Pub. by Intl Biog). Biblio Dist.

Watkins, Susan M. Conversations with Seth, Vol. 1. LC 80-17760. 1980. 10.95 (ISBN 0-13-172007-4). P-H.

Watkins, T. F., et al. Chemical Warfare, Pyrotechnics & the Fireworks Industry. 1968. 16.50 (ISBN 0-08-012811-4); pap. 7.75 (ISBN 0-08-012810-6). Pergamon.

Watkins, T. H. John Muir's America. (Illus.). 160p. 1981. pap. 12.95 (ISBN 0-912856-64-5). Graphic Arts Ctr.

Watkins, Vernon. I That Was Born in Wales: A New Selection from the Poems of Vernon Watkins. Watkins, Gwen & Pryor, R., eds. 1976. bds. 8.00 (ISBN 0-7083-0615-2). Verry.

Watkins, W. Sheet Metal Fabrication. (Illus.). 1971. pap. text ed. 22.30x (ISBN 0-444-20124-6, Pub. by Applied Science). Burgess-Intl Ideas.

Watkins, W. P., ed. see International Cooperative Alliance.

Watkins, Wayne. Hypothalamic Releasing Factors, Vol. 1. 1977. 19.20 (ISBN 0-88831-002-1). Eden Med Res.

Watkins, Wayne B. Hypothalamic Releasing Factors, Vol. 2, 1977. Horrobin, David F., ed. (Annual Research Reviews Ser.). 1978. 21.60 (ISBN 0-88831-033-1). Eden Med Res.

Watkins, William J. Suburban Wilderness. (Illus.). 192p. 1981. 9.95 (ISBN 0-399-12552-3). Putnam.

Watkins, William J. & Cavalieri, Grace. Per-Se Award Plays, 1969: Special Issue 5. 38p. pap. 1.00 (ISBN 0-912292-06-7). The Smith.

Watkins, William J., jt. auth. see Brown, Tom.

Watkinson, R. J., ed. Developments in Biodegradation of Hydrocarbons, Vol. 1. (Illus.). 1978. text ed. 45.50x (ISBN 0-85334-751-4, Pub. by Applied Science). Burgess-Intl Ideas.

Watkins-Pitchford, Denys J. Countryside. LC 66-97721. (Pegasus Books: No. 1). (Illus.). 1964. 7.50x (ISBN 0-234-77773-7). Intl Pubns Serv.

Watling, E. F., tr. see Sophocles.

Watling, Roy. How to Identify Mushrooms to Genus V. Using Cultural & Developmental Features. 1981. pap. price not set. Mad River.

Watling, Roy & Gregory, Norma. Census Catalogue of World Members of the Bolbitiaceae. (Bibliotheca Mycologica). 300p. 1981. lib. bdg. 40.00x (ISBN 3-7682-1279-3, Pub. by Cramer Germany). Lubrecht & Cramer.

Watling, Roy, ed. A Literature Guide to the Identification of Mushrooms. 120p. (Orig.). 1980. pap. 6.75. Mad River.

Watling, T. & Morley, J. Successful Commodity Futures Trading. 2nd ed. 244p. 1974. text ed. 29.50x (ISBN 0-220-66340-8, Pub. by Busn Bks England). Renouf.

Watling, T. F., jt. auth. see Taylor, W. J.

Watling, Tom. Plan for Promotion: Advancement & the Manager. 237p. 1977. text ed. 19.75x (ISBN 0-220-66327-0, Pub. by Busn Bks England). Renouf.

Watney, Bernard. English Blue & White Porcelain of the Eighteenth Century. 2nd ed. 1973. 41.00 (ISBN 0-571-04796-3, Pub. by Faber & Faber). Merrimack Bk Serv.

--Longton Hall Porcelain. 1957. 22.00 (ISBN 0-571-06580-5, Pub. by Faber & Faber). Merrimack Bk Serv.

Watney, John. Boat Electrics. LC 80-68680. (Illus.). 160p. 1981. 24.50 (ISBN 0-7153-7957-7). David & Charles.

--Mervyn Peake. LC 76-17422. (Illus.). 1977. 10.95 o.p. (ISBN 0-312-53025-0). St Martin.

Watrous, Livingston V. Lasithi, A History of Settlement on a Highland Plain in Crete. (Hesperia Ser.: Suppl. XVIII). 1981. price not set (ISBN 0-87661-518-3). Am Sch Athens.

Watson. I Believe in the Church. pap. 4.95. Eerdmans.

--Marine Electrical Practice. 5th ed. 1981. text ed. price not set (ISBN 0-408-00498-3). Butterworth.

Watson, ed. see Grosicki.

Watson, A., et al. The Generic Names of Moths of the World. Vol. II. Noctuoidea: Arctiidae, Ctenuchidae, Dioptidae, Lymantriidae, Notodontidae, Thaumetopoeidae & Thyretidae. Nye, I. W., ed. (Illus.). xiv, 228p. 1980. 58.00x (ISBN 0-565-00811-0). Sabbot-Natural Hist Bks.

Watson, A. H., jt. auth. see Munby, Denys.

Watson, A. H., ed. Nursery Rhymes. (Childrens Illustrated Classics Ser). (Illus.). 1975. Repr. of 1958 ed. 9.00x o.p. (ISBN 0-460-05041-9, Pub. by J. M. Dent England). Biblio Dist.

Watson, A. H., ed. see Munby, D. L.

Watson, A. Shaw. Aquaculture & Algae Culture-Processes & Products. LC 79-17067. (Food Technology Review: No. 53). (Illus.). 1980. 32.00 (ISBN 0-8155-0779-8). Noyes.

Watson, Adam. Toleration in Religion & Politics. LC 80-65746. (Second Annual Distinguished Cria Lecture on Morality & Foreign Policy Ser.). 1980. pap. 4.00 (ISBN 0-87641-218-5). Coun Rel & Intl.

Watson, Alan. Rome of the Twelve Tables: Persons & Property. LC 75-3481. 235p. 1975. 18.00 (ISBN 0-691-03548-2). Princeton U Pr.

Watson, Alan D. Burke County: A Brief History. (Illus., Orig.). 1979. pap. 2.00 (ISBN 0-86526-130-X). NC Archives.

--Edgecombe Country: A Brief History. (Illus.). 1979. pap. 2.00 (ISBN 0-86526-127-X). NC Archives.

Watson, Aldren A., jt. auth. see Watson, Ernest W.

Watson, Alice S. Troubled Waters. 6.95 (ISBN 0-8062-1587-9). Carlton.

Watson, Andrew, ed. Mao Zedong & the Political Economy of the Border Region. LC 78-67434. (Publications of the Contemporary China Institute). (Illus.). 1980. 29.95 (ISBN 0-521-22551-5); pap. 11.95 (ISBN 0-521-29547-5). Cambridge U Pr.

Watson, Andrew G., jt. ed. see Parkes, M. B.

Watson, Burton. Early Chinese Literature. LC 62-17552. (Companions to Asian Studies). 1962. 20.00x (ISBN 0-231-02579-3); pap. 4.95 (ISBN 0-231-08671-7). Columbia U Pr.

Watson, Burton, ed. & tr. Basic Writings of Mo Tzu, Hsun Tzu, & Han Fei Tzu. LC 67-16170. (Records of Civilization, Sources & Studies: No. 74). 1967. 16.00x (ISBN 0-231-02515-7). Columbia U Pr.

Watson, Burton, jt. ed. see Sato, Hiroaki.

Watson, Burton, tr. from Chinese. Chinese Lyricism: Shih Poetry from the Second to Twelfth Century. LC 71-109252. (Companions to Asian Studies). 1971. 16.00x (ISBN 0-231-03464-4); pap. 5.00 (ISBN 0-231-03465-2). Columbia U Pr.

--Chinese Rhyme-Prose: Poems in the Fu Form from the Han & Six Dynasties Period. LC 75-159674. 1971. 12.50x (ISBN 0-231-03553-5); pap. 2.95 o.p. (ISBN 0-231-03554-3). Columbia U Pr.

Watson, Burton, tr. Courtier & Commoner in Ancient China: Selections from the History of Former Han by Pan Ku. LC 73-18003. 272p. 1974. 17.50x (ISBN 0-231-03765-1); pap. 6.50x (ISBN 0-231-08354-8). Columbia U Pr.

--Japanese Literature in Chinese: Poetry and Prose in Chinese by Japanese Writers, 2 vols. 132p. Vol. 1 1975. 12.50x (ISBN 0-231-03986-7); Vol. 2 1976. 15.00x (ISBN 0-231-04146-2). Columbia U Pr.

--Records of the Grand Historian of China, 2 vols. Incl. Vol. 1. Early Years of the Han Dynasty, 209 to 141 B.C. o.p. (ISBN 0-231-08933-3); Vol. 2. The Age of Emperor Wu, 140 to c. 100 B.C (ISBN 0-231-08934-1). LC 60-13348. (Records of Civilization: Sources & Studies: No. 6). (Illus.). 1961. 22.50x ea. Columbia U Pr.

Watson, Burton, tr. from Chinese. Records of the Historian. LC 70-89860. (Translations from the Oriental Classics). Orig. Title: Chapters from the Shih Chi of Ssu-Ma Ch'ien. 1970. pap. text ed. 8.50x (ISBN 0-231-03321-4). Columbia U Pr.

Watson, Burton, tr. Su Tung-P'o: Selections from a Sung Dynasty Poet. LC 65-13619. 1965. 12.50x (ISBN 0-231-02798-2); pap. 6.00x (ISBN 0-231-02799-0). Columbia U Pr.

Watson, Burton, tr. see Chuang Tzu.

Watson, Burton, tr. see Han, Li & Tzu-Kuang, Hsu.

Watson, Burton, tr. see Han Fei Tzu.

Watson, Burton, tr. see Ikeda, Daisaku.

Watson, Burton, tr. see Lu, Yu.

Watson, Burton, jt. tr. see Sato, Hiroaki.

Watson, C. E. Results-Oriented Management: How to Effectively Get Things Done. 1981. pap. write for info. (ISBN 0-201-08355-8). A-W.

Watson, Charles E. Managing for Results: How to Efecttively Get Things Done. LC 80-24047. 208p. 1981. pap. text ed. price not set. A-W.

Watson, Clyde. Binary Numbers. LC 75-29161. (Young Math Ser.). (Illus.). (gr. 1-4). 1977. PLB 7.89 (ISBN 0-690-00993-3, TYC-J). T Y Crowell.

--Father Fox's Pennyrhymes. LC 71-146291. (Illus.). (gr. k-3). 1971. 8.95 (ISBN 0-690-29213-9, TYC-J); PLB 8.79 (ISBN 0-690-29214-7). T Y Crowell.

--Quips & Quirks. LC 75-4678. (Illus.). 64p. (gr. 3-7). 1975. 5.95 (ISBN 0-690-00733-7, TYC-J). T Y Crowell.

Watson, Colin. Plaster Sinners. LC 80-1989. (Crime Club Ser.). 192p. 1981. 9.95 (ISBN 0-385-17338-5). Doubleday.

Watson, D. S., jt. auth. see Burns, A. E.

Watson, David. Creo en la Evangelizacion. Schwieters, Elsa S., tr. from Eng. (Serie Creo). 235p. (Orig., Span.). 1979. pap. 3.95 (ISBN 0-89922-133-5). Edit Caribe.

--Is Anyone There? Answers About God. 120p. 1981. pap. 3.50 (ISBN 0-87788-395-5). Shaw Pubs.

Watson, David, jt. ed. see Timms, Noel.

Watson, David L. & Tharp, Roland G. Self Directed Behavior: Self-Modification for Personal Adjustment. 3rd ed. LC 80-24411. 300p. 1981. text ed. 10.95 (ISBN 0-8185-0443-9). Brooks-Cole.

Watson, Diana C. & Hurtado, Hernan. Vocabulary Building: Syllabus, Level III. 1973. pap. text ed. 5.25 (ISBN 0-89420-007-0, 270043); cassette recordings 69.20 (ISBN 0-89420-194-8, 270000). Natl Book.

Watson, Diana C. & Watson, Malcolm. Vocabulary Building: Syllabus, Level IV. 1975. pap. text ed. 5.35 (ISBN 0-89420-039-9, 270053); cassette recordings 68.90 (ISBN 0-89420-195-6, 270200). Natl Book.

Watson, Donald, tr. see Navarre, Yves.

Watson, Donald S. & Getz, Malcolm. Price Theory & Its Uses. 5th ed. LC 80-82461. (Illus.). 480p. 1981. text ed. 18.95 (ISBN 0-395-30056-8); write for info. instr's manual (ISBN 0-395-30057-6). HM.

--Price Theory in Action. 4th ed. 448p. 1981. pap. text ed. 9.95 (ISBN 0-395-30058-4); write for info. instr's manual (ISBN 0-395-30057-6). HM.

Watson, Donald S. & Holman, Mary A. Price Theory & Its Uses. 4th ed. LC 76-14003. (Illus.). 1976. text ed. 18.50 (ISBN 0-395-24422-6); inst. manual 1.25 (ISBN 0-395-24423-4). HM.

Watson, Donald S., ed. Price Theory in Action: A Book of Readings. 3rd ed. LC 72-85910. 450p. (Orig.). 1973. pap. text ed. 12.50 (ISBN 0-395-15073-6, 3-58884). HM.

Watson, E. see Bowen, D. Q.

Watson, E. Bradlee & Pressey, Benfield, eds. Contemporary Drama, Fifteen Plays. Incl. Hedda Gabler. Ibsen, Henrik; Importance of Being Earnest. Wilde, Oscar; Uncle Vanya. Chekhov, Anton; Dream Play. Strindberg, August; Man & Superman. Shaw, George B; Riders to the Sea. Synge, John M; Henry Fourth. Pirandello, Luigi; Ah, Wilderness. O'Neill, Eugene; Blood Wedding. Gracia Lorca, Federico; Murder in the Cathedral. Eliot, T. S; Purple Dust. O'Casey, Sean; Skin of Our Teeth. Wilder, Thornton; Come Back, Little Sheba. Inge, William; Crucible. Miller, Arthur; Look Homeward, Angel. Frings, Keti. 577p. 1959. pap. text ed. 10.95x (ISBN 0-684-41478-3, ScribC). Scribner.

Watson, E. Vernon. British Mosses & Liverworts. 2nd ed. LC 68-22665. (Illus.). 1968. 50.00 (ISBN 0-521-06741-3). Cambridge U Pr.

Watson, E. W. & Blanco, Miquel A. Cuatro Dramas De Navidad. 1977. pap. 0.65 (ISBN 0-311-08224-6). Casa Bautista.

Watson, Edward B., jt. auth. see Fried, William.

Watson, Edward W. The Church of England. LC 80-22643. (Home University Library of Modern Knowledge: No. 90). 192p. 1981. Repr. of 1961 ed. lib. bdg. 25.00x (ISBN 0-313-22683-0, WAEN). Greenwood.

Watson, Elizabeth, jt. auth. see Lamb, Warren.

Watson, Elizabeth E. Tell Me About Jesus. 1980. pap. 3.50 (ISBN 0-570-03484-1, 56-1705). Concordia.

Watson, Eric V. Structure & Life of Bryopytes. 3rd ed. 1971. pap. text ed. 7.50 (ISBN 0-09-109301-5, Hutchinson U Lib). Humanities.

Watson, Ernest W. & Watson, Aldren A. The Watson Drawing Book. 1981. pap. 9.95 (ISBN 0-442-20054-4). Van Nos Reinhold.

Watson, F. R. Developments in Mathematics Teaching. (Changing Classroom). 1976. text ed. 9.75x (ISBN 0-7291-0085-5); pap. text ed. 4.75x (ISBN 0-7291-0080-4). Humanities.

Watson, Foster. The Beginnings of the Teaching of Modern Subjects in England. 1978. Repr. of 1909 ed. 19.00x o.p. (ISBN 0-85409-704-X). Charles River Bks.

--Old Grammar Schools. (Illus.). 150p. 1968. 29.50x (ISBN 0-7146-1449-1, F Cass Co). Biblio Dist.

Watson, Foster, ed. English Writers on Education, Fourteen Eighty to Sixteen Hundred & Three. LC 67-18716. 1967. Repr. of 1906 ed. 20.00x (ISBN 0-8201-1048-5). Schol Facsimiles.

Watson, G. N. Complex Integration & Cauchy's Theorem. (Cambridge Tracts in Mathematics & Mathematical Physics Ser.: No. 15). 1960. Repr. of 1914 ed. 7.50 o.s.i. (ISBN 0-02-854490-0). Hafner.

Watson, George. Concise Cambridge Bibliography of English Literature, 600-1950. 2nd ed. (Orig.). 1965. 45.00 (ISBN 0-521-04504-5); pap. 12.50x (ISBN 0-521-09265-5). Cambridge U Pr.

Watson, George & McGaw, Dickinson. Statistical Inquiry: Elementary Statistics for the Political, Social & Policy Sciences. LC 79-12109. 1980. text ed. 18.95 (ISBN 0-471-02087-7); tchrs'. manual avail. (ISBN 0-471-05730-4). Wiley.

Watson, George, jt. auth. see McGaw, Dickinson L.

Watson, George, ed. see Coleridge, Samuel T.

Watson, George N. Theory of Bessel Functions. pap. text ed. 29.95x (ISBN 0-521-09382-1). Cambridge U Pr.

Watson, George N., jt. auth. see Whittaker, Edmund T.

Watson, Gerald H. Incongruities, Inconsistencies, Absurdities in Hegel's Conception of the Universe. (Illus.). 1980. 37.75 (ISBN 0-89266-220-4). Am Classical Coll Pr.

Watson, Geralyn, jt. auth. see Huse, Dennis.

Watson, Goodwin B. What Psychology Can We Trust. LC 61-15927. 1961. pap. 2.25x (ISBN 0-8077-2308-8). Tchrs Coll.

Watson, Harold M. Claudel's Immortal Heroes: A Choice of Deaths. LC 73-160572. 1971. 14.50 (ISBN 0-8135-0695-6). Rutgers U Pr.

Watson, Henry B., jt. auth. see Weaver, Robert B.

Watson, Hugh J. Computer Simulation in Business. 400p. 1981. text ed. 16.95 (ISBN 0-471-03638-2). Wiley.

Watson, Hugh J. & Carroll, Archie B., eds. Computers for Business: A Book of Readings. 1980. pap. 10.50x (ISBN 0-256-02289-5). Business Pubns.

Watson, Ivan. What Shall I Film? 1975. 9.95 o.p. (ISBN 0-85242-432-9, Pub. by Fountain). Morgan.

Watson, J., jt. auth. see McCormack, R. M.

Watson, J. D. Molecular Biology of the Gene. 3rd ed. LC 75-14791. 1976. 23.95 (ISBN 0-8053-9609-8). Benjamin-Cummings.

Watson, J. N. Victorian & Edwardian Field Sports. 1979. 19.95 (ISBN 0-7134-1484-7, Pub. by Batsford England). David & Charles.

Watson, J. Steven. Reign of George Third, Seventeen Sixty to Eighteen Fifteen. (Oxford History of England Ser). 1960. 33.00x (ISBN 0-19-821713-7). Oxford U Pr.

Watson, J. Throck. Introduction to Mass Spectrometry: Biomedical, Environmental & Forensic Applications. LC 74-21989. 1976. 27.00 (ISBN 0-89004-056-7). Raven.

Watson, James. Liberal Studies in Further Education: An Informal Survey. (General Ser.). 72p. 1973. pap. text ed. 12.00x (ISBN 0-85633-023-X, NFER). Humanities.

--Your Book of Stamps. (Your Book Ser.). (Illus.). 1966. 3.95 o.p. (ISBN 0-571-06647-X, Pub. by Faber & Faber). Merrimack Bk Serv.

Watson, James D. The Double Helix: A Norton Critical Edition. Stent, Gunther S., ed. 1981. write for info. (ISBN 0-393-01245-X); pap. text ed. 5.95x (ISBN 0-393-95075-1). Norton.

--Double Helix: Being a Personal Account of the Discovery of the Structure of DNA. LC 68-11211. (Illus.). 1968. 7.95 (ISBN 0-689-10285-2); pap. 5.95 (ISBN 0-689-70602-2, 261). Atheneum.

Watson, James D. & Tooze, John, eds. Recombinant DNA: A Scrapbook Edited by James D. Watson & John Tooze. (Illus.). 1981. text ed. price not set (ISBN 0-7167-1292-X). W H Freeman.

Watson, James L. Asian & African Systems of Slavery. 1980. 22.75 (ISBN 0-520-04031-7). U of Cal Pr.

--Emigration & the Chinese Lineage: The 'Mans' in Hong Kong & London. 1975. 17.50x (ISBN 0-520-02647-0). U of Cal Pr.

Watson, James L., ed. Between Two Cultures: Migrants & Minorities in Britain. 1977. 36.00x (ISBN 0-631-18300-0, Pub. by Basil Blackwell); pap. 14.00x (ISBN 0-631-18710-3). Biblio Dist.

Watson, Jane. Animal Dictionary. (Illus.). (ps-2). 1960. PLB 4.57 o.p. (ISBN 0-307-60533-7, Golden Pr). Western Pub.

--Birds. (Illus.). 24p. (ps-4). 1958. PLB 5.00 (ISBN 0-307-60184-6, Golden Pr). Western Pub.

--Dinosaurs. (ps-3). 1959. PLB 5.00 (ISBN 0-307-60355-5, Golden Pr). Western Pub.

Watson, Jane W. Alternate Energy Sources. LC 78-10872. (First Bks.). (Illus.). (gr. 4 up). 1979. PLB 6.45 s&l (ISBN 0-531-02252-8). Watts.

--Conservation of Energy. (First Books Ser.). (Illus.). (gr. 4 up). 1978. PLB 6.45 s&l (ISBN 0-531-01404-5). Watts.

--Deserts of the World: Future Threat or Promise? (Illus.). 136p. (gr. 10-12). 1981. 12.95 (ISBN 0-399-20785-6). Philomel.

--The First Americans: Tribes of North America. (An I Am Reading Bk.). (Illus.). (gr. 1-4). 1980. 4.95 (ISBN 0-394-84194-8); PLB 5.99 (ISBN 0-394-94194-2). Pantheon.

--Whales. (Big Picture Bk.). (Illus.). (ps-k). 1979. PLB 7.62 (ISBN 0-307-60824-7, Golden Pr); pap. 1.95 (ISBN 0-307-10824-4). Western Pub.

Watson, Janet. Rocks & Minerals. 2nd rev. ed. (Introducing Geology Ser.). (Illus.). pap. text ed. 4.95x (ISBN 0-04-551031-8). Allen Unwin.

Watson, Janet, jt. auth. see Read, H. H.

Watson, Jean, ed. The Family Library Series, 3 bks. Incl. The Pilgrim's Progress: In Modern English. Bunyan, John. 6.95 (ISBN 0-310-38810-4); The Princess & Curdie. MacDonald, George; The Princess & the Goblin. MacDonald, George. (gr. 3 up). 1980. Set. slipcased 19.85 (ISBN 0-310-42718-5). Zondervan.

Watson, Jean, ed. see MacDonald, George.

Watson, Jeannette E. Medical-Surgical Nursing & Related Physiology. 2nd ed. LC 78-64732. (Illus.). 1043p. 1979. text ed. 22.00 (ISBN 0-7216-9136-6). Saunders.

Watson, Joellen & Gorvine, Beverly, eds. Maternal-Newborn Nursing: Poetest Self-Assessment & Review. LC 78-50597. (Nursing: Pretest Self-Assessment & Review Ser.). 1978. pap. 6.95 (ISBN 0-07-051570-0). McGraw-Pretest.

Watson, John. Kant & His English Critics: A Comparison of Critical & Empirical Philosophy. Beck, Lewis W., ed. LC 75-32046. (The Philosophy of Immanuel Kant Ser.: Vol. 10). 1977. Repr. of 1881 ed. lib. bdg. 37.00 (ISBN 0-8240-2334-X). Garland Pub.

--The Massage & Bodywork Resource Guide. (Illus.). 360p. (Orig.). 1981. pap. 6.95 (ISBN 0-913300-13-6). Unity Pr.

--The Philosophy of Kant Explained. Beck, Lewis W., ed. LC 75-32047. (Philosophy of Immanual Kant Ser.: Vol. 11). 1977. Repr. of 1908 ed. lib. bdg. 40.00 (ISBN 0-8240-2335-8). Garland Pub.

Watson, John C. Patient Care & Special Procedures in Radiologic Technology. 4th ed. LC 74-1115. 360p. 1974. text ed. 17.95 (ISBN 0-8016-5358-4). Mosby.

Watson, John L. English: Franco, Slav & Flank Defence. (Contemporary Chess Openings Ser.). (Illus.). 112p. 1981. 19.50 (ISBN 0-7134-2690-X, Pub. by Batsford England). David & Charles.

Watson, John S., tr. see Quintilian.

Watson, K. L. Slate Waste: Engineering & Environmental Aspects. (Illus.). xii, 195p. 1980. 37.50x (ISBN 0-85334-880-4, Pub. by Applied Science). Burgess-Intl Ideas.

Watson, Katherine, tr. see Beurdeley, Cecile & Beurdeley, Michel.

Watson, Katherine, tr. see Schneeberger, Pierre-F.

Watson, L. S., Jr. Child Behavior Modification: A Manual for Teachers, Nurses & Parents. 1973. pap. text ed. 9.25 (ISBN 0-08-017061-7). Pergamon.

Watson, Lewis & Watson, Sharon. How to Start a Homestead Mail Order Business. (Illus.). pap. cancelled o.s.i. (ISBN 0-686-02631-4). Stonehouse.

Watson, Lillian E., ed. Light from Many Lamps. 1980. pap. write for info. (ISBN 0-671-83507-6). PB.

Watson, Liselotte B., jt. auth. see Brittin, Burdick H.

Watson, Louis H. Watson's Classic Book on the Play of the Hand at Bridge. Fry, Sam, Jr., ed. 1959. pap. 3.95 (ISBN 0-06-463209-1, EH 209, EH). Har-Row.

Watson, Malcom, jt. auth. see Watson, Diana C.

Watson, Miller. Basic Dog Training. (Illus.). 1979. 2.95 (ISBN 0-87666-673-X, KW-022). TFH Pubns.

Watson, Nancy D. The Birthday Goat. LC 73-3389. (Illus.). 40p. (ps-3). 1974. 6.95 (ISBN 0-690-00145-2, TYC-J); PLB 6.79 (ISBN 0-690-00146-0). T Y Crowell.

Watson, Naomi. Energize with Isometric Quickies. LC 77-76947. (Illus., Orig.). 1977. 8.95 o.p. (ISBN 0-918766-06-0); pap. 4.95 (ISBN 0-918766-02-8). Butterfly Pr.

Watson, P. Building the Medieval Cathedrals. LC 74-19525. (Introduction to the History of Mankind). 48p. 1976. pap. 3.95 limp bdg. (ISBN 0-521-08711-2). Cambridge U Pr.

Watson, Patty J., et al. Explanation in Archeology: An Explicit Scientific Approach. LC 73-158340. (Illus.). 1971. 15.00x (ISBN 0-231-03544-6). Columbia U Pr.

Watson, Paul M. Debt & the Developing Countries: New Problems & New Actors. LC 78-57185. (Development Papers: No. 26). 88p. 1978. pap. 1.50 (ISBN 0-686-28673-1). Overseas Dev Council.

Watson, Pauline. My Turn, Your Turn. LC 77-25306. (Illus.). (ps-2). Date not set. 6.95g o.p. (ISBN 0-13-608703-5). P-H. Postponed.

--Wriggles: The Little Wishing Pig. LC 78-5855. (Illus.). (gr. k-3). 1978. 7.95 (ISBN 0-395-28828-2, Clarion). HM.

Watson, Pauline & Cricket Magazine Editors. Cricket's Cookery. LC 77-3637. (Illus.). (gr. 1-6). 1977. 2.95 (ISBN 0-394-83540-9, BYR); PLB 3.99 (ISBN 0-394-93540-3). Random.

Watson, Peter G. & Hazleman, Brian L. The Sclera & Systemic Disorders. LC 76-26776. (Major Problems in Ophthalmology Ser.: Vol. 2). (Illus.). 1976. text ed. 24.00 (ISBN 0-7216-9134-X). Saunders.

Watson, Philip S. & Lehmann, Helmut T., eds. Luther's Works, Vol. 33: Career of the Reformer III. new ed. LC 55-9893. 1972. 10.95 (ISBN 0-8006-0333-8, 1-333). Fortress.

Watson, Richard. An Apology for Christianity in a Series of Letters Addressed to Edward Gibbon. Wellek, Rene, ed. LC 75-25132. (British Philosophers & Theologians of the 17th & 18th Centuries Ser.). 1977. lib. bdg. 42.00 (ISBN 0-8240-1765-X). Garland Pub.

Watson, Richard A. Promise & Performance of American Democracy. 4th ed. 500p. 1981. text ed. 12.95 (ISBN 0-471-07964-2). Wiley.

Watson, Richard A. & Fitzgerald, Michael R. Promise & Performance of American Democracy: National Editon. 4th ed. 570p. 1981. text ed. 14.95 (ISBN 0-471-08380-1). Wiley.

--Promise & Performance of American Democracy: State Edition. 4th ed. 650p. 1981. text ed. 16.95 (ISBN 0-471-08381-X). Wiley.

Watson, Richard L., Jr., ed. The United States & the Contemporary World, 1945-1962. LC 65-11901. (Orig.). 1965. pap. text ed. 3.25 o.s.i. (ISBN 0-02-934000-4). Free Pr.

Watson, Robert. Night-Blooming Cactus. LC 80-65999. 1980. 10.00 (ISBN 0-689-11090-1); pap. 5.95. Atheneum.

Watson, Robert, jt. auth. see Langford, Herbert G.

Watson, Robert I. R. I. Watson's Selected Papers on the History of Psychology. Brozek, Josef & Evans, Rand B., eds. LC 76-11675. 409p. 1978. text ed. 25.00x (ISBN 0-87451-130-5). U Pr of New Eng.

Watson, Rowan, tr. see Metzger, Therese & Metzger, Mendel.

Watson, Sam D., Jr. Dogs for Police Service: Programming & Training. (Illus.). 100p. 1972. 12.75 (ISBN 0-398-02025-6). C C Thomas.

Watson, Sara R. V. Sackville-West. (English Authors Ser.: No. 134). lib. bdg. 10.95 (ISBN 0-8057-1472-3). Twayne.

Watson, Sharon, jt. auth. see Watson, Lewis.

Watson, Simon. The Partisan. LC 74-20582. 144p. (gr. 5 up). 1975. 4.95 o.s.i. (ISBN 0-02-792500-5). Macmillan.

Watson, Tex. Will You Die for Me? 1978. 7.95 o.p. (ISBN 0-8007-0912-8); 2.50 o.p. (ISBN 0-8007-8361-1, Spire Bks). Revell.

Watson, Theo F., et al. Practical Insect Pest Management: A Self-Instructional Manual. (Illus.). 1976. pap. text ed. 9.95x (ISBN 0-7167-0558-3). W H Freeman.

Watson, Thomas. The Beatitudes. 7.95 o.p. (ISBN 0-686-12491-X). Banner of Truth.

--A Body of Divinity. 1978. 9.95 (ISBN 0-85151-145-7). Banner of Truth.

--A Divine Cordial. (Summit Ser.). 96p. 1981. pap. 2.45 (ISBN 0-8010-9646-4). Baker Bk.

--Lord's Prayer. 1978. 9.95 (ISBN 0-85151-145-7). Banner of Truth.

--The Ten Commandments. 1976. 9.95 (ISBN 0-85151-146-5). Banner of Truth.

Watson, Thomas, jt. auth. see Andrews, Bart.

Watson, Thomas, et al. R C R A-Hazardous Waste Handbook. 850p. 1980. 65.00 (ISBN 0-86587-086-1). Gov Insts.

Watson, Thomas E. Handbook of Politics & Economics. (Studies in Populism). 1980. lib. bdg. 75.00 (ISBN 0-686-68879-1). Revisionist Pr.

--Life & Speeches of Thomas E. Watson. (Studies in Populism). 1980. lib. bdg. 75.00 (ISBN 0-686-68880-5). Revisionist Pr.

--Mr. Watson's Editorials on the War Issues. (Studies in Populism). 1980. lib. bdg. 69.95 (ISBN 0-686-68881-3). Revisionist Pr.

--Prose Miscellanies. (Studies in Populism). 1980. lib. bdg. 69.95 (ISBN 0-686-68882-1). Revisionist Pr.

--The Roman Catholic Hierarchy. (Studies in Populism). 1980. lib. bdg. 69.95 (ISBN 0-686-68883-X). Revisionist Pr.

--Sketches: Historical, Literary, Biographical, Economic. (Studies in Populism). 1980. lib. bdg. 75.00 (ISBN 0-686-68884-8). Revisionist Pr.

--Socialists & Socialism. (Studies in Populism). 1980. lib. bdg. 69.95 (ISBN 0-686-68885-6). Revisionist Pr.

Watson, W. Tribal Cohesion in a Money Economy: A Study of the Mambwe People of Zambia. (Institute for African Studies). (Illus.). 286p. 1971. pap. text ed. 13.00x (ISBN 0-7190-1037-3). Humanities.

Watson, W., jt. auth. see Susser, Mervyn W.

Watson, W. E. Cell Biology of Brain. LC 76-1921. 1976. 48.95 o.p. (ISBN 0-470-15042-4). Halsted Pr.

Watson, Wendy. Jamie's Story. (Illus.). 32p. (gr. 1-4). 1981. 6.95 (ISBN 0-399-20789-9); lib. bdg. 6.99 (ISBN 0-399-61177-0). Philomel.

Watson, William. Ancient Chinese Bronzes. 2nd ed. (Illus.). 1977. 39.00 (ISBN 0-571-04917-6, Pub. by Faber & Faber). Merrimack Bk Serv.

--Watson's Textile Design & Color. 7th ed. Grosicki, Z. J., ed. 1977. text ed. 35.95 (ISBN 0-408-70515-9). Butterworths.

Watson, William C. Physiological Psychology: An Introduction. LC 80-82838. (Illus.). 592p. 1981. text ed. 16.95 (ISBN 0-395-30221-8); price not set instr's manual (ISBN 0-395-30222-6); study guide 6.95 (ISBN 0-395-30223-4). HM.

Watson, William D., Jr., jt. auth. see Ridker, Ronald G.

Watson, William H. Understanding Physics Today. 1963. 27.50 (ISBN 0-521-06745-6). Cambridge U Pr.

Watson, Wreford J. A Social Geography of the United States. (Illus.). 1979. 26.00 (ISBN 0-582-48196-1); pap. text ed. 11.95 (ISBN 0-582-48197-X). Longman.

Watson de Barros, Leda, jt. auth. see Sutton, Joan L.

Watt, Alan. Evolution of Australian Foreign Policy (1938-1965) 44.00 (ISBN 0-521-06747-2); pap. 12.95x (ISBN 0-521-09552-2). Cambridge U Pr.

Watt, Alan, jt. auth. see McGregor, Jim.

Watt, D. C. Greenwich Forum VI: Britain & the Sea: the Challenges for Shipping in the 1990's. 1981. text ed. write for info. (ISBN 0-86103-049-4, Westbury Hse). Butterworths.

Watt, D. C., ed. Greenwich Forum V: Europe & the Sea: the Cause for & Against a New International Regime for the North Sea and Its Approaches. 1980. text ed. 52.00 (ISBN 0-86103-039-7). Butterworths.

Watt, D. E. A Biographical Dictionary of Scottish Graduates to A. D. 1410. 1977. 98.00x (ISBN 0-19-822447-8). Oxford U Pr.

Watt, David A., jt. auth. see Findlay, William.

Watt, Donald, ed. Aldous Huxley: The Critical Heritage. (The Critical Heritage Ser.). 1975. 30.00x (ISBN 0-7100-8114-6). Routledge & Kegan.

Watt, Donald C. Too Serious a Business: European Armed Forces & the Coming of the Second World War. LC 74-82853. 1975. 16.50x (ISBN 0-520-02829-5). U of Cal Pr.

Watt, George W., et al. Chemistry. (Illus.). 1964. 15.95x (ISBN 0-393-09511-8, NortonC); pap. labaratory manual. 9.95x (ISBN 0-393-09626-2). Norton.

Watt, Gordon. The Meaning of the Cross. 1970. pap. 1.25. Chr Lit.

Watt, Homer A., et al. Outlines of Shakespeare's Plays. rev. ed. (Orig.). 1969. pap. 3.95 (ISBN 0-06-460025-4, CO 25, COS). Har-Row.

Watt, Ian. Conrad in the Nineteenth Century. 1980. 15.95 (ISBN 0-520-03683-2); pap. 7.95 (ISBN 0-520-04405-3). U of Cal Pr.

--Conrad in the Nineteenth Century. 1981. pap. 7.95 (ISBN 0-520-04405-3, CAL 507). U of Cal Pr.

Watt, Ian, ed. British Novel: Scott Through Hardy. LC 72-96559. (Goldentree Bibliographies in Language & Literature Ser.). (Orig.). 1973. pap. 6.95x (ISBN 0-88295-533-0). AHM Pub.

Watt, J. A. Church & the Two Nations in Medieval Ireland. LC 72-120196. (Cambridge Studies in Medieval Life & Thought: Vol. 3). (Illus.). 1970. 42.00 (ISBN 0-521-07738-9). Cambridge U Pr.

Watt, James, jt. auth. see Silver, Robert S.

Watt, James C. Chinese Jades from Han to Ch'ing. LC 80-20115. (Illus.). 236p. 1980. 22.50 (ISBN 0-87848-057-9). Asia Soc.

Watt, James C., ed. The Translation of Art: Essays on Chinese Painting & Poetry. LC 76-28572. (Renditions Ser.). (Illus.). 218p. 1977. 15.00 (ISBN 0-295-95535-X). U of Wash Pr.

Watt, John R. The District Magistrate in Late Imperial China. LC 79-187299. (East Asian Institute Ser). 384p. 1972. 20.00x (ISBN 0-231-03535-7). Columbia U Pr.

Watt, Norman F., jt. auth. see White, Robert W.

Watt, Robert. Bibliography of Robert Watt. LC 68-28119. 1968. Repr. of 1950 ed. 15.00 (ISBN 0-8103-3323-6). Gale.

Watt, Ruth. Love Unveiled. 192p. (YA) 1976. 5.95 (ISBN 0-685-62025-5, Avalon). Bouregy.

Watt, W. M. Islamic Political Thought. 186p. 1980. pap. 6.50x (ISBN 0-85224-403-7, Pub. by Edinburgh U Pr Scotland). Columbia U Pr.

Watt, W. Montgomery. Islam & the Integration of Society. 1961. 13.95x o.s.i. (ISBN 0-8101-0240-4). Northwestern U Pr.

--Muhammad at Medina. 1956. 24.95x (ISBN 0-19-826513-1). Oxford U Pr.

--Muhammad: Prophet & Statesman. 255p. 1974. pap. 5.95 (ISBN 0-19-881078-4, GB409, GB). Oxford U Pr.

Wattenbarger, James L. & Cage, Bob N. More Money for More Opportunity: Financial Support of Community College Systems. LC 74-3608. (Higher Education Ser.). 224p. 1974. 11.95x o.p. (ISBN 0-87589-233-7). Jossey-Bass.

Wattenmaker, Beverly & Wilson, Virginia. A Guidebook for Teaching English As a Second Language. 224p. 1980. text ed. 19.95 (ISBN 0-205-06976-2). Allyn.

--A Guidebook for Teaching Foreign Language: Spanish, French, & German. 312p. 1980. text ed. 17.95 (ISBN 0-205-06846-4). Allyn.

Wattenmaker, Richard J. The Art of Charles Prendergast. LC 68-9480. (Illus.). 1968. pap. 3.00 (ISBN 0-87846-141-8, Pub. by Mus Fine Arts Boston). C E Tuttle.

Watters, Barbara. Horary Astrology & the Judgement of Events. 1973. 13.50 o.s.i. (ISBN 0-685-42026-4). Arcane Pubns.

--Sex & the Outer Planets. 1971. 4.95 o.s.i. (ISBN 0-912356-03-0). Arcane Pubns.

Watters, Garnette, jt. auth. see Courtis, Stuart A.

Watters, Mary. Illinois in the Second World War: Vol. 2, The Production Front. 1952. 5.00 (ISBN 0-912154-19-5). Ill St Hist Lib.

Watters, R. F. Koro: Economic Development & Social Change in Fiji. 1969. 16.50x o.p. (ISBN 0-19-821546-0). Oxford U Pr.

Watters, Ron. Ski Camping. LC 79-22843. (Illus., Orig.). 1979. pap. 7.95 (ISBN 0-87701-165-6). Chronicle Bks.

Watterson, David G., jt. auth. see Schuerger, James M.

Watterson, Henry. Marse Henry: An Autobiography, 2 vols. (American Newspapermen 1790-1933 Ser.). (Illus.). 629p. 1974. Repr. of 1919 ed. Set. 37.00x (ISBN 0-8464-0002-2). Beekman Pubs.

Watterson, John S. The Egypt-Israel Treaty & the Peace-War Prospects for the World. (Illus.). 1979. deluxe ed. 59.75 (ISBN 0-930008-40-5). Inst Econ Pol.

--Thomas Burke Restless Revolutionary. LC 79-3875. 302p. 1980. text ed. 18.50 (ISBN 0-8191-0943-6); pap. text ed. 10.75 (ISBN 0-8191-0944-4). U Pr of Amer.

Watt-Evans, Lawrence. The Seven Altars of Dusarra. 240p. 1981. pap. 2.50 (ISBN 0-345-29264-2, Del Rey). Ballantine.

Watts. Infection in Surgery: Basic & Clinical Aspects. 1981. text ed. 65.00 (ISBN 0-443-02246-1). Churchill.

--A Walk Through Leicester. 1967. Repr. of 1804 ed. text ed. 5.00x (ISBN 0-7185-1073-9, Leicester). Humanities.

Watts, A. D., jt. auth. see McNair, Arnold D.

Watts, A. E., tr. see Ovid.

Watts, A. G. Counselling at Work. 92p. 1977. text ed. 7.40x (ISBN 0-7199-0925-2, Pub. by Bedford England); pap. text ed. 4.40x (ISBN 0-7199-0924-4, Pub. by Bedford England). Renouf.

--Diversity & Choice in Higher Education. 1972. 22.50x (ISBN 0-7100-7400-X). Routledge & Kegan.

Watts, Alan. Meditation. 1976. pap. 2.95 (ISBN 0-515-05842-4). Jove Pubns.

Watts, Alan W. Two Hands of God. 1969. pap. 3.95 (ISBN 0-02-068110-0, Collier). Macmillan.

Watts, Alan W., ed. see Perry, John W.

Watts, Anthony. U-Boat Hunters. (Nagel Encyclopedia Guides). 1980. 12.95 (ISBN 0-356-08244-X, Pub. by MacDonald & Jane's England). Hippocrene Bks.

Watts, B. K. Elements of Finance for Managers. (Illus.). 256p. 1976. pap. 12.95x (ISBN 0-7121-0551-4, Pub. by Macdonald & Evans England). Intl Ideas.

Watts, C. T. & Davies, L. Cunninghame Graham. LC 78-18107. (Illus.). 1979. 32.50 (ISBN 0-521-22467-5). Cambridge U Pr.

Watts, C. T., ed. Joseph Conrad's Letters to R. B. Cunninghame Graham. LC 69-16288. (Illus.). 1969. 42.00 (ISBN 0-521-07213-1). Cambridge U Pr.

Watts, Cynthia. Just Right for You. (Hello World Ser.). 1977. pap. 1.65 (ISBN 0-8163-0284-7). Pacific Pr Pub Assn.

--Parable of the Happy Animals. (Hello Worlds Ser.). 1976. pap. 1.65 (ISBN 0-8163-0295-2). Pacific Pr Pub Assn.

--Who Goes to Bed. (Hello World Ser.). 1977. pap. 1.65 (ISBN 0-8163-0291-X). Pacific Pr Pub Assn.

Watts, Denis. Athletics: Jumping & Vaulting. (Pelham Pictorial Sports Instruction Ser.). (Illus.). 1979. 9.95 (ISBN 0-7207-0919-9). Transatlantic.

Watts, Denis, jt. auth. see LeMasurier, John.

Watts, Denis, jt. auth. see Ward, Ian.

Watts, Derek A. Cardinal De Retz: The Ambiguities of a Seventeenth-Century Mind. 308p. 1980. text ed. 39.95x (ISBN 0-19-815762-2). Oxford U Pr.

Watts, Donald G., jt. auth. see Jenkins, Gwilym M.

Watts, Elizabeth. Towards Dance & Art. (Illus.). 1978. 14.95 (ISBN 0-86019-027-7). Transatlantic.

Watts, Elizabeth S. Biology of the Living Primates. (Elements of Anthropology Ser). 80p. 1975. pap. text ed. 3.50x o.p. (ISBN 0-697-07538-9). Wm C Brown.

Watts, Emily S. The Poetry of American Women from 1632 to 1945. LC 76-43282. 1977. text ed. 13.95 o.p. (ISBN 0-292-76435-9); pap. 7.95x (ISBN 0-292-76450-2). U of Tex Pr.

Watts, Franklin. Let's Find Out About Christmas. (Let's Find Out Bks). (Illus.). (gr. k-3). 1967. PLB 4.47 o.p. (ISBN 0-531-00010-9). Watts.

--Let's Find Out About Easter. LC 69-12595. (Let's Find Out Bks). (Illus.). (gr. k-3). 1969. PLB 4.47 o.p. (ISBN 0-531-00018-4). Watts.

Watts, George B., jt. auth. see Cole, Arthur H.

Watts, Gilbert S. The Complete Guide for the Everyday Use of Gardeners, Fruit Growers, Poultrymen & Farmers on the Maketing of Their Products Directly to the Consumer. (Illus.). 156p. Date not set. Repr. of 1926 ed. deluxe ed. 37.45 (ISBN 0-89901-013-X). Found Class Reprints.

--How to Make a Million Dollars from a Fruit & Vegetables Roadside Market. (Illus.). 1977. Repr. 39.75 (ISBN 0-89266-054-6). Am Classical Coll Pr.

Watts, H. D. The Large Industrial Enterprise: Some Spatial Perspectives. (Geography & Environment Ser.). (Illus.). 303p. 1980. 44.00x (ISBN 0-7099-0267-0, Pub. by Croom Helm Ltd England). Biblio Dist.

Watts, Harold H. Aldous Huxley. LC 68-24289. (English Authors Ser.: No. 79). 1969. lib. bdg. 9.95 (ISBN 0-8057-1284-4). Twayne.

Watts, Harriet. How to Start Your Own Preschool Playgroup. LC 72-91198. (Illus.). 160p. 1973. 5.00x o.p. (ISBN 0-87663-177-4). Universe.

Watts, Henry E. Life of Miguel De Cervantes. LC 79-141743. 1971. Repr. of 1891 ed. 15.00 (ISBN 0-8103-3631-6). Gale.

Watts, Isaac. Reliquiae Juveniles: Miscellaneneous Thoughts in Prose & Verse. LC 68-17018. 1968. Repr. of 1734 ed. 38.00x (ISBN 0-8201-1049-3). Schol Facsimiles.

Watts, Isaac see Bunyan, John.

Watts, J. McK., et al. Infection in Surgery: Basic & Clinical Aspects. (Symposium Ser.). (Illus.). 488p. 1981. lib. bdg. 65.00 (ISBN 0-443-02246-1). Churchill.

Watts, John. The Supervision of Construction: A Guide to Site Inspection. (Illus.). 208p. 1980. 38.00 (ISBN 0-7134-2173-8, Pub. by Batsford England). David & Charles.

--Teaching. 1973. 11.95 (ISBN 0-7153-6481-2). David & Charles.

Watts, John, ed. The Countesthorpe Experience. (Unwin Education Bks). 1977. text ed. 19.50x (ISBN 0-04-373003-5). Allen Unwin.

Watts, John D. Lists of Words Occurring Frequently in the Hebrew Bible. (Heb, & Eng). 1960. pap. 1.95 (ISBN 0-8028-1214-7). Eerdmans.

Watts, John D. W. Obadiah. Date not set. pap. 4.95 (ISBN 0-88469-138-1). BMH Bks.

Watts, L. & Nisbet, J. Legibility in Children's Books: A Review of Research. (General Ser.). 100p. 1974. pap. text ed. 12.00x (ISBN 0-85633-034-5, NFER). Humanities.

Watts, L., III. Fine Art of Baseball: A Complete Guide to Strategy, Skills, & Systems. 2nd ed. (Illus.). 1973. 15.95 (ISBN 0-13-316968-5). P-H.

Watts, Lawrence. A Wonderful Money Making Opportunity for Everyone: Roadside Marketing for Maximal Profits. (Illus.). 1980. 39.75 (ISBN 0-89266-214-X). Am Classical Coll Pr.

Watts, Leslie. Flower & Vegetable Plant Breeding. (Orig.). 1980. pap. 22.50 (ISBN 0-901361-35-6, Pub. by Grower Bks England). Intl Schol Bk Serv.

Watts, Lisa & Tyler, Jenny. The Children's Book of the Earth. LC 77-13212. (Children's Guides). (Illus.). (gr. 3 up). 1978. PLB 6.95 (ISBN 0-88436-466-6). EMC.

Watts, Lisa, jt. auth. see Tyler, Jenny.

Watts, Mabel. Boy Who Listened to Everyone. LC 63-8178. (Illus.). (gr. k-3). 1963. 5.95 o.s.i. (ISBN 0-8193-0030-6, Four Winds). Schol Bk Serv.

--King & the Whirlybird. LC 69-12605. (Illus.). (gr. k-3). 1969. 5.95 o.s.i. (ISBN 0-8193-0289-9, Four Winds); PLB 5.41 o.s.i. (ISBN 0-8193-0290-2). Schol Bk Serv.

--Little Red Riding Hood. (Illus.). 24p. (ps-3). 1977. Repr. of 1972 ed. PLB 5.00 (ISBN 0-307-60232-X, Golden Pr). Western Pub.

--The Narrow Escapes of Solomon Smart. LC 66-10021. (Illus.). (ps-3). 1966. 5.95 o.s.i. (ISBN 0-8193-0149-3, Four Winds); PLB 5.41 o.s.i. (ISBN 0-8193-0150-7). Schol Bk Serv.

--Where Is the Keeper? (Tell-a-Tale Readers). (Illus.). (gr. k-3). 1979. PLB 4.77 (ISBN 0-307-68469-5, Whitman). Western Pub.

--While the Horses Galloped to London. LC 72-8096. (Illus.). 48p. (gr. k-3). 1971. 5.95 o.s.i. (ISBN 0-8193-0652-5, Four Winds); PLB 5.41 o.s.i. (ISBN 0-8193-0653-3). Schol Bk Serv.

--Zoo Friends Are at Our School Today! (A Tell-a-Tale Reader Ser.). (gr. k-3). 1979. PLB 4.77 (ISBN 0-307-68423-7, Golden Pr). Western Pub.

Watts, Mabel, jt. auth. see Werth, Kurt.

Watts, Marjorie-Ann. Mulroy's Magic. (Illus.). (ps-5). 1972. 6.50 (ISBN 0-571-09645-X, Pub. by Faber & Faber). Merrimack Bk Serv.

--Zebra Goes to School. LC 80-2688. (Illus.). 32p. (gr. k-2). 1981. 9.95 (ISBN 0-233-97241-2). Andre Deutsch.

Watts, Martin, jt. auth. see Major, J. Kenneth.

Watts, May T. Reading the Landscape of America. rev. ed. (Illus.). 288p. 1975. 12.95 o.s.i. (ISBN 0-02-624400-4). Macmillan.

Watts, Michael R. The Dissenters: From the Reformation to the French Revolution, Vol. 1. (Illus.). 1978. 49.00x (ISBN 0-19-822460-5). Oxford U Pr.

Watts, Mimi, tr. see Pellicani, Luciano.

Watts, Peter, tr. see Ibsen, Henrik.

Watts, R. K. Point Defects in Crystals. LC 76-43013. 1977. 35.50 (ISBN 0-471-92280-3, Pub by Wiley-Interscience). Wiley.

Watts, S. I., jt. auth. see Watts, S. J.

Watts, S. J. & Watts, S. I. From Border to Middle Shire: Northumberland 1586-1625. (Illus.). 256p. 1975. text ed. 20.00x (ISBN 0-7185-1127-1, Leicester). Humanities.

Watts, Theodore F., ed. Energy Fact Book, 1976. LC 75-45508. (Illus.). 200p. 1976. 8.95 (ISBN 0-916646-00-9); pap. 4.95 (ISBN 0-916646-01-7). Tetra Tech.

Watts, Thomas D. The Societal Learning Approach: A New Approach to Social Welfare Policy & Planning in America. LC 80-69231. 140p. 1981. perfect bdg. 11.95 (ISBN 0-86548-058-3). Century Twenty One.

Watts, Virginia. The Single Parent. 1976. 7.95 (ISBN 0-8007-0823-7). Revell.

Watts, Walter F., jt. ed. see Mall, David.

Watts, William & Free, Lloyd A. State of the Union III. LC 77-18653. (Illus.). 1978. 15.95x (ISBN 0-669-01507-5). Lexington Bks.

Watts, William, et al. Japan, Korea & China. LC 78-7128. 1979. 17.95 (ISBN 0-669-02470-8). Lexington Bks.

Watzlawick, Paul. How Real Is Real? 1976. 10.00 o.p. (ISBN 0-394-49853-4). Random.

Watzlawick, Paul & Weakland, John H., eds. The Interactional View: Studies at the Mental Research Institute, Palo Alto, 1965-1974. 1977. 18.95x (ISBN 0-393-01131-3). Norton.

Wauer, Roland H. Naturalist's Big Bend. LC 78-21776. (Illus.). 158p. 1980. 10.45 (ISBN 0-89096-069-0); pap. 5.95 (ISBN 0-89096-070-4). Tex A&M Univ Pr.

Waugaman, Charles A. Cheyenne Artist: The Story of Richard West. LC 70-130779. (Bold Believers Ser). (Orig.). 1970. pap. 0.95 o.p. (ISBN 0-377-84211-7). Friend Pr.

Waugh, Albert E. Sundials, Their Theory & Construction. (Illus.). 8.00 (ISBN 0-8446-4835-3). Peter Smith.

Waugh, Alec. My Brother Evelyn & Other Portraits. 1968. 6.95 o.p. (ISBN 0-374-21680-0). FS&G.

--Pleasure. LC 79-53467. (Short Story Index in Reprint Ser.). Date not set. Repr. of 1921 ed. 24.50x (ISBN 0-8486-5013-1). Core Collection. Postponed.

--Wines & Spirits. LC 68-55300. (Foods of the World Ser). (Illus.). (gr. 6 up). 1968. PLB 14.94 (ISBN 0-8094-0061-8, Time-Life). Silver.

--Wines & Spirits. (Foods of the World Ser). (Illus.). 1968. 14.95 (ISBN 0-8094-0034-0). Time-Life.

Waugh, Alice. Interior Design. 1967. spiral bdg. 5.95 o.p. (ISBN 0-8087-2305-7). Burgess.

Waugh, Auberon. A Little Order: A Selection from His Journalism. 240p. 1980. 11.95 (ISBN 0-316-92632-9). Little.

Waugh, Carol A. & Larsen, Judith L. The Roller Skating: The Sport of a Lifetime. (Illus.). 1979. 9.95 (ISBN 0-02-062446-8, Collier); pap. 3.95 (ISBN 0-02-029950-8, Collier). Macmillan.

Waugh, Charles, jt. ed. see Greenberg, Martin.

Waugh, Charles G. & Greenberg, Martin H. Baseball Three Thousand. 240p. (gr. 7 up). 1981. 9.95 (ISBN 0-525-66732-6). Elsevier-Nelson.

Waugh, Charles G. & Greenberg, Martin H., eds. The Fantastic Cornell Woolrich. (Alternatives Ser.). 416p. Date not set. price not set (ISBN 0-8093-1008-2). S Ill U Pr.

Waugh, Charles G., jt. ed. see Greenberg, Martin H.

Waugh, Coulton. How to Paint with a Knife. LC 70-145666. (Illus.). 1971. 21.95 (ISBN 0-8230-3880-7). Watson-Guptill.

--Landscape Painting with a Knife. LC 74-11148. 192p. 1974. 21.95 o.p. (ISBN 0-8230-2632-9). Watson-Guptill.

Waugh, Evelyn. The Letters of Evelyn Waugh. Amory, Mark, ed. LC 80-17818. 684p. 1980. 25.00 (ISBN 0-89919-021-9). Ticknor & Fields.

--A Little Order: A Selection from His Journalism. Gallagher, Donat, ed. 224p. 1981. 12.95 (ISBN 0-316-92633-7). Little.

Waugh, Hillary. Finish Me off. 1978. pap. 1.75 (ISBN 0-505-51324-2). Tower Bks.

--Madman at My Door. 1979. pap. 2.25 (ISBN 0-380-47159-0, 47159). Avon.

Waugh, Kenneth, jt. auth. see Bush, Wilma J.

Waugh, Linda R. Roman Jakobson's Science of Language. (PDR Press Publications on Roman Jakobson: No. 2). (Orig.). 1977. pap. text ed. 10.25x (ISBN 90-316-0112-8). Humanities.

Waugh, Linda R., jt. auth. see Jakobson, Roman.

Waugh, Mary. The Shell Book of Country Parks. LC 80-68695. (Illus.). 224p. 1981. 19.95 (ISBN 0-7153-7963-1). David & Charles.

Waugh, Norah. Corsets & Crinolines. LC 69-11134. (Illus.). 1954. 11.95 o.s.i. (ISBN 0-87830-020-1); pap. 10.95 (ISBN 0-87830-526-2). Theatre Arts.

--Cut of Men's Clothes: 1600-1900. LC 64-21658. (Illus.). 1964. 19.95 (ISBN 0-87830-025-2). Theatre Arts.

--Cut of Women's Clothes: 1600-1930. LC 68-13408. (Illus.). 1968. 32.45 (ISBN 0-87830-026-0). Theatre Arts.

Wavell, Bruce B. The Living Logos: A Philosophico-Religious Essay in Free Verse. LC 77-18478. 1978. pap. text ed. 8.75x (ISBN 0-8191-0324-1). U Pr of Amer.

Wawrzkowicz, Peter. In the Shadow of Hammer & Sickle. Date not set. 6.95 (ISBN 0-8062-1657-3). Carlton.

Wax, Murray L., ed. When Schools Are Desegregated: Problems & Possibilities for Students, Educators, Parents & the Community. 300p. 1982. 19.95 (ISBN 0-87855-376-2). Transaction Bks. Postponed.

Wax, Murray L. & Cassell, Joan, eds. Federal Regulations: Ethical Issues & Social Research. (AAAS Selected Symposium: No. 36). 1979. lib. bdg. 22.50x (ISBN 0-89158-487-0). Westview.

Waxer, Peter H. Nonverbal Aspects of Psychotherapy. LC 78-71280. 1978. 19.95 (ISBN 0-03-046721-7). Praeger.

Waxman, Bruce, jt. auth. see Stacy, Ralph W.

Waxman, Chaim I. The Stigma of Poverty: A Critique of Poverty Theories & Policies. LC 77-5760. 1977. text ed. 12.75 (ISBN 0-08-021800-8); pap. text ed. 4.95 (ISBN 0-08-021798-2). Pergamon.

Waxman, Meyer. A History of Jewish Literature, 5 vols. in 6. Set. boxed 50.00 o.p. (ISBN 0-498-08640-2, Yoseloff); 10.00 ea. o.p. Vol. 1 (ISBN 0-498-08913-4). Vol. 2 (ISBN 0-498-08921-5). Vol. 3 (ISBN 0-498-08917-7). Vol. 4, Pt. 1 (ISBN 0-498-08912-6). Vol. 4, Pt. 2 (ISBN 0-498-08922-3). Vol. 5 (ISBN 0-498-08885-5). A S Barnes.

Waxman, Meyer, et al. Blessed Is the Daughter. 7th ed. LC 65-12053. (Illus.). 1980. 10.95 (ISBN 0-88400-064-8). Shengold.

Waxman, Stephanie. What Is a Girl? What Is a Boy? LC 76-42451. (Illus.). 48p. (ps-12). 1976. 6.95 (ISBN 0-915238-11-X); pap. 4.95 (ISBN 0-915238-10-1). Peace Pr.

Waxman, Stephen G., ed. Physiology & Pathobiology of Axons. LC 77-17751. 1978. 41.00 (ISBN 0-89004-215-2). Raven.

Waxter, Julia B. Science Cookbook. LC 79-57431. 1981. pap. 6.95 (ISBN 0-8224-6292-3). Pitman Learning.

Way, Arthur S. Letters of Paul, Hebrews & Psalms. 468p. 1981. text ed. 12.95 (ISBN 0-8254-4016-5). Kregel.

Way, Brian. Audience Participation: Theatre for Young People. 1980. pap. 7.95 (ISBN 0-87440-000-7). Bakers Plays.

--Development Through Drama. (Orig.). 1967. pap. text ed. 4.95x (ISBN 0-391-00296-1). Humanities.

Way, Charles W. Van see Van Way, Charles W. & Buerk, Charles A.

Way, E. Leong, ed. Endogenous & Exogenous Opiate Agonists & Antagonists: Proceedings of the International Narcotic Club Conference, 11-15 June 1979, North Falmouth, Massachusetts, USA. (Book Supplement to Pergamon Journal Life Sciences). (Illus.). 600p. 1980. 66.00 (ISBN 0-08-025488-8). Pergamon.

Way, H. Frank. Criminal Justice & the American Constitution. 1980. text ed. 17.95 (ISBN 0-87872-238-6). Duxbury Pr.

--Liberty in the Balance. 5th, rev. ed. (Foundations of American Government & Political Science Ser.). 144p. 1981. pap. text ed. 6.95 (ISBN 0-07-068661-0, C). McGraw.

Way, Lawrence W., jt. ed. see Dunphy, J. Englebert.

Way, Margaret. Blue Lotus. (Harlequin Romances Ser.). (Orig.). 1980. pap. 1.25 o.p. (ISBN 0-373-02328-6, Pub. by Harlequin). PB.

--Flamingo Park. (Harlequin Romances). 192p. 1981. pap. 1.25 (ISBN 0-373-02400-2, Pub. by Harlequin). PB.

--The Golden Puma. (Harlequin Romances Ser.). 192p. 1980. pap. 1.25 o.p. (ISBN 0-373-02357-X, Pub. by Harlequin). PB.

--Lord of the High Valley. (Harlequin Romances Ser.). 192p. (Orig.). 1981. pap. 1.25 (ISBN 0-373-02387-1, Pub. by Harlequin). PB.

Wayas, Joseph. Nigeria's Leadership Role in Africa. 1979. text ed. 26.00x (ISBN 0-333-26295-6). Humanities.

Wayburn, Ned. The Art of Stage Dancing. LC 80-69259. (Belvedere Bk.). (Illus.). 382p. 1980. pap. 9.95 (ISBN 0-87754-250-3). Chelsea Hse.

Wayburn, Peggy, jt. auth. see Miller, Mike.

Wayland, H. Lincoln, ed. see Muller, George.

Wayman & Plum. Secrets & Surprises. (gr. k-8). 1977. 7.95 (ISBN 0-916456-13-7, GA70). Good Apple.

Wayman, Alex. Calming the Mind & Discerning the Real. Wayman, Alex, tr. from Sanskrit. (Translations from the Oriental Classics Ser.). 1978. 30.00x (ISBN 0-231-04404-6). Columbia U Pr.

--Yoga of the Guhyasamajatantra. 1977. 24.95 (ISBN 0-89684-003-4, Pub. by Motilal Banarsidass India). Orient Bk Dist.

Wayman, Alex & Wayman, Hideko, trs. from Chinese. The Lion's Roar of Queen Srimala. 160p. 1974. 17.50x (ISBN 0-231-03726-0). Columbia U Pr.

Wayman, Hideko, jt. tr. see Wayman, Alex.

Wayman, Joe & Mitchell, Don. Imagination & Me Book. (gr. k-8). 1976. 5.95 (ISBN 0-916456-02-1, GA54). Good Apple.

Wayman, Joe, jt. auth. see Mitchell, Don.

Wayman, Joe, et al. Anything Can Happen Book. (gr. k-8). 1976. 5.95 (ISBN 0-916456-06-4, GA55). Good Apple.

Wayman, Patrick A., ed. Transactions of the International Astronomical Union, Vol. XVIIB. 536p. 1980. PLB 68.50 (ISBN 90-277-1159-3). Kluwer Boston.

Wayman, Tom. Introducing Tom Wayman, Selected Poems 1973-80. LC 80-20260. (Ontario Review Press Poetry Ser.). 144p. 1980. 10.95 (ISBN 0-86538-003-1); pap. 5.95 (ISBN 0-86538-004-X). Ontario Rev NJ.

Wayment, Hilary, tr. see Ayrout, Henry H.

Waymouth, Charity, et al, eds. The Growth Requirements of Vertebrate Cells in Vitro. (Illus.). 480p. Date not set. price not set (ISBN 0-521-23019-5). Cambridge U Pr.

Wayne, Doreen. The Healthy Gourmet: Low Calorie-Low Cholesterol-Low Cost Cookery. 1979. 14.95x (ISBN 0-8464-0055-3). Beekman Pubs.

Wayner, Julie. His Gentle Voice. 112p. 1976. 2.95 (ISBN 0-930756-18-5, 4230-WA1). Women's Aglow.

Wayre, Philip. The Private Life of the Otter. 1979. 17.95 (ISBN 0-7134-0833-2, Pub. by Batsford England). David & Charles.

Ways, M., et al. The Future of Business Global Issues in the Eighties & Nineties. (Orig.). 1979. 18.25 (ISBN 0-08-022477-6); pap. 8.75 (ISBN 0-08-022476-8). Pergamon.

Waywell, T. G., tr. see Lavigne, Marie.

Waz, Joseph W., Jr. Reverse the Charges: How to Save Dollars on Your Phone Bill. 1980. pap. 3.50 (ISBN 0-9603466-5-1). NCCB.

We, Editors. German Military Uniforms & Insignia, 1933-1945. LC 68-6985. (Illus.). 1967. 8.95 o.p. (ISBN 0-911964-00-2). Paladin Ent.

Wead, George & Lellis, Geore. Film: Form & Function. LC 80-82804. (Illus.). 512p. 1981. pap. text ed. 12.95 (ISBN 0-395-29740-0). HM.

Wead, George & Lellis, George. The Film Career of Buster Keaton. Gottesman, Ronald, ed. (Three Director Set). 1978. pap. 7.80 (ISBN 0-913178-57-8). Redgrave Pub Co.

Wead, R. Douglas. The Iran Crisis. (Orig.). 1980. pap. 2.95 (ISBN 0-88270-433-8). Logos.

Weakland, John H., jt. ed. see Watzlawick, Paul.

Weakland, Rembert. Walking on the Wings of the Wind. 144p. (Orig.). 1980. pap. 2.95 (ISBN 0-8091-2334-7). Paulist Pr.

Weakley, Brenda. A Beginner's Handbook of Biological Transmission Electron Microscopy. (Illus.). 272p. (Orig.). 1981. pap. 16.50 (ISBN 0-443-02091-4). Churchill.

Weaks, M. C. Captain Elias Pelletreau, Long Island Silversmith. 1966. pap. 3.95 (ISBN 0-911660-04-6). Yankee Peddler.

Weal, Elke C & Weal, John A, eds. Combat Aircraft of World War II. LC 77-961. 1977. 9.98 o.s.i. (ISBN 0-02-624660-0). Macmillan.

Weal, John A, jt. ed. see Weal, Elke C.

Weale, Albert. Equality & Social Policy. (International Library of Welfare & Philosophy). 1978. 16.00 (ISBN 0-7100-8770-5); pap. 7.95 (ISBN 0-7100-8771-3). Routledge & Kegan.

Weale, Anne. The Girl from the Sea. (Harlequin Presents Ser.). 192p. 1981. pap. 1.50 (ISBN 0-373-10408-1, Pub. by Harlequin). PB.

Weales, Gerald. Jumping-off Place: American Drama of the 1960's. 1969. 6.95 o.s.i. (ISBN 0-02-624670-8). Macmillan.

Weales, Gerald, ed. see Miller, Arthur.

Wear, Jennifer & Holmes, King. How to Have Intercourse Without Getting Screwed. LC 76-41190. 1976. pap. 4.95 (ISBN 0-914842-12-9). Madrona Pubs.

Wearin, Otha. Before the Colors Fade. 5.95 o.p. (ISBN 0-87069-007-8). Wallace-Homestead.

Wearing, J. P. American & British Theatrical Biography: A Directory. LC 78-31162. 1013p. 1979. 40.00 (ISBN 0-8108-1201-0). Scarecrow.

--The London Stage, Nineteen Hundred to Nineteen Nine: A Calendar of Plays & Players, 2 vols. LC 80-28353. 1202p. 1981. Set. 50.00 (ISBN 0-8108-1403-X). Scarecrow.

--The London Stage 1890-1899: A Calendar of Plays & Players, 2 vols. LC 76-1825. 1242p. 1976. Set. 47.50 (ISBN 0-8108-0910-9). Scarecrow.

Wearing, J. P., jt. ed. see Conolly, Leonard W.

Wearing-King, R. The English Sixth Form College: An Educational Concept. 1969. pap. 5.50 o.p. (ISBN 0-08-013214-6). Pergamon.

Wearne, S. H. Principles of Engineering Organization. (Illus.). 1973. pap. text ed. 11.95x (ISBN 0-7131-3290-6). Intl Ideas.

Wearne, S. H., ed. Control of Engineering Projects. (Illus.). 1974. pap. 12.95x (ISBN 0-7131-3330-9). Intl Ideas.

Weart, Spencer & Szilard, Gertrude W., eds. Leo Szilard: His Version of the Facts. Selected Works & Correspondence. (Illus.). 1978. 20.00x (ISBN 0-262-19168-7); pap. 7.95 (ISBN 0-262-69070-5). MIT Pr.

Weary, Gifford, jt. auth. see Harvey, John H.

Weatherall, David J. Medicine Nineteen Seventy-Eight. LC 78-58440. 1978. 24.50 (ISBN 0-471-04888-7, Pub. by Wiley Medical). Wiley.

Weatherall, Donald M., jt. auth. see Quinn, Daniel.

Weatherbee, Donald E. Ancient Indonesia: And Its Influence in Modern Times. LC 74-3004. (First Bks. Ser). (Illus.). 96p. (gr. 5-10). 1974. PLB 6.45 (ISBN 0-531-02732-5). Watts.

Weatherby, J. Goliath. 288p. (Orig.). 1981. pap. 2.75 (ISBN 0-553-14593-2). Bantam.

Weatherby, W. J. Conversations with Marilyn. 1977. pap. 1.75 o.p. (ISBN 0-345-25568-2). Ballantine.

Weatherford, John W. Collective Bargaining & the Academic Librarian. LC 76-45424. 1976. 10.00 (ISBN 0-8108-0983-4). Scarecrow.

Weatherford, Marion T. Arlington: Child of the Columbia. LC 77-80362. (Illus.). 280p. 1977. pap. 6.95 (ISBN 0-87595-056-6). Oreg Hist Soc.

Weatherford, Richard M., ed. Stephen Crane: The Critical Heritage. (The Critical Heritage Ser.). 362p. 1973. 30.00x (ISBN 0-7100-7636-3). Routledge & Kegan.

Weatherhead, A. Kingsley. A Reading of Henry Green. LC 61-8767. 180p. 1961. 11.00 (ISBN 0-295-73902-9). U of Wash Pr.

Weatherhead, Leslie. Will of God. 1976. pap. 1.25 (ISBN 0-89129-165-2). Jove Pubns.

Weatherhead, Leslie D. Christian Agnostic. 1972. Repr. of 1965 ed. 3.50 o.p. (ISBN 0-687-06977-7, Apex). Abingdon.

--Psychology, Religion & Healing. (Series D). 1959. pap. 5.95 (ISBN 0-687-34885-4, Apex). Abingdon.

--Time for God. 1981. pap. 1.75 (ISBN 0-687-42113-6). Abingdon.

--The Will of God. 56p. 1974. Repr. large print 6.95 o.p. (ISBN 0-687-45575-8); gift ed. 4.95 o.p. (ISBN 0-687-45573-1). Abingdon.

Weatherhead, R. G. FRP Technology. (Illus.). xvii, 460p. 1980. 70.00x (ISBN 0-85334-886-3). Burgess-Intl Ideas.

Weatherhill, Craig. Belerion: Ancient Sites of Land's End. 96p. 1980. 15.00x (ISBN 0-906720-01-X, Pub. by Hodge England). State Mutual Bk.

Weatherman, H. M. Colored Glassware of the Depression Era 1970. (Illus.). 240p. 1981. 12.00 (ISBN 0-913074-00-4). Weatherman.

Weatherman, Hazel M. Decorated Tumbler "PriceGuy". 128p. 1979. pap. 3.75 (ISBN 0-913074-13-6). Weatherman.

Weathers, Thomas & Hunter, Claud. Fundamentals of Electricity & Automotive Electrical Systems. (Illus.). 256p. 1981. text ed. 16.95 (ISBN 0-13-337030-5). P-H.

Weathers, Tom & Hunter, Claud. Diesel Engines for Automobiles & Small Trucks. 300p. 1981. text ed. 16.95 (ISBN 0-8359-1288-4); instr's. manual free (ISBN 0-8359-1289-2). Reston.

Weathers, Winston. An Alternative Style: Options in Compostition. 144p. 1980. text ed. 6.19x (ISBN 0-686-69598-4). Hayden.

--Mezzo Cammin. (Orig.). 1981. pap. 4.50x (ISBN 0-912484-20-9). Joseph Nichols.

Weatherspoon, Ricky, jt. auth. see Wall, Joan.

Weaver, jt. auth. see Hudson.

Weaver, Ann A. Getting Ready to Cook. (gr. 7-12). 1974. pap. 2.80 (ISBN 0-8224-3383-4); tchrs' manual free (ISBN 0-8224-7677-0). Pitman Learning.

--Planning Meals & Shopping. (Young Homemakers at Work Ser). (Special Education Ser. for slow learners). (gr. 7-12,RL 2.5). 1970. pap. 2.80 (ISBN 0-8224-5450-5); tchrs.' manual free (ISBN 0-8224-7676-2). Pitman Learning.

--Young Homemaker's Cookbook. (gr. 7 up). 1974. pap. 2.80 (ISBN 0-8224-7675-4); tchrs' manual free (ISBN 0-8224-7678-9). Pitman Learning.

Weaver, Ann A., jt. auth. see Hudson, Margaret W.

Weaver, Barbara N. & Bishop, Wiley L. The Corporate Memory: A Profitable, Practical Approach to Information Management & Retention. LC 74-7410. (Systems & Controls for Financial Management Ser.). 257p. 1974. 29.50 (ISBN 0-471-92323-0, Pub. by Wiley-Interscience). Wiley.

Weaver, Barry. Collected Words. Date not set. 4.75 (ISBN 0-8062-1607-7). Carlton.

Weaver, Carl H. Human Listening. LC 75-182878. (Speech Communication Ser.). 1972. pap. text ed. 4.50 (ISBN 0-672-61234-8, SC18). Bobbs.

Weaver, Clifford L. & Babcock, Richard F. City Zoning. LC 79-90347. 328p. (Orig.). 1980. pap. 16.95 (ISBN 0-918286-17-4). Planners Pr.

Weaver, Clyde, jt. auth. see Friedmann, John.

Weaver, Constance, jt. auth. see Malmstrom, Jean.

Weaver, D. A., jt. auth. see Ferry, Ted S.

Weaver, Frederick S. Class, State & Industrial Structure: The Historical Process of South American Industrial Growth. LC 79-6571. (Contributions in Economics & Economic History: No. 32). (Illus.). xiv, 247p. 1980. lib. bdg. 28.50 (ISBN 0-313-22114-6, WCI/). Greenwood.

Weaver, Harriett. Beloved Was Bahamas. LC 74-76442. 184p. (gr. 4-6). 1974. 6.95 (ISBN 0-8149-0740-7). Vanguard.

Weaver, Harriett E. Adventures in the Redwoods. LC 75-3912. (Illus.). 1975. pap. 3.95 (ISBN 0-87701-060-9). Chronicle Bks.

--Frosty: A Raccoon to Remember. (gr. 5-7). 1977. pap. 1.95 (ISBN 0-671-42094-1). Archway.

Weaver, Helen, tr. see Artaud, Antonin.

Weaver, Helen, tr. see Leduc, Violette.

Weaver, Horace R., ed. The International Lesson Annual, 1980-81. (Orig.). 1980. pap. 4.50 o.p. (ISBN 0-687-19144-0). Abingdon.

--The International Lesson Annual 1981-1982. 448p. (Orig.). 1981. pap. 4.50 (ISBN 0-687-19145-9). Abingdon.

Weaver, John. Los Angeles: The Enormous Village. 2nd ed. Orig. Title: El Pueblo Grande. (Illus.). 240p. 1980. 15.00 (ISBN 0-88496-158-3); pap. 8.95 (ISBN 0-88496-153-2). Capra Pr.

Weaver, John T. Forty Years of Screen Credits Nineteen Twenty-Nine to Nineteen Sixty-Nine, 2 Vols. LC 76-12592. 1970. Set. 45.00 (ISBN 0-8108-0299-6). Scarecrow.

--Twenty Years of Silents, Nineteen Hundred & Eight to Nineteen Twenty-Eight. LC 73-157729. 514p. 1971. lib. bdg. 20.50 (ISBN 0-8108-0299-6). Scarecrow.

Weaver, Kathleen, ed. Film Programmer's Guide to 16mm Rentals. 3rd ed. 1980. pap. 21.25 (ISBN 0-934456-02-X). Reel Res.

Weaver, M. William Carlos Williams. LC 77-149431. (Illus.). 1977. 38.00 (ISBN 0-521-08072-X); pap. 8.50x (ISBN 0-521-29195-X). Cambridge U Pr.

Weaver, Mabel E. & Koehler, Vera J. Programmed Mathematics of Drugs & Solutions: Nineteen Seventy-Nine Revision with Intravenous Rate Calculations & Mathematics Pretest. LC 79-10790. 1979. pap. text ed. 4.95x (ISBN 0-397-54232-1). Lippincott.

Weaver, Mary J., ed. Letters from a "Modernist". The Letters from George Tyrrell to Wilfrid Ward, 1893-1908. LC 80-28372. 230p. 1981. 30.00 (ISBN 0-915762-12-9). Patmos Pr.

Weaver, Michael K., jt. auth. see Kirkpatrick, James M.

Weaver, Muriel P. The Aztecs, & Their Presecessors: Archaeology of Mesoamerica. 2nd ed. (Studies in Archaeology). 1981. write for info. (ISBN 0-12-785936-5). Acad Pr.

Weaver, P. R. Familia Caesaris: A Social Study of the Emperor's Freedmen & Slaves. LC 76-171686. (Illus.). 1972. 42.95 (ISBN 0-521-08340-0). Cambridge U Pr.

Weaver, Patricia C., jt. auth. see Weaver, Robert G.

Weaver, Paul H. see Commission on Critical Choices.

Weaver, Peter. Strategies for the Second Half of Life. 1981. pap. 3.50 (ISBN 0-451-09814-5, E9814, Signet Bks). NAL.

Weaver, Raymond, ed. The Shorter Novels of Herman Melville. 1977. pap. 2.50 (ISBN 0-449-30798-0, Prem). Fawcett.

Weaver, Richard. In Praise of Jesus. 1981. 4.95 (ISBN 0-8062-1711-1). Carlton.

Weaver, Richard L., II. Understanding Interpersonal Communication. 2nd ed. 1981. pap. text ed. 10.95x (ISBN 0-673-15436-X). Scott F.

--Understanding Interpersonal Communication. 1978. pap. 9.95x (ISBN 0-673-15089-5). Scott F.

Weaver, Rip. Structural Drafting Workbook. (Illus.). 112p. 1980. pap. text ed. 9.95. Gulf Pub.

Weaver, Robert, ed. Canadian Short Stories. (Ser. 3). 1978. pap. 6.95x (ISBN 0-19-540291-X). Oxford U Pr.

Weaver, Robert B. Our Flag & Other Symbols of Americanism. 76p. (gr. 7-8). 1972. pap. 0.50 (ISBN 0-912530-09-X); test 0.10 (ISBN 0-685-47428-3). Patriotic Educ.

Weaver, Robert B. & Watson, Henry B. The Key to the Constitution of the United States. 6th ed. LC 79-64230. 67p. 1979. pap. 1.00 (ISBN 0-912530-12-X). Patriotic Educ.

Weaver, Robert G. & Weaver, Patricia C. Persuasive Writing: A Manager's Guide to Effective Letters & Reports. LC 76-7178. 1977. 12.95 (ISBN 0-02-934020-9). Free Pr.

Weaver, Robert J. Plant Growth Substances in Agriculture. LC 71-166964. (Plant Science Ser.). (Illus.). 1972. text ed. 39.95x (ISBN 0-7167-0824-8). W H Freeman.

Weaver, Sally M. Making Canadian Indian Policy: The Hidden Agenda 1968-1970. (Studies in the Structure of Power). 352p. 1980. 25.00x (ISBN 0-8020-5504-4); pap. 10.00 (ISBN 0-8020-6403-5). U of Toronto Pr.

Weaver, Suzanne. Decision to Prosecute: Organization & Public Policy in the Antitrust Division. 208p. 1980. 17.50 (ISBN 0-262-23085-2); pap. 5.95 (ISBN 0-262-73053-7). MIT Pr.

Weaver, W., tr. see Gadda, Carlo Emilio.

Weaver, Warren, jt. auth. see Shannon, Claude E.

Weaver, William. The Golden Century of Italian Opera: From Rossini to Puccini. (Illus.). 256p. 1980. 27.50 (ISBN 0-500-01240-7). Thames Hudson.

Weaver, William & Hume, Paul. Puccini: The Man & His Music. LC 77-6323. 1977. 8.95 o.p. (ISBN 0-525-18610-7). Dutton.

Weaver, William, tr. see Calvino, Italo.

Webb, A. E. & Weeden, R. Unemployment, Vacancies & the Rate of Change of Earnings: Regional Rates of Growth of Employment. (National Inst. of Economic & Social Research, Regional Papers: No. 3). 1974. pap. 13.95 (ISBN 0-521-09895-5). Cambridge U Pr.

Webb, Adrian L. Income Redistribution & the Welfare State. 125p. 1971. pap. text ed. 6.25x (Pub. by Bedford England). Renouf.

Webb, Augustus D. New Dictionary of Statistics: A Complement to the Fourth Edition of Mulhall's Dictionary of Statistics. LC 68-18017. 1971. Repr. of 1911 ed. 44.00 (ISBN 0-8103-3988-9). Gale.

Webb, Barbara, jt. ed. see Cook, Peter.

Webb, Barbara O. Families Sharing God. 48p. 1981. pap. 3.50 (ISBN 0-8170-0900-0). Judson.

Webb, Beatrice. Beatrice Webb's American Diary, Eighteen Ninety-Eight. Shannon, David, ed. (Illus.). 1963. 17.50 (ISBN 0-299-02851-8). U of Wis Pr.

--My Apprenticeship. LC 79-15437. 1980. 49.95 (ISBN 0-521-22941-3); pap. 15.95 (ISBN 0-521-29731-1). Cambridge U Pr.

Webb, Bernard L. Mass Merchandising of Automobile Insurance. 309p. 1969. pap. 10.00 o.p. (ISBN 0-88245-007-7). Merritt Co.

Webb, Bernice L. Poetry on the Stage William Poel Producer of Verse Drama. (Salzburg Institute for English Literature Poetic Drama Studies: 45). (Orig.). 1979. pap. text ed. 25.00x (ISBN 0-391-01726-8). Humanities.

Webb, Brian. Suizer Diesel Locomotives of British Rail. 1978. 16.95 (ISBN 0-7153-7514-8). David & Charles.

Webb, Brian & Duncan, John. AC Electric Locomotives of the British Rail. (Illus.). 1979. 17.95 (ISBN 0-7153-7663-2). David & Charles.

Webb, Byron H. & Whittier, Earle O. By-Products from Milk. 2nd ed. (Illus.). 1971. 32.00 o.p. (ISBN 0-87055-085-3). AVI.

Webb, Byron H., et al, eds. Fundamentals of Dairy Chemistry. 2nd ed. 1974. text ed. 45.00 (ISBN 0-87055-143-4). AVI.

Webb, C. deB. & Wright, J. B., eds. A Zulu King Speaks: Statements Made by Cetshwayo Kampande on the History & Customs of His People. (Killie Campbell Africana Library Reprint: No. 3). (Illus.). 1979. text ed. 21.00x (ISBN 0-86980-153-8). Verry.

Webb, Charles. The Investor's Guide to American Convertible & Special-Interest Automobiles, 1946-1976. LC 77-84592. (Illus.). 1979. 25.00 (ISBN 0-498-02183-1). A S Barnes.

Webb, D. A. An Irish Flora. (Illus.). 14.95. Dufour.

Webb, David. Teaching Modern Languages. LC 74-82025. (Teaching Ser.). 1975. 17.95 (ISBN 0-7153-6858-3). David & Charles.

Webb, David M. The Old Woman and the Bird. LC 79-55781. (Illus.). 45p. (gr. 3-8). 1981. 6.95 (ISBN 0-935054-04-9). Webb-Newcomb.

Webb, David S. The Burge & Minnechaduza Clarendonian Mammalian Faunas of Northcentral Nebraska. (U. C. Publ. in Geological Sciences: Vol. 78). 1969. pap. 10.95x (ISBN 0-520-09181-7). U of Cal Pr.

Webb, Donald G. Investigation of Safe & Money Chest Burglary. (Illus.). 124p. 1975. 16.75 (ISBN 0-398-03270-X). C C Thomas.

Webb, Eugene. The Plays of Samuel Beckett. LC 72-2901. (Washington Paperback Ser., No. 71). 160p. 1972. 10.50 (ISBN 0-295-95202-4); pap. 2.95 (ISBN 0-295-95314-4). U of Wash Pr.

Webb, George J., jt. auth. see Mason, Lowell.

Webb, Graham, jt. auth. see Axenrod, Theodore.

Webb, Henry J. Elizabethan Military Science: The Books & the Practice. (Illus.). 1965. 25.00x (ISBN 0-299-03810-6). U of Wis Pr.

Webb, Herschel. An Introduction to Japan. 2nd ed. LC 57-9552. 1957. pap. 5.00x (ISBN 0-231-08505-2). Columbia U Pr.

--Japanese Imperial Institution in the Tokugawa Period. LC 68-11912. (East Asian Institute Ser). 1968. 17.50x (ISBN 0-231-03120-3). Columbia U Pr.

Webb, J. A., jt. auth. see Moore, P. D.

Webb, J. P., jt. auth. see Smith, B. L.

Webb, James. The Occult Establishment. LC 75-22157. (Illus.). 541p. 1976. 22.50 o.p. (ISBN 0-912050-56-X, Library Pr). Open Court.

--A Sense of Honor. LC 80-25852. 81. 10.95 (ISBN 0-13-806646-9). P-H.

Webb, Jan. Ferrari Dino 206GT, 246GT & GTS. (AutoHistory Ser.). (Illus.). 128p. 1980. 12.95 (ISBN 0-85045-365-8, Pub. by Osprey England). Motorbooks Intl.

Webb, John N. Migratory-Casual Worker. LC 73-165690. (FDR & the Era of the New Deal Ser.). 1971. Repr. of 1937 ed. lib. bdg. 15.00 (ISBN 0-306-70339-4). Da Capo.

--Transient Unemployed. LC 71-166337. (FDR & the Era of the New Deal Ser.). 1971. Repr. of 1935 ed. lib. bdg. 15.00 (ISBN 0-306-70335-1). Da Capo.

Webb, John N., jt. auth. see Brown, Malcolm.

Webb, Kempton. Changing Face of Brazil. 1974. 22.50x (ISBN 0-231-03767-8). Columbia U Pr.

Webb, Kempton, jt. auth. see James, Preston E.

Webb, Kenneth & Hatry, Harry P. Obtaining Citizen Feedback: The Application of Citizen Surveys to Local Governments. 1973. pap. 3.50 (ISBN 0-87766-055-7, 18000). Urban Inst.

Webb, Lance. Onesimus. 374p. 1980. pap. 5.95 (ISBN 0-8407-5742-5). Nelson.

Webb, Lesley. Making a Start on Child Study. (Blackwell's Practical Guides Ser.). (Illus.). 1975. pap. 6.25x (ISBN 0-631-16480-4, Pub. by Basil Blackwell). Biblio Dist.

--Purpose & Practice in Nursery Education. 1974. pap. 9.25x (ISBN 0-631-15240-7, Pub. by Basil Blackwell). Biblio Dist.

Webb, Lyme. Poems from Life Within. 1981. 4.95 (ISBN 0-8062-1648-4). Carlton.

Webb, M. G. & Ricketts, Martin J. The Economics of Energy. LC 79-18708. 1980. 25.95x (ISBN 0-470-26841-7). Halsted Pr.

Webb, Mary. Gone to Earth. 288p. 1979. o. p. 18.00x (ISBN 0-686-28504-2, Pub. by Duckworth); pap. 4.50x (ISBN 0-7156-1339-1). Biblio Dist.

--Precious Bane. 290p. 1978. o. p. 18.00x (ISBN 0-686-28566-2, Pub. by Duckworth); pap. 4.50x (ISBN 0-7156-1336-7). Biblio Dist.

Webb, P. K., jt. auth. see Whorwood, R. W.

Webb, Philip C. & Grove, Joseph. The Question Whether a Jew, Born Within the British Dominions, Was, Before the Making of the Late Act of Parliament, a Person Capable by Law, to Purchase & Hold Lands to Him and His Heirs. Berkowitz, David S. & Thorne, Samuel E., eds. LC 77-86671. (Classics of English Legal History in the Modern Era Ser.: Vol. 48). 169p. 1979. lib. bdg. 40.00 (ISBN 0-8240-3097-4). Garland Pub.

Webb, R. G. Reptiles of Oklahoma. LC 69-16716. (Stovall Museum Publication Ser.: No. 2). (Illus.). 1975. pap. 8.95 (ISBN 0-8061-0896-7). U of Okla Pr.

Webb, R. W., jt. auth. see Norris, R. M.

Webb, Ralph, Jr. Interpersonal Speech Communication: Principles & Practices. (Illus.). 320p. 1975. pap. text ed. 14.95 (ISBN 0-13-475103-5). P-H.

Webb, Richard. These Came Back. (Orig.). 1976. pap. 1.75 (ISBN 0-89129-039-7). Jove Pubns.

Webb, Richard C., jt. ed. see Frank, Charles R., Jr.

Webb, Robert H. Elementary Wave Optics. 1969. text ed. 22.95 (ISBN 0-12-739550-4). Acad Pr.

Webb, Robert H., tr. see Aristophanes.

Webb, Robert K. British Working Class Reader Seventeen-Ninety to Eighteen Forty-Eight: Literacy & Social Tension. LC 55-27828. Repr. of 1955 ed. lib. bdg. 13.50x (ISBN 0-678-00578-8). Kelley.

Webb, Robert N. The Colony of Rhode Island. LC 70-189517. (First Bks). (Illus.). 96p. (gr. 5-8). 1972. PLB 6.45 (ISBN 0-531-00778-2). Watts.

--Hannibal: Invader from Carthage. LC 68-10512. (Biography Ser). (gr. 7 up). 1968. PLB 5.90 o.p. (ISBN 0-531-00881-9). Watts.

--James Watt: Inventor of the Steam Engine. LC 74-93767. (Biography Ser). (Illus.). (gr. 7 up). 1970. PLB 5.90 o.p. (ISBN 0-531-00940-8). Watts.

--Jean Jacques Rousseau: The Father of Romanticism. LC 76-93947. (Biography Ser). (Illus.). (gr. 7 up). 1970. PLB 6.90 (ISBN 0-531-00941-6). Watts.

--Raid on Harper's Ferry, October 17, 1859: A Brutal Skirmish Widens the Rift Between North & South. LC 78-131151. (Focus Bks). (Illus.). (gr. 7 up). 1971. PLB 4.90 o.p. (ISBN 0-531-01020-1). Watts.

--Simon Bolivar: The Liberator. LC 66-12146. (Biography Ser). (gr. 7 up). 1966. PLB 5.90 o.p. (ISBN 0-531-00856-8). Watts.

Webb, Ross A. Benjamin Helm Bristow: Border State Politician. LC 74-80089. (Illus.). 384p. 1969. 14.50x (ISBN 0-8131-1182-X). U Pr of Ky.

Webb, Samuel C. Managerial Economics. LC 75-31039. (Illus.). 608p. 1976. text ed. 20.95 (ISBN 0-395-20589-1); solutions manual 2.75 (ISBN 0-395-20590-5). HM.

Webb, Sherman. Practical Pointer Training. (Illus.). 1974. 9.95 (ISBN 0-87691-131-9). Winchester Pr.

Webb Society. Webb Society Deep-Sky Observer's Handbook: Vol. III: Open & Globular Clusters. Jones, Kenneth G., ed. LC 78-31260. (Illus.). 224p. 1980. pap. 8.95 (ISBN 0-89490-034-X). Enslow Pubs.

Webb, Sydney J. Nutrition, Time & Motion in Metabolism & Genetics. (Illus.). 426p. 1976. 39.75 (ISBN 0-398-03158-4). C C Thomas.

Webb, Timothy. The Violet in the Crucible: Shelley & Translation. 1977. 43.00x (ISBN 0-19-812059-1). Oxford U Pr.

Webb, Vincent J., jt. auth. see Roberg, Roy R.

Webb, Walter P. Divided We Stand: The Crisis of a Frontierless Democracy. LC 79-1598. 1981. Repr. of 1944 ed. 16.00 (ISBN 0-88355-903-X). Hyperion Conn.

--The Great Frontier. 1964. 14.95 (ISBN 0-292-73253-8); pap. 7.95 (ISBN 0-292-72706-2). U of Tex Pr.

--Talks on Texas Books: A Collection of Book Reviews. Friend, Llerena B., ed. LC 76-84083. 1970. 6.00 (ISBN 0-87611-024-3). Tex St Hist Assn.

--Texas Rangers. new ed. 1965. 14.95 (ISBN 0-292-73400-X). U of Tex Pr.

Webb, Walter P. & Carroll, H. Bailey, eds. Handbook of Texas. Incl. 1952. 55.00 (ISBN 0-87611-013-8); Vol. 3. Branda, Eldon S., ed. (Vol. 3 is sold both as a part of the 3 vol. set & by itself). 1976. supplement 35.00 (ISBN 0-87611-027-8). LC 76-55058. Three Vol. Set. 85.00 (ISBN 0-87611-036-7). Tex St Hist Assn.

Webb, Watts R. Surgery in Acute Coronary Problems. (Illus.). 68p. 1974. pap. 9.95 o.p. (ISBN 0-683-08888-2, Pub. by Williams & Wilkins). Krieger.

Webb, Wilfred M. The Heritage of Dress: Being Notes on the History & Evolution of Clothes. LC 70-141749. (Illus.). 1971. Repr. of 1912 ed. 18.00 (ISBN 0-8103-3398-8). Gale.

Webb, William S. Indian Knoll. LC 73-18473. (Illus.). 280p. 1974. Repr. of 1946 ed. 14.50x (ISBN 0-87049-150-4). U of Tenn Pr.

Webb, William S. & Snow, Charles E. The Adena People. LC 75-10598. (Illus.). 420p. 1974. Repr. of 1945 ed. 16.50x (ISBN 0-87049-159-8). U of Tenn Pr.

Webber, B. M., jt. auth. see Mayfield, J. M.

Webber, Bonnie L. A Formal Approach to Discourse Anaphora. Hankamer, Jorge, ed. LC 78-67737. (Outstanding Dissertations in Linguistics Ser.). 1979. lib. bdg. 24.00 (ISBN 0-8240-9670-3). Garland Pub.

Webber, Diane, jt. auth. see Webber, Joe.

Webber, Frederick R. Church Symbolism: An Explanation of the More Important Symbols of the Old & New Testament, the Primitive, the Mediaeval & the Modern Church. rev. 2nd ed. LC 79-107627. (Illus.). 1971. Repr. of 1938 ed. 28.00 (ISBN 0-8103-3349-X). Gale.

Webber, Jeanette & Grumman, Joan. Woman As Writer. (Illus., LC 77-074379). 1978. pap. text ed. 10.50 (ISBN 0-395-26438-3). HM.

Webber, Joan M., ed. see Oberg, Arthur.

Webber, Joe & Webber, Diane. Naked & Together. 5.95 (ISBN 0-910550-06-9). Elysium.

Webber, Kathie. Kathie Webber's Book of Autumn Cooking. (Illus.). 1978. 14.95 (ISBN 0-241-89820-X, Pub. by Hamish Hamilton England). David & Charles.

--Kathie Webber's Book of Spring Cooking. (Illus.). 1978. 14.95 (ISBN 0-241-89818-8, Pub. by Hamish Hamilton England). David & Charles.

--Kathie Webber's Book of Summer Cooking. (Illus.). 1978. 14.95 (ISBN 0-241-89819-6, Pub. by Hamish Hamilton England). David & Charles.

--Kathie Webber's Book of Winter Cooking. 1979. 14.95 (ISBN 0-241-89821-8, Pub. by Hamish Hamilton England). David & Charles.

Webber, Kathleen, ed. see Heine, Heinrich.

Webber, M. J. Information Theory & Urban Spatial Structure. 394p. 1979. 80.00x (ISBN 0-85664-665-2, Pub. by Croom Helm Ltd England). Biblio Dist.

Webber, Margaret S. Language Skills for Exceptional Learners. 275p. 1981. text ed. write for info. (ISBN 0-89443-343-1). Aspen Systems.

Webber, Patrick J., ed. High Altitude Geocology. (AAAS Selected Symposium Ser.: No. 12). (Illus.). 1979. lib. bdg. 21.50x (ISBN 0-89158-440-4). Westview.

Webber, Ross. Mangement Pragmatics. 1979. pap. 10.50x (ISBN 0-256-02232-1). Irwin.

Webber, Ross A. Management: Basic Elements of Managing Organizations. rev ed. 1979. text ed. 19.50 (ISBN 0-256-02234-8). Irwin.

--Time Is Money! Tested Tactics That Conserve Time for Top Executives. LC 80-1032. (Illus.). 1980. 10.95 (ISBN 0-02-934030-6). Free Pr.

Webber, Ross D. To Be a Manager. 1981. 18.95x (ISBN 0-256-02520-7). Irwin.

Webber, Toni. Your Stable, Its Construction & Management. 1976. 8.50 (ISBN 0-7207-0846-X, Pub. by Michael Joseph). Merrimack Bk Serv.

Webber, Winslow L. Books About Books. LC 73-18456: 1974. Repr. of 1937 ed. 22.00 (ISBN 0-8103-3690-1). Gale.

Webel, A. A German-English Dictionary of Technical, Scientific & General Terms. 3rd ed. 1969. Repr. of 1952 ed. 37.50 (ISBN 0-7100-2258-1). Routledge & Kegan.

Weber. All-Pro Baseball Stars 1980. (gr. 7-12). 1980. pap. 1.25 (ISBN 0-590-31537-4, Schol Pap). Schol Bk Serv.

--TV Olympics Program Guide. (gr. 7-12). Date not set. pap. cancelled o.p. (ISBN 0-590-30362-7, Schol Pap). Schol Bk Serv.

Weber & McLean. Electrical Measurement Systems for Biological & Physical Scientists. 1976. 19.95 (ISBN 0-201-04593-1). A-W.

Weber, Albert, jt. ed. see Willinger, Herman.

Weber, Andrew & Rice, Tim. Evita: The Lgend of Eva Peron, 1919-1952. 1979. pap. 5.95 (ISBN 0-380-46433-0, 46433). Avon.

Weber, Annina N., ed. Discussion. LC 78-19533. (Illus.). 1980. pap. 14.95 (ISBN 0-915570-13-0). Oolp Pr.

Weber, Arnold R. Inpursuit of Price Stability: The Wage Price Freeze of 1971. LC 73-11346. (Studies in Wage-Price Policy: Studies in Wage Price Policy). 137p. 1973. 10.95 (ISBN 0-8157-9264-6); pap. 4.95 (ISBN 0-8157-9263-8). Brookings.

Weber, Arnold R. & Mitchell, Daniel J. B. The Pay Board's Progress: Wage Controls in Phase II. (Studies in Wage-Price Policy). 1978. 16.95 (ISBN 0-8157-9266-2); pap. 7.95 (ISBN 0-8157-9265-4). Brookings.

Weber, Arnold R., jt. ed. see Hartman, Robert W.

Weber, B., ed. Diabetic Angiopathy in Children. (Pediatric & Adolescent Endocrinology Ser.: Vol. 9). (Illus.). viii, 422p. 1981. 114.00 (ISBN 3-8055-1574-X). S Karger.

Weber, Brom see Crane, Hart.

Weber, Bruce. All-Pro Basketball Stars 1979. rev. ed. (gr. 7-12). 1979. pap. 1.25 o.p. (ISBN 0-590-12064-6, Schol Pap). Schol Bk Serv.

Weber, Carl J. Fore-Edge Painting: A Historical Survey of a Curious Art in Book Decoration. LC 66-26931. (Illus.). 1966. 25.00 o.p. (ISBN 0-8178-3811-2). Harvey.

Weber, Carol, ed. see Wilensky, Julius M.

Weber, Catherine. Coulter's Woman. (Orig.). 1980. pap. 1.95 (ISBN 0-532-23199-6). Manor Bks.

Weber, Daniel. Return to Black River Camp. (Illus.). 60p. (Orig.). 1980. pap. 5.00 (ISBN 0-934996-11-3). Am Stud Pr.

Weber, Darrell J. & Hess, W. M. The Fungal Spore: Form & Function. LC 75-38889. 895p. 1976. 46.75 (ISBN 0-471-92332-X, Pub. by Wiley-Interscience). Wiley.

Weber, Darrell J., jt. auth. see Weete, John D.

Weber, David C., jt. auth. see Rogers, Rutherford D.

Weber, David J. The Taos Trappers: The Fur Trade in the Far Southwest. 260p. 1980. pap. 6.95 (ISBN 0-8061-1702-8). U of Okla Pr.

Weber, David J., ed. Foreigners in Their Native Land: Historical Roots of the Mexican Americans. LC 73-77858. 1979. pap. 7.50x (ISBN 0-8263-0279-3). U of NM Pr.

--New Spain's Far Northern Frontier: Essays on Spain in the American West, 1540-1821. LC 78-21428. 296p. 1979. pap. 9.95x (ISBN 0-8263-0499-0). U of NM Pr.

Weber, Dennis. Affair on the Rhine. 1981. pap. 1.95 (ISBN 0-8439-0906-4, Leisure Bks). Nordon Pubns.

Weber, Dick & Alexander, Roland. Weber on Bowling: The Complete Guide to Getting Your Game Together. LC 80-23649. 1981. 12.95 (ISBN 0-13-947937-6). P-H.

Weber, Donald A., jt. ed. see Stevens, Elliot L.

Weber, Dudley L, et al. Autopsy Pathology Procedure & Protocol. (Illus.). 136p. 1973. 21.75 (ISBN 0-398-02625-4). C C Thomas.

Weber, E. A. The Practical Photographer. 1974. 17.95 o.p. (ISBN 0-85242-002-1, Pub. by Fountain). Morgan.

Weber, Edwin J., jt. auth. see Weber, Gloria Hansen.

Weber, Eric. How to Pick up Girls. 1981. 4.95 (ISBN 0-914094-00-9). Green Hill.

Weber, Eugen. Europe Since Seveteen Fifteen: A Modern History. (Illus.). 790p. 1972. pap. text ed. 12.95x (ISBN 0-393-09404-9). Norton.

--Modern History of Europe: Men, Cultures, & Societies from the Renaissance to the Present. LC 77-133957. (Illus.). 1971. 17.95x (ISBN 0-393-09981-4). Norton.

--The Nationalist Revival in France. (California Library Reprint Series: No. 7). 1968. 21.50x (ISBN 0-520-01321-2). U of Cal Pr.

Weber, Eugen, ed. see Du Gard, Roger.

Weber, Eugen, jt. ed. see Rogger, Hans.

Weber, Eugene, jt. ed. see Spaethling, Robert.

Weber, Evelyn. Kindergarten: Its Encounter with Educational Thought in America. LC 70-75202. 1969. pap. 8.25x (ISBN 0-8077-2315-0). Tchrs Coll.

Weber, Evelyn, jt. ed. see Shapiro, Edna K.

Weber, G., ed. Advances in Enzyme Regulation: Proceedings of the 17th Symposium on Regulation of Enzyme Activity & Synthesis in Normal & Neoplastic Tissues, Indiana University School of Medicine, Indianapolis, 2-3 October 1978, Vol. 17. (Illus.). 1979. 110.00 (ISBN 0-08-024424-6). Pergamon.

Weber, George H. & Haberlein, Bernard J., eds. Residential Treatment of Emotionally Disturbed Children. LC 78-189948. (Child Care Ser). 350p. 1973. text ed. 24.95 (ISBN 0-87705-067-8). Human Sci Pr.

Weber, George H. & McCall, George J., eds. Social Scientists As Advocates: Views from the Applied Disciplines. LC 77-26798. (Sage Focus Editions: Vol. 4). 1978. 18.95x (ISBN 0-8039-0943-8); pap. 9.95x (ISBN 0-8039-0944-6). Sage.

Weber, Gerda & Weber, Herman. Lenin Chronology. 226p. 1981. lib. bdg. 22.50 (ISBN 0-87196-515-1). Facts on File.

Weber, Gloria H., et al. Notetaking & Study Skills. (gr. 10-12). 1977. 11.20x (ISBN 0-912036-27-3); wkbk. 5.76x (ISBN 0-912036-28-1); instrs'. manual 1.76x (ISBN 0-912036-29-X); profiles pkg. of 25 5.88x (ISBN 0-912036-30-3). Forkner.

Weber, Gloria Hansen & Weber, Edwin J. Guided Study in Forkner Shorthand. 1974. pap. 5.32x (ISBN 0-912036-21-4). Forkner.

Weber, Hans, jt. auth. see Bloomberg, Marty.

Weber, Hans-Ruedi. The Cross: Tradition & Interpretation of the Crucifixion of Jesus in the World of the New Testament. 1978. pap. 6.95 o.p. (ISBN 0-8028-1739-4). Eerdmans.

--Salty Christians. 1963. pap. 0.75 (ISBN 0-8164-2062-9). Crossroad NY.

Weber, Harry, tr. see Eikhenbaum, Boris.

Weber, Harry B., ed. The Modern Encyclopedia of Russian & Soviet Literature: Mersh, Vol. 1. 1977. 31.50 (ISBN 0-87569-070-X). Academic Intl.

--Modern Encyclopedia of Russian & Soviet Literature: Mersh, Vol. 3. 1979. 31.50 (ISBN 0-685-96303-9). Academic Intl.

Weber, Harry B. see Wieczynski, Joseph L.

Weber, Heinrich. Lehrbuch der Algebra, Vols. 1, 2, & 3. 3rd ed. LC 61-6890. 1979. Repr. of 1962 ed. Set. text ed. 85.00 (ISBN 0-8284-0144-6). Chelsea Pub.

Weber, Helen I. Nursing Care of the Elderly. (Illus.). 240p. 1980. text ed. 12.95 (ISBN 0-8359-5035-2); pap. 11.95 (ISBN 0-8359-5034-4). Reston.

Weber, Herman, jt. auth. see Weber, Gerda.

Weber, J. R. How to Use Your Apple II Computer. LC 80-70465. (IDM's How to Use Your Microcomputer Ser.). 250p. (gr. 10-12). 1981. 19.95 (ISBN 0-938862-02-2); pap. 14.95 (ISBN 0-938862-03-0). Five Arms Corp.

--How to Use Your PET Computer. (IDM's How to Use Your Microcomputer Ser.). 250p. (gr. 10-12). 1981. 14.95 (ISBN 0-9604892-7-4); pap. 12.95 (ISBN 0-9604892-8-2). Five Arms Corp.

--How to Use Your TRS-80 Model II Computer. LC 80-70467. (IDM's How to Use Your Microcomputer Ser.). 250p. (gr. 10-12). 1981. 19.95 (ISBN 0-938862-00-6); pap. 14.95 (ISBN 0-938862-01-4). Five Arms Corp.

Weber, J. Sherwood. Good Reading: A Guide for Serious Readers. rev. ed. 1980. pap. 3.50 (ISBN 0-451-61909-9, ME1909, Ment). NAL.

Weber, J. W., jt. ed. see Stocker, F.

Weber, James A. Grow or Die: The Over-Population Myth. 1977. 11.95 o.p. (ISBN 0-87000-367-4). Arlington Hse.

Weber, Jeffrey. Beautiful Legs: You Can Have Them. LC 80-67533. 1980. cancelled (ISBN 0-9604892-2-3). Five Arms Corp.

Weber, Jeffrey R. Camera Repair Simplified. LC 80-65475. 112p. (Orig.). 1980. pap. text ed. 9.95 (ISBN 0-9604892-0-7). Five Arms Corp.

--Computerized Accounts Payable System: Manual & Source Code for Microcomputers. (International Data Management Computerized Accounting System Ser.). 144p. 1981. pap. 29.95 (ISBN 0-9604892-5-8). Five Arms Corp.

--Computerized Accounts Receivable System: Manual & Source Code for Microcomputers. (International Data Management Computerized Accounting System Ser.). 144p. 1981. pap. 29.95 (ISBN 0-9604892-4-X). Five Arms Corp.

--Computerized General Ledger System: Manual & Source Code for Microcomputers. (International Data Management Computerized Accounting System Ser.). 144p. 1981. pap. 29.95 (ISBN 0-9604892-6-6). Five Arms Corp.

--Computerized Payroll System: Manual & Source Code for Microcomputers. (International Data Management Computerized Accouting System Ser.). 144p. 1981. pap. 29.95 (ISBN 0-9604892-3-1). Five Arms Corp.

--Muscle Builders: Twelve-Week Bodybuilding Course. LC 80-66788. 112p. (gr. 10-12). 1980. pap. text ed. 11.95 (ISBN 0-9604892-1-5). Five Arms Corp.

Weber, Lenora M. Angel in Heavy Shoes: A Katie Rose Story. LC 68-13589. (gr. 7-11). 1968. 10.95 (ISBN 0-690-09189-3, TYC-J). T Y Crowell.

--Beany & the Beckoning Road. LC 52-7645. (gr. 5 up). 1952. 10.95 (ISBN 0-690-12313-2, TYC-J). T Y Crowell.

--Beany Has a Secret Life. LC 55-5839. (gr. 5 up). 1955. 10.95 (ISBN 0-690-12384-1, TYC-J). T Y Crowell.

--Beany Malone. LC 48-1943. (gr. 5 up). 1948. 10.95 (ISBN 0-690-12455-4, TYC-J). T Y Crowell.

--Bright Star Falls. LC 59-11398. (gr. 5 up). 1959. 10.95 (ISBN 0-690-16005-4, TYC-J). T Y Crowell.

--Come Back, Wherever You Are. LC 69-13643. (Beany Malone Ser). (gr. 7 up). 1969. 10.95 (ISBN 0-690-20123-0, TYC-J). T Y Crowell.

--Don't Call Me Katie Rose. LC 64-13909. (gr. 5 up). 1964. 10.95 (ISBN 0-690-24241-7, TYC-J). T Y Crowell.

--Hello My Love, Goodbye. LC 77-132306. (Stacy Belford Story Ser). (gr. 6 up). 1971. 10.95 (ISBN 0-690-37697-9, TYC-J). T Y Crowell.

--How Long Is Always? LC 75-1937. (gr. 7 up). 1970. 10.95 (ISBN 0-690-40680-0, TYC-J). T Y Crowell.

--Meet the Malones. LC 43-12453. (gr. 5 up). 1943. 10.95 (ISBN 0-690-52999-6, TYC-J). T Y Crowell.

--New & Different Summer. LC 66-11951. (gr. 5 up). 1966. 10.95 (ISBN 0-690-58040-1, TYC-J). T Y Crowell.

--Pick a New Dream. LC 61-10488. (gr. 7-11). 1961. 10.95 (ISBN 0-690-62016-0, TYC-J). T Y Crowell.

Weber, Loraine J. & Covino, Willam A. GED Writing Skills Test Preparation Guide: High School Equivalency Examination. (Cliffs Test Preparation Ser.). 151p. (Orig.). (gr. 10 up). 1981. pap. 3.95 (ISBN 0-8220-2015-7). Cliffs.

Weber, M. Ancient Judaism. LC 52-8156. 1967. pap. text ed. 7.95 (ISBN 0-02-934130-2). Free Pr.

Weber, M. see Von Wiesner, J. & Von Regel, C.

Weber, Marianne. Max Weber: A Biography. Zohn, Harry, ed. & tr. LC 74-23904. 719p. 1975. 31.50 (ISBN 0-471-92333-8, Pub. by Wiley-Interscience). Wiley.

Weber, Marsha I., jt. auth. see Montero, Darell.

Weber, Max. Basic Concepts in Sociology. 1980. pap. 3.95 (ISBN 0-8065-0304-1). Lyle Stuart.

--The City. LC 58-6492. 1958. 12.95 (ISBN 0-02-934200-7); pap. text ed. 4.95 (ISBN 0-02-934210-4). Free Pr.

--General Economic History. (Social Science Classics Ser.). 1981. text ed. 19.95 (ISBN 0-87855-317-7); pap. text ed. 7.95 (ISBN 0-87855-690-7). Transaction Bks.

--Max Weber on Methodology of the Social Sciences. 1949. text ed. 10.95 (ISBN 0-02-934360-7). Free Pr.

--Protestant Ethic & the Spirit of Capitalism. rev. ed. 1977. pap. 3.95 o.p. (ISBN 0-684-15502-8, SL756, ScribT). Scribner.

--Rational & Social Foundations of Music. Martindale, Don, et al, trs. LC 56-12134. 198p. 1958. Repr. lib. bdg. 12.95x (ISBN 0-8093-0015-X). S Ill U Pr.

--Rational & Social Foundations of Music. Martindale, Don, et al, trs. LC 56-12134. (Arcturus Books Paperbacks). 1969. pap. 6.95 (ISBN 0-8093-0355-8). S Ill U Pr.

--Religion of China. 1951. 8.95 o.s.i. (ISBN 0-02-934440-9); pap. text ed. 5.95 o.s.i. (ISBN 0-02-934450-6). Free Pr.

--Roscher & Knies: The Logical Problems of Historical Economics. Oakes, Guy, tr. & intro. by. LC 75-6315. 1975. 14.95 (ISBN 0-02-934050-0). Free Pr.

--Theory of Social & Economic Organization. Parsons, Talcott, tr. 1947. 15.95 (ISBN 0-02-934920-6); pap. text ed. 6.95 (ISBN 0-02-934930-3). Free Pr.

Weber, Michael & Lloyd, Anne. The American City. (Illus.). 463p. 1975. pap. text ed. 11.95 (ISBN 0-8299-0036-5); instrs.' manual avail. (ISBN 0-8299-0580-4). West Pub.

Weber, Michael, jt. auth. see Haeger, John.

Weber, Nancy, jt. auth. see Smith, Alexander H.

Weber, Nelva M. How to Plan Your Own Home Landscape. LC 75-33535. (Illus.). 320p. 1976. 13.95 (ISBN 0-685-62625-3). Bobbs.

--How to Plan Your Own Home Landscape. LC 75-33535. (Illus.). 1979. pap. 10.95 (ISBN 0-672-52599-2). Bobbs.

Weber, O., ed. Audiovisual Market Place A Multimedia Guide 1981: A Multimedia Guide. 11th ed. LC 69-18201. 1981. pap. 32.50 (ISBN 0-8352-1333-1). Bowker.

Weber, Paul, ed. see Nurbaksh, Javad.

Weber, Paul J. & Gilbert, Dennis A. Private Churches & Public Money: Church-Government Fiscal Relations. LC 80-1793. (Contributions to the Study of Religion: No. 1). (Illus.). 256p. 1981. lib. bdg. 27.95 (ISBN 0-313-22484-6, WCM/). Greenwood.

Weber, R., et al, eds. Biblia Sacra Iuxta Vulgatam Versionem 2nd ed. 1975. 32.00 (ISBN 3-438-05302-0, 71686). United Bible.

Weber, Ralph E., jt. auth. see Hachey, Thomas.

Weber, Ralph E., jt. auth. see Hachey, Thomas E.

Weber, Robert L. Pioneers of Science: Nobel Prize Winners in Physics. Lenihan, J. M., ed. 285p. 1980. 23.00 (ISBN 0-9960020-1-4, Pub. by a Hilger England). Heyden.

Weber, Robert L., jt. auth. see Strother, G. K.

Weber, Robert L. A Random Walk in Science: An Anthology. LC 74-75874. (Illus.). 224p. 1974. 16.50x (ISBN 0-8448-0574-2). Crane-Russak Co.

Weber, Ronald. The Literature of Fact: Literary Nonfiction in American Writing. LC 80-16323. viii, 181p. 1980. 15.00x (ISBN 0-8214-0558-6). Ohio U Pr.

Weber, Ronald E., jt. auth. see Uslaner, Eric M.

Weber, Rudolf, ed. Biochemistry of Animal Development, 3 vols. Incl. Vol. 1. Descriptive Biochemistry of Early Development. 1965. 52.50 (ISBN 0-12-740601-8); Vol. 2. Biochemical Control Mechanisms & Adaptations in Development. 1967. 48.75 (ISBN 0-12-740602-6); Vol. 3. 1975. 39.50 (ISBN 0-12-740603-4). Set. 118.75 (ISBN 0-685-23207-7). Acad Pr.

Weber, Samuel, ed. Electronic Circuits Notebook: Proven Designs for Systems Applications. LC 80-29479. (Electronic Magazine Bks.). (Illus.). 344p. (Orig.). 1981. professional 14.95 (ISBN 0-07-606720-3, R-026). McGraw.

Weber, Samuel, ed. see Electronics Magazine.

Weber, Thad L. Alarm Systems & Theft Prevention. LC 73-78572. 384p. 1973. 17.95 (ISBN 0-913708-11-9). Butterworths.

Weber, Timothy P. The Future Explored. 1978. pap. 3.95 (ISBN 0-88207-763-5). Victor Bks.

--Living in the Shadow of the Second Coming: American Premillennialism 1875-1925. 1979. 15.95 (ISBN 0-19-502494-X). Oxford U Pr.

Weber, W. M. Covered Bridges in Indiana. LC 77-84376. 14.95 o.p. (ISBN 0-87359-012-0). Northwood Inst.

Weber, Walter. Health Hazards from Pigeons, Starlings & English Sparrows. LC 79-55324. Date not set. 13.00 (ISBN 0-913702-10-2). Thomson Pub Ca.

Weber, William H., III. Socioeconomic Methods in Educational Analysis. LC 74-28195. (Illus.). 125p. 1975. text ed. 13.60x (ISBN 0-8077-2449-1); pap. text ed. 7.50x (ISBN 0-8077-2448-3). Tchrs Coll.

Weber, William J. Wild Orphan Friends. LC 76-11738. (Illus.). 160p. (gr. 5 up). 1980. pap. 3.50 (ISBN 0-03-056822-6). HR&W.

--Wild Orphan Friends. LC 76-11738. (Illus.). 160p. (gr. 5 up). 1976. 6.95 o.p. (ISBN 0-03-017536-4). HR&W.

Webman, Jerry A., jt. ed. see Nathan, Richard P.

Webster, ed. see Sophocles.

Webster, Bob. The South Texas Garden Book. 140p. (Orig.). 1980. pap. 10.95 (ISBN 0-931722-03-9). Corona Pub.

Webster, Bruce, ed. The Acts of David II, 1329-71. 550p. 1981. 55.00x (ISBN 0-85224-395-2, Pub. by Edinburgh U Pr Scotland). Columbia U Pr.

Webster, C. C. & Wilson, P. N. Agriculture in the Tropics. 2nd ed. LC 74-40086. (Tropical Agriculture Ser.). (Illus.). 540p. 1980. text ed. 32.00 (ISBN 0-582-46814-0). Longman.

Webster, Charles, ed. The Intellectual Revolution of the Seventeenth Century. (Past & Present Ser.). 452p. 1975. 25.00 (ISBN 0-7100-7844-7). Routledge & Kegan.

Webster, Charles, et al. William Harvey & His Age: The Professional & Social Context of the Discovery of Circulation. LC 78-20526. 1979. 12.50x (ISBN 0-8018-2213-0). Johns Hopkins.

Webster, Christopher D., et al, eds. Autism: New Directions in Research & Education. LC 79-19732. (Pergamon Policy Studies). 1980. 24.50 (ISBN 0-08-025083-1). Pergamon.

Webster, Daniel. The Papers of Daniel Webster: Correspondence, Volume 1, 1798-1824. Wiltse, Charles M. & Moser, Harold D., eds. LC 73-92705. (Papers of Daniel Webster: Series 1, Correspondence). (Illus.). 544p. 1974. text ed. 27.50x (ISBN 0-87451-096-1). U Pr of New Eng.

--The Papers of Daniel Webster: Correspondence, Vol. 2, 1825-1829. Wiltse, Charles M. & Moser, Harold D., eds. LC 73-92705. (The Papers of Daniel Webster: Series 1, Correspondence). (Illus.). 587p. 1976. text ed. 27.50x (ISBN 0-87451-120-8). U Pr of New Eng.

--The Papers of Daniel Webster, Correspondence, Vol. 3: 1830-1834. Wiltse, Charles M. & Allen, David G., eds. LC 73-92705. (Papers of Daniel Webster: Series 1, Correspondence). (Illus.). 573p. 1977. text ed. 27.50x (ISBN 0-87451-131-3). U Pr of New Eng.

Webster, David. Body Building: An Illustrated History. (Illus.). 1981. Repr. lib. bdg. 10.95 (ISBN 0-668-04898-0). Arco.

--How to Do a Science Project. LC 73-12214. (First Bks). (Illus.). 72p. (gr. 4 up). 1974. PLB 6.45 (ISBN 0-531-00817-7). Watts.

--Let's Find Out About Mosquitoes. LC 74-4154. (Let's Find Out Bks). (Illus.). 48p. (gr. k-3). 1974. PLB 4.47 o.p. (ISBN 0-531-02740-6). Watts.

--Photo Fun: An Idea Book for Shutterbugs. LC 72-8112. (Illus.). 96p. (gr. 4 up). 1973. PLB 5.90 o.p. (ISBN 0-531-02620-5). Watts.

--Science Projects with Eggs. LC 76-15015. 72p. (gr. 4-6). 1976. PLB 6.45 (ISBN 0-531-01212-3). Watts.

--Track Watching. LC 75-180167. (Illus.). 96p. (gr. 4 up). 1972. PLB 5.88 o.p. (ISBN 0-531-02030-4). Watts.

Webster, David, jt. auth. see Gardner, Robert.

Webster, Douglas B. & Webster, Molly. Comparative Vertebrate Morphology. 1974. text ed. 23.95 (ISBN 0-12-740850-9). Acad Pr.

Webster, E. M. Whirlwinds in the Plain: Ludwig Leichardt - Friends, Foes & History. 484p. 1980. 40.00x (ISBN 0-522-84181-3, Pub. by Melbourne U Pr Australia). Intl Schol Bk Serv.

Webster, Elizabeth J. Professional Approaches with Parents of Handicapped Children. 292p. 1976. 16.75 (ISBN 0-398-03521-0). C C Thomas.

Webster, Frank. The New Photography. 1981. 29.95 (ISBN 0-7145-3798-5); pap. 14.95 (ISBN 0-7145-3801-9). Riverrun NY.

Webster, Frederick E., Jr. Curso de Mercadotecnica. (Span.). 1977. pap. text ed. 9.00 (ISBN 0-06-317070-1, IntlDept). Har-Row.

--Marketing Communication: Modern Promotional Strategy. 694p. 1971. 24.95 (ISBN 0-8260-9230-6). Wiley.

Webster, Frederick E., Jr., jt. auth. see Davis, Kenneth R.

Webster, G. D. Chester Through Derry Conodonts & Stratigraphy of Northern Clark & Southern Lincoln Counties, Nevada. (U. C. Publ. in Geological Sciences: Vol. 79). 1969. pap. 8.00x (ISBN 0-520-09182-5). U of Cal Pr.

Webster, Gary D. Bibliography & Index of Paleozoic Crinoids, Nineteen Forty-Two to Nineteen Sixty-Eight. LC 73-76885. (Memoir: No. 137). 180p. 1973. 19.75x (ISBN 0-8137-1137-1). Geol Soc.

Webster, Geral S. How to Bring up a Child to Become a Financial Leader. (A Human Development Library Bk.). (Illus.). 113p. 1981. 31.75 (ISBN 0-89266-294-8). Am Classical Coll Pr.

Webster, Grady L., jt. auth. see Deghan, Bijan.

Webster, Graham. Boudica: The British Revolt Against Rome A.D. 60. 1978. 33.00 (ISBN 0-7134-1064-7, Pub. by Batsford England). David & Charles.

--The Roman Invasion of Britain. (Illus.). 224p. 1980. 14.00x (ISBN 0-389-20107-3). B&N.

Webster, Harriet, jt. auth. see Webster, Jonathan.

Webster, Harvey C. After the Trauma: Representative British Novelists Since 1920. LC 74-119815. 216p. 1970. 10.50x (ISBN 0-8131-1224-9). U Pr of Ky.

Webster, Helen. Bulletins from a War. (Illus.). 46p. (Orig.). 1980. pap. 5.95 (ISBN 0-915380-11-0). Word Works.

Webster, Henry K. Who Is the Next. LC 75-46005. (Crime Fiction Ser). 1976. Repr. of 1931 ed. lib. bdg. 17.50 (ISBN 0-8240-2397-8). Garland Pub.

--Who Is the Next? LC 80-8720. 320p. 1981. pap. 2.25 (ISBN 0-06-080539-0, P/539, PL). Har-Row.

Webster, Hutton. Rest Days, the Christian Sunday, the Jewish Sabbath & Their Historical & Anthropological Prototypes. LC 68-58165. 1968. Repr. of 1916 ed. 24.00 (ISBN 0-8103-3342-2). Gale.

Webster, J. B. & Boahen, A. A. The Revolutionary Years: West Africa Since Eighteen Hundred. (The Growth of African Civilization Ser.). (Illus.). 1981. pap. text ed. 5.95 (ISBN 0-582-60332-3). Longman.

Webster, J. B., ed. Chronology, Migration & Drought in Interlacustrine Africa. LC 78-7050. (Dalhousie African Studies). 1979. text ed. 44.50x (ISBN 0-8419-0377-8, Africana); pap. text ed. 22.45x (ISBN 0-8419-0388-3, Africana). Holmes & Meier.

Webster, Jean. Daddy Long Legs. (gr. 7 up). 1980. pap. 1.95 (ISBN 0-448-17147-3, Tempo). G&D.

Webster, Joanne. Love Genie. (gr. 9-12). 1980. 8.95 (ISBN 0-525-66699-0). Elsevier-Nelson.

Webster, John. Duchess of Malfi. Hopper, Vincent F. & Lahey, Gerald B., eds. (gr. 9 up). 1962. 4.75 (ISBN 0-8120-5030-4); pap. text ed. 2.95 (ISBN 0-8120-0058-7). Barron.

--Introduction to Fungi. 2nd ed. LC 79-52856. (Illus.). 1980. 79.50 (ISBN 0-521-22888-3); pap. 21.95x (ISBN 0-521-29699-4). Cambridge U Pr.

--Sex Is for Giving. (Illus.). 1968. 5.95 (ISBN 0-910550-12-3). Elysium.

--White Devil. Mulryne, J. R., ed. LC 68-20771. (Regents Renaissance Drama Ser). 1969. 9.95x (ISBN 0-8032-0287-3); pap. 2.95x (ISBN 0-8032-5288-9, BB 233, Bison). U of Nebr Pr.

Webster, John & Ford, John. Selected Plays. 1953. 6.00x (ISBN 0-460-00899-4, Evman); pap. 3.50 (ISBN 0-460-01899-X). Dutton.

Webster, John, tr. see Esser, Karl.

Webster, John G. Medical Instrumentation: Application & Design. LC 77-76419. (Illus.). 1978. text ed. 29.95 (ISBN 0-395-25411-6); sol. manual 2.00 (ISBN 0-395-25412-4). HM.

Webster, John G., jt. auth. see Jacobson, Bertil.

Webster, John G., jt. ed. see Cook, Albert M.

Webster, Jonathan & Webster, Harriet. The Underground Marketplace. LC 80-54401. (Illus.). 208p. 1981. text ed. 12.50x (ISBN 0-87663-348-3); pap. 6.95 (ISBN 0-87663-555-9). Universe.

Webster, Josh. The Beckoning. (Orig.). 1980. pap. 2.95 (ISBN 0-440-10943-4). Dell.

Webster, Marie D. Quilts: Their Story & How to Make Them. LC 75-174137. (Tower Bks). (Illus.). xviii, 178p. 1972. Repr. of 1915 ed. 18.00 (ISBN 0-8103-3111-X). Gale.

Webster, Mary. Essentials of Higher Physics. 1978. pap. text ed. 9.50x o.p. (ISBN 0-435-68836-7). Heinemann Ed.

Webster, Molly, jt. auth. see Webster, Douglas B.

Webster, Murray, Jr. & Sobieszek, Barbara. Sources of Self Evaluation: A Formal Theory of Significant Others & Social Influence. LC 74-5066. 189p. 1974. 24.50 (ISBN 0-471-92440-7, Pub. by Wiley-Interscience). Wiley.

Webster, Ned. The Big White Puzzle Book. 1980. pap. 7.95 o.p. (ISBN 0-89903-001-7). Caroline Hse.

Webster, Noah. Collection of Essays & Fugitiv Writings on Moral, Historical, Political, & Literary Subjects. LC 77-22094. 1977. Repr. of 1790 ed. 45.00x (ISBN 0-8201-1297-6). Schol Facsimiles.

--A Pay-off in Switzerland. LC 77-74271. 1977. 6.95 o.p. (ISBN 0-385-13246-8). Doubleday.

Webster, Peter, jt. auth. see Swanson, Carl P.

Webster, Polly. My Private Life. (Illus.). (gr. 6-10). 5.00 o.p. (ISBN 0-8313-0104-X). Lantern.

Webster, Prentice. A Treatise on the Law of Citizenship in the United States. xxiii, 338p. 1980. Repr. of 1891 ed. lib. bdg. 30.00 (ISBN 0-8377-1307-2). Rothman.

Webster, Prentiss. Law of Naturalization in the United States of America & of Other Countries. xx, 403p. 1981. Repr. of 1895 ed. lib. bdg. 32.50x (ISBN 0-8377-1309-9). Rothman.

Webster, R. K., jt. ed. see Mulvey, T.

Webster, Richard A. Industrial Imperialism in Italy, 1908-1915. LC 74-76393. 480p. 1975. 31.50x (ISBN 0-520-02724-8). U of Cal Pr.

Webster, Robert. Gemmologists' Compendium. 6th rev. ed. Jobbins, Allan, ed. 256p. 1980. 14.95 (ISBN 0-442-23885-1). Van Nos Reinhold.

Webster, T. B. Life in Classical Athens. 1978. 19.95 (ISBN 0-7134-1279-8, Pub. by Batsford England). David & Charles.

Webster, T. B., ed. see Dale, A. M.

Wechsberg, Joseph. Cooking of Vienna's Empire. LC 68-25883. (Foods of the World Ser). (Illus.). (gr. 6 up). 1968. PLB 14.94 (ISBN 0-8094-0059-6, Time-Life). Silver.

--Cooking of Vienna's Empire. (Foods of the World Ser). (Illus.). 1968. 14.95 (ISBN 0-8094-0032-4). Time-Life.

--Looking for a Bluebird. LC 73-16801. (Illus.). 210p. 1974. Repr. of 1945 ed. lib. bdg. 19.75x (ISBN 0-8371-7234-9, WELO). Greenwood.

Wechsler, Ben L., jt. auth. see Whitehouse, Gary E.
Wechsler, Charles. Minnesota: State of Beauty. (Illus.). 96p. 1981. pap. 10.95 (ISBN 0-931714-12-5). Nodin Pr.
Wechsler, Harold. The Qualified Student: A History of Selective College Admission in America. LC 76-47692. 1977. 26.95 (ISBN 0-471-92441-5, Pub. by Wiley-Interscience). Wiley.
Wechsler, Henry. Explorations in Nursing Research. Kibrick, Anne, ed. LC 79-719. 1979. text ed. 24.95 (ISBN 0-87705-379-0); pap. text ed. 12.95 (ISBN 0-87705-399-5). Human Sci Pr.
--A Guide to Medical Schools & Medical School Admission. Date not set. write for info. (ISBN 0-88410-723-X). Ballinger Pub.
--Handbook of Medical Specialities. LC 74-19051. 1976. text ed. 24.95 (ISBN 0-87705-232-8); pap. text ed. 9.95 (ISBN 0-87705-292-1). Human Sci Pr.
Wechsler, Henry, et al, eds. The Horizons of Health. 1977. 18.50 (ISBN 0-674-40630-3); pap. 6.95 (ISBN 0-674-40631-1). Harvard U Pr.
Wechsler, James & Lavine, Harold. War Propoganda & the United States. LC 72-147476. (Library of War & Peace; the Character & Causes of War). lib. bdg. 38.00 (ISBN 0-8240-0268-7). Garland Pub.
Wechsler, James, jt. auth. see Lavine, Harold.
Wecht, Cyril H. Legal Medicine 1980. (Illus.). 320p. 1980. text ed. 27.50 (ISBN 0-7216-9142-0). Saunders.
Wecht, Cyril H., jt. auth. see Perper, Joshua A.
Wecht, Cyril H., ed. Legal Medicine Annual: 1975. (Illus.). 350p. 1975. text ed. 28.50 o.p. (ISBN 0-8385-5653-1). ACC.
--Legal Medicine Annual 1978. (Illus.). 1978. 34.50 (ISBN 0-8385-5656-6). ACC.
Weck, A. L. De see De Weck, A. L.
Weck, Alain L. De see De Weck, Alain L., et al.
Weckselmann, David & Bevan, Elizabeth. Tunde et Ses Amis, 2 bks. 1962-65. text ed. 2.25x ea. Vol. 1 (ISBN 0-521-06757-X). Vol. 2 (ISBN 0-521-06758-8). Cambridge U Pr.
Weckstein, Donald T., jt. auth. see Aronson, Robert H.
Weckstein, Joyce. Racquetball "For Women". 3rd ed. LC 75-39292. (Illus.). 1975. pap. 2.50 (ISBN 0-9600980-1-1, 9600980). J R Weckstein.
Wedderburn, K. W. & Davies, P. L. Employment Grievances & Disputes Procedures in Great Britain. LC 71-84788. 1969. 25.00x (ISBN 0-520-01408-1). U of Cal Pr.
Weddington, D. Patterns for Practical Communications: Composition Package. 1977. text ed. 180.00 (ISBN 0-13-653881-9); tchrs manual 10.00 (ISBN 0-13-653865-7). P-H.
--Patterns for Practical Communications: Sentence Package. 1977. text ed. 180.00 (ISBN 0-13-653790-1); script sentences 13.00 (ISBN 0-13-653816-9). P-H.
Weddington, Doris C. Patterns for Practical Communications: Combined Sentence & Composition Packages. 1976. 40 wkbks.,20 cassettes,2 scripts,2 tchrs' manuals 350.00 (ISBN 0-13-653899-1). P-H.
Weddle, A. J. Marine Engineering Systems: An Introduction for Merchant Navy Officers. (Illus.). 1976. text ed. 16.50x (ISBN 0-434-92233-1). Sheridan.
Weddle, Ferris. Tall Like a Pine. LC 74-17072. (Illus.). 128p. (gr. 4-7). 1974. 5.95g o.p. (ISBN 0-8075-7757-X). A Whitman.
Weddle, Robert S. San Juan Bautista: Gateway to Spanish Texas. (Illus.). 1968. 17.95 (ISBN 0-292-73306-2). U of Tex Pr.
--Wilderness Manhunt: The Spanish Search for La Salle. LC 72-1579. (Illus.). 286p. 1973. 14.95 (ISBN 0-292-79000-7). U of Tex Pr.
Weddon, Willah. How to Heat & Eat with Woodburning Stoves. (Illus.). 128p. 1980. pap. 4.95 (ISBN 0-932296-06-8). Eberly Pr.
Wedeck, Harry E. Classics of Greek Literature. LC 63-11490. 1963. 6.00 (ISBN 0-8022-1826-1). Philos Lib.
Wedekind see Bentley, Eric.
Wedekind, Frank. The Lulu Plays. Spender, Stephen, tr. from Ger. (Illus.). 1977. pap. 5.95 (ISBN 0-7145-0868-3). Riverrun NY.
--Lulu Plays & Other Sex Tragedies. Spender, Stephen, tr. 1979. pap. 5.95 (ISBN 0-7145-0868-3). Riverrun NY.
--Spring Awakening. Osborn, Tom, tr. from Ger. 1979. pap. 4.95 (ISBN 0-7145-0634-6). Riverrun NY.
Wedel, Kenneth, et al. Social Services by Government Contract. 22.95 (ISBN 0-03-052161-0). Praeger.
Wedel, Waldo R. Prehistoric Man on the Great Plains. (Illus.). 1961. 15.95 (ISBN 0-8061-0501-1). U of Okla Pr.
Wedell, E. G. Structures of Broadcasting: A Symposium. 108p. 1970. 27.00x (ISBN 0-686-63741-0, Pub. by Manchester U Pr England). State Mutual Bk.
Wedertz. Bodie 1859-1900. LC 72-96763. pap. 8.95 (ISBN 0-912494-20-4). Chalfant Pr.
Wedgewood, Cicely V. World of Rubens. LC 67-27679. (Library of Art Ser.). (Illus.). (gr. 6 up). 1967. 12.96 (ISBN 0-8094-0269-6, Pub. by Time-Life). Silver.
Wedgeworth, Robert, ed. ALA Yearbook 1979. LC 76-647548. 1979. text ed. 45.00 (ISBN 0-8389-0292-8). ALA.
Wedgwood, Barbara & Wedgwood, Hensleigh. The Wedgwood Circle: 1730-1897; Four Generations of Wedgwoods & Their Friends. LC 80-65213. (Illus.). 408p. 1980. 22.50 (ISBN 0-89860-038-3). Eastview.
Wedgwood, C. V. Velvet Studies. 159p. 1980. Repr. of 1946 ed. lib. bdg. 15.00 (ISBN 0-89987-861-X). Darby Bks.
Wedgwood, Cicely V. Poetry & Politics Under the Stuarts. 1960. 32.00 (ISBN 0-521-06762-6). Cambridge U Pr.
--World of Rubens. (Library of Art). (Illus.). 1967. 15.95 (ISBN 0-8094-0240-8). Time-Life.
Wedgwood, Hensleigh, jt. auth. see Wedgwood, Barbara.
Wedgwood, James I. The Larger Meaning of Religion. 80p. 1981. pap. text ed. 3.70 (ISBN 0-918980-10-0). St Alban Pr.
Wedlake, G. E. SOS: The Story of Radio Communication. LC 73-91529. (Illus.). 240p. 1974. 14.50x (ISBN 0-8448-0270-0). Crane-Russak Co.
Wedlock, Bruce D. & Roberge, James K. Electronic Components & Measurements. 1969. ref. ed. 22.95 (ISBN 0-13-250464-2). P-H.
Wee, George C. Atlas of Improved Surgical Procedures for Common Foot Disorders: Ingrown Toenail & Hammertoe. (Illus.). 80p. 1972. 8.75 (ISBN 0-398-02498-7). C C Thomas.
Weeber, Stanley C., jt. auth. see Roebuck, Julian.
Weed, Clarence M. An Introduction to the Art & Science of Collecting Butterflies. (Illus.). 1980. Repr. of 1917 ed. 41.75 (ISBN 0-89901-003-2). Found Class Reprints.
Weed, James A. National Estimates of Marriage Dissolution & Suvivorship. Cox, Klaudia, ed. (Ser. 3, No. 19). 50p. 1980. pap. text ed. 1.75 (ISBN 0-8406-0196-4). Natl Ctr Health Stats.
Weed, Libby, jt. auth. see Weed, Michael.
Weed, Michael. Letters of Paul to the Ephesians, Colossians, & Philemon. Ferguson, Everett, ed. LC 79-134688. (The Living Word Commentary Ser.: Vol. 11). 1971. 7.95 (ISBN 0-8344-0055-3). Sweet.
Weed, Michael & Weed, Libby. Bible Handbook: A Guide for Basic Bible Learning. LC 73-91023. 1978. student's ed. 2.95 (ISBN 0-8344-0101-0); pocket ed. 2.95 (ISBN 0-686-65381-5); gift ed. o.s.i. 2.95 (ISBN 0-8344-0103-7). Sweet.
--Bible Handbook for Young Learners. LC 73-91023. (Illus.). 236p. (gr. 3-8). 1974. kivar 5.95 o.p. (ISBN 0-8344-0082-0). Sweet.
Weeden, Hester E., ed. see Schuster, Edgar H.
Weeden, Hester E., ed. see Stanford, Gene.
Weeden, R; see Cheshire, P. D.
Weeden, R., jt. auth. see Webb, A. E.
Weeden, William B. War Government, Federal & State, 1861-65. LC 75-87685. (Law, Politics & History Ser.). 1972. Repr. of 1906 ed. lib. bdg. 39.50 (ISBN 0-306-71707-7). Da Capo.
Weedon, William B. Economic & Social History of New England 1620-1789, 2 Vols. 1963. Set. text ed. 25.00x (ISBN 0-391-00493-X). Humanities.
Weedy, B. M. Electric Power Systems. 2nd ed. LC 71-37109. 453p. 1972. 20.50 o.p. (ISBN 0-471-92445-8, Pub. by Wiley-Interscience). Wiley.
--Electric Power Systems. 3rd ed. LC 79-40081. 27.50 (ISBN 0-471-27584-0, Pub. by Wiley-Interscience). Wiley.
Weeghman, Richard, ed. see Aviation Consumer.
Weekes, Claire. Hope & Help for Your Nerves. LC 69-12957. 1968. 8.95 o.p. (ISBN 0-8015-3576-X). Dutton.
--Peace from Nervous Suffering. 1972. 7.95 o.p. (ISBN 0-8015-5802-6); pap. 3.95 o.p. (ISBN 0-8015-5804-2). Dutton.
Weekley, Ernest. Etymological Dictionary of Modern English, 2 Vols. 1967. pap. text ed. 6.00 ea.; Vol. 1. pap. text ed. (ISBN 0-486-21873-2); Vol. 2. pap. text ed. (ISBN 0-486-21874-0). Dover.
--Jack & Jill: A Study in Our Christian Names. LC 74-148925. 1974. Repr. of 1939 ed. 15.00 (ISBN 0-8103-3649-9). Gale.
Weeks, Albert. The Troubled Detente. LC 75-27166. 1976. 12.00 (ISBN 0-8147-9166-2). NYU Pr.
Weeks, Albert, jt. auth. see London, Herbert I.
Weeks, Claire. Agoraphobia. 1977. 8.95 (ISBN 0-8015-0111-3, Hawthorn). Dutton.
Weeks, Dorothy. The Jar Garden. LC 76-428. (Illus.). 64p. (Orig.). 1976. pap. 3.95 (ISBN 0-912800-26-7). Woodbridge Pr.
Weeks, John. Pyramids. (Introduction to the History of Mankind Ser.). (Illus.). 1971. 3.95 (ISBN 0-521-07240-9). Cambridge U Pr.
--A Superman of Letters: R. Reginald & the Borgo Press. LC 80-11112. 64p. 1981. lib. bdg. 8.95x (ISBN 0-89370-811-9); pap. 2.95x (ISBN 0-89370-911-5). Borgo Pr.
Weeks, John, jt. auth. see Hogg, Ivan V.
Weeks, John R. Population: An Introduction to Concepts & Issues. 1978. text ed. 17.95x (ISBN 0-534-00549-7). Wadsworth Pub.
--Teenage Marriages: A Demographic Analysis. LC 76-5330. (Studies in Population & Urban Demography Ser.: No. 2). (Illus.). 192p. (Orig.). 1976. lib. bdg. 16.50 (ISBN 0-8371-8898-9, WTM/). Greenwood.
Weeks, Kent M. Ombudsmen Around the World: A Comparative Chart. 2nd ed. LC 78-17224. 1978. pap. 7.00x (ISBN 0-87772-258-7). Inst Gov Stud Berk.
Weeks, Kent R., jt. auth. see Harris, James E.
Weeks, Lewis E., jt. auth. see Berman, Howard J.
Weeks, Lewis E., jt. auth. see Berman, Howard W.
Weeks, Lewis E. & Berman, Howard J., eds. Economics in Health Care. LC 77-10860. 1977. text ed. 25.00 (ISBN 0-89443-026-2). Aspen Systems.
Weeks, Lewis E., ed. see Bellin, Lowell E.
Weeks, Lewis E., et al. Financing of Health Care - An Inquiry Anthology. LC 79-13436. (Illus.). 1979. pap. text ed. 14.00 (ISBN 0-914904-34-5); pap. text ed. 17.00 (ISBN 0-914904-35-3). Health Admin Pr.
Weeks, Paul M. Acute Bone & Joint Injuries of the Hand & Wrist: A Clinical Guide to Management. (Illus.). 299p. 1980. text ed. 37.50 (ISBN 0-8016-5373-8). Mosby.
Weeks, Paul M. & Wray, R. Christie. Management of Acute Hand Injuries: A Biological Approach. 2nd ed. LC 78-5718. 1978. text ed. 48.50 (ISBN 0-8016-5371-1). Mosby.
Weeks, Philip & Gidney, James B. Subjugation & Dishonor: A Brief History of the Travail of the Native Americans. LC 79-28713. (Orig.). 1980. 12.50 (ISBN 0-89874-076-2); pap. 5.95 (ISBN 0-686-66018-8). Krieger.
Weeks, Robert P., ed. Machines & the Man: A Sourcebook on Automation. LC 61-6338. (Illus., Orig.). 1961. pap. text ed. 5.95x (ISBN 0-89197-282-X). Irvington.
Weeks, Stephen B. Church & State in North Carolina. Repr. of 1893 ed. pap. 7.00 (ISBN 0-384-66391-5). Johnson Repr.
Weeks, Thelma E. Slow Speech Development of a Bright Child. LC 73-23019. (Illus.). 1974. 17.95 (ISBN 0-669-91876-8). Lexington Bks.
Weeks, Townsend E., jt. auth. see Gordon, Julius.
Weeks, William W., et al, eds. A Manual of Structured Experiences for Cross-Cultural Learning. LC 79-100422. 1977. pap. text ed. 5.95 (ISBN 0-933934-05-X). Intercult Pr.
Weems, Ann. Reaching for Rainbows: Resources for Creative Worship. 1980. pap. write for info. (ISBN 0-664-24355-X). Westminster.
Weems, David B. Twenty One Custom Speaker Enclosure Projects You Can Build. (Illus.). 240p. (Orig.). 1980. 12.95 (ISBN 0-8306-9962-7); pap. 7.95 (ISBN 0-8306-1234-3, 1234). TAB Bks.
Weems, Mason L. The Life of Washington the Great, Repr. Of 1806 Ed. 5th, rev. ed. Bd. with The Eclectic First Reader. McGuffey, William H. Repr. of 1836 ed. LC 75-32156. (Classics of Children's Literature, 1621-1932: Vol. 21). 1976. PLB 38.00 (ISBN 0-8240-2270-X). Garland Pub.
Weems, Robert E. Panoply. 100p. 1979. 4.95 (ISBN 0-8059-2624-0). Dorrance.
Weemshall, H., jt. auth. see Henshaw, Paul.
Weeney, L. Mac, tr. see Ussher, Arland.
Weenink, Allan D. Art of Church Canvass. LC 78-69998. 1978. pap. 4.95 (ISBN 0-87983-172-3). Keats.
Weeraratne, Victor. Springs of Freedom in Czechoslovakia. (Illus.). 1970. 5.95 o.p. (ISBN 0-8158-0048-7). Chris Mass.
Weerman, F., jt. ed. see Zonneveld, W.
Weernink, Wim O. La Lancia: Seventy Years of Excellence. (Illus.). 1979. 49.95 (ISBN 0-900549-42-4). Motorbooks Intl.
Weese, Harry, jt. auth. see Goldenberg, Leon.
Weesner, Frances M., jt. ed. see Krishna, Kumar.
Weetall, Howard, jt. ed. see Luderer, Albert.
Weete, John D. & Weber, Darrell J. Lipid Biochemistry of Fungi & Other Organisms. 400p. 1980. 45.00 (ISBN 0-306-40570-9, Plenum Pr). Plenum Pub.
Weever, John. Ancient Funerall Monuments Within the United Monarchie of Great Britaine, Ireland & the Islands Adjacent. LC 79-84145. (Englsh Experience Ser.). 910p. 1979. Repr. of 1631 ed. lib. bdg. 125.00 (ISBN 90-221-0961-5). Walter J Johnson.
Weevers, Theodor. Poetry of the Netherlands in Its Euroean Context: 1170-1930. 1960. text ed. 20.00x (ISBN 0-485-11041-5, Athlone Pr). Humanities.
Weg, Ruth B. Nutrition & the Later Years. LC 77-91696. 1978. pap. 6.50 (ISBN 0-88474-042-0). USC Andrus Geron.
Wegbreit, Ben. Studies in Extensible Programming Languages. LC 79-7309. (Outstanding Dissertations in the Computer Sciences Ser.: Vol. 23). 425p. 1980. lib. bdg. 36.00 (ISBN 0-8240-4423-1). Garland Pub.
Wegelin, C. American Novel: Background Readings & Criticism. LC 76-136274. 1972. pap. text ed. 6.95 o.s.i. (ISBN 0-02-934590-1). Free Pr.
Wegen, Ron. Where Can the Animals Go. LC 77-15001. (Illus.). (gr. k-3). 1978. 7.95 (ISBN 0-688-80137-4); PLB 7.63 (ISBN 0-688-84137-6). Greenwillow.
Wegen, Ronald. Sand Castle. LC 75-30707. (gr. k-3). 1977. 6.25 (ISBN 0-688-80033-5); PLB 6.00 (ISBN 0-688-84033-7). Greenwillow.
Wegener, Alfred. Origin of Continents & Oceans. Biram, John, tr. (Illus.). 1966. pap. 4.50 (ISBN 0-486-61708-4). Dover.
Wegener, Bernd, ed. Social Attitudes & Psychophysical Measurement. 432p. 1981. professional reference text 24.95 (ISBN 0-89859-083-3). L Erlbaum Assocs.
Weger, Karl-Heinz. Karl Rahner: An Introduction to His Theology. 1980. 10.95 (ISBN 0-8164-0127-6). Crossroad NY.
Weger, Karl-Heinz, jt. auth. see Rahner, Karl.
Wegg, Jervis. The Decline of Antwerp Under Philip of Spain. LC 78-20500. 1981. Repr. of 1924 ed. 26.50 (ISBN 0-88355-876-9). Hyperion Conn.
Weggalaer, Jan. Amsterdam: Capital City of the Netherlands. (Q Books: Famous Cities). (Illus.). (gr. 3-6). 1978. 3.95 (ISBN 0-8467-0446-3, Pub. by Two Continents). Hippocrene Bks.
Wegler, R., ed. Insecticides: Biochemical & Biological Methods, Natural Products. (Chemie der Pflanzenschutz und Schaedlingsbekaempfungsmittel). 500p. 1981. 152.30 (ISBN 0-387-10307-4). Springer-Verlag.
Wegman & DePrist. Statistical Analysis of Weather Modification Experiments. 184p. 1980. write for info. (ISBN 0-8247-1177-7). Dekker.
Wegner, Daniel M. & Vallacher, Robin R. Implicit Psychology: An Introduction to Social Cognition. (Illus.). 1978. 7.95x (ISBN 0-19-502228-9); pap. text ed. 6.95x (ISBN 0-19-502229-7). Oxford U Pr.
Wegner, P. Programming with Ada: An Introduction by Means of Graduated Examples. 1980. 13.95 (ISBN 0-13-730697-0). P-H.
Wegner, Robert & Sayles, Leonard. Cases in Organizational & Administrative Behavior. LC 71-158913. 1972. pap. text ed. 10.95 (ISBN 0-13-118562-4). P-H.
Wegner, Susan, ed. see Moon, Warren G.
Wegsheider, Sharon. Another Chance: Hope & Health for Alcoholic Families. 1980. 12.95 (ISBN 0-8314-0059-5). Sci & Behavior.
Wegst, Audrey V., ed. Nuclear Medicine Science Syllabus. LC 78-68703. 1978. loose-leaf text 33.00 (ISBN 0-932004-01-6). Soc Nuclear Med.
Wehle, Harry B. American Minatures Seventeen Thirty to Eighteen Fifty: One Hundred & Seventy-Three Portraits. LC 71-87684. (Library of American Art Ser.). 1970. Repr. of 1927 ed. lib. bdg. 27.50 (ISBN 0-306-71708-5). Da Capo.
Wehman, Henry J. see Miller, Pierre.
Wehman, Paul. Competitive Employment: New Horizons for Severely Disabled Individuals. LC 80-24926. (Illus.). 278p. (Orig.). 1981. pap. text ed. 13.95 (ISBN 0-933716-12-5). P H Brookes.
--Competitive Employment: New Horizons for Severely Disabled Individuals. 210p. 1980. pap. 13.95 (ISBN 0-933716-12-5). P H Brookes.
--Helping the Mentally Retarded Acquire Play Skills: A Behavioral Approach. (Illus.). 244p. 1977. 17.50 (ISBN 0-398-03604-7). C C Thomas.
Wehman, Paul H. Curriculum Design for Severely & Profoundly Handicapped. LC 78-23704. 1979. text ed. 14.95x (ISBN 0-87705-365-0). Human Sci Pr.
Wehmeyer, Lillian B. Images in a Crystal Ball: World Futures in Novels for Young People. 1981. lib. bdg. 18.50x (ISBN 0-87287-219-X). Libs Unl.
--The School Librarian As Educator. LC 76-41303. 250p. 1976. lib. bdg. 17.50x (ISBN 0-87287-165-7). Libs Unl.
--The School Library Volunteer. LC 75-12586. (Illus.). 128p. 1975. lib. bdg. 10.00x (ISBN 0-87287-110-X). Libs Unl.
Wehner, R., ed. Information Processing in the Visual Systems of Arthropods. LC 72-91887. 340p. 1973. pap. 25.10 (ISBN 0-387-06020-0). Springer-Verlag.

Wehner, Walter L. Rhythmic Sightsinging. LC 78-66281. 1979. pap. text ed. 7.50 (ISBN 0-8191-0687-9). U Pr of Amer.

Wehr, M. Russell, et al. Physics of the Atom. 3rd ed. LC 77-77752. (Physics Ser.). (Illus.). 1978. text ed. 19.95 (ISBN 0-201-08587-9). A-W.

Wehr, Paul. Conflict Regulation. 1979. lib. bdg. 22.00x (ISBN 0-89158-351-3); pap. 8.50x (ISBN 0-89158-352-1). Westview.

Wehr, Paul & Washburn, Michael. Peace & World Order Systems: Teaching & Research. LC 75-23614. (Sage Library of Social Research: Vol. 25). 1976. 18.00x (ISBN 0-8039-0552-1); pap. 8.95x (ISBN 0-8039-0553-X). Sage.

Wehrle, Edmund S., jt. auth. see Lach, Donald F.

Wehrli, K. Division. (Michigan Arithmetic Program Ser.). (gr. 4). 1976. wkbk. 7.00 (ISBN 0-89039-180-7). Ann Arbor Pubs.

Wehrli, K., jt. ed. see Steele, B.

Wehrli, Kitty. Addition, Ten to Twenty. (Michigan Arithmetic Program Ser.). (gr. 2). 1977. wkbk. 7.00 (ISBN 0-89039-105-X). Ann Arbor Pubs.

--Cues & Comprehension: Level 1. (Ann Arbor Tracking Program Ser.). (gr. 2). 1976. wkbk. 5.00 (ISBN 0-89039-168-8). Ann Arbor Pubs.

--Cues & Comprehension: Level 2. (Ann Arbor Tracking Program Ser.). (gr. 2). 1976. wkbk. 5.00 (ISBN 0-89039-169-6). Ann Arbor Pubs.

--Cues & Comprehension: Level 3. (Ann Arbor Tracking Progam Ser.). (gr. 2). 1976. wkbk. 5.00 (ISBN 0-89039-170-X). Ann Arbor Pubs.

--Cues & Comprehension: Level 4. (gr. 2). 1976. wkbk. 5.00 (ISBN 0-89039-171-8). Ann Arbor Pubs.

--Michigan Arithmetic Program,Multiplication, Level 2: Consuable Edition. (gr. 3). 1975. 7.00 (ISBN 0-89039-132-7). Ann Arbor Pubs.

--Multiple Tracking: Math 2: A Self-Instruction Workbook for Visual Accuracy,Resuable Edition. (gr. 1). 1971. wkbk. 6.00 (ISBN 0-89039-033-9). Ann Arbor Pubs.

--Multiplication,Level 1: Consumable Edition. (Michigan Arithmetic Program Ser.). (gr. 3). 1975. Repr. wkbk 7.00 (ISBN 0-89039-094-0). Ann Arbor Pubs.

--Number Tracking: Math 1: A Self-Instruction Workbook for Visual Accuracy, Resuable Edition. (gr. 1). 1971. wkbk. 5.00 (ISBN 0-89039-031-2). Ann Arbor Pubs.

--Numbers & Numerals. (Michigan Arithmetic Program). (ps-2). 1976. 1.00 (ISBN 0-89039-199-8); wkbk. 5.00 (ISBN 0-89039-102-5). Ann Arbor Pubs.

--Subtraction 10-0. (Michigan Arithmetic Program Ser.). (gr. 2-3). 1976. wkbk. 7.00 (ISBN 0-89039-176-9). Ann Arbor Pubs.

--Subtraction 20-10, Levels 1 & 2. (Michigan Arithmetic Program). (gr. 2-3). 1976. Level 1. wkbk 7.00x ea. Level 2. Ann Arbor Pubs.

--Thought Tracking Level Four: Questions & Answers. (gr. 2 up). 1976. wkbk. 5.00x (ISBN 0-89039-192-0). Ann Arbor Pubs.

--Thought Tracking Level One: Simple Phrases. (gr. 2). 1976. wkbk. 5.00 (ISBN 0-89039-186-6). Ann Arbor Pubs.

--Thought Tracking Level Three: Simple Sentences. (gr. 2). 1976. wkbk. 5.00 (ISBN 0-89039-190-4). Ann Arbor Pubs.

--Thought Tracking Level Two: Sequential Phrases. (gr. 2). wkbk. 5.00 (ISBN 0-89039-188-2). Ann Arbor Pubs.

--Visual & Transfer Skill Mastery, 2 levels. (Michigan Arithmetic Program Ser.). 1976. wkbk. 7.00x ea.; Levels 1 & 2. (ISBN 0-89039-948-4). Ann Arbor Pubs.

Wehrly, Max. Mobile Homes, 2 pts. LC 72-79132. (Illus.). 80p. 1972. Set. pap. 4.75 (ISBN 0-87420-068-7). An Analysis Of Characteristics. An Analysis Of Communities. Urban Land.

Wehrum, Victoria. The American Theatre. LC 73-9972. (First Bks.). (Illus.). 72p. (gr. 5-8). 1974. PLB 4.90 o.p. (ISBN 0-531-00792-8). Watts.

Wei, C. C., jt. auth. see Goren, Charles H.

Wei, Cho-Min. The Political Principles of Mencius. (Studies in Chinese Government & Law). 99p. 1977. Repr. of 1916 ed. 11.50 (ISBN 0-89093-063-5). U Pubns Amer.

Wei, Tan Tai. The Concept of Education, Educational Conceptions, & Liberal Education. LC 77-18470. 1978. pap. text ed. 7.50x (ISBN 0-8191-0418-3). U Pr of Amer.

Weibel, Kathryn N. Mirror Mirror: Images of Women in Popular Culture. LC 76-47835. 1977. pap. 3.95 (ISBN 0-385-11131-2, Anch). Doubleday.

Weich, I. Edward. Real Estate. (Orig.). 1967. pap. 3.95 (ISBN 0-06-460060-2, CO 60, COS). Har-Row.

Weicher, John C. Housing: Federal Policies & Programs. 1980. pap. 6.25 (ISBN 0-8447-3378-4). Am Enterprise.

Weichsel, Paul M., jt. auth. see Paley, Hiram.

Weick, Friedhelm & Brown, Leslie. Birds of Prey of the World: A Coloured Guide to Identification of All the Diurnal Species Order Falconiformes. (Illus.). 159p. (Orig.). 1980. 48.00 (ISBN 3-490-08518-3). Parey Sci Pubs.

Weick, Karl E. Social Psychology of Organizing. 2nd ed. LC 79-10015. (Topics in Social Psychology Ser.). 1979. pap. text ed. 7.95 (ISBN 0-201-08591-7). A-W.

Weide, Alexander, jt. auth. see Yonker, Donald Y.

Weidenaar, Dennis J. & Weiler, Emanuel T. Economics: An Introduction to the World Around You. 2nd ed. LC 78-67942. (Economics Ser.). (Illus.). 1979. text ed. 14.95 (ISBN 0-201-08517-8); instr's manual avail. (ISBN 0-201-08516-X). A-W.

--Introduction to the World Around You: Student Tutor, Alternate Edition. (Economics Ser.). pap. text ed. 7.95 (ISBN 0-201-08518-6). A-W.

Weidenaar, Reynold H. & Zeller, Ann. A Sketchbook of Michigan. (Illus.). 128p. 1980. 15.95 (ISBN 0-8010-9620-0). Baker Bk.

Weidenbaum, Murray. Business, Government, & the Public. LC 76-23088. (Illus.). 1977. 16.95 (ISBN 0-13-099317-4). P-H.

Weidenborner, Stephen, jt. auth. see Caruso, Domenick.

Weidenbruch, Peter P., jt. auth. see Sobeloff, Jonathan.

Weidener, F. W., jt. ed. see Rose, J.

Weidenhan, Joseph L. Baptismal Names. 4th ed. LC 68-26618. 1968. Repr. of 1931 ed. 24.00 (ISBN 0-8103-3136-5). Gale.

Weidenmuller, H. A., jt. auth. see Norenberg, W.

Weidenreich, Franz. The Brain & Its Role in the Phylogenetic Transformation of the Human Skull. LC 78-72707. Repr. of 1941 ed. 19.50 (ISBN 0-404-18278-X). AMS Pr.

Weider, Joe. The Best of Joe Weider's Muscle & Fitness Bodybuilding Nutrition & Training Programs. (Illus.). 1981. 12.95 (ISBN 0-8092-5917-6); pap. 5.95 (ISBN 0-8092-5916-8). Contemp Bks.

--The Best of Joe Weider's Muscle & Fitness Training Tips & Routines. (Illus.). 1981. 12.95 (ISBN 0-8092-5911-7); pap. 5.95 (ISBN 0-8092-5910-9). Contemp Bks.

--The Best of Joe Weider's Muscle & Fitness: The Worlds's Leading Bodybuilders Answer Your Questions. (Illus.). 1981. 12.95 (ISBN 0-8092-5914-1); pap. 5.95 (ISBN 0-8092-5912-5). Contemp Bks.

Weider, Robert S. & Hall, George. The Great American Convertible: An Affectionate Guide. LC 77-72416. 1977. pap. 6.95 (ISBN 0-385-13123-2, Dolp). Doubleday.

Weidert, Alfons. Componential Analysis of Lushai Phonology. (Current Issues in Linguistics Theory: No. 2). 1979. text ed. 23.00x (ISBN 0-391-01640-7). Humanities.

Weidhaas, Ernest. Architectural Drafting & Design. 3rd ed. 1977. text ed. 18.50x o.p. (ISBN 0-205-05624-5); tchr's manual avail. o.p. (ISBN 0-205-05625-3). Allyn.

Weidhass, Ernest H. Architectural Drafting & Construction. 560p. 1981. text ed. 24.95; instr's hdbk. avail. Allyn.

Weidhass, Ernest R. Architectural Drafting & Construction. 560p. 1974. text ed. 18.50x o.p. (ISBN 0-205-04221-X); instr's hndbk avail. o.p. (ISBN 0-205-04222-8). Allyn.

Weidhorn, Manfred. Winston Churchill. (English Authors Ser.: No. 264). 1979. lib. bdg. 12.50 (ISBN 0-8057-6760-6). Twayne.

Weidhorn, Manfred, jt. auth. see Nass, Stanley.

Weidling, Philip. The Secret of the Old Bridge. (gr. 6-8). 1975. 4.95 o.p. (ISBN 0-87482-044-8). Wake-Brook.

Weidman, Bette S. & Martin, Linda B. Nassau County, Long Island, in Early Photographs, 1869-1940. (Illus.). 144p. (Orig.). 1981. pap. price not set (ISBN 0-486-24136-X). Dover.

Weidman, Bette S., jt. ed. see Black, Nancy B.

Weidman, Jerome. Counselors-at-Law. LC 78-14712. 408p. 1980. 12.95 (ISBN 0-385-12880-0). Doubleday.

Weidman, Judith L., ed. Women Ministers: How Women Are Redifining Traditional Roles. LC 80-8345. 192p. (Orig.). 1981. pap. 5.95 (ISBN 0-06-069291-X, RD 345, HarpR). Har-Row.

Weidner, Edward W., ed. see Hutchins, John G. B.

Weidner, James H. Rusky -- Poetry & Prose Vignettes. LC 80-68817. 104p. (Orig.). 1980. pap. 5.95 (ISBN 9-0701-7619-X). Foris Pubns.

Weidner, Richard T & Sells, Robert L. Elementary Physics: Classical & Modern. 1975. text ed. 26.95x (ISBN 0-205-04647-9, 7346476); instr's. man. free (ISBN 0-205-04648-7). Allyn.

Weidner, Richard T., jt. auth. see Carr, Herman Y.

Weidner, Richard T., et al. Elementary Classical Physics, 2 vols. 2nd ed. 1973. text ed. 22.95x combined edition o.p. (ISBN 0-685-27996-0, 737574); Vol. 1. text ed. 20.95x o.p. (ISBN 0-205-03597-3, 7335970); Vol. 2. text ed. 20.95x o.p. (ISBN 0-205-03598-1, 7335989). Vol. 2. sol. man. 4.95 o.p. (ISBN 0-205-04010-1, 7340109). Allyn.

Weigall, Arthur. Life & Times of Akhnaton, Pharaoh of Egypt. LC 79-115209. 1971. Repr. of 1922 ed. 14.50 o.p. (ISBN 0-8046-1102-5). Kennikat.

Weigan, John F. & Thomas, Sydney F. Complications of Diagnostic Radiology. (Illus.). 576p. 1973. 35.75 (ISBN 0-398-02501-0). C C Thomas.

Weigand, Dennis A. Dermatology Continuing Education Review. 2nd. ed. Olson, Robert L., ed. 1980. pap. 14.50 (ISBN 0-87488-341-5). Med Exam.

Weigand, Dennis A., ed. Dermatology. 4th ed. (Medical Examination Review Book: Vol. 21). 1980. pap. 18.00 (ISBN 0-87488-127-7). Med Exam.

Weigand, George. Getting Ready for College: How to Settle Down & Make the Grade. 1981. pap. text ed. 2.25 (ISBN 0-8120-2080-4). Barron.

Weigand, J., ed. Implementing Teacher Competencies: Positive Approaches to Personalizing Education. 1977. pap. text ed. 11.95 (ISBN 0-13-451930-2). P-H.

Weigand, James E., ed. Developing Teacher Competencies. LC 70-149972. (Illus.). 1971. pap. text ed. 11.95 (ISBN 0-13-205278-4). P-H.

Weigand, Phil C., jt. ed. see Hinton, Thomas B.

Weigel, James, Jr. Mythology. 210p. 1973. pap. 2.95 (ISBN 0-8220-0865-3). Cliffs.

Weigel, John A. B.F. Skinner. (World Leaders Ser.: No. 64). 1977. lib. bdg. 9.95 (ISBN 0-8057-7713-X). Twayne.

--Colin Wilson. LC 74-28137. (English Authors Ser.: No. 181). 1975. lib. bdg. 10.95 (ISBN 0-8057-1575-4). Twayne.

--Lawrence Durrell. 1966. pap. 1.25 o.p. (ISBN 0-525-47185-5). Dutton.

--Lawrence Durrell. (English Authors Ser.: No. 29). 1965. lib. bdg. 10.95 (ISBN 0-8057-1180-5). Twayne.

Weigel, Richard D., jt. auth. see Melko, Matthew.

Weigelin, E. & Lobstein, A. Ophthalmodynamometry. 1963. 10.75 o.s.i. (ISBN 0-02-854630-X). Hafner.

Weiger, John G. Cristobal De Virues. (World Authors Ser.: No. 497 (Spain)). 1978. 12.95 (ISBN 0-8057-6338-4). Twayne.

--The Individuated Self: Cervantes & the Emergence of the Individual. LC 78-13019. xvi, 183p. 1979. 12.95x (ISBN 0-8214-0396-6). Ohio U Pr.

--The Valencian Dramatists of Spain's Golden Age. LC 75-25558. (World Authors Ser.: Spain: No. 371). 1976. lib. bdg. 12.50 (ISBN 0-8057-6219-1). Twayne.

Weigert, Andrew J. A Sociology of Everyday Life. 272p. 1981. pap. text ed. 10.95 (ISBN 0-582-28199-7). Longman.

Weigh, Iris. Someone to Love. (Aston-Hall Romances Ser.). 192p. (Orig.). Date not set. pap. 1.75 (ISBN 0-523-41131-6). Pinnacle Bks.

Weigh, Ken S. Russo-Chinese Diplomacy. LC 79-2845. 382p. 1981. Repr. of 1928 ed. 29.50 (ISBN 0-8305-0021-9). Hyperion Conn.

Weight, Harold O. & Weight, Lucile. Rhyolite - Death Valley's Ghost City of Golden Dreams. 8th ed. 1978. pap. 1.50 o.p. (ISBN 0-912714-04-2). Calico Pr.

--Rhyolite-Death Valley's Ghost City of Golden Dreams. 9th ed. 1980. pap. 1.95. Calico Pr.

Weight, Lucile, jt. auth. see Weight, Harold O.

Weight Watchers International. Weight Watchers Holiday & Party Cookbook. 1980. 12.95 (ISBN 0-453-01005-9, TE-5). NAL.

Weightman, Doreen, tr. see Guehenno, Jean.

Weightman, Doreen, tr. see Levi-Strauss, Claude.

Weightman, John, tr. see Guehenno, Jean.

Weightman, John, tr. see Levi-Strauss, Claude.

Weightman, John, intro. by. Masterworks of the French Cinema. Incl. The Italian Straw Hat. Claire, Rene; Grand Illusion. Renoir, Jean; La Ronde. Ophuls, Max; The Wages of Fear. Clouzot, Henri-Georges. LC 73-21853. (Icon Editions: Masterworks Film Ser). (Illus.). 312p. 1974. pap. 4.95 o.s.i. (ISBN 0-06-430051-X, IN-51, HarpT). Har-Row.

Weigl, Egon. Neuropsychology & Neurolinguistics. (Janua Linguarum, Ser. Maior: No. 78). 1980. text ed. 75.00x (ISBN 90-279-7956-1). Mouton.

Weigle, Luther A see Gabriel, Ralph H.

Weigle, Marta. Jacks & Jack Games: Follow My Fancy. Davis, Jessica H., ed. LC 71-81735. (Orig.). (gr. 1-6). 1970. pap. 2.00 (ISBN 0-486-22081-8). Dover.

Weigle, Oscar, ed. Great Big Joke & Riddle Book. LC 79-129734. (Illus.). 224p. (gr. 1-5). 1981. 6.95 (ISBN 0-448-02584-1); PLB 10.15 (ISBN 0-448-03167-1). G&D.

Weigley, R. F. History of the United States Army. 1967. 14.95 (ISBN 0-02-625640-1). Macmillan.

Weigley, Russell F. The American Way of War: A History of United States Military Strategy & Policy. LC 72-91169. 708p. 1973. 14.95 (ISBN 0-02-625650-9). Macmillan.

--American Way of War: A History of U. S. Military Strategy & Policy. LC 77-74434. (Wars of the United States Ser.). (Illus.). 602p. 1977. pap. 7.95x (ISBN 0-253-28029-X). Ind U Pr.

Weigley, Russell F., ed. The American Military: Readings in the History of the Military in American Society. (Themes & Social Forces in American History Ser). (Orig.). 1969. pap. text ed. 6.95 (ISBN 0-201-08594-1). A-W.

Weigner, Gladys, jt. auth. see Moosbrugger, Bernhard.

Weigold, Marilyn. The American Mediterranean. 1974. 12.95 o.p. (ISBN 0-8046-9064-2). Kennikat.

Weih, Starr, jt. auth. see Scott, Leroy.

Weihe, W. H., jt. ed. see Tromp, S. W.

Weihofen, Henry. Legal Services & Community Mental Health Centers. 74p. 1969. pap. 3.00 (ISBN 0-685-24859-3, P229-0). Am Psychiatric.

--Legal Writing Style. 2nd ed. LC 79-23662. 332p. 1980. text ed. 11.95 (ISBN 0-8299-2066-8). West Pub.

Weihrich, Heinz, jt. auth. see O'Donnell, Harold K.

Weijnen, A., ed. Atlas Linguarum Europae-Ale. 216p. 1980. text ed. 22.50 (ISBN 90-232-1697-0). Humanities.

Weik, Martin H. Fiber Optics & Lightwave Communications Standard Dictionary. 320p. 1980. text ed. 18.50 (ISBN 0-442-25658-2). Van Nos Reinhold.

--Standard Dictionary of Computers & Information Processing. rev., 2nd ed. 1977. 22.50 (ISBN 0-8104-5099-2). Hayden.

Weiker, Walter F. Modernization in Turkey Nineteen Twenty-Three to Nineteen Seventy-Nine. LC 80-24514. 250p. 1980. text ed. 24.00x (ISBN 0-8419-0503-7). Holmes & Meier.

Weil. Candy Egg Bunny. (gr. 2-3). 1980. pap. 3.50 incl. record (ISBN 0-590-24001-3, Schol Pap). Schol Bk Serv.

Weil, C., jt. ed. see Sen, R. N.

Weil, G. L. Trade Policy in the Seventies. LC 73-4787. 1969. pap. 1.00 (ISBN 0-527-02847-9). Kraus Repr.

Weil, Henri. The Order of Words in the Ancient Languages Compared with That of the Modern Languages. (Amsterdam Classics in Linguistics Ser.: No. 14). 1979. text ed. 25.75x (ISBN 90-272-0871-9). Humanities.

Weil, John L. A Neurophysiological Model of Emotional & Intentional Behavior. (Illus.). 204p. 1974. 22.75 (ISBN 0-398-02497-9). C C Thomas.

Weil, Judith. Christopher Marlowe. LC 76-26586. 1977. 34.00 (ISBN 0-521-21554-4). Cambridge U Pr.

Weil, Lisl. Fat Ernest. LC 72-8095. (Illus.). 48p. (gr. k-3). 1973. 5.95 o.s.i. (ISBN 0-8193-0656-8, Four Winds); PLB 5.41 o.s.i. (ISBN 0-8193-0657-6). Schol Bk Serv.

--The Funny Old Bag. LC 73-13564. (Illus.). 48p. (ps-3). 1974. 5.95 o.s.i. (ISBN 0-8193-0717-3, Four Winds); PLB 5.41 o.s.i. (ISBN 0-8193-0718-1). Schol Bk Serv.

--Gertie & Gus. LC 77-4757. (Illus.). (gr. k-4). 1977. 5.95 o.s.i. (ISBN 0-8193-0911-7, Four Winds); PLB 5.41 o.s.i. (ISBN 0-8193-0912-5). Schol Bk Serv.

--Golden Spinning Wheel. LC 69-20614. (Illus.). (gr. k-3). 1969. 4.95g o.s.i. (ISBN 0-686-66482-5). Macmillan.

--Melissa's Friend Fabrizzio. (gr. k-2). 1967. 3.95g o.s.i. (ISBN 0-02-792450-5). Macmillan.

--Owl & Other Scrambles. LC 80-13742. (Illus.). (ps-3). 1980. PLB 8.95 (ISBN 0-525-36527-3, Unicorn). Dutton.

--Ralphi Rhino. LC 73-92448. (Illus.). 32p. (ps-3). 1974. 4.95 o.s.i. (ISBN 0-8027-6176-3); PLB 4.85 o.s.i. (ISBN 0-8027-6177-1). Walker & Co.

--Walt & Pepper. LC 73-22183. (Illus.). 40p. (ps-3). 1974. 5.95 o.s.i. (ISBN 0-8193-0758-0, Four Winds). Schol Bk Serv.

Weil, Marsha & Joyce, Bruce. Information Processing Models of Teaching: Expanding Your Teaching Repertoire. LC 77-5414. (Illus.). 1978. ref. ed. 14.95 (ISBN 0-13-464552-9); pap. text ed. 10.95 (ISBN 0-13-464545-6). P-H.

--Social Models of Teaching: Expanding' Your Teaching Repetoire. LC 77-5448. (Illus.). 1978. 14.95 (ISBN 0-13-815944-0); pap. 10.95 (ISBN 0-13-815936-X). P-H.

Weil, Marsha, jt. auth. see Joyce, Bruce.

Weil, Marsha, et al. Personal Models of Teaching: Expanding Your Teaching Repertoire. LC 77-7738. (Illus.). 1978. ref 13.95 (ISBN 0-13-657767-9); pap. text ed. 9.95 (ISBN 0-13-657759-8). P-H.

Weil, N. A. see Ordway, Frederick I., 3rd.

Weil, Raymond, jt. auth. see Fordyce, Jack K.

Weil, Robert & Fitzgerald, James. The Yankee Quizbook. LC 80-1654. (Illus.). 144p. 1981. pap. 5.95 (ISBN 0-385-17178-1, Dolp). Doubleday.

Weil, Rudolf, ed. see Andersen, Hans C.

Weil, Simone. Iliad or the Poem of Force. LC 57-6026. 1956. pap. 1.25x (ISBN 0-87574-091-X). Pendle Hill.

--Lectures on Philosophy. Price, H., tr. from Fr. LC 77-26735. 1978. 32.95 (ISBN 0-521-22005-X); pap. 7.50 (ISBN 0-521-29333-2). Cambridge U Pr.

--Oppression & Liberty. Wills, Arthur & Petrie, John, trs. from Fr. LC 72-92284. 216p. 1973. 12.00x o.p. (ISBN 0-87023-120-0); pap. 4.95 (ISBN 0-87023-251-7). U of Mass Pr.

Weil, Susanne & Singer, Barry. Steppin' Out: A Guide to Live Music in Manhattan. LC 79-23812. (Illus.). 160p. 1980. lib. bdg. 10.25 o.p. (ISBN 0-914788-24-8). East Woods.

Weil, William B., Jr. Fluid & Electrolyte Metabolism in Infants & Children: A Unified Approach. 1978. 32.00 (ISBN 0-8089-1028-0). Grune.

Weiler, Anton, jt. ed. see Alberigo, Giuseppe.

Weiler, Beverly. Santa's Christmas Tree. LC 79-54318. (A Once-Upon-a-Time Book). (Illus.). 64p. (gr. k-5). 1980. 7.95g (ISBN 0-9604572-0-8). Great Western.

Weiler, Emanuel T., jt. auth. see Weidenaar, Dennis J.

Weiler, Eugene. Jesus: A Pictorial History of the New Testament. (Illus.). 160p. 1980. pap. 10.95 (ISBN 0-8245-2287-7). Crossroad NY.

Weiler, Gershon. Mauthner's Critique of Language. LC 76-114605. 1971. 42.00 (ISBN 0-521-07861-X). Cambridge U Pr.

Weiler, Kathi, jt. auth. see Kernicki, Jeanette.

Weiler, Lawrence D., jt. ed. see Platt, Alan.

Weiler, Nicholas W. Reality & Career Planning: A Guide for Personal Growth. (Illus.). 224p. 1977. text ed. 13.95 (ISBN 0-201-08572-0); pap. text ed. 7.95 (ISBN 0-201-08570-4). A-W.

Weilerstein, Sadie R. K'ton Ton in Israel. (Illus.). (ps-3). 1964. 3.50 o.p. (ISBN 0-685-06932-X). Bloch.

Weill, Alix. Tutu: The True Story of a Budgie. LC 79-21793. (Illus., Orig.). 1979. pap. 3.95 (ISBN 0-89127-056-6). Omni Pubs.

Weill, Francis W. Ultrasonography of Digestive Diseases. LC 77-13046. (Illus.). 1978. 57.50 (ISBN 0-8016-5374-6). Mosby.

Weill, Gus. A Woman's Eyes. 208p. 1976. pap. 1.50 o.p. (ISBN 0-345-24774-4). Ballantine.

Weill, Herman N. European Diplomatic History 1815-1914: Documents & Interpretations. LC 74-171719. 1972. 15.00 o.p. (ISBN 0-682-47375-8, University); pap. 5.00 o.p. (ISBN 0-682-47327-8). Exposition.

Weil-Malherbe, Hans & Szara, Stephen I. Biochemistry of Functional & Experimental Psychoses. (Amer. Lec. in Living Chemistry Ser.). (Illus.). 424p. 1971. 26.75 (ISBN 0-398-02435-9). C C Thomas.

Weiman, Eiveen. Which Way Courage. LC 80-36725. 144p. (gr. 4-7). 1981. PLB 8.95 (ISBN 0-689-30835-3). Atheneum.

Weimar, Karl S. & Hoffmeister, Werner G. Practice & Progress: A German Grammar for Review & Reference. 1970. text ed. 14.95x (ISBN 0-471-00619-X); tapes avail. (ISBN 0-471-00621-1). Wiley.

Weimar, Karl S., ed. Thirty-Six German Poems. LC 50-14279. 1950. pap. text ed. 4.75 (ISBN 0-395-05524-5, 3-59405). HM.

Weimer, David L. Improving Prosecution? The Inducement & Implementartion of Innovations for Prosecution Management. LC 79-6190. (Contributions in Political Science: No. 49). (Illus.). xv, 237p. 1980. lib. bdg. 25.00 (ISBN 0-313-22247-9, WEP/). Greenwood.

Weimer, Jan, jt. auth. see Olmstead, Marty.

Weimer, Walter B. & Palermo, David, eds. Cognition & the Symbolic Processes, Vol. 2. 426p. 1981. professional ref. text 24.95 (ISBN 0-89859-066-3). L Erlbaum Assocs.

Wei-Ming, Tu. Humanity & Self-Cultivation Essays in Confucian Thought. 1980. text ed. 22.50 (ISBN 0-89581-600-8, Asian Humanities). Lancaster-Miller.

Wein, Horst. Science of Hockey. 2nd ed. Belchamber, David, tr. (Illus.). 22.00 (ISBN 0-7207-1149-5). Transatlantic.

Wein, Jacqueline. Roommate. 1980. pap. 2.25 (ISBN 0-451-09160-4, E9160, Sig). NAL.

Weinaug, Catherine. Puppet Parables for Children's Church. (Paperback Program Ser.). 88p. 1980. pap. 3.45 (ISBN 0-8010-9638-3). Baker Bk.

Weinbaum, Helen, tr. see Ellenberger, W., et al.

Weinbaum, Paul. Statue of Liberty: Heritage of America. DenDooven, Gweneth R., ed. LC 78-78122. (Illus.). 1979. 7.95 (ISBN 0-916122-64-6); pap. 3.00 (ISBN 0-916122-63-8). K C Pubns.

Weinberg, jt. auth. see Cary.

Weinberg, Alvin M. & Wigner, Eugene P. Physical Theory of Neutron Chain Reactors. LC 58-8507. (Illus.). 1958. 30.00x (ISBN 0-226-88517-8). U of Chicago Pr.

Weinberg, Alyce T. Spirits of Frederick. LC 79-54039. (Illus.). 73p. (Orig.). 1979. pap. 3.95x (ISBN 0-9604552-0-5). A T Weinberg.

Weinberg, Arthur & Weinberg, Lila. Clarence Darrow: The Sentimental Rebel. 1980. 17.95 (ISBN 0-399-11936-1). Putnam.

Weinberg, Bernard, jt. auth. see Dargan, E. Preston.

Weinberg, Bernard, ed. French Poetry of the Renaissance. LC 64-19796. (Arcturus Books Paperbacks). 260p. (Fr). 1964. pap. 6.95 (ISBN 0-8093-0135-0). S Ill U Pr.

Weinberg, Bernd, jt. auth. see Shedd, Donald P.

Weinberg, C. Education & Social Problems. LC 72-129289. 1971. pap. text ed. 4.50 o.s.i. (ISBN 0-02-934950-8). Free Pr.

Weinberg, Carl. Social Foundations of Educational Guidance. LC 68-24440. 1969. text ed. 12.95 (ISBN 0-02-934970-2). Free Pr.

Weinberg, Daniela. Peasant Wisdom: Cultural Adoption in a Swiss Village. (Illus.). 226p. 1975. 21.50x (ISBN 0-520-02789-2). U of Cal Pr.

Weinberg, F. J., ed. Combustion Institute European Symposium: Papers Presented at Symposium Held at the University of Sheffield, Sept., 1973. 1974. 94.50 (ISBN 0-12-742350-8). Acad Pr.

Weinberg, Frank, jt. auth. see Partington, A. M.

Weinberg, Frank F., jt. auth. see Warner, James C.

Weinberg, George. Self Creation. 1978. pap. 2.50 (ISBN 0-380-43521-7, 43521). Avon.

--Self Creation. LC 77-10375. 1978. 8.95 o.p. (ISBN 0-312-71232-4). St Martin.

--Society & the Healthy Homosexual. 160p. 1973. pap. 1.95 (ISBN 0-385-05083-6, Anch). Doubleday.

Weinberg, George H., et al. Statistics: An Intuitive Approach. 4th ed. 384p. 1980. text ed. 15.95 (ISBN 0-8185-0426-9). Brooks-Cole.

Weinberg, George M. & Schumaker, John A. Statistics: An Intuitive Approach. 3rd ed. LC 73-85595. 1974. text ed. 15.95 (ISBN 0-8185-0113-8); solutions manual avail. (ISBN 0-685-42226-7). Brooks-Cole.

Weinberg, Gerald, ed. see Marcus, Robert.

Weinberg, Gerhard L. The Foreign Policy of Hitler's Germany: Starting World War II, 1937-1939. LC 79-26406. 1980. 44.00x (ISBN 0-226-88511-9). U of Chicago Pr.

Weinberg, H. Barbara. The Decorative Work of John la Farge. LC 76-23654. (Outstanding Dissertations in the Fine Arts - 2nd Series - American). (Illus.). 1977. Repr. of 1972 ed. lib. bdg. 84.00 (ISBN 0-8240-2736-1). Garland Pub.

Weinberg, H. Barbara, ed. The Masterpieces of the Centennial International Exhibition. Illustrated, 3 vols. Incl. Vol. 1. Fine Art. Strahan, Edward; Vol. 2. Industrial Art. Smith, Walter; Vol. 3. History, Mechanics, Science. Wilson, Joseph M. LC 75-28867. (Art Experience in Late 19th Century America Ser.: Vol. 3). (Illus.). 1976. Repr. of 1876 ed. Set. lib. bdg. 172.00 (ISBN 0-8240-2227-0). Garland Pub.

Weinberg, H. Barbara, ed. see Benjamin, S. G.

Weinberg, H. Barbara, ed. see Champney, Benjamin.

Weinberg, H. Barbara, ed. see Cook, Clarence.

Weinberg, H. Barbara, ed. see Irving, Washington, et al.

Weinberg, H. Barbara, ed. see Jarves, James J.

Weinberg, H. Barbara, ed. see Koehler, S. R.

Weinberg, H. Barbara, ed. see Robinson, Frank T.

Weinberg, H. Barbara, jt. ed. see Saint-Gaudens, Homer.

Weinberg, H. Barbara, ed. see Sheldon, G. W.

Weinberg, H. Barbara, ed. see Simmons, Edward.

Weinberg, H. Barbara, ed. see Trumble, Alfred.

Weinberg, H. Barbara, ed. see Van Rensselaer, Mariana G.

Weinberg, Harry L. Levels of Knowing & Existence: Studies in General Semantics. LC 73-80740. 1973. pap. 5.50x (ISBN 0-910780-07-2). Inst Gen Semantics.

Weinberg, Herman. The Lubitsch Touch: A Critical Study. 2nd ed. LC 76-44119. (Illus.). 1977. pap. 4.00 o.p. (ISBN 0-486-23483-5). Dover.

Weinberg, Joel S. College Reading: Skills & Practice. LC 77-78585. (Illus.). 1978. pap. text ed. 10.95 (ISBN 0-395-25319-5); inst. manual 0.45 (ISBN 0-395-25320-9). HM.

Weinberg, Judity W., jt. auth. see Weinberg, Lee S.

Weinberg, Julius R. Abstraction, Relation, & Induction: Three Essays in the History of Thought. 1965. 17.50x (ISBN 0-299-03540-9). U of Wis Pr.

--Ideas & Concept. (Aquinas Lectures Ser). 1970. 6.95 (ISBN 0-87462-135-6). Marquette.

--Ockham, Descartes, & Hume: Self Knowledge, Substance, & Causality. Courtenay, William J., ed. 1977. 22.50 (ISBN 0-299-07120-0). U of Wis Pr.

Weinberg, Julius R. & Yandell, Keith. Problems in Philosophical Inquiry. LC 73-148058. 1971. 29.50x (ISBN 0-03-083380-9); pap. text ed. 18.95x (ISBN 0-89197-905-0). Irvington.

Weinberg, Julius R. & Yandell, Keith E., eds. Metaphysics. LC 73-148058. 1971. pap. text ed. 9.75x (ISBN 0-03-085668-X). Irvington.

Weinberg, Larry, adapted by. The Legend of the Lone Ranger Storybook. LC 80-5751. (Movie Storybooks). (Illus.). 64p. (gr. 3-7). 1981. PLB 6.99 o.p. (ISBN 0-394-94683-9); pap. 5.95 boards o.p. (ISBN 0-394-84683-4). Random.

Weinberg, Lee S. & Weinberg, Judity W. Law & Society: An Interdisciplinary Introduction. LC 80-5229. 495p. 1980. pap. text ed. 21.50 (ISBN 0-8191-1055-8). U Pr of Amer.

Weinberg, Leonard, jt. auth. see Siegel, Richard L.

Weinberg, Lila, jt. auth. see Weinberg, Arthur.

Weinberg, Lynn G., jt. auth. see Weinberg, Richard.

Weinberg, Martha. Managing the State. 1977. text ed. 16.00x (ISBN 0-262-23077-1); pap. text ed. 5.95x (ISBN 0-262-73048-0). MIT Pr.

Weinberg, Martha W., jt. ed. see Burnham, Walter D.

Weinberg, Martin S., jt. ed. see Rubington, Earl.

Weinberg, Martin S., et al, eds. The Solution of Social Problems: Five Perspectives. 2nd ed. 240p. 1981. pap. text ed. 7.95x (ISBN 0-19-502787-6). Oxford U Pr.

Weinberg, Meyer. Afro-American History: Separate or Interracial. 1968. pap. 0.90 (ISBN 0-685-38477-2). Integrated Ed Assoc.

--Illinois Divorce, Separate Maintenance & Annulment, with Forms. 2nd ed. 1969. with suppl. 25.00 (ISBN 0-672-82919-3, Bobbs-Merrill Law); 1976 suppl. 10.00 (ISBN 0-672-82804-9). Michie.

--Race & Place: A Legal History of the Neighborhood School. 1968. pap. 3.60 (ISBN 0-912008-06-7). Integrated Ed Assoc.

Weinberg, Meyer, compiled by. The Education of Poor & Minority Children: A World Bibliography, 2 vols. LC 80-29441. 1981. lib. bdg. 95.00 (ISBN 0-313-21996-6, WEC/). Greenwood.

Weinberg, Meyer, ed. Education of the Minority Child: A Comprehensive Bibliography of 10,000 Selected Entries. 1970. 12.95 o.p. (ISBN 0-685-38479-9); pap. 5.95 o.p. (ISBN 0-912008-01-6). Integrated Ed Assoc.

--Learning Together. LC 64-19114. 1964. pap. 3.75 (ISBN 0-912008-00-8). Integrated Ed Assoc.

Weinberg, Michael A. Emeralds (Poetry) facsimile ed. (Illus.). 25p. 1971. write for info. (ISBN 0-9601014-0-3). Weinberg.

Weinberg, Michael A., compiled by. Effortless Childbirth...No Such Thing?-a Bibliography. 57p. (Orig.). 1980. text ed. 3.50 (ISBN 0-9601014-9-7). Weinberg.

Weinberg, Paul J. European Labor & Multinationals. LC 78-9449. (Praeger Special Studies). 1978. 21.95 (ISBN 0-03-044256-7). Praeger.

Weinberg, Richard & Weinberg, Lynn G. Parent Perogatives: How to Handle Teacher Misbehavior & Other School Disorders. LC 78-23718. 1979. 12.95 (ISBN 0-88229-442-3). Nelson-Hall.

Weinberg, Richard A., jt. auth. see Boehm, Ann E.

Weinberg, Robert. The Annotated Guide to Robert E. Howard's Sword & Sorcery. LC 80-19169. 160p. 1980. Repr. of 1976 ed. lib. bdg. 13.95x (ISBN 0-89370-030-4). Borgo Pr.

Weinberg, Robert, ed. The Death Dealers. LC 80-8667. 80p. 1980. lib. bdg. 11.95 (ISBN 0-89370-099-1); pap. 5.95 (ISBN 0-89370-097-5). Borgo Pr.

--The Phantom Detective. LC 80-8668. 80p. 1980. Repr. of 1979 ed. lib. bdg. 11.95 (ISBN 0-89370-085-1); pap. 5.95 (ISBN 0-89370-084-3). Borgo Pr.

--The Weird Tales Story. LC 77-73602. 1977. 17.50 (ISBN 0-913960-16-0). Fax Collect.

Weinberg, Roger & Cheuk, Shu L. Introduction to Dental Statistics. LC 80-36706. 185p. (Orig.). 1980. 18.00 (ISBN 0-8155-0813-1). Noyes.

Weinberg, S. Kirson. Social Problems in Modern Urban Society. 2nd ed. 1970. text ed. 17.95 (ISBN 0-13-817528-4). P-H.

Weinberg, Sanford, jt. auth. see Colburn, William.

Weinberg, Sanford B., jt. auth. see Baird, John E., Jr.

Weinberg, Sharon L. & Goldberg, Kenneth P. Basic Statistics for Education & the Behavioral Sciences. LC 78-56433. (Illus.). 1979. text ed. 18.75 (ISBN 0-395-26853-2); inst. manual 0.80 (ISBN 0-395-26854-0). HM.

Weinberg, Stanley L. Biology: An Inquiry into the Nature of Life. rev. ed. 644p. 1974. text ed. 14.80x o.p. (ISBN 0-205-04487-5); instr's manual avail. o.p. (ISBN 0-205-04488-3). Allyn.

Weinberg, Stanley L. & Stoltze, Herbert J. Action Biology. new ed. 1977. 15.12 (ISBN 0-205-05525-7, 6755259); tchrs'. guide 9.92 (ISBN 0-205-05534-6, 6755348). Allyn.

--Action Biology. (gr. 9-12). 1974. 15.12 (ISBN 0-205-04139-6, 6741398); tchrs'. guide 9.92 (ISBN 0-205-04140-X, 6741401). Allyn.

--Children & Ancestors. (Action Biology Ser.). (gr. 9-12). 1974. pap. text ed. 3.20 (ISBN 0-205-04143-4, 6741436). Allyn.

--Doing Their Thing. (Action Biology Ser). (gr. 9-12). 1974. pap. text ed. 3.20 (ISBN 0-205-04146-9, 6741460). Allyn.

--Food. (Action Biology Ser.). (gr. 9-12). 1974. pap. text ed. 3.20 (ISBN 0-205-04144-2, 6741444). Allyn.

--The Invisible World. (Action Biology Ser.). (gr. 9-12). 1974. pap. text ed. 3.20 (ISBN 0-205-04145-0, 6741452). Allyn.

--Keeping Alive. (Action Biology Ser.). (gr. 9-12). 1974. pap. text ed. 3.20 (ISBN 0-205-04141-8, 674141X). Allyn.

--Reproduction. (Action Biology Ser.). (gr. 9-12). 1974. pap. text ed. 3.20 (ISBN 0-205-04142-6, 6741428). Allyn.

Weinberg, Stanley L. & Stolze, Herbert J. Ecology. (Action Biology Ser.). (gr. 9-12). 1974. pap. text ed. 3.20 (ISBN 0-205-04147-7, 6741479). Allyn.

Weinberg, Steve. The Secrets of Washington Journalists. 1981. 12.50 (ISBN 0-87491-424-8). Acropolis.

Weinberg, Steven. Gravitation & Cosmology; Principles & Applications of the General Theory of Relativity. LC 78-37175. 750p. 1972. 34.95 (ISBN 0-471-92567-5). Wiley.

Weinberg, Thomas. Looking Down Dark Holes & Climbing Mountains. (Illus.). 150p. (Orig.). 1979. pap. 6.95 (ISBN 0-9603484-0-9, Dist. by Bookpeople). Gordons & Weinberg.

Weinberg, Victor. Structured Analysis. LC 78-105808. 1978. pap. 19.00 (ISBN 0-917072-05-7). Yourdon.

--Structured Analysis. (Illus.). 1980. text ed. 25.95 (ISBN 0-13-854414-X). P-H.

Weinberger, Andrew D. Freedom & Protection: The Bill of Rights. LC 72-6217. 180p. 1972. Repr. of 1962 ed. lib. bdg. 12.75x (ISBN 0-8371-6474-5, WEFP). Greenwood.

Weinberger, Dorothy. Songs in the Night. 1981. 4.75 (ISBN 0-8062-1699-9). Carlton.

Weinberger, Eliot, tr. see Paz, Octavio.

Weinberger, Emily K., jt. auth. see Krawitt, Laura P.

Weinberger, Hans F. First Course in Partial Differential Equations: With Complex Variables & Transform Methods. 1965. 28.95 (ISBN 0-471-00623-8). Wiley.

Weinberger, J., ed. see Bacon, Francis.

Weinberger, Norman S. The Art of the Photogram: Photography Without a Camera. LC 78-20702. (Illus.). 1981. 19.95 (ISBN 0-8008-0371-X, Pentalic). Taplinger.

Weine, Franklin S. Endodontic Therapy. 2nd ed. LC 75-38723. (Illus.). 1976. 37.50 (ISBN 0-8016-5382-7). Mosby.

Weine, Ruth, ed. see Curran, June.

Weiner & Green. Barron's How to Prepare for the Test of Standard Written English. 1981. pap. 4.95 (ISBN 0-8120-2095-2). Barron.

Weiner, jt. auth. see Brownstein.

Weiner, Arlene W. The Iron Age. Orgel, Stephen, ed. LC 78-66846. (Renaissance Drama Ser.). 1979. lib. bdg. 35.00 (ISBN 0-8240-9728-9). Garland Pub.

Weiner, Bill. Quiet Desperation. 1980. 10.95 (ISBN 0-686-65059-X). Lyle Stuart.

Weiner, Charles, jt. ed. see Smith, Alice K.

Weiner, Charles A., et al. Famous Firsts for Teachers. 1976. pap. text ed. 1.75x (ISBN 0-8134-1844-5, 1844). Interstate.

Weiner, Donald D. & Spina, John F. The Sinusoidal Analysis & Modeling of Weakly Nonlinear Circuits: With Application to Nonlinear Interference Effects. (Electrical-Computer Science & Engineering Ser.). 304p. 1980. text ed. 27.50 (ISBN 0-442-26093-8). Van Nos Reinhold.

Weiner, Dora B. Raspail, Scientist & Reformer. LC 68-19761. (Illus.). 1968. 20.00x (ISBN 0-231-03059-2). Columbia U Pr.

Weiner, Dora B., ed. & tr. see Pinel, Philippe.

Weiner, Douglas. Tibetan & Himalayan Woodblock Prints. (Illus., Orig.). 1974. pap. 6.00 (ISBN 0-486-22988-2). Dover.

Weiner, Egon. Art & Human Emotions. (Illus.). 104p. 1975. 9.75 (ISBN 0-398-03265-3). C C Thomas.

Weiner, Ellis. The Great Muppet Caper. 96p. 1981. pap. 8.95 (ISBN 0-553-01304-1). Bantam.

Weiner, Harold M., jt. ed. see Schmidt, Frances.

Weiner, Herbert, et al, eds. Brain, Behavior, & Bodily Disease. (Association of Research in Nervous & Mental Disease (ARNMD) Research Publications Ser.: Vol. 59). 388p. 1980. text ed. 37.00 (ISBN 0-89004-480-5). Raven.

Weiner, Homer. Spacewater Blues. 1981. 12.95. Sonica Pr.

Weiner, Irving B. Clinical Methods in Psychology. LC 75-28366. (Personality Processes Ser). 678p. 1976. 35.95 (ISBN 0-471-92576-4, Pub. by Wiley-Interscience). Wiley.

--Psychological Disturbance in Adolescence. (Personality Processes Ser.). 400p. 1970. 29.50 (ISBN 0-471-92568-3, Pub. by Wiley-Interscience). Wiley.

Weiner, Irving B., jt. auth. see Elkind, David.

Weiner, J. S. The Piltdown Forgery. (Illus.). 240p. 1981. pap. 4.00 (ISBN 0-486-24075-4). Dover.

Weiner, J. S. & Huizinga, J., eds. The Assessment of Population Affinities in Man. 192p. 1972. 28.00x (ISBN 0-19-857352-9). Oxford U Pr.

Weiner, J. S. & Weiner, J. S., eds. Physiological Variation & Its Genetic Basis: Proceedings, Vol. 17. (Society for the Study of Human Biology, Symposia). 1977. 24.95 (ISBN 0-470-99314-6). Halsted Pr.

Weiner, J. S., jt. ed. see Maule, H. G.

Weiner, Jack, jt. auth. see Pollock, Vera.

Weiner, Janet. How to Organize & Run a Film Society. (Illus.). 192p. 1973. pap. 3.95 o.s.i. (ISBN 0-02-012900-9, Collier). Macmillan.

Weiner, Jerome H., jt. auth. see Boley, Bruno A.

Weiner, M. L. Personality: The Human Potential. 200p. 1973. 21.00 (ISBN 0-08-016946-5). Pergamon.

Weiner, Marcella B., jt. auth. see Starr, Bernard D.

Weiner, Marcella B., et al. Working with the Aged. (Illus.). 1978. pap. 10.95 ref. ed. (ISBN 0-13-967570-1). P-H.

Weiner, Melissa. Prescott: A Pictorial History. Friedman, Donna R., ed. (Illus.). 208p. 1981. pap. write for info. (ISBN 0-89865-092-5). Donning Co.

Weiner, Melvin L. The Cognitive Unconscious: A Piagetian Approach to Psychotherapy. LC 75-12937. (Illus.). 202p. 1975. 15.95x (ISBN 0-915662-01-9). Intl Psych Pr.

Weiner, Michael. Man's Useful Plants. LC 74-18469. (Illus.). 160p. (gr. 7 up). 1976. 9.95 (ISBN 0-02-792600-1, 79260). Macmillan.

--The People's Herbal. (Orig.). 1981. pap. 8.95 (ISBN 0-446-97574-5). Warner Bks.

Weiner, Michael A. Plant a Tree: A Working Guide to Re-Greening America. LC 73-19048. (Illus.). 224p. 1975. 15.95 o.s.i. (ISBN 0-02-625660-6). Macmillan.

--Plant a Tree Book: A Working Guide to Re-Greening America. (Illus.). 224p. 1975. pap. 6.95 o.s.i. (ISBN 0-02-063780-2, Collier). Macmillan.

--The Sceptical Nutritionist. 256p. 1981. 9.95 (ISBN 0-02-625620-7). Macmillan.

--The Taster's Guide to Beer: Brews & Breweries of the World. LC 76-30364. 1977. 17.95 (ISBN 0-02-625600-2, 62560). Macmillan.

Weiner, Mitchel. Barron's Verbal Aptitude Workbook for College Entrance Examinations. rev. ed. (gr. 10-12). 1979. pap. text ed. 3.75 (ISBN 0-8120-2074-X). Barron.

--Verbal Aptitude Workbook for College Entrance Examinations. (gr. 10-12). 1979. pap. text ed. 3.75 (ISBN 0-8120-2074-X). Barron.

Weiner, Mitchel, jt. auth. see Brownstein, Samuel C.

Weiner, Myron F. Therapist Disclosure: The Use of Self in Psychotherapy. 1978. 18.95 (ISBN 0-409-95070-X). Butterworths.

Weiner, Norman L. The Roles of the Police in Urban Society: Conflicts & Consequences. LC 76-14958. 1976. pap. text ed. 3.95 (ISBN 0-672-61365-4). Bobbs.

Weiner, Peter. Making the Media Revolution: A Handbook of Video-Tape Production. LC 72-92867. (Illus.). 224p. 1973. 12.95 (ISBN 0-02-625690-8). Macmillan.

Weiner, Richard. News Bureaus in the U. S. 6th ed. LC 80-83995. 186p. 1981. 25.00 (ISBN 0-913046-01-9). Public Relations.

--Professional's Guide to Publicity. LC 78-52626. 1978. 9.50 (ISBN 0-913046-36-1); pap. 6.50 o.p. (ISBN 0-913046-07-8). Public Relations.

Weiner, Richard & Colasurdo, James F. College Alumni Publications. 190p. 1980. 20.00 (ISBN 0-913046-12-4). Public Relations.

--College Alumni Publications. LC 80-81159. 1980. 20.00 (ISBN 0-913046-12-4). Public Relations.

Weiner, Robert T. & Ellen, Rose, Jr. Bible Studies on the Overcoming Life II. 134p. 1976. 3.95 (ISBN 0-686-68912-7). Maranatha Hse.

Weiner, Robert T. & Weiner, Rose E. Bible Studies on the Overcoming Life. 110p. 1976. 3.95 (ISBN 0-686-68913-5). Maranatha Hse.

Weiner, Robert T., Jr., jt. auth. see Weiner, Rose E.

Weiner, Rose E. & Weiner, Robert T., Jr. Bible Studies for the Preparation of the Bride. 195p. 1980. 4.95 (ISBN 0-686-68911-9). Maranatha Hse.

Weiner, Rose E., jt. auth. see Weiner, Robert T.

Weiner, S. & Palmer, R. The Writing Lab. 1974. pap. 11.95 (ISBN 0-02-479620-4, 47962). Macmillan.

Weiner, Samuel, jt. ed. see Robins, Philip K.

Weiner, Sandra. It's Wings That Make Birds Fly: The Story of a Boy. LC 68-12658. (Illus.). (gr. 1-4). 1968. PLB 5.99 (ISBN 0-394-91266-7). Pantheon.

Weiner, Sheila L. Ajanta: Its Place in Buddhist Art. (Illus.). 1977. 22.50x (ISBN 0-520-02878-3). U of Cal Pr.

Weiner, William J., ed. Respiratory Dysfunction in Neurologic Disease. LC 80-68262. (Illus.). 344p. 1980. monograph 32.50 (ISBN 0-87993-152-3). Futura Pub.

Weinerman, Chester S. Practical Law: A Layperson's Handbook. LC 77-26164. 1978. 13.95 (ISBN 0-13-691113-7, Spec); pap. 4.95 (ISBN 0-13-691105-6, Spec). P-H.

Weinert, jt. auth. see Palmer.

Weinfeld, Nanci R. Helpful Hints & Tricks for New Moms & Dads (& Not So New) LC 79-57188. (Illus.). 88p. (Orig.). 1980. pap. 3.95 (ISBN 0-9603964-0-3). DJD Prods.

--Helpful Hints & Tricks for New Moms & Dads. LC 80-53669. (Illus.). 96p. (Orig.). 1981. pap. 3.95 (ISBN 0-528-88041-1). Rand.

Weingart, John R., jt. auth. see Levine, Arthur E.

Weingarten, Henry. The Study of Astrology, Vol. II. Date not set. pap. 7.95 (ISBN 0-88231-030-5). ASI Pubs Inc. Postponed.

Weingartner, James J. Crossroads of Death: The Story of the Malmedy Massacre & Trial. LC 77-91771. 1979. 16.95x (ISBN 0-520-03623-9). U of Cal Pr.

Weingartner, Rudolf H., ed. The Unity of the Platonic Dialogue: The Cratylus, the Protagras, the Parmenides. 1973. pap. 4.50 (ISBN 0-672-61310-7, LLA224). Bobbs.

Weingartner, Rudolph H. The Unity of the Platonic Dialogue: The Cratylus, the Protagoras, the Parmenides. LC 73-186244. 1973. text ed. 24.00x (ISBN 0-672-51658-6). Irvington.

Weingartner, Thomas. Stalin und der Aufstieg Hitlers: Die Deutschlandpolitik der Kommunistischen Internationale, 1929-1934. (Beitraege zur auswaertigen und international Politik, No. 4). (Ger). 1970. 23.55x (ISBN 3-11-002702-X). De Gruyter.

Weingerb, N. L. see Weissberger, A.

Weingreen, Jacob. Classical Hebrew Composition. 1957. 13.95x (ISBN 0-19-815423-2). Oxford U Pr.

--Practical Grammar for Classical Hebrew. 2nd ed. 1959. 11.95x (ISBN 0-19-815422-4). Oxford U Pr.

Weinhaus, Ann K. Chicken at the Window. LC 78-19482. (Illus.). 32p. (gr. k-3). 1981. 8.95 (ISBN 0-06-026390-3, HarpJ); PLB 8.79g (ISBN 0-06-026391-1). Har-Row.

Weinhold, Barry, jt. auth. see Andresen, Gail.

Weinhouse, Sidney & Klein, George, eds. Advances in Cancer Research, Vol. 34. (Serial Publication Ser.). 1981. write for info. (ISBN 0-12-006634-3). Acad Pr.

Weinhouse, Sidney see Greenstein, Jesse P. & Haddow, Alexander.

Weinhouse, Sidney, jt. ed. see Klein, George.

Weininger, Otto. Physical Attraction & the Theory of Homosexuality. (Illus.). 1979. deluxe ed. 49.85 (ISBN 0-930582-36-5). Gloucester Art.

--Play & Education: The Basic Tool for Early Childhood Learning. 196p. 1979. 15.75 (ISBN 0-398-03845-7). C C Thomas.

Weinland, James D. How to Improve Your Memory. (Orig.). 1957. pap. 3.50 (ISBN 0-06-463273-3, EH 273, EH). Har-Row.

--How to Think Straight. (Quality Paperback: No. 81). (Orig.). 1975. pap. 3.95 (ISBN 0-8226-0081-1). Littlefield.

Weinlein, Gregg T. Choosing a Sports Camp for Your Child. (Illus.). 1980. cancelled (ISBN 0-8092-7376-4); pap. 6.95 (ISBN 0-8092-7375-6). Contemp Bks.

Weinman, Marjorie S. see Weinman, Marjorie W. & Sharmat, Mitchell.

Weinman, Marjorie W. & Sharmat, Mitchell. Day I Was Born. (Illus.). (ps-2). 1980. PLB 7.95 (ISBN 0-525-28560-1). Dutton.

Weinreb, Lloyd L. Criminal Law, Cases, Comment & Questions. 3rd ed. LC 80-14620. (University Casebook Ser.). 894p. 1980. text ed. write for info. (ISBN 0-88277-008-X). Foundation Pr.

--Denial of Justice: Criminal Process in the United States. LC 76-27222. 1979. pap. text ed. 6.95 (ISBN 0-02-934870-6). Free Pr.

Weinreich, Beatrice S., ed. see Weinreich, Uriel.

Weinreich, Uriel. On Semantics. Labov, William & Weinreich, Beatrice S., eds. LC 78-65114. 1979. 28.50x (ISBN 0-8122-7759-7). U of Pa Pr.

Weinsheimer, Joel, ed. Jane Austen Today. LC 75-11447. 187p. 1975. 13.00x (ISBN 0-8203-0382-8). U of Ga Pr.

Weinsier, Roland L. Handbook of Clinical Nutrition: Clinicians Manual for the Diagnosis & Management of Nutritional Problems. (Illus.). 231p. 1980. pap. text ed. 10.95 (ISBN 0-8016-5406-8). Mosby.

Weinstein, A., jt. auth. see Marsden, J.

Weinstein, Abraham, jt. auth. see Roethel, Louis.

Weinstein, Alan. Lectures on Symplectic Manifolds. LC 77-3399. (Conference Board of the Mathematical Sciences Ser.: No. 29). 1979. Repr. of 1977 ed. with corrections 6.80 (ISBN 0-8218-1679-9, CBMS29). Am Math.

Weinstein, Alan, jt. auth. see Marsden, Jerrold.

Weinstein, Allen. Freedom & Crisis: An American History. 972p. 1981. text ed. 18.95 (ISBN 0-394-32415-3). Random.

--Freedom & Crisis: An American History, 2 vols. 3rd ed. 1981. Vol. 1, 498p. pap. text ed. 12.95 (ISBN 0-394-32611-3); Vol. 2, 539p. pap. text ed. 12.95 (ISBN 0-394-32612-1). Random.

Weinstein, Allen & Wilson, R. Jackson. Freedom & Crisis, 2 vols. 2nd ed. 1978. Single Vol. pap. text ed. 17.95x (ISBN 0-394-31217-1); pap. 12.95 ea.; Vol. 1. (ISBN 0-394-31219-8); Vol. 2. (ISBN 0-394-31223-6); wkbks. 4.95 ea. Vol. 1 (ISBN 0-394-32294-0). Vol. 2 (ISBN 0-394-32295-9). Random.

Weinstein, Allen & Gatell, Frank O., eds. Segregation Era, Eighteen Sixty Three to Nineteen Fifty Four. (gr. 9-12). 1970. 4.95x (ISBN 0-19-500657-7); pap. 4.50x (ISBN 0-19-501099-X). Oxford U Pr.

Weinstein, Alvin S., et al. Products Liability & the Reasonably Safe Product: A Guide for Management, Design & Marketing. LC 78-8749. 1978. 23.00 (ISBN 0-471-03904-7, Pub. by Wiley-Interscience). Wiley.

Weinstein, Arnold. Fictions of the Self: 1550-1800. LC 80-7558. 344p. 1981. 20.00 (ISBN 0-691-06448-2); pap. 9.95 ltd. ed. (ISBN 0-691-10107-8). Princeton U Pr.

Weinstein, Bernard L. & Firestine, Robert E. Regional Growth & Decline in the United States: The Rise of the Sunbelt & the Decline of the Northeast. LC 77-25447. (Praeger Special Studies). 1978. 22.50 (ISBN 0-275-23950-0). Praeger.

Weinstein, Brian. Gabon: Nation-Building on the Ogooue. (Illus.). 1967. 17.00x (ISBN 0-262-23023-2). MIT Pr.

Weinstein, David, jt. auth. see Deitch, Lillian.

Weinstein, Deena. Bureaucratic Opposition: Challenging Abuses at the Workplace. (Pergamon Policy Studies). 1979. 17.75 (ISBN 0-08-023903-X); pap. 6.95 (ISBN 0-08-023902-1). Pergamon.

Weinstein, Edwin A. & Friedland, Robert P., eds. Hemi-Inattention & Hemisphere Specialization. LC 77-5278. (Advances in Neurology Ser.: Vol. 18). 1977. 15.50 (ISBN 0-89004-115-6). Raven.

Weinstein, Florence, ed. & intro. by. Crocheting Tablecloths & Placemats. LC 74-21221. (Illus.). 160p. 1975. pap. 4.00 (ISBN 0-486-20659-9). Dover.

Weinstein, Franklin B. U.S.-Japan Relations & the Security of East Asia: The Next Decade. LC 77-13752. (Special Studies on International Relations & U.S. Foreign Policy Ser.). 1978. lib. bdg. 14.00x o.p. (ISBN 0-89158-053-0); pap. text ed. 9.75x (ISBN 0-89158-067-0). Westview.

Weinstein, Fred. The Dynamics of Nazism: Leadership, Ideology & the Holocaust. LC 80-514. (Studies in Social Discontinuity Ser.). 1980. 13.50 (ISBN 0-12-742480-6). Acad Pr.

Weinstein, Fred & Platt, Gerald M. The Wish To Be Free: Society, Psyche, & Value Change. LC 71-83291. 1969. 18.50x (ISBN 0-520-01398-0); pap. 0.85x o.p. (ISBN 0-520-02493-1). U of Cal Pr.

Weinstein, Gerald, et al. Education of the Self: A Trainer's Manual. LC 76-9529. (Mandala Series in Education). 155p. 1976. pap. text ed. 9.95 (ISBN 0-916250-16-4). Irvington.

Weinstein, James. The Corporate Ideal in the Liberal State: 1900-1918. LC 80-22211. xvii, 263p. 1981. Repr. of 1968 ed. lib. bdg. 25.00x (ISBN 0-313-22709-8, WECI). Greenwood.

--Corporate Ideal in the Liberal State: Nineteen Hundred to Nineteen Eighteen. 1969. pap. 5.95x (ISBN 0-8070-5457-7, BP327). Beacon Pr.

Weinstein, Leo. Hippolyte Taine. (World Authors Ser.: France: No. 139). lib. bdg. 10.95 (ISBN 0-8057-2878-3). Twayne.

Weinstein, Malcolm S. Health in the City: Environmental & Behavioral Influences. (Habitat Text Ser.). (Illus.). 1980. 11.00 (ISBN 0-08-023375-9). Pergamon.

Weinstein, Marion. Positive Magic. rev. ed. (Illus.). 320p. 1981. pap. 5.95 (ISBN 0-919345-00-X). Cerridwen & Co.

Weinstein, Matt & Goodman, Joel. Playfair: Everybody's Guide to Noncompetitive Play. LC 80-12591. (Orig.). 1980. pap. 8.95 (ISBN 0-915166-50-X). Impact Pubs Cal.

Weinstein, Milton C. & Fineberg, Harvey V. Clinical Decision Analysis. (Illus.). 400p. 1980. text ed. 215.00 (ISBN 0-7216-9166-8). Saunders.

Weinstein, Paul A., ed. Featherbedding & Technological Change. (Studies in Economics). 1965. pap. text ed. 2.95 o.p. (ISBN 0-669-25924-1). Heath.

Weinstein, Robert A. Grays Harbor: 1885-1913. (Large Format Ser.). (Illus.). 1978. pap. 7.95 o.p. (ISBN 0-14-004890-1). Penguin.

--Grays Harbor: 1885-1913. (Illus.). 1978. 16.95 o.p. (ISBN 0-670-34833-3, Studio). Viking Pr.

Weinstein, S. & Walker, M. Annual Accounting Review: Vol. 1 1979. 265p. 1979. lib. bdg. 35.50 (ISBN 3-7186-0009-9). Harwood Academic.

Weinstein, Stephen, jt. auth. see Prc Energy Analysis Company.

Weinstein, Warren. Historical Dictionary of Burundi. LC 76-13594. (African Historical Dictionaries Ser.: No. 8). 1976. 18.00 (ISBN 0-8108-0962-1). Scarecrow.

Weinstein, Warren & Grotpeter, John J. Pattern of African Decolonialization-a New Interpretation. LC 73-83839. (Foreign & Comoarative Studies-Eastern African Ser.: No. 10). 123p. 1973. pap. 4.50x (ISBN 0-915984-07-5). Syracuse U Foreign Comp.

Weinstein, Warren & Schire, Robert. Political Conflict & Ethnic Strategies: A Case Study of Burundi. LC 76-22649. (Foreign & Comparative Studies-Eastern African Ser.: No. 23). 68p. 1976. pap. text ed. 4.50x (ISBN 0-915984-20-2). Syracuse U Foreign Comp.

Weinstein, Warren, ed. Chinese & Soviet Aid to Africa. LC 74-3512. (Special Studies). (Illus.). 316p. 1975. text ed. 32.50 (ISBN 0-275-09050-7). Praeger.

Weinstein, Warren & Henriksen, Thomas H., eds. Soviet & Chinese Aid to African Nations. LC 79-21128. (Praeger Special Studies). 1980. 20.95 (ISBN 0-03-052756-2). Praeger.

Weinstock, E. B. & Arthur, Robert P. New Gothic Restaurant. 1978. pap. text ed. 9.25 (ISBN 0-8191-0369-1). U Pr of Amer.

Weinstock, H., jt. auth. see Jones, A.

Weinstock, Herbert. Chopin: The Man & His Music. (Music Ser.). (Illus.). xiv, 336p. 1981. Repr. of 1949 ed. lib. bdg. 27.50 (ISBN 0-306-76081-9). Da Capo.

Weinstock, Herbert, ed. see Huneker, James G.

Weinstock, Herbert, tr. see Chavez, Carlos.

Weinstock, Irwin T. & Torgerson, Paul E. Management: An Integrated Approach. LC 71-162354. (Illus.). 1972. text ed. 18.95 (ISBN 0-13-548396-4). P-H.

Weinstock, Robert. Calculus of Variations. pap. text ed. 5.00 (ISBN 0-486-63069-2). Dover.

Weinstock, Ruth. The Graying of the Campus. LC 78-69846. 160p. 1978. 14.00 (ISBN 0-89192-247-4); pap. 8.00 (ISBN 0-89192-290-3). Interbk Inc.

Weinstock, Stephen M. & Wirtschafter, Jonathan D. A Decision-Oriented Manual of Retinoscopy. (Illus.). 116p. 1976. 16.50 (ISBN 0-398-03397-8); pap. 10.75 (ISBN 0-398-03406-0). C C Thomas.

Weinswig, Melvin H. Use & Misuse of Drugs Subject to Abuse. LC 72-83815. 1973. 8.50 (ISBN 0-672-53712-5); pap. 6.10 (ISBN 0-672-63712-X). Pegasus.

Weintraub, Andrew, et al, eds. The Economic Growth Controversy. LC 73-75076. 200p. 1973. 12.00 o.p. (ISBN 0-87332-038-7). M E Sharpe.

Weintraub, Benjamin. What Every Credit Executive Should Know About Chapter Eleven of the Bankruptcy Code. LC 80-82081. 133p. 1980. pap. 9.50 (ISBN 0-934914-32-X). NACM.

Weintraub, Daniel J. & Walker, Edward L. Perception. LC 66-26288. (Basic Concepts in Psychology Ser). (Orig.). 1966. pap. text ed. 5.95 (ISBN 0-8185-0310-6); perceptual demonstration kit, 1972 15.95 (ISBN 0-8185-0049-2). Brooks-Cole.

Weintraub, E. R. Microfoundations. LC 78-16551. (Cambridge Surveys of Economic Literature Ser.). 1979. 26.50 (ISBN 0-521-22305-9); pap. 7.95x (ISBN 0-521-29445-2). Cambridge U Pr.

Weintraub, Hyman G. Andrew Furuseth, Emancipator of the Seamen. (Institute of Industrial Relations, UC Berkeley). 1959. 18.50x (ISBN 0-520-01322-0). U of Cal Pr.

Weintraub, Rodelle, ed. see Shaw, George B.

Weintraub, Russell J. Commentary on the Conflict of Laws. 2nd ed. LC 80-10480. (University Textbook Ser.). 655p. 1980. write for info. (ISBN 0-88277-000-4). Foundation Pr.

Weintraub, Sidney. Capitalism's Inflation & Unemployment Crisis. LC 77-73955. (Economics Ser.). (Illus.). 7.95 (ISBN 0-201-08502-X). A-W.

--Classical Keynesianism: Monetary Theory & the Price Level. LC 72-2573. (Illus.). 190p. 1961. Repr. lib. bdg. 18.75x (ISBN 0-8371-6421-4, WECK). Greenwood.

--Keynes, Keynesians, & Monetarists. LC 77-20307. (Illus.). 1978. pap. 9.95x (ISBN 0-8122-7741-4). U of Pa Pr.

Weintraub, Sidney, jt. auth. see Cline, William R.

Weintraub, Stanley. Biography & Truth. LC 67-28300. (Composition & Rhetoric Ser.). 1967. pap. 2.50 (ISBN 0-672-60901-0, CR15). Bobbs.

--The London Yankees: Portraits of American Writers & Artists in England, 1894-1914. Ellenboger, Eileen, tr. LC 78-22276. 1979. 14.95 (ISBN 0-15-152978-7). HarBraceJ.

Weintraub, Stanley, ed. The Portable Bernard Shaw. (Viking Portable Library Ser: P90). 1977. pap. 5.95 (ISBN 0-14-015090-0). Penguin.

--The Portable Oscar Wilde. rev. ed. 1981. 14.95 (ISBN 0-670-76743-3). Viking Pr.

Weintraub, Stanley, ed. see Hichens, Robert.

Weintraub, Stanley, ed. see Shaw, Bernard.

Weintraub, Stanley, ed. see Shaw, George B.

Weintraub, Walter. Verbal Behavior: Adaption & Psychopathology. LC 80-27021. 224p. 1981. text ed. price not set (ISBN 0-8261-2660-X); pap. text ed. price not set (ISBN 0-8261-2661-8). Springer Pub.

Weintz, Caroline & Weintz, Walter. The Discount Guide for Travelers Over Fifty-Five. 1981. pap. 5.95 (ISBN 0-525-93175-9). Dutton.

Weintz, Walter, jt. auth. see Weintz, Caroline.

Weinzweig, Helen. Basic Black with Pearls. (Anansi Fiction Ser.: No. 41). 136p. (Orig.). 1980. pap. 7.95 (ISBN 0-88784-079-5, Pub. by Hse Anansi Pr Canada). U of Toronto Pr.

--Basic Black with Pearls. LC 80-22304. 135p. 1981. 7.95 (ISBN 0-688-00397-4). Morrow.

--Passing Ceremony. LC 72-95751. (Anansi Fiction Ser.: No. 24). 120p. 1973. pap. 4.95 (ISBN 0-88784-325-5, Pub. by Hse Anansi Pr Canada). U of Toronto Pr.

Weinzweig, Marjorie, jt. auth. see Bishop, Sharon.

Wei-Ping, W. Chinese Acupuncture. 7.50 o.p. (ISBN 0-685-47283-3). Weiser.

Weir. Handbook of Experimental Immunology: Application of Immunological Methods, Vol. 3. 3rd ed. 1978. pap. 45.25 (ISBN 0-632-00186-0, Blackwell Scientific). Mosby.

--Three Day Challenge. (gr. 3-5). pap. 1.25 o.p. (ISBN 0-590-11929-X, Schol Pap). Schol Bk Serv.

Weir, A. J. General Integration & Measure. LC 73-91620. (Illus.). 344p. 1974. 35.50 (ISBN 0-521-20407-0); pap. 13.95 (ISBN 0-521-29715-X). Cambridge U Pr.

--Lebesgue Integration & Measure. LC 72-83584. (Illus.). 220p. (Orig.). 1973. 37.95 (ISBN 0-521-08728-7); pap. 14.95x (ISBN 0-521-09751-7). Cambridge U Pr.

Weir, Albert E., ed. see Bachmann, Alberto.

Weir, Alison, jt. auth. see Raven, Susan.

Weir, D., jt. auth. see Butterworth, E.

Weir, D. M., ed. Handbook of Experimental Immunology: Cellular Immunology, Vol. 2. 3rd ed. 1978. pap. 45.25 (ISBN 0-632-00176-3, Blackwell Scientific). Mosby.

Weir, LaVada. Advanced Skateboarding: A Complete Guide to Skatepark Riding & Other Tips for the Better Skateboarder. (Illus.). (gr. 4 up). 1980. pap. 2.95 (ISBN 0-671-33040-3). Wanderer Bks.

--Advanced Skateboarding: A Complete Guide to Skateboard Riding & Other Tips for the Better Skateboarder. LC 79-16801. (Illus.). 128p. (gr. 10 up). 1980. PLB 7.79 (ISBN 0-671-33011-X). Messner.

--Breaking Point. LC 74-641. (Laurie Newman Adventures Ser). 32p. (gr. 3-9). 1974. 5.95 (ISBN 0-87191-337-2). Creative Ed.

--Chaotic Kitchen. LC 74-858. (Laurie Newman Adventures Ser). 32p. (gr. 3-9). 1974. 5.95 (ISBN 0-87191-334-8). Creative Ed.

--Edge of Fear. LC 74-859. (Laurie Newman Adventures Ser). 32p. (gr. 3-9). 1974. 5.95 (ISBN 0-87191-338-0). Creative Ed.

--Grass Skiing: A Complete Beginner's Book. (Illus.). 128p. (gr. 4-6). 1981. PLB 7.29 (ISBN 0-686-69301-9). Messner.

--The Horse-Flambeau. LC 74-860. (Laurie Newman Adventures Ser). 32p. 1974. 5.95 (ISBN 0-87191-335-6). Creative Ed.

--Laurie Loves a Horse. LC 74-643. (Laurie Newman Adventures Ser). 32p. (gr. 7-9). 1974. 5.95 (ISBN 0-87191-352-6). Creative Ed.

--A Long Distance. LC 74-971. (Laurie Newman Adventures Ser). 32p. (gr. 3-9). 1974. 5.95 (ISBN 0-87191-333-X). Creative Ed.

--Men! LC 74-974. (Laurie Newman Adventures Ser). 32p. (gr. 3-9). 1974. 5.95 (ISBN 0-87191-336-4). Creative Ed.

--The New Girl. LC 74-824. (Laurie Newman Adventures Ser). 32p. (gr. 3-9). 1974. 5.95 (ISBN 0-87191-351-8). Creative Ed.

--The Roller Skating Book. LC 79-19653. (Illus.). 128p. (gr. 4 up). 1979. PLB 8.29 (ISBN 0-671-33048-9). Messner.

Weir, Mary, jt. auth. see Mumford, Enid.

Weir, Maurice D. Calculator Clout: Programming Methods for Your Programmable. (Illus.). 256p. 1981. text ed. 17.95 (ISBN 0-13-110411-X, Spec); pap. text ed. 8.95 (ISBN 0-13-110403-9, Spec). P-H.

Weir, Robert F., ed. Death in Literature. 432p. 1980. 25.00x (ISBN 0-231-04936-6); pap. 10.00x (ISBN 0-231-04937-4). Columbia U Pr.

Weis, Elizabeth, jt. ed. see Byron, Stuart.

Weis, Ina J. The Design of Library Areas & Buildings. (Architecture Ser.: Bibliography: A-413). 80p. 1981. pap. 12.00. Vance Biblios.

Weis, P. Nationality & Statelessness in International Law. rev. ed. 400p. 1979. 62.50x (ISBN 90-286-0329-8). Sijthoff & Noordhoff.

Weisband, Edward, jt. auth. see Franck, Thomas M.

Weisbecker, Joe. Home Computers Can Make You Rich. 1980. pap. 6.50 (ISBN 0-8104-5177-8). Hayden.

Weisberg, D. Kelly. Women & the Law: The Social Historical Perspective. 600p. 1981. text ed. 24.95x (ISBN 0-87073-586-1); pap. text ed. 9.95x (ISBN 0-87073-587-X). Schenkman.

Weisberg, Gabriel P. Traditions & Revisions: Themes from the History of Sculpture. LC 75-26708. (Illus.). 162p. 1975. pap. 10.00x (ISBN 0-910386-23-4, Pub. by Cleveland Mus Art). Ind U Pr.

Weisberg, Gabriel P. & Talbot, William S. Chardin & the Still-Life Tradition in France. LC 79-63386. (Themes in Art Ser.). (Illus.). 128p. (Orig.). 1979. pap. 7.95x (ISBN 0-910386-51-X, Pub. by Cleveland Mus Art). Ind U Pr.

Weisberg, Gabriel P. & Zakon, Ronnie L. Between Past & Present: French, English, & American Etching 1850-1950. LC 76-53113. (Themes in Art Ser.). (Illus.). 78p. pap. 4.95x (ISBN 0-910386-33-1, Pub. by Cleveland Mus Art). Ind U Pr.

Weisberg, Herbert F. & Bowen, Bruce D. An Introduction to Survey Research & Data Analysis. LC 76-39975. (Illus.). 1977. text ed. 18.95x (ISBN 0-7167-0485-4); pap. text ed. 9.95x (ISBN 0-7167-0484-6). W H Freeman.

Weisberg, Herbert F., jt. auth. see Bowen, Bruce D.

Weisberg, Herbert F., jt. ed. see Niemi, Richard G.

Weisberg, Joseph S. Meteorology: The Earth & Its Weather. LC 75-26094. (Illus.). 320p. 1976. text ed. 17.95 (ISBN 0-395-20673-1); inst. manual 1.50 (ISBN 0-395-20674-X); slides 11.25 (ISBN 0-395-24686-5). HM.

--Meteorology: The Earth & Its Weather. 2nd ed. (Illus.). 432p. 1981. text ed. 18.95 (ISBN 0-395-29516-5); instr's manual avail. (ISBN 0-395-29517-3). HM.

Weisberg, S. Applied Linear Regression. LC 80-10378. (Probability & Mathematical Statistics: Applied Probability & Statistics Section). 1980. 24.95 (ISBN 0-471-04419-9, Pub. by Wiley-Interscience). Wiley.

Weisberger, Bernard A. Age of Steel & Steam, Eighteen Seventy-Seven to Eighteen Ninety. LC 63-8572. (Life History of the United States Ser.). (Illus.). (gr. 5 up). 1974. PLB 9.96 (ISBN 0-8094-0556-3, Pub. by Time-Life). Silver.

--The American Newspaperman. LC 61-8647. (Chicago History of American Civilization Ser.). (Illus.). 1961. lib. bdg. 10.00x o.s.i. (ISBN 0-226-89138-0). U of Chicago Pr.

--New Industrial Society. LC 68-8953. 1969. pap. text ed. 8.95x (ISBN 0-471-92723-6). Wiley.

--Reaching for Empire, 1890-1901. LC 63-8572. (Life History of the United States). (Illus.). (gr. 5 up). 1974. lib. bdg. 9.96 (ISBN 0-685-72982-6, Pub. by Time-Life). Silver.

Weisberger, Bernard A. & Nevins, Allan. Captains of Industry. (American Heritage Junior Library). (Illus.). (gr. 5 up). 1966. 9.95 (ISBN 0-8281-0398-4, Dist. by Har-Row); PLB 12.89 (ISBN 0-06-026379-2). Am Heritage.

Weisberger, Bernard A., jt. auth. see Gardner, Joseph L.

Weisberger, Calvin L., jt. auth. see Sprengelmeyer, James.

Weisberger, Eleanor. Your Young Child & You: How to Manage Growing-up Problems in the Years from One to Five. rev. ed. 1979. pap. 4.95 (ISBN 0-87690-329-4). Dutton.

Weisbord, M., et al. Improving Police Department Management Through Problem Solving Task Forces: A Case in Organization Development. 1974. 7.95 (ISBN 0-201-04122-7). A-W.

Weisbord, Marvin R. Organizational Diagnosis: A Workbook of Theory. LC 77-93328. 1978. pap. text ed. 8.95 (ISBN 0-201-08357-4). A-W.

Weisbord, Vera B. Radical Life. LC 76-28276. (Illus.). 352p. 1977. 15.00x (ISBN 0-253-34773-4). Ind U Pr.

Weisbrod, Burton A. The Voluntary Non-Profit Sector: An Economic Analysis. LC 77-9132. 1977. 21.00 (ISBN 0-669-01772-8). Lexington Bks.

Weisbrod, Burton A., et al. Disease & Economic Development: The Impact of Parasitic Diseases in St. Lucia. LC 72-7997. 224p. 1973. 27.50x (ISBN 0-299-06340-2). U of Wis Pr.

--Public Interest Law: An Economic & Institutional Analysis. 1978. 36.50x (ISBN 0-520-03355-8); pap. 9.50 (ISBN 0-520-03568-2). U of Cal Pr.

Weischer, Bernd M. & Wilson, Peter L., trs. from Persian. Heart's Witness: The Sufi Quatrains of Awhaduddin Kirmani. LC 78-72535. 1979. 11.50 (ISBN 0-87773-719-3). Great Eastern.

Weise, Frieda O., ed. Health Statistics: A Guide to Information Sources. LC 80-12039. (Health Affairs Information Guide Ser.: Vol. 4). 1980. 30.00 (ISBN 0-8103-1412-6). Gale.

Weisenburger, Francis P. Life of John McLean. LC 76-150296. (American Constitutional & Legal History Ser.). 1971. Repr. of 1937 ed. lib. bdg. 29.50 (ISBN 0-306-70106-5). Da Capo.

Weisenfeld, Murray. Runner's Repair Manual. 192p. 1981. pap. 4.95 (ISBN 0-312-69597-7). St Martin.

Weiser, Bruce. Dispatch from Cadiz. (Chenevix Ser.: No. 2). 1981. pap. 2.25 (ISBN 0-8439-0826-2, Leisure Bks). Nordon Pubns.

Weiser, David K. The Prose Style of John Jewel. (Salzburg Studies in English Literature, Elizabethan & Renaissance Studies: No. 9). 194p. 1973. pap. text ed. 25.00x (ISBN 0-391-01562-1). Humanities.

Weiser, Francis X. Handbook of Christian Feasts & Customs. LC 58-10908. 1958. 9.50 o.p. (ISBN 0-15-138435-5). HarBraceJ.

Weiser, H. H., et al. Practical Food Microbiology & Technology. 2nd ed. 1971. 19.50 o.p. (ISBN 0-87055-064-0). AVI.

Weiser, Irwin H., jt. auth. see Zulauf, Sander W.

Weiser, Marjorie P. & Arbeiter, Jean S. Womanlist. LC 80-65983. (Illus.). 512p. 1981. 19.95 (ISBN 0-689-11083-9); pap. 10.95 (ISBN 0-689-11113-4). Atheneum.

Weiser, Marjorie P., ed. Ethnic America. (Reference Shelf Ser.: Vol. 50, No. 2). 1978. 6.25 (ISBN 0-8242-0623-1). Wilson.

Weiser, Nora, ed. Open to the Sun: An Anthology of Latin American Poets. 1980. 8.50 o.p. (ISBN 0-912288-16-7). Caroline Hse.

Weiser, Reuben. Regina, the German Captive, or, True Piety Among the Lowly. LC 75-7093. (Indian Captivities Ser.: Vol. 69). 1977. Repr. of 1856 ed. lib. bdg. 44.00 (ISBN 0-8240-1693-9). Garland Pub.

Weiser, Thomas, tr. see Barth, Karl.

Weisfeldt, Myron L., ed. The Aging Heart: Its Function & Response to Stress. (Aging Ser.: Vol. 12). 324p. 1980. 32.00 (ISBN 0-89004-307-8, 382). Raven.

Weisgard, Leonard, jt. auth. see Joslin, Sesyle.

Weisgerber, Bill, jt. auth. see Baker, Dan.

Weisgerber, Jean. Faulkner & Dostoevsky: Influence & Confluence. McWilliams, Dean, tr. from Fr. LC 72-85537. xxii, 383p. 1974. 16.00 (ISBN 0-8214-0149-1). Ohio U Pr.

Weisgerber, Robert A. A Special Educator's Guide to Vocational Training. (Illus.). 224p. 1980. text ed. 16.50 (ISBN 0-398-03938-0). C C Thomas.

Weisgerber, Robert A., et al. Training the Handicapped for Productive Employment. 450p. 1980. text ed. 29.50 (ISBN 0-89443-331-8). Aspen Systems.

Weishahn, Mel, jt. auth. see Gearheart, Bill R.

Weishahn, Mel W., jt. auth. see Gearheart, Bill R.

Weisheipl, James A. Development of Physical Theory in the Middle Ages. 1971. 5.95 o.p. (ISBN 0-472-09181-6). U of Mich Pr.

Weisheipl, James A., ed. see Aquinas, Thomas.

Weisheipl, James A., O.P. Friar Thomas B Aquino: His Life, Thought & Works. LC 73-80801. 480p. 1974. 10.00 o.p. (ISBN 0-385-01299-3). Doubleday.

Weisheit, E. Sixty-One Worship Talks for Children. rev. ed. LC 68-20728. (gr. 3-6). 1975. pap. 3.95 (ISBN 0-570-03714-X, 12-2616). Concordia.

Weisheit, Eldon. A Sermon Is More Than Words. (Preacher's Workshop Ser.). 48p. 1977. pap. 2.25 (ISBN 0-570-07407-X, 12-2679). Concordia.

--Sixty One Gospel Talks for Children: With Suggested Objects for Illustration. LC 70-96217. 1969. pap. 3.95 (ISBN 0-570-03713-1, 12-2615). Concordia.

Weiskel, Timothy C. French Colonial Rule & the Baule Peoples: Resistance & Collaboration, 1889-1911. (Oxford Studies in African Affairs Ser.). (Illus.). 352p. 1981. 42.50x (ISBN 0-19-822715-9). Oxford U Pr.

Weiskopf, Don, jt. auth. see Allen, George.

Weiskopf, Don, jt. auth. see Alston, Walter.

Weiskopf, Donald C. A Guide to Recreation & Leisure. 362p. 1975. text ed. 19.95x (ISBN 0-205-04589-8, 6245897). Allyn.

Weiskopf, Donald C., jt. auth. see Bush, Jim.

Weiskopf, Herm & Pezzano, Chuck. Sports Illustrated: Bowling. LC 80-7887. (Illus.). 160p. 1981. pap. 5.95 (ISBN 0-690-02006-6, CN 866, CN). Har-Row.

Weiskopf, Herman. The Perfect Game. LC 77-19111. (Illus.). 1978. text ed. 15.95 o.p. (ISBN 0-13-657015-1). P-H.

Weiskopf, Tom. Go for the Flag. 1969. pap. 3.50 (ISBN 0-8015-3018-0, Hawthorn). Dutton.

Weisler, Jules. Physical Science: Intermediate Level. (gr. 7-10). 1971. wkbk. 7.17 (ISBN 0-87720-009-2). AMSCO Sch.

--Review Text in Physical Science: Intermediate Level. (gr. 7-10). 1970. pap. text ed. 6.17 (ISBN 0-87720-007-6). AMSCO Sch.

Weisman, Avery D. On Dying & Denying: A Psychiatric Study of Terminality. LC 79-174268. 208p. 1972. text ed. 22.95 (ISBN 0-87705-068-6). Human Sci Pr.

Weisman, Herman. Technical Report Writing. 2nd ed. (Speech Ser). 192p. 1975. pap. text ed. 9.95 (ISBN 0-675-08791-0). Merrill.

Weisman, Herman M. Information Systems, Services & Centers. LC 72-1156. (Information Sciences Ser.). 265p. 1972. 22.95 (ISBN 0-471-92645-0, Pub. by Wiley-Interscience). Wiley.

Weisman, John. Dark Room. 1981. pap. 2.50 (E9724, Sig). NAL.

--Evidence. Date not set. pap. 2.25 (ISBN 0-686-69452-X, E9724, Sig). NAL. Postponed.

Weisman, M. H. Rheumatic Disease. 1981. text ed. price not set (ISBN 0-443-08100-X). Churchill.

Weisman, Michael. Rheumetic Disease. (Illus.). 288p. 1981. lib. bdg. 25.00 (ISBN 0-443-08100-X). Churchill.

Weismandel, Michael B. Ten Questions to the Zionists or, Zionist Complicity in Nazi War Atrocities. 1980. lib. bdg. 59.95 (ISBN 0-686-68886-4). Revisionist Pr.

Weismann, Donald L. Jelly Was the Word. (Illus.). 8.50 o.p. (ISBN 0-8363-0124-2). Jenkins.

Weisner, Stan, jt. auth. see Terrell, Paul.

Weiss. Home Maintenance. (gr. 9-12). 1978. text ed. 10.60 (ISBN 0-87002-199-0); student guide 2.60 (ISBN 0-87002-239-3); tchr's guide avail. Bennett IL.

Weiss & Klass. Case Studies in Regulation: Revolution & Reform. 1981. pap. text ed. 9.95 (ISBN 0-316-92893-3). Little.

Weiss & Mann. Human Biology & Behavior. 3rd ed. 1981. text ed. 16.95 (ISBN 0-316-92891-7); training manual free (ISBN 0-316-92892-5). Little.

Weiss, Al. Ninja: Clan of Death. (Orig.). 1981. pap. 2.50 (ISBN 0-671-43046-7). PB.

Weiss, Ann E. The Nuclear Question. LC 80-8806. (Illus.). 192p. (gr. 7 up). 1981. 10.95 (ISBN 0-15-257596-0, HJ). HarBraceJ.

--Polls & Surveys: A Look at Public Opinion Research. (Impact Bks.). (Illus.). (gr. 7 up). 1979. PLB 6.90 s&l (ISBN 0-531-02859-3). Watts.

Weiss, Beno & Perez, Louis C. Juan De la Cueva's los Inventores De las Cosas: A Critical Edition & Study. LC 80-83466. 220p. 1980. text ed. 17.50x (ISBN 0-271-00279-4). Pa St U Pr.

Weiss, Bernard. Digital Computers in the Behavioral Laboratory. (Century Psychology Ser.). (Illus.). 1979. Repr. of 1973 ed. text ed. 22.50x o.p. (ISBN 0-8290-0058-5). Irvington.

Weiss, Bernard, jt. ed. see Merigan, William.

Weiss, Carol H. Evaluating Action Programs: Readings in Social Action & Education. 1972. pap. text ed. 14.95x (ISBN 0-205-03247-8, 813247X). Allyn.

--Evaluation Research: Methods of Assessing Program Effectiveness. (Methods of Social Science Ser). (Illus.). 176p. 1972. pap. text ed. 10.95 (ISBN 0-13-292193-6). P-H.

--Using Social Research for Public Policy-Making. LC 75-42954. (Policy Studies Organization Ser.). 1977. 22.95 (ISBN 0-669-00498-7). Lexington Bks.

Weiss, Carol H. & Barton, Allen H., eds. Making Bureaucracies Work. LC 80-12774. (Sage Focus Editions: Vol. 22). (Illus.). 309p. 1980. 18.95x (ISBN 0-8039-1413-X); pap. 9.95x (ISBN 0-8039-1414-8). Sage.

Weiss, Caroline, et al. Creative Cooking Sugar Free. (Illus.). 1979. pap. 2.50 (ISBN 0-686-65551-6). Budlong.

--Gourmet Cookbook for Those Interested in Weight Control. (Illus.). 1979. pap. 2.50 (ISBN 0-686-65552-4). Budlong.

Weiss, Charles, Jr., jt. ed. see Ramesh, Jairam.

Weiss, Clara. Astrological Keys to Self Realization & Self Actualization. 1980. pap. 4.95 (ISBN 0-87728-509-8). Weiser.

Weiss, Curtis E. & Lillywhite, Gordon. Clinical Management of Articulation Disorders. LC 80-17348. (Illus.). 303p. 1980. pap. text ed. 11.95 (ISBN 0-8016-5391-6). Mosby.

Weiss, Curtis E. & Lillywhite, Harold S. Communicative Disorders: Prevention & Early Intervention. 2nd ed. (Illus.). 398p. 1981. pap. text ed. 12.50 (ISBN 0-8016-5389-4). Mosby.

Weiss, D., jt. auth. see Kuhn, G.

Weiss, David. Physician Extraordinary. 512p. 1975. 8.95 o.s.i. (ISBN 0-440-05916-X). Delacorte.

--The Venetian. LC 76-18940. 1976. 9.95 o.p. (ISBN 0-688-03098-X). Morrow.

Weiss, David W., jt. ed. see Zuckerman, Avivah.

Weiss, E. see Arber, W., et al.

Weiss, Edda. Deutsch: Erleben Wir Es! 2nd ed. Saslow, Joan, ed. LC 80-16484. (Illus.). 344p. (Ger.). (gr. 10). 1980. text ed. 14.64 (ISBN 0-07-069215-7, W); tchrs. ed. 15.96 (ISBN 0-07-069216-5); wkbk. 4.26 (ISBN 0-07-069217-3); tests 69.00 (ISBN 0-07-069218-1); tapes 404.00 (ISBN 0-07-097815-8); cassettes 381.80 (ISBN 0-07-097816-6); filmstrips 113.36 (ISBN 0-07-097817-4). McGraw.

Weiss, Edith, jt. auth. see Weiss, Hal.

Weiss, Edward C., ed. The Many Faces of Information Science. LC 77-12103. (AAAS Selected Symposium Ser.: No. 3). (Illus.). 1978. lib. bdg. 16.00x (ISBN 0-89158-430-7). Westview.

Weiss, Edwin. Algebraic Number Theory. 2nd ed. LC 76-5803. xii, 275p. 1976. 11.95 (ISBN 0-8284-0293-0). Chelsea Pub.

--First Course in Algebra & Number Theory. 1971. text ed. 21.95 (ISBN 0-12-743150-0). Acad Pr.

Weiss, Elizabeth & Wolfson, Rita. Cholesterol Counter. (Health Ser.). (Orig.). 1973. pap. 1.50 (ISBN 0-515-05689-8, P3208). Jove Pubns.

Weiss, Elizabeth & Wolfson, Rita P. The Gourmet's Low-Cholesterol Cookbook. 1974. pap. 2.25 o.p. (ISBN 0-515-05690-1, V3458). Jove Pubns.

Weiss, Elizabeth S. & Wolfson, Rita P. Protein Planner. 1974. pap. 1.00 o.s.i. (ISBN 0-515-03301-4, P3301). Jove Pubns.

Weiss, Ellen. Millicent Maybe. LC 78-13144. (Easy-Read Story Bks.). (Illus.). (gr. k-3). 1979. 3.95 (ISBN 0-531-02382-6); PLB 6.45 s&l (ISBN 0-531-02299-4). Watts.

--Millicent Maybe. 1980. pap. 1.50 (ISBN 0-380-49197-4, 49197, Camelot). Avon.

--Things to Make & Do for Christmas. (Things to Make & Do Bks.). (gr. k-3). 1980. PLB 7.90 (ISBN 0-531-02293-5, C02); pap. 3.95 (ISBN 0-531-02145-9). Watts.

Weiss, Fredric. The Antic Spectre: Satire in Early Gothic Novels. Varma, Devendra P., ed. LC 79-8489. (Gothic Studies & Dissertations Ser.). 1980. lib. bdg. 25.00x (ISBN 0-405-12664-6). Arno.

Weiss, G., ed. Hazardous Chemicals Data Book. LC 80-21634. (Environmental Health Review: No. 4). 1188p. 1981. 64.00 (ISBN 0-8155-0831-X). Noyes.

Weiss, G. Christian. Perfect Will of God. 1950. pap. 1.50 (ISBN 0-8024-6468-8). Moody.

Weiss, Guido & Wainger, Steve, eds. Harmonic Analysis in Euclidean Spaces, 2 pts. LC 79-12726. (Proceedings of Symposia in Pure Mathematics: Vol. 35). 1979. Set. 44.40 (ISBN 0-8218-1436-2); Pt. 1. 26.00 (ISBN 0-686-67540-1, PSPUM 35, 1); Pt. 2. pap. 24.00 (ISBN 0-8218-1438-9, PSPUM 35, 2). Am Math.

Weiss, H. Structure & Application of Galvanomagnetic Devices. 1969. 60.00 (ISBN 0-08-012597-2). Pergamon.

Weiss, Hal & Weiss, Edith. Catering Handbook. (Illus.). 1971. 16.95 (ISBN 0-8104-9452-3). Hayden.

Weiss, Harold & McGrath, J. B. Technically Speaking: Oral Communication for Engineers, Scientists & Technical Personnel. 1963. 16.75x (ISBN 0-07-069085-5, C). McGraw.

Weiss, Harry B. A Book About Chapbooks: The People's Literature of Bygone Times. LC 69-20399. (Illus.). x, 149p. Repr. of 1969 ed. 18.00 (ISBN 0-8103-5028-9). Gale.

Weiss, Harvey. Ceramics, from Clay to Kiln. LC 64-13583. (Beginning Artist's Library Ser.). (gr. 5-9). 1964. PLB 7.95 o.p. (ISBN 0-201-09153-4, A-W Childrens). A-W.

--How to Be an Inventor. LC 79-7823. (Illus.). 96p. (gr. 5 up). 1980. 8.95 (ISBN 0-690-04052-0, TYC-J); PLB 8.79 (ISBN 0-690-04053-9). T Y Crowell.

--How to Make Your Own Books. LC 73-17267. (Illus.). (gr. 5-12). 1974. 9.95 (ISBN 0-690-00400-1, TYC-J). T Y Crowell.

--How to Run a Railroad: Everything You Need to Know About Model Trains. LC 76-18128. (Illus.). (gr. 5 up). 1977. 9.95 (ISBN 0-690-01304-3, TYC-J). T Y Crowell.

--Model Airplanes & How to Build Them. LC 74-19451. (Illus.). 80p. (gr. 5 up). 1975. 9.95 (ISBN 0-690-00594-6, TYC-J). T Y Crowell.

--Model Cars & Trucks & How to Build Them. LC 44-7403. (Illus.). 80p. (gr. 5 up). 1974. 10.95 (ISBN 0-690-00414-1, TYC-J). T Y Crowell.

--Motors & Engines & How They Work. LC 69-11828. (Illus.). (gr. 5-9). 1969. 10.95 (ISBN 0-690-56478-3, TYC-J). T Y Crowell.

--Pencil, Pen, & Brush. (Illus.). (gr. 4-6). 1974. pap. 1.50 (ISBN 0-590-02229-6, Schol Pap). Schol Bk Serv.

--Ship Models & How to Build Them. LC 72-7562. (Illus.). (gr. 5-9). 1973. 10.95 (ISBN 0-690-73270-8, TYC-J). T Y Crowell.

Weiss, Herman. The Sound of Dreams. 288p. (Orig.). 1981. pap. 2.50 (ISBN 0-380-76976-X, 76976). Avon.

Weiss, Hugh. Week in Daniel's World: France. LC 69-18809. (Face to Face Books Ser). (Illus.). (gr. k-3). 1969. 4.95g (ISBN 0-685-16355-5, CCPr); text ed. 1.36 o.p. (ISBN 0-02-792610-9, CCPr). Macmillan.

Weiss, Ila. Sanford Robinson Gifford (1823-1880) LC 76-23655. (Outstanding Dissertations in the Fine Arts - American). (Illus.). 1977. Repr. of 1968 ed. lib. bdg. 80.00 (ISBN 0-8240-2737-X). Garland Pub.

Weiss, Iris R. & Place, Carol, eds. Women Scientists Roster. 143p. (Orig.). 1979. pap. 3.50 (ISBN 0-87355-015-3). Natl Sci Tchrs.

Weiss, Irving, ed. see De Chazal, Malcolm.

Weiss, James. Monarch Notes on Conrad's Heart of Darkness & the Secret Sharer. (Orig.). pap. 1.95 (ISBN 0-671-00817-X). Monarch Pr.

Weiss, Jeffery. Great Kitchens. 96p. 1981. pap. 9.95 (ISBN 0-312-34605-0). St Martin.

Weiss, Jeffrey. Cornerstone Collector's Guide to Wicker. 128p. 1981. 7.95 (ISBN 0-346-12535-9). Cornerstone.

--Cornerstone's Collector's Guide to Glass. 128p. 1981. 7.95 (ISBN 0-346-12534-0). Cornerstone.

--Great Bathrooms. 96p. 1981. pap. 9.95 (ISBN 0-312-34486-4). St Martin.

--Kitchen Antiques. LC 80-7831. (Illus.). 128p. (Orig.). 1980. pap. 8.95 (ISBN 0-06-090813-0, CN 813, CN). Har-Row.

--Pine. LC 80-7832. (Illus.). 128p. (Orig.). 1980. pap. 8.95 (ISBN 0-06-090814-9, CN 814, CN). Har-Row.

Weiss, Jeffrey & Gault, Lila. Small Houses. 1980. pap. 7.95 (ISBN 0-446-97346-7). Warner Bks.

Weiss, Jeffrey, jt. auth. see Wise, Herbert H.

Weiss, Joan T. The Lemonade Lady. LC 80-50703. (Illus.). 123p. (Orig.). (gr. 1-3). 1980. pap. 4.95 (ISBN 0-936822-00-7). Peppertree.

Weiss, Johannes. Jesus' Proclamation of the Kingdom of God. Keck, Leander E., ed. Hiers, Richard H. & Holland, David L., trs. from Ger. LC 79-135267. (Lives of Jesus Ser). 160p. (Orig.). 1971. pap. 3.95 (ISBN 0-8006-0153-X, 1-153). Fortress.

Weiss, John. Life & Correspondence of Theodore Parker, 2 Vols. LC 76-106987. (American Public Figures Ser). 1864. Set. lib. bdg. 85.00 (ISBN 0-306-71874-X). Da Capo.

--The Whitetail Deer Hunter's Handbook. (Illus.). 1979. 12.95 (ISBN 0-87691-279-X). Winchester Pr.

Weiss, John D. Training a Dog to Live in Your Home. LC 80-67749. (Housebreaking Chewing Ser.: Bk. One). (Illus.). 84p. (Orig., Prog. Bk.). 1980. pap. 6.95 (ISBN 0-686-64627-4). Animal Owners.

Weiss, John M., jt. auth. see Mills, Richard G.

Weiss, Jonathan, jt. auth. see Weiss, Paul.

Weiss, Karl, ed. The Prison Experience: An Anthology. LC 75-32920. 352p. (gr. 6 up). 1976. 9.95 o.p. (ISBN 0-440-06017-6). Delacorte.

--Under the Mask: An Anthology About Prejudice in America. LC 71-176035. (gr. 7 up). 1972. 7.95 o.s.i. (ISBN 0-440-09171-3). Delacorte.

Weiss, Ken. The Movie Collector's Catalog. (Illus.). 160p. (Orig.). 1977. pap. 5.95 (ISBN 0-938350-50-1). Cummington Pub.

Weiss, Kenneth L. & Kurland, David J. Drug Laws & the Rights That Protect You. (Orig.). 1980. pap. (ISBN 0-671-41362-7, Fireside). S&S.

Weiss, L. E., et al. Structural Features of the Laksevag Gneiss. (Geological Survey of Norway Ser: No. 334, Bulletin 43). 1978. pap. 12.00x (ISBN 82-00-31368-9, Dist. by Columbia U Pr). Universitet.

Weiss, Leatie. Funny Feet. (Easy-Read Story Books Ser.). (Illus.). (gr. k-3). 1978. PLB 6.45 s&l (ISBN 0-531-01348-0). Watts.

--Heather's Feathers. LC 76-12624. (Easy-Read Storybooks). (Illus.). 32p. (gr. k-3). 1976. 3.95 o.p. (ISBN 0-531-02475-X); PLB 4.90 o.p. (ISBN 0-531-01204-2). Watts.

Weiss, Lee D., jt. auth. see Uslander, Arlene.

Weiss, Leon. Cells & Tissues of the Immune System: Structure, Functions, Interactions. (Foundations of Immunology Ser). (Illus.). 1972. ref. ed. 22.95x (ISBN 0-13-121772-0). P-H.

Weiss, Leonard. Economics & Society. 2nd ed. 576p. 1981. text ed. 18.95 (ISBN 0-471-03160-7). Wiley.

--Trade Liberalization & the National Interest, Vol. II. LC 80-80932. (Significant Issues Ser.: No. 2). 60p. 1980. 5.95 (ISBN 0-89206-016-6). CSI Studies.

Weiss, Leonard, et al. Lymphatic System Metastasis. (Medical Publications Ser.). 1980. lib. bdg. 55.00 (ISBN 0-8161-2142-7). G K Hall.

Weiss, Leonard W. Case Studies in American Industry. 3rd ed. LC 78-31149. (Introduction to Economics Ser.). 1980. pap. text ed. 10.50 (ISBN 0-471-03159-3). Wiley.

--Economics & Society. LC 74-18054. 576p. 1975. 18.95 (ISBN 0-471-92704-X, Pub. by Wiley-Hamilton). Wiley.

Weiss, M., ed. see Makhlis, F. A.

Weiss, Malcolm E. Blindness. (gr. 4 up). 1980. PLB 6.45 (ISBN 0-531-02939-5). Watts.

--Solomon Grundy, Born on Oneday: A Finite Arithmetic Puzzle. LC 76-26560. (Young Math Ser.). (Illus.). (gr. k-3). 1977. PLB 7.89 (ISBN 0-690-01275-6, TYC-J). T Y Crowell.

--Storms: From the Inside Out. LC 73-5396. (Illus.). 96p. (gr. 4-6). 1973. PLB 5.79 o.p. (ISBN 0-671-32612-0). Messner.

Weiss, Mark, jt. auth. see Schumann, G. Berry.

Weiss, Martin D. The Great Money Panic: A Guide for Survival & Action. (Illus.). 256p. 1981. 15.95 (ISBN 0-87000-502-2). Arlington Hse.

Weiss, N. A. & Yoseloff, M. L. Finite Mathematics. LC 74-20001. (Illus.). ix, 628p. 1975. text ed. 17.95x (ISBN 0-87901-039-8). Worth.

Weiss, Nathan, et al, eds. Practical Points in Allergy. 2nd. ed. 1979. pap. 14.75 (ISBN 0-87488-731-3). Med Exam.

Weiss, Neil & Hassett, Matthew. Introductory Statistics. LC 80-23520. (Statistics Ser.). (Illus.). 672p. 1981. text ed. 17.95 (ISBN 0-201-09507-6). A-W.

Weiss, Nicki. Menj! LC 80-15955. (Read-Alone Bk.). (Illus.). 48p. (gr. 1-3). 1981. 5.95 (ISBN 0-688-80306-7); PLB 5.71 (ISBN 0-688-84306-9). Greenwillow.

Weiss, Paul. Beyond All Appearances. LC 74-5484. 413p. 1974. 18.95x (ISBN 0-8093-0617-4). S Ill U Pr.

--God We Seek. LC 64-13476. 267p. 1964. 10.95x (ISBN 0-8093-0133-4). S Ill U Pr.

--God We Seek. LC 72-11838. (Arcturus Books Paperbacks). 1973. pap. 7.95 (ISBN 0-8093-0628-X). S Ill U Pr.

--Making of Men. LC 67-10046. 167p. 1967. 10.95x (ISBN 0-8093-0264-0). S Ill U Pr.

--Making of Men. LC 67-10046. (Arcturus Books Paperbacks). 167p. 1969. pap. 7.95 (ISBN 0-8093-0405-8). S Ill U Pr.

--Man's Freedom. LC 67-23318. (Arcturus Books Paperbacks). 335p. 1967. pap. 8.95 (ISBN 0-8093-0277-2). S Ill U Pr.

--Modes of Being. LC 57-11877. 626p. 1958. lib. bdg. 19.95x (ISBN 0-8093-0012-5); deluxe ed. 25.00x 2 vols. boxed (ISBN 0-8093-0013-3). S Ill U Pr.

--Modes of Being. LC 57-11877. (Arcturus Books Paperbacks). 626p. 1968. pap. 11.95x (ISBN 0-8093-0294-2). S Ill U Pr.

--Our Public Life. LC 59-9852. 256p. 1966. 10.95x (ISBN 0-8093-0219-5). S Ill U Pr.

--Our Public Life. LC 59-9852. (Arcturus Books Paperbacks). 256p. 1966. pap. 7.95 (ISBN 0-8093-0220-9). S Ill U Pr.

--Philosophy in Process. Incl. Vol. 1. June 24, 1955 - December 25, 1960. 800p. 1966 (ISBN 0-8093-0190-3); Vol. 2. December 26, 1960-March 6, 1964. 736p. 1966. o.p. (ISBN 0-8093-0231-4); Vol. 3. March-November 1964. 700p. 1968 (ISBN 0-8093-0329-9); Vol. 4. November 26, 1964-September 2, 1965. 634p. 1969 (ISBN 0-8093-0401-5); Vol. 5. September 3, 1965-August 27, 1968. 832p. 1971 (ISBN 0-8093-0465-1); Vol. 6. August 28, 1968-May 22, 1971. 761p. 1975 (ISBN 0-8093-0678-6); Vol. 7. April 13, 1975 - June 21, 1976. 643p. 1978 (ISBN 0-8093-0821-5). LC 63-14293. 25.00x ea. S Ill U Pr.

--Reality. LC 67-11699. 318p. 1967. lib. bdg. 11.95x (ISBN 0-8093-0243-8). S Ill U Pr.

--Reality. LC 67-11699. (Arcturus Books Paperbacks). 318p. 1967. pap. 8.95 (ISBN 0-8093-0244-6). S Ill U Pr.

--Sport: A Philosophic Inquiry. LC 69-15326. 286p. 1969. 10.95x (ISBN 0-8093-0358-2). S Ill U Pr.

--Sport: A Philosophic Inquiry. LC 69-15326. (Arcturus Books Paperbacks). 286p. 1971. pap. 7.95 (ISBN 0-8093-0501-1). S Ill U Pr.

--World of Art. LC 61-5168. (Arcturus Books Paperbacks). 204p. 1964. pap. 5.95 (ISBN 0-8093-0112-1). S Ill U Pr.

--You, I, & the Others. LC 79-13375. 432p. 1980. 25.95 (ISBN 0-8093-0923-8). S Ill U Pr.

Weiss, Paul & Weiss, Jonathan. Right & Wrong: A Philosophical Dialogue Between Father & Son. LC 73-12702. (Arcturus Books Paperbacks). 222p. 1974. pap. 5.95 (ISBN 0-8093-0658-1). S Ill U Pr.

Weiss, Richard, jt. auth. see Spector, Leo.

Weiss, Richard, jt. ed. see Nash, Gary B.

Weiss, Richard M. Dealing with Alcoholism in the Workplace, Report No. 784. (Illus.). vii, 59p. (Orig.). 1980. pap. 15.00 (ISBN 0-8237-0220-0). Conference Bd.

Weiss, Rita. Crocheting Afgans. (Illus.). 1979. pap. 1.50 (ISBN 0-486-23883-0). Dover.

--Crocheting Edgings. (Illus.). 48p. 1980. pap. 1.75 (ISBN 0-486-24031-2). Dover.

--Design & Chart Your Own Needlepoint. (Dover Needlework Ser.). (Illus.). 48p. (Orig.). 1976. pap. 2.95 (ISBN 0-486-23301-4). Dover.

--Early American Iron-on Transfer Patterns for Crewel & Embroidery. (Needlework Ser.). pap. 1.75 (ISBN 0-486-23162-3). Dover.

--Floral Doilies for Crocheting. (Illus.). 1979. pap. 1.75 (ISBN 0-486-23789-3). Dover.

--Tatting Doilies & Edgings. (Illus.). 50p. (Orig.). 1980. pap. 2.00 (ISBN 0-486-24051-7). Dover.

Weiss, Rita, ed. Crocheting Doilies. LC 76-24565. (Illus.). 48p. 1976. pap. 1.75 (ISBN 0-486-23424-X). Dover.

--Floral Iron-on Transfer Patterns. LC 75-21351. (Needlework Ser.). 48p. (Orig.). 1976. pap. 1.75 (ISBN 0-486-23248-4). Dover.

Weiss, Roberto. Renaissance Discovery of Classical Antiquity. 1969. text ed. 18.25x (ISBN 0-631-11690-7). Humanities.

Weiss, Ruth. Light & Other Poems. LC 76-23153. (Illus.). 1976. 10.00 o.p. (ISBN 0-914024-23-X); pap. 3.00 (ISBN 0-914024-25-6). SF Arts & Letters.

Weiss, Seymour N. How to Raise & Train a Border Terrier. (Illus., Orig.). pap. 1.79 o.p. (ISBN 0-87666-249-1, DS1060). TFH Pubns.

--How to Raise & Train a Lakeland Terrier. (Orig.). 1966. pap. 2.00 (ISBN 0-87666-333-1, DS1096). TFH Pubns.

--How to Raise & Train a Skye Terrier. (Orig.). pap. 1.79 o.p. (ISBN 0-87666-395-1, DS1119). TFH Pubns.

Weiss, Sidney J., jt. auth. see Van Scott, Timothy.

Weiss, Stanley, jt. auth. see Singer, Stuart R.

Weiss, Stephen M., et al, eds. Perspectives on Behavioral Medicine 1980, Vol. I. (Serial Publication). 1981. price not set (ISBN 0-12-532101-5). Acad Pr.

Weiss, Theodore. Fireweeds: Poems. 1976. 9.95 o.s.i. (ISBN 0-02-625750-5). Macmillan.

--Fireweeds: Poems. 1976. pap. 5.95 o.s.i. (ISBN 0-02-071000-3, Collier). Macmillan.

--World Before Us: Poems 1950-1970. LC 71-119143. 1970. 9.95 (ISBN 0-02-625720-3). Macmillan.

Weiss, Theodore J. Food Oils & Their Uses. (Illus.). 1970. lib. bdg. 27.50 (ISBN 0-87055-093-4). AVI.

Weiss, Thomas, jt. auth. see Bateman, Fred.

Weiss, Thomas G. International Bureaucracy: An Analysis of the Operation of Functional Global International Secretariats. LC 75-2. 160p. 1975. 19.95x (ISBN 0-669-99341-7). Lexington Bks.

Weiss, Thomas G. & Jordan, Robert S. The World Food Conference & Global Problem Solving. LC 75-19830. (Special Studies). 1976. text ed. 19.50 o.p. (ISBN 0-275-55840-1). Praeger.

Weiss, Ulrich & Edwards, John. Biosynthesis of Aromatic Compounds. LC 78-1496. 1980. 35.00 (ISBN 0-471-92690-6, Pub by Wiley-Interscience). Wiley.

Weiss, Volker, jt. ed. see Burke, John J.

Weiss, William. Home Maintenance: A Guide to Taking Better Care of Your House. (Illus.). 1978. 12.95 o.p. (ISBN 0-684-15594-X, ScribT). Scribner.

Weissberg, Robert. Public Opinion & Popular Government. (Illus.). 320p. 1976. pap. 10.95 (ISBN 0-13-737908-0). P-H.

Weissberger, A. Technique of Organic Chemistry. Incl. Vol. 2. Catalytic, Photochemical & Electrolytic Reactions. 2nd ed. 1956. 42.00 (ISBN 0-470-92862-X); Vol. 3, Pt. 2. Laboratory Engineering. 1957. 36.95 (ISBN 0-470-92928-6). (All other vols. in set o.p., Pub. by Wiley-Interscience). Wiley.

Weissberger, A. & Perry, E. S. Techniques of Chemistry: Vol. 13 Laboratory Engineering & Manipulations. 3rd ed. 531p. 1979. 47.50 (ISBN 0-471-03275-1). Wiley.

Weissberger, A. see Perry, Edward S.

Weissberger, A., ed. Techniques of Chemistry. Incl. Vol. 1. Physical Methods of Chemistry, 5 pts. Rossiter, B. 1971-72; Pt. 1A. Components of Scientific Instruments. 40.50 (ISBN 0-471-92724-4); Pt. 2A. Electrochemical Methods. 68.00 (ISBN 0-471-92727-9); Pt. 3A. o.p. (ISBN 0-471-92729-5); Pt. 1B. Automatic Recording & Control, Computers in Chemical Research. 36.50 (ISBN 0-471-92725-2); Pt. 2B. o.p. (ISBN 0-471-92728-7); Pt. 3B. Spectroscopy & Spectometry in Infrared, Visible & Ultraviolet. 62.50 (ISBN 0-471-92731-7); Pt. 3C. Polarimetry. 47.95 (ISBN 0-471-92732-5); Pt. 3D. X-Ray, Nuclear, Molecular Beam & Radioactivity Methods. 62.95 (ISBN 0-471-92733-3); Pt. 4. Determination of Mass, Transport & Electrical-Magnetic Properties. 54.50; Pt. 5. o.p. (ISBN 0-471-92734-1); Pt. 6. Supplement & Cumulative Index. LC 75-29544. 256p. 1976. 31.50 (ISBN 0-471-92899-2); Vol. 2. Organic Solvents: Physical Properties & Methods of Purification. 3rd ed. Riddick, John A. & Bunger, William B. LC 72-114919. 1971. **Pt. 1. 60.50 (ISBN 0-471-92726-0); Vol. 3. Photochromism. Brown, G. H. LC 45-8533. 1971. 93.00 (ISBN 0-471-92894-1); Vol. 4. Elucidation of Organic Structures by Physical & Chemical Methods, 3 pts. Bentley, K. W. & Kirby, G. W. 1972-73. Pt. 1. 57.00 (ISBN 0-471-92896-8); Pt. 2. 58.00 (ISBN 0-471-92897-6); Pt. 3. o.p. (ISBN 0-471-92898-4); Vol. 5. Techniques of Electroorganic Synthesis, 2 pts. Weingerb, N. L., ed. Pt. 1. 84.50; Pt. 2. 75.00 (ISBN 0-471-93272-8); Vol. 6. Investigation of Rates & Mechanisms of Reactions, 2 pts. 3rd ed. Lewis, E. S., ed. LC 73-8850. 1974. Pt. 1. 77.00 (ISBN 0-471-93095-4); Pt. 2. 52.50 (ISBN 0-471-93127-6); Vol. 7. Membranes in Separations. Hwang, S. T. & Kammermeyer, K. LC 74-2218. 1975. 60.50 (ISBN 0-471-93268-X); Vol. 10. Applications of Biochemical Systems in Organic Chemistry, 2 pts. Jone, Bryan J., et al, eds. 1976. Pt. 1. 45.00 (ISBN 0-471-93267-1); Pt. 2. 50.00 (ISBN 0-471-93270-1). Pub. by Wiley-Interscience). Wiley.**

Weissberger, Arnold & Hsu, Hsien-Wen. Separations by Centrifugal Phenomena. (Techniques of Chemistry Ser.: Vol. 16). 400p. 49.50 (ISBN 0-471-05564-6, Pub. by Wiley-Interscience). Wiley.

Weissbluth, Mitchel. Atoms & Molecules: Student Edition. 1980. lib ed 24.50 (ISBN 0-12-744452-1). Acad Pr.

Weisser, Otto & Landa, S. Sulphide Catalysts, Their Properties & Applications. Sofr, Ota, tr. 506p. 1973. text ed. 75.00 (ISBN 0-08-017556-2). Pergamon.

Weissglass, Julian. Exploring Elementary Mathematics: A Small-Group Approach for Teaching. LC 79-14931. (Mathematical Sciences Ser.). (Illus.). 1979. text ed. 15.95x (ISBN 0-7167-1027-7); instr's manual 3.95x (ISBN 0-7167-1223-7). W H Freeman.

Weisskopf, T., jt. auth. see MacEwan, A.

Weissler, Arlene & Weissler, Paul. A Woman's Guide to Fixing the Car. (Illus.). 128p. 1973. 6.95 o.s.i. (ISBN 0-8027-0416-6); pap. 3.95 (ISBN 0-8027-7091-6). Walker & Co.

Weissler, Paul. Automotive Air Conditioning. (Illus.). 1981. text ed. 13.95 (ISBN 0-8359-0261-7); pap. 12.95 (ISBN 0-8359-0260-9); solutions manual free. Reston.

Weissler, Paul, jt. auth. see Weissler, Arlene.

Weissman, Clark. LISP One-Point-Five Primer. (Orig.). 1967. pap. 16.95x (ISBN 0-8221-1050-4). Dickenson.

Weissman, Cynthia. Breakfast for Sammy. LC 77-13869. (Illus.). 32p. (gr. k-3). 1978. 6.95 (ISBN 0-590-07503-9, Four Winds). Schol Bk Serv.

Weissman, Frances. Helen & All. (Orig.). 1980. pap. 3.95 (ISBN 0-89260-192-2). Hwong Pub.

Weissman, Gerald, et al, eds. Proceedings. LC 78-55809. (Advances in Inflammation Research Ser.: Vol. 1). 1979. text ed. 67.00 (ISBN 0-89004-337-X). Raven.

Weissman, Irving, et al. Essential Concepts in Immunology. LC 78-57262. 1978. 10.95 (ISBN 0-8053-4406-3). Benjamin-Cummings.

Weissman, Jerry. The Zodiac Killer. (Orig.). 1979. pap. 2.25 o.p. (ISBN 0-523-40529-4). Pinnacle Bks.

Weissman, Stuart L., jt. ed. see Abt, Lawrence E.

Weissmann, Gerald, ed. Advances in Inflammation Research, Vol. 2. 1981. text ed. price not set (ISBN 0-89004-582-8). Raven.

Weissmann, Heidi see Freeman, Leonard.

Weisstein, Ulrich J., ed. see Ritchie, J. M.

Weisstub, David N. & Gostin, Larry O. International Casebook on Law & Psychiatry. (Law & Psychiatry Ser.). Date not set. price not set (ISBN 0-08-023158-6). Pergamon.

Weisstub, David N., ed. Law & Psychiatry in the Canadian Context. 1980. 60.00 (ISBN 0-08-023134-9). Pergamon.

--Law & Psychiatry: Proceedings of an International Symposium Held at Clarke Institute of Psychiatry, Toronto, Canada, Feb. 1977. LC 78-9436. 125p. 1978. 19.00 (ISBN 0-08-023133-0). Pergamon.

Weist, Lois A. What's Cooking in Towne & Country USA, Vol. I. (Special Collectors' Keepsake Ser.). (Illus.). 240p. 1979. 14.99 (ISBN 0-938166-00-X). Weist Pub OH.

--What's Cooking in Towne & Country USA, Vol. II. (Special Collectors' Keepsake Ser.). (Illus.). 250p. 1979. 14.99 (ISBN 0-938166-01-8). Weist Pub OH.

Weist, Tom. A History of the Cheyenne People. (Indian Culture Ser.). (Illus.). 1977. write for info. (ISBN 0-89992-506-5); pap. write for info. (ISBN 0-89992-507-3). Mt Coun Indian.

Weistart, John C. & Lowell, Cym H. The Law of Sports. 1979. 40.00 (ISBN 0-672-82337-3, Bobbs-Merrill Law). Michie.

Weister, Wallace. Insecure Heart & Other Poems. 1980. 4.00 o.p. (ISBN 0-8062-1127-X). Carlton.

Weisz, Frank B. SuperTrust. rev. ed. LC 78-72975. 1980. 14.95 (ISBN 0-87863-179-8). Farnswth Pub.

Weisz, George, jt. ed. see Fox, Robert.

Weisz, H. Microanalysis by the Ring Oven Technique. 2nd ed. 1970. 25.00 (ISBN 0-08-015702-5). Pergamon.

Weisz, Paul B. Elements of Zoology. 1968. text ed. 16.00 o.p. (ISBN 0-07-069103-7, C); instructor's manual 2.00 o.p. (ISBN 0-07-069104-5); study guide by Brenner 7.50 o.p. (ISBN 0-07-007639-1). McGraw.

Weit, Erwin. At the Red Summit: Interpreter Behind the Iron Curtain. 256p. 1973. 6.95 o.s.i. (ISBN 0-02-625780-7). Macmillan.

Weitenkampf, Frank. American Graphic Art. LC 74-6198. 1974. Repr. of 1912 ed. 20.00 (ISBN 0-8103-4020-8). Gale.

Weitenkampf, Frank, ed. Political Caricature in the United States in Separately Published Cartoons. LC 79-137698. (Illus.). 1971. Repr. of 1953 ed. 15.00 (ISBN 0-87104-506-0, Co-Pub. by Arno). NY Pub Lib.

Weitenkampf, Frank, ed. see New York Public Library.

Weithas, Art, ed. Twenty Years of Award Winners from the Society of Illustrators. (Illus.). 352p. 1981. 45.00 (ISBN 0-8038-7224-0, Visual Communication). Hastings.

Weitz, C. Introduction to Physical Anthropology & Archaeology. 1979. pap. 13.95 (ISBN 0-13-492637-4); pap. 5.95 study guide & wkbk. (ISBN 0-13-492645-5). P-H.

Weitz, C., jt. auth. see Miller, E.

Weitz, John & Mahlin, Everett. Man in Charge. 192p. 1974. 6.95 o.s.i. (ISBN 0-02-625770-X). Macmillan.

Weitz, M. Twentieth-Century Philosophy: The Analytic Tradition. LC 66-10366. 1966. pap. text ed. 6.95 (ISBN 0-02-934990-7). Free Pr.

Weitz, Morris, tr. see Hanslick, Edward.

Weitz, Raanan. From Peasant to Farmer: A Revolutionary Strategy for Development. LC 76-170926. (Twentieth Century Fund Study). 1971. 17.50x (ISBN 0-231-03592-6). Columbia U Pr.

Weitz, Shirley. Nonverbal Communication: Readings with Commentary. 2nd ed. (Illus.). 1978. text ed. 15.95x (ISBN 0-19-502447-8); pap. text ed. 9.95x (ISBN 0-19-502448-6). Oxford U Pr.

Weitzel, G., jt. ed. see Voelter, W.

Weitzman, Cay. Distributed Micro Minicomputer Systems: Structure, Implementation & Application. (Illus.). 1980. text ed. 24.95 (ISBN 0-13-216481-7). P-H.

--Minicomputer Systems: Structure, Implementation, & Application. (Illus.). 384p. 1974. 24.95 (ISBN 0-13-584227-1). P-H.

Weitzman, David. Traces: A Field Guide to the History on Your Doorstep. (Illus.). 1980. 17.95 (ISBN 0-684-16107-9, ScribT). Scribner.

--Underfoot: A Guide to Exploring and Preserving America's Past. LC 76-11475. (Illus.). 192p. 1976. pap. 4.95 encore ed. (ISBN 0-684-16205-9, ScribT). Scribner.

Weitzman, Lenore J. The Marriage Contract: Couples, Lovers & the Law. 1980. 14.95 (ISBN 0-13-558403-5, Spec); pap. 5.95 (ISBN 0-13-558395-0). P-H.

Weitzmann, C. F. History of Pianoforte-Playing & Pianoforte-Literature. LC 74-90209. (Music Reprint Ser). 1969. Repr. of 1897 ed. lib. bdg. 29.50 (ISBN 0-306-71817-0). Da Capo.

Weitzmann, Kurt. Byzantine Liturgical Psalters & Gospels. 322p. 1980. 200.00x (ISBN 0-86078-064-3, Pub. by Variorum England). State Mutual Bk.

--Late Antique-Early Christian Painting. LC 76-16444. (Magnificent Paperback Art Ser.). 128p. 1977. 19.95 (ISBN 0-8076-0830-0); pap. 9.95 (ISBN 0-8076-0831-9). Braziller.

Wei Wu-Wei. Posthumous Pieces. 245p. 1981. pap. 5.00 (ISBN 0-85656-027-8). Great Eastern.

--The Tenth Man. 246p. 1981. pap. 6.00 (ISBN 0-85656-013-8). Great Eastern.

--Unwordly Wise. 88p. 1981. 6.50 (ISBN 0-85656-103-7). Great Eastern.

Weizenbaum, Joseph. Computer Power & Human Reason: From Judgment to Calculation. LC 75-19305. (Illus.). 1976. 14.00x o.p. (ISBN 0-7167-0464-1); pap. text ed. 8.95x (ISBN 0-7167-0463-3). W H Freeman.

Weizman Institute of Science, Rehovot, Israel, Feb. 1980 & Littauer, U. Z. Drug Receptors in the Central Nervous System - Based on a Workshop Sponsored by the European Molecular Biology Organization: Proceedings. 350p. 1980. 43.00 (ISBN 0-471-27893-9, Pub. by Wiley-Interscience). Wiley.

Weizsaecker, C. C. Barriers to Entry: A Theoretical Treatment. (Lecture Notes in Economics & Mathematical Systems Ser.: Vol. 185). (Illus.). 220p. 1981. pap. 19.00 (ISBN 0-387-10272-8). Springer-Verlag.

Wekerle, Gerda R., et al, eds. New Space for Women. (Westview Special Studies in Women in Contemporary Society). 352p. 1980. lib. bdg. 28.50x (ISBN 0-89158-775-6). Westview.

Welber, Robert. Winter Picnic. LC 77-77418. (Illus.). (gr. 7 up). 1970. PLB 5.99 o.s.i. (ISBN 0-394-90444-3). Pantheon.

Welborn, C. A. Red River Controversy. 6.95 (ISBN 0-685-48787-3). Nortex Pr.

Welborn, David M. Governance of Federal Regulatory Agencies. LC 77-8012. 1977. 11.50x (ISBN 0-87049-216-0). U of Tenn Pr.

Welborn, Don. On the Subject of Tongues: From the New Testament. 56p. pap. 0.35 (ISBN 0-937396-48-6). Walterick Pubs.

Welborn, Peggy, jt. auth. see Kelly, Dan H.

Welburn, Tyler. Structured COBOL: Fundamentals & Style. (Illus.). 640p. (Orig.). 1981. pap. text ed. price not set (ISBN 0-87484-543-2). Mayfield Pub.

Welch, et al, eds. Facets of Taoism: Essays in Chinese Religion. LC 77-28034. 307p. 1981. pap. 7.95x (ISBN 0-300-02673-0). Yale U Pr.

Welch, Alford T., ed. see Gatje, Helmut.

Welch, Anthony. Shah 'Abbas & the Arts of Isfahan. LC 73-76938. (Illus.). 152p. 1973. 19.95 (ISBN 0-87848-041-2). Asia Soc.

Welch, Claude E. & Hedberg, Stephen E. Polypoid Lesions of the Gastrointestinal Tract. 2nd ed. (Mpcs Ser.: Vol. 2). (Illus.). 220p. 1975. text ed. 16.00 (ISBN 0-7216-9171-4). Saunders.

Welch, Denton. Maiden Voyage. 1981. Repr. of 1943 ed. 12.95 (ISBN 0-8290-0358-4). Irvington.

--A Voice Through a Cloud. 1981. Repr. of 1950 ed. 12.95 (ISBN 0-8290-0357-6). Irvington.

Welch, E. The Peripatetic University, Cambridge Local Lectures, 1873-1973. LC 72-91961. (Illus.). 204p. 1973. 26.50 (ISBN 0-521-20152-7). Cambridge U Pr.

Welch, E. B. Ecological Effects of Waste Water. LC 78-11371. 1980. 32.50 (ISBN 0-521-22495-0); pap. 9.95x (ISBN 0-521-29525-4). Cambridge U Pr.

Welch, Finis. Minimum Wages: Issues & Evidence. 1978. pap. 4.25 (ISBN 0-8447-3308-3). Am Enterprise.

Welch, Holmes & Seidel, Anna, eds. Facets of Taoism: Essays in Chinese Religion. LC 77-28034. 1979. 27.50x (ISBN 0-300-01695-6). Yale U Pr.

Welch, James. The Death of Jim Loney. LC 79-1712. 192p. 1981. pap. 2.25 (ISBN 0-06-080538-2, P 538, PL). Har-Row.

--Winter in the Blood. LC 74-5985. 192p. 1981. pap. 2.25 (ISBN 0-06-080537-4, P 537, PL). Har-Row.

Welch, Jeffrey. Liturature & Film: An Annotated Bibliography, 1900 to 1977. LC 80-8509. 350p. 1981. lib. bdg. 40.00 (ISBN 0-8240-9478-6). Garland Pub.

Welch, John F., ed. Van Sickle's Modern Airmanship. 5th ed. 896p. 1980. text ed. 24.95 (ISBN 0-442-25793-7). Van Nos Reinhold.

Welch, June. All Hail the Might State. (Illus.). 1979. 14.95 (ISBN 0-87244-048-6). Texian.

Welch, June R. The Colleges of Texas. (Illus.). 230p. 1981. 17.95 (ISBN 0-912854-11-1). GLA Pr.

--The Texas Courthouse Revisited. (Illus.). Date not set. 14.95g (ISBN 0-685-96874-X). GLA Pr. Postponed.

Welch, June R., illus. The Texas Senator. 1978. 13.95 (ISBN 0-912854-10-3). GLA Pr.

Welch, Karen K. & Cole, Joan W. Little Trolley Books. (Crossties Ser.). (gr. k-2). 1977. Set. pap. text ed. 119.85 54 bks. (ISBN 0-8332-1126-9); dupl. masters 30.99 (ISBN 0-8332-1129-3); tchrs'. guide 0.78 (ISBN 0-8332-1127-7). Economy Co.

Welch, Karen K., et al. Grand Central Books. (Crossties Ser.). (gr. k-2). 1977. 10 copies 249.90 (ISBN 0-8332-1113-7); tchrs' manual 4.89 (ISBN 0-8332-1124-2); dupl. masters 30.99 (ISBN 0-8332-1129-3). Economy Co.

Welch, Kenneth R., jt. auth. see Harding, Keith A.

Welch, Lew. How I Work As a Poet & Other Essays - Plays - Stories. Allen, Donald, ed. & intro. by. LC 73-84119. 66p. 1973. 5.00 (ISBN 0-912516-07-0); pap. 5.00 o.p. (ISBN 0-912516-06-2). Grey Fox.

--I Remain: The Letters of Lew Welch with the Correspondence of His Friends, Volume 2. Allen, Donald, ed. LC 79-21574. 208p. 1980. 12.00 (ISBN 0-912516-41-0); pap. 5.95 (ISBN 0-912516-42-9). Grey Fox.

Welch, Martha M. Sunflower! LC 80-1008. (Illus.). 64p. (gr. 2-5). 1980. PLB 6.95 (ISBN 0-396-07885-0). Dodd.

Welch, Mary, tr. Mais Que Passarinhos. (Portugese Bks.). (Port.). 1979. 1.25 (ISBN 0-8297-0801-4). Life Pubs Intl.

--Mas Que Pajarillos. (Spanish Bks.). (Span.). 1977. 1.60 (ISBN 0-8297-0749-2). Life Pubs Intl.

--Nous Valons Plus Que Des Passereaux. (French Bks.). (Fr.). 1979. 1.75 (ISBN 0-8297-0843-X). Life Pubs Intl.

Welch, Mary S. The Family Wilderness Handbook. (Orig.). 1973. pap. 1.65 o.p. (ISBN 0-345-23253-4). Ballantine.

Welch, Mary Scott. Networking. 304p. 1981. pap. 2.95 (ISBN 0-446-93578-6). Warner Bks.

Welch, Paul S. Limnology. 2nd ed. (Illus.). 1952. text ed. 25.00 o.p. (ISBN 0-07-069179-7, C). McGraw.

Welch, Paula D. & Lerch, Harold A. Handbook of American Physical Education & Sport. write for info. C C Thomas.

Welch, Reuben. We Really Do Need to Listen. LC 78-50098. (Illus.). 1978. 5.95 (ISBN 0-914850-30-X); pap. 2.50 (ISBN 0-914850-69-5); pap. text ed. 1.50 study guide (ISBN 0-686-67968-7). Impact Tenn.

--When You Run Out of Fantastic-Persevere. LC 76-20999. 1976. pap. text ed. 1.50 study guide (ISBN 0-914850-30-X); pap. text ed. 1.50 study guide (ISBN 0-686-67577-0); pap. text ed. 1.50 study guide (ISBN 0-686-67578-9). Impact Tenn.

Welch, Robert. Blue Book of the John Birch Society. LC 74-29425. 1961. 4.00 (ISBN 0-88279-215-6); pap. 2.00 pocketsize (ISBN 0-88279-106-0). Western Islands.

--Irish Poetry from Moore to Yeats. 248p. 1980. text ed. 23.25x (ISBN 0-901072-93-1). Humanities.

Welch, Ronald. Zulu Warrior. LC 74-78244. (gr. 3-8). 1974. 5.95 (ISBN 0-7153-6555-X). David & Charles.

Welch, Ruth, ed. Neighbors & Other People: More of the Best of Douglass Welch. LC 77-20285. (Illus.). 1977. pap. 4.95 (ISBN 0-914842-24-2). Madrona Pubs.

--Squirrel Cage: The Best of Douglass Welch. LC 76-45418. (Illus.). 1976. pap. 4.95 (ISBN 0-914842-15-3). Madrona Pubs.

Welch, S. M. & Croft, B. A. The Design of Biological Monitoring Systems for Pest Management. LC 79-10960. 1980. pap. 19.95x (ISBN 0-470-26632-5). Halsted Pr.

Welch, Stuart C. Indian Drawings & Painted Sketches: 16th Through 19th Centuries. LC 75-29780. (Illus.). 144p. 1976. 17.50 (ISBN 0-87848-046-3). Asia Soc.

--A King's Book of Kings. 200p. 1981. 50.00 (ISBN 0-87099-028-4, 494208). NYGS.

--Wonders of the Age: Masterpieces of Early Safavid Painting, 1501-1576. LC 79-2480. 223p. 1979. pap. 12.95 (ISBN 0-916724-38-7). Fogg Art.

Welch, Susan, jt. auth. see Karnig, Albert.

Welch, Susan & Peters, John G., eds. Legislative Reform & Public Policy. LC 77-5046. (Special Studies). 1977. text ed. 21.95 o.p. (ISBN 0-275-24540-3). Praeger.

Welch, Thomas R., jt. auth. see Krugman, Richard D.

Welch, W. Evert, jt. auth. see Plossl, George W.

Welch, W. W., jt. auth. see Husher, R. W.

Welch, William. Government & Common Sense: Citizens Guide to Political Thinking. (Littlefield, Adams Quality Paperback Ser.: No. 362). 224p. (Orig.). 1981. pap. 4.95 (ISBN 0-8226-0362-4). Littlefield.

Welcher, Jeanne K. John Evelyn. (English Authors Ser.: No. 144). lib. bdg. 10.95 (ISBN 0-8057-1184-8). Twayne.

Welcome, John. Neck or Nothing. (Illus.). 1970. lib. bdg. 5.95 o.p. (ISBN 0-571-08466-4, Pub. by Faber & Faber). Merrimack Bk Serv.

--Run for Cover. 1972. pap. 0.95 o.p. (ISBN 0-06-087027-3, HW). Har-Row.

Welcomme, Robin L. Fisheries Ecology of Floodplain Rivers. (Illus.). 1979. text ed. 50.00 (ISBN 0-582-46310-6). Longman.

Welder, G. Chemisorption: An Experimental Approach. Klemperer, D., tr. 1977. text ed. 24.95 (ISBN 0-408-10611-5). Butterworths.

Welding Institute of Canada, Toronto, Ontario, ed. Pipeline & Energy Plant Piping--Design & Construction: Proceedings of the International Conference on Pipeline & Energy Plant Piping, Calgary, Alberta, Nov. 10-13, 1980. (Illus.). 360p. 1980. 40.00 (ISBN 0-08-025368-7). Pergamon.

Weldon, Fay. Puffball. LC 80-14585. 1980. 10.95 (ISBN 0-671-44809-9). Summit Bks.
Weldon, T. D. States & Morals: A Study in Political Conflicts. 1973. pap. 4.95 (ISBN 0-685-30027-7). Transatlantic.
Weldon, Wilson O. Christmas: More Than a Season. LC 80-51313. 75p. (Orig.). 1980. pap. 1.95x (ISBN 0-8358-0402-X). Upper Room.
Weldy, Norma J. Body Fluids & Electrolytes: A Programmed Presentation. 3rd ed. (Illus.). 1980. pap. 8.50 (ISBN 0-8016-5383-5). Mosby.
Welford, A. T. & Birren, James E. Decision Making & Age. Stein, Leon, ed. LC 79-8699. (Growing Old Ser.). (Illus.). 1980. Repr. of 1969 ed. lib. bdg. 14.00x (ISBN 0-405-12810-X). Arno.
Welford, A. T., ed. Man Under Stress. LC 74-5440. 140p. 1974. 15.95 (ISBN 0-470-93315-1). Halsted Pr.
Welford, A. T. & Houssiadas, L., eds. Contemporary Problems in Perception. 1970. 18.50x (ISBN 0-85066-039-4). Intl Ideas.
Welke, Elton, jt. auth. see Dudley, Donald L.
Welke, Janice H., ed. EDP Institute, August 22-25, 1976: Proceedings. 1977. pap. 8.75 (ISBN 0-89154-054-7). Intl Found Employ.
--Fund Advisors Institute, August 1976: Proceedings. 1976. pap. 10.50 (ISBN 0-89154-053-9). Intl Found Employ.
Welker, Carole E., jt. auth. see Scheib, Ida.
Welker, David. Theatrical Direction. 1971. text ed. 17.95 (ISBN 0-205-03220-6, 4832205). Allyn.
--Theatrical Set Design: The Basic Techniques. 1969. text ed. 13.95x o.p. (ISBN 0-205-02222-7, 4822226). Allyn.
--Theatrical Set Design: The Basic Techniques. 2nd ed. 1979. text ed. 19.95 (ISBN 0-205-06451-5). Allyn.
Welkowitz, Joan, et al. Introductory Statistics for the Behavioral Sciences. 316p. 1976. 15.95 (ISBN 0-12-743260-4); wkbk. 5.95 (ISBN 0-12-743267-1); ans. key 2.00 (ISBN 0-12-743268-X). Acad Pr.
Welkowitz, Walter, ed. Bioengineering: Proceedings of the Ninth Northeast Conference, March, 1981, Rutgers University, Piscataway, New Jersey. (Illus.). 432p. 1981. pap. 60.00 (ISBN 0-08-027207-X). Pergamon.
Wellach, Donald F. Proteins of Animal Cell Plasma Membranes, Vol. 1. 1978. 19.20 (ISBN 0-88831-011-0). Eden Med Res.
Welland, Dennis. Mark Twain in England. 1978. text ed. 21.00x (ISBN 0-391-00553-7). Humanities.
Wellbery, David E., tr. see Schwarz, Egon.
Wellburn. Post-Natal Depression. 1980. text ed. 19.50x (ISBN 0-7190-0792-5). Humanities.
Wellek, Rene. Four Critics: Croce, Valery, Lukacs, & Ingarden. LC 80-54429. (The Walker-Ames Lecture Ser.). 104p. 1981. 8.95 (ISBN 0-295-95800-6). U of Wash Pr.
--A History of Modern Criticism: 1750-1950: Volume 1 - the Later Eighteenth Century. 358p. Date not set. pap. price not set (ISBN 0-521-28295-0). Cambridge U Pr.
--A History of Modern Criticism: 1750-1950: Volume 2 - the Romantic Age. 460p. Date not set. pap. price not set (ISBN 0-521-28296-9). Cambridge U Pr.
Wellek, Rene, ed. Anti-Scepticism: Henry Lee. LC 75-11231. (British Philosophers & Theologians of the 17th & 18th Centuries Ser.). 1977. lib. bdg. 42.00 (ISBN 0-8240-1784-6). Garland Pub.
--The Divine Legation of Moses, 4 vols. 2nd ed. LC 75-11264. (British Philosophers & Theologians of the 17th & 18th Centuries Ser.: Vol. 62). 1978. Set. lib. bdg. 168.00 (ISBN 0-8240-1813-3); lib. bdg. 42.00 ea. Garland Pub.
--Dostoevsky: A Collection of Critical Essays. 1962. pap. 2.95 o.p. (ISBN 0-13-218784-1, Spec). P-H.
--James Burnett Monboddo (1714-1799) Antient Metaphysics, 6 Vol., 1779-99. LC 75-11236. (British Philosophers & Theologians of the 17th & 18th Centuries Ser.). 1977. lib. bdg. 42.00 (ISBN 0-8240-1789-7). Garland Pub.
--John Leland. LC 75-11232. (British Philosophers & Theologians of the 17th & 18th Centuries Ser.). 1978. lib. bdg. 42.00 (ISBN 0-8240-1785-4). Garland Pub.
Wellek, Rene, ed. see Beattie, James.
Wellek, Rene, ed. see Bentley, Richard.
Wellek, Rene, ed. see Blaguy, John.
Wellek, Rene, ed. see Bolingbroke, Henry Viscount.
Wellek, Rene, ed. see Bramhall, John.
Wellek, Rene, ed. see Browne, Peter.
Wellek, Rene, ed. see Chubb, Thomas.
Wellek, Rene, ed. see Collier, Arthur.
Wellek, Rene, ed. see Collins, Anthony.
Wellek, Rene, ed. see Cudworth, Ralph.
Wellek, Rene, ed. see Culverwel, Nathanael.
Wellek, Rene, ed. see Cumberland, Richard.
Wellek, Rene, ed. see Digby, Sir Kenelm.
Wellek, Rene, ed. see Ferguson, Adam.
Wellek, Rene, ed. see Gildon, Charles.
Wellek, Rene, ed. see Glanvill, Joseph.
Wellek, Rene, ed. see Glanville, Joseph.
Wellek, Rene, ed. see Jenyns, Soame.
Wellek, Rene, ed. see Kames, Henry H.
Wellek, Rene, ed. see Law, Edmund.
Wellek, Rene, ed. see Mayne, Zachary.
Wellek, Rene, ed. see Middleton, Conyers.
Wellek, Rene, ed. see More, Henry.
Wellek, Rene, ed. see Nitsch, Friedrich A.
Wellek, Rene, ed. see Norris, John.
Wellek, Rene, ed. see Paley, William.
Wellek, Rene, ed. see Price, Richard.
Wellek, Rene, ed. see Priestley, Joseph.
Wellek, Rene, ed. see Reid, Thomas.
Wellek, Rene, ed. see Sherlock, Thomas.
Wellek, Rene, ed. see Smith, John.
Wellek, Rene, ed. see Stanley, Thomas.
Wellek, Rene, ed. see Tindal, Matthew.
Wellek, Rene, ed. see Toland, John.
Wellek, Rene, ed. see Tucker, Abraham.
Wellek, Rene, ed. see Warburton, William.
Wellek, Rene, ed. see Watson, Richard.
Wellek, Rene, ed. see Willich, Anthony F.
Wellek, Rene, ed. see Wollaston, William.
Wellek, Rene, ed. see Woolston, Thomas.
Weller, Charles & Boylan, Brian R. How to Live with Hypoglycemia. 1977. pap. 2.25 (ISBN 0-515-05979-X). Jove Pubns.
Weller, E. J., ed. see Follette, Daniel.
Weller, George. Story of Submarines. (gr. 5-8). 1962. PLB 5.99 (ISBN 0-394-90402-8). Random.
Weller, John, jt. ed. see Ranger, T. O.
Weller, Michael. Cancer. 1971. pap. 3.95 o.p. (ISBN 0-571-09765-0, Pub. by Faber & Faber). Merrimack Bk Serv.
Weller, Milton W. The Island Waterfowl. new ed. (Illus.). 144p. 1980. text ed. 11.95 (ISBN 0-8138-1310-7). Iowa St U Pr.
Weller, P. F. & Supple, J. H. Chemistry: Elementary Principles. 1971. 17.95 (ISBN 0-201-08596-8). A-W.
Weller, R. O. & Navarro, J. Cervos. Pathology of Peripheral Nerves: A Practical Approach. (Postgraduate Pathology Ser.). 1977. 39.95 (ISBN 0-407-00073-9). Butterworths.
Weller, Richard, ed. Humanistic Education. LC 77-71196. 1977. 19.50x (ISBN 0-685-78478-9); text ed. 17.50x (ISBN 0-8211-2256-8). McCutchan.
Weller, Richard H. Verbal Communication in Instructional Supervision. LC 70-161300. (Illus.). 1971. text ed. 11.50x (ISBN 0-8077-2322-3). Tchrs Coll.
Weller, Richard H., ed. see Symposium on Educational Research,14th.
Weller, Robert C., jt. auth. see Smith, Myron J., Jr.
Weller, Robert H., jt. ed. see Poston, Dudley L., Jr.
Weller, Walter J. Assembly Level Programming for Small Computers. LC 75-13436. (Illus.). 256p. 1975. 18.95 (ISBN 0-669-00049-3). Lexington Bks.
Welles, E. R. Legend of Sleepy Hollow, Rip Van Winkle, President Van Buren & Brown. 1973. pap. 2.00x (ISBN 0-913692-10-7). Learning Inc.
Welles, Kenneth B. K-2-FDOS: A Floppy Disk Operating System for the 8080. (Orig.). 1979. pap. 20.00 (ISBN 0-07-069206-8, BYTE Bks). McGraw.
Welles, Patricia. Members Only. 1981. 12.95 (ISBN 0-87795-270-1). Arbor Hse.
Welles, S. P. & Cosgriff, John. A Revision of the Labyrinthodont Family Capitosauridae & a Description of Parotosaurus Peabodyi N. Sp. from the Wupatki Member of the Moenkopi Formation of Northern Arizona. (U. C. Publ. in Geological Sciences: Vol. 54). 1965. pap. 7.50x (ISBN 0-520-09155-8). U of Cal Pr.
Welles, S. P. & Estes, Richard. Hadrokkosaurus Bradyi from the Upper Moenkopi Formation of Arizona with a Review of the Brachyopid Labyrinthodonts. (U. C. Publ. in Geological Sciences: Vol. 84). 1969. pap. 7.50x (ISBN 0-520-09188-4). U of Cal Pr.
Wellesley, Kenneth. The Long Year A.D. 69. LC 76-5390. 1977. 24.50 o.p. (ISBN 0-89158-609-1). Westview.
Wellesley, William L. A View of the Court of Chancery. 110p. 1980. Repr. of 1830 ed. lib. bdg. 15.00x (ISBN 0-8377-1303-X). Rothman.
Welle-Strand. Motoring in Norway. new ed. (Illus.). 1975. pap. 6.00x (ISBN 0-89918-411-1, N411). Vanous.
Welle-Strand, E. Angling in Norway. (Illus.). 1972. pap. 5.00x (ISBN 0-89918-510-X, N-510). Vanous.
Wellesz, Egon. Arnold Schonberg. Kerridge, W. H., tr. LC 69-12698. (Music Ser). (Ger). 1969. Repr. of 1925 ed. lib. bdg. 19.50 (ISBN 0-306-71226-1). Da Capo.
Wellesz, Egon see Abraham, Gerald, et al.
Wellesz, Egon see Abraham, Gerald.
Wellhausen, Julius. Prolegomena to the History of Ancient Israel. 9.00 (ISBN 0-8446-3147-7). Peter Smith.
Welling, William. Photography in America: The Formative Years, 1839-1900. LC 77-1983. (Illus.). 1977. 29.95 o.s.i. (ISBN 0-690-01421-X, TYC-T). T Y Crowell.
Wellington, A. Apple Pie. 1979. 5.95 (ISBN 0-13-038745-2). P-H.
Wellington, Harry H. Labor & the Legal Process. LC 68-27769. 1968. 24.00x (ISBN 0-300-01038-9); pap. 5.95x o.p. 1969 (ISBN 0-300-01183-0, Y216). Yale U Pr.
Wellington, Harry H. & Winter, Ralph K. Unions & the Cities. LC 79-179327. (Studies of Unionism in Government). 1972. 14.95 (ISBN 0-8157-9294-8); pap. 5.95 (ISBN 0-8157-9293-X). Brookings.
Wellington, Paul A., ed. Loneliness. 1980. pap. 2.50 (ISBN 0-8309-0287-2). Herald Hse.
--Parenting Alone. 1980. pap. 2.50 (ISBN 0-8309-0297-X). Herald Hse.
--Planning to Stay Together. 1980. pap. 4.00 (ISBN 0-8309-0308-9). Herald Hse.
--Rules & Resolutions, Nineteen Eighty. LC 74-84765. 1980. 7.50 (ISBN 0-8309-0136-1). Herald Hse.
Wellington, V. K. V. K. Wellington Koo's Foreign Policy: Some Selected Documents. King, Wuncz, ed. (Studies in Chinese History & Civilization). 141p. 1977. Repr. of 1931 ed. 16.00 (ISBN 0-89093-071-6). U Pubns Amer.
Wellisch, Hans H. The Conversion of Scripts: Its Nature, History, & Utilization. LC 77-2205. 1978. 38.95 (ISBN 0-471-01620-9, Pub. by Wiley-Interscience). Wiley.
Wellisch, Hans H., ed. Indexing & Abstracting: A Guide to International Sources. LC 80-11907. 398p. 1980. 22.75 (ISBN 0-87436-300-4). Abc-
Wellman, Carl. Morals & Ethics. 328p. 1975. pap. 8.95x (ISBN 0-673-05013-0). Scott F.
Wellman, D. T., ed. Portraits of White Racism. LC 76-47187. 1977. 29.95 (ISBN 0-521-21514-5); pap. 7.95x (ISBN 0-521-29179-8). Cambridge U Pr.
Wellman, Frederick L. Dictionary of Tropical American Crops & Their Diseases. LC 77-8558. 1977. 24.00 (ISBN 0-8108-1071-9). Scarecrow.
--Tropical American Plant Disease. LC 71-175527. (Neotropical Phytopathology Problems). (Illus.). 1972. 32.50 (ISBN 0-8108-0459-X). Scarecrow.
Wellman, John D., jt. auth. see Marans, Robert W.
Wellman, Manley W. After Dark. LC 80-650. (Double D Science Ficion Ser.). 192p. 1980. 8.95 (ISBN 0-385-15604-9). Doubleday.
Wellman, Manley W. & Wellman, Wade. Sherlock Holmes' War of the Worlds. 208p. (Orig.). 1975. pap. 1.25 o.s.i. (ISBN 0-446-76982-7). Warner Bks.
Wellman, Manly. Brave Horse. LC 68-24439. (Young Readers Ser.). (Illus., Orig.). (gr. 4-7). 1968. 3.95 o.p. (ISBN 0-910412-81-2). Williamsburg.
Wellman, Manly W. The Beyonders. (Orig.). 1977. pap. 1.50 o.s.i. (ISBN 0-446-88202-X). Warner Bks.
Wellman, Paul I. The Female: A Novel of Another Time. 3.95 o.p. (ISBN 0-686-67650-5). Doubleday.
Wellman, Wade, jt. auth. see Wellman, Manley W.
Wellmer, Albrecht. Critical Theory of Society. LC 70-150309. 1971. pap. 3.50 (ISBN 0-8164-9189-5); o.p. (ISBN 0-8164-9189-5, Continuum). Continuum.
Wellnitz, Marcus Von see Von Wellnitz, Marcus.
Wells. The Empire of the Ants & Other Stories. (gr. 7-12). pap. 1.25 (ISBN 0-590-11845-5, Schol Pap). Schol Bk Serv.
Wells, A. F. Structural Inorganic Chemistry. 4th ed. (Illus.). 1120p. 1975. text ed. 84.00x (ISBN 0-19-855354-4). Oxford U Pr.
Wells, Albert. As Touching the Holy. (Direction Bks.). (Orig.). 1980. pap. 2.45 (ISBN 0-8010-9637-5). Baker Bk.
Wells, Andy J. Audio Servicing: Text/Lab Manual. 1st ed. (Illus.). 144p. 9.95 (ISBN 0-07-069247-5). McGraw.
--Audio Servicing: Theory & Practice. 1st ed. (Illus.). 240p. (Orig.). pap. text ed. 13.95 (ISBN 0-07-069246-7, G); lab manual 9.95 (ISBN 0-07-069247-5). McGraw.
Wells, Anna M. Murderer's Choice. 256p. 1981. pap. text ed. 2.25 (ISBN 0-06-080534-X, P 534, PL). Har-Row.
Wells, Archibald H. The Moral Function of Education. (Illus.). 1980. 33.45 (ISBN 0-89266-226-3). Am Classical Coll Pr.
Wells, Arnold, jt. auth. see Witkowski, Edward.
Wells, B. K., jt. auth. see Start, K. B.
Wells, Barry T. Hot Air Ballooning. LC 80-80504. (Free Time Fun Ser.). (Illus.). 56p. (gr. 5 up). 1981. lib. bdg. 6.79 (ISBN 0-8178-0003-4). Harvey.
Wells, C. M. The German Policy of Augustus: An Examination of the Archaeological Evidence. (Illus.). 340p. 1972. 28.50x (ISBN 0-19-813162-3). Oxford U Pr.
Wells, Calvin. Man in His World. (Illus.). 1971. text ed. 9.00x (ISBN 0-212-98383-0). Humanities.
Wells, Carolyn. Carolyn Wells' Book of American Limericks. LC 77-174140. (Tower Bks). (Illus.). viii, 91p. 1972. Repr. of 1925 ed. 18.00 (ISBN 0-8103-3929-3). Gale.
--Parody Anthology. 1967. pap. 2.50 o.p. (ISBN 0-486-21844-9). Dover.
--Parody Anthology. LC 67-14060. 1968. Repr. of 1904 ed. 15.00 (ISBN 0-8103-3224-8). Gale.
Wells, Claudia E. Whiskers, the Bank Mouse. LC 77-10823. (Illus.). (gr. 1-4). 1981. pap. write for info. (ISBN 0-930506-01-4). Popcorn Pubs.
Wells, D. A. Recent Economic Changes. LC 69-16654. (American Scene Ser.). 1970. Repr. of 1889 ed. lib. bdg. 49.50 (ISBN 0-306-71143-5). Da Capo.
Wells, David. The Prophetic of George Tyrrell. LC 79-27097. (American Academy of Religion Monograph: No. 22). 12.00x (ISBN 0-89130-375-8, 01 00 22); pap. 7.50x (ISBN 0-89130-376-6). Scholars Pr CA.
Wells, David A., jt. ed. see Price, Glanville.
Wells, David A., ed. see Timbs, John.
Wells, Dean F. The Ghosts of Rowan Oak: William Faulkner's Ghost Stories for Children. LC 80-52628. (Illus.). 64p. 1980. 9.95. Yoknapatawpha.
Wells, Dean F. & Cole, Hunter, eds. Mississippi Heroes, Vol. 1. LC 80-19704. (Illus.). 250p. 1980. 15.00 (ISBN 0-87805-128-7). U Pr of Miss.
Wells, Dee. Jane. 1975. pap. 1.95 (ISBN 0-380-00222-1, 38356). Avon.
Wells, Dorothy P., ed. Child Abuse: An Annotated Bibliography. LC 79-21641. 458p. 1980. 20.00 (ISBN 0-8108-1264-9). Scarecrow.
Wells, Elaine F. The Lords of Castle Weirwyck. 256p. (Orig.). 1980. pap. 1.95 (ISBN 0-89083-668-X). Zebra.
--Run, Ellen, Run. (YA) 1978. 5.95 (ISBN 0-685-87348-X, Avalon). Bouregy.
Wells, Ellen B., ed. Horsemanship: A Guide to Information Sources. LC 79-16046. (Sports, Games, & Pastimes Information Guide Ser.: Vol. 4). 1979. 30.00 (ISBN 0-8103-1444-4). Gale.
Wells, F. V. Perfumery Technology. 2nd ed. 400p. 1981. 110.00 (ISBN 0-470-26958-8). Halsted Pr.
Wells, F. V., jt. auth. see Billot, Marcel.
Wells, G. A. Did Jesus Exist? (Skeptic's Bookshelf Ser.). 241p. 1975. 13.95 (ISBN 0-87975-086-3). Prometheus Bks.
--The Plays of Grillparzer. 1969. 16.50 (ISBN 0-08-012950-1); pap. 7.75 (ISBN 0-08-012949-8). Pergamon.
Wells, G. L. Process Engineering with Economic Objective. 1974. 18.95x (ISBN 0-249-44116-0). Intl Ideas.
--Safety in Process Plant Design. 276p. 1980. 59.95x (ISBN 0-470-26907-3). Halsted Pr.
Wells, G. L. & Robson, P. M. Computation for Process Engineers. 1974. 19.95x (ISBN 0-249-44126-8). Intl Ideas.
Wells, G. R. Comprehensive Transport Planning. 157p. 1975. 39.50x (ISBN 0-85264-233-4, Pub. by Griffin England). State Mutual Bk.
--Highway Planning Techniques: The Balance of Cost & Benefit. 150p. 1971. 35.00x (ISBN 0-85264-196-6, Pub. by Griffin England). State Mutual Bk.
--Traffic Engineering: An Introduction. 190p. 1979. 34.50x (ISBN 0-85264-254-7, Pub. by Griffin England). State Mutual Bk.
Wells, Gordon, et al. Learning Through Interaction. LC 80-41113. (Language at Home & at School Ser.: Vol. 1). (Illus.). 200p. Date not set. text ed. 39.50 (ISBN 0-521-23774-2); pap. text ed. 10.95 (ISBN 0-521-28219-5). Cambridge U Pr.
Wells, H. G. Best Science Fiction Stories. 7.50 (ISBN 0-8446-3149-3). Peter Smith.
--The Complete Short Stories. LC 79-145813. 1971. 14.95 (ISBN 0-312-15855-6, C4000). St Martin.
--Early Writings in Science & Science Fiction. Philmus, Robert M. & Hughes, David, eds. LC 73-91673. 1975. 18.50x (ISBN 0-520-02679-9). U of Cal Pr.
--The Invisible Man. pap. 1.25 o.p. (ISBN 0-445-08417-0). Popular Lib.
--The Invisible Man: A Fantastic Sensation. LC 80-10547. 279p. 1981. Repr. lib. bdg. 10.00x (ISBN 0-8376-0457-5). Bentley.
--The Island of Doctor Moreau. LC 80-110. 1981. Repr. of 1960 ed. lib. bdg. 10.00x (ISBN 0-8376-0431-1). Bentley.
--Modern Utopia. LC 67-26614. 1967. pap. 5.95x (ISBN 0-8032-5213-7, BB 393, Bison). U of Nebr Pr.
--Outline of History, 4 vols. 1920. Repr. 125.00 (ISBN 0-403-03082-X). Somerset Pub.
--Outline of History: Being a Plain History of Life & Mankind. rev. ed. LC 75-139072. 1971. 15.95 (ISBN 0-385-02420-7). Doubleday.

--Things to Come. (Science Fiction Ser). 184p. 1975. Repr. of 1935 ed. lib. bdg. 12.50 (ISBN 0-8398-2318-5). Gregg.

--The Time Machine & the War of the Worlds: A Critical Edition. McConnell, Frank D., ed. (Illus.). 1977. pap. text ed. 4.95x (ISBN 0-19-502164-9). Oxford U Pr.

--Tono-Bungay. LC 77-28027. 1978. 13.95x (ISBN 0-8032-4702-8); pap. 4.25x (ISBN 0-8032-9701-7, BB669, Bison). U of Nebr Pr.

--War of the Worlds. (Literature Ser). (gr. 7-12). 1970. pap. text ed. 3.33 (ISBN 0-87720-742-9). AMSCO Sch.

--The War of the Worlds & the Time Machine. pap. 1.95 (ISBN 0-385-08274-6, Dolphin). Doubleday.

Wells, Harold C. & Canfield, Jack. One Hundred Ways to Enhance Self Concepts in the Classroom: Handbook for Teachers & Parents. (Illus.). 288p. 1976. 14.95 (ISBN 0-13-636951-0); pap. 10.95 (ISBN 0-13-636944-8). P-H.

Wells, Haru, tr. see Paterson, Katherine.

Wells, Henry W. Introduction to Wallace Stevens. LC 75-45395. 218p. 1976. Repr. of 1964 ed. lib. bdg. 18.75x (ISBN 0-8371-8736-2, WEWS). Greenwood.

Wells, Herman B. Being Lucky: Reminiscences & Reflections. LC 80-7493. 512p. 1980. 17.50x (ISBN 0-253-11556-6). Ind U Pr.

Wells, Ida B., jt. auth. see Addams, Jane.

Wells, J. The Rat. 1966. pap. text ed. 6.50x o.p. (ISBN 0-435-60939-4). Heinemann Ed.

Wells, Jack E., et al, eds. Review of Basic Sciences & Clinical Dentistry, 2 vols. Incl. Vol. 1. Basic Science. 262p. text ed. 27.50 (ISBN 0-06-142657-1); Vol. 2. Clinical Dentistry. 466p. text ed. 42.50 (ISBN 0-06-142658-X). (Illus.). 1400p. 1980. text ed. write for info. (Harper Medical). Har-Row.

Wells, James S. Plant Propagation Practices. (Illus.). 1955. 12.95 (ISBN 0-02-625900-1). Macmillan.

Wells, Joel, ed. Pilgrim's Regress: Cartoons from the CRITIC. (Illus.). 1979. 10.95 (ISBN 0-88347-093-4). Thomas More.

Wells, John. Situational Supervision for Banks. 1977. text ed. 8.95 (ISBN 0-201-08514-3). A-W.

--Situational Supervision for Business. 1977. pap. text ed. 8.95 (ISBN 0-201-08515-1). A-W.

Wells, Joseph, jt. ed. see How, Walter W.

Wells, Kenneth. Light & Electron Microscopic Studies of Ascobolus Stercorarius: Aseus & Ascosporeontogeny. (U. C. Publ. in Botany: Vol. 62). 1972. pap. 8.50x (ISBN 0-520-09420-4). U of Cal Pr.

Wells, Kenneth M., jt. auth. see Weston, Paul B.

Wells, L. T., jt. auth. see Vernon, R.

Wells, Lawrence. Ole Miss Football: A Photo History. LC 79-92411. (Illus.). 1980. 24.95 (Pub. by Sports Yearbook). Yoknapatawpha.

Wells, Louis T. & Vernon, Raymond. Manager in the International Economy. 4th ed. (Illus.). 1981. text ed. 18.95 (ISBN 0-13-549550-4). P-H.

Wells, Louis T., Jr. & Vernon, Raymond. Economic Environment of International Business. 3rd ed. (Illus.). 272p. 1981. text ed. 13.95 (ISBN 0-13-224329-6). P-H.

Wells, M. Computing Systems Hardware. LC 75-27263. (Cambridge Computer Science Texts Ser.: No. 6). (Illus.). 225p. 1976. 16.95x (ISBN 0-521-29034-1). Cambridge U Pr.

Wells, Malcolm. Gentle Architecture. (Illus.). 192p. 1981. 22.50 (ISBN 0-07-069245-9, P&RB). McGraw.

Wells, Malcolm, jt. auth. see Anderson, Bruce.

Wells, Marian. When Love Is Not Enough. LC 79-4534. 1979. pap. 3.50 (ISBN 0-87123-646-X, 210646). Bethany Fell.

Wells, P. N. T. & Ziskin, Marvin, eds. New Techniques & Instrumentation in Ultrasound. (Clinics in Diagnostic Ultrasound Ser.). (Illus.). 224p. 1980. text ed. 20.50 (ISBN 0-443-08075-5). Churchill.

Wells, P. S. Culture Contact & Culture Change. LC 80-40212. (New Studies in Archaeology). (Illus.). 195p. 1981. 24.95 (ISBN 0-521-22808-5). Cambridge U Pr.

Wells, Paul R. James Barr & the Bible: Critique of a New Liberalism. 1980. pap. 12.00 (ISBN 0-87552-546-6). Presby & Reformed.

Wells, R. O., jt. auth. see Resnikoff, H. L.

Wells, Reuben F. With Caesar's Legions. LC 60-16709. (Illus.). (gr. 7-11). 1951. 8.50x (ISBN 0-8196-0110-1). Biblo.

Wells, Robert. Winter's Task. 63p. (Orig.). 1980. pap. 7.95 (ISBN 0-85635-210-1, Pub. by Carcanet New England Pr). Persea Bks.

Wells, Rosemary. The Fog Comes on Little Pig Feet. (gr. 7 up). 1973. pap. 1.50 o.p. (ISBN 0-380-01192-1, 48249). Avon.

--Leave Well Enough Alone. (gr. 7-10). 1980. pap. 1.95 (ISBN 0-686-42687-8). Archway.

--Stanley & Rhoda. LC 78-51874. (Illus.). 40p. (ps-2). 1981. pap. 2.95 (ISBN 0-8037-7995-X, Pied Piper Bk). Dial.

--Timothy Goes to School. LC 80-20785. (Illus.). 32p. (ps-2). 1981. 7.50 (ISBN 0-8037-8948-3); PLB 7.28 (ISBN 0-8037-8949-1). Dial.

Wells, S., jt. ed. see Muir, K.

Wells, S., jt. ed. see Spencer, T. J.

Wells, S. H., et al. Pharmacological Testing in a Correctional Institution. 76p. 1975. 11.75 (ISBN 0-398-03202-5). C C Thomas.

Wells, Sara J., et al. Manual of Cardiovascular Assessment. 1981. pap. text ed. 14.95 (ISBN 0-8359-4233-3). Reston.

Wells, Sidney W., ed. Shakespeare: Select Bibliographical Guides. 384p. 1974. text ed. 18.95x (ISBN 0-19-871026-7); pap. text ed. 9.95x (ISBN 0-19-871032-1). Oxford U Pr.

Wells, Stanley. Shakespeare: The Writer & His Work. (Illus.). 1979. 8.95 (ISBN 0-684-15983-X, ScribT); pap. 1.95 encore ed. (ISBN 0-684-16932-0, ScribT). Scribner.

Wells, Stanley, ed. English Drama (Excluding Shakespeare) Select Bibliographical Guides. 320p. 1975. text ed. 18.95x (ISBN 0-19-871034-8); pap. text ed. 9.50x (ISBN 0-19-871028-3). Oxford U Pr.

Wells, Stuart. Instructional Technology in Developing Countries: Decision Making Processes in Education. LC 76-24371. (Illus.). 1976. text ed. 23.95 (ISBN 0-275-23750-8). Praeger.

Wells, Susan. Mend Your Own China & Glass. (Illus.). 80p. 1976. 9.50 (ISBN 0-7135-1875-8); pap. 8.95 (ISBN 0-7135-1883-9). Transatlantic.

Wells, Ted & Lamb, Lowry. Scientific Sailboat Racing. rev. ed. LC 79-13553. 1979. 10.95 (ISBN 0-396-07690-4). Dodd.

Wells, Thomas H. The Technique of Electronic Music. 2nd ed. LC 78-8819. (Illus.). 1981. text ed. 25.00 (ISBN 0-02-872830-0). Schirmer Bks.

Wells, Tom H. Confederate Navy: A Study in Organization. LC 72-169496. 1971. 12.50 o.p. (ISBN 0-8173-5105-1). U of Ala Pr.

Wells, Walter. Communications in Business. 2nd ed. 1977. 18.95x (ISBN 0-534-00502-0). Wadsworth Pub.

Wells, William D., ed. see Attitude Research Conference, October, 1974, San Francisco.

Wells, William K. Effigies. (Orig.). 1980. pap. 2.95 (ISBN 0-440-12245-7). Dell.

Wellstone, Paul D. How the Rural Poor Got Power: Narrative of a Grass-Roots Organizer. LC 77-22109. 240p. 1980. pap. text ed. 6.50x (ISBN 0-87023-139-1). U of Mass Pr.

Wellstone, Paul D., jt. auth. see Casper, Barry M.

Wellwarth, George. The Theater of Protest & Paradox: Developments in Avant-Garde Drama. rev. ed. LC 64-16901. 1971. 15.00x (ISBN 0-8147-0432-8); pap. 3.95x (ISBN 0-8147-0433-6). NYU Pr.

Welmers, William E. African Language Structures. LC 70-186108. 1974. 30.00x (ISBN 0-520-02210-6). U of Cal Pr.

--Grammar of Vai. (Publ. in Linguistics Ser: Vol. 84). 1977. pap. 10.75x (ISBN 0-520-09555-3). U of Cal Pr.

Welmers, William E; see Bishop, G. Reginald, Jr.

Wels, Byron. Fire & Theft Security Systems. 2nd ed. (Illus.). 1976. 8.95 o.p. (ISBN 0-8306-6956-6, 956); pap. 5.95 (ISBN 0-8306-5956-0). TAB Bks.

Welsch, Clifford W., ed. see Cshl Banbury Center Report 8 - Hormones & Breast Cancer, et al.

Welsch, Glenn A. Budgeting: Profit Planning & Control. 4th ed. (Illus.). 656p. 1976. 21.95x (ISBN 0-13-085712-2). P-H.

--Cases in Profit Planning & Control. 1970. pap. text ed. 9.95 (ISBN 0-13-118471-7). P-H.

Welsch, Glenn A. & Anthony, Robert N. Fundamentals of Financial Accounting. rev ed. 1977. text ed. 19.00 (ISBN 0-256-01907-X); working papers 6.50 (ISBN 0-256-01958-4); practice set 5.95 (ISBN 0-256-01959-2); study guide 6.00 (ISBN 0-256-01957-6). Irwin.

Welsch, Glenn A. & Harrison, Walter T., Jr. Plaid for Intermediate Accounting, 2 vols. 1977. Vol. 1. pap. 5.50 (ISBN 0-256-02005-1, 01-0776-02); Vol. 2. pap. 4.95 (ISBN 0-256-01988-6, 01-0880-02). Learning Syst.

Welsch, Glenn A., jt. auth. see Anthony, Robert N.

Welsch, Glenn A., et al. Intermediate Accounting. 5th ed. (Illus.). 1979. text ed. 23.95 (ISBN 0-256-02178-3); pap. 6.50x working papers 1-14 (ISBN 0-256-02180-5); pap. 6.50x working papers 15-25 (ISBN 0-256-02181-3); pap. 4.95 study guide (ISBN 0-256-02179-1). Irwin.

--Intermediate Accounting. (Second canadian edition). 1978. text ed. 23.95 (ISBN 0-256-01984-3). Irwin.

Welsch, Janice R., jt. ed. see Conger, Syndy M.

Welsch, Roger. Omaha Tribal Myths & Trickster Tales. LC 80-22636. 350p. 1981. 15.95 (ISBN 0-8040-0700-4, 0700S, SB). Swallow.

Welsford, Enid. Spenser: Fowre Hymnes & Epithalamion: a Study of Edmund Spenser's Doctrine of Love. 1967. 16.50x o.p. (ISBN 0-631-10500-X, Pub. by Basil Blackwell). Biblio Dist.

Welsh, A. N. The Skills of Management. 247p. 1981. 14.95 (ISBN 0-8144-5670-7). Am Mgmt.

Welsh, Alexander. Reflections on the Hero As Quixote. LC 80-8584. 256p. 1981. 15.00x (ISBN 0-691-06465-2). Princeton U Pr.

Welsh, Charles. Bookseller of the Last Century. LC 79-179343. (English Book Trade). Repr. of 1885 ed. lib. bdg. 17.50x (ISBN 0-678-00883-3). Kelley.

Welsh, David, tr. see Buczkowski, Leopold.

Welsh, David, tr. see Konwicki, Tadeusz.

Welsh, Elizabeth, tr. see Von Franz, Marie-Louise.

Welsh, Elizabeth M., et al. Outline of Basic Nursing Care. (Illus.). 1975. pap. text ed. 11.95x (ISBN 0-433-35220-5). Intl Ideas.

Welsh, J. & Elder, J. Introduction to Pascal. 1979. 15.95 (ISBN 0-13-491522-4). P-H.

Welsh, James M., jt. auth. see Brock, D. Heyward.

Welsh, James M., jt. auth. see Kramer, Steven P.

Welsh, James R. Fundamentals of Plant Genetics & Breeding. LC 80-14638. 450p. 1981. text ed. 23.95 (ISBN 0-471-02862-2). Wiley.

Welsh, Robert C., jt. auth. see Benton, Curtis D., Jr.

Welsh, Robert P. Piet Mondrian's Early Career: The Naturalistic Periods. LC 76-23659. (Outstanding Disserations in the Fine Arts Ser.). 1977. lib. bdg. 56.00x (ISBN 0-8240-2738-8). Garland Pub.

Welsh, Stan. Utah Two. (Illus.). 128p. 1981. 27.50 (ISBN 0-912856-65-3). Graphic Arts Ctr.

Welsh, Stuart C. Room for Wonder: Indian Painting During the British Period, 1760 to 1880. LC 78-50093. (Illus.). 192p. 1981. pap. 14.95 (ISBN 0-917418-60-3). Agrinde Pubns. Postponed.

Welsh, William, ed. Survey Research & Public Attitudes in Eastern Europe & the Soviet Union. LC 79-27902. (Pergamon Policy Studies). 550p. Date not set. 47.51 (ISBN 0-08-025958-8). Pergamon.

Welsh, William A., ed. Studying Politics. LC 77-189929. 272p. 1973. pap. 5.95 o.p. (ISBN 0-275-84150-2). Praeger.

Welsome, John. Grand National. 1978. pap. 1.95 o.p. (ISBN 0-449-23578-5, Crest). Fawcett.

Welter, Barbara. Dimity Convictions: The American Woman in the Nineteenth Century. LC 76-8305. 230p. 1976. 12.95x (ISBN 0-8214-0352-4); pap. 5.95x (ISBN 0-8214-0358-3). Ohio U Pr.

Welter, Paul R. The Nursing Home: A Caring Community Staff Manuel. 96p. 1981. pap. 2.95 (ISBN 0-8170-0935-3). Judson.

--The Nursing Home: A Caring Community-Trainers' Manual. 176p. 1981. pap. 9.95 (ISBN 0-8170-0934-5). Judson.

Welter, Rush. The Mind of America, 1820-1860. 576p. 1975. 20.00x (ISBN 0-231-02963-2); pap. 10.00x (ISBN 0-231-08351-3). Columbia U Pr.

--Popular Education & Democratic Thought in America. LC 62-19909. 1963. 25.00x (ISBN 0-231-02560-2); pap. 12.50x (ISBN 0-231-08563-X). Columbia U Pr.

Welter, Rush, ed. American Writings on Popular Education: The 19th Century. LC 73-151611. (American Heritage Ser). 1971. 13.50 (ISBN 0-672-51508-3, AHS-81); pap. 7.95 (ISBN 0-672-60134-6). Bobbs.

Weltman, Gershon & Zuckerman, Marvin, trs. Yiddish Sayings Mama Never Taught You. LC 73-79282. (Perivale Translation Ser.: No. 2). 99p. 1976. pap. 4.95 (ISBN 0-912288-04-3). Perivale Pr.

Weltner, Linda. Beginning to Feel the Magic. 168p. (gr. 6 up). 1981. 8.95 (ISBN 0-316-93052-0). Little.

Weltner, Linda R. The New Voice. LC 80-70414. 192p. Date not set. 12.95 (ISBN 0-8070-3248-4); pap. 5.95 (ISBN 0-8070-3249-2, BP 621). Beacon Pr.

Welty, Edwin C., Jr., jt. auth. see Axelrod, Herbert R.

Welty, Eudora. Bride of the Innisfallen & Other Stories. LC 55-5248. 1972. pap. 3.95 (ISBN 0-15-614075-6, HB227, Harv). HarBraceJ.

--Collected Stories of Eudora Welty. LC 80-7947. 576p. 1980. 17.50 (ISBN 0-15-118994-3). HarBraceJ.

--Losing Battles. LC 78-58857. 416p. 1978. pap. 2.45 (ISBN 0-394-72668-5, Vin). Random.

--The Optimist's Daughter. 208p. Date not set. pap. 2.95 (ISBN 0-394-72667-7, Vin). Random.

--Ponder Heart. LC 54-5248. (Illus.). 1954. 6.95 o.p. (ISBN 0-15-173073-3). HarBraceJ.

Welty, Eudora, jt. auth. see Spencer, Elizabeth.

Welty, James R. Engineering Heat Transfer, SI Version. LC 78-5179. 1978. text ed. 29.95 (ISBN 0-471-02860-6). Wiley.

Welty, James R., et al. Fundamentals of Momentum, Heat & Mass Transfer. 2nd ed. LC 76-16813. 897p. 1976. text ed. 31.95 (ISBN 0-471-93354-6). Wiley.

Welty, Paul T. The Asians: Their Heritage & Their Destiny. 5th ed. LC 76-27357. 1976. pap. text ed. 6.50 scp (ISBN 0-397-47359-1, HarpC). Har-Row.

Welvaart, K., et al, eds. Colorectal Cancer. (Boerhaave Series for Postgraduate Medical Education: No. 18). (Illus.). 290p. 1981. PLB 58.00 (ISBN 90-6021-465-X, Pub. by Leiden U Pr). Kluwer Boston.

Welzen, J. Van see Van Welzen, J.

Wempner, Gerald. Mechanics of Solids with Application to Thin Bodies. (Mechanics of Elastics & Viscoelastic Solids). 620p. 1980. 35.00x (ISBN 90-286-0880-X). Sijthoff & Noordhoff.

Wen, C. Y. & Lee, E. Stanley, eds. Coal Conversion Technology. LC 79-12975. (Energy Science & Technology: No. 2). (Illus.). 1979. text ed. 32.50 (ISBN 0-201-08300-0). A-W.

Wenburg, John R., jt. auth. see Wilmot, William W.

Wende & Devlin. Old Witch Rescues Halloween. (gr. 3-4). 1980. pap. 3.50 incl. record (ISBN 0-590-24006-4, Schol Pap). Schol Bk Serv.

Wende, John R., jt. auth. see Sandberg, Karl C.

Wendel, Natalja. Born in April. LC 74-31096. 1975. 7.95 (ISBN 0-8119-0245-5). Fell.

Wendel, Robert L., jt. auth. see Saucier, Weems A.

Wendel, Tim. Going for the Gold. new ed. (Illus.). 228p. 1980. 10.00 (ISBN 0-88208-116-0). Lawrence Hill.

Wendell, Barrett. Cotton Mather, 30 vols. LC 80-23335. (American Men & Women of Letters). Orig. Title: Cotton Mather: the Puritan Priest. 328p. 1981. pap. 5.95 (ISBN 0-87754-166-3). Chelsea Hse.

--English Composition. 316p. 1980. Repr. of 1903 ed. lib. bdg. 30.00 (ISBN 0-8495-5654-6). Arden Lib.

--Literary History of America. LC 68-30589. 1968. Repr. of 1900 ed. 26.00 (ISBN 0-8103-3226-4). Gale.

Wendell, Berry. A Part. 96p. 1980. 12.50 (ISBN 0-86547-007-3); pap. 6.00 (ISBN 0-86547-008-1). N Point Pr.

Wendell, Carolyn. Alfred Bester. (Starmont Reader's Guide: No. 6). 80p. 1981. Repr. lib. bdg. 9.95x (ISBN 0-89370-037-1). Borgo Pr.

--Reader's Guide to Alfred Bester. Schlobin, Roger C., ed. LC 80-19655. (Reader's Guide to Contemporary Science Fiction & Fantasy Authors Ser.: Vol. 6). (Illus., Orig.). 1980. pap. text ed. 3.95 (ISBN 0-916732-08-8). Starmont Hse.

Wendell, Charles. The Evolution of the Egyptian National Image: From Its Origins to Ahmad Lufti al-Sayyid. 1973. 30.00x (ISBN 0-520-02111-8). U of Cal Pr.

Wendell, Hasan & Al-Banna, Hasan. Five Tracts of Hasan Al-Banna: A Selection from the Majmu'at Rasa'il Al-'imam Al-Shahid Hasan Al-Banna. LC 77-83119. (Publications in Near Eastern Studies: Vol. 20). 1978. pap. 11.50x (ISBN 0-520-09584-7). U of Cal Pr.

Wender, Dorothea, tr. from Latin. Roman Poetry from the Republic to the Silver Age. LC 79-28219. 160p. 1980. 9.95x (ISBN 0-8093-0963-7). S Ill U Pr.

Wender, Herbert. Southern Commercial Conventions Eighteen Thirty-Seven to Eighteen Fifty-Nine. LC 79-1601. 1981. Repr. of 1930 ed. 19.50 (ISBN 0-88355-904-8). Hyperion Conn.

Wender, Paul H. Minimal Brain Dysfunction in Children. LC 77-142142. (Personality Processes Ser). 1971. 26.50 (ISBN 0-471-93362-7). Wiley.

Wenders, John T., ed. see Mountain States Telephone & Telegraph Company.

Wendland, E. H. Of Other Gods & Other Spirits. 1977. pap. 4.95 (ISBN 0-8100-0034-2, 12-1711). Northwest Pub.

Wendland, Ernst H. To Africa with Love. 1974. pap. 6.25 (ISBN 0-8100-0033-4, 12N1710). Northwest Pub.

Wendland, Michael F. The Arizona Project: How a Team of Investigative Reporters Got Revenge on Deadline. 1978. 9.95 o.p. (ISBN 0-8362-0728-9). Andrews & McMeel.

Wendland, W., jt. auth. see Haack, W.

Wendlandt, Wesley W., jt. auth. see Geanangel, Russell A.

Wendt, F. W., et al, eds. Mechanics of Composite Materials: International Conference on the Mechanics & Chemistry & Solid Propellants. 1970. 105.00 (ISBN 0-08-006421-3). Pergamon.

Wendt, Ingrid, jt. auth. see Hedges, Elaine.

Wendt, John F., ed. see International Symposium on Gas-Flow and Chemical Lasers, 2nd, Rhode-St-Genese, Belgium, Sept. 11-15, 1978.

Wendt, Lloyd & Kogan, Herman. Give the Lady What She Wants: The Story of Marshall Fields & Company. LC 52-7501. (Illus.). 1979. pap. 3.95 (ISBN 0-89708-020-3). And Bks.

Wendt, Paul F. Real Estate Appraisal: Review & Outlook. LC 72-97939. 276p. 1974. 14.95x (ISBN 0-8203-0317-8). U of Ga Pr.

Wendzel, Robert L. International Politics: Policymakers & Policymaking. LC 80-36681. 500p. 1981. text ed. 16.95 (ISBN 0-471-05046-6). Wiley.

Weng, Virginia, jt. auth. see Jagendorf, M. A.
Weng, Will. Will Weng's Crossword Puzzles: Fifty Original Sunday-Sized Crossword Puzzles, Vol. 7. 64p. 1980. 3.95 (ISBN 0-8129-0933-X). Times Bks.
--Will Weng's Holiday Puzzles: Fifty Original Sunday-Size Crossword Puzzles with Holiday Themes. 64p. 1980. 3.95 (ISBN 0-8129-0934-8). Times Bks.
Weng, Will, ed. Will Weng's Crossword Puzzles, No. 5. Date not set. pap. cancelled (ISBN 0-8129-0812-0). Times Bks. Postponed.
Wenger, Eliezer. Chagaynu, Vols. 1 & 2. (Illus.). 104p. (gr. 4 up). 1975. Set. pap. text ed. 3.00 (ISBN 0-89655-100-8); wkbk. 0.50 (ISBN 0-89655-101-6); answer key 0.25 (ISBN 0-89655-102-4). BRuach HaTorah.
--Jewish Book of Lists & Summaries, Vol. 2. (gr. 5 up). 1979. pap. 1.00 (ISBN 0-89655-141-5). BRuach HaTorah.
Wenger, J. C. The Family Faith. (No. 10). 72p. 1981. pap. 0.95 (ISBN 0-686-69151-2). Herald Pr.
Wenger, Nanette K. & Hellerstein, H. K. Rehabilitation of the Coronary Patient. LC 78-12531. 1978. 28.00 (ISBN 0-471-93369-4, Pub. by Wiley Medical). Wiley.
Wengrov, Charles. The Book of Sabbath. (Illus.). 1962. 3.00 (ISBN 0-914080-43-1). Shulsinger Sales.
Wenham, Edward, jt. auth. see Ensko, Stephen G.
Wenham, John W. Elements of New Testament Greek. 1966. text ed. 7.50x (ISBN 0-521-09842-4); key 2.50x (ISBN 0-521-06769-3). Cambridge U Pr.
Wenham, Lynette. The Cook & Carry Book. (Illus.). 160p. (Orig.). 1980. pap. 8.95 (ISBN 0-589-01275-4, Pub. by Reed Bks Australia). C E Tuttle.
Weniger, Del. Cacti of the Southwest: Texas, New Mexico, Oklahoma, Arkansas, & Louisiana. (Spencer Foundation Ser.: No. 4). (Illus.). 1970. 29.50 o.p. (ISBN 0-292-70000-8). U of Tex Pr.
Wenk, Arthur B. Claude Debussy & the Poets. LC 74-82854. 1976. 31.50x (ISBN 0-520-02827-9). U of Cal Pr.
Wenk, Edward, Jr. Margins for Survival: Overcoming Political Limits in Steering Technology. LC 78-40932. (Illus.). 1979. 30.00 (ISBN 0-08-023373-2); pap. 13.25 (ISBN 0-08-023372-4). Pergamon.
Wenk, Ernst & Harlow, Nora. Dropout. LC 79-66854. (Dialogue Bks). 128p. (Orig.). 1980. pap. 5.75 (ISBN 0-89881-007-8). Intl Dialogue Pr.
Wenkam, Robert. Kauai, & the Park Country of Hawaii. Brower, Kenneth, ed. (Illus.). 1969. pap. 3.95 o.p. (ISBN 0-345-21557-5). Ballantine.
--Kauai: Hawaii's Garden Island. (Illus.). 1979. 25.00 (ISBN 0-528-81040-5). Rand.
Wenner, Jann. Lennon Remembers. pap. 1.25 o.p. (ISBN 0-445-08191-0). Popular Lib.
Wenner, Manfred W. North Yemen. (Nations of the Contemporary Middle East Ser.). 128p. 1981. lib. bdg. 16.50x (ISBN 0-89158-774-8). Westview.
Wennerstrom, Mary H. Anthology of Twentieth Century Music. 1969. pap. 18.50 (ISBN 0-13-038489-5). P-H.
Wenniger, Mary A. Collagraph Printmaking. (Illus.). 184p. 1980. pap. 10.95 (ISBN 0-8230-0666-2). Watson-Guptill.
Wenninger, M. J. Polyhedron Models. LC 69-10200. (Illus.). 1971. 27.50 (ISBN 0-521-06917-3); pap. 11.95x (ISBN 0-521-09859-9). Cambridge U Pr.
Wenninger, Magnus J. Spherical Models. LC 78-58806. 1979. 22.50 (ISBN 0-521-22279-6); pap. 9.95 (ISBN 0-521-29432-0). Cambridge U Pr.
Wennrich, Peter. Anglo-American & German Abbreviations in Environmental Protection. 624p. 1979. 60.00 (ISBN 0-89664-096-5, Pub. by K G Saur). Gale.
Wenrich, Ralph C. & Wenrich, William J. Leadership in Administration of Vocational & Technical Education. LC 73-86161. 1974. text ed. 20.95 (ISBN 0-675-08878-X). Merrill.
Wenrich, Wes W., et al. Self-Directed Systemic Desensitization. LC 76-9019. (Illus.). 95p. (Orig.). 1980. pap. 7.00 (ISBN 0-917472-05-5). F Fournies.
Wenrich, William J., jt. auth. see Wenrich, Ralph C.
Wensinger, Arthur S., tr. see Gropius, Walter.
Wensley, G. F., jt. auth. see Keay, F.
Went, A. E. Atlantic Salmon: Its Future. 272p. 1980. 52.50x (ISBN 0-85238-103-4, Pub. by Fishing News England). State Mutual Bk.
Went, Frits W. Plants. LC 63-20048. (Life Nature Library). (Illus.). (gr. 5 up). 1963. PLB 8.97 o.p. (ISBN 0-8094-0626-8, Pub. by Time-Life). Silver.
Went, H. A. The Behaviour of Centrioles & the Structure & Formation of the Achromatic Figure. (Protoplasmatologia: Vol. 6, Pt. G1). (Illus.). 1966. pap. 30.70 o.p. (ISBN 0-387-80783-7). Springer-Verlag.
Went, R. W., et al. Phytohormones. (Landmark Reprint in Plant Science Ser.). 1937. text ed. 22.50 (ISBN 0-86598-004-7). Allanheld.
Wentink, S. & Koch, S. UV Curing in Screen Printing for Printed Circuits & the Graphic Arts. 1980. 92.00 (ISBN 0-936840-00-5). Tech Marketing.
Wentling, Tim L. & Lawson, Tom E. Evaluating Occupational Education & Training Programs. 356p. 1975. text ed. 17.95x o.p. (ISBN 0-205-05048-4, 2250489L). Allyn.
Wentworth, Donald R., jt. auth. see Brue, Stanley L.
Wentworth, Eric, ed. Federal Affairs Handbook Nineteen Seventy-Nine to Nineteen Eighty. rev. ed. 1979. pap. 27.50 (ISBN 0-89964-044-3). CASE.
Wentworth, Felix. Handbook of Physical Distribution. 1977. 36.00x o.p. (ISBN 0-8464-0470-2). Beekman Pubs.
Wentworth, Frank L. Aspen on the Roaring Fork. Collman, Russ & Meyers, Stanna, eds. (Illus.). 1976. 30.00 o.p. (ISBN 0-913582-15-8). Sundance.
Wentworth, Harold & Flexner, Stuart B. Dictionary of American Slang. 2nd ed. LC 75-8644. 766p. 1975. 14.95 (ISBN 0-690-00670-5, TYC-T). T Y Crowell.
Wentworth, Michael J. James Tissot, Catalogue: Raisonne of His Prints. (Illus.). 1978. 20.00 (ISBN 0-685-67986-1). Minneapolis Inst Arts.
Wentworth, Patricia. The Fingerprint. 240p. 1980. pap. 1.95 (ISBN 0-553-13948-7). Bantam.
--Poison in the Pen. 208p. 1980. pap. 1.95 (ISBN 0-553-14237-2). Bantam.
Wentworth, Sally. Garden of Thorns. (Harlequin Romances Ser.). 192p. 1980. pap. 1.25 o.p. (ISBN 0-373-02361-8, Pub. by Harlequin). PB.
--Race Against Love. (Harlequin Presents Ser.). 192p. (Orig.). 1981. pap. 1.50 (ISBN 0-373-10414-6, Pub. by Harlequin). PB.
--Say Hello to Yesterday. (Harlequin Presents Ser.). 192p. 1981. pap. 1.50 (ISBN 0-373-10426-X, Pub. by Harlequin). PB.
--Set the Stars on Fire. (Harlequin Presents Ser.). 192p. 1980 (ISBN 0-373-10389-1, Pub. by Harlequin). pap. 1.50 (ISBN 0-686-68314-5). PB.
Wentworth, Wayne, jt. auth. see Becker, Ralph.
Wentworth, Wayne E., jt. auth. see Becker, Ralph S.
Wentz, Abdel R. & Lehmann, eds. Luther's Works, Vol. 36: Word & Sacrament II. LC 55-9893. 400p. 1959. 16.95 (ISBN 0-8006-0336-2, 1-336). Fortress.
Wentz, Bud. Paper Movie Machines. 1975. pap. 3.50 (ISBN 0-912300-57-4, 57-4). Troubador Pr.
Wentz, Frank M. Principles & Practice of Periodontics: With an Atlas of Treatment. (American Lecture in Dentistry). (Illus.). 320p. 1978. 42.75 (ISBN 0-398-03672-1). C C Thomas.
Wentz, Walter B. Cases in Marketing Research. 290p. 1975. pap. text ed. 10.95 scp (ISBN 0-06-047008-9, HarpC). Har-Row.
--Marketing. (Illus.). 1979. text ed. 18.50 (ISBN 0-8299-0227-9); study guide 6.95 (ISBN 0-8299-0263-5); instr.' manual avail. (ISBN 0-8299-0581-2). West Pub.
Wentzel, Kenneth B. Hospice Means Hope. 1980. 9.95 (ISBN 0-89182-020-5); pap. text ed. 4.95 (ISBN 0-89182-030-2). Charles River Bks.
Wentzell, Melinda & Holland, D. K. Optricks. (Illus.). 40p. 1973. pap. 2.25 (ISBN 0-912300-34-5, 34-5). Troubador Pr.
--Optricks Two. (Illus.). 40p. 1974. pap. 2.25 (ISBN 0-912300-51-5, 51-5). Troubador Pr.
Wentzlaff-Eggebert, Friedrich-Wilhelm. Belehrung und Verkuendigung: Schriften zur deutschen Literatur vom Mittelalter bis zur Neuzeit. Dick, Manfred & Kaiser, Gerhard, eds. 344p. 1975. 85.30x (ISBN 3-11-005714-X). De Gruyter.
Wenzel, Bill. Do I Have a Girl for You? 1978. pap. 1.50 (ISBN 0-505-51232-7). Tower Bks.
Wenzel, David. Kingdom of the Dwarfs. Walsh, Robb. (Illus.). 144p. (Orig.). 1980. pap. 8.95 (ISBN 0-87818-017-6). Centaur.
Wenzel, George. Blueprint for Restaurant Success. 1973. 21.50 (ISBN 0-8436-2001-3). CBI Pub.
Wenzel, Gerhard, jt. auth. see Nitzsche, Werner.
Wenzel, Gertrude. Granny. (Illus.). 272p. 1981. 12.50 (ISBN 0-682-49694-4). Exposition.
Wenzel, K., jt. ed. see Stringer, Peter.
Wenzel, William J. Motivation Training Manual. 272p. 1970. 22.50 (ISBN 0-8436-0599-5). CBI Pub.
Wenzel, William, Jr. Wenzel's Menu Maker. 2nd ed. LC 79-13732. 1979. 99.95 (ISBN 0-8436-2135-4). CBI Pub.
Wepman, Dennis, et al. The Life: The Lore & Folk Poetry of the Black Hustler. LC 76-12047. 1976. 15.00 (ISBN 0-8122-7710-4); pap. 5.95x (ISBN 0-8122-1089-1). U of Pa Pr.
Wepner, Gabriella. Basic Mathematics. 1981. write for info. Franklin Inst Pr.
Werble, Beatrice, jt. auth. see Grinker, Roy R., Sr.
Werblowsky, Zui. Beyond Tradition & Modernity: Changing Religions in a Changing World. (Jordan Lectures in Comparative Religion, 11th Ser.). 146p. 1976. text ed. 16.25x (ISBN 0-485-17411-1, Athlone Pr). Humanities.
Werder, Hans. Zum Problem der Begabung und Intelligenz. (Psychologische Praxis: Vol. 55). 190p. 1980. pap. 17.00 (ISBN 3-8055-1123-X). S Karger.
Werevka, Robert, Jr. & Seller, Charles E. Hanger Eighteen. 176p. (Orig.). 1980. pap. 2.25 (ISBN 0-553-14473-1). Bantam.
Werf, Tjeerd van der see Van der Werf, Tjeerd.
Werfel, Franz. Jacobowsky & der Oberst. Arlt, Gustave O., ed. (Illus., Orig., Ger.). 1961. pap. text ed. 3.95x (ISBN 0-89197-250-1). Irvington.
Werff, T. J. Van Der see Collins, R. & Van Der Werff, T. J.
Wergin, Joseph P. How to Win at Cribbage. 1980. 10.95 (ISBN 0-87691-304-4). Winchester Pr.
Werhare, P., jt. auth. see Donaldson, T.
Werkmeister, W. H., ed. Facets of Plato's Philosophy. 1976. pap. text ed. 21.75x (ISBN 90-232-1362-9). Humanities.
Werkmeister, William H. A History of Philosophical Ideas in America. LC 80-24507. xvi, 599p. 1981. Repr. of 1949 ed. lib. bdg. 49.75x (ISBN 0-313-22743-8, WEHI). Greenwood.
Werler, John E., jt. auth. see Tennant, Alan.
Werley, Judith G., ed. The Artist... & the Legend: A Visit to China Is Remembered & the Legends Unfold... LC 74-81927. (Illus.). (gr. 7 up). 1974. 20.00x (ISBN 0-933652-09-7). Domjan Studio.
Werlich, David P. Peru: A Short History. LC 77-17107. (Illus.). 447p. 1978. 24.95 (ISBN 0-8093-0830-4). S Ill U Pr.
Werlich, R. Russian Orders, Decorations & Medals. 2nd ed. (Illus.). 1981. 36.00 (ISBN 0-685-90818-6). Quaker.
Werlin, Mark, jt. auth. see Werlin, Marvin.
Werlin, Marvin & Werlin, Mark. The St. Clair Summer. 1981. 13.95 (ISBN 0-453-00395-8, H395). NAL.
--The Savior. 1980. pap. 2.75 (ISBN 0-440-17748-0). Dell.
Wermuth, Mary L. Images of Michigan. LC 80-80509. (gr. 6-8). 1981. text ed. 15.65 (ISBN 0-910726-12-4). Hillsdale Educ.
Wermuth, Paul G. Bayard Taylor. (U. S. Authors Ser.: No. 228). 1973. lib. bdg. 10.95 (ISBN 0-8057-0718-2). Twayne.
Wernecke, Herbert. When Loved Ones Are Called Home. (Ultra Bks Ser). 3.95 (ISBN 0-8010-9504-2); pap. 1.50 (ISBN 0-8010-9513-1). Baker Bk.
Werner, jt. auth. see Wilson.
Werner, A. E., jt. auth. see Plenderleith, H. J.
Werner, Alfred. Degas Pastels. (Illus.). 1977. pap. 8.95 o.p. (ISBN 0-8230-1276-X). Watson-Guptill.
Werner, Chalmers, ed. see Ball, J. Dyer.
Werner, Charles. Reading to Learn: A Unit Approach. LC 74-30264. 400p. 1975. pap. 12.95 (ISBN 0-87909-701-9); instrs'. manual avail. Reston.
Werner, Dietrich, ed. The Biology of Diatoms. LC 76-55574. (Botanical Monographs: Vol. 13). 1977. 48.50x (ISBN 0-520-03400-7). U of Cal Pr.
Werner, Donald L., ed. Light & Lens: Methods of Photography. LC 73-84659. (Illus.). 80p. 1973. pap. 8.00 (ISBN 0-87100-043-1, Pub. by Hudson River Mus). Pub Ctr Cult Res.
Werner, E. T. Chinese Weapons. Alston, Pat, ed. (Series 308). (Illus.). 1972. pap. 4.95 (ISBN 0-89750-036-9). Ohara Pubns.
Werner, Eric. The Sacred Bridge. (Music Reprint Ser.). 1979. Repr. of 1959 ed. lib. bdg. 42.50 (ISBN 0-306-79581-7). Da Capo.
Werner, Gary. Burning Wood. (Illus.). 1980. softcover 6.00 (ISBN 0-686-64446-8); lib. bdg. 10.00 (ISBN 0-915262-53-3). S J Durst.
Werner, Gottfried, jt. auth. see Fischer, Helmut A.
Werner, Hofmann. Turning Points in Twentieth Century Art: 1890-1917. (Illus.). 1966. 15.00 o.s.i. (ISBN 0-8076-0456-9). Braziller.
Werner, Jack, ed. see Shaw, George B.
Werner, Jane. Animal Friends. (ps-3). 1953. PLB 4.57 o.p. (ISBN 0-307-60560-4, Golden Pr). Western Pub.
--The Fuzzy Duckling. (ps-1). 1949. PLB 5.00 (ISBN 0-307-60557-4, Golden Pr). Western Pub.
--The Fuzzy Duckling. (ps-1). 1949. 1.95 (ISBN 0-307-10841-4, Golden Pr); PLB 7.62 (ISBN 0-307-60841-7). Western Pub.
--Smokey the Bear. (Illus.). (ps-3). 1955. PLB 5.00 (ISBN 0-307-60481-0, Golden Pr). Western Pub.
--The Tall Book of Make-Believe. (Tall Bks.). (Illus.). 92p. (gr. k-3). 1980. 5.95 (ISBN 0-06-026505-1, HarpJ); PLB 6.89 (ISBN 0-06-026506-X). Har-Row.
Werner, Joan K. Neuroscience: A Clinical Perspective. LC 79-64779. (Illus.). 225p. 1980. text ed. 13.95 (ISBN 0-7216-9116-1). Saunders.
Werner, Mario, ed. Microtechniques for the Clinical Laboratory: Concepts & Applications. LC 75-34373. 1976. 51.50 (ISBN 0-471-93370-8, Pub. by Wiley Medical). Wiley.
Werner, Mario, jt. ed. see Goldberg, David M.
Werner, O. James. Manual for Prison Law Libraries. (A. A. L. L. Publication Ser.: No. 12). 117p. 1976. text ed. 12.50x (ISBN 0-8377-0110-4). Rothman.
Werner, Oswald. On the Limits of Social Science Theory. (PDR Press Publication in Ethnoscience Ser.: No. 1). 1975. pap. text ed. 1.00x o.p. (ISBN 90-316-0045-8). Humanities.
Werner, Percy. Sales Tax Strategies of Wisconsin Businesses. Fischer-Williams, M., ed. LC 80-65336. 94p. (Orig.). 1980. pap. 12.75 (ISBN 0-936400-01-3). Gearhart-Edwards.
Werner, Peter H. & Burton, Elsie. Learning Through Movement: Teaching Cognitive Content Through Physical Activities. LC 78-11895. (Illus.). 1979. pap. text ed. 10.95 (ISBN 0-8016-5415-7). Mosby.
Werner, Peter H. & Rini, Lisa. Perceptual Motor Development Equipment: Inexpensive Ideas & Activities. LC 75-43744. 160p. 1976. text ed. 12.50 (ISBN 0-471-93371-6). Wiley.
Werner, Raymond J., jt. auth. see Kratovil, Robert.
Werner, Robert G. Freshwater Fishes of New York State: A Field Guide. (Illus.). 270p. 1980. 20.00s (ISBN 0-8156-2233-3); pap. 11.95 (ISBN 0-8156-2222-8). Syracuse U Pr.
Werner, Ruth M. Public Financing of Voluntary Agency Foster Care Programs. LC 76-54383. (Orig.). 1976. pap. 3.95 (ISBN 0-87868-163-9). Child Welfare.
Werner, S. Benson, jt. auth. see Austin, Donald F.
Werner, Sarah, et al. Atlas of Neonatal Electroencephalography. LC 77-83692. 1977. 81.00 (ISBN 0-89004-080-X). Raven.
Werner-Beland, Jean A. Grief Response for the Critically Ill. (Illus.). 1980. text ed. 13.95 (ISBN 0-8359-2591-9); pap. text ed. 9.95 (ISBN 0-8359-2590-0). Reston.
Wernham, R. B. The Making of Elizabethan Foreign Policy, 1558-1603. (Illus.). 120p. 1981. 15.50x (ISBN 0-520-03966-1); pap. 3.95x (ISBN 0-520-03974-2, CAMPUS 244). U of Cal Pr.
Wernick, J. H., jt. auth. see Shay, J. L.
Wernick, Robert. Blitzkreig. LC 76-25750. (World War II). (Illus.). (gr. 6 up). 1976. PLB 14.94 (ISBN 0-8094-2455-X, Pub by Time-Life). Silver.
--Blitzkrieg. Time-Life Books, ed. (World War II Ser.). 1976. 12.95 (ISBN 0-8094-2454-1). Time-Life.
--The Family. (Human Behavior Ser.). 1974. 9.95 (ISBN 0-8094-1908-4); lib. bdg. avail. (ISBN 0-685-50862-5). Time-Life.
--The Family. LC 74-17706. (Human Behavior Ser.). (Illus.). 1974. lib. bdg. 9.99 o.p. (ISBN 0-686-51075-5). Silver.
--The Monument Builders. (The Emergence of Man Ser.). (Illus.). 160p. 1973. 9.95 (ISBN 0-8094-1312-4); lib. bdg. avail. (ISBN 0-685-48123-9). Time-Life.
--The Monument Builders. LC 73-88012. (gr. 6 up). 1973. PLB 9.63 o.p. (ISBN 0-8094-1313-2, Pub. by Time-Life). Silver.
--The Vikings. (The Seafarers Ser.). (Illus.). 1979. lib. bdg. 14.94 (ISBN 0-686-50990-0). Silver.
Wernick, Saul. The Hero. (Orig.). 1981. pap. write for info. (ISBN 0-671-82689-1). PB.
Werning, David & Werning, Mary K. The Mistake Proof Earth Shelter Handbook. (Illus.). 160p. 1981. price not set (ISBN 0-89196-087-2, Domus Bks); pap. price not set. Quality Bks IL.
Werning, Mary K., jt. auth. see Werning, David.
Wernstedt, Frederick L. & Spencer, Joseph E. The Philippine Island World: A Physical, Cultural & Regional Geography. (California Library Reprint Ser.). 1978. 38.50x (ISBN 0-520-03513-5). U of Cal Pr.
Weron, A., ed. Probability Theory an Vector Spaces II: Proceedings. (Lecture Notes in Mathematics Ser.: Vol. 828). 324p. 1981. pap. 19.50 (ISBN 0-387-10253-1). Springer-Verlag.
Werry, John S., jt. auth. see Quay, Herbert C.
Wersba, Barbara. Twenty-Six Starlings Will Fly Through Your Mind. LC 77-3811. (Illus.). 40p. 1980. 8.95 (ISBN 0-06-026376-8, HarpJ); PLB 8.79 (ISBN 0-06-026377-6). Har-Row.
Wershow, Harold J. Controversial Issues in Gerontology. 1981. text ed. price not set (ISBN 0-8261-3100-X); pap. text ed. price not set (ISBN 0-8261-3101-8). Springer Pub.

Werstein, Irving. Boxer Rebellion: Anti-Foreign Terror Seizes China. LC 79-172448. (World Focus Bks). (Illus.). (gr. 7 up). 1971. PLB 4.90 o.p. (ISBN 0-531-02150-5). Watts.
--Land & Liberty: The Mexican Revolution (1910-1919) (Illus.). 192p. (gr. 7 up). 1971. 5.95 o.p. (ISBN 0-8092-8692-0); PLB avail o.p. (ISBN 0-685-28674-6). Contemp Bks.
--Many Faces of the Civil War. LC 61-14461. (Illus.). (gr. 7 up). 1961. PLB 4.79 o.p. (ISBN 0-671-32484-5). Messner.
--Strangled Voices: The Story of the Haymarket Affair. LC 76-89595. (Illus.). (gr. 5-9). 1970. 4.95g o.s.i. (ISBN 0-02-792560-9). Macmillan.
Wert, James E. & Henderson, Glenn V. Financing Business Firms. 6th ed. 1979. text ed. 18.95 (ISBN 0-256-02182-1). Irwin.
Wert, William F. Van see Van Wert, William F.
Wert, William Van see Van Wert, William.
Wertelecki, Wladimir & Plato, Chris C., eds. Dermatoglyphics Fifty Years Later. LC 79-2595. (Alan R. Liss Ser.: Vol. 15, No. 6). 1979. 76.00 (ISBN 0-8451-1031-4). March of Dimes.
Wertenbaker, Charles. Before They Were Men. Repr. of 1931 ed. 8.00x o.p. (ISBN 0-685-84015-8). Va Bk.
Wertenbaker, Lael. World of Picasso. (Library of Art). (Illus.). 1967. 15.95 (ISBN 0-8094-0242-4). Time-Life.
--World of Picasso. LC 67-30587. (Library of Art Ser.). (Illus.). (gr. 6 up). 1967. 12.96 (ISBN 0-8094-0271-8, Pub. by Time-Life). Silver.
Wertenbaker, Lael, jt. auth. see Rosenthal, Jean.
Werth, Alexander. France & Munich. LC 68-9632. 1969. Repr. of 1939 ed. 14.25 (ISBN 0-86527-071-6). Fertig.
--The Twilight of France, 1933-1940. 21.00 (ISBN 0-86527-199-2). Fertig.
Werth, Kurt & Watts, Mabel. Molly & the Giant. LC 72-6076. (Illus.). 48p. (gr. k-3). 1973. 5.95 o.s.i. (ISBN 0-8193-0638-X, Four Winds); PLB 5.41 o.s.i. (ISBN 0-8193-0639-8). Schol Bk Serv.
Wertham, F. Sign for Cain. 1966. 12.95 (ISBN 0-02-625970-2). Macmillan.
Wertheim, Arthur F. Radio Comedy. LC 78-10679. (Illus.). 1979. 19.95 (ISBN 0-19-502481-8). Oxford U Pr.
Wertheim, Arthur Frank. The New York Little Renaissance: Iconoclasm, Modernism, & Nationalism in American Culture, 1908-1917. LC 75-21805. 1976. 17.50x (ISBN 0-8147-9164-6). NYU Pr.
Wertheim, S., jt. auth. see Gross, Theodore L.
Wertheim, Willem F. Indonesian Society in Transition: A Study of Social Change. LC 78-14150. 1981. Repr. of 1959 ed. 27.50 (ISBN 0-88355-823-8). Hyperion Conn.
--Indonesian Society in Transition: A Study of Social Change. LC 80-19660. (Illus.). xiv, 394p. 1980. Repr. of 1959 ed. lib. bdg. 29.75x (ISBN 0-313-22578-8, WEIO). Greenwood.
Wertheimer, A. A Pharmacy Practice. 2nd ed. 1981. 24.50 (ISBN 0-8391-0801-X). Univ Park.
Wertheimer, Barbara M. & Nelson, Ann H. Trade Union Women: A Study of Their Participation in New York City Locals. LC 74-32398. (Special Studies). (Illus.). 206p. 1975. text ed. 24.95 (ISBN 0-275-05850-6). Praeger.
Wertheimer, Douglas, jt. auth. see Freeman, R. B.
Wertheimer, Leonard. Books in Other Languages. 4th ed. 1979. pap. 40.00 (ISBN 0-89664-147-3, Pub. by K G Saur). Gale.
Wertheimer, Micheal, jt. auth. see Bauer, Marianne.
Wertheimer, Richard F., II & Zedlewski, Sheila R. The Impact of Demographic Change on the Distribution of Earned Income & the AFDC Program: 1979-1985. (An Institute Paper). 96p. 1977. pap. 3.50 (ISBN 0-87766-179-0, 16200). Urban Inst.
Werther, William & Davis, Keith. Personnel Management. (Illus.). 528p. (Orig.). text ed. 18.95x (ISBN 0-07-069436-2); instructor's manual & test bank. write for info. (ISBN 0-07-069437-0). McGraw.
Werthman, Michael S., jt. ed. see Cantor, Norman F.
Wertsch, James V., tr. from Rus. The Concept of Activity in Soviet Psychology. 1981. 30.00 (ISBN 0-87332-158-8). M E Sharpe.
Wertsman, Vladimir, ed. The Romanians in America & Canada: A Guide to Information Sources. LC 80-191. (Gale Information Guide Library, Ethnic Information Guide Ser.: Vol. 5). 175p. 1980. 30.00 (ISBN 0-8103-1417-7). Gale.
Wertsman, Vladimir, jt. ed. see Sokolyszyn, Aleksander.
Wertz, J. E., jt. auth. see Henderson, B.
Wertz, Richard W., ed. Readings on Ethical & Social Issues in Biomedicine. 320p. 1973. pap. 11.95 ref. ed. (ISBN 0-13-755884-8). P-H.
Wery, Mary K., jt. auth. see Soltow, Martha J.
Werz, James R., ed. Spacecraft Attitude Determination & Control. (Astrophysics & Space Science Library: No. 73). 858p. 1980. PLB 52.00 (ISBN 90-277-0959-9, Pub. by D. Reidel); pap. 28.95 (ISBN 90-277-1204-2). Kluwer Boston.
Wesche, Alice M. Runs Far, Son of the Chichimecs. (gr. 3-7). 1981. pap. 5.95 (ISBN 0-89013-133-3). Museum NM Pr.
Weschler, Judith. Cezanne in Perspective. (Artists in Perspective Ser). (Illus.). 192p. 1975. 8.95 o.p. (ISBN 0-13-123356-4, Spec); pap. 1.95 o.p. (ISBN 0-13-123349-1). P-H.
Weslager, C. A. The Delaware Indians: A History. (Illus.). 576p. 1972. 35.00 (ISBN 0-8135-0702-2). Rutgers U Pr.
--Delawares: A Critical Bibliography. LC 78-3250. (The Newberry Library Center for the History of the American Indian Bibliographical Ser.). 96p. 1978. pap. 4.95x (ISBN 0-253-31680-4). Ind U Pr.
--The English on the Delaware: Sixteen Ten to Sixteen Eighty-Two. 1967. 19.50 (ISBN 0-8135-0548-8). Rutgers U Pr.
--The Log Cabin in America: From Pioneer Days to the Present. (Illus.). 1969. 23.00 (ISBN 0-8135-0596-8). Rutgers U Pr.
Weslager, Clinton A. Dutch Explorers, Traders & Settlers in the Delaware Valley. LC 61-5543. 1964. 10.00x o.p. (ISBN 0-8122-7262-5). U of Pa Pr.
Wesley, Claire, jt. auth. see Wesley, Frank.
Wesley, Edgar B. Our United States...Its History in Maps. rev. ed. (Illus.). 96p. 1980. pap. text ed. 9.10x (ISBN 0-87453-001-6, 81001). Denoyer.
Wesley, Frank & Sullivan, Edith. Human Growth & Development: Psychological Maturation & Socialization. LC 79-21929. 1980. text ed. 19.95x (ISBN 0-87705-445-2); pap. text ed. 9.95x (ISBN 0-87705-446-0). Human Sci Pr.
Wesley, Frank & Wesley, Claire. Sex-Role Psychology. LC 77-1308. 1977. text ed. 22.95 (ISBN 0-87705-307-3); pap. 8.95 (ISBN 0-87705-357-X). Human Sci Pr.
Wesley, George. Spare the Rod. LC 78-57982. 1978. pap. text ed. 9.00 (ISBN 0-8191-0660-7). U Pr of Amer.
Wesley, George R. A History of Hysteria. LC 79-51464. 1979. pap. text ed. 9.00 (ISBN 0-8191-0751-4). U Pr of Amer.
--A Primer of Misbehavior: An Introduction to Abnormal Psychology. LC 70-185995. 216p. 1972. 12.95 (ISBN 0-911012-21-4). Nelson-Hall.
--A Primer of Misbehavior: An Introduction to Abnormal Psychology. (Quality Paperback: No. 262). 203p. 1975. pap. 3.50 (ISBN 0-8226-0262-8). Littlefield.
Wesley, James. Diamond Range. 192p. (YA) 1975. 5.95 (ISBN 0-685-52911-8, Avalon). Bouregy.
--Showdown at Eureka. (YA) 1978. 5.954 (ISBN 0-685-85782-4, Avalon). Bouregy.
--Showdown at the MB Ranch. 192p. (YA) 1976. 5.95 (ISBN 0-685-66575-5, Avalon). Bouregy.
Wesley, James P. Ecophysics: The Application of Physics to Ecology. (Illus.). 368p. 1974. 26.75 (ISBN 0-398-02959-8); pap. 18.50 (ISBN 0-398-03077-4). C C Thomas.
Wesley, Roland. So You Think You Want to Be in the Helping Profession As a Community Organizer. LC 80-65603. 135p. 1981. perfect bdg. 11.50 (ISBN 0-86548-059-1). Century Twenty One.
Wesley-Smith, P. The Unequal Treaty Eighteen Ninety-Seven to Nineteen Ninety-Seven. (East Asian Historical Monographs). (Illus.). 296p. 26.00 (ISBN 0-19-580436-8). Oxford U Pr.
Wesling, Donald. The Chances of Rhyme: Device & Modernity. 1980. 14.75x (ISBN 0-520-03861-4). U of Cal Pr.
Wesling, Donald, jt. auth. see Engberg, Robert.
Wesolowki, Wlodsimierz. Classes, Strata & Power. (International Library of Sociology). 1979. 20.00 (ISBN 0-7100-8845-0). Routledge & Kegan.
Wesolowski, Wlodzimierz, et al, eds. Social Mobility in Comparative Perspective. Bogdan W., tr. LC 79-313623. (Illus.). 319p. 1978. 27.50x (ISBN 0-8002-2284-9). Intl Pubns Serv.
Wesolowsky, George O. Multiple Regression & Analysis of Variance: An Introduction for Computer Users in Management & Economics. LC 76-5884. 1976. 31.95 (ISBN 0-471-93373-2, Pub. by Wiley-Interscience). Wiley.
Wessel, Andrew E. Computer-Aided Information Retrieval. LC 74-32146. (Information Sciences Ser). 208p. 1975. text ed. 23.95 (ISBN 0-471-93376-7, Pub. by Wiley-Interscience). Wiley.
--Implementation of Complex Information Systems. LC 79-9892. (Information Sciences Ser.). 1979. 23.95 (ISBN 0-471-02661-1, Pub. by Wiley-Interscience). Wiley.
--The Social Use of Information: Ownership & Access. LC 76-18211. (Information Sciences Ser.). 1976. 25.50 (ISBN 0-471-93377-5, Pub. by Wiley-Interscience). Wiley.
Wessel, Helen, ed. see Dick-Read, Grantly.
Wessel, Janet A., jt. auth. see MacIntyre, Christine M.
Wessel, Milton R. Freedom's Edge: The Computer Threat to Society. (Illus.). 200p. 1974. pap. 8.95 (ISBN 0-201-08543-7). A-W.
Wessel, Milton R., jt. auth. see Gilchrist, Bruce.
Wessell, Nils, jt. ed. see Kirk, Grayson.
Wessells, Katharine T. Golden Song Book. (Illus.). (gr. 1-2). 1945. PLB 9.15 o.p. (ISBN 0-307-65708-6, Golden Pr). Western Pub.
Wessells, Michael G., jt. auth. see Donahoe, John W.
Wessells, Norman K. Tissue Interactions & Development. LC 76-42696. 1977. pap. text ed. 12.95 (ISBN 0-8053-9620-9). Benjamin-Cummings.
Wessells, Norman K., intro. by. Vertebrate Structures & Functions: Readings from Scientific American. LC 73-17004. (Illus.). 1974. text ed. 19.95x (ISBN 0-7167-0890-6); pap. text ed. 9.95x (ISBN 0-7167-0889-2). W H Freeman.
Wesselow, M. R. De see De Wesselow, M. R.
Wessels, N. K. & Center, Elizabeth M., eds. Vertebrates: A Laboratory Text. (Illus.). 250p. 1975. pap. 10.75 (ISBN 0-913232-26-2). W Kaufmann.
Wessler, Richard L., jt. auth. see Wessler, Ruth A.
Wessler, Ruth A. & Wessler, Richard L. The Principles & Practice of Rational-Emotive Therapy. LC 80-8319. (Social & Behavioral Science Ser.). 1980. text ed. 14.95x (ISBN 0-87589-473-9). Jossey-Bass.
Wesson, Donald R. & Smith, David E. Barbiturates: Their Use, Misuse & Abuse. LC 76-41079. 224p. 1977. text ed. 16.95 (ISBN 0-87705-249-2); pap. 8.95 (ISBN 0-87705-314-6). Human Sci Pr.
Wesson, Robert. The Aging of Communism. LC 80-1600. 180p. 1980. 19.95 (ISBN 0-03-057053-0). Praeger.
Wesson, Robert, ed. The Soviet Union: Looking to the 1980s. (Special Project Ser.). 298p. 1980. 25.00 (ISBN 0-8179-4251-3). Hoover Inst Pr.
Wesson, Robert G. Communism & Communist Systems. 1978. pap. 10.50 ref. (ISBN 0-13-153437-8). P-H.
--Foreign Policy for a New Age. LC 76-13999. (Illus.). 1976. pap. text ed. 17.95 (ISBN 0-395-24652-0). HM.
--The Imperial Order. 1967. 32.50x (ISBN 0-520-01325-5). U. of Cal Pr.
--Lenin's Legacy: The Story of the CPSU. Staar, Richard F., ed. LC 77-92341. (Publications Ser. No. 192: Histories of Ruling Communist Parties). 1978. pap. 7.50 (ISBN 0-8179-6922-5). Hoover Inst Pr.
--State Systems: International Pluralism, Politics, & Culture. LC 77-84945. 1978. 17.95 (ISBN 0-02-934940-0). Free Pr.
West, tr. see Mueller, F. Max.
West, Aille X. Trucks at the Track. (Pal Paperbacks, - Pal Skills II Ser.). (Illus.). (gr. 5-12). 1980. pap. text ed. 1.25 (ISBN 0-8374-6806-X). Xerox Ed Pubns.
West, Allan M. The National Education Association: The Power Base for Education. LC 80-66130. 1980. 15.95 (ISBN 0-02-934880-3). Free Pr.
West, Amanda W. Glenrose Calling. 1979. pap. 2.50 (ISBN 0-515-05081-4). Jove Pubns.
West, Anthony J. The American Family Christian Philosophy of Life. (Illus.). 1979. 37.75 (ISBN 0-89266-203-4). Am Classical Coll Pr.
West, B. B., et al. Food for Fifty. 6th ed. LC 78-21921. 1979. text ed. 21.95 (ISBN 0-471-02688-3). Wiley.
West, Betty M. Diabetic Menus, Meals & Recipes. LC 76-53412. 1978. 8.95 (ISBN 0-385-04651-0). Doubleday.
West, Bill. West Arms Library of Big-5, U. S. Arms Manufacturers, 5 vols. (Illus.). 1977. Set. 149.00 (ISBN 0-685-27896-4). Vol. 1 (ISBN 0-911614-12-5). Vol. 2 (ISBN 0-911614-07-9). Vol. 3 (ISBN 0-911614-08-7). Vol. 4 (ISBN 0-911614-10-9). Vol. 5 (ISBN 0-911614-05-2). B West.
West, Bill W., jt. auth. see Mietus, Norbert J.
West, Celeste, ed. Feminist Erotica. (Illus., Orig.). 1981. 20.00 (ISBN 0-685-96697-6). Booklegger Pr.
West, Charles C. Power to Be Human: Toward a Secular Theology. 1971. 7.95 o.s.i. (ISBN 0-02-626060-3). Macmillan.
West, Christopher J. Inflation: A Management Guide to Company Survival. 155p. 1976. 26.50 (ISBN 0-470-15087-4). Halsted Pr.
West, D. & Woodman, T., eds. Creative Imitation & Latin Literature. LC 79-1181. 1980. 36.00 (ISBN 0-521-22668-6). Cambridge U Pr.
West, D., jt. ed. see Woodman, A. J.
West, D. J. & Farrington, D. P. The Delinquent Way of Life. LC 76-41090. 1977. 18.00x (ISBN 0-8448-1033-9). Crane-Russak Co.
West, David & Wood, Glenn. Personal Financial Management. LC 75-172124. 80p. (Orig.). 1972. text ed. 18.95 (ISBN 0-395-12428-X, 3-59690); tchr's. manual. pap. 1.75 (ISBN 0-395-13495-1, 3-59691). HM.
West, E. G. Non-Public School Aid: The Law, Economics & Politics of American Education. LC 75-31289. 256p. 1976. 18.95x (ISBN 0-669-00337-9). Lexington Bks.
West, Edith, jt. auth. see Fraser, Dorothy M.
West, Edwin G. & Miller, Roger L. Canadian Economics Today, Vol. 1: The Macro View. 1978. pap. text ed. 11.50 scp (ISBN 0-685-86365-4, HarpC); tchr's ed. avail. (ISBN 0-06-385472-4); scp study guide 6.50 (ISBN 0-06-385474-0). Har-Row.
West, Elliott, jt. ed. see Morris, Margaret F.
West, Elliott, jt. ed. see Philp, Kenneth R.
West, Elmer H. How to Sell a Dealership. 64p. (Orig.). 1980. pap. 7.95 (ISBN 0-682-49645-6). Exposition.
West, Emerson R. Profiles of the Presidents. LC 80-10455. 328p. 1980. 7.95 (ISBN 0-87747-800-7). Deseret Bk.
West, F. J. Justiciarship in England 1066-1232. (Cambridge Studies in Medieval Life & Thought: No. 12). 1966. 42.95 (ISBN 0-521-06772-3). Cambridge U Pr.
West, G. D. Index of Proper Names in French Arthurian Verse Romances, 1150-1300. LC 70-443975. (Romance Ser). 1969. 15.00x o.p. (ISBN 0-8020-5226-6). U of Toronto Pr.
West, Geoffrey. All About Your Cat's Health. (All About Ser.). (Illus.). 176p. 1980. 16.50 (ISBN 0-7207-1277-7, Pub. by Michael Joseph). Merrimack Bk Serv.
West, Geoffrey, ed. Black's Veterinary Dictionary. 13th ed. (Illus.). 906p. 1979. 27.50x (ISBN 0-389-20125-1). B&N.
West, Helen L. Adopted Four & Had One More. 1968. 3.50 o.p. (ISBN 0-8272-0001-3). Bethany Pr.
West, Henry, jt. auth. see Feinberg, Joel.
West, Herbert B. Stay with Me Lord: A Man's Prayers. LC 73-17914. 1974. 4.95 (ISBN 0-8164-0255-8). Crossroad NY.
West, J., ed. Alternatives in Development: Is Europe Responding to Third World Needs? 1974. text ed. 19.50 (ISBN 0-08-018169-4). Pergamon.
West, J. B. & Kotz, Mary L. Upstairs at the White House. (Illus.). 416p. 1974. pap. 2.95 (ISBN 0-446-93953-6). Warner Bks.
West, J. M. Basic Corrosion & Oxidation. 247p. 1981. 69.95 (ISBN 0-470-27080-2). Halsted Pr.
West, James. Plainville, USA. LC 45-1863. 1945. pap. 5.00x (ISBN 0-231-08514-1). Columbia U Pr.
West, James L., ed. Gyascutus: Studies in Antebellum Southern Humorous & Sporting Writings. (Costerus New Ser.: No. 5-6). 1978. pap. text ed. 20.00x (ISBN 90-6203-522-1). Humanities.
West, James L., jt. ed. see Hoge, James O.
West, James L., III, et al, eds. see Dreiser, Theodore.
West, Jane. The Advantage of Education; or, the History of Maria Williams, 2 vols. Luria, Gina, ed. (The Femnist Controversy in England, 1788-1810 Ser.). 1974. lib. bdg. 50.00 ea. Garland Pub.
--A Gossip's Story, & a Legendary Tale, 2 vols. Luria, Gina, ed. LC 73-22192. (The Feminist Controversy in England, 1788-1810 Ser.). 1974. lib. bdg. 50.00 ea. (ISBN 0-8240-0884-7). Garland Pub.
--Letters to a Young Lady, in Which the Duties & Character of Women Are Considered, 3 vols. Luria, Gina, ed. (The Feminist Controversy in England, 1788-1810 Ser.). 1974. lib. bdg. 50.00 ea. (ISBN 0-8240-0885-5). Garland Pub.
--A Tale of the Times, 3 vols. (The Feminist Controversy in England, 1788-1810 Ser.). 1974. Set. lib. bdg. 114.00 (ISBN 0-8240-0886-3); lib. bdg. 50.00 ea. Garland Pub.
West, Jane, ed. see Schnessel, Michael.
West, Jerry. The Windfalls of Kent. 128p. 1980. 24.75x (ISBN 0-7050-0065-6, Pub. by Skilton & Shaw England). State Mutual Bk.
West, Jessamyn. Double Discovery. LC 80-7948. 1980. 11.95 (ISBN 0-15-126402-3). HarBraceJ.
--The Massacre at Fall Creek. 320p. 1976. pap. 1.95 o.p. (ISBN 0-449-22771-5, C2771, Crest). Fawcett.
West, John F. & Roberts, Bruce. This Proud Land: The Blue Ridge Mountains. LC 74-20051. (Illus., Orig.). 1974. 4.50 (ISBN 0-87461-960-2). McNally.
West, K., ed. see Driscoll, P., et al.
West, K., ed. see Sullivan, George E. & Cox, Warren.
West, K., et al, eds. see Sullivan, George E. & Cox, Warren.
West, Kathleene. No Warning. 1977. 2.50 (ISBN 0-918116-11-2). Jawbone Pr.
West, L. J., jt. ed. see Siegel, R. K.

West, Larry E. The Saint Gall Passion Play. 1976. 11.50 o.s.i. (ISBN 0-686-23383-2). Classical Folia.
West, Leonard. Acquisition of Typewriting Skills. LC 68-24228. 1969. pap. 16.00 (ISBN 0-8224-2089-9). Pitman Learning.
West, Leonard J. Modern College Typewriting: A Basic Course. (Illus.). 1977. text ed. 7.95 spiral bdg. (ISBN 0-15-560550-X, HC); instructor's manual avail. (ISBN 0-15-560551-8); kit of student supplies 3.75 (ISBN 0-686-68519-9); timing tapes avail. (ISBN 0-15-560555-0); transparency masters avail.; Student's ProgramedGuide 3.95 (ISBN 0-686-68520-2). HarBraceJ.
West, M. L. Textual Criticism & Editorial Technique. 150p. 1973. 22.00 (ISBN 3-5190-7402-8); pap. 16.75 (ISBN 3-519-07401-X); pap. 16.30 (ISBN 0-686-66955-X). Adler.
West, Mae. Goodness Had Nothing to Do with It. (A Belvedere Bk.). 312p. 1981. pap. 6.95 (ISBN 0-87754-301-1). Chelsea Hse.
West, Martin. Studies in Greek Elegy & Iambus. LC 73-93168. (Untersuchungen zur antiken Literatur & Geschichte, Vol. 14). ix, 198p. 1974. 57.10x (ISBN 3-11-004585-0). De Gruyter.
West, Martin, jt. auth. see Whisson, M. G.
West, Morris. The Navigator. LC 76-5504. 1976. 8.95 o.p. (ISBN 0-688-03061-0). Morrow.
--The Salamander. 1981. pap. 2.95 (ISBN 0-671-42432-7). PB.
West, Muriel. The Devil & John Webster. (Salzburg Studies in English Literature, Jacobean Drama Studies: No. 11). 319p. 1974. pap. text ed. 25.00x (ISBN 0-391-01563-X). Humanities.
West, Nathanael. The Dream Life of Balso Snell. Bd. with Cool Million. 179p. 1963. pap. 4.95 (ISBN 0-374-50292-7, N244). FS&G.
--Miss Lonelyhearts. Bd. with Day of the Locust. LC 62-16924. pap. 3.95 (ISBN 0-8112-0215-1, NDP125). New Directions.
West, Nick. Alfred Hitchcock & the Three Investigators in the Mystery of the Coughing Dragon. LC 74-117549. (Three Investigator's Ser: No. 14). (Illus.). (gr. 4-7). 1970. 2.95 (ISBN 0-394-81411-8, BYR); PLB 5.39 (ISBN 0-394-91411-2). Random.
West, Owen. The Funhouse. 288p. 1980. pap. 2.75 (ISBN 0-515-05726-6). Jove Pubns.
West, Paul. The Very Rich Hours of Count von Stauffenberg. LC 79-2662. 320p. 1980. 12.95 (ISBN 0-06-014593-5, HarpT). Har-Row.
West, Peggy J., ed. Growing with Television: A Study of Biblical Values & the Television Experience - Adult Leader's Guide. 32p. 1980. pap. 2.95 (ISBN 0-8164-2272-9). Seabury.
West, R. E., jt. auth. see Kreith, Frank.
West, R. G. Pleistocene Geology & Biology. 2nd ed. LC 76-28353. (Illus.). 1977. pap. text ed. 18.95x (ISBN 0-582-44620-1). Longman.
--The Pre-Glacial Pleistocene of the Norfolk & Suffolk Coasts. LC 77-90191. (Illus.). 1980. 95.00 (ISBN 0-521-21962-0). Cambridge U Pr.
West, R. G. see Bowen, D. Q.
West, R. G., jt. ed. see Walker, D.
West, Ralph E. Sea-Change: An Anthology of Short Stories. 228p. (Orig.). (gr. 11-12). 1980. pap. text ed. 4.50x (ISBN 0-88334-126-3). Ind Sch Pr.
West, Ralph E., ed. Kaleidoscope: A Variety of Short Stories. (gr. 9-11). 1970. pap. text ed. 3.95x (ISBN 0-88334-030-5). Ind Sch Pr.
West, Raymond O., ed. Public Health & Preventive Medicine. 6th ed. (Medical Examination Review Book Ser.: Vol .6). 1975. spiral bdg. 8.50 (ISBN 0-87488-106-4). Med Exam.
West, Rebecca. Birds Fall Down. 1980. pap. 2.50 (ISBN 0-446-91189-5). Warner Bks.
--The Judge. (Virago Modern Classic). 430p. 1981. pap. 6.95 (ISBN 0-8037-3996-6). Dial.
West, Richard, et al. Discourse Concerning Treasons & Bills of Attainder. Berkowitz, David S. & Thorne, Samuel E., eds. LC 77-89246. (Classics of English Legal History in the Modern Era Ser.: Vol. 77). 273p. 1979. lib. bdg. 40.00 (ISBN 0-8240-3176-8). Garland Pub.
West, Richard C. Tolkien Criticism: An Annotated Checklist. rev. ed. 1981. Repr. of 1970 ed. write for info. Kent St U Pr.
West, Richard R., jt. auth. see Tinic, Seha M.
West, Robert. The Oxocarbons. LC 80-515. (Organic Chemistry Ser.). 1980. 32.00 (ISBN 0-12-744580-3). Acad Pr.
West, Robert C., jt. auth. see Augelli, John P.
West, Robert H. The Invisible World. 275p. 1980. Repr. of 1939 ed. lib. bdg. 30.00 (ISBN 0-8482-7063-0). Norwood Edns.
--Shakespeare & the Outer Mystery. LC 68-56300. 216p. 1968. 10.00x (ISBN 0-8131-1166-8). U Pr of Ky.
West, Robert M. Review of the North American Eocene & Oligocene Apatemyidae (Mammalia: Insectivora) (Special Publications: No. 3). (Illus.). 42p. 1973. pap. 2.00 (ISBN 0-89672-028-4). Tex Tech Pr.
West, Serene. Very Practical Meditation. LC 79-20249. (Orig.). 1980. pap. 4.95 (ISBN 0-89865-006-2, Unilaw). Donning Co.
West, Stanley A. & Macklin, June. The Chicano Experience. (Special Studies in Contemporary Social Issues). 1979. lib. bdg. 26.50x (ISBN 0-89158-489-7). Westview.
West, Stephen, ed. see Los Angeles County Museum of Art Curatorial Staff.
West, Stephen G. & Wicklund, Robert A. A Primer of Social Psychological Theories. LC 80-16292. 320p. 1980. text ed. 14.95 (ISBN 0-8185-0395-5). Brooks-Cole.
West, T. F., jt. auth. see Davidson Pratt, J.
West, T. S. Analytical Chemistry - Part 1. (Mtp International Review of Science-Physical Chemistry Ser. 1: Vol. 12). (Illus.). 1981. Set. 29.50, index vol. 12.50 (ISBN 0-685-02107-6). Univ Park.
--Analytical Chemistry - Part 2. (Mtp International Review of Science-Physical Chemistry Ser. 1: Vol. 13). (Illus.). 1981. Set. 29.50, index vol. 12.50 (ISBN 0-685-02109-2). Univ Park.
West, Theodora L. Continental Short Story: An Existential Approach. LC 69-11184. (Orig.). 1969. pap. 7.70 o.p. (ISBN 0-672-63024-9). Odyssey Pr.
West, Tom. Hard Trail to Santa Fe. 205p. (Orig.). 1980. pap. 1.95 (ISBN 0-89083-676-0). Zebra.
West, Trudy. Fireplace in the Home. LC 74-81060. (Illus.). 160p. 1976. 16.95 (ISBN 0-7153-6751-X). David & Charles.
--Timber-Frame House in England. (Illus.). Date not set. 8.95 (ISBN 0-8038-0245-5). Hastings.
West, Victor, jt. auth. see Osborne, Ernest L.
West Virginia Trial Lawyers Association. Trial Tactics. 466p. 1966. 12.00 (ISBN 0-913338-21-4). Trans-Media Pub.
West, Wallace. Everlasting Exiles. (YA) 5.95 (ISBN 0-685-07431-5, Avalon). Bouregy.
West, William. Symbolaeographia, Which May Be Termed the Art, Description, or Image of Instruments Covenants, Contracts, 2 vols. Berkowitz, David S. & Thorne, Samuel E., eds. LC 77-86629. (Classics of English Legal History in the Modern Era Ser.: Vol. 85). 1979. Set. lib. bdg. 110.00 (ISBN 0-8240-3072-9); lib. bdg. 55.00 ea. Garland Pub.
--Symbolaeographia Which Termed the Art, Description of Instruments, Covenants, Contracts, Etc. LC 74-28892. (English Experience Ser.: No. 768). 1975. Repr. of 1590 ed. 43.00 (ISBN 90-221-0768-X). Walter J Johnson.
West, William G., ed. How to Survive Stress (In This Mad Mad World) (Illus.). 108p. (Orig.). 1980. pap. 6.00 (ISBN 0-914778-35-8). Phoenix Bks.
West, William R. & Stremnel, Stephen H. Exploring, Visualizing, Communicating: A Composition Text. (Ser. in English Composition). 1979. pap. text ed. 7.95 (ISBN 0-13-297556-4). P-H.
Westacott, Hugh D. The Walker's Handbook. (Illus., Orig.). 1979. pap. 5.95 (ISBN 0-14-046267-8). Penguin.
Westall, Robert. Devil on the Road. LC 79-10427. (gr. 6 up). 1979. 7.95 (ISBN 0-688-80227-3); lib. bdg. 7.63 (ISBN 0-688-84227-5). Greenwillow.
--Fathom Five. LC 80-11223. 256p. (gr. 7 up). 1980. 8.95 (ISBN 0-688-80286-9); PLB 8.59 (ISBN 0-688-84286-0). Greenwillow.
--The Machine Gunners. LC 76-13630. (gr. 5-9). 1976. 8.25 (ISBN 0-688-80055-6); PLB 7.92 (ISBN 0-688-84055-8). Greenwillow.
--The Watch House. LC 77-19088. (gr. 5-9). 1978. 7.95 (ISBN 0-688-80149-8); PLB 7.63 (ISBN 0-688-84149-X). Greenwillow.
--The Wind Eye. LC 77-5162. (gr. 5-9). 1977. 8.25 (ISBN 0-688-80114-5); PLB 7.92 (ISBN 0-688-84114-7). Greenwillow.
Westaway, K. M., ed. see Plautus.
Westbeau, Georges. Little Tyke. LC 56-13322. 115p. pap. 4.95 (ISBN 0-8163-0048-8, 12480-0). Pacific Pr Pub Assn.
Westberg, Granger. Ante la Perdida De un Ser Querido. Rodriguez, Jorge A., tr. 1980. Repr. of 1978 ed. 0.95 (ISBN 0-311-46081-X). Casa Bautista.
Westbrook, A., jt. auth. see Ratti, O.
Westbrook, James. Aim for a Job in Restaurants & Food Service. LC 68-26145. (Aim High Vocational Guidance Ser.). (Illus.). (gr. 7 up). 1978. PLB 5.97 (ISBN 0-8239-0099-1). Rosen Pr.
Westbrook, James H. Aim for a Job in Restaurants & Food Service. LC 70-114136. (Career Guidance Ser). 1971. pap. 3.50 (ISBN 0-668-02229-9). Arco.
Westbrook, Max. Walter Van Tilburg Clark. (U. S. Authors Ser.: No. 155). 1970. lib. bdg. 10.95 (ISBN 0-8057-0148-6). Twayne.
Westbrook, Max, jt. auth. see Handy, William J.
Westbrook, Perry D. Acres of Flint: Sarah Orne Jewett & Her Contemporaries. rev. ed. LC 80-20501. 204p. 1981. 12.50 (ISBN 0-8108-1357-2). Scarecrow.
--John Burroughs. (U. S. Authors Ser.: No. 227). 1974. lib. bdg. 10.95 (ISBN 0-8057-0117-6). Twayne.
--William Bradford. (United States Authors Ser.). 1978. lib. bdg. 12.50 (ISBN 0-8057-7243-X). Twayne.
Westbrook, Wayne W. Wall Street in the American Novel. LC 79-47997. (The Gotham Library Ser.). 224p. 1980. 20.00x (ISBN 0-8147-9194-8); pap. 8.00x (ISBN 0-8147-9195-6). NYU Pr.
Westburg, John E. What's Creative About Creative Writing? pap. 3.00 (ISBN 0-87423-018-7). Westburg.
Westbury, Ian & Bellack, Arno A., eds. Research into Classroom Processes: Recent Developments & Next Steps. LC 70-170131. 280p. 1971. text ed. 14.25x (ISBN 0-8077-2327-4). Tchrs Coll.
Westbury, Lord. Handlist of Italian Cookery Books 1475-1860. (Illus.). pap. 30.00x o.p. (ISBN 0-685-08674-7). Corner.
Westby-Gibson. Education in a Dynamic Society: A Contemporary Sourcebook. 1972. 8.95 (ISBN 0-201-08537-2). A-W.
Westby-Gibson, Dorothy, ed. Social Foundations of Education. LC 67-15060. 1967. pap. text ed. 3.50 o.s.i. (ISBN 0-02-935200-2). Free Pr.
Westcott, Alvin M. & Smith, James A. Creative Teaching of Mathematics in the Elementary School. 2nd ed. 1978. pap. text ed. 11.50 (ISBN 0-205-06051-X). Allyn.
Westcott, Brooke F. Commentary on Epistle to the Hebrews. (Gr). 1950. 9.95 (ISBN 0-8028-3289-X). Eerdmans.
--Saint Paul's Epistle to the Ephesians. 1978. 9.75 (ISBN 0-686-12958-X). Klock & Klock.
Westcott, Nadine B. I Know an Old Lady Who Swallowed a Fly. (Illus.). 32p. (gr. k-3). 1980. 8.95 (ISBN 0-316-93128-4, Pub. by Atlantic Monthly Pr); pap. 4.95 (ISBN 0-316-93127-6). Little.
Westcott, Ray D., jt. auth. see Fessler, George R.
Westcott, William D. How to Raise & Train a Keeshond. (Orig.). pap. 2.00 (ISBN 0-87666-326-9, DS1091). TFH Pubns.
Westefeld, Albert. Getting Started: Urban Youth in the Labor Market. LC 77-166952. (FDR & the Era of the New Deal Ser.). 1971. Repr. of 1943 ed. lib. bdg. 19.50 (ISBN 0-306-70358-0). Da Capo.
Westenfelder, M., ed. Malformations of the External Genitalia. (Monographs in Paediatrics: Vol. 12). (Illus.). 200p. 1981. soft cover 60.00 (ISBN 3-8055-1509-X). S Karger.
Westenholz, Aage. Literary & Lexical Texts & the Earliest Administrative Documents from Nippur. (Bibliotheca Mesopotamica Ser.: Vol. 1). (Illus.). 200p. 1975. 18.50 (ISBN 0-89003-008-1); pap. 12.00 (ISBN 0-686-68506-7). Undena Pubns.
Westerberg, A. W., et al. Process Flowsheeting. LC 78-51682. (Illus.). 1979. 29.50 (ISBN 0-521-22043-2). Cambridge U Pr.
Westerberg, Christine. The Cap That Mother Made. LC 76-48301. (Illus.). (ps-2). 1977. 6.95 (ISBN 0-13-113365-9); pap. 2.50 (ISBN 0-13-113274-1). P-H.
Westerberg, Kermit B., tr. see Ljungmark, Lars.
Westerby, Herbert. History of Pianoforte Music. LC 78-87624. (Music Ser). 1970. Repr. of 1924 ed. lib. bdg. 29.50 (ISBN 0-306-71809-X). Da Capo.
Westergaard, Peter. Introduction to Tonal Theory. 448p. 1976. pap. text ed. 16.00x (ISBN 0-393-09342-5). Norton.
Westerhoff, John H. Will Our Children Have Faith? 1976. 6.95 (ISBN 0-8164-0319-8). Crossroad NY.
Westerhoff, John H. & Neville, Gwen K. Learning Through Liturgy. 1978. 8.95 (ISBN 0-8164-0406-2). Crossroad NY.
Westerhoff, John H. & Willimon, William H. Liturgy & Learning Through the Life Cycle. 176p. 1980. 9.95 (ISBN 0-8164-0471-2). Seabury.
Westerhoff, John H., III. Inner Growth-Outer Change: An Educational Guide to Church Renewal. (Orig.). pap. 4.95 (ISBN 0-8164-2213-3). Crossroad NY.
Westerhoff, John H., 3rd. Bringing up Children in the Christian Faith. 108p. (Orig.). 1980. pap. 4.95 (ISBN 0-03-056203-1). Winston Pr.
Westerlund, Gunnar & Sjostrand, Sven-Erik. Organizational Myths. 1979. text ed. 11.95 (ISBN 0-06-318074-X, IntlDept). Har-Row.
Westerman, Claus & Lessing, Erich. The Bible: A Pictorial History. (Illus.). 1976. 14.95 (ISBN 0-8164-1216-2); pap. 8.95 (ISBN 0-8164-1220-0). Crossroad NY.
Westermann, Claus. Blessing: In the Bible & the Life of the Church, No. 3. Brueggemann, Walter & Donahue, John R., eds. Crim, Keith, tr. from Ger. LC 78-54564. (Overtures to Biblical Theology Ser.). 144p. 1978. pap. 5.95 (ISBN 0-8006-1529-8, 1-1529). Fortress.
--Creation. Scullion, John J., tr. from Ger. LC 74-75730. 144p. (Orig.). 1974. pap. 3.25 o.p. (ISBN 0-8006-1072-5, 1-1072). Fortress.
--Genesis Accounts of Creation. Wagner, Norman E., ed. LC 64-11858. (Facet Ser.). 1964. pap. 1.35 o.p. (ISBN 0-8006-3007-6, 1-3007). Fortress.
--Praise & Lament in the Psalms. rev. enl. ed. Crim, Keith & Soulen, Richard, trs. from German. 1981 (ISBN 0-8042-1791-2). pap. 9.50 (ISBN 0-8042-1792-0). John Knox.
--The Promises to the Fathers: Studies on the Patriarchal Narratives. Green, David E., tr. from Ger. LC 79-7395. Orig. Title: Die Verheissungen an Die Vater. 208p. 1980. 12.95 (ISBN 0-8006-0580-2, 1-580). Fortress.
--The Structure of the Book of Job: A Form-Critical Analysis. Muenchow, Charles A., tr. from Ger. LC 80-2379. 160p. 1981. 14.95 (ISBN 0-8006-0651-5, 1-651). Fortress.
Western Institute of Drug Problems Summer School, 3rd Annual & Blachly, Paul H. Progress in Drug Abuse: Proceedings. 336p. 1972. pap. 19.75 spiral o.p. (ISBN 0-398-02233-X). C C Thomas.
Western, John. Outcast Capetown. (Illus.). 352p. 1981. 20.00 (ISBN 0-8166-1025-8). U of Minn Pr.
Western, Leone N. The Gold Key to Writing Your Life History. LC 80-83026. (Illus.). 124p. 1981. pap. 7.95 (ISBN 0-918146-20-8). Peninsula WA.
Western Publishing Co. Editors, ed. New Grosset Road Atlas of the United States, Canada, & Mexico. (Illus., Orig.). Date not set. pap. 3.95 (ISBN 0-448-16282-2). G&D.
Western Publishing Editors. Betty Crocker's Starting Out. 512p. 1980. pap. 2.95 (ISBN 0-553-10528-0). Bantam.
Western Writers of America. Water Trails West. LC 77-82973. 1978. 12.95 o.p. (ISBN 0-385-12709-X). Doubleday.
--Water Trails West. 1979. pap. 3.50 (ISBN 0-380-47688-6, 47688, Discus). Avon.
--The Women Who Made the West. LC 79-8442. (Illus.). 1980. 10.95 (ISBN 0-385-15801-7). Doubleday.
Westernhagen, C. Von see Von Westernhagen, C.
Westers, Jacqueline, ed. Christmas Programs for the Church, No. 12. (Special-Day Program Bks). 64p. (Orig.). 1979. pap. 2.75 (ISBN 0-87239-252-X, 8612). Standard Pub.
--Easter Programs for the Church, No. 6. 1977. pap. 2.75 (ISBN 0-87239-159-0, 8718). Standard Pub.
Westfall, Gloria. French Official Publications. LC 80-40418. (Guides to Official Publications: Vol. 6). (Illus.). 223p. 1980. 35.00 (ISBN 0-08-021838-5). Pergamon.
Westfall, Gloria, jt. auth. see Kohler, Carolyn.
Westfall, Minter J., jt. auth. see Needham, James G.
Westfall, R. S. The Construction of Modern Science. LC 77-84001. (History of Science Ser.). (Illus.). 1978. 21.95 (ISBN 0-521-21863-2); pap. 7.95x (ISBN 0-521-29295-6). Cambridge U Pr.
--Never at Rest: A Biography of Isaac Newton. LC 77-84001. (Illus.). 850p. 1981. 49.50 (ISBN 0-521-23143-4). Cambridge U Pr.
Westgate, Douglas G. Office Procedures 2000. 512p. 1977. text ed. 15.27 (ISBN 0-7715-0897-2); tchr's. manual 39.93 (ISBN 0-7715-0898-0). Forkner.
Westhaeffer, Paul J. History of the Cumberland Valley Railroad. LC 79-178. (Illus.). 1979. 21.50 (ISBN 0-933954-00-X). Natl Rail Hist Soc DC Corp.
Westheimer, David. Von Ryan's Return. LC 80-24232. 481p. 1980. Repr. of 1980 ed. large print ed. 12.95 (ISBN 0-89621-253-X). Thorndike Pr.
Westin, Alan F., ed. Whistle-Blowing! Loyalty & Dissent in the Corporation. LC 80-15800. 192p. 1980. 12.50 (ISBN 0-07-069483-4, P&RB). McGraw.
Westin, Alan P. & Mahoney, Barry. The Trial of Martin Luther King. LC 74-9945. (Apollo Eds.). (Illus.). 1976. pap. 4.95 o.s.i. (ISBN 0-8152-0421-3, TYC-T). T Y Crowell.
Westin, Helen. Introducing the Song Sheet. LC 75-40331. (Illus.). 176p. 1976. 14.95 o.p. (ISBN 0-8407-4325-4). Nelson.
Westin, Jeane. Making Do: How Women Survived the Thirties. LC 75-170. 360p. 1976. 9.95 o.p. (ISBN 0-695-80593-2). Follett.
Westing, Harold J. Make Your Sunday School Grow Through Evaluation. 120p. 1976. pap. 1.95 o.p. (ISBN 0-88207-464-4). Victor Bks.
--Super Superintendent: A Layman's Guide to Sunday School Management. LC 80-66721. (Accent Teacher Training Ser.). 160p. (Orig.). 1980. pap. 3.95 (ISBN 0-89636-057-1). Accent Bks.
Westing, J. H., et al. Purchasing Management: Materials in Motion. 4th ed. LC 75-38969. 624p. 1976. text ed. 26.50 (ISBN 0-471-93632-4). Wiley.
Westlake, D., jt. auth. see Tenn, William.
Westlake, Donald. Castle in the Air. 288p. 1981. pap. 2.50 (ISBN 0-449-24382-6, Crest). Fawcett.

--Up Your Banners: A Novel. 1969. 16.95 (ISBN 0-02-626120-0). Macmillan.
Westlake, Donald E. Enough. 1978. pap. 1.75 o.p. (ISBN 0-449-23768-0, Crest). Fawcett.
Westlake, H. D. Individuals in Thucydides. LC 68-23918. 1968. 49.50 (ISBN 0-521-07246-8). Cambridge U Pr.
Westland, Lynn. Iron Trail to Stirrup. 192p. (YA) 1975. 5.95 (ISBN 0-685-55330-2, Avalon). Bouregy.
Westland, Pamela. The Sixty-Minute Cookbook. (Illus.). 224p. 1981. 23.00 (ISBN 0-571-11554-3, Pub. by Faber & Faber); pap. 7.50 (ISBN 0-571-11555-1). Merrimack Bk Serv.
--The Yoghurt Cookbook. (Illus.). 175p. 1980. 19.95 (ISBN 0-241-89763-7, Pub. by Hamish Hamilton England). David & Charles.
Westley, Bruce. News Editing. 3rd ed. LC 79-88796. (Illus.). 1980. text ed. 17.75 (ISBN 0-395-27993-3). HM.
Westley, Bruce H. News Editing. 2nd ed. LC 79-170163. (Illus.). 1972. text ed. 16.95 o.p. (ISBN 0-395-05529-6, 3-59706). HM.
Westley, Bruce H., jt. auth. see Stempel, Guido H., III.
Westley, Richard, jt. auth. see May, William.
Westley, William A. Violence & the Police: A Sociological Study of Law, Custom, & Morality. 1970. 12.50x o.p. (ISBN 0-262-23042-9); pap. 4.95 (ISBN 0-262-73027-8, 187). MIT Pr.
Westley, William A. & Epstein, Nathan B. The Silent Majority: Families of Emotionally Healthy College Students. LC 77-75937. (Higher Education Ser). 1969. 11.95x o.p. (ISBN 0-87589-039-3). Jossey-Bass.
Westling, Louise. The Evolution of Michael Krayton's Idea. (Salzburg Studies in Literature, Elizabethan & Renaissance Studies: No. 37). 187p. 1974. pap. text ed. 25.00x (ISBN 0-391-01564-8). Humanities.
Westmacott, Richard, jt. auth. see Tourbier, Joachim.
Westman, Jack C., ed. Individual Differences in Children. LC 72-10131. (Personality Processes Ser.). 368p. 1973. 31.00 (ISBN 0-471-93690-1, Pub. by Wiley-Interscience). Wiley.
Westman, Paul. Jesse Jackson: I Am Somebody. LC 80-20521. (Taking Part Ser.). 48p. (gr. 3 up). 1980. PLB 6.95 (ISBN 0-87518-203-8). Dillon.
--Neil Armstrong: Space Pioneer. LC 80-10832. (The Achievers Ser.). (Illus.). (gr. 4-9). 1980. PLB 5.95g (ISBN 0-8225-0479-0). Lerner Pubns.
Westman, Robert S., ed. The Copernican Achievement. 1976. 22.75x (ISBN 0-520-02877-5). U of Cal Pr.
Westminster Assembly. Shorter Catechism with Scripture Proofs. Date not set. 0.75 (ISBN 0-686-28948-X). Banner of Truth.
Westoff, Charles F., jt. auth. see Cohen, Wilbur J.
Westoff, Leslie A. Breaking Out of the Middle-Age Trap. 1980. 11.95 (ISBN 0-453-00378-8, H378). NAL.
Westoll, T. S., ed. see Royal Society of London.
Weston. Plaid for Financial Management. rev ed. 1981. write for info. (ISBN 0-256-02135-X, 06-0848-02). Learning Syst. Postponed.
--Plaid for Financial Management. 1975. pap. 5.50 (ISBN 0-256-01285-7, 06-0848-00). Learning Syst.
Weston, Alan. Survey of Allied Health Professions. (Illus.). 224p. pap. text ed. 12.95 (ISBN 0-933014-63-5). College-Hill.
Weston, Alan J. Communicative Disorders: An Appraisal. (Illus.). 432p. 1972. 19.75 (ISBN 0-398-02437-5). C C Thomas.
Weston, Anthony. The Chinese Revolution. Yapp, Malcolm, et al, eds. (World History Ser.). (Illus.). 32p. (gr. 10). 1980. Repr. of 1977 ed. lib. bdg. 5.95 (ISBN 0-89908-139-8); pap. text ed. 1.95 (ISBN 0-89908-114-2). Greenhaven.
Weston, Burns H., jt. ed. see Reisman, W. Michael.
Weston, Burns H., et al. International Law & World Order: An Introductory Problem-Oriented Coursebook. LC 80-15873. (American Casebook Ser.). 1195p. 1980. text ed. 23.95 (ISBN 0-8299-2097-8). West Pub.
Weston, Carolyn. Rouse the Demon. 1976. 6.95 o.p. (ISBN 0-394-40703-2). Random.
Weston, Corin & Greenberg, Janelle R. Subjects & Sovereigns: The Grand Controversy Over Legal Sovereignty in Stuart England. LC 80-40588. 400p. Date not set. 39.50 (ISBN 0-521-23272-4). Cambridge U Pr.
Weston, Edward G., jt. auth. see Griffith, John L.
Weston, G. J., jt. auth. see Sherwin, E.
Weston, George F., Jr. Boston Ways: High, by, & Folk. rev. ed. Raymond, Charlotte C., ed. LC 74-213. (Illus.). 352p. 1974. 10.00 o.p. (ISBN 0-8070-5180-2); pap. 3.95 (ISBN 0-8070-5181-0, BP520). Beacon Pr.
Weston, Glen E., jt. ed. see Oppenheim, S. Chesterfield.
Weston, J. D. & Godwin, Herbert J. Some Exercises in Pure Mathematics. (Orig.). pap. 6.95x (ISBN 0-521-09561-1). Cambridge U Pr.
Weston, J. Fred & Brigham, Eugene F. Managerial Finance. 7th ed. LC 80-65811. 1088p. 1981. text ed. 20.95 (ISBN 0-03-058186-9). Dryden Pr.
Weston, J. Fred & Sorge, Bart W. International Managerial Finance. 1972. text ed. 18.95 (ISBN 0-256-01390-X). Irwin.
Weston, J. Fred, jt. auth. see Copeland, Thomas E.
Weston, Jessie L. From Ritual to Romance. McLaughlin, Mary M., tr. 7.50 (ISBN 0-8446-3162-0). Peter Smith.
--From Ritual to Romance. LC 57-3633. 1957. pap. 2.95 (ISBN 0-385-09334-9, A125, Anch). Doubleday.
Weston, Paul B. Combat Shooting for Police. 2nd ed. (Police Science Ser.). (Illus.). 184p. 1978. 12.75 (ISBN 0-398-03747-7). C C Thomas.
--The New Handbook of Handgunning. (Illus.). 112p. 1980. 12.95 (ISBN 0-398-04092-3). C C Thomas.
--The Police Traffic Control Function. 4th ed. (Illus.). 420p. 1978. 16.25 (ISBN 0-398-03764-7). C C Thomas.
Weston, Paul B. & Wells, Kenneth M. The Administration of Justice. 4th ed. (Illus.). 240p. 1981. text ed. 14.95 (ISBN 0-686-69272-1). P-H.
Weston, Penelope B. Framework for the Curriculum. (Monographs in Curriculum Studies: No. 2). 1977. pap. text ed. 18.00x (ISBN 0-85633-137-6, NFER). Humanities.
--Negotiating the Curriculum: A Study in Secondary Schooling. (Monographs in Curriculum Study: No. 4). 302p. 1980. pap. text ed. 29.00x (ISBN 0-85633-186-4, NFER). Humanities.
Weston, Ralph & Schwarz, Harold. Chemical Kinetics. (Fundamental Topics in Physical Chemistry Ser). (Illus.). 1972. ref. ed. 17.95 (ISBN 0-13-128660-9). P-H.
Weston, Sophie. An Undefended City. (Harlequin Romances Ser.). 192p. 1980. pap. 1.25 o.p. (ISBN 0-373-02362-6, Pub. by Harlequin). PB.
Weston, Susan B. Wallace Stevens: An Introduction to the Poetry. LC 77-1594. (Twentieth Century American Poets Ser.). 1977. 15.00x (ISBN 0-231-03990-5). Columbia U Pr.
Westover, Frederic & Westover, Margaret. How to Raise & Train an Irish Wolfhound. (Orig.). pap. 2.00 (ISBN 0-87666-324-2, DS1089). TFH Pubns.
Westover, Margaret, jt. auth. see Westover, Frederic.
Westphal, Albert. Protozoa. (Illus.). 1976. 35.00x (ISBN 0-216-90216-9). Intl Ideas.
Westphal, Barbara. Man Called Pedro. LC 75-25227. (Destiny Ser.). 1975. pap. 4.95 (ISBN 0-8163-0214-6, 13075-7). Pacific Pr Pub Assn.
Westphal, Chester, jt. auth. see Westphal, Wilma.
Westphal, F. Art of Philosophy: An Introductory Reader. LC 78-38042. (Illus.). 352p. 1972. pap. text ed. 11.95 (ISBN 0-13-048025-8). P-H.
Westphal, Fred A. Activity of Philosophy: A Concise Introduction. (Philosophy Ser). 1969. pap. text ed. 10.95 (ISBN 0-13-003608-0). P-H.
Westphal, Katherine. Dragons & Other Creatures: Chinese Embrodiery of Katherine Westphal. (Lancaster-Miller Art Ser.). (Illus.). 1980. 8.95 (ISBN 0-89581-012-3). Lancaster-Miller.
Westphal, Wilma & Westphal, Chester. Feathers in the Wind, Bk. 2. (Orion Ser.). 160p. 1981. pap. price not set (ISBN 0-8127-0322-7). Southern Pub.
Westphal, Wilma R. Feathers in the Wind, Bk. 1. (Orion Ser.). 160p. 1981. pap. write for info. (ISBN 0-8127-0309-X). Southern Pub.
Westreich, Budd, ed. see Directory of Private Presses & Letterpress Printers & Publishers.
Westrom, Robert. Dialects for the Actor. 69p. (Orig.). 1978. pap. 2.95 (ISBN 0-938230-01-8). Westrom.
--Monologues for the Actor. 60p. (Orig.). 1978. pap. 2.50 (ISBN 0-938230-02-6). Westrom.
--Scenes for the Actor. 76p. (Orig.). 1979. pap. 2.95 (ISBN 0-938230-03-4). Westrom.
--Speech for the Actor. rev. ed. (Illus.). 87p. (Orig.). 1978. pap. 3.50 (ISBN 0-938230-00-X). Westrom.
Westrup, J. A. Bach Cantatas. LC 70-80507. (BBC Music Guides: No. 3). (Illus.). 60p. (Orig.). 1969. pap. 2.95 (ISBN 0-295-95017-X). U of Wash Pr.
--Purcell. rev. ed. (The Master Musicians Ser.). (Illus.). 325p. 1980. 19.75 (ISBN 0-460-03177-5, Pub. by J M Dent England). Biblio Dist.
Westrup, J. A. see Abraham, Gerald.
Westrup, J. A., ed. see Fellowes, Edmund H.
Westrup, J. A., ed. see Walker, Ernest.
Westshore, Inc. Doing Business with the Russians. (Praeger Special Studies). 1979. 20.95 (ISBN 0-03-048456-1). Praeger.
Westwood, Gwen. Forgotten Bride. (Harlequin Romances Ser.). 192p. 1980. pap. 1.25 o.p. (ISBN 0-373-02363-4, Pub. by Harlequin). PB.
Westwood, Jennifer. Stories of Charlemagne. LC 74-12435. (gr. 6 up). 1976. 9.95 (ISBN 0-87599-213-7). S G Phillips.
Westwood, John. Railways at War. LC 80-25429. 224p. 1981. 17.50 (ISBN 0-8310-7138-9). Howell-North.
Westwood, Melvin N. Temperate-Zone Pomology. LC 77-26330. (Illus.). 1978. text ed. 29.95x (ISBN 0-7167-0196-0). W H Freeman.
Wetering, Jan Van de see Van de Wetering, Jan.
Wetherbee, Helen & White, Bruce D. Cases & Materials on Pharmacy Law. LC 80-14608. 612p. 1980. text ed. 17.95 (ISBN 0-8299-2091-9). West Pub.
Wetherbee, Winthrop, ed. & tr. The Cosmographia of Bernardus Silvestris. (Records of Civilization, Sources & Studies: Sources & Studies). 176p. 1973. 15.00x (ISBN 0-231-03673-6). Columbia U Pr.
Wethered, Vernon D. Medical Radiesthesia & Radionics: An Introduction. 1980. 30.00x (ISBN 0-85207-109-4, Pub. by Daniel Co England). State Mutual Bk.
--Medical Radiesthesia & Radionics: An Introduction. 196p. 1957. 11.95x (ISBN 0-8464-1032-X). Beekman Pubs.
--The Practice of Medical Radiesthesia. 150p. 1977. 9.15x (ISBN 0-8464-1040-0). Beekman Pubs.
Wetherell, June. The Privateer's Woman. 1978. pap. 1.95 o.p. (ISBN 0-523-40186-8). Pinnacle Bks.
--Tawny McShane. 1979. pap. 2.25 o.p. (ISBN 0-523-40340-2). Pinnacle Bks.
Wetherill, G. B. Sequential Methods in Statistics. 2nd ed. LC 74-16164. 240p. 1975. text ed. 12.95 o.p. (ISBN 0-470-93709-2). Halsted Pr.
Wetherill, G. B., jt. auth. see Hine, J.
Wetherill, G. W., et al, eds. Annual Review of Earth & Planetary Sciences, Vol. 9. LC 72-82137. (Illus.). 1981. 20.00 (ISBN 0-8243-2009-3). Annual Reviews.
Wetherill, P. M. The Literary Text: An Examination of Critical Methods. 1974. 20.00x (ISBN 0-520-02709-4). U of Cal Pr.
Wetlesen, Jon. Spinoza's Philosophy of Man: Proceedings. 1978. pap. 22.00x (ISBN 82-00-05240-0, Dist. by Columbia U Pr.). Universitet.
Wetmore, Alexander. The Birds of the Republic of Panama, 3 pts. Incl. Part 1. Tinamidae (Tinamous) to Rynchopidae (Skimmers) (Illus.). 483p. 1965. 17.50x (ISBN 0-87474-063-0); Part 2. Columbidae (Pigeons) to Picidae (Woodpeckers) (Illus.). 605p. 20.00x (ISBN 0-87474-064-9); Part 3. Passeriformes: Dendrocolaptidae (Woodcreepers) to Oxyruncidae (Sharpbills) 631p. 1965. 20.00x (ISBN 0-87474-122-X). LC 66-61061. (Illus.). 1968. Smithsonian.
Wetmore, Helen C. Buffalo Bill, Last of the Great Scouts: The Life Story of Colonel William F. Cody. LC 65-13258. (Illus.). 1965. pap. 2.95 (ISBN 0-8032-5215-3, BB 315, Bison). U of Nebr Pr.
Wetmore, Monroe N. Index Verborum Catullianus. 1912. 37.50x (ISBN 0-685-89758-3). Elliots Bks.
Wetmore, Reagh. Drownproofing Techniques for Floating, Swimming & Open Water Survival. (Illus., Orig.). 1981. pap. 7.95 (ISBN 0-8289-0410-3). Greene.
Wetterau, Bruce. The Last Crossword Dictionary. (Orig.). 1981. pap. 3.50 (ISBN 0-451-09910-9, E9910). NAL.
Wetterer, Margaret K. The Mermaid's Cape. LC 80-20338. (Illus.). 32p. (gr. 1-4). 1981. 8.95 (ISBN 0-689-50197-8, McElderry Bk). Atheneum.
Wettig, Gerhard. Broadcasting & Detente. LC 77-72285. 1977. 14.95x (ISBN 0-312-10588-6). St Martin.
Wettlaufer, George & Wettlaufer, Nancy. The Craftsman's Survival Manual: Making a Full or Part-Time Living from Your Crafts. (Creative Handcrafts Ser.). 1974. 9.95 o.p. (ISBN 0-13-188789-0, Spec); pap. 3.45 o.p. (ISBN 0-13-188771-8, Spec). P-H.
Wettlaufer, Nancy, jt. auth. see Wettlaufer, George.
Wettstone, Eugene, ed. Gymnastics Safety Manual: The Official Manual of the United States Gymnastics Safety Association. 2nd ed. LC 79-65860. (Illus.). 1979. text ed. 11.95x (ISBN 0-271-00242-5); pap. text ed. 7.95x (ISBN 0-271-00244-1). Pa St U Pr.
Wetzel, Charles M. Trout Flies: Naturals & Imitations. (Illus.). 154p. 1979. 15.00 (ISBN 0-8117-1739-9). Stackpole.
Wetzel, Guy F. Automotive Diagnosis & Tune-up. new ed. (gr. 9-12). 1974. text ed. 17.16 (ISBN 0-87345-100-7). McKnight.
Wetzel, Heinz, jt. ed. see Genno, Charles N.
Wetzel, Ralph, jt. auth. see Tharp, Roland.
Weverka, Robert. Circle of Iron. (Orig.). 1979. pap. 1.95 o.s.i. (ISBN 0-446-89928-3). Warner Bks.
Wewer, William, jt. ed. see Winkler, Stanley.
Wexelblat, Richard L., ed. History of Programming Languages. LC 80-518. (ACM Monograph Ser.). 1980. write for info. (ISBN 0-12-745040-8). Acad Pr.
Wexford, Jane. Monarch Notes on Turgenev's Fathers & Sons. (Orig.). pap. 2.25 (ISBN 0-671-00877-3). Monarch Pr.
Wexler, David A. & Rice, Laura N. Innovations in Client-Centered Therapy. LC 74-10538. (Personality Processes Ser). 1974. 34.95 (ISBN 0-471-93715-0, Pub. by Wiley-Interscience). Wiley.
Wexler, David B. Mental Health Law: Major Issues. 265p. 1981. 25.00 (ISBN 0-306-40538-5, Plenum Pr). Plenum Pub.
Wexler, H., jt. auth. see Scorer, R. S.
Wexler, Howard A. & Poole, Catherine A. Pediatric Radiology Case Studies. 1977. spiral bdg. 17.50 (ISBN 0-87488-064-5). Med Exam.
Wexler, Jean S., jt. auth. see King, Louise T.
Wexler, Jerome. Secrets of the Venus's Fly Trap. LC 80-2775. (Illus.). 64p. (gr. 2-5). 1981. PLB 6.95 (ISBN 0-396-07941-5). Dodd.
Wexler, Jerome, jt. auth. see Selsam, Millicent E.
Wexler, Joyce P. Laura Riding's Pursuit of Truth. LC 76-51688. xii, 169p. 1980. 14.00x (ISBN 0-8214-0364-8). Ohio U Pr.
Wexler, M. & Adler, L. Help the Patient Tell His Story. 1971. pap. 7.95 (ISBN 0-87489-080-2). Med Economics.
Wexler, Murray, jt. auth. see Enelow, Allen J.
Wexler, Philip. The Sociology of Education: Beyond Equality. LC 75-35994. (Studies in Sociology). 64p. 1976. pap. text ed. 3.50 (ISBN 0-672-61338-7). Bobbs.
Wexler, Susan S. The Story of Sandy. rev. ed. 176p. (RL 10). Date not set. pap. 1.50 (ISBN 0-451-08102-1, W8102, Sig). NAL.
Wexler, Victor G., jt. ed. see Gay, Peter.
Wexley, Kenneth A. & Yukl, Gary A. Organizational Behavior & Personal Psychology. 1977. pap. 11.50 (ISBN 0-256-01884-7). Irwin.
Wexley, Kenneth N., jt. auth. see Latham, Gary P.
Weyand, Clint. Surviving Popular Psychology: Debriefing the Me Degeneration. 148p. (Orig.). 1980. pap. 3.95 (ISBN 0-686-28854-8). Being Bks.
Weydemeyer, Winton. A Grange Master's America: In Defense of Freedom. 272p. 1981. 12.50 (ISBN 0-682-49677-4). Exposition.
Weydenthal, Jan B. de see De Weydenthal, Jan B.
Weydt, Harald, ed. Die Partikein der Deutschen Sprache. 1979. 105.00x (ISBN 3-11-007833-3). De Gruyter.
Weygandt, Cornelius. A Century of the English Novel. 1980. Repr. of 1925 ed. write for info. (ISBN 0-89760-916-6). Telegraph Bks.
Weygandt, Jerry J., jt. auth. see Kieso, Donald E.
Weyl, Hermann. Space, Time, Matter. 1922. pap. text ed. 4.50 (ISBN 0-486-60267-2). Dover.
--Theory of Groups & Quantum Mechanics. 1950. pap. text ed. 5.50 (ISBN 0-486-60269-9). Dover.
Weyl, Hermann, et al. Das Kontinuum und Andere Monographien, 4 vols. in 1. Incl. Kantinuum; Mathematische Analyse Des Raumproblems; Neuere Funktionentheorie. Landau; Hypothesen. Reimann. LC 72-81808. 14.95 (ISBN 0-8284-0134-9). Chelsea Pub.
Weyl, Peter K. Oceanography: An Introduction to the Marine Environment. 1970. 21.95 (ISBN 0-471-93744-4). Wiley.
Weyl, Richard. Geology of Central America, Vol. 15. 2nd ed. (Beitraege Zur Regionalen Geologie der Erde). (Illus.). 371p. 1980. lib. bdg. 88.85x (ISBN 3-443-11015-0). Lubrecht & Cramer.
Weyland, J. The Principles of Population & Production. 493p. 1971. Repr. of 1816 ed. 38.00x (ISBN 0-7165-1777-9, Pub. by Irish Academic Pr Ireland). Biblio Dist.
Weyland, Jack. Punch & Cookies Forever. LC 80-84566. 150p. 1981. 5.95 (ISBN 0-88290-173-7). Horizon Utah.
Weyman, Darrell. Tectonic Processes. (Process in Physical Geography Ser.: No. 4). (Illus.). 128p. (Orig.). 1981. pap. text ed. 8.95x (ISBN 0-04-551044-X, 2653). Allen Unwin.
Weyman, Darrell & Weyman, Valerie. Landscape Processes: An Introduction to Geomorphology. (Processes in Physical Geography Ser). (Illus.). 1977. pap. text ed. 6.95x (ISBN 0-04-551026-1). Allen Unwin.
Weyman, Valerie, jt. auth. see Weyman, Darrell.
Weymouth, Lally & Glaser, Milton. America in Eighteen Seventy-Six: The Way We Were. 1976. pap. 7.95 (ISBN 0-394-71616-7, V-616, Vin); pap. 7.95 (ISBN 0-394-71616-7). Random.
Weymouth, R. F. New Testament in Modern Speech. 3rd ed. LC 78-9536. 1978. kivar 10.95 (ISBN 0-8254-4025-4). Kregel.
Weyr, Tom, tr. see Vandenberg, Philipp.
Wezel, A. L. van see Hennessen, W. & Van Wezel, A. L.

Whale, John. Politics of the Media. LC 77-88395. (Political Issues of Modern Britain). 1977. text ed. 13.00x (ISBN 0-391-00550-2). Humanities.
Whale, John S. Christian Doctrine. 1941. 19.95 (ISBN 0-521-06774-X); pap. 5.95x (ISBN 0-521-09642-1). Cambridge U Pr.
Whalen, Charles W. Your Right to Know: How the Free Flow of News Depends on the Journalist's Right to Protect His Sources. 1973. 8.95 o.p. (ISBN 0-394-48732-X). Random.
Whalen, Edward L., jt. ed. see Tuckman, Howard P.
Whalen, G., jt. auth. see Graf, R.
Whalen, Harold B. & Nickerson, Robert L. Getting Paid: Practical Credit Collection Techniques for Business & Industry. LC 80-82730. (Illus.). 135p. (Orig.). 1980. pap. 10.00 (ISBN 0-937788-00-7). Kalum Pr.
Whalen, Philip. Enough Said: Poems 1974-1979. LC 80-16530. 96p. 1980. ltd. ed. 35.00 (ISBN 0-912516-48-8); pap. 4.95 (ISBN 0-912516-49-6). Grey Fox.
--Off the Wall: Interviews with Philip Whalen. Allen, Donald, ed. LC 77-1511. (Writing Ser.: No. 37). 1978. pap. 3.50 (ISBN 0-87704-035-4). Four Seasons Foun.
--Scenes of Life at the Capital. LC 72-163756. 74p. (Orig.). 1971. 7.00 (ISBN 0-912516-10-0); pap. 2.50 (ISBN 0-912516-00-3). Grey Fox.
Whalen, Richard E., jt. ed. see Gorski, Roger A.
Whalen, William J., jt. auth. see Arden, Kelvin J.
Whaley. Problems & Materials on Negotiable Instruments. Date not set. text ed. price not set (ISBN 0-316-93214-0). Little.
Whaley, Donald L. Psychological Testing & the Philosophy of Measurement. 58p. 1973. pap. text ed. 7.00 (ISBN 0-914474-02-2). F Fournies.
Whaley, Donald L. & Malott, Richard. Elementary Principles of Behavior. (Orig.). 1971. pap. text ed. 15.95 (ISBN 0-13-259499-4). P-H.
Whaley, Donald L., jt. auth. see Malott, Richard W.
Whaley, Donald L., jt. auth. see O'Banion, Daniel.
Whaley, Lucille F. & Wong, Donna. Nursing Care of Infants & Children. LC 78-31225. (Illus.). 1979. text ed. 27.95 (ISBN 0-8016-5417-3). Mosby.
Whaley, Lucille F., jt. auth. see Wong, Donna L.
Whalley, B. H. Production Management Handbook. 512p. 1980. text ed. 49.25x (ISBN 0-566-02133-1, Pub. by Gower Pub Co England). Renouf.
--Production Management Handbook. 1980. text ed. 49.25x (ISBN 0-566-02133-1, Pub. by Gower Pub Co England). Renouf.
Whalley, Paul. Butterflies. (Illus.). 128p. 1980. 8.95 (ISBN 0-600-31456-1). Transatlantic.
Whalon, Marion K., ed. Performing Arts Research: A Guide to Information Sources. LC 75-13828. (Performing Arts Information Guide Ser.: Vol. 1). 240p. 1976. 30.00 (ISBN 0-8103-1364-2). Gale.
Wharey, James B., ed. see Bunyan, John.
Wharton, Anne H. Through Colonial Doorways. LC 70-141040. 1970. Repr. of 1893 ed. 15.00 (ISBN 0-8103-3588-3). Gale.
Wharton, C., ed. see Commission of the European Communities.
Wharton, Edith. The Age of Innocence. LC 68-27785. 1968. lib. rep. ed. 17.50x (ISBN 0-684-14659-2, ScribT); pap. 4.95 (ISBN 0-684-71925-8, SL201, ScribT). Scribner.
--The Custom of the Country. 1976. lib.rep.ed. 17.50x (ISBN 0-684-14655-X, ScribT); pap. 5.95 (ISBN 0-684-71926-6, SL 62, ScribT). Scribner.
--The Edith Wharton Omnibus. (Encore Edition). 1978. 4.95 (ISBN 0-684-16933-9, ScribT). Scribner.
--Ethan Frome. lib. rep. ed. 1911. 12.50x (ISBN 0-684-15326-2, ScribT); pap. 2.45 (ISBN 0-684-71927-4, SL8, ScribT); text ed. 4.40 (ISBN 0-684-51564-4, ScribC); pap. text ed. 2.92 (ISBN 0-684-51565-2, ScribC). Scribner.
--Ghost Stories of Edith Wharton. LC 76-25402. 256p. 1973. lib. rep. ed. 17.50x (ISBN 0-684-14829-3, ScribT). Scribner.
--The Ghost Stories of Edith Wharton. 1976. pap. 1.75 o.p. (ISBN 0-445-08507-X). Popular Lib.
--The House of Mirth. 1976. lib. rep. ed. 17.50x (ISBN 0-684-14658-4, ScribT); pap. 4.95 (ISBN 0-684-71928-2, SL 41, ScribT). Scribner.
--The House of Mirth. 1981. pap. 2.95 (ISBN 0-425-04611-7). Berkley Pub.
--The House of Mirth. Lewis, R. W. B., ed. LC 77-77299. (Gotham Library). 335p. 1977. 15.00x (ISBN 0-8147-4976-3); pap. 6.00x (ISBN 0-8147-4977-1). NYU Pr.
--Italian Villas & Their Gardens. LC 76-10659. (Architecture & Decorative Arts Ser.). 1976. lib. bdg. 39.50 (ISBN 0-306-70817-5); pap. 8.95 (ISBN 0-306-80048-9). Da Capo.
--The Reef. lib. rep. ed. LC 65-21879. 1970. 17.50x (ISBN 0-684-15557-5, ScribT). Scribner.
--Short Stories of Edith Wharton, 1910-1937. 1975. lib. rep. ed. 30.00x (ISBN 0-684-14420-4, ScribT). Scribner.
--Summer. 1981. pap. 2.75 (ISBN 0-425-04610-9). Berkley Pub.
Wharton, H. T., tr. see Sappho.
Wharton, Mary E. & Bowen, Edward L. The Horse World of the Bluegrass, Vol. 1. Denbo, Bruce F. & Wharton, Mary E., eds. 246p. 1980. 30.00 (ISBN 0-934554-00-5). Host Assoc.
Wharton, Mary E., ed. see Wharton, Mary E. & Bowen, Edward L.
Wharton, William. Birdy. 1979. pap. 2.50 (ISBN 0-380-47282-1, 47282). Avon.
--Dad. LC 80-2725. 416p. 1981. 12.95 (ISBN 0-394-51097-6). Knopf.
Wharton, William H. Texas, a Brief Account. pap. 4.50 wrappers (ISBN 0-8363-0093-9). Jenkins.
Whatcom Museum of History & Art. Arts of a Vanished Era. LC 68-9204. (Whatcom Museum Ser.). (Illus.). 64p. 1968. pap. 5.00 (ISBN 0-295-95576-7). U of Wash Pr.
--Green Gold Harvest: A History of Logging & Its Products. LC 72-10060. (Whatcom Museum Ser.). (Illus.). 78p. 1969. pap. 5.00 (ISBN 0-295-95577-5). U of Wash Pr.
--Whatcom Seascapes: The Influence of the Sea on Whatcom County. LC 77-140515. (Whatcom Museum Ser.). (Illus.). 80p. 1970. pap. 5.00 (ISBN 0-295-95578-3). U of Wash Pr.
Whately, Richard. Elements of Rhetoric. Ehninger, Douglas, ed. LC 63-14292. (Landmarks in Rhetoric & Public Address Ser). 509p. 1963. Repr. of 1846 ed. 12.95x (ISBN 0-8093-0101-6). S Ill U Pr.
Whately, William. A Bride-Bush, or a Wedding Sermon. LC 74-28893. (English Experience Ser.: No. 769). 1975. Repr. of 1617 ed. 5.00 (ISBN 90-221-0769-8). Walter J Johnson.
Whatley, A., ed. International & Comparative Librarianship Group (CLG) Handbook. 1977. pap. 7.95x (ISBN 0-85365-790-4, Pub. by Lib Assn England). Oryx Pr.
Whatley, Arthur & Kelley, Lane. Personnel Management in Action: Skill Building Experiences. (Management Ser). (Illus.). 1977. pap. text ed. 11.95 (ISBN 0-8299-0123-X); instrs.' manual avail. (ISBN 0-8299-0582-0). West Pub.
Whatley, Arthur A., jt. auth. see Kelley, Nelson L.
Whatley, H. A., ed. Librarianship & Information, Nineteen Seventy-One to Nineteen Seventy-Five. 1977. 32.50x (ISBN 0-85365-099-3, Pub. by Lib Assn England). Oryx Pr.
Whatley, Jo Ann. Banking & Finance Careers. (Career Concise Guides Ser.). (Illus.). (gr. 7 up). 1978. PLB 6.45 s&l o.s.i. (ISBN 0-531-01346-4). Watts.
Whattam, Al, ed. see Redenbaugh, Al.
Whealon, Terry O., jt. ed. see Fuller, Jack W.
Wheat, E. Love Life for Every Married Couple. 288p. 1980. pap. 5.95 (ISBN 0-310-42511-5). Zondervan.
Wheat Flour Institute. Winning Sandwiches for Menu Makers. Thomas, Kathleen M., ed. LC 76-45621. (Illus.). 1976. 18.95 (ISBN 0-8436-2123-0). CBI Pub.
Wheat, Patte. By Sanction of the Victim. LC 78-63000. 1978. pap. 6.50 (ISBN 0-931328-02-0). Timely Bks.
Wheatcroft, Andrew. The Tennyson Album: A Biography in Original Photographs. (Illus.). 200p. 1980. 25.00 (ISBN 0-7100-0494-X). Routledge & Kegan.
Wheatcroft, Andrew, jt. auth. see Keegan, John.
Wheatcroft, Andrew, jt. ed. see Best, Geoffrey.
Wheatcroft, G. S., ed. Value Added Tax in the Enlarged Common Market. LC 73-2294. 140p. 1973. 15.95 (ISBN 0-470-93754-8). Halsted Pr.
Wheatcroft, Harry, jt. auth. see Hessayon, D. G.
Wheatcroft, John. Ordering Demons. LC 78-75343. Date not set. cancelled o.p. (ISBN 0-498-02383-4). A S Barnes. Postponed.
Wheatcroft, Mildred. Revolution in British Management Education. 1971. 12.00x o.p. (ISBN 0-8464-0795-7). Beekman Pubs.
Wheatley, David. Psychopharmacology in Family Practice. (Illus.). 1973. 17.95x (ISBN 0-433-35680-4). Intl Ideas.
Wheatley, David, ed. Stress & the Heart. 2nd ed. 430p. 1981. 39.50 (ISBN 0-89004-520-8). Raven.
--Stress & the Heart: Interactions of the Cardiovascular System, Behavioral State, & Psychotropic Drugs. LC 76-55064. 1977. 19.00 (ISBN 0-89004-151-2). Raven.
Wheatley, Dennis & Links, Jay. Who Killed Robert Prentice? 117p. 1980. 17.95 (ISBN 0-686-64567-7). Mayflower Bks.
Wheatley, Edward W., jt. auth. see Fox, Edward J.
Wheatley, G. A., jt. auth. see Lewis, G. M.
Wheatley, George. Pony Riders Book. 1970. 7.50x (ISBN 0-87556-407-0). Saifer.
--The Young Rider's Companion. (Adult & Young Adult Bks.). (Illus.). 120p. (gr. 4 up). 1981. PLB 14.95 (ISBN 0-8225-0767-6). Lerner Pubns.
Wheatley, Grayson, jt. auth. see Townsend, Neal R.
Wheatley, Henry B. Dedication of Books to Patron & Friend. LC 68-30615. 1968. Repr. of 1887 ed. 15.00 (ISBN 0-8103-3316-3). Gale.
--Literary Blunders. LC 68-30616. 1969. Repr. of 1893 ed. 18.00 (ISBN 0-8103-3317-1). Gale.
--London, Past & Present: A Dictionary of Its History Associations & Traditions, 3 Vols. LC 68-17956. 1968. Repr. of 1891 ed. Set. 78.00 (ISBN 0-8103-3499-2). Gale.
Wheatley, Henry B., ed. see Percy, Thomas.
Wheatley, James & Edge, Hoyt L. Philosophical Dimension of Parapsychology. (Illus.). 520p. 1976. 39.75 (ISBN 0-398-03310-2). C C Thomas.
Wheatley, P. J. Determination of Molecular Structure. 2nd, rev. ed. 264p. 1981. pap. 5.00 (ISBN 0-486-64068-X). Dover.
Wheatley, Paul. The Golden Khersonese. LC 73-1841. (Illus.). 388p. 1973. Repr. of 1961 ed. lib. bdg. 33.25x (ISBN 0-8371-6808-2, WHGH). Greenwood.
Wheaton, B. R., jt. auth. see Heilbron, J. L.
Wheaton, Elsie C. Geneva of Erstwhile. 1981. 5.95 (ISBN 0-8062-1674-3). Carlton.
Wheaton, F. W. Aquacultural Engineering. LC 77-22876. (Ocean Engineering Ser.). 1977. 47.50 (ISBN 0-471-93755-X, Pub by Wiley-Interscience). Wiley.
Wheaton, Henry. Elements of International Law. LC 78-157426. (American Constitutional & Legal History Ser). 360p. 1972. Repr. of 1836 ed. lib. bdg. 39.50 (ISBN 0-306-70206-1). Da Capo.
--Enquiry into the Validity of the British Claim to a Right of Visitation & Search of the American Vessels Suspected to Be Engaged in the African Slave-Trade. LC 78-91668. Repr. of 1842 ed. 11.75x (ISBN 0-8371-2072-1). Negro U Pr.
Wheaton, William C., ed. Interregional Movements & Regional Growth. (Papers on Public Economics Ser.: Vol. 2). 253p. (Orig.). 1980. pap. 7.50 (ISBN 0-87766-257-6, 26600). Urban Inst.
Wheble, B. S., jt. ed. see Clay, C. J.
Whedon, Julia. Good Sport. LC 79-7670. 216p. 1981. 10.95 (ISBN 0-385-15528-X). Doubleday.
Whedon, Peggy. Always on Sunday. 1980. 12.95 (ISBN 0-393-01407-X). Norton.
Wheelan, Susan & Silberman, Melvin. How to Discipline Without Feeling Guilty. 1980. 10.95 (ISBN 0-8015-3645-6, Hawthorn). Dutton.
Wheele, Steven J. Van Der see Van der Weele, Steven.
Wheeler, Alwynne. Fishes of the World: Illustrated Dictionary. Fraser, Thomas B., ed. LC 75-6972. (Illus.). 400p. 1975. 12.98 o.s.i. (ISBN 0-02-626180-4, 62618). Macmillan.
Wheeler, Arthur L. Catullus & the Traditions of Ancient Poetry. (Sather Classical Lectures: Vol. 9). 1974. 20.00x (ISBN 0-520-02640-3). U of Cal Pr.
Wheeler, Brandon W., jt. auth. see Crowdis, David G.
Wheeler, Charles B. Design of Poetry. 1967. 6.50x (ISBN 0-393-04256-1); pap. 6.95x (ISBN 0-393-09707-2, NortonC). Norton.
Wheeler, David R. Control Yourself. LC 75-15259. 180p. 1976. 12.95 (ISBN 0-88229-207-2). Nelson-Hall.
Wheeler, Douglas L. Republican Portugal: A Political History, 1910-1926. LC 77-15059. (Illus.). 1978. 20.00 (ISBN 0-299-07450-1). U of Wis Pr.
Wheeler, E. R., jt. auth. see Wheeler, R. E.
Wheeler, Ed. R., jt. auth. see Wheeler, Ruric E.
Wheeler, Gary L. & Strang, David M. Tiny Mouse. 1980. pap. 2.75 (ISBN 0-937172-10-3). JLJ Pubs.
--Tiny Mouse. (Orig.). 1980. pap. 2.75 (ISBN 0-937172-10-3). JLJ Pubs.
Wheeler, Gerald R. Counterdeterrence: A Report on Juvenile Sentencing & Effects of Prisonization. LC 77-26975. 1978. 15.95 (ISBN 0-88229-315-X). Nelson-Hall.
Wheeler, Gerald W. Deluge. LC 78-8404. (Flame Ser.). 1978. pap. 0.95 (ISBN 0-8127-0191-7). Southern Pub.
Wheeler, Gershon. Introduction to Microwaves. (Illus.). 1963. ref. ed. 18.95 (ISBN 0-13-487843-4). P-H.
Wheeler, Grace. Microwave Cooking My Way. new ed. LC 80-53591. 240p. 1980. 7.95 (ISBN 0-914488-25-2). Rand-Tofua.
--Microwave Cooking My Way: It's a Matter of Time. Rand, Elizabeth, ed. LC 80-53591. (Illus.). 240p. 1981. plastic comb bound 7.95 (ISBN 0-914488-25-2). Rand-Tofua.
Wheeler, Harvey, ed. Beyond the Punitive Society: Operant Conditioning, Social & Political Aspects. LC 73-1269. (Illus.). 1973. pap. text ed. 9.95x (ISBN 0-7167-0775-6). W H Freeman.
Wheeler, Helen. Womanhood Media: Current Resources About Women. LC 72-7396. 1972. 10.00 (ISBN 0-8108-0549-9). Scarecrow.
--Womanhood Media Supplement: Additional Current Resources About Women. LC 72-7396. 1975. 18.00 (ISBN 0-8108-0858-7). Scarecrow.
Wheeler, Hugh & Sondheim, Stephen. Sweeney Todd, The Demon Barber of Fleet Street. LC 79-18468. 1979. 7.95 (ISBN 0-396-07776-5). Dodd.
Wheeler, James E. & Galliart, William F. An Appraisal of Interperiod Income Tax Allocation. LC 74-84803. 1974. 10.00 o.p. (ISBN 0-910586-10-1). Finan Exec.
Wheeler, James O. & Muller, Peter O. Economic Geography. LC 80-21536. 450p. 1981. text ed. 20.95 (ISBN 0-471-93760-6). Wiley.
Wheeler, James O., jt. auth. see Brunn, Stanley D.
Wheeler, John, jt. auth. see Kuhaulua, Jesse.
Wheeler, John A., jt. auth. see Taylor, Edwin F.
Wheeler, Joseph. The Santiago Campaign Eighteen Ninety-Eight. LC 70-137930. 1970. Repr. of 1898 ed. 15.00 o.p. (ISBN 0-8046-1492-X). Kennikat.
Wheeler, K. The Railroaders. LC 73-84316. (Old West Ser.). (Illus.). (gr. 5 up). 1973. kivar 12.96 (ISBN 0-8094-1467-8, Pub. by Time-Life). Silver.
Wheeler, Kathleen. Sources, Processes & Methods in Coleridge's Biographia Literaria. LC 79-41683. 240p. 1980. 39.50 (ISBN 0-521-22690-2). Cambridge U Pr.
Wheeler, Keith. The Alaskans. (Old West Ser.). (Illus.). (gr. 5 up). 1977. 12.96 (ISBN 0-8094-1506-2, Pub. by Time-Life). Silver.
--The Chroniclers. (Old West Ser.). (Illus.). 1976. 12.95 (ISBN 0-8094-1529-1). Time-Life.
--The Chroniclers. LC 75-34961. (The Old West). (Illus.). (gr. 5 up). 1976. kivar 12.96 (ISBN 0-8094-1531-3, Pub. by Time-Life). Silver.
--The Railroaders. (The Old West Ser.). (Illus.). 1973. 12.95 (ISBN 0-8094-1466-X). Time-Life.
--The Scouts. (Old West Ser.). (Illus.). 1978. 12.95 (ISBN 0-8094-2304-9). Time-Life.
--The Scouts. LC 78-1364. (The Old West Ser.). (Illus.). 1978. lib. bdg. 12.96 (ISBN 0-686-51081-X). Silver.
--The Townsmen. (The Old West Ser). (Illus.). 240p. 1975. 12.95 (ISBN 0-8094-1488-0). Time-Life.
--Townsmen. LC 74-2180. (Old West Ser.). (Illus.). 240p. (gr. 5 up). 1975. lib. bdg. 12.96 kivar (ISBN 0-8094-1490-2). Silver.
--War Under the Pacific. Time-Life Books Editors, ed. (World War Two Ser.). (Illus.). 208p. 1980. 13.95 (ISBN 0-8094-3375-3). Time-Life.
Wheeler, Keith & Time-Life Editors. The Alaskans. new ed. (Old West Ser.). 1977. 12.95 (ISBN 0-8094-1504-6). Time-Life.
Wheeler, Ladd, ed. Review of Personality & Social Psychology: No. 1. (Illus.). 352p. 1980. 20.00 (ISBN 0-8039-1457-1). Sage.
--Review of Personality & Social Psychology: No. 1. (Illus.). 352p. 1980. pap. 9.95 (ISBN 0-8039-1458-X). Sage.
Wheeler, Ladd, et al. Interpersonal Influence. 2nd ed. 1978. pap. text ed. 10.95 (ISBN 0-205-06061-7). Allyn.
Wheeler, Leslie, ed. Loving Warriors: Selected Letters of Lucy Stone & Henry B. Blackwell, 1853-1893. (Illus.). 1981. 19.95. Dial.
Wheeler, Leslie J. Principles of Cinematography. 4th ed. 1978. 17.95 o.p. (ISBN 0-85242-080-3, Pub. by Fountain). Morgan.
Wheeler, Lora J., ed. International Business & Foreign Trade. LC 67-31263. (Management Information Guide Ser.: No. 14). 1968. 30.00 (ISBN 0-8103-0814-2). Gale.
Wheeler, Marcus & Unbegaun, B. O., eds. The Oxford-Russian-English Dictionary. 919p. 1972. 45.00 (ISBN 0-19-864111-7). Oxford U Pr.
Wheeler, Margaret F., jt. auth. see Volk, Wesley A.
Wheeler, Mark C. Britain & the War for Yugoslavia, Nineteen Forty to Nineteen Forty-Three. (East European Monographs: No. 64). 1980. 18.50x (ISBN 0-914710-57-5). East Eur Quarterly.
Wheeler, Max. Phonology of Catalan. 1979. 42.25x (ISBN 0-631-11621-4, Pub. by Basil Blackwell England). Biblio Dist.
Wheeler, Michael, ed. Divided Children. 223p. 1981. pap. 4.95 (ISBN 0-14-005777-3). Penguin.
Wheeler, Monroe, intro. by. Looking South: Latin American Art in New York Collections. (Illus.). 60p. 1972. pap. 2.00 o.p. (ISBN 0-913456-14-4). Interbk Inc.

Wheeler, Mortimer. Indus Civilization. 3rd ed. LC 22-11272. (Illus.). 1968. 32.50 (ISBN 0-521-06958-0); pap. 8.50x (ISBN 0-521-09538-7). Cambridge U Pr.
--Roman Art & Architecture. (World of Art Ser.). (Illus.). 1964. pap. 9.95 (ISBN 0-19-519921-9). Oxford U Pr.
Wheeler, Penney E. The Appearing. LC 79-16298. (Orion Ser.). 1979. pap. 2.95 (ISBN 0-8127-0231-X). Southern Pub.
Wheeler, Penny E. With Long Life. LC 78-13748. (Crown Ser.). 1978. pap. 4.50 (ISBN 0-8127-0192-5). Southern Pub.
Wheeler, R. Man, Nature & Art. 1968. 18.75 (ISBN 0-08-012690-1); pap. 9.25 (ISBN 0-08-012689-8). Pergamon.
Wheeler, R. & Whitcomb, H. Judicial Administration: Text & Readings. 1977. text ed. 15.95 (ISBN 0-13-511675-9). P-H.
Wheeler, R. E. & Wheeler, E. R. Mathematics: An Everyday Language. LC 78-13072. 1979. text ed. 19.95x (ISBN 0-471-03423-1); student supplement 7.50 (ISBN 0-471-04924-7); tchrs. manual 2.85 (ISBN 0-471-05409-7). Wiley.
Wheeler, Richard. Sherman's March. LC 78-3321. (Illus.). 1978. 11.95 o.p. (ISBN 0-690-01746-4, TYC-T). T Y Crowell.
--The Siege of Vicksburg. LC 77-14258. (Illus.). 1978. 12.95 o.p. (ISBN 0-690-01427-9, TYC-T). T Y Crowell.
--Voices of Seventeen Seventy Six. LC 72-78277. (Illus.). 384p. 1972. 12.95 o.s.i. (ISBN 0-690-86422-1, TYC-T). T Y Crowell.
--Voices of Seventeen Seventy-Six. 1975. pap. 1.95 (ISBN 0-449-30742-5, C742, Prem). Fawcett.
--Voices of the Civil War. LC 75-33705. (Illus.). 416p. 1976. 15.95 o.s.i. (ISBN 0-690-01090-7, TYC-T). T Y Crowell.
--We Knew Stonewall Jackson. LC 76-58009. (Illus.). 1977. 9.95 (ISBN 0-690-01289-6, TYC-T). T Y Crowell.
--We Knew William Tecumseh Sherman. LC 77-4334. (Illus.). 1977. 8.95 o.p. (ISBN 0-690-01426-0, TYC-T). T Y Crowell.
Wheeler, Richard P. Shakespeare's Development & Problem Comedies: Turn & Counter-Turn. 275p. 1981. 18.50x (ISBN 0-520-03902-5). U of Cal Pr.
Wheeler, Richard S. Bushwack. LC 78-7772. 1978. 7.95 o.p. (ISBN 0-385-14281-1). Doubleday.
--Children of Darkness: Some Heretical Reflections on the Kid Cult. 1973. 7.95 o.p. (ISBN 0-87000-208-2). Arlington Hse.
Wheeler, Robert R. & Whited, Maurine. Oil from Prospect to Pipeline. 4th ed. 157p. 1981. pap. 6.95 (ISBN 0-87201-635-8). Gulf Pub.
Wheeler, Robert W. Jim Thorpe: The World's Greatest Athlete. LC 78-58080. (Illus.). 320p. 1981. pap. 5.95 (ISBN 0-8061-1745-1). U of Okla Pr.
Wheeler, Robinetta T., jt. ed. see Bower, Fay L.
Wheeler, Ruric. Modern Mathematics: An Elementary Approach, Alternative Edition. 585p. 1981. text ed. 18.95 (ISBN 0-8185-0413-7). Brooks-Cole.
Wheeler, Ruric E. Modern Mathematics: An Elementary Approach. 5th ed. 625p. 1981. text ed. 19.95 (ISBN 0-8185-0430-7). Brooks-Cole.
Wheeler, Ruric E. & Peeples, W. D. Finite Mathematics: An Introduction to Mathematical Models. LC 73-89593. (Contemporary Undergrad Math Ser). 1974. text ed. 18.95 (ISBN 0-8185-0117-0); instr's. manual o.p. (ISBN 0-685-46781-3). Brooks-Cole.
--Modern Mathematics with Applications to Business & the Social Sciences. 2nd ed. LC 74-21453. (Contemporary Undergraduate Mathematics Ser.). 1976. text ed. 16.95x o.p. (ISBN 0-685-67043-0); instructor's manual avail. o.p. (ISBN 0-685-67044-9). Brooks-Cole.
Wheeler, Ruric E. & Peeples, W. D., Jr. Finite Mathematics: With Applications to Business & the Social Sciences. LC 80-13916. 550p. 1980. text ed. 19.95 (ISBN 0-8185-0418-8). Brooks-Cole.
--Modern Mathematics with Applications to Business & the Social Sciences. 3rd ed. LC 79-18636. 1980. text ed. 18.95 (ISBN 0-8185-0366-1). Brooks-Cole.
Wheeler, Ruric E. & Wheeler, Ed. R. Programmed Study of Number Systems. (Contemporary Undergrad Math Ser). (Prog. Bk.). 1972. pap. text ed. 8.95 (ISBN 0-8185-0402-5). Brooks-Cole.
Wheeler, Russell C. Atlas of Tooth Form. 4th ed. LC 69-17806. (Illus.). 1969. 16.00 (ISBN 0-7216-9276-1). Saunders.
Wheeler, Ruth & Coffin, Harold G. Dinosaurs. LC 78-50443. (Panda Ser.). 1978. pap. 4.95 (ISBN 0-8163-0195-6, 04340-6). Pacific Pr Pub Assn.
Wheeler, Ruth L. Story of Birds of North America. LC 65-14630. (Story of Science Ser.). (Illus.). (gr. 5-10). 1965. PLB 7.29 (ISBN 0-8178-3542-3). Harvey.
Wheeler, S., jt. auth. see Brim, Q. G.
Wheeler, Stanton, jt. ed. see Rothman, David.
Wheeler, Thomas G. All Men Tall. LC 70-77313. (gr. 8 up). 1969. 9.95 (ISBN 0-87599-157-2). S G Phillips.
--Fanfare for the Stalwart. LC 67-22813. (gr. 8 up). 1967. 9.95 (ISBN 0-87599-139-4). S G Phillips.
--Loose Chippings. LC 69-11990. (Illus.). (YA) 1969. 9.95 (ISBN 0-87599-152-1). S G Phillips.
--Lost Threshold. LC 68-16349. (Illus.). (gr. 7 up). 1968. 9.95 (ISBN 0-87599-140-8). S G Phillips.
Wheeler, Tony. Across Asia on the Cheap. 3rd ed. (Illus.). 1979. pap. 4.95 o.p. (ISBN 0-908086-02-4). Hippocrene Bks.
--Australia, Travel Survival Kit. (Illus.). 1979. pap. 3.95 (ISBN 0-908086-04-0). Hippocrene Bks.
--New Zealand, a Travel Survival Kit. (Illus.). 1977. pap. 2.95 o.p. (ISBN 0-9598080-9-4, Pub. by Two Continents). Hippocrene Bks.
--South-East Asia: On a Shoestring. (Illus., Orig.). 1978. pap. 3.95 (ISBN 0-8467-0473-0, Pub. by Two Continents). Hippocrene Bks.
Wheeler, W. H. Wet Fire. (Pacesetter Ser.). (Illus.). 64p. (gr. 4 up). 1978. PLB 7.95 (ISBN 0-516-02174-5). Childrens.
Wheeler, William & Hayward, Charles. Woodcarving. LC 74-6469. (Drake Home Craftsman Ser.). (Illus.). 124p. 1972. 8.95 o.p. (ISBN 0-8069-8793-6); pap. 5.95 (ISBN 0-8069-8790-1). Sterling.
Wheeler, William & Hayward, Charles H. Wood Carving. rev. ed. (Illus.). 1979. pap. 5.95 (ISBN 0-8069-8790-1). Sterling.
Wheeler, William A. Explanatory & Pronouncing Dictionary of the Noted Names of Fictions. LC 66-25811. 1966. Repr. of 1889 ed. 18.00 (ISBN 0-8103-0165-2). Gale.
--Familiar Allusions: A Hand-Book of Miscellaneous Information. LC 66-24371. 1966. Repr. of 1882 ed. 26.00 (ISBN 0-8103-0166-0). Gale.
--Who Wrote It. LC 68-30667. 1968. Repr. of 1881 ed. 15.00 (ISBN 0-8103-3228-0). Gale.
Wheeler, William M. Ants: Their Structure, Development, & Behavior. rev. ed. LC 10-8253. (Columbia Biological Ser.: No. 9). (Illus.). 1960. 35.00x (ISBN 0-231-00121-5). Columbia U Pr.
Wheeler-Bennett, J. W. Information on the Renunciation of War 1927-1928. LC 72-89272. 192p. 1973. Repr. of 1928 ed. 15.50 (ISBN 0-8046-1761-9). Kennikat.
Wheeler-Bennett, John W. Disarmament & Security Since Locarno, 1925-1931. 22.00 (ISBN 0-86527-045-7). Fertig.
--Pipe Dream of Peace: The Story of the Collapse of Disarmament. LC 76-80601. 1971. Repr. 19.00 (ISBN 0-86527-151-8). Fertig.
Wheeler-Voegelin, Erminie. Chipewa Indians I: Red Lake & Pembina Chippewa. (American Indian Ethnohistory Ser: North Central & Northeastern Indians). (Illus.). lib. bdg. 42.00 (ISBN 0-8240-0808-1). Garland Pub.
--Indians of Northwest Ohio: An Ethnohistorical Report on the Wyandot, Potawatomi, Ottawa & Chippewa of Northwest Ohio. Horr, David A., ed. (North Central & Northeastern Indians - American Indian Ethnohistory Ser.). 1974. lib. bdg. 42.00 (ISBN 0-8240-0799-9). Garland Pub.
--Miami, Wea, & El-River Indians of Southern Indian. Horr, David A., ed. (American Indian Ethnohistory Ser.). 1974. lib. bdg. 42.00 (ISBN 0-8240-0806-5). Garland Pub.
Wheeler-Voegelin, Erminie, jt. auth. see Steward, Julian H.
Wheeler-Voegelin, Erminie, et al. California Indians Three. Horr, David A., ed. (American Indian Ethnohistory Ser.). 1978. lib. bdg. 42.00 (ISBN 0-8240-0773-5). Garland Pub.
--Chippewa Indians V. Horr, David A., ed. (American Indian Ethnohistory Ser.). 1978. lib. bdg. 42.00 (ISBN 0-8240-0812-X). Garland Pub.
Wheeless, Clifford R., Jr. Atlas of Pelvic Surgery. LC 80-27140. (Illus.). 400p. 1981. text ed. write for info. (ISBN 0-8121-0727-6). Lea & Febiger.
Wheelis, Allen. Illusionless Man: Some Fantasies & Meditations on Disillusionment. 1971. pap. 2.95x o.p. (ISBN 0-06-131927-9, TB1927, Torch). Har-Row.
--On Not Knowing How to Live. LC 75-4294. 128p. (YA) 1975. 5.95 o.s.i. (ISBN 0-06-014562-5, HarpT). Har-Row.
Wheelis, M., jt. auth. see Segel, W.
Wheelock, Arthur K., Jr. Perspecture, Optics, & Delft Artists Around 1650. LC 76-23661. (Outstanding Dissertations in the Fine Arts - 17th Century). (Illus.). 1977. Repr. of 1973 ed. lib. bdg. 56.00 (ISBN 0-8240-2740-X). Garland Pub.
Wheelock, Walt. Beaches of Baja. (Illus.). 1972. 2.50 (ISBN 0-910856-28-1). La Siesta.
--Ropes, Knots & Slings for Climbers. rev. ed. (Illus.). 1967. wrappers 1.50 (ISBN 0-910856-00-1). La Siesta.
Wheelock, Walt, ed. Desert Peaks Guide One. rev. ed. (Illus.). 1964. wrappers 1.95 (ISBN 0-910856-03-6). La Siesta.
Wheelock, Warren, jt. auth. see Sheldon, William D.
Wheelock, Warren H., jt. auth. see Sheldon, William.
Wheelwright, Jane. The Death of a Woman. 288p. 1981. 12.95 (ISBN 0-312-18744-0). St Martin.
Wheelwright, Philip, ed. & tr. Presocratics. LC 66-12944. (Orig.). 1966. pap. 7.50 (ISBN 0-672-63091-5). Odyssey Pr.
Wheelwright, Philip, ed. Way of Philosophy. rev. ed. 1960. 13.20 o.p. (ISBN 0-672-63217-9). Odyssey Pr.
Wheelwright, Philip & Fuss, Peter, eds. Five Philosophers. LC 63-14019. 1963. pap. 7.50 (ISBN 0-672-63035-4). Odyssey Pr.
Wheelwright, Philip, ed. see Aristotle.
Wheelwright, Steven C. & Makridakis, Spyros. Forecasting Methods for Management. 3rd ed. LC 79-23476. (Systems & Controls for Financial Management Ser.). 300p. 1980. 28.95 (ISBN 0-471-05630-8, Pub by Ronald Pr). Wiley.
--Forecasting Methods for Management. 2nd ed. LC 76-42294. (Systems & Controls for Financial Management Ser). 1977. 27.95 o.p. (ISBN 0-471-02225-X, Pub. by Wiley-Interscience). Wiley.
Wheelwright, Steven C., jt. auth. see Makridakis, Spyros.
Whelan, A. & Brydson, J. A., eds. Developments with Thermosetting Plastics. LC 74-34013. 198p. 1975. 29.95 (ISBN 0-470-93772-6). Halsted Pr.
Whelan, A. & Craft, J. L., eds. Developments in Injection Molding, Vol. 1. (Illus.). 1978. text ed. 51.40x (ISBN 0-85334-798-0, Pub. by Applied Science). Burgess-Intl Ideas.
Whelan, Donald J., ed. Handbook for Development Officers at Independent Schools. 1979. pap. 21.50 (ISBN 0-89964-045-1). CASE.
Whelan, Elizabeth. Boy or Girl? LC 76-44667. (Illus.). 1977. 7.95 o.p. (ISBN 0-672-52276-4). Bobbs.
Whelan, Elizabeth M. A Baby?...Maybe: A Guide to Making the Most Fateful Decision of Your Life. rev. ed. LC 79-55437. 256p. 1980. 11.95 (ISBN 0-672-52628-X); pap. 8.95 (ISBN 0-672-52629-8). Bobbs.
Whelan, Michael. Wonderworks: Science Fiction & Fantasy Art. Freas, Polly & Freas, Kelly, eds. LC 79-12575. (Illus.). 1979. 13.95 (ISBN 0-915442-75-2, Starblaze); pap. 7.95 (ISBN 0-915442-74-4, Starblaze); collector's edition 30.00 (ISBN 0-915442-83-3). Donning Co.
Whelan, W. J., ed. see Conference on Recombinant DNA, Committee on Genetic Experimentation (COGENE) & the Royal Society of London, Wye College, Kent, UK, April, 1979.
Whelton. The Aminoglycosides: Microbiology, Use & Toxicology. Date not set. price not set (ISBN 0-8247-1364-8). Dekker.
Wherlock, Julia. The Fire Bride. (Orig.). 1980. pap. write for info. (ISBN 0-671-41295-7). PB.
Wherrett, B. S., ed. see National Quantum Electronics Conference, 4th, Heriot-Watt University Edinburgh, 1979.
Wherry, Joseph H. Indian Masks & Myths of the West. (Apollo Eds.). 288p. 1974. pap. 3.50 o.s.i. (ISBN 0-8152-0358-6, A358, TYC-T). T Y Crowell.
--The Totem Pole Indians. (Apollo Eds.). 1974. pap. 3.50 o.s.i. (ISBN 0-8152-0359-4, A-359, TYC-T). T Y Crowell.
Whetham, Edith J. & Currie, Jean I., eds. Economics of African Countries. LC 69-12931. (Illus.). 1969. 30.50 (ISBN 0-521-07070-8); pap. 11.95x (ISBN 0-521-09534-4). Cambridge U Pr.
Whethan, Edith J. & Curie, Jean I., eds. Reading in the Applied Economics of Africa, 2 vols, Vol. 1, Micro-Economics. pap. 11.95x (ISBN 0-521-09437-2). Vol. 2, Macro-Economics. pap. 11.95x (ISBN 0-521-09438-0). Cambridge U Pr.
Whetstone, G. W. & Grigoriev, V. J., eds. Hydrologic Information Systems. LC 72-90686. (Studies & Reports in Hydrology). (Illus.). 72p. (Orig.). 1973. pap. 9.25 (ISBN 92-3-100957-5, U289, UNESCO). Unipub.
Whetten, Lawrence L. Current Research in Comparative Communism: An Analysis & Bibliographic Guide to the Soviet System. LC 76-19553. 1976. text ed. 22.95 (ISBN 0-275-23550-5). Praeger.
--Germany East & West: Conflicts, Collaboration & Confrontation. LC 79-3713. 244p. 1981. 17.50x (ISBN 0-8147-9193-X). NYU Pr.
--Germany's Ostpolitik: Relations Between the Federal Republic & the Warsaw Pact Countries. 1971. pap. 6.50x o.p. (ISBN 0-19-285051-2). Oxford U Pr.
Whetten, N. L., jt. auth. see Zimmerman, C. C.
Whichcote, Benjamin. The Works, 4 vols. LC 75-11265. (British Philosophers & Theologians of the 17th & 18th Centuries: Vol. 64). 1977. Repr. of 1751 ed. Set. lib. bdg. write for info. (ISBN 0-8240-1814-1); lib. bdg. 42.00 ea. Garland Pub.
Whicher, George F., ed. William Jennings Bryan & the Campaign of 1896. (Problems in American Civilization Ser.). 1953. pap. text ed. 4.95x o.p. (ISBN 0-669-24000-1). Heath.
Whicher, George F., ed. see Thoreau, Henry D.
Whicher, Stephen E. Freedom & Fate: An Inner Life of Ralph Waldo Emerson. 2nd ed. LC 74-84742. 1969. 10.00 o.p. (ISBN 0-8122-7045-2). U of Pa Pr.
Whidden, Angela, ed. Come Me Sacaras De Este Apuro, Senor? (Span.). 1979. pap. 1.75 (ISBN 0-8297-0553-8). Vida Pubs.
Whidden, Angela, ed. see Cho, Paul Y.
Whidden, Angela, jt. ed. see Marosi, Esteban.
Whidden, Angela, ed. see Winley, Jesse.
Whiffen, D. H., ed. Expression of Results in Quantum Chemistry. new ed. 1978. pap. text ed. 6.60 o.p. (ISBN 0-08-022367-2). Pergamon.
--Manual of Symbols & Terminology for Physiochemical Quantities & Units. 1979. pap. text ed. 10.25 (ISBN 0-08-022386-9). Pergamon.
Whiffen, Marcus & Koeper, Frederick. American Architecture: A History, 1607-1976. 600p. 1981. text ed. 20.00 (ISBN 0-262-23105-0). MIT Pr.
Whigham, Peter, tr. see Meleager.
Whiiler, C. E. & Kenyon, J. D. An Introduction to the Principles & Practice of Homoeopathy. 371p. 1957. 17.95x (ISBN 0-8464-1027-3). Beekman Pubs.
Whimbey, Arthur & Lochhead, Jack. Developing Mathematical Skills. (Illus.). 448p. 1981. text ed. 11.95 (ISBN 0-07-069517-2, C). McGraw.
Whinney, Margaret & Gunnis, Rupert. The Collection of Models by John Flaxman at University College, London: A Catalogue & Introduction. 1967. text ed. 11.50x (ISBN 0-485-11088-1, Athlone Pr). Humanities.
Whinston, Andrew B., jt. auth. see Haseman, William D.
Whipkey, Harry E. Guide to the Manuscript Groups in the Pennsylvania State Archives. 1977. 7.00 (ISBN 0-911124-84-5). Pa Hist & Mus.
Whipkey, Harry E., ed. see Simonett, Martha L.
Whipkey, K. L. & Whipkey, Mary N. The Power of Calculus. 3rd ed. LC 78-24067. 1979. 18.50 (ISBN 0-471-03140-2); tchrs. manual 2.00 (ISBN 0-471-05500-X). Wiley.
Whipkey, Kenneth L., et al. Power of Mathematics: Applications to Management & the Social Sciences. LC 77-27365. 1978. text ed. 18.95 (ISBN 0-471-93785-1); tchrs. manual 4.50 (ISBN 0-471-03760-5); study guide 7.95 (ISBN 0-471-03759-1). Wiley.
--The Power of Mathematics: Applications to the Management & the Social Sciences. 2nd ed. LC 80-19576. 512p. 1981. text ed. 19.95 (ISBN 0-471-07709-7). Wiley.
Whipkey, Mary N., jt. auth. see Whipkey, K. L.
Whipkey, Mary N., et al. The Power of Relevant Mathematics: The Basic Concept. (Illus.). 1977. text ed. 17.95 (ISBN 0-13-687202-6). P-H.
Whipp, Thresa, ed. Pipeline Rates on Gasoline & Petroleum Products. 700p. pap. 95.00 (ISBN 0-686-28100-4). CSG Pr.
Whipple, A. B. The Clipper Ships. Time-Life Bks, ed. (The Seafarers Ser.). (Illus.). 176p. 1980. 14.95 (ISBN 0-8094-2677-3). Time-Life.
--Fighting Sail. new ed. Time-Life Books, ed. (Seafarers Ser.). (Illus.). 1978. 13.95 (ISBN 0-8094-2654-4). Time-Life.
--Vintage Nantucket. LC 78-7107. (Illus.). 1978. 8.95 (ISBN 0-396-07517-7). Dodd.
Whipple, A. B. & Time-Life Books Editors. The Mediterranean. (World War II Ser). (Illus.). 208p. 1981. 13.95 (ISBN 0-8094-3383-4). Time-Life.
Whipple, A. B., jt. auth. see Time-Life Books Editors.
Whipple, Alan L. Research & the Library: A Student Guide to Basic Techniques. 120p. (Orig.). (gr. 8-11). 1974. pap. text ed. 2.95x (ISBN 0-88334-062-3). Ind Sch Pr.
Whipple, Alan L., jt. auth. see Fraser, Theodore P.
Whipple, Bishop. Bishop Whipple's Southern Diary. Shippee, Lester B., ed. LC 68-13637. (American Scene Ser). (Illus.). 1969. lib. bdg. 25.00 (ISBN 0-306-70987-2). Da Capo.
Whipple, Cal. Fighting Sail. LC 78-52043. (The Seafarers Ser.). (Illus.). 1978. lib. bdg. 11.97 (ISBN 0-686-50985-4). Silver.
--The Whalers. (The Seafarers Ser.). (Illus.). 1979. lib. bdg. 11.97 (ISBN 0-686-50991-9). Silver.
Whipple, G. M., tr. see Stern, William L.
Whipple, Jane, ed. see Bothwell, Jean.

Whipple, L. Story of Civil Liberty in the United States. LC 72-107419. (Civil Liberties in American History Ser). 1970. Repr. of 1927 ed. lib. bdg. 35.00 (ISBN 0-306-71879-0). Da Capo.
Whipple, Leland, jt. auth. see Villard, Kenneth L.
Whipple, Leon. Our Ancient Liberties. LC 73-175723. (Civil Liberties in American History Ser.). 1972. Repr. lib. bdg. 15.00 (ISBN 0-306-70419-6). Da Capo.
Whipple, William J. Planning of Water Quality Systems. LC 76-47336. 1977. 23.95 (ISBN 0-669-01144-4). Lexington Bks.
Whisenand, jt. auth. see Shanahan.
Whisenand, P. M. Police Supervision: Theory & Practice. 2nd ed. (Illus.). 576p. 1976. 17.95 (ISBN 0-13-686311-6). P-H.
Whisenand, Paul M. Crime Prevention. (Criminal Justice Ser.). 419p. 1977. text ed. 16.50 (ISBN 0-205-05548-6, 825595-4); instructor's manual free (ISBN 0-205-05596-6). Allyn.
Whisenand, Paul M. & Ferguson, R. Fred. The Managing of Police Organizations. 2nd ed. (Illus.). 1978. text ed. 18.95 (ISBN 0-13-550731-6). P-H.
Whisenhunt, Donald W. The Environment & the American Experience: A Historian Looks at the Ecological Crisis. LC 74-80068. (National University Publications). 1974. 12.95 (ISBN 0-8046-9071-5). Kennikat.
Whisenhunt, Donald W., ed. see Fell, John.
Whishaw, Ian Q., jt. auth. see Kolb, Bryan.
Whisker, James B. The Citizen Soldier & United States Military Policy. 7.50 (ISBN 0-88427-035-1); pap. 4.95 (ISBN 0-88427-036-X). Green Hill.
--Dictionary of Concepts. LC 80-15591. 285p. 1980. pap. 7.95 (ISBN 0-471-07716-X). Wiley.
--The Right to Hunt. 156p. 1981. 7.95 (ISBN 0-88427-042-4, Dist. by Caroline Hse). North River.
Whisler, Walter W., jt. auth. see Voris, Harold C.
Whisnant, David E. James Boyd. (U. S. Authors Ser.: No. 199). lib. bdg. 10.95 (ISBN 0-8057-0080-3). Twayne.
Whissen, Thomas R. Isak Dineser's Aesthetics. LC 73-83272. 144p. 1974. 10.00 (ISBN 0-8046-9059-6). Kennikat.
Whisson, M. G. & West, Martin. Religion & Social Change in Southern Africa: Anthropological Essays in Honour of Monica Wilson. 1977. text ed. 18.00x (ISBN 0-949968-44-7). Verry.
Whistell, Ray L. Kinesics & Context. 1975. pap. 1.95 o.p. (ISBN 0-345-24841-4). Ballantine.
Whisteside, Robert L., jt. auth. see Whiteside, David.
Whistler, James A. The Gentle Art of Making Enemies. 8.50 (ISBN 0-8446-3168-X). Peter Smith.
Whistler, Roy L. & Paschall, Eugene F., eds. Starch: Chemistry & Technology, 2 vols. Incl. Vol. 1. Fundamental Aspects. 1965. 55.25 (ISBN 0-12-746261-9); Vol. 2. Industrial Aspects. 1967. 67.50 (ISBN 0-12-746262-7). Acad Pr.
Whistler, Roy L. & Wolfrom, Melville L., eds. Methods in Carbohydrate Chemistry, 8 vols. Incl. Vol. 1. Analysis & Preparation of Sugars. 1962. 55.25 (ISBN 0-12-746201-5); Vol. 2. Reactions of Carbohydrates. 1963. 55.25 (ISBN 0-12-746202-3); Vol. 3. Cellulose. 1963. 52.50 (ISBN 0-12-746203-1); Vol. 4. Starch. 1964. 52.50 (ISBN 0-12-746204-X); Vol. 5. General Polysaccharides. 1965. 52.50 (ISBN 0-12-746205-8); Vol. 6. 1971. 55.25 (ISBN 0-12-746206-6); Vol. 7. 46.50 (ISBN 0-12-746207-4); Vol. 8. 1980. 38.50 (ISBN 0-12-746208-2). Acad Pr.
Whiston, Charles F., ed. see Fenelon, Francois.
Whiston, Lionel. Through the Eyes of Love. 1981. pap. 4.95 (ISBN 0-8499-2929-6). Word Bks.
Whiston, William, tr. see Josephus, Flavius.
Whitaker, Arthur P. Documents Relating to the Commercial Policy of Spain with Florida. limited ed. 1921. 85.00x o.p. (ISBN 0-685-69882-3). Elliots Bks.
--Spanish-American Frontier, 1783-1795: The Westward Movement & the Spanish Retreat in the Mississippi Valley. LC 27-23368. (Illus.). 1969. pap. 2.95x (ISBN 0-8032-5216-1, BB 398, Bison). U of Nebr Pr.
--U. S. & the Independence of Latin America, 1800-1830. 1964. pap. 3.95 o.p. (ISBN 0-393-00271-3, Norton Lib). Norton.
Whitaker, Ben. Biharis in Bangladesh. (Minority Rights Group: No. 11). 1972. pap. 2.50 (ISBN 0-89192-100-1). Interbk Inc.
Whitaker, Carl A. & Malone, Thomas P. The Roots of Psychotherapy. LC 80-24437. (Brunner Mazel Classics in Psychoanalysis & Psychotherapy: No. 9). 272p. 1981. Repr. 17.50 (ISBN 0-87630-265-7). Brunner-Mazel.
Whitaker, Carl A., jt. auth. see Napier, Augustus Y.
Whitaker, George O. & Meyers, Joan. Dinosaur Hunt. LC 65-12614. (Illus.). (gr. 5-8). 1965. 5.95 o.p. (ISBN 0-15-223501-9, HJ). HarBraceJ.
Whitaker, Haiganoosh & Whitaker, Harry A., eds. Studies in Neurolinguistics, 2 vols. LC 75-13100. (Perspectives in Neurolinguistics & Psycholinguistics). 1976-79. Vol. 1. 32.50, subscription 29.00 (ISBN 0-12-746301-1); Vol. 2. 29.00, subscription 26.50 (ISBN 0-12-746302-X); Vol. 3. 28.00, subscription 21.50 (ISBN 0-12-746303-8); Vol. 4. 28.50, by subscription 24.50 (ISBN 0-12-746304-6). Acad Pr.
Whitaker, Harold & Halas, John. Timing for Animation. LC 80-41303. (Illus.). 144p. 1981. 25.00 (ISBN 0-240-50871-8). Focal Pr.
Whitaker, Harry A., jt. ed. see Whitaker, Haiganoosh.
Whitaker, Jennifer S., ed. Africa & the United States: Vital Interests. LC 77-92753. 1978. 15.00x (ISBN 0-8147-9181-6); pap. 7.00x (ISBN 0-8147-9182-4). NYU Pr.
Whitaker, John. Personal Marriage Contract. LC 76-9623. (Illus.). 1976. 5.95 o.p. (ISBN 0-917278-02-X); pap. 3.95 o.p. (ISBN 0-685-73029-8). OK Street.
Whitaker, John O., Jr. The Audubon Field Guide to North American Mammals. LC 79-3525. (Illus.). 752p. 1980. 9.95 (ISBN 0-394-50762-2). Knopf.
Whitaker, John O., Jr., jt. auth. see Hamilton, William J., Jr.
Whitaker, John R. & Tannenbaum, Steven R., eds. Food Proteins. (Illus.). 1977. lib. bdg. 39.00 (ISBN 0-87055-230-9). AVI.
Whitaker, Keith, jt. auth. see Learmouth, John.
Whitaker, Linton A. & Randall, Peter, eds. Symposium on Reconstruction of Jaw Deformity. LC 78-4867. (Symposia of the Educational Foundaion of the American Society of Plastic & Reconstructive Surgeons, Inc. Ser.). 1978. text ed. 54.50 (ISBN 0-8016-5610-9). Mosby.
Whitaker, Norman. Process Instrumentation Primer. 128p. 1980. 27.50 (ISBN 0-87814-128-6). Pennwell Pub.
Whitaker, Pamela, jt. auth. see Wallas, James.
Whitaker, Rogers E. M., jt. auth. see Ball, Don, Jr.
Whitaker, Romulus. Common Indian Snakes: A Field Guide. (Illus.). 154p. (Orig.). 1979. pap. text ed. 4.00x (ISBN 0-333-90198-3). R Curtis Bks.
Whitaker, Thomas. The Design of Piled Foundations. 2nd ed. 224p. 1976. text ed. 27.00 (ISBN 0-08-019706-X); pap. text ed. 14.75 (ISBN 0-08-019705-1). Pergamon.
Whitaker, Thomas R. William Carlos Williams. LC 68-24297. (U. S. Authors Ser.: No. 139). 1968. lib. bdg. 10.95 (ISBN 0-8057-0816-2). Twayne.
Whitbourne, Susan K., jt. auth. see Hulicka, Irene M.
Whitburn, Joel. Top Pop Records, Nineteen Fifty-Five to Nineteen Seventy-Two. new ed. (Record Research Ser.). (Illus., Orig.). 1973. pap. text ed. 30.00 o.p. (ISBN 0-89820-000-8). Record Research.
--Top Pop Records, 1975. 40p. (Orig.). 1976. pap. text ed. 10.00 o.p. (ISBN 0-89820-006-7). Record Research.
--Top Pop Records, 1977. 36p. (Orig.). 1978. pap. text ed. 10.00 o.p. (ISBN 0-89820-008-3). Record Research.
--Top Pop Records,Nineteen Seventy-Three. new ed. (Record Research Ser.). (Orig.). pap. text ed. 10.00 o.p. (ISBN 0-89820-004-0). Record Research.
Whitby, W. M. & Anderson, R. R., eds. Fianza Satisfecha: Attributed to Lope De Vega. 1971. 42.00 (ISBN 0-521-07912-8). Cambridge U Pr.
Whitby-Strevens, C., jt. auth. see Richards, M.
Whitcomb, David K. Externalities & Welfare. LC 71-172174. (Columbia Studies in Economics: No. 6). 144p. 1972. 20.00x (ISBN 0-231-03586-1). Columbia U Pr.
Whitcomb, H., jt. auth. see Wheeler, R.
Whitcomb, Howard R., jt. auth. see Barry, Donald D.
Whitcomb, John C. The Early Earth. 1972. pap. 3.95 (ISBN 0-8010-9524-7). Baker Bk.
Whitcomb, John C., jt. auth. see Davis, John J.
Whitcomb, M. A., jt. auth. see Griffinn, S. G.
Whitcomb, Michael, ed. Aspen Epicure. (Epicure Library). (Orig.). 1979. pap. 2.50 (ISBN 0-89716-050-9). Peanut Butter.
Whitcomb, Selden L. Chronological Outlines of American Literature. LC 68-30590. 1968. Repr. of 1894 ed. 18.00 (ISBN 0-8103-3227-2). Gale.
Whitcombe, Elizabeth. Agrarian Conditions in Northern India, Vol. 1, The United Provinces Under British Rule, 1860-1900. LC 75-129027. (Center for South & Southeast Asia Studies, UC Berkeley). (Illus.). 1972. 22.75x (ISBN 0-520-01706-4). U of Cal Pr.
Whitcut, Janet. Learning with LDOCE. (Illus.). 1979. pap. text ed. 2.75x (ISBN 0-582-55607-4); cassette 7.50x (ISBN 0-582-55629-5). Longman.
White. Atoms, Peace & Vitamin C: Linus Pauling. 1980. PLB 9.95 (ISBN 0-8027-6390-1); 8.95 (ISBN 0-8027-6389-8). Walker & Co.
--Charlotte's Web. (Illus.). (gr. 5). Date not set. pap. cancelled (ISBN 0-590-30271-X, Schol Pap). Schol Bk Serv.
--Clinical Oral Periatrics. 148p. 1981. 68.00 (ISBN 0-931386-32-2). Quint Pub Co.
White & Denny. Sealing Mechanisms of Flexible Packings. 1947. 16.00. BHRA Fluid.
White, jt. auth. see Dodd.
White, tr. see Eikhenbaum, Boris.
White, et al. Bridge Maintenance: Inspection & Evaluation. 272p. 1981. 32.75 (ISBN 0-8247-1086-X). Dekker.
White, A., jt. ed. see Hemmings, J. A. G.
White, A. T., jt. auth. see Biggs, N. L.
White, Al. The Mickey Mouse Book. (ps-1). 1965. PLB 5.38 (ISBN 0-307-68914-X, Golden Pr). Western Pub.
--The Winnie-the-Pooh Book. (Illus.). (ps-1). 1965. PLB 5.38 (ISBN 0-307-68927-1, Golden Pr). Western Pub.
White, Alistair. El Salvador. (Illus.). 1973. lib. bdg. 19.75x (ISBN 0-510-39523-6). Westview.
White, Anne. Dayspring: Words of Personal Prophecy for Daily Devotions. LC 71-160700. 180p. 1971. pap. 4.95 (ISBN 0-912106-21-2). Logos.
--Visiting Museums. 1968. 6.50 (ISBN 0-571-08741-8, Pub. by Faber & Faber). Merrimack Bk Serv.
White, Anne S. All in All. 128p. (Orig.). 1980. pap. 2.50 (ISBN 0-9605178-0-4). Victorious Ministry.
White, Anne T. Prehistoric America. (Landmark Ser: No. 38). (Illus.). (gr. 4-6). 1951. PLB 5.99 (ISBN 0-394-90311-0, BYR). Random.
--Rocks All Around Us. (gr. 3-6). 1959. 2.95 o.p. (ISBN 0-394-80109-1, BYR). Random.
White, Antonia. Beyond the Glass. (Virago Modern Classic). 286p. 1981. pap. 5.95 (ISBN 0-686-69081-8). Dial.
--Frost in May. (Virago Modern Classic). 221p. 1980. pap. 4.95 (ISBN 0-8037-2697-X). Dial.
--The Lost Traveller. (Virago Modern Classic). 314p. 1980. pap. 5.95 (ISBN 0-8037-4935-X). Dial.
--The Sugar House. (Virago Modern Classic Ser.). 256p. 1981. pap. 5.95 (ISBN 0-686-69334-5). Dial.
White, Antonia, tr. see Colette.
White, Arnold. Efficiency & Empire. Searle, G. R., ed. LC 70-131993. (Society & Victorians: No. 15). 315p. 1973. Repr. of 1901 ed. text ed. 17.25x (ISBN 0-901759-42-2). Humanities.
White, Augustus A. & Panjabi, Manohar. Clinical Biomechanics of the Spine. LC 78-15708. (Illus.). 1978. 51.75 (ISBN 0-397-50388-1). Lippincott.
White, B. Joseph, jt. ed. see Hill, Ray.
White, B. T. German Tanks & Armoured Vehicles 1914-1945. LC 68-26167. (Illus.). 1966. lib. bdg. 3.50 o. p. o.p. (ISBN 0-668-01783-X); pap. 1.95 o.p. (ISBN 0-668-01784-8). Arco.
--Tanks & Other AFVS: 1911-1918. 1917. 8.95 (ISBN 0-02-265400-3). Macmillan.
--Tanks & Other Armored Fighting Vehicles 1942-1945. LC 75-28306. (Macmillan Color Ser.). (Illus.). 176p. 1976. 6.95 o.s.i. (ISBN 0-02-626550-8, 62655). Macmillan.
White, Barbara E., ed. Impressionism in Perspective. LC 77-21780. (Artists in Perspective Ser.). (Illus.). 1978. 10.95 o.p. (ISBN 0-13-452037-8); pap. 5.95 o.p. (ISBN 0-13-452029-7). P-H.
White, Barbara N., jt. auth. see White, Sheldon.
White, Benjamin. Silver: Its History & Romance. LC 71-174144. (Illus.). xxviii, 325p. 1972. Repr. of 1920 ed. 24.00 (ISBN 0-8103-3930-7). Gale.
White, Benjamin V. & White, Helen. The Excitement of Change: A Book of Personal Growth. 190p. 1975. 7.95 (ISBN 0-8164-1206-5). Crossroad NY.
White, Bill. Build Your Own Woodburning Furnace. LC 78-66818. (Illus.). 1978. pap. 3.50 (ISBN 0-9601794-2-9). FireBuilders.
--Convert Your Oil Furnace to Wood. 2nd ed. LC 76-58642. (Illus.). 1977. 3.50 (ISBN 0-9601794-1-0). FireBuilders.
White, Bouck. The Book of Daniel Drew. 1980. pap. 6.95 (ISBN 0-8065-0745-4). Lyle Stuart.
White, Bruce D., jt. auth. see Wetherbee, Helen.
White, Bruce L., et al. Experience & Environment: Major Influences on the Development of the Young Child, Vol. II. LC 72-10354. (Early Childhood Education Ser.). (Illus.). 1978. ref. ed. 25.95x (ISBN 0-13-294819-2). P-H.
White, Burton L. The First Three Years of Life. 1978. pap. 4.95 (ISBN 0-380-01893-4, 37234). Avon.
--A Parent's Guide to the First Three Years. LC 80-21924. 1980. 10.95 (ISBN 0-13-649905-8). P-H.
White, Burton L., et al. The Origins of Human Competence. LC 77-81793. 1979. 19.95 (ISBN 0-669-01943-7). Lexington Bks.
White, C. C. & Holland, Ada M. No Quittin' Sense. (Illus.). 1969. 9.95x (ISBN 0-292-70002-4); pap. 5.95 (ISBN 0-292-75508-2). U of Tex Pr.
White, C. Langdon, et al. Regional Geography of Anglo-America. 5th ed. (Illus.). 1979. text ed. 20.95 (ISBN 0-13-770883-1). P-H.
--Essentials of College Geography. LC 58-6374. (Illus.). 1958. text ed. 18.95x (ISBN 0-89197-553-5); pap. text ed. 8.95x (ISBN 0-89197-752-X). Irvington.
White, C. M. Bases of Modern Librarianship. 1964. 22.00 (ISBN 0-08-010627-7). Pergamon.
White, Carl. Historical Introduction to Library Education: Problems & Progress to 1951. LC 75-28086. 1976. 13.50 (ISBN 0-8108-0874-9). Scarecrow.
White, Carol. Energy Potential: Toward a New Electromagnetic Field Theory. Cleary, James, tr. 1978. pap. 7.95 (ISBN 0-918388-04-X, QC665.E4W45, Univ Edns). New Benjamin.
--The New Dark Ages Conspiracy: Britain's Plot to Destroy Civilization. LC 80-23546. (Illus.). 400p. (Orig.). 1980. pap. 4.95 (ISBN 0-933488-05-X). New Benjamin.
White, Caroline. Patrons & Partisans: A Study of Politics in Two Southern Italian Comuni. LC 79-53406. (Cambridge Studies in Social Anthropology: No. 31). (Illus.). 1980. 19.95 (ISBN 0-521-22872-7). Cambridge U Pr.
White, Chelsea C., jt. auth. see Sage, Andrew P.
White, Christopher, jt. ed. see Spannaus, Nancy B.
White, Claire N. Biography & Other Poems. LC 80-2069. 96p. 1981. 9.95 (ISBN 0-385-15799-1). Doubleday.
White, Claire Nicolas, tr. see Mulisch, Harry.
White, Colin. Edmund Dulac. (Encore Edition). (Illus.). 1975. 10.95 o.p. (ISBN 0-684-15470-6, ScribT). Scribner.
White, Curtis. Heretical Songs. LC 79-3848. 1981. 9.95 (ISBN 0-914590-62-6); pap. 4.95 (ISBN 0-914590-63-4). Fiction Coll.
White, D. How to Find Out About Iron & Steel. 1970. 16.00 (ISBN 0-08-015790-4); pap. 9.50 (ISBN 0-08-015789-0). Pergamon.
--A Modern Introduction to Chemistry. 1967. pap. 3.45 o.p. (ISBN 0-08-012164-0). Pergamon.
White, D. C. & Thorson, John. The Kinetics of Muscle Contraction. 1975. pap. text ed. 11.25 (ISBN 0-08-018149-X). Pergamon.
White, D. M. Predicacion Expositiva. Estrello, Francisco E., tr. Orig. Title: The Excellence of Exposition. 1980. 3.25 (ISBN 0-311-42061-3). Casa Bautista.
White, D. N. Recent Advances in Perinatal Pathology & Physiology: Ultra Sound in Biomedicine Research Ser, Vol. 4. (Research Studies Press Ser.). 264p. 1981. 54.00 (ISBN 0-471-27925-0, Pub. by Wiley-Interscience). Wiley.
White, D. O., jt. auth. see Burnet, F. Macfarlane.
White, Dan. Play to Win: A Profile of Princeton Basketball Coach Pete Carril. LC 77-20143. 1978. 8.95 o.p. (ISBN 0-13-683904-5). P-H.
White, Dan, jt. auth. see Muse, Bill.
White, Dan S., jt. ed. see Maier, Charles S.
White, David J., jt. auth. see Gillett, John M.
White, David M., jt. ed. see Dexter, Lewis A.
White, De Vere. Tom Moore. 1979. 22.50 (ISBN 0-241-89622-3, Pub. by Hamish Hamilton England). David & Charles.
White, Donald & Vroman, H. William. Action in Organizations: Cases & Experiences in Organizational Behavior. 1977. pap. text ed. 12.95 (ISBN 0-205-05599-0, 085599-5); instr's manual o.p. Allyn.
White, Donald D. Contemporary Perspectives in Organizational Behavior. 500p. 1981. price not set (ISBN 0-205-07350-6); free (ISBN 0-205-07351-4). Allyn. Postponed.
White, Donald D. & Vroman, H. William. Action in Organizations. 500p. 1981. price not set (ISBN 0-205-07353-0); instructor manual free (ISBN 0-205-07354-9). Allyn. Postponed.
White, Donald F., jt. auth. see McHose, Allen I.
White, Donald R., ed. see Pink, A. W.
White, Doris, jt. auth. see Picken, Mary B.
White, Dorothy, tr. see Pope John XXIII.
White, Dorothy, et al. Fundamentals: The Foundations of Nursing. 324p. 1972. 16.95 (ISBN 0-13-331991-1). P-H.
White, Douglas M. The Excellence of Exposition: Practical Procedure in Expository Preaching. 1977. 4.25 (ISBN 0-87213-938-7). Loizeaux.
White, E. B. Letters of E.B. White. Incl. Essays of E.B. White. 1979. Box Set. pap. 12.95 o.p. (ISBN 0-06-090736-3; CN 736, CN). Har-Row.
--The Points of My Compass. LC 62-15742. 1979. pap. 2.95 (ISBN 0-06-080475-0, P 475, PL). Har-Row.
--Second Tree from the Corner. LC 53-11864. 1954. 12.95 o.p. (ISBN 0-06-014590-0, HarpT). Har-Row.

White, E. B., ed. see White, Katherine S.

White, E. E. Experiences of a Special Indian Agent. rev. ed. (Western Frontier Library: No. 29). (Illus.). 1966. 5.95 o.p. (ISBN 0-8061-0680-8). U of Okla Pr.

White, E. G. Conflict of the Ages. 1940. pap. 28.95 set (ISBN 0-8163-0293-6). Pacific Pr Pub Assn.

--Signs of the Times Articles, Vol. 1. 1976. 26.00 (ISBN 0-8163-0220-0, 05391-8). Pacific Pr Pub Assn.

--Signs of the Times Articles, Vol. 2. 1977. 26.00 (ISBN 0-8163-0166-2, 05392-6). Pacific Pr Pub Assn.

--Signs of the Times Articles, Vol. 3. 1977. 26.00 (ISBN 0-8163-0167-0, 05393-4). Pacific Pr Pub Assn.

White, E. N. Maintenance Planning, Control & Documentation. 1979. text ed. 35.25x (ISBN 0-566-02144-7, Pub. by Gower Pub Co England). Renouf.

White, Earl. Nourishing Self Esteem: A Parent Handbook for Nurturing Love. (Illus.). 95p. (Orig.). 1981. pap. text ed. 5.00 (ISBN 0-686-69561-5). Whitenwife Pubns.

White, Edmund. The First Men. (The Emergence of Man Ser.). (Illus.). 1973. 9.95 (ISBN 0-8094-1259-4); lib. bdg. avail. (ISBN 0-685-28794-7). Time-Life.

--The First Men. LC 73-93968. (The Emergence of Man Ser.). (Illus.). 1973. lib. bdg. 9.63 o.p. (ISBN 0-686-51072-0). Silver.

--Forgetting Elena. 192p. 1976. pap. 1.50 o.p. (ISBN 0-445-03145-X). Popular Lib.

--States of Desire. 320p. 1981. pap. 3.95 (ISBN 0-553-14544-4). Bantam.

White, Edward M. The Pop Culture Tradition. 240p. (Orig.). 1972. pap. text ed. 4.95x (ISBN 0-393-09969-5). Norton.

--Writer's Control of Tone. 1970. pap. text ed. 4.95x (ISBN 0-393-09894-X, NortonC). Norton.

White, Edwin & Battye, Marguerite. Acting & Stage Movement. LC 63-10202. 1978. pap. text ed. 2.95 o.p. (ISBN 0-668-04386-5). Arco.

White, Elizabeth W. Anne Bradstreet: The Tenth Muse. 1971. 17.95 (ISBN 0-19-501440-5). Oxford U Pr.

White, Ellen G. The Acts of the Apostles. 633p. 1911. deluxe ed. 9.50 (ISBN 0-8163-0033-X, 01092-6); pap. 5.25 (ISBN 0-8163-0034-8, 01093-4). Pacific Pr Pub Assn.

--Can We Know God? (Uplook Ser.). 1970. pap. 0.75 (ISBN 0-8163-0067-4, 03035-3). Pacific Pr Pub Assn.

--Christ in His Sanctuary. LC 70-94869. (Dimension Ser.). 1969. pap. 5.95 (ISBN 0-8163-0128-X, 03254-0). Pacific Pr Pub Assn.

--Colporteur Ministry. 1953. 3.25 (ISBN 0-8163-0110-7, 03431-4); pap. 2.25 (ISBN 0-8163-0111-5, 03430-6). Pacific Pr Pub Assn.

--Counsels on Education. 1968. deluxe ed. 6.50 (ISBN 0-8163-0112-3, 03555-0); pap. 4.50 (ISBN 0-8163-0113-1, 035568). Pacific Pr Pub Assn.

--Counsels on Health & Instruction to Medical Missionary Workers. 1951. deluxe ed. 7.50 (ISBN 0-8163-0114-X, 03561-8). Pacific Pr Pub Assn.

--Counsels to Parents, Teachers & Students Regarding Christian Education. 1943. Repr. of 1913 ed. deluxe ed. 6.95 (ISBN 0-8163-0115-8, 03591-5). Pacific Pr Pub Assn.

--The Desire of Ages. 1940. 5.95 (ISBN 0-8163-0029-1, 04259-8); pap. 0.95 newsprint ed. (ISBN 0-8163-0030-5, 04261-4); pap. 3.50 (ISBN 0-8163-0031-3, 04254-9); deluxe ed. 9.50 (ISBN 0-8163-0032-1, 04257-2). Pacific Pr Pub Assn.

--Education. 324p. 1952. 6.50 (ISBN 0-8163-0042-9, 05151-6); pap. 4.50 o.p. (ISBN 0-8163-0043-7, 05152-4). Pacific Pr Pub Assn.

--The Great Controversy. 1950. 5.95 (ISBN 0-8163-0035-6, 07886-5); deluxe ed. 9.50 (ISBN 0-8163-0036-4, 07882-4); pap. 0.95 (ISBN 0-8163-0037-2, 07887-3). Pacific Pr Pub Assn.

--How to Get Along with Others. (Uplook Ser.). 1964. pap. 0.75 (ISBN 0-8163-0072-0, 08835-1). Pacific Pr Pub Assn.

--The Master's Immortal Sermon. 96p. 1971. pap. 0.95 o.p. (ISBN 0-8163-0056-9, 13325-6). Pacific Pr Pub Assn.

--Medical Ministry. 1963. pap. 6.50 (ISBN 0-8163-0157-3, 13371-0); pap. 5.95 deluxe ed. (ISBN 0-8163-0158-1, 13370-2). Pacific Pr Pub Assn.

--Ministry of Healing. 1942. pap. 4.95 o.p. (ISBN 0-8163-0123-9, 13541-8); pap. 6.50 deluxe ed. (ISBN 0-8163-0124-7, 13540-0). Pacific Pr Pub Assn.

--Patriarchs & Prophets. 805p. 1958. deluxe ed. 9.50 (ISBN 0-8163-0038-0, 16082-0); pap. 5.95 (ISBN 0-8163-0039-9, 16083-8). Pacific Pr Pub Assn.

--Prophets & Kings. 752p. deluxe ed. 9.50 (ISBN 0-8163-0040-2, 16642-1); pap. 5.95 (ISBN 0-8163-0041-0, 16643-9). Pacific Pr Pub Assn.

--Selected Messages, Vol. III. 1980. Christian Home Library Ed. 5.95 (ISBN 0-8280-0055-7, 19275-7); Shield Ser. Ed. 4.50 (ISBN 0-8280-0056-5, 19276-5); Special Ed. pap. 2.95 (ISBN 0-8280-0057-3, 19277-3). Review & Herald.

--Selected Messages, 3 vols. 1980. Set. pap. 7.95 (ISBN 0-8280-0059-X, 19269-0). Review & Herald.

--Steps to Christ. LC 56-7169. 134p. 1956. 4.95 (ISBN 0-8163-0045-3, 19543-8); pap. 0.95 (ISBN 0-8163-0046-1, 19547-9). Pacific Pr Pub Assn.

--Steps to Jesus. 128p. 1980. 3.95 (ISBN 0-8127-0316-2); pap. 1.95 (ISBN 0-8127-0318-9). Southern Pub.

--Temperance. 1949. pap. 4.50 (ISBN 0-8163-0150-6, 20101-4); pap. 6.50 deluxe ed. (ISBN 0-8163-0151-4, 20100-4). Pacific Pr Pub Assn.

--Testimonies for the Church, 9 vols. 1948. 5.95 ea. (ISBN 0-8163-0152-2); Set. 52.95 (ISBN 0-8163-0153-0, 20140-0). Pacific Pr Pub Assn.

--Thoughts from the Mount of Blessing. LC 56-7170. 172p. 1956. 4.95 (ISBN 0-8163-0047-X, 20401-6). Pacific Pr Pub Assn.

--What to Do with Doubt. 31p. 1970. pap. 0.75 (ISBN 0-8163-0079-8, 23265-2). Pacific Pr Pub Assn.

--Why Be a Christian? 32p. 1970. pap. 0.75 (ISBN 0-8163-0081-X, 23615-8). Pacific Pr Pub Assn.

--Your Mind & Your Health. 31p. 1964. pap. 0.75 (ISBN 0-8163-0083-6, 24505-0). Pacific Pr Pub Assn.

White, Elliott. Sociobiology & Human Politics. LC 79-3016. 1981. price not set (ISBN 0-669-03602-1). Lexington Bks.

White, Eric W. The Rise of English Opera. LC 78-87683. (Music Ser.). (Illus.). 374p. 1972. Repr. of 1951 ed. lib. bdg. 27.50 (ISBN 0-306-71709-3). Da Capo.

White, Eugene E. Puritan Rhetoric: The Issue of Emotion in Religion. LC 76-181987. (Landmarks in Rhetoric & Public Address Ser.). 229p. 1972. 10.95x (ISBN 0-8093-0563-1). S Ill U Pr.

White, Florence W. Linus Pauling: Scientist & Crusader. (Illus.). 96p. (gr. 5-9). 1980. 8.95 (ISBN 0-8027-6389-8); PLB 9.85 (ISBN 0-8027-6390-1). Walker & Co.

White, Frank M. Elementary Fluid Mechanics. (Illus.). 1979. text ed. 21.95 (ISBN 0-07-069667-5, C); write for info solution manual (ISBN 0-07-069668-3). McGraw.

White, Fred, jt. auth. see Collins, Bobby.

White, Freda. Ways of Aquitaine. (Illus.). 172p. 1980. 8.95 o.p. (ISBN 0-571-08445-1, Pub by Faber & Faber). Merrimack Bk Serv.

White, Frederick A. Our Acoustic Environment. LC 75-8888. 501p. 1975. 37.50 (ISBN 0-471-93920-X, Pub. by Wiley-Interscience). Wiley.

White, George. A Digest of All the Laws at Present in Existence Respecting Masters & Work People. Berkowitz, David S. & Thorne, Samuel E., eds. LC 77-89205. (Classics of English Legal History in the Modern Era Ser.: Vol. 59). 159p. 1979. lib. bdg. 40.00 (ISBN 0-8240-3158-X). Garland Pub.

White, George R. Concrete Technology. 3rd ed. LC 76-5304. 1977. pap. text ed. 6.00 (ISBN 0-8273-1095-1); instructor's guide 1.75 (ISBN 0-8273-1092-7). Delmar.

White, Gifford, ed. Eighteen-Forty Census of the Republic of Texas. 19.50 (ISBN 0-8363-0029-7). Jenkins.

White, Gilbert F., ed. Environmental Effects of Complex River Development: International Experience. LC 77-3943. (Westview Special Studies in Natural Resources & Energy Management). (Illus.). 1977. lib. bdg. 20.00 o.p. (ISBN 0-89158-249-5). Westview.

White, Gordon. Party & Professionals: The Political Role of Teachers in Contemporary China. 350p. 1981. 25.00 (ISBN 0-87332-188-X). M E Sharpe.

White, Gordon & Hyman, Merv. Coach Tom Cahill: Man for the Corps. (Illus.). (gr. 7 up). 1969. 5.95 o.s.i. (ISBN 0-02-626510-9). Macmillan.

White, Gordon E., jt. auth. see Jugenheimer, Donald W.

White, Gordon S., Jr., jt. auth. see Hymen, Mervin D.

White, Gwen. Perspective: A Guide for Artists, Architects & Designers. 1974. pap. 16.95 (ISBN 0-7134-2873-2, Pub. by Batsford England). David & Charles.

White, H. J., jt. ed. see Wordsworth, J.

White, H. P. The Continuing Conurbation: Change & Development in Greater Manchester. 224p. 1980. text ed. 30.75x (ISBN 0-566-00248-5, Pub. by Gower Pub Co England). Renouf.

--Forgotten Railways of South East England. (Forgotten Railways Ser.). 1976. 14.95 (ISBN 0-7153-7286-6). David & Charles.

--A Regional History of the Railways of Great Britain: Greater London, Vol. 3. (Illus.). 1971. 19.95 (ISBN 0-7153-5337-3). David & Charles.

--A Regional History of the Railways of Great Britain: Southern England, Vol. 2. (Regional History of the Railways of Great Britain Ser.). (Illus.). 1974. 16.95 (ISBN 0-7153-4070-0). David & Charles.

White, H. P. & Gleave, M. B. An Economic Geography of West Africa. (Advanced Economic Geography Ser.). 1971. pap. text ed. 16.50x (ISBN 0-7135-1721-2). Westview.

White, H. Roy. The Meaning & Significance of Christian Hope. 1981. 5.95 (ISBN 0-533-04536-3). Vantage.

White, Hardin Q., Jr., et al. Celebration of the Gospel. 1978. 3.95 (ISBN 0-687-04800-1). Abingdon.

White, Hayden. Metahistory: The Historical Imagination in Nineteenth-Century Europe. LC 73-8110. 462p. 1974. 22.50x (ISBN 0-8018-1469-3); pap. 6.95 (ISBN 0-8018-1761-7). Johns Hopkins.

White, Hayden V. The Greco-Roman Tradition. (White Ser). 158p. 1973. pap. text ed. 9.50 scp (ISBN 0-06-047064-X, HarpC). Har-Row.

White, Heather. Essays in Hellenistic Poetry. (London Studies in Classical Philology: Vol. 5). 81p. 1981. pap. text ed. 17.25x (ISBN 90-70265-52-4, Pub. by Gieben Holland). Humanities.

White, Helen. Jesse Hill Ford: An Annotated Checklist of His Published Works & of His Papers. (Mississippi Valley Collection Bulletin, No. 7). (Illus.). 55p. 1974. pap. 5.95x (ISBN 0-87870-083-8). Memphis St Univ.

White, Helen, jt. auth. see White, Benjamin V.

White, Herbert S., jt. auth. see Fry, Bernard M.

White, Howard D., ed. Reader in Machine-Readable Social Data. LC 77-92432. (Readers Er. in Librarianship & Information Science: Vol. 24). 1978. lib. bdg. 21.00 (ISBN 0-910972-70-2). IHS-PDS.

White, Iain, tr. see Brandell, Gunnar.

White, Irvin L., et al. North Sea Oil & Gas: Implications for Future United States Development. LC 73-21222. (Illus.). 176p. (Orig.). 1973. pap. 5.95x (ISBN 0-8061-1182-8). U of Okla Pr.

White, J. F. The Cambridge Movement. LC 79-50916. (Illus.). 1979. 29.95 (ISBN 0-521-06781-2). Cambridge U Pr.

White, J. M., jt. auth. see Hyatt, E. C.

White, James. The Aliens Among Us. 224p. 1981. pap. 2.25 (ISBN 0-345-29171-9, Del Rey). Ballantine.

--Hospital Station. 1979. pap. 2.25 (ISBN 0-345-29613-3). Ballantine.

--John Butler Yeats & the Irish Renaissance. (New Yeats Papers Ser: No. 5). 1972. pap. text ed. 4.50x (ISBN 0-85105-234-7, Dolmen Pr). Humanities.

--Major Operation. 192p. 1981. pap. 2.25 (ISBN 0-345-29381-9). Ballantine.

--Monsters & Medics. (A Del Rey Bk.). 1977. pap. 1.50 o.p. (ISBN 0-345-25623-9). Ballantine.

--Star Surgeon. 160p. (Orig.). 1981. pap. 1.95 (ISBN 0-345-29169-7, Del Rey). Ballantine.

--Your Home Computer. LC 77-73316. (Illus., Orig.). 1977. pap. 10.95 (ISBN 0-918138-05-1). Dilithium Pr.

White, James C. & Sweet, William H. Pain & the Neurosurgeon: A Forty-Year Experience. (Illus.). 1032p. 1969. text ed. 52.75 (ISBN 0-398-02058-2). C C Thomas.

White, James D. Talking with a Child: What to Say After "Hello" What's Your Name, How Old Are You, Where Do You Go to School, When's Your Birthday, Well That's Nice. 1976. 8.95 o.s.i. (ISBN 0-02-626570-2). Macmillan.

White, James J. & Summers, Robert S. Handbook of the Law Under the Uniform Commercial Code. 2nd ed. LC 79-27189. (Hornbook Ser.). 1287p. 1980. text ed. 19.95 (ISBN 0-8299-2082-X). West Pub.

White, Jane. Benjamin's Open Day. 192p. 1979. 16.95 (ISBN 0-241-89978-8, Pub. by Hamish Hamilton England). David & Charles.

White, Jane N. & Burnett, Collins W. Higher Education Bibliography. 1981. price not set (ISBN 0-912700-80-7). Oryx Pr.

White, Jay C. Pilots & Aircraft Owners Legal Guide. 3rd ed. 1979. pap. 9.95 (ISBN 0-911721-57-6, Pub. by Taxlogs Unlimited); pap. 5.95 (ISBN 0-686-65933-3). Taxlogs.

White, Jeremy J. Central Administration in Nigeria, Nineteen Fourteen to Nineteen Fifty-One: The Problem of Polarity. 250p. 1981. 39.00x (ISBN 0-686-28430-5, Pub. by Irish Academic Pr Ireland). Biblio Dist.

White, Jerry. Rothschild Buildings: Life in an East End Tenement Block 1887-1920. (History Workshop Ser.). 1980. 30.00 (ISBN 0-7100-0429-X); pap. 15.00 (ISBN 0-686-65998-8). Routledge & Kegan.

White, Jerry & White, Mary. Christian in Mid-Life. LC 80-83388. (Orig.). 1980. pap. 4.95 (ISBN 0-89109-448-2). NavPress.

White, Jerry E. & White, Mary E. Your Job: Survival or Satisfaction. 1976. 4.95 (ISBN 0-310-34321-[illegible] Zondervan.

White, John. The Iron Sceptre. (Illus.). 404p. (Orig.). (gr. 4-7). 1981. pap. 7.95 (ISBN 0-87784-589-1). Inter-Varsity.

White, John & Morison, Margaret P. Western Towns & Buildings. 364p. 1980. 22.50x (ISBN 0-85564-156-8, Pub. by U of West Australia). Intl Schol Bk Serv.

White, John, jt. auth. see Gordon, Peter.

White, John, ed. Kundalini, Evolution & Enlightenment. LC 78-1226. 1979. pap. 4.50 (ISBN 0-385-14095-9, Anch). Doubleday.

--What Is Meditation? LC 73-81126. 280p. 1974. pap. 2.95 (ISBN 0-385-07638-X, Anch). Doubleday.

White, John & Krippner, Stanley, eds. Future Science: Life Energies & the Physics of Paranormal Phenomena. LC 76-23808. 600p. 1977. pap. 4.50 (ISBN 0-385-11203-3, Anch). Doubleday.

White, John B. A Study of the Language of Love in the Song of Songs & Ancient Egyptian Poetry. LC 77-13399. (Society of Biblical Literature. Dissertation Ser.: Vol. 38). 1978. pap. 7.50 (ISBN 0-89130-192-5, 060138). Scholars Pr Ca.

White, John B., jt. auth. see Hawkins, Gerald S.

White, John D. Analysis of Music. 1976. 15.50 (ISBN 0-13-033233-X). P-H.

White, John H., Jr. Early American Locomotives. LC 79-188951. (Illus.). 142p. (Orig.). 1972. pap. 5.00 (ISBN 0-486-22772-3). Dover.

White, John L. The Form & Function of the Body of the Greek Letter in the Non-Literary Papyri & in Paul the Apostle. LC 75-33088. (Society of Biblical Literature. Dissertation Ser.). (Illus.). 1975. pap. 7.50 (ISBN 0-89130-048-1, 060102). Scholars Pr Ca.

--The Form & Structure of the Official Petition: A Study in Greek Epistolography. LC 72-87889. (Society of Biblical Literature. Dissertations Ser.: No. 5). (Illus.). 1972. pap. 9.00 (ISBN 0-89130-161-5, 060105). Scholars Pr Ca.

White, John M. Physical Chemistry Laboratory Experiments. (Illus.). 576p. 1975. ref. ed. 17.95 (ISBN 0-13-665927-6). P-H.

White, John S. Monarch Notes on Remarque's All Quiet on the Western Front. (Orig.). pap. 1.75 (ISBN 0-671-00861-7). Monarch Pr.

White, John S., ed. see Plutarch.

White, John T. Hedgerow. LC 80-81264. (Illus.). 48p. 1980. 13.95 (ISBN 0-688-03683-X). Morrow.

White, John W. The Coming World Dictator. 144p. (Orig.). 1981. pap. 2.50 (ISBN 0-87123-042-9, 200042). Bethany Fell.

--What Does It Mean to Be Born Again? (Orig.). 1977. pap. 1.95 (ISBN 0-87123-641-9, 200641). Bethany Fell.

White, John W., tr. Retorno. (Portugese Bks.). (Port.). 1979. 1.40 (ISBN 0-8297-0684-4). Life Pubs Intl.

White, John Warren, 1939-, ed. Frontiers of Consciousness. 1975. pap. 2.95 (ISBN 0-380-00393-7, 48850). Avon.

White, John Wesley. Man from Krypton: The Gospel According to Superman. LC 78-73455. 1978. pap. 2.25 (ISBN 0-87123-384-3, 200384). Bethany Fell.

White, Jon M. Death by Dreaming. 160p. 1981. 10.95 (ISBN 0-918222-27-3). Apple Wood.

White, Joseph L. The Limits of Trade Union Militancy: The Lancashire Textile Workers, 1910-1914. LC 77-87965. (Contributions in Labor History: No. 5). (Illus.). 1978. lib. bdg. 17.95 (ISBN 0-313-20029-7, WLT/). Greenwood.

White, K. D. Farm Equipment of the Roman World. LC 73-82450. (Illus.). 248p. 1975. 58.00 (ISBN 0-521-20333-3). Cambridge U Pr.

White, K. J., jt. ed. see Payne, C. J.

White, Karol. What to Do When You Think You Can't Have a Baby. LC 80-1730. (Illus.). 216p. 1981. 11.95 (ISBN 0-385-15446-1). Doubleday.

White, Katherine S. Onward & Upward in the Garden. White, E. B., ed. 384p. 1979. 12.95 (ISBN 0-374-22654-7). FS&G.

--Onward & Upward in the Garden. White, E. B., ed. 1981. pap. 6.95 (ISBN 0-374-51629-4). FS&G.

White, Kay & Joshua, Joan. Practical Guide to the Dogs. 1976. 11.95 (ISBN 0-600-37046-1). Transatlantic.

White, Ken. Bookstore Planning & Design. (Illus.). 192p. 1982. 34.50 (ISBN 0-07-069851-1). McGraw.

White, Kenneth, tr. see Lambert, Jean-Clarence.

White, Kenneth S. Man's New Shapes: French Avant-Garde Drama's Metamorphoses. LC 79-62911. 1979. pap. text ed. 6.50 (ISBN 0-8191-0717-4). U Pr of Amer.

--Savage Comedy Since King Ubu: A Tangent to "The Absurd". 1977. pap. text ed. 6.75x (ISBN 0-8191-0152-4). U Pr of Amer.

White, Kenneth S., ed. Savage Comedy: Structure of Humor. 1978. pap. text ed. 11.75x (ISBN 90-6203-310-5). Humanities.

White, L. J., ed. Hostiles & Horse Soldiers. LC 72-80262. 1972. 10.95 o.p. (ISBN 0-87108-061-3). Pruett.

White, L. P. Aerial Photography & Remote Sensing for Soil Survey. (Monographs on Soil Survey). (Illus.). 1977. 24.00x (ISBN 0-19-854509-6). Oxford U Pr.

White, Landeg, jt. auth. see Vail, Leroy.

White, Laurence B., Jr. & Broekel, Ray. The Surprise Book: Seventy-Seven Stupendously Silly Practical Jokes You Can Play on Your Friends. (Illus.). 96p. 1981. 7.95a (ISBN 0-385-15832-7); PLB (ISBN 0-385-15833-5). Doubleday.

White, Lawrence J. Reforming Regulation: Processes & Problems. (Illus.). 240p. 1981. text ed. 13.95 (ISBN 0-13-770115-2); pap. text ed. 8.95 (ISBN 0-13-770107-1). P-H.

White, Lawrence J., jt. auth. see Goldberg, Lawrence G.

White, Lazarus & Prentis, Edmund A., eds. Cofferdams. 2nd rev & enl. ed. LC 50-10778. 1956. 22.50x (ISBN 0-231-01777-4). Columbia U Pr.

White, Leonard D. New Horizons in Public Administration. 1946. 9.50 o.p. (ISBN 0-8173-4800-X). U of Ala Pr.

--The Republican Era, 1869-1901. 1958. 9.95 (ISBN 0-02-626860-4). Macmillan.

White, Leslie A. The Concept of Cultural Systems: A Key to Understanding Tribes & Nations. LC 75-33003. 192p. 1975. 15.00x (ISBN 0-231-03961-1). Columbia U Pr.

White, Leslie A. & Dillingham, Beth. The Concept of Culture. LC 72-88749. (Basic Concepts in Anthropology Ser.). pap. 3.25 o.p. (ISBN 0-8087-2333-2). Burgess.

White, Louise G., jt. auth. see Bryant, Coralie.

White, Lynn, Jr. Medieval Religion & Technology: Collected Essays. LC 77-83113. (Center for Medieval & Renaissance Studies, UCLA: No. 13). 1978. 26.50x (ISBN 0-520-03566-6). U of Cal Pr.

--Medieval Technology & Social Change. 1966. pap. 4.95 (ISBN 0-19-500266-0, GB). Oxford U Pr.

--The Transformation of the Roman World: Gibbon's Problem After Two Centuries. (UCLA Center for Medieval & Renaissance Studies). 1966. 11.00 o.p. (ISBN 0-520-01334-4); pap. 4.95x (ISBN 0-520-02491-5). U of Cal Pr.

White, Lynn T., 3rd. Careers in Shanghai: The Social Guidance of Personal Energies in a Developing Chinese City, 1949-1966. 1978. 20.00x (ISBN 0-520-03361-2). U of Cal Pr.

White, M. J. Animal Cytology & Evolution. 3rd ed. LC 79-190418. (Illus.). 1000p. 1973. 105.00 (ISBN 0-521-07071-6); pap. 29.95x (ISBN 0-521-29227-1). Cambridge U Pr.

White, M. P. Some Texas Fusulinidae. (Illus.). 106p. 1932. 0.75 (BULL 3211). Bur Econ Geology.

White, Margaret J., jt. auth. see Warner, James A.

White, Mark. Obeserver's Book of Big Bands. (Observer Bks.). (Illus.). 1978. 3.95 (ISBN 0-684-15593-1, ScribT). Scribner.

White, Mary. How to Do Beadwork. (Illus.). 160p. 1972. pap. 3.00 (ISBN 0-486-20697-1). Dover.

--How to Make Baskets. LC 72-162523. Repr. of 1902 ed. 15.00 (ISBN 0-8103-3064-4). Gale.

--More Baskets & How to Make Them. LC 76-162524. Repr. of 1912 ed. 18.00 (ISBN 0-8103-3065-2). Gale.

White, Mary, jt. auth. see White, Jerry.

White, Mary C., compiled by. Prayers by & for the Elderly. 1979. 0.60 (ISBN 0-686-28787-8). Forward Movement.

White, Mary E., jt. auth. see White, Jerry E.

White, Mary S. Touch & Tell. LC 62-7103. (Illus.). (ps). 1962. bds. 0.60 (ISBN 0-8054-4126-3). Broadman.

White, Maynard P., intro. by. Clarence White. (Aperture History of Photography Ser.: No. 11). (Illus.). 1979. over boards 8.95 (ISBN 0-89381-019-3). Aperture.

White, Mel. Lust: The Other Side of Love. 1978. 7.95 (ISBN 0-8007-0932-2). Revell.

White, Melvin R., jt. auth. see Coger, Leslie I.

White, Merry. Pasta & Noodles. 288p. 1981. pap. 5.95 (ISBN 0-14-046504-9). Penguin.

White, Michael J. Modes of Speciation. LC 77-10955. (Biology Ser.). (Illus.). 1978. text ed. 33.95x (ISBN 0-7167-0284-3). W H Freeman.

--Urban Renewal & the Changing Residential Structure of the City. (Illus.). 225p. (Orig.). 1980. pap. text ed. write for info. (ISBN 0-89836-029-3). Comm & Family.

White, Minor, ed. Octave of Prayer. LC 72-87368. (Aperture Vol. 17, No. 1). (Illus.). 96p. 1972. 12.50 o.p. (ISBN 0-912334-36-3); pap. 8.50 o.p. (ISBN 0-912334-37-1). Aperture.

White, Morton. The Philosophy of the American Revolution. LC 77-18081. (American Social Thought Ser.). 1978. 17.95x (ISBN 0-19-502381-1). Oxford U Pr.

--The Philosophy of the American Revolution. 321p. 1981. pap. 6.95 (ISBN 0-19-502891-0, GB 625, OPB). Oxford U Pr.

--Pragmatism & the American Mind: Essays & Reviews in Philosophy & Intellectual History. 288p. 1973. 15.95 (ISBN 0-19-501623-8). Oxford U Pr.

White, Morton, ed. Documents in the History of American Philosophy: From Jonathan Edward to John Dewey. 1972. text ed. 10.95x (ISBN 0-19-501556-8); pap. text ed. 8.95x (ISBN 0-19-501555-X). Oxford U Pr.

White, Moseqelle, ed. see Ivey, Jean.

White, Mosezelle, ed. see Williams, Hobie L.

White, Mrs. N. D. see Janney, Abel.

White, Nelson C. Abbott H. Thayer, Painter & Naturalist. 1969. 35.00x (ISBN 0-87233-015-X). Bauhan.

White, Nicholas P. A Companion to Plato's Republic. LC 78-70043. 1979. 16.50 (ISBN 0-915144-56-5); pap. text ed. 7.95 (ISBN 0-915144-92-1). Hackett Pub.

White, Norval & Willensky, Elliot, eds. AIA Guide to New York City. rev. ed. 1978. pap. 12.95 (ISBN 0-02-000980-1, Collier). Macmillan.

White, Owen R. & Haring, Norris G. Exceptional Teaching: Individually Planned Educations. 2nd ed. (Special Education Ser.). 368p. 1980. text ed. 17.95 (ISBN 0-675-08156-4); instructor's manual 3.95 (ISBN 0-686-63188-9). Merrill.

White, P. D., jt. auth. see Gertler, M.

White, Patrick. A Fringe of Leaves. 1977. pap. 1.95 (ISBN 0-380-01826-8, 36160). Avon.

White, Paul. Fairs & Circuses. (Junior Reference Ser.). (Illus.). 64p. (gr. 7 up). 1972. 7.95 (ISBN 0-7136-1323-8). Dufour.

--Getting About in Towns. (Junior Reference Ser.). (Illus.). 64p. (gr. 7 up). 7.95 (ISBN 0-7136-1691-1). Dufour.

--Janet at School. LC 77-26681. (John Day Bk.). (Illus.). (gr. k-4). 1978. PLB 7.89 (ISBN 0-381-99557-7, TYC-J). T Y Crowell.

--Shops & Markets. (Junior Reference Ser.). (Illus.). 64p. (gr. 7 up). 1971. 7.95 (ISBN 0-7136-1155-3). Dufour.

White, Paul B. & Beckley, Helen. Hotel Reception. 3rd ed. (Illus.). 1978. pap. 12.95x (ISBN 0-7131-0191-1). Intl Ideas.

White, Paul D. Symposium: Major Advances in Cardiovascular Therapy. 400p. 1973. 37.50 (ISBN 0-685-78090-2, Pub. by Williams & Wilkins). Krieger.

White, Peter, ed. Benjamin Tompson, Colonial Bard: A Critical Edition. LC 79-21367. (Illus.). 230p. 1980. text ed. 16.75x (ISBN 0-271-00250-6). Pa St U Pr.

White, Peter A. Portrait of County Durham. LC 67-95176. (Portrait Bks.). (Illus.). 1967. 10.50x (ISBN 0-7091-2420-1). Intl Pubns Serv.

White, Phillip D., jt. ed. see Slater, Charles C.

White, R. E. Introduction to the Principles & Practice of Soil Science. LC 79-14361. 198p. 1979. pap. 22.95x (ISBN 0-470-26717-8). Halsted Pr.

White, R. J., ed. see Stephen, James F.

White, R. W. The Abnormal Personality. 5th ed. LC 80-22055. 1981. text ed. 21.95 (ISBN 0-471-04599-3); tchrs'. manual avail. (ISBN 0-471-05342-2). Wiley.

White, Randy. Motherlode. (Illus.). 1977. cancelled o.p. (ISBN 0-912950-35-8); pap. 4.50 o.p. (ISBN 0-912950-36-6). Blue Oak.

White, Ray L. Gore Vidal. (U. S. Authors Ser.: No. 135). 1968. lib. bdg. 10.95 (ISBN 0-8057-0760-3). Twayne.

White, Reginald J. Short History of England. (Illus.). 1967. 38.50 (ISBN 0-521-06784-7); pap. 10.50x (ISBN 0-521-09439-9). Cambridge U Pr.

White, Rhea A. Surveys in Parapsychology. LC 76-119. 496p. 1976. 21.00 (ISBN 0-8108-0906-0). Scarecrow.

White, Rhea A. & Dale, Laura A. Parapsychology: Sources of Information. LC 73-4853. 1973. 10.00 (ISBN 0-8108-0617-7). Scarecrow.

White, Richard. Land Use, Environment, & Social Change: The Shaping of Island County, Washington. LC 79-4845. (Illus.). 246p. 1980. 12.95 (ISBN 0-295-95691-7). U of Wash Pr.

White, Richard M. The Entrepreneur's Manual: Business Start-Ups, Spin-Offs, & Innovative Management. LC 76-55520. 1976. 17.50 (ISBN 0-8019-6454-7). Chilton.

White, Richard N., et al. Structural Engineering, Vol. 3: Behavior of Members & Systems. LC 75-174772. 544p. 1974. text ed. 27.50 (ISBN 0-471-94072-0). Wiley.

--Structural Engineering, Combined Edition, 2 vols. in 1. LC 76-202. 570p. 1976. text ed. 27.95 (ISBN 0-471-94067-4). Wiley.

--Structural Engineering, Vol. 1: Introduction to Design Concepts & Analysis. 2nd ed. LC 75-174772. 288p. 1976. text ed. 21.95 (ISBN 0-471-94066-6). Wiley.

White, Robb. Deathwatch. LC 75-157637. (gr. 9-12). 1972. 6.95a o.p. (ISBN 0-385-02510-6); PLB (ISBN 0-385-02612-9). Doubleday.

--Fire Storm. (gr. 5-9). 1979. 7.95a (ISBN 0-385-14630-2); PLB (ISBN 0-385-14631-0). Doubleday.

--The Long Way Down. LC 77-79561. (gr. 7-12). 1977. PLB 5.95 (ISBN 0-385-13149-6); PLB (ISBN 0-385-13149-6). Doubleday.

White, Robert B., Jr., ed. English Literary Journal to Nineteen Hundred: A Guide to Information Sources. LC 73-16998. (American Literature English Literature & World Literatures in English Information Guide Ser.: Vol. 8). 250p. 1977. 30.00 (ISBN 0-8103-1228-X). Gale.

White, Robert C. Sewell's Dog's Medical Dictionary. 1976. cased 14.00 (ISBN 0-7100-8365-3); pap. 6.95 (ISBN 0-7100-8366-1). Routledge & Kegan.

White, Robert H., jt. auth. see Rodrigues, Raymond J.

White, Robert W. & Watt, Norman F. The Abnormal Personality. 4th ed. 640p. 1973. 20.95 o.p. (ISBN 0-471-06929-9); instructors' manual avail. o.p. (ISBN 0-471-07532-9). Wiley.

White, Robin, et al. America II: Special Issue 21. pap. 1.00 o.p. (ISBN 0-685-78394-4). The Smith.

White, Roger. Absent with Cause: Lessons of Truancy. (Routledge Education Bks.). 300p. (Orig.). 1980. pap. 18.00 (ISBN 0-7100-0665-9). Routledge & Kegan.

--Another Song, Another Season: Poems & Portrayals. 1979. 8.50 (ISBN 0-85398-087-X, 7-32-36, Pub. by G Ronald England); pap. 3.95 (ISBN 0-85398-088-8, 7-32-37, Pub. by G Ronald England). Baha'i.

White, Roger & Brockington, Dave. In & Out of School: The ROSLA Community Education Project. 1978. 15.00 (ISBN 0-7100-8888-4). Routledge & Kegan.

White, Ronald V. Teaching Written English. (Practical Language Teaching Series). (Illus., Orig.). 1980. pap. text ed. 6.95x (ISBN 0-04-371068-9, 2372). Allen Unwin.

White, Ruthe. Be the Woman You Want to Be. LC 77-88190. 1978. pap. 3.95 (ISBN 0-89081-114-8, 1148). Harvest Hse.

White, Sarah H., jt. auth. see McGarry, Daniel D.

White, Sarah L., jt. auth. see White, William.

White, Sheila J., jt. ed. see Teller, Virginia.

White, Sheldon & White, Barbara N. Childhood: Pathways of Discovery. (Life Cycle Ser.). 1979. pap. text ed. 4.95 scp (ISBN 0-06-384743-4, HarpC). Har-Row.

White, Sheryl. Beautiful Indiana. Shangle, Robert D., ed. LC 80-26310. (Illus.). 72p. 1980. 14.95 (ISBN 0-89802-160-X); pap. 7.95 (ISBN 0-89802-159-6). Beautiful Am.

--Beautiful Kentucky. Shangle, Robert D., ed. LC 80-25924. (Illus.). 72p. 1980. 14.95 (ISBN 0-915796-67-8); pap. 7.95 (ISBN 0-915796-66-X). Beautiful Am.

White, Sheryl & Shangle, Robert D., eds. Mormon: One Hundred & Fifty Years. (Illus.). 72p. 1980. 14.95 (ISBN 0-89802-177-4); pap. 7.95 (ISBN 0-89802-201-0). Beautiful Am.

White, Sidney H. Sidney Howard. (United States Authors Ser.: No. 288). 1977. lib. bdg. 12.50 (ISBN 0-8057-7191-3). Twayne.

White, Stephen L. Managing Health & Human Service Programs: A Guide for Managers. LC 80-1057. (Illus.). 1981. 17.95 (ISBN 0-02-934550-2). Free Pr.

White, Stewart E. Arizona Nights. 1976. lib. bdg. 15.75x (ISBN 0-89968-124-7). Lightyear.

--Daniel Boone: Wilderness Scout. 1976. lib. bdg. 14.75x (ISBN 0-89968-125-5). Lightyear.

--The Magic Forest. 1976. lib. bdg. 9.95x (ISBN 0-89968-126-3). Lightyear.

--The Silent Places. 1976. lib. bdg. 14.25x (ISBN 0-89968-123-9). Lightyear.

White, T. H. Darkness at Pemberley. LC 77-20549. 1978. pap. 3.75 (ISBN 0-486-23613-7). Dover.

--Mistress Masham's Repose. (Children's Literature Ser.). 1980. PLB 9.95 (ISBN 0-8398-2615-X). Gregg.

White, T. P. Ordnance Survey of the United Kingdom. 1975. pap. text ed. 15.00x (ISBN 90-6041-118-8). Humanities.

White, Ted. By Furies Possessed. 1980. pap. write for info. (ISBN 0-671-83308-1). PB.

--Club Operations & Management. LC 79-11864. (Illus.). 1979. text ed. 15.95 (ISBN 0-8436-0783-1). CBI Pub.

--The Secret of the Marauder Satellite. 1978. pap. 1.75 o.p. (ISBN 0-425-03888-2, Dist. by Putnam). Berkley Pub.

White, Ted & Bischoff, Dave. Forbidden World. 1978. pap. 1.50 o.p. (ISBN 0-445-04328-8). Popular Lib.

White, Thelma, jt. auth. see DeVore, Sally.

White, Theodore H. Caesar at the Rubicon: A Play About Politics. LC 77-11796. 1978. 8.95 o.s.i. (ISBN 0-06-014602-8, HarpT). Har-Row.

--In Search of History. 720p. 1981. pap. cancelled (ISBN 0-446-96729-7). Warner Bks.

--Making of the President Nineteen Sixty. LC 79-25849. (gr. 10 up). 1961. 10.00 o.p. (ISBN 0-689-10291-7). Atheneum.

--Making of the President Nineteen Sixty. 1967. pap. 2.00 (ISBN 0-451-61874-2, ME1874, Ment). NAL.

--The Making of the President, Nineteen Sixty. LC 79-25849. 1980. pap. 8.95 (ISBN 0-689-70600-6, 259). Atheneum.

--Making of the President Nineteen Sixty-Four. 1966. pap. 1.75 o.p. (ISBN 0-451-61255-8, ME1255, Ment). NAL.

White, Theodore H. & Jacoby, Annalee. Thunder Out of China. LC 74-31228. vi, 331p. 1975. Repr. of 1946 ed. lib. bdg. 32.50 (ISBN 0-306-70699-7). Da Capo.

--Thunder Out of China. 345p. 1980. pap. 7.95 (ISBN 0-306-80128-0). Da Capo.

White, Thomas T. & Harrison, R. Cameron. Reoperative Gastrointestinal Surgery. 2nd ed. 1979. text ed. 38.50 (ISBN 0-316-93604-9). Little.

White, Thurman J., jt. ed. see Taylor, Benjamin J.

White, Vernon S., ed. see Sawmill Clinic, 5th, Portland, Oregon, March 1975.

White, Virginia. Grants for the Arts. 275p. 1980. 19.50 (ISBN 0-306-40270-X, Plenum Pr). Plenum Pub.

White, W. A. Insanity & the Criminal Law. (Historical Foundations of Forensic Psychiatry & Psychology Ser.). 281p. 1980. Repr. of 1923 ed. lib. bdg. 25.00 (ISBN 0-306-76069-X). Da Capo.

White, W. A., jt. auth. see Wiese, B. R.

White, Wain L., ed. Surgery: PreTest Self-Assessment & Review. LC 77-78445. (Clinical Sciences: PreTest Self-Assessment & Review Ser.). (Illus.). 1978. pap. 9.95 (ISBN 0-07-051605-7). McGraw-Pretest.

White, Wallace F. Language of the Health Sciences: A Lexical Guide to Word Parts, Word Roots, & Their Meanings. LC 77-9310. 1977. pap. 12.95 (ISBN 0-471-02159-8, Pub. by Wiley Medical). Wiley.

White, Warren T., et al. Machine Tools & Machining Practices, 2 vols. LC 76-27863. 1977. Vol. 1. text ed. 25.95 (ISBN 0-471-94035-6); Vol. 2. text ed. 25.95 (ISBN 0-471-94036-4). Wiley.

White, William & White, Sarah L. A Terrarium in Your Home. LC 76-19807. (Illus.). (gr. 7 up). 1976. 6.95 o.p. (ISBN 0-8069-3732-7); PLB 6.69 o.p. (ISBN 0-8069-3733-5). Sterling.

White, William, jt. auth. see Cody, William J., Jr.

White, William, ed. see Hemingway, Ernest.

White, William A. Autobiography of William Allen White. 1946. 6.95 o.s.i. (ISBN 0-02-627100-1). Macmillan.

--A Certain Rich Man. LC 79-104763. (Novel As American Social History Ser.). 446p. 1970. 10.00x (ISBN 0-8131-1206-0); pap. 4.50 (ISBN 0-8131-0127-1). U Pr of Ky.

White, William C. Chinese Jews: A Compilation of Matters Relating to the Jews of K'ai-feng Fu. abr., 2nd ed. 9.95 (ISBN 0-8037-1252-9). Dial.

White, William D. U. S. Tactical Air Power: Missions, Forces, & Costs. (Studies in Defense Policy). 121p. 1974. pap. 3.95 (ISBN 0-8157-9371-5). Brookings.

White, William H. The Autobiography of Mark Rutherford, Dissenting Minister, 1881. Wolff, Robert L., ed. Bd. with Mark Rutherford's Deliverance, 1885. LC 75-1514. (Victorian Fiction Ser.). 1975. lib. bdg. 66.00 (ISBN 0-8240-1587-8). Garland Pub.

--Catherine Furze, 1893. Wolff, Robert L., ed. Bd. with Clara Hopgood, 1896. LC 75-1516. (Victorian Fiction Ser.). 1975. lib. bdg. 66.00 (ISBN 0-8240-1589-4). Garland Pub.

--The Revolution in Tanner's Lane, 1887. Wolff, Robert L., ed. Bd. with Miriam's Schooling, Eighteen Ninety. LC 75-1515. (Victorian Fiction Ser.). 1975. lib. bdg. 66.00 (ISBN 0-8240-1588-6). Garland Pub.

White, William J. Airships for the Future. rev. ed. LC 76-19768. (Illus.). (YA) 1978. 12.95 (ISBN 0-8069-0090-3); PLB 11.69 (ISBN 0-8069-0091-1). Sterling.

White, William, Jr. The American Chameleon. LC 76-51162. (Nature Ser.). (Illus.). (gr. 7 up). 1977. 7.95 (ISBN 0-8069-3532-4); PLB 7.49 (ISBN 0-8069-3533-2). Sterling.

--The Angelfish: Its Life Cycle. LC 75-14511. (Colorful Nature Ser.). (Illus.). 64p. (gr. 5 up). 1975. 9.95 (ISBN 0-8069-3482-4); PLB 9.29 (ISBN 0-8069-3483-2). Sterling.

--Cycle of the Seasons. LC 76-51172. (Living Nature Ser.). (gr. 4 up). 1977. 7.95 (ISBN 0-8069-3580-4); PLB 7.49 (ISBN 0-8069-3581-2). Sterling.

--An Earthworm Is Born. LC 75-14512. (Nature Ser.). (Illus.). 96p. (gr. 5 up). 1975. 7.95 (ISBN 0-8069-3530-8); PLB 7.49 (ISBN 0-8069-3531-6). Sterling.

--Edge of the Ocean. LC 78-80953. (Living Nature Ser.). (Illus.). (gr. 6 up). 1977. 7.95 (ISBN 0-8069-3582-0); PLB 7.49 (ISBN 0-8069-3583-9). Sterling.

--Forest & Garden. LC 76-19799. (Living Nature Ser.). (Illus.). (gr. 7 up). 1976. 7.95 (ISBN 0-8069-3578-2); PLB 7.49 (ISBN 0-8069-3579-0). Sterling.

--A Frog Is Born. LC 72-81037. (Nature Ser.). (Illus.). 96p. (gr. 5 up). 1972. 6.95 o.p. (ISBN 0-8069-3522-7); PLB 6.69 o.p. (ISBN 0-8069-3523-5). Sterling.

--The Guppy: Its Life Cycle. LC 73-83441. (Colorful Nature Ser.). 64p. (gr. 5 up). 1974. 9.95 (ISBN 0-8069-3476-X); PLB 9.29 (ISBN 0-8069-3477-8). Sterling.

--A Mosquito Is Born. LC 77-93319. (Sterling Nature Series). (Illus.). (gr. 5 up). 1978. 7.95 (ISBN 0-8069-3534-0); PLB 7.49 (ISBN 0-8069-3535-9). Sterling.

--A Turtle Is Born. (Illus.). 96p. (gr. 5 up). 1973. 6.95 o.p. (ISBN 0-8069-3528-6); PLB 6.69 o.p. (ISBN 0-8069-3529-4). Sterling.

White, William, Jr., ed. A Laboratory Handbook of Photomacrography. 1981. write for info. Franklin Inst Pr.

White, William L., jt. auth. see Light, J. O.

White, William M. Sweet Wild World: Thoreau on Birds & Small Creatures. (Illus.). 146p. (Orig.). 1981. 10.00 (ISBN 0-85699-112-0); pap. 6.95 (ISBN 0-85699-115-5). Chatham Pr.

White, Willie W. The Greatest Work in the World. rev. ed. 1975. pap. 3.95 (ISBN 0-89900-108-4). College Pr Pub.

Whitebird, J., ed. see Bright, Susan.

Whitebird, Joanie. And Then There Was. LC 78-63429. (Illus., Orig.). Date not set. pap. cancelled o.p. (ISBN 0-930138-06-6). Harold Hse.

Whitebread, Charles. Standards Relating to Transfer Between Courts. (Juvenile Justice Standards Project Ser.). 1980. softcover 5.95 (ISBN 0-88410-818-X); casebound 12.50 (ISBN 0-88410-230-0). Ballinger Pub.

--Standards Relating to Transfer Between Courts. LC 76-17798. (Juvenile Justice Standards Project Ser.). 1977. soft cover 5.95 o.p. (ISBN 0-88410-780-9); 12.50, casebound o.p. Ballinger Pub.

Whitebread, Charles H. Criminal Procedure: An Analysis of Constitutional Cases & Concepts. LC 80-14619. (University Textbook Ser.). 644p. 1980. text ed. write for info. (ISBN 0-88277-006-3). Foundation Pr.

Whitebread, Charles H., jt. auth. see Bonnie, Richard J.

Whitechurch, Canon V. Stories of the Railway. (Illus.). 1977. cased 12.00 (ISBN 0-7100-8635-0). Routledge & Kegan.

Whited, Maurine, jt. auth. see Wheeler, Robert R.

Whited, N. W. Automotive Oscilloscope. LC 76-3937. (Illus.). 88p. (gr. 10-12). 1977. pap. 5.40 (ISBN 0-8273-1033-1). Delmar.

White Eagle. The Gentle Brother. 1968. 3.95 (ISBN 0-85487-002-4). De Vorss.

--Golden Harvest. 1958. 3.50 (ISBN 0-85487-017-2). De Vorss.

--Heal Thyself. 1962. 3.95 (ISBN 0-85487-015-6). De Vorss.

--The Living Word of St. John. new ed. 208p. 1979. 13.95 (ISBN 0-85487-044-X). De Vorss.

--Morning Light. 1957. 3.50 (ISBN 0-85487-018-0). De Vorss.

--The Quiet Mind. 1972. 3.50 (ISBN 0-85487-009-1). De Vorss.

--Spiritual Unfoldment One. 1942. 5.95 (ISBN 0-85487-012-1). De Vorss.

--Sunrise. 1958. 3.50 (ISBN 0-85487-016-4). De Vorss.

--Wisdom from White Eagle. 5.95 (ISBN 0-85487-004-0). De Vorss.

Whitefield, Edwin. Hudson River Houses: Edwin Whitefield's the Hudson River & Rail Road Illustrated. LC 80-22371. (Illus.). 96p. 1981. 14.50 (ISBN 0-88427-043-2, Dist. by Caroline Hse). North River.

--Hudson River Houses: Edwin Whitefield's the Hudson River & Railroad Illustrated. 1980. 14.95 (ISBN 0-88427-043-2). Caroline Hse.

Whitefield, George. George Whitefield's Journals. 1978. 14.95 (ISBN 0-85151-147-3). Banner of Truth.

--Journals of George Whitefield, 1737-1741. LC 73-81363. (Illus.). 1969. Repr. of 1905 ed. 52.00x (ISBN 0-8201-1069-8). Schol Facsimiles.

Whitefield, Goerge. George Whitefield's Letters: 1734-1742. 1976. 14.95 (ISBN 0-85151-239-9). Banner of Truth.

Whitehead, Albert C. Standard Bearer: A Story of Army Life in the Time of Caesar. (Illus.). (gr. 7-11). 1943. 8.50x (ISBN 0-8196-0116-0). Biblo.

Whitehead, Alfred N. Concept of Nature. 32.95 (ISBN 0-521-06787-1); pap. 8.95x (ISBN 0-521-09245-0). Cambridge U Pr.

--Dialogues of Alfred North Whitehead. LC 76-49903. (Illus.). 1977. Repr. of 1954 ed. lib. bdg. 27.75x (ISBN 0-8371-9341-9, WHDI). Greenwood.

--Modes of Thought. LC 38-33184. 1968. pap. text ed. 3.95 (ISBN 0-02-935210-X). Free Pr.

--Nature & Life. LC 34-9604. (Illus.). 1969. Repr. of 1934 ed. lib. bdg. 10.75x (ISBN 0-8371-0751-2, WHNL). Greenwood.

Whitehead, Alfred N. & Russell, Bertrand. Principia Mathematica, 3 Vols. Set. 270.00 (ISBN 0-521-06791-X). Cambridge U Pr.

--Principia Mathematica to Fifty-Six. 2nd ed. 1925-27. pap. 19.95x (ISBN 0-521-09187-X). Cambridge U Pr.

Whitehead, Barbara. The Caretaker Wife. 1979. pap. 1.95 o.p. (ISBN 0-425-04038-0). Berkley Pub.

Whitehead, Bruce & Whitehead, Charlotte. Montana Bound: An Activity Approach to Teaching Montana History. (Illus.). 180p. (gr. 5-6). 1980. pap. text ed. 7.95x (ISBN 0-87108-235-7). Pruett.

Whitehead, Charles E., ed. see Ballesteros, Antonio M.

Whitehead, Charlotte, jt. auth. see Whitehead, Bruce.

Whitehead, Christine, tr. see Lora, G.

Whitehead, E. A. The Foursome. 1972. 7.50 (ISBN 0-571-09878-9, Pub. by Faber & Faber); pap. 4.95 (ISBN 0-571-09879-7). Merrimack Bk Serv.

--The Sea Anchor. (Orig.). 1975. pap. 4.95 (ISBN 0-571-10640-4, Pub. by Faber & Faber). Merrimack Bk Serv.

Whitehead, Eric. First Book of Ice Hockey. LC 69-12390. (First Bks). (Illus.). (gr. 4-6). 1969. PLB 4.90 o.p. (ISBN 0-531-00557-7). Watts.

--The Patricks: Hockey's Royal Family. LC 79-6879. (Illus.). 288p. 1980. 11.95 (ISBN 0-385-15662-6). Doubleday.

Whitehead, Evelyn E. & Whitehead, James D. Christian Life Patterns: The Psychological Challenges & Religious Invitations of Adult Life. LC 78-22543. 1979. 9.95 (ISBN 0-385-15130-6). Doubleday.

Whitehead, Evelyn E., jt. auth. see Whitehead, James D.

Whitehead, F., ed. Le Chanson De Roland. (French Texts Ser.). 1975. pap. text ed. 9.95x (ISBN 0-631-00390-8, Pub. by Basil Blackwell). Biblio Dist.

Whitehead, George. Growing for Showing. (Illus.). 176p. 1981. pap. 7.95 (ISBN 0-571-11706-6, Pub. by Faber & Faber). Merrimack Bk Serv.

Whitehead, Graham. Enquiry Learning in Social Studies. (Australian Council for Educational Research Ser.: No. 101). (Illus.). 1978. pap. 25.00x (ISBN 0-85563-164-3). Verry.

Whitehead, Harold. Administration of Marketing & Selling. 19.50x (ISBN 0-392-07566-0, SpS). Soccer.

Whitehead, Henry. The Village Gods of South India: 1921. LC 78-74275. (Oriental Religions Ser.: Vol. 10). 188p. 1980. lib. bdg. 22.00 (ISBN 0-8240-3907-6). Garland Pub.

Whitehead, James D. & Whitehead, Evelyn E. Method in Ministry: Theological Reflection and Christian Ministry. 240p. 1980. 12.95 (ISBN 0-8164-0455-0). Seabury.

Whitehead, James D., jt. auth. see Whitehead, Evelyn E.

Whitehead, K. D., jt. auth. see Likoudis, James.

Whitehead, Kenneth. Hunting & Stalking Deer Throughout the Ages. LC 79-56462. (Illus.). 241p. 1980. 53.00 (ISBN 0-7134-2083-9, Pub. by Batsford England). David & Charles.

Whitehead, L., ed. see Lora, G.

Whitehead, Lana E. Incredible Swimfants! LC 77-75712. 1979. 9.95 (ISBN 0-9604096-0-2). Family YMCA Stanislaus.

Whitehead, Laurence, jt. ed. see Foxley, Alejandro.

Whitehead, N. Conditioning for Sport. 128p. 1980. 12.95 (ISBN 0-8069-9110-0, Pub. by EP Publishing England); pap. 5.95 (ISBN 0-8069-9112-7). Sterling.

Whitehead, N. J. Track Athletics. (Sports Library). (Illus.). 1979. 12.95 (ISBN 0-8069-9156-9); pap. 6.95 (ISBN 0-8069-9158-5). Sterling.

Whitehead, O. Z. Some Early Baha'is of the West. (Illus.). 1976. 9.95 (ISBN 0-85398-065-9, 7-32-20, Pub. by George Ronald England); pap. 5.50 (ISBN 0-85398-067-5, 7-32-21, Pub. by George Ronald England). Baha'i.

Whitehead, P. C., jt. auth. see Frankel, B. G.

Whitehead, Paul, jt. auth. see Brook, Robert.

Whitehead, Peter, tr. see Budker, Paul.

Whitehead, R., jt. auth. see Bamman, H.

Whitehead, R. A. Kaleidoscope of Steam Wagons. (Illus.). 1979. 15.00x (ISBN 0-906116-10-4). Intl Pubns Serv.

--A Kaleidoscope of Traction Engines. (Illus.). 1980. 20.00x (ISBN 0-906116-20-1). Intl Pubns Serv.

--Steam in the Village. 1977. 14.50 o.p. (ISBN 0-7153-7449-4). David & Charles.

Whitehead, R. J., jt. auth. see Bamman, Henry A.

Whitehead, Robert. Children's Literature: Strategies of Teaching. (Orig.). 1968. pap. text ed. 10.95 (ISBN 0-13-132589-2). P-H.

--First Book of Eagles. LC 68-24609. (First Bks). (Illus.). (gr. 4-6). 1968. PLB 4.90 o.p. (ISBN 0-531-00517-8). Watts.

Whitehead, Robert & Teason, James. First Book of Bears. LC 66-10585. (First Bks). (Illus.). (gr. 4-6). 1966. PLB 4.90 o.p. (ISBN 0-531-00481-3). Watts.

Whitehead, Robert J. Rabbits & Hares. (First Bks.). (Illus.). 72p. (gr. 4-6). 1976. PLB 6.45 (ISBN 0-531-00338-8). Watts.

Whitehead, Ruth. Mother Tree. LC 75-142155. (Illus.). (gr. 3-6). 1971. 6.50 o.p. (ISBN 0-8164-3045-4, Clarion). HM.

Whitehead, Stanley B. The Observer's Book of House Plants. (Illus.). 1977. 2.95 (ISBN 0-684-14943-5, ScribT). Scribner.

Whitehead, T. P. Quality Control in Clinical Chemistry. LC 76-44522. (Quality Control Methods in the Clinical Laboratory Ser). 1977. text ed. 26.95 (ISBN 0-471-94075-5, Pub. by Wiley Medical). Wiley.

Whitehead, Willis F., jt. auth. see Carrington, Hereward.

Whitehill, James. Enter the Quiet: Everyone's Way to Meditation. LC 79-2996. (Illus.). 192p. (Orig.). 1980. pap. 5.95 (ISBN 0-06-069365-7, RD 312). Har-Row.

Whitehill, Walter, jt. auth. see King, Ernest.

Whitehill, Walter M. Boston in the Age of John Fitzgerald Kennedy. (Centers of Civilization Ser.: No. 19). xvi, 208p. 1966. 4.95 o.p. (ISBN 0-8061-0681-6). U of Okla Pr.

--Boston Public Library: A Centennial History. (Published by Harvard University). 1956. 4.75. Boston Public Lib.

--Spanish Romanesque Architecture of the Eleventh Century. 1941. 45.00x (ISBN 0-19-817167-6). Oxford U Pr.

Whitehill, Walter M., intro. by. Paul Revere's Boston 1735-1818. LC 74-21766. (Illus.). 300p. 1975. 29.50 (ISBN 0-87846-088-8, 694622). NYGS.

Whitehill, Walter M., et al, eds. Boston Furniture of the Eighteenth Century. LC 74-8139. 1975. 25.00x o.p. (ISBN 0-685-56093-7, Colonial Soc. of Massachusetts). U Pr of Va.

Whitehorne, P., tr. see Macchiavelli, Niccolo.

Whitehouse, Albert. Home Brewing: An Illustrated Guide. LC 80-68689. (Illus.). 1981. 12.95 (ISBN 0-7153-7985-2). David & Charles.

Whitehouse, D. G., jt. auth. see Roberts, J.

Whitehouse, David & Whitehouse, Ruth. Archaeological Atlas of the World. (Illus.). 1975. text ed. 27.95x (ISBN 0-7167-0274-6); pap. 14.95x (ISBN 0-7167-0273-8). W H Freeman.

Whitehouse, Gary E. & Wechsler, Ben L. Applied Operations Research: A Survey. LC 76-16545. 1976. 22.95x (ISBN 0-471-02552-6); solutions manual avail. (ISBN 0-685-66900-9). Wiley.

Whitehouse, Jack E., jt. auth. see Becker, Harold K.

Whitehouse, N. D., jt. auth. see Benson, Rowland S.

Whitehouse, Rith. Your Book of Archaeology. (gr. 6 up). 1979. 6.95 (ISBN 0-571-11255-2, Pub. by Faber & Faber). Merrimack Bk Serv.

Whitehouse, Ruth, jt. auth. see Whitehouse, David.

Whitehouse, W. A. Creation, Science, & Theology: Essays in Response to Karl Barth. 272p. (Orig.). 1981. pap. 10.95 (ISBN 0-8028-1870-6). Eerdmans.

Whitehouse, Wilfrid & Yanagisawa, Eizo, trs. Lady Nijo's Own Story: The Candid Diary of a 13th Century Japanese Imperial Court Concubine. LC 73-93503. 1974. 10.00 o.p. (ISBN 0-8048-1117-2). C E Tuttle.

Whitehurst, D. D., ed. Coal Liquefaction Fundamentals. LC 80-20585. (ACS Symposium Ser.: No. 139). 1980. 38.00 (ISBN 0-8412-0587-6). Am Chemical.

Whitehurst, D. D., et al. Coal Liquefaction: The Chemistry & Technology of Thermal Process. 1980. 19.50 (ISBN 0-12-747080-8). Acad Pr.

Whitehurst, Grover J. & Vasta, Ross F. Child Behavior. LC 76-14009. (Illus.). 1977. text ed. 19.50 (ISBN 0-395-24446-3); test item manual 1.00 (ISBN 0-395-24447-1); wkbk. 6.75 (ISBN 0-395-25794-8). HM.

Whitehurst, Robert N., jt. auth. see Libby, Roger W.

Whitelaw, J. S., jt. auth. see Cumberland, K. B.

Whitelaw, R. R. Marketing & Economics. 1969. 23.00 (ISBN 0-08-006583-X); pap. 11.25 (ISBN 0-08-006582-1). Pergamon.

Whitelaw, Thomas A. Introduction to Abstract Algebra. (Illus.). 1978. pap. text ed. 16.95x (ISBN 0-216-90488-9). Intl Ideas.

Whiteley, Bruce. Tina. 192p. 1979. 9.95 (ISBN 0-679-51378-7). McKay.

Whiteley, C. H. Introduction to Metaphysics. LC 77-1892. (Repr. of 1950 ed.). 1977. text ed. 13.00x (ISBN 0-391-00711-4). Humanities.

--Mind in Action: An Essay in Philosophical Psychology. (Oxford Paperbacks University Ser). 128p. 1973. pap. 3.95x o.p. (ISBN 0-19-888092-8). Oxford U Pr.

Whiteley, D. E. Thessalonians. (New Clarendon Bible Ser). (Illus.). 1969. 6.95x (ISBN 0-19-836906-9). Oxford U Pr.

Whiteley, John M. The History of Counseling Psychology. LC 79-23441. 1980. pap. text ed. 8.95 (ISBN 0-8185-0370-X). Brooks-Cole.

Whiteley, John M. & Fretz, Bruce R. The Present & Future of Counseling Psychology. LC 80-315. (Counseling Psychology Ser.). 256p. (Orig.). 1980. pap. text ed. 8.95 (ISBN 0-8185-0396-3). Brooks-Cole.

Whiteley, Robert J. Geophysical Case Study of the Woodlawn Orebody, New South Wales Australia. LC 79-42637. (Illus.). xviii, 592p. 1980. 80.00 (ISBN 0-08-023996-X). Pergamon.

Whitelock, Dorothy. From Bede to Alfred: Studies in Early Anglo-Saxon Literature & History. 368p. 1980. 75.00x (ISBN 0-86078-066-X, Pub. by Variorum England). State Mutual Bk.

Whitelocke, Lester T. An Analytical Concordance of the Books of the Apocrypha. LC 78-61389. 1978. pap. text ed. 16.75 ea.; Vol. 1. (ISBN 0-8191-0603-8); Vol. 2. (ISBN 0-8191-0604-6). U Pr of Amer.

Whitely, J. Stuart & Gordon, John. Group Approaches in Psychiatry. (Social & Psychological Aspects of Medical Practice Ser.). 1979. 20.00x (ISBN 0-7100-8970-8). Routledge & Kegan.

Whitely, Jon. Ingres. (Illus.). 15.95 (ISBN 0-8467-0250-9, Pub. by Two Continents); pap. text ed. 9.95 (ISBN 0-8467-0249-5). Hippocrene Bks.

Whitely, Opal, jt. auth. see Boulton, Jane.

Whiteman, A. L., ed. see Symposia in Pure Mathematics-Pasadena-1963.

Whiteman, Anne, et al, eds. Statesmen, Scholars & Merchants: Essays in Eighteenth-Century History. 396p. 1973. 24.95x (ISBN 0-19-822378-1). Oxford U Pr.

Whiteman, Marcia F., ed. Reactions to Ann Arbor: Vernacular Black English & Education. 104p. (Orig.). 1980. pap. text ed. 5.95 (ISBN 0-87281-125-5). Ctr Appl Ling.

Whiteman, Maxwell. Copper for America: The Hendricks Family & a National Industry, 1755-1939. LC 79-153446. 1971. 23.00 (ISBN 0-8135-0587-5). Rutgers U Pr.

--Gentlemen in Crisis: The First Century of the Union League of Philadelphia, 1862-1962. LC 75-13693. (Illus.). 372p. 1975. 12.00 (ISBN 0-915810-00-X). Union League PA.

Whitener, Barbara, jt. auth. see Wortham, Jim.

Whitern, Wilfred H., jt. auth. see Axelrod, Herbert R.

Whitern, Wilfred L. Livebearers. (Illus.). 93p. 1979. 2.95 (ISBN 0-87666-518-0, KW-049). TFH Pubns.

Whitesell, Faris D. & Perry, Lloyd M. Variety in Your Preaching. 1954. 10.95 (ISBN 0-8007-0335-9). Revell.

Whiteside, Abby. Indispensables of Piano Playing. LC 61-18671. 12.50 (ISBN 0-684-10653-1, ScribT). Scribner.

--Mastering the Chopin Etudes & Other Essays. LC 79-85263. 1969. 12.50 (ISBN 0-684-10654-X, ScribT). Scribner.

Whiteside, Andrew G. The Socialism of Fools: Georg Ritter Von Schonerer & Austrian Pan-Germanism. 512p. 1975. 32.50x (ISBN 0-520-02434-6). U of Cal Pr.

Whiteside, Conon D. EDP Systems for Credit Management. LC 74-156330. 1971. 23.95 (ISBN 0-471-94080-1, Pub. by Wiley-Interscience). Wiley.

Whiteside, D. T., ed. see Newton, Isaac.

Whiteside, D. T., et al, eds. see Newton, Isaac.

Whiteside, David & Whisteside, Robert L. How to Win Over Yourself and Other People, Assertiveness Techniques and Traits. LC 76-16856. 1976. 7.95 (ISBN 0-8119-0270-6). Fell.

Whiteside, Karen. Brother Mouky & the Falling Sun. LC 79-2014. (Illus.). 32p. (gr. k-3). 1980. 7.95 (ISBN 0-06-026407-1, HarpJ); PLB 7.89 (ISBN 0-06-026408-X). Har-Row.

Whiteside, Robert. Animal Language. LC 80-14822. (Illus.). 112p. 1981. 9.95 (ISBN 0-8119-0297-8, 111). Fell.

--Face Language. LC 74-4418. 1974. 9.95 (ISBN 0-8119-0231-5). Fell.

Whiteside, Thomas. Alone Through the Dark Sea. LC 64-12964. 1964. 5.00 o.s.i. (ISBN 0-8076-0275-2). Braziller.

--Computer Capers: Tales of Electronic Thievery, Embezzlement, & Fraud. LC 77-25184. 1978. 9.95 (ISBN 0-690-01743-X, TYC-T). T Y Crowell.

--Twiggy & Justin. (Photos). 1968. 4.50 o.p. (ISBN 0-374-27980-2). FS&G.

Whitesitt, J. Eldon. Boolean Algebra & Its Applications. 1961. 14.95 (ISBN 0-201-08660-3). A-W.

--Principles of Modern Algebra. 2nd ed. LC 74-184163. 1973. text ed. 14.95 (ISBN 0-201-08706-5). A-W.

Whiteway, Catherine E., jt. auth. see Elward, Margaret.

Whitfield, Danny J. Historical & Cultural Dictionary of Vietnam. (Historical & Cultural Dictionaries of Asia Ser.: No. 7). 1976. 15.00 o.p. (ISBN 0-8108-0887-0). Scarecrow.

Whitfield, Francis J., tr. see Hjelmslev, Louis.

Whitfield, I. C. Electrical Installations Technology. 1968. 25.00 (ISBN 0-08-012704-5); pap. text ed. 11.25 (ISBN 0-08-012703-7). Pergamon.

Whitfield, Jane S. Whitfield's University Rhyming Dictionary. Stillman, Frances, ed. (Apollo Eds.). pap. 3.95 (ISBN 0-8152-0080-3, A80, TYC-T). T Y Crowell.

Whitfield, Richard C. Education for Family Life: Some New Policies for Child Care. 161p. 1980. pap. text ed. 10.00 (ISBN 0-340-25524-2). Verry.

Whitfield, Stephen J. Into the Dark: Hannah Arendt & Totalitarianism. 352p. 1980. 18.95 (ISBN 0-87722-188-X). Temple U Pr.

--Scott Nearing: Apostle of American Radicalism. 1974. 15.00x (ISBN 0-231-03816-X). Columbia U Pr.

Whitfield, Susan, jt. auth. see Davis, Bertha.

Whitfield, Thomas. From Night to Sunlight. LC 80-68874. 1980. pap. 4.95 (ISBN 0-8054-5291-5). Broadman.

Whitfield, Vallie. History of Pleasant Hill, California. 1981. 15.00 (ISBN 0-930920-15-5). Whitfield.

Whitford, Frank. Eduardo Paolozzi. (Tate Gallery Art Ser.). (Illus.). 1977. 3.95 o.p. (ISBN 0-8120-5144-0). Barron.

--Egon Schiele: World of Art. (Illus.). 288p. 1981. 17.95 (ISBN 0-19-520245-7); pap. 9.95 (ISBN 0-19-520246-5). Oxford U Pr.

--Grosz. (Oresko-Jupiter Art Bks). (Illus.). 96p. 1981. 17.95 (ISBN 0-933516-88-6, Pub. by Oresko-Jupiter England). Hippocrene Bks.

--Japanese Prints & Western Painters. LC 76-45182. (Illus.). 1977. 35.00 (ISBN 0-02-627180-X, 62718). Macmillan.

Whitford, L. A. & Schumacher, George. Manual of Freshwater Algae. 15.00 (ISBN 0-916822-01-X). Sparks Pr.

Whitford, Robert H. Physics Literature. 2nd ed. LC 68-12636. 1968. 11.50 (ISBN 0-8108-0112-4). Scarecrow.

Whitin, T. M., jt. auth. see Hadley, George.

Whiting, Allen S. China & the United States: What Next? (Headline Ser.: 230). (Illus.). 1976. pap. 2.00 (ISBN 0-87124-035-1, 76-4299). Foreign Policy.

--Chinese Domestic Politics & Foreign Policy in the 1970s. LC 78-31865. (Michigan Papers in Chinese Studies: No. 36). (Orig.). 1979. pap. text ed. 4.00 (ISBN 0-89264-036-7). U of Mich Ctr Chinese.

Whiting, Charles. Death of a Division. LC 80-5717. (Illus.). 176p. 1981. 11.95 (ISBN 0-8128-2760-0). Stein & Day.

Whiting, Charles G. Paul Valery. (Athlone French Poets Ser.). 1978. text ed. 22.50x (ISBN 0-485-14609-6, Athlone Pr); pap. text ed. 10.75x (ISBN 0-485-12209-X). Humanities.

--Valery: Jeune Poete. (Yale Romantic Studies). 1960. pap. 27.50x (ISBN 0-685-69883-1). Elliots Bks.

Whiting, Charles G., ed. see Valery, Paul.

Whiting, D. P. International Trade & Payments. (Illus.). 160p. 1978. pap. 11.95x (ISBN 0-7121-0952-8). Intl Ideas.

Whiting, Ella K., ed. The Poems of John Audelay. (EETS, OS Ser.: No. 184). Repr. of 1931 ed. 16.00 (ISBN 0-527-00183-X). Kraus Repr.

Whiting, Frank M. An Introduction to the Theatre. 4th ed. 1978. text ed. 18.50 scp (ISBN 0-06-047089-5, HarpC). Har-Row.

Whiting, Gertrude. Old-Time Tools & Toys of Needlework. 1970. pap. 6.00 (ISBN 0-486-22517-8). Dover.

Whiting, John. Chapman's Log & Owner's Manual. 128p. 1980. 12.95 (ISBN 0-87851-801-0); deluxe ed. 75.00 (ISBN 0-87851-801-0). Hearst Bks.

Whiting, Larry & Rogers, David, eds. University of Texas, Institute of Texan Cultures: Univ. of Texas, Institute of Texan Cultures. (Illus.). 1978. pap. text ed. 6.95x (ISBN 0-8138-1875-3). Iowa St U Pr.

Whiting, M. C., tr. see Kagan, Henri.

Whiting, Robert. The Chrysanthemum & the Bat. LC 76-27708. (Illus.). 352p. 1977. 10.00 (ISBN 0-396-07317-4). Dodd.

Whiting, Thomas A. Be Good to Yourself. LC 80-27304. 128p. 1981. 6.95 (ISBN 0-687-02800-0). Abingdon.

Whiting, U. H., tr. see Kagan, Henri.

Whiting, William. War Powers Under the Constitution of the United States. LC 70-169640. (American Constitutional & Legal History Ser). 1972. Repr. of 1871 ed. lib. bdg. 59.50 (ISBN 0-306-70361-0). Da Capo.

Whitinger, Robert G. Indiana Small Claims. 180p. 1980. 20.00 (ISBN 0-87215-326-6). Michie.

Whitlach, John. Shoot-Out at Dawn--An Arizona Tragedy. De Mente, Boye, ed. (Illus.). 176p. (Orig.). 1980. pap. 6.95 (ISBN 0-914778-37-4). Phoenix Bks.

Whitley, Craig. Recipes for Runners: A Complete Nutrition Guide for Runners. (Illus.). 272p. 1981. cancelled (ISBN 0-913276-34-0). Stone Wall Pr.

Whitley, David S., et al, eds. Inland Chumash Archaeological Investigations. (Monographs: Vol. XV). (Illus.). 258p. 1980. pap. 7.00 (ISBN 0-917956-18-4). UCLA Arch.

Whitley, Kathleen, jt. auth. see Clayton, Barbara.

Whitley, Richard, ed. Social Processes of Scientific Development. 1974. 22.50x (ISBN 0-7100-7705-X). Routledge & Kegan.

Whitley, William T. Gilbert Stuart. LC 77-87680. (Library of American Art Ser). 1932. lib. bdg. 27.50 (ISBN 0-306-71712-3). Da Capo.

Whitlock, Brand. The Buckeyes: Politics & Abolitionism in an Ohio Town, 1836-1845. Miller, Paul W., ed. LC 76-8306. (Illus.). 273p. 1977. 12.95 (ISBN 0-8214-0222-6). Ohio U Pr.

--The Turn of the Balance. LC 76-104765. (The Novel As American Social History). 650p. 1970. 10.00x (ISBN 0-8131-1213-3). U Pr of Ky.

Whitlock, Dave, jt. auth. see Boyle, Robert H.

Whitlock, Dorothy, et al, eds. Ireland in Early Medieval Europe. LC 80-40325. (Studies in Memory of Kathleen Hughes). (Illus.). 400p. Date not set. price not set (ISBN 0-521-23547-2). Cambridge U Pr.

Whitlock, F. A. Psychophysiological Aspects of Skin Disease, Vol. 8. LC 76-20942. (Illus.). 1976. 22.00 (ISBN 0-7216-9301-6). Saunders.

Whitlock, Herbert P. Story of the Gems. (Illus.). (gr. 9 up). 13.95 o.s.i. (ISBN 0-87523-053-9). Emerson.

Whitlock, Linda J., jt. auth. see Whitlock, Robert R.

Whitlock, Pamela, jt. auth. see Hull, Katharine.

Whitlock, Quentin, ed. see Association for Programmed Learning & Educational Technology Conference, 1979.

Whitlock, Ralph. Chimpanzees. LC 77-13965. (Animals of the World Ser.). (Illus.). (gr. 4-5). 1977. PLB 10.65 (ISBN 0-8172-1077-6). Raintree Pubs.

--A Closer Look at Butterflies & Moths. (Closer Look at Ser.). (Illus.). (gr. 4-7). 1978. PLB 6.90 (ISBN 0-531-01425-8); pap. 1.95 (ISBN 0-531-02488-1). Watts.

--Everyday Life of the Maya. 1976. 19.95 (ISBN 0-7134-3232-2, Pub. by Batsford England). David & Charles.

--Penguins. LC 77-14042. (Animals of the World Ser.). (Illus.). (gr. 4-8). 1977. PLB 10.65 (ISBN 0-8172-1078-4). Raintree Pubs.

--Spiders. Brenner, Barbara, ed. LC 76-14935. (Illus.). 80p. (gr. 4 up). 1976. PLB 6.95 o.p. (ISBN 0-8172-0325-7). Raintree Pubs.

Whitlock, Richard. A Calendar of Country Customs. 1978. 19.95 (ISBN 0-7134-0571-6). David & Charles.

Whitlock, Robert R. & Whitlock, Linda J. The Sunnyside of Chords: An Encyclopedia of Chord & Scale Diagrams for Fingerboard Instruments. LC 78-71087. (Illus.). 240p. 1979. pap. 22.00 (ISBN 0-9602178-0-0). Pattecky Music.

Whitlow, Roger. Black American Literature: A Critical History. LC 73-75525. 1973. 14.95x (ISBN 0-88229-100-9). Nelson-Hall.

Whitman, Alan. Christian Occasions: A Photographic Study of Unusual Styles of Religion in American Life. LC 77-76286. 1979. pap. 6.95 (ISBN 0-385-12597-6, Dolp). Doubleday.

Whitman, Alfred. Print-Collector's Handbook. LC 72-177279. (Tower Bks). (Illus.). xii, 152p. 1972. Repr. of 1901 ed. 24.00 (ISBN 0-8103-3938-2). Gale.

Whitman, John. The Best Free Attractions in the East. Grooms, Kathe, ed. (The Best Free Attractions Ser.). (Illus., Orig.). 1981. pap. 3.95 (ISBN 0-915658-35-6). Meadowbrook Pr.

--The Best Free Attractions in the Midwest. Grooms, Kathe, ed. (The Best Free Attractions Ser.). (Illus.). 200p. 1981. pap. 3.95 (ISBN 0-915658-37-2). Meadowbrook Pr.

--The Best Free Attractions in the South. Grooms, Kathe, ed. (The Best Free Attractions Ser.). (Illus.). 200p. 1981. pap. 3.95 (ISBN 0-915658-38-0). Meadowbrook Pr.

--The Best Free Attractions in the West. Grooms, Kathe, ed. (The Best Free Attractions Ser.). (Illus.). 200p. 1981. pap. 3.95 (ISBN 0-915658-36-4). Meadowbrook Pr.

--The Uncommon Guide to Europe. LC 77-10376. (Illus.). 1978. 13.95 o.p. (ISBN 0-312-82862-4); pap. 5.95 o.p. (ISBN 0-312-82863-2). St Martin.

--Whitman's off Season Travel Guide to Europe: Europe at Its Best from September to May. LC 73-91600. 352p. 1975. 17.50 o.p. (ISBN 0-312-86905-3); pap. 6.95 o.p. (ISBN 0-312-86940-1). St Martin.

--Whitman's Restaurant Guide to Minnesota. (Illus.). 1976. pap. 1.00 (ISBN 0-685-78748-6). Nodin Pr.

--Whitman's Travel Guide to Minnesota. (Illus.). 1977. pap. 1.00 (ISBN 0-685-88678-6). Nodin Pr.

Whitman, Malcolm D. Tennis Origins & Mysteries. LC 68-58970. 1968. Repr. of 1932 ed. 18.00 (ISBN 0-8103-3542-5). Gale.

Whitman, Mark. The Films of Clint Eastwood. Castell, David, ed. (The Films of...Ser.). (Illus.). (gr. 7-12). 1978. Repr. of 1973 ed. PLB 5.95 (ISBN 0-912616-75-X). Greenhaven.

--The Films of James Dean. Castell, David, ed. (The Films of...Ser.). (Illus.). (gr. 7-12). 1978. Repr. of 1974 ed. PLB 5.95 (ISBN 0-912616-88-1). Greenhaven.

Whitman, Martin & Shubik, Martin. The Aggressive Conservative Investor. LC 78-21593. 1979. 17.95 (ISBN 0-685-67576-9). Random.

Whitman, Nancy C. & Braun, Frederick G. The Metric System: A Laboratory Approach for Teachers. LC 77-22793. 1978. pap. text ed. 11.50 (ISBN 0-471-02763-4). Wiley.

Whitman, Robert. Simplified Guide to Estate Planning & Administration. 192p. 1981. pap. 6.95 (ISBN 0-671-09136-0). Monarch Pr.

Whitman, Robert F. Beyond Melancholy: John Webster & the Tragedy of Darkness. (Salzburg Studies in English Literature, Jacobean Drama Studies: No. 4). 1973. pap. text ed. 25.00x (ISBN 0-391-01565-6). Humanities.

Whitman, Robert F., ed. see Shaw, George B.

Whitman, Robert V., jt. auth. see Lambe, T. William.

Whitman, Ruth. An Anthology of Modern Yiddish Poetry. LC 66-25551. 141p. 1979. pap. 4.95. Workmen's Circle.

--Permanent Address: New Poems 1973-1980. LC 80-66182. 72p. 1980. pap. 4.95 (ISBN 0-914086-30-8). Alicejamesbook.

--Tamsen Donner: A Woman's Journey. LC 77-90508. 80p. 1977. pap. 4.95 (ISBN 0-914086-20-0). Alicejamesbooks.

Whitman, Sarah H. Edgar Poe & His Critics. 81p. 1967. pap. 2.50 (ISBN 0-910120-03-X). Americanist.

Whitman, Sarah H. P. Edgar Poe & His Critics. LC 80-26202. 105p. Repr. of 1949 ed. 9.00x (ISBN 0-686-69559-3). Gordian.

Whitman, Walt. A Choice of Whitman's Verse. Hall, Donald, ed. 1968. 4.95 o.p. (ISBN 0-571-08403-6, Pub. by Faber & Faber); pap. 4.95 (ISBN 0-571-08613-6). Merrimack Bk Serv.

--The Correspondence, 5 vols. Miller, Edwin H., ed. Incl. Vol. 1. 1842-1867. 394p. 1961 (ISBN 0-8147-0435-2); Vol. 2. 1868-1875. 372p. 1961 (ISBN 0-8147-0436-0); Vol. 3. 1876-1885. 473p. 1964 (ISBN 0-8147-0437-9); Vol. 4. 1886-1889. 458p. 1969 (ISBN 0-8147-0438-7); Vol. 5. 1890-1892. 365p. 1969 (ISBN 0-8147-0439-5). LC 60-15980. (Illus.). 25.00x ea. NYU Pr.

--The Early Poems & the Fiction. Brasher, Thomas L., ed. LC 60-15980. (Illus.). 1963. 25.00x (ISBN 0-8147-0441-7). NYU Pr.

--Leaves of Grass. 1971. pap. 1.95 (ISBN 0-451-51395-9, CJ1395, Sig Classics). NAL.

--Leaves of Grass. Bradley, Sculley & Blodgett, Harold W., eds. (Critical Editions Ser.). 500p. 1973. pap. text ed. 12.95x (ISBN 0-393-09388-3). Norton.

--Leaves of Grass. Cowley, Malcolm, ed. (Poets Ser). 1976. pap. 2.25 (ISBN 0-14-042199-8). Penguin.

--Leaves of Grass: Comprehensive Reader's Edition. Blodgett, Harold W. & Bradley, Sculley, eds. LC 60-15980. (Illus.). 1965. 24.50x (ISBN 0-8147-0440-9). NYU Pr.

--Poems of Walt Whitman. Powell, Lawrence C., ed. & compiled by. LC 64-20689. (Apollo Eds.). (Illus.). 1971. pap. 1.95 o.p. (ISBN 0-8152-0312-8, A312, TYC-T). T Y Crowell.

--Prose Works Eighteen Ninety-Two, 2 vols. Stovall, Floyd, ed. Incl. Vol. 1. Specimen Days. 358p. 1963 (ISBN 0-8147-0442-5); Vol. 2. Collect & Other Prose. 445p. 1964 (ISBN 0-8147-0443-3). LC 60-15980. (Illus.). 25.00x ea. NYU Pr.

--Walt Whitman: Leaves of Grass: A Textual Variorum of the Printed Poems, 1855-1892, 3 Vols. Bradley, Sculley, et al, eds. LC 78-65727. (The Collected Writings of Walt Whitman Ser.). 944p. 1980. 125.00x set (ISBN 0-8147-1024-7); Vol. 1 (ISBN 0-8147-1014-X); Vol. 2 (ISBN 0-8147-1015-8); Vol. 3 (ISBN 0-8147-1016-6). NYU Pr.

Whitmore. Giftedness, Conflict & Underachievement. 478p. 1980. text ed. 18.95 (ISBN 0-205-06870-7, 2468700). Allyn.

Whitmore, et al. Self-Correcting Problems in Statistics. text ed. 12.95 (ISBN 0-205-02617-6, 1626175). Allyn.

Whitmore, Allen P. The Major Characters of Lord Byron's Plays. (Salzburg Studies in English Literature, Poetic Drama & Poetic Theory: No. 6). 145p. 1974. pap. text ed. 25.00x (ISBN 0-391-01566-4). Humanities.

Whitmore, D. A. & Ibbetson, J. The Management of Motivation & Renumeration. 230p. 1977. text ed. 29.50x (ISBN 0-220-66319-X, Pub. by Busn Bks England). Renouf.

Whitmore, Dennis A. Work Study & Related Management Services. 3rd ed. LC 68-135711. (Illus.). 336p. 1968. 12.50x (ISBN 0-434-92253-6). Intl Pubns Serv.

Whitmore, G. A. & Findlay, M. C., eds. Stochastic Dominance. LC 76-55111. (Illus.). 1978. 21.95x (ISBN 0-669-01310-2). Lexington Bks.

Whitmore, John K., jt. ed. see Hall, Kenneth R.

Whitmore, R. L. Rheology of the Circulation. LC 68-18535. 232p. 1968. 32.00 (ISBN 0-08-012661-8). Pergamon.

Whitmore, Richard. Victorian & Edwardian Crime & Punishment. 1978. 17.95 (ISBN 0-7134-0348-9, Pub. by Batsford England). David & Charles.

Whitmore, William H. Family Tree Ancestral Tablets. 1955. pap. 7.75 (ISBN 0-8048-0684-5). C E Tuttle.

Whitmoyer, C. W., Sr. Your Health Is What You Make It: A Guide for Diet, Vitamin Supplementation, Cholesterol Control, Exercise, Mental Health, and Longevity. 1972. 10.00 o.p. (ISBN 0-682-47522-X, Banner). Exposition.

Whitnah, Dorothy L. Guide to the Golden Gate National Recreation Area. Winnett, Thomas, ed. LC 76-57009. (Illus., Orig.). 1978. pap. 5.95 (ISBN 0-911824-54-5). Wilderness.

--Point Reyes. Winnett, Thomas, ed. LC 79-57597. (Illus., Orig.). 1981. pap. 6.95 (ISBN 0-911824-95-2). Wilderness.

Whitney, jt. auth. see Dubbs.

Whitney, Alex, ed. McKay's Big Book of Cowboys & Cowgirls. (gr. 4 up). Date not set. cancelled (ISBN 0-679-20540-3). McKay.

--McKay's Big Book of Dinosaurs. (gr. 4 up). Date not set. cancelled (ISBN 0-679-20536-5). McKay.

--McKay's Big Book of Model Trains. (gr. 4 up). Date not set. cancelled (ISBN 0-679-20539-X). McKay.

--McKay's Big Book of Villains. (gr. 4 up). 7.95 o.p. (ISBN 0-679-20535-7). McKay.

Whitney, Arthur H. Colloquial Hungarian. 2nd ed. (Trubner's Colloquial Manuals). (Illus.). 1977. pap. 7.95 (ISBN 0-7100-8550-8). Routledge & Kegan.

Whitney, Blair. John G. Neihardt. LC 76-6543. (U. S. Authors Ser.: No. 270). lib. bdg. 10.95 (ISBN 0-8057-7170-0). Twayne.

Whitney, David C. Colonial Spirit of '76. 1974. 39.00 (ISBN 0-87827-200-3). Ency Brit Ed.

--Easy Book of Fractions. LC 70-100093. (First Steps to Math Ser). (Illus.). (gr. 4-6). 1970. PLB 4.47 o.p. (ISBN 0-531-01842-3). Watts.

--The Easy Book of Numbers & Numerals. LC 73-6695. (First Steps to Math Ser). (Illus.). (gr. 2-4). 1973. PLB 6.45 (ISBN 0-531-02597-7). Watts.

--The Easy Book of Sets. LC 70-39841. (First Steps to Math Ser). (Illus.). 48p. (gr. 3-5). 1972. PLB 6.45 (ISBN 0-531-02554-3). Watts.

--First Book of Facts & How to Find Them. LC 66-12152. (First Bks). (Illus.). (gr. 4-6). 1966. PLB 4.90 o.p. (ISBN 0-531-00527-5). Watts.

--Let's Find Out About Milk. LC 67-14832. (Let's Find Out Bks). (Illus.). (gr. k-3). 1967. PLB 4.47 o.p. (ISBN 0-531-00033-8). Watts.

--Let's Find Out About Subtraction. LC 68-11890. (Let's Find Out Bks). (Illus.). (gr. k-3). 1968. PLB 4.47 o.p. (ISBN 0-531-00045-1). Watts.

Whitney, Eleanor N. & Hamilton, Eva M. Understanding Nutrition. (Illus.). 1977. text ed. 18.50 (ISBN 0-8299-0052-7); instrs.' manual avail. (ISBN 0-8299-0583-9). West Pub.

--Understanding Nutrition. 2nd ed. (Illus.). 650p. 1981. text ed. 18.95 (ISBN 0-8299-0419-0). West Pub.

Whitney, Eleanor N., jt. auth. see Hamilton, Eva M.

Whitney, Elinor, jt. auth. see Mahoney, Bertha.

Whitney, Frederick A. The Law of Modern Commercial Practices, 2vols. 2nd ed. LC 65-4288. 1965. 85.00 (ISBN 0-686-14490-2). Lawyers Co-Op.

Whitney, George D., jt. auth. see Whitney, Leon F.

Whitney, Hassler. Complex Analytic Varieties. 1972. 20.95 (ISBN 0-201-08653-0). A-W.

Whitney, Leon F. All About Guppies. (Orig.). pap. 5.95 (ISBN 0-87666-083-9, PS603). TFH Pubns.

--Birth Control Today: A Practical Approach to Intelligent Family Planning. (Illus.). 1962. pap. 0.95 o.s.i. (ISBN 0-02-078350-7, Collier). Macmillan.

--Breed Your Dog. (Orig.). 1962. pap. 2.00 (ISBN 0-87666-255-6, DS1021). TFH Pubns.

--Groom Your Dog. (Orig.). 1962. pap. 2.00 (ISBN 0-87666-313-7, DS1023). TFH Pubns.
--Keep Your Pigeons Flying. 2nd ed. (Illus.). 1968. 9.95 o.p. (ISBN 0-571-04649-5, Pub. by Faber & Faber). Merrimack Bk Serv.
Whitney, Leon F. & Whitney, George D. The Complete Book of Cat Care. rev. ed. LC 79-7216. (Illus.). 1980. 9.95 (ISBN 0-385-14707-4). Doubleday.
Whitney, Leon F., D.V.M. Training You to Train Your Cat. LC 68-14215. 1968. 5.95 o.p. (ISBN 0-385-08381-5). Doubleday.
Whitney, Maurice. Backgrounds in Music Theory. 1954. pap. 5.95 (ISBN 0-02-872870-X). Schirmer Bks.
--One Hundred Fifty Progressive Exercises for Melodic Dictation. (For use with Backgrounds in Music Theory). 1954. pap. 1.95 (ISBN 0-02-872880-7). Schirmer Bks.
Whitney, Norman see Milne, John.
Whitney, Phyllis. Fire & the Gold. (YA) (RL 7). 1974. pap. 1.50 (ISBN 0-451-07320-7, W7320, Sig). NAL.
--Poinciana. 1981. lib. bdg. 15.95 (ISBN 0-8161-3148-1, Large Print Bks). G K Hall.
--Silverhill. 1978. pap. 2.25 (ISBN 0-449-24094-0, Crest). Fawcett.
--Turquoise Mask. 1980. pap. 2.50 (ISBN 0-449-23470-3, Crest). Fawcett.
Whitney, Phyllis A. Blue Fire. 1981. pap. 2.25 (ISBN 0-449-24083-5, Crest). Fawcett.
--Columbella. 256p. 1981. pap. 2.50 (ISBN 0-449-22919-X, Crest). Fawcett.
--Columbella. 1978. pap. 1.75 o.p. (ISBN 0-449-22919-X, Crest). Fawcett.
--Domino. 1980. pap. 2.75 (ISBN 0-449-24350-8, Crest). Fawcett.
--The Golden Unicorn. 320p. 1977. pap. 2.25 (ISBN 0-449-23104-6, Crest). Fawcett.
--Listen for the Whisperer. LC 76-168682. 1972. 5.95 o.p. (ISBN 0-385-03354-0). Doubleday.
--A Long Time Coming. (RL 7). 1976. pap. 1.50 (ISBN 0-451-09310-0, W9310, Sig). NAL.
--Lost Island. 1978. pap. 2.25 (ISBN 0-449-23886-5, Crest). Fawcett.
--The Red Carnelian. (Orig.). 1974. pap. 1.75 o.s.i. (ISBN 0-446-84670-8). Warner Bks.
--Snowfire. 1978. pap. 2.25 (ISBN 0-449-24246-3, Crest). Fawcett.
--Spindrift. 320p. 1978. pap. 2.25 (ISBN 0-449-22746-4, Crest). Fawcett.
--The Winter People. 1978. pap. 1.95 (ISBN 0-449-23681-1, Crest). Fawcett.
Whitney, Roy P. The Story of Paper. (TAPPi Press Reports). (Illus.). 28p. 1980. pap. 9.99 (ISBN 0-89852-385-0, 01-01-R085). Tappi.
Whitney, Stephen, ed. see Evans, Craig.
Whitney, Susan. Dr. Gloom's Monster Jokes & Puzzles. (Dr. Gloom Activity Ser.). (Illus.). 64p. (gr. 4-6). pap. 1.95 (ISBN 0-15-224223-6, VoyB). HarBraceJ.
--Dr. Gloom's Outer Space Jokes & Puzzles. (Dr. Gloom's Activity Ser.). (Illus.). 64p. (gr. 4-6). pap. 1.95 (ISBN 0-15-224225-2, VoyB). HarBraceJ.
Whitney, Thomas P., tr. from Rus. In a Certain Kingdom: Twelve Russian Fairy Tales. LC 79-165106. (gr. 3-6). 1972. 5.95 o.s.i. (ISBN 0-02-792680-X). Macmillan.
--Marko the Rich & Vasily the Unlucky. LC 73-6043. (Illus.). 32p. (gr. 1-4). 1974. 5.95g o.s.i. (ISBN 0-02-792710-5). Macmillan.
Whitney, Thomas P., tr. see Solzhenitsyn, Alexandr I.
Whitney, William D. Life & Growth of Language. LC 79-53017. 1980. pap. text ed. 5.00 (ISBN 0-486-23866-0). Dover.
--Roots, Verb Forms & Primary Derivatives of the Sanskrit Language. (American Oriental Ser.: Vol. 30). 1945. 9.00x (ISBN 0-686-00014-5). Am Orient Soc.
Whitooma, Mary B. Tee-Bo & the Persnickety Prowler. (Tee-Bo Bks.). (gr. 4 up). 1978. pap. 1.25 (ISBN 0-307-21583-0, Golden Pr). Western Pub.
--Tee-Bo in the Great Hort Hunt. (Tee-Bo Bks.). (gr. 4 up). 1978. pap. 1.25 (ISBN 0-307-21584-9, Golden Pr). Western Pub.
Whitrow, G. J. The Natural Philosophy of Time. 2nd ed. (Illus.). 288p. 1980. 39.50x (ISBN 0-19-858212-9). Oxford U Pr.
Whitrow, G. J., ed. Einstein: The Man & His Achievement. LC 72-98113. 94p. 1973. pap. 2.25 (ISBN 0-486-22934-3). Dover.
Whitsett, Dan D. Does Prayer Make a Difference? (Prayers in My Life Ser.: Ser. I). 1974. pap. 1.00x (ISBN 0-8358-0312-0). Upper Room.
Whitson, Gary, ed. Nuclear-Cytoplasmic Interactions in the Cell Cycle. (Cell Biology Ser.). 1980. 39.00 (ISBN 0-12-747750-0). Acad Pr.
Whitson, Skip. The Elegant Homes of America One Hundred Years Ago, 2 vols. (Sun Historical Ser.). (Illus.). 1977. Vol. 1. pap. 3.50 (ISBN 0-89540-046-4, SB-046); Vol. 2. pap. 3.50 (ISBN 0-89540-047-2, SB-047). Sun Pub.
Whitson, William W. Foreign Policy & U. S. National Security: Major Postelection Issues. LC 76-2070. (Praeger Special Studies Ser.). 384p. 1976. text ed. 32.50 (ISBN 0-275-56540-8); pap. text ed. 11.95 (ISBN 0-275-85700-X). Praeger.
Whittaker, Albert H., jt. auth. see Selleck, Henry B.
Whittaker, C. R., jt. ed. see Garnsey, P. D.
Whittaker, David. Stereochemistry & Mechanism. (Oxford Chemistry Ser.). (Illus.). 108p. 1973. pap. text ed. 11.50x (ISBN 0-19-855405-2). Oxford U Pr.
Whittaker, E. J. Crystallography: An Introduction for Earth Science (and Other Solid State) Students. LC 80-41188. (Illus.). 240p. 1981. 33.00 (ISBN 0-686-69443-0); pap. 19.50 (ISBN 0-08-023804-1). Pergamon.
Whittaker, Edmund T. & Watson, George N. A Course of Modern Analysis. 4th ed. 1927. 74.50 (ISBN 0-521-06794-4); pap. text ed. 19.95x (ISBN 0-521-09189-6). Cambridge U Pr.
Whittaker, Gerald F., ed. Community Revitalization. 1979. pap. 5.00 o.p. (ISBN 0-87712-192-3). U Mich Busn Div Res.
--Survival in the Face of Crises: Selected Proceedings of the Fifth National Symposium of the Black Economy. 1976. pap. 3.50 o.p. (ISBN 0-87712-174-5). U Mich Busn Div Res.
Whittaker, James B. Strategic Planning in a Rapidly Changing Environment. LC 77-4538. 1978. 19.95 (ISBN 0-669-01484-2). Lexington Bks.
Whittaker, James K. & Trieschman, Albert E., eds. Children Away from Home: A Sourcebook in Residential Treatment. LC 72-140014. 1972. 24.95x (ISBN 0-202-36010-5). Aldine Pub.
Whittaker, Lou, jt. ed. see Press, Larry.
Whittaker, P. A. & Danks, Susan M. Mitochondria: Structure, Function & Assembly. new ed. (Integrated Themes in Biology Ser.). (Illus.). 1979. pap. text ed. 10.95 (ISBN 0-582-44382-2). Longman.
Whittaker, W. Gillies. The Cantatas of Johann Sebastian Bach, Sacred & Secular, 2 vols. 1978. pap. 21.00x (ISBN 0-19-315238-X). Oxford U Pr.
Whittal, Yvonne. The Man from Amazibu Bay. (Harlequin Romances Ser.). 192p. 1980. pap. 1.25 o.p. (ISBN 0-373-02358-8, Pub. by Harlequin). PB.
Whittall, Arnold, tr. see Von Westernhagen, C.
Whittall, Mary, tr. see Dahlhaus, Carl.
Whittall, Mary, tr. see Von Westernhagen, C.
Whittemore, Colin T. Lactation of the Dairy Cow. LC 79-40442. (Longman Handbooks in Agriculture Ser.). (Illus.). 94p. 1980. pap. text ed. 9.95 (ISBN 0-582-45079-9). Longman.
--Pig Production: The Scientific & Practical Principles. (Longman Handbooks in Agriculture Ser.). (Illus.). 160p. (Orig.). 1980. pap. text ed. 13.50 (ISBN 0-582-45590-1). Longman.
Whittemore, Edward. Jerusalem Poker. 1978. 10.95 o.p. (ISBN 0-03-018516-5). HR&W.
Whittemore, Hank. Find the Magician! LC 80-5510. 276p. 1980. 11.95 (ISBN 0-670-31738-1). Viking Pr.
Whittemore, L. H. Peroff: The Man Who Knew Too Much. 368p. 1976. pap. 1.95 o.p. (ISBN 0-345-25104-0). Ballantine.
Whittemore, Margaret. Chimney Swifts & Their Relatives. 176p. 1981. pap. 5.95 (ISBN 0-912542-02-0). Nature Bks Pub.
--Historic Kansas. 1954. pap. 5.95 (ISBN 0-686-14876-2). Flint Hills.
Whittemore, Reed. The Poet As Journalist: Life at the New Republic. LC 76-14897. 220p. 1976. 8.95 o.p. (ISBN 0-915220-16-4). New Republic.
Whittemore, Richard. Nicholas Murray Butler & Public Education 1862-1911. LC 78-122749. 1970. text ed. 13.75x (ISBN 0-8077-2336-3). Tchrs Coll.
Whitten, D. J. & Lanier, Roy H. Whitten-Lanier Debate. pap. 4.95 (ISBN 0-89315-356-7). Lambert Bk.
Whitten, Norman E., Jr. & Szwed, John F. Afro-American Anthropology: Contemporary Perspectives on Theory & Research. LC 79-93109. 1970. 15.95 (ISBN 0-02-935260-6). Free Pr.
Whitten, Phillip. Readings in Sociology: Contemporary Perspectives. 2nd ed. 1979. pap. text ed. 9.50 scp (ISBN 0-06-045503-9, HarpC). Har-Row.
Whitten, Ralph U., jt. auth. see Bridwell, Randall.
Whittenburg, Clarice & Stinneford, Carol. Wyoming's People. 2nd ed. 1978. pap. 5.75x (ISBN 0-933472-12-9). Johnson Colo.
Whittick, Arnold. Symbols for Designers. LC 71-175760. (Illus.). xvi, 168p. 1972. Repr. of 1935 ed. 26.00 (ISBN 0-8103-3119-5). Gale.
Whittier, Bob. Most Common Boat Maintenance Problems. (Illus.). 256p. 1981. lib. bdg. 12.95 (ISBN 0-668-04877-8, 4877). Arco.
Whittier, Earle O., jt. auth. see Webb, Byron H.
Whitting, C. E., tr. see Ibn Al-Tiqtaqa.
Whitting, C. E., tr. see Ibn Al-Titaka.
Whitting, G. C. see Von Wiesner, J. & Von Regel, C.
Whittingham, Richard. Joe D: On the Street with a Chicago Homicide Cop. 288p. 1980. pap. 5.95 (ISBN 0-89505-040-4). Argus Comm.
--Just About Anything Can Be Moved. LC 80-22669. (On the Move Ser.). 48p. (gr. 3-6). 1981. PLB 9.25 (ISBN 0-516-03889-3). Childrens.
Whittinghill, Dick & Page, Don. Did You Whittinghill This Morning? The Madcap Adventures of a Hollywood Disc Jockey. LC 76-6294. (Illus.). 1976. 7.95 o.p. (ISBN 0-8092-8064-7). Contemp Bks.
Whittington, Harry. Charro! 1981. pap. 1.75 (ISBN 0-449-14189-6, GM). Fawcett.
--Dry Gultch Town. 128p. (gr. 7 up). Date not set. pap. 1.50 (ISBN 0-686-26923-3, Tempo). G&D.
--Rampage. 1978. pap. 1.95 o.p. (ISBN 0-449-14074-1, GM). Fawcett.
Whittington, Lloyd R. Whittington's Dictionary of Plastics. 2nd rev. ed. LC 78-73776. 1978. 25.00 (ISBN 0-87762-267-1). Technomic.
Whittle, Amberys, ed. see Stickney, Trumbull.
Whittle, Elizabeth & Dockery, F. A. One Turn of Seasons. LC 80-65203. (Illus.). 64p. (Orig.). 1980. pap. 5.95x perfect bound (ISBN 0-9604046-0-0). E Whittle & F A Dockery.
Whittle, Frank. Gas Turbine Aero-Thermodynamics: With Special Reference to Aircraft Propulsion. LC 80-41372. 240p. 1981. 30.00 (ISBN 0-08-026719-X); pap. 17.50 (ISBN 0-08-026718-1). Pergamon.
Whittle, G. Newcastle & Carlisle Railway. LC 79-52378. (Illus.). 1979. 19.95 (ISBN 0-7153-7855-4). David & Charles.
Whittle, R. & Yarwood, J. Experimental Physics for Students. LC 73-15219. 400p. 1974. text ed. 18.95x o.p. (ISBN 0-470-94131-6). Halsted Pr.
Whittlesey, Derwent S. Environmental Foundations of European History. (Perspectives in European History Ser.: No. 38). xiii, 160p. 1980. Repr. of 1949 ed. lib. bdg. 15.00x (ISBN 0-87991-074-7). Porcupine Pr.
Whittlesey, W. R. & Sonneck, O. G. Catalogue of First Editions of Stephen C. Foster. LC 76-155233. (Music Ser). 1971. Repr. of 1915 ed. lib. bdg. 15.00 (ISBN 0-306-70162-6). Da Capo.
Whittock, Trevor. Reading of the Canterbury Tales. (Orig.). 1969. 49.50 (ISBN 0-521-06795-2); pap. 11.95 (ISBN 0-521-09557-3). Cambridge U Pr.
Whitton, B. A. River Ecology. LC 75-10884. 735p. 1975. 57.50x (ISBN 0-520-03016-8). U of Cal Pr.
Whitton, Blair, ed. Bliss Toys & Dollhouses: Eighty Nine Illustrations, Including the Complete 1911 Catalog. (Illus.). 1979. pap. 2.75 (ISBN 0-486-23790-7). Dover.
Whitton, K. S. Advanced Nacherzahlungen. 1969. 4.10 (ISBN 0-08-013065-8); pap. 3.00 (ISBN 0-08-013064-X). Pergamon.
Whitton, Kenneth S. The Theatre of Friedrich Durrenmatt. (Illus.). 200p. 1978. text ed. 20.75x (ISBN 0-391-01694-6). Humanities.
Whitton, Margaret. The Jumeau Doll. (Illus.). 96p. (Orig.). 1980. pap. 6.00 (ISBN 0-486-23954-3). Dover.
Whittow, John. Disasters: The Anatomy of Environmental Hazards. LC 79-5236. (Illus.). 405p. 1981. pap. 9.95 (ISBN 0-8203-0542-1). U of Ga Pr.
Whitty & Zangwill. Amnesia. 2nd ed. 1977. 19.95 (ISBN 0-407-00056-9). Butterworths.
Whitty, Geoff, jt. auth. see Gleeson, Denis.
Whitwell, David. A New History of Wind Music. 1980. pap. 9.00 (ISBN 0-686-15899-7). Instrumentalist Co.
Whitwell, R. J., jt. ed. see David, Henry W.
Whitworth, George C. An Anglo-Indian Dictionary: A Glossary of Indian Terms Used in English and of Such English & Other Than Indian Terms As Have Obtained Special Meanings in India. 1977. Repr. of 1885 ed. 13.50 o.p. (ISBN 0-8364-0380-0). South Asia Bks.
Whitworth, John McKelvie. God's Blueprints. 1975. 25.00x (ISBN 0-7100-8002-6). Routledge & Kegan.
Whitworth, Reginald. The Cinema & Theatre Organ. (Illus.). 144p. 1981. pap. 15.00x (ISBN 0-913746-14-2). Organ Lit.
--The Cinema & Theatre Organ: A Comprehensive Description of This Instrument, Its Constituent Parts, & Its Use. (Illus.). 144p. 1981. pap. 15.00x (ISBN 0-913746-14-2). Organ Lit.
Wholeben, Brent E. The Design, Implementation & Evaluation of Mathematical Modeling Procedures for Decisioning Among Educational Alternatives. LC 80-5437. 474p. 1980. lib. bdg. 24.50 (ISBN 0-8191-1093-0); pap. text ed. 15.50 (ISBN 0-8191-1094-9). U Pr of Amer.
Wholey, Ellen J., jt. auth. see Wallower, Lucille.
Wholey, Ellen J., ed. see Wallower, Lucille.
Wholey, Joseph S. Evaluation: Promise & Performance. (An Institute Paper). 226p. 1979. pap. 7.50 (ISBN 0-87766-250-9, 25100). Urban Inst.
--Zero-Base Budgeting & Program Evaluation. LC 77-4610. 1978. 15.95 (ISBN 0-669-01730-2). Lexington Bks.
Whorlow, R. W. Rheological Techniques. LC 79-40992. (Physics in Medicine & Biology Ser.). 447p. 1980. 89.95x (ISBN 0-470-26736-4). Halsted Pr.
Whorwood, R. W. & Webb, P. K. Transmission Planning of Telephone Networks. (IEE Telecommunications Ser.). 256p. 1981. price not set. Inst Elect Eng. Postponed.
Who's Cooking What Editors, ed. Who's Cooking What in Illinois. 1978. 10.00 o.p. (ISBN 0-533-03440-X). Vantage.
Whybray, R. N. Isaiah Forty to Sixty-Six. Clements, Ronald E., ed. (New Century Bible Commentary). 320p. (Orig.). 1981. pap. 7.95 (ISBN 0-8028-1884-6). Eerdmans.
--Thanksgiving for a Liberated Prophet: An Interpretation of Isaiah Chapter Fifty-Three. (JSOT Supplement Ser.: No. 4). 184p. 1978. text ed. 29.95x (ISBN 0-905774-09-4, Pub. by JSOT Pr England); pap. text ed. 16.95x (ISBN 0-905774-04-3, Pub. by JSOT Pr England). Eisenbrauns.
Whyburn, Gordon T. Analytic Topology. LC 63-21794. (Colloquium Pbns. Ser.: Vol. 28). 1980. Repr. of 1971 ed. 26.00 (ISBN 0-8218-1028-6, COLL-28). Am Math.
--Open Mappings in Locally Compact Spaces. LC 52-42839. (Memoirs: No. 1). 1969. pap. 4.40 (ISBN 0-8218-1201-7, MEMO-1). Am Math.
Whyburn, William M., jt. auth. see Daus, Paul H.
Whymper, Edward. Scrambles Amongst the Alps in the Years Eighteen Sixty to Eighteen Sixty-Nine. (Illus.). 176p. 1981. pap. 5.95 (ISBN 0-89815-043-4). Ten Speed Pr.
Whyte, A. Commentary on the Shorter Catechism. (Handbook for Bible Classes Ser.). 213p. pap. text ed. 8.95 (ISBN 0-567-28144-2). Attic Pr.
Whyte, Alexander. Walk, Conversation, & Character of Christ. (Religious Heritage Reprint Library). 339p. 1975. Repr. of 1905 ed. 7.95 o.p. (ISBN 0-8010-9568-9). Baker Bk.
--Whyte's Bible Characters. (Illus.). 1968. 16.95 (ISBN 0-310-34410-7). Zondervan.
Whyte, Ann V. & Burton, Ian. Environmental Risk Assessment: Scope 15. LC 79-42903. (Physics in Medicine & Biology Ser.). 157p. 1980. 30.00 (ISBN 0-471-27701-0, Pub. by Wiley-Interscience). Wiley.
Whyte, Anthony J. & Wise, Herbert A. The Planet Pluto. LC 79-23998. 1980. 19.50 (ISBN 0-08-024648-6). Pergamon.
Whyte, H. A. Kiss of Satan. 1973. pap. 1.25 o.p. (ISBN 0-88368-030-0). Whitaker Hse.
Whyte, Karen. Kid's Natural Foods Party & Picnic Color & Cookbook. (Illus.). 40p. (gr. 1-8). 1979. pap. 2.25 (ISBN 0-912300-13-2). Troubador Pr.
Whyte, Karen C. The Complete Sprouting Cookbook. LC 72-92942. (Illus.). 120p. 1973. pap. 4.95 (ISBN 0-912300-28-0, 28-0). Troubador Pr.
--The Complete Yogurt Cookbook. 160p. 1976. pap. 1.95 (ISBN 0-345-27725-2). Ballantine.
Whyte, Kay. Design in Embroidery. (Illus.). 240p. 1969. 14.75 (ISBN 0-8231-4008-3). Branford.
Whyte, Lancelot L. Essay on Atomism: From Democritus to 1960. LC 61-14236. 1961. 12.50x (ISBN 0-8195-3019-0, Pub. by Wesleyan U Pr). Columbia U Pr.
--The Universe of Experience: A World View Beyond Science & Religion. 1974. pap. 3.45x o.p. (ISBN 0-06-131821-3, TB1821, Torch). Har-Row.
Whyte, M. B., jt. auth. see Prins, H. A.
Whyte, Mal. North American Sealife Coloring Album. (Wildlife Ser.). (Illus.). 1973. pap. 3.50 (ISBN 0-912300-27-2, 27-2). Troubador Pr.
Whyte, Malcolm, ed. Once Upon a Time. (Illus.). 40p. (gr. 1-8). 1979. pap. 2.25 (ISBN 0-912300-16-7). Troubador Pr.
--Pyramid Puzzles. (Illus.). 40p. (Orig.). (gr. 1-12). 1979. pap. 2.25 (ISBN 0-89844-003-3). Troubador Pr.
Whyte, Martin K. Small Groups & Political Rituals in China. 1974. 20.00x (ISBN 0-520-02499-0); pap. 5.95x (ISBN 0-520-03053-2). U of Cal Pr.
Whyte, Martin K., jt. auth. see Parish, William L.
Whyte, Norrie. Motor Cycle Racing Champions. LC 75-295936. 1976. 7.95 (ISBN 0-668-03910-8). Arco.
Whyte, R. O. Grasslands of the Monsoon. (Illus.). 1969. 7.95 o.p. (ISBN 0-571-08583-0, Pub. by Faber & Faber). Merrimack Bk Serv.
--Milk Production in Developing Countries. (Illus.). 1967. 10.95 o.p. (ISBN 0-571-08089-8, Pub. by Faber & Faber). Merrimack Bk Serv.

Whyte, W. S. Basic Metric Surveying. 2nd ed. (Illus.). 312p. 1976. pap. 18.50 (ISBN 0-408-00197-6). Transatlantic.
--Building Regulations Explained & Illustrated. (Illus.). 1979. 26.95x (ISBN 0-8464-0050-2). Beekman Pubs.

Whyte, W. S. & Powell-Smith, Vincent. The Building Regulations Explained & Illustrated. 5th ed. 299p. 1978. text ed. 34.00 (ISBN 0-246-11273-5, Pub. by Granada England). Renouf.

Whyte, William H., Jr. Securing Open Space for Urban America: Conservation Easements. (Illus.). 1959. pap. 4.75 (ISBN 0-87420-036-9). Urban Land.

Whytes, Larry K. The Philosophical Foundations of Education. (Illus.). 127p. 1980. deluxe ed. 39.75 (ISBN 0-89266-237-9). Am Classical Coll Pr.

Whytt, Robert. Works of Robert Whytt. Bd. with Memoirs on the Nervous System. Hall, Marshall; Memoirs. Cabanis, Pierre J; Two Essays. Hall, G. S. & DuBois-Reymond, E.. (Contributions to the History of Psychology Ser., Vol. I, Pt. E: Physiological Psychology). 1978. Repr. of 1768 ed. 30.00 (ISBN 0-89093-174-7). U Pubns Amer.

Wiarda, Howard J. Corporaism & National Development in Latin America. (Westview Replica Edition Ser.). 325p. 1981. lib. bdg. 27.00x (ISBN 0-86531-031-9). Westview.
--Corporatism & National Development in Latin America. (Replica Edition Ser.). 325p. 1981. lib. bdg. 27.00x (ISBN 0-86531-031-9). Westview.

Wiarda, Howard J., ed. The Continuing Struggle for Democracy in Latin America. LC 79-13551. (Westview Special Studies on Latin America). 26.50x (ISBN 0-89158-663-6). Westview.

Wiat, Philippa. Lion Without Claws. LC 77-73019. 1978. 7.95 o.p. (ISBN 0-312-48736-3). St Martin.

Wibberley, Leonard. Attar of the Ice Valley. LC 68-13683. 176p. (gr. 7 up). 1968. 3.95 (ISBN 0-374-30451-3). FS&G.
--The Crime of Martin Coverly. LC 79-28538. 184p. (gr. 4 up). 1980. 8.95 (ISBN 0-374-31656-2). FS&G.
--Guarneri: Story of a Genius. LC 74-8142. 160p. (gr. 7 up). 1974. 5.95 (ISBN 0-374-32822-6). FS&G.
--Leopard's Prey. LC 78-149225. 192p. (gr. 7 up). 1971. 4.50 o.p. (ISBN 0-374-34378-0). FS&G.
--The Mouse That Saved the West. LC 80-25567. 192p. 1981. 8.95 (ISBN 0-688-00364-8). Morrow.

Wibberley, Mary. A Dangerous Man. (Harlequin Romances Ser.). (Orig.). 1980. pap. text ed. 1.25 o.p. (ISBN 0-373-02340-5, Pub. by Harlequin). PB.
--Dangerous Marriage. (Harlequin Romances Ser.). 192p. 1980. pap. 1.25 o.p. (ISBN 0-373-02364-2, Pub. by Harlequin). PB.
--Debt of Dishonour. (Harlequin Presents Ser.). 192p. 1980. pap. 1.50 (ISBN 0-373-10390-5, Pub. by Harlequin). PB.
--A Dream of Thee. (Harlequin Presents Ser.). 192p. 1981. pap. 1.50 (ISBN 0-373-10419-7, Pub. by Harlequin). PB.
--Gold to Remember. (Harlequin Presents Ser.). 192p. 1981. pap. 1.50 (ISBN 0-373-10432-4, Pub. by Harlequin). PB.
--Man of Power. (Harlequin Romances Ser.). 192p. (Orig.). 1981. pap. 1.25 (ISBN 0-373-02388-X, Pub. by Harlequin). PB.
--The Moon Dancers. (Alpha Books). 80p. 1978. pap. text ed. 2.25x (ISBN 0-19-424162-9). Oxford U Pr.

Wiberg, Hugh. Backyard Vegetable Gardening for the Beginner. LC 70-171918. 1971. 5.00 o.p. (ISBN 0-682-47329-4, Banner). Exposition.

Wichita Falls Poetry Society. Reflections: An Anthology. 3.95 o.p. (ISBN 0-685-48828-4). Nortex Pr.

Wichmann, K. Pocket Dictionary of the German & English Languages. 1952. 12.00 (ISBN 0-7100-2290-5). Routledge & Kegan.

Wichterman, Catherine, adapted by. Lost Horizon. (Contemporary Motivators Ser.). (Illus.). 32p. (Orig.). 1979. pap. text ed. 1.25 (ISBN 0-88301-309-6). Pendulum Pr.

Wick, Barbara H., jt. auth. see Throop, Sara.

Wick, Denis. Trombone Technique. 160p. 1971. pap. 7.75 (ISBN 0-19-318704-3). Oxford U Pr.

Wick, John D. Automatic Generation of Assemblers. LC 79-50822. (Outstanding Dissertations in the Computer Sciences). 1980. lib. bdg. 25.00 (ISBN 0-8240-4418-5). Garland Pub.

Wicka, Donna K. & Falk, Mervyn L. Advice to Parents of a Cleft Palate Child. (Illus.). 68p. 1970. pap. 7.75 photocopy ed. spiral (ISBN 0-398-02061-2). C C Thomas.

Wickelgren, Wayne A. Cognitive Psychology. (Illus.). 1979. ref. ed. 19.95 (ISBN 0-13-139543-2). P-H.
--Learning & Memory. (Experimental Psychology Ser.). 1977. 18.95 (ISBN 0-13-527663-2). P-H.

Wickelgren, Wayne E. How to Solve Problems: Elements of the Theory of Problems & Problem Solving. LC 73-15787. (Psychology Ser.). (Illus.). 1974. pap. text ed. 8.95x (ISBN 0-7167-0845-0). W H Freeman.

Wickens, G. M. Arabic Grammar. LC 77-82523. 180p. 1980. write for info. (ISBN 0-521-21885-3); pap. 12.95 (ISBN 0-521-29301-4). Cambridge U Pr.

Wickens, J. Themes in U.S. History. 2nd ed. 1973. pap. 7.95x (ISBN 0-02-478960-7, 47896). Macmillan.

Wickens, James F. Colorado in the Great Depression. Freidel, Frank, ed. LC 78-62518. (Modern American History Ser.: Vol. 20). 1979. lib. bdg. 30.00 (ISBN 0-8240-3643-3). Garland Pub.

Wicker, Elmus R., jt. auth. see Boughton, James M.

Wicker, Kevin. Two Hundred Brilliancies. LC 80-54188. (Illus.). 144p. 1981. 15.00 (ISBN 0-668-05214-7, 5214). Arco.

Wicker, Kevin, jt. auth. see Moles, John.

Wicker, Tom. A Time to Die. (Illus.). 448p. Date not set. pap. 2.50 (ISBN 0-345-28993-5). Ballantine.

Wickers, David. The Complete Urban Farmer: How to Grow Your Own Fruits & Vegetables in Town. (Handbooks Ser). 1978. pap. 2.95 o.p. (ISBN 0-14-046288-0). Penguin.

Wickert, Frederic R. & McFarland, Dalton E., eds. Measuring Executive Effectiveness. LC 67-18987. (Illus.). 1967. 24.50x (ISBN 0-89197-298-6). Irvington.

Wickes, George. Americans in Paris. (Illus.). xvi, 302p. 1980. pap. 6.95 (ISBN 0-306-80127-2). Da Capo.

Wickes, George, ed. Henry Miller & the Critics. LC 63-14289. (Crosscurrents-Modern Critiques Ser.). 212p. 1963. 12.95 (ISBN 0-8093-0102-4). S Ill U Pr.

Wickham, E. C., ed. see Horace.

Wickham, Geoffrey. Rapid Perspective. (gr. 10 up). 6.95 (ISBN 0-85458-050-6); pap. 3.75 (ISBN 0-85458-051-4). Transatlantic.

Wickham, Glynne. Early English Stages, Vol. III: Plays & Their Makers to 1576. (Early English Stages Ser.). 1980. 22.50x o.p. (ISBN 0-231-08938-4). Columbia U Pr.

Wickham, Glynne W. Early English Stages: 1300 to 1660, 2 vols. Incl. 1300 to 1576. Vol. 1. 20.00x o.p. (ISBN 0-231-08935-X); 1576 to 1660. Vol. 2, Pt. 1. 30.00x (ISBN 0-231-08936-8); Vol. 2, Pt. 2. 30.00x (ISBN 0-231-08937-6). (Illus.). 1959. Columbia U Pr.

Wickland, Carl A. Thirty Years Among the Dead. LC 80-19669. 390p. 1980. Repr. of 1974 ed. lib. bdg. 12.95x (ISBN 0-89370-625-6). Borgo Pr.

Wicklein, John. Electronic Nightmare: The New Communications & Freedom. LC 80-54199. 320p. 1981. 15.95 (ISBN 0-670-50658-3). Viking Pr.
--The New Communications & Freedom. 1981. 14.95 (ISBN 0-670-50658-3). Viking Pr.

Wicklund, Millie Mae. The Marisol Poems. 1981. pap. 1.50. Ghost Dance.

Wicklund, Robert A., jt. auth. see West, Stephen G.

Wickman, Peter, ed. Readings in Social Problems: Contemporary Perspectives. 1977-1978 ed. (Contemporary Perspective Readers Ser.). 1977. pap. text ed. 10.50 scp (ISBN 0-06-047053-4, HarpC); inst. manual free (ISBN 0-06-367163-8). Har-Row.

Wickman, Peter, et al. Criminology: Perspectives on Crime & Criminality. 1980. text ed. 17.95 (ISBN 0-669-01600-4); instr's guide free (ISBN 0-669-01922-4). Heath.

Wickramasekera, Ian, ed. Biofeedback, Behavior Therapy, & Hypnosis: Potentiating the Verbal Control of Behavior for Clinicians. LC 76-18294. 384p. 1976. 24.95x (ISBN 0-88229-193-9); pap. 13.95x (ISBN 0-88229-579-9). Nelson-Hall.

Wicks, Harry. How to Plan, Buy or Build Your Leisure Home. (Illus.). 544p. 1976. 12.95 (ISBN 0-87909-345-5). Reston.

Wicks, Keith. Stars & Planets. (gr. 2-4). 1980. PLB 6.45 (ISBN 0-531-03247-7). Watts.

Wicks, Robert, jt. auth. see Platt, Jerome.

Wicks, Robert G. & Keough, Lawrence. Society, Systems & Man: Selections for Reading & Composition. LC 75-161496. 1972. text ed. 10.50 (ISBN 0-471-94290-1). Wiley.

Wicks, Robert J. Counseling Strategies & Intervention Techniques for the Human Services. LC 76-55408. 1977. pap. 6.50 scp (ISBN 0-397-47365-6, HarpC). Har-Row.
--Human Services: New Careers & Roles in the Helping Professions. (Illus.). 248p. 1978. 15.50 (ISBN 0-398-03777-9). C C Thomas.
--International Corrections. LC 77-8721. 1979. 21.00 (ISBN 0-669-01638-1). Lexington Bks.

Wicks, Robert J. & Josephs, Ernest H., Jr. Practical Psychology of Leadership for Criminal Justice Officers: A Basic Programmed Text. 128p. 1973. pap. 8.75 (ISBN 0-398-02783-8). C C Thomas.
--Techniques in Interviewing for Law Enforcement & Corrections Personnel: A Programmed Text. 152p. 1977. pap. 10.75 (ISBN 0-398-03677-2). C C Thomas.

Wicks, Robert J., jt. auth. see DeCato, Clifford M.

Wicks, Susanne B., jt. auth. see Humm, Harold J.

Wickstead, James M. How to Win at Stud Poker. (Gamblers Book Shelf). 1968. pap. 2.95 (ISBN 0-89650-509-X). Gamblers.

Wickstrom, Lois. Food Conspiracy Cookbook & Member's Manual. (Illus.). 215p. 1973. 3.50 (ISBN 0-916176-01-0). Sproing.

Wickstrom, Lois, ed. see Carr, Jayge, et al.

Wickstrom, Lois, ed. see Joseph, Alaine, et al.

Wickstrom, Lois, ed. see Lorrah, Jean, et al.

Wickstrom, Ralph & Larson, Charles. Racquetball: Paddle Ball Fundamentals. LC 78-172488. 96p. 1972. pap. text ed. 5.95 (ISBN 0-675-09173-X). Merrill.

Wickwar, J. W. Witchcraft & the Black Art: A Book Dealing with the Psychology & Folklore of the Witches. LC 71-151817. 1971. Repr. of 1925 ed. 26.00 (ISBN 0-8103-3692-8). Gale.

Wiczyk, Arlene Z., ed. A Treasury of Needlework Projects from Godey's Lady's Book. LC 72-3698. (Illus.). 320p. 1972. pap. 3.95 o.p. (ISBN 0-668-02692-8). Arco.

Widder, Keith R. Dr. William Beaumont: The Mackinac Years. (Illus.). 40p. (Orig.). 1975. pap. 1.50 (ISBN 0-911872-15-9). Mackinac Island.

Widder, Keith R., jt. auth. see Armour, David A.

Widdicombe, J. G., ed. Respiratory Pharmacology, 3 vols. (International Encyclopedia of Pharmacology & Therapeutics: Section 104). Date not set. Set. 135.00 (ISBN 0-08-022673-6). Pergamon.

Widdowson, H. G. Discovering Discourse. (Orig.). 1979. pap. text ed. 5.95x (ISBN 0-19-451355-6); ed. 8.95xtchr's (ISBN 0-19-451356-4). Oxford U Pr.

Widdowson, H. G., jt. auth. see Allen, J. P.

Widdowson, H. G., ed. Exploring Funcions. (Reading & Thinking in English Ser.). 136p. 1979. pap. text ed. 5.95x (ISBN 0-19-451353-X); tchr's. ed. 8.95x (ISBN 0-19-451354-8). Oxford U Pr.
--Reading & Thinking in English: Discourse in Action. (Reading & Thinking in English Ser.). (Illus.). 128p. 1980. pap. 5.95 (ISBN 0-19-451357-2); 10.95 (ISBN 0-19-451358-0). Oxford U Pr.
--Reading & Thinking in English: Exploring Functions. (Reading & Thinking in English Ser.). (Illus.). 132p. 1979. pap. text ed. 5.95 o.p. (ISBN 0-19-451353-X); tchr's ed. 8.95 o.p. (ISBN 0-19-451354-8). Oxford U Pr.

Widdowson, Henry G. Stylistics & the Teaching of Literature. (Applied Linguistics & Language Study). (Illus.). 144p. 1975. pap. text ed. 8.75x (ISBN 0-582-55076-9). Longman.

Widdowson, J. D., jt. auth. see Stork, F. C.

Widener, Don. Jack Lemmon: An Authorized Biography. (Illus.). 256p. 1975. 9.95 o.s.i. (ISBN 0-02-628200-3). Macmillan.

Widengren, Geo. Iran & Islam. (Jordon Lectures in Comparative Religion Ser: No. 10). 160p. 1979. cancelled (ISBN 0-485-17410-3, Athlone Pr). Humanities.

Widenor, William C. Henry Cabot Lodge & the Search for an American Foreign Policy. 1980. 18.50 (ISBN 0-520-03778-2). U of Cal Pr.

Wider Opportunities for Women, Inc. Suit Yourself...Shopping for a Job. Kaplan, Roberta, ed. LC 80-53209. (Illus.). 52p. (Orig.). 1980. pap. text ed. 5.00 (ISBN 0-934966-02-8). WOW Inc.

Widick, B. J., jt. auth. see Howe, I.

Widick, B. J., ed. Auto Work & Its Discontents. LC 76-16095. (Policy Studies in Employment & Welfare: No. 25). (Illus.). 128p. 1976. 8.00x o.p. (ISBN 0-8018-1856-7); pap. 3.95x (ISBN 0-8018-1857-5). Johns Hopkins.

Widicus, Wilbur W. & Stitzel, Thomas E. Personal Investing. rev. ed. 1976. text ed. 15.50x o.p. (ISBN 0-256-01832-4). Irwin.

Widimsky, J., ed. Pulmonary Embolism. (Progress in Respiration Research: Vol. 13). (Illus.). viii, 192p. 1980. 87.00 (ISBN 3-8055-0487-X). S Karger.

Widing, Thomas L. Budget Shoppers' Guide to Metropolitan New York. new ed. (Orig.). 1977. pap. 3.50 o.p. (ISBN 0-917908-02-3). Hamilton Hse.
--Budget Shopper's Guide to the Delaware Valley. rev. ed. LC 80-84929. 160p. (Orig.). 1981. pap. 3.95 (ISBN 0-917908-03-1). Hamilton Hse.
--Budget Shoppers' Guide to the Delaware Valley. LC 76-43532. (Orig.). 1976. pap. 2.95 o.p. (ISBN 0-917908-01-5). Hamilton Hse.

Widmayer, Charles E. Hopkins of Dartmouth: The Story of Ernest Martin Hopkins & His Presidency of Dartmouth College. LC 77-153864. (Illus.). 320p. 1977. text ed. 27.50x (ISBN 0-87451-145-3). U Pr of New Eng.

Widmer, Kingsley. Henry Miller. (U. S. Authors Ser.: No. 44). 1963. lib. bdg. 10.95 (ISBN 0-8057-0504-X). Twayne.

Widmer, Mary Lou. Night Jasmine. 1980. pap. 2.75 (ISBN 0-440-16558-X). Dell.

Widmer, Pat. Pat Widmer's Dog Training Book. 1980. 4.98 (ISBN 0-679-50781-7). McKay.

Widmer, Patricia P. Pat Widmer's Dog Training Book. 1980. pap. 2.25 (ISBN 0-451-09348-8, E9348, Sig). NAL.
--Pat Widmer's Dog Training Book: Straight Talk for Owners of City & Suburban Dogs. (Illus.). 1977. 4.98 o.p. (ISBN 0-679-50781-7). McKay.

Widney, Bette W. Mystery of the Wheat Pirates. LC 65-17375. (gr. 4 up). 1968. 5.95 (ISBN 0-8149-0437-8). Vanguard.

Widom, Joanne M. & Edelstein, Stuart J. Chemistry: An Introduction to General, Organic, & Biological Chemistry. LC 80-23816. (Illus.). 1981. text ed. 22.95x (ISBN 0-7167-1224-5); instr's. manual avail.; study guide 4.95x. W H Freeman.

Widroe, Harvey J. Human Behavior & Brain Function. (Illus.). 132p. 1975. 10.75 (ISBN 0-398-03271-8). C C Thomas.

Widtsoe, John A. Discourses of Brigham Young. 497p. pap. 2.50 (ISBN 0-87747-788-4). Deseret Bk.

Wiebe, Robert H. The Segmented Society: An Introduction to the Meaning of America. 1975. 12.95 (ISBN 0-19-501839-7). Oxford U Pr.

Wiebers, Jacob & Rogers, Wallace. Study Guide to Accompany Essential Human Anatomy & Physiology. 2nd ed. 1980. pap. text ed. 7.95x (ISBN 0-673-15323-1). Scott F.

Wiechmann, Ulrich E. Marketing Management in Multinational Firms: The Consumer Packaged Goods Industry. LC 75-19831. (Special Studies). 1976. text ed. 22.95 (ISBN 0-275-55850-9). Praeger.

Wieck, Fred, tr. see Richter, Liselotte.

Wieckert, Jeanne E. & Bell, Irene W. Classroom Skills Through Games for the Middle School, Vol. 1. (Illus.). 300p. 1981. lib. bdg. 17.50x (ISBN 0-87287-227-0). Libs Unl.
--Classroom Skills Through Games for the Middle School, Vol. 2. (Illus.). 250p. 1981. lib. bdg. 17.50x (ISBN 0-87287-236-X). Libs Unl.

Wieckert, Jeanne E., jt. auth. see Bell, Irene W.

Wiecks, Tom. The Best Cookin' in the Country. LC 79-91262. (Illus., Orig.). 1979. pap. 6.95 (ISBN 0-935566-00-7). Barleycorn.

Wieczynski, Joseph L. Modern Encyclopedia of Russian & Soviet History: Mersh, Vols. 6 & 7. 1978. Set. 30.50 ea. (ISBN 0-685-92172-7). Academic Intl.

Wieczynski, Joseph L., ed. The Modern Encyclopedia of Russian & Soviet History: Mersh. Incl. Vol. 1 (ISBN 0-87569-064-5); Vol. 2 (ISBN 0-87569-065-3); Vol. 3; Vol. 4. 1977; Vol. 5. 1977; Vol. 19. 1980. 30.50; Vol. 4. Weber, Harry B., ed. 1980. 31.50 (ISBN 0-87569-038-6). 30.50 ea. Academic Intl.
--Modern Encyclopedia of Russian & Soviet History: Mersh, Vol. 8. 1978. 30.50 (ISBN 0-685-03450-X). Academic Intl.
--Modern Encyclopedia of Russian & Soviet History: Mersh, 50 vols, Vols. 9, 10 & 11. 1979. 30.50 (ISBN 0-685-92201-4). Academic Intl.
--Modern Encyclopedia of Russian & Soviet History: Mersh, Vols. 12-13. 1979. 30.50 (ISBN 0-686-65389-0). Academic Intl.
--Modern Encyclopedia of Russian & Soviet History: Mersh, Vols. 14, 30.50 ea.; Vols. 15,16,17,18. 1980 30.50 ea. Academic Intl.

Wiedekehr, Dietrich. Belief in Redemption: Explorations in Doctrine from the New Testament to Today. Moiser, Jeremy, tr. from Ger. LC 78-24088. Orig. Title: Glaube an Erlosung. 120p. 1981. pap. 5.95 (ISBN 0-8042-0476-4). John Knox.

Wiedemann, H. G., ed. see International Conference on Thermal Analysis, 3rd, Davos, Switzerland, 23-28 August 1971.

Wieder, Charles. Fear & Force Versus Education. LC 77-11235. 1978. pap. 4.95 (ISBN 0-8283-1706-2). Branden.

Wieder, H. H. Intermetallic Semiconducting Films. LC 76-80293. 1970. 50.00 (ISBN 0-08-013367-3). Pergamon.

Wieder, Sol. The Foundations of Quantum Theory. 1973. text ed. 22.95 (ISBN 0-12-749050-7). Acad Pr.

Wiederhold, Gio. Database Design. (Computer Science Ser.). 1977. text ed. 25.95 (ISBN 0-07-070130-X, C); write for info. instructor's manual (ISBN 0-07-070131-8). McGraw.

Wiederholt, J. Lee, et al. The Resource Teacher: A Guide to Effective Practices. 1978. pap. text ed. 10.95 (ISBN 0-205-05970-8); ring binder 29.95 (ISBN 0-205-05971-6). Allyn.

Wiegel, Robert L. Oceanographical Engineering. 1964. ref. ed. 34.95 (ISBN 0-13-629600-9). P-H.

Wiegel, Robert L., et al. Earthquake Engineering. (Civil Engineering Ser). 1969. ref. ed. 34.95 (ISBN 0-13-222646-4). P-H.

Wiegele. Biopolitics: Search for a More Human Political Science. LC 79-16252. (Westview Special Studies). 1979. lib. bdg. 18.50x (ISBN 0-89158-691-1); pap. text ed. 8.00x (ISBN 0-89158-751-9). Westview.

Wieger, L. Chinese Characters, Their Origin, Etymology, History, Classification & Signification. 2nd ed. Davrout, L., tr. 1927. pap. 10.00 (ISBN 0-486-21321-8). Dover.

Wiegerink, Ronald & Pelosi, John W., eds. Developmental Disabilities: The DD Movement. LC 79-15516. 184p. (Orig.). 1979. pap. text ed. 10.50 (ISBN 0-933716-02-8). P H Brookes.

--Developmental Disabilities: The DD Movement. 182p. 1979. pap. 10.50 (ISBN 0-933716-02-8). P H Brookes.

Wiegner, Kathleen. Freeway Driving. 1981. pap. 4.00 (ISBN 0-914610-23-6). Hanging Loose.

Wieland. How to Prepare for the Regents Competency Examination in Mathematics. 1981. pap. 6.95 (ISBN 0-8120-2246-7). Barron.

Wieland, Angelo. Barron's How to Prepare for the Competency Examination in Mathematics. (gr. 7-12). 1981. pap. text ed. 5.95 (ISBN 0-8120-2246-7). Barron.

Wieland, George F. Improving Health Care Management: Organization Development & Organization Change. (Illus.). 528p. 1981. text ed. write for info. (ISBN 0-914904-49-3). Health Admin Pr.

Wieland, George F. & Ullrich, Robert A. Organizations: Behavior, Design, & Change. 1976. text ed. 16.95x o.p. (ISBN 0-256-01847-2). Irwin.

Wieland, James & Force, Edward. Corgi Toys: The Ones with Windows. (Illus.). 1981. 8.95 (ISBN 0-87938-123-X). Motorbooks Intl.

Wieland, Robert. Eighteen Eighty-Eight Message. LC 80-10807. (Horizon Ser.). 1980. pap. 4.50 (ISBN 0-8127-0283-2). Southern Pub.

Wieland, Robert J. The Backward Prayer. (Uplook Ser.). 32p. 1971. pap. 0.75 (ISBN 0-8163-0064-X, 02042-0). Pacific Pr Pub Assn.

Wielens, J. B., et al. Geological Survey of Norway, No. 359, Bulletin 56. (Illus.). 60p. 1981. pap. 14.00x. Universitet.

Wieler, Hank, jt. auth. see Smith, Duane A.

Wieman, Harold. Morro Bay Meanderings. LC 72-2793. (Illus.). 1975. pap. 3.50 (ISBN 0-914598-12-0). Padre Prods.

Wieman, Henry N. Man's Ultimate Commitment. LC 58-5488. (Arcturus Books Paperbacks). 1963. pap. 3.25 o.p. (ISBN 0-8093-0084-2). S Ill U Pr.

--Religious Experience & Scientific Method. 387p. 1971. Repr. of 1927 ed. lib. bdg. 11.95x (ISBN 0-8093-0537-2). S Ill U Pr.

--Religious Experience & Scientific Method. (Arcturus Books Paperbacks). 387p. 1971. pap. 9.95 (ISBN 0-8093-0530-5). S Ill U Pr.

--Seeking a Faith for a New Age. Hepler, Cedric L., ed. LC 74-34052. 1975. 15.00 (ISBN 0-8108-0795-5). Scarecrow.

--Source of Human Good. LC 63-2226. 318p. 1964. lib. bdg. 10.95x (ISBN 0-8093-0116-4). S Ill U Pr.

--Source of Human Good. LC 63-2226. (Arcturus Books Paperbacks). 318p. 1974. pap. 2.95 (ISBN 0-8093-0117-2). S Ill U Pr.

Wiemers, Eugene. Materials Availability Handbook. (Occasional Papers Ser.: No. 149). 1981. pap. 3.00 (ISBN 0-686-69450-3). U of Ill Lib Sci.

Wienandt, Elwyn A. Choral Music of the Church. (Music Reprint Ser.). xi, 494p. 1980. Repr. of 1965 ed. lib. bdg. 32.50 (ISBN 0-306-76002-9). Da Capo.

Wienandt, Elwyn A. & Young, Robert H. Anthem in England & America. LC 76-76225. 1970. 15.95 (ISBN 0-02-935230-4). Free Pr.

Wiencke, Gustav K. & Lehman, Helmut T., eds. Luther's Works: Devotional Writing II, Vol. 43. LC 55-9893. 1968. 15.95 (ISBN 0-8006-0343-5, 1-343). Fortress.

Wiener, A. Patterns of Control in Post-Industrial Society: Magnificent Myth. 1978. text ed. 45.00 (ISBN 0-08-021474-6); pap. text ed. 15.00 (ISBN 0-08-023100-4). Pergamon.

Wiener, A. W. Mental Health for the Nonprofessional. 88p. 1980. 9.75 (ISBN 0-398-04010-9); pap. 5.95 (ISBN 0-398-04011-7). C C Thomas.

Wiener, Daniel N., jt. auth. see Stieper, Donald R.

Wiener, Daniel P. Reclaiming the West: The Coal Industry & Surface Mined Lands. LC 80-81777. 1980. pap. 75.00 (ISBN 0-918780-16-0). Inform.

Wiener, Harvey & Bazerman, Charles. Reading Skills Handbook. LC 77-74097. (Illus.). 1977. pap. text ed. 8.25 (ISBN 0-395-24556-7); inst. manual 0.45 (ISBN 0-395-24558-3). HM.

Wiener, Harvey S. Creating Compositions. 3rd ed. Butcher, Phillip A., ed. (Illus.). 448p. 1981. pap. text ed. 9.95x (ISBN 0-07-070160-1, C); instructor's manual 3.95x (ISBN 0-07-070161-X). McGraw.

--The Writing Room: A Resource Book for Teachers of English. 352p. 1981. pap. 7.95 (ISBN 0-19-502826-0). Oxford U Pr.

--The Writing Room: A Resource Book for Teachers of English. 352p. 1981. pap. text ed. 7.95x (ISBN 0-19-502826-0). Oxford U Pr.

Wiener, Harvey S. & Bazerman, Charles. English Skills Handbook: Reading & Writing. LC 76-14015. (Illus.). 1976. pap. text ed. 8.25 (ISBN 0-395-20595-6); instructor's manual 0.75 (ISBN 0-395-20669-3). HM.

Wiener, Joan & Glick, Joyce. A Motherhood Book: Adventures in Pregnancy, Birth & Being a Mother. 160p. (Orig.). 1974. pap. 1.95 o.s.i. (ISBN 0-02-078400-7, Collier). Macmillan.

Wiener, Leo. The History of Yiddish Literature in the Nineteenth Century. LC 73-136773. 440p. 1973. Repr. of 1899 ed. 14.50 o.p. (ISBN 0-87203-032-6). Hermon.

Wiener, Martin. English Culture & the Decline of the Industrial Spirit, 1850-1980. (Illus.). 256p. Date not set. 15.95 (ISBN 0-521-23418-2). Cambridge U Pr.

Wiener, Martin, ed. see Rothman, David, et al.

Wiener, Matthew B., jt. auth. see Romano, Joseph A.

Wiener, Morton & Mehrabian, Albert. Language Within Language: Immediacy, a Channel in Verbal Communication. LC 68-15231. (Century Psychology Ser.). 1968. 20.00x (ISBN 0-89197-267-6); pap. text ed. 8.95x (ISBN 0-89197-268-4). Irvington.

Wiener, Moshe. Glory of the King's Daughter: Kvuda Bas Melech. 280p. (Orig., Hebrew & Eng.). 1980. 8.95 (ISBN 0-9605406-0-1); pap. 6.95 (ISBN 0-9605406-1-X). M Wiener.

Wiener, Norbert. Cybernetics: Or Control & Communication in the Animal & the Machine. 2nd ed. (Illus., Orig.). 1961. 17.50x (ISBN 0-262-23007-0); pap. 5.95 (ISBN 0-262-73009-X). MIT Pr.

--Fourier Integral & Certain of Its Applications. 1933. pap. text ed. 3.50 (ISBN 0-486-60272-9). Dover.

Wiener, Philip. Evolution & the Founders of Pragmatism. 304p. 1972. pap. 5.95x (ISBN 0-8122-1043-3, Pa Paperbks). U of Pa Pr.

Wiener, Philip P., ed. Dictionary of the History of Ideas. 1980. pap. 100.00 5-volume boxed edition (ISBN 0-686-61145-4). Scribner.

Wiener, Philip P. & Fisher, John, eds. Violence & Aggression in the History of Ideas. 288p. 1974. pap. 4.95x o.p. (ISBN 0-8135-0772-3). Rutgers U Pr.

Wiener, Philip P., ed. see Nakamura, Hajime.

Wiener, Philip P., ed. see Peirce, Charles S.

Wiener, Solomon. The College Graduate Guide for Scoring High on Employment Tests. 160p. (Orig.). 1981. pap. 4.95 (ISBN 0-686-69227-6). Monarch Pr.

--Handy Book of Commonly Used American Idioms. (gr. 9 up). 1958. pap. text ed. 1.95 (ISBN 0-88345-061-5, 17395). Regents Pub.

--The High School Graduate Guide for Scoring High on Civil Service Tests. 160p. (Orig.). (gr. 12). 1981. pap. 4.95 (ISBN 0-671-42776-8). Monarch Pr.

--How to Take Simple Tests for Civil Service Jobs & Score Higher. 160p. (Orig.). 1981. pap. 4.95 (ISBN 0-671-42777-6). Monarch Pr.

--Manual De Modismos Americanos Mas Comunes. (gr. 9 up). 1958. pap. text ed. 1.95 (ISBN 0-88345-097-6, 17403). Regents Pub.

Wiener, Solomon, et al. Marketing & Advertising Careers. (Career Concise Guides Ser). (Illus.). (gr. 7 up). 1977. PLB 6.45 (ISBN 0-531-01307-3). Watts.

Wienpahl, P. Zen Diary. 6.95 o.p. (ISBN 0-685-47284-1). Weiser.

Wier, Bernice, jt. auth. see Wallower, Lucille.

Wier, Dara. The Eight-Step Grapevine. LC 80-65699. (Poetry Ser.). 1980. 9.95 (ISBN 0-915604-37-X); pap. 4.95 (ISBN 0-915604-38-8). Carnegie-Mellon.

Wier, Ester. Easy Does It. LC 65-17375. (Illus.). (gr. 4-7). 1965. 5.95 (ISBN 0-8149-0438-6). Vanguard.

--Loner. (Illus.). (gr. 7-9). 1963. 5.95 o.p. (ISBN 0-679-20097-5). McKay.

--Rumptydoolers. LC 64-16260. (Illus.). (gr. 4-7). 5.95 (ISBN 0-8149-0439-4). Vanguard.

Wiercinski, F. J; see Small, J.

Wiersbe, Warren. The Annotated Pilgrim's Progress. 1980. 6.95 (ISBN 0-8024-0229-1). Moody.

--Be Complete. 160p. 1981. pap. 3.50 (ISBN 0-88207-257-9). Victor Bks.

Wiersbe, Warren W. A Basic Library for Bible Students. (Orig.). 1981. pap. 2.95 (ISBN 0-8010-9641-3). Baker Bk.

--Be a Real Teen. 128p. (Orig.). (YA) 1971. pap. 1.50 (ISBN 0-8024-6047-X). Moody.

--Be Free. 160p. 1975. pap. 2.95 (ISBN 0-88207-716-3). Victor Bks.

--Be Joyful. LC 74-76328. 1974. pap. 2.95 (ISBN 0-88207-705-8). Victor Bks.

--Be Mature. 1978. pap. 2.95 (ISBN 0-88207-771-6). Victor Bks.

--Be Ready. 1979. pap. 2.95 (ISBN 0-88207-782-1). Victor Bks.

--Be Real. LC 72-77014. 190p. 1972. pap. 2.95 (ISBN 0-88207-046-0). Victor Bks.

--Be Rich. 176p. 1976. pap. 2.95 (ISBN 0-88207-730-9). Victor Bks.

--Be Right. 1977. pap. 2.95 (ISBN 0-88207-729-5). Victor Bks.

--Listening to the Giants. 1979. 11.95 (ISBN 0-8010-9618-9). Baker Bk.

--Meet Yourself in the Parables. 1979. pap. 2.95 (ISBN 0-88207-790-2). Victor Bks.

Wiersbe, Warren W., ed. see Marchant, James.

Wierwille, V. P. Power for Abundant Living. 1980. 6.95 (ISBN 0-910068-01-1). Devin.

Wierzbicka, Anna. The Case for Surface Case. (Linguistica Extranea: Studia: No. 9). 201p. 1980. 13.50 (ISBN 0-89720-027-6); pap. 7.50 (ISBN 0-89720-028-4). Karoma.

Wiese, B. R. & White, W. A. Padre Island National Seashore-a Guide to the Geology, Natural Environments & History of a Texas Barrier Island. Date not set. price not set (GB 17). Bur Econ Geology.

Wiese, B. Von see Von Wiese, B.

Wiese, Gunther. Untersuchungen Zu Den Prosaschriften Henry Vaughans. (Salburg Studies in English Literature, Elizabethan & Renaissance: No. 72). 1978. pap. text ed. 25.00x (ISBN 0-391-01568-0). Humanities.

Wiesel, Elie. Dawn. 1973. pap. 1.95 (ISBN 0-380-01132-8, 42663, Bard). Avon.

--Gates of the Forest. 1969. pap. 2.75 o.s.i. (ISBN 0-380-01206-5, 51821, Bard). Avon.

--Images from the Bible: The Paintings of Shalom of Safed, the Words of Elie Wiesel. LC 79-51032. (Illus.). 1980. 35.00 (ISBN 0-87951-107-9); limited, signed 400.00 (ISBN 0-87951-108-7). Overlook Pr.

--The Testament. 1981. 12.95 (ISBN 0-671-44833-1). Summit Bks.

Wieseltier, Leon, tr. see Klein, Robert.

Wiesen, Allen E. Positive Therapy: Making the Very Best of Everything. LC 76-14849. 288p. 1977. 14.95 (ISBN 0-88229-269-2); pap. 7.95 (ISBN 0-88229-463-6). Nelson-Hall.

Wiesen-Cooke, Blanche. Women & Support Networks. (Out & Out Pamphlet Ser.). pap. 2.00 (ISBN 0-918314-10-0). Out & Out.

Wiesenfarth, Joseph. George Eliot: A Writer's Notebook, 1854-1879, Collected Writings. LC 80-23271. Date not set. write for info. (ISBN 0-8139-0887-6). U Pr of Va.

Wiesenfeld, Cheryl, et al, eds. Women See Women. (Illus.). 176p. 1976. 12.50 o.s.i. (ISBN 0-690-00965-8, TYC-T); pap. 6.95 o.s.i. (ISBN 0-690-00972-0, TYC-T). T Y Crowell.

Wiesenthal, Eleanor & Wiesenthal, Ted. Let's Find Out About Eskimos. LC 70-87929. (Let's Find Out Bks). (Illus.). (gr. k-3). 1969. PLB 4.47 o.p. (ISBN 0-531-00061-3). Watts.

--Let's Find Out About Rivers. LC 79-150732. (Let's Find Out Bks). (Illus.). (gr. k-3). 1971. PLB 4.47 o.p. (ISBN 0-531-00074-5). Watts.

Wiesenthal, Simon. Sails of Hope: The Secret Mission of Christopher Columbus. Winston, Richard & Winston, Clara, trs. from Ger. LC 73-2126. (Illus.). 256p. 1973. 5.95 o.s.i. (ISBN 0-02-628400-6). Macmillan.

Wiesenthal, Ted, jt. auth. see Wiesenthal, Eleanor.

Wieser-Benedetti, Hans, jt. auth. see Grenier, Lise.

Wiesley, Keith, jt. auth. see Platt, Deborah L.

Wiesley, Keith, ed. see Lakey, Harold.

Wiesmann, Susan, tr. see Bittlinger, Arnold.

Wiesner, J. Von see Von Wiesner, J. & Von Regel, C.

Wiesner, Jerome, et al. The Telephone's First Century & Beyond. 1977. 10.00 o.s.i. (ISBN 0-690-01485-6, TYC-T). T Y Crowell.

Wiesner, William. Hansel & Gretel. LC 78-154302. (Illus.). (gr. k-3). 1971. 6.50 (ISBN 0-395-28829-0, Clarion). HM.

--Magic Tales & Magic Tricks. LC 73-19269. (Encore Ser.). (Illus.). 64p. (gr. 2-6). 1974. 4.95 (ISBN 0-684-16587-2, ScribJ). Scribner.

--The Riddle Pot. 128p. (ps-2). 1977. PLB 5.95 (ISBN 0-525-38285-2); pap. 1.50 o.p. (ISBN 0-525-45033-5). Dutton.

--Turnabout. LC 72-190380. (Illus.). 40p. (ps-3). 1972. 5.95 (ISBN 0-395-28832-0, Clarion). HM.

Wiesner, William, compiled by. How Silly Can You Be? A Book of Jokes. LC 74-4044. (gr. 2-6). 1974. 6.95 (ISBN 0-395-28830-4, Clarion). HM.

Wiesnet, Eugen, jt. auth. see Lubkoll, Hans-Georg.

Wiessner, John, Jr. Pot of Gold: A Juvenile Fantasy Novel. 160p. (gr. 5). 1981. 5.95 (ISBN 0-8059-2769-7). Dorrance.

Wiest, Roger De see De Wiest, Roger J.

Wiffen, Jeremiah H. Julia Alpinula; with the Captive of Stamboul, & Other Poems, Repr. Of 1820 Ed. Reiman, Donald H., ed. Bd. with The Echo of Antiquity. the Past & the Future. (Poems. LC 75-31273. (Romantic Context Ser.: Poetry 1789-1830: Vol. 119). 1979. lib. bdg. 47.00 (ISBN 0-8240-2219-X). Garland Pub.

--Poems by Three Friends. (Thomas Raffles, Baldwin Brown, & J. H. Wiffen), Repr. Of 1813 Ed. Reiman, Donald H., ed. Bd. with Aonian Hours, & Other Poems. Repr. of 1819 ed. LC 75-31272. (Romantic Ser.: Poetry 1789-1830). 1979. lib. bdg. 47.00 (ISBN 0-8240-2218-1). Garland Pub.

Wigder, H. Neil. Dr. Wigder's Guide to Over-the-Counter Drugs. 1979. 8.95 o.p. (ISBN 0-312-90489-4). St Martin.

Wigfield, W. MacDonald. The Monmouth Rebellion: A Social History Including the Complete Text of "Wade's Narrative," 1685 & "a Guide to the Battlefield of Sidgemoor". (Illus.). 176p. 1980. 24.50x (ISBN 0-389-20149-9). B&N.

Wiggin, K. D. & Smith, N. A. The Story Hour. 185p. 1980. Repr. PLB 20.00 (ISBN 0-8492-8803-7). R West.

Wiggin, Kate D. Rebecca of Sunnybrook Farm. LC 75-32202. (Classics of Children's Literature, 1621-1932: Vol. 63). (Illus.). 1976. Repr. of 1902 ed. PLB 38.00 (ISBN 0-8240-2312-9). Garland Pub.

Wiggin, Maurice. Troubled Waters. 10.95x (ISBN 0-392-06465-0, SpS). Soccer.

Wiggins. Rebecca of Sunnybrook Farm. (gr. 4-6). 1973. pap. 1.25 (ISBN 0-590-04487-7, Schol Pap). Schol Bk Serv.

Wiggins, Arthur W. Physical Science with Environmental Applications. 384p. 1974. text ed. 17.75 (ISBN 0-395-17072-9); instructors' manual .75 (ISBN 0-395-17852-5); study guide 5.00 (ISBN 0-395-17071-0); Set. 20-35mm slides 11.75 (ISBN 0-395-18187-9). HM.

Wiggins, David. Truth, Invention & the Meaning of Life. 1976. pap. 2.50x o.p. (ISBN 0-8476-6067-2). Rowman.

Wiggins, James D. & English, Dori. Affective Education: A Methods & Techniques Manual for Growth. 1977. pap. text ed. 8.00 (ISBN 0-8191-0217-2). U Pr of Amer.

Wiggins, Jerry S., et al. Principles of Personality. LC 75-28729. 1976. text ed. 19.95 (ISBN 0-201-08618-2). A-W.

--The Psychology of Personality. 1971. 20.95 (ISBN 0-201-08636-0); instr's manual 3.25 (ISBN 0-201-08637-9); test items 3.25 (ISBN 0-201-08638-7). A-W.

Wiggins, Kate & Smith, Nora, eds. Arabian Nights. 1974. pap. 3.95 o.p. (ISBN 0-684-13809-3, SL523, ScribT). Scribner.

Wiggins, Marianne. Went South. 1980. 9.95 (ISBN 0-440-09420-8). Delacorte.

Wiggins, Norman A., jt. auth. see Stephenson, Gilbert T.

Wiggins, Peter Desa, tr. Satires of Ludovico Ariosto: A Renaissance Autobiography. LC 74-80810. xiv, 187p. 1976. 12.95x (ISBN 0-8214-0171-8). Ohio U Pr.

Wiggins, Walt. Ernest Berke: Paintings & Sculptures of the Old West. (Pintores Press Art Book Series: No. 2). (Illus.). 144p. 1980. 50.00 (ISBN 0-934116-03-2). Pintores Pr.

Wiggins, Walter. From "Wiggins Wonders" Comes Psychic Phenomena. 1981. 8.95 (ISBN 0-533-04235-6). Vantage.

Wigginton, Dave, jt. auth. see Glubetich, Dave.

Wigginton, Dave, ed. see Glubetich, Dave.

Wigginton, Eliot. Foxfire Books, Bks. 1-3. (Illus.). 1312p. 1975. Set. pap. 20.85 (ISBN 0-385-11253-X, Anch). Doubleday.

--Foxfire Six: Shoemaking, Gourd Banjos & Song-Bows, 100 Toys & Games, Wooden Locks, a Water-Powered Sawmill & Other Affairs of Just Plain Living. LC 79-6541. (Illus.). 512p. 1980. 14.95 (ISBN 0-385-15271-X, Anchor Pr); pap. 7.95 (ISBN 0-385-15272-8). Doubleday.

Wigginton, Eliot, ed. The Foxfire Book: Hog Dressing, Log Cabin Building, Mt. Crafts, Foods Planting by the Signs, Snake Lore, Hunting Tales, Faith Healing, Moonshining & Other Affairs of Plain Living. 320p. 1972. 10.95 (ISBN 0-385-07350-X, Anch); pap. 5.95 (ISBN 0-385-07353-4, Anch). Doubleday.

--Foxfire Five. LC 78-55859. 1979. 12.95 (ISBN 0-385-14307-9, Anchor Pr); pap. 7.95 (ISBN 0-385-14308-7). Doubleday.

--Foxfire Four. LC 76-50803. 1977. 12.95 (ISBN 0-385-12086-9, Anchor Pr); pap. 7.95 (ISBN 0-385-12087-7, Anch). Doubleday.

--Foxfire Three. LC 73-9183. 512p. 1975. 10.00 (ISBN 0-385-02265-4, Anchor Pr); pap. 7.95 (ISBN 0-385-02272-7, Anch). Doubleday.

--Foxfire Two. LC 70-163087. 12.95 (ISBN 0-385-02254-9, Anchor Pr); pap. 7.95 (ISBN 0-385-02267-0, Anch). Doubleday.

--I Wish I Could Give My Son a Wild Raccoon. LC 76-5343. 1976. pap. 4.95 (ISBN 0-385-11391-9, Anchor Pr). Doubleday.

Wigginton, F. Peter. Residential Real Estate Practice. LC 78-832. 1978. text ed. 18.95 (ISBN 0-672-97102-X). Bobbs.

Wigglesworth, V. B. Insect Hormones. (Illus.). 1970. text ed. 11.95x (ISBN 0-7167-0688-1). W H Freeman.

Wight, Fred H. Manners & Customs of Bible Lands. 1953. 9.95 (ISBN 0-8024-5175-6). Moody.

--Usos y Costumbres De las Tierras Biblica. 336p. (Span.). 1981. pap. 7.95 (ISBN 0-8024-9043-3). Moody.

Wight, Frederick S. The Potent Image: Art in the Western World from Cave Paintings to the 1970's. 512p. 1976. pap. 9.95 o.s.i. (ISBN 0-02-000970-4, Collier). Macmillan.

Wight, Martin. Systems of States. Bull, Hedley, intro. by. 1977. text ed. 18.25x (ISBN 0-7185-1153-0, Leicester). Humanities.

Wight, O. W., ed. & tr. see De Chateaubriand, Francois R.

Wight, Oliver W. Production & Inventory Management in the Computer Age. LC 74-7127. 300p. 1974. 18.95 (ISBN 0-8436-0732-7). CBI Pub.

Wight, Russell B., ed. see Edwin Gould Foundation For Children.

Wightman, David. Toward Economic Cooperation in Asia. 1963. 42.50x (ISBN 0-685-69884-X). Elliots Bks.

Wightman, Margaret. Faces of Germany: An Introduction to the German People. (Illus.). 1971. 14.95x (ISBN 0-245-50399-4). Intl Ideas.

Wightman, Ralph. Portrait of Dorset. LC 66-4364. (Portrait Bks.). (Illus.). 1966. 10.50x (ISBN 0-7091-6446-7). Intl Pubns Serv.

Wightman, W. P. Science in a Renaissance Society. 1972. text ed. 8.00x (ISBN 0-09-111650-3, Hutchinson U Lib); pap. text ed. 3.50x (ISBN 0-09-111651-1). Humanities.

Wightman, Wilfred E. The Lacy Family in England & Normandy, 1066-1194. LC 80-2206. 1981. Repr. of 1966 ed. 37.50 (ISBN 0-404-18794-3). AMS Pr.

Wightman, William P. Science & the Renaissance, 2 vols. Incl. Vol. 1. Introduction to the Study of the Emergence of the Sciences in the Sixteenth Century; Vol. 2. Annotated Bibliography of the Sixteenth Century Books Relating to the Sciences in the Library of the University of Aberdeen. (Books Relating to the Sciences in the Library of Aberdeen). 1962. Set. 27.25 o.s.i. (ISBN 0-02-854830-2). Hafner.

Wigman, Mary. The Language of Dance. Sorell, Walter, tr. from Ger. LC 66-13118. (Illus.). 118p. (Orig.). 1975. pap. 9.95 (ISBN 0-8195-6037-5, Pub. by Wesleyan U Pr). Columbia U Pr.

Wigmore, Ann. Be Your Own Doctor: Let Living Food Be Your Medicine. 176p. pap. text ed. 1.95. Hippocrates.

--From Fat to Fit. 2nd ed. 96p. 1977. pap. 1.95. Hippocrates.

--Healthy Children: Nature's Way. 120p. pap. 1.95. Hippocrates.

--How to Grow Living Foods in Seven Days. pap. text ed. write for info. Hippocrates.

--New Naturama: Living Textbook. 400p. pap. text ed. 12.95. Hippocrates.

--Recipes for Life. Kimball, Betsy, ed. (Illus.). 181p. pap. text ed. 7.95. Hippocrates.

--Spiritual Diet. (Health Digest Ser.: No. 152). 64p. pap. 1.50. Hippocrates.

--Spiritual-Physical Survival Through Sprouting. (Health Digest Ser.: No. 153). 63p. pap. 1.50. Hippocrates.

--Why Suffer? (Illus.). 173p. pap. text ed. 2.95. Hippocrates.

--You Are Your Own Healer. 207p. pap. 1.95. Hippocrates.

Wigmore, John H. & Simmons, D. B. Notes on Land Tenure & Local Institutions in Old Japan. (Studies in Japanese History & Civilization). 1979. 21.00 (ISBN 0-89093-223-9). U Pubns Amer.

Wigmore-Beddoes, Dennis G. Yesterday's Radicals: A Study of the Affinity Between Unitarianism & Broad Church Anglicanism in the Nineteenth Century. 182p. Repr. of 1971 ed. 10.00 (ISBN 0-227-67751-X). Attic Pr.

Wigner, E. P., jt. ed. see Salam, A.

Wigner, Eugene P. Symmetries & Reflections. LC 79-89843. 1979. pap. text ed. 9.50 (ISBN 0-918024-16-1). Ox Bow.

Wigner, Eugene P., jt. auth. see Weinberg, Alvin M.

Wignjowijoto, Hortojo, jt. auth. see Lindholm, Richard W.

Wigod, Jacob. The Darkening Chamber: The Growth of Tragic Consciousness in Keats. (Salzburg Studies in English Literature, Romantic Reassessment: No. 22). 231p. 1972. pap. text ed. 25.00x (ISBN 0-391-01567-2). Humanities.

Wigoder, Geoffrey & Karpman, Itzhak, eds. The New Standard Jewish Encyclopedia. LC 76-21965. 1977. 29.95 o.p. (ISBN 0-385-12519-4). Doubleday.

Wigutoff, Sharon, jt. ed. see Bracken, Jeanne.

Wihlborg, Clas G., jt. ed. see Levich, Richard M.

Wiig, Elisabeth & Semel, Eleanor. Language Disabilities in Children & Adolescents. new ed. 1976. text ed. 18.50 (ISBN 0-675-08614-0). Merrill.

Wiig, Elisabeth H. & Semel, Eleanor M. Language Assessment & Intervention for the Learning Disabled. (Special Education Ser.). 464p. 1980. text ed. 17.95 (ISBN 0-675-08180-7). Merrill.

Wiig, Karl M., jt. auth. see Mansvelt-Beck, Frederick W.

Wijngaert, Christine van den see Van den Wijngaert, Christine.

Wikler, Abraham. Opioid Dependence--Mechanisms & Treatment. 300p. 1980. 27.50 (ISBN 0-306-40591-1, Plenum Pr). Plenum Pub.

Wikler, Janet. How to Study & Learn. (First Bks.). (Illus.). (gr. 4-6). 1978. PLB 6.45 s&l (ISBN 0-531-01409-6). Watts.

Wikler, Madeline, jt. auth. see Saypol, Judyth R.

Wikler, Norma, jt. auth. see Fabe, Marilyn.

Wiksell, Wesley. Do They Understand You? 1960. 4.95 o.s.i. (ISBN 0-02-628480-4). Macmillan.

Wikstrom, Nelson. Councils of Governments: A Study of Political Incrementalism. LC 76-28784. 1977. 14.95 (ISBN 0-88229-322-2). Nelson-Hall.

Wilan, jt. auth. see Seyler.

Wilander. Paris Album. (Illus.). 160p. (Polyglot.). 1974. 45.00 o.p. (ISBN 2-03-079902-5, 2651). Larousse.

Wilansky, Albert. Topology for Analysis. 400p. 1981. Repr. of 1970 ed. lib. bdg. price not set (ISBN 0-89874-343-5). Krieger.

--Topology for Analysis. 1970. text ed. 28.50 o.p. (ISBN 0-471-00633-5). Wiley.

Wilber, Charles G. Ballistic Science for the Law Enforcement Officer. (Illus.). 324p. 1977. 30.75 (ISBN 0-398-03579-2). C C Thomas.

--Beryllium--A Potential Environmental Contaminant. (Illus.). 128p. 1980. 14.75. (ISBN 0-398-04118-0). C C Thomas.

--Biological Aspects of Water Pollution. (Illus.). 308p. 1971. text ed. 31.75 (ISBN 0-398-02062-0). C C Thomas.

--Contemporary Violence: A Multidisciplinary Examination. (Illus.). 176p. 1975. 14.75 (ISBN 0-398-03457-5). C C Thomas.

--Forensic Biology for the Law Enforcement Officer. (Illus.). 392p. 1974. 25.75 (ISBN 0-398-03174-6). C C Thomas.

--Medicolegal Investigation of the President John F. Kennedy Murder. (Illus.). 336p. 1978. 19.50 (ISBN 0-398-03679-9). C C Thomas.

Wilber, Charles K. Political Economy of Development. 1973. pap. text ed. 7.50 o.p. (ISBN 0-394-31756-4). Random.

Wilber, Charles K., jt. ed. see Jameson, Kenneth P.

Wilber, Donald N. The Land & People of Ceylon. rev. ed. LC 72-15668. (Portraits of the Nations Ser.). (Illus.). (gr. 6 up). 1972. 8.79 (ISBN 0-397-31399-3). Lippincott.

Wilber, George L., ed. Poverty: A New Perspective. LC 74-7884. (Illus.). 208p. 1975. 14.00x (ISBN 0-8131-1321-0). U Pr of Ky.

Wilber, Gordon O. & Pendered, Norman C. Industrial Arts in General Education. 4th ed. 1973. text ed. 20.50 scp (ISBN 0-685-51244-4, HarpC). Har-Row.

Wilbers, Stephen. The Iowa Writers' Workshop: Origins, Emergence & Growth. LC 80-20190. 148p. 1981. 12.50 (ISBN 0-87745-098-6); pap. 7.95 (ISBN 0-87745-105-2). U of Iowa Pr.

Wilbert, Johannes, ed. Enculturation in Latin America: An Anthology. new ed. LC 76-620078. (Latin American Studies: Vol. 37). (Orig.). 1976. pap. 13.95 (ISBN 0-87903-028-3). UCLA Lat Am Ctr.

--Folk Literature of the Yamana Indians: Martin Gusinde's Collection of Yamana Narratives. LC 76-20026. 1977. 20.00x (ISBN 0-520-03299-3). U of Cal Pr.

Wilbert, Johannes, ed. see Nettleford, Rex.

Wilbert, Warren N. Teaching Christian Adults. 280p. 1980. 9.95 (ISBN 0-8010-9636-7). Baker Bk.

Wilbourn, Carole C. The Inner Cat: A New Approach to Cat Behavior. LC 77-20189. (Illus.). 204p. 1980. pap. 4.95 (ISBN 0-8128-6081-0). Stein & Day.

Wilbur, Alan. Growing Unusual Vegetables. 1980. pap. 4.50 (ISBN 0-7153-7904-6). David & Charles.

Wilbur, C. Keith. The New England Indians. LC 78-61713. (Illus.). 1978. pap. 8.95 (ISBN 0-87106-004-3); pap. 8.95 (ISBN 0-87106-040-X). Globe Pequot.

Wilbur, C. Keith M. D. Revolutionary Medicine, Seventeen Hundred to Eighteen Hundred. LC 80-82790. (Illus.). 96p. (Orig.). 1980. pap. 8.95 (ISBN 0-87106-041-8). Globe Pequot.

Wilbur, C. Martin. Sun Yat-Sen: Frustrated Patriot. LC 76-18200. 384p. 1976. 22.50x (ISBN 0-231-04036-9). Columbia U Pr.

Wilbur, Charles K., jt. ed. see Jegen, Mary E.

Wilbur, Henry W. President Lincoln's Attitude Toward Slavery & Emancipation. 1914. 12.00x (ISBN 0-8196-0267-1). Biblo.

Wilbur, Karl M. & Yonge, C. M., eds. Physiology of Mollusca, Vol. 2. 1966. Vol. 1. 55.00 (ISBN 0-12-751302-7). Acad Pr.

Wilbur, L. Perry. Build a Second Income Writing Articles. 224p. 1981. pap. text ed. 7.95 (ISBN 0-471-08426-3). Wiley.

Wilbur, Leslie, et al. Improving College English Skills. rev. ed. 448p. 1972. pap. 8.95x (ISBN 0-673-07655-5). Scott F.

Wilbur, Liz, ed. Publication Design Thirteen Plus Fourteen. new ed. (Illus.). 500p. 1980. 49.50 o.s.i. (ISBN 0-8038-5888-4, Visual Communication). Hastings.

--Publication Design Twelve. Date not set. 24.95 o.p. (ISBN 0-8038-6756-5). Hastings.

Wilbur, Marguerite E. Thomas Jefferson: The Apostle of Liberty. 416p. 1962. 6.95 o.p. (ISBN 0-87140-809-0). Liveright.

Wilbur, Terence. Prolegomena to a Grammar of Basque. (Current Issues in Linguistic Theory). 1980. text ed. 28.50x (ISBN 90-272-0909-X). Humanities.

Wilbur, William H. Making of George Washington. 2nd ed. LC 73-85936. 1974. pap. 1.95 (ISBN 0-912530-02-2). Patriotic Educ.

Wilburn, Jean A. Biddle's Bank: The Crucial Years. 1967. 15.00x (ISBN 0-231-02981-0). Columbia U Pr.

Wilburn, Michael D. & Gladstone, Robert M. Optimizing Development Profits in Large Scale Real Estate Projects. LC 72-79135. (Technical Bulletin Ser.: No. 67). (Illus.). 1972. pap. 9.75 (ISBN 0-87420-067-9). Urban Land.

Wilby. Concrete for Structural Engineers. 1977. 29.95 (ISBN 0-408-00256-5). Butterworths.

Wilby, C. B. Design Graphs for Concrete Shell Roofs. (Illus.). xii, 148p. 1980. 37.50x (ISBN 0-85334-899-5). Burgess-Intl Ideas.

Wilby, C. B. & Khwaja, I. Concrete Shell Roofs. LC 77-391. 1977. 59.95 (ISBN 0-470-99088-0). Halsted Pr.

Wilby, Lee D. The Buffalo People. (The Making of America Ser.). (Orig.). 1981. pap. 2.75 (ISBN 0-440-00776-3). Dell.

Wilbye, John. The Second Set of Madrigales to 3. 4. 5. & 6. Parts Apt Both for Voyals & Voyces. LC 73-6171. (English Experience Ser.: No. 633). 1973. Repr. of 1609 ed. 27.00 (ISBN 90-221-0633-0). Walter J Johnson.

Wilcher, Marshall E. Environmental Cooperation in the North Atlantic Area. LC 79-3423. 1980. pap. text ed. 9.00 (ISBN 0-8191-0890-1). U Pr of Amer.

Wilcken, Ulrich. Alexander the Great. Borza, Eugene N., ed. Richards, G. C., tr. 1967. pap. 7.95 (ISBN 0-393-00381-7, Norton Lib). Norton.

Wilckens, Leslie Von see Von Wilckens, Leonie.

Wilcock, Gordon, jt. auth. see Gray, J. Muir.

Wilcock, John, jt. auth. see Pepper, Elizabeth.

Wilcock, M. I Saw Heaven Opened: The Message of Revelation. LC 74-31845. (Bible Speaks Today Ser.). 1975. pap. 5.25 (ISBN 0-87784-774-6). Inter-Varsity.

Wilcock, Michael. Savior of the World. Motyer, J. A. & Stott, John R., eds. LC 79-2720. (Bible Speaks Today Ser.). (Orig.). 1979. pap. 4.75 (ISBN 0-87784-599-9). Inter-Varsity.

Wilcock, W. L. see Marton, L.

Wilcockson, John. The Bicycle Book: The Total Illustrated Guide to Bicycles & Bicycling. Holzer, E., ed. (Illus.). 184p. 1980. 14.95 (ISBN 0-88421-156-8). Butterick Pub.

Wilcomb, E., compiled by. The American Indian & the United States: A Documentary History, 4 vols. LC 72-10259. 1973. Set. lib. bdg. 175.00 (ISBN 0-313-20137-4). Greenwood.

Wilcox. Growth Mechanisms & Silicon Nitride. Date not set. price not set (ISBN 0-8247-1368-0). Dekker.

--Lead Tin Telluride, Silver Halides & Czochralski Growth. Date not set. price not set (ISBN 0-8247-1354-0). Dekker.

Wilcox & Sutton. Understanding Death & Dying. 2nd ed. 1981. 10.95 (ISBN 0-88284-122-X). Alfred Pub.

Wilcox, B. & Eustace, P. J. Tooling up for Curriculum Review. 101p. 1981. pap. text ed. 23.50x (ISBN 0-85633-210-0, NFER). Humanities.

Wilcox, Clair. Toward Social Welfare: An Analysis of Programs & Proposals Attacking Poverty, Insecurity, & Inequality of Opportunity. 1969. text ed. 16.00 (ISBN 0-256-00589-3). Irwin.

Wilcox, Collin. Aftershock. 1979. pap. 1.75 o.s.i. (ISBN 0-515-05184-5). Jove Pubns.

--Doctor, Lawyer. (Mystery Ser.). 192p. 1981. pap. 1.95 (ISBN 0-515-05194-2). Jove Pubns.

--Long Way Down. 1979. pap. 1.75 (ISBN 0-515-05195-0). Jove Pubns.

Wilcox, Daniel. I'm My Mommy-I'm My Daddy. 24p. (ps). 1975. 1.95 (ISBN 0-307-10499-0, Golden Pr); PLB 7.62 (ISBN 0-307-60499-3). Western Pub.

Wilcox, David R., ed. see Wine Adsisory Bloard.

Wilcox, Delos F. Government by All the People. LC 72-1117. (American Constitutional & Legal History Ser.). 338p. 1972. Repr. of 1932 ed. lib. bdg. 32.50 (ISBN 0-306-70502-8). Da Capo.

Wilcox, Dennis J. Mass Media in Black Africa: Philosophy & Control. LC 74-30713. (Illus.). 188p. 1975. text ed. 18.95 o.p. (ISBN 0-275-05990-1). Praeger.

Wilcox, Dennis L., jt. ed. see Nolte, Lawrence W.

Wilcox, Donald J. In Search of God & Self: Renaissance & Reformation Thought. 1975. pap. text ed. 9.25 (ISBN 0-395-17178-4). HM.

Wilcox, Elliot. The Failure of the Greatest 20th Century Conspiracy for the Economic & Political Restructuring of the World: The Unexpected, Incredible Developments Resulting from Such a Failure. (Illus.). 207p. 1976. 55.00 (ISBN 0-89266-003-1). Am Classical Coll Pr.

Wilcox, Francis O., ed. China & the Great Powers: Relations with the U. S., the Soviet Union & Japan. LC 74-1736. (Special Studies). 96p. 1974. text ed. 15.95 o.p. (ISBN 0-275-08770-0). Praeger.

Wilcox, Francis O. & Frank, Richard A., eds. The Constitution & the Conduct of Foreign Policy. LC 75-23999. (Special Studies). 166p. 1976. text ed. 23.95 (ISBN 0-275-55860-6); pap. text ed. 8.95 (ISBN 0-275-89480-0). Praeger.

Wilcox, Fred, ed. The Grass Roots: An Anti-Nuke Sourcebook. LC 80-11762. (Illus.). 192p. 1980. 13.95 (ISBN 0-89594-032-9); pap. 6.95 (ISBN 0-89594-031-0). Crossing Pr.

Wilcox, Glade. Basic Electronics. LC 60-7871. 412p. 1960. 12.50 o.p. (ISBN 0-685-72304-6, Pub. by HR&W). Krieger.

Wilcox, L. R., jt. auth. see Kershner, R. B.

Wilcox, Laird M. Astrology, Mysticism & the Occult: A Critical Bibliography of Debunking Books & Articles. 1980. pap. 9.95 (ISBN 0-933592-09-4). Edit Res Serv.

--Bibliography on Espionage, Subversion, Destabilization & Problems of Counterintelligence & Internal Security. 1980. pap. text ed. 9.95 (ISBN 0-933592-14-0). Edit Res Serv.

--Bibliography on Political Psychology: Ideological Belief Systems, Propaganda, Persuasion & Forms of Resistance Against Them. 1980. pap. text ed. 9.95 (ISBN 0-933592-15-9). Edit Res Serv.

--Bibliography on Terriorism, Assassination, Kidnapping, Bombing, Guerilla Warfare & Countermeasures Against Them. 1980. pap. text ed. 8.95 (ISBN 0-933592-13-2). Edit Res Serv.

--Bibliography on the American Left. 1980. pap. 9.95 (ISBN 0-933592-05-1). Edit Res Serv.

--Bibliography on the American Right. 1980. pap. 9.95 (ISBN 0-933592-04-3). Edit Res Serv.

--Directory of the American Right. 1980. pap. 12.95 (ISBN 0-933592-06-X). Edit Res Serv.

--Mini-Manual on Nuclear War Survival. 1980. pap. cancelled (ISBN 0-933592-12-4). Edit Res Serv.

--One Hundred Secret Hiding Places in Your Home. (Orig.). 1980. pap. 3.00 (ISBN 0-933592-11-6). Edit Res Serv.

Wilcox, M. Basic Algebra. new ed. (gr. 9-10). 1977. pap. text ed. 12.12 (ISBN 0-201-08573-9, Sch Div); tchr's ed. 15.36 (ISBN 0-201-08574-7). A-W.

Wilcox, M., jt. auth. see Ellis, E. E.

Wilcox, Mary M. Developmental Journey: A Guide to the Development of Logical & Moral Reasoning & Social Perspective. LC 79-1340. 1979. 10.95 (ISBN 0-687-10510-2). Abingdon.

Wilcox, Pamela. Between Hell & Charing Cross. 1978. 13.50 (ISBN 0-04-920051-8). Allen Unwin.

Wilcox, R. Dictionary of Costume. 1979. 45.00 (ISBN 0-7134-0856-1, Pub. by Batsford England). David & Charles.

Wilcox, R. Paul, jt. auth. see Knight, C. Gregory.

Wilcox, R. Turner. Folk & Festival Costume of the World. lib. rep. ed. LC 65-23986. (Illus.). 1965. 25.00x (ISBN 0-684-15379-3, ScribT). Scribner.

--Mode in Costume. LC 58-12732. (Illus.). 1942. Repr. of 1942 ed. lib. rep. ed. 25.00x (ISBN 0-684-15165-0, ScribT). Scribner.

Wilcox, Robert K. Fatal Glimpse. 1981. pap. 2.25 (ISBN 0-8439-0899-8, Leisure Bks). Nordon Pubns.

Wilcox, Roger P. Oral Reporting in Business & Industry. 1967. text ed. 17.95 (ISBN 0-13-639302-0). P-H.

Wilcox, Sandra & Sutton, Marilyn. Understanding Death & Dying. 2nd ed. LC 76-30406. (Illus.). 1977. 10.95 (ISBN 0-88284-051-7); pap. 9.95x (ISBN 0-88284-052-5). Alfred Pub.

Wilcox, Tamara. Bats, Cats, & Sacred Cows. LC 77-10834. (Myth, Magic & Superstition Ser.). (Illus.). (gr. 4-5). 1977. PLB 9.65 (ISBN 0-8172-1026-1). Raintree Pubs.

--Mysterious Detectives: Psychics. LC 77-14315. (Great Unsolved Mysteries Ser.). (Illus.). (gr. 4-5). 1977. PLB 9.65 (ISBN 0-8172-1061-X). Raintree Pubs.

Wilcox, Thomas W. The Anatomy of College English. LC 72-11970. (Higher Education Ser.). 1973. 10.95x o.p. (ISBN 0-87589-163-2). Jossey-Bass.

Wilcox, Walter W. The Farmer in the Second World War. LC 72-2389. (FDR & the Era of the New Deal Ser). 426p. 1973. Repr. of 1947 ed. lib. bdg. 39.50 (ISBN 0-306-70474-9). Da Capo.

Wilcox, Walter W., et al. Economics of American Agriculture. 3rd ed. (Illus.). 512p. 1974. ref. ed. 19.95 (ISBN 0-13-229666-7). P-H.

Wilcox, Wayne A. Pakistan: The Consolidation of a Nation. LC 63-9873. 1963. 17.50x (ISBN 0-231-02589-0). Columbia U Pr.

Wilczynski, J. Economics & Politics of East-West Trade. 10.00x o.p. (ISBN 0-8464-0351-X). Beekman Pubs.

Wilczynski, Jozef. The Multinationals & East-West Relations: Towards Transideological Collaboration. LC 76-2080. 1976. 28.50x (ISBN 0-89158-540-0). Westview.

Wild, A. E., jt. ed. see Balls, M.

Wild, Cynthia, jt. auth. see Blatt, Sidney J.

Wild, J. P. Textile Manufacture in the Northern Roman Provinces. LC 74-77294. (Cambridge Classical Studies). (Illus.). 1970. 26.50 (ISBN 0-521-07491-6). Cambridge U Pr.

Wild, Jocelyn, jt. auth. see Wild, Robin.

Wild, Peter. Jeanne d'Arc. LC 78-13043. (A Raccoon Book). 1980. pap. 4.95 signed ed (ISBN 0-918518-16-4); pap. 3.95 (ISBN 0-918518-12-1). St Luke TN.

--Pioneer Conservationists of Eastern America. 1981. 15.95 (ISBN 0-87842-126-2); pap. 7.95 (ISBN 0-87842-124-6). Mountain Pr.

Wild, Ray. Concepts for Operations Management. LC 77-7232. 1978. 46.25 (ISBN 0-471-99539-8, Pub. by Wiley-Interscience); pap. 20.75 (ISBN 0-471-99543-6). Wiley.

--Operations Management: A Policy Framework. (Illus.). 1979. 35.00 (ISBN 0-08-022504-7); pap. 15.00 (ISBN 0-08-022505-5). Pergamon.

Wild, Robin & Wild, Jocelyn. How Animals Work for Us. rev. ed. LC 73-157991. (Finding-Out Book). (Illus.). 64p. (gr. 2-4). 1974. PLB 6.95 (ISBN 0-8193-0707-6). Enslow Pubs.

Wild, Victor. How to Take & Sell Erotic Photographs: Secrets of the Masters. 126p. (Orig.). 1981. pap. 9.95 (ISBN 0-938444-00-X). Wildfire Pub.

--The Science of Revolution: Fundamentals of Marxism-Leninism, Mao Tse Tung Thought & the Line of the Revolutionary Communist Party, Usa. 352p. (Orig.). 1981. 17.95 (ISBN 0-89851-035-X); pap. 5.95 (ISBN 0-89851-036-8). RCP Pubns.

Wildasin, John, jt. auth. see Altland, Millard.

Wildavsky, Aaron. How to Limit Government Spending. 197p. 1980. 8.95 (ISBN 0-686-69040-0). U of Cal Pr.

Wildavsky, Aaron, jt. auth. see Caiden, Naomi.

Wildavsky, Aaron, jt. auth. see Heclo, Hugh.

Wildavsky, Aaron, jt. auth. see Polsby, Nelson.

Wildavsky, Aaron, jt. auth. see Pressman, Jeffrey L.

Wilde, Alan. Horizons of Assent: Modernism, Postmodernism, & the Ironic Imagination. LC 80-22576. 224p. 1981. text ed. 15.00x (ISBN 0-8018-2449-4). Johns Hopkins.

Wilde, Daniel U. An Introduction to Computing: Problem-Solving Algorithms & Data Structures. LC 72-5754. (Illus.). 448p. 1973. ref. ed. 18.95 (ISBN 0-13-479519-9). P-H.

Wilde, Douglass & Beightler, C. Foundations of Optimization. 1967. 22.95 o.p. (ISBN 0-13-330035-8). P-H.

Wilde, Douglass J. Globally Optimal Design. LC 78-2933. 1978. 29.95 (ISBN 0-471-03898-9, Pub. by Wiley-Interscience). Wiley.

Wilde, Jane F. Ancient Cures, Charms & Usages of Ireland. LC 74-137347. 1970. Repr. of 1890 ed. 20.00 (ISBN 0-8103-3599-9). Gale.

Wilde, Jennifer. Love's Tender Fury. 512p. (Orig.). 1976. pap. 2.95 (ISBN 0-446-93904-8). Warner Bks.

Wilde, Johannes. Michelangelo: Six Lectures by Johannes Wilde. Shearman, John & Hirst, Michael, eds. (Oxford Studies in the History of Art & Architecture). (Illus.). 1979. pap. 12.95x (ISBN 0-19-817346-6). Oxford U Pr.

Wilde, Larry. The Complete Doctor's Joke Book. 208p. (Orig.). 1981. pap. 1.95 (ISBN 0-553-14751-X). Bantam.

--The Last Official Jewish Joke Book. 192p. (Orig.). 1980. pap. 1.95 (ISBN 0-553-14349-2). Bantam.

--The Last Official Polish Joke Book. (Illus.). 1977. pap. 1.95 (ISBN 0-523-41468-4). Pinnacle Bks.

--More of the Official Polish Italian Joke Book. 224p. (Orig.). 1975. pap. 1.95 (ISBN 0-523-41424-2). Pinnacle Bks.

--More the Official Jewish-Irish Joke Book. (Larry Wilde Bestselling Humor Ser.). 1979. pap. 1.95 (ISBN 0-523-41423-4). Pinnacle Bks.

--More: The Official Republican-Democrat Joke Book. 224p. (Orig.). 1980. pap. 1.95 o.p. (ISBN 0-523-40705-X). Pinnacle Bks.

--More: The Official Sex Maniac's Joke Book. 176p. (Orig.). 1981. pap. 1.95 (ISBN 0-553-14623-8). Bantam.

--The Official Democrat-Republican Joke Book. 224p. (Orig.). 1976. pap. 1.50 o.p. (ISBN 0-523-40535-9). Pinnacle Bks.

--The Official Dirty Joke Book. (Illus.). 1978. pap. 1.95 (ISBN 0-523-41421-8). Pinnacle Bks.

--The Official Golfers Joke Book. 1977. pap. 1.95 (ISBN 0-523-41469-2). Pinnacle Bks.

--The Official Italian Joke Book. rev. ed. 160p. 1981. pap. 1.75 (ISBN 0-523-41196-0). Pinnacle Bks.

--The Official Jewish Irish Jokebook. (Orig.). 1974. pap. 1.95 (ISBN 0-523-41257-6). Pinnacle Bks.

--The Official Polish Joke Book. rev. ed. 160p. 1981. pap. 1.75 (ISBN 0-523-41195-2). Pinnacle Bks.

Wilde, Mary P. The Best of Ethnic Home Style Cooking. LC 80-50406. 240p. 1981. 10.95 (ISBN 0-87477-138-2). J P Tarcher.

Wilde, Meta C. & Borsten, Orin. A Loving Gentleman. 1977. pap. 1.95 o.s.i. (ISBN 0-515-04421-0). Jove Pubns.

Wilde, Oscar. The Annotated Oscar Wilde. (Illus.). 320p. Date not set. 25.00 (ISBN 0-89835-052-2). Abaris Bks.

--Ballad of Reading Gaol. (Illus.). 1978. pap. 3.50 o.p. (ISBN 0-904526-26-7, Journeyman Press). Carrier Pigeon.

--Essays & Lectures. Stansky, Peter & Shewan, Rodney, eds. LC 76-17753. (Aesthetic Movement & the Arts & Crafts Movement Ser.). 1978. Repr. of 1908 ed. lib. bdg. 44.00x (ISBN 0-8240-2455-9). Garland Pub.

--First Collected Edition of the Works of Oscar Wilde, 15 Vols. Ross, Robert, ed. 1969. Repr. of 1922 ed. Set. 225.00x o.p. (ISBN 0-06-497659-9). B&N.

--The Happy Prince & Other Tales. Lurie, Alison & Schiller, Justin G., eds. Incl. A House of Pomergranates. LC 75-32193. (Classics of Children's Literature 1621-1932 Ser.). PLB 38.00 (ISBN 0-8240-2304-8). Garland Pub.

--The Happy Prince & Other Tales. LC 79-3512. (Illus.). 1980. pap. 6.95 (ISBN 0-394-73881-0). Shambhala Pubns.

--Importance of Being Earnest. pap. 2.00 (ISBN 0-8283-1442-X, 13, IPL). Branden.

--The Nightingale & the Rose. (Illus.). 32p. (gr. 4 up). 1981. 9.95 (ISBN 0-19-520231-7). Oxford U Pr.

--Picture of Dorian Gray. (Literature Ser). (gr. 10-12). 1970. pap. text ed. 3.50 (ISBN 0-87720-734-8). AMSCO Sch.

--The Picture of Dorian Gray. Murray, Isobel M., ed. (Oxford English Novels Ser.). 256p. 1974. 13.50x (ISBN 0-19-255368-2). Oxford U Pr.

--The Picture of Dorian Gray. 1976. pap. 2.95 (ISBN 0-460-01198-7, Evman). Dutton.

--Plays & Prose Writings & Poems. 1955. 12.95x (ISBN 0-460-00858-7, Evman); pap. 4.95 (ISBN 0-460-01858-2). Dutton.

--Salome. 1962. pap. 2.50 (ISBN 0-8283-1466-7, 65). Branden.

--Selected Letters of Oscar Wilde. Hart-Davis, Rupert, ed. 1979. 19.95 (ISBN 0-19-212205-3). Oxford U Pr.

--Wit & Humor of Oscar Wilde. Redman, Alvin, ed. 1959. pap. 3.50 (ISBN 0-486-20602-5). Dover.

Wilde, Oscar see Salerno, Henry F.

Wilde, Oscar see Watson, E. Bradlee & Pressey, Benfield.

Wilde, Robert. Practical & Decorative Concrete. LC 77-2833. (Illus.). 144p. 1977. 13.95 (ISBN 0-912336-38-2); pap. 6.95 (ISBN 0-912336-39-0). Structures Pub.

Wilde, Sergius A. Russia of the Tsars & Poets. LC 76-12944. 1976. pap. 4.95 o.p. (ISBN 0-8158-0342-7). Chris Mass.

Wilde, William H. Henry Kendall. LC 75-41479. (World Authors Ser.: Australia: No. 387). 1976. lib. bdg. 12.50 (ISBN 0-8057-6229-9). Twayne.

Wilde, William H., jt. ed. see Andrews, Barry G.

Wildemann, E. De. Prodrome De la Flore Algologique Des Indes Neerlandaises et Partie Des Territoires De Borneo Etc. 193p. 1978. lib. bdg. 55.00x (ISBN 3-87429-145-6). Lubrecht & Cramer.

Wilden, Anthony, et al. Myths of Information: Technology & Postindustrial Culture. Woodward, Kathleen, ed. LC 80-23653. (Theories of Contemporary Culture Ser.: Vol. 3). 276p. (Orig.). 1980. 15.95 (ISBN 0-930956-12-5); pap. 6.95 (ISBN 0-930956-13-3). Coda Pr.

Wilden, Theodore. Exchange of Clowns. 228p. 1981. 11.95 (ISBN 0-316-94051-8). Little.

--To Die Elsewhere. LC 76-21748. 1976. 7.95 o.p. (ISBN 0-15-190480-4). HarBraceJ.

--To Die Elsewhere. 1978. pap. 1.95 o.s.i. (ISBN 0-515-04468-7). Jove Pubns.

Wilder, Anne. Wilder Musings. 64p. 1981. 5.00 (ISBN 0-682-49725-8). Exposition.

Wilder, B. Joseph & Bruni, Joseph. Seizure Disorders: A Pharmacological Approach to Treatment. 1981. text ed. price not set (ISBN 0-89004-539-9). Raven.

Wilder, Barbara & Iribe, Maybelle. Pates for Kings & Commoners. 1977. 7.95 o.p. (ISBN 0-8015-5781-X, Hawthorn); pap. 3.95 (ISBN 0-8015-5782-8, Hawthorn). Dutton.

Wilder, C. S. Hospital & Surgical Insurance Coverage United States 1974. Stevenson, Taloria, ed. (Ser.10, No. 117). 1977. pap. text ed. 1.50 (ISBN 0-8406-0109-3). Natl Ctr Health Stats.

Wilder, Charles S. Limitation of Activity & Mobility Due to Chronic Conditions, U. S., 1972. LC 74-12431. (Data from the Health Interview Survey Ser. 10: No. 96). 54p. 1975. pap. text ed. 1.15 (ISBN 0-8406-0024-0). Natl Ctr Health Stats.

--Persons Injured & Disability Days by Detailed Type & Class of Accident, U. S., 1971 & 1972. Shipp, Audrey M., ed. LC 75-35509. (Ser. 10: No. 105). 53p. 1976. pap. text ed. 1.25 (ISBN 0-8406-0055-0). Natl Ctr Health Stats.

Wilder, Cherry. The Luck of Brin's Five. 224p. 1980. pap. 2.25 (ISBN 0-671-41637-5). PB.

Wilder, Claudyne & Rogers, William I. Taking Charge: Personal Effectiveness in Organizations. LC 79-9513. 1980. pap. text ed. 9.95 (ISBN 0-201-08624-7). A-W.

Wilder, David E., jt. ed. see Sieber, Sam D.

Wilder, Edna. Secrets of Eskimo Skin Sewing. LC 76-3783. (Illus., Orig.). 1976. pap. 6.95 (ISBN 0-88240-026-6). Alaska Northwest.

Wilder, Laura I. Little House on the Prairie. (YA) 1975. pap. 1.50 (ISBN 0-06-080357-6, P357, PL). Har-Row.

--On the Banks of Plum Creek. (Little House Ser.). (gr. 1-5). 1976. pap. 1.25 o.p. (ISBN 0-06-080393-2, P393, PL). Har-Row.

Wilder, Raymond I. Mathematics As a Cultural System. (Foundations & Philosophy of Science & Technology Ser.). 170p. 1981. 25.00 (ISBN 0-08-025796-8). Pergamon.

Wilder, Raymond L. Introduction to the Foundations of Mathematics. LC 80-12446. 346p. 1980. Repr. of 1965 ed. pap. 19.50 (ISBN 0-89874-170-X). Krieger.

Wilder, Thornton. The Alcestiad or a Life in the Sun. 1979. pap. 2.25 (ISBN 0-380-41855-X, 41855, Bard). Avon.

--Heaven's My Destination. pap. 2.50 (ISBN 0-380-00331-7, 49395, Bard). Avon.

--The Long Christmas Dinner & Other Plays in One Act. 1980. pap. 2.50 (ISBN 0-380-50245-3, 50245, Bard). Avon.

--Theophilus North. 352p. 1981. pap. 3.95 (ISBN 0-380-00160-8, 53108, Bard). Avon.

--Three Plays by Thornton Wilder. 1976. pap. 2.25 (ISBN 0-686-68405-2, 48231, Bard). Avon.

Wilder, Thornton see Watson, E. Bradlee & Pressey, Benfield.

Wilder, Warren F., jt. auth. see Giese, Frank S.

Wilders, John, ed. see Butler, Samuel.

Wilder-Smith, A. W. Man's Origin, Man's Destiny. LC 74-28508. 320p. 1975. pap. 5.95 (ISBN 0-87123-356-8, 210356). Bethany Fell.

Wildes, Harry E. Voice of the Lord: A Biography of George Fox. LC 64-10896. 1964. 11.50x o.p. (ISBN 0-8122-7431-8). U of Pa Pr.

--William Penn. LC 73-1857. 512p. 1974. 14.95 o.s.i. (ISBN 0-02-628570-3). Macmillan.

Wildhorn, Sorrel, jt. auth. see Kakalik, James.

Wildi, Ernst. Hasselblad Manual. (Illus.). 468p. 1980. 34.95 (ISBN 0-240-51042-9). Focal Pr.

Wildi, Theodore. Electrical Power Technology. 704p. 1981. write for info. solns. manual (ISBN 0-471-07764-X); price not set solns. manual (ISBN 0-471-09239-8). Wiley.

Wilding, Gary. Marin County Speaks Out: "Quips-Quotes-Opinions of the 'real' People" 1980. LC 79-93227. 300p. (Orig.). 1980. pap. 5.95 (ISBN 0-936092-02-5, 103). Harbinger Pr.

--Other Voices in American Poetry, 1980. LC 80-81203. 184p. 1981. pap. 7.95 (ISBN 0-936092-01-7, 102). Harbinger Pr.

--Young Voices in American Poetry-1980. LC 79-92559. 304p. (Orig.). 1980. pap. text ed. 7.95 (ISBN 0-936092-00-9, 101). Harbinger Pr.

Wilding, L. A. Greek for Beginners. (gr. 7-12). text ed. 8.95 (ISBN 0-571-10402-9). Transatlantic.

Wilding, Michael. Political Fictions. 1980. 25.00x (ISBN 0-7100-0457-5). Routledge & Kegan.

--West Midland Underground. 1975. 7.95x; pap. 4.25x (ISBN 0-7022-0991-0). U of Queensland Pr.

Wilding, Michael, ed. see Miller, John.

Wilding, Paul, jt. auth. see George, Victor.

Wilding, R. W. Key to Latin Course for Schools, Part I. 1966. 2.95 o.p. (ISBN 0-571-06632-1, Pub. by Faber & Faber). Merrimack Bk Serv.

--Key to Latin Course for Schools, Part II. 1966. 2.95 o.p. (ISBN 0-571-06633-X, Pub. by Faber & Faber). Merrimack Bk Serv.

Wilding, Suzanne, ed. Horse Tales. LC 76-13052. (Illus.). (YA) 1976. 7.95 (ISBN 0-312-39200-1). St Martin.

Wilding-White, Ted. All About UFO's. LC 77-17599. (World of the Unknown Ser). (Illus.). (gr. 4-5). 1978. PLB 6.95 (ISBN 0-88436-468-2). EMC.

Wildlife Education, Ltd. Birds of Prey. (Zoobooks). (Illus.). 20p. (Orig.). 1980. pap. 1.00 (ISBN 0-937934-01-1). Wildlife Educ.

--Elephants. (Zoobooks). (Illus.). 20p. (Orig.). 1980. pap. 1.00 (ISBN 0-937934-00-3). Wildlife Educ.

--Orangutans. (Zoobooks). (Illus.). 20p. (Orig.). 1980. pap. 1.00 (ISBN 0-937934-02-X). Wildlife Educ.

Wildlife Management Institute. Big Game of North America. rev. ed. Gilbert, Douglas L., ed. LC 78-14005. (Illus.). 512p. 1979. 24.95 (ISBN 0-8117-0244-8). Stackpole.

Wildlife Society. Wildlife Management Techniques Manual. 4th ed. Schemnitz, Sanford D., ed. LC 80-19970. (Illus.). 722p. 1980. 20.00 (ISBN 0-933564-08-2). Wildlife Soc.

Wildlife Society Elementary Education Committee, jt. ed. see Horwitz, Eleanor.

Wildlife Society, Inc. A Manual of Wildlife Conservation. Teague, Richard D., ed. LC 72-143895. (Illus.). 206p. (Orig.). 1971. pap. text ed. 4.25 (ISBN 0-933564-01-5). Wildlife Soc.

Wildman, Emily. Crochet, Step by Step. (Step by Step Craft Ser). 1972. PLB 9.15 o.p. (ISBN 0-307-62009-3, Golden Pr); pap. 2.95 (ISBN 0-307-42009-4). Western Pub.

Wildman, Eugene. Montezuma's Ball. LC 74-112037. 183p. 1970. 8.95x (ISBN 0-8040-0211-8); pap. 4.50 (ISBN 0-8040-0212-6). Swallow.

--Nuclear Love. LC 70-189193. 85p. 1972. 6.50 (ISBN 0-8040-0568-0); pap. 3.75 (ISBN 0-8040-0569-9). Swallow.

Wildman, Eugene, ed. Experiments in Prose. LC 70-77128. (Illus.). 351p. 1969. 13.95x (ISBN 0-8040-0103-0); pap. 5.95x (ISBN 0-8040-0104-9). Swallow.

Wildman, Faye. A Race for Love. 192p. (Orig.). 1980. pap. 1.50 (ISBN 0-671-57048-X). S&S.

--Rain Lady. 192p. (Orig.). 1980. pap. 1.50 (ISBN 0-671-57029-3). S&S.

Wildman, Frederick S., Jr. A Wine Tour of France. (Illus.). 320p. 1972. 9.95 o.p. (ISBN 0-688-00088-6). Morrow.

Wildman, George, illus. The Popeye Mix or Match Storybook. LC 80-52869. (Mix or Match Ser.). (Illus.). 9p. (ps-3). 1981. spiral wire 3.50 (ISBN 0-394-84585-4). Random.

Wildman, Manfred, ed. see Gross, William & Matsch, Lee A.

Wildonie, Herrandv. The Tales & Songs of Herrand von Wildonie. Thomas, J. W., tr. LC 76-183354. (Studies in Germanic Languages and Literatures: No. 4). 88p. 1972. 7.25x (ISBN 0-8131-1267-2). U Pr of Ky.

Wildridge, Thomas T. Grotesque in Church Art. LC 68-30633. 1969. Repr. of 1899 ed. 15.00 (ISBN 0-8103-3077-6). Gale.

Wildsmith, Alan. Northern Phantom. (gr. 6 up). 1979. PLB 8.95 (ISBN 0-233-97002-9). Andre Deutsch.

Wildsmith, Brian. Animal Games. (Illus.). 24p. (ps-3). 1981. 5.95 (ISBN 0-19-279731-X). Oxford U Pr.

--Animal Homes. (Illus.). 24p. (ps-3). 1981. 5.95 (ISBN 0-19-279732-8). Oxford U Pr.

--Animal Shapes. (Illus.). 24p. (ps-3). 1981. 5.95 (ISBN 0-19-279733-6). Oxford U Pr.

--Animal Tricks. (Illus.). 24p. (ps-3). 1981. 5.95 (ISBN 0-19-279743-3). Oxford U Pr.

--Brian Wildsmith's ABC. (Illus.). (gr. k-3). 1963. PLB 5.95 (ISBN 0-531-01525-4). Watts.

--Brian Wildsmith's Fishes. LC 68-12046. (Illus.). (gr. k-3). 1968. PLB 5.95 o.p. (ISBN 0-531-01528-9). Watts.

--The Lazy Bear. LC 73-8398. (Illus.). 32p. (gr. k-3). 1974. PLB 5.95 o.p. (ISBN 0-531-01559-9). Watts.

--The Little Wood Duck. LC 72-3828. (Illus.). 32p. (gr. k-3). 1973. PLB 5.95 o.p. (ISBN 0-531-02593-4). Watts.

--Professor Noah's Spaceship. (Illus.). 32p. (ps-3). 1980. 9.95 (ISBN 0-19-279741-7). Oxford U Pr.

--Seasons. (Illus.). 24p. (ps-3). 1981. 5.95 (ISBN 0-19-279730-1). Oxford U Pr.

--Squirrels. LC 74-6193. (Illus.). 32p. (gr. k-3). 1975. PLB 5.95 o.p. (ISBN 0-531-02754-6). Watts.

Wildt, Albert R. & Vahtola, Olli. Analysis of Covariance. LC 78-64331. (University Papers Ser.: Quantitative Applications in the Social Sciences No. 12). 1978. pap. 3.50x (ISBN 0-8039-1164-5). Sage.

Wile, B. Couples Therapy: A Nontraditional Approach. 240p. 1981. 22.50 (ISBN 0-471-07811-5, Pub. by Wiley Interscience). Wiley.

Wilen, Sam & Jacques, J. Enantiomers, Racemates & Resolutions. Collet, Andre, ed. 350p. 1981. 35.00 (ISBN 0-471-08058-6, Pub. by Wiley-Interscience). Wiley.

Wilensky. Intraocular Lenses. (Illus.). 19.50 (ISBN 0-8385-4304-9). ACC.

Wilensky, Gail R. & Holahan, John. National Health Insurance: Costs & Distributional Effects. 1972. pap. 3.50 o.p. (ISBN 0-87766-035-2, 70008). Urban Inst.

Wilensky, Harold L. The Welfare State & Equality: Structural & Ideological Roots of Public Expenditures. 1975. pap. 5.95x (ISBN 0-520-02908-9). U of Cal Pr.

Wilensky, Julius M. Cruising Guide to the Abacos & the Northern Bahamas. rev. 2nd ed. Weber, Carol, ed. LC 80-50792. (Illus.). 220p. 1980. pap. 17.25 (ISBN 0-918752-03-5). Wescott Cove.

Wilentz, Joan S., jt. auth. see Nelson, Charles.

Wiles, David K. Energy, Winter, & Schools: Chronology of Decision Crisis. (Politics of Education Ser.). (Illus.). 1979. 18.95 (ISBN 0-669-02544-5). Lexington Bks.

Wiles, Domini. Death Flight. 1978. pap. 1.95 o.s.i. (ISBN 0-515-04719-8). Jove Pubns.

Wiles, G. P. Paul's Intercessory Prayers. (Society for New Testament Studies Monographs: No. 24). 360p. 1974. 47.50 (ISBN 0-521-20274-4). Cambridge U Pr.

Wiles, Jon & Bondi, Joseph. Curriculum Development: A Guide to Practice Elementary Education. 1979. text ed. 16.95 (ISBN 0-675-08315-X). Merrill.

Wiles, Jon & Bondi, Joseph, Jr. Supervision: A Guide to Practice. (Educational Administration Ser.: No. C21). 350p. 1980. text ed. 15.95 (ISBN 0-675-08168-8). Merrill.

Wiles, Jon W. & Bondi, Joseph, Jr. The Essential Middle School. (Illus.). 432p. Date not set. text ed. 16.95 (ISBN 0-675-08086-X). Merrill.

Wiles, Julian. Tradd Street Follies. LC 76-45729. 1978. 6.50 (ISBN 0-937684-08-2). Tradd St Pr.

Wiles, M. & Santer, M., eds. Documents in Early Christian Thought. LC 74-31807. 304p. 1976. 36.00 (ISBN 0-521-20669-3); pap. 8.50x (ISBN 0-521-09915-3). Cambridge U Pr.

Wiles, M. F. What Is Theology? 1977. 7.95x (ISBN 0-19-213525-2); pap. 4.50x (ISBN 0-19-289066-2). Oxford U Pr.

Wiles, Maurice F. Making of Christian Doctrine. 1967. 23.95 (ISBN 0-521-06803-7); pap. 7.95x (ISBN 0-521-09962-5). Cambridge U Pr.

Wiles, P., ed. Prediction of Communist Economic Performance. LC 75-123677. (Soviet & East European Studies). (Illus.). 1971. 37.50 (ISBN 0-521-07885-7). Cambridge U Pr.

Wiles, Peter. Economic Institutions Compared. LC 76-6175. 608p. 1977. 34.95 (ISBN 0-470-15083-1). Halsted Pr.

Wiles, Timothy J. The Theater Event: Modern Theories of Performance. Gottschalk, Fruma, tr. LC 80-12206. 1980. lib. bdg. 17.50x (ISBN 0-226-89801-6). U of Chicago Pr.

Wiley, Bell I. The Life of Billy Yank. LC 75-162619. 1978. pap. 8.95 (ISBN 0-8071-0476-0). La State U Pr.

Wiley, Bell I., ed. Slaves No More: Letters from Liberia, 1833-1869. LC 79-4015. (Illus.). 360p. 1980. 21.50x (ISBN 0-8131-1388-1). U Pr of Ky.

Wiley, Bell I., ed. see Akin, Warren.

Wiley, Bell I., ed. see Dawson, Francis W.

Wiley, Bowman G. The Clear Synthesis: A Study of William Wordsworth's Stylistic Development As a Descriptive Poet from 1793 to 1808. (Salzburg Studies in English Literature, Romantic Reassessment: No. 16). 1974. pap. text ed. 25.00x (ISBN 0-391-01571-0). Humanities.

Wiley, Constance & Wiley, Wilson. Boxers. Foyle, Christina, ed. (Foyle's Handbks). (Illus.). 1973. 3.95 (ISBN 0-685-55794-4). Palmetto Pub.

Wiley, Dean. Money Management in the Casino. (Gambler's Book Shelf). pap. 2.95 (ISBN 0-89650-584-7). Gamblers.

--Understanding Gambling Systems. (Gambler's Book Shelf). 64p. 1975. pap. 2.95 (ISBN 0-89650-554-5). Gamblers.

Wiley, E. O., ed. see Armstrong, Barry L. & Murphy, James B.

Wiley, E. O., ed. see Nowak, Ronald M.

Wiley, Edward. Death's Pale Flag. 1981. pap. 1.95 (ISBN 0-8439-0859-9, Leisure Bks). Nordon Pubns.

Wiley, Edward O. Phylogenetics: Theory & Practice of Phylogenetic Systematics. 552p. 1981. price not set (ISBN 0-471-05975-7, Pub. by Wiley-Interscience). Wiley.

Wiley, Jack. Acrobatics Book. LC 78-58043. (Illus.). 187p. 1978. pap. 5.95 (ISBN 0-89037-141-5). Anderson World.

--Boat Living. LC 76-5201. (Illus.). 1976. 9.95 (ISBN 0-87742-078-5). Intl Marine.

--Modifying Fiberglass Boats. LC 74-25164. (Illus.). 200p. 1975. 12.50 (ISBN 0-87742-048-3). Intl Marine.

--Women's Gymnastics. LC 79-64732. (Illus.). 176p. (Orig.). 1980. pap. 7.95 (ISBN 0-89037-223-3). Anderson World.

Wiley, M., ed. Estuarine Processes, 2 vols. Vol. 1. 1976. 35.00 (ISBN 0-12-751801-0); Vol. 2. 1977. 31.50 (ISBN 0-12-751802-9). Acad Pr.

Wiley, Paul F., jt. auth. see Neunhoeffer, Hans.

Wiley, Paul L., compiled by. British Novel: Conrad to the Present. LC 79-178291. (Goldentree Bibliographies in Language & Literature Ser). (Orig.). 1973. pap. 6.95x (ISBN 0-88295-530-6). AHM Pub.

Wiley, Paul L. & Orel, Harold, eds. British Poetry, Eighteen Eighty to Nineteen Twenty: Edwardian Voices. LC 73-79174. 1969. 29.50x (ISBN 0-89197-049-5); pap. text ed. 16.95x (ISBN 0-89197-050-9). Irvington.

Wiley, Robert J. Real Estate Accounting & Mathematics Handbook. LC 80-12990. (Real Estate for Professional Practitioners Ser.). 1980. 26.95 (ISBN 0-471-04812-7, Pub by Ronald Pr). Wiley.

--Real Estate Investment: Analysis & Strategy. LC 75-14950. 1976. 21.95 (ISBN 0-8260-9432-5). Ronald Pr.

Wiley, Virginia, jt. auth. see Huenefeld, John.

Wiley, Wilson, jt. auth. see Wiley, Constance.

Wilf. Programming for a Digital Computer in the Fortran Language. 1969. 6.50 (ISBN 0-201-08639-5). A-W.

Wilf, H. S., jt. ed. see Ralston, Anthony.

Wilf, Herbert S. Mathematics for the Physical Sciences. 1978. pap. text ed. 4.50 (ISBN 0-486-63635-6). Dover.

Wilford, D. Sykes. Monetary Policy & the Open Economy: Mexico's Experience. LC 77-14386. (Praeger Special Studies). 1977. 22.95 (ISBN 0-03-028156-3). Praeger.

Wilford, D. Sykes, jt. ed. see Putnam, Bluford H.

Wilford, John N. The Mapmakers. LC 80-2716. (Illus.). 448p. 1981. 20.00 (ISBN 0-394-46194-0). Knopf.

Wilford, John N., ed. Scientists at Work: The Creative Process of Scientific Research. LC 78-18256. (Illus.). 1979. 9.95 (ISBN 0-396-07603-3). Dodd.

Wilgen, John K., jt. auth. see Feld, Werner J.

Wilgocka-Okon, Barbara, jt. auth. see Okon, Wincenty.

Wilgus, A. Curtis. Historiography of Latin America: A Guide to Historical Writing, 1500-1800. 1975. 18.00 (ISBN 0-8108-0859-5). Scarecrow.

--Latin America Fourteen Ninety-Two to Nineteen Forty-Two: A Guide to Historical & Cultural Development Before World War Two. 1973. Repr. of 1941 ed. 27.50 (ISBN 0-8108-0595-2). Scarecrow.

--Latin America, Spain & Portugal: A Selected & Annotated Bibliographical Guide to Books Published 1954-1974. LC 76-58355. 1977. 40.00 (ISBN 0-8108-1018-2). Scarecrow.

Wilgus, A. Curtis, ed. Caribbean: British, Dutch, French, United States. LC 51-12532. (Caribbean Conference Ser: Vol. 8). 1958. 9.00 o.p. (ISBN 0-8130-0248-6). U Presses Fla.

Wilgus, A. Curtis, ed. see Hedrick, Basil C. & Hedrick, Anne K.

Wilgus, A. Curtis, ed. see Rasmussen, R. Kent.

Wilgus, D. K. & Sommer, Carol, eds. Folklore International: Essays in Traditional Literature, Belief, & Custom in Honor of Wayland Debs Hand. LC 67-16249. (Illus.). xiv, 259p. Repr. of 1967 ed. 20.00 (ISBN 0-8103-5023-8). Gale.

Wilgus, Karna S. Latin American Books: An Annotated Bibliography. 80p. 1974. pap. 3.00 o.p. (ISBN 0-913456-84-5, Pub. by Ctr Inter-Am Rel). Interbk Inc.

Wilhelm. The Kaiser's Memoirs, 1888-1918. Ybarra, Thomas R., tr. from Ger. LC 74-22349. 366p. 1977. Repr. of 1922 ed. 22.50 (ISBN 0-86527-113-5). Fertig.

Wilhelm, Donald. Creative Alternatives to Communism: Guidelines for the Future. 188p. 1980. 12.95x (ISBN 0-8290-0298-7); pap. 6.95x (ISBN 0-8290-0299-5). Irvington.

--Creative Alternatives to Communism: Guidelines for Tomorrow's World. 1977. text ed. 13.00x (ISBN 0-333-21852-3); pap. text ed. 4.00x (ISBN 0-333-21856-6). Humanities.

--Emerging Indonesia. (Illus.). 192p. 1980. 25.00x (ISBN 0-389-20105-7). B&N.

Wilhelm, Glenda & Wilhelm, Tim. The Bicycle Touring Book. (Illus.). 228p. 1980. 12.95 (ISBN 0-87857-295-3); pap. 9.95 (ISBN 0-87857-307-0). Rodale Pr Inc.

Wilhelm, Hellmut. Heaven, Earth, & Man in the Book of Changes: Seven Eranos Lectures. LC 76-7801. (Publications on Asia of the School of International Studies: No. 28). 248p. 1977. 15.00 (ISBN 0-295-95516-3); pap. 8.95 (ISBN 0-295-95692-5). U of Wash Pr.

Wilhelm, James J., ed. Medieval Song: An Anthology of Hymns & Lyrics. 1971. pap. 3.95 o.p. (ISBN 0-525-47297-5). Dutton.

Wilhelm, Kate. The Clewiston Test. 1980. pap. write for info. (ISBN 0-671-83503-3). PB.

--The Clewiston Test. LC 75-31683. 256p. 1976. 8.95 o.p. (ISBN 0-374-12500-7). FS&G.

--The Infinity Box: A Collection of Speculative Fiction. LC 74-15894. 318p. (YA) 1975. 8.95 o.s.i. (ISBN 0-06-014653-2, HarpT). Har-Row.

--A Sense of Shadow. 1981. 9.95 (ISBN 0-686-69061-3). HM.

--Somerset Dreams & Other Fictions. LC 77-11776. 1978. 9.95 o.s.i. (ISBN 0-06-014649-4, HarpT). Har-Row.

--Where Late the Sweet Birds Sang. LC 75-6379. 260p. (YA) 1976. 10.00 o.p. (ISBN 0-06-014654-0, HarpT). Har-Row.

Wilhelm, Paul. Travels in North America, 1822-1824. Lottinville, Savoie, ed. Nitske, W. Robert, tr. (Illus.). 1974. pap. text ed. 9.95 (ISBN 0-8061-1501-7). U of Okla Pr.

Wilhelm, R. Dwight. Two Ways to Look South: A Guide to Latin America. (Orig.). 1980. pap. 2.25 (ISBN 0-377-00098-1). Friend Pr.

Wilhelm, Tim, jt. auth. see Wilhelm, Glenda.

Wilhelmsen, Frederick. Citizens of Rome: Reflections from the Life of a Roman Catholic. 12.95 (ISBN 0-89385-010-1); pap. 4.95 (ISBN 0-89385-005-5). Green Hill.

Wilhelmsen, Frederick D. Christianity & Political Philosophy. LC 77-22754. 243p. 1978. 14.50 (ISBN 0-8203-0431-X). U of Ga Pr.

Wilhite, J. Porter. Modern Churches & the Church. 4.95 (ISBN 0-89315-155-6). Lambert Bk.

Wilhite, J. Portert & Dew, James F. Wilhite-Dew Debate. pap. 2.50 (ISBN 0-89315-355-9). Lambert Bk.

Wilhite, J. Portr. Trail Blazers. 4.95 (ISBN 0-89315-302-8). Lambert Bk.

Wilhite, Robert & Mishler, Clifford. Standard Guide to U. S. Coin & Paper Money Valuations. 6th ed. LC 79-67100. (Illus.). 1979. pap. 1.95 o.s.i. (ISBN 0-87341-051-3). Krause Pubns.

Wilhoit, G. Cleveland & De Bock, Harold, eds. Mass Communication Review Yearbook, Vol. 1. (Illus.). 751p. 1980. 35.00x (ISBN 0-8039-1186-6). Sage.

Wilhoit, J. C., Jr. Elementary Partial Differential Equations for Engineers & Scientists. LC 78-62181. 1978. pap. text ed. 11.00 (ISBN 0-8191-0501-5). U Pr of Amer.

Wiliams, Guy. Instructions to Young Collectors. 9.75x (ISBN 0-392-07941-0, SpS). Soccer.

Wilings, David R. Understanding Management. 320p. 1979. text ed. 14.35 (ISBN 0-7715-5728-0); instr's. manual 7.41 (ISBN 0-7715-5730-2). Forkner.

Wilk, Chester A. Everything You Should Know About Chiropractic. LC 80-53014. 1980. write for info. Wilk Pub.

Wilk, Christopher. Thonet: One Hundred Fifty Years of Furniture. (Furniture & Design Ser.). 1980. 18.95 (ISBN 0-8120-5384-2). Barron.

Wilk, Max. Get Out & Get Under. 1981. 12.95 (ISBN 0-393-01425-8). Norton.

--The Golden Age of Television. 1976. 10.00 o.p. (ISBN 0-440-02950-3). Delacorte.

Wilke, G., jt. auth. see Jolly, P. W.

Wilken, Paul H., jt. auth. see Blalock, Hubert M., Jr.

Wilken, Robert L. The Myth of Christian Beginnings. LC 80-11884. 218p. 1980. pap. text ed. 4.95 (ISBN 0-268-01348-9). U of Notre Dame Pr.

Wilken, Robert L., jt. auth. see Meeks, Wayne A.

Wilkenfeld, Jonathan, et al. Foreign Policy Behavior: The Interstate Behavior Analysis Model. LC 80-13161. (Illus.). 288p. 1980. 22.50 (ISBN 0-8039-1476-8). Sage.

Wilken-Jensen, K. Lexikon Allergologicum. 1965. 15.00 (ISBN 0-08-011838-0). Pergamon.

Wilkens, Robert. Black Sabbath. 4.95 o.p. (ISBN 0-685-46130-0). Vantage.

Wilkerson, Cynthia. The Fast Life. 1979. pap. 2.25 (ISBN 0-505-51350-1). Tower Bks.

Wilkerson, David. Beyond the Cross & the Switchblade. 1974. 5.95 o.p. (ISBN 0-912376-08-2). Chosen Bks Pub.

--Beyond the Cross & the Switchblade. (Orig.). pap. 1.75 (ISBN 0-89129-151-2). Jove Pubns.

--The Christian Maturity Manual. rev. ed. LC 79-169590. 1977. 2.95 (ISBN 0-8307-0496-5, 5200121). Regal.

--Cross & the Switchblade. 1976. pap. 1.50 (ISBN 0-89129-197-0). Jove Pubns.

--The End Times New Testament. pap. 3.95 o.p. (ISBN 0-912376-11-2). Chosen Bks Pub.

--Have You Felt Like Giving up Lately? 1980. pap. 4.95 (ISBN 0-8007-5042-X). Revell.

--Hey, Preach, You're Comin' Through. 1975. pap. 1.25 (ISBN 0-89129-064-8, PV064). Jove Pubns.

--I'm Not Mad at God. 1967. pap. 2.25 (ISBN 0-87123-245-6, 200245). Bethany Fell.

--Little People. (gr. 8-12). 1969. pap. 1.25 o.p. (ISBN 0-685-19670-4). Jove Pubns.

--Man Have I Got Problems. 1973. pap. 1.25 o.s.i. (ISBN 0-515-04668-X). Jove Pubns.

--The Pocket Promise Book. gift ed. LC 72-86208. 96p. 1981. imitation leather 3.95 (ISBN 0-8307-0782-4). Regal.

--Promesas de Jesus. Orig. Title: Jesus Person Pocket Promise Book. 95p. (Span.). 1974. pap. 1.95 (ISBN 0-89922-027-4). Edit Caribe.

--Purple Violet Squish. (gr. 9 up). 1970. pap. 0.95 o.s.i. (ISBN 0-89129-179-2). Jove Pubns.

--Racing Toward Judgement. (Orig.). pap. 1.50 (ISBN 0-89129-035-4). Jove Pubns.

--Twelve Angels from Hell. (gr. 9 up). 1967. pap. 1.25 o.s.i. (ISBN 0-89129-082-6). Jove Pubns.

--Vision. (Orig.). 1974. pap. 1.75 o.s.i. (ISBN 0-515-05294-9). Jove Pubns.

--When in Doubt...Faith It. LC 72-83844. (Illus.). 64p. (Orig.). 1972. pap. 0.95 o.p. (ISBN 0-8307-0168-0, 50-066-00). Regal.

Wilkerson, David, ed. Jesus Person Pocket Promise Book. LC 72-86208. 96p. pap. 1.95 (ISBN 0-8307-0191-5, 50-078-01); gift ed. imitation leather 3.95. Regal.

Wilkerson, David, tr. La Cruz y el Punal. (Spanish Bks.). 1979. 1.90 (ISBN 0-8297-0522-8). Life Pubs Intl.

--Depois De a Cruz E O Punhal. (Portuguese Bks.). 1979. 1.40 (ISBN 0-8297-0731-X). Life Pubs Intl.

--Despues De la Cruz y el Punal. (Spanish Bks.). (Span.). 1978. 1.75 (ISBN 0-8297-0537-6). Life Pubs Intl.

--Hombre, Si Que Tengo Problemas. (Spanish Bks.). (Span.). 1978. 1.50 (ISBN 0-8297-0576-7). Life Pubs Intl.

--Homem, Estou Cheio De Problemas. (Portugese Bks.). (Port.). 1979. 1.40 (ISBN 0-8297-0815-4). Life Pubs Intl.

--Jesucristo, Roca Firme. (Spanish Bks.). (Span.). 1978. 1.60 (ISBN 0-8297-0577-5). Life Pubs Intl.

--Jesus Cristo, a Rocha Firme. (Portuguese Bks.). 1979. 1.40 (ISBN 0-8297-0669-0). Life Pubs Intl.

--Poder De la Alabanza. (Spanish Bks.). (Span.). 1978. 1.90 (ISBN 0-8297-0444-2). Life Pubs Intl.

--Respuesta a la Alabanza. (Spanish Bks.). (Span.). 1979. 1.80 (ISBN 0-8297-0446-9). Life Pubs Intl.

--La Vision. (Spanish Bks.). (Span.). 1979. 1.65 (ISBN 0-8297-0608-9). Vida Pub.

--La Vision. (French Bks.). (Fr.). 1979. 1.95 (ISBN 0-686-28823-8). Vida Pub.

Wilkerson, David, et al. Cross & the Switchblade. 1970. pap. 2.25 (ISBN 0-515-05844-0). Jove Pubns.

Wilkerson, Dick, jt. auth. see Wilkerson, Michael.

Wilkerson, Don & Manuel, David. Hell-Bound. LC 78-60735. 199p. 1978. pap. 2.95 (ISBN 0-932260-03-9). Rock Harbor.

Wilkerson, Don, jt. auth. see Torres, Victor.

Wilkerson, Frederick. British & American Flintlocks. (Country Life Collectors Guides Ser). 1972. 4.95 (ISBN 0-600-43590-3). Transatlantic.

Wilkerson, Gwen & Schonauer, Betty. In His Strength. LC 77-92619. 1978. pap. 3.45 (ISBN 0-8307-0619-4, 54-089-03). Regal.

Wilkerson, Gwen, tr. En Su Fuerza. (Spanish Bks.). (Span.). 1979. 1.50 (ISBN 0-8297-0910-X). Life Pubs Intl.

--Par Sa Force. (French Bks.). (Fr.). 1979. 1.85 (ISBN 0-8297-0927-4). Life Pubs Intl.

Wilkerson, H., jt. auth. see Feng, G.

Wilkerson, M. & Van Der Zee, J. Life in the Peace Zone: An American Company Town. 1971. pap. 3.95 o.s.i. (ISBN 0-02-096850-7, Collier). Macmillan.

Wilkerson, Michael & Wilkerson, Dick. Someone Cry for the Children: The Unsolved Girl Scout Murders of Oklahoma & the Case of Gene Leroy Hart. 256p. 1981. 10.95 (ISBN 0-8037-8283-7). Dial.

Wilkes, G. A., ed. The Complete Plays of Ben Johnson, Vol.1. 428p. 1980. 89.00 (ISBN 0-19-812599-2). Oxford U Pr.

--The Complete Plays of Ben Jonson, Vol. 2. 448p. 1981. 89.00 (ISBN 0-19-812601-8). Oxford U Pr.

--The Tempest. (The Challis Shakespeare Ser.). 1981. pap. 3.50x (ISBN 0-686-68845-7, Pub. by Sydney U Pr Australia). Intl Schol Bk Serv.

Wilkes, J. Herman Cortes, Conquistador in Mexico. (Introduction to the History of Mankind Ser.). (Illus.). 48p. (gr. 5-11). 1974. pap. 3.95 (ISBN 0-521-20424-0). Cambridge U Pr.

--The London Police in the Nineteenth Century. LC 76-57247. (Cambridge Introduction to the History of Mankind Ser.). (Illus.). 1977. 3.95 (ISBN 0-521-21406-8). Cambridge U Pr.

--Roman Army. (Introduction to the History of Mankind Ser). (Illus.). (gr. 4 up). 1973. 3.95 (ISBN 0-521-07243-3). Cambridge U Pr.

Wilkes, Kathleen. Physicalism. (Studies in Philosophical Psychology). 1978. text ed. 12.50x (ISBN 0-391-00741-6). Humanities.

Wilkes, Kenneth. Radio & Radar in Sail & Power Boats. 120p. 1980. 15.00x (ISBN 0-245-53191-2, Pub. by Nautical England). State Mutual Bk.

Wilkes, Lyall. John Dobson, Architect & Landscape Gardener. 144p. 1980. 30.00 (ISBN 0-85362-181-0). Routledge & Kegan.

Wilkes, M. V. & Needham, R. M. The Cambridge CAP Computer & Its Operating System. (Operating & Programming System Ser.: Vol. 6). 1979. 16.95 (ISBN 0-444-00357-6, North Holland); pap. 9.95 (ISBN 0-444-00358-4). Elsevier.

Wilkes, P. Solid State Theory in Metallurgy. LC 72-180020. (Illus.). 480p. (Orig.). 1973. 68.50 (ISBN 0-521-08454-7); pap. 19.95x (ISBN 0-521-09699-5). Cambridge U Pr.

Wilkes, Paul. Six American Families. (Orig.). 1977. pap. 1.95 (ISBN 0-8164-2142-0). Crossroad NY.

Wilkes, Peter, ed. Christianity Challenges the University. 108p. 1981. pap. 3.95 (ISBN 0-87784-474-7). Inter Varsity.

Wilkie, James W. The Mexican Revolution: Federal Expenditure & Social Change Since 1910. 2nd rev ed. LC 74-103072. 1970. 21.50x (ISBN 0-520-01919-9); pap. 5.50x (ISBN 0-520-01869-9, CAMPUS36). U of Cal Pr.

Wilkie, James W., ed. Statistical Abstract of Latin America 1981, Vol. 21. LC 56-63569. 1981. lib. bdg. price not set (ISBN 0-87903-239-1). UCLA Lat Am Ctr.

Wilkie, James W., et al, eds. Contemporary Mexico: Papers of the Fourth International Congress of Mexican History. 1976. 42.50x (ISBN 0-520-02798-1); pap. 16.75x (ISBN 0-520-02871-6, CAMPUS 144). U of Cal Pr.

Wilkie, Jane. Confessions of an Ex-Fan Magazine Writer. LC 80-780. (Illus.). 324p. 1981. 12.95 (ISBN 0-385-15921-8). Doubleday.

Wilkie, W. E. The Cardinal Protectors of England, Rome & the Tudors Before the Reformation. LC 73-82462. 224p. 1974. 35.50 (ISBN 0-521-20332-5). Cambridge U Pr.

Wilkin, Binnie T. Survival Themes in Fiction for Children & Young People. LC 77-14295. 1978. 12.00 (ISBN 0-8108-1048-4). Scarecrow.

Wilkin, David. Caring for the Mentally Handicapped Child. 192p. 1980. 30.00x (ISBN 0-85664-648-2, Pub. by Croom Helm England). State Mutual Bk.

Wilkin, Eloise, illus. Baby Listens. (Baby's First Golden Bks.). (Illus.). 8p. (ps). Date not set. 1.25 (ISBN 0-307-10754-X, Golden Pr). Western Pub.

--Baby Looks. (Baby's First Golden Bks.). (Illus.). 8p. (ps). Date not set. 1.25 (ISBN 0-307-10753-1, Golden Pr). Western Pub.

--Baby's First Christmas. LC 80-80710. (Board Bks). (Illus.). 14p. (ps). 1980. 2.95 (ISBN 0-394-84575-7). Random.

--Eloise Wilkin Four Baby's First Golden Books, 4 bks. (Illus.). (ps). Date not set. boxed set 4.95 (ISBN 0-307-13650-7, Golden Pr). Western Pub.

--How Big Is Baby? (Baby's First Golden Bks.). (Illus.). 8p. (ps). Date not set. 1.25 (ISBN 0-307-10756-6, Golden Pr). Western Pub.

--The Little Book. (Baby's First Golden Bks.). (Illus.). 8p. (ps). Date not set. 1.25 (ISBN 0-307-10755-8, Golden Pr). Western Pub.

--My Goodnight Book. (Golden Sturdy Shape Bk). (Illus.). 14p. 1981. 2.95 (ISBN 0-307-12258-1, Golden Pr). Western Pub.

--Six Little Golden Books by Eloise Wilkin, 6 bks. (Illus.). Date not set. boxed set 4.50 (ISBN 0-307-15517-X, Golden Pr). Western Pub.

Wilkin, Esther. To You from Me. (Golden Book of Picture Postcards Ser.). (Illus.). (ps-4). 1977. pap. 0.95 o.p. (ISBN 0-307-11102-4, Golden Pr). Western Pub.

Wilkin, Leon O., Jr., jt. auth. see Lewis, Benjamin.

Wilkin, Refna. Dental Health. LC 76-9871. (First Books Ser.). (Illus.). 72p. (gr. 4-6). 1976. PLB 4.90 o.p. (ISBN 0-531-00321-3). Watts.

Wilkin, Robert N. The Spirit of the Legal Profession. viii, 178p. 1981. Repr. of 1938 ed. lib. bdg. 18.50x (ISBN 0-8377-1308-0). Rothman.

Wilkinks, Ronald J. The Emerging Church. (To Live Is Christ Ser.). 1981. pap. 4.10 (ISBN 0-697-01760-5). Wm C Brown.

Wilkins. The Unwanted Adventure of Harold Greenhouse. (gr. 3-5). pap. 0.95 o.p. (ISBN 0-590-05410-4, Schol Pap). Schol Bk Serv.

Wilkins, Alfred T., Jr. & Dunn, Joseph. The Real Race. LC 80-85152. (Illus.). 210p. 1981. 10.95 (ISBN 0-938694-04-9). Jordan & Co.

Wilkins, Austin H. Ten Million Acres of Timber: The Remarkable Story of Forest Protection in the Maine Forestry District 1909-1972. (Illus.). xxiv, 312p. 1978. 10.00 (ISBN 0-931474-02-7); pap. 8.95 (ISBN 0-931474-03-5). TBW Bks.

Wilkins, Bruce. Outdoor Recreation. (Brighton Ser. in Recreation & Leisure Studies). 1981. text ed. 15.95x (ISBN 0-89832-015-1). Brighton Pub Co.

Wilkins, D. A. Linguistics in Language Teaching. 250p. 1972. 12.50x o.p. (ISBN 0-262-23060-7). MIT Pr.

--Notional Syllabuses. 1977. pap. text ed. 6.50x (ISBN 0-19-437071-2). Oxford U Pr.

Wilkins, Dennis A., jt. auth. see Jones, David A.

Wilkins, Eliza G. Know Thyself in Greek & Latin Literature. Taran, Leonardo, ed. LC 78-66584. (Ancient Philosophy Ser.: Vol. 28). 111p. 1979. lib. bdg. 13.00 (ISBN 0-8240-9572-3). Garland Pub.

Wilkins, Ernest H., jt. auth. see Nitze, William A.

Wilkins, Ernest J. Impacto Hispanico: Lectures Contemporaneas. LC 78-14336. 1979. pap. text ed. 8.95 (ISBN 0-471-03537-8). Wiley.

Wilkins, Ernest J., jt. auth. see Hansen, Terrence L.

Wilkins, Frances. Growing up During the Norman Conquest. LC 79-56440. (Growing up Ser.). (gr. 7-9). 1980. text ed. 14.95 (ISBN 0-7134-3360-4, Pub. by Batsford England). David & Charles.

--Growing up in Roman Britain. (Growing up Ser.). (Illus.). 72p. (gr. 7 up). 1980. text ed. 14.95 (ISBN 0-7134-0773-5, Pub. by Batsford England). David & Charles.

Wilkins, Francis. Growing up Between the Wars. (Growing Up Ser.). 1979. 16.95 (ISBN 0-7134-0775-1, Pub. by Batsford England). David & Charles.

--Growing up in Tudor Times. (Growing up). 1977. 16.95 (ISBN 0-7134-0479-5, Pub. by Batsford England). David & Charles.

Wilkins, Gregory L. African Influence in the United Nations, 1967-1975: The Politics & Techniques of Gaining Compliance to U. N. Principles & Resolutions. LC 80-5735. 263p. (Orig.). 1981. lib. bdg. 19.25 (ISBN 0-8191-1424-3); pap. text ed. 10.50 (ISBN 0-8191-1425-1). U Pr of Amer.

Wilkins, Kay S., ed. Women's Education in the United States: A Guide to Information Sources. LC 79-54691. (Education Information Guide Ser.: Vol. 4). 1979. 30.00 (ISBN 0-8103-1410-X). Gale.

Wilkins, Leslie T., jt. ed. see Carter, Robert M.

Wilkins, Lester. How to Build Plastic Ship Models. Angle, Burr, ed. LC 80-82496. (Illus.). 64p. (Orig.). 1980. pap. 6.25 (ISBN 0-89024-552-5). Kalmbach.

Wilkins, Nigel. One Hundred Ballades. LC 69-10342. 1969. 42.00 (ISBN 0-521-07146-1). Cambridge U Pr.

Wilkins, Robert H. Cerbral Arterial Spasm: Proceedings of Second International Workshop. (Illus.). 706p. 1981. write for info. (ISBN 0-683-09086-0). Williams & Wilkins.

Wilkins, Robert P. & Wilkins, Wynona H. North Dakota. (States & the Nation Ser.). (Illus.). 1977. 12.95 (ISBN 0-393-05655-4, Co-Pub by AASLH). Norton.

Wilkins, Ronald J. Achieving Social Justice: A Christian Perspective. (To Live Is Christ Ser.). 1981. pap. text ed. 4.10 (ISBN 0-697-01775-3). Wm C Brown.

--Challenge! rev. ed. (To Live Is Christ Ser). 1978. pap. 4.10 (ISBN 0-697-01683-8). Wm C Brown.

--Christian Faith: The Challenge of the Call. 72p. 1978. pap. 3.00 (ISBN 0-697-01688-9); tchr's. manual 3.50 (ISBN 0-697-01689-7). Wm C Brown.

--Focus on Faith in Jesus. (To Live in Christ Ser.). 1980. pap. 3.75 (ISBN 0-697-01719-2); parish ed. 3.00 (ISBN 0-697-01720-6). Wm C Brown.

--The Jesus Book: Short Ed. (To Live Is Christ Ser.). 112p. 1979. pap. 3.00 (ISBN 0-697-01695-1). Wm C Brown.

--Reading the New Testament. (To Live Is Christ Ser). 160p. 1978. pap. 3.80 extended study (ISBN 0-697-01672-2); pap. 3.00 short edition (ISBN 0-697-01673-0). Wm C Brown.

--Religion in North America. (To Live Is Christ Ser.). 208p. 1979. pap. text ed. 4.10 (ISBN 0-697-01701-X). Wm C Brown.

--The Religions of the World. rev. ed. (To Live Is Christ Ser.). 240p. 1979. pap. 4.25 (ISBN 0-697-01715-X). Wm C Brown.

--Understanding Christian Morality. (To Live Is Christ Ser). 256p. 1977. pap. 4.25 (ISBN 0-697-01660-9). Wm C Brown.

--Understanding Christian Morality: Short Edition. (To Live Is Christ Ser.). 112p. 1977. pap. 3.25 (ISBN 0-697-01661-7). Wm C Brown.

--Understanding Christian Worship: Extended Edition. (To Live Is Christ Ser.). 216p. 1977. pap. 4.10 (ISBN 0-697-01662-5). Wm C Brown.

--Understanding Christian Worship: Short Edition. (To Live Is Christ Ser.). 80p. 1977. pap. 3.00 (ISBN 0-697-01663-3); tchr's ed. 3.50 (ISBN 0-697-01669-2). Wm C Brown.

--Understanding the Bible: Extended Edition. (To Live Is Christ Ser). 212p. 1977. pap. 4.10 (ISBN 0-697-01658-7). Wm C Brown.

Wilkins, Rose, ed. see Wongrey, Jan.

Wilkins, Sophie, tr. see Cobler, Sebastian.

Wilkins, Thurman. Cherokee Tragedy. LC 73-92077. 1970. 10.00 o.s.i. (ISBN 0-02-628670-X). Macmillan.

Wilkins, Tony. Do-It-Yourself Home Projects. (Illus.). 1971. 5.75 o.p. (ISBN 0-258-96782-X). Transatlantic.

Wilkins, W. J. Modern Hinduism: An Account of the Religion & Life of the Hindus. 2nd ed. 1975. text ed. 12.50x (ISBN 0-7007-0046-3). Humanities.

Wilkins, Wynona H., jt. auth. see Wilkins, Robert P.

Wilkinson. Uniforms & Weapons of the Crimean War. pap. 14.95 (ISBN 0-7134-0666-6). David & Charles.

Wilkinson, et al. Clinical Anesthesia: Case Selections from the University of California, San Francisco. LC 79-23938. (Illus.). 1980. 37.50 (ISBN 0-8016-3423-7). Mosby.

Wilkinson, B. The High Middle Ages in England, 1154-1377. LC 77-8490. (Conference on British Studies Bibliographical Handbooks). 1978. 15.50x (ISBN 0-521-21732-6). Cambridge U Pr.

Wilkinson, Barry. Diverting Adventures of Tom Thumb. LC 74-140867. (Illus.). (gr. 3-6). 1969. 4.95 o.p. (ISBN 0-15-201620-1, HJ). HarBraceJ.

Wilkinson, Bertie. Later Middle Ages in England: 1216-1485. LC 73-78343. (History of England Ser.). 1977. pap. text ed. 11.50x (ISBN 0-582-48032-9). Longman.

Wilkinson, Bruce W. Trends in Canada's Mineral Trade. 64p. (Orig.). 1978. pap. text ed. 3.50x (ISBN 0-686-63145-5, Pub. by Ctr Resource Stud Canada). Renouf.

Wilkinson, Bud. Sports Illustrated Football Defense. 1973. 5.95 (ISBN 0-397-00833-3); pap. 2.95 (ISBN 0-397-00993-3). Lippincott.

--Sports Illustrated Football Quarterback. LC 75-17678. (Sports Illustrated Ser). (Illus.). 1976. 5.95 (ISBN 0-397-01097-4); pap. 2.95 (ISBN 0-397-01105-9). Lippincott.

Wilkinson, Bud & Sports Illustrated Editors. Sports Illustrated Football Offense. LC 72-2924. (Illus.). 1972. 5.95 (ISBN 0-397-00834-1); pap. 2.95 (ISBN 0-397-00910-0, LP-69). Lippincott.

Wilkinson, Burke. Cardinal in Armor: The Story of Richelieu & His Times. (gr. 7 up). 1966. 4.50g o.s.i. (ISBN 0-02-792930-2). Macmillan.

--Young Louis Fourteenth: The Early Years of the Sun King. LC 70-89596. (Illus.). (gr. 7 up). 1970. 4.95g o.s.i. (ISBN 0-02-792960-4). Macmillan.

Wilkinson, C. H., ed. see Carew, Bampfylde-Moore.

Wilkinson, C. W. & Clarke, Peter B. Communicating Through Letters & Reports. 7th ed. 1980. 17.95x (ISBN 0-256-02270-4). Irwin.

Wilkinson, Catherine. The Hospital of Cardinal Tavera Toledo. LC 76-23660. (Outstanding Dissertations in the Fine Arts Ser.). (Illus.). 1977. lib. bdg. 63.00x (ISBN 0-8240-2739-6). Garland Pub.

Wilkinson, Charles F., jt. auth. see Coggins, George C.

Wilkinson, D., ed. Proceedings of the International School of Nuclear Physics, Erice, 2-14 Sept. 1976. (Progress in Particle & Nuclear Physics Ser.: Vol. 1). 1979. 81.00 (ISBN 0-08-020327-2). Pergamon.

Wilkinson, D. R., jt. ed. see Bakker, Jan.

Wilkinson, David. Deadly Quarrels: Lewis F. Richardson & the Statistical Study of War. 1980. 18.50 (ISBN 0-520-03829-0). U of Cal Pr.

Wilkinson, Denys, ed. Progress in Particle & Nuclear Physics, Vol. 3. 1980. 81.00 (ISBN 0-08-025020-3). Pergamon.

--Progress in Particle & Nuclear Physics, Vol. 4. (Illus.). 600p. 1980. 81.00 (ISBN 0-08-025039-4). Pergamon.

Wilkinson, Doris Y. & Taylor, Ronald L., eds. The Black Male in America: Perspectives on His Status in Contemporary Society. LC 76-44310. 1977. 18.95 (ISBN 0-88229-227-7); pap. 9.95 (ISBN 0-88229-409-1). Nelson-Hall.

Wilkinson, Elizabeth, jt. auth. see Henderson, Marjorie.

Wilkinson, Elizabeth M., ed. see Mann, Thomas.

Wilkinson, Endymion P. Studies in Chinese Price History. LC 78-24799. (The Modern Chinese Economy Ser.). 285p. 1980. lib. bdg. 31.00 (ISBN 0-8240-4257-3). Garland Pub.

Wilkinson, Faye, jt. auth. see Walton, Sally.

Wilkinson, Frank. Bygones. 540p. 1981. 14.95 (ISBN 0-399-12572-8). Putnam.

Wilkinson, Frederick. Collecting Military Antiques. LC 74-15858. (Illus.). 192p. 1976. 14.95 o.s.i. (ISBN 0-06-014661-3, HarpT). Har-Row.

Wilkinson, Frederick, jt. ed. see Windrow, Martin.

Wilkinson, Gene L. Media in Instruction: Sixty Years of Research. 52p. (Orig.). 1980. pap. 5.95 (ISBN 0-89240-041-2, 0-89240-041-2). Assn Ed Comm Tech.

Wilkinson, Geoffrey, jt. auth. see Cotton, Albert F.

Wilkinson, Hiran P. Family in Classical China. (Studies in Chinese History & Civilization). 239p. 1977. Repr. of 1926 ed. 19.50 (ISBN 0-89093-085-6). U Pubns Amer.

Wilkinson, J., jt. auth. see Goudie, A.

Wilkinson, J. B. Laredo & the Rio Grande Frontier. LC 75-27031. (Illus.). 476p. 1975. 14.95 o.p. (ISBN 0-8363-0134-X). Jenkins.

Wilkinson, J. C. Water & Tribal Settlements in South-East Arabia: A Study of Aflaj of Oman. (Oxford Research Studies in Geography). (Illus.). 1977. 37.50x (ISBN 0-19-823217-9). Oxford U Pr.

Wilkinson, J. F. Don't Raise Your Child to Be a Fat Adult. 1981. Repr. pap. 2.50 (ISBN 0-451-09902-8, E9902, Sig). NAL.

Wilkinson, J. Harvie, ed. From Brown to Bakke: The Supreme Court & School Integration, 1954-1978. (A Galaxy Book: No. 634). 378p. 1981. pap. 6.95 (ISBN 0-19-502897-X). Oxford U Pr.

Wilkinson, J. Harvie, 3rd. Harry Byrd & the Changing Face of Virginia Politics, 1945-1966. LC 68-22731. (Illus.). 410p. 1968. 10.95x (ISBN 0-8139-0239-8). U Pr of Va.

Wilkinson, James H. Algebraic Eigenvalue Problem. (Monographs on Numerical Analysis Ser). 1965. 79.00x (ISBN 0-19-853403-5). Oxford U Pr.

Wilkinson, John F., jt. auth. see Taylor, Gerard W.

Wilkinson, Joseph W. Accounting with the Computer: A Practice Case & Simulation. 3rd ed. 1975. pap. text ed. 8.95 (ISBN 0-256-01659-3). Irwin.

Wilkinson, Jule. Complete Book of Cooking Equipment. 2nd ed. LC 80-16554. 336p. 1980. 21.50 (ISBN 0-8436-2186-9). CBI Pub.

--Country, Colonial Themes. 1969. pap. 10.95 (ISBN 0-8436-0515-4). CBI Pub.

--Seasoning Cookbook. LC 80-14412. (Illus.). 208p. 1980. spiral bd. 16.95 (ISBN 0-8436-2188-5). CBI Pub.

--Three C's of Atmosphere. 1971. pap. 8.95 (ISBN 0-686-69418-X). CBI Pub.

Wilkinson, Jule & Amendola, Joseph. Professional Chef's Baking Recipes. (Illus.). 1974. pap. 8.95 (ISBN 0-8436-0526-X). CBI Pub.

Wilkinson, Jule, ed. The Anatomy of Food Service Design 1. LC 75-5730. (Illus.). 224p. 1975. 21.50 (ISBN 0-8436-0569-3). CBI Pub.

--Anatomy of Food Service Design 2. LC 75-5730. (Illus.). 1978. 21.50 (ISBN 0-8436-2105-2). CBI Pub.

--Making the Most of Fruit on Foodservice Menus. LC 76-51342. (Foodservice Menu Planning Ser.). (Illus.). 1977. 15.95 (ISBN 0-8436-2150-8). CBI Pub.

--Selected Recipes from Ivy Award Winners. 272p. 1976. 16.95 (ISBN 0-8436-2069-2). CBI Pub.

--Special Atmosphere Themes for Foodservice. LC 78-184740. 1972. 10.95 (ISBN 0-8436-0536-7). CBI Pub.

Wilkinson, Jule, ed. see Snider, Nancy.

Wilkinson, L., jt. auth. see Waterson, A. P.

Wilkinson, L. P. Georgics of Virgil. LC 75-79058. 1969. 55.00 (ISBN 0-521-07450-9); pap. 12.50 (ISBN 0-521-29323-5). Cambridge U Pr.

--Golden Latin Artistry. 1963. 42.00 (ISBN 0-521-06807-X). Cambridge U Pr.

--Horace & His Lyric Poetry. 1957. pap. 6.95 (ISBN 0-521-09527-1). Cambridge U Pr.

Wilkinson, L. P., ed. & tr. Letters of Cicero: A Selection in Translations. 1966. text ed. 4.50x (ISBN 0-09-078690-4, Hutchinson U Lib). Humanities.

Wilkinson, Linda. Cinnamon Clouds. LC 78-55222. 1979. padded gift ed. 8.95 (ISBN 0-89081-139-3, 1393). Harvest Hse.

--Peppermint Dreams. gift ed. LC 77-81667. 1977. lib. bdg. 8.95 (ISBN 0-89081-070-2). Harvest Hse.

Wilkinson, Loren, ed. Earthkeeping: Christian Stewardship of Natural Resources. 2nd ed. (Orig.). 1980. pap. 10.95 (ISBN 0-8028-1834-X). Eerdmans.

Wilkinson, M., jt. auth. see Russell, R. R.

Wilkinson, Martin. Children & Divorce. (Practice of Social Work Ser.: No. 6). 288p. 1981. 25.00x (ISBN 0-631-12514-0, Pub. by Basil Blackwell England); pap. 12.50x (ISBN 0-631-12524-8). Biblio Dist.

Wilkinson, Norman B. Bibliography of Pennsylvania History. LC 58-9079. 1957. 10.00 (ISBN 0-911124-07-1). Pa Hist & Mus.

Wilkinson, Paul. Political Terrorism. LC 74-18470. 1976. pap. text ed. 12.95 (ISBN 0-470-98957-2). Halsted Pr.

--Terrorism & the Liberal State. LC 78-53992. 1979. pap. 6.00x usa (ISBN 0-8147-9184-0). NYU Pr.

--Terrorism & the Liberal State. LC 77-12115. 1978. 18.95 (ISBN 0-470-99313-8). Halsted Pr.

Wilkinson, Philip, jt. auth. see Grace, Clive.

Wilkinson, R. E. & Jaques, Harry E. How to Know the Weeds. 3rd ed. (Picture Key Nature Ser.). 256p. 1979. cloth ed. write for info. (ISBN 0-697-04764-4); wire coil bdg. write for info. (ISBN 0-697-04765-2). Wm C Brown.

Wilkinson, Robert E. Camps: Their Planning & Management. (Illus.). 299p. 1981. text ed. 15.95 (ISBN 0-8016-5550-1). Mosby.

Wilkinson, Sarah. Reuven Rubin. LC 72-166215. (Contemporary Art & Artists Ser.). (Illus.). 252p. 1974. 65.00 o.p. (ISBN 0-8109-0463-2); ltd. ed. signed 500.00 o.p. (ISBN 0-686-67060-4). Abrams.

Wilkinson, Sylvia. Can-Am. (World of Racing Ser.). (Illus.). 48p. (gr. 4 up). 1981. PLB 9.25 (ISBN 0-516-04710-8). Childrens.

--Endurance Cars. (World of Racing Ser.). (Illus.). 48p. (gr. 4 up). 1981. PLB 9.25 (ISBN 0-516-04712-4). Childrens.

--Stock Cars. (World of Racing Ser.). (Illus.). 48p. (gr. 4 up). 1981. PLB 9.25 (ISBN 0-516-04715-9). Childrens.

--Super Vee. (World of Racing Ser.). (Illus.). 48p. (gr. 4 up). 1981. PLB 9.25 (ISBN 0-516-04714-0). Childrens.

Wilkinson, Tate. The Wandering Patentee, 4 vols. in 2 vols. facsimile ed. 1973. Repr. of 1795 ed. Set. 20.00x o.p. (ISBN 0-85967-123-2, Pub. by Scolar Pr England). Biblio Dist.

Wilkinson, Theon. Two Monsoons. (Illus.). 240p. 1976. 13.50x (ISBN 0-7156-1015-5, Pub. by Duckworth England). Biblio Dist.

Wilkinson-Latham, Christopher, jt. auth. see Wilkinson-Latham, Robert.

Wilkinson-Latham, Robert. Cycles in Color. (Illus.). 1978. 11.95 (ISBN 0-7137-0853-0, Pub. by Blandford Pr England). Sterling.

Wilkinson-Latham, Robert & Wilkinson-Latham, Christopher. Cavalry Uniforms of Britain & the Commonwealth. (Color Ser.). (Illus.). 1969. 9.95 (ISBN 0-7137-0134-X, Pub by Blandford Pr England). Sterling.

--Infantry Uniforms of Britain & the Commonwealth in Color, 1855-1939. LC 79-95304. (World Uniforms in Color Ser). 1971. 8.90 (ISBN 0-02-628730-7). Macmillan.

Wilkomirsky, I., jt. auth. see Coudurier, L.

Wilks, I. Asante in the Nineteenth Century. LC 74-77834. (African Studies: No. 13). (Illus.). 872p. 1975. 69.50 (ISBN 0-521-20463-1). Cambridge U Pr.

Wilks, John. Properties of Liquid & Solid Helium. (International Series of Monographs on Physics). 1967. 74.00x (ISBN 0-19-851245-7). Oxford U Pr.

Wilks, Mark & Hammick, Murry. Historical Sketches of the South Indian History, 4 vols. Incl. Vol. 1. 453p; Vol. 2. 397p; Vol. 3. 335p; Vol. 4. 482p. 1980. Repr. of 1817 ed. 24.50 (ISBN 0-89684-265-7, Pub. by Cosmo Pubns India). Orient Bk Dist.

Wilks, Rick J. & Millyard, Anne W. Getting Along. LC 80-65478. 1978. pap. 4.40 (ISBN 0-8224-3377-X). Pitman Learning.

Wilks, Robin J. Principles of Radiological Physics. (Illus.). 528p. 1981. pap. text ed. 37.50 (ISBN 0-443-02035-3). Churchill.

Wilks, Ronald, tr. see Chekhov, Anton.

Wilks, Ronald, tr. see Gorky, Maxim.

Will & Nicholas. Chaga. LC 55-7615. (Illus.). (gr. k-3). 1945. 4.95 o.p. (ISBN 0-15-215894-4, HJ). HarBraceJ.

Will, Ed. Red Blood at White River. (Orig.). 1980. pap. 1.75 (ISBN 0-532-23143-0). Manor Bks.

Will, Frederic. The Fact of Literature: Three Essays on Public Material. 215p. (Orig.). 1973. pap. text ed. 20.00x (ISBN 9-0620-3377-6). Humanities.

--From a Year in Greece. (Illus.). 1967. 11.50 (ISBN 0-292-73664-9). U of Tex Pr.

--The Generic Demands of Greek Literature. 1976. pap. text ed. 14.25x (ISBN 90-6203-447-0). Humanities.

--Herondas. (World Authors Ser.: Greece: No. 227). lib. bdg. 10.95 (ISBN 0-8057-2420-6). Twayne.

Will, George F. The Pursuit of Happiness, & Other Sobering Thoughts. LC 77-6898. 1978. 10.95 o.s.i. (ISBN 0-06-014663-X, HarpT). Har-Row.

Will, George F. & Hyde, George E. Corn Among the Indians of the Upper Missouri. LC 64-63592. 323p. 1964. 14.50x (ISBN 0-8032-0892-8); pap. 3.95 (ISBN 0-8032-5846-1, BB 195, Bison). U of Nebr Pr.

Will, James E. Must Walls Divide? The Creative Witness of the Churches in Europe. (Orig.). 1981. pap. 3.75 (ISBN 0-377-00106-6). Friend Pr.

Will, Margaret T. Recycled Buildings: A Bibliography of Adaptive Use Literature Since Nineteen Seventy. (Architecture Ser.: Bibliography A-154). 71p. 1979. pap. 7.50 (ISBN 0-686-26957-8). Vance Biblios.

Will, Paul J., et al. Public Education Religion Studies: An Overview. Taylor, Mark, ed. LC 80-12237. (Aids for the Study of Religion Ser.). 1981. write for info. (ISBN 0-89130-401-0); pap. write for info. (ISBN 0-89130-402-9). Scholars Pr CA.

Will, R. Ted, jt. auth. see Hasty, Ronald W.

Will, Robin. Adventures in Oregon Country. Shangle, Robert D., ed. LC 79-28595. 64p. Date not set. pap. 4.95 (ISBN 0-89802-064-6). Beautiful Am.

--Adventures in Washington Country. Shangle, Robert D., ed. (Illus.). 64p. 1981. pap. 4.95 (ISBN 0-89802-065-4). Beautiful Am.

--Beautiful Dallas. Shangle, Robert D., ed. LC 80-18361. (Illus.). 72p. 1980. 14.95 (ISBN 0-89802-098-0); pap. 7.95 (ISBN 0-89802-097-2). Beautiful Am.

--Beautiful Minnesota. 72p. 1978. write for info. (ISBN 0-915796-61-9); pap. write for info. (ISBN 0-915796-60-0). Beautiful Am.

--Beautiful Nevada. Shangle, Robert D., ed. (Illus.). 72p. 1981. 14.95 (ISBN 0-89802-101-4); pap. 7.95 (ISBN 0-89802-100-6). Beautiful Am.

--Beautiful Ohio. LC 78-9935. 72p. 1980. 14.95 (ISBN 0-915796-77-5); pap. 7.95 (ISBN 0-915796-76-7). Beautiful Am.

--Beautiful Portland. Shangle, Robert D., ed. LC 79-778. 72p. 1979. 14.95 (ISBN 0-915796-91-0); pap. 7.95 (ISBN 0-915796-90-2). Beautiful Am.

--Beautiful Tennessee. (Illus.). 72p. 1981. 14.95 (ISBN 0-89802-103-0); pap. 7.95 (ISBN 0-89802-102-2). Beautiful Am.

--Beautiful Texas. Shangle, Robert D., ed. LC 78-23422. (Illus.). 72p. 1978. 14.95 (ISBN 0-915796-75-9); pap. 7.95 (ISBN 0-915796-74-0). Beautiful Am.

--Beautiful Yosemite National Park. LC 79-15850. (Illus.). 80p. 14.95 (ISBN 0-89802-069-7); pap. 7.95 (ISBN 0-89802-068-9). Beautiful Am.

Will, Thomas E. Telecommunications Structure & Management in the Executive Branch of Government: 1900-1970. 1978. lib. bdg. 25.50x (ISBN 0-89158-286-X). Westview.

Will, W. Marvin, jt. ed. see Millett, Richard.

Willan, Ann. Entertaining: Complete Menus for All Occasions. (Illus.). 216p. 1981. 22.50 (ISBN 0-7134-3408-2, Pub. by Batsford England). David & Charles.

Willan, Anne. LaVarenne's Basic French Cookery. (Orig.). 1980. 12.95 (ISBN 0-89586-086-4); pap. 7.95 (ISBN 0-89586-056-2). H P Bks.

--LaVarenne's Basic French Cookery. 1980. 12.95 (ISBN 0-89586-086-4). H P Bks.

--Paris Kitchen: An Introduction to the La Varenne Cooking School. LC 80-27346. (Illus.). 288p. 1981. price not set (ISBN 0-688-00411-3). Morrow.

Willans, Geoffrey & Searle, Ronald. Molesworth Back in the Jug Agane. (Illus.). 1959. 4.95 o.s.i. (ISBN 0-8149-0235-9). Vanguard.

--Molesworth's Guide to the Atommic Age. (Illus.). 4.95 o.s.i. (ISBN 0-8149-0234-0). Vanguard.

Willard, Barbara. The Iron Lily. LC 74-7195. 176p. (gr. 5-7). 1974. PLB 5.95 o.p. (ISBN 0-525-32592-1). Dutton.

--Richleighs of Tantamount. LC 67-16229. (Illus.). (gr. 6-8). 1966. 5.50 o.p. (ISBN 0-15-266750-4, HJ). HarBraceJ.

--Surprise Island. (Illus.). 112p. (gr. 3-6). 1981. 7.95 (ISBN 0-525-66734-2). Elsevier-Nelson.

Willard, Barbara, ed. Happy Families. LC 73-22433. (Illus.). 256p. (gr. 5 up). 1974. 6.95g o.s.i. (ISBN 0-02-793010-6). Macmillan.

Willard, Beatrice L. & Raese, Jon W. Plant Sociology of Alpine Tundra, Trail Ridge, Rocky Mountain National Park, Colorado. LC 79-26590. (CSM Quarterly Ser.: Vol. 74, No. 4). (Illus.). 119p. 1979. pap. 10.00x (ISBN 0-686-63162-5). Colo Sch Mines.

Willard, Charlotte. Frank Lloyd Wright. LC 71-188775. (Illus.). (gr. 7 up). 1972. 8.95 (ISBN 0-02-793070-X). Macmillan.

Willard, Dan E. Predicate-Oriented Database Search Algorithms. LC 79-50230. (Outstanding Dissertations in the Computer Sciences). 1980. lib. bdg. 34.00 (ISBN 0-8240-4405-3). Garland Pub.

Willard, Frances E. & Livermore, Mary A. American Women: American Women: Fifteen Hundred Biographies with Over Fourteen Hundred Portraits, 2 vols. LC 73-7985. Orig. Title: Woman of the Century. 824p. 1974. Repr. of 1897 ed. Set. 68.00 (ISBN 0-8103-3225-6). Gale.

Willard, Hildegard, jt. auth. see Bower, Wilma.

Willard, Hobarth, et al. Instrumental Methods of Analysis. 6th ed. Date not set. text ed. price not set (ISBN 0-442-24502-5). D Van Nostrand.

Willard, Mildred W. The Ice Cream Cone. (Beginning to Read Ser). (Illus.). 32p. (gr. 1-3). 1973. 2.50 o.p. (ISBN 0-695-80418-9); PLB 3.39 o.p. (ISBN 0-695-40418-0). Follett.

Willard, Nancy. Carpenter of the Sun. 55p. 1974. 6.95 o.p. (ISBN 0-87140-602-0); pap. 2.50 o.p. (ISBN 0-87140-098-7). Liveright.

--The Marzipan Moon. LC 80-24221. (Illus.). 48p. (ps-3). 1981. pap. 4.95 (ISBN 0-15-252963-2, VoyB). HarBraceJ.

--The Marzipan Moon. LC 80-24221. (Illus.). 48p. (ps-3). 1981. 9.95 (ISBN 0-15-252962-4, HJ). HarBraceJ.

Willard, Stephen. General Topology. LC 74-100890. 1970. text ed. 19.95 (ISBN 0-201-08707-3). A-W.

Willardson, R. K. & Beer, A. C., eds. Semiconductors & Semimetals. Incl. Vol. 1. Physics of III-V Compounds. 1967. 52.75 (ISBN 0-12-752101-1); Vol. 2. Physics of III-V Compounds. 1966. 52.75 (ISBN 0-12-752102-X); Vol. 3. Optical Properties of III-V Compounds. 1967. 52.75 (ISBN 0-12-752103-8); Vol. 4. Physics of III-V Compounds. 1968. 52.75 (ISBN 0-12-752104-6); Vol. 5. Infrared Detectors. 1970. 52.75 (ISBN 0-12-752105-4); Vol. 6. Injection Phenomena. 1970. 52.75 (ISBN 0-12-752106-2); Vol. 7A. Semiconductor Applications & Devices. 1971. 52.75 (ISBN 0-12-752107-0); Vol. 7B. Applications & Devices. 1971. 52.75 (ISBN 0-12-752147-X); Vol. 8. Techniques for Studying Semiconducting Materials. 1971. 52.75 (ISBN 0-12-752108-9); Vol. 9. Modulation Techniques. 1972. 52.75 (ISBN 0-12-752109-7); Vol. 10. 1975. 52.75 (ISBN 0-12-752110-0); Vol. 11. 1976. 52.75 (ISBN 0-685-23206-9); Vol. 12. 1977. 50.50 (ISBN 0-12-752112-7). Acad Pr.

Willardson, R. K., et al, eds. Semiconductors & Semimetals: Cadmium Telluride. 1978. Vol. 13. 28.00 (ISBN 0-12-752113-5); Vol. 14. 1979. 32.00 (ISBN 0-12-752114-3). Acad Pr.

Willardson, Robert & Beer, A. C., eds. Semiconductors & Semimetals: Contacts, Junctions, Emitters, Vol. 15. 1981. price not set (ISBN 0-12-752115-1). Acad Pr.

Willauer, George J., Jr., ed. A Lyme Miscellany, 1776-1976. LC 76-41483. 1977. 20.00x (ISBN 0-8195-5009-4, Pub. by Wesleyan U Pr). Columbia U Pr.

Willbanks, Ray. Randolph Stow. (World Authors Ser.: No. 472). 1978. lib. bdg. 12.50 (ISBN 0-8057-6313-9). Twayne.

Willbern, York. Withering Away of the City. LC 63-19642. 136p. 1964. 7.00 o.p. (ISBN 0-8173-4709-7). U of Ala Pr.

Willcock, G. D., ed. see Puttenham, G.

Willcock, Malcolm M. A Companion to the "Iliad". Lattimore, Richmond, tr. LC 75-20894. (Illus.). 302p. 1976. 15.00x (ISBN 0-226-89854-7). U of Chicago Pr.

--A Companion to the "Iliad". LC 75-20894. 1976. pap. 6.95 (ISBN 0-226-89855-5, P677, Phoen). U of Chicago Pr.

Willcocks, Arthur J. Creation of the National Health Service. (Orig.). 1967. text ed. 6.00x (ISBN 0-7100-4021-0); pap. 2.75x (ISBN 0-7100-4024-5). Humanities.

Willcocks, David, ed. Hymns for Choirs. 1976. pap. 5.00 (ISBN 0-19-353556-4). Oxford U Pr.

Willcox, Alfred B., et al. Introduction to Calculus One & Two. 1971. lib. bdg. 24.95 (ISBN 0-395-05543-1, 3-60410). HM.

Willcox, Isobel. Acrobats & Ping-Pong: Young China's Games, Sports, & Amusements. LC 80-22176. (Illus.). 160p. (gr. 4 up). 1981. PLB 8.95 (ISBN 0-396-07917-2). Dodd.

Willcox, L. C., tr. see Girdoux, Jean.

Willcox, Sheila. The Event Horse. LC 73-5923. (Illus.). 160p. 1973. 9.95 (ISBN 0-397-01000-1). Lippincott.

Willcox, William B. see Smith, Lacey B.

Willcutt, J. Robert & Ball, Kenneth R. The Musical Instrument Collector. Brines, Steven F., ed. LC 78-68088. (Illus.). pap. 8.95 (ISBN 0-933224-00-1). Bold Strummer Ltd.

Wille, Fred. The ABC's of Creativity & Language Arts: Teacher's Edition. (gr. 2-8). 1978. 9.95 (ISBN 0-916456-30-7, GA85). Good Apple.

Wille, Lutz & Obladen, Michael. Neonatal Intensive Care: Principles & Guidelines. (Illus.). 300p. 1981. pap. 28.40 (ISBN 0-387-10462-3). Springer-Verlag.

Wille, Wayne, pref. by. The World Book Year Book. LC 62-4818. (Illus.). 608p. (gr. 6-12). 1980. PLB write for info. (ISBN 0-7166-0481-7). World Bk-Childcraft.

Willebrink, George A. The Dossier of Flaubert's un Coeur Simple. 1976. pap. text ed. 37.25x (ISBN 90-6203-409-8). Humanities.

Willeford, George. Cosmetic Surgery May Be for You. (Illus.). 1979. 7.95 (ISBN 0-88319-048-6); pap. 4.50 (ISBN 0-88319-049-4). Shoal Creek Pub.

Willemain, Thomas R. & Larson, Richard C., eds. Urban Public Safety Systems Volume IV. LC 77-80341. (Illus.). 1977. 21.95 (ISBN 0-669-01483-4). Lexington Bks.

Willemen, Paul, jt. auth. see Johnston, Claire.

Willems, Nicholas, et al. Strength of Materials. (Illus.). 576p. 1981. text ed. write for info. (ISBN 0-07-070297-7, C); write for info. solutions manual (ISBN 0-07-070298-5). McGraw.

Willemsen, Eleanor W. Understanding Infancy. LC 78-21181. (Psychology Ser.). (Illus.). 1979. text ed. 16.95x (ISBN 0-7167-1002-1); pap. text ed. 8.95x (ISBN 0-7167-1001-3). W H Freeman.

--Understanding Statistical Reasoning: How to Evaluate Research Literature in the Behavioral Sciences. LC 73-13647. (Psychology Ser.). (Illus.). 1974. text ed. 19.95x (ISBN 0-7167-0838-8); pap. text ed. 9.95x (ISBN 0-7167-0837-X). W H Freeman.

Willener, A. Videology & Utopia: Explorations in a New Medium. (Orig.). 1976. pap. 15.00 (ISBN 0-7100-8435-8). Routledge & Kegan.

Willensky, Elliot, jt. ed. see White, Norval.

Willer, David & Willer, Judith. Systematic Empiricism: Critique of a Pseudoscience. (General Sociology Ser.). (Illus.). 176p. 1973. 13.95 (ISBN 0-13-880351-X). P-H.

Willer, Judith, jt. auth. see Willer, David.

Willerding, M. F. Elementary Mathematics: Its Structure & Concepts. 2nd ed. LC 71-100328. 1970. text ed. 21.95 o.p. (ISBN 0-471-94665-6). Wiley.

Willerding, Margaret F. College Algebra & Trigonometry. 2nd ed. LC 74-22391. 613p. 1975. text ed. 20.95 (ISBN 0-471-94671-0). Wiley.

--Modern Intermediate Algebra. 2nd ed. LC 74-16160. 368p. 1975. text ed. 21.95 (ISBN 0-471-94667-2); instructor's manual avail. (ISBN 0-471-94672-9). Wiley.

Willerding, Margaret F. & Engelsohn, H. S. Mathematics: The Alphabet of Science. 3rd ed. LC 76-48913. 376p. 1977. 21.95 (ISBN 0-471-94653-2); instructors' manual avail. (ISBN 0-471-02388-4). Wiley.

Willerding, Margaret F. & Hoffman, Stephen. College Algebra. LC 72-165951. 1971. text ed. 18.50 o.p. (ISBN 0-471-94657-5). Wiley.

Willerman, Lee. The Psychology of Individual & Group Differences. LC 78-9865. (Psychology Ser.). (Illus.). 1979. text ed. 18.95x (ISBN 0-7167-0292-4). W H Freeman.

Willerman, Lee & Turner, R. Gerald, eds. Readings About Individual & Group Differences. LC 78-13079. (Psychology Ser.). (Illus.). 1979. text ed. 17.95x (ISBN 0-7167-1015-3); pap. text ed. 8.95x (ISBN 0-7167-1014-5). W H Freeman.

Willert, James. The Terry Letters: Private Letters of General Alfred Howe Terry to His Sisters During the Eighteen Seventy-Six Indian War. (Illus.). 78p. 1980. 20.00x (ISBN 0-930798-03-1). J Willert.

Willerton, P. F. Basic Shiphandling for Masters, Mates & Pilots. 152p. 1981. 17.50x (ISBN 0-540-07333-4). Sheridan.

Willet, C. S. Gas Lasers. 1974. text ed. 90.00 (ISBN 0-08-017803-0). Pergamon.

Willet, Shelagh M. & Ambrose, David. Lesotho. (World Bibliographical Ser.: No. 3). 600p. 1980. write for info. (ISBN 0-903450-11-9). Abc-Clio.

Willett, Frank. African Art. (World of Art Ser.). (Illus.). 1971. pap. 9.95 (ISBN 0-19-519948-0). Oxford U Pr.

Willett, John. The Singer in the Stone. (gr. 5-8). 1981. 6.95 (ISBN 0-395-30374-5). HM.

Willett, Ralph. A Memoir on the Origin of Printing. Lew, Irving, ed. (Bibliographical Reprint Ser.). 1980. Repr. of 1820 ed. ltd. ed. 25.00 (ISBN 0-89782-032-0). Battery Pk.

Willett, Roderick & Grattan, Gurney A. Rough Shooting. 3rd ed. (Illus.). 1975. 15.95 o.p. (ISBN 0-571-04850-1, Pub. by Faber & Faber). Merrimack Bk Serv.

Willett, Thomas D. International Liquidity Issues. 1980. pap. 5.25 (ISBN 0-8447-3388-1). Am Enterprise.

Willett, Thomas D., jt. auth. see Officer, Lawrence H.

Willette, R. E., jt. ed. see Stillman, R. C.

Willetts, H. J., jt. auth. see Byrde, R. J.

Willetts, H. T., tr. see Pope John Paul II.

Willetts, R. F. The Civilization of Ancient Crete. 1978. 31.50x (ISBN 0-520-03406-6). U of Cal Pr.

Willey, Basil. Cambridge & Other Memories Nineteen Twenty to Nineteen Fifty-Three. 1968. text ed. 5.25x (ISBN 0-7011-1430-4). Humanities.

--Eighteenth Century Background: Studies on the Idea of Nature in the Thought of the Period. LC 40-31307. 1941. 20.00x (ISBN 0-231-01234-9). Columbia U Pr.

--More Nineteenth-Century Studies: A Group of Honest Doubters. LC 80-40635. 304p. 1981. pap. 9.95 (ISBN 0-521-28067-2). Cambridge U Pr.

--Nineteenth Century Studies: Coleridge to Mathew Arnold. LC 49-50265. 1949. 20.00x (ISBN 0-231-01789-8). Columbia U Pr.

--Nineteenth-Century Studies; Coleridge to Matthew Arnold. LC 80-40634. 288p. 1981. pap. 9.95 (ISBN 0-521-28066-4). Cambridge U Pr.

--Seventeenth Century Background: Studies in the Thought of the Age in Relation to Poetry & Religion. LC 34-21849. 1942. 20.00x (ISBN 0-231-01395-7). Columbia U Pr.

Willey, David. Rome. LC 80-50997. (Rand McNally Pocket Guide Ser.). (Illus.). 1980. pap. 3.95 (ISBN 0-528-84309-5). Rand.

Willey, David, tr. see Fischer, Georges.

Willey, Gordon, ed. Excavations at Seibal. LC 74-77554. (Peabody Museum Memoirs Ser.: No. 13-1&2). (Illus.). 1975. pap. 40.00 (ISBN 0-87365-685-7). Peabody Harvard.

Willey, Gordon R. The Altar De Sacrificios Excavations: General Summary & Conclusions. LC 73-77202. (Peabody Museum Papers: Vol. 64, No. 3). 1973. pap. text ed. 10.00 (ISBN 0-87365-185-5). Peabody Harvard.
--The Artifacts of Altar De Sacrificios. LC 72-93407. (Peabody Museum Papers: Vol. 64, No. 1). pap. text ed. 25.00 (ISBN 0-87365-183-9). Peabody Harvard.
--Introduction to American Archaeology, Vol. 1: North & Middle America. 1966. text ed. 26.95 (ISBN 0-13-477836-7). P-H.
--Introduction to American Archaeology, Vol. 2: South America. (Illus.). 1971. text ed. 26.95 (ISBN 0-13-477851-0). P-H.
--Pre-Columbian Archaeology: Readings from Scientific American. LC 79-26329. (Illus.). 1980. text ed. 19.95x (ISBN 0-7167-1182-6); pap. text ed. 9.95x (ISBN 0-7167-1183-4). W H Freeman.
Willey, Gordon R. & Sabloff, Jeremy A. A History of American Archaeology. 2nd ed. LC 79-23114. (Illus.). 1980. text ed. 16.95x (ISBN 0-7167-1122-2); pap. text ed. 8.95x (ISBN 0-7167-1123-0). W H Freeman.
Willey, Gordon R. & Smith, A. Ledyard. The Ruins of Altar De Sacrificios, Department of Peten, Guatemala: An Introduction. LC 74-82521. (Peabody Museum Papers: Vol. 62, No. 1). 1969. pap. 10.00 (ISBN 0-87365-177-4). Peabody Harvard.
Willey, Keith. When the Sky Fell Down. 231p. 1980. 13.95x (ISBN 0-00-216434-5, Pub. by W Collins Australia). Intl Schol Bk Serv.
Willey, Keith & Smith, Robin. Red Centre: The Landscape and People of Outback Australia. (Illus.). 106p. 1976. 12.00 (ISBN 0-584-97049-8). Transatlantic.
Willey, R. C., jt. auth. see Haxby, J. A.
Willey, Raymond C. Modern Dowsing: The Dowser's Handbook. LC 75-18220. (Illus.). 1975. pap. 6.00 (ISBN 0-89861-005-2). Esoteric Pubns.
Willgoose, Carol. The Curriculum in Physical Education. 3rd ed. (Illus.). 1979. ref. ed. 17.95 (ISBN 0-13-196303-1). P-H.
William Fox Mining Journal Books Ltd. Tin: The Working of a Commodity Agreement. 418p. 1980. 21.00x (ISBN 0-900117-05-2, Pub. by Mining Journal England). State Mutual Bk.
William, Lester. Morality, Anyone? 1975. 7.95 o.p. (ISBN 0-87000-297-X). Arlington Hse.
William, Raymond. Keywords: A Vocabulary of Culture & Society. 1976. pap. 4.95 (ISBN 0-19-519855-7, GB). Oxford U Pr.
William-Ellis, Annabel. Fairy Tales from East & West. (Illus., Orig.). 1978. pap. 2.95 (ISBN 0-8467-0535-4, Pub. by Two Continents). Hippocrene Bks.
William Of Ockman. Philosophical Writings. Boehner, Philotheus, tr. LC 64-16710. pap. 4.95 (ISBN 0-672-60431-0, LLA193). Bobbs.
William Of St. Tierry. The Nature & Dignity of Love. Elder, E. R., ed. Davis, Thomas X., tr. from Lat. (Cistercian Fathers Ser.: No. 30). Orig. Title: De natura et dignitate amoris. 1981. write for info. (ISBN 0-87907-330-6). Cistercian Pubns.
Williams, jt. auth. see Friese, John F.
Williams, jt. auth. see Penland.
Williams, jt. auth. see Ventolo.
Williams & Belov, eds. Titanium & Titanium Alloys: Scientific & Technological Aspects, 3 vols. 1981. 195.00 (ISBN 0-306-40191-6, Plenum Pr). Plenum Pub.
Williams, A. Britain & France in the Middle East & North Africa. 1969. 6.95 (ISBN 0-312-09765-4). St Martin.
Williams, A. F. & Lom, W. L. Liquified Petroleum Gases: A Guide to Properties, Applications & Usage of Propane & Butane. LC 73-15141. (Illus.). 403p. 1973. 65.95 (ISBN 0-470-94850-7). Halsted Pr.
Williams, A. F., jt. auth. see Lom, W. L.
Williams, A. H., jt. auth. see Eales, R. G.
Williams, A. L., et al. Introduction to Chemistry. 2nd ed. 1973. text ed. 18.95 o.p. (ISBN 0-201-08738-3); instr's manual o.p. 2.50 (ISBN 0-201-08744-8). A-W.
Williams, Aaron. The Use of Radar Imagery in Climatological Research. LC 73-82275. (CCG Resource Papers Ser.: No. 21). (Illus.). 1973. pap. text ed. 4.00 (ISBN 0-89291-068-2). Assn Am Geographers.
Williams, Alan. Holy of Holies. 1980. 12.95 (ISBN 0-89256-147-5). Rawson Wade.
Williams, Alan & Anderson, Robert. Efficiency in the Social Services. (Aspects of Social Policy Ser.). 1975. 14.00x (ISBN 0-631-16570-3, Pub. by Basil Blackwell); pap. 12.50x (ISBN 0-631-16580-0). Biblio Dist.
Williams, Alan, jt. auth. see Sugden, Robert.
Williams, Alfred. Folksongs of the Upper Thames. LC 68-31150. 1968. Repr. of 1923 ed. 18.00 (ISBN 0-8103-3421-6). Gale.
--Life in a Railway Factory: London Nineteen Fifteen. LC 79-56941. 1980. lib. bdg. 28.00 (ISBN 0-8240-0126-5). Garland Pub.
Williams, Alise D., jt. auth. see Davis, Frank.
Williams, Allan & Marshall, William. The Man Who Gave the Beatles Away. (Illus.). 1975. 9.95 o.s.i. (ISBN 0-02-629050-2). Macmillan.
Williams, Alvin M., Jr. Conversations at Little Gidding. LC 78-85741. (Illus.). 1970. 58.00 (ISBN 0-521-07680-3). Cambridge U Pr.
Williams, Amelia W. & Barker, Eugene C., eds. Writings of Sam Houston, Eighteen Thirteen to Eighteen Thir y-Six, 8 Vols. Set. 145.00 (ISBN 0-685-13280-3). Jenkins.
Williams, Ann, ed. Prophecy & Millenarianism. (Illus.). 1981. text ed. 60.00 (ISBN 0-582-36136-2). Longman.
Williams, Ann M., ed. Looking at... Important Topics in the Social Studies. LC 80-22709. 90p. (Orig.). 1980. pap. 6.95 (ISBN 0-89994-250-4). Soc Sci Ed.
Williams, Arthur B. Handbook of Electronic Filter Design. 1980. write for info. (ISBN 0-07-070430-9). McGraw.
Williams, Arthur L., et al. Introduction to Chemistry. 3rd ed. (Chemistry Ser.). (Illus.). 896p. 1981. text ed. 21.95 (ISBN 0-201-08726-X). A-W.
--General Chemistry. 2nd ed. LC 73-18784. 1974. text ed. 14.95 (ISBN 0-201-08743-X); instr. manual 2.50 (ISBN 0-201-08744-8). A-W.
--Introduction to Laboratory Chemistry: General. 2nd ed. LC 77-79451. (Chemistry Ser.). 1978. pap. text ed. 8.50 (ISBN 0-201-08458-9). A-W.
--Introduction to Laboratory Chemistry: Organic & Biochemistry. 2nd ed. LC 77-81204. (Chemistry Ser.). 1978. pap. text ed. 8.50 (ISBN 0-201-08459-7). A-W.
Williams, Arthur V., Jr., et al, eds. Self-Assessment of Current Knowledge in Nephrology. 2nd ed. 1976. 14.00 (ISBN 0-87488-280-X). Med Exam.
Williams, B. If He's My Brother. 1980. pap. 2.50 (ISBN 0-13-450627-8). P-H.
Williams, B., jt. auth. see Smart, J. J.
Williams, B. A. Problems of the Self: Philosophical Papers, 1956-1972. 240p. 1973. 35.50 (ISBN 0-521-20225-6); pap. 9.95x (ISBN 0-521-29060-0). Cambridge U Pr.
Williams, B. J. Evolution & Human Origins: An Introduction to Physical Anthropology. 2nd ed. (Illus.). 1979. text ed. 12.95 scp (ISBN 0-06-047121-2, HarpC). Har-Row.
Williams, B. R., ed. Science & Technology in Economic Growth: Proceedings of a Conference Held by the International Economic Association at St. Anton, Austria. LC 72-14227. (International Economic Association Ser.). 1973. 26.95 (ISBN 0-470-94679-2). Halsted Pr.
Williams, Barbara. Breakthrough: Women in Archaeology. LC 80-7687. (Breakthrough Ser.). (Illus.). 190p. (gr. 5 up). 1981. 9.95 (ISBN 0-8027-6406-1). Walker & Co.
--Chester Chipmunk's Thanksgiving. LC 77-20812. (Illus.). (gr. k-3). 1978. PLB 7.95 (ISBN 0-525-27655-6). Dutton.
--Cornzapoppin! Popcorn Recipes & Party Ideas for All Occasions. LC 75-28329. (Illus.). 160p. (gr. 6-12). 1976. 5.95 o.p. (ISBN 0-03-015166-X); pap. 2.95 (ISBN 0-03-053526-3). HR&W.
--Guess Who's Coming to My Tea Party. LC 77-10548. (ps-1). 1978. 5.95 o.p. (ISBN 0-03-021541-2). HR&W.
--Seven True Elephant Stories. (Illus.). (gr. 3-6). 1977. 6.95 (ISBN 0-8038-6746-8). Hastings.
--So What If I'm a Sore Loser? LC 80-24783. (Illus.). 48p. (ps-3). 1981. 8.95 (ISBN 0-15-277260-X, HJ). HarBraceJ.
--A Valentine for Cousin Archie. LC 80-181. (Illus.). 32p. (gr. k-3). 1981. PLB 8.95 (ISBN 0-525-41930-6). Dutton.
--Women in Archaeology. 174p. 1981. 9.95. Walker & Co.
Williams, Barbara A., jt. auth. see Giles, Carl H.
Williams, Basil. Whig Supremacy, 1714-1760. 2nd ed. Stuart, C. H., ed. (Oxford History of England Ser.). 1962. 33.00x (ISBN 0-19-821710-2). Oxford U Pr.
Williams, Benjamin H. Economic Foreign Policy of the United States. 1967. Repr. 19.00 (ISBN 0-86527-051-1). Fertig.
Williams, Bill. A Sampler on Sampling. LC 77-23839. (Probability & Mathematical Statistics Ser.). 1978. 19.95 (ISBN 0-471-03036-8, Pub. by Wiley-Interscience). Wiley.
Williams, Bill, jt. auth. see Lipscombe, Joan.
Williams, Bill, illus. Winnie the Pooh All Year Long. (Golden Sturdy Shape Bks.). (Illus.). 14p. 1981. 2.95 (ISBN 0-307-12260-3, Golden Pr). Western Pub.
Williams, Bill R. & Crotts, Gwen. Man's Mathematical Models: Fundamental Concepts for the Nonmathematician. LC 73-93104. 1975. 15.95 (ISBN 0-88229-110-6). Nelson-Hall.
Williams, Brad. Legendary Women of the West. (Illus.). (gr. 7 up). 1978. 7.95 o.p. (ISBN 0-679-20776-7). McKay.
Williams, Brian. Exploring Under the Sea. (Explorer Books). (Illus.). (gr. 3-5). 1979. 2.95 (ISBN 0-531-09133-3); PLB 6.45 s&l (ISBN 0-531-09118-X). Watts.
--Exploring War & Weapons. (Explorer Books). (Illus.). (gr. 3-5). 1979. 2.95 (ISBN 0-531-09132-5); PLB 6.45 s&l (ISBN 0-531-09117-1). Watts.
--Inventions & Discoveries. (Skylark Bks.). (Illus.). (gr. 5 up). 1979. 4.95 (ISBN 0-685-65720-5); PLB 7.90 s&l (ISBN 0-531-09112-0). Watts.
Williams, Brian, jt. auth. see Storrer, Philip.
Williams, Bruce, jt. auth. see Gray, Virginia.
Williams, C. A. Outlines of Chinese Symbolism & Art Motives. LC 76-40397. 472p. 1976. pap. 6.00 (ISBN 0-486-23372-3). Dover.
Williams, C. Abdy. Story of Notation. LC 69-16797. 1968. Repr. of 1903 ed. 18.00 (ISBN 0-8103-3557-3). Gale.
--Story of Organ Music. LC 69-16789. 1968. Repr. of 1905 ed. 15.00 (ISBN 0-8103-3558-1). Gale.
Williams, C. Arthur, Jr. & Heins, Richard M. Risk Management & Insurance. 4th ed. (Insurance Ser.). (Illus.). 672p. 1980. text ed. 19.95 (ISBN 0-07-070564-X, C); instructor's manual 5.95 (ISBN 0-07-070565-8). McGraw.
Williams, C. B. Style & Vocabulary: Numerical Studies. 1970. 8.75 o.s.i. (ISBN 0-02-854850-7). Hafner.
Williams, C. F. The Story of the Organ. LC 78-90250. (Illus.). 328p. 1972. Repr. of 1903 ed. 18.00 (ISBN 0-8103-3067-9). Gale.
Williams, C. J. What Is Truth. LC 75-23533. 120p. 1976. 21.50 (ISBN 0-521-20967-6). Cambridge U Pr.
Williams, C. K., tr. see Sophocles.
Williams, C. N. & Chew, W. Y. Tree & Field Crops of the Wetter Regions of the Tropics. (Intermediate Tropical Agriculture Series). (Illus.). 262p. 1981. pap. text ed. 5.95x (ISBN 0-582-60319-6). Longman.
Williams, Carol E., jt. ed. see Pearson, Paul H.
Williams, Carol T. & Wolfe, Gary K. Elements of Research: A Guide for Writers. LC 78-12170. (Illus.). 1979. pap. text ed. 5.95 (ISBN 0-88284-070-3). Alfred Pub.
Williams, Cecil B. Henry Wadsworth Longfellow. (U. S. Authors Ser.: No. 68). 1964. lib. bdg. 9.95 (ISBN 0-8057-0456-6). Twayne.
Williams, Charles. All Hallows' Eve. 274p. 1981. pap. 5.95 (ISBN 0-8028-1215-5). Eerdmans.
--Witchcraft. (Orig.). pap. 3.95 o.p. (ISBN 0-452-00400-4, F400, Mer). NAL.
--Works. Incl. War in Heaven. pap. 3.95 (ISBN 0-8028-1219-8); Many Dimensions. pap. 3.95 (ISBN 0-8028-1221-X); The Place of the Lion. pap. 2.95 (ISBN 0-8028-1222-8); Shadows of Ecstacy. pap. 3.95 (ISBN 0-8028-1223-6); Descent into Hell. pap. 3.95 (ISBN 0-8028-1220-1). 1965. pap. 24.50 boxed set (ISBN 0-8028-1215-5). Eerdmans.
Williams, Charles R. Life of Rutherford Birchard Hayes, 2 Vols. LC 79-87678. (American Scene Ser). 1970. Repr. of 1914 ed. lib. bdg. 85.00 (ISBN 0-306-71714-X). Da Capo.
Williams, Christine L. Primary Prevention of Chronic Disease Beginning in Childhood. 250p. 1981. 18.50 (ISBN 0-87527-237-1). Green.
Williams, Christopher. Origins of Form. (Illus.). 160p. (Orig.). 1980. pap. 12.00 (ISBN 0-8038-5394-7). Hastings.
Williams, Chuck. Mount St. Helens: A Changing Landscape. (Illus.). 128p. 27.50 (ISBN 0-912856-63-7). Graphic Arts Ctr.
Williams, Claudette. Blades of Passion. 1978. pap. 1.95 o.p. (ISBN 0-449-23481-9, Crest). Fawcett.
--Cassandra. 1979. pap. 2.25 o.p. (ISBN 0-449-23895-4, Crest). Fawcett.
--Desert Rose...English Moon. 256p. (Orig.). 1981. pap. 2.50 (ISBN 0-449-24388-5, Crest). Fawcett.
--Myriah. 1978. pap. 1.50 o.p. (ISBN 0-449-23577-7, Crest). Fawcett.
--Sassy. 1977. pap. 1.50 o.p. (ISBN 0-449-23371-5, Crest). Fawcett.
--Spring Gambit. 1979. pap. 1.75 o.p. (ISBN 0-449-23891-1, Crest). Fawcett.
--Sunday's Child. 1979. pap. 1.75 o.p. (ISBN 0-449-23986-1, Crest). Fawcett.
Williams, Colin W. New Directions in Theology Today. LC 68-22647. (New Directions in Theology Today: Vol. 4). 1968. pap. 3.25 (ISBN 0-664-24834-9). Westminster.
Williams, Connie. Fire Service Reference Guide Addendum: 502a. 1978. pap. text ed. 1.50 (ISBN 0-87939-026-3). Intl Fire Serv.
Williams, Connie E., ed. see IFSTA Committee.
Williams, Curtis A. & Chase, Merrill W., eds. Methods in Immunology & Immunochemistry, 5 vols. Vol. 1. 1968. 49.25, subscription 39.25 (ISBN 0-12-754401-1); Vol. 2. 1968. 42.25, subscription 39.25 (ISBN 0-12-754402-X); Vol. 3. 1971. 49.25, by subscription 42.25 (ISBN 0-12-754403-8); Vol. 4 1977. 49.25, subscription 42.25 (ISBN 0-12-754404-6); Vol. 5 1976. 49.25, subscription 42.25 (ISBN 0-12-754405-4). Acad Pr.
Williams, D. A. & Jones, G. Liquid Fuels. 1963. pap. 9.75 (ISBN 0-08-010385-5). Pergamon.
Williams, D. A., jt. auth. see Dyson, J. E.
Williams, D. F. Fundamental Aspects of Biocompatibility, 2 vols. (Biocompatability Ser.: Vol. 1). 1981. 56.95 (ISBN 0-8493-5581-8); Vol. 2, 272p. 69.95 (ISBN 0-8493-5588-5). CRC Pr.
Williams, D. F., jt. auth. see Hastings, G. W.
Williams, D. F., ed. Systemic Aspects of Biocompatibility. 1981. Vol. 1. 69.95 (ISBN 0-8493-5585-0); Vol. 2. 59.95 (ISBN 0-8493-5589-3). CRC Pr.
Williams, D. G. & Aalami, B. Thin Plate Design for In-Plane Loading. (Constrado Monographs). 210p. 1980. 44.95x (ISBN 0-470-26834-4). Halsted Pr.
Williams, D. I. Urology. (Operative Surgery Ser.). 1977. 119.00 (ISBN 0-407-00612-5). Butterworths.
Williams, D. L., jt. auth. see Harden, B. M.
Williams, D. S., ed. The Modern Diesel: Development & Design. 14th ed. 248p. 1973. 24.00 (ISBN 0-408-00260-3). Transatlantic.
Williams, D. Z., ed. The Monster in the Mirror: Studies in Nineteenth-Century Realism. 1978. 34.50x (ISBN 0-19-713433-5). Oxford U Pr.
Williams, Dakin. The Bar Bizarre. 270p. 1980. write for info. (ISBN 0-86629-009-5). Sunrise MO.
Williams, Daniel D. The Minister & the Care of Souls. LC 76-62929. (Orig.). 1977. pap. 4.95 (ISBN 0-06-318071-5, RD 213, HarpR). Har-Row.
Williams, David. The Burning Wood. (Anansi Fiction Ser.: No. 34). 204p. 1975. 12.95 (ISBN 0-88784-435-9, Pub. by Hse Anansi Pr Canada); pap. 6.95 (ISBN 0-88784-054-X). U of Toronto Pr.
--Genesis & Exodus: A Portrait of the Benson Family. 1979. 27.00 (ISBN 0-241-10190-5, Pub. by Hamish Hamilton England). David & Charles.
--George Meredith: His Life & Lost Love. 1978. 25.00 (ISBN 0-241-89630-4, Pub. by Hamish Hamilton England). David & Charles.
--Second Sight. 1979. pap. 1.75 o.s.i. (ISBN 0-515-04708-2). Jove Pubns.
Williams, David, ed. see Williams, Judith B.
Williams, David A. David C. Broderick: A Political Portrait. LC 79-85342. 1969. 10.00 (ISBN 0-87328-035-0). Huntington Lib.
Williams, David A., jt. auth. see Haas, Richard.
Williams, David J. Polymer Science & Engineering. (Physical & Chemical Engineering Sciences Ser). (Illus.). 1971. ref. ed. 29.95 (ISBN 0-13-685636-5). P-H.
Williams, Dick. God Thoughts. 1970. pap. 1.65 (ISBN 0-8164-2026-2, SP66). Crossroad NY.
Williams, Don, jt. auth. see Verbsky, Ray.
Williams, Donald & Woods, Thomas J. Basic Calculus with Applications. 1979. text ed. 19.95x (ISBN 0-534-00685-X). Wadsworth Pub.
Williams, Donald R. Modern Mathematics for Business Decision-Making. 2nd ed. 1978. text ed. 19.95x (ISBN 0-534-00558-6). Wadsworth Pub.
Williams, Dorian. Book of Horses. LC 70-164017. (Illus.). 1971. 8.95 (ISBN 0-397-00888-0). Lippincott.
--Equestrianism. (Illus.). 237p. 1980. 19.95 (ISBN 0-8069-9228-X, Pub by Guinness Superlatives England). Sterling.
--Great Riding Schools of the World. LC 74-14906. (Illus.). 320p. 1975. 12.98 o.s.i. (ISBN 0-02-629060-X). Macmillan.
--The Horseman's Companion. 574p. 1980. 15.00 (ISBN 0-312-39217-6). St Martin.
--Show Jumper. LC 70-101235. (Illus.). 1968. pap. 1.95 o.p. (ISBN 0-668-02817-3). Arco.
Williams, Doris & Griggs, Patricia. Preparing for the Messiah. (Griggs Educational Resources Ser.). 1979. pap. 4.95 (ISBN 0-687-33920-0). Abingdon.
Williams, Doyle Z., jt. ed. see Needles, Belverd E., Jr.
Williams, Dudley & Spangler, John. General Physics. Date not set. text ed. price not set (ISBN 0-442-26155-1). D Van Nostrand.
Williams, Dudley, jt. auth. see Shortley, George.
Williams, Dudley see Marton, L.
Williams, Duncan. To Be or Not to Be: A Question of Survival. (International Library Ser.). 1976. pap. text ed. 8.25 (ISBN 0-08-019934-8). Pergamon.
--Trousered Apes: The Influence of Literature on Contemporary Society. 160p. 1972. 6.95 o.p. (ISBN 0-87000-182-5). Arlington Hse.

Williams, E. N. Eighteenth-Century Constitution: Documents & Commentary. (English Constitutional History Ser). 47.95 (ISBN 0-521-06810-X); pap. 14.95x (ISBN 0-521-09123-3). Cambridge U Pr.
--The Penguin Dictionary of English & European History 1485-1789. 480p. 1980. pap. 6.95 (ISBN 0-14-051084-2). Penguin.
Williams, E. T. & Palmer, Helen M., eds. The Dictionary of National Biography, 1951-1960. 7th suppl ed. 1176p. 1971. 65.00x (ISBN 0-19-865206-2). Oxford U Pr.
Williams, E. W. Modern Law Enforcement & Police Science. (Illus.). 408p. 1967. lexotone 37.50 (ISBN 0-398-02071-X). C C Thomas.
Williams, Earl J., jt. auth. see Tanner, C. Kenneth.
Williams, Earl P., Jr. The Amtrak Story: A Pictorial History. 1979. pap. 5.50 (ISBN 0-685-80663-4). Maryland Hist Pr.
Williams, Edward. Back to Basics Mathematics, 3 vols. Incl. Vol. 1. From Addition to Division. LC 78-21490 (ISBN 0-8120-0691-7); Vol. 2. Improving Skills with Fractions (ISBN 0-8120-0692-5); Vol. 3. Decimals, Percents & Other Matter (ISBN 0-8120-0693-3). LC 78-21490. (Math Ser.). 1979. pap. text ed. 4.75 ea. Barron.
Williams, Edward & Cohen, Jacob. Survival Math. (gr. 9-12). 1981. pap. 4.95 (ISBN 0-8120-2012-X). Barron. Postponed.
Williams, Edward, jt. auth. see Burns, Arthur.
Williams, Edward E., jt. auth. see Gisborne, Maria.
Williams, Edward H., jt. auth. see Hoag, Ernest B.
Williams, Edward J. Latin American Christian Democratic Parties. LC 67-13159. 1967. 15.00x (ISBN 0-87049-073-7). U of Tenn Pr.
--The Rebirth of the Mexican Petroleum Industry: Developmental Directions & Policy Implications. LC 79-1546. 240p. 1979. 20.95 (ISBN 0-669-02908-4). Lexington Bks.
Williams, Edward R., jt. auth. see House, Peter W.
Williams, Edwin B. New College Spanish & English Dictionary. (gr. 7-12). 1968. pap. text ed. 7.17 (ISBN 0-87720-511-6). AMSCO Sch.
Williams, Edwina D. & Freeman, Lucy. Remember Me to Tom. 2nd ed. 336p. 1980. pap. 5.95 (ISBN 0-86629-006-0). Sunrise MO.
Williams, Effie. The Man of His Counsel. 112p. pap. 1.00. Faith Pub Hse.
Williams, Effie M. The Infidel Doctor of Salem. 52p. pap. 0.40; pap. 1.00 3 copies. Faith Pub Hse.
--The Revival in Tin Town. 84p. pap. 0.75. Faith Pub Hse.
--Trials & Triumphs of Eva Grant. 94p. pap. 1.00. Faith Pub Hse.
Williams, Efie M. Just Mary. 96p. pap. 0.75. Faith Pub Hse.
Williams, Elaine, jt. auth. see Olson, Joan.
Williams, Elizabeth see Janeway, James.
Williams, Elizabeth S. Venereal Disease. new ed. Burnes, Alan J., ed. (Urban America Ser.). (Illus.). 64p. (Orig.). (gr. 6-10). 1969. pap. 0.95 o.p. (ISBN 0-88301-022-4). Pendulum Pr.
Williams, Elma. Ride a Cock Horse. 1972. 8.95 (ISBN 0-7181-0930-9). Transatlantic.
Williams, Emlyn. Headlong. LC 80-51775. 300p. 1981. 12.95 (ISBN 0-670-36439-8). Viking Pr.
Williams, Emma I., ed. A West Tennessee Rebel: The Diary of Robert H. Cartmell, 1853-1866. (Illus.). 1981. 16.95x (ISBN 0-87870-096-X). Memphis St Univ. Postponed.
Williams, Emmett. Anthology of Concrete Poetry. 10.00. Green Hill.
Williams, Eric E. British Historians & the West Indies. LC 72-76470. 238p. 1972. text ed. 19.50x (ISBN 0-8419-0088-4, Africana). Holmes & Meier.
--Education in British West Indies. 1968. pap. 6.00 (ISBN 0-685-20859-1). Univ Place.
--From Columbus to Castro: The History of the Caribbean, 1492-1969. LC 75-138773. (Illus.). 1971. 13.95x (ISBN 0-06-014668-0, HarpT). Har-Row.
--History of the People of Trinidad & Tobago. 10.95 (ISBN 0-685-20593-2). Transatlantic.
--Inward Hunger: The Education of a Prime Minister. LC 70-170729. 352p. 1972. 10.00x (ISBN 0-226-89920-9). U of Chicago Pr.
--Negro in the Caribbean. LC 74-103458. (Studies in Black History & Culture, No. 54). 1970. Repr. lib. bdg. 17.95 (ISBN 0-8383-1190-3). Haskell.
--Negro in the Caribbean. LC 71-88421. Repr. of 1942 ed. 7.50x (ISBN 0-8371-1809-3); pap. 3.95 (ISBN 0-8371-8987-X). Negro U Pr.
Williams, Ernest S. Systematic Theology, 3 vols. Incl. Vol. 1. 6.95 (ISBN 0-88243-665-1, 02-0665); pap. 4.95 (ISBN 0-88243-643-0, 02-0643); Vol. 2. 6.95 (ISBN 0-88243-666-X, 02-0666); pap. 4.95 (ISBN 0-88243-644-9, 02-0644); Vol. 3. 6.95 (ISBN 0-88243-667-8, 02-0667); pap. 4.95 (ISBN 0-88243-645-7, 02-0645). 1953. Set. 18.95 (ISBN 0-88243-668-6, 02-0668); Set. pap. 13.50 (ISBN 0-88243-650-3, 02-0650). Gospel Pub.
Williams, Ernest W., Jr., jt. auth. see Fair, Marvin L.
Williams, Ernest W., Jr., jt. auth. see Sletmo, Gunnar K.
Williams, Ervin, ed. Participative Management: Concepts, Theory, & Implementation. LC 76-13650. 285p. 1976. 14.95 (ISBN 0-88406-102-7). Ga St U Busn Pub.
Williams, Esther, tr. see Skhi-Igumen, John.
Williams, Ethel L. & Brown, Clifton F. Howard University Bibliography of African & Afro-American Religious Studies: With Locations in American Libraries. LC 76-5604. 1977. 29.00 (ISBN 0-8420-2080-2). Scholarly Res Inc.
Williams, Evan & Sheehan, Larry. You Can Hit the Golf Ball Farther. LC 79-50544. (Illus.). 127p. 1979. 9.95 (ISBN 0-914178-26-1, 24922); pap. 5.95 (ISBN 0-914178-29-6, 24964). Golf Digest.
Williams, F., jt. ed. see Libby, P. A.
Williams, F. Donald. Private Thoughts. 1980. 4.00 o.p. (ISBN 0-8062-1198-9). Carlton.
Williams, F. J., jt. auth. see Freund, John E.
Williams, Forman A. Combustion Theory. 2nd ed. (Illus.). 1981. write for info. (ISBN 0-201-08652-2, Adv Bk Prog). A-W.
Williams, Forrest, tr. see Sartre, Jean-Paul.
Williams, Frances, ed. Why the Poor Pay More. (Illus.). 1977. text ed. 16.00x (ISBN 0-333-23643-2); pap. text ed. 7.75x (ISBN 0-333-23644-0). Humanities.
Williams, Frances L. Matthew Fontaine Maury, Scientist of the Sea. (Illus.). 1963. 32.50 (ISBN 0-8135-0433-3). Rutgers U Pr.
Williams, Frankwood E. Adolescence Studies in Mental Hygiene. 279p. 1980. Repr. lib. bdg. 25.00 (ISBN 0-89984-511-8). Century Bookbindery.
Williams, Frederick. Language & Speech: Introductory Perspectives. 1972. pap. text ed. 8.95 (ISBN 0-13-522789-5). P-H.
Williams, Frederick & Holstein, J. E. Introduction to Probability. 1967. text ed. 3.00x spiral bdg (ISBN 0-87543-061-9). Lucas.
Williams, Frederick C., ed. Nuclear Nonproliferation: The Spent Fuel Problem. Deese, David A. (Pergamon Policy Studies). 1980. 33.00 (ISBN 0-08-023887-4). Pergamon.
Williams, G. H., ed. Advances in Free Radical Chemistry, 4 vols. 1967-75. Vol. 2. 49.25 (ISBN 0-12-017002-7); Vol. 3. 49.25 (ISBN 0-12-017003-5); Vol. 4. 49.25 (ISBN 0-12-017004-3); Vol. 5. 49.25 (ISBN 0-12-017005-1). Acad Pr.
Williams, G. Walton. The Winter Folk. 3.95 (ISBN 0-932298-11-7). Green Hill.
Williams, Gareth. Computational Linear Algebra with Models. 2nd ed. 1978. text ed. 20.95 (ISBN 0-205-05998-8); write for info instr's man (ISBN 0-205-05999-6). Allyn.
--Finite Mathematics with Models. 1976. text ed. 17.80x (ISBN 0-205-04913-3); instr's manual free (ISBN 0-205-04914-1). Allyn.
--Mathematics with Applications in the Management, Natural, & Social Sciences. 656p. 1981. text ed. 22.00 (ISBN 0-205-07188-0, 567188-4); tchrs'. ed. avail. (ISBN 0-205-07189-9). Allyn.
--Practical Finite Mathematics. 1979. text ed. 17.80 (ISBN 0-205-06525-2, 566525-6). Allyn.
Williams, Gareth, jt. auth. see Smith, David.
Williams, Garth. Baby Animals. (ps-1). 1956. PLB 4.57 o.p. (ISBN 0-307-60517-5, Golden Pr). Western Pub.
--Baby Farm Animals. (Big Picture Bk.). 24p. (gr. 1-3). 1953. 1.95 (ISBN 0-307-10545-8, Golden Pr); PLB 7.62 (ISBN 0-307-60545-0). Western Pub.
--Baby Farm Animals. (Big Picture Bk.). (Illus.). 24p. (ps-3). 1977. Repr. of 1958 ed. PLB 5.00 (ISBN 0-307-60545-0, Golden Pr). Western Pub.
--Big Golden Animal ABC. (gr. k-2). 1957. 1.95 (ISBN 0-307-10457-5, Golden Pr); PLB 7.62 (ISBN 0-307-60457-8). Western Pub.
Williams, Garth, illus. Animal Friends Everywhere! (Golden Storytime Bks.). (Illus.). (ps). 1980. pap. 4.50 boxed set (ISBN 0-307-15514-5, Golden Pr). Western Pub.
--Three Bedtime Stories. (Illus.). (gr. k-3). 1958. 1.95 o.p. (ISBN 0-307-10392-7, Golden Pr); PLB 7.15 o.p. (ISBN 0-307-60392-X). Western Pub.
Williams, Gary M., jt. ed. see Borek, Carmia.
Williams, Gene B. The Homeowner's Pest Extermination Handbook. LC 77-4204. (Illus.). 1978. lib. bdg. 6.95 o.p. (ISBN 0-668-04316-4, 4316); pap. 2.95 o.p. (ISBN 0-668-04321-0, 4321). Arco.
Williams, Geoffrey, jt. auth. see Barrett, James.
Williams, George H. The Mind of John Paul II: Origins of His Thought & Action. 352p. 1980. 14.95 (ISBN 0-8164-0473-9). Seabury.
--The Polish Brethren. (Harvard Theological Studies: No. 30). 16.00; pap. 11.00 (ISBN 0-89130-201-8). Scholars Pr CA.
Williams, George H., et al. Thomas Hooker: Writings in England & Holland, Sixteen Twenty-Six to Sixteen Thirty-Three. LC 75-30570. (Harvard Theological Review & Studies). 1975. pap. 12.00 (ISBN 0-89130-310-3, 020028). Scholars Pr CA.
Williams, George M. The Quest for Meaning of Svami Vivekananda: A Study of Religious Change. LC 74-10906. (The Religious Quest Ser: Vol. 1). (Illus.). 158p. 1974. lib. bdg. 14.95x (ISBN 0-914914-02-2); pap. text ed. 5.50x (ISBN 0-914914-00-6). New Horizons.
Williams, George S. Nursery Crops & Landscape Designs for Agri-Business Studies. LC 75-10482. 1975. 9.65 (ISBN 0-8134-1717-1); text ed. 7.25x (ISBN 0-685-65744-2). Interstate.
Williams, George W., jt. auth. see Turner, Robert K., Jr.
Williams, George W., ed. see Middleton, Thomas & Rowley, William.
Williams, Gerald. Digital Technology. LC 76-47660. 1977. text ed. 18.95 (ISBN 0-574-21500-X, 13-4500); instr's guide avail. (ISBN 0-574-21501-8, 13-4501); lab. manual 4.95 (ISBN 0-574-21502-6, 13-4502). SRA.
Williams, Gerry, et al. Studio Potter Book. 1979. 22.50 (ISBN 0-442-29461-1). Litton Educ Pub.
Williams, Gertrude & Gordon, Sol, eds. Clinical Child Psychology: Current Practices & Future Perspectives. LC 73-13511. 632p. 1974. text ed. 29.95 (ISBN 0-87705-125-9). Human Sci Pr.
Williams, Gladys. Children & Their Books. 2nd rev. ed. 1981. pap. 3.95x (ISBN 0-7156-0535-6, Pub. by Duckworth England). Biblio Dist.
Williams, Gordon. Change & Decline: Roman Literature in the Early Empire. LC 76-24598. (Sather Classical Lectures: No. 45). 1978. 17.75x (ISBN 0-520-03333-7). U of Cal Pr.
Williams, Gordon F. Children with Chronic Arthritis: A Primer for Patients & Parents. LC 80-14190. 350p. 1981. 22.50 (ISBN 0-88416-273-7, 273). PSG Pub.
Williams, Gurney. Ghosts & Poltergeists. (Illus.). (gr. 4-6). 1979. PLB 6.45 s&l (ISBN 0-531-02214-5). Watts.
--True Escape & Survival Stories. LC 77-1421. (Illus.). (gr. 4-6). 1977. PLB 6.90 (ISBN 0-531-00119-9). Watts.
--Twins. (First Bks.). (Illus.). (gr. 4 up). 1979. PLB 6.45 s&l (ISBN 0-531-02265-X). Watts.
Williams, Gurney, 3rd. Writing Careers. (Career Concise Guides Ser.). (Illus.). 96p. (gr. 7 up). 1976. PLB 4.90 o.p. (ISBN 0-531-01130-5). Watts.
Williams, Guy R. Working with Leather. (Illus.). 1967. 7.95 o.s.i. (ISBN 0-87523-161-6). Emerson.
Williams, Guy St. John see St. John Williams, Guy & Hyland, Francis.
Williams, Gwyn. The Land Remembers. 1977. 14.95 (ISBN 0-571-10323-5, Pub. by Faber & Faber). Merrimack Bk Serv.
Williams, Gwyn, ed. & tr. Welsh Poems: Sixth Century to 1600. 1974. 11.95x (ISBN 0-520-02603-9). U of Cal Pr.
Williams, Gwyn, ed. Welsh Poems: Sixth Century to 1600. 1973. pap. 2.95 o.p. (ISBN 0-571-10379-0, Pub. by Faber & Faber). Merrimack Bk Serv.
Williams, Gwyn A. Artisans & Sans-Culottes. LC 69-14476. (Foundations of Modern History Ser). 1969. pap. text ed. 3.95x (ISBN 0-393-09832-X, NortonC). Norton.
Williams, H. A. The Simplicity of Prayer: A Discussion of the Methods & Results of Christian Prayer. LC 77-78649. 80p. 1977. pap. 2.50 (ISBN 0-8006-1315-5, 1-1315). Fortress.
Williams, H. B., jt. auth. see Andrew, William G.
Williams, H. B., jt. auth. see Andrews, William G.
Williams, H. Page. X-Rated Marriages. 1977. pap. 2.95 o.p. (ISBN 0-88270-242-4). Logos.
Williams, Harold, ed. see Swift, Jonathan.
Williams, Harold H. Book Clubs & Printing Societies of Great Britain & Ireland. LC 68-26622. 1971. Repr. of 1929 ed. 22.00 (ISBN 0-8103-3749-5). Gale.
Williams, Harold R. see Peterson, Wallace C.
Williams, Harriet B., ed. Serology, Immunology & Blood Banking. (Functional Mdical Laboratory Manual). (Illus.). 1978. pap. text ed. 10.00 (ISBN 0-87055-266-X). AVI.
Williams, Harry. Streets of the Kings. LC 80-50035. 1980. 8.95 (ISBN 0-533-04584-3). Vantage.
--Twins of Ceylon. (Twins Ser). (Illus.). (gr. 6-9). 1965. 6.00 (ISBN 0-8023-1108-3). Dufour.
Williams, Haydn M. The Fiction of Ruth Prawer Jhabvala. (Writers Workshop Greybird Book Ser.). 60p. 1975. 12.00 (ISBN 0-88253-540-4); pap. text ed. 4.80 (ISBN 0-88253-539-0). Ind-US Inc.
--Studies in Modern Indian Fiction in English, 2 vols. (Greybird Book). 182p. 1975. Set. text ed. 24.00 (ISBN 0-88253-652-4); Set. pap. text ed. 15.00 (ISBN 0-88253-651-6). Ind-US Inc.
Williams, Heathcote. The Immortalist. 1980. pap. 3.95 (ISBN 0-7145-3714-4). Riverrun NY.
Williams, Helen, jt. ed. see Abercrombie, V. T.
Williams, Helen E. High-Low Consensus. LC 80-19794. 1980. pap. 15.50 (ISBN 0-87272-088-8). Brodart.
--Independent Reading, K-Three. LC 80-20423. 1980. pap. 17.25 (ISBN 0-87272-089-6). Brodart.
Williams, Helen M. Julia, a Novel, 2 vols. (The Feminist Controveersy in England, 1788-1810 Ser.). 1974. Set. lib. bdg. 76.00 (ISBN 0-8240-0887-1); lib. bdg. 50.00 ea. Garland Pub.
Williams, Henry M., Jr. & Shim, Chang. Asthma - Discussions in Patient Management. 1976. spiral bdg. 8.00 o.p. (ISBN 0-87488-876-X). Med Exam.
Williams, Hobie L. The American Artists Today in Black, Vol. I. White, Mosezelle & Roberts, Bobby, II, eds. 87p. (Orig.). 1981. pap. text ed. 7.95x (ISBN 0-936026-11-1). R&M Pub Co.
--The American Artists Today in Black, Vol. II. White, Mosezelle & Roberts, Bobby, II, eds. 103p. (Orig.). Date not set. pap. text ed. 8.95 (ISBN 0-936026-12-X). R&M Pub Co.
Williams, Howel, et al. Petrography: An Introduction to the Study of Rocks in Thin Sections. LC 54-5872. (Geology Ser.). (Illus.). 1954. 26.95x (ISBN 0-7167-0206-1). W H Freeman.
Williams, Howell & Curtis, G. H. The Sutter Buttes of California: A Study of Plio-Pleistocene Volcanism. (Library Reprint Ser.: No. 97). 1979. Repr. of 1977 ed. 11.95x (ISBN 0-520-03808-8). U of Cal Pr.
Williams, Howell, et al. Geologic Reconnaissance of Southeastern Guatemala. (U. C. Publ. in Geological Sciences: Vol. 50). 1964. pap. 7.50x (ISBN 0-520-09150-7). U of Cal Pr.
Williams, I. Emyr Humphreys. (Writers of Wales). 1980. pap. 9.00 (ISBN 0-7083-0750-7). Verry.
Williams, I. P. Matrices for Scientists. 1972. text ed. 8.00x (ISBN 0-09-110250-2, Hutchinson U Lib); pap. text ed. 3.25x (ISBN 0-09-110251-0). Humanities.
Williams, Ioan. The Criticism of Henry Fielding. 1970. 30.00 (ISBN 0-7100-6596-5). Routledge & Kegan.
--Novel & Romance, 1700-1800: A Documentary Record. 1970. 40.00x (ISBN 0-7100-6595-7). Routledge & Kegan.
Williams, Ion M. Thackeray. LC 78-78852. (Literary Critiques Ser.). (Illus., Orig.). 1969. lib. bdg. 4.95 o.p. (ISBN 0-668-01952-2). Arco.
Williams, Irving G. Rise of the Vice-Presidency. 5.00 (ISBN 0-8183-0204-6). Pub Aff Pr.
Williams, J. Complex Numbers. (Problem Solvers Ser.). (Illus.). 1972. pap. text ed. 4.95x o.p. (ISBN 0-04-512019-6). Allen Unwin.
Williams, J., ed. Carbon Dioxide, Climate & Society: Proceedings of an IIASA Workshop, Feb. 1978. 1978. text ed. 45.00 (ISBN 0-08-023252-3). Pergamon.
Williams, J., et al. Aperture: No. 77. 1977. pap. 9.50 (ISBN 0-89381-013-4). Aperture.
Williams, J. B. The Lives of Philip & Matthew Henry. 1974. 14.95 (ISBN 0-85151-178-3). Banner of Truth.
Williams, J. D. Teaching Technique in Primary Maths. (Exploring Education Ser). (Illus.). 1971. pap. text ed. 5.75x (ISBN 0-391-02082-X, NFER). Humanities.
Williams, J. E. Literature in Celtic Countries. (Taliesin Congress Lectures). 218p. 1979. pap. text ed. 10.00x o.p. (ISBN 0-686-64124-8). Verry.
Williams, J. E., jt. auth. see Pressman, R. S.
Williams, J. G. Stress Analysis of Polymers. 2nd rev. ed. LC 80-40144. (Ellis Horwood Ser. in Engineering Science). 360p. 1980. 77.95x (ISBN 0-470-26964-2). Halsted Pr.
Williams, J. N. Steam Generation. 1969. text ed. 25.00x (ISBN 0-04-621013-X). Allen Unwin.
Williams, J. R. IFR by the Book: Techniques of Instrument Flight. (Illus.). 1980. pap. 5.95 (ISBN 0-911721-83-5, Pub. by Gen. Avn. Press). Aviation.
--Snowing in Paradise. (Orig.). 1980. pap. 2.25 (ISBN 0-532-23147-3). Manor Bks.
Williams, J. R., et al. Ethanol, Methanol, & Gasohol. (Illus.). 200p. 1981. 18.75 (ISBN 0-250-40382-X). Ann Arbor Science.
Williams, J. Rodman. Gift of the Holy Spirit Today. (Orig.). 1980. pap. 6.95 (ISBN 0-88270-413-3). Logos.
Williams, J. SerVaas. Abram & Sarai. LC 80-69805. (Illus.). 350p. 1981. 12.95 (ISBN 0-938280-01-5). Corinth Hse.
Williams, J. W. The Big Ranch Country. 10.95 (ISBN 0-685-48783-0). Nortex Pr.
Williams, Jay. A Bag Full of Nothing. LC 73-22186. (Illus.). 40p. (ps-3). 1974. 5.95 o.s.i. (ISBN 0-8193-0774-2, Four Winds); PLB 5.41 o.s.i. (ISBN 0-8193-0725-4). Schol Bk Serv.
--The Burglar Next Door. LC 76-12422. (Illus.). 128p. (gr. 3-7). 1976. 6.95 (ISBN 0-590-07436-9, Four Winds). Schol Bk Serv.

--Everyone Knows What a Dragon Looks Like. LC 74-13121. (Illus.). 32p. (gr. k-3). 1976. 9.95 (ISBN 0-590-07284-6, Four Winds); pap. 5.95 (ISBN 0-590-07751-1). Schol Bk Serv.
--Forgetful Fred. LC 73-12965. (Illus.). 40p. (ps-3). 1974. 5.95 o.s.i. (ISBN 0-8193-0719-X, Four Winds); PLB 5.41 o.s.i. (ISBN 0-8193-0720-3). Schol Bk Serv.
--The Hero from Otherwhere. (YA) (gr. 7-9). pap. 1.75 (ISBN 0-671-56076-X). PB.
--King with Six Friends. LC 68-21078. (Illus.). (gr. k-3). 1968. 5.95 o.s.i. (ISBN 0-8193-0341-0, Four Winds); PLB 5.41 o.s.i. (ISBN 0-8193-0342-9). Schol Bk Serv.
--The Magic Grandfather. LC 78-22285. (Illus.). 160p. (gr. 3-7). 1979. 8.95 (ISBN 0-590-07588-8, Four Winds). Schol Bk Serv.
--Practical Princess. LC 69-12606. (Illus.). (gr. k-3). 1969. PLB 5.95 o.s.i. (ISBN 0-8193-0233-3, Four Winds); PLB 5.41 o.s.i. (ISBN 0-8193-0234-1). Schol Bk Serv.
--The Practical Princess & Other Liberating Fairy Tales. LC 78-6998. (Illus.). 112p. 1978. lib. bdg. 8.95 (ISBN 0-590-07725-2, Four Winds); PLB 7.61 (ISBN 0-8193-0969-9). Schol Bk Serv.
--A Present from a Bird. LC 72-153786. (Illus.). (gr. k-3). 1971. 5.95 o.s.i. (ISBN 0-8193-0500-6, Four Winds); PLB 5.41 o.s.i. (ISBN 0-8193-0501-4). Schol Bk Serv.
--The Reward Worth Having. LC 76-56135. (Illus.). 32p. (gr. k-3). 1977. 6.95 (ISBN 0-590-07342-7, Four Winds). Schol Bk Serv.
--School for Sillies. LC 71-77785. (gr. k-3). 1969. 5.95 o.s.i. (ISBN 0-8193-0305-4, Four Winds); PLB 5.41 o.s.i. (ISBN 0-8193-0306-2). Schol Bk Serv.
--The Surprising Things Maui Did. LC 79-5069. (Illus.). 40p. (gr. k-3). 1979. 9.95 (ISBN 0-590-07553-5, Four Winds). Schol Bk Serv.
--The Time of the Kraken. LC 77-5696. (YA) 1978. 7.95g o.s.i. (ISBN 0-590-07501-2, Four Winds). Schol Bk Serv.
--To Catch a Bird. 1968. 3.95g o.s.i. (ISBN 0-02-793040-8, CCPr). Macmillan.
--The Water of Life. LC 79-19438. (Illus.). 40p. (gr. k-3). 1980. 8.95 (ISBN 0-590-07530-6, Four Winds). Schol Bk Serv.
--The Wicked Tricks of Tyl Uilenspiegel. LC 77-7884. (Illus.). 64p. (gr. 1-5). 1978. 8.95 (ISBN 0-590-07478-4, Four Winds). Schol Bk Serv.
--World of Titian. (Library of Art). (Illus.). 1968. 15.95 (ISBN 0-8094-0245-9). Time-Life.
--World of Titian. LC 68-28257. (Library of Art Ser.). (Illus.). (gr. 6 up). 1968. 12.96 (ISBN 0-8094-0274-2, Pub. by Time-Life). Silver.
--The Youngest Captain. LC 72-629. 48p. (gr. k-3). 1972. 5.95 o.s.i. (ISBN 0-8193-0594-4, Four Winds); PLB 5.41 o.s.i. (ISBN 0-8193-0595-2). Schol Bk Serv.
Williams, Jay & Abrashkin, Raymond. Danny Dunn & the Anti-Gravity Paint, No. 7. (Illus.). (gr. 4-6). 1979. pap. 1.75 (ISBN 0-671-42060-7). Archway.
--Danny Dunn & the Automatic House. (gr. 4-7). 1965. PLB 6.95 o.p. (ISBN 0-07-070533-X, GB). McGraw.
--Danny Dunn & the Automatic House: No. 12. (Illus.). (gr. 4-6). 1979. pap. 1.75 (ISBN 0-671-29977-8). PB.
--Danny Dunn & the Heat Ray: No. 14. (Illus.). (gr. 4-6). pap. 1.75 (ISBN 0-671-29969-7). PB.
--Danny Dunn & the Smallifying Machine, No. 1. (Danny Dunn Ser.: No. 1). (Illus.). (gr. 4-6). 1979. pap. 1.75 (ISBN 0-671-41496-8). Archway.
--Danny Dunn & the Voice from Space, No. 12. (Illus.). (gr. 4-6). 1979. pap. 1.95 (ISBN 0-671-42684-2). Archway.
--Danny Dunn & the Weather Machine, No. 10. (Illus.). (gr. 4-6). 1979. pap. 1.75 (ISBN 0-671-42888-8). Archway.
--Danny Dunn on a Desert Islanda: No. 15. (gr. 4-6). 1979. pap. 1.75 (ISBN 0-671-29976-X). PB.
--Danny Dunn on the Ocean Floor. (gr. 4-7). 1964. PLB 6.95 o.p. (ISBN 0-07-070524-0, GB). McGraw.
--Danny Dunn on the Ocean Floor, No. 9. (Illus.). (gr. 4-6). 1979. pap. 1.75 (ISBN 0-671-41855-6). Archway.
--Danny Dunn, Time Traveler, No. 8. (gr. 4-6). 1979. pap. 1.75 (ISBN 0-671-42451-3). Archway.
Williams, Jay & Smith, Lacey B. Spanish Armada. LC 66-25994. (Horizon Caravel Bks). (Illus.). 153p. (gr. 5 up). 1966. 9.95 (ISBN 0-8281-0399-2, Dist. by Har-Row); PLB 6.89 o.p. (ISBN 0-06-026541-8). Am Heritage.
Williams, Jay G. Judaism. LC 80-51551. 204p. 1981. pap. 5.50 (ISBN 0-8356-0540-X, Quest). Theos Pub Hse.
--Understanding the Old Testament. LC 74-162825. (gr. 10 up). 1972. pap. 5.75 (ISBN 0-8120-0424-8). Barron.
Williams, Jeanette T. Learning to Write, or Writing to Learn? (General Ser.). (Illus.). 1977. pap. text ed. 7.75x (ISBN 0-85633-128-7, NFER). Humanities.
Williams, Jeanne. San Patricio. 1980. pap. write for info. (ISBN 0-671-82732-4). PB.
Williams, Jerome. Oceanography. LC 72-2336. (First Bks). (Illus.). 96p. (gr. 7-12). 1972. PLB 4.90 o.p. (ISBN 0-531-00775-8). Watts.
Williams, Jerome & Williams, Lelia. Science Puzzles. (Illus.). (gr. 4-6). 1979. PLB 6.90 s&l (ISBN 0-531-02876-3). Watts.
Williams, Joe, jt. auth. see Monkhouse, Frank.
Williams, Joey. The Bachelor's Pad Cookbook. LC 80-69572. (Illus.). 183p. 1980. pap. 7.95 (ISBN 0-938280-00-7). Corinth Hse.
Williams, John. Archery for Beginners. LC 75-35000. (Illus.). 192p. 1976. pap. 5.95 o.p. (ISBN 0-8092-8288-7). Contemp Bks.
--Atlas of Weapons & War. LC 76-3515. (John Day Bk.). 1976. 12.95 o.s.i. (ISBN 0-381-98291-2, TYC-T). T Y Crowell.
--Cross-Country Ski Trails in the Rockies. 1978. 11.95 o.p. (ISBN 0-8092-7573-2); pap. 5.95 (ISBN 0-8092-7572-4). Contemp Bks.
--The Films of Charlton Heston. Castell, David, ed. (The Films of...Ser.). (Illus.). (gr. 7-12). 1978. Repr. of 1974 ed. PLB 5.95 (ISBN 0-912616-80-6). Greenhaven.
--The Films of Roger Moore. Castell, David, ed. (The Films of...Ser.). (Illus.). (gr. 7-12). 1979. Repr. of 1974 ed. PLB 5.95 (ISBN 0-912616-89-X). Greenhaven.
--The Holy Spirit, Lord & Life-Giver: A Biblical Introduction to the Doctrine of the Holy Spirit. LC 79-27891. 1980. 8.50 (ISBN 0-87213-950-6); pap. 5.75 (ISBN 0-87213-951-4). Loizeaux.
--The Holy Table, Name & Thing, More Patiently, Properly, & Literally Used Under the New Treatment, Than That of an Altar. LC 79-84146. (English Experience Ser.: No.962). 244p. 1979. Repr. of 1637 ed. lib. bdg. 22.00 (ISBN 90-221-0962-3). Walter J Johnson.
--An Introduction to Hunting. (Illus.). pap. 5.25 (ISBN 0-85131-200-4, Dist. by Sporting Book Center). J A Allen.
--The Redeemed Captive, Returning to Zion. LC 75-7024. (Indian Captivities Ser.: Vol. 5). 1976. Repr. of 1707 ed. lib. bdg. 44.00 (ISBN 0-8240-1629-7). Garland Pub.
--Study Guide for the Holy Spirit, Lord & Life-Giver. (Illus.). 1980. pap. text ed. 3.25 (ISBN 0-87213-952-2). Loizeaux.
--The Yankee. (Orig.). 1981. pap. 2.95 (ISBN 0-440-19779-1). Dell.
Williams, John, jt. auth. see Woods, Gerald.
Williams, John A. The Junior Bachelor Society. LC 75-32297. 7.95 o.p. (ISBN 0-385-09455-8). Doubleday.
--West Virginia. (States & the Nation Ser). (Illus.). 1976. 12.95 (ISBN 0-393-05590-6, Co-Pub by AASLH). Norton.
Williams, John A., ed. Themes of Islamic Civilization. 1971. 22.75x (ISBN 0-520-01685-8). U of Cal Pr.
Williams, John B. New Zealand Journal, 1842-1844, of John B. Williams of Salem, Massachusetts. Kenny, Robert W., ed. (Illus.). 120p. 1956. 10.00 (ISBN 0-87057-041-2, Pub. by Brown U Pr). Univ Pr of New England.
Williams, John J. Survival Guns & Ammo: Raw Meat. (Illus.). 1979. pap. 19.00 (ISBN 0-686-24791-4). Consumertronics.
Williams, John S. Consecrated Ingenuity: The Shakers & Their Inventions. (Illus.). 1957. 1.00 (ISBN 0-937942-01-4). Shaker Mus.
--The Revolutionary War & Issachar Bates. 1960. 1.00 (ISBN 0-937942-02-2). Shaker Mus.
--Shaker Religious Concept. (Illus.). 1959. 1.25 (ISBN 0-937942-04-9). Shaker Mus.
--The Shakers: A Brief Summary. 1977. 1.00 (ISBN 0-937942-07-3). Shaker Mus.
Williams, John W., jt. auth. see Lewis, Phillip.
Williams, Jon. The Privateer. (Orig.). 1981. pap. 2.75 (ISBN 0-440-16811-2). Dell.
Williams, Jon L. Operant Learning: Procedures for Changing Behavior. LC 72-91088. (Core Bks in Psychology Ser). 1973. text ed. 10.95 o.p. (ISBN 0-8185-0058-1). Brooks-Cole.
Williams, Joseph J. Hebrewisms of West Africa: From Nile to Niger with the Jews. LC 67-19534. (Illus.). 1930. 17.50x (ISBN 0-8196-0194-2). Biblo.
Williams, Joseph M. New English: Structure, Form & Style. LC 76-76225. 1970. text ed. 10.95 (ISBN 0-02-935310-6). Free Pr.
--Style: Ten Lessons in Clarity & Grace. 1981. text ed. 8.95x (ISBN 0-673-15393-2). Scott F.
Williams, Joyce E. Black Community Control: A Study of Transition in a Texas Ghetto. LC 72-85984. (Special Studies in U.S. Economic, Social & Political Issues). 1973. 29.50x (ISBN 0-89197-681-7). Irvington.
Williams, Juanita H., ed. Psychology of Women: Selected Readings. 1979. pap. text ed. 9.95x (ISBN 0-393-09068-X). Norton.
Williams, Judith B. British Commercial Policy & Trade Expansion, 1750-1850. Davis, Ralph & Williams, David, eds. 512p. 1972. 39.50x (ISBN 0-19-822360-9). Oxford U Pr.
Williams, Karel. From Pauperism to Poverty. 500p. 1981. 60.00 (ISBN 0-7100-0698-5). Routledge & Kegan.
Williams, Kathleen. Spenser's World of Glass: A Reading of The Faerie Queen. (California Library Reprint Series: No. 34). 1973. 18.50x (ISBN 0-520-02369-2). U of Cal Pr.
Williams, Keith. The Book of the Wood Stove. (Illus.). 152p. 1980. 14.95 (ISBN 0-7153-7926-7). David & Charles.
Williams, Ken. Statistics & Urban Planning. LC 75-23011. 189p. 1975. 21.50 (ISBN 0-686-65294-0, Pub. by Wiley). Krieger.
Williams, Kenneth P. Lincoln Finds a General, 4 vols. 1949. 8.50 ea. o.s.i. Vol. 1. Vol. 2. Vol. 3. Vol. 4. Macmillan.
Williams, Kit. Masquerade. LC 80-14127. (Illus.). 32p. 1980. 9.95 (ISBN 0-8052-3747-X). Schocken.
Williams, L. A. Secondary Schools for American Youth. 529p. 1980. Repr. of 1944 ed. lib. bdg. 25.00 (ISBN 0-89984-524-X). Century Bookbindery.
Williams, L. O. Hydrogen Power: An Introduction to Hydrogen Energy & Its Applications. LC 80-40434. (Illus.). 200p. 1980. 27.00 (ISBN 0-08-024783-0); pap. 11.00 (ISBN 0-08-025422-5). Pergamon.
Williams, L. Pearce. The Origins of Field Theory. LC 80-5710. 160p. 1980. lib. bdg. 15.50 (ISBN 0-8191-1175-9); pap. text ed. 7.50 (ISBN 0-8191-1176-7). U Pr of Amer.
Williams, Lalla, jt. auth. see Moorman, Ruth.
Williams, Lelia, jt. auth. see Williams, Jerome.
Williams, Leonard. Challenge to Survival. LC 76-51920. 170p. 1977. 12.00x (ISBN 0-8147-9172-7). NYU Pr.
Williams, Leslie. A Bear in the Air. LC 80-10290. (Illus.). 28p. (gr. k up). 1980. 7.95 (ISBN 0-916144-54-2). Stemmer Hse.
Williams, Leslie P. Selected Correspondence of Michael Faraday, 2 Vols. LC 77-138377. (Illus.). 1971. Set. 150.00 (ISBN 0-521-07475-4). Cambridge U Pr.
Williams, Lester F. Self-Assessment of Current Knowledge in General Surgery. 2nd ed. 1974. spiral bdg. 12.00 o.p. (ISBN 0-87488-250-8). Med Exam.
Williams, Letty. Little Red Hen: La Pequena Gallina Roja. LC 78-75684. (Illus., Eng. & Span.). (ps-3). 1969. 6.95 o.p.; pap. 1.25 (ISBN 0-13-537894-X). P-H.
Williams, Lewis T. & Lefkowitz, Robert J. Receptor Binding Studies in Adrenergic Pharmacology. LC 78-3011. 1978. 19.50 (ISBN 0-89004-164-4). Raven.
Williams, Lloyd B. & Gray, Allan W. Calculus: Combined Differential & Integral: Syllabus. 1973. text ed. 16.00 (ISBN 0-89420-059-3, 122210); cassette recordings 140.95 (ISBN 0-89420-130-1, 350500). Natl Book.
--Calculus: Differential Syllabus, Pt. 1. 1973. text ed. 9.25 (ISBN 0-89420-057-7, 122202); cassette recordings 89.20 (ISBN 0-89420-131-X, 350510). Natl Book.
Williams, Lloyd H. Pirates of Colonial Virginia. LC 73-78670. (Illus.). 1972. Repr. of 1937 ed. 15.00 (ISBN 0-8103-3817-3). Gale.
Williams, Lois, jt. auth. see Wink, Richard L.
Williams, Louis N. Black Psychology: Compelling Issues & Views. LC 78-60627. 1978. pap. text ed. 7.50 (ISBN 0-8191-0562-7). U Pr of Amer.
Williams, M. Practical Handgun Ballistics. (Illus.). 232p. 1980. 17.50 (ISBN 0-398-04032-X). C C Thomas.
Williams, M. M. Nuclear Safety. (Illus.). 1979. pap. 18.50 (ISBN 0-08-024752-0). Pergamon.
--Progress in Nuclear Energy: The Role of the Boltzmann Transport Equation in Radiation Damage Calculations, Vol. 3, No. 1. LC 77-25743. (Progress in Nuclear Energy Ser.). (Illus.). 66p. 1979. pap. 39.00 (ISBN 0-08-024243-X). Pergamon.
--Random Processes in Nuclear Reactors. LC 74-4066. 1974. text ed. 42.00 (ISBN 0-08-017920-7). Pergamon.
Williams, M. M., ed. Progress in Nuclear Energy, Vol. 3, No. 2. (Illus.). 92p. 1979. pap. 39.00 (ISBN 0-08-024253-7). Pergamon.
--Progress in Nuclear Energy, Vol. 3, No. 3. 96p. 1979. pap. 39.00 (ISBN 0-08-024844-6). Pergamon.
--Reactor Noise - Smorn II: Proceedings of the 2nd Specialists' Meeting on Reactor Noise 1977. 1978. pap. text ed. 182.00 (ISBN 0-686-68044-8). Pergamon.
--Reactor Noise. an International Symposium: Special Multi Issue of Journal of Annals of Nuclear Energy. 400p. 1976. pap. text ed. 55.00 (ISBN 0-08-019895-3). Pergamon.
Williams, M. M. & Sher, R., eds. Progress in Nuclear Energy: New Series. (Illus.). 1977. Vol. 1, No. 1. pap. text ed. 27.00 (ISBN 0-08-022118-1); Vol. 1, Nos. 2-4. pap. text ed. o.p. (ISBN 0-685-81147-6); Vol. 2, No. 1. pap. text ed. 27.00 (ISBN 0-08-022710-4). Pergamon.
Williams, M. M. R., ed. Progress in Nuclear Energy, 3 vols. (Illus.). 252p. 1979. Set. 97.00 (ISBN 0-08-024875-6). Pergamon.
Williams, M. Monier. Dictionary of English & Sanskrit. LC 73-495007. 1971. Repr. of 1851 ed. 17.50x (ISBN 0-8002-0172-8). Intl Pubns Serv.
Williams, M. R., jt. auth. see Maurer, H. A.
Williams, Margery. The Velveteen Rabbit. (gr. 1-9). 1975. pap. 1.95 (ISBN 0-380-00255-8, 43257, Camelot). Avon.
--The Velveteen Rabbit. (Illus.). 44p. 1981. pap. 2.25 (54148, Camelot). Avon.
--The Velveteen Rabbit: Or How Toys Become Real. (Illus.). 50p. (Orig.). (gr. k-12). 1981. PLB 12.90 (ISBN 0-89471-127-X); pap. 3.95 (ISBN 0-89471-128-8). Running Pr.
Williams, Marianne M. A Grammar of Tuscarora. LC 75-25124. (American Indian Linguistics Ser.). 1976. lib. bdg. 42.00 (ISBN 0-8240-1974-1). Garland Pub.
Williams, Martha E., ed. The Annual Review of Information Science & Technology, Vol. 11, 1976. LC 66-25096. (Illus.). 1976. 42.50 (ISBN 0-87715-212-8). Knowledge Indus.
--Annual Review of Information Science & Technology, Vol. 13. LC 66-25096. 1978. 42.50 (ISBN 0-914236-21-0). Knowledge Indus.
--Annual Review of Information Science & Techology 1979, Vol. 14. LC 66-25096. 1979. 42.50 (ISBN 0-914236-44-X). Knowledge Indus.
--Computer-Readable Data Bases: A Directory & Data Sourcebook. LC 66-46249. 1979. softcover 95.00 (ISBN 0-914236-45-8). Knowledge Indus.
Williams, Martin. Jazz Masters in Transition: 1957-1969. (The Roots of Jazz Ser.). 1980. Repr. of 1970 ed. 25.00 (ISBN 0-306-79612-0). Da Capo.
--Jazz Masters of New Orleans. (The Roots of Jazz Ser.). 1978. Repr. of 1967 ed. lib. bdg. 22.50 (ISBN 0-306-77541-7). Da Capo.
--The Smithsonian Experience. (Illus.). 1978. 19.95 (ISBN 0-89599-000-8). Norton.
Williams, Martin, ed. The Art of Jazz: Ragtime to Bebop. (Da Capo Quality Paperbacks Ser.). 248p. 1981. pap. 6.95 (ISBN 0-306-80134-5). Da Capo.
--Jazz Panorama. (The Roots of Jazz Ser.). 1979. Repr. of 1962 ed. lib. bdg. 22.50 (ISBN 0-306-79574-4). Da Capo.
Williams, Martin, jt. ed. see Blackbeard, Bill.
Williams, Mary C. Sources of Unity in Ben Jonson's Comedy. (Salzburg Studies in English Literature, Jacobean Drama Studies: No. 22). 230p. 1972. pap. text ed. 25.00x (ISBN 0-391-01572-9). Humanities.
Williams, Mary F. History of the San Francisco Committee of Vigilance of 1851. LC 71-87676. (American Scene Ser.). 1969. Repr. of 1921 ed. lib. bdg. 49.50 (ISBN 0-306-71716-6). Da Capo.
--The Public School & Finances. LC 80-20771. (The Education of the Public & the Public School Ser.). 64p. 1980. pap. 2.50 (ISBN 0-8298-0414-5). Pilgrim NY.
Williams, Mary F., ed. Government in the Classroom: Dollars & Power in the Classroom. LC 78-74964. 1979. 21.95 (ISBN 0-03-052751-1). Praeger.
Williams, Mary R. All About the Labrador. 1975. 8.95 o.p. (ISBN 0-7207-0842-7, Pub. by Michael Joseph). Merrimack Bk Serv.
--The Dual Purpose Labrador. 1969. 8.95 (ISBN 0-7207-0242-9, Pub. by Michael Joseph). Merrimack Bk Serv.
Williams, Masha. White Among the Reds. 224p. 1980. 25.00x (ISBN 0-85683-044-5, Pub. by Shepheard-Walwyn England). State Mutual Bk.
Williams, Mason, jt. auth. see Skillen, Charles R.
Williams, Melvin H. Drugs & Athletic Peformance. 212p. 1974. 14.75 (ISBN 0-398-03064-2). C C Thomas.
Williams, Merryn. Thomas Hardy & Rural England. LC 72-318. 1972. 17.50x (ISBN 0-231-03674-4). Columbia U Pr.
Williams, Michael. Draining of the Somerset Levels. LC 73-75830. (Illus.). 1970. 57.50 (ISBN 0-521-07486-X). Cambridge U Pr.
--Farm Tractors in Color. LC 74-20544. (Macmillan Color Ser.). (Illus.). 208p. 1975. 8.95 (ISBN 0-02-629300-5, 62930). Macmillan.
--Wales: A Study from the Air. 1975. pap. text ed. 6.95x o.p. (ISBN 0-435-34921-X). Heinemann Ed.
Williams, Michael & Bell, Stephen. Using the Urban Environment. 1972. pap. text ed. 3.95x o.p. (ISBN 0-435-80065-5). Heinemann Ed.
Williams, Michael, jt. auth. see Glen, Ann.
Williams, Michael D. Music for Viola. LC 78-70022. (Detroit Studies in Music Bibliography Ser.: No. 42). 1979. 16.50 (ISBN 0-911772-95-2). Info Coord.
Williams, Michael Z., jt. auth. see Filippone, Samuel R.

Williams, Mike. Rugby Sevens. 1975. 8.95 o.p. (ISBN 0-571-10523-8, Pub. by Faber & Faber); pap. 5.50 (ISBN 0-571-10679-X). Merrimack Bk Serv.
Williams, Miller. Why God Permits Evil. LC 77-8711. 1977. 9.95 (ISBN 0-8071-0377-2); pap. 4.95 (ISBN 0-8071-0378-0). La State U Pr.
Williams, Miller & McPherson, James A. Railroad: Trains & Train People. 1976. pap. 7.95 (ISBN 0-394-73237-5). Random.
--Railroad: Trains & Train People. 1976. 15.00 o.p. (ISBN 0-394-49857-7, BYR). Random.
Williams, Miller, jt. auth. see Ciardi, John.
Williams, Miller, ed. Contemporary American Poetry. (Illus.). 256p. 1972. pap. text ed. 7.95 (ISBN 0-394-31625-8). Random.
--Ozark, Ozark: A Hillside Reader. 200p. 1981. 15.95 (ISBN 0-8262-0331-0). U of Mo Pr.
Williams, Miller, tr. see Belli, Giuseppe G.
Williams, Morris, tr. Le Comportement Du Croyant. (French Bks.). (Fr.). 1979. write for info. (ISBN 0-8297-0833-2). Life Pubs Intl.
--La Justicia De Dios. (Spanish Bks.). (Span.). 1977. 2.50 (ISBN 0-8297-0759-X). Life Pubs Intl.
--Publiez Sa Justice. (French Bks.). (Fr.). 1979. 2.50 (ISBN 0-8297-0839-1). Life Pubs Intl.
Williams, Moyra. Breed of Horses. LC 75-134731. 1971. text ed. 15.00 (ISBN 0-08-007123-6). Pergamon.
Williams, N., jt. auth. see Kuzmanovic, B. O.
Williams, Neville. All the Queen's Men. (Elizabeth & Her Courtiers). (Illus.). 272p. 1972. 12.95 o.s.i. (ISBN 0-02-629110-X). Macmillan.
--The Cardinal & the Secretary: Thomas Wolsey & Thomas Cromwell. (Illus.). 288p. 1976. 9.95 o.s.i. (ISBN 0-02-629070-7). Macmillan.
--Elizabeth First. LC 74-187567. 224p. 1972. 4.95 o.p. (ISBN 0-385-01104-0). Doubleday.
--Henry Eighth & His Court. Roberts, Ray, ed. LC 70-125407. (Illus.). 1971. 12.95 o.s.i. (ISBN 0-02-629100-2). Macmillan.
--The Sea Dogs. LC 75-10503. (Illus.). 280p. 1975. 15.00 o.s.i. (ISBN 0-02-629120-7). Macmillan.
Williams, Norman. Terror at Tenerife. 1977. pap. 3.50 (ISBN 0-89728-058-X, 683641). Omega Pubns OR.
Williams, Nyal Z. & Tsukamoto, Jack T., eds. Library Instruction & Faculty Development. (Library Orientation Ser.: No. 11). 1980. 10.00 (ISBN 0-87650-125-0). Pierian.
Williams, Ora. American Black Women in the Arts & Social Sciences: A Bibliographic Survey. rev. ed. LC 77-17055. (Illus.). 1978. 10.00 (ISBN 0-8108-1096-4). Scarecrow.
Williams, Oscar, ed. The Mentor Book of Major British Poets. pap. 2.95 (ISBN 0-451-61876-9, ME1876, Ment). NAL.
Williams, Oscar & Honig, eds. The Mentor Book of Major American Poets. pap. 2.50 (ISBN 0-451-61773-8, ME1773, Ment). NAL.
Williams, P., ed. see Society for Psychosomatic Research, 22nd, Royal College of Physicians, London, Nov. 27-28 1978.
Williams, P. C. Low Back & Neck Pain: Causes & Conservative Treatment. (Illus.). 96p. 1980. pap. 6.95 (ISBN 0-398-03193-2). C C Thomas.
Williams, P. F. Beginner's Guide to Lightweight Camping. (Beginners Guide Ser.). 1975. 8.95 o.p. (ISBN 0-7207-0818-4, Pub. by Michael Joseph). Merrimack Bk Serv.
Williams, Pat, jt. auth. see Hill, Douglas.
Williams, Patricia, ed. see Rabineau, Phyllis.
Williams, Paul. Das Energi. LC 73-80135. 160p. 1980. pap. 4.95 (ISBN 0-934558-00-0). Entwhistle Bks.
--Das Energi. 1978. pap. 2.50 (ISBN 0-446-91955-1). Warner Bks.
--Das Energi. 1976. pap. 3.95 o.p. (ISBN 0-446-87250-4). Warner Bks.
--Heart of Gold. 1981. pap. 4.95 (ISBN 0-9601428-8-6); 9.95 (ISBN 0-934558-10-8). Entwhistle Bks.
Williams, Paul H. Antenna Theory & Design. 15.95x (ISBN 0-392-07549-0, SpS). Soccer.
Williams, Paul L. The Moral Philosophy of Peter Abelard. LC 80-5604. 191p. 1980. lib. bdg. 17.75 (ISBN 0-8191-1137-6); pap. text ed. 9.00 (ISBN 0-8191-1138-4). U Pr of Amer.
Williams, Paul L., ed. Christian Faith in a Neo-Pagan Society: Proceedings of the Fellowship of Catholic Scholara. LC 81-80229. 128p. (Orig.). 1981. pap. 5.95 (ISBN 0-937374-02-4); pap. text ed. 4.50 (ISBN 0-937374-03-2). NE Bks.
Williams, Paul L. & Moore, Jerry R., eds. Criterion-Referenced Testing for the Social Studies, No. 64. LC 80-84889. (Bulletin Ser.). 1980. pap. write for info. (ISBN 0-87986-034-0). Coun Soc Studies.
Williams, Paul N. Investigative Reporting & Editing. LC 77-4855. (Illus.). 1978. 14.50 (ISBN 0-13-504662-9). P-H.
Williams, Paul O. Breaking of Northwall. 288p. 1981. pap. 2.25 (ISBN 0-345-29259-6, Del Rey). Ballantine.
--The Ends of the Circle. 208p. (Orig.). 1981. pap. 2.25 (ISBN 0-345-29551-X, Del Rey). Ballantine.
Williams, Paul V. Primitive Religion & Healing: A Study of Folk Medicine in North East Brazil. (Folklore Society Mistletoe Ser.). (Illus.). 212p. 1979. 32.50x (ISBN 0-8476-6222-5). Rowman.
Williams, Penry. The Tudor Regime. 1979. 45.00x (ISBN 0-19-822491-5). Oxford U Pr.
Williams, Peter. European Organ, 1450-1850. LC 78-57080. (Illus.). 336p. 1978. Repr. of 1966 ed. 27.50x (ISBN 0-253-32083-6). Ind U Pr.
--New History of the Organ: From the Greeks to the Present Day. LC 79-2176. (Illus.). 264p. 1980. 27.50x (ISBN 0-253-15704-8). Ind U Pr.
--The Organ Music of J. S. Bach, 2 vols. LC 77-71431. (Illus.). Vol. 1, 01/1981. 72.00 (ISBN 0-521-21723-7); Vol. 2. 57.50 (ISBN 0-521-21517-X). Cambridge U Pr.
Williams, Peter W. Popular Religions in America. (P-H Studies on Religions Ser.). 1980. pap. text ed. 9.95 (ISBN 0-13-686113-X). P-H.
Williams, Petra. Flow Blue China: An Aid to Identification. LC 77-171985. (Illus.). 225p. 1971. 12.95x o.p. (ISBN 0-914736-01-9). Fountain Hse East.
--Flow Blue China, an Aid to Identification. rev. ed. LC 80-70461. (Illus.). 234p. 1981. 12.95x (ISBN 0-914736-07-8). Fountain Hse East.
--Flow Blue China & Mulberry Ware Similarity & Value Guide. rev. ed. LC 80-68848. (Illus.). 220p. 1980. 12.95x (ISBN 0-914736-06-X). Fountain Hse East.
Williams, Philip. Crisis Management: Confrontation & Diplomacy in the Nuclear Age. 1976. 24.95 (ISBN 0-470-98899-1). Halsted Pr.
--French Politicians & Elections, 1951-1968. (Illus.). 1970. 41.50 (ISBN 0-521-07709-5); pap. 12.50x (ISBN 0-521-09608-1). Cambridge U Pr.
--Wars, Plots & Scandals in Post-War France. LC 77-96105. 1970. 31.95 (ISBN 0-521-07741-9). Cambridge U Pr.
Williams, Philip M. Hugh Gaitskell: A Political Biography. 1979. 47.50x (ISBN 0-389-20032-8). B&N.
Williams, Phillip G. Free Cleveland: A Guide to Leisure Fun in the Cleveland, Ohio, Area. LC 80-82977. (Illus.). 1981. pap. text ed. 7.95 (ISBN 0-936284-00-5). P Gaines Co.
Williams, R., jt. ed. see Axton, Marie.
Williams, R. A. D. & Kruk, Z. L. An Introduction to the Biochemistry & Pharmacology of Antibiotics. 128p. 1980. 25.00x (ISBN 0-85664-857-4, Pub. by Croom Helm England). State Mutual Bk.
Williams, R. E., intro. by. Aviation Europe Nineteen Eighty-One. 34th ed. (Illus.). 170p. 1980. pap. 27.50x (ISBN 0-85499-888-8). Intl Pubns Serv.
Williams, R. F. The Shoot Apex & Leaf Growth. (Illus.). 280p. 1975. 35.50 (ISBN 0-521-20453-4). Cambridge U Pr.
Williams, R. Hal. Years of Decision: American Politics in the 1890's. LC 78-6407. (Critical Episodes in American Politics Ser). 1978. pap. text ed. 8.95 (ISBN 0-471-94878-0). Wiley.
Williams, R. J., jt. auth. see Phillips, C. S.
Williams, R. L. & Karacan, I. Sleep Disorders: Diagnosis & Treatment. LC 78-18896. 1978. 42.95 (ISBN 0-471-94682-6, Pub. by Wiley-Medical). Wiley.
Williams, R. Ora, ed. An Alice Dunbar-Nelson Reader. LC 78-58596. 1978. pap. text ed. 10.50 (ISBN 0-8191-0543-0). U Pr of Amer.
Williams, R. T., jt. auth. see Morrison, John S.
Williams, Rachel, jt. auth. see Spellmann, Charles M.
Williams, Ralph, tr. Escuela Dominical, Corazon De la Iglesia. (Spanish Bks.). 1979. 1.30 (ISBN 0-8297-0550-3). Life Pubs Intl.
Williams, Ralph C., Jr. Rheumatoid Arthritis. LC 74-4594. (Major Problems in Internal Medicine Ser.: Vol. 4). (Illus.). 255p. 1974. text ed. 14.50 (ISBN 0-7216-9417-9). Saunders.
Williams, Ralph G., ed. & tr. from Lat. The De Arta Poetica of Marco Girolamo Vida. 288p. 1976. 22.50x (ISBN 0-231-03959-X). Columbia U Pr.
Williams, Ralph M. Phonetic Spelling for College Students. LC 80-24084. 180p. 1980. Repr. of 1960 ed. lib. bdg. 27.50x (ISBN 0-313-22650-4, WIPS). Greenwood.
Williams, Raymond. Keywords: A Vocabulary of Culture & Society. 288p. 1976. Repr. 14.95 (ISBN 0-19-519854-9, 464). Oxford U Pr.
--Marxism & Literature. (Marxist Introductions Ser.). 1977. 12.95x (ISBN 0-19-876056-6). Oxford U Pr.
--Problems in Materialism & Culture: Selected Essays. 288p. 1981. 19.50x (ISBN 0-8052-7093-0, Pub. by NLB England); pap. 8.75 (ISBN 0-8052-7092-2). Schocken.
Williams, Redford B., jt. auth. see Gentry, W. Doyle.
Williams, Reese, ed. Hotel. 320p. 1980. 12.95 (ISBN 0-934378-13-4); pap. 6.95 (ISBN 0-934378-00-2). Tanam Pr.
Williams, Rex. Snooker -How to Become a Champion. 1976. 4.25 o.p. (ISBN 0-86002-136-X). Transatlantic.
Williams, Richard. The Loggers. (The Old West). (Illus.). (gr. 5 up). 1976. kivar 12.96 (ISBN 0-8094-1527-5, Pub. by Time-Life). Silver.
--The Northwest Coast. LC 73-87559. (American Wilderness Ser). (Illus.). (gr. 6 up). 1973. lib. bdg. 11.97 (ISBN 0-8094-1193-8, Pub. by Time-Life). Silver.
--The Northwest Coast. (The American Wilderness Ser.). (Illus.). 240p. 1974. 12.95 (ISBN 0-8094-1192-X). Time-Life.
Williams, Richard E. Called & Chosen: The Story of Mother Rebecca Jackson & the Philadelphia Shakers. LC 80-25498. (ATLA Monograph Ser.: No. 17). 193p. 1981. 11.00 (ISBN 0-8108-1382-3). Scarecrow.
Williams, Richard L. The Cascades. (The American Wilderness Ser.). (Illus.). 1974. 12.95 (ISBN 0-8094-1245-4). Time-Life.
--The Cascades. LC 74-13323. (American Wilderness). (Illus.). (gr. 6 up). 1974. PLB 11.97 (ISBN 0-8094-1246-2, Pub. by Time-Life). Silver.
--The Loggers. (The Old West Ser.). (Illus.). 1976. 12.95 (ISBN 0-8094-1525-9). Time-Life.
Williams, Richard L. & Moffat, Gene H. Occupational Alcoholism Programs. (Illus.). 296p. 1975. 24.75 (ISBN 0-398-03282-3). C C Thomas.
Williams, Robert. Hub: Champion of the Cutting Horses. (Illus.). 64p. 1975. 7.95 (ISBN 0-89015-104-0). Nortex Pr.
Williams, Robert B. & Venturini, Joseph L. School Vandalism: Cause & Cure. LC 80-69230. 130p. 1981. perfect bdg. 9.50 (ISBN 0-86548-060-5). Century Twenty One.
Williams, Robert H. The Old Corps. (Illus.). 160p. Date not set. 25.95 (ISBN 0-87021-504-3). Naval Inst Pr. Postponed.
Williams, Robert H., jt. auth. see Ross, Marc H.
Williams, Robert H., ed. Textbook of Endocrinology. 5th ed. LC 73-76190. (Illus.). 1138p. 1974. text ed. 35.00 (ISBN 0-7216-9397-0). Saunders.
--Toward a Solar Civilization. (Illus.). 264p. 1980. 15.00x (ISBN 0-262-23089-5); pap. 6.95 (ISBN 0-262-73054-5). MIT Pr.
Williams, Robert L. Educational Alternatives for Colonized People: Models for Liberation. (Illus.). 128p. 1974. 9.95 (ISBN 0-8046-7077-3). Kennikat.
Williams, Robert L., et al. Electroencephalography (EEG) of Human Sleep: Clinical Applications. LC 73-20032. 192p. 1974. 34.50 (ISBN 0-471-94686-9, Pub. by Wiley Medical). Wiley.
Williams, Robert M., ed. Ucla Business Forecast for the Nation & California in 1980. 1980. 35.00 (ISBN 0-686-52633-3). UCLA Busn Forecasting.
Williams, Robley C. & Fisher, Harold W. An Electron Micrographic Atlas of Viruses. (Illus.). 152p. 1974. 22.75 (ISBN 0-398-03153-3). C C Thomas.
Williams, Rod. How to Immigrate Without a Lawyer. 200p. 1980. pap. 19.95 (ISBN 0-89260-198-1). Hwong Pub.
Williams, Roger. Key into the Language of America. 5th ed. LC 70-157500. Repr. of 1643 ed. 18.00 (ISBN 0-8103-3723-1). Gale.
--The Nuclear Power Decisions: British Policies, 1953-1978. 365p. 1980. 49.00x (ISBN 0-7099-0265-4, Pub. by Croom Helm Ltd England). Biblio Dist.
Williams, Roger J. Alcoholism: The Nutritional Approach. 1959. pap. 3.45 (ISBN 0-292-70301-5). U of Tex Pr.
--Nutrition in a Nutshell. LC 62-15322. pap. 2.50 (ISBN 0-385-03031-2, C396, Dolp). Doubleday.
--The Prevention of Alcoholism Through Nutrition. 176p. (Orig.). 1981. pap. 2.50 (ISBN 0-553-14502-9). Bantam.
--You Are Extraordinary. 1967. 6.95 o.p. (ISBN 0-394-45316-6). Random.
Williams, Roger J. & Kalita, Dwight K., eds. A Physician's Handbook on Orthomolecular Medicine. LC 77-8304. 1977. text ed. 19.95 (ISBN 0-08-021533-5). Pergamon.
Williams, Roger L. French Revolution of 1870-1871. (Revolutions in the Modern World Ser.). 1969. pap. 5.95x (ISBN 0-393-09837-0, NortonC). Norton.
Williams, Roger M. Sing a Sad Song: The Life of Hank Williams. LC 80-15520. (Music in American Life Ser.). 275p. 1981. 18.95 (ISBN 0-252-00844-8); pap. 7.95 (ISBN 0-252-00861-8). U of Ill Pr.
Williams, Rosa M., ed. Restoration: Our Philosophy Through Inspired Poems. LC 79-66586. 1980. 6.50x (ISBN 0-9602366-1-9); pap. 4.50x (ISBN 0-686-65878-7). Sooty-Face.
Williams, Rosalie I., compiled by. Institute of Jamaica, Kingston, Jamaican National Bibliography, 1964-1974. LC 80-11767. 1981. lib. bdg. 120.00 (ISBN 0-527-45166-5). Kraus Intl.
Williams, Rowan. Christian Spirituality: A Theological History from the New Testament to Luther & St. John of the Cross. LC 80-82190. 193p. 1980. 15.00 (ISBN 0-8042-0660-0); pap. 7.50 (ISBN 0-8042-0508-6). John Knox.
Williams, Roy, jt. auth. see Padfield, Harland.
Williams, Roy, ed. see Follette, Daniel.
Williams, Royson V. Acoustic Emission. 140p. 1980. 29.00 (ISBN 0-9960020-0-6, Pub. by a Hilger England). Heyden.
Williams, Russ. Nothing New Under the Sun. 1981. 7.95 (ISBN 0-8062-1585-2). Carlton.
Williams, S. A. Salesmanship. (Teach Yourself Ser.). 1974. pap. 2.95 o.p. (ISBN 0-679-10485-2). McKay.
Williams, S. T., jt. auth. see Gray, T. R.
Williams, S. T., ed. see Irving, Washington.
Williams, Sam K. Jesus' Death As Saving Event the Background & Origin of a Concept. LC 75-28341. (Harvard Dissertations in Religion). 1975. pap. 9.00 (ISBN 0-89130-029-5, 020102). Scholars Pr Ca.
Williams, Sarkey V., jt. auth. see Eisenberg, John M.
Williams, Selma R. Divine Rebel: The Life of Anne Marbury Hutchinson. LC 80-20109. 256p. 1981. 12.95 (ISBN 0-03-055846-8). HR&W.
Williams, Shirley. The Peacock Poems (& Others) LC 75-12531. (Wesleyan Poetry Program: Vol. 79). 87p. (Orig.). 1975. pap. 4.95 (ISBN 0-8195-1079-3, Pub. by Wesleyan U Pr). Columbia U Pr.
Williams, Stanley T see Gabriel, Ralph H.
Williams, Stephen. Caddoan Indians One. Horr, David A., ed. (American Indian Ethnohistory Ser.). 1978. lib. bdg. 42.00 (ISBN 0-8240-0763-8). Garland Pub.
Williams, Stephen, ed. The Waring Papers: The Collected Works of Antonio J. Waring. LC 67-27476. (Papers of the Peabody Museum Ser.). 1977. pap. 20.00 (ISBN 0-87365-169-3). Peabody Harvard.
Williams, Stephen J. Issues in Health Services. LC 79-22066. (Ser. in the Health Services). 1980. 17.95 (ISBN 0-471-04679-5, Pub. by Wiley-Med). Wiley.
--A Welsh Grammar. 184p. 1980. pap. text ed. 20.00 (ISBN 0-7083-0737-X). Verry.
Williams, Strephon K. Jungian-Senoi Dreamwork Manual. 302p. (Orig.). 1980. pap. 14.95 o.p. (ISBN 0-918572-04-5). Journey Pr.
Williams, Sue R. Essentials of Nutrition & Diet Therapy. 2nd ed. LC 77-18733. (Illus.). 1978. pap. text ed. 13.95 (ISBN 0-8016-5571-4). Mosby.
--Mowry's Basic Nutrition & Diet Therapy. 6th ed. LC 79-26165. (Illus.). 1980. pap. text ed. 9.50 (ISBN 0-8016-5556-0). Mosby.
--Nutrition & Diet Therapy. 4th ed. (Illus.). 875p. 1981. text ed. 19.95 (ISBN 0-8016-5554-4). Mosby.
--Self-Study Guide for Nutrition & Diet Therapy. 2nd ed. 1978. pap. text ed. 8.50 (ISBN 0-8016-5573-0). Mosby.
Williams, Sunnie. The Nomie Book: Growing up from Shy. (Illus.). 104p. (Orig.). (gr. 3-6). 1981. pap. 5.95 (ISBN 0-9605444-0-2). Wee Smile.
Williams, T. B., jt. auth. see Thorold, H.
Williams, T. Franklin, ed. Rehabilitation of the Aged. 1981. price not set (ISBN 0-89004-417-1, 471). Raven.
Williams, T. Harry. The History of American Wars: From Colonial Times to World War I. LC 80-2717. 1981. 20.00 (ISBN 0-394-51167-0). Knopf.
--A History of American Wars: From Colonial Times to World War I. LC 80-2717. 512p. 1981. 20.00 (ISBN 0-394-51167-0). Knopf.
--Lincoln & the Radicals. (Illus.). 1941. pap. 8.95x (ISBN 0-299-00274-8). U of Wis Pr.
--The Union Restored, 1861-1876. LC 63-8572. (Life History of the United States). (Illus.). (gr. 5 up). 1974. PLB 9.96 (ISBN 0-8094-0555-5, Pub. by Time-Life). Silver.
--The Union Sundered, 1849-1865. LC 63-8572. (Life History of the United States). (Illus.). (gr. 5 up). 1974. PLB 9.96 (ISBN 0-8094-0554-7, Pub. by Time-Life). Silver.
Williams, T. Harry, ed. With Beauregard in Mexico. LC 69-19760. (American Scene Ser.). 1969. Repr. of 1956 ed. lib. bdg. 17.50 (ISBN 0-306-71255-5). Da Capo.
Williams, Tennessee. In the Bar of the Tokyo Hotel & Other Plays. LC 78-159743. (The Theatre of Tennessee Williams: Vol. VII). 352p. 1981. 17.95 (ISBN 0-8112-0795-1). New Directions.
--One Arm & Other Stories. LC 57-31974. pap. 5.95 (ISBN 0-8112-0223-2, NDP237). New Directions.

--Small Craft Warnings. LC 72-80978. 1972. pap. 4.95 (ISBN 0-8112-0460-X). New Directions.
--Streetcar Named Desire. LC 48-5556. 1980. pap. 3.95 (ISBN 0-8112-0765-X, NDP501). New Directions.
--A Streetcar Named Desire. 1973. pap. 1.75 (ISBN 0-451-07595-1, E9372, Sig). NAL.
--Tennessee Williams' Letters to Donald Windham. 1976. 110.00x (ISBN 0-917366-01-8). S Campbell.
--Twenty Seven Wagons Full of Cotton. 3rd ed. LC 53-12488. 1966. pap. 4.95 (ISBN 0-8112-0225-9, NDP217). New Directions.
--Twenty-Seven Wagons Full of Cotton & Other Short Stories. LC 78-159743. (The Theatre of Tennessee Williams: Vol. VI). 288p. 1981. 17.95 (ISBN 0-8112-0794-3). New Directions.
Williams, Terence H., jt. auth. see Gluhbegovic, Nedzad.
Williams, Terrell G. Consumer Behavior: Concepts & Strategies. 600p. pap. text ed. 14.36 (ISBN 0-8299-0420-4). West Pub.
Williams, Theodore P. & Baker, B. N., eds. The Effect of Constant Light on Visual Processes. LC 79-26293. 465p. 1980. 45.00 (ISBN 0-306-40328-5, Plenum Pr). Plenum Pub.
Williams, Thomas. The Hair of Harold Roux. 384p. 1975. pap. 1.95 o.p. (ISBN 0-345-25300-0). Ballantine.
--Town Burning. 1970. 6.95 o.p. (ISBN 0-394-44918-5). Random.
--Whipple's Castle. LC 68-58852. 1969. 8.95 o.p. (ISBN 0-394-45170-8). Random.
Williams, Thomas & Somers, John. Excellency & Praeheminence of the Law of England. Berkowitz, David S. & Thorne, Samuel E., eds. LC 77-86674. (Classics of English Legal History in the Modern Era Ser.: Vol. 50). 357p. 1979. lib. bdg. 40.00 (ISBN 0-8240-3099-0). Garland Pub.
Williams, Thomas A. & Johnson, James H. Mental Health in the Twenty-First Century. LC 78-20270. 208p. 1979. 21.95x (ISBN 0-669-02718-9). Lexington Bks.
Williams, Thomas A., jt. auth. see Anderson Sweeney, David R.
Williams, Thomas E. Self-Assessment of Current Knowledge in Pediatric Hematology & Oncology. 1974. 15.00 (ISBN 0-87488-277-X). Med Exam.
Williams, Thomas R. The Dunsun: A North Borneo Society. Spindler, George & Spindler, Louise, eds. (Case Studies in Cultural Anthropology). 114p. pap. text ed. 6.95x (ISBN 0-8290-0310-X). Irvington.
Williams, Trevor, et al. School, Work, & Career 17-Year-Olds in Australia. (Australian Council for Educational Research Monograph: No. 6). 167p. 1980. pap. text ed. 22.50 (ISBN 0-85563-206-2). Verry.
Williams, Ursula M. The Nine Lives of Island MacKenzie. LC 80-670265. 128p. (gr. 3-7). 1980. 8.95 (ISBN 0-7011-0227-6, Pub. by Chatto, Bodley Head & Jonathan). Merrimack Bk Serv.
Williams, Ursula Vaughan see Vaughan Williams, Ursula.
Williams, Vera B. Three Days on a River in a Red Canoe. LC 80-23893. (Illus.). 32p. (gr. k-3). 1981. 8.95 (ISBN 0-688-80307-5); PLB 8.59 (ISBN 0-688-84307-7). Greenwillow.
Williams, Virginia R., et al. Basic Physical Chemistry for the Life Sciences. 3rd ed. LC 77-13374. (Illus.). 1978. text ed. 23.95x (ISBN 0-7167-0027-1); answer bk. avail. (ISBN 0-685-87690-X). W H Freeman.
Williams, W. E., ed. A Book of English Essays. 1981. pap. 3.95 (ISBN 0-14-043153-5). Penguin.
Williams, W. H. H. L. Mencken. (United States Authors Ser.: No. 297). 1977. lib. bdg. 10.95 (ISBN 0-8057-7200-6). Twayne.
Williams, W. M. Occupational Choice: A Selection of Papers from the Sociological Review. 1974. pap. text ed. 12.50x (ISBN 0-04-371026-3). Allen Unwin.
Williams, W. P. & Van Zandt, Joseph H. How to Start Your Own Magazine. 1979. 12.95 o.p. (ISBN 0-8092-7444-2); pap. 4.95 (ISBN 0-8092-7443-4). Contemp Bks.
Williams, Walley, jt. auth. see Urban, John.
Williams, Walter. The Implementation Perspctive: A Guide for Mananging Social Service Delivery Programs. 1980. 11.50 (ISBN 0-520-04054-6); pap. 3.95 (ISBN 0-520-04063-5). U of Cal Pr.
--The Mr. Bill Show. 80p. pap. 2.50 (ISBN 0-671-42039-9). PB.
Williams, Walter, jt. ed. see Rossi, Peter H.
Williams, Walter E. & Reed, James H. Fundamentals of Business Mathematics. 2nd ed. 580p. 1981. text ed. write for info. (ISBN 0-697-08049-8); wkbk avail. (ISBN 0-697-08056-0); instrs' manual avail. (ISBN 0-697-08057-9). Wm C Brown.
--Fundamentals of Business Mathematics. 1977. text ed. 14.95x o.p. (ISBN 0-697-08015-3); wkbk 7.95x o.p. (ISBN 0-697-08019-6); instructor's manual 4.00 o.p. (ISBN 0-686-67790-0). Wm C Brown.
Williams, Walter L., ed. Southeastern Indians Since the Removal Era. LC 78-10490. (Illus.). 270p. 1979. 18.50x (ISBN 0-8203-0464-6); pap. 6.00 (ISBN 0-8203-0483-2). U of Ga Pr.
Williams, Wick, ed. see DuPont, Elizabeth N.
Williams, Wiley J., jt. auth. see Cheney, Frances N.
Williams, William A. Some Presidents: Wilson to Nixon. 1972. pap. 1.95 o.p. (ISBN 0-686-66886-3, 70227). Random.
Williams, William C. In the Money. LC 40-35170. (Stecher Trilogy: Vol. 2). 1967. pap. 2.45 (ISBN 0-8112-0231-3, NDP240). New Directions.
--Many Loves & Other Plays. Incl. Many Loves; A Dream of Love; Tituba's Children; The First President; The Cure. LC 61-9334. 1961. pap. 9.95 (ISBN 0-8112-0232-1, NDP191). New Directions.
Williams, William J. General Semantics & the Social Sciences. LC 71-155970. 1972. 8.50 o.p. (ISBN 0-8022-2055-X). Philos Lib.
Williams-Ellis, Amabel & Stobbs, William. Life in England: A Pictorial History, 2 vols. Incl. Pt. 2. Tudor England. o.p. (ISBN 0-685-32717-5); Pt. 3. Seventh Century England (ISBN 0-216-87195-6); Pt. 4. Hanoverian England. o.p. (ISBN 0-685-32718-3); Pt. 5. Waterloo to 1914. o.p. (ISBN 0-685-32719-1); Pt. 6. Modern Times (ISBN 0-216-87198-0). (Illus.). 1970. 5.00 ea. o.p. Dufour.
Williams-Ellis, Annabel. Fairy Tales from Everywhere. (Illus., Orig.). 1978. pap. 2.95 (ISBN 0-8467-0533-8, Pub. by Two Continents). Hippocrene Bks.
--Fairy Tales from Here & There. (Illus., Orig.). 1978. pap. 2.95 (ISBN 0-8467-0536-2, Pub. by Two Continents). Hippocrene Bks.
--Fairy Tales from Near & Far. (Illus., Orig.). 1978. pap. 2.95 (ISBN 0-8467-0534-6, Pub. by Two Continents). Hippocrene Bks.
Williams-Heller, Ann. Nature's Own Vegetable Cookbook. LC 73-183557. Orig. Title: Cooked to Your Taste. 234p. 1972. pap. 1.45 o.p. (ISBN 0-668-02586-7). Arc Bks.
Williamson, et al. Social Problems: The Contemporary Debates. 3rd ed. 1981. pap. text ed. 9.95 (ISBN 0-316-94362-2); test bank avail. (ISBN 0-316-94363-0). Little.
Williamson, Ann P., jt. auth. see Robb, George P.
Williamson, Charles C. The Williamson Reports of Nineteen Twenty-One & Nineteen Twenty-Three: Including Training for Library Work & Training for Library Service. LC 78-25204. 1971. 13.50 (ISBN 0-8108-0417-4). Scarecrow.
Williamson, Clark M. God Is Never Absent. 1977. pap. 2.50 (ISBN 0-8272-1230-5). Bethany Pr.
Williamson, Daniel R. Feature Writing for Newspapers. 1975. 12.50 (ISBN 0-8038-2312-6); pap. text ed. 6.95x (ISBN 0-8038-2313-4). Hastings.
Williamson, Edmund G. & Biggs, Donald A. Student Personnel Work: A Program of Development Relationships. LC 74-28492. 384p. 1975. text ed. 24.50 (ISBN 0-471-94880-2). Wiley.
Williamson, G. & Payne, W. J. An Introduction to Animal Husbandry in the Tropics. 3rd ed. (Tropical Agriculture Ser.). (Illus.). 1978. text ed. 31.00x (ISBN 0-582-46813-2). Longman.
Williamson, G. I. The Shorter Catechism: A Study Manual, 2 vols. Vol. 1. pap. 3.75 (ISBN 0-87552-539-3); Vol. 2. pap. 3.75 (ISBN 0-87552-540-7). Presby & Reformed.
--Westminster Confession of Faith: A Study Manual. 5.50 (ISBN 0-87552-538-5). Presby & Reformed.
Williamson, Geoffrey A., tr. see Josephus, Flavius.
Williamson, H. D. The Year of the Koala. LC 75-12704. 1975. 8.95 o.p. (ISBN 0-684-14351-8, ScribT). Scribner.
Williamson, H. D., jt. auth. see Douglas, S. W.
Williamson, H. G. Israel in the Book of Chronicles. LC 76-11096. 1977. 34.00 (ISBN 0-521-21305-3). Cambridge U Pr.
Williamson, Harold F., et al. The American Petroleum Industry, 2 vols. Incl. Vol. 1. The Age of Illumination, 1859 to 1899; Vol. 2. The Age of Energy, 1899 to 1959. LC 80-22253. (Northwestern University Studies in Business History). (Illus.). 1981. lib. bdg. 125.00x set (ISBN 0-313-22788-X, WIAC). Greenwood.
--The American Petroleum Industry: The Age of Illumination, 1859-1899; the Age of Energy, 1899-1959, 2 vols. LC 80-22253. (Northwestern University Studies in Business History). (Illus.). 1981. Repr. of 1959 ed. Set. lib. bdg. 125.00x (ISBN 0-313-22788-8, WIAC). Greenwood.
Williamson, Henry. Salar the Salmon. (Illus., Orig.). 1973. pap. 6.95 (ISBN 0-571-04811-0, Pub. by Faber & Faber). Merrimack Bk Serv.
Williamson, Henry H., Jr. To Be Self-Evident. 280p. 1980. 8.95 (ISBN 0-533-04016-7). Vantage.
Williamson, J., jt. auth. see Newell, Gordon.
Williamson, J. N. Horror House. LC 80-85113. 304p. (Orig.). 1981. pap. 2.95 (ISBN 0-87216-832-8). Playboy Pbks.
Williamson, Jack. The Humanoid Touch. 2nd ed. 224p. 1981. pap. 2.25 (ISBN 0-553-14598-3). Bantam.
--The Power of Blackness. LC 75-29508. 192p. (YA) 1976. 6.95 o.p. (ISBN 0-399-11467-X, Dist. by Putnam). Berkley Pub.
--Seetee. 1979. pap. 1.95 (ISBN 0-515-05150-0). Jove Pubns.
Williamson, Jack, jt. auth. see Pohl, Frederick.
Williamson, Jack, jt. auth. see Pohl, Frederik.
Williamson, James A. Great Britain & the Commonwealth. 3rd ed. 1965. text ed. 5.50x (ISBN 0-7136-0844-7). Humanities.
--The Tudor Age. (A History of England). (Illus.). 496p. 1979. pap. text ed. 13.95 (ISBN 0-582-49074-X). Longman.
Williamson, Janet A. Current Perspectives in Nursing Education, Vol. 2. LC 75-32544. (Current Perspectives Ser.). (Illus.). 1978. 11.95 (ISBN 0-8016-5578-1); pap. 9.50 (ISBN 0-8016-5579-X). Mosby.
Williamson, Janet A., et al. Intensive Care Nursing Continuing Education Review. 1977. spiral bdg. 6.00 o.p. (ISBN 0-87488-399-7). Med Exam.
Williamson, Jeffrey G. & Lindert, Peter H. American Inequality: A Macroeconomic History. (Institute for Research on Poverty Monograph). 1980. 29.50 (ISBN 0-12-757160-4). Acad Pr.
Williamson, Joel. New People: Miscegenation & Mulattoes in the United States. LC 80-65201. 1980. 16.95 (ISBN 0-02-934790-4). Free Pr.
Williamson, Joel R., ed. Origins of Segregation. (Problems in American Civilization Ser.). 1968. pap. text ed. 4.95x o.p. (ISBN 0-669-46201-2). Heath.
Williamson, John. The Failure of World Monetary Reform, 1971-74. LC 77-71278. 221p. 1977. 15.00x (ISBN 0-8147-9173-5); pap. 6.00x (ISBN 0-8147-9174-3). NYU Pr.
Williamson, John D. & Danaher, Kate. Self-Care in Health. 1978. lib. bdg. 22.50 (ISBN 0-85664-484-6). N Watson.
Williamson, Karina, ed. see Smart, Christopher.
Williamson, Kenneth D., Jr., jt. ed. see Cox, Kenneth E.
Williamson, Kenneth L., jt. auth. see Fieser, Louis F.
Williamson, L. Keith, jt. auth. see Smith, R. Dennis.
Williamson, Lamar, Jr., jt. auth. see Beck, Madeline H.
Williamson, Liz, ed. see Fischer-Munstermann, Uta.
Williamson, M. F., jt. auth. see Evans, R. G.
Williamson, Margaret. First Book of Birds. (First Bks). (Illus.). (gr. 4-6). 1951. PLB 4.90 o.p. (ISBN 0-531-00484-8). Watts.
--Social Worker. 1964. 3.95 o.s.i. (ISBN 0-02-629950-X). Macmillan.
Williamson, Nancy E. Sons or Daughters: A Cross Cultural Survey of Parental Preferences. LC 76-26888. (Sage Library of Social Research: Vol. 31). 1976. 18.00x (ISBN 0-8039-0673-0); pap. 8.95x (ISBN 0-8039-0674-9). Sage.
Williamson, Oliver E. Markets & Hierarchies - Analysis & Antitrust Implications: A Study in the Economics of Internal Organization. LC 74-27597. (Illus.). 1975. 17.95 (ISBN 0-02-935360-2). Free Pr.
Williamson, Porter B. Patton's Principles. LC 77-70779. (Illus.). 1979. 9.95 (ISBN 0-918356-04-0); pap. 5.95 (ISBN 0-918356-03-2). MSC Inc.
Williamson, Richard & Trotter, Hale. Multivariable Mathematics: Linear Algebra, Calculus, Differential Equations. 2nd ed. (Illus.). 1979. ref. 23.95 (ISBN 0-13-604850-1). P-H.
Williamson, Richard, et al. Calculus of Vector Functions. 3rd ed. LC 75-167788. (Illus.). 576p. 1972. ref. ed. 23.95 (ISBN 0-13-112367-X). P-H.
Williamson, Robert C. Marriage & Family Relations. 2nd ed. LC 70-37027. 1972. text ed. 18.95 (ISBN 0-471-94905-1). Wiley.
Williamson, Robert C., et al. Social Psychology. LC 80-52451. 550p. 1981. text ed. 14.95 (ISBN 0-87581-264-3). Peacock Pubs. Postponed.
Williamson, Samuel. Origins of a Tragedy. (Problems in Civilization Ser.). (Orig.). 1981. pap. text ed. 3.95x (ISBN 0-88273-409-1). Forum Pr MO.
Williamson, Samuel J. Fundamentals of Air Pollution. LC 75-186842. 1973. text ed. 23.95 (ISBN 0-201-08629-8). A-W.
Williamson, Stanley. The Munich Air Disaster. (Illus.). 1973. 8.95 o.p. (ISBN 0-85181-005-5, Pub. by Faber & Faber). Merrimack Bk Serv.
Williamson, Tony. The Samson Strike. 256p. 1981. pap. 2.50 (ISBN 0-445-04643-0). Popular Lib.
Williamson, Yvonne M. Research Methodology & Its Application to Nursing. 360p. 1981. 13.95 (ISBN 0-471-03313-8, Pub. by Wiley Med). Wiley.
Williams-Wood, Cyril. Staffordshire Pot Lids & Their Potters. 1972. 26.00 o.p. (ISBN 0-571-09826-6, Pub. by Faber & Faber). Merrimack Bk Serv.
Willianson, Jack. Brothers to Demons, Brothers to Gods. 1981. pap. 2.25 (ISBN 0-425-04529-3). Berkley Pub.
Williard. The Highest Hit. (gr. 4-6). Date not set. pap. cancelled (ISBN 0-590-30051-2, Schol Pap). Schol Bk Serv.
Willich, Anthony F. Elements of Critical Philosophy. Wellek, Rene, ed. LC 75-11266. (British Philosophers & Theologians of the 17th & 18th Centuries: Vol. 65). 1977. Repr. of 1798 ed. lib. bdg. 42.00 (ISBN 0-8240-1815-X). Garland Pub.
Willie, Charles V. The Sociology of Urban Education: Desegregation & Integration. LC 78-4403. (Illus.). 1978. 18.95 (ISBN 0-669-02348-5). Lexington Bks.
Willie, Charles V. & Beker, Jerome. Race Mixing in Public Schools. LC 73-10947. (Special Studies in U.S. Economic, Social & Political Issues). 1973. 20.00x (ISBN 0-275-28812-9); pap. text ed. 8.95x (ISBN 0-89197-915-8). Irvington.
Willie, Charles V. & Edmonds, Ronald R., eds. Black Colleges in America. LC 78-17147. 1978. pap. text ed. 8.95x (ISBN 0-8077-2528-5). Tchrs Coll.
Willier, Robert A., jt. auth. see Unruh, Adolph.
Williford, Miriam, ed. Source Directory: Assistance to Third World Broadcasters. LC 79-3610. 1979. loose leaf 5.95 (ISBN 0-916584-14-3). Ford Found.
Willig, George & Bergman, Drew. Going It Alone. LC 78-69672. (Illus.). 160p. 1979. 12.95 (ISBN 0-385-14725-2); pap. 6.95 (ISBN 0-385-14726-0). Doubleday.
Willig, P. Lichtstreifen. 141p. 1973. pap. 5.75 (ISBN 0-08-016281-9); pap. text ed. 3.30 (ISBN 0-08-017826-X). Pergamon.
Willig, Robert D. Welfare Analysis of Policies Affecting Prices & Products. LC 78-75051. (Outstanding Dissertations in Economics). 1980. lib. bdg. 20.00 (ISBN 0-8240-4129-1). Garland Pub.
Willigen, John Van see Van Willigen, John.
Willigen, John Van see Abbott, Susan & Van Willigen, John.
Willimon, William H. Integrative Preaching: The Pulpit at the Center. LC 80-39628. (Abingdon Preacher's Library). 112p. (Orig.). 1981. pap. 4.95 (ISBN 0-687-19129-7). Abingdon.
Willimon, William H., jt. auth. see Westerhoff, John H.
Willims, Michael A., tr. see Dibelius, Martin.
Willing, Jules Z. The Reality of Retirement: The Inner Experience of Becoming a Retired Person. 224p. 1981. 10.95 (ISBN 0-688-00298-6); pap. 6.95 (ISBN 0-688-00394-X). Morrow.
Willinger, Herman & Weber, Albert, eds. Echerichia coli Infections in Domestic Animals. (Advances in Veterinary Medicine Ser.: Vol. 29). (Illus.). 86p. (Orig.). 1979. pap. text ed. 25.90 (ISBN 3-489-77916-9). Parey Sci Pubs.
Willingham, Calder. End As a Man. LC 47-1581. 8.95 (ISBN 0-8149-0238-3). Vanguard.
--Eternal Fire. LC 63-7498. 1962. 8.95 (ISBN 0-8149-0237-5). Vanguard.
--Providence Island. LC 68-8088. 10.00 (ISBN 0-8149-0236-7). Vanguard.
--Rambling Rose. 1972. 6.95 o.p. (ISBN 0-440-07229-3). Delacorte.
Willings, David. The Creatively Gifted: Recognising & Developing the Creative Personality. 184p. 30.00x (ISBN 0-85941-120-6, Pub. by Woodhead-Faulkner England). State Mutual Bk.
Willis, A. H., jt. auth. see Rosenauer, N.
Willis, A. T. Anaerobic Bacteriology: Clinical & Laboratory Practice. 3rd ed. 1977. 24.95 (ISBN 0-407-00081-X). Butterworths.
Willis, Alden T., jt. auth. see Johnston, Carol L.
Willis, Arthur J. & George, W. N. The Architect in Practice. 333p. 1974. text ed. 26.50x (ISBN 0-258-96959-8, Pub. by Granada England). Renouf.
Willis, Arthur J. & Willis, Christopher J. Practice & Procedure for the Quantity Surveyor. 8th ed. 239p. 1980. text ed. 30.00x (ISBN 0-246-11172-0, Pub. by Granada England); pap. text ed. 16.75x (ISBN 0-246-11242-5, Pub. by Granada England). Renouf.
Willis, Avery T., Jr. Indonesian Revival: Why Two Million Came to Christ. LC 77-12811. (Illus.). 1977. pap. 6.95 (ISBN 0-87808-428-2). William Carey Lib.
Willis, B. T. Chemical Applications of Thermal Neutron Scattering. (Harwell Ser.). (Illus.). 328p. 1973. 45.00x (ISBN 0-19-851709-2). Oxford U Pr.

Willis, B. T. & Pryor, A. W. Thermal Vibrations in Crystallography. LC 73-94357. (Illus.). 280p. 1975. 49.50 (ISBN 0-521-20447-X). Cambridge U Pr.

Willis, Charles D. Blueprint Reading for Commercial Construction. LC 77-87887. 1979. pap. 10.40 (ISBN 0-8273-1654-2); instructor's guide 2.25 (ISBN 0-8273-1655-0). Delmar.

Willis, Christopher. Problem-Solving in General Chemistry. LC 76-14004. (Illus.). 1977. pap. text ed. 9.50 (ISBN 0-395-24532-X). HM.

Willis, Christopher J., jt. auth. see Willis, Arthur J.

Willis, Cleve E., jt. ed. see Field, Barry C.

Willis, David L., jt. auth. see Wang, Chih H.

Willis, Dean, jt. ed. see Naib, Zuther M.

Willis, Donald C. Horror & Science Fiction Films: A Checklist. LC 72-3682. 1972. 21.00 (ISBN 0-8108-0508-1). Scarecrow.

Willis, Earl T. Education & First Principles: A Historical Perspective. LC 80-16408. ix, 132p. 1980. 12.74 (ISBN 0-8130-0646-5). U Presses Fla.

--Educational & First Principles: A Historical Perspective. LC 80-16406. 1980. 12.75 (ISBN 0-8130-0646-5). U Presses Fla.

Willis, Ellen. Beginning to See the Light: Pieces of a Decade. LC 80-22890. 320p. 1981. 12.95 (ISBN 0-394-51137-9). Knopf.

Willis, F. Roy. Western Civilization, an Urban Perspective, 3 vols. Incl. Vol. 1. From the Rise of Athens Through the Late Middle Ages (ISBN 0-669-89235-1); Vol. 2. From 1300 Through 1815 (ISBN 0-669-89243-2); Vol. 3. From 1815 to the Contemporary Age. o.p. (ISBN 0-669-89250-5). 1973. pap. text ed. 7.95x ea. o.p.; instructors' manual free o.p. (ISBN 0-669-84913-8). Heath.

--Western Civilization: An Urban Perspective, 2 vols. 3rd ed. (Vol. 1, 688 pp.:vol. 2, 560 pp.). 1981. Vol. 1. pap. text ed. 12.95 (ISBN 0-669-03364-2); Vol. 2. pap. text ed. 12.95 (ISBN 0-669-03365-0); instructor's guide (ISBN 0-669-03366-9). Heath.

--Western Civilization: An Urban Perspective, 2 vols. 2nd ed. 1977. pap. text ed. 12.95x ea. o.p.; Vol. 1. (ISBN 0-669-00455-3); Vol. 2. (ISBN 0-669-00463-4); instructor's manual free o.p. (ISBN 0-669-00471-5). Heath.

Willis, George, ed. Qualitative Evaluation Concepts & Cases in Curriculum Criticism. LC 77-23647. (Education Ser.). 1978. 21.50 (ISBN 0-8211-2257-6); text ed. 19.50 ten copies (ISBN 0-685-04974-4). McCutchan.

Willis, Hulton. Modern Descriptive English Grammar. 1972. text ed. 13.95 scp (ISBN 0-352-15125-0, HarpC). Har-Row.

Willis, Irene, jt. auth. see Richards, Arlene K.

Willis, J. C. A Dictionary of the Flowering Plants & Ferns Vol. 1: Generie & Family Names. 8th ed. LC 72-83581. 1300p. 1973. 90.00 (ISBN 0-521-08699-X). Cambridge U Pr.

Willis, J. F., jt. auth. see Primack, M. L.

Willis, J. H. Drug Dependence. 2nd ed. (Illus.). 1974. 7.95 (ISBN 0-571-04861-7, Pub. by Faber & Faber); pap. 3.95 (ISBN 0-571-04862-5). Merrimack Bk Serv.

Willis, J. R. William Empson. LC 74-76254. (Columbia Essays on Modern Writers Ser.: No. 39). 1969. pap. 2.00 (ISBN 0-231-03131-9, MW39). Columbia U Pr.

Willis, James, tr. see Petit, Paul.

Willis, James F. & Primack, Martin L. Explorations in Economics. LC 76-13973. (Illus.). 1977. text ed. 19.95 (ISBN 0-395-24524-9); inst. manual 3.00 (ISBN 0-395-24525-7); wkbk. 6.95 (ISBN 0-395-24757-8); test bank 4.50 (ISBN 0-395-24526-5). HM.

Willis, James F., jt. auth. see Primack, Martin L.

Willis, Jean. Historical Dictionary of Uruguay. LC 74-14630. (Latin American Historical Dictionaries Ser.: No. 11). 1974. 11.00 (ISBN 0-8108-0766-1). Scarecrow.

Willis, Jenny, ed. British Tourist Authority Guide to the North of England. (Illus.). 158p. 1980. bds. 20.00x (ISBN 0-7099-0384-7, Pub. by Croom Helm Ltd England). Biblio Dist.

Willis, Jerry. Peanut Butter & Jelly Guide to Computers. LC 78-70238. 225p. 1978. pap. 8.95 (ISBN 0-918398-13-4). Dilithium Pr.

Willis, Jerry & Danley, William, Jr. Nailing Jelly to a Tree. 275p. 1981. pap. 12.95 (ISBN 0-918398-42-8). Dilithium Pr.

Willis, Jerry & Miller, Merl. Computers for Everybody. 140p. 1981. pap. 4.95 (ISBN 0-918398-49-5). Dilithium Pr.

Willis, Jerry W., et al. Guiding the Psychological & Educational Growth of Children. (Illus.). 232p. 1976. 15.50 (ISBN 0-398-03273-4); pap. 9.75 (ISBN 0-398-03274-2). C C Thomas.

Willis, John. Theatre World: Vol. 36, 1979-80. Aymar, Brandt, ed. (Illus.). 288p. 1981. 18.95 (ISBN 0-517-54264-1). Crown.

Willis, John R. God's Frontiersmen: The Yale Band in Illinois. LC 79-65011. 1979. pap. text ed. 10.00 (ISBN 0-8191-0781-6). U Pr of Amer.

Willis, John T. Genesis. LC 78-52455. (Living Word Commentary Ser.: Vol. 2). 1979. 13.95 (ISBN 0-8344-0098-7). Sweet.

--Isaiah. Jones, David G., ed. (Living Word Commentary - Old Testament Ser.). 465p. 1980. 13.95 (ISBN 0-8344-0115-0). Sweet.

Willis, John V. Talent Manual for Carpenters, Millwrights & Pile Drivers: Gr. 1st. Year of Apprenticeship Through 4 Years Training. (Illus.). 100p. 1970. 5.50 (ISBN 0-686-63616-3). J V Willis.

Willis, Larryanne. Chappaquiddick Decision. (Illus., Orig.). 1980. pap. 2.95 (ISBN 0-937980-00-5). Better Bks.

Willis, Leydel J. Yesterday, Today, & Tomorrow: Yesterday, Book One of a Trilogy. new ed. 1976. 4.95 (ISBN 0-8187-0021-1). Clodele.

Willis, M. B., jt. auth. see Preston, T. R.

Willis, Malcolm B. Canine Genetics: A Definitive Study. LC 80-10188. (Illus.). 464p. 1980. 49.95 (ISBN 0-686-61139-X, 4936-9). Arco.

Willis, Mark A. Perspectives Drawing with the Computer. pap. text ed. 14.95 (ISBN 0-87567-041-5). Entelek.

Willis, Mary. People of That Book. Van Dolson, Bobbie J., ed. 128p. 1981. pap. price not set (ISBN 0-8280-0033-6). Review & Herald.

Willis, Maud. The Bionic Woman: Welcome Home Jamie. 1976. pap. 1.25 o.p. (ISBN 0-425-03230-2). Berkley Pub.

Willis, Melvin D. Boatbuilding & Repairing with Fiberglass. LC 74-176120. (Illus.). 1972. 12.50 (ISBN 0-87742-018-1). Intl Marine.

Willis, Paul E. Learning to Labour: How Working Class Kids Get Working Class Jobs. (Illus.). 1977. 21.00 (ISBN 0-566-00150-0, 00730-7, Pub. by Saxon Hse England). Lexington Bks.

--Profane Culture. 1978. 19.00x (ISBN 0-7100-8789-6). Routledge & Kegan.

Willis, Peter. Charles Bridgeman & the English Landscape Garden. (Studies in Architecture: Vol. 17). (Illus.). 1978. 100.00 o.p. (ISBN 0-8390-0223-8). Allanheld & Schram.

Willis, R. F., ed. Vibrational Spectroscopy of Adsorbates. (Springer Series in Chemical Physics: Vol. 15). (Illus.). 200p. 1981. 29.50 (ISBN 0-387-10429-1). Springer-Verlag.

Willis, Roy, ed. The Interpretation of Symbolism. LC 75-4111. (Association of Social Anthropologists Studies: No. 2). 181p. 1975. 24.95 (ISBN 0-470-94920-1). Halsted Pr.

Willis, Roy G., ed. There Was a Certain Man: Spoken Art of the Fipa. (Library of African Literature). 1979. 24.00x (ISBN 0-19-815146-2). Oxford U Pr.

Willis, Sherry L., jt. auth. see Peters, Donald L.

Willis, Stephen C. Luigi Cherubini: The Middle Years, Seventeen Ninety-Five to Eighteen Fifteen. Buelow, George, ed. (Studies in Musicology). 303p. 1981. 29.95 (ISBN 0-8357-1118-8, Pub. by UMI Res Pr). Univ Microfilms.

Willis, Ted. Man-Eater. LC 76-25009. 1977. 7.95 o.p. (ISBN 0-688-03124-2). Morrow.

Willis, Thayer, et al. The Last Frontiers. 480p. 1973. 7.95 o.p. (ISBN 0-385-04286-8). Doubleday.

Willis, William D., Jr. & Grossman, Robert G. Medical Neurobiology. (Illus.). 611p. 1981. text ed. 29.50 (ISBN 0-8016-5584-6). Mosby.

Willis, William D., Jr., jt. ed. see Pinsker, Harold.

Willison, G. O. The Bearded Collie. (Foyle's Handbks). 1971. 3.95 (ISBN 0-685-55805-3). Palmetto Pub.

Willison, Marilyn M. Diary of a Divorced Mother. 192p. 1981. pap. 2.50 (ISBN 0-553-14501-0). Bantam.

Williston, Glenn R. Appreciation of Literary Forms: Middle Level. (Comprehension Skills Ser.). (Illus.). 64p. 1976. pap. text ed. 2.40x (ISBN 0-89061-070-3, CB7M). Jamestown Pubs.

--Drawing a Conclusion: Middle Level. (Comprehension Skills Ser.). (Illus.). 64p. (gr. 6-8). 1976. pap. text ed. 2.40x (ISBN 0-89061-067-3, CB-4M). Jamestown Pubs.

--Isolating Details & Recalling Specific Facts. (Comprehension Skills Ser.). (Illus.). 64p. (gr. 6-12). 1976. Middle Level. pap. text ed. 2.40x (ISBN 0-89061-072-X, CB9M); Advanced Level. pap. text ed. 2.40x (ISBN 0-89061-020-7, CB9A). Jamestown Pubs.

--Making a Judgment: Middle Level. (Comprehension Skills Ser.). (Illus.). 64p. (gr. 6-8). 1976. pap. text ed. 2.40x (ISBN 0-89061-065-7, CB2M). Jamestown Pubs.

--Making an Inference: Middle Level. (Comprehension Skills Ser.). (Illus.). 64p. (gr. 6-8). 1976. pap. text ed. 2.40x (ISBN 0-89061-068-1, CB5M). Jamestown Pubs.

--Recognizing Tone: Middle Level. (Comprehension Skill Ser.). (Illus.). 64p. (gr. 6-8). 1976. pap. text ed. 2.40x (ISBN 0-89061-069-X, CB6M). Jamestown Pubs.

--Retaining Concepts & Organizing Facts: Middle Level. (Comprehension Skills Ser.). (Illus.). 64p. (gr. 6-8). 1976. pap. text ed. 2.40x (ISBN 0-89061-071-1, CB8M). Jamestown Pubs.

--Understanding Characters: Middle Level. (Comprehension Skills Ser.). (Illus.). 64p. (gr. 6-8). 1976. pap. text ed. 2.40x (ISBN 0-89061-066-5, CB3M). Jamestown Pubs.

--Understanding the Main Idea: Middle Level. (Comprehension Skills Ser.). (Illus.). 64p. (gr. 6-8). 1976. pap. text ed. 2.40x (ISBN 0-89061-064-9, CB1M). Jamestown Pubs.

Williston, Glenn R., jt. auth. see Giroux, James A.

Willman. Electronic Music for Young People. write for info. (ISBN 0-87628-210-9). Ctr Appl Res.

Willmer, E. N. Cells & Tissues in Culture: Methods, Biology, & Physiology, 3 Vols. 1965-1967. Vol. 1. 98.00, by subscription 69.00 (ISBN 0-12-757601-0); Vol. 2. 98.00, by subscription 69.00 (ISBN 0-12-757602-9); Vol. 3. 98.00, by subscription 69.00 (ISBN 0-12-757603-7). Acad Pr.

Willmer, Edward N. Cytology & Evolution. rev. ed. 1970. 55.00 o.s.i. (ISBN 0-12-757652-5). Acad Pr.

Willmore, T. J. Introduction to Differential Geometry. (Illus.). 1959. 19.50x (ISBN 0-19-853125-7). Oxford U Pr.

Willmott, A. John, jt. auth. see Schmidt, Frank W.

Willmott, A. S., jt. auth. see Nuttall, D. L.

Willmott, Alan S. & Fowles, Diane E. The Objective Interpretation of Test Performance: The Rasch Model Applied. (General Ser.). (Illus.). 94p. 1974. pap. text ed. 11.25x (ISBN 0-85633-041-8, NFER). Humanities.

Willmott, Ned & Pimlott, John. Strategy & Tactics of War. (Illus.). 240p. 1980. 16.95 (ISBN 0-85685-503-0). Quality Bks IL.

Willmott, Peter, jt. auth. see Young, Michael.

Willmott, W. E. Political Structure of the Chinese Community in Cambodia. (Monographs on Social Anthropology Ser: No. 42). (Illus.). 1970. text ed. 18.75x (ISBN 0-391-00114-0, Athlone Pr). Humanities.

Willner, Natalie. Bring Back Romance. 1979. pap. 1.95 o.p. (ISBN 0-425-04023-2). Berkley Pub.

Willock, Colin. Africa's Rift Valley. (The World's Wild Places Ser). (Illus.). 184p. 1974. 12.95 (ISBN 0-8094-2009-0). Time-Life.

--Africa's Rift Valley. (The World's Wild Places Ser.). (Illus.). 1974. lib. bdg. 11.97 (ISBN 0-686-51014-3). Silver.

--The Angler's Encyclopaedia. 1975. 14.95 (ISBN 0-7207-0639-4, Pub. by Michael Joseph). Merrimack Bk Serv.

--Gorilla. LC 77-10372. 1978. 10.00 o.p. (ISBN 0-312-34035-4). St Martin.

Willougby, Lee D. The Homesteaders. (The Making of America Ser.). (Orig.). 1981. pap. 2.75 (ISBN 0-440-03628-3). Dell.

Willoughby, Alan. The Alcohol Troubled Person. LC 79-1173. 1979. 14.95 (ISBN 0-88229-425-3); pap. 7.95 (ISBN 0-88229-680-9). Nelson-Hall.

--What Is Love. Jordan, Alton, ed. (Elephant Ser.). (Illus.). (gr. k-3). 1975. PLB 3.50 (ISBN 0-89868-018-2, Read Res); pap. text ed. 1.75 (ISBN 0-89868-051-4). ARO Pub.

Willoughby, Alana. Boots. Jordan, Alton, ed. (I Can Read Underwater Bks). (Illus.). (gr. k-3). 1974. PLB 3.50 (ISBN 0-89868-006-9, Read Res); pap. text ed. 1.75 (ISBN 0-89868-039-5, Read Rest). ARO Pub.

--Christmas. Jordan, Alton, ed. (Holidays Ser.). (Illus.). (gr. k-3). 1977. PLB 3.50 (ISBN 0-89868-025-5, Read Res); pap. text ed. 1.75 boxed (ISBN 0-89868-058-1, Read Res). ARO Pub.

--The Little Mouse. Jordan, Alton, ed. (I Can Read Underwater Bks). (Illus.). (gr. k-3). 1974. PLB 3.50 (ISBN 0-89868-007-7, Read Res); text ed. 1.75 softbd. (ISBN 0-89868-040-9). ARO Pub.

--My Dolly. Wasserman, Dan, ed. (Ten Word Bks.). (Illus.). (gr. k-1). 1979. PLB 4.50 (ISBN 0-89868-075-1); pap. 1.95 (ISBN 0-89868-086-7). ARO Pub.

--Rain: I Can Read Underwater Bks. Jordan, Alton, ed. (gr. k-3). 1974. PLB 3.50 (ISBN 0-89868-003-4, Read Res); pap. text ed. 1.75 (ISBN 0-89868-036-0). ARO Pub.

--Spring. Jordan, Alton, ed. (Elephant Ser.). (Illus.). (gr. k-3). 1975. PLB 3.50 (ISBN 0-89868-019-0, Read Res); pap. text ed. 1.75 (ISBN 0-89868-052-2). ARO Pub.

--Thanksgiving. Jordan, Alton, ed. (Holidays Ser.). (Illus.). (gr. k-3). PLB 3.50 (ISBN 0-89868-024-7, Read Res); pap. text ed. 1.75 (ISBN 0-89868-057-3). ARO Pub.

Willoughby, Amanda. The Alaskans. 1980. pap. 2.75 (ISBN 0-440-00199-4). Dell.

--The Texans. 1980. pap. 2.75 (ISBN 0-440-08665-5). Dell.

Willoughby, Charles C. Indian Antiquities of the Kennebec Valley. Spiess, Arthur E., ed. (Occasional Publications in Mane Archaeology: No. 1). (Illus.). 160p. 1980. 22.00 (ISBN 0-913764-13-2). Maine St Mus.

--Indian Antiquities of the Kennebec Valley. (Illus.). 1980. 22.00 (ISBN 0-913764-13-2). Maine St Mus.

Willoughby, L. A., ed. see Schiller, Johann.

Willoughby, Larry. Austin: A Pictorial History. Friedman, Donna R., ed. (Illus.). 208p. 1981. pap. write for info. (ISBN 0-89865-078-X). Donning Co.

Willoughby, Lee D. The Frontier Healers. (The Making of America Ser.). (Orig.). 1981. pap. 2.75 (ISBN 0-440-02608-3). Dell.

--Golden Staters. 1980. pap. 2.75 (ISBN 0-440-03020-X). Dell.

--The Land Grabbers. 1981. pap. 2.75 (ISBN 0-440-04762-5). Dell.

--The River People. 1981. pap. 2.75 (ISBN 0-440-07248-4). Dell.

Willoughby, Malcolm F. The U. S. Coast Guard in World War II. LC 79-6163. (Navies & Men Ser.). (Illus.). 1980. Repr. of 1957 ed. lib. bdg. 35.00x (ISBN 0-405-13081-3). Arno.

Willoughby, Robert J., jt. auth. see Loken, Newton C.

Willrich, Mason. Energy & World Politics. LC 75-12058. 1978. pap. text ed. 7.95 (ISBN 0-02-935800-0). Free Pr.

Willrich, Mason & Lester, Richard K. Radioactive Waste: Management & Regulation. LC 77-80228. 1977. 17.95 (ISBN 0-02-934560-X). Free Pr.

Willrich, Mason & Rhinelander, John B. SALT: The Moscow Agreements & Beyond. LC 73-10698. (Illus.). 1975. pap. text ed. 7.95 (ISBN 0-02-935470-6). Free Pr.

Wills, Antoinette. Crime & Punishment in Revolutionary Paris. LC 80-654. (Contributions in Legal Studies: No. 15). (Illus.). xxi, 227p. 1981. lib. bdg. 32.50 (ISBN 0-313-21494-8, WCP/). Greenwood.

Wills, Arthur, tr. see Weil, Simone.

Wills, B. A. Mineral Processing Technology: An Introcution to the Practical Aspects of Ore Treatment & Mineral Recovery. 2nd ed. LC 80-41698. (International Series on Materials Science & Technology: Vol. 29). (Illus.). 450p. 1981. 60.00 (ISBN 0-08-027322-X); pap. 20.00 (ISBN 0-08-027323-8). Pergamon.

Wills, Christopher. Genetic Variability. (Illus.). 350p. 1981. text ed. 45.00x (ISBN 0-19-857570-X). Oxford U Pr.

Wills, F. H. Fundamentals of Layout. LC 78-166431. 1971. lib. bdg. 11.50x (ISBN 0-88307-595-4). Gannon.

--Fundamentals of Layout for Newspaper & Magazine Advertising, for Page Design of Publications & Brochures. LC 78-166431. (Illus.). 1971. pap. 3.50 (ISBN 0-486-21279-3). Dover.

Wills, G. Marketing Through Research. 1967. 28.00 (ISBN 0-08-012620-0); pap. 14.50 (ISBN 0-08-012619-7). Pergamon.

Wills, Garry. At Button's. 1979. 8.95 o.p. (ISBN 0-8362-6108-9). Andrews & McMeel.

--Explaining America: The Federalist. LC 79-6542. 336p. 1981. 14.95 (ISBN 0-385-14689-2). Doubleday.

Wills, Gordon. Strategic Issues in Marketing. LC 74-14910. 239p. 1974. 20.95 (ISBN 0-470-94958-9). Halsted Pr.

Wills, Gordon, jt. auth. see Hayhurst, Roy.

Wills, J. B., jt. ed. see Leakey, C. L.

Wills, J. Robert. Directing in the Theatre: A Casebook. LC 80-19432. 149p. 1980. 10.00 (ISBN 0-8108-1348-3); instr's manual avail. Scarecrow.

Wills, John E., Jr., jt. auth. see Spence, Jonathan.

Wills, Ludmilla M. Le Regard Contemplatif Chez Valery et Mallarme. (Orig., Fr.). 1976. pap. text ed. 14.50x (ISBN 90-620-3407-1). Humanities.

Wills, Maralys. Manbirds: Hang Gliders & Hang Gliding. 320p. 1981. 17.95 (ISBN 0-13-551101-1). P-H.

Wills, Philip. On Being a Bird. 1977. 13.50 (ISBN 0-7153-7426-5). David & Charles.

Wills, R. D., ed. see COSPAR, Twenty-Second Plenary Meeting, Bangalore, India, 1979.

Wills, Richard H. The Institutionalized Severely Retarded: A Study of Activity & Interaction. (Illus.). 208p. 1973. 13.75 (ISBN 0-398-02755-2). C C Thomas.

Wills, Russell, jt. auth. see Hendricks, C. G.

Wills, Tom T., compiled by. The Giant Quiz Book. 256p. 1981. pap. 6.95 (ISBN 0-89104-207-5). A & W Pubs.

Wills, Walter J. An Introduction to Agri-Business Management. 2nd ed. LC 78-62100. 1979. 14.65 (ISBN 0-8134-2055-5, 2055); text ed. 11.00x (ISBN 0-685-34807-5). Interstate.

--Introduction to Grain Marketing. LC 74-155289. 155p. 1972. 11.65 (ISBN 0-8134-1299-4, 1299); text ed. 8.75x (ISBN 0-685-25881-5). Interstate.

Willsberger, Johann. The History of Photography. LC 76-24894. 1977. 13.95 (ISBN 0-385-12664-6). Doubleday.

Willsmer, Ray L. The Basic Arts of Marketing. 230p. 1976. text ed. 22.00x (ISBN 0-220-66307-6, Pub. by Busn Bks England). Renouf.

Willsmore, Heidy. Macrame: A Comprehensive Study. (Illus.). 1979. 23.00 (ISBN 0-571-11310-9, Pub. by Faber & Faber). Merrimack Bk Serv.
Willson, A. L., ed. Dimension: A Reader of German Literature Since Nineteen Sixty-Eight. 320p. 1981. 9.95 (ISBN 0-8264-0042-6). Continuum.
Willson, A. Leslie, tr. see Grass, Guenter.
Willson, Alan N., Jr. Nonlinear Networks: Theory & Analysis. LC 74-19558. (IEEE Selected Reprint Ser.). 397p. 1975. 14.50 (ISBN 0-471-94953-1, Pub. by Wiley-Interscience). Wiley.
Willson, Amos L. Mythical Image: The Ideal of India in German Romanticism. LC 65-19449. 1964. 14.75 o.p. (ISBN 0-686-66407-8). Duke.
Willson, J. D., jt. auth. see Heckert, J. Brooks.
Willson, J. Robert & Carrington, Elsie R. Obstetrics & Gynecology. 6th ed. LC 78-31642. (Illus.). 1979. text ed. 34.50 (ISBN 0-8016-5595-1). Mosby.
Willson, James D. & Campbell, John B. Controllership: The Work of the Managerial Accountant. 3rd ed. 800p. Date not set. write for info. (ISBN 0-471-05711-8). Wiley.
--Controllership: The Work of the Managerial Accountant. 3rd ed. 800p. 1981. 29.95 (ISBN 0-471-05711-8). Ronald Pr.
Willumeit, H. P., ed. see IAVSD-Symposium Held at the Technical University Berlin, 6th, September 1979.
Willums, Jan-Olaf, ed. New Concepts in Air Pollution Research. LC 73-19210. 184p. 1974. pap. 21.95 (ISBN 0-470-94956-2). Halsted Pr.
Willwerth, James. Badge of Madness. 1978. pap. 1.75 o.p. (ISBN 0-449-23487-8, Crest). Fawcett.
Willymat, William. The Loyal Subjects Looking-Glasse. LC 73-38231. (English Experience Ser.: No. 495). 76p. 1972. Repr. of 1604 ed. 6.00 (ISBN 90-221-0495-8). Walter J Johnson.
Wilm, Emil C. Immanuel Kant, Seventeen Hundred Twenty-Four to Nineteen Twenty-Four. 88p. 1980. Repr. of 1925 ed. lib. bdg. 20.00 (ISBN 0-8482-7062-2). Norwood Edns.
Wilmer, Lambert A; see Poe, Edgar Allan.
Wilmer, Valerie. As Serious As Your Life. (Illus.). 296p. (Orig.). 1980. 14.95 (ISBN 0-88208-112-8); pap. 7.95 (ISBN 0-88208-113-6). Lawrence Hill.
--The Face of Black Music. LC 76-18115. (Photography Ser.). 1976. lib. bdg. 18.50 (ISBN 0-306-70756-X); pap. 7.95 (ISBN 0-306-80039-X). Da Capo.
Wilmerding, John. American Art. (Pelican History of Art Ser.: No. 40). 1976. 40.00 o.p. (ISBN 0-670-11678-5). Viking Pr.
--American Masterpieces from the National Gallery of Art. LC 80-15192. (Illus.). 180p. 1980. 32.50 (ISBN 0-933920-10-5). Hudson Hills.
--Audubon, Homer, Whistler, & the 19th Century America. (Illus.). 1975. Repr. 5.95 o.p. (ISBN 0-88308-011-7). Lamplight Pub.
Wilmerding, L., Jr. James Monroe: Public Claimant. LC 60-11525. 1960. 4.00 (ISBN 0-910294-26-7). Brown Bk.
Wilmerding, Lucius, Jr. The Electoral College. 1958. 15.00 (ISBN 0-8135-0294-2). Rutgers U Pr.
Wilmeth, Don B. The Language of American Popular Entertainment: A Glossary of Argot, Slang, & Terminology. LC 80-14795. 296p. 1981. lib. bdg. 29.95 (ISBN 0-313-22497-8, WEN/). Greenwood.
Wilmeth, Don B., ed. American & English Popular Entertainment: A Guide to Information Sources. LC 79-22869. (Performing Arts Information Guide Ser.: Vol. 7). 1980. 30.00 (ISBN 0-8103-1454-1). Gale.
--American Stage to World War I: A Guide to Information Sources. LC 78-53488. (Performing Arts Information Guide Ser.: Vol. 4). 1978. 30.00 (ISBN 0-8103-1392-8). Gale.
Wilmington, Michael, jt. auth. see McBride, Joseph.
Wilmore, Gayraud S. Secular Relevance of the Church. (Orig.). 1962. pap. 1.25 o.s.i. (ISBN 0-664-24410-6). Westminster.
Wilmore, Jack H. Athletic Training & Physical Fitness: Physiological Principles & Practices of the Conditioning Process. new ed. 1977. text ed. 19.95 (ISBN 0-205-05630-X). Allyn.
Wilmore, Jack H., jt. auth. see Behnke, Albert R., Jr.
Wilmore, Sylvia B. Crows, Jays, Ravens (& Their Relatives) (Illus.). 1979. 6.95 (ISBN 0-87666-878-3, PS-779). TFH Pubns.
Wilmot, John. Inspired Principles of Prophetic Interpretation. 1975. 9.95 o.p. (ISBN 0-685-54809-0). Reiner.
--The Letters of John-Wilmot, Earl of Rochester. Treglown, Jeremy, ed. LC 80-20592. 1980. lib. bdg. 26.00x (ISBN 0-226-81181-6). U of Chicago Pr.
Wilmot, Norah M. Cooking for One. (Illus.). 1975. pap. 2.95 (ISBN 0-914842-03-X). Madrona Pubs.
Wilmot, Philip D. & Slingerland, Aart. Technology Assessment & the Oceans. LC 77-73026. 1977. lib. bdg. 46.50x (ISBN 0-89158-725-X). Westview.
Wilmot, William W. & Wenburg, John R. Communication Involvement: Personal Perspectives. LC 80-16247. 452p. 1981. Repr. of 1974 ed. lib. bdg. write for info. (ISBN 0-89874-185-8). Krieger.
Wilms, Barbara. Crunchy Bananas & Other Great Recipes Kids Can Cook. LC 74-31139. (Illus.). 112p. (ps-3). 1975. pap. 4.95 o.s.i. (ISBN 0-87905-507-3). Sagamore Bks.
Wilmshurst, John. Fundamentals & Practice of Marketing. 1978. pap. 14.95x (ISBN 0-434-92263-3). Intl Ideas.
Wilner, Eleanor. Aya. LC 79-4753. 1979. lib. bdg. 8.00x (ISBN 0-87023-277-0); pap. 3.95 (ISBN 0-87023-278-9). U of Mass Pr.
Wilpert, Bernhard, ed. see Heller, Frank A.
Wilshaw, T. R., jt. auth. see Lawn, B. R.
Wilsing, N., jt. auth. see Kupka, I.
Wilsing, Weston C. Office Machines: A College Course. 1974. pap. text ed. 9.50x o.p. (ISBN 0-256-00596-6). Irwin.
Wilske, Kenneth R., et al. Therapeutic Program for the Patient with Arthritis. 3rd ed. 54p. Date not set. pap. 5.00 (ISBN 0-9601944-3-6). Mason Clinic.
Wilson. A Monographic Revision of the Heliothripinae of the World - Thysanoptera. (Memoirs Ser: No. 23). (Illus.). 354p. 1974. 25.00 (ISBN 0-686-17150-0). Am Entom Inst.
Wilson & Werner. Simplified Stair Layout. 2nd ed. LC 70-188808. 64p. 1973. pap. 3.40 (ISBN 0-8273-0103-0). Delmar.
Wilson, jt. auth. see Rosewall.
Wilson, et al. Human Sexuality: A Text with Readings. 2nd ed. 1980. pap. text ed. 11.16 (ISBN 0-8299-0328-3); study guide 4.95 (ISBN 0-8299-0322-4); instrs.' manual avail. (ISBN 0-8299-0584-7). West Pub.
Wilson, A. Latin Dictionary. (Teach Yourself Ser.). 1974. pap. 2.95 o.p. (ISBN 0-679-10204-3). McKay.
Wilson, A., ed. see Moore, N.
Wilson, A., ed. see Savage, A. W.
Wilson, A., ed. see Tunley, M.
Wilson, A., ed. see Wallis, M.
Wilson, A., ed. see Yorke, D. A.
Wilson, A., tr. see Horne, Herbert P., et al.
Wilson, A. G. & Kirby, M. J. Mathematics for Geographers & Planners. 2nd ed. (Contemporary Problems in Geography Ser.). (Illus.). 424p. 1980. text ed. 36.00x (ISBN 0-19-874114-6); pap. text ed. 19.95x (ISBN 0-19-874115-4). Oxford U Pr.
Wilson, A. G. & Kirkby, M. J. Mathematical Methods for Geographers & Planners. (Illus.). 344p. 1975. text ed. 19.00x o.p. (ISBN 0-19-874022-0); pap. text ed. 7.50x o.p. (ISBN 0-19-874023-9). Oxford U Pr.
Wilson, A. J. Elements of X-Ray Crystallography. 1970. 20.95 (ISBN 0-201-08698-0). A-W.
Wilson, A. N. The Laird of Abbotsford: A View of Sir Walter Scott. 214p. 1980. text ed. 24.95x (ISBN 0-19-211756-4). Oxford U Pr.
Wilson, Alice, et al. Flashback!-I Didn't Know That. (Orig.). 1980. playscript 2.50 (ISBN 0-87602-236-0). Anchorage.
Wilson, Amy A., et al. Deviance & Social Control in Chinese Society. LC 76-12886. (Special Studies). 1977. text ed. 26.95 (ISBN 0-275-56470-3); pap. 11.95 (ISBN 0-275-89650-1). Praeger.
Wilson, Andrew. Ever-Victorious Army: A History of the Chinese Campaign Under Lt. Col. C. G. Gordon & of the Suppression of the T'ai P'ing Rebellion. (Studies in Chinese History & Civilization). 395p. 1977. 24.75 (ISBN 0-89093-078-3). U Pubns Amer.
Wilson, Angus. Setting the World on Fire. 312p. 1980. 12.95 (ISBN 0-670-63502-2). Viking Pr.
--The Wild Garden or Speaking of Writing. 1963. 12.95x (ISBN 0-520-01346-8); pap. 1.25 (ISBN 0-520-01347-6, CAL112). U of Cal Pr.
Wilson, Ann C., jt. auth. see Smith, David W.
Wilson, Ann Q. Houston: A Pictorial History. Friedman, Donna R., ed. (Illus.). 205p. Date not set. pap. price not set (ISBN 0-89865-087-9). Donning Co.
Wilson, Anna. Enjoying Embroidery. LC 74-32170. (Illus.). 120p. 1975. 10.25 o.p. (ISBN 0-8231-4032-6). Branford.
Wilson, Anton R., jt. auth. see Shea, Robert J.
Wilson, Arnold T. The Persian Gulf: An Historical Sketch from the Earliest Times to the Beginning of the Twentieth Century. LC 79-2888. (Illus.). 327p. 1981. Repr. of 1928 ed. 27.50 (ISBN 0-8305-0055-3). Hyperion Conn.
Wilson, B. K. Path Through the Woods. (Illus.). (gr. 6-10). 1958. 8.95 (ISBN 0-87599-128-9). S G Phillips.
Wilson, Barbara. Taking Sides. (Orig.). 1981. pap. 4.95 (ISBN 0-931188-09-1). Seal Pr WA.
--Talk & Contact. LC 77-52008. 76p. (Orig.). 1978. pap. 3.00 (ISBN 0-931188-01-6). Seal Pr WA.
Wilson, Barry R. & Gillett, Keith. A Field Guide to Australian Shells. (Illus.). 288p. 1979. 25.75 (ISBN 0-589-50120-8, Pub. by Reed Books Australia). C E Tuttle.
Wilson, Barry W., intro. by. Birds: Readings from Scientific American. LC 79-26134. (Illus.). 1980. text ed. 19.95x (ISBN 0-7167-1206-7); pap. 9.95x (ISBN 0-7167-1207-5). W H Freeman.
Wilson, Betty L., jt. ed. see Wilson, William K.
Wilson, Bob. Soccer. (Pelham Pictorial Sports Instructors Ser.). 1977. 8.95 (ISBN 0-7207-0793-5). Transatlantic.
Wilson, Bonnie, ed. see Clark, Merrian E.
Wilson, Brent D. Disinvestment of Foreign Subsidiaries. Dufey, Gunter, ed. (Research for Business Decisions). 112p. 1980. 19.95 (ISBN 0-8357-1132-3, Pub. by UMI Res Pr). Univ Microfilms.
Wilson, Bryan. Contemporary Transformations of Religion. 1979. pap. text ed. 4.50x (ISBN 0-19-875045-5). Oxford U Pr.
--The Noble Savages: An Essay on Charisma-the Rehabilitation of a Concept. LC 74-81444. (Quantum Bk Ser.). 1975. 11.95x (ISBN 0-520-02815-5). U of Cal Pr.
--Youth Culture & the Universities. 1970. 6.95 o.p. (ISBN 0-571-09233-0, Pub. by Faber & Faber). Merrimack Bk Serv.
Wilson, Bryan R., ed. Rationality. 1977. pap. 13.50x (ISBN 0-631-09900-X, Pub by Basil Blackwell). Biblio Dist.
Wilson, C. Applied Statistics for Engineers. (Illus.). 1972. pap. text ed. 22.30x (ISBN 0-85334-529-5, Pub. by Applied Science). Burgess-Intl Ideas.
--Case Studies in Quantitative Management. 1972. text ed. 14.95x (ISBN 0-7002-0166-1). Intl Ideas.
Wilson, C., jt. auth. see Alexander, L. G.
Wilson, C., jt. auth. see Alexis, Marcus.
Wilson, C. B., jt. ed. see Coppock, J. T.
Wilson, Carroll L., ed. Coal Bridge to the Future, Vol. 1. (World Coal Study: Vol. 1). 1980. 12.95 (ISBN 0-88410-099-5). Ballinger Pub.
--Future Coal Prospects: Country & Regional Assessments, Vol. 2. 1980. 37.50 (ISBN 0-88410-098-7). Ballinger Pub.
Wilson, Carter. A Green Tree & a Dry Tree. LC 79-184534. (Illus.). 320p. 1972. 7.95 o.s.i. (ISBN 0-02-630130-X). Macmillan.
Wilson, Carter, tr. see Abrey, Emilo.
Wilson, Charis. California & the West. LC 78-66677. (Illus.). 1978. 25.00 (ISBN 0-89381-034-7); ltd. ed. with print 300.00 (ISBN 0-89381-037-1). Aperture.
--Edward Weston: Nudes. LC 77-80022. (Illus.). 1977. 25.00 (ISBN 0-89381-020-7); ltd ed 350.00 (ISBN 0-89381-025-8); pap. 14.95 (ISBN 0-89381-026-6). Aperture.
Wilson, Charis, ed. Cole Weston: 18 Photographs. (Illus.). 56p. 1981. pap. 19.95 (ISBN 0-87905-084-5). Peregrine Smith.
Wilson, Charles. Queen Elizabeth & the Revolt of the Netherlands. LC 76-119009. 1970. 18.50x (ISBN 0-520-01744-7). U of Cal Pr.
--The Transformation of Europe, 1558-1648. LC 75-17283. 1976. 30.00x (ISBN 0-520-03075-3). U of Cal Pr.
Wilson, Charles H., Sr. Education for Negroes in Mississippi Since Nineteen Hundred & Ten. 1974. 20.00 (ISBN 0-89020-011-4). Brown Bk.
Wilson, Charles M., jt. auth. see Nitske, W. Robert.
Wilson, Charles R. Laboratory Investigations in General Biology, Vol. 2. 80p. 1978. pap. text ed. 6.95 o.p. (ISBN 0-8403-1816-2). Kendall-Hunt.
Wilson, Chris & Press, Max. Catamaran Sailing to Win. LC 73-3767. (Illus.). 160p. 1976. 7.95 o.p. (ISBN 0-498-01392-8). A S Barnes.
Wilson, Christine C. & Hovey, Wendy R. Cesarean Childbirth: A Handbook for Parents. rev., expanded ed. LC 78-22792. (Illus.). 312p. (Orig.). 1980. pap. 6.95 (ISBN 0-385-15154-3, Dolp). Doubleday.
Wilson, Clifford A. Rocks, Relics & Biblical Reliability. (Probe Ser.). 1977. pap. 4.95 (ISBN 0-310-35701-2). Zondervan.
Wilson, Colin. Anti-Sartre: With an Essay on Camus. LC 80-24098. (Milford Series: Popular Writers of Today: Vol. 34). 64p. (Orig.). 1981. lib. bdg. 8.95x (ISBN 0-89370-149-1); pap. text ed. 2.95x (ISBN 0-89370-249-8). Borgo Pr.
--New Pathways in Psychology. 280p. 1974. pap. 1.95 o.p. (ISBN 0-451-61315-5, MJ1315, Ment). NAL.
--The Philosopher's Stone. 320p. 1974. pap. 1.95 o.s.i. (ISBN 0-446-89442-7). Warner Bks.
--The Quest for Wilhelm Reich. LC 78-22774. 288p. 1981. 12.95 (ISBN 0-385-01845-2, Anchor Pr). Doubleday.
--Starseekers. LC 80-1273. 256p. 1981. 15.95 (ISBN 0-385-17253-2). Doubleday.
--Stature of Man. Repr. of 1959 ed. lib. bdg. 17.50x (ISBN 0-8371-0273-1, WISM). Greenwood.
Wilson, Colin, jt. ed. see Grant, John.
Wilson, Curtis. William Heytesbury: Medieval Logic & the Rise of Mathematical Physics. (Medieval Science Pubns., No. 3). 1956. 20.00x (ISBN 0-299-01350-2). U of Wis Pr.
Wilson, D. Broadcasting-Vision & Sound. 1968. 4.50 (ISBN 0-08-012849-1). Pergamon.
--The Communicators & Society. 1968. pap. 3.50 (ISBN 0-08-012977-3). Pergamon.
--History of South & Central Africa. 1975. pap. text ed. 8.95x (ISBN 0-521-20559-X). Cambridge U Pr.
--Modern Practice in Servo Design. 1970. 60.00 (ISBN 0-08-015812-9). Pergamon.
Wilson, D., jt. auth. see Swift, William.
Wilson, D., ed. Mao Tse-Tung in the Scales of History. LC 76-57100. (Contemporary China Institute Publications Ser.). 1977. 36.50 (ISBN 0-521-21583-8); pap. 8.95 (ISBN 0-521-29190-9). Cambridge U Pr.
Wilson, D. A., jt. auth. see Sagay, J. O.
Wilson, D. B., ed. French Renaissance Scientific Poetry. (Renaissance Library). 1974. text ed. 18.75x (ISBN 0-485-13808-5, Athlone Pr); pap. text ed. 10.00x (ISBN 0-485-12808-X). Humanities.
Wilson, D. E. & Gardner, A. L., eds. Proceedings: Fifth International Bat Research Conference. 434p. (Orig.). 1980. pap. 16.00 (ISBN 0-89672-083-7). Tex Tech Pr.
Wilson, D. L., jt. auth. see Lester, J. C.
Wilson, D. R., ed. Aerial Reconnaissance for Archaeology. 158p. 1980. pap. 29.95x (ISBN 0-900312-29-7, Pub. by Coun Brit Arch England). Intl Schol Bk Serv.
Wilson, D. S. The Natural Selection of Population & Communities. 1980. 16.95 (ISBN 0-8053-9560-1). A-W.
Wilson, Dana L. Boston English. (Illus.). 1976. pap. 1.95 (ISBN 0-8220-1633-8). Centennial.
--Boston English Illustrated. (Illus.). 1976. pap. 1.95 o.p. (ISBN 0-686-65384-X). Cliffs.
Wilson, Daniel J. Arthur O. Lovejoy & the Quest for Intelligibility. LC 79-25902. xvii, 248p. 1980. 18.00x (ISBN 0-8078-1431-8). U of NC Pr.
Wilson, David. Roman Frontiers of Britain. 1967. 3.95x o.p. (ISBN 0-435-32966-9). Heinemann Ed.
--Your Book of Men in Space. (Your Book Ser.). (Illus.). 1976. 6.95 (ISBN 0-571-10937-3, Pub. by Faber & Faber). Merrimack Bk Serv.
Wilson, David, tr. from German. Christian Rohlfs: Watercolors, Drawings & Prints. 80p. 1968. 5.00 (ISBN 0-88397-018-X). Intl Exhibit Foun.
Wilson, David A. Al Hadj: The Pilgrimage. 100p. (Orig.). 1981. pap. 4.00 (ISBN 0-934852-22-7). Lorien Hse.
Wilson, David H. & Hall, Malcolm H. Casualty Officer's Handbook. 4th ed. (Illus.). 1979. text ed. 29.95 (ISBN 0-407-00140-9). Butterworths.
Wilson, David M. The Archaeology of Anglo-Saxon England. (Illus.). 532p. Date not set. pap. price not set (ISBN 0-521-28390-6). Cambridge U Pr.
Wilson, David M., ed. The Northern World: The History & Heritage of Northern Europe, A. D. 400-1100. (Illus.). 248p. 1980. 40.00 (ISBN 0-686-62715-6, 1365-8). Abrams.
Wilson, Derek. England in the Age of Thomas More. (Illus.). 1980. text ed. 15.50x (ISBN 0-246-10943-2). Humanities.
--England in the Age of Thomas More. 1979. 17.95x (ISBN 0-8464-0106-1). Beekman Pubs.
--Sweet Robin: A Biography of Robert Dudley, Earl of Leicester, 1533-1588. (Illus.). 304p. 1981. 54.00 (ISBN 0-241-10149-2, Pub. by Hamish Hamilton England). David & Charles.
--The World Encompassed: Francis Drake & His Great Voyage. LC 77-3782. (Illus.). 1978. 12.95 o.s.i. (ISBN 0-06-014679-6, HarpT). Har-Row.
Wilson, Derek, jt. auth. see Shaman, Margaret.
Wilson, Don. Secrets of Our Spaceship Moon. 1979. pap. 1.95 o.s.i. (ISBN 0-440-17847-9). Dell.
Wilson, Donald R. The Dreams of Donald Roller Wilson. (Illus.). 1979. pap. 9.95 (ISBN 0-8015-0353-1, Hawthorn). Dutton.
Wilson, Doric. Forever After. LC 80-82802. 80p. (Orig.). 1980. pap. 3.95 (ISBN 0-935672-01-X). JH Pr.
Wilson, Doris B. & Wilson, Wilfred. Human Anatomy. (Illus.). 1978. 21.95x (ISBN 0-19-502310-2). Oxford U Pr.
Wilson, Dorothy C. Apostle of Sight: The Story of Victor Rambo. 255p. 1980. 7.95 (ISBN 0-915684-54-3). Christian Herald.
--Granny Brand, Her Story. LC 76-16721. (Illus.). 1976. 6.95 o.p. (ISBN 0-915684-11-X); pap. 3.50 o.p. (ISBN 0-915684-27-6). Christian Herald.
--Lincoln's Mothers. LC 80-950. 432p. 1981. 13.95 (ISBN 0-385-15146-2, Galilee). Doubleday.
Wilson, Douglas, jt. auth. see Drew, Leslie.
Wilson, Sir Duncan. Tito's Yugoslavia. LC 79-11009. 1980. 29.95 (ISBN 0-521-22655-4). Cambridge U Pr.

Wilson, Dwayne & Haley, John. Oklahoma Supplement for Modern Real Estate Practice. 130p. (Orig.). 1981. pap. 7.95 (ISBN 0-88462-327-0). Real Estate Ed Co.

Wilson, E. B., Jr., et al. Molecular Vibrations: The Theory of Infrared & Raman Vibrational Spectra. (Illus.). 1980. pap. text ed. 6.00 (ISBN 0-486-63941-X). Dover.

Wilson, E. D., et al. Principles of Nutrition. 4th ed. LC 78-11710. 1979. text ed. 21.95 (ISBN 0-471-02695-6); tchrs. manual avail. (ISBN 0-471-04786-4); wkbk. 6.95 (ISBN 0-471-05766-5). Wiley.

Wilson, E. M., jt. auth. see Norton, F. J.

Wilson, E. O. & Eisner, T. Life on Earth. 2nd ed. LC 78-4656. (Illus.). 1978. text ed. 18.95x (ISBN 0-87893-936-9); student study guide 6.95x (ISBN 0-87893-679-3). Sinauer Assoc.

Wilson, Earl. Sinatra. LC 75-44193. (Illus.). 450p. 1976. 9.95 o.s.i. (ISBN 0-02-630090-7, 63009). Macmillan.

Wilson, Edmund. The Thirties. Edel, Leon, ed. 800p. 1980. 17.50 (ISBN 0-374-27572-6). FS&G.

--To the Finland Station: A Study in the Writing & Acting of History. LC 53-3591. 1953. pap. 3.95 (ISBN 0-385-09281-4, A6, Anch). Doubleday.

Wilson, Edmund, ed. see Bishop, John Peale.

Wilson, Edward. Diary of the Discovery Expedition to the Antarctic Regions, 1901-1904. 1967. text ed. 25.00x (ISBN 0-7137-0431-4). Humanities.

Wilson, Edward L., jt. auth. see Bathe, Klaus-Jurgen.

Wilson, Edward M. & Cruickshank, Don W. Samuel Pepys's Spanish Plays. 160p. 1981. 74.00 (ISBN 0-19-721793-1). Oxford U Pr.

Wilson, Edward M., ed. Solitudes of Don Luis De Gongora. 1965. 32.00 (ISBN 0-521-06814-2). Cambridge U Pr.

Wilson, Edward O. & Bossert, William H. Primer of Population Biology. LC 73-155365. (Illus.). 192p. (Orig.). 1971. pap. text ed. 6.50x (ISBN 0-87893-926-1). Sinauer Assoc.

Wilson, Edward O., intro. by. Ecology, Evolution, & Population Biology: Readings from Scientific American. LC 73-17448. (Illus.). 1974. text ed. 19.95x (ISBN 0-7167-0888-4); pap. text ed. 9.95x (ISBN 0-7167-0887-6). W H Freeman.

Wilson, Edward O. see Eisner, Thomas.

Wilson, Eldred D. Arizona Gold Placers & Placering. (Illus.). 148p. 1980. pap. 5.95 (ISBN 0-89632-003-0). Del Oeste.

Wilson, Elinor. Jim Beckwourth: Black Mountain Man & War Chief of the Crows. 248p. 1980. pap. 6.95 (ISBN 0-8061-1555-6). U of Okla Pr.

Wilson, Ellen, jt. auth. see Agle, Nan H.

Wilson, Erica. The Craft of Blackwork & Whitework. (Illus.). 96p. 1976. pap. 4.95 o.p. (ISBN 0-684-14496-4, SL617). Scribner.

--Craft of Crewel Embroidery. LC 62-9637. (Illus.). 1971. pap. 5.95 (ISBN 0-684-12501-3, SL211, ScribT). Scribner.

--The Craft of Silk & Gold Thread Embroidery & Stumpwork. (Illus.). 1977. pap. 4.95 o.p. (ISBN 0-684-15067-0, ScribT). Scribner.

--Erica Wilson's Embroidery Book. LC 78-123841. (Illus.). 224p. 1973. 17.50 o.p. (ISBN 0-684-13018-1, ScribT). Scribner.

--Needleplay. LC 75-6036. (Encore Edition). 1975. 5.95 (ISBN 0-684-16556-2, ScribT). Scribner.

Wilson, Eunice. History of Shoe Fashion. LC 75-89994. (Illus.). pap. 8.95 (ISBN 0-87830-548-3). Theatre Arts.

Wilson, Eunice & Gile, Joanne. Fashion Bags. 1979. 14.95 (ISBN 0-7134-1073-6). David & Charles.

Wilson, Evan M. Decision on Palestine: How the U. S. Came to Recognize Israel. LC 78-59867. (Publications Ser.: 218). (Illus.). 244p. 1979. 14.95 (ISBN 0-8179-7181-5). Hoover Inst Pr.

Wilson, Everett, jt. auth. see Goldsmid, Charles.

Wilson, F., jt. auth. see Barnes, D.

Wilson, F. Paul. Healer. 1977. pap. 1.50 o.s.i. (ISBN 0-440-13569-9). Dell.

Wilson, Florence & Neuhauser, Duncan. Health Services in the U. S. rev. ed. Date not set. price not set (ISBN 0-88410-713-2). Ballinger Pub.

Wilson, Forbes. The Conquest of Cooper Mountain. LC 80-69369. 1981. 14.95 (ISBN 0-689-11153-3). Atheneum.

Wilson, Forrest. Emerging Form in Architecture: Conversations with Lev Zetlin. LC 75-8912. (Illus.). 224p. 1975. 21.50 (ISBN 0-8436-0150-7). CBI Pub.

Wilson, Fran. Where Mountains Wait. 192p. (Orig.). 1980. pap. 1.50 (ISBN 0-671-57009-9). S&S.

Wilson, Frances, ed. & tr. The Love of Krishna: The Krsnakarnamrta of Lilasuka Bilvamangala. LC 74-153426. (Haney Foundation Ser.). 448p. 1975. 15.00x (ISBN 0-8122-7655-8). U of Pa Pr.

Wilson, Francis. Labour in the South African Gold Mines 1936-1969. LC 77-161290. (African Studies: No. 6). 1972. 38.50 (ISBN 0-521-08303-6). Cambridge U Pr.

Wilson, Francis, ed. Farm Labour in South Africa. Kooy, Alide. pap. 21.00 o.p. (ISBN 0-949968-91-9). Verry.

Wilson, Frank. Kelp for Better Health & Vitality. 1979. pap. 1.95 o.s.i. (ISBN 0-7225-0367-9). Newcastle Pub.

Wilson, Frank A. Food Fit for Humans. 1980. 15.00x (ISBN 0-85207-132-9, Pub. by Daniel Co England). State Mutual Bk.

--Food Fit for Humans. 1975. 7.25x (ISBN 0-8464-1011-7). Beekman Pubs.

Wilson, Frank E. Faith & Practice. (Orig.). 1941. pap. 4.95 o.p. (ISBN 0-8192-1082-X). Morehouse.

Wilson, Frank P. Shakespearian & Other Studies. Gardner, Helen, ed. 1969. 26.00x (ISBN 0-19-811677-2). Oxford U Pr.

Wilson, Fred, ed. Classical Chess Matches, 1907-1913. LC 74-79463. (Illus.). viii, 227p. (Orig.). 1975. pap. 3.00 o.p. (ISBN 0-486-23145-3). Dover.

Wilson, Fred M. You Have Retinal Detachment: A Guide for Patients. (Illus.). 136p. 1978. 9.75 (ISBN 0-398-03700-0). C C Thomas.

Wilson, Frieberger, jt. auth. see Wilson, Saul.

Wilson, G. Three Hundred Years of American Drama & Theatre. (Illus.). 1972. ref. ed. 19.95 (ISBN 0-13-920314-1). P-H.

Wilson, G. T., jt. auth. see Rachman, S. J.

Wilson, G. Terence & O'Leary, K. Daniel. Principles of Behavior Therapy. (Ser. in Social Learning Theory). (Illus.). 1980. text ed. 18.95 (ISBN 0-13-701102-4). P-H.

Wilson, G. Terence, jt. auth. see Kazdin, Alan E.

Wilson, G. Terence, jt. auth. see O'Leary, K. Daniel.

Wilson, Gabriel H., ed. Current Radiology, Vol. 1. (Illus.). 1978. 35.00x (ISBN 0-89289-100-9). HM Prof Med Div.

--Current Radiology, Vol. 2. 1979. 40.00x (ISBN 0-89289-107-6). HM Prof Med Div.

Wilson, Gahan. Packrat Press Books. 1978. pap. 1.25 (ISBN 0-440-43824-1, YB). Dell.

Wilson, Geoffrey. Ephesians. 1978. pap. 2.95 (ISBN 0-85151-263-1). Banner of Truth.

--First & Second Thessalonians. 1975. pap. 2.45 (ISBN 0-85151-227-5). Banner of Truth.

--First Corinthians. 1978. pap. 3.95. Banner of Truth.

--Galatians. 1979. pap. 3.50 (ISBN 0-85151-294-1). Banner of Truth.

--Hebrews. 1976. pap. 3.95 (ISBN 0-85151-099-X). Banner of Truth.

--Romans. 254p. 1977. pap. 4.25 (ISBN 0-85151-238-0). Banner of Truth.

--Second Corinthians. 1979. pap. 3.95 (ISBN 0-85151-295-X). Banner of Truth.

Wilson, Geoffrey B. Colossians & Philemon. (Wilson'a New Testament Commentaries). 111p. (Orig.). 1980. pap. 3.95 (ISBN 0-85151-313-1). Banner of Truth.

Wilson, Glenn & Gosselin, Chris. Sexual Variations: Fetishism, Sadomasochism & Transvestism. 1981. 12.95 (ISBN 0-671-24624-0). S&S.

Wilson, Glenn & Nias, David. The Mystery of Love: How the Science of Sexual Attraction Can Work for You. 1980. pap. cancelled (ISBN 0-553-10876-X). Bantam.

Wilson, Glenn, jt. ed. see Cook, Mark.

Wilson, Gloria. More Scottish Fishing Craft & Their Work: Their Work in Great Lining, Small Lining, Seining, Pair Trawling, Drifting, Potting & Trawling. (Illus.). 170p. 8.75 (ISBN 0-85238-048-8, FN). Unipub.

Wilson, Gordon C. Three Stories. 1980. 3.00 (ISBN 0-933292-09-0); pap. 1.50 (ISBN 0-933292-06-6). Arts End.

Wilson, H. N. An Approach to Chemical Analysis, 2 vols. 1966. Set. 25.00 (ISBN 0-08-011543-8); Set. pap. 12.75 (ISBN 0-08-011542-X). Pergamon.

Wilson, H. T. The American Ideology: Science, Technology & Organization As Modes of Rationality. (International Library of Sociology Ser.). 1977. 28.00x (ISBN 0-7100-8501-X). Routledge & Kegan.

Wilson, Harold. The Governance of Britain. LC 76-47262. (Illus.). 1977. 10.95 o.p. (ISBN 0-06-014676-1, HarpT). Har-Row.

Wilson, Harriet & Herbert, G. W. Parents & Children in the Inner City. (Direct Editions Ser.). (Orig.). 1978. pap. 16.00 (ISBN 0-7100-8715-2). Routledge & Kegan.

Wilson, Harris W. & Hoeveler, Diane L., eds. English Prose & Criticism in the Nineteenth Century: A Guide to Information Sources. LC 74-11527. (American Literature, English Literature, & World Literature in English Info. Guide Ser.: Vol. 18). 1979. 30.00 (ISBN 0-8103-1235-2). Gale.

Wilson, Helen. Gold Fever. (Illus.). 1979. pap. 7.25 (ISBN 0-913814-27-X). Nevada Pubns.

Wilson, Helen V. Helen Van Pelt Wilson's African Violet Book. 1970. 11.95 (ISBN 0-8015-3852-1, Hawthorn); pap. 5.95 (ISBN 0-8015-3858-0, Hawthorn). Dutton.

Wilson, Helen V., ed. see Davenport, Elaine.

Wilson, Helen Van Pelt. Color for Your Winter Yard & Garden. LC 77-13822. (Encore Edition). (Illus.). 1978. 4.95 (ISBN 0-684-16557-0, ScribT). Scribner.

Wilson, Henry S. The Imperial Experience in Sub-Saharan Africa. LC 76-9489. (Europe & the World in the Age of Expansion: Vol. 8). 1977. 20.00x (ISBN 0-8166-0797-4); pap. 3.45x (ISBN 0-8166-0854-7). U of Minn Pr.

Wilson, Holly S. & Kneisl, Carol R. Psychiatric Nursing. LC 78-7775. 1979. 22.95 (ISBN 0-201-08340-X, 08340, M&N Div); wkbk. 7.95 (ISBN 0-201-08342-6); instr's guide 3.95 (ISBN 0-685-94886-2, 08341). A-W.

Wilson, I. H., ed. Low-Energy Ion Beams Nineteen Eighty. (Institute of Physics Conference Ser.: No. 54). 1981. 85.00 (ISBN 0-9960033-4-7, Pub. by a Hilger England). Heyden.

Wilson, Ian. The Shroud of Turin: The Burial Cloth of Jesus Christ. LC 79-1942. (Illus.). 1979. pap. 4.50 (ISBN 0-385-15042-3, Im). Doubleday.

Wilson, J. The Assessment of Morality. (General Ser.). 1973. pap. text ed. 10.00x (ISBN 0-85633-012-4, NFER). Humanities.

--Moral Education & the Curriculum. 1969. 9.75 o.p. (ISBN 0-08-013897-7); pap. 5.25 o.p. (ISBN 0-08-013898-5). Pergamon.

--Octavio Paz. LC 78-18108. 1979. 32.50 (ISBN 0-521-22306-7); pap. 9.95x (ISBN 0-521-29509-2). Cambridge U Pr.

Wilson, J., jt. auth. see Rudden, M. N.

Wilson, J. D. Diagnostic Immunology & Serology: A Clinician's Guide. Simpson, Sandra I., ed. 161p. 1980. pap. text ed. 14.95 (ISBN 0-909337-01-2). ADIS Pr.

Wilson, J. G. & Perry, G. E. Cosmic Rays. LC 75-38743. (Wykeham Science Ser.: No. 40). 1976. 8.60x (ISBN 0-8448-1167-X). Crane Russak Co.

Wilson, J. J., jt. auth. see Petersen, Karen.

Wilson, J. L. Carbonate Facies in Geologic History. (Illus.). 485p. 1975. 44.60 o.p. (ISBN 0-387-07236-5). Springer-Verlag.

Wilson, J. M. & Newcombe, R. J. Experiments in Physical Chemistry. 3rd ed. Date not set. 48.01 (ISBN 0-08-023808-4); pap. 18.01 (ISBN 0-08-023807-6). Pergamon.

Wilson, J. P. Inflation, Deflation, Reflation: Managemnent & Accounting in Economic Uncertainty. 345p. 1980. text ed. 36.75x (ISBN 0-220-67015-3, Pub. by Busn Bks England). Renouf.

Wilson, J. Q. Negro Politics. LC 60-10906. 1960. pap. 2.95 o.s.i. (ISBN 0-02-935400-5); pap. 2.95 (ISBN 0-02-935390-4). Free Pr.

Wilson, J. R. Emotion & Object. LC 76-179160. 240p. 1972. 23.95 (ISBN 0-521-08450-4). Cambridge U Pr.

Wilson, J. R., et al. Experiments in Physical Chemistry. 2nd rev. ed. 1968. 41.00 (ISBN 0-08-012541-7). Pergamon.

Wilson, J. R., et al, eds. Experiments in Physical Chemistry. 2nd rev. ed. Newcombe, R. J. & Denaro, A. R. LC 68-18536. 1978. 16.25 (ISBN 0-08-023798-3). Pergamon.

Wilson, J. S., ed. Multinational Enterprises. 1974. 40.00 (ISBN 9-0286-0124-4). Heinman.

Wilson, J. Tuzo, intro. by. Continents Adrift & Continents Aground: Readings from Scientific American. LC 76-46564. (Illus.). 1976. pap. text ed. 9.95x (ISBN 0-7167-0280-0). W H Freeman.

Wilson, J. Walter & Plunkett, Orda A. The Fungous Diseases of Man. 1965. 28.50x (ISBN 0-520-01344-1). U of Cal Pr.

Wilson, James. Canada's Indians. (Minority Rights Group: No. 21). 1974. pap. 2.50 (ISBN 0-89192-107-9). Interbk Inc.

--The Original Americans: US Indians. (Minority Rights Group Ser.: No. 31). 28p. 1976. pap. 2.50 (ISBN 0-89192-128-1). Interbk Inc.

Wilson, James G. & Newall, A. B. General & Inorganic Chemistry. 2nd ed. (Illus.). 1971. text ed. 19.95x (ISBN 0-521-07073-2). Cambridge U Pr.

Wilson, James M. & Muckersie, John R. Structured Questions in Physics. 1975. pap. text ed. 5.25x o.p. (ISBN 0-435-67681-4). Heinemann Ed.

Wilson, James Q. American Government: Institutions & Policies. 1979. text ed. 16.95 (ISBN 0-669-01621-7); student handbk. 4.95 (ISBN 0-669-02521-6); inst. guide free to adopters (ISBN 0-669-02531-3); test item file free to adopters (ISBN 0-669-02522-4). Heath.

Wilson, Jane A; see Brown, O. Z.

Wilson, Jane B. The Story Experience. LC 79-13888. 177p. 1979. 10.00 (ISBN 0-8108-1224-X). Scarecrow.

Wilson, Jean. Crusader for Christ (Billy Graham) (gr. 6-9). 1973. pap. 1.95 (ISBN 0-87508-602-0). Chr Lit.

--Entertainments for Elizabeth I. (Studies in Elizabethean & Renaissance Culture Ser. II). 179p. 1980. 27.50x (ISBN 0-8476-6820-7). Rowman.

Wilson, Jeanne, jt. auth. see Ross, Dave.

Wilson, Jerome D. & Ricketson, William F. Thomas Paine. (United States Authors Ser: No. 301). 1978. lib. bdg. 9.95 (ISBN 0-8057-7206-5). Twayne.

Wilson, Jerry D. Physics: Concepts & Aplications. 2nd ed. (Illus.). 884p. 1981. text ed. 22.95 (ISBN 0-669-03373-1); instr's guide avail. (ISBN 0-669-01948-8); student guide 7.95 (ISBN 0-669-03362-6); lab guide 12.95 (ISBN 0-669-01947-X). Heath.

--Physics: Concepts & Applications. 1977. text ed. 20.95x o.p. (ISBN 0-669-96180-9); instructor's manual free o.p. (ISBN 0-669-00243-7). Heath.

Wilson, Jim. Go Preach the Kingdom Heal the Sick. 127p. pap. text ed. 4.75 (ISBN 0-227-67659-9). Attic Pr.

--Growth in Prayer. 1961. pap. 3.25 (ISBN 0-227-67475-8). Attic Pr.

--Healing Through the Power of Christ. 1969. pap. 3.25 (ISBN 0-227-67478-2). Attic Pr.

--Meditation & the Fulness of Life: An Exposition of Romans 9-11. 1974. pap. 4.75 (ISBN 0-227-67810-9). Attic Pr.

--Purpose. 80p. pap. text ed. 3.25 (ISBN 0-227-67707-2). Attic Pr.

Wilson, Joan H., jt. auth. see Sachs, Albie.

Wilson, Joe F. The United States, Chile & Peru in the Tacna & Arica Plebiscite. LC 78-66124. (Orig.). 1979. pap. text ed. 11.50 (ISBN 0-8191-0685-2). U Pr of Amer.

Wilson, John. Becky. LC 66-10507. (Illus.). (gr. k-3). 1967. 6.79 (ISBN 0-690-12669-7, TYC-J). T Y Crowell.

--Bright Lightu. 6.95 o.p. (ISBN 0-8062-1232-2). Carlton.

--Educational Theory & the Preparation of Teachers. (General Ser.). 200p. 1975. pap. text ed. 15.25x (ISBN 0-85633-080-9, NFER). Humanities.

--Fantasy & Commonsense in Education. LC 79-10938. 134p. 1979. 18.95x (ISBN 0-470-26707-0). Halsted Pr.

--Indian Caste, 2 vols. 1976. Repr. of 1877 ed. Set. 30.00x o.p. (ISBN 0-88386-914-4). South Asia Bks.

--The Isle of Palms, & Other Poems. Reiman, Donald H., ed. LC 75-31275. (Romantic Context Ser.: Poetry 1789-1830: Vol. 121). 1978. Repr. of 1812 ed. lib. bdg. 47.00 (ISBN 0-8240-2221-1). Garland Pub.

--Language & the Pursuit of Truth. 1956. 22.95 (ISBN 0-521-06821-5); pap. 4.95x (ISBN 0-521-09421-6). Cambridge U Pr.

--Love, Sex, Feminism. LC 79-24902. 1980. 18.95 (ISBN 0-03-056103-5). Praeger.

--Philosophy & Educational Research. (NFER General Ser.). (Orig.). 1979. pap. text ed. 13.75x (ISBN 0-85633-005-1). Humanities.

--Philosophy & Practical Education. (Students Library of Education). 1977. 16.50x (ISBN 0-7100-8675-X). Routledge & Kegan.

--Preface to the Philosophy of Education. (International Library of the Philosophy of Education). 1979. 26.00x (ISBN 0-7100-0283-1). Routledge & Kegan.

--Religion in American Society: The Effective Presence. LC 77-16808. 1978. ref. ed. 17.95 (ISBN 0-13-773259-7). P-H.

--Specimens of the British Critics. LC 78-12061. 1979. 34.00x (ISBN 0-8201-1326-3). Schol Facsimiles.

--Thinking with Concepts. 1970. 26.95 (ISBN 0-521-06825-8); pap. 5.95x (ISBN 0-521-09601-4). Cambridge U Pr.

Wilson, John & Arnold, Carroll. Dimensions of Public Communication. 272p. 1976. pap. text ed. 10.95x (ISBN 0-205-04917-6, 4849175); instructor's manual free (ISBN 0-205-04918-4). Allyn.

Wilson, John & International Agency for the Prevention of Blindness. World Blindness & Its Prevention. 104p. 1980. text ed. 17.95x (ISBN 0-19-261249-2). Oxford U Pr.

Wilson, John & Parsons, C. Basic Latin Vocabulary. 1960. text ed. 5.95 (ISBN 0-312-06825-5). St Martin.

Wilson, John, jt. auth. see Oliver, Eric.

Wilson, John, jt. ed. see Oliver, Eric.

Wilson, John A., jt. auth. see Robeck, Mildred C.

Wilson, John D. Fortunes of Falstaff. 1943. 23.95 (ISBN 0-521-06830-4); pap. 6.95 (ISBN 0-521-09246-9). Cambridge U Pr.

--Manuscript of Shakespeare's Hamlet, 2 Vols. 1934. Set. 60.00 (ISBN 0-521-06833-9). Cambridge U Pr.

--What Happens in Hamlet. 3rd ed. 1951. 49.50 (ISBN 0-521-06835-5); pap. 10.50x (ISBN 0-521-09109-8, 109). Cambridge U Pr.

Wilson, John F. Practice & Theory of Electrochemical Machining. 266p. 1981. Repr. of 1971 ed. lib. bdg. write for info. (ISBN 0-89874-229-3). Krieger.

Wilson, John F. & Mulder, John M. Religion in American History: Interpretive Essays. 448p. 1978. text ed. 14.95 (ISBN 0-13-771998-1); pap. text ed. 11.95 (ISBN 0-13-771980-9). P-H.
Wilson, John H., ed. see Crowne, John.
Wilson, John O. After Affluence: Resolving the Middle Class Crisis. LC 80-7752. 192p. 1980. 9.95 (ISBN 0-06-250970-5, HarpR). Har-Row.
Wilson, John P. The Rights of Adolescents in the Mental Health System. LC 77-4542. 1978. 24.95 (ISBN 0-669-01485-0). Lexington Bks.
Wilson, John R. Mind. LC 64-23096. (Life Science Library). (Illus.). (gr. 5 up). 1969. PLB 8.97 o.p. (ISBN 0-8094-0465-6, Pub. by Time-Life). Silver.
Wilson, Jose. American Cooking: The Eastern Heartland. (Foods of the World Ser.). (Illus.). 1971. 14.95 (ISBN 0-8094-0052-9). Time-Life.
--American Cooking: The Eastern Heartland. LC 70-150960. (Foods of the World Ser.). (gr. 6 up). 1971. lib. bdg. 14.94 (ISBN 0-8094-0079-0, Pub. by Time-Life). Silver.
Wilson, Jose, jt. auth. see Groff, Betty.
Wilson, Joseph M; see Weinberg, H. Barbara.
Wilson, Joseph T. Presenting Folk Culture: A Handbook on Folk Festival Organization & Management. Udall, Lee, ed. Date not set. write for info. (ISBN 0-87049-300-0). U of Tenn Pr. Postponed.
Wilson, Josephine M., jt. auth. see Pauk, Walter.
Wilson, Josleen. The Passionate Amateur's Guide to Archaeology in the United States. (Illus.). 448p. 1981. pap. 12.95 (ISBN 0-02-098670-X, Collier). Macmillan.
Wilson, Josleen, jt. auth. see Feinman, Max L.
Wilson, Josleen, jt. auth. see Thodes, Sonya.
Wilson, Joyce. Complete Indoor Exercise Book. LC 79-642299. (Illus.). 160p. (Orig.). 1980. pap. cancelled (ISBN 0-89037-178-4). Anderson World.
Wilson, K. Costumes & Uniforms. 1980. pap. 3.95 (ISBN 0-931064-26-0). Starlog Pr.
Wilson, Katherine M. The Real Rhythm in English Poetry. 171p. 1980. Repr. of 1929 ed. lib. bdg. 25.00 (ISBN 0-89987-860-1). Darby Bks.
Wilson, Kax. A History of Textiles. (Illus.). 1979. lib. bdg. 30.00 (ISBN 0-89158-491-9); text ed. 18.00x (ISBN 0-89158-491-9). Westview.
Wilson, Keith. The Policy of the Entente: The Determinants of British Foreign Policy, 1904-1914. 1981. text ed. 15.00 (ISBN 0-391-02198-2). Humanities.
Wilson, Ken, jt. auth. see Case, Doug.
Wilson, Ken, ed. Game Climbers Play: A Selection of One Hundred Mountaineering Articles. (Sierra Club Paperback Library). (Illus.). 688p. 1980. pap. 9.95 o.p. (ISBN 0-87156-301-0). Sierra.
--Games Climbers Play: A Collection of Mountaineering Writing. LC 80-15374. (Sierra Club Paperback Library). (Illus.). 688p. 1980. pap. 9.95 (ISBN 0-87156-301-0). Sierra.
Wilson, Kenneth D., ed. Prospects for Growth: Changing Expectations for the Future. LC 77-14567. (Praeger Special Studies). 1977. 24.95 (ISBN 0-03-041446-6); pap. 11.95 (ISBN 0-03-041441-5). Praeger.
Wilson, Kieth. Retablos. (Illus.). 32p. (Orig.). 1980. pap. 3.00 (ISBN 0-88235-042-0). San Marcos.
Wilson, L. B., jt. auth. see Page, E. S.
Wilson, L. Craig. School Leadership Today: Strategies for the Educator. new ed. 1978. text ed. 18.95 (ISBN 0-205-06019-6). Allyn.
Wilson, L. D., jt. auth. see Leibholz, S. W.
Wilson, Lanford. Balm in Gilead & Other Plays. Incl. Balm in Gilead; Home Free; Ludlow Fair. 116p. (Orig.). 1965. pap. 4.50 (ISBN 0-8090-1208-1, New Mermaid). Hill & Wang.
--Hot l Baltimore. (Mermaid Dramabook). 145p. 1973. 7.95 (ISBN 0-8090-5544-9); pap. 4.50 (ISBN 0-8090-1230-8). Hill & Wang.
--The Rimers of Eldritch & Other Plays. Incl. The Rimers of Eldritch; This Is the Rill Speaking; Wandering; Days Ahead; The Madness of Lady Bright. 122p. (Orig.). 1967. pap. 3.95 (ISBN 0-8090-1214-6, New Mermaid). Hill & Wang.
Wilson, LaVisa C. Caregiver Training for Child Care: A Multimedia Program. (Elementary Education Ser.). 1977. pap. text ed. 7.95 (ISBN 0-675-08482-2); instr's manual 3.95 (ISBN 0-686-67613-0). Merrill.
Wilson, Lawrence, tr. see Jetzinger, Franz.
Wilson, Leland. Silver City. 96p. (Orig.). 1980. pap. 3.95 (ISBN 0-87178-790-3). Brethren.
Wilson, Leslie E. A Delphinid (Mammalia: Cetacea) from the Miocene of Palos Verdes Hills, California. (U. C. Publ. in Geological Sciences: Vol. 103). 1973. pap. 7.00x (ISBN 0-520-09458-1). U of Cal Pr.
Wilson, Lionel. The First Stunt Stars of Hollywood. LC 78-14465. (Famous Firsts Ser.). (Illus.). 1978. lib. bdg. 7.35 (ISBN 0-686-50002-4). Silver.
Wilson, Logan. American Academics: Then & Now. (Illus.). 1979. pap. text ed. 15.95x (ISBN 0-19-502482-6). Oxford U Pr.
Wilson, Loring D. The Handy Sportsman. 1976. 12.95 (ISBN 0-87691-213-7). Winchester Pr.
--The Handy Sportsman. (Stoeger Bks). 1977. pap. 5.95 o.p. (ISBN 0-695-80848-6). Follett.
Wilson, M. Curtis, et al. Practical Insect Pest Management: Insects of Man's Household & Health, No. 5. LC 77-82251. (Illus.). 1977. 6.95x (ISBN 0-917974-07-7). Waveland Pr.
--Practical Insect Pest Management: Insects of Ornamental Plants, No. 4. LC 77-82602. (Illus.). 1977. 6.50x (ISBN 0-917974-06-9). Waveland Pr.
--Practical Insect Pest Management. rev. ed. (Insects of Livestock & Agronomic Crops Ser: No.2). (Illus.). 208p. 1980. pap. text ed. 7.95x (ISBN 0-917974-39-5). Waveland Pr.
--Practical Insect Pest Management: Insects of Vegetables & Fruits, No. 3. LC 77-71174. 1977. 5.95x (ISBN 0-917974-05-0). Waveland Pr.
Wilson, M. T. The Management of Marketing. LC 80-23617. 141p. 1981. 29.95 (ISBN 0-470-27074-8). Halsted Pr.
--Managing Sales Force. (Illus.). 184p. 1970. 19.50 (ISBN 0-7161-0048-7). Herman Pub.
Wilson, Major L. Space, Time, & Freedom. LC 74-287. 309p. 1974. lib. bdg. 17.50x (ISBN 0-8371-7373-6, WIT/). Greenwood.
Wilson, Malcolm & Henderson, M. D. British Rust Fungi. 68.00 (ISBN 0-521-06839-8). Cambridge U Pr.
Wilson, Margaret. Tirso De Molina. (World Authors Ser.: No. 445). 1977. lib. bdg. 12.50 (ISBN 0-8057-6281-7). Twayne.
Wilson, Margery. God: Here & Now. 1978. pap. 4.95 (ISBN 0-87707-207-8). CSA Pr.
Wilson, Mark, ed. The Best of Henry Longhurst. LC 78-69793. 208p. 1978. 8.50 (ISBN 0-914178-22-9, 24574). Golf Digest.
Wilson, Mary, jt. auth. see Young, Biloine W.
Wilson, Merlin R., jt. auth. see Topilow, Arthur A.
Wilson, Mitchell. Energy. rev. ed. LC 63-21614. (Life Science Library). (Illus.). (gr. 5 up). 1969. PLB 8.97 o.p. (ISBN 0-8094-0460-5, Pub. by Time-Life). Silver.
Wilson, Mona. Jane Austin & Some Contemporaries. 304p. 1980. Repr. of 1938 ed. lib. bdg. 20.00 (ISBN 0-8492-2973-1). R West.
Wilson, Mona, jt. auth. see Howarth, Edward G.
Wilson, Monica. Religion & the Transformation of Society: A Study in Social Change in Africa. LC 73-134622. (Scott Holland Memorial Lecturers of 1969 Ser). (Illus.). 1971. 19.95 (ISBN 0-521-07991-8). Cambridge U Pr.
Wilson, Morrow & Fremon, Suzanne, eds. Rural America. (Reference Shelf Ser.). 1976. 6.25 (ISBN 0-8242-0597-9). Wilson.
Wilson, Morrow & Wilson, Suzanne, eds. Drugs in American Life. (Reference Shelf Ser: Vol. 47, No. 1). 1975. 6.25 (ISBN 0-8242-0569-3). Wilson.
Wilson, N. G. Saint Basil on the Value of Greek Literature. (Illus.). 75p. 1975. 17.95x (ISBN 0-7156-0872-X, Pub. by Duckworth England). Biblio Dist.
Wilson, N. G., jt. auth. see Reynolds, L. D.
Wilson, Nelly. Bernard-Lazare. LC 77-82524. 1979. 42.00 (ISBN 0-521-21802-0). Cambridge U Pr.
Wilson, O. Progressive Exercises in Physics to Ordinary Level. 3rd ed. 1971. pap. text ed. 3.95x o.p. (ISBN 0-435-67937-6). Heinemann Ed.
Wilson, O. W. Police Planning. 2nd ed. (Illus.). 562p. 1977. 21.75 (ISBN 0-398-02081-7). C C Thomas.
Wilson, Ostis B. The Plan of Salvation. 64p. pap. 0.50. Faith Pub Hse.
Wilson, P. L. & Pourjavady, N. Kings of Love. LC 78-62008. 1979. 18.00 (ISBN 0-87773-733-9). Great Eastern.
Wilson, P. N., jt. auth. see Webster, C. C.
Wilson, P. S. Interest & Discipline in Education. (Students Library of Education). 1971. 12.50x (ISBN 0-7100-7049-7); pap. 6.50 (ISBN 0-7100-7908-7). Routledge & Kegan.
Wilson, Patricia P. Household Equipment: Selection & Management. LC 75-31023. (Illus.). 384p. 1976. text ed. 18.95 (ISBN 0-395-20596-4); resource manual 5.00 (ISBN 0-395-20597-2). HM.
Wilson, Patrick. Public Knowledge, Private Ignorance: Toward a Library & Information Policy. LC 76-52327. (Contributions in Librarianship & Information Sciences: No. 10). 1977. lib. bdg. 15.00x (ISBN 0-8371-9485-7, WPN/). Greenwood.
--Two Kinds of Power: An Essay on Bibliographic Control. (California Library Reprint Ser.). 1978. 17.50x (ISBN 0-520-03515-1). U of Cal Pr.
Wilson, Paul, jt. auth. see Waldron, Ellis.
Wilson, Paul, tr. see Mlynar, Zdenek.
Wilson, Paul R. Public Housing for Australia. (Illus.). 1976. 10.95x (ISBN 0-7022-1363-2); pap. 7.90x (ISBN 0-7022-1363-2). U of Queensland Pr.
Wilson, Paul R. & Brown, J. W. Crime & the Community. 1973. pap. 6.00x (ISBN 0-7022-0839-6). U of Queensland Pr.
Wilson, Paul T. & Becke, Donna, eds. Money & Information for Mental Health: Descriptive Directory of Federal & Private Resources. 1971. pap. 3.50 o.p. (ISBN 0-685-24849-6, 174). Am Psychiatric.
Wilson, Pauline. Community Elite & the Public Library: Uses of Information in Leadership. LC 76-15336. (Contributions in Librarianship & Information Science: No. 18). 1977. lib. bdg. 16.95 (ISBN 0-8371-9031-2, WCE/). Greenwood.
Wilson, Peter. Forty Games for Frivolous People. (Illus.). 1979. pap. 3.95 (ISBN 0-8256-3154-8, Quick Fox). Music Sales.
--Simplified Swahili. 328p. (Orig.). 1981. pap. text ed. 8.95x (ISBN 0-582-62358-8). Longman.
Wilson, Peter, jt. auth. see Fry, Eric C.
Wilson, Peter J. The Promising Primate: Anthropological Specualtions on Human Evolution. 224p. 1980. write for info. Yale U Pr.
Wilson, Peter L., jt. ed. see Ibish, Yusuf.
Wilson, Peter L., tr. see Nasr, Seyyed H.
Wilson, Peter L., jt. tr. see Weischer, Bernd M.
Wilson, Philip K., et al. Cardiac Rehabilitation, Adult Fitness & Exercise Testing. LC 80-16556. (Illus.). 462p. 1981. text ed. 29.50 (ISBN 0-8121-0687-3). Lea & Febiger.
Wilson, R., jt. ed. see Hadgraft, C.
Wilson, R. A., tr. see Ebeling, Gerhard.
Wilson, R. A., tr. see Klink, Johanna L.
Wilson, R. G. Gentlemen Merchants. LC 79-149804. 271p. 1971. lib. bdg. 15.00x (ISBN 0-678-06785-6). Kelley.
Wilson, R. G., jt. auth. see Campbell, R. H.
Wilson, R. Jackson, jt. auth. see Weinstein, Allen.
Wilson, R. M. Management Controls & Marketing Planning. 224p. 1979. 21.95x (ISBN 0-470-26673-2); pap. 21.95 (ISBN 0-470-27053-5). Halsted Pr.
Wilson, R. M., jt. auth. see Broer, M. R.
Wilson, R. McL., jt. ed. see Best, E.
Wilson, R. W. & Wright, D. F. A Field Approach to Biology. 1972. pack 6.50x o.p. (ISBN 0-435-59940-2). Heinemann Ed.
Wilson, Ramsay J. Land Surveying. 2nd ed. (Illus.). 480p. 1977. pap. 14.95x (ISBN 0-7121-1242-1, Pub. by Macdonald & Evans England). Intl Ideas.
Wilson, Renate, jt. ed. see Jones, George F.
Wilson, Rex L. Bottles on the Western Frontier. (Illus.). 1981. price not set (ISBN 0-8165-0414-8). U of Ariz Pr.
Wilson, Richard. Health Effects of Fossil Fuel Burning: Assessment & Mitigation. 1980. 30.00 (ISBN 0-88410-714-0). Ballinger Pub.
Wilson, Richard & Crouch, Edmond. Risk-Benefit Analysis. Date not set. price not set (ISBN 0-88410-667-5). Ballinger Pub.
Wilson, Richard & Jones, William. Energy, Ecology & the Environment. 353p. 1974. 10.95 (ISBN 0-12-757550-2). Acad Pr.
Wilson, Richard W. The Moral State: A Study of the Political Socialization of Chinese & American Children. LC 73-2333. 1974. 19.95 (ISBN 0-02-935410-2). Free Pr.
Wilson, Richard W. & Schochet, Gordon J., eds. Moral Development & Politics. LC 79-15922. 1980. 26.95 (ISBN 0-03-044231-1). Praeger.
Wilson, Richard W., et al. Value Change in Chinese Society. LC 77-83479. (Praeger Special Studies). 1979. 26.95 (ISBN 0-03-023046-2). Praeger.
Wilson, Robert, jt. ed. see Robinson, Keith.
Wilson, Robert A. Feminine Forever. LC 66-11166. (Illus.). 224p. 1966. 8.95 (ISBN 0-87131-049-X). M Evans.
--The Illuminati Papers. LC 80-16641. 160p. 1980. pap. 7.95 (ISBN 0-915904-52-7). And-Or Pr.
--Masks of the Illuminati. (Orig.). 1981. pap. 2.95 (ISBN 0-671-82585-2). PB.
Wilson, Robert A. & Schulz, David A. Urban Sociology. (P-H Ser. in Sociology). (Illus.). 1978. ref. ed. 17.95 (ISBN 0-13-939520-2). P-H.
Wilson, Robert A., jt. auth. see Shea, Robert J.
Wilson, Robert C. Crooked Tree. 1981. pap. 2.75 (ISBN 0-425-04842-X). Berkley Pub.
Wilson, Robert C., et al. College Professors & Their Impact on Students. LC 74-26553. 256p. 1975. 18.95 (ISBN 0-471-94961-2, Pub. by Wiley-Interscience). Wiley.
Wilson, Robert E. see Heat Transfer & Fluid Mechanics Institute.
Wilson, Robert F. Fluids, Electrolytes, & Metabolism. 148p. 1975. pap. 11.50 (ISBN 0-398-02643-2). C C Thomas.
Wilson, Robert H., jt. auth. see Garn, Harvey A.
Wilson, Robert L. The Book of Colt Engraving. 2nd ed. (Illus.). 560p. 1980. 50.00 (ISBN 0-917714-30-X). Beinfeld Pub.
--Shaping the Congregation. LC 80-22228. (Into Our Third Century Ser.). 144p. (Orig.). 1981. pap. 3.95 (ISBN 0-687-38334-X). Abingdon.
Wilson, Robert M. Diagnostic & Remedial Reading for Classroom & Clinic. 4th ed. (Illus.). 448p. 1981. text ed. 17.95 (ISBN 0-675-08048-7); instr's. manual 3.95 (ISBN 0-686-69489-9). Merrill.
Wilson, Robert M. & Hall, Marryanne. Programmed Work Attack. 3rd ed. 1979. text ed. 6.95 (ISBN 0-675-08286-2). Merrill.
Wilson, Robert M., jt. auth. see Gambrell, Linda B.
Wilson, Robert M., et al. Programmed Reading for Teachers. (Elementary Education Ser.: No. C22). 280p. 1980. pap. text ed. 10.95 (ISBN 0-675-08285-4). Merrill.
Wilson, Robert N., et al. Readings in Medical Sociology. 448p. Date not set. text ed. 12.95 (ISBN 0-669-03945-4). Heath. Postponed.
Wilson, Robert S. Investor's Guide to Investing in Multiple Dwellings. LC 76-4381. 1976. 16.95x (ISBN 0-669-00648-3). Lexington Bks.
--Trolley Trails Through the West: Southern California, Vol. 8. (Illus., Orig.). 1980. pap. 4.00 (ISBN 0-934944-08-3). Wilson Bros.
Wilson, Robert W., et al. Innovation, Competition & Government Policy in the Semiconductor Industry. LC 80-8317. 1980. 21.95 (ISBN 0-669-03995-0). Lexington Bks.
Wilson, Ron. The Hedgerow Book. LC 78-75251. 1979. 17.95 (ISBN 0-7153-7728-0). David & Charles.
--How the Body Works. LC 78-54636. (Illus.). (gr. 5-7). 1979. 8.95 (ISBN 0-88332-096-7, 8049). Larousse.
Wilson, Rowena. Man in a Million. (Candlelight Romance Ser.). (Orig.). Date not set. pap. 1.50 (ISBN 0-440-15528-2). Dell.
Wilson, Ruby E. Frank J. North: Pawnee Scout, Commander & Pioneer. (Illus.). 1981. 15.00 (ISBN 0-8040-0767-5). Swallow. Postponed.
Wilson, S. Pop. LC 77-80183. (Modern Movements in Art Ser.). 1978. pap. 1.95 (ISBN 0-8120-0883-9). Barron.
Wilson, Samuel, ed. Mission Handbook: North American Protestant Ministries Overseas. 1980. 22.50 (ISBN 0-912552-34-4). MARC.
Wilson, Samuel, et al. Readings in Human Sexuality. LC 75-4362. (Illus.). 252p. 1975. pap. text ed. 8.50 (ISBN 0-8299-0050-0). West Pub.
Wilson, Samuel, Jr., jt. auth. see Huber, Leonard.
Wilson, Saul & Wilson, Frieberger. Nung Grammar. (SIL Publications in Linguistics Ser.). 150p. 1980. write for info. (ISBN 0-88312-081-X); price not set microfiche (ISBN 0-88312-481-5). Summer Inst Ling.
Wilson, Scott. The Plumber's Bible. LC 76-42420. (Homeowner's Bible Ser.). (Illus.). 160p. 1981. pap. 4.95 (ISBN 0-385-11211-4). Doubleday.
Wilson, Shirley A., jt. auth. see Ladley, Betty A.
Wilson, Sidney R. & Soules, Eugene H. Did I Say That? (Editing Your First Draft) 1976. pap. 3.25 (ISBN 0-86589-005-6). Individual Learn.
Wilson, Simon. British Art: From Holbein to the Present Day. LC 79-89630. (Illus.). 1980. 10.00 (ISBN 0-8120-5373-7). Barron.
--The Surrealists. (Tate Gallery: Little Art Books Ser.). (Illus.). 1977. pap. 1.95 (ISBN 0-8120-0861-8). Barron.
Wilson, Sloan. The Greatest Crime. (Adventure & Suspense Ser.). 11.50 (ISBN 0-87795-296-5). Arbor Hse.
--Ice Brothers. 1981. pap. 2.95. Avon.
--Ice Brothers. 544p. 1981. pap. 2.95 (ISBN 0-380-53611-0, 53611). Avon.
Wilson, Snoo. Pignight & Blowjob. 1980. pap. 4.95 (ISBN 0-7145-3509-5). Riverrun NY.
Wilson, Stanley. Fuchsias. 1977. pap. 10.95 (ISBN 0-571-11047-9, Pub. by Faber & Faber). Merrimack Bk Serv.
Wilson, Stanley D. & Marsal, Raul. Current Trends in Design & Construction of Embankment Dams. 136p. 1979. pap. text ed. 11.75 (ISBN 0-87262-197-9). Am Soc Civil Eng.
Wilson, Stephen R. Informal Groups: An Introduction. (P-H Ser. in Sociology). 1978. ref. ed. 17.95 (ISBN 0-13-464636-3). P-H.
Wilson, Suanna J. Confidentiality in Social Work: Issues & Principles. LC 77-18475. 1980. pap. text ed. 9.95 (ISBN 0-02-934850-1). Free Pr.
--Recording: Guidelines for Social Workers. LC 79-7636. 241p. 1980. 19.95 (ISBN 0-02-935940-6). Free Pr.
--Recording: Working Guidelines for Social Workers. LC 79-7636. 1980. 19.95 (ISBN 0-02-935940-6); pap. text ed. 9.95 (ISBN 0-02-935810-8). Free Pr.
Wilson, Suzanne, jt. ed. see Wilson, Morrow.
Wilson, T. D. An Introduction to Chain Indexing. (Library & Information Science Ser.). 107p. 1971. 11.00 (ISBN 0-208-01069-6, Linnet). Shoe String.
Wilson, Terry C. Researcher's Guide to Statistics: Glossary & Decision Map. LC 78-56267. 1978. pap. text ed. 7.25 (ISBN 0-8191-0519-8). U Pr of Amer.

Wilson, Theodore A. The Marshall Plan: Nineteen Forty Seven-Nineteen Fifty One. LC 77-89364. (Headline Ser.: 236). (Illus., Orig.). 1977. pap. 2.00 (ISBN 0-87124-042-4). Foreign Policy.
--WW 2. LC 74-11680. 1975. pap. text ed. 6.50x o.p. (ISBN 0-684-13987-1, ScribC). Scribner.
Wilson, Theodore A., jt. auth. see Merli, Frank J.
Wilson, Thomas. Discourse on Usury. Tawney, R. H., ed. LC 65-31641. Repr. of 1925 ed. 25.00x (ISBN 0-678-05095-3). Kelley.
Wilson, Thomas & Skinner, Andrew S., eds. The Market & the State: Essays in Honour of Adam Smith. 1977. 37.50x (ISBN 0-19-828406-3). Oxford U Pr.
Wilson, Thomas, jt. ed. see Skinner, Andrew S.
Wilson, Thomas C., jt. auth. see Shortt, Joseph.
Wilson, Thomas F., jt. ed. see Boulding, Kenneth E.
Wilson, Tom. Encore! Encore! A New Ziggy Treasury. (Illus.). (gr. 4 up). 1979. 12.95 (ISBN 0-8362-1150-2); pap. 8.95 (ISBN 0-8362-1151-0). Andrews & McMeel.
--It's a Ziggy World. (Alligator Bks). (Illus.). 96p. 1974. pap. 2.50 (ISBN 0-8362-0575-8). Andrews & McMeel.
--Life Is Just a Bunch of Ziggys. LC 73-9101. (Alligator Bks.). (Illus.). 96p. (Orig.). 1973. pap. 2.50 (ISBN 0-8362-0551-0). Andrews & McMeel.
--Never Get Too Personally Involved with Your Own Life. (Illus.). 96p. (Orig.). 1975. pap. 2.50 o.p. (ISBN 0-8362-0623-1). Andrews & McMeel.
--Plants Are Some of My Favorite People. (Illus.). 96p. (Orig.). 1976. pap. 2.50 (ISBN 0-8362-0674-6). Andrews & McMeel.
--Promises to Myself: Ziggy's Thirty-Day Ledger of I Owe Me's. (Alligator Bks). 1975. pap. 2.50 (ISBN 0-8362-0643-6). Andrews & McMeel.
--This Book Is for the Birds. (Illus.). 1978. pap. 2.50 (ISBN 0-8362-1110-3). Andrews & McMeel.
--A Ziggy Christmas. 48p. (gr. 4 up). 4.95 (ISBN 0-8362-1161-8). Andrews & McMeel.
--Ziggy's Door Openers. 20p. (gr. 4 up). 1980. pap. 4.95 (ISBN 0-8362-1914-7). Andrews & McMeel.
--Ziggys of the World Unite. new ed. (Illus.). 96p. (Orig.). 1976. pap. 2.50 (ISBN 0-8362-0673-8). Andrews & McMeel.
Wilson, Trevor, ed. Political Diaries of C. P. Scott, 1911-1928. LC 75-110993. 512p. 1970. 22.50 (ISBN 0-8014-0569-6). Cornell U Pr.
Wilson, Valerie, ed. RBP Pattern Resource Book. (Illus.). 1975. wire spiral 3.25 (ISBN 0-87227-016-5). Reg Baptist.
Wilson, Violet. Sewing Without Tears. LC 78-38767. (Encore Edition). (Illus.). 1972. 3.95 o.p. (ISBN 0-684-15471-4, ScribT). Scribner.
Wilson, Virginia, jt. auth. see Wattenmaker, Beverly.
Wilson, W. Ker. Vibration Engineering. 292p. 1959. 65.00x (ISBN 0-85264-023-4, Pub. by Griffin England). State Mutual Bk.
Wilson, Wesley M. Know Your Job Rights. LC 75-28954. 180p. 1976. 8.95 o.p. (ISBN 0-87094-115-1). Dow Jones-Irwin.
--Labor Law Handbook. 1963. with 1976 suppl. 22.50 (ISBN 0-672-82866-9, Bobbs-Merrill Law); 1976 suppl. 12.00 (ISBN 0-672-82776-X). Michie.
Wilson, Wilfred, jt. auth. see Wilson, Doris B.
Wilson, William. With Their Whole Strength. LC 80-2084. 128p. (gr. 6 up). 1981. pap. 2.75 (ISBN 0-385-17435-7, Im). Doubleday.
Wilson, William E. Guillen de Castro. (World Authors Ser.: Spain: No. 253). 1973. pap. 10.95 (ISBN 0-8057-2202-5). Twayne.
--Indiana: A History. LC 66-22445. (Illus.). 256p. 1966. 12.50x (ISBN 0-253-14150-8); pap. 6.95x (ISBN 0-253-28305-1). Ind U Pr.
Wilson, William E., jt. auth. see Garcia-Prada, Carlos.
Wilson, William H. The Golden Age: Dutch Seventeenth Century Portraiture. LC 80-53473. (Illus.). 175p. (Orig.). 1980. pap. 8.00 (ISBN 0-916758-03-6). Ringling Mus Art.
Wilson, William H., jt. auth. see Robinson, Franklin W.
Wilson, William J. The Declining Significance of Race: Blacks & Changing American Institutions. 2nd ed. 1980. pap. 5.95 (ISBN 0-226-90129-7, P900, Phoen). U of Chicago Pr.
--Power, Racism & Privilege: Race Relations in Theoretical & Sociohistorical Perspectives. LC 72-87160. 1976. pap. text ed. 6.95 (ISBN 0-02-935580-X). Free Pr.
Wilson, William K. & Wilson, Betty L., eds. Directory of Research Grants, 1981. 360p. 1981. pap. 37.50 (ISBN 0-912700-92-0). Oryx Pr.
Wilson, William S., tr. see Yamamoto, Tsunetomo.
Wilson, Woodrow. The Papers of Woodrow Wilson, Vol. 18-33. Link, Arthur S., ed. Incl. Vol. 18. 1908-1909. 1974. 30.00x (ISBN 0-691-04631-X); Vol. 19. Jan.-July 1910. 1975. 30.00x (ISBN 0-691-04633-6); Vol. 20. Jauary 12 - July 15, 1910. 1975. 30.00 (ISBN 0-691-04635-2); Vol. 21. July-Nov. 1910. 1976. 30.00 (ISBN 0-691-04636-0); Vol. 22. 1911. 1976-1977. 30.00 (ISBN 0-691-04638-7); Vol. 23. 1911-1912. 1976-1977. 30.00 (ISBN 0-691-04643-3); Vol. 24. January-August, 1912. (Illus.). 1977. text ed. 30.00 (ISBN 0-691-04645-X); Vol. 25. August - November, 1912. (Illus.). 1978. text ed. 30.00 (ISBN 0-691-04650-6); Vol. 26. Contents & Index, Vols. 14-25. 1980. 25.00 (ISBN 0-691-04664-6); Vol. 27. January - June 1913. (Illus.). 1978. 30.00 (ISBN 0-691-04652-2); Vol. 28. 1913. (Illus.). 1978. text ed. 30.00 (ISBN 0-691-04653-0); Vol. 29. 1913-1914. 1979. 30.00x (ISBN 0-691-04659-X); Vol. 30. May - December 1914. 30.00x (ISBN 0-691-04663-8); Vol. 31. September - December 1914. 1979. 30.00x (ISBN 0-691-04666-2); **Vol. 32. 1979. 30.00x (ISBN 0-691-04667-0); Vol. 33. April - July 1915. (Illus.). 30.00x (ISBN 0-691-04668-9). LC 66-10880. Princeton U Pr.**
Wilson-Barnett, Jenifer. Stress in Hospital. (Illus.). 136p. 1980. pap. text ed. 8.95x (ISBN 0-443-01879-0). Churchill.
Wilson-Kastner, Patricia. Coherence in a Fragmented World: Jonathan Edwards' Theology of the Holy Spirit. LC 78-62667. 1978. pap. text ed. 6.75 (ISBN 0-8191-0587-2). U Pr of Amer.
Wilstach, Paul. Tidewater Maryland. LC 76-92686. (Illus.). 1969. 10.00 (ISBN 0-87033-137-X, Pub. by Tidewater). Cornell Maritime.
Wilt, Alan F. The French Riviera Campaign of August Nineteen Forty-Four. LC 80-23041. 1981. price not set (ISBN 0-8093-1000-7). S Ill U Pr.
Wilt, Fred, ed. How They Train, Vol. 2: Long Distances. 2nd ed. LC 73-76248. (Illus.). 128p. (Orig.). 1973. 5.00 o.p. (ISBN 0-911520-58-9); pap. 4.00 o.p. (ISBN 0-911520-46-5). Tafnews.
--How They Train, Vol.1: Middle Distances. 2nd ed. LC 73-76247. (Illus.). 128p. 1973. pap. 4.00 (ISBN 0-911520-38-4). Tafnews.
--The Jumps: Contemporary Theory, Technique & Training. LC 73-189447. 160p. 1972. pap. 6.50 o.p. (ISBN 0-911520-35-X). Tafnews.
Wilt, Judith. Ghosts of the Gothic: Austen, Eliot, & Lawrence. LC 80-7559. 1980. 18.50 (ISBN 0-691-06439-3). Princeton U Pr.
Wiltgen, R. M. The Founding of the Roman Catholic Church in Oceania 1825-1850. LC 78-74665. (Illus.). 610p. 1980. text ed. 36.95 (ISBN 0-7081-0835-0, 0572). Bks Australia.
Wilton. Turner in the British Museum: Drawings & Watercolours. Date not set. pap. 7.95 (ISBN 0-8120-0905-3). Barron. Postponed.
Wilton, Andrew. Turner & the Sublime. (Illus.). 192p. 1981. 40.00 (ISBN 0-930606-24-8, 06188-4, Pub. by British Museum). U of Chicago Pr.
--Turner Watercolors. LC 77-79293. (Illus.). 195p. (Orig.). 1977. pap. 12.00 (ISBN 0-88397-002-3). Intl Exhibit Foun.
Wilton, George W. Fingerprints: History, Law & Romance. LC 70-164057. 1971. Repr. of 1938 ed. 20.00 (ISBN 0-8103-3755-X). Gale.
Wilton, Keri M. & Boersma, Frederic J. Eye Movements, Surprise Reactions & Cognitive Development. (Modern Approaches to the Diagnosis & Instruction of Multi-Handicapped Children: Vol. 13). 78p. 1973. text ed. 17.75 (ISBN 90-237-4117-X, Pub. by Swets Pub Serv Holland). Swets North Am.
Wilton, McKinley & Wilton, Norman, eds. Wilton's Wonderland of Cake Decorating. 1960. 12.95 (ISBN 0-912696-00-1). Wilton.
Wilton, Norman, jt. ed. see Wilton, McKinley.
Wiltse, Charles M., ed. see Webster, Daniel.
Wiltse, David, ed. Best Tennis Humor: It Only Hurts When I Serve. (Illus.). 1980. 9.95 (ISBN 0-914178-37-7, Pub. by Tennis Mag). Golf Digest.
Wiltse, David & Tennis Magazine, eds. It Only Hurts When I Serve: Best Tennis Humor. LC 80-66687. (Tennis Magazine Bks.). (Illus.). 192p. 1980. 9.95 (ISBN 0-914178-37-7, 41419-4). Golf Digest.
Wiltsee, Ernest A. The Pioneer Miner & the Pack Mule Express. LC 76-4134. (Illus.). 160p. 1976. Repr. 35.00x (ISBN 0-88000-084-8). Quarterman.
Wiltshire, David. The Social & Political Thought of Herbert Spencer. (Oxford Historical Monographs). 1978. 29.95x (ISBN 0-19-821873-7). Oxford U Pr.
Wilwerding, Walter J. Animal Drawing & Painting. (Illus.). 1966. pap. 4.50 (ISBN 0-486-21716-7). Dover.
Wimberly, Vera. Please Listen God! (Illus.). (gr. k-3). 1977. pap. 2.50 (ISBN 0-570-03467-1, 56-1299). Concordia.
Wimer, Sally. The Snowmobiler's Companion. LC 72-1235. (Illus.). 1972. 9.95 o.p. (ISBN 0-684-13080-7, ScribT). Scribner.
Wimmert, Robert J. Computer Programming Techniques: Fortran Language, Vol. 2. 1978. pap. text ed. 9.95 o.p. (ISBN 0-8403-1282-2). Kendall-Hunt.
Wimp, J., jt. ed. see Robson, E.
Wimp, Jet. Sequence Transformations & Their Applications. LC 80-68564. (Mathematics in Science & Engineering Ser.). 1981. price not set (ISBN 0-12-757940-0). Acad Pr.
Wimsatt, James I. Allegory & Mirror: Tradition & Structure in Middle English Literature. LC 71-101376. 1970. 20.00x (ISBN 0-672-63502-X). Irvington.
Wimsatt, W. K., ed. Literary Criticism, Idea & Act: The English Institute, 1939-1972. 1974. 30.00x (ISBN 0-520-02585-7). U of Cal Pr.
Wimsatt, W. K., jt. ed. see Brady, Frank.
Wimsatt, William A., ed. Biology of Bats. Vol. 1, 1970. 48.50, by subscription 41.75 (ISBN 0-12-758001-8). Vol. 2, 1971. 49.50, by subscription 42.50 (ISBN 0-12-758002-6). Acad Pr.
Wimsatt, William K. Hateful Contraries: Studies in Literature & Criticism. LC 65-11823. 280p. 1965. 11.00x (ISBN 0-8131-1099-8); pap. 4.50 (ISBN 0-8131-0110-7, KP110). U Pr of Ky.
--The Verbal Icon: Studies in the Meaning of Poetry. LC 54-7479. 320p. 1967. pap. 5.00x (ISBN 0-8131-0111-5). U Pr of Ky.
Winans, A. D., ed. see Fowler, Gene.
Winans, A. D., ed. see Micheline, Jack.
Winans, Edgar V. Shambala: The Constitution of a Traditional State. (Illus.). 1962. 20.00x (ISBN 0-520-01348-4). U of Cal Pr.
Winans, Robert B. A Descriptive Checklist of Book Catalogues Separately Printed America. 1981. 35.00 (ISBN 0-912296-47-X, Dist. by U Pr of Va). Am Antiquarian.
Winant, Lewis. Firearms Curiosa. LC 54-7114. (Illus.). 1961. 9.95 o.p. (ISBN 0-686-15793-1). Ray Riling.
Winawer, Sidney J., et al, eds. Colorectal Cancer: Prevention, Epidemiology, & Screening. (Progress in Cancer Research & Therapy). 432p. 1980. 39.50 (ISBN 0-89004-447-3). Raven.
Winber, Gloria K. Better Eating Habits - A Step by Step Approach. (Illus.). 170p. (Orig.). pap. 5.95. Winfoto.
Winbery, Carlton L., jt. auth. see Brooks, James A.
Winblad, Martha. Anna Olsson: A Child of the Prarie. (Illus.). 1978. pap. 10.00. W a Linder.
Winbolt, Samuel E. Latin Hexametre Verse. Commager, Steele, ed. LC 77-70818. (Latin Poetry Ser.). 1978. lib. bdg. 27.50 (ISBN 0-8240-2982-8). Garland Pub.
Winbury, Martin & Abiko, Yasushi, eds. Ischemic Myocardium & Antianginal Drugs. (Perspectives in Cardiovascular Research Ser.: Vol. 3). 1979. 25.00 (ISBN 0-89004-380-9). Raven.
Winch, D. Adam Smith's Politics. LC 77-82525. (Studies in the History & Theory of Politics Ser.). 1978. 32.95 (ISBN 0-521-21827-6); pap. 10.50x (ISBN 0-521-29288-3). Cambridge U Pr.
Winch, D., jt. auth. see Howson, S.
Winch, Peter. Idea of a Social Science & Its Relation to Philosophy. LC 77-112410. (Studies in Philosophical Psychology). 1970. pap. text ed. 5.25x (ISBN 0-391-00061-6). Humanities.
Winch, Peter, ed. Studies in the Philosophy of Wittgenstein. (International Library of Philosophy & Scientific Method). 1969. text ed. 18.25x (ISBN 0-7100-6393-8). Humanities.
Winch, Peter, tr. see Wittgenstein, Ludwig.
Winch, Robert F. Mate Selection: A Study of Complementary Needs. (Reprints in Sociology Ser). lib. bdg. 26.50x (ISBN 0-697-00215-2); pap. text ed. 8.95x (ISBN 0-89197-842-9). Irvington.
Winch, Robert F., et al. Familial Organization. LC 77-2434. (Illus.). 1978. 17.95 (ISBN 0-02-935340-8). Free Pr.
Winchell, Mark R. Joan Didion. (United States Authors Ser.: No. 370). 1980. lib. bdg. 8.95 (ISBN 0-8057-7308-8). Twayne.
Winchester, A. M. Genetics: A Survey of the Principles of Heredity. 5th ed. LC 76-14001. (Illus.). 1977. text ed. 18.95 (ISBN 0-395-24557-5); inst. manual & solutions 1.75 (ISBN 0-395-24559-1); twenty transparencies 7.75 (ISBN 0-395-24560-5). HM.
--Human Genetics. 3rd ed. 1979. pap. text ed. 7.95 (ISBN 0-675-08314-1). Merrill.
Winchester, Alice, jt. auth. see Lipman, Jean.
Winchester, Stanley. The Practice. pap. 1.50 o.s.i. (ISBN 0-440-17081-8). Dell.
Winckel, Fritz. Music, Sound & Sensation: A Modern Exposition. Binkley, Thomas, tr. (Illus.). 1967. pap. text ed. 3.50 (ISBN 0-486-21764-7). Dover.
Winckelmann, J. J. Versuch Einer Allegorie, Repr. Of 1766 Ed. Bd. with De L'Allegorie. Winckelmann, J. J. Repr. of 1799 ed. LC 75-27890. (Renaissance & the Gods Ser.: Vol. 44). (Illus.). 1976. lib. bdg. 73.00 (ISBN 0-8240-2093-6). Garland Pub.
Winckler, Paul A., ed. History of Books & Printing: A Guide to Information Sources. LC 79-13006. (Books, Publishing & Libraries Information Guide Ser.: Vol. 2). 1979. 30.00 (ISBN 0-8103-1408-8). Gale.
Wincor, R. Copyright, Patents & Trademarks. 1980. 5.95 (ISBN 0-379-11138-1). Oceana.
Wind, Edgar. Giorgione's Tempesta, with Comments on Giorgione's Poetic Allegories. 1969. 19.95x o.p. (ISBN 0-19-817165-X). Oxford U Pr.
--Pagan Mysteries in the Renaissance. 2nd ed. 1968. 19.95 o.p. (ISBN 0-571-04634-7, Pub. by Faber & Faber). Merrimack Bk Serv.
Wind, Herbert W. Golf Quiz. LC 80-66690. (Illus.). 192p. (Orig.). 1980. pap. 8.95 (ISBN 0-914178-41-5, 41416-X). Golf Digest.
Wind, Yoram, ed. see Annual Attitude Research Conference, 7th, Hilton Head, S.C., Feb. 1976.
Wind, Yoram, et al. New-Product Forecasting: Models & Applications. LC 80-8388. 1981. price not set (ISBN 0-669-04102-5). Lexington Bks.
Windal, Floyd & Corley, Robert. The Accounting Professional: Ethics, Responsibility, & Liability. (Illus.). 1980. text ed. 21.95 (ISBN 0-13-003020-1). P-H.
Winder, Alan A. & Loda, Charles J. Introduction to Acoustical Space Time Information Processing. (Illus.). 200p. 1980. pap. 14.95 (ISBN 0-932146-04-X). Peninsula.
Winder, Alvin E., jt. auth. see Appley, Dee G.
Winder, Blanche, ed. Stories of King Arthur. (Classics Ser). (gr. 4 up). pap. 1.50 (ISBN 0-8049-0167-8, CL-167). Airmont.
Winder, Jack. Hands. Jordan, Alton, ed. (Elephant Ser.). (Illus.). (gr. k-3). 1975. PLB 3.50 (ISBN 0-89868-020-4, Read Res); pap. text ed. 1.75 (ISBN 0-89868-053-0). ARO Pub.
--Listening. Jordan, Alton, ed. (Elephant Ser.). (Illus.). (gr. k-3). 1975. PLB 3.50 (ISBN 0-89868-021-2, Read Res); text ed. 1.75 soft bd. (ISBN 0-89868-054-9). ARO Pub.
--Presidents Day. Jordan, Alton, ed. (Holdays Ser.). (Illus.). (gr. k-3). 1977. PLB 3.50 (ISBN 0-89868-028-X, Read Res); pap. text ed. 1.75 (ISBN 0-89868-061-1). ARO Pub.
--What Are Faces for? Jordan, Alton, ed. (Buppet Series). (Illus.). (gr. k-3). 1981. PLB 4.50 (ISBN 0-89868-096-4, Read Res); pap. text ed. 1.95 (ISBN 0-89868-107-3). ARO Pub.
--Your Face. Jordan, Alton, ed. (I Can Read Underwater Bks). (Illus.). (gr. k-3). 1974. PLB 3.50 (ISBN 0-89868-008-5, Read Res); pap. text ed. 1.75 (ISBN 0-89868-041-7). ARO Pub.
Winders, P. Understanding Hamlet. pap. 4.30 o.p. (ISBN 0-08-018304-2). Pergamon.
Windham, Donald. Stone in the Hourglass. 1981. ltd. ed. 15.00 (ISBN 0-917366-05-0). S Campbell.
--Tanaquil. LC 77-73864. 1977. 8.95 o.p. (ISBN 0-03-022566-3). HR&W.
--Tanaquil: The Hardest Thing of All. (Illus.). 1972. limited ed 75.00x (ISBN 0-917366-05-0). S Campbell.
Windhorst, Dorothy, jt. ed. see Terry, William D.
Windle. The Spinal Cord & It's Reaction to Traumatic Injury. 448p. 1980. 45.00 (ISBN 0-8247-6688-1). Dekker.
Windle, William F., jt. auth. see Rasmussen, Grant L.
Windlesham. Broadcasting in a Free Society. (Mainstream Ser.). 172p. 1980. 19.50x (ISBN 0-631-11371-1, Pub. by Basil Blackwell). Biblio Dist.
Windmiller, et al. Moral Development & Socialization. 320p. 1980. text ed. 16.95 (ISBN 0-205-06844-8, 2468441). Allyn.
Windom, H. L. & Duce, R. A. Marine Pollutant Transfer. (Illus.). 1976. 25.95 (ISBN 0-669-00855-9). Lexington Bks.
Windrow, M. & Gembleton. Model Soldiers. (Illus.). 1976. 4.95 o.p. (ISBN 0-85059-234-8). Aztex.
Windrow, Martin. Uniforms of the French Foreign Legion 1831-1981. (Illus.). 160p. 1981. 19.95 (ISBN 0-7137-1010-1, Pub. by Blandford Pr England). Sterling.
Windrow, Martin & Mason, F. K. Concise Dictionary of Military Biography: 200 Names in Land Warfare 10th-20th Centuries. 337p. 1975. 18.00x o.p. (ISBN 0-8464-0271-8). Beekman Pubs.
Windrow, Martin & Wilkinson, Frederick, eds. The Universal Soldier: Fourteen Studies in Campaign Life, A.D. 43-1944. (Illus.). 1977. 12.45 o.p. (ISBN 0-85112-176-4). Presidio Pr.
Windsor, Duane. Fiscal Zoning in Suburban Communities. LC 78-20632. (Illus.). 208p. 1979. 21.00 (ISBN 0-669-02751-0). Lexington Bks.
Windsor, Pamela. At Passion's Tide. 240p. (Orig.). 1980. pap. 2.25 (ISBN 0-515-05639-1). Jove Pubns.

--Rebel's Rapture. 1979. pap. 1.95 o.p. (ISBN 0-425-04129-8). Berkley Pub.

Windsor, Patricia. Killing Time. LC 80-7926. 196p. (YA) (gr. 7 up). 1980. 8.95 (ISBN 0-06-026549-3, HarpJ); PLB 8.79 (ISBN 0-06-026550-7). Har-Row.

Windsor, Philip & Roberts, Adam. Czechoslovakia, Nineteen Sixty-Eight. LC 70-79086. 1969. 20.00 (ISBN 0-231-03306-0); pap. 3.50 (ISBN 0-686-63930-8). Columbia U Pr.

Windt, Gaye De see DeWindt, Gaye.

Wine Adsisory Bloard. Gourmet Wine Cooking the Easy Way. 3rd ed. Wilcox, David R., ed. (Illus.). 1980. 5.95 (ISBN 0-932664-01-6). Wine Appreciation.

Wine Advisory Board. Easy Recipes of California Winemakers. Jacobs, Marjorie K., ed. (Illus.). 1970. 5.95 (ISBN 0-932664-05-9). Wine Appreciation.

--Epicurean Recipes of California Winemakers. Bottrell, Donna, ed. (Illus.). 1978. 5.95 (ISBN 0-932664-00-8). Wine Appreciation.

--Favorite Recipes of California Winemakers. Hecker, Lee, ed. (Illus.). 1963. 5.95 (ISBN 0-932664-03-2). Wine Appreciation.

Wine, J. Floyd. A History of Calvary Church of the Brethren. LC 72-95960. (Illus.). 1972. pap. 3.95 (ISBN 0-9604350-1-8). J F Wine.

Wine, J. Floyd, jt. auth. see Wine, Jacob D.

Wine, Jacob D. & Wine, J. Floyd. The Wine Family in America, Section 3. LC 53-4352. (Illus.). 1971. 16.00 (ISBN 0-9604350-0-X). J F Wine.

Wine, M. L., ed. see Marston, John.

Winecoff, H. Larry & Kelly, Eugene W., Jr. Teachers Free of Prejudice? 1969. 1.25 (ISBN 0-685-59508-0). Integrated Ed Assoc.

Winefield, Helen & Peay, Marilyn. Behaviourial Science in Medicine. 357p. 1980. 40.00x (Pub. by Beaconsfield England). State Mutual Bk.

Winefordner, J. D., ed. Trace Analysis: Spectroscopic Methods for Elements. LC 75-41460. (Chemical Analysis Ser.: Vol. 46). 1976. 40.00 (ISBN 0-471-95401-2, Pub. by Wiley-Interscience). Wiley.

Wineman, David, jt. auth. see Redl, Fritz.

Winer, Alfred D., jt. ed. see Schwert, George W.

Wines, Roger, ed. Leopold Von Ranke: The Secret of World History; Selected Writings on the Art & Science of History. LC 80-65600. 160p. 1981. 17.50 (ISBN 0-8232-1050-2); pap. 7.50 (ISBN 0-8232-1051-0). Fordham.

Winetrout, Kenneth. Arnold J. Toynbee. (World Leaders Ser.: No. 47). 1975. lib. bdg. 10.95 (ISBN 0-8057-3725-1). Twayne.

Winey, Michael J., jt. auth. see Dunkelman, Mark H.

Winfield, Ian. Learning to Teach Practical Skills: A Self-Instruction Guide. 1979. 13.50 (ISBN 0-85038-198-3, Pub. by Kogan Pg.). Nichols Pub.

Winfield, Mike, jt. auth. see Caddell, Laurie.

Winfree, Waverly K., ed. Laws of Virginia: Being a Supplement to Hening's the Statutes at Large. 486p. 1971. 15.00x o.p. (ISBN 0-88490-025-8, Virginia State Library). U Pr of Va.

Winfrey, Dorman H. Seventy-Five Years of Texas History: The Texas State Historical Association, 1897-1972. 38p. (YA) 1975. 17.50 (ISBN 0-8363-0131-5). Jenkins.

Winfrey, Dorman H., intro. by. Discovery of the Mississippi. LC 74-19562. 208p. 1975. Repr. of 1844 ed. 1.50 o.p. (ISBN 0-88319-020-6). Shoal Creek Pub.

Winfrey, Laurie P. Pig Appeal. (Illus.). 96p. Date not set. postponed 15.95 (ISBN 0-8027-0668-1); pap. 9.95 (ISBN 0-8027-7166-1). Walker & Co. Postponed.

Wing, Charles, compiled by. Evils of the Factory System Demonstrated by Parliamentary Evidence. LC 67-19730. Repr. of 1837 ed. 27.50x (ISBN 0-678-05096-1). Kelley.

Wing, J. K. & Brown, G. W. Institutionalism & Schizophrenia. LC 75-118068. (Illus.). 1970. 32.50 (ISBN 0-521-07882-2). Cambridge U Pr.

Wing, J. K. & Hailey, Anthea M., eds. Evaluating a Community Psychiatric Service: The Camberwell Register 1964-1971. (Nuffield Publications). (Illus.). 468p. 1972. 24.95x o.p. (ISBN 0-19-721372-3). Oxford U Pr.

Wing, J. K. & Olsen, Rolf, eds. Community Care for the Mentally Disabled. (Illus.). 1979. pap. text ed. 14.95x (ISBN 0-19-261146-1). Oxford U Pr.

Wing, J. K., et al. Measurement & Classification of Psychiatric Symptoms. LC 73-89008. (Illus.). 224p. 1974. 27.50 (ISBN 0-521-20382-1). Cambridge U Pr.

Wing, Jennifer, jt. auth. see Patai, Raphael.

Wing, Lorna, ed. Early Childhood Autism. 2nd ed. 314p. 1976. text ed. 30.00 (ISBN 0-08-017177-X); pap. text ed. 12.75 (ISBN 0-08-017178-8). Pergamon.

Wing, Milton G., jt. auth. see Bellman, Richard.

Wing, R. L. The I Ching Workbook. LC 77-15142. 1979. pap. 7.95 (ISBN 0-385-12838-X). Doubleday.

Wingard, Lemual B., et al, eds. Enzyme Engineering: Future Directions. 535p. 1980. 59.50 (ISBN 0-306-40442-7, Plenum Pr). Plenum Pub.

Wingate, Isabel. Textile Fabrics & Their Selection. 7th ed. 1976. 19.95 (ISBN 0-13-912840-9). P-H.

Wingate, John. Red Mutiny. LC 77-14717. 1978. 7.95 o.p. (ISBN 0-312-66661-6). St Martin.

Wingate, John W., et al. Retail Merchandise Management. LC 73-168617. (Illus.). 1972. ref. ed. 18.95 (ISBN 0-13-778753-7). P-H.

Wingate, Marcel E. Stuttering: Theory & Treatment. 2nd ed. (Speech & Hearing Series). 384p. 1981. text ed. 18.50x (ISBN 0-8290-0359-2). Irvington.

Wingate, Phillip J. Bandages of Soft Illusion. LC 79-65281. (Illus.). 98p. 1979. 11.75 (ISBN 0-935968-06-7); pap. 8.75 o.s.i. (ISBN 0-935968-10-5). Holly Pr.

Wingate, William. Bloodbath. 240p. 1981. pap. 2.50 (ISBN 0-553-14707-2). Bantam.

--Fireplay. 1978. pap. 1.95 o.s.i. (ISBN 0-515-04782-1). Jove Pubns.

Wingell. Experiencing Music. 1981. 15.95 (ISBN 0-88284-116-5); instr's. manual free (ISBN 0-88284-131-9); wkbk. 4.95 (ISBN 0-88284-117-3); record set 30.00 (ISBN 0-88284-132-7). Alfred Pub.

Winger, Bernard J. Cases in Financial Management. LC 80-11532. (Finance Ser.). 115p. 1981. pap. 8.50 (ISBN 0-88244-224-4). Grid Pub.

--Cases in Managerial Economics. LC 78-27382. (Grid Series in Economics). 1979. pap. text ed. 7.95 (ISBN 0-88244-183-3). Grid Pub.

Winger, Bernard J., jt. auth. see Seo, K. K.

Winger, Martin. Electronic Calculator Handbook for Pilots. (Illus.). Date not set. spiral bdg. 3.95 (ISBN 0-911721-77-0, Pub. by Winger). Aviation.

Wingert, Paul S. Primitive Art: Its Traditions & Styles. (Illus.). 1965. pap. 5.95 (ISBN 0-452-00545-0, F545, Mer). NAL.

Winget, Lynn W., jt. auth. see Savaiano, Eugene.

Winget, Lynn W., jt. auth. see Saviano, Eugene.

Wingfield, Anthony, jt. auth. see Devereux, Robert.

Wingfield, Sheila. Admissions: Poems Nineteen Seventy-Four to Nineteen Seventy-Seven. 1977. text ed. 13.00x (ISBN 0-85105-334-3, Dolmen Pr). Humanities.

--Her Storms: Selected Poems 1938-1977. 1977. text ed. 19.50x (ISBN 0-85105-335-1, Dolmen Pr). Humanities.

Wingfield Digby, Cornelia, tr. see Spuhler, Friedrich.

Wingfield Digby, George, tr. see Spuhler, Friedrich.

Wingfield-Stratford, Esme. Those Earnest Victorians. 8.00 (ISBN 0-8446-0966-8). Peter Smith.

Wingo, John W. & Holloway, Gordon F., eds. An Appraisal of Speech Pathology & Audiology: A Symposium. (Illus.). 220p. 1973. 16.75 (ISBN 0-398-02771-4). C C Thomas.

Wingo, Max G. Philosophies of American Education. 1974. text ed. 15.95x (ISBN 0-669-84400-4). Heath.

Wingrave, Helen & Harrold, Robert. Spanish Dancing. (Illus., Orig.). 1978. pap. 2.95 (ISBN 0-8467-0449-8, Pub. by Two Continents). Hippocrene Bks.

Wingren, Gustaf. Creation & Gospel: The New Situation of European Theology. LC 78-78183. (Toronto Studies in Theology: Vol. 2). lii, 189p. 1979. soft cover 19.95x (ISBN 0-88946-994-6). E Mellen.

Wingrove, C. Ray, jt. auth. see Rooke, M. Leigh.

Wingrove, C. Ray, jt. ed. see Barry, John R.

Wingrove, G. A. The Model Cars of Gerald Wingrove. (Illus.). 1979. 42.95 (ISBN 0-904568-12-1, Pub. by Eyre Methuen England). Motorbooks Intl.

Wingrove, Gerald A. The Techniques of Ship Modelling. (Illus.). 133p. 1974. 12.50x (ISBN 0-85242-366-7). Intl Pubns Serv.

Winick, Charles, jt. auth. see Brill, Leon.

Winick, Charles, jt. auth. see Roe, Clifford.

Winick, Charles, ed. Deviance & Mass Media. LC 78-16024. (Sage Annual Reviews of Studies in Deviance: Vol. 2). 1978. 20.00x (ISBN 0-8039-1040-1); pap. 9.95x (ISBN 0-8039-1041-X). Sage.

Winick, Charles, ed. see DeLeeuw, Hendrik.

Winick, Charles, ed. see Hall, Gladys.

Winick, Charles, ed. see Hayward, C.

Winick, Charles, ed. see Marchant, James.

Winick, Charles, ed. see Segilman, E. R.

Winick, Herman & Doniach, Seb, eds. Synchrotron Radiation Research. (Illus.). 740p. 1980. 65.00 (ISBN 0-306-40363-3, Plenum Pr). Plenum Pub.

Winick, M. Nutrition & the Killer Diseases. (Current Concepts in Nutrition Ser.: Vol. 10). 200p. 1981. 24.95 (ISBN 0-471-09130-8, Pub. by Wiley-Interscience). Wiley.

Winick, Myron. Hunger Disease: Studies by the Jewish Physicians in the Warsaw Ghetto. LC 78-26397. (Current Concepts in Nutrition Ser.: Vol. 7). 1979. 20.50 (ISBN 0-471-05003-2, Pub. by Wiley-Interscience). Wiley.

--Nutrition & Cancer. LC 77-22650. (Current Concepts in Nutrition: Vol. 6). 1977. 27.50 (ISBN 0-471-03394-4, Pub. by Wiley-Interscience). Wiley.

--Nutrition & Gastroenterology. LC 80-16169. (Vol. 9). 221p. 1980. 32.50 (ISBN 0-471-08173-6, Pub. by Wiley Interscience). Wiley.

--Nutritional Disorders of American Women. LC 76-54393. (Current Concepts in Nutrition Ser.: Vol. 5). 1977. 25.95 (ISBN 0-471-02393-0, Pub. by Wiley-Interscience). Wiley.

Winick, Myron, ed. Nutrition & Development. LC 72-5097. (Current Concepts in Nutrition Ser.: Vol. 1). 320p. 1972. 32.50 (ISBN 0-471-95440-3, Pub. by Wiley-Interscience). Wiley.

--Nutrition & Fetal Development. (Current Concepts in Nutrition, Vol. 2). 240p. 1974. 26.50 (ISBN 0-471-95435-7, Pub. by Wiley-Interscience). Wiley.

--Nutritional Management of Genetic Disorders, Vol. 8. LC 79-16192. (Current Concepts in Nutrition Ser.). 1979. 28.50 (ISBN 0-471-05781-9, Pub. by Wiley-Interscience). Wiley.

Winick, Steven D. Rhythm: An Annotated Bibliography. LC 74-14582. 1974. 10.00 (ISBN 0-8108-0767-X). Scarecrow.

Winik, Marion. Nonstop. (Cedar Rock Poetry Ser.). 1981. pap. 3.50 (ISBN 0-930024-13-3). Cedar Rock.

Winikoff, B., jt. ed. see Segal, S. J.

Winitz, Harris, ed. The Comprehension Approach to Foreign Language Instruction. (Illus.). 352p. (Orig.). 1981. pap. text ed. 14.95 (ISBN 0-88377-181-0). Newbury Hse.

Wink, Richard. Fundamentals of Music. LC 76-20867. (Illus.). 1977. pap. text ed. 14.50 (ISBN 0-395-20598-0). HM.

Wink, Richard L. & Williams, Lois. Invitation to Listening. 2nd ed. LC 75-31007. (Illus.). 352p. 1976. text ed. 14.95 (ISBN 0-395-18651-X); instructor's manual 1.25 (ISBN 0-395-18778-8); of six LP records 18.75 set (ISBN 0-395-19372-9). HM.

Wink, Walter. Transforming Bible Study: A Leader's Guide. LC 80-16019. 176p. 1980. pap. 6.50 (ISBN 0-687-42499-2). Abingdon.

Winkel, David E. & Prosser, Franklin P. The Art of Digital Design: An Introduction to Top-Down Design. (Illus.). 1980. text ed. 25.95 (ISBN 0-13-046607-7). P-H.

Winkelman, Jack L. Essentials of Basic Life Support. (Orig.). 1981. pap. text ed. write for info. (ISBN 0-8087-2385-5). Burgess.

Winkelman, N. William, Jr. The Placebo Response: An Experimental & Theoretical Model. Date not set. 20.00 (ISBN 0-87630-229-0). Brunner-Mazel. Postponed.

Winkfield, Trevor, tr. see Roussel, Raymond.

Winkle, Gary M., jt. auth. see Cook, John W.

Winkle, Ted Van see Van Winkle, Ted.

Winkle, Van see Heyne & Van Winkle.

Winkler. Magnetic Garnets. 1980. write for info. (ISBN 0-9940013-3-9, Pub. by Vieweg & Sohn Germany). Heyden.

Winkler, Anthony & McCuen, Jo Ray. Sentences, Paragraphs, & Short Essays. 256p. 1980. pap. text ed. 8.95 (ISBN 0-574-22060-7, 13-5060); instr's. guide avail. (ISBN 0-574-22061-5, 13-5061). SRA.

Winkler, Anthony C., jt. auth. see McCuen, JoRay.

Winkler, Erhard M. Engineering Geology Case Histories: Decay & Preservation of Stone, No. 11. LC 58-2632. 1978. pap. 10.00x (ISBN 0-8137-4011-8). Geol Soc.

Winkler, Franz E. Man: The Bridge Between Two Worlds. LC 80-82064. 268p. 1980. pap. 4.95 (ISBN 0-913098-32-9). Myrin Institute.

Winkler, Gabriele. Prayer Attitude in the Eastern Church. 1978. pap. 1.25 (ISBN 0-937032-01-8). Light & Life Pub Co MN.

Winkler, Gershon. The Golem of Prague. (Illus.). 1980. 12.95 (ISBN 0-910818-24-X); pap. 9.95 (ISBN 0-910818-25-8). Judaica Pr.

Winkler, H. G. Petrogenesis of Metamorphic Rocks. 4th ed. LC 76-3443. 1976. pap. 14.10 o.p. (ISBN 0-387-07473-2). Springer-Verlag.

Winkler, Ruthild, jt. auth. see Eigen, Manfred.

Winkler, Stanley, jt. auth. see Magnus, Wilhelm.

Winkler, Stanley & Wewer, William, eds. Computers, Law & Public Policy. LC 80-69245. (Executive Information Ser.). 400p. Date not set. price not set (ISBN 0-88283-030-9). AFIPS Pr.

Winkless, Nels, III & Browning, Iben. Climate & the Affairs of Men. 2nd ed. 1980. flexible cover 10.00 (ISBN 0-87034-059-X). Fraser Pub Co.

Winklessless, Nels & Browning, Iben. Robots on Your Doorstep: A Book About Thinking Machines. LC 78-50710. 1978. pap. 7.95 (ISBN 0-89661-000-4). Robotics Pr.

Winklevoss, Howard E. Pension Mathematics: With Numerical Illustrations. 1977. 12.00x (ISBN 0-256-01886-3). Irwin.

Winks, Robin. An American's Guide to Britain. LC 77-23341. 1977. pap. 6.95 (ISBN 0-684-15189-8, ScribT). Scribner.

Winks, Robin W. Canadian-West Indian Union: A Forty Year Minuet. 1968. pap. text ed. 4.00x (ISBN 0-485-17611-4, Athlone Pr). Humanities.

Winks, Robin W., ed. Historian As Detective: Essays on Evidence. 1970. pap. 6.95x (ISBN 0-06-131933-3, TB1933, Torch). Har-Row.

--Slavery: A Comparative Perspective: Readings on Slavery from Ancient Times to the Present. LC 72-84386. 240p. 1972. 10.00x (ISBN 0-8147-9156-5); pap. 5.00x (ISBN 0-8147-9157-3). NYU Pr.

Winkworth, D. W. Maunsell's Nelsons. (Steam Past Ser.). (Illus.). 128p. 1980. 17.50 (ISBN 0-04-385079-0, 2407). Allen Unwin.

Winky-Lotz, H. I Owe My Life to Jesus -- You Also? An Autobiography Charismatic. (Illus.). 210p. 1980. 11.95 (ISBN 0-936112-00-X); pap. 7.95 (ISBN 0-936112-01-8). Willyshe Pub.

--A Woman for President, Foundation of the Federation of the Goths, Stretching from Iran to Norway. (Historical Novel, Europe About 175 B. C. to 95 B. C. Ser.: Vol. I). (Illus.). 312p. 1980. 14.55 (ISBN 0-936112-02-6); pap. 11.25 (ISBN 0-936112-09-3). Willyshe Pub.

--A Woman for President, the Roots of "Cinderella" of Our Fairy Tale. (Historical Novel, Europe About 95 B. C. to 57 B. C. Ser.: Vol. II). (Illus.). 245p. 1980. 14.55 (ISBN 0-936112-08-5); pap. 11.25 (ISBN 0-936112-03-4). Willyshe Pub.

Winky-Lotz, Hildegard. Cerebral Palsy, Spina Bifida: No Cause for Life Long Handicap. (Illus.). 85p. Date not set. pap. 4.40 (ISBN 0-936112-04-2). Willyshe Pub. Postponed.

Winley, Jesse. Fe Incommovible. Marosi, Esteban & Whidden, Angela, eds. Lacy, Susana B., tr. 218p. (Span.). 1980. pap. 1.60 (ISBN 0-8297-0979-7). Vida Pubs.

Winlund, Edmond. ChartGuide for Southern California 1980-81. rev. ed. LC 74-29812. (Illus.). 138p. (Orig.). 1979. pap. 17.25 (ISBN 0-938206-00-1). ChartGuide.

Winn, Albert C. A Sense of Mission: Guidance from the Gospel of John. 1981. pap. price not set (ISBN 0-664-24365-7). Westminster.

Winn, Albert C., jt. auth. see Burgess, Joseph A.

Winn, Charles S. & Walsh, L. A. Exploring Transportation Occupations. (Careers in Focus Ser.). 1976. text ed. 5.32 (ISBN 0-07-071023-6, G); tchr's. manual & key 3.30 (ISBN 0-07-071024-4); wksheet booklet 13.28 (ISBN 0-07-071054-6). McGraw.

Winn, Edward B. Le see Le Winn, Edward B.

Winn, H. E. & Olla, B. L. Behavior of Marine Animals, Vols. 1-3. Incl. Vol. 1. Invertebres. 244p. 1972. 27.50 (ISBN 0-306-37571-0); Vol. 2. Vertebrates. 259p. 1972. 27.50 (ISBN 0-306-37572-9); Vol. 3. Cetaceans. 460p. 1978. 37.50 (ISBN 0-306-37573-7). LC 79-16775 (Plenum Pr). Plenum Pub.

Winn, James A. Unsuspected Eloquence: A History of the Relations Between Poetry & Music. LC 80-27055. 384p. 1981. 18.95x (ISBN 0-300-02615-3). Yale U Pr.

Winn, Lela P. The Marsh: A Century of Cranberries. 144p. 1981. 7.50 (ISBN 0-682-49697-9). Exposition.

Winn, Marie. The Sick Book: Questions & Answers About Hiccups & Mumps, Sneezes & Bumps & Other Things That Go Wrong with Us. LC 75-34470. (Illus.). 160p. (gr. 2-6). 1976. 9.95 (ISBN 0-590-07259-5, Four Winds). Schol Bk Serv.

Winn, Paul R., jt. auth. see Johnson, Ross H.

Winnen, Betty L. Personal Poetry of Love & Life. 1981. 4.50 (ISBN 0-8062-1638-7). Carlton.

Winner, Irene. Slovenian Village: Zerovnica. LC 77-127367. (Illus.). 267p. 1971. 14.00x (ISBN 0-87057-128-1, Pub. by Brown U Pr). Univ Pr of New England.

Winner, Irene P. & Rmiker-Sebeok, Jean, eds. Semiotics of Culture. (Approaches to Semiotics: No. 53). 1979. text ed. 51.75x (ISBN 90-279-7988-X). Mouton.

Winner, Ken & Jones, Roger. Windsurfing with Ken Winner: A Complete Illustrated Guide to a Fast-Growing Sport. LC 80-8399. (Illus.). 136p. (Orig.). 1981. pap. 8.95 (ISBN 0-06-250971-3, CN 4007, CN). Har-Row.

Winner, Thomas G., ed. Tvorcheskie Raboty Uchenikov Tolstogo V Yasnoi Polyane. LC 72-2453. (Slavic Reprint Ser: No. 10). 136p. (Rus.). 1974. pap. 4.00 (ISBN 0-87057-135-4, Pub. by Brown U Pr). Univ Pr of New England.

Winner, Viola H. Henry James & the Visual Arts. LC 73-109223. (Illus.). 202p. 1970. 10.95x (ISBN 0-8139-0285-1). U Pr of Va.

Winner, Walter, ed. Airman's Information Manual: Nineteen Eighty-One. 304p. 1981. pap. 5.50 (ISBN 0-911721-86-X). Aviation.

Winnett, Thomas. Sierra North. 3rd ed. LC 75-38175. (Trail Guide Ser). (Illus., Orig.). 1976. pap. 8.95 (ISBN 0-911824-46-4). Wilderness.

Winnett, Thomas & Roberts, Ed. High Sierra Hiking Guide to Blackcap Mountain. 2nd ed. LC 74-27684. (High Sierra Hiking Guide Ser: Vol. 3). (Illus., Orig.). 1976. pap. 3.95 (ISBN 0-911824-36-7). Wilderness.

Winnett, Thomas, ed. High Sierra Hiking Guide to Mt. Abbot. 2nd ed. LC 73-100114. (High Sierra Hiking Guide Ser: Vol. 2). (Illus., Orig.). 1973. pap. 3.95 (ISBN 0-911824-08-1). Wilderness.

Winnett, Thomas, ed. see Fawcett, Ken.

Winnett, Thomas, ed. see Felzer, Ron.

Winnett, Thomas, ed. see Jenkins, J. C.

Winnett, Thomas, ed. see Linkhart, Luther.

Winnett, Thomas, ed. see Mazel, David.

Winnett, Thomas, ed. see Pierce, Robert & Pierce, Margaret.

Winnett, Thomas, ed. see Robinson, John W.

Winnett, Thomas, ed. see Schaffer, Jeff P., et al.

Winnett, Thomas, ed. see Schaffer, Jeffrey P.

Winnett, Thomas, ed. see Selters, Andrew.

Winnett, Thomas, ed. see Smith, Robert.

Winnett, Thomas, ed. see Whitnah, Dorothy L.

Winnick, Karen B. Patch and the Strings. LC 76-56446. 1977. 6.95 o.p. (ISBN 0-397-31749-2). Lippincott.

Winnick, R. H. & Thompson, Lawrence. Robert Frost: The Later Years, 1938-1963. 1977. 17.95 o.p. (ISBN 0-686-67554-1). HR&W.

Winnicott, D. W. The Child, the Family & the Outside World. lib. bdg. 8.50x o.p. (ISBN 0-88307-484-2). Gannon.
--The Child, the Family, & the Outside World. 240p. 1964. pap. 1.95 o.p. (ISBN 0-14-020668-X, Pelican). Penguin.

Winnie, Robert E., et al. Jobs & Earnings for State Citizens: Monitoring the Outcomes of State Economic Development & Employment & Training Programs. (An Institute Paper). 146p. 1977. pap. 4.00 (ISBN 0-87766-208-8, 19900). Urban Inst.

Winnig. Das Roemerzimmer. (Easy Reader, A). pap. 2.90 (ISBN 0-88436-041-5, GEA110053). EMC.

Winny, J., ed. see Chaucer, Geoffrey.

Winny, James. A Preface to Donne. (Preface Bks). (Illus.). 1977. pap. text ed. 5.95x (ISBN 0-582-31504-2). Longman.

Winogrand, Garry. Stock Photographs: The Fort Worth Fat Stock Show & Rodeo. (Illus.). 128p. Date not set. 19.95 (ISBN 0-292-72433-0). U of Tex Pr.

Winokur, Alice, jt. auth. see Gipe, George.

Winokur, Stephen. A Primer of Verbal Behavior: An Operant View. (Prentice Hall Experimental Psychology Ser). (Illus.). 192p. 1976. text ed. 13.95 (ISBN 0-13-700609-8). P-H.

Winold, A. & Rehm, J. Introduction to Music Theory. 2nd ed. 1979. pap. 15.95 (ISBN 0-13-489666-1). P-H.

Winold, A., jt. auth. see DeLone, R. P.

Winold, Allen, jt. auth. see Robinson, Ray.

Winquist, Charles E. The Communion of Possibility. LC 75-859. (The Religions Quest Ser: Vol. 2). 160p. 1975. lib. bdg. 17.50x (ISBN 0-914914-05-7); pap. text ed. 6.95x (ISBN 0-914914-04-9). New Horizons.
--Practical Hermeneutics. LC 79-22848. (Scholars Press General Ser.: No. 1). 12.00x (ISBN 0-89130-363-4); pap. 7.50x (ISBN 0-89130-364-2). Scholars Pr CA.

Winqvist, T., jt. auth. see Jansson, B.

Winsberg, Fred. Clinical Ultrasound Review, Vol. 1. LC 80-19595. (Annual Review of Ultrasound). 300p. 1980. 32.00 (ISBN 0-471-05738-X, Pub. by Wiley Med). Wiley.

Winship, Barbara J., jt. auth. see Kelley, Jan D.

Winship, Florence S., illus. Fifty Favorite Rhymes of Mother Goose. (Illus.). 24p. (gr. k-1). 1976. PLB 7.15 o.p. (ISBN 0-307-69053-9, Golden Pr). Western Pub.

Winskell, Cyril, jt. auth. see Barnett, Winston.

Winslade, B. A. J. & Melvil, Dewey. Dewey Decimal Classification for British Schools: Introduction. 3rd ed. 1977. 5.50x (ISBN 0-910608-18-0). Forest Pr.

Winslow, jt. auth. see Lowney.

Winslow, Anna G. Diary of Anna Green Winslow, a Boston Schoolgirl of 1771. Earle, Allic M., ed. LC 71-124586. (Illus.). 1970. Repr. of 1894 ed. 15.00 (ISBN 0-8103-3586-7). Gale.

Winslow, Donald J. Life-Writing: A Glossary of Terms in Biography, Autobiography, & Related Forms. (Biography Monographs Ser.). 64p. (Orig.). pap. 4.50x (ISBN 0-8248-0748-0). U Pr of Hawaii.

Winslow, Eugene. Afro-American Seventy Six. LC 75-23936. (Illus.). 80p. 1975. 8.95 (ISBN 0-910030-20-0); pap. 5.95 (ISBN 0-910030-21-9). Afro-Am.

Winslow, F. H., jt. ed. see Pappas, S. Peter.

Winslow, Marjorie. Mud Pies & Other Recipes. (Illus.). (gr. k-2). 1961. 5.95 o.s.i. (ISBN 0-02-793080-7). Macmillan.
--Mud Pies & Other Recipes. LC 61-10336. (Illus.). 48p. (ps-3). 1973. pap. 1.95 o.s.i. (ISBN 0-02-045440-6, Collier). Macmillan.

Winslow, Octavius. Personal Declension & Revival of Religion in the Soul. 1978. pap. 2.95 (ISBN 0-85151-261-5). Banner of Truth.
--The Work of the Holy Spirit. pap. 12.95 o.p. (ISBN 0-85151-279-8). Banner of Truth.

Winslow, Pauline. Copper Gold. 1981. pap. 2.25 (ISBN 0-440-11130-7). Dell.

Winslow, Robert W. Crime in a Free Society. 3rd ed. 1977. pap. text ed. 13.95x (ISBN 0-8221-0192-0). Dickenson.

Winslow, Ron, jt. auth. see Silverman, Milton J.

Winsnes, Thore S., ed. The Geological Development of Svalbard During the Precambrian, Lower Palaeozoic, & Devonian. (Norsk Polarinstitutt Skrifter: Vol. 167). (Illus.). 323p. 1980. pap. text ed. 30.00x (ISBN 82-90307-03-9). Universitet.

Winsor, Bill. Texas in the Confederacy: Military Installations, Economy & People. LC 78-68432. (Illus.). 1978. 12.50 (ISBN 0-912172-24-X). Hill Jr Coll.

Winsor, P. A., jt. ed. see Gray, G. W.

Winsor, Ricker, ed. see Callahan, Harry.

Winspear, Violet. A Girl Possessed. (Harlequin Presents Ser.). 192p. 1981. pap. 1.50 (ISBN 0-373-10420-0, Pub. by Harlequin). PB.

Winstedt, E. O., ed. see Nepos, Cornelius.

Winston, Brian. The Terrors & Horrors of a Haunted House. 1981. 6.95 (ISBN 0-533-04574-6). Vantage.

Winston, Clara, tr. see Andersen, Hans C.

Winston, Clara, tr. see Herlin, Hans.

Winston, Clara, tr. see Hesse, Hermann.

Winston, Clara, tr. see Jung, C. G.

Winston, Clara, tr. see Kooiker, Leonie.

Winston, Clara, tr. see Messegue, Maurice.

Winston, Clara, tr. see Wiesenthal, Simon.

Winston, Daoma. Emerald Station. 1974. pap. 1.95 (ISBN 0-380-00738-X, 38281). Avon.
--The Lotteries. 1981. pap. 2.75 (ISBN 0-671-41277-9). PB.
--Mills of the Gods. 1980. pap. write for info. (ISBN 0-671-81601-2). PB.
--Mira. LC 80-68544. 288p. 1981. 11.95 (ISBN 0-87795-300-7). Arbor Hse.

Winston Editorial Staff, ed. Joy Three. rev. ed. (The Joy Ser.). (gr. 3). 1977. pap. text ed. 4.50 (ISBN 0-03-017671-9); tchr's ed. 5.95 (ISBN 0-03-004196-1). Winston Pr.

Winston, Ellen E., jt. auth. see Woofter, Thomas Jackson.

Winston, George P. John Fiske. (U. S. Authors Ser.: No. 197). lib. bdg. 10.95 (ISBN 0-8057-0256-3). Twayne.

Winston, Henry. Class, Race & Black Liberation. LC 77-923. 1977. 8.00 (ISBN 0-7178-0484-4); pap. 2.75 o.p. (ISBN 0-7178-0491-7). Intl Pub Co.

Winston, Kathryn, jt. auth. see Adams, Carolyn.

Winston, Krishna, tr. see Schlemmer, Oskar.

Winston, Mary, jt. auth. see Eshelman, Ruthe.

Winston, Patrick H. & Horn, Berthold K. Lisp. (Illus.). 300p. 1981. pap. text ed. 13.95 (ISBN 0-201-08329-9). A-W.

Winston Press Editorial Staff. Joy Six. rev. ed. (Joy Religious Ser.). 1979. pap. 4.50 (ISBN 0-03-008331-1, 665); teacher's ed 5.95 (ISBN 0-03-049536-9). Winston Pr.

Winston Press Editorial Staff, ed. The Christmas Pageant. (Illus.). 1979. 7.95 (ISBN 0-03-046356-4). Winston Pr.

Winston, R. Working Your Way Through College. 1979. pap. 7.95 (ISBN 0-930204-04-2). Lord Pub.

Winston, Richard & Bober, Harry. Charlemagne. LC 68-13721. (Horizon Caravel Bks). (Illus.). 153p. (gr. 6 up). 1968. 9.95 (ISBN 0-8281-0475-1, Dist. by Har-Row); PLB 12.89 (ISBN 0-06-026543-4). Am Heritage.

Winston, Richard, tr. see Andersen, Hans C.

Winston, Richard, tr. see Herlin, Hans.

Winston, Richard, tr. see Hesse, Hermann.

Winston, Richard, tr. see Jung, C. G.

Winston, Richard, tr. see Kooiker, Leonie.

Winston, Richard, tr. see Wiesenthal, Simon.

Winston, Richard, tr. see Wunderlich, Hans G.

Winston, Sandra. The Entrepreneurial Woman. 240p. 1980. pap. 2.95 (ISBN 0-553-13479-5). Bantam.

Winston, Stephanie. Getting Organized. 1980. pap. 5.95 (ISBN 0-446-97806-X). Warner Bks.
--Getting Organized: Time & Paperwork. 1980. pap. 2.50 (ISBN 0-446-97564-8). Warner Bks.

Winter, Arthur. Life & Death Decisions. 88p. 1980. text ed. 11.50 (ISBN 0-398-03957-7). C C Thomas.
--Moment of Death: A Symposium. (Illus.). 100p. 1969. 9.50 (ISBN 0-398-02090-6). C C Thomas.

Winter, Arthur, ed. Surgical Control of Behavior: A Symposium. (Illus.). 100p. 1971. 11.25 (ISBN 0-398-02091-4). C C Thomas.

Winter, C. Chester & Morel, Alice. Nursing Care of Patients with Urologic Diseases. 4th ed. LC 76-14837. (Illus.). 1977. pap. 16.95 (ISBN 0-8016-5607-9). Mosby.

Winter, Catherine. I Share God's Special Meal: My First Communion Book. 1977. 6.95 o.p. (ISBN 0-03-021251-0, 892). Winston Pr.

Winter, Colin. Namibia. (Orig.). 1977. pap. 4.95 o.p. (ISBN 0-8028-1664-9). Eerdmans.

Winter, David. How to Walk with God. LC 99-78727. Orig. Title: Now What. (Illus.). 1969. pap. 1.95 (ISBN 0-87788-594-X). Shaw Pubs.

Winter, David A. Biomechanics of Human Movement. LC 79-12660. (Biomedical Engineering & Health Systems Ser.). 1979. 22.95 (ISBN 0-471-03476-2, Pub. by Wiley-Interscience). Wiley.

Winter, David G. The Power Motive. LC 72-92869. 1973. 17.95 (ISBN 0-02-935460-9). Free Pr.

Winter, David J. Abstract Lie Algebras. 1972. 20.00x (ISBN 0-262-23051-8). MIT Pr.

Winter, E. G. World Chess Champions. (Illus.). 208p. 1981. 14.51 (ISBN 0-08-024094-1); pap. 8.51 (ISBN 0-08-024117-4). Pergamon.

Winter, Ella. And Not to Yield: An Autobiography. LC 63-15320. 5.95 o.p. (ISBN 0-15-106820-8). HarBraceJ.

Winter, Ella, tr. see Kohler, Wolfgang.

Winter, Elmer L. Your Future in Your Own Business. LC 79-114130. 188p. 1975. pap. 3.50 (ISBN 0-668-02236-1). Arco.

Winter, Francis De see Bereny, Justin A.

Winter, Francis de see De Winter, Francis.

Winter, Garry, ed. Crafts & Hobbies. rev. ed. LC 64-21342. (Illus.). 1971. lib. bdg. 3.95 o.p. (ISBN 0-668-01212-9). Arco.

Winter, George D. Evaluation of Biomaterials. LC 79-42730. (Advances in Biomaterials Ser.). 1980. 135.00 (ISBN 0-471-27658-8, Pub. by Wiley-Interscience). Wiley.

Winter, Gibson. Being Free: Reflections on America's Cultural Revolution. 1970. 4.95 o.p. (ISBN 0-02-630500-3); pap. 1.95 (ISBN 0-685-04267-7). Macmillan.

Winter, Gordon. Country Camera, Eighteen Forty-Four to Nineteen Fourteen: Rural Life As Depicted in Photographs from the Early Days of Photography to the Outbreak of the First World War. LC 76-148407. (Illus.). 1971. Repr. of 1966 ed. 15.00 (ISBN 0-8103-3399-6). Gale.

Winter, Herbert R. & Bellows, Thomas J. People & Politics. 2nd ed. LC 80-20518. 525p. 1981. text ed. 16.95 (ISBN 0-471-08153-1). Wiley.

Winter, J. M., ed. War & Economic Development. LC 74-82219. (Illus.). 320p. 1975. 41.00 (ISBN 0-521-20535-2). Cambridge U Pr.

Winter, M. Mind Your Own Business, Be Your Own Boss. 1980. 12.95 (ISBN 0-13-583468-6); pap. 6.95 (ISBN 0-13-583450-3). P-H.

Winter, Mary, jt. auth. see Morris, Earl W.

Winter, Michael. Society & Religion in Early Ottoman Egypt. 230p. 1981. 19.95 (ISBN 0-87855-351-7). Transaction Bks.

Winter, Michelle de see De Winter, Michelle.

Winter, Paula. The Bear & the Fly. (Illus.). (ps-k). Date not set. pap. 1.50 (ISBN 0-590-31568-4). Schol Bk Serv.
--Sir Andrew. (Illus.). 32p. (gr. k-2). 1980. PLB 7.95 (ISBN 0-517-53911-X). Crown.

Winter, Ralph K. Government & the Corporation. 1978. pap. 4.25 (ISBN 0-8447-3313-X). Am Enterprise.

Winter, Ralph K., jt. auth. see Wellington, Harry H.

Winter, Robert. The California Bungalow. LC 80-14078. (Illus.). 96p. 1980. 14.95 (ISBN 0-912158-85-9). Hennessey.

Winter, Robert & Carr, Bruce, eds. Beethoven, Performers & Critics: The International Beethoven Congress Detroit, 1977. (Illus.). 228p. 1981. 16.95 (ISBN 0-8143-1658-1). Wayne St U Pr.

Winter, Rolf. Quantum Physics. 1979. text ed. 23.95x (ISBN 0-534-00697-3). Wadsworth Pub.

Winter, Ruth. Feet First: The Complete Guide to Foot Care. (Orig.). 1981. pap. 6.95 (ISBN 0-87701-204-0). Chronicle Bks.
--The Fragile Bond. 208p. 1976. 7.95 o.s.i. (ISBN 0-02-630510-0). Macmillan.
--The Smell Book: Scent, Sex & Society. LC 76-18783. (Illus.). 1976. 7.95 o.p. (ISBN 0-397-01163-6). Lippincott.
--Triumph Over Tension. 1978. pap. 1.50 (ISBN 0-441-82411-0). Charter Bks.

Winter, Thelma F. Art & Craft of Ceramic Sculpture. LC 73-20150. (Illus.). 269p. 1973. 28.95 (ISBN 0-470-95475-2). Halsted Pr.

Winter, W. T. Divorce & You. 1963. 2.50 o.s.i. (ISBN 0-02-630540-2). Macmillan.

Winter, Willard W. Studies in First & Second Samuel. LC 70-1508. (The Bible Study Textbook Ser.). 1967. 15.00 (ISBN 0-89900-011-8). College Pr Pub.
--Studies in Joshua, Judges, Ruth. (The Bible Study Textbook Ser.). (Illus.). 1969. 15.00 (ISBN 0-89900-010-X). College Pr Pub.

Winter, William. Brief Chronicles, 3 pts. in 1. LC 72-130085. (Dunlap Society Ser.: Nos. 7, 8, 10). 1971. Repr. of 1889 ed. 33.50 (ISBN 0-8337-3826-7). B Franklin.

Winter, William, jt. auth. see McEntee, Howard G.

Winter, William H., ed. see Johnson, Overton.

Winterboer, Ronald D., jt. auth. see Beneke, Raymond R.

Winterbotham, Ann V. Treasury of Traditional Stained Glass Designs. (Illus.). 80p. (Orig.). 1981. pap. price not set (ISBN 0-486-24084-3). Dover.

Winterbotham, R. Lord of Nardos. 5.95 (ISBN 0-685-07443-9, Avalon). Bouregy.

Winterbottom, M., ed. see Tacitus.

Winterbottom, Michael, ed. see Gildas.

Winterburn, Roy, ed. see Association for Educational & Training Technology.

Wintercross, Paul W. The Absolutely Definite Philosophy for the Intelligence of Contemporary Man. (Illus.). 1980. deluxe ed. 39.75 (ISBN 0-89266-221-2). Am Classical Coll Pr.

Winterfield, Henry. Star Girl. (gr. 2-7). 1976. pap. 1.25 o.s.i. (ISBN 0-380-00659-6, 28506, Camelot). Avon.

Winterich, John T. Early American Books & Printing. LC 74-3022. 1974. Repr. of 1935 ed. 22.00 (ISBN 0-8103-3661-8). Gale.

Winternitz, tr. see Mueller, F. Max.

Winternitz, Emanuel. Musical Instruments & Their Symbolism in Western Art. (Illus.). 1979. 27.50x (ISBN 0-300-02324-3); pap. 10.95 (ISBN 0-300-02376-6). Yale U Pr.

Winternitz, Milton C. Pathology of Influenza. (Illus.). 1920. 100.00x (ISBN 0-685-69886-6). Elliots Bks.

Winters, Arthur A. & Goodman, Stanley. Fashion Sales Promotion Handbook. 3rd ed. 1967. pap. text ed. 8.95 (ISBN 0-672-96040-0); tchr's manual 5.00 (ISBN 0-672-96041-9). Bobbs.

Winters, Bonnie, jt. auth. see Berger, Evelyn.

Winters, Donald L. Farmers Without Farms: Agricultural Tenancy in Nineteenth-Century Iowa. LC 78-4021. (Contributions in American History Ser.: No. 79). (Illus.). 1978. lib. bdg. 17.50 (ISBN 0-313-20408-X, WFL/). Greenwood.

Winters, Donna, jt. auth. see Jensen, William E.

Winters, John D. The Civil War in Louisiana. LC 63-9647. 552p. 1979. 25.00 (ISBN 0-8071-0834-0). La State U Pr.

Winters, Jon. The Drakov Memoranda. 1977. pap. 2.25 (ISBN 0-380-47563-4, 47563). Avon.

Winters, Kay. The Teacher's CopeBook: End the Year Better Than You Started. LC 80-81682. 1980. pap. 8.95 (ISBN 0-8224-6767-4). Pitman Learning.

Winters, L. Alan. An Econometric Model of the Export Sector. (Cambridge Studies in Applied Econometrics). 192p. Date not set. price not set (ISBN 0-521-23720-3). Cambridge U Pr.

Winters, Robert W. & Hasselmeyer, Eileen G. Intravenous Nutrition in the High Risk Infants. LC 74-26712. (Clinical Pediatrics, Maternal & Child Health Ser). 528p. 1975. 48.95 (ISBN 0-471-95500-0, Pub. by Wiley Medical). Wiley.

Winters, Shelley. Shelley Also Known As Shirley. 512p. 1981. pap. 3.50 (ISBN 0-345-29506-4). Ballantine.

Winters, Stanley A. & Cox, Eunice W. Competency-Based Instruction for Exceptional Children. (Illus.). 160p. 1976. pap. 16.75 (ISBN 0-398-03402-8). C C Thomas.

Winters, Stanley B., ed. From Riot to Recovery: Newark After Ten Years. LC 79-66424. 1979. text ed. 22.25 (ISBN 0-8191-0822-7); pap. text ed. 15.75 (ISBN 0-8191-0823-5). U Pr of Amer.

Winters, Thomas A., jt. auth. see Nelson, Gayle L.

Winters, Tobey L. Deepwater Ports in the United States: An Economic & Environmental Impact Study. LC 76-12885. (Special Studies). 1977. text ed. 27.50 (ISBN 0-275-23250-6). Praeger.

Winters, W. D., et al. A Stereotaxic Brain Atlas for Macaca Nemestrina. LC 69-16743. (Illus.). 1969. 45.00x (ISBN 0-520-01445-6). U of Cal Pr.

Winters, Yvor. Collected Poems. 146p. 1960. pap. 4.95x (ISBN 0-8040-0047-6, 10). Swallow.
--Early Poems of Yvor Winters Nineteen-Twenty to Nineteen-Twenty-Eight. LC 66-25962. 148p. 1966. 4.95x (ISBN 0-8040-0072-7). Swallow.
--Forms of Discovery: Critical & Historical Essays on the Forms of the Short Poem in English. LC 66-30433. 378p. 1967. 8.95 o.p. (ISBN 0-8040-0118-9); pap. 7.95x (ISBN 0-8040-0119-7). Swallow.
--Function of Criticism: Problems & Exercises. LC 57-1652. 220p. 1957. pap. 5.95x (ISBN 0-8040-0130-8, 83). Swallow.
--In Defense of Reason. LC 47-2236. 611p. 1947. pap. 12.95x (ISBN 0-8040-0151-0, 69). Swallow.

Winters, Yvor & Fields, Kenneth, eds. Quest for Reality: An Anthology of the Short Poems in English. LC 78-75739. 199p. 1969. 10.00x o.p. (ISBN 0-8040-0257-6); pap. 4.95x (ISBN 0-8040-0258-4). Swallow.

Wintersgill, Donald. English Antiques: The Age of Elegance 1700-1830. LC 75-4162. (Illus.). 272p. 1975. 18.00 o.p. (ISBN 0-688-02931-0). Morrow.

Winterton, Bert W. The Processes of Heredity. 304p. (Orig.). 1980. pap. 10.95 (ISBN 0-8403-2166-X). Kendall-Hunt.
Winterton, R. H. Thermal Design of Nuclear Reactors. LC 80-41187. (Illus.). 200p. 30.00 (ISBN 0-08-024215-4); pap. 15.00 (ISBN 0-08-024214-6). Pergamon.
Winther, Oscar O. Old Oregon Country: A History of Frontier Trade, Transportation, & Travel. LC 50-63368. (Illus.). 1969. pap. 3.95 (ISBN 0-8032-5218-8, BB 388, Bison). U of Nebr Pr.
--The Transportation Frontier: Trans-Mississippi West, 1865-1890. LC 64-10639. (Histories of the American Frontier Ser.). (Illus.). 238p. 1974. pap. 6.50x (ISBN 0-8263-0317-X). U of NM Pr.
Winther, Sophus K. Take All to Nebraska. LC 75-11672. vi, 306p. 1976. 12.50x (ISBN 0-8032-0861-8); pap. 4.50 (ISBN 0-8032-5831-3, BB 611, Bison). U of Nebr Pr.
Winthrop, Elizabeth. Miranda in the Middle. (Skylark Ser.). 128p. 1981. pap. cancelled (ISBN 0-553-15073-1). Bantam.
--Sloppy Kisses. LC 80-13673. (Illus.). 32p. (gr. k-3). 1980. PLB 7.95 (ISBN 0-02-793210-9). Macmillan.
Winthrop, John. Life & Letters of John Winthrop, 2 Vols. Winthrop, Robert C., ed. LC 72-152833. (American Public Figures Ser). 1971. Repr. of 1864 ed. Set. lib. bdg. 75.00 (ISBN 0-306-70147-2). Da Capo.
Winthrop, Robert C., ed. see Winthrop, John.
Winthrop, Theodore. Canoe & Saddle. 2nd ed. (Illus.). 1981. pap. 5.95 (ISBN 0-8323-0380-1). Binford.
Wintle, Justin. Makers of Modern Culture. 704p. 1981. 34.95 (ISBN 0-87196-493-7). Facts on File.
Wintner, Claude E. Strands of Organic Chemistry: A Series of Lectures. LC 78-60358. 1979. pap. text ed. 6.95 (ISBN 0-8162-9661-8). Holden-Day.
Winton, Alison. Proust's Additions, 2 vols. Incl. Vol. 1. (ISBN 0-521-21610-9); Vol. 2. (ISBN 0-521-21611-7). LC 76-58869. 1977. 68.00 set (ISBN 0-521-21612-5). Cambridge U Pr.
Winton, Calhoun, ed. see Steele, Richard.
Winton, Dorothy de see De Winton, Dorothy.
Winton, John. Air Power at Sea: Nineteen Thirty-Nine to Nineteen Forty-Five. LC 76-41384. (Illus.). 1977. 12.95 o.s.i. (ISBN 0-690-01222-5, TYC-T). T Y Crowell.
--Find, Fix & Strike! The Fleet Air Arm at War 1939-45. (Illus.). 192p. 1981. 28.50 (ISBN 0-7134-3488-0, Pub. by Batsford England). David & Charles.
--Sink the Haguro! The Last Destroyer of the Second World War. (Illus.). x, 182p. 1978. 19.50 (ISBN 0-85422-152-2). Shoe String.
Winton, R. C., jt. auth. see Dummer, Geoffrey W.
Winton, W. M. & Adkins, W. S. The Geology of Tarrant County. (Illus.). 122p. 1919. 0.50 (BULL 1931). Bur Econ Geology.
Wintz, Paul, jt. auth. see Gonzalez, Rafael C.
Winward, Walter. Hammerstrike. 304p. 1981. pap. 2.95 (ISBN 0-553-13317-9). Bantam.
--Seven Minutes Past Midnight. 1980. 12.95 (ISBN 0-671-24932-0). S&S.
Winwood, Stevie. Stevie Winwood & His Friends. 1971. pap. 2.95 o.s.i. (ISBN 0-02-061940-5, Collier). Macmillan.
Wionczek, Miguel S. International Indebtedness & World Economic Stagnation. 135p. 1981. 17.50 (ISBN 0-08-024702-4). Pergamon.
Wionczek, Miguel S., jt. ed. see Thomas, D. Babatunde.
Wiplinger, Peter P. Borders-Grenzen. Kuhner, Herbert, tr. LC 77-18422. (Bilingual Poetry Ser.: No. 1). (Ger.). 1977. 10.00x (ISBN 0-89304-022-3, CCC112); signed o.p. 10.50x (ISBN 0-89804-038-8); special signed ed. o.p. 25.00 (ISBN 0-89304-024-X); pap. 4.50x (ISBN 0-89304-023-1); pap. 6.50x signed ltd. ed. o.p. (ISBN 0-89304-039-8). Cross Cult.
Wippel, John F. The Metaphysical Thought of Godfrey of Fontaines: A Study in Late Thirteenth Century Philosophy. 1980. text ed. write for info. (ISBN 0-8132-0556-5, Dist. by Isbs). Intl Schol Bk Serv.
Wippel, John F. & Wolter, Allen B., eds. Medieval Philosophy: From St. Augustine to Nicholas of Cusa. LC 69-10043. 1969. pap. text ed. 7.95 (ISBN 0-02-935650-4). Free Pr.
Wippern, Ronald F. Cases in Modern Financial Management: Public & Private Sector Perspectives. 1980. 17.95x (ISBN 0-256-02363-8). Irwin.
Wippler, Migene. Dreams and What They Mean. pap. 2.25. Merit Pubns.
Wire, Gertrude. Chasing Gold: For Fun & Profit. LC 78-62651. (Illus.). 210p. 1980. 9.95 (ISBN 0-86533-003-4). Amber Crest.
Wiren, Gary. Golf. (Sport Ser). (Illus.). (gr. 10 up). 1971. text ed. 4.95 ref. ed. o.p. (ISBN 0-13-358028-8); pap. 3.95 ref. ed. (ISBN 0-13-358010-5). P-H.
Wiren, Gary, et al. The New Golf Mind. 164p. 1981. pap. 4.95 (ISBN 0-346-12478-6). Cornerstone.
Wires, Richard. Studying Civilizations Past & Present, Vol. 1. 8th ed. 1981. pap. text ed. 5.95x study guide (ISBN 0-673-15502-1). Scott F.
Wirsen, Claes, et al. Child Is Born: The Drama of Life Before Birth. 1969. pap. 6.95 (ISBN 0-440-51214-X, Dell Trade Pbks). Dell.
Wirsing, Marie E. Teaching & Philosophy: A Synthesis. LC 79-47998. 238p. 1980. pap. text ed. 9.25 (ISBN 0-8191-0994-0). U Pr of Amer.
Wirsing, Nancy, jt. auth. see Wirsing, Robert G.
Wirsing, Robert G. Protection of Minorities: Comparative Perspectives. (Pergamon Policy Studies). 300p. Date not set. 39.51 (ISBN 0-08-025556-6). Pergamon.
Wirsing, Robert G. & Wirsing, Nancy. Ancient India & Its Influence on Modern Times. LC 73-6740. (First Bks.). (gr. 4-6). 1973. PLB 4.90 o.p. (ISBN 0-531-00806-1). Watts.
Wirsing, Robert G., ed. Protection of Ethnic Minorities: Comparative Perspectives. LC 80-25618. (Pergamon Policy Studies on International Politices Ser.). 350p. 1981. 39.50 (ISBN 0-08-025556-6). Pergamon.
Wirszubski, Chaim. Libertas As a Political Idea at Rome. (Cambridge Classical Studies). 1950. 17.95 (ISBN 0-521-06848-7). Cambridge U Pr.
Wirt, Frederick & Kirst, Michael. Political & Social Foundations of Education. 2nd ed. LC 75-20297. 1975. 17.50 (ISBN 0-8211-1016-0); text ed. 15.75x (ISBN 0-685-57428-8). McCutchan.
Wirt, Frederick M. Power in the City: Decision Making in San Francisco. LC 73-90662. 1975. 19.95 (ISBN 0-520-02654-3); pap. 6.95 (ISBN 0-520-03640-9). U of Cal Pr.
Wirt, Frederick M., ed. The Polity of the School. LC 74-26311. (Politics of Education Ser.). 384p. 1975. 22.95 (ISBN 0-669-97618-0). Lexington Bks.
Wirt, Frederick M., jt. ed. see Gove, Samuel K.
Wirt, John G., et al. R & D Management: Methods Used by Federal Agencies. LC 74-27510. 288p. 1975. 15.00x o.p. (ISBN 0-669-97642-3). Lexington Bks.
Wirt, Sherwood. The Confessions of Augustine in Modern English. 1977. pap. 4.95 (ISBN 0-310-34641-X). Zondervan.
--A Thirst for God. 176p. 1980. 6.95 (ISBN 0-310-34640-1). Zondervan.
Wirth, Arthur G. Education in the Technological Society: The Vocational-Liberal Studies Controversy in the Early Twentieth Century. LC 81-618. 272p. 1980. lib. bdg. 18.75 (ISBN 0-8191-1222-4); pap. text ed. 10.50 (ISBN 0-8191-1223-2). U Pr of Amer.
Wirth, Conrad L. Parks, Politics & the People. LC 79-6709. (Illus.). 450p. 1980. 19.95 (ISBN 0-8061-1605-6). U of Okla Pr.
Wirth, Dick & Young, Jerry. Ballooning: The Complete Guide to Riding the Winds. LC 80-5281. (Illus.). 168p. 1980. 20.00 (ISBN 0-394-51338-X). Random.
Wirth, Louis & Bernet, Eleanor H., eds. Local Community Fact Book of Chicago. LC 50-5597. (Illus.). 1950. pap. 7.00x o.s.i. (ISBN 0-226-90243-9). U of Chicago Pr.
Wirth, Niklaus. Systematic Programming: An Introduction. (Illus.). 208p. 1973. 22.95 (ISBN 0-13-880369-2). P-H.
Wirth, Niklavs. Algorithms Plus Data Structures Equals Programs. (Illus.). 400p. 1976. 23.95 (ISBN 0-13-022418-9). P-H.
Wirth, Willis W. & Atchley, William R. A Review of the North American Leptoconops (Diptera: Ceratopogonidae) (Graduate Studies: No. 5). (Illus., Orig.). 1973. pap. 3.00 (ISBN 0-89672-012-8). Tex Tech Pr.
Wirtschafter, Jonathan D., jt. auth. see Weinstock, Stephen M.
Wirtschaftsverlag, Hoppenstedt, ed. Who Makes Machinery Nineteen Seventy-Eight (West Germany) 40th ed. 1978. pap. 15.00x o.p. (ISBN 3-87362-001-4). Intl Pubns Serv.
Wirtz, Willard. The Boundless Resource: A Prospectus for an Education-Work Policy. LC 75-30556. 1975. 8.95 o.p. (ISBN 0-915220-07-5); pap. 3.95 o.p. (ISBN 0-915220-10-5). New Republic.
Wirz, H. J. & Smolderen, J. J. Numerical Methods in Fluid Dynamics. (McGraw-Hill - Hemisphere Series in Thermal & Fluids Engineering). (Illus.). 1978. text ed. 37.50 (ISBN 0-07-071120-8, C). McGraw.
Wisbey, R. A. Computer in Literary & Linguistic Research. LC 70-152645. (Publications of the Literary & Linguistic Computing Centre: No. 1). 1971. 49.50 (ISBN 0-521-08146-7). Cambridge U Pr.
Wisch, Nathaniel, ed. Comprehensive. 3rd ed. (Medical Examination Review Books: Vol. 1). 1972. spiral bdg. 15.00 (ISBN 0-87488-101-3). Med Exam.
Wisch, Nathaniel, et al, eds. Internal Medicine Specialty Board Review. 6th ed. 1978. spiral bdg. 16.50 (ISBN 0-87488-303-2). Med Exam.
--Medicine. 6th ed. (Medical Examination Review Books: Vol. 2). 1980. pap. 8.50 o.p. (ISBN 0-87488-102-1). Med Exam.
Wischnitzer, S. Introduction to Electron Microscopy. 2nd ed. LC 77-93757. 1970. 19.50 (ISBN 0-08-006944-4). Pergamon.
Wischnitzer, Saul. Atlas & Dissection Guide for Comparative Anatomy: Lab Manual. 3rd ed. (Illus.). 1979. pap. 9.95x (ISBN 0-7167-0197-9); individual exercises 0.50 ea. W H Freeman.
--Barron's Guide to Medical, Dental & Allied Health Science Careers. rev. ed. 286p. 1981. pap. text ed. 6.50 (ISBN 0-8120-2281-5). Barron.
--Barron's Guide to Medical, Dental & Allied Health Science Careers. rev. ed. LC 76-41772. (gr. 12). 1977. pap. 6.50 (ISBN 0-8120-0719-0). Barron.
--Introduction to Electron Microscopy. 3rd ed. LC 80-15266. 320p. 1980. 19.75 (ISBN 0-08-026298-8). Pergamon.
--Outline of Human Anatomy. (Illus.). 404p. 1972. 11.75 (ISBN 0-398-02655-6). C C Thomas.
Wisdom, John. Philosophy & Psychoanalysis. 1969. pap. 14.25x (ISBN 0-631-04410-8, Pub. by Basil Blackwell). Biblio Dist.
--Problems of Mind & Matter. (Orig.). 26.95 (ISBN 0-521-08508-X); pap. 6.95x (ISBN 0-521-09197-7). Cambridge U Pr.
Wisdom, Linda. Dancer in the Shadows. 192p. (Orig.). 1980. pap. 1.50 (ISBN 0-671-57049-8). S&S.
Wisdom, Robert. My Life in Christ. LC 78-68607. 1980. 5.95 (ISBN 0-533-04175-9). Vantage.
Wisdom, William, jt. auth. see Leblanc, Hugues.
Wise, A., jt. auth. see Monie, J.
Wise, Aaron N. Trade Secrets & Know-How Throughout the World, 5 vols. rev. ed. 1977. looseleaf 265.00 (ISBN 0-87632-128-7). Boardman.
Wise, Alan F. Water, Sanitary & Waste Services for Buildings. (Mitchell's Building Construction Ser.). 156p. 1979. pap. 13.95x (ISBN 0-470-26888-3). Halsted Pr.
Wise, Arthur & Wise, Nicola. Blood Red Rose. LC 80-84375. 272p. 1981. pap. 2.50 (ISBN 0-87216-815-8). Playboy Pbks.
Wise, Burton L. Preoperative & Postoperative Care in Neurological Surgery. 2nd ed. (Illus.). 208p. 1978. 19.75 (ISBN 0-398-03825-2). C C Thomas.
Wise, Charles, jt. ed. see Fredericksson, H. George.
Wise County Historical Survey Committee. History of Wise County: A Link with the Past. Gregg, Rosalie, ed. (Illus.). 515p. 1974. 25.00 (ISBN 0-89015-076-1). Nortex Pr.
Wise, David. Spectrum. LC 80-17418. 336p. 1981. 13.95 (ISBN 0-670-66219-4). Viking Pr.
Wise, David B. Automobile Archaeology. (Illus.). 160p. 1981. 35.95 (ISBN 0-85059-455-3). Aztex.
Wise, E. M. & Mueller, G. O. Studies in Comparative Criminal Law. (Criminal Law Education & Research Center Ser.). (Illus.). 338p. 1975. 25.75 (ISBN 0-398-03168-1). C C Thomas.
Wise, E. M., jt. auth. see Mueller, Gerhard O.
Wise, Felicity. A Williamsburg Hornbook. LC 73-16301. (Illus.). 128p. 1973. op (ISBN 0-8117-1896-4); pap. 3.95 (ISBN 0-8117-1203-6). Stackpole.
Wise, Francis H. Youth & Drugs. (Illus.). Date not set. price not set. Wise Pub.
Wise, Francis H. & Wise, Joyce M. Arithmetic Series, 10 bks. Incl. Bk. 3. An Adding XV. 1979 (ISBN 0-915766-45-0); Vol. 2. Arithmetic Books 6-10. 1979; Bk. 4. Subtraction. 1980; Bk. 5. Column. 1980; Bk. 6. Multiply. 1980; Bk. 7. Division. 1980; Bk. 8. Fractions. 1980; Bk. 9. Carry. 1980; Bk. 10. Borrow. 1980. (Illus.). 105p. (gr. k-2). pap. 1.50 ea. Wise Pub.
Wise, Gene. American Historical Explanations. rev. ed. 415p. 1980. 20.00x (ISBN 0-8166-0954-3); pap. 8.95x (ISBN 0-8166-0957-8). U of Minn Pr.
Wise, Gilbert J., jt. auth. see Morel, Alice.
Wise, Herbert A., jt. auth. see Whyte, Anthony J.
Wise, Herbert H. & Weiss, Jeffrey. Made with Oak. (Illus.). 96p. 1975. pap. 6.95 (ISBN 0-8256-3052-5, Quick Fox). Music Sales.
Wise, Jennings C. & Deloria, Vine, Jr. Red Man in the New World Drama. 1971. 12.95 (ISBN 0-02-630550-X). Macmillan.
Wise, John S. A Treatise on American Citizenship. (Studies in Constitutional Law). viii, 340p. 1981. Repr. of 1906 ed. lib. bdg. 30.00x (ISBN 0-8377-1306-4). Rothman.
Wise, Joyce M., jt. auth. see Wise, Francis H.
Wise, Leonard. The Diggstown Ringers. LC 77-27722. 1978. 10.00 o.p. (ISBN 0-385-13126-7). Doubleday.
Wise, M. J. & Rawstron, E. M. R. O. Buchanan & Economic Geography. (Advanced Edonoic Geography Ser.). 1973. lib. bdg. 20.00x (ISBN 0-7135-1766-2). Westview.
Wise, M. J., jt. auth. see Smith, Wilfred.
Wise, Mark B., jt. auth. see Trainor, Lynn.
Wise, Melvin J. The All-Sufficiency of the Gospel. 5.95 (ISBN 0-89315-000-2). Lambert Bk.
--Glorifying God & Other Sermons. 4.95 (ISBN 0-89315-076-2). Lambert Bk.
Wise, Nicola, jt. auth. see Wise, Arthur.
Wise, S. F. Canadian Airmen & the First World War: The Official History of the Royal Canadian Air Force, Vol. 1. 980p. 1980. 35.00 (ISBN 0-8020-2379-7). U of Toronto Pr.
--Canadians in the British Flying Service, Nineteen Fourteen to Nineteen Eighteen. 1980. 35.00 o.p. (ISBN 0-8020-2379-7). U of Toronto Pr.
Wise, Sheldon. Essentials of Management. LC 79-88238. (The ALA ESP Ser.). (Illus.). v, 110p. (Orig.). 1979. pap. text ed. 6.25 (ISBN 0-934270-06-6). Am Lang Acad.
Wise, Sheldon, jt. auth. see Annand, William S.
Wise, Sidney, jt. auth. see Preston, Richard A.
Wise, Susan & Piper, David. European Portraits Sixteen Hundred to Nineteen Hundred in The Art Institute of Chicago. LC 78-57638. (Illus.). 183p. (Orig.). 1978. pap. 10.00x (ISBN 0-86559-029-X). Art Inst Chi.
Wise, Susan, jt. ed. see Keefe, John W.
Wise, Terence. Ten Sixty Six, Year of Destiny. 1980. text ed. 19.50x (ISBN 0-85045-320-8). Humanities.
--The Wars of the Crusades. 1980. text ed. 19.50x (ISBN 0-85045-300-3). Humanities.
Wise, William. Fresh, Canned, & Frozen: Food from Past to Future. LC 74-145599. (Finding-Out Books for Science & Social Studies, Grades 1-4). (Illus.). (gr. 2-4). 1971. PLB 6.95 (ISBN 0-8193-0482-4, Pub. by Parents). Enslow Pubs.
--Massacre at Mountain Meadows: An American Legend & a Monumental Crime. LC 76-16014. 1976. 11.95 o.s.i. (ISBN 0-690-01174-1, TYC-T). T Y Crowell.
--Monster Myths of Ancient Greece. (Illus.). 48p. (gr. 7-11). 1981. PLB 6.99 (ISBN 0-399-61143-6). Putnam.
--Off We Go: A Book of Transportation. LC 73-168483. (Finding-Out Book). (Illus.). 64p. (gr. 3-4). 1972. PLB 6.95 (ISBN 0-8193-0532-4). Enslow Pubs.
Wiseberg, Laurie S. & Scoble, Harry M. North American Human Rights Directory 1980. 188p. (Orig.). 1980. pap. 12.00 (ISBN 0-912048-20-4). Garrett Pk.
Wiseley, William. A Tool of Power: The Political History of Money. LC 76-57701. 300p. 1977. 28.95 (ISBN 0-471-02235-7, Pub. by Wiley-Interscience). Wiley.
Wisely, Rae & Sanders, Gladys. The Independent Woman. 192p. 1981. 9.95 (ISBN 0-87477-176-5). J P Tarcher.
Wisely, William H. The American Civil Engineer, Eighteen Fifty-Two to Nineteen Seventy-Four. LC 74-17792. 464p. 1974. text ed. 20.00 (ISBN 0-87262-000-X). Am Soc Civil Eng.
Wiseman, A. Topics in Enzyme & Fermentation Biotechnology, Vol. 5. 300p. 1980. 95.00 (ISBN 0-470-27089-6). Halsted Pr.
Wiseman, A. J., jt. auth. see Lockhart, J. A.
Wiseman, Alan. Handbook of Enzyme Biotechnology. LC 75-2466. 275p. 1975. 68.95 (ISBN 0-470-95617-8). Halsted Pr.
--Topics in Enzyme & Fermentation Biotechnology, VI, Vol. 6. LC 76-25441. 1977. 29.95 (ISBN 0-470-98896-7). Halsted Pr.
Wiseman, Alan, ed. Topics in Enzyme & Fermentation Biotechnology, Vol. 2. LC 76-25441. 1978. 37.95 (ISBN 0-470-99318-9). Vol. 2. Halsted Pr.
--Topics in Enzyme & Fermentation Biotechnology, Vol. 4. (Topics in Enzyme & Fermentation Biotechnology Ser.). 242p. 1980. 69.95x (ISBN 0-470-26922-7). Halsted Pr.
Wiseman, Ann. Bread Sculpture: The Edible Art. LC 75-26909. (Illus.). 96p. (Orig.). 1975. 3.95 (ISBN 0-912238-74-7); pap. 2.95 (ISBN 0-912238-72-0). One Hund One Prods.
--Making Musical Things. (Illus.). 64p. (gr. 2 up). 1979. 8.95 (ISBN 0-684-16114-1). Scribner.
--Rug Hooking & Rag Tapestries. 1981. pap. 7.95 (ISBN 0-442-20658-5). Van Nos Reinhold.
Wiseman, Ann S. Finger Paint & Pudding Prints. LC 80-14353. (Illus.). 32p. (gr. k-3). 1980. PLB 5.95 (ISBN 0-201-08346-9, 8346, A-W Childrens). A-W.
Wiseman, Bernard. Iglook's Seal. LC 76-23410. (gr. 1-4). 1977. 5.95 (ISBN 0-396-07396-4). Dodd.
--Little New Kangaroo. LC 72-92444. (Ready-to-Read Ser.). (Illus.). 40p. (gr. k-3). 1973. 7.95 (ISBN 0-02-793220-6). Macmillan.
--Morris Has a Cold. LC 77-12030. (gr. 1-4). 1978. 6.95 (ISBN 0-396-07522-3). Dodd.
--Oscar Is a Mama. LC 79-24737. (Bernard Wiseman Bks.). (Illus.). (gr. k-4). 1980. PLB 5.49 (ISBN 0-8116-6081-8). Garrard.

--Penny's Poodle Puppy, Pickle. LC 79-26403. (Bernard Wiseman Bks.). (Illus.). (gr. k-4). 1980. PLB 5.49 (ISBN 0-8116-6080-X). Garrard.
--Tails Are Not for Painting. Wiseman, Bernard, tr. LC 79-18373. (Bernard Wiseman Bks.). (Illus.). 32p. (gr. k-4). 1980. PLB 5.49 (ISBN 0-8116-6078-8). Garrard.
Wiseman, D. J., jt. auth. see Harrison, R. K.
Wiseman, D. J., ed. Peoples of Old Testament Times. (Illus.). 419p. 1973. 23.95x (ISBN 0-19-826316-3). Oxford U Pr.
Wiseman, David. Jeremy Visick. (gr. 5 up). 1981. 7.95 (ISBN 0-395-30449-0). HM.
Wiseman, Douglas C. Practical Approach to Adapted Physical Education. (Physical Education Ser.). (Illus.). 544p. 1981. text ed. 17.95 (ISBN 0-201-08347-7). A-W.
Wiseman, E. J. Victorian Do-It-Yourself. LC 76-40807. 1977. 5.95 (ISBN 0-7153-7307-2). David & Charles.
Wiseman, Herbert V. Local Government at Work: A Case Study of a County Borough. (Library of Political Science). 1967. text ed. 5.75x (ISBN 0-7100-5128-X); pap. 2.75x (ISBN 0-7100-5117-4). Humanities.
Wiseman, Jack, jt. auth. see Peacock, Alan T.
Wiseman, James. Stobi: A Guide to the Excavations. (Illus.). 100p. Date not set. pap. 4.75x (ISBN 0-292-77505-9). U of Tex Pr.
Wiseman, James & Mano-Zissi, Djordje, eds. Studies in the Antiquities of Stobi. (Illus.). 300p. Date not set. 15.00x (ISBN 0-292-77506-7). U of Tex Pr.
Wiseman, Nicholas P. Fabiola; or, the Church of the Catacombs, 1854. Wolff, Robert L., ed. LC 75-454. (Victorian Fiction Ser). 1975. lib. bdg. 66.00 (ISBN 0-8240-1533-9). Garland Pub.
Wiseman, Rex. The Okara Mask. 1979. pap. 1.95 (ISBN 0-505-51434-6). Tower Bks.
Wiseman, Robert. Spatial Aspects of Aging. Natoli, Salvatore J., ed. LC 78-59103. (Resource Papers for College Geography Ser.). (Illus.). 1979. pap. text ed. 4.00 (ISBN 0-89291-133-6). Assn Am Geographers.
Wiseman, T. P. Cinna, the Poet & Other Roman Essays. 224p. 1974. text ed. 14.50x (ISBN 0-7185-1120-4, Leicester). Humanities.
Wiser, Charlotte, jt. auth. see Wiser, William.
Wiser, Charlotte V. Four Families of Karimpur. LC 78-1557. (Foreign & Comparative Studies-South Asian Ser.: No. 3). (Illus.). 1978. pap. text ed. 6.50x (ISBN 0-915984-78-4). Syracuse U Foreign Comp.
Wiser, William. Disappearances. LC 79-55616. 1980. 11.95 (ISBN 0-689-11062-6). Atheneum.
Wiser, William & Wiser, Charlotte. Behind Mud Walls, Nineteen Thirty to Nineteen Sixty: With a Sequel: the Village in 1970. rev. ed. 1972. 15.75x (ISBN 0-520-02093-6); pap. 3.95 (ISBN 0-520-02101-0, CAL91). U of Cal Pr.
Wish, John R., et al. The Consumer: The Art of Buying Wisely. LC 77-13030. (Illus.). 1978. text ed. 15.95 (ISBN 0-13-169102-3). P-H.
Wishard, Bill & Wishard, Laurie. Men's Rights: A Handbook for the 80's. LC 80-20194. 264p. 1980. 12.95 (ISBN 0-89666-011-7); pap. 6.95 (ISBN 0-89666-012-5). Cragmont Pubns.
Wishard, Laurie & Wishard, William R. Adoption: The Grafted Tree. 1980. 12.95 o.p. (ISBN 0-686-28219-1). Caroline Hse.
Wishard, Laurie, jt. auth. see Wishard, Bill.
Wishard, William R. Credit & Borrowing in Illinois. LC 79-13022. 1981. pap. 6.95 (ISBN 0-89666-005-2, Dist. by Caroline Hse.). Cragmont Pubns.
--Credit & Borrowing in New York. LC 79-12957. 1981. pap. 6.95 (ISBN 0-89666-004-4, Dist. by Caroline Hse.). Cragmont Pubns.
Wishard, William R. & Felder, Frederick E. Credit & Borrowing in Texas: Consumers' Rights & Duties. LC 78-15355. 1978. pap. 6.95 (ISBN 0-89666-001-X). Cragmont Pubns.
Wishard, William R., jt. auth. see Wishard, Laurie.
Wishart, B. J., jt. auth. see Reichman, L.
Wishbone, Lipton Kitchens. Not for Salads Only from Wishbone. (Orig.). Date not set. price not set (ISBN 0-87502-081-X). Benjamin Co.
Wishon, George E. & Burks, Julia M. Let's Write English. rev. ed. 430p. (gr. 9-12). 1980. pap. text ed. 5.20 (ISBN 0-278-47520-5); tchrs. ed. 1.20 (ISBN 0-278-47522-1). Litton Educ Pub.
Wishy, Bernard. Child & the Republic: The Dawn of Modern American Child Nurture. LC 67-26223. 1972. 10.00x (ISBN 0-8122-7556-X); pap. 5.95x (ISBN 0-8122-1026-3, Pa Paperbks). U of Pa Pr.
Wishy, Bernard, tr. see Vossler, Otto.
Wishy, Bernard W., ed. Western World in the Twentieth Century. LC 61-8987. (gr. 9 up). 1961. 20.00x (ISBN 0-231-02489-4). Columbia U Pr.
Wiskemann, Elizabeth. Europe of the Dictators Nineteen Nineteen to Nineteen Forty-Five. LC 80-66913. (History of Europe Ser.; Cornell Paperbacks Ser.). 287p. 1980. pap. 5.95 (ISBN 0-8014-9210-6). Cornell U Pr.
Wisland, Milton V. Psychoeducational Diagnosis of Exceptional Children. (Illus.). 408p. 1977. 19.75 (ISBN 0-398-02843-5). C C Thomas.
Wisler, Chester O. & Brater, E. F. Hydrology. 2nd ed. LC 59-14981. 1959. 23.95 (ISBN 0-471-95634-1). Wiley.
Wisler, G. Clifton. My Brother the Wind. LC 78-14690. 1979. 7.95 o.p. (ISBN 0-385-14822-4). Doubleday.
--Winter of the Wolf. (gr. 6 up). 1980. 7.95 (ISBN 0-525-66716-4). Elsevier-Nelson.
Wisner, Bill. How to Catch Saltwater Fish. LC 72-89130. 600p. 1973. 10.00 o.p. (ISBN 0-385-07217-1). Doubleday.
Wisner, Bill, jt. auth. see Mundus, Frank.
Wisner, Robert J., ed. see Smith, Karl J.
Wisner, William L., jt. auth. see Cook, Joseph J.
Wisse, Ruth, jt. ed. see Howe, Irving.
Wisse, Ruth R. A Shtetl & Other Yiddish Novellas. LC 73-10252. (Library of Jewish Studies). 368p. 1973. 6.95x o.p. (ISBN 0-87441-201-3). Behrman.
Wisser, jt. auth. see McCarr.
Wissler, Clark. Indians of the United States: Four Centuries of Their History & Culture. LC 66-12215. 1966. 7.95 (ISBN 0-385-00757-4); pap. 2.95 o.p. (ISBN 0-385-02019-8). Doubleday.
Wissler, Clark see Gabriel, Ralph H.
Wissman, Ruth. Dreamer Beware. 1978. pap. 1.50 o.p. (ISBN 0-445-04167-6). Popular Lib.
Wister, Fanny K. Fanny, the American Kemble: Her Journals & Unpublished Letters. LC 72-80474. 227p. 1972. 10.00x (ISBN 0-932068-00-6). South Pass Pr.
Wister, Owen. Virginian. (Illus.). 1925. 12.95 (ISBN 0-02-630580-1); large print ed. 9.95 (ISBN 0-02-489480-X). Macmillan.
--The West of Owen Wister: Selected Short Stories. LC 74-175805. 1972. 9.95x (ISBN 0-8032-0808-1); pap. 1.95 (ISBN 0-8032-5760-0, BB 546, Bison). U of Nebr Pr.
Wistreich, George, jt. auth. see Kane, Rosalyn.
Wistreich, George A. & Lechtman, Max D. Microbiology & Human Disease. 3rd ed. 1981. text ed. 21.95x (ISBN 0-02-470910-7). Macmillan.
Wistrich, Robert. Trotsky: Fate of a Revolutionary. LC 80-6163. 235p. 1981. 14.95 (ISBN 0-8128-2774-0). Stein & Day.
--Trotsky: Fate of a Revolutionary. 235p. 1980. 19.00x (ISBN 0-8476-3105-2). Rowman.
Wistrich, Robert, ed. The Left Against Zion: Communism, Israel & the Middle East. 309p. 1979. 24.00x (ISBN 0-85303-193-2, Pub by Vallentine Mitchell England); pap. 9.95x (ISBN 0-85303-199-1). Biblio Dist.
Wiswall, F. L. Development of Admiralty, Jurisdiction & Practice Since 1800. LC 77-108113. (Illus.). 1971. 35.50 (ISBN 0-521-07751-6). Cambridge U Pr.
Wiswell, Phil. I Hate Charades & Forty-Nine Other New Games. LC 80-54341. (Illus.). 128p. 1981. 5.95 (ISBN 0-8069-4582-6); lib. bdg. 6.69 (ISBN 0-8069-4583-4). Sterling.
Wiswell, Tom & Leopold, Jules. The Wonderful World of Checkers & Draughts. LC 78-69631. (Illus.). 1981. 9.95 (ISBN 0-498-02258-7). A S Barnes.
Wiswesser, ed. Pesticide Index. 5th ed. LC 76-21894. 1976. 20.00 (ISBN 0-686-15427-4). Entomol Soc.
Wit, Dorothy De see De Wit, Dorothy.
Wit, H. C. De see De Wit, H. C.
Wit, Joost de see De Wit, Joost & Barkan, Stanley H.
Witbeck, Alan R., jt. auth. see Allsen, Philip E.
Witbeck, Alan R., jt. auth. see Alsen, Philip E.
Witchell, F. C. Roses for Every Garden. (Leisure Plan Bks). 1971. pap. 2.95 (ISBN 0-600-44178-4). Transatlantic.
Witemeyer, Hugh. The Poetry of Ezra Pound: Forms & Renewal, 1908-1920. 1969. 16.50x (ISBN 0-520-01542-8). U of Cal Pr.
Withee, John. Growing & Cooking Beans. Orcutt, Georgia, ed. LC 79-57179. 144p. (Orig.). 1980. pap. 7.95 (ISBN 0-911658-05-X, 3070). Yankee Bks.
Wither, George. Collection of Emblemes: Ancient & Moderne. (Illus.). 303p. 1973. Repr. of 1633 ed. 30.00x (ISBN 0-85967-134-8, Pub. by Scolar Pr England). Biblio Dist.
Witherall, William O., jt. auth. see De Vos, George A.
Withers, Bruce & Vipond, Stanley. Irrigation: Design & Practice. 2nd ed. LC 80-66673. (Illus.). 300p. 1980. soft cover 12.95 (ISBN 0-8014-9874-0). Cornell U Pr.
Withers, Carl. Eenie-Meenie-Minie-Mo & Other Counting-Out Rhymes. (Illus.). 1970. pap. 1.75 (ISBN 0-486-22414-7). Dover.
Withers, E. N. Standards for Library Service: An International Survey. (Documentation, Libraries & Archives, Studies & Research Ser., No. 6). 421p. (Orig.). 1974. pap. 19.75 (ISBN 92-3-101177-4, U637, UNESCO). Unipub.
Withers, H. R., jt. ed. see Meyn, Rodney E.
Withers, Richard S. Transport of Charged Aerosols. LC 78-74993. (Outstanding Dissertations on Energy Ser.). 1979. lib. bdg. 38.00 (ISBN 0-8240-3993-9). Garland Pub.
Withers, William. The Corporations & Social Change. Dillon, Mary E., ed. & intro. by. LC 73-189865. (The Politics of Government Ser.). 155p. (Orig.). 1972. pap. 2.50 o.p. (ISBN 0-8120-0446-9). Barron.
Witherspoon, Gary, jt. auth. see Callaway, Sydney M.
Witherspoon, Herbert. Singing. (Music Reprint Ser.). (Illus.). 126p. 1980. Repr. of 1925 ed. lib. bdg. 15.00 (ISBN 0-306-76001-0). Da Capo.
Witherspoon, James D. The Functions of Life: A Laboratory Guide for Animal Physiology. LC 71-100892. 1970. pap. text ed. 9.95 (ISBN 0-201-08717-0). A-W.
Witherspoon, Robert E., et al. Mixed Use Development: New Ways of Land Use. LC 75-37217. (Technical Bulletin Ser: No. 71). (Illus.). 1976. pap. 22.00 (ISBN 0-87420-071-7). Urban Land.
Withiam, Jack, Jr., jt. auth. see Neubert, Christopher.
Withington, Eleanor, ed. see Cleveland, John.
Withington, Frederic G. The Use of Computers in Business Organizations. 2nd ed. LC 76-139162. (Technology Ser). (Illus.). 1971. text ed. 12.95 (ISBN 0-201-08643-3). A-W.
Withington, W. A. & Fisher, Margaret, eds. Southeast Asia. LC 78-54259. (World Cultures Ser). (Illus.). (gr. 5 up). 1979. text ed. 9.95 1-4 copies o.p. (ISBN 0-88296-134-9); text ed. 7.96 5 or more o.p. (ISBN 0-685-14505-0); tchrs' ed 8.94 o.p. (ISBN 0-88296-369-4). Fideler.
Withner, C. L. The Orchids: Scientific Survey. (Illus.). 1959. 27.50 (ISBN 0-8260-9485-6, Pub. by Wiley-Interscience). Wiley.
Withner, Carl L., ed. The Orchids: Scientific Studies. LC 73-20496. (Illus.). 624p. 1974. 40.50 (ISBN 0-471-95715-1, Pub. by Wiley-Interscience). Wiley.
Withrow, Frank B. & Nygren, Carolyn J. Language Curriculum & Materials for the Handicapped Learner. 1976. text ed. 17.95 (ISBN 0-675-08615-9). Merrill.
Witkin, Herman A. & Goodenough, Donald R. Cognitive Styles: Essence & Origins- Field Dependence & Field Independence. (Psychological Issues Monograph: No. 51). (Illus.). 130p. 1981. text ed. 15.00x (ISBN 0-8236-1003-9, 00-1003). Intl Univs Pr.
Witkin, Lee D. & London, Barbara. The Photograph Collector's Guide. 448p. 1981. pap. 19.95 (ISBN 0-8212-1124-2). NYGS.
Witkowski, Edward & Wells, Arnold. Economics of Agricultural Production. LC 78-22717. 1979. text ed. 15.95 (ISBN 0-88284-072-X). Alfred Pub.
Witmark, Isidore & Goldberg, Isaac. Story of the House of Witmark: From Ragtime to Swingtime. LC 76-20707. (Roots of Jazz Ser.). 1975. Repr. of 1939 ed. lib. bdg. 29.50 (ISBN 0-306-70686-5). Da Capo.
Witmer, Enos E. Space-Time & Microphysics: A New Synthesis. LC 79-66152. 1979. pap. text ed. 9.00 (ISBN 0-8191-0794-8). U Pr of Amer.
Witmer, Lightner. Nearing Case: Limitation of Academic Freedom at the Univ. of Penn. by Act of the Board of Trustees, June 14, 1915. LC 71-122163. (Civil Liberties in American Liberty Ser.). 123p. 1974. Repr. of 1915 ed. lib. bdg. 17.50 (ISBN 0-306-71978-9). Da Capo.
Witney, F., jt. auth. see Sloane, A. A.
Witney, Fred, jt. auth. see Tyler, Benjamin.
Witney, K. P. The Jutish Forest: A Study of the Weald of Kent from 450 to 1380 AD. (Illus.). 1976. text ed. 37.75x (ISBN 0-485-11165-9, Athlone Pr). Humanities.
Witsen, Betty Van see Van Witsen, Betty.
Witt, Bud. How to Start a Business in Your Home & Gro. LC 47-332. 208p. (Orig.). (gr. 12). 1980. pap. text ed. 12.00 (ISBN 0-9604932-0-4). B Witt.
Witt, Gary, jt. auth. see Shook, Georg.
Witt, Glen L & Hankinson, Ken. Boat Building with Plywood. 2nd ed. 1978. text ed. 14.95 (ISBN 0-686-08738-0). Glen-L Marine.
Witt, Glen L. & Hankinson, Ken. Inboard Motor Installations. 2nd rev. ed. (Illus.). 1978. text ed. 13.95 (ISBN 0-686-08739-9). Glen-L Marine.
Witt, I., ed. New Methods for the Analysis of Coagulation Using Chromogenic Substrates. 275p. 1977. text ed. 52.50x (ISBN 3-11007-116-9). De Gruyter.
Witt, Paul W., ed. Technology & the Curriculum. LC 68-9689. 1968. pap. text ed. 5.25x (ISBN 0-8077-2342-8). Tchrs Coll.
Witt, Robert E. Indian Summer & More. 64p. 1981. 5.00 (ISBN 0-682-49668-5). Exposition.
Witt, Robert W. Mirror Within a Mirror: Ben Jonson & the Play-Within. (Salzburg Studies in English Literature Jacobean Drama Studies: No. 46). 154p. 1976. pap. text ed. 25.00x (ISBN 0-391-01574-5). Humanities.
--Of Comfort & Despair: Shakespeare's Sonnet Sequence. (SSEL Elizabethan & Renaissance Studies: N0. 77). 1979. pap. text ed. 25.00x (ISBN 0-391-01620-2). Humanities.
Witt, Ronald G., jt. auth. see Kohl, Benjamin G.
Witt, Shirley H. The Tuscaroras. LC 75-189730. (Illus.). (gr. 5up). 1972. 6.95 (ISBN 0-02-793270-2, CCPr). Macmillan.
Witt, Susan. Susan Witt's Classics for Needlepoint. LC 80-84410. (Illus.). 160p. 1981. 17.95 (ISBN 0-8487-0525-4). Oxmoor Hse.
Wittcoff, Harold & Reuben, Bryan G. Industrial Organic Chemicals in Perspective: Technology, Formulation & Use, Pt. 2. 1980. 45.00 (ISBN 0-471-05780-0, Pub. by Wiley-Interscience). Wiley.
Witte. Statistics. LC 78-57922. 315p. 1980. text ed. 16.95 (ISBN 0-03-055231-1, HoltC); wkbk. 6.95 (ISBN 0-03-055236-2). HR&W.
Witte, Edwin E. Development of the Social Security Act. 1962. 25.00x (ISBN 0-299-02540-3); pap. 7.95x (ISBN 0-299-02544-6). U of Wis Pr.
Witte, Eve, jt. auth. see Witte, Pat.
Witte, John C. Loving the Days. LC 78-7629. (Wesleyan Poetry Program: Vol. 93). 1978. pap. 10.00x (ISBN 0-8195-2093-4, Pub. by Wesleyan U Pr); pap. 4.95 (ISBN 0-8195-1093-9). Columbia U Pr.
Witte, John F. Democracy, Authority, & Alienation in Work: Workers' Participation in an American Corporation. LC 80-16241. (Illus.). 1980. lib. bdg. 20.00x (ISBN 0-226-90420-2). U of Chicago Pr.
Witte, Mike, jt. auth. see McGraw, Tug.
Witte, Pat & Witte, Eve. Who Lives Here? (Golden Touch & Feel Bk). (Illus.). 1961. 3.95 (ISBN 0-307-12147-X, Golden Pr). Western Pub.
Witte, W., ed. see Mann, Thomas.
Witten, David M., et al. Emmett's Clinical Urography, 3 vols. 4rd ed. LC 76-19614. (Illus.). 1977. Set. 110.00 (ISBN 0-685-04797-0); Vol. 1. (ISBN 0-7216-9472-1); Vol. 2. (ISBN 0-7216-9473-X); Vol. 3. (ISBN 0-7216-9474-8). Saunders.
Wittenberger. Animal Social Behavior. (Illus.). 748p. 1981. text ed. price not set (ISBN 0-87872-295-5). Duxbury Pr.
Wittenborn, Dirk. Eclipse. LC 77-24285. 1977. 8.95 (ISBN 0-396-07383-2). Dodd.
Wittenborn, J. R. Response to Meprobamate-A Predictive Analysis. LC 70-107228. 1970. 13.50 (ISBN 0-911216-11-1). Raven.
Wittenborn, J. R., et al, eds. Psychopharmacology & the Individual Patient. LC 71-116996. 1970. 19.00 (ISBN 0-911216-13-8). Raven.
Wittenborn, J. R., et al, eds. see Rutgers Symposium on Drug Abuse.
Wittenborn, J. R., et al, eds. see Rutgers Symposium on Drug Abuse, 2nd.
Witter, Barbara. The Christmas Lamb. (Illus.). (gr. k-6). 1977. pap. 1.50 o.p. (ISBN 0-917726-18-9). Hunter Bks.
Wittgenstein, Ludwig. Blue & Brown Books. pap. 3.95 (ISBN 0-06-090451-8, CN451, CN). Harper Row.
--Culture & Value. Von Wright, G. H., ed. Winch, Peter, tr. LC 80-15234. 1980. 20.00x (ISBN 0-226-90432-6). U of Chicago Pr.
--Notebooks: 1914-1916. Anscombe, G. E. & Von Wright, G. H., eds. Anscombe, G. E., tr. 1969. Repr. of 1961 ed. 24.50x (ISBN 0-631-06220-3, Pub. by Basil Blackwell). Biblio Dist.
--Philosophical Grammar. Kenny, A. J., tr. 1974. 27.50x (ISBN 0-520-02664-0); pap. 6.95 (ISBN 0-520-03725-1). U of Cal Pr.
--Philosophical Remarks. Rhees, Rush, et al, eds. LC 80-14296. 1980. pap. 8.95 (ISBN 0-226-90431-8, P912, Phoen). U of Chicago Pr.
--Philosophische Grammatik. Rhees, Rush, ed. 1969. 20.00x o.p. (ISBN 0-631-12350-4, Pub. by Basil Blackwell). Biblio Dist.
--Remarks on Colour. Anscombe, G. E., ed. McAlister, Linda L. & Schattle, Margarete, trs. from Ger. 1978. 14.50x (ISBN 0-520-03357-4); pap. 2.95 (ISBN 0-520-03727-8, CAL 406). U of Cal Pr.
--Remarks on the Philosophy of Psychology, Vol. 1. Anscombe, G. E. & Von Wright, G. H., eds. LC 80-52781. 408p. 1980. lib. bdg. 35.00x (ISBN 0-226-90433-4). U of Chicago Pr.
--Remarks on the Philosophy of Psychology, Vol. 2. Von Wright, G. H. & Nyman, Heikki, eds. Luckhardt, C. G. & Aue, A. E., trs. LC 80-52781. 1980. lib. bdg. 27.50x (ISBN 0-226-90434-2). U of Chicago Pr.
--Tractatus Logico-Philosophicus. Pears, D. F. & McGuinness, B. F., trs. from Ger. 114p. 1972. text ed. 15.00x (ISBN 0-391-00359-3); pap. text ed. 3.50x. Humanities.
--Zettel. Anscombe, G. E. M. & Von Wright, G. H., eds. Anscombe, G. E. M., tr. 1967. 16.75x (ISBN 0-520-01355-7); pap. 4.95x (ISBN 0-520-01635-1, CAL189). U of Cal Pr.
Wittig, Arno. Schaum's Outline of Psychology of Learning. (Schaum's Outline Ser.). (Illus.). 1980. pap. 6.95 (ISBN 0-07-071192-5). McGraw.

Wittig, J. Alice. U. S. Government Publications for the School Media Center. LC 79-24798. 1979. lib. bdg. 11.50 (ISBN 0-87287-214-9). Libs Unl.

Wittig, Monique. The Lesbian Body. LC 75-7738. 1975. 5.95 o.p. (ISBN 0-688-02900-0). Morrow.

Wittig, S., et al. Participating Reader. 1978. pap. 9.50 (ISBN 0-13-650200-8). P-H.

Wittig, Susan. Stylistic & Narrative Structures in the Middle English Romances. 1977. 15.95x o.p. (ISBN 0-292-77541-5). U of Tex Pr.

Wittig, Susan, tr. see Uspensky, Boris.

Wittikoff, Douglas. The Desperate Alternatives of the Soviet Leaders in the Face of the Incipient Break-up of the Communist Empire. (The Major Currents in Contemporary World History Library Ser.). (Illus.). 143p. 1981. 69.85 (ISBN 0-930008-81-2). Inst Econ Pol.

Wittke, Carl. The First Fifty Years: The Cleveland Museum of Art 1916-1966. LC 66-21227. (Illus.). 176p. 1966. 10.00x (ISBN 0-910386-09-9, Pub. by Cleveland Mus Art). Ind U Pr.

--History of English Parliamentary Privilege. LC 74-87623. (Law, Politics, & History Ser). 1969. Repr. of 1921 ed. lib. bdg. 25.00 (ISBN 0-306-71810-3). Da Capo.

--Irish in America. LC 68-9259. 1968. pap. 2.95 (ISBN 0-8077-2345-2). Tchrs Coll.

Wittke, Carl F. Tambo & Bones: A History of the American Minstrel Stage. LC 69-10174. 1968. Repr. of 1930 ed. lib. bdg. 19.75x (ISBN 0-8371-0276-6, WIAM). Greenwood.

Wittke, J. P., jt. auth. see Dicke, Robert H.

Wittkofski, Joseph. The Pastoral Use of Hypnotic Technique. 128p. 1971. pap. 7.95 spiral (ISBN 0-398-02101-5). C C Thomas.

Wittkopf, Eugene R., jt. auth. see Kegley, Charles W., Jr.

Wittkower, Eric D., jt. auth. see Dongier, Maurice.

Wittkower, Rudolf. Art & Architecture in Italy Sixteen Hundred to Seventeen Fifty. (Pelican History of Art). (Illus.). 664p. 1980. pap. 19.95 (ISBN 0-14-056116-1). Penguin.

--Palladio & Palladianism. LC 73-90463. (Illus.). 192p. 1975. 22.50 o.s.i. (ISBN 0-8076-0735-5). Braziller.

Wittliff, James L. & Dapunt, Otto. Steroid Receptors & Hormone Dependent Neoplasia. (Illus.). 320p. 1979. 46.75 (ISBN 0-89352-043-8). Masson Pub.

Wittliff, William D., jt. ed. see Crawford, Ann.

Wittman, Debbie D. The Birth of the Baha'i Faith. (Illus., Orig.). (gr. 5-9). 1980. pap. 1.00 (ISBN 0-87743-146-9, 7-52-55). Baha'i.

Wittman, George. A Matter of Intelligence. LC 75-11669. 252p. 1975. 7.95 o.s.i. (ISBN 0-02-630850-9). Macmillan.

--The Role of American Intelligence Organizations. (Reference Shelf Ser.). 1976. 6.25 (ISBN 0-8242-0599-5). Wilson.

Wittmann, E. Grundfragen Des Mathematikunterrichts. 202p. (Ger.). 1978. pap. 13.50 (ISBN 3-528-48332-6). Birkhauser.

Wittner, Lawrence S. Rebels Against War: The American Peace Movement 1941-1960. LC 69-19464. (Contemporary American History Ser.: No. 1). 1969. 22.50x (ISBN 0-231-03220-X); pap. 6.00 o.p. (ISBN 0-231-08641-5). Columbia U Pr.

Witton, Dorothy. Our World: Mexico. LC 72-81387. (Illus.). (gr. 4-6). 1969. PLB 4.29 o.p. (ISBN 0-671-32138-2). Messner.

Wittreich, Joseph A., Jr. Angel of Apocalypse: Blake's Idea of Milton. LC 74-27316. 328p. 1975. 30.00x (ISBN 0-299-06800-5). U of Wis Pr.

Wittreich, Joseph A., Jr., ed. Milton & the Line of Vision. LC 75-12215. (Illus.). 288p. 1975. 27.50x (ISBN 0-299-06910-9). U of Wis Pr.

--Nineteenth-Century Accounts of William Blake by Benjamin Heath Malkin, Henry Crabb Robinson, John Thomas Smith, Allan Cunningham, Frederick Tatham, & William Butler Yeats. LC 78-133330. 1970. 30.00x (ISBN 0-8201-1085-X). Schol Facsimiles.

Wittreich, Joseph A., Jr., jt. ed. see Curran, Stuart.

Wittrock, Merlin C., jt. auth. see Pirozzolo, Francis J.

Wittrock, Merlin C., ed. Learning & Instruction. LC 76-18038. (Readings in Educational Research Ser.). 1977. 25.00 (ISBN 0-8211-2255-X); text ed. 22.50 ten or more copies (ISBN 0-685-52960-6). McCutchan.

Wittrup. Laboratory Manual for Human Anatomy & Physiology. 1981. cancelled; instr's guide cancelled. Burgess.

Wittrup, Robert C. Human Anatomy & Physiology Laboratory Manual with Cat Dissections. (Orig.). 1981. write for info. (ISBN 0-8087-2384-7). Burgess.

Witts, F. E. The Diary of a Cotswold Parson. Verey, David, ed. (Illus.). 192p. 1980. text ed. 19.25x (ISBN 0-686-64329-1). Humanities.

Witts, L. J. Stomach & Anaemia. 1966. text ed. 4.25x (ISBN 0-485-26317-3, Athlone Pr). Humanities.

Witts, Max M., jt. auth. see Thomas, Gordon.

Wittschiebe, Charles E. God Invented Sex. LC 74-78047. (Anvil Ser.). 256p. 1974. pap. 5.95 (ISBN 0-8127-0081-3, 07366-8). Southern Pub.

Wittwer, S. H. & Honma, S. Greenhouse Tomatoes, Lettuce & Cucumbers. (Illus.). 225p. 1979. 15.00x (ISBN 0-87013-210-5). Mich St U Pr.

Witty, Ken. A Day in the Life of an Illustrator. LC 80-54100. (Illus.). 32p. (gr. 4 up). 1980. PLB 5.89 (ISBN 0-89375-448-X); pap. 2.50 (ISBN 0-89375-449-8). Troll Assocs.

Witty, Ken, jt. auth. see Witty, Margot.

Witty, Margot & Witty, Ken. A Day in the Life of a Meteorologist. LC 80-54098. (Illus.). 32p. (gr. 4 up). 1980. PLB 5.89 (ISBN 0-89375-450-1); pap. 2.50 (ISBN 0-89375-451-X). Troll Assocs.

Witty, Paul. How to Become a Better Reader. 1962. text ed. 10.07 (ISBN 0-574-30086-4, 3-0086); pap. text ed. 10.07 (ISBN 0-574-30086-4, 3-0086); student record book 0.87 (ISBN 0-574-30089-9, 3-0089). SRA.

Witty, Paul A., et al. Teaching of Reading: A Developmental Process. 1966. text ed. 8.95x o.p. (ISBN 0-669-20305-X). Heath.

Witwer, Daniel B., jt. auth. see Pacifico, Carl R.

Witz, Isaac & Hanna, M. G., eds. Contemporary Topics in Immunobiology: Volume 10, "in Situ" Expression of Tumor Immunity, Vol. 10. 330p. 1980. 32.50 (ISBN 0-306-40387-0, Plenum Pr). Plenum Pub.

Witzenman, Herbert. The Virtues: Die Tugenden. Aldan, Daisy, tr. 1975. 3.95 (ISBN 0-913152-17-X). PLB 5.95 (ISBN 0-685-52245-8). Folder Edns.

Witzke, P. T., jt. auth. see McHale, T. J.

Witzke, Paul T., jt. auth. see McHale, Thomas J.

Witzky, Herbert K. The Labor-Management Relations Handbook: For Hotels, Motels, Restaurants & Institutions. LC 75-37532. 224p. 1976. 14.95 (ISBN 0-8436-2083-8). CBI Pub.

Wixom, Hartt, jt. auth. see Rees, Clair.

Wixom, William D. Renaissance Bronzes: From Ohio Collections. LC 75-30966. (Illus.). 196p. 1975. pap. 15.00x (ISBN 0-910386-24-2, Pub. by Cleveland Mus Art). Ind U Pr.

Wixon, Rufus & Cox, Robert G. Principles of Accounting. 2nd ed. LC 69-14676. 827p. 1969. 25.95 (ISBN 0-8260-9500-3); instructors' manual avail. (ISBN 0-471-07488-8). Wiley.

Wlson, Renate. Inside Outward Bound. (Illus.). 208p. 1981. pap. 7.95 (ISBN 0-914788-41-8). East Woods.

Wm. C. Brown Education Division Staff. Mystery, Value & Awareness: Aids for Understanding Religions of the World. (To Live Is Christ Ser.). 28p. (Orig.). 1979. wkbk. 10.95 (ISBN 0-697-01736-2). Wm C Brown.

--Pluralism, Similarities, & Contract: Aids to Understanding Religion in North America. (To Live Is Christ Ser.). 28p. (Orig.). 1979. wkbk. 10.95 (ISBN 0-697-01735-4). Wm C Brown.

Wodarski, John S. Behavioral Social Work: An Introduction. LC 78-26356. 1979. text ed. 24.95x (ISBN 0-87705-375-8); pap. text ed. 9.95x (ISBN 0-87705-395-2). Human Sci Pr.

Woddis, Jack. Africa: The Way Ahead. LC 64-17900. 1963. 4.00 (ISBN 0-910294-13-5). Brown Bk.

--Introduction to Neo-Colonialism. (Orig.). 1968. pap. 1.95 (ISBN 0-7178-0102-0, LNW). Intl Pub Co.

Wodehouse, Lawrence, ed. American Architects from the Civil War to the First World War: A Guide to Information Sources. LC 73-17525. (Art & Architecture Information Guide Ser.: Vol. 3). 380p. 1976. 30.00 (ISBN 0-8103-1269-7). Gale.

--American Architects from the First World War to the Present: A Guide to Information Sources. LC 74-10259. (Art & Architecture Information Guide Ser.: Vol. 4). 380p. 1977. 30.00 (ISBN 0-8103-1270-0). Gale.

--British Architects, Eighteen Forty-Nineteen Seventy-Six: A Guide to Information Sources. LC 78-54116. (Art & Architecture Information Guide Ser.: Vol. 8). 1978. 30.00 (ISBN 0-8103-1393-6). Gale.

--Indigenous Architecture Worldwide: A Guide to Information Sources. LC 79-26580. (Art & Architecture Information Guide Ser.: Vol. 12). 1980. 30.00 (ISBN 0-8103-1450-9). Gale.

Wodehouse, P. G. Carry on Jeeves. 240p. 1975. pap. 2.95 (ISBN 0-14-001174-9). Penguin.

--The Inimitable Jeeves. 224p. 1975. pap. 2.95 (ISBN 0-14-000933-7). Penguin.

--Lord Emsworth & Others. 224p. 1975. pap. 2.95 (ISBN 0-14-002568-5). Penguin.

--Pigs Have Wings. 1977. pap. 1.95 o.p. (ISBN 0-345-25516-X). Ballantine.

Wodsedalek, J. E., ed. General Zoology Laboratory Guide: Shortversion. 8th ed. Lytle, Charles F. 237p. 1981. write for info. wire coil. Wm C Brown.

Woehr, Richard, et al. Pasaporte, First Year Spanish. LC 79-26709. 1980. text ed. 17.95 (ISBN 0-471-02758-8); tchr's ed. (ISBN 0-471-04193-9); wkbk (ISBN 0-471-02759-6); tapes (ISBN 0-471-05837-8). Wiley.

Woelcken, Fritz. Der Literarische Mord. Bleiler, E. F., ed. LC 78-60827. (Fiction of Popular Culture Ser.: Vol. 19). 1979. lib. bdg. 38.00 (ISBN 0-8240-9649-5). Garland Pub.

Woelfel, James W. Augustinian Humanism: Studies in Human Bondage & Earthly Grace. LC 79-5376. 1979. pap. text ed. 7.50 (ISBN 0-8191-0874-X). U Pr of Amer.

Woelfflin, Heinrich. Sense of Form in Art. LC 57-12877. (Illus., Orig.). pap. 4.95 (ISBN 0-8284-0153-5). Chelsea Pub.

Woellner, Elizabeth H. Requirements for Certification: Of Teachers, Counselors, Librarians, Administrators for Elementary Schools, Secondary Schools, Junior Colleges, 1981-82. 45th ed. (Illus.). 240p. 1981. lib. bdg. price not set (ISBN 0-226-90466-0, A43-1905). U of Chicago Pr.

Woerden, Hugo Van see Van Woerden, Hugo, et al.

Woerkom, Dorothy O. Van see Van Woerkom, Dorothy O.

Woerkom, Dorothy Van see Van Woerkom, Dorothy O.

Woerz-Busekros, A. Algebras in Genetics. (Lecture Notes in Biomathematics: Vol. 36). 237p. 1980. pap. 16.00 (ISBN 0-387-09978-6). Springer-Verlag.

Woessner, Nina, jt. auth. see Sheldon, William D.

Woessner, Nina C., jt. auth. see Sheldon, William.

Woessner, Warren, jt. auth. see Stephens, Jim.

Wofford, Harris. Of Kennedys & Kings: Making Sense of the Sixties. 496p. 1980. 17.50 (ISBN 0-374-22432-3). FS&G.

Wofford, Vera D. Hale County, Facts & Folklore. 18.00 (ISBN 0-686-68989-5). Pioneer Bk Tx.

Wogen, Norris L. The Shadow of His Hand. LC 74-21059. 1974. pap. 2.25 (ISBN 0-87123-533-1, 210533). Bethany Fell.

Wohl, Anthony S., ed. see Mearns, Andrew, et al.

Wohl, G., jt. auth. see Edwards, A.

Wohl, Gary, jt. auth. see Edwards, Audrey.

Wohl, Gerald. Structured COBOL: A Direct Approach. 1979. pap. text ed. 13.95 (ISBN 0-574-21230-2, 13-4230); instr's guide avail. (ISBN 0-574-21231-0, 13-4231). SRA.

Wohl, James P. The Nirvana Contracts. 1979. pap. 1.75 o.s.i. (ISBN 0-515-04691-4). Jove Pubns.

Wohl, Paul. Gun Trader's Guide. 8th ed. (Stoeger Bks). (Illus.). 1977. pap. 7.95 o.p. (ISBN 0-695-80843-5). Follett.

Wohlgelernter, Maurice. Frank O'connor: An Introductory Study. LC 76-45085. 1977. 15.00x (ISBN 0-231-04194-2). Columbia U Pr.

Wohlgemuth, M. Song of Zion. 1977. 5.00 o.p. (ISBN 0-682-48946-8). Exposition.

Wohlrabe, Raymond A. Exploring the World of Leaves. LC 75-15865. (Illus.). 160p. (gr. 7 up). 1976. 10.95 (ISBN 0-690-00511-3, TYC-J). T Y Crowell.

Wohlrabe, Raymond A. & Krusch, Werner E. Land & People of Venezuela. (Portraits of the Nations Ser). (Illus.). (gr. 7-9). 1963. PLB 8.79 o.p. (ISBN 0-397-30464-1). Lippincott.

Wohlwill, J. F., jt. ed. see Altman, Irwin.

Woillet, M. J. Appropriate Technology: Scope for Co-Operation Among the Countries of the West African Economic Community. International Labour Office, Geneva, ed. ii, 104p. (Orig.). 1980. pap. 5.70 (ISBN 92-2-102359-1). Intl Labour Office.

Woiwode, Larry. Beyond the Bedroom Wall. 1976. pap. 2.95 (ISBN 0-380-00684-7, 47670, Bard). Avon.

Wojcicki, Ryszard. Topics in the Formal Methodology of Empirical Sciences. Jansen, Ewa, tr. from Polish. (Synthese Library: No. 135). 1980. lib. bdg. 50.00 (ISBN 90-277-1004-X, D. Reidel Pub). Kluwer Boston.

Wojciechowska, Maria. Shadow of a Bull. (Illus.). (gr. 5 up). 1972. pap. 2.95 (ISBN 0-689-70298-1, Aladdin). Atheneum.

Wojciechowski, Andrzej, tr. see Barron, Stephanie, et al.

Wojciechowski, Bohdan W. Chemical Kinetics for Chemical Engineers. 2nd ed. (Illus.). 333p. 1981. pap. text ed. 11.95 (ISBN 0-88408-130-3). Sterling Swift.

Wojciechowski, Jercy A., ed. Conceptual Basis of the Classification of Knowledge: Proceedings of the Ottawa Conference. 503p. 1978. text ed. 58.00 (ISBN 0-89664-016-7, Pub. by K G Saur). Gale.

Wojciechowski, Margot J. Federal Mineral Policies, Nineteen Forty-Five to Seventy-Five: A Survey of Federal Activities That Affected the Canadian Mineral Industry. 87p. (Orig.). 1979. pap. 3.50x (ISBN 0-686-63135-8, Pub. by Ctr Resource Stud Canada). Renouf.

Wojcik, Jan. Muted Consent: A Casebook in Modern Medical Ethics. LC 77-89472. (Science & Society: a Purdue University Series in Science, Technology, & Human Values: Vol. 1). 176p. 1978. pap. 3.25 (ISBN 0-931682-02-9). Purdue Univ Bks.

Wojna, Ryszard, tr. Poland: The Country & Its People. LC 80-451948. 208p. (Orig.). 1979. pap. 6.00x (ISBN 0-8002-2278-4). Intl Pubns Serv.

Wojniechowski, William V. & Neff, Paula E. Comprehensive Review of Respiratory Therapy. 400p. 1981. 15.95 (ISBN 0-471-08408-5, Pub. by Wiley Med). Wiley.

Wojowasito, Soewojo. A Kawi Lexicon. Mills, Roger F., ed. LC 78-57221. (Michigan Papers on South & Southeast Asia: No. 17). 636p. (Orig.). 1980. pap. 13.00x (ISBN 0-89148-017-X). Ctr S&SE Asian.

Wojslaw, Charles F. Integrated Circuits: Theory & Applications. (Illus.). 1978. text ed. 18.95 (ISBN 0-87909-379-X); students manual avail. Reston.

Wojtyla, Karol. Fruitful & Responsible Love. (Orig.). 1979. pap. 2.95 (ISBN 0-8164-2237-0). Crossroad NY.

--Sign of Contradiction. 1980. pap. 3.95 (ISBN 0-8164-2048-3). Crossroad NY.

--Sign of Contradiction. 1979. 8.95 (ISBN 0-8164-0433-X). Crossroad NY.

Wojtyla, Karol see John Paul, Pope.

Wolandt, Gerd. Idealismus und Faktizitaet. 287p. 1971. 41.75x (ISBN 3-11-002375-X). De Gruyter.

Wolanin, Mary O. & Phillips, Linda R. Confusion: Prevention & Care. (Illus.). 415p. 1980. pap. text ed. 18.95 (ISBN 0-8016-5629-X). Mosby.

Wolanin, Ron, jt. auth. see Grossman, Irwin.

Wolanin, Thomas R. Presidential Advisory Commissions: Truman to Nixon. LC 74-27317. 368p. 1975. 27.50 (ISBN 0-299-06860-9). U of Wis Pr.

Wolanin, Thomas R., jt. auth. see Gladieux, Lawrence E.

Wolansky, William D., et al. Fundamentals of Fluid Power. LC 76-13963. (Illus.). 1976. text ed. 21.50 (ISBN 0-395-18956-X); inst. manual 2.25 (ISBN 0-395-18955-1). HM.

Wolbarsht, Myron, jt. auth. see Sliney, David.

Wolberg, Arlene R. The Psychoanalytic Psychotherapy of the Borderline Patient. (Illus.). 350p. 1981. text ed. 30.00 (ISBN 0-86577-022-0). Thieme-Stratton.

Wolberg, Lewis R. & Aronson, Marvin L., eds. Group & Family Therapy: 1980: An Overview. LC 72-10881. 432p. 1980. 25.00 (ISBN 0-87630-238-X). Brunner-Mazel.

Wolburg, H. Axonal Transport, Degeneration, & Regeneration in the Visual System of the Goldfish. (Advances in Anatomy, Embryology & Cell Biology Ser.: Vol. 67). (Illus.). 100p. 1981. pap. 28.50 (ISBN 0-387-10336-8). Springer-Verlag.

Wolck, I. D., ed. Subject Catalogue-Africa, 3 vols. Incl. Vol. 2. Politics; Vol. 3. Literature; Vol. 4. Social & Cultural Anthropology. 1979. Set. 110.00 (ISBN 0-89664-073-6, Pub. by K G Saur); 68.00 ea. Gale.

Wolcott, Leon O., jt. auth. see Gaus, John M.

Wolcott, Mark W., ed. Ambulatory Surgery & the Basics of Emergency Surgical Care. (Illus.). 640p. 1981. pap. text ed. 39.50 (ISBN 0-397-50480-2). Lippincott.

Wolcott, Roger, ed. see Prescott, W. H.

Wold, Erling, jt. auth. see Wold, Margaret.

Wold, Jo A. Well, Why Didn't You Say So? LC 75-8584. (Self Starter Bks.). 32p. (gr. k-2). 1975. 6.50g (ISBN 0-8075-8724-9). A Whitman.

Wold, Joanne. Tell Them My Name Is Amanda. Rubin, Caroline, ed. LC 77-14297. (Concept Books Ser.). (Illus.). 32p. (gr. k-3). 1977. 6.50g (ISBN 0-8075-7768-5). A Whitman.

Wold, Margaret & Wold, Erling. Bible Readings for Couples. LC 80-65541. 112p. (Orig.). 1980. pap. 2.95 (ISBN 0-686-61283-3, 10-0676). Augsburg.

Wold, Susan J. School Nursing: A Framework for Practice. (Illus.). 530p. 1981. pap. text ed. 15.95 (ISBN 0-8016-5611-7). Mosby.

Wold, Tina & Frost, John. Men & Women Use... Menus. LC 80-68806. 120p. (Orig.). 1980. pap. 5.95 (ISBN 0-9604802-0-X). Frost Art.

Woldum, Thomas & Gadbois, Robert. Harold Sets a Record. LC 77-1690. (Books by Children for Children). (Illus.). (gr. 2-5). 1977. PLB 6.45 (ISBN 0-87191-612-6). Creative Ed.

Wolensky, Robert P. & Miller, Edward J., eds. The Small City & Regional Community: Proceeding of the Nineteen Eighty Conference, Vol. 3. viii, 450p. (Orig.). 1980. pap. text ed. 11.50 (ISBN 0-932310-02-8). UWSP Found Pr.

Wolf. Intrepretation of Electrophoretic Patterns of Serum Proteins, Lipoproteins, Isoenzymes, & Hemoglobins. 1981. price not set (ISBN 0-89352-035-7). Masson Pub.

--Journey in Faith. pap. 6.95 (ISBN 0-8164-5646-1); leader's guide 0.95 (ISBN 0-8164-5645-3). Crossroad NY.

Wolf, Alexander, et al. Beyond the Couch: Dialogues in Teaching & Learning Psychoanalysis in Groups. LC 70-11256. 1970. 25.00x (ISBN 0-87668-029-5). Aronson.

Wolf, Aline D. A Book About Anna: For Children & Their Parents. (Illus.). 56p. (Orig.). 1981. pap. write for info. (ISBN 0-9601016-4-0). Parent-Child Pr.

--Una Guia Para Padres Al a Montessori. (Illus., Sp.). 1979. 5.00 (ISBN 0-9601016-3-2). Parent-Child Pr.

--Look at the Child. LC 78-58153. (Illus.). 1978. 4.95 (ISBN 0-9601016-2-4). Parent-Child Pr.

--A Parents' Guide to the Montessori Classroom. (Illus.). 1980. 3.50x (ISBN 0-9601016-0-8). Parent-Child Pr.

--Tutoring Is Caring -- You Can Help Someone to Read. LC 76-15777. (Illus.). 1976. spiral bdg. 12.50 (ISBN 0-9601016-1-6). Parent-Child Pr.

Wolf, Alison, jt. auth. see Wallace, Ruth A.

Wolf, Allan C., jt. auth. see Hornbrook, John F.

Wolf, Alvin. Lobbies & Lobbyists: In Whose Best Interest? Fraenkel, Jack, ed. (Crucial Issues in American Government Ser.). (gr. 9-12). 1976. pap. text ed. 4.96 (ISBN 0-205-04909-5, 7649096). Allyn.

Wolf, Alvin & Zevin, Jack. Participation, Protest & Apathy: A Question of Involvement? (Crucial Issues in American Government). (gr. 9-12). 1978. pap. text ed. 4.96 (ISBN 0-205-05522-2, 7655223). Allyn.

Wolf, Arthur P. & Huang, Chieh-Shan. Marriage & Adoption in China, 1845-1945. LC 78-66182. 1980. 18.95x (ISBN 0-8047-1027-9). Stanford U Pr.

Wolf, Barbara & Wolf, Jack. Professional Picture Framing for the Amateur. LC 73-86764. (Illus.). 168p. 1974. pap. 4.95 (ISBN 0-8306-2674-3, 674). TAB Bks.

Wolf, Bernard. Connie's New Eyes. (Illus.). (YA) (gr. 7-9). 1978. pap. 1.25 (ISBN 0-671-29897-6). PB.

--Michael & the Dentist. LC 80-12343. (Illus.). 48p. (ps-3). 1980. 7.95 (ISBN 0-590-07637-X, Four Winds). Schol Bk Serv.

Wolf, Beverly, jt. auth. see Barry, Ruth.

Wolf, Beverly H. The Ways of My Grandmothers. 224p. 1981. pap. 5.95. Morrow.

--The Ways of My Grandmothers. LC 79-91645. 224p. 1980. 9.95 (ISBN 0-688-03665-1). Morrow.

Wolf, Burton, jt. auth. see Rice, William.

Wolf, Carolyn & Wolf, Richard. Basic Library Skills: A Short Course. 110p. 1981. lib. bdg. write for info (ISBN 0-89950-018-8). McFarland & Co.

Wolf, Carolyn E. & Folk, Karen R. Indians of North & South America: A Bibliography Based on the Collection at the Willard E. Yager Library-Museum Hartwick College, Oneonta, N.Y. LC 77-1759. 1977. 27.50 (ISBN 0-8108-1026-3). Scarecrow.

Wolf, Christa. A Model Childhood. Molinaro, Ursule & Rappolt, Hedwig, trs. from Ger. 416p. 1980. 17.50 (ISBN 0-374-21170-1). FS&G.

--The Quest for Christa T. 185p. 1970. 4.95 (ISBN 0-374-51534-4). FS&G.

Wolf, Dave & Bruns, Bill. Great Moments in Pro Basketball. (gr. 5-9). 1968. PLB 3.69 (ISBN 0-394-90872-4, BYR). Random.

Wolf, David. Foul: The Connie Hawkins Story. LC 71-117279. 1972. 7.95 o.p. (ISBN 0-03-086021-0). HR&W.

Wolf, Deborah G. The Lesbian Community, LC 77-93478. 1979. 10.95 (ISBN 0-520-03657-3); pap. 4.95 (ISBN 0-520-04248-4, CAL 484). U of Cal Pr.

Wolf, Dieter. Spin Temperature & Nuclear Spin Relaxation in Matter: Basic Principles & Applications. (International Series of Monographs on Physics). (Illus.). 480p. 1979. text ed. 34.95x (ISBN 0-19-851295-3). Oxford U Pr.

Wolf, Donald D., ed. One Thousand & One Helpful Family Hints. (Illus.). 256p. (Orig.). 1980. pap. 9.95 (ISBN 0-8326-2246-X, 7030). Delair.

Wolf, Donald D., ed. see Demske, Dick.

Wolf, E., jt. auth. see Born, M.

Wolf, Eleanor P. Trial & Error: The Detroit School Segregation Case. 400p. 1981. 19.95 (ISBN 0-8143-1673-5). Wayne St U Pr.

Wolf, Elliott, ed. Seattle Epicure. (Epicure Ser.). 160p. (Orig.). 1979. pap. 4.95 (ISBN 0-89716-026-6). Peanut Butter.

--Sun Valley: Ketchum Epicure. 1978. pap. 2.50 (ISBN 0-89716-030-4). Peanut Butter.

Wolf, Eric A. Anthropology. 113p. 1974. pap. 2.95x (ISBN 0-393-09290-9). Norton.

Wolf, Eric R. Peasants. (Illus., Orig.). 1966. pap. 6.95 ref. ed. (ISBN 0-13-655456-3). P-H.

Wolf, George, jt. auth. see Ehrlich, David.

Wolf, George D. The Fair Play Settlers of the West Branch Valley, 1769 to 1784: A Study of Frontier Ethnography. (Illus., Orig.). 1969. 5.00 (ISBN 0-911124-31-4); pap. 3.00 (ISBN 0-911124-30-6). Pa Hist & Mus.

--William Warren Scranton: Pennsylvania Statesman. LC 80-21736. (Illus.). 160p. 1981. 16.50x (ISBN 0-271-00278-6, Keystone Bks). Pa St U Pr.

Wolf, H. F. Silicon Semiconductor Data. 1969. 105.00 (ISBN 0-08-013019-4). Pergamon.

Wolf, Harold. Personal Finance. 6th ed. 700p. 1981. 19.95 (ISBN 0-205-07298-4, 1072986); tchr's ed. free (ISBN 0-205-07299-2, 1072994). Allyn.

Wolf, Harold A. Personal Finance. 5th ed. 1978. text ed. 18.95 o.p. (ISBN 0-205-06047-1, 1060473); instr's man. avail. o.p. (ISBN 0-205-06048-X, 1060481). Allyn.

Wolf, Harvey J. & Frangia, George W. Behavioral Applications in Public Management: A Reader. LC 79-63852. (Illus.). 1979. pap. text ed. 7.75 (ISBN 0-8191-0744-1). U Pr of Amer.

Wolf, Howard. Forgive the Father: A Memoir of Changing Generations. LC 78-14396. 1978. 8.95 o.p. (ISBN 0-915220-44-X). New Republic.

Wolf, J. J. Studies in Stock Speculation, 2 vols. Repr. of 1967 ed. Vol. 1. flexible cover 5.00 (ISBN 0-87034-017-4); Vol. 2. flexible cover 5.00 (ISBN 0-87034-018-2). Fraser Pub Co.

Wolf, Jack, jt. auth. see Wolf, Barbara.

Wolf, James M. The Results of Treatment in Cerebral Palsy. 344p. 1969. pap. 26.25 spiral (ISBN 0-398-02104-X). C C Thomas.

Wolf, James M. & Anderson, Robert. The Multiply Handicapped Child. 488p. 1973. pap. 19.00 spiral (ISBN 0-398-02105-8). C C Thomas.

Wolf, James R. Guide to the Continental Divide Trail: Wyoming, Vol. 3. LC 76-17632. (Guide to the Continental Divide Trail Ser.). (Illus., Orig.). 1980. pap. 9.95 (ISBN 0-934326-03-7). Continent Divide.

Wolf, Jerome. Ferment in Labor. Krinsky, Fred & Boskin, Joseph, eds. (Insight Series: Studies in Contemporary Issues). (Illus.). 128p. 1968. pap. text ed. 4.95x (ISBN 0-02-479150-4, 47915). Macmillan.

Wolf, Joan. A London Season. (Orig.). 1981. pap. 1.95 (ISBN 0-451-09570-7, J9570, Sig). NAL.

Wolf, John. The Vivitar Guide. (Illus.). 144p. 1980. 12.95 (ISBN 0-87165-065-7); pap. 7.95 (ISBN 0-87165-066-5). Ziff-Davis Pub.

Wolf, John K. Classical Brain Stem Syndromes: Translations of the Original Papers with Notes on the Evolution of Clinical Neuroanatomy. (Illus.). 186p. 1971. text ed. 13.75 (ISBN 0-398-02170-8). C C Thomas.

--Practical Clinical Neurology. LC 79-91846. 1980. pap. 13.75 (ISBN 0-87488-728-3). Med Exam.

Wolf, John Q. Life in the Leatherwoods. Wolf, John Q., Jr., ed. LC 74-3412. 1974. 9.95 (ISBN 0-87870-020-X); pap. 3.95 o.p. (ISBN 0-87870-021-8). Memphis St Univ.

Wolf, Joseph. Classification & Fourier Inversion for Parabolic Subgroups with Square Integrable Nilradical. LC 79-21155. (Memoirs: No. 225). 1979. 7.60 (ISBN 0-8218-2225-X). Am Math.

Wolf, Joyce. An Ecology Alphabet. (Illus.). (gr. 3-6). 1981. PLB price not set (ISBN 0-671-42692-3). Messner.

Wolf, Katherine M. & Auerbach, Aline B. As Your Child Grows: The First 18 Months. rev. ed. 27p. 1976. pap. 1.50 (ISBN 0-686-12269-0). Jewish Bd Family.

Wolf, Larry L., jt. auth. see McNaughton, S. J.

Wolf, Leonard. A Dream of Dracula. 1977. pap. 1.95 o.p. (ISBN 0-445-08567-3). Popular Lib.

Wolf, Mary A. Mom's Tried & True Recipes for Family Prayer. (Illus., Orig.). 1981. pap. 3.25 (ISBN 0-89570-199-5). Claretian Pubns.

Wolf, Myron. Blue Book Illustrated Price Guide to Collectable Cameras, 1839-1981: 2nd Silver Issue. 2nd ed. (Illus.). 224p. 1980. pap. 14.95 (ISBN 0-9604352-0-4). Photo Memorabilia.

Wolf, P., jt. auth. see Brinker, R.

Wolf, P., ed. Tumor Associated Markers: The Importance of Identification in Clinical Medicine. LC 79-87540. (Illus.). 208p. 1979. 25.50 (ISBN 0-89352-065-9). Masson Pub.

Wolf, Patricia, tr. see Boulle, Pierre.

Wolf, Paul L. Interpretation of Biochemical Multitest Profiles: An Analysis of 100important Conditions. LC 76-54053. (Illus.). 296p. 1977. 25.00 (ISBN 0-89352-002-0). Masson Pub.

Wolf, Paul L., et al. Methods & Techniques in Clinical Chemistry. LC 78-39685. 400p. 1972. 29.95 (ISBN 0-471-95900-6, Pub. by Wiley Medical). Wiley.

--Practical Clinical Enzymology: Techniques & Interpretations & Biochemical Profiling. LC 80-12468. 592p. 1981. Repr. of 1973 ed. lib. bdg. price not set (ISBN 0-89874-162-9). Krieger.

Wolf, Peter. Land: Power & Wealth. (Illus.). 1981. 17.95 (ISBN 0-394-50437-2). Pantheon.

Wolf, Ray. Rodale Plans Insulating Window Shade. (Illus.). 86p. 1980. 14.95 (ISBN 0-87857-311-9). Rodale Pr Inc.

Wolf, Ray, ed. Rodale Plans Solar Growing Frame. (Illus.). 80p. 1980. pap. 14.95 (ISBN 0-87857-305-4). Rodale Pr Inc.

Wolf, Ray, ed. see Hoffman, Jim.

Wolf, Richard, jt. auth. see Wolf, Carolyn.

Wolf, Richard C., ed. see Brauer, Jerald C.

Wolf, Richard M. Evaluation in Education: Foundations of Competency Assessment & Program Review. LC 78-25743. 1979. 19.95 (ISBN 0-03-049116-9). Praeger.

Wolf, Richard M., jt. auth. see Tyler, Ralph W.

Wolf, Robert E., tr. see Baumstark, Reinhold.

Wolf, Robert E., tr. see Vogt, Paul.

Wolf, Ronald H. & Mund, Vernon A. Business & Government. 1980. text ed. 19.95 (ISBN 0-89894-006-0). Advocate Pub Group.

Wolf, Ruth S., tr. see Verlaine, Paul.

Wolf, Sheldon M., et al. Neurology Case Studies. 2nd ed. 1975. spiral bdg. 13.75 (ISBN 0-87488-006-8). Med Exam.

Wolf, Stanley. Guide to Electronic Measurements & Laboratory Practice. (Illus.). 560p. 1973. ref. ed. 22.95 (ISBN 0-13-369587-5). P-H.

Wolf, Stewart. Social Environment & Health. LC 80-50868. (The Jessie & John Danz Lecture Ser.). (Illus.). 112p. 1981. 8.95 (ISBN 0-295-95777-8). U of Wash Pr.

Wolf, Stewart & Goodell, Helen. Behavioral Science in Clinical Medicine. (Illus.). 256p. 1976. 19.75 (ISBN 0-398-03444-3). C C Thomas.

Wolf, Stewart, et al. Occupational Health As Human Ecology. (Illus.). 128p. 1978. 14.75 (ISBN 0-398-03793-0). C C Thomas.

Wolf, Stewart, et al, eds. Structure & Function of the Circulation, Vol. 1. 825p. 1980. 75.00 (ISBN 0-306-40278-5). Plenum Pub.

Wolf, Walter, jt. auth. see Tubis, Manuel.

Wolf, William. Healers, Gurus, Spiritual Guide. LC 76-2180. 1969. pap. 6.50 (ISBN 0-933900-07-4). Foun Human Under.

Wolf, William B. Conversations with Chester I. Barnard. LC 72-619666. (ILR Paperback Ser.: No. 12). 1973. pap. 6.25 special bdg. (ISBN 0-87546-280-4); pap. 3.25 (ISBN 0-87546-047-X). NY Sch Indus Rel.

Wolf, William D. The Reform of the Fallen World: The Virtuous Prince in Jonsonian Tragedy & Comedy. (Salzburg Studies in English Literature, Jacobean Drama Studies: No. 27). 1973. pap. text ed. 25.00x (ISBN 0-391-01575-3). Humanities.

Wolf, William J., compiled by. Thomas Traherne's Centuries of Meditation. 1980. 1.60 (ISBN 0-686-28796-7). Forward Movement.

Wolfart, H. Christoph & Carroll, Janet F. Meet Cree: A Guide to the Cree Language. 160p. 1981. 12.50x (ISBN 0-8032-4716-8). U of Nebr Pr.

Wolfbein, Seymour. Education & Training for Full Employment. LC 67-23754. 1967. 20.00x (ISBN 0-231-02946-2). Columbia U Pr.

Wolfe. House of Lim: Study of a Chinese Farm Family. 1960. pap. text ed. 6.95 (ISBN 0-13-394973-7). P-H.

Wolfe, Alan. The Limits of Legitimacy: Political Contradictions of Contemporary Capitalism. LC 76-51567. 1980. pap. text ed. 9.95 (ISBN 0-02-934860-9). Free Pr.

Wolfe, Arthur D. & Naffziger, Frederick J. Legal Perspectives of American Business Associations. LC 76-5614. (Law Ser.). 1977. text ed. 20.95 o.p. (ISBN 0-88244-109-4). Grid Pub.

Wolfe, Bertram D. Revolution & Reality: Essays on the Origin of the Soviet System. LC 80-16178. (Illus.). 422p. 1981. 19.00x (ISBN 0-8078-1453-9); pap. 11.00x (ISBN 0-8078-4073-4). U of NC Pr.

--Strange Communists I Have Known. LC 65-14401. 232p. 1981. pap. 7.95 (ISBN 0-8128-6120-5). Stein & Day.

Wolfe, Betty. The Banner Book. LC 74-80378. (Illus.). 96p. 1974. 6.95 (ISBN 0-8192-1173-7). Morehouse.

Wolfe, Charles K. Tennessee Strings: The Story of Country Music in Tennessee. LC 77-8052. (Tennessee Three Star Bks. Ser.). (Illus.). 1977. lib. bdg. 8.50x (ISBN 0-87049-295-0); pap. 3.50. U of Tenn Pr.

Wolfe, Charles K., Jr., jt. auth. see Kepler, James.

Wolfe, D. M., jt. auth. see Blood, Robert O., Jr.

Wolfe, David, et al. The Child Management Program for Abusive Parents. (Illus.). 192p. (Orig.). 1981. pap. write for info. (ISBN 0-89305-035-0). Anna Pub.

Wolfe, David B. Condominium & Homeowners Associations That Work. LC 78-67831. (Illus.). 136p. 1978. pap. text ed. 19.50 (ISBN 0-87420-583-2). Urban Land.

Wolfe, Douglas A., ed. Fate & Effects of Petroleum Hydrocarbons in Marine Organisms & Ecosystems. LC 77-76464. 1977. text ed. 67.00 (ISBN 0-08-021613-7). Pergamon.

Wolfe, Gary K., jt. auth. see Williams, Carol T.

Wolfe, Gene. The Claw of the Conciliator. (The Book of the New Sun Ser.: Vol. II). 1981. 12.95 (ISBN 0-671-41370-8). S&S.

--The Devil in a Forest. LC 76-5318. 224p. (gr. 7 up). 1976. 6.95 o.p. (ISBN 0-695-80667-X); PLB 6.99 o.p. (ISBN 0-695-40667-1). Follett.

--Gene Wolfe's Book of Days. LC 80-1074. (Science Fiction Ser.). 192p. 1981. 9.95 (ISBN 0-385-15991-9). Doubleday.

--The Shadow of the Torturer. 1981. pap. 2.50 (ISBN 0-671-82825-8). PB.

Wolfe, James H. & Couloumbis, Theo. A. Introduction to International Relations: Power & Justice. (Illus.). 1978. text ed. 16.95 (ISBN 0-13-485300-8). P-H.

Wolfe, John H. & Phelps, E. R. Mechanics' Vest Pocket Reference Book. 1945. 6.95 (ISBN 0-13-572024-9). P-H.

Wolfe, John N. Mammography. (Illus.). 168p. 1967. 17.50 (ISBN 0-398-02107-4). C C Thomas.

--Xeroradiography: Breast Calcifications. (Illus.). 184p. 1977. 29.50 (ISBN 0-398-03551-2). C C Thomas.

--Xeroradiography: Uncalcified Breast Masses. (Illus.). 208p. 1977. 36.75 (ISBN 0-398-03504-0). C C Thomas.

Wolfe, Kenneth C. Cooking for the Professional Chef: A Structured Approach. LC 76-5300. 1976. pap. text ed. 12.00 (ISBN 0-8273-0390-4); instructor's guide 1.60 (ISBN 0-8273-0391-2). Delmar.

Wolfe, Linda. Cooking of the Caribbean Islands. (Foods of the World Ser). (Illus.). 1970. 14.95 (ISBN 0-8094-0044-8). Time-Life.

--Cooking of the Caribbean Islands. LC 75-108615. (Foods of the World Ser.). (Illus.). (gr. 6 up). 1970. PLB 14.94 (ISBN 0-8094-0071-5, Pub. by Time-Life). Silver.

Wolfe, Linde. Private Practices. 1981. pap. 3.25 (ISBN 0-440-17185-7). Dell.

Wolfe, Louis. Disaster Detectives. (Illus.). 160p. (gr. 8-12). 1981. PLB price not set (ISBN 0-671-34042-5). Messner.

--Disease Detectives. (Illus.). (gr. 4-6). 1979. PLB 6.90 s&l (ISBN 0-531-02921-2). Watts.

Wolfe, Martin. The Economic Causes of Imperialism. LC 77-38965. (Major Issues in History Ser.). 1972. pap. text ed. 6.95x o.p. (ISBN 0-471-95951-0). Wiley.

Wolfe, Maxine G. & Goldsmith, Margot. Practical Pregnancy. LC 79-22003. (Illus.). 320p. (Orig.). 1980. 12.50 (ISBN 0-446-51204-4); pap. 5.95 (ISBN 0-446-97032-8). Warner Bks.

Wolfe, Morris. Aurora: New Canadian Writing Nineteen Eighty. LC 80-719. 312p. 1981. pap. 9.95 (ISBN 0-385-15771-1). Doubleday.

Wolfe, Morris, ed. Aurora: Canadian Writing in 1978. LC 78-1227. 1979. pap. 7.95 (ISBN 0-385-13646-3). Doubleday.

Wolfe, Peter. Graham Greene the Entertainer. LC 72-188700. (Crosscurrents-Modern Critiques Ser.). 191p. 1972. 11.95 (ISBN 0-8093-0580-1). S Ill U Pr.

Wolfe, Rinna. The Singing Pope: The Story of Pope John Paul II. (Illus.). 128p. (gr. 6-8). 1980. 8.95 (ISBN 0-8164-0472-0). Seabury.

Wolfe, Robert L. The Truck Book. LC 80-15683. (Illus.). 32p. (ps-3). 1981. PLB 5.95 (ISBN 0-87614-125-4). Carolrhoda Bks.

Wolfe, S. Anthony, tr. see Tessier, Paul A.

Wolfe, Sidney, jt. auth. see Coley, Chris.

Wolfe, Stephen. Biology of the Cell. 1972. 24.95x (ISBN 0-534-00106-8). Wadsworth Pub.

--Biology: The Foundations. 1977. 18.95x (ISBN 0-534-00490-3). Wadsworth Pub.

Wolfe, Susan J., jt. ed. see Stanley, Julia P.

Wolfe, Thomas. Hills Beyond. 1941. 12.50 o.s.i. (ISBN 0-06-014700-8, HarpT). Har-Row.

--Look Homeward Angel. 1929. pap. 5.95 (ISBN 0-684-71941-X, ScribT). Scribner.

--Of Time & the River, 2 vols. (Contemporary Classics). 1971. pap. 9.95 set (ISBN 0-684-16649-6, SL284, ScribT). Scribner.

--Of Time & the River. 1935. lib.rep.ed. 17.50x o.p. (ISBN 0-684-14739-4, ScribT). Scribner.

Wolfe, Thomas E., jt. auth. see Allen, Robert D.

Wolfe, Tom. In Our Time. (Illus.). 1980. 12.95 (ISBN 0-374-17576-4). FS&G.

--The Right Stuff. 384p. 1980. pap. 3.50 (ISBN 0-553-13828-6). Bantam.

Wolfe, W. Dean & Goulding, Daniel J., eds. Articulation & Learning: New Dimensions in Research, Diagnostics, & Therapy. 2nd ed. (Illus.). 350p. 1980. text ed. 23.75 (ISBN 0-398-04007-9). C C Thomas.

Wolfe, W. L. & Zissis, G. J., eds. The Infrared Handbook. LC 77-90786. (Illus.). 1978. 25.00 (ISBN 0-9603590-0-1). Environ Res Inst.

Wolfe, Walter B., tr. see Adler, Alfred.

Wolfe, Walter G. & Sabiston, David C., Jr. Pulmonary Embolism. LC 79-66047. (Major Problems in Clinical Surgery Ser.: Vol. 25). (Illus.). 180p. 1980. text ed. 17.00 (ISBN 0-7216-9584-1). Saunders.

Wolfe Howe, De M. see Howe, M. De Wolfe.

Wolfel, H., ed. see Marguerre, K.

Wolfendale, E., et al, eds. M O S Integrated Circuit Design. LC 72-1927. 120p. 1973. 24.95 (ISBN 0-470-95947-9). Halsted Pr.

Wolfenden, E. P. Hiligaynon Reference Grammar. McKaughan, Howard P., ed. LC 79-152473. (PALI Language Texts: Philippines). (Orig.). 1971. pap. text ed. 6.00x o.p. (ISBN 0-87022-867-6). U Pr of Hawaii.

Wolfensberger, Wolf. The Origin & Nature of Our Institutional Models. 3.50 (ISBN 0-937540-03-X, HPP-4). Human Policy Pr.

Wolfenstein, Eugene V. The Victims of Democracy: Malcolm X & the Black Revolution. 600p. 1981. 20.00 (ISBN 0-520-03903-3). U of Cal Pr.

Wolfenstine, Manfred R. The Manual of Brands & Marks. Adams, Ramon F., ed. LC 68-31379. (Illus.). 355p. 1981. 24.95 (ISBN 0-8061-0867-3). U of Okla Pr.

Wolfers, Elsie E. & Evansen, Virginia B. Organizations, Clubs, Action Groups: How to Start Them, How to Run Them. 256p. 1981. 11.95 (ISBN 0-312-58791-0). St Martin.

Wolfers, Michael. Black Man's Burden Revisited. LC 74-82176. 192p. 1975. 18.95 (ISBN 0-312-08330-0). St Martin.

--Poems from Angola. (African Writers Ser.). 1980. pap. text ed. 5.50x (ISBN 0-435-90215-6). Heinemann Ed.

Wolff, Barbara. Evening Gray, Morning Red: A Handbook of American Weather Wisdom. LC 76-15640. (Ready to Read Ser.). (Illus.). (gr. 1-4). 1976. 8.95 (ISBN 0-02-793320-2, 79332). Macmillan.

Wolff, Bernard. Friends & Friends of Friends. (Illus.). 1978. pap. 8.95 o.p. (ISBN 0-525-47519-2). Dutton.

Wolff, Caryl, jt. auth. see Wolff, Sydney.

Wolff, Charles R., jt. auth. see Shapiro, Eli.

Wolff, Christian. Preliminary Discourse on Philosophy in General. Blackwell, Richard, tr. LC 63-20239. (Orig.). 1963. pap. 2.50 (ISBN 0-672-60395-0, LA167). Bobbs.

Wolff, George. Theodore Roethke. (United States Authors Ser.: No. 390). 1981. lib. bdg. 9.95 (ISBN 0-8057-7323-1). Twayne.

Wolff, Gerald. Kansas-Nebraska Bill: Party, Section, & the Origin of the Civil War. 1980. lib. bdg. 69.95 (ISBN 0-87700-255-X). Revisionist Pr.

Wolff, H., ed. see Calvino, Italo.

Wolff, Hans J. Roman Law: An Historical Introduction. 1976. pap. 5.95x (ISBN 0-8061-1296-4). U of Okla Pr.

Wolff, Hans W. Hosea. Hanson, Paul D., ed. Stansell, Gary, tr. from Ger. LC 70-179634. (Hermeneia: a Critical & Historical Commentary on the Bible). Orig. Title: Dodekapropheton-Hosea. 292p. 1973. 19.95 (ISBN 0-8006-6004-8, 20-6004). Fortress.

Wolff, Hans W., Jr. Joel & Amos. McBride, Dean, ed. Janzen, Waldemar, tr. from Fr. LC 75-76932. (Hermeneia: a Critical & Historical Commentary on the Bible). 416p. 1977. 22.95 (ISBN 0-8006-6007-2, 20-6007). Fortress.

Wolff, Helen, ed. see Sciascia, Leonardo.

Wolff, Henry, tr. see Mauriac, Claude.

Wolff, Janet. Hermeneutic Philosophy & the Sociology of Art. (International Library of Sociology). 1975. 20.00x (ISBN 0-7100-8048-4). Routledge & Kegan.

--Hermeneutic Philosophy & the Sociology of Art: An Approach to Some of the Epistemological Problems of the Sociology of Art & Literature. (International Library of Sociology). 150p. 1981. pap. 12.50 (ISBN 0-7100-0682-9). Routledge & Kegan.

Wolff, Janet, jt. ed. see Routh, Jane.

Wolff, Jurgen, jt. auth. see Lipe, Dewey.

Wolff, Kurt. Emotional Rehabilitation of the Geriatric Patient. 248p. 1970. 16.75 (ISBN 0-398-02111-2). C C Thomas.

Wolff, Kurt H. Trying Sociology. 448p. 1974. 26.50 (ISBN 0-471-95940-5, Pub. by Wiley-Interscience). Wiley.

Wolff, Kurt H., ed. see Mannheim, Karl.

Wolff, Kurt H., tr. see Simmel, Georg.

Wolff, Luverne, jt. auth. see Hagen, Elizabeth.

Wolff, Manfred E. Burger's Medicinal Chemistry: The Basis of Medicinal Chemistry, 3 pts. 4th ed. LC 78-10791. 1980. Pt. 1. 33.95 (ISBN 0-471-01570-9, Pub. by Wiley-Interscience); Pt. 2. 100.00 (ISBN 0-471-01571-7); Pt. 3. write for info. (ISBN 0-471-01572-5). Wiley.

Wolff, Marianne, jt. ed. see Fenoglio, Cecilia M.

Wolff, Michael, jt. auth. see Dyos, H. J.

Wolff, Michael, et al, eds. The Waterloo Directory of Victorian Periodicals. 1203p. 1980. 215.00 (ISBN 0-08-026079-9). Pergamon.

Wolff, Miles, Jr. Season of the Owl. LC 80-51607. 192p. 1980. 10.95 (ISBN 0-8128-2744-9). Stein & Day.

--Seasons of the Owl. LC 80-51788. 256p. 1981. cancelled (ISBN 0-8128-2750-3). Stein & Day.

Wolff, P. A., jt. auth. see Platzman, P. M.

Wolff, Peter. Breakthroughs in Mathematics. 2.75 o.p. (ISBN 0-452-25010-2, Z5010, Plume). NAL.

Wolff, Peter, jt. auth. see Warntz, William.

Wolff, Peter, ed. Planning for Better Learning. (Clinics in Developmental Medicine Ser. No. 33). 159p. 1969. 15.50 (ISBN 0-685-24741-4). Lippincott.

Wolff, Peter, ed. see Simon, Yves.

Wolff, Pierre. May I Hate God. LC 78-70815. 1979. pap. 2.45 (ISBN 0-8091-2180-8). Paulist Pr.

Wolff, Robert. Animals of Europe. LC 77-78379. (Illus.). (gr. 3-9). 1969. PLB 12.00 (ISBN 0-87460-092-8). Lion.

--Animals of the Americas. LC 73-78378. (Illus.). (gr. 3-9). 1969. PLB 12.00 (ISBN 0-87460-093-6). Lion.

--Philosophy: A Modern Encounter. LC 76-25427. 1976. text ed. 12.50 (ISBN 0-13-663385-4); pap. text ed. 14.50 (ISBN 0-13-663377-3). P-H.

Wolff, Robert E., ed. see Maxwell, William H.

Wolff, Robert J. Seeing Red. LC 67-24052. (Illus.). (gr. 1-5). 1967. reinforced bdg. 5.95 o.p. (ISBN 0-684-12826-8, ScribJ). Scribner.

Wolff, Robert L. The Balkans in Our Time. rev. ed. 1978. pap. text ed. 8.95x (ISBN 0-393-09010-8). Norton.

--Gains & Losses. (Victorian Fiction Ser). Orig. Title: Faith & Doubt in Victorian England. 1975. lib. bdg. 66.00 (ISBN 0-8240-1617-3). Garland Pub.

--The Golden Key: A Study of the Fiction of George MacDonald. 1961. 34.50x (ISBN 0-686-51395-9). Elliots Bks.

--Studies in the Latin Empire of Constantinople. 412p. 1980. 60.00x (ISBN 0-902089-99-4, Pub. by Variorum England). State Mutual Bk.

--William Carleton, Irish Peasant Novelist: A Preface to His Fiction. LC 79-4399. 200p. 1980. lib. bdg. 18.00 (ISBN 0-8240-3527-5). Garland Pub.

Wolff, Robert L., ed. Aurora Floyd, 3 vols. LC 79-50468. (Mary Elizabeth Braddon Ser.: Vol. 1). 1979. Set. lib. bdg. 96.00 (ISBN 0-8240-4350-2); lib. bdg. 38.00 ea. Garland Pub.

--Priests & People: A No-Rent Romance. (Ireland-Nineteenth Century Fiction Ser.: Vol. 77). 1979. lib. bdg. 126.00 (ISBN 0-8240-3526-7); lib. bdg. 46.00 ea. Garland Pub.

Wolff, Robert L., ed. see Adderly, James G.

Wolff, Robert L., ed. see Allingham, William.

Wolff, Robert L., ed. see Arnold, William D.

Wolff, Robert L., ed. see Banim, John & Banim, Michael.

Wolff, Robert L., ed. see Barry, William F.

Wolff, Robert L., ed. see Bayley, Ada E.

Wolff, Robert L., ed. see Besant, Walter.

Wolff, Robert L., ed. see Brew, Margaret W.

Wolff, Robert L., ed. see Buchanan, Robert.

Wolff, Robert L., ed. see Butler, Samuel.

Wolff, Robert L., ed. see Carleton, William.

Wolff, Robert L., ed. see Charles, Elizabeth.

Wolff, Robert L., ed. see Conybeare, William J.

Wolff, Robert L., ed. see Corelli, Marie.

Wolff, Robert L., ed. see Craigie, Pearl M.

Wolff, Robert L., ed. see Craik, Dinah M.

Wolff, Robert L., ed. see Crowe, Eyre E.

Wolff, Robert L., ed. see Crows, Eyre E.

Wolff, Robert L., ed. see Davies, Charles M.

Wolff, Robert L., ed. see Dering, Edward H.

Wolff, Robert L., ed. see Disraeli, Benjamin.

Wolff, Robert L., ed. see Douglas, Gertrude.

Wolff, Robert L., ed. see Edgar, A. H.

Wolff, Robert L., ed. see Edgeworth, Maria.

Wolff, Robert L., ed. see Edgeworth, Marie.

Wolff, Robert L., ed. see Eliot, George.

Wolff, Robert L., ed. see Froude, James A.

Wolff, Robert L., ed. see Fullerton, Georgiana.

Wolff, Robert L., ed. see Gaskell, Elizabeth C.

Wolff, Robert L., ed. see Gissing, George.

Wolff, Robert L., ed. see Gould, Frederick J.

Wolff, Robert L., ed. see Gresley, William.

Wolff, Robert L., ed. see Guyton, Emma J. W.

Wolff, Robert L., ed. see Hall, Anna Maria.

Wolff, Robert L., ed. see Harris, Elizabeth F.

Wolff, Robert L., ed. see Heygate, William E.

Wolff, Robert L., ed. see Howitt, William.

Wolff, Robert L., ed. see Humphreys, Mrs. Desmond.

Wolff, Robert L., ed. see Ingelow, Jean.

Wolff, Robert L., ed. see Jewsbury, Geraldine E.

Wolff, Robert L., ed. see Kennedy, Grace.

Wolff, Robert L., ed. see Kingsley, Charles.

Wolff, Robert L., ed. see Lawless, Emily.

Wolff, Robert L., ed. see Linton, Eliza L.

Wolff, Robert L., ed. see Long, Catherine.

Wolff, Robert L., ed. see Longueville, Thomas de.

Wolff, Robert L., ed. see MacDonald, George.

Wolff, Robert L., ed. see Mallock, W. H.

Wolff, Robert L., ed. see Maturin, Charles R.

Wolff, Robert L., ed. see Maxwell, William H.

Wolff, Robert L., ed. see Moore, George.

Wolff, Robert L., ed. see Newman, John H.

Wolff, Robert L., ed. see Oliphant, Margaret O.

Wolff, Robert L., ed. see Oliphant, Margaret W.

Wolff, Robert L., ed. see Owenson, Lady Morgan S.

Wolff, Robert L., ed. see Paget, Francis E.

Wolff, Robert L., ed. see Pater, Walter.

Wolff, Robert L., ed. see Reade, William W.

Wolff, Robert L., ed. see Robinson, Frederick W.

Wolff, Robert L., ed. see Schreiner, Olive.

Wolff, Robert L. see Setton, Kenneth M.

Wolff, Robert L., ed. see Sewell, William.

Wolff, Robert L., ed. see Shorthouse, Joseph H.

Wolff, Robert L., ed. see Sinclair, Catherine.

Wolff, Robert L., ed. see Skene, Felicia.

Wolff, Robert L., ed. see Smith, Frederick R.

Wolff, Robert L., ed. see Sydney Owenson, Lady Morgan.

Wolff, Robert L., ed. see Tonna, Charlotte E.

Wolff, Robert L., ed. see Trollope, Anthony.

Wolff, Robert L., ed. see Trollope, Frances M.

Wolff, Robert L., ed. see Ward, Mary A.

Wolff, Robert L., ed. see White, William H.

Wolff, Robert L., ed. see Wiseman, Nicholas P.

Wolff, Robert L., ed. see Yonge, Charlotte.

Wolff, Robert L., ed. see Yonge, Charlotte M.

Wolff, Robert Lee, ed. see Buchanan, Robert.

Wolff, Robert P. About Philosophy. (Illus.). 352p. 1976. text ed. 16.95 (ISBN 0-13-000836-2). P-H.

--About Philosophy. 2nd ed. (Illus.). 448p. 1981. text ed. 15.95 (ISBN 0-13-000695-5). P-H.

--Kant's Theory of Mental Activity, a Commentary on the Transcendental Analytic of the Critique of Pure Reason. 8.00 (ISBN 0-8446-4054-9). Peter Smith.

Wolff, Robert P., ed. Introductory Philosophy. 1979. text ed. 17.50 (ISBN 0-13-500876-X). P-H.

Wolff, Robert P., ed. see Kant, Immanuel.

Wolff, Ruth. Crack in the Sidewalk. LC 65-23039. (John Day Bk.). (YA) 1965. 6.95 o.p. (ISBN 0-381-98201-7, A16460, TYC-T). T Y Crowell.

Wolff, Sonia. What Did They Do to Miss Lily. 288p. 1981. 12.95 (ISBN 0-06-014861-6, HarpT). Har-Row.

--What They Did to Miss Lily. LC 80-8709. 288p. 1981. 12.95 (ISBN 0-06-014861-6, HarpT). Har-Row.

Wolff, Sydney & Wolff, Caryl. Games Without Words: Activities for Thinking Teachers & Thinking Children. (Illus.). 120p. 1977. pap. text ed. 12.50 (ISBN 0-398-03062-6). C C Thomas.

Wolff, Werner. The Dream, Mirror of Conscience: A History of Dream Interpretation from 2000 B.C. & a New Theory of Dream Synthesis. LC 70-152618. (Illus.). 348p. 1972. Repr. of 1952 ed. lib. bdg. 27.50x (ISBN 0-8371-6053-7, WODR). Greenwood.

Wolffe, Lenard L. New Zoning Landmarks in Planned Unit Developments. LC 68-59421. (Technical Bulletin Ser: No. 62). (Orig.). 1968. pap. 4.75 (ISBN 0-87420-062-8). Urban Land.

Wolffheim, Nelly. Psychology in the Nursery School. Hannam, Charles L., tr. LC 77-162630. 143p. 1972. Repr. of 1953 ed. lib. bdg. 16.00x (ISBN 0-8371-6197-5, WONS). Greenwood.

Wolfflin, Heinrich. Principles of Art History: The Problem of the Development of Style in Later Art. (Illus.). 8.50 (ISBN 0-8446-3205-8). Peter Smith.

Wolfgang, Charles F. Helping Active and Passive Preschoolers Through Play. (Elementary Education Ser.). 1977. pap. text ed. 7.50 (ISBN 0-675-08550-0). Merrill.

Wolfgang, Charles H. & Glickman, Carl D. Solving Discipline Problems: Strategies for Classroom Teachers. 288p. 1980. text ed. 17.95 (ISBN 0-205-06888-X). Allyn.

Wolfgang, Leonhard. Child of the Revolution. 2nd ed. Woodhouse, C. M., tr. from Ger. 448p. 1980. pap. text ed. 13.00x (ISBN 0-906133-26-2). Humanities.

Wolfgang, Martin E., ed. Prisons: Present & Possible. LC 77-3860. 1979. 18.95 (ISBN 0-669-01674-8). Lexington Bks.

Wolfgang, Marvin E. & Lambert, Richard D., eds. Social Effects of Inflation. (The Annals of the American Academy of Political & Social Science: No. 456). 250p. 1981. 7.50 (ISBN 0-87761-264-1); pap. 6.00 (ISBN 0-87761-265-X). Am Acad Pol Soc Sci.

Wolfgang, Marvin E., et al. Sociology of Crime & Delinquency. 2nd ed. LC 73-96041. 1970. pap. text ed. 16.95 (ISBN 0-471-95955-3). Wiley.

Wolfinger, R. Politics of Progress. 1974. pap. text ed. 11.95 (ISBN 0-13-685024-3). P-H.

Wolfinger, R., ed. Readings on Congress. 1971. pap. 9.95 o.p. (ISBN 0-13-761254-0). P-H.

Wolfinger, R. E., et al. Dynamics of American Politics. 1976. text ed. 16.95 (ISBN 0-13-221168-8); pap. 4.95 study guide & wkbk. (ISBN 0-13-221176-9). P-H.

Wolfinger, Raymond, et al. Dynamics of American Politics. 2nd ed. (Illus.). 1980. text ed. 17.95 (ISBN 0-13-221143-2); study guide & wkbk. 4.95 (ISBN 0-13-221127-0). P-H.

Wolfle, Dael, ed. see Carnegie Commission on Higher Education.

Wolfman, Bernard. Federal Income Taxation of Business Enterprise. 1095p. 1971. 24.50 (ISBN 0-316-95113-7); pap. 1979 suppl. o.p. (ISBN 0-316-95114-5). Little.

Wolfman, Bernard, et al. Dissent Without Opinion: The Behavior of Justice William O. Douglas in Federal Tax Cases. LC 74-16827. 224p. 1975. 14.00x (ISBN 0-8122-7682-5). U of Pa Pr.

Wolfort, Francis G., ed. Acute Hand Injuries: A Multispecialty Approach. LC 79-90896. 1980. text ed. 27.50 (ISBN 0-316-95112-9). Little.

Wolfowitz, Jacob. Coding Theorems of Information Theory. 2nd ed. (Ergebnisse der Mathematik und Ihrer Grenzgebiete: Vol. 31). 1964. 17.30 o.p. (ISBN 0-387-03124-3). Springer-Verlag.

Wolfram, E., ed. Colloid & Surface Science: Proceedings of an International Conference, Budapest, 1975. LC 76-44624. 1977. text ed. 34.00 (ISBN 0-08-021570-X). Pergamon.

Wolfram, Eddie. History of Collage. (Illus.). 176p. 1976. 16.95 o.s.i. (ISBN 0-02-630870-3). Macmillan.

Wolfram, Walt. The Linguist in Speech Pathology. (Language in Education Ser.: No. 2). 1978. pap. 2.95 (ISBN 0-87281-078-X). Ctr Appl Ling.

--Speech Pathology & Dialect Difference. (Dialects & Educational Equity Ser.: No. 3). 1979. pap. 2.50 (ISBN 0-87281-122-0). Ctr Appl Ling.

Wolfram, Walt & Christian, Donna. Appalachian Speech. LC 76-15079. 1976. pap. 8.75x (ISBN 0-87281-050-X). Ctr Appl Ling.

--Dialogue on Dialects. (Dialects & Educational Equity Ser.: No. 1). 1979. pap. 2.50 (ISBN 0-87281-120-4). Ctr Appl Ling.

--Exploring Dialects. (Dialects & Educational Equity Ser.: No. 2). 1979. pap. 2.50 (ISBN 0-87281-121-2). Ctr Appl Ling.

Wolfram, Walt, et al. Reading & Dialect Differences. (Dialects & Educational Equity Ser.: No. 4). pap. 2.50 (ISBN 0-87281-123-9). Ctr Appl Ling.

Wolfrom, Melville see Pigman, Ward & Wolfrom, Melville L.

Wolfrom, Melville L., jt. ed. see Pigman, Ward.

Wolfrom, Melville L. see Pigman, Ward & Wolfrom, Melville L.

Wolfrom, Melville L., jt. ed. see Whistler, Roy L.

Wolfshutz, Hans, jt. ed. see Best, Alan D.

Wolfskill, G. & Hudson, J. A. All but the People. 1969. 7.95 o.s.i. (ISBN 0-02-630900-9). Macmillan.

Wolfson, Alice, jt. auth. see Meyer, Ursula.

Wolfson, Jerome H., jt. auth. see Bass, Lee W.

Wolfson, Murray. Karl Marx. 1969. pap. 3.00 (ISBN 0-231-03146-7, 108). Columbia U Pr.

--Reappraisal of Marxian Economics. LC 66-14790. 1966. 17.50x (ISBN 0-231-02880-6). Columbia U Pr.

Wolfson, Rita, jt. auth. see Weiss, Elizabeth.

Wolfson, Rita P., jt. auth. see Weiss, Elizabeth.

Wolfson, Rita P., jt. auth. see Weiss, Elizabeth S.

Wolgemuth, Kathleen D. Hawaii's Super Shopper. LC 80-83398. 128p. (Orig.). 1980. pap. 3.50 (ISBN 0-9604798-0-5). Island Writers.

Wolins, Martin. Selecting Foster Parents: The Ideal & the Reality. LC 63-19855. 1964. 17.50x (ISBN 0-231-02514-9). Columbia U Pr.

Wolke, Robert L. Chemistry Explained. (Illus.). 1980. text ed. 18.95 (ISBN 0-13-129163-7). P-H.

Wolken, Jerome J. Euglena: An Experimental Organism for Biochemical & Biophysical Studies. LC 67-13378. 204p. 1967. 19.50 (ISBN 0-306-50086-8, Plenum Pr). Plenum Pub.

Wolkers, Jan. A Rose of Flesh. Scott, John, tr. LC 67-12383. 1963. 4.50 o.p. (ISBN 0-8076-0403-8). Braziller.

Wolkin, Rachel, jt. auth. see Barcus, F. Earle.

Wolkoff, Judie. Where the Elf King Sings. LC 80-15298. 160p. (gr. 5-7). 8.95 (ISBN 0-87888-169-7). Bradbury Pr.

Wolkonsky, Catherine & Poltoratzky, Marianna. Handbook of Russian Roots. LC 61-1403. (Columbia Slavic Studies). 1961. 25.00x (ISBN 0-231-02117-8). Columbia U Pr.

Wolkstein, Diane. Lazy Stories. LC 75-25781. (Illus.). 32p. (gr. 1-5). 1976. 6.95 o.p. (ISBN 0-8164-3135-3, Clarion). HM.

--White Wave: A Chinese Tale. LC 78-4781. (Illus.). (gr. 2 up). 1979. 6.95 (ISBN 0-690-03893-3, TYC-J); PLB 6.89 (ISBN 0-690-03894-1). T Y Crowell.

Woll. American Government: Readings & Cases. 7th ed. 1981. pap. text ed. 8.95 (ISBN 0-316-95143-9); tchrs'. manual free (ISBN 0-316-95144-7). Little.

--Behind the Scenes in American Government. 3rd ed. 1981. pap. text ed. 7.95 (ISBN 0-316-95137-4); tchrs'. manual free. Little.

Woll, Allen L. The Latin Image in American Film. LC 77-620044. (Latin American Studies Ser: Vol. 39). 1978. pap. text ed. 4.75 o.p. (ISBN 0-87903-039-9). UCLA Lat Am Ctr.

--The Latin Image in American Film. rev. ed. LC 80-620041. (Latin American Studies: Vol. 50). 1981. pap. price not set (ISBN 0-87903-050-X). UCLA Lat Am Ctr.

Woll, Peter. Administrative Law: The Formal Process. (California Library Reprint Ser: No. 58). 1974. 19.50x (ISBN 0-520-02802-3). U of Cal Pr.

--American Bureaucracy. 2nd ed. 1977. 12.50x (ISBN 0-393-05615-5); pap. 5.95x (ISBN 0-393-09141-4). Norton.

Wollack, Anne, jt. auth. see Hutchinson, G. Evelyn.

Wollard, Joy J. Nutritional Management of the Cancer Patient. LC 78-68523. 1979. text ed. 17.50 (ISBN 0-89004-357-4); pap. text ed. 12.00 (ISBN 0-685-94934-6). Raven.

Wollaston, Thomas A. The Incredible Conditions of the World in the Year 2000: An Astonishing Forecast. (Illus.). 131p. 1981. 67.85 (ISBN 0-930008-74-X). Inst Econ Pol.

Wollaston, William. The Religion of Nature Delineated. Wellek, Rene, ed. LC 75-11267. (British Philosophers & Theologians of the 17th & 18th Centuries Ser.). 1978. Repr. of 1722 ed. lib. bdg. 42.00 (ISBN 0-8240-1816-8). Garland Pub.

Wolle, Muriel S. The Bonanza Trail: Ghost Towns & Mining Camps of the West. (Illus.). 510p. 1953. Repr. pap. 14.95 (ISBN 0-8040-0685-7, SB). Swallow.

--Timberline Tailings: Tales of Colorado's Ghost Town & Mining Camps. LC 76-17740. (Illus.). 337p. 1976. 19.95 (ISBN 0-8040-0739-X). Swallow.

Wollemann, Marie, jt. ed. see Vizi, E. S.

Wollenberg, Charles M. All Deliberate Speed: Segregation & Exclusion in California Schools, 1855-1975. 1977. 14.95x (ISBN 0-520-03191-1); pap. 3.50 (ISBN 0-520-03728-6). U of Cal Pr.

Woller, Jim, jt. auth. see Pashdag, John.

Wollheim, Donald A., ed. The Nineteen Eighty-One Annual World's Best SF. (Science Fiction Ser.). 1981. pap. 2.50 (ISBN 0-87997-617-9, UE1617). DAW Bks.

Wollheim, Richard. Art & Its Objects. 2nd ed. LC 79-20790. 1980. 29.50 (ISBN 0-521-22898-0); pap. 8.95 (ISBN 0-521-29706-0). Cambridge U Pr.

--A Family Romance. 256p. 1969. 5.95 o.p. (ISBN 0-374-15292-6). FS&G.

--Sigmund Freud. 316p. Date not set. pap. price not set (ISBN 0-521-28385-X). Cambridge U Pr.

Wollheim, Richard, ed. see Stokes, Adrian.

Wollstonecraft, Mary. Letters Written During a Short Residence in Sweden, Norway, & Denmark. Poston, Carol H., ed. LC 75-38056. (Illus.). xxiv, 202p. 1976. 11.50x (ISBN 0-8032-0862-6); pap. 4.95 (ISBN 0-8032-5832-1, BB 613, Bison). U of Nebr Pr.

--Mary, a Fiction. Luria, Gina, ed. (The Feminist Controversy in England, 1788-1810 Ser.). 1974. lib. bdg. 50.00 (ISBN 0-8240-0888-X). Garland Pub.

--Posthumous Works, 4 vols. Godwin, William, ed. (The Feminist Controversy in England, 1788-1810 Ser.). 1974. Set. lib. bdg. 200.00 (ISBN 0-8240-0889-8); lib. bdg. 50.00 ea. Garland Pub.

--Thoughts on the Education of Daughters: With Reflections on Female Conduct, in the More Important Duties of Life. Luria, Gina, ed. (The Feminist Controversy in England, 1788-1810 Ser.). 1974. lib. bdg. 50.00 (ISBN 0-8240-0890-1). Garland Pub.

--A Vindication of the Rights of Woman: With Strictures on Political & Moral Subjects. (The Feminist Controversy in England, 1788-1810 Ser.). 1974. lib. bdg. 50.00 (ISBN 0-8240-0891-X). Garland Pub.

Wollstonecraft, Mary see Day, Thomas.

Wollstonecraft, Mary, ed. Female Reader. LC 79-27565. 1980. 47.00x (ISBN 0-8201-1347-6). Schol Facsimiles.

Wolman, B. B., ed. Psychological Aspects of Gynecology & Obstetrics. 1978. 22.50 (ISBN 0-87489-009-8). Med Economics.

Wolman, Baron. Profiles. LC 74-81290. (Illus.). 1974. deluxe ed. 15.00 signed, ltd., numbered (ISBN 0-916290-02-6); pap. 5.95 (ISBN 0-916290-01-8). Squarebooks.

Wolman, Baron, jt. auth. see Owens, Richard.

Wolman, Benjamin B. Handbook of Parapsychology. 1070p. 1981. pap. text ed. 17.95 (ISBN 0-442-26479-8). Van Nos Reinhold.

--The International Directory of Psychology. LC 78-27868. (Illus.). 313p. 1979. 19.95 (ISBN 0-306-40209-2, Plenum Pr). Plenum Pub.

Wolman, Benjamin B. & Knapp, Susan. Contemporary Theories & Systems in Psychology. rev., 2nd ed. 690p. 1981. 42.50 (ISBN 0-306-40515-6, Plenum Pr); pap. 17.95 (ISBN 0-306-40530-X). Plenum Pub.

Wolman, Benjamin B., ed. Clinical Diagnosis of Mental Disorders: A Handbook. LC 78-14969. (Illus.). 933p. 1978. 50.00 (ISBN 0-306-31141-0, Plenum Pr). Plenum Pub.

--Handbook of General Psychology. LC 74-166142. (Illus.). 1088p. 1973. ref. ed. 65.00 (ISBN 0-13-378141-0). P-H.

--Handbook of Treatment of Mental Disorders in Childhood & Adolescence. LC 77-7928. (Illus.). 1978. ref. ed. 45.00 (ISBN 0-13-382234-6). P-H.

Wolman, Benjamon B. & Money, John. Handbook of Human Sexuality. (Illus.). 1980. text ed. 36.95 (ISBN 0-13-378422-3). P-H.

Wolman, Judith. Bad Willie. LC 78-74876. (Illus.). (gr. k-3). Date not set. 3.50 (ISBN 0-89799-175-3); pap. price not set (ISBN 0-89799-176-1). Dandelion Pr. Postponed.

--The Camping Trip. LC 78-73534. (Illus.). (gr. 1-4). Date not set. price not set (ISBN 0-89799-152-4); pap. price not set (ISBN 0-89799-070-6). Dandelion Pr. Postponed.

--Jesus Performs Miracles. LC 78-64419. (Illus.). (gr. k-5). 1979. 3.50 (ISBN 0-89799-119-2); pap. 1.50 (ISBN 0-89799-034-X). Dandelion Pr.

--Rapunzel. LC 78-74131. (Illus.). (gr. 2-5). Date not set. price not set (ISBN 0-89799-168-0); pap. price not set (ISBN 0-89799-167-2). Dandelion Pr. Postponed.

Wolman, Y. Peptides Nineteen Seventy-Four: Proceedings of the Thirteenth European Peptide Symposium, Israel, April, 1974. LC 75-8603. 1975. 44.95 (ISBN 0-470-95957-6). Halsted Pr.

Wolohojian, Albert M., tr. from Armenian. Romance of Alexander the Great. LC 74-84593. (Records of Civilization Ser: No. 82). 1969. 17.50x (ISBN 0-231-03297-8). Columbia U Pr.

Woloszyn, Tony. Fifty Poems for Men & Mice. 1981. 4.95 (ISBN 0-8062-1594-1). Carlton.

Wolotkiewicz, Rita. College Administrator's Handbook. 280p. 1980. text ed. 19.95 (ISBN 0-205-06873-1). Allyn.

Wolpe, Annmarie, jt. ed. see Kuhn, Annette.

Wolpe, Howard. Urban Politics in Nigeria: A Study of Port Harcourt. 1975. 28.50x (ISBN 0-520-02451-6). U of Cal Pr.

Wolpe, Joseph. The Practice of Behavior Therapy. 2nd ed. LC 72-11653. 1974. text ed. 19.75 (ISBN 0-08-017089-7); pap. text ed. 8.75 (ISBN 0-08-017090-0). Pergamon.

--Theme & Variations: A Behavior Therapy Casebook. 200p. 1976. text ed. 21.00 (ISBN 0-08-020422-8); pap. text ed. 12.75 (ISBN 0-08-020421-X). Pergamon.

Wolpers, C. Gallensteine Im Roentgenbild. (Illus.). 66p. 1980. soft cover 20.50 (ISBN 3-8055-2031-X). S Karger.

Wolpert, J., et al. Metropolitan Neighborhoods: Participation & Conflict Over Change. LC 72-75260. (CCG Resource Papers Ser.: No. 16). (Illus.). 1972. pap. text ed. 4.00 (ISBN 0-89291-063-1). Assn Am Geographers.

Wolpert, Stanley. A New History of India. LC 76-42678. (Illus.). 1977. 19.95 (ISBN 0-19-502153-3); pap. 8.95x (ISBN 0-19-502154-1). Oxford U Pr.

Wolpert, Stanley A. Morley & India 1906-1910. 1967. 20.00x (ISBN 0-520-01360-3). U of Cal Pr.

--Tilak & Gokhale: Revolution & Reform in the Making of Modern India. (California Library Reprint Ser.). 1977. 22.75x (ISBN 0-520-03339-6). U of Cal Pr.

Wolpert, Vladimir M. Synthetic Polymers & the Paper Industry. LC 76-6719. (A Pulp & Paper Book). (Illus.). 1977. 42.50 (ISBN 0-87930-056-6). Miller Freeman.

Wolpin, M. D. Military Indoctrination & United States Imperialism. (Occasional Papers: No. 13). 1973. 1.50 o.p. (ISBN 0-686-05790-2). Am Inst Marxist.

--U.S. Intervention in Latin America: An Annotated Bibliography. (Bibliographical Ser.: No. 8). 1972. 1.25 (ISBN 0-89977-030-4). Am Inst Marxist.

Wolpin, Miles D. Militarism & Social Revolution in the Third World. 256p. 1981. text ed. 25.00 (ISBN 0-86598-021-7). Allanheld.

Wolpoff, Milford H. Paleoanthropology. 416p. 1980. text ed. 17.95 (ISBN 0-394-32197-9). Knopf.

Wolseley, Garnet. American Civil War: An English View. Rawley, James A., ed. LC 64-22632. 1964. 9.95 (ISBN 0-8139-0242-8). U Pr of Va.

Wolseley, P. A., jt. auth. see Haslam, S. M.

Wolseley, Pat. A Field Key to the Flowering Plants of Iceland. 60p. 1980. pap. 8.95x (ISBN 0-906191-42-4, Pub. by Thule Pr England). Intl Schol Bk Serv.

Wolski, Thomas R., jt. auth. see Houpt, Katherine A.

Wolstenholme, E. E. Elementary Vectors: SI Units. 3rd ed. LC 77-30311. 1978. text ed. 7.50 (ISBN 0-08-021679-X); pap. text ed. 4.20 (ISBN 0-08-021654-4); tchr's. ed. 2.55 (ISBN 0-08-021655-2). Pergamon.

Wolter, Allan, tr. see Duns Scotus, John.

Wolter, Allen B., jt. ed. see Wippel, John F.

Wolter, Annette & Teubner, Christian. On Tasting Best of Baking. (Orig.). 1980. 14.95 (ISBN 0-89586-041-4); pap. 9.95 (ISBN 0-89586-071-6). H P Bks.

Wolter, Carlo. Figure Skating. (First Books). (Illus.). (gr. 4 up). 1977. s&l 6.45 (ISBN 0-531-00396-5). Watts.

Wolter, Ulf, ed. Rudolf Bahro: Critical Responses. Vale, Michel, tr. from Ger., Fr., Ital. LC 80-5453. 1980. 22.50 (ISBN 0-87332-159-6). M E Sharpe.

Wolters, J. Stochastic Dynamic Properties of Linear Econometric Models. (Lecture Notes in Economics & Mathematical Systems: Vol. 182). (Illus.). 154p. 1981. pap. 15.00 (ISBN 0-387-10240-X). Springer Verlag.

Wolters, Raymond. Negroes & the Great Depression: The Problem of Economic Recovery. Kutler, Stanley E., ed. LC 78-95510. (Contributions in American History: No. 6). 1970. lib. bdg. 19.95 (ISBN 0-8371-2341-0, WON/); pap. 3.95 (ISBN 0-8371-5961-X). Greenwood.

Wolters, Richard A. City Dog. 1975. 8.95 (ISBN 0-87690-148-8). Dutton.

--Family Dog. rev. ed. 1975. 8.95 (ISBN 0-87690-173-9). Dutton.

--Gun Dog. Revolutionary Rapid Training Method. (Illus.). 1961. 11.95 (ISBN 0-525-12005-X). Dutton.

--Living on Wheels: The Secrets of a Safe, Happy, & Comfortable Living in a Motor Home. 1973. 8.95 (ISBN 0-87690-100-3). Dutton.

--Water Dog. 1964. 11.95 (ISBN 0-525-23021-1). Dutton.

Wolterstorff, Nicholas. Educating for Responsible Action. 152p. (Orig.). 1980. pap. 6.95 (ISBN 0-8028-1857-9). Eerdmans.

Woltjer, Lodewijk, ed. Galaxies & the Universe: Lectures. LC 68-20445. (Vetlesen Symposium, 1966). (Illus.). 1968. 15.00x (ISBN 0-231-03110-6). Columbia U Pr.

Woltz, Phebe M. & Arlen, Richard T. College Accounting: An Introduction. 1979. text ed. 12.95 (ISBN 0-07-071551-3, C); tests 7.95 (ISBN 0-07-071555-6); exams 7.95 (ISBN 0-07-071567-X); practice sets 1 4.95 (ISBN 0-07-071553-X); practice set 2 6.50 (ISBN 0-686-52289-3); transparencies, avail. (ISBN 0-07-074795-4) (ISBN 0-07-071552-1). working papers & solutions guide avail. (ISBN 0-07-071556-4). McGraw.

Wolverton, Ruth. Build-It Book of Learning Plaything. (Illus.). 1977. pap. 6.95 (ISBN 0-8306-6915-9, 915). TAB Bks.

Wolvin, Andrew D., jt. auth. see Berko, Roy M.

Wolz, Carl. Bugaku: Japanese Court Dance. LC 76-101136. (D (Monographs), No. 1). (Illus.). viii, 181p. (Orig.). 1971. pap. text ed. 9.00x (ISBN 0-913360-03-1). Asian Music Pub.

Womach, Merrill & Womach, Virginia, trs. Provado Pelo Fogo. (Portugese Bks.). (Port.). 1979. 1.25 (ISBN 0-8297-0842-1). Life Pubs Intl.

Womach, Virginia, jt. tr. see Womach, Merrill.

Womack, David. Alive in Christ. (Radiant Life Ser.). 1975. pap. 1.95 (ISBN 0-88243-888-3, 02-0888, Radiant Books); teacher's ed 2.50 (ISBN 0-88243-162-5, 32-0162). Gospel Pub.

--Breaking the Stained-Glass Barrier. LC 72-11366. 1973. 5.95 o.p. (ISBN 0-06-069680-X, HarpR). Har-Row.

Womack, David A. The Pyramid Principle. LC 76-46312. 1977. pap. 3.50 (ISBN 0-87123-462-9, 210462). Bethany Fell.

Womack, Lester. The Commercial Mauser 'ninety-Eight Sporting Rifle. Angevine, Jay B., Jr., ed. (Illus.). 72p. 1981. 20.00x (ISBN 0-9605530-0-2). Womack Assoc.

Womack, Merril & Womack, Virginia, trs. Probado Por Fuego. (Spanish Bks.). (Span.). 1977. 1.60 (ISBN 0-8297-0773-5). Life Pubs Intl.

Womack, Morris. Church Through the Ages, Pt. 1. (Living Word Paperback Ser.). (Orig.). 1965. Pt. 1. pap. 2.25 (ISBN 0-8344-0052-9). Sweet.

Womack, Virginia, jt. tr. see Womack, Merril.

Women in Transition, Inc. Women in Transition: A Feminist Handbook on Separation & Divorce. LC 75-15728. (Illus.). 1975. pap. 8.95 o.p. (ISBN 0-684-14257-0, SL591, ScribT). Scribner.

Women's Aglow Editors. Reflections: Anthology. 216p. 1979. pap. 6.95 (ISBN 0-930756-48-7, 4230-AD1). Women's Aglow.

Women's Club of Havana. Flowering Plants from Cuban Gardens. (Illus.). 1958. 12.95 (ISBN 0-87599-131-9). S G Phillips.

Women's Co-Operative Guild. Maternity: Letters from Working-Women, Collected by the Women's Co-Operative Guild with a Preface by the Right Hon. Herbert Samuel, M.P., London 1915. LC 79-56940. (The English Working Class Ser.). 1980. lib. bdg. 20.00 (ISBN 0-8240-0127-3). Garland Pub.

Women's Studies Group Centre for Contemporary Cultural Studies. Women Take Issue: Aspects of Women's Subordination. (Illus.). 1979. text ed. 17.00x (ISBN 0-09-133600-7, Hutchinson U Lib); pap. text ed. 8.50x (ISBN 0-09-133601-5, Hutchinson U Lib). Humanities.

Women's Work Force. National Directory of Women's Employment Programs: Who They Are; What They Do. LC 79-117218. (Illus.). 1979. 7.50 (ISBN 0-934966-00-1). WOW Inc.

Wonder, John P., jt. auth. see Espinosa, Aurelio M.

Wonderlin, Richard P., jt. auth. see Lakela, Olga.

Wonderly, William L. Bible Translations for Popular Use. 1968. 1.50 (ISBN 0-8267-0004-7, 08509). United Bible.

Wondersmith, Grant. Inspiration for All Time. LC 78-55989. (Illus.). 1978. softcover 12.95 o.p. (ISBN 0-930490-06-1). Future Shop.

Wong, Alex, jt. auth. see Ramey, Emmett.

Wong, Donna, jt. auth. see Whaley, Lucille F.

Wong, Donna L. & Whaley, Lucille F. Clinical Handbook of Pediatric Nursing. (Illus.). 316p. 1981. pap. text ed. 10.95 (ISBN 0-8016-5545-5). Mosby.

Wong, Douglas L. The Deceptive Hands of Wing Chu. LC 76-55613. (Illus.). 112p. 1977. pap. 4.95 (ISBN 0-86568-027-2). Unique Pubns.

--Kung-Fu: The Way of Life. LC 76-55617. (Illus.). 112p. 1975. pap. 4.95 (ISBN 0-86568-028-0). Unique Pubns.

--Shaolin Fighting. LC 76-55613. (Illus.). 1975. pap. 4.95 (ISBN 0-86568-031-0). Unique Pubns.

Wong, Edward T., jt. auth. see Stoll, Robert R.

Wong, H. Y. Handbook of Essential Formulae & Data on Heat Transfer for Engineers. LC 77-5681. (Illus.). 1977. pap. text ed. 14.50x (ISBN 0-582-46050-6). Longman.

Wong, Harry. Dynamic Tension. LC 80-53545. (Illus.). 144p. 1980. pap. 5.95 (ISBN 0-86568-013-2). Unique Pubns.

Wong, Herbert H. & Vessel, Matthew F. My Goldfish. LC 69-15803. (Illus.). (gr. k-2). 1969 (ISBN 0-201-08720-0, A-W Childrens). PLB 6.95 tchrs' manual o.p. (ISBN 0-685-05057-2). A-W.

--My Ladybug. LC 69-15802. (Illus.). (gr. k-2). 1969. PLB 6.95 (ISBN 0-201-08721-9, A-W Childrens) (ISBN 0-685-05058-0). A-W.

--Our Terrariums. LC 69-15805. (Illus.). (gr. k-2). 1969. PLB 6.95 (ISBN 0-201-08722-7, A-W Childrens). A-W.

Wong, J. Y. Yeh Ming-Ch'en. LC 75-18119. (Studies in Chinese History Literature and Institutions Ser.). (Illus.). 268p. 1976. 49.50 (ISBN 0-521-21023-2). Cambridge U Pr.

Wong, Jade S. No Chinese Stranger. LC 73-14301. (Illus.). 378p. (YA) 1975. 10.95 o.s.i. (ISBN 0-06-014732-6, HarpT). Har-Row.

Wong, K. C., jt. auth. see Cracknell, A. P.

Wong, Ming, jt. auth. see Huard, Pierre.

Wong, Nellie, et al. Dreams in Harrisson Railroad Park. 2 nd ed. Brodine & LaPalma, eds. (Illus.). 1978. 3.75 o.p. (ISBN 0-932716-09-1). Kelsey St Pr.

Wong, Paul. China's Higher Leadership in the Socialist Transition. LC 76-7179. 1976. 25.00 (ISBN 0-02-935600-8). Free Pr.

Wong, Shirleen S. Kung Tzu-Chen. (World Authors Ser.: China: No. 370). 1975. lib. bdg. 12.50 (ISBN 0-8057-6184-5). Twayne.

Wong, Siu-Lun. Sociology & Socialism in Contemporary China. (International Library of Sociology). 1979. 18.00 (ISBN 0-7100-0089-8). Routledge & Kegan.

Wong, Stanford. Professional Blackjack. rev. ed. LC 80-82350. (Illus.). 240p. 1980. 19.95 (ISBN 0-935926-03-8). Pi Yee Pr.

--Stanford Wong's Blackjack Newsletters, 1980, Vol. 2. (Stanford Wong's Blackjack Newsletters Ser.). (Illus.). 222p. Date not set. pap. 29.95 (ISBN 0-935926-05-4). Pi Yee Pr.

--Winning Without Counting. LC 80-10723. (Illus.). 237p. 1980. 50.00 (ISBN 0-935926-01-1). Pi Yee Pr.

Wong, Stanley. The Foundations of Paul Samuelson's Revealed Preference Theory: A Study by the Method of Rational Reconstruction. 1978. 30.00x (ISBN 0-7100-8643-1). Routledge & Kegan.

Wong, Theodore R. Chronological Tables of the Chinese Dynasties. Lyman, E. R., ed. (Studies in Chinese History & Civilization). 103p. 1977. Repr. of 1902 ed. 12.00 (ISBN 0-89093-092-9). U Pubns Amer.

Wong, Timothy C. Wu Ching-Tzu. (World Authors Ser.: No. 495). 1978. lib. bdg. 13.50 (ISBN 0-8057-6336-8). Twayne.

Wong, Warren, ed. see Brauer, Richard.

Wong, Yau-Chuen & Ng, Kung-Fu. Partially Ordered Topological Vector Spaces. (Oxford Mathematical Monographs Ser.). 217p. 1974. 39.00x (ISBN 0-19-853523-6). Oxford U Pr.

Wong-Fraser, Agatha S. Symmetry & Selectivity in the U. S. Defense Policy: A Grand Design or a Major Mistake? LC 80-5610. 172p. 1980. lib. bdg. 17.50 (ISBN 0-8191-1182-1); pap. text ed. 8.95 (ISBN 0-8191-1183-X). U Pr of Amer.

Wongrey, Jan. Southern Vegetable Cookbook. Roberts, Del & Wilkins, Rose, eds. LC 80-50790. (Illus.). 152p. 1981. 5.95 (ISBN 0-87844-045-3). Sandlapper Store.

Wonnacott, Paul. Macroeconomics. rev. ed. 1978. text ed. 18.95 (ISBN 0-256-02032-9). Irwin.

Wonnacott, Ronald J. & Wonnacott, Thomas H. Econometrics. 2nd ed. LC 78-31257. (Probability & Mathematical Statistics Ser.). 1979. text ed. 26.95 (ISBN 0-471-95981-2); solutions manual (ISBN 0-471-07837-9). Wiley.

Wonnacott, Ronald J., jt. auth. see Wonnacott, Thomas H.

Wonnacott, Ronald J., jt. auth. see Wonnacott, Thomas J.

Wonnacott, Thomas H. & Wonnacott, Ronald J. Introductory Statistics. 3rd ed. (Wiley Ser. in Probability & Mathematical Statistics). 1977. text ed. 24.95 (ISBN 0-471-95982-0). Wiley.

--Introductory Statistics for Business & Economics. 2nd ed. LC 76-55773. (Probability & Mathematical Statistics Ser.). 1977. text ed. 24.50 (ISBN 0-471-95980-4, Pub. by Wiley-Hamilton). Wiley.

Wonnacott, Thomas H., jt. auth. see Wonnacott, Ronald J.

Wonnacott, Thomas J. & Wonnacott, Ronald J. Statistics: Discovering Its Power. 448p. 1981. text ed. 16.95 (ISBN 0-471-01412-5). Wiley.

Won Sul Lee. Beyond Ideology: A Christian Response to Sociopolitical Conflict in Asia. 1979. pap. 4.95 o.p. (ISBN 0-89107-163-6, Cornerstone Bks). Good News.

Woo, Juliana J., jt. auth. see Szilard, Paula.

Wood. Fundamentals of Psychological Research. 3rd ed. text ed. 17.95 (ISBN 0-316-95169-2); training manual free (ISBN 0-316-95170-6). Little.

--Reviews of Diagnosis: Oral Medicine, Radiology & Treatment Planning. LC 79-15358. 1979. pap. 15.95 (ISBN 0-8016-5614-1). Mosby.

Wood, A. A Theory of Pay. LC 78-1038. 1978. 29.95 (ISBN 0-521-22073-4). Cambridge U Pr.

--A Theory of Profits. 192p. 1975. 27.50 (ISBN 0-521-20768-1). Cambridge U Pr.

Wood, A. D., jt. auth. see Burghes, D. N.

Wood, A. S., jt. auth. see Blaiklock, E. M.

Wood, A. Skevington. The Burning Heart: John Wesley, Evangelist. LC 78-52837. 1978. pap. 4.95 (ISBN 0-87123-043-7, 210043). Bethany Fell.

Wood, Alan, jt. auth. see Naylor, John.

Wood, Alan, jt. ed. see Wood, David.

Wood, Albert E. The Oligocene Rodents of North America, Vol. 70, Pt. 5. 1980. 8.00 (ISBN 0-87169-705-X). Am Philos.

Wood, Alexander. The Physics of Music. 7th ed. Bowsher, J. M., ed. LC 80-20967. (Illus.). xiv, 258p. 1981. Repr. of 1975 ed. lib. bdg. 28.50x (ISBN 0-313-22644-X, WOPM). Greenwood.

--Problems in Physical Chemistry. 170p. 1974. pap. text ed. 8.50x (ISBN 0-19-855134-7). Oxford U Pr.

Wood, Allen. Karl Marx. (The Arguments of the Philosophers Ser.). 280p. 1981. 25.00 (ISBN 0-7100-0672-1). Routledge & Kegan.

Wood, Allen W., tr. see Kant, Immanuel.

Wood, Audrey. The Moon Flute. 40p. (Orig.). 1980. pap. 6.95 (ISBN 0-914676-44-X). Green Tiger.

Wood, B. J. & Fraser, D. G. Elementary Thermodynamics for Geologists. (Illus.). 1976. pap. text ed. 14.95x (ISBN 0-19-859927-7). Oxford U Pr.

Wood, Barbara. Children & Communication: Verbal & Non-Verbal Language Development. LC 75-22452. (Speech Communication Ser.). (Illus.). 336p. 1976. text ed. 15.95x (ISBN 0-13-131896-9). P-H.

--Childsong. LC 80-1821. 288p. 1981. 12.95 (ISBN 0-385-15560-3). Doubleday.

--Hounds & Jackals. LC 77-12888. (Romantic Suspense Ser.). 1978. 7.95 o.p. (ISBN 0-385-12972-6). Doubleday.

--Hounds & Jackals. 1979. pap. 1.95 (ISBN 0-380-48538-9, 48538). Avon.

--Yesterday's Child. 272p. 1981. pap. 2.50 (ISBN 0-380-50765-X, 50765). Avon.

Wood, Barbara S. Children & Communication: Verbal & Nonverbal Language Development. 2nd ed. (Illus.). 320p. 1981. text ed. 15.95 (ISBN 0-13-131920-5). P-H.

Wood, Bari. The Tribe. 1981. 12.95 (ISBN 0-453-00393-1, H393). NAL.

Wood, Barry. Complete Home Insulation. (Illus.). 1979. 14.95 (ISBN 0-7153-7799-X). David & Charles.

Wood, Basil Charles. The What, When, & Where Guide to Northern California. LC 75-2858. 144p. 1977. pap. 4.95 (ISBN 0-385-05052-6). Doubleday.

--The What, When & Where Guide to Southern California. rev. ed. LC 78-3264. 1979. pap. 3.95 (ISBN 0-385-14043-6). Doubleday.

Wood, Bernard. The Evolution of Early Man. (Illus.). 1978. 12.95 o.p. (ISBN 0-8467-0560-5, Pub. by Two Continents). Hippocrene Bks.

Wood, Bernard D. Applications of Thermodynamics. 3rd ed. (Mechanical Engineering Ser.). 1981. text ed. write for info. A-W.

--Applications of Thermodynamics. (Mechanical Engineering Ser). 1969. text ed. 21.95 o.p. (ISBN 0-201-08740-5). A-W.

Wood, Bruce. The Process of Local Government Reform: 1966 - 1974. (New Local Government Ser.). 1976. text ed. 25.00x (ISBN 0-04-350052-8). Allen Unwin.

Wood, Bryce. San Juan Island: Coastal Place Names & Cartographic Nomenclature. LC 80-17728. (Sponsor Ser.). 280p. (Orig.). 1980. pap. 20.75 (ISBN 0-8357-0526-9, SS-00132). Univ Microfilms.

--The United States & Latin America Wars, 1932-1942. LC 65-25493. 1966. 25.00x (ISBN 0-231-02868-7). Columbia U Pr.

Wood, C. M., et al. The Geography of Pollution: A Study of Greater Manchester. 150p. 1974. 27.00x (ISBN 0-7190-0564-7, Pub. by Manchester U Pr England). State Mutual Bk.

Wood, Charles E. Building Your Dream Boat. (Illus.). 1981. price not set (ISBN 0-87033-259-7, 2597). Cornell Maritime.

Wood, Charles L., et al. The Secondary School Principal: Manager & Supervisor. 1978. text ed. 18.95 (ISBN 0-205-06165-6, 2361655). Allyn.

Wood, Charles M. The Formation of Christian Understanding: An Essay in Theological Hermeneutics. (Orig.). 1981. pap. price not set (ISBN 0-664-24373-8). Westminster.

--Theory & Religious Understanding: A Critique of the Hermeneutics of Joachim Wach. LC 75-26839. (American Academy of Religion. Dissertation Ser.). 1975. pap. 7.50 (ISBN 0-89130-026-0, 010112). Scholars Pr Ca.

Wood, Charles R. Milwaukee Road-West. 2nd ed. LC 72-77009. (Illus.). 192p. 1981. 19.95 (ISBN 0-87564-511-9). Superior Pub.

Wood, Charles T., tr. see Gert, Bernard.

Wood, Christine. Coping with Crisis. 32p. 1980. 0.75 (ISBN 0-930756-52-5, 4240-CC). Women's Aglow.

Wood, Christopher. James Bond & Moonraker. (Orig.). 1979. pap. 2.25 (ISBN 0-515-05344-9). Jove Pubns.

--North to Rabaul. 320p. 1980. pap. 2.75 (ISBN 0-345-28782-7). Ballantine.

--The Spy Who Loved Me. 1977. pap. 1.75 o.s.i. (ISBN 0-446-84544-2). Warner Bks.

--Victorian Panorama: Paintings of Victorian Life. 1977. 41.00 (ISBN 0-571-10780-X, Pub. by Faber & Faber). Merrimack Bk Serv.

Wood, Christopher, ed. Dictionary of Victorian Painters. 2nd ed. (Illus.). 764p. 1978. 95.00 (ISBN 0-902028-72-3, Pub. by Antique Collectors Club England). Gale.

Wood, Clement, ed. Complete Rhyming Dictionary. 1936. 8.95 (ISBN 0-385-00046-4). Doubleday.

Wood, Clement & Goddard, Gloria, eds. Complete Book of Games. 1938. 8.95 o.p. (ISBN 0-385-00041-3). Doubleday.

Wood, Clement, ed. see Buckle, Henry T.

Wood, D. Grammar & L Formas: An Introduction. (Lecture Notes in Computer Science: Vol. 91). 314p. 1980. pap. 19.50 (ISBN 0-387-10233-7). Springer-Verlag.

Wood, D. F., jt. auth. see Elwell, W. T.

Wood, D. L. Studies on Host Selection by Ips confusus (LeConte) (Coleoptera: Scolytidae), with Special Reference to Hopkins' Host Selection Principle. (U. C. Publ. in Entomology: Vol. 27.3). 1963. pap. 2.00x o.p. (ISBN 0-520-09092-6). U of Cal Pr.

Wood, David & Wood, Alan, eds. The Times Guide to the European Parliament. (Illus.). 360p. 1980. 45.00x (ISBN 0-930466-30-6). Meckler Bks.

Wood, Debby. Oh, God, Not Another Beautiful Day! LC 80-69857. (Illus.). 128p. 1980. pap. 3.95 (ISBN 0-89305-032-6). Anna Pub.

Wood, Deborah. The Mistress of Soundcliff Manor. 528p. (Orig.). 1980. pap. 2.95 (ISBN 0-89083-652-3). Zebra.

Wood, Denis, compiled by. Poets in the Garden. (Illus.). 127p. 1979. 15.00 (ISBN 0-7195-3562-X). Transatlantic.

Wood, Dennis W. Principles of Animal Physiology. 2nd ed. LC 74-4090. (Contemporary Biology Ser.). 329p. 1975. 19.50 o.p. (ISBN 0-444-19534-3); pap. text ed. 18.95 (ISBN 0-444-19533-5). Univ Park.

Wood, Derek. This Modern World. 1976. pap. text ed. 8.95x (ISBN 0-435-31951-5). Heinemann Ed.

Wood, Donald F. & Johnson, James C. Contemporary Transportation. 641p. 1980. 18.95 (ISBN 0-87814-112-X). Pennwell Pub.

--Readings in Contemporary Transportation. 256p. 1980. 11.95 (ISBN 0-87814-126-X). Pennwell Pub.

Wood, Dorothy, jt. auth. see Wood, Frances.

Wood, Douglas & Byrne, James. International Business Finance. LC 80-23951. 400p. 1981. text ed. 47.50x (ISBN 0-8419-0663-7). Holmes & Meier.

Wood, E. F. & Szollosi-Nagy, A., eds. Real-Time Forecasting Control of Water Resource Systems: Proceedings of a IIASA Workshop, October, 1979. (IIASA Proceedings Ser: Vol. 8). 1980. 58.00 (ISBN 0-08-024486-6). Pergamon.

Wood, E. G. Added Value: The Key to Prosperity. 148p. 1978. text ed. 22.00x (ISBN 0-220-66349-1, Pub. by Busn Bks England). Renouf.

--Bigger Profits for the Smaller Firm. 2nd ed. 211p. 1978. pap. text ed. 12.25x (ISBN 0-220-66350-5, Pub. by Busn Bks England). Renouf.

--Costing Matters for Managers. 199p. 1974. text ed. 24.50x (Pub. by Busn Bks England). Renouf.

Wood, E. J. Inshore Dinghy Fishing. (Leisure Plan Bks). pap. 2.95 (ISBN 0-600-40083-2). Transatlantic.

--The Living Ocean. 250p. 1980. 29.00x (ISBN 0-85664-026-3, Pub. by Croom Helm England). State Mutual Bk.

Wood, Edward J. Curiosities of Clocks & Watches from the Earliest Times. LC 70-174149. (Illus.). x, 443p. 1974. Repr. of 1866 ed. 20.00 (ISBN 0-8103-3984-6). Gale.

Wood, Elizabeth A. Crystals and Light: An Introduction to Optical Crystallography. LC 76-27458. (Illus.). 156p. 1977. pap. text ed. 3.00 (ISBN 0-486-23431-2). Dover.

Wood, Elizabeth C., jt. auth. see Becker, Paul.

Wood, Ellen. Mind & Politics: An Approach to the Meaning of Liberal & Socialist Individualism. LC 74-153556. 224p. 1972. 18.50x (ISBN 0-520-02029-4). U of Cal Pr.

Wood, Ernest, ed. Zen Dictionary. LC 62-12828. 1962. 4.75 o.p. (ISBN 0-8022-1925-X). Philos Lib.

Wood, F., jt. auth. see Sahade, J.

Wood, Forrest G. Black Scare: The Racist Response to Emancipation & Reconstruction. 1968. 19.50x (ISBN 0-520-01361-1); pap. 2.45 (ISBN 0-520-01664-5, CAL190). U of Cal Pr.

Wood, Frances & Wood, Dorothy. America, Land of Wonders. LC 72-3155. (Illus.). 192p. (gr. 5 up). 1973. 5.95 (ISBN 0-396-06529-5). Dodd.

--At Home in the Wild. LC 76-534619. (gr. 6-9). 1977. 5.95 (ISBN 0-396-07429-4). Dodd.

Wood, Fred M. Fire in My Bones. 2nd ed. 1981. pap. 3.50 (ISBN 0-8054-1219-0). Broadman.

Wood, Ge-Zay. Shantung Question: A Study in Diplomacy & World Politics. (Studies in Chinese History Civilization). 1977. 21.50 (ISBN 0-89093-089-9). U Pubns Amer.

Wood, Geoffrey E. see Griffiths, Brian.

Wood, Gerald L., ed. Animal Facts & Feats. LC 76-51163. (Guinness Family Ser.). 1977. 17.95 (ISBN 0-8069-0104-7); lib. bdg. 15.99 (ISBN 0-8069-0105-5). Sterling.

Wood, Geraldine. Saudi Arabia. (First Bks). (Illus.). (gr. 4-6). 1978. PLB 6.45 s&l (ISBN 0-531-02234-X). Watts.

Wood, Glenn, jt. auth. see West, David.

Wood, Gordon S., ed. The Rising Glory of America, 1760-1820. LC 75-151798. (American Culture Ser). (Illus.). 1971. 8.95 o.s.i. (ISBN 0-8076-0611-1); pap. 4.95 (ISBN 0-8076-0610-3). Braziller.

Wood, H. Graham, jt. auth. see Burgess, Robert H.

Wood, Henry J. Pelargoniums. (Illus.). 1966. 9.95 o.p. (ISBN 0-571-06888-X, Pub. by Faber & Faber). Merrimack Bk Serv.

Wood, Houston, jt. auth. see Mehan, Hugh.

Wood, Ira, jt. auth. see Piercy, Marge.

Wood, J. B. The Gun Digest Book of Firearms Assembly: Centerfire Rifles, Pt. IV. 288p. 1980. pap. 8.95 (ISBN 0-695-81420-6). Follett.

--Gun Digest Book of Firearms Assembly-Disassembly: Automatic Pistols, Pt. I. (Illus.). 320p. 1979. pap. 8.95 (ISBN 0-695-81315-3). Follett.

--Gun Digest Book of Firearms Assembly-Disassembly: Part V, Shotguns. 1980. pap. 8.95 (ISBN 0-695-81510-5). DBI.

--Gun Digest Book of Firearms Assembly-Disassembly: Revolvers, Pt. II. 320p. 1979. pap. 8.95 (ISBN 0-695-81316-1). Follett.

--The Gun Digest Book of Firearms Assembly-Disassembly: Rimfire Rifles, Pt. III. 288p. 1980. pap. 8.95 (ISBN 0-695-81419-2). Follett.

Wood, Jacqueline, jt. auth. see Gilchrist, Joelyn.

Wood, James. A Black Horse Running. LC 74-30874. 1977. 7.95 (ISBN 0-8149-0757-1). Vanguard.

--Friday Run. LC 76-141319. 1969. 6.95 (ISBN 0-8149-0672-9). Vanguard.

--Three Blind Mice. LC 73-188691. 1973. 6.95 (ISBN 0-8149-0705-9). Vanguard.

Wood, James H., ed. Neurobiology of Cerebrospinal Fluid, I. 750p. 1980. 69.50 (ISBN 0-306-40369-2, Plenum Pr). Plenum Pub.

Wood, Jerome H., Jr. Conestoga Crossroads: Lancaster, Pennsylvania, 1730-1790. 1979. 11.00 (ISBN 0-911124-98-5). Pa Hist & Mus.

Wood, Jesse H. & Keenan, Charles. Quimica General. (Span.). 1970. 8.00 (ISBN 0-06-317050-7, IntlDept). Har-Row.

Wood, John, tr. see Moliere, Jean B.

Wood, John E., ed. see Wood, Mel.

Wood, John R. & Serres, Jean. Diplomatic Ceremonial & Protocol. 1970. 30.00x (ISBN 0-231-03138-6). Columbia U Pr.

Wood, John R., jt. auth. see Hippler, Arthur E.

Wood, John R., jt. auth. see Jones, Dorothy M.

Wood, John W., ed. see Munson, Kenneth.

Wood, June. Introductory Algebra. 3rd ed. (Mathematics Ser.). 1977. text ed. 17.95 (ISBN 0-675-08511-X); instr's manual 3.95 (ISBN 0-686-67527-4). Merrill.

Wood, June & Outcalt, David. Elementary Algebra for College Students: A Revision of a First Course in Algebra. (Mathematics Ser.). 1977. text ed. 15.95 (ISBN 0-675-08510-1); instructor's manual 3.95 (ISBN 0-685-74280-6). Merrill.

Wood, Katherine D., jt. auth. see Palmer, Gladys L.

Wood, L. F. How Love Grows in Marriage. 1974. pap. 2.95 o.p. (ISBN 0-8015-3660-X). Dutton.

Wood, L. J., jt. auth. see Lee, Trevor R.

Wood, Laurence W. Pentecostal Grace: A Theology of Christian Experience. 256p. 1980. pap. text ed. 8.95 (ISBN 0-937336-00-9). F Asbury Pub Co.

Wood, Leland Foster. Harmony in Marriage. 1979. 3.95 (ISBN 0-8007-1087-8). Revell.

Wood, Leon J. A Commentary on Daniel. 320p. 1972. 12.95 (ISBN 0-310-34710-6). Zondervan.

--Genesis: A Study Guide Commentary. 160p. 1975. pap. 3.50 (ISBN 0-310-34743-2). Zondervan.

--Survey of Israel's History. LC 70-120041. (Illus.). 1970. text ed. 12.95 (ISBN 0-310-34760-2). Zondervan.

Wood, Louis A. History of Farmers' Movements in Canada: The Origins & Development of Agrarian Protest, 1872-1924. LC 73-91559. (Social History of Canada Ser.). 1975. pap. 6.50 (ISBN 0-8020-6193-1); pap. 6.50. U of Toronto Pr.

Wood, Lucille. Rhythms to Reading, 12 bks. new ed. Incl. Autumn (ISBN 0-8372-0622-7); Camping in the Mountains (ISBN 0-8372-0618-9); December Holidays (ISBN 0-8372-0620-0); Easter Lady (ISBN 0-8372-0623-5); February Holidays (ISBN 0-8372-0613-8); Halloween (ISBN 0-8372-0621-9); Harbor & the Sea (ISBN 0-8372-0617-0); Spring Secret (ISBN 0-8372-0615-4); Springtime Walk (ISBN 0-8372-0614-6); A Summer Day on the Farm (ISBN 0-8372-0616-2); Winter Days (ISBN 0-8372-0612-X); Zoo & the Circus (ISBN 0-8372-0619-7). (ps-3). 1973. text ed. 6.60 ea.; text ed. 15.96 picture songbk. (ISBN 0-8372-0743-6); lp records 8.49 ea.; cassettes 8.97 ea. of bks, records & songbook in bkshelf container 189.00 set, cassette ed. (ISBN 0-8372-0959-5); filmstrip sets, with spirit masters, cassettes, & tchr's guide avail. (ISBN 0-685-29087-5). Bowmar-Noble.

Wood, Lucille, jt. auth. see McLaughlin, Roberta.

Wood, M., tr. see Nicod, Jean.

Wood, M. W. The History of Alameda County, California. facsimile ed. (Illus.). 1000p. Repr. of 1883 ed. simulated lea. 22.50 (ISBN 0-910740-09-7). Holmes.

Wood, Marcia D., jt. auth. see Thompson, Ann M.

Wood, Margaret. The Ninth Windmill Book of One-Act Plays. 1977. pap. text ed. 3.25x o.p. (ISBN 0-435-23959-7). Heinemann Ed.

Wood, Margaret I., jt. auth. see Robertson, Elizabeth C.

Wood, Margaret M. Paths of Loneliness: The Individual Isolated in Modern Society. LC 53-8218. 1953. pap. 5.00x (ISBN 0-231-08503-6). Columbia U Pr.

Wood, Marion M., jt. auth. see Larwood, Laurie.

Wood, Marion N. Delicious & Easy Rice Flour Recipes: A Sequel to Gourmet Food on a Wheat-Free Diet. 160p. 1972. pap. 8.50 (ISBN 0-398-02441-3). C C Thomas.

--Gourmet Food on a Wheat-Free Diet. 128p. 1979. 10.75 (ISBN 0-398-02117-1). C C Thomas.

Wood, Matthew T., jt. auth. see Burkes, E. Jeff.

Wood, Mel. The Big Illusion. Wood, John E., ed. (Illus.). 73p. 1981. 20.00 (ISBN 0-9604644-0-9). Sheephead Bks.

Wood, Merle. The Davis Family: A Personal Recordkeeping Practice Set. 2nd ed. (Illus.). (gr. 10-12). 1981. 6.28 (ISBN 0-07-071623-4, G). McGraw.

Wood, Michael. Fish Cookery. (Illus.). 5.95x o.p. (ISBN 0-8464-0417-6). Beekman Pubs.

--Stendhal. Hough, Graham, ed. LC 73-164669. (Novelists & Their World Ser). 1971. 14.50x (ISBN 0-8014-0680-3); pap. 4.95 (ISBN 0-8014-9124-X). Cornell U Pr.

Wood, Miriam. Congressman Jerry L. Pettis. LC 77-80683. (Destiny Ser.). 1977. pap. 4.95 (ISBN 0-8163-0279-0). Pacific Pr Pub Assn.

--The Little Missionary Truck That Could Do Anything. (Penguin Ser.). 1980. 4.50 (ISBN 0-8280-0050-6, 12450-3). Review & Herald.

--Those Happy Golden Years. 1980. 6.95 (ISBN 0-8280-0062-X, 20380-2). Review & Herald.

Wood, Nancy. Many Winters. LC 74-3554. 80p. (gr. 6 up). 1974. 7.95 (ISBN 0-385-02226-3); limited edition 25.00 (ISBN 0-385-07107-8). Doubleday.
--When Buffalo Free the Mountains. LC 76-42412. (Illus.). 256p. (gr. 10-12). 1980. 14.95 (ISBN 0-385-01474-0). Doubleday.
Wood, Nathan R. The Trinity in the Universe. LC 78-5483. Orig. Title: Secret of the Universe. 1978. Repr. 6.95 (ISBN 0-8254-4013-0). Kregel.
Wood, Norman K., ed. Treatment Planning: A Pragmatic Approach. LC 78-18375. (Illus.). 1978. 21.95 (ISBN 0-8016-5615-X). Mosby.
Wood, Oliver G., Jr. & Barksdale, William C. How to Borrow Money. 144p. 1981. text ed. 13.95 (ISBN 0-442-25204-8). Van Nos Reinhold.
Wood, P., jt. auth. see Jackson, D. D.
Wood, P. W. The Twisted Cubic, with Some Account of the Metrical Properties of the Cubic Hyperbla. (Cambridge Tracts in Mathematics & Mathematical Physics Ser: No. 14). (Illus.). 1960. Repr. of 1913 ed. 7.50 o.s.i. (ISBN 0-02-854980-5). Hafner.
Wood, Pamela. The Salt Book. LC 76-53419. 480p. 1977. pap. 5.95 (ISBN 0-385-11423-0, Anchor Pr); pap. 5.95 (ISBN 0-385-11423-0, Anch). Doubleday.
Wood, Pamela, ed. Salt Two: Boatbuilding, Sailmaking, Island People, River Driving, Bean Hold Beans, Wooden Paddles, & More Yankee Doings. LC 80-553. (Illus.). 448p. 1980. 14.95 (ISBN 0-385-14346-X, Anchor Pr); pap. 7.95. Doubleday.
Wood, Patrick M., jt. auth. see Sutton, Antony C.
Wood, Paul & Schwartz, Bernard. How to Get Your Children to Do What You Want Them to Do. LC 76-54846. 1977. 7.95 o.p. (ISBN 0-13-409797-1). P-H.
Wood, Paul W. Stained Glass Crafting. rev. ed. LC 67-27750. (Illus.). (gr. 10 up). 1971. 8.95 (ISBN 0-8069-5094-3); PLB 8.29 (ISBN 0-8069-5095-1). Sterling.
--Starting with Stained Glass. (Little Craft Book Ser.). (Illus.). 48p. (gr. 6 up). 1973. 4.95 o.p. (ISBN 0-8069-5244-X); PLB 5.89 o.p. (ISBN 0-8069-5245-8). Sterling.
--Working with Stained Glass. LC 80-54350. (Illus.). 104p. 1981. 9.95; lib. bdg. 9.29 (ISBN 0-8069-5441-8); pap. 5.95 (ISBN 0-8069-8966-1). Sterling.
Wood, Peter. The Caribbean Isles. (The American Wilderness Ser). (Illus.). 184p. 1975. 12.95 (ISBN 0-8094-1213-6). Time-Life.
--Caribbean Isles. LC 74-24663. (American Wilderness Ser.). (Illus.). 184p. (gr. 6 up). 1975. lib. bdg. 11.97 (ISBN 0-8094-1214-4). Silver.
--The Spanish Main. (The Seafarers Ser.). (Illus.). 1979. lib. bdg. 11.97 (ISBN 0-8094-2720-6); kivar bdg. 9.96 (ISBN 0-8094-2721-4). Silver.
--Switching Power Converters. 464p. 1981. text ed. 26.50 (ISBN 0-442-24333-2). Van Nos Reinhold.
Wood, Peter, jt. auth. see Jackson, D.
Wood, Peter, jt. auth. see Kulicke, Barbara.
Wood, Peter H. Black Majority: Negroes in Colonial South Carolina from 1670 Through the Stono Rebellion. 384p. 1975. pap. 4.95 (ISBN 0-393-00777-4, Norton Lib). Norton.
Wood, Phyllis A. This Time Count Me In. LC 80-15068. (A Highway Bk.). 1980. 8.95 (ISBN 0-664-32665-X). Westminster.
Wood, R. & Skurnik, L. S. Item Banking. (General Ser.). (Illus.). 184p. 1969. pap. text ed. 15.00x (ISBN 0-901225-10-X, NFER). Humanities.
Wood, Renate. Points of Entry. 20p. (Orig.). 1981. pap. price not set (ISBN 0-936600-01-2). Riverstone Foothills.
Wood, Reuben E. Introduction to Chemical Thermodynamics. LC 79-84475. (Illus.). 1970. text ed. 34.50x (ISBN 0-89197-238-2); pap. text ed. 18.95x (ISBN 0-89197-798-8). Irvington.
Wood, Robert. Pleasure Packing. (Encore Edition). 1972. pap. 1.95 (ISBN 0-684-16935-5, SL577, ScribT). Scribner.
Wood, Robert C. The Necessary Majority: Middle America & the Urban Crisis. LC 70-183228. (Radner Lecture Ser). 108p. 1972. 12.50x (ISBN 0-231-03617-5). Columbia U Pr.
Wood, Robert E., jt. auth. see Mandell, Muriel.
Wood, Robert S. Desolation Wilderness. 2nd rev. ed. (Illus.). 256p. 1975. pap. 4.95 (ISBN 0-89815-044-2). Ten Speed Pr.
--Mountain Cabin. LC 76-30878. (Illus.). 1977. pap. 4.95 o.p. (ISBN 0-87701-090-0). Chronicle Bks.
--Pleasure Packing for the Eighties. 2nd rev. ed. (Illus.). 256p. 1981. pap. 6.95 (ISBN 0-89815-035-3). Ten Speed Pr.
Wood, Rulon K. Community Resources. Duane, James E., ed. LC 80-20963. (The Instructional Media Library: Vol. 2). (Illus.). 96p. 1981. 13.95 (ISBN 0-87778-162-1). Educ Tech Pubns.
Wood, Ruzena. The Palace of the Moon & Other Tales from Czechoslovakia. LC 80-2687. (Illus.). 144p. (gr. 2-7). 1981. 9.95 (ISBN 0-233-97206-4). Andre Deutsch.
Wood, Samuel see Newbery, F.
Wood, Susan. Bazaar. LC 80-14985. 64p. 1981. 10.95 (ISBN 0-03-057856-6, Owl Bk); pap. 5.95 (ISBN 0-03-057709-8). HR&W.
Wood, T. M. George Du Maurier: The Satirist of the Victorians. 198p. 1980. Repr. of 1913 ed. lib. bdg. 35.00 (ISBN 0-89760-913-1). Telegraph Bks.
Wood, Thomas. An Institute of the Laws of England: Or Laws of England in Their Natural Order According to Common Use. Berkowitz, David S. & Thorne, Samuel E., eds. LC 77-86569. (Classics of English Legal History in the Modern Era Ser.: Vol. 71). 1979. lib. bdg. 55.00 (ISBN 0-8240-3058-3). Garland Pub.
Wood, V., jt. auth. see Pilch, Michael.
Wood, W. B. Biochemistry: A Problems Approach. 2nd ed. 1981. 12.95; solutions manual 3.95. Benjamin-Cummings.
Wood, W. B., et al. Biochemistry: A Problems Approach. 1974. 12.95 o.p. (ISBN 0-8053-9850-3); tchr's suppl. 2.50 o.p. (ISBN 0-8053-9853-8); research games suppl. 1.75 o.p. (ISBN 0-8053-9854-6). Benjamin-Cummings.
Wood, W. G., jt. auth. see Martin, D. G.
Wood, W. Raymond & Liberty, Margot, eds. Anthropology on the Great Plains. LC 79-28369. (Illus.). viii, 306p. 1980. 25.00x (ISBN 0-8032-4708-7). U of Nebr Pr.
Wood, Wendy. The Silver Chanter: Traditional Scottish Tales & Legends. LC 80-670272. (Illus.). 108p. (gr. 4-7). 1980. 10.95 (ISBN 0-7011-2448-2, Pub. by Chatto Bodley Jonathan). Merrimack Bk Serv.
Wood, William see Gabriel, Ralph H.
Wood, William see Johnson, Allen & Nevins, Allan.
Wood, William A. Electronic Journalism. LC 67-25305. 1967. 15.00x (ISBN 0-231-02875-X). Columbia U Pr.
Wood, William B. & Sticht, Frank D. Heart & Vascular Systems Basic Sciences. 2nd ed. 1977. spiral bdg. 11.50 (ISBN 0-87488-212-5). Med Exam.
Woodall, Irene R. Comprehensive Dental Hygiene Care. LC 80-15145. (Illus.). 506p. 1980. text ed. 19.95 (ISBN 0-8016-5624-9). Mosby.
--Leadership, Management & Role Delineation: Issues for the Dental Team. LC 77-8533. (Illus.). 1977. pap. 13.95 (ISBN 0-8016-5621-4). Mosby.
Woodard, Gloria, jt. auth. see MacCann, Donnarae.
Woodard, Gloria, jt. ed. see MacCann, Donnarae.
Woodard, James & Purdy, Linda. One to Ten Count Again. (Illus.). (ps). 1972. PLB 5.51 (ISBN 0-914844-07-5). J Alden.
Woodard, Kim. The International Energy Relations of China. LC 77-92949. (Illus.). 744p. 1980. 50.00x (ISBN 0-8047-1008-2). Stanford U Pr.
Woodard, Thomas K. & Greenstein, Blanche. Crib Quilts: And Other Small Wonders. Nelson, Cyril T., ed. (Illus.). 144p. 1981. 27.95 (ISBN 0-525-20565-9); pap. 15.95 (ISBN 0-525-47628-8). Dutton.
Woodason, V. J. Scale Model Aircraft in Wood. (Illus.). 64p. (Orig.). 1978. pap. 5.00x (ISBN 0-905418-27-1). Intl Pubns Serv.
Woodberry, George E. Edgar Allan Poe. LC 80-19049. (American Men & Women of Letters Ser.). 360p. 1980. pap. 5.95 (ISBN 0-87754-152-3). Chelsea Hse.
--History of Wood-Engraving. LC 69-17490. 1969. Repr. of 1883 ed. 15.00 (ISBN 0-8103-3890-4). Gale.
--Nathaniel Hawthorne, 30 vols. LC 80-23480. (American Men & Women of Letters Ser.). 304p. 1981. pap. 4.95 (ISBN 0-87754-154-X). Chelsea Hse.
--Nathaniel Hawthorne. LC 67-23888. 1967. Repr. of 1902 ed. 20.00 (ISBN 0-8103-3043-1). Gale.
Woodbine. Antibiotics & Antibiosis in Agriculture. LC 77-30021. (Nottingham Easter School Ser.). 1978. text ed. 64.95 (ISBN 0-408-70917-0). Butterworths.
Woodbine, M., ed. Problems of Listeriosis: Proceedings of the 5th International Symposium. (Illus.). 320p. 1975. text ed. 16.25x (ISBN 0-7185-1143-3, Leicester). Humanities.
Woodbridge, F. J. The Son of Apollo: Themes of Plato. 272p. (gr. 7 up). 1972. Repr. of 1929 ed. 12.50x (ISBN 0-8196-0278-7). Biblo.
Woodbridge, George. Reform Bill of 1832. LC 78-107301. (AHM Europe Since 1500 Ser.). (Orig.). 1970. pap. 5.95x (ISBN 0-88295-772-4). AHM Pub.
Woodbridge, George, jt. auth. see DeBartolo, Dick.
Woodbridge, George, jt. auth. see Meglin, Nick.
Woodbridge, George, jt. auth. see Siegel, Larry.
Woodbridge, Hensley C. Reuben Dario: A Selective Classified & Annotated Bibliography. LC 74-30490. 1975. 12.00 (ISBN 0-8108-0790-4). Scarecrow.
Woodbridge, Hensley C., compiled by. Benito Perez Galdos: A Selective Annotated Bibliography. LC 75-2045. 333p. 1975. 15.00 (ISBN 0-8108-0800-5). Scarecrow.
Woodbridge, Homer E. G. B. Shaw: Creative Artist. LC 63-14294. (Arcturus Books Paperbacks). 193p. 1965. pap. 1.65 (ISBN 0-8093-0159-8). S Ill U Pr.
Woodbridge, Sally, ed. Bay Area Houses. (Illus.). 1979. pap. 13.95 (ISBN 0-19-502527-X, GB568, GB). Oxford U Pr.
Woodbridge, Sally, et al. Bay Area Houses. LC 76-9261. (Illus.). 1976. 39.95 (ISBN 0-19-502084-7). Oxford U Pr.
Woodbridge, Sally B. & Montgomery, Roger. A Guide to Achitecture in Washington State: An Environmental Perspective. LC 80-51076. (Illus.). 500p. 1980. 25.00 (ISBN 0-295-95761-1); pap. 12.95 (ISBN 0-295-95779-4). U of Wash Pr.
Woodburn, John H. Taking Things Apart & Puttings Things Together. LC 76-20448. 1976. 6.00 o.p. (ISBN 0-8412-0314-8); pap. 2.50 (ISBN 0-8412-0314-8). Am Chemical.
Woodburn, Margaret. Social Implications of Spina Bifida. (General Ser.). (Illus.). 285p. 1975. pap. text ed. 23.50x (ISBN 0-85633-061-2, NFER). Humanities.
Woodbury, Angus M., et al. A Survey of Vegetation in the Curecanti Reservoir Basins. (University of Utah Anthropological Papers: No. 56). 1962. pap. 8.00x (ISBN 0-87480-173-7). U of Utah Pr.
Woodbury, D. M., et al, eds. Antiepileptic Drugs. LC 70-181310. (Illus.). 1972. 31.50 (ISBN 0-911216-29-4). Raven.
Woodbury, Dixon M., jt. auth. see Aird, Robert B.
Woodbury, Marda. Selecting Materials for Instruction: Issues & Policies. LC 79-18400. (Illus.). 1979. lib. bdg. 22.50 (ISBN 0-87287-197-5). Libs Unl.
--Selecting Materials for Instruction: Media & the Curriculum. LC 79-18400. (Illus.). 1980. lib. bdg. 22.50 (ISBN 0-87287-212-2). Libs Unl.
--Selecting Materials for Instruction: Subject Areas & Implementation. LC 79-18400. (Illus.). 1980. lib. bdg. 22.50x (ISBN 0-87287-213-0). Libs Unl.
Woodbury, Richard B. Alfred V. Kidder. LC 72-10082. (Leaders of Modern Anthropology Ser.). 225p. 1973. 15.00x (ISBN 0-231-03484-9); pap. 5.00x (ISBN 0-231-03485-7). Columbia U Pr.
Woodbury, Robert A., et al. Pharmacology Review. 4th ed. 1981. pap. 8.50 (ISBN 0-87488-205-2). Med Exam.
Woodbury, Thomas C., jt. auth. see Grange, William J.
Woodcock, Alexander. Catastrophe Theory. 1980. pap. 2.75 (ISBN 0-380-48397-1, 48397). Avon.
Woodcock, Alexander & Davis, Monte. Castastrophe Theory. 1979. pap. 2.75 (ISBN 0-380-48397-1, 48397). Avon.
Woodcock, George. Dawn & the Darkest Hour: A Study of Aldous Huxley. 1972. 9.95 (ISBN 0-571-08939-9, Pub. by Faber & Faber). Merrimack Bk Serv.
--Herbert Read: The Stream & the Source. 1972. 11.95 (ISBN 0-571-08656-X, Pub. by Faber & Faber). Merrimack Bk Serv.
--Incas & Other Men: Travels in the Andes. (Illus., Orig.). 1965. pap. 4.95 (ISBN 0-571-06118-4, Pub. by Faber & Faber). Merrimack Bk Serv.
--Into Tibet: The Early British Explorers. (Great Travellers Ser.). (Illus.). 1971. 6.95 o.p. (ISBN 0-571-08394-3, Pub. by Faber & Faber). Merrimack Bk Serv.
--The Kestrel & Other Poems of Past & Present. 54p. 1980. signed ed 14.95x (ISBN 0-904461-40-8, Pub. by Ceolfrith Pr England); pap. 5.95x (ISBN 0-904461-39-4). Intl Schol Bk Serv.
--The World of Canadian Writing: Critiques & Recollections. LC 80-15497. 312p. 1981. pap. price not set (ISBN 0-295-95808-1). U of Wash Pr.
Woodcock, George, ed. The Anarchist Reader. 1977. text ed. 23.75x (ISBN 0-391-00709-2). Humanities.
--Poets & Critics: Essays from Canadian Literature 1966-1974. 256p. 1974. pap. 7.50x (ISBN 0-19-540224-3). Oxford U Pr.
Woodcock, Mike. Team Development Manual. LC 78-20789. 1979. 24.95x (ISBN 0-470-26636-8). Halsted Pr.
Woodcock, Mike & Francis, Dave. Unblocking Your Organization. LC 78-62929. Orig. Title: People at Work. 254p. 1979. pap. 15.50 (ISBN 0-88390-148-X). Univ Assocs.
Wooden, John, et al. The Wooden-Sharman Method: A Guide to Winning Basketball. (Illus.). 128p. 1975. 9.95 o.s.i. (ISBN 0-02-631300-6). Macmillan.
Wooden, John R. Practical Modern Basketball. 2nd ed. LC 79-13731. 1980. text ed. 17.95 (ISBN 0-471-05865-3). Wiley.
Wooden, Kenneth, ed. The Children of Jonestown. (Paperbacks Ser.). 1980. pap. 4.95 (ISBN 0-07-071641-2, GB). McGraw.
Woodfield, A. Teleology. LC 75-44574. (Illus.). 240p. 1976. 32.95 (ISBN 0-521-21102-6). Cambridge U Pr.
Woodfin, Mrs. A. The Auction: A Modern Novel, 1760, 2 vols. in 1. Shugrue, Michael F., ed. (The Flowering of the Novel, 1740-1775 Ser: Vol. 54). 1974. lib. bdg. 50.00x (ISBN 0-8240-1153-8). Garland Pub.
Woodfin, Yandall. With All Your Mind. 272p. 1980. pap. 8.95 (ISBN 0-687-45839-0). Abingdon.
Woodford, Jim, jt. auth. see Stirling, David.
Woodford, Peggy. Mozart: His Life & Times. (Illustrated Lives & Times of the Composers). (Illus.). 1978. 9.95 (ISBN 0-8467-0419-6, Pub. by Two Continents); pap. 5.95 (ISBN 0-8467-0420-X). Hippocrene Bks.
--Rise of the Raj. (Illus.). 1978. text ed. 22.25x (ISBN 0-391-00867-6). Humanities.
--Schubert, His Life & Times. expanded ed. (Illus.). 192p. Repr. of 1978 ed. 19.95 (ISBN 0-87666-640-3). Paganiniana Pubns.
--Schubert: His Life & Times. LC 78-53223. (Life & Times of the Composer Ser.). (Illus.). 1978. 16.95 (ISBN 0-8467-0489-7, Pub. by Two Continents); pap. 5.95 (ISBN 0-8467-0462-5). Hippocrene Bks.
Woodford, Protase E. & Kernan, Doris. Bridges to English, Bk. 1. Rebisz, J., ed. LC 80-21012. (Illus.). 144p. 1980. pap. text ed. 5.64 (ISBN 0-07-034481-7, W); write for info. tchrs. ed. (ISBN 0-07-034482-5); wkbk. 3.52 (ISBN 0-07-034483-3); cassettes avail. (ISBN 0-07-034484-1); cue cards avail. (ISBN 0-07-034485-X); tests avail. (ISBN 0-07-034486-8). McGraw.
Woodford, Susan. The Parthenon. (Cambridge Introduction to the History of Mankind Ser.). Date not set. pap. price not set (ISBN 0-521-22629-5). Cambridge U Pr.
Woodforde, John. Bricks: To Build a House with. (Illus.). 240p. 1975. 15.00 (ISBN 0-7100-8105-7). Routledge & Kegan.
--Observer's Book of Furniture. (Observer Bks.). (Illus.). 1977. 3.95 o.p. (ISBN 0-684-15217-7, ScribT). Scribner.
--The Story of the Bicycle. (Illus.). 1977. pap. 4.95 (ISBN 0-7100-8644-X). Routledge & Kegan.
--The Truth About Cottages. (Illus.). 1979. pap. 6.95 (ISBN 0-7100-0165-7). Routledge & Kegan.
Woodgate, H. S. Planning by Network. 330p. 1977. text ed. 24.50x (ISBN 0-220-66312-2, Pub. by Busn Bks England). Renouf.
Woodger, J. H., tr. see Tarski, Alfred.
Woodhall, Maureen. Cost-Benefit Analysis in Educational Planning. (Fundamentals of Educational Planning Ser., No. 13). (Orig.). 1970. pap. 6.00 (ISBN 92-803-1038-0, U105, UNESCO). Unipub.
--Economic Aspects of Education. (General Ser). 130p. (Orig.). 1972. pap. text ed. 8.00x (ISBN 0-85633-011-6, NFER). Humanities.
Woodham-Smith, Cecil. Great Hunger. 1980. pap. 8.95 (ISBN 0-525-47643-1). Dutton.
Woodhead, Daniel & Beene, Wayne, eds. A Dictionary of Iraqi Arabic: Arabic-English. (Richard Slade Harrell Arabic Ser). 509p. 1967. pap. 8.50 (ISBN 0-87840-003-6). Georgetown U Pr.
Woodhead-Faulkner, ed. The City Directory 1980-81: An Investors Chronicle Guide to Financial & Professional Services Allied to the City of London. 432p. 1980. 45.00x (ISBN 0-85941-135-4, Pub. by Woodhead-Faulkner England); pap. 36.00x (ISBN 0-85941-136-2). State Mutual Bk.
Woodhead, H. G., et al. Extraterritoriality in China: The Case Against Abolition. LC 78-74343. 189p. (The growth & decline of rural industrial enterprise in North China. Extent & effects of industrialization in China the modern Chinese economy). 1980. lib. bdg. 22.00 (ISBN 0-8240-4280-8). Garland Pub.
Woodhead, Martin. Intervening in Disadvantage: A Challenge for Nursery Education. (General Ser.). (Orig.). 1976. pap. text ed. 8.25x (ISBN 0-85633-095-7, NFER). Humanities.
Woodhead, Martin, ed. An Experiment in Nursery Education. (Orig.). 1976. pap. text ed. 13.75x (ISBN 0-85633-122-8, NFER). Humanities.
Woodhead, R. W., jt. auth. see Anderson, S. D.
Woodhead, Ronald W., jt. auth. see Halpin, Daniel W.
Woodhouse, Barbara. Book of Dogs. 7.50x (ISBN 0-392-06367-0, SpS). Soccer.
--Dog Training My Way. LC 72-82833. (Illus.). 128p. 1981. pap. 5.95 (ISBN 0-8128-6082-9). Stein & Day.
Woodhouse, C. M., tr. see Wolfgang, Leonhard.
Woodhouse, Frederick. Opera for Amateurs. 1951. 6.95 (ISBN 0-234-77225-5). Dufour.

Woodhouse, J. Castiglione: A Reassessment of the Courtier. (Writers of Italy: No. 7). 229p. 1979. 12.50x (ISBN 0-85224-346-4, Pub. by Edinburgh U Pr Scotland). Columbia U Pr.
Woodhouse, J. M. Science for Textile Designers. 1975. 14.95 o.p. (ISBN 0-236-31047-X, Pub. by Paul Elek); pap. 9.95x (ISBN 0-236-31048-8). Merrimack Bk Serv.
Woodhouse, Mark. Preface to Philosophy. 2nd ed. 1979. pap. text ed. 6.95x (ISBN 0-534-00738-4). Wadsworth Pub.
Woodhouse, Nicholas. Geometric Quantization. (Oxford Mathematical Monographs). (Illus.). 400p. 1980. 74.00 (ISBN 0-19-853528-7). Oxford U Pr.
Woodhouse, Robert. History of the Calculus of Variations in the 18th Century. LC 64-20969. 7.95 (ISBN 0-8284-0177-2). Chelsea Pub.
Woodhouse, S. C. English-Greek Dictionary: A Vocabulary of the Attic Language. 1971. Repr. of 1910 ed. 45.00 (ISBN 0-7100-2324-3). Routledge & Kegan.
Woodin, J. C. & Hayes, Louis. Home & Building Maintenance. 14.00 (ISBN 0-87345-466-9). McKnight.
Wooding, Charles J. Evolving Culture: A Cross-Cultural Study of Surinam, West Africa & the Caribbean. LC 80-5612. 343p. 1981. lib. bdg. 21.75 (ISBN 0-8191-1377-8); pap. text ed. 12.00 (ISBN 0-8191-1378-6). U Pr of Amer.
Woodiwiss, Kathleen E. The Flame & the Flower. 1976. pap. 2.50 (ISBN 0-380-00525-5, 46276). Avon.
Woodland, A. W., ed. Petroleum & the Continental Shelf of North-West Europe, Vol. I: Geology. LC 75-14329. 501p. 1975. 65.95 (ISBN 0-470-95993-2). Halsted Pr.
Woodland, Les. Cycle Racing: Training to Win. (Illus.). 144p. 1976. 12.50 (ISBN 0-7207-0788-9). Transatlantic.
--Dope: The Use of Drugs in Sport. LC 80-66086. (Illus.). 164p. 1980. 22.50 (ISBN 0-7153-7894-5). David & Charles.
Woodley, Richard. Ark of Doom. 1978. pap. 1.50 o.s.i. (ISBN 0-440-15927-X). Dell.
--Deadly Encounter. 192p. (Orig.). 1980. pap. 1.95 (ISBN 0-515-04844-5). Jove Pubns.
--It's Alive. 1977. pap. 1.95 (ISBN 0-345-27465-2). Ballantine.
--The Jazz Singer. 192p. (Orig.). 1980. pap. 2.25 (ISBN 0-553-13236-9). Bantam.
--Killer Spores. 1978. pap. 1.50 o.s.i. (ISBN 0-440-15926-1). Dell.
--Man from Atlantis: No. 1. 1977. pap. 1.50 o.s.i. (ISBN 0-440-15368-9). Dell.
--Man from Atlantis: No. 2. pap. 1.50 o.s.i. (ISBN 0-440-15369-7). Dell.
--One Last Season. (Orig.). 1981. pap. 2.95 (ISBN 0-440-16698-5). Dell.
--Slap Shot. 1977. pap. 1.50 o.p. (ISBN 0-425-03339-2). Berkley Pub.
Woodman, A. J., ed. Velleius Paterculus, the Tiberian Narrative. LC 76-22985. (Classical Texts & Commentaries Ser: No. 19). 1977. 49.50 (ISBN 0-521-21397-5). Cambridge U Pr.
Woodman, A. J. & West, D., eds. Quality & Pleasure in Latin Poetry. 184p. 1975. 28.50 (ISBN 0-521-20532-8). Cambridge U Pr.
Woodman, Bill. Fish & Moose News. LC 79-27794. (Illus.). 128p. 1980. pap. 6.95 (ISBN 0-396-07825-7). Dodd.
--Whose Birthday Is It? Anderson, Jennifer, ed. LC 79-2776. (Illus.). 48p. 1980. 7.95 (ISBN 0-690-04005-9, TYC-J); PLB 7.89 (ISBN 0-690-04006-7). T Y Crowell.
Woodman, Natalie J. & Lenna, Harry R. Counseling with Gay Men & Women: A Guide for Facilitating Positive Life-Styles. LC 80-8002. (Social & Behavioral Science Ser.). 1980. text ed. 12.95x (ISBN 0-87589-468-2). Jossey-Bass.
Woodman, Ross G. Apocalyptic Vision in the Poetry of Shelley. LC 64-5257. 1964. 15.00x o.p. (ISBN 0-8020-5136-7). U of Toronto Pr.
Woodman, T., jt. ed. see West, D.
Woodmansee, Keith. Shot History of Aviation. LC 65-14328. 1965. 4.95 o.p. (ISBN 0-8168-8400-5); pap. 4.95 o.p. (ISBN 0-8168-8404-8). Aero.
Woodman-Smith, Cecil. Queen Victoria. 1974. pap. 1.75 o.s.i. (ISBN 0-440-17318-3). Dell.
Woodress, James. Willa Cather: Her Life & Art. LC 71-124673. (Illus.). 228p. 1975. pap. 3.50 (ISBN 0-8032-5815-1, BB 600, Bison). U of Nebr Pr.
Woodress, James, ed. American Fiction, Nineteen Hundred to Nineteen-Fifty: A Guide to Information Sources. LC 73-17501. (American Literature, English Literature, & World Literatures in English Information Guide Ser.: Vol. 1). 246p. 1974. 30.00 (ISBN 0-8103-1201-8). Gale.
Woodrew, Greta. On a Slide of Light. 224p. 1981. 12.95 (ISBN 0-02-631390-1). Macmillan.
Woodring, Carl. Virginia Woolf. LC 66-19554. (Columbia Essays on Modern Writers Ser.: No. 18). (Orig.). 1966. pap. 2.00 (ISBN 0-231-02829-6, MW18). Columbia U Pr.
Woodring, Carl R. Politics in the Poetry of Coleridge. 1961. 25.00 (ISBN 0-299-02440-7). U of Wis Pr.
Woodroffe. The Adventures of the Hole Eating Duck Tinker. 1980. cancelled (ISBN 0-8120-5395-8). Barron.
Woodroffe, John. Introduction to Tantra Shastra. 7.50 (ISBN 0-89744-114-1, Pub. by Ganesh & Co. India). Auromere.
--Principles of Tantra, 2 vols. 1979. 29.50 (ISBN 0-89744-129-X, Pub. by Ganesh & Co India). Auromere.
--Sakti & Sakta. 16.95 (ISBN 0-89744-116-8, Pub. by Ganesh & Co. India). Auromere.
--The World As Power. new ed. Bd. with Mahamaya: Power As Consciousness. Woodroffe, John & Mukhyopadhyaya, Pramatha N.. 1974. 13.95 (ISBN 0-89744-119-2, Pub. by Ganesh & Co. India). Auromere.
Woodroffe, John, tr. Great Liberation (Mahanirvana Tantra) 7.95 o.p. (ISBN 0-89744-113-3, Pub. by Ganesh & Co. India). Auromere.
Woodroof, J. G. Peanuts: Production, Processing, Products. 2nd ed. (Illus.). 330p. 1973. text ed. 29.50 (ISBN 0-87055-135-3). AVI.
--Tree Nuts. 2nd ed. (Illus.). 1979. lib. bdg. 54.00 (ISBN 0-87055-254-6). AVI.
Woodroof, J. G. & Luh, B. S. Commercial Fruit Processing. (Illus.). 710p. 1975. lib. bdg. 27.00 (ISBN 0-87055-178-7). AVI.
Woodroof, J. G. & Phillips, G. Frank. Beverages: Carbonated & Noncarbonated. rev. ed. (Illus.). 1981. text ed. 45.00 (ISBN 0-87055-381-X). AVI.
--Beverages: Carbonated & Noncarbonated. rev. ed. (Illus.). 1981. lib. bdg. 45.00 (ISBN 0-87055-381-X). AVI.
Woodroof, J. G., jt. auth. see Luh, B. S.
Woodroof, Jasper G. Coconuts: Production, Processing, Products. 2nd ed. (Illus.). 1979. lib. bdg. 28.50 (ISBN 0-87055-276-7). AVI.
Woodroof, Jasper G., jt. auth. see Tressler, Donald K.
Woodroof, M. G., 3rd & Fonseca, John R. Automobile Insurance & No-Fault Law. LC 74-76324. 1974. 47.50 (ISBN 0-686-14511-9). Lawyers Co-Op.
Woodroofe, Kathleen. From Charity to Social Work in England & the United States. LC 65-49593. 1962. pap. 6.50 (ISBN 0-8020-6118-4). U of Toronto Pr.
Woodrow, Ralph. Babylon Mystery Religion: Ancient & Modern. (Illus.). 1966. 3.00 (ISBN 0-916938-00-X). R Woodrow.
Woodruff, A. Bond. Directed Readings: Introduction to Psychology. 2nd ed. 144p. 1980. pap. text ed. 5.95 (ISBN 0-8403-2243-7). Kendall-Hunt.
Woodruff, A. W. see Lincicome, David R.
Woodruff, D. P. The Solid-Liquid Interface. LC 72-91362. (Solid State Science Ser.). (Illus.). 150p. 1973. 29.95 (ISBN 0-521-20123-3). Cambridge U Pr.
--The Solid-Liquid Interface. LC 72-91362. (Cambridge Solid State Science). (Illus.). 182p. 1980. pap. 11.95 (ISBN 0-521-29971-3). Cambridge U Pr.
Woodruff, David S., jt. auth. see Atchley, W. R.
Woodruff, H. Charles. Shortwave Listerner's Guide. 8th ed. LC 79-67132. 1980. pap. 5.95 (ISBN 0-672-21655-8). Bobbs.
Woodruff, Leroy L. Cooking the Dutch Oven Way. (Illus.). 144p. 1980. pap. 4.95 (ISBN 0-934802-01-7). Ind Camp Supply.
Woodruff, Michael F. The Interaction of Cancer & Host: Its Therapeutic Significance. 1980. 46.50 (ISBN 0-8089-1265-8). Grune.
Woodruff, Robert B., et al, eds. Marketing Management Perspectives & Applications. 1976. pap. text ed. 9.95x o.p. (ISBN 0-256-01843-X). Irwin.
Woodruff, Una. Inventorum Natura. LC 79-63799. (Illus.). 128p. 1981. pap. 8.95 (ISBN 0-06-090815-7, CN 815, CN). Har-Row.
Woodruff, William. America's Impact on the World: A Study of the Role of the U. S. in the World Economy 1750-1970. LC 74-23474. 296p. 1975. 19.95 (ISBN 0-470-95963-0). Halsted Pr.
Woods, jt. auth. see Fogel, Catherine I.
Woods, A. E. & Aurand, L. W. Laboratory Manual in Food Chemistry. (Illus.). 1977. pap. text ed. 11.00 (ISBN 0-87055-220-1). AVI.
Woods, A. E., jt. auth. see Aurand, Leonard W.
Woods, Archie L., jt. auth. see Quanbeck, B. Alton H.
Woods, Bill, jt. auth. see Woods, Erin.
Woods, Cedric S. Freshwater Life in Ireland. 1974. 7.00x (ISBN 0-7165-2280-2, Pub. by Irish Academic Pr Ireland); pap. 2.50x (ISBN 0-7165-2281-0). Biblio Dist.
Woods, Charles, ed. see Fielding, Henry.
Woods, Clyde M. Living Way Commentary, 2 vols. Incl. Vol. 1. Geh-Exodus. pap. 6.95 (ISBN 0-89315-139-4); Vol. 2. Lev., Num., Devt. pap. 6.95 (ISBN 0-89315-140-8). vols. 1 & 2 combined 12.95 (ISBN 0-89315-141-6). Lambert Bk.
Woods, David L. My Job, My Boss, & Me. LC 80-19829. 144p. 1980. pap. 5.95 (ISBN 0-534-97982-3). Lifetime Learn.
Woods, Donald. Asking for Trouble. LC 80-69643. 1981. 11.95 (ISBN 0-689-11159-2). Atheneum.
Woods, Douglas & Burrows, James C. World Aluminum-Bauxite Market. LC 78-19455. 1980. 24.50 (ISBN 0-03-044356-3). Praeger.
Woods, Erin & Woods, Bill. Bicycling the Backroads of Southwest Washington. LC 80-14682. (Illus., Orig.). 1980. pap. 6.95 (ISBN 0-916890-91-0). Mountaineers.
Woods, Fred. Folk Revival: The Rediscovery of a National Music. (Illus.). 1979. 9.95 (ISBN 0-7137-0970-7, Pub by Blandford Pr England); pap. 4.95 (ISBN 0-7137-0993-6). Sterling.
Woods, Gerald & Williams, John. Creative Techniques in Landscape Photography. LC 80-8396. (Illus.). 200p. 1981. 18.95 (ISBN 0-06-014835-7, HarpT). Har-Row.
Woods, Geraldine. Drug Use & Drug Abuse. (First Bks.). (Illus.). (gr. 4 up). 1979. s&l 6.45 (ISBN 0-531-02941-7). Watts.
Woods, Geraldine & Woods, Harold. Is James Bond Dead? LC 80-13633. (gr. 4-10). 1980. pap. 1.95 (ISBN 0-88436-763-0). EMC.
Woods, Guy N. John. 1981. 8.95 (ISBN 0-89225-207-3). Gospel Advocate.
Woods, H. F. Topics in Therapeutics, No. 6. 1980. lib. bdg. 25.00 (ISBN 0-8161-2222-9, Hall Medical). G K Hall.
Woods, H. G. At the Temple Church. (Scholar As Preacher Ser.). 252p. Repr. of 1911 ed. 7.75 (ISBN 0-567-04406-8). Attic Pr.
Woods, Harold, jt. auth. see Woods, Geraldine.
Woods, Henry. The Negligence Case: Comparative Fault, Vol. 1. LC 78-51108. 1978. 47.50. Lawyers Co-Op.
Woods, Herb. Galveston - Houston Electric Railway. (Special Ser.: No. 22). (Illus.). 84p. 1976. pap. 6.00 o.p. (ISBN 0-916374-23-8). Interurban.
Woods, Hubert. Durability in Concrete Construction. (Monograph: No. 4). 1968. 13.25 (ISBN 0-685-85138-9, M-4) (ISBN 0-685-85139-7). ACI.
Woods, J. E. Mathematical Economics: Topics in Multi-Sectoral Economics. (Modern Economics Ser.). (Illus.). 1978. pap. text ed. 19.95 (ISBN 0-582-44675-9). Longman.
Woods, J. H., tr. Yoga System of Patanjali. (Harvard Oriental Ser.: Vol. 17). 1972. 15.00x o.p. (ISBN 0-8426-0470-7). Verry.
Woods, James H. Yoga-System of Patanjali. 1977. pap. 8.50 (ISBN 0-89684-344-0, Pub. by Motilal Banarsidass India). Orient Bk Dist.
Woods, Jeff. DUKW: Two & One Half Ton Six by Six Amphibian. (MV - Ser.: No. 2). (Illus., Orig.). 1978. pap. 3.95 o.s.i. (ISBN 0-686-53150-7). Beachcomber Bks. Postponed.
Woods, John B., et al. Student Teaching: The Entrance to Professional Physical Education. 1973. pap. text ed. 9.50 (ISBN 0-12-763050-3). Acad Pr.
Woods, John E. The Aqquyunlu: Clan, Confederation, & Empire. LC 74-27613. (Studies in Middle Eastern History: No. 3). 1976. 27.50x (ISBN 0-88297-011-9). Bibliotheca.
Woods, Katherine, tr. see De Saint-Exupery, Antoine.
Woods, Katherine, tr. see Saint-Exupery, Antoine de.
Woods, Katherine, tr. see Saint-Exupery, Antoine De.
Woods, L. B. A Decade of Censorship in America: The Threat to Classrooms & Libraries, 1966-1975. LC 79-20960. 195p. 1979. 11.00 (ISBN 0-8108-1260-6). Scarecrow.
Woods, L. C. The Thermodynamics of Fluid Systems. (Oxford Engineering Science Ser). (Illus.). 350p. 1975. 58.00x (ISBN 0-19-856125-3). Oxford U Pr.
Woods, Loren. Fishes. (Beginning Science Bks). (gr. 2-4). 2.50 o.p. (ISBN 0-695-82890-8). Follett.
Woods, Loren P. Tropical Fish. LC 74-118956. (Beginning-to-Read Bks). (Illus.). (gr. 2-4). 1971. PLB 2.97 o.p. (ISBN 0-695-40175-0); pap. 1.50 o.p. (ISBN 0-695-30175-6). Follett.
Woods, M. E., jt. auth. see Hollis, F.
Woods, M. J. The Poet & the Natural World in the Age of Gongora. (Modern Languages & Literature Monographs). 1978. 37.50x (ISBN 0-19-815533-6). Oxford U Pr.
Woods, Marjorie B. Your Wedding: How to Plan & Enjoy It. 1972. pap. 2.75 (ISBN 0-515-05843-2). Jove Pubns.
Woods, Mary L. & Moe, Alden J. Analytic Reading Inventory. 2nd ed. (Illus.). 160p. 1981. spiral bdg. 7.95 (ISBN 0-675-08059-2). Merrill.
Woods, Michael. Mounting & Framing Pictures. 1978. 17.95 (ISBN 0-7134-0743-3). David & Charles.
Woods, Nancy F. Human Sexuality in Health & Illness. 2nd ed. LC 78-11511. (Illus.). 1979. pap. 10.95 (ISBN 0-8016-5619-2). Mosby.
Woods, Nellie B., compiled by. The Healings of the Bible. 1975. pap. 1.95 o.p. (ISBN 0-8015-3349-X). Dutton.
Woods, Pamela. Papercraft. (Illus.). 173p. 1980. 12.95 (ISBN 0-312-59583-2). St Martin.
Woods, Peter, ed. Teacher Strategies: Exploration in the Sociology of the School. 282p. 1980. 28.00x (ISBN 0-7099-0115-1, Pub. by Croom Helm Ltd). Biblio Dist.
Woods, Peter E. The Divided School. (Education Bks). 1979. 25.00x (ISBN 0-7100-0124-X). Routledge & Kegan.
Woods, R. A. Biochemical Genetics. 2nd ed. LC 79-41695. 80p. 1980. pap. 5.95 (ISBN 0-412-13160-9, 6340). Methuen Inc.
Woods, Ralph. Pocketful of Prayers. 1976. pap. 1.50 (ISBN 0-89129-217-9). Jove Pubns.
Woods, Ralph L. Government Guides to Health & Nutrition. (Orig.). 1975. pap. 1.25 o.s.i. (ISBN 0-515-03654-4, V3654). Jove Pubns.
Woods, Ralph L., ed. Third Treasury of the Familiar. LC 79-109455. 1970. 10.95 o.s.i. (ISBN 0-02-631420-7). Macmillan.
--Treasury of the Familiar. 1942. 16.95 (ISBN 0-02-631490-8). Macmillan.
Woods, Randall B. A Black Odyssey: John Lewis Waller & the Promise of American Life, 1878-1900. LC 80-18965. (Illus.). 272p. 1981. 20.00x (ISBN 0-7006-0207-0). Regents Pr KS.
Woods, Richard. Another Kind of Love: Homosexuality & Spirituality. LC 77-27729. 1978. pap. 1.95 (ISBN 0-385-14312-5, Im). Doubleday.
--Mysterion. 372p. 1981. 14.95 (ISBN 0-88347-127-2). Thomas More.
--Occult Revolution: A Christian Meditation. 1971. pap. 2.95 (ISBN 0-8164-2584-1). Crossroad NY.
Woods, Richard D. Reference Materials on Mexican Americans: An Annotated Bibliography. LC 76-10663. 197p. 1976. 10.00 (ISBN 0-8108-0963-X). Scarecrow.
Woods, Richard G., ed. Future Dimensions of World Food & Populations. (Winrock Ser.). 425p. 1981. lib. bdg. 22.50x (ISBN 0-86531-160-9). Westview.
Woods, Richard S., ed. Audit Decisions in Accounting Practice. 350p. 1973. 11.50 (ISBN 0-8260-9575-5, 98631, Pub. by Wiley-Hamilton). Wiley.
Woods, Robert. Population Analysis in Geography. (Illus.). 1979. pap. text ed. 15.95x (ISBN 0-582-48696-3). Longman.
Woods, Sara. Cry Guilty. 192p. 1981. 9.95 (ISBN 0-312-17802-6). St Martin.
--Weep for Her. 224p. 1981. 9.95 (ISBN 0-312-86019-6). St Martin.
Woods, Sherwyn M., jt. ed. see Marmor, Judd.
Woods, Shirley E. Ottawa: The Capital of Canada. LC 79-6101. 256p. 1981. 19.95 (ISBN 0-385-14722-8). Doubleday.
Woods, Shirley E., Jr. The Squirrels of Canada. (Illus.). 208p. 1981. lib. bdg. 29.95 (ISBN 0-660-10344-3, 56511-4, Pub. by Natl Mus Canada). U of Chicago Pr.
--The Squirrels of Canada. (Illus.). 208p. 21.95 (ISBN 0-660-10344-3, 56512-2, Pub. by Natl Mus Canada). U of Chicago Pr.
Woods, Stuart. Chiefs: A Novel. 1981. 15.95 (ISBN 0-393-01461-4). Norton.
Woods, Sylvia & Owen, Ray. Old English Sheepdogs. (Illus.). 224p. 1981. 22.00 (ISBN 0-571-11620-5, Pub. by Faber & Faber). Merrimack Bk Serv.
Woods, T. F., jt. auth. see Adams, Roger G.
Woods, Thomas J., jt. auth. see Williams, Donald.
Woods, W. A., ed. see Bradshaw, P.
Woods, William. A Mermaid in Nikoli. 1967. 4.95 o.p. (ISBN 0-8090-6895-8). Hill & Wang.
Woods, William A. Semantics for a Question-Answering System. LC 79-50824. (Outstanding Dissertations in the Computer Sciences Ser.: Vol. 27). 1980. lib. bdg. 31.00 (ISBN 0-8240-4419-3). Garland Pub.
Woodside, Alexander B. Community & Revolution in Modern Vietnam. LC 75-18429. (Illus.). 418p. 1976. pap. text ed. 14.75 (ISBN 0-395-20367-8). HM.
Woodside, Arch G., jt. auth. see DeLozier, M. Wayne.
Wood-Smith, F. G., jt. auth. see Vickers, M. D.
Woodson, Meg. Following Joey Home. 160p. 1980. pap. 3.95 (ISBN 0-310-34861-7). Zondervan.
Woodson, Robert. A Summons to Life: Mediating Structures & the Prevention of Youth Crime. 150p. 1981. 16.50 (ISBN 0-88410-826-0). Ballinger Pub.
Woodson, T. T. Introduction to Engineering Design. 1966. text ed. 17.00 o.p. (ISBN 0-07-071760-5, C); instructor's manual 1.50 o.p. (ISBN 0-07-071761-3). McGraw.
Woodson, Wesley E. & Conover, Donald W. Human Engineering Guide for Equipment Designers. 2nd rev ed. (Illus.). 1965. 30.00x (ISBN 0-520-01363-8). U of Cal Pr.
Woodstone, Arthur. Inside Nixon's Head. pap. 1.95 o.p. (ISBN 0-445-08576-2). Popular Lib.

Woodsworth, James S. My Neighbor: A Study of City Conditions, a Plan for Social Service. LC 77-163839. (Social History of Canada Ser.). (Illus.). xix, 216p. 1972. pap. 5.00 (ISBN 0-8020-6126-5). U of Toronto Pr.
--Strangers Within Our Gates. LC 76-163836. (Social History of Canada Ser.). 1972. pap. 6.50 (ISBN 0-8020-6149-4). U of Toronto Pr.
Woodward & Bernstein, Carl. Final Days. 1976. pap. 2.50 (ISBN 0-380-00844-0, 31104). Avon.
Woodward, A. Smith, ed. see Von Zittel, K. A.
Woodward, Arthur E. & Bovey, Frank, eds. Polymer Characterization by ESR & NMR. LC 80-21840. (ACS Symposium Ser.: No. 142). 1980. 32.00 (ISBN 0-8412-0594-9). Am Chemical.
Woodward, Bob & Armstrong, Scott. The Brethren. 1980. pap. 3.50 (ISBN 0-380-52183-0, 52183). Avon.
Woodward, Bob, jt. auth. see Bernstein, Carl.
Woodward, C. Vann. Responses of the Presidents to Charges of Misconduct. 1974. 10.00 o.p. (ISBN 0-440-05923-2). Delacorte.
--The Strange Career of Jim Crow. 3rd rev. ed. 256p. 1974. pap. 4.95 (ISBN 0-19-501805-2, GB). Oxford U Pr.
--Tom Watson: Agrarian Rebel. 1963. pap. 7.95 (ISBN 0-19-500707-7, GB). Oxford U Pr.
Woodward, C. Vann, ed. Mary Chesnut's Civil War. LC 80-36661. (Illus.). 960p. 1981. 29.95x (ISBN 0-300-02459-2). Yale U Pr.
Woodward, Calvin A. Growth of a Party System in Ceylon. LC 76-89465. (Illus.). 338p. 1969. 12.50x (ISBN 0-87057-115-X, Pub. by Brown U Pr). Univ Pr of New England.
Woodward, D., tr. see Bablet, Denis.
Woodward, Dolores M. Mainstreaming the Learning Disabled Adolescent: A Manual of Strategies & Materials. 200p. 1981. text ed. write for info. (ISBN 0-89443-299-0). Aspen Systems.
Woodward, F. Managing the Transport Services Function. 336p. 1978. text ed. 25.25x (ISBN 0-566-02032-7, Pub. by Gower Pub Co England). Renouf.
Woodward, Grace S. Cherokees. (Civilization of the American Indian Ser.: No. 65). (Illus.). 1979. Repr. of 1963 ed. 14.95 (ISBN 0-8061-0554-2). U of Okla Pr.
Woodward, H. W. Art, Feat & Mystery: The Story of Thomas Webb & Sons, Glassmakers. 61p. 1978. 25.00x (ISBN 0-9506439-0-4, Pub. by Mark & Moody England). State Mutual Bk.
Woodward, Hiram W., ed. Barabudur: History & Significance of a Buddhist Monument. Gomez, Luis O. 1981. 20.00 (ISBN 0-89581-151-0). Lancaster-Miller.
Woodward, J. F. Quantitative Methods in Construction Management & Design. (Illus.). 1976. 27.50x (ISBN 0-333-17720-7); pap. text ed. 18.50x (ISBN 0-333-18602-8). Scholium Intl.
Woodward, James B. Electric Load Modeling. LC 78-75001. (Outstanding Dissertations on Energy). 1980. lib. bdg. 32.00 (ISBN 0-8240-3981-5). Garland Pub.
Woodward, Jean. Valley of Romance. 192p. (YA) 1976. 5.95 (ISBN 0-685-66572-0, Avalon). Bouregy.
Woodward, Joan. Industrial Organization: Theory & Practice. 2nd ed. (Illus.). 324p. 1981. 42.00 (ISBN 0-19-874122-7); pap. 20.00 (ISBN 0-19-874123-5). Oxford U Pr.
Woodward, John. To Do the Sick No Harm: A Study of the British Voluntary Hospital System to 1875. (International Library of Social Policy Ser.). 1978. pap. 8.95 (ISBN 0-7100-8911-2). Routledge & Kegan.
Woodward, John B. Low Speed Marine Diesel. (Ocean Engineering: a Wiley Ser.). 368p. 1981. 33.50 (ISBN 0-471-06335-5, Pub.by Wiley-Interscience). Wiley.
Woodward, John C., jt. auth. see Diamond, Robert M.
Woodward, Kathleen. The Late Poems of Eliot Pound, Stevens & Williams. 193p. 1980. 14.50 (ISBN 0-8142-0306-X). Ohio St U Pr.
Woodward, Kathleen, ed. see Wilden, Anthony, et al.
Woodward, Kenneth L., jt. auth. see Kornhaber, Arthur.
Woodward, L. A. Introduction to the Theory of Molecular Vibrations & Vibrational Spectroscopy. (Illus.). 370p. 1972. 37.50x (ISBN 0-19-855352-8). Oxford U Pr.
--Molecular Statistics for Students of Chemistry. (Illus.). 232p. 1975. 28.00x (ISBN 0-19-855357-9). Oxford U Pr.
Woodward, L. T. I Am a Nymphomaniac. 1975. pap. 1.50 o.p. (ISBN 0-685-52177-X, LB254DK, Leisure Bks). Nordon Pubns.
Woodward, Llewellyn. Age of Reform, Eighteen Fifteen to Eighteen Seventy. 2nd ed. 1962. 33.00x (ISBN 0-19-821711-0). Oxford U Pr.
Woodward, Marcus. Leaves from Gerard's Herball. (Illus.). 1969. pap. 4.50 (ISBN 0-486-22343-4). Dover.
Woodward, Mary A., compiled by. That Ye May Heal: A Manual for Individual & Group Study of Meditation for Healing, from the Edgar Cayce Records. rev. ed. 53p. 1970. pap. 2.50 (ISBN 0-87604-075-X). ARE Pr.
Woodward, Nancy H. If Your Child Is Drinking... What You Can Do to Fight Alcohol Abuse at Home, at School, & in the Community. 360p. 1981. 11.95 (ISBN 0-399-12457-8). Putnam.
--Teas of the World. (Illus.). 128p. 1980. pap. 7.95 (ISBN 0-02-082870-5, Collier). Macmillan.
Woodward, R. B. & Hoffmann, R. The Conservation of Orbital Symmetry. LC 79-63636. (Illus.). 1970. 14.70 (ISBN 3-5272-5325-4); pap. 7.70 (ISBN 3-5272-5324-6). Verlag Chemie.
Woodward, Ralph, jt. auth. see Ross, Corinne M.
Woodward, Ralph L., Jr. Belize. (World Bibliographical Ser.: No. 21). 1980. write for info. (ISBN 0-903450-41-0). Abc-Clio.
Woodward, Ralph L., Jr., ed. Positivism in Latin America, 1850-1960. LC 72-152809. (Problems in Latin American Civilization Ser.). 1971. pap. text ed. 4.95x o.p. (ISBN 0-669-52431-X). Heath.
--Tribute to Don Bernardo De Galvez. LC 80-116160. (Illus.). xxviii, 148p. 1979. 14.95x (ISBN 0-917860-04-7). Historic New Orleans.
Woodward, Richard S., tr. see Duboscq, Genevieve.
Woodward, Robert H. The Craft of Prose. 5th ed. 432p. 1979. pap. text ed. 7.95x (ISBN 0-534-00781-3). Wadsworth Pub.
Woodward, Robert H. & Clark, James J., eds. Social Rebel in American Literature. LC 68-21801. (Orig.). 1968. pap. 8.95 (ISBN 0-672-63115-6). Odyssey Pr.
Woodward, Thomas. Turning Things Upside Down: A Theological Workbook. 128p. 1975. 4.50 (ISBN 0-8164-0279-5). Crossroad NY.
Woodward, V. H. see Bowers, J.
Woodward, William E. Bunk: Prelude to Depression. LC 76-22715. (The Social & Intellectual History of American 1920's Ser.). 1976. Repr. of 1923 ed. lib. bdg. 29.50 (ISBN 0-306-70846-9). Da Capo.
Woodward, William H. Vittorino Da Feltre & Other Humanist Educators. LC 63-22510. (Orig.). 1964. text ed. 9.75 (ISBN 0-8077-2359-2); pap. text ed. 5.50x (ISBN 0-8077-2356-8). Tchrs Coll.
Woodward, William H., ed. Desiderius Erasmus Concerning the Aim & Method of Education. LC 64-18613. (Orig.). 1964. text ed. 9.75 (ISBN 0-8077-2350-9); pap. text ed. 4.25x (ISBN 0-8077-2347-9). Tchrs Coll.
--Studies in Education During the Age of the Renaissance 1400 to 1600. LC 67-17748. (Orig.). 1967. pap. text ed. 5.25x (ISBN 0-8077-2353-3). Tchrs Coll.
Woodworth, Floyd. Hacia la Meta. (Spanish Bks.). 1977. 1.60 (ISBN 0-8297-0562-7). Life Pubs Intl.
Woodworth, Floyd, tr. Escalera De la Predicacion. (Spanish Bks.). 1978. 1.80 (ISBN 0-686-28804-1). Life Pubs Intl.
Woody, D. W. The Kids of Mischief Island. 1981. 4.75 (ISBN 0-8062-1693-X). Carlton.
Woody, J. D., jt. auth. see Woody, R. H.
Woody, Jeanine. Abortion? 1977. pap. 1.95 o.p. (ISBN 0-917726-10-3). Hunter Bks.
Woody, R. H. & Woody, J. D. Sexual, Marital, & Familial Relations. (Illus.). 312p. 1973. 16.50 (ISBN 0-398-02803-6). C C Thomas.
Woody, Robert H. Bodymind Liberation: Achieving Holistic Health. 172p. 1980. 15.50 (ISBN 0-398-04055-9). C C Thomas.
--Getting Custody: Winning the Last Battle of a Marital War. 1978. 10.95 (ISBN 0-02-631570-X). Macmillan.
--Legal Aspects of Mental Retardation: A Search for Reliability. 144p. 1974. 12.75 (ISBN 0-398-03243-2). C C Thomas.
--More Than a Job: How to Win at Working. LC 80-18914. 160p. (gr. 7 up). 1980. PLB 8.29 (ISBN 0-671-34048-4). Messner.
--The Use of Massage in Facilitating Holistic Health. (Illus.). 136p. 1980. text ed. 12.50 (ISBN 0-398-03954-2). C C Thomas.
Wooff, Terence. Developments in Art Teaching. (Changing Classroom). (Illus.). 1976. text ed. 9.75x (ISBN 0-7291-0039-1); pap. text ed. 4.75x (ISBN 0-7291-0034-0). Humanities.
Woofter, T. J., Jr. Landlord & Tenant on the Cotton Plantation. LC 77-165691. (FDR & the Era of the New Deal Ser.). 1971. Repr. of 1936 ed. lib. bdg. 27.50 (ISBN 0-306-70337-8). Da Capo.
Woofter, Thomas Jackson & Winston, Ellen E. Seven Lean Years. LC 79-39479. (FDR & the Era of the New Deal Ser). 1972. Repr. of 1939 ed. lib. bdg. 20.00 (ISBN 0-306-70463-3). Da Capo.
Wool, I. G. see Harris, Robert S., et al.
Woolams, Stan, jt. auth. see Brown, Michael.
Woolard, Wilma L. Combined School - Public Libraries: A Survey with Conclusions & Recommendations. LC 80-36742. 204p. 1980. 11.00 (ISBN 0-8108-1335-1). Scarecrow.
Wooldridge, D. Letter Assembly in Printing. (Library of Printing Technology). Date not set. 18.95 (ISBN 0-8038-4274-0). Hastings.
Wooldridge, E. T., Jr. The P-Eighty Shooting Star: Evolution of a Jet Fighter. LC 79-17648. (Famous Aircraft of the National Air & Space Museum Ser.: Bk. 3). (Illus.). 110p. 1979. pap. 6.95 (ISBN 0-87474-965-4). Smithsonian.
Wooldridge, P. J. & Leonard, R. C. Methods of Clinical Experimentation to Improve Patient Care. LC 77-11072. (Illus.). 1978. pap. text ed. 10.00 (ISBN 0-8016-5622-2). Mosby.
Wooler, Richard G. Marine Transportation of LNG (Liquefied Natural Gas) & Related Products. LC 75-23457. (Illus.). 348p. 1975. 18.00x (ISBN 0-87033-193-0). Cornell Maritime.
Woolery, Arlo. The Art of Valuation. LC 78-5471. 1978. 15.95 (ISBN 0-669-02340-X). Lexington Bks.
Wooley, Bryan. November Twenty-Second. 448p. 1981. 12.95 (ISBN 0-87223-690-0). Seaview Bks.
Woolf. The Letters of Virginia Woolf: Nineteen Thirty-Six to Nineteen Forty-One, Vol. VI. Nicholson, Nigel & Trautmann, Joanne, eds. LC 75-25538. 576p. 1980. 19.95 (ISBN 0-15-150929-8). HarBraceJ.
Woolf, Charlotte. Hindsight. Campbell, Dennis, ed. 312p. 1981. 20.00 (ISBN 0-89182-035-3). Charles River Bks.
Woolf, Colin R. The Clinical Core of Respiratory Medicine. (Illus.). 224p. 1981. pap. text ed. write for info (ISBN 0-397-50501-9). Lippincott.
Woolf, Daniel J., tr. see Beringer, Johann B.
Woolf, Harry. Albert Einstein Centennial Celebration. (Illus.). 400p. 1980. text ed. 43.50 (ISBN 0-201-09924-1). A-W.
Woolf, Harry, ed. Quantification: A History of the Meaning of Measurement in the Natural & Social Sciences. 1961. text ed. 28.50x (ISBN 0-672-60844-8); pap. text ed. 10.95x (ISBN 0-89197-913-1). Irvington.
Woolf, Leonard. Economic Imperialism. LC 68-9627. 1970. Repr. of 1920 ed. 12.25 (ISBN 0-86527-053-8). Fertig.
--Empire & Commerce in Africa. LC 67-24602. 1968. 20.00 (ISBN 0-86527-058-9). Fertig.
--War for Peace. LC 75-148376. (Library of War & Peace; the Character & Causes of War). lib. bdg. 38.00 (ISBN 0-8240-0465-5). Garland Pub.
Woolf, Neville. Pathology of Atherosclerosis. Crawford, T., ed. (Postgraduate Pathology Ser.). 1981. price not set (ISBN 0-407-00125-5). Butterworths.
Woolf, Neville & Anthony, P. P. Recent Advances in Histopathology. 10th ed. (Illus.). 1979. pap. text ed. 32.00 (ISBN 0-443-01783-2). Churchill.
Woolf, Robert. Behind Closed Doors. (RL 7). 1977. pap. 1.95 o.p. (ISBN 0-451-07423-8, J7423, Sig). NAL.
Woolf, Virginia. The Diary of Virginia Woolf: Vol. 2, 1920-1924. LC 78-23882. 1980. pap. 5.95 (ISBN 0-15-626037-9, Harv). HarBraceJ.
--The Diary of Virginia Woolf: Volume Four 1931-1935. Bell, Ann O. & McNeillie, Andrew, eds. 1981. price not set. HarBraceJ.
--Melymbrosia: Being a Scholar's Edition of the Earliest Extant Version of "the Voyage Out". DeSalvo, Louise A., ed. 432p. 1981. 20.00 (ISBN 0-87104-277-0). NY Pub Lib.
Woolfolk. The Girl Cried Murder. (gr. 7-12). pap. 0.95 o.p. (ISBN 0-590-05810-X, Schol Pap). Schol Bk Serv.
--Who Killed Daddy? (gr. 7-12). 1980. pap. 1.25 (ISBN 0-590-30032-6, Schol Pap). Schol Bk Serv.
Woolfolk, Anita & Nicolich, Lorraine. Educational Psychology for Teachers. (Illus.). 1980. text ed. 17.95 (ISBN 0-13-240598-9); pap. 6.95 studyguide & wkbk. (ISBN 0-13-240556-3). P-H.
Woolfolk, Doug, ed. see Ditto, Tanya.
Woolfolk, Doug, ed. see McIntyre, Bill.
Woolfolk, Doug, ed. see Tenney, Frank F., Jr.
Woolfolk, Doug, ed. see Valentine, Orpha.
Woolfolk, Joanna. Honeymoon for Life: How to Live Happily Ever After. LC 77-15966. 252p. 1981. pap. 6.95 (ISBN 0-8128-6102-7). Stein & Day.
Woolfolk, William. The Sendai. 288p. 1981. pap. 2.75 (ISBN 0-445-04628-7). Popular Lib.
Woolfson, M. M. Introduction to X-Ray Crystallography. LC 69-16289. (Illus.). 1970. 57.50 (ISBN 0-521-07440-1); pap. 17.50x (ISBN 0-521-29343-X). Cambridge U Pr.
Woolfson, Marion. Prophets in Babylon: Jews in the Arab World. LC 80-670264. 304p. 1980. 38.00 (ISBN 0-571-11458-X, Pub. by Faber & Faber). Merrimack Bk Serv.
Woolgar, Jack. Hot on Ice. LC 65-15106. (Pilot Book Ser). (Illus.). 128p. (gr. 3-5). 1965. 6.95g (ISBN 0-8075-3383-1). A Whitman.
--Mystery in the Desert. (gr. 6-8). 1967. 4.25 o.p. (ISBN 0-8313-0107-4); PLB 6.19 (ISBN 0-685-13778-3). Lantern.
Woolham, Frank, et al. Aviary Birds in Color. (Illus.). 1974. 11.95 (ISBN 0-7137-0707-0, Pub by Blandford Pr England). Sterling.
Woollam, W. G. Shipping Terms & Abbreviations: Maritime-Insurance-International Trade. LC 62-22181. 1963. 5.00x (ISBN 0-87033-107-8). Cornell Maritime.
Woollard, A. G. Progress: A Christian Doctrine? 96p. 1973. pap. 1.95 o.p. (ISBN 0-8170-0576-5). Judson.
Woollett, Mick. Lightweight Bikes. (Illus.). 64p. 1981. pap. 5.95 (Pub. by Batsford England). David & Charles.
Woollett, Mike. Bike & Superbike. (Illus.). 64p. 1980. pap. 5.95 (ISBN 0-7134-0540-6, Pub. by Batsford England). David & Charles.
Woolley, Catherine. Cathy Leonard Calling. (Illus.). (gr. 3-7). 1961. 7.75 o.p. (ISBN 0-688-21154-2). Morrow.
--Cathy's Little Sister. (Illus.). (gr. 3-7). 1964. 8.25 (ISBN 0-688-21155-0). Morrow.
--Ginnie & the New Girl. (Illus.). (gr. 3-7). 1954. 6.75 o.p. (ISBN 0-688-21336-7). Morrow.
--Ginnie Joins In. (Illus.). (gr. 3-7). 1951. 6.95 (ISBN 0-688-21341-3). Morrow.
--Libby Shadows a Lady. LC 74-2029. (Illus.). 192p. (gr. 3-7). 1974. PLB 7.92 (ISBN 0-688-31787-1). Morrow.
--Libby's Uninvited Guest. LC 70-108722. (Illus.). (gr. 3-7). 1970. 8.25 (ISBN 0-688-21809-1). Morrow.
--Look Alive, Libby. (Illus.). (gr. 3-7). 1962. 8.25 (ISBN 0-688-21754-0). Morrow.
--A Room for Cathy. (Illus.). (gr. 3-7). 1956. PLB 7.92 (ISBN 0-688-31687-5). Morrow.
Woolley, Charles L. The Development of Sumerian Art. LC 80-24292. (Illus.). 140p. 1981. Repr. of 1935 ed. lib. bdg. 35.00x (ISBN 0-8371-4373-X, WOSA). Greenwood.
--Digging up the Past. 2nd ed. LC 77-13325. (Illus.). 1977. Repr. of 1954 ed. lib. bdg. 17.50x (ISBN 0-8371-9853-4, WODU). Greenwood.
Woolley, David E. & Evanson, John M. Collagenase in Normal & Pathological Connective Tissues. LC 79-19557. 1980. 46.00 (ISBN 0-471-27668-5, Pub. by Wiley-Interscience). Wiley.
Woolley, Diana. Advertising Law Handbook. 2nd ed. 106p. 1976. text ed. 21.00x (ISBN 0-220-66306-8, Pub. by Busn Bks England). Renouf.
Woolley, LeGrand H. Medical-Dental Terminology: Syllabus. 2nd ed. 1974. pap. text ed. 6.10 (ISBN 0-89420-003-8, 217705); cassette recordings 177.70 (ISBN 0-89420-162-X, 196700). Natl Book.
Woolley, Leonard. Spadework in Archaeology. 1953. 4.75 o.p. (ISBN 0-8022-1932-2). Philos Lib.
Woolley, Leslie. Drainage Details in SI Metric. (Illus.). 1978. 13.50x (ISBN 0-7198-2520-2). Intl Ideas.
Woolley, Persia. The Custody Handbook. LC 79-10862. 1980. pap. 5.95 (ISBN 0-671-44841-2). Summit Bks.
Woolner, Frank. Trout Hunting. 1977. 12.95 (ISBN 0-87691-196-3). Winchester Pr.
Woolner, Frank, jt. auth. see Lyman, Henry.
Woolner, Lionel R., ed. The Hunting of the Hare. (Illus.). 6.10 (ISBN 0-85131-122-9, Dist. by Sporting Book Center). J A Allen.
Woolner, Lionel R., tr. see De Vezins, Elie.
Woolrich, Willis R. Handbook of Refrigerating Engineering, 2 vols. 4th ed. Incl. Vol. 1. Fundamentals. 460p. 1965 (ISBN 0-87055-054-3); Vol. 2. Applications. 434p. 1966 (ISBN 0-87055-055-1). (Illus.). 29.00 ea. o.p. AVI.
Woolrich, Willis R. & Hallowell, Elliot R. Cold & Freezer Storage Manual. LC 76-115688. (Illus.). 1970. 28.00 o.p. (ISBN 0-87055-074-8). AVI.
Woolsey, Raymond H. & Anderson, Ruth. Harry Anderson: The Man Behind the Paintings. LC 76-15700. (Illus.). 1976. 7.95 (ISBN 0-8280-0047-6). Review & Herald.
Woolsey, Sarah C. What Katy Did. LC 75-32177. (Classics of Children's Literature, 1621-1932: Vol. 40). (Illus.). 1976. Repr. of 1873 ed. PLB 38.00 (ISBN 0-8240-2289-0). Garland Pub.
Woolson, jt. auth. see Nichols.
Woolston, Thomas. Discourses on the Miracles of Our Savior. Wellek, Rene, ed. LC 75-11268. (British Philosophers & Theologians of the 17th & 18th Centuries Ser.: Vol. 67). 565p. 1979. lib. bdg. 42.00 (ISBN 0-8240-1778-1); lib. bdg. 2700.00 set of 101 vols. (ISBN 0-686-60102-5). Garland Pub.
Woosley, Hugh, jt. auth. see Caviella, Patrick.
Woosnam, Phil & Gardner, Paul. Sports Illustrated Soccer. LC 72-5629. (Illus.). 96p. 1972. 5.95 (ISBN 0-397-00908-9); pap. 2.95 (ISBN 0-397-00909-7, LP-70). Lippincott.
Wooster, Ralph A. Politicians, Planters, & Plain Folk: Courthouse & Statehouse in the Upper South, 1850-1860. LC 75-32339. 204p. 1975. 12.50x (ISBN 0-87049-166-0). U of Tenn Pr.

Wooster, Ralph A. & Calvert, Robert A., eds. Texas Vistas: Selections from the Southwestern Historical Quarterly. LC 80-52706. 1980. 11.95 (ISBN 0-87611-047-2); pap. 6.50 (ISBN 0-87611-048-0). Tex St Hist Assn.

Wooten, James. Dasher, the Roots & the Rising of Jimmy Carter. LC 77-25272. 1978. 11.95 (ISBN 0-671-40004-5). Summit Bks.

Wooten, Jean W., jt. auth. see Godfrey, Robert K.

Wooten, William, jt. auth. see Drooyan, Irving.

Wooton, Anthony. Insects Are Animals Too. LC 77-91775. 13.50 (ISBN 0-7153-7534-2). David & Charles.

Wooton, Graham, jt. ed. see Ehrlich, Stanislaw.

Wooton, William & Drooyan, Irving. Intermediate Algebra. 5th ed. 1979. text ed. 17.95x (ISBN 0-534-00704-X); study guide 5.95x (ISBN 0-534-00787-2); solutions for students 4.95x (ISBN 0-534-00739-2). Wadsworth Pub.

Wooton, William, jt. auth. see Drooyan, Irving.

Wooton, William, jt. auth. see Green, Tom.

Wooton, William, et al. Modern Trigonometry. rev. ed. 1979. text ed. 15.64 (ISBN 0-395-21687-7, 2-60824); instructor's guide & solutions, pap. 7.40 (ISBN 0-395-21688-5, 2-60825). HM.

Wootters, John. The Complete Book of Practical Handloading. (Illus.). 1976. 13.95 (ISBN 0-87691-215-3). Winchester Pr.

--A Guide to Hunting in Texas. LC 79-19642. 1979. pap. 5.95 (ISBN 0-88415-369-X). Pacesetter Pr.

Wootton, Barbara. Crime & Penal Policy. 1978. text ed. 25.00x (ISBN 0-04-364011-7); pap. text ed. 9.95x (ISBN 0-04-364013-3). Allen Unwin.

--Social Foundations of Wage Policy. 1962. pap. text ed. 9.50x o.p. (ISBN 0-04-331034-6). Allen Unwin.

Wootton, Graham. Pressure Politics in Contemporary Britain. LC 77-26372. 1978. 21.95x (ISBN 0-669-02167-9). Lexington Bks.

Wootton, Lutian R., et al, eds. Trends & Issues Affecting Curriculum: Programs and Practices. LC 80-5784. 281p. 1980. lib. bdg. 18.75 (ISBN 0-8191-1224-0); pap. text ed. 10.75 (ISBN 0-8191-1225-9). U Pr of Amer.

Wootton, Richard. Honky Tonkin' A Travel Guide to American Music. 3rd ed. LC 80-503. (Illus.). 192p. 1980. lib. bdg. 10.25 o.p. (ISBN 0-914788-26-4). East Woods.

Woozley, A. D. Theory of Knowledge: An Introduction. (Repr. of 1949 ed). 1964. pap. text ed. 8.25x (ISBN 0-09-044571-6, Hutchinson U Lib). Humanities.

Wopko, Jensma. Sing for Our Execution: Poems. (Illus.). 1973. pap. 10.00 (ISBN 0-86975-021-6, Pub by Ravan Press). Three Continents.

Worakwinto, Thongyoy. A Village Ordination. Silcock, T. H., tr. from Thai. (Scandinavian Inst. of Asian Studies Monographs: No. 25). (Illus.). 1976. pap. text ed. 9.25x (ISBN 0-7007-0092-7). Humanities.

Worboye, jt. auth. see Pavitt.

Worboys, Anne. Run Sara Run. 288p. 1981. 10.95 (ISBN 0-684-16818-9). Scribner.

--The Way of the Tamarisk. 216p. 1975. 6.95 o.s.i. (ISBN 0-440-05990-9). Delacorte.

Worcester, Donald B., jt. auth. see Boyd, Maurice.

Worcester, Donald E. Brazil: From Colony to World Power. LC 73-1328. (Illus.). 1977. encore edition 3.95 (ISBN 0-684-15011-5, ScribC); pap. text ed. 3.95x (ISBN 0-684-13391-1, ScribC). Scribner.

--The Chisholm Trail. LC 80-12412. xx, 201p. 1981. 14.50 (ISBN 0-8032-4710-9). U of Nebr Pr.

Worcester, J. H., Jr. David Livingstone. pap. 2.25 (ISBN 0-8024-4782-1). Moody.

Worcester, Tom & Cary, James. Portrait of Washington D. C. LC 79-55979. (Portrait of America Ser.). (Illus., Orig., Photos by robert reynolds). 1980. pap. 6.95 (ISBN 0-912856-55-6). Graphic Arts Ctr.

Worchel, S. & Goethals, G. Adjustment & Human Relations. 592p. 1981. text ed. 16.95 (ISBN 0-394-32226-6); wkbk. 6.95 (ISBN 0-394-32737-3). Knopf.

Worchel, Stephen & Cooper, Joel. Understanding Social Psychology. rev. ed. 1979. text ed. 18.50x (ISBN 0-256-02200-3); study guide 3.95 (ISBN 0-256-02223-2). Dorsey.

Worden, A. B., ed. see Ludlow, Edmund.

Worden, B. The Rump Parliament, 1648-1653. LC 73-77264. 500p. 1974. 41.95 (ISBN 0-521-20205-1); pap. 14.95 (ISBN 0-521-29213-1). Cambridge U Pr.

Worden, William L. Cargoes: Matson's First Century in the Pacific. 208p. 1981. 12.95 (ISBN 0-8248-0708-1). U Pr of Hawaii.

Wordingham, J. A. & Reboul, P. Dictionary of Plastics. (Quality Paperback: No. 174). 1967. pap. 2.95 (ISBN 0-8226-0174-5). Littlefield.

Wordsworth, Amy. The Big Red Puzzle Book. 1980. pap. 7.95 o.p. (ISBN 0-89903-002-5). Caroline Hse.

Wordsworth, Christopher. Scholae Academicae: Some Account of Studies at English Universities in the 18th Century. LC 79-93271. Repr. of 1877 ed. 22.50x (ISBN 0-678-05085-6). Kelley.

Wordsworth, Dorothy. Journals of Dorothy Wordsworth. Moorman, Mary, ed. (Oxford Paperbacks Ser). 1971. pap. 5.95x (ISBN 0-19-281103-7). Oxford U Pr.

Wordsworth, J & White, H. J., eds. Novum Testamentum Latine: Editio Minor. 1980. Repr. of 1920 ed. 2.95 (ISBN 0-564-02119-9, 71700). United Bible.

Wordsworth, J. C., ed. see Thucydides.

Wordsworth, Nat. Understanding Microcomputers & Small Computer Systems. (Da Capo Quality Paperbacks Ser.). (Illus.). 312p. 1981. pap. 8.95 (ISBN 0-306-80143-4). Da Capo.

Wordsworth, William. Benjamin the Waggoner by William Wordsworth. Betz, Paul, ed. (Illus.). 336p. 1981. 35.00 (ISBN 0-8014-1270-6). Cornell U Pr.

--A Choice of Wordsworth's Verse. Thomas, R. S., ed. 1971. 5.95 o.p. (ISBN 0-571-09258-6, Pub. by Faber & Faber); pap. 3.95 (ISBN 0-571-09259-4). Merrimack Bk Serv.

--Poetical Works with Introd. & Notes. new rev ed. Hutchinson, Thomas & De Selincourt, Ernest, eds. (Oxford Standard Authors Ser.). 810p. 1950. 23.95 (ISBN 0-19-254152-8); pap. 8.95x (ISBN 0-19-281052-9, OPB). Oxford U Pr.

--Prelude, Bks. 1-4. Yarker, P. M., ed. (Routledge English Texts). 1968. 7.50x (ISBN 0-7100-6096-3); pap. 3.95 (ISBN 0-7100-6097-1). Routledge & Kegan.

--The Prelude: A Parallel Text. Maxwell, J. C., ed. (Poets Ser.). 1977. pap. 3.95 (ISBN 0-14-042214-5). Penguin.

--Prelude: Or, Growth of a Poet's Mind. De Salincourt, Ernest, ed. (Oxford Standard Authors Ser). 1960. 21.00 (ISBN 0-19-254153-6). Oxford U Pr.

--The Prose Works of William Wordsworth, 3 vols. Owen, W. J. & Worthington, Jane, eds. (Oxford English Texts Ser.). 1355p. 1974. 125.00x (ISBN 0-19-812436-8). Oxford U Pr.

--The Ruined Cottage & the Pedlar. Butler, James, ed. LC 78-58066. (Cornell Wordsworth Ser.). (Illus.). 1978. 38.00x (ISBN 0-8014-1153-X). Cornell U Pr.

--Selected Poems. 12.95 (ISBN 0-19-250189-5, WC 189). Oxford U Pr.

--Works of Wordsworth. rev. new ed. (Cambridge Editions Ser.). Date not set. 15.00 (ISBN 0-395-18496-7). HM. Postponed.

Worgol, George. From Magic to Metaphor. LC 79-56752. (Orig.). 1980. pap. 8.95 (ISBN 0-8091-2280-4). Paulist Pr.

Worick, W. & Schaller, W. Alcohol, Tobacco & Drugs: Their Use & Abuse. 1977. pap. 8.95 (ISBN 0-13-021436-1). P-H.

Work, Henry C. Songs. LC 73-5099. (Earlier American Music Ser.: Vol. 19). (Illus.). 180p. 1974. Repr. of 1884 ed. lib. bdg. 25.00 (ISBN 0-306-70586-9). Da Capo.

Work, James A., ed. see Sterne, Laurence J.

Working Group Meeting on Energy Planning Program & Committee on Natural Resources, Fifth. Proceedings. (Energy Resources Development Ser.: No. 20). 151p. 1980. pap. 12.00 (ISBN 0-686-68966-6, UN79/2F11, UN). Unipub.

Working Group Meeting on Energy Planning & Committee on Natural Resources. Proceedings, Fifth Session. (Energy Resources Development Ser: No. 20). 151p. 1980. pap. 12.00 (UN79-2F11, UN). Unipub.

Working Party No. 3, Economic Policy Committee. The Balance of Payments Adjustment Process. 32p. 1966. 0.80 o.p. (ISBN 0-686-14785-5). OECD.

Workman, Harold. Introduction to Polymer Painting. (Illus.). 1967. 4.50 o.p. (ISBN 0-8231-7027-6). Branford.

Workman, Lewis C., jt. auth. see Harper, Floyd S.

Workman, M., tr. see Bartels, H.

Workman, Pat. What Happened to My Bread. 1981. 3.95 (ISBN 0-932298-12-5). Green Hill.

Works, Jan, jt. ed. see Works, Pat.

Works, John A., Jr. Pilgrims in a Strange Land: Hausa Communities in Chad. LC 76-23138. 1976. 17.50x (ISBN 0-231-03976-X). Columbia U Pr.

Works, Pat. The Art of Freefall Relative Work. rev. ed. LC 75-21405. 1979. 14.95 (ISBN 0-930438-04-3); pap. 7.95 (ISBN 0-930438-01-9). RWU Parachuting.

Works, Pat & Works, Jan, eds. United We Fall. LC 77-84030. 17.95 (ISBN 0-930438-03-5); pap. 11.95 (ISBN 0-930438-02-7). RWU Parachuting.

Workshop Held in the Leeuwenhorst Congress Centre Noordwijkerhout, Nov. 23-25, 1979. Epilepsy & Behavior Nineteen Seventy-Nine: Proceedings. Kulig, B. M., ed. 1980. text ed. 21.00 (ISBN 90-265-0332-6, Pub by Swets Pub Serv Holland). Swets North Am.

Workshop of the Phenomenon Known As 'El Nino' Proceedings. 284p. 1980. pap. 22.50 (ISBN 92-3-101509-5, U1019, UNESCO). Unipub.

Workshop on Chemical Aspects of Rice Grain Quality. Proceedings. 390p. 1979. pap. 20.50 (R027, IRRI). Unipub.

Workshop on the Genetic Conservation of Rice. Proceedings. 54p. 1978. pap. 7.50 (R034, IRRI). Unipub.

Workshop on the Interfaces Between Agriculture, Nutrition, & Food Science, 1977. Proceedings. 143p. 1979. pap. 7.25 (R087, IRRI). Unipub.

Worland, Peter B. Introduction to Basic Programming: A Structured Approach. LC 78-56436. (Illus.). 1979. pap. text ed. 11.95 (ISBN 0-395-26775-7); solutions manual 0.60 (ISBN 0-395-26776-5). HM.

World Almanac Editors. The World Almanac Book of Buffs, Masters, Mavens & Uncommon Experts. LC 80-8179. 1980. 12.50 (ISBN 0-13-967836-0). P-H.

--The World Almanac Book of Who. LC 80-81180. 1980. 12.50 (ISBN 0-13-967844-1). P-H.

World Association Of World Federalists - Youth And Student Division - 6th Intl. Study Conference. World Peace Through World Economy. 1968. pap. text ed. 5.75x (ISBN 0-391-02070-6). Humanities.

World Book Childcraft International, Inc. Best-Loved Bible Stories: Old Testament & New Testament, 2 vols. LC 79-55309. (Illus.). 90p. (gr. 4-8). 1980. write for info. (ISBN 0-7166-2059-6). World Bk-Childcraft.

World Book-Childcraft International Staff. The Bug Book. (Illus.). 304p. (gr. k-6). 1981. price not set (ISBN 0-7166-0681-X). World Bk-Childcraft.

World Book-Childcraft International Inc., ed. Childcraft-the How & Why Library, 15 vols. Incl. Vol. 1. Poems & Rhymes; Vol. 2. Stories & Fables; Vol. 3. Children Everywhere; Vol. 4. World & Space; Vol. 5. About Animals; Vol. 6. The Green Kingdom; Vol. 7. How Things Work; Vol. 8. About Us; Vol. 9. Holidays & Birthdays; Vol. 10. Places to Know; Vol. 11. Make & Do; Vol. 12. Look & Learn; Vol. 13. Mathemagic; Vol. 14. About Me; Vol. 15. Guide for Parents. (Illus.). (gr. k-6). 1981. PLB write for info. (ISBN 0-7166-0181-8). World Bk Child.

World Book-Childcraft International, Inc. Christmas in France. LC 80-50994. (Around the World Christmas Program Ser.). (Illus.). 80p. (ps-9). 1980. write for info. (ISBN 0-7166-3106-7). World Bk-Childcraft.

World Book-Childcraft International. Science Year, the World Book Science Annual. LC 65-21776. (Illus.). 432p. (gr. 7-12). 1980. PLB 11.95 (ISBN 0-7166-0581-3); text ed. 10.95 (ISBN 0-686-27566-7). World Bk Childcraft.

World Book-Childcraft International, Inc. Staff. Today Nineteen Eighty. LC 76-27228. (World Book Today Yearly Diaries Ser.). 1979. 8.95 (ISBN 0-7166-2031-6). World Bk-Childcraft.

World Book-Childcraft International, Inc. Today, 1981: A Personal Record & Reference Book. LC 76-27228. (World Book Today Yearly Diaries Ser.). (Illus.). 192p. 1980. write for info. (ISBN 0-7166-2032-4). World Bk-Childcraft.

World Book-Childcraft International. The World Book Encyclopedia, 22 vols. rev. ed. LC 79-84167. (Illus.). (gr. 4-12). 1980. Set. PLB write for info. (ISBN 0-7166-0080-3). World Bk-Childcraft.

World Book-Childcraft International, Inc. The World Book Illustrated Home Medical Encyclopedia, 4 vols. LC 79-56907. (Illus.). 1038p. 1980. write for info. (ISBN 0-7166-2060-X). World Bk-Childcraft.

World Book Encyclopedia Inc Staff. Today 1979. (World Book Today Yearly Diaries Ser.). 1978. 8.95 o.p. (ISBN 0-7166-2028-6). World Bk-Chilcraft.

World Congress on Pain, 1st, Florence, 1975. Advances in Pain Research & Therapy: Proceedings, Vol. 1. Bonica, John J. & Albe-Fessard, Denise, eds. LC 75-32095. 1976. 87.50 (ISBN 0-89004-090-7). Raven.

World Congress on Pain, 2nd, Montreal, Aug. 1978. Proceedings. Bonica, John J., et al, eds. LC 79-87468. (Advances in Pain Research & Therapy Ser.: Vol. 3). 1979. text ed. 84.00 (ISBN 0-89004-270-5). Raven.

World Congress on Special Education, 1st. Abstracts of Presentations: Abstracts of Presentations. Fink, Albert H., ed. LC 78-74018. 318p. 1978. pap. 5.00 o.p. (ISBN 0-86586-001-7). Coun Exc Child.

World Council of Churches. Classified Catalog of the Ecumenical Movement: First Supplement. (Library Catalogs-Supplements Ser.). 1981. lib. bdg. 95.00 (ISBN 0-686-69558-5). G K Hall.

World Environment & Resources Council (WERC) Brussels, Apr. 1976. The Environment of Human Settlements: Human Well-Being in Cities, Vol. 2. Laconte, Pierre, et al, eds. LC 76-5192. 1977. text ed. 75.00 (ISBN 0-685-74703-4). Pergamon.

World Health Organization. Waste Discharge into the Marine Environment: Principles & Guidelines. LC 80-40899. (Illus.). 544p. 1980. 75.00 (ISBN 0-08-026194-9). Pergamon.

World Hydrogen Energy Conference, 2nd, Zurich, Aug. 1978. Hydrogen Energy System: Proceedings, 4 vols. Veziroglu, T. N. & Seifritz, W., eds. LC 78-40507. 1978. Set. text ed. 410.00 (ISBN 0-08-023224-8). Pergamon.

World Hydrogen Energy Conference, 3rd, Tokyo, Japan 23-26 June 1980, et al. Hydrogen Energy Progress: Proceedings, 4 vols. Veziroglu, T. N., et al, eds. LC 80-40559. (Advances in Hydrogen Energy: 2). (Illus.). 2500p. 1981. 385.00 set (ISBN 0-08-024729-6). Pergamon.

World Meteorological Congress, Eighth. Proceedings. 261p. 1980. pap. 30.00 (ISBN 92-63-10547-2, W472, WMO). Unipub.

World Peace Through Law Centre. The Athens World Conference, 1963: Proceedings. 890p. 1964. 12.50x o.p. (ISBN 0-8002-0674-6). Intl Pubns Serv.

World Petroleum Congress, 9th, Japan, 1975. Proceedings. Applied Science Publishers Ltd., ed. Incl. Vol. 1. Introduction; Vol. 2. Geology; Vol. 3. Exploration & Transportation; Vol. 4. Drilling & Production; Vol. 5. Processing & Storage; Vol. 6. Conservation & Safety; Vol. 7. Index. (Illus.). 1975. 745.00 set (ISBN 0-85334-670-4). Intl Ideas.

World Print Council. Paper-Art & Technology. (Illus., Orig.). 1980. pap. 11.50 (ISBN 0-87701-162-1). Chronicle Bks.

World Shakespeare Congress, Vancouver, August 1971. Shakespeare Nineteen Seventy-One: Proceedings. Leech, Clifford & Margeson, John M., eds. LC 72-86265. 1972. 15.00x o.p. (ISBN 0-8020-1906-4); pap. 5.95 o.p. (ISBN 0-8020-6259-8). U of Toronto Pr.

Worldmark Press Ltd. The Worldmark Encyclopedia of the States. Sachs, Moshe, ed. LC 80-8218. (Illus.). 700p. 1981. pre-july 54.95 (ISBN 0-06-014733-4, HarpT); 54.95. Har-Row.

Worley, Ann, jt. auth. see Judd, Rue.

Worley, Richard, jt. auth. see Gant, Norman F.

Wormald, R. D. & Lyne, G. M. Rogues' Gallery. (Lat). 1939. text ed. 7.95x (ISBN 0-521-06869-X). Cambridge U Pr.

Wormer, Joe Van see Van Wormer, Joe.

Wormhoudt, Arthur, tr. from Classical Arabic. Dhikra Al Tanisi. (Arab Translation Ser.: No. 53). (Illus.). 1981. pap. 6.50x (ISBN 0-916358-09-7). Wormhoudt.

Wormhoudt, Arthur, tr. Dhikra Ibn Al Hajjaj. (Arab Translation Ser.: No. 55). (Illus.). 160p. pap. 6.50x (ISBN 0-916358-04-6). Wormhoudt.

Wormhoudt, Arthur, tr. from Arabic. Diwan 'Abdallah ibn al Mu'tazz. (Arab Translation Ser.: No. 38). 1978. pap. 6.50 (ISBN 0-916358-88-7). Wormhoudt.

--Diwan Al Gazal: Love Poems by Abu Nuwas & Abu Tammam. (Arab Translation Ser.: No. 48). 180p. 1980. pap. 6.50 (ISBN 0-916358-98-4). Wormhoudt.

--Diwan al Mutanabbi, Farsiyyat. (Arab Translation Ser.: No. 37). 1978. pap. 6.50 (ISBN 0-916358-87-9). Wormhoudt.

--Diwan al Mutanabbi, Misriyyat. (Arab Translation Ser.: No. 36). 1978. pap. 6.50 (ISBN 0-916358-86-0). Wormhoudt.

--Diwan al Mutanabbi: Selections. (Arab Translation Ser.: No. 1). 1968. pap. 2.50 (ISBN 0-916358-51-8). Wormhoudt.

--Diwan al Mutanabbi, Shawmiyyat, 3 pts. (Arab Translation Ser.: No. 31-33). 1978. pap. 6.50 ea. Pt. 1 (ISBN 0-916358-81-X). Pt. 2 (ISBN 0-916358-82-8). Pt. 3 (ISBN 0-916358-83-6). Wormhoudt.

--Diwan al Mutanabbi, Shawmiyyat, 2 pts. (Arab Translation Ser.: No. 34-35). 1978. pap. 6.50 ea. Pt. 1 (ISBN 0-916358-84-4). Pt. 2 (ISBN 0-916358-85-2). Wormhoudt.

--Diwan Jarwal Ibn Malik Ibn Makhzum Al 'absi Called Al Hutaia. (Arab Translation Ser.: No. 46). 175p. pap. 6.50x (ISBN 0-916358-96-8). Wormhoudt.

--Diwan Ka'b ibn Zuhair & Akhbar Majnun. (Arab Translation Ser.: No. 18). 1975. pap. 6.50 (ISBN 0-916358-68-2). Wormhoudt.

Wormhoudt, Arthur, tr. from Classical Arabic. The Diwan of Abu Tayyib Al Mutanabbi: Complete with Comments. (Arab Translation Ser.: No. 52). 200p. 1981. pap. 6.50x (ISBN 0-916358-07-0). Wormhoudt.

--The Diwan of Muslim ibn al Walid. (Arab Translation Ser.: No. 54). (Illus.). 175p. 1980. pap. 6.50 (ISBN 0-916358-02-X). Wormhoudt.

Wormhoudt, Arthur, tr. Poems from the Diwan of al Mutanabbi. (Arab Translation Ser.: No. 1). 85p. 1968. pap. 2.50 (ISBN 0-916358-51-8). Wormhoudt.

Wormhoudt, Arthur, tr. from Classical Arabic. Selections from the Quran. (Arab Translation Ser.: No. 51). 175p. 1981. pap. 6.50x (ISBN 0-916358-03-8). Wormhoudt.

Wormhoudt, Arthur, tr. see Al Ma 'arri, Abu 'Ala.

Wormhoudt, Arthur, tr. see Al Tha'alibi.

Wormhoudt, Arthur, tr. see Jarir & Farazdag.

Wormhoudt, Arthur, tr. see Ma'Arri, Abu Ala Al.

Wormhoudt, Pearl S. Building the Voice As an Instrument with a Studio Reference Handbook. (Illus., Orig.). 1981. pap. text ed. 8.95 (ISBN 0-916358-08-9). Wormhoudt.

Wormington, H. M. Prehistoric Indians of the Southwest. (Popular Ser.: No. 7). (Illus.). 192p. 1947. pap. 4.75 o.p. (ISBN 0-916278-15-8). Denver Mus Natl Hist.

Wormington, H. M. & Neal, Arminta. The Story of Pueblo Pottery. 4th ed. (Museum Pictorial: No. 2). 1974. pap. 1.10 o.p. (ISBN 0-916278-31-X). Denver Mus Natl Hist.

Wormser, Richard. The Black Mustanger. (Illus.). (gr. 5-9). 1971. 7.25 (ISBN 0-688-21104-6); PLB 6.96 (ISBN 0-688-31104-0). Morrow.

--Gone to Texas. (Illus.). (gr. 5-9). 1970. 8.25 (ISBN 0-688-21354-5). Morrow.

--On the Prod. 1978. pap. 1.25 o.p. (ISBN 0-449-14031-8, GM). Fawcett.

Wormsley, K. G. Duodenal Ulcer, Vol. 1. 1977. 14.40 (ISBN 0-904406-53-9). Eden Med Res.

Wormuth, Francis D. Essays in Law & Politics. Nelson, Dalmas H. & Sklar, Richard L., eds. (National University Pubns. Multi-Disciplinary Studies in the Law). 1978. 16.50 (ISBN 0-8046-9211-4). Kennikat.

Wormuth, John H. The Biogeography, & Numerical Taxonomy of the Oegopsid Squid Family: Ommastrephidae in the Pacific Ocean. (Bulletin of the Scipps Institution of Oceanography Ser.: Vol. 23). 1977. pap. 9.00x (ISBN 0-520-09540-5). U of Cal Pr.

Worner, Karl H. Stockhausen: Life & Work. Hopkins, Bill, ed. & tr. LC 76-174460. (Illus.). 1973. 17.95x (ISBN 0-520-02143-6); pap. 3.95 (ISBN 0-520-03272-1). U of Cal Pr.

Worner, Roger B. Student Diagnosis, Placement, & Prescription: A Criterion-Referenced Approach. LC 76-26432. (Illus.). 256p. 1977. 10.95x (ISBN 0-253-35526-5). Ind U Pr.

Woronoff, Jon. Organizing African Unity. LC 72-16716. 703p. 1979. lib. bdg. 19.00 (ISBN 0-8108-0321-6). Scarecrow.

--West African Wager: Houphouet Versus Nkrumah. LC 72-5155. 1972. 13.00 (ISBN 0-8108-0523-5). Scarecrow.

Worp, K. A., jt. auth. see Bagnall, Roger S.

Worrall, Arthur L. Quakers in the Colonial Northeast. LC 79-63086. 248p. 1980. text ed. 12.50 (ISBN 0-87451-174-7). U Pr of New Eng.

Worrall, J., ed. see Lakatos, E.

Worrall, J., ed. see Lakatos, I.

Worrall, J., ed. see Lakatos, Imre.

Worrall, Nick. Sudan. (Illus.). 136p. 1980. 30.00 (ISBN 0-7043-2242-0, Pub. by Quqrtet England). Horizon.

Worrall, W. E. Clays & Ceramic Raw Materials. LC 75-12684. 203p. 1975. 29.95 (ISBN 0-470-96085-X). Halsted Pr.

Worrel, J. W. Directory of Music Companies: United States & Foreign. pap. 4.50 o.p. (ISBN 0-686-15898-9). Instrumental Co.

Worrell, Albert C., jt. auth. see Sinden, J. A.

Worrell, Estelle A. Children's Costume in America Sixteen Hundred & Seven to Nineteen Ten. (Illus.). 224p. 1981. 25.00 (ISBN 0-684-16645-3, ScribT). Scribner.

Worrell, George E. How to Take the Worry Out of Witnessing. LC 76-13342. 96p. 1976. pap. 2.75 (ISBN 0-8054-5568-X). Broadman.

Worring, Raymond, jt. auth. see Hibbard, Whitney.

Worsfold, W. Basil. Palestine of the Mandate. (Return to Zion Ser.). (Illus.). xii, 275p. 1980. Repr. of 1925 ed. lib. bdg. 20.00x (ISBN 0-87991-138-7). Porcupine Pr.

Worsley, Dale. The Focus Changes of August Pervico. LC 80-19515. 192p. 1980. 10.00 (ISBN 0-8149-0841-1). Vanguard.

Worsley, F. A. Shackleton's Boat Journey. 1978. pap. 1.95 o.s.i. (ISBN 0-515-04486-5). Jove Pubns.

Worsley, Peter. Two Blades of Grass: Rural Cooperatives in Agricultural Modernization. 1971. text ed. 21.00x (ISBN 0-7190-0444-6). Humanities.

Worst, Edward. Foot Treadle Loom Weaving. rev ed. (Illus.). 1975. pap. 4.95 (ISBN 0-88930-011-9, Pub. by Cloudburst Canada). Madrona Pubs.

Worstell, Emma V. Jump the Rope Jingles. (gr. k up). 1967. 4.95g o.s.i. (ISBN 0-02-793400-4). Macmillan.

Worster, Donald. Dust Bowl: The Southern Plains in the 1930's. (Illus.). 1979. 16.95 (ISBN 0-19-502550-4). Oxford U Pr.

--Nature's Economy. LC 78-8220. 1979. pap. 4.95 (ISBN 0-385-14345-1, Anch). Doubleday.

Worsthorne, Simon T. Venetian Opera in the Seventeenth Century. 1954. 36.00x (ISBN 0-19-816116-6). Oxford U Pr.

Worstman, Gail L. The Natural Fast Food Cookbook. LC 80-19474. 160p. 1980. pap. 5.95 (ISBN 0-914718-52-5). Pacific Search.

Worswick, G. David, ed. The Concept & Measurement of Involuntary Unemployment. LC 75-42385. 1976. 38.50x (ISBN 0-89158-527-3). Westview.

Wortabet & Porter. Arabic-English; English-Arabic Dictionary. 1979. 15.00 (ISBN 0-685-96662-3). Intl Bk Ctr.

Wortabet, John. Arabic-English Pocket Dictionary. 1980. pap. 5.50x. Intl Bk Ctr.

--English-Arabic; Arabic-English Dictionary. 1979. pap. 15.00x. Intl Bk Ctr.

--English-Arabic Pocket Dictionary. 1980. pap. 5.50x. Intl Bk Ctr.

Wortabet, William. Arabic-English Dictionary. 1968. 18.00x (ISBN 0-685-72027-6). Intl Bk Ctr.

Worth, B. H. Income Tax Law for Ministers & Religious Workers. 1979. pap. 2.95 o.p. (ISBN 0-8010-9631-6). Baker Bk.

Worth, B. J. Income Tax Handbook for Ministers & Religious Workers: 1981 Edition for Preparing 1980 Returns. 60p. (Orig.). 1980. pap. 2.95 (ISBN 0-8010-9642-1). Baker Bk.

Worth, C. A., ed. see Stigant, S. Austin & Franklin, A. C.

Worth, Dean S. A Bibliography of Russian Word-Formation. 1977. soft cover 14.95 (ISBN 0-89357-041-9). Slavica.

--A Dictionary of Western Kamchadal. (U. C. Publ. in Linguistics: Vol. 59). 1969. pap. 10.00x (ISBN 0-520-09256-2). U of Cal Pr.

Worth, Fred L. The Complete Unabridged Super Trivia Encyclopedia. 1978. pap. 3.50 (ISBN 0-446-96905-2). Warner Bks.

--Thirty Years of Rock & Roll Trivia. 288p. (Orig.). 1980. pap. 2.50 (ISBN 0-446-91494-0). Warner Bks.

Worth, Fred L., jt. auth. see Strauss, David P.

Worth, Katharine. The Irish Drama of Europe from Yeats to Beckett. LC 78-18909. 1978. text ed. 32.50x (ISBN 0-391-00891-9, Athlone Pr). Humanities.

Worth, Katharine, ed. Beckett the Shape Changer. 1975. 15.00 (ISBN 0-7100-8123-5). Routledge & Kegan.

Worth, Leslie. Laying a Watercolour Wash. (Leisure Arts Painting Ser.). (Illus.). 32p. 1980. pap. 2.50 (ISBN 0-8008-4574-9, Pentalic). Taplinger.

--Painting Sea & Sky in Watercolor. (Leisure Arts Painting Ser.). (Illus.). 32p. 1980. pap. 2.50 (ISBN 0-8008-6206-6, Pentalic). Taplinger.

--Working with Watercolour. (Leisure Arts Painting Ser.). (Illus.). 32p. 1980. pap. 2.50 (ISBN 0-8008-8546-5, Pentalic). Taplinger.

Worth, Thomas. Basic for Everyone. (Illus.). 368p. 1976. 13.95 (ISBN 0-13-061481-5); pap. write for info. P-H.

--Cobol for Beginners. (Illus.). 1977. pap. text ed. 13.95 (ISBN 0-13-139378-2). P-H.

Worth, Veryl M. Willow Pattern China: With Separate Price Guide. 2nd ed. (Illus.). 1981. pap. 9.95. Worth Co.

Wortham, Anne. The Other Side of Racism: A Philosophical Study of Black Consciousness. 237p. 1981. 12.50 (ISBN 0-8142-0318-3). Ohio St U Pr.

Wortham, Jim & Whitener, Barbara. Forget the Gas Pumps-Make Your Own Fuel. LC 79-90459. (Illus., Orig.). 1979. lib. bdg. 12.95 (ISBN 0-915216-72-8); pap. 4.95 (ISBN 0-915216-43-4). Love Street.

Wortham, John D. Genesis of British Egyptology, 1549-1906. LC 78-160509. (Illus.). 1971. 9.95x o.p. (ISBN 0-8061-0981-5). U of Okla Pr.

Wortham, Thomas, et al, eds. Selected Letters of W. D. Howells, 1892-1901, Vol. 4. (Critical Editions Program Ser.). 1981. lib. bdg. 30.00 (ISBN 0-8057-8530-2). Twayne.

Worthen, Amy N. & Reed, Sue W. The Etchings of Jacques Bellange. (Illus.). 1976. pap. 6.00 (ISBN 0-87846-094-2, Pub. by Desmoines Art Center). Mus Fine Arts Boston.

Worthing, Charles R., ed. The Pesticide Manual. 6th ed. 655p. 1979. 59.95x (ISBN 0-901436-44-5, Pub. by Brit Crop Protection England). Intl Schol Bk Serv.

Worthingham, Catherine, jt. auth. see Daniels, Lucille.

Worthington, Arthur M. Study of Splashes. (gr. 10 up). 1963. 6.25g o.s.i. (ISBN 0-02-793570-1). Macmillan.

Worthington, Barton. The Nile. LC 78-62991. (Rivers of the World Ser.). (Illus.). 1978. lib. bdg. 7.95 (ISBN 0-686-51136-0). Silver.

Worthington, Bonnie & Taylor, Lynda. Nutrition During Pregnancy & Breast Feeding. (Illus.). 1980. pap. 2.50. Budlong.

Worthington, E. B., ed. The Evolution of IBP, Vol. 1. LC 75-2722. (International Biological Programme Ser.). (Illus.). 276p. 1975. 49.50 (ISBN 0-521-20736-3). Cambridge U Pr.

Worthington, E. Barton, ed. Arid Land Irrigation in Developing Countries: Environmental Problems & Effects. 1977. text ed. 105.00 (ISBN 0-08-021588-2). Pergamon.

Worthington, George. In Search of World Records. LC 80-82032. (gr. 10-12). 1980. 12.95 (ISBN 0-938282-01-8); pap. 9.95 (ISBN 0-938282-02-6). Hang Gliding.

Worthington, Greville. A Bibliography of the Waverly Novels. 143p. 1980. Repr. of 1931 ed. lib. bdg. 30.00 (ISBN 0-8495-5655-4). Arden Lib.

Worthington, Jane, ed. see Wordsworth, William.

Worthington, Robin. Helping Children Meet Change. (Uplook Ser.). 1978. pap. 0.75 (ISBN 0-8163-0200-6, 08493-9). Pacific Pr Pub Assn.

--Mom, I Can't Decide. (Uplook Ser.). 32p. 1973. pap. 0.75 (ISBN 0-8163-0075-5, 13640-8). Pacific Pr Pub Assn.

Worthington-Roberts, Bonnie S. Contemporary Developments in Nutrition. LC 80-21557. (Illus.). 603p. 1980. pap. text ed. 17.95 (ISBN 0-8016-5627-3). Mosby.

Worthington-Roberts, Bonnie S., et al. Nutrition in Pregnancy & Lactation. (Illus.). 296p. 1981. pap. text ed. 11.95 (ISBN 0-8016-5626-5). Mosby.

Worthley, John A. Public Administration & Legislatures: Experimentation & Exploration. LC 75-23150. 256p. 1976. 16.95 (ISBN 0-88229-233-1). Nelson-Hall.

Worthley, John A. & Ludwin, William G., eds. Zero-Base Budgeting in State & Local Government: Current Experiences & Cases. LC 79-10162. 1979. 20.95 (ISBN 0-03-049121-5). Praeger.

Worthley, William J. Sourcebook of Articulation Activities. 1981. pap. text ed. price not set. Little.

Wortis, Joseph. Fragments of an Analysis with Freud. LC 54-9792. 224p. 1975. 6.95 o.p. (ISBN 0-07-071903-9, SP); pap. 3.50 o.p. (ISBN 0-07-071904-7). McGraw.

Wortis, Joseph, ed. Mental Retardation & Developmental Disabilities, Vol. XII. LC 73-647002. 200p. 1981. 20.00 (ISBN 0-87630-263-0). Brunner-Mazel.

--Mental Retardation & Developmental Disabilities: An Annual Review. Incl. Vol. 5. 1973. o.p. (ISBN 0-87630-068-9); Vol. 6. 1974 (ISBN 0-685-57356-7); Vol. 7. 1975 (ISBN 0-685-57357-5); Vol. 8. 1976 (ISBN 0-685-57358-3); Vol. 9. 1977; Vol. 10. 1978; Vol. 11. LC 73-647002. 1979 (ISBN 0-87630-214-2). LC 75-86629. Vols. 6-11. 20.00 ea. Brunner-Mazel.

Wortman, Camille, jt. auth. see Loftus, Elizabeth.

Wortman, Leon. Successful Small Business Management. (AMACOM Executive Books). 1978. pap. 5.95 (ISBN 0-8144-7503-5). Am Mgmt.

Wortman, Leon A. Effective Management for Engineers & Scientists. 264p. 1981. 17.95 (ISBN 0-471-05523-9, Ronald Pr). Wiley.

Wortman, Max S., jt. auth. see Hodgetts, Richard M.

Wortman, Richard. Crisis of Russian Populism. 1967. 26.95 (ISBN 0-521-06913-0). Cambridge U Pr.

Wortman, Tunis. Treatise Concerning Political Enquiry & the Liberty of the Press. LC 78-122162. (Civil Liberties in American History Ser). 1970. Repr. of 1800 ed. lib. bdg. 35.00 (ISBN 0-306-71967-3). Da Capo.

Woshinsky, Oliver H. The French Deputy: Incentives & Behavior in the National Assembly. LC 73-7960. (Illus.). 256p. 1973. 17.95 o.p. (ISBN 0-669-90159-8). Lexington Bks.

Woudenberg, Paul. Lincoln & Continental: The Postwar Years. LC 80-12242. (Marques of America Ser.). (Illus.). 152p. 1980. 18.95 (ISBN 0-87938-063-2). Motorbooks Intl.

Woudhuysen, Jan. Tarot Therapy. LC 80-51556. 203p. 1980. 10.00 (ISBN 0-87477-141-2). J P Tarcher.

Woudstra, Marten H. The Book of Joshua. LC 80-23413. (New International Commentary on the Old Testament). 400p. 1981. 16.95 (ISBN 0-8028-2356-4). Eerdmans.

Wouk, Herman. City Boy. 1980. pap. write for info. (ISBN 0-671-41511-5). PB.

--City Boy: The Adventures of Herbie Bookbinder. LC 69-10961. 1969. 8.95 (ISBN 0-385-04072-5). Doubleday.

--The Lomokome Papers. (Illus.). 113p. 1976. Repr. of 1968 ed. lib. bdg. 12.95x (ISBN 0-89244-086-4). Queens Hse.

--This Is My God. LC 79-78741. 1959. 10.95 (ISBN 0-385-02158-5). Doubleday.

--This Is My God. 1980. pap. write for info. (ISBN 0-671-41512-3). PB.

Woy, James B., ed. Business Trends & Forecasting Information Sources. LC 65-28351. (Management Information Guide Ser.: No. 9). 1965. 30.00 (ISBN 0-8103-0809-6). Gale.

--Investment Information: A Detailed Guide to Selected Sources. LC 79-118791. (Management Information Guides Ser.: No. 19). 1970. 30.00 (ISBN 0-8103-0819-3). Gale.

Wozniak, John M. English Composition in Eastern Colleges 1850-1940. LC 78-59125. (Illus.). 1978. pap. text ed. 11.75 (ISBN 0-8191-0549-X). U Pr of Amer.

Wozniak, John S. Contact, Negotiation, & Conflict: An Ethnohistory of the Eastern Dakota, 1819-1839. LC 78-62248. 1978. pap. text ed. 9.00 (ISBN 0-8191-0569-4). U Pr of Amer.

Wragg, David. A Dictionary of Aviation. LC 74-75382. 1974. 9.95 (ISBN 0-8119-0236-6). Fell.

--Flight Before Flying. LC 73-93897. (Illus.). 1974. 9.95 (ISBN 0-8119-0233-1). Fell.

Wragg, David W. Speed in the Air. LC 74-7456. 1975. 9.95 (ISBN 0-8119-0246-3). Fell.

Wragg, E. C. Teaching Teaching. LC 74-82023. 1975. 17.95 (ISBN 0-7153-6857-5). David & Charles.

Wragg, H., jt. auth. see Duckitt, M.

Wraight, A. D. & Stern, Virginia. In Search of Christopher Marlowe: A Pictorial Biography. LC 65-20820. (Illus.). 1965. 15.00 (ISBN 0-8149-0213-8). Vanguard.

Wraith, R. E. & Hutchesson, P. G. Administrative Tribunals. (Royal Institute of Public Administration). 1973. text ed. 49.95x (ISBN 0-04-347002-5). Allen Unwin.

Wraith, R. E. & Lamb, G. B. Public Inquiries As an Instrument of Government. (Royal Institute of Public Administration). 1971. text ed. 42.50x (ISBN 0-04-351037-X). Allen Unwin.

Wrangel, Alexis. The Last Great Cavalry Battles. (Illus.). 180p. 1981. 15.00 (ISBN 0-88254-518-3). Hippocrene Bks.

Wrangell, Ferdinand P. Russian-America, Statistical & Ethnographical Information. Pierce, Richard A., ed. Sadouski, Mary, tr. from Ger. (Materials for the Study of Alaska History: No. 15). (Illus.). 1980. 16.50 (ISBN 0-919642-79-9). Limestone Pr.

Wrangham, Elizabeth. The Communications Revolution. Yapp, Malcolm, et al, eds. (World History Ser.). (Illus.). 32p. (gr. 10). 1980. Repr. of 1977 ed. lib. bdg. 5.95 (ISBN 0-89908-134-7); pap. text ed. 1.95 (ISBN 0-89908-109-6). Greenhaven.

Wrangham, Elizabeth, et al. The Family. Yapp, Malcolm, et al, eds. (World History Ser.). (Illus.). 32p. (gr. 10). 1980. lib. bdg. 5.95 (ISBN 0-89908-148-7); pap. text ed. 1.95 (ISBN 0-89908-123-1). Greenhaven.

Wrangles, Alan, ed. The Complete Guide to Sea Angling. (Illus.). 16.95 (ISBN 0-7153-5886-3). David & Charles.

Wratchford, Eugene P. Brain Research & Personhood: A Philosophical Theological Inquiry. LC 79-51466. 1979. pap. text ed. 8.60 o.p. (ISBN 0-8191-0749-2). U Pr of Amer.

Wrathall, Celia, jt. auth. see Miller, Webb.

Wray, Eje, ed. see Taylor, R. D.

Wray, Monika J., et al. Unified Vocational Preparation: An Evaluation of the Pilot Programme. (Report of the National Foundation for Educational Research in England & Wales). 289p. 1980. pap. text ed. 19.25x (ISBN 0-85633-199-6). Humanities.

Wray, R. Christie, jt. auth. see Weeks, Paul M.

Wrede, Robert C. Introduction to Vector & Tensor Analysis. 418p. 1972. pap. text ed. 6.00 (ISBN 0-486-61879-X). Dover.

Wrede, Stuart, tr. see Aalto, Alvar.

Wrede, William. Messianic Secret. Greig, J. C., tr. 1972. 20.00 (ISBN 0-227-67717-X). Attic Pr.

Wren, Christopher S. Winner Got Scars Too: The Life & Legends of Johnny Cash. 1974. pap. 1.25 o.p. (ISBN 0-345-23731-5). Ballantine.

Wren, Daniel A. Evolution of Management Thought. 2nd ed. LC 78-10959. (Management & Administration Ser.). 1979. text ed. 22.95 (ISBN 0-471-04695-7). Wiley.

Wren, Daniel A. & Voich, Dan, Jr. Principles of Management: Process & Behavior. 2nd ed. LC 75-43472. 1976. 21.95x (ISBN 0-8260-9640-9, Pub. by Wiley-Hamilton). Wiley.

Wren, David N. Every First Monday: A History of Canton, Texas. 7.95 (ISBN 0-685-48793-8). Nortex Pr.

Wren, M. K. Phoenix I. (Orig.). 1981. pap. 2.75 (ISBN 0-425-04746-6). Berkley Pub.

--Seasons of Death. (Crime Club Ser.). 192p. 1981. 9.95 (ISBN 0-385-17413-6). Doubleday.

--Shadow of the Swan. 1981. pap. text ed. 2.75 (ISBN 0-425-04747-4). Berkley Pub.

Wren, Percival C. Beau Geste. 1976. lib. bdg. 17.75x (ISBN 0-89968-135-2). Lightyear.

--Beau Ideal. 1976. lib. bdg. 16.75x (ISBN 0-89968-136-0). Lightyear.

--Beau Sabreur. 1976. lib. bdg. 16.75x (ISBN 0-89968-136-0). Lightyear.

Wren, R. C. Potter's New Cyclopaedia of Botanical Drugs & Preparations. 1980. text ed. 23.95x (ISBN 0-8464-1039-7). Beekman Pubs.

Wren, Robert M. Achebe's World: The Historical & Cultural Context of Chinua Achebe's Novels. (Illus.). 240p. (Orig.). 1980. 18.00x (ISBN 0-89410-005-X); pap. 9.00x (ISBN 0-89410-006-8). Three Continents.

Wren, Thomas, intro. by. The Personal Universe: Essays in Honor of John Macmurray. 120p. 1975. Repr. text ed. 8.00x (ISBN 0-391-00398-4). Humanities.

Wrenn, C. Gilbert. The World of the Contemporary Counselor. LC 72-4800. 368p. (Orig.). 1973. pap. text ed. 10.95 (ISBN 0-395-13901-5, 3-60800). HM.

Wrenn, C. Gilbert & Larsen, Robert P. Studying Effectively. 1955. pap. 0.65x (ISBN 0-8047-1071-6). Stanford U Pr.

Wrenn, C. Gilbert, jt. auth. see Schwarzrock, Shirley.

Wrenn, C. L. The English Language. Date not set. Repr. of 1949 ed. lib. bdg. 22.50 (ISBN 0-89760-901-8). Telegraph Bks.

Wrenn, Catherine B., jt. auth. see Kreith, Frank.

Wrenn, Charles L. W. B. Yeats: A Literary Study. 50p. 1980. Repr. of 1920 ed. lib. bdg. 10.00 (ISBN 0-8492-2998-7). R West.

Wrenn, John H. John Dos Passos. (U. S. Authors Ser.: No. 9). 1961. lib. bdg. 10.95 (ISBN 0-8057-0208-3). Twayne.

Wrenn, Marie-Claude. You're the Only One Here Who Doesn't Look Like a Doctor: Portrait of a Woman Surgeon. LC 77-7871. 1977. 9.95 o.p. (ISBN 0-690-01420-1, TYC-T). T Y Crowell.

Wrentz, Susie R. The Saint & the Sinner. LC 79-66397. 1980. 7.95 (ISBN 0-533-04389-1). Vantage.

Wreszin, Michael. Superfluous Anarchist: Albert Jay Nock. LC 75-154339. (Illus.). 196p. 1971. 8.50 (ISBN 0-87057-130-3). Univ Pr of New England.

Wreszin, Michael, jt. ed. see Warren, Frank A.

Wreto, Tore. Johan Ludvig Runeberg. (World Author Ser.: No, 503). 1981. lib. bdg. 14.95 (ISBN 0-8057-6344-9). Twayne.

Wrich, James T. The Employee Assistance Program. rev. ed. 1980. 7.95. Hazelden.

--The Employee Assistance Program. 1974. pap. 2.95 (ISBN 0-89486-097-6). Hazelden.

Wriggins, W. Howard. Ruler's Imperative: Strategies for Political Survival in Asia & Africa. LC 73-90431. (Southern Asian Institute Publications Ser.). 1969. 17.50x (ISBN 0-231-03314-1). Columbia U Pr.

Wriggins, W. Howard & Adler-Karlsson, Gunnar. Reducing Global Inequities. (Nineteen Eighties Project (Council on Foreign Relations)). 1978. text ed. 10.95 o.p. (ISBN 0-07-071925-X, P&RB); pap. text ed. 5.95 o.p. (ISBN 0-07-071926-8). McGraw.

Wriggins, W. Howard & Guyot, James F., eds. Population, Politics, & the Future of Southern Asia. 400p. 1973. 15.00x (ISBN 0-231-03756-2); pap. 7.00x (ISBN 0-231-03757-0). Columbia U Pr.

Wright & New. Introductory Algebra. 298p. 1981. text ed. 16.95 (ISBN 0-205-07310-7, 5673100); free tchr's ed. (ISBN 0-205-07311-5); free student's guide (ISBN 0-205-07312-3). Allyn.

Wright & Sims. Community Nutrition. 1981. pap. text ed. 11.95 (ISBN 0-686-69107-5). Duxbury Pr.

Wright & Tate. Economic Concepts & Systems Analysis: An Introduction for Public Managers. 1973. 8.95 (ISBN 0-201-08745-6). A-W.

Wright, A., jt. auth. see Byrne, D.

Wright, A., et al. Games for Language Learning. pap. 7.95 (ISBN 0-521-22170-6). Cambridge U Pr.

Wright, A. E. & Moseley, F. Ice Ages: Ancient & Modern; Geological Journal Special Issue, No. 6. (Liverpool Geological Society & the Manchester Geological Association). 320p. 1980. 51.95 (ISBN 0-471-27753-3, Pub. by Wiley-Interscience). Wiley.

Wright, A. J., jt. auth. see Golden, Dean W.

Wright, Al G. & Newcomb, Stanley. Bands of the World. 14.00 (ISBN 0-686-15894-6). Instrumentalist Co.

Wright, Andrew. Visual Materials for the Language Teacher. (Handbooks for Language Teachers Ser.). (Illus.). 192p. 1975. pap. text ed. 7.50x (ISBN 0-582-52267-6). Longman.

Wright, Anne, ed. see Shaw, George B.

Wright, Arthur F., ed. Perspctives on the T'ang. Twitchett. LC 72-91310. 542p. 1981. pap. 10.95x (ISBN 0-300-02674-9). Yale U Pr.

Wright, B. A., ed. see Milton, John.

Wright, Barbara, ed. see Fromentin, Eugene.

Wright, Barbara, tr. see Arrabal, Fernando.

Wright, Barbara, tr. see Cixous, Helen.

Wright, Barbara, tr. see Queneau, Raymond.

Wright, Barbara, tr. see Topor, Roland.

Wright, Barbara, tr. see Tzara, Tristan.

Wright, Benjamin D. & Stone, Mark H. Best Test Design. LC 79-88489. 1979. 19.00. Mesa Pr IL.

Wright, Benjamin D., jt. ed. see David, Thomas G.

Wright, Benjamin F. Five Public Philosophies of Walter Lippmann. LC 73-6696. 168p. 1973. 12.95x o.p. (ISBN 0-292-72407-1). U of Tex Pr.

Wright, Betty R. The Cat Who Stamped His Feet. (Eager Readers Ser.). (Illus.). (gr. k-3). 1975. PLB 5.00 (ISBN 0-307-60806-9, Golden Pr). Western Pub.

--The Day Our TV Broke Down. LC 80-14434. (Life & Living from a Child's Point of View Ser.). (Illus.). 32p. (gr. k-5). 1980. PLB 9.65 (ISBN 0-8172-1365-1). Raintree Pubs.

--I Like Being Alone. LC 80-25513. (Life & Living from a Child's Point of View Ser.). (Illus.). (gr. k-5). 1981. PLB 9.65 (ISBN 0-8172-1367-8). Raintree Child.

--I Want to Read. (Illus.). (ps-2). 1965. 1.95 (ISBN 0-307-10879-1, Golden Pr); PLB 7.62 (ISBN 0-307-60879-4). Western Pub.

--My New Mom & Me. LC 80-25529. (Life & Living from a Child's Point of View Ser.). (Illus.). (gr. k-5). 1981. PLB 9.65 (ISBN 0-8172-1368-6). Raintree Child.

--My Sister Is Different. LC 80-25508. (Life & Living from a Child's Point of View Ser.). (Illus.). 32p. (gr. k-5). 1981. PLB 9.65 (ISBN 0-8172-1369-4). Raintree Child.

--The Rabbit's Adventure. (Young Reader Ser.). (Illus.). (gr. k-3). 1979. PLB 5.00 (ISBN 0-307-60164-1, Golden Pr). Western Pub.

--Roger' Upside-Down Day. (Tell-a-Tale Reader). 32p. (ps-3). 1980. PLB 4.77 (ISBN 0-307-68481-4, Golden Pr). Western Pub.

--This Room Is Mine: A Story About Sharing. (Tell-a-Tale Readers). (Illus.). (gr. k-3). 1977. PLB 4.77 (ISBN 0-307-68643-4, Whitman). Western Pub.

--Why Do I Daydream? LC 80-25561. (Life & Living from a Child's Point of View Ser.). (Illus.). 32p. (gr. k-5). 1981. PLB 9.65 (ISBN 0-8172-1371-6). Raintree Child.

Wright, Billie. Four Seasons North: A Journal of Life in the Alaskan Wilderness. LC 79-138774. (Illus.). 288p. (YA) 1973. 9.95 o.p. (ISBN 0-06-014756-3, HarpT). Har-Row.

Wright, Brooks. The Artist & the Unicorn. 1978. 16.95 (ISBN 0-89062-058-X). Rockland County Hist.

Wright, C. D., intro. by see Benitez, Zuleyka.

Wright, Carol. The Holiday Cook: Recipes & Shopping Away from Home. LC 80-68682. (Illus.). 160p. 1981. 14.50 (ISBN 0-7153-8017-6). David & Charles.

--Hotel. LC 78-61229. (Careers Ser.). (Illus.). 1979. lib. bdg. 7.95 (ISBN 0-686-51121-2). Silver.

Wright, Charles. Bloodlines. LC 74-2196. (Wesleyan Poetry Program: Vol. 77). 80p. 1975. pap. 4.95 (ISBN 0-8195-1077-7, Pub. by Wesleyan U Pr). Columbia U Pr.

--China Trace. LC 77-74604. (The Wesleyan Poetry Program: Vol. 88). 1977. pap. 10.00x (ISBN 0-8195-2088-8, Pub. by Wesleyan U Pr); pap. 4.95 (ISBN 0-8195-1088-2). Columbia U Pr.

--Dead Color. (Fine Press Poetry Ser.). (Illus.). 20p. 1980. fabriano covers, signed 45.00 (ISBN 0-931356-04-0). Seluzicki Poetry.

--The Grave of the Right Hand. LC 76-105510. (Wesleyan Poetry Program: Vol. 51). Orig. Title: Lost Displays. 1970. 10.00x (ISBN 0-8195-2051-9, Pub. by Wesleyan U Pr). Columbia U Pr.

--Hard Freight. LC 73-6014. (Wesleyn Poetry Program: Vol. 69). 1973. pap. 4.95 (ISBN 0-8195-1069-6, Pub. by Wesleyan U Pr). Columbia U Pr.

Wright, Charles & St. John, David. Wright: A Profile. (Profile Editions Ser.). (Illus.). 1979. pap. 4.00 o.p. (ISBN 0-931238-06-4); pap. 8.00 signed & lettered o. p. o.p. (ISBN 0-931238-07-2). Grilled Flowers Pr.

Wright, Charles & Neil, Charles, eds. The Protestant Dictionary: Containing Articles on the History, Doctrines, & Practices of the Christian Church. LC 73-155436. 1971. Repr. of 1933 ed. 32.00 (ISBN 0-8103-3388-0). Gale.

Wright, Chris & Bisson, Roy. Motorcycling Fundamentals. (Fundamentals: A Series on Getting It Right First Time). (Illus.). 80p. (Orig.). 1979. pap. 10.25 (ISBN 0-589-50081-3, Pub. by Reed Books Australia). C E Tuttle.

Wright, Christopher. The Dutch Painters: One Hundred Seventeenth Century Masters. LC 77-21988. (Illus.). 1978. 14.95 (ISBN 0-8120-5163-7). Barron.

--Vermeer. (Illus.). 1977. 15.95 (ISBN 0-8467-0254-1, Pub. by Two Continents); pap. 9.95 (ISBN 0-8467-0253-3). Hippocrene Bks.

--The Welfare State. (Illus.). 72p. (gr. 9-12). 1981. 14.95 (ISBN 0-7134-2375-7, Pub. by Batsford England). David & Charles.

Wright, Christopher, compiled by. Paintings in Dutch Museums: An Index of Oil Paintings in Public Collections in the Netherlands. (Illus.). 591p. 1980. 75.00x (ISBN 0-85667-077-4, Pub. by Sotheby Parke Bernet England). Biblio Dist.

Wright, D., ed. History of Nepal. Singh, M. S., tr. 1972. Repr. of 1877 ed. 18.00 (ISBN 0-8426-0478-2). Verry.

Wright, D. F., jt. auth. see Wilson, R. W.

Wright, D. F., ed. see Jenkins, Peter.

Wright, D. Franklin & Lindgren, Kenneth E. Elementary Algebra for College Students. 1971. text ed. 14.95x o.p. (ISBN 0-669-52134-5); instructor's guide free o.p. (ISBN 0-669-52142-6). Heath.

--Elementary Functions: Pre-Calculus Mathematics. 1973. text ed. 15.95x o.p. (ISBN 0-669-84285-0); instructor's guide free o.p. (ISBN 0-669-84798-4). Heath.

--Intermediate Algebra for College Students. LC 74-146711. (Illus.). 1971. text ed. 15.95x o.p. (ISBN 0-669-61754-7); instructor's manual free o.p. (ISBN 0-669-61762-8). Heath.

Wright, D. Franklin & New, Bill D. Intermediate Algebra. new ed. 450p. 1981. text ed. 16.75 (ISBN 0-205-07185-6, 567185-X); tchrs'. ed. avail. (ISBN 0-205-07186-4). Allyn.

Wright, Daniel, ed. History of Nepal. 1972. 9.50x (ISBN 0-685-89512-2). Himalaya Hse.

Wright, Dare. Edith & the Duckling. LC 80-1664. (Illus.). 48p. (ps-3). 1981. 8.95a (ISBN 0-385-17100-5); PLB (ISBN 0-385-17101-3). Doubleday.

--Look at a Gull. (Illus.). (gr. k-3). 1967. PLB 4.99 (ISBN 0-394-91628-X, BYR). Random.

Wright, David. To the Gods the Shades. (Poetry Ser.). 1979. 9.95 o.s.i. (ISBN 0-85635-181-4, Pub. by Carcanet New Pr England). Persea Bks.

Wright, David, jt. ed. see Heath-Stubbs, John.

Wright, David H. Co-Operatives & Community. 118p. 1979. pap. text ed. 8.75x (ISBN 0-7199-0952-X, Pub. by Bedford England). Renouf.

Wright, David M. The Creation of Purchasing Power: A Study in the Problem of Economic Stabilization. xiv, 251p. 1980. Repr. of 1942 ed. lib. bdg. 17.50x (ISBN 0-87991-072-0). Porcupine Pr.

Wright, David W., jt. auth. see Cragan, John F.

Wright, Dorothy. The Complete Book of Baskets & Basketry. (Encore Edition). (Illus.). 1978. 3.95 (ISBN 0-684-16558-9, ScribT). Scribner.

Wright, Dudley. The Book of Vampires. 1973. Repr. of 1924 ed. 15.00 (ISBN 0-685-32597-0). Gale.

Wright, Edmund. The Ironic Discourse: An Interdisciplinary Approach. (Harvester Studies in Philosophy: No. 19). 1980. text ed. write for info. (ISBN 0-391-01807-8). Humanities.

Wright, Elizabeth M. Rustic Speech & Folklore. LC 68-18011. 1968. Repr. of 1913 ed. 18.00 (ISBN 0-8103-3294-9). Gale.

Wright, Elizabeth M., jt. auth. see Wright, Joseph.

Wright, Ellen, ed. see Wright, Richard.

Wright, Elliott. Holy Company: Christian Heros & Heroines. 1980. 11.95 (ISBN 0-02-631590-4). Macmillan.

Wright, Elliott, jt. auth. see Lynn, Robert W.

Wright, Elvera G. Driblets from the Pen of E. G. W. LC 80-52185. (Illus.). 65p. 1981. 5.95 (ISBN 0-533-04747-1). Vantage.

Wright, Esmond. Benjamin Franklin: A Profile. 227p. 1970. pap. 6.95 o.p. (ISBN 0-8090-4657-1). Hill & Wang.

Wright, Esmond, ed. American Profiles. LC 68-90664. (Selections from History Today Ser.: No. 7). (Illus.). 1969. pap. 3.95 (ISBN 0-05-001534-6). Dufour.

--American Themes. LC 68-88949. (Selections from History Today Ser.: No. 1). (Illus.). 1969. 5.00 (ISBN 0-05-001529-X); pap. 3.95 (ISBN 0-685-09156-2). Dufour.

--A Tug of Loyalties: Anglo-American Relations 1765-85. (Institute of U. S. Studies Monographs Ser: No. 2). 92p. 1975. pap. text ed. 7.50x (ISBN 0-485-12902-7, Athlone Pr). Humanities.

Wright, F. A., ed. Lempriere's Classical Dictionary. new rev. ed. 1969. Repr. of 1788 ed. 21.00 (ISBN 0-7100-1734-0). Routledge & Kegan.

Wright, F. A., jt. tr. see Pott, J. A.

Wright, Forrest J. Two Gringos Visit South America. Bd. with A Journey to Bhutan. LC 79-67523. (Illus.). 1980. 6.95 (ISBN 0-533-04475-8). Vantage.

Wright, Frances W. Coastwise Navigation. (Illus.). 1980. pap. 7.50 (ISBN 0-87033-260-0). Cornell Maritime.

Wright, Francis S., jt. auth. see Swaiman, Kenneth F.

Wright, Frank L. Three-Quarters of a Century of Drawings. (Illus.). 1981. 27.50 (ISBN 0-8180-0031-7); pap. 17.50 (ISBN 0-8180-0032-5). Horizon.

--Writings & Buildings. Kaufmann, Edgar & Raeburn, Ben, eds. (Illus.). 7.95 (ISBN 0-8180-0021-X). Horizon.

Wright, Fred, et al, eds. Forensic Psychology & Psychiatry. LC 80-17982. (N.Y. Academy of Sciences Annals: Vol. 347). 364p. 1980. 58.00 (ISBN 0-89766-084-6). NY Acad Sci.

Wright, Freire & Foreman, Michael. Borrowed Feathers & Other Fables. LC 77-79844. (ps-3). 1978. 3.95 (ISBN 0-394-83730-4, BYR); PLB 4.99 (ISBN 0-394-93730-9). Random.

Wright, Friere & Foreman, Michael. Seven in One Blow. (Pictureback Ser.). (Illus.). 32p. (ps-3). 1981. PLB 4.99 (ISBN 0-394-93805-4); pap. 1.25 (ISBN 0-686-68750-7). Random.

Wright, G., jt. auth. see Moskowitz, H.

Wright, G. H. Von see Wittgenstein, Ludwig.

Wright, G. H. Von see Von Wright, G. H.

Wright, G. N. An Historical Guide to the City of Dublin. 2nd ed. 260p. 1981. Repr. of 1825 ed. 20.00x (ISBN 0-906127-21-1, Pub. by Irish Academic Pr Ireland). Biblio Dist.

Wright, Gavin, ed. The Political Economy of the Cotton South. (Illus.). 1978. 10.95 (ISBN 0-393-05686-4); pap. 5.95x (ISBN 0-393-09038-8). Norton.

Wright, Geoffrey N. The Yorkshire Dales. 1977. 14.95 (ISBN 0-7153-7454-0). David & Charles.

Wright, Georg H. Von see Von Wright, Georg H.

Wright, George N. Total Rehabilitation. LC 80-81957. 830p. 1980. text ed. 32.50 (ISBN 0-316-95628-7). Little.

Wright, George T. W. H. Auden. LC 68-24302. (U. S. Authors Ser.: No. 144). 1969. lib. bdg. 10.95 (ISBN 0-8057-0028-5). Twayne.

Wright, Gerald Z. Behavior Management in Dentistry for Children. LC 74-31840. (Illus.). 266p. 1975. text ed. 25.00 o.p. (ISBN 0-7216-9608-2). Saunders.

Wright, Gordon. France in Modern Times. 3rd ed. 1981. 24.95 (ISBN 0-393-01455-X). Norton.

--France in Modern Times. 3rd ed. 500p. 1981. 24.95 (ISBN 0-393-95153-7); 12.95 (ISBN 0-393-95153-7). Norton.

--The Reshaping of French Democracy. LC 68-9654. 1970. Repr. of 1948 ed. 15.00 (ISBN 0-86527-167-4). Fertig.

Wright, Gordon, jt. auth. see Herold, J. Christopher.

Wright, Gordon, frwd. by. George H. Morris Teaches Beginners How to Ride: A Clinic for Instructors, Parents, & Students. LC 79-7224. (Illus.). 144p. 1981. 10.95 (ISBN 0-385-14226-9). Doubleday.

Wright, H. Beric. Executive Ease & Dis-Ease. LC 75-1072. 1975. 19.95 (ISBN 0-470-96450-2). Halsted Pr.

Wright, H. C. Elementary Semiconductor Physics. 21.95 (ISBN 0-442-30198-7). Litton Educ Pub.

Wright, H. M., tr. see Chesneaux, Jean.

Wright, H. M., tr. see Coedes, G.

Wright, H. Norman. How to Be a Better-Than-Average In-Law. 1981. pap. 3.95 (ISBN 0-88207-342-7). Victor Bks.

--Marital Counseling: A Biblical Behavioral Cognitive Approach. 370p. 1981. 16.95 (ISBN 0-938786-00-8). Chr Marriage.

--The Pillars of Marriage. LC 78-68849. 1979. pap. 4.95 (ISBN 0-8307-0698-4, 5412501); leader's guide 9.95 (ISBN 0-8307-0699-2, 5202418). Regal.

Wright, H. W. Running for the Exit. (Illus., Orig.). 1981. pap. 6.95 (ISBN 0-89407-035-5). Strawberry Hill.

Wright, Harold, tr. see Tanikawa, Shuntaro.

Wright, Helen L. Metropolitan Opera House. 1980. pap. 14.95. Greylock Pubs.

--Metropolitan Opera House. 1979. write for info. Immediate Pr.

Wright, Henry B. The Campaign of Plataea: Campaign of Plataea: September, Four Hundred & Seventy-Nine B.C. 1904. pap. 27.50x (ISBN 0-685-89737-0). Elliots Bks.

Wright, Henry T., III. An Early Town on the Deh Luran Plain: Excavations at Tepe Farukhabad. (Memoirs Ser.: No. 13). 1980. pap. write for info. (ISBN 0-932206-87-5). U Mich Mus Anthro.

Wright, Herbert E. & Frey, D. G., eds. The Quaternary of the United States. (Illus.). 1965. 45.00x (ISBN 0-691-08021-6). Princeton U Pr.

Wright, Inez. The Birthmark. 7.50 o.p. (ISBN 0-8062-1231-4). Carlton.

Wright, Ione S. & Nekhom, Lisa M. Historical Dictionary of Argentina. LC 78-7918. (Latin American Historical Dictionaries: No. 17). 1978. 37.50 (ISBN 0-8108-1144-8). Scarecrow.

Wright, J. B., jt. ed. see Webb, C. deB.

Wright, J. Leitch, Jr. The Only Land They Knew: The Tragic Story of the American Indians in the Old South. LC 80-1854. (Illus.). 1981. 16.95 (ISBN 0-02-935790-X). Free Pr.

Wright, J. Patrick. On a Clear Day You Can See General Motors. 304p. 1980. pap. 2.95 (ISBN 0-380-51722-1, 51722). Avon.

Wright, J. Stafford. La Mente y lo Desconocido. Gilchrist, James S., tr. from Eng. LC 76-9906. 228p. (Orig., Span.). 1976. pap. 3.50 (ISBN 0-89922-070-3). Edit Caribe.

Wright, James. The Branch Will Not Break. LC 63-8858. (Wesleyan Poetry Program: Vol. 18). (Orig.). 1963. pap. 4.95 (ISBN 0-8195-1018-1, Pub. by Wesleyan U Pr). Columbia U Pr.

--Collected Poems. LC 70-142727. 1971. 15.00x (ISBN 0-8195-4031-5, Pub. by Wesleyan U Pr); pap. 6.95 (ISBN 0-8195-6022-7). Columbia U Pr.
--Historia Histronica: An Historical Account of the English Stage. Bd. with Roscius Anglicanus: An Historical Review of the Stage. Downes, John. LC 70-170465. (The English Stage Ser.: Vol. 38). lib. bdg. 50.00 (ISBN 0-8240-0621-6). Garland Pub.
--Saint Judas. LC 59-12481. (Wesleyan Poetry Program: Vol. 4). (Orig.). 1959. 10.00x (ISBN 0-8195-2004-7, Pub. by Wesleyan U Pr). Columbia U Pr.
--Shall We Gather at the River. LC 68-27545. (Wesleyan Poetry Program: Vol. 43). 1968. 10.00x (ISBN 0-8195-2043-8, Pub. by Wesleyan U Pr); pap. 4.95 (ISBN 0-8195-1043-2). Columbia U Pr.
Wright, James A. I See the Wind. LC 74-81875. 70p. 1974. pap. 5.00 o.p. (ISBN 0-8283-1574-4). Branden.
Wright, Jay. Double Invention of Komo. (U. T. Poetry Ser.: No. 5). (Illus.). 120p. 1980. 10.95 (ISBN 0-292-71525-0); pap. 6.95 (ISBN 0-292-71526-9). U. of Tex Pr.
Wright, Jeni. The Encyclopedia of Asian Cooking. (Illus.). 224p. 1980. 20.00 (ISBN 0-7064-0990-6); pap. 9.95 (ISBN 0-7064-1354-7). Mayflower Bks.
Wright, John. Military Collections at the Essex Institute. (E. I. Museum Booklet Ser.). (Illus.). 64p. 1981. pap. text ed. 4.95 (ISBN 0-88389-104-2). Essex Inst.
Wright, John H., jt. auth. see Sharf, Frederic A.
Wright, John P. Vital Spark. 1974. text ed. 9.95x o.p. (ISBN 0-435-68945-2). Heinemann Ed.
Wright, John S. & Dimsdale, Parks B. Pioneers in Marketing. LC 73-620235. 162p. 1974. pap. 8.95 (ISBN 0-88406-016-0). Ga St U Busn Pub.
Wright, Jonathan R. Above Parties: The Political Attitudes of the German Protestant Church Leadership 1918-1933. (Oxford Historical Monographs Ser.). 216p. 1974. 22.50x (ISBN 0-19-821856-7). Oxford U Pr.
Wright, Jonathan W. Introduction to Forest Genetics. 1976. 29.50 (ISBN 0-12-765250-7). Acad Pr.
Wright, Joseph. Grammar of the Gothic Language & the Gospel of St. Mark. 2nd ed. 1954. 24.95x (ISBN 0-19-811922-4). Oxford U Pr.
Wright, Joseph & Wright, Elizabeth M. Old English Grammar. 3rd ed. 1925. 26.00x (ISBN 0-19-811923-2). Oxford U Pr.
Wright, Joseph L. The Adventures of Davy & Bartholomew. LC 78-66284. (Illus., Orig.). (gr. 3-6). 1979. pap. 1.95 (ISBN 0-9602290-1-9). Delanie Way.
Wright, Judith, ed. New Land, New Language: An Anthology of Australian Verse. 1958. pap. 5.95x (ISBN 0-19-550298-1). Oxford U Pr.
Wright, K. G., jt. auth. see Culyer, A. J.
Wright, Kathleen. Other Americans: Minorities in American History. 1976. pap. 1.75 o.p. (ISBN 0-449-30674-7, X674, Prem). Fawcett.
Wright, Kathryn S. Let the Children Paint. 4.50 (ISBN 0-8164-0162-4); film strip 4.50 (ISBN 0-685-20292-5). Crossroad NY.
--Let the Children Sing: Music in Religious Education. LC 73-17915. 1974. 7.95 (ISBN 0-8164-0256-6). Crossroad NY.
Wright, Kevin N., ed. Crime & Criminal Justice in a Declining Economy. LC 80-26623. 128p. 1981. lib. bdg. 20.00 (ISBN 0-89946-046-1). Oelgeschlager.
Wright, Kieth C. Library & Information Services for Handicapped Individuals. LC 78-26472. 1979. lib. bdg. 17.50x (ISBN 0-87287-129-0). Libs Unl.
Wright, Kit. Soundings. 1975. pap. text ed. 4.95x o.p. (ISBN 0-435-14911-3). Heinemann Ed.
Wright, Lance, jt. ed. see Boyne, D. A.
Wright, Larry. Teleological Explanations: An Etiological Analysis of Goals & Functions. LC 75-17284. 1976. 15.95x (ISBN 0-520-02086-3). U. of Cal Pr.
Wright, Lawrence. Clean & Decent: The Fascinating History of the Bathroom & the Water Closet. 224p. (Orig.). 1980. pap. 7.95 (ISBN 0-7100-0647-0). Routledge & Kegan.
--Home Fires Burning: The History of Domestic Heating & Cooking. 1964. 15.00 (ISBN 0-7100-2332-4). Routledge & Kegan.
Wright, Len. Your Book of Badminton. (gr. 4 up). 1972. 6.95 (ISBN 0-571-09890-8). Transatlantic.
Wright, Leonard, Jr. Thinking Man's Guide to Trout Angling. 1972. 6.95 o.p. (ISBN 0-525-21740-1). Dutton.
Wright, Leonard M. Fishing the Dry Fly As a Living Insect: An Unorthodox Method. (Illus.). 1972. 6.95 o.p. (ISBN 0-525-21740-1). Dutton.
Wright, Leonard M., Jr. Fly-Fishing Heresies. (Illus.). 1975. 8.95 o.p. (ISBN 0-87691-203-X). Winchester Pr.
Wright, Leonard M., Jr., jt. auth. see Migel, Michael J.
Wright, Leonard T. Principles of Investments: Text & Cases. 2nd ed. LC 76-5618. (Finance & Real Estate Ser.). 1977. text ed. 19.95 o.p. (ISBN 0-88244-083-7). Grid Pub.
Wright, Logan. Parent Power. 240p. 1981. pap. 2.95 (ISBN 0-553-14654-8). Bantam.
Wright, Louis B. The American Heritage History of the Thirteen Colonies. LC 67-23814. (Illus.). 384p. 1967. 27.50 (ISBN 0-8281-0299-6, Dist. by Scribner); Bo555d. deluxe ed. 32.50 slipcased (ISBN 0-8281-0304-6, Dist. by Scribner). Am Heritage.
--The American Heritage History of the Thirteen Colonies. LC 67-23814. (Illus.). 384p. 1981. pap. 12.95 (ISBN 0-8281-0429-8, Dist. by Scribner). Am Heritage.
--The First Gentlemen of Virginia: Intellectual Qualities of the Early Colonial Ruling Class. LC 40-247. pap. 3.95 (ISBN 0-8139-0247-9). U Pr of Va.
--South Carolina. (States & the Nation). (Illus.). 225p. 1976. pap. 12.95 (ISBN 0-393-05560-4, Co-Pub by AASLH). Norton.
Wright, Louis B., ed. Cultural Life of the American Colonies. (New American Nation Ser.). pap. 5.95x (ISBN 0-06-133005-1, TB3005, Torch). Har-Row.
Wright, Louis B. & Fowler, Elaine, eds. The Moving Frontier: North America Seen Through the Eyes of Its Pioneer Discoverers. (Illus.). 1972. 10.00 o.p. (ISBN 0-440-05874-0). Delacorte.
--West & by North. 1971. 10.00 o.s.i. (ISBN 0-440-09490-9). Delacorte.
Wright, Louis B., ed. see Beverley, Robert.
Wright, Louis B., ed. see Shakespeare, William.
Wright, M. R., ed. Empedocles - the Extant Fragments. LC 80-17923. 416p. 1981. text ed. 45.00 (ISBN 0-300-02475-4). Yale U Pr. Postponed.
Wright, Marion I. & Sullivan, Robert J. The Rhode Island Atlas. (Illus.). 192p. (Orig., Contains considerable text). 1981. pap. write for info. (ISBN 0-917012-19-4). RI Pubns Soc.
Wright, Mary. Cornish Guernsey & Knit-Frocks. 72p. 1980. 10.00x (ISBN 0-906720-05-2, Pub. by Hodge England). State Mutual Bk.
Wright, Michael, ed. Complete Book of Gardening. 1980. pap. 9.95 (ISBN 0-446-87239-3). Warner Bks.
Wright, Michael & Walters, Sally, eds. The Book of the Cat. LC 80-23570. (Illus.). 256p. 1981. 24.95 (ISBN 0-671-44753-X); pap. 9.95 (ISBN 0-671-41624-3). Summit Bks.
Wright, Milburn D., jt. auth. see Pederson, Carlton A.
Wright, Mildred S. Jasper County, Texas Cemeteries. LC 76-44116. (Illus.). 1979. pap. 22.75 (ISBN 0-917016-05-X). M S Wright.
--Josiah W. Wilson & Lydia Melinda Wilson & Slasham Valley, St. Clair County, Alabama Kinfolk. LC 79-56809. (Illus.). 1979. 28.75 (ISBN 0-917016-14-9); pap. 18.75 (ISBN 0-917016-15-7). M S Wright.
--William Harper Wright: His Ancestry & Descendants & Allied Lines of Stone's River, Tennessee. LC 80-52849. (Illus.). 183p. 1980. 35.00 (ISBN 0-917016-16-5); accopress 25.00 (ISBN 0-917016-17-3). M S Wright.
Wright, Moorehead, ed. Theory & Practice of the Balance of Power 1486-1914. (Rowman & Littlefield University Librry). 152p. 1975. 12.50x (ISBN 0-87471-407-9). Rowman.
Wright, Moorhead, jt. ed. see Booth, Ken.
Wright, Muriel H. Guide to the Indian Tribes of Oklahoma. (Civilization of the American Indian Ser.: No. 33). (Illus.). 1979. Repr. of 1951 ed. 12.50 (ISBN 0-8061-0238-1). U of Okla Pr.
Wright, Myron A. Business of Business: Private Enterprise & Public Affairs. 1967. 9.50 o.p. (ISBN 0-07-072057-6, P&RB). McGraw.
Wright, Nancy D. & Allen, Gene P., eds. The National Directory of State Agencies, 1980-1981. 718p. 1975. text ed. 62.50 (ISBN 0-87815-032-3). Info Resources.
Wright, Naomi. Everwidening Circle: A Workable Plan for Women's Bible Studies. LC 77-18361. 1978. pap. 3.95 (ISBN 0-930014-17-0). Multnomah.
Wright, Nathalia. Horatio Greenough: The First American Sculptor. LC 62-11261. 1963. 9.50x o.p. (ISBN 0-8122-7324-9). U of Pa Pr.
Wright, Nathalia, ed. Letters of Horatio Greenough, American Sculptor. LC 77-176417. (Illus.). 516p. 1972. 37.50x (ISBN 0-299-06070-5). U of Wis Pr.
Wright, Norman. An Answer to in-Law Relationships. (Orig.). pap. 1.25 (ISBN 0-89081-076-1). Harvest Hse.
--An Answer to Loneliness. (Orig.). pap. 1.25 (ISBN 0-89081-077-X). Harvest Hse.
--An Answer to Parent-Teen Relationships. (Orig.). pap. 1.25 (ISBN 0-89081-075-3). Harvest Hse.
--An Answer to Submission & Decision Making. pap. 1.25 (ISBN 0-89081-078-8). Harvest Hse.
--The Family That Listens. 1978. pap. 3.95 (ISBN 0-88207-633-7). Victor Bks.
--Help! I'm a Camp Counselor. LC 68-18057. (Orig.). 1969. pap. 2.95 (ISBN 0-8307-0032-3, 50-015-28). Regal.
Wright, Norman & Inmon, Marvin. Guidebook to Dating, Waiting & Choosing a Mate. LC 78-26913. 1978. pap. 3.95 (ISBN 0-89081-150-4, 1504). Harvest Hse.
Wright, Norman E. Building an American Pedigree: A Guide to Family & Local History Research. 2nd, rev. ed. (Illus.). 1981. pap. text ed. 12.95 (ISBN 0-8425-1863-0). Brigham.
--Preserving Your American Heritage: A Guide to Family & Local History. rev. ed. (Illus.). 1981. pap. text ed. 12.95 (ISBN 0-8425-1863-0). Brigham.
Wright, Norman H. & Inmon, Marvin N. Preparing for Parenthood. LC 79-92949. 192p. 1980. pap. 4.95 (ISBN 0-8307-0743-3, 5412218); wkbk. 10.95 (ISBN 0-8307-0755-7, 80-50263). Regal.
Wright, O. The Modal System of Arab & Persian Music A.D. 1250-1300. (Illus.). 292p. 1976. 95.00x (ISBN 0-19-713575-7). Oxford U Pr.
Wright, O., jt. auth. see Plossl, G.
Wright, P. H. & Poquette, Radnor J. Highway Engineering. 4th ed. LC 78-13643. 1979. text ed. 30.95 (ISBN 0-471-07260-5); solutions manual avail. (ISBN 0-471-05981-1). Wiley.
Wright, Patricia. Journey into Fire. 1978. pap. 2.50 o.s.i. (ISBN 0-446-81525-X). Warner Bks.
--Shadow of the Rock. 384p. 1979. pap. 2.50 (ISBN 0-380-49064-1, 49064). Avon.
--The Storms of Fate. LC 80-1695. 504p. 1981. 13.95 (ISBN 0-385-17117-X). Doubleday.
Wright, Peter. Cockney Dialect. 192p. 1981. 22.50 (ISBN 0-7134-2242-4, Pub. by Batsford England). David & Charles.
--Language at Work. 1968. pap. text ed. 6.95x o.p. (ISBN 0-435-10975-8). Heinemann Ed.
Wright, Peter H. Rome, England, the United States & the Forces for the Decline & the Death of the Empires. (A Science of Man Library Bk.). 1978. deluxe ed. 43.65 (ISBN 0-930008-14-6). Inst Econ Pol.
Wright, Philip A. Old Farm Implements. LC 73-168335. (Illus.). 112p. 1975. 11.95 (ISBN 0-7153-6801-X). David & Charles.
Wright, Quincy. International Law & the United Nations. LC 74-27430. 1976. Repr. of 1960 ed. lib. bdg. 16.00x (ISBN 0-8371-7900-9, WRIL). Greenwood.
Wright, R. C. & Hort, N. D. The Complete Handbook of Plant Propagation. (Illus.). 192p. 1975. 14.95 (ISBN 0-02-631580-7). Macmillan.
Wright, R. T. & Jensen, T. R. Manufacturing. LC 76-5892. (Illus.). 1976. Set. text ed. 10.64 (ISBN 0-87006-203-4); lab manual 4.00 (ISBN 0-87006-281-6). Goodheart.
Wright, R. Thomas & Jensen, Thomas R. Manufacturing Laboratory Manual. 192p. 1980. 4.00 (ISBN 0-87006-292-1). Goodheart.
Wright, Richard. Eight Men. (gr. 10 up). 1969. pap. 1.50 o.s.i. (ISBN 0-515-02034-6, V2034). Jove Pubns.
--Richard Wright Reader. Wright, Ellen & Fabre, Michel, eds. LC 77-76690. (Illus.). 1978. 15.95 o.s.i. (ISBN 0-06-014737-7, HarpT); pap. 7.95 (ISBN 0-06-014736-9, TD-292, HarpT). Har-Row.
--White Man, Listen! LC 78-17905. 1978. Repr. of 1957 ed. lib. bdg. 17.75x (ISBN 0-313-20533-7, WRWM). Greenwood.
Wright, Richard & Wright, Rochelle. Canoe Routes: British Columbia. (Illus.). 160p. (Orig.). 1977. pap. 6.95 (ISBN 0-916890-61-9). Mountaineers.
--Canoe Routes: Yukon Territory. (Illus.). 122p. (Orig.). 1977. pap. 6.95 (ISBN 0-916890-60-0). Mountaineers.
Wright, Richard A. African Philosophy: An Introduction. 2nd ed. LC 78-65457. 1978. pap. 10.00 (ISBN 0-8191-0505-8). U Pr of Amer.
Wright, Richard B. The Weekend Man. 1971. 6.95 o.p. (ISBN 0-374-28740-6). FS&G.
--The Weekend Man. 1972. pap. 1.75 o.p. (ISBN 0-451-08245-1, E8245, Sig). NAL.
Wright, Rita & Anderson, Mildred, eds. Texas Trade & Professional Associations (1981 Edition) rev. ed. 75p. (Orig.). 1981. pap. 5.00 (ISBN 0-686-69074-5). U of Tex Busn Res.
Wright, Robert. Building Bicycle Wheels. LC 75-35277. (Illus.). 48p. 1980. pap. 1.95 (ISBN 0-89037-106-7). Anderson World.
Wright, Robert C. Frederick Manfred. (United States Authors Ser.: No. 336). 1979. lib. bdg. 13.50 (ISBN 0-8057-7247-2). Twayne.
Wright, Robert G. Mosaics of Organization Character. LC 74-76943. 1975. lib. bdg. 11.50 (ISBN 0-8046-9297-1); pap. text ed. 5.95 (ISBN 0-8046-9278-5). Kennikat.
Wright, Robert G., jt. ed. see Hipple, Theodore W.
Wright, Robert L., Jr., jt. auth. see Foster, Arthur R.
Wright, Rochelle, jt. auth. see Wright, Richard.
Wright, Roy D., jt. auth. see Gist, Noel P.
Wright, Roy J. & Wagner, Richard M. Eighteen Ninety-Five to Nineteen Eleven. (Cincinnati Streetcars: No.5). 1971. pap. 4.75 o.s.i. (ISBN 0-914196-10-3). Trolley Talk.
--Nineteen-Twelve to Nineteen Twenty-Two. (Cincinnati Streetcars: No.6). 1973. pap. 4.95 o.s.i. (ISBN 0-914196-14-6). Trolley Talk.
Wright, Roy J., jt. auth. see Wagner, Richard M.
Wright, Samuel. The Music Machine. LC 97-9200. (Illus.). (gr. 3-6). 1979. pap. 2.95 (ISBN 0-87123-707-5, 210707). Bethany Fell.
Wright, Scott. Count of Van Rheeden Castle. 1976. pap. 1.25 o.p. (ISBN 0-445-08474-X). Popular Lib.
Wright, Sean & Farrell, John. Sherlock Holmes Cookbook. LC 75-10547. (Illus.). 1975. 8.95 o.p. (ISBN 0-8473-1003-5). Sterling.
Wright, Sharon & Fontes, Rick. Elements. (Orig.). 1979. pap. 5.00 o.p. (ISBN 0-930138-07-4). Harold Hse.
Wright, Sheila, jt. ed. see Bray, Jean.
Wright, Stanley. Kiangsi Native Trade & Its Taxation. LC 78-74332. (The Modern Chinese Economy Ser.). 201p. 1980. lib. bdg. 22.00 (ISBN 0-8240-4258-1). Garland Pub.
Wright, Susan, jt. auth. see Kahn, Jack.
Wright, T. Anglo-Saxon & English Vocabularies, 2 Vols. Set. 125.00 (ISBN 0-685-05174-9). Adler.
Wright, T. H. The Sermon on the Mount for to-Day. 298p. Repr. of 1927 ed. 4.95 (ISBN 0-567-02296-X). Attic Pr.
Wright, Thomas. Biographia Britannica Literaria, 2 vols. LC 68-22061. 1968. Repr. of 1842 ed. Set. 40.00 (ISBN 0-8103-3154-3). Gale.
--Homes of Other Days: A History of Domestic Manners & Sentiments in England During the Middle Ages. LC 67-23902. (Social History References Ser.). (Illus.). 1968. Repr. of 1871 ed. 15.00 (ISBN 0-8103-3263-9). Gale.
--The Life of Charles Dickens. 392p. 1980. Repr. of 1935 ed. lib. bdg. 45.00 (ISBN 0-8492-2999-5). R West.
--Narratives of Sorcery & Magic, from the Most Authentic Sources. LC 73-177421. 1974. Repr. of 1851 ed. 28.00 (ISBN 0-8103-3821-1). Gale.
--Passions of the Minde in Generall. LC 78-139807. 1971. Repr. of 1604 ed. 16.00 o.p. (ISBN 0-252-00147-8). U of Ill Pr.
--Romance of the Shoe. LC 68-26624. 1968. Repr. of 1922 ed. 22.00 (ISBN 0-8103-3543-3). Gale.
--Songs & Ballads, with Other Short Poems, Chiefly of the Reign of Philip & Mary. 214p. 1980. Repr. of 1860 ed. lib. bdg. 45.00 (ISBN 0-8495-5827-1). Arden Lib.
Wright, Tom. The Gardens of Britain, Four: Kent, Sussex & Surrey. 1978. 24.00 (ISBN 0-7134-1281-X, Pub. by Batsford England). David & Charles.
Wright, Vincent. The Government & Politics of France. LC 78-9274. 1978. text ed. 24.45x (ISBN 0-8419-0409-X); pap. text ed. 9.75x (ISBN 0-8419-0410-3). Holmes & Meier.
Wright, W. A., ed. see Ascham, R.
Wright, Waldo C. Business Correspondence. Incl. 1967. 3rd ed. text ed. 10.50 (ISBN 0-672-96007-9); 1963. tchr's manual 6.67 (ISBN 0-685-58241-8). Bobbs.
Wright, Walter. Gravity Is a Push. 1979. 6.95 (ISBN 0-8062-1263-2). Carlton.
Wright, Walter F. Art & Substance in George Meredith: A Study in Narrative. LC 80-14417. vii, 211p. 1980. Repr. of 1953 ed. lib. bdg. 19.00x (ISBN 0-313-22514-1, WRAS). Greenwood.
Wright, Walter F., ed. see Conrad, Joseph.
Wright, Will. Sixguns & Society. 1975. 12.50x o.p. (ISBN 0-520-02753-1); pap. 5.95 (ISBN 0-520-03491-0). U of Cal Pr.
Wright, William. The Brontes in Ireland. LC 76-29146. (Illus.). 1981. Repr. of 1894 ed. 10.00 (ISBN 0-916620-12-3). Portals Pr.
--Grammar of the Arabic Language, 2 Vols. 3rd ed. 1933-1967. Vol. 1. 42.00 (ISBN 0-521-06875-4); Vol. 2. pap. text ed. 27.50x (ISBN 0-521-09455-0). Cambridge U Pr.
--Heiress: The Rich Life of Marjorie Merriweather Post. LC 77-26168. (Illus.). 1978. 12.50 o.p. (ISBN 0-915220-36-9). New Republic.
Wright, William, jt. auth. see Pavarotti, Luciano.
Wright, William, tr. A Briefe Relation of the Persecution Lately Made Against the Catholike Christians in Japonia. Taken Out of the Annuall Letters of the Soc. of Jesus. LC 75-26238. (English Experience Ser.: No. 159). 1969. Repr. of 1619 ed. 35.00 (ISBN 90-221-0159-2). Walter J Johnson.
Wright, William E. Serf, Seigneur & Sovereign: An Agrarian Reform in Eighteenth-Century Bohemia. LC 66-29653. 1966. 8.95x (ISBN 0-8166-0411-8). U of Minn Pr.
Wright, William H. The Grizzly Bear: The Narrative of a Hunter-Naturalist. LC 77-1772. (Illus.). 1977. 15.50x (ISBN 0-8032-0927-4); pap. 4.95 (ISBN 0-8032-5865-8, BB 646, Bison). U of Nebr Pr.

Wright, Winthrop R. British-Owned Railways in Argentina: Their Effect on the Growth of Economic Nationalism, 1854-1948. (Latin American Monographs: No. 34). 358p. 1974. 15.00 (ISBN 0-292-70710-X). U of Tex Pr.

Wright, Wm. Grammar of the Arabic Language. 1974. 25.00 (ISBN 0-685-77114-8). Intl Bk Ctr.

Wrighter, Carl P. I Can Sell You Anything. 1975. pap. 2.25 (ISBN 0-345-28462-3). Ballantine.

Wrightman, Lawrence S., jt. auth. see Stang, David J.

Wrightsman, Dwayne. An Introduction to Monetary Theory & Policy. 2nd ed. LC 75-22767. (Illus.). 1976. 14.95 o.s.i. (ISBN 0-02-935510-9); pap. text ed. 9.95 (ISBN 0-02-935560-5). Free Pr.

Wrightsman, Dwayne, jt. auth. see Robinson, Roland I.

Wrightsman, Lawrence & Deaux, Kay. Social Psychology in the Eighties. 3rd ed. LC 80-23440. 760p. 1980. 18.95 (ISBN 0-8185-0415-3). Brooks-Cole.

Wrightsman, Lawrence S., et al. Psychology: A Scientific Study of Human Behavior. 5th ed. LC 78-59674. (Illus.). 1979. text ed. 17.95 (ISBN 0-8185-0280-0). Brooks-Cole.

Wrightson, Keith & Levine, David. Poverty & Piety in an English Village: Terling, 1525-1700. LC 78-1102. (Studies in Social Discontinuity Ser.). 1979. 17.00 (ISBN 0-12-765950-1). Acad Pr.

Wrightson, Patricia. Feather Star. LC 63-7901. (Illus.). (gr. 7 up). 1963. 4.95 o.p. (ISBN 0-15-227501-0, HJ). HarBraceJ.

--Journey Behind the Wind. LC 80-25005. (gr. 7 up). 1981. 8.95 (ISBN 0-689-50198-6, McElderry Bk). Atheneum.

Wrigley, C. W., jt. auth. see Fitzsimmons, R. W.

Wrigley, Denis. The Little Giant James. (Dinosaur Ser.). (Illus.). (gr. k-3). 1978. pap. 7.25 pack of 5 o.p. (ISBN 0-85122-076-2, Pub. by Dino Pub); pap. 1.45 ea. o.p. Merrimack Bk Serv.

Wrigley, E. A., ed. The Study of Nineteenth Century Society. LC 71-174258. (Illus.). 512p. 1972. 46.50 (ISBN 0-521-08412-1). Cambridge U Pr.

Wrigley, E. A., jt. ed. see Abrams, P.

Wrigley, Elizabeth S., jt. ed. see Davies, David W.

Wrigley, J., jt. auth. see Straugham, R.

Wrigley, Jack, ed. see Rudduck, J. & Kelly, P.

Wrigley, Neil & Bennett, Robert J., eds. Quantitative Geography in Britain: Retrospect & Prospect. 448p. 1981. price not set (ISBN 0-7100-0731-0). Routledge & Kegan.

Wrinkle, Ted. British Columbia. Shangle, Robert D., ed. LC 78-10233. (Illus.). 72p. 1977. 14.95 (ISBN 0-915796-44-9); pap. 7.95 (ISBN 0-915796-43-0). Beautiful Am.

Wriston, Henry M. Policy Perspectives. LC 64-17776. 178p. 1964. 7.50 (ISBN 0-87057-081-1). Univ Pr of New England.

--Wriston Speaking: A Selection of Addresses. LC 57-11230. 263p. 1957. 8.50 (ISBN 0-87057-048-X). Univ Pr of New England.

Writers Collective, tr. from Ital. It's Scary Sometimes. LC 77-17641. (gr. 4-8). 1978. 8.95 (ISBN 0-87705-366-9). Human Sci Pr.

Writers Program, Virginia. Dinwiddie County, "the Country of the Apamatica.". LC 73-3659. (American Guide Ser.). 1942. Repr. 16.00 (ISBN 0-404-57955-8). AMS Pr.

Wrobleski, Henry M. & Hess, Karen M. Introduction to Law Enforcement & Criminal Justice. (Criminal Justice Ser.). (Illus.). 1979. text ed. 17.95 (ISBN 0-8299-0250-3); instrs.' manual avail. (ISBN 0-8299-0602-9). West Pub.

Wrobleski, William J., jt. auth. see Spirey, W. Allen.

Wrone, David R. see Guth, DeLloyd J.

Wrong, Dennis H. Power: Its Forms, Bases, & Uses. LC 78-24703. (Orig.). 1979. pap. 5.95 (ISBN 0-06-090702-9, CN 702, CN). Har-Row.

--Power: Its Forms, Bases, & Uses. 1979. text ed. 28.50 o.p. (ISBN 0-06-136181-X, Torch Lib). Har-Row.

--Skeptical Sociology. LC 76-18843. 1976. 20.00x (ISBN 0-231-04014-8). Columbia U Pr.

Wroten, William H. Assateague. LC 72-79769. (Illus.). 1972. pap. 2.00 (ISBN 0-87033-168-X, Pub. by Tidewater). Cornell Maritime.

Wroth, Lawrence C. Colonial Printer. (Illus.). 1964. pap. 3.95 (ISBN 0-8139-0250-9). U Pr of Va.

Wroth, Lawrence C., jt. auth. see Berger, Josef.

Wroth, William. The Chapel of Our Lady of Talpa. 1979. pap. 7.50. Taylor Museum.

Wrottesley, John. Great Northern Railway, Vol. III. (Illus.). 192p. 1981. 30.00 (ISBN 0-7134-3835-5, Pub. by Batsford England). David & Charles.

--The Great Northern Railway: Expansion & Competition, Vol. 2. 1979. 30.00 (ISBN 0-7134-1592-4, Pub. by Batsford England). David & Charles.

--The Great Northern Railway: Origins & Development, Vol. 1. 1979. 30.00 (ISBN 0-7134-1590-8, Pub. by Batsford England). David & Charles.

Wroughton, John, jt. auth. see Cook, Chris.

Wruble, Lawrence D., et al, eds. Gastroenterology. 3rd ed. Lewis, Myron & Levinson, Michael. (Medical Examination Review Book: Vol.22). 1977. spiral bdg. 16.50 (ISBN 0-87488-141-2). Med Exam.

Wu, C. S., jt. ed. see Hughes, Vernon.

Wu, Chun-hsi. Dollars, Dependents, & Dogma: Overseas Chinese Remittances to Communist China. LC 67-24368. (Publications Ser.: No. 55). 1967. 10.00 (ISBN 0-8179-1551-6). Hoover Inst Pr.

Wu, Chun-hsi, jt. auth. see Wu, Yuan-li.

Wu, Fu-Mei C. Richard M. Nixon, Communism & China. LC 78-69834. 1978. pap. text ed. 9.50 (ISBN 0-8191-0578-3). U Pr of Amer.

Wu-hi. Introduction to Chinese Literature. LC 66-12729. 332p. 1966. 12.50x (ISBN 0-253-33090-4); pap. 4.95x (ISBN 0-253-33091-2). Ind U Pr.

Wu, Joseph S. Clarification & Enlightenment: Essays in Comparative Philosophy. LC 78-62175. 1978. pap. text ed. 9.75 o.p. (ISBN 0-8191-0425-6). U Pr of Amer.

Wu, Kuo-Cheng. Ancient Chinese Political Theories. (Studies in Chinese Government & Law). 340p. 1977. Repr. of 1928 ed. 24.00 (ISBN 0-89093-068-6). U Pubns Amer.

Wu, Nelson I. Chinese & Indian Architecture. LC 63-7513. (Great Ages of World Architecture Ser). 1963. 7.95 o.p. (ISBN 0-8076-0210-8); pap. 3.95 o.p. (ISBN 0-8076-0339-2). Braziller.

Wu, Nesa & Coppins, Richard. Linear Programming & Extensions. (Industrial Engineering & Management Science Ser.). (Illus.). 480p. 1981. 25.95 (ISBN 0-07-072117-3, C); solutions manual 8.95 (ISBN 0-07-072118-1). McGraw.

Wu, Ruth. Behavior & Illness. (Scientific Foundations of Nursing Practice Ser.). (Illus.). 224p. 1973. pap. 11.95 ref. ed. (ISBN 0-13-074138-8). P-H.

Wu, Theodore Y., et al, eds. Swimming & Flying in Nature. LC 75-33753. 1975. Vol. 1, 420p. 45.00 (ISBN 0-306-37088-3, Plenum Pr); Vol. 2, 583p. 45.00 (ISBN 0-306-37089-1). Plenum Pub.

Wu, Tien Hsing. Soil Mechanics. 2nd ed. 464p. 1976. text ed. 25.95x (ISBN 0-205-04863-3, 2748630). Allyn.

Wu, Yel-Chiang, jt. auth. see Hilton, Peter.

Wu Yuan-li. As Peking Sees Us: People's War in the United States & Communist China's America Policy. LC 70-88765. (Studies: No. 25). (Illus.). 1969. pap. 3.00 (ISBN 0-8179-3252-6). Hoover Inst Pr.

Wu, Yuan-li. Economic Development & the Use of Energy Resources in Communist China. LC 63-15122. (Publications Ser.: No. 30). 275p. 1963. 10.00 (ISBN 0-8179-1301-7). Hoover Inst Pr.

--Spatial Economy of Communist China: A Study on Industrial Location and Transportation. LC 67-20739. (Publications Ser.: No. 56). 1967. 12.00 (ISBN 0-8179-1561-3). Hoover Inst Pr.

--The Steel Industry in Communist China. LC 64-8250. (Publications Ser.: No. 36). 334p. 1965. 10.00 (ISBN 0-8179-1361-0). Hoover Inst Pr.

--The Strategic Land Ridge: Peking's Relations with Thailand, Maylaysia, Singapore, & Indochina. LC 75-12597. (Publications Ser.: No.147). 1975. 5.95 (ISBN 0-8179-6471-1). Hoover Inst Pr.

--U.S. Policy & Strategic Interests in the Western Pacific. LC 74-33204. 1975. 16.50x (ISBN 0-8448-0622-6); pap. 7.50x (ISBN 0-8448-0714-1). Crane-Russak Co.

Wu, Yuan-li & Wu, Chun-hsi. Economic Development in Southeast Asia: The Chinese Dimension. LC 79-2455. (Publication Ser.: No. 209). 232p. 1980. pap. text ed. 8.95 (ISBN 0-8179-7092-4). Hoover Inst Pr.

Wu, Yuan-li, ed. Arms Control Arrangements for the Far East. LC 67-20822. (Publications Ser.: No. 54). 1967. pap. 5.00 (ISBN 0-8179-1542-7). Hoover Inst Pr.

--Communist China & Arms Control: A Contingency Study, 1967-1976. LC 68-54095. (Publications Ser.: No. 78). (Illus.). 1968. pap. 5.00 (ISBN 0-8179-1782-9). Hoover Inst Pr.

Wuasten, J. & Plumpe, J., eds. St. Augustine, Faith, Hope & Charity. Arand, Louis A., tr. (Ancient Christian Writers Ser.: No. 3). 165p. 1947. 8.95 (ISBN 0-8091-0045-2). Paulist Pr.

Wubben, Pamela G. Drying Foods Naturally: A Handbook for Preserving Foods & Using Them Later. 80p. 1980. pap. 4.50 (ISBN 0-935442-01-4). One Percent.

--The Food Dryer Handbook. 55p. 1980. pap. 3.50 (ISBN 0-935442-02-2). One Percent.

--Genealogy for Children. 65p. (ps-7). 1981. pap. 7.95 (ISBN 0-935442-03-0). One Percent.

--The Rhubarb Cookbook. LC 79-66754. (Illus.). 65p. 1979. 4.95 (ISBN 0-935442-00-6). One Percent.

--View from the Out House: The Joke's on the Bureaucrat. 100p. 1980. pap. 3.33 (ISBN 0-935442-04-9). One Percent.

--Wood Stove Cookery. 50p. 1981. pap. 3.75 (ISBN 0-935442-05-7). One Percent.

Wucherer, Ruth. How to Sell Your Crafts. (Illus.). 192p. 1975. pap. 4.95 o.p. (ISBN 0-8069-8406-6). Sterling.

Wu-Chi, Liu. Su Man-Shu. (World Authors Ser.: China: No. 191). lib. bdg. 10.95 (ISBN 0-8057-2870-8). Twayne.

Wu Ching-Tsu. The Scholars. silk 14.95 (ISBN 0-8351-0316-1). China Bks.

Wuebben, Paul, et al. The Experiment As a Social Occassion. 330p. 1974. 12.00x o.p. (ISBN 0-87709-720-8); pap. 5.95x o.p. (ISBN 0-87709-220-6). Boyd & Fraser.

Wuehrmann, Arthur H. & Manson-Hing, Lincoln R. Dental Radiology. 5th ed. (Illus.). 500p. 1981. text ed. 27.50 (ISBN 0-8016-5643-5). Mosby.

Wuertz-Schaefer, Karin. Hiking Virginia's National Forests. LC 77-70414. (Illus.). 204p. 1977. lib. bdg. 10.25 (ISBN 0-914788-05-1). East Woods.

Wuest, Kenneth S. The Fullness of the Spirit. 1975. pap. 2.50 (ISBN 0-8024-2897-5). Moody.

--Word Studies in the Greek New Testament, for the English Reader, 16 bks. Incl. Bk. 1. Golden Nuggets. pap. 2.25 (ISBN 0-8028-1242-2); Bk. 2. Bypaths. pap. 2.95 (ISBN 0-8028-1318-6); Bk. 3. Treasures. pap. 2.95 (ISBN 0-8028-1243-0); Bk. 4. Untranslatable Riches. pap. 2.25 (ISBN 0-8028-1241-4); Bk. 5. Studies in Vocabulary. pap. 2.45 (ISBN 0-8028-1240-6); Bk. 6. Great Truths to Live by. pap. 3.45 (ISBN 0-8028-1246-5); Bk. 7. Mark. pap. 3.95 (ISBN 0-8028-1230-9); Bk. 8. Romans. pap. 3.95 (ISBN 0-8028-1231-7); Bk. 9. Galatians. pap. 2.95 (ISBN 0-8028-1232-5); Bk. 10. Ephesians & Colossians. pap. 3.95 (ISBN 0-8028-1233-3); Bk. 11. Philippians. pap. 2.25 (ISBN 0-8028-1234-1); Bk. 12. The Pastoral Epistles. pap. 3.95 (ISBN 0-8028-1236-8); Bk. 13. Hebrews. pap. 2.95 (ISBN 0-8028-1235-X); Bk. 14. First Peter. pap. 2.45 (ISBN 0-8028-1237-6); Bk. 15. In These Last Days. pap. 3.95 (ISBN 0-8028-1238-4); Bk. 16. Prophetic Light in the Present Darkness. pap. 2.95 (ISBN 0-8028-1239-2). Set. 50.00 (ISBN 0-8028-2280-0). Eerdmans.

Wuethrich, Hans U. Das Konsonantensystem der deutschen Hochsprache. (Studia Linguistica Germanica, Vol. 11). 203p. 1974. 38.25x (ISBN 3-11-004735-7). De Gruyter.

Wujek, E. D. & Rupp, R. F. Diatoms of the Tittabawassee River, Michigan. (Bibliotheca Phycologica: No. 50). (Illus.). 160p. 1981. pap. text ed. 25.00x (ISBN 3-7682-1271-8, Pub. by Cramer Germany). Lubrecht & Cramer.

Wulf, Helen H. Aphasia, My World Alone. rev. ed. 144p. 1979. 9.50x. Wayne St U Pr.

Wulf, Kathleen. I'm Glad I'm Little. LC 76-16535. (Illus.). (ps-2). 1976. 5.50 (ISBN 0-913778-53-2). Childs World.

Wulf, W. A., et al. Hydra-CMMP: An Experimental Computer System. (Advanced Computer Science Ser.). (Illus.). 351p. 1980. text ed. 29.95 (ISBN 0-07-072120-3, C). McGraw.

Wulf, William, et al. Fundamental Structures of Computer Science. LC 79-12374. 1981. text ed. 21.95 (ISBN 0-201-08725-1). A-W.

Wulff, J., ed. Structure & Properties of Materials, 4 vols. Incl. Vol. 1. Structures. Moffatt, G. W., et al. 236p (ISBN 0-471-61265-0); Vol. 3. Mechanical Behavior. Hayden, H. W., et al. 247p (ISBN 0-471-36469-X); Vol. 4. Electronic Properties. Rose, R. M., et al. 306p (ISBN 0-471-73548-5). 1964-66. Set. pap. 31.50 (ISBN 0-471-96495-6). Wiley.

Wulff, Keith M., ed. Regulation of Scientific Inquiry: Societal Concerns with Research. (AAAS Selected Symposium: No. 37). 1979. lib. bdg. 22.50x (ISBN 0-89158-492-7). Westview.

Wulffson, Don L. The Invention of Ordinary Things. LC 80-17498. (Illus.). 96p. (gr. 3 up). 1981. 6.95 (ISBN 0-688-41978-X); PLB 6.67 (ISBN 0-688-51978-4). Morrow.

Wunder, Dietrich, intro. by. Directory of the West German Chemical Industry-Firmenhandbuch Chemische Industrie, 1979 to 1981, 2 vols. 10th ed. 512p. 1979. 115.00x (ISBN 3-430-12758-0). Intl Pubns Serv.

Wunderlich, Bernard. Macromolecular Physics: Crystals, Structure, Morphology & Defects. 1973. Vol. 1, 1973. 52.75 (ISBN 0-12-765601-4); Vol. 2, 1976. 62.75 (ISBN 0-12-765602-2). Acad Pr.

Wunderlich, D. Foundations of Linguistics. Lass, R., tr. from Ger. LC 77-82526. (Cambridge Studies in Linguistics Monographs: No. 22). 1979. 59.95 (ISBN 0-521-22007-6); pap. 17.50x (ISBN 0-521-29334-0). Cambridge U Pr.

Wunderlich, Elinor. Easy Whole-Food Recipes. LC 80-81655. (Orig.). 1980. pap. 3.95 (ISBN 0-910812-26-8). Johnny Reads.

Wunderlich, Hans G. The Secret of Crete. Winston, Richard, tr. LC 74-12403. (Illus.). 320p. 1974. 8.95 o.p. (ISBN 0-02-631600-5). Macmillan.

Wunderlich, Klaus & Gloede, Wolfgang. Nature As Constructor. Varecha, Vladimir, tr. from Ger. LC 80-18311. (Illus.). 196p. 1979. 40.00x (ISBN 0-8002-2424-8). Intl Pubns Serv.

Wunderlich, Ray C. Allergy, Brains, & Children Coping. new ed. LC 72-96304. (Illus.). 170p. 1973. 9.25 (ISBN 0-910812-12-8); pap. 6.90 (ISBN 0-910812-13-6). Johnny Reads.

Wunderlich, Ray C., Jr. Explanatory Notes to Accompany Wunder-Form No. 11: Health & Developmental Questionnaire. new ed. 1974. pap. 1.55 (ISBN 0-910812-16-0). Johnny Reads.

--Fatigue: What Causes It, What It Does to You, What You Can Do About It. new ed. (Illus.). 59p. 1976. pap. 2.10 (ISBN 0-910812-18-7). Johnny Reads.

--Kids, Brains, & Learning: What Goes Wrong-Prevention & Treatment. LC 76-79767. (Illus.). 534p. 1970. 13.75 (ISBN 0-910812-03-9); pap. 9.85 (ISBN 0-910812-04-7). Johnny Reads.

Wunderluch, Klaus & Gloede, Wolfgang. Nature As Constructor. Varecha, Vladimir, tr. from Ger. LC 80-18311. (Illus.). 196p. 1981. 19.95 (ISBN 0-668-05102-7, 5102). Arco.

Wundram, Manfred. Art of the Renaissance. LC 73-175861. (History of Art Ser.). (Illus.). 196p. 1972. 8.95x o.s.i. (ISBN 0-87663-170-7). Universe.

Wundt, Wilhelm M. Elements of Folk Psychology: Outlines of Psychological History of the Development of Mankind. Schaub, E. L., tr. from German. (Contributions to the History of Psychology Ser.). 1980. Repr. of 1916 ed. 30.00 (ISBN 0-89093-317-0). U Pubns Amer.

--Lectures on Human & Animal Psychology. Creighton, J., tr. from German. (Contributions to the History of Psychology D, I, Comparative Psychology Ser.). 1978. Repr. of 1894 ed. 30.00 (ISBN 0-89093-170-4). U Pubns Amer.

Wunsch, Carol, jt. ed. see Warren, Bruce A.

Wuolle, A. Finnish-English, English-Finnish Dictionary, 2 Vols. 11th ed. 1978-79. Set. 35.00 (ISBN 951-0-09469-2). Finnish-Eng (ISBN 9-5100-8500-6). Eng.-Finnish (ISBN 951-0-08500-6). Heinman.

Wuolle, A., ed. Finnish-English-Finnish Pocket Dictionary. 1978. pap. text ed. 9.50x (ISBN 9-5100-7468-3, F559). Vanous.

Wuolle, Aino. Finnish Small Dictionary: Finnish-English, Vol. 2. 11th ed. 1976. text ed. 20.00x (ISBN 9-5100-0074-4, F558). Vanous.

Wuorinen, Charles. Simple Composition. (Music Ser.). 1979. pap. text ed. 13.95x (ISBN 0-582-28059-1). Longman.

Wurgaft, Lewis D. The Activists: Kurt Hiller & the Politics of Action on the German Left, 1914-1933. (Transactions Ser.: Vol. 67, Pt. 8). 1977. 12.00 (ISBN 0-87169-678-9). Am Philos.

Wurm, Klaus. Substanz und Qualitaet: Ein Beitrag zur Interpretation der plotinischen Traktate Vi 1, 2, und 3. LC 72-81572. (Quellen und Studien zur Philosophie, Vol. 5). 276p. 1973. 41.75x (ISBN 3-11-001899-3). De Gruyter.

Wurmbrand, Richard. Reaching Toward the Heights. 1977. pap. 5.95 (ISBN 0-310-35471-4). Zondervan.

Wurtman, Judith J. Eating Your Way Through Life. LC 77-84121. 1979. text ed. 14.50 (ISBN 0-89004-280-2); pap. text ed. 10.50 (ISBN 0-685-99040-0). Raven.

Wurtman, Judith J., jt. ed. see Wurtman, Richard J.

Wurtman, Richard J. & Wurtman, Judith J., eds. Control of Feeding Behavior, & Biology of the Brain in Protein-Calorie Malnutrition. LC 75-14593. (Nutrition & the Brain Ser: Vol. 2). 1977. 31.50 (ISBN 0-89004-046-X). Raven.

--Determinants of the Availability of Nutrients to the Brain. LC 75-14593. (Nutrition & the Brain Ser: Vol. 1). 1977. 31.50 (ISBN 0-89004-045-1). Raven.

--Nutrition & the Brain: Disorders of Eating & Nutrients in Treatment of Brain Diseases. (Nutrition & the Brain Ser.: Vol. 3). 1979. text ed. 32.00 (ISBN 0-89004-245-4). Raven.

--Nutrition & the Brain: Toxic Effects of Food Constituents on the Brain. LC 79-2073. (Nutrition & the Brain Ser.: Vol. 4). 1979. text ed. 25.00 (ISBN 0-89004-246-2). Raven.

Wurzer, Karl. Five-Minute Feasts. Leedham, L., ed. (Illus.). 176p. 1980. 12.95 (ISBN 0-88421-157-6). Butterick Pub.

Wust, Klaus. The Virginian Germans. LC 69-17334. Repr. of 1975 ed. 10.95x (ISBN 0-8139-0256-8). U Pr of Va.

Wuster, Eugene, ed. The Road to Infoterm. (Infoterm Ser.: Vol. 1). 144p. 1974. pap. text ed. 25.00 (ISBN 3-7940-5501-2, Pub. by K G Saur). K G Saur.

Wuthnow, Robert. The Consciousness Reformation. 1976. 18.95x (ISBN 0-520-03138-5). U of Cal Pr.
--Experimentation in American Religion: The New Mysticisms & Their Implications for the Churches. 1978. 18.95 (ISBN 0-520-03446-5). U of Cal Pr.
Wu Wei-P'Ing. Chinese Acupuncture. Chancellor, Philip, tr. from Fr. 184p. 1962. text ed. 10.35x (ISBN 0-8464-0999-2). Beekman Pubs.
Wyant, Frank R. The United States, OPEC & Multinational Oil. LC 77-217. 1977. 21.95x (ISBN 0-669-01433-8). Lexington Bks.
Wyant, Linsley & Stakkestad, James. First Course in Algebra. (Page-Ficklin Math Ser). 1976. pap. 12.95 (ISBN 0-8087-3710-4). Burgess.
Wyatt, David H. Essential of International Trade. LC 79-88237. (The ALA ESP Ser.). (Illus.). v, 205p. (Orig.). 1979. pap. text ed. 10.00 (ISBN 0-934270-07-4). Am Lang Acad.
Wyatt, G. Language Learning & Communication Disorders in Children. LC 68-28371. (Illus.). 1969. 15.95 (ISBN 0-02-935550-8). Free Pr.
Wyatt, Isabel. King Beetle-Tamer & Other Lighthearted Wonder Tales. LC 79-21245. (Illus.). 160p. (gr. 3-12). 1980. 9.95 (ISBN 0-89742-029-2); pap. 6.95 (ISBN 0-89742-028-4). Dawne-Leigh.
Wyatt, James C. Moniseur Jones. 1980. 7.95 (ISBN 0-533-04457-X). Vantage.
Wyatt, John. The Shining Levels: The Story of a Man Who Went Back to Nature. LC 74-9642. 1974. 6.95 o.p. (ISBN 0-397-01037-0). Lippincott.
Wyatt, L. M. Materials of Construction for Steam Power Plant. (Illus.). 1976. 63.30x (ISBN 0-85334-661-5). Intl Ideas.
Wyatt, Molly M. Sharing God's Love with Others. 1979. pap. 3.50 (ISBN 0-570-07795-8, 56-1333). Concordia.
Wyatt, Olive M. Teach Yourself Lip-Reading. (Illus.). 172p. 1974. 8.75 (ISBN 0-398-02128-7). C C Thomas.
Wyatt, Oliver H. & Dew-Hughes, D. Metals, Ceramics & Polymers. LC 70-178286. (Illus.). 500p. 1974. 86.50 (ISBN 0-521-08238-2); pap. 24.50x (ISBN 0-521-09834-3). Cambridge U Pr.
Wyatt, R. J. The Austin. LC 80-68896. (Illus.). 256p. 1981. 38.00 (ISBN 0-7153-7948-8). David & Charles.
Wyatt, Richard J., jt. auth. see Slaby, Andrew E.
Wyatt, Stanley P. Principles of Astronomy. 3rd ed. 1977. text ed. 20.95 (ISBN 0-205-05679-2, 7356794); answer bk. o.p. avail. (ISBN 0-205-05680-6). Allyn.
Wyatt, Stanley P. & Kaler, James B. Principles of Astronomy: A Short Version. 592p. 1974. pap. text ed. 16.95x o.p. (ISBN 0-205-04205-8, 7342055). Allyn.
--Principles of Astronomy: A Short Version. 550p. 1981. text ed. 18.95 (ISBN 0-205-07315-8); instructor's manual free (ISBN 0-205-07316-6). Allyn.
Wyatt, Thomas. Poetry of Sir Thomas Wyatt: A Selection & Study by E. M. W. Tillyard. Repr. of 1929 ed. 19.00 (ISBN 0-403-08614-0). Somerset Pub.
Wyatt, Wes. Wes Wyatt System of Seminar Selling. LC 80-67857. 1980. 19.95 (ISBN 0-87863-018-X). Farnswth Pub.
Wyatt, Will. The Secret of the Sierra Madre: The Man Who Was B. Traven. LC 79-8570. (Illus.). 384p. 1980. 14.95 (ISBN 0-385-15600-6). Doubleday.
Wyatt, William E. General Architectural Drafting. (gr. 10-12). 1976. text ed. 17.68 (ISBN 0-87002-072-2); student guide 3.00 (ISBN 0-87002-166-4); drafting masters 10.88 (ISBN 0-87002-189-3). Bennett IL.
Wyatt, William F., Jr. Indo-European. LC 73-83140. (Haney Foundation Ser). 1970. 7.50x (ISBN 0-8122-7594-2). U of Pa Pr.
Wybar, Kenneth. Ophthalmology: (Concise Medical Textbook) 2nd ed. (Illus.). 1974. text ed. 14.50 (ISBN 0-02-859840-7). Macmillan.
Wybourne, Brian G. Classical Groups for Physicists. LC 73-17363. 416p. 1974. 33.95 (ISBN 0-471-96505-7, Pub. by Wiley-Interscience). Wiley.
Wycherley, William. Country Wife. Fujimura, Thomas H., ed. LC 65-10542. (Regents Restoration Drama Ser). 1965. 9.50x (ISBN 0-8032-0371-3); pap. 2.45x (ISBN 0-8032-5371-0, BB 250, Bison). U of Nebr Pr.
--Plain Dealer. Hughes, Leo, ed. LC 67-10670. (Regents Restoration Drama Ser). 1967. 9.95x (ISBN 0-8032-0372-1); pap. 3.50x (ISBN 0-8032-5372-9, BB 263, Bison). U of Nebr Pr.
--The Plays of William Wycherley. Friedman, Arthur, ed. (Oxford English Texts Ser.). 1979. 79.00x (ISBN 0-19-811861-9). Oxford U Pr.
Wyckoff, D. Daryl. Organizational Formality & Performance in the Motor Carrier Industry. LC 74-298. (Illus.). 1974. 15.95 (ISBN 0-669-91710-9). Lexington Bks.
--Railroad Management. LC 75-5237. 1976. 18.95x (ISBN 0-669-99770-6). Lexington Bks.
--Truck Drivers in America. LC 78-24793. (Illus.). 1979. 16.95 (ISBN 0-669-02818-5). Lexington Bks.
Wyckoff, D. Daryl & Maister, David H. The Domestic Airline Industry. LC 76-54612. (Lexington Casebook Series in Industry Analysis). 1977. 18.95 (ISBN 0-669-01307-2); instructors manual free (ISBN 0-669-01843-0). Lexington Bks.
--Owner-Operators: Independent Trucker. LC 74-23978. (Illus.). 1975. 15.95x (ISBN 0-669-96800-5). Lexington Bks.
--The U. S. Motor-Carrier Industry. (Lexington Casebook Series in Industry Analysis). (Illus.). 1977. 18.95x (ISBN 0-669-01113-4); instructors manual free (ISBN 0-669-01454-0). Lexington Bks.
Wyckoff, D. Daryl & Sasser, W. Earl. The Chain-Restaurant Industry. LC 77-2048. (Lexington Casebook Series in Industry Analysis). 1978. 19.95x (ISBN 0-669-01440-0); instructors manual free (ISBN 0-669-03248-4). Lexington Bks.
Wyckoff, Elizabeth see Euripides.
Wyckoff, Hogie. Solving Problems Together. LC 80-1003. 272p. 1980. pap. 7.95 (ISBN 0-394-17739-8, E 767, Ever). Grove.
--Solving Women's Problems: Through Awareness, Action, & Contact. pap. 4.95 (ISBN 0-394-17003-2, E668, Ever). Grove.
Wyckoff, James. Rogue Sheriff. 1977. pap. 1.25 o.s.i. (ISBN 0-440-14138-9). Dell.
Wyckoff, Jerome. Rock, Time, & Landforms. LC 66-10662. (Illus.). 1966. 13.50 o.s.i. (ISBN 0-06-072110-3, HarpT). Har-Row.
--The Story of Geology: Our Changing Earth Through the Ages. (Illus.). 1976. PLB 13.77 (ISBN 0-307-67750-8, Golden Pr). Western Pub.
Wyckoff, Ralph W. Crystal Structures, 5 vols, Vols. 1-2, 4-6. 2nd ed. LC 48-9169. 1963-71. Vol. 1. 33.00x o.p. (ISBN 0-470-96860-5); Vol. 2. 47.00 o.p. (ISBN 0-470-96862-1); Vol. 4. 48.95x o.p. (ISBN 0-470-96866-4); Vol. 5. 62.95x (ISBN 0-470-96868-0); Vol. 6, Pt. 1. 43.50x o.p. (ISBN 0-471-96869-2); Vol. 6, Pt. 2. 65.00x o.p. (ISBN 0-471-96870-6, Pub. by Wiley-Interscience). Wiley.
--Crystal Structures, Vol. 3. 989p. 1981. Repr. of 1951 ed. lib. bdg. write for info. (ISBN 0-88275-800-4). Krieger.
Wyckoff, Richard D. Determining & Exploiting the Long-Term of the Market. (New Stock Market Library). (Illus.). 1979. 59.75 (ISBN 0-89266-196-8). Am Classical Coll Pr.
--The Fundamental Rules of Successful Investing. (Illus.). 121p. 1981. 57.85 (ISBN 0-918968-85-2). Inst Econ Finan.
--Studies in Tape Reading. (The New Stock Market Library). (Illus.). 1978. Repr. of 1921 ed. 125.45 (ISBN 0-89266-134-8). Am Classical Coll Pr.
Wyckoff, Vertrees J. Tobacco Regulations in Colonial Maryland. LC 78-64291. (Johns Hopkins University. Studies in the Social Sciences. Extra Volumes.: 22). Repr. of 1936 ed. 21.00 (ISBN 0-404-61391-8). AMS Pr.
Wycliffe, John. Latin Works, 36 Vols. Buddensieg, Rudolf, et al, eds. Set. 1075.00 (ISBN 0-384-69800-X); 23.75 ea. Johnson Repr.
Wycoff, James. Famous Guns That Won the West. LC 68-16740. (Illus.). 1975. pap. 2.00 o.p. (ISBN 0-668-03829-2). Arco.
Wyden, Peter, jt. auth. see Bach, George R.
Wydenthal, Jan B. de see De Weydenthal, Jan B.
Wydeville, A. & Rivers, Earl, trs. from Fr. Here Endeth the Book Named the Dictes or Sayengis of the Philosophres. LC 79-84100. (English Experience Ser.: No. 920). 160p. (Eng.). 1979. Repr. of 1477 ed. lib. bdg. 25.00 (ISBN 90-221-0920-8). Walter J Johnson.
Wydro, Kenneth. Flying Solo: The New Art of Living Single. LC 77-27287. 1978. 8.95 o.p. (ISBN 0-399-12151-X, Pub. by Berkley Pub). Berkley Pub.
--Think on Your Feet: The Art of Thinking & Speaking Under Pressure. 192p. 1981. text ed. 11.95 (ISBN 0-13-917815-5, Spec); pap. text ed. 4.95 (ISBN 0-13-917807-4, Spec). P-H.
Wydro, Kenneth, jt. auth. see Wydro, Luigi.
Wydro, Luigi & Wydro, Kenneth. The Luigi Jazz Dance Technique. LC 80-1091. (Illus.). 192p. Date not set. pap. 12.95 (ISBN 0-385-15588-3, Dolph). Doubleday.
Wykeham, Nicholas. Farm Machines. LC 78-20396. (Machine World Ser.). (Illus.). (gr. 2-4). 1979. PLB 9.95 (ISBN 0-8172-1328-7). Raintree Pubs.
Wykeham, Peter. Fighter Command: A Study of Air Defence 1914-1960. Gilbert, James, ed. LC 79-7303. (Flight: Its First Seventy-Five Years Ser.). (Illus.). 1979. Repr. of 1960 ed. lib. bdg. 24.00x (ISBN 0-405-12209-8). Arno.
Wykoff, Frank C. Macroeconomics: Theory, Evidence & Policy. (Illus.). 1976. 18.95 (ISBN 0-13-543959-0). P-H.
--Macroeconomics: Theory, Evidence & Policy. 2nd ed. (Illus.). 640p. 1981. 19.95 (ISBN 0-13-543967-1). P-H.
Wykoff, George S. & Shaw, Harry. Harper Handbook of College Composition. 4th ed. LC 69-10552. (Illus.). 1969. text ed. 10.50 scp (ISBN 0-06-047261-8, HarpC); scp wkbk. 6.95 (ISBN 0-06-047262-6); instructor's guide & key to selected exercises avail. (ISBN 0-06-367263-4). Har-Row.
Wykstra, R. A. Education & the Economics of Human Capital. LC 75-153078. 1971. 15.95 (ISBN 0-02-935610-5). Free Pr.
--Human Capital Formation & Manpower Development. LC 71-153077. 1971. 13.95 o.s.i. (ISBN 0-02-935630-X). Free Pr.
Wyland, Johanna L. Your Paths in Ink Graphoanalysis & the Personality. (Illus.). 112p. 1980. 6.95 (ISBN 0-682-49604-9). Exposition.
Wyld, Henry C. The Universal English Dictionary. 1960. 45.00 (ISBN 0-7100-2333-2). Routledge & Kegan.
Wylder, Robert C., jt. auth. see Roloff, Joan G.
Wylder, Robert C., jt. ed. see Purcell, Mary.
Wylen, G. J. Van see Sonntag, R. E. & Van Wylen, G. J.
Wylen, G. J. Van see Van Wylen, G. J.
Wylen, Gordon J. An see Van Wylen, Gordon J. & Sonntag, Richard E.
Wylen, Gordon J. Van see Van Wylen, Gordon J. & Sonntag, Richard E.
Wylen, Gordon Van see Van Wylen, Gordon.
Wyler, Rose. First Book of Science Experiments. LC 76-132066. (First Bks). (Illus.). (gr. 4-6). 1971. PLB 4.90 o.p. (ISBN 0-531-00623-9). Watts.
--Real Science Riddles. (Illus.). (gr. 1-4). 1971. 5.95g (ISBN 0-8038-6320-9). Hastings.
--What Happens If... ? (gr. k-3). 1976. pap. 1.25 o.p. (ISBN 0-590-09845-4, Schol Pap). Schol Bk Serv.
Wyler, Rose & Ames, Gerald. Funny Magic: Easy Tricks for the Young Magician. LC 73-39866. (Illus.). 56p. (gr. k-3). 1972. 5.95 o.s.i. (ISBN 0-8193-0584-7, Four Winds); PLB 5.41 o.s.i. (ISBN 0-8193-0585-5). Schol Bk Serv.
--Funny Number Tricks: Easy Magic with Arithmetic. LC 76-3439. 48p. (ps-2). 1976. 5.95 o.s.i. (ISBN 0-8193-0846-3, Four Winds); PLB 5.41 o.s.i. (ISBN 0-8193-0847-1). Schol Bk Serv.
Wyler, Rose & Baird, Eva-Lee. Nutty Number Riddles. LC 74-33695. (gr. 3-5). 1977. PLB 5.95 (ISBN 0-385-00685-3). Doubleday.
Wyler, Rose, jt. auth. see Ames, Gerald.
Wyler, Rose, jt. auth. see Baird, Eva-Lee.
Wylie, Edwin, jt. auth. see Balmer, Philip.
Wylie, Elinor. Mr. Hodge & Mr. Hazard. 256p. 1980. Repr. of 1928 ed. lib. bdg. 20.00 (ISBN 0-89760-924-7). Telegraph Bks.
--The Orphan Angel. 337p. 1980. Repr. of 1926 ed. lib. bdg. 20.00 (ISBN 0-89984-506-1). Century Bookbindery.
Wylie, Harry L. & Harty, James Q., eds. Office Management Handbook. 2nd ed. (Illus.). 1958. 37.50 (ISBN 0-8260-9680-8). Ronald Pr.
Wylie, James. The Sign of Dawn. abr. ed. LC 80-52009. (Illus.). 372p. 1981. 14.95 (ISBN 0-670-64462-5). Viking Pr.
Wylie, Joanne. The Creative Guide for Preschool Teachers. 1966. pap. 10.50 (ISBN 0-685-93229-X). Bobbs.
Wylie, Jonathan & Margolin, David. The Ring of Dancers: Images of Faroese Culture. 1980. text ed. 19.95x (ISBN 0-8122-7783-X). U of Pa Pr.
Wylie, Joseph C. Military Strategy: A General Theory of Power Control. LC 80-36885. vii, 111p. 1980. Repr. of 1967 ed. lib. bdg. 17.50x (ISBN 0-313-22679-2, WYMS). Greenwood.
Wylie, L. & Begue, A. Les Francais. 1970. 14.95 o.p. (ISBN 0-13-530634-5). P-H.
Wylie, Laura. The Night Visitor. 1979. pap. 1.95 o.p. (ISBN 0-523-40398-4). Pinnacle Bks.
Wylie, Laura J. Studies in the Revolution of English Criticism. 212p. 1980. Repr. of 1903 ed. text ed. 25.00 (ISBN 0-8492-2997-9). R West.
Wylie, Laurence & Stafford, Rick. Beaux Gestes: A Guide to French Body Talk. (Illus.). 1977. 8.95 o.p.; pap. 3.95 (ISBN 0-525-03025-5). Dutton.
Wylie, Laurence see Bree, Germaine.
Wylie, Max. Four Hundred Miles from Harlem: Courts, Crime, & Correction. 288p. 1972. 6.95 o.s.i. (ISBN 0-02-631900-4). Macmillan.
Wylie, Philip. The Disappearance. 1978. pap. 2.25 o.s.i. (ISBN 0-446-82837-8). Warner Bks.
Wylie, Philip & Balmer, Edwin. After Worlds Collide. 192p. 1963. pap. 2.25 (ISBN 0-446-92813-5). Warner Bks.
Wylie, R. D., frwd. by. Materials Technology - An Interamerican Approach. 1968. pap. 27.00 o.p. (ISBN 0-685-06528-6, H00034). ASME.
Wylie, Raymond F. The Emergence of Maoism: Mao-Tse-Tung, Ch'en Po-Ta, & the Search for Chinese Theory, 1935-1945. LC 79-64221. 368p. 1980. 25.00x (ISBN 0-8047-1051-1). Stanford U Pr.
Wylie, Samuel & McKenzie, John L. Advent-Christmas. LC 74-76924. (Proclamation 1: Aids for Interpreting the Lessons of the Church Year, Ser. A). 64p. 1974. pap. 1.95 (ISBN 0-8006-4061-6, 1-4061). Fortress.
Wylie, Shaun, jt. auth. see Hilton, Peter J.
Wyllie, Ethel K. Today's Custom Tailoring. 1979. text ed. 15.80 (ISBN 0-87002-245-8); tchr's guide 3.40 (ISBN 0-87002-210-5). Bennett IL.
Wyllie, G. A. Elementary Statistical Mechanics. 1970. pap. text ed. 3.00x (ISBN 0-09-101321-6, Hutchinson U Lib). Humanities.
Wyllie, Irvin G. Self-Made Man in America. 1966. pap. text ed. 7.95 (ISBN 0-02-935670-9). Free Pr.
Wyllie, John. A Pocket Full of Dead. LC 77-89882. 1978. 6.95 o.p. (ISBN 0-385-13483-5). Doubleday.
Wyllie, Peter J. Dynamic Earth: Textbook in Geosciences. LC 73-155909. (Illus.). 1971. 31.95 (ISBN 0-471-96889-7, Pub. by Wiley-Interscience). Wiley.
Wyllie, Peter J., ed. Ultramafic & Related Rocks. LC 78-12080. 484p. (Orig.). 1979. Repr. of 1967 ed. 35.00 (ISBN 0-88275-755-5). Krieger.
Wyllie, Robert W. The Spirit Seekers: New Religious Movements in Southern Ghana. Cherry, Conrad, ed. LC 79-20486. (Studies in Religion: No. 21). 139p. 13.50 (ISBN 0-89130-355-3); pap. 9.00 (ISBN 0-89130-356-1). Scholars Pr CA.
Wyly, Thomas J., jt. ed. see Hoffman, W. Michael.
Wyman, Alvin C., et al. Radiologic Transverse Anatomy of the Human Thorax, Abodomen, & Pelvis. 1978. text ed. 45.00 (ISBN 0-316-96250-3). Little.
Wyman, Donald. Dwarf Shrubs: Maintenance-Free Woody Plants for Today's Gardens. (Illus.). 160p. 1975. 9.95 o.s.i. (ISBN 0-02-632040-1). Macmillan.
--Ground Cover Plants. (Illus.). 1956. 5.95 o.s.i. (ISBN 0-02-632030-4). Macmillan.
--Ground Cover Plants. (Illus.). 192p. 1976. pap. 3.95 o.s.i. (ISBN 0-02-064020-X, Collier). Macmillan.
--The Saturday Morning Gardener: A Guide to Once-a-Week Maintenance. rev. ed. LC 73-11833. (Illus.). 256p. 1974. pap. 2.95 o.s.i. (ISBN 0-02-063950-3, Collier). Macmillan.
--Trees for American Gardens. rev. & enl. ed. 1965. 16.95 (ISBN 0-02-632200-5). Macmillan.
Wyman, Harold E., jt. auth. see Cohan, Avery B.
Wyman, Jeffries, jt. auth. see Edsall, John T.
Wyman, Walker D. Nothing but Prairie & Sky: Life on the Dakota Range in the Early Days. (Western Frontier Library: No. 45). 1954. 5.95 (ISBN 0-8061-0287-X). U of Okla Pr.
--Wild Horse of the West. LC 66-17457. (Illus.). 1962. pap. 2.45 (ISBN 0-8032-5223-4, B*B 144, Bison). U of Nebr Pr.
Wymer, J. J. see Bowen, D. Q.
Wymer, John. Gazetteer of Mesolithics Sites in England & Wales. 1980. pap. 27.60 (ISBN 0-900312-49-1, Pub. by GEO Abstracts England). State Mutual Bk.
--Lower Palaeolithic Archaeology in Britain: As Represented by the Thames Valley. LC 67-30791. (Illus.). 1969. text ed. 25.50x (ISBN 0-212-35964-9). Humanities.
Wymer, Norman. Your Book of Television. (Your Book Ser.). (Illus.). 1966. 4.95 o.p. (ISBN 0-571-06791-3, Pub. by Faber & Faber). Merrimack Bk Serv.
Wymer, Raymond G. & Vondra, Benedict L., Jr., eds. Light Water Reactor Nuclear Fuel Cycle. 256p. 1981. 64.95 (ISBN 0-8493-5687-3). CRC Pr.
Wynar, Anna T., jt. auth. see Wynar, Lubomyr R.
Wynar, Bohdan S. Best Reference Books: Titles of Lasting Value Selected from American Reference Books Annual 1970-1976. LC 76-45781. 448p. 1976. lib. bdg. 22.50 (ISBN 0-87287-163-0). Libs Unl.
--Economic Thought in Kievan Rus. 128p. (Ukrainian.). 1975. pap. 7.50x (ISBN 0-87287-162-2). Ukrainian Acad.
Wynar, Bohdan S., ed. American Reference Books Annual 1972. 3rd ed. LC 75-120328. 1972. 30.00x o.p. (ISBN 0-87287-049-9). Libs Unl.
--American Reference Books Annual 1975. 6th ed. LC 75-120328. 904p. 1975. lib. bdg. 30.00x o.p. (ISBN 0-87287-114-2). Libs Unl.
--American Reference Books Annual 1977, Vol. 8. LC 75-120328. 1977. lib. bdg. 30.00x o.p. (ISBN 0-87287-144-4). Libs Unl.
--American Reference Books Annual 1978, Vol. 9. LC 75-120328. 1978. lib. bdg. 35.00x o.p. (ISBN 0-87287-185-1). Libs Unl.
--Reference Books in Paperback: An Annotated Guide. 2nd ed. LC 76-44238. 1976. PLB 18.50x (ISBN 0-87287-166-5). Libs Unl.
Wynar, Bohdan S. & Depp, Roberta J., eds. Colorado Bibliography. LC 80-13752. 1980. lib. bdg. 60.00x (ISBN 0-87287-211-4). Libs Unl.

Wynar, Bohdan S., jt. ed. see Holte, Susan.

Wynar, Bohdan S., et al. Introduction to Cataloging & Classification. 6th ed. LC 80-16462. (Library Science Text Ser.). 1980. lib. bdg. 25.00x (ISBN 0-87287-220-3); pap. text ed. 15.50x (ISBN 0-87287-221-1). Libs Unl.

Wynar, Bohdan S., et al, eds. American Reference Books Annual 1980, Vol. 11. LC 75-120328. 1980. lib. bdg. 45.00x (ISBN 0-87287-217-3). Libs Unl.

--American Reference Books Annual 1981, Vol. 12. LC 75-12038. 800p. 1981. lib. bdg. 45.00x (ISBN 0-87287-250-5). Libs Unl.

--Dictionary of American Library Biography. LC 77-28791. 1978. lib. bdg. 85.00x (ISBN 0-87287-180-0). Libs Unl.

Wynar, Christine G. The Ukrainian American Index: The Ukrainian Weekly, Nineteen Seventy-Nine. 119p. (Orig.). 1980. pap. 9.50 (ISBN 0-934760-02-0). Ukrainian Res.

Wynar, Christine L. Guide to Reference Books for School Media Centers. LC 73-87523. 473p. 1973. lib. bdg. 19.50- (ISBN 0-87287-069-3). Libs Unl.

--Index to American Reference Books Annual, 1975-79: A Cumulative Index of Subjects, Authors & Titles. 1979. lib. bdg. 35.00x (ISBN 0-87287-199-1). Libs Unl.

Wynar, Lubomyr R. Encyclopedic Directory of Ethnic Organizations in the United States. LC 75-28150. 440p. 1975. lib. bdg. 25.00x (ISBN 0-87287-120-7). Libs Unl.

Wynar, Lubomyr R. & Buttlar, Lois. Ethnic Film & Filmstrip Guide for Libraries & Media Centers: A Selective Filmography. LC 80-18056. 277p. 1980. lib. bdg. 25.00x (ISBN 0-87287-233-5). Libs Unl.

Wynar, Lubomyr R. & Wynar, Anna T. Encyclopedic Directory of Ethnic Newspapers & Periodicals in the United States. 2nd rev. ed. LC 76-23317. 248p. 1976. PLB 20.00x (ISBN 0-87287-154-1). Libs Unl.

Wynar, Lubomyr R., jt. auth. see Buttlar, Lois.

Wynar, Lubomyr R., jt. auth. see Murfin, Marjorie E.

Wynar, Lubomyr R., ed. Habsburgs & Zaporozhian Cossacks: The Diary of Erich Lassota Von Steblau 1594. Subtelny, Orest, tr. from Ger. LC 75-15543. Orig. Title: Tagebuch des Erich Lassota Von Steblau. (Illus.). 152p. 1975. 15.00x (ISBN 0-87287-119-3). Ukrainian Acad.

Wynd, Oswald. The Ginger Tree. LC 77-6892. 1977. 10.95 o.p. (ISBN 0-06-014729-6, HarpT). Har-Row.

Wynder. The Lamp in the Window. 1970. pap. 1.25. Chr Lit.

Wynder, Ernest L. & Hoffman, Dietrich, eds. Tobacco & Tobacco Smoke. 1967. 64.00 (ISBN 0-12-767450-0). Acad Pr.

Wyndham, John. Day of the Triffids. 192p. 1981. pap. 2.50 (ISBN 0-449-23721-4, Crest). Fawcett.

--Trouble with Lichen. 1977. pap. 1.50 o.p. (ISBN 0-345-25847-9). Ballantine.

Wyndham, Lee. Bonnie. LC 60-50701. 5.95 o.p. (ISBN 0-385-07919-2). Doubleday.

--Candy Stripers. LC 58-11487. (gr. 7up). 1958. PLB 5.79 o.p. (ISBN 0-671-32052-1). Messner.

--Russian Tales of Fabulous Beasts & Marvels. LC 76-77797. (Illus.). 96p. (gr. 4 up). 1969. 5.95 o.s.i. (ISBN 0-8193-0303-8, Four Winds); PLB 5.41 o.s.i. (ISBN 0-8193-0304-6). Schol Bk Serv.

Wyndham, Lee, jt. auth. see Mara, Thalia.

Wyndham, Roger P. The Secret Love Story of Napoleon & Madame Walewska. (An Essential Knowledge Library Bk). 1979. plastic spiral bdg. 24.00 (ISBN 0-89266-169-0). Am Classical Coll Pr.

Wyne, Marvin D. & O'Connor, Peter D. Exceptional Children: A Developmental View. 1979. pap. text ed. 16.95x (ISBN 0-669-95786-0). Heath.

Wynia, G. W. The Politics of Latin American Development. LC 77-87395. (Illus.). 1978. 32.95 (ISBN 0-521-21922-1); pap. 9.95x (ISBN 0-521-29310-3). Cambridge U Pr.

Wynia, Gary W. Politics & Planners: Economic Development Policy in Central America. 296p. 1972. 21.50x (ISBN 0-299-06210-4). U of Wis Pr.

Wynkoop, Sally. Government Reference Books, '70-71: A Biennial Guide to U.S. Government Publications. 2nd ed. LC 76-146307. 250p. 1972. 8.50 o.p. (ISBN 0-87287-062-6). Libs Unl.

--Subject Guide to Government Reference Books. LC 72-83382. 1972. 18.50 (ISBN 0-87287-025-1). Libs Unl.

Wynkoop, William M. Three Children of the Universe: Emerson's Views of Shakespeare, Bacon, & Milton. LC 80-2548. 1981. Repr. of 1966 ed. 25.50 (ISBN 0-404-19272-6). AMS Pr.

Wynmalen, Henry. Equitation. (Illus.). 21.85 (ISBN 0-85131-138-5, Dist. by Sporting Book Center). J A Allen.

--Horse Breeding & Stud Management. (Illus.). 20.10 (ISBN 0-85131-139-3, Dist. by Sporting Book Center). J A Allen.

--The Horse in Action. LC 73-78531. (Illus.). 64p. 1974. 10.00 o.p. (ISBN 0-668-03313-4). Arco.

Wynn, ed. Obstetrics & Gynecology Annual: 1974, Vol. 3. (Illus.). 1974. 22.50 o.p. (ISBN 0-8385-7178-6). ACC.

--Obstetrics & Gynecology Annual: 1975, Vol. 4. (Illus.). 1975. 26.50 o.p. (ISBN 0-8385-7179-4). ACC.

--Obstetrics & Gynecology Annual: 1976, Vol. 5. (Illus.). 1976. 28.50 o.p. (ISBN 0-8385-7180-8, A7180-1). ACC.

Wynn, Arthur, jt. auth. see Wynn, Margaret.

Wynn, Graeme. Timber Colony: A Historical Geography of Early Nineteenth Century New Brunswick. 248p. 1980. 20.00x (ISBN 0-8020-5513-3); pap. 7.50 (ISBN 0-8020-6407-8). U of Toronto Pr.

Wynn, Margaret & Wynn, Arthur. Prevention of Handicap & the Health of Women. (Inequality in Society Ser.). (Illus.). 1979. 27.00 (ISBN 0-7100-0284-X). Routledge & Kegan.

Wynn, Peter. Foam Sandwich Boatbuilding. LC 72-87223. (Illus.). 128p. 1972. 9.95 o.p. (ISBN 0-87742-027-0). Intl Marine.

Wynn, R. F. & Holden, K. An Introduction to Applied Econometric Analysis. LC 74-3665. 245p. 1974. text ed. 26.95 (ISBN 0-470-96898-2). Halsted Pr.

Wynn, Ralph M., ed. Obstetrics & Gynecology Annual 1978, Vol. 7. (Illus.). 1978. 33.50 (ISBN 0-8385-7182-4). ACC.

--Obstetrics & Gynecology Annual 1979, Vol. 8. (Illus.). 1979. 29.50 (ISBN 0-8385-7183-2). ACC.

--Obstetrics & Gynecology Annual 1980. (Obstetrics & Gynecology Ser.). 390p. 1980. 29.50x (ISBN 0-8385-7186-7). ACC.

--Obstetrics & Gynecology Annual, 1981. (Obstetrics & Gynecology Annual Series). 1981. 33.50 (ISBN 0-8385-7188-3). ACC.

Wynne, E. G., jt. auth. see Pedder, I. J.

Wynne, Edward. The Politics of School Accountibility. LC 74-190055. 300p. 1972. 17.50x (ISBN 0-8211-2250-9); text ed. 15.75x (ISBN 0-685-24960-3). McCutchan.

--Social Security: A Reciprocity System Under Pressure. (Westview Special Studies in Contemporary Social Issues). 220p. 1980. lib. bdg. 18.50x (ISBN 0-89158-930-9). Westview.

Wynne, Edward A. Looking at Schools: Good, Bad, & Indifferent. LC 79-2798. 272p. 1980. 23.95 (ISBN 0-669-03292-1). Lexington Bks.

Wynne, George. Reinforced Concrete. 1981. text ed. 19.95 (ISBN 0-8359-6638-0); instrs'. manual avail. (ISBN 0-8359-6639-9). Reston.

Wynne, John. Crime Wave. 1981. 12.95. Riverrun NY.

Wynne, Michael. Hoofmarks. LC 80-51728. 270p. Date not set. pap. price not set (ISBN 0-89526-673-3). Regnery-Gateway. Postponed.

Wynne, Michael J., jt. auth. see Bold, Harold C.

Wynne, Pamela. Rainbow in the Spray. (Barbara Cartland's Library of Love: Vol. 13). 218p. 1980. 12.95x (ISBN 0-7156-1473-8, Pub. by Duckworth England). Biblio Dist.

Wynne, Ronald D., jt. auth. see Phillips, Joel.

Wynne-Jones, Tim. Odd's End. 1980. 11.95 (ISBN 0-316-96308-9). Little.

Wynn-Parry, C. B. Rehabilitation of the Hand. 4th rev. ed. LC 80-41761. (Illus.). 1981. text ed. price not set (ISBN 0-407-38502-9). Butterworths.

Wynorski, James. They Came from Outer Space. LC 80-2249. 336p. 1981. 11.95 (ISBN 0-385-18502-2). Doubleday.

Wynter, Andrew. Curiosities of Civilization. LC 67-23949. (Social History Reference Ser.: No. 11). 1968. Repr. of 1860 ed. 15.00 (ISBN 0-8103-3264-7). Gale.

--Our Social Bees. LC 67-23950. (Social History Reference Ser.). (Illus.). 1969. Repr. of 1861 ed. 15.00 (ISBN 0-8103-3265-5). Gale.

--Subtle Brains & Lissom Fingers. 3rd ed. LC 67-27868. (Social History Reference Ser.). (Illus.). 1968. Repr. of 1863 ed. 15.00 (ISBN 0-8103-3267-1). Gale.

Wynter, C. I. Chemical Analyses for Medical Technologists. (Illus.). 232p. 1975. 19.75 (ISBN 0-398-03236-X); pap. 13.50 (ISBN 0-398-03238-6). C C Thomas.

Wyon, Olive. Prayer. LC 78-2965. 72p. 1978. pap. 1.75 (ISBN 0-8006-1335-X, 1-1335). Fortress.

Wyrick-Spirduso, Waneen, jt. auth. see Locke, Lawrence F.

Wyrwicka, Wanda. The Mechanisms of Conditioned Behavior: A Critical Look at the Phenomena of Conditioning. (Illus.). 192p. 1972. 15.50 (ISBN 0-398-02444-8). C C Thomas.

Wyse, Bonita W., jt. auth. see Hansen, R. Gaurth.

Wyse, Lois. Grandfathers Are to Love. LC 67-18466. (Illus.). (gr. k-1). 1967. 2.50 o.s.i. (ISBN 0-8193-0165-5, Four Winds); boxed set with Grandmothers Are to Love 5.00 o.s.i. (ISBN 0-685-48750-4). Schol Bk Serv.

--Grandmothers Are to Love. LC 67-18465. (Illus.). (gr. k-1). 1967. 2.50 o.s.i. (ISBN 0-8193-0167-1, Four Winds); boxed set with Grandfathers Are to Love 5.00 o.s.i. (ISBN 0-685-48749-0). Schol Bk Serv.

Wyse, Lois, jt. auth. see Carter, John M.

Wyse Jackson, Robert. Story of Limerick. 1974. pap. 1.75 (ISBN 0-85342-376-8). Irish Bk Ctr.

Wysinger, Vossa E. The Celestial Democracy. LC 66-24014. 1966. text ed. 12.00 (ISBN 0-686-24366-8); pap. text ed. 9.00 (ISBN 0-686-24367-6). V E Wysinger.

Wysong, Patricia, jt. auth. see Strain, Barbara.

Wysor, Bettie. A Stranger's Eyes. 352p. (Orig.). 1981. pap. 2.75 (ISBN 0-515-05564-6). Jove Pubns.

Wyss, J. R. The Swiss Family Robinson. (Childrens Illustrated Classics Ser). (Illus.). 350p. 1977. Repr. of 1957 ed. 9.00x (ISBN 0-460-05008-7, Pub. by J. M. Dent England). Biblio Dist.

Wyss, Max, ed. Earthquake Prediction & Rock Mechanics. (Contributions to Current Research in Geophysics: Vol. 1). 1975. text ed. 60.00x (ISBN 3-7643-0809-5). Renouf.

Wyss, Orville & Eklund, C. E. Microorganisms & Man. LC 70-146674. 1971. text ed. 19.95x (ISBN 0-471-96900-1). Wiley.

Wyszecki, Gunter, jt. auth. see Judd, Deane B.

X

Xan, Erna O. Wisconsin My Home. 232p. 1976. 15.00 (ISBN 0-299-00711-1); pap. 5.25 (ISBN 0-299-00714-6). U of Wis Pr.

Xanthos, Paul. Handbook for Organization & Conduct of Tennis Clinics & Teacher Training Workshops. (Illus.). 39p. 1974. 2.95 (ISBN 0-938822-03-9). USTA.

Xanthos, Paul, jt. auth. see Johnson, Joan D.

Xenakis, Christopher. The Gay Cliche. pap. 4.95 (ISBN 0-933656-06-8). Trinity Pub Hse.

Xhafer, Anita. The Powder Box Lady. (Illus.). 32p. (ps-6). 1981. 10.95 (ISBN 0-19-554263-0). Oxford U Pr.

Xirau, Ramon, jt. ed. see Fromm, Erich.

Xu Liangying & Fan Dianian. Science & Socialist Construction in China. Perrolle, Pierre M., ed. Hsu, John C., tr. from Chinese. 250p. 25.00 (ISBN 0-87332-189-8). M E Sharpe.

Y

Y. W. C. A. World Fellowship Committee - Tokyo. Japanese Etiquette: An Introduction. LC 59-9828. (Illus.). (gr. 7 up). 1959. pap. 4.75 (ISBN 0-8048-0290-4). C E Tuttle.

Yablon, Isadore G. Injuries to the Ankle. (Illus.). 320p. 1981. lib. bdg. 30.00 (ISBN 0-443-08095-X). Churchill.

Yablonsky, Lewis. Psychodrama. 300p. Date not set. pap. text ed. 11.95 (ISBN 0-89876-016-X). Gardner Pr.

Yabrov, Alexander. Interferon & Non-Specific Resistance. LC 80-13677. 376p. 1980. 39.95 (ISBN 0-87705-497-5). Human Sci Pr.

Yacenko, Miquel. Antologia Poetica De Miguel Yacenko. Date not set. pap. 1.65 (ISBN 0-311-08756-6). Casa Bautista.

Yachnin, Stanley, jt. auth. see Piomelli, Sergio.

Yachnin, Stanley, jt. ed. see Piomelli, Sergio.

Yacht. Clear & Simple Guide to Touch Typing. (Clear & Simple Guides Ser.). (Illus.). 96p. (Orig.). 1981. pap. 5.95 (ISBN 0-671-42223-5). Monarch Pr.

Yackel, James W., jt. auth. see Moore, David S.

Yadav, C. S. Land Use in Big Cities: A Study of Delhi. 1979. text ed. 21.25x (ISBN 0-391-01840-X). Humanities.

Yadav, Rajendra. The Flirt. Ratan, Jai, tr. from Hindi. Orig. Title: Kulta. 100p. 1975. pap. 1.50 (ISBN 0-88253-769-5). Ind-US Inc.

Yadava, J. S. & Vinayshil, Gautam, eds. The Communication of Ideas. 256p. 1980. text ed. 15.75x (ISBN 0-391-02128-1). Humanities.

Yaeger, Randolph O. Renaissance New Testament, 20 vols. Incl. Vol. 1 (ISBN 0-88289-957-0); Vol. 2 (ISBN 0-88289-657-1); Vol. 3 (ISBN 0-88289-357-2); Vol. 4 (ISBN 0-88289-857-4); Vol. 5 (ISBN 0-88289-257-6); Vol. 6 (ISBN 0-88289-757-8). 3360p. 1980. each 19.95. Pelican.

Yaffe, Sumner J., ed. Pediatric Pharmacology: Therapeutic Principles in Practice. 1980. 44.50 (ISBN 0-8089-1251-8). Grune.

Yaffe, Sumner J., jt. ed. see Schwarz, Richard A.

Yager, E. Ben, jt. auth. see Langenderfer, Harold Q.

Yager, Edwin G., jt. auth. see Michalak, Donald F.

Yager, Joseph A., jt. auth. see Steinberg, Eleanor B.

Yager, Joseph A., ed. Nonproliferation & U. S. Foreign Policy. LC 80-20483. 464p. 1980. 22.95 (ISBN 0-8157-9674-9); pap. 8.95 (ISBN 0-8157-9673-0). Brookings.

Yagiela, John A., jt. auth. see Jastak, J. Theodore.

Yaglom, I. M. Complex Numbers in Geometry. 1967. 30.50 o.p. (ISBN 0-12-768150-7). Acad Pr.

Yahr, M. D., ed. Current Concepts in the Treatment of Parkinsonism. LC 74-79191. 1974. 24.50 (ISBN 0-911216-83-9). Raven.

Yahr, Melvin D., ed. The Basal Ganglia. LC 75-25114. (Association for Research in Nervous & Mental Disease Research Publications: Vol. 55). 1976. 48.00 (ISBN 0-89004-099-0). Raven.

Yahr, Melvin D. & Purpura, Dominick P., eds. Neurophysiological Basis of Normal & Abnormal Motor Activities. LC 67-28247. 1967. 37.50 (ISBN 0-911216-04-9). Raven.

Yahuda, Michael B. China's Role in World Affairs. LC 78-19218. 1978. 20.00 (ISBN 0-312-13358-8). St Martin.

Yahue, Kathryn. Photo Filters & Lens Attachments. (Petersen's Photographic Library). (Illus.). 160p. 1981. pap. 8.95 (ISBN 0-8227-4044-3). Petersen Pub.

Yakovlev, Nikolai N., jt. auth. see Sivachev, Kolai V.

Yakowitz, Sidney J. Computational Probability & Simulation. LC 77-3002. (Applied Mathematics & Computation Ser.: No. 12). 1977. text ed. 28.50 (ISBN 0-201-08892-4, Adv Bk Prog); pap. text ed. 16.50 (ISBN 0-201-08893-2). A-W.

Yale Committee on Human Sexuality. Student Guide to Sex on Campus. pap. 1.00 (ISBN 0-451-04607-2, N4607, Sig). NAL.

Yale, Irving. Podiatric Medicine. 2nd ed. (Illus.). 368p. 1980. 39.00 (ISBN 0-683-09318-5). Williams & Wilkins.

Yale, Paul B. Geometry & Symmetry. LC 67-28042. 1968. 17.95x (ISBN 0-8162-9964-1). Holden-Day.

Yale Univ. Library. List of Newspapers in Library of Yale. (Yale Historical Pubs., Miscellany Ser.: No. II). 1916. 42.50x (ISBN 0-685-69889-0). Elliots Bks.

Yale University Index Staff, ed. see Henderson, Virginia.

Yalkowsky & Sinkula. Physical Chemical Properties of Drugs. 384p. 1980. 45.00 (ISBN 0-8247-1008-8). Dekker.

Yallop, David. The Day the Laughter Stopped. LC 75-40810. (Illus.). 1976. 12.50 o.p. (ISBN 0-312-18410-7). St Martin.

Yallop, H. J. Explosion Investigation. 280p. 1980. 15.00x (ISBN 0-7073-0272-2, Pub. by Scottish Academic Pr Scotland). Columbia U Pr.

Yalman, Nur. Under the Bo Tree: Studies in Caste, Kinship & Marriage in the Interior of Ceylon. 1967. 20.00x (ISBN 0-520-01368-9); pap. 5.95x (ISBN 0-520-02054-5, CAMPUS62). U of Cal Pr.

Yalom, Irvin D. Existential Psychotherapy. LC 80-50553. 524p. 1980. 18.50 (ISBN 0-465-02147-6). Basic.

Yalouris, Nicholas M. & Rhomiopoulou, Katerina, eds. The Search for Alexander: An Exhibition. 1980. 22.50 (ISBN 0-8212-1108-0, 779105); pap. 12.95 (ISBN 0-8212-1117-X, 779113). NYGS.

Yamada, Abbot S., jt. auth. see Covell, Jon Carter.

Yamada, C. F., ed. Decorative Arts of Japan. LC 63-22011. (Illus.). 1963. 85.00 (ISBN 0-87011-006-3). Kodansha.

Yamada, Chisaburoh F., ed. Dialogue in Art: Japan & the West. LC 73-79772. (Illus.). 334p. 1976. 60.00 (ISBN 0-87011-214-7). Kodansha.

Yamada, Nakaba. Ghenko: The Mongol Invasion of Japan. (Studies in Japanese History & Civilization). 1979. Repr. of 1916 ed. 25.00 (ISBN 0-89093-254-9). U Pubns Amer.

Yamada, Sadami. Animal Sumi-E in Three Weeks. LC 65-27100. (Illus.). 32p. pap. 3.50 (ISBN 0-87040-006-1). Japan Pubns.

--Complete Sumi-E Techniques. LC 66-24010. 1966. pap. 10.95 (ISBN 0-87040-361-3). Japan Pubns.

--Landscape Sumi-E in Three Weeks. LC 65-27102. (Illus.). 32p. pap. 3.50 (ISBN 0-87040-075-4). Japan Pubns.

--Sumi-E in Three Weeks. LC 64-17024. (Illus.). 32p. 1964. pap. 3.50 (ISBN 0-87040-121-1). Japan Pubns.

Yamada, Yoshimitsu. The New Aikido. 1981. 25.00 (ISBN 0-8184-0301-2). Lyle Stuart.

Yamada, Yosi-Aki & Eastlake, F. Warrington. Heroic Japan: A History of the War Between China & Japan. (Studies in Japanese History & Civilization). 1979. Repr. of 1897 ed. 40.50 (ISBN 0-89093-291-3). U Pubns Amer.

Yamaguchi. Recent Advances on the Lacrimal System. Date not set. 47.50 (ISBN 0-89352-140-X). Masson Pub.

Yamaguchi, Gosei. The Fundamentals of Goju-Ryu Karate. Alston, Pat, ed. LC 72-80830. (Ser.112). (Illus.). 1972. pap. text ed. 7.95 (ISBN 0-89750-007-5). Ohara Pubns.

Yamaguchi, Susumu. The Mahayana Way to Buddhahood. Buddhist Books International, tr. from Japanese. 1981. 9.95 (ISBN 0-914910-11-6); pap. 6.95 (ISBN 0-914910-12-4). Buddhist Bks.

Yamakawa, Reiko, tr. see O'Hara, Betsy.

Yamamoto, Kaoru, ed. Child & His Image: Self Concept in the Early Years. LC 72-163283. (Illus., Orig.). 1972. pap. text ed. 10.95 (ISBN 0-395-12571-5, 3-60986). HM.

--Children in Time & Space. LC 79-91. 1979. pap. text ed. 9.95 (ISBN 0-8077-2553-6). Tchrs Coll.

Yamamoto, Tsunetomo. Hagakure: The Book of the Samurai. Wilson, William S., tr. from Jap. LC 78-71315. 1978. 9.95 (ISBN 0-87011-378-X). Kodansha.

Yamamura, Henry I., et al, eds. Neurotransmitter Receptor Binding. LC 78-3010. 1978. 21.00 (ISBN 0-89004-231-4). Raven.

Yamamura, Kozo. Economic Policy in Postwar Japan: Growth Versus Economic Democracy. (Center for Japanese & Korean Studies, UC Berkeley). 1967. 21.50x (ISBN 0-520-01369-7). U of Cal Pr.

Yamamura, Sakae. Theory of Linear Induction Motors. 2nd ed. LC 78-21550. 1979. 28.95 (ISBN 0-470-26583-3). Halsted Pr.

Yamane, Taro. Estadistica Aplicada. 3rd ed. (Span.). 1974. 12.50 o.p. (ISBN 0-06-319775-8, IntlDept). Har-Row.

--Estadistica Con Problemas. (Span.). 1979. pap. text ed. 13.00 (ISBN 0-06-319777-4, Pub. by HarLA Mexico). Har-Row.

--Statistics: An Introductory Analysis. 3rd ed. (Illus.). 1973. text ed. 21.95 scp (ISBN 0-06-047313-4, HarpC); scp problems manual 6.50 (ISBN 0-06-047319-3); solutions manual free (ISBN 0-06-367313-4). Har-Row.

Yamanouchi, H. The Search for Authenticity in Modern Japanese Literature. LC 77-84815. 1978. 29.95 (ISBN 0-521-21856-X). Cambridge U Pr.

--The Search for Authenticity in Modern Japanese Literature. LC 77-84815. 214p. 1980. pap. 10.95 (ISBN 0-521-29974-8). Cambridge U Pr.

Yamanushi, Toshiko. The Nutcracker. Tresselt, Alvin, tr. from Japanese. LC 74-5809. Orig. Title: Kurmi- wari Ningyo. (Illus.). 40p. (ps-2). 1974. Repr. 5.95 o.s.i. (ISBN 0-8193-0743-2, Four Winds); PLB 5.41 o.s.i. (ISBN 0-8193-0744-0). Schol Bk Serv.

Yamaoka, Haruo. Meditation Gut Enlightenment: The Way of Hara. 1976. pap. 2.50 o.p. (ISBN 0-89346-001-X). Heian Intl.

Yamashiro, Stanley M., jt. auth. see Grodins, Fred S.

Yamashita, Yasumasa, et al. An Atlas of Representative Stellar Spectra. LC 78-535. 1978. 69.95 (ISBN 0-470-26315-6). Halsted Pr.

Yamauchi, Edwin. Archaeology of New Testament Cities in Western Asia Minor. LC 80-66991. (Baker Studies in Biblical Archaeology). 160p. 1980. pap. 7.95 (ISBN 0-8010-9915-3). Baker Bk.

--Harper's World of the New Testament. LC 80-8606. (Illus.). 144p. (Orig.). 1981. pap. 9.95 (ISBN 0-06-069708-3, HarpR). Har-Row.

Yamazaki, Mikio, jt. ed. see Uraguchi, Kenji.

Yamazaki, W. T. Soft Wheat: Production, Breeding, Milling, & Uses. LC 80-65826. (The AACC Monograph: Vol. VI). 352p. 1980. 36.00 (ISBN 0-913250-17-1). Am Assn Cereal Chem.

Yamey, B. S., jt. auth. see Goss, B.

Yamori, Yukio, et al. Prophylactic Approach to Hypertensive Disease: Symposium. (Perspectives in Cardiovascular Research Ser.: Vol. 4). 1979. 58.50 (ISBN 0-89004-339-6). Raven.

Yampolsky, Philip B., tr. Platform Sutra of the Sixth Patriarch. LC 67-11847. (Records of Civilization, Studies & Sources: No. 76). 1967. 18.00x (ISBN 0-231-02994-2); pap. 10.00x (ISBN 0-231-08361-0). Columbia U Pr.

Yampolsky, Philip B., tr. from Jap. Zen Master Hakuin: Selected Writings. LC 75-145390. (Records of Civilization, Studies & Sources: No. 86). 1971. 17.50x (ISBN 0-231-03463-6). Columbia U Pr.

Yamrus, John. Someone Else's Dreams. LC 80-70611. (Illus.). 60p. (Orig.). 1981. pap. 3.75 (ISBN 0-930090-13-6); pap. 10.00 special ltd. ed. Applezaba.

Yanagisawa, Eizo, jt. tr. see Whitehouse, Wilfrid.

Yanarella, Ernest J. The Missile Defense Controversy: Strategy, Technology, & Politics, 1955-1972. LC 76-46034. 1977. 18.00x (ISBN 0-8131-1355-5). U Pr of Ky.

Yance, Becky & Linedecker, Cliff. My Life with Elvis. LC 77-10377. (Illus.). 1977. 3.98 (ISBN 0-312-55834-1). St Martin.

Yance, Norman A. Religion Southern Style: Southern Baptists & Society in Histoical Pspective. LC 78-61185. (Special Studies Ser.: No. 4). 1978. 3.95 (ISBN 0-932180-03-5). Assn Baptist Profs.

Yancey, Philip. Where Is God When It Hurts. 1977. 6.95 (ISBN 0-310-35410-2); pap. 4.95 (ISBN 0-310-35411-0). Zondervan.

--Where Is God When It Hurts? A Study Guide. (Orig.). 1978. pap. 1.95 (ISBN 0-310-35431-5). Zondervan.

Yancey, Phillip, jt. auth. see Brand, Paul.

Yancy, Becky & Linedecker, Cliff. My Life with Elvis. (Illus.). 1978. pap. 2.50 o.s.i. (ISBN 0-446-81927-1). Warner Bks.

Yancy, Wallace. The Dream Dictionary. 1981. 6.95 (ISBN 0-8062-1685-9). Carlton.

Yanda, Bill & Fisher, Rick. The Food & Heat Producing Solar Greenhouse. rev. ed. LC 79-91276. (Illus.). 208p. (Orig.). 1980. pap. 8.00 (ISBN 0-912528-20-6). John Muir.

Yanda, Susan, jt. auth. see Yanda, W. F.

Yanda, W. F. & Yanda, Susan. An Attached Solar Greenhouse. (Sp. & Eng.). 1976. pap. 2.00 (ISBN 0-89016-028-7). Lightning Tree.

Yandell, Keith, jt. auth. see Weinberg, Julius R.

Yandell, Keith E., jt. ed. see Weinberg, Julius R.

Yandell, M. D. National Parkways, Zion & Bryce Canyon National Parks. (Illus.). 64p. 1972. 2.95. Zion.

Yandle, Bruce, jt. auth. see Ulbrich, Holley H.

Yandle, Bruce, Jr., jt. auth. see Macauley, Hugh, Jr.

Yando, Regina & Seitz, Victoria. Intellectual & Personality Characteristics of Children: Social-Class & Ethnic-Group Differences. 136p. 1979. profess./reference text 12.95 (ISBN 0-89859-001-9). Erlbaum Assocs.

Yanev, Peter. Peace of Mind in Earthquake Country: How to Save Your Home & Life. LC 74-7406. (Illus.). 320p. 1974. 9.95 (ISBN 0-87701-050-1); pap. 5.95 (ISBN 0-87701-049-8). Chronicle Bks.

Yaney, Joseph P. Personnel Management: Reaching Organizational & Human Goals. new ed. (Business Ser). 448p. 1975. text ed. 17.95 (ISBN 0-675-08760-0); instructor's manual 3.95 (ISBN 0-685-50978-8). Merrill.

Yaney, Joseph P., jt. auth. see Stern, D. Nordlinger.

Yang, Martin C. A Chinese Village: Taitou, Shantung Province. LC 45-4581. 1945. pap. 6.00x (ISBN 0-231-08561-3). Columbia U Pr.

Yang, Richard & Lazzerini, Edward J. The Chinese World. LC 77-81184. (World of Asia Ser.). (Illus., Orig.). 1978. pap. 3.95 (ISBN 0-88273-504-7). Forum Pr MO.

Yang, Rita, jt. auth. see Lee, Kaiman.

Yang Ywing-Ming. Shaolin Chin Na. LC 80-53546. (Illus.). 144p. (Orig.). 1980. pap. 6.95 (ISBN 0-86568-012-4). Unique Pubns.

Yankaskas, Bonnie C., jt. ed. see Gold, Ronald.

Yankee, Herbert W. Manufacturing Processes. LC 78-13059. (Illus.). 1979. 26.95 (ISBN 0-13-555557-4). P-H.

Yankelovich, Daniel. The New Morality: A Profile of American Youth in the Seventies. 176p. (Orig.). 1974. pap. 2.95 (P&RB). McGraw.

Yankowitz, Susan. Silent Witness. 1976. 7.95 o.p. (ISBN 0-394-49943-3). Knopf.

Yannacone, Victor J., Jr., et al. Environmental Rights & Remedies, 2 vols. LC 79-118365. 1972. 90.00 (ISBN 0-686-14502-X). Lawyers Co-Op.

Yannarella, Philip A. & Aluri, Rao. U. S. Government Scientific & Technical Periodicals. LC 75-38740. 1976. 12.00 (ISBN 0-8108-0888-9). Scarecrow.

Yannatos, James. Explorations in Musical Materials: A Working Approach to Making Music. (Illus.). 1978. pap. text ed. 14.50 (ISBN 0-13-295956-9). P-H.

Yannela, Donald & Roch, John, trs. American Prose to Eighteen Twenty: A Guide to Information Sources. LC 79-63741. (American Literature, English Literature, & World Literatures in English Information Guide Ser.: Vol. 21). 600p. 1979. 30.00 (ISBN 0-8103-1361-8). Gale.

Yannopoulos, G., jt. ed. see Shlaim, A.

Yannopoulos, G. N., jt. auth. see Shlaim, A.

Yanouzas, John N., jt. auth. see Veiga, John F.

Yanov, Alexander. The Russian New Right: Right-Wing Ideologies in the Contemporary USSR. Dunn, Stephen P., tr. from Rus. LC 78-620020. (Research Ser: No. 35). 1978. pap. 4.50x (ISBN 0-87725-135-5). U of Cal Intl St.

Yanovsky, Elias. Food Plants of the North American Indians. 1980. lib. bdg. 49.95 (ISBN 0-8490-3108-7). Gordon Pr.

Yanovsky, V. S. Of Light & Sounding Brass. Levitin, Isabella, tr. from Rus. LC 72-83353. 296p. 1972. 8.95 (ISBN 0-8149-0719-9). Vanguard.

Yanowitch, Murray. Social & Economic Inequality in the Soviet Union: Six Studies. LC 77-71634. 1977. 15.00 o.p. (ISBN 0-87332-105-7); pap. 6.95 (ISBN 0-87332-148-0). M E Sharpe.

Yanowitch, Murray, jt. auth. see Silverman, Bertram.

Yanson, I. K., jt. auth. see Kulik, I. O.

Yao, James S., jt. auth. see Neiman, Harvey L.

Yao, James S., jt. ed. see Bergan, John J.

Yao, James T., jt. auth. see Nicolaides, A. N.

Yao Hsin-Nung. The Malice of Empire. Ingalls, Jeremy, tr. & intro. by. LC 69-19942. 1970. 15.75x (ISBN 0-520-01560-6). U of Cal Pr.

Yao-wen, Li, jt. auth. see Kendall, Carol.

Yapp, M. E., jt. auth. see Parry, V. J.

Yapp, Malcolm. The Ancient Near East. Killingray, Margaret, et al, eds. (World History Ser.). (Illus.). 32p. (gr. 10). 1980. Repr. of 1977 ed. lib. bdg. 5.95 (ISBN 0-89908-025-1); pap. text ed. 1.95 (ISBN 0-89908-000-6). Greenhaven.

--British Raj & Indian Nationalism. Killingray, Margaret & O'Connor, Edmund, eds. (World History Ser.). (Illus.). 32p. (gr. 10). 1980. Repr. of 1977 ed. lib. bdg. 5.95 (ISBN 0-89908-228-9); pap. text ed. 1.95 (ISBN 0-89908-203-3). Greenhaven.

--Chingis Khan & the Mongol Empire. Killingray, Margaret & O'Connor, Edmund, eds. (World History Ser.). (Illus.). 32p. (gr. 10). 1980. Repr. of 1977 ed. lib. bdg. 5.95 (ISBN 0-89908-030-8); pap. text ed. 1.95 (ISBN 0-89908-005-7). Greenhaven.

--Gandhi. Killingray, Margaret & O'Connor, Edmund, eds. (World History Ser.). (Illus.). 32p. (gr. 10). 1980. Repr. of 1977 ed. lib. bdg. 5.95 (ISBN 0-89908-128-2); pap. text ed. 1.95 (ISBN 0-89908-103-7). Greenhaven.

--The Growth of the State. Killingray, Margaret & O'Connor, Edmund, eds. (Greenhaven World History Ser.). (Illus.). 32p. (gr. 10). 1980. Repr. of 1977 ed. lib. bdg. 5.95 (ISBN 0-89908-229-7); pap. text ed. 1.95 (ISBN 0-89908-204-1). Greenhaven.

--Ibn Sina & the Muslim World. Killingray, Margaret & O'Connor, Edmund, eds. (World History Ser.). (Illus.). 1980. lib. bdg. 5.95 (ISBN 0-89908-037-5); pap. text ed. 1.95 (ISBN 0-89908-012-X). Greenhaven.

--Nationalism. Killingray, Margaret & O'Connor, Edmund, eds. (World History Ser.). (Illus.). 32p. (gr. 10). 1980. Repr. of 1977 ed. lib. bdg. 5.95 (ISBN 0-89908-227-0); pap. text ed. 1.95 (ISBN 0-89908-202-5). Greenhaven.

Yapp, Malcolm, ed. see Addison, John, et al.

Yapp, Malcolm, ed. see Duckworth, John, et al.

Yapp, Malcolm, ed. see Harrison, John, et al.

Yapp, Malcolm, ed. see Heater, Derek & Owen, Gwyneth.

Yapp, Malcolm, ed. see Killingray, David.

Yapp, Malcolm, ed. see Killingray, Margaret.

Yapp, Malcolm, ed. see O'Connor, Edmund.

Yapp, Malcolm, ed. see Painter, Desmond.

Yapp, Malcolm, ed. see Painter, Desmond & Shepard, John.

Yapp, Malcolm, ed. see Pearson, Eileen.

Yapp, Malcolm, ed. see Tames, Richard.

Yapp, Malcolm, jt. auth. see Read, James.

Yapp, Malcolm, et al, eds. see Addison, John, et al.

Yapp, Malcolm, et al, eds. see Amey, Peter.

Yapp, Malcolm, et al, eds. see Amey, Peter, et al.

Yapp, Malcolm, et al, eds. see Amey, Peter.

Yapp, Malcolm, et al, eds. see Byres, Terence.

Yapp, Malcolm, et al, eds. see Clifford, Alan.

Yapp, Malcolm, et al, eds. see Cripwell, Kenneth.

Yapp, Malcolm, et al, eds. see Garrett, Sean.

Yapp, Malcolm, et al, eds. see Guyatt, John.

Yapp, Malcolm, et al, eds. see Kanitkar, Helen & Kanitkar, Hemant.

Yapp, Malcolm, et al, eds. see Killingray, David.

Yapp, Malcolm, et al, eds. see Killingray, David, et al.

Yapp, Malcolm, et al, eds. see Killingray, David.

Yapp, Malcolm, et al, eds. see Killingray, Margaret.

Yapp, Malcolm, et al, eds. see Knox, D. M.

Yapp, Malcolm, et al, eds. see Knox, Diana.

Yapp, Malcolm, et al, eds. see Nicholson, Alasdair.

Yapp, Malcolm, et al, eds. see O'Connor, Edmund.

Yapp, Malcolm, et al, eds. see Painter, Desmond.

Yapp, Malcolm, et al, eds. see Tames, Richard.

Yapp, Malcolm, et al, eds. see Townson, Duncan.

Yapp, Malcolm, et al, eds. see Weston, Anthony.

Yapp, Malcolm, et al, eds. see Wrangham, Elizabeth.

Yapp, Malcolm, et al, eds. see Wrangham, Elizabeth, et al.

Yapp, Martin, ed. see Booth, Martin, et al.

Yapp, Michael, jt. ed. see Taylor, David.

Yapp, W. B. & Smith, M. I. Production, Pollution, Protection. (Wykeham Science Ser.: No. 19). 1972. 9.95x (ISBN 0-8448-1121-1). Crane-Russak Co.

Yaqub, Adil. Elementary Functions. 368p. 1975. text ed. 17.50 (ISBN 0-395-17093-1); instructors manual pap. 2.25 (ISBN 0-395-17871-1). HM.

Yaqub, Adil & Moore, Hal G. Elementary Linear Algebra with Applications. LC 79-18743. (Mathematics Ser.). 1980. text ed. 17.50 (ISBN 0-201-08825-8). A-W.

Yarber, Robert, jt. ed. see Hurtik, Emil.

Yarber, Robert E., jt. auth. see Hogins, James B.

Yarborough, Charlotte. The Condor Conspiracy. (Orig.). 1980. pap. 1.75 (ISBN 0-8439-0739-8, Leisure Bks). Nordon Pubns.

Yarborough, Larry. Being Joyous. LC 72-96151. pap. 0.50 tchr's guide (ISBN 0-8054-5318-0). Broadman.

Yarbro, Adela, tr. see Dibelius, Martin & Conzelmann, Hans.

Yarbro, Charles Q. Sins of Omission. 1980. pap. 2.25 (ISBN 0-451-09165-5, E9165, Sig). NAL.

Yarbro, Chelsea Q. Dead & Buried. (Orig.). 1980. pap. 2.75 (ISBN 0-446-95886-7). Warner Bks.

--Messages from Michael. LC 80-82567. 288p. 1980. pap. 2.50 (ISBN 0-87216-766-6). Playboy Pbks.

--The Palace: A Historical Horror Novel. LC 78-3996. 1979. 9.95 o.p. (ISBN 0-312-59474-7). St Martin.

--Path of the Eclipse. 518p. 1981. 13.95 (ISBN 0-312-59802-5). St Martin.

Yarbro, John & Bornstein, Richard, eds. Oncologic Emergencies. (Clinical Oncology Monographs). 1980. write for info. (ISBN 0-8089-1317-4). Grune.

Yarbrough, Camille. Cornrows. (Illus.). 48p. (Orig.). (gr. k-3). 1981. pap. 2.95 (ISBN 0-698-20529-4, Peppercorn). Coward.

Yarbrough, Raymond B. Electrical Engineering Review Manual. 2nd ed. LC 80-81797. (Engineering Review Manual Ser.). (Illus.). 443p. 1980. pap. 24.50 (ISBN 0-936754-00-1); wkbk. 7.00 (ISBN 0-936754-03-6). Prof Engine.

Yardley & Goldman. Mucosal Biopsies in Gastroenterology. 1981. text ed. write for info. (ISBN 0-443-08059-3). Churchill.

Yardley, Alice. Exploration & Language. LC 72-95335. 152p. 1973. 3.25 o.p. (ISBN 0-590-07330-3, Citation). Schol Bk Serv.

--Learning to Adjust. LC 73-81973. 144p. 1973. 3.25 o.p. (ISBN 0-590-07348-6, Citation). Schol Bk Serv.

--Reaching Out. LC 72-95335. 112p. 1973. 3.25 o.p. (ISBN 0-590-07328-1, Citation). Schol Bk Serv.

--Senses & Sensitivity. LC 72-95335. 144p. 1973. 3.25 o.p. (ISBN 0-590-07329-X, Citation). Schol Bk Serv.

--Structure in Early Learning. LC 73-94155. 1974. 3.25 o.p. (ISBN 0-590-07395-8, Citation). Schol Bk Serv.

--The Teacher of Young Children. LC 72-95336. 112p. 1973. 3.25 o.p. (ISBN 0-590-07326-5, Citation). Schol Bk Serv.

--Young Children Thinking. 144p. 1973. 3.25 o.p. (ISBN 0-590-07331-1, Citation). Schol Bk Serv.

Yardley, D. C., jt. auth. see Hanbury, H. G.

Yardley, Edward. The Supernatural in Romantic Fiction. 1979. 28.50 o.p. (ISBN 0-685-94350-X). Porter.

Yardley, John H. & Morson, Basil C., eds. Inflammatory & Neoplastic Disease of the Gastrointestinal Tract, No. 18. International Academy of Pathology. 1977. 26.00 (ISBN 0-683-09317-7). Williams & Wilkins.

Yards, A. Mafia-Syndicate: Organized Crime - the Government Within the Government. LC 76-23355. 202p. 1977. pap. 4.95 (ISBN 0-686-22703-4). A Yards.

Yardumian, Charles. The Problem of Cheating in Schools: Its Psychological Meaning & the Future of the American Society. (American Culture Library Bk.). (Illus.). 107p. 1981. 29.95 (ISBN 0-89266-293-X). Am Classical Coll Pr.

Yarington, C. T., Jr., ed. Otolaryngology Case Studies. 2nd ed. 1974. spiral bdg. 14.00 (ISBN 0-87488-021-1). Med Exam.

Yarington, David J. Surviving in College. 1977. pap. text ed. 7.50 (ISBN 0-672-61372-7); tchr's manual 2.50 (ISBN 0-672-61373-5). Bobbs.

Yariv, Amnon. Quantum Electronics. 2nd ed. LC 75-1392. 544p. 1975. text ed. 34.95 (ISBN 0-471-97176-6). Wiley.

Yariv, Fran P. The Hallowing. (Orig.). pap. 2.50 (ISBN 0-515-05192-6). Jove Pubns.

--Last Exit. 256p. (Orig.). 1981. pap. 2.50 (ISBN 0-515-05416-X). Jove Pubns.

Yarker, K. A. International Marketing. 178p. 1976. text ed. 23.50x (ISBN 0-220-66298-3, Pub. by Busn Bks England). Renouf.

Yarker, P. M., ed. see Wordsworth, William.

Yarmish, Joshua, jt. auth. see Yarmish, Rina.

Yarmish, Rina & Yarmish, Joshua. Assembly Language Fundamentals, 360-370. LC 79-64125. 1979. text ed. 18.95 (ISBN 0-201-08798-7). A-W.

Yarnall, Agnes. An Attempted Evocation of the Civil War. 93p. 1980. 8.95 (ISBN 0-8059-2749-2). Dorrance.

--Hesperides & Other Poems. LC 80-66609. (Illus.). 64p. 1978. 4.95 (ISBN 0-8059-2485-X). Dorrance.

Yarnall, Sophia. The Clark Inheritance: A Coal Country Saga. LC 80-54812. 224p. 1981. 11.95 (ISBN 0-8027-0679-7). Walker & Co.

Yarnell, Allen. Democrats & Progressives: The 1948 Presidential Election As a Test of Postwar Liberalism. 1974. 16.95x (ISBN 0-520-02539-3). U of Cal Pr.

Yaron. Salinity in Irrigation & Water Resources. 448p. 1981. 49.75 (ISBN 0-8247-6741-1). Dekker.

Yaroslavskii, L. P. & Merzlyakov, N. S. Methods of Digital Holography. 250p. 1980. 45.00 (ISBN 0-306-10963-8, Consultants). Plenum Pub.

Yarrow, Leon J., jt. auth. see Shereshefsky, Pauline M.

Yarrow, P. J., ed. see Hugo, Victor.

Yarry, Mark R. The Fastest Game in Town: Commodities. 192p. 1981. 9.95 (ISBN 0-13-307884-1). P-H.

Yartz, Frank, et al. Progress & the Crisis of Man. LC 75-44451. 144p. 1976. 14.95 (ISBN 0-88229-165-3). Nelson-Hall.

Yarwood, Doreen. The British Kitchen. (Illus.). 192p. 1981. 28.95 (ISBN 0-7134-1430-8, Pub. by Batsford England). David & Charles.

--Costume of the Western World. 192p. 1980. 17.50x. St Martin.

--Encyclopedia of World Costume. (Illus.). 1978. 27.50 (ISBN 0-684-15805-1, ScribT). Scribner.

--English Costume from the Second Century BC to the Present Day. 1973. 30.00 (ISBN 0-7134-0853-7, Pub. by Batsford England). David & Charles.

--The English Home. 1979. 30.00 (ISBN 0-7134-0805-7, Pub. by Batsford England). David & Charles.

--European Costume. 1975. 53.00 (ISBN 0-7134-3020-6, Pub. by Batsford England). David & Charles.

--Outline of English Costume. 1972. 19.95 (ISBN 0-7134-0852-9, Pub. by Batsford England). David & Charles.

Yarwood, J., jt. auth. see Whittle, R.

Yarwood, J., ed. Vacuum & Thin Film Technology. 1978. text ed. 40.00 (ISBN 0-08-022112-2). Pergamon.

Yarwood, J., ed. see Israeli Vacuum Congress, Fifth, Israel, April 1978.

Yarwood, Y., jt. auth. see Close, K. J.

Yashinskaya, F. I., ed. see Babaevsky, P. G., et al.

Yashiro, Nobutaka. Asian Electrical & Electronics Trades Directory 1979-80. Hirayama, T. & Takalashi, Y., eds. (Illus.). 1979. pap. 140.00x (ISBN 0-8002-0350-X). Intl Pubns Serv.

Yasser, Joseph. A Theory of Evolving Tonality. LC 74-34376. (Music Reprint Ser). (Illus.). x, 381p. 1975. Repr. of 1932 ed. lib. bdg. 35.00 (ISBN 0-306-70729-2). Da Capo.

Yater, Verna V. Mainstreaming of Children with a Hearing Loss: Practical Guidelines & Implications. (Illus.). 304p. 1977. 28.50 (ISBN 0-398-03586-5); pap. 19.25 (ISBN 0-398-03589-X). C C Thomas.

Yates. The First Twenty-Five Years: A Review of the NFER 1946-71. 1971. pap. text ed. 3.00x (ISBN 0-901225-82-7, NFER). Humanities.

Yates, Alfred, ed. Current Problems of Teacher Education. (International Studies in Education). (Orig.). 1971. pap. 9.25 (ISBN 0-685-02838-0, U145, UNESCO). Unipub.

Yates, Anthony P., jt. auth. see Goldfarb, I. William.

Yates, Aubrey J. Biofeedback & the Modification of Behavior. LC 79-400. (Illus.). 524p. 1980. 24.50 (ISBN 0-306-40226-2, Plenum Pr). Plenum Pub.

--Theory & Practice in Behavior Therapy. LC 74-30018. (Personality Processes Ser). 336p. 1975. 23.95 (ISBN 0-471-97230-4, Pub. by Wiley-Interscience). Wiley.

Yates, B. How to Find Out About Physics. 1965. 15.00 (ISBN 0-08-011289-7); pap. 7.00 (ISBN 0-08-011288-9). Pergamon.

--How to Find Out About the United Kingdom Cotton Industry. 1967. 13.75 (ISBN 0-08-012360-0); pap. 6.25 (ISBN 0-08-012361-9). Pergamon.

Yates, B. T. Improving Effectiveness & Reducing Costs in Mental Health. (Illus.). 240p. 1980. 19.75 (ISBN 0-398-03971-2). C C Thomas.

Yates, Brock. Dead in the Water. 224p. 1975. 7.95 o.p. (ISBN 0-374-13544-4). FS&G.

Yates, David O. What the Bible Says About Your Personality. LC 80-7759. 192p. (Orig.). 1980. pap. 5.95 (ISBN 0-06-069711-3, RD 333, HarpR). Har-Row.

Yates, Donald A., ed. see Borges, Jorge L.

Yates, Dorothy. Family Tree. 1967. 4.50 o.p. (ISBN 0-374-15320-5). FS&G.

Yates, Douglas. Franz Grillparzer, a Critical Biography. 188p. 1980. Repr. of 1946 ed. lib. bdg. 22.50 (ISBN 0-8482-3111-2). Norwood Edns.

Yates, Douglas, ed. see Grillparzer, Franz.

Yates, Douglas T., jt. auth. see Nelson, Richard R.

Yates, Elizabeth. A Book of Hours. 1976. 5.95 (ISBN 0-685-89238-7); pap. 2.95 (ISBN 0-8164-0900-5). Crossroad NY.

--Carolina's Courage. (Illus.). (gr. 3-5). 1964. PLB 7.50 o.p. (ISBN 0-525-27480-4). Dutton.

--My Diary - My World. LC 80-24977. (Illus.). (gr. 5-9). 1981. 8.95 (ISBN 0-664-32675-7). Westminster.

--Sarah Whitcher's Story. 2nd ed. (Illus.). 93p. (gr. 4-8). 1979. pap. 2.65x (ISBN 0-915892-11-1). Regional Ctr Educ.

--We, the People. (Bicentennial Historiettes). (Illus.). 64p. (gr. 7-8). 1976. text ed. 4.95x (ISBN 0-914378-06-6); pap. text ed. 0.95x (ISBN 0-915892-18-9). Regional Ctr Educ.

--Your Prayers & Mine. (Illus.). (gr. 7-9). 1954. 3.95 o.p. (ISBN 0-395-07212-3). HM.

Yates, Elizabeth, ed. see Tregarthen, Enys.

Yates, Frances A. The Occult Philosophy in the Elizabethan Age. (Illus.). 1979. 20.00 (ISBN 0-7100-0320-X). Routledge & Kegan.

--The Rosicrucian Enlightenment. (Illus.). 286p. 1972. 22.50 (ISBN 0-7100-7380-1). Routledge & Kegan.

--Shakespeare's Last Plays. 1975. 15.00 (ISBN 0-7100-8100-6). Routledge & Kegan.

Yates, Frank. Sampling Methods for Censuses & Surveys. 3rd, rev. ed. 1965. 20.75 o.s.i. (ISBN 0-02-855500-7). Hafner.

Yates, Gayle G. What Women Want: The Ideologies of the Movement. 224p. 1975. 12.50x (ISBN 0-674-95077-1); pap. 3.95 (ISBN 0-674-95079-8). Harvard U Pr.

Yates, J. G. Fluidized Bed Reactors. 1981. text ed. price not set. Butterworth.

Yates, Jack & Thorold, Henry. Lincolnshire: A Shell Guide. (Shell Guide Ser.). (Illus.). 1968. 14.95 (ISBN 0-571-06297-0, Pub. by Faber & Faber). Merrimack Bk Serv.

Yates, James R., jt. auth. see Hencley, Stephan P.

Yates, Joanne C. My Fears Are Gone. 1978. pap. 2.95 (ISBN 0-89728-047-4, 704083). Omega Pubns OR.

Yates, Kyle M. Essentials of Biblical Hebrew. rev. ed. Owens, J. J., ed. 1955. 8.00x (ISBN 0-06-069710-5, HarpR). Har-Row.

Yates, Kyle M. & Owens, J. J. Nociones Esenciales Del Hebreo Biblico. Daglio, S. Daniel, tr. 1980. Repr. of 1978 ed. 5.25 (ISBN 0-311-42056-7). Casa Bautista.

Yates, Madelein, jt. auth. see Miklowitz, Gloria D.

Yates, Madeleine. Earth Power: The Story of Geothermal Energy. LC 79-25155. (Illus.). 64p. (gr. 4-7). 1980. 7.95g (ISBN 0-687-11450-0). Abingdon.

Yates, Maria S. see Knorre, Marty, et al.

Yates, Norris W. Robert Benchley. LC 68-24296. (U. S. Authors Ser.: No. 138). 1968. lib. bdg. 10.95 (ISBN 0-8057-0048-X). Twayne.

Yates, Peter. The Garden Prospect. 1980. 15.00 (ISBN 0-912330-41-4); pap. 9.50 (ISBN 0-912330-42-2). Jargon Soc.

--The Garden Prospect: Selected Poems of Peter Yates. 1980. 15.00 (ISBN 0-912330-41-4); pap. 9.50 (ISBN 0-912330-42-2). Jargon Soc.

--Twentieth Century Music: Its Evolution from the End of the Harmonic Era into the Present Era of Sound. LC 80-23310. xv, 367p. 1981. Repr. of 1967 ed. lib. bdg. 28.75x (ISBN 0-313-22516-8, YATC). Greenwood.

Yates, Richard. Eleven Kinds of Loneliness: Short Stories. LC 72-603. 230p. 1962. Repr. lib. bdg. 19.75x (ISBN 0-8371-5727-7, YALO). Greenwood.

Yates, Robert & Gordon, Mildred. Male Reproductive System: Fine Structure Analysis by Scanning & Transmission Electron Microscopy. LC 77-71435. (Illus.). 214p. 1977. 47.75 (ISBN 0-89352-004-7). Masson Pub.

Yates, W. E. Grillparzer: A Critical Introduction. LC 77-158550. 1972. 47.50 (ISBN 0-521-08241-2). Cambridge U Pr.

Yates, W. E., ed. see Grillparzer, F.

Yatiswarananda, Swami. The Divine Life. 1935. 2.25 o.p. (ISBN 0-87481-442-1). Vedanta Pr.

--Meditation & Spiritual Life. 700p. 1980. 18.95 (ISBN 0-87481-403-0). Vedanta Pr.

Yatsimirskii, K. B. Kinetic Methods of Analysis. Harvey, P. J., tr. 1966. 25.00 (ISBN 0-08-011364-8); pap. 8.25 (ISBN 0-08-013827-6). Pergamon.

Yavari, Brigitta. There Is a Love: A Beautifully Designed Tribute to Christ by a Talented European Illustrator. 1972. pap. 4.50 o.p. (ISBN 0-88270-006-5). Logos.

Yaverbaum, L. H., ed. Technology of Metal Powders: Recent Developments. LC 80-31. (Chemical Technology Review: No. 153). (Illus.). 400p. 1980. 45.00 (ISBN 0-8155-0794-1). Noyes.

Yawkey, Thomas D., et al. Language Arts & the Young Child. LC 80-52447. 270p. 1981. pap. text ed. 7.50 (ISBN 0-87581-263-5). Peacock Pubs.

Yaziji, Ibrahim. Naj Atu Ur-Ra'ld wa-Shar Atu al-Warid Fi al-Mutaradifi. (Arabic.). 1970. 23.00x (ISBN 0-685-72052-7). Intl Bk Ctr.

Ybarra, Thomas R., tr. see Wilhelm.

Ybarra-Frausto, T., jt. auth. see Sommers, J.

Y'Blood, William T. Red Sun Setting: The Battle of the Philippine Sea. 208p. 1981. 18.95 (ISBN 0-87021-532-9). Naval Inst Pr.

Ydur, Rudy. How Not to Write. 64p. 1981. 5.00 (ISBN 0-930592-06-9). Lumeli Pr.

Yeadon, David. Backroads of Southern Europe. LC 80-8222. (Illus.). 256p. 1981. 15.00 (ISBN 0-06-014779-2, CN 838, HarpT); pap. 6.95 (ISBN 0-06-090838-6). Har-Row.

--Hidden Corners of Britain. (Illus.). 1981. 19.95 (ISBN 0-393-01460-6). Norton.

--Hidden Corners of New England. LC 75-42072. (Funk & W Bk.). (Illus.). 224p. 1976. 12.50 o.s.i. (ISBN 0-308-10240-1, TYC-T); pap. 6.95 o.s.i. (ISBN 0-308-10241-X, TYC-T). T Y Crowell.

--Hidden Corners of the Mid-Atlantic States. LC 76-30417: (Funk & W Bk.). (Illus.). 1977. 12.95 o.s.i. (ISBN 0-308-10286-X, TYC-T); pap. 6.95 o.s.i. (ISBN 0-308-10297-5, TYC-T). T Y Crowell.

--When the Earth Was Young. LC 76-42430. 1978. pap. 5.95 o.p. (ISBN 0-385-12466-X). Doubleday.

Yeager, D. & Gourley, R. Introduction to Electron & Electromechanical Devices. 1976. 20.95 (ISBN 0-13-481408-8). P-H.

Yeager, Ernest & Salkind, Alvin J., eds. Techniques of Electrochemistry. LC 73-37940. 464p. Vol. 1, 1972. 50.00 (ISBN 0-471-97700-4, Pub. by Wiley-Interscience); Vol. 2, 1973. 43.00 (ISBN 0-471-97701-2); Vol. 3, 1978. 34.95 (ISBN 0-471-02919-X). Wiley.

Yeager, Frederick, jt. auth. see Seitz, Neil.

Yeager, Joseph C., jt. auth. see Raudsepp, Eugene.

Yeager, L. Dayle & Baker, Glenn E. Wood Technology Student's Manual. 176p. 1977. pap. text ed. 6.95 (ISBN 0-672-97107-0). Bobbs.

Yeager, L. Dayle, jt. auth. see Baker, Glenn E.

Yeager, Leland B. Proposals for Government Credit Allocation. 1977. pap. 2.75 (ISBN 0-8447-3281-8). Am Enterprise.

Yeager, Leland B. & Tuerck, David G. Foreign Trade & U. S. Policy: The Case for Free International Trade. LC 75-19832. (Praeger Special Studies Ser.). 275p. 1976. text ed. 29.95 (ISBN 0-275-56270-0); pap. text ed. 11.95 (ISBN 0-275-89510-6). Praeger.

Yeager, Peter C., jt. auth. see Clinard, Marshall B.

Yeager, Randolph O., ed. The Renaissance New Testament, Vol. 7. 1981. 19.95 (ISBN 0-88289-457-9). Pelican.

Yeager, Robert C. Losing It: The Economic Fall of the Middle Class. 224p. 1980. 10.95 (ISBN 0-07-072256-0, GB). McGraw.

Yeager, Trisha. The California Beauty Book: A Total Guide to Bringing Out Your Natural Beauty. (Illus.). 240p. 1981. pap. 9.95 (ISBN 0-936602-11-2). Harbor Pub CA.

Yeakel, M. H., jt. auth. see Von Prince, K.

Yeaple, F. Hydraulic & Pneumatic Power & Control: Design, Performance, Application. 1966. 29.50 o.p. (ISBN 0-07-072257-9, P&RB). McGraw.

Yearns, W. Buck & Barrett, John G., eds. North Carolina Civil War Documentary. LC 79-17604. (Illus.). xvii, 365p. 1980. 17.95x (ISBN 0-8078-1407-5). U of NC Pr.

Yearns, Wilfred B., ed. Papers of Thomas Jordan Jarvis, Vol. 1, 1869-1882. (Illus.). 1969. 10.00 (ISBN 0-86526-045-1). NC Archives.

Yearsley, Ann. The Royal Captives: A Fragment of Secret History, 4 vols. Luria, Gina, ed. (The Feminist Controversy in England, 1788-1810 Ser.). 1974. Set. lib. bdg. write for info. (ISBN 0-8240-0892-8); lib. bdg. 50.00 ea. Garland Pub.

Yearsley, Macleod. Folklore of Fairy-Tale. LC 68-31517. 1968. Repr. of 1924 ed. 18.00 (ISBN 0-8103-3457-7). Gale.

Yearsley, Percival M. Doctors in Elizabethan Drama. 128p. 1980. Repr. of 1933 ed. lib. bdg. 20.00 (ISBN 0-8495-6101-9). Arden Lib.

Yearwood, Lennox S., ed. Black Organizations: Issues on Survival Techniques. LC 79-5500. 286p. 1980. pap. 9.50 (ISBN 0-8191-0898-7); 18.50 (ISBN 0-8191-0897-9). U Pr of Amer.

Yeates, Donald, jt. ed. see Daniels, Alan.

Yeates, Maurice. North American Urban Patterns. LC 80-17708. (Scripta Series in Geography). 168p. 1980. 27.95 (ISBN 0-470-27017-9, Pub. by Halsted Pr). Wiley.

Yeates, N. T., et al. Animal Science: Reproduction, Climate, Meat & Wool. 2296p. 1975. text ed. 32.00 (ISBN 0-08-018209-7). Pergamon.

Yeates, Sybil. Development of Hearing. (Studies in Developmental Pediatrics Ser.: Vol. 2). 240p. 1981. text ed. 17.50 (ISBN 0-88416-378-4). PSG Pub.

Yeatman, E. F. On the Green. 50p. 1980. Repr. of 1894 ed. lib. bdg. 10.00 (ISBN 0-8414-9767-2). Folcroft.

Yeats see Bentley, Eric.

Yeats, J. B. Letters from Bedford Park: A Selection from the Correspondence of John Butler Yeats, 1890-1901. Murphy, William M., ed. 77p. (Hand printed limited ed). 1972. text ed. 13.00x (ISBN 0-391-01593-1). Humanities.

Yeats, Jack B. Ah Well: A Romance in Perpetuity, & "and to You Also". 1974. 15.00 (ISBN 0-7100-7665-7). Routledge & Kegan.

--The Charmed Life. 1974. 16.00 (ISBN 0-7100-7667-3). Routledge & Kegan.

--Verses. 1981. pap. text ed. 6.00 (ISBN 0-391-01592-3). Humanities.

Yeats, W. B. Nineteen One to Nineteen Eight. Samhain, ed. 324p. Repr. of 1970 ed. 35.00x (ISBN 0-7146-2101-3, F Cass Co). Biblio Dist.

--Uncollected Prose: Early Reviews & Articles 1897-1939, Vol. 1. LC 74-101295. 1975. 30.00x (ISBN 0-231-02845-8). Columbia U Pr.

--Uncollected Prose: Later Reviews, Articles & Other Miscellaneous Prose, 1897-1939, Vol. 2. Frayne, John P. & Johnson, Colton, eds. LC 74-101295. 543p. 1976. 30.00x (ISBN 0-231-03660-4). Columbia U Pr.

Yeats, W. B., tr. see Patanjali, Swami S.

Yeats, William B. Collected Poems. definitive 2nd ed. 1956. 14.95 (ISBN 0-02-632690-6). Macmillan.

--A Tower of Polished Black Stones. Clarke, David R. & Mayhew, George P., eds. (Dolmen Editions Ser.: No. II). 1971. text ed. 18.00x (ISBN 0-85105-192-8, Dolmen Pr). Humanities.

--Tribute to Thomas Davis. 55p. 1980. Repr. of 1947 ed. lib. bdg. 8.50 (ISBN 0-8492-3121-3). R West.

--Variorum Edition of the Plays of W. B. Yeats. Alspach, R. K., ed. 1966. 40.00 (ISBN 0-02-501720-9). Macmillan.

--Variorum Edition of the Poems of W. B. Yeats. Allt, P., ed. 1957. 19.95 (ISBN 0-02-501560-5). Macmillan.

--W. B. Yeats. 49p. 1980. Repr. of 1927 ed. lib. bdg. 6.50 (ISBN 0-8495-6126-4). Arden Lib.

Yeats, William B. & Kinsella, T. Davis, Mangan, Ferguson: Tradition & the Irish Writer. (Tower Ser. of Anglo Irish Studies). 1970. pap. text ed. 1.75 (ISBN 0-85105-166-9, Dolmen Pr). Humanities.

Yeats, William B; see Salerno, Henry F.

Yeats, William B., ed. Fairy & Folk Tales of the Irish Peasantry. 416p. 1973. 12.95 (ISBN 0-02-632640-X). Macmillan.

Yeats, William B., et al. W. B. Yeats & the Designing of Ireland's Coinage. Cleeve, Brian, ed. (New Yeats Papers Ser.: No. 3). 1972. pap. text ed. 3.75x (ISBN 0-85105-221-5, Dolmen Pr). Humanities.

Yeazell, Ruth B. Language & Knowledge in the Late Novels of Henry James. LC 75-46538. viii, 144p. 1980. lib. bdg. 6.00x (ISBN 0-226-95095-6). U of Chicago Pr.

Yeazell, Ruth B., ed. The Death & Letters of Alice James: Selected Correspondence. (Illus.). 200p. 1980. 12.95 (ISBN 0-520-03745-6). U of Cal Pr.

Yedidiah, S. Centrifugal Pump Problems. 232p. 1980. 35.00 (ISBN 0-87814-131-6). Pennwell Pub.

Yedlin, T., ed. Women in Eastern Europe & the Soviet Union. 250p. 27.50 (ISBN 0-03-055311-3). Praeger.

Yee, Chiang. Men of the Burma Road. (Illus.). (gr. 4-6). 4.50 (ISBN 0-685-20604-1). Transatlantic.

Yee, Diane, jt. auth. see Low, Jennie.

Yee, Janice C. God's Meekest Angels. (Illus.). (gr. k-6). 1980. pap. 1.75 (ISBN 0-686-60162-9); pap. 1.05 (ISBN 0-686-66043-9). Pi Pr. Postponed.

--This Gift I Present of Poetry from Hawaii. 3rd ed. (Poetry Gift Ser.). (Illus.). 54p. 1980. pap. 5.00. Pi Pr.

Yee, Min S. & Layton, Thomas N. In My Father's House. 384p. 1981. 13.95 (ISBN 0-03-053396-1). HR&W.

Yefimov, N. V. Quadratic Forms & Matrices: An Introductory Approach. (Eng.). 1964. pap. 10.50 o.p. (ISBN 0-12-769956-2). Acad Pr.

Yeh, R., ed. Current Trends in Programming Methodology: Program Validation, Vol. 2. 1977. 21.95x (ISBN 0-13-195719-8). P-H.

Yeh, Raymond T., jt. ed. see Chandy, K.

Yeh Ch'ing. Inside Mao Tse-Tung's Thought: An Analytical Blueprint of His Actions by a Former Top Chinese Communist Leader. Pan, Stephen, ed. Tsuan, T. H. & Mortensen, Ralph, trs. from Chinese. 1975. 12.50 o.p. (ISBN 0-682-48339-7). Exposition.

Yehl, Joan K. & Bandlow, Richard F. P. O. W. E. R. The Reading - Writing Connection. (Illus.). 320p. 1981. pap. text ed. 8.95 (ISBN 0-675-08064-9); instr's. manual 3.95 (ISBN 0-686-69497-X). Merrill.

Yeivin, Israel. Introduction to the Tiberian Masorah. LC 79-24755. (Society of Biblical Literature Masoretic Studies: No. 5). pap. 10.50x (ISBN 0-89130-374-X, 06 05 05). Scholars Pr Ca.

Yelland, M., jt. ed. see Coward, R. E.

Yelland, M., jt. ed. see Downing, J. C.

Yellen, Barry, jt. ed. see Schlossberg, Julian.

Yellin, David. Special: Fred Freed & the Television Documentary. LC 72-80909. (Illus.). 242p. 1973. 9.95 o.s.i. (ISBN 0-02-632970-0). Macmillan.

Yellowitz, Irwin, ed. Essays in the History of New York City: A Memorial to Sidney Pomerantz. (National University Pubns. Interdisciplinary Urban Ser.). 1978. 13.95 (ISBN 0-8046-9208-4). Kennikat.

Yellow Robe, Rose. Album of the American Indian. LC 73-134657. (Picture Albums Ser). (Illus.). (gr. 4-6). 1969. PLB 5.90 o.p. (ISBN 0-531-01506-8). Watts.

Yelton, Donald C. Brief American Lives: Four Studies in Collective Biography. LC 77-29102. 1978. 12.00 (ISBN 0-8108-1114-6). Scarecrow.

Yemel'yan ov, V. S. & Yevstyukin, A. I. Metallurgy of Nuclear Fuels. 1969. 94.00 (ISBN 0-08-012073-3). Pergamon.

Yen, Ernest Y. Review & Assessment in Family Practice. 288p. 1980. pap. 12.95x (ISBN 0-8385-2539-3). ACC.

Yen, Isabella Y. English for Speakers of Mandarin Chinese. (English As a Foreign Language Ser.). 356p. 1981. text & cassettes 85.00x (ISBN 0-87950-603-2); cassettes 80.00 (ISBN 0-686-69430-9). text ed. 10.00x (ISBN 0-87950-301-7). Spoken Lang Serv.

Yen, Teh Fu & Walsh, Don, eds. Energy & Resource Development of Continental Margins. LC 80-14813. (Illus.). 238p. 1980. 33.00 (ISBN 0-08-025127-7). Pergamon.

Yen, Wendy M., jt. auth. see Allen, Mary J.

Yeni-Komshian, Grace H., et al, eds. Child Phonology: Vol. I Production. LC 79-8867. (Perspectives in Neurolinguistics Psycho-Linguistics Ser.). 1980. write for info. (ISBN 0-12-770601-1). Acad Pr.

--Child Phonology: Vol. 2, Perception. (Perspectives in Neurolinguistics & Psycholinguistics Ser.). 1980. 24.00 (ISBN 0-12-770602-X). Acad Pr.

Yenser, Stephen. Circle to Circle: The Poetry of Robert Lowell. LC 74-79778. 400p. 1976. 23.75x (ISBN 0-520-02790-6). U of Cal Pr.

Yeo, C. A., jt. auth. see Heichelheim, Fritz M.

Yeoman, John. Bear's Water Picnic. LC 70-116757. (Illus.). (gr. k-3). 1971. 4.95g o.s.i. (ISBN 0-02-793640-6). Macmillan.

--Beatrice & Vanessa. LC 74-13122. (Illus.). 32p. (gr. k-2). 1975. 5.95 o.s.i. (ISBN 0-02-793660-0). Macmillan.

--Mouse Trouble. LC 72-95190. (Illus.). 32p. (ps-3). 1973. 7.95 (ISBN 0-02-793600-7). Macmillan.

--Sixes & Sevens. LC 79-147893. (Illus.). 32p. (ps-1). 1974. pap. 1.25 o.s.i. (ISBN 0-02-045720-0, 04572, Collier). Macmillan.

--The Wild Washerwoman. LC 78-32147. (Illus.). (gr. k-3). 1979. 8.95 (ISBN 0-688-80219-2); PLB 8.59 (ISBN 0-688-84219-4). Greenwillow.

--The Young Performing Horse. LC 78-6304. (Illus.). 40p. (ps-3). 1978. 5.95 (ISBN 0-590-07726-0, Four Winds); PLB 5.41 (ISBN 0-8193-0971-0). Schol Bk Serv.

Yeoman, John & Blake, Quentin. Sixes & Sevens. (Illus.). (gr. k-3). 1971. 7.95 (ISBN 0-02-793610-4). Macmillan.

Yeoman, R. S. A Catalog of Modern World Coins. 1979. pap. 5.95 o.p. (ISBN 0-307-09053-1, Golden Pr). Western Pub.

--A Guide Book of United States Coins. 1979. 4.95 (ISBN 0-307-09051-5, Golden Pr). Western Pub.

--Handbook of United States Coins. 1979. 3.50 (ISBN 0-307-09050-7, Golden Pr). Western Pub.

Yeomans, John. The Twenty Best Sights of Sydney. 128p. 1980. pap. 4.95x (ISBN 0-686-68862-7, Pub. by W Collins Australia). Intl Schol Bk Serv.

Yeomans, K. A., jt. auth. see Davis, E. W.

Yeomans, William N. Jobs '79. 1979. pap. 3.95 o.p. (ISBN 0-425-04197-2). Berkley Pub.

Yep, Lawrence. Seademons. LC 77-3809. 1977. 8.95 o.p. (ISBN 0-06-014771-7, HarpT). Har-Row.

Yepes, Jose A. The Challenge of Venezuelan Democracy. 175p. 1981. 19.95 (ISBN 0-87855-401-7); text ed. 19.95 (ISBN 0-686-68055-3). Transaction Bks.

Yepsen, Roger B., ed. see Hill, Lewis.

Yepsen, Roger B., Jr., ed. Home Food Systems: Rodale's Catalog of Methods & Tools for Producing, Processing & Preserving Naturally Good Foods. (Illus.). 512p. 1981. 18.95 (ISBN 0-87857-325-9); pap. 15.95 (ISBN 0-87857-320-8). Rodale Pr Inc.

Yerby, Frank. Hail the Conquering Hero. 1980. pap. 2.95 o.s.i. (ISBN 0-440-13456-0). Dell.

Yerby, Lorees see Corrigan, Robert W.

Yereance, Robert A. Strangers, All Strangers. 1981. 10.95 (ISBN 0-87949-151-5). Ashley Bks.

Yergin, Angela S. East-West Technology Transfer: European Perspectives. LC 80-80363. (The Washington Papers: No. 75). (Illus.). 88p. 1980. pap. 3.50x (ISBN 0-8039-1463-6). Sage.

Yergin, Daniel, jt. ed. see Stobaugh, Robert.

Yerian & Cameron, eds. Weird Gardens. (gr. 4-6). Date not set. pap. cancelled (ISBN 0-590-30025-3, Schol Pap). Schol Bk Serv.

Yerian, Theo, jt. auth. see Piper, Joanne.

Yerian, Theo, jt. auth. see Salser, Carl W.

Yerian, Theodore & Salser, Carl W. Punctuation: Syllabus. 2nd ed. 1972. pap. text ed. 5.35 (ISBN 0-89420-020-8, 357498); cassette recordings 55.20 (ISBN 0-89420-178-6, 357500). Natl Book.

Yerian, Theodore, jt. auth. see Salser, Carl W.

Yerkes, Robert M. Mental Life of Monkeys & Apes. LC 79-22241. (History of Psychology Ser.). 1979. 30.00x (ISBN 0-8201-1341-7). Schol Facsimiles.

Yermakov, Nick. Journey to Flesh. (Orig.). 1981. pap. 2.25 o.p. (ISBN 0-425-04588-9). Berkley Pub.

Yermanos, D. M., tr. see Malecot, Gustave.

Yermokov, Nichol. Last Communion. (Orig.). 1981. pap. price not set (ISBN 0-451-09822-6, Signet Bks). NAL.

Yescombe, E. R. Plastics & Rubbers: World Sources of Information. 1976. 79.20x (ISBN 0-85334-675-5). Intl Ideas.

Yeshurun, Avoth. The Syrian-African Rift & Other Poems. Amichai, Yehuda & Mandelbaum, Allen, eds. Schimmel, Harold, tr. 160p. 1980. 11.95 (ISBN 0-8276-0181-6, 464); pap. 7.95 (ISBN 0-8276-0182-4, 463). Jewish Pubn.

Yesudian, Selvarajan & Haich, Elisabeth. Yoga & Health. LC 54-6039. (Illus.). 1954. 8.95 o.p. (ISBN 0-06-007590-2, HarpT). Har-Row.

Yetman, Norman R. & Steele, C. Hoy. Majority & Minority: The Dynamics of Ethnic & Racial Relations. 2nd ed. 660p. 1975. text ed. 13.60 (ISBN 0-205-04815-3, 8148155). Allyn.

Yett, Donald, et al. A Forecasting & Policy Simulation Model of the Health Care Sector: The HRRC Prototype Microeconomic Model. LC 74-15534. (Human Resources Research Center Monographs). (Illus.). 1979. 21.50 (ISBN 0-669-94250-2). Lexington Bks.

Yett, Donald E. & Levine, Daniel. Mental Health Expenditures & Funding Through 1985. LC 74-15534. (Human Resources Research Center Monographs). Date not set. cancelled o.p. (ISBN 0-669-94250-2). Lexington Bks.

Yeung, Ellen, tr. see Hsiao Hung.

Yevstyukin, A. I., jt. auth. see Yemel'yan ov, V. S.

Yevtushenko, Evgeny. Yevtushenko: Selected Poems. 1962. 5.50 o.p. (ISBN 0-525-23922-7). Dutton.

Yevtushenko, Yevgeny. The Poetry of Yevgeny Yevtushenko. bilingual ed. 312p. 1981. pap. 8.95 (ISBN 0-7145-0482-3, Pub. by M. Boyars). Merrimack Bk Serv.

Yezzo, Dominick. A G.I.'s Vietnam Diary. LC 73-17193. 96p. (gr. 7 up). 1974. PLB 5.90 (ISBN 0-531-02684-1). Watts.

Yglesias, Helen. Sweetsir. 1981. 13.95 (ISBN 0-671-25092-2). S&S.

Yi-Fu Tuan. Man & Nature. LC 71-182310. (CCG Resource Papers Ser.: No. 10). (Illus.). 1971. pap. text ed. 4.00 (ISBN 0-89291-057-7). Assn Am Geographers.

Yih, C. S., ed. Advances in Applied Mechanics, Vol. 20. (Serial Pub.). 1980. 31.50 (ISBN 0-12-002020-3); microfiche ed. 22.00 (ISBN 0-12-002051-3); 22.00 (ISBN 0-12-002052-1). Acad Pr.

Yih, Chia-Shun see Von Mises, Richard & Von Karman, Theodore.

Yin, John. The Government of the Soviet Union: A Constitutional Approach, Vol. 1. LC 80-82427. (Orig.). 1980. pap. 29.50 (ISBN 0-913124-41-9). Nordland Pub.

Yinon, Jehuda & Zitrin, Shmuel. The Analysis of Explosives. (Pergamon Ser. in Analytic Chemistry: Vol. 3). (Illus.). 300p. 1981. 60.00 (ISBN 0-08-023846-7); pap. 25.00 (ISBN 0-08-023845-9). Pergamon.

Yip, Ka-Che. Religion, Nationalism & Chinese Students: The Anti-Christian Movement of 1922-1927. (Studies on East Asia). (Illus.). 133p. 1980. pap. 7.50 (ISBN 0-914584-15-4). West Wash Univ.

Yip, Sidney, jt. auth. see Boon, Jean P.

Yip, Wai-Lim. Chinese Poetry: Major Modes & Genres. LC 74-76394. 1976. 23.75x (ISBN 0-520-02727-2). U of Cal Pr.

Yizze, James P., jt. auth. see Munem, Mustafa.

Ylvisaker, J. The Gospels Then. 1977. Repr. 16.95 (ISBN 0-8100-0052-0). Northwest Pub.

Ynamuno. La Tia Tula. D'Entremont, E., ed. 1975. pap. 7.50 (ISBN 0-13-522870-0). P-H.

Yoakum, James D., compiled by. American Pronghorn Antelope. LC 79-89207. (Illus.). 244p. (Orig.). 1979. pap. 4.50 (ISBN 0-933564-05-8). Wildlife Soc.

Yochelson, Ellis L., ed. The Scientific Ideas of G.K. Gilbert. LC 80-67676. (Special Paper Ser.: No. 183). (Illus., Orig.). 1980. pap. write for info. (ISBN 0-8137-2183-0). Geol Soc.

Yochem, Barbara & Shelby, Peggy. Inner Shooting. 128p. 1981. 6.95 (ISBN 0-938826-03-4); pap. 3.95 (ISBN 0-938826-02-6). By by Products.

Yockey. Imperium. 1962. 20.00 (ISBN 0-911038-52-3); pap. 6.00 (ISBN 0-911038-10-8). Noontide.

Yockey, Ross, jt. auth. see Bookspan, Martin.

Yocum. The Holy Way. pap. 5.95 (ISBN 0-686-12915-6). Schmul Pub Co.

Yocum, Glenn A., jt. ed. see Buck, Harry M.

Yoder, D. Personnel Management & Industrial Relations. 6th ed. 1970. 19.95 (ISBN 0-13-659201-5). P-H.

Yoder, Glee. Our Unfolding World. 13.95 o.p. (ISBN 0-685-61336-4). Brethren.

Yoder, H. S., Jr. Generation of Basaltic Magma. LC 76-29672. 1976. text ed. 8.25 o.p. (ISBN 0-685-75493-6); pap. text ed. 6.25 (ISBN 0-309-02504-4). Natl Acad Pr.

Yoder, John H. The Politics of Jesus. 176p. 1972. pap. 4.95 (ISBN 0-8028-1485-9). Eerdmans.

Yoder, Jon A. Upton Sinclair. LC 74-78450. (Modern Literature Ser.). 160p. 1975. 10.95 (ISBN 0-8044-2989-8). Ungar.

Yoder, Pat S., jt. auth. see Tobin, Helen M.

Yoder, Paul V., jt. auth. see Teller, Edward.

Yoder, R. A. Emerson & the Orphic Poet in America. LC 76-24599. 1978. 17.50x (ISBN 0-520-03317-5). U of Cal Pr.

Yoder, Walter E., jt. ed. see Hostetler, Lester.

Yodfat, Aryeh & Arnon-Ohanna, Yuval. P. L. O. Strategy & Tactics. 1981. write for info. (ISBN 0-312-61761-5). St Martin.

Yoeli, M., jt. auth. see Brzozowski, J. A.

Yoffey, J. M. & Coortice, F. C. Lymphatics, Lymph & the Lymphomyeloid Complex. 1971. 98.00 (ISBN 0-12-772050-2). Acad Pr.

Yogi Vithaldas. Yoga System of Health. 1981. pap. 3.95 (ISBN 0-686-69341-8). Cornerstone.

Yohalem, Alice M. Women Returning to Work: Policies & Progress in Five Countries. LC 79-55819. (LandMark Studies). (Illus.). 304p. 1980. text ed. 25.00 (ISBN 0-916672-51-4). Allanheld.

Yohalem, Alice M., jt. auth. see Ginzberg, Eli.

Yohannan, John D., jt. ed. see Hamalian, Leo.

Yohe, Gary W. A Comparison of Price Controls & Quantity Controls Under Uncertainty. LC 78-75060. (Outstanding Dissertations in Economics Ser.), 1979. lib. bdg. 28.00 (ISBN 0-8240-4137-2). Garland Pub.

Yoke, Carl. Roger Zelazny. LC 80-19170. (Starmont Reader's Guide Ser.: No. 2). 111p. 1980. Repr. of 1979 ed. lib. bdg. 9.95x (ISBN 0-89370-033-9). Borgo Pr.

Yokell, Michael, jt. auth. see Taylor, June.

Yokell, Michael D. The Economics of Solar & Non-Renewable Energy Technologies. 1981. write for info (ISBN 0-88410-619-5). Ballinger Pub.

--Environmental Benefits & Costs of Solar Energy. LC 79-3688. 1980. 16.95 (ISBN 0-669-03468-1). Lexington Bks.

Yoken, Melvin B. Claude Tillier. LC 75-22346. (World Author Ser.: France: No. 376). 1976. lib. bdg. 10.95 (ISBN 0-8057-6222-1). Twayne.

Yoken, Melvin B., tr. see Bosquet, Alain.

Yokley, E. C. The Law of Subdivisions. 1963. with 1980 suppl. 50.00 (ISBN 0-87215-061-5); 1980 suppl 25.00 (ISBN 0-87215-344-4). Michie.

--Municipal Corporations, 4 vols. 3rd ed. 1956. with 1980 cum. suppl. 175.00 (ISBN 0-87215-063-1); 1980 cum suppl seperately 90.00 (ISBN 0-87215-340-1). Michie.

Yokogawa, Ken'Ichi, tr. see Kimura, Gibun.

Yokoi, Yuho & Victoria, Daizen. Zen Master Dogen: An Introduction with Selected Writings. LC 75-33200. (Illus.). 220p. 1976. 9.75 (ISBN 0-8348-0116-7); pap. 4.75 (ISBN 0-8348-0112-4). Weatherhill.

Yokota, Takezo, tr. see Kawase, Kozyun.

Yolen, Jane. The Boy Who Had Wings. LC 73-17010. (Illus.). (ps-4). 1974. PLB 9.89 (ISBN 0-690-15900-5, TYC-J). T Y Crowell.

--The Boy Who Spoke Chimp. LC 79-27259. (Capers Ser.). (Illus.). 128p. (gr. 3-6). 1981. pap. 4.99 (ISBN 0-394-94467-4); PLB 8.99 (ISBN 0-394-84467-X). Knopf.

--Brothers of the Wind. (Illus.). 1981. 10.955 (ISBN 0-399-20787-2). Philomel.

--Friend: The Story of George Fox & the Quakers. LC 74-171865. 192p. (gr. 7 up). 1972. 6.95 (ISBN 0-395-28932-7, Clarion). HM.

--The Giants Go Camping. LC 78-17928. (Illus.). (gr. 1-3). 1979. 6.95 (ISBN 0-395-28834-7, Clarion). HM.

--The Gift of Sarah Barker. LC 80-26443. 156p. (gr. 7 up). 1981. 9.95 (ISBN 0-670-64580-X). Viking Pr.

--The Girl Who Cried Flowers: And Other Tales. LC 80-26140. (Illus.). 64p. 1981. pap. 5.95 (ISBN 0-8052-0666-3). Schocken.

--The Girl Who Cried Flowers & Other Tales. LC 73-8903. (Illus.). 64p. (gr. 3-6). 1974. 9.95 (ISBN 0-690-00216-5, TYC-J); PLB 7.89 (ISBN 0-690-00217-3). T Y Crowell.

--The Girl Who Loved the Wind. LC 71-171012. (Illus.). (gr. k-3). 1972. 9.95 (ISBN 0-690-33100-2, TYC-J); PLB 9.89 (ISBN 0-690-33101-0). T Y Crowell.

--How Beastly! A Menagerie of Nonsense Poems. LC 79-22416. (Illus.). 48p. (gr. 4-6). 1980. 7.95 (ISBN 0-529-05421-3). Philomel.

--An Invitation to the Butterfly Ball. LC 75-19191. (Illus.). 40p. (ps-3). 1976. 5.95 o.s.i. (ISBN 0-8193-0799-8, Four Winds); PLB 5.41 o.s.i. (ISBN 0-8193-0800-5). Schol Bk Serv.

--The Little Spotted Fish. LC 74-14819. 32p. (ps-4). 1975. 7.95 (ISBN 0-395-28835-5, Clarion). HM.

--The Moon Ribbon, & Other Tales. LC 75-34462. (Illus.). 64p. (gr. 3-7). 1976. 8.95 (ISBN 0-690-01044-3, TYC-J). T Y Crowell.

--The Rainbow Rider. LC 73-19700. (Illus.). (ps-3). 1974. 8.79 (ISBN 0-690-00311-0, TYC-J). T Y Crowell.

--Ring Out! A Book of Bells. LC 74-4043. (gr. 4-7). 1974. 6.95 (ISBN 0-395-28886-X, Clarion). HM.

--The Seeing Stick. LC 75-6946. (Illus.). (gr. k up). 1977. 8.95 (ISBN 0-690-00455-9, TYC-J); PLB 8.79 (ISBN 0-690-00596-2). T Y Crowell.

--Shirlick Holmes & the Case of the Wandering Wardrobe. (Illus.). 80p. (gr. 9-12). 1981. 7.95 (ISBN 0-698-20498-0). Coward.

--The Sultan's Perfect Tree. LC 76-18096. (Illus.). (ps-4). 1977. 5.95 o.s.i. (ISBN 0-8193-0864-1, Four Winds); PLB 5.41 o.s.i. (ISBN 0-8193-0865-X). Schol Bk Serv.

--The Transfigured Hart. LC 75-2377. (Illus.). (gr. 4 up). 1975. 7.95 (ISBN 0-690-00736-1, TYC-J). T Y Crowell.

--Uncle Lemon's Spring. LC 80-22145. (Illus.). (gr. 2-6). 1981. PLB 8.95 (ISBN 0-525-41830-X). Dutton.

--Zoo Two Thousand: Twelve Stories of Science Fiction & Fantasy Beasts. LC 72-97773. (gr. 6 up). 1973. 7.95 (ISBN 0-395-28934-3, Clarion). HM.

Yolen, Jane, compiled by. Rounds About Rounds. (Illus.). (gr. 4-6). 1977. PLB 9.90 (ISBN 0-531-00125-3). Watts.

--Shape Shifters: Fantasy & Science Fiction Tales About Humans Who Can Change Their Shapes. LC 77-13646. (gr. 6 up). 1978. 8.95 (ISBN 0-395-28933-5, Clarion). HM.

Yolen, Jane H. The Giants' Farm. LC 76-58317. (Illus.). (ps-3). 1977. 6.95 (ISBN 0-395-28834-7, Clarion). HM.

--Witch Who Wasn't. (Illus.). (gr. k-3). 1964. 4.95g o.s.i. (ISBN 0-02-793650-3). Macmillan.

Yolton, J. W., ed. The Locke Reader. LC 76-9181. 1977. 29.95 (ISBN 0-521-21282-0); pap. 9.95x (ISBN 0-521-29084-8). Cambridge U Pr.

Yolton, John W. Locke & the Compass of Human Understanding. LC 76-112477. 1970. 29.95 (ISBN 0-521-07838-5). Cambridge U Pr.

Yonan, Grazia P., jt. auth. see Valenti, Tony.

Yonck, Barbara. Candle Crafts. (Illus.). (gr. 4-8). 1981. PLB 7.95 (ISBN 0-87460-376-5). Lion.

Yonemura, Ann. Japanese Lacquer. LC 79-19719. (Illus., Orig.). 1979. pap. 12.00 (ISBN 0-934686-35-1). Freer.

Yonemura, Margaret. Developing Language Programs for Young Disadvantaged Children. LC 79-75451. 1969. pap. 4.50x (ISBN 0-8077-2364-9). Tchrs Coll.

Yoneyama, Kyoko. The Collection of Stuffed Dolls from a Fancy World. (Illus.). 1977. 11.50 (ISBN 0-87040-401-6). Japan Pubns.

Yonezawa, Yoshio, et al. Arts of China: Paintings in Chinese Museums. LC 68-17454. (Arts of China Ser: Vol. 3). (Illus.). 1970. 75.00 (ISBN 0-87011-128-0). Kodansha.

Yong, Robert F. Starfinder. 208p. 1980. pap. 2.25 (ISBN 0-671-83282-4). PB.

Yonge, C. M., jt. ed. see Wilbur, Karl M.

Yonge, Charlotte. The Daisy Chain. LC 75-32169. (Classics of Children's Literature, 1621-1932: Vol. 33). (Illus.). 1977. Repr. of 1868 ed. PLB 38.00 (ISBN 0-8240-2282-3). Garland Pub.

--The Heir of Redclyffe. Wolff, Robert L., ed. LC 75-476. (Victorian Fiction Ser.). 1975. Repr. of 1853 ed. lib. bdg. 66.00 (ISBN 0-8240-1554-1). Garland Pub.

Yonge, Charlotte M. Abbeychurch; or, Self-Control & Self-Conceit, 1844. Wolff, Robert L., ed. Bd. with The Castle-Builders; or, the Deferred Confirmation, 1854. LC 75-470. (Victorian Fiction Ser.). 1975. lib. bdg. 66.00 (ISBN 0-8240-1548-7). Garland Pub.

--The Clever Woman of the Family, 1865. Wolff, Robert L., ed. LC 75-1523. (Victorian Fiction Ser.). 1975. lib. bdg. 66.00 (ISBN 0-8240-1595-9). Garland Pub.

--History of Christian Names. 1966. Repr. of 1884 ed. 24.00 (ISBN 0-8103-3139-X). Gale.

--Hopes & Fears: Or, Scenes from the Life of a Spinster, 2 vols. in 1. LC 79-8221. Repr. of 1860 ed. 44.50 (ISBN 0-404-62173-2). AMS Pr.

--Magnum Bonum; or, Mother Carey's Brood, 1879. Wolff, Robert L., ed. (Victorian Fiction Ser). 1975. lib. bdg. 66.00 (ISBN 0-8240-1598-3). Garland Pub.

Yonge, Maurice, jt. ed. see Stoddart, D. R.

Yonisuke, Ikeda. JFCC Catalogue of Cultures. 3rd ed. 320p. 1980. 35.00x (ISBN 0-89955-221-8, Pub. by JSSP Japan). Intl Schol Bk Serv.

Yonker, Donald Y. & Weide, Alexander. Soccer: Coaching to Win. LC 77-92311. 1978. pap. 5.95 (ISBN 0-8015-6909-5, Hawthorne). Dutton.

Yoo, Yushin. Books on Buddhism: An Annotated Subject Guide. LC 76-2706. 263p. 1976. 11.00 o.p. (ISBN 0-8108-0913-3). Scarecrow.

--Buddhism: A Subject Index to Periodical Articles in English, 1728-1971. LC 73-8679. 1973. 10.00 (ISBN 0-8108-0557-X). Scarecrow.

Yorburg, Betty. Sexual Identity: Sex Roles & Social Change. LC 80-22489. 240p. 1981. Repr. text ed. 8.50 (ISBN 0-89874-265-X). Krieger.

Yorburg, Betty G. The Changing Family: A Sociological Perspective. LC 72-7284. 1973. 17.50x (ISBN 0-231-03461-X); pap. 6.00x (ISBN 0-231-08317-3). Columbia U Pr.

--Utopia & Reality: A Collective Portrait of American Socialists. LC 72-79573. 1969. 20.00x (ISBN 0-231-03268-4). Columbia U Pr.

Yorgason, Blaine M. Massacre at Salt Creek. LC 78-22744. 1979. 8.95 (ISBN 0-385-15200-0). Doubleday.

Yorinks, Arthur. Louis the Fish. LC 80-16855. (Illus.). 32p. (ps-3). 1980. 9.95 (ISBN 0-374-34658-5). FS&G.

York, Alexander. Back to Basics Natural Beauty Handbook. 1978. pap. text ed. 1.95 (ISBN 0-515-04536-5). Jove Pubns.

York, Alexandra. Lose Ten Years in Ten Days. (Illus.). 192p. 1981. 10.95 (ISBN 0-02-633270-1). Macmillan.

York, Carol B. Febold Feboldson, the Fix It Farmer. new ed. LC 79-66321. (Illus.). 48p. (gr. 4-6). 1980. lib. bdg. 4.89 (ISBN 0-89375-312-2); pap. 1.50 (ISBN 0-89375-311-4). Troll Assocs.

--The Look-Alike Girl. LC 80-22102. 96p. (gr. 4 up). 1980. 7.95 (ISBN 0-8253-0016-9). Beaufort Bks NY.

--Mystery at Dark Wood. LC 70-175801. (Illus.). 128p. (gr. 4-7). 1972. PLB 5.95 o.p. (ISBN 0-531-02038-X). Watts.

--The Mystery of the Spider Doll. LC 72-6073. (Illus.). 96p. (gr. 4-6). 1973. PLB 5.88 o.p. (ISBN 0-531-02601-9). Watts.

--Stray Dog. LC 80-28779. 128p. (gr. 4 up). 1981. 7.95 (ISBN 0-8253-0046-0). Beaufort Bks NY.

--Takers & Returners. (gr. 5 up). 1979. pap. 1.50 (ISBN 0-448-17100-7, Tempo). G&D.

--The Witch Lady Mystery. (gr. 4-6). 1977. pap. 1.25 (ISBN 0-590-11917-6, Schol Pap). Schol Bk Serv.

York, D. & Farquhar, R. M. The Earth's Age & Geochronology. 1972. pap. 14.50 (ISBN 0-08-016387-4). Pergamon.

York, Dorothy. Blacks' Survival for the Nineteen Eighties & Beyond. LC 80-50646. 63p. (Orig.). 1980. pap. 3.95 o.p. (ISBN 0-934616-07-8). Valkyrie Pr.

York, Herbert F., intro. by. Arms Control: Readings from Scientific American. LC 73-4963. (Illus.). 1973. text ed. 19.95x (ISBN 0-7167-0880-9); pap. text ed. 9.95x (ISBN 0-7167-0879-5). W H Freeman.

York, Jeremy. Murder Came Late. (Cock Robin Mystery Ser.). 1969. 8.95 (ISBN 0-02-633230-2). Macmillan.

York, Judith. Peek-a-Boo! (Illus.). (ps). 1979. 2.50 (ISBN 0-525-69503-6, Gingerbread). Dutton.

York, Kenneth H. & Bauman, John A. Cases & Materials on Remedies. 3rd ed. LC 78-23510. (American Casebook Ser.). 1250p. 1979. text ed. 23.95 (ISBN 0-8299-2021-8). West Pub.

York, Lyle. Effective Communication in Real Estate Management. LC 79-67426. 183p. 1979. 18.00 (ISBN 0-913652-21-0). Realtors Natl.

York, Robert. The Swords of December. LC 78-24026. 1979. 8.95 o.p. (ISBN 0-684-16142-7, ScribT). Scribner.

Yorke, D. A. Marketing the Library Service. Wilson, A., ed. (Management Pamphlet Ser.). 1977. 3.95x (ISBN 0-85365-590-1, Pub. by Lib Assn England). Oryx Pr.

Yorke, Margaret. The Cost of Silence. LC 77-79964. 1977. 6.95 o.s.i. (ISBN 0-8027-5379-5). Walker & Co.

--The Scent of Fear. 224p. 1981. 9.95 (ISBN 0-312-70048-2). St Martin.

Yorke, R. Electric Circuit Theory. LC 80-41323. (Applied Electricity & Electronics Ser.). (Illus.). 272p. 1981. 30.00 (ISBN 0-08-026133-7); pap. 15.00 (ISBN 0-08-026132-9). Pergamon.

Yorke, Susan. Agency House, Malaya. 1962. 3.95 o.p. (ISBN 0-374-10253-8). FS&G.

Yorkey, Richard C., et al. English for International Communication: InterCom, Bk. 1. (Illus.). 200p. 1981. pap. text ed. price not set (ISBN 0-278-49201-0); price not set tchr's. ed. (ISBN 0-278-49216-9); price not set wkbk (ISBN 0-278-49230-4); price not set audio prog. (ISBN 0-278-49245-2). Litton Educ Pub.

Yorkis, Paul. Greenberg's Price Guide to American Flyer S Gauge Trains 1945-1966. LC 80-67942. (Illus., Orig.). 1980. 19.95 (ISBN 0-89778-225-9); pap. cancelled. Greenberg Pub Co.

Yorkis, Paul G. & Walsh, Jim. Greenberg's Guide to American Flyer's Gauge. 160p. 1980. pap. 19.95 (ISBN 0-442-21209-7). Van Nos Reinhold.

Yorks, Lyle. A Radical Approach to Job Enrichment. LC 75-44481. 176p. 1976. 12.95 (ISBN 0-8144-5412-7). Am Mgmt.

Yoseloff, M. L., jt. auth. see Weiss, N. A.

Yoshida, Ken'Ichi. Total-Life Exercise Book: The Official Japanese Physical Fitness Guide. (Illus.). 336p. 1980. pap. 8.95 (ISBN 0-02-082880-2, Collier). Macmillan.

Yoshida, Yasuo, et al. Japanese for Beginners. (gr. 12). 1977. 19.95 (ISBN 0-8120-5189-0). Barron.

Yoshihara, Kunio. Japanese Economic Development: A Short Introduction. (Illus.). 168p. 1979. text ed. 9.95x (ISBN 0-19-580439-2). Oxford U Pr.

Yoshihashi, Takehiko. Conspiracy at Mukden: The Rise of the Japanese Military. LC 80-13747. (Yale Studies in Political Science: No. 9). (Illus.). xvi, 274p. 1980. Repr. of 1963 ed. lib. bdg. 22.50x (ISBN 0-313-22443-9, YOCO). Greenwood.

Yoshii, Zensaku, et al. Atlas of Electron Scanning Microscopy in Microbiology. (Illus.). 240p. 1976. 55.00 o.p. (ISBN 0-683-09325-8). Williams & Wilkins.

Yoshikawa, jt. auth. see Cohan.

Yoshino, Yozo. Japanese Abacus Explained. (Illus.). pap. 3.50 o.p. (ISBN 0-486-21109-6). Dover.

Yoshiyuki, Junnosuke. The Dark Room. Bester, John, tr. from Japanese. LC 75-11390. 170p. 1980. pap. 3.95 (ISBN 0-87011-361-5). Kodansha.

Yosida, K. Functional Analysis. 5th ed. (Grundlehren der Mathematischen Wissenschaften: Vol. 123). 1978. 34.10 o.p. (ISBN 0-387-08627-7). Springer-Verlag.

--Functional Analysis. 6th ed. (Grundlehren der Mathematischen Wissenschaften Ser.: Vol. 123). 501p. 1980. 39.00 (ISBN 0-387-10210-8). Springer-Verlag.

Yosso, Mel. Transculture; Universal Heritage: Sixty-Five Timeless Allegories. 160p. 1980. pap. 6.50 (ISBN 0-935862-00-5). Transculture Inc.

Yost, David S., ed. NATO's Strategic Options: Arms Control & Defense. (Pergamon Policy Studies on International Politics). (Illus.). 275p. 1981. 30.00 (ISBN 0-08-027184-7). Pergamon.

Yost, Frank H., jt. auth. see Johnson, Alvin W.

Yost, H. T., jt. auth. see Hexter, W.

Yost, Nellie S. Call of the Range. LC 66-30428. 437p. 1966. 16.95 (ISBN 0-8040-0028-X, SB). Swallow.

--Medicine Lodge: The Story of a Kansas Frontier Town. LC 79-132588. (Illus.). 237p. 1970. 8.95 o.p. (ISBN 0-8040-0198-7, SB); pap. 4.95 (ISBN 0-8040-0199-5). Swallow.

Yost, Nellie S., jt. auth. see Leakey, John.

Yost, Nellie S., jt. auth. see Snyder, A. B.

Yost, Nellie S., ed. see Lemmon, Ed.

Yott, Donald H. Conjunctions: An in Depth Delineation. 1981. pap. 6.95 (ISBN 0-87728-524-1). Weiser.

--Man & Metaphysics. 1980. pap. 5.95 (ISBN 0-87728-488-1). Weiser.

Youcha, Geraldine. A Dangerous Pleasure. LC 78-53486. 1978. 10.95 o.p. (ISBN 0-8015-1922-5). Dutton.

Youdale, Peter J. Managing Your Sales Office. 1975. 18.00x o.p. (ISBN 0-8464-0601-2). Beekman Pubs.

Youden, W. J. Statistical Methods for Chemists. LC 76-51742. 136p. 1977. Repr. of 1951 ed. 8.50 o.p. (ISBN 0-88275-509-9). Krieger.

Youdim, M. B. Aromatic Amino Acid Hydroxylases & Mental Disease. LC 79-40642. 1980. 79.50 (ISBN 0-471-27606-5, Pub. by Wiley-Interscience). Wiley.

Youdim, M. B. & Lovenberg, W., eds. Essays in Neurochemistry & Neuropharmacology, Vol. 5. Sharman, D. F. & Lagnado, J. R., trs. 152p. 1981. 47.00 (ISBN 0-471-27879-3, Pub. by Wiley-Interscience). Wiley.

Youdim, M. B., et al, eds. Essays in Neurochemistry & Neuropharmacology, 4 vols. LC 76-21043. 1977-80. Vol. 1. 37.95 (ISBN 0-471-99424-3, Pub. by Wiley-Interscience); Vol. 2. 30.75 (ISBN 0-471-99516-9); Vol. 3. 33.50 (ISBN 0-471-99613-0, Pub. by Wiley-Interscience); Vool. 4. 67.50 (ISBN 0-471-27645-6). Wiley.

Youings, Joyce. The Dissolution of the Monasteries. (Historical Problems: Studies & Documents). 1971. pap. text ed. 9.95x (ISBN 0-04-942090-9). Allen Unwin.

Youldon. Circus. (ps-2). 1980. cancelled (ISBN 0-531-04167-0); PLB cancelled (ISBN 0-531-03525-5). Watts.

--Zoo. (ps-2). 1980. PLB cancelled (ISBN 0-531-03526-3); PLB 5.90 (ISBN 0-531-04168-9). Watts.

Youldon, Gillian. Alphabet. (All A-Board Bks). 16p. (ps-2). 1981. 3.50 (ISBN 0-686-69397-3). Watts.

--Colors. (Picture Play Ser.). (Illus.). (ps-2). 1979. 2.95 (ISBN 0-531-02387-7); PLB 5.90 s&l (ISBN 0-531-00439-2). Watts.

--Homes. (All A-Board Bks). (Illus.). 16p. (ps-2). 1981. 3.50 (ISBN 0-531-02539-X). Watts.

--Numbers. (Picture Play Ser.). (Illus.). (ps-2). 1979. 3.50 (ISBN 0-531-02388-5); PLB 5.90 s&l (ISBN 0-531-00440-6). Watts.

--Opposites. (ps-2). 1980. 3.50 (ISBN 0-531-02127-0, C16); PLB 5.90 (ISBN 0-531-03416-X, B26). Watts.

--Shapes. (Picture Play Ser.). (Illus.). (ps-2). 1979. 3.50 (ISBN 0-531-02389-3); PLB 5.45 s&l (ISBN 0-531-00441-4). Watts.

--Sizes. (Picture Play Ser.). (Illus.). (ps-2). 1979. 3.50 (ISBN 0-531-02390-7); PLB 5.45 s&l (ISBN 0-531-00442-2). Watts.

--Time. (ps-2). 1980. 3.50 (ISBN 0-531-02128-9, C17); PLB 5.90 (ISBN 0-531-03417-8, C03). Watts.

Youldos, Gillian. Counting. (All a-Board Bks. Ser.). (ps-2). 1980. 3.50 (ISBN 0-531-02142-4). Watts.

Youmans, Guy P., et al. The Biologic & Clinical Basis of Infectious Diseases. 2nd ed. LC 78-65974. (Illus.). 849p. 1980. pap. text ed. 22.50 (ISBN 0-7216-9647-3). Saunders.

Young. Personal Selling. 1978. 19.95 (ISBN 0-03-020836-X). Dryden Pr.

Young, A. Nursing the Law. 1981. text ed. 19.80 (ISBN 0-06-318181-9, Pub. by Har-Row Ltd England); pap. text ed. 10.45 (ISBN 0-686-69150-4). Har-Row.

--Tropical Soils & Soil Survey. LC 75-19573. (Geographical Studies: No. 9). 1976. 65.50 (ISBN 0-521-21054-2). Cambridge U Pr.

--Tropical Soils & Soil Survey. LC 75-19573. (Cambridge Geographical Studies: No. 9). 468p. Date not set. pap. 15.95 (ISBN 0-521-29768-0). Cambridge U Pr.

Young, A. P. & Griffiths, L. Automobile Electrical & Electronic Equipment. 9th ed. Fardon, G. E., ed. (Illus.). 1980. 24.95 (ISBN 0-408-00463-0). Butterworths.

Young, Al. Ask Me Now. 1980. 11.95 (ISBN 0-07-072360-5). McGraw.

--Geography of the Near Past. LC 75-21624. 1976. 6.95 o.p. (ISBN 0-03-013876-0); pap. 3.95 o.p. (ISBN 0-03-013881-7). HR&W.

--Snakes. 160p. 1981. pap. 5.95 (ISBN 0-916870-34-0). Creative Arts Bk.

Young, Alan. Sea Angling for Beginners. (Angler's Library). 1978. 4.50 o.p. (ISBN 0-257-65229-9, 8003, Dist. by Arco). Barrie & Jenkins.

--Sea Angling: Modern Methods, Baits & Tackle. (Angler's Library). 1978. 4.50 o.p. (ISBN 0-257-65228-0, 8004, Dist. by Arco). Barrie & Jenkins.

Young, Alan R. Henry Peachman. (English Authors Ser.: No. 251). 1979. lib. bdg. 10.95 (ISBN 0-8057-6732-0). Twayne.

Young, Alexander. Chronicles of the First Planters of the Colony of Massachusetts Bay, 1623-1636. LC 78-87667. (Law, Politics & History Ser.). 1970. Repr. of 1846 ed. lib. bdg. 55.00 (ISBN 0-306-71759-X). Da Capo.

--Pricing Decisions: A Practical Guide to Interdivisional Transfer Pricing Policy. 223p. 1979. text ed. 36.75x (ISBN 0-220-67002-1, Pub. by Busn Bks England). Renouf.

--The Sogo Shosha: Japanese Multi-National Trading Companies. LC 78-18935. (Westview Special Studies in International Economics). 1979. lib. bdg. 25.50x (ISBN 0-89158-425-0). Westview.

Young, Alfred, jt. auth. see Grace, John A.

Young, Alida E. Land of the Iron Dragon. LC 77-16892. (gr. 9 up). 1978. PLB 7.95 (ISBN 0-385-13568-8). Doubleday.

Young, Allen, jt. auth. see Jay, Karla.

Young, Alvin L., jt. auth. see Bovey, Rodney W.

Young, Amy R. By Death or Divorce...It Hurts to Lose. LC 78-51382. 1976. pap. 1.95 (ISBN 0-89636-004-0). Accent Bks.

--It Only Hurts Between Paydays. LC 75-17366. (Illus.). 1975. pap. 2.25 (ISBN 0-916406-09-1). Accent Bks.

Young, Andrew D. & Provenzo, Eugene F., Jr. The History of the St. Louis Car Company. (Illus.). 304p. 1981. Repr. of 1978 ed. 27.50 (ISBN 0-8310-7114-1). A S Barnes.

--The History of the St. Louis Car Company. (Illus.). 304p. 1981. Repr. of 1978 ed. 27.50 (ISBN 0-8310-7114-1). Howell-North.

Young, Andrew M., et al. The Paintings of James McNeill Whistler, 2 vols. LC 80-5214. (Studies in British Art Ser.). (Illus.). 670p. 1980. 150.00 (ISBN 0-300-02384-7); prepub. 125.00 pre-Dec (ISBN 0-686-62784-9). Yale U Pr.

Young, Anne. Collie Guide. 6.98 o.p. (ISBN 0-385-01573-9). Doubleday.

Young, Anthony, jt. auth. see Riley, Denis R.

Young, Arthur. The Adventures of Emmera; or, the Fair American, 1767, 2 vols. in 1. Shugrue, Michael F., ed. (The Flowering of the Novel, 1740-1775 Ser: Vol. 80). 1974. lib. bdg. 50.00 (ISBN 0-8240-1179-1). Garland Pub.

Young, Arthur C., ed. see Gissing, George R.

Young, Arthur M. The Reflexive Universe: Evolution of Consciousness. 1976. 15.95 o.s.i. (ISBN 0-440-05925-9, Sey Lawr); pap. 6.95 (ISBN 0-440-05924-0). Delacorte.

--Socialist & Labour Movement in Japan. (Studies in Japanese History & Civilization). 145p. 1979. Repr. of 1921 ed. 18.00 (ISBN 0-89093-268-9). U Pubns Amer.

Young, Arthur P. Books for Sammies: The American Library Association During World War I. (Beta Phi Mu Chapbook Ser.: No. 15). (Illus.). 175p. 1981. write for info. (ISBN 0-910230-15-3). Beta Phi Mu.

Young, Barbara E., jt. ed. see Bennett, Dean B.

Young, Betty. Silky Terrier. (Illus.). 1970. pap. 2.00 (ISBN 0-87666-393-5, DS1044). TFH Pubns.

Young, Biloine W. & Wilson, Mary. How Carla Saw the Shalako God. (Illus.). 28p. (gr. 1-4). 1972. 1.50 o.p. (ISBN 0-8309-0088-8). Independence Pr.

--Jenny Redbird Finds Her Friends. (Illus.). 28p. (gr. 1-4). 1972. 1.50 o.p. (ISBN 0-8309-0087-X). Independence Pr.

--Medicine Man Who Went to School. (Illus.). 28p. (gr. 1-4). 1972. 1.50 o.p. (ISBN 0-8309-0086-1). Independence Pr.

Young, Blanche A., jt. auth. see Rees, Alan M.

Young, Bob. How to Stay Healthy While Traveling: A Guide to Today's World Traveler. LC 80-5320. (Illus.). 119p. (Orig.). 1980. pap. 4.95 (ISBN 0-915520-31-1). Ross-Erikson.

Young, Bob & Young, Jan. Where Tomorrow? (YA) (gr. 7-9). 1969. pap. 0.75 (ISBN 0-671-29535-7). PB.

Young, Bob, jt. auth. see Chapman, Geoff.

Young, Bob, jt. auth. see Levidow, Les.

Young, Brian. George-Etienne Cartier: Montreal Bourgeois. (Illus.). 200p. 1981. 23.95x (ISBN 0-7735-0370-6); pap. 10.95x (ISBN 0-7735-0371-4). McGill-Queens U Pr.

Young, Brian J. Promoters & Politicians: The North-Shore Railways in the History of Quebec, 1854-1885. 1978. 17.50x (ISBN 0-8020-5377-7). U of Toronto Pr.

Young, Bruce K., ed. Perinatal Medicine Today: Proceedings. LC 80-17343. (Progress in Clinical & Biological Research Ser.: Vol. 44). 244p. 1980. 20.00 (ISBN 0-8451-0044-0). A R Liss.

Young, Burt. Uncle Joe Shannon. 1979. pap. 2.25 o.p. (ISBN 0-523-40572-3). Pinnacle Bks.

Young, Carl B., Jr. First Aid for Emergency Crews: A Manual on Emergency First Aid Procedures for Ambulance Crews, Law Enforcement Officers, Fire Service Personnel, Wrecker Drivers, Hospital Staffs, Industry, Nurses. (Illus.). 192p. 1970. 10.75 (ISBN 0-398-02134-1). C C Thomas.

Young, Carrie. Green Broke. 224p. 1981. 8.95 (ISBN 0-396-07953-9). Dodd.

Young, Charles R. The Royal Forests of Medieval England. LC 78-65109. (The Middle Ages Ser.). (Illus.). 1979. 15.00x (ISBN 0-8122-7760-0). U of Pa Pr.

Young, Chester V. The Magic of a Powerful Memory. rev. & abr. ed. LC 80-70955. 254p. 1981. Repr. of 1971 ed. 10.95 (ISBN 0-8119-0416-4). Fell.

Young, Christa G., jt. auth. see Garner, Kathryn F.

Young, Christine A. From 'Good Order' to Glorious Revolution: Salem, Massachusetts, Sixteen Twenty-Eight to Sixteen Eighty-Nine. Berkhofer, Robert, ed. (Studies in American History & Culture). 273p. 1980. 27.95 (ISBN 0-8357-1101-3, Pub. by UMI Res Pr). Univ Microfilms.

Young, Clara G. Workbook for Learning Medical Terminology Step by Step. LC 79-11068. (Illus.). 1979. 10.50 (ISBN 0-8016-5658-3). Mosby.

Young County Historical Survey Committee. Centennial History of Graham. 7.95 o.p. (ISBN 0-685-48797-0). Nortex Pr.

Young, Crawford. Politics in the Congo: Decolonization & Independence. 1965. 25.00x (ISBN 0-691-03050-2); pap. 6.50 o.p. (ISBN 0-691-00005-0, 73). Princeton U Pr.

--The Politics of Cultural Pluralism. LC 74-27318. 1976. 35.00 (ISBN 0-299-06740-8). U of Wis Pr.

--Politics of Cultural Pluralism. (Illus.). 1979. pap. 7.95 (ISBN 0-299-06744-0). U of Wis Pr.

Young, Curtiss L. Lyrics: You Touched My Heart. 1979. 4.00 o.p. (ISBN 0-8062-1228-4). Carlton.

Young, D., ed. Developmental Neurobiology of Arthropods. (Illus.). 200p. 1973. 47.50 (ISBN 0-521-20229-9). Cambridge U Pr.

Young, D. M., jt. auth. see Hageman, L. A.

Young, D. W. Heterocyclic Chemistry. LC 75-11739. (Illus.). 1976. pap. text ed. 12.50x (ISBN 0-582-44253-2). Longman.

Young, Daniel G., jt. auth. see Strathdee, Elizabeth D.

Young, David, jt. auth. see Callahan, Neal.

Young, David, jt. auth. see Dalferes, Clayelle.

Young, David M. Iterative Solution of Large Linear Systems. 1971. 49.90 o.s.i. (ISBN 0-12-773050-8). Acad Pr.

Young, David M. & Gregory, Robert T. A Survey of Numerical Mathematics, Vol. 1. LC 78-168767. 1972. text ed. 21.95 (ISBN 0-201-08773-1). A-W.

--A Survey of Numerical Mathematics, Vol. 2. LC 78-168767. 1973. text ed. 22.95 (ISBN 0-201-08774-X). A-W.

Young, David P., ed. Twentieth Century Interpretations of Henry Fourth, Pt. 2. LC 68-23698. (Twentieth Century Interpretations Ser). (YA) 1968. pap. 1.25 o.p. (ISBN 0-13-386987-3, Spec). P-H.

Young, David W. The Managerial Process in Human Service Agencies. LC 78-19767. (Praeger Special Studies). 1979. 27.95 (ISBN 0-03-047081-1). Praeger.

Young, Dean & Raymond, Jim. Blondie, No. 2. (Blondie Cartoon Ser.). 128p. (Orig.). (gr. 3 up). 1981. pap. 1.50 (Tempo). G&D.

Young, Desmond. Rommel, the Desert Fox. LC 51-9112. (Illus.). 1951. lib. bdg. 9.87 o.p. (ISBN 0-06-014776-8, HarpT). Har-Row.

Young, Don, jt. auth. see Francis, Dave.

Young, Donald. The Great American Desert. LC 80-21183. (Illus.). 64p. (gr. 4 up). 1980. PLB 7.29 (ISBN 0-671-33054-3). Messner.

Young, Donald F., et al. Essentials of Mechanics. (Illus.). 576p. 1974. text ed. 9.25 (ISBN 0-8138-1110-4). Iowa St U Pr.

Young, Donald R. Physical Performance, Fitness & Diet. (Amer. Lec. Environmental Studies). (Illus.). 128p. 1977. 13.50 (ISBN 0-398-03642-X). C C Thomas.

Young, Dorothy W. Life & Letters of J. Alden Weir. LC 76-146157. (Library of American Art Ser.). 1971. Repr. of 1960 ed. lib. bdg. 29.50 (ISBN 0-306-70097-2). Da Capo.

Young, Douglas. Edinburgh in the Age of Sir Walter Scott. (Centers of Civilization Ser.: No. 17). 1965. 5.95 o.p. (ISBN 0-8061-0661-1). U of Okla Pr.

--A Strange Judgment. Hunting, Constance, ed. (Orig.). 1981. pap. 4.95 (ISBN 0-913006-23-8). Puckerbrush.

Young, E., ed. The Capture & Care of Wild Animals. LC 75-21985. (Illus.). 224p. 1976. 20.00 o.p. (ISBN 0-88359-010-7). R Curtis Bks.

Young, E., jt. ed. see Derber, M.

Young, E. C. The New Penguin Dictionary of Electronics. 1979. pap. 5.95 (ISBN 0-14-051074-5). Penguin.

Young, E. J. In the Beginning. 1976. pap. 2.45 (ISBN 0-85151-235-6). Banner of Truth.

Young, Ed, jt. auth. see Ziner, Feenie.

Young, Edgar B. Lincoln Center: The Building of an Institution. 320p. 1980. 24.95 (ISBN 0-8147-9656-7). NYU Pr.

Young, Edwin H. The Lord Is... LC 80-68750. 1981. pap. 3.25 (ISBN 0-8054-1526-2). Broadman.

Young, Edwin H., jt. auth. see Brownell, Lloyd E.

Young, Eleanor. Crewel Embroidery. (Career Concise Guides Ser.). (Illus.). 96p. (gr. 6 up). 1976. PLB 6.45 (ISBN 0-531-00341-8). Watts.

Young, Eleanor R. Fathers, Fathers, Fathers. (Early Childhood Bk.). (Illus.). (ps-2). PLB 4.95 o.p. (ISBN 0-513-01108-0). Denison.

--First Book of Pearls. LC 72-104031. (First Bks). (Illus.). (gr. 4-6). 1970. PLB 4.90 o.p. (ISBN 0-531-00691-3). Watts.

--Needlepoint. (Career Concise Guides Ser.). (Illus.). 96p. (gr. 6 up). 1976. PLB 4.90 o.p. (ISBN 0-531-02779-1). Watts.

--Venereal Disease. LC 73-8758. (Career Concise Guides Ser.). (gr. 7-12). 1973. text ed. 4.90 o.p. (ISBN 0-531-02642-6). Watts.

Young, Elinore W. How to Raise & Train a Bedlington Terrier. (Orig.). 1966. pap. 2.00 (ISBN 0-87666-245-9, DS1052). TFH Pubns.

Young, Ellin. Help Yourself to Understand Nineteen Eighty-One. 1980. pap. 2.95 (ISBN 0-87728-512-8). Weiser.

Young, Eoin & Hunt, James. James Hunt Against All Odds. 1978. 9.95 o.p. (ISBN 0-525-13625-8). Dutton.

Young, Eric. Bartolome Bermejo. 1975. 42.00 (ISBN 0-236-31041-0, Pub. by Paul Elek). Merrimack Bk Serv.

Young, Fay. The Awakening. 64p. 1981. 5.00 (ISBN 0-682-49701-0). Exposition.

Young, Frances M. Thankfulness Unites: The History of the United Thank Offering. 1979. 1.75 (ISBN 0-686-28795-9). Forward Movement.

Young, Freddie & Petzold, Paul. Work of the Motion Picture Cameraman. (Library of Film & Television Practice). Date not set. 16.50 (ISBN 0-8038-8061-8). Hastings.

Young, G. M. Last Essays: Scott, Newman, Push Kiv, Hardy. 288p. 1980. Repr. of 1950 ed. lib. bdg. 20.00 (ISBN 0-8495-6149-3). Arden Lib.

Young, G. S., jt. auth. see Hocking, John G.

Young, George. Digital Electronics: A Hands-on Learning Approach. (gr. 12). 1980. pap. 8.95 (ISBN 0-8104-5668-0). Hayden.

Young, George, ed. see Richler, Mordecai.

Young, George M. Today & Yesterday: Tennyson, Burke, Thackeray, Shakespeare. 312p. 1980. lib. bdg. 15.00 (ISBN 0-8482-3125-2). Norwood Edns.

--Victorian England: Portrait of an Age. 2nd ed. 1964. pap. 7.95 (ISBN 0-19-500259-8, GB). Oxford U Pr.

Young, George M., Sr. Nikolai Fedorov: An Introduction. LC 78-78119. 400p. 1980. 29.50 (ISBN 0-913124-29-X). Nordland Pub.

Young, Gordon D., ed. Ugarit in Retrospect. 1981. text ed. price not set (ISBN 0-931464-07-2). Eisenbrauns.

Young, Grace C. & Young, William H. Beginner's Book of Geometry. LC 76-114211. Orig. Title: First Book of Geometry. (gr. 1-5). 1970. Repr. of 1905 ed. text ed. 9.50 (ISBN 0-8284-0231-0). Chelsea Pub.

Young, Harben B., et al. Height & Weight of Children in Relation to Socioeconomic Status: Tunisia & the United States. Shipp, Audrey, ed. 50p. Date not set. pap. text ed. 1.75 (ISBN 0-8406-0206-5). Natl Ctr Health Stats.

Young, Harold C. Planning, Programming, Budgeting Systems in Academic Libraries: An Exploratory Study of PPBS in University Libraries Having Membership in the Association of Research Libraries. LC 76-10667. 180p. 1976. 26.00 (ISBN 0-8103-0264-0). Gale.

Young, Harold C., jt. ed. see Young, Margaret L.

Young, Harold C., jt. ed. see Young, Margaret Labash.

Young, Harold C., jt. ed. see Young, Margarey Labash.

Young, Harry F. Prince Lichnowsky & the Great War. LC 75-11448. (Illus.). 256p. 1977. 15.00x (ISBN 0-8203-0385-2). U of Ga Pr.

Young, Helen. A Throne for Sesame. LC 78-74757. (Illus.). (ps-2). 1979. 7.95 (ISBN 0-233-96871-7). Andre Deutsch.

--What Difference Does It Make, Danny? LC 80-65665. (Illus.). 96p. (gr. 1-6). 1980. 7.95 (ISBN 0-233-97248-X). Andre Deutsch.

--Wide Awake Jake. LC 74-19424. (Illus.). 32p. (gr. k-3). 1975. 6.75 o.p. (ISBN 0-688-22024-X); PLB 6.48 o.p. (ISBN 0-688-32024-4). Morrow.

Young, Henry L. Memoirs of a Castrato. 1981. 7.95 (ISBN 0-533-04707-2). Vantage.

Young, Howard, jt. auth. see Coles, Clarence.

Young, Howard T. Victorious Expression: A Study of Four Contemporary Spanish Poets, Unamuno, Machado, Jimenez, & Lorca. 1964. 15.00x (ISBN 0-299-03140-3); pap. 6.95x (ISBN 0-299-03144-6). U of Wis Pr.

Young, Ian. Male Homosexual in Literature: A Bibliography. LC 75-25611. 1975. 11.00 (ISBN 0-8108-0861-7). Scarecrow.

Young, Ian, ed. On the Line: New Gay Fiction. 224p. 1981. 11.95 (ISBN 0-89594-048-5); pap. 5.95 (ISBN 0-89594-049-3). Crossing Pr.

Young, J. M. & Buchanan, N. J. Accounting for Pensions. 160p. 1980. 39.00x (ISBN 0-85941-124-9, Pub. by Woodhead-Faulkner England). State Mutual Bk.

Young, J. Terry. Compelled by the Cross. LC 80-66768. 1981. 2.95 (ISBN 0-8054-5282-6). Broadman.

Young, J. Z. Programs of the Brain. (Illus.). 334p. 1981. pap. 6.95 (ISBN 0-19-286019-4, GB 641, GB). Oxford U Pr.

Young, James C. Medical Choice in a Mexican Village. 200p. 1981. 19.50 (ISBN 0-8135-0895-9). Rutgers U Pr.

Young, James H. Medical Messiahs: A Social History of Health Quackery in Twentieth-Century America. 1967. 20.00x (ISBN 0-691-04526-7); pap. 6.95 (ISBN 0-691-00579-6). Princeton U Pr.

Young, James J. Growing Through Divorce. LC 79-90993. (Paths of Life Ser.). 60p. (Orig.). 1979. pap. 2.45 (ISBN 0-8091-2267-7). Paulist Pr.

Young, James J., ed. Ministering to the Divorced Catholic. LC 78-61731. 1978. pap. 6.95 (ISBN 0-8091-2142-5). Paulist Pr.

Young, James S. Washington Community: Eighteen Hundred - Eighteen Twenty-Eight. LC 66-14080. 1966. 17.50x (ISBN 0-231-02901-2). Columbia U Pr.

Young, James S., et al, eds. United States Congressional Directories, 1789-1840. 400p. 1973. 25.00x (ISBN 0-231-03365-6). Columbia U Pr.

Young, James W. How to Become an Advertising Man. LC 79-56393. (Advertising Publications Ser). 100p. 1963. pap. text ed. 4.95 (ISBN 0-87251-001-8). Crain Bks.

Young, Jan, jt. auth. see Young, Bob.

Young, Jay, jt. auth. see Ledbetter, Elaine.

Young, Jean I., tr. see Sturluson, Snorri.

Young, Jeffrey T. Classical Theories of Value: From Smith to Sraffa. 1978. lib. bdg. 18.00 o.p. (ISBN 0-89158-287-8). Westview.

Young, Jerrald F. Decision Making for Small Business Management. 256p. 1981. Repr. of 1977 ed. lib. bdg. price not set (ISBN 0-89874-346-X). Krieger.

--Decision Making for Small Business Management. LC 76-25970. 1977. text ed. 16.95 (ISBN 0-471-97938-4); instrs'. manual avail. (ISBN 0-471-02426-0). Wiley.

Young, Jerry, jt. auth. see Wirth, Dick.

Young, Jimmy. Pubs That Welcome Children. LC 79-56580. (Illus.). 96p. 1980. 5.95 (ISBN 0-7153-7965-8). David & Charles.

--Services on & off the Motorways. 1978. 5.95 (ISBN 0-7153-7609-8). David & Charles.

--A Short History of Ale. LC 79-52373. (Illus.). 1979. 7.50 (ISBN 0-7153-7839-2). David & Charles.

Young, Joanne B., jt. auth. see Lewis, Taylor B., Jr.

Young, Jock, jt. ed. see Cohen, Stanley.

Young, John. Designing with Glass Reinforced Cement. 1979. 12.50x (ISBN 0-85139-017-X, Pub. by Architectural Pr). Nichols Pub.

--Great Northern Suburban. 1977. 19.95 (ISBN 0-7153-7477-X). David & Charles.

Young, John & Newton, Jan. Capitalism & Human Obsolescence: Corporate Control vs. Individual Survival in Rural America. LC 78-71099. (LandMark Study). 272p. 1981. text ed. 21.50 (ISBN 0-916672-22-0). Allanheld.

Young, John, jt. auth. see Bush, Grace.

Young, John, ed. see Carson, Alexander.

Young, John E. & Bush, Grace A. Geometry for Elementary Teachers. LC 77-155559. 300p. 1971. text ed. 17.95x (ISBN 0-8162-9984-6); instr's manual 2.50 (0-8162-9994). Holden-Day.

Young, John V. Ghost Towns of the Santa Cruz Mountains. Gant, Michael S., ed. LC 79-90223. (Illus.). 156p. Date not set. pap. 4.95 (ISBN 0-934136-06-8, Paper Vision). Western Tanager. Postponed.

Young, John W. Play Direction for the High School Theatre. LC 73-78885. 1973. 9.95 (ISBN 0-8046-9040-5); pap. 4.95 (ISBN 0-8046-9085-5). Kennikat.

Young, John Z. Anatomy of the Nervous System of Octopus Vulgaris. (Illus.). 1971. 69.00x (ISBN 0-19-857340-5). Oxford U Pr.

--Life of Vertebrates. 2nd ed. 1962. 14.95x (ISBN 0-19-501109-0). Oxford U Pr.

--Model of the Brain. 1964. 24.50x (ISBN 0-19-857333-2). Oxford U Pr.

Young, John Z. & Hobbs, M. J. The Life of Mammals: Their Anatomy & Physiology. 2nd ed. (Illus.). 528p. 1975. text ed. 39.00x (ISBN 0-19-857156-9). Oxford U Pr.

Young, Jordan M. Brazilian Revolution of Nineteen Thirty & the Aftermath. 1967. 11.00 (ISBN 0-8135-0545-3). Rutgers U Pr.

Young, Joseph & Young, Lucille, eds. Nineteen Eighty-One Federal Employees' Almanac. 156p. (Orig.). 1981. pap. 2.75 (ISBN 0-910582-01-7). Fed Employees.

Young, Joy. Christian Home Birth: A Preparation for Spirit, Soul & Body. (Illus.). 208p. (Orig.). 1980. pap. 6.00x (ISBN 0-686-28082-2). J Young.

Young, K., et al, eds. The MRCGP Study Book. 150p. 1981. PLB 36.90 (ISBN 0-906141-13-3, Pub. by Update Books Ltd); pap. 31.50 (ISBN 0-686-28845-9). Kluwer Boston.

Young, Karl, ed. see Seler, Eduard.

Young, Katherine A., jt. auth. see Young, Virgil M.

Young, Keith. Geology: The Paradox of Earth & Man. 416p. 1975. text ed. 20.50 (ISBN 0-395-05561-X); instructor's manual 1.25 (ISBN 0-395-18267-0). HM.

Young, Ken. Local Politics & the Rise of the Party. 256p. 1975. text ed. 19.50x (ISBN 0-7185-1140-9, Leicester). Humanities.

Young, Kenneth see Swan, Michael.

Young, Kevin, et al. Malaysia: Growth & Equity in a Multiracial Society. LC 79-3677. (A World Bank Country Economic Report Ser.). (Illus.). 368p. 1980. text ed. 25.00 (ISBN 0-8018-2384-6); pap. text ed. 7.95 (ISBN 0-8018-2385-4). Johns Hopkins.

Young, Kimball. Source Book Fro Sociology. 639p. 1980. Repr. of 1935 ed. lib. bdg. 45.00 (ISBN 0-8495-6105-1). Arden Lib.

Young, L. C., jt. auth. see Ursell, H. D.

Young, Larry C., jt. auth. see Farnsworth, B. A.

Young, Lesley. Queen Victoria. (Profiles Ser.). (Illus.). 64p. (gr. 3-6). 1981. 7.95 (ISBN 0-241-10480-7, Pub. by Hamish Hamilton England). David & Charles.

Young, Linda L. Basic Skills for Nursing Assistants. 128p. 1980. wire coil & shrink wrap 9.95 (ISBN 0-8403-2219-4). Kendall-Hunt.

Young, Lois H. Dimensions for Happening. LC 76-144081. 1971. pap. 2.50 o.p. (ISBN 0-8170-0506-4). Judson.

Young, Lorelle & Bielefeld, Carole. Hometrics. (Illus.). (gr. 7 up). 1977. pap. 4.95 (ISBN 0-933358-01-6). Enrich.

Young, Louise B., ed. Exploring the Universe. 2nd ed. (Illus.). 1971. 12.95x (ISBN 0-19-501381-6); pap. 10.95 o.p. (ISBN 0-19-501380-8). Oxford U Pr.

--Mystery of Matter. 1965. pap. 9.95x (ISBN 0-19-501265-8). Oxford U Pr.

--Population in Perspective. 1968. pap. 8.95x (ISBN 0-19-501111-2). Oxford U Pr.

Young, Lucille, jt. ed. see Young, Joseph.

Young, M. D. Differences Between States in Arid Law Administration. 1980. 13.00x (ISBN 0-643-00336-3, Pub. by CSJRO Australia). State Mutual Bk.

Young, Margaret B. First Book of American Negroes. (First Bks). (Illus.). (gr. 4-6). 1967. PLB 6.45 (ISBN 0-531-00592-5); pap. 1.25 (ISBN 0-531-02306-0). Watts.

--Picture Life of Martin Luther King, Jr. LC 67-20866. (Picture Life Bks). (Illus.). (gr. k-3). 1968. PLB 6.45 (ISBN 0-531-00981-5). Watts.

--Picture Life of Thurgood Marshall. LC 79-131154. (Picture Life Bks). (Illus.). (gr. k-3). 1971. PLB 4.90 o.p. (ISBN 0-531-00984-X). Watts.

Young, Margaret L. & Young, Harold C., eds. Dictionary of Special Libraries & Information Centers, 3 vols. 6th ed. Incl. Vol. 1. Special Libraries & Information Centers in the United States & Canada (ISBN 0-8103-0258-6); Vol. 2. Geographic-Personnel Index (ISBN 0-8103-0259-4); Vol. 3. New Special Libraries (ISBN 0-8103-0260-8). 1000p. 1981. price not set. Gale.

--Subject Directory of Special Libraries & Information Centers, 5 vols. 5th rev. ed. Incl. Vol. 1. Business & Law Libraries (ISBN 0-8103-0300-0); Vol. 2. Education & Information Science Libraries, Including Audiovisual, Picture, Publishing, Rare Book, & Recreational Libraries (ISBN 0-8103-0301-9); Vol. 3. Health Sciences Libraries, Including All Aspects of Basic & Applied Medical Sciences (ISBN 0-8103-0302-7); Vol. 4. Social Sciences & Humanities Libraries, Including Aera-Ethnic, Art, Geography-Map, History, Music Religion-Theology, Theatre, & Urban-Regional Planning Libraries (ISBN 0-8103-0303-5); Vol. 5. Science & Technology Libraries Including Agriculture, Energy, Environment-Conservation, & Food Sciences Libraries (ISBN 0-8103-0304-3). LC 79-21711. 163p. 1979. Set. 280.00 set (ISBN 0-8103-0299-3); 68.00 ea. Gale.

Young, Margaret L., et al, eds. Directory of Special Libraries & Information Centers: Vol. 2-Geographic & Personnel Indexes. 5th ed. LC 79-16788. 1979. 92.00 (ISBN 0-8103-0298-5). Gale.

--Directory of Special Libraries & Information Centers: Vol. 3-New Special Libraries. 5th ed. 1979. pap. text ed. 110.00 (ISBN 0-8103-0281-0). Gale.

Young, Margaret Labash & Young, Harold C., eds. Subject Directory of Special Libaries & Information Centers, 5 vol. set. 6th ed. 1981. Set. 350.00 (ISBN 0-8103-0305-1). Gale.

--Subject Directory of Special Libaries and Information Centers: Education & Information Science Libraries, Including Audiovisual, Picture, Publishing, Rare Book, & Recreational Libaries, Vol. 2. 6th ed. 1981. 80.00 (ISBN 0-8103-0307-8). Gale.

--Subject Directory of Special Libaries & Information Services: Science & Technology Libraries, Including Agriculture, Energy, Environment-Conservation & Food, Vol. 5. 6th ed. 1981. 80.00 (ISBN 0-8103-0309-4). Gale.

--Subject Directory of Special Libraries & Information Centers: Health Science Libraries, Including All Aspects of Basic & Pplied Medical Sciences, Vol. 3. 6th ed. 1981. 80.00 (ISBN 0-8103-0308-6). Gale.

Young, Margaret Labash & Ypung, Harold C., eds. Subject Directory of Special Libraries & Info. Centers: Business & Law Libaries, Vol. 1. 6th ed. 1981. 80.00 (ISBN 0-8103-0306-X). Gale.
Young, Margarey Labash & Young, Harold C., eds. Subject Directory of Special Libaries & Information Centers: Social Sciences & Humanities Libraries, Including Area-Ethic, Art, Geography-Map, History, Music, Religion, Theology, Theatre, Urban-Regional Planning Libraries, Vol. 4. 6th ed. 1981. 80.00 (ISBN 0-8103-0309-4). Gale.
Young, Martin. The Travellers' Guide to Corfu & the Other Ionian Islands. LC 77-363313. (Travellers' Guide Ser.). (Illus.). 1979. 9.95 (ISBN 0-224-01307-6, Pub. by Chatto Bodley Jonathan). Merrimack Bk Serv.
Young, Mary. Collector's Guide to Paperdolls. (Illus.). 1980. pap. 9.95 (ISBN 0-89145-133-1). Collector Bks.
Young, Maryann. Besieged by Love. (Candelight Romance Ser.). (Orig.). Date not set. pap. 1.50 (ISBN 0-440-10581-1). Dell.
Young, Melissa L., jt. auth. see Bruntjen, Scott.
Young, Michael. The Imaginary Friend. LC 77-9925. (Moods & Emotions Ser.). (Illus.). (gr. k-3). 1977. PLB 8.95 (ISBN 0-8172-0960-3). Raintree Pubs.
Young, Michael & McGeeney, Patrick. Learning Begins at Home: A Study of a Junior School & Its Parents. 1968. text ed. 10.00x (ISBN 0-7100-6529-9). Humanities.
Young, Michael & Willmott, Peter. The Symmetrical Family. LC 73-7009. 1974. 10.00 o.p. (ISBN 0-394-48727-3). Pantheon.
Young, Michael W., ed. see Malinowski, Bronislaw.
Young, Miriam. If I Drove a Tractor. LC 72-5142. (Illus.). 32p. (gr. k-3). 1973. 7.75 (ISBN 0-688-41338-2); PLB 7.44 o.p. (ISBN 0-688-51338-7). Lothrop.
--If I Drove a Train. LC 70-177317. (Illus.). 32p. (gr. k-3). 1972. PLB 7.44 (ISBN 0-688-51601-7). Lothrop.
--If I Flew a Plane. LC 79-101481. (Illus.). (gr. k-3). 1970. PLB 7.44 o.p. (ISBN 0-688-51043-4). Lothrop.
--Jellybeans for Breakfast. LC 68-21082. (Illus.). (gr. k-3). 1968. 5.95 o.s.i. (ISBN 0-8193-0339-9, Four Winds); PLB 5.41 o.s.i. (ISBN 0-8193-0340-2). Schol Bk Serv.
--King Basil's Birthday. LC 73-182288. (gr. k-4). 1973. PLB 5.90 (ISBN 0-531-02594-2). Watts.
--Miss Suzy. LC 64-10363. (Illus.). (gr. k-3). 1964. 5.95 o.s.i. (ISBN 0-8193-0092-6, Four Winds); PLB 5.41 o.s.i. (ISBN 0-8193-0093-4). Schol Bk Serv.
--Miss Suzy's Birthday. LC 73-22187. (Illus.). (ps-3). 1974. 5.95 o.s.i. (ISBN 0-8193-0764-5, Four Winds); PLB 5.41 o.s.i. (ISBN 0-8193-0765-3). Schol Bk Serv.
--Miss Suzy's Easter Surprise. LC 80-17315. (Illus.). 48p. (ps-3). 1980. Repr. of 1972 ed. 8.95 (ISBN 0-590-07777-5, Four Winds). Schol Bk Serv.
--No Place for Mitty. LC 75-35606. 128p. (gr. 3-7). 1976. 5.95 (ISBN 0-685-62044-1, Four Winds). Schol Bk Serv.
--The Secret of Stone House Farm. LC 63-15405. (Illus.). (gr. 5-7). 1966. pap. 0.60 o.p. (ISBN 0-15-679994-4, AVB48, VoyB). HarBraceJ.
--So What If It's Raining! LC 75-19340. (Illus.). 40p. (ps-3). 1976. 5.95 o.s.i. (ISBN 0-8193-0803-X, Four Winds); PLB 5.41 o.s.i. (ISBN 0-8193-0804-8). Schol Bk Serv.
Young, Morris, ed. see Houdini, Harry.
Young, Morris N., jt. auth. see Gibson, Walter B.
Young, N., jt. auth. see Evans, F. C.
Young, Nancy, jt. auth. see Hope, Karol.
Young, Nat. Nat Young's Book of Surfing: The Fundamentals & Adventures of Board-Riding. (Illus.). 90p. 1979. 17.95 (ISBN 0-589-50130-5, Pub. by Reed Books Australia). C E Tuttle.
Young Nations Conference, Sydney, 1976. Paradise Postponed: Essays on Research & Development in the South Pacific: Proceedings. Mamak, Alexander & McCall, Grant, eds. 1979. text ed. 29.00 (ISBN 0-08-023005-9); pap. text ed. 11.00 (ISBN 0-08-023004-0). Pergamon.
Young, Nigel. An Infantile Disorder? The Crisis & Decline of the New Left. LC 76-30272. 1978. lib. bdg. 27.50x (ISBN 0-89158-549-4). Westview.
Young, Nora. An Alaskan Christmas & Other Stories. 150p. 1981. 8.95 (ISBN 0-918270-10-3). That New Pub.
Young, Oran R. Natural Resources & the State: The Political Economy of Resource Management. 1981. 16.50 (ISBN 0-520-04285-9). U of Cal Pr.
Young, P. Great Ideas in Music. 6.25 (ISBN 0-08-007072-8). Pergamon.
Young, P., jt. auth. see Kemp, J. F.
Young, Patrick. Drifting Continents, Shifting Seas: An Introduction to Plate Tectonics. (Impact Bks). (Illus.). 96p. (gr. 7 up). 1976. PLB 4.90 o.p. (ISBN 0-531-00848-7). Watts.
Young, Paul. Datsun Tune-up for Everybody. (Illus.). 1980. pap. 7.95 (ISBN 0-89815-026-4). Ten Speed Pr.
--Honda Tune-up for Everybody. (Illus.). 144p. (Orig.). 1981. pap. 7.95 (ISBN 0-89815-031-0). Ten Speed Pr.
Young, Paul T. Understanding Your Feelings & Emotions. (Illus.). 192p. 1976. pap. 4.95 o.p. (ISBN 0-13-936500-1, Spec). P-H.
Young People's Science Encyclopedia Editors. Young People's Science Dictionary, 2 vols. LC 67-17925. (Illus.). (gr. 4 up). 1979. lib. bdg. 15.95 (ISBN 0-516-00274-0). Childrens.
Young, Percy M. The Choral Tradition. rev. ed. 400p. 1981. pap. 8.95 (ISBN 0-393-00058-3). Norton.
--A Critical Dictionary of Composers & Their Music. LC 78-66927. (Encore Music Editions Ser.). 1981. Repr. of 1954 ed. 27.50 (ISBN 0-88355-771-1). Hyperion Conn.
--Handbook of Choral Technique. (Student's Music Library Ser). 1953. 6.95 (ISBN 0-234-77213-1). Dufour.
--Messiah, a Study in Interpretation. 1961. 6.95 (ISBN 0-234-77215-8). Dufour.
Young, Percy M., ed see Tchaikovsky, Piotr I.
Young, Perry D., jt. auth. see Kopay, David.
Young, Peter. Short History of World War Two, 1939-1945. (Apollo Eds.). (Illus.). pap. 5.50 (ISBN 0-8152-0181-8, A181, TYC-T). T Y Crowell.
Young, Phillip. The Look of Music: Rare Musical Instruments, 1500-1900. (Illus.). 240p. 1980. 35.00 (ISBN 0-295-95784-0); pap. 16.95 (ISBN 0-295-95785-9). U of Wash Pr.
Young, Phillip T. Twenty-Five Hundred Historical Woodwind Instruments: An Inventory of the Major Collections. (Illus.). 1981. lib. bdg. price not set (ISBN 0-918728-17-7). Pendragon NY.
Young, Phyllis. Playing the String Game: Strategies for Teaching Cello & Strings. (Illus.). 1978. 15.00x o.p. (ISBN 0-292-73814-5); pap. text ed. 9.95x (ISBN 0-292-73815-3). U of Tex Pr.
Young, Richard. Schooling of the Western Horse. (Illus.). 15.75 (ISBN 0-85131-182-2). J A Allen.
Young, Richard A. & Cross, Frank L., eds. Operation & Maintenance for Air Particulate Control Equipment. LC 80-65506. (Illus.). 184p. 1980. 37.50 (ISBN 0-250-40367-6). Ann Arbor Science.
Young, Richard M., jt. ed. see Klein, Lawrence R.
Young, Robert. Young's Analytical Concordance to the Bible. 1955. 19.95 (ISBN 0-8028-8084-3); pap. 19.95 (ISBN 0-8028-8085-1). Eerdmans.
Young, Robert E., jt. auth. see Pritzker, Alan B.
Young, Robert H., jt. auth. see Wienandt, Elwyn A.
Young, Robert M. An Introduction to Nonharmonic Fourier Series. LC 79-6807. (Pure & Applied Ser.). 1980. 32.00 (ISBN 0-12-772850-3). Acad Pr.
Young, Robert W. & Morgan, William. The Navajo Language: A Grammar & Colloquial Dictionary. LC 79-56812. 1980. 35.00x (ISBN 0-8263-0536-9). U of NM Pr.
Young, Roger. Modern Cooking Equipment & Its Applicaions. (Illus.). 1979. 18.50x (ISBN 0-7198-2684-5). Intl Ideas.
Young, Roland. British Parliament. 1962. 11.95x o.s.i. (ISBN 0-8101-0246-3). Northwestern U Pr.
Young, Roland, ed. Through Masailand with Joseph Thomson. (Illus.). 1962. 10.95x o.s.i. (ISBN 0-8101-0248-X). Northwestern U Pr.
Young, Roland A. Congressional Politics in the Second World War. LC 70-38757. (FDR & the Era of the New Deal Ser). 282p. 1972. Repr. of 1956 ed. lib. bdg. 29.50 (ISBN 0-306-70442-0). Da Capo.
Young, S. Electronics in the Life Sciences. LC 73-8083. 198p. 1973. 17.95 (ISBN 0-470-97943-7). Halsted Pr.
Young, Stanley P. The Bobcat of North America: Its History, Life Habits, Economic Status & Control, with List of Currently Recognized Subspecies. LC 77-14021. (Illus.). 1978. 12.95x (ISBN 0-8032-0977-0); pap. 3.50 (ISBN 0-8032-5894-1, BB 663, Bison). U of Nebr Pr.
Young, Stanley P. & Jackson, Hartley H. The Clever Coyote. LC 77-14026. (Illus.). 1978. 19.50x (ISBN 0-8032-0976-2); pap. 5.50 (ISBN 0-8032-5893-3, BB 662, Bison). U of Nebr Pr.
Young, Stella, jt. auth. see Bryan, Nonobah G.
Young, Stella, ed. Navajo Native Dyes: Their Preparation & Use. LC 76-43671. (Indian Affairs Ser.: No. 2). (Illus.). Repr. of 1940 ed. 11.50 (ISBN 0-404-15504-9, E99). AMS Pr.
Young, Stephen B. & Orgel, Stephen, eds. Match at Midnight (1633) LC 79-54324. (Renaissance Drama Second Ser.). 270p. 1980. lib. bdg. 30.00 (ISBN 0-8240-4481-9). Garland Pub.
Young, Steven C. The Frame Structure in Tudor & Stuart Drama. (Salzburg Studies in English Literature, Elizabethan & Renaissance Studies: No. 6). 189p. (Orig.). 1976. pap. text ed. 25.00x (ISBN 0-391-01577-X). Humanities.
Young, T. D., et al. The Literature of the South. rev. ed. 1968. 17.95x (ISBN 0-673-05660-0). Scott F.
Young, T. R. New Sources of Self. 124p. 1972. text ed. 12.25 (ISBN 0-08-016672-5). Pergamon.
Young, Thomas. Linear Integrated Circuits. (Kosow Electrical Ser.). 464p. 1981. text ed. 18.95 (ISBN 0-471-97941-4). Wiley.
Young, Thomas D. & Inge, M. Thomas. Donald Davidson. (U. S. Authors Ser.: No. 190). lib. bdg. 10.95 (ISBN 0-8057-0188-5). Twayne.
Young, Thomas D. & Hindle, John J., eds. The Correspondence of John Peale Bishop & Allen Tate. LC 80-5186. 1981. price not set (ISBN 0-8131-1443-8). U Pr of Ky.
Young, Trudee. Georges Simenon: A Checklist of His "Maigret" & Other Mystery Novels & Short Stories in French & in English Translations. LC 76-14410. (Author Bibliographies Ser.: No. 29). 1976. 10.00 (ISBN 0-8108-0964-8). Scarecrow.
Young Viewers of Zoom. Zoom Catalog. (Illus.). 1972. lib. bdg. 5.69 (ISBN 0-394-92532-7); pap. 3.50 (ISBN 0-394-82532-2). Random.
Young, Viola M. Pseudomonas Aeruginosa: Ecological Aspects & Patient Colonization. LC 76-56919. 1977. 12.50 (ISBN 0-89004-149-0). Raven.
Young, Virgil M. & Young, Katherine A. Story of Idaho Teacher's Aid Booklet. rev. ed. LC 80-51706. 1980. 15.00 (ISBN 0-89301-055-3). U Pr of Idaho.
Young, W. Ogg & Ray's Essentials of American National Government. 10th ed. 1969. pap. 12.95 (ISBN 0-13-633651-5). P-H.
Young, Walter J. Stamp Collecting A-Z. LC 80-27181. (Illus.). 150p. 1981. 9.95 (ISBN 0-498-02479-2). A S Barnes.
Young, William, tr. St. Ignatius's Own Story. 1980. Repr. 3.95 (ISBN 0-8294-0359-0). Loyola.
Young, William F., jt. auth. see Farnsworth, E. Allan.
Young, William G. & Sedano, Heddie O. Atlas of Oral Pathology. LC 80-29439. (Illus.). 256p. 1981. 25.00x (ISBN 0-8166-1040-1). U of Minn Pr.
Young, William H., jt. auth. see Young, Grace C.
Young, William H., ed. see Ogg, Frederic A. & Ray, P. Orman.
Young, William J., jt. auth. see Cuff, David J.
Youngberg, Norma. Nyla & the White Crocodile. LC 65-18680. (Destiny Ser.). 1977. pap. 4.95 (ISBN 0-8163-0306-1, 14640-7). Pacific Pr Pub Assn.
Youngberg, Norma, jt. auth. see Hill, Beth.
Youngberg, Norma R. Singer on the Sand. LC 64-17655. (Panda Ser). 1974. pap. 4.95 (ISBN 0-8163-0213-8, 19356-5). Pacific Pr Pub Assn.
Youngberg, Norma R., jt. auth. see Kreye, Eric.
Youngblood, Ronald. How It All Began: (Genesis 1-11) LC 80-50539. (Bible Commentary for Laymen Ser.). 160p. 1980. pap. 2.50 (ISBN 0-8307-0675-5, S342103). Regal.
Youngdale, James M. Populism: A Psychohistorical Perspective. (National University Publications Ser. in American Studies). 1975. 17.50 (ISBN 0-8046-9102-9, Natl U). Kennikat.
Younger, Richard D. People's Panel: The Grand Jury in the United States, 1634-1941. LC 63-12993. 263p. 1965. Repr. of 1963 ed. 10.00 (ISBN 0-87057-076-5). Univ Pr of New England.
Younghusband, Eileen. Social Work & Social Change. (National Institute Social Services Library). 1964. pap. text ed. 4.95x o.p. (ISBN 0-04-360022-0). Allen Unwin.
Youngman, Henny. Henny Youngman's Bar Bets, Bar Jokes, Bar Tricks. LC 73-90951. (Illus.). 168p. 1974. 5.95 (ISBN 0-8065-0404-8). Citadel Pr.
--Henny Youngman's Big Blue Bamboozle. 1978. pap. 1.95 o.p. (ISBN 0-523-40349-6). Pinnacle Bks.
--Henny Youngman's Five Hundred All-Time Greatest One-Liners. 160p. (Orig.). 1981. pap. 1.95 (ISBN 0-523-41142-1). Pinnacle Bks.
Youngman, M. B., et al. Analysing Jobs. 168p. 1978. text ed. 26.50x (ISBN 0-566-02089-0, Pub. by Gower Pub Co England). Renouf.
Youngman, W. & Randall, C. Growing Your Trees. Date not set. 33.50 (ISBN 0-686-26730-3, 37). Am Forestry.
Youngquist, Walter. Investing in Natural Resources. 2nd ed. LC 80-67667. 264p. 1980. 14.95 (ISBN 0-87094-221-2). Dow Jones-Irwin.
Young Rifai, Marlene A., ed. Justice & Older Americans. LC 76-52764. (Illus.). 1977. 19.95 (ISBN 0-669-01333-1). Lexington Bks.
Youngs, F. A. The Proclamations of the Tudor Queens. LC 75-30442. 304p. 1976. 46.50 (ISBN 0-521-21044-5). Cambridge U Pr.
Youngs, J. W. Representation Problem for Frechet Surfaces. LC 52-42839. (Memoirs: No. 8). 1980. pap. 9.20 (ISBN 0-8218-1208-4, MEMO-8). Am Math.
Youngs, Robert W. What It Means to Be a Christian. 1977. pap. 3.50 o.p. (ISBN 0-8015-8520-1). Dutton.
Youngs, T. William. American Essays, 2 vols. (Orig.). 1981. Vol. 1. pap. text ed. 8.95 ea. (ISBN 0-316-97727-6). Vol. 2 (ISBN 0-316-97729-2). training manual free (ISBN 0-316-97728-4). Little.
Youngsberg, Norma, jt. auth. see Quimby, Paul.
Youngstrom, Karl A., jt. auth. see Diedrich, William M.
Younie, William J. Instructional Approaches to Slow Learning. LC 67-21694. 1967. pap. text ed. 5.75x (ISBN 0-8077-2365-7). Tchrs Coll.
Younker, Lucas & Fried, D. V. Animal Doctor. 1976. pap. 2.50 (ISBN 0-515-05888-2). Jove Pubns.
Younker, Lucas & Fried, John J. Animal Doctor: The Making of a Veterinarian. 256p. 1981. pap. 2.50. Jove Pubns.
Younker, Richard. On Site: The Construction of a High-Rise. LC 79-7889. (Illus.). (gr. 5-12). 1980. 7.95 (ISBN 0-690-04003-2, TYC-J); PLB 7.89 (ISBN 0-690-04004-0). T Y Crowell.
Yourcenar, Marguerite. Coup De Grace. Frick, Grace, tr. from Fr. 151p. 1957. 15.00 (ISBN 0-374-13052-3). FS&G.
--Coup De Grace. Frick, Grace, tr. from Fr. 1981. pap. 5.95 (ISBN 0-374-51631-6). FS&G.
Yourdan, Edward. Techniques of Program Structure & Design. (Illus.). 384p. 1976. 23.95 (ISBN 0-13-901702-X). P-H.
Yourdon, E., ed. Structured Walkthroughs. 2nd ed. 1980. 13.95 (ISBN 0-13-855221-5). P-H.
Yourdon, Edward. Design of on-Line Computer Systems. (Illus.). 576p. 1972. ref. ed. 24.95 (ISBN 0-13-201301-0). P-H.
Yourdon, Edward & Constantine, Larry L. Structured Design. 2nd ed. LC 78-24465. 599p. 1978. pap. 21.00 (ISBN 0-917072-11-1). Yourdon.
Yourdon, Edward, jt. auth. see Lister, Timothy R.
Yourdon, Edward, et al. Learning to Program in Structured COBOL: Part 1. 2nd ed. LC 78-63350. 252p. 1978. pap. 12.00 (ISBN 0-917072-12-X). Yourdon.
Yourgrau, Wolfgang & Mandelstam, Stanley. Variational Principles in Dynamics & Quantum Theory. 3rd ed. LC 78-73521. 1979. pap. text ed. 4.00 (ISBN 0-486-63773-5). Dover.
Yourgrau, Wolfgang & Merwe, Alwyn Van Der, eds. Perspectives in Quantum Theory. LC 78-74119. 1979. pap. text ed. 5.00 (ISBN 0-486-63778-6). Dover.
Yousef, Fathi S., jt. auth. see Condon, John C.
Youth Hostels Association. Standard Youth Hosteler's Guide to Europe. rev. ed. (Illus.). 498p. 1981. 6.95 (ISBN 0-02-098950-4, Collier). Macmillan.
Youth Hostels Association Service. Youth Hostel Association Services. (Illus.). 512p. 1973. pap. 2.95 o.s.i. (ISBN 0-02-040900-1, Collier). Macmillan.
Youth with a Mission. The Singing Word: Youth with a Mission Songbook. enl &rev. 2nd ed. (Illus.). 280p. 1974. plastic spiral bd. 5.95 (ISBN 0-87123-505-6, 280505). Bethany Fell.
Yoxall, H. W. The Wines of Burgundy: The International Wire & Food Society's Guide. LC 78-57582. (Illus.). 192p. 1980. pap. 5.95 (ISBN 0-8128-6091-8). Stein & Day.
Ypung, Harold C., jt. ed. see Young, Margaret Labash.
Yrigoyen, Charles, Jr. & Bricker, George H., eds. Catholic & Reformed: Selected Writings of John Williamson Nevin. LC 78-2567. (Pittsburgh Original Texts & Translations: No. 3). 1978. pap. text ed. 9.50 (ISBN 0-915138-37-9). Pickwick.
Yrigoyen, Charles, Jr. & Bricker, George H, eds. Reformed & Catholic: Selected Theological Writings of Phillip Schaff. LC 79-17391. (Pittsburgh Original Texts & Translations Ser: No. 4). 1979. pap. text ed. 12.95 (ISBN 0-915138-40-9). Pickwick.
Ysseldyke, James, jt. auth. see Salvia, John.
Ysseldyke, James E., jt. auth. see Salvia, John.
Yu, Andrew B., jt. auth. see Shargel, Leon.
Yu, Anthony C., ed. Journey to the West, Vol. 3. LC 75-27896. 1980. lib. bdg. 30.00x (ISBN 0-226-97147-3). U of Chicago Pr.
Yu, Elena, jt. ed. see Nandi, Proshanta.
Yu, Francis T. Optics & Information Theory. LC 76-23135. 1976. 21.50 (ISBN 0-471-01682-9, Pub. by Wiley-Interscience). Wiley.
Yu, Frederick T. C., jt. ed. see Davison, W. Phillips.
Yu, George T., jt. auth. see Scalapino, Robert A.
Yu, George T., ed. Intra-Asian International Relations. LC 77-24382. (Westview Special Studies on China & East Asia-South & Southeast Asia). 1978. lib. bdg. 20.00x (ISBN 0-89158-125-1). Westview.

Yu, Paul N. & Goodwin, John F., eds. Progress in Cardiology, Vol. 9. LC 77-157474. (Illus.). 193p. 1980. text ed. 15.00 (ISBN 0-8121-0728-4). Lea & Febiger.

Yu, Pauline. Poetry of Wang Wei: New Translations & Commentary. LC 79-3623. (Chinese Literature in Translation Ser.). 288p. Date not set. 27.50x (ISBN 0-253-17772-3); pap. 9.95x (ISBN 0-253-20252-3). Ind U Pr.

Yu, S. C. The Structure of Accounting Theory. LC 76-10355. 1976. pap. 9.00 (ISBN 0-8130-0405-5). U Presses Fla.

Yu, T. S., jt. auth. see Fu, K. S.

Yu, Tsao. Thunderstorm. 1978. 4.95 (ISBN 0-8351-0554-7). China Bks.

Yu, Tzong-shian, jt. ed. see Hou, Chi-Ming.

Yu, Ying-shih. Trade & Expansion in Han China. 1967. 20.00x (ISBN 0-520-01374-3). U of Cal Pr.

Yuan, Nathan S. Crossing the Rubicon: The Story of a Chinese Refugee Family. 115p. 1980. 5.95 (ISBN 0-8059-2731-X). Dorrance.

Yuan, Shao. Foundations of Fluid Mechanics. 1967. text ed. 26.95x (ISBN 0-13-329813-2). P-H.

Yuan-Cheng Fung, see Fung, Yuan-Cheng.

Yuan Kao, ed. see Heckner, Fritz.

Yuasa, Nobuyuki, tr. from Jap. The Zen Poems of Ryokan. LC 80-8585. (Princeton library of Asian Translations). (Illus.). 196p. 1981. 17.50x (ISBN 0-691-06466-0). Princeton U Pr.

Yuasa, Nobuyuki, tr. see Issa.

Yudelson, J. & Kitchin, M., eds. California Solar Business Directory. 194p. 1980. pap. 12.00 (ISBN 0-89934-045-8, V055-PD). Solar Energy Info.

Yudkin, John. Lose Weight, Feel Great. (Illus.). 219p. 1974. pap. 1.75 (ISBN 0-915962-02-0). Larchmont Bks.

Yudkin, John, ed. Diet of Man: Needs & Wants. (Illus.). 1978. text ed. 57.00x (ISBN 0-85334-750-6, Pub. by Applied Science). Burgess-Intl Ideas.

Yudkin, M. & Offord, R. A Guidebook to Biochemistry: A New Edition of a Guidebook to Biochemistry by K. Harrison. 3rd ed. LC 70-153012. (Illus.). 1971. 32.50 (ISBN 0-521-08195-5); pap. text ed. 11.95x (ISBN 0-521-09654-5). Cambridge U Pr.

Yudkin, Michael & Offord, Robin. Biochemistry. 1975. text ed. 22.95 (ISBN 0-395-17199-7); instructors manual 1.00 (ISBN 0-395-18266-2); slides (set of 20 35-mm) 11.25 (ISBN 0-395-18189-5). HM.

--Comprehensible Biochemistry. LC 73-85212. (Illus.). 576p. 1973. text ed. 23.00x (ISBN 0-582-44251-6). Longman.

--A Guidebook to Biochemistry. rev. 4th ed. LC 79-41606. (Illus.). 200p. 1980. 53.50 (ISBN 0-521-23084-5); pap. 15.95 (ISBN 0-521-29794-X). Cambridge U Pr.

Yudof, Mark G., jt. auth. see Kirp, David L.

Yuen, Aubrey. Geometric & Positional Tolerancing Reference & Work Book. 2nd ed. 90p. 1973. perfect bnd 7.95x (ISBN 0-912702-07-9). Global Eng.

Yuen, Aubrey, ed. Geometric & Positional Tolerancing Reference & Work Book. 1973. 7.95x (ISBN 0-912702-07-9). Global Eng.

Yuen, C. K., jt. auth. see Beauchamp, K. G.

Yuhas, John M., et al, eds. Biology of Radiation Carcinogenesis. LC 74-14486. 1976. 34.50 (ISBN 0-89004-010-9). Raven.

Yui, Tsunehiko, jt. auth. see Hirschmeier, Johannes.

Yuill, G. M. The Treatment of Renal Failure. 214p. 1975. 12.00x (ISBN 0-7190-0628-7, Pub. by Manchester U Pr England). State Mutual Bk.

Yukl, Gary. Leadership in Organizations. (Illus.). 336p. 1981. text ed. 16.95 (ISBN 0-13-527176-2). P-H.

Yukl, Gary A., jt. auth. see Wexley, Kenneth A.

Yukoff, George, jt. auth. see Schecter, David.

Yule, John-David. Concise Encyclopedia of the Sciences. 1981. 29.95 (ISBN 0-87196-491-0). Facts on File.

Yule, W. & Carr, J., eds. Behaviour Modification for the Mentally Handicapped. 304p. 1980. 30.00x (ISBN 0-85664-841-8, Pub. by Croom Helm England). State Mutual Bk.

Yule, William, et al. A Neuropsychiatric Study in Childhood. (Clinics in Developmental Medicine Ser.: Nos. 35 & 36). 272p. 1970. 21.00 (ISBN 0-685-24728-7). Lippincott.

Yulsman, Jerry. Complete Book of Thirty-Five-mm Photography. LC 75-45425. (Illus.). 224p. (YA) 1976. 8.95 (ISBN 0-698-10734-9). Coward.

Yumoto, John M. Samurai Sword: A Handbook. LC 58-7497. (Illus.). 1958. 11.00 (ISBN 0-8048-0509-1). C E Tuttle.

Yunck, John A., tr. from Fr. Eneas: A Twelfth-Century French Romance. (Record of Civilization, Sources & Studies: No. 93). 272p. 1974. 12.50x (ISBN 0-231-03823-2). Columbia U Pr.

Yung, K. K., compiled by. National Portrait Gallery: Complete Illustrated Catalogue. (Illus.). 650p. 1980. 49.50x (ISBN 0-312-15777-0). St Martin.

Yung, Victor S. The Great Wok Cookbook. 256p. 1974. 7.95 o.p. (ISBN 0-8402-1310-7). Nash Pub.

Yung C. Shang. Aquaculture Economics: Basic Concepts & Methods of Analysis. (Westview Special Studies in Agricultural Sciences). 140p. 1981. lib. bdg. 17.50x (ISBN 0-86531-047-5). Westview.

Yung-Ping Chen, jt. ed. see Scholen, Kenneth.

Yunik, Maurice. Design of Modern Transistor Circuits. (Illus.). 384p. 1973. 18.95x o.p. (ISBN 0-13-201285-5). P-H.

Yunker, Mary J. Guinness World Records Comprehension Module Program II. LC 78-730959. (gr. 4-8). 1978. pap. text ed. 175.00 (ISBN 0-89290-110-1, CM-72). Soc for Visual.

Yura. Nursing Leadership: Theory & Process. 2nd ed. (Illus.). 1980. pap. 11.95 (ISBN 0-8385-7028-3). ACC.

Yurick, Ann G., et al. The Aged Person & the Nursing Process. 550p. 1980. text ed. 16.95 (ISBN 0-8385-0082-X). ACC.

Yurick, Sol. Richard A. LC 80-66497. 1981. 11.95 (ISBN 0-87795-272-8). Arbor Hse.

Yurka, Blanche. Bohemian Girl: Blanche Yurka's Theatrical Life. LC 79-81449. xii, 306p. 1970. 11.95 (ISBN 0-8214-0071-1). Ohio U Pr.

Yushin Yoo. Bong Nam & the Pheasants. LC 79-15749. (Illus.). (ps-2). 1979. 6.95 (ISBN 0-13-079665-4); PLB 7.95 (ISBN 0-13-079657-3). P-H.

Yusuf, A. The Holy Quran. (Arabic & Eng.). 14.95 (ISBN 0-686-63572-8). Intl Bk Ctr.

Yuyama Akira, ed. Prajna - Paramita - Guna - Samcaya - Gatha. LC 75-32910. 285p. 1976. 49.50 (ISBN 0-521-21081-X). Cambridge U Pr.

Yvon, J. Correlations & Entropy in Classical Statistical Mechanics. 1969. 26.00 (ISBN 0-08-012755-X). Pergamon.

Z

Zabalza, A., et al. The Economics of Teacher Supply. LC 78-967. (Illus.). 1979. 49.50 (ISBN 0-521-22078-5). Cambridge U Pr.

Zabeeh, Farhang. Understanding Human: A New Synthesis. LC 78-65843. 1979. pap. 10.25 (ISBN 0-8191-0670-4). U Pr of Amer.

Zabel, James A. Nazism & the Pastors. LC 75-30607. (American Academy of Religion. Dissertation Ser.: No. 14). 1976. pap. 7.50 (ISBN 0-89130-040-6, 010114). Scholars Pr Ca.

Zabih, Sepehr. The Communist Movement in Iran. 1966. 21.75x (ISBN 0-520-01377-8). U of Cal Pr.

--Iran's Revolutionary Upheaval: An Interpretive Essay. new ed. LC 79-53696. (Orig.). 1979. 9.95x (ISBN 0-931290-18-X); pap. 5.95x (ISBN 0-686-66195-8). Alchemy Bks.

Zabinski, Michael P., jt. auth. see Harms, Edward.

Zabka, John R. Personnel Management & Human Relations. 1st ed. LC 73-142500. 1971. 12.30 o.p. (ISBN 0-672-96095-8); tchrs' manual 6.67 o.p. (ISBN 0-672-96097-4); wkbk 6.75 o.p. (ISBN 0-672-96096-6). Bobbs.

Zabolotskii, N. Stolbtsy. (Rus.). 1974. pap. 3.50 (ISBN 0-88233-191-4). Ardis Pubs.

Zaborowski, Leon M. & Hill, John W. Chemical Problems for Changing Times. 1973. pap. text ed. 3.95 o.p. (ISBN 0-8087-2600-5). Burgess.

Zabre, Alfonso T. Guide to the History of Mexico. (Illus.). 9.50 o.p. (ISBN 0-8363-0039-4). Jenkins.

Zabriskie, Francis. Horace Greeley: The Editor. (American Newspapermen 1790-1933 Ser.). 398p. 1974. Repr. of 1890 ed. 19.50x o.s.i. (ISBN 0-8464-0000-6). Beekman Pubs.

Zabriskie, George A. Summerdog Comes Home. (Illus.). 1980. pap. 1.75 (ISBN 0-380-75259-X, 75259, Camelot). Avon.

Zabriskie, John. Clinical Immunology of the Heart. (Perspectives in Clinical Immunology Ser.). 230p. 1981. 32.50 (ISBN 0-471-02676-X, Pub. by Wiley Med). Wiley.

Zabriskie, John B., jt. ed. see Read, Stanley E.

Zabronski, Ann, jt. auth. see Peebles Press International.

Zabrowski, Edward K. Soccer Statistics Made Easy: A Guide to Rating & Predicting Player & Team Performance. (Illus.). viii, 81p. 1979. 5.95 (ISBN 0-9604994-0-7). Crossbar Ent.

Zaccarelli, Bro. Herman E. & Maggiore, Josephine. Nursing Home Menu Planning, Food Purchasing & Management. LC 73-182087. 1972. 15.95 (ISBN 0-8436-0541-3). CBI Pub.

Zachar, Irwin J., ed. Plays As Experience: One-Act Plays for the Secondary Schools. rev. ed. LC 62-13411. 1962. pap. 7.50 (ISBN 0-672-73228-9). Odyssey Pr.

Zachariah, Gerald, jt. auth. see McKenzie, Bruce A.

Zachariah, K. C. & Conde, Julian. Migration in West Africa: The Demographic Aspects. (World Bank Research Publication Ser.). (Illus.). 256p. 1980. 16.95 (ISBN 0-19-520186-8); pap. 6.95 (ISBN 0-19-520187-6). Oxford U Pr.

Zacharias, Donald W., ed. In Pursuit of Peace: Speeches of the Sixties. 6.00 (ISBN 0-8446-0298-1). Peter Smith.

Zacharias, Gerhard. The Satanic Cult. Trollope, Christine, tr. (Illus.). 208p. (Ger.). 1980. 22.50x (ISBN 0-04-133008-0, 2370). Allen Unwin.

Zacharias, Lee. Helping Muriel Make It Through the Night-Stories. LC 75-18047. 128p. 1976. pap. 4.95 (ISBN 0-8071-0166-4); pap. 3.95 (ISBN 0-8071-0177-X). La State U Pr.

Zachary, Elizabeth. Hotel Destiny. (Grand Hotel Ser.: No. 1). Orig. Title: The Adlon, Berlin. (Orig.). 1981. pap. 2.75 (ISBN 0-515-06046-1). Jove Pubns.

Zachary, Elizabeth, jt. auth. see Zachary, Hugh.

Zachary, Hugh. Bloodrush. 1981. pap. 1.95 (ISBN 0-8439-0857-2, Leisure Bks). Nordon Pubns.

--Murder in White. 1981. pap. 1.95 (ISBN 0-8439-0876-9, Leisure Bks). Nordon Pubns.

Zachary, Hugh & Zachary, Elizabeth. Of Love & Battle. 480p. (Orig.). 1981. pap. 2.75 (ISBN 0-345-28610-3). Ballantine.

Zachel, Fred. Cocaine & Blue Eyes. 1979. pap. 2.25 o.p. (ISBN 0-425-04456-4). Berkley Pub.

Zacher, Mark W. Dag Hammarskjold's United Nations. LC 71-101593. (International Organization Ser.: No. 7). 1969. 20.00x (ISBN 0-231-03275-7). Columbia U Pr.

--International Conflicts & Collective Security: 1946-1977. LC 78-19775. (Praeger Special Studies). 1979. 25.95 (ISBN 0-03-044261-3). Praeger.

Zack, Carol, jt. auth. see Gregorich, Barbara.

Zackler, Jack & Brandstadt, Wayne, eds. The Teenage Pregnant Girl. (Illus.). 336p. 1975. 17.50 (ISBN 0-398-03152-5). C C Thomas.

Zacklin, Ralph. The United Nations & Rhodesia: A Study in International Law. LC 74-1751. (Special Studies). (Illus.). 202p. 1974. text ed. 21.50 o.p. (ISBN 0-275-09260-7). Praeger.

Zacks, S. Parametric Statistical Inference: Basic Theory & Modern Approaches. LC 80-41715. (I.S. in Nonlinear Mathematics Series; Theory & Applications: Vol. 4). 400p. 1981. 48.00 (ISBN 0-08-026468-9); pap. 19.70 (ISBN 0-08-026467-0). Pergamon.

Zadan, Craig. Sondheim & Company. 1976. pap. 4.35 o.s.i. (ISBN 0-380-00607-3, 28639). Avon.

Zadeh, Norman. Winning Poker Systems. LC 74-5234. (Illus.). 228p. 1974. 8.95 o.p. (ISBN 0-13-961292-0); pap. 3.95 o.p. (ISBN 0-13-961284-X). P-H.

Zadig, Ernest A. The Complete Book of Pleasure Boat Engines. LC 79-24306. (Illus.). 320p. 1980. 17.95 (ISBN 0-13-157636-4). P-H.

Zadoks, Jan C. & Schein, Richard D. Epidemiology & Plant Disease Management. (Illus.). 1979. text ed. 22.95x (ISBN 0-19-502451-6); pap. text ed. 9.95x (ISBN 0-19-502452-4). Oxford U Pr.

Zadrazil, S., ed. see FEBS Symposium on DNA, Liblice, 24-29 September, 1979.

Zadunaisky, Jose A. & Davson, Hugh, eds. Current Topics in Eye Research, Vol. 2. (Serial Publication). 1980. 35.00 (ISBN 0-12-153002-7). Acad Pr.

Zaehner, R. C., ed. Hindu Scriptures. 1976. 8.95x (Evman); pap. 5.95 (Evman). Dutton.

Zaehner, Robert C. Hinduism. 1962. pap. 4.95 (ISBN 0-19-500383-7, GB172, GB). Oxford U Pr.

--Zurvan: A Zoroastrian Dilemma. 1973. Repr. of 1955 ed. 19.50x (ISBN 0-8196-0280-9). Biblo.

Zaetz, Jay L. Occupational Activities Training Manual: For Severely Retarded Adults. (Illus.). 124p. 1969. photocopy ed. spiral 12.50 (ISBN 0-398-02138-4). C C Thomas.

--Organization of Sheltered Workshop Programs for the Mentally Retarded Adult. (Illus.). 248p. 1971. 24.75 (ISBN 0-398-02158-9). C C Thomas.

Zaevolkow, E., jt. ed. see Gustason, G.

Zafferano, George J. Handball Basics. LC 76-19798. 1977. 9.95 (ISBN 0-8069-4104-9); PLB 9.29 (ISBN 0-8069-4105-7). Sterling.

Zaffo, George. Giant Nursery Book of Things That Work. LC 67-10020. (gr. k-1). 1967. PLB 7.95 (ISBN 0-385-06412-8). Doubleday.

Zafforoni, Joseph, jt. auth. see Navarra, John G.

Zaffuto, Anthony A. Alphagenics. 1975. pap. 1.75 o.s.i. (ISBN 0-446-59899-2). Warner Bks.

Zafiratos, C. Physics. LC 75-14034. 911p. 1976. 27.95x (ISBN 0-471-98104-4); instructor's manual avail. (ISBN 0-471-01854-6). Wiley.

Zagaris, Bruce. Foreign Investment in the United States. LC 79-20638. (Praeger Special Studies Ser.). (Illus.). 334p. 1980. 26.95 (ISBN 0-03-052401-6). Praeger.

Zagat, I. R., ed. see Zagat, Samuel.

Zagat, Samuel. Jewish Life on New York's Lower East Side: Drawings & Paintings, 1912-1962. Zagat, I. R., ed. (Illus.). 1972. 25.00 (ISBN 0-911268-09-X). Rogers Bk.

Zaglits, Oscar. Man, Religion & Science. Date not set. 10.95 (ISBN 0-533-04808-7). Vantage.

Zagora, Edward. Eye Injuries. (Illus.). 618p. 1970. text ed. 59.75 (ISBN 0-398-02139-2). C C Thomas.

Zagoria, Donald S. Vietnam Triangle: Moscow, Peking, Hanoi. LC 67-25501. (Illus., Orig.). 1967. 8.95 (ISBN 0-672-53607-2). Pegasus.

Zahar, Renate. Frantz Fanon: Colonialism & Alienation. Feuser, Willfried F., tr. from Ger. LC 74-7783. (Modern Reader Paperback Ser). 144p. 1976. pap. 5.00 (ISBN 0-85345-374-8, PB-3748). Monthly Rev.

Zahavy, Tzvee. The Traditions of Eleazar Ben Azariah. LC 76-46373. (Brown University. Brown Judaic Studies: No. 2). 1977. pap. 9.00 (ISBN 0-89130-095-3, 140002). Scholars Pr Ca.

Zahavy, Zev. Whence & Wherefore: The Cosmological Destiny of Man Scientifically & Philosophically Considered. LC 77-84786. 1978. 7.50 o.p. (ISBN 0-498-02190-4). A S Barnes.

Zahl, Peter-Paul, et al. Doors: Poems-1981. 128p. 1981. 8.95 (ISBN 0-87376-037-9). Red Dust.

Zahlan, A. B., ed. see United Nations Economic Commission for Western Asia, Natural Resources, Science & Technology Division.

Zahn, C. T. C Notes: A Guide to the C Programming Language. LC 78-63290. (Orig.). 1979. pap. 16.50 (ISBN 0-917072-13-8). Yourdon.

Zahn, Carl F., compiled by. The Fine Arts Cookbook, Two. (Illus.). 195p. 1981. 14.95 (ISBN 0-8436-2211-3). CBI Pub.

Zahn, Frank. Macroeconomic Theory & Policy. (Illus.). 320p. 1975. 17.95 (ISBN 0-13-542555-7). P-H.

Zahn, Gordon C. In Solitary Witness: The Life & Death of Franz Jagerstatter. 1981. Repr. of 1964 ed. 18.95x (ISBN 0-03-047535-X). Irvington.

Zahn, Theodor. Introduction to the New Testament, 3 vols. 1977. 48.00 (ISBN 0-686-12975-X). Klock & Klock.

Zahorski, Kenneth J., jt. ed. see Boyer, Robert M. Z.

Zahradnik, Raymond L. Theory & Techniques of Optimization for Practicing Engineers. LC 70-146261. 1971. pap. 9.95 (ISBN 0-8436-0311-9). CBI Pub.

Zaichkowsky, Lionard D., et al. Growth & Development: The Child in Physical Activity. LC 79-23443. 1980. pap. text ed. 10.95 (ISBN 0-8016-5663-X). Mosby.

Zaide, Sonia M., jt. ed. see Pritchard, R. John.

Zaidenberg, Arthur. Drawing All Animals. (Funk & W Bk.). (Illus.). 176p. 1974. pap. 6.95 (ISBN 0-308-10108-1, F99, TYC-T). T Y Crowell.

--Drawing the Figure from Top to Toe. (Funk & W Bk.). (Illus.). 176p. 1974. pap. 6.95 (ISBN 0-308-10107-3, F98, TYC-T). T Y Crowell.

--How to Draw Portraits: A Book for Beginners. LC 62-11216. (Illus.). (gr. 7-9). 5.95 (ISBN 0-8149-0442-4). Vanguard.

--How to Draw with Pen & Brush. LC 65-17376. (Illus.). (gr. 6-9). 1965. 5.95 (ISBN 0-8149-0441-6). Vanguard.

--How to Paint in Oil: A Book for Beginners. LC 56-7892. (Illus.). (gr. 7-9). 1954. 5.95 (ISBN 0-8149-0444-0). Vanguard.

--How to Paint with Water Colors: A Book for Beginners. LC 66-28885. (Illus.). (gr. 5 up). 1968. 5.95 (ISBN 0-8149-0440-8). Vanguard.

--The Lively Way to Modeling Sculpture: A Book for Beginners. LC 74-134676. (Illus.). (gr. 9 up). Date not set. 4.95 (ISBN 0-8149-0446-7). Vanguard. Postponed.

Zaika, V. E. Specific Production of Aquatic Invertebrates. Gollek, B., ed. Mercado, A., tr. from Rus. LC 73-12320. 154p. 1973. 39.95 (ISBN 0-470-98111-3). Halsted Pr.

Zaikov, G. E., jt. auth. see Bochkov, A. E.

Zaimis, Eleanor, ed. Nerve Growth Factor & Its Antiserum. (Illus.). 384p. 1972. text ed. 24.00x (ISBN 0-485-11132-2, Athlone Pr). Humanities.

Zaimont, Judith L. & Famera, Karen, eds. Contemporary Concert Music by Women: A Directory of the Composers & Their Works. LC 80-39572. (Illus.). 320p. 1981. lib. bdg. 25.00 (ISBN 0-313-22921-X, ZCM/). Greenwood.

Zaimovsky, S. G. Russian-English, English-Russian Dictionary. pap. 6.00 (ISBN 0-685-20192-9, 069-0). Saphrograph.

Zainaldin, Jamil S., jt. auth. see Presser, Stephen B.

Zainnuddin. Songs of Indonesia. 1970. pap. text ed. 3.50x (ISBN 0-686-65419-6, 00508). Heinemann Ed.

Zaionchkovsky, P. A. The Russian Autocracy Under Alexander III. Jones, David R., ed. & tr. (Russian Series: Vol. 22). 1976. 21.50 (ISBN 0-87569-067-X). Academic Intl.
Zaionchkovsky, Peter A. The Russian Autocracy in Crisis, 1878-1882. 1979. 26.50 (ISBN 0-87569-031-9). Academic Intl.
Zais, James P., et al. Modifying Section Eight: Implications from Experiments with Housing Allowances. (An Institute Paper). 61p. 1979. pap. 4.50 (ISBN 0-87766-240-1, 24100). Urban Inst.
Zajac, A., jt. auth. see Hecht, E.
Zajda, Joseph I. Education in the USSR. (International Studies in Education & Social Change). (Illus.). 200p. 1980. 29.00 (ISBN 0-08-025807-7); pap. 12.00 (ISBN 0-08-025806-9). Pergamon.
Zak, Therese A., ed. see Corwin, Sheila.
Zak, Therese A., ed. see Learning Achievement Corp.
Zak, Therese A., ed. see Learning Achievement Corporation.
Zak, Vladimir, jt. auth. see Korchnoi, Viktor.
Zakas, Spiros. Furniture in Twenty Four Hours. 1976. 10.95 o.s.i. (ISBN 0-02-633390-2). Macmillan.
Zakhoder, Boris. How a Piglet Crashed the Christmas Party. LC 70-155750. (Illus.). (gr. k-3). 1971. PLB 7.92 o.p. (ISBN 0-688-51622-X). Lothrop.
Zakin, Helen J. French Cistercian Grisaille Glass. LC 78-74385. (Outstanding Dissertations in the Fine Arts, Fourth Ser.). 1979. lib. bdg. 44.00 (ISBN 0-8240-3971-8). Garland Pub.
Zakin, Richard. Electric Kiln Ceramics: A Potter's Guide to Clay & Glazes. LC 80-68274. (Illus.). 256p. 1981. 24.50 (ISBN 0-686-69517-8). Chilton.
Zakkar, Suhail. Emirate of Aleppo. (Arab Background Ser.). 1971. 20.00x (ISBN 0-685-77108-3). Intl Bk Ctr.
Zakon, Ronnie L. The Artist & the Studio: In the Eighteenth & Nineteenth Centuries. LC 78-51885. (Themes in Art Ser.). (Illus.). 68p. 1978. pap. 4.95x (ISBN 0-910386-40-4, Pub. by Cleveland Mus Art). Ind U Pr.
Zakon, Ronnie L., jt. auth. see Weisberg, Gabriel P.
Zakrajsek, Dorothy & Carnes, Lois. Learning Experiences: An Approach to Teaching Physical Education. 208p. 1981. write for info. (ISBN 0-697-07098-0). Wm C Brown.
Zakreski, L. A. The Budget Backpacker. 1977. 11.95 (ISBN 0-87691-189-0). Winchester Pr.
Zakrevsky, A. D., jt. ed. see Gavrilov, M. A.
Zakus, Sharron. Clinical Skills & Assisting Techniques for the Medical Assistant. (Illus.). 536p. 1981. pap. text ed. 15.95 (ISBN 0-8016-5672-9). Mosby.
Zakusov, V. V. Pharmacology of Central Synapses. (Illus.). 1980. 48.00 (ISBN 0-08-020549-6). Pergamon.
Zaky, A. A. & Hawley, R. Dielectric Solids. (Solid-State Physics Ser.). 1970. pap. 5.00 (ISBN 0-7100-6604-X). Routledge & Kegan.
Zakythinos, D. A. The Making of Modern Greece: From Byzantium to Independence. Johnstone, K. R., tr. from Greek. 235p. 1976. 21.50x o.p. (ISBN 0-87471-796-5). Rowman.
Zalatimo, Suleiman & Sleeman, Phillip. A Systems Approach to Learning Environents. 1975. pap. 12.40 (ISBN 0-913178-68-3). Redgrave Pub Co.
Zalaznick, Charles. Real Estate Development & Construction Financing 1980: Course Handbook. LC 80-80907. (Real Estate Law & Practice Course Handgook Ser.). 716p. 1980. pap. text ed. 25.00 (ISBN 0-686-68829-5, N4-4349). PLI.
Zalba, Serapio R., jt. ed. see Schwartz, William.
Zalben, Jane B. Oh, Simple! (Illus.). 32p. (ps up). 1981. 8.95 (ISBN 0-374-35604-1). FS&G.
--Oliver & Alison's Week. LC 80-17300. (Illus.). 32p. (gr. k-3). 1980. 9.95 (ISBN 0-374-35618-1). FS&G.
--Will You Count the Stars Without Me? (Illus.). 32p. 1979. 8.95 (ISBN 0-374-38433-9). FS&G.
Zaldivar, Gladys. Fabulacion De Enea-the Keeper of the Flame. Rivers, Elias L., tr. from Eng. & Span. (Coleccion Vortex). 67p. pap. 14.95 (ISBN 0-89729-200-6). Ediciones.
Zale, Eric M., ed. Proceedings of the Conference on Language & Language Behavior. LC 68-28144. 1968. 30.00x (ISBN 0-89197-906-9). Irvington.
Zaleski, M. B., ed. see International Convocation on Immunology, 7th, Niagra Falls, N. Y., July 1980, et al.
Zalewski, Leon, jt. auth. see Lunetta, Vincent.
Zaleznik, Abraham. Human Dilemmas of Leadership. LC 66-11480. 1966. 10.00x o.p. (ISBN 0-06-037160-9, HarpT). Har-Row.
Zalk, Sue, jt. auth. see Bittman, Sam.
Zalkind, Ronald. Getting Ahead in the Music Business. LC 79-7366. 1979. 15.00 (ISBN 0-02-872990-0); pap. 6.95 (ISBN 0-02-873000-3). Schirmer Bks.
Zalkind, Ronald, jt. auth. see Lambert, Dennis.
Zalkind, S., jt. auth. see Costello, Timothy.
Zalkind, Sheldon S., jt. ed. see Kalt, Neil C.
Zall, P. M., ed. Ben Franklin Laughing: Anecdotes from Original Sources by & About Benjamin Franklin. 1980. 9.95 (ISBN 0-520-04026-0). U of Cal Pr.
--Nest of Ninnies & Other English Jestbooks of the Seventeenth Century. LC 70-88091. 1970. 11.75x (ISBN 0-8032-0723-9). U of Nebr Pr.
Zall, P. M., ed. see Franklin, Benjamin.
Zall, Paul M., ed. Ben Franklin Laughing: Anecdotes from Original Sources by & About Benjamin Franklin. 216p. 1981. 12.95 (ISBN 0-520-04026-0). U of Cal Pr.
Zallen, Eugenia M., jt. auth. see Zallen, Harold.
Zallen, Harold & Zallen, Eugenia M. Ideas Plus Dollars: Research Methodology & Funding. LC 75-46502. (Illus.). 387p. 1976. 17.25 (ISBN 0-915582-00-7); microfiche 12.00 (ISBN 0-915582-01-5). Academic World.
Zallen, Harold & Zellen, Eugenia M. Ideas Plus Dollars: Research Methodology & Funding. 2nd ed. LC 79-55737. (Illus.). 1980. 12.95. Academic World.
Zaller, Robert. The Parliament of 1621: A Study in Constitutional Conflict. LC 77-104106. 1971. 20.00x (ISBN 0-520-01677-7). U of Cal Pr.
Zallinger, Peter. Prehistoric Animals. (Pictureback Ser.). (Illus.). 32p. (ps-3). 1981. PLB 4.99 (ISBN 0-394-93737-6); pap. 1.25 (ISBN 0-394-83737-1). Random.
Zalman Amit, jt. auth. see Sutherland, E. Ann.
Zaltman, G. & Wallendorf, M. Consumer Behavior: Basic Findings & Management Implications. LC 78-23335. 1979. text ed. 23.95x (ISBN 0-471-98126-5); tchrs. manual avail. (ISBN 0-471-04862-3). Wiley.
Zaltman, Gerald & Duncan, Robert. Strategies for Planned Change. LC 76-39946. 1977. 25.95 (ISBN 0-471-98131-1, Pub. by Wiley-Interscience). Wiley.
Zaltman, Gerald & Sikorski, Linda. Dynamic Educational Change: Models, Strategies, Tactics, & Management. LC 76-19645. (Illus.). 1977. 17.95 (ISBN 0-02-935750-0). Free Pr.
Zaltman, Gerald, jt. auth. see Levy, Sidney J.
Zaltman, Gerald, jt. auth. see Wallendorf, Melanie.
Zaltman, Gerald, jt. ed. see King, William R.
Zaltman, Gerald, et al. Innovations & Organizations. LC 73-5873. 224p. 1973. 18.95 (ISBN 0-471-98129-X, Pub. by Wiley-Interscience). Wiley.
Zamansky, H., jt. ed. see Frankel, F. H.
Zambotti, Geno, et al. College Chemistry in the Laboratory. 1980. 7.25 (ISBN 0-8403-1888-X). Kendall-Hunt.
Zambucka, Kristin. Ano' Ano: The Seed. pap. 8.50. Mawa Pub.
Zameeruddin, Qazi & Khanna, V. K. Solid Geometry. 1977. 15.00 (ISBN 0-7069-0560-1, Pub. by Vikas India). Advent Bk.
Zameeruddin, Qazi, et al. Business Mathematics. 600p. 1980. text ed. 18.95x (ISBN 0-7069-0752-3, Pub. by Vikas India). Advent Bk.
--Elementary Mathematics. 1975. 10.50 (ISBN 0-7069-0388-9, Pub. by Vikas India). Advent Bk.
Zamiatin, Eugeny. Navodenie. (Rus.). 1977. pap. 8.00 (ISBN 0-88233-240-6). Ardis Pubs.
Zamm, Alfred. Why Your House May Be Hazardous to Your Health. 1980. 9.95 (ISBN 0-671-24128-1). S&S.
Zammattio, Carlo, et al. Leonardo the Scientist. LC 80-18436. (Illus.). 192p. 1980. 9.95 (ISBN 0-07-007933-1). McGraw.
Zamoff, Richard B. Guide to the Assessment of Day Care Services & Needs at the Community Level. 1971. pap. 3.00 o.p. (ISBN 0-87766-072-7, 10007). Urban Inst.
Zamora, et al. Pet Basic I: Training Your Pet. 1981. 14.95 (ISBN 0-8359-5525-7); pap. 7.95 (ISBN 0-8359-5524-9). Reston.
Zampaglione, Gerardo. The Idea of Peace in Antiquity. Dunn, Richard, tr. from Italian. Orig. Title: Idea Della Pace Nel Mondo Antico. 344p. 1973. text ed. 20.00x (ISBN 0-8290-0341-X). Irvington.
Zamyatnin, A. A., jt. auth. see Gorbachev, V. M.
Zand, Dale. Management in a Knowledge Society. Newton, William R., ed. (Illus.). 224p. Date not set. 12.95 (ISBN 0-07-072743-0, P&RB). McGraw.
Zand, P., jt. auth. see Shepherd, W.
Zanden, James W. Human Development. 2nd ed. 665p. 1981. text ed. 16.95 (ISBN 0-394-32370-X); wkbk. 6.95 (ISBN 0-394-32371-8). Knopf.
Zanden, James W. Vander see Vander Zanden, James W.
Zander, Alvin. Groups at Work: Unresolved Issues in the Study of Organizations. LC 77-82918. (Social & Behavioral Science Ser). 1977. text ed. 11.95x (ISBN 0-87589-347-3). Jossey-Bass.
Zander, Hans. Harmonica Man. (gr. 1-3). 1977. pap. 1.50 (ISBN 0-590-10350-4, Schol Pap). Schol Bk Serv.
Zander, Karen S. Primary Nursing: Development & Management. LC 79-28837. 361p. 1980. text ed. 25.95 (ISBN 0-89443-170-6). Aspen Systems.
Zander, Karen S. & Bower, Kathleen A., eds. A Practical Manual for Patient-Teaching. LC 78-7039. 1978. pap. text ed. 15.95 (ISBN 0-8016-5678-8). Mosby.
Zander, Michael. Cases & Materials on the English Legal System. 3rd ed. (Law in Context Ser.). xxvii, 476p. 1980. 47.95x (ISBN 0-297-77822-6, Pub. by Weidenfeld & Nicholson England). Rothman.
--Cases & Materials on the English Legal System. (Law in Context Ser.). 484p. 1973. 19.50x o.p. (ISBN 0-297-99547-2). Rothman.
--The Law-Making Process. (Law in Context Ser.). 332p. 1980. 40.00x (ISBN 0-297-77750-5, Pub. by Weidenfeld & Nicolson England). Rothman.
Zanderer, Leo, jt. ed. see Salzman, Jack.
Zandi, I., ed. Advances in Solid-Liquid Flow in Pipes & Its Application. LC 77-120000. 1971. 50.00 (ISBN 0-08-015767-X). Pergamon.
Zandin, K., ed. Most Work Measurement Systems. (Industrial Engineering Ser.). 222p. 1980. 19.50 (ISBN 0-8247-6899-X). Dekker.
Zandt, Townes Van see Van Zandt, Townes.
Zane, Polly. The Jack Sprat Cookbook: Good Eating on a Low-Cholesterol, Low-Saturated-Fat Diet. LC 72-79701. 512p. 1980. pap. 6.95 (ISBN 0-06-090803-3, CN 803, CN). Har-Row.
--The Jack Sprat Cookbook, or Good Eating on a Low-Cholesterol Diet. LC 72-79701. (Illus.). 510p. 1973. 12.95 o.p. (ISBN 0-06-014801-2, HarpT). Har-Row.
Zaner, Richard M. The Context of Self: A Phenomenological Inquiry Using Medicine As a Clue. LC 80-18500. (Continental Thought Ser.: Vol. 1). (Illus.). xiv, 282p. 1981. 16.95x (ISBN 0-8214-0443-1); pap. 8.95x (ISBN 0-8214-0600-0). Ohio U Pr.
--The Way of Phenomenology: Criticism As a Philosophical Discipline. LC 77-114178. (Traditions in Philosophy Ser). 1970. pap. 5.50 (ISBN 0-672-63611-5). Pegasus.
--The Way of Phenomenology: Criticism As a Philosophical Discipline. LC 77-114178. 1970. 18.95x (ISBN 0-672-53611-0). Irvington.
Zang, Barbara, ed. How to Get Help for Kids: A Reference Guide to Services for Handicapped Children. 245p. 1980. pap. 29.95 (ISBN 0-915794-18-7). Gaylord Prof Pubns.
Zanger, Henry. Electronic Systems-Theory & Applications. LC 76-18714. (Illus.). 1977. text ed. 20.95 (ISBN 0-13-252155-5). P-H.
Zangwill, jt. auth. see Whitty.
Zangwill, Israel. Children of the Ghetto. x1893 ed. (Victorian Library Ser). (Illus.). 448p. 1977. Repr. of 1893 ed. text ed. 15.75x (ISBN 0-7185-5028-5, Leicester). Humanities.
Zangwill, O., ed. see International Symposium Held at St. Ode, Belgium, Oct. 1-3, 1979.
Zangwill, Willard I. Success with People: The Theory Z Approach to Mutual Achievement. 1976. pap. text ed. 10.95 (ISBN 0-256-01864-2). Irwin.
Zanjani, Sally S. The Unspiked Rail: Memoir of a Nevada Rebel. LC 80-39920. (Lancehead Ser.). (Illus.). xv, 357p. 1981. price not set (ISBN 0-87417-064-8). U of Nev Pr.
Zankel, Harry T. Stroke Rehabilitation: A Guide to the Rehabilitation of an Adult Patient Following a Stroke. (Illus.). 300p. 1971. text ed. 29.75 photocopy ed. spiral (ISBN 0-398-02446-4). C C Thomas.
Zann, Leon P. Living Together in the Sea. (Illus.). 416p. 1980. 20.00 (ISBN 0-87666-500-8, H-990). TFH Pubns.
Zannes, Estelle. Communication: The Widening Circle. LC 80-15150. (Speech Ser.). 324p. 1981. pap. text ed. 10.95 (ISBN 0-201-08997-1). A-W.
Zant, James H., jt. auth. see Keller, M. Wiles.
Zant, Mayphine V. Ballroom Dancing. (Illus.). 1978. 12.95 o.p. (ISBN 0-679-50796-5); pap. 6.95 o.p. (ISBN 0-679-50797-3). McKay.
Zant, Nancy Van see Van Zant, Nancy.
Zant, William Van see Van Zant, William.
Zanten, David Van see Van Zanten, David.
Zanzig, Thomas. Sharing the Christian Message: A Program Manual for Volunteer Catechists, Tenth Grade. 1977. pap. 9.95 (ISBN 0-88489-089-9); duplicating masters 4.95 (ISBN 0-88489-129-1). St Marys.
--Sharing the Christian Message: A Program Manual for Volunteer Catechists, 11th & 12th Grade. (Illus.). (gr. 11-12). 1979. pap. 38.00 (ISBN 0-88489-110-0); spiritmasters 9.95 (ISBN 0-88489-130-5). St Marys.
--Sharing the Christian Message: A Program Manual for Volunteer Catechist, Ninth Grade. 1977. pap. 9.95 (ISBN 0-88489-086-4); duplicating masters 4.95 (ISBN 0-88489-128-3). St Mary's.
--Understanding Your Faith: An Introduction to Catholic Christianity for Freshmen. LC 80-50258. (Illus.). 192p. (gr. 9). 1980. pap. text ed. 5.20x (ISBN 0-88489-115-1); tchr's guide 5.00x (ISBN 0-88489-122-4); spiritmasters 9.95 (ISBN 0-88489-131-3). St Mary's.
Zanzucchi, Anne M. Family Portrait, from a Mother's Diary. Szczesniak, Lenny, tr. from It. LC 81-80031. Orig. Title: Giorno per Giorno. 100p. 1981. pap. 2.95 (ISBN 0-911782-19-2). New City.
Zapata, Luis. Adonis Garcia: A Picaresque Novel. Lacey, E. A., tr. from Span. 192p. (Orig.). 1981. 20.00 (ISBN 0-917342-79-8); pap. 7.95 (ISBN 0-917342-79-8). Gay Sunshine.
Zapf, Hermann. About Alphabets. 1970. pap. 3.95 o.p. (ISBN 0-262-74003-6, 146). MIT Pr.
Zapp, E., jt. auth. see Pataki, L.
Zapp, Holly & Zapp, Ivar. The Story of Creation. LC 75-2799. 1975. pap. 2.50 o.p. (ISBN 0-88270-119-3). Logos.
Zapp, Ivar, jt. auth. see Zapp, Holly.
Zappalorti, Robert. Drawing Sharp Focus Still Lifes. 192p. 1981. 18.95 (ISBN 0-8230-1435-5). Watson-Guptill.
Zappia, V, et al, eds. Biochemical & Pharmacological Roles of Adenosylmethionine & the Central Nervous System: Proceedings of an International Round Table on Adenosylmethionine & the Central Nervous System, Naples, Italy, May 1978. (Illus.). 1979. 35.00 (ISBN 0-08-024929-9). Pergamon.
Zappler, Georg. Behind the Scenes at the Zoo. LC 76-42418. 1977. PLB 5.95 (ISBN 0-385-09514-7). Doubleday.
Zappler, Lisbeth. Nature's Oddballs. LC 76-42419. (gr. 7-9). 1978. PLB 5.95 (ISBN 0-385-08355-6). Doubleday.
Zappolo, Aurora. Discharge from Nursing Homes: 1977 National Nursing Home Survey. Cox, Klaudia, ed. (Ser. 13: No. 54). 60p. 1981. pap. 1.75 (ISBN 0-8406-0216-2). Natl Ctr Health Stats.
Zappulli, Cesare. The Power of Goodness. 1980. 3.00 (ISBN 0-8198-5800-5); pap. 2.00 (ISBN 0-8198-5801-3). Dghtrs St Paul.
Zar, Jerrold H. Biostatistical Analysis. (Illus.). 608p. 1974. ref. ed. 23.95 (ISBN 0-13-076984-3). P-H.
Zaranka, William. A Mirror Driven Through Nature: Vagrom Champ Bk. (No. 18). 48p. 1981. pap. 3.95 (ISBN 0-935552-00-6). Sparrow Pr.
Zarate, Stella G. Woman of the Maya. 1978. 7.50 o.p. (ISBN 0-682-49053-9). Exposition.
Zarb, Frank G., jt. auth. see Fabozzi, Frank J.
Zarb, George A., jt. auth. see Hickey, Judson C.
Zarb, George A., et al. Prosthodontic Treatment for Partially Edentulous Patients. 1978. text ed. 29.95 (ISBN 0-8016-5677-X). Mosby.
Zarbock, Barbara. The Complete Book of Rug Hooking. LC 71-83216. (Illus.). 128p. 1972. pap. 5.95 o.p. (ISBN 0-8069-8630-1). Sterling.
Zaremba, Joseph, ed. Mathematical Economics & Operations Research: A Guide to Information Sources. LC 73-17586. (Economics Information Guide Ser.: Vol. 10). 1978. 30.00 (ISBN 0-8103-1298-0). Gale.
--Statistics & Econometrics: A Guide to Information Sources. (Economics Information Guide Ser.: Vol. 15). 650p. 1980. 30.00 (ISBN 0-8103-1466-5). Gale.
Zaremba, M., jt. ed. see Laskiewicz, H. J.
Zaret, Thomas M. Predation & Freshwater Communities. LC 80-5399. (Illus.). 208p. 1980. text ed. 15.00x (ISBN 0-300-02349-9). Yale U Pr.
Zaretskei, Ze'Ev V. Mass Spectrometry of Steroids. LC 75-38916. 1976. 30.95 (ISBN 0-470-15225-7). Halsted Pr.
Zaretsky, Eli. Capitalism, the Family & Personal Life. 1976. pap. 3.95 (ISBN 0-06-090538-7, CN538, CN). Har-Row.
Zarian, Gostan. The Traveller & His Road. Baliozian, Ara, tr. from Armenian. LC 80-22809. 160p. (Orig.). 1981. pap. 5.95 (ISBN 0-935102-04-3). Ashod Pr.
Zaric, Z., ed. Heat & Mass Transfers in Flows with Separated Regions. LC 72-85858. 232p. 1975. pap. text ed. 29.00 (ISBN 0-08-017156-7). Pergamon.
Zaric, Z., ed. see International Advanced Course & Workshop on Thermal Effluent Disposal from Power Generation, Aug. 23-28, 1976, Dubrovnik, Yugoslavia.
Zariski, Oscar. Oscar Zariski, 4 vols. Lipman, J. & Teissier, B., eds. (Mathematicians of Our Time Ser.). 1979. Vol. 1. text ed. 32.50x (ISBN 0-262-08049-4); Vol. 2. text ed. 32.50x (ISBN 0-262-01038-0); Vol. 3. text ed. 40.00x (ISBN 0-262-24021-1). MIT Pr.
Zarit, Steven H., ed. Readings in Aging and Death: Contemporary Perspectives. (Contemporary Perspectives Readers Ser.). 1977. pap. text ed. 9.50 scp (ISBN 0-06-047056-9, HarpC); instructor's manual avail. (ISBN 0-685-75417-0). Har-Row.

Zarlenga, Peter. The Orator. LC 79-55798. (Illus.). 1980. 12.95 (ISBN 0-916728-28-5). Bks in Focus.
Zarlenga, Stephen A., ed. see Katz, Howard S.
Zarnecki, G. Art of the Medieval World: Architecture, Sculpture, Painting, the Sacred Arts. 1976. 21.95 (ISBN 0-13-047514-9). P-H.
Zaro, Joan S. A Guide for Beginning Psychotherapists. LC 77-76080. 1977. 27.50 (ISBN 0-521-21687-7); pap. 7.95 (ISBN 0-521-29230-1). Cambridge U Pr.
Zaroulis, N. L. The Poe Papers. 1978. pap. 1.75 o.s.i. (ISBN 0-515-04457-1). Jove Pubns.
Zaroulis, Nancy. Call the Darkness Light. 1980. pap. 2.95 (ISBN 0-451-09291-0, E9291, Sig). NAL.
Zarrella, John. Operating Systems: Concepts & Principles. LC 79-122639. (Microprocessor Software Engineering Concepts Ser.). (Illus., Orig.). 1979. pap. 7.95 (ISBN 0-935230-00-9). Microcomputer Appns.
--System Architecture. LC 80-82932. (Microprocessor Software Engineering Concepts Ser.). (Illus.). 240p. (Orig.). 1980. pap. 9.95 (ISBN 0-935230-02-5). Microcomputer Appns.
--Word Processing & Text Editing. LC 80-114189. (Microprocessor Software Engineering Concepts Ser.). (Illus.). 1980. pap. 7.95 (ISBN 0-935230-01-7). Microcomputer Appns.
Zarren, H. S. The Respiratory System: Disease, Diagnosis, Treatment. (Clinical Monographs Ser.). (Illus.). 1973. pap. 7.95 (ISBN 0-87618-056-X). R J Brady.
Zarren, Harvey. Health, Infection & Diseases. (Illus.). 1975. pap. 7.95 (ISBN 0-87618-064-0). R J Brady.
Zarrilli, Phillip B., ed. Martial Arts in Actor Training. 1981. 13.95x (ISBN 0-89676-052-9); pap. 10.00x (ISBN 0-89676-053-7). Drama Bk.
Zarrop, M. B. Optimal Experiment Design for Dynamic System Identification. (Lecture Notes in Control & Information Sciences: Vol. 21). 197p. 1980. pap. 14.50 (ISBN 0-387-09841-0). Springer-Verlag.
Zartman, I. William. Politics of Trade Negotiations Between Africa & the European Economic Community. LC 76-120765. (Center for International Studies, NYU Ser.). 1971. 13.50 (ISBN 0-691-05642-0). Princeton U Pr.
Zartman, I. William, ed. Elites in the Middle East. 270p. 1980. 24.95 (ISBN 0-03-055961-8). Praeger.
Zaruba, J. R. Questions & Answers on the Rules of the Road. 3rd ed. (Illus.). 1979. pap. text ed. 7.50x (ISBN 0-87033-262-7). Cornell Maritime.
Zashin, Elliot M. Civil Disobedience & Democratic Theory. LC 74-122283. 1972. 7.95 o.s.i. (ISBN 0-02-935710-1). Free Pr.
Zaslavsky, Robert. Platonic Myth & Platonic Writing. LC 80-5563. 306p. 1981. lib. bdg. 20.50 (ISBN 0-8191-1381-6); pap. text ed. 11.50 (ISBN 0-8191-1382-4). U Pr of Amer.
Zasloff, Joseph J. & Brown, MacAlister. Communist Indochina & U. S. Foreign Policy: Forging New Relations. LC 77-28462. 1978. lib. bdg. 24.00x (ISBN 0-89158-150-2). Westview.
Zasloff, Joseph J., jt. auth. see Langer, Paul F.
Zaslow, David. A Rose by Any Other Name. (Illus.). 96p. (Orig.). Date not set. pap. 5.00 (ISBN 0-89411-002-0). Onset Pubns.
Zassenhaus, Hans J. Theory of Groups. 2nd ed. LC 56-13058. 12.95 (ISBN 0-8284-0053-9). Chelsea Pub.
Zastrow, Charles H. Introduction to Social Welfare Institutions: Social Problems, Services, & Current Issues. 1978. 17.95x (ISBN 0-256-02090-6). Dorsey.
Zaten, David Van see Egbert, Donald D.
Zatuchni, Gerald, et al. Vaginal Contraception: New Developments. (PARFR Series on Fertility Regulation). (Illus.). 384p. 1980. text ed. 17.50 (ISBN 0-06-142901-5, Harper Medical). Har-Row.
Zatuchni, Gerald I., et al. Research Frontiers in Fertility Regulation. (Illus.). 416p. 1981. text ed. write for info. (ISBN 0-06-142902-3, Harper Medical). Har-Row.
Zaturenska, Marya. The Hidden Waterfall. LC 73-91288. 72p. 1974. 6.95 (ISBN 0-8149-0738-5). Vanguard.
Zaturenska, Marya, jt. auth. see Gregory, Horace.
Zaturenska, Marya, ed. see Rossetti, Christina.
Zaturenska, Marya, ed. see Teasdale, Sara.
Zatz, Joel L. Pharmaceutical Calculations. 2nd ed. LC 80-23382. 375p. 1981. 15.00 (ISBN 0-471-07757-7, Pub. by Wiley-Interscience). Wiley.
Zauberman, Alfred. Topics in Trade Coordination in Planned Economics. 108p. 1980. text ed. 32.50x (ISBN 0-8419-5085-7). Holmes & Meier.
Zauder, Howard L., jt. ed. see Stehling, Linda C.
Zaum, Marjorie. All About Cats As Pets. (Illus.). 64p. (gr. 3-5). 1981. PLB 6.97 (ISBN 0-686-69306-X). Messner.
Zauner, Lou, jt. auth. see Zauner, Phyllis.
Zauner, Phyllis. The Train Whistle's Echo: Story of Western Railroading. (Western Mini-Histories Ser.). (Illus.). 64p. (Orig.). 1980. pap. 3.00 (ISBN 0-936914-05-X). Zanel Pubns.
Zauner, Phyllis & Zauner, Lou. San Francisco, the Way It Was Then & Now. (Western Mini-Histories Ser.). (Illus.). 64p. (Orig.). 1980. pap. 3.00 (ISBN 0-936914-04-1). Zanel Pubns.
Zauner, Renate. Speaking of: Children's Posture Problems & the Injuries They Cause. Ray, Susan, tr. from Ger. LC 80-687464. (The Medical Adviser Ser.). (Illus.). 1980. pap. 3.95 (ISBN 0-8326-2244-3, 7459). Delair.
Zaustinsky, E. M. Spaces with Non-Symmetric Distance. LC 52-42839. (Memoirs: No. 34). 1978. pap. 5.20 (ISBN 0-8218-1234-3, MEMO-34). Am Math.
Zavala, Albert & Paley, James J., eds. Personal Appearance Identification. (Illus.). 352p. 1972. pap. 23.75 (ISBN 0-398-02447-2). C C Thomas.
Zavala, Silvio. The Defence of Human Rights in Latin America (16th to 18th Centuries) 1964. pap. 2.50 (ISBN 92-3-100571-5, U152, UNESCO). Unipub.
Zavarin, Valentina, tr. see Uspensky, Boris.
Zavarzadeh, Mas ud. The Mythopoeic Reality: The Postwar American Nonfiction Novel. 271p. 1980. pap. 5.95 (ISBN 0-252-00645-3). U of Ill Pr.
Zavatsky, Bill. Theories of Rain & Other Poems. LC 74-34537. 1975. 10.00 (ISBN 0-915342-08-1); pap. 4.00 (ISBN 0-915342-03-0). SUN.
Zavodskaya, I. S., et al. Neurogenic Heart Lesions. LC 80-40436. (Illus.). 150p. 1980. 58.00 (ISBN 0-08-025482-9). Pergamon.
Zavoral, Nolan & Sanders, Peter. In the Chutes. LC 75-22008. (The Venture Ser, a Reading Incentive Program). (Illus.). 76p. (gr. 7-12,RL 4.5-6.5). 1975. text ed. 23.25 ea. pack of 5 (ISBN 0-8172-0243-9, Raintree Editions). Follett.
Zawadiwsky, Christine. The World at Large. 1978. pap. 24.00 o.p. (ISBN 0-931460-06-9). Bieler.
Zawadzki, W., ed. Narrow Gap Semiconductors: Physics & Applications. (Lecture Notes in Physics Ser.: Vol. 133). 572p. 1981. pap. 37.20 (ISBN 0-387-10261-2). Springer-Verlag.
Zawodny, J. K. Death in the Forest: The Story of the Katyn Forest Massacre. LC 62-16639. (Illus.). 235p. 1980. text ed. 14.00 (ISBN 0-268-00849-3); pap. text ed. 7.95 (ISBN 0-268-00850-7). U of Notre Dame Pr.
Zayas, Zoila de see De Zayas, Zoila.
Zayas-Bazan, Eduardo, tr. see Montaner, Carlos A.
Zaydan, Jirji. Umayyads & Abbasids. Margoliuth, D. S., tr. from Arabic. LC 79-2889. 325p. 1981. Repr. of 1907 ed. 26.50 (ISBN 0-8305-0056-1). Hyperion Conn.
Zbar, Paul B., jt. auth. see Electronic Industries Association.
Zbinden, G., ed. Fine Needle Aspiration Biopsy of the Rat Liver - Cytological, Cytochemical & Biochemical Methods: Proceedings of a Workshop on Technique & Application of Fine Needle Aspiration Biology in Experimental Toxicology, Zurich, 1979. (Illus.). 70p. 1980. 29.00 (ISBN 0-08-025508-6). Pergamon.
Zbinden, G. & Gross, F., eds. Pharmacological Methods in Toxicology. 1979. text ed. 160.00 (ISBN 0-08-024900-0); pap. text ed. 80.00 (ISBN 0-08-021544-0). Pergamon.
Zderad, Loretta T., jt. auth. see Paterson, Josephine G.
Zea, Leopoldo. Latin-American Mind. Abbott, James H. & Dunham, Lowell, trs. (Illus.). 1970. 14.95x o.p. (ISBN 0-8061-0563-1); pap. 6.95x o.p. (ISBN 0-8061-1278-6). U of Okla Pr.
Zearfoss, Dr. Robert Foreword by see Baylis, Fred S.
Zebroff, Kareen & Zebroff, Peter. Yoga for Kids. LC 78-52346. (Illus.). (gr. 7 up). 1978. 7.95 (ISBN 0-8069-4128-6); PLB 7.49 (ISBN 0-8069-4129-4). Sterling.
Zebroff, Peter, jt. auth. see Zebroff, Kareen.
Zebrowski, George. The Best of Thomas M. Scortia. LC 80-2349. 288p. 1981. 11.95 (ISBN 0-385-14695-7). Doubleday.
Zecher, Richard, jt. auth. see Phillips, Susan.
Zechlin, Katharina. Creative Enamelling & Jewelry-Making. Kuttner, Paul, tr. LC 65-20877. (gr. 10 up). 1965. 6.95 (ISBN 0-8069-5062-5); PLB 6.69 (ISBN 0-8069-5063-3). Sterling.
--Games You Can Build Yourself. LC 74-82327. (Illus.). 64p. (gr. 6 up). 1975. 9.95 (ISBN 0-8069-5308-X); PLB 9.29 (ISBN 0-8069-5309-8). Sterling.
--Making Games in Wood. LC 80-54353. (Illus.). 80p. 1981. pap. 6.95 (ISBN 0-8069-8996-3). Sterling.
Zechman, Roberta, jt. auth. see Radeloff, Deanna J.
Zechmann. Grilling. 1981. 8.95 (ISBN 0-8120-5399-0). Barron.
Zechner, L. see Von Wiesner, J. & Von Regel, C.
Zeck, Gerry & Zeck, Pam. Sternwheel Paddleboats. (Illus.). 32p. (gr. k-3). Date not set. PLB 5.95 (ISBN 0-87614-143-2). Carolrhoda Bks.
Zeck, Pam, jt. auth. see Zeck, Gerry.
Zeder, Melinda A., jt. ed. see Meadow, Richard H.
Zeder, Susan. Ozma of Oz: A Tale of Time. (Orig.). 1981. playscript 2.00 (ISBN 0-87602-233-6). Anchorage.
Zedlewski, Sheila R., jt. auth. see Wertheimer, Richard F., II.
Zee, David S., jt. auth. see Leigh, R. John.
Zee, John Van Der see Van Der Zee, John.
Zee, John Van Der see Van Der Zee, John & Jacobson, Boyd.
Zee, Karen Van Der see Van Der Zee, Karen.
Zee Karen Van, Der see Van Der Zee, Karen.
Zeeman, E. C. Catastrophe Theory: Selected Papers (1972-1977) LC 77-21459. 1977. text ed. 33.50 (ISBN 0-201-09014-7, Adv Bk Prog); pap. text ed. 21.50 (ISBN 0-201-09015-5). A-W.
Zeevy, Rechavam, ed. see Har-El, Menashe.
Zegel, Jon M. The Shelf Book: Complete Do-It-Yourself Systems for Building Shelves in Living Rooms, Kitchens, Closets, Basements, Garages, Etc. LC 77-12366. (Illus.). 1977. lib. bdg. 12.90 (ISBN 0-89471-001-X); pap. 5.95 (ISBN 0-89471-000-1). Running Pr.
Zegger, Hrisey D. May Sinclair. (English Authors Ser: No. 192). 1976. lib. bdg. 12.50 (ISBN 0-8057-6666-9). Twayne.
Zeggeren, F. Van see Van Zeggeren, F. & Storey, S. H.
Zegveld, Walter, jt. auth. see Rothwell, Roy.
Zehavi, A. M., ed. The Complete Junior Encyclopedia of Transportation. LC 72-11310. (Illus.). 288p. (gr. 3 up). 1973. PLB 8.87 o.p. (ISBN 0-531-02596-9). Watts.
--Handbook of the World's Religions. LC 73-9283. (gr. 7-12). 1973. PLB 9.90 o.p. (ISBN 0-531-02644-2). Watts.
Zehery, Miklos, tr. see Racz, Attila.
Zehr, Paul M. God Dwells with His People. 216p. 1981. pap. 7.95 (ISBN 0-8361-1939-8). Herald Pr.
Zehr, Wilmer, jt. auth. see Campion, Michael.
Zehring, John W. Careers in State & Local Government. LC 80-67448. (Illus.). 236p. 1980. pap. 10.95 (ISBN 0-912048-15-8). Garrett Pk.
--Preparing for Work. 1980. pap. 2.50 (ISBN 0-88207-582-9). Victor Bks.
Zehring, Karen. The Corporate Finance Sourcebook, 1979. 1979. 79.50 o.p. (ISBN 0-07-072775-9, P&RB). McGraw.
Zeidenstein, Sondra, ed. Learning About Rural Women. (Studies in Family Planning Ser.: Vol. 10, Nos. 11-12). 118p. (Orig.). 1979. pap. 2.50. Population Coun.
Zeidner, Lisa. Customs. LC 80-21478. 288p. 11.95 (ISBN 0-394-51475-0). Knopf.
Zeig, Jeffrey K., ed. see Erickson, Milton H.
Zeiger, Arthur, jt. auth. see Waldhorn, Arthur.
Zeigler, jt. auth. see Dye.
Zeigler, B. P., et al, eds. see Symposium on Modelling & Simulation Methodology, Israel, August 1978.
Zeigler, Earle F. Problems in the History & Philosophy of Physical Education & Sport. LC 68-18594. (Foundations of Physical Education Series). (Orig.). 1969. pap. 7.95 ref. ed. (ISBN 0-13-716787-3). P-H.
Zeigler, Earle F., ed. History of Physical Education & Sport. LC 78-9066. (P-H Foundations of Physical Education & Sport Ser.). (Illus.). 1979. ref. ed. 15.95 (ISBN 0-13-391656-1). P-H.
Zeigler, Earle F. & Spaeth, Marcia J., eds. Administrative Theory & Practice in Physical Education & Athletics. (Illus.). 496p. 1975. 17.95 (ISBN 0-13-008581-2). P-H.
Zeigler, L., jt. auth. see Van Dallen, H.
Zeigler, Mildred. Onward & Upward. 60p. 1981. pap. 4.00 (ISBN 0-86629-027-3). Sunrise MO.
Zeigler, Sherilyn & Johnson, J. Douglas. Creative Strategy & Tactics in Advertising: A Managerial Approach to Copywriting & Production. LC 80-23899. (Advertising Ser.). 360p. 1981. text ed. 19.95 (ISBN 0-88244-229-5). Grid Pub.
Zeigler, Sherilyn K. & Howard, Herbert H. Broadcast Advertising: A Comprehensive Working Textbook. LC 78-50048. (Advertising & Journalism Ser.). 1978. pap. text ed. 10.50 (ISBN 0-88244-167-1). Grid Pub.
Zeiler, Michael D. & Harzem, Peter, Advances in Analysis of Behaviour: Reinforcement & the Organisation of Behaviour, Vol. 1. LC 78-31697. (Wiley Series on Advances in Analysis of Behaviour). 1980. 55.00 (ISBN 0-471-27573-5, Pub. by Wiley-Interscience). Wiley.
Zeiler, Michael D., jt. auth. see Harzem, Peter.
Zeiller, Warren. Tropical Marine Invertebrates of Southern Florida & the Bahama Islands. LC 74-2467. (Illus.). 144p. 1974. 32.95x (ISBN 0-471-98153-2, Pub. by Wiley-Interscience). Wiley.
Zeine, Zeine N. Arab-Turkish Relations & the Emergence of Arab Nationalism. LC 80-25080. 156p. 1981. Repr. of 1958 ed. lib. bdg. 19.75x (ISBN 0-313-22705-5, ZEAT). Greenwood.
Zeines, Ben. Transistor Circuit Analysis & Application. (Illus.). 448p. 1976. 18.95x o.p. (ISBN 0-87909-837-6); instrs' manual avail. o.p. Reston.
Zeisel, John. Inquiry by Design: Tools for Environment - Behavior. LC 80-14292. (Basic Concepts in Environment & Behavior Ser.). (Orig.). 1980. pap. text ed. 8.95 (ISBN 0-8185-0375-0). Brooks-Cole.
Zeisel, William, jt. ed. see Rosof, Patricia J.
Zeiss, P. Anthony & Smith, Noel T. Broadcast Announcer's License Manual: A Guide to FCC Third Class Exam. (Illus.). (gr. 10 up). 1976. pap. 7.15 (ISBN 0-8104-0826-0). Hayden.
Zeitlin, Irving. Ideology & the Development of Sociological Theory. 1968. text ed. 17.95 (ISBN 0-13-449561-6). P-H.
--Rethinking Sociology: A Critique of Contemporary Theory. (Sociology Ser.). 300p. 1973. 17.95 (ISBN 0-13-778654-9). P-H.
Zeitlin, Irving M. Ideology & the Development of Sociological Theory. 2nd ed. (P-H Ser. in Sociology). (Illus.). 336p. 1981. text ed. 17.95 (ISBN 0-13-449769-4). P-H.
--The Social Condition of Humanity: An Introduction to Sociology. 432p. 1981. pap. text ed. 11.95x (ISBN 0-19-502734-5). Oxford U Pr.
Zeitlin, Marian F., jt. ed. see Austin, James E.
Zeitlin, Patty. A Song Is a Rainbow: Body Movement, Music, & Rythym Instruments in the Nursery School & Kindergarten. 336p. (Orig.). pap. 12.95 (ISBN 0-8302-8196-7). Goodyear.
Zeitlin, S., ed. The Book of Judith. 15.00 (ISBN 0-685-55556-9, Pub. by Dropsie U Pr). Ktav.
Zeitlin, Shirley. Kindergarten Screening. (Illus.). 304p. 1976. 19.75 (ISBN 0-398-03574-1). C C Thomas.
Zeitlin, Solomon. Who Crucified Jesus? 1976. pap. 4.95 (ISBN 0-8197-0013-4). Bloch.
Zeitz. Private Urban Renewal: A Different Residential Trend. LC 78-19568. (Illus.). 1979. 15.95 (ISBN 0-669-02627-1). Lexington Bks.
Zekman, Pamela, jt. auth. see Smith, Zay N.
Zekowski, Arlene & Berne, Stanley. Cardinals & Saints. LC 58-11713. 1958. 75.00 (ISBN 0-913844-10-1). Am Canadian.
Zekowski, Arlene, jt. auth. see Berne, Stanley.
Zelany, Roger. The Changing Land. 224p. 1981. pap. 2.50 (ISBN 0-345-25389-2, Del Rey). Ballantine.
--My Name Is Legion. 224p. (Orig.). 1981. pap. 2.25 (Del Rey). Ballantine.
Zelayeta, Elena. Elena's Secrets of Mexican Cooking. 1968. pap. 4.95 (ISBN 0-385-00197-5, Dolp). Doubleday.
Zelaznak, Shirley. Backpacking. Schroeder, Howard, ed. LC 79-27800. (Back to Nature). (Illus.). (gr. 3-5). 1980. lib. bdg. 5.95 (ISBN 0-89686-069-8). Crestwood Hse.
Zelazny, Jack. Jack of Shadows. pap. 1.75 (ISBN 0-451-09370-4, E9370, Sig). NAL.
Zelazny, Roger. Changeling. 1980. pap. 6.95 (ISBN 0-441-10256-5). Ace Bks.
--The Courts of Chaos. 1979. pap. 1.75 (ISBN 0-380-47175-2, 47175). Avon.
--Creatures of Light & Darkness. 1976. pap. 1.50 (ISBN 0-380-01122-0, 35956). Avon.
--The Dream Master. 192p. 1975. pap. 1.95 (ISBN 0-441-16705-5). Ace Bks.
--The Dream Master. (Science Fiction Ser.). 1976. Repr. of 1966 ed. lib. bdg. 10.00 (ISBN 0-8398-2345-2). Gregg.
--Four for Tomorrow. 192p. 1973. pap. 1.95 (ISBN 0-441-24904-3). Ace Bks.
--The Hand of Oberon. 1977. pap. 1.75 (ISBN 0-380-01664-8, 51318). Avon.
--Isle of the Dead. (Science Fiction Ser.). 208p. 1976. Repr. of 1969 ed. lib. bdg. 11.00 (ISBN 0-8398-2346-0). Gregg.
--Lord of Light. 1976. pap. 2.25 (ISBN 0-380-01403-3, 44834). Avon.
--My Name Is Legion. LC 75-44242. 224p. (Orig.). 1976. pap. 2.25 (ISBN 0-345-29522-6). Ballantine.
--This Immortal. 192p. 1975. pap. 2.25 (ISBN 0-441-80696-1). Ace Bks.
Zeldin, David. Educational Ideas of Charles Fourier. LC 67-31331. 1969. 22.50x (ISBN 0-678-05019-8). Kelley.
Zeldin, Dick. A Tennis Guide to the USA: Where to Play in the Most Traveled Cities. 1980. pap. 7.95 (ISBN 0-531-09922-9, C25). Watts.
Zeldin, Mary-Barbara. Freedom & the Critical Undertaking: Essays on Kant's Later Critiques. LC 80-17553. (Sponsor Ser.). 346p. (Orig.). 1980. pap. 21.75 (ISBN 0-8357-0525-0, SS-00143). Univ Microfilms.
Zeldin, Theodore. France, Eighteen Forty-Eight to Nineteen Forty-Five: Ambition & Love. 1979. pap. 8.95 (ISBN 0-19-285090-3, GB 587, GB). Oxford U Pr.

--France Eighteen Forty-Eight to Nineteen Forty-Five: Politics & Anger. (Illus.). 1979. pap. 8.95 (ISBN 0-19-285082-2, GB578, GB). Oxford U Pr.
--France Eighteen Forty-Eight to Nineteen Forty-Five: Taste & Corruption. 448p. 1980. pap. 8.95 (ISBN 0-19-285100-4, GB 620). Oxford U Pr.
--France 1848-1945: Ambition, Love & Politics, Vol. 1. (Oxford History of Modern Europe Ser.). (Illus.). 828p. 1973. 45.00x (ISBN 0-19-822104-5). Oxford U Pr.
--France, 1848-1945: Intellect, Taste, & Anxiety, Vol. 2. (Oxford History of Modern Europe Ser.). 1977. text ed. 49.50x (ISBN 0-19-822125-8). Oxford U Pr.
Zeldin, Theodore, ed. Conflicts in French Society: Anticlericalism, Education & Morals in the Nineteenth Century. (St. Anthony's Publications). 1971. text ed. 17.95x o.p. (ISBN 0-04-301023-7). Allen Unwin.
Zeldis, Chayym, ed. May My Words Feed Others: An Anthology of Verse & Fiction from the Reconstructionist Magazine. LC 72-6377. 284p. 1973. 12.95 o.p. (ISBN 0-498-01249-2). A S Barnes.
Zelenev, Y. V., jt. ed. see Bartenev, G. M.
Zeleny, Jindrich. The Logic of Marx. Carver, Terrell, ed. 251p. 1980. 27.50x (ISBN 0-8476-6767-7). Rowman
Zeleny, Lawrence. Bluebird: How You Can Help Its Fight for Survival. LC 74-22832. (Midland Bks.: No. 212). (Illus.). 192p. 1976. pap. 4.95x (ISBN 0-253-20212-4). Ind U Pr.
Zeleny, Milan. Multiple Criteria Decision Making. 1981. write for info instrs.' manual (ISBN 0-07-072795-3, C); price not set instr's manual (ISBN 0-07-072796-1). McGraw.
Zeleny, Milan, ed. Autopoiesis, Dissipative Structures & Spontaneous Social Orders. (AAAS Selected Symposium Ser.: No. 55). 150p. 1980. lib. bdg. 20.00x (ISBN 0-86531-035-1). Westview.
Zelermyer, William. Invasion of Privacy. LC 59-15386. 1956. 10.00x (ISBN 0-8156-0017-8). Syracuse U Pr.
Zelevansky, Paul. The Book of Takes. 1976. 15.00 (ISBN 0-9605610-0-5). Zartscorp.
--The Case for the Burial of Ancestors, Bk. 1. 1981. 25.00 (ISBN 0-9605610-3-X); pap. 15.00 (ISBN 0-9605610-2-1). Zartscorp.
Zeleznak, Shirley. Camping. Schroeder, Howard, ed. LC 80-425. (Back to Nature Sports Ser.). (Illus.). 1980. lib. bdg. 5.95 (ISBN 0-89686-071-X). Crestwood Hse.
--Jogging. Schroeder, Howard, ed. (Back to Nature Ser.). (Illus.). (gr. 3-5). 1979. lib. bdg. 5.95 (ISBN 0-89686-068-X). Crestwood Hse.
Zelickson, Sue, et al, eds. Minnesota Heritage Cookbook. LC 79-52859. (Illus.). 1979. 6.00 (ISBN 0-9602796-0-1). Am Cancer Minn.
Zeligs, Rose. Children's Experience with Death. 264p. 1974. 14.75 (ISBN 0-398-02984-9). C C Thomas.
Zelinsky, Daniel. First Course in Linear Algebra. 2nd ed. 1973. text ed. 18.95 (ISBN 0-12-779060-8). Acad Pr.
Zelinsky, Paul O. The Maid & the Mouse & the Odd-Shaped House. LC 80-2774. (Illus.). 32p. (ps-2). 1981. PLB 9.95 (ISBN 0-396-07938-5). Dodd.
Zelinsky, Wilbur. The Cultural Geography of the United States. LC 72-4503. (Illus.). 176p. 1973. pap. 6.95 ref. ed. (ISBN 0-13-195495-4). P-H.
--Prologue to Population Geography. (Illus.). 1966. pap. 8.95 ref. ed. (ISBN 0-13-730788-8). P-H.
Zelizer, Viviana. Morals & Markets. LC 78-31205. 1979. 17.50x (ISBN 0-231-04570-0). Columbia U Pr.
Zelkind, Irving & Sprug, Joseph. Time Research: 1172 Studies. 1974. 10.00 (ISBN 0-8108-0768-8). Scarecrow.
Zelko, L. International Value-International Prices. LC 80-50648. 153p. 1980. 17.50 (ISBN 90-286-0040-X). Sijthoff & Noordhoff.
Zelkowitz, Marvin V., et al. Principles of Software Engineering & Design. LC 78-27315. (Illus.). 1979. text ed. 22.95 (ISBN 0-13-710202-X). P-H.
Zell, Hans, ed. Reader's Guide to Contemporary African Literature. 2nd, rev ed. 300p. 1981. text ed. 20.00x (ISBN 0-686-69153-9, Africana); pap. text ed. 10.00x (ISBN 0-8419-0640-8). Holmes & Meier.
Zellen, Eugenia M., jt. auth. see Zallen, Harold.
Zeller, Ann, jt. auth. see Weidenaar, Reynold H.
Zeller, Eduard. Outlines of the History of Greek Philosophy. 1980. Repr. of 1931 ed. text ed. 4.50 (ISBN 0-486-23920-9). Dover.
Zeller, Hubert Van see Van Zeller, Hubert.
Zeller, Richard A., jt. auth. see Carmines, Edward G.
Zellers, Margaret. Austria...the Inn Way. 162p. 1981. 4.95 (ISBN 0-937334-01-4). Berkshire Traveller.
--Caribbean...the Inn Way. rev. ed. 240p. 1980. 4.95 (ISBN 0-937334-00-6). Berkshire Traveller.
--Fielding's Caribbean, 1981. rev. ed. LC 79-64015. 1981. Fieldingflex 10.95 (ISBN 0-688-03713-5). Fielding.
Zelles, T., ed. Saliva & Salivation: Proceedings of a Satellite Symposium to the 28th International Congress of Physiological Held at Szekesfehervar, Hungary, 1980. LC 80-41878. (Advances in Physiological Sciences: Vol. 28). (Illus.). 500p. 1981. 60.00 (ISBN 0-08-027349-1). Pergamon.
Zelmer, A. C. Community Media Handbook. 2nd ed. LC 79-12989. (Illus.). 430p. 1979. 16.50 (ISBN 0-8108-1223-1). Scarecrow.
Zelon, Helen, ed. Focus on Health: Issues & Events of 1979. LC 80-1719. (News in Print Ser.). (Illus.). 1980. lib. bdg. 24.95x (ISBN 0-405-12879-7). Arno.
Zelonky, Joy. I Can't Always Hear You. LC 79-23891. (Life & Living from a Child's Point of View Ser.). (Illus.). (gr. k-5). 1980. PLB 9.65 (ISBN 0-8172-1355-4). Raintree Child.
--My Best Friend Moved Away. LC 79-24111. (Life & Living from a Child's Point of View Ser.). (Illus.). (gr. k-5). 1980. PLB 9.65 (ISBN 0-8172-1353-8). Raintree Child.
Zelter, M. Exploring Shorthand. 96p. 1980. text ed. 4.60 (ISBN 0-7715-0735-6). Forkner.
Zeltner, Gerda. Das Ich Ohne Gewaehr: Gegenwartsautoren Aus der Schweiz. (Ger.). 1980. pap. 13.00 (ISBN 3-288-04743-8, Pub. by Insel Verlag Germany). Suhrkamp.
Zeltner, Philip M., jt. ed. see Mulvaney, Robert J.
Zelzany, Roger. Isle of the Dead. 192p. 1976. pap. 1.95 (ISBN 0-441-37469-7). Ace Bks.
Zemach, Harve. Judge. LC 79-87209. (Illus.). 48p. (ps-3). 1969. 9.95 (ISBN 0-374-33960-0). FS&G.
--A Penny a Look: An Old Story. LC 71-161373. (Illus.). (ps-3). 1971. 6.95 (ISBN 0-374-35793-5). FS&G.
Zemach, Margot. Jake & Honeybunch Go to Heaven. (Illus.). 40p. (ps up). Date not set. 10.95 (ISBN 0-374-33652-0). FS&G.
Zemach, Margot, retold by. & illus. It Could Always Be Worse: A Yiddish Folk Tale. LC 76-53895. 32p. (ps-3). 1977. 7.95 (ISBN 0-374-33650-4). FS&G.
Zeman, Z. & Zoubek, J., eds. East-West Trade 1975: International Yearbook. 170p. 1976. text ed. 140.00 (ISBN 0-08-019504-0). Pergamon.
Zeman, Z. A. Gentlemen Negotiators: A Diplomatic History of World War One. LC 70-108149. 1971. 9.95 o.s.i. (ISBN 0-02-633450-X). Macmillan.
Zeman, Zbynek. The Masaryks: The Making of Czechoslovakia. LC 76-2316. (Illus.). 230p. 1976. text ed. 19.50x (ISBN 0-06-497968-7). B&N.
Zemansky, Mark & Dittman, Richard. Heat & Thermodynamics. 6th ed. (Illus.). 560p. 1981. text ed. 22.95 (ISBN 0-07-072808-9, C). McGraw.
Zemansky, Mark W. Temperatures Very Low & Very High. 144p. 1981. pap. price not set (ISBN 0-486-24072-X). Dover.
Zemel, Carol M. The Formation of a Legend: van Gogh Criticism, Eighteen Ninety to Nineteen Twenty. Kuspit, Donald B., ed. (Studies in Fine Arts: Criticism). 280p. 1981. 27.95 (ISBN 0-8357-1094-7, Pub. by UMI Res Pr). Univ Microfilms.
Zemel, Z. & Hyslop, N. St. G., eds. Biometeorology: Proceedings of the Eighth International Biometeorological Congress 9-15 September 1979.Supplement to Volume 24 of the International Journal of Biometeorology, No.7, Pt.1. vi, 150p. 1980. pap. text ed. 44.75 (ISBN 90-265-0349-0). Swets North Am.
Zemel, Z., ed. see Eighth International Biometeorological Congress 9-15 September 1979.
Zemelman, Steven. Making Sense of It: Patterns in English Grammar. 1980. pap. text ed. 6.95 (ISBN 0-13-547570-8). P-H.
Zemelman Merino, Hugo, jt. auth. see Petras, James.
Zemlin, W. R. Speech & Hearing Science. 2nd ed. (Illus.). 704p. 1981. text ed. 23.95 (ISBN 0-13-827378-2). P-H.
Zempel, Edward N., jt. auth. see Verkler, Linda A.
Zempel, Edward N. & Verkler, Linda A., eds. A First Edition? Statements of Selected North American, British Commonwealth, & Irish Publishers on Their Methods of Designating First Editions. LC 77-89503. 1977. 12.50 (ISBN 0-930358-00-7); pap. 7.95 (ISBN 0-930358-01-5). Spoon River.
Zenderland, Leila, ed. Recycling the Past: Popular Uses of American History. LC 77-20306. 1978. 15.00 o.p. (ISBN 0-8122-7740-6); pap. 5.95x (ISBN 0-8122-1095-6). U of Pa Pr.
Zenger, Sharon & Zenger, Weldon. Writing & Evaluating Curriculum Guide. LC 73-77593. 1973. pap. 3.95 o.p. (ISBN 0-8224-7506-5). Pitman Learning.
Zenger, Weldon, jt. auth. see Zenger, Sharon.
Zenkovsky, Serge A. Pan-Turkism & Islam in Russia. LC 60-5399. (Russian Research Center Studies: No. 36). 1960. 17.50x (ISBN 0-674-65350-5). Harvard U Pr.
Zenos, A. C. The Son of Man. (Short Course Ser.). 145p. Repr. of 1914 ed. 2.95 (ISBN 0-567-08312-8). Attic Pr.
Zentmyer, Earl. The Ebony Image. Date not set. 12.95 (ISBN 0-87949-133-7). Ashley Bks.
Zentmyer, George A., ed. Phytophthora Cinna Moni & the Diseases It Causes. (Monograph Ser.: No. 10). 96p. 1980. 8.00 (ISBN 0-89054-030-6). Am Phytopathol Soc.
Zentner, Carola. Twins. LC 75-2914. (Illus.). 128p. 1975. 11.95 (ISBN 0-7153-6997-0). David & Charles.
Zentner, Judith P., jt. auth. see Murray, Ruth B.
Zentner, Wendy W. The Victorian Cookery Book. LC 79-66496. (Victorian Ser.: Vol. 1). (Illus., Orig.). 1979. pap. 7.95 (ISBN 0-934950-01-6). Zentner Pubns.
Zenz, Carl, ed. Developments in Occupational Medicine. (Illus.). 448p. 1980. 45.75. Year Bk Med.
--Occupational Medicine: Principles & Practical Applications. (Illus.). 944p. 1975. 65.00 (ISBN 0-8151-9864-7). Year Bk Med.
Zenz, Gary L. Purchasing & the Management of Materials. 5th ed. 600p. 1981. text ed. 21.95 (ISBN 0-471-06091-7); tchrs.' ed. avail. (ISBN 0-471-08935-4). Wiley.
Zepke, Brent E. Business Statistics: An Introduction. Cone, Nancy, ed. LC 78-21440. (College Outline Ser.). 192p. (Orig.). pap. text ed. 4.95 (ISBN 0-06-460180-3, CO 180, COS). Har-Row.
--Law for Non-Lawyers. (Littlefield, Adams Quality Paperbacks: No. 355). 336p. (Orig.). 1981. pap. 4.95 (ISBN 0-8226-0355-1). Littlefield.
Zepp, Ira G., Jr. & Palmer, Melvyn D., eds. Drum Major for a Dream: Poetic Tributes to Martin Luther King, Jr. 1976. 12.00 (ISBN 0-89253-801-5); flexible cloth 8.00 (ISBN 0-89253-802-3). Ind-US Inc.
Zerchykov, Ross, jt. auth. see Stanton, Jim.
Zerchykov, Ross, jt. ed. see Davies, Don.
Zerchykov, Ross, et al. Leading the Way: State Mandates for School Advisory Council in California, Florida, & South Carolina. 175p. (Orig.). 1980. pap. 6.00 (ISBN 0-917754-15-8). Inst Responsive.
Zerman, Melvyn B. Beyond a Reasonable Doubt: Understanding the American Jury System. 9.95 (ISBN 0-690-04094-6). T y Crowell.
Zerna, Wolfgang, jt. auth. see Green, Albert E.
Zerne, Winnie. Maria, Daughter of Shadow. LC 73-89474. (Desting Ser.). 1976. pap. 4.95 (ISBN 0-8163-0224-3, 13211-8). Pacific Pr Pub Assn.
Zernich, Theodore, ed. Careers in the Visual Arts: Options, Training & Employment. 64p. 1980. 4.75 (ISBN 0-686-27493-8). Natl Art Ed.
Zeron, Edward. What Catholics Should Know About Jews: And Other Christians. 1980. pap. 3.25 (ISBN 0-697-01739-7). Wm C Brown.
Zerov, Mykola. Do Dzherel: Istorychno-Literaturni Ta Krytychni Statti. LC 68-53064. (Ukra.). 1967. text ed. 15.00 (ISBN 0-918884-15-2). Slavia Lib.
Zerwick, Chloe. A Short History of Glass. (Illus.). 95p. 1981. pap. price not set (ISBN 0-486-24158-0). Dover.
--A Short History of Glass. LC 79-57251. (Illus.). 96p. 1980. pap. 5.00 (ISBN 0-87290-072-X). Corning.
Zesch, Lindy. TCG Survey 1977. 1978. pap. 4.00 o.p. (ISBN 0-930452-06-2, Pub. by Theatre Comm). Pub Ctr Cult Res.
Zetterling, Mai. Bird of Passage. LC 76-13050. 1976. 7.95 o.p. (ISBN 0-312-08120-0). St Martin.
Zettl, Herbert. Television Production Handbook. 3rd ed. 1976. 19.95x (ISBN 0-534-00414-8); 6.95x (ISBN 0-534-00530-6). Wadsworth Pub.
Zettler, Howard E., ed. Ologies & Isms: A Thematic Dictionary. LC 78-8328. 1978. 30.00 (ISBN 0-8103-1014-7). Gale.
Zettler, Howard G., ed. Ologies & Isms: A Thematic Dictionary. 2nd ed. 300p. 1981. 28.00 (ISBN 0-8103-1055-4). Gale.
Zeuthen, Peter, jt. auth. see Jul, Mogens.
Zevin, Jack, jt. auth. see Wolf, Alvin.
Zevin, Schlomo Y. A Treasury of Chassidic Tales: On the Torah, Vol. 2. Kaploun, Uri, tr. (Art Scroll Judaica Classics). 352p. 1980. 11.95 (ISBN 0-89906-902-9); pap. 8.95 (ISBN 0-89906-903-7); gift box ed. 25.95 (ISBN 0-89906-904-5). Mesorah Pubns.
Zeydel, E. H., ed. see Storm, Theodor.
Zeydel, Edwin H., tr. Vagabond Verse: Secular Latin Poems of the Middle Ages. LC 66-13794. 1966. 9.95x o.p. (ISBN 0-8143-1288-8). Wayne St U Pr.
Zey-Ferrell, Mary & Aiken, Michael. Complex Organizations: Critical Perspectives. pap. text ed. 11.95 (ISBN 0-673-15269-3). Scott F.
Zeyher, Lewis R. Production Manager's Handbook of Formulas & Tables. 1972. 27.95 o.p. (ISBN 0-13-724427-4). P-H.
Zeyl, Donald J., ed. see Grube, G. M.
Zeylancius. Ceylon. 1970. 19.95 (ISBN 0-236-17657-9, Pub. by Paul Elek). Merrimack Bk Serv.
Zeylmans. The Secret Worldian Epos. 1980. pap. 2.25. St George Bk Serv.
Zezza, Carol. The Love Potion. 1978. pap. 1.95 o.s.i. (ISBN 0-515-04629-9). Jove Pubns.
Zgusta, Ladislav, ed. Theory & Methodology in Lexicography. 1980. pap. 5.75 (ISBN 0-686-64344-5). Hornbeam Pr.
Zhdanov, G. S. Crystal Physics. 1966. 48.00 (ISBN 0-12-779650-9). Acad Pr.
Zhdanov, Valentin S., jt. auth. see Vikhert, Anatolii M.
Zheleznyakov, V. V. Radio Emission of the Sun & Planets. LC 75-76797. 1970. 115.00 (ISBN 0-08-013061-5). Pergamon.
Zheng Shifeng, et al. China. LC 80-23641. (Illus.). 230p. 1980. 50.00 (ISBN 0-07-056830-8); until Dec. 1980 50.00 (ISBN 0-686-64507-3). McGraw.
Zhirmunsky, Victor, jt. auth. see Chadwick, Nora K.
Zhishman, Joseph. Das Ehrerecht der Orientalischen Kirche. LC 80-2367. 1981. Repr. of 1864 ed. 63.50 (ISBN 0-404-18918-0). AMS Pr.
Zhukov, Marshal G. Memoirs of Marshal G. Zhukov. 1971. 15.00 o.p. (ISBN 0-440-05571-7, Sey Lawr). Delacorte.
Zhukovitskii, E. M., jt. auth. see Gershuni, G. Z.
Ziadeh, Nicola. Origins of Nationalism in Tunsia. (Arab Background Ser.). Repr. of 1969 ed. 8.00x (ISBN 0-685-77110-5). Intl Bk Ctr.
--Syria & Lebanon. (Arab Background Ser.). 1968. 14.00x (ISBN 0-685-77109-1). Intl Bk Ctr.
Zich, A. The Rising Sun. LC 76-52547. (World War II Ser.). (Illus.). (gr. 6 up). 1977. 14.94 (ISBN 0-8094-2463-0, Pub. by Time-Life). Silver.
Zich, Arthor, ed. The Rising Sun. (World War II Ser.). 1977. 12.95 (ISBN 0-8094-2462-2). Time-Life.
Zichella, L. & Pancheri, P., eds. Psychoneuroendocrinology in Reproduction. (Developments in Endocrinology Ser.: Vol. 5). 602p. 1979. 59.50 (ISBN 0-444-80172-3, North Holland). Elsevier.
Zichichi, A., ed. Theory & Phenomenology in Particle Physics, 2 pts. 1969. Pt. A. 49.00 (ISBN 0-12-780571-0); Pt. B. 53.75 (ISBN 0-12-780572-9); Set. 83.50 (ISBN 0-685-05147-1). Acad Pr.
Zichichi, Antonio, ed. The New Aspects of Subnuclear Physics. (The Subnuclear Ser.: Vol. 16). 800p. 1981. 75.00 (ISBN 0-306-40459-1, Plenum Pr). Plenum Pub.
Zickgraf, Cordula. I Am Learning to Live Because You Must Die: A Hospital Diary. Scheidt, David L., tr. from Ger. LC 80-2371. 144p. 1981. pap. 6.95 (ISBN 0-8006-1434-8, 1-1434). Fortress.
Zickler, Joyce K., jt. auth. see Levitan, Sar A.
Zide, Donna C. Lost Splendor. 464p. (Orig.). 1980. pap. 2.50 (ISBN 0-446-91274-3). Warner Bks.
--Savage in Silk. (Orig.). 1978. pap. 2.50 (ISBN 0-446-81878-X). Warner Bks.
Ziebell, Beth. Wellness: An Arthritis Reality. LC 80-84001. 144p. 1981. pap. text ed. 6.95 (ISBN 0-8403-2329-8). Kendall-Hunt.
Ziebur, Allen D., jt. auth. see Fisher, Robert C.
Zief, Morris & Mitchell, James W. Contamination Control in Trace Element Analysis. LC 76-16837. (Chemical Analysis Ser.: Vol. 47). 336p. 1976. 37.50 (ISBN 0-471-61169-7, Pub. by Wiley-Interscience). Wiley.
Ziegelmann, H., jt. auth. see Schmid, E. W.
Ziegelmueller, George W. & Dause, Charles A. Argumentation: Inquiry & Advocacy. LC 74-7358. (Speech Communications Ser.). (Illus.). 336p. 1975. 14.95 (ISBN 0-13-046029-X). P-H.
Ziegenhagen, Eduard A. Victims, Crime, & Social Control. LC 75-19833. (Praeger Special Studies). 1977. text ed. 21.95 (ISBN 0-275-56560-2). Praeger.
Zieger, Robert H. Republicans & Labor, 1919-1929. LC 77-80087. 320p. 1969. 14.50x (ISBN 0-8131-1180-3). U Pr of Ky.
Ziegler. War, Peace & International Relations. 2nd ed. 1981. pap. text ed. 8.95 (ISBN 0-316-98493-0). Little.
Ziegler, A. Doctor's Administrative Program, 6 vols. Incl. Dap 1. Patient Contract & Public Relations (ISBN 0-87489-150-7); Dap 2. Bookkeeping & Tax Reports (ISBN 0-87489-151-5); Dap 3. Insurance & Third-Party-Payable Claims (ISBN 0-87489-152-3); Dap 4. Correspondence (ISBN 0-87489-153-1); Billing & Collections; Dap 6. Patient Records Control (ISBN 0-87489-155-8). 1978. Set. write for info. (ISBN 0-87489-158-2); Ea. Vol. write for info.
--Insurance & Third-Party-Payable Claims. (Illus.). 1979. pap. 12.00 (ISBN 0-87489-152-3). Med Economics.

--Patient Records Control. (Illus.). 1979. pap. 12.00 (ISBN 0-87489-155-8). Med Economics.
Ziegler, A. C., jt. auth. see Lidicker, W. Z., Jr.
Ziegler, Alan. The Writing Workshop. (Orig.). 1981. pap. 6.00 (ISBN 0-915924-11-0). Tchrs & Writers Coll.
Ziegler, Daniel J., jt. auth. see Hjelle, Larry A.
Ziegler, E. K. Simple Living. 1975. pap. 1.25 (ISBN 0-89129-078-8, PV078). Jove Pubns.
Ziegler, Edward, jt. ed. see Pfafflin, James.
Ziegler, Edward K. Tapestry of Grace. 158p. (Orig.). 1980. pap. 5.95 (ISBN 0-87178-834-9). Brethren.
Ziegler, Frank, tr. see Bekker, Cajus.
Ziegler, J. F., jt. auth. see Littmark, U.
Ziegler, James F., ed. Helium: Stopping Powers & Ranges in All Elemental Matter. LC 77-13219. 1977. text ed. 40.00 (ISBN 0-08-021606-4). Pergamon.
Ziegler, James F., jt. ed. see Andersen, Hans H.
Ziegler, Jean. Switzerland Exposed. (Allison & Busby Motive Ser.). 180p. 1981. pap. 7.95 (ISBN 0-8052-8077-4, Pub. by Allison & Busby England). Schocken.
Ziegler, P. Thomas, jt. auth. see Romans, John R.
Ziegler, Philip. Omdurman. 1974. 7.95 o.p. (ISBN 0-394-48936-5). Knopf.
Ziegler, Richard, jt. auth. see Flaherty, Patrick F.
Ziegler, Richard S., jt. auth. see Flaherty, Patrick F.
Ziegler, Ronald, ed. Wilderness Waterways: A Guide to Information Sources. LC 78-10410. (Sports, Games, & Pastimes Information Guide Ser.: Vol. 1). 1979. 30.00 (ISBN 0-8103-1434-7). Gale.
Ziegler, Sandra. Our Christmas Handbook. (Illus.). 112p. pap. 5.95 (ISBN 0-89565-180-7, 3041). Standard Pub.
--Service Project Ideas. (Ideas Ser.). (Illus.). 1977. pap. text ed. 1.75 (ISBN 0-87239-122-1, 7962). Standard Pub.
Ziegler, Sandy. Friends. Buerger, Jane, ed. 1980. 5.95 (ISBN 0-89565-174-2, 4931). Standard Pub.
Ziegler, Thomas W. Transport in High Resistance Epithelia, Vol. 1, 1977. Horrobin, D., ed. 1978. 21.60 (ISBN 0-88831-012-9). Eden Med Res.
Ziehn, Bernhard. Canonic Studies. Stevenson, Ronald, ed. 1977. 12.50x (ISBN 0-8008-1232-8, Crescendo). Taplinger.
Ziek, Nona M., jt. auth. see De Rodriquez, Judy Z.
Ziel, Albert Van Der see Van Der Ziel, Albert.
Ziel, Aldert Van Der see Van Der Ziel, Aldert.
Zielhuis, R. L., ed. see Commission of the European Communities.
Zielinski, J., jt. auth. see Kaserand, Michael.
Zielstorff, Rita. Computers in Nursing. LC 80-80813. (Nursing Administration Ser.). 1980. pap. text ed. 10.95 (ISBN 0-913654-66-3). Nursing Res.
Zieman, Nancy L., ed. see Hellyer, Barbara.
Ziemel, E. V., jt. auth. see Michelson, M. J.
Ziemer, Rodger E. & Tranter, William. Principles of Communciations: Systems Modulation & Noise. LC 75-25015. (Illus.). 736p. 1976. text ed. 27.50 (ISBN 0-395-20603-0); solutions manual 4.30 (ISBN 0-395-20604-9). HM.
Ziemke, Earl, jt. auth. see Time-Life Books Editors.
Zienkiewicz, O. C. The Finite Element Method. 3rd ed. (Illus.). 1978. text ed. 34.95 (ISBN 0-07-084072-5, C). McGraw.
Zienkiewicz, O. C., ed. see Lewis, R. W. & Morgan, K.
Zieschang, H., et al. Surfaces & Planar Discontinuous Groups: Revised & Expanded Translation. (Lecture Notes in Mathematics Ser.: Vol. 835). 334p. 1981. pap. 19.50 (ISBN 0-387-10024-5). Springer-Verlag.
Zietlow, Paul. Moments of Vision: The Poetry of Thomas Hardy. LC 73-85184. 304p. 1974. text ed. 16.50x (ISBN 0-674-58215-2). Harvard U Pr.
Zieve, Philip D. & Levin, Jack. Disorders of Hemostasis. LC 76-1252. (Major Problems in Internal Medicine Ser.: Vol. 10). 1976. text ed. 14.50 (ISBN 0-7216-9685-6). Saunders.
Zif, J., jt. auth. see Izraeli, D.
Ziff, Dolores & Filoromo, Tina. Nurse Recruitment: Strategies for Success. LC 80-14829. 1980. text ed. 25.00 (ISBN 0-89443-164-1). Aspen Systems.
Ziff, Gil. Tibet: Being the Recollections & Adventures of the Hermit Yungdrung, Called Small Ears. 348p. 1981. pap. 4.95 (ISBN 0-517-54436-9); 18-copy prepack 89.10 (ISBN 0-517-54440-7). Crown.
Ziff, Larzer. The American 1890s: Life & Times of a Lost Generation. LC 79-14754. 1979. 17.95x (ISBN 0-8032-4900-4); pap. 5.95x (ISBN 0-8032-9900-1, BB 711, Bison). U of Nebr Pr.
--Literary Democracy: The Declaration of Cultural Independence in America 1837-1861. 1981. 17.95 (ISBN 0-670-43026-9). Viking Pr.
Ziff, Larzer, ed. see Hawthorne, Nathaniel.
Ziff, Norman D. Paul Delaroche: A Study in 19th Century French History Painting. LC 76-23663. (Outstanding Dissertations in the Fine Arts - 19th Century). (Illus.). 1977. Repr. of 1974 ed. lib. bdg. 56.00 (ISBN 0-8240-2741-8). Garland Pub.
Zifing, Lawrence & Kim, C. I. An Introduction to Asian Politics. (Illus.). 1977. text ed. 16.95 (ISBN 0-13-478081-7). P-H.
Ziglar, Zig. Confessions of a Happy Christian. LC 78-6729. (gr. 6 up). 1978. 8.95 (ISBN 0-88289-196-0). Pelican.
Zigler, Edward F. & Child, Irvin L. Socialization & Personality Development. LC 73-190612. 1973. pap. text ed. 9.95 (ISBN 0-201-08791-X). A-W.
Zigmond, Maurice L. Kawaiisu Mythology: An Oral Tradition of South-Central California. (Anthropological Papers: No. 18). (Illus.). 252p. (Orig.). 1980. pap. 11.95 (ISBN 0-87919-089-2). Ballena Pr.
Zigrosser, Carl. The Expressionists. 1957. 12.50 o.p. (ISBN 0-8076-0040-7). Braziller.
--Multum in Parvo: An Essay in Poetic Imagination. LC 65-19325. (Illus.). 1965. 5.00 o.s.i. (ISBN 0-8076-0309-0). Braziller.
Zijderveld, Anton C. On Cliches: The Supersedure of Meaning by Function in Modernity. (International Library of Sociology). 1979. 18.00 (ISBN 0-7100-0186-X). Routledge & Kegan.
Zijl, J. B. van see Van Zijl, J. B.
Zikmund, Barbara B., jt. ed. see Manschreck, Clyde L.
Zikmund, Joseph & Dennis, Deborah E., eds. Suburbia: A Guide to Information Sources. LC 78-10523. (Urban Studies Information Guide Ser: Vol. 9). 1979. 30.00 (ISBN 0-8103-1435-5). Gale.
Zikmund, William & Lundstrom, William J. A Collection of Outstanding Cases in Marketing Management. (Illus.). 1979. pap. text ed. 12.95 (ISBN 0-8299-0234-1); instrs.' manual avail. (ISBN 0-8299-0585-5). West Pub.
Zikorus, Frederick J. Mechanical Estimating of Water & Waste Treatment Plants. LC 80-65512. (Illus.). 300p. Date not set. 75.00 (ISBN 0-250-40370-6). Ann Arbor Science. Postponed.
Zilbert, Edward R. Albert Speer & the Nazi Ministry of Arms: Economic Institutions & Industrial Production in the German War Economy. LC 76-17030. 304p. 1981. 19.50 (ISBN 0-686-69379-5). Fairleigh Dickinson.
Zilczer, Judith. The Noble Buyer: John Quinn, Patron of the Avant-Garde. LC 78-2041. (Illus.). 198p. 1978. 25.00 (ISBN 0-87474-998-0). Smithsonian.
Zile, Judy A. Van see Van Zile, Judy A.
Zill, Dennis G., et al. The Basic Math for Calculus. 1978. text ed. 18.95x (ISBN 0-534-00568-3). Wadsworth Pub.
--College Mathematics for Students of Business & the Social Sciences. 1977. text ed. 19.95x (ISBN 0-534-00467-9). Wadsworth Pub.
--College Algebra & Trigonometry. 1979. text ed. 18.95x (ISBN 0-534-00612-4). Wadsworth Pub.
Ziller, R. C. The Social Self. 320p. 1973. text ed. 23.00 (ISBN 0-08-017030-7); pap. text ed. 10.75 (ISBN 0-08-017250-4). Pergamon.
Zillman, Donald N., jt. auth. see Schoenfeld, Clarence A.
Zillman, Lawrence J., ed. Shelley's "Prometheus Unbound". A Variorum Edition. LC 59-9913. (Illus.). 812p. 1959. 17.50 (ISBN 0-295-73931-2). U of Wash Pr.
Zils, Michael, ed. Directory of North & South American Universities, Vol. 24. 1978. 58.00 (ISBN 0-89664-001-9, Pub. by K G Saur). Gale.
--International Directory of Booksellers. 1978. 120.00 (ISBN 0-89664-014-0, Pub. by K G Saur). Gale.
--Publishers' International Directory. 798p. 1979. 140.00 (ISBN 0-89664-100-7, Pub. by K G Saur). Shoe String.
--World Guide to Scientific Associations & Learned Societies. 3rd ed. (Handbook of International Documentation & Information Ser.: Vol. 13). 400p. 1981. 150.00 (ISBN 3-598-20517-1, Dist. by Gale Research). K G Saur.
--World Guide to Trade Associations. 2nd ed. (Handbook of International Documentation & Information Ser.: Vol. 12). 845p. 1980. 180.00 (ISBN 3-598-20513-9, Dist by Gale Research Co.). K G Saur.
Zilva, Joan F. & Pannall, P. R. Clinical Chemistry in Diagnosis & Treatment. 3rd ed. (Illus.). 1979. pap. 24.95 (ISBN 0-8151-9869-8). Year Bk Med.
Zim, Herbert S. Alligators & Crocodiles. rev. ed. LC 78-6615. (gr. 4-6). 1978. PLB 6.67 (ISBN 0-688-32170-4). Morrow.
--The Big Cats. new rev. ed. LC 76-819. (Illus.). 64p. (gr. 3-7). 1976. PLB 6.48 (ISBN 0-688-32072-4). Morrow.
--Blood. (Illus.). (gr. 3-7). 1968. PLB 6.48 (ISBN 0-688-31109-1). Morrow.
--Bones. (Illus.). (gr. 3-7). 1969. PLB 6.48 (ISBN 0-688-31115-6). Morrow.
--Codes & Secret Writing. (Illus.). (gr. 5-9). 1948. PLB 6.48 (ISBN 0-688-31178-4). Morrow.
--Comets. (Illus.). (gr. 3-7). 1957. PLB 6.48 (ISBN 0-688-31180-6). Morrow.
--Corals. (Illus.). (gr. 3-7). 1966. PLB 6.48 (ISBN 0-688-31186-5). Morrow.
--Diamonds. (Illus.). (gr. 3-7). 1959. PLB 6.48 (ISBN 0-688-31236-5). Morrow.
--Dinosaurs. (Illus.). (gr. 3-7). 1954. PLB 6.48 (ISBN 0-688-31239-X). Morrow.
--Elephants. (Illus.). (gr. 3-7). 1946. PLB 6.48 (ISBN 0-688-31262-4). Morrow.
--Frogs & Toads. (Illus.). (gr. 3-7). 1950. PLB 6.48 (ISBN 0-688-31316-7). Morrow.
--Golden Hamsters. (Illus.). (gr. 3-7). 1951. 6.48 (ISBN 0-688-31353-1). Morrow.
--Goldfish. (Illus.). (gr. 3-7). 1947. PLB 6.48 (ISBN 0-688-31340-X). Morrow.
--The Great Whales. (Illus.). (gr. 3-7). 1951. PLB 6.48 (ISBN 0-688-31360-4). Morrow.
--Homing Pigeons. (Illus.). (gr. 3-7). 1949. PLB 6.48 (ISBN 0-688-31398-1). Morrow.
--Little Cats. LC 77-20257. (Illus.). (gr. 3-7). 1978. 6.95 (ISBN 0-688-22149-1); PLB 6.67 (ISBN 0-688-32149-6). Morrow.
--Medicine. LC 74-4299. (Illus.). 64p. (gr. 3-7). 1974. 6.25 o.p. (ISBN 0-688-21786-9); PLB 6.48 (ISBN 0-688-31786-3). Morrow.
--Mice, Men & Elephants. LC 42-36123. (Illus.). (gr. 7-9). 5.95 o.p. (ISBN 0-15-253305-2, HJ). HarBraceJ.
--Monkeys. (Illus.). (gr. 3-7). 1955. PLB 6.48 (ISBN 0-688-31517-8). Morrow.
--Our Senses & How They Work. (Illus.). (gr. 3-7). 1956. PLB 6.48 (ISBN 0-688-31550-X). Morrow.
--Owls. rev. ed. (Illus.). (gr. 3-7). 1977. PLB 6.48 (ISBN 0-688-32109-7). Morrow.
--Rabbits. (Illus.). (gr. 3-7). 1948. PLB 6.48 (ISBN 0-688-31566-6). Morrow.
--Sharks. (Illus.). (gr. 4-6). 1966. PLB 6.00 (ISBN 0-688-26810-2). Morrow.
--Snakes. (Illus.). (gr. 3-7). 1949. PLB 6.48 (ISBN 0-688-31549-6). Morrow.
--The Sun. rev. ed. LC 74-34461. (Illus.). 64p. (gr. 3-7). 1975. PLB 6.48 (ISBN 0-688-32033-3). Morrow.
--Things Around the House. (Illus.). (gr. 1 up). 1954. PLB 6.00 o.p. (ISBN 0-688-31571-2). Morrow.
--The Universe. rev. ed. (Illus.). 64p. (gr. 3-7). 1973. PLB 6.48 (ISBN 0-688-31976-9); pap. 1.25 (ISBN 0-688-25096-3). Morrow.
--Waves. (Illus.). (gr. 3-7). 1967. PLB 6.48 (ISBN 0-688-31479-1). Morrow.
--What's Inside of Animals. (Illus.). (gr. 11 up). 1953. PLB 6.96 (ISBN 0-688-26518-9). Morrow.
--What's Inside of Engines. (Illus.). (gr. 1 up). 1953. PLB 6.96 (ISBN 0-688-31554-2). Morrow.
--What's Inside of Me. (Illus.). (ps-3). 1952. PLB 6.96 (ISBN 0-688-21551-3). Morrow.
--What's Inside of Plants. (Illus.). (ps-3). 1952. PLB 6.96 (ISBN 0-688-31490-2). Morrow.
--What's Inside the Earth. (Illus.). (gr. 1 up). 1953. PLB 6.96 (ISBN 0-688-31475-9). Morrow.
--Your Brain & How It Works. LC 78-168479. (Illus.). 64p. (gr. 3-7). 1972. PLB 6.48 (ISBN 0-688-31922-X). Morrow.
--Your Food & You. (Illus.). (gr. 4-8). 1957. PLB 6.48 (ISBN 0-688-31568-2). Morrow.
--Your Heart & How It Works. (Illus.). (gr. 3-7). 1959. PLB 6.48 (ISBN 0-688-31552-6). Morrow.
--Your Skin. LC 78-10878. (Illus.). (gr. 4-6). 1979. 6.95 (ISBN 0-688-22178-5); PLB 6.67 (ISBN 0-688-32178-X). Morrow.
--Your Stomach & Digestive Tract. LC 72-6734. (Illus.). 64p. (gr. 3-7). 1973. 6.00 o.p. (ISBN 0-688-21838-5); PLB 6.48 (ISBN 0-688-31838-X). Morrow.
Zim, Herbert S. & Gabrielson, Ira N. Birds. (Golden Guide Ser). (Illus.). 1956. PLB 9.15 (ISBN 0-307-63505-8, Golden Pr); pap. 1.95 (ISBN 0-307-24490-3). Western Pub.
Zim, Herbert S. & Krantz, Lucretia. Commercial Fishing. LC 73-4931. (Illus.). 64p. (gr. 3-7). 1973. 6.75 (ISBN 0-688-20091-5); PLB 6.48 (ISBN 0-688-30091-X); pap. 1.25 (ISBN 0-688-05267-3). Morrow.
--Crabs. LC 73-16328. (Illus.). 64p. (gr. 3-7). 1974. 6.25 o.p. (ISBN 0-688-20114-8); PLB 6.48 (ISBN 0-688-30114-2). Morrow.
--Sea Stars & Their Kin. LC 75-17633. (Illus.). 64p. (gr. 3-7). 1976. PLB 6.96 (ISBN 0-688-32053-8) (ISBN 0-688-22053-3). Morrow.
--Snails. LC 74-16262. (Illus.). 64p. (gr. 3-7). 1975. 6.75 (ISBN 0-688-22012-6); PLB 6.48 (ISBN 0-688-32012-0). Morrow.
Zim, Herbert S. & Skelly, James R. Cargo Ships. (How Things Work). (Illus.). (gr. 3-7). 1970. PLB 5.71 (ISBN 0-688-31143-1). Morrow.
--Eating Places. LC 74-14949. (Illus.). 64p. (gr. 3-7). 1975. 6.00 o.p. (ISBN 0-688-22011-8); PLB 6.00 (ISBN 0-688-32011-2). Morrow.
--Hoists, Cranes, & Derricks. LC 74-79098. (How Things Work Ser). (Illus.). (gr. 3-7). 1974. PLB 6.48 (ISBN 0-688-31395-7); pap. 1.25 (ISBN 0-688-26395-X). Morrow.
--Machine Tools. LC 69-10403. (How Things Work Ser., No. 1). (Illus.). (gr. 3-7). 1960. PLB 6.48 (ISBN 0-688-31555-0); pap. 1.25 (ISBN 0-688-26555-3). Morrow.
--Metric Measure. LC 74-702. (Illus.). 64p. (gr. 3-7). 1974. PLB 6.48 (ISBN 0-688-30118-5). Morrow.
--Pipes & Plumbing Systems. LC 73-14589. (Illus.). 64p. (gr. 3-7). 1974. 6.75 (ISBN 0-688-20101-6); PLB 6.48 (ISBN 0-688-30101-0); pap. 1.25 (ISBN 0-688-25101-3). Morrow.
--Tractors. LC 78-189893. (Illus.). 64p. (gr. 3-7). 1974. PLB 6.48 (ISBN 0-688-31782-0); pap. 1.25. Morrow.
--Trucks. LC 75-107973. (Illus.). (gr. 3-7). 1974. PLB 6.48 (ISBN 0-688-31565-8); pap. 1.25 (ISBN 0-688-26565-0). Morrow.
Zim, Herbert S. & Skelly, James R., eds. Telephone Systems. LC 74-151937. (How Things Work Ser). (Illus.). (gr. 3-7). 1974. 5.75 o.p. (ISBN 0-688-21781-8); PLB 6.48 (ISBN 0-688-31781-2); pap. 1.25 (ISBN 0-688-26781-5). Morrow.
Zim, Herbert S., ed. see Hoffmeister, Donald F.
Zima, Peter V., ed. Semiotics & Dialects: Ideology & the Text. (Linguistic & Literary Studies in Eastern Europe Ser.: No. 5). 400p. 1980. text ed. 45.75x (ISBN 90-272-1505-7). Humanities.
Ziman, J. M. Electrons & Phonons. (International Series of Monographs on Physics). 1960. 67.00x (ISBN 0-19-851235-X). Oxford U Pr.
--The Force of Knowledge. LC 75-23529. (Illus.). 368p. 1976. 41.50 (ISBN 0-521-20649-9); pap. 14.95x (ISBN 0-521-09917-X). Cambridge U Pr.
--Models of Disorder. LC 77-82527. (Illus.). 1979. 71.50 (ISBN 0-521-21784-9); pap. 19.95 (ISBN 0-521-29280-8). Cambridge U Pr.
--Principles of the Theory of Solids. 2nd ed. (Illus.). 456p. 1972. text ed. 33.95 (ISBN 0-521-08382-6); pap. 15.95x (ISBN 0-521-29733-8). Cambridge U Pr.
--Reliable Knowledge. LC 78-3792. (Illus.). 1979. 23.95 (ISBN 0-521-22087-4). Cambridge U Pr.
Ziman, John. Teaching & Learning About Science & Society. LC 80-40326. (Illus.). 148p. 1980. 22.50 (ISBN 0-521-23221-X). Cambridge U Pr.
Ziman, John M. Elements of Advanced Quantum Theory. LC 69-16290. (Illus.). 1969. 32.95 (ISBN 0-521-07458-4); pap. 14.95 (ISBN 0-521-09949-8). Cambridge U Pr.
--Physics of Metals, Vol. 1: Electrons. LC 69-10436. (Illus.). 1969. 49.50 (ISBN 0-521-07106-2). Cambridge U Pr.
--Public Knowledge: An Essay Concerning the Social Dimension of Science. 1968. 23.95 (ISBN 0-521-06894-0); pap. 7.95x (ISBN 0-521-09519-0). Cambridge U Pr.
Ziman, Larry, ed. Urthkin, Prose, Verse One. 1978. pap. 3.95 (ISBN 0-933456-00-X). L Ziman.
--Urthkin Prose, Verse Two. (Illus.). 1979. pap. 3.95 (ISBN 0-933456-01-8). L Ziman.
Zimansky, Curt A., ed. see Vanbrugh, John.
Zimbal, Samuel F. & Levy, Wilbert J. Reading Comprehension: Workbook Lessons & Tests. rev. ed. (gr. 7-10). 1969. text ed. 8.75 (ISBN 0-87720-363-6); pap. text ed. 4.42 (ISBN 0-87720-362-8); wkbk. 5.33 (ISBN 0-87720-323-7); tchrs' ed. 3.35 (ISBN 0-87720-324-5). AMSCO Sch.
Zimbardo, Philip. Shyness. 1978. pap. 2.25 (ISBN 0-515-04587-X). Jove Pubns.
Zimbardo, Philip & Maslach, Christina. Psychology for Our Times: Readings. 2nd ed. 1977. pap. 7.95x (ISBN 0-673-15052-6). Scott F.
Zimbardo, Philip G. Essentials of Psychology & Life. 10th ed. 1979. text ed. 17.95x (ISBN 0-673-15184-0). Scott F.
--Psychology & Life. 10th ed. 1979. text ed. 18.95x (ISBN 0-673-15183-2). Scott F.
Zimbardo, Philip G., jt. auth. see Dempsey, David.
Zimelman, Nathan. Positively No Pets Allowed. LC 80-377. (Illus.). 32p. (gr. k-2). 1980. 7.95g (ISBN 0-525-37560-0). Dutton.
--Walls Are to Be Walked. (gr. k-3). 1977. PLB 6.95 o.p. (ISBN 0-525-42175-0). Dutton.
Zimen, E., ed. The Red Fox: Symposium on Behavior & Ecology. (Biogeographica Ser.: Vol. 18). 286p. 1980. lib. bdg. 73.50 (ISBN 0-686-28665-0, Pub. by Dr. W. Junk). Kluwer Boston.
Zimen, Erik. The Wolf: A Species in Danger. 1981. 13.95 (ISBN 0-440-09619-7). Delacorte.
Zimering, Stanley, jt. auth. see Saltman, Jules.
Zimet, Melvin. Decentralization & School Effectiveness. LC 73-78731. 1973. text ed. 9.25x (ISBN 0-8077-2399-1); pap. text ed. 6.50x (ISBN 0-8077-2420-3). Tchrs Coll.

Zimikes, Martha R. Iron-on Transfers from a Treasury of Needlework Designs: Ready-to-Use Patterns for Needlepoint & Embroidery. 96p. 1981. pap. 9.95 (ISBN 0-442-23119-9). Van Nos Reinhold.

Zimmer, A. B. Employing the Handicapped: A Practical Compliance Manual. 530p. 1981. 19.95 (ISBN 0-8144-5525-5). Am Mgmt.

Zimmer, Basil G., jt. auth. see Hawley, Amos H.

Zimmer, K. G. Quantitative Radiation Biology. Griffith, H. D., tr. (Illus.). 1961. 10.75 o.s.i. (ISBN 0-02-855800-6). Hafner.

Zimmer, Norma. Norma. 1976. 7.95 o.p. (ISBN 0-8423-4717-8); with cassette o.p. 8.95 (ISBN 0-685-80877-7); pap. 2.95 (ISBN 0-685-80878-5). Tyndale.

Zimmer, Norma, jt. auth. see Lawrence, Carol.

Zimmer, Rudolf A. Applications in Technology of Right Triangular Trigonometry: Unit 5. 64p. 1980. pap. text ed. 4.95 (ISBN 0-8403-2278-X). Kendall-Hunt.

Zimmer, Rudolph A. Basic Trigonometry with Applications in Technology. LC 80-82834. 256p. 1980. pap. text ed. 10.95 (ISBN 0-8403-2273-9). Kendall-Hunt.

--Primary Trigonometric Ratios: Unit 3. 49p. 1980. pap. text ed. 4.50 (ISBN 0-8403-2276-3). Kendall-Hunt.

--Secondary (Reciprocal) Trigonometric Ratios: Unit 4. 49p. 1980. pap. text ed. 4.50 (ISBN 0-8403-2277-1). Kendall-Hunt.

Zimmer, Stefan. Die Satzstellung des Finiten Verbs im Tocharischen. (Janua Linguarum, Ser. Practica: No. 238). 108p. 1976. pap. text ed. 26.25x (ISBN 90-279-3461-4). Mouton.

Zimmerer, Thomas W., jt. auth. see Preston, Paul.

Zimmerli, Walther. Ezekiel One. Cross, Frank M., Jr. & Baltzer, Klaus, eds. LC 75-21540. (Hermenia: a Critical & Historical Commentary on the Bible). 558p. 1979. 32.95 (ISBN 0-8006-6008-0, 20-6008). Fortress.

Zimmerman, jt. ed. see Kaufman.

Zimmerman, Andrea. Yetta the Trickster. LC 78-6164. (Illus.). (gr. 1-4). 1978. 6.95 (ISBN 0-395-28836-3, Clarion). HM.

Zimmerman, Bill. Airlift to Wounded Knee. LC 76-3138. (Illus.). 348p. 1976. 13.95 (ISBN 0-8040-0691-1). Swallow.

Zimmerman, C. C. & Whetten, N. L. Rural Families on Relief. LC 70-165606. (FDR & the Era of the New Deal Ser.). 1971. Repr. of 1938 ed. lib. bdg. 17.50 (ISBN 0-306-70349-1). Da Capo.

Zimmerman, Caroline. How to Break into the Media Professions. 216p. 1981. 11.95 (ISBN 0-385-15933-1). Doubleday.

--How to Break into the Media Professions. LC 79-6665. 1981. pap. 5.95 (ISBN 0-385-15934-X, Dolp). Doubleday.

Zimmerman, Caroline A. Your Child Can Be a Model. (Illus.). 224p. 1981. 13.95 (ISBN 0-8015-9110-4, Hawthorn). Dutton.

Zimmerman, Diane, ed. see Lockerbie, D. Bruce.

Zimmerman, Elizabeth. Knitting Without Tears. LC 70-140776. (Illus.). 1973. pap. 7.95 (ISBN 0-684-13505-1, SL466, ScribT). Scribner.

Zimmerman, Fred W. Exploring Woodworking. LC 79-12354. (Illus.). 1979. text ed. 9.96 (ISBN 0-87006-276-X); wkbk. 3.20 (ISBN 0-87006-281-6). Goodheart.

--Leathercraft. LC 77-8007. (Illus.). 1977. text ed. 4.80 (ISBN 0-87006-234-4). Goodheart.

Zimmerman, Gary, jt. auth. see Irving, Hancock.

Zimmerman, Gloria, jt. auth. see Ngo, Bach.

Zimmerman, Gordon I. Public Speaking Today. (Illus.). 1979. pap. text ed. 11.50 (ISBN 0-8299-0259-7); instrs.' manual avail. (ISBN 0-8299-0586-3). West Pub.

Zimmerman, Gordon I., et al. Speech Communication: A Contemporary Introduction. (Illus.). 1977. pap. text ed. 11.50 (ISBN 0-8299-0055-1); instrs.' manual avail. (ISBN 0-8299-0587-1). West Pub.

Zimmerman, H. Robots. 1979. pap. 7.95 (ISBN 0-931064-12-0). Starlog Pr.

--Spaceships. 1980. pap. 7.95 (ISBN 0-931064-23-6). Starlog Pr.

Zimmerman, Harry, ed. Progress in Neuropathology, Vol. IV. (Vol 4). 1979. 41.00 (ISBN 0-89004-388-4). Raven.

Zimmerman, Henry A. Intravascular Catherization. (Illus.). 1304p. 1972. pap. 57.50 spiral (ISBN 0-398-02148-1). C C Thomas.

Zimmerman, Howard. Robots. LC 79-63382. 1979. pap. 7.95 (ISBN 0-931064-12-0). Starlog.

--Spaceships. enl. ed. 1980. pap. 7.95 (ISBN 0-931064-23-6). O'Quinn Studio.

Zimmerman, Howard, ed. Spaceships. (Illus.). (gr. 3 up). 1977. pap. 2.95 (ISBN 0-931064-00-7). Starlog.

Zimmerman, Howard, ed. see Naha, Ed.

Zimmerman, Howard, ed. see Skotak, Robert & Holton, Scot.

Zimmerman, Hyman J. Hepatotoxicity: The Adverse Effects of Drugs & Other Chemicals on the Liver. (Illus.). 1978. 54.50 (ISBN 0-8385-3725-1). ACC.

Zimmerman, Jack. Hospice. 300p. 1981. price not set (ISBN 0-8067-2211-8). Urban & S.

Zimmerman, John W., jt. auth. see Tregoe, Benjamin B.

Zimmerman, Joseph F. State & Local Government. 3rd ed. (Illus., Orig.). pap. 4.95 (ISBN 0-06-460181-1, CO 181, COS). Har-Row.

--State & Local Government. 2nd ed. LC 70-124363. (Illus., Orig.). 1970. pap. 4.95 o.p. (ISBN 0-06-460112-9, 112, COS). Har-Row.

Zimmerman, Joseph F., jt. auth. see Prescott, Frank W.

Zimmerman, Karl, jt. auth. see Cook, Roger.

Zimmerman, Marjorie. The Castle Mystery. LC 77-78494. (Illus.). (gr. 3-6). 1977. pap. 1.95 o.p. (ISBN 0-89191-080-8, 15289). Cook.

Zimmerman, Martha. How to Celebrate the Feasts. (Illus.). 160p. (Orig.). 1981. pap. 4.95 (ISBN 0-87123-228-6, 210228). Bethany Fell.

Zimmerman, Martin B. The U. S. Coal Industry: The Economics of Policy Change. 256p. 1982. text ed. 27.50. MIT Pr.

Zimmerman, Marvin. Contemporary Problems of Democracy. 1972. text ed. 7.50x (ISBN 0-391-00223-6). Humanities.

Zimmerman, Mary K. Passage Through Abortion: The Personal & Social Reality of Women's Experiences. LC 77-12742. (Praeger Special Studies). 1977. 24.95 (ISBN 0-03-029816-4). Praeger.

Zimmerman, Michael. Eclipse of the Self: The Development of Heidegger's Concept of Authenticity. LC 80-19042. xxx, 331p. 1981. 18.95x (ISBN 0-8214-0570-5); pap. 9.95 (ISBN 0-8214-0601-9). Ohio U Pr.

Zimmerman, Mildred K., jt. auth. see Zimmerman, O. T.

Zimmerman, Morris, et al, eds. Percursor Processing in the Biosynthesis of Proteins. LC 80-16863. 449p. 1980. 79.00x (ISBN 0-89766-072-2). NY Acad Sci.

Zimmerman, O. T. & Lavine, Irvin. Chemical Engineering Costs. 1950. 19.50 (ISBN 0-686-20565-0). Indus Res Serv.

--Chemical Engineering Laboratory Equipment. 2nd ed. 1955. 17.50 (ISBN 0-686-20566-9). Indus Res Serv.

--Conversion Factors & Tables. 3rd ed. 1961. 13.80 (ISBN 0-686-20568-5). Indus Res Serv.

--Handbook of Material Trade Names, with Supplements 1, 2, 3, & 4. 1953-65. 175.00 (ISBN 0-686-20569-3). Indus Res Serv.

--Psychrometric Tables & Charts. 2nd ed. 1964. 28.00 (ISBN 0-686-20570-7). Indus Res Serv.

Zimmerman, O. T. & Zimmerman, Mildred K. College Placement Directory. 4th ed. 1965. 19.50 (ISBN 0-686-20567-7). Indus Res Serv.

Zimmerman, Paul. Last Season of Weeb Ewbank. 1974. 10.00 o.p. (ISBN 0-374-18462-3). FS&G.

Zimmerman, Robert. Medical Radiographic Techniques. LC 74-18672. (Allied Health Ser). 1975. pap. 8.35 (ISBN 0-672-61392-1). Bobbs.

Zimmerman, Thomas J. Focus on Life Student Project Book. rev ed. (To Live Is Christ Ser.). 40p. 1976. wkbk. 1.65 (ISBN 0-697-01655-2). Wm C Brown.

Zimmerman, Waldo. Condemned to Life: The Plight of the Unwanted Child. 260p. (Orig.). 1980. pap. 3.95 (ISBN 0-89260-181-7). Hwong Pub.

Zimmerman, Walter J. Coin Collectors Fact Book. LC 73-77839. (Illus.). 192p. 1973. lib. bdg. 5.95 o. p. (ISBN 0-668-02991-9); pap. 3.95 (ISBN 0-668-02992-7). Arco.

Zimmerman, William. How to Tape Instant Oral Biographies: Instant Oral Biographies. LC 79-56828. (Illus.). 96p. (Orig.). 1981. pap. price not set (ISBN 0-935966-00-5, 100). Guarionex Pr.

Zimmerman, William, jt. auth. see Ruthven, John A.

Zimmermann, E. & George, R., eds. Narcotics & the Hypothalamus. LC 74-83453. 1974. 27.00 (ISBN 0-911216-87-1). Raven.

Zimmermann, Georges D. Songs of Irish Rebellion: Political Street Ballads & Rebel Songs, 1780-1900. LC 67-21410. 342p. Repr. of 1967 ed. 15.00 (ISBN 0-8103-5025-4). Gale.

Zimmermann, Karl R. CZ: The Story of the California Zephyr. (Illus.). 1975. 10.95 o.s.i. (ISBN 0-931726-01-8). Delford Pr.

--A Decade of D & H. (Illus.). 1978. pap. 6.95 o.s.i. (ISBN 0-931726-02-6). Delford Pr.

Zimmermann, M. H., jt. ed. see Tomlinson, P. B.

Zimmermann, Odo J., tr. see Gregorius I.

Zimmermann, Paul. Rock Strata & the Bible Record. LC 78-111692. 1970. 7.50 (ISBN 0-570-03206-7, 15-2103). Concordia.

Zimmermann, Ulrich & Eigel, Christine, eds. Ploetzlich Brach der Schulrat in Traenen Aus: Verstaendigungstexte Von Schuelern und Lehrern. (Edition Suhrkamp). 429p. (Orig.). 1980. pap. text ed. 6.50 (ISBN 3-518-10429-2, Pub. by Insel Verlag Germany). Suhrkamp.

Zimmerman-Stidham, Susan, jt. auth. see Gandy, Charles.

Zimmernman, Fred W. Upholstering Methods. LC 80-25308. (Illus.). 196p. 1981. text ed. 12.00 (ISBN 0-87006-313-8). Goodheart.

Zimolzak, Chester & Stansfield, Charles. The Human Landscape: Geography & Culture. 1979. text ed. 19.95 (ISBN 0-675-08290-0); instructor's manual 3.95 (ISBN 0-685-96155-9). Merrill.

Zinberg, Norman E., ed. Alternate States of Consciousness. LC 76-46722. (Illus.). 1979. pap. text ed. 7.95 (ISBN 0-02-935930-9). Free Pr.

Zinc Development Assoc., London, ed. see International Galvanizing Conference Madrid 1976.

Zindel, Bonnie, jt. auth. see Zindel, Paul.

Zindel, Paul. The Pigman's Legacy. LC 79-2684. 192p. (YA) (gr. 7 up). 1980. 8.95 (ISBN 0-06-026853-0, HarpJ); PLB 8.79 (ISBN 0-06-026854-9). Har-Row.

Zindel, Paul & Zindel, Bonnie. A Star for the Latecomer. 160p. (gr. 6 up). 1981. pap. 1.95 (ISBN 0-553-14335-2). Bantam.

Ziner, Feenie & Young, Ed. Cricket Boy: A Chinese Tale Retold. LC 76-51999. (gr. 3 up). 1977. PLB 6.95 (ISBN 0-385-12507-0); PLB (ISBN 0-385-12507-0). Doubleday.

Zingale, Nancy, jt. auth. see Flanigan, William H.

Zingale, Nancy H., jt. auth. see Flanigan, William H.

Zingg, Ernst J., jt. auth. see Mayor, Georges.

Zinggeler, Jeff, et al, illus. Read & Learn with Beth, the Traveler. (Read & Learn Ser.). (Illus.). 88p. (gr. 3-5). 1979. pap. 2.95 (ISBN 0-675-01056-X). Merrill.

Zink, David, jt. auth. see Zink, Joan.

Zink, David D. Leslie Stephen. (English Authors Ser.: No. 142). lib. bdg. 10.95 (ISBN 0-8057-1512-6). Twayne.

Zink, Harriet R. Emerson's Use of the Bible. 75p. 1980. Repr. of 1935 ed. lib. bdg. 15.00 (ISBN 0-8495-6206-6). Arden Lib.

Zink, Joan & Zink, David. You Are the Mystery. LC 76-44601. (Illus.). 1976. 7.95 o.p. (ISBN 0-87707-178-0). CSA Pr.

Zink, R. A., jt. ed. see Brendel, W.

Zinkgraf, June, jt. auth. see Bauman, Toni.

Zinkiewicz, Crystal. The Anytime Book for Busy Families. LC 79-67098. 1979. spiral bdg. 4.95x (ISBN 0-8358-0378-3). Upper Room.

Zinkin, Taya. Write Right. 128p. 1980. pap. 4.95 (ISBN 0-08-024566-8). Pergamon.

Zinkowski, Nicholas B. Commercial Oilfield Diving. nd ed. LC 78-7214. (Illus.). 1978. 19.00x (ISBN 0-87033-235-X). Cornell Maritime.

Zinn, Donald J. The Handbook for Beach Strollers: From Maine to Cape Hatteras. LC 75-1921. (Illus.). 128p. 1975. pap. 5.95 (ISBN 0-87106-055-8). Globe Pequot.

Zinn, Howard. Postwar America: 1945-1971. LC 72-88273. (History of American Society Ser). 260p. (Orig.). 1973. pap. 5.95 (ISBN 0-672-60936-3). Bobbs.

Zinn, Howard, ed. New Deal Thought. LC 66-16755. (Orig.). 1966. pap. 8.50 (ISBN 0-672-60112-5). Bobbs.

Zinn, Keith M. The Pupil. (Illus.). 152p. 1972. 14.95 (ISBN 0-398-02320-4). C C Thomas.

Zinn, Walter, jt. auth. see Solomon, Herbert.

Zinner, Ellen & McMahon, Joan. How to Conduct a One-Day Conference on Death Education. (Thanatology Service Ser.). 50p. 1980. 7.95 (ISBN 0-930194-04-7). Highly Specialized.

Zinner, Ellen S. & Steele, Stephen F., eds. Forum for Death Education & Counseling: Selected Proceedings from the First National Conference. 298p. (Orig.). 1979. pap. 11.95 (ISBN 0-536-03314-5). Ginn Custom.

Zinner, Paul E., ed. National Communism & Popular Revolt in Eastern Europe: A Selection of Documents on Events in Poland & Hungary Feb. - Nov., 1956. LC 57-13560. (Orig.). 1956. pap. 10.00x (ISBN 0-231-02200-X). Columbia U Pr.

Zinnes, Dina A. Contemporary Research in International Relations: A Perspective & a Critical Assessment. LC 75-11290. (Illus.). 1976. 25.00 (ISBN 0-02-935730-6). Free Pr.

Zinnes, Dina A. & Gillespie, John V., eds. Mathematical Models in International Relations. LC 75-25000. (Special Studies). (Illus.). 1976. text ed. 45.00 (ISBN 0-275-55870-3). Praeger.

Zinnes, Dina A., jt. ed. see Gillispie, John V.

Zinnes, Harriet, ed. see Pound, Ezra.

Zinnes, Joseph L., jt. auth. see Auerbach, Carl.

Zinngrabe. Sheet Metal Blueprint Reading: For the Building Trades. LC 79-2748. 1980. 10.00 (ISBN 0-8273-1352-7); instructor's guide 1.65 (ISBN 0-8273-1353-5). Delmar.

Zinngrabe, C. J. & Schumacher, F. W. Practical Layout for Sheet Metal Shop. LC 75-6063. 1975. pap. text ed. 7.40 (ISBN 0-8273-0224-X); instructor's guide 1.60 (ISBN 0-8273-0225-8). Delmar.

--Safety for Sheet Metal Workers. LC 76-49325. (gr. 9-12). 1977. pap. 3.80 (ISBN 0-8273-1614-3); tchr's guide 0.75 (ISBN 0-8273-1615-1). Delmar.

--Sheet Metal Hand Processes. LC 73-2159. 1974. 7.40 (ISBN 0-8273-0220-7); instructor's guide 1.50 (ISBN 0-8273-0221-5). Delmar.

--Sheet Metal Machine Processes. LC 73-2160. 1975. pap. text ed. 7.40 (ISBN 0-8273-0222-3); instructor's guide 1.60 (ISBN 0-8273-0223-1). Delmar.

Zinsser, William K. On Writing Well: An Informal Guide to Writing Nonfiction. 2nd ed. 1980. text ed. 8.50 scp (ISBN 0-06-047396-7, HarpC); pap. text ed. write for info. (ISBN 0-06-047395-9). Har-Row.

Zinszer, Paul H., jt. ed. see Lusch, Robert F.

Zintz, Miles V. Corrective Reading. 4th ed. 470p. 1981. text ed. write for info. (ISBN 0-697-06187-6). Wm C Brown.

Zintz, Walter. Nova Venturion's Bootstrap Venture Manual. 1981. softcover 14.50 (ISBN 0-915254-08-5). Nova Venturion.

--Nova Venturion's Handbook for Non-Salesmen. 1981. softcover 12.50 (ISBN 0-915254-09-3). Nova Venturion.

--The Teaching Job Hunt. LC 73-88726. 27p. 1973. pap. 3.00 o.p. (ISBN 0-915254-05-0, 05-0). Nova Venturion.

Ziolkowski, Theodore. Disenchanted Images: A Literary Iconology. 1977. text ed. 16.50 (ISBN 0-691-06334-6). Princeton U Pr.

Ziolkowski, Theodore, tr. see Hesse, Hermann.

Ziolkowski, Yetta, tr. see Hesse, Hermann.

Zion, Gene. The Plant Sitter. (Illus.). (gr. k-3). 1972. pap. 1.50 (ISBN 0-590-08752-5, Schol Pap). Schol Bk Serv.

Zionts, Stanley. Linear & Integer Programming. (Illus.). 528p. 1974. text ed. 21.95 (ISBN 0-13-536763-8). P-H.

Zipser, Arthur. Working Class Giant: The Life of William Z. Foster. (Orig.). 1981. 11.00 (ISBN 0-7178-0590-5); pap. 4.25 (ISBN 0-7178-0582-4). Intl Pub Co.

Zipser, Arthur, ed. see Foster, William Z.

Zireau, Lillee. Beekeeping. LC 77-185674. (Handicraft Ser.: Bk. 6). (Illus.). 32p. (Orig.). (gr. 7-12). 1971. lib. bdg. 2.45 incl. catalog cards (ISBN 0-87157-906-5); pap. 1.25 vinyl laminated covers (ISBN 0-87157-406-3). SamHar Pr.

Ziring, Lawrence. Pakistan: The Enigma of Political Development. (Illus.). 256p. 1980. lib. bdg. 28.50x (ISBN 0-89158-982-1, Pub. by Dawson Pub). Westview.

Ziring, Lawrence, ed. The Subcontinent in World Politics: India, Its Neighbors & the Great Powers. LC 78-19468. (Praeger Special Studies). 1978. 24.95 (ISBN 0-03-042921-8). Praeger.

Zirkoff, Boris De see Blavatsky, Helena P.

Zisk, Betty. Political Research: A Methodological Sampler. 352p. 1981. pap. text ed. 8.95 (ISBN 0-669-02338-8). Heath.

Ziskin, Jay. Coping with Psychiatric & Psychological Testimony, 2 vols. 3rd ed. Incl. Vol. 1. 429p. 50.00 (ISBN 0-9603630-2-5); Vol. 2. 577p. write for info. (ISBN 0-9603630-3-3). 1981. Set. 80.00 (ISBN 0-9603630-4-1). Law & Psych.

--Coping with Psychiatric & Psychological Testimony. 2nd ed. LC 75-1743. 1975. 30.00 o.p. (ISBN 0-9603630-0-9). Law & Psych.

--Supplement to Coping with Psychiatric & Psychological Testimony. 1977. 9.50 o.p. (ISBN 0-9603630-1-7). Law & Psych.

Ziskin, Marvin, jt. ed. see Wells, P. N. T.

Zissis, G. J., jt. ed. see Wolfe, W. L.

Zissos, D. Problems & Solutions in Logic Design. 2nd ed. (Illus.). 1980. 29.95x (ISBN 0-19-859362-7). Oxford U Pr.

Zistel, Era. Good Companions. 1981. pap. 1.75 (ISBN 0-451-09813-7, E9813, Signet Bks). NAL.

--Hi Fella. LC 77-8583. (Illus.). 1977. 6.95 o.p. (ISBN 0-397-01241-1). Lippincott.

Zistel, Eva. Good Companions. large print ed. LC 80-29117. 1981. Repr. of 1980 ed. 7.95 (ISBN 0-89621-265-3). Thorndike Pr.

Zitner, Rosalind & Hayden, Shelby. Our Youngest Parents: A Study of the Use of Support Services by Adolescent Mothers. (Orig.). 1980. pap. text ed. 4.95 (ISBN 0-87868-144-2). Child Welfare.

Zitner, Sheldon P., et al. Preface to Literary Analysis. 1964. pap. 6.95x (ISBN 0-673-05216-8). Scott F.

Zito, George V. Population & Its Problems. LC 79-581. 1979. text ed. 22.95 (ISBN 0-87705-396-0); pap. text ed. 9.95 (ISBN 0-87705-414-2). Human Sci Pr.

Zito, Mario. How to Avoid Pitfalls & Pratfalls in English. LC 79-3810. 1980. pap. text ed. 11.25 (ISBN 0-8191-0930-4). U Pr of Amer.

Zitrin, Shmuel, jt. auth. see Yinon, Jehuda.

Ziv, Avner. Counselling the Intellectually Gifted Child. 1977. pap. text ed. 4.50x (ISBN 0-8077-8021-9). Tchrs Coll.

Zivin, Gail. The Development of Self-Regulation Through Private Speech. LC 78-27615. (Origins of Behavior Ser.). 1980. 29.50 (ISBN 0-471-98380-2, Pub by Wiley-Interscience). Wiley.

Zizmor, Jonathan & Foreman, John. Super Hair. 1978. pap. 1.95 o.p. (ISBN 0-425-03878-5, Dist. by Putnam). Berkley Pub.

--Super Skin. LC 75-28443. 224p. 1976. 8.95 (ISBN 0-690-01078-8, TYC-T). T Y Crowell.

--SuperHair: The Doctor's Book of Beautiful Hair. LC 77-22817. (Illus.). (YA) 1978. 7.95 o.p. (ISBN 0-399-12005-X, Pub. by Berkley Pub). Berkley Pub.

Zlatkovich, Charles P. Texas Railroads: A Record of Construction & Abandonment. (Research Monograph). 100p. (Orig.). 1981. pap. 7.00 (ISBN 0-87755-248-7). U of Tex Busn Res.

Zlobin, Vladimir. A Difficult Soul: Zinaida Gippius. Karlinsky, Simon, ed. (Documentary Studies in Modern Russian Poetry). 200p. 1980. 14.50x (ISBN 0-520-03867-3). U of Cal Pr.

Zlot, William, et al. Elementary Algebra. (Sourcebook of Fundamental Mathematics Ser.). 156p. 1973. pap. 6.50 (ISBN 0-685-91066-0, Pub. by W & W). Krieger.

Zlotowitz, Bernard, jt. auth. see Luka, Ronald.

Zlotowitz, Meir. Bereishis-Genesis, Vol. 5. (Art Scroll Tanach Ser.). 1980. 14.95 (ISBN 0-89906-358-6); pap. 11.95 (ISBN 0-89906-359-4). Mesorah Pubns.

--Bereishis-Genesis: Vol. 4, Vayeitzei-Vayishlach. (Art Scroll Tanach Ser.). 400p. 1979. 13.95 (ISBN 0-89906-356-X); pap. 11.25 (ISBN 0-89906-357-8). Mesorah Pubns.

Zlutnik, Steven, jt. ed. see Katz, Roger C.

Znamierowski, Nell. Weaving, Step by Step. (Step by Step Craft Ser). 1967. PLB 9.15 o.p. (ISBN 0-307-62002-6, Golden Pr); pap. 2.95 (ISBN 0-307-42002-7). Western Pub.

Znaniecki, Florian. Social Relations & Social Roles. (Reprints in Sociology Ser). lib. bdg. 28.50x (ISBN 0-697-00219-5); pap. 8.95x (ISBN 0-89197-940-9). Irvington.

Znosko-Borovsky, Eugene. Art of Chess Combination: A Guide for All Players of the Game. Sergeant, Philip W., tr. (Illus.). 1936. pap. 3.50 (ISBN 0-486-20583-5). Dover.

Zobel, Jan, ed. San Francisco Bay Area People's Yellow Pages. 5th ed. (Illus.). 1981. pap. 4.95. SF Bay Area.

Zobel, Jan, ed. see Mary, Donnis, et al.

Zobell, Albert, Jr., compiled by. Discourse Cameos. 67p. 1973. 0.75 o.p. (ISBN 0-87747-497-4). Deseret Bk.

Zodhiates, Spiros. Formula for Happiness. 256p. (Orig.). 1980. pap. 8.75 (ISBN 0-89957-046-1). AMG Pubs.

Zoega, Geir T. Concise Dictionary of Old Icelandic. 1910. 34.50x (ISBN 0-19-863108-1). Oxford U Pr.

Zoellner, Robert. The Salt-Sea Mastodon: A Reading of Moby-Dick. 1973. 17.50x (ISBN 0-520-02339-0). U of Cal Pr.

Zoerb, Alice A. My Life Memories. 1978. 10.95 (ISBN 0-9602888-0-5). Heritage Rec.

Zoeteman, B. C. Sensory Assessment of Water Quality. (Pergamon Series on Environmental Science: Vol. 2). (Illus.). 160p. 1980. 33.00 (ISBN 0-08-023848-3). Pergamon.

Zogner, L. see Wallis, H.

Zohar, Danah. Israel. LC 77-88352. (Countries Ser.). (Illus.). 1978. lib. bdg. 7.95 (ISBN 0-686-51152-2). Silver.

Zohary, M. Geobotanical Foundations of the Middle East. 762p. 1973. text ed. 255.00 (ISBN 90-265-0157-9, Pub. by Swets Pub Serv Holland). Swets North Am.

Zohn, David A. & Mennell, John M. Musculoskeletal Pain: Principles of Physical Diagnosis & Physical Treatment. 1976. 19.95 (ISBN 0-316-98893-6). Little.

Zohn, H., ed. Der Farbenvolle Untergang: Osterreichisches Lesebuck. 1971. pap. 9.50 (ISBN 0-13-199000-4). P-H.

Zohn, Harry, ed. & tr. see Weber, Marianne.

Zokeisha. Baby Animals. (Puppet Story Board Bks.). (Illus.). 12p. (ps-k). Date not set. boards 2.95 (ISBN 0-671-42645-1, Little Simon). S&S.

--Bedtime Stories. (Puppet Story Board Bks.). (Illus.). 12p. (ps-k). Date not set. boards 2.95 (ISBN 0-671-42644-3, Little Simon). S&S.

--Kittens. (Puppet Story Board Bks.). (Illus.). 12p. (ps-k). Date not set. boards 2.95 (ISBN 0-686-69451-1, Little Simon). S&S.

--Little Nursery Rhymes. (Puppet Story Board Bks.). (Illus.). 12p. (ps-k). Date not set. boards 2.95 (ISBN 0-671-42642-7, Little Simon). S&S.

--Mother Goose. (Puppet Story Board Bks.). (Illus.). 12p. (ps-k). Date not set. boards 2.95 (ISBN 0-671-42643-5, Little Simon). S&S.

--What Time Is It? (Puppet Story Board Bks.). (Illus.). 12p. (ps-k). Date not set. boards 2.95 (ISBN 0-671-42646-X, Little Simon). S&S.

Zola, Emile. Abee Mouret's Sin. 1957. 12.95 (ISBN 0-236-30808-4, Pub. by Paul Elek). Merrimack Bk Serv.

--Beast in Man. 1956. 13.95 (ISBN 0-236-31007-0, Pub. by Paul Elek). Merrimack Bk Serv.

--Claude's Confession. Cox, George D., tr. from Fr. 1979. Repr. of 1882 ed. 16.50 (ISBN 0-86527-030-9). Fertig.

--Earth. 1960. 13.95 (ISBN 0-236-30863-7, Pub. by Paul Elek). Merrimack Bk Serv.

--Germinal. Ellis, Havelock, tr. 1964. 5.00x o.p. (ISBN 0-460-00897-8, Evman); pap. op o.p. (ISBN 0-460-01897-3, EP1897). Dutton.

--Kill. 1957. 13.95 (ISBN 0-236-30899-8, Pub. by Paul Elek). Merrimack Bk Serv.

--Lettres Inedites a Henry Ceard. Salvan, Albert J., ed. LC 59-10016. (Brown University Studies: No. 22). 174p. (Orig., Fr.). 1959. pap. 4.00x (ISBN 0-87057-060-9). Univ Pr of New England.

--A Love Affair. 1957. 13.95 (ISBN 0-236-30905-6, Pub. by Paul Elek). Merrimack Bk Serv.

--Madeleine Ferat. 1957. 13.95 (ISBN 0-236-30907-2, Pub. by Paul Elek). Merrimack Bk Serv.

--Masterpiece. 1968. pap. 5.95 (ISBN 0-472-06145-3, 145, AA). U of Mich Pr.

--The Mysteries of Marseilles. Vizetelly, E., tr. from Fr. viii, 384p. 1976. Repr. of 1895 ed. 21.50 (ISBN 0-86527-280-8). Fertig.

--Nana. Holden, George, tr. (Classics Ser.). 1972. pap. 3.95 (ISBN 0-14-044263-4). Penguin.

--Priest in the House. 1957. 13.95 (ISBN 0-236-30964-1, Pub. by Paul Elek). Merrimack Bk Serv.

--Restless House. 1971. 13.95 (ISBN 0-236-30967-6, Pub. by Paul Elek). Merrimack Bk Serv.

--Three Faces of Love. Gant, R., tr. LC 67-29442. 6.95 (ISBN 0-8149-0247-2). Vanguard.

--Zest for Life. 1959. 13.95 (ISBN 0-236-31013-5, Pub. by Paul Elek). Merrimack Bk Serv.

Zola, Irene, et al, eds. see Siegmond, Warren E.

Zolar. Everything You Want to Know About Astrology, Numerology, How to Win. LC 72-3135. (Zolar's Everything You Want to Know Ser.). 224p. 1972. pap. 1.50 (ISBN 0-668-02656-1). Arc Bks.

--Everything You Want to Know About Dreams, Lucky Numbers, Omens, Oils & Incense. LC 70-188859. (Zolar's Everything You Want to Know Ser.). 226p. 1972. pap. 1.95 (ISBN 0-668-02600-6). Arc Bks.

Zolbrod, Paul G., jt. ed. see Tobias, Richard C.

Zoll, Allen A., III. Explorations in Managing. (Illus.). 356p. 1974. text ed. 14.95 o.p. (ISBN 0-201-08812-6); pap. text ed. 9.95 (ISBN 0-201-08814-2). A-W.

Zoll, Allen A., 3rd. Dynamic Management Education. 2nd ed. 1969. 21.95 (ISBN 0-201-08800-2). A-W.

Zoll, Don. Western Riding: Your Self-Teaching Guide. 1979. 9.95 o.p. (ISBN 0-679-51452-X). McKay.

Zoller, Robert. The Lost Key to Prediction: The Arabic Parts in Astrology. 350p. 1980. pap. 8.95 (ISBN 0-89281-013-0). Inner Tradit.

Zoller, W. H., jt. auth. see Gordon, G. E.

Zollers, Frances E. & Foreman, Gail H. Business Law: A Practical Approach. LC 76-44036. 1978. pap. text ed. 10.80 (ISBN 0-8273-1431-0); instructor's guide 1.60 (ISBN 0-8273-1432-9). Delmar.

Zollinger, Peter. The Political Creature: An Evolutionary Reorientation. LC 67-27525. 1967. 7.50 o.s.i. (ISBN 0-8076-0432-1). Braziller.

Zollinger, Robert M. & Coleman, David W. The Influences of Pancreatic Tumors on the Stomach. (Beaumont Lecture Ser.). (Illus.). 224p. 1974. text ed. 22.50 (ISBN 0-398-02683-1). C C Thomas.

Zollschan, G. K. & Hirsch, W. Social Change: Explorations, Diagnosis, & Conjectures. LC 75-8736. 1976. text ed. 22.50 (ISBN 0-470-98408-2); pap. text ed. 10.50x (ISBN 0-470-98409-0). Halsted Pr.

Zolna, Ed & Conklin, Mike. Mastering Softball. (Mastering Ser.). (Illus.). 1981. 12.95 (ISBN 0-8092-7184-2); pap. 5.95 (ISBN 0-8092-7183-4). Contemp Bks.

Zolotas, Xenophon. International Monetary Issues & Development Policies. LC 77-90142. 1977. 22.50x (ISBN 0-8147-9654-0). NYU Pr.

Zolotow, Charlotte. I Have a Horse of My Own. (gr. 4-7). 7.95 (ISBN 0-690-04046-6). T Y Crowell.

--If You Listen. LC 79-2688. (An Ursula Nordstrom Bk.). (Illus.). 32p. (ps-3). 1980. 8.95 (ISBN 0-06-027049-7, HarpJ); PLB 8.79 (ISBN 0-06-027050-0). Har-Row.

--The Little Black Puppy. (Eager Readers Ser.). (gr. k-3). 1975. PLB 5.00 (ISBN 0-307-60804-2, Golden Pr). Western Pub.

--One Step, Two... rev. ed. LC 80-11749. (Illus.). 32p. (gr. k-1). 1981. 7.95 (ISBN 0-688-51971-7); PLB 7.63 (ISBN 0-686-68921-6). Morrow.

Zolotow, Charlotte, jt. auth. see Shaw, Ray.

Zoltan, J. Atlas der chirurgischen Schnitt--und Nahttechnik. 2nd ed. (Illus.). 176p. 1980. 69.00 (ISBN 3-8055-0439-X). S Karger.

Zolten, J. Jerome, jt. auth. see Phillips, Gerald M.

Zolynas, Al. The New Physics. LC 79-65337. (Wesleyan Poetry Program: Vol. 97). 1979. 10.00x (ISBN 0-8195-2097-7, Pub. by Wesleyan U Pr); pap. 4.95 (ISBN 0-8195-1097-1). Columbia U Pr.

Zon, Raphael, ed. see Pennsylvania University Bicentennial Conference.

Zondag, Jack & Oosterman, Gordon. Building British Canada. 1978. 3.05 (ISBN 0-87463-336-2). Chr Sch Intl.

Zondag-Hamaker, Karen. Astro-Psychology. 1980. pap. 7.95 (ISBN 0-87728-465-2). Weiser.

Zondergeld, Rein, jt. auth. see Krichbaum, Jorg.

Zondervan Staff. Zondervan Expanded Concordance. 1968. 19.95 o.p. (ISBN 0-310-35010-7). Zondervan.

Zoneraich, Samuel. Diabetes & the Heart. (Illus.). 320p. 1978. 35.75 (ISBN 0-398-03644-6). C C Thomas.

--Non-Invasive Methods in Cardiology. (Illus.). 596p. 1975. text ed. 59.75 (ISBN 0-398-03107-X). C C Thomas.

Zong, In Sob, compiled by. & tr. Folk Tales from Korea. 176p. 1979. write for info. (ISBN 0-930878-15-9). Hollym Intl.

Zonker, Patricia. Murdercycles. LC 78-12855. (Illus.). 1978. 13.95 (ISBN 0-88229-553-5); pap. 7.95 (ISBN 0-88229-610-8). Nelson-Hall.

Zonneveld, W. & Weerman, F., eds. Linguisitcs in the Netherlands 1977-1979. (Publications in Language Sciences: No. 1). 483p. 1980. pap. text ed. write for info. (ISBN 90-70176-09-2). Humanities.

Zonneveld, Wim. A Formal Theory of Exceptions in Generative Phonology. (Illus.). 1978. pap. text ed. 23.00x (ISBN 0-685-92395-9). Humanities.

Zook, jt. auth. see Royce.

Zook, Ardith. Captain Gaius Sees a Miracle. 1980. pap. 0.79 (ISBN 0-570-06133-4, 59-1251, Arch Bk). Concordia.

Zook, David H., Jr. & Higham, Robin. A Short History of Warfare. LC 65-28533. (Illus.). 12.50 o.p. (ISBN 0-685-59133-6, H-587). Hippocrene Bks.

Zook, Wayne H. Constructing & Manufacturing Wood Products. (Illus.). 434p. (gr. 9-12). 1974. 15.96 (ISBN 0-87345-048-5). McKnight.

Zoological Society of London - 17th Symposium. Some Recent Developments in Comparative Medicine. 1967. 55.50 (ISBN 0-12-613317-4). Acad Pr.

Zoological Society Of London - 20th Symposium. Echinoderm Biology. Millot, N., ed. 1968. 34.00 (ISBN 0-12-613320-4). Acad Pr.

Zoological Society of London - 29th Symposium. Conservation & Productivity of Natural Waters. Edwards, R. W. & Garrod, D. J., eds. 1972. 45.00 o.s.i. (ISBN 0-12-613329-8). Acad Pr.

Zoological Society of London - 30th Symposium. Diseases of Fish. Mawdesley-Thomas, Lionel E., ed. 1972. 50.50 o.s.i. (ISBN 0-12-613330-1). Acad Pr.

Zoost, Brenda L. Van see Van Zoost, Brenda L.

Zopf, Paul E., Jr. Cultural Accumulation in Latin America. LC 79-48091. 393p. 1980. text ed. 20.00 (ISBN 0-8191-1012-4); pap. text ed. 12.25 (ISBN 0-8191-1013-2). U Pr of Amer.

--Sociocultural Systems. LC 78-62250. 1978. 17.75 (ISBN 0-8191-0567-8). U Pr of Amer.

Zopf, Paul E., Jr., jt. auth. see Smith, T. Lynn.

Zophy, Jonathan W., ed. The Holy Roman Empire: A Dictionary Handbook. LC 79-8282. (Illus.). xxvii, 551p. 1980. lib. bdg. 45.00 (ISBN 0-313-21457-3, ZHR/). Greenwood.

Zorab, P. A. Scoliosis & Muscle. (Clinics in Developmental Medicine Ser., Research Monographs: Vol. 4A). 220p. 1974. 26.00 o.p. (ISBN 0-685-59047-X). Lippincott.

Zorach, Cecile. English Grammar for Students of German. LC 80-82773. 1980. pap. 4.50 (ISBN 0-934034-02-8). Olivia & Hill.

Zorgniotti, A. W. & Rossi, G. Vasculogenic Impotence. (Illus.). 344p. 1980. 39.75 (ISBN 0-398-03982-8). C C Thomas.

Zorina, Vera. Dancer's Choice: The Ballet in Music & Pictures. Date not set. 27.00 (ISBN 0-03-057982-1, HarpT). Har-Row.

Zorita, Alonso De see De Zorita, Alonso.

Zorn, J. D. Brass Ensemble Methods for Music Educators. 1977. pap. text ed. 13.95x (ISBN 0-534-00503-9). Wadsworth Pub.

Zorn, Jay & Hanshumaker, James. Fundammentals Learning Through Making Music. Feldstein, Sandy, ed. LC 79-25768. 1980. pap. 13.50 (ISBN 0-88284-105-X). Alfred Pub.

Zorn, John W. The Essential Delsarte. LC 68-12619. 1968. 10.00 (ISBN 0-8108-0044-6). Scarecrow.

Zorn, Robert L. Speed Reading. LC 79-2744. (Everyday Handbook Ser.: EH-502). 128p. (Orig.). 1980. pap. 3.50 (ISBN 0-06-463502-3, EH 502, EH). Har-Row.

Zorn, Stephen, jt. auth. see Radetzki, Marian.

Zornosa, Jesus. Percutaneous Needle Biopsies: A Radiological Approach. (Illus.). 200p. 1981. lib. bdg. write for info. (ISBN 0-683-09400-9). Williams & Wilkins.

Zornow, Edith, jt. auth. see Goldstein, Ruth M.

Zorro, Harold W. Doctor Death: Twelve Must Die. LC 80-8666. 80p. 1980. lib. bdg. 11.95 (ISBN 0-89370-083-5); pap. 5.95 (ISBN 0-89370-082-7). Borgo Pr.

Zoshchenko, Mikhail. Rasskazy, 1921-1930. (Rus.). 1980. pap. 5.00 (ISBN 0-88233-591-X). Ardis Pubs.

Zosimos Of Panopolis. On the Letter Omega. Jackson, Howard, tr. from Greek. LC 78-18264. (Society of Biblical Literature. Texts & Translations. Graeco-Roman Religion Ser.: No. 5). 1978. pap. 4.50 (ISBN 0-89130-250-6, 060214). Scholars Pr Ca.

Zoss, Joel. Chronicle. (Orig.). 1980. pap. write for info. (ISBN 0-671-41458-5). PB.

Zotos, John. Mathematical Models of the Chemical, Physical & Mathematical Properties of Engineering Alloys. LC 76-22228. 1977. 28.95 (ISBN 0-669-00884-2). Lexington Bks.

Zotterman, Y. Touch, Tickle & Pain, 2 vols. LC 70-91702. Vol. 1. 1969. 23.00 (ISBN 0-08-015532-4); Vol. 2. 1971. 25.00 (ISBN 0-08-016052-2). Pergamon.

Zotterman, Y., ed. see Hirsch, C.

Zotterman, Yngve, jt. auth. see Emmelin, N.

Zotterman, Yngve, ed. Olfaction & Taste. (Vol. 1). 1963. text ed. 24.75 o.p. (ISBN 0-08-009814-2). Pergamon.

Zottoli, Robert A. Introduction of Marine Environments. 2nd ed. 1978. pap. text ed. 11.50 (ISBN 0-8016-5694-X). Mosby.

Zoubek, C., jt. auth. see Leslie, L. Et Al.

Zoubek, Charles E., jt. auth. see Leslie, Louis A.

Zoubek, J., jt. ed. see Zeman, Z.

Zouche, Robert C. Visits to Monasteries in the Levant. LC 80-2200. 1981. Repr. of 1916 ed. 45.00 (ISBN 0-404-18989-X). AMS Pr.

Zouwen, J. van der, jt. ed. see Geyer, R. F.

Zschoche, Donna A. Mosby's Comprehensive Review of Critical Care. 2nd ed. LC 80-16790. (Illus.). 959p. 1980. text ed. 25.95 (ISBN 0-8016-5697-4). Mosby.

Zsoldos, L., jt. auth. see Kovacs, T.

Zube, Ervin H. Environmental Evaluation: Perception & Public Policy. LC 80-11860. (Basic Concepts in Environment & Behavior Ser.). (Orig.). 1980. pap. text ed. 6.95 (ISBN 0-8185-0377-7). Brooks-Cole.

Zubek, John P., ed. Sensory Deprivation: Fifteen Years of Research. LC 69-12143. (Century Psychology Ser.). (Illus.). 1969. 26.50x (ISBN 0-89197-400-8); pap. text ed. 8.95x (ISBN 0-89197-401-6). Irvington.

Zubenko, Ivan. Zirka. 2nd, rev. ed. 171p. (Ukrainian.). 1980. pap. text ed. 6.00 (ISBN 0-686-63323-7). Slavia Lib.

Zuber, Cecil J. Squash for Players & Coaches. (Illus.). 128p. 1980. 16.95 (ISBN 0-13-839910-7, Spec); pap. 6.95 (ISBN 0-13-839902-6). P-H.

Zuber, O. The Languages of Theatre: Problems in the Translation & Transposition of Drama. LC 79-41711. 178p. 1980. 32.50 (ISBN 0-08-025246-X). Pergamon.

Zuber, Rene. Who Are You Monsieur Gurdjieff? Koralek, Jenny, tr. 80p. 1980. pap. 7.50 (ISBN 0-7100-0674-8). Routledge & Kegan.

Zuber, Richard L. North Carolina During Recontruction. (Illus.). 1975. pap. 1.00 (ISBN 0-86526-089-3). NC Archives.

Zuber, William P. My Eighty Years in Texas. Mayfield, Janis B., ed. (Personal Narratives of the West Ser: No. 6). 285p. 1971. 9.95 o.p. (ISBN 0-292-70050-4); pap. 4.95 o.p. (ISBN 0-292-75022-6). U of Tex Pr.

Zuberbuhler, J. R. Clinical Diagnosis in Pediatric Cardiology. (Modern Pediatric Cardiology Ser.). (Illus.). 192p. 1981. text ed. 50.00 (ISBN 0-686-28921-8). Churchill.

--Clinical Diagnosis in Pediatric Cardiology. (Modern Pediatric Cardiology Ser.). (Illus.). 192p. 1981. 50.00 (ISBN 0-443-01889-8). Churchill.

Zubov, V. P. Leonardo Da Vinci. Kraus, David, tr. LC 67-27096. (Illus.). 1968. 16.50x (ISBN 0-674-52450-0). Harvard U Pr.

Zubrick, James W. Work in the Hood: The First Entertaining Organic Chemistry Laboratory Guide. LC 80-69113. (Illus.). 120p. (Orig.). 1980. pap. 4.50 (ISBN 0-937926-00-0). Scienspot.

Zubrow, E. Prehistoric Carrying Capacity: A Model. LC 74-8415. 1975. 7.95 o.p. (ISBN 0-8465-8779-3, 58779). Benjamin-Cummings.

Zubrow, Ezra B., et al, eds. New World Archaeology: Theoretical & Cultural Transformations: Readings from Scientific American. LC 74-7028. (Illus.). 1974. text ed. 20.95x (ISBN 0-7167-0503-6); pap. text ed. 10.95x (ISBN 0-7167-0502-8). W H Freeman.

Zubrowski, Bernie. A Children's Museum Activity Book: Ball-Point Pens. LC 78-31622. (Children's Museum Bks.). (Illus.). (gr. 5-7). 1979. 6.95g (ISBN 0-316-98882-0); pap. 3.95 (ISBN 0-316-98883-9). Little.

Zucchi, Jacopo see Baldini, Baccio.

Zucher, E. The Buddhist Conquest of China: The Spread & Adaptation of Buddhism in Early Medieval China, 2 vols. 470p. 1973. Set. text ed. 73.00x (ISBN 0-391-01961-9). Humanities.

Zuck, Barbara A. A History of Musical Americanism. Buelow, George, ed. (Studies in Musicology). 412p. 1980. 34.95 (ISBN 0-8357-1109-9, Pub. by UMI Res Pr). Univ Microfilms.

Zucker, C., jt. auth. see Kushner, M.

Zucker, David H. Stage & Image in the Plays of Christopher Marlowe. (Salzburg Studies in English Literature, Elizabethan & Renaissance Studies: No. 7). 188p. 1972. pap. text ed. 25.00x (ISBN 0-391-01578-8). Humanities.

Zucker, H. Problems of Psychotherapy. LC 67-19235. 1967. 12.95 (ISBN 0-02-935700-4). Free Pr.

Zucker, Martine, jt. auth. see Manning, Peter K.

Zucker, Mitchell H. Electronic Circuits for the Behavioral & Biomedical Sciences: A Reference Book of Useful Solid-State Circuits. LC 76-81921. (Illus.). 1969. text ed. 22.95x (ISBN 0-7167-0918-X). W H Freeman.

Zucker, Ralph. FilmRow Executive BlackBook. 400p. 1981. pap. write for info. (ISBN 0-686-27694-9). Filmrow Pubns.

--Filmrow: The Executive BlackBook of the Theatrical Motion Picture Marketing Business. 400p. (Orig.). 1981. write for info. Filmrow Pubns.

Zuckerland, Victor. Sound & Symbol, 2 vols. Incl. Vol. 1. Music & the External World. Trask, W. R., tr. 1956. 20.00 (ISBN 0-691-09828-X); pap. 5.95 (ISBN 0-691-01759-X, 183); Vol. 2. Man the Musician. Guterman, Norbert, tr. 450p. 1973. 22.00 (ISBN 0-691-09925-1); pap. 5.95 (ISBN 0-691-01812-X). LC 55-11489. (Bollingen Ser.: Vol. 44). Set. 37.50 (ISBN 0-686-64022-5). Princeton U Pr.

Zuckerman. The Social Life of Monkeys & Apes. 2nd ed. (Illus.). 496p. 1980. 55.00 (ISBN 0-7100-0691-8). Routledge & Kegan.

Zuckerman, et al. A New System of Anatomy: Being a Dissector's Guide & Atlas. 2nd ed. (Illus.). 650p. 1981. pap. text ed. 29.50x (ISBN 0-19-263136-5). Oxford U Pr.

Zuckerman, A., ed. Dynamic Aspects of Host-Parasite Relationships, Vol. 2. LC 70-189940. 225p. 1976. 41.95 (ISBN 0-470-98430-9). Halsted Pr.

Zuckerman, Arthur J. A Jewish Princedom in Feudal France 768-900. LC 72-137392. (Studies in Jewish History, Culture, & Institutions: No. 2). 435p. 1972. 27.50x (ISBN 0-231-03298-6). Columbia U Pr.

Zuckerman, Avivah & Weiss, David W., eds. Dynamic Aspects of Host Parasite Relationships, Vol.1. 1973. 31.00 (ISBN 0-12-782001-9). Acad Pr.

Zuckerman, Harriet. Scientific Elite: Nobel Laureates in the United States. LC 76-26444. (Illus.). 1977. 14.95 (ISBN 0-02-935760-8); pap. text ed. 7.95 (ISBN 0-02-935880-9). Free Pr.

Zuckerman, Herbert S., jt. auth. see Niven, Ivan.

Zuckerman, J. J., ed. see Atkinson, G.

Zuckerman, Lawrence, et al. A Parent's Guide to Children: The Challenge. LC 77-90090. (Illus., Orig.). 1978. pap. 2.75 (ISBN 0-8015-5734-8, Hawthorn). Dutton.

Zuckerman, Lord, ed. Great Zoos of the World: Their Origins & Significance. (Illus.). 230p. 1980. lib. bdg. 35.00x (ISBN 0-89158-985-6). Westview.

Zuckerman, Marilyn. Monday Morning Movie. LC 80-51924. (Illus.). 56p. (Orig.). 1980. write for info. (ISBN 0-935694-03-X); pap. 10.00 (ISBN 0-935694-04-8). St Edns.

Zuckerman, Martin. Arithmetic Without Trumpets or Drums. 1978. pap. text ed. 16.95 (ISBN 0-205-06163-X); instr's man. avail. (ISBN 0-205-05916-3). Allyn.

Zuckerman, Martin M. Algebra & Trigonometry: A Straightforward Approach. 1980. text ed. 15.95x (ISBN 0-393-95020-4); wkbk. 4.95x (ISBN 0-393-95037-9); instr's manual avail. (ISBN 0-393-95046-8). Norton.

--Basic Mathematics. 520p. 1980. text ed. 14.95 (ISBN 0-442-21911-3); instr's. manual 2.50 (ISBN 0-442-23264-0). Van Nos Reinhold.

--Elementary Algebra Without Trumpets or Drums. 448p. 1976. text ed. 17.80x (ISBN 0-205-04895-1); instructor's manual free (ISBN 0-685-57481-4); student wkbk 6.95 (ISBN 0-205-05824-8). Allyn.

Zuckerman, Marvin, jt. tr. see Weltman, Gershon.

Zuckerman, Michael. Peaceable Kingdoms: New England Towns in the Eighteenth Century. 1978. pap. 5.95 (ISBN 0-393-00895-9, N895, Norton Lib). Norton.

Zuckerman, Solly. From Apes to Warlords. LC 77-3783. (Illus.). 1978. 22.50 o.s.i. (ISBN 0-06-014807-1, HarpT). Har-Row.

Zuckerman, Solly, ed. Ovary. 2nd ed. Incl. Vol. 1. General Aspects. 1977. 49.00 (ISBN 0-12-782601-7); Vol. 2. Physiology. 1977. 53.50 (ISBN 0-12-782602-5); Vol. 3. Regulation of Oogenesis & Sleriodogenesis. 1978. 45.00 (ISBN 0-12-782603-3). 1977. Acad Pr.

Zuckrow, Edward. The Death of Horn & Hardart: Special Issue 15. pap. 1.00 o.p. (ISBN 0-685-78396-0). The Smith.

Zucrow, Maurice J. & Hoffman, Joe D. Gas Dynamics, 2 vols. LC 76-6855. 768p. Vol. 1. text ed. 44.95 (ISBN 0-471-98440-X); Vol. 2. text ed. 44.95 (ISBN 0-471-01806-6). Wiley.

Zuercher, K. & Krebs, A. Hautnebenwirkungen interner Arzneimittel: Cutaneous Side Effects of Systemic Drugs. (Illus.). 1980. pap. 50.50 (ISBN 3-8055-0019-X). S Karger.

Zuesse, Evan M. Ritual Cosmos: The Sanctification of Life in African Religions. LC 79-13454. x, 256p. 1980. 18.00x (ISBN 0-8214-0398-2). Ohio U Pr.

Zuidema, George D., jt. auth. see Shackelford, Richard T.

Zuidema, George D., ed. The Johns Hopkins Atlas of Human Functional Anatomy. rev., 2nd ed. LC 79-25191. 1980. text ed. 17.50x (ISBN 0-8018-2363-3); pap. text ed. 10.95x (ISBN 0-8018-2364-1). Johns Hopkins.

Zuilen, A. J. The Life Cycle of Magazines: A Historical Study of the Decline & Fall of the General Interest Mass Audience Magazines in the United States, During the Period 1946-1972. 1977. pap. text ed. 28.50x (ISBN 90-6296-041-3). Humanities.

Zuk. Family Therapy. rev. ed. 1981. 19.95x (ISBN 0-87705-430-4); pap. 12.95x (ISBN 0-87705-955-1). Human Sci Pr.

Zuk, William. Concepts of Structure. 80p. 1972. Repr. of 1963 ed. 7.50 o.p. (ISBN 0-88275-072-0). Krieger.

Zukav, Gary. The Dancing Wu Li Masters: An Overview of the New Physics. LC 78-25827. (Illus.). 1979. 12.95 (ISBN 0-688-03402-0); pap. 6.95 (ISBN 0-688-08402-8). Morrow.

Zuker-Bujanowska, Liliana. Liliana's Journal: Warsaw 1939-1945. (Illus.). 176p. 1980. 9.95 (ISBN 0-8037-4997-X). Dial.

Zukin, S. Beyond Marx & Tito. LC 74-12978. (Illus.). 272p. 1975. 29.95 (ISBN 0-521-20630-8). Cambridge U Pr.

Zukofsky, Louis. A Test of Poetry. 1981. 12.95 (ISBN 0-393-01446-0); pap. 4.95 (ISBN 0-393-00050-8). Norton.

Zukoski, Theodore. Passageways. 1981. 4.95 (ISBN 0-8062-1672-7). Carlton.

Zukowsky, John. The Plan of Chicago: 1909-1979. LC 79-55997. (Illus.). 52p. (Orig.). 1979. pap. 4.95x (ISBN 0-86559-039-7). Art Inst Chi.

Zulaika, Joseba. Terranova: The Ethos & Luck of Deep-Sea Fishermen. LC 80-20931. (Illus.). 160p. 1981. text ed. 14.50x (ISBN 0-89727-016-9). Inst Study Human.

Zulauf, Sander W. & Cifelli, Edward M. Index of American Periodical Verse: 1976. LC 73-3060. 1978. 20.00 (ISBN 0-8108-1082-4). Scarecrow.

--Index of American Periodical Verse: 1977. LC 73-3060. 1979. lib. bdg. 20.00 (ISBN 0-8108-1169-3). Scarecrow.

Zulauf, Sander W. & Weiser, Irwin H. Index of American Periodical Verse, 1971. LC 73-3060. 1973. 20.00 (ISBN 0-8108-0606-1). Scarecrow.

--Index of American Periodical Verse 1972. LC 73-3060. 1974. 20.00 (ISBN 0-8108-0698-3). Scarecrow.

--Index of American Periodical Verse: 1973. LC 73-3060. 1975. 20.00 (ISBN 0-8108-0778-5). Scarecrow.

--Index of American Periodical Verse: 1974. LC 73-3060. 1976. 20.00 (ISBN 0-8108-0872-2). Scarecrow.

--Index of American Periodical Verse: 1975. LC 73-3060. 1977. 20.00 (ISBN 0-8108-0965-6). Scarecrow.

Zulch, Joan C., ed. see Rose, Noel R., et al.

Zulfo, Ismat H. Karari. xv, 252p. 1980. 10.50 (ISBN 0-208-09495-4, SSC). Shoe String.

Zulke, Frank. Through the Eyes of Social Science. 2nd ed. 336p. 1981. pap. text ed. 7.95x (ISBN 0-917974-54-9). Waveland Pr.

Zulli, Floyd. The Joy of Reading: A Personal Introduction to Great Books. LC 75-171904. 192p. (gr. 7 up). 1972. PLB 5.88 o.p. (ISBN 0-531-00430-9). Watts.

Zuman, P., jt. auth. see Meites, L.

Zumberge, James H. & Nelson, Clemens A. Elements of Physical Geology. LC 75-26843. 432p. 1976. text ed. 20.50x (ISBN 0-471-98674-7). Wiley.

Zumwalt, Betty. Ketchup Pickles Sauces: 19th Century Food in Glass. (Illus.). 480p. 1980. 25.00x (ISBN 0-686-28760-6). M West Pubs.

Zundell, George. Hydration & Intermolecular Interaction: Infrared Investigations with Polyelectrolyte Membranes. 1970. 48.00 (ISBN 0-12-782850-8). Acad Pr.

Zunin, Leonard & Zunin, Natalie. Contact: The First Four Minutes. 1972. 7.95 o.p. (ISBN 0-8402-1288-7). Nash Pub.

--Contact: The First Four Minutes. 1975. pap. 2.50 (ISBN 0-345-28662-6). Ballantine.

Zunin, Natalie, jt. auth. see Zunin, Leonard.

Zunker, Vernon G. Career Counseling. LC 80-23030. 357p. 1980. text ed. 16.95 (ISBN 0-8185-0428-5). Brooks-Cole.

Zunser, Miriam S. Yesterday: A Memoir of a Russian-Jewish Family. Leider, Emily W., ed. LC 78-2150. (Illus.). 1978. 11.95 o.s.i. (ISBN 0-06-014810-1, HarpT). Har-Row.

Zupko, Ronald E. British Weights & Measures: A History from Antiquity to the Seventeenth Century. 1977. 21.50 (ISBN 0-299-07340-8, 734). U of Wis Pr.

--Dictionary of English Weights & Measures from Anglo-Saxon Times to the Nineteenth Century. LC 68-14038. 1968. 25.00x (ISBN 0-299-04870-5). U of Wis Pr.

Zupnick, Elliot. Foreign Investment in the U. S. Costs & Benefits. LC 80-66684. (Headline Ser.: No. 249). (Illus.). 80p. (Orig.). 1980. pap. 2.00 (ISBN 0-87124-061-0). Foreign Policy.

Zuppinger, A., et al, eds. High Energy Electrons in Radiation Therapy. (Illus.). 130p. 1980. pap. 28.40 (ISBN 0-387-10188-8). Springer-Verlag.

Zurayk, Constantine, tr. see Miskawayh, Ali.

Zurbuchen, Mary S. Introduction to Old Javanese Language and Literature: A Kawi Prose Anthology. LC 76-16235. (Michigan Series in South & Southeast Asian Languages & Linguistics: No. 3). 150p. 1976. pap. 5.00x (ISBN 0-89148-053-6). Ctr S&SE Asian.

Zurcher, Arnold J., jt. auth. see Smith, Edward C.

Zur Heide, Karl Gert see Gert zur Heide, Karl.

Zusman, Jack & Davidson, David L., eds. Organizing the Community to Prevent Suicide. 112p. 1971. 11.50 (ISBN 0-398-02448-0). C C Thomas.

--Practical Aspects of Mental Health Consultation. (Illus.). 176p. 1972. 11.75 (ISBN 0-398-02449-9). C C Thomas.

Zusne, Leonard & Jones, Warren H. Anomalistic Psychology. LC 80-17345. 502p. 1981. text ed. 29.95 (ISBN 0-89859-068-X). L Erlbaum Assocs.

Zussman, J., ed. Physical Methods in Determinative Mineralogy. 2nd ed. 1978. 73.50 (ISBN 0-12-782960-1). Acad Pr.

Zuver, Jean. Getting Your Shape in Shape: A New Weight Conditioning Program for Women. LC 80-26725. (Illus.). 128p. 1981. 7.95 (ISBN 0-498-02536-5). A S Barnes.

Zuwaylif, Fadil H. Applied Business Statistics. 1974. text ed. 17.95 (ISBN 0-201-08906-8). A-W.

--General Applied Statistics. 3rd ed. LC 78-67937. 1979. text ed. 15.95 (ISBN 0-201-08994-7). A-W.

Zuwaylif, Fadil H., et al. Management Science: An Introduction. LC 78-5827. (Management & Administration Ser.). 1979. text ed. 24.95 (ISBN 0-471-98675-5); sol. manual avail. (ISBN 0-471-03222-0). Wiley.

Zuwiyya, Jalal. The Near East(South-West Asia & North Africa) A Bibliographic Study. LC 72-13364. 1973. 13.50 (ISBN 0-8108-0583-9). Scarecrow.

Zuyev, Yu. S., jt. auth. see Bartenev, G. M.

Zuylen, Guirne Van see Van Zuylen, Guirne.

Zuzanek, Jiri. Work & Leisure in the Soviet Union: A Time-Budget Analysis. 1980. 29.95 (ISBN 0-03-056292-9). Praeger.

Zvegintzov, Catherine, tr. see Denikin, Anton I.

Zvelebil, K. Introduction to the Historical Grammar of the Tamil Language. (Oriental Institute Czechoslovakia Dissertationes Orientales, Vol. 25). 1970. 6.00x o.p. (ISBN 0-685-27140-4). Paragon.

Zwager, Louise H. The English Philosophic Lyric. 208p. 1980. Repr. of 1931 ed. lib. bdg. 30.00 (ISBN 0-8495-6225-2). Arden Lib.

Zwar, Desmond. The Bio-Adventures: The Drama of Medical Research. LC 80-6168. 288p. 1981. 14.95 (ISBN 0-8128-2807-0). Stein & Day.

Zweden, J. Van see Van Zweden, J.

Zweig. Novellen. (Easy Reader, C). pap. 3.75 (ISBN 0-88436-042-3, GEA201053). EMC.

Zweig, Ellen, jt. ed. see Vincent, Stephen.

Zweig, Gunter, ed. Analytical Methods for Pesticides, Plant Growth Regulators & Food Additives, 10 vols. Incl. Vol. 1. Principles, Methods & General Applications. 1963. 62.75 (ISBN 0-12-784301-9); Vol. 2. Insecticides. 1964. 62.75 (ISBN 0-12-784302-7); Vol. 3. Fungicides, Nematocides & Soil Fumigants, Rodenticides, & Food & Feed Additives. 1964. 36.50 (ISBN 0-12-784303-5); Vol. 4. Herbicides (Plant Growth Regulators) 1964. 36.50 (ISBN 0-12-784304-3); Vol. 5. 1967. 60.00 (ISBN 0-12-784305-1); Vol. 6. 68.50 (ISBN 0-12-784306-X); Vol. 7. Thin-Layer & Liquid Chromatography & Analysis of Pesticides of International Importance. 1974. o.s.i (ISBN 0-12-784307-8); Vol. 8. Government Regulations, Pheromone Analyses, Additional Pesticides. Zweig, Gunter & Sharma, Joseph, eds. 1976. 62.75 (ISBN 0-12-784308-6); Vol. 10. Newer & Updated Methods. Zweig, Gunter & Sharma, Joseph, eds. 1978. 48.00 (ISBN 0-12-784310-8); Vol. 11. 1980. 46.00 (ISBN 0-12-784311-6). Set. 514.00. Acad Pr.

Zweig, Gunter & Sherma, Joseph, eds. Handbook of Chromatography, CRC, 2 vols. LC 76-163067. (Handbook Ser). 400p. 1972. Vol. 1, 784p. 59.95 (ISBN 0-8493-0561-6); Vol. 2, 343p. 49.95 (ISBN 0-87819-562-9). CRC Pr.

Zweig, Paul. The Heresy of Self-Love: A Study of Subversive Individualism. LC 79-5482. 288p. 1980. 17.50x (ISBN 0-691-06431-8); pap. 4.95 (ISBN 0-691-01371-3). Princeton U Pr.

--Lautreamont: The Violent Narcissus. LC 78-189562. 1972. 10.00 (ISBN 0-8046-9021-9, Natl U). Kennikat.

--Muktananda: Selected Essays. LC 76-9994. 1977. pap. 5.95 (ISBN 0-06-069860-8, RD185, HarpR). Har-Row.

Zweig, Stefan. The World of Yesterday. LC 43-5821. (Illus.). xxvi, 455p. 1964. pap. 6.25x (ISBN 0-8032-5224-2, BB 181, Bison). U of Nebr Pr.

Zweig, Stefan, jt. auth. see Strauss, Richard.

Zweigert, Konrad & Kropholler, Jan. Law of Copyright, Competition & Industrial Property. Kolle, Gert & Hallstein, Hans P., eds. (Sources of International Uniform Law Ser.: Vol. III-A First Supplement). 1340p. 1980. 175.00x (ISBN 9-0286-0099-X). Sijthoff & Noordhoff.

Zwerdling, Daniel. Workplace Democracy. LC 79-2025. 1979. pap. 5.95 (ISBN 0-06-090733-9, CN-733, CN). Har-Row.

Zwerin, Raymond A. But This Night Is Different. (Illus.). 48p. (ps-1). 1981. text ed. 7.95x (ISBN 0-8074-0032-7, 102561). UAHC.

--For One Another: Jewish Organizations That Help Us All. (Illus.). (gr. 6). 1975. text ed. 6.00 (ISBN 0-8074-0136-6, 141420); tchr's. guide o.p. 5.00 (ISBN 0-685-48915-9, 201421). UAHC.

Zwerin, Raymond A., jt. auth. see Marcus, Audrey F.

Zwerling, Israel see Andolfi, Maurizio.

Zwick, Earl J., jt. auth. see Rector, Robert E.

Zwick, Edward, ed. Literature & Liberalism: An Anthology of Sixty Years of the New Republic. LC 76-2448. 1976. 15.00 o.p. (ISBN 0-915220-06-7, 23097); pap. 5.95 o.p. (ISBN 0-915220-31-8). New Republic.

Zwick, George. Beginner's Guide to TV Repair. 2nd ed. (Illus.). 1979. 10.95 (ISBN 0-8306-9758-6); pap. 5.95 (ISBN 0-8306-1013-8, 1013). TAB Bks.

--Everyman's Guide to Auto Maintenance. LC 73-78200. (Illus.). 192p. 1973. pap. 4.95 (ISBN 0-8306-2648-4); pap. 4.95 (ISBN 0-8306-2648-4, 648). TAB Bks.

Zwicker, Steven N. Dryden's Political Poetry: The Typology of King & Nation. LC 70-188832. 154p. 1972. 8.00x (ISBN 0-87057-134-6, Pub. by Brown U Pr). Univ Pr of New England.

Zwicky, Arnold M., et al. Language Development, Grammer, & Semantics: The Contribution of Linguistics to Bilingual Education. LC 79-57530. (Bilingual Ed. Ser.: No. 7). 89p. 1980. text ed. 6.50x (ISBN 0-87281-111-5). Ctr Appl Ling.

Zwienen, John Van see Van Zwienen, John.

Zwierlein, Frederick K. Religion in the New Netherland, 1623-1664. LC 72-120851. (Civil Liberties in American History Ser). 1970. Repr. of 1910 ed. lib. bdg. 35.00 (ISBN 0-306-71960-6). Da Capo.

Zwinger, Ann. Beyond the Aspen Grove. (Nature Library). (Illus.). 384p. (Orig.). 1981. pap. 5.95 (ISBN 0-06-090842-4, CN 842, CN). Har-Row.

Zwingli, Ulrich. The Accompt Rekenynge & Confession of the Faith of Huldrik Zwinglius. Cotsforde, Thomas, tr. from Latin. LC 79-84148. (The English Experience: No. 964). Orig. Title: Swinglische Bekenntuis. 156p. 1979. Repr. of 1555 ed. lib. bdg. 11.50 (ISBN 90-221-0964-X). Walter J Johnson.

--Selected Writings. Jackson, Samuel M., tr. from Ger. LC 72-80383. (Sources of Medieval History Ser.). (Eng.). 1972. 12.50x o.p. (ISBN 0-8122-7670-1); pap. 3.95x (ISBN 0-8122-1049-2, Pa Paperbks). U of Pa Pr.

Zwirner, E. & Zwirner, K. Phonometrie, Teil 1: Grundfragen der Phonometrie. 3rd ed. Zwirner, E. & Ezawa, K., eds. (Bibliotheca Phonetica Ser.: No. 3). (Illus.). vi, 218p. 1981. pap. 49.75 (ISBN 3-8055-2370-X). S Karger.

Zybert, Richard. Notebook on Time. LC 80-50741. (Illus.). 60p. (Orig.). 1981. pap. 4.95 (ISBN 0-9604260-0-0). Zybert.

Zygmund, A. Trigonometric Series. LC 77-82528. 1977. 79.50 (ISBN 0-521-07477-0). Cambridge U Pr.

Zyla, Wolodymyr T., ed. Albert Camus' Literary Milieu: Arid Lands. Aycock, Wendell M. (Proceedings of the Comparative Literature Symposium: Vol. VIII). (Illus., Orig.). 1976. 6.00 (ISBN 0-89672-050-0). Tex Tech Pr.

--From Surrealism to the Absurd. (Proceedings of the Comparative Literature Symposium: Vol. III). (Illus.). 5.00 o.s.i. (ISBN 0-89672-045-4). Tex Tech Pr.

Zyskind, Harold & Sternfeld, Robert. The Voiceless University: An Argument for Intellectual Autonomy. LC 78-132822. (Higher Education Ser.). 1971. 11.95x o.p. (ISBN 0-87589-103-9). Jossey-Bass.

Zyskind, Sara. Stolen Years. (Adult & Young Adult Bks.). 192p. (gr. 4 up). 1981. PLB 9.95 (ISBN 0-8225-0766-8). Lerner Pubns.

Zysman, John. Political Strategies for Industrial Order: State, Market, & Industry in France. 1977. 20.00x (ISBN 0-520-02889-9). U of Cal Pr.

TITLE INDEX

A

A A C C Technical Guide to Key Cereal & Making Ingredients. Norm Betz. LC 80-68710. 138p. 1980. write for info. (ISBN 0-913250-18-X). Am Assn Cereal Chem.

A. A. Milne. Thomas B. Swann. (English Authors Ser.: No. 113). lib. bdg. 10.95 (ISBN 0-8057-1396-4). Twayne.

A & P: Past, Present & Future. Ed. by Lee Dyer. (Illus.). 4.95 o.p. (ISBN 0-911790-06-3). Prog Grocer.

A Arithma Games Fractions & Mixed Numbers. (gr. 3-7). 1980. pap. 7.20 (ISBN 0-913688-49-5). Pawnee Pub.

A B C Book of Early Americana. Eric Sloane. LC 63-18657. (gr. 1 up). 1963. 4.95a (ISBN 0-385-04663-4); PLB o.p. (ISBN 0-385-05169-7). Doubleday.

A B C of Buses. Dorothy E. Shuttlesworth. (ps-1). PLB 4.95 o.p. (ISBN 0-385-01999-8). Doubleday.

A B C of Music: A Short Practical Guide to the Basic Essentials of Rudiments, Harmony, & Form. Imogen Holst. (Orig.). 1963. 8.95x (ISBN 0-19-317103-1). Oxford U Pr.

A B C Phonics & Faces. James Neal Blake. (Illus.). 84p. 1972. pap. 9.75 (ISBN 0-398-02528-2). C C Thomas.

A B C Pictionary. (Children's Library of Picture Bks.). (Illus.). 10p. (ps). 1979. 1.95 (ISBN 0-89346-180-6, Pub. by Froebel-Kan Japan). Heian Intl.

A B C Rhymes. Carl Memling. (Illus.). (ps-3). 1970. PLB 4.57 o.p. (ISBN 0-307-60543-4, Golden Pr). Western Pub.

A B C's of Integrated Circuits. Rufus P. Turner. LC 70-143034. (Illus., Orig.). 1971. pap. 3.50 o.p. (ISBN 0-672-20823-7, 20823). Sams.

A B C's of Library Promotion. 2nd ed. Steve Sherman. LC 79-24232. 252p. 1980. 12.00 (ISBN 0-8108-1274-6). Scarecrow.

A B C's of Poker. Frank R. Wallace. 1980. pap. cancelled (ISBN 0-911752-31-5). I & O Pub.

A B C's of Small Boat Sailing. Lincoln Clark & Alice Clark. LC 63-13079. (YA) pap. 2.50 (ISBN 0-385-06690-2, C424, Dolp). Doubleday.

A. Bronson Alcott: His Life & Philosophy, 2 Vols. Franklin B. Sanborn & William T. Harris. LC 65-23481. 1893. Set. 15.00x (ISBN 0-8196-0161-6). Biblo.

A. C. Bradley & His Influence in Twentieth-Century Shakespeare Criticism. Katherine Cooke. 1972. 22.00x (ISBN 0-19-812024-9). Oxford U Pr.

A. C. Goodwin. Museum of Fine Arts, Boston, Department of Fine Arts. (Illus.). 1974. pap. 2.00 o.p. (ISBN 0-87846-084-5). Mus Fine Arts Boston.

A Capella Music in the Public Workshop of the Church. Everett Ferguson. LC 72-76963. (Way of Life Ser: No. 125). 1972. pap. text ed. 2.95 (ISBN 0-89112-125-0) Bibl Res Pr.

A. D. Janelle Viglini. 1975. 12.50 o.p. (ISBN 0-685-54022-7, 0-911156-15-6). Porter.

A. D. Hope. Joy H. Hooton. (Australian Bibliographies Ser.). 286p. 1979. text ed. 12.95x (ISBN 0-19-550523-9). Oxford U Pr.

A. E. Housman. Tom B. Haber. (English Authors Ser.: No. 46). 1967. lib. bdg. 10.95 (ISBN 0-8057-1272-0). Twayne.

A. E. Housman: A Collection of Critical Essays. Ed. by Christopher Ricks. (Twentieth Century Views Ser). 1968. 10.05 (ISBN 0-13-395913-9, Spec); pap. 1.95 (ISBN 0-13-395905-8, STC83, Spec). P-H.

A. E. Housman: The Scholar-Poet. Perceval Graves. 15.95 (ISBN 0-684-16106-0). Scribner.

A. E. S. Contributions to the Irish Statesman. Ed. by Henry Summerfield. (Collected Edition of the Writings of G. W. Russell II). 1979. text ed. 52.00x (ISBN 0-391-01121-9). Humanities.

A. E.'s Paintings. Marion B. Motley. (Collected Edition of the Writings of G. W. Russell Ser.: No. 8). 1980. text ed. write for info. (ISBN 0-391-01201-0). Humanities.

A for Anything. Damon Knight. 1980. pap. 1.95 (ISBN 0-380-48553-2, 48553). Avon.

A. G. Daniels. John J. Robertson. LC 77-80687. (Dimension Ser.). 1977. pap. 5.95 (ISBN 0-8163-0276-6). Pacific Pr Pub Assn.

A. Hoen on Stone: E. Weber & Co. and A. Hoen & Co. Exhibition Catalogue. Lois B. McCauley. LC 79-87284. (Illus.). 1969. 4.50 (ISBN 0-938420-02-X). Md Hist.

A. I. B. S. Directory of Bioscience Departments & Facilities in the United States & Canada. 2nd ed. Ed. by Peter Gray. LC 75-33761. 1975. 43.50 (ISBN 0-12-786589-6). Acad Pr.

A Is for Aloha. Stephanie Feeney. (Illus.). 64p. (ps-k). 1980. 7.95 (ISBN 0-8248-0722-7). U Pr of Hawaii.

A. J. Foyt: Championship Auto Racer. Julian May. LC 75-28934. (Sports Close-up Ser.). (gr. 3-9). 1975. PLB 5.95 o.p. (ISBN 0-913940-33-X); pap. 2.95 o.p. (ISBN 0-913940-99-2). Crestwood Hse.

A J Handbook of Building Structure. 2nd ed. Allan Hodgkinson. (Illus.). 428p. (Orig.). 1980. pap. 37.50x (ISBN 0-85139-273-3). Intl Pubns Serv.

A la Decouverte De L'arabie. Jacqueline Pirenne. (Arabia Past & Present Ser.: Vol. 14). (Fr.). 32.50 (ISBN 0-902675-53-2). Oleander Pr.

A la New Orleans: Restaurant Recipes. Michael Grady. (Orig.). 1980. pap. 6.50 (ISBN 0-937070-02-5). Crabtree.

A la San Francisco: Restaurant Recipes. Catherine G. Crabtree. (Illus.). 240p. (Orig.). 1980. pap. 6.50 (ISBN 0-937070-01-7). Crabtree.

A-Level Physics: Electricity & Semiconducters, Vol.3. 2nd ed. M. Chapple. (Illus.). 288p. (Orig.). 1980. pap. text ed. 11.95x (ISBN 0-7121-0158-6). Intl Ideas.

A Level Physics: Mechanics & Heat, Vol. 1. 2nd ed. M. Chapple. (Illus.). 336p. (Orig.). 1979. pap. text ed. 10.95x (ISBN 0-7121-0154-3, Pub. by Macdonald & Evans England). Intl Ideas.

A Level Physics: Wave Motion-Sound & Light, Vol. 2. 2nd ed. M. Chapple. (Illus.). 240p. (Orig.). 1979. pap. text ed. 10.95x (ISBN 0-7121-0155-1, Pub. by Macdonald & Evans England). Intl Ideas.

A los Que Dios Ha Juntado En Matrimonio. David R. Mace. 1978. pap. 1.80 (ISBN 0-311-40036-1, Edit Mundo). Casa Bautista.

A. Mitchell Palmer: Politician. Stanley Coben. LC 79-180787. (Civil Liberties in American History Ser). (Illus.). 352p. 1972. Repr. of 1963 ed. lib. bdg. 35.00 (ISBN 0-306-70208-8). Da Capo.

A Partir del Eden. Kathryn Lindskoog. Tr. by Julio Orozco from Eng. LC 77-73843. 144p. (Orig., Span.). 1977. pap. 2.50 (ISBN 0-89922-092-4). Edit Caribe.

A Plus Guide to Good Grades. Colligan. (gr. 7-12). 1980. pap. 1.50 (ISBN 0-590-30001-6, Schol Pap). Schol Bk Serv.

A. R. Ammons. Alan Holder. (United States Authors Ser.: No. 303). 1978. lib. bdg. 12.50 (ISBN 0-8057-7208-1). Twayne.

A. R. Shands, Jr. Birthday Celebration Issue. Association of Bone & Joint Surgeons. Ed. by Marshall R. Urist. (Clinical Orthopaedics Ser., Vol. 76). 1971. 15.00 (ISBN 0-685-22854-1). Lippincott.

A to Z Horoscope Maker & Delineator. 13th, rev. ed. Llewellyn George. Ed. by Marylee Bytheriver. (Illus.). 600p. (Orig.). 1981. 17.95 (ISBN 0-87542-263-2). Llewellyn Pubns.

A to Z No-Cook Cookbook. Felipe R. Lombardi. LC 72-79753. 1975. 5.95 (ISBN 0-910294-12-7). Brown Bk.

A to Z No-Cook Cookbook. Felipe Rojas-Lombardi. (Illus.). 64p. (gr. k-6). 1974. 3.95 o.p. (ISBN 0-307-15784-9, Golden Pr); PLB 9.15 o.p. (ISBN 0-307-65784-1). Western Pub.

A to Z of Sales Management. John Fenton. 168p. 1981. 14.95 (ISBN 0-8144-5655-3). Am Mgmt.

A Traves De la Biblia. Tr. by Myer Pearlman. (Spanish Bks.). 1977. 4.25 (ISBN 0-8297-0501-5); pap. 3.25 (ISBN 0-686-28805-X). Life Pubs Intl.

A Vida Da Celula. OAS General Secretariat Deparment of Scientific & Technological Affairs. (Serie De Biologia: No. 5). (Illus.). 117p. (Orig.). Repr. of 1968 ed. 2.00 (ISBN 0-8270-1141-5). OAS.

A-Z Industrial Salesmanship. John Fenton. 1975. text ed. 16.95x (ISBN 0-434-90559-3); pap. text ed. 9.95x (ISBN 0-434-90560-7). Intl Ideas.

A-Z London Map. Automobile Association British Tourist Authority. (Illus.). 1981. pap. write for info. (ISBN 0-85039-021-4, Pub. by Auto Assn-British Tourist Authority England). Merrimack Bk Serv.

A-Z of Astronomy. Patrick Moore. (Encore Edition). (Illus.). 1977. pap. 1.95 (ISBN 0-684-16913-4, SL700, ScribT). Scribner.

A-Z of Clinical Chemistry. W. Hood. LC 80-23908. 386p. 1980. 19.95 (ISBN 0-470-27029-2). Halsted Pr.

A-Z of Space. Peter Fairley. (Illus.). 58p. (gr. 7-12). 1975. 6.95 (ISBN 0-298-12044-5). Transatlantic.

A-Z Visitors' London Atlas & Guide. Automobile Association & British Tourist Authority. (Illus.). 96p. 1981. pap. write for info. (ISBN 0-85039-107-5, Pub. by Auto Assn-British Tourist Authority England). Merrimack Bk Serv.

AA -BTA Where to Go in Britain. Automobile Association & British Tourist Authority. (Illus.). 224p. 1981. write for info. (ISBN 0-86145-028-0, Pub. by Auto Assn-British Tourist Authority England). Merrimack Bk Serv.

AA-BTA Book of London. (Illus.). 196p. 1980. pap. 17.95 (ISBN 0-86145-020-5, Pub. by B T A). Merrimack Bk Serv.

AA BTA Touring Map of Great Britain. rev. ed. pap. 2.50 (ISBN 0-86145-000-0, Pub. by B T A). Merrimack Bk Serv.

AA Camping & Caravanning in Britain. rev. ed. Automobile Association. (Illus.). 256p. 1981. pap. write for info. (ISBN 0-86145-041-8, Pub. by Auto Assn-British Tourist Authority England). Merrimack Bk Serv.

AA Camping & Caravanning in Europe. rev. ed. Automobile Assication. (Illus.). 416p. 1981. pap. write for info. (Pub. by Auto Assn-British Tourist Authority England). Merrimack Bk Serv.

AA Guesthouses & Inns in Britain. rev. ed. Automobile Association. (Illus.). 264p. 1981. pap. write for info. (ISBN 0-86145-042-6, Pub. by Auto Assn-British Tourist Authority England). Merrimack Bk Serv.

AA Guesthouses, Farmhouses & Inns in Europe. rev. ed. 256p. 1980. pap. 8.95 o.p. (ISBN 0-901088-97-8, Pub. by B T A). Merrimack Bk Serv.

AA Guesthouses, Farmhouses & Inns in Europe. rev. ed. Automobile Association. (Illus.). 256p. 1981. pap. write for info. (Pub. by Auto Assn-British Tourist Authority England). Merrimack Bk Serv.

AA Guide to Camping & Caravanning in Britain. rev. ed. 272p. 1980. pap. 8.95 o.p. (ISBN 0-86145-007-8, Pub. by B T A). Merrimack Bk Serv.

AA Guide to Camping & Caravanning in Europe. rev. ed. 400p. 1980. pap. 8.95 o.p. (ISBN 0-901088-93-5, Pub. by B T A). Merrimack Bk Serv.

AA Guide to Guesthouses, Farmhouses & Inns in Britain. rev. ed. 256p. 1980. pap. 8.95 o.p. (ISBN 0-86145-008-6, Pub. by B T A). Merrimack Bk Serv.

AA Hotels & Restaurants in Britain. rev. ed. 576p. 1980. pap. 10.95 o.p. (ISBN 0-86145-006-X, Pub. by B T A). Merrimack Bk Serv.

AA Hotels & Restaurants in Britain. rev. ed. Automobile Association. (Illus.). 600p. 1981. pap. write for info. (ISBN 0-86145-040-X, Pub. by Auto Assn-British Tourist Authority England). Merrimack Bk Serv.

AA Ireland: Where to Go, What to Do. Automobile Association. (Illus.). 204p. 1981. pap. write for info. (ISBN 0-86145-035-3, Pub. by Auto Assn-British Tourist Authority England). Merrimack Bk Serv.

AA London Map. rev. ed. pap. 2.50 (ISBN 0-901088-99-4, Pub. by B T A). Merrimack Bk Serv.

AA Motoring in Europe. rev. ed. Automobile Association. (Illus.). 416p. 1981. pap. write for info. (Pub. by Auto Assn-British Tourist Authority England). Merrimack Bk Serv.

AA Motoring in Western Europe. rev. ed. 400p. 1980. pap. 9.95 o.p. (ISBN 0-901088-98-6, Pub. by B T A). Merrimack Bk Serv.

AA Motorists' Atlas of Great Britain. British Tourist Authority. (Illus.). 1979. 12.95 (ISBN 0-09-211480-6, Pub. by BTA). Merrimack Bk Serv.

AA Motorists' Map of Northern England. British Tourist Authority. 1979. pap. 2.50 (ISBN 0-905522-31-1, Pub. by B T a). Merrimack Bk Serv.

AA Nine Hundred & Ninety-Nine Places to Eat in Britain for Around Five Pounds. rev. ed. 256p. 1980. pap. 5.95 o.p. (ISBN 0-86145-019-1, Pub. by B T A). Merrimack Bk Serv.

AA Road Atlas of New Zealand. Automobile Associations of New Zealand. LC 77-372880. (Illus.). 1975. 15.00x (ISBN 0-600-07347-5). Intl Pubns Serv.

AA Self Catering in Britain. rev. ed. Automobile Association. (Illus.). 272p. 1981. pap. write for info. (ISBN 0-86145-043-4, Pub. by Auto Assn-British Tourist Authority England). Merrimack Bk Serv.

AA Stately Homes, Museums, Castles & Gardens. rev. ed. 256p. 1980. pap. 8.95 o.p. (ISBN 0-86145-010-8, Pub. by B T A). Merrimack Bk Serv.

AA Stately Homes, Museums, Castles & Gardens. rev. ed. Automobile Association. (Illus.). 272p. 1981. pap. price not set (ISBN 0-86145-044-2, Pub. by Auto Assn-British Tourist Authority England). Merrimack Bk Serv.

AA The Motorists' Atlas of Western Europe. Automobile Association. (Illus.). Date not set. pap. price not set (ISBN 0-86145-029-9, Pub. by Auto Assn-British Tourist Authority England). Merrimack Bk Serv.

AA Touring Guide to England. British Tourist Authority. (Illus.). 1979. 23.95 (ISBN 0-09-125890-1, Pub. by B T A). Merrimack Bk Serv.

AA Touring Guide to Ireland. British Tourist Authority. (Illus.). 1979. 23.95 (ISBN 0-09-127020-0, Pub. by B T A). Merrimack Bk Serv.

AA Touring Guide to Scotland. British Tourist Authority. (Illus.). 1979. 23.95 (ISBN 0-09-125870-7, Pub. by B T A). Merrimack Bk Serv.

AA Touring Guide to Wales. British Tourist Authority. (Illus.). 1979. 23.95 (ISBN 0-09-125880-4, Pub. by B T A). Merrimack Bk Serv.

AA Touring Map of Western Europe. Automobile Association. (Illus.). Date not set. pap. price not set (ISBN 0-86145-001-9). Merrimack Bk Serv.

AA Town Plans. rev. ed. 224p. 1980. pap. 10.50 (ISBN 0-86145-003-5, Pub. by B T A). Merrimack Bk Serv.

AACTE Directory 1980. American Association of College for Teacher Education. 118p. (Orig.). 1980. pap. text ed. 6.00 (ISBN 0-89333-020-5). AACTE.

A&P Mechanics Airframe Written Examination Questions. Federal Aviation Administration. (Aviation Maintenance Training Course Ser.). (Illus.). 113p. 1979. pap. 3.75 (ISBN 0-89100-158-1, EA-AC65-20). Aviation Maintenance.

A&P Mechanic's Certification Guide. 4th ed. Federal Aviation Administration. (Aviation Maintenance Training Course Ser.). 64p. 1976. pap. 2.50 (ISBN 0-89100-082-8, EA-AC65-2D). Aviation Maintenance.

A&P Mechanics General Handbook Study Guide. Dale Crane. (Aviation Maintenance Training Course Ser.). (Illus.). 172p. 1977. pap. text ed. 6.00 (ISBN 0-89100-072-0, EA-65-9ASG). Aviation Maintenance.

A&P Mechanics General Written Examination Questions. Federal Aviation Administration. (Aviation Maintenance Training Course Ser.). 88p. 1979. pap. 3.75 (ISBN 0-89100-157-3, EA-AC65-20). Aviation Maintenance.

A&P Mechanics Powerplant Handbook Study Guide. Dale Crane. (Aviation Maintenance Training Course Ser.). 161p. 1978. pap. 6.00 (ISBN 0-89100-073-9, EA-65-12ASG). Aviation Maintenance.

A&P Mechanics Powerplant Written Examination Questions. Federal Aviation Administration. (Aviation Maintenance Training Course Ser.). (Illus.). 99p. 1979. pap. 3.75 (ISBN 0-89100-159-X, EA-AC65-22). Aviation Maintenance.

Aaron Copland. Arthur Berger. LC 79-136055. (Illus.). 1971. Repr. of 1953 ed. lib. bdg. 16.50x (ISBN 0-8371-5205-4, BEAC). Greenwood.

Aaron Ladner Lindsley: Founder of Alaska Missions. 9p. Repr. pap. 1.00 (ISBN 0-8466-0050-1, SJS50). Shorey.

Aaron to Zuverink: A Nostalgic Look at the Baseball Players of the Fifties. Rich Marazzi & Len Fiorito. LC 80-5893. 352p. 1981. 14.95 (ISBN 0-8128-2775-9). Stein & Day.

Aaron's Rod. D. H. Lawrence. 1976. pap. 2.95 (ISBN 0-14-000755-5). Penguin.

Aau Directory 1981. softcover 4.00 (ISBN 0-685-59728-8). AAU Pubns.

Aau Official Code 1981. softcover 4.00 (ISBN 0-685-59727-X). AAU Pubns.

Aau Official Competitive Swimming Rules 1981. 1981. softcover 3.50 (ISBN 0-685-59732-6). AAU Pubns.

Aau Official Diving Rules 1981. 1981. softcover 3.50 (ISBN 0-685-59729-6). AAU Pubns.

Aau Official Junior Olympics Handbook 1981. softcover 2.00 (ISBN 0-685-59730-X). AAU Pubns.

Aau Official Karate Rules 1981. 1977. softcover 3.50 (ISBN 0-685-59754-7). AAU Pubns.

Aau Official Synchronized Swimming Handbook 1981. 1981. softcover 3.50 (ISBN 0-685-59733-4). AAU Pubns.

Aau Official Track & Field Rules 1980. 1977. softcover 3.00 (ISBN 0-685-59756-3). AAU Pubns.

Aau Official Wrestling Handbook 1980. softcover 6.00 (ISBN 0-685-59758-X). AAU Pubns.

Ab Initio Calculations: Methods & Applications in Chemistry. P. Carsky & M. Urban. (Lecture Notes in Chemistry: Vol. 16). (Illus.). 247p. 1980. pap. 21.00 (ISBN 0-387-10005-9). Springer-Verlag.

Ab Initio Calculations on Diatomic Molecules. Ed. by Robert S. Mulliken. W. C. Ermler. 1977. 28.50 (ISBN 0-12-510750-1). Acad Pr.

Ab Initio Valence Calculations in Chemistry. D. B. Cook. LC 73-15144. 1974. 37.95 (ISBN 0-470-17000-X). Halsted Pr.

Ab Urbe Condita, 5 vols. Livy. Incl. Vol. 1. Books 1-5. 2nd ed. Ed. by R. M. Ogilvie et al. 1974. 18.50x (ISBN 0-19-814661-2); Vol. 2. Books 6-10. Ed. by R. S. Conway et al. 1920. 18.50x (ISBN 0-19-814621-3); Vol. 3. Books 21-25. Ed. by R. S. Conway & S. K. Johnson. 1929. 24.00x (ISBN 0-19-814622-1); Vol. 4. Books 26-30. Ed. by R S. Conway & S. K. Johnson. 1934. 22.50x (ISBN 0-19-814623-X); Vol. 5. Books 31-35. Ed. by Alexander H. McDonald. 1965. 18.50x (ISBN 0-19-814646-9). (Oxford Classical Texts Ser.). Oxford U Pr.

ABA Standards for Criminal Justice, 4 vols. American Bar Association. 1980. Set. 195.00 (ISBN 0-316-03709-5); 50.00 ea. Little.

Abacus. Jesse Dilson. (Illus.). (gr. 5-8). 1969. 6.95 (ISBN 0-312-00105-3); pap. 4.95 (ISBN 0-312-00140-1). St Martin.

Abacus in Modern Math. Robert F. Arnold. Date not set. price not set (ISBN 0-685-46523-3). Pacific Bks.

Abandon Yourself to Love. Renee Locks & Joseph McHugh. LC 80-67343. (Illus.). 112p. 1981. 4.95 (ISBN 0-89087-304-6). Celestial Arts.

Abandoned. G. D. Griffiths. LC 74-18131. 96p. (gr. 4 up). 1975. 4.95 o.p. (ISBN 0-695-80537-1); lib. ed. 4.98 o.p. (ISBN 0-695-40537-3). Follett.

Abandoned. Edwin Silberstang. LC 80-1071. 312p. 1981. 10.95 (ISBN 0-385-15978-1). Doubleday.

Abandoned for Love. Caroline Courtney. 224p. (Orig.). 1981. pap. 1.75 (ISBN 0-446-94298-7). Warner Bks.

Abandoned Music Room. William Pillin. (Illus.). 60p. 1975. pap. 2.00 o.p. (ISBN 0-87711-059-X). Kayak.

Abandonment to Divine Providence. Jean-Pierre De Caussade. LC 74-2827. 120p. 1975. pap. 1.95 (ISBN 0-385-02544-0, Im). Doubleday.

Abba Eban: An Autobiography. Abba Eban. 1977. 15.00 (ISBN 0-394-49302-8); lmtd. ed. 25.00 (ISBN 0-394-42644-4). Random.

Abba: Guides to Wholeness & Holiness East & West. Ed. by John R. Sommerfeldt. (Cistercian Studies Ser.: No. 38). 1981. price not set (ISBN 0-87907-838-3). Cistercian Pubns.

Abbasid Revolution. M. A. Shaban. 1979. 32.00 (ISBN 0-521-07849-0); pap. 11.95 (ISBN 0-521-29534-3). Cambridge U Pr.

Abbe C. Georges Bataille. George Bataille. Date not set. 10.00 (ISBN 0-89396-017-9). Urizen Bks.

Abbess of Crewe. Muriel Spark. 1977. pap. 1.95 o.s.i. (ISBN 0-14-004074-9). Penguin.

Abbey Court. Marcella Thum. LC 76-3136. 1976. 7.95 o.p. (ISBN 0-385-12040-0). Doubleday.

Abbey Lubbers, Banshees & Boggarts: An Illustrated Encyclopedia of Fairies. Katharine M. Briggs. LC 79-1897. 1979. 10.00 (ISBN 0-394-50806-8). Pantheon.

Abbeychurch; or, Self-Control & Self-Conceit, 1844. Charlotte M. Yonge. Ed. by Robert L. Wolff. Bd. with Castle-Builders; or, the Deferred Confirmation, 1854. LC 75-470. (Victorian Fiction Ser.). 1975. lib. bdg. 66.00 (ISBN 0-8240-1548-7). Garland Pub.

Abbeys, Ghosts & Castles: A Guide to the Folk History of the Middle Rhine. Beverley D. Eddy. 1979. 8.95 o.p. (ISBN 0-8062-1205-5). Carlton.

Abbot. Walter Scott. 1969. 5.00x o.p. (ISBN 0-460-00124-8, Evman). Dutton.

Abbot's House. Laura Conway. 256p. 1975. pap. 1.25 o.p. (ISBN 0-445-00328-6). Popular Lib.

Abbott H. Thayer, Painter & Naturalist. Nelson C. White. 1969. 35.00x (ISBN 0-87233-015-X). Bauhan.

Abbreviations Guide to French Forms in Justice & Administration. Georg Leistner. 191p. 1975. 17.25 (ISBN 3-7940-3016-8, Pub. by K G Saur). Shoe String.

Abbreviations in Medicine. Albrecht Schertl. 204p. 1977. pap. 20.00 (ISBN 3-7940-7017-8, Pub. by K G Saur). Gale.

Abbreviations in Medicine. 4th ed. Edwin B. Steen. 1978. pap. 10.95 (ISBN 0-02-859430-4). Macmillan.

Abbreviations in National & International Standardization. Artur Buechner. LC 70-587455. 175p. 1971. pap. 30.00x (ISBN 3-486-33611-8). Intl Pubns Serv.

Abbreviations in the African Press, a Transdex Book. new ed. Macmillan Information Division. 1973. 15.00 o.s.i. (ISBN 0-02-468060-5). Macmillan Info.

Abbreviations in the Latin American Press, a Transdex Book. new ed. Macmillan Information Division. 1973. 15.00 o.s.i. (ISBN 0-02-468050-8). Macmillan Info.

Abbreviations of Names of Journals. 1980. 1.00 (ISBN 0-8218-0000-0, ABBR). Am Math.

Abby Mandel's Cuisinart Classroom. Abby Mandel. Ed. by Ruth McElheny. (Illus.). 288p. (Orig.). 1980. pap. 12.50 (ISBN 0-936662-03-4). Cuisinart Cooking.

ABC. (Block Bk.). (Illus.). (ps). 1981. 2.50 (ISBN 0-686-69364-7, Golden Pr). Western Pub.

ABC. Walt Disney Productions. (ps-1). 1979. PLB 6.08 (ISBN 0-307-61080-2, Golden Pr); pap. 1.95 o.p. (ISBN 0-307-11080-X). Western Pub.

ABC Around the House. Sharon Holaves. (Little Golden Reader Ser.). (Illus.). (gr. k-3). 1979. PLB 5.00 (ISBN 0-307-60176-5, Golden Pr). Western Pub.

ABC Book About Christmas. J. M. Stifle. 1981. pap. 2.95 (ISBN 0-570-04053-1, 56-1714). Concordia.

ABC Book About Jesus. J. M. Stifle. 1981. pap. 2.95 (ISBN 0-570-04054-X, 56-1715). Concordia.

ABC Book of Hi-Fi-Audio Projects. George D. Leon. (Illus.). 1977. pap. 5.95 (ISBN 0-8306-6921-3, 921). TAB Bks.

ABC-Buch Kinderlogik, 2 vols. Karl P. Moritz. Ed. by Horst Guenther. (Ger.). Repr. of 1793 ed. text ed. 50.70 (ISBN 3-458-04938-X, Pub. by Insel Verlag Germany). Suhrkamp.

ABC De Puerto Rico. De Matos Freyre. 1966. 8.95 (ISBN 0-87751-005-9, Pub by Troutman Press). E Torres & Sons.

ABC Frieze. Michael Spink. (Illus.). (ps-1). 1980. pap. 4.95 (ISBN 0-224-61538-6, Pub. by Chatto Bodley Jonathan). Merrimack Bk Serv.

ABC Mazes. Waneta B. Bullock & Ganelle Loveless. (Educational Ser.). (Illus.). (gr. k-1). 1979. pap. 3.50 (ISBN 0-89039-244-7). Ann Arbor FL.

ABC Monday Night Football Book. 1980. pap. cancelled (ISBN 0-201-00058-X). A-W.

ABC of a Summer Pond. new ed. Judith C. Friedman. LC 73-92631. (Illus.). (gr. k-4). 1975. 5.45 (ISBN 0-910812-14-4); pap. 2.35 (ISBN 0-910812-15-2). Johnny Reads.

ABC of Children's Names. Doris Ewen & Mary Ewen. (Illus.). 30p. (ps-4). Date not set. pap. cancelled (ISBN 0-914676-41-5). Green Tiger.

ABC of Ecology. Harry Milgrom. LC 74-20654. (Illus.). 32p. (gr. k-3). 1976. pap. 1.95 o.s.i. (ISBN 0-02-044740-X, 04474, Collier). Macmillan.

ABC of Poultry Raising: A Complete Guide for the Beginner or Expert. J. H. Florea. 8.00 (ISBN 0-8446-5186-9). Peter Smith.

ABC of Relativity. 3rd ed. Bertrand Russell. 1969. text ed. 7.50x o.p. (ISBN 0-04-521001-2, 2041). Allen Unwin.

ABC of Stock Speculation & the Anticipation of the Wave Theory. S. A. Nelson. (New Stock Market Library Ser.). 1978. Repr. of 1903 ed. 57.50 (ISBN 0-89266-097-X). Am Classical Coll Pr.

ABC Play with Me. Donna Kelly. (Golden Book for Early Childhood Ser.). (Illus.). (gr. k-3). 1979. PLB 5.38 (ISBN 0-307-68822-4, Golden Pr). Western Pub.

ABC Science Experiments. Harry Milgrom. LC 75-116788. (Illus.). (gr. k-3). 1970. 5.95g o.s.i. (ISBN 0-02-766980-7). Macmillan.

ABC Triplets at the Zoo. DeLage. PLB 5.49 (ISBN 0-8116-4357-3). Garrard.

ABCDEFGHIJKLMNOPQRSTUVWXYZ in Eng & French. Beatrice Rich. (Illus.). 64p. (gr. k-2). 1981. PLB 7.95 (ISBN 0-87460-353-6). Lion.

ABC's. (Ladybird Stories Ser.). (Illus., Arabic.). 2.50x (ISBN 0-686-53060-8). Intl Bk Ctr.

ABC's of Bureaucracy. Robert B. Jansen. LC 78-1840. 1978. 13.95 (ISBN 0-88229-331-1). Nelson-Hall.

ABC's of Capacitors. 3rd ed. William F. Mullin. LC 77-90500. 1978. pap. 5.60 (ISBN 0-672-21498-9). Sams.

ABC's of Creativity & Language Arts: Teacher's Edition. Fred Wille. (gr. 2-8). 1978. 9.95 (ISBN 0-916456-30-7, GA85). Good Apple.

ABC's of Faith, 2 bks. Francine M. O'Connor & Kathryn Boswell. (gr. 1-4). 1979. Bk. 1. pap. 1.50 (ISBN 0-89243-113-X); Bk. 2. pap. 1.50 (ISBN 0-89243-114-8). Liguori Pubns.

ABC's of FETS. 2nd ed. Rufus P. Turner. LC 77-99108. 1978. pap. 3.95 o.p. (ISBN 0-672-21510-1). Sams.

ABC's of Fo'c'sle Living. A. K. Larssen & Sig Jaeger. LC 76-17265. (Illus.). 1976. pap. 3.95 (ISBN 0-914842-11-0). Madrona Pubs.

ABC's of FORTRAN Programming. Michael J. Merchant. 1979. pap. text ed. 14.95x (ISBN 0-534-00634-5). Wadsworth Pub.

ABC's of Hydraulic Circuits. John M Storer & Harry L Stewart. LC 73-83372. (Illus., Orig.). 1973. pap. 4.50 o.p. (ISBN 0-672-21003-7). Sams.

ABC's of Investing Your Retirement Funds. C. Colburn Hardy. 1978. 22.50 (ISBN 0-87489-008-X). Med Economics.

ABC's of Italian Wines. John D. Sarles. LC 80-51642. (Illus.). 200p. (Orig.). Date not set. 10.95 (ISBN 0-9604488-1-0); pap. 9.95 (ISBN 0-9604488-0-2). Wine Bks. Postponed.

ABC's of Mobile Home & Recreation Vehicle Park Investments. David Nulsen & Robert H. Nulsen. 1980. 24.95 o.s.i. (ISBN 0-87593-040-9). Trail-R.

ABC's of Real Estate Exchanging. Louise Lynch. 1981. text ed. 12.95 (ISBN 0-8359-0015-0); instrs'. manual avail. (ISBN 0-8359-0016-9). Reston.

ABC's of Sex. (Illus.). 4.95 (ISBN 0-910550-25-5). Centurion Pr.

ABC's of Shortcut Sewing. (Illus.). 96p. 1976. pap. 1.50 (ISBN 0-918178-03-7). Simplicity.

ABC's of Sports Injuries. James H. McMaster. LC 80-20636. 1981. lib. bdg. write for info. (ISBN 0-88275-890-X). Krieger.

ABC's of Video Therapy. Michael T. Greelis & Betsy S. Haarmann. (Illus.). 96p. 1980. pap. text ed. 7.00 (ISBN 0-87879-243-0). Acad Therapy.

ABC's of What a Girl Can Be. Vivian S. Epstein. (Illus.). 32p. (ps-3). 1980. pap. 3.95 (ISBN 0-9601002-2-9). V S Epstein.

Abd al-Qadir & the Algerians: Resistance to the French & Internal Consolidation. Raphael Danziger. LC 76-18061. 1977. text ed. 34.50x (ISBN 0-8419-0236-4, Africana). Holmes & Meier.

Abdeker; or, the Art of Preserving Beauty, 1754. A. Le Camus. Ed. by Michael F. Shugrue. (Flowering of the Novel, 1740-1775 Ser: Vol. 41). 1974. lib. bdg. 50.00 (ISBN 0-8240-1140-6). Garland Pub.

Abdomen. Ed. by Alavi Abass & Peter Arger. LC 80-24363. (Multiples Imaging Procedures Ser.). 1980. 44.50 (ISBN 0-8089-1306-9). Grune.

Abdominal Gray Scale Ultrasonography. Barry B. Goldberg. LC 77-5889. (Wiley Series in Diagnostic & Therapeutic Radiology). 1977. 45.00 (ISBN 0-471-01510-5, Pub. by Wiley Medical). Wiley.

Abdominal Operations, 2 vols. 8th ed. Maingot. 1980. 142.00 (ISBN 0-8385-0044-7). ACC.

Abdominal Operations, 2 vols. 7th ed. Rodney Maingot. 2802p. 1979. Set. 142.00x (ISBN 0-8385-8779-8). ACC.

Abdominal Surgery: An Atlas of Operative Techniques. Pietro Valdoni. Tr. by George Nardi. LC 75-40641. (Illus.). 1976. text ed. 70.00 (ISBN 0-7216-8950-7). Saunders.

Abdominal Ultrasound in the Cancer Patient. Donn J. Brascho & Thomas H. Shawker. LC 80-15838. (Diagnostic & Therapeutic Radiology Ser.). 380p. 1980. 39.50 (ISBN 0-471-01742-6, Pub. by WileyMed). Wiley.

Abdu'l-Baha: The Centre of the Covenant of Baha'u'llah. H. M. Balyuzi. (Illus.). 1971. 11.95 (ISBN 0-85398-029-2, 7-31-36, Pub. by George Ronald England); pap. 5.95 (ISBN 0-85398-043-8, 7-31-37, Pub. by G Ronald England). Baha'i.

Abe Lincoln's Beard. Jan Wahl. LC 75-156045. (Illus.). (ps-3). 1971. PLB 4.58 o.s.i. (ISBN 0-440-00413-6, Sey Lawr). Delacorte.

ABE Staff Training. Hy Hoffman & Jules Pagano. 58p. 1971. 4.00 (ISBN 0-685-63816-2). Adult Ed.

Abecedario Biblico. (Spanish Bks.). 1978. 1.30 (ISBN 0-8297-0494-9). Life Pubs Intl.

Abecedary. Christopher Logue. (Illus.). 1979. 7.50 (ISBN 0-224-01562-1, Pub. by Chatto Bodley Jonathan). Merrimack Bk Serv.

Abee Mouret's Sin. Emile Zola. 1957. 12.95 (ISBN 0-236-30808-4, Pub. by Paul Elek). Merrimack Bk Serv.

Abel Being Dead, Yet Speaketh. John Norton. LC 78-8184. 1978. Repr. of 1658 ed. 20.00 (ISBN 0-8201-1310-7). Schol Facsimiles.

Abel Gance. Steven P. Kramer & James M. Welsh. (Theatrical Arts Ser.). 1978. lib. bdg. 12.50 (ISBN 0-8057-9254-6). Twayne.

Abel's Island. William Steig. LC 75-35918. (Illus.). 128p. (gr. 4 up). 1976. 7.95 (ISBN 0-374-30010-0). FS&G.

Abel's Island. William Steig. 128p. (gr. 4-6). 1981. pap. 1.95 (ISBN 0-553-15060-X, Skylark). Bantam.

Abenteuer Eines Brotbeutels und Andere Geschichten. Heinrich Boll. Ed. by Richard Plant. (Ger). 1958. pap. 2.25x o.p. (ISBN 0-393-09459-6, NortonC). Norton.

Aberdeen Coalition, 1852-1855: A Study in Mid-Nineteenth-Century Party Politics. J. B. Conacher. LC 68-10148. (Illus.). 1968. 64.00 (ISBN 0-521-04711-0). Cambridge U Pr.

Aberdeenshire Peasant Life: William Alexander-Scottish Peasant Life. Ed. by Ian Carter. (Library of Peasant Studies: No. 5). 1981. 28.00x (ISBN 0-7146-3087-X, F Cass Co). Biblio Dist.

Aberrant Development in Infancy: Human & Animal Studies. Ed. by Norman R. Ellis. LC 75-9657. 287p. 1975. 16.50 (ISBN 0-470-23859-3, Pub. by Wiley). Krieger.

Aberration of Starlight. Gilbert Sorrentino. 1981. pap. 3.95 (ISBN 0-14-005879-6). Penguin.

Aberration of Starlight. Gilbert Sorrentino. LC 80-5280. 224p. 1980. 8.95 (ISBN 0-394-51189-1). Random.

Abhijnana Sakuntalam of Kalidasa. 4th ed. Tr. by C. R. Devadhar. 1972. pap. 4.95 (ISBN 0-89684-164-2). Orient Bk Dist.

Abhinavagupta on Indian Aesthetics. Y. S. Walimbe. 1980. 9.50x (ISBN 0-8364-0624-9, Pub. by Ajanta). South Asia Bks.

Abiding Appalachia: Where Mountain & Atom Meet. Marilou B. Thompson. LC 78-12970. (Illus.). 1978. 8.95 (ISBN 0-918518-09-1); pap. 6.95 (ISBN 0-918518-15-6). St Luke TN.

Abigail. Lois T. Henderson. LC 80-65429. 256p. 1980. 8.95 (ISBN 0-915684-62-4). Christian Herald.

Abigail Adams & Her Times. Laura E. Richards. LC 78-143631. 1971. Repr. of 1917 ed. 18.00 (ISBN 0-8103-3640-5). Gale.

Abigull. Toni A. Snow. LC 80-82792. (Illus.). 48p. (Orig.). (gr. 1-6). 1980. pap. 2.95 (ISBN 0-932384-12-9). Tashmoo.

Abilities of Young Children. Council for Exceptional Children & Ruth A. Martinson. 1967. 3.50 o.p. (ISBN 0-86586-000-9). Coun Exc Child.

Ability Grouping: Homogenous Vs. Hetergoneous. Ed. by Anthony Pugliese. 39p. 1977. pap. 9.00 o.p. (ISBN 0-686-00900-2, D-107). Essence Pubns.

Ability Grouping of Public School Students: Legal Aspects of Tracking Methods. Bryson & Bentley. 300p. 1980. 15.00 (ISBN 0-87215-332-0). Michie.

Ability Grouping: The Banbury Enquiry. David Newbold. (General Ser.). (Illus.). 1977. pap. text ed. 16.00x (ISBN 0-85633-142-2, NFER). Humanities.

Abingdon Clergy Income Tax Guide, 1979. 7th ed. Compiled by Price Waterhouse & Co. 1978. pap. 2.95 o.p. (ISBN 0-687-00390-3). Abingdon.

Abingdon Clergy Income Tax Guide, 1981 Edition for 1980 Returns. Ed. by Price Waterhouse & Co. (Orig.). 1980. pap. 2.95 (ISBN 0-687-00394-6). Abingdon.

Abingdon Clergy Income Tax Guide, 1980. Rev. by Price Waterhouse & Co. (Orig.). 1979. pap. 2.95 o.p. (ISBN 0-687-00392-X). Abingdon.

Able Seaman & Lifevoatman: All Grades. rev. ed. Ed. by Richard A. Block. (Illus.). 338p. 1978. pap. 21.00 (ISBN 0-934114-04-8). Marine Educ.

Able to Learn? the Pursuit of Culture-Fair Assessment. Seamus Hegarty & Dorothy Lucas. (General Ser.). 1979. pap. text ed. 10.00x (ISBN 0-85633-173-2, NFER). Humanities.

ABMS Non-Ferrous Metal Data Publication. annual ed. American Bureau of Metal Statistics Inc. 1978. 25.00 (ISBN 0-685-91837-8). Am Bur Metal.

ABMS Non-Ferrous Metal Data Publication: 1974 Yearbook. rev. ed. Compiled by American Bureau of Metal Statistics Staff. LC 21-15719. 1975. 25.00 (ISBN 0-910064-08-3). Am Bur Metal.

ABMS Non-Ferrous Metal Data Publication: 1975 Yearbook. rev. ed. Ed. by American Bureau of Metal Statistics Staff. LC 21-15719. 1976. 25.00 (ISBN 0-910064-09-1). Am Bur Metal.

ABMS Non-Ferrous Metal Data Publication: 1976 Year Book. rev. ed. Ed. by American Bureau of Metal Statistics Staff. LC 21-15719. 1977. 25.00 (ISBN 0-910064-10-5). Am Bur Metal.

Abnormal Behavior: A Guide to Information Sources. Ed. by Henry Leland & Marilyn W. Deutsch. LC 80-65. (Psychology Informationguide Ser.: Vol. 5). 261p. 1980. 30.00 (ISBN 0-8103-1416-9). Gale.

Abnormal Behavior: Psychology's View. Frank B. McMahon. 1976. 20.95 (ISBN 0-13-000711-0). P-H.

Abnormal Neuronal Discharges. Ed. by N. Chalazonitis & M. Boisson. LC 76-58750. 1978. 38.00 (ISBN 0-89004-238-1). Raven.

Abnormal Personality. 5th ed. R. W. White. LC 80-22055. 1981. text ed. 21.95 (ISBN 0-471-04599-3); tchrs'. manual avail. (ISBN 0-471-05342-2). Wiley.

Abnormal Personality. 4th ed. Robert W. White & Norman F. Watt. 640p. 1973. 20.95 o.p. (ISBN 0-471-06929-9); instructors' manual avail. o.p. (ISBN 0-471-07532-9). Wiley.

Abnormal Personality Through Literature. Sue Stone & Alan Stone. (Orig.). 1966. pap. text ed. 11.95 (ISBN 0-13-000786-2). P-H.

Abnormal Postural Reflex Activity Caused by Brain Lesions. 2nd ed. Berta Bobath. (Illus.). 1976. pap. 7.50 (ISBN 0-433-03332-0). Heinman.

Abnormal Postural Reflex Activity Caused by Brain Lesions. 2nd ed. Berta Bobath. 1973. pap. 11.00x (ISBN 0-433-03332-0). Intl Ideas.

Abnormal Psychology. Henry E. Adams. 750p. Date not set. text ed. price not set. Wm C Brown.

Abnormal Psychology. Sheldon Cashdan. LC 70-39029. (Foundations of Modern Psychology). (Illus.). 160p. 1972. ref. ed. 12.95x (ISBN 0-13-000802-8); pap. 7.95x ref. ed. (ISBN 0-13-000794-3). P-H.

Abnormal Psychology. Walter J. Coville et al. (Orig.). 1960. pap. 3.95 (ISBN 0-06-460094-7, CO 94, COS). Har-Row.

Abnormal Psychology. David C. Rimm & John W. Somervill. 696p. 1977. 18.95 (ISBN 0-12-588840-6). Acad Pr.

Abnormal Psychology: An Experimental Clinical Approach. 2nd ed. Gerald C. Davison & John M. Neale. LC 77-13940. 1978. text ed. 21.95x (ISBN 0-471-19923-0); tchrs. manual avail. (ISBN 0-471-01731-0); study guide 7.95 (ISBN 0-471-03401-0); tests avail. (ISBN 0-471-03772-9). Wiley.

Abnormal Psychology & Modern Life. 6th ed. James C. Coleman et al. 1979. text ed. 21.95x (ISBN 0-673-15213-8); pap. 6.95x student's guide (ISBN 0-673-15283-9). Scott F.

Abnormal Psychology: Current Perspectives. 2nd ed. Communications Research Machines, Inc. 1976. text ed. 18.95 o.p. (ISBN 0-394-31062-4). Random.

Abnormal Psychology: Perspectives on Human Variance. Michael J. Mahoney. 1980. text ed. 20.95 scp (ISBN 0-397-47410-5, HarpC); scp study guide 8.95 (ISBN 0-397-47411-3); instr's manual avail. (ISBN 0-397-47410-5). Har-Row.

Abnormal Psychology: Problem of Maladaptive Behavior. 2nd ed. I. G. Sarason. (Illus.). 1976. 21.95 o.p. (ISBN 0-13-001123-1); pap. 7.50 readings o.p. (ISBN 0-13-756759-6). P-H.

Abnormal Psychology: The Problem of Maladaptive Behavior. 3rd ed. Irwin G. Sarason & Barbara R. Sarason. (Century Psychology Ser.). (Illus.). 1980. text ed. 21.95 (ISBN 0-13-001107-X). P-H.

Aboard the USS Florida: 1863-65. William F. Keeler. Ed. by Robert W. Daly. LC 79-6112. (Navies & Men Ser.). 1980. Repr. of 1968 ed. lib. bdg. 20.00x (ISBN 0-405-13041-4). Arno.

Abolitionism: A New Perspective. Gerald Sorin. LC 79-143981. (New Perspectives in American History). 187p. 1972. pap. 7.95 (ISBN 0-275-84140-5). Praeger.

Abolitionists: The Growth of a Dissenting Minority. Merton L. Dillon. 1979. pap. 4.95 (ISBN 0-393-00957-2). Norton.

Abolitionists: The Growth of a Dissenting Minority. Merton L. Dillon. Ed. by Moses Rischin. LC 73-15096. (American Minorities Ser). (Illus.). 300p. (gr. 12). 1974. 10.00 (ISBN 0-87580-044-0); pap. 4.00 (ISBN 0-87580-513-2). N Ill U Pr.

Abominable Snow Mad. (Mad Ser.: No. 52). (Illus.). 1979. pap. 1.75 (ISBN 0-446-94446-7). Warner Bks.

Abominable Snowcreature. Stephen Rudley. (Illus.). (gr. 5 up). 1978. PLB 7.45 s&l (ISBN 0-531-02212-9). Watts.

Abomination of Desolation in Biblical Eschatology. Desmond Ford. LC 79-64195. 1979. pap. text ed. 11.50 (ISBN 0-8191-0757-3). U Pr of Amer.

Aboriginal Men of High Degree. 2nd ed. A. P. Elkin. LC 77-87170. (Illus.). 1978. 15.95x (ISBN 0-312-00167-3). St Martin.

Aboriginal Place Names of New York. William M. Beauchamp. LC 68-17915. 333p. 1972. Repr. of 1907 ed. 21.00 (ISBN 0-8103-3231-0). Gale.

Aboriginal Students in Victoria. M. De Lemos. (ACER Research Monograph: No. 3). 1979. pap. 18.00 (ISBN 0-85563-193-7). Verry.

Aboriginal Subsistence Technology on the Southeastern Coastal Plain During the Late Prehistoric Period. Lewis H. Larson. LC 80-16279. (Ripley P. Bullen Monographs in Anthropology & History: No. 2). (Illus.). 1980. 20.00 (ISBN 0-8130-0675-9). U Presses Fla.

Aboriginal Tribes of Australia: Their Terrain, Environmental Controls, Distribution, Limits, & Proper Names. Norman B. Tindale. (Illus.). 1975. 82.50x (ISBN 0-520-02005-7). U of Cal Pr.

Aborigines. Ross-Larson. LC 75-190188. (Illus.). (gr. 5-12). 1972. PLB 5.95 o.p. (ISBN 0-87191-210-4). Creative Ed.

Abortion. Malcolm Potts et al. LC 76-27907. (Illus.). 1977. 66.00 (ISBN 0-521-21442-4); pap. 17.95x (ISBN 0-521-29150-X). Cambridge U Pr.

Abortion? Jeanine Woody. 1977. pap. 1.95 o.p. (ISBN 0-917726-10-3). Hunter Bks.

Abortion: An Annotated Indexed Bibliography. Ed. by Maureen Muldoon. (Studies in Women & Religion: Vol. 3). 1980. 39.95x (ISBN 0-88946-972-5). E Mellen.

Abortion & Moral Theory. L. W. Sumner. LC 80-8578. 264p. 1981. 16.50x (ISBN 0-691-07262-0); pap. 4.95x (ISBN 0-691-02017-5). Princeton U Pr.

Abortion & Social Justice. Ed. by Thomas Hilgers & Dennis J. Horan. LC 72-6690. (Illus.). 320p. 1973. pap. 3.95 o.p. (ISBN 0-8362-0542-1). Andrews & McMeel.

Abortion & Sterilization: Medical & Social Aspects. Jane E. Hodgson. 1981. write for info. (ISBN 0-8089-1344-1). Grune.

Abortion & the Evangelical. John J. Davis. LC 80-82736. (Nordland Series in Contemporary American Social Problems). 150p. (Orig.). 1980. pap. 7.95 (ISBN 0-913124-43-5). Nordland Pub.

Abortion & the Moral Degeneration of the American Medical Profession. Vivian De Danois. (Science of Man Library Bk). 92p. 1975. 41.50 (ISBN 0-913314-56-0). Am Classical Coll Pr.

Abortion: A/Biblical Approach. Harold Warnke. 1980. 2.75 (ISBN 0-8100-0116-0). Northwest Pub.

Abortion Controversy. 2nd ed. Betty Sarvis & Hyman Rodman. 200p. 1974. 17.50x (ISBN 0-231-03871-2); pap. 6.00x (ISBN 0-231-03865-8). Columbia U Pr.

Abortion Decision. David Granfield. LC 69-12185. 1969. 6.95 o.p. (ISBN 0-385-03304-4). Doubleday.

Abortion in a Crowded World: The Problem of Abortion with Special Reference to India. S. Chandrasekhar. LC 73-19750. (John Danz Lecture Ser.). 150p. 1974. 10.50 (ISBN 0-295-95317-9). U of Wash Pr.

Abortion in America: The Origins & Evolution of National Policy. James C. Mohr. 1978. 15.95 (ISBN 0-19-502249-1). Oxford U Pr.

Abortion in Context: A Select Bibliography. Charles J. Dollen. 1970. 10.00 (ISBN 0-8108-0337-2). Scarecrow.

Abortion Law Reformed. Madeleine Simms & Keith Hindell. (Contemporary Issues Ser: No. 3). 1971. text ed. 11.50x (ISBN 0-391-01941-4). Humanities.

Abortion: Mercy or Murder? James Londis. LC 79-25126. (Better Living Ser.). 1980. pap. 0.95 (ISBN 0-8127-0257-3). Southern Pub.

Abortion Parley. Ed. by James T. Burtchaell. 420p. 1980. 20.00 (ISBN 0-8362-3600-9). Andrews & McMeel.

Abortion Parley. Ed. by James T. Burtchaell. 360p. 1980. cancelled. ACC.

Abortion Politics: Private Morality & Public Policy. Frederick S. Jaffe et al. LC 80-17035. 224p. 1980. 14.95 (ISBN 0-07-032189-2, P&RB). McGraw.

Abortion Revolution. Allen Quist. 1980. 4.95 (ISBN 0-8100-0115-2). Northwest Pub.

Abortion Today. Jules Saltman & Stanley Zimering. 192p. 1973. pap. 10.50 (ISBN 0-398-02672-6). C C Thomas.

About Aging: A Catalog of Films. 4th ed. Compiled by Mildred V. Allyn. LC 79-64804. 1979. pap. 5.50 (ISBN 0-88474-091-9). USC Andrus Geron.

About Alphabets. Hermann Zapf. 1970. pap. 3.95 o.p. (ISBN 0-262-74003-6, 146). MIT Pr.

About Animals. Richard Scarry. (Golden Look-Look Bks.). (Illus.). 1976. limp bdg. 0.95 (ISBN 0-307-11822-3, Golden Pr); PLB 5.38 (ISBN 0-307-61822-6). Western Pub.

About Antiques. Ella S. Bowles. LC 70-174011. (Tower Bks). (Illus.). 1971. Repr. of 1929 ed. 18.00 (ISBN 0-8103-3921-8). Gale.

About Bedsores. Marian E. Miller & Marvin L. Sachs. LC 74-3385. 1974. text ed. 8.50 (ISBN 0-397-54186-4); pap. text ed. 7.50 (ISBN 0-397-54156-2). Lippincott.

About Bees & Honey. Althea. (ps-2). 1979. pap. 1.75 available in 5-pk (ISBN 0-85122-187-4, Pub. by Dinosaur Pubns). Merrimack Bk Serv.

About Belonging. Molly Cone. (Shema Storybooks: No. 3). (Illus.). 64p. (Orig.). (gr. 1-2). 1972. pap. 5.00 (ISBN 0-8074-0125-0, 101083). UAHC.

About David. Susan B. Pfeffer. LC 80-65837. 176p. (gr. 8-12). 1980. 8.95 (ISBN 0-440-00093-9). Delacorte.

About Diabetes & the Diet. John B. Lust. 1980. pap. 1.95 (ISBN 0-87904-046-7). Lust.

About Divorce: Eighty-Two Questions & Answers. rev. ed. Lawyers & Judges Publishing Staff. 1978. pap. 0.95 (ISBN 0-88450-052-7, 6110-B). Lawyers & Judges.

About God. Molly Cone. (Shema Storybooks: No. 4). (Illus.). 64p. (gr. 1-2). 1973. pap. 5.00 (ISBN 0-8074-0126-9, 101084). UAHC.

About Grams. Alma Gilleo. LC 77-23285. (Metric Bk.). (Illus.). (gr. 1-4). 1977. 5.50 (ISBN 0-913778-84-2); pap. 2.75 (ISBN 0-89565-061-4). Childs World.

About Hebrew Manuscripts. Elkan N. Adler. LC 78-136769. (Illus.). 1971. Repr. of 1905 ed. 12.50 (ISBN 0-87203-025-3). Hermon.

About Herbs: Nature's Medicine. Benedict Lust. 1980. pap. 1.95 (ISBN 0-87904-045-9). Lust.

About Honey: Nature's Elixir for Health. P Norris. 1980. pap. 1.95 (ISBN 0-87904-043-2). Lust.

About Learning. Molly Cone. (Shema Primary Ser: No. 2). (Illus., Orig.). (gr. 1). 1972. pap. 5.00 (ISBN 0-8074-0127-7, 101082). UAHC.

About Liters. Alma Gilleo. LC 77-23260. (Metric Bk.). (Illus.). (gr. 1-4). 1977. 5.50 (ISBN 0-913778-85-0); pap. 2.75 (ISBN 0-89565-062-2). Childs World.

About Me. Jane B. Moncure. LC 76-16556. (Illus.). (ps-2). 1976. 5.50 (ISBN 0-913778-52-4). Childs World.

About Meters. Alma Gilleo. LC 77-23261. (Metric Bk.). (Illus.). (gr. 1-4). 1977. 5.50 (ISBN 0-913778-86-9); pap. 2.75 (ISBN 0-89565-063-0). Childs World.

About New York. Francis X. Clines. LC 80-16080. 288p. 1980. 12.95 (ISBN 0-07-011384-X). McGraw.

About Old Story-Tellers. Donald G. Mitchell. LC 75-159859. 1971. Repr. of 1877 ed. 20.00 (ISBN 0-8103-3732-0). Gale.

About Our Dogs. A. Broxton Smith. 17.50x (ISBN 0-392-06336-0, SpS). Soccer.

About Our Schools. Alec Clegg. (Illus.). 160p. 1981. 24.50x (ISBN 0-631-12881-6, Pub. by Basil Blackwell); pap. 9.95 (ISBN 0-631-12832-8). Biblio Dist.

About Philosophy. Robert P. Wolff. (Illus.). 352p. 1976. text ed. 16.95 (ISBN 0-13-000836-2). P-H.

About Philosophy. 2nd ed. Robert P. Wolff. (Illus.). 448p. 1981. text ed. 15.95 (ISBN 0-13-000695-5). P-H.

About Plants: Topics in Plant Biology. Frederick C. Steward. LC 66-10506. (Biology Ser). (Orig.). 1966. pap. 7.95 (ISBN 0-201-07284-X). A-W.

About Prostate Trouble. Benedict Lust. 1980. pap. 1.95 (ISBN 0-87904-042-4). Lust.

About Raw Juices. John B. Lust. 1980. pap. 1.95 (ISBN 0-87904-047-5). Lust.

About Scientific Fasting. Linda B. Hazzard. 1980. pap. 1.95 (ISBN 0-87904-044-0). Lust.

About the Food You Eat. Seymour Simon. Date not set. price not set. McGraw.

About the House. Joyce Flynn. 6.95 (ISBN 0-916752-08-9). Green Hill.

About the Thermometer. Alma Gilleo. LC 77-23182. (Metric Book). (Illus.). (gr. 1-4). 1977. PLB 5.50 (ISBN 0-913778-87-7); pap. 2.75 (ISBN 0-89565-064-9). Childs World.

About Thinking. W. Ward Fearnside. 1980. pap. text ed. 10.30 (ISBN 0-13-000844-3). P-H.

About Time! A Woman's Guide to Time Management. Alec MacKenzie & Kay C. Waldo. (McGraw-Hill Paperback Ser.). 224p. (Orig.). 1981. pap. price not set (ISBN 0-07-044651-2, GB). McGraw.

About to Teach: An Introduction to Method in Teaching. Souper. 1976. 16.00x (ISBN 0-7100-8311-4); pap. 8.95 (ISBN 0-7100-8315-7). Routledge & Kegan.

About Wise Men & Simpletons: Twelve Tales from Grimm. Grimm Brothers. Tr. by Elizabeth Shub from Ger. LC 79-146628. (Illus.). (gr. 3-6). 1971. 8.95 (ISBN 0-02-737290-1). Macmillan.

About Your Deposition: Ninety-Five Questions & Answers. rev. ed. Lawyers & Judges Publishing Staff. 1979. pap. 0.95 (ISBN 0-88450-051-9, 6109-B). Lawyers & Judges.

Above Every Name: The Lordship of Christ & Social Systems. Ed. by Thomas E. Clark. LC 80-82082. (Woodstock Studies). 256p. (Orig.). 1980. pap. 7.95 (ISBN 0-8091-2338-X). Paulist Pr.

Above Parties: The Political Attitudes of the German Protestant Church Leadership 1918-1933. Jonathan R. Wright. (Oxford Historical Monographs Ser.). 216p. 1974. 22.50x (ISBN 0-19-821856-7). Oxford U Pr.

Above Suspicion. Helen MacInnes. 1978. pap. 2.25 (ISBN 0-449-23833-4, Crest). Fawcett.

Above the Battle: War-Making in America from Appomattox to Versailles. Thomas C. Leonard. (Illus.). 1978. 15.95 (ISBN 0-19-502239-4). Oxford U Pr.

Above Timberline: A Wildlife Biologist's Rocky Mountain Journal. Dwight Smith. Ed. by Alan Anderson, Jr. LC 80-7618. (Illus.). 1981. 13.95 (ISBN 0-394-40037-2). Knopf.

Abracadaver. Peter Lovesey. 1981. pap. 2.95 (ISBN 0-14-005803-6). Penguin.

Abracatabby. Catherine Hiller. (Illus.). 64p. (gr. 6-9). 1981. PLB 6.99 (ISBN 0-698-30727-5). Coward.

Abraham. Gordon Stowell. Tr. by S. D. de Lerin from English. (Libros Pescaditos Sobre Perssonajes Biblicos). (Illus.). 1980. pap. 0.40 (ISBN 0-311-38511-7, Edit Mundo). Casa Bautista.

Abraham. Gordon Stowell. (Illus.). 24p. (Orig.). (ps-2). 1975. pap. 0.39 o.p. (ISBN 0-8307-0340-3, 56-009-01). Regal.

Abraham & the Contemporary Mind. Silvano Arieti. LC 80-68187. 187p. 1981. 11.95 (ISBN 0-465-00005-3). Basic.

Abraham Fornander: A Biography. Eleanor H. Davis. LC 78-31368. 1979. 0.95 (ISBN 0-8248-0459-7). U Pr of Hawaii.

Abraham, Friend of God. Gordon Lindsay. (Old Testament Ser.). 1.25 (ISBN 0-89985-126-6). Christ Nations.

Abraham: Friend of God. Amos Miller. LC 73-6406. 1973. 7.95x o.p. (ISBN 0-685-32288-2). Jonathan David.

Abraham Isaac Kook: The Lights of Penitance, Lights of Holiness. the Moral Principles. Essays, Letters & Poems. Tr. by Ben Zion Bokser. (Classics of Western Spirituality). 1978. 11.95 (ISBN 0-8091-0278-1); pap. 7.95 (ISBN 0-8091-2159-X). Paulist Pr.

Abraham Joshua Herschel. Byron Sherwin. LC 78-71051. (Makers of Contemporary Theology Ser.). 1979. pap. 3.45 (ISBN 0-8042-0466-7). John Knox.

Abraham Lincoln. David D. Anderson. (U. S. Authors Ser.: No. 153). 1970. lib. bdg. 9.95 (ISBN 0-8057-0452-3). Twayne.

Abraham Lincoln. rev. ed. D. W. Brogan. 145p. 1974. 16.00x (ISBN 0-7156-0865-7, Pub. by Duckworth England). Biblio Dist.

Abraham Lincoln. Bella Koral. (Illus.). (gr. k-3). 1952. 1.95 o.p. (ISBN 0-394-80625-5, BYR). Random.

Abraham Lincoln & the Union. Oscar Handlin & Lilian Handlin. (Library of American Biography). 224p. (Orig.). 1980. 10.95 (ISBN 0-316-34315-3); pap. 4.95 (ISBN 0-316-34314-5). Little.

Abraham Lincoln Encyclopedia. Mark E. Neely, Jr. (Illus.). 448p. 1981. write for info (ISBN 0-07-046145-7, P&RB). McGraw.

Abraham Lincoln Joke Book. De Reginiers. (gr. 3-5). 1980. pap. 1.25 (ISBN 0-590-30968-4, Schol Pap). Schol Bk Serv.

Abraham Lincoln, the Prairie Years & the War Years, 3 Vols. Carl Sandburg. Set. pap. 6.95 (ISBN 0-440-30008-8, LE). Dell.

Abraham Lincoln's World. Genevieve Foster. (Illus.). (gr. 5-11). 1944. lib. rep. ed. 20.00x (ISBN 0-684-14855-2, ScribJ). Scribner.

Abraham Rattner. Abraham Rattner. Ed. by Allen Leepa. LC 79-133447. (Contemporary Artists Ser.). (Illus.). 196p. 1974. 65.00 o.p. (ISBN 0-8109-0429-2). Abrams.

Abraham Sacrifiant: Tragedie Francoise (Geneve, 1550) Theodore de Beze. (Classiques De la Renaissance En France: No. 2). 1970. 15.30 (ISBN 90-2796-344-4). Mouton.

Abraham: The First Hebrew. Aaron Gerber. 180p. 1981. 12.50 (ISBN 0-89962-208-9). Todd & Honeywell.

Abraham Was Their Father. A. Warren Matthews. LC 81-146. vii, 266p. 1981. 19.50 (ISBN 0-86554-005-5). Mercer Univ Pr.

Abram & Sarai. J. SerVaas Williams. LC 80-69805. (Illus.). 350p. 1981. 12.95 (ISBN 0-938280-01-5). Corinth Hse.

Abrasive Methods Engineering, Vol. 2. Francis T. Farago. LC 76-14970. (Illus.). 508p. 1980. 55.00 (ISBN 0-8311-1134-8). Indus Pr.

Abridged Thermodynamic & Thermochemical Tables in S. I. Units. F. D. Hamblin. 1971. 11.25 (ISBN 0-08-016456-0); pap. 5.75 (ISBN 0-08-016457-9). Pergamon.

Abridgement of Mental Philosophy. Thomas Upham. LC 79-10925. (History of Psychology Ser.). 1979. Repr. of 1861 ed. lib. bdg. 57.00x (ISBN 0-8201-1331-X). Schol Facsimiles.

Abridgement of the Lord Coke's Commentary on Littleton. Humphrey Davenport. Ed. by David S. Berkowitz & Samuel E. Thorne. LC 77-89239. (Classics of English Legal History in the Modern Era Ser.: Vol. 74). 484p. 1979. lib. bdg. 40.00 (ISBN 0-8240-3173-3). Garland Pub.

Absent & Present. Chester Kallman. LC 63-8859. (Wesleyan Poetry Program: Vol. 17). (Orig.). 1963. 10.00x (ISBN 0-8195-2017-9, Pub. by Wesleyan U Pr); pap. 4.95x (ISBN 0-8195-1017-3). Columbia U Pr.

Absent with Cause: Lessons of Truancy. Roger White. (Routledge Education Bks.). 300p. (Orig.). 1980. pap. 18.00 (ISBN 0-7100-0665-9). Routledge & Kegan.

Absentee. Maria Edgeworth. Ed. by Robert L. Wolff. (Ireland: Nineteenth Century Fiction Ser.). 1979. lib. bdg. 46.00 (ISBN 0-8240-3453-8). Garland Pub.

Absolute & die Wirklichkeit in Schellings Philosophie: Mit der Erstedition einer Handschrift aus dem Berliner Schelling-Nachlass. Barbara Loer. LC 73-93164. (Quellen & Studien zur Philosophie, Vol. 7). (Illus.). viii, 288p. 1974. 60.59x (ISBN 3-11-004329-7). De Gruyter.

Absolute Differential Calculus: Calculus of Tensors. Tullio Levi-Civita. Ed. by Enrico Persico. Tr. by Marjorie Long from Italian. LC 76-27497. (Illus.). 480p. 1977. pap. text ed. 6.50 (ISBN 0-486-63401-9). Dover.

Absolute Measurements in Electricity & Magnetism. 2nd ed. Andrew Gray. (Illus.). 1921. pap. text ed. 6.00 (ISBN 0-486-61787-4). Dover.

Absolute Nothingness: Foundations for a Buddhist-Christian Dialogue. Hans Waldenfels. Tr. by James W. Heisig from Ger. Orig. Title: Absolutes Nichts. 214p. 1980. pap. 7.95 (ISBN 0-8091-2316-9). Paulist Pr.

Absolute Poor. Jane W. Jacqz. 54p. 1974. pap. 1.00 (ISBN 0-89192-073-0). Interbk Inc.

Absolute Stellungnahmen: Eine Ontologische Untersuchung Uber das Wesen der Religion. Kurt Stavenhagen. Ed. by Maurice Natanson. LC 78-66740. (Phenomenology Ser.: Vol. 13). 234p. 1979. lib. bdg. 23.00 (ISBN 0-8240-9557-X). Garland Pub.

Absolute Surrender. Andrew Murray. pap. 1.50 (ISBN 0-8024-0560-6). Moody.

Absolute Surrender. Andrew Murray. 128p. 1981. pap. 2.50 (ISBN 0-88368-093-9). Whitaker Hse.

Absolute Unlawfulness of the Stage Entertainment Fully Demonstrated. William Law. Bd. with Stage Defended. John Dennis; Law Outlaw'd: A Short Reply to Mr. Law's Long Declamation Against the Stage. LC 75-170493. (English Stage Ser.: Vol. 49). lib. bdg. 50.00 (ISBN 0-8240-0632-1). Garland Pub.

Absolute Zero: Being the Second Part of the Bagthorpe Saga. Helen Cresswell. LC 77-12675. (gr. 5 up). 1978. 7.95 (ISBN 0-02-725550-6, 72555). Macmillan.

Absolutely Definite Philosophy for the Intelligence of Contemporary Man. Paul W. Wintercross. (Illus.). 1980. deluxe ed. 39.75 (ISBN 0-89266-221-2). Am Classical Coll Pr.

Absolutely Mad Inventions. A. E. Brown & H. A. Jeffcott, Jr. Orig. Title: Beware of Imitations. (Illus.). 1970. pap. 2.00 (ISBN 0-486-22596-8). Dover.

Absolutes in Moral Theology? Ed. by Charles E. Curran. LC 75-3988. 320p. 1976. Repr. of 1968 ed. lib. bdg. 25.00x (ISBN 0-8371-7450-3, CUMT). Greenwood.

Absorption & Distribution of Drugs. L. Saunders. (Illus.). 1974. text ed. 14.95 o.s.i. (ISBN 0-02-859150-X). Macmillan.

Absorption-Desorption Phenomena. Ed. by F. Ricca. 1972. 31.50 (ISBN 0-12-587750-1). Acad Pr.

Absorption, Distribution, Transformation & Excretion of Drugs. Peter K. Knoefel et al. (Illus.). 220p. 1972. 18.75 (ISBN 0-398-02518-5). C C Thomas.

Absorption from the Intestine. F. Verzar & E. J. McDougall. 1968. Repr. of 1936 ed. 18.00 o.s.i. (ISBN 0-02-854200-2). Hafner.

Absorption of Light & Ultraviolet Radiation: Fluorescence & Phosphorescence Emission. George Schenk. (Instrumentation Ser., Vol. 4). 324p. 1973. pap. text ed. 11.95x o.p. (ISBN 0-205-03720-8). Allyn.

Absorption of Polymers. Yu. S Lipatov & L. M. Sergeeva. Ed. by D. Slutzkin. Tr. by R. Kondor from Rus. LC 74-12194. 177p. 1974. 28.95 (ISBN 0-470-54040-0). Halsted Pr.

Absorption Spectra, Vols. 18 & 19. Lang. 1974. Vol. 18. 55.25 (ISBN 0-12-436318-0); Vol. 19. 55.25 (ISBN 0-12-436319-9). Acad Pr.

Absorption Spectra in the Ultraviolet & Visible Region. Ed. by L. Lang. Incl. Vols. 3-4. 1962-63. 52.25 ea. Vol. 3 (ISBN 0-12-436303-2). Vol. 4 (ISBN 0-12-436304-0); Vol. 5. 1965. 52.25 (ISBN 0-12-436305-9); Vols. 6-12. 1966-73. 55.25 ea. Vol. 6 (ISBN 0-12-436306-7). Vol. 7 (ISBN 0-12-436307-5). Vol. 8 (ISBN 0-12-436308-3). Vol. 9 (ISBN 0-12-436309-1). Vol. 10 (ISBN 0-12-436310-5). Vol. 11. (ISBN 0-12-436311-3); Vol. 12. (ISBN 0-12-436312-1); Index to Volumes. 1969. 21.00 (ISBN 0-12-436356-3); Vols. 13-15. 1970. 52.25 ea. Vol. 13 (ISBN 0-12-426313-5). Vol. 14 (ISBN 0-12-436314-8). Vol. 15 (ISBN 0-12-436315-6); Index to Volumes 11-15. 1971. 27.00 (ISBN 0-686-57637-3); Vols. 16-17. 1972-73. 55.25 ea. Vol. 16 (ISBN 0-12-436316-4). Vol. 17 (ISBN 0-12-436317-2). Acad Pr.

Absorption Spectroscopy of Organic Molecules. V. M. Parikh. LC 72-3460. 1974. pap. text ed. 16.95 (ISBN 0-201-05708-5). A-W.

Abstract Algebra: A First Course. Larry J. Goldstein. LC 72-12790. (Illus.). 1973. 21.95x (ISBN 0-13-000851-6). P-H.

Abstract Algebra: A First Course. Dan Saracino. LC 79-18692. (Illus.). 1980. text ed. 17.95 (ISBN 0-201-07391-9). A-W.

Abstract Algebra: An Active Learning Approach. Neil A. Davidson & Frances F. Gulick. LC 75-19537. (Illus.). 1976. text ed. 19.50 (ISBN 0-395-20663-4); inst. manual 1.75 (ISBN 0-395-20664-2). HM.

Abstract & Linear Algebra. D. M. Burton. 1972. text ed. 16.95 o.p. (ISBN 0-201-00738-X). A-W.

Abstract Currents in Ecuadorian Art. annual Jacqueline Barnitz. (Illus.). 48p. 1977. pap. text ed. 3.00 (ISBN 0-89192-235-0). Interbk Inc.

Abstract Expressionism. A. Everitt. LC 77-80188. (Modern Movements in Art Ser.). 1978. pap. 1.95 (ISBN 0-8120-0880-4). Barron.

Abstract Inference. Ulf Grenander. LC 80-22016. (Probability & Mathematical Statistics Ser.). 528p. 1980. 30.00 (ISBN 0-471-08267-8, Pub. by Wiley Interscience). Wiley.

Abstract Journal, 1790-1920: Origin, Development & Diffusion. Bruce M. Manzer. LC 77-24143. 1977. 15.00 (ISBN 0-8108-1047-6). Scarecrow.

Abstract Lie Algebras. David J. Winter. 1972. 20.00x (ISBN 0-262-23051-8). MIT Pr.

Abstract of British Historical Statistics. Brian R. Mitchell & P. Deane. (Department of Applied Economics Monographs: No. 17). 1962. 68.50 (ISBN 0-521-05738-8). Cambridge U Pr.

Abstract of the Answers & Returns: The Census Report for 1801, 2 vols. Great Britain, Census Office. LC 79-366591. 1981. Repr. of 1802 ed. Set. lib. bdg. 90.00x (ISBN 0-678-05225-5). Vol. 1, Enumeration. Vol. 2, Parish Registers. Kelley.

Abstract of the Original Titles of Record in the General Land Office of Texas. Repr. of 1838 ed. 17.50 (ISBN 0-685-13268-4). Jenkins.

Abstract Painting: Its Origin & Meaning. Adrian Heath. 1953. 3.75 (ISBN 0-85458-828-0). Transatlantic.

Abstract Software Specifications. Ed. by D. Bjorner. (Lecture Notes in Computer Sciences: Vol. 86). 567p. 1980. pap. 31.00 (ISBN 0-387-10007-5). Springer-Verlag.

Abstraction & Artifice in Twentieth Century Art. Harold Osborne. (Illus.). 1979. 24.95x (ISBN 0-19-817359-8). Oxford U Pr.

Abstraction, Relation, & Induction: Three Essays in the History of Thought. Julius R. Weinberg. 1965. 17.50x (ISBN 0-299-03540-9). U of Wis Pr.

Abstracts. American Heart Association, Scientific Sessions, 52nd. (AHA Monograph: No. 65). 1979. pap. 8.00 (ISBN 0-686-58031-1). Am Heart.

Abstracts. International Association of Logopedics & Phoniatrics, 18th Congress, Washington, D.C. August, 1980. Ed. by E. Loebell. (Journal: Folia Phoniatrica: Vol. 32, No. 3). 110p. 1980. soft cover 19.75 (ISBN 3-8055-1249-X). S Karger.

Abstracts. Symposium on the Mechanisms of Vasodilation. Ed. by P. M. Vanhoutte. (Journal: Blood Vessels: Vol. 17, No. 3). 56p. 1980. soft cover 22.25 (ISBN 3-8055-1252-X). S Karger.

Abstracts & Indexes in Science & Technology: A Descriptive Guide. Dolores Owen & Marguerite Hanchey. LC 74-1345. 1974. 10.00 (ISBN 0-8108-0709-2). Scarecrow.

Abstracts of Methods Used to Assess Fish Quality. S. Jhaveri et al. (Marine Technical Report Ser.: No. 69). 3.00 (ISBN 0-938412-00-0). URI MAS.

Abstracts of Microbiological Methods. Ed. by V. B. Skerman. LC 69-16128. 1969. 81.00 o.p. (ISBN 0-471-79385-X, Pub. by Wiley-Interscience). Wiley.

Abstracts of Presentations: Abstracts of Presentations. World Congress on Special Education, 1st. Ed. by Albert H. Fink. LC 78-74018. 318p. 1978. pap. 5.00 o.p. (ISBN 0-86586-001-7). Coun Exc Child.

Abstracts of the Annual Meeting of the American Society for Microbiology-1978. 1978. 10.00 (ISBN 0-914826-32-8). Am Soc Microbio.

Abstracts of the International Conference on Renal Transport of Organic Substances Held in Innsbruck, July, 1980. Ed. by S. Silbernagel. (Journal: Renal Physiology: Vol. 2, No. 3). (Illus.). 62p. 1980. pap. 17.00 (ISBN 3-8055-1641-X). S Karger.

Abstracts of the Proceedings of the Twelfth Cancer Congress, Buenos Aires, 1978. International Cancer Congress, 12th, Buenos Aires, 5-11 October 1978. Ed. by O. Estevez & R. Chacon. LC 79-40032. (Advances in Medical Oncology, Research & Education: Vol. 12). 1979. 205.00 (ISBN 0-08-024378-9). Pergamon.

Abstracts of the Second International Congress on Child Abuse & Neglect. International Congress on Child Abuse & Neglect, 2nd, London 1978. Ed. by A. White Franklin. LC 78-41195. 1979. 30.00 (ISBN 0-08-023438-0). Pergamon.

Abstracts of Vital Records from Raleigh, North Carolina, Newspapers 1820-1829, Vol. 2. Lois S. Neal. LC 79-13328. (Abstracts of Vital Records from Raleigh, North Carolina, Newspapers 1799-1915 Ser.). (Illus.). 940p. 1980. 50.00 (ISBN 0-87152-296-9). Reprint.

Abstracts of Wills & Estates, Barbour County, Ala. Eighteen Fifty-Two to Eighteen Fifty-Six, Vol. 3. Helen S. Foley. 122p. 1976. pap. 12.50 (ISBN 0-89308-183-3). Southern Hist Pr.

Absurd Alphabedtime Stories. Julius Hunter. (Illus.). (gr. k-4). 1976. 1.50 (ISBN 0-8272-0012-9). Bethany Pr.

Absurd Convictions, Modest Hopes: Conversation After Prison. Daniel Berrigan & Lee Lockwood. 256p. 1973. pap. 1.95 o.p. (ISBN 0-394-71912-3, Vin). Random.

Absurd Hero in American Fiction: Updike, Styron, Bellow, Salinger. 2nd, rev. ed. David D. Galloway. 288p. 1981. text ed. 22.50x (ISBN 0-292-70356-2); pap. text ed. 8.95x (ISBN 0-292-70355-4). U of Tex Pr.

Absurdity, Insecurity & Despair. James Park. (Existential Freedom Ser.: No. 8). 1975. pap. 2.00x (ISBN 0-89231-008-1). Existential Bks.

Abu Ali: Three Tales of the Middle East. Dorothy O. Van Woerkom. LC 76-8401. (Ready to Read Ser.). (Illus.). (gr. 1-4). 1976. 7.95 (ISBN 0-02-791310-4, 79131). Macmillan.

Abu Wahab Caper. Ross H. Spencer. 1980. pap. 1.95 (ISBN 0-686-69269-1, 76356). Avon.

Abuse & Maltreatment of the Aged. Jordan I. Kosberg. 400p. Date not set. text ed. 30.00 (ISBN 0-88416-353-9). PSG Pub.

Abuse of Central Stimulants. Ed. by Folke Sjoqvist & Malcolm Tottie. LC 72-116704. (Illus.). 1969. 13.50 (ISBN 0-911216-28-6). Raven.

Abuse of Power: The War Between Downing Street & the Media from Lloyd George to James Callaghan. James Margach. (Illus.). 1978. 15.95 (ISBN 0-491-02044-9). Transatlantic.

Abuse on Wall Street: Conflicts of Interest in the Securities Markets. Twentieth Century Fund. LC 79-8295. (Illus.). 1980. lib. bdg. 35.00 (ISBN 0-89930-001-4, TWC/, Quorum Bks). Greenwood.

Abusing Family. Rita Justice & Blair Justice. LC 76-6478. 1976. text ed. 19.95 (ISBN 0-87705-294-8); pap. 8.95 (ISBN 0-87705-315-4). Human Sci Pr.

Abysmal Failure of the German Philosophers. Paul B. Gardiner. (Illus.). 157p. 1981. 39.75 (ISBN 0-89266-285-9). Am Classical Coll Pr.

Abyss Deep Enough: The Letters of Heinrich Von Kleist with a Selection of Essays & Anecdotes. Heinrich von Kleist. Ed. & tr. by Philip B. Miller. 288p. 1981. 16.95 (ISBN 0-525-05479-0); pap. 8.95 o.p. (ISBN 0-525-03008-5). Dutton.

Abyss Deep Enough: The Letters of Heinrich Von Kleist with a Selection of Essays & Anecdotes. Ed. by Philip B. Miller. 288p. 1981. 16.95 (ISBN 0-525-05479-0). Dutton.

Abyss of Time: Changing Conceptions of the Earth's Antiquity After the 16th Century. Claude C. Allbritton, Jr. LC 79-57131. (Illus.). 272p. 1980. text ed. write for info. (ISBN 0-87735-341-7). Freeman C.

Abyssinian Difficulty: The Emperor Theodorus & the Magdala Campaign, 1867-68. Darrell Bates. (Illus.). 256p. 27.50x (ISBN 0-19-211747-5). Oxford U Pr.

AC Circuit Analysis. Noble L. Lockhart & Ora E. Rice. LC 75-27997. 1976. pap. 8.00 (ISBN 0-8273-1136-2); instructors guide 1.60 (ISBN 0-8273-1137-0). Delmar.

AC Electric Locomotives of the British Rail. Brian Webb & John Duncan. (Illus.). 1979. 17.95 (ISBN 0-7153-7663-2). David & Charles.
Academic Adaptations: Higher Education Prepares for the 1980's & 1990's. Verne A. Stadtman. LC 80-8000. (Carnegie Council Ser.). 1980. text ed. 15.95x (ISBN 0-87589-480-1). Jossey-Bass.
Academic Administrator Grid: A Guide to Developing Effective Management Teams. Robert R. Blake et al. LC 80-8908. (Higher Education Ser.). 1981. text ed. price not set (ISBN 0-87589-492-5). Jossey-Bass.
Academic American Encyclopedia, 21 vols. 1980. Set. 400.00 (ISBN 0-933880-00-6). Arete.
Academic Degree Structures: Innovative Approaches. Carnegie Commission On Higher Education. 1970. 10.95 o.p. (ISBN 0-07-010010-1, P&RB). McGraw.
Academic Degrees. Walter C. Eells & Harold A. Haswell. LC 70-128397. Repr. of 1960 ed. 15.00 (ISBN 0-8103-3015-6). Gale.
Academic Equitation. Decarpentry. Tr. by Nicole Bartle from Fr. (Illus.). Repr. of 1949 ed. pap. 5.25 (ISBN 0-85131-036-2, Dist. by Sporting Book Center). J A Allen.
Academic Freedom in the Age of the College. Richard Hofstadter. LC 61-2329. 1955. pap. 7.00 (ISBN 0-231-08511-7). Columbia U Pr.
Academic Freedom in the Age of the University. Walter P. Metzger. LC 61-2328. 1955. pap. 6.00x (ISBN 0-231-08512-5). Columbia U Pr.
Academic Gamesmanship: Student-Oriented Change in Higher Education. Alexander W. Astin. LC 76-12520. (Illus.). 1976. text ed. 22.95 (ISBN 0-275-56720-6). Praeger.
Academic Janus: The Private College & Its Faculty. Reece McGee. LC 70-149913. (Higher Education Ser.). 1971. 13.95x o.p. (ISBN 0-87589-097-0). Jossey-Bass.
Academic Library: Essays in Honor of Guy R. Lyle. Evan I. Farber & Ruth Walling. LC 74-2098. 1974. 10.00 (ISBN 0-8108-0712-2). Scarecrow.
Academic Library Services for Handicapped Students in the U. S. Carol H. Thomas & James L. Thomas. 350p. 1981. text ed. 45.00x (ISBN 0-912700-95-5). Oryx Pr.
Academic Melting Pot: Catholics & Jews in American Higher Education. Carnegie Commission on Higher Education. Ed. by Stephen Steinberg. LC 73-9656. (Illus.). 208p. 1974. 10.95 o.p. (ISBN 0-07-010067-5, P&RB). McGraw.
Academic Power: Patterns of Authority in Seven National Systems of Higher Education. John H. Van De Graaff et al. LC 78-17172. (Praeger Special Studies). 1978. 23.95 (ISBN 0-03-045531-6). Praeger.
Academic Rewards in Higher Education. Ed. by Darrell R. Lewis & William E. Becker. LC 79-11692. 1979. 19.50 (ISBN 0-88410-189-4). Ballinger Pub.
Academic Ropes: A Perceptual-Motor Academic Program. Tom Hall. Ed. by Frank Alexander & Diane Alexander. (Illus.). 89p. (Orig.). 1981. pap. 5.95 (ISBN 0-915256-08-8). Front Row.
Academic Skills: A Handbook for Working Adults Returning to School. Rebecca Thatcher. 1976. pap. 1.50 (ISBN 0-87546-248-0). NY Sch Indus Rel.
Academic Study of Religion: Nineteen Seventy-Five: Public Schools Religion-Studies: 1975. Anne Carr et al. LC 75-26653. (American Academy of Religion. Section Papers). 1975. pap. 4.00 (ISBN 0-89130-023-6, 010917). Scholars Pr Ca.
Academic Study of Religion: Proceedings. Ed. by Anne Carr. LC 74-14212. (American Academy of Religion. Section Papers). 1974. pap. 4.50 (ISBN 0-88420-115-5, 010911). Scholars Pr Ca.
Academic System in American Society. Carnegie Commission on Higher Education. Ed. by Alain Touraine. LC 73-3322. (Illus.). 336p. 1974. 15.95 o.p. (ISBN 0-07-010054-3, P&RB). McGraw.
Academic Transformation: Seventeen Institutions Under Pressure. Carnegie Commission on Higher Education. Ed. by David Riesman & Verne Stadtman. (Illus.). 512p. 1973. 16.95 o.p. (ISBN 0-07-010049-7, P&RB). McGraw.
Academie Imperiale De Musique: Histoire Litteraire, Musicale, Politique et Galant De Ce Theatre, De 1645 a 1855, 2 vols. Francois H. Blaze. LC 80-2258. 1981. Repr. of 1855 ed. 95.00 (ISBN 0-404-18804-4). AMS Pr.
Academies of Art, Past & Present. Nikolaus Pevsner. LC 78-87379. (Illus.). 332p. 1973. Repr. of 1940 ed. lib. bdg. 30.00 (ISBN 0-306-71603-8). Da Capo.
Academy Awards. Art Sarno. (Illus.). 1980. lib. bdg. 14.95 (ISBN 0-912076-37-2); pap. 9.95 (ISBN 0-912076-38-0). ESE Calif.
Academy Awards Best Actor Oscar Winners. Robert Osborne. 1977. pap. 4.95 (ISBN 0-912076-03-8). ESE Calif.
Academy Awards Best Actress Oscar Winners. Robert Osborne. 1977. pap. 4.95 (ISBN 0-912076-02-X). ESE Calif.
Academy Awards Best Picture Oscar Winners. Robert Osborne. 1977. pap. 4.95 (ISBN 0-912076-05-4). ESE Calif.
Academy Awards Nineteen Eighty-One Oscar Annual. Art Sarno. (Illus.). 1981. lib. bdg. 14.95 (ISBN 0-912076-43-7); pap. 9.95 (ISBN 0-912076-44-5). ESE Calif.
Academy Awards, Nineteen Seventy-Four: Oscar Annual. Robert Osborne. (Illus.). 96p. 1974. 11.95 (ISBN 0-912076-14-3). ESE Calif.
Academy Awards Nineteen Seventy-Six Oscar Annual. Robert Osborne. (Illus.). 1976. lib. bdg. 11.95 (ISBN 0-912076-23-2); pap. 4.95 (ISBN 0-912076-22-4). ESE Calif.
Academy Awards Nineteen Seventy-Three Oscar Annual. annual Robert Osborne. (Illus.). 96p. 1973. 11.95 (ISBN 0-912076-11-9). ESE Calif.
Acadia, Maine, & New Scotland: Marginal Colonies in the Seventeenth Century. John G. Reid. 320p. 1981. 27.50x (ISBN 0-8020-5508-7). U of Toronto Pr.
Acadia: The Georgraphy of Early Nova Scotia to 1760. Andrew H. Clark. (Illus.). 470p. 1968. 27.50x (ISBN 0-299-05080-7). U of Wis Pr.
Acadia: The Story Behind the Scenery. Robert Rothe. Ed. by Gweneth R. DenDooven. LC 78-78121. (Illus.). 1979. 7.95 (ISBN 0-916122-58-1); pap. 3.00 (ISBN 0-916122-57-3). K C Pubns.
Accelerated Strength Testing. 1978. 23.25 (SP-56); 17.25. ACI.
Accelerating Learning: The Use of Suggestion in the Classroom. Allyn Prichard & Jean Taylor. 176p. 1980. pap. text ed. 7.00 (ISBN 0-87879-249-X). Acad Therapy.
Accelerating Population Stabilization Through Social & Economic Progress. Robert S. McNamara. (Development Papers: No. 24). 64p. 1977. pap. 1.50 (ISBN 0-686-28675-8). Overseas Dev Council.
Accent & Rhythm: Prosodic Features of Latin & Greek. W. Sidney Allen. LC 72-91361. (Studies in Linguistics). 432p. 1973. 57.50 (ISBN 0-521-20098-9). Cambridge U Pr.
Accentual Symmetry in Virgil. William F. Knight. Ed. by H. Steele Commager. LC 77-70820. (Latin Poetry Ser.). 1979. Repr. of 1939 ed. lib. bdg. 13.00 (ISBN 0-8240-2971-2). Garland Pub.
Accentuation in Dutch: An Experimental Linguistic Study. A. Van Katwijk. 188p. 1974. pap. text ed. 13.00x (ISBN 90-232-1209-6). Humanities.
Acceptanc Establishing the Covenant, Vol. 8. 250p. Date not set. 11.95. Maznaim.
Acceptance Sampling in Quality Control. Shilling. Date not set. price not set (ISBN 0-8247-1347-8). Dekker.
Access Policy & Procedures & the Law in U. S. Higher Education. Larry G. Simon et al. (Access to Higher Education Ser.: No. 6). 124p. 1978. pap. 6.00 (ISBN 0-89192-215-6, Pub. by Intl Coun Ed Dev). Interbk Inc.
Access: The Guide to a Better Life for Disabled Americans. Lilly Bruck. 252p. 1978. 12.95 (ISBN 0-394-50133-0); pap. 5.95 (ISBN 0-394-73455-6). Random.
Access to Ambulatory Care & the U. S. Economy. Frank A. Sloan & Judith D. Bentkover. LC 78-19537. 1979. 17.95 (ISBN 0-669-02510-0). Lexington Bks.
Access to Higher Education: Two Perspectives. James A. Perkins. 84p. 1978. pap. 2.50 (ISBN 0-89192-219-9, Pub. by Intl Coun Ed Dev). Interbk Inc.
Access to Home Care. 1980. 3.00. Comm Coun Great NY.
Access to Law: The Second Seminar on Australian Lawyers & Social Change. Ed. by J. Golding et al. 336p. (Orig.). 1980. pap. text ed. 16.95 (ISBN 0-7081-1305-2, 0581). Bks Australia.
Access to Power: Cross-National Studies of Women & Elites. Ed. by Cynthia F. Epstein & Rose L. Coser. (Illus.). 280p. 1980. text ed. 27.50x (ISBN 0-04-301118-7, 2523). Allen Unwin.
Access to the Past: Museum Programs & Handicapped Visitors. Alice P. Kenney. x, 131p. (Orig.). 1980. pap. 7.95 (ISBN 0-910050-45-7). AASLH.
Accessible City. Wilfred Owen. 150p. 1972. 10.95 (ISBN 0-8157-6770-6); pap. 4.95 (ISBN 0-8157-6769-2). Brookings.
Accessory Glands of the Male Reproductive Tract. Ed. by E. S. Hafez & Elinor Spring-Mills. LC 79-89654. (Perspectives in Human Reproduction Ser.: Vol. 6). (Illus.). 1979. 34.00 (ISBN 0-250-40268-8). Ann Arbor Science.
Accident. Carol Carrick. LC 76-3532. (Illus.). 32p. (ps-3). 1976. 7.95 (ISBN 0-395-28774-X, Clarion). HM.
Accident. Hila Colman. LC 80-20509. 160p. (gr. 7-9). 1980. 7.95 (ISBN 0-688-22238-2); PLB 7.63 (ISBN 0-688-32238-7). Morrow.
Accident Action: The Essential Family Guide to Home Safety & First Aid. Tony Smith & Richard V. Lee. Ed. by Bill Breckon. (Illus.). 1979. 9.95 o.p. (ISBN 0-670-10206-7, Studio). Viking Pr.
Accident at Three Mile Island: The Human Dimensions. Ed. by David L. Sills et al. 200p. (Orig.). 1981. lib. bdg. 20.00x (ISBN 0-86531-165-X); pap. text ed. 12.00x (ISBN 0-86531-187-0). Westview.
Accident at Three Mile Island: The Need for Change, the Legacy of TMI. Ed. by John G. Kemeny. (Illus.). 201p. 1981. 33.00 (ISBN 0-08-025949-9); pap. 25.00 (ISBN 0-08-025946-4). Pergamon.
Accident Causation. Society of Automotive Engineers. 1980. 15.00. Soc Auto Engineers.
Accident Compensation. Terence G. Ison. 240p. 1981. 37.50x (ISBN 0-7099-0249-2, Pub. by Croom Helm Ltd England). Biblio Dist.
Accident or Suicide: Destruction by Automobile. Norman Tabachnick et al. 288p. 1973. 16.75 (ISBN 0-398-02819-2). C C Thomas.
Accidental Century. Michael Harrington. 1965. 12.95 (ISBN 0-02-548200-9). Macmillan.
Accidental or Incendiary. Richard D. Fitch & Edward A. Porter. 224p. 1975. 14.75 (ISBN 0-398-00582-6). C C Thomas.
Accidents & Disasters: Causes & Countermeasures. A. L. Thygerson. (Illus.). 1977. 16.95x (ISBN 0-13-000968-7). P-H.
Accidents & Emergencies: A Practical Handbook for Personal Use. 3rd ed. R. H. Hardy. (Illus.). 240p. 1981. text ed. 14.95x (ISBN 0-19-261321-9). Oxford U Pr.
Accidents, Compensation & the Law. 3rd ed. P. S. Atiyah. (Law in Context Ser.). xxiv, 695p. 1980. 47.00x (ISBN 0-297-77754-8, Pub. by Weidenfeld & Nicolson England). Rothman.
Accommodation of Utility Plant Within the Rights of Way of Urban Streets & Highways. Compiled By American Society of Civil Engineers. (ASCE Manual & Report on Engineering Practice Ser.: No. 14). 116p. 1974. pap. text ed. 18.00 (ISBN 0-87262-207-X). Am Soc Civil Eng.
Accompt Rekenynge & Confession of the Faith of Huldrik Zwinglius. Ulrich Zwingli. Tr. by Thomas Cotsforde from Latin. LC 79-84148. (English Experience: No. 964). Orig. Title: Swinglische Bekenntuis. 156p. 1979. Repr. of 1555 ed. lib. bdg. 11.50 (ISBN 90-221-0964-X). Walter J Johnson.
According to Mork: The World As Mork Sees It. Bruce Kraus. (Illus.). 1980. pap. cancelled (ISBN 0-671-41486-0). Wanderer Bks.
According to Promise. C. H. Spurgeon. pap. 2.25 (ISBN 0-686-26192-5). Pilgrim Pubns.
Account of a Meeting with Denizens of Another World. William R. Looseley. 1980. 7.95 (ISBN 0-312-00233-5). St Martin.
Account of the British Settlement of Aden in Arabia. F. M. Hunter. 232p. 1968. 28.50x (ISBN 0-7146-1986-8, F Cass Co). Biblio Dist.
Account of the Cultivation & Manufacture of Tea in China. Samuel Ball. LC 78-74309. (Modern Chinese Economy Ser.). 382p. 1980. lib. bdg. 38.00 (ISBN 0-8240-4250-6). Garland Pub.
Account of the Discoveries of the Portuguese in the Interior of Angola & Mozambique. Thomas E. Bowdich. LC 74-15013. Repr. of 1824 ed. 21.00 (ISBN 0-404-12008-3). AMS Pr.
Account of the English Dramatick Poets. Gerard Langbaine. LC 71-170468. (English Stage Ser.: Vol. 20). lib. bdg. 50.00 (ISBN 0-8240-0603-8). Garland Pub.
Account of the Expenses of John of Brabant & Thomas & Henry of Lancaster. (Camden Society Ser.: Vol. 55). 1853. 27.00 (ISBN 0-685-13335-4). Johnson Repr.
Account of the History of Stranger's Fever in Charleston, 1699-1876. M. Foster Farley. LC 78-66421. 1978. pap. text ed. 9.00 (ISBN 0-8191-0320-9). U Pr of Amer.
Account of the Life, Opinions, & Writings of John Milton. Thomas Keightley. 484p. 1980. Repr. of 1855 ed. lib. bdg. 50.00 (ISBN 0-8492-1495-5). R West.
Account of the Mutiny on H. M. S. Bounty. William Bligh. Ed. by Robert Bowman. 224p. 1980. text ed. write for info. (ISBN 0-391-02095-1). Humanities.
Account of the Polynesian Race: Its Origin & Migration, 3 vols. in 1. Abraham Fornander. LC 69-13505. (Illus.). 1980. Repr. of 1878 ed. Set. 37.50 (ISBN 0-8048-0002-2). C E Tuttle.
Accountability: A State, a Process, or a Product? Ed. by William Gephart. LC 74-84288. 82p. 1975. pap. 3.50 (ISBN 0-87367-702-1). Phi Delta Kappa.
Accountability & Quality Assurance. Jack Greenspan. LC 80-11308. (Illus.). 288p. 1980. text ed. 29.95 (ISBN 0-89303-007-4). Charles.
Accountability for School Psychologists: Selected Readings. Thomas N. Fairchild. 1978. pap. text ed. 9.75 (ISBN 0-8191-0371-3). U Pr of Amer.
Accountability for Teachers & School Administrators. Ed. by Allan C. Ornstein. LC 72-95012. 1973. pap. 4.95 (ISBN 0-8224-0055-3). Pitman Learning.
Accountability in Education. Ed. by Tony Becher & Stuart Maclure. (General Ser.). (Illus.). 1978. pap. text ed. 20.00x (ISBN 0-85633-167-8, NFER). Humanities.
Accountants Cost Handbook. 2nd ed. R. I. Dickey. 1050p. 1960. 39.50 (ISBN 0-471-06519-6). Wiley.
Accountants Guide to Management Techniques. Ed. by Stanley Oliver. 500p. 1975. 25.00 o.s.i. (ISBN 0-7161-0231-5). Herman Pub.
Accountants' Handbook. 6th ed. Lee J. Seidler & Douglas R. Carmichael. 1700p. 1981. 75.00 (ISBN 0-471-05505-0). Ronald Pr.
Accounting: A Management Approach. 6th ed. Gordon Shillinglaw et al. 1979. 20.95 (ISBN 0-256-02175-9). Irwin.
Accounting: A Self-Instruction Guide to Procedures & Theory. Morton D. Bluestone. (Illus.). 208p. 1973. pap. 2.95 o.s.i. (ISBN 0-02-008160-X, Collier). Macmillan.
Accounting: A Survey. Henry E. Riggs. 1981. text ed. 18.95 (ISBN 0-07-052851-9, C); write for info instrs.' manual (ISBN 0-07-052852-7). McGraw.
Accounting: An Information Systems Approach. John W. Buckley & Kevin M. Lightner. LC 72-93646. text ed. 19.95 (ISBN 0-8221-0097-5). CBI Pub.
Accounting & Analytical Methods. Richard Mattessich. LC 64-22113. 1978. Repr. of 1964 ed. text ed. 20.00 (ISBN 0-914348-21-3). Scholars Bk.
Accounting & Computer Systems. Clifton & Lucey. 1977. 22.50x o.p. (ISBN 0-8464-0107-X). Beekman Pubs.
Accounting & Reporting Practices of Private Foundations: A Critical Evaluation. Jack Traub. LC 77-5344. (Special Studies). 1977. text ed. 26.50 (ISBN 0-275-24530-6). Praeger.
Accounting Book of Readings. 2nd ed. Gerhard Mueller. LC 73-115174. 1977. pap. 10.95 (ISBN 0-03-089908-7). Dryden Pr.
Accounting Essentials. Neal Margolis & N. Paul Harmon. LC 72-4756. (Self-Teaching Guides Ser.). 320p. 1972. pap. text ed. 7.95 (ISBN 0-471-56867-8). Wiley.
Accounting, Evaluation & Economic Behavior. Raymond J. Chambers. LC 66-13944. 1975. Repr. of 1966 ed. text ed. 13.00 (ISBN 0-914348-15-9). Scholars Bk.
Accounting, Finance, & Taxation: A Basic Guide for Small Business. C. Richard Baker & Rick S. Hayes. LC 79-16481. 1980. 22.50 (ISBN 0-8436-0784-X). CBI Pub.
Accounting-Financial Report, 2 pts. Ed. by Steven Langer. Incl. Pt. 1. Public Accounting Firms (ISBN 0-916506-48-7); Pt. 2. Industry, Government, Education, Non-Profit (ISBN 0-916506-49-5). 1980. pap. 60.00 ea. Abbot Langer Assocs.
Accounting-Financial Report: Industry-Government-Education-Non-Profit, Pt. II. 2nd ed. Ed. by Steven Langer. 1981. pap. 75.00 (ISBN 0-916506-61-4). Abbott Langer Assocs.
Accounting-Financial Report: Public Accounting Firms, Pt. I. 2nd ed. Ed. by Steven Langer. 1981. pap. 75.00 (ISBN 0-916506-60-6). Abbott Langer Assocs.
Accounting Flows: Income, Funds & Cash. Robert K. Jaedicke & Robert T. Sprouse. (Orig.). 1965. pap. 9.95x ref. ed. (ISBN 0-13-002352-3). P-H.
Accounting for a Simplified Firm Owning Depreciable Assets: Seventeen Essays & a Synthesis Based on a Common Case. Ed. by Robert R. Sterling & Arthur L. Thomas. LC 79-18604. 1979. text ed. 15.00 (ISBN 0-914348-27-2). Scholars Bk.
Accounting for Advertising Assets. Dale L. Flesher. 1979. pap. 4.50 (ISBN 0-938004-01-8). U MS Bus Econ.
Accounting for Business. 2nd ed. John R. Cerepak. LC 73-85889. 832p. 1974. text ed. 18.95 (ISBN 0-675-08881-X); Vols. 1-14 Ea. 6.50 ea. (ISBN 0-675-08823-2); Vols. 15-27. 6.50 ea. (ISBN 0-675-08822-4). Merrill.
Accounting for Changing Prices: Replacement Cost & General Price Level Adjustments. James A. Largay & J. L. Livingstone. LC 76-7491. (Accounting, Management & Information Systems Ser.). 1976. text ed. 24.95 (ISBN 0-471-54210-5). Wiley.
Accounting for Construction Management. J. B. Goodlad. 1975. 16.95x (ISBN 0-434-90680-8). Intl Ideas.
Accounting for Decision Making. Denzil Y. Causey. LC 77-78479. (Accounting Ser.). 1978. text ed. 19.95 o.p. (ISBN 0-88244-156-6). Grid Pub.
Accounting for Economic Events. Edgar O. Edwards et al. LC 79-22971. 1979. text ed. 26.00 (ISBN 0-914348-28-0). Scholars Bk.
Accounting for Government & Nonprofit Entities. 6th ed. Leon E. Hay. 1980. 22.95x (ISBN 0-256-02329-8). Irwin.
Accounting for Industrial Management. R. Sidebotham. 1964. 25.00 (ISBN 0-08-009892-4); pap. 12.75 (ISBN 0-08-009891-6). Pergamon.

Accounting for Inflation: Stating a True Financial Position. R. McGee. 15.95 (ISBN 0-13-002337-X); pap. 7.95 (ISBN 0-13-002329-9). P-H.

Accounting for Lawyers. 3rd ed. E. Faris. LC 75-12479. (Illus.). 1975. 23.00 (ISBN 0-672-82026-9, Bobbs-Merrill Law). Michie.

Accounting for Life Insurance Companies. Charles Van House & Rogers Hammond. 1969. text ed. 10.50 (ISBN 0-256-00570-2). Irwin.

Accounting for Management Analysis. Li. 1964. 18.95 (ISBN 0-675-09814-9). Merrill.

Accounting for Managerial Analysis. 3rd ed. James M. Fremgen. (Illus.). 1976. text ed. 18.95 (ISBN 0-256-01777-8). Irwin.

Accounting for Managerial Decision Making. 2nd ed. D. T. Decoster et al. LC 77-15785. (Accounting & Information Systems Ser.). 1978. pap. text ed. 14.50 (ISBN 0-471-02204-7). Wiley.

Accounting for Multinational Enterprises. Dhia D. Alhashim & James W. Robertson. LC 77-13732. (Key Issues Lecture Ser). 1978. 13.95 (ISBN 0-672-97209-3); pap. 7.95 (ISBN 0-672-97183-6). Bobbs.

Accounting for Nonfinancial Managers. Merwin Leven. LC 80-19502. 175p. 1980. 50.00 (ISBN 0-932648-16-9). Boardroom.

Accounting for Pensions. J. M. Young & N. J. Buchanan. 160p. 1980. 39.00x (ISBN 0-85941-124-9, Pub. by Woodhead-Faulkner England). State Mutual Bk.

Accounting for Price Level Changes. R. S. Gynther. 1966. 13.75 (ISBN 0-08-011712-0); pap. 10.75 (ISBN 0-08-011711-2). Pergamon.

Accounting for Research & Development. J. Batty. 237p. 1976. text ed. 23.50x (Pub. by Busn Bks England). Renouf.

Accounting for Slower Economic Growth: The United States in the 1970s. Edward F. Denison. LC 79-20341. 212p. 1979. 18.95 (ISBN 0-8157-1802-0); pap. 8.95 (ISBN 0-8157-1801-2). Brookings.

Accounting for the Cost of Interest. Robert N. Anthony. LC 75-12484. 128p. 1975. 15.95 (ISBN 0-669-00027-2). Lexington Bks.

Accounting for the Distrubutive Trades. 2nd ed. E. Hicks & A. Teasdale. 1975. pap. text ed. 16.50x (ISBN 0-685-83680-0). Intl Ideas.

Accounting for the Middle Manager. Dale L. Flesher & Tonya K. Flesher. 462p. 1980. 16.95 (ISBN 0-442-23875-4). Van Nos Reinhold.

Accounting for United States Economic Growth: 1929-1969. Edward F. Denison. LC 74-278. 355p. 1974. 18.95 (ISBN 0-8157-1804-7); pap. 7.95 (ISBN 0-8157-1803-9). Brookings.

Accounting Fundamentals: A Self-Instructional Approach. 2nd ed. Stephen Moscove. 1980. pap. text ed. 10.95 (ISBN 0-8359-0061-4); wkbk. 7.95 (ISBN 0-8359-0070-3); instr's. manual avail. (ISBN 0-8359-0062-2). Reston.

Accounting Fundamentals for Non-Financial Executives. Allen Sweeny. LC 78-173320. 1972. 11.95 (ISBN 0-8144-5286-8). Am Mgmt.

Accounting Goes Public. Morton Levy. LC 77-81445. 1977. 13.95 (ISBN 0-8122-7733-3). U of Pa Pr.

Accounting Graffiti. Martin L. Gosman. LC 75-4144. (Illus.). 152p. 1975. pap. text ed. 6.95 (ISBN 0-8299-0058-6). West Pub.

Accounting Handbook for Non-Accountants. 2nd ed. Clarence B. Nickerson. LC 79-1368. 1979. 27.50 (ISBN 0-8436-0765-3). CBI Pub.

Accounting in Business. 4th ed. R. J. Bull. LC 80-49870. (Illus.). 448p. 1980. text ed. 34.95 (ISBN 0-408-10669-7); pap. text ed. 19.95 (ISBN 0-408-10670-0). Butterworths.

Accounting in Business Decisions: Theory, Method, & Use. 3rd ed. Homer A. Black et al. (Illus.). 752p. 1973. 19.95x (ISBN 0-13-001545-8); accounting forms 4.95x (ISBN 0-13-001644-6); practice case 2.95x (ISBN 0-13-001230-0). P-H.

Accounting in Perspective. Ed. by Robert R. Sterling & William F. Bentz. LC 78-26732. 1979. text ed. 13.00 (ISBN 0-914348-25-6). Scholars Bk.

Accounting Information Sources. Rosemary Demarest. LC 70-120908. (Management Information Guide Ser.: No. 18). 1970. 30.00 (ISBN 0-8103-0818-5). Gale.

Accounting Information Systems. James O. Hicks, Jr. & Wayne E. Leininger. 500p. 1981. text ed. 15.96 (ISBN 0-8299-0384-4). West Pub.

Accounting Information Systems. Richard Lindhe & Steven D. Grossman. 500p. 1980. text ed. 18.95x (ISBN 0-931920-23-X). Dame Pubns.

Accounting Information Systems: A Book of Readings. James R. Davis & Barry E. Cushing. LC 78-74681. pap. 8.95 (ISBN 0-201-01099-2). A-W.

Accounting Information Systems & Business Organizations. 2nd ed. Barry E. Cushing. LC 77-83024. (Illus.). 1978. text ed. 19.95 (ISBN 0-201-01016-X). A-W.

Accounting Information Systems: Concepts & Practice for Effective Decision Making Systems. Stephen A. Moscove & Mark G. Simkin LC 80-15445. (Wiley Ser. in Accounting & Information Systems). 560p. 1981. 23.95 (ISBN 0-471-03369-3); tchr's manual avail. (ISBN 0-471-03371-5). Wiley.

Accounting: Its Principles & Problems. Henry R. Hatfield. LC 78-12596. 1971. Repr. of 1927 ed. text ed. 15.00 (ISBN 0-914348-02-7). Scholars Bk.

Accounting, Legal & Tax Aspects of Corporate Acquisitions. Joseph R. Guardino. 1973. 27.95 o.p. (ISBN 0-13-002105-9). P-H.

Accounting Made Simple. Joseph Peter Simini. LC 66-12174. pap. 3.50 (ISBN 0-385-02032-5, Made). Doubleday.

Accounting Manual for Catholic Elementary & Secondary Schools. rev. ed. J. Alfred Moroni & Francis J. Lahey. 86p. 1969. 4.00. Natl Cath Educ.

Accounting Measurements for Financial Reports. William J. Vatter. 1971. text ed. 13.95x o.p. (ISBN 0-256-00628-8). Irwin.

Accounting Methods for Non-Profit Organizations. Bessie Chukuocha. 1981. 6.95 (ISBN 0-8062-1650-6). Carlton.

Accounting Mission. Frank S. Bray. LC 73-84525. 1973. Repr. of 1951 ed. text ed. 10.00 (ISBN 0-914348-01-9). Scholars Bk.

Accounting Policy Formation: The Role of Corporate Management. Lauren Kelly-Newton. (A-W Paperback Accounting Ser.). 200p. 1980. pap. text ed. 4.95 (ISBN 0-201-05291-1). A-W.

Accounting Practice & Procedure. Arthur L. Dickinson. LC 73-13487. 1975. Repr. of 1918 ed. text ed. 13.00 (ISBN 0-914348-17-5). Scholars Bk.

Accounting Practices for Hotels, Motels, & Restaurants. Paul Dittmer. LC 79-142507. 1971. text ed. 17.95 (ISBN 0-672-96062-1); tchr's manual 5.00 (ISBN 0-672-26064-6); wkbk., 1972 9.95 (ISBN 0-672-96063-X). Bobbs.

Accounting Practices in OECD Member Countris. OECD. (International Investment & Multinational Enterprises). (Illus.). 250p. (Orig.). 1980. pap. text ed. 13.50x (ISBN 92-64-12076-9). OECD.

Accounting Practices in the Petroleum Industry. Robert H. Irving, Jr. & Verden R. Draper. 1958. 16.50 o.p. (ISBN 0-8260-4685-1). Ronald Pr.

Accounting Principles. 4th ed. Robert N. Anthony & James S. Reece. 1979. text ed. 17.95x (ISBN 0-256-02147-3). Irwin.

Accounting Principles. Roger H. Hermanson et al. 1980. 18.95x (ISBN 0-256-02258-5); study guide 6.95x (ISBN 0-256-02262-3); working papers, bk. 5.95x (ISBN 0-256-02263-1); working papers, bk. 2 avail. (ISBN 0-256-02264-X); practice set no. 1 avail. (ISBN 0-256-02305-0); practice set no. 2 avail. (ISBN 0-256-02306-9); practice set no. 3 avail. (ISBN 0-256-02383-2). Business Pubns.

Accounting Principles. 2nd ed. Ronald Thacker. (Illus.). 1979. text ed. 19.95 (ISBN 0-13-002766-9). P-H.

Accounting Principles: A Multimedia Program. Dudley Curry & Robert Frame. LC 72-95544. 1973. Modules 1-15. pap. text ed. 15.95 (ISBN 0-675-08992-1); Modules 16-30. pap. text ed. 16.95x (ISBN 0-675-08924-7); media: audiocassettes & filmstrips for modules 1-15 325.00, 2-7 sets, 280.00 ea., 8-15 sets 247.50 ea., 16 or more sets, 197.50 ea. (ISBN 0-675-08930-1); media: audiocassettes & filmstrips for modules 16-30 325.00, 2-7 sets, 280.00 ea., 8-15 sets 247.50 ea., 16 or more sets, 197.50 ea. (ISBN 0-675-08908-5). test 3.95 (ISBN 0-686-66866-9). Merrill.

Accounting: Principles & Applications, 3 pts. 4th ed. Horace R. Brock & Charles E. Palmer. LC 80-16713. (College Accounting Instructional System Ser.). (Illus.). 1981. One Vol. Ed. text ed. 16.95x (ISBN 0-07-008090-9, G); Pt. 1. pap. text ed. 9.50x (ISBN 0-07-008092-5); Pt. 2. pap. text ed. 9.50x (ISBN 0-07-008093-3); Pt. 3. pap. text ed. 9.50x (ISBN 0-07-008094-1); wkbk. 5.45 (ISBN 0-07-008096-8); Pt. 2, Individualized Performance Guide. 5.95 (ISBN 0-07-008096-8); Course Management & solutions manual 10.00 (ISBN 0-07-008101-8); tests avail. (ISBN 0-07-008098-4). McGraw.

Accounting Principles & Reporting Practices for Certain Nonprofit Oragnizations. 1979. pap. 4.00 (SOP 78-10). Am Inst CPA.

Accounting Principles Workbook. 5th ed. James S. Reece & Robert N. Anthony. 1979. pap. text ed. 6.95 (ISBN 0-256-02171-6). Irwin.

Accounting Problems & How to Solve Them. Joseph Schabacker & Paul Schroeder. (Orig.). 1952. pap. 2.95 (ISBN 0-06-460085-8, CO 85, COS). Har-Row.

Accounting Problems of Multinational Enterprises. Elwood L. Miller. LC 78-20273. (Illus.). 1979. 21.00 (ISBN 0-669-02712-X). Lexington Bks.

Accounting Profession. John W. Buckley & Marlene H. Buckley. LC 74-8880. (Management, Accounting & Information Systems Ser.). 192p. 1974. 15.95 o.p. (ISBN 0-471-11610-6); pap. 8.95 (ISBN 0-471-11609-2). Wiley.

Accounting Professional: Ethics, Responsibility, & Liability. Floyd Windal & Robert Corley. (Illus.). 1980. text ed. 21.95 (ISBN 0-13-003020-1). P-H.

Accounting Responses to Changing Prices: Experimentation with Four Models. 1980. pap. 14.00. Am Inst CPA.

Accounting Simplified: An Inroductory Text. Gayle A. Stelter & Ambrose S. Kodet. 1981. write for info. (ISBN 0-672-97177-1); tchrs. manual avail. (ISBN 0-672-97180-1); working papers avail. (ISBN 0-672-97179-8). Bobbs.

Accounting Systems of U. S. Government Agencies. Thomas Canada. 1980. 15.20 (ISBN 0-87771-013-9). Grad School.

Accounting: Text & Cases. 6th ed. Robert N. Anthony & James S. Reece. 1979. text ed. 19.95x (ISBN 0-256-02148-1). Irwin.

Accounting: The Basis for Business Decisions. 5th ed. Walter B. Meigs & Robert F. Meigs. Ed. by M. Singer & D. Mason. (Illus.). 1216p. 1980. text ed. 20.95 (ISBN 0-07-041551-X, C); study guide 7.50 (ISBN 0-07-041552-8); Learning Objectives avail. (ISBN 0-07-041565-X); practice set 1 6.50 (ISBN 0-07-041558-7); practice set 2 6.50 (ISBN 0-07-041559-5); comp. exam guide free (ISBN 0-07-041557-9); overhead transpariencies 375.00 (ISBN 0-07-074714-8); Chapters 1-28. wksheets A 6.95 ea. (ISBN 0-07-041560-9); Chapters 1-28. wksheets B 6.95 ea. McGraw.

Accounting: The Canadian Scene. Art Guthrie et al. 144p. 1980. pap. text ed. 8.95 (ISBN 0-8403-2234-8). Kendall-Hunt.

Accounting Theory. 3rd. ed. Eldon S. Hendriksen. 1977. text ed. 19.95 (ISBN 0-256-01901-0). Irwin.

Accounting Theory. Kenneth S. Most. LC 76-41424. (Accounting Ser.). 1977. text ed. 19.50 (ISBN 0-88244-142-6). Grid Pub.

Accounting Theory. William A. Paton. LC 73-84526. 1973. Repr. of 1962 ed. text ed. 15.00 (ISBN 0-914348-06-X). Scholars Bk.

Accounting Theory: Text & Readings. Levi D. McCullers & Richard G. Schroeder. LC 78-570. (Wiley Ser. in Accounting & Information Systems). 1978. text ed. 23.95x (ISBN 0-471-58364-2). Wiley.

Accounting Two. James A. Cashin & Joel L. Lerner. (Schaum's Outline Ser.). 1974. pap. text ed. 4.95 o.p. (ISBN 0-07-010212-0, SP). McGraw.

Accounting with the Computer: A Practice Case & Simulation. 3rd ed. Joseph W. Wilkinson. 1975. pap. text ed. 8.95 (ISBN 0-256-01659-3). Irwin.

Accounts for the Year. Jon Lindsey. 1981. 8.95 (ISBN 0-533-04793-5). Vantage.

Accounts Payable: CBM-PET Edition. Lon Poole. 200p. (Orig.). 1980. pap. cancelled (ISBN 0-931988-42-X). Osborne-McGraw.

Accounts Receivable & Inventory Lending: How to Establish & Operate a Department. David A. Robinson. LC 77-5322. (Illus.). 1977. 36.00 o.p. (ISBN 0-87267-029-5). Bankers.

Accounts Receivable & Inventory Lending: How to Establish & Operate a Department. 2nd ed. David A. Robinson. LC 80-21097. (Illus.). 1981. text ed. 43.00 (ISBN 0-87267-036-8). Bankers.

Accounts Receivable: CBM-PET Edition. Ed. by Lon Poole. 200p. (Orig.). 1980. pap. cancelled (ISBN 0-931988-43-8). Osborne-McGraw.

Accoutrement Plates North & South, 1861-1865. 2nd enl. ed. William G. Gavin. LC 74-24432. (Illus.). 400p. 1975. casebound 22.00 o.p. (ISBN 0-87387-068-9); pap. 15.00 o.p. (ISBN 0-87387-050-6). Shumway.

Acculturation: The Study of Culture Contact. Melville J. Herskovits. 7.00 (ISBN 0-8446-1235-9). Peter Smith.

Acculturation: Theory, Models & Some New Findings. Ed. by Amado M. Padilla. LC 79-21617. (AAAS Selected Symposium Ser.: No. 39). (Illus.). 165p. 1980. lib. bdg. 17.00x (ISBN 0-89158-859-0). Westview.

Accumulation of Nitrate. Committee on Nitrate Accumulation. vii, 106p. 1972. pap. text ed. 6.00 (ISBN 0-309-02038-7). Natl Acad Pr.

Accurate Rifle. Warren Page. 11.95 (ISBN 0-87691-102-5). Winchester Pr.

Accursed. Paul Boorstin. 1977. pap. 1.75 o.p. (ISBN 0-451-07745-8, E7745, Sig). NAL.

Ace of the Iron Cross. Ernst Udet. Ed. by Stanley M. Ulanoff. Tr. by Richard K. Riehn from Ger. LC 80-26156. (Air Combat Classics). (Illus.). 256p. 1981. 9.95 (ISBN 0-668-05161-2); pap. 5.95 (ISBN 0-668-05163-9). Arco.

ACEC International Engineering Directory: 1980-1981. American Consulting Engineers Council. 1980. 10.00 (ISBN 0-686-60619-1). Am Consul Eng.

ACEC Membership Directory, 1980-1981. American Consulting Engineers Council. 1980. 25.00 (ISBN 0-686-60620-5). Am Consul Eng.

Aceite. Harlan Wade. Tr. by Mamie M. Contreras from Eng. LC 78-26613. (Book About Ser.). (Illus., Sp.). (gr. k-3). 1979. PLB 7.30 (ISBN 0-8172-1485-2). Raintree Pubs.

Acension of Christ. William Milligan. Date not set. 12.50 (ISBN 0-86524-061-2). Klock & Klock.

Aceptado Por Dios. John Blanchard. 2.50 (ISBN 0-686-12564-9). Banner of Truth.

Aces & Aircraft of World War One. Christopher Campbell. (Illus.). 128p. 1981. 24.95 (Pub. by Blandford Pr England). Sterling.

Aces & Eights. Loren D. Estleman. LC 80-2447. (Double D Western Ser.). 192p. 1981. 9.95 (ISBN 0-385-17469-1). Doubleday.

Aces, Heroes & Daredevils of the Air. LeRoy Hayman. 160p. (gr. 8-12). 1981. PLB price not set (ISBN 0-671-34049-2). Messner.

Aces Wild. E. Jefferson Clay. Bd. with Badge for Brazos. 1980. pap. 2.25 (ISBN 0-505-51470-2). Tower Bks.

Acetelyne Based Chemicals from Coal & Other Natural Sources. Tedeschi. Date not set. price not set (ISBN 0-8247-1358-3). Dekker.

Acetylcholine: An Approach to the Molecular Mechanism of Action. M. J. Michelson & E. V. Ziemel. LC 73-11271. 252p. 1974. text ed. 49.00 (ISBN 0-08-017159-1). Pergamon.

Acetylsalicylic Acid: New Uses for an Old Drug. Ed. by H. J. Barnett et al. 1981. text ed. price not set (ISBN 0-89004-647-6). Raven.

ACFTL Nineteen Seventy-Nine: Abstracts of Presented Papers. (Language in Education Ser.: No. 25). 1980. pap. 5.95 (ISBN 0-87281-113-1). Ctr Appl Ling.

Acharnians. Aristophanes. Ed. by Charles E. Graves. (Gr.). 1905. text ed. 6.50x (ISBN 0-521-04045-0). Cambridge U Pr.

Achebe's World: The Historical & Cultural Context of Chinua Achebe's Novels. Robert M. Wren. (Illus.). 240p. (Orig.). 1980. 18.00x (ISBN 0-89410-005-X); pap. 9.00x (ISBN 0-89410-006-8). Three Continents.

Achievement. Antonius H. Gunneweg & Walter Schmithals. Tr. by David Smith. LC 80-26977. (Biblical Encounter Ser.). 208p. (Orig.). 1981. pap. 7.95 (ISBN 0-687-00690-2). Abingdon.

Achievement in Mathematics, 2 vols. Rudd Crawford et al. (Mathematics Program). (gr. 7-8). 1974. Vol. 1. text ed. 14.60 (ISBN 0-205-03976-6, 563976X); Vol. 2. text ed. 14.60 (ISBN 0-205-04225-2, 5642256); tchrs'. guide for vol. 1 10.96 (ISBN 0-205-03977-4, 5639778); tchrs'. guide for vol. 2 10.96 (ISBN 0-205-04226-0, 5642264). Allyn.

Achievement in Secondary School: Attitudes, Personality & School Success. R. Sumner & F. W. Warburton. (General Ser.). 208p. (Orig.). 1972. pap. text ed. 17.50x (ISBN 0-901225-76-2, NFER). Humanities.

Achievement of C. S. Lewis: A Reading of His Fiction. Thomas Howard. LC 80-14188. (Wheaton Literary Ser.). 200p. 1980. pap. 5.95 (ISBN 0-87788-004-2). Shaw Pubs.

Achievement of Isaac Bashevis Singer. Ed. by Marcia Allentuck. LC 69-19747. (Crosscurrents-Modern Critique Ser.). 197p. 1969. 9.95 (ISBN 0-8093-0383-3). S Ill U Pr.

Achievement of William Faulkner. Michael Millgate. LC 78-16318. 1978. 15.00x (ISBN 0-8032-3054-0); pap. 4.95 (ISBN 0-8032-8102-1, BB 680, Bison). U of Nebr Pr.

Achievement-Related Motives in Children. Ed. by Charles P. Smith. LC 75-81045. 1969. 8.75x (ISBN 0-87154-811-9). Russell Sage.

Achievement, Stress & Anxiety. Ed. by Heinz W. Krohne & Lothar Laux. LC 79-28840. (Clinical & Community Psychology Ser.). (Illus.). 448p. Date not set. text ed. 24.95 (ISBN 0-89116-187-2). Hemisphere Pub. Postponed.

Achievers. Gerald D. Bell. LC 73-79581. 200p. 1973. pap. 8.95 (ISBN 0-914616-00-5). Preston-Hill.

Achieving Better Classroom Discipline. Robert C. Hawley & Isabel L. Hawley. LC 80-67946. 128p. (Orig.). 1981. pap. 9.95 (ISBN 0-913636-11-8). Educ Res MA.

Achieving Classroom Communication Through Self Analysis. Theodore Parson. 1976. kit (instructor's manual, worktext, audiotape cassettes, instruction sheets) 21.50leader's (ISBN 0-574-23040-8, 13-6040); group leader's manual 4.95 (ISBN 0-574-23042-4, 13-6042); worktext 8.95 (ISBN 0-574-23041-6, 13-6041); studio kit (worktext, audiotape, instruction sheet) 17.50 (ISBN 0-574-23045-9, 3-6045); pre-recorded audiotape cassette 9.95 (13-6043). SRA.

Achieving Social Justice: A Christian Perspective. Ronald J. Wilkins. (To Live Is Christ Ser.). 1981. pap. text ed. 4.10 (ISBN 0-697-01775-3). Wm C Brown.

Achieving Society. David C. McClelland. LC 69-11373. 1967. pap. text ed. 8.95 (ISBN 0-02-920510-7). Free Pr.

Achieving Success in Manufacturing Management. Charles Hoitash. LC 80-51544. (Manufacturing Update Ser.). (Illus.). 260p. 1980. 29.00 (ISBN 0-87263-055-2). SME.
Achieving the Aim. M. M. Botvinnik. (Illus.). 230p. 1981. 19.00 (ISBN 0-08-024120-4); pap. cancelled (ISBN 0-08-024119-0). Pergamon.
Achitophel, or Toe Picture of a Wicked Politician. Nathanael Carpenter. LC 79-84094. (English Experience Ser.: No. 914). 76p. 1979. Repr. of 1629 ed. lib. bdg. 9.00 (ISBN 90-221-0914-3). Walter J Johnson.
ACI Detailing Manual. 1980. 44.95 (SP-66). ACI.
ACI Manual of Concrete Inspection. 6th ed. ACI Committee 311. 1975. 17.95 (ISBN 0-685-85096-X, SP-2) (ISBN 0-685-85097-8). ACI.
ACI Manual of Concrete Practice, 3 pts. Incl. Pt. 1. 1978. 35.00 (ISBN 0-685-85453-1) (ISBN 0-685-85454-X); Pt. 2. 1978. 35.00 (ISBN 0-685-85455-8) (ISBN 0-685-85456-6); Pt. 3. 1978. 29.95 (ISBN 0-685-85457-4) (ISBN 0-685-85458-2). 88.00 set (ISBN 0-685-85451-5) (ISBN 0-685-85452-3). ACI.
ACI Manual of Concrete Practice, 5 pts. Incl. Pt. 1. 29.92; Pt. 2. 29.95; Pt. 3. 29.95; Pt. 4. 29.95; Pt. 5. 29.95. 1980. ACI.
ACI Ten Year Index: 1959-1968. 1970. 15.75 (ISBN 0-685-85156-7, I-10) (ISBN 0-685-85157-5). ACI.
ACI 55-Year Index: 1905-1959. 1960. 18.25 (ISBN 0-685-85154-0, I-55) (ISBN 0-685-85155-9). ACI.
Acid-Base Homeostasis & Its Disorders. Martin A. Tuller. 98p. 1971. spiral bdg. 6.00 (ISBN 0-87488-601-5). Med Exam.
Acid-Base Status of the Blood. 4th ed. Ole Siggaard-Andersen. 230p. 1974. 22.50 (ISBN 87-16-01567-3). Krieger.
Acid-Base Titration in Non-Aqueous Solvents. new ed. James S. Fritz. 156p. 1973. pap. text ed. 10.95x o.p. (ISBN 0-205-03735-6). Allyn.
Acid Rain. Compiled By American Society of Civil Engineers et al. 76p. 1980. pap. text ed. 17.50 (ISBN 0-87262-202-9). Am Soc Civil Eng.
Ackerman & Del Ragato's Cancer: Diagnosis, Treatment, & Prognosis. 5th ed. Juan A. Del Regato & Harlan J. Spjut. LC 76-26170. (Illus.). 1977. pap. 69.50 (ISBN 0-8016-1250-0). Mosby.
Ackerman's Surgical Pathology. 6th ed. Juan Rosai. (Illus.). 1450p. 1981. text ed. 97.50 (ISBN 0-8016-0045-6). Mosby.
ACLU & the Wagner Act: An Inquiry into the Depression-Era Crisis of American Liberalism. Cletus E. Daniel. LC 80-22450. (Cornell Studies in Industrial & Labor Relations: No. 20). 146p. 1981. 13.50 (ISBN 0-87546-082-8); pap. 7.95 (ISBN 0-87546-083-6). NY Sch Indus Rel.
ACLU on Trial. William H. McIlhany. 1976. 8.95 o.p. (ISBN 0-87000-337-2). Arlington Hse.
ACLU 1976 Policy Guide. American Civil Liberties Union. LC 78-19573. (Orig.). 1978. pap. 13.95 (ISBN 0-669-01683-7); 1979 supplement 12.95 (ISBN 0-669-02624-7). Lexington Bks.
Acne: And Related Disorders of Complexion & Scalp. Arthur Bobroff. 136p. 1964. pap. 12.75 photocopy ed. spiral (ISBN 0-398-00183-9). C C Thomas.
Acnes: Clinical Features, Pathogenesis & Treatment. W. J. Cunliffe & J. A. Cotterill. LC 75-21145. (Major Problems in Dermatology Ser.: Vol. 6). (Illus.). 306p. 1975. 30.00 (ISBN 0-7216-2785-4). Saunders.
Acoma. Tryntje V. Seymour. portfolio 295.00 (ISBN 0-915998-05-X). Lime Rock Pr.
Acoma Grammar & Texts. W. R. Miller. (U. C. Publ. in Linguistics: Vol. 40). 1965. pap. 9.00x (ISBN 0-520-09234-1). U of Cal Pr.
Acorn Sprout & His Forest Friends. (Illus.). 23p. (Orig.). (gr. 1-4). 1980. pap. 1.25 (ISBN 0-89323-010-3). BMA Pr.
Acoustic Emission. Ed. by R. W. Nichols. (Illus.). 1976. text ed. 33.60x (ISBN 0-85334-681-X, Pub. by Applied Science). Burgess-Intl Ideas.
Acoustic Emission. Royson V. Williams. 140p. 1980. 29.00 (ISBN 0-9960020-0-6, Pub. by a Hilger England). Heyden.
Acoustic Guitar: Adjustment, Care, Maintenance, & Repair, Vol. I. Don E. Teeter. LC 74-5962. (Illus.). 250p. 1975. 22.50 (ISBN 0-8061-1219-0). U of Okla Pr.
Acoustic Guitar: Adjustment, Care, Maintenance, & Repair, Vol. II. Don E. Teeter. LC 79-5962. (Illus.). 208p. 1980. 20.00 (ISBN 0-8061-1607-2). U of Okla Pr.
Acoustic Nerve Tumors: Early Diagnosis & Treatment. 2nd ed. J. Lawrence Pool et al. (Illus.). 252p. 1970. 18.75 (ISBN 0-398-01507-4). C C Thomas.
Acoustic Phonetics: A Course of Basic Reading. D. B. Fry. (Illus.). 1976. 35.00 (ISBN 0-521-21393-2). Cambridge U Pr.
Acoustical Imaging, Vol. 8. Ed. by A. F. Metherell. 1980. 59.50. (ISBN 0-306-40171-1, Plenum Pr). Plenum Pub.
Acoustical Oceanography: Principles & Applications. Clarence S. Clay & Herman Medwin. LC 77-1133. (Ocean Engineering Ser.). 1977. text ed. 39.50 (ISBN 0-471-16041-5, Pub. by Wiley-Interscience). Wiley.
Acoustical Studies of Mandarin Vowels & Tones. J. M. Howie. LC 74-19529. (Princeton-Cambridge Studies in Chinese Linguistics: No. 6). (Illus.). 281p. 1976. 64.00 (ISBN 0-521-20732-0). Cambridge U Pr.
Acoustics: An Introducton to Its Physical Principles & Applications. Allan D. Pierce. (Illus.). 656p. 1981. text ed. 28.95x (ISBN 0-07-049961-6, C); write for info solutions manual (ISBN 0-07-049962-4). McGraw.
Acoustics, Design & Practice, Vol. 1. Ram Lal Suri. 1966. 25.00x (ISBN 0-210-27067-5). Asia.
Acoustics, Noise & Buildings. 4th ed. P. H. Parkin et al. LC 79-670251. 1979. 24.00 (ISBN 0-571-04952-4, Pub. by Faber & Faber); pap. 15.95 (ISBN 0-571-04953-2, Pub. by Faber & Faber). Merrimack Bk Serv.
ACP States Yearbook, 1980 to 1981. 670p. 1981. pap. 257.25 (ISBN 2-8029-0014-5, ED13, Edns Delta). Unipub.
Acquaintances. Arnold J. Toynbee. 1967. 14.95 (ISBN 0-19-500189-3). Oxford U Pr.
Acquired Bleeding Disorders in Children: Abnormalities of Hemostasis. Lusher. (Monographs in Pediatric Hematology-Oncology: Vol. 3). 1981. price not set (ISBN 0-89352-127-2). Masson Pub.
Acquiring Arithmetic Skills. 2nd ed. W. F. Hunter et al. (gr. 8-12). 1976. 5.80 (ISBN 0-07-031321-0, W); tchr's manual 6.64 (ISBN 0-07-031325-3). McGraw.
Acquisition & Corporate Development: A Contemporary Perspective for the Manager. James W. Bradley & Donald H. Korn. LC 79-7719. (Arthur D. Little Bk.). (Illus.). 1981. price not set (ISBN 0-669-03170-4). Lexington Bks.
Acquisition & Development of Language. Paula Menyuk. LC 79-135023. (Current Research in Developmental Psychology Ser). 1971. 16.95x (ISBN 0-13-003087-2). P-H.
Acquisition of Foreign Materials for U.S. Libraries. Theodore Samore. LC 73-4314. 1973. 13.00 (ISBN 0-8108-0614-2). Scarecrow.
Acquisition of Maya Phonology: Variation in Yucatec Child Language. Stephen H. Straight. LC 75-25123. (American Indian Linguistics Ser.). 1976. lib. bdg. 42.00 (ISBN 0-8240-1973-3). Garland Pub.
Acquisition of Phonology. N. V. Smith. LC 72-95409. 228p. 1973. 29.95 (ISBN 0-521-20154-3). Cambridge U Pr.
Acquisition of Typewriting Skills. Leonard West. LC 68-24228. 1969. pap. 16.00 (ISBN 0-8224-2089-9). Pitman Learning.
Acquisition Search Programs. Jerold L. Freier. LC 80-26356. 1981. pap. 3.95 (ISBN 0-87576-094-5). Pilot Bks.
Acquisitions & Mergers. G. D. McCarthy. 1963. 29.95 (ISBN 0-8260-5810-8, Pub. by Wiley-Interscience). Wiley.
Acquittal. John Wainwright. 1980. pap. 1.95 (ISBN 0-425-04578-1). Berkley Pub.
Acquitted! Message from the Cross. Sakae Kubo. LC 74-28685. (Stories That Win Ser.). 1975. pap. 0.95 o.p. (ISBN 0-8163-0190-5, 01070-2). Pacific Pr Pub Assn.
Acres of Diamonds. Conwell. 1975. 4.95 (ISBN 0-8007-1075-4). Revell.
Acres of Diamonds. Russell H. Conwell. 1972. pap. 1.75 (ISBN 0-515-05650-2, V2762). Jove Pubns.
Acres of Flint: Sarah Orne Jewett & Her Contemporaries. rev. ed. Perry D. Westbrook. LC 80-20501. 204p. 1981. 12.50 (ISBN 0-8108-1357-2). Scarecrow.
Acrobatics Book. Jack Wiley. LC 78-58043. (Illus.). 187p. 1978. pap. 5.95 (ISBN 0-89037-141-5). Anderson World.
Acrobats & Ping-Pong: Young China's Games, Sports, & Amusements. Isobel Willcox. LC 80-22176. (Illus.). 160p. (gr. 4 up). 1981. PLB 8.95 (ISBN 0-396-07917-2). Dodd.
Acronyms, Initialisms, & Abbreviations Dictionary, Vol. 1. 7th ed. Ed. by Ellen T. Crowley. 1500p. 1980. 75.00 (ISBN 0-8103-0504-6). Gale.
Acropolis. R. J. Hopper. LC 76-134880. (Illus.). 1971. 10.00 o.s.i. (ISBN 0-02-553980-9). Macmillan.
Across a Billion Years. Robert Silverberg. (Orig.). 1980. pap. 1.95 o.p. (ISBN 0-425-04627-3). Berkley Pub.
Across America on the Yellow Brick Road. Virginia M. Madden. (Illus.). 1980. pap. 8.95 (ISBN 0-937760-00-5). Crow Canyon.
Across Asia on the Cheap. 3rd ed. Tony Wheeler. (Illus.). 1979. pap. 4.95 o.p. (ISBN 0-908086-02-4). Hippocrene Bks.
Across Five Aprils. Irene Hunt. 192p. 1981. pap. 1.95 (ISBN 0-448-17032-9, Tempo). G&D.
Across South America. Hiram Bingham. (Latin America in the 20th Century Ser.). 1976. Repr. of 1911 ed. lib. bdg. 32.50 (ISBN 0-306-70834-5). Da Capo.
Across the Barricades. Joan Lingard. LC 72-8915. 160p. (gr. 7 up). 1973. 7.95 o.p. (ISBN 0-525-66280-4). Elsevier-Nelson.
Across the Board: Three Harper Novels of Suspense. Dick Francis. Incl. Enquiry; Flying Finish; Blood Sport. LC 74-15869. 1975. 14.95 o.s.i. (ISBN 0-06-011318-9, HarpT). Har-Row.
Across the Bridges or Life by the South London River-Side, London Nineteen Eleven. Alexander Paterson. LC 79-56967. (English Working Class Ser.). 1980. lib. bdg. 25.00 (ISBN 0-8240-0118-4). Garland Pub.
Across the Chichimec Sea: Papers in Honor of J. Charles Kelley. Ed. by Carroll L. Riley & Basil C. Hedrick. LC 78-802. (Illus.). 336p. 1978. 19.95x (ISBN 0-8093-0829-0). S Ill U Pr.
Across the Generations: Old People & Young Volunteers. Roger Hadley et al. (National Institute Social Services Library). 1975. text ed. 35.00x (ISBN 0-04-300052-5); text ed. 11.95x (ISBN 0-04-300053-3). Allen Unwin.
Across the Golden Gate: California's North Coast, Wine Country & Redwoods. Alan Magary & Kerstin F. Magary. LC 78-2149. (Illus.). 320p. (Orig.). 1980. pap. 6.95 (ISBN 0-06-090821-1, CN 821, CN). Har-Row.
Across the Great Divide. Kerry Allyne. (Harlequin Romances Ser.). (Orig.). 1980. pap. 1.25 o.p. (ISBN 0-373-02323-5, Pub. by Harlequin). PB.
Across the High Technology Threshold: The Case of Synthetic Rubber. Robert Solo. 130p. 1980. Repr. of 1959 ed. lib. bdg. 17.50 (ISBN 0-8482-6222-0). Norwood Edns.
Across the Pastures. Dorothea B. Morse. 1981. 8.95 (ISBN 0-8062-1592-5). Carlton.
Across the Rhine. Franklin M. Davis. Ed. by Time-Life Books. (World War II Ser.). (Illus.). 208p. 1980. 13.95 (ISBN 0-8094-2542-4). Time-Life.
Across the Rio Grande. Jake Logan. LC 75-23640. (John Slocum Ser.: No. 4). 224p. 1975. pap. 1.50 (ISBN 0-87216-702-X). Playboy Pbks.
Across the River & into the Trees. Ernest Hemingway. LC 75-100353. 1950. lib. rep. ed. 15.00x (ISBN 0-684-15313-0, ScribT); pap. 4.95 (ISBN 0-684-71795-6, SL 202). Scribner.
Across the Sea from Galway. Leonard E. Fisher. LC 75-9513. (Illus.). 112p. (gr. 3-7). 1975. 6.95g o.s.i. (ISBN 0-590-07345-1, Four Winds). Schol Bk Serv.
Across the Years. Virginius Dabney. LC 77-15147. 1978. 10.00 o.p. (ISBN 0-385-12247-0). Doubleday.
ACT (American College Testing) Jerry Bobrow & William A. Covino. Date not set. pap. text ed. cancelled. Cliffs.
Act Natural. Bruce Hugman. 95p. 1977. text ed. 9.90x (ISBN 0-7199-0933-3, Pub. by Bedford England). Renouf.
Act Now: Plays & Ways to Make Them. Nellie McCaslin. LC 75-25557. (Illus.). 134p. (gr. 4-7). 1975. 9.95 (ISBN 0-87599-216-1). S G Phillips.
Act of Contrition. Jeffrey Sobosan. LC 79-54695. 128p. 1979. pap. 2.95 (ISBN 0-87793-189-5). Ave Maria.
Act of Love. Celia Dale. 1977. pap. 1.75 (ISBN 0-505-51211-4). Tower Bks.
Act of Loving. Robert Russell. LC 67-19287. 1967. 9.95 (ISBN 0-8149-0195-6). Vanguard.
Act of Marriage. Tim LaHaye & Beverly LaHaye. 1976. o. p. 7.95 (ISBN 0-310-27060-X); pap. 5.95 (ISBN 0-310-27061-8); pap. 2.95 (ISBN 0-310-27062-6). Zondervan.
Act of Marriage. Tim LaHaye & Beverly LaHaye. 316p. 1981. pap. 2.95. Zondervan.
Act of Reading: A Theory of Aesthetic Response. Wolfgang Iser. LC 78-58296. 1979. 15.00x o.p. (ISBN 0-8018-2101-0); pap. 5.95 (ISBN 0-8018-2371-4). Johns Hopkins.
Act of Vengeance. Trevor Armbrister. 1980. pap. 2.75 (ISBN 0-446-85707-6). Warner Bks.
Act of War. Brian Callison. 1977. 7.95 o.p. (ISBN 0-525-05023-X). Dutton.
Act of Will. Roberto Assagioli. 1974. pap. 4.50 (ISBN 0-14-003866-3). Penguin.
Act of Writing. Ed. by Jessie Rehder & Wallace Kaufman. LC 68-21800. 1969. pap. 6.95 (ISBN 0-672-63002-8). Odyssey Pr.
Act of Writing & Reading: A Combined Text. Alan Casty. (Orig.). 1966. pap. text ed. 8.95x (ISBN 0-13-003780-X). P-H.
Act Two: Mid-Career Job Changes. Nancy C. Baker. LC 79-56027. 256p. 1980. 10.00 (ISBN 0-8149-0833-0). Vanguard.
Act Yourself: How to Stop Playing Roles & Unmask Your True Feeings. Jo Loudin. (Illus.). 1979. 9.95 (ISBN 0-13-003715-X, Spec); pap. 3.95 (ISBN 0-13-003707-9). P-H.
Actaeon Homeward: A Novel. Robert Emmitt. LC 78-60621. (Writers West Book). 1979. 8.95 o.p. (ISBN 0-8040-9014-9); pap. 4.50 o.p. (ISBN 0-8040-9010-6). Swallow.
Actas y Documentos: Resoluciones Aprobadas. Septimo Periodo Extraordinario de Sesiones. Washington, D.C. 22 de Mayo de 1979. Ed. by OAS Department of Publication. 266p. 1980. pap. text ed. 15.00 (ISBN 0-8270-1171-7). OAS.
Actas y Documentos Segunda Conferencia Especializada Interamericana Sobre Derecho Internacional Privado, 3 vols. OAS General Secretariat. (CIDIP-II Ser.: Vols. 1-3). 1980. Vol. 1, 455p. pap. text ed. 25.00 (ISBN 0-8270-1113-X); Vol. 2, 547p. pap. text ed. 25.00 (ISBN 0-8270-1114-8); Vol. 3, 469p. pap. text ed. 25.00 (ISBN 0-8270-1115-6). OAS.
Actas Y Documentos Segunda Conferencia Especializada Interamerica Sobre Derecho Internacional Privado, Vol. 1. OAS General Secretariat Office of Development & Codification of International Law. (International Law). 455p. 1980. lib. bdg. 25.00 (ISBN 0-8270-1113-X). OAS.
Actas Y Documentos Segunda Conferencia Especializada Interamericana Sobre Derecho Internacional Privado, Vol. 2. OAS General Secretatiat Office of Development & Codification of International Law. (International Law Ser.). 450p. 1980. text ed. 25.00 (ISBN 0-8270-1114-8). OAS.
Actas Y Documentos Segunda Conferencia Especializada Interamericana Sobre Derecho Internacional Privado, Vol. 3. OAS General Secretariat Office of Development & Codification of Inernational Law. (International Law Ser.). 469p. 1980. text ed. 25.00 (ISBN 0-8270-1115-6). OAS.
Actas y Documentos: Textos Certificados De las Resoluciones, Vol. 2. Extraordinario De Sesiones, Segundo Periodo, Washington, D. C., Del 24 Al 25 De Agosto De 1970. (General Assembly Ser.). (Span., Eng., Fr., & Port.). pap. 2.00 o.p. (ISBN 0-8270-0895-3). OAS.
Actas y Documentos, Vol. II, Primera Parte: Actas Textuales De las Sesiones Plenarias, Informes De los Relatores y Documentos Varios. (General Assembly Ser.). 1976. 3.00 o.p. (ISBN 0-8270-0990-9). OAS.
Actas y Documentos, Vol. II, Primera Parte: Quinto Periodo Ordinario de Sesiones. Wash. D.C., del 8 al 19 de Mayo de 1975. Actas de las Sesiones Plenarias. (General Assembly Ser.). 1976. 5.00 (ISBN 0-8270-0980-1). OAS.
Actas y Documentos, Vol. II, Segunda Parte: Actas De la Comision General y Actas Resumidas De las Comisiones I, II, III, y IV, y Anexos. (General Assembly Ser.). 1976. 10.00 (ISBN 0-8270-0985-2). OAS.
Actas y Documentos, Vol. II, Segunda Parte: Actas Textuales De las Sesiones De la Comision General y Actas Resumidas De las Sesiones De las Comisiones Primer, Segunda, Tercery y Cuarta. (General Assembly Ser.). 1976. 3.00 o.p. (ISBN 0-685-88867-3). OAS.
Actas y Documentos Vol. 1, Sexto Periodo: Ordinario De Sesiones. Santiago, Chile, del 4 al 18 de Junio de 1976. Textos certificados de las resoluciones en espanol. (General Assembly Ser.). 1976. 3.00 (ISBN 0-8270-0995-X). OAS.
Actas y Documentos, Vol 1: Textos Certificados De las Resoluciones y Declaraciones. (General Assembly Ser.). 1975. 3.00 o.p. (ISBN 0-685-88865-7). OAS.
Actes de la Commune de Paris pendant la Revolution, 9 vols. Commune de Paris, 1789-1794. (Second Ser.). Repr. of 1955 ed. Set. 479.25 (ISBN 0-404-52630-6); 53.25 ea. AMS Pr.
Actes de la Commune de Paris pendant la Revolution, 10 vols. Commune de Paris, 1789-1794. (First Ser.). Repr. of 1942 ed. Set. 532.50 (ISBN 0-404-52620-9); 53.25 ea. AMS Pr.
ACTH & LPH in Health & Disease. Ed. by T. B. Van Wimersma Greidanus & L. H. Rees. (Frontiers of Hormone Research Ser.: Vol. 8). (Illus.). 200p. 1981. 60.00 (ISBN 3-8055-1977-X). S Karger.
Acting & Stage Movement. Edwin White & Marguerite Battye. LC 63-10202. 1978. pap. text ed. 2.95 o.p. (ISBN 0-668-04386-5). Arco.
Acting & the Stage. David Taylor. (Greek & Roman Topics Ser.). (Illus.). 1978. pap. text ed. 3.95x (ISBN 0-04-930008-3). Allen Unwin.
Acting in Opera. George E. Shea. (Music Reprint Ser.: 1980). (Illus.). 1980. Repr. of 1915 ed. lib. bdg. 14.50 (ISBN 0-306-76004-5). Da Capo.
Acting on Principle: An Essay in Kantian Ethics. Onora Nell. LC 74-20647. 192p. 1975. 15.00x (ISBN 0-231-03848-8). Columbia U Pr.
Acting Out. 2nd ed. Ed. by Lawrence E. Abt & Stuart L. Weissman. LC 76-53942. 1976. Repr. 25.00x (ISBN 0-87668-287-5). Aronson.

Acting-Out Child: Coping with Classroom Disruption. Hill M. Walker. 1979. pap. text ed. 10.95 (ISBN 0-205-06576-7); pap. text ed. 9.95 (ISBN 0-205-06569-4). Allyn.

Acting: The Creative Process. 3rd ed. Hardie Albright & Arnita Albright. 432p. 1980. pap. text ed. 13.95x (ISBN 0-534-00744-9). Wadsworth Pub.

Acting: The First Six Lessons. Richard Boleslavsky. 1949. 5.95 (ISBN 0-87830-000-7). Theatre Arts.

Actinomycosis of the Thorax. George E. Farrell. (Illus.). 144p. 1981. 16.50- (ISBN 0-87527-205-3). Green.

Action: A Handbook of Classroom Ideas to Motivate the Teaching of Elementary Physical Education. (Spice Ser). 1978. 6.50 (ISBN 0-89273-106-0). Educ Serv.

Action & Interpretation. Ed. by C. Hookway & P. Pettit. LC 77-7875. 178p. 1980. 22.95 (ISBN 0-521-21740-7); pap. 9.95x (ISBN 0-521-29908-X). Cambridge U Pr.

Action & Responsibility. Ed. by Michael Bradie & Myles Brand. (Bowling Green Studies in Applied Philosophy: Vol. 2). 140p. 1980. text ed. 15.00 (ISBN 0-935756-02-7); pap. text ed. 10.00 (ISBN 0-935756-03-5). BGSU Dept Phil.

Action at a Distance in Physics & Cosmology. Fred Hoyle & J. V. Narlikar. LC 74-4158. (Astronomy & Astrophysics Ser.). (Illus.). 1974. text ed. 31.95x (ISBN 0-7167-0346-7). W H Freeman.

Action Biology. new ed. Stanley L. Weinberg & Herbert J. Stoltze. 1977. 15.12 (ISBN 0-205-05525-7, 6755259); tchrs'. guide 9.92 (ISBN 0-205-05534-6, 6755348). Allyn.

Action Biology. Stanley L. Weinberg & Herbert J. Stoltze. (gr. 9-12). 1974. 15.12 (ISBN 0-205-04139-6, 6741398); tchrs'. guide 9.92 (ISBN 0-205-04140-X, 6741401). Allyn.

Action by the European Community Through Its Financial Instruments-Documentation. 316p. 1980. pap. 25.00 (ISBN 2-8029-0023-4, ED11, Edns Delta). Unipub.

Action! Camera! Super-Eight Cassette Film Making for Beginners. Rick Carrier & David Carroll. LC 78-162739. (Illus.). 78p. 1972. 7.95 (ISBN 0-684-12490-4). Scribner.

Action Centered Leadership. John Adair. 1979. text ed. 26.00x (ISBN 0-566-02143-9, Pub. by Gower Pub Co England). Renouf.

Action Emotion & Will. Anthony Kenny. 1963. pap. text ed. 8.50x (ISBN 0-391-00272-4). Humanities.

Action in Affirmation: Towards an Unambiguous Profession of Nursing. Jerome P. Lysaught. (Illus.). 224p. 1981. pap. text ed. 13.95 (ISBN 0-07-039271-4, HP). McGraw.

Action in Organizations. Donald D. White & H. William Vroman. 500p. 1981. price not set (ISBN 0-205-07353-0); instructor manual free (ISBN 0-205-07354-9). Allyn. Postponed.

Action in Organizations: Cases & Experiences in Organizational Behavior. Donald White & H. William Vroman. 1977. pap. text ed. 12.95 (ISBN 0-205-05599-0, 085599-5); instr's manual o.p. Allyn.

Action, Knowledge & Reality: Studies in Honor of Wilfrid Sellars. Hector-Neri Castaneda. LC 74-8419. 374p. 1975. text ed. 26.50 (ISBN 0-672-61213-5). Bobbs.

Action Now! A Citizen's Guide to Better Communities. Richard W. Poston. LC 76-949. 270p. 1976. 11.85x (ISBN 0-8093-0760-X); pap. 7.95 (ISBN 0-8093-0763-4). S Ill U Pr.

Action of the Tiger: The Four Hundred & Thirty Seventh Troop Carrier Group in World War II. Frank Guild, Jr. LC 80-65181. (Aviation Ser.: No. 2). (Illus.). 177p. 1980. Repr. 15.00 (ISBN 0-89839-028-1). Battery Pr.

Action Proposal. rev. ed. Marcia Federbush. 1974. pap. 1.20 o.p. (ISBN 0-685-56767-2). Know Inc.

Action Rhymes for Preschoolers. Marie Frost. (Peter Panda Ser.). 1977. pap. 1.25 (ISBN 0-87239-142-6, 42034). Standard Pub.

Action Stations Two: Military Airfields of Lincolnshire & the East Midlands. Bruce B. Halpenny. (Illus.). 232p. 1981. 37.95 (ISBN 0-85059-484-7). Aztex.

Action Stories of Yesterday & Today. Ralph Cutlip. (Orig.). (gr. 7-12). 1971. pap. text ed. 4.58 (ISBN 0-87720-351-2). AMSCO Sch.

Action Techniques for the Take-Charge Sales Manager. David C. Carter. 1974. 10.95 o.p. (ISBN 0-13-003376-6). P-H.

Action Theory for Public Administration. Michael M. Harmon. (Longman Professional Studies in Public Administration). 256p. (Orig.). 1981. text ed. 22.50 (ISBN 0-582-28254-3); pap. text ed. 9.95 (ISBN 0-582-28255-1). Longman.

Action with the Elderly: A Handbook for Relatives & Friends. Kenneth M. Keddie. 1978. text ed. 23.00 (ISBN 0-08-021442-8); pap. text ed. 9.75 (ISBN 0-08-021441-X). Pergamon.

Actions of Finite Groups on the Hyperfinite Type II (to the First Power) Factor. Vaughan Jones. LC 80-22560. (Memoirs Ser.: No. 237). 4.40 (ISBN 0-8218-2237-3, MEMO-237). Am Math.

Activation Analysis: Principles & Applications. Ed. by J. M. Lenihan & S. J. Thompson. (Illus.). 1966. 32.00 (ISBN 0-12-443650-1). Acad Pr.

Active Filter Design Handbook: For Use with Programmable Pocket Calculators & Minicomputers. G. S. Moschytz. 296p. 1981. 49.95 (ISBN 0-471-27850-5, Pub. by Wiley-Interscience). Wiley.

Active Filters. Electronics Magazine. LC 79-17479. (Illus.). 133p. 1980. pap. text ed. 5.95 (ISBN 0-07-606622-3, R-003). McGraw.

Active Galactic Nuclei. Ed. by C. Hazard & S. Mitton. LC 78-67426. 1979. 38.50 (ISBN 0-521-22494-2). Cambridge U Pr.

Active Games & Contests. 2nd ed. R. H. Donnelly et al. 672p. 1958. 17.50 (ISBN 0-471-07088-2). Wiley.

Active Games & Contests. 2nd ed. R. J. Donnelly et al. (Illus.). (gr. 7 up). 1958. 17.50 (ISBN 0-8260-2795-4). Ronald Pr.

Active Inductorless Filters. Sanjit K. Mitra. LC 70-179914. (IEEE Press Selected Reprint Ser). 1971. 15.95 (ISBN 0-471-61177-8, Pub. by Wiley-Interscience); pap. text ed. 7.95 o.p. (ISBN 0-471-61176-X). Wiley.

Active Learning Experiences for Teaching Elementary School Mathematics. Harold H. Lerch. (Illus.). 592p. 1981. pap. text ed. price not set (ISBN 0-395-29764-8). HM.

Active Learning: Games to Enhance Academic Abilities. Bryant J. Cratty. (Physical Education Ser). (Illus.). 1971. pap. text ed. 9.50 (ISBN 0-13-003491-6). P-H.

Active Network Theory. S. S. Haykin. 1970. 24.95 (ISBN 0-201-02680-5). A-W.

Active Oxygen in Medicine. Anne P. Autor. Date not set. text ed. cancelled (ISBN 0-89004-410-4). Raven.

Active Psychotheraphy. new ed. Harold Greenwald. LC 73-22473. 384p. 1974. Repr. 25.00x (ISBN 0-87668-136-4). Aronson.

Active Review of French: Selected Patterns, Vocabulary & Pronunciation Problems for Speakers of English. Robert L. Politzer & Michio P. Hagiwara. LC 63-155633. 1963. pap. 14.95x (ISBN 0-471-00438-3); tapes avail. (ISBN 0-471-00439-1). Wiley.

Active Society. Amitai Etzioni. LC 61-14107. 1971. 13.25 o.s.i. (ISBN 0-02-909590-5); pap. text ed. 10.95 (ISBN 0-02-909580-8). Free Pr.

Active Solar Energy System Design Practice Manual: Preliminary Field Experience. The Ehrenkrantz Group & Mueller Associates Inc. 230p. 1981. pap. 24.50 (ISBN 0-89934-091-1). Solar Energy Info.

Active Touch-The Mechanism of Recognition of Objects by Manipulation: A Multidisciplinary Approach. Ed. by G. Gordon. 1978. text ed. 59.00 (ISBN 0-08-022647-7); pap. text ed. 34.00 (ISBN 0-08-022667-1). Pergamon.

Active Transport Through Animal Cell Membranes. P. G. Le Fevre. (Protoplasmatologia: Vol. 8, Pt. 7a). (Illus.). 1955. pap. 33.70 o.p. (ISBN 0-387-80387-4). Springer-Verlag.

Active Years for Your Aging Dog. Bernard Hershhorn. LC 78-52966. (Illus.). 1978. 12.50 (ISBN 0-8015-4599-4, Hawthorn). Dutton.

Activists: Kurt Hiller & the Politics of Action on the German Left, 1914-1933. Lewis D. Wurgaft. (Transactions Ser.: Vol. 67, Pt. 8). 1977. 12.00 (ISBN 0-87169-678-9). Am Philos.

Activities & Games for Successful Teaching. Ivan D. Muse & David A. Squires. (Illus.). 1977. pap. 14.95x o.p. (ISBN 0-8425-0635-7). Brigham.

Activities & Projects: India in Color. Claude Soleillant. LC 77-79499. (Activities & Projects Ser.). (Illus.). (gr. 2 up). 1977. 9.95 (ISBN 0-8069-4550-8); PLB 9.29 (ISBN 0-8069-4551-6). Sterling.

Activities & Readings in Learning & Development. Margaret M. Clifford & Myrna Grandgenett. LC 80-84892. (Illus.). 256p. 1981. pap. text ed. price not set (ISBN 0-395-29924-1). HM.

Activities for Intellectually Handicapped Children. Michael Ahrens. LC 76-357014. 1975. 6.10x (ISBN 0-7233-0423-8). Intl Pubns Serv.

Activities for Succeeding in the World of Work. Grady Kimbrell & Ben S. Vineyard. 1975. pap. 4.64 (ISBN 0-87345-526-6). McKnight.

Activities for Teaching Metrics in Kindergarden. Sam E. Brown. LC 77-95155. 1978. pap. text ed. 7.00 (ISBN 0-8191-0462-0). U Pr of Amer.

Activities for the Aged & Infirm: A Handbook for the Untrained Worker. Toni Merrill. (Illus.). 392p. 1979. 16.50 (ISBN 0-398-01294-6). C C Thomas.

Activities for the Christian Family Handbook (Paths of Life) Gaynell B. Cronin. 1980. 2.45 (ISBN 0-8091-2273-1). Paulist Pr.

Activities for the Maintenance of Computational Skills. Bonnie Litwiller & David Duncan. 1980. pap. 3.20 (ISBN 0-87353-169-8). NCTM.

Activities for Trainers: Fifty Useful Designs. Cyril R. Mill. LC 80-50465. 240p. 1980. pap. 16.50 (ISBN 0-88390-159-5). Univ Assocs.

Activities Handbook for Energy Education. Gerald Krockover & Alfred Devito. (Illus.). 192p. (Orig.). 1981. pap. 10.95 (ISBN 0-8302-2717-2). Goodyear.

Activities Handbook for Teachers of Young Children. 3rd ed. Doreen Croft & Robert D. Hess. LC 79-90365. 1980. pap. text ed. 10.95 (ISBN 0-395-28698-0). HM.

Activities Handbook for Teaching with the Hand Held Calculator. Bitter & Mikesell. 1979. text ed. 14.65 (ISBN 0-205-06713-1, 2367130). Allyn.

Activities of OECD in 1975. Organization for Economic Cooperation & Development, Secretary General. 1976. 5.00 o.p. (ISBN 92-64-11522-6). OECD.

Activities of Some Centres Engaged in Research & Information Programmes in the Field of Youth. 212p. 1980. pap. 15.00 (UN80-4-2, UN). Unipub.

Activities of Transnational Corporations in the Industrial, Mining & Military Sectors of Southern Africa. 79p. 1980. pap. 7.00 (ISBN 0-686-68940-2, UN80/2A3, UN). Unipub.

Activities Therapy. Anne C. Mosey. LC 73-79286. 193p. 1973. 12.50 (ISBN 0-911216-41-3). Raven.

Activity Approach to Elementary Concepts of Mathematics. Douglas B. Smith & William R. Topp. (Mathematics Ser.). (Illus.). 150p. 1981. pap. text ed. price not set (ISBN 0-201-07694-2). A-W.

Activity Coefficients in Electrolyte Solutions, 2 vols. Ricardo M. Pytkowicz. 1979. Vol. 2, 336p. 69.95 (ISBN 0-8493-5411-0); Vol. 2. 74.95 (ISBN 0-8493-5412-9). CRC Pr.

Activity Conscientiousness & Personality. A. Leontiev. 1978. 23.95 (ISBN 0-13-003533-5). P-H.

Activity Costing & Input-Output Accounting. George J. Staubus. (Willard J. Graham Ser. in Accounting). 1971. pap. text ed. 6.95x o.p. (ISBN 0-256-00543-5). Irwin.

Activity Networks: Project Planning & Control by Network Models. F. E. Elmaghraby. LC 77-9501. 443p. 1977. 37.95 (ISBN 0-471-23869-4, Pub. by Wiley-Interscience). Wiley.

Activity of Children. P. M. Pickard. 1965. text ed. 4.75x (ISBN 0-582-32420-3). Humanities.

Activity of Philosophy: A Concise Introduction. Fred A. Westphal. (Philosophy Ser). 1969. pap. text ed. 10.95 (ISBN 0-13-003608-0). P-H.

Acton & Gladstone. Owen Chadwick. 1976. pap. text ed. 6.50x (ISBN 0-485-14122-1, Athlone Pr). Humanities.

Actor & His Body. Litz Pisk. LC 76-8369. (Illus.). 1976. 8.65 (ISBN 0-87830-008-2); pap. 4.75 (ISBN 0-87830-553-X). Theatre Arts.

Actor at Work. 3rd ed. Robert Benedetti. (Illus.). 1981. text ed. 14.95 (ISBN 0-13-003673-0). P-H.

Actor at Work. rev. & enl ed. Robert L. Benedetti. (Illus.). 272p. 1976. 14.95 (ISBN 0-13-003665-X). P-H.

Actor Guide to the Talkies, 1949-1964, 2 vols. Richard B. Dimmitt. LC 67-12057. 1967. Set. 45.00 (ISBN 0-8108-0000-4). Scarecrow.

Actor Prepares. Constantin Stanislavski. 1948. 9.95 (ISBN 0-87830-001-5). Theatre Arts.

Actor Training 3. Linda Smith et al. Ed. by Richard Brown. LC 72-90200. 112p. 1976. pap. text ed. 3.95x o.p. (ISBN 0-910482-76-4). Drama Bk.

Actors' Analects. Ed. by Charles W. Dunn. (Studies in Oriental Culture Ser). (Illus.). 1970. 17.00x (ISBN 0-231-03391-5). Columbia U Pr.

Actors & Systems: The Politics of Collective Action. Michel Crozier & Erhard Friedberg. Tr. by Arthur Goldhammer. LC 80-13803. 272p. 1980. lib. bdg. 25.00x (ISBN 0-226-12183-6). U of Chicago Pr.

Actors Guide to Monologues, Vol. I. rev ed. Jane Grumbach & Robert Emerson. LC 74-23335. 35p. 1972. pap. text ed. 2.95x (ISBN 0-910482-41-1). Drama Bk.

Actor's Guide to Monologues, Vol. 2. rev ed. Jane Grumbach & Robert Emerson. LC 73-21893. 1981. pap. 2.95x (ISBN 0-89676-043-X). Drama Bk.

Actors Guide to Scenes. Jane Grumbach & Robert Emerson. LC 73-75346. 28p. 1973. pap. text ed. 2.95x (ISBN 0-910482-42-X). Drama Bk.

Actor's Guide to the Talkies, Nineteen Sixty-Five to Nineteen Seventy-Four. Andrew A. Aros. LC 77-21589. 1977. 32.50 (ISBN 0-8108-1052-2). Scarecrow.

Actors Life: Journals, 1956-1976. Charlton Heston. 1978. 12.95 o.p. (ISBN 0-525-05030-2, Henry Robbins Book). Dutton.

Actor's Manual. The Beverly Hills Bar Association Barristers Committee. 1981. pap. 9.95 (ISBN 0-8015-0040-0, Hawthorn). Dutton.

Actor's Manual: A Practical Legal Guide. Beverly Hills Bar Association. Barristers Committee for the Arts. Compiled by Norman Beil et al. 288p. 1981. 13.95 (ISBN 0-8015-0040-0); pap. 9.95 (ISBN 0-8015-0041-9). Dutton.

Actors on Acting. Joanmarie Kalter. LC 79-65062. (Illus.). 1981. pap. 7.95 (ISBN 0-8069-8976-9). Sterling.

Actors on Acting: Performing in Theatre & Film Today. Joanmarie Kalter. LC 79-65062. (Illus.). 1979. 12.95 (ISBN 0-8069-7026-X); lib. bdg. 11.69 (ISBN 0-8069-7027-8). Sterling.

Actors' Television Credits Nineteen Fifty to Nineteen Seventy-Two. James R. Parish. LC 73-9914. 1973. 25.00 (ISBN 0-8108-0673-8). Scarecrow.

Actors' Television Credits: Supplement 1. James R. Parish. LC 77-10741. 1978. 19.50 (ISBN 0-8108-1053-0). Scarecrow.

Actor's Ways & Means. Michael Redgrave. 1979. pap. 4.85 (ISBN 0-87830-516-5). Theatre Arts.

Acts. Jerome Crowe. Ed. by Wilfrid Harrington & Donald Senior. (New Testament Message Ser.: Vol. 8). 204p. 1980. 9.95 (ISBN 0-89453-131-X); pap. 4.95 (ISBN 0-89453-196-4). M Glazier.

Acts. Gerald Dye. (Double Trouble Puzzles Ser.). (Illus.). 1977. pap. 1.25 (ISBN 0-87239-151-5, 2822). Standard Pub.

Acts. H. A. Ironside. 9.95 (ISBN 0-87213-351-6). Loizeaux.

Acts. Irving L. Jensen. (Bible Self-Study Ser). 1970. pap. 2.25 (ISBN 0-8024-1044-8). Moody.

Acts. Gerhard Krodel. LC 80-2395. (Proclamation Commentaries: the New Testament Witnesses for Preaching). 128p. (Orig.). 1981. pap. 3.95 (ISBN 0-8006-0585-3, 1-585). Fortress.

Acts. R. H. Smith. LC 70-98297. (Concordia Commentary Ser). 1970. 10.95 (ISBN 0-570-06283-7, 15-2059). Concordia.

Acts, Vol. 2, Chapts. 13-28. T. M. Lindsay. (Handbooks for Bible Classes). 165p. 1950. text ed. 3.50 (ISBN 0-567-08117-6). Attic Pr.

Acts, a Study Guide. John Timmer. (Revelation Ser. for Adults). 1981. pap. text ed. 1.45 (ISBN 0-933140-20-7). Bd of Pubns CRC.

Acts, Adventures of the Early Church. Keith L. Brooks. (Teach Yourself the Bible Ser). 1961. pap. 1.75 (ISBN 0-8024-0125-2). Moody.

Acts: An Exposition, Vol. 3. W. A. Criswell. 320p. 1980. 10.95 (ISBN 0-310-22900-6, 9413). Zondervan.

Acts & the History of Earliest Christianity. Martin Hengel. LC 79-8893. 160p. 1980. 8.95 (ISBN 0-8006-0630-2, 1-630). Fortress.

Acts of David II, 1329-71. Ed. by Bruce Webster. 550p. 1981. 55.00x (ISBN 0-85224-395-2, Pub. by Edinburgh U Pr Scotland). Columbia U Pr.

Acts of Knowledge: Pope's Later Poems. Fredric V. Bogel. LC 78-75194. 285p. 1981. 18.50 (ISBN 0-8387-2380-2). Bucknell U Pr.

Acts of Light: Emily Dickinson. Emily Dickinson. Ed. by Jane Langton. 188p. 1980. 24.95 (ISBN 0-8212-1098-X, 006505); deluxe ed. 50.00 (ISBN 0-8212-1118-8, 006513DXLE). NYGS.

Acts of the Apostles, 2 vols. in 1. J. A. Alexander. (Banner of Truth Geneva Series Commentaries). 1980. 19.95 (ISBN 0-85151-309-3). Banner of Truth.

Acts of the Apostles. E. M. Blaiklock. (Tyndale New Testament Commentary). 1959. pap. 2.65 o.p. (ISBN 0-8028-1404-2). Eerdmans.

Acts of the Apostles. Don DeWelt. LC 79-53712. (Pictorial New Testament Ser.). (Illus.). 1979. 7.95 (ISBN 0-89900-200-5). College Pr Pub.

Acts of the Apostles. I. Howard Marshall. (Tyndale New Testament Commentaries Ser.). (Orig.). 1980. pap. 6.95 (ISBN 0-8028-1423-9). Eerdmans.

Acts of the Apostles. Ellen G. White. 633p. 1911. deluxe ed. 9.50 (ISBN 0-8163-0033-X, 01092-6); pap. 5.25 (ISBN 0-8163-0034-8, 01093-4). Pacific Pr Pub Assn.

Acts of the Apostles, Pt. I. Anthony L. Ash. LC 79-63269. (Living Word Commentary Ser.: Vol. 6). 1979. 7.95 (ISBN 0-8344-0069-3). Sweet.

Acts of the Apostles, Pt. 2. Rick Oster. LC 79-63268. (Living Word Commentary Ser.: Vol. 6). 1979. 7.95 (ISBN 0-8344-0099-5). Sweet.

Acts of the International Symposium on Rock Art. Ed. by Sverre Marstrander. (Illus., Six articles are in German). 1978. 20.50x (ISBN 82-00-14194-2, Dist. by Columbia U Pr.). Universitet.

Acts-Revelation. Matthew Henry. (Commentary on the Whole Bible Ser: Vol. 6). 1192p. 12.00 (ISBN 0-8007-0202-6). Revell.

Acts Six: One to Eight: Four. Earl Richard. LC 78-12926. (Society of Biblical Literature. Dissertation Ser.: No. 41). (Orig.). 1978. pap. 9.00 (ISBN 0-89130-261-1, 060141). Scholars Pr Ca.

Acts Story. G. Raymond Carlson. (Radiant Life Ser). 1975. pap. 1.50 (ISBN 0-88243-913-8, 02-0913); teacher's ed 2.50 (ISBN 0-88243-184-6, 0184). Gospel Pub.

Acts: Then & Now. Henry Jacobsen. LC 72-96738. 224p. 1973. pap. 3.95 (ISBN 0-88207-239-0). Victor Bks.

Acts: 14 Lessons, Vol. 1. Bernice C. Jordan. (Footsteps of Faith Ser.). (gr. 3-9). 1954. pap. text ed. 1.95 (ISBN 0-86508-039-9); figures 7.95 (ISBN 0-86508-040-2). BCM Inc.

Acts: 15 Lessons, Vol. 2. Bernice C. Jordan. (Footsteps of Faith Ser.). (gr. 3-9). 1954. pap. text ed. 1.95 (ISBN 0-86508-041-0); figures 7.95 (ISBN 0-86508-042-9). BCM Inc.

Actualidad Hispanica. Guillermina M. Supervia et al. (gr. 7-12). 1972. text ed. 14.80 (ISBN 0-205-03046-7, 4230469); tchrs'. guide 4.96 (ISBN 0-205-03047-5, 4230477). Allyn.

Actualite et Avenir: A Guide to France & to French Conversation. Oscar A. Haac & Arthur Bieler. LC 74-30489. (Illus.). 256p. 1975. pap. text ed. 9.50 (ISBN 0-13-003855-5). P-H.

Actualizations: You Don't Have to Rehearse to Be Yourself. Stewart Emery. LC 77-76276. 1978. pap. 5.95 (ISBN 0-385-13122-4, Dolp). Doubleday.

Actualizations: You Don't Have to Rehearse to Be Yourself. Stewart Emery. Ed. by Neal Rogin. 222p. 1980. Repr. of 1978 ed. 14.95 (ISBN 0-8290-0222-7). Irvington.

Actuarial Aspects of Pension Security. William F. Marples. 1965. text ed. 8.50x o.p. (ISBN 0-256-00655-5). Irwin.

Actuarial Assesment of Child & Adolescent Personality: An Interpretive Guide for the Personality Inventory for Children Profile. David Lachar & Charles Gdowski. LC 79-66985. 186p. 1979. text ed. 19.75x (ISBN 0-87424-305-X). Western Psych.

Acupressure Way of Health: Jin Shin Do. Iona M. Teeguarden. (Illus., Orig.). 1978. pap. 9.95 (ISBN 0-87040-421-0). Japan Pubns.

Acupuncture- the Scientific Evidence & Far-Eastern Medicine. Kim Bonghan et al. (Illus.). pap. write for info. (ISBN 0-916508-15-3). Happiness Pr.

Acupuncture: An International Bibliography. Billy K. Tam & Mariam S. Tam. LC 73-5772. 1973. 10.00 (ISBN 0-8108-0625-8). Scarecrow.

Acupuncture & the Life Energies. Sidney Rose-Neil. 160p. 1981. pap. 8.95 (ISBN 0-88231-121-2). ASI Pubs Inc.

Acupuncture Anesthesia in the People's Republic of China: A Trip Report of the American Acupuncture Anesthesia Study Group. Committee on Scholarly Communication with the People's Republic of China. LC 76-22856. 1976. pap. 5.75 (ISBN 0-309-02517-6). Natl Acad Pr.

Acupuncture for Physicians. Teruo Matsumoto. (Illus.). 224p. 1974. 19.75 (ISBN 0-398-02958-X). C C Thomas.

Acupuncture Handbook. D. Lawson-Wood & J. Lawson-Wood. 6.00 o.p. (ISBN 0-685-36226-4). Weiser.

Acupuncture Handbook. J. Lawson-Wood & D. Lawson-Wood. 141p. 1973. 6.75x (ISBN 0-8464-0989-5). Beekman Pubs.

Acupuncture Medicine. Yoshiaki Omura. LC 79-1944. 1981. 19.95 (ISBN 0-87040-491-1). Japan Pubns.

Acupuncture: Science or Charlatanism? Cesar M. Pinto. (Illus.). 440p. 1978. 14.95 (ISBN 0-8059-2433-7). Dorrance.

Acupuncture, the Ancient Chinese Art of Healing. Felix Mann. (Illus.). 7.25 (ISBN 0-8446-4583-4). Peter Smith.

Acupuncture Vitality & Revival Points. D. Lawson-Wood & J. Lawson-Wood. 56p. 1975. 6.00x (ISBN 0-8464-0990-9). Beekman Pubs.

Acute Abdomen in Infancy & Childhood. John G. Raffensperger et al. LC 71-130975. (Illus., Span. ed. avail). 1970. 13.00 o.p. (ISBN 0-397-50259-1). Lippincott.

Acute Ambulatory Care for the House Officer. Norman Diamond. (House Officer Ser.). (Illus.). 200p. 1981. price not set softcover (ISBN 0-683-02504-X). Williams & Wilkins.

Acute Bone & Joint Injuries of the Hand & Wrist: A Clinical Guide to Management. Paul M. Weeks. (Illus.). 299p. 1980. text ed. 37.50 (ISBN 0-8016-5373-8). Mosby.

Acute Cardiovascular Failure. Dennis Greenbaum & Stanley Gianelli, Jr. (Clinics in Critical Care Medicine Ser.). (Illus.). 224p. 1981. lib. bdg. 22.50 (ISBN 0-443-08111-5). Churchill.

Acute Geriatric Medicine. Davis Coakley. 290p. 1981. pap. 27.50 (ISBN 0-88416-354-7). PSG Pub.

Acute Geriatric Medicine. Ed. by Davis Coakley. 256p. 1980. 30.00 (Pub. by Croom Helm England). State Mutual Bk.

Acute Grief & the Funeral. Ed. by Vanderlyn R. Pine et al. (Illus.). 328p. 1976. 21.75 (ISBN 0-398-03434-6). C C Thomas.

Acute Hand Injuries: A Multispecialty Approach. Ed. by Francis G. Wolfort. LC 79-90896. 1980. text ed. 27.50 (ISBN 0-316-95112-9). Little.

Acute Hemiplegias & Hemisyndromes in Childhood. Ed. by Werner Isler. (Clinics in Developmental Medicine, Vol, 41-42). 1971. 25.50 (ISBN 0-685-27034-3). Lippincott.

Acute Leukemias. Thomas F. Necheles. (Clinical Monographs in Hematology: Vol. 1). (Illus.). 1979. pap. 14.75 (ISBN 0-913258-57-1). Thieme-Stratton.

Acute Myocardial Infarction. McBride & Moses. 1979. pap. 6.95 (ISBN 0-8385-0049-8). ACC.

Acute Myocardial Infarction: Reaction and Recovery. Rue L. Cromwell et al. LC 76-49883. (Illus.). 1977. text ed. 12.95 o.p. (ISBN 0-8016-1079-6). Mosby.

Acute Pancreatic & Hepatic Dysfunction. Marsha E. Orr. Ed. by R. Craig Percy. (Fleschner Series in Critical Care Nursings). (Illus.). 175p. (Orig.). 1981. pap. text ed. 9.95 (ISBN 0-937878-04-9). Fleschner.

Acute Renal Failure. Barry M. Brenner & Jay H. Stein. (Contemporary Issues in Nephrology: Vol. 6). (Illus.). 320p. 1980. text ed. 35.00 (ISBN 0-443-08116-6). Churchill.

Acute Renal Failure. Ed. by Antoine Chapman. (Clinics in Critical Care Medicine). 224p. 1980. text ed. 29.50x (ISBN 0-443-01930-4). Churchill.

Acute Respiratory Care. Kathy L. Emanuelsen & Mary J. Densmore. Ed. by R. Craig Percy. (Fleschner Series in Critical Care Nursing). (Illus.). 190p. (Orig.). 1981. pap. text ed. 9.95 (ISBN 0-937878-01-4). Fleschner.

Acute Respiratory Tract Diseases: Prevention & Treatment. Hobart A. Reiman. LC 74-8610. 154p. 1975. 15.00 (ISBN 0-8463-0152-0). Krieger.

Ad Propertii Carmina Commentarius Criticus, Zutpen. P. J. Enk. Ed. by Steele Commager. LC 77-70813. (Latin Poetry Ser.). 1978. Repr. of 1911 ed. lib. bdg. 48.50 (ISBN 0-8240-2954-2). Garland Pub.

Ad Valorem Appraisers: The New Professionals. LC 72-76987. (ASA Monograph Ser.: No. 6). 1975. 5.00 (ISBN 0-937828-15-7). Am Soc Appraisers.

Ada or Ardor: A Family Chronicle. Vladimir Nabokov. (McGraw-Hill Paperback Ser.). 612p. 1980. pap. 6.95 (ISBN 0-07-045723-9, GB). McGraw.

ADA Programming Structures: With an Introduction to Structured Concurrent Programming. George Cherry. 400p. 1981. text ed. 15.95 (ISBN 0-8359-0151-3). Reston.

Adages (One to Five Hundred, Vol. 31. Erasmus. Tr. by Margaret M. Phillips & R. A. Mynors. (Collected Works of Erasmus). 1981. 35.00x (ISBN 0-8020-2373-8). U of Toronto Pr.

Adalbert Stifter. Margaret Gump. (World Authors Ser.: Austria: No. 274). 1974. lib. bdg. 10.95 (ISBN 0-8057-2864-3). Twayne.

Adam & His Work: A Bibliography of Sources by & About Paul Goodman (Nineteen Eleven to Nineteen Seventy-Two) Tom Nicely. LC 79-11662. (Scarecrow Author Bibliographies: No. 42). 362p. 1979. 19.00 (ISBN 0-8108-1219-3). Scarecrow.

Adam & the Qabalistic Tree. Z'Ev Ben Shimon Halevi. 1980. pap. 7.95 (ISBN 0-87728-263-3). Weiser.

Adam Bede. George Eliot. 1960. 12.95x (ISBN 0-460-00027-6, Evman); pap. 4.95 (ISBN 0-460-01027-1). Dutton.

Adam Clarke's Commentary on the Entire Bible. Ed. by Ralph Earle. 22.95 (ISBN 0-8010-2321-1). Baker Bk.

Adam Experiment. Geoffrey Simmons. 1979. pap. 2.25 o.p. (ISBN 0-425-04492-0). Berkley Pub.

Adam Kok's Griquas. R. Ross. (African Studies: No. 21). (Illus.). 1977. 24.95 (ISBN 0-521-21199-9). Cambridge U Pr.

Adam or Ape: A Sourcebook of Discoveries About Early Man. Ed. by L. S. Leakey & William S. Bestor. 540p. 1981. text ed. 15.95x (ISBN 0-87073-700-7); pap. text ed. 8.95x (ISBN 0-87073-701-5). Schenkman.

Adam Sleep. Winfred Van Atta. 192p. 1981. pap. 2.25 (ISBN 0-380-53744-3, 53744). Avon.

Adam Smith, Malthus & Marx. Terence Byres. Ed. by Malcolm Yapp et al. (World History Ser.). (Illus.). 32p. (gr. 10). 1980. Repr. of 1977 ed. lib. bdg. 5.95 (ISBN 0-89908-046-4); pap. text ed. 1.95 (ISBN 0-89908-021-9). Greenhaven.

Adam Smith's Politics. D. Winch. LC 77-82525. (Studies in the History & Theory of Politics Ser.). 1978. 32.95 (ISBN 0-521-21827-6); pap. 10.50x (ISBN 0-521-29288-3). Cambridge U Pr.

Adam Unregenerate: Selected Lyric Poems. George B. Saul. LC 77-23070. 1977. 11.95 (ISBN 0-916144-13-5); pap. 5.95 (ISBN 0-916144-14-3). Stemmer Hse.

Adams - Jefferson, 2 vols. Incl. Vol. 1. Adams: An American Dynasty. Francis Russell. LC 76-924. 374p (ISBN 0-8281-0350-X); Jefferson: A Revealing Biography. Page Smith. LC 76-3593. 310p (ISBN 0-8281-0315-1). (Illus.). 1976. Boxed Set. 32.50 (ISBN 0-8281-0379-8, 3062D). Am Heritage.

Adams County, 2 vols. Dorothy W. Creigh. Incl. Study of the Great Plains. 1972. 25.00 (ISBN 0-934858-00-4); The/People. 1971. 25.00 (ISBN 0-934858-01-2). (Illus.). Set. 45.00 (ISBN 0-934858-02-0). Adams County.

Adam's Daughter. Gertrude Samuels. LC 77-101. (gr. 7 up). 1977. 8.95 (ISBN 0-690-01322-1, TYC-J). T Y Crowell.

Adam's Eden. Faith Baldwin. LC 76-29898. 1977. 7.95 o.p. (ISBN 0-03-018896-2). HR&W.

Adam's Key. Eleanor F. Lattimore. LC 76-13013. (Illus.). (gr. 2-5). 1976. PLB 6.96 (ISBN 0-688-32089-9). Morrow.

Adam's New Friend & Other Stories from the Bible. David Bartlett & Carol Bartlett. 96p. 1980. pap. 4.95 (ISBN 0-8170-0882-9). Judson.

Adams One-Fifty. Compiled by Ramon F. Adams. LC 76-8959. (Illus.). 100p. 1976. 30.00 (ISBN 0-8363-0143-9). Jenkins.

Adams' Physical Diagnosis. 16th ed. John Burnside. (Illus.). 275p. 1981. write for info. soft cover (1137-5). Williams & Wilkins.

Adams' Revolvers. W. H. Chamberlain & A. W. Taylerson. 1978. 29.95 o.p. (ISBN 0-214-20089-2, 8011, Dist. by Arco). Barrie & Jenkins.

Adam's World: San Francisco. Kathleen Fraser & Miriam Levy. LC 71-150801. (Illus.). (gr. k-2). 1971. 5.75g o.p. (ISBN 0-8075-0174-3). A Whitman.

Adanson: The Bicentennial of Michel Adanson's "Familles des plantes", 2 vols. Ed. by G. H. Lawrence. (Illus.). 1965. Vol. 1. 19.00 (ISBN 0-913196-23-1); Vol. 2. 15.00 (ISBN 0-686-65641-5); Vol. 1. soft cover 17.00 (ISBN 0-913196-25-8); Vol. 2. soft cover 13.00 (ISBN 0-913196-26-6). Hunt Inst Botanical.

Adapt the Living. Albert Cook. LC 80-17828. 83p. 1981. 8.95 (ISBN 0-8040-0350-5); pap. 4.50 (ISBN 0-8040-0359-9). Swallow.

Adapt the Living. Albert S. Cook. LC 80-17828. 85p. 1981. 8.95 (ISBN 0-8040-0350-5); pap. 4.50 (ISBN 0-8040-0359-9). Swallow.

Adaptable Man. Janet Frame. LC 65-19327. 1965. 4.95 o.s.i. (ISBN 0-8076-0302-3). Braziller.

Adaptation & Education in Japan. Mobuo Shimahara. LC 79-9929. 1979. 22.95 (ISBN 0-03-049206-8). Praeger.

Adaptation & Intelligence: Organic Selection & Phenocopy. Jean Piaget. Tr. by Steward Eames. LC 79-25592. 130p. 11.00 (ISBN 0-226-66777-4). U of Chicago Pr.

Adaptation in Cultural Evolution: An Approach to Medical Anthropology. Alexander Alland. LC 78-100666. 1970. 17.50x (ISBN 0-231-03229-3); pap. 6.00x (ISBN 0-231-03997-2). Columbia U Pr.

Adaptation in Schizophrenia: The Theory of Segmental Set. David Shakow. LC 79-14979. (Personality Processes Ser.). 1979. 22.95 (ISBN 0-471-05756-8, Pub. by Wiley-Interscience). Wiley.

Adaptational Psychodynamics Motivation & Control. Sandor Rado. Ed. by Jean Jameson & Henriette Klein. LC 70-82528. 1969. 25.00 (ISBN 0-87668-018-X). Aronson.

Adaptations of Scientists & Organizations. Howard M. Vollmer. LC 75-18091. (Science & Technology Management Ser., No. 2). Date not set. price not set (ISBN 0-685-52882-0). Pacific Bks.

Adapted Physical Education & Recreation: A Multidisciplinary Approach. 2nd ed. Claudine Sherrill. 1981. 15.95x (ISBN 0-697-07176-6). Wm C Brown.

Adaptibility of the Vascular Wall: Proceedings. Ed. by Z. Reinis. (Illus.). 650p. 1980. 87.40 (ISBN 0-387-09907-7). Springer-Verlag.

Adaptive Arrays. J. E. Hudson. (IEE Electromagnetic Waves Ser.). 1981. price not set (Pub. by Peregrinus England). Inst Electrical.

Adaptive Behavior Curriculum (ABC) Prescriptive Behavior Analyses for Moderately, Severely, & Profoundly Handicapped Persons, Vol. 1. Dorothy Popovich & Sandra L. Laham. 336p. (Orig.). 1980. pap. text ed. 13.95 (ISBN 0-933716-13-3). P H Brookes.

Adaptive Behavior Curriculum: Prescriptive Behavioral Analyses for Moderately, Severely, & Profoundly Handicapped Students, Vol. 1. Dorothy Popovich & Sandra L. Loham. 336p. 1981. pap. text ed. 13.95 (ISBN 0-933716-13-3). P H Brookes.

Adaptive Behavior Curriculum: Thirty-Five Hundred Prescriptive Behavior Analyses for Moderately, Severely, & Profoundly Handicapped Students. Dorothy Popovich & Sandra L. Laham. 230p. 1980. pap. 13.95 (ISBN 0-933716-13-3). P H Brookes.

Adaptive Development. Margaret Pollack. (Studies in Developmental Pediatrics Ser: Vol. 3). 240p. 1981. text ed. 17.50 (ISBN 0-88416-380-6). PSG Pub.

Adaptive Environmental Assessment & Management. Ed. by C. S. Holling. LC 78-8523. (IIASA International Series on Applied Systems Analysis). 1978. 24.75 (ISBN 0-471-99632-7, Pub. by Wiley-Interscience). Wiley.

Adaptive Growth. Richard J. Goss. 1965. 39.00 (ISBN 0-12-292750-8). Acad Pr.

Adaptive Learning: Behavior Modification with Children. Ed. by Beatrice A. Ashem & Ernest G. Poser. LC 72-156903. 460p. 1975. pap. 15.00 (ISBN 0-08-017683-6). Pergamon.

Adaptive Optics & Short Wavelength Sources. Ed. by Stephen Jacobs et al. LC 78-17486. (Physics of Quantum Electronics: Vol. 6). (Illus.). text ed. cancelled o.s.i. (ISBN 0-201-05686-0, Adv Bk Prog). A-W.

Adaptive Radiation in Prehistoric Panama. Olga F. Linares & Anthony J. Ranere. Ed. by Lorna Condon. (Peabody Museum Monograph: No. 5). (Orig.). 1980. pap. text ed. 20.00 (ISBN 0-87365-905-8). Peabody Harvard.

Adaptive Use. W. Paul O'Mara et al. LC 78-56054. (Illus.). 246p. 1978. 26.25 (ISBN 0-87420-582-4). Urban Land.

Add a Few Sprouts. Martha H. Oliver. LC 75-10539. (Pivot Original Health Bk). 128p. (Orig.). 1975. pap. 1.95 (ISBN 0-87983-104-9). Keats.

Add-a-Room. Consumer Guide. 1980. pap. 8.95 (ISBN 0-686-60943-3, 25270); pap. 7.95 (ISBN 0-686-60944-1, 25271). S&S.

Add Spice to Your Travels. Bill MacRobbie. (Illus.). 196p. 1980. pap. 4.95 (ISBN 0-9605244-0-1). B Sales.

Add Years to Your Heart. Max Warmbrand. 1969. pap. 2.50 (ISBN 0-515-05720-7, N2046). Jove Pubns.

Added Value: The Key to Prosperity. E. G. Wood. 148p. 1978. text ed. 22.00x (ISBN 0-220-66349-1, Pub. by Busn Bks England). Renouf.

Addict to Yearning: Inspirational Philosophy & Religion. Merle Lighton. 1952. 5.00 (ISBN 0-910892-00-8, 910892). Lighton Pubns.

Addicted Society. Joel Fort. LC 80-8918. 256p. 1981. pap. 3.95 (ISBN 0-394-17889-0, B454, BC). Grove.

Addicted to Mediocrity. Franky Schaeffer. (Illus.). 128p. 1981. pap. 4.95 (ISBN 0-89107-214-4). Good News.

Addicted to Suicide: A Woman Struggling to Live. Mary Savage. 1980. text ed. 12.50x (ISBN 0-87073-906-9); pap. text ed. 5.95x (ISBN 0-87073-907-7). Schenkman.

Addiction: An Artificially Induced Drive. Nils Bejerot. (Illus.). 96p. 1972. 12.50 (ISBN 0-398-02527-4). C C Thomas.

Addiction & Brain Damage. Ed. by Derek Richter. 320p. 1980. 45.00x (Pub. by Croom Helm England). State Mutual Bk.

Addiction & Society. Nils Bejerot. (Illus.). 272p. 1970. text ed. 27.50 (ISBN 0-398-00126-X). C C Thomas.

Addiction Experience. Stanton Peele. 1980. pap. 1.50. Hazelden.

Addiction Research & Treatment Converging Trends: Proceedings. Coatesville-Jefferson Conference on Addiction, 1st, October 1977. Ed. by E. L. Gottheil et al. LC 78-23703. 1978. 18.25 (ISBN 0-08-023025-3). Pergamon.

Addictions: Issues & Answers. Jerome Jaffe et al. (Life Cycle Ser.). 1979. pap. text ed. 4.95 scp (ISBN 0-06-384748-5, HarpC). Har-Row.

Addictive Behaviors: Treatment of Alcoholism, Drug Abuse, Smoking & Obesity. William R. Miller. (Illus.). 275p. 1980. 36.00 (ISBN 0-08-025203-6). Pergamon.

Addie's Year. Rosalie Kelly. LC 80-26566. 160p. (gr. 5 up). 1981. 7.95 (ISBN 0-8253-0028-2). Beaufort Bks NY.

Adding a Dimension. Isaac Asimov. 1975. pap. 1.50 (ISBN 0-380-00278-7, 36871). Avon.

Adding Eye Appeal to Foods. Bruce H. Axler. 1974. pap. 3.70 o.p. (ISBN 0-672-96115-6). Bobbs.

Adding on. (Home Repair & Improvement Ser.). (Illus.). 1979. lib. bdg. 11.97 (ISBN 0-686-51041-0). Silver.

Adding Room, Saving Energy--Upstairs, Downstairs, Sideways. William M. Cowan. (Illus.). 1979. 14.95 (ISBN 0-02-528540-8, Collier); pap. 7.95 (ISBN 0-02-000280-7, Collier). Macmillan.

Addison & the White Corpuscles: An Aspect of Nineteenth-Century Biology. L. J. Rather. LC 71-149940. (Wellcome Institute of the History of Medicine). 1972. 17.50x (ISBN 0-520-01972-5). U of Cal Pr.

Addison Wesley General Mathematics: Level One. Paul Anderson et al. 1980. text ed. 13.40 (ISBN 0-201-03825-0, Sch Div); tchr's. manual 15.28 (ISBN 0-201-03826-9, Sch Div); tests & d.m. avail. A-W.

Addison-Wesley Reading Program: Placement Tests. Pleasant Rowland. (Addison-Wesley Reading Program Ser.). (gr. k-3). 1979. 8.36 (ISBN 0-201-20870-9, Sch Div). A-W.

Addison-Wesley Science Experience Records Books, Gr. 3-6. Verne Rockcastle et al. (Addison-Wesley Science Program Ser.). (gr. 1-6). 1980. 3.12 (Sch Div). Gr. 3 (ISBN 0-201-05383-7). Gr. 4. l.p. 3.92 (ISBN 0-201-05384-5); Gr. 5. l.p. 4.72 (ISBN 0-201-05385-3); Gr. 6. l.p. 4.72 (ISBN 0-201-05386-1). A-W.

Addisoniana. 242p. 1980. Repr. of 1803 ed. lib. bdg. 75.00 (ISBN 0-8492-3207-4). R West.

Addition & Subtraction. Philip Lutgendorf. LC 79-730038. (Illus.). 1978. pap. text ed. 99.00 (ISBN 0-89290-092-X, A508-SATC). Soc for Visual.

Addition & Subtraction Learning Module. Daniel Quinn & Donald M. Weatherall. (ps). 1974. pap. text ed. 330.25 (ISBN 0-89290-131-4, CM-52). Soc for Visual.

Addition & Subtraction with a Happy Ending. Steve Marcy & Janis Marcy. (Illus.). (gr. 4-7). 1976. wkbk. 4.75 (ISBN 0-88488-051-6). Creative Pubns.

Addition, Ten to Twenty. Kitty Wehrli. (Michigan Arithmetic Program Ser.). (gr. 2). 1977. wkbk. 7.00 (ISBN 0-89039-105-X). Ann Arbor Pubs.

Addition, Zero to Ten. (Michigan Arithmetic Program Ser.). 1976. wkbk. 7.00 (ISBN 0-89039-946-8). Ann Arbor Pubs.

Additional Adventures of Messrs. Box & Cox: A Continuation of the Dramatic History of Box & Cox. W. S. Gilbert. Ed. by Ralph MacPhail, Jr. Bd. with Penelope Anne. F. C. Burnand. LC 75-304933. (Illus.). 74p. 1974. pap. 7.50x (ISBN 0-9601580-0-6). Parenthesis Pr.

Additional Applied Mathematics. L. Harwood Clarke & F. G. Norton. 1972. pap. text ed. 6.25x o.p. (ISBN 0-435-51183-1). Heinemann Ed.

Additional Pure Mathematics. L. Harwood Clarke. 1970. pap. text ed. 11.50x o.p. (ISBN 0-435-51177-7). Heinemann Ed.

Additions Aux Dictionnaires Arabes (Arabic-French) E. Fagnan. 1969. 17.00x (ISBN 0-685-72024-1). Intl Bk Ctr.

Additive Migration from Plastics into Food. T. R. Crompton. 1979. 54.00 (ISBN 0-08-022465-2). Pergamon.

Address Book of Some Assemblies of Christians (Current) 1981. pap. 3.95 (ISBN 0-937396-03-6). Walterick Pubs.

Address Book with Riddles, Rhymes, Tales & Tongue Twisters. Monika Beisner. (Illus.). 1979. 6.95 (ISBN 0-374-30053-4). FS&G.

Addresses of the Philadelphia Society for the Promotion of National Industry. Mathew Carey. Ed. by Michael Hudson. Bd. with Essay on Expediency & Practicability of Improving or Creating Home Markets for the Sale of Agricultural Productions & Raw Materials. George Tibbits. (Neglected American Economists Ser.). 1974. lib. bdg. 50.00 (ISBN 0-8240-1000-0). Garland Pub.

Adelaide Crapsey. Edward Butscher. (United States Authors Ser.: No. 337). 1979. lib. bdg. 11.95 (ISBN 0-8057-7273-1). Twayne.

Adelaide of Brunswick. x1954 ed. Marquis De Sade. Tr. by Hobart Ryland. LC 72-11856. 1973. 10.00 (ISBN 0-8108-0574-X). Scarecrow.

Adelante! A Cultural Approach to Intermediate Spanish. 2nd ed. Eduardo Neale-Silva & Robert L. Nicholas. 1980. text ed. 15.95x (ISBN 0-673-15412-2); pap. text ed. 5.95x wkbk. (ISBN 0-673-15440-8). Scott F.

Adelardo Lopez De Ayala. Edward V. Coughlin. (World Authors Ser.: No. 466). 1977. lib. bdg. 12.50 (ISBN 0-8057-6303-1). Twayne.

Adelbert Ames, 1835-1933. Blanche A. Ames. (Illus.). 1964. 15.00 (ISBN 0-87266-000-1). Argosy.

Adeline Mowbray; or, the Mother & Daughter: A Tale, 3 vols. Amelia Opie. Ed. by Gina Luria. (Feminist Controversy in England, 1788-1810). 1974. lib. bdg. 50.00 ea. (ISBN 0-8240-0874-X). Garland Pub.

Adeline Schlime. Tatjana Hauptmann. (Illus.). 32p. (gr. k-3). 1980. 10.95 (ISBN 0-03-057979-1). HR&W.

Adena People. William S. Webb & Charles E. Snow. LC 75-10598. (Illus.). 420p. 1974. Repr. of 1945 ed. 16.50x (ISBN 0-87049-159-8). U of Tenn Pr.

Adenine Arabinoside: An Antiviral Agent. Ed. by D. Pavan-Langston et al. LC 75-4087. 425p. 1975. 34.50 (ISBN 0-89004-024-9). Raven.

ADF Fundamentals. Frank Harris. (Avionics Technician Training Course Ser.). (Illus.). 185p. 1980. pap. 6.95 (ISBN 0-89100-120-4). Aviation Maintenance.

Adhesive Bonding. J. Shields. (Engineering Design Guides Ser.). (Illus.). 1974. pap. 9.95x (ISBN 0-19-859130-6). Oxford U Pr.

Adhesive Bonding of Wood. M. L. Selbo. LC 77-88958. (Drake Home Craftsman Ser.). (Illus.). 1978. pap. 5.95 (ISBN 0-8069-8104-0, 000900). Sterling.

Adhesive Technology: Developments Since 1977. Ed. by S. Torrey. LC 79-25936. (Chemical Technology Review Ser.: No. 148). (Illus.). 1980. 54.00 (ISBN 0-8155-0787-9). Noyes.

Adhesives: Adherends, Adhesion. 2nd ed. Nicholas J. De Lollis. LC 79-1371. 280p. 1980. Repr. of 1970 ed. lib. bdg. 26.50 (ISBN 0-88275-981-7). Krieger.

Adi-Granth: The Japji. Guru Nanak. Tr. by Sangat Singh from Punjabi. 128p. (Orig.). 1974. pap. 2.25 (ISBN 0-88253-317-7). Ind-US Inc.

Adios, Amor Mio. Terry C. Thomas. Tr. by Sara Bautista from Eng. LC 77-79933. 202p. (Orig., Span.). 1977. pap. 2.50 (ISBN 0-89922-089-4). Edit Caribe.

Adios, Bandido! E. Jefferson Clay. Bd. with Desparados on the Loose. 1980. pap. 2.25 (ISBN 0-505-51459-1). Tower Bks.

Adirondack Album, No. 1. Barney Fowler. (Illus.). 200p. (Orig.). 1981. pap. 10.25 (ISBN 0-9605556-1-7). Outdoor Assocs.

Adirondack Album, No. 2. Barney Fowler. (Illus.). 200p. (Orig.). 1980. pap. 10.25 (ISBN 0-9605556-0-9). Outdoor Assocs.

Adirondack Canoe Waters: North Flow. 2nd ed. Paul Jamieson. LC 80-26774. (Illus.). 300p. (Orig.). 1981. pap. 8.95 (ISBN 0-935272-13-5). ADK Mtn Club.

Adirondack Guide-Boat. Kenneth Durant & Helen Durant. LC 80-80778. (Illus.). 224p. 1980. 30.00 (ISBN 0-87742-125-0). Intl Marine.

Adirondack Railroads, Real & Phantom. Harold K. Hochschild. (Illus.). 20p. 1962. pap. 3.00 (ISBN 0-8156-8020-1, Pub. by Adirondack Museum). Syracuse U Pr.

Adirondack Rock & Ice Climbs. Thomas R. Rosecrans. (Illus.). 124p. 1978. lib. bdg. 9.25 o.p. (ISBN 0-914788-17-5). East Woods.

Adirondack Sampler, II: Backpacking Trips in the Adirondacks. Bruce Wadsworth. (Orig.). 1981. pap. 6.95 (ISBN 0-935272-15-1). Adk Mtn Club.

Adirondack Voices: Woodsmen & Woods Lore. Robert D. Bethke. LC 80-24054. (Music in American Life Ser.). (Illus.). 180p. 1981. 12.50 (ISBN 0-252-00829-4). U of Ill Pr.

Aditi & Other Deities in the Veda. M. P. Pandit. 1979. 3.95 (ISBN 0-89744-960-6). Auromere.

Adjunct to Understanding Data Processing: The Course on Modern Data Processing & Accounting Procedures. William G. Moore. 1979. pap. text ed. 2.99 (ISBN 0-934488-01-0). Williams Ent.

Adjustable Diet Cookbook. rev. ed. Suzy Chapin. LC 75-26762. (Funk & W Bk.). 1976. 8.95 (ISBN 0-308-10222-3, TYC-T). T Y Crowell.

Adjustment: A Longitudinal Study. D. Magnusson et al. LC 75-11593. 1975. 17.95 (ISBN 0-470-56347-8). Halsted Pr.

Adjustment & Human Relations. S. Worchel & G. Goethals. 592p. 1981. text ed. 16.95 (ISBN 0-394-32226-6); wkbk. 6.95 (ISBN 0-394-32737-3). Knopf.

Adjustment & Personality. 4th ed. James M. Sawrey & Charles W. Telford. 608p. 1975. text ed. 14.95x o.p. (ISBN 0-205-04642-8, 7946422). Allyn.

Adjustment Assistance: American Jobs & Trade with the Developing Countries. Charles R. Frank, Jr. LC 73-84869. (Development Papers: No. 13). 50p. 1973. pap. 1.00 (ISBN 0-686-28678-2). Overseas Dev Council.

Adjustment, Behavior, & Personality. 2nd ed. Leonard D. Goodstein & Richard I. Lanyon. LC 78-62553. (Illus.). 1979. text ed. 17.95 (ISBN 0-201-02455-1); wkbk. 6.50 (ISBN 0-201-02456-X). A-W.

Adjustment: Fulfilling Human Potentials. Nicholas S. DiCaprio. (Illus.). 1980. text ed. 14.95 (ISBN 0-13-004101-7). P-H.

Adjustment in the Urban System: The Tasman Bridge Collapse & Its Effects on Metropolitan Hobart. Trevor R. Lee & L. J. Wood. 85p. 1980. pap. 13.50 (ISBN 0-08-026810-2). Pergamon.

Adjustment: Models & Mechanisms. I. Tucker. 1970. text ed. 18.95 (ISBN 0-12-702850-1). Acad Pr.

Adjustment of the Blind. Hector Chevigny & Sydell Braverman. 1950. 37.50x (ISBN 0-685-89731-1). Elliots Bks.

Adjustment to Empire: The New England Colonies in the Era of the Glorious Revolution, 1675-1715. Richard R. Johnson. (Illus.). 448p. 1981. 29.50 (ISBN 0-8135-0907-6). Rutgers U Pr.

Adjustment to Retirement: A Cross-National Study. Ed. by R. J. Havinghurst et al. (Orig.). 1969. text ed. 11.50x (ISBN 90-232-0011-X). Humanities.

Adjustment to Work. Ed. by John G. Cull & Richard E. Hardy. (Amer. Lec. Social & Rehabilitation Psychology). 360p. 1973. pap. 32.75 photocopy ed. spiral (ISBN 0-398-02799-4). C C Thomas.

Adler Book of Puzzles & Riddles: Or, Sam Loyd Up-To-Date. Irving Adler & Peggy Adler. LC 62-14898. (Illus.). (gr. 3-6). 1962. PLB 7.89 (ISBN 0-381-99977-7, A00800, JD-J). John Day.

Adler's Physiology of the Eye. 7th ed. Robert A. Moses. LC 80-16862. (Illus.). 747p. 1980. text ed. 41.00 (ISBN 0-8016-3541-1). Mosby.

Adler's Physiology of the Eye: Clinical Application. 6th ed. Robert A. Moses. LC 74-28483. 800p. 1975. text ed. 36.50 (ISBN 0-8016-3540-3). Mosby.

Administering Agricultural Development in Asia: A Comparative Analysis of Four National Programs. new ed. Richard W. Gable & J. Fred Springer. LC 76-41210. (Illus.). 1977. lib. bdg. 32.00x (ISBN 0-89158-206-1). Westview.

Administering Britain. Brian Smith & Jeffery Stanyer. 288p. 1976. 24.00x (ISBN 0-85520-139-8, Pub. by Martin Robertson England). Biblio Dist.

Administering Britain: A Guidebook to Administrative Institutions. Brian C. Smith & Jeffrey Stanyer. 288p. 1981. pap. 9.95x (ISBN 0-85520-374-9, Pub. by Martin Robertson England). Biblio Dist.

Administering Change in Schools. Robert G. Owens & Carl R. Steinhoff. (Illus.). 192p. 1976. Ref. Ed. 14.95 (ISBN 0-13-004929-8). P-H.

Administering Education: International Challenge. Ed. by Meredydd Hughes. (Illus.). 320p. 1975. pap. text ed. 20.75x (ISBN 0-485-12026-7, Athlone Pr). Humanities.

Administering Human Resources: A Behavioral Approach to Educational Administration. Ed. by Francis M. Trusty. LC 71-146311. (Orig.). 1971. 19.75x (ISBN 0-8211-1903-6); text ed. 17.75x (ISBN 0-685-04200-6). McCutchan.

Administering Medications. Phyllis T. Bayt. (Health Occupations Ser.). 1981. pap. write for info. (ISBN 0-672-61522-3). Bobbs.

Administracao Do Tempo. Tr. by Ted W. Engstrom & R. A. McKenzie. (Portugese Bks.). (Port.). 1979. 1.40 (ISBN 0-8297-0637-2). Life Pubs Intl.

Administracion De una Revolucion: La Reforma Del Poder Ejecutivo En Puerto Rico Bajo el Gobernador Tugwell, 1941-1946. Charles T. Goodsell. 5.00 o.p. (ISBN 0-8477-2206-6); pap. 3.75 (ISBN 0-8477-2207-4). U of PR Pr.

Administration: A Bibliography on Historical Organization Practices, Vol. 5. Frederick L. Rath & Merrilyn R. O'Connell. 250p. 1980. text ed. 14.95x (ISBN 0-910050-44-9). AASLH.

Administration for Development in Africa. 61p. 1979. 8.00 (ISBN 0-914970-15-1, CM 001, Conch Mag). Unipub.

Administration in Music Education. Robert W. House. LC 72-4564. (Contemporary Perspective in Music Education Ser). (Illus.). 192p. 1973. pap. text ed. 9.95 (ISBN 0-13-005132-2). P-H.

Administration in the Federated Malay States: Eighteen Ninety-Six-Nineteen Twenty. Jagjit S. Sidhu. (East Asian Historical Monographs). 250p. 1980. 25.00 (ISBN 0-19-580432-5). Oxford U Pr.

Administration in the Human Sciences: A Normative Systems Approach. Paul Abels & Michael J. Murphy. (P-H Ser. in Social Work). (Illus.). 256p. 1981. text ed. 16.95 (ISBN 0-686-68604-7). P-H.

Administration in the Public Sector. 2nd ed. Harold J. Gortner. LC 80-19757. 400p. 1981. text ed. 15.95 (ISBN 0-471-06320-7). Wiley.

Administration of Activity Therapy Service. Gerald S. O'Morrow. (Illus.). 440p. 1976. 22.50 (ISBN 0-398-01425-6). C C Thomas.

Administration of Archives. J. H. Hodson. LC 72-163642. 224p. 1972. 42.00 (ISBN 0-08-016676-8). Pergamon.

Administration of Athletic Programs: A Managerial Approach. J. Frank Broyles & Robert D. Hay. (Illus.). 1979. ref. 17.95 (ISBN 0-13-005249-3). P-H.

Administration of Civil Justice in England & Wales. R. W. Vick & C. F. Schoolbred. LC 67-31508. 1968. 23.00 (ISBN 0-08-013299-5); pap. 8.75 (ISBN 0-08-013285-5). Pergamon.

Administration of Federal Work Relief. A. W. MacMahon et al. LC 73-167845. (FDR & the Era of the New Deal Ser.). 408p. 1971. Repr. of 1941 ed. lib. bdg. 39.50 (ISBN 0-306-70326-2). Da Capo.

Administration of Ghana's Foreign Relations 1957-65: A Personal Memoir. Michael Dei-Anang. (Commonwealth Papers Ser: No. 17). 96p. 1975. pap. text ed. 8.75x (ISBN 0-485-17617-3, Athlone Pr). Humanities.

Administration of Government Documents Collections. Rebekah M. Harleston & Carla J. Stoffle. LC 74-81960. 1974. lib. bdg. 15.00x (ISBN 0-87287-086-3). Libs Unl.

Administration of High School Athletics. 6th ed. Charles E. Forsythe & Irwin A. Keller. (Illus.). 1977. 17.95x (ISBN 0-13-005710-X). P-H.

Administration of Intramural & Recreational Activities: Everyone Can Participate. John A. Colgate. LC 77-9265. 1978. text ed. 18.95 (ISBN 0-471-01728-0). Wiley.

Administration of Justice. 4th ed. Paul B. Weston & Kenneth M. Wells. (Illus.). 240p. 1981. text ed. 14.95 (ISBN 0-686-69272-1). P-H.

Administration of Justice in India. T. K. Mann. 1979. text ed. 13.50x (ISBN 0-391-01854-X). Humanities.

Administration of Justice in Norway. Ed. by Royal Norwegian Ministry of Justice. 96p. 1981. pap. 12.00x (ISBN 82-00-05501-9). Universitet.

Administration of Marketing & Selling. Harold Whitehead. 19.50x (ISBN 0-392-07566-0, SpS). Soccer.

Administration of Mental Health Services. 2nd ed. Saul Feldman. (Illus.). 544p. 1980. 49.75 (ISBN 0-398-03942-9). C C Thomas.

Administration of Mineral Exploration in the Yukon & Northwest Territories. Katherine A. Graham et al. 60p. (Orig.). 1979. pap. text ed. 3.00x (ISBN 0-686-63144-7, Pub. by Ctr Resource Stud Canada). Renouf.

Administration of PE & Athletics. 2nd ed. Reuben B. Frost & Stanley J. Marshall. 432p. 1981. text ed. 17.25 (ISBN 0-697-07171-5). Wm C Brown.

Administration of Physical Education for Women. Dudley Ashton. (Illus.). 1968. 10.50 o.p. (ISBN 0-8260-0545-4). Wiley.

Administration of Physical Education & Athletic Programs. 7th ed. Charles A. Bucher. LC 78-11952. (Illus.). 1979. text ed. 17.95 (ISBN 0-8016-0851-1). Mosby.

Administration of Public Employee Retirement Systems: Georgia & the Nation. Archibald L. Patterson. 100p. (Orig.). 1981. pap. price not set (ISBN 0-89854-073-9). U of GA Inst Govt.

Administration of Recreation, Parks, & Leisure Services. 2nd ed. Lynn S. Rodney & Robert F. Joalson. 496p. 1981. text ed. 17.95 (ISBN 0-471-05806-8). Wiley.

Administration of Schools for Young Children. Phyllis Click. (Early Childhood Education Ser.). 148p. 1975. pap. 7.20 o.p. (ISBN 0-8273-0575-3); instructor's guide 1.45 o.p. (ISBN 0-8273-0576-1). Delmar.

Administration of Schools for Young Children. 2nd ed. Phyllis Click. LC 79-55285. (Early Childhood Education Ser.). 176p. 1981. pap. text ed. 10.60 (ISBN 0-8273-1575-9); instr's. guide 1.80 (ISBN 0-8273-1576-7). Delmar.

Administration of Solvent Deceased Estates in Queensland. W. A. Lee. 1973. pap. 2.50x (ISBN 0-7022-0856-6). U of Queensland Pr.

Administration of the Colonies. T. Pownall. LC 79-146155. (Era of the American Revolution Ser). 1971. Repr. of 1768 ed. lib. bdg. 39.50 (ISBN 0-306-70123-5). Da Capo.

Administration: The Word & the Science. A. Dunsire. LC 73-7176. 262p. 1973. text ed. 13.95 (ISBN 0-470-22752-4). Halsted Pr.

Administrative Action: The Techniques of Organization & Management. 2nd ed. William H. Newman. 1963. ref. ed. 19.95x (ISBN 0-13-007195-1). P-H.

Administrative Appraisal of the NLRB. 3rd ed. Edward B. Miller. 165p. 1980. pap. 10.50 (ISBN 0-89546-013-0). Indus Res Unit-Wharton.

Administrative Aspects of Education for Librarianship: A Symposium. Ed. by Mary B. Cassata & Herman L. Totten. LC 75-15726. 425p. 1975. 17.50 (ISBN 0-8108-0829-3). Scarecrow.

Administrative Behavior. 2nd ed. H. A. Simon. 1957. 5.95 o.s.i. (ISBN 0-02-610990-5). Macmillan.

Administrative Behavior. 3rd ed. Herbert A. Simon. LC 75-18009. 1976. 17.95 (ISBN 0-02-928970-X); pap. text ed. 8.95 (ISBN 0-02-929000-7). Free Pr.

Administrative Control & Executive Action. 2nd ed. Bernhard C. Lemke & J. Don Edwards. LC 71-161870. 564p. 1971. text ed. 21.95 (ISBN 0-675-09792-4). Merrill.

Administrative Control of Aliens. William C. Van Vleck. LC 70-148084. (Civil Liberties in American History Ser.). Repr. of 1932 ed. lib. bdg. 29.50 (ISBN 0-306-70126-X). Da Capo.

Administrative Directory, 1980. LC 80-17018. 6.00 (ISBN 0-8218-0070-1). Am Math.

Administrative Feedback: Monitoring Subordinates' Behavior. Herbert Kaufman. 1973. 9.95 (ISBN 0-8157-4838-8); pap. 3.95 (ISBN 0-8157-4837-X). Brookings.

Administrative Functions of the French Conseil D' Etat. Margherita Rendel. (LSE Research Monograph: No. 6). 1970. bds. 17.00x (ISBN 0-297-00042-X). Humanities.

Administrative Justice & Supplementary Benefits. Melvin Herman. 68p. 1972. pap. text ed. 5.00x (ISBN 0-7135-1711-5, Pub. by Bedford England). Renouf.

Administrative Law Casebook. Bernard Schwartz. 1977. 21.50 (ISBN 0-316-77563-0). Little.

Administrative Law: The Formal Process. Peter Woll. (California Library Reprint Ser.: No. 58). 1974. 19.50x (ISBN 0-520-02802-3). U of Cal Pr.

Administrative Law Treatise. 2nd ed. Kenneth C. Davis. LC 77-86317. 1977. 47.50 o.p. (ISBN 0-686-22900-2). Lawyers Co-Op.

Administrative Law 1981. Gould Editorial Staff. 1981. pap. text ed. 6.50x (ISBN 0-87526-190-6). Gould.

Administrative Manager. Harold Smith & William Baker. LC 78-6085. 1978. text ed. 16.95 (ISBN 0-574-20030-4, 13-3030); instr's guide avail. (ISBN 0-574-20031-2, 13-3031); study guide 6.50 (ISBN 0-574-20032-0, 13-3032). SRA.

Administrative Medical Assistant. Bonnie J. Lindsey. 184p. 1979. pap. text ed. 9.95 (ISBN 0-87619-435-8). R J Brady.

Administrative Office Management. H. Webster Johnson & William G. Savage. 1968. 16.95 (ISBN 0-201-03325-9). A-W.

Administrative Office Management: A Practical Approach. Majorie P. Leaming & Robert J. Motley. 1979. text ed. 14.95x (ISBN 0-697-08030-7); instr. manual 4.00 (ISBN 0-685-91852-1). Wm C Brown.

Administrative Organization. John M. Pfiffner & F. Sherwood. 1960. 19.95x (ISBN 0-13-008615-0). P-H.

Administrative Policy: Text & Cases in Strategic Management. 2nd ed. Richard M. Hodgetts & Max S. Wortman. LC 78-24528. (Management Ser.). 712p. 1979. text ed. 22.95 (ISBN 0-471-03605-6); case notes avail. (ISBN 0-471-05041-5). Wiley.

Administrative Politics & Social Change. Louis C. Gawthrop. LC 76-145413. (American Politics Ser). 1971. pap. text ed. 5.95 (ISBN 0-312-00455-9). St Martin.

Administrative Practices in Boys & Girls Interscholastic Athletics. John H. Healey & William A. Healey. (Illus.). 616p. 1976. 37.75 (ISBN 0-398-03475-3). C C Thomas.

Administrative Practices in Concrete Construction. Portland Cement Association. LC 74-28259. (National Concrete Technology Curriculum Project Ser). 230p. 1975. text ed. 25.95 (ISBN 0-471-67433-8). Wiley.

Administrative Process. James M. Landis. LC 73-17952. 160p. 1974. Repr. lib. bdg. 17.50x (ISBN 0-8371-7284-5, LAAP). Greenwood.

Administrative Process. 2nd ed. Stephen P. Robbins. (Illus.). 1980. text ed. 21.95 (ISBN 0-13-007385-7); study guide 7.95 (ISBN 0-13-007369-5). P-H.

Administrative Process. 2nd ed. Glen O. Robinson et al. LC 80-114. (American Casebook Ser.). 997p. 1980. text ed. 21.95 (ISBN 0-8299-2085-4). West Pub.

Administrative Process: Integrating Theory & Practice. Stephen P. Robbins. 512p. 1976. 18.95 o.p. (ISBN 0-13-007419-5); 6.50 o.p. study guide (ISBN 0-13-007393-8). P-H.

Administrative Secrecy in Developed Countries. Ed. by Donald C. Rowat. LC 78-16376. (International Institute of Administrative Sciences Ser.). 1979. 21.50x (ISBN 0-231-04596-4). Columbia U Pr.

Administrative Theory & Practice in Physical Education & Athletics. Ed. by Earle F. Zeigler & Marcia J. Spaeth. (Illus.). 496p. 1975. 17.95 (ISBN 0-13-008581-2). P-H.

Administrative Training & Development: A Comparative Study of East Africa, Zambia, Pakistan, & India. Ed. by Bernard Schaffer. LC 73-21501. 456p. 1974. text ed. 29.95 o.p. (ISBN 0-275-28736-X). Praeger.

Administrative Tribunals. R. E. Wraith & P. G. Hutchesson. (Royal Institute of Public Administration). 1973. text ed. 49.95x (ISBN 0-04-347002-5). Allen Unwin.

Administrator & Educational Facilities. Jack Davis & E. E. Loveless. LC 80-1445. 272p. 1981. lib. bdg. 19.00 (ISBN 0-8191-1391-3); pap. text ed. 10.50 (ISBN 0-8191-1392-1). U Pr of Amer.

Administrator: Cases on Human Aspects in Management. 5th ed. John D. Glover et al. 1973. text ed. 19.50 (ISBN 0-256-00170-7). Irwin.

Administrator's Collection. Annual Ed. annual ed. LC 77-23776. 72p. 1978. pap. 6.25 (ISBN 0-87258-238-8, 1088). Am Hospital.

Administrator's Handbook on Designing Programs for the Gifted & Talented. Ed. by June B. Jordan & John A. Grossi. LC 80-68984. 144p. 1980. pap. 9.75 (ISBN 0-86586-112-9). Coun Exc Child.

Administrator's Manual for Plastics Education. Robert S. Krolick. LC 78-8937. 1978. pap. 5.95 (ISBN 0-672-97186-0). Bobbs.

Admirable & Indefatigable Adventures of the Nine Pious Pilgrims... Written in America. Richard Franck. LC 72-170515. (Foundations of the Novel Ser.: Vol. 11). lib. bdg. 50.00 (ISBN 0-8240-0523-6). Garland Pub.

Admiral Byrd. (gr. 1). 1974. pap. text ed. 2.80 (ISBN 0-205-03876-X, 8038767); tchrs'. guide 12.00 (ISBN 0-205-03866-2, 803866X). Allyn.

Admiral Halsey's Story. William Halsey & J. Bryan. (Politics & Strategy of World War II Ser.). 1976. Repr. of 1917 ed. lib. bdg. 27.50 (ISBN 0-306-70770-5). Da Capo.

Admiral of the Fleet. R. Hough. LC 72-77970. (Illus.). 1970. 8.95 o.s.i. (ISBN 0-02-554480-2). Macmillan.

Admiral of the Fleet, Earl Beatty: The Last Naval Hero. Stephen Roskill. LC 80-19778. 1981. 19.95 (ISBN 0-689-11119-3). Atheneum.

Admiralty Law of the Supreme Court. 3rd ed. Herbert R. Baer. 1978. 50.00 (ISBN 0-87215-216-2); 1980 supplement 12.50 (ISBN 0-87215-339-8). Michie.

Admiralty Officials Sixteen Sixty-Eighteen Seventy. Compiled by J. C. Sainty. (No. 4). 159p. 1975. text ed. 19.50x (ISBN 0-485-17144-9, Athlone Pr). Humanities.

Admission to Higher Education: A Select Annotated Bibliography. Ed. by Bruce Choppin & Patricia Fara. 1972. pap. text ed. 3.25x (ISBN 0-901225-89-4, NFER). Humanities.

Admissions: Poems Nineteen Seventy-Four to Nineteen Seventy-Seven. Sheila Wingfield. 1977. text ed. 13.00x (ISBN 0-85105-334-3, Dolmen Pr). Humanities.

Admit Impediment. Marie Ponsot. LC 80-2727. (Knopf Poetry Ser.: No. 5). 1981. 10.95 (ISBN 0-394-51450-5); pap. 5.95 (ISBN 0-394-74845-X). Knopf.

Adobes in the Sun. Morley Baer et al. LC 72-85173. (Illus.). 144p. 1980. pap. 8.95 (ISBN 0-87701-168-0). Chronicle Bks.

Adolescence. 2nd ed. Robert E. Grinder. LC 77-7239. 1978. text ed. 20.95x (ISBN 0-471-32767-0); 2.00 (ISBN 0-471-03798-2). Wiley.

Adolescence: A Psychological Perspective. 2nd ed. Dorothy Rogers. LC 77-16639. (Illus.). 1978. pap. text ed. 8.95 (ISBN 0-8185-0249-5); test items upon adoption of text free (ISBN 0-685-85040-4). Brooks-Cole.

Adolescence: A Report. Joint Commission on Mental Health of Children. Ed. by Irene M. Josselyn. LC 78-127300. 1971. 12.50 o.p. (ISBN 0-06-012231-5, HarpT). Har-Row.

Adolescence: A Social Psychological Analysis. 2nd ed. Hans Sebald. 1977. pap. text ed. 15.95 (ISBN 0-13-008599-5). P-H.

Adolescence: An Introduction. John W. Santrock. 600p. 1981. pap. text ed. write for info. (ISBN 0-697-06635-5); instrs.' manual avail. (ISBN 0-697-06640-1). Wm C Brown.

Adolescence & Breakdown. Ed. by Simon Meyerson. (Tavistock Clinic of Human Relations Studies). 1975. text ed. 17.95x (ISBN 0-04-150053-9); pap. text ed. 11.50x (ISBN 0-04-150054-7). Allen Unwin.

Adolescence & Individuality: A Conceptual Approach to Adolescent Psychology. Judith E. Gallatin. 364p. 1975. pap. text ed. 15.50 scp (ISBN 0-06-042227-0, HarpC); instructor's manual free (ISBN 0-06-362233-5). Har-Row.

Adolescence & Youth: Psychological Development in a Changing World. 2nd ed. John J. Conger. (Illus.). 1977. text ed. 20.50 scp (ISBN 0-06-041362-X, HarpC). Har-Row.

Adolescence: Generation Under Pressure. John Conger. (Life Cycle Ser.). 1979. pap. text ed. write for info. (ISBN 0-06-384744-2, HarpC). Har-Row.

Adolescence in Literature. Thomas W. Gregory. LC 77-17719. (English & Humanities Ser.). 1978. pap. text ed. 10.95 (ISBN 0-582-28045-1). Longman.

Adolescence of P One. Thomas J. Ryan. 1977. 10.95 (ISBN 0-02-606500-2). Macmillan.

Adolescence Studies in Mental Hygiene. Frankwood E. Williams. 279p. 1980. Repr. lib. bdg. 25.00 (ISBN 0-89984-511-8). Century Bookbindery.

Adolescence: The Crises of Adjustment. Ed. by Simon Meyerson. (Tavistock Clinic of Human Relations Studies). 1975. text ed. 12.50x o.p. (ISBN 0-04-150051-2); pap. text ed. 11.50x (ISBN 0-04-150052-0). Allen Unwin.

Adolescence: Theory & Experience. new ed. Edward A. Dreyfus. 256p. 1976. pap. text ed. 11.95 (ISBN 0-675-08679-5). Merrill.

Adolescence Today: Sex Roles & the Search for Identity. David R. Matteson. 1975. pap. text ed. 10.95x (ISBN 0-256-01731-X). Dorsey.

Adolescent & Mood Disturbance. Harvey Golombek. 1981. 22.50 (ISBN 0-8236-0085-8). Intl Univs Pr.

Adolescent As Individual: Issues & Insights. Carol J. Guardo. 352p. 1975. pap. text ed. 10.95 (ISBN 0-06-042228-9, HarpC). Har-Row.

Adolescent Dermatology. Lawrence M. Solomon et al. LC 77-78574. (Major Problems in Clinical Pediatrics Ser.: Vol. 19). (Illus.). 1978. text ed. 39.50 (ISBN 0-7216-8492-0). Saunders.

Adolescent Development & the Life Tasks. Guy J. Manaster. 1977. text ed. 17.50x (ISBN 0-205-05547-8); instructor's manual free (ISBN 0-205-05553-2). Allyn.

Adolescent Development in Contemporary Society. Jeannette Haviland & Hollis Scarborough. 1980. text ed. 16.95 (ISBN 0-442-25862-3). D Van Nostrand.

Adolescent: Development, Relationships, & Culture. 3rd ed. F. Phillip Rice. 700p. 1981. text ed. 17.95 (ISBN 0-205-07303-4, 2473038); free tchr's ed. (ISBN 0-205-07304-2). Allyn.

Adolescent Diaries of Karen Horney. Karen Horney. LC 80-50552. (Illus.). 271p. 1980. 12.95 (ISBN 0-465-00055-X). Basic.

Adolescent Gap: Research Findings on Drug Using & Non-Drug Using Teens. Edward M. Scott. (Illus.). 160p. 1972. 9.75 (ISBN 0-398-02403-0). C C Thomas.

Adolescent Girls at Risk. Harold Marchant & Helen M. Smith. 1977. text ed. 16.50 (ISBN 0-08-018914-8); pap. text ed. 7.00 (ISBN 0-08-020634-4). Pergamon.

Adolescent Gynecology. F. P. Heald. 173p. 1966. 10.50 o.p. (ISBN 0-683-03891-5, Pub. by Williams & Wilkins). Krieger.

Adolescent Health. Brent Q. Hafer et al. 1978. pap. text ed. 10.95 (ISBN 0-89832-009-7). Brighton Pub.

Adolescent Immaturity: Prevention & Treatment. I. Newton Kugelmass. (American Lectures in Living Chemistry Ser.). (Illus.). 320p. 1973. text ed. 17.50 (ISBN 0-398-02707-2). C C Thomas.

Adolescent in Psychotherapy. Donald J. Holmes. 337p. 1964. 15.95 (ISBN 0-316-37060-6). Little.

Adolescent Medicine Case Studies. George D. Comerci et al. LC 78-61736. 1979. pap. 18.00 (ISBN 0-87488-053-X). Med Exam.

Adolescent Medicine in Primary Care. Walter R. Anyan. LC 78-16772. 1978. 19.50 (ISBN 0-471-03976-4, Pub. by Wiley Medical). Wiley.

Adolescent Medicine: Principles & Practice. I. Newton Kugelmass. (American Lectures in Living Chemistry Ser.). (Illus.). 584p. 1975. 31.75 (ISBN 0-398-03288-2). C C Thomas.

Adolescent-Parental Separation. Michael V. Bloom. LC 79-13928. 177p. 1980. 22.95 (ISBN 0-470-26739-9). Halsted Pr.

Adolescent Patients in Transition: Impact & Outcome of Psychiatric Hospitalization. Mollie C. Grob & Judith E. Singer. LC 73-22379. 224p. 1974. text ed. 19.95 (ISBN 0-87705-137-2). Human Sci Pr.

Adolescent Pregnancy Prevention: School-Community Cooperation. Constance H. Shapiro. (Illus.). 144p. 1981. price not set (ISBN 0-398-04463-5); pap. price not set (ISBN 0-398-04464-3). C C Thomas.

Adolescent Prejudice. Charles Y. Glock et al. LC 74-15824. (Patterns of American Prejudice Ser.). (Illus.). 248p. 1975. 12.50x o.p. (ISBN 0-06-011567-X, HarpT). Har-Row.

Adolescent Psychiatry, Vol. 8. Sherman C. Feinstein & Peter L. Giovacchini. LC 70-147017. 544p. 1981. lib. bdg. 25.00x (ISBN 0-226-24053-3). U of Chicago Pr.

Adolescent Separation Anxiety, Vol. 1. Henry G. Hansburg. LC 79-21797. 208p. 1980. Repr. of 1972 ed. lib. bdg. 6.95 (ISBN 0-89874-042-8). Krieger.

Adolescent Separation Anxiety: Separation Disorders, Vol. 2. Henry G. Hansburg. LC 79-21798. (Orig.). 1980. lib. bdg. 8.95 (ISBN 0-89874-043-6). Krieger.

Adolescent Sexuality: A Study of Attitudes & Behavior. Helen F. Antonovsky et al. LC 80-8337. 176p. 1980. 18.95 (ISBN 0-669-04030-4). Lexington Bks.

Adolescent Society. James S. Coleman. LC 61-14725. 1971. pap. text ed. 4.95 (ISBN 0-02-906410-4). Free Pr.

Adolescent Suicide: With a New Preface. Jerry Jacobs. 1980. text ed. 18.00x o.p. (ISBN 0-8290-0113-1); pap. text ed. 8.95x (ISBN 0-8290-0114-X). Irvington.

Adolescent Thieves. K. S. Shukla. 1979. text ed. 15.00x (ISBN 0-391-01925-2). Humanities.

Adolescents. Guy Le Francois. 1976. text ed. 18.95x (ISBN 0-534-00433-4). Wadsworth Pub.

Adolescents & Morality: A Study of Some Moral Values & Dilemmas of Working Adolescents in the Context of a Changing Climate of Opinion. Emanuel M. Eppel & M. Eppel. (International Library of Sociology & Social Reconstruction Ser.). (Illus.). 1966. text ed. 8.50x (ISBN 0-7100-3455-5). Humanities.

Adolescents & Youth. 4th ed. Dorothy Rogers. (Illus.). 544p. 1981. text ed. 18.95 (ISBN 0-13-008748-3). P-H.

Adolescents with Behavior Problems: Strategies for Teaching, Counseling & Parent Involvement. abr. ed. Jones. 1980. text ed. 10.50 (ISBN 0-205-06824-3). Allyn.

Adolescents with Behavior Problems: Strategies for Teaching, Counseling & Parent Involvement. Vernon F. Jones. 353p. 1979. 16.95 (ISBN 0-205-06801-4). Allyn.

Adolf Hitler. John Toland. 1056p. 1981. pap. 9.95 (ISBN 0-345-29470-X). Ballantine.

Adolf Hitler: Faces of a Dictator. Heinrich Hoffmann. LC 68-24392. 1969. 9.50 (ISBN 0-15-103551-2). HarBraceJ.

Adolphe. Benjamin Constant. (Classiques Larousse). (Illus., Fr.). pap. 2.95 (ISBN 0-685-13793-7, 59). Larousse.

Adolphe Appia: Prophet of the Modern Theatre; a Profile. Walther R. Volbach. LC 68-27547. (Illus.). 1968. 20.00x (ISBN 0-8195-3094-8, Pub. by Wesleyan U Pr). Columbia U Pr.

Adolphe Monad's Farewell. Adolphe Monad. 1962. pap. 1.95 (ISBN 0-686-12506-1). Banner of Truth.

Adolphe Thiers. Rene Albrecht-Carrie. (World Leaders Ser.: No. 67). 1977. lib. bdg. 12.50 (ISBN 0-8057-7717-2). Twayne.

Adonis Garcia: A Picaresque Novel. Luis Zapata. Tr. by E. A. Lacey from Span. 192p. (Orig.). 1981. 20.00 (ISBN 0-917342-79-8); pap. 7.95 (ISBN 0-917342-79-8). Gay Sunshine.

Adopt Your Way to Inheritance & Gift Tax Savings. Charles P. Moriarty. LC 80-23202. 1980. 12.95 (ISBN 0-916076-31-8). Writing.

Adopted Four & Had One More. Helen L. West. 1968. 3.50 o.p. (ISBN 0-8272-0001-3). Bethany Pr.

Adopted in Love: Contemporary Studies in Romans. Burton H. Throckmorton, Jr. LC 77-22143. 1978. pap. 3.95 (ISBN 0-8164-1230-8). Crossroad NY.

Adopting Older Children. Alfred Kadushin. LC 71-125918. 1970. 16.00x (ISBN 0-231-03322-2). Columbia U Pr.

Adoption Adviser. Joan McNamara. 256p. 1975. 9.95 o.p. (ISBN 0-8015-0068-0, Hawthorn); pap. 5.95 (ISBN 0-8015-0069-9). Dutton.

Adoption in Brief: Research & Other Literature in the United States, Canada & Great Britain 1966-72, an Annotated Bibliography. Alan A. Jacka. (General Ser.). 72p. 1973. pap. text ed. 6.25x (ISBN 0-85633-015-9, NFER). Humanities.

Adoption of Black Children. Dawn Day. LC 77-18585. (Illus.). 1979. 17.95 (ISBN 0-669-02107-5). Lexington Bks.

Adoption of Innovation by Local Government. Richard D. Bingham. LC 75-41922. 1976. 22.95 (ISBN 0-669-00484-7). Lexington Bks.

Adoption: The Grafted Tree. Laurie Wishard & William R. Wishard. 1980. 12.95 o.p. (ISBN 0-686-28219-1). Caroline Hse.

Adora. Bertrice Small. (Orig.). 1980. pap. 2.50 (ISBN 0-345-28493-3). Ballantine.

Adrenal Androgens. Ed. by A. R. Genazzani et al. 400p. 1980. text ed. 35.00 (ISBN 0-89004-488-0). Raven.

Adrenal Cortex: Physiological Function & Disease. Don H. Nelson. LC 79-64776. (MPIM Ser.: Vol. 18). (Illus.). 281p. 1980. text ed. 29.00 (ISBN 0-7216-6733-3). Saunders.

Adrenal Gland. Ed. by Vivian H. James. LC 77-85870. 1979. 34.50 (ISBN 0-89004-297-7). Raven.

Adrenal Medulla of Rats: Comparative Physiology, Histology, & Pathology. Samuel Thompson et al. (Illus.). 112p. 1980. 18.75 (ISBN 0-398-04091-5). C C Thomas.

Adrenoceptors & Catecholamine Action. George Kunos. (Neurotransmitter Receptors Ser.: Vol. 1). 300p. 1981. 29.50 (ISBN 0-471-05725-8, Pub. by Wiley-Interscience). Wiley.

Adrienne Rich's Poetry. Ed. by Barbara Gelpi & Albert Gelpi. (Critical Editions Ser). 150p. 1975. 7.95 (ISBN 0-393-04399-1); pap. text ed. 4.95x (ISBN 0-393-09241-0). Norton.

Adsorption & Adsorbents, No. 1. Ed. by D. N. Strazhesko. Tr. by A. Barouch from Rus. LC 73-17749. 237p. 1973. 39.95 (ISBN 0-470-83324-6). Halsted Pr.

Adsorption of Inorganics at Solid Liquid Interfaces. Rubin Anderson. 1981. text ed. 39.95 (ISBN 0-250-40226-2, Dist. by Butterworths). Ann Arbor Science.

Adsorptive Bubble Separation Techniques. Robert Lemlich. 1972. 48.50 (ISBN 0-12-443350-2). Acad Pr.

Adult Access to Education & New Careers; A Handbook for Action. Ed. by Harvey B. Schmelter & Carol B. Aslanian. 141p. (Orig.). 1980. pap. 9.75 (ISBN 0-87447-125-7, 001257). College Bd.

Adult & Child Care: A Client Approach to Nursing. 2nd ed. Janet M. Barber et al. LC 76-26637. (Illus.). 1977. 26.95 (ISBN 0-8016-0444-3). Mosby.

Adult & Immature Tabanidae (Diptera) of California. Woodrow W. Middlekauff & Robert S. Lane. (Bulletin of the California Insect Survey Ser.: Vol. 22). 1980. pap. 10.50 (ISBN 0-520-09604-5). U of Cal Pr.

Adult & the Nursery School Child. 2nd ed. Margaret I. Fletcher. LC 59-4886. (Illus.). 1974. 7.50x o.p. (ISBN 0-8020-2167-0). U of Toronto Pr.

Adult Aphasia. Harvey Halpern. LC 72-189018. (Studies in Communicative Disorders Ser). 1972. pap. 3.50 (ISBN 0-672-61280-1). Bobbs.

Adult Development. John Dacey. 1981. text ed. write for info. (ISBN 0-8302-0114-9). Goodyear.

Adult Development & Aging. David F. Hultsch & Francine Deutsch. (Illus.). 448p. 1980. 18.95 (ISBN 0-07-031156-0, C); instr's manual 4.95 (ISBN 0-07-031157-9). McGraw.

Adult Education. Annette W. Jaffee. LC 80-84834. 220p. 1981. 12.95 (ISBN 0-86538-007-4). Ontario Rev. NJ.

Adult Education & the Burden of the Future. Leon McKenzie. LC 78-50845. 1978. pap. text ed. 7.50 (ISBN 0-8191-0470-1). U Pr of Amer.

Adult Education Dissertation Abstracts Nineteen Sixty-Eight to Sixty Nine. Ed. by Stanley M. Grabowski & Nehume League. 1972. 7.50 o.p. (ISBN 0-88379-001-7). Adult Ed.

Adult Education Dissertation Abstracts 1963-19. Ed. by Roger DeCrow. Nehume League. 1970. write for info. Adult Ed.

Adult Education for Social Change. T. V. Rao & Anil Bhatt. 1980. 15.00x (ISBN 0-8364-0648-6, Pub. by Manohar India). South Asia Bks.

Adult Education Procedures: A Handbook of Tested Patterns for Effective Participation. Paul Bergevin et al. 1963. pap. 3.95 (ISBN 0-8164-2000-9, SP29). Crossroad NY.

Adult English One. John Chapman. (Illus.). 1978. pap. 7.50 (ISBN 0-13-008821-8). P-H.

Adult English Three. John Chapman. 1978. pap. 7.50 (ISBN 0-13-008862-5). P-H.

Adult English Two. John Chapman. (Illus.). 1978. pap. 7.50 (ISBN 0-13-008839-0). P-H.

Adult Guide to Beginning Piano & Basic Musicianship. Milton Friedman. (Illus.). 1979. pap. 11.50 ref. (ISBN 0-13-008797-1). P-H.

Adult Hemiplegia. 2nd ed. Berta Bobath. 1978. pap. 11.00x (ISBN 0-433-03334-7). Intl Ideas.

Adult Homemaking. University of Missouri - Home Economics Resource Unit. text ed. 2.00x spiral bdg. (ISBN 0-87543-021-X). Lucas.

Adult Learner on Campus: A Guide for Instructors & Administrators. Jerry W. Apps. 288p. 1981. 17.95 (ISBN 0-695-81577-6, Assn Pr). Follett.

Adult Learning: A Design for Action: A Comprehensive International Survey. Ed. by Bud L. Hall & Roby Kidd. 1978. text ed. 52.00 (ISBN 0-08-022245-5); pap. text ed. 15.00 (ISBN 0-08-023007-5). Pergamon.

Adult Learning: Psychological Research & Applications. Michael J. A. Howe. LC 76-44226. 256p. 1977. 35.75 (ISBN 0-471-99458-8, Pub. by Wiley-Interscience). Wiley.

Adult Learning Today: A New Role for the Universities. Caroline Ellwood. LC 75-38420. (Sage Studies in Social & Educational Change: Vol. 4). 1977. 18.00x (ISBN 0-8039-9979-8); pap. 9.95x (ISBN 0-8039-9853-8). Sage.

Adult Life of Toulouse Lautrec by Henri Toulouse Lautrec. Kathy Acker. LC 78-58942. 1978. pap. text ed. 4.50 (ISBN 0-931106-21-4). Printed Matter.

Adult Literacy in Britain: An Annotated Bibliography. Ed. by W. Hay. 1978. 9.75x (ISBN 0-85365-811-0, Pub. by Lib Assn England). Oryx Pr.

Adult Medicine. Elizabeth Laird. (Modern Practical Nursing Ser.: No. 9). 1972. pap. 9.95x (ISBN 0-433-19050-7). Intl Ideas.

Adult Nursing. Jack Rudman. (College Proficiency Examination Ser.: CLEP-35). (Cloth bdg. avail. on request). pap. 9.95 (ISBN 0-8373-5435-8). Natl Learning.

Adult Postoperative Chest. Myron Melamed et al. (Illus.). 396p. 1977. 41.75 (ISBN 0-398-03476-1). C C Thomas.

Adult Tooth Movement in General Dentistry. Allan Schlossberg. LC 74-4588. (Illus.). 244p. 1975. text ed. 22.50 o.p. (ISBN 0-7216-7957-9). Saunders.

Adult Vacation Bible School. Incl. pap. 1.95 saddlewire, adult member (ISBN 0-8054-3821-1); pap. 2.10 saddlewire, adult teacher (ISBN 0-8054-3822-X); Ages 4-5. pap. 0.70 saddlewire, pupil (ISBN 0-8054-3813-0); pap. 1.75 saddlewire, teacher (ISBN 0-8054-3814-9); Ages 6-8. (gr. 1-3). pap. 0.70 saddlewire, pupil (ISBN 0-8054-3815-7); pap. 1.75 saddlewire, teacher (ISBN 0-8054-3816-5); Ages 9-11. pap. 0.70 saddlewire, pupil (ISBN 0-8054-3817-3); pap. 1.75 saddlewire, teacher (ISBN 0-8054-3818-1); Planbook, 1981. pap. 0.80 saddlewire (ISBN 0-8054-3811-4); Youth. (gr. 7-12). pap. 0.85 saddlewire, pupil (ISBN 0-8054-3819-X); pap. 2.05 saddlewire, teacher (ISBN 0-8054-3820-3). 1980. Broadman.

Adult Vocational ESL. Jo Ann Crandall. (Language in Education Ser.: No. 22). 51p. 1979. pap. 5.95 (ISBN 0-87281-108-5). Ctr Appl Ling.

Adult Western, No. 4. 1980. pap. write for info. (ISBN 0-671-83435-5). PB.

Adult Years. Wilbur Bradbury. LC 75-18649. (Human Behavior). (Illus.). (gr. 5 up). 1975. PLB 11.97 (ISBN 0-8094-1942-4, Pub. by Time-Life). Silver.

Adult Years: An Introduction to Aging. Dorothy Rogers. (Illus.). 1979. text ed. 18.95 (ISBN 0-13-008987-7). P-H.

Adultery Accepted. (Illus.). 4.95 (ISBN 0-910550-26-3). Centurion Pr.

Adultery & Other Private Matters: Your Right to Personal Freedom in Marriage. Lonny Myers & Hunter Leggitt. LC 75-4701. (Illus.). 224p. 1975. 13.95 (ISBN 0-911012-51-6). Nelson-Hall.

Adulthood & Aging: An Interdisciplinary Developmental View. 2nd ed. Douglas C. Kimmel. LC 79-24037. 1980. text ed. 18.95x (ISBN 0-471-05229-9); tchrs. manual avail. (ISBN 0-471-05237-X). Wiley.

Adults & Their Parents in Family Therapy. Lee Headley. 193p. 1977. 14.95 (ISBN 0-306-31087-2, Plenum Pr). Plenum Pub.

Adults As Learners: Increasing Participation & Facilitating Learning. K. Patricia Cross. LC 80-26985. (Higher Education Series). 1981. text ed. price not set (ISBN 0-87589-491-7). Jossey-Bass.

Adults Teaching Adults: Principles & Strategies. John R. Verduin, Jr. et al. 1977. 16.95 (ISBN 0-89384-015-7). Learning Concepts.

Advaita & Visistadvaita. 2nd ed. S. M. Chari. 1976. 7.50 (ISBN 0-8426-0886-9). Orient Bk Dist.

Advaitic Sadhana. S. S. Cohen. 1976. 7.50 (ISBN 0-8426-0989-X). Orient Bk Dist.

Advance Locator for Capitol Hill, 1981: With Biographical Material. 19th ed. Ed. by Charles B. Brownson. LC 59-13987. (Congressional Staff Directory Ser.). 1981. pap. 9.00. Congr Staff.

Advanced Abacus: Japanese Theory & Practice. Takashi Kojima. LC 62-15064. (Illus.). 160p. 1963. pap. 5.25 (ISBN 0-8048-0003-0). C E Tuttle.

Advanced Accounting. Floyd A. Beams. 1979. text ed. 21.95 (ISBN 0-13-010124-9). P-H.

Advanced Accounting. 4th ed. Charles H. Griffin et al. 1980. 22.95x (ISBN 0-256-02328-X). Irwin.

Advanced Accounting. Andrew A. Haried et al. LC 78-21944. (Accounting & Information Systems Ser.). 1979. 22.95 (ISBN 0-471-02374-4); tchrs. manual (ISBN 0-471-05298-1); working papers (ISBN 0-471-05345-7); checklist avail. (ISBN 0-471-05964-1); test avail. (ISBN 0-471-05874-2). Wiley.

Advanced Accounting: An Organizational Approach. 4th ed. Norton M. Bedford et al. LC 78-6961. (Accounting & Information Systems Ser.). 1979. text ed. 26.95 (ISBN 0-471-02927-0); solutions manual avail. (ISBN 0-471-04275-7). Wiley.

Advanced Accounting Part 1: Syllabus. W. R. Singleton & E. R. Johansson. 1977. pap. text ed. 8.55 (ISBN 0-89420-016-X, 352050); cassette recordings 255.10 (ISBN 0-89420-124-7, 352000). Natl Book.

Advanced Accounting Part 2: Syllabus. W. R. Singleton & E. R. Johansson. 1977. pap. text ed. 8.55 (ISBN 0-89420-017-8, 352060); cassette recordings 257.20 (ISBN 0-89420-124-7, 352000). Natl Book.

Advanced Accounting: Theory & Practice. James B. Cameron et al. LC 78-69529. (Illus.). 1979. text ed. 21.75 (ISBN 0-395-27446-X); inst. manual 3.00 (ISBN 0-395-27497-4); student check sheets 2.00 (ISBN 0-395-27497-4). HM.

Advanced Algebra & Calculus Made Simple. William R. Gondin & Bernard Sohmer. 1959. pap. 3.95 (ISBN 0-385-00438-9, Made). Doubleday.

Advanced Analysis with the Sharp 5100 Scientific Calculator. J. M. Smith. LC 79-22505. 1979. 7.95 (ISBN 0-471-07753-4, Pub. by Wiley-Interscience). Wiley.

Advanced & Extra Class Amateur License Q & A Manual. 2nd ed. M. Tepper. (gr. 10 up). 1978. pap. 7.25 (ISBN 0-8104-5814-4). Hayden.

Advanced & High-Temperature Gas-Cooled Reactors. (Illus., Orig.). 1968. pap. 55.75 (ISBN 92-0-050768-9, IAEA). Unipub.

Advanced Ansi,COBOL Disk-Tape Programming Efficiencies. Gary B. Shelly & Thomas J. Cashman. LC 74-21838. 1975. pap. text ed. 11.95x (ISBN 0-88236-105-8). Anaheim Pub Co.

Advanced Aquarist Guide. Ghadially, F. N., Dr. 6.98 o.p. (ISBN 0-385-01556-9). Doubleday.

Advanced Atlas of Histology. W. H. Freeman & Brian Bracegirdle. (Heinemann Biology Atlases Ser.). 1976. text ed. 16.95x (ISBN 0-435-60317-5). Heinemann Ed.

Advanced Bacterial Genetics. Ed. by R. Davis et al. 150p. (Orig.). 1980. lab manual 24.00x (ISBN 0-87969-130-1). Cold Spring Harbor.

Advanced BASIC: Applications & Problems. James S. Coan. Ed. by J. Haag. (Computer Programming Ser.). 1976. text ed. 13.25x (ISBN 0-8104-5856-X); pap. text ed. 10.75x (ISBN 0-8104-5855-1). Hayden.

Advanced Bass Tackle & Boats. A. D. Livingston. LC 75-15557. (Illus.). 240p. 1975. 9.95 o.p. (ISBN 0-397-01100-8). Lippincott.

Advanced Calculus. Charles Dixon. 192p. 1981. 36.00 (ISBN 0-471-27913-7, Pub. by Wiley-Interscience); pap. 17.95 (ISBN 0-471-27914-5). Wiley.

Advanced Calculus. 2nd ed. Wilfred Kaplan. LC 77-184161. 1973. text ed. 23.95 (ISBN 0-201-03611-8). A-W.

Advanced Calculus. Lynn H. Loomis & Shlomo Sternberg. 1968. 25.95 (ISBN 0-201-04305-X). A-W.

Advanced Calculus. John M. Olmsted. (Illus.). 1961. text ed. 23.95 (ISBN 0-13-010983-5). P-H.

Advanced Calculus. 2nd ed. Angus E. Taylor & Robert W. Mann. (Illus.). 900p. 1972. text ed. 26.95x (ISBN 0-471-00587-8). Wiley.

Advanced Calculus: An Introduction to Analysis. 3rd ed. Watson Fulks. LC 78-5268. 1978. text ed. 27.95 (ISBN 0-471-02195-4); solns. manual 3.00 (ISBN 0-471-05125-X). Wiley.

Advanced Calculus: An Introduction to Modern Analysis. Ed. by Voxman et al. 1981. 55.00 (ISBN 0-8247-6949-X). Dekker.

Advanced Calculus for Applications. 2nd ed. Francis B. Hildebrand. (Illus.). 816p. 1976. 26.95 (ISBN 0-13-011189-9). P-H.

Advanced Calculus: Functions of Several Variables. R. Sikorski. 1969. 15.95 (ISBN 0-02-852280-X). Hafner.

Advanced Calculus of Several Variables. C. H. Edwards. 1973. 22.95 (ISBN 0-12-232550-8). Acad Pr.

Advanced Calculus with Linear Analysis. Joseph R. Lee. 1972. text ed. 20.95 (ISBN 0-12-440750-1). Acad Pr.

Advanced Capitalist System: A Revisionist View. Lynn Turgeon. LC 80-51202. 192p. 1980. 15.00 (ISBN 0-87332-171-5); pap. 7.95 (ISBN 0-87332-172-3). M E Sharpe.

Advanced Cell Biology. Ed. by Lagar M. Schwartz & Miguel M. Azar. 1168p. 1981. text ed. 39.50 (ISBN 0-442-27471-8). Van Nos Reinhold.

Advanced Chemical Methods for Soil & Clay Minerals Reasearch. Ed. by J. W. Stucki & L. Banwart. 488p. 1980. lib. bdg. 58.00 (Pub. by D. Reidel). Kluwer Boston.

Advanced Christian Training. Jean Gibson. (Believer's Bible Lessons Ser.). (Orig.). Date not set. pap. 5.95 (ISBN 0-937396-04-4). Walterick Pubs. Postponed.

Advanced Concepts & Techniques in the Study of Snow & Ice Resources. U. S. National Committee for the International Hydrological Decade. Compiled by H. Santeford & J. Smith. x, 789p. 1974. pap. 15.25 (ISBN 0-309-02235-5). Natl Acad Pr.

Advanced Concepts in Ocean Measurements for Marine Biology. Ed. by Ferdinand Diemer et al. LC 79-24801. (Belle Baruch Library Ser.: Vol. 10). (Illus.). 572p. 1980. text ed. 27.50x (ISBN 0-87249-388-1). U of SC Pr.

Advanced Criminal Trial Tactics - for Prosecution & Defense Course Handbook. (Litigation & Administrative Practice Course Handbook Ser., 1977-78: Vol. 96). 1978. pap. 20.00 o.p. (ISBN 0-685-59695-8, C4-4121). PLI.

Advanced Custom Rod Building. Dale P. Clemens. (Illus.). 1978. 16.95 (ISBN 0-87691-258-7). Winchester Pr.

Advanced Data-Transmission Systems. A. P. Clark. LC 76-55018. 1977. 29.95 (ISBN 0-470-99029-5). Halsted Pr.

Advanced Designs for the Woodcarver. Richard A. Dabrowski. LC 77-94903. (Illus.). 1979. spiral bdg. 10.15 (ISBN 0-918036-04-6). Woodcraft Supply.

Advanced Developing Countries As Export Competitors in Third World Markets: The Brazilian Experience, Vol. II. William G. Tyler. LC 80-67710. (Significant Issues Ser.: No. 9). 88p. 1980. 5.95 (ISBN 0-89206-022-0). CSI Studies.

Advanced Developing Countries: Emerging Actors in the World Economy. John A. Mathieson. LC 79-91996. (Development Papers: No. 28). 72p. 1979. pap. 3.00 (ISBN 0-686-28672-3). Overseas Dev Council.

Advanced Dictation & Transcription. Frances A. Greer & W. M. Mitchell. 384p. 1974. 9.45 o.p. (ISBN 0-911744-27-4). Intl Educ Systems.

Advanced Drilling Techniques. William Maurer. 576p. 1980. 45.00 (ISBN 0-87814-117-0). Pennwell Pub.

Advanced Driver. Joe Kells. LC 77-85033. (Illus.). 1978. 16.95 (ISBN 0-7153-7494-X). David & Charles.

Advanced Economics. 2nd ed. G. L. Thirkettle. 160p. (Orig.). 1976. pap. text ed. 10.00x (ISBN 0-7121-0164-0, Pub. by Macdonald & Evans England). Intl Ideas.

Advanced Educational Psychology. S. S. Chauhan. 1978. 18.95 (ISBN 0-7069-0572-5, Pub. by Vikas India). Advent Bk.

Advanced Electric Circuits. A. M. Brookes. 1966. text ed. 17.50 (ISBN 0-08-011610-8); pap. text ed. 7.75 (ISBN 0-08-011609-4). Pergamon.

Advanced English Practice. 2nd ed. B. D. Graver. 1971. pap. text ed. 3.50x with key o.p. (ISBN 0-19-432190-8). Oxford U Pr.

Advanced First Aid Afloat. 2nd ed. Peter F. Eastman. LC 72-78241. (Illus.). 1974. pap. 6.00 (ISBN 0-87033-169-8). Cornell Maritime.

Advanced First Aid & Emergency Care. 2nd ed. American National Red Cross. LC 79-53479. (American Red Cross Bks.). (Illus.). 1980. pap. 3.00 (ISBN 0-385-15737-1). Doubleday.

Advanced First Aid for All Outdoors. Peter F. Eastman. LC 76-44658. (Illus.). 1976. pap. 6.00 (ISBN 0-87033-223-6). Cornell Maritime.

Advanced French, 2 pts. Foreign Service Institute. 567p. 1980. Pt. A. text & cassettes 170.00x (ISBN 0-88432-067-7, Audio-Forum); Pt. B. text & cassettes 160.00 (ISBN 0-88432-068-5). J Norton Pubs.

Advanced French. Katherine L. O'Brien et al. 365p. 1965. 18.50x (ISBN 0-471-00400-6). Wiley.

Advanced French Unseens. R. J. LeGrand. 1970. pap. text ed. 4.95x o.p. (ISBN 0-435-37536-9). Heinemann Ed.

Advanced Gas Turbine Systems for Automobiles. Society of Automotive Engineers. 1980. 18.00 (ISBN 0-89883-236-5). Soc Auto Engineers.

Advanced General Psychology. Russell W. Levanway. LC 70-145878. 1972. 17.75x (ISBN 0-88295-206-4). AHM Pub.

Advanced General Statistics. B. C. Erricker. 358p. 1971. 19.50x (ISBN 0-8448-0078-3). Crane-Russak Co.

Advanced Geological Map Interpretation. Frank Moseley. LC 79-11243. 1979. pap. 10.95x (ISBN 0-470-26708-9). Halsted Pr.

Advanced German Course. Foreign Service Institute. 375p. 1980. plus 18 audio-cassettes 160.00x (ISBN 0-88432-043-X, G160). J Norton Pubs.

Advanced Guide to Coin Collecting. Howard Linecar. (Illus.). 1970. 9.95 o.p. (ISBN 0-7207-0224-0, Pub. by Michael Joseph). Merrimack Bk Serv.

Advanced Harmony: Theory & Practice. 2nd ed. Robert W. Ottman. LC 72-173655. (Illus.). 304p. 1972. text ed. 17.50 (ISBN 0-13-012955-0). P-H.

Advanced Hockey for Women. Brenda Reed & Freda Walker. (Illus.). 182p. 1976. 18.50 (ISBN 0-571-09881-9). Transatlantic.

Advanced Immigration 1980. (Litigation & Administrative Course Handbook Ser. 1979-80: Vol. 158). 1980. pap. 25.00 (ISBN 0-685-63713-1, H4-4822). PLI.

Advanced in Sewage Treatment. Institute of Civil Engineers, UK. 88p. 1980. 60.00x (ISBN 0-901948-70-5, Pub. by Telford England). State Mutual Bk.

Advanced Industrial Selling. David A. Stumm. 426p. 1981. 17.95 (ISBN 0-8144-5665-0). Am Mgmt.

Advanced Investment Strategies. Thomas C. Noddings. LC 78-62631. 1978. 17.50 (ISBN 0-87094-170-4). Dow Jones-Irwin.

Advanced Laboratory Manual for Nutrition Research. G. Krishna & S. K. Ranjhan. 150p. 1980. text ed. 13.95 (ISBN 0-7069-1125-3, Pub by Vikas India). Advent Bk.

Advanced Laboratory Manual: Nutrition Research. G. Krishna & S. K. Rajhan. 176p. 1980. text ed. 15.00 (ISBN 0-7069-1125-3, Pub. by Vikas India). Advent Bk.

Advanced Lapidary Techniques. Herbert Scarfe. 1979. 27.00 (ISBN 0-7134-0398-5, Pub. by Batsford England). David & Charles.

Advanced Level Physics Questions. A. C. Jarvis & C. Gregory. 1974. pap. text ed. 4.95x o.p. (ISBN 0-435-68230-X). Heinemann Ed.

Advanced Level Vectors. A. P. Armit. 1973. pap. text ed. 5.95x o.p. (ISBN 0-435-51036-3). Heinemann Ed.

Advanced Masonry Skills. Richard T. Kreh. LC 77-78176. 1978. pap. text ed. 11.44 (ISBN 0-8273-1636-4); instructor's guide 1.60 (ISBN 0-8273-1637-2). Delmar.

Advanced Mass Spectrometry: Applications in Organic & Analytical Chemistry. U. P. Schlunegger. (Illus.). 150p. 1980. 32.00 (ISBN 0-08-023842-4). Pergamon.

Advanced Mathematics: An Introductory Course. Richard Brown & David Robbins. (gr. 11-12). 1978. text ed. 16.28 (ISBN 0-395-25553-8); instrs'. guide & solns. 9.40 (ISBN 0-395-25554-6). HM.

Advanced Mathematics for Engineers. Wilfred Kaplan. LC 80-19492. (Mathematics Ser.). (Illus.). 960p. 1981. text ed. 22.95 (ISBN 0-201-03773-4). A-W.

Advanced Mechanics of Materials. 3rd ed. Arthur P. Boresi et al. LC 77-28283. 1978. text ed. 35.50 (ISBN 0-471-08892-7). Wiley.

Advanced Mechanics of Materials. 2nd ed. High Ford & J. M. Alexander. 1977. 34.95 (ISBN 0-470-99065-1). Halsted Pr.

Advanced Medicine - XI: Proceedings of the 11th Annual Symposium on Advanced Medicine 1975. Ed. by A. F. Lant. (Illus.). 450p. (Orig.). 1975. pap. text ed. 30.00x (ISBN 0-8464-0112-6). Beekman Pubs.

Advanced Metal Working Technologies, GB-052. Business Communications Co. 1979. 750.00 (ISBN 0-89336-230-1). BCC.

Advanced Methods for Sheet Metal Work. 6th ed. William Cookson. (Illus.). 1975. 21.00x (ISBN 0-291-39427-2). Intl Ideas.

Advanced Nacherzahlungen. K. S. Whitton. 1969. 4.10 (ISBN 0-08-013065-8); pap. 3.00 (ISBN 0-08-013064-X). Pergamon.

Advanced Negligence Trial Strategy 1978, Vol. 120. (Litigation & Administrative Practice Course Handbook Series 1978-79). 1978. pap. 20.00 o.p. (ISBN 0-685-90301-X, H4-3872). PLI.

Advanced Number Theory. Harvey Cohn. (Illus.). 1980. pap. 5.00 (ISBN 0-486-64023-X). Dover.

Advanced Ozone Technology: Proceedings. Symposium on Advanced Ozone Technology, Toronto Canada, May 1978. Ed. by Aharon Netzer. text ed. cancelled o.s.i. (ISBN 0-918650-11-9). Intl Ozone.

Advanced Pilot Manual. 3rd ed. (Pilot Training Ser.). (Illus.). 480p. 1981. text ed. 18.25 (ISBN 0-88487-068-5, S314298). Jeppesen Sanderson.

Advanced Pilot's Flight Manual. 4th ed. William K Kershner. (Illus.). 246p. 1976. pap. 13.95 (ISBN 0-8138-1300-X). Iowa St U Pr.

Advanced Pipe & Tube Welding. Ed. by F. W. Copleston et al. (Engineering Craftsmen: No. F21). (Illus.). 1970. spiral bdg. 28.50x (ISBN 0-85083-131-8). Intl Ideas.

Advanced Play at Bridge. H. W. Kelsey. LC 68-87519. 1979. 11.95 (ISBN 0-571-08300-5, Pub. by Faber & Faber). Merrimack Bk Serv.

Advanced Play at Bridge. H. W. Kelsey. 192p. 1981. pap. 6.95 (ISBN 0-571-11677-9, Pub. by Faber & Faber). Merrimack Bk Serv.

Advanced Plumbing. Harry Slater. LC 79-89242. (Construction Ser.). 1981. pap. text ed. 6.60 (ISBN 0-8273-1111-7); instructor's guide 1.60 (ISBN 0-8273-1112-5). Delmar.

Advanced Plumbing. Harry Slater & Lee Smith. LC 79-89242. 1981. pap. 6.60 (ISBN 0-8273-1106-0); instructor's guide 1.60 (ISBN 0-8273-1112-5). Delmar.

Advanced Plumbing. 3rd ed. Harry Slater & Lee Smith. 198p. 1980. 8.95 (ISBN 0-442-23873-8). Van Nos Reinhold.

Advanced Practical Geography. 5th ed. Arthur Guest. 1977. text ed. 14.95x (ISBN 0-435-35356-X). Heinemann Ed.

Advanced Problems & Methods for Space Flight Optimization. B. F. De Veubeke. 1969. 46.00 (ISBN 0-08-013290-1). Pergamon.

Advanced Process Control. W. Harmon Ray. (Chemical Engineering Ser.). (Illus.). 1980. text ed. 29.50 (ISBN 0-07-051250-7, C). McGraw.

Advanced Programming & Problem Solving with Pascal. Schneider & Bruell. 480p. 1981. text ed. 22.95 (ISBN 0-471-07876-X). Wiley.

Advanced Programming Techniques: A Second Course in Programming Using Fortran. Ed. by Charles E. Hughes et al. 287p. 1978. text ed. 19.95 (ISBN 0-471-02611-5). Wiley.

Advanced Quilting. Elsie Svennas. (Illus.). 144p. 1980. 16.95 (ISBN 0-684-16612-7, ScribT). Scribner.

Advanced Radio Control. Edward L. Safford, Jr. LC 65-22390. (Illus., Orig.). 1965. 7.95 (ISBN 0-8306-4122-X, 122); pap. 4.95 (ISBN 0-8306-5122-5). TAB Bks.

Advanced Reactors: Physics, Design, & Economics: Proceedings, International Conference, Atlanta, Georgia, Sept. 1974. Ed. by J. M. Kallfelz & R. A. Karam. LC 75-4642. 864p. 1975. text ed. 46.00 (ISBN 0-08-019610-1). Pergamon.

Advanced Real Estate Primer. 20th ed. George R. Fessler & Ray D. Westcott. 336p. pap. 7.95 (ISBN 0-935810-04-8). Primer Pubs.

Advanced River Rafting. Cecil Kuhne. LC 80-14073. (Illus.). 224p. (Orig.). 1980. pap. 4.95 (ISBN 0-89037-183-0). Anderson World.

Advanced Rockcraft. Royal Robbins. (Illus.). 1973. wrappers 3.95 (ISBN 0-910856-56-7). La Siesta.

Advanced Science Bookshelf. (Classroom Libraries). (gr. 7-9). 148.63 o.p. (ISBN 0-531-00729-4). Watts.

Advanced Skateboarding: A Complete Guide to Skatepark Riding & Other Tips for the Better Skateboarder. LaVada Weir. (Illus.). (gr. 4 up). 1980. pap. 2.95 (ISBN 0-671-33040-3). Wanderer Bks.

Advanced Skateboarding: A Complete Guide to Skateboard Riding & Other Tips for the Better Skateboarder. LaVada Weir. LC 79-16801. (Illus.). 128p. (gr. 10 up). 1980. PLB 7.79 (ISBN 0-671-33011-X). Messner.

Advanced Social Studies Library. (Classroom Libraries). (gr. 7-9). 140.00 o.p. (ISBN 0-531-00727-8). Watts.

Advanced Software Design Techniques. Robert J. Rader. (Illus.). 172p. text ed. 16.50 (ISBN 0-89433-046-2). Petrocelli.

Advanced Soil Physics. Don Kirkham & W. L. Powers. LC 74-153083. 1972. 53.50 (ISBN 0-471-48875-5, Pub. by Wiley-Interscience). Wiley.

Advanced Spanish Course. K. L. Mason. 1967. text ed. 11.40 (ISBN 0-08-012272-8); pap. text ed. 8.00 (ISBN 0-08-012271-X). Pergamon.

Advanced Spanish, Part B. Foreign Service Institute. 614p. 1980. plus 12 audio-cassettes 135.00x (ISBN 0-88432-058-8, S 153). J Norton Pubs.

Advanced Spanish, Pt. A. Foreign Service Institute. 699p. 1980. plus 16 audio cassettes 155.00x (ISBN 0-88432-057-X, S 131). J Norton Pubs.

Advanced Statistical Mechanics. R. K. Pathria. 1972. text ed. 50.00 (ISBN 0-08-016747-0); pap. text ed. 24.00 (ISBN 0-08-018994-6). Pergamon.

Advanced Stories for Reproduction. Leslie A. Hill. 62p. 1965. pap. 2.50x (ISBN 0-19-432543-1). Oxford U Pr.

Advanced Strength of Materials. Enrico Volterra & J. H. Gaines. 1971. ref. ed. 27.95 (ISBN 0-13-013854-1). P-H.

Advanced Study of Gymnastics. John Salmela. (Illus.). 288p. 1976. 27.50 (ISBN 0-398-03438-9). C C Thomas.

Advanced Techniques in Ophthalmic Microsurgery: Corneal Surgery, Vol. II. Louis J. Girard. LC 78-31773. (Illus.). 305p. 1980. text ed. 82.50 (ISBN 0-8016-1835-5). Mosby.

Advanced Techniques, Proceedings of a Conference Held in Chicago, Sept. 27-28, 1978: Advanced Techniques, Proceedings of the Conference Held in Chicago, Sept. 27-28, 1977. Ed. by Gerald J. Moyar & Walter D. Pilkey. LC 78-1678. 484p. 55.00 (ISBN 0-08-022153-X). Pergamon.

Advanced Technobiology. Ed. by B. Rybak. 712p. 1979. 56.00x (ISBN 90-286-0299-2). Sijthoff & Noordhoff.

Advanced Teeline. I. C. Hill & James Hill. 1972. pap. text ed. 5.50x o.p. (ISBN 0-435-45334-3); practical exercises 3.25x o.p. (ISBN 0-435-45337-8). Heinemann Ed.

Advanced Tennis. rev ed. Paul Metzler. LC 68-18790. (Illus.). 192p. (gr. 5 up). 1972. 8.95 (ISBN 0-8069-4000-X); PLB 8.29 (ISBN 0-8069-4001-8). Sterling.

Advanced Theory of Statistics, 3 vols. 3rd ed. M. G. Kendall & A. Stuart. Incl. Vol. 1. Distribution Theory. xii, 439p. 1969. o.p. (ISBN 0-02-847660-3); Vol. 2. Statistical Inference & Statistical Relationship. ix, 690p. 1974. 0.p. o.s.i. (ISBN 0-02-847670-0); Vol. 3. Design & Analysis, & Time-Series. (Illus.). x, 557p. 1976. 49.50 o.s.i. (ISBN 0-02-847640-9). Hafner.

Advanced Theory of Statistics, 3 vols. 4th ed. M. G. Kendall & A. Stuart. Incl. Vol. 1. Distribution Theory. 4th ed. 1977. 41.25 (ISBN 0-02-847630-1); Vol. 2. Statistical Inference & Statistical Relationship. th ed. 1979. 59.95 (ISBN 0-02-847820-7); Vol. 3. Design & Analysis, & Time Series. 3rd ed. (Illus.). 1976. 55.00 (ISBN 0-02-847640-9). Hafner.

Advanced Value Clarification. Howard Kirschenbaum. LC 76-50695. 188p. (Orig.). 1977. pap. 12.95 (ISBN 0-88390-132-3). Univ Assocs.

Advanced Watch & Clock Repair. H. G. Harris. (Illus.). 9.95 (ISBN 0-87523-181-0). Wallace-Homestead.

Advanced Will Drafting 1980. (Tax Law & Estate Planning Course Handbook Ser. 1979-80: Vol. 109). 1980. pap. 25.00 (ISBN 0-685-85311-X, D4-5125). PLI.

Advanced Wiring. LC 78-1105. (Home Repair & Improvement Ser.). (Illus.). 1978. lib. bdg. 11.97 (ISBN 0-686-51034-8). Silver.

Advanced Wiring. (Home Repair & Improvement Ser.). 1978. 10.95 (ISBN 0-8094-2398-7). Time-Life.

Advanced Woodwork & Furniture Making. Feirer & Hutchings. 1978. text ed. 15.36 (ISBN 0-87002-205-9); student guide 3.96 (ISBN 0-87002-269-5); visual masters 14.40 (ISBN 0-87002-148-6). Bennett IL.

Advancement of Learning. Francis Bacon. Ed. by G. W. Kitchin. (Rowman & Littlefield University Library). 246p. 1973. 11.50x (ISBN 0-87471-664-0); pap. 6.50x (ISBN 0-87471-665-9). Rowman.

Advancement of Learning, Bk. 1. Francis Bacon. Ed. by William Armstrong. 154p. 1975. text ed. 10.75x (ISBN 0-485-13605-8, Athlone Pr). Humanities.

Advances & Controversies in Cardiology. Ed. by Ephraim Donoso. (Current Cardiovascular Topics: Vol. VI). (Illus.). 350p. 1981. text ed. 35.00 (ISBN 0-86577-024-7). Thieme-Stratton.

Advances & Technical Standards in Neurosurgery, Vol. 5. Ed. by H. Krayenbuehl et al. LC 74-10499. (Illus.). 1978. 46.00 (ISBN 0-387-81441-8). Springer-Verlag.

Advances & Technical Standards in Neurosurgery, Vol. 7. Ed. by H. Krayenbuehl et al. (Illus.). 270p. 1980. 57.90 (ISBN 0-387-81592-9). Springer-Verlag.

Advances in Agronomy, Vol. 33. Ed. by N. C. Brady. 1980. write for info. (ISBN 0-12-000733-9); lib. ed. 54.00 (ISBN 0-12-000786-X); microfiche 29.00 (ISBN 0-12-000787-8). Acad Pr.

Advances in Agronomy: Vol. 32, Cumulative Index for Volumes 1-30. Ed. by Albert S. Hunter. 1980. 18.50 (ISBN 0-12-000732-0); lib ed. 24.00 (ISBN 0-12-000784-3); microfiche ed. 13.00 (ISBN 0-12-000785-1). Acad Pr.

Advances in Allergology & Applied Immunology: Proceedings. International Congress of Allergology, 10th, Jerusalem, Israel, Nov. 1979. Ed. by A. Oehling et al. (Illus.). 680p. 1980. 145.00 (ISBN 0-08-025519-1). Pergamon.

Advances in Analysis of Behaviour: Reinforcement & the Organisation of Behaviour, Vol. 1. Michael D. Zeiler & Peter Harzem. LC 78-31697. (Wiley Series on Advances in Analysis of Behaviour). 1980. 55.00 (ISBN 0-471-27573-5, Pub. by Wiley-Interscience). Wiley.

Advances in Animal & Comparative Physiology: Proceedings of the 28th International Congress of Physiological Sciences, Budapest, 1980. G. Pethes & V. L. Frenyo. LC 80-41894. (Advances in Physiological Sciences: Vol. 20). (Illus.). 400p. 1981. 50.00 (ISBN 0-08-027341-6). Pergamon.

Advances in Applied Mechanics. Ed. by Richard Von Mises & Theodore Von Karman. Incl. Vol. 1. 1948. 44.00 (ISBN 0-12-002001-7); Vol. 2. 1951. 44.00 (ISBN 0-12-002002-5); Vol. 3. 1953. 44.00 (ISBN 0-12-002003-3); Vol. 4. Ed. by H. L. Dryden et al. 1956. 44.00 (ISBN 0-12-002004-1); Vol. 5. 1958. 44.00 (ISBN 0-12-002005-X); Vol. 6. 1960. 44.00 (ISBN 0-12-002006-8); Vol. 7. 1962. 44.00 (ISBN 0-12-002007-6); Vol. 8. 1964. 44.00 (ISBN 0-12-002008-4); Vol. 9. Ed. by G. Kuerti. 1966. 44.00 (ISBN 0-12-002009-2); Vol. 10. Fascicle 1. 1967. o.s.i. **(ISBN 0-12-002091-2); Vol. 11. Ed. by Chia-Sun Yih. 1971. 44.00 (ISBN 0-12-002011-4); Vol. 12. 1972. 44.00 (ISBN 0-12-002012-2); Vol. 13. 1973. 48.00 (ISBN 0-12-002013-0); Vol. 16. Ed. by Chia-Shun Yih. 1976. 51.75 (ISBN 0-12-002016-5); lib ed 66.50 (ISBN 0-12-002043-2); microfiche 337.25 (ISBN 0-686-66621-6); Vol. 17. Ed. by Chia-Shun Yih. 1977. 51.75 (ISBN 0-12-002017-3); lib. ed 66.50 (ISBN 0-12-002045-9); microfiche 37.25 (ISBN 0-686-66622-4); Vol. 18. Ed. by Chia-Shun Yih. 1979. 43.50 (ISBN 0-12-002018-1); lib. ed. 56.50 (ISBN 0-12-002047-5); microfiche 31.50 (ISBN 0-12-002048-3). LC 48-8503. Acad Pr.**

Advances in Applied Mechanics, Vol. 20. Ed. by C. S. Yih. (Serial Pub.). 1980. 31.50 (ISBN 0-12-002020-3); microfiche ed. 22.00 (ISBN 0-12-002051-3); 22.00 (ISBN 0-12-002052-1). Acad Pr.

Advances in Applied Microbiology. Ed. by Wayne W. Umbreit. Incl. Vol. 1. 1959. 48.00 (ISBN 0-12-002601-5); Vol. 2. 1960. 48.00 (ISBN 0-12-002602-3); Vol. 3. 1961. o.s.i. (ISBN 0-12-002603-1); Vol. 4. 1962. 48.00 (ISBN 0-12-002604-X); Vol. 5. 1963. 48.00 (ISBN 0-12-002605-8); Vol. 6. 1964. o.s.i. (ISBN 0-12-002606-6); Vol. 7. 1965. 48.00 o.s.i. (ISBN 0-12-002607-4); Vol. 8. 1966. (ISBN 0-12-002608-2); Vol. 9. 1968. 48.00 (ISBN 0-12-002609-0); Vol. 10. Ed. by D. Perlman & W. Umbreit. 1968. 48.00 (ISBN 0-12-002610-4); Vol. 11. Ed. by D. Perlman. 1969. 48.00 (ISBN 0-12-002611-2); Vol. 12. Ed. by D. Perlman & W. Umbreit. 1970. 48.00 (ISBN 0-12-002612-0); Vol. 13. Ed. by D. Perlman & W. Umbreit. 1970. 48.00 (ISBN 0-12-002613-9); Vol. 14. Ed. by D. Perlman & W. Umbreit. 1971. 48.00 (ISBN 0-12-002614-7); Vol. 15. Ed. by D. Perlman. 1972. 48.00 (ISBN 0-12-002615-5); Vol. 16. Ed. by David Perlman. 1973. 48.00 (ISBN 0-12-002616-3); Vol. 21. Ed. by David Perlman. 1977. 39.00 (ISBN 0-12-002621-X); Vol. 22. Ed. by David Perlman. 1977. 37.50 (ISBN 0-12-002622-8); Vol. 23. Ed. by David Perlman. 1978. 29.50 (ISBN 0-12-002623-6); Vol. 24. Ed. by David Perlman. 1978. 31.50 (ISBN 0-12-002624-4); Vol. 25. 1979. 31.00 (ISBN 0-12-002625-2); Vol. 26. 1980. 29.50 (ISBN 0-12-002626-0). Acad Pr.

Advances in Applied Microbiology, Vol. 27. Ed. by D. Perlman & A. I. Laskin. (Serial Publication). 1981. 26.00 (ISBN 0-12-002627-9). Acad Pr.

Advances in Applied Solid State Science, Supplement, 2A: Silicon Integrated Circuits. Ed. by D. Kahng. (Serial Publication). 1981. price not set (ISBN 0-12-002954-5); price not set lib. ed. (ISBN 0-12-002955-3); price not set microfiche ed. (ISBN 0-12-002956-1). Acad Pr.

Advances in Archaeological Methods & Theory, Vol. 3. Ed. by Michael B. Schiffer. (Serial Publication). 1980. 39.50 (ISBN 0-12-003103-5). Acad Pr.

Advances in Atomic & Molecular Physics, Vols. 1-14. Ed. by D. R. Bates et al. Incl. Vol. 1. 1965. 50.00 (ISBN 0-12-003801-3); Vol. 2. 1966. 50.00 (ISBN 0-12-003802-1); Vol. 3. 1968. 50.00 (ISBN 0-12-003803-X); Vol. 4. 1968. 50.00 (ISBN 0-12-003804-8); Vol. 5. 1969. 50.00 (ISBN 0-12-003805-6); Vol. 6. 1970. 50.00 (ISBN 0-12-003806-4); Vol. 7. 1971. 50.00 (ISBN 0-12-003807-2); Vol. 8. 1972. 50.00 (ISBN 0-12-003808-0); Vol. 9. 1974. 50.00 (ISBN 0-12-003809-9); Vol. 10. 1974. 50.00 (ISBN 0-12-003810-2); Vol. 11. 1976. 67.00 (ISBN 0-686-66770-0); lib ed. 86.25 (ISBN 0-12-003874-9); microfiche 47.75 (ISBN 0-12-003875-7); Vol. 12. 1976. 59.00 (ISBN 0-12-003812-9); lib ed. 76.00 (ISBN 0-12-003876-5); microfiche 42.25 (ISBN 0-12-003877-3); Vol. 13. 1978. 58.00 (ISBN 0-12-003813-7); lib ed. 74.50 (ISBN 0-12-003878-1); microfiche 36.00 (ISBN 0-12-003879-X); Vol. 14. 1979. 48.50 (ISBN 0-12-003814-5); lib ed. 62.50 (ISBN 0-12-003880-3); microfiche 35.00 (ISBN 0-12-003881-1). Acad Pr.

Advances in Atomic & Molecular Physics, Vol. 16. Ed. by Sir David R. Bates & Benjamin Bederson. LC 65-18423. 1980. write for info. (ISBN 0-12-003816-1); lib. bdg. 61.50 (ISBN 0-12-003884-6); microfiche ed. 33.50 (ISBN 0-12-003885-4). Acad Pr.

Advances in Behavioral Pharmacology, Vol. 2. Ed. by Travis Thompson & Peter B. Dews. LC 74-10187. 1979. 25.50 (ISBN 0-12-004702-0); library ed. 33.00 (ISBN 0-12-004772-1); microfiche 18.00 (ISBN 0-12-004773-X). Acad Pr.

Advances in Behaviour Research & Therapy, Vol. 2. Ed. by S. Rachman. (Illus.). 186p. 1980. 84.00 (ISBN 0-08-027110-3). Pergamon.

Advances in Biochemical Psychopharmacology, Vol. 24. Ed. by F. Cattabeni et al. 680p. 1980. text ed. 62.50 (ISBN 0-89004-375-2). Raven.

Advances in Biological Psychiatry, Vol. 6. Ed. by D. Kemali. (Illus.). 128p. 1981. pap. 48.00 (ISBN 3-8055-2420-X). S Karger.

Advances in Biomedical Engineering, Pt. I. Cooney. 360p. 1980. 35.00 (ISBN 0-8247-6925-2). Dekker.

Advances in Biomedical Engineering. Ed. by R. M. Kenedi. Incl. Vol. 1. 1971. 34.50 (ISBN 0-12-004901-5); Vol. 2. Ed. by J. H. Brown & James F. Dickson, 3rd. 1972. 48.00 (ISBN 0-12-004902-3); Vol. 3. 1973. 48.00 (ISBN 0-12-004903-1). Acad Pr.

Advances in Biomedical Engineering, Pt. 2. Ed. by David O. Cooney. (Biomedical Engineering & Instrumentation Ser.: Vol. 6). (Illus.). 368p. 1980. 39.50 (ISBN 0-8247-6994-5). Dekker.

Advances in Biophysics, 12 vols, Vols. 7-12. Ed. by M. Kotani. (Illus.). Vols. 7-10. 19.50 ea. Vol. 7, 1975 (ISBN 0-8391-0104-X). Vol. 8, 1975 (ISBN 0-8391-0105-8). Vol. 9, 1977 (ISBN 0-8391-0106-6). Vol. 10, 1978 (ISBN 0-8391-0107-4). Vols. 11 & 12. 29.50 ea. Vol. 11, 1979 (ISBN 0-8391-0108-2). Vol. 12, 1979 (ISBN 0-8391-0109-0). Vol. 13. 39.50 (ISBN 0-8391-0110-4). Univ Park.

Advances in Cancer Research. Incl. Vol. 19. 1974. 47.00 (ISBN 0-12-006619-X); Vol. 20. 1974. 47.00 (ISBN 0-12-006620-3); Vol. 21. 1976. 47.00 (ISBN 0-12-006621-1); Vol. 22. 1975. 47.00 (ISBN 0-12-006622-X); Vol. 23. 1976. 48.50 (ISBN 0-12-006623-8); Vol. 24. 1977. 48.50 (ISBN 0-12-006624-6); Vol. 25. 1977. 48.50 (ISBN 0-12-006625-4). (Serial Publication). Acad Pr.

Advances in Cancer Research. Ed. by Jesse P. Greenstein & Alexander Haddow. Incl. Vol. 1. 1953. 47.00 (ISBN 0-12-006601-7); Vol. 2. 1954. 47.00 (ISBN 0-12-006602-5); Vol. 3. 1955. 47.00 (ISBN 0-12-006603-3); Vol. 4. 1956. 47.00 (ISBN 0-12-006604-1); Vol. 5. 1958. 47.00 (ISBN 0-12-006605-X); Vol. 6. Ed. by Alexander Haddow & Sidney Weinhouse. 1962. 47.00 (ISBN 0-12-006606-8); Vol. 7. 1963. 47.00 (ISBN 0-12-006607-6); Vol. 8. 1964. 47.00 (ISBN 0-12-006608-4); Vol. 9. 1965. 47.00 (ISBN 0-12-006609-2); Vol. 10. 1967. 47.00 (ISBN 0-12-006610-6); Vol. 11. 1969. 47.00 (ISBN 0-12-006611-4); Vol. 12. Ed. by George Klein & Sidney Weinhouse. 1969. 47.00 (ISBN 0-12-006612-2); Vol. 13. 1970. 47.00 (ISBN 0-12-006613-0); Vol. 14. 1971. 47.00 (ISBN 0-12-006614-9); Vol. 15. 1972. 47.00 (ISBN 0-12-006615-7); Vol. 16. 1972. 47.00 (ISBN 0-12-006616-5); Vol. 17. 1973. 47.00 (ISBN 0-12-006617-3); Vol. 18. 1973. 47.00 (ISBN 0-12-006618-1). Acad Pr.

Advances in Cancer Research, Vol. 31. Ed. by George Klein & Sidney Weinhouse. LC 52-13360. 1980. 35.00 (ISBN 0-12-006631-9). Acad Pr.

Advances in Cancer Research, Vol. 32. Ed. by George Klein & Sidney Weinhouse. 1980. 36.00 (ISBN 0-12-006632-7). Acad Pr.

Advances in Cancer Research, Vol. 33. Ed. by George Klein & Sidney Weinhouse. 1980. 37.50 (ISBN 0-12-006633-5). Acad Pr.

Advances in Cancer Research, Vol. 34. Ed. by Sidney Weinhouse & George Klein. (Serial Publication Ser.). 1981. write for info. (ISBN 0-12-006634-3). Acad Pr.

Advances in Carbohydrate Chemistry. Ed. by Ward Pigman & Melville L. Wolfrom. Incl. Vol. 1. 1945 (ISBN 0-12-007201-7); Vol. 2. 1946 (ISBN 0-12-007202-5); Vol. 3. 1948 (ISBN 0-12-007203-3); Vol. 4. 1949 (ISBN 0-12-007204-1); Vol. 5. Ed. by C. S. Hudson & S. M. Cantor. 1950 (ISBN 0-12-007205-X); Vol. 6. 1951 (ISBN 0-12-007206-8); Vol. 7. Ed. by C. S. Hudson et al. 1952 (ISBN 0-12-007207-6); Vol. 8. Ed. by C. S. Hudson & Melville Wolfrom. 1953 (ISBN 0-12-007208-4); Vol. 9. Ed. by Melville L. Wolfrom & R. Stuart Tipson. 1954 (ISBN 0-12-007209-2); Vol. 10. 1955 (ISBN 0-12-007210-6); Vol. 11. 1956 (ISBN 0-12-007211-4); Vol. 12. 1957 (ISBN 0-12-007212-2); Vol. 13. 1958 (ISBN 0-12-007213-0); Vol. 14. 1959 (ISBN 0-12-007214-9); Vol. 15. 1960 (ISBN 0-12-007215-7); Vol. 16. 1962 (ISBN 0-12-007216-5); Vol. 17. 1963 (ISBN 0-12-007217-3); Vol. 18. 1963 (ISBN 0-12-007218-1); Vol. 19. 1964 (ISBN 0-12-007219-X); Vol. 20. 1965 (ISBN 0-12-007220-3); Vol. 21. 1967 (ISBN 0-12-007221-1); Vol. 22. 1967 (ISBN 0-12-007222-X); Vol. 23. 1968 (ISBN 0-12-007223-8); Vol. 24. 1970 (ISBN 0-12-007224-6); Vol. 25. 1971. 49.50 (ISBN 0-12-007225-4); Vol. 26. Ed. by Stuart R. Tipson & Derek Horton. 1971. 49.50 (ISBN 0-12-007226-2); Vol. 27. 1972. 49.50 (ISBN 0-12-007227-0); Vol. 28. 1973. 58.00 (ISBN 0-12-007228-9); Vol. 29. 1974. 58.00 (ISBN 0-12-007229-7). Vols. 1-19. 49.50 ea.; Vols. 20-24. 49.50 ea. Acad Pr.

Advances in Carbohydrate Chemistry & Biochemistry, Vol. 38. Dereck Horton & R. Stuart Tipson. 1981. write for info. (ISBN 0-12-007238-6); lib. bdg. write for info. (ISBN 0-12-007288-2); write for info. microfiche (ISBN 0-12-007289-0). Acad Pr.

Advances in Carbohydrate Chemistry & Biochemistry, Vol. 39. Ed. by R. Stuart Tipson & Derek Horton. (Serial Publication Ser.). write for info. Acad Pr.

Advances in Cardiology, Vol. 28. Ed. by H. Abel. (Illus.). 240p. 1980. 66.00 (ISBN 3-8055-1185-X). S Karger.

Advances in Cardiovascular Nursing. Edward R. Diethrich. LC 79-9375. 150p. 1979. pap. text ed. 19.95 (ISBN 0-87619-457-9). R J Brady.

Advances in Catalysis, Vol. 27. Ed. by D. D. Eley et al. 1979. 47.00 (ISBN 0-12-007827-9); lib ed. 60.00 (ISBN 0-12-007880-5); microfiche 35.50 (ISBN 0-12-007881-3). Acad Pr.

Advances in Catalysis, Vol. 29. Ed. by D. D. Eley et al. LC 49-7755. 1980. 45.00 (ISBN 0-12-007829-5); lib. bdg. 58.50 (ISBN 0-12-007884-8); microfiche ed. 31.50 (ISBN 0-12-007885-6). Acad Pr.

Advances in Catalysis & Related Subjects, Vol. 29. W. G. Frankenburg et al. Date not set. 45.00 (ISBN 0-12-007829-5). Acad Pr.

Advances in Catering Technology. Ed. by G. Glew. (Illus.). xii, 450p. 1980. 99.00x (ISBN 0-85334-844-8). Burgess-Intl Ideas.

Advances in Cell Culture, Vol. I. Ed. by Karl Maramorosh. (Serial Publication Ser.). 1981. write for info. (ISBN 0-12-007901-1). Acad Pr.

Advances in Cell Culture, Vol. 2. Ed. by Karl Maramorosh. (Serial Publication). 1981. price not set (ISBN 0-12-007902-X). Acad Pr.

Advances in Cellular Neurobiology, Vol. 1. Ed. by S. Fedoroff & L. Hertz. 1980. 39.50 (ISBN 0-12-008301-9). Acad Pr.

Advances in Cellular Neurobiology, Vol. 2. Ed. by S. Federoff & L. Hertz. 1981. write for info. (ISBN 0-12-008302-7). Acad Pr.

Advances in Chemical Engineering. Ed. by Thomas B. Drew & John W. Hoopes, Jr. Incl. Vol. 1. 1956. 52.50 (ISBN 0-12-008501-1); Vol. 2. 1958. 52.50 (ISBN 0-12-008502-X); Vol. 3. Ed. by Thomas B. Drew et al. 1962. 52.50 (ISBN 0-12-008503-8); Vol. 4. 1963. 52.50 (ISBN 0-12-008504-6); Vol. 5. 1964. 52.50 (ISBN 0-12-008505-4); Vol. 6. 1966. 52.50 (ISBN 0-12-008506-2); Vol. 7. 1968. 52.50 (ISBN 0-12-008507-0); Vol. 8. 1970. 52.50 (ISBN 0-12-008508-9); Vol. 9. 1974. 52.50 (ISBN 0-12-008509-7). Acad Pr.

Advances in Chemical Engineering, Vol. 10. Thomas B. Drew & John W. Hoopes. (Serial Publication). 1978. 43.50 (ISBN 0-12-008510-0). Acad Pr.

Advances in Chemical Physics, Vol. 26. Ed. by I. Prigogine. 317p. 1974. 32.50 (ISBN 0-471-69931-4). Krieger.

Advances in Chemical Physics, Vols. 27, 31-37, 43-44 & 46. Ed. by I. Prigogine & Stuart A. Rice. Incl. Vol. 27. 50.50 (ISBN 0-471-69932-2); Vol. 31. 45.50 (ISBN 0-471-69933-0); Vol. 32. 35.95 (ISBN 0-471-69934-9); Vol. 33. 41.95 (ISBN 0-471-69935-7); Vol. 34. 41.50 (ISBN 0-471-69936-5); Vol. 35. 42.50 (ISBN 0-471-69937-3); Vol. 36. 52.50 (ISBN 0-471-02274-8); Vol. 37. 40.50 (ISBN 0-471-03459-2); Vol. 43. 1980. 36.50 (ISBN 0-471-05741-X); Vol. 44. 1980. 65.00 (ISBN 0-471-06025-9); Vol. 46. 432p. 1980. 42.50 (ISBN 0-471-08295-3). LC 58-9935 (Pub. by Wiley-Interscience). Wiley.

Advances in Chemical Physics, Vol. 48. I. Prigogine & Stuart A. Rice. (Advances in Chemical Physics Ser.). 530p. 1981. 53.00 (ISBN 0-471-08294-5, Pub. by Wiley-Interscience). Wiley.

Advances in Chemical Radio-Sensitization. (Illus.). 156p. (Orig.). 1975. pap. 10.75 (ISBN 92-0-111474-5, IAEA). Unipub.

Advances in Child Development & Behavior. Ed. by Hayne Reese. Incl. Vol. 1. 1964. 36.00 (ISBN 0-12-009701-X); Vol. 2. Ed. by Lewis P. Lipsitt & Charles G Spiker. 1965. 36.00 (ISBN 0-12-009702-8); Vol. 3. 1967. 36.00 (ISBN 0-12-009703-6); Vol. 4. Ed. by Lewis P Lipsitt & Hayne W. Reese. 1969. 36.00 (ISBN 0-12-009704-4); Vol. 5. 1970. 36.00 (ISBN 0-12-009705-2); Vol. 6. 1971. 36.00 (ISBN 0-12-009706-0); Vol. 7. 1973. 32.50 (ISBN 0-12-009707-9); Vol. 8. 1974. 32.50 (ISBN 0-12-009708-7); Vol. 9. 1974. 32.50 (ISBN 0-12-009709-5); Vol. 10. 1975. 32.50 (ISBN 0-12-009710-9); lib. ed. 43.00 (ISBN 0-12-009774-5); microfiche 23.50 (ISBN 0-12-009775-3); Vol. 11. 1976. 32.50 (ISBN 0-12-009711-7); lib ed. 43.00 (ISBN 0-12-009776-1); microfiche 23.50 (ISBN 0-12-009777-X); Vol. 12. 1978. 28.00 (ISBN 0-12-009712-5); lib ed. 36.00 (ISBN 0-12-009778-8); microfiche 19.50 (ISBN 0-12-009779-6); Vol. 13. 1979. 26.00 (ISBN 0-12-009713-3); lib ed. 33.50 (ISBN 0-12-009780-X); microfiche 18.50 (ISBN 0-12-009781-8). LC 63-23237. Acad Pr.

Advances in Child Development & Behavior, Vol. 15. Ed. by H. W. Reese & L. P. Lipsitt. 1980. 28.00 (ISBN 0-12-009715-X); lib. bdg. 36.50 (ISBN 0-12-009784-2); microfiche ed. 19.50 (ISBN 0-12-009785-0). Acad Pr.

Advances in Chromatography, Vol. 17. Giddings et al. 1979. 36.00 (ISBN 0-8247-6902-3). Dekker.

Advances in Chromatography, Vol. 19. Giddings. 336p. Date not set. 39.75. Dekker.

Advances in Civil Engineering Through Engineering Mechanics: Proceedings. American Society of Civil Engineers, Conference, North Carolina State Univ., May 1977. 640p. 1977. pap. text ed. 36.00 (ISBN 0-87262-087-5). Am Soc Civil Eng.

Advances in Clinical Chemistry, Vol. 20. Ed. by Oscar Bodansky & Latner. 1978. 42.50 (ISBN 0-12-010320-6); lib ed. 47.25 (ISBN 0-12-010380-X); microfiche 27.00 (ISBN 0-12-010381-8). Acad Pr.

Advances in Clinical Chemistry, Vol. 21. Ed. by A. L. Latner & Morton K. Schwartz. LC 58-12341. (Serial Publication). 1980. 29.00 (ISBN 0-12-010321-4); library ed. 37.50 (ISBN 0-12-010382-6); microfiche 20.50 (ISBN 0-12-010383-4). Acad Pr.

Advances in Clinical Cytology. Leopold G. Koss & Dulcie V. Coleman. LC 80-49874. 380p. 1980. text ed. 66.95 (ISBN 0-407-00174-3). Butterworths.

Advances in Clinical Psychoanalysis. John E. Gedo. (Illus.). 250p. 1981. text ed. 29.95 (ISBN 0-8236-0125-0, 00-0125). Intl Univs Pr.

Advances in Comparative Physiology & Biochemistry. Ed. by O. Lowenstein. Incl. Vol. 5. 1974. 40.50 (ISBN 0-12-011505-0); Vol. 6. 1975. 42.50 (ISBN 0-12-011506-9); lib. ed. 52.00 (ISBN 0-12-011574-3); microfiche 29.00 (ISBN 0-12-011575-1). Acad Pr.

Advances in Comparative Physiology & Biochemistry, Vols. 1-4. Ed. by O. E. Lowenstein. 52.50 ea. Vol. 1, 1962 (ISBN 0-12-011501-8). Vol. 2 (ISBN 0-12-011502-6). Vol. 3. o.s.i (ISBN 0-12-011503-4). Vol. 4, 1971 (ISBN 0-12-011504-2). Acad Pr.

Advances in Comparative Physiology & Biochemistry, Vol. 7. Ed. by O. Lowenstein. 1978. 42.50 (ISBN 0-12-011507-7); lib. ed. 54.00 (ISBN 0-12-001576-5); microfiche 31.00 (ISBN 0-12-011577-8). Acad Pr.

Advances in Composite Materials. Ed. by G. Piatti. (Illus.). 1978. text ed. 91.10x (ISBN 0-85334-770-0, Pub. by Applied Science). Burgess-Intl Ideas.

Advances in Composite Materials: Proceedings of the Third International Conference on Composite Materials, Paris, France, 26-29 August, 1980. Ed. by A. R. Bunsell et al. LC 80-40997. 2000p. 1980. 200.00 (ISBN 0-08-026717-3). Pergamon.

Advances in Computer Communications. rev. ed. Ed. by Wesley W. Chu. LC 75-31381. (Illus.). 1977. pap. 27.00 o.p. (ISBN 0-685-79343-5). Artech Hse.

Advances in Concrete Slab Technology: Materials Design, Construction & Finishing. R. K. Dhir & J. G. Munday. 1980. 115.00 (ISBN 0-08-023256-6). Pergamon.

Advances in Consumer Research: Proceedings of 1979 Meeting, Vol. VII. Ed. by Gerald Olson. softcover 21.00 (ISBN 0-915552-05-1). Assn Consumer Res.

Advances in Control & Dynamic Systems: Theory & Application, Vol. 17. Ed. by C. T. Leondes. (Serial Publication). 1981. price not set (ISBN 0-12-012717-2). Acad Pr.

Advances in Cryogenic Engineering (Materials, Vol. 26. Ed. by A. F. Clark & R. P. Reed. 720p. 1981. 59.50 (ISBN 0-306-40531-8, Plenum Pr). Plenum Pub.

Advances in Cyclic Nucleotide Research, Vol. 4. Ed. by Paul Greengard & G. Alan Robison. LC 71-181305. 498p. 1974. 39.00 (ISBN 0-911216-76-6). Raven.

Advances in Cyclic Nucleotide Research, Vol. 6. Ed. by P. Greengard & G. A. Robison. LC 71-181305. 368p. 1975. 34.50 (ISBN 0-89004-042-7). Raven.

Advances in Cyclic Nucleotide Research, Vol. 7. Ed. by Paul Greengard & G. Alan Robison. LC 71-181305. 1976. 34.50 (ISBN 0-89004-107-5). Raven.

Advances in Cyclic Nucleotide Research, Vol. 8. Ed. by Paul Greengard & G. Alan Robison. LC 71-181305. 1977. 43.50 (ISBN 0-89004-169-5). Raven.

Advances in Cyclic Nucleotide Research, Vol. 11. Ed. by Paul Greengard & G. Alan Robison. LC 71-181305. 1979. text ed. 39.00 (ISBN 0-89004-363-9). Raven.

Advances in Cyclic Nucleotide Research, Vol. 13. Ed. by G. Alan Robison & Paul Greengard. 352p. 1980. text ed. 38.00 (ISBN 0-89004-471-6). Raven.

Advances in Cyclic Nucleotide Research Series, 2 vols. Ed. by P. Greengard & G. A. Robison. Incl. Vol. 2. New Assay Methods for Cyclic Nucleotides. 145p. 1972. 19.00 (ISBN 0-911216-21-9); Vol. 3. 250p. 1973. 32.00 (ISBN 0-911216-38-3). LC 71-181305. Raven.

Advances in Cyclic Nucleotide Research: Proceedings. International Conference on Cyclic Amp, 2nd, July, 1974. Ed. by G. I. Drummond et al. LC 74-24679. (Advances in Cyclic Nucleotide Research Ser.: Vol. 5). 1975. 67.00 (ISBN 0-89004-021-4). Raven.

Advances in Cyclic Nucleotide Research: Proceedings, Vol. 9. International Conference on Cyclic Nucleotide, 3rd, New Orleans, la., July 1977. Ed. by William J. George & Louis Ignarro. LC 77-84555. 1978. 72.50 (ISBN 0-89004-240-3). Raven.

Advances in Cytopharmacology, Vol. 1. International Symposium on Cell Biology & Cytopharmacology, First. Ed. by F. Clementi & B. Ceccarelli. LC 70-84115. (Illus.). 1971. 48.00 (ISBN 0-911216-09-X). Raven.

Advances in Data Communications Management, Vol. 1. Ed. by Thomas A. Rullo. 225p. 1980. 29.50 (ISBN 0-85501-605-1). Heyden.

Advances in Data Processing Management, Vol. 1. Ed. by Thomas A. Rullo. 225p. 1980. 27.50 (ISBN 0-85501-601-9). Heyden.

Advances in Desert & Arid Land Technology & Development, Vol. 2. A. Bishay & W. B. McGinnies. 350p. 1981. price not set (ISBN 3-7186-0002-1). Harwood Academic.

Advances in Developmental Psychology, Vol. 1. Ed. by Michael E. Lamb & Ann L. Brown. (Advances in Developmental Psychology Ser.). 400p. 1981. prof. ref. 24.95 (ISBN 0-89859-094-9). L Erlbaum Assocs.

Advances in Distributed Processing Management, Vol. 1. Ed. by Thomas A. Rullo. 225p. 1980. 32.50 (ISBN 0-85501-604-3). Heyden.

Advances in Drug Research. Ed. by N. J. Harper & A. B. Simmonds. Incl. Vol. 1. 1964. 28.00 (ISBN 0-12-013301-6); Vol. 2. 1966. 28.00 (ISBN 0-12-013302-4); Vol. 3. 1966. 29.50 (ISBN 0-12-013303-2); Vol. 5. 1970. o.s.i. (ISBN 0-12-013305-9); Vol. 6. 1972. 18.65 o.s.i. (ISBN 0-12-013306-7); Vol. 7. 1974. 32.50 (ISBN 0-12-013307-5). Acad Pr.

Advances in Drying, Vol. 1. Ed. by Arun S. Mujumdar. LC 80-10432. (Illus.). 301p. 1980. text ed. 55.00 (ISBN 0-89116-185-6). Hemisphere Pub.

Advances in Ecological Research. Ed. by J. B. Cragg. Vol. 1 1963. 29.00 o.s.i. (ISBN 0-12-013901-4); Vol. 2 1965. 35.50 (ISBN 0-12-013902-2); Vol. 3 1966. 45.00 (ISBN 0-12-013903-0); Vol. 4 1967. 43.00 (ISBN 0-12-013904-9); Vol. 6 1969. 32.50 (ISBN 0-12-013906-5); Vol. 7 1971. 34.00 (ISBN 0-12-013907-3); Vol. 8 1974. 57.50 (ISBN 0-12-013908-1); Vol. 9 1975. 55.00 (ISBN 0-12-013909-X); Vol. 10, 1978. 24.50 (ISBN 0-12-013910-3). Acad Pr.

Advances in Ecological Research, Vol. 11. Ed. by J. B. Cragg. 1981. 66.50 (ISBN 0-12-013911-1). Acad Pr.

Advances in Electrochemistry & Electrochemical Engineering. Ed. by Heinz Gerischer & Charles W. Tobias. LC 61-15021. Vol. 10, 1977. 42.50 (ISBN 0-471-87527-9, Pub. by Wiley-Interscience); Vol. 11, 1978. 37.50 (ISBN 0-471-87528-7). Wiley.

Advances in Electrochemistry & Electrochemical Engineering, Vol. 12. Heinz Gerischer. Ed. by Charles W. Tobias. 40404p. 1981. write for info. (ISBN 0-471-87530-9, Pub. by Wiley-Interscience). Wiley.

Advances in Electronic & Electron Physics, Vol. 55. Ed. by L. Marton & Claire Marton. (Serial Publication). 1981. 47.50 (ISBN 0-12-014655-X); lib. bdg. 62.00 (ISBN 0-12-014710-6); microfiche ed. 33.50 (ISBN 0-12-014711-4). Acad Pr.

Advances in Electronic Circuit Packaging, Vol. 4. Ed. by M. A. Marese. 490p. 1964. 25.00 (ISBN 0-306-37014-X, Plenum Pr). Plenum Pub.

Advances in Electronic Circuit Packaging, Vol. 5. Ed. by L. L. Rosine. 297p. 1965. 25.00 (ISBN 0-686-64908-7, Plenum Pr). Plenum Pub.

Advances in Electronics & Electron Physics. Ed. by L. Marton. Incl. Vols. 1-5. 1948-53. 49.50 ea. Vol. 1 (ISBN 0-12-014501-4). Vol. 2 (ISBN 0-12-014502-2). Vol. 3 (ISBN 0-12-014503-0). Vol. 4 (ISBN 0-12-014504-9). Vol. 5 (ISBN 0-12-014505-7); Vols. 6-8. 1954-56. 49.50 ea. Vol. 6 (ISBN 0-12-014506-5). Vol. 7 (ISBN 0-12-014507-3). Vol. 8 (ISBN 0-12-014508-1); Vols. 9-10. 1957-58. 49.50 ea. Vol. 9 (ISBN 0-12-014509-X). Vol. 10 (ISBN 0-12-014510-3); Vol. 11. 1959. 49.50 (ISBN 0-12-014511-1); Vol. 12. Proceedings. Symposium on Photo-Electronic Image Devices - 1st. Ed. by J. D. McGee & W. L. Wilcock. 1960. 36.50 (ISBN 0-12-014512-X); Vols. 13-15. 1960-61. 49.50 ea. Vol. 13 (ISBN 0-12-014513-8). Vol. 14 (ISBN 0-12-014514-6). Vol. 15 (ISBN 0-12-014515-4); Vol. 16. Proceedings. Symposium on Photo-Electronic Image Devices - 2nd. Ed. by J. D. McGee et al. 1962. 68.00 (ISBN 0-12-014516-2); Vol. 17. 1963. 49.50 (ISBN 0-12-014517-0); Vol. 18. 1963. 49.50 (ISBN 0-12-014518-9); Vol. 19. 1964. 49.50 (ISBN 0-12-014519-7); Vols. 20-21. 1965-66. 49.50 ea. Vol. 20 (ISBN 0-12-014520-0). Vol. 21 (ISBN 0-12-014521-9); Vol. 22. Proceedings. Symposium on Photo-Electronic Image Devices - 3rd. Ed. by J. D. McGee et al. 1966. Pt. A. 69.00 (ISBN 0-12-014522-7); Pt. B. 41.00 (ISBN 0-12-014542-1); Vol. 23. 1967. 49.50 (ISBN 0-12-014523-5); Vol. 24. 1968. 49.50 (ISBN 0-12-014524-3); Vol. 25. 1968. 49.50 (ISBN 0-12-014525-1); Vol. 26. 1969. 49.50 (ISBN 0-12-014526-X); Vol. 27. 1970. 49.50 (ISBN 0-12-014527-8); Vol. 28. Proceedings. Symposium on Photo-Electronic Image Devices - 4th. Ed. by J. D. McGee et al. 1969. Pt. A. 76.00 (ISBN 0-12-014528-6); Pt. B, 1970. 77.50 (ISBN 0-12-014548-0); Vol. 29. 1970. 49.50 (ISBN 0-12-014529-4); Vol. 30. 1971. 49.50 (ISBN 0-12-014530-8); Vol. 31. 1972. 49.50 (ISBN 0-12-014531-6); Vol. 32. 1973. 49.50 (ISBN 0-12-014532-4); Vol. 33. Proceedings. Symposium on Photo-Electronic Image Devices - 5th. Ed. by J. D. McGee et al. 1972. Pt. A, 1972. 58.00, o.s.i. (ISBN 0-12-014533-2); Pt. A. 84.00 (ISBN 0-12-014533-2). Pt. B, 1973. Acad Pr.

Advances in Electronics & Electron Physics, Vols. 34 & 35. Ed. by L. Marton. Vol. 34, 1973. 51.50 (ISBN 0-12-014534-0); Vol. 35, 1974. 51.50 (ISBN 0-12-014535-9). Acad Pr.

Advances in Electronics & Electron Physics: Supplements. Ed. by L. Marton. Incl. Suppl. 1. Electroluminescence & Related Effects. Henry F. Ivey. 1963. 44.00 (ISBN 0-12-014561-8); Suppl. 2. Optical Masers. George Birnbaum. 1964. 40.50 (ISBN 0-12-014562-6); Suppl. 3. Narrow Angle Electron Guns & Cathode Ray Tubes. Hilary Moss. 1968. 33.00 (ISBN 0-12-014563-4); Suppl. 5. Linear Ferrite Devices for Microwave Applications. W. H. Von Aulock & C. E. Fay. 1969. 41.00 (ISBN 0-12-014565-0); Suppl. 6. Electron Probe Microanalysis. A. J. Tousimis & L. Marton. 1969. 52.75 (ISBN 0-12-014566-9); Suppl. 7. Quadruples in Electron Lens Design. P. W. Hawkes. 1970. 49.00 (ISBN 0-12-014567-7); Suppl. 9. Sequency Theory Foundations & Applications. Ed. by Henning F. Harmuth. 1977. 52.75 (ISBN 0-12-014569-3); Suppl. 11. Acoustic Imaging with Electronic Circuits. Ed. by Henning F. Harmuth. 1979. 32.00 (ISBN 0-12-014571-5). Acad Pr.

Advances in Electronics & Electron Physics, Supplement 13A: Applied Charged Particle Optics. L. Marton. 1980. 41.00 (ISBN 0-12-014573-1). Acad Pr.

Advances in Electronics & Electron Physics, Supplement 14: Nonsinusoidal Waves for Radar & Radio Communication. Ed. by C. Marton & H. F. Harmuth. (Serial Publication Ser.). 1981. write for info. (ISBN 0-12-014575-8). Acad Pr.

Advances in Environmental Science & Engineering, Vol. 4. Ed. by James Pfafflin & Edward Ziegler. 240p. 1981. write for info. (ISBN 0-677-16250-2). Gordon.

Advances in Environmental Science & Technology. Ed. by James N. Pitts, Jr. & Robert L. Metcalf. LC 69-18013. 1977. Vol. 4. 30.95 o.p. (ISBN 0-471-69087-2); Vol. 7. 43.50 (ISBN 0-471-01365-X, Pub. by Wiley-Interscience). Wiley.

Advances in Enzyme Regulation: Proceedings of the 17th Symposium on Regulation of Enzyme Activity & Synthesis in Normal & Neoplastic Tissues, Indiana University School of Medicine, Indianapolis, 2-3 October 1978, Vol. 17. Ed. by G. Weber. (Illus.). 1979. 110.00 (ISBN 0-08-024424-6). Pergamon.

Advances in Enzymology. F. F. Nord. Incl. Vol. 14. 1953. 28.50 (ISBN 0-470-64647-0); Vol. 15. 1954. 31.50 (ISBN 0-470-64680-2); Vol. 23. 1961. 34.00 (ISBN 0-470-64944-5); Vol. 25. 1963. 34.00 (ISBN 0-470-64948-8). LC 41-9213 (Pub. by Wiley-Interscience). Wiley.

Advances in Enzymology & Related Areas of Molecular Biology. Ed. by Alton Meister. Incl. Vol. 36, 1972 (ISBN 0-471-59171-8). Vol. 37, 1973 (ISBN 0-471-59172-6). Vol. 38, 1973 (ISBN 0-471-59173-4). Vol. 39, 1973 (ISBN 0-471-59174-2). Vol. 40, 1974 (ISBN 0-471-59175-0). Vol. 41, 1974 (ISBN 0-471-59176-9); Vol. 42, 1975 (ISBN 0-471-59177-7). Vol. 43, 1975 (ISBN 0-471-59178-5). LC 41-9213. (Pub. by Wiley-Interscience). Wiley.

Advances in Enzymology & Related Areas of Molecular Biology. Ed. by Alton Meister. Vol. 45, 1977. 36.50 (ISBN 0-471-02726-X, Pub. by Wiley-Interscience); Vol. 46, 1978. 41.50 (ISBN 0-471-02993-9); Vol. 47, 1978. 42.50 (ISBN 0-471-04116-5); Vol. 51, 1980, 225p. 29.50 (ISBN 0-471-05653-7). Wiley.

Advances in Enzymology & Related Areas of Molecular Biology, Vol. 52. Alton Meister. 350p. 1981. 27.50 (ISBN 0-471-08120-5, Pub. by Wiley-Interscience). Wiley.

Advances in Ephemeroptera Biology. Ed. by John F. Flannagan & K. Eric Marshall. 556p. 1980. 49.50 (ISBN 0-306-40357-9, Plenum Pr). Plenum Pub.

Advances in Epileptology: Eleventh International Epilepsy Symposium. Ed. by Raffaele Canger et al. 510p. 1980. text ed. 48.00 (ISBN 0-89004-510-0). Raven.

Advances in Epileptology: Proceedings. Epilepsy International Symposium, 10th. Ed. by Juhn Wade & J. Kiffin Penry. 594p. 1980. text ed. 52.00 (ISBN 0-89004-511-9). Raven.

Advances in Epileptology Research. Ed. by J. Kiffin Penry & Mogens Dam. (Twelfth Eplilepsy International Symposium, Copenhagen, Denmark). 1981. text ed. price not set (ISBN 0-89004-611-5). Raven.

Advances in Epileptology, 1977: Psychology, Pharmacotherapy & New Diagnostic Approaches. Ed. by H. Meinardi & A. J. Rowan. 468p. 1978. pap. text ed. 37.75 (ISBN 90-265-0273-7, Pub. by Swets Pub Serv Holland). Swets North Am.

Advances in European Geothermal Research. Ed. by A. S. Strub & P. Ungemach. 1096p. 1980. lib. bdg. 63.00 (ISBN 90-277-1138-0, Pub. by D. Reidel). Kluwer Boston.

Advances in Experimental Social Processes, Vol. 2. Clayton P. Alderfer & Cary L. Cooper. 1980. 41.75 (ISBN 0-471-27623-5, Pub. by Wiley-Interscience). Wiley.

Advances in Experimental Social Psychology. Ed. by Leonard Berkowitz. Incl. Vol. 2. 1966. 31.00 (ISBN 0-12-015202-9); Vol. 3. 1967. 31.00 (ISBN 0-12-015203-7); Vol. 4. 1969. 31.00 (ISBN 0-12-015204-5); Vol. 5. 1971. 31.00 (ISBN 0-12-015205-3); Vol. 6. 1972. 31.00 (ISBN 0-12-015206-1); Vol. 7. 1974. 31.00 (ISBN 0-12-015207-X); Vol. 8. 1975. 31.00 (ISBN 0-12-015208-8); microfiche 22.50 (ISBN 0-12-015275-4); Vol. 10. 1977. 31.00 (ISBN 0-12-015210-X); lib ed. 40.50 (ISBN 0-12-015278-9); microfiche 22.50 (ISBN 0-12-015279-7); Vol. 11. 1978. 26.50 (ISBN 0-12-015211-8). LC 64-23452. Acad Pr.

Advances in Experimental Social Psychology, Vol. 13. Ed. by Leonard Berkowitz. (Serial Publication Ser.). 1980. 22.50 (ISBN 0-12-015213-4); lib. ed. 29.50 (ISBN 0-12-015284-3); microfiche 16.00 (ISBN 0-12-015285-1). Acad Pr.

Advances in Factor Analysis & Structural Equation Models. Karl G. Joreskog & Dag Sorbom. LC 79-52433. 1979. 25.00 (ISBN 0-89011-535-4). Abt Assoc.

Advances in Family Psychiatry, Vol. 2. John G. Howells. LC 101. 1980. text ed. 29.95 (ISBN 0-8236-0101-3). Intl Univs Pr.

Advances in Fish Science & Technology. 512p. 1980. pap. 95.00 (ISBN 0-85238-108-5, FN 87, FN). Unipub.

Advances in Fish Science & Technology. J. J. Connell. 77p. 1980. 100.00x (ISBN 0-686-64734-3, Pub. by Fishing News England). State Mutual Bk.

Advances in Fish Science & Technology. Ed. by J. J. Connell. 528p. 1980. cloth 118.50x (ISBN 0-85238-108-5, Pub. by Fishing News England). State Mutual Bk.

Advances in Food Research, Vols. 1-24. Ed. by E. M. Mrak et al. Incl. Vol. 1. 1948 (ISBN 0-12-016401-9); Vol. 2. 1949 (ISBN 0-12-016402-7); Vols. 3-5. 1951-54. Vol. 3 (ISBN 0-12-016403-5). Vol. 4 (ISBN 0-12-016404-3). Vol. 5 (ISBN 0-12-016405-1); Vol. 6. 1955 (ISBN 0-12-016406-X); Vols. 7-8. 1957-58. Vol. 7 (ISBN 0-12-016407-8). Vol. 8 (ISBN 0-12-016408-6); Vol. 9. Ed. by C. O. Chichester et al. 1960 (ISBN 0-12-016409-4); Vols. 11-13. 1963-64. Vol. 10. o.s.i (ISBN 0-12-016410-8). Vol. 11 (ISBN 0-12-016411-6). Vol. 12 (ISBN 0-12-016412-4). Vol. 13 (ISBN 0-12-016413-2); Vol. 14. 1965 (ISBN 0-12-016414-0); Vol. 15. 1967 (ISBN 0-12-016415-9); Vol. 16. 1968. o.s.i (ISBN 0-12-016416-7); Vol. 17. 1969 (ISBN 0-12-016417-5); Vol. 18. 1970 (ISBN 0-12-016418-3); Vol. 19. 1971 (ISBN 0-12-016419-1); Vol. 20. 1973 (ISBN 0-12-016420-5); Vol. 21. 1975 (ISBN 0-12-016421-3). lib ed. 59.50 (ISBN 0-686-66766-2); microfiche 33.50 (ISBN 0-12-016485-X); Vol. 22. 1976 (ISBN 0-12-016422-1). lib ed. 59.50 (ISBN 0-686-66767-0); microfiche 33.50 (ISBN 0-12-016487-6); Vol. 23. 1977. 43.50 (ISBN 0-12-016423-X); lib ed. 46.50 (ISBN 0-12-016488-4); microfiche 27.00 (ISBN 0-12-016489-2); Vol. 24. 1978. 40.00 (ISBN 0-12-016424-8). Vols. 1-22. 46.50 ea. Acad Pr.

Advances in Food Research, Vol. 26. Ed. by C. O. Chichester et al. LC 48-7808. 1980. 31.00 (ISBN 0-12-016426-4); lib. ed. 40.50 (ISBN 0-12-016494-9); microfiche 21.50 (ISBN 0-12-016495-7). Acad Pr.

Advances in Food Research: Supplements. Ed. by E. M. Mrak & G. F. Stewart. Incl. Suppl. 1. Phenolic Substances in Grapes & Wine & Their Significance. V. L. Singleton & P. Esau. 1969. 37.50 (ISBN 0-12-016461-2); Suppl. 2. Chemical Constituents of Citrus Fruits. J. F. Kefford & B. V. Chandler. 1970. 31.50 (ISBN 0-12-016462-0); Suppl. 3. Advances in the Chemistry of Plant Pigments. Ed. by O. Chichester. 1972. 31.50 (ISBN 0-12-016463-9). Acad Pr.

Advances in Fracture Research: Proceedings of the 5th International Conference on Fracture, 1981, Cannes, France. D. Francois. LC 80-41879. (International Series on the Strength & Fracture of Materials & Structures). 3000p. 1981. 450.00 (ISBN 0-08-025428-4); pap. 375.00 (ISBN 0-08-024776-8). Pergamon.

Advances in Free Radical Chemistry, 4 vols. Ed. by G. H. Williams. 1967-75. Vol. 2. 49.25 (ISBN 0-12-017002-7); Vol. 3. 49.25 (ISBN 0-12-017003-5); Vol. 4. 49.25 (ISBN 0-12-017004-3); Vol. 5. 49.25 (ISBN 0-12-017005-1). Acad Pr.

Advances in General & Cellular Pharmacology. Ed. by Toshio Narahashi & C. Paul Bianchi. Incl. Vol. 1. 252p. 1976. 29.50 (ISBN 0-306-35071-8); Vol. 2. 195p. 1977. 24.50 (ISBN 0-306-35072-6). Plenum Pr). Plenum Pub.

Advances in Genetics. Ed. by M. Demerec. Incl. Vol. 1. 1947 (ISBN 0-12-017601-7); Vol. 2. 1948 (ISBN 0-12-017602-5); Vol. 3. 1950 (ISBN 0-12-017603-3); Vol. 4. 1951 (ISBN 0-12-017604-1); Vol. 5. 1953 (ISBN 0-12-017605-X); Vol. 6. 1954 (ISBN 0-12-017606-8); Vol. 7. 1955 (ISBN 0-12-017607-6); Vol. 8. 1956 (ISBN 0-12-017608-4); Vol. 9. 1958 (ISBN 0-12-017609-2); Vol. 10. Ed. by E. W. Caspari & J. M. Thoday. 1961 (ISBN 0-12-017610-6); Vol. 11. 1962 (ISBN 0-12-017611-4); Vol. 12. 1964 (ISBN 0-12-017612-2); Vol. 13. 1965 (ISBN 0-12-017613-0); Vol. 14. Ed. by E. W. Caspari. 1968 (ISBN 0-12-017614-9); Vol. 15. Ed. by E. W. Caspari. 1970 (ISBN 0-12-017615-7); Vol. 16. Ed. by E. W. Caspari. 1971 (ISBN 0-12-017616-5); Vol. 17. Genetics of Tribolium & Related Species. 1973. 48.50 (ISBN 0-12-017617-3); Vol. 18. 1976. 52.50 (ISBN 0-12-017618-1); Vol. 19. 1977. 55.00 (ISBN 0-12-017619-X); Suppl. 1. Genetics of Tribolium & Related Species. Alexander Sokoloff. 1966. 33.00 (ISBN 0-12-017661-0). Vols. 1-16. 48.00 ea. Acad Pr.

Advances in Geometric Programming. Ed. by Mordecai Avriel. (Mathematical Concepts & Methods in Science & Engineering Ser.: Vol. 21). 470p. 1980. 39.50 (ISBN 0-306-40381-1, Plenum Pr). Plenum Pub.

Advances in Geophysics, 19 vols. Ed. by H. E. Landsberg. Incl. Vol. 1. 1952 (ISBN 0-12-018801-5); Vol. 2. 1955 (ISBN 0-12-018802-3); Vol. 3. 1956 (ISBN 0-12-018803-1); Vol. 4. Ed. by H. E. Landsberg & J. Van Mieghen. 1958 (ISBN 0-12-018804-X); Vol. 5. 1958 (ISBN 0-12-018805-8); Vol. 6. Atmospheric Diffusion & Air Pollution: Proceedings. Ed. by F. N. Frenkiel & P. A. Sheppard. 1959 (ISBN 0-12-018806-6); Vol. 7. 1961 (ISBN 0-12-018807-4); Vol. 8. 1961 (ISBN 0-12-018808-2); Vol. 9. 1962 (ISBN 0-12-018809-0); Vol. 10. 1964 (ISBN 0-12-018810-4); Vol. 11. 1965 (ISBN 0-12-018811-2); Vol. 12. 1967 (ISBN 0-12-018812-0); Vol. 13. 1969 (ISBN 0-12-018813-9); Vol. 14. 1970 (ISBN 0-12-018814-7); Vol. 15. 1971 (ISBN 0-12-018815-5); Suppl. 1. Biometeorological Methods. R. E. Munn. 1966. 30.50 (ISBN 0-12-018861-9); Vol. 16. 1973 (ISBN 0-12-018816-3); Vol. 17. 1974 (ISBN 0-12-018817-1); Vol. 18A. 1974. 33.00 (ISBN 0-12-018818-X); Vol. 19. 1976. 48.00 (ISBN 0-12-018819-8). Vols. 1-17. 52.50 ea. Acad Pr.

Advances in Geophysics: Vol. 22 Estuarine Physics & Chemistry-Studies in Long Island Sound. Ed. by Barry Saltzman. 1980. 44.50 (ISBN 0-12-018822-8); lib. ed. 58.00 (ISBN 0-12-018880-5); microfiche 31.00 (ISBN 0-12-018881-3). Acad Pr.

Advances in Heat Transfer, 14 vols. Ed. by Thomas F. Irvine, Jr. & James P. Hartnett. Incl. Vol. 1. 1964. 51.00 (ISBN 0-12-020001-5); Vol. 2. 1965. 51.00 (ISBN 0-12-020002-3); Vol. 3. 1966. 51.00 (ISBN 0-12-020003-1); Vol. 4. 1967. 51.00 (ISBN 0-12-020004-X); Vol. 5. 1968. 55.25 (ISBN 0-12-020005-8); Vol. 6. 1970. 55.25 (ISBN 0-12-020006-6); Vol. 7. 1970. 51.00 (ISBN 0-12-020007-4); Vol. 8. 1972. 51.00 (ISBN 0-12-020008-2); Vol. 9. 1973. 51.00 (ISBN 0-12-020009-0); Vol. 10. 1974. 51.00 (ISBN 0-12-020010-4); Vol. 11. 1975. 59.00 (ISBN 0-12-020011-2); lib. bdg. 75.50 (ISBN 0-12-020074-0); microfiche 42.25 (ISBN 0-12-020075-9); Vol. 12. 1976. 49.00 (ISBN 0-12-020012-0); lib. bdg. 63.00 (ISBN 0-12-020076-7); microfiche 55.50 (ISBN 0-12-020077-5); Vol. 13. 1977. 49.00 (ISBN 0-12-020013-9); lib. bdg. 63.00 (ISBN 0-12-020078-3); microfiche 35.50 (ISBN 0-12-020079-1); Vol. 14. 1979. 43.00 (ISBN 0-12-020014-7); lib. bdg. 55.00 (ISBN 0-12-020080-5); microfiche 31.00 (ISBN 0-12-020081-3). Acad Pr.

Advances in Heterocyclic Chemistry, Vols. 1-16, 22-24. Ed. by A. R. Katritzky. Incl. Vol. 1. 1963. 51.50 (ISBN 0-12-020601-3); Vol. 2. 1963. 51.50 (ISBN 0-12-020602-1); Vol. 3. 1964 (ISBN 0-12-020603-X); Vol. 4. 1965 (ISBN 0-12-020604-8); Vol. 5. 1965 (ISBN 0-12-020605-6); Vol. 6. Ed. by A. R. Katritzky & A. J. Boulton. 1966 (ISBN 0-12-020606-4); Vol. 7. 1966. o.s.i. (ISBN 0-12-020607-2); Vol. 8. 1967 (ISBN 0-12-020608-0); Vol. 9. 1968 (ISBN 0-12-020609-9); Vol. 10. 1969. o.s.i. (ISBN 0-12-020610-2); Vol. 11. 1970 (ISBN 0-12-020611-0); Vol. 12. 1970 (ISBN 0-12-020612-9); Vol. 13. 1971. o.s.i. (ISBN 0-12-020613-7); Vol. 14. 1972 (ISBN 0-12-020614-5); Vol. 15. 1973 (ISBN 0-12-020615-3); Vol. 16. 1974 (ISBN 0-12-020616-1); Vol. 22. 1978. 48.00 (ISBN 0-12-020622-6); lib ed. 62.50 (ISBN 0-12-020682-X); microfiche 35.00 (ISBN 0-12-020683-8); Vol. 23. 52.50 (ISBN 0-12-020623-4); lib ed. 67.50 (ISBN 0-12-020684-6); microfiche 37.50 (ISBN 0-12-020685-4); Vol. 24. 1979. 51.00 (ISBN 0-12-020624-2); info. lib ed. 65.50 (ISBN 0-12-020686-2); microfiche 33.50 (ISBN 0-12-020687-0). Vols. 1-16. 51.50 ea. Acad Pr.

Advances in Heterocyclic Chemistry, Vol. 25. Ed. by Alan R. Katritzky. 1980. 41.00 (ISBN 0-12-020625-0); lib ed. 53.50 (ISBN 0-12-020689-7); microfiche 28.50 (ISBN 0-12-020690-0). Acad Pr.

Advances in Heterocyclic Chemistry, Vol. 27. Ed. by A. R. Katritzky & A. J. Boulton. (Serial Publication). 1980. 49.50 (ISBN 0-12-020627-7); lib. bdg. 64.50 (ISBN 0-12-020728-1); microfiche ed. 34.50 (ISBN 0-12-020729-X). Acad Pr.

Advances in Heterocyclic Chemistry, Vol. 28. Ed. by A. R. Katritzky. (Serial Publication Ser.). 1981. write for info. (ISBN 0-12-020628-5); lib. ed. (ISBN 0-12-020730-3); microfiche ed. (ISBN 0-12-020731-1). Acad Pr.

Advances in High Voltage Insulation & Arc Interruption in SF & Vacuum. Motukuru S. Naidu & Venktesh N. Maller. Date not set. 35.00 (ISBN 0-08-024726-1). Pergamon.

Advances in Human Clinical Nutrition. Ed. by Joseph J. Vitale. (Illus.). 236p. 1981. text ed. 24.50 (ISBN 0-88416-219-2). PSG Pub.

Advances in Immunology, Vols. 1-30. Ed. by W. H. Taliaferro & J. H. Humphrey. Incl. Vol. 1. 1961. (ISBN 0-12-022401-1); Vol. 2. 1963 (ISBN 0-12-022402-X); Vol. 3. Ed. by F. J. Dixon, Jr. & J. H. Humphrey. 1963 (ISBN 0-12-022403-8); Vol. 4. 1964 (ISBN 0-12-022404-6); Vol. 5. 1966 (ISBN 0-12-022405-4); Vol. 6. 1967. o.s.i. (ISBN 0-12-022406-2); Vol. 7. Ed. by F. J. Dixon, Jr. & Henry G. Kunkel. 1967. (ISBN 0-12-022407-0); Vol. 8. 1968 (ISBN 0-12-022408-9); Vol. 9. 1968 (ISBN 0-12-022409-7); Vol. 10. 1969 (ISBN 0-12-022410-0); Vol. 11. 1969. (ISBN 0-12-022411-9); Vol. 12. 1970 (ISBN 0-12-022412-7); Vol. 13. 1971 (ISBN 0-12-022413-5); Vol. 14. 1971 (ISBN 0-12-022414-3); Vol. 15. 1972 (ISBN 0-12-022415-1); Vol. 16. 1973 (ISBN 0-12-022416-X); Vol. 17. 1973 (ISBN 0-12-022417-8); Vol. 18. 1974 (ISBN 0-12-022418-6); Vol. 19. 1974 (ISBN 0-12-022419-4); Vol. 20. 1975 (ISBN 0-12-022420-8); Vol. 21. 1975 (ISBN 0-12-022421-6); Vol. 22. 1976 (ISBN 0-12-022422-4); Vol. 23. 1976 (ISBN 0-12-022423-2); Vol. 24. 1976 (ISBN 0-12-022424-0); Vol. 25. 1978. 32.00 (ISBN 0-12-022425-9); Vol. 26. Ed. by Henry G. Kunkel & E. J. Dixon. 1978. 35.00 (ISBN 0-12-022426-7); Vol. 27. 1979. 32.50 (ISBN 0-12-022427-5); Vol. 28. 1980. 37.50 (ISBN 0-12-022428-3); Vol. 29. 1980. 35.00 (ISBN 0-12-022429-1). LC 61-17057. Vol. 1-24. 43.50 (ISBN 0-686-66773-5). Acad Pr.

Advances in Immunology, Vol. 29. Ed. by Henry G. Kunkel & Frank J. Dixon. (Serial Pub.). 1980. 35.00 (ISBN 0-12-022429-1). Acad Pr.

Advances in Immunology, Vol. 30. Ed. by H. G. Kunkel & F. J. Dixon. 1980. 35.00 (ISBN 0-12-022430-5). Acad Pr.

Advances in Infancy Research. Ed. by Lewis P. Lipsitt. 300p. 1981. price not set (ISBN 0-89391-045-7). Ablex Pub.

Advances in Inflammation Research, Vol. 2. Ed. by Gerald Weissmann. 1981. text ed. price not set (ISBN 0-89004-582-8). Raven.

Advances in Inorganic Chemistry & Radiochemistry. Ed. by H. J. Emeleus & A. G. Sharpe. Incl. Vol. 1. 1959. 52.50 (ISBN 0-12-023601-X); Vol. 2. 1960. 52.50 (ISBN 0-12-023602-8); Vol. 3. 1961. 52.50 (ISBN 0-12-023603-6); Vol. 4. 1962. 52.50 (ISBN 0-12-023604-4); Vol. 5. 1963. 52.50 (ISBN 0-12-023605-2); Vol. 6. 1964. 52.50 (ISBN 0-12-023606-0); Vol. 7. 1965. 52.50 (ISBN 0-12-023607-9); Vol. 8. 1966. 52.50 (ISBN 0-12-023608-7); Vol. 9. 1966. 52.50 (ISBN 0-12-023609-5); Vol. 10. 1968. 52.50 (ISBN 0-12-023610-9); Vol. 11. 1968. 52.50 (ISBN 0-12-023611-7); Vol. 12. 1970. 49.25 (ISBN 0-12-023612-5); Vol. 13. 1970. 49.25 (ISBN 0-12-023613-3); Vol. 14. 1972. 49.25 (ISBN 0-12-023614-1); Vol. 15. 1972. 49.25 (ISBN 0-12-023615-X); Vol. 16. 1974. 47.00 (ISBN 0-12-023616-8); Vol. 20. 1977. 47.00 (ISBN 0-12-023620-6); lib ed. 60.25 (ISBN 0-12-023680-X); microfiche 34.00 (ISBN 0-12-023681-8); Vol. 21. 1978. 37.00 (ISBN 0-12-023621-4); lib ed. 47.50 (ISBN 0-12-023682-6); microfiche 27.00 (ISBN 0-12-023683-4); Vol. 22. 1979. 51.50 (ISBN 0-12-023622-2); lib. ed. 65.50 (ISBN 0-12-023684-2); microfiche 36.50 (ISBN 0-12-023685-0). Acad Pr.

Advances in Inorganic Chemistry & Radiochemistry, Vol. 23. Ed. by H. J. Emeleus & A. G. Sharpe. 1980. 51.00 (ISBN 0-12-023623-0); lib. ed. 66.50 (ISBN 0-12-023686-9); microfilm ed. 35.75 (ISBN 0-12-023687-7). Acad Pr.

Advances in Inorganic Chemistry & Radiochemistry, Vol. 24. Ed. by H. J. Emeleus & A. G. Sharpe. (Serial Publication Ser.). 1981. write for info. (ISBN 0-12-023624-9). Acad Pr.

Advances in Insect Population Control by the Sterile-Male Technique. (Technical Reports Ser.: No. 44). (Illus., Orig.). 1965. pap. 7.50 (ISBN 92-0-115065-2, IAEA). Unipub.

Advances in International Maternal & Child Health, Vol. 1. Ed. by D. B. Jelliffe & E. F. Jelliffe. 250p. 1981. text ed. 45.00x (ISBN 0-19-261281-6). Oxford U Pr.

Advances in Legume Science. Ed. by R. J. Summerfield & A. H. Bunting. (Illus.). xvi, 667p. 1980. pap. 38.50x (ISBN 0-85521-223-3, Pub by Brit Mus Nat Hist England). Sabbot-Natural Hist Bks.

Advances in Librarianship, 8 vols. Ed. by Michael J. Harris & Melvin J. Voight. Incl. Vol. 1. 294p. 1970. 37.50 (ISBN 0-12-785001-5); Vol. 2. 388p. 1971. 37.50 (ISBN 0-12-785002-3); Vol. 3. 275p. 1972. 37.50 (ISBN 0-12-785003-1); Vol. 4. 1974. 37.50 (ISBN 0-12-785004-X); Vol. 5. 1975. 37.50 (ISBN 0-12-785005-8); lib ed. 48.00 (ISBN 0-12-785012-0); microfiche 27.50 (ISBN 0-12-785013-9); Vol. 6. 1976. 28.50 (ISBN 0-12-785006-6); lib ed. 35.50 (ISBN 0-12-785014-7); microfiche 21.00 (ISBN 0-12-785015-5); Vol. 7. 1977. lib ed. 45.00 (ISBN 0-12-785016-3); 35.50 (ISBN 0-12-785007-4); microfiche 25.50 (ISBN 0-12-785017-1); Vol. 8. 25.50 (ISBN 0-12-785008-2); lib. ed. 32.50 (ISBN 0-12-785018-X); microfiche 19.00 (ISBN 0-12-785019-8). LC 79-88675. Acad Pr.

Advances in Librarianship, Vol. 10. Ed. by Michael H. Harris. 1980. 23.00 (ISBN 0-12-785010-4); lib. bdg. 30.00 (ISBN 0-12-785023-6); microfiche ed. 16.00 (ISBN 0-12-785024-4). Acad Pr.

Advances in Lipid Research, Vols. 1-16. Ed. by R. Paoletti & D. Kritchevsky. Incl. Vol. 1. 1964. 52.00 (ISBN 0-12-024901-4); Vol. 2. 1964. 52.00 (ISBN 0-12-024902-2); Vol. 3. 1965. 52.00 (ISBN 0-12-024903-0); Vol. 4. 1967. 52.00 (ISBN 0-12-024904-9); Vol. 5. 1967. 52.00 (ISBN 0-12-024905-7); Vol. 6. 1968. 52.00 (ISBN 0-12-024906-5); Vol. 7. 1969. 52.00 (ISBN 0-12-024907-3); Vol. 8. 1970. 52.00 (ISBN 0-12-024908-1); Vol. 9. 1971. 52.00 (ISBN 0-12-024909-X); Vol. 10. 1972. 52.00 (ISBN 0-12-024910-3); Vol. 11. 1973. 52.00 (ISBN 0-12-024911-1); Vol. 12. 1974. 52.00 (ISBN 0-12-024912-X); Vol. 13. 1975. 52.00 (ISBN 0-12-024913-8); Vol. 14. 1976. 52.00 (ISBN 0-12-024914-6); lib ed. 67.00 (ISBN 0-12-024974-X); microfiche 37.50 (ISBN 0-12-024975-8); Vol. 15. 1977. 45.50 (ISBN 0-12-024915-4); lib ed. 58.00 (ISBN 0-12-024976-6); microfiche 33.00 (ISBN 0-12-024977-4); Vol. 16. 1978. 42.50 (ISBN 0-12-024916-2); lib. ed. 54.00 (ISBN 0-12-024979-0); microfiche 31.00 (ISBN 0-12-024979-0). LC 63-22330. Acad Pr.

Advances in Lipid Research, Vol. 17. Ed. by David Kritchevsky & Rodolfo Paoletti. LC 63-22330. (Serial Publication). 1980. 31.00 (ISBN 0-12-024917-0); lib ed. 40.50 (ISBN 0-12-024980-4); microfiche 20.50 (ISBN 0-12-024981-2). Acad Pr.

Advances in Liquid Crystal Research & Applications: Proceedings of the Third Liquid Crystal Conference of the Socialist Countries, Budapest, 27-31 August 1979. Ed. by L. Bata. 1000p. 1981. 170.00 (ISBN 0-08-026191-4). Pergamon.

Advances in Management Education. John Beck & Charles Cox. LC 80-40117. 1980. 47.50 (ISBN 0-471-27775-4, Pub. by Wiley-Interscience). Wiley.

Advances in Manufacturing Systems - Research & Development. J. Peklenik. 196p. 1972. text ed. 50.00 (ISBN 0-08-016497-8). Pergamon.

Advances in Marine Biology. Ed. by F. S. Russell. Incl. Vol. 12. 1974. 62.00 (ISBN 0-12-026112-X); Vol. 13. 1976. 62.00 (ISBN 0-12-026113-8); Vol. 14. Ed. by D. H. Cushing. 1976. 66.50 (ISBN 0-12-026114-6). (Serial Publication). Acad Pr.

Advances in Maritime Economics. Ed. by R. O. Goss. LC 76-1135. (Illus.). 1977. 49.50 (ISBN 0-521-21232-4). Cambridge U Pr.

Advances in Materials Technology in the Americas, 2 vols. Ed. by I. Le May. Incl. Vol. 1. Materials Recovery & Utilization: Bk. No. H00161, MD1; Vol. 2. Materials Processing & Performance: Bk. No. H00162, MD2. 1980. Set. 30.00. ASME.

Advances in Mechanics & Physics of Surfaces. R. M. Latanision & R. Courtel. 262p. 1981. 35.50 (ISBN 3-7186-0026-9). Harwood Academic.

Advances in Metabolic Disorders. Incl. Vol. 7. Ed. by R. Levine & R. Luft. 1974. 48.00 (ISBN 0-12-027307-1); Vol. 8. Somatomedins & Some Other Growth Factors. Ed. by R. Levine & R. Luft. 1975. 50.00 (ISBN 0-12-027308-X); lib. ed. 64.25 (ISBN 0-12-027384-5); microfiche 36.00 (ISBN 0-12-027385-3); Vol. 9. International Studies in the Epidemiology of Diabetes. Ed. by R. Levine & P. Bennett. 1978. 51.50 (ISBN 0-12-027309-8); 1978. lib. ed. 66.00 (ISBN 0-12-027386-1); microfiche 37.00 (ISBN 0-12-027387-X). (Serial Publication). Acad Pr.

Advances in Metabolic Disorders, Vols. 1-6. Ed. by R. Levine & R. Luft. Incl. Vol. 1. 1964 (ISBN 0-12-027301-2); Vol. 2. 1965. o.s.i. (ISBN 0-12-027302-0); Vol. 3. 1968 (ISBN 0-12-027303-9); Vol. 4. 1970 (ISBN 0-12-027304-7); Vol. 5. 1971 (ISBN 0-12-027305-5); Vol.6. 1972 (ISBN 0-12-027306-3). 48.00 ea. Acad Pr.

Advances in Microbial Ecology, Vol. 2. Ed. by M. Alexander. (Illus.). 311p. 1978. 24.50 (ISBN 0-306-38162-1, Plenum Pr). Plenum Pub.

Advances in Microbial Physiology. Ed. by A. H. Rose et al. Incl. Vol. 1. 1967. o.p. (ISBN 0-12-027701-8); Vol. 2. 1968. 29.50 (ISBN 0-12-027702-6); Vol. 3. 1969. 34.50 (ISBN 0-12-027703-4); Vol. 4. 1970. 49.00 (ISBN 0-12-027704-2); Vol. 5. 1970. o.s.i (ISBN 0-12-027705-0); Vol. 6. 1971. 51.00 (ISBN 0-12-027706-9); Vol. 7. Ed. by A. H. Rose & D. W. Tempest. 1972. 43.00 (ISBN 0-12-027707-7); Vol. 8. 1972. 37.50 (ISBN 0-12-027708-5); Vol. 9. 1973. 35.00 (ISBN 0-12-027709-3); Vol. 10. 1973. 41.50 (ISBN 0-12-027710-7); Vol. 14. 1977. 57.50 (ISBN 0-12-027714-X); Vol. 15. 1977. 61.50 (ISBN 0-12-027715-8); Vol. 16. 1978. 52.00 (ISBN 0-12-027716-6); Vol. 17. 1978. 55.50 (ISBN 0-12-027717-4). Acad Pr.

Advances in Modern Toxicology: New Concepts in Safety Evaluation, 2 pts, Vol. 1. M. A. Mehlman & R. Shapiro. LC 76-27277. 1976. Pt. 1. 24.50x (ISBN 0-470-98919-X); Pt. 2. 24.50x (ISBN 0-470-26382-2). Halsted Pr.

Advances in Modern Toxicology: Vol. 4, Dermatoxicology & Pharmacology. Ed. by F. N. Marzulli & H. I. Maibach. 592p. 1977. 37.50x o.p. (ISBN 0-470-99063-5). Halsted Pr.

Advances in Neuroblastoma Research. Ed. by Audrey E. Evans. (Progress in Cancer Research & Therapy Ser.: Vol. 12). 360p. 1980. 38.00 (ISBN 0-89004-459-7, 516). Raven.

Advances in Neurotoxicology: Proceedings of the International Congress on Neurotoxicology, Varese, 27-30 September 1979. Ed. by L. Manzo. (Illus.). 404p. 1980. 69.00 (ISBN 0-08-024953-1). Pergamon.

Advances in Nuclear Science & Technology, Vol. 8. Ed. by E. J. Henley & H. H. Kouts. (Serial Publication). 1975. 48.00 (ISBN 0-12-029308-0). Acad Pr.

Advances in Nuclear Science & Technology, Vol. 12. Ed. by Martin Becker et al. 350p. 1980. 39.50 (ISBN 0-306-40315-3, Plenum Pr). Plenum Pub.

Advances in Nutritional Research, Vols. 1-3. Ed. by Harold H. Draper. Incl. Vol. 1. 362p. 1977. 27.50 (ISBN 0-306-34321-5); Vol. 2. 264p. 1979. 27.50 (ISBN 0-306-40213-0); Vol. 3. 300p. 1980. 32.50 (ISBN 0-306-40415-X). Plenum Pub. (Illus., Plenum Pr). Plenum Pub.

Advances in Occlusion: Diagnoisis & Treatment. Ed. by Harry C. Lundeen & Charles H. Gibbs. 1981. write for info. (ISBN 0-88416-168-4). PSG Pub.

Advances in Ophthalmology, Vol. 41. Ed. by E. B. Streiff. (Illus.). xvii, 216p. 1980. 96.00 (ISBN 3-8055-0375-X). S Karger.

Advances in Ophthalmology, Vol. 42. Ed. by E. B. Streiff. (Illus.). 200p. 1980. 60.00 (ISBN 3-8055-1025-X). S Karger.

Advances in Organic Geochemistry: Proceedings. P. A. Schenck. 1969. 96.00 (ISBN 0-08-006628-3). Pergamon.

Advances in Organic Geochemistry, 1969: Proceedings. Ed. by G. D. Hobson. 1970. 82.00 (ISBN 0-08-012758-4). Pergamon.

Advances in Organic Geochemistry 1979: Proceedings of the 9th International Meeting on Organic Geochemistry Held at Newcastle-Upon-Tyne, England, Sept. 1979. Ed. by A G. Douglas & J. R. Maxwell. LC 80-41078. (International Ser. in Earth Sciences: Vol. 36). (Illus.). 750p. 1980. 150.00 (ISBN 0-08-024017-8). Pergamon.

Advances in Pain Research & Therapy: Proceedings, Vol. 1. World Congress on Pain, 1st, Florence, 1975. Ed. by John J. Bonica & Denise Albe-Fessard. LC 75-32095. 1976. 87.50 (ISBN 0-89004-090-7). Raven.

Advances in Perinatal Medicine, Vol. 1. Ed. by Aubrey Milunsky et al. 450p. 1981. 35.00 (ISBN 0-306-40482-6, Plenum Pr). Plenum Pub.

Advances in Pesticide Science: Proceedings, 3 vols. International Congress of Pesticide Chemistry, 4th, Zurich, 1978. Ed. by H. Geissbuehler et al. 1979. Set. text ed. 225.00 (ISBN 0-08-022349-4). Pergamon.

Advances in Pharmacology & Chemotherapy, Vol. 17. Ed. by Robert J. Schnitzer et al. 1980. 36.00 (ISBN 0-12-032917-4); lib. ed. 47.00 (ISBN 0-12-032984-0); microfiche ed. 25.00 (ISBN 0-12-032985-9). Acad Pr.

Advances in Pharmacology & Therapeutics, 10 vols. new ed. Ed. by J. R. Boissier et al. (Illus.). 1979. Set. text ed. 650.00 o.p. (ISBN 0-08-022680-9). Pergamon.

Advances in Photochemistry. James N. Pitts et al. LC 66-13592. Vol. 10, 1977. 38.50 (ISBN 0-471-02145-8, Pub. by Wiley-Interscience); Vol. 11, 1979. 43.95 (ISBN 0-471-04797-X); Vol. 12, 1980. 42.50 (ISBN 0-471-06286-3). Wiley.

Advances in Physical & Biological Radiation Detectors. (Illus.). 742p. (Orig.). 1972. pap. 52.50 (ISBN 92-0-020171-7, ISP269, IAEA). Unipub.

Advances in Physical Organic Chemistry. Ed. by Victor Gold. Incl. Vol. 1. 1963. 59.00 (ISBN 0-12-033501-8); Vol. 2. 1964. 40.50 (ISBN 0-12-033502-6); Vol. 3. 1965. 39.00 (ISBN 0-12-033503-4); Vol. 4. 1966. 49.50 (ISBN 0-12-033504-2); Vol. 5. 1967. 54.00 (ISBN 0-12-033505-0); Vol. 6. 1968. 50.00 (ISBN 0-12-033506-9); Vol. 7. 1969. 48.50 (ISBN 0-12-033507-7); Vol. 8. 1970. 58.50 (ISBN 0-12-033508-5); Vol. 9. 1972. 41.00 (ISBN 0-12-033509-3); Vol. 10. 1973. 34.50 (ISBN 0-12-033510-7). Acad Pr.

Advances in Polyamine Research, 2 vols. Ed. by Robert A. Campbell et al. LC 77-83687. 1978. Vol. 1. 34.50 (ISBN 0-89004-189-X); Vol. 2. 41.00 (ISBN 0-89004-194-6). Raven.

Advances in Polyamine Research, Vol. 3. Ed. by Claudio M. Caldarera et al. 1981. text ed. price not set (ISBN 0-89004-621-2). Raven.

Advances in Polymer Science. Ed. by Z. A. Rogovin. Tr. by N. Kaner from Rus. LC 74-13580. 331p. 1974. 48.95 (ISBN 0-470-73132-X). Halsted Pr.

Advances in Polymer Science, Vols. 1-14. Ed. by H. J. Cantow et al. Incl. Vol. 1. (Illus.). iv, 612p. 1958-60. o.p. (ISBN 0-685-24350-8); Vol. 2. (Illus.). iv, 607p. 1960-61. o.p. (ISBN 0-685-24351-6); Vol. 3. (Illus.). iv, 711p. 1961-64. o.p. (ISBN 0-685-24352-4); Vol. 4. (Illus.). iv, 509p. 1965-67. o.p. (ISBN 0-685-24353-2); Vol. 5, 1 vol. ed. (Illus.). iv, 619p. 1967-68. 155.80 (ISBN 0-387-04034-X); Vol. 6, 1 vol. ed. (Illus.). iii, 574p. 1969-70. 147.00 (ISBN 0-387-04401-9); Vol. 7, 1 vol. ed. (Illus.). 600p. 1970. 155.80 (ISBN 0-387-05342-5); Vol. 8. (Illus.). 1971. 77.90 (ISBN 0-387-05483-9); Vol. 9. (Illus.). 1972. 93.30 (ISBN 0-387-05484-7); Vol. 10. (Illus.). 1972. 56.70 (ISBN 0-387-05838-9); Vol. 11. 1973. 57.90 (ISBN 0-387-06054-5); Vol. 12. (Illus.). 1973. 50.80 (ISBN 0-387-06431-1); Vol. 13. (Illus.). 1974. 30.70 (ISBN 0-387-06552-0); Vol. 14. (Illus.). 1974. 37.80 (ISBN 0-387-06649-7). Springer-Verlag.

Advances in Preconcentration & Dehydration of Foods. Ed. by Arnold Spicer. LC 74-9512. 526p. 1974. 69.95 (ISBN 0-470-81591-4). Halsted Pr.

Advances in Preparation & Characterization of Multiphase Polymer Systems. R. J. Ambrose & S. L. Aggarwal. (Journal of Polymer Science Symposium: No. 60). 1977. 18.95 (ISBN 0-471-04714-7). Wiley.

Advances in Programming Non-Numerical Applications to Computing Machines. Ed. by L. Fox. 1965. 16.80 o.p. (ISBN 0-08-011356-7). Pergamon.

Advances in Prostaglandin & Thromboxane Research, 2 vols. Ed. by B. Samuelsson & R. Paoletti. LC 75-14588. 1976. Vol. 1. 52.00 (ISBN 0-89004-050-8); Vol. 2. 53.50 (ISBN 0-89004-074-5). Raven.

Advances in Prostaglandin & Thromboxane Research, Vols. 6-8. Ed. by Bengt Samuelsson et al. 1980. Set. text ed. 173.00 (ISBN 0-89004-452-X); text ed. 59.50 ea. Vol. 6 (ISBN 0-89004-452-X). Vol. 7 (ISBN 0-89004-513-5). Vol. 8 (ISBN 0-89004-514-3). Raven.

Advances in Protein Chemistry, Vol. 34. Ed. by C. B. Anfinsen et al. (Serial Publication). 1981. price not set (ISBN 0-12-034234-0); price not set lib. ed. (ISBN 0-12-034284-7); price not set microfiche. Acad Pr.

Advances in Protoplast Research: Proceedings. International Protoplast Symposium, 5th, July 1979, Szeged, Hungary. Ed. by L. Ferenczy & G. L. Farks. LC 79-41251. 550p. 1980. 84.00 (ISBN 0-08-025528-0). Pergamon.

Advances in Psychobiology, Vol. 3. A. H. Riesen & R. F. Thompson. LC 70-178148. 1976. 37.50 (ISBN 0-471-72173-5). Wiley.

Advances in Psychotherapy of the Borderline Patient. Joseph LeBoit & Attilio Capponi. LC 79-50292. Date not set. 35.00x (ISBN 0-87668-365-0). Aronson.

Advances in Quantum Chemistry, Vols. 1-11. Ed. by Per-Olov Lowdin. Incl. Vol. 1. 1964. 49.25 (ISBN 0-12-034801-2); Vol. 2. Vol. 2, 1966. 49.25 (ISBN 0-12-034802-0); Vol. 3. 1967. 49.25 (ISBN 0-12-034803-9); Vol. 4. 1968. 49.25 (ISBN 0-12-034804-7); Vol. 5. 1970. 49.25 (ISBN 0-12-034805-5); Vol. 6. 1972. 49.25 (ISBN 0-12-034806-3); Vol. 7. Vol. 7, 1973. 49.25 (ISBN 0-12-034807-1); Vol. 8. 1974. 49.25 (ISBN 0-12-034808-X); Vol. 9. 1975. 55.00 (ISBN 0-12-034809-8); Vol. 10. 1977. 50.00 (ISBN 0-686-66780-8); Vol. 11. 1979. 50.50 (ISBN 0-12-034811-X). Acad Pr.

Advances in Quantum Chemistry, Vol. 12. Ed. by Per-Olov Lowdin. LC 64-8029. 1980. 48.00 (ISBN 0-12-034812-8). Acad Pr.

Advances in Radiation Biology, Vol. 7. Ed. by J. T. Lett & Howard Edler. 1978. 52.50 (ISBN 0-12-035407-1); lib. ed. 67.50 (ISBN 0-12-035478-0); microfiche 34.50 (ISBN 0-12-035479-9). Acad Pr.

Advances in Radiation Biology, Vol. 9. Ed. by J. T. Lett & H. I. Adler. (Serial Publication Ser.). 1981. write for info. (ISBN 0-12-035409-8). Acad Pr.

Advances in Radiation Protection & Dosimetry. Ed. by Ralph H. Thomas & Victor Perez-Mendez. (Ettore Najorana International Science Ser., Life Sciences: Vol. 2). 650p. 1980. 69.50 (ISBN 0-306-40468-0). Plenum Pub.

Advances in Radiation Protection Monitoring. 778p. 1980. pap. 97.50 (ISBN 92-0-020279-9, ISP494, IAEA). Unipub.

Advances in Reproductive Physiology, Vol. 6. Ed. by Marcus W. Bishop. 1973. 39.95x o.p. (ISBN 0-236-17670-6, Pub. by Paul Elek). Merrimack Bk Serv.

Advances in Research & Technology of Seeds, Pt. 5. 115p. 1981. pap. 25.00 (ISBN 90-220-0746-4, PDC 215, Pudoc). Unipub.

Advances in Road Vehicle Aerodynamics. 1973. pap. 42.00 (ISBN 0-900983-26-4, Dist. by Air Science Co.). BHRA Fluid.

Advances in Rock Mechanics: Proceedings, Vol. 2, Pts. A & B. International Society for Rock Mechanics, 3rd Congress. xxxii, 1505p. 1974. 33.75 (ISBN 0-309-02246-0). Natl Acad Pr.

Advances in San Juan Basin Paleontology. Ed. by Spencer Lucas & Keith Rigby, Jr. 440p. 1981. 27.50x (ISBN 0-8263-0554-7). U of NM Pr.

Advances in Satellite Meteorology, Vol. 2. Ed. by N. K. Vinnichenko & A. G. Gorelik. Tr. by M. Levi from Rus. 1974. text ed. 26.95 (ISBN 0-470-90836-X). Halsted Pr.

Advances in School Management. T. Bush et al. 1980. text ed. 23.65 (ISBN 0-06-318167-3, IntlDept); pap. text ed. 13.10 (ISBN 0-06-318168-1). Har-Row.

Advances in School Psychology, Vol. 1. Thomas R. Kratochwill. (Advances in School Psychology Ser.). 368p. 1981. profess. & reference 24.95 (ISBN 0-89859-076-0). L Erlbaum Assocs.

Advances in Sex Hormone Research, Vol. 4. Ed. by John A. Thomas. Radhey L. Singhal. LC 79-25717. (Illus.). 1980. text ed. 32.50 (ISBN 0-8067-1914-1). Urban & S.

Advances in Shock Research: Proceedings, Vol. 1. Papers from the First Annual Conference on Shock, Airlie, Va., June 1978. Ed. by Allan M. Lefer & Leena M. Mela. LC 79-63007. 288p. 1979. 30.00x (ISBN 0-8451-0600-7). A R Liss.

Advances in Shock Research: Proceedings, Vol. 2. Papers from the First Annual Conference on Shock, Airlie, Va. June 1978. Ed. by William Schumer et al. LC 79-63007. 308p. 1979. 30.00x (ISBN 0-8451-0601-5). A R Liss.

Advances in Shock Research: Proceedings, Vol. 3. Papers from the Second Annual Conference on Shock, Williamsburg, Va. June 1979. Ed. by Allan M. Lefer & Thomas M. Saba. LC 79-63007. 316p. 1980. 34.00x (ISBN 0-8451-0602-3). A R Liss.

Advances in Shock Research: Proceedings, Vol. 4. Papers from the Second Annual Conference on Shock, Williamsburg, Va., June 1979. Ed. by John J. Spitzer & Bryan E. Marshall. LC 79-63007. 232p. 1980. 26.00x (ISBN 0-8451-0603-1). A R Liss.

Advances in Shock Research, Vol. 5: Proceedings, Part One. Third Annual Conference on Shock, Lake of the Ozarks, Missouri, June 1980. Ed. by Allan M. Lefer. LC 79-63007. 150p. 1981. 26.00x (ISBN 0-8451-0604-X). A R Liss.

Advances in Shock Research, Vol. 6: Proceedings, Part Two. Third Annual Conference on Shock, Lake of the Ozarks, Missouri, June 1980 et al. Ed. by William Schumer & John J. Spitzer. LC 79-63007. 150p. 1981. 26.00x (ISBN 0-8451-0605-8). A R Liss.

Advances in Smoking of Foods. Ed. by Rutkowski. 1977. text ed. 27.00 (ISBN 0-08-022002-9). Pergamon.

Advances in Solid-Liquid Flow in Pipes & Its Application. Ed. by I. Zandi. LC 77-120000. 1971. 50.00 (ISBN 0-08-015767-X). Pergamon.

Advances in Solid State Physics: Festkoerper Probleme, Vols. 9-15. Ed. by O. Madelung & H. J. Queisser. Vol. 9. 1969. 60.00 (ISBN 0-08-015543-X). Vol. 10. 1971. 40.00 (ISBN 0-08-017563-5); Vol. 11. 1971. 30.00 (ISBN 0-08-017593-7); Vol. 12. 1972. 66.00 (ISBN 0-08-017285-7); Vol. 13, 1973. 42.50 (ISBN 0-08-017293-8); Vol. 14, 1974. 42.50 (ISBN 0-08-018206-2); Vol. 15, 1975. 55.00 (ISBN 0-08-019894-5). Pergamon.

Advances in Solid State Science, Supplement 2B: Silicon Integrated Circuits. Ed. by Dawon Kahng. (Serial Publication). 1981. price not set (ISBN 0-12-002957-X); price not set lib. ed. (ISBN 0-12-002958-8); microfiche ed. (ISBN 0-12-002959-6). Acad Pr.

Advances in Space Science & Technology, Vols. 1-11. Ed. by Frederick I. Ordway, 3rd. Incl. Vols. 1-7. 1959-65. 49.00 ea. Vol. 1 (ISBN 0-12-037301-7). Vol. 2. o.p. (ISBN 0-12-037302-5). Vol. 3 (ISBN 0-12-037303-3). Vol. 4 (ISBN 0-12-037304-1). Vol. 5. o.p. (ISBN 0-12-037305-X). Vol. 6 (ISBN 0-12-037306-8). Vol. 7 (ISBN 0-12-037307-6); Vol. 8. 1966. 40.00 (ISBN 0-12-037308-4); Vol. 9. 1967. 40.00 (ISBN 0-12-037309-2); Vol. 10. 1970. 49.00 (ISBN 0-12-037310-6); Vol. 11. 1972. 57.00 (ISBN 0-12-037311-4); Suppl. 1. Space Carrier Vehicles: Design, Development & Testing of Launching Rockets. O. H. Lange & R. J. Stein. 1963. 43.50 (ISBN 0-12-037361-0); Suppl. 2. Lunar & Planetary Surface Conditions. N. A. Weil. 1965. 43.50 (ISBN 0-12-037362-9). Acad Pr.

Advances in Stereotactic & Functional Neurosurgery Four: Proceedings. F. J. Gillingham. (Acta Neurochirurgica Supplementum: Vol. 30). (Illus.). 444p. 1981. pap. 146.40 (ISBN 0-387-90501-4). Springer-Verlag.

Advances in Steroid Biochemistry & Pharmacology, Vols. 1-7. Ed. by M. H. Briggs & G. A. Christie. Incl. Vol. 1. 71.50 (ISBN 0-12-037501-X); Vol. 2. 66.50 (ISBN 0-12-037502-8); Vol. 3. 1972. 35.50 (ISBN 0-12-037503-6); Vol. 4. 1974. 45.00 (ISBN 0-12-037504-4); Vol. 5. 1976. 51.50 (ISBN 0-12-037505-2); Vol. 6. 1978. 24.50 (ISBN 0-12-037506-0); Vol. 7. 1980. 23.00 (ISBN 0-12-037507-9). Acad Pr.

Advances in the House-Tree-Person Technique: Variations & Applications. Ed. by John N. Buck & Emanuel F. Hammer. LC 66-29864. (Illus.). 1969. 22.50x o.p. (ISBN 0-87424-302-5). Western Psych.

Advances in the Management of Cleft Palate. Edwards et al. (Illus.). 1981. text ed. 30.00 (ISBN 0-443-01601-1). Churchill.

Advances in the Study of Behavior, Vol. 11. Ed. by Jay S. Rosenblatt et al. 1980. 35.00 (ISBN 0-12-004511-7). Acad Pr.

Advances in the Teaching of Modern Languages, Vol. 2. Ed. by G. Mathieu. 1966. 23.00 (ISBN 0-08-011840-2). Pergamon.

Advances in Transport Processes, Vol. I. A. S Mujumdar. 263p. 1980. 27.95x (ISBN 0-470-26957-X). Halsted Pr.

Advances in Vacuum Science & Technology: Proceedings. Israeli Vacuum Congress, Fifth, Israel, April 1978. Ed. by J. Yarwood & Y. Margoninski. 1979. pap. 13.00 (ISBN 0-08-024238-3). Pergamon.

Advances in Veterinary Science & Comparative Medicine. Ed. by C. A. Brandly & E. L. Jungherr. Incl. Vol. 13. 1969. 52.00 (ISBN 0-12-039213-5); Vol. 14. 1970. 52.00 (ISBN 0-12-039214-3); Vol. 15. 1971. 52.00 (ISBN 0-12-039215-1); Vol. 16. 1972. 52.50 (ISBN 0-12-039216-X); Vol. 17. 1973. 55.50 (ISBN 0-12-039217-8); Vol. 18. 1974. 47.00 (ISBN 0-12-039218-6); Vol. 19. 1976. 48.00 (ISBN 0-12-039219-4); lib. ed. 61.50 (ISBN 0-12-039274-7); microfiche 34.50 (ISBN 0-12-039275-5); Vol. 20. 1976. 47.00 (ISBN 0-12-039220-8); lib ed. 60.25 (ISBN 0-12-039276-3); microfiche 34.00 (ISBN 0-12-039277-1); Vol. 21. 1977. 52.75 (ISBN 0-12-039221-6); lib ed. 67.75 (ISBN 0-12-039278-X); microfiche 38.00 (ISBN 0-12-039279-8); Vol. 22. 1978. 43.50 (ISBN 0-12-039222-4); lib ed. 50.00 (ISBN 0-12-039280-1); microfiche 31.50 (ISBN 0-12-039281-X). LC 53-7098. Acad Pr.

Advances in Virus Research, Vol. 26. Ed. by Max A. Lauffer et al. (Serial Publication). 1981. write for info. (ISBN 0-12-039826-5). Acad Pr.

Advances in Vitreous Surgery. Alexander R. Irvine & Conor O'Malley. (Illus.). 736p. 1976. 66.75 (ISBN 0-398-03391-9). C C Thomas.

Advances in X-Ray Analysis, Vol. 23. Ed. by John S. Rhodes et al. 400p. 1980. 45.00 (ISBN 0-306-40435-4). Plenum Pub.

Advances in X-Ray Spectroscopy: A Reference Text in Honour of Professor Y Cauchois. Ed. by C. Bonnelle & C. Mande. (Illus.). 400p. 1981. 60.00 (ISBN 0-08-025266-4). Pergamon.

Advancing Paul Newman. Eleanor Bergstein. 320p. 1976. pap. 1.75 o.p. (ISBN 0-445-08438-3). Popular Lib.

Advantage of Education; or, the History of Maria Williams, 2 vols. Jane West. Ed. by Gina Luria. (Femnist Controversy in England, 1788-1810 Ser.). 1974. lib. bdg. 50.00 ea. Garland Pub.

Advantage of Lyric: Essays on Feeling in Poetry. Barbara Hardy. LC 76-47167. 152p. 1977. 10.95x (ISBN 0-253-30130-0). Ind U Pr.

Advantage Tennis: Racket Work, Tactics & Logic. Jack M. Barnaby. (Illus.). 300p. 1975. text ed. 17.95 (ISBN 0-205-04686-X, 6246869). Allyn.

Advent & Event. John Brokhoff & Barbara Brokhoff. 88p. (Orig.). 1980. pap. text ed. 3.65 (ISBN 0-89536-453-0). CSS Pub.

Advent-Christmas. Frederick H. Borsch & Davie Napier. Ed. by Elizabeth Achtemeier et al. LC 79-7377. (Proclamation 2: Aids for Interpreting the Lessons of the Church Year, Ser. A). 64p. (Orig.). 1980. pap. 2.50 (ISBN 0-8006-4091-8, 1-4091). Fortress.

Advent-Christmas. Reginald H. Fuller. Ed. by Elizabeth Achtemeier et al. LC 79-7377. (Proclamation 2: Aids for Interpreting the Lessons of the Church Year, Ser. C). 64p. 1979. pap. 2.50 (ISBN 0-8006-4079-9, 1-4079). Fortress.

Advent-Christmas. Thor Hall & James L. Price. LC 74-24899. (Proclamation 1: Aids for Interpreting the Lessons of the Church Year, Ser. B). 64p. 1974. pap. 1.95 (ISBN 0-8006-4071-3, 1-4071). Fortress.

Advent-Christmas. David B. Watermulder & Gerhard Krodel. LC 73-79329. (Proclamation 1: Aids for Interpreting the Lessons of the Church Year, Ser. C). 64p. 1973. pap. 1.95 (ISBN 0-8006-4051-9, 1-4051). Fortress.

Advent-Christmas. Samuel Wylie & John L. McKenzie. LC 74-76924. (Proclamation 1: Aids for Interpreting the Lessons of the Church Year, Ser. A). 64p. 1974. pap. 1.95 (ISBN 0-8006-4061-6, 1-4061). Fortress.

Advent Devotion. 1980. 1.95 (ISBN 0-8100-0128-4). Northwest Pub.

Advent Event. Herbert Skelly & Margaret Skelly. 32p. (Orig.). 1973. pap. 3.25 (ISBN 0-8192-1148-6); kit 13.95 (ISBN 0-8192-1283-0). Morehouse.

Advent of American Democracy. Leonard L. Richards. 1977. pap. 7.95x (ISBN 0-673-07904-X). Scott F.

Advent of Christ. Victor Mohr. 116p. Date not set. pap. 4.95 (ISBN 0-934616-16-7). Valkyrie Pr.

Advent of Divine Justice. Shoghi Effendi. LC 63-21643. 9.00 (ISBN 0-87743-044-6, 7-08-01); pap. 4.00 (ISBN 0-87743-045-4, 7-08-02). Baha'i.

Advent of War, Nineteen Thirty-Nine to Nineteen Forty. Roy Douglas. LC 78-12266. 1979. 21.95 (ISBN 0-312-00650-0). St Martin.

Adventismo Del Septimo Dia. D. M. Canright. Tr. by F. G. Correa. Date not set. pap. 1.20 (ISBN 0-311-05601-6). Casa Bautista.

Adventist Education at the Crossroads. Raymond S. Moore. LC 76-1147. (Dimension Ser.). 1976. pap. 5.95 (ISBN 0-8163-0230-8, 01104-9). Pacific Pr Pub Assn.

Adventistas Del Septimo Dia y Sus Doctrinas. (Spanish Bks.). 1978. write for info. (ISBN 0-8297-0887-1). Life Pubs Intl.

Adventure. Borden Deal. LC 77-74297. 1978. 8.95 o.p. (ISBN 0-385-05227-8). Doubleday.

Adventure at Beaver Falls. Erling Calkins. LC 79-15601. (Crown Ser.). (gr. 5-8). 1979. 4.50 (ISBN 0-8127-0223-9). Southern Pub.

Adventure at Murray's: A Strange Shopping Trip. David Roberts & Robert Gadbois. LC 77-1646. (Books by Children for Children). 1977. PLB 6.45 (ISBN 0-87191-611-8). Creative Ed.

Adventure in Diplomacy. Kenneth Pendar. LC 76-5479. (World War II Ser.). 1976. Repr. of 1945 ed. lib. bdg. 22.50 (ISBN 0-306-70774-8). Da Capo.

Adventure in the Wilderness: The American Journals of Louis Antoine De Bougainville 1756-1760. Louis A. De Bougainville. Tr. by Edward P. Hamilton. (American Exploration & Travel Ser.: No. 42). 1964. 18.95 o.p. (ISBN 0-8061-0596-8). U of Okla Pr.

Adventure of Living. Paul Tournier. LC 65-20459. 256p. 1976. pap. 4.95 (ISBN 0-06-068294-9, RD 260, HarpR). Har-Row.

Adventure of Making Money. Ken Davis & Tom Taylor. LC 79-24749. (Illus., Orig.). (gr. 5-10). 1980. pap. 2.95 (ISBN 0-916392-47-3). Oak Tree Pubns.

Adventure of Man. Arthur S. Gregor. (gr. 7 up). 1966. 4.95g o.s.i. (ISBN 0-02-736970-6). Macmillan.

Adventure of the Eleven Cuff-Buttons. James F. Thierry. 1979. pap. 6.50 (ISBN 0-915230-14-3). Rue Morgue.

Adventure of the Lost Manuscripts & One Other. Edmund L. Pearson. (Illus.). 40p. (Orig.). 1974. pap. 4.00 o.p. (ISBN 0-915230-05-4). Rue Morgue.

Adventure of the Peerless Peer. Philip J. Farmer. 112p. 1974. 5.50 o.p. (ISBN 0-915230-06-2). Rue Morgue.

Adventure on Padre Island. Aleda Renken. LC 75-5945. (Haley Adventure Bks.). 96p. (gr. 3-7). 1975. pap. 2.50 (ISBN 0-570-07231-X, 39-1029). Concordia.

Adventure Stories for Boys. Frank Morrison. (Upper Grade Bk.). (Illus.). (gr. 4-6). PLB 4.50 o.p. (ISBN 0-513-00485-8). Denison.

Adventure Together: Teacher's Manual. W. Imbiorski. 60p. 1974. pap. 3.00. Buckley Pubns.

Adventure Travel. Patricia Dickerman. LC 79-57153. 256p. 1980. 7.95 (ISBN 0-913216-03-8). Berkshire Traveller.

Adventure Travel, North America. Pat Dickerman. LC 77-25745. (Illus.). 1978. 9.95 o.p. (ISBN 0-690-01750-2, TYC-T); pap. 5.95 (ISBN 0-690-01751-0, TYC-T). T Y Crowell.

Adventure with Flowers. Elizabeth T. Billington. LC 66-15814. (Illus.). (gr. 5-9). 1966. 6.95 (ISBN 0-7232-6021-4). Warne.

Adventure with Foods & Health. Ross Brockman. 1978. 4.95 (ISBN 0-533-02994-5). Vantage.

Adventurers. Ernest Haycox. 286p. 1975. Repr. of 1954 ed. lib. bdg. 6.95 o.p. (ISBN 0-89190-971-0). Am Repr-Rivercity Pr.

Adventurers for God. Clarence W. Hall. LC 75-36730. 1976. pap. 1.95 o.p. (ISBN 0-06-063571-1, HJ 18, HarpR). Har-Row.

Adventures & Discourses of Captain John Smith. John Ashton. LC 76-78108. (Illus.). 1969. Repr. of 1883 ed. 15.00 (ISBN 0-8103-3565-4). Gale.

Adventures & Philosophy of a Pennsylvania Dutchman: An Autobiography in a Broad Setting. Homer T. Rosenberger. LC 79-165295. (Illus.). 665p. 1971. lib. bdg. 15.00 (ISBN 0-917264-03-7). Rose Hill.

Adventures & Recollections of Walter P. Lane, a San Jacinto Veteran Containing Sketches of the Texan, Mexican, & Civil Wars with Several Indian Fights Thrown In. Walter P. Lane. (Illus.). 15.00 (ISBN 0-8363-0001-7). Jenkins.

Adventures, Blizzards & Coastal Calamities. Edward R. Snow. LC 78-23316. (Illus.). 1978. 8.95 (ISBN 0-396-07634-3). Dodd.

Adventures in Being a Parent: Family Enrichment Ideas for Busy Parents. Shirley Pollock. (Orig.). 1981. pap. 3.50 (ISBN 0-87239-458-1, 2971). Standard Pub.

Adventures in California Country. Lee Foster. Ed. by Robert D. Shangle. LC 79-28673. (Illus.). 64p. 1981. pap. 4.95 (ISBN 0-89802-063-8). Beautiful Am.

Adventures in Christian Living & Learning: A Resource Book for Use with Retarded Persons, Pt. 2. Ed. by Doris Monroe. (Cooperative Ser: Curriculum Materials for the Mentally Retarded). (Illus., Orig.). (gr. 6-10). 1970. pap. 1.25 ea. o.p. (ISBN 0-8042-1140-X); tchrs' ed. 2.50 ea. o.p. (ISBN 0-8042-1141-8). John Knox.

Adventures in Christian Living & Learning, Pt. 2. LaDonna Bogardus. (Orig.). 1970. pap. 2.50 tchrs' bk. (ISBN 0-687-00904-9); pap. 2.25 pupils' bk (ISBN 0-687-00905-7). Abingdon.

Adventures in Darkness. Tom Sullivan & Derek Gill. (Illus.). 160p. (RL 5). Date not set. pap. 1.95 o.p. (ISBN 0-686-68444-3, J9376-3, Sig). NAL.

Adventures in Error. Vilhjalmur Stefansson. LC 71-121210. 1970. Repr. of 1936 ed. 15.00 (ISBN 0-8103-3838-6). Gale.

Adventures in Existing-Light Photography. rev. ed. (Code No. AC-44). (Illus.). 1980. pap. 4.00 (ISBN 0-87985-251-8). Eastman Kodak.

Adventures in Faith: Studies in the Life of Abraham. Martin R. DeHaan. 1979. pap. 3.95 (ISBN 0-310-23251-1). Zondervan.

Adventures in Food, Natural Cooking Made Easy: How to Cook Better for Less Without Adding Oil or Sugar. Ruth M. Fenton. (Orig.). 1980. pap. 6.95 (ISBN 0-934178-01-1). Christian Success.

Adventures in High Fantasy. Jeffery Dillow. 1981. 15.95 (ISBN 0-8359-0165-3); pap. 13.95 (ISBN 0-8359-0164-5). Reston.

Adventures in Italian Cooking. James K. McNair. Ed. by Ortho Books Editorial Staff. LC 80-66345. (Illus.). 96p. (Orig.). 1981. pap. 4.95 (ISBN 0-917102-89-4). Ortho.

Adventures in Italian Cooking. James K. McNair. Ed. by Ortho Books Editorial Staff. LC 80-66345. (Illus.). 96p. (Orig.). 1981. pap. 4.95 (ISBN 0-917102-89-4, Ortho Bks). Chevron Chem.

Adventures in Living Judaism: Identity, Bk. 1. 1976. Bk. 1. 3.50 (ISBN 0-8074-0030-0, 145050); Survival Bk. 2. 7.50 (ISBN 0-8074-0031-9, 145051). UAHC.

Adventures in Living Storybooks, 12. 79.50 (ISBN 0-87827-137-6). Ency Brit Ed.

Adventures in Making: Romance of Crafts Around the World. Seon Manley. LC 59-12397. (Illus.). (gr. 7 up). 1959. 7.95 (ISBN 0-8149-0361-4). Vanguard.

Adventures in Mexican Cooking. Ortho Books Editorial Staff. LC 78-57893. (Illus.). 1979. pap. text ed. 4.95 (ISBN 0-917102-71-1). Ortho.

Adventures in Nameless Valley Ranch. Sharon Todd. Ed. by Bobbie J. Van Dolson. 96p. 1981. pap. price not set (ISBN 0-8280-0032-8). Review & Herald.

Adventures in Oregon Country. Robin Will. Ed. by Robert D. Shangle. LC 79-28595. 64p. Date not set. pap. 4.95 (ISBN 0-89802-064-6). Beautiful Am.

Adventures in Oriental Cooking. Ed. by Ortho Books Editorial Staff. LC 76-29252. 1977. 4.95 (ISBN 0-917102-24-X). Ortho.

Adventures in Pennsylvania. H. Bess Shires & Rita N. March. (gr. 5-6). 1976. pap. 3.50 (ISBN 0-931992-12-5). Penns Valley.

Adventures in Prayer. Marshall. 1976. 1.95 (ISBN 0-8007-8269-0). Revell.

Adventures in Public Service. Ed. by Ferdinand Kuhn & Delia Kuhn. LC 63-21855. 3.95 (ISBN 0-8149-0137-9). Vanguard.

Adventures in Stitches. Mariska Karasz. LC 59-10899. (Funk & W Bk.). (Illus.). 128p. 1975. pap. 5.95 o.s.i. (ISBN 0-308-10177-4, F-118, TYC-T). T Y Crowell.

Adventures in Stitches & More Adventures, Fewer Stitches. Mariska Karasz. (Funk & W Bk.). (Illus.). (gr. 7 up). 1959. 9.95 o.s.i. (ISBN 0-308-70181-X, TYC-T); pap. 5.95 o.s.i. (ISBN 0-308-10177-4). T y Crowell.

Adventures in the Land of Canaan. R. L. Berry. 128p. pap. 1.00. Faith Pub Hse.

Adventures in the Redwoods. Harriett E. Weaver. LC 75-3912. (Illus.). 1975. pap. 3.95 (ISBN 0-87701-060-9). Chronicle Bks.

Adventures in the Skin Trade & Other Stories. Dylan Thomas. LC 55-7367. 1955. 4.50 (ISBN 0-8112-0779-X, NDP183); pap. 3.75 (ISBN 0-8112-0202-X, NDP183). New Directions.

Adventures in the Supernormal: A Personal Memoir. Eileen J. Garrett. 1949. 4.95 o.p. (ISBN 0-912326-02-6). Garrett-Helix.

Adventures in the Unknown Interior of America. Cabeza De Vaca. Ed. & tr. by Cyclone Covey. 152p. 1972. pap. 1.25 o.s.i. (ISBN 0-02-031580-5, Collier). Macmillan.

Adventures in Urban Reading Series. Jacqueline Low & Yves Jacot. Incl. Choosing Sides (ISBN 0-8224-9401-9); Daydreamer (ISBN 0-8224-9406-X); Dope Pusher (ISBN 0-8224-9402-7); Good Joss Means Good Luck (ISBN 0-8224-9403-5). (gr. 4-8). 1974. pap. 2.00 ea. Pitman Learning.

Adventures in Washington Country. Robin Will. Ed. by Robert D. Shangle. (Illus.). 64p. 1981. pap. 4.95 (ISBN 0-89802-065-4). Beautiful Am.

Adventures in Wine Cookery. 2nd ed. California Winemakers. Ed. by Donna Bottrell et al. (Wine Cookbook Ser.). (Illus.). 128p. 1980. pap. 5.95 (ISBN 0-932664-10-5). Wine Appreciation.

Adventures of a Bank-Note, Seventeen Seventy to Seventeen Seventy-One, 4 vols. in 2. Thomas Bridges. Ed. by Michael F. Shugrue. (Flowering of the Novel, 1740-1775 Ser: Vol. 90). 1974. lib. bdg. 50.00 ea. (ISBN 0-8240-1189-9). Garland Pub.

Adventures of a Brownie, Repr. Of 1872 Ed. Dinah M. Mulock. Bd. with Little Lame Prince. Repr. of 1875 ed. LC 75-32175. (Classics of Children's Literature, 1621-1932: Vol. 38). (Illus.). 1977. PLB 38.00 (ISBN 0-8240-2287-4). Garland Pub.

Adventures of a Bystander. Peter F. Drucker. LC 78-2120. 344p. 1980. pap. 5.95 (ISBN 0-06-090774-6, CN 774, CN). Har-Row.

Adventures of a Cheap Antiquer. Arline Beitler. 1979. pap. 1.95 (ISBN 0-380-42804-0, 43804). Avon.

Adventures of a Cork-Screw, Seventeen Seventy-Five. Ed. by Michael F. Shugrue. (Flowering of the Novel, 1740-1775 Ser: Vol. 107). 1974. lib. bdg. 50.00 (ISBN 0-8240-1206-2). Garland Pub.

Adventures of a Jesuit, Seventeen Seventy-One, 2 vols. in 1. Ed. by Michael F. Shugrue. (Flowering of the Novel, 1740-1775 Ser: Vol. 94). 1974. lib. bdg. 50.00 (ISBN 0-8240-1193-7). Garland Pub.

Adventures of a Kidnapped Orphan, Seventeen Forty-Seven. Ed. by Michael F. Shugrue. (Flowering of the Novel, 1740-1775 Ser: Vol. 21). 1974. lib. bdg. 50.00 (ISBN 0-8240-1120-1). Garland Pub.

Adventures of a Letter. G. Warren Schloat, Jr. (Illus.). 48p. (gr. 3-7). 1949. reinforced bdg. 5.95 o.p. (ISBN 0-684-13479-9, ScribJ). Scribner.

Adventures of a Little Rag Doll. 1980. 4.95 (ISBN 0-8351-0764-7); pap. 2.50 (ISBN 0-8351-0757-4). China Bks.

Adventures of a Roving Playhouse. Anne C. Boise. 1981. 4.95 (ISBN 0-533-04550-9). Vantage.

Adventures of an Author: Written by Himself and a Friend, 2 vols. in 1. Ed. by Michael F. Shugrue. (Flowering of the Novel, 1740-1775 Ser: Vol. 77). 1974. lib. bdg. 50.00 (ISBN 0-8240-1176-7). Garland Pub.

Adventures of Barney Bean. Martha Bee. (Illus.). 1977. 6.95 o.p. (ISBN 0-533-02890-6). Vantage.

Adventures of Being a Wife. Mrs. Norman V. Peale. 1977. pap. 1.95 o.p. (ISBN 0-449-23439-8, Crest). Fawcett.

Adventures of Big-Foot Wallace. John C. Duval. Ed. by Mabel Major & Rebecca S. Lee. LC 36-334. 1966. pap. 4.50 (ISBN 0-8032-5053-3, BB 343, Bison). U of Nebr Pr.

Adventures of Caleb Williams. William Gidwin. LC 80-2481. 1981. Repr. of 1926 ed. 49.50 (ISBN 0-404-19115-0). AMS Pr.

Adventures of Captain Al Scabbard, No. 1. Lawrence J. Crabb, Jr. & Lawrence J. Crabb, Sr. 128p. (Orig.). (gr. 6-8). 1981. pap. 1.95 (ISBN 0-8024-0280-1). Moody.

Adventures of Captain Al Scabbard, No. 2. Lawrence J. Crabb, Jr. & Lawrence J. Crabb, Sr. 128p. (Orig.). (gr. 6-8). 1981. pap. 1.95 (ISBN 0-8024-0281-X). Moody.

Adventures of Captain William Walrus. Michael Duplaix. (ps-3). 1972. PLB 7.62 o.p. (ISBN 0-307-64545-2, Golden Pr). Western Pub.

Adventures of Carlo Pittore. C. S. Stanley. (Illus.). 18p. 1979. pap. 10.00 (ISBN 0-934376-01-8). Pittore Euforico.

Adventures of Crawfish-Man. Timothy Edler. (Tim Edler's Tales from the Atchafalaya Ser.). (Illus.). 40p. (gr. k-8). 1979. 5.00x (ISBN 0-931108-04-7). Little Cajun.

Adventures of Creighton Holmes. Ned Hubbell. 1979. pap. 1.95 o.p. (ISBN 0-445-04350-4). Popular Lib.

Adventures of D. W. Griffith. Karl Brown. Ed. by Kevin Brownlow. (Illus.). 251p. 1973. 10.00 (ISBN 0-374-10093-4). FS&G.

Adventures of Dan & Mark. S. Norman Strandholt. (gr. 1-4). 1978. 4.00 o.p. (ISBN 0-682-49070-9). Exposition.

Adventures of David Simple, 1744, 2 vols. in 1. 2nd ed. Sarah Fielding. Ed. by Michael F. Shugrue. (Flowering of the Novel, 1740-1775 Ser: Vol. 14). 1974. lib. bdg. 50.00 (ISBN 0-8240-1113-9). Garland Pub.

Adventures of Davy & Bartholomew. Joseph L. Wright. LC 78-66284. (Illus., Orig.). (gr. 3-6). 1979. pap. 1.95 (ISBN 0-9602290-1-9). Delanie Way.

Adventures of Egbert the Easter Egg. Richard Armour. (Illus.). (gr. k-3). 1965. PLB 7.95 o.p. (ISBN 0-07-002236-4, GB). McGraw.

Adventures of Emmera; or, the Fair American, 1767, 2 vols. in 1. Arthur Young. Ed. by Michael F. Shugrue. (Flowering of the Novel, 1740-1775 Ser: Vol. 80). 1974. lib. bdg. 50.00 (ISBN 0-8240-1179-1). Garland Pub.

Adventures of Eovaai, Princess of Ijaveo. Elizabeth Haywood. LC 70-170595. (Foundations of the Novel Ser.: Vol. 65). lib. bdg. 50.00 (ISBN 0-8240-0577-5). Garland Pub.

Adventures of Ferdinand Count Fathom. Tobias Smollet. Ed. by Damian Grant. (Oxford English Novels Ser). 1971. 14.95x (ISBN 0-19-255321-6). Oxford U Pr.

Adventures of Gerard. new ed. Arthur Conan Doyle. 15.95 (ISBN 0-7195-3226-4). Transatlantic.

Adventures of Healing: How to Use New Testament Practices & Receive New Testament Results. rev. ed. Donald W. Bartow. 371p. 1981. pap. 5.95 (ISBN 0-938736-02-7). Life Enrich.

Adventures of Herbilee & Harbilee Hitlow. Buck Scribbs. Ed. by Sam Garner. 72p. (Orig.). 1980. pap. 2.95 (ISBN 0-935440-00-3). October Pr.

Adventures of Huckleberry Finn. 2nd ed. Samuel L. Clemens. Ed. by Sculley Bradley & Richmond C. Beatty. LC 76-30648. (Critical Eidtions). 1977. 15.00 (ISBN 0-393-04454-8); pap. 4.95x (ISBN 0-393-09146-5). Norton.

Adventures of Huckleberry Finn. Mark Twain. (Literature Ser). (gr. 7-12). 1969. pap. text ed. 3.75 (ISBN 0-87720-701-1). AMSCO Sch.

Adventures of Huckleberry Finn. Mark Twain. Ed. by Leo Marx. LC 66-30699. 1967. 6.50 o.p. (ISBN 0-672-51108-8, LL4); pap. 5.75 (ISBN 0-672-60969-X, LL4). Bobbs.

Adventures of Huckleberry Finn. Mark Twain. (gr. 7 up). 1962. 5.95g o.s.i. (ISBN 0-02-789550-5). Macmillan.

Adventures of Huckleberry Finn. rev. ed. Mark Twain. Ed. by Robert J. Dixson. (American Classics Ser.: Bk. 9). (gr. 9-12). 1973. pap. 2.75 (ISBN 0-88345-205-7, 18128); cassettes 40.00 (ISBN 0-685-38990-1); tapes 40.00 (ISBN 0-685-38991-X). Regents Pub.

Adventures of Huckleberry Finn: Twentieth Century Interpretations. C. Simpson. 1968. 7.95 o.p. (ISBN 0-13-013995-5, Spec). P-H.

Adventures of Huckleberry Finn with Reader's Guide. Mark Twain. (Amsco Literature Program). (gr. 9-12). 1972. pap. text ed. 4.58 (ISBN 0-87720-816-6); with model ans. 2.95 (ISBN 0-87720-916-2). AMSCO Sch.

Adventures of Jack Wander, 1766. Ed. by Michael F. Shugrue. (Flowering of the Novel, 1740-1775 Ser: Vol. 73). 1974. lib. bdg. 50.00 (ISBN 0-8240-1172-4). Garland Pub.

Adventures of Jules De Grandin: Phantom Fighter. (Seabury Quinn Ser.: No. 1). 1976. pap. 1.25 o.p. (ISBN 0-445-00394-4). Popular Lib.

Adventures of Kama Pua'a. Guy Buffet & Pam Buffet. Ed. by Ruth Tabrah. LC 72-76459. (Illus.). (gr. 1-7). 1972. 5.95 (ISBN 0-89610-003-0). Island Her.

Adventures of King Midas. Lynne R. Banks. (Illus.). 1976. 9.00x o.p. (ISBN 0-460-06752-4, Pub. by J. M. Dent England). Biblio Dist.

Adventures of Lindamira, a Lady of Quality. Bd. with Jilted Bridegroom: The London Coquet. LC 72-170507. LC 79-170506. (Foundations of the Novel Ser.: Vol. 5). lib. bdg. 50.00 (ISBN 0-8240-0517-1). Garland Pub.

Adventures of Little Mouk. Wilhelm Hauff. Tr. by Elizabeth Shub. LC 74-4420. (Illus.). 36p. (gr. k-3). 1975. 6.95g o.s.i. (ISBN 0-02-743400-1). Macmillan.

Adventures of Little Rabbit. Anne-Marie Dalmais. (ps-2). 1972. PLB 9.15 o.p. (ISBN 0-307-63633-X, Golden Pr). Western Pub.

Adventures of Long John Silver. Denis Judd. (YA) 1978. pap. 1.75 (ISBN 0-380-42275-1, 42275). Avon.

Adventures of Miss Bigley & Her Little Store. Ellen Shire. (gr. k-3). 1971. 4.95 o.s.i. (ISBN 0-8027-6003-1); PLB 4.85 o.s.i. (ISBN 0-8027-6004-X). Walker & Co.

Adventures of Mr. George Edwards, a Creole, 1751. John Hill. Ed. by Michael F. Shugrue. (Flowering of the Novel, 1740-1775 Ser: Vol. 34). 1974. lib. bdg. 50.00 (ISBN 0-8240-1133-3). Garland Pub.

Adventures of Moshie Cat. Helen Griffiths. (gr. 4-6). 1977. pap. 1.25 o.s.i. (ISBN 0-671-29816-X). Archway.

Adventures of Mrs. Pussycat. (Illus.). (gr. k-3). 1972. PLB 5.95 o.p. (ISBN 0-13-014142-9); pap. 1.95 o.p. (ISBN 0-13-014126-7). P-H.

Adventures of Oliver Twist. Charles Dickens. (World's Classics Ser: No. 8). 12.95 (ISBN 0-19-250008-2). Oxford U Pr.

Adventures of Oxymel Classic, Esq., Once an Oxford Scholar, 1768. Ed. by Michael F. Shugrue. (Flowering of the Novel, 1740-1775 Ser: Vol. 82). 1974. lib. bdg. 50.00 (ISBN 0-8240-1181-3). Garland Pub.

Adventures of Picklock Holes. R. C. Lehmann. (Illus.). 64p. 1975. 10.00 o.p. (ISBN 0-915230-07-0); pap. 5.00 o.p. (ISBN 0-915230-08-9). Rue Morgue.

Adventures of Pinocchio. C. Collodi. Tr. by Carol Della Chiesa. (Illus.). (gr. 3-5). 1972. pap. 1.50 o.s.i. (ISBN 0-02-042740-9, Collier). Macmillan.

Adventures of Pinocchio. rev. ed. Carlo Collodi. Tr. by Carol D. Chiesa. LC 25-26908. (Illus.). (gr. k-5). 1969. deluxe ed. 19.95 (ISBN 0-02-722820-7). Macmillan.

Adventures of Pryderi: Taken from the Mabinogion. W. Griffith. 1962. 7.50x (ISBN 0-7083-0418-4). Verry.

Adventures of Rivella. Mary D. Manley. Bd. with Adventures & Surprizing Deliverances of James Dubourdieu & His Wife Who Were Taken by Pyrates. Ambrose Evans. LC 73-170534. LC 70-170533. (Foundations of the Novel Ser.: Vol. 22). lib. bdg. 50.00 (ISBN 0-8240-0534-1). Garland Pub.

Adventures of Robin Hood. Roger L. Green. (Orig.). (gr. 2-5). 1956. pap. 2.50 (ISBN 0-14-030101-1, Puffin). Penguin.

Adventures of Sherlock Holmes. Arthur Conan Doyle. (gr. 10 up). pap. 2.25 (ISBN 0-425-04869-1, Medallion). Berkley Pub.

Adventures of Sherlock Holmes. facsimile ed. Arthur Conan Doyle. (Illus.). 328p. 1975. pap. 3.95 o.p. (ISBN 0-89104-023-4). A & W Pubs.

Adventures of Spider. Joyce C. Arkhurst. (Illus.). (gr. 2-6). 1964. 7.95 (ISBN 0-316-05106-3). Little.

Adventures of Sylvia Hughes, Written by Herself 1761. Ed. by Michael F. Shugrue. (Flowering of the Novel, 1740-1775 Ser: Vol. 56). 1974. lib. bdg. 50.00 (ISBN 0-8240-1155-4). Garland Pub.

Adventures of Telemachus, 2 vols. Fenelon & Francois De Salignac De La Mothe. Ed. by Ronald Paulson. LC 78-60835. (Novel 1720-1805 Ser.: Vol. 1). 1979. lib. bdg. 31.00 (ISBN 0-8240-3650-6). Garland Pub.

Adventures of the Black Hand Gang. Press. (gr. 3-5). 1980. pap. 1.25 (ISBN 0-590-30000-8, Schol Pap). Schol Bk Serv.

Adventures of the Black Hand Gang. Hans J. Press. Tr. by Barbara Littlewood from Ger. LC 77-5950. (Illus.). (gr. 2-5). 1977. PLB 6.95 (ISBN 0-13-013938-6). P-H.

Adventures of the Hole Eating Duck Tinker. Woodroffe. 1980. cancelled (ISBN 0-8120-5395-8). Barron.

Adventures of the S. S. Happiness Crew: Cap'n Joshua's Dangerous Dilemma. June Dutton. (Illus.). 1980. 4.95 (ISBN 0-915696-36-3). Determined Prods.

Adventures of the Superkids, Bk. 1. Pleasant Rowland. (Addison-Wesley Reading Program). (gr. 1). 1979. pap. text ed. 6.40 (ISBN 0-201-20600-5, Sch Div); six skillbks 4.72 (ISBN 0-201-20601-3); tchr. guides in binder 38.50 (ISBN 0-201-20602-1); end-of-level tests 20.32. A-W.

Adventures of Tim Rabbit. Alison Uttley. (Illus.). (ps-5). 1945. 6.95 (ISBN 0-571-05676-8, Pub. by Faber & Faber). Merrimack Bk Serv.

Adventures of Tom Sawyer. Samuel L. Clemens. LC 58-13029. (Great Il. Classics). (Illus.). (gr. 7 up). 1979. 8.95 (ISBN 0-396-07743-9). Dodd.

Adventures of Tom Sawyer. Mark Twain. (Literature Ser). (gr. 7-12). 1969. pap. text ed. 3.42 (ISBN 0-87720-702-X). AMSCO Sch.

Adventures of Tom Sawyer. holiday ed. Mark Twain. (Illus.). 10.00 o.p. (ISBN 0-06-014465-3, HarpT); PLB 7.87 o.p. (ISBN 0-06-014427-0). Har-Row.

Adventures of Tom Sawyer. Mark Twain. (Illus.). (gr. 5-8). 1962. 3.95g o.s.i. (ISBN 0-02-789630-7). Macmillan.

Adventures of Tom Sawyer. Mark Twain. LC 78-2796. (Raintree's Illustrated Classics). (Illus.). (gr. 5-8). 1978. PLB 9.65 (ISBN 0-8393-6205-6). Raintree Child.

Adventures of Tom Sawyer. Mark Twain. Ed. by John C. Gerber et al. Incl. Tom Sawyer Abroad; Tom Sawyer Detective. (Iowa-California Works of Mark Twain). 1980. 27.50 (ISBN 0-520-03353-1). U of Cal Pr.

Adventures of Ulysses. Gerald Gottlieb. (World Landmark Ser.: No. 40). (Illus.). (gr. 5-9). 1959. PLB 4.39 o.p. (ISBN 0-394-90540-7, BYR). Random.

Adventures on Library Shelves. M. Ringstad. LC 68-16398. (Illus.). (gr. 2 up). 1967. PLB 7.99 prebound (ISBN 0-87783-156-4); pap. 2.75 (ISBN 0-686-66511-2). Oddo.

Adventures Through the Bible. rev. ed. Dana Eynon. 176p. (gr. 3-6). 1980. pap. 6.95 (ISBN 0-87239-378-X, 3234). Standard Pub.

Adventures with a Straw. Harry Milgrom. (Illus.). (ps-2). 1967. lib. bdg. 7.95 o.p. (ISBN 0-525-25229-0). Dutton.

Adventures with a Texas Naturalist. Roy Bedichek. (Illus.). 1961. pap. 7.95 (ISBN 0-292-70311-2). U of Tex Pr.

Adventures with Aeneas. George M. Singleton. (Lat). (gr. 7-9). 1969. 4.95 (ISBN 0-312-00665-9). St Martin.

Adventures with Collage. Jan Beany. LC 79-128406. (Illus.). (gr. 5-9). 1970. 6.95 (ISBN 0-7232-6033-8). Warne.

Adventures with God. Ed. by Harry N. Huxhold. LC 66-15551. 1966. pap. 5.50 (ISBN 0-570-03736-0, 12-2640). Concordia.

Adventures with Paper. A. Van Breda. 1955. 6.50 (ISBN 0-571-06982-7, Pub. by Faber & Faber). Merrimack Bk Serv.

Adventures with Words, 2 bks. Joseph Bellafiore. (gr. 9-12). 1971. Bk. 1. wkbk. 5.25 (ISBN 0-87720-353-9); Bk. 2. wkbk 5.25 (ISBN 0-87720-355-5). AMSCO Sch.

Adventuring. Raphael Hayes. (Orig.). 1979. pap. 1.75 o.s.i. (ISBN 0-515-04804-6, Jove). Jove Pubns.

Adventuring in Archaeology. Cottie A. Burland. LC 63-11556. (Illus.). (gr. 4-8). 1963. 6.95 (ISBN 0-7232-6029-X). Warne.

Adventuring in the Church. William Backus et al. pap. 4.85 (ISBN 0-933350-08-2); tchrs' ed. 1.95 (ISBN 0-933350-58-9). Morse Pr.

Adventurous Decade: Comic Strips in the Thirties. Ron Goulart. 1975. 8.95 o.p. (ISBN 0-87000-252-X). Arlington Hse.

Adventurous Future. Paul H. Bowman. 296p. 1959. 3.75 o.p. (ISBN 0-87178-011-9). Brethren.

Adventurous Simplicissimus. H. J. Von Grimmelshausen. Tr. by A. T. Goodrick. LC 62-8406. (Illus.). 1962. pap. 3.95x (ISBN 0-8032-5077-0, BB 134, Bison). U of Nebr Pr.

Adventurous World of Paris Nineteen Hundred to Nineteen Fourteen. Nigel Gosling. LC 78-52477. (Illus.). 1978. 17.95 o.p. (ISBN 0-688-03366-0). Morrow.

Adverbes en Chinois Moderne. V. Alleton. (Materiaux Pour L'etude De L'extreme-Orient Moderne et Contemporain, Etudes Linguistiques: No. 4). 1972. pap. 24.10x (ISBN 90-2796-989-2). Mouton.

Adverbs & Comparatives: An Analytical Bibliography. Conrad Sabourin. (Library & Information Sources in Linguistics: No. 2). 1979. text ed. 31.50x (ISBN 0-391-01647-4). Humanities.

Adversaries: America, Russia and the Open World 1941-1962. Michael Balfour. 224p. 1981. price not set (ISBN 0-7100-0687-X). Routledge & Kegan.

Adverse Mechanical Tension of the Central Nervous System: An Analysis of Cause & Effect. Alf Breig. LC 77-88852. 1978. 84.50 (ISBN 0-471-04137-8, Pub. by Wiley Medical). Wiley.

Adverse Selection in the Labor Market. Bruce C. Greenwald. LC 78-75052. (Outstanding Dissertations in Economics Ser.). 1979. lib. bdg. 30.00 (ISBN 0-8240-4130-5). Garland Pub.

Advertised Orgy. (Illus.). pap. 5.00 (ISBN 0-910550-27-1). Centurion Pr.

Advertisements for Myself. Norman Mailer. 540p. 1981. pap. 6.95 (ISBN 0-399-50538-5, Perigee). Putnam.

Advertising. William H. Bolen. LC 80-18915. (Wiley Ser in Marketing). 600p. 1981. text ed. 19.95 (ISBN 0-471-03486-X). Wiley.

Advertising. 4th ed. Dunn. 1978. 21.95 (ISBN 0-03-014341-1). Dryden Pr.

Advertising. 4th ed. Albert W. Frey & Jean C. Halterman. 593p. 1970. 24.50x (ISBN 0-8260-3245-1, 33291). Wiley.

Advertising. 2nd ed. Maurice I. Mandell. 1974. 18.95 o.p. (ISBN 0-13-014472-X). P-H.

Advertising. 3rd ed. Maurice I. Mandell. (Illus.). 1980. text ed. 21.95 (ISBN 0-13-014449-5). P-H.

Advertising. 2nd ed. David S. Nicholl. LC 74-152834. (Illus.). 196p. 1978. 13.50x (ISBN 0-7121-0166-7). Intl Pubns Serv.

Advertising: A Behavioral Approach for Managers. Edmund W. Faison. LC 79-21379. (Wiley Series in Marketing). 1980. text ed. 21.95 (ISBN 0-471-04956-5); tchrs.' manual avail. (ISBN 0-471-07768-2). Wiley.

Advertising Agency & Studio Skills. 3rd ed. Tom Cardamone. 160p. 1981. 10.95 (ISBN 0-8230-0151-2). Watson-Guptill.

Advertising Agency & Studio Skills: A Guide to the Preparation of Art & Mechanicals for Reproduction. rev. ed. Tom Cardamone. (Illus.). 1970. 9.95 o.p. (ISBN 0-8230-0150-4). Watson-Guptill.

Advertising & Competition. Jules Backman. LC 67-17108. (Illus.). 1967. 12.00x (ISBN 0-8147-0020-9). NYU Pr.

Advertising & Economic Behaviour. Keith Cowling et al. 202p. 1975. text ed. 35.00x o.p. (ISBN 0-8419-5006-7). Holmes & Meier.

Advertising & Free Speech. Ed. by Allen Hyman & M. Bruce Johnson. LC 77-5272. 1977. 14.95 (ISBN 0-669-01604-7). Lexington Bks.

Advertising & Marketing Research: A New Methodology. B. Stuart Tolley. LC 77-1120. 1977. 21.95x (ISBN 0-88229-179-3). Nelson-Hall.

Advertising & Press Annual of Sothern Africa, 1980. Ed. by F. M. Botha. LC 52-41681. (Illus.). 278p. 1980. 62.50x (ISBN 0-8002-2727-1). Intl Pubns Serv.

Advertising & Public Relations for a Small Business. Diane Bellavance. (Illus.). 80p. 1980. pap. 5.95 (ISBN 0-9605276-0-5). DBA Bks.

Advertising & the Practice of Marketing. Kenneth E. Runyon. (Marketing & Management Ser.). 1979. text ed. 19.95 (ISBN 0-675-08311-7); instructor's manual 3.95 (ISBN 0-686-67275-5); transparencies 3.95 (ISBN 0-686-67276-3). Merrill.

Advertising Art. Tony Hinwood. 16.95 (ISBN 0-7153-5694-1). David & Charles.

Advertising Campaigns: Formulation & Tactics. 2nd ed. Leon Quera. LC 76-42684. (Advertising & Journalism Ser.). 1977. text ed. 20.95 (ISBN 0-88244-130-2). Grid Pub.

Advertising Controversy: Evidence on the Economic Effects of Advertising. Mark S. Albion & Paul Farris. 224p. 1980. 19.95 (ISBN 0-86569-057-X). Auburn Hse.

Advertising Copywriting. 4th ed. Philip W. Burton. LC 77-81533. (Advertising Ser.). 1978. text ed. 20.95 (ISBN 0-88244-159-0). Grid Pub.

Advertising Dolls. Joleen Robison & Kay Sellers. (Illus.). 1980. pap. 9.95 (ISBN 0-89145-134-X). Collector Bks.

Advertising for a Small Business. Jeffrey Feinman. Date not set. cancelled (ISBN 0-671-96123-3); pap. 2.95 (ISBN 0-346-12416-2). Cornerstone.

Advertising Giveaways to Baskets. Time-Life Books Editors. LC 77-99201. (Encyclopedia of Collectibles Ser.). (Illus.). 1978. lib. bdg. 10.98 (ISBN 0-686-50972-2). Silver.

Advertising: How to Write the Kind That Works. David L. Malickson & John W. Nason. LC 76-18310. (Illus.). 320p. 1977. 12.50 (ISBN 0-684-14770-X, ScribT); pap. 7.95 (ISBN 0-684-14771-8, SL679, ScribT). Scribner.

Advertising in the Marketplace. John D. Burke. (Illus.). 454p. 1973. text ed. 16.95 (ISBN 0-07-009031-9, G); instructors' manual & key 4.00 (ISBN 0-07-009032-7). McGraw.

Advertising Law Anthology, Vol. Philip A. Garon. LC 73-87656. 1981. 59.95 (ISBN 0-686-69402-3). Intl Lib.

Advertising Law Anthology: 1973, Vol. I-VI. Ed. by Philip A. Garon. LC 73-87656. (National Law Anthology Ser.). 1973. 59.95 ea.; Vol. 1, 1973. (ISBN 0-914250-01-9). Vol.II, 1974 (ISBN 0-914250-07-8). Vol. III, 1975 (ISBN 0-914250-09-4). Vol. IV, 1976 (ISBN 0-914250-11-6). Vol. V, 1977-78 (ISBN 0-914250-15-9). Vol. VI, 1979 (ISBN 0-914250-18-3). Vol VII, 1980-81 (ISBN 0-914250-22-1). complete set 344.90 (ISBN 0-914250-05-1). Intl Lib.

Advertising Law Handbook. 2nd ed. Diana Woolley. 106p. 1976. text ed. 21.00x (ISBN 0-220-66306-8, Pub. by Busn Bks England). Renouf.

Advertising Layout Basics: Ad Kit 4. Larry Notman. 220p. 1981. pap. 4.00x (ISBN 0-918488-09-5). Newspaper Serv.

Advertising Management. C. Gilligan & G. Crowther. 1976. 33.00x (ISBN 0-86003-500-X, Pub. by Allan Pubs England); pap. 16.50x (ISBN 0-86003-600-6). State Mutual Bk.

Advertising Management: Test & Cases. Robert L. Anderson & Thomas E. Barry. (Marketing & Management Ser.). 1979. text ed. 18.95 (ISBN 0-675-08302-8); instructor's manual 3.95 (ISBN 0-685-60799-2). Merrill.

Advertising Media. Donald W. Jugenheimer & Peter B. Turk. LC 79-23007. (Grid Ser. in Advertising-Journalism). 1980. text ed. 17.95 (ISBN 0-88244-210-4). Grid Pub.

Advertising Principles & Problems. 5th ed. Charles J. Dirksen & Arthur Kroeger. 1977. text ed. 17.95x (ISBN 0-256-01925-8). Irwin.

Advertising Procedure. 6th ed. D. Kleppner. 1973. 16.95 o.p. (ISBN 0-13-018069-6). P-H.

Advertising Procedure. 7th ed. Otto Kleppner & Norman Govoni. LC 78-5728. 1979. 21.00 (ISBN 0-13-018119-6). P-H.

Advertising Pure & Simple. Hank Seiden. (AMACOM Executive Bks). 1978. pap. 5.95 (ISBN 0-8144-7510-8). Am Mgmt.

Advertising Research. Tom Cannon. 1973. pap. text ed. 11.00x (ISBN 0-7002-0220-X). Intl Ideas.

Advertising Strategy: A Communication Theory Approach. Larry Percy & John R. Rossiter. LC 79-25228. 314p. 1980. 26.50 (ISBN 0-03-055906-5). Praeger.

Advertising: The Economic Implications. Tom Cannon. 1974. text ed. 16.95x (ISBN 0-685-83689-4). Intl Ideas.

Advertising: Theory & Practice. 10th ed. Charles H. Sandage et al. 1979. text ed. 18.95 (ISBN 0-256-02174-0). Irwin.

Advertising: Three Thousand B. C. to Nineteen Hundred A.D. Maurice Annenberg. LC 77-75421. 1969. 20.00 o.p. (ISBN 0-916526-02-X). Maran Pub.

Advertising Today. 2nd ed. Frank Jefkins. 1977. text ed. 27.50x (ISBN 0-7002-0263-3); pap. text ed. 16.95x (ISBN 0-7002-0265-X). Intl Ideas.

Advertising Today. J. Douglas Johnson. LC 78-15897. 416p. 1978. pap. text ed. 15.95 (ISBN 0-574-19355-3, 13-2355); instr's guide avail. (ISBN 0-574-19356-1, 13-2356). SRA.

Advertising Yearbook. Ed. by Crain Books Staff. 1981. price not set (ISBN 0-87251-056-5). Crain Bks.

Advertising Your Way to Success: How to Create Best-Selling Advertisements in All Media. Cort Sutton. (Illus.). 208p. 1981. text ed. 18.95 (ISBN 0-686-68610-1, Spec); pap. text ed. 9.95 (ISBN 0-13-018135-8, Spec). P-H.

Advice About Buying a Car, Car Maintenance, Car Repair. (Home Adviser Ser.). 80p. (Orig.). 1981. pap. 1.95 (ISBN 0-8326-2405-5, 7053). Delair.

Advice About Drugs, Food, Fitness. (Home Adviser Ser.). 80p. (Orig.). 1981. pap. 1.95 (ISBN 0-8326-2408-X, 7050). Delair.

Advice About First Aid, High Blood Pressure, Heart Attack. (Home Adviser Ser.). 80p. (Orig.). 1981. pap. 1.95 (ISBN 0-8326-2404-7, 7054). Delair.

Advice About Household Appliances, Cooking, Entertaining. (Home Adviser Ser.). 80p. (Orig.). 1981. pap. 1.95 (ISBN 0-8326-2403-9, 7052). Delair.

Advice About Insurance, Credit, Budgeting. (Home Adviser Ser.). 80p. (Orig.). 1981. pap. 1.95 (ISBN 0-8326-2407-1, 7051). Delair.

Advice About Tools & Home Repair. (Home Adviser Ser.). 80p. (Orig.). 1981. pap. 1.95 (ISBN 0-8326-2406-3, 7055). Delair.

Advice Among Masters: The Ideal in Slave Management in the Old South. Ed. by James O. Breeden. LC 79-54054. (Contributions in Afro-American & African Studies: No. 51). (Illus.). xxvi, 350p. 1980. lib. bdg. 25.00 (ISBN 0-313-20658-9, BRS/). Greenwood.

Advice from the Soccer Pros. David Faries. LC 79-64730. (Illus.). 166p. 1980. pap. 4.95 (ISBN 0-89037-219-5). Anderson World.

Advice How to Plant Tobacco in England. LC 72-6032. (English Experience Ser.: No. 559). 1973. Repr. of 1615 ed. 6.00 (ISBN 90-221-0559-8). Walter J Johnson.

Advice to a Young Scientist. P. B. Medawar. LC 79-1676. 128p. 1981. pap. 3.95 (ISBN 0-06-090810-6, CN 810, CN). Har-Row.

Advice to Parents of a Cleft Palate Child. Donna K. Wicka & Mervyn L. Falk. (Illus.). 68p. 1970. pap. 7.75 photocopy ed. spiral (ISBN 0-398-02061-2). C C Thomas.

Advice to Young Men. William Cobbett. 352p. 1980. 16.50x (ISBN 0-19-212212-6). Oxford U Pr.

Advise & Consent. Allen Drury. LC 59-9137. 1959. 12.95 (ISBN 0-385-05419-X). Doubleday.

Advise & Consent. Allen Drury. 1972. pap. 2.50 (ISBN 0-380-01007-0, 35543). Avon.

Advising Ministers: A Case Study of the South West Economic Planning Council. Brian C. Smith. (Library of Political Studies). 1969. text ed. 7.25x (ISBN 0-7100-6371-7). Humanities.

Advising Schools: A Handbook for Concerned Citizens. W. James Popham. 1977. pap. 7.95 (ISBN 0-932166-00-8). Instruct Object.

Advisor Handbook for Counterinsurgency: Field Manual 31-73. U.S. Army. (Illus.). 1977. pap. 5.00 o.p. (ISBN 0-87364-091-8). Paladin Ent.

Advisory Jurisdiction of the International Court. Dharma Pratap. 310p. 1972. text ed. 39.50x (ISBN 0-19-825302-8). Oxford U Pr.

Advocacy. S. C. Consul & C. Chandra. 1967. 5.50x o.p. (ISBN 0-210-26934-0). Asia.

Advocacy Advertising & Large Corporations: Social Conflict, Big Business Image, the News Media, and Public Policy. S. Prakash Sethi. LC 76-6770. 1976. 25.95 o.p. (ISBN 0-669-00678-5). Lexington Bks.

Advocacy & Age: Issues, Experiences, Strategies. Ed. by Paul A. Kerschner. LC 76-22321. 1976. 4.50 (ISBN 0-88474-035-8). USC Andrus Geron.

Advocacy & Objectivity: A Crisis in the Professionalization of American Social Science, 1865-1905. Mary O. Furner. LC 73-86403. 376p. 1975. 19.50x (ISBN 0-8131-1309-1). U Pr of Ky.

Advocacy Conference: Proceedings. 1978. 4.00 (ISBN 0-86671-039-6). Comm Coun Great NY.

Advocate Guide to Gay Health. R. D. Fenwick. (Illus.). 1978. 10.95 o.p. (ISBN 0-525-05050-7). Dutton.

AEG Manual Two: General Electrical Engineering. 8th ed. LC 67-24080. (Illus.). 1972. 25.00x (ISBN 3-87087-023-0). Intl Pubns Serv.

Aegean Turkey. George E. Bean. (Illus.). 1980. 17.50 o.p. (ISBN 0-393-01328-6). Norton.

Aegean World. Alfred Nawrath. (Illus.). 1978. 25.00 o.p. (ISBN 0-88331-097-X, Joseph Binns Bk). McKay.

AElfric's Catholic Homilies: The Second Series Text. AElfric. Ed. by Malcolm Godden. (Early English Text Soc., Supplementary Ser.: No. 5). (Illus.). 480p. 1979. text ed. 49.50x (ISBN 0-19-722405-9). Oxford U Pr.

Aelita. Alexei Tolstoy. Tr. by Antonina W. Bouis from Rus. (Best of Soviet Science Fiction Ser.). 156p. 1981. 9.95 (ISBN 0-02-619200-4). Macmillan.

Aelred of Rievaulx: A Study. Aelred Squire. (Cistercian Studies Ser.: No. 50). 192p. 1981. price not set (ISBN 0-87907-950-9); pap. price not set. Cistercian Pubns.

Aeneid. 2nd ed. Vergil. Ed. & tr. by Frank O. Copley. LC 74-28088. (LLA Ser). 350p. 1975. pap. text ed. 6.95 (ISBN 0-672-61370-0). Bobbs.

Aeneid. Virgil. 1957. 5.00x o.p. (ISBN 0-460-00161-2, Evman). Dutton.

Aeneid. Virgil. Tr. by William F. Knight. (Classics Ser.). (Orig.). 1956. pap. 2.95 (ISBN 0-14-044051-8). Penguin.

Aeneid for Boys & Girls. Alfred J. Church. (gr. 6 up). 1962. 4.95g o.s.i. (ISBN 0-02-718400-5). Macmillan.

Aeneid of Virgil. Rolfe Humphries. 1951. pap. 4.95 (ISBN 0-684-71816-2, SL6, ScribT). Scribner.

Aeneid of Virgil. Virgil. 1953. pap. 2.95 (ISBN 0-385-09318-7, A20, Anch). Doubleday.

Aeneidos: Liber Quartus. Virgil. Ed. by R. G. Austin. 1955. 14.50x (ISBN 0-19-872020-3). Oxford U Pr.

Aeneidos: Liber Secundus. Virgil. Ed. by R. G. Austin. 1964. 18.95x (ISBN 0-19-872018-1); pap. 13.95x (ISBN 0-19-872106-4). Oxford U Pr.

Aeneidos: Libri VII & VIII. Virgil. Ed. by John D. Christie. (Lat.). 1978. text ed. 36.00x (ISBN 0-19-713309-6). Oxford U Pr.

Aeolic Style in Architecture: A Survey of Its Development in Palestine, the Halikarnassos Peninsula, & Greece, 1000-500 B.C. Philip P. Betancourt. LC 76-45890. (Illus.). 1977. text ed. 30.00 (ISBN 0-691-03922-4). Princeton U Pr.

Aeration of Activated Sludge in Sewage Treatment. D. L. Gibbon. LC 74-8138. 126p. 1975. text ed. 23.00 (ISBN 0-08-018156-2). Pergamon.

Aere Perennius. David G. Fratter. (Lat. & Eng.). 1969. 4.95 (ISBN 0-312-00735-3). St Martin.

Aerial America: From Sea to Shining Sea. Aerial Photo. Date not set. 3.95 (ISBN 0-936672-11-0). Aerial Photo.

Aerial Models. Dorothy Diamond. LC 77-82978. (Teaching Primary Science Ser.). 1978. pap. text ed. 6.95 (ISBN 0-356-05074-2). Raintree Child.

Aerial Photo Interpretation. G. Barry Sully. 1971. pap. text ed. 10.95x (ISBN 0-435-34865-5). Heinemann Ed.

Aerial Photography & Remote Sensing for Soil Survey. L. P. White. (Monographs on Soil Survey). (Illus.). 1977. 24.00x (ISBN 0-19-854509-6). Oxford U Pr.

Aerial Photography: The Story of Aerial Mapping & Reconnaissance. Grover Heiman, Jr. (U. S. Air Force Academy Ser.). (Illus.). 192p. 1972. 5.95 o.s.i. (ISBN 0-02-550770-2). Macmillan.

Aerial Reconnaissance for Archaeology. Ed. by D. R. Wilson. 158p. 1980. pap. 29.95x (ISBN 0-900312-29-7, Pub. by Coun Brit Arch England). Intl Schol Bk Serv.

Aero Album, 8 vols. Kenn C. Rust & Paul Matt. Incl. Vol. 5. 1968. pap. o.p. (ISBN 0-8168-0104-5); Vol. 6. 1968. (ISBN 0-8168-0105-3); Vol. 7. 1968. (ISBN 0-8168-0106-1); Vol. 8. 1968. pap. (ISBN 0-8168-0107-X). 1.50 ea. Aero.

Aero Armor Series, Vol. 11. Uwe Feist. LC 79-91946. (Illus.). 1979. pap. 3.95 (ISBN 0-8168-2040-6). Aero.

Aero-Armor Series, Vol. 12. Uwe Feist. LC 80-66353. 52p. 1980. pap. 3.95 (ISBN 0-8168-2044-9). Aero.

Aero Armor Series, Vol. 13. Uwe Feist. 52p. 1981. pap. 3.95 (ISBN 0-8168-2046-5). Aero.

Aero Armor Series, Vol. 14. Uwe Feist. LC 80-66353. (Orig.). 1981. pap. 3.95 (ISBN 0-8168-2048-1). Aero.

Aero-Hydrodynamics of Sailing. C. A. Marchaj. LC 79-27724. (Illus.). 1980. 40.00 (ISBN 0-396-07739-0). Dodd.

Aero Pictorial, No. 6. Uwe Feist. 100p. 1980. 6.95 (ISBN 0-8168-0320-X). Aero.

Aero Pictorial, Vol. 5: Luftwaffe in WW II - Pt. 2. Uwe Feist. LC 68-28679. 100p. 1980. pap. 6.95 (ISBN 0-8168-0316-1). Aero.

Aerobatics. Don Berliner. LC 80-10914. (Superwheels & Thrill Sports Bks.). (Illus.). 48p. (gr. 4 up). 1980. PLB 6.95 (ISBN 0-8225-0436-7). Lerner Pubns.

Aerobatics Today. Bob O'Dell. (Illus.). 224p. 1980. 12.95 (ISBN 0-312-00759-0). St Martin.

Aerobic Gram-Negative Bronchopneumonias: Proceedings. Symposium on Aerobic Gram-Negative Bronchopneumonias, Brussels, Sep. 22, 1978. Ed. by J. Kalstersky et al. LC 79-42759. (Illus.). 120p. 1980. 29.00 (ISBN 0-08-025533-7). Pergamon.

Aerobic Nutrition: The Long-Life Plan for Ageless Health & Vigor. Donald Mannerberg & Jane Roth. 1981. 14.95 (ISBN 0-8015-0070-2). Dutton.

Aerodynamic Theory: A General View of Progress, 6 vols. Ed. by W. Fredrick Durand. Incl. Vol. 1. Mathematical Aids, Fluid Mechanics, Historical Sketch. 12.00 (ISBN 0-8446-0603-0); Vol. 2. General Aerodynamic Theory, Perfect Fluids. 12.00 (ISBN 0-8446-0604-9); Vol. 3. Theory of Single Burbling, Mechanics of Viscous Fluids, Etc. 12.00 (ISBN 0-8446-0605-7); Vol. 4. Applied Airfoil Theory, Airplane Body Drag & Influence, Etc. 12.00 (ISBN 0-8446-0606-5); Vol. 5. Dynamics of the Airplane, Airplane Performance. 12.00 (ISBN 0-8446-0607-3); Vol. 6. Airplanes As a Whole, Aerodynamics of Airships, Etc. 12.00 (ISBN 0-8446-0739-8). Set. 72.00 (ISBN 0-8446-0602-2). Peter Smith.

Aerodynamics. L. J. Clancy. LC 73-15266. 1975. text ed. 27.95 (ISBN 0-470-15837-9). Halsted Pr.

Aerodynamics. Theodore Von Karman. (Illus.). 1964. pap. 3.95 o.p. (ISBN 0-07-067602-X, SP). McGraw.

Aerodynamics, Aeronautics, & Flight Mechanics. Barnes W. McCormick. LC 79-11073. 1979. text ed. 30.95 (ISBN 0-471-03032-5). Wiley.

Aerodynamics & Ventilation of Vehicle Tunnels Review & Bibliography. Ed. by B. R. Pursall & A. L. King. (BHRA Fluid Engineering Ser.: Vol. 2). 1977. pap. 52.00 (ISBN 0-900983-62-0, Dist. by Air Science Co.). BHRA Fluid.

Aerodynamics for Engineers. John J. Bertin & Michael L. Smith. (Illus.). 1979. text ed. 29.95 (ISBN 0-13-018234-6). P-H.

Aerodynamics for Naval Aviators. 2nd ed. H. R. Hurt, Jr. (Pilot Training Ser.). (Illus.). 416p. 1975. pap. 9.95 (ISBN 0-89100-182-4, E*A-182-4). Aviation Maintenance.

Aerodynamics of the Airplane. Hermann T. Schlichting & Erich A. Truckenbrodt. (Illus.). 1979. text ed. 54.50 (ISBN 0-07-055341-6). McGraw.

Aeroelasticity. R. L. Bisplinghoff et al. 1955. 34.95 (ISBN 0-201-00595-6). A-W.

Aeroelasticity of Plates & Shells. E. H. Dowell. (Mechanics: Dynamical System Ser.: No. 1). 154p. 1978. 25.00x (ISBN 90-286-0404-9). Sijthoff & Noordhoff.

Aerofilms Book of England from the Air. Ed. by Stuart Booth. (Illus.). 1979. 14.95 (ISBN 0-7137-0965-0, Pub by Blandford Pr England). Sterling.

Aeromarine Origins. H. F. King. (Illus.). 1966. 5.50 o.p. (ISBN 0-370-00058-7). Aero.

Aeromodeller Annual, 1978-79. LC 51-16366. (Illus., Orig.). 1978. pap. 10.00x (ISBN 0-85242-626-7). Intl Pubns Serv.

Aeromodelling. R. H. Warring. 9.75x (ISBN 0-392-07177-0, LTB). Soccer.

Aeronautics at the Mid-Century. Jerome C. Hunsaker. 1952. 24.50x (ISBN 0-685-89732-X). Elliots Bks.

Aeronautics in the Union & Confederate Armies: With a Survey of Military Aeronautics Prior to 1861, Vol. I. Frederick S. Haydon. Ed. by James Gilbert. LC 79-7271. (Flight: Its First Seventy-Five Years Ser.). (Illus.). 1979. Repr. of 1941 ed. lib. bdg. 38.00x (ISBN 0-405-12181-4). Arno.

Aeronauts. Time-Life Books Editors & Donald D. Jackson. (Epic of Flight Ser.). (Illus.). 176p. 1980. 12.95 (ISBN 0-8094-3268-4). Time-Life.

Aeronca C-Two: The Story of the Flying Bathtub. Jay P. Spenser. LC 78-606098. (Famous Aircraft of the National Air & Space Museum Ser.: No. 2). (Illus.). 72p. 1978. pap. 5.95 (ISBN 0-87474-879-8). Smithsonian.

Aeronomy. P. M. Banks & G. Kockarts. Incl. Pt. A. 1973. 47.00 (ISBN 0-12-077801-7); Set. 38.50 (ISBN 0-12-077801-7); Pt. B. 1973. 48.00 (ISBN 0-12-077802-5). Set. 39.50 (ISBN 0-12-077802-5). Acad Pr.

Aeroplane or a Grave. Brian Peachment. 1976. pap. 1.55 (ISBN 0-08-017841-3). Pergamon.

Aerosol Microphysics I: Particle Interactions. Ed. by W. H. Marlow. (Topics in Current Physics: Vol. 16). (Illus.). 180p. 1980. 31.90 (ISBN 0-387-09866-6). Springer-Verlag.

Aerosol Science. Ed. by Charles N. Davies. 1967. 64.50 o.s.i. (ISBN 0-12-205650-7). Acad Pr.

Aerosols, Airways & Asthma. Ed. by J. Trautlein. 121p. 1981. text ed. 20.00 (ISBN 0-89335-059-1). Spectrum Pub.

Aerosols: Anthropogenic & Natural, Sources & Transport. Ed. by Theo J. Kneip & Paul J. Lioy. LC 80-12891. (N.Y. Academy of Sciences Annals: Vol. 338). 618p. Date not set. 108.00x (ISBN 0-89766-064-1); pap. price not set (ISBN 0-89766-065-X). NY Acad Sci.

Aerospace Projects for Young Children. Jane A. Caballero. (Illus.). 109p. (Orig.). 1979. pap. 9.95 (ISBN 0-89334-052-9). Humanics Ltd.

Aerostructures, Selected Papers of Nicholas J. Hoff. Ed. by R. B. Testa. LC 77-164024. 1971. 32.00 (ISBN 0-08-016834-5). Pergamon.

Aes & Pecunia Records of Roman Currency Down to 269 B. C. H. Mattingly. Date not set. pap. 3.00 (ISBN 0-916710-51-3). Obol Intl.

Aeschylean Drama. Michael Gagarin. LC 74-30520. 1976. 18.00x (ISBN 0-520-02943-7). U of Cal Pr.

Aeschylean Tragedy. Herbert W. Smyth. LC 67-19531. 1969. Repr. of 1924 ed. 8.50x (ISBN 0-8196-0235-3). Biblo.

Aeschylus: A Collection of Critical Essays. Ed. by M. McCall, Jr. 1972. 8.95 o.p. (ISBN 0-13-018317-2, STC99, Spec); pap. 1.95 o.p. (ISBN 0-13-018309-1). P-H.

Aeschylus' "Prometheus Bound" A Literary Commentary. D. J. Conacher. 128p. 1980. 20.00x (ISBN 0-8020-2391-6); pap. 7.50 (ISBN 0-8020-6416-7). U of Toronto Pr.

Aeschylus' Supplices: Play & Trilogy. A. F. Garvie. LC 69-10195. 1969. 48.00 (ISBN 0-521-07182-8). Cambridge U Pr.

Aeschylus: The Oresteia. Tr. by F. Raphael & K. McLeish. LC 78-6013. (Greek & Roman Authors Ser.). 1979. 14.95 (ISBN 0-521-22060-2); pap. 4.50 (ISBN 0-521-29344-8). Cambridge U Pr.

Aesculapius Comes to the Colonies. Maurice R. Gordon. LC 70-101590. (Illus.). 1969. Repr. of 1949 ed. 17.50. Argosy.

Aesculapius in Latin America. Aristides A. Moll. LC 76-101589. (Illus.). 1969. Repr. of 1944 ed. 17.50. Argosy.

Aesop: His Book. Ruth J. Heffelfinger. 1973. 6.95 (ISBN 0-87018-074-6). Ross.

Aesthetes: A Sourcebook. Ian Small. (Illus.). 1979. 21.00x (ISBN 0-7100-0145-2); pap. 9.95 (ISBN 0-7100-0146-0). Routledge & Kegan.

Aesthetic. Benedetto Croce. Tr. by Douglas Ainslie. LC 78-58500. 544p. 1979. pap. 7.50 (ISBN 0-87923-255-2, Nonpareil Bk.). Godine.

Aesthetic Aspects of Civil Engineering Design. 120p. 1980. pap. 25.00x (ISBN 0-901948-13-6, Pub. by Telford England). State Mutual Bk.

Aesthetic Plastic Surgery, 2 vols. Thomas D. Rees. (Illus.). 1168p. 1980. Vol. 1. text ed. 75.00 (ISBN 0-7216-7519-0); Vol. 2. text ed. 85.00 (ISBN 0-7216-7521-2); Set. text ed. 160.00 (ISBN 0-7216-7522-0). Saunders.

Aesthetic Plastic Surgery. Ed. by Richard B. Stark. LC 80-80594. 1980. text ed. 55.00 (ISBN 0-316-81085-1). Little.

Aesthetic Quality: A Contextualistic Theory of Beauty. Stephen C. Pepper. LC 79-110052. 239p. Repr. of 1937 ed. lib. bdg. 19.75x (ISBN 0-8371-4437-X, PEAQ). Greenwood.

Aesthetic Rhinoplasty. Jack H. Sheen. LC 78-27554. (Illus.). 1978. text ed. 87.50 (ISBN 0-8016-4575-1). Mosby.

Aesthetic Surgery: Trouble - How to Avoid It & How to Treat It. Ed. by Eugene H. Courtiss. LC 78-4958. 1978. text ed. 42.50 (ISBN 0-8016-1060-5). Mosby.

Aesthetic Theories of Kant, Hegel & Schopenhauer. Israel Knox. 1978. Repr. of 1936 ed. text ed. 12.50x (ISBN 0-391-00929-X). Humanities.

Aesthetics: A Critical Anthology. George Dickie & R. J. Sclafani. LC 76-28127. (Illus.). 1977. text ed. 15.95 (ISBN 0-312-00910-0). St Martin.

Aesthetics: An Introduction. George Dickie. (Traditions in Philosophy Ser). 1971. pap. 4.95 (ISBN 0-672-63500-3). Pegasus.

Aesthetics & Art Theory. Harold Osborne. (Illus.). 1970. pap. 4.95 o.p. (ISBN 0-525-47258-4). Dutton.

Aesthetics & Language. Ed. by William Elton. 1970. 24.00x (ISBN 0-631-04610-0, Pub. by Basil Blackwell). Biblio Dist.

Aesthetics of Pianoforte-Playing. Adolf Kullak. LC 69-16652. (Music Reprint Ser.). 340p. 1972. Repr. of 1893 ed. lib. bdg. 27.50 (ISBN 0-306-71095-1). Da Capo.

Aesthetics: Problems in the Philosophy of Criticism. 2nd ed. Monroe C. Beardsley. (Illus.). 688p. 1981. 25.00 (ISBN 0-915145-09-X); pap. text ed. 14.50 (ISBN 0-915145-08-1). Hackett Pub.

Afanasy Fet. Lydia Lotman. (World Author Ser.: Russia: No. 279). 1976. lib. bdg. 12.50 (ISBN 0-8057-2309-9). Twayne.

AFDC Foster Care: Problems & Recommendations. Winford Oliphant. LC 74-75319. (Orig.). 1974. pap. 1.75 o.p. (ISBN 0-87868-121-3). Child Welfare.

Affair. C. P. Snow. (Hudson River Edition). 1960. 17.50x (ISBN 0-684-15317-3, ScribT). Scribner.

Affair at Honey Hill. Berry Fleming. 104p. 1981. 5.95 (ISBN 0-9604810-2-8). Cotton Lane.

Affair of Sorcerers. George Chesbro. 1980. pap. 2.25 (ISBN 0-451-09243-0, E9243, Sig). NAL.

Affair of Strangers. John Crosby. 272p. 1976. pap. 1.95 o.s.i. (ISBN 0-446-89280-7). Warner Bks.

Affair on the Rhine. Dennis Weber. 1981. pap. 1.95 (ISBN 0-8439-0906-4, Leisure Bks). Nordon Pubns.

Affair Prevention. Peter Kreitler et al. 256p. 1981. 10.95 (ISBN 0-02-566710-6). Macmillan.

Affairs: How to Cope with Extra-Marital Relationships. Tony Lake. 224p. 1981. 10.95 (ISBN 0-13-018671-6, Spec); pap. 5.95 (ISBN 0-13-018663-5). P-H.

Affairs of Daura: History & Change in a Hausa State, 1800-1958. M. G. Smith. LC 73-80825. 1978. 35.00x (ISBN 0-520-02502-4). U of Cal Pr.

Affairs of Love. Glenna Finley. 1980. pap. 1.75 (ISBN 0-451-09409-3, E909, Sig). NAL.

Affairs of State: Public Life in Late Nineteenth Century America. Morton Keller. LC 76-21676. 1979. 20.00 (ISBN 0-674-00721-2, Belknap Pr); pap. 7.50 (ISBN 0-674-00710-7). Harvard U Pr.

Affairs of the Generals. Hans H. Kirst. 1980. pap. 2.50 o.p. (ISBN 0-449-24258-7, Crest). Fawcett.

Affairs of the Heart. Nora Powers. 192p. (Orig.). 1980. pap. 1.50 (ISBN 0-671-57003-X). S&S.

Affairs of the Mind: The Salon in Europe & America from the 18th to the 20th Century. Peter Quennell. (Illus.). 1980. 14.95 o.p. (ISBN 0-915220-57-1). New Republic.

Affect & Memory: A Reformulation. S. Dutta & R. N. Kanunga. LC 75-8628. 148p. 1975. text ed. 25.00 (ISBN 0-08-018270-4). Pergamon.

Affectionate Cousins: T. Sturge Moore & Maria Appia. Sylvia Legge. (Illus.). 288p. 1980. text ed. 24.50x (ISBN 0-19-211761-0). Oxford U Pr.

Affectionately, Dad. Ed. by Roger H. Crook. LC 80-67461. 1981. 5.95 (ISBN 0-8054-5641-4). Broadman.

Affective Correlates of Learning Disabilities. James W. Chapman & Frederic J. Boersma. (Modern Approaches to the Diagnosis & Instruction of Multihandicapped Children Ser.: Vol. 15). 108p. 1980. text ed. 22.50 (ISBN 90-265-0341-5, Pub. by Swets Pub Serv Holland). Swets North Am.

Affective Education: A Methods & Techniques Manual for Growth. James D. Wiggins & Dori English. 1977. pap. text ed. 8.00 (ISBN 0-8191-0217-2). U Pr of Amer.

Affective Education for Special Children & Youth. Ed. by William C. Morse et al. LC 80-65499. 128p. (Orig.). pap. 6.75 (ISBN 0-86586-104-8). Coun Exc Child.

Afferent Innervation of the Heart. A. Y. Khabarova. LC 62-15548. 175p. 1963. 25.00 (ISBN 0-306-10656-6, Consultants). Plenum Pub.

Affiches De la Commune De Paris, 1793-1794. Intro. by Albert Soboul. (Fr.). 1976. Repr. lib. bdg. 550.00x o.p. (ISBN 0-8287-1326-X). Clearwater Pub.

Affidavits of Genius: Edgar Allan Poe & the French Critics, 1847-1924. Jean Alexander. LC 79-154033. 1971. 14.50 (ISBN 0-8046-9015-4, Natl U). Kennikat.

Affinal Relationship System of the Australian Aborigines in the Port Keats District. Johannes Falkenberg & Aslaug Falkenberg. 224p. 1981. pap. 23.00x. Universitet.

Affine Representations of Grothendieck Groups & Applications to Rickart C -Algebras & Aleph O-Continuous Regular Rings. K. R. Goodearl et al. (Memoirs: No. 234). 1980. 6.00 (ISBN 0-8218-2234-9). Am Math.

Affine Sets & Affine Groups. D. G. Northcott. LC 79-41595. (London Mathematical Society Lecture Note Ser.: No. 39). 1980. pap. 26.95x (ISBN 0-521-22909-X). Cambridge U Pr.

Affinities of Orpheus. Edwin Honig. (Illus.). 1976. pap. 4.50 (ISBN 0-914278-10-X). Copper Beech.

Affinity. Katherine Hale. 1978. pap. 1.95 (ISBN 0-380-40907-0, 40907). Avon.

Affinity & Matter: Elements of Chemical Philosophy, 1800-1865. Trevor H. Levere. 248p. 1971. 28.00x (ISBN 0-19-858134-3). Oxford U Pr.

Affinity Chromatography. William H. Scouten. (Chemical Analysis Ser.). 344p. 1981. 39.50 (ISBN 0-471-02649-2, Pub. by Wiley-Interscience). Wiley.

Affinity Chromatography: Proceedings of an International Symposium Held in Vienna, 1977. Ed. by O. Hoffman-Ostenhof et al. LC 78-40289. 1978. text ed. 60.00 (ISBN 0-08-022632-9). Pergamon.

Affirmation. Christopher Priest. 240p. 1981. 10.95 (ISBN 0-684-16957-6, ScribT). Scribner.

Affirmative Action Compliance Kit: Eed Dictionary. Peter Reid. 1980. pap. 10.00 (ISBN 0-917386-35-3). Exec Ent.

Affirmative Action Compliance Kit: Reference Guide. Peter Reid. 1980. pap. 15.00 (ISBN 0-917386-34-5). Exec Ent.

Affirmative Action Compliance Kit: Working Manual. Peter Reid. 1980. pap. 75.00 (ISBN 0-917386-33-7). Exec Ent.

Affirmative Action Plan Workbook for Federal Contractors. 2nd ed. Pepper. 1979. pap. 45.00 (ISBN 0-917386-31-0). Exec Ent.

Affluence, Altruism, & Atrophy: The Decline of the Welfare State. Morris Silver. LC 79-3528. 200p. 1980. 17.00x (ISBN 0-8147-7810-0). NYU Pr.

Affluence & Anxiety: America Since Nineteen Forty-Five. 2nd ed. Carl N. Degler. 210p. 1975. pap. 7.95x (ISBN 0-673-07956-2). Scott F.

Affluent Worker, in the Class Structure. John H. Goldthorpe et al. (Studies in Sociology: No. 3). 1969. 29.95 (ISBN 0-521-07231-X); pap. 9.95x (ISBN 0-521-09533-6). Cambridge U Pr.

Affluent Worker: Industrial Attitudes. John H. Goldthorpe et al. LC 68-21192. (Cambridge Studies in Sociology: No. 1). 1968. 24.00 (ISBN 0-521-07109-7); pap. 9.95x (ISBN 0-521-09466-6). Cambridge U Pr.

Affronts, Insults, & Indignities. Morris Mandel. LC 74-6568. 180p. 1975. 8.95 o.p. (ISBN 0-685-50514-6, 0-8246-0180). Jonathan David.

Afganistan: Key to a Continent. John C. Griffiths. 200p. 1981. 16.00 (ISBN 0-86531-080-7). Westview.

Afghan Hound: A Definitive Study. Margaret Niblock. LC 79-57391. (Illus.). 448p. 1980. 49.95 (ISBN 0-668-04934-0, 4934-0). Arco.

Afghan Hounds. Beverly Pisano. (Illus.). 125p. 1980. 2.95 (ISBN 0-87666-682-9, KW-077). TFH Pubns.

Afghan Hounds: A Complete Guide. Daphne Gie. 1978. 19.95 (ISBN 0-7153-7423-0). David & Charles.

Afghani & Abduh: An Essay on Religious Unbelief & Political Activism in Modern Islam. Elie Kedourie. 1966. text ed. 7.50x (ISBN 0-391-01942-2). Humanities.

Afghanistan. Photos by Roland Michaud & Sabrina Michaud. LC 80-51192. (Illus.). 144p. 1980. 45.00 (ISBN 0-86565-009-8). Vendome.

Afghanistan: A Study of Political Developments in Central and Southern Asia. 5th ed. William K. Fraser-Tytler, Sr. LC 80-1931. 1981. 42.50 (ISBN 0-404-18962-8). AMS Pr.

Afghanistan in Crisis. K. P. Misra. 1981. 20.00x (ISBN 0-7069-1305-1, Pub. by Vikas India). Advent Bk.

Afghanistan, Nineteen Hundred to Nineteen Twenty Three: A Diplomatic History. Ludwig W. Adamec. 1967. 20.00x (ISBN 0-520-00002-1). U of Cal Pr.

Afghanistan: 1980 Edition. Louis Dupree. LC 76-154993. (Illus.). 784p. 1980. 35.00 (ISBN 0-691-00023-9); pap. 9.95. Princeton U Pr.

AFIPS Proceedings, Vol. 46. National Computer Conference, 1977. Ed. by Robert R. Korfhage. LC 55-44701. (Illus.). xiv, 1026p. 1977. 60.00 (ISBN 0-88283-007-4). AFIPS Pr.

AFIPS Proceedings, Vol. 47. National Computer Conference, 1978. Ed. by Sakti P. Ghosh & Leonard Y. Liu. LC 55-44701. (Illus.). xxxiv, 1300p. 1978. 60.00 (ISBN 0-88283-006-6). AFIPS Pr.

AFIPS Proceedings, Vol. 48. National Computer Conference, 1979. Ed. by Richard E. Merwin. LC 55-44701. (Illus.). xi, 1114p. 1979. 60.00 (ISBN 0-88283-005-8). AFIPS Pr.

AFIPS Proceedings, Vol. 49. National Computer Conference, 1980. Ed. by Donald B. Medley. LC 80-66206. (Illus.). 1980. 60.00 (ISBN 0-88283-003-1). AFIPS Pr.

Afloat & Ashore: A Sea Tale. James F. Cooper. 549p. 1980. Repr. of 1844 ed. lib. bdg. 18.25x (ISBN 0-89968-212-X). Lightyear.

Afloat in a Sunken Forest; or, with Frank Reade Jr. on a Submarine Cruise. Ed. by E. F. Bleiler. (Frank Reade Library: Vol. 8). 1980. lib. bdg. 44.00 (ISBN 0-8240-3547-X). Garland Pub.

Afloat in America. Charles Hadfield & Alice M. Hadfield. LC 79-52986. (Illus.). 1979. 13.50 (ISBN 0-7153-7910-0). David & Charles.

Afocha: A Link Between Community & Administration in Harar Ethiopia. Peter Koehn & Sidney R. Waldron. LC 78-27903. (Foreign & Comparative Studies-African Ser.: No. XXXI). (Illus.). 120p. 1979. pap. 7.00x (ISBN 0-915984-53-9). Syracuse U Foreign Comp.

Afraid, No. 137. Barbara Cartland. 160p. (Orig.). 1981. pap. 1.75 (ISBN 0-553-14509-6). Bantam.

Afraid to Ride. Clarence W. Anderson. (Illus.). (gr. 3-7). 1962. 4.95g o.s.i. (ISBN 0-02-701440-1). Macmillan.

Africa. 5th ed. H. R. Jarrett. (Illus.). 624p. (Orig.). 1979. pap. text ed. 24.00x (ISBN 0-7121-0153-5, Pub by MacDonald & Evans England). Intl Ideas.

Africa. rev ed. Benjamin E. Thomas et al. LC 76-17679. (World Cultures Ser). (Illus.). (gr. 6 up). 1978. text ed. 9.95 ea. 1-4 copies o.p. (ISBN 0-88296-142-X); text ed. 7.96 ea. 5 or more copies o.p.; tchrs'. guide 8.94 o.p. (ISBN 0-686-67612-2). Fideler.

Africa, A Modern History: Eighteen Hundred to Nineteen Seventy Five. J. O. Sagay & D. A. Wilson. LC 79-16594. (Illus.). 1980. text ed. 22.50x (ISBN 0-8419-0542-8, Africana); pap. text ed. 13.95x (ISBN 0-8419-0543-6, Africana). Holmes & Meier.

Africa A to Z. Robert S. Kane. LC 75-175386. 408p. 1972. 9.95 o.p. (ISBN 0-385-02679-X). Doubleday.

Africa Administration, 1 vol. Walter Z. Duic. 1978. 95.00 set (ISBN 0-89664-017-5, Pub. by K G Saur). Gale.

Africa & International Crisis. Robert W. Brown et al. LC 77-17820. (Foreign & Comparative Studies-Eastern Africa Ser.: No. 22). 106p. 1976. pap. text ed. 4.50x (ISBN 0-915984-19-9). Syracuse U Foreign Comp.

Africa & South America. rev. ed. William D. Allen et al. LC 77-87337. (World Cultures Ser). (Illus.). (gr. 6 up). 1978. text ed. 12.43 ea. 1-4 copies, 5 or more 9.94 (ISBN 0-88296-166-7); tchrs'. guide 8.94 (ISBN 0-88296-369-4). Fideler.

Africa & the Communist World. Ed. by Zbigniew Brzezinski. LC 63-17816. (Publications Ser.: No. 32). 272p. 1963. 10.00 (ISBN 0-8179-1322-X). Hoover Inst Pr.

Africa & the Islands. 4th ed. R. J. Church et al. LC 77-3459. 1977. pap. text ed. 14.95 (ISBN 0-470-99085-6). Halsted Pr.

Africa & the United States: Vital Interests. Ed. by Jennifer S. Whitaker. LC 77-92753. 1978. 15.00x (ISBN 0-8147-9181-6); pap. 7.00x (ISBN 0-8147-9182-4). NYU Pr.

Africa & the Victorians: The Official Mind of Imperialism. R. Robinson et al. 1967. pap. text ed. 13.50x (ISBN 0-333-05552-7). Humanities.

Africa & the West: Intellectual Responses to European Culture. Ed. by Philip D. Curtin. LC 77-176409. 274p. 1972. 25.00 (ISBN 0-299-06121-3); pap. 7.95x (ISBN 0-299-06124-8). U of Wis Pr.

Africa & Unity: The Evolution of Pan-Africanism. Vincent B. Thompson. 412p. 1969. pap. text ed. 12.00x (ISBN 0-582-64522-0). Humanities.

Africa: Apostolic Pilgrimage. Pope John Paul II. 1980. 8.00 (ISBN 0-8198-0708-7); pap. 7.00 (ISBN 0-8198-0709-5). Dghtrs St Paul.

Africa Below the Sahara. rev. ed. Stephen Marvin. (World Studies Inquiry Ser.). (gr. 7-12). 1979. pap. text ed. 6.04 (ISBN 0-201-42665-X, Sch Div); tchr's ed. 2.76 (ISBN 0-201-42666-8). A-W.

Africa Contemporary Record, Vol. 9. Ed. by Colin Legum. LC 70-7957. (Illus.). 1977. 125.00x (ISBN 0-8419-0158-9, Africana). Holmes & Meier.

Africa Contemporary Record, Vol. 10. Ed. by Colin Legum. LC 70-7957. 1979. 125.00x (ISBN 0-8419-0159-7, Africana). Holmes & Meier.

Africa Contemporary Record, Vol. 11. Ed. by Colin Legum. LC 70-7957. 1980. 125.00x (ISBN 0-8419-0160-0, Africana). Holmes & Meier.

Africa Contemporary Record, Vol. 12. Colin Legum. LC 70-7957. 1400p. 1981. text ed. 125.00x (ISBN 0-8419-0550-9, Africana). Holmes & Meier.

Africa Contemporary Record: Annual Survey & Documents. Ed. by Colin Legum. Incl. Vol. 1. 1968-69. 904p (ISBN 0-8419-0150-3); Vol. 2. 1969-70. 1213p (ISBN 0-8419-0151-1); Vol. 3. 1970-71. 1065p (ISBN 0-8419-0152-X); Vol. 4. 1971-1972. 1100p (ISBN 0-8419-0153-8); Vol. 5. 1972-73. Ed. by Colin Legum (ISBN 0-8419-0154-6). LC 70-7957. 125.00 ea. (Africana). Holmes & Meier.

Africa Contemporary Record: 1973-74, Vol. 6. Ed. by Colin Legum. LC 70-7957. (Illus.). 1200p. 1974. 125.00x (ISBN 0-8419-0155-4, Africana). Holmes & Meier.

Africa Contemporary Record: 1974-75, Vol. 7. Ed. by Colin Legum. LC 70-7957. (Illus.). 1100p. 1975. 125.00x (ISBN 0-8419-0156-2, Africana). Holmes & Meier.

Africa Faces the World. Richard A. Fredland. LC 80-81101. (Scholarly Monograph Ser.). 212p. 1980. pap. 15.00 (ISBN 0-8408-0502-0); pap. text ed. 15.00 o.p. (ISBN 0-686-64869-2). Carrollton Pr.

Africa from Early Times to Eighteen Hundred. Ed. by P. J. McEwan. (Readings in African History Ser). 1968. 22.00x (ISBN 0-19-215661-6). Oxford U Pr.

Africa: From Mystery to Maze, Vol. XI. Commission on Critical Choices & Helen Kitchen. LC 75-44729. (Critical Choices for Americans Ser.). 1976. 22.95 (ISBN 0-669-00425-1). Lexington Bks.

Africa Guide. 1979. pap. 16.95 o.p. (ISBN 0-528-84229-3). Rand.

Africa Guide, Nineteen Eighty-One. 5th ed. Ed. by Graham Hancock. (Annual Review Ser.). (Illus.). 1981. pap. 24.95 (ISBN 0-528-84517-9). Rand.

Africa in the Iron Age. R. A. Oliver & B. M. Fagan. LC 74-25639. (Illus.). 300p. 1975. 29.95 (ISBN 0-521-20598-0); pap. 7.95x (ISBN 0-521-09900-5). Cambridge U Pr.

Africa in the United Nations. Thomas Hovet, Jr. (African Studies Ser.: No. 10). (Illus.). 1963. 14.95x o.s.i. (ISBN 0-8101-0124-6). Northwestern U Pr.

Africa in the Wider World. D. Brokensha & M. Crowder. 1967. 25.00 (ISBN 0-08-012673-1); pap. 13.25 (ISBN 0-08-012672-3). Pergamon.

Africa in U. S. Schools, K-12: A Survey. Susan J. Hall. 39p. (Orig.). 1978. pap. text ed. 4.00 (ISBN 0-89192-292-X). Interbk Inc.

Africa Independent. Keesing's Publication Ltd. LC 70-162750. (Keesing's Research Reports Ser.). 1971. 10.00 o.p. (ISBN 0-684-12532-3, ScribT). Scribner.

Africa Must Unite. Kwame Nkrumah. LC 70-140209. 1970. 6.95 (ISBN 0-7178-0295-7); pap. 2.95 (ISBN 0-7178-0296-5). Intl Pub Co.

Africa: Problems in Economic Development. J. S. Uppal & Louis K. Salkever. LC 78-169240. 1972. 17.95 (ISBN 0-02-932910-8). Free Pr.

Africa: Regional Study. rev. ed. Hyman Kublin. 1974. pap. 6.60 (ISBN 0-395-17716-2). HM.

Africa Remembered: Narratives by West Africans from the Era of the Slave Trade. Ed. by Philip D. Curtin. (Illus.). 1968. 25.00 (ISBN 0-299-04281-2); pap. 8.95 (ISBN 0-299-04284-7). U of Wis Pr.

Africa: Selected Readings. rev. ed Hyman Kublin. 1974. pap. 6.60 (ISBN 0-395-17743-X). HM.

Africa Since Eighteen Hundred. 2nd ed. R. Oliver & A. Atmore. LC 70-189595. (Illus.). 340p. 1972. 29.95 (ISBN 0-521-08522-5); pap. 8.95x (ISBN 0-521-29240-9). Cambridge U Pr.

Africa Since Eighteen Hundred. 3rd ed. R. Oliver & A. Atmore. (Illus.). 396p. Date not set. price not set (ISBN 0-521-23485-9); pap. price not set (ISBN 0-521-29975-6). Cambridge U Pr.

Africa Sketches. Ed. by Gerald Hartwig. (Illus.). 64p. (gr. 7-10). 1980. 2.20 ea.; of 9 17.00 set (ISBN 0-686-28127-6). Ctr Intl Stud Duke.

Africa South of the Sahara: The Challenge to Western Security. L. H. Gann & Peter Duignan. LC 80-82750. (Publication Ser.: No. 238). 155p. 1980. pap. 9.95 (ISBN 0-8179-7382-6). Hoover Inst Pr.

Africa South of the Sahara 1979-80. 9th ed. LC 78-112271. (Illus.). 1325p. 1979. 75.00x o.p. (ISBN 0-905118-37-5). Intl Pubns Serv.

Africa South of the Sahara 1980-1981. 10th ed. LC 78-112271. 1396p. 1980. 90.00x (ISBN 0-905118-49-9). Intl Pubns Serv.

Africa That Never Was: Four Centuries of British Writing About Africa--an Anthropological View Contrasting the Africa of Fact & the Africa of Fiction. Dorothy Hammond & Alta Jablow. LC 78-77035. 251p. 1978. text ed. 28.50x (ISBN 0-8290-0151-4); pap. text ed. 12.95x (ISBN 0-8290-0152-2). Irvington.

Africa: The Climatic Background. B. W. Thompson. (Studies in the Development of African Resources). (Illus.). 72p. 1975. pap. 5.25x o.p. (ISBN 0-19-575253-8). Oxford U Pr.

Africa: The Way Ahead. Jack Woddis. LC 64-17900. 1963. 4.00 (ISBN 0-910294-13-5). Brown Bk.

Africa: Tribal Art of Forest & Savanna. Arnold Bamert. (Illus.). 332p. 1980. 60.00 (ISBN 0-500-23318-7). Thames Hudson.

Africa 1974: Turning Points in American Policy. Susan J. Hall. 1974. pap. 1.50 (ISBN 0-89192-074-9). Interbk Inc.

African Administrators in Action. rev. ed. A. H. M. Kirk-Greene. 1981. 29.50x (ISBN 0-7146-3134-5, F Cass Co). Biblio Dist.

African Adventures. (Animal Picture Bks.). (Illus.). 10p. (ps). 1979. 1.95 (ISBN 0-89346-173-3, A49). Heian Intl.

African Agricultural Research Capabilities. Board on Agriculture & Renewable Resources. LC 74-22370. 1974. pap. 9.00 o.p. (ISBN 0-309-02241-X). Natl Acad Pr.

African Agriculture & Rural Development, 5 vols. Ed. by Margot A. Bellamy. Incl. Vol. 1. General. 33p (ISBN 0-85198-359-6); Vol. 2. North & Northeast Africa. 33p (ISBN 0-85198-360-X); Vol. 3. East Africa. 60p (ISBN 0-85198-361-8); Vol. 4. South & Central Africa. 37p (ISBN 0-85198-363-4); Vol. 5. West Africa. 70p (ISBN 0-85198-362-6). (Annotated Bibliography Ser.: B., 1970 to 1974). 1975. Set. pap. 67.50x (ISBN 0-8002-2412-4). Intl Pubns Serv.

African Aims & Attitudes: Selected Documents. Ed. by M. Minogue & J. Molloy. LC 74-76567. 404p. 1974. 39.50 (ISBN 0-521-20426-7); pap. text ed. 12.95x (ISBN 0-521-09851-3). Cambridge U Pr.

African American Workshop. Lucille Wallower & Marilyn M. Porter. LC 76-52052. (gr. 3-4). 1977. pap. 4.60 (ISBN 0-931992-00-1); answerbook 0.40 (ISBN 0-931992-19-2). Penns Valley.

African & Afro-American History. Jack Rudman. (College Proficiency Examination Ser.: CLEP-36). (Cloth bdg. avail. on request). pap. 9.95 (ISBN 0-8373-5436-6). Natl Learning.

African & Ancient Mexican Art: The Loran Collection. Eric Loran et al. LC 74-84681. (Illus.). 1974. pap. 4.95 (ISBN 0-88401-004-X, Pub. by Fine Arts Mus). C E Tuttle.

African & Black American Studies. Alexander S. Birkos & Lewis A. Tambs. LC 74-31262. (Academic Writer's Guide to Periodicals Ser.: Vol. 3). 205p. 1975. lib. bdg. 13.50x o.p. (ISBN 0-87287-109-6). Libs Unl.

African Animal in Rennaissance Literature & Art. Joan B. Lloyd. (Oxford Studies in the History of Art & Architecture Ser). (Illus.). 1971. 27.00x (ISBN 0-19-817180-3). Oxford U Pr.

African Animals of William R. Leigh. Forrest Fenn. (Illus.). 32p. (Orig.). 1980. pap. 10.00 (ISBN 0-937634-01-8). Fenn Gall Pub.

African-Arab Conflict in the Sudan. Dunstan M. Wai. LC 80-15410. 240p. 1981. text ed. 20.00x (ISBN 0-8419-0631-9, Africana). Holmes & Meier.

African Art. Frank Willett. (World of Art Ser.). (Illus.). 1971. pap. 9.95 (ISBN 0-19-519948-0). Oxford U Pr.

African Art in Cultural Perspective: An Introduction. new ed. William Bascom. (Illus.). 192p. 1973. 7.95x (ISBN 0-393-04368-1); pap. 4.95x (ISBN 0-393-09375-1). Norton.

African Art in Motion: Icon & Act in the Collection of Katherine Coryton White. Robert F. Thompson. (Illus.). 1974. 35.00 (ISBN 0-520-03844-4); pap. 14.95 (ISBN 0-520-03843-6). U of Cal Pr.

African Art in Needlework: Needlework Motifs Inspired by African Culture. Leslie Tillett. LC 78-3320. (Illus.). 1979. 20.95 o.s.i. (ISBN 0-690-01404-X, TYC-T); pap. 9.95 o.s.i. (ISBN 0-690-01793-6, TYC-T). T Y Crowell.

African Art in Washington Collections. (Illus.). 60p. 1972. pap. 4.00 (ISBN 0-89192-230-X). Interbk Inc.

African Artisan: Education & the Informal Sector in Kenya. Kenneth King. LC 76-58316. 1977. pap. text ed. 8.75x (ISBN 0-8077-8023-5). Tchrs Coll.

African-Asian Reading Guide for Children & Young Adults. Jeanette K. Hotchkiss. LC 74-37530. 1976. 10.00 o.p. (ISBN 0-8108-0886-2). Scarecrow.

African Assertion: A Critical Anthology of African Literature. Ed. by Austin J. Shelton, Jr. LC 67-18742. (Orig.). (gr. 9-12). 1968. pap. 5.00 o.p. (ISBN 0-672-63004-4). Odyssey Pr.

African Authors: A Companion to Black African Writing 1300-1973, Vol. 1. Ed. by Donald E. Herdeck. LC 73-172338. (Illus.). 605p. 1973. 48.00 (ISBN 0-685-53608-4, Pub. by Black Orpheus Press). Gale.

African Boundaries: A Legal & Diplomatic Encyclopedia. Ian Brownlie. 1979. 160.00x (ISBN 0-520-03795-2). U of Cal Pr.

African Businessmen & Social Change in Zambia. Andrew A. Beveridge & Anthony R. Oberschall. LC 79-83978. 1979. 22.50x (ISBN 0-691-03121-5). Princeton U Pr.

African Calliope. Edward Hoagland. 256p. 1981. pap. 4.95 (ISBN 0-14-005806-0). Penguin.

African Capitalism: A Case Study in Nigerian Entrepreneurship. E. Wayne Nafzinger. LC 76-48484. (Publication Ser: No. 169). (Illus.). 1977. 8.95 (ISBN 0-8179-6691-9). Hoover Inst Pr.

African Christianity. Adrian Hastings. 1977. 6.95 (ISBN 0-8164-0336-8). Crossroad NY.

African Cichlids of Lakes Malawi & Tanganyika. Herbert R. Axelrod. (Illus.). 224p. 1973. 14.95 (ISBN 0-87666-515-6, PS-703). TFH Pubns.

African Cities & Towns Before the European Conquest. Richard W. Hull. LC 76-16038. (Illus.). 1976. 10.95x (ISBN 0-393-05581-7); pap. 4.95x (ISBN 0-393-09166-X). Norton.

African Cooking. Laurens Van Der Post. (Foods of the World Ser). (Illus.). 1970. 14.95 (ISBN 0-8094-0046-4). Time-Life.

African Cooking. Laurens Van Der Post. LC 77-119620. (Foods of the World Ser.). (Illus.). (gr. 6 up). 1970. PLB 14.94 (ISBN 0-8094-0073-1, Pub. by Time-Life). Silver.

African Countries & Cultures. 1981. 12.50 (ISBN 0-679-20507-1). McKay.

African Development & Europe. T. Burley & P. Tregear. 1970. 19.50 (ISBN 0-08-006669-0); pap. 9.75 (ISBN 0-08-006670-4). Pergamon.

African Development Bank: Problems of International Cooperation. Kwame D. Fordwor. LC 80-24607. (Pergamon Policy Studies on International Development). 300p. 1980. 30.00 (ISBN 0-08-026339-9). Pergamon.

African Dimension in Latin American Societies, Vol. 3. Franklin W. Knight. LC 73-11732. (Latin American Ser.). (Illus.). 180p. 1974. 9.95 o.s.i. (ISBN 0-02-564200-6). Macmillan.

African Dimensions: Essays in Honor of William O. Brown. Ed. by Mark Karp. LC 74-84802. (African Studies Center Ser). 224p. 1975. text ed. 10.00x (ISBN 0-8419-8717-3, Africana). Holmes & Meier.

African Elite: The Big Men of a Small Town. Joan Vincent. LC 79-132691. (Illus.). 1971. 22.50x (ISBN 0-231-03353-2); pap. text ed. 10.00x (ISBN 0-231-08332-7). Columbia U Pr.

African Experience in Spanish America: 1502 to the Present Day. L. B. Rout. LC 75-9280. (Latin American Studies: No. 23). (Illus.). 276p. 1976. 39.50 (ISBN 0-521-20805-X); pap. 9.95x (ISBN 0-521-29010-4). Cambridge U Pr.

African Experiment in Nation Building: The Bilingual Cameroon Republic. Ed. by Ndiva Kofele-Kale. (Westview Special Studies on Africa). 1980. lib. bdg. 26.50x (ISBN 0-89158-685-7). Westview.

African Fables, Bk. 2. Eudene Keidel. (Illus.). 112p. 1981. pap. 3.25 (ISBN 0-8361-1945-2). Herald Pr.

African Fishes of Lake Kariba. Eugene K. Balon. (Illus.). 144p. 1974. 4.95 (ISBN 0-87666-073-1, PS-706). TFH Pubns.

African Folktales. Paul Radin. (Bollingen Ser., Vol. 32). 1970. pap. 6.95 o.p. (ISBN 0-691-01762-X). Princeton U Pr.

African Furniture & Household Objects. Roy Sieber. LC 79-5340. (Illus.). 240p. 1980. 37.50x (ISBN 0-253-11927-8); pap. 20.00x (ISBN 0-253-28242-X). Ind U Pr.

African Heritage Cookbook. Helen Mendes. (Illus.). 1970. 7.95 o.s.i. (ISBN 0-02-584210-2). Macmillan.

African History & Societies to 1914, a Critical Survey of Relevant Books with Special References to West Africa. Ed. by Victor N. Low. Incl. Vol. 1. Africa at Large; Vol. 2. West Africa Region by Region. 1700p. 1981. 65.00x ea (ISBN 0-7146-3056-X, F Cass Co). Biblio Dist.

African Husbandman. William Allan. LC 75-17188. (Illus.). 1977. Repr. of 1965 ed. lib. bdg. 33.50x (ISBN 0-8371-8287-5, ALAH). Greenwood.

African Index to Continental Periodical Literature: Covering 1978, No. 3. 1980. 62.50 (Dist. by Gale Research Co.). K G Saur.

African Influence in the United Nations, 1967-1975: The Politics & Techniques of Gaining Compliance to U. N. Principles & Resolutions. Gregory L. Wilkins. LC 80-5735. 263p. (Orig.). 1981. lib. bdg. 19.25 (ISBN 0-8191-1424-3); pap. text ed. 10.50 (ISBN 0-8191-1425-1). U Pr of Amer.

African Insect Life. 2nd ed. Sydney H. Skaife. Ed. by John Ledger. (Illus.). 1980. 35.00 o.p. (ISBN 0-684-16335-7, ScribT). Scribner.

African Iron Age. P. L. Shinnie. 1971. 29.00x (ISBN 0-19-813158-5). Oxford U Pr.

African Kingdoms. Basil Davidson. LC 66-25647. (Great Ages of Man). (Illus.). (gr. 6 up). 1966. PLB 11.97 (ISBN 0-8094-0371-4, Pub. by Time-Life). Silver.

African Kingdoms. Basil Davidson. (Great Ages of Man Ser). (Illus.). 1971. 12.95 (ISBN 0-8094-0349-3). Time-Life.

African Kingdoms. Lucy Mair. (Illus.). 1977. text ed. 22.50x (ISBN 0-19-821698-X); pap. text ed. 9.95x (ISBN 0-19-874075-1). Oxford U Pr.

African Kingships in Perspective: Political Change & Modernization in Monarchical Settings. Ed. by Rene Lemarchand. 325p. 1977. 32.50x (ISBN 0-7146-3027-6, F Cass Co). Biblio Dist.

African Labourer. G. St. Orde Browne. 240p. 1967. Repr. of 1933 ed. 24.00x (ISBN 0-686-26224-7, F Cass Co). Biblio Dist.

African Language Literatures South of the Sahara: An Introduction. Albert S. Gerard. LC 79-3103. (Illus.). 396p. 1981. 30.00x (ISBN 0-914478-65-6); pap. 12.00x (ISBN 0-914478-66-4). Three Continents.

African Language Structures. William E. Welmers. LC 70-186108. 1974. 30.00x (ISBN 0-520-02210-6). U of Cal Pr.

African Literature: A Critical View. David Cook. 1978. pap. text ed. 9.95x (ISBN 0-582-64211-6). Longman.

African Literature in French. Dorothy S. Blair. LC 75-39374. (Illus.). 1976. 49.50 (ISBN 0-521-21195-6). Cambridge U Pr.

African Literature Today: Myth, History & the Contemporary Writer, Vol. 11. Ed. by Eldred D. Jones. LC 72-75254. 240p. 1980. text ed. 33.50x (ISBN 0-8419-0577-0, Africana); pap. text ed. 18.00x (ISBN 0-8419-0652-1). Holmes & Meier.

African Metropolis. Andrew Hake. LC 75-4266. 1977. 22.50 (ISBN 0-312-00980-1). St Martin.

African Microfilms at the E. S. Bird Library, Syracuse University: An Annotated Guide. David L. Easterbrook & Kenneth P. Lohrentz. (Foreign & Comparative Studies-African Special Publications Ser.: No.7). 72p. 1975. pap. 3.50x. Syracuse U Foreign Comp.

African Middle Ages. R. Oliver & A. Atmore. (Illus.). 245p. Date not set. price not set (ISBN 0-521-23301-1); pap. price not set (ISBN 0-521-29894-6). Cambridge U Pr.

African Millionaire: Episodes in the Life of the Illustrious Colonel Clay. Grant Allen. 1980. pap. 4.50 (ISBN 0-486-23992-6). Dover.

African Nationalism. 2nd ed. Ndabaningi Sithole. LC 68-133467. (Illus.). 1968. 10.50x (ISBN 0-19-215631-4); pap. 3.95x (ISBN 0-19-501053-1). Oxford U Pr.

African Nationalism & Militarism & Military Ascendancy. 85p. 1979. 8.00 (ISBN 0-914970-13-5, CM 003, Conch Mag). Unipub.

African Nexus: Black American Perspectives on the European Partitioning of Africa, 1880-1920. Sylvia M. Jacobs. LC 80-660. (Contributions in Afro-American & African Studies: No. 55). (Illus.). 264p. 1981. lib. bdg. 27.50 (ISBN 0-313-22312-2, JEP/). Greenwood.

African One-Party States. Ed. by C. M. Carter. LC 62-19165. 1962. 12.75 (ISBN 0-910294-14-3). Brown Bk.

African Pastureland Ecology. (FAO Pasture & Fodder Crop Studies: No. 7). 203p. 1981. pap. 11.00 (ISBN 92-5-100873-6, F2099, FAO). Unipub.

African Personality. 29p. 1980. pap. 5.00 (ISBN 92-808-0136-8, TUNU 062, UNC). Unipub.

African Perspectives on South Africa: Collection of Speeches, Articles & Doucuments, Vol. I. Ed. by Hendrik W. Van Der Merwe & Nancy C. J. Charton. LC 78-20359. (Publications Ser.: No. 176). 1978. pap. 9.95 (ISBN 0-8179-6762-1). Hoover Inst Pr.

African Philosophy: An Introduction. 2nd ed. Richard A Wright. LC 78-65457. 1978. pap. 10.00 (ISBN 0-8191-0505-8). U Pr of Amer.

African Poetry. H. U. Beier. (Illus., Orig.). 1966. 10.95 (ISBN 0-521-04140-6); pap. 5.50x (ISBN 0-521-04141-4). Cambridge U Pr.

African Poison Murders. Elspeth Huxley. LC 80-8717. 288p. 1981. pap. 2.25 (ISBN 0-06-080540-4, P/540, PL). Har-Row.

African Policy Crossroads. Jane W. Jacaz. (Illus.). 68p. (Orig.). 1979. pap. text ed. 3.00 (ISBN 0-89192-315-2). Interbk Inc.

African Politics & Society. R. L. Markovitz. LC 79-88119. 1970. pap. text ed. 9.95 (ISBN 0-02-920070-9). Free Pr.

African Politics in South Africa: Parties & Issues. D. A. Kotze. LC 75-6050. 350p. 1975. 29.95 (ISBN 0-312-01015-X). St Martin.

African Popular Literature. E. Obiechina. 28.50 (ISBN 0-521-20015-6); pap. 11.50x (ISBN 0-521-09744-4). Cambridge U Pr.

African Reaction to Missionary Education. Edward H. Berman. LC 74-22497. (Orig.). 1975. pap. text ed. 9.95x (ISBN 0-8077-2445-9). Tchrs Coll.

African Realities. Kenneth L. Adelman. LC 80-15828. 1980. 16.50x (ISBN 0-8448-1376-1). Crane-Russak Co.

African Refugees & the Law. Ed. by Goran Melander & Peter Nobel. (Scandinavian Institute of African Studies, Uppsala). 1978. text ed. 11.50 (ISBN 0-8419-9736-5). Holmes & Meier.

African Roots of Jazz. Fredrick Kaufman & John P. Guckin. LC 78-8470. 148p. 1979. 14.95 (ISBN 0-88284-065-7); pap. 7.95 (ISBN 0-686-64874-9). Alfred Pub.

African Rural, Urban Migration, the Movement to Ghana's Towns. John C. Caldwell. LC 69-17496. 1969. 16.00x (ISBN 0-231-03269-2). Columbia U Pr.

African School. Kitt Elliott. LC 78-111128. 1970. 22.50x (ISBN 0-521-07722-2). Cambridge U Pr.

African Slave Trade. rev. enl. ed. Basil Davidson. 312p. 1981. 12.50 (ISBN 0-686-69142-3, Pub. by Atlantic Monthly Pr); pap. 6.95 (ISBN 0-686-69143-1). Little.

African Social Studies. Ed. by G. Gutkind. 1979. 24.50 o.p. (ISBN 0-685-67796-6). Porter.

African Socialism in Two Countries. Ahmed Mohiddin. 231p. 1981. 25.00x (ISBN 0-389-20170-7). Barron.

African Societies. Lucy Mair. LC 73-93398. (Illus.). 236p. 1974. 27.50 (ISBN 0-521-20442-9); pap. 8.95x (ISBN 0-521-09854-8). Cambridge U Pr.

African States & the Military: Past & Present. Ed. by Boniface I. Obichere. 1980. 27.50x (ISBN 0-7146-3135-3, F Cass Co). Biblio Dist.

African Studies Since 1945: A Tribute to Basil Davidson. Ed. by Christopher Fyfe. 1976. text ed. 15.00x o.p. (ISBN 0-8419-6700-8). Holmes & Meier.

African Survey. Alan C. Best & Harm J. Blij. LC 76-44520. 1977. text ed. 23.95 (ISBN 0-471-20063-8). Wiley.

African Systems of Kinship & Marriage. Ed. by Alfred R. Radcliff-Brown. 1950. pap. 14.95x (ISBN 0-19-724147-6). Oxford U Pr.

African Theatre Today. Martin Banham. (Theatre Today Ser). 1976. pap. 4.95 (ISBN 0-685-50819-6, Pitman Pub); pap. 4.95 o.p. Columbia U Pr.

African Traditional Religion. Geoffrey Parrinder. LC 75-39900. 160p. 1976. pap. 3.95x o.p. (ISBN 0-06-066472-X, RD150, HarpR). Har-Row.

African Upheavals Since Independence. Grace S. Ibingira. (Westview Special Studies on Africa). 1980. lib. bdg. 25.00x (ISBN 0-89158-585-0). Westview.

African Urban Kinsman: The Ga of Central Accra. Marion D. Kilson. LC 74-79128. 1975. 21.95 (ISBN 0-312-01050-8). St Martin.

African Violets. 5th ed. Sunset Editors. LC 76-46656. (Illus.). 80p. 1977. pap. 2.95 (ISBN 0-376-03056-9, Sunset Bks). Sunset-Lane.

African Violets & Other Gesneriads for Modern Living. M. Jane Helmer. (Modern Living Ser.). (Illus.). 80p. (Orig.). 1978. pap. 2.95 (ISBN 0-89484-006-1, 10108). Merchants Pub Co.

African Voices: An Anthology of Native African Writings. Ed. by Peggy Rutherford. LC 60-9719. 1959. 8.95 (ISBN 0-8149-0196-4). Vanguard.

African Wise Sayings. Ed. by Linus A. Bassey. 1980. pap. write for info. African Policy.

African Women: Their Struggle for Economic Independence. Christine Obbo. 240p. 1980. text ed. 18.95 (ISBN 0-905762-33-9, Pub. by Zed Pr); pap. 7.95. Lawrence Hill.

African Worlds. Ed. by Daryll Forde. 1954. pap. 11.50x (ISBN 0-19-724156-5). Oxford U Pr.

African Writers on African Writing. Ed. by G. D. Killam. 1973. pap. text ed. 4.25x o.s.i. (ISBN 0-8101-0420-2). Northwestern U Pr.

African (Yoruba) Case Studies in the Application of Metaphysical, Herbal, & Occult Therapies. F. O. Esho. (Traditional Healing Ser.: Vol. 4). (Illus.). 1981. 22.50x (ISBN 0-932426-03-4); pap. text ed. 12.50x (ISBN 0-932426-07-7). Trado-Medic.

Africana Byways. Anna H. Smith. (Illus.). 1976. 14.00 (ISBN 0-949937-19-3). Munger Africana Lib.

Africanderisms. Charles Pettman. LC 68-18007. 1968. Repr. of 1913 ed. 28.00 (ISBN 0-8103-3289-2). Gale.

Africanisation, Nationalisation & Inequality. P. Daniel. LC 78-31563. (DAE-Industrial Relations & Labour Ser.). 1979. 35.50 (ISBN 0-521-22719-4); pap. 15.50x (ISBN 0-521-29623-4). Cambridge U Pr.

Africanity: The Cultural Unity of Black Africa. Jacques Maquet. Tr. by Joan Rayfield. 1972. 14.95 (ISBN 0-19-519701-1). Oxford U Pr.

Africanization of the Labor Market: Educational & Occupational Segmentations in the Camerouns. Remi Clignet. LC 75-13145. 1976. 20.00x (ISBN 0-520-03019-2). U of Cal Pr.

Africans Abroad: A Documentary History of the Black Diaspora in Asia, Latin America, and the Caribbean in the Age of Slavery. Ed. by Graham W. Irwin. LC 77-457. 1977. 25.00x (ISBN 0-231-03936-0); pap. 10.00 (ISBN 0-231-03937-9). Columbia U Pr.

Africans: An Ethnological Account. H. Schneider. 1981. pap. 9.95 (ISBN 0-13-018648-1). P-H.

Africans & Seminoles: From Removal to Emancipation. Daniel F. Littlefield, Jr. LC 77-86. (Contributions in Afro-American & African Studies: No. 32). 1977. lib. bdg. 17.95x (ISBN 0-8371-9529-2, LAS/). Greenwood.

Africans in European Eyes-the Portrayal of Black Africans in Fourteenth & Fifteenth Century Europe. Peter A. Mark. LC 74-25878. (Foreign & Comparative Studies-Eastern African Ser.: No. 16). 98p. 1975. pap. 4.50x (ISBN 0-915984-13-X). Syracuse U Foreign Comp.

Africa's Industrial Future. Richard Bailey. LC 76-30919. 1977. text ed. 25.00x (ISBN 0-89158-726-8). Westview.

Africa's International Relations: The Diplomacy of Dependency & Change. Ali A. Mazrui. LC 77-595. 1978. text ed. 13.50 (ISBN 0-89158-671-7). Westview.

Africa's Rift Valley. Colin Willock. (World's Wild Places Ser). (Illus.). 184p. 1974. 12.95 (ISBN 0-8094-2009-0). Time-Life.

Africa's Rift Valley. Colin Willock. (World's Wild Places Ser.). (Illus.). 1974. lib. bdg. 11.97 (ISBN 0-686-51014-3). Silver.

Africa's Rough Road: Problems of Change & Development. Absolom L. Vilakazi et al. 1977. pap. text ed. 9.50x (ISBN 0-8191-0113-3). U Pr of Amer.

Afrika Korps. A. J. Barker. LC 78-70063. (Illus.). 192p. 1979. 17.95 o.p. (ISBN 0-89196-017-1, Domus Bks). Quality Bks IL.

Afrikaans Pocket Dictionary. 4.50 (ISBN 0-685-36172-1). Heinman.

Afrikaner Politics in South Africa, 1934-1948. Newell M. Stultz. (Perspectives on Southern Africa: Vol. 13). 1974. 18.00x (ISBN 0-520-02452-4). U of Cal Pr.

Afro-American Anthropology: Contemporary Perspectives on Theory & Research. Norman E. Whitten, Jr. & John F. Szwed. LC 79-93109. 1970. 15.95 (ISBN 0-02-935260-6). Free Pr.

Afro-American Arts of the Suriname Rain Forest. Sally Price & Richard Price. (Illus.). 240p. 1981. 37.50 (ISBN 0-520-04345-6, CAL 516); pap. 14.95 (ISBN 0-520-04412-6). U of Cal Pr.

Afro-American Authors. Ed. by William Adams et al. LC 74-160035. (Multi-Ethnic Literature Ser.). (Illus.). 165p. (gr. 10-12). 1971. pap. text ed. 5.32 (ISBN 0-395-12700-9, 2-40591); inst guide 5.84 (ISBN 0-395-24042-5). HM.

Afro-American Authors, American Indian Authors, Mexican-American Authors: Instructor's Guide. Ed. by William Adams. (Multo-Ethnic Literature Ser.). 1976. 5.32 (ISBN 0-395-24042-5). HM.

Afro-American Fiction, Eighteen Fifty-Three to Nineteen Seventy-Six: A Guide to Information Sources. Ed. by Edward Margolies & David Bakish. LC 73-16976. (American Literature, English Literature, & World Literatures in English Information Guide Ser.: Vol. 25). 1979. 30.00 (ISBN 0-8103-1207-7). Gale.

Afro-American History, Past to Present. Ed. by Henry N. Drewry & Cecelia H. Drewry. LC 74-136591. 585p. (gr. 9-12). 1971. pap. text ed. 8.95x o.p. (ISBN 0-684-41232-2, ScribC). Scribner.

Afro-American History: Separate or Interracial. Meyer Weinberg. 1968. pap. 0.90 (ISBN 0-685-38477-2). Integrated Ed Assoc.

Afro-American History: Sources for Research. Ed. by Robert L. Clarke. (Illus.). 450p. 1981. 19.50 (ISBN 0-88258-018-3). Howard U Pr.

Afro-American Literature & Culture, Nineteen Forty-Five to Nineteen Seventy-Three: A Guide to Information Sources. Ed. by Charles D. Peavy. LC 73-17561. (American Studies Information Guide Ser.: Vol. 6). 1979. 30.00 (ISBN 0-8103-1254-9). Gale.

Afro-American Literature: Drama. Ed. by William Adams et al. (Afro-American Literature Ser). (gr. 9-12). 1970. pap. 5.32 (ISBN 0-395-01973-7, 2-00200). HM.

Afro-American Literature: Fiction. Ed. by William Adams et al. (Afro-American Literature Ser). (gr. 9-12). 1970. pap. 5.32 (ISBN 0-395-01977-X, 2-00204). HM.

Afro-American Literature: Nonfiction. Ed. by William Adams et al. (Afro-American Literature Ser). (gr. 9-12). 1970. pap. 5.32 (ISBN 0-395-01979-6, 2-00206). HM.

Afro-American Literature: Poetry. Ed. by William Adams et al. (Afro-American Literature Ser). (gr. 10-12). 1970. pap. 5.32 (ISBN 0-395-01975-3, 2-00202). HM.

Afro-American Poetry & Drama, Seventeen Sixty to Nineteen Seventy-Five: A Guide to Information Sources. Ed. by Genevieve E. Fabre et al. LC 74-11518. (American Literature, English Literature, & World Literature in English Information Guide Ser.: Vol. 17). 1979. 30.00 (ISBN 0-8103-1208-5). Gale.

Afro-American Seventy Six. Eugene Winslow. LC 75-23936. (Illus.). 80p. 1975. 8.95 (ISBN 0-910030-20-0); pap. 5.95 (ISBN 0-910030-21-9). Afro-Am.

Afro-American Slaves: Community or Chaos? Ed. by Randall M. Miller. 128p. (Orig.). 1981. pap. 5.50 (ISBN 0-89874-078-9). Krieger.

Afro-American Tradition in Decorative Arts. John M. Vlach. LC 77-19326. (Illus.). 184p. 1978. pap. 12.00x (ISBN 0-910386-39-0, Pub. by Cleveland Mus Art). Ind U Pr.

Afro-American Writing: An Anthology of Prose & Poetry, 2 vols. Ed. by Richard A. Long & Eugenia W. Collier. LC 72-83827. 1972. 22.50x set (ISBN 0-8147-4954-2); pap. 10.00x set (ISBN 0-8147-4955-0). NYU Pr.

Afro-Arab Relations in the New World Order. E. C. Chibwe. LC 77-90935. 1978. 19.95 (ISBN 0-312-01063-X). St Martin.

Afro-Argentines of Buenos Aires, 1800-1900. G. Reid Andrews. LC 80-5105. 336p. 1980. 21.50 (ISBN 0-299-08290-3). U of Wis Pr.

Afro-Asian Culture Studies. rev. ed. Erwin Rosenfeld & Harriet Geller. LC 76-16066. (gr. 7-12). 1976. text ed. 9.75 o.p. (ISBN 0-8120-5122-X); pap. text ed. 5.50 o.p. (ISBN 0-8120-0648-8). Barron.

Afro-Asian Dimension of Brazilian Foreign Policy, 1956-1972. Wayne A. Selcher. LC 73-19968. (Latin American Monographs 2: No. 13). 1974. 11.00 (ISBN 0-8130-0384-9). U Presses Fla.

Afro-Asian Group in the U.N. D. N. Sharma. 1969. 10.00x o.p. (ISBN 0-8426-1518-0). Verry.

Afro-Asian, Japanese, & Euro-American Contributions to Mankind & Civilization Yestermorrow, Vol. 1. Yoshitaka Horiuchi et al. 1981. 9.50 (ISBN 0-533-04486-3). Vantage.

Afro-Asian World: A Cultural Understanding. rev. ed. Edward R. Kolevzon. (gr. 7-12). 1972. text ed. 16.80 (ISBN 0-205-03298-2, 7832982); tchrs'. guide 4.40 (ISBN 0-205-03299-0, 7832990); wkbk. & tchrs'. ed. 5.12 ea. (7822960, 7822979); tests & tchrs'. ed. 4.80 ea. (ISBN 0-205-02294-4, 7822944, 7822952). Allyn.

Afro-Asian World: A Cultural Understanding. Edward R. Kolevzon. (gr. 7-12). 1978. text ed. 16.80 (ISBN 0-205-05608-3, 7856083); 14.12 (ISBN 0-205-02294-4). Allyn.

Afrocommunism. David Ottaway & Marina Ottaway. LC 80-24289. (New Library of African Affairs Ser.). 320p. 1981. text ed. 25.00x (ISBN 0-8419-0664-5, Africana). Holmes & Meier.

After a - Level? A Study of the Transition from School to Higher Education. B. H. Choppin et al. (General Ser.). 1972. pap. text ed. 3.75x (ISBN 0-85633-008-6, NFER). Humanities.

After Affluence: Resolving the Middle Class Crisis. John O. Wilson. LC 80-7752. 192p. 1980. 9.95 (ISBN 0-06-250970-5, HarpR). Har-Row.

After Afghanistan: The Long Haul Safeguarding Security & Independence in the Third World. The Atlantic Council's Working Group on Security Affairs et al. (Atlantic Council Policy Paper Ser.). 71p. 1980. pap. text ed. 6.50x (Pub. by Atlantic Council of the U.S.). Westview.

After Amin: The Bloody Pearl. Michael L. Richardson. LC 80-23249. (Illus.). 224p. (Orig.). 1980. pap. 4.95 (ISBN 0-9604968-0-7, 737). Majestic Bks.

After Auschwitz: Essays in Contemporary Judaism. Richard J. Rubenstein. (Orig.). pap. 6.95 (ISBN 0-672-61150-3). Bobbs.

After Babel: Aspects of Language & Translation. George Steiner. 512p. 1975. 27.50 (ISBN 0-19-212196-0). Oxford U Pr.

After Claude. Iris Owens. 224p. 1974. pap. 1.50 o.p. (ISBN 0-446-78427-3). Warner Bks.

After Dark. Manley W. Wellman. LC 80-650. (Double D Science Ficion Ser.). 192p. 1980. 8.95 (ISBN 0-385-15604-9). Doubleday.

After Death-Life in God. Norman Pittenger. 96p. 1980. 4.95 (ISBN 0-8164-0108-X). Crossroad NY.

After-Dinner Gardening Book: The Avocado-Gift Edition. Richard W. Langer. (Illus.). 198p. 1974. 9.95 o.s.i. (ISBN 0-02-567940-6). Macmillan.

After-Dinner Laughter. Ed. by Sylvia L. Boehm. LC 76-51166. 1977. 7.95 (ISBN 0-8069-0102-0); lib. bdg. 7.49 (ISBN 0-8069-0103-9). Sterling.

After Einstein: Proceedings. Einstein Centennial Celebration, Memphis State University, March 14-16, 1979. Ed. by Peter Barker & Cecil G. Shugart. LC 80-27347. (Illus.). 1981. 24.95x (ISBN 0-87870-095-1). Memphis St Univ. Postponed.

After Eli. Terry Kay. 288p. 1981. 10.95 (ISBN 0-395-30854-2). HM.

After Everything: Western Intellectual History Since 1945. Roland N. Stromberg. LC 74-24980. 250p. (Orig.). 1975. 14.95 (ISBN 0-312-01085-0); pap. text ed. 6.95 (ISBN 0-312-01120-2). St Martin.

After Fifty Cookbook: A Treasury of Creative Recipes for 1 or 2, Retired People, or Those on Special Diets. Donna M. Hamilton. LC 74-16551. 377p. 1974. 13.50 (ISBN 0-8040-0667-9). Swallow.

After Hard Guns. Eli Mitchell. 272p. (Orig.). 1980. pap. 1.95 (ISBN 0-89083-699-X). Zebra.

After Hiroshima: America Since Nineteen Forty-Five. Albert C. Ganley et al. (Illus.). 320p. (Orig.). (gr. 11-12). 1979. pap. text ed. 4.75x (ISBN 0-88334-121-2). Ind Sch Pr.

After Industrial Society? The Emerging Self-Service Economy. J. Gershuny. 1978. text ed. 20.75x (ISBN 0-391-00837-4); pap. text ed. 7.75x (ISBN 0-391-00847-1). Humanities.

After Leningrad: From the Caucasus to the Rhine, August 9, 1942-March 25, 1945. Elena Skrjabina. Ed. by Norman Luxenburg. LC 78-18872. (Illus.). 197p. 1978. 14.95 (ISBN 0-8093-0856-8). S Ill U Pr.

After Mao What? Jagdish P. Jain. LC 75-31534. 1976. 24.50x (ISBN 0-89158-528-1). Westview.

After More Black Coffee. Robert I. Gannon. 1964. 3.50 o.p. (ISBN 0-374-10196-5). FS&G.

After Ninety. Imogen Cunningham. LC 77-73306. (Illus.). 112p. 1977. 20.00 (ISBN 0-295-95559-7); pap. 10.95 (ISBN 0-295-95673-9). U of Wash Pr.

After Pa Was Shot. Judy Alter. (gr. 7-9). 1978. PLB 7.63 (ISBN 0-688-32136-4). Morrow.

After Plastic Surgery: Adaptation & Adjustment. Frances C. Macgregor. LC 79-11808. (Praeger Special Studies Ser.). 160p. 1980. 19.95 (ISBN 0-03-052131-9). Praeger.

After Polygamy Was Made a Sin: The Social History of Christian Polygamy. John Cairncross. 1974. 18.00x (ISBN 0-7100-7730-0). Routledge & Kegan.

After San Jacinto: The Texas-Mexican Frontier, 1836-1841. Joseph M. Nance. (Illus.). 1962. 25.00x (ISBN 0-292-73156-6). U of Tex Pr.

After Scholarships, What: Sixteen Ways to Reduce Your College Costs. Compiled by Peterson's Guides Editors. 400p. 1981. pap. 8.00 (ISBN 0-87866-129-8). Petersons Guid.

After Seven Years. Raymond Moley. LC 71-168390. (FDR & the Era of the New Deal Ser.). 446p. 1972. Repr. of 1939 ed. lib. bdg. 42.50 (ISBN 0-306-70327-0). Da Capo.

After Strange Fruit: Changing Literary Tastes in Post-World-War II Boston. P. Albert Duhamel. write for info. Boston Public Lib.

After Suicide. Samuel E. Wallace. LC 73-9793. 269p. 1973. 21.95 (ISBN 0-471-91865-2, Pub. by Wiley-Interscience). Wiley.

After the Apocalypse. W. Randolph Fox. (Orig.). 1980. pap. 1.95 (ISBN 0-532-23118-X). Manor Bks.

After the Big Bang. Paula Randall. 105p. (Orig.). 1980. pap. 3.95 (ISBN 0-89260-186-8). Hwong Pub.

After the Crash: America in the Great Depression. John Rublowsky. LC 73-9019. (Illus.). (gr. 7-12). 1970. 4.95g o.s.i. (ISBN 0-02-777930-0, CCPr). Macmillan.

After the Cross. Hugh Schonfield. LC 80-27856. 128p. 1981. 7.95 (ISBN 0-498-02549-7). A S Barnes.

After the Elm. Ed. by Brian Clouston & Kathy Stansfield. (Illus.). 186p. 1980. text ed. 24.50x (ISBN 0-8419-6107-7). Holmes & Meier.

After the Fall. Arthur Miller. (Plays Ser). 1968. pap. 2.50 o.p. (ISBN 0-670-00231-3). Penguin.

After the Festival. March Cost. LC 66-28883. 1966. 7.95 (ISBN 0-8149-0049-6). Vanguard.

After the First Death. Donald Taylor. LC 72-93479. 176p. 1973. 5.95 o.p. (ISBN 0-8076-0675-8). Braziller.

After the Flowers Have Gone. Beatrice Decker & Gladys Kooiman. 160p. 1973. 5.95 o.p. (ISBN 0-310-23240-6). Zondervan.

After the Genteel Tradition: American Writers 1910-1930. rev. ed. Ed. by Malcolm Cowley. LC 64-11608. (Crosscurrents-Modern Critiques Ser.). 220p. 1964. 11.95 (ISBN 0-8093-0118-0). S Ill U Pr.

After the Goat Man. Betsy Byars. (gr. 3-5). 1975. pap. 1.75 (ISBN 0-380-00437-2, 53314, Camelot). Avon.

After the Gold Rush. Archie Satterfield. LC 76-13642. (Illus.). 1976. 8.95 o.p. (ISBN 0-397-01142-3). Lippincott.

After the Guns Fall Silent. Mohamed Sid-Ahmed. LC 76-24997. 1976. 19.95 (ISBN 0-312-01155-5). St Martin.

After the Hunt. Alfred Frankenstein. LC 68-31417. (Illus.). 1975. 45.00 (ISBN 0-520-02936-4). U of Cal Pr.

After the Last Heartbeat. Tom Scarinci. LC 79-55679. 1980. 8.95 (ISBN 0-915684-55-1). Christian Herald.

After the Lesson Plan: Realities of High School Teaching. Amy P. Emmers. 1981. pap. 7.95 (ISBN 0-8077-2605-2). Tchrs Coll.

After the Odyssey. Gillian Bottomley. (Studies in Society & Culture). 1980. 22.95x (ISBN 0-7022-1399-3). U of Queensland Pr.

After the Omen. Frank Allnutt. 1978. pap. 1.95 (ISBN 0-89728-002-4, 704481). Omega Pubns OR.

After the Reformation: Essays in Honor of J. H. Hexter. Ed. by Barbara C. Malament. LC 79-5254. 256p. 1980. 30.00x (ISBN 0-8122-7774-0). U of Pa Pr.

After the Revival--What? Robert L. Sumner. 1980. pap. 3.95 (ISBN 0-87398-026-3). Bibl Evang Pr.

After the Sun Sets. Charlotte Huber et al. (Wonder-Story Books Ser). (gr. 3). text ed. 10.28 (ISBN 0-06-517503-4, SchDept). Har-Row.

After the Trauma: Representative British Novelists Since 1920. Harvey C. Webster. LC 74-119815. 216p. 1970. 10.50x (ISBN 0-8131-1224-9). U Pr of Ky.

After the Wake: An Essay on the Contemporary Avant-Garde. Christopher Butler. (Illus.). 192p. 1980. 24.00 (ISBN 0-19-815766-5). Oxford U Pr.

After the War. H. R. Coursen. (Illus.). 1980. 12.95 (ISBN 0-918606-06-3); pap. 7.95 (ISBN 0-918606-05-5). Heidelberg Graph.

After the Wedding. Hila Colman. LC 75-11587. 192p. (gr. 7 up). 1975. PLB 6.96 (ISBN 0-688-32043-0). Morrow.

After Therapy What? Thomas C. Oden et al. (Illus.). 224p. 1974. text ed. 16.75 (ISBN 0-398-03105-3). C C Thomas.

After Tito What? K. Krishna Moorthy. (Illus.). 225p. 1980. text ed. 12.50x (ISBN 0-391-02063-3). Humanities.

After Virtue. Alasdair MacIntyre. LC 80-53073. 320p. 1981. text ed. 15.95 (ISBN 0-268-00662-8). U of Notre Dame Pr.

After Winter, Spring. Nita Schuh. 1978. pap. 2.95 o.p. (ISBN 0-88270-284-X). Logos.

After Worlds Collide. Philip Wylie & Edwin Balmer. 192p. 1963. pap. 2.25 (ISBN 0-446-92813-5). Warner Bks.

After You've Said Goodbye: How to Recover After Ending a Relationship. Trudy Helmlinger. 1977. 8.95 (ISBN 0-8467-0214-2, Pub. by Two Continents). Hippocrene Bks.

After You've Said I Do. Dwight H. Small. 1976. pap. 1.75 (ISBN 0-89129-213-6). Jove Pubns.

Afterimages: Zen Poems of Shinkichi Takahashi. Shinkichi Takahashi. LC 77-132582. 127p. 1970. 8.95 (ISBN 0-8040-0512-5). Swallow.

Aftermath of Colonialism. Ed. by Nancy L. Hoepli. 206p. 1973. 6.25 (ISBN 0-8242-0470-0). Wilson.

Aftermath of Rape. Thomas W. McCahill & Linda C. Meyer. LC 79-1952. (Illus.). 288p. 1979. 22.95 (ISBN 0-669-03018-X). Lexington Bks.

Aftermath of the Napoleonic Wars. Hans G. Schenk. 1968. 16.50 (ISBN 0-86527-000-7). Fertig.

Afternoon of an Author. F. Scott Fitzgerald. (Hudson River Edition Ser.). 1981. write for info. (ISBN 0-684-16469-8, ScribT). Scribner.

Aftershock. David Howell. 192p. (Orig.). 1981. pap. 2.50 (ISBN 0-515-05454-2). Jove Pubns.

Aftershock. Collin Wilcox. 1979. pap. 1.75 o.s.i. (ISBN 0-515-05184-5). Jove Pubns.

Aftershocks: A Tale of Two Victims. David H. Bain. 320p. 1980. 10.95 (ISBN 0-416-00681-7). Methuen Inc.

Afterwards. Patricia Cumming. LC 73-94068. 64p. 1974. pap. 4.95 (ISBN 0-914086-02-2). Alicejamesbooks.

Afterwords: Novelists on Their Novels. Ed. by Thomas McCormack. LC 68-28208. 1969. 7.95 o.s.i. (ISBN 0-06-012903-4, HarpT). Har-Row.

AG Aviation. Miles E. Gibson. pap. 7.00 (ISBN 0-685-46361-3, Pub. by Diversified). Aviation.

AG Pilot & Chemicals. Miles E. Gibson. pap. 7.00 (ISBN 0-685-46362-1, Pub. by Diversified). Aviation.

AG Pilot Employment Guide. Miles E. Gibson. pap. 7.00 (ISBN 0-685-46363-X, Pub. by Diversified). Aviation.

Agadir. Artur Lundkvist. Tr. by William Jay Smith & Leif Sjoberg. LC 80-15978. (International Poetry Ser.: Vol. 2). (Illus.). xiii, 57p. 1980. 10.95 (ISBN 0-8214-0444-X); pap. 5.95 (ISBN 0-8214-0561-6). Ohio U Pr.

Again Calls the Owl. Margaret Craven. 1981. pap. 2.25 (ISBN 0-440-10074-7). Dell.

Against All Odds. Tom Helms. LC 78-3302. 1978. 10.95- (ISBN 0-690-01763-4, TYC-T). T Y Crowell.

Against All Odds. John K. Jacobs. (gr. 7 up). 1967. 8.95g (ISBN 0-02-747580-8). Macmillan.

Against All Odds. F. A. Jameson. Ed. by Pat McCarthy. (Pal Paperbacks Ser., Kit B). (Illus., Orig.). (gr. 7-12). 1974. pap. text ed. 1.25 (ISBN 0-8374-3504-8). Xerox Ed Pubns.

Against Behaviouralism: A Critique of Behavioural Science. Edmund Ions. 165p. 1977. 22.50x (ISBN 0-87471-864-3). Rowman.

Against Infinity. Ed. by E. Robson & J. Wimp. 1979. 17.00; pap. 8.95. Primary Pr.

Against Julian. St. Augustine. (Fathers of the Church Ser.: Vol. 35). 21.00 (ISBN 0-8132-0035-0). Cath U Pr.

Against Odds. Basil Heatter. 160p. 1970. write for info. (ISBN 0-374-30170-0). FS&G.

Against Taffy Sinclair Club. Betsy Haynes. 112p. (gr. 3-6). 1981. pap. 1.50 (ISBN 0-553-15108-8). Bantam.

Against the Academicians. Saint Augustine. Tr. by Sr. M. Patricia Garvey. 1957. pap. 5.95 (ISBN 0-87462-202-6). Marquette.

Against the Age: An Introduction to William Morris. Peter Faulkner. (Illus.). 192p. 1980. text ed. 28.50 (ISBN 0-04-809012-3, 2524). Allen Unwin.

Against the Clock: The Story of Ray Buker, Sr., Olympic Runner & Missionary Statesman. Eric S. Fife. (Illus.). 224p. (Orig.). 1981. pap. 5.95 (ISBN 0-310-24351-3). Zondervan.

Against the Fall of Night. Arthur C. Clarke. 1978. pap. 1.75 o.s.i. (ISBN 0-515-04832-1). Jove Pubns.

Against the Falling Evil. James McMichael. LC 72-17187. (New Poetry Ser.: No. 43). 55p. 1971. o.p 5.00 (ISBN 0-8040-0552-4); pap. 3.25 (ISBN 0-8040-0620-2). Swallow.

Against the Stream. James Hanley. 256p. 1981. 10.95 (ISBN 0-8180-0629-3). Horizon.

Against the Tide: Watchman Nee. Angus Kinnear. 1974. pap. 2.95 (ISBN 0-87508-408-7). Chr Lit.

Against the World for the World: The Hartford Appeal & the Future of American Religion. Peter Berger & Richard J. Neuhaus. 180p. 1976. pap. 3.95 (ISBN 0-8164-2121-8). Crossroad NY.

Agamemnon. Aeschylus. Tr. by Gilbert Murray. 1920. pap. text ed. 3.95x (ISBN 0-04-882002-4). Allen Unwin.

Agamemnon. Aeschylus & Aeschylus. Tr. by Hugh Lloyd-Jones from Greek. 1979. 20.00x (ISBN 0-7156-1365-0, Pub. by Duckworth England); pap. text ed. 6.75x (ISBN 0-7156-1367-7, Pub. by Duckworth England). Biblio Dist.

Agapology: The Rational Love Philosphy, Guide of Life. Wilmon H. Sheldon. 1965. 4.95 o.p. (ISBN 0-8158-0184-X). Chris Mass.

Agaricales in Modern Taxonomy. 3rd & rev. ed. R. Singer. 1975. 125.00 o.s.i. (ISBN 3-7682-0143-0). Lubrecht & Cramer.

Agatha. Kathleen Tynan. 1979. pap. 2.25 (ISBN 0-345-27586-1). Ballantine.

Agatha Christie Crossword Puzzle Book. Randall Toye & Judith H. Gaffney. 132p. (Orig.). 1981. pap. 6.95 (ISBN 0-686-69122-9). HR&W.

Agatha Crumm. Bill Hoest. (Orig.). 1980. pap. 1.50 (ISBN 0-451-09422-0, W9422, Sig). NAL.

Agathiae Myrinaei Historiarum Libri quinque. Agathias. Ed. by Rudolfus Keydell. (Corpus Fontium Historiae Byzantinae Ser. Berolinensis Vol. 2). 232p. (Lat). 1967. 48.25x (ISBN 3-11-001348-7). De Gruyter.

Agaton Sax & Lispington's Grandfather Clock. Nils-Olof Franzen. (gr. 2-7). 1979. PLB 8.95 (ISBN 0-233-96964-0). Andre Deutsch.

Agaton Sax & the Big Rig. Nils-Olof Franzen. LC 80-2693. (Illus.). 128p. (gr. 2-7). 1981. 8.95 (ISBN 0-233-96754-0). Andre Deutsch.

Agaton Sax & the Big Rig. Nils-Olof Franzen. LC 80-2693. 128p. (gr. 2-7). 1981. 8.95 (ISBN 0-233-96754-0). Andre Deutsch.

Agaton Sax & the Diamond Thieves. Nils-Clof Franzen. LC 79-64183. (Illus.). (gr. 2-7). 1980. 7.95 (ISBN 0-233-95724-3). Andre Deutsch.

Age & Grace. William Fournier & Sarah A. O'Malley. (Orig.). 1980. 6.95 (ISBN 0-8146-1127-3). Liturgical Pr.

Age & Sex in Human Societies: A Biosocial Perspective. Pierre Van den Berghe. 7.95x (ISBN 0-534-00311-7). Wadsworth Pub.

Age, Generation & Time: Some Features of East African Age Organizations. Ed. by P. T. Baxter & Uri Almagor. LC 78-18952. (Illus.). 1978. 25.00 (ISBN 0-312-01172-5). St Martin.

Age in Society. Ed. by Anne Foner. LC 76-41105. (Sage Contemporary Social Science Issues: Vol. 30). 1976. 4.95x (ISBN 0-8039-0731-1). Sage.

Age, Learning Ability & Intelligence. Ed. by Richard L. Sprott. 176p. 1980. text ed. 15.00 (ISBN 0-442-27895-0). Van Nos Reinhold.

Age of Absolutism, Sixteen Sixty to Eighteen Fifteen. Max Beloff. 1971. Repr. of 1954 ed. text ed. 11.50x (ISBN 0-09-020271-6, Hutchinson U Lib). Humanities.

Age of Alexander. Plutarch. Tr. by Ian Scott-Kilvert. (Classics Ser). 1973. pap. 3.95 (ISBN 0-14-044286-3). Penguin.

Age of Augustus. Donald Earl. 1968. 19.95 o.p. (ISBN 0-236-40026-6, Pub. by Paul Elek); pap. 7.95 o.p. (ISBN 0-236-31130-1). Merrimack Bk Serv.

Age of Balfour & Baldwin: 1902-1940. John Ramsden. (History of the Conservative Party). (Illus.). 1978. text ed. 40.00x (ISBN 0-582-50714-6). Longman.

Age of Bureaucracy. Wolfgang J. Mommsen. 1977. pap. 3.95x o.p. (ISBN 0-06-131862-0, TB 1862, Torch). Har-Row.

Age of Cameras. Edward Holmes. 1978. 24.95 o.p. (ISBN 0-85242-346-2, Pub. by Fountain). Morgan.

Age of Catherine de Medici. J. E. Neale. 1978. pap. 6.50 (ISBN 0-224-60566-6, Pub. by Chatto Bodley Jonathan). Merrimack Bk Serv.

Age of Change, from Nineteen Forty-Five. William E. Leuchtenburg. LC 63-8572. (Life History of the United States). (Illus.). (gr. 5 up). 1974. PLB 9.96 (ISBN 0-8094-0561-X, Pub. by Time-Life). Silver.

Age of Charlemagne. Edward Rice. 112p. 1963. 2.95 (ISBN 0-374-29492-5). FS&G.

Age of Civil War & Reconstruction, 1830-1900: A Book of Interpretative Essays. rev. ed. Ed. by Charles Crowe. 1975. pap. text ed. 12.50x (ISBN 0-256-01528-7). Dorsey.

Age of Enlightenment. 2nd ed. Otis E. Fellows & Norman L. Torrey. LC 73-147121. 1971. text ed. 17.95 (ISBN 0-13-018465-9). P-H.

Age of Enlightenment. Peter Gay. LC 66-18266. (Great Ages of Man). (Illus.). (gr. 6 up). 1966. PLB 11.97 (ISBN 0-8094-0368-4, Pub. by Time-Life). Silver.

Age of Enlightenment: An Anthology of Eighteenth Century Texts, 2 vols. Ed. by Simon Eliot & Beverly Stern. 1980. Vol. 1. 23.50x; Vol. 2. 23.50x. B&N.

Age of Exploration. John R. Hale. LC 66-20552. (Great Ages of Man). (Illus.). (gr. 6 up). 1966. PLB 11.97 (ISBN 0-8094-0369-2, Pub. by Time-Life). Silver.

Age of Faith. Anne Fremantle. (Great Ages of Man Ser). (Illus.). 1965. 12.95 (ISBN 0-8094-0343-9). Time-Life.

Age of Fishes: The Development of the Most Successful Vertebrate. Joy O. Spoczynska. LC 75-18750. 1976. 10.00 o.p. (ISBN 0-684-14495-6, ScribT). Scribner.

Age of German Liberation, 1795-1815. Friedrich Meinecke. Tr. by Peter Paret & Helmut Fischer. LC 74-79767. Orig. Title: Das Zeitalter der Deutschen Erhebung. 1977. 20.00x (ISBN 0-520-02792-2); pap. 4.95x (ISBN 0-520-03454-6). U of Cal Pr.

Age of Giant Corporations: A Microeconomic History of American Business, 1914-1970. Robert Sobel. LC 72-835. (Contributions in Economics & Economic History). 1972. lib. bdg. 15.00 (ISBN 0-8371-6404-4, SAB/); pap. 3.45 (ISBN 0-8371-7339-6). Greenwood.

Age of Great Cities. R. Vaughan. 384p. 1971. Repr. of 1843 ed. 25.00x (ISBN 0-7165-1597-0, Pub. by Irish Academic Pr Ireland). Biblio Dist.

Age of Horace Walpole in Caricature: An Exhibition of Satirical Prints & Drawings from the Collection of W. S. Lewis. John C. Riely. 48p. 1981. pap. text ed. 5.00x (ISBN 0-300-03509-8, 73-88450). Yale U Pr.

Age of Ideology: Political Thought 1750 to the Present. 2nd ed. Isaac Kramnick & Frederick Watkins. (Foundations of Modern Political Science Ser.). 1979. pap. 6.95 ref. ed. (ISBN 0-13-018499-3). P-H.

Age of Imperialism. L. Magdoff. 1979. 24.50 o.p. (ISBN 0-685-67797-4). Porter.

Age of Industrialism in America. Frederick C. Jaher. LC 68-14107. 1968. 10.95 o.s.i. (ISBN 0-02-915970-9). Free Pr.

Age of Innocence. Edith Wharton. LC 68-27785. 1968. lib. rep. ed. 17.50x (ISBN 0-684-14659-2, ScribT); pap. 4.95 (ISBN 0-684-71925-8, SL201, ScribT). Scribner.

Age of Innovation: The World of Electronics, 1930-2000. Electronics Magazine Editors. LC 80-14816. (Illus.). 274p. 1980. text ed. 18.50 (ISBN 0-07-606688-6, R-013). McGraw.

Age of Jewett: Charles Coffin Jewett & American Librarianship, 1841-1868. Ed. by Michael H. Harris. LC 75-14205. (Heritage of Librarianship Ser: No. 1). 166p. 1975. lib. bdg. 20.00x (ISBN 0-87287-113-4). Libs Unl.

Age of Kings. Charles Blitzer. LC 67-23412. (Great Ages of Man). (Illus.). (gr. 6 up). 1967. PLB 11.97 (ISBN 0-8094-0376-5, Pub. by Time-Life). Silver.

Age of Louis the Fourteenth. Francois M. De Voltaire. 1958. 6.00x (ISBN 0-460-00780-7, Evman); pap. 2.95 o.p. (ISBN 0-460-01780-2). Dutton.

Age of MacDiarmid: Essays on Hugh MacDiarmid & His Influence on Contemporary Scotland. Ed. by P. H. Scott & A. C. Davis. 268p. 1981. 22.50x (ISBN 0-389-20199-5). B&N.

Age of Mammals. Bjorn Kurten. LC 79-177479. (Illus.). 1972. 17.50x (ISBN 0-231-03624-8). Columbia U Pr.

Age of Mammals. Bjorn Kurten. (Illus.). 1972. pap. 7.50 (ISBN 0-231-03647-7). Columbia U Pr.

Age of Milton: Backgrounds to Seventeenth-Century Literature. Ed. by C. A. Patrides. Raymond B. Waddington. (Illus.). 438p. 1980. 33.50x (ISBN 0-389-20051-4); pap. 14.00x (ISBN 0-389-20052-2). B&N.

Age of Nationalism and Reform, 1850-1890. Norman Rich. (Illus.). 1977 10.95x (ISBN 0-393-05607-4); pap. 4.95 1976 (ISBN 0-393-09183-X). Norton.

Age of Peel. Ed. by Norman Gash. 1969. pap. 5.95x (ISBN 0-312-01260-8). St Martin.

A.G.E. of Planets. Alan J. O'Hara. 1981. 8.95 (ISBN 0-533-04638-6). Vantage.

Age of Plantagenet & Valois. Kenneth Fowler. 1967. 19.95 o.p. (ISBN 0-236-30832-7, Pub. by Paul Elek). Merrimack Bk Serv.

Age of Plunder. W. G. Hoskins. LC 75-43647. (Social & Economic History of England Ser.). (Illus.). 1976. pap. text ed. 9.95x (ISBN 0-582-48544-4). Longman.

Age of Porfirio Diaz: Selected Readings. Ed. by Carlos A. Gil. LC 76-57535. (Illus.). 191p. 5.95 (ISBN 0-8263-0284-X). U of NM Pr.

Age of Progress. Samuel C. Burchell. (Great Ages of Man Ser). (Illus.). 1966. 12.95 (ISBN 0-8094-0351-X). Time-Life.

Age of Realism. Ed. by F. W. Hemmings. 1978. Repr. of 1974 ed. text ed. 27.50x (ISBN 0-391-00817-X). Humanities.

Age of Reason, Pt. 1. 2nd ed. Thomas Paine. Ed. by Alburey Castell. 1957. pap. 2.50 (ISBN 0-672-60167-2, LLA5). Bobbs.

Age of Reform, Eighteen Fifteen to Eighteen Seventy. 2nd ed. Llewellyn Woodward. 1962. 33.00x (ISBN 0-19-821711-0). Oxford U Pr.

Age of Reform: From Bryan to F. D. R. Richard Hofstadter. 328p. Date not set. pap. 3.95 (ISBN 0-394-70095-3, Vin). Random.

Age of Religious Wars, Fifteen Fifty-Nine to Seventeen Fifteen. 2nd ed. Richard S. Dunn. (Illus.). 1979. 18.95 (ISBN 0-393-05694-5); pap. text ed. 5.95x (ISBN 0-393-09021-3). Norton.

Age of Revolution & Reaction, 1789-1850. Charles Breunig. (Illus.). 1977. 12.95 (ISBN 0-393-05612-0); pap. 5.95x (ISBN 0-393-09143-0). Norton.

Age of Steam. 25.00 (ISBN 0-685-83311-9). Chatham Pub CA.

Age of Steam & Steel. Kenneth Neill. (Illus.). 1976. pap. 4.95x o.p. (ISBN 0-7171-0786-8). Irish Bk Ctr.

Age of Steel & Steam, Eighteen Seventy-Seven to Eighteen Ninety. Bernard A. Weisberger. LC 63-8572. (Life History of the United States Ser.). (Illus.). (gr. 5 up). 1974. PLB 9.96 (ISBN 0-8094-0556-3, Pub. by Time-Life). Silver.

Age of Stonehenge. Colin Burgess. (History in the Landscape Ser.). (Illus.). 402p. 1980. 25.00x (ISBN 0-460-04254-8, Pub. by J M Dent England). Biblio Dist.

Age of Tennyson. Hugh Walker. 309p. 1980. Repr. of 1932 ed. lib. bdg. 25.00 (ISBN 0-89760-914-X). Telegraph Bks.

Age of the Cathedrals: Art & Society, 980-1420. Georges Duby. Tr. by Eleanor Levieux & Barbara Thompson. LC 80-22769. (Illus.). 1981. price not set (ISBN 0-226-16769-0). U of Chicago Pr.

Age of the Economic Revolution: 1876-1900. 2nd ed. Carl N. Degler. 1977. pap. 7.95x (ISBN 0-673-07967-8). Scott F.

Age of the Economist. 3rd ed. Daniel R. Fusfeld. 1977. pap. 7.95x (ISBN 0-673-15071-2). Scott F.

Age of the Gods. Christopher Dawson. LC 68-9653. (Illus., Maps, Tabs). 1971. Repr. of 1928 ed. 18.50 (ISBN 0-86527-001-5). Fertig.

Age of the Grand Tour. Anthony Burgess & Francis Haskell. 1967. ltd. ed. 50.00 o.p. (ISBN 0-236-30811-4, Pub. by Paul Elek). Merrimack Bk Serv.

Age of the Mad Dragons: Steam Locomotives in North America. Douglas Waitley. LC 80-27242. (Illus.). 192p. (gr. 6 up). 1981. 10.95 (ISBN 0-8253-0029-0). Beaufort Bks NY.

Age of the Molecule: Chemistry in the World & Society. Frank W. Dobbs. 337p. 1976. text ed. write for info. (ISBN 0-06-041659-9, HarpC); instructor's manual free (ISBN 0-06-361640-8). Har-Row.

Age of Transition: Britain in the Nineteenth Twentieth Centuries. D. F. MacDonald. 1967. 16.95 (ISBN 0-312-01330-2). St Martin.

Age of Urban Reform: New Perspectives on the Progressive Era. Ed. by Michael H. Ebner & Eugene M. Tobin. LC 77-4959. (National University Pubns., Interdisciplinary Urban Ser.). 1977. 15.00 (ISBN 0-8046-9192-4); pap. text ed. 8.95 (ISBN 0-8046-9204-1). Kennikat.

Age of Velikovsky. C. J. Ransom. LC 76-22381. (Illus.). 1977. 12.95 (ISBN 0-917994-01-9). Kronos Pr.

Age of Western Expansion. The Educational Research Council. (Human Adventure Concepts & Inquiry Ser). (gr. 6). 1975. pap. text ed. 7.20 (ISBN 0-205-04452-2, 804452X); tchrs'. guide 5.20 (ISBN 0-205-04453-0, 8044538). Allyn.

Age Structure of the Corporate System. William L. Crum. (Institute of Business & Economic Research, UC Berkeley). (Illus.). 1953. 14.00x (ISBN 0-520-00281-4). U of Cal Pr.

Aged in the Community: Managing Senility & Deviance. Dwight Frankfather. LC 77-8327. (Praeger Special Studies). 1977. text ed. 22.95 (ISBN 0-03-021936-1); pap. 9.95 (ISBN 0-03-021931-0). Praeger.

Aged Person & the Nursing Process. Ann G. Yurick et al. 550p. 1980. text ed. 16.95 (ISBN 0-8385-0082-X). ACC.

Aged Poor in England & Wales, London 1894. Charles Booth. LC 79-56948. (English Working Class Ser.). 1980. lib. bdg. 40.00 (ISBN 0-8240-0103-6). Garland Pub.

Aged, the Family, & the Community. Minna Field. LC 79-164500. 304p. 1972. 17.50x (ISBN 0-231-03348-6). Columbia U Pr.

Ageing & Stabilisation of Polymers. Ed. by A. S. Kuz'Minskii. Tr. by B. N. Leyland from Rus. (Illus.). 1971. text ed. 48.50x (ISBN 0-444-20076-2, Pub. by Applied Science). Burgess-Intl Ideas.

Ageism: Prejudice & Discrimination Against the Elderly. Jack Levin & William Levin. 168p. 1980. pap. text ed. 7.95x (ISBN 0-534-00881-X). Wadsworth Pub.

Agencies & Children: A Child Welfare Network's Investment in Its Clients. Deborah Shapiro. 240p. 1976. text ed. 12.50x (ISBN 0-231-03578-0). Columbia U Pr.

Agency & Partnership, Cases, Materials & Problems. J. Dennis Hynes. (Contemporary Legal Eucation Ser.). 1975. 20.00 (ISBN 0-672-81769-1, Bobbs-Merrill Law). Michie.

Agency Company Relationships in Manpower Operations for the Hard to Employ. Louis A. Ferman & Roger Manela. 1973. pap. 6.50x (ISBN 0-87736-329-3). U of Mich Inst Labor.

Agency House, Malaya. Susan Yorke. 1962. 3.95 o.p. (ISBN 0-374-10253-8). FS&G.

Agency Law of U. S., 1981. Gould Editorial Staff. 1981. pap. text ed. 5.75x (ISBN 0-87526-191-4). Gould.

Agency-Partnership - Cases & Materials. 4th ed. Roscoe T. Steffen & Thomas R. Kerr. LC 79-28206. (American Casebook Ser.). 859p. 1980. text ed. 21.95 (ISBN 0-8299-2077-3). West Pub.

Agenda for the Eighties. Ed. by Coral Bell. LC 80-65340. 256p. 1980. pap. text ed. 18.95 (ISBN 0-7081-1086-X, 0469, Pub. by ANUP Australia). Bks Australia.

Agenda for the Nation. Ed. by Kermit Gordon. 1968. 15.95 (ISBN 0-8157-3210-4). Brookings.

Agent of Love. Jillian Kearny. 1979. pap. 1.75 (ISBN 0-446-94003-8). Warner Bks.

Agent Secret. M. E. Mountjoy. (Illus., Fr.). (gr. 7-9). 1969. pap. 4.95 (ISBN 0-312-01400-7). St Martin.

Agent's & Buyer's Guide: Annual Edition 1980. rev ed. Editors of the Fire Casualty & Surety Bulletins. 540p. 1980. pap. 10.50 (ISBN 0-87218-305-X). Natl Underwriter.

Agent's & Buyer's Guide, Nineteen Seventy-Nine. 32nd ed. Fire, Casualty & Surety Bulletins Editors. LC 77-92759. 1979. spiral bdg 9.50 o.p. (ISBN 0-87218-300-9). Natl Underwriter.

Agent's Legal Responsibility. Ronald T. Anderson. LC 80-83690. 168p. 1980. text ed. 12.75 (ISBN 0-87218-307-6). Natl Underwriter.

Agents of Influence. Palma Harcourt. 1978. 7.95 o.s.i. (ISBN 0-8027-5374-4). Walker & Co.

Ager's Way to Easy Elegance: Ager the Butler's Guide to Clothes Care, Managing the Table, Running Your Home & Other Graces. Stanley Ager & Fiona St. Auby. LC 80-673. 176p. 1980. 14.95 (ISBN 0-672-52665-4). Bobbs.

Ages & Stages. Donald G. Macrae. (Auguste Camte Memorial Institute Lecture Ser.: No. 9). 1973. pap. text ed. 2.50x o.p. (ISBN 0-485-19109-1, Athlone Pr). Humanities.

Ages of Mathematics: Western Mathematics Comes of Age, Vol. 3. Cynthia C. Cook. LC 76-10336. (Illus.). (YA) (gr. 10 up). 1977. 5.95 o.p. (ISBN 0-385-11218-1); PLB (ISBN 0-385-11219-X). Doubleday.

Ages of Woman: Female Lives in American History. Goodfriend. (Orig.). 1981. pap. text ed. 7.95 (ISBN 0-316-32005-6). Little.

Aggregate & Industry-Level Productivity Analysis. Ali Dogramaci & Nabil R. Adam. (Productivity Analysis Studies: Vol. 2). 204p. 1981. lib. bdg. 25.00 (ISBN 0-89838-037-5, Pub. by Martinus Nijhoff). Kluwer Boston.

Aggregate Data: Analysis & Interpretation. Ed. by Edgar F. Borgatta & David J. Jackson. LC 79-23909. 1980. 18.50 (ISBN 0-8039-1428-8); pap. 8.95 (ISBN 0-8039-1429-6). Sage.

Aggregate Economic Analysis. 5th ed. Joseph P. McKenna. LC 76-19362. 1977. text ed. 17.95 (ISBN 0-03-089707-6). Dryden Pr.

Aggression. Ed. by Shervert Frazier. (ARNMD Research Publications Ser.: Vol. 52). 1974. 34.50 (ISBN 0-683-00246-5). Raven.

Aggression: A Social Learning Analysis. Albert Bandura. (P-H Social Learning Ser). (Illus.). 368p. 1973. ref. ed. 17.95 (ISBN 0-13-020743-8). P-H.

Aggression & Anti-Social Behaviour in Childhood & Adolescence. Ed. by L. Hersov et al. 1977. pap. text ed. 11.25 (ISBN 0-08-021810-5). Pergamon.

Aggression & Behavior Change: Biological & Social Processes. Ed. by Seymour Feshbach & Adam Fraczek. LC 79-17934. (Praeger Special Studies Ser.). (Illus.). 316p. 1979. 26.95 (ISBN 0-03-052446-6). Praeger.

Aggression & Crimes of Violence. Jeffrey H. Goldstein. Ed. by Robert Lana & Ralph Rosnow. (Reconstruction of Society Ser). (Illus.). 208p. 1975. 12.95 (ISBN 0-19-501935-0); pap. 3.95x (ISBN 0-19-501936-9). Oxford U Pr.

Aggression & Evolution. Ed. by Charlotte M. Otten. LC 79-179422. 1973. text ed. 7.50 o.p. (ISBN 0-471-00407-3). Wiley.

Aggression: Myths & Models. Knud S. Larsen. LC 76-5882. 416p. 1976. 19.95x (ISBN 0-911012-71-0); pap. 9.95x (ISBN 0-88229-452-0). Nelson-Hall.

Aggressive Behavior & the Rosenzweig Picture-Frustration Study. Saul Rosenzweig. LC 78-18200. (Praeger Special Studies). 1978. 22.95 (ISBN 0-03-045656-8). Praeger.

Aggressive Campaign for Automatic Commodity Trading. Joseph Hadad. 1980. 65.00. Windsor.

Aggressive Child. Fritz Redl & David Wineman. 1957. 16.95 (ISBN 0-02-925870-7). Free Pr.

Aggressive Conservative Investor. Martin Whitman & Martin Shubik. LC 78-21593. 1979. 17.95 (ISBN 0-685-67576-9). Random.

Agincourt. Christopher Hibbert. 1978. 22.50 (ISBN 0-7134-1150-3, Pub. by Batsford England). David & Charles.

Aging. Helen Lancaster. 1980. pap. 2.50 (ISBN 0-8309-0290-2). Herald Hse.

Aging: A Christian Approach. Barbara A. Brown. 1980. 0.65 (ISBN 0-686-28771-1). Forward Movement.

Aging, Ageism, & Society. Georgia Barrow & Patricia Smith. (Illus.). 1979. pap. text ed. 13.95 (ISBN 0-8299-0237-6); instrs.' manual avail. (ISBN 0-8299-0458-1). West Pub.

Aging: Aging in Muscle, Vol. 6. Ed. by George Kaldor & William J. DiBattista. LC 78-4356. 1978. 22.00 (ISBN 0-89004-097-4). Raven.

Aging & Exercise. Everett L. Smith & Karl Stoedefalke. 1981. pap. text ed. 8.95 (ISBN 0-89490-040-4). Enslow Pubs.

Aging & Health: Biologic & Social Perspectives. Cary S. Kart et al. LC 77-88690. 1978. 16.95 (ISBN 0-201-03600-2, M&N Div). A-W.

Aging & Income: Programs & Prospects for the Elderly. Ed. by Barbara R. Herzog. LC 78-2510. 1978. 24.95 (ISBN 0-87705-369-3). Human Sci Pr.

Aging & Reproductive Physiology, Vol. 2. Ed. by E. S. Hafez. LC 75-36279. (Perspectives in Human Reproductions Ser.). 1976. 24.00 (ISBN 0-250-40108-8). Ann Arbor Science.

Aging & Retirement. Anne Foner & Karen Schwab. LC 80-24765. (Social Gerontology Ser.). 192p. (Orig.). 1981. pap. text ed. 8.95 (ISBN 0-8185-0444-7). Brooks-Cole.

Aging & Social Policy: Leadership Planning. Patricia L. Kasschau. LC 78-15481. 1978. 29.95 (ISBN 0-03-046411-0). Praeger.

Aging & the Aged: An Annotated Bibliography & Research Guide. Linna F. Place et al. (Westview Guides to Library Research). 175p. 1980. lib. bdg. 17.50x (ISBN 0-89158-934-1). Westview.

Aging & the Aged: Problems, Opportunities, Challenges. Ed. by David E. Flesner & Edwin D. Freed. LC 80-5869. 368p. 1980. lib. bdg. 21.00 (ISBN 0-8191-1267-4); pap. text ed. 12.75 (ISBN 0-8191-1268-2). U Pr of Amer.

Aging Better. E. V. Cowdry. (Illus.). 500p. 1972. pap. 19.75 spiral, photocopy ed. (ISBN 0-398-02263-1). C C Thomas.

Aging: Communication Processes & Disorders. Ed. by Daniel S. Beasley & G. A. Davis. 1980. 29.50 (ISBN 0-8089-1281-X). Grune.

Aging, Death, & the Completion of Being. Ed. by David D. Van Tassel. LC 78-65111. (Illus.). 1979. 22.00 (ISBN 0-8122-7757-0); pap. 11.95x (ISBN 0-8122-1102-2). U of Pa Pr.

Aging from Birth to Death: Interdisciplinary Perspectives. Ed. by Matilda W. Riley. (AAAS Selected Symposium: No. 30). (Illus.). 1979. lib. bdg. 20.00x (ISBN 0-89158-363-7). Westview.

Aging Game: Success, Sanity, & Sex After 60. Barbara G. Anderson. 252p. 1981. pap. 4.95 (ISBN 0-07-001761-1). McGraw.

Aging Gut & What to Do About It. Texter. 1981. write for info. Masson Pub.

Aging Heart: Its Function & Response to Stress. Ed. by Myron L. Weisfeldt. (Aging Ser.: Vol. 12). 324p. 1980. 32.00 (ISBN 0-89004-307-8, 382). Raven.

Aging, Immunity & Arthritic Diseases. Ed. by Marguerite Kay et al. (Aging Ser.: Vol. 13). 275p. 1980. text ed. 27.00 (ISBN 0-89004-382-5). Raven.

Aging in America. 2nd ed. Kart & Manard. 1981. 10.95 (ISBN 0-88284-121-1). Alfred Pub.

Aging in America & Other Cultures. Gerhard Falk et al. LC 80-83627. 135p. 1981. perfect bdg. 11.50 (ISBN 0-86548-034-6). Century Twenty One.

Aging in America: Readings in Social Gerontology. Ed. by Cary S. Kart & Barbara Manard. LC 76-2051. 250p. 1976. pap. text ed. 10.95 (ISBN 0-88284-035-5). Alfred Pub.

Aging in Contemporary Society. Ed. by Ethel Shanas. LC 73-89942. (Sage Contemporary Social Science Issues: No. 6). 1974. 4.95x (ISBN 0-8039-0338-3). Sage.

Aging in Culture & Society: Comparative Viewpoints & Strategies. Ed. by Christine L. Frey. LC 79-13198. 29.95 (ISBN 0-03-052726-0). Praeger.

Aging in Mass Society. Jan Hendricks & Davis Hendricks. 420p. 1981. ref. ed. 15.95 (ISBN 0-87626-017-2). Winthrop.

Aging in Modern Society. Ed. by Alexander Simon & Leon J. Epstein. 1968. pap. 7.50 (ISBN 0-685-24866-6, P023-0). Am Psychiatric.

Aging in the Nineteen-Eighties: Psychological Issues. Ed. by Leonard Poon. LC 80-18515. 1980. 19.50. Am Psychol.

Aging Is a Family Affair. Bumagin & Hirn. 1981. 10.95 (ISBN 0-690-01823-1). Lippincott & Crowell.

Aging-Its Chemistry: Proceedings of the Third Arnold O. Beckman Conference in Clinical Chemistry. Ed. by A. A. Dietz & G. F. Grannis. LC 80-65825. 448p. 1980. 31.95 (ISBN 0-915274-10-8). Am Assn Clinical Chem.

Aging Nervous System. Ed. by Gabe J. Maletta & Francis J. Pirozzolo. LC 79-21167. (Advances in Neurogerontology: Vol. 1). 344p. 1980. 28.95 (ISBN 0-03-052136-X). Praeger.

Aging of Communism. Robert Wesson. LC 80-1600. 180p. 1980. 19.95 (ISBN 0-03-057053-0). Praeger.

Aging of Connective Tissue. David A. Hall. 1976. 28.00 (ISBN 0-12-319150-5). Acad Pr.

Aging of the Brain & Dementia. Ed. by L. Amaducci et al. (Aging Ser.). 1980. text ed. 35.00 (ISBN 0-89004-457-0). Raven.

Aging Parents. Ed. by Pauline K. Ragan. LC 78-66073. 1979. pap. 6.00 (ISBN 0-88474-087-0). USC Andrus Geron.

Aging Phenomena: Relationships Among Different Levels of Organization. Ed. by T. Makinodan et al. (Advances in Experimental Medicine & Biology: Vol. 129). 330p. 1980. 37.50 (ISBN 0-306-40460-5, Plenum Pr). Plenum Pub.

Aging Process: A Health Perspective. Molly S. Wantz & John E. Gay. (Sociology Ser.). (Illus.). 320p. 1981. pap. text ed. 10.95 (ISBN 0-87626-008-3). Winthrop.

Aging: Prospects & Issues. rev. ed. Ed. by Richard H. Davis. 1980. 10.00 (ISBN 0-88474-097-8). USC Andrus Geron.

Aging: Prospects & Issues. 3rd rev. ed. Ed. by Richard H. Davis. LC 80-53413. 427p. 1981. pap. 10.00 (ISBN 0-88474-097-8). USC Andrus Geron.

Aging Reproductive System. Ed. by Edward L. Schneider. LC 77-83693. (Aging Ser: Vol. 4). 1978. 34.50 (ISBN 0-89004-176-8). Raven.

Aging: The Fulfillment of Life. Henri J. M. Nouwen & Walter J. Gaffney. LC 74-1773. 160p. 1974. 2.45 (ISBN 0-385-00918-6, Im). Doubleday.

Aglow in the Kitchen. 160p. 1976. 3.95 (ISBN 0-930756-21-5, 4230-AC). Women's Aglow.

Agnes' Cardboard Piano. Linda P. Silbert & Alvin J. Silbert. (Little Twirps, TM Understanding People Bks.). (Illus.). (gr. k-4). 1978. pap. 2.25 (ISBN 0-89544-054-7). Silbert Bress.

Agnes Martin. Suzanne Delehanty et al. (Illus.). 1976. pap. 8.00 (ISBN 0-88454-010-3). U of Pa Contemp Art.

Agnes Nixon's All My Children Book III: The Lovers. Rosemarie Santini. (Orig.). pap. 2.50 (ISBN 0-515-04896-8). Jove Pubns.

Agnes Nixon's All My Children: Erica, Bk. II. Rosemarie Santini. 224p. (Orig.). 1980. pap. 2.25 (ISBN 0-515-04895-X). Jove Pubns.

Agnes Nixon's All My Children: Tara & Philip, Bk. 1. Rosmarie Santini. 250p. (Orig.). 1980. pap. 2.25 (ISBN 0-515-04892-5). Jove Pubns.

Agni. Robert E. Miller. (Writers Workshop Redbird Ser.). 1975. 8.00 (ISBN 0-88253-492-0); pap. text ed. 4.80 (ISBN 0-88253-491-2). Ind-US Inc.

Agni: The Vedic Ritual of the Fire Altar, 2 vols. Fritz Staal. (Illus.). 1982. 250.00 (ISBN 0-89581-450-1). Lancaster-Miller.

Agni Yoga. (Agni Yoga Ser.). 1954. flexible cover 8.00x o.p. (ISBN 0-933574-04-5). Agni Yoga Soc.

Agnolo Gaddi. Bruce Cole. (Oxford Studies in History of Art & Archetecture). (Illus.). 1977. 52.00x (ISBN 0-19-817339-3). Oxford U Pr.

Agnostic Island: A Tale. Frederick J. Gould. Ed. by Robert L. Wolff. Bd. with Individualist. W. H. Mallock. Repr. of 1899 ed. LC 75-1536. (Victorian Fiction Ser.). 1975. lib. bdg. 66.00 (ISBN 0-8240-1608-4). Garland Pub.

Agnostic Who Dared to Search. Viggo B. Olsen. 64p. 1975. pap. 0.95 (ISBN 0-8024-0139-2). Moody.

Agony & Promise: Current Issues in Higher Education 1969. Ed. by G. Kerry Smith. LC 73-92897. (Higher Education Ser.). 1969. 12.95x o.p. (ISBN 0-87589-049-0). Jossey-Bass.

Agony at Easter: The Nineteen Sixteen Irish Uprising. Thomas M. Coffey. (Illus.). 1969. 6.95 o.s.i. (ISBN 0-02-526650-0). Macmillan.

Agoraphobia. Claire Weeks. 1977. 8.95 (ISBN 0-8015-0111-3, Hawthorn). Dutton.

Agrarian Change in the Scottish Highlands: The Role of the Highlands & Islands Development Board in the Agricultural Economy of the Crofting Counties. John Bryden & George Houston. 152p. 1976. bds. 24.50x (ISBN 0-85520-151-7, Pub. by Martin Robertson England). Biblio Dist.

Agrarian China: Selected Source Materials from Chinese Authors. Tr. by R. H. Tawney from Chinese. (Studies in Chinese History & Civilization). 257p. 1977. Repr. of 1938 ed. 18.75 (ISBN 0-89093-084-8). U Pubns Amer.

Agrarian Conditions in Northern India, Vol. 1, The United Provinces Under British Rule, 1860-1900. Elizabeth Whitcombe. LC 75-129027. (Center for South & Southeast Asia Studies, UC Berkeley). (Illus.). 1972. 22.75x (ISBN 0-520-01706-4). U of Cal Pr.

Agrarian Development in Peasant Economies. E. S. Clayton. 1964. 16.50 (ISBN 0-08-010562-9); pap. 7.25 o.p. (ISBN 0-08-010561-0). Pergamon.

Agrarian Egalitarianism, Land Tenures & Land Reforms in South Asia. Mushtaqur Rahman & Iowa State University Research Foundation. 224p. 1980. pap. text ed. 9.95 (ISBN 0-8403-2343-3). Kendall-Hunt.

Agrarian History of England & Wales, Vol. 1, Pt. 1: Prehistory. Ed. by S. Piggott. LC 66-19763. (Agrarian History of England & Wales Ser.). Date not set. 64.50 (ISBN 0-521-08741-4). Cambridge U Pr.

Agrarian Policies in Communist Europe: A Critical Introduction. Ed. by Karl-Eugen Wadekin. LC 79-55000. (Studies in East European & Soviet Russian Agrarian Policy: Vol. 1). 250p. 1981. text ed. 22.50 (ISBN 0-916672-40-9). Allanheld.

Agrarian Policy of the Russian Socialist-Revolutionary Party. Maureen Perrie. LC 76-644. (Soviet & East European Studies Ser.). 1977. 27.50 (ISBN 0-521-21213-8). Cambridge U Pr.

Agrarian Populism & the Mexican State: The Struggle for Land in Sonora. Steven E. Sanderson. 1981. 18.50x (ISBN 0-520-04056-2). U of Cal Pr.

Agrarian Radicalism in Veracruz, 1920-38. Heather F. Salamini. LC 77-26106. (Illus.). 1978. 15.00x (ISBN 0-8032-0952-5). U of Nebr Pr.

Agrarian Reform & Peasant Organization on the Ecuadorian Coast. M. R. Redcliff. (Univ. of London Institute of Latin American Studies Monographs: No. 8). (Illus.). 1978. text ed. 25.75x (ISBN 0-485-17708-0, Athlone Pr). Humanities.

Agrarian Reform in Latin America: An Annotated Bibliography. LC 74-29076. (Land Economics Monograph Ser. No. 5). 500p. 1974. 32.00 (ISBN 0-299-95030-1); pap. 15.00 (ISBN 0-299-95034-4). U of Wis Pr.

Agrarian Reform in Latin American. Robert J. Alexander. LC 73-11733. (Latin American Ser.: Vol. 2). 120p. 1974. 5.95 o.s.i. (ISBN 0-02-500770-X). Macmillan.

Agrarian Relations in India. Arvind Dass. 1980. 18.50x (ISBN 0-8364-0648-6, Pub. by Manohar India). South Asia Bks.

Agrarian Revolution: Social Movements & Export Agriculture in the Underdeveloped World. Jeffery M. Paige. LC 74-25601. 1978. pap. text ed. 8.95 (ISBN 0-02-923550-2). Free Pr.

Agrarian Socialism: The Cooperative Commonwealth Federation in Saskatchewan: A Study in Political Sociology. rev. ed. Seymour M. Lipset. 1971. 10.00 o.p.; pap. 6.95x (ISBN 0-520-02056-1, CAMPUS64). U of Cal Pr.

Agrarian Structure & Peasant Politics in Scandinavia. Oivind Osterud. 1978. pap. 19.00x (ISBN 82-00-01702-8, Dist. by Columbia U Pr.). Universitet.

Agrarian Structure in Latin America. Solon Barraclough & Juan Collarte. LC 72-7020. 272p. 1973. 21.95 o.p. (ISBN 0-669-83006-2). Lexington Bks.

Agrarian Structure of Bangladesh: Impediments to Development. F. Tomasson Jannuzi & James T. Peach. (Westview Special Studies on China & East Asia). 1980. lib. bdg. 20.00x (ISBN 0-89158-682-2). Westview.

Agrarianism in American Literature. Ed. by M. Thomas Inge. LC 68-31706. (Prospectives in American Literature Ser). 1969. pap. 8.95 (ISBN 0-672-63005-2). Odyssey Pr.

Agreements Registered with the International Atomic Energy Agency. (Legal Ser.: No. 3). 1978. pap. 20.50 (ISBN 92-0-176078-7, ISP 485, IAEA). Unipub.

Agribusiness in the Americas: The Political Economy of Corporate Agriculture. Roger Burbach & Patricia Flynn. LC 79-3869. 256p. 1980. 16.50 (ISBN 0-85345-535-X); pap. 6.50 (ISBN 0-85345-536-8). Monthly Rev.

Agribusiness Management. W. David Downey & John K. Trocke. (Illus.). 480p. 1980. text ed. 17.95 (ISBN 0-07-017645-0, C); study guide 5.95 (ISBN 0-07-017646-9); study guide 7.95 (ISBN 0-07-017649-3). McGraw.

Agribusiness Management Resource Materials. Ed. by J. D. Drilon. Incl. Vol. I. Introduction to Agribusiness Management. LC 72-170364. 236p. 1973. 13.50 (ISBN 0-685-56587-4, APO1); Vol. II. Agribusiness (Asian Case Studies) 748p. 1971. Pt. 2. 13.50 (ISBN 0-685-56589-0, APO8); Vol. III. 1975. 29.00 (ISBN 0-685-56590-4, APO10). APO). Unipub.

Agribusiness: Management Resources Materials, Advanced Agribusiness Course & Seminar Materials, Vol. III. 1976. 21.75 o.p. (ISBN 92-833-1034-9, APO 12, APO). Unipub.

Agricola & the Germania. Tacitus. Tr. by Hugh Mattingly. (Classics Ser). 1971. pap. 2.50 (ISBN 0-14-044241-3). Penguin.

Agricultural Administration in Andhra Pradesh: A Study of the Process of Implementation of Intensive Agricultural Development Programmes. K. Seshadri. (Illus.). 302p. 1974. lib. bdg. 13.50 o.p. (ISBN 0-88253-490-4). InterCulture.

Agricultural & Food Chemistry: Past, Present, Future. Roy Teranishi. (Illus.). 1978. lib. bdg. 36.50 (ISBN 0-87055-231-7). AVI.

Agricultural & Rural Development in Indonesia. Ed. by Gary E. Hansen. (Special Studies in Social, Political, & Economic Development). 312p. 1981. lib. bdg. 20.00x (ISBN 0-86531-124-2). Westview.

Agricultural & Urban Considerations in Irrigation & Drainage. Compiled By American Society of Civil Engineers. 808p. 1974. pap. text ed. 32.50 (ISBN 0-87262-067-0). Am Soc Civil Eng.

Agricultural Botany 1: Dicotyledonous Crops. 3rd ed. N. T. Gill & K. C. Vear. (Illus.). 268p. 1980. 45.00x (ISBN 0-7156-1250-6, Pub. by Duckworth England). Biblio Dist.

Agricultural Botany 2: Monocotyledonous Crops. 3rd ed. N. T. Gill & K. C. Vear. Rev. by A. D. Barnard. (Illus.). 259p. 1980. 45.00x (ISBN 0-7156-1251-4, Pub by Duckworth England). Biblio Dist.

Agricultural Chemical Books, 4 bks. W. T. Thompson. Incl. Bk. 1. Insecticides, Acaracides & Ovicides; Bk. 2. Herbicides; Vol. 3. Fumigants, Growth Regulators, Repellents, Rodenticides (ISBN 0-913702-08-0); Bk. 4. Fungicides. LC 64-24795. 1976. 13.50 ea. Thomson Pub CA.

Agricultural Chemicals, Book 1: Insecticides. rev. ed. W. T. Thomson. 240p. 1981. pap. 13.50 (ISBN 0-913702-13-7). Thomson Pub Ca.

Agricultural Chemicals, Book 2: Herbicides. rev. ed. W. T. Thomson. 260p. 1981. pap. 13.50 (ISBN 0-913702-12-9). Thomson Pub Ca.

Agricultural Cooperative Credit in South East Asia. International Cooperative Alliance. 7.25x (ISBN 0-210-33926-8). Asia.

Agricultural Credit for Small Farm Development: Policies & Practices. David D. Bathrick. (Westview Special Studies in Social, Political, & Economic Development). (Illus.). 1981. lib. bdg. 17.50x (ISBN 0-86531-037-8). Westview.

Agricultural Decision Making: Anthropological Contributions to Rural Development. Ed. by Peggy F. Barlett. LC 80-513. (Studies in Anthropology Ser.). 1980. 28.00 (ISBN 0-12-078880-2). Acad Pr.

Agricultural Development in Africa: Issues of Public Policy. Robert H. Bates & Michael F. Lofchie. LC 79-24914. 464p. 1980. 36.95 (ISBN 0-03-056173-6). Praeger.

Agricultural Development in Asia. Ed. by R. T. Shand. LC 76-92678. 1969. 22.75x (ISBN 0-520-01554-1). U of Cal Pr.

Agricultural Development of Jordan. Oddvar Aresvik. LC 75-8399. 1976. 41.95 (ISBN 0-275-00450-3). Praeger.

Agricultural Development of Turkey. Oddvar Aresvik. LC 74-3575. (Illus.). 244p. 1975. text ed. 19.95 o.p. (ISBN 0-275-28851-X). Praeger.

Agricultural Development Strategy in the Developing Countries. Ed. by Judit Kiss. (Studies on Developing Countries: No. 103). (Illus.). 156p. (Orig.). 1979. pap. 12.50x (ISBN 963-301-060-8). Intl Pubns Serv.

Agricultural Ecology: An Analysis of World Food Production Systems. George W. Cox & Michael D. Atkins. LC 78-25745. (Illus.). 1979. text ed. 29.95x (ISBN 0-7167-1046-3). W H Freeman.

Agricultural Ecology of Savanna: A Study of West Africa. J. M. Kowal & A. H. Kassam. LC 77-30412. (Illus.). 1979. 59.00x (ISBN 0-19-859462-3). Oxford U Pr.

Agricultural Economics. Casavant & Infanger. 1981. text ed. 17.95 (ISBN 0-8359-0184-X); instr's. manual free (ISBN 0-8359-0184-X). Reston.

Agricultural Economics. John W. Goodwin. (Illus.). 400p. 1977. text ed. 15.95 (ISBN 0-87909-020-0); instructor's manual free. Reston.

Agricultural Economics & Agribusiness: An Introduction. Gail L. Cramer & Clarence W. Jensen. LC 78-11713. 1979. text ed. 23.95 (ISBN 0-471-04429-6); tchrs. manual avail. (ISBN 0-471-04430-X). Wiley.

Agricultural Economics & Rural Sociology: A Multilingual Thesaurus. Ed. by Commission of European Communities Directorate-General for Research Science & Documentation. 1979. 4 vols. & index 160.00 (ISBN 0-89664-035-3, Pub. by K G Saur). Gale.

Agricultural Energetics. Richard C. Fluck & C. Direlle Baird. (Illus.). 1980. text ed. 19.50 (ISBN 0-87055-346-1). AVI.

Agricultural Enterprises Management in an Urban-Industrial Society: A Guide to Information Sources. Ed. by Portia Christian. LC 76-27856. (Management Information Guide: No. 34). 1978. 30.00 (ISBN 0-8103-0834-7). Gale.

Agricultural Exports, Farm Income, & the Eisenhower Administration. Trudy H. Peterson. LC 79-15825. 1979. 15.95x (ISBN 0-8032-3659-X). U of Nebr Pr.

Agricultural Extension: A Field Study. Arun Mukhopadhyay. 1971. 10.00 o.p. (ISBN 0-88386-197-6). South Asia Bks.

Agricultural Finance. 7th ed. Warren F. Lee et al. Ed. by Aaron G. Nelson & William G. Murray. 1980. text ed. 17.50 (ISBN 0-8138-0050-1). Iowa St U Pr.

Agricultural Finance. 6th ed. Aaron G. Nelson et al. (Illus.). 1973. text ed. 12.50x o.p. (ISBN 0-8138-0050-1). Iowa St U Pr.

Agricultural Finance: An Introduction to Micro & Macro Concepts. John B. Penson, Jr. & David A. Lins. (Illus.). 1980. text ed. 20.95 (ISBN 0-13-018903-0). P-H.

Agricultural Fluctuations in Europe: From the Thirteen to the Twentieth Centuries. Wilhelm Abel. Tr. by Olive Ordish. LC 80-5072. 1980. 40.00 (ISBN 0-312-01465-1). St Martin.

Agricultural Geography. Majid Husain. (Illus.). 1980. text ed. 17.50x (ISBN 0-391-01931-7). Humanities.

Agricultural Geography. W. B. Morgan & R. J. Munton. 165p. 1972. 13.95 (ISBN 0-312-01470-8). St Martin.

Agricultural Geography. Leslie Symons. (Advanced Economic Geography Ser.). 1979. lib. bdg. 28.50x (ISBN 0-89158-499-4). Westview.

Agricultural Geography: Problems in Modern Geography. John R. Tarrant. 1980. 28.00 (ISBN 0-7153-6286-0). David & Charles.

Agricultural Growth in Japan, Taiwan, Korea, & the Philippines. 404p. 1979. 11.00 (APO82, APO). Unipub.

Agricultural Insect Pests of the Tropics. D. S. Hill. (Illus.). 584p. 1975. 60.00 (ISBN 0-521-20261-2); pap. 19.95 (ISBN 0-521-29441-X). Cambridge U Pr.

Agricultural Insurance: Theory & Practice & Application to Developing Countries. 2nd ed. P. K. Ray. (Illus.). 360p. Date not set. 86.01 (ISBN 0-08-025787-9). Pergamon.

Agricultural Involution: The Processes of Ecological Change in Indonesia. Clifford Geertz. 1963. 16.50x (ISBN 0-520-00458-2); pap. 4.25x (ISBN 0-520-00459-0, CAMPUS11). U of Cal Pr.

Agricultural Land-Use in Punjab: A Spatial Analysis. Gurdev S. Gosal & B. S. Ojha. (Illus.). 87p. 1967. 7.50x (ISBN 0-8002-0430-1). Intl Pubns Serv.

Agricultural Law: Principles & Cases. Donald L. Uchtmann & J. W. Looney. (Illus.). 624p. 1981. text ed. 24.95 (ISBN 0-07-065746-7). McGraw.

Agricultural Marketing for Developing Countries: Proceedings, Vol. 2. International Conference on Marketing Systems for Developing Countries. Ed. by D. N. Izaeli & F. Messner. 1977. 39.95 (ISBN 0-470-15095-5). Halsted Pr.

Agricultural Marketing System. James Rhodes. LC 77-95339. (Agricultural Economics Ser.). 1978. text ed. 20.95 (ISBN 0-88244-170-1). Grid Pub.

Agricultural Mathematics. Roger Higgs et al. 1981. 10.50 o.p. (ISBN 0-685-40545-1); pap. 6.95x o.p. (ISBN 0-8134-2130-6); ans. bk. 1.00x o.p. (ISBN 0-8134-2131-4, 2131). Interstate.

Agricultural Mathematics. 2nd ed. Roger Higgs et al. 1981. 9.25 (ISBN 0-8134-2130-6); pap. 5.95x; ans. bk. 1.00x (ISBN 0-8134-2131-4, 2131). Interstate.

Agricultural Mission of Churches & Land-Grant Universities: Papers. Ed. by Dieter Hessel & Dieter Hissel. 1979. pap. text ed. 7.50 (ISBN 0-8138-0920-7). Iowa St U Pr.

Agricultural Physics. C. W. Rose. 1966. 16.50 (ISBN 0-08-011885-2); pap. 12.00 (ISBN 0-08-011884-4). Pergamon.

Agricultural Policies in the USSR & Eastern Europe. Ronald A. Francisco & Betty A. Laird. (Westview Special Studies on the Soviet Union & Eastern Europe Ser.). (Illus.). 332p. 1980. lib. bdg. 26.50x (ISBN 0-89158-687-3). Westview.

Agricultural Policy in an Affluent Society. Ed. by Vernon W. Ruttan et al. (Problems of the Modern Economy Ser.). 1969. 7.50x (ISBN 0-393-05274-5, NortonC); pap. text ed. 5.95x (ISBN 0-393-09839-7). Norton.

Agricultural Policy in Developing Countries. Ed. by N. Islam. LC 74-108. (International Economic Association Ser.). 1974. 40.95 (ISBN 0-470-42875-9). Halsted Pr.

Agricultural Problems in India. P. C. Bansil. 1977. 18.95 (ISBN 0-7069-0363-3, Pub. by Vikas India). Advent Bk.

Agricultural Problems of India. 2nd ed. P. C. Bansil. LC 75-903617. 608p. 1975. 11.50x (ISBN 0-7069-0363-3). Intl Pubns Serv.

Agricultural Process Engineering. 3rd ed. S. M. Henderson & R. L. Perry. (Illus.). 1976. pap. text ed. 20.50 (ISBN 0-87055-300-3). AVI.

Agricultural Product Prices. William G. Tomek & Kenneth L. Robinson. (Illus.). 392p. 1972. 16.50x (ISBN 0-8014-0748-6). Cornell U Pr.

Agricultural Product Prices. 2nd ed. William G. Tomek & Kenneth L. Robinson. LC 80-16085. 400p. 1981. 19.50x (ISBN 0-8014-1337-0). Cornell U Pr.

Agricultural Production Economics & Resource-Use. M. Upton. (Illus.). 1976. 45.00x (ISBN 0-19-859452-6). Oxford U Pr.

Agricultural Production Efficiency. Board on Agriculture & Renewable Resources. LC 74-28314. 1975. pap. 9.00 (ISBN 0-309-02310-6). Natl Acad Pr.

Agricultural Production in Communist China, Nineteen Forty-Nine to Nineteen Sixty-Five. Kang Chao. LC 70-121766. (Illus.). 1970. 27.50 (ISBN 0-299-05770-4). U of Wis Pr.

Agricultural Project Design & Evaluation in an Island Community. Alan Bollard. (Development Studies Centre - Monograph: No. 15). (Illus., Orig.). 1980. pap. 13.95 (ISBN 0-7081-1071-1, 0537, Pub. by ANUP Australia). Bks Australia.

Agricultural Research for Development. M. H. Arnold. 368p. 1976. 57.50 (ISBN 0-521-21051-8). Cambridge U Pr.

Agricultural Revolution. J. D. Chambers & G. E. Mingay. 1975. 22.50 (ISBN 0-7134-1350-6, Pub. by Batsford England); pap. 14.50 (ISBN 0-7134-1358-1). David & Charles.

Agricultural Revolution. Margaret Killingray. Ed. by Malcolm Yapp & Edmund O'Connor. (World History Ser.). (Illus.). 32p. (gr. 10). 1980. Repr. of 1977 ed. lib. bdg. 5.95 (ISBN 0-89908-131-2); pap. text ed. 1.95 (ISBN 0-89908-106-1). Greenhaven.

Agricultural Revolution: Changes in Agriculture Sixteen Fifty to Eighteen Eighty. Ed. by G. E. Mingay. (Documents in Economic History). 1977. text ed. 18.25x (ISBN 0-7136-1703-9). Humanities.

Agricultural Revolution in South Lincolnshire. David B. Grigg. (Cambridge Studies in Economic History). 1966. 41.50 (ISBN 0-521-05152-5). Cambridge U Pr.

Agricultural Statistics: A Handbook for Developing Countries. N. M. Idaikkadar. (Illus.). 1979. text ed. 28.00 (ISBN 0-08-023388-0); pap. text ed. 11.50 (ISBN 0-08-023387-2). Pergamon.

Agricultural Supply Response: A Survey of the Econometric Evidence. Hossein Askari & John T. Cummings. LC 76-23376. 1976. 49.95 (ISBN 0-275-23260-3). Praeger.

Agricultural Testament. Albert Howard. (Illus.). 253p. 1973. 7.95 (ISBN 0-87857-060-8). Rodale Pr Inc.

Agriculture. Byron J. Alpers & Mitchell L. Afrow. (Shoptalk - Vocational Reading Skills). (gr. 9-12). 1978. pap. text ed. 5.12 (ISBN 0-205-05818-3, 4958187); 5.40 (ISBN 0-205-05824-8, 4958241). Allyn.

Agriculture. Hugh D. Clout. (Studies in Contemporary Europe). (Illus.). 64p. (Orig.). 1971. pap. text ed. 2.50x (ISBN 0-333-12293-3). Humanities.

Agriculture, a New Approach. P. H. Hainsworth. Ed. by Bargyla & Gylver Rateaver. LC 74-33125. (Conservation Gardening & Farming Ser: Ser. C). 1976. pap. 13.00 (ISBN 0-9600698-5-2). Rateavers.

Agriculture & Allied Terminology Dictionary: English-Arabic with Arabic Glossary. Chihabi. Ed. by A. Khatib. 40.00x (ISBN 0-686-65470-6). Intl Bk Ctr.

Agriculture & General Education. (Educational Studies & Documents: No. 2). (Illus.). 56p. (Orig.). 1972. pap. 2.50 (ISBN 92-3-100926-5, U9, UNESCO). Unipub.

Agriculture & the Economic Development of Low Income Countries. Y. S. Brenner. LC 77-146701. (Publications of the Institute of Social Studies Paperbacks: No. 2). 254p. 1972. pap. text ed. 12.25x (ISBN 90-2791-713-2). Mouton.

Agriculture & the European Community. John S. Marsh & Pamela J. Swanney. (Studies on Contemporary Europe). (Illus.). 96p. (Orig.). 1980. text ed. 15.95x (ISBN 0-04-338092-1, 2525); pap. text ed. 6.95x (ISBN 0-04-338093-X, 2526). Allen Unwin.

Agriculture & the Industrial Revolution. E. L. Jones. LC 74-2400. 1974. 19.95 (ISBN 0-470-44870-9). Halsted Pr.

Agriculture & the Planning Process. A. S. Hearne et al. 250p. 1980. text ed. 24.75x o.p. (ISBN 0-686-66037-4). Renouf.

Agriculture & the State in Ancient Mesopotamia: An Introduction to Problems of Land Tenure. Maria deJ Ellis. (Occasional Publications of the Babylonian Fund: Vol. 1). 1976. 20.00 (ISBN 0-934718-28-8). Univ Mus of U PA.

Agriculture: Capitalist & Socialist. Jack Dunman. 1975. text ed. 13.00x (ISBN 0-85315-330-2). Humanities.

Agriculture Careers. Gene Gurney & Clare Gurney. (Career Concise Guides Ser.). (Illus.). (gr. 7 up). 1978. PLB 6.45 s&l (ISBN 0-531-01418-5). Watts.

Agriculture, Economics & Resource Management. 2nd ed. Milton M. Snodgrass & Tim Wallace. (Illus.). 1980. text ed. 18.95 (ISBN 0-13-018820-4). P-H.

Agriculture in African Secondary Schools. James R. Sheffield et al. 124p. 1976. pap. 3.50 (ISBN 0-89192-125-7). Interbk Inc.

Agriculture in Development Theory. Ed. by Lloyd G. Reynolds. LC 74-20085. 528p. 1975. 30.00x (ISBN 0-300-01805-3); pap. 6.95x (ISBN 0-300-02188-7). Yale U Pr.

Agriculture in Eastern Europe & the Soviet Union: Comparative Studies. Ed. by Karl-Eugen Wadekin. LC 80-636. (Studies in East European & Soviet Russian Agrarian Policy: Vol. 3). 450p. 1980. text ed. 45.00 (ISBN 0-916672-42-5). Allanheld.

Agriculture in France on the Eve of the Railway Age. Hugh Clout. (Illus.). 239p. 1980. 28.50x (ISBN 0-389-20017-4). B&N.

Agriculture in Iraq During the Third Century. Husam Samarraie. (Arab Background Ser.). 1972. 14.00x (ISBN 0-685-77104-0). Intl Bk Ctr.

Agriculture in Secondary Schools: Case Studies of Botswana, Kenya & Tanzania. James R. Sheffield et al. LC 76-11330. 124p. (Orig.). 1976. pap. 1.75 (ISBN 0-686-66072-2). AAI.

Agriculture in the Republic of Ireland. Gillmor. 1977. 15.00 (ISBN 0-686-28201-9, Pub. by Kaido Hungary). Heyden.

Agriculture in the Third World: A Spatial Analysis. W. B. Morgan. LC 77-24064. (Advanced Economic Geopraphies Ser.). (Illus.). 1978. lib. bdg. 32.50x (ISBN 0-89158-820-5). Westview.

Agriculture in the Tropics. 2nd ed. C. C. Webster & P. N. Wilson. LC 74-40086. (Tropical Agriculture Ser.). (Illus.). 540p. 1980. text ed. 32.00 (ISBN 0-582-46814-0). Longman.

Agriculture in the United States: A Documentary History, 3 vols. Wayne Rasmussen. 1975. Set. 135.00 o.p. (ISBN 0-394-47320-5). Random.

Agriculture in Western Australia. G. H. Burvill. 397p. 1980. 21.00x (ISBN 0-85564-154-1, Pub. by Univ Western Australia). Intl Schol Bk Serv.

Agriculture: People & the Land. Educational Research Council. (Concepts & Inquiry Ser). (gr. 4). 1975. pap. text ed. 7.24 (ISBN 0-205-04436-0, 8044368); tchrs'. guide 7.24 (ISBN 0-205-04437-9, 8044376). Allyn.

Agriculture: Producers Rationality & Technical Change. Sipra Dasgupta. 196p. 1972. lib. bdg. 8.25x (ISBN 0-210-22517-3). Asia.

Agriculture: Toward Two Thousand Twentieth Session. 257p. 1981. pap. 18.50 (F2093, FAO). Unipub.

Agrippa D'aubigne. Keith Cameron. (World Authors Ser.: France: No. 443). 1977. lib. bdg. 12.50 (ISBN 0-8057-6280-9). Twayne.

Agris Forestry. (FAO Forestry Paper: No. 15). 138p. 1980. pap. 8.50 (ISBN 92-5-000810-4, F 1876, FAO). Unipub.

Agro-Climatic Classification for Evaluating Cropping Systems Potentials in Southeast Asian Rice Growing Regions. 10p. pap. 5.00 (R112, IRRI). Unipub.

Agro-Industrial Complexes & Types of Agriculture in Eastern Siberia. Shotski. 1979. 14.00 (ISBN 0-9960016-2-X, Pub. by Kaido Hungary). Heyden.

Agro-Industrial Complexes & Types of Agriculture in Eastern Siberia. V. P. Shotski. Tr. by Bela Kecskes from Rus. (Geography of World Agriculture Ser.: Vol. 8). (Illus.). 131p. 1979. 13.50x (ISBN 963-05-1845-7). Intl Pubns Serv.

Agrochemicals in Soils: Selected Papers. Soil Chemistry, Soil Fertility & Soil Clay Mineralogy Commissions of the International Society of Soil Science, 13-18 July 1976, Jerusalem. Ed. by A. Banin & U. Kafkafi. LC 79-41750. 500p. 1980. 79.00 (ISBN 0-08-025914-6). Pergamon.

Agropolitics in the European Community: Interest Groups & the Common Agricultural Policy. William F. Averyt, Jr. LC 77-10619. 1977. 21.95 (ISBN 0-03-039666-2). Praeger.

Agua. Harlan Wade. Tr. by Mamie M. Contreras from Eng. LC 78-26818. (Book About Ser.). Orig. Title: Water. (Illus., Sp.). (gr. k-3). 1979. PLB 7.30 (ISBN 0-8172-1490-9). Raintree Pubs.

Agustin Moreto. James A. Castaneda. (World Authors Ser.: Spain: No. 308). 1974. lib. bdg. 12.50 (ISBN 0-8057-2633-0). Twayne.

Ah Well: A Romance in Perpetuity, & "and to You Also". Jack B. Yeats. 1974. 15.00 (ISBN 0-7100-7665-7). Routledge & Kegan.

Aha! Insight. Martin Gardner. LC 78-51259. (Illus.). 1978. pap. text ed. 7.95x (ISBN 0-89454-001-7). W H Freeman.

Ahapius Honcharenko & the Alaska Hearald: The Editor's Life & an Analysis of His Newspaper. Wasyl Luciw. LC 65-923. pap. text ed. 6.00 (ISBN 0-918884-10-1). Slavia Lib.

Ahavat Chesed - Love Mercy: Reader. Abraham Shumsky & Adaia Shumsky. (Mah Tov Hebrew Teaching Ser.: Bk. 2). (Illus.). (gr. 4 up). 1970. text ed. 5.00 (ISBN 0-8074-0175-7, 405304); tchrs'. guide 3.50 (ISBN 0-8074-0176-5, 205305); wkbk. 3.50 (ISBN 0-8074-0177-3, 405303). UAHC.

Ahead of Myself: Confessions of a Professional Psychic, Shawn Robbins As Told to Milton Pierce. As told to Shawn Robbins. LC 80-20486. 80. 9.95 (ISBN 0-13-004002-9). P-H.

Ahhh! said Stork. Gerald Rose. (Illus.). 1977. 7.95 (ISBN 0-571-11097-5, Pub. by Faber & Faber). Merrimack Bk Serv.

Ahimsa: Dynamic Compassion. Nat Altman. LC 80-51548. 150p. (Orig.). 1981. pap. 4.95 (ISBN 0-8356-0537-X, Quest). Theos Pub Hse.

Ahmadiyah Movement: A History & Perspective. Spencer Lavan. LC 74-901627. ix, 220p. 1974. 10.00x o.p. (ISBN 0-88386-455-X). South Asia Bks.

Ahmedabad: A Study in Indian Urban History. K. L. Gillion. 1968. 18.75x (ISBN 0-520-00473-6). U of Cal Pr.

Ahora Brillan las Estrellas. Paquita Berio. 134p. (Orig., Span.). 1981. pap. 2.50 (ISBN 0-89922-201-3). Edit Caribe.

AIA Guide to New York City. rev. ed. Ed. by Norval White & Elliot Willensky. 1978. pap. 12.95 (ISBN 0-02-000980-1, Collier). Macmillan.

Aid & Dependence: British Aid to Malawi. Kathryn Morton. 188p. 1975. 21.00x o.p. (ISBN 0-8419-5501-8). Holmes & Meier.

Aid & Inequality in Kenya: British Development Assistance to Kenya. Gerald Holtham & Arthur Hazelwood. 1976. text ed. 25.00x o.p. (ISBN 0-8419-5508-5). Holmes & Meier.

Aid & Influence: The Case of Bangladesh. Ed. by Just Faaland. LC 80-13481. 1980. 25.00 (ISBN 0-312-01492-9). St Martin.

Aid As Obstacle: Twenty Questions About Our Foreign Aid & the Hungry. David H. Kinley et al. (Illus., Orig.). 1980. pap. 4.95 (ISBN 0-935028-07-2). Inst Food & Develop.

Aid to Africa. I. M. Little. 1964. 3.30 o.p. (ISBN 0-08-010938-1). Pergamon.

Aid to Africa: A Policy Outline for the Nineteen Seventies. Paul Streeten. LC 74-180854. (Special Studies in International Economics & Development). 1972. 24.50x (ISBN 0-275-28263-5). Irvington.

Aid to Russia: Nineteen Forty-One to Nineteen Forty-Six. George C. Herring. LC 72-10545. (Contemporary American History Ser). 1976. pap. 9.00x (ISBN 0-231-08348-3). Columbia U Pr.

Aid to Russia, Nineteen Forty-One to Nineteen Forty-Six: Strategy, Diplomacy, the Origins of the Cold War. George C. Herring, Jr. 364p. 1973. 22.50x (ISBN 0-231-03336-2). Columbia U Pr.

Aid to State Board Examinations in Cosmetology. Florence E. Wall. 1975. pap. 5.00 (ISBN 0-912126-08-6, 1268-00). Keystone Pubns.

Aida: Verdi. William Mannn. Ed. by William Mann & Roger Parker. Tr. by Edmund Tracey. 1980. pap. 4.95 (ISBN 0-7145-3770-5). Riverrun NY.

Aids & Adaptations. Ursula Keeble. 320p. 1979. pap. text ed. 14.90x (ISBN 0-7199-0963-5, Pub. by Bedford England). Renouf.

Aids & Their Application. British Horse Society & Pony Club. 1976. pap. 3.25 (ISBN 0-8120-0760-3). Barron.

Aids to Anaesthesia, Vol. 1: Basic Sciences. M. J. Harrison et al. (Illus.). 224p. 1980. pap. 15.00x (ISBN 0-443-01688-7). Churchill.

Aids to Ethics & Professional Conduct for Student Radiologic Technologists. 2nd ed. James Ohnysty. 176p. 1979. 11.75 (ISBN 0-398-01419-1). C C Thomas.

Aids to Goatkeeping. Corl A. Leach. Date not set. 10.00 (ISBN 0-686-26686-2). Dairy Goat.

Aids to Nursing Diagnosis. 3rd ed. Marie M. Seedor. (Nursing Education Monograph: No. 6). 1980. pap. 8.95 (ISBN 0-397-54120-1, Pub. by Columbia U Pr). Lippincott.

Aids to Nursing Diagnosis: A Programmed Unit in Fundamentals of Nursing. 3rd ed. Marie M. Seedor. 378p. (Orig.). 1980. pap. text ed. 8.50 (ISBN 0-8077-2630-3). Tchrs Coll.

Aids to Nursing Judgement: A Programed Unit in Fundamentals of Nursing. Marie M. Seedor. LC 76-189024. 401p. 1972. pap. text ed. 8.00x (ISBN 0-8077-2126-3). Tchrs Coll.

Aids to Nursing Judgment. 2nd ed. Marie M. Seedor. (Nursing Education Monograph Ser, No. 6). 1972. pap. 7.25 o.p. (ISBN 0-397-54120-1, Pub. by Columbia U Pr). Lippincott.

Aids to Oral Pathology & Diagnosis. R. A. Cawson. (Dental Ser.). (Illus.). 144p. 1981. pap. text ed. 8.75 (ISBN 0-443-01871-5). Churchill.

Aids to Psycholinguistic Teaching. 2nd ed. Wilma J. Bush & Marian T. Giles. (Special Education Ser.). 1977. text ed. 17.95 (ISBN 0-675-08525-X). Merrill.

Aids to Sexual Stimulation. (Illus.). pap. 5.00 (ISBN 0-910550-28-X). Centurion Pr.

Aids to Teaching & Learning. H. E. Coppen. 1969. 22.00 (ISBN 0-08-012905-6); pap. 10.75 (ISBN 0-08-012904-8). Pergamon.

Aids to Undergraduate Medicine. 3rd ed. J. L. Burton. (Aids to... Ser.). (Illus.). 1980. pap. text ed. 7.50 (ISBN 0-443-02159-7). Churchill.

Aiiieeeee! Frank Chin et al. 320p. 1975. pap. 3.95 o.p. (ISBN 0-385-01243-8, Anch). Doubleday.

Aikido & Jiu Jitsu Holds & Locks. Bruce Tegner. LC 70-99026. (Orig.). 1969. pap. 2.95 o.p. (ISBN 0-87407-009-0). Thor.

Aim for a Job As Electronic Technician. John E. Keefe. LC 67-11254. (Aim High Vocational Guidance Ser). (gr. 7up). 1978. PLB 5.97 (ISBN 0-8239-0451-2). Rosen Pr.

Aim for a Job in Air Conditioning & Refrigeration. Donald F. Daly. LC 70-114141. (Career Guidance Ser). 1971. pap. 3.50 (ISBN 0-668-02224-8). Arco.

Aim for a Job in Appliance Repair. James Hahn & Lynn Hahn. (Aim High Ser.). 128p. 1981. lib. bdg. 5.97 (ISBN 0-8239-0541-1). Rosen Pr.

Aim for a Job in Automotive Service. James J. Bradley. LC 76-114140. (Career Guidance Ser.). 138p. 1971. pap. 3.50 (ISBN 0-668-02226-4). Arco.

Aim for a Job in Automotive Service. Dawson Taylor & James Bradley. LC 68-11891. (Aim High Vocational Guidance Ser.). (Illus.). (gr. 7 up). 1977. PLB 5.97 (ISBN 0-8239-0091-6); PLB 5.97 large type ed. o.p. (ISBN 0-8239-0165-3). Rosen Pr.

Aim for a Job in Drafting. Fred J. Delong. LC 68-10505. (Aim High Vocational Guidance Ser.). (gr. 7 up). 1976. PLB 5.97 (ISBN 0-8239-0365-6). Rosen Pr.

Aim for a Job in Hospital Work. W. Richard Kirk. LC 74-114137. (Career Guidance Ser.). 124p. 1971. pap. 3.50 (ISBN 0-668-02230-2). Arco.

Aim for a Job in Restaurants & Food Service. James Westbrook. LC 68-26145. (Aim High Vocational Guidance Ser.). (Illus.). (gr. 7 up). 1978. PLB 5.97 (ISBN 0-8239-0099-1). Rosen Pr.

Aim for a Job in Restaurants & Food Service. James H. Westbrook. LC 70-114136. (Career Guidance Ser). 1971. pap. 3.50 (ISBN 0-668-02229-9). Arco.

Aim for a Job in the Bakery Industry. Desmond H. O'Connell. LC 71-114139. (Career Guidance Ser). 1971. pap. 3.50 (ISBN 0-668-02227-2). Arco.

Aim for a Job in the Building Trades. Donald F. Daly. LC 72-110289. (Aim High Vocational Guidance Ser.). (Illus.). (gr. 7 up). 1970. PLB 5.97 o.p. (ISBN 0-8239-0213-7). Rosen Pr.

Aim for a Star. Helen Lowrie Marshall. 1966. 2.95 (ISBN 0-385-08258-4). Doubleday.

Aim of a Lady. Laura Matthews. (Orig.). 1980. pap. 1.75 (ISBN 0-446-94341-X). Warner Bks.

Aims, Activities & Fields of Competence of National Tourist Organisations, 3 pts. 2nd ed. International Union of Offical Travel Organisations. 505p. 1974. Set. 35.00x o.p. (ISBN 0-8002-0324-0). Intl Pubns Serv.

Aims & Methods of Scholarship in Modern Languages & Literatures. 2nd ed. Ed. by James Thorpe. 81p. (Orig.). 1970. pap. 3.75x o.p. (ISBN 0-87352-013-0). Modern Lang.

Aims & Methods of Scientific Research. R. Hodes. (No. 9). 1.00 (ISBN 0-89977-011-8). Am Inst Marxist.

Aims & Methods of Vegetation Ecology. Dieter Mueller-Dombois & Heinz Ellenberg. LC 74-5492. 432p. 1974. text ed. 25.95 (ISBN 0-471-62290-7). Wiley.

Aims in Education. Ed. by T. H. Hollins. 1966. text ed. 14.50x (ISBN 0-7190-0038-6). Humanities.

Aims, Influences & Change in the Primary School Curriculum. Ed. by P. H. Taylor. (General Ser.). 143p. 1975. pap. text ed. 16.50x (ISBN 0-85633-072-8, NFER). Humanities.

AIMS Information About Aptitudes. rev. ed. Brenda H. Smith & Irvin C. Shambaugh. 201p. 1980. pap. 10.00 (ISBN 0-9602710-1-5). Aptitude Inventory.

Aims of Education. L. M. Brown. LC 76-120600. 1970. pap. text ed. 8.75x (ISBN 0-8077-1129-2). Tchrs Coll.

Aims, Role & Deployment of Staff in the Nursery. Phillip Clift et al. (Report of the National Foundation for Educational Research in England & Wales). 224p. 1980. pap. text ed. 18.75x (ISBN 0-85633-197-X). Humanities.

Ainsley's New Complete Guide to Harness Racing. rev. ed. Tom Ainsley. 1981. Repr. of 1971 ed. 17.95 (ISBN 0-671-25257-7). S&S.

Ainsworth & Bisby's Dictionary of the Fungi, Including the Lichens. 6th ed. G. C. Ainsworth. LC 74-883641. (Illus.). 673p. 1971. 27.50x (ISBN 0-85198-075-9). Intl Pubns Serv.

Ainsworth Rand Spofford: Bookman & Librarian. J. Cole. Ed. by Michael H. Harris. LC 75-31517. (Heritage of Librarianship: No. 2). 208p. 1975. PLB 20.00x (ISBN 0-87287-117-7). Libs Unl.

Ain't Misbehavin: The Story of Fats Waller. Ed Kirkeby. LC 75-14123. (Roots of Jazz). 248p. 1975. lib. bdg. 22.50 (ISBN 0-306-70683-0); pap. 4.95 (ISBN 0-306-80015-2). Da Capo.

Ain't We Got Fun: Essays, Lyrics, & Stories of the Twenties. Ed. by Barbara H. Solomon. 1980. pap. 2.95 (ISBN 0-451-61846-7, ME 1846, Ment). NAL.

Ainu of the Northwest Coast of Southern Sakhalin. Emiko Ohnuki-Tierney. Ed. by George Spindler & Louise Spindler. (Case Studies in Cultural Anthropology). (Illus.). 144p. pap. text ed. 4.95x (ISBN 0-8290-0276-6). Irvington.

Air Aces of the Nineteen Fourteen to Nineteen Eighteen War. Bruce Robertson. LC 59-13378. (Harleyford Ser). (Illus.). 1959. 18.95 (ISBN 0-8168-6350-4). Aero.

Air Around Us. T. J. Chandler. LC 70-78676. (gr. 4-9). 5.95 o.p. (ISBN 0-385-06766-6). Doubleday.

Air Conditioning & Mechanical Trades: Preparing for the Contractor's License Examination. John Gladstone. LC 74-18258. (Illus.). 425p. 1980. pap. 18.95 (ISBN 0-930644-04-2). Engineers Pr.

Air Conditioning & Refrigeration. William H. Severns & Julian R. Fellows. LC 58-7908. 1958. text ed. 28.95x (ISBN 0-471-77781-1). Wiley.

Air Conditioning & Ventilation of Buildings, Vol. 1. 2nd ed. D. J. Croome & B. M. Roberts. LC 79-40965. (International Ser. in Heating, Ventilation & Refrigeration: Vol. 14). (Illus.). 1981. 60.00 (ISBN 0-08-024779-2). Pergamon.

Air Conditioning for Building Engineers & Managers. Seymour G. Price. 1970. 25.00 (ISBN 0-8311-3001-6). Indus Pr.

Air Conditioning: Home & Commercial. Roland Palmquist. LC 77-71586. 1977. 10.95 (ISBN 0-672-23288-X). Audel.

Air Conditioning Principles & Systems: An Energy Approach. Edward G. Pita. LC 80-18958. 608p. 1981. text ed. 19.95 (ISBN 0-471-04214-5). Wiley.

Air Conditioning Testing & Balancing: A Field Practice Manual. John Gladstone. 1974. cancelled (ISBN 0-685-92593-5). Engineers Pr.

Air-Cooled Automotive Engines. J. Mackerle. 518p. 1972. 59.00x (ISBN 0-85264-205-9, Pub. by Griffin England). State Mutual Bk.

Air Filters for Use at Nuclear Facilities. P. Linder. (Technical Reports Ser.: No. 122). (Illus.). 76p. (Orig.). 1970. pap. 6.50 (ISBN 92-0-125670-1, IDC122, IAEA). Unipub.

Air Force Colors: Nineteen Twenty-Six to Nineteen Forty-Two. 1980. pap. 7.95 (ISBN 0-89747-091-5). Squad Sig Pubns.

Air Force: From Balloons to Space Ships. Helen Doss. (Illus.). 64p. (gr. 4-6). 1981. PLB 6.97 (ISBN 0-686-69305-1). Messner.

Air Force Mafia. Peter James. 1974. 9.95 o.p. (ISBN 0-87000-289-9). Arlington Hse.

Air Force Officer's Guide. 25th, rev. ed. A. J. Kinney. (Illus.). 416p. 1981. pap. 10.95 (ISBN 0-8117-2055-1). Stackpole.

Air Force One. Edwin Corley. 1979. pap. 2.50 o.s.i. (ISBN 0-440-10063-1). Dell.

Air Force One. Edwin Corley. LC 77-82618. 1978. 8.95 o.p. (ISBN 0-385-11402-8). Doubleday.

Air Gun. John Walker. (Illus.). 144p. 1981. 19.95 (ISBN 0-8117-0046-1). Stackpole.

Air in Danger: Ecological Perspectives of the Atmosphere. Georg Breuer. Tr. by P. Fabian from Ger. LC 79-18820. (Illus.). 180p. 1980. 24.95 (ISBN 0-521-22417-9); pap. 7.95 (ISBN 0-521-29483-5). Cambridge U Pr.

Air Is All Around You. Franklyn Branley. LC 62-7738. (Let's-Read-& Find-Out Science Bk). (Illus.). (gr. k-3). 1962. PLB 7.89 (ISBN 0-690-05356-8, TYC-J). T Y Crowell.

Air of Mars: And Other Stories of Time & Space. Ed. & tr. by Mirra Ginsburg. LC 75-34279. 160p. (gr. 5 up). 1976. 6.95 o.s.i. (ISBN 0-02-736160-8, 73616). Macmillan.

Air Photography & Coastal Problems. Ed. by Mohamed T. El-Ashry. (Benchmark Papers in Geology: Vol. 38). 1977. 43.50 (ISBN 0-12-786410-5). Acad Pr.

Air Pollution. Ed. by R. E. Bryson & J. E. Kutzbach. LC 68-54859. (CCG Resource Papers Ser.: No. 2). (Illus.). 1968. pap. text ed. 4.00 (ISBN 0-89291-049-6). Assn Am Geographers.

Air Pollution. Homer W. Parker. (Illus.). 1977. 26.95x (ISBN 0-13-021006-4). P-H.

Air Pollution. R. S. Scorer. 1968. 27.00 (ISBN 0-08-013345-2); pap. 13.25 (ISBN 0-08-012275-2). Pergamon.

Air Pollution. D. J. Spedding. (Oxford Chemistry Ser.). (Illus.). 90p. 1974. pap. text ed. 8.95x (ISBN 0-19-855464-8). Oxford U Pr.

Air Pollution & Athmospheric Diffusion. Ed. by M. E. Berlyand. LC 73-1982. 221p. 1974. Vol. 1. 27.95 (ISBN 0-470-07034-X); Vol. 2. 36.95 (ISBN 0-470-07038-2). Halsted Pr.

Air Pollution & Forests. W. H. Smith. (Springer Series on Environmental Management). (Illus.). 400p. 1981. 39.80 (ISBN 0-387-90501-4). Springer-Verlag.

Air Pollution & the Lung. Ed. by E. F. Aharonson et al. LC 76-3488. 313p. 1976. 64.95 (ISBN 0-470-15049-1). Halsted Pr.

Air Pollution Control: Measuring & Monitoring Air Pollutants, Pt. III. Ed. by Werner Strauss. LC 79-28773. (Environmental Science & Technology, a Wiley-Interscience Series of Texts & Monographs). 1978. 42.00 (ISBN 0-471-83323-1, Pub by Wiley-Interscience). Wiley.

Air Pollution, Human Health, & Public Policy. Charles T. Stewart. LC 78-13818. 1979. 16.50 (ISBN 0-669-02670-0). Lexington Bks.

Air Pollution Offsets: Trading Selling & Banking. Richard A. Liroff. LC 80-66464. 54p. (Orig.). 1980. pap. 5.00 (ISBN 0-89164-061-4). Conservation Foun.

Air Pollution: Threat & Response. David A. Lynn. LC 74-12799. (Illus.). 400p. 1976. text ed. 9.95 (ISBN 0-201-04355-6). A-W.

Air Power at Sea: Nineteen Thirty-Nine to Nineteen Forty-Five. John Winton. LC 76-41384. (Illus.). 1977. 12.95 o.s.i. (ISBN 0-690-01222-5, TYC-T). T Y Crowell.

Air Power in the Next Generation. E. J. Feuchtwanger & R. A. Mason. 1979. text ed. 26.00x (ISBN 0-333-23609-2). Humanities.

Air Quality. George Tolley et al. (Environmental Policy Ser.: Vol. II). 1981. write for info. (ISBN 0-88410-626-8). Ballinger Pub.

Air Quality & Smoke from Urban & Forest Fires. Committee on Fire Research, National Research Council. LC 76-8356. (Illus.). 1976. pap. 10.25 (ISBN 0-309-02500-1). Natl Acad Pr.

Air Raid Pearl Harbor: The Story of December 7, 1941. Theodore Taylor. LC 76-132303. (Illus.). (gr. 5-8). 1971. 8.95 (ISBN 0-690-05373-8, TYC-J). T Y Crowell.

Air Resource Management Primer. Compiled By American Society of Civil Engineers. 280p. 1973. pap. text ed. 16.75 (ISBN 0-87262-055-7). Am Soc Civil Eng.

Air Rights & Highways. rev. ed. Real Estate Research Corporation. LC 79-97085. (Technical Bulletin Ser.: No. 64). (Illus.). 1969. pap. 4.75 (ISBN 0-87420-064-4). Urban Land.

Air Supported Structures. Compiled By American Society of Civil Engineers. 104p. 1979. pap. text ed. 11.00 (ISBN 0-87262-196-0). Am Soc Civil Eng.

Air Taxi Charter & Rental Directory of North America & Connection Points of Commuter Airlines with Other Scheduled Air Carriers. Joseph Payton. LC 75-648387. 100p. 1980. pap. 15.00 perfect bdg (ISBN 0-9603908-0-4). Aircraft Chart & Rent.

Air Time. Ronald Seidle. 1977. text ed. 17.95 (ISBN 0-205-05602-4, 485602-3). Allyn.

Air Track Physics: A First Semester Laboratory Manual. Harold J. Metcalf. 49p. 1980. pap. text ed. 4.95 (ISBN 0-8403-2286-0). Kendall-Hunt.

Air Traffic Control Communications Manual. Deborah J. Balter. Date not set. pap. 14.95. Aviation.

Air Transport Economics in the Supersonic Era. 2nd, new ed. H. Alan Stratford. LC 72-84866. 1973. 22.50 (ISBN 0-312-01610-7). St Martin.

Air Transportation. 7th ed. Robert M. Kane & Allen D. Vose. (Illus.). 1979. perfect bdg. 11.95 (ISBN 0-8403-2037-X). Kendall Hunt.

Air Transportation Nineteen Seventy-Five & Beyond: A Systems Approach. Ed. by William W. Seifert & B. A. Schriever. 1968. 23.00x (ISBN 0-262-19042-7). MIT Pr.

Air Travel Answers. Larry M. Minear. Ed. & illus. by Beulah F. Minear. LC 79-52955. (Illus.). 1979. 2.10 (ISBN 0-934268-00-2). Aerofacts.

Air Travel from the Beginning. Alma Gilleo. LC 77-24134. (From the Beginning Ser.). (Illus.). (gr. 1-4). 1977. PLB 5.50 (ISBN 0-89565-002-9). Childs World.

Air War in Europe. Ronald Bailey. (World War II Ser.). 1979. 12.95 (ISBN 0-8094-2494-0). Time-Life.

Air War in Europe. Ronald Bailey. (World War II Ser.). (Illus.). 1979. lib. bdg. 14.94 (ISBN 0-686-51053-4). Silver.

Air War, Nineteen Thirty-Nine to Nineteen Forty-Five. R. J. Overy. LC 80-6200. 288p. 1981. 16.95 (ISBN 0-8128-2792-9). Stein & Day.

Air War: One Volume Edition. Edward Jablonski. LC 78-8213. 1979. 19.95 (ISBN 0-385-14279-X). Doubleday.

Air War Over Korea. Robert Jackson. LC 74-19687. 1975. 9.95 o.p. (ISBN 0-684-14193-0, ScribT). Scribner.

Air War Southeast Asia, Nineteen Sixty-One to Nineteen Seventy-Three: An Annotated Bibliography & 16mm Film Guide. Myron J. Smith, Jr. LC 79-21046. 316p. 1979. 16.50 (ISBN 0-8108-1261-4). Scarecrow.

Air Warfare. Hubert R. Allen. LC 76-19593. (Pegasus Books: No. 18). 1968. 7.50x (ISBN 0-234-77156-9). Intl Pubns Serv.

Airborne: A Sentimental Journey. William F. Buckley, Jr. (Illus.). 1976. 12.95 o.s.i. (ISBN 0-02-518040-1, 51804). Macmillan.

Airborne at War. Napier Crookenden. (Illus.). 1978. 14.95 o.p. (ISBN 0-684-15658-X, ScribT). Scribner.

Airborne for Pleasure: A Guide to Flying, Gliding, Ballooning & Parachuting. Albert Morgan. LC 74-20449. (Illus.). 128p. 1975. 9.95 o.p. (ISBN 0-7153-6477-4). David & Charles.

Airbrush Book: Art, History, & Technique. Seng-gye T. Curtis & Christopher Hunt. 160p. 1980. 24.95 (ISBN 0-442-21213-5). Van Nos Reinhold.

Aircraft Piston Engines: From the Manly Baltzer to the Continental Tiara. Herschel Smith. (Aviation Ser.). (Illus.). 264p. 1981. 18.95 (ISBN 0-07-058472-9, P&RB). McGraw.

Aircraft. Christopher Tunney. LC 79-64384. (Question & Answer Books). (Illus.). 36p. (gr. 3-6). 1980. PLB 5.95g (ISBN 0-8225-1176-2). Lerner Pubns.

Aircraft Aerobatics. Christopher Tunney. LC 79-64384. (Question & Answer Books). (Illus.). (gr. 3-6). 1980. PLB 5.95g o.p. (ISBN 0-8225-1176-2). Lerner Pubns.

Aircraft Alive: Aviation & Air Traffic for Enthusiasts. Chris McCallister. LC 79-56459. 144p. 1980. 19.95 (ISBN 0-7134-1914-8, Pub. by Batsford England). David & Charles.

Aircraft at Work. Mary Elting. LC 64-14511. (Illus.). (gr. 4-6). 1964. PLB 5.49 (ISBN 0-8178-3522-9). Harvey.

Aircraft Carriers of the U. S. Navy. Stefan Terzibaschitcsch. (Illus.). 336p. 1980. 35.00 (ISBN 0-8317-0109-9). Mayflower Bks.

Aircraft Dynamic Stability & Response. A. W. Babister. (Illus.). 230p. 1980. 41.00 (ISBN 0-08-024769-5); pap. 17.00 (ISBN 0-08-024768-7). Pergamon.

Aircraft Electricity & Electronics. rev. ed. Ralph D. Bent & James L. McKinley. (Aviation Technology Ser.). (Illus.). 432p. 1981. pap. text ed. 16.95x (ISBN 0-07-004793-6, G). McGraw.

Aircraft, Engines & Airmen: A Selective Review of the Periodical Literature, 1930-1969. A. Hanniball. LC 70-171927. 1972. 27.50 (ISBN 0-8108-0430-1). Scarecrow.

Aircraft Erecting. Ed. by T. Airey et al. (Engineering Craftsmen: No. H34). (Illus.). 1977. spiral bdg. 26.00x (ISBN 0-85083-413-9). Intl Ideas.

Aircraft Fabric Covering. Dale Crane. (Aviation Maintenance Training Course Ser.). (Illus.). 54p. 1978. pap. 4.95 (ISBN 0-89100-077-1, EA-ADF). Aviation Maintenance.

Aircraft Fatigue: Design, Operational & Economic Aspects. Ed. by J. Y. Mann & I. S. Milligan. LC 71-125094. 570p. 1972. 73.00 (ISBN 0-08-017526-0). Pergamon.

Aircraft Fire Protection & Rescue Procedures: 206. 2nd ed. Ed. by Connie Williams & Jerry Laughlin. LC 78-52898. (Illus.). 1978. pap. text ed. 7.00 (ISBN 0-87939-025-5). Intl Fire Serv.

Aircraft for the Royal Air Force. Michael J. F. Bowyer. (Illus.). 160p. 1980. 27.00 (ISBN 0-571-11515-2, Pub. by Faber & Faber). Merrimack Bk Serv.

Aircraft Fuel Metering Systems. Dale Crane. (Aviation Maintenance Training Course Ser.). (Illus.). 70p. 1975. pap. 5.95 (ISBN 0-89100-057-7, EA-FMS). Aviation Maintenance.

Aircraft Gas Turbine Engine Technology. 2nd ed. Irwin Treager. (Illus.). 1978. pap. text ed. 22.75 (ISBN 0-07-065158-2, G). McGraw.

Aircraft Governors. Frank Delp. (Aviation Technician Training Course Ser.). 96p. (Orig.). 1980. pap. text ed. 4.95 (ISBN 0-89100-119-0). Aviation Maintenance.

Aircraft Industry Dynamics: An Analysis of Competition, Capital & Labor. Barry Bluestone & Peter Jordan. 180p. 1981. 19.95 (ISBN 0-86569-053-7). Auburn Hse.

Aircraft of the Indian Air Force, 1933-73. Pushpindar Singh. LC 74-903552. (Illus.). 186p. 1974. 21.00x (ISBN 0-8002-0433-6). Intl Pubns Serv.

Aircraft of the Vietnam War. Lou Drendel. LC 79-113405. (Famous Aircraft Ser.). (Illus.). 64p. 1980. pap. 4.95 (ISBN 0-8168-5651-6). Aero.

Aircraft Painting & Finishing. Dale Crane & Neal Carlson. (Aviation Maintenance Training Course Ser.). (Illus.). 67p. 1980. pap. 5.95 (ISBN 0-89100-152-2, E*A-A*P-2). Aviation Maintenance.

Aircraft Pavement Design. Institute of Civil Engineers. 114p. 1980. 79.00x (ISBN 0-901948-04-7, Pub. by Telford England). State Mutual Bk.

Aircraft Technical Dictionary. 2nd ed. Dale Crane et al. (Aviation Maintenance Training Course Ser.). Date not set. pap. price not set (ISBN 0-89100-124-7). Aviation Maintenance.

Aircraft That Work for Us. Tony Freeman. LC 80-23078. (On the Move Ser.). (Illus.). 48p. (gr. 3-6). 1981. PLB 9.25 (ISBN 0-516-03888-5). Childrens.

Aircraft Versus Submarine. Alfred Price. LC 74-75792. 1973. 15.50 (ISBN 0-87021-802-6). Naval Inst Pr.

Aircraft Woodwork. Ruth Spencer. 1972. pap. 3.95 o.p. (ISBN 0-8306-2204-7, 2204). TAB Bks.

Airdale Terrier. Irene E. Hayes. Ed. by Christina Foyle. (Foyle's Handbks). 1973. 3.95 (ISBN 0-685-55814-2). Palmetto Pub.

Aires. Julia Parker. (Pocket Guides to Astrology Ser.). (Orig.). 1980. pap. write for info. (ISBN 0-671-25551-7, Fireside). S&S.

Airframe & Powerplant Mechanics Certification Guide: Ac 65-2d. Federal Aviation Administration. pap. 2.50 (ISBN 0-685-46348-6). Aviation.

Airframe & Powerplant Mechanics Powerplant Handbook: Ac 65-12a. Federal Aviation Administration. pap. 8.75x (ISBN 0-89100-079-8). Aviation Maint.

Airframe & Systems Fitting. 2nd ed. Ed. by C. J. Green et al. (Engineering Craftsmen: No. H9). (Illus.). 1973. spiral bdg. 14.95x (ISBN 0-85083-218-7). Intl Ideas.

Airframe Logbook. Aviation Maintenance Publishers. 77p. 1975. pap. 4.95 (ISBN 0-89100-190-5, E*A-A*F*L-1). Aviation Maintenance.

Airframe Mechanics Manual. rev. ed. Ed. by Pan American Navigation Service Staff. LC 79-138652. (Zweng Manual Ser.). (Illus.). 1977. soft cover 15.95 (ISBN 0-87219-017-X). Pan Am Nav.

Airguide Traveler: Bahamas, Florida, Florida Keys, & Sea Islands. Airguide. (Illus.). 1980. pap. 11.00 (ISBN 0-911721-89-4). Aviation.

Airlift to Wounded Knee. Bill Zimmerman. LC 76-3138. (Illus.). 348p. 1976. 13.95 (ISBN 0-8040-0691-1). Swallow.

Airline Builders. Oliver E. Allen. Ed. by Time-Life Books. (Epic of Flight Ser.). (Illus.). 175p. 1981. 13.95 (ISBN 0-8094-3283-8). Time Life.

Airline Competition: A Study of the Effects of Competition on the Quality & Price of Airline Service & the Self-Sufficiency of the United States Domestic Airlines. F. W. Gill & G. L. Bates. 1970. 51.00 (ISBN 0-08-018738-2). Pergamon.

Airline Guide to Stewardess & Steward Careers: 1979-1980. Alexander C. Morton. (Illus.). 1979. lib. bdg. 9.00 o.p. (ISBN 0-668-04346-6); pap. 6.95 o.p. (ISBN 0-668-04350-4). Arco.

Airline Job Kit. Jon M. LeRette. (Illus.). 82p. 1980. pap. text ed. 3.50 (ISBN 0-686-28722-3). Airline Job.

Airline Pilots: A Study in Elite Unionization. George E. Hopkins. LC 71-152699. (Illus.). 1971. 11.00x (ISBN 0-674-01275-5). Harvard U Pr.

Airline Price Policy: A Study of Airline Passenger Fares. P. W. Cherington. 1970. Repr. of 1958 ed. 40.00 (ISBN 0-08-018739-0). Pergamon.

Airline Skier: 1977-78. C. R. Goeldner. 77p. 1978. 15.00 (ISBN 0-89478-045-X). U CO Busn Res Div.

Airline Transport Pilot: Airplane (Air Carrier) Written Test Guide. Federal Aviation Administration. (Pilot Training Ser.). (Illus.). 189p. 1979. pap. 5.95 (ISBN 0-89100-199-9, EA-AC-61-87). Aviation Maintenance.

Airline Transport Pilot, Airplane, Answer Book. Ed. by Wallace E. Manning. (Aviation Test Prep Ser.). 1979. pap. 10.95 o.p. (ISBN 0-911721-42-8, Pub. by AvTest). Aviation.

Airline Transport Pilot Course: Mach IV. Jeppesen Sanderson. (Illus.). 390p. 1977. write for info. 3-ring binder (ISBN 0-88487-003-0, JE304913). Jeppesen Sanderson.

Airline Transport Pilot Rating Course. (Pilot Training Ser.). (Illus.). 310p. (Orig.). 1981. price not set (ISBN 0-88487-073-1, JS304127). Jeppesen Sanderson.

Airliners Between the Wars Nineteen Nineteen to Nineteen Thirty Nine, Vol. 14. Kenneth Munson. LC 76-160081. (Pocket Encyclopedia of World Aircraft in Color Ser.). (Illus.). 176p. 1972. 8.95 (ISBN 0-02-588000-4). Macmillan.

Airliners Since Nineteen Forty-Six. 2nd. rev. ed. K. Munson. 1975. 9.95 (ISBN 0-02-588180-9). Macmillan.

Airliners Since Nineteen Forty-Six. rev. ed. Kenneth Munson. LC 76-186444. (Pocket Encyclopedia of World Aircraft in Color Ser.). (Illus.). 192p. 1972. 5.95 o.s.i. (ISBN 0-02-588160-4). Macmillan.

Airlines in Transition. Nawal K. Taneja. LC 80-8735. 1981. 23.95 (ISBN 0-669-04345-1). Lexington Bks.

Airlines Traffic Forecasting. Nawal K. Taneja. LC 78-874. (Illus.). 1978. 22.95 (ISBN 0-669-02186-5). Lexington Bks.

Airman's Information Manual. Federal Aviation Administration. (Pilot Training Ser.). (Illus.). 327p. 1980. pap. 4.95 (ISBN 0-89100-149-2, EA-149-2). Aviation Maintenance.

Airman's Information Manual: Nineteen Eighty-One. Ed. by Walter Winner. 304p. 1981. pap. 5.50 (ISBN 0-911721-86-X). Aviation.

Airman's Information Manual, 1981. Aero Staff. LC 70-186849. 256p. 1981. pap. write for info. (ISBN 0-8168-1360-4). Aero.

Airmart Hardware Digest: AN, MS, & NAS. Airmart. Date not set. pap. 4.95. Aviation.

Airplane. (Activity Bks.). 1980. 2.95 (ISBN 0-8431-0669-7). Price Stern.

Airplane Book. Bob Ottum. (ps-1). 1972. PLB 5.38 (ISBN 0-307-68936-0, Golden Pr). Western Pub.

Airplane Performance, Stability & Control. Courtland D. Perkins & R. E. Hage. 1949. 29.95 (ISBN 0-471-68046-X). Wiley.

Airplanes. (MacDonald Educational Ser.). (Illus., Arabic.). 3.50x (ISBN 0-686-53080-2). Intl Bk Ctr.

Airplanes & Balloons. Howard W. Kanetzke. LC 77-27532. (Read About Science Ser.). (Illus.). (gr. k-3). 1978. PLB 9.95 (ISBN 0-8393-0090-5). Raintree Child.

Airport. Arthur Reed. LC 78-61230. (Careers Ser.). (Illus.). 1978. lib. bdg. 7.95 (ISBN 0-686-51119-0). Silver.

Airport, Aircraft & Airline Security. Kenneth C. Moore. LC 76-45104. (Illus.). 1976. 19.95 (ISBN 0-913708-26-7). Butterworths.

Airport City: Development Concepts for the Twenty-First Century. rev. ed. McKinley Conway. LC 80-65254. (Illus.). 227p. 1980. 29.00x (ISBN 0-910436-14-2). Conway Pubns.

Airport Confidential. Brian Moynahan. LC 79-24395. 1980. 15.95 (ISBN 0-671-40111-4); pap. 6.95 (ISBN 0-671-40119-X). Summit Bks.

Airport Economic Planning. Ed. by George P. Howard. 688p. 1974. 23.00x (ISBN 0-262-08072-9). MIT Pr.

Airport Guide. 2nd ed. Randall L. Voight. 1981. pap. 7.95 (ISBN 0-930318-01-3). Intl Res Eval.

Airport Noise Pollution: A Bibliography of Its Effects on People & Property. Richard L. King. LC 73-3370. 1973. 13.50 (ISBN 0-8108-0610-X). Scarecrow.

Airports— the Challenging Future. Institute of Civil Engineers, UK. 256p. 1980. 79.00x (ISBN 0-7277-0017-0, Pub. by Telford England). State Mutual Bk.

Airports for the Eighties. Institute of Civil Engineers. 220p. 1980. 80.00x (ISBN 0-901948-72-1, Pub. by Telford England). Sate Mutual Bk.

Airports for the Future. Institute of Civil Engineers. 129p. 1980. 60.00x (ISBN 0-901948-36-5, Pub. by Telford England). State Mutual Bk.

Airports of Mexico & Central America. Arnold D. Senterfitt. (Illus.). 1980. pap. 24.95 (Pub. by Senterfitt). Aviation.

Airports of Mexico & Centro America. 15th ed. Arnold D. Senter Fitt. (Illus.). 560p. (Orig.). 1980. pap. 24.95 (ISBN 0-937260-00-2). Senterfitt.

Airports of the World. John Stroud. (Putnam Aeronautical Bks.). (Illus.). 576p. 1981. 55.00 (ISBN 0-370-30037-8, Pub. by Chatto Bodley Jonathan). Merrimack Bk Serv.

Airports: Today's Small Field, Tomorrow's Neighborhood Nightmare. Dick Amann. 1981. 45.00 (ISBN 0-917194-05-5). Prog Studies.

Airships for the Future. rev. ed. William J. White. LC 76-19768. (Illus.). (YA) 1978. 12.95 (ISBN 0-8069-0090-3); PLB 11.69 (ISBN 0-8069-0091-1). Sterling.

Airways of America. Ed. by Poyntz Tyler. (Reference Shelf Ser.). 1958. 6.25 (ISBN 0-8242-0063-2). Wilson.

Airways: The Call of the Sky. Paul Buddee. (Australian Life Ser.: No. 4). 1979. pap. 6.95x (ISBN 0-85091-055-2, Pub. by Lothian). Intl Schol Bk Serv.

Ait Ayash of the High Moulouya Plain: Rural Social Organization in Morocco. John P. Chiapuris. (Anthropological Papers Ser.: No. 69). 1980. pap. 6.00x (ISBN 0-932206-83-2). U Mich Mus Anthro.

Aitareya Aranyaka. Ed. by Arthur B. Keith. 396p. 1969. Repr. of 1909 ed. text ed. 22.50x (ISBN 0-19-815442-9). Oxford U Pr.

AJ Handbook of Building Structure. 2nd ed. Ed. by Alan Hodgkinson. LC 75-301801. (Illus.). 360p. 1980. 32.50x (ISBN 0-85139-273-3). Intl Pubns Serv.

Ajanta: Its Place in Buddhist Art. Sheila L. Weiner. (Illus.). 1977. 22.50x (ISBN 0-520-02878-3). U of Cal Pr.

Akan Weights & the Gold Trade. Timothy H. Garrard. (Legon History Ser.). (Illus.). 1980. text ed. 50.00 (ISBN 0-582-64631-6). Longman.

Akbar. M. Mujeeb. (gr. 6-9). 1969. pap. 1.00 (ISBN 0-88253-350-9). Ind-US Inc.

Akbar & the Mughal Empire. John Harrison et al. Ed. by Malcolm Yapp & Margaret Killingray. (Greenhaven World History Ser.). (Illus.). 32p. (gr. 10). lib. bdg. 5.95 (ISBN 0-89908-031-6); pap. text ed. 1.95 (ISBN 0-89908-006-5). Greenhaven.

Akers' Simple Library Cataloging. 6th, completely rev. ed. Arthur Curley & Jana Varlejs. LC 76-26897. 1977. 11.00 (ISBN 0-8108-0978-8). Scarecrow.

Akimba & the Magic Cow. pap. 2.95 incl. record (ISBN 0-686-68470-2, Schol Pap). Schol Bk Serv.

Akkadien de Boghaz-Koi. Rene Labat. LC 78-72748. (Ancient Mesopotamian Texts & Studies). 1979. Repr. of 1932 ed. 37.50 (ISBN 0-685-91790-8). Ams Pr.

Akkumulation: Abhaengigkeit und Unterentwicklung. Andre G. Frank. (Edition Suhrkamp: 706). 256p. (Orig., Ger.). 1980. pap. text ed. 6.50 (ISBN 3-518-10706-2, Pub. by Insel Verlag Germany). Suhrkamp.

Akrilica: Poemas 1978-1980. Juan F. Herrera. Ed. by Francisco X. Alarcon. LC 80-83765. (Hand-Size Poetry Ser.: No. 1). (Illus.). 48p. (Orig.). 1981. pap. cancelled (ISBN 0-938254-00-6). Poetasumanos.

Akron-Canton Epicure. Bob Andrea. (Epicure Ser.). 1981. pap. 4.95 (ISBN 0-89716-080-0). Peanut Butter.

Aktil's Big Swim. Inga Moore. (Illus.). 32p. (ps-3). 1980. 10.95 (ISBN 0-19-554250-9). Oxford U Pr.

Aktuelle Perspektiven der Lithiumprophylaxe: Current Perspectives in Lithium Prophilaxis. Ed. by P. Berner et al. (Bibliotheca Psychiatrica: No. 161). (Illus.). vi, 294p. 1981. pap. 90.00 (ISBN 3-8055-1753-X). S Karger.

Akwe-Shavante Society. David Maybury-Lewis. (Illus.). 392p. 1974. pap. write for info. Oxford U Pr.

Al-Anon's Twelve Steps & Twelve Traditions. Al-Anon Family Group Headquarters. 140p. 5.00 (ISBN 0-910034-24-9). Al-Anon.

Al-Arif: A Dictionary of Grammatical Terms-Arabic-English, English-Arabic. Pierre Cachia. 1974. 12.00x (ISBN 0-685-72025-X). Intl Bk Ctr.

Al Bate! William D. Sheldon. Tr. by Nancy Phipps from Eng. (Breakthrough Ser.). (gr. 7-12). 1976. pap. text ed. 4.80 (ISBN 0-205-04873-0, 5248736); tchrs'. guide 2.40 (ISBN 0-205-05635-0, 5256356). Allyn.

Al Bowlly. Sid Colin & Tony Staveacre. 1979. 24.00 (ISBN 0-241-10057-7, Pub. by Hamish Hamilton England). David & Charles.

Al Capone. Fred D. Pasley. (Illus., Orig.). 1968. pap. 3.95 o.p. (ISBN 0-571-06726-3, Pub. by Faber & Faber). Merrimack Bk Serv.

Al-Fakhr: On the Systems of Government and the Moslem Dynasties. Ibn Al-Titaka. Tr. by C. E. Whitting. LC 80-2201. 1981. Repr. of 1947 ed. 35.00 (ISBN 0-404-18968-7). AMS Pr.

Al-Fakhri: On the Systems of Government & the Moslem Dynasties. Ibn Al-Tiqtaqa. Tr. by C. E. Whitting. LC 79-2869. 326p. 1981. Repr. of 1947 ed. 26.50 (ISBN 0-8305-0041-3). Hyperion Conn.

Al-Farabi on the Perfect State: Abu Nast al-Farabi's "the Principles of the Views of the Citizens of the Best State". Ed. by Richard Walzer. 1981. 45.00x (ISBN 0-19-824505-X). Oxford U Pr.

Al-Ghazali on Islamic Guidance. M. A. Quasem. 124p. 1980. 9.95x (ISBN 0-89955-208-0, Pub. by M A Quasem Malaysia); pap. 6.95x (ISBN 0-89955-209-9). Intl Schol Bk Serv.

Al Ghazali: On the Duties of Brotherhood. Tr. by Muhtar Holland. LC 76-8057. 96p. 1979. pap. 5.95 (ISBN 0-87951-083-8). Overlook Pr.

Al-Hadiyati 'l-Hamidiyah: Kurdish-Arabic Dictionary. M. Mokri. 1975. 18.00x. Intl Bk Ctr.

Al Hadj: The Pilgrimage. David A. Wilson. 100p. (Orig.). 1981. pap. 4.00 (ISBN 0-934852-22-7). Lorien Hse.

Al Jaffee: Dead or Alive. Al Jaffee. 1980. pap. 1.75 (ISBN 0-451-09494-8, E9494, Sig). NAL.

Al Jaffee Fowls His Nest. Al Jaffee. 1981. pap. 1.95 (ISBN 0-451-09741-6, J9741). NAL.

Al Jaffee Hogs the Show. Al Jaffee. (Orig.). 1981. pap. price not set (ISBN 0-451-09908-7, Sig). NAL.

Al Jaffee Sinks to a New Low. Al Jaffee. (Orig.). 1978. pap. 1.50 (ISBN 0-451-09009-8, W9009, Sig). NAL.

Al Jaffee's Mad Book of Magic & Other Dirty Tricks. Al Jaffee. (Mad Ser.). (Illus.). 1976. pap. 1.75 (ISBN 0-446-94406-8). Warner Bks.

Al Jaffee's Mad Inventions. Al Jaffee. (Mad Ser.). (Illus., Orig.). 1978. pap. 1.75 (ISBN 0-446-94407-6). Warner Bks.

Al Jolson: You Ain't Heard Nothing Yet. Robert Oberfirst. LC 80-16736. 1980. 8.95 (ISBN 0-498-02500-4). A S Barnes.

Al-Manar: An English-Arabic Dictionary. Hasan Karmi. text ed. 12.00x (ISBN 0-685-77119-9). Intl Bk Ctr.

Al Margen de la Vida: Poblacion y Pobreza en America Central. J. Mayone Stycos. LC 72-90916. Orig. Title: Margin of Life. (Illus., Span.). 1974. pap. text ed. 6.95x (ISBN 0-89197-653-1). Irvington.

Al Naqaid. Jarir & Farazdag. Tr. by Arthur Wormhoudt from Arabic. (Arab Translation Ser.: No. 7). 1974. pap. 6.50 (ISBN 0-916358-57-7). Wormhoudt.

Al Raychard's Fly Fishing in Maine. Al Raychard. LC 80-12126. (Illus.). 176p. (Orig.). 1980. pap. 6.95 (ISBN 0-89621-055-3). Thorndike Pr.

Al Ubell's Energy-Saving Guide. Al Ubell. (Orig.). 1980. pap. 4.95 (ISBN 0-446-97666-0). Warner Bks.

Al Who? J. Alastair Haig. LC 80-52617. 270p. (Orig.). 1980. pap. 4.95 (ISBN 0-932260-05-5). Rock Harbor.

ALA Accreditation Process, 1973-1976: A Survey of Library Schools Whose Programs Were Evaluated Under the 1972 Standards for Accreditation. Russell E. Bidlack. LC 77-21153. 1977. pap. 5.00 o.p. (ISBN 0-8389-3205-3). ALA.

A'la Aspen: Restaurant Recipes. rev. ed. Catherine G. Crabtree. pap. 6.50 (ISBN 0-937070-05-X). Crabtree.

ALA Filing Rules. Filing Committee of the Resources & Technical Services Division American Library Association. LC 80-22186. 62p. 1980. pap. 3.50 (ISBN 0-8389-3255-X). ALA.

ALA TOEFL Course. 2nd ed. William S. Annand & Sheldon Wise. (Orig.). 1980. Set Includes Tchrs.' Handbk, Classwork Bk, Homework Bk. pap. text ed. write for info. (ISBN 0-934270-00-7). Antiquary Pr.

A'la Vail: Restaurant Recipes. Catherine G. Crabtree. LC 80-67564. pap. 6.50 (ISBN 0-937070-03-3). Crabtree.

Ala y Trino: Pajaros De Puerto Rico Libro De Ninos Para Colorear. Ester Feliciano-Mendoza & Felix Rodriquez-Baez. LC 79-24763. (Orig., Span.). 1980. pap. write for info. (ISBN 0-8477-3600-8). U of PR Pr.

ALA Yearbook 1979. Ed. by Robert Wedgeworth. LC 76-647548. 1979. text ed. 45.00 (ISBN 0-8389-0292-8). ALA.

Alaawich. Lucy Arvidson. 1978. 2.00 (ISBN 0-686-25512-7). Malki Mus Pr.

Alabad a Dios. Mary F. Carson & Arlo D. Duba. Tr. by Justo L. Gonzalez from Eng. 86p. (Orig., Span.). 1979. pap. 2.50 (ISBN 0-89922-155-6). Edit Caribe.

Alabama. 28.00 (ISBN 0-89770-076-7). Curriculum Info Ctr.

Alabama - Coushatta (Creek) Indians. Incl. Alabama - Coushatta Indians: Ethnological Report & Statement of Testimony. Daniel Jacobson; Ethnological Analysis of Documents Relating to the Alabama & Coushatta Tribes of the State of Texas. Howard Martin; A History of Polk County, Texas, Indians. Ralph H. Marsh. (American Indian Ethnohistory Ser: Southern & Southeast Indians). (Illus.). lib. bdg. 42.00 (ISBN 0-8240-0758-1). Garland Pub.

Alabama, a Bicentennial History. Virginia V. Hamilton. (States & the Nation Ser.). (Illus.). 1977. 12.95 (ISBN 0-393-05621-X). Norton.

Alabama Brown. Lorinda Hagen. (Orig.). 1980. pap. 2.25 (ISBN 0-505-51564-4). Tower Bks.

Alabama Historical Sketches. Thomas C. McCorvey. Ed. by G. B. Johnston. LC 60-16695. 254p. 1971. 9.95x (ISBN 0-8139-0377-7). U Pr of Va.
Alabama's Covered Bridges. Tom Sangster & Dess L. Sangster. LC 80-68408. (Illus.). 100p. (Orig.). 1980. pap. 20.00 (ISBN 0-938252-00-3); includes 13 lithographs 29.50, 1st 500 numbered & signed by artist Tom Sangster (ISBN 0-686-69146-6). Coffeetable.
Alabama's State & Local Government. David L. Martin. LC 75-1714. (Government Ser.). 1975. perfect bdg. 6.95 (ISBN 0-8403-1121-4). Kendall Hunt.
Alabanza En Accion. Tr. by Merlin Carothers. (Spanish Bks.). (Span.). 1979. 1.60 (ISBN 0-8297-0490-6). Life Pubs Intl.
Aladdin. (Ladybird Stories Ser.). (Illus., Arabic.). 3.50 (ISBN 0-686-53068-3). Intl Bk Ctr.
Aladdin & the Wonderful Lamp. Harold G. Shane. Ed. by William Clark. (Hero Legends Bk). (Illus.). 16p. (gr. 3-5). 1980. pap. 22.00 ten bks & one cass. (ISBN 0-89290-080-6, BC15-3). Soc for Visual.
Aladore. Henry Newbolt. Ed. by R. Reginald & Douglas Menville. LC 80-19114. (Newcastle Forgotten Fantasy Library: Vol. 5). 363p. 1980. Repr. of 1975 ed. lib. bdg. 10.95x (ISBN 0-89370-504-7). Borgo Pr.
Alain Resnais. John F. Kriedl. (Theatrical Art Ser.). 1978. 12.50 (ISBN 0-8057-9256-2). Twayne.
Alain Resnais. James Monaco. (Illus.). 1979. pap. 6.95 (ISBN 0-19-520038-1, GB540, GB). Oxford U Pr.
Alain Robbe-Grillet. Bruce A. Morrissette. LC 65-26337. (Columbia Essays on Modern Writers Ser.: No. 11). (Orig.). pap. 2.00 (ISBN 0-231-02682-X, MW11). Columbia U Pr.
Alain Robbe-Grillet: An Annotated Bibliography of Critical Studies, 1953-1972. Dale W. Fraizer. LC 73-13874. (Author Bibliographies Ser.: No. 13). 1973. 10.00 (ISBN 0-8108-0645-2). Scarecrow.
Alakananda. Monika Varma. 1976. 8.00 (ISBN 0-89253-823-6); flexible cloth 4.80 (ISBN 0-89253-824-4). Ind-US Inc.
Alamo. John M. Myers. LC 48-5208. (Illus.). 240p. 1973. 10.95x (ISBN 0-8032-0884-7); pap. 3.25 (ISBN 0-8032-5779-1, BB 566, Bison). U of Nebr Pr.
Alan & the Animal Kingdom. Isabelle Holland. (YA) 1980. pap. 1.50 (ISBN 0-440-90382-3, LFL). Dell.
Alan Chadwick's Enchanted Garden. Tom Cuthbertson. (Illus.). 1978. pap. 7.50 o.p. (ISBN 0-525-47509-5). Dutton.
Alan Mendelsohn, the Boy from Mars. Daniel M. Pinkwater. LC 78-12052. (gr. 4-7). 1979. PLB 9.95 (ISBN 0-525-25360-2). Dutton.
Alan Mendelsohn: The Boy from Mars. Daniel M. Pinkwater. 224p. (gr. 5-8). 1981. pap. 1.95 (ISBN 0-553-14522-3). Bantam.
Alan Oken's Complete Astrology. Alan Oken. 640p. 1980. pap. 9.95 (ISBN 0-553-01262-2). Bantam.
Alan Paton. Edward Callan. LC 67-25207. (World Authors Ser.: South Africa: No. 40). 1968. lib. bdg. 10.95 (ISBN 0-8057-2686-1). Twayne.
Alan Sillitoe. Allen R. Penner. LC 72-161822. (English Authors Ser.: No. 141). lib. bdg. 10.95 (ISBN 0-8057-1496-0). Twayne.
Alan the Animal Kingdom. Isabelle Holland. LC 76-55371. 1977. 9.95 (ISBN 0-397-31745-X). Lippincott.
Alarm. Joseph Alleine. 1978. pap. 2.45 (ISBN 0-85151-081-7). Banner of Truth.
Alarm Systems & Theft Prevention. Thad L. Weber. LC 73-78572. 384p. 1973. 17.95 (ISBN 0-913708-11-9). Butterworths.
Alarms & Diversions. James Thurber. LC 80-8401. 367p. 1981. pap. 4.95 (ISBN 0-06-090830-0, CN 830, CN). Har-Row.
Alarms and Excursions in Arabia. Bertram Thomas. LC 80-1911. 1981. Repr. of 1931 ed. 36.00 (ISBN 0-404-18986-5). AMS Pr.
Alaryngeal Speech. William M. Diedrich & Karl A. Youngstrom. (Illus.). 232p. 1977. 18.75 (ISBN 0-398-00451-X). C C Thomas.
Alas, Alas for England: What Went Wrong with Britain. Louis Heren. 192p. 1981. 22.50 (ISBN 0-241-10538-2, Pub. by Hamish Hamilton England). David & Charles.
Alas, Alas, That Great City & Other Essays. Tom Robison. (Illus.). 65p. 1980. pap. 2.50 (ISBN 0-918700-05-1). Duverus Pub.
Alasdair MacColla & the Highland Problem in the Seventeenth Century. D. Stevenson. 1980. text ed. 39.00x (ISBN 0-85976-055-3). Humanities.
Alasia Problems. L. Hellbing. (Studies in Mediterranean Archaeology: No. 57). 1979. pap. text ed. 35.00x (ISBN 9-1850-5890-4). Humanities.
Alaska. 23.00 (ISBN 0-89770-077-5). Curriculum Info Ctr.
Alaska: A Geography. Roger W. Pearson & Donald F. Lynch. 300p. 1981. lib. bdg. 35.00x (ISBN 0-89158-903-1); text ed. 20.00x (ISBN 0-89158-903-1). Westview.
Alaska: A Guide to Alaska, Last American Frontier. LC 72-84457. 1939. 40.00 (ISBN 0-403-02154-5). Somerset Pub.
Alaska Almanac: Facts About Alaska. 4th rev. ed. Alaska Magazine Staff et al. (Illus.). 1979. pap. 3.95 o.p. (ISBN 0-88240-135-1). Alaska Northwest.
Alaska & the Eskimos. (gr. 2). 1974. pap. text ed. 5.80 (ISBN 0-205-03883-2, 803883X); tchrs'. guide 5.80 (ISBN 0-205-04229-5, 8042292). Allyn.
Alaska-Energy Lands: The Inside Story. P. M. Ivey et al. LC 79-5457. 300p. 1980. 12.95 (ISBN 0-918270-06-5). That New Pub.
Alaska in Pictures. Sterling Publishing Company Editors. LC 58-13382. (Visual Geography Ser). (Orig.). (gr. 6 up). 1966. PLB 4.99 (ISBN 0-8069-1001-1); pap. 2.95 (ISBN 0-8069-1000-3). Sterling.
Alaska: Past & Present. 3rd ed. Clarence C. Hulley. LC 80-25274. (Illus.). 477p. 1981. Repr. of 1970 ed. lib. bdg. 39.75x (ISBN 0-313-22845-0, HUAL). Greenwood.
Alaska Pipeline. Virginia O. Shumaker. LC 79-13696. (Illus.). 64p. (gr. 3-5). 1979. PLB 7.29 (ISBN 0-671-32975-8). Messner.
Alaska Reindeer Herdsmen: A Study of Native Management in Transition. Dean F. Olson. LC 71-631923. (Institute of Social, Economic & Government Research Ser.: No. 22). (Illus.). 172p. 1969. pap. 5.00 (ISBN 0-295-95119-2). U of Wash Pr.
Alaska Shippers Guide. (Illus.). 208p. 1980. 19.95 (ISBN 0-88240-147-5). Alaska Northwest.
Alaska Statutes, 11 vols. 1980. write for info. (ISBN 0-87215-143-3). Michie.
Alaska: The Great Land. Mike Miller & Peggy Wayburn. (Illus.). 128p. 1975. pap. 7.95 o.p. (ISBN 0-684-14125-6, SL576, ScribT). Scribner.
Alaska, Travel Guide. Norma Spring. LC 71-77497. (Illus.). 1970. 6.95 o.s.i. (ISBN 0-685-14593-X). Macmillan.
Alaska: Travel Guide. 3rd ed. Sunset Editors. LC 77-90724. (Illus.). 112p. 1978. pap. 5.95 (ISBN 0-376-06035-2, Sunset Bks). Sunset-Lane.
Alaska Treaty. David H. Miller. (Materials for the Study of Alaska History Ser.: No. 18). (Illus.). 1981. 16.50x (ISBN 0-919642-94-2). Limestone Pr.
Alaskan Christmas & Other Stories. Nora Young. 150p. 1981. 8.95 (ISBN 0-918270-10-3). That New Pub.
Alaskan Energy Potential & Constraints to Development. Ed. by Clarice Feldman & Bettina Silber. LC 79-91022. (Americans for Energy Independence Energy Policy Ser.). (Orig.). 1979. pap. 5.00 (ISBN 0-934458-01-4). Americans Energy Ind.
Alaskan Journey. Helen P. Jochum. LC 80-51526. (Illus.). 153p. 1980. 10.00. Jochum.
Alaskans. Keith Wheeler. (Old West Ser.). (Illus.). (gr. 5 up). 1977. 12.96 (ISBN 0-8094-1506-2, Pub. by Time-Life). Silver.
Alaskans. new ed. Keith Wheeler & Time-Life Editors. (Old West Ser.). 1977. 12.95 (ISBN 0-8094-1504-6). Time-Life.
Alaskans. Amanda Willoughby. 1980. pap. 2.75 (ISBN 0-440-00199-4). Dell.
Alaska's Agriculture: An Analysis of Developmental Problems. Wayne Burton. LC 79-175624. (Institute of Social & Economic Research Ser.: No. 30). 276p. 1971. pap. 5.00 (ISBN 0-295-95198-2). U of Wash Pr.
Albanians: Europe's Forgotten Survivors. Anton Logoreci. LC 77-14985. 1978. lib. bdg. 22.50x (ISBN 0-89158-827-2). Westview.
Albany: Birth of a Prison--End of an Era. Roy D. King & Kenneth W. Elliott. (International Library of Social Policy Ser.). 1978. 25.00 (ISBN 0-7100-8727-6). Routledge & Kegan.
Alba's Medical Technology Board Examination Review, Vol. I. 9th ed. Alba. (Illus.). 1980. pap. text ed. 20.00 (ISBN 0-910224-05-6). Berkeley Sci.
Alba's Medical Technology Board Examination Review, Vol. II. 4th ed. Alba. LC 72-172446. (Illus.). 1978. pap. text ed. 17.00 (ISBN 0-910224-02-1). Berkeley Sci.
Albatros D.Va: German World War I Fighter. Robert C. Mikesh. LC 80-36711. (Famous Aircraft of the National Air & Space Museum Ser.: No. 4). (Illus.). 115p. (Orig.). 1980. pap. 7.95 (ISBN 0-87474-633-7). Smithsonian.
Alben W. Barkley: Senate Majority Leader & Vice President. Polly Ann Davis. Ed. by Frank Freidel. LC 78-62380. (Modern American History Ser.: Vol. 6). 1979. lib. bdg. 30.00 (ISBN 0-8240-3630-1). Garland Pub.
Albert & the Green Bottle. Gerald Rose & Elizabeth Rose. (Illus.). (ps-5). 1972. 6.95 (ISBN 0-571-09873-8, Pub. by Faber & Faber). Merrimack Bk Serv.
Albert Camus. Carol Petersen. Tr. by Alexander Gode. LC 68-31455. (Modern Literature Ser.). 1969. 10.95 (ISBN 0-8044-2691-0); pap. 3.45 (ISBN 0-8044-6646-7). Ungar.
Albert Camus. Phillip H. Rhein. (World Authors Ser.: France: No. 69). 1969. lib. bdg. 9.95 (ISBN 0-8057-2196-7). Twayne.
Albert Camus' Literary Milieu: Arid Lands. Ed. by Wolodymyr T. Zyla. Wendell M. Aycock. (Proceedings of the Comparative Literature Symposium: Vol. VIII). (Illus., Orig.). 1976. 6.00 (ISBN 0-89672-050-0). Tex Tech Pr.
Albert Camus Nineteen Eighty. Raymond Gay-Crosier. LC 80-22240. 330p. (Orig., Fr.). 1981. pap. 16.00 (ISBN 0-8130-0691-0). U Presses Fla.
Albert D. Kirwan: A Man for All Seasons. Frank F. Mathias. LC 74-18936. (Illus.). 208p. 1975. 13.00x (ISBN 0-8131-1325-3). U Pr of Ky.
Albert Einstein Autobiographical Notes: A Centennial Edition. Ed. by Paul A. Schilpp. LC 78-13925. 1979. 10.95 (ISBN 0-87548-352-6). Open Court.
Albert Einstein Centennial Celebration. Harry Woolf. (Illus.). 400p. 1980. text ed. 43.50 (ISBN 0-201-09924-1). A-W.
Albert Einstein: Four Commemorative Lectures. Intro. by Albert C. Lewis. 1980. 3.50 (ISBN 0-87959-093-9). U of Tex Hum Res.
Albert Einstein, the Human Side: New Glimpses from His Archives. Helen Dukas & Banesh Hoffman. LC 78-70289. 168p. 1981. pap. 3.95 (ISBN 0-691-02368-9). Princeton U Pr.
Albert Einstein: World Scientist. Irving Gerber. 1979. of 10 6.75 set (ISBN 0-87594-185-0). Book Lab.
Albert Einstein's Special Theory of Relativity: Discovery (1905) & Early Interpretation (1905-1911) LC 79-27495. (Illus.). 450p. 1980. text ed. 36.50 (ISBN 0-201-04680-6); pap. 24.50 (ISBN 0-201-04679-2). A-W.
Albert Gallatin. Henry Adams. LC 80-25555. (American Statesmen Ser.). 695p. 1981. pap. 8.95 (ISBN 0-87754-194-9). Chelsea Hse.
Albert Inskip Dickerson: Selected Writings. Albert I. Dickerson. LC 74-84230. (Illus.). 232p. 1974. text ed. 10.00x (ISBN 0-87451-107-0). U Pr of New Eng.
Albert Maltz. Jack Salzman. (United States Authors Ser.: No. 311). 1978. lib. bdg. 12.50 (ISBN 0-8057-7228-6). Twayne.
Albert Shaw of the Review of Reviews: An Intellectual Biography. Lloyd J. Graybar. LC 73-80464. (Illus.). 256p. 1974. 14.00x (ISBN 0-8131-1300-8). U Pr of Ky.
Albert Speer & the Nazi Ministry of Arms: Economic Institutions & Industrial Production in the German War Economy. Edward R. Zilbert. LC 76-17030. 304p. 1981. 19.50 (ISBN 0-686-69379-5). Fairleigh Dickinson.
Albert the Great: Commemorative Essays. Ed. by Francis J. Kovach & Robert W. Shahan. LC 79-6713. 250p. 1980. 12.95x (ISBN 0-8061-1666-8). U of Okla Pr.
Alberti's Church of San Sebastiano in Mantua. Richard E. Lamoureux. Ed. by Sydney J. Freedberg. LC 78-74370. (Oustanding Dissertations in the Fine Arts Ser.). (Illus.). 1979. lib. bdg. 38.00 (ISBN 0-8240-3958-0). Garland Pub.
Alberto Moravia. Jane E. Cottrell. LC 73-84599. (Modern Literature Ser.). 174p. 1974. 10.95 (ISBN 0-8044-2131-5). Ungar.
Alberto Moravia. Luciano Rebay. LC 77-126544. (Columbia Essays on Modern Writers Ser.: No. 52). (Orig.). 1970. pap. 2.00 (ISBN 0-231-02762-1, MW52). Columbia U Pr.
Albi Angel. Shirley A. Maloney. (gr. k-4). 1977. pap. 5.95 (ISBN 0-570-03466-3, 56-1298). Concordia.
Albion in China: The First British Football Tour to China in Pictures. D. Kingsley & F. Taylor. (Illus.). 1979. pap. 9.00 (ISBN 0-08-024496-3). Pergamon.
Albion W. Small. George Christakes. (World Leaders Ser.: No. 68). 1978. lib. bdg. 12.50 (ISBN 0-8057-7718-0). Twayne.
Albor: Mediaeval & Renaissance Dawn-Songs in the Iberian Peninsula. D. Empaytaz De Croome. LC 80-23767. (Sponsor Ser.). 106p. (Orig.). 1980. pap. 12.75 (ISBN 0-8357-0531-5, SS-00144). Univ Microfilms.
Albrecht Altdorfer: Four Centuries of Criticism. Reinhild Janzen. Ed. by Donald B. Kuspit. (Studies in Fine Arts: Criticism). 208p. 1980. 24.95 (ISBN 0-8357-1120-X, Pub. by UMI Res Pr). Univ Microfilms.
Albrecht Duerer: Master Printmaker. Eleanor A. Sayre. LC 77-183708. (Illus.). 320p. 1972. 27.50 (ISBN 0-87846-005-5); pap. 10.00 o.p. (ISBN 0-685-24672-8). Mus Fine Arts Boston.
Albucasis on Surgery & Instruments: A Definitive Edition of the Arabic Text, with English Translation & Commentary. Ed. by Martin S. Spink & Geoffrey Lewis. LC 68-10498. (Welcome Institute of the History of Medicine & Near Eastern Center UCLA). (Illus.). 1973. 67.50x (ISBN 0-520-01532-0). U of Cal Pr.
Album Ex Medicorum: 115 American & European Book Plates. Wasyl Luciw. 1961. 15.00 o.p. (ISBN 0-685-89026-0). Slavia Lib.
Album of American History, 3 vols. rev. ed. James T. Adams. LC 74-91746. (gr. 5 up). 1969. Set. 165.00 (ISBN 0-684-16848-0, ScribR). Scribner.
Album of Automobile Racing. William Butterworth. (Picture Albums Ser.). (Illus.). 1977. PLB 7.90 s&l (ISBN 0-531-02909-3). Watts.
Album of Chinese Americans. Betty L. Sung. LC 76-45185. (Picture Albums Ser.). (Illus.). (gr. 4-6). 1977. PLB 5.90 s&l o.p. (ISBN 0-531-00366-3). Watts.
Album of Colonial America. Leonard Ingraham. LC 71-75721. (Picture Albums Ser). (Illus.). (gr. 4-6). 1969. PLB 5.90 o.p. (ISBN 0-531-01507-6). Watts.
Album of Great Science Fiction Films. Frank Manchel. (Picture Albums Ser.). (gr. 5 up). 1976. PLB 7.90 (ISBN 0-531-00345-0). Watts.
Album of Indian Sculpture. C. Sivaramamurti. (Illus.). 1979. pap. 10.00 (ISBN 0-89744-194-X). Auromere.
Album of Irish Americans. Gene Murphy & Tim Driscoll. LC 73-13994. (Picture Albums Ser.). (Illus.). 96p. (gr. 5-8). 1974. PLB 5.90 o.p. (ISBN 0-531-01519-X). Watts.
Album of Martin Luther King Jr. Jeanne A. Rowe. LC 73-110474. (Picture Albums Ser). (Illus.). 1970. PLB 7.90 (ISBN 0-531-01509-2). Watts.
Album of Nazism. William L. Katz. LC 78-12723. (Picture Album Ser.). (Illus.). (gr. 5 up). 1979. PLB 7.90 s&l (ISBN 0-531-01500-9). Watts.
Album of Puerto Ricans in the United States. Stuart J. Brahs. LC 73-5936. (Picture Albums Ser). (Illus.). 96p. (gr. 4-6). 1973. PLB 5.90 o.p. (ISBN 0-531-01517-3). Watts.
Album of Reconstruction. William L. Katz. LC 73-21933. (Picture Album Ser). (Illus.). 96p. (gr. 4-7). 1974. PLB 5.90 o.p. (ISBN 0-531-02701-5). Watts.
Album of Reptiles. Tom McGowen. (gr. 3-7). 1978. 5.95 (ISBN 0-528-82001-X); PLB 5.97 o.p. (ISBN 0-528-80014-0). Rand.
Album of Sharks. Tom McGowen. LC 77-5172. (Illus.). (gr. 5-7). 1977. 5.95 (ISBN 0-528-82023-0); PLB 5.97 o.p. (ISBN 0-528-80212-7). Rand.
Album of Television. Carol A. Emmers. (gr. 5 up). 1980. PLB 7.90 (ISBN 0-531-01503-3, A15). Watts.
Album of the American Cowboy. John Malone. LC 79-151886. (Picture Albums Ser). (Illus.). (gr. 4-6). 1971. PLB 5.90 o.p. (ISBN 0-531-01512-2). Watts.
Album of the American Indian. Rose Yellow Robe. LC 73-134657. (Picture Albums Ser). (Illus.). (gr. 4-6). 1969. PLB 5.90 o.p. (ISBN 0-531-01506-8). Watts.
Album of the Civil War. William L. Katz. LC 73-11031. (Picture Albums Ser.). (Illus.). 96p. (gr. 4-7). 1974. PLB 7.90 (ISBN 0-531-01518-1). Watts.
Album of the Depression. William Katz. (Picture Albums Ser.). (Illus.). (gr. 5 up). 1978. PLB 7.90 s&l (ISBN 0-531-02914-X). Watts.
Album of the Fifties. Edmund Lindop. (Illus.). (gr. 6 up). 1978. PLB 7.90 s&l (ISBN 0-531-01505-X). Watts.
Album of the Italian American. Salvatore J. LaGumina. LC 72-6275. (Picture Albums Ser.). (Illus.). 96p. (gr. 4 up). 1972. PLB 5.90 o.p. (ISBN 0-531-01514-9). Watts.
Album of the Jews in America. Yuri Suhl. LC 72-5475. (Picture Albums Ser). (Illus.). 96p. (gr. 4 up). 1972. PLB 5.90 o.p. (ISBN 0-531-01513-0). Watts.
Album of Women in American History. Leonard W. Ingraham & Claire R. Ingraham. LC 72-6138. (Picture Albums Ser.). (Illus.). 96p. (gr. 4 up). 1972. PLB 5.90 o.p. (ISBN 0-531-01515-7). Watts.
Album of World War I. Dorothy Hoobler & Thomas Hoobler. (Picture Albums Ser). (Illus.). 96p. (gr. 5 up). 1976. PLB 7.90 (ISBN 0-531-01169-0). Watts.
Album of World War II. Dorothy Hoobler & Thomas Hoobler. (Picture Albums Ser.). (Illus.). (gr. 5 up). 1977. PLB 7.90 s&l (ISBN 0-531-02911-5). Watts.
Albumin: Structure, Function & Uses. Ed. by Victor Rosenoer et al. 1977. text ed. 57.00 (ISBN 0-08-019603-9). Pergamon.
Albuquerque. Jeannine D. Van Eperen. 386p. 1980. 15.95 (ISBN 0-937268-02-X); pap. 8.95 (ISBN 0-937268-01-1). Alpha Printing.
Alcaeus. Hubert Martin, Jr. (World Authors Ser.: Greece: No. 210). lib. bdg. 10.95 (ISBN 0-8057-2016-2). Twayne.
Alceste: The Tradgeie of Alceste & Eliza. Tr. by Francisco Bracciolini. LC 79-84082. (English Experience Ser.: No. 902). 80p. 1979. Repr. of 1638 ed. lib. bdg. 9.00 (ISBN 90-221-0902-X). Walter J Johnson.
Alcestiad or a Life in the Sun. Thornton Wilder. 1979. pap. 2.25 (ISBN 0-380-41855-X, 41855, Bard). Avon.

Alcestis. Euripides. Ed. by A. M. Dale. (Plays of Euripides Ser.). 1954. pap. 11.50x (ISBN 0-19-872097-1). Oxford U Pr.

Alcestis. Euripides. Tr. by William Arrowsmith. (Greek Tragedy in New Translations Ser). 1973. 10.95 (ISBN 0-19-501861-3). Oxford U Pr.

Alcestis. Euripides. Tr. by Gilbert Murray. 1915. pap. text ed. 3.95x (ISBN 0-04-882025-3). Allen Unwin.

Alchemical Active Imagination. Marie-Louise Von Franz. (Seminar Ser.). (Orig.). 1979. pap. text ed. 8.50 (ISBN 0-88214-114-7). Spring Pubns.

Alchemical Society. Journal, Vols. 1-3 In 1. LC 79-8591. Repr. of 1915 ed. 29.50 (ISBN 0-404-18445-6). AMS Pr.

Alchemist. Ben Jonson. Ed. by John I. McCollum, Jr. 1965. 5.75 (ISBN 0-8120-5001-0); pap. 1.95 (ISBN 0-8120-0019-6). Barron.

Alchemist. 1967 ed. Ben Jonson. Ed. by J. B. Steane. text ed. 5.95x (ISBN 0-521-06945-9). Cambridge U Pr.

Alchemist & the Other Poems. James R. Bagley. 1980. 5.50 (ISBN 0-8233-0318-7). Golden Quill.

Alchemy: A Bibliography of English Language Writings. Alan Pritchard. 400p. 1980. 75.00x (ISBN 0-7100-0472-9). Routledge & Kegan.

Alchemy, Ancient & Modern. H. Stanley Redgrove. (Illus.). 141p. 1980. 20.00 (ISBN 0-89005-344-8). Ares.

Alchemy: Ancient & Modern. Herbert S. Redgrove. LC 79-8624. Repr. of 1922 ed. 23.50 (ISBN 0-404-18490-1). AMS Pr.

Alchemy & Other Chemical Achievements of the Ancient Orient. Masumi Chikashige. LC 79-8602. Repr. of 1936 ed. 20.00 (ISBN 0-404-18456-1). AMS Pr.

Alchemy & the Alchemists, 3 vols. Reuben S. Clymer. LC 79-8603. Repr. of 1907 ed. Set. 79.50 (ISBN 0-404-18457-X). AMS Pr.

Alchemy Connection. Alfred Sylvester. 1980. 6.75 (ISBN 0-8062-1459-7). Carlton.

Alchemy, Its Science & Romance. John E. Mercer. LC 79-8617. (Illus.). Repr. of 1921 ed. 27.50 (ISBN 0-404-18481-2). AMS Pr.

Alchemy, Medicine, & Religion in the China of A. D. 320: The Nei P'ien of Ko Hung (Pao-p'u tzu) Tr. by James R. Ware from Chinese. 416p. 1981. pap. price not set (ISBN 0-486-24088-6). Dover.

Alchemy of Awareness. Lorraine Sinkler. LC 76-62957. 1977. 6.95 o.p. (ISBN 0-06-067387-7, HarpR). Har-Row.

Alchemy of Happiness. Inayat Khan. (Sufi Message of Hazrat Inayat Khan Ser.: Vol. 6). 1979. 6.95 (ISBN 90-6077-953-3, Pub. by Servire BV Netherlands). Hunter Hse.

Alchemy: Pre-Egyptian Legacy, Millennial Promise. Ed. by Richard Grossinger. (Io Ser.: No. 26). (Illus., Orig.). 1979. pap. 8.95 (ISBN 0-913028-62-2). North Atlantic.

Alchemy: The Philosopher's Stone. Allison Coudert. LC 79-67688. (Illus.). 1980. pap. 9.95 (ISBN 0-394-73733-4). Shambhala Pubns.

Alcholism: Development, Consequences & Interventions. Nada J. Estes & M. Edith Heinemaann. LC 77-1676. (Illus.). 1977. pap. text ed. 12.95 (ISBN 0-8016-1529-1). Mosby.

Alcholism: Its Causes & Cure. Harry Milt. LC 76-8476. 192p. 1976. 8.95 o.p. (ISBN 0-684-14667-3, ScribT). Scribner.

Alcohol -- What It Is, What It Does. Judith S. Seixas. LC 76-43344. (Read-Alone Bk.). (Illus.). 56p. (gr. 1-3). 1981. pap. 2.95 (ISBN 0-688-00462-8). Greenwillow.

Alcohol Abuse & Rehabilitation Approaches. Ed. by John G. Cull & Richard E. Hardy. (American Lecture in Social & Rehabilitation Psychology Ser.). (Illus.). 220p. 1974. text ed. 18.75 (ISBN 0-398-03017-0). C C Thomas.

Alcohol Abuse Prevention: A Comprehensive Guide for Youth Organization. Boys' Clubs of America et al. (Illus., Orig.). Date not set. pap. 10.00 (ISBN 0-9604288-0-1). Boys Clubs.

Alcohol & Abnormal Protein Biosynthesis, Biochemical & Clinical. Ed. by M. A. Rothschild et al. 550p. 1976. text ed. 46.00 (ISBN 0-08-017708-5). Pergamon.

Alcohol & Alcoholism. Roberta Evans. LC 76-13228. (First Bks. Ser.). (Illus.). 96p. (gr. 4-6). 1976. PLB 6.45 (ISBN 0-531-00334-5). Watts.

Alcohol & Alcoholism, Vol. I. Keith B. Rix. Ed. by D. F. Horrobin. (Alcohol Research Review Ser.). 250p. 1980. Repr. of 1977 ed. 24.95x (ISBN 0-87705-960-8). Human Sci Pr.

Alcohol & Alcoholism. Royal College of Psychiatrists. LC 79-20712. 1979. 15.95 (ISBN 0-02-927510-5). Free Pr.

Alcohol & Aldehyde Metabolizing Systems. Ed. by Ronald Thurman. (Advances in Experimental Medicine & Biology Ser.). 335p. 1980. 75.00 (ISBN 0-306-40476-1, Plenum Pr). Plenum Pub.

Alcohol & Aldehyde Metabolizing Systems, 3 vols. Ed. by Ronald G. Thurman et al. (Johnson Foundation Colloquia Ser.). 1974-78. Vol. 1. 38.50 (ISBN 0-12-691450-8); Vol. 2. 41.00 (ISBN 0-12-691402-8); Vol. 3. 41.00 (ISBN 0-12-691403-6); Set. 98.00. Acad Pr.

Alcohol & Behavior: An Activated Education Approach, No. 1. Darwin Dennison et al. LC 79-25741. 1980. pap. text ed. 7.95 (ISBN 0-8016-1252-7). Mosby.

Alcohol & Drug Abuse & the Law, Vol. 27. I. Sloan. 1980. 5.95 (ISBN 0-379-11137-3). Oceana.

Alcohol & Drugs: Similarities & Differences. Joel Solomon & Kim Keeley. 1981. write for info. (ISBN 0-88416-306-7). PSG Pub.

Alcohol & the Diet. Daphne A. Roe. (Illus.). 1979. lib. bdg. 17.50 (ISBN 0-87055-316-X). AVI.

Alcohol & the Elderly: A Comprehensive Bibliography. Grace M. Barnes et al. LC 80-1786. xvii, 138p. 1980. lib. bdg. 25.00 (ISBN 0-313-22132-4, BAE/). Greenwood.

Alcohol & the Family. Ed. by Jim Orford & Judith Harwin. 200p. 1980. 25.00x (Pub. by Croom Helm England). State Mutual Bk.

Alcohol & the Family: Three Sure Ways to Solve the Problem. Frank. 1978. pap. 1.50 (ISBN 0-89243-086-9). Liguori Pubns.

Alcohol & the Jews: A Cultural Study of Drinking & Sobriety. Charles R. Snyder. LC 77-24885. (Arcturus Books Paperbacks). 240p. 1978. pap. 6.95 (ISBN 0-8093-0846-0). S Ill U Pr.

Alcohol As a Crutch. Shirley Schwarzrock & C. Gilbert Wrenn. (Coping with Ser.). (Illus.). (gr. 7-12). 1971. pap. text ed. 1.30 (ISBN 0-913476-17-X). Am Guidance.

Alcohol Dependence. B. D. Hore. (Postgraduate Psychiatry Ser). 1976. 17.95 (ISBN 0-407-00082-8). Butterworths.

Alcohol Dependence & Smoking Behavior. Griffith Edwards et al. LC 75-30137. 280p. 1976. 23.95 (ISBN 0-347-01127-6, 00368-9, Pub. by Saxon Hse). Lexington Bks.

Alcohol Detoxification Programs: Treatment Instead of Jail. H. H. Siegel. (Illus.). 110p. 1973. 11.75 (ISBN 0-398-02820-6). C C Thomas.

Alcohol Economy: What's Ahead. 1980. 850.00 (ISBN 0-89336-263-8, C-030). BCC.

Alcohol Fuel Book. Robert Gaither. (Illus.). 55p. (Orig.). Date not set. pap. price not set (ISBN 0-89196-084-8, Domus Bks). Quality Bks IL.

Alcohol Fuels Information Series, Vol. 5: Gasohol. Ed. by Justin Bereny. Date not set. price not set (ISBN 0-89934-033-4, B942-SS); pap. price not set (ISBN 0-89934-034-2, B042-SS). Solar Energy Info.

Alcohol Fuels Information Series, Vol. 6: Ethanol. Ed. by Justin Bereny. Date not set. price not set (ISBN 0-89934-035-0, B943-SS); pap. price not set (ISBN 0-89934-036-9, B043-SS). Solar Energy Info.

Alcohol Fuels Information Series, Vol. 7: Methanol. Ed. by Justin Bereny. Date not set. price not set (ISBN 0-89934-037-7, B944-SS); pap. price not set (ISBN 0-89934-038-5, B044-SS). Solar Energy Info.

Alcohol Fuels Information Series, Vol. 1: U. S. Government Overviews, Gasohol: the Alcohol Fuel Issue Brief; Gasohol: a Technical Memorandum; Will Gasohol Help Power America's Future? the Report of the Alcohol Fuels Policy Review; Ed. by Justin Bereny & Linda Kittle. LC 80-51918. 1980. 49.95 (ISBN 0-89934-031-8, B941-SS); pap. 34.95 (ISBN 0-89934-032-6, B041-SS). Solar Energy Info.

Alcohol Problems in Employment. Ed. by Brian Hore. 200p. 1980. 35.00x (Pub. by Croom Helm England). State Mutual Bk.

Alcohol Problems in Employment. Ed. by Brian Hore & Michael Plant. 200p. 1981. 35.00x (ISBN 0-7099-1202-1, Pub. by Croom Helm LTD England). Biblio Dist.

Alcohol: The Beloved Enemy. Jack Van Impe & Roger F. Campbell. 1980. 7.95 (ISBN 0-8407-5192-3). Nelson.

Alcohol: The Delightful Poison. Alice Fleming. LC 74-22629. (Illus.). 160p. (gr. 5 up). 1975. 7.95 o.s.i. (ISBN 0-440-01796-3); PLB 7.45 (ISBN 0-440-02524-9). Delacorte.

Alcohol, Tobacco & Drugs: Their Use & Abuse. W. Worick & W. Schaller. 1977. pap. 8.95 (ISBN 0-13-021436-1). P-H.

Alcohol Troubled Person. Alan Willoughby. LC 79-1173. 1979. 14.95 (ISBN 0-88229-425-3); pap. 7.95 (ISBN 0-88229-680-9). Nelson-Hall.

Alcoholic Employee: A Handbook of Helpful Guidelines. Ashton Brisolara. LC 78-15763. 318p. 1978. text ed. 18.95 (ISBN 0-87705-327-8). Human Sci Pr.

Alcoholic in Your Life. Jo Coudert. 288p. 1974. pap. 2.25 o.s.i. (ISBN 0-446-92240-4). Warner Bks.

Alcoholic in Your Life. Jo Coudert. LC 70-185955. 264p. 1981. pap. 6.95 (ISBN 0-8128-6121-3). Stein & Day.

Alcoholic Priests: A Sociological Study. Andrew A. Sorensen. 1977. 8.95 (ISBN 0-8164-0317-1). Crossroad NY.

Alcoholics Anonymous. 3rd, rev. ed. LC 76-4029. 575p. 1976. 5.65 (ISBN 0-916856-00-3). AAWS.

Alcoholics Anonymous Comes of Age: A Brief History of A. A. LC 57-10949. 333p. 1957. 5.75 (ISBN 0-916856-02-X). AAWS.

Alcoholics Victorious. Jerry G. Dunn. pap. 3.00 (ISBN 0-8024-0200-3). Moody.

Alcoholism. Alvin Silverstein & Virginia B. Silverstein. LC 75-17938. 128p. (gr. 5-8). 1975. 7.95 (ISBN 0-397-31648-8); pap. 3.50 (ISBN 0-397-31649-6, LSC-39). Lippincott.

Alcoholism - One Family's Story. Jane Doe. 1978. pap. 2.50 (ISBN 0-8309-0231-7). Herald Hse.

Alcoholism - Whose Responsibility? Coordinator's Guide. American Hospital Association. 1972. loose-leaf bdg 18.50 o.p. (ISBN 0-87258-082-2, 1225). Am Hospital.

Alcoholism & Affective Disorders: Clinical, Genetic, & Biochemical Studies with Emphasis on Alcohol-Lithium Interaction. new ed. Ed. by Donald W. Goodwin & Carlton K. Erickson. (Illus.). 1979. 29.95 (ISBN 0-89335-073-7). Spectrum Pub.

Alcoholism & Driving. Carl J. Bridge. (Illus.). 96p. 1972. 10.75 (ISBN 0-398-02243-7). C C Thomas.

Alcoholism & Health. Ed. by Sharon V. Davidson. LC 80-12354. 216p. 1980. text ed. 24.50 (ISBN 0-89443-292-3). Aspen Systems.

Alcoholism & Society. Morris E. Chafetz & Harold W. Demone, Jr. 1962. 14.95 (ISBN 0-19-500504-X). Oxford U Pr.

Alcoholism & Treatment. David J. Armor et al. LC 77-17421. (Personality Processes Ser.). 1978. 23.50 (ISBN 0-471-02558-5, Pub. by Wiley-Interscience). Wiley.

Alcoholism Counseling: Issues for an Emerging Profession. Stephen K. Valle. (Illus.). 184p. 1979. 15.75 (ISBN 0-398-03877-5). C C Thomas.

Alcoholism: Interdisciplinary Approaches to an Enduring Problem. Ed. by Ralph E. Tarter & A. Arthur Sugerman. 880p. 1976. text ed. 33.50 (ISBN 0-201-08146-6, Adv Bk Prog); pap. text ed. 21.50 (ISBN 0-201-08145-8, Adv Bk Prog). A-W.

Alcoholism: New Knowledge & New Responses. G. Edwards & M. Grant. 368p. 1980. 35.00x (Pub. by Croom Helm England). State Mutual Bk.

Alcoholism Skid Row & the Police. Allen Z. Gammage et al. 96p. 1972. photocopy ed. spiral 9.75 (ISBN 0-398-02288-7). C C Thomas.

Alcoholism: The Hidden Addiction. Ebbe C. Hoff. LC 74-13014. 1975. 7.95 (ISBN 0-8164-0248-5). Crossroad NY.

Alcoholism: The Nutritional Approach. Roger J. Williams. 1959. pap. 3.45 (ISBN 0-292-70301-5). U of Tex Pr.

Alcoholism: The Total Treatment Approach. Ed. by Ronald J. Catanzaro. (Illus.). 528p. 1977. text ed. 34.50 (ISBN 0-398-00295-9). C C Thomas.

Alcoholism Treatment, Vol. 2. Cedric Smith. Ed. by D. F. Horrobin. (Alcoholism Research Review Ser.). 107p. 1980. Repr. of 1978 ed. 14.95x (ISBN 0-87705-968-3). Human Sci Pr.

Alcoholism Treatment in Transition. Ed. by Griffith Edwards. 336p. 1980. 35.00x (Pub. by Croom Helm England). State Mutual Bk.

Alcoholisms in Perspective. Marcus Grant & Paul Gwinner. 176p. 1980. 27.00x (ISBN 0-85664-790-X, Pub. by Croom Helm England). State Mutual Bk.

Alcohols & Derivatives, 2 vols. Ed. by J. Tremolieres. 1970. Set. 82.00 (ISBN 0-08-006937-1). Pergamon.

Alcohols As Motor Fuels. Society of Automotive Engineers. 1980. 29.95 (ISBN 0-89883-107-5). Soc Auto Engineers.

Alcools. Guillaume Apollinaire. Tr. & annotations by Anne Hyde Greet. 1966. 16.00x (ISBN 0-520-00028-5); pap. 3.75 (ISBN 0-520-00029-3, CAL121). U of Cal Pr.

Alcools. Guillaume Apollinaire. Ed. by Garnet Rees. (French Poets Ser.). 192p. 1975. text ed. 19.75x (ISBN 0-485-14708-4, Athlone Pr); pap. text ed. 10.00x (ISBN 0-485-12708-3, Athlone Pr). Humanities.

Alcuin & Beowulf: An Eighth-Century View. W. F. Bolton. 1978. 16.00 (ISBN 0-8135-0865-7). Rutgers U Pr.

ALD - a New Test for Aphasia. Lon Emerick. 27.00 (ISBN 0-686-69371-X). Northern Mich.

Aldo Ice Cream. Johanna Hurwitz. LC 80-24371. (Illus.). 128p. (gr. 4-6). 1981. 6.95 (ISBN 0-688-00375-3); PLB 6.67 (ISBN 0-688-00376-1). Morrow.

Aldo Rossi in America: Nineteen Seventy-Six to Nineteen Seventy-Nine. Peter D. Eisenman & Aldo Rossi. Ed. by Kenneth Frampton. Tr. by Diane Ghirardo from Ital. (IAUS Exhibition Catalogues Ser.). (Illus.). 64p. 1979. pap. 10.00 (ISBN 0-932628-02-8). IAUS.

Aldosterone. Edith Glaz & Paul Vecsei. LC 70-138666. 628p. 1971. 87.00 (ISBN 0-08-013368-1). Pergamon.

Aldous Huxley. Keith M. May. 1972. text ed. 15.50x (ISBN 0-236-17682-X). Humanities.

Aldous Huxley. Harold H. Watts. LC 68-24289. (English Authors Ser.: No. 79). 1969. lib. bdg. 9.95 (ISBN 0-8057-1284-4). Twayne.

Aldous Huxley: A Collection of Critical Essays. Ed. by Robert E. Kuehn. (Twentieth Century Views Ser.). 192p. 1974. 10.95 (ISBN 0-13-448514-9, Spec); pap. 2.45 o.p. (ISBN 0-13-448506-8, Spec). P-H.

Aldous Huxley: An Annotated Bibliography. Eben E. Bass. LC 79-7907. (Garland Reference Library of Humanities). 275p. 1981. 30.00 (ISBN 0-8240-9525-1). Garland Pub.

Aldous Huxley: Novelist. C. S. Ferns. 1980. text ed. 35.00x (ISBN 0-485-11194-2, Athlone Pr). Humanities.

Aldous Huxley: The Critical Heritage. Ed. by Donald Watt. (Critical Heritage Ser.). 1975. 30.00x (ISBN 0-7100-8114-6). Routledge & Kegan.

Aldous Huxley: Vedantic & Buddhistic Influences. Kishore Gandhi. 256p. 1980. text ed. write for info. (ISBN 0-391-02024-2). Humanities.

Aldrich Report on Men. Peggy Aldrich. 1977. pap. text ed. 1.95 (ISBN 0-505-51158-4, BT51158). Tower Bks.

Alec Forbes of Howglen, 1865. George MacDonald. Ed. by Robert L. Wolff. LC 75-1509. (Victorian Fiction Ser.). 1975. lib. bdg. 66.00 (ISBN 0-8240-1583-5). Garland Pub.

Alechinsky - Catalogue of the Prints 1946-1972: Les Estampes. 1977. pap. 59.95 (ISBN 0-8120-0955-X). Barron.

Alechinsky a la Ligne. 1977. pap. 21.95 (ISBN 0-8120-0956-8). Barron.

Aleck Maury, Sportsman: A Novel. Caroline Gordon. LC 80-14493. (Lost American Fiction Ser.). 312p. 1980. 12.95 (ISBN 0-8093-0972-6); pap. 6.95 (ISBN 0-8093-0988-2). S Ill U Pr.

Alef Bet Fun. Lillian Abramson & Jessie Robinson. (Illus.). (gr. 2-4). 1957. pap. 2.75x (ISBN 0-8197-0028-2). Bloch.

Alegebra; Beginning: Syllabus. 2nd ed. Al Gray. 1976. pap. text ed. 6.90 (ISBN 0-89420-033-X, 367015); cassette recordings 164.00 (ISBN 0-89420-125-5, 367007). Natl Book.

Alejandro Casona, Playwright. Harold K. Moon. (Charles E. Merrill Monograph Series in the Humanities & Social Sciences: Vol. 2, No. 1). 1970. pap. 1.50 o.p. (ISBN 0-8425-0216-5). Brigham.

Alejandro Obregon. Juan G. Ponce. (Illus.). 1970. pap. 2.00 (ISBN 0-913456-09-8). Interbk Inc.

Alekhine's Defence. R. G. Eales & A. H. Williams. 1973. 15.95 (ISBN 0-7134-0366-7, Pub. by Batsford England). David & Charles.

Aleksandr Blok: a Biography, Vol. I: The Distant Thunder, 1880-1908. Avril Pyman. (Illus.). 1979. 29.50x (ISBN 0-19-211714-9). Oxford U Pr.

Aleksandra Kollontai: Socialism, Feminism, & the Bolshevik Revolution. Beatrice Farnsworth. LC 79-67775. (Illus.). xii, 448p. 1980. 28.50x (ISBN 0-8047-1073-2). Stanford U Pr.

Aleph Solution. Sandor Frankel & Webster Mews. 1981. pap. 2.50 (ISBN 0-425-04654-0). Berkley Pub.

Alesandro Manzoni. Bernard Wall. 1954. 24.50 (ISBN 0-686-51343-6). Elliots Bks.

Alessandro Manzoni. Gian P. Barricelli. LC 76-16481. (World Authors Ser: No. 411). 1976. lib. bdg. 11.95 (ISBN 0-8057-6251-5). Twayne.

Alessandro Scarlatti: An Introduction to His Operas. Donald J. Grout. 1979. 14.00x (ISBN 0-520-03682-4). U of Cal Pr.

Aleut & Eskimo Art: Tradition & Innovation in South Alaska. Dorothy J. Ray. LC 79-56591. (Illus.). 224p. 1981. 29.95 (ISBN 0-295-95709-3). U of Wash Pr.

Aleut Bibliography. Dorothy M. Jones & John R. Wood. LC 74-620054. 192p. 1976. pap. 15.00 (ISBN 0-295-95529-5). U of Wash Pr.

Alex Comfort. Arthur E. Salmon. (English Authors Ser.: No. 237). 1978. lib. bdg. 12.50 (ISBN 0-8057-6708-8). Twayne.

Alex in Wonderland. Dave Schansberg. (Illus.). 64p. (Orig.). (gr. 1-6). 1980. pap. 3.95 (ISBN 0-89542-941-1). Ideals.

Alex in Wonderland. David Schansberg. (Illus.). 1980. 7.95g (ISBN 0-516-09201-4). Childrens.

Alexander. Harold Littledale. LC 64-10365. (Illus.). (gr. k-3). 1964. 5.95 o.s.i. (ISBN 0-8193-0086-1, Four Winds). Schol Bk Serv.

Alexander. Duncan Townson. Ed. by Margaret Killingray et al. (World History Ser.). (Illus.). 32p. (gr. 10). 1980. Repr. of 1977 ed. lib. bdg. 5.95 (ISBN 0-89908-039-1); pap. text ed. 1.95 (ISBN 0-89908-014-6). Greenhaven.

Alexander Alekhine. Alexander Kotov. 1975. 18.95 (ISBN 0-7134-2963-1, Pub. by Batsford England). David & Charles.

Alexander & the Greeks. Victor Ehrenberg. Tr. by Ruth Fraenkel Von Velson from Ger. LC 79-4913. 1981. Repr. of 1938 ed. 12.50 (ISBN 0-88355-963-3). Hyperion Conn.

Alexander Blok: An Anthology of Essays & Memoirs. Ed. by Lucy Vogel. 1981. 17.50 (ISBN 0-88233-487-5). Ardis Pubs.

Alexander Blok As Man & Poet. Kornei Chukovsky. Tr. by Burgin & O'Connor. 1981. 22.00 (ISBN 0-88233-491-3). Ardis Pubs.

Alexander Blok: Selected Poems. Ed. by Avril Pyman. LC 67-31506. 388p. 1972. text ed. 30.00 (ISBN 0-08-012185-3). Pergamon.

Alexander Botts: Great Stories from the Saturday Evening Post. LC 77-90937. 1977. 5.95 (ISBN 0-89387-011-0). Sat Eve Post.

Alexander Gumberg & Soviet-American Relations, 1917-1933. James K. Libbey. LC 77-73704. 248p. 1978. 17.00x (ISBN 0-8131-1361-X). U Pr of Ky.

Alexander Hamilton. Henry C. Lodge. LC 80-22082. (American Statesmen Ser.). 310p. 1981. pap. 4.95 (ISBN 0-87754-179-5). Chelsea Hse.

Alexander Hamilton: A Biography in His Own Words. Alexander Hamilton. Ed. by Mary-Jo Kline. LC 72-92140. (Founding Fathers Ser.). (Illus.). 416p. (YA) 1973. 15.00 o.s.i. (ISBN 0-06-012417-2, HarpT). Har-Row.

Alexander Hamilton: A Concise Biography. Broadus Mitchell. LC 75-16899. (Illus.). 384p. 1976. 17.95x (ISBN 0-19-501979-2). Oxford U Pr.

Alexander Hamilton & Aaron Burr. Anna Crouse & Russell Crouse. (Landmark Ser.: No. 85). 1963. PLB 5.99 (ISBN 0-394-90385-4, BYR). Random.

Alexander Harkin: Dealer in Dry Goods & Groceries. Jeffrey A. Hess. LC 77-23425. (Minnesota Historic Sites Pamphlet Ser.: No. 14). (Illus.). 1977. pap. 2.00 (ISBN 0-87351-115-8). Minn Hist.

Alexander Herzen & the Role of the Intellectual Revolutionary. E. Acton. LC 78-56747. 1979. 22.95 (ISBN 0-521-22166-8). Cambridge U Pr.

Alexander James Dallas, Lawyer-Politician-Financier. Raymond Walters. LC 75-86582. (American Scene Ser.). 1969. Repr. of 1943 ed. lib. bdg. 27.50 (ISBN 0-306-71814-6). Da Capo.

Alexander Kuprin. Nicholas J. Luker. (World Authors Ser.: No. 481). 1978. lib. bdg. 12.50 (ISBN 0-8057-6322-8). Twayne.

Alexander Pope. Donald B. Clark. (English Authors Ser.: No. 41). 1966. lib. bdg. 10.95 (ISBN 0-8057-1452-9). Twayne.

Alexander Pope. Y. Gooneratne. LC 76-4758. (British Authors Ser). 160p. 1976. 27.50 (ISBN 0-521-21127-1); pap. 7.95x (ISBN 0-521-29051-1). Cambridge U Pr.

Alexander Porter, Whig Planter of Old Louisiana. Wendell H. Stephenson. LC 69-19761. (American Scene Ser.). 1969. Repr. of 1934 ed. lib. bdg. 17.50 (ISBN 0-306-71254-7). Da Capo.

Alexander Pushkin. Walter N. Vickery. (World Authors Ser.: Russia: No. 82). lib. bdg. 9.95 (ISBN 0-8057-2726-4). Twayne.

Alexander Pushkin Symposium II. Ed. by Andrej Kodjak et al. (New York University Slavic Papers Ser.: Vol. III). (Illus.). 131p. (Orig.). 1980. pap. 8.95 (ISBN 0-89357-067-2). Slavica.

Alexander Ramsey & the Politics of Survival. Marx Swanholm. LC 77-23371. (Minnesota Historic Sites Pamphlet Ser.: No. 13). (Illus.). 1977. pap. 2.00 (ISBN 0-87351-114-X). Minn Hist.

Alexander Solzhenitsyn. Steven Allaback. 1979. pap. 2.50 (ISBN 0-446-71926-9). Warner Bks.

Alexander Solzhenitsyn. Andrej Kodjak. (Twayne's World Author Ser.: No. 479). 1978. lib. bdg. 9.95 (ISBN 0-8057-6320-1). Twayne.

Alexander Technique. Wilfred Barlow. 1980. pap. 4.95 (ISBN 0-446-97280-0). Warner Bks.

Alexander Technique: Joy in the Life of Your Body. Judith Stransky & Robert B. Stone. LC 80-26380. (Illus.). 224p. 1981. 14.95 (ISBN 0-8253-0000-2). Beaufort Bks NY.

Alexander, the Great. (MacDonald Educational Ser.). (Illus., Arabic.). 3.50 (ISBN 0-686-53096-9). Intl Bk Ctr.

Alexander the Great, 2 vols. W. W. Tarn. LC 78-74533. (Illus.). 1979. Vol. 1. 23.50 (ISBN 0-521-22584-1); Vol. 1. pap. 6.95x (ISBN 0-521-29563-7); Vol. 2. 48.00 (ISBN 0-521-22585-X). Cambridge U Pr.

Alexander the Great. Ulrich Wilcken. Ed. by Eugene N. Borza. Tr. by G. C. Richards. 1967. pap. 7.95 (ISBN 0-393-00381-7, Norton Lib). Norton.

Alexander the Great & the Greeks: The Epigraphic Evidence. A. J. Heisserer. LC 79-6712. (Illus.). 350p. 1980. 29.95x (ISBN 0-8061-1612-9). U of Okla Pr.

Alexander the Great & the Logistics of the Macedonian Army. Donald W. Engels. LC 76-52025. 1978. 18.00x (ISBN 0-520-03433-3); pap. 4.95 (ISBN 0-520-04272-7, CAL 472). U of Cal Pr.

Alexander the Great: King, Commander, & Statesman. Nicholas G. Hammond. LC 80-18573. (Illus.). 358p. 1981. 24.00 (ISBN 0-8155-5058-8). Noyes.

Alexander, Who Used to Be Rich, Last Sunday. Judith Viorst. 1980. pap. 1.95 (ISBN 0-689-70476-3, Aladdin). Atheneum.

Alexander Woollcott. Wayne Chatterton. (United States Authors Ser.: No. 305). 1978. lib. bdg. 12.50 (ISBN 0-8057-7210-3). Twayne.

Alexander's Bridge. Willa Cather. LC 76-56439. 1977. pap. 3.95 (ISBN 0-8032-5863-1, BB 635, Bison). U of Nebr Pr.

Alexander's Care of the Patient in Surgery. 6th ed. Marie J. Rhodes & Barbara J. Gruendemann. LC 77-26054. (Illus.). 1978. text ed. 29.95 (ISBN 0-8016-0431-1). Mosby.

Alexander's Gate, Gog & Magog & the Inclosed Nations. Andrew R. Anderson. 1932. 7.50 o.p. (ISBN 0-910956-07-3). Medieval.

Alexandra Kollontai: The Lonely Struggle of the Woman Who Defied Lenin. Cathy Porter. (Illus.). 553p. 1980. 14.95 (ISBN 0-8037-0129-2). Dial.

Alexandre Dumas, Pere. Richard S. Stowe. (World Authors Ser.: No. 388). 1976. lib. bdg. 9.95 (ISBN 0-8057-6230-2). Twayne.

Alexandre Dumas: The King of Romance. F. W. Hemmings. (Illus.). 1980. 12.95 (ISBN 0-684-16391-8, ScribT). Scribner.

Alexandre-Gabriel Decamps (1803-1860, 2 vols. Dewey F. Mosby. LC 76-23651. (Outstanding Dissertations in the Fine Arts - 2nd Series - 19th Century). (Illus.). 1977. Repr. of 1973 ed. Set. lib. bdg. 128.00 (ISBN 0-8240-2714-0). Garland Pub.

Alexandria: A History & a Guide. new ed. E. M. Forster. LC 74-78549. 243p. 1974. 11.95 (ISBN 0-87951-023-4). Overlook Pr.

Alexandria Quartet. Lawrence Durrell. Incl. Justine; Balthazar; Mountolive; Clea. 1961. Set. pap. 15.95 (ISBN 0-525-47795-0). Dutton.

Alexandria, the Ambivalent. Kathryn Kimbrough. (Saga of the Phenwick Women Ser.: No. 36). 256p. 1981. pap. 2.25 (ISBN 0-445-04655-4). Popular Lib.

Alexis Lichine's New Encyclopedia of Wines & Spirits. 3rd ed. Alexis Lichine. LC 80-22385. (Illus.). 736p. 1981. 29.95 (ISBN 0-394-51781-4). Knopf.

Alexi's Secret Mission. Anita Deyneka. LC 74-29466. (Illus.). 128p. (Orig.). (gr. 3-7). 1975. pap. 1.95 (ISBN 0-912692-58-8). Cook.

Alex's Bed. Mary Dickinson. (Illus.). (ps-1). 1980. 7.95 (ISBN 0-233-97207-2). Andre Deutsch.

Alexsandr Solzhenitsyn. John B. Dunlop et al. 1975. pap. 5.95 o.s.i. (ISBN 0-02-050550-7, Collier). Macmillan.

Alfonso Martinez De Toledo. E. Michael Gerli. LC 76-4556. (World Authors Ser: No. 398). 1976. lib. bdg. 12.50 (ISBN 0-8057-9239-2). Twayne.

Alfonso Reyes y la Literatural Espanola. Jorge Luis Morales. (Mante y Palabra Ser.). 193p. (Span.). 1980. 6.25 (ISBN 0-8477-0558-7); pap. 5.00 (ISBN 0-8477-0559-5). U of PR Pr.

Alfonso X of Castile, Patron of Literature & Learning. Evelyn S. Procter. LC 80-10508. (Norman Macoll Lectures: 1949). vi, 149p. 1980. Repr. of 1951 ed. lib. bdg. 19.50x (ISBN 0-313-22347-5, PRAL). Greenwood.

Alford Waters. Emanuel Skolnick. LC 80-17192. (Story of an American Indian Ser.). (Illus.). 64p. (gr. 5 up). 1980. PLB 6.95 (ISBN 0-87518-201-1). Dillon.

Alford's Greek Testament, 4 vols. Henry A. Alford. 1980. Repr. 75.00 (ISBN 0-8010-0158-7). Baker Bk.

Alfred Adler: The Man & His Work. Hertha Ogler. 1972. pap. 1.75 o.p. (ISBN 0-451-61165-9, ME1165, Ment). NAL.

Alfred Bester. Carolyn Wendell. (Starmont Reader's Guide: No. 6). 80p. 1981. Repr. lib. bdg. 9.95x (ISBN 0-89370-037-1). Borgo Pr.

Alfred Doblin. Wolfgang Kort. LC 73-16222. (World Author Ser.: Germany: No. 290). 1974. lib. bdg. 10.95 (ISBN 0-8057-2266-1). Twayne.

Alfred G. Graebner Memorial High School Handbook of Rules & Regulations: A Novel. Ellen Conford. (YA) (gr. 7-9). 1977. pap. 1.75 (ISBN 0-671-56043-3). PB.

Alfred Goes House Hunting. Bill Binzen. LC 73-81425. 32p. (gr. 1-4). 1974. 5.95a o.p. (ISBN 0-385-04820-3); PLB (ISBN 0-385-08223-1). Doubleday.

Alfred Hitchcock & the Three Investigators in the Mystery of the Moaning Cave. William Arden. Ed. by Alfred Hitchcock. LC 68-23677. (Three Investigators Ser.: No. 10). (Illus.). (gr. 4-7). 1968. 2.95 (ISBN 0-394-81423-1, BYR); PLB 5.39 (ISBN 0-394-91423-6); pap. 1.95 (ISBN 0-394-83773-8). Random.

Alfred Hitchcock & the Three Investigators in the Mystery of the Shrinking House. William Arden. Ed. by Alfred Hitchcock. (Three Investigators Ser.: No. 18). (Illus.). (gr. 4-7). 1972. 2.95 (ISBN 0-394-82482-2, BYR); PLB 5.39 (ISBN 0-394-92482-7); pap. 1.95 (ISBN 0-394-83777-0). Random.

Alfred Hitchcock & the Three Investigators in the Mystery of the Deadly Double. William Arden. LC 78-55960. (Illus.). (gr. 4-7). 1978. 2.95 (ISBN 0-394-83902-1, BYR); PLB 5.39 (ISBN 0-394-93902-6); pap. 1.95 (ISBN 0-394-84491-2). Random.

Alfred Hitchcock & the Three Investigators in the Mystery of the Dead Man's Riddle. William Arden. LC 74-4934. (Three Investigators Ser.). (Illus.). 160p. (gr. 4-7). 1974. 2.95 (ISBN 0-394-82927-1, BYR); PLB 5.39 (ISBN 0-394-92927-6); pap. 1.95 (ISBN 0-394-84451-3). Random.

Alfred Hitchcock & the Three Investigators in the Mystery of the Dancing Devil. William Arden. LC 76-8134. (Illus.). (gr. 4-7). 1976. 2.95 (ISBN 0-394-83289-2, BYR); PLB 5.39 (ISBN 0-394-93289-7). Random.

Alfred Hitchcock & the Three Investigators in the Mystery of the Fiery Eye. Robert Arthur. LC 77-28860. (Three Investigators Ser.: No. 7). (Illus.). (gr. 4-8). 1967. 2.95 (ISBN 0-394-81661-7, BYR); PLB 5.39 (ISBN 0-394-91661-1); pap. 1.95 (ISBN 0-394-83770-3). Random.

Alfred Hitchcock & the Three Investigators in the Mystery of the Green Ghost. Robert Arthur. Ed. by Alfred Hitchcock. (Three Investigators Ser.: No. 4). (Illus.). (gr. 4-8). 1965. 2.95 (ISBN 0-394-81228-X, BYR); PLB 5.39 (ISBN 0-394-91228-4); pap. 1.95 (ISBN 0-394-84258-8). Random.

Alfred Hitchcock & the Three Investigators in the Mystery of the Silver Spider. Robert Arthur. (Three Investigators Ser.: No. 8). (Illus.). (gr. 4-8). 1967. 2.95 (ISBN 0-394-81663-3, BYR); PLB 5.39 (ISBN 0-394-91663-8); pap. 1.95 (ISBN 0-394-83771-1). Random.

Alfred Hitchcock & the Three Investigators in the Mystery of the Screaming Clock. Robert Arthur. Ed. by Alfred Hitchcock. LC 68-23676. (Three Investigators Ser.: No. 9). (Illus.). (gr. 4-7). 1968. 2.95 (ISBN 0-394-81288-3, BYR); PLB 5.39 (ISBN 0-394-91288-8); pap. 1.95 (ISBN 0-394-83772-X). Random.

Alfred Hitchcock & the Three Investigators in the Mystery of the Stuttering Parrot. Robert Arthur. Ed. by Alfred Hitchcock. (Three Investigators Ser.: No. 1). (Illus.). (gr. 4-8). 1964. 2.95 (ISBN 0-394-81243-3, BYR); PLB 5.39 (ISBN 0-394-91243-8); pap. 1.95 (ISBN 0-394-83767-3). Random.

Alfred Hitchcock & the Three Investigators in the Mystery of the Talking Skull. Robert Arthur. Ed. by Alfred Hitchcock. LC 69-20274. (Three Investigators Ser.: No. 11). (Illus.). (gr. 4-7). 1969. 2.95 (ISBN 0-394-81380-4, BYR); PLB 5.39 (ISBN 0-394-91380-9); pap. 1.95 (ISBN 0-394-83774-6). Random.

Alfred Hitchcock & the Three Investigators in the Mystery of the Vanishing Treasure. Robert Arthur. Ed. by Alfred Hitchcock. (Three Investigators Ser.: No. 5). (Illus.). (gr. 4-8). 1966. 2.95 (ISBN 0-394-81550-5, BYR); PLB 5.39 (ISBN 0-394-91550-X); pap. 1.95 (ISBN 0-394-84452-1). Random.

Alfred Hitchcock & the Three Investigators in the Mystery of the Whispering Mummy. Robert Arthur. Ed. by Alfred Hitchcock. (Three Investigators Ser.: No. 3). (Illus.). (gr. 4-8). 1965. 2.95 (ISBN 0-394-81220-4, BYR); PLB 5.39 (ISBN 0-394-91220-9); pap. 1.95 (ISBN 0-394-83768-1). Random.

Alfred Hitchcock & the Three Investigators in the Mystery of the Flaming Footprints. M. V. Carey. Ed. by Alfred Hitchcock. (Three Investigators Ser.: No. 15). (Illus.). (gr. 4-7). 1971. 2.95 (ISBN 0-394-82296-X, BYR); PLB 5.39 (ISBN 0-394-92296-4); pap. 1.95 (ISBN 0-394-83776-2). Random.

Alfred Hitchcock & the Three Investigators in the Mystery of the Magic Circle. M. V. Carey. LC 78-55915. (Alfred Hitchcock & the Three Investigators Ser.: No. 27). (Illus.). (gr. 4-7). 1978. 2.95 (ISBN 0-394-83607-3, BYR); PLB 5.39 (ISBN 0-394-93607-8); pap. 1.95 (ISBN 0-394-84490-4). Random.

Alfred Hitchcock & the Three Investigators in the Mystery of Monster Mountain. M. V. Carey. Ed. by Alfred Hitchcock. (Three Investigators Ser.: No. 20). (Illus.). (gr. 4-7). 1973. 2.95 (ISBN 0-394-82664-7, BYR); PLB 5.39 (ISBN 0-394-92664-1); pap. 1.95 (ISBN 0-394-84259-6). Random.

Alfred Hitchcock & the Three Investigators in the Mystery of the Invisible Dog. M. V. Carey. LC 75-8073. (Three Investigators Ser.: No. 23). (Illus.). 160p. (gr. 4-7). 1975. 2.95 (ISBN 0-394-83105-5, BYR); PLB 5.39 (ISBN 0-394-93105-X); pap. 1.95 (ISBN 0-394-84492-0). Random.

Alfred Hitchcock & the Three Investigators in the Mystery of Death Trap Mine. M. V. Carey. LC 76-8135. (Illus.). (gr. 4-7). 1976. 2.95 (ISBN 0-394-83321-X, BYR); PLB 5.39 (ISBN 0-394-93321-4); pap. 1.95 (ISBN 0-394-84449-1). Random.

Alfred Hitchcock & the Three Investigators in the Mystery of the Laughing Shadow. Ed. by Alfred Hitchcock. (Three Investigators Ser.: No. 12). (Illus.). (gr. 4-7). 1969. 2.95 (ISBN 0-394-81492-4, BYR); PLB 5.39 (ISBN 0-394-91492-9); pap. 1.95 (ISBN 0-394-83775-4). Random.

Alfred Hitchcock & the Three Investigators in the Mystery of the Coughing Dragon. Nick West. LC 74-117549. (Three Investigator's Ser: No. 14). (Illus.). (gr. 4-7). 1970. 2.95 (ISBN 0-394-81411-8, BYR); PLB 5.39 (ISBN 0-394-91411-2). Random.

Alfred Hitchcock & the Three Investigators in the Secret of Phantom Lake. William Arden. Ed. by Alfred Hitchcock. (Three Investigators Ser.: No. 19). (Illus.). (gr. 4-7). 1973. 2.95 (ISBN 0-394-82651-5, BYR); PLB 5.39 (ISBN 0-394-92651-X); pap. 1.95 (ISBN 0-394-84257-X). Random.

Alfred Hitchcock & the Three Investigators in the Secret of Skeleton Island. Robert Arthur. Ed. by Alfred Hitchcock. (Three Investigators Ser.: No. 6). (Illus.). (gr. 4-9). 1966. 2.95 (ISBN 0-394-81552-1, BYR); PLB 5.39 (ISBN 0-394-91552-6); pap. 1.95 (ISBN 0-394-83769-X). Random.

Alfred Hitchcock & the Three Investigators in the Secret of Terror Castle. Robert Arthur. Ed. by Alfred Hitchcock. (Three Investigators Ser.: No. 2). (Illus.). (gr. 4-8). 1964. 2.95 (ISBN 0-394-81241-7, BYR); PLB 5.39 (ISBN 0-394-91241-1); pap. 1.95 (ISBN 0-394-83766-5). Random.

Alfred Hitchcock & the Three Investigators in the Secret of the Haunted Mirror. M. V. Carey. LC 74-5750. (Alfred Hitchcock & the Three Investigators). (Illus.). 160p. (gr. 4-7). 1974. 2.95 (ISBN 0-394-82820-8, BYR); PLB 5.39 (ISBN 0-394-92820-2); pap. 1.95 (ISBN 0-394-84450-5). Random.

Alfred Hitchcock & the Three Investigators, 4 bks. Illus. by Harry Kane. Incl. Mystery of the Fiery Eye. Robert Arthur. LC 77-28860; Mystery of the Moaning Cave. William Arden. LC 77-28731; Mystery of the Silver Spider. Robert Arthur. LC 77-19355; Secret of Terror Castle. Robert Arthur. LC 77-29129. (gr. 4-7). 1978. Boxed Set. pap. 6.00 (ISBN 0-394-84005-4, BYR). Random.

Alfred Hitchcock Presents Scream Along with Me. Ed. by Alfred Hitchcock. 1977. pap. 1.25 o.s.i. (ISBN 0-440-13633-4). Dell.

Alfred Hitchcock Presents: Sixteen Skeletons from My Closet. Alfred Hitchcock. 1976. pap. 1.25 o.s.i. (ISBN 0-440-18011-2). Dell.

Alfred Hitchcock Presents Slay Ride. Alfred Hitchcock. 1977. pap. 1.50 o.s.i. (ISBN 0-440-13641-5). Dell.

Alfred Hitchcock Presents: The Master's Choice. Ed. by Alfred Hitchcock. 1979. 10.00 (ISBN 0-394-50419-4, BYR). Random.

Alfred Hitchcock's Monster Museum. Ed. by Alfred Hitchcock. (gr. 6-11). 1965. 4.95 (ISBN 0-394-81230-1, BYR); PLB 6.99 (ISBN 0-394-91230-6). Random.

Alfred Hitchcock's Solve-Them-Yourself Mysteries. Ed. by Alfred Hitchcock. (Illus.). (gr. 6-9). 1963. 5.95 (ISBN 0-394-81242-5, BYR); PLB 6.99 (ISBN 0-394-91242-X). Random.

Alfred Hitchcock's Spellbinders in Suspense. Alfred Hitchcock. (Illus.). (gr. 7-11). 1967. 4.95 o.s.i. (ISBN 0-394-81665-X, BYR); PLB 6.99 o.s.i. (ISBN 0-394-91665-4). Random.

Alfred Hitchcock's Tales to Be Read with Caution. 1979. 9.95 (ISBN 0-8037-0343-0). Davis Pubns.

Alfred Hitchcock's Tales to Fill You with Fear & Trembling. Ed. by Eleanor Sullivan. 350p. 1980. 9.95 (ISBN 0-8037-0392-9). Dial.

Alfred Hitchcock's Tales to Make Your Hair Stand on End. Ed. by Eleanor Sullivan. 348p. 1981. 10.95 (ISBN 0-8037-0028-8). Davis Pubns.

Alfred Hitchcock's Tales to Make Your Teeth Chatter. Ed. by Eleanor Sullivan. 348p. 1980. 9.95 (ISBN 0-8037-0173-X). Davis Pubns.

Alfred Jarry: Nihilism & the Theatre of the Absurd. Maurice M. LaBelle. LC 79-3009. (Gotham Library). 1980. 15.00x (ISBN 0-8147-4995-X); pap. 7.00x (ISBN 0-8147-4996-8). NYU Pr.

Alfred Jensen: Paintings & Diagrams from the Years 1957-1977. Ed. by Karen L. Spaulding. LC 77-83756. (Illus.). 1978. pap. 12.00 (ISBN 0-914782-15-0, Pub. by Albright-Knox Art Gallery). C E Tuttle.

Alfred Kroeber. Julian Steward. LC 72-8973. (Leaders of Modern Anthropology Ser.). 225p. 1973. 15.00x (ISBN 0-231-03489-X); pap. 4.00x (ISBN 0-231-03490-3). Columbia U Pr.

Alfred Kroeber: A Personal Configuration. Theodora Kroeber. LC 71-94983. (Illus.). 1970. 14.50 (ISBN 0-520-01598-3); pap. 4.95 (ISBN 0-520-03720-0). U of Cal Pr.

Alfred North Whitehead's Early Philosophy of Space & Time. Janet A. Fitzgerald. LC 79-63849. (Illus.). 1979. 9.50 (ISBN 0-8191-0747-6). U Pr of Amer.

Alfred Steiglitz, Photographer. Doris Bry. 1974. 15.00 (ISBN 0-87846-035-7); pap. 5.00 (ISBN 0-87846-147-7). Mus Fine Arts Boston.

Alfred Stieglitz & the American Avant-Garde. William I. Homer. LC 76-50068. (Illus.). 1977. 17.50 (ISBN 0-8212-0676-1, 031917); pap. 9.95 o.p. (ISBN 0-8212-0755-5). NYGS.

Alfred Stieglitz Talking: Notes on Some of His Conversations, 1925-1931 with a Foreward. Ed. by Herbert J. Seligmann. 161p. 1981. text ed. 15.00x (ISBN 0-300-03510-1, 66-20942). Yale U Pr.

Alfred Tennyson. James Kissane. (English Authors Ser.: No. 110). lib. bdg. 9.95 (ISBN 0-8057-1544-4). Twayne.

Alfred, the Little Bear. Bill Binzen. LC 78-99465. (gr. 1-3). 1970. PLB 5.95 (ISBN 0-385-08967-8). Doubleday.

Alfred V. Kidder. Richard B. Woodbury. LC 72-10082. (Leaders of Modern Anthropology Ser.). 225p. 1973. 15.00x (ISBN 0-231-03484-9); pap. 5.00x (ISBN 0-231-03485-7). Columbia U Pr.

Alfred Waterhouse & the Natural History Museum. Mark Girouard. LC 80-53742. (Illus.). 1981. 12.95x (ISBN 0-300-02578-5). Yale U Pr.

Alfred William Pollard: A Selection of His Essays. Compiled by Fred W. Roper. LC 76-25547. (Great Bibliographers Ser.: No. 2). 252p. 1976. 12.00 (ISBN 0-8108-0958-3). Scarecrow.

Alfred's Alphabet Antics. Elizabeth Gregory. (Illus.). 1981. 6.95 (ISBN 0-933184-07-7); pap. 4.95 (ISBN 0-933184-08-5). Flame Intl.

Algae. 2nd ed. V. J. Chapman & D. J. Chapman. 500p. 1975. 19.95 (ISBN 0-312-01715-4). St Martin.

Algae of the Western Great Lakes Area. G. W. Prescott. 1962. text ed. 24.95x o.p. (ISBN 0-697-04552-8). Wm C Brown.

Algae: The Grass of Many Waters. 2nd ed. Lewis H. Tiffany. (Illus.). 216p. 1968. 11.75 (ISBN 0-398-01926-6). C C Thomas.

Algal Assays & Monitoring Eutrophication. Ed. by P. Marvan et al. (Illus.). 253p. (Orig.). 1979. pap. 35.00x (ISBN 3-510-65091-3). Intl Pubns Serv.

Algal Cultures & Phytoplankton Ecology. 2nd ed. G. E. Fogg. LC 74-27308. 144p. 1975. 15.00 (ISBN 0-299-06760-2). U of Wis Pr.

Algebra, 2 vols. P. M. Cohn. LC 73-2780. Vol. 1, 1974, 384p. 34.25 (ISBN 0-471-16430-5, Pub. by Wiley-Interscience); Vol. 2, 1977. 29.95 (ISBN 0-471-01823-6); Vol. 1. pap. 15.95 (ISBN 0-471-16431-3). Wiley.

Algebra. Harley Flanders & Justin J. Price. 1975. text ed. 15.95 (ISBN 0-12-259666-8); instr.s' manual 3.00 (ISBN 0-12-259669-2). Acad Pr.

Algebra. Serge A. Lang. 1965. 23.95 (ISBN 0-201-04177-4). A-W.

Algebra. Florence Lovaglia. (Span.). 1974. pap. 7.40 (ISBN 0-06-315513-3, IntlDept). Har-Row.

Algebra. rev. ed. Gerald E. Moore. 1970. pap. 3.95 (ISBN 0-06-460038-6, CO 38, COS). Har-Row.

Algebra. Kaj L. Nielsen & Charlotte M. Gemmel. LC 69-18677. (Rapid Reviews Ser.). pap. text ed. 3.95 (ISBN 0-8220-1760-1). Cliffs.

Algebra, Vol. 1. L. Redei. 1966. 72.00 (ISBN 0-08-010954-3). Pergamon.

Algebra: A First Course. John Baley et al. 432p. 1979. pap. text ed. 15.95x (ISBN 0-534-00727-9). Wadsworth Pub.

Algebra: A Modern Approach. Kaj L. Nielsen. LC 68-26403. (Illus., Orig.). 1969. pap. 4.50 (ISBN 0-06-460064-5, CO 64, COS). Har-Row.

Algebra, a Modern Introduction, 12 vols. Mervin L. Keedy & Marvin L. Bittinger. **Incl. Whole Numbers, Addition & Subtraction. 2.68 o.p. (ISBN 0-201-03635-5); Whole Numbers, Multiplication & Division. 2.68 o.p. (ISBN 0-201-03636-3); Operations of the Numbers of Arthmetic. 2.68 o.p. (ISBN 0-201-03637-1); Decimals & Percent. 2.68 o.p. (ISBN 0-201-03638-X); Measures, Ratio & Averages. 2.68 o.p. (ISBN 0-201-03639-8); The Numbers of Ordinary Arithmetic & Algebra. 2.68 o.p. (ISBN 0-201-03640-1); Rational Numbers, Albegra & Solving Equations. 2.68 o.p. (ISBN 0-201-03641-X); Polynomials. 2.68 o.p. (ISBN 0-201-03642-8); Functions & Basic Geometry. 2.68 o.p. (ISBN 0-201-03643-6); Linear Equations & Systems of Equations. 2.68 o.p. (ISBN 0-201-03644-4); Polynomials in Several Variables & Fractional Equations. 1.60 o.p. (ISBN 0-201-03645-2); Roots, Radicals & Quadratic Equations. 2.68 o.p. (ISBN 0-201-03646-0); tchrs' manual 4.04 o.p. (ISBN 0-201-03647-9). 1976. tchr's manual 4.04 o.p. (ISBN 0-201-03647-9).** A-W.

Algebra: An Incremental Approach, Vol. I. John H. Saxon, Jr. (Illus.). 1980. pap. 15.95 ref. (ISBN 0-13-021600-3). P-H.

Algebra: An Introductory Course. Morris Bramson. (gr. 9 up). 1978. wkbk 7.25 (ISBN 0-87720-240-0). AMSCO Sch.

Algebra & Calculus for Business. Thomas Dyckman & L. Joseph Thomas. (Illus.). 464p. 1974. text ed. 18.95 (ISBN 0-13-021758-1). P-H.

Algebra & Geometry for Teachers. Charles Brumfiel & Irvin Vance. LC 70-93983. (Mathematics Ser). 1970. text ed. 16.95 (ISBN 0-201-00667-7); instr's manual 1.25 (ISBN 0-201-00668-5). A-W.

Algebra & Its Applications: A Problem Solving Approach. Clifford W. Sloyer. LC 72-10087. 1970. text ed. 11.95 (ISBN 0-201-07041-3). A-W.

Algebra & Triginometry: A Precalculus Approach. Max A. Sobel & Norbert Lerner. (Illus.). 1979. ref. ed. 17.95 (ISBN 0-13-021709-3). P-H.

Algebra & Trigonometry. Harley Flanders & Justin J. Price. 1975. text ed. 17.95 (ISBN 0-12-259665-X); tchr's manual 3.00 (ISBN 0-12-259668-4). Acad Pr.

Algebra & Trigonometry. Walter Fleming & Dale Varberg. (Illus.). 1980. text ed. 18.95 (ISBN 0-13-021824-3); study guide 6.95 (ISBN 0-13-021881-2). P-H.

Algebra & Trigonometry. 2nd ed. Margaret L. Lial & Charles D. Miller. 1980. text ed. 18.95x (ISBN 0-673-15272-3). Scott F.

Algebra & Trigonometry. Arnold J. Steffensen & L. M. Johnson. 1980. pap. text ed. 16.95 (ISBN 0-673-15371-1). Scott F.

Algebra & Trigonometry: A Functions Approach. 2nd ed. Mervin L. Keedy & Marvin L. Bittinger. LC 77-79461. (Illus.). 1978. pap. text ed. 16.95 (ISBN 0-201-03870-6); instructor's manual 5.95 (ISBN 0-201-03871-4); test booklet with answers 3.00 (ISBN 0-201-03872-2); dianostic test 0.35 (ISBN 0-201-03749-1). A-W.

Algebra & Trigonometry: A Skills Approach. Nanney & Cable. 600p. 1980. text ed. 17.80 (ISBN 0-205-06917-7, 5669170); study guide avail. (ISBN 0-205-06919-3, 5669197). Allyn.

Algebra & Trigonometry: A Straightforward Approach. Martin M. Zuckerman. 1980. text ed. 15.95x (ISBN 0-393-95020-4); wkbk. 4.95x (ISBN 0-393-95037-9); instr's manual avail. (ISBN 0-393-95046-8). Norton.

Algebra & Trigonometry for College Students. Nancy Myers. 650p. 1980. pap. text ed. 16.95 (ISBN 0-442-25758-9); instr's. manual avail. (ISBN 0-442-25701-5). Van Nos Reinhold.

Algebra & Trigonometry: For College Students. Richard S. Paul & Ernest F. Haeusler, Jr. (Illus.). 1978. ref. 17.95 (ISBN 0-87909-031-6); instructor's manual free. Reston.

Algebra & Trigonometry Refresher for Calculus Students. Loren C. Larson. LC 79-20633. (Mathematical Sciences Ser.). (Illus.). 1979. pap. 6.95x (ISBN 0-7167-1110-9). W H Freeman.

Algebra & Trigonometry with Analytic Geometry. Arthur B. Simon. LC 78-23409. (Mathematical Sciences Ser.). (Illus.). 1979. text ed. 18.95x (ISBN 0-7167-1016-1); solutions manual avail. W H Freeman.

Algebra & Trigonometry with Calculators. Marshall Hestenes & Richard Hill. (Illus.). 512p. 1981. text ed. 17.95 (ISBN 0-13-021857-X). P-H.

Algebra der Logik, 5 vols. in 3. 2nd ed. Ernst Schroeder. LC 63-11315. 2192p. (Ger.). 1980. Set. 75.00 (ISBN 0-8284-0171-3). Chelsea Pub.

Algebra for College Students. Bernard Kolman & Arnold Shapiro. 1980. text ed. 17.95 (ISBN 0-12-417880-4); instr's manual 3.00 (ISBN 0-12-417885-5). Acad Pr.

Algebra for College Students. Nancy Myers. 446p. 1979. pap. text ed. 13.95 (ISBN 0-442-25625-6). Van Nos Reinhold.

Algebra for College Students: An Intermediate Approach. 2nd ed. Max A. Sobol & Norbert Lerner. 1980. text ed. 16.95 (ISBN 0-13-021584-8). P-H.

Algebra for the Trades: A Guided Approach. Robert A. Carman. 1980. pap. text ed. write for info. (ISBN 0-471-05966-8). Wiley.

Algebra: Groups, Rings, & Other Topics. McCoy & Berger. 1977. text ed. 23.05 (ISBN 0-205-05699-7). Allyn.

Algebra I. Isidore Dressler. (gr. 9). 1966. text ed. 10.67 (ISBN 0-87720-208-7). AMSCO Sch.

Algebra I: Rings, Modules & Categories. C. Faith. (Grundlehren der Mathematischen Wissenschaften Ser.: Vol. 190). 610p. 1981. 48.00 (ISBN 0-387-05551-7). Springer-Verlag.

Algebra II - Trigonometry: Final Preliminary Edition. Sherman K. Stein & Calvin D. Crabill. (Illus.). (gr. 11-12). 1976. text ed. 11.95x (ISBN 0-7167-0469-2); solutions key avail. (ISBN 0-685-65024-3). W H Freeman.

Algebra, Number Theory, & Their Applications. Ed. by A. N. Andrianov et al. (Trudy Steklov: No. 148). Date not set. 88.00 (ISBN 0-8218-3046-5). Am Math.

Algebra of Abu Kamil, in a Commentary by Mordecai Finzi. Abukamil Shuja Ibn Aslam. Tr. by Martin Levey. (Publications in Medieval Science No. 10). 1966. 24.50x (ISBN 0-299-03800-9). U of Wis Pr.

Algebra of Invariants. John A. Grace & Alfred Young. LC 65-11860. 1965. 13.95. Chelsea Pub.

Algebra of Quantics. 2nd ed. Edwin B. Elliott. LC 63-11320. 11.95 (ISBN 0-8284-0184-5). Chelsea Pub.

Algebra of Random Variables. Melvin D. Springer. LC 78-9315. (Wiley Ser. in Probability & Mathematical Statistics: Applied Section). 1979. 32.95 (ISBN 0-471-01406-0, Pub. by Wiley-Interscience). Wiley.

Algebra One: A Two Part Course. Richard Johnson et al. (gr. 9-12). 1977. First Book. text ed. 12.56 (ISBN 0-201-14300-3, Sch Div); Second Book. text ed. 12.56 (ISBN 0-201-14302-X); Course A. tchr's guide 16.32 (ISBN 0-201-14301-1); Course B. tchr's guide 16.32 (ISBN 0-201-14303-8). A-W.

Algebra One Review Guide. Isidore Dressler. (Illus., Orig.). (gr. 9). 1966. pap. text ed. 5.00 (ISBN 0-87720-207-9). AMSCO Sch.

Algebra, Part One: Elements of Mathematics. Nicholas Bourbaki. (Chapters 1-3). 1973. 57.50 (ISBN 0-201-00639-1, Adv Bk Prog). A-W.

Algebra Programmed, Pt. 2. 2nd ed. Robert H. Alwin & Robert D. Hackworth. (Illus.). 1978. pap. text ed. 10.95 (ISBN 0-13-022020-5). P-H.

Algebra Programmed, Pt. 4. Robert H. Alwin & R. Hackworth. LC 73-76042. (Illus.). 1971. pap. 9.50 (ISBN 0-13-022178-3). P-H.

Algebra Programmed, Pt. 1. 2nd ed. Robert H. Alwin & Robert D. Hackworth. (Illus.). 1978. pap. text ed. 10.95 (ISBN 0-13-022038-8). P-H.

Algebra Review. Charles Denlinger & Elaine Denlinger. 116p. 1978. pap. text ed. 2.50 (ISBN 0-12-059568-0). Acad Pr.

Algebra Text: Elementary. Robert H. Alwin et al. (Illus.). 424p. 1974. pap. 15.95x ref. ed. (ISBN 0-13-022293-3). P-H.

Algebra Text: Intermediate. Robert H. Alwin et al. (Illus.). 1974. pap. 15.95 ref. ed. (ISBN 0-13-022400-6). P-H.

Algebra Two & Trigonometry: A Modern Integrated Course. Isidore Dressler & Barnett Rich. (gr. 11-12). 1972. text ed. 12.50 (ISBN 0-87720-221-4); pap. text ed. 7.53 (ISBN 0-87720-220-6). AMSCO Sch.

Algebra Two, Ring Theory. C. Faith. LC 72-96724. (Grundlehren der Mathematischen Wissenschaften: Vol. 191). 1976. 49.80 o.p. (ISBN 0-387-05705-6). Springer-Verlag.

Algebraic & Analytic Aspects of Operator Algebras. Irving Kaplansky. LC 74-145635. (CBMS Regional Comference Series in Mathematics: Vol. 1). 1980. Repr. of 1970 ed. 6.40 (ISBN 0-8218-1650-0, CBMS-1). Am Math.

Algebraic & Arithmetic Structures: A Concrete Approach for Elementary School Teachers. Max S. Bell et al. LC 75-2807. (Illus.). 1976. text ed. 16.95 (ISBN 0-02-902270-3). Free Pr.

Algebraic & Geometric Topology, 2 pts. Ed. by R. J. Milgram. LC 78-14304. (Proceedings of Symposia in Pure Mathematics: Vol. 32). 1980. Repr. of 1978 ed. Set. 34.00 (ISBN 0-8218-1432-X, PSPUM 32.1); 20.00 (32.2); 20.00 (ISBN 0-8218-1433-8). Am Math.

Algebraic Cobordism & K-Theory. V. P. Snaith. LC 79-17981. (Memoirs Ser.: No. 221). 1979. 7.60 (ISBN 0-8218-2221-7). Am Math.

Algebraic Eigenvalue Problem. James H. Wilkinson. (Monographs on Numerical Analysis Ser). 1965. 79.00x (ISBN 0-19-853403-5). Oxford U Pr.

Algebraic Extensions of Fields. 2nd ed. Paul J. McCarthy LC 75-41499. ix, 166p. 1976. 9.50 (ISBN 0-8284-1284-7). Chelsea Pub.

Algebraic Geometry-Arcata 1974: Proceedings, Vol. 29. Symposia in Pure Mathematics, Humboldt State University, Arcata, Calif., July 29-August 16, 1974. Ed. by Robin Hartstone. LC 75-9530. 1979. Repr. of 1979 ed. with corrections 32.40 (ISBN 0-8218-1429-X, PSPUM-29). Am Math.

Algebraic Graph Theory. N. L. Biggs. LC 73-86042. (Tracts in Mathematics Ser.: No. 67). (Illus.). 180p. 1974. 28.95x (ISBN 0-521-20335-X). Cambridge U Pr.

Algebraic Logic. Paul R. Halmos. LC 61-17955. 1962. 9.95 (ISBN 0-8284-0154-3). Chelsea Pub.

Algebraic Methods in Business, Economics, & the Social Sciences: A Short Course. Gerald Freilich & Frederick P. Greenleaf. (Mathematics Ser.). (Illus.). 1977. pap. text ed. 7.95x (ISBN 0-7167-0470-6). W H Freeman.

Algebraic Number Theory. I. N. Stewart & D. O. Tall. LC 78-31625. 200p. 1979. pap. 14.95 (ISBN 0-412-16000-5, Pub. by Chapman & Hall). Methuen Inc.

Algebraic Number Theory. 2nd ed. Edwin Weiss LC 76-5803. xii, 275p. 1976. 11.95 (ISBN 0-8284-0293-0). Chelsea Pub.

Algebraic Numbers. P. Ribenboim. LC 74-37174. (Pure & Applied Mathematics Ser.). 360p. 1972. 35.50 (ISBN 0-471-71804-1, Pub. by Wiley-Interscience). Wiley.

Algebraic Potential Theory. Maynard Arsove & Heinz Leutwiler. LC 79-24384. (Memoirs of the American Mathematical Society Ser.). 1980. 7.60 (ISBN 0-8218-2226-8). Am Math.

Algebraic Structure of Group Rings. Donald S. Passman. LC 77-4898. (Pure & Applied Mathematics Ser.). 1977. 45.00 (ISBN 0-471-02272-1, Pub. by Wiley-Interscience). Wiley.

Algebraic Structures. Serge A. Lang. 1967. 12.95 (ISBN 0-201-04173-1). A-W.

Algebraic Structures of Symmetric Domains. Ichiro Satake. LC 80-7551. (Publications of the Mathematical Society of Japan Ser.: No. 14). 315p. 1981. 39.50x (ISBN 0-691-08271-5). Princeton U Pr.

Algebraic Theory of Semigroups, 2 Vols. A. H. Clifford & G. B. Preston. LC 61-15686. (Mathematical Surveys Ser.: Vol. 7). 1977. Repr. of 1961 ed. Vol. 1. with corrections 16.40 (ISBN 0-8218-0271-2, SURV-7-1); Vol. 2. with corrections 19.20 (ISBN 0-8218-0272-0, SURV-7.2). Am Math.

Algebraic Topology. Solomon Lefschetz. LC 41-6147. (Colloquium Pbns. Ser.: Vol. 27). 1980. 31.60 (ISBN 0-8218-1027-8, COLL-27). Am Math.

Algebraic Topology. C. R. Maunder. LC 79-41610. (Illus.). 1980. 59.50 (ISBN 0-521-23161-2); pap. 22.95 (ISBN 0-521-29840-7). Cambridge U Pr.

Algebraic Topology: A Student's Guide. John F. Adams. LC 75-163178. (London Mathematical Lecture Note Ser.: No. 4). (Illus.). 1972. 23.95x (ISBN 0-521-08076-2). Cambridge U Pr.

Algebraic Topology: Aarhus Nineteen Seventy-Eight. Ed. by J. L. Dupont & J. H. Madsen. (Lecture Notes in Mathematics: Vol. 763). 695p. 1980. pap. 33.60 (ISBN 0-387-09721-X). Springer-Verlag.

Algebraische Funktionen. Kurt Hensel & G. Landsberg. LC 65-11624. (Ger). 1965. 29.50 (ISBN 0-8284-0179-9). Chelsea Pub.

Algebraische Theorie der Koerper. Ernst Steinitz. LC 51-10623. 1976. text ed. 9.95 (ISBN 0-8284-0077-6). Chelsea Pub.

Algebraische Zahlen. 2nd ed. Erich Hecke. LC 50-3732. (Ger). 1970. 11.95 (ISBN 0-8284-0046-6). Chelsea Pub.

Algebraische Zahlen. 2nd ed. Edmund Landau. (Ger). 8.95 (ISBN 0-8284-0062-8). Chelsea Pub.

Algebras in Genetics. A. Woerz-Busekros. (Lecture Notes in Biomathematics: Vol. 36). 237p. 1980. pap. 16.00 (ISBN 0-387-09978-6). Springer-Verlag.

Algebro - Geometric & Lie Theoretic Tecniques in Systems Theory: Part A. Robert Herman. (Interdisciplinary Mathematics Ser.: No. 13). 1977. 22.00 (ISBN 0-915692-17-1). Math Sci Pr.

Algebroid Curves in Positive Characteristic. A. Campillo. (Lecture Notes in Mathematics Ser.: Vol. 813). 168p. 1980. pap. text ed. 11.80 (ISBN 0-387-10022-9). Springer-Verlag.

Algemene Winkler Prins Encyclopedie, 14 vols. (Dutch.). 1975-1977. 725.00 set. Pergamon.

Algenvegetation Des Golfes Von Neapel. Georg Funk. (Pubbl. d. Stazione Zool. di Napoli). (Illus., Ger.). Repr. of 1927 ed. lib. bdg. 95.40 (ISBN 3-87429-142-1). Lubrecht & Cramer.

Alger Hiss: The True Story. John C. Smith. 1977. pap. 2.95 o.p. (ISBN 0-14-004427-2). Penguin.

Algerbra. T. W. Hungerford. (Graduate Texts in Mathematics: Vol. 73). 526p. 1981. 24.00 (ISBN 0-387-90518-9). Springer-Verlag.

Algerbraic Geometry I: Complex Projective Varieties. I. D. Mumford. (Grundlehren der Mathematischen Wissenschaften: Vol. 221). (Illus.). 200p. 1981. 18.90 (ISBN 0-387-07603-4). Springer-Verlag.

Algeria. Richard Lawless. (World Bibliographical Ser.: No. 19). 1981. write for info. (ISBN 0-903450-32-1). Abc-Clio.

Algeria: The Politics of a Socialist Revolution. David Ottaway & Marina Ottaway. LC 70-83210. (Illus.). 1970. 20.00x (ISBN 0-520-01655-6). U of Cal Pr.

Algerine Captive. Royall Tyler. LC 67-10272. 1967. Repr. of 1797 ed. 48.00x (ISBN 0-8201-1046-9). Schol Facsimiles.

Algernon C. Swinburne. John A. Cassidy. (English Authors Ser.: No. 10). lib. bdg. 10.95 (ISBN 0-8057-1524-X). Twayne.

Algiers in the Age of the Corsairs. William Spencer. (Centers of Civiization Ser.: Vol. 34). 184p. 1981. pap. 3.95 (ISBN 0-8061-1705-2). U of Okla Pr.

ALGOL Sixty & FORTRAN IV. R. A. Vowels. 1974. pap. 9.95 o.p. (ISBN 0-471-91192-5). Wiley.

ALGOL Sixty-Eight. A. D. McGettrick. LC 77-1104. (Computer Science Texts Ser.: No. 8). (Illus.). 1978. 47.95 (ISBN 0-521-21412-2); pap. 16.95x (ISBN 0-521-29143-7). Cambridge U Pr.

Algonquin. Dion Henderson. (gr. 3 up). 1979. pap. 1.25 (ISBN 0-307-21618-7, Golden Pr). Western Pub.

Algonquin Cat. Val Schaffner. (Illus.). 1980. 9.95 (ISBN 0-440-00073-4). Delacorte.

Algonquin Legends of New England. Charles G. Leland. LC 68-31217. 1968. Repr. of 1884 ed. 22.00 (ISBN 0-8103-3468-2). Gale.

Algorithmic Aesthetics: Computer Models for Criticism & Design in the Arts. George Stiny & James Gips. 1979. 18.50x (ISBN 0-520-03467-8). U of Cal Pr.

Algorithms in SNOBOL 4. James F. Gimpel. LC 75-33850. 487p. 1976. 30.00 (ISBN 0-471-30213-9, Pub. by Wiley-Interscience). Wiley.

Algorithms Plus Data Structures Equals Programs. Niklavs Wirth. (Illus.). 400p. 1976. 23.95 (ISBN 0-13-022418-9). P-H.

Alhambra: A Cycle of Studies on the Eleventh Century in Moorish Spain. Fredrick P. Bargebuhr. 1968. 100.00x (ISBN 3-11-000524-7). De Gruyter.

Ali Baba. (Ladybird Stories Ser.). (Illus., Arabic.). 2.50x (ISBN 0-686-53067-5). Intl Bk Ctr.

Ali, the Fighting Prophet. Gilbert Odd. 1975. 8.95 o.p. (ISBN 0-7207-0845-1, Pub. by Michael Joseph). Merrimack Bk Serv.

Alias Jimmy Valentine. O'Henry. Ed. by Walter Pauk & Raymond Harris. (Jamestown Classics Ser.). (Illus.). 37p. (gr. 6-12). 1979. pap. text ed. 1.60x (ISBN 0-89061-192-0, 409); tchrs. ed. 3.00 (ISBN 0-89061-194-7). Jamestown Pubs.

Alias the Buffalo Doctor. Jean Cummings. LC 80-81714. (Illus.). 266p. 1981. 11.95 (ISBN 0-8040-0815-9). Swallow.

Alias William Shakespeare? Claud W. Sykes. 221p. 1980. Repr. of 1947 ed. lib. bdg. 25.00 (ISBN 0-89987-764-8). Century Bookbindery.

Alice. Kirill Bulychev. Tr. by Mirra Ginsburg. LC 76-47539. (Illus.). (gr. 3-6). 1977. 8.95 (ISBN 0-02-736520-4, 73652). Macmillan.

Alice-All-By-Herself. Elizabeth Coatsworth. (Illus.). (gr. 4-6). 1966. 4.95g o.s.i. (ISBN 0-02-719060-9). Macmillan.

Alice B. Toklas Cook Book. Alice B. Toklas. 1954. pap. 2.50 (ISBN 0-385-09439-6, A196, Anch). Doubleday.

Alice Cooper. Steve Demorest. (Circus Magazine Rock Ser.: No. 1). (Illus.). 192p. 1974. pap. 1.50 o.p. (ISBN 0-445-03046-1). Popular Lib.

Alice Doesn't Live Here Anymore. Robert Getchell. 128p. 1975. pap. 1.50 o.s.i. (ISBN 0-446-88418-9). Warner Bks.

Alice Dunbar-Nelson Reader. Ed. by R. Ora Williams. LC 78-58596. 1978. pap. text ed. 10.50 (ISBN 0-8191-0543-0). U Pr of Amer.

Alice in Wonderland. (Illustrated Junior Library). (Illus.). 304p. 1981. pap. 4.95 (ISBN 0-448-11004-0). G&D.

Alice in Wonderland. Lewis Carroll. Ed. by Donald J. Gray. (Critical Editions Ser). (Illus.). 1971. 10.00 (ISBN 0-393-04343-6); pap. 4.95x (ISBN 0-393-09977-6). Norton.

Alice in Wonderland & Through the Looking Glass. Lewis Carroll. 1965. 12.95x (ISBN 0-460-00836-6, Evman); pap. 2.95 (ISBN 0-460-01836-1). Dutton.

Alice in Wonderland Meets White Rabbit. Walt Disney. (Illus.). (ps-3). 1977. PLB 5.00 (ISBN 0-307-60019-X, Golden Pr). Western Pub.

Alice Through the Looking Glass. pap. 4.95 (ISBN 0-517-50136-8). Potter.

Alice's Adventures in Wonderland. L. Carroll. Bd. with Through the Looking Glass. (Illus.). 285p. 1966. 6.95 (ISBN 0-312-01821-5). St Martin.

Alice's Adventures in Wonderland. L. Carroll. (Illus.). 285p. (gr. 4 up). 1969. pap. 2.25 o.p. (ISBN 0-312-01785-5, Papermac). St Martin.

Alice's Adventures in Wonderland. Lewis Carroll. Bd. with Through the Looking Glass. (Classics Ser.). (gr. 5 up). pap. 1.50 (ISBN 0-8049-0079-5, CL-79). Airmont.

Alice's Adventures in Wonderland. Lewis Carroll & Sir John Tenniel. LC 77-77324. (Illus.). (gr. 5 up). 1977. 7.95 (ISBN 0-312-01821-5). St Martin.

Alice's Adventures in Wonderland & Through the Looking Glass. Lewis Carroll. LC 78-3389. (Raintree's Illustrated Classics). (Illus.). (gr. 5-8). 1978. PLB 9.65 (ISBN 0-8393-6208-0). Raintree Child.

Alicia & Her Nacional Ballet De Cuba. Walter Terry. LC 79-7879. (Illus.). 192p. 1981. pap. 10.95 (ISBN 0-385-14956-5, Anch). Doubleday.

Alicia's Trump. Joseph Mathewson. 224p. (Orig.). 1980. pap. 2.25 (ISBN 0-380-76521-7, 76521). Avon.

Alicyclic Chemistry. F. J. McQuillin. (Chemistry Texts Ser). (Illus.). 1972. 34.95 (ISBN 0-521-08216-1); pap. 11.95x (ISBN 0-521-09659-6). Cambridge U Pr.

Alicyclic Chemistry, Vols. 2-6. Ed. by W. Parker. Incl. Vols. 2 & 3. 1972 Literature. LC 72-82047. Vol. 2, 1974. 49.50 (ISBN 0-85186-522-4); Vol. 3, 1973 Literature. 66.00 (ISBN 0-85186-552-6); Vol. 4. 1974 Literature. LC 72-82047. 1976. 75.50 (ISBN 0-85186-582-8); Vol. 5. 1975 Literature. 1977. 77.00 (ISBN 0-85186-612-3); Vol. 6. 1976 Literature. 1978. 79.75 (ISBN 0-85186-632-8). LC 72-82047. Am Chemical.

Alien. Victor Besaw. 1979. pap. 1.75 o.p. (ISBN 0-449-14197-7, GM). Fawcett.

Alien. George Leonard. LC 76-49397. 256p. 1980. pap. 2.25 (ISBN 0-87216-746-1). Playboy Pbks.

Alien Animals: A Worldwide Investigation. Janet Bord & Colin Bord. 248p. Date not set. pap. 6.95 (ISBN 0-13-021998-3). P-H. Postponed.

Alien Atlas. C. M. Alexander. (Orig.). 1980. pap. 1.95 (ISBN 0-532-23189-9). Manor Bks.

Alien Christ. Roy C. DeLamotte. LC 80-5902. 276p. 1980. lib. bdg. 18.75 (ISBN 0-8191-1304-2); pap. text ed. 10.50 (ISBN 0-8191-1305-0). U Pr of Amer.

Alien Doctors: Foreign Medical Graduates in American Hospitals. Rosemary Stevens et al. LC 77-12934. (Health, Medicine & Society Ser.). 1978. 26.95 (ISBN 0-471-82455-0, Pub. by Wiley-Interscience). Wiley.

Alien Encounter. Flanna Devin. 1981. pap. 1.95 (ISBN 0-8439-0898-X, Leisure Bks). Nordon Pubns.

Alien Encounters. Ed. by Jan H. Finder. 256p. 1981. 11.95 (ISBN 0-8008-0168-7). Taplinger.

Alien Immigrants to England. William Cunningham. LC 72-94541. (Illus.). Repr. of 1897 ed. lib. bdg. 22.50x (ISBN 0-678-05098-8). Kelley.

Alien in Their Midst: Images of the Jews in English Literature. Esther L. Panitz. LC 78-75183. 150p. 1981. 10.50 (ISBN 0-8386-2318-2). Fairleigh Dickinson.

Alien Invasion: The Origins of the Aliens Act of 1905. Bernard Gainer. LC 72-80307. 302p. 1972. 17.50x (ISBN 0-8448-0050-3). Crane-Russak Co.

Alien Minds. E. Everett Evans. 1976. Repr. of 1955 ed. lib. bdg. 11.95 (ISBN 0-88411-981-5). Amereon Ltd.

Alien Starships. Yoong Bae. (Illus.). 32p. 1980. pap. 3.50 (ISBN 0-89844-014-9). Troubador Pr.

Alien Under American Law. A. Peter Mutharika. LC 80-18236. 575p. 1980. looseleaf 85.00 (ISBN 0-379-20341-3). Oceana.

Alien Way. Gordon Dickson. 1977. pap. 1.75 o.s.i. (ISBN 0-446-84552-3). Warner Bks.

Alien Wisdom: The Limits of Hellenization. A. D. Momigliano. LC 75-10237. 140p. 1976. 23.95 (ISBN 0-521-20876-9). Cambridge U Pr.

Alienacion y Agresion En Juan Goytisolo En Senas De Identidad y Reivindicacion Del Conde Don Julian. Jose Ortega. 1973. 10.50 (ISBN 0-88303-012-8); pap. 7.50 (ISBN 0-685-73216-9). E Torres & Sons.

Alienated Affections. Seymour Kleinberg. 320p. 1981. 13.95 (ISBN 0-312-01857-6). St Martin.

Alienation. Burl Hogins & Gerald Bryant, Jr. 1970. pap. text ed. 3.95x (ISBN 0-02-474950-8, 47495). Macmillan.

Alienation. 2nd ed. B. Ollman. LC 76-4234. (Studies in the History & Theory of Politics). 1977. 29.95 (ISBN 0-521-21281-2); pap. 8.50x (ISBN 0-521-29083-X). Cambridge U Pr.

Alienation. Richard Schacht. LC 70-116252. 1971. pap. 1.95 o.p. (ISBN 0-385-04791-6, Anch). Doubleday.

Alienation & Identification. Morton A. Kaplan. LC 76-8146. 1976. 14.95 (ISBN 0-02-916790-6). Free Pr.

Alienation As a Social Phenomenon. Adam Schaff. Date not set. 48.00 (ISBN 0-08-021807-5). Pergamon.

Alienation: Concept, Term, & Meaning. Ed. by Frank A. Johnson. LC 72-7702. 1973. 25.00 (ISBN 0-12-785381-2). Acad Pr.

Alienation in Contemporary Society: A Multidisciplinary Examination. Ed. by Roy S. Bryce-Laporte & Claudewell S. Thomas. LC 76-18123. (Special Studies). (Illus.). 420p. 1976. text ed. 29.95 o.p. (ISBN 0-275-09800-1). Praeger.

Aliens. E. Naha. 1977. pap. 7.95 (ISBN 0-931064-03-1). Starlog Pr.

Aliens Among Us. James White. 224p. 1981. pap. 2.25 (ISBN 0-345-29171-9, Del Rey). Ballantine.

Alik the Detective. Anatoli Aleksin. Tr. by Bonnie Carey from Russ. (gr. 7-9). 1977. 8.25 (ISBN 0-688-22117-3); PLB 7.92 (ISBN 0-688-32117-8). Morrow.

Alimentary Tract Radiology: Abdominal Imaging, Vol. 3. Alexander R. Margulis & H. Joachim Burhenne. LC 72-14444. (Illus.). 1979. text ed. 87.50 (ISBN 0-8016-3134-3). Mosby.

Alimentary Tract Roentgenology, Vols. 1 & 2. 2nd ed. Ed. by Alexander R. Margulis & H. Joachim Burhenne. LC 72-14444. 1689p. 1973. Set. 157.50 (ISBN 0-8016-3131-9); Vol.1. 74.75 (ISBN 0-8016-3149-1); Vol. 2. 74.75 (ISBN 0-8016-3150-5). Mosby.

Aline. Carole Klein. (Illus.). 1980. pap. 2.95 (ISBN 0-446-93526-3). Warner Bks.

Aliphatic, Alicyclic, & Saturated Heterocyclic Chemistry: 1970-1971 Literature, Vol. 1 In 3 Pts. Ed. by W. Parker. LC 72-83454. 1973. pt. 1 30.25 (ISBN 0-85186-502-X); pt. 2 44.00 (ISBN 0-685-55721-9); pt. 3 44.00 (ISBN 0-685-55722-7). Am Chemical.

Aliphatic Nucleophilic Substitution. S. R. Hartshorn. LC 72-96675. (Chemistry Texts Ser.). (Illus.). 150p. 1973. 32.50 (ISBN 0-521-20177-2); pap. 11.95x (ISBN 0-521-09801-7). Cambridge U Pr.

Alive & Aware: Improving Communications in Relationships. Sherod Miller et al. LC 75-27948. (Illus.). 1975. 8.95 o.p. (ISBN 0-917340-01-9); pap. text ed. 7.95 (ISBN 0-917340-02-7); tchrs. manual o.p. 3.95 (ISBN 0-917340-03-5); couple workbook o.p. 3.95 (ISBN 0-917340-04-3); student workbook o.p. 3.95 (ISBN 0-917340-05-1). Interpersonal Comm.

Alive & Growing Teacher. Clark E. Moustakas. 1959. 4.00 o.p. (ISBN 0-685-77550-X). Philos Lib.

Alive & Taking Names. Colette Inez. LC 77-86351. 74p. 1977. 8.95 (ISBN 0-8214-0377-X); pap. 4.95 (ISBN 0-8214-0393-1). Ohio U Pr.

Alive in Christ. David Womack. (Radiant Life Ser.). 1975. pap. 1.95 (ISBN 0-88243-888-3, 02-0888, Radiant Books); teacher's ed 2.50 (ISBN 0-88243-162-5, 32-0162). Gospel Pub.

Alive: The Story of the Andes Survivors. Piers P. Read. 1975. pap. 2.50 (ISBN 0-380-00321-X, 51714). Avon.

Alive with the Spirit. Martin Franzmann. 94p. 1974. pap. 2.95 (ISBN 0-570-03174-5, 12-2577). Concordia.

Aliways to Rice Garden: A Case Study of the Intensification of Rice Farming in Camarines Sur, Philippines. (IRRI Research Paper Ser.: No. 36). 23p. 1979. pap. 5.00 (R076, IRRI). Unipub.

Aliya. Brenda L. Segal. 1979. pap. 1.95 (ISBN 0-515-04773-2). Jove Pubns.

Alkaline-Earth Sulfates in All Solvents: Solubilities of Solids. J. W. Lorimer. (IUPAC Solubility Data Ser.: Vol. 6). 1981. 100.00 (ISBN 0-08-023916-1). Pergamon.

Alkaline Storage Batteries. S. Uno Falk & A. J. Salkind. LC 77-82980. (Electrochemical Society Ser.). 1969. 60.00 (ISBN 0-471-25362-6, Pub. by Wiley-Interscience). Wiley.

Alkaloid Chemistry. Manfred Hesse. 384p. 1981. 22.50 (ISBN 0-471-07973-1, Pub. by Wiley-Interscience). Wiley.

Alkaloids: Chemistry & Physiology. Ed. by R. H. Manske et al. Incl. Vol. 1. 1965. 62.00 (ISBN 0-12-469501-9); Vol. 2. 1952. 62.00 (ISBN 0-12-469502-7); Vol. 3. 1965. 55.25 (ISBN 0-12-469503-5); Vol. 4. 1965. 52.50 (ISBN 0-12-469504-3); Vol. 5. Pharmacology. 1965. 52.50 (ISBN 0-12-469505-1); Vol. 6. Supplement to Volumes 1 & 2. 1965. 52.50 (ISBN 0-12-469506-X); Vol. 7. Supplement to Volumes 2, 3, 4 & 5. 1960. 59.00 (ISBN 0-12-469507-8); Vol. 8. The Indole Alkaloids. 1965. 72.25 (ISBN 0-12-469508-6); Vol. 9. 1967. 64.25 (ISBN 0-12-469509-4); Vol. 10. 1968. 64.25 (ISBN 0-12-469510-8); Vol. 11. 1968. 64.25 (ISBN 0-12-469511-6); Vol. 12. 1970. 64.25 (ISBN 0-12-469512-4); Vol. 13. 1971. 55.25 (ISBN 0-12-469513-2); Vol. 14. 1973. 68.50 (ISBN 0-12-469514-0); Vol. 15. 1975. 55.25 (ISBN 0-12-469515-9); Vol. 16. 1977. 73.00 (ISBN 0-12-469516-7); Vol. 17. 1979. 58.00 (ISBN 0-12-469517-5). Acad Pr.

Alkema's Complete Guide to Creative Art for Young People. Chester J. Alkema. LC 70-167654. (Illus.). 1971. 16.95 (ISBN 0-8069-5188-5); PLB 14.99 (ISBN 0-8069-5189-3). Sterling.

Alkoholkonsum und Alkoholismus als didaktisches Problem. F. Kicherer. (Psychologische Praxis Ser.: Band 54). (Illus.). vi, 146p. 1980. pap. 17.50 (ISBN 3-8055-0957-X). S Karger.

All About Action Photography. David Hodgson. (Illus.). 1976. 18.00 (ISBN 0-7207-0888-5). Transatlantic.

All About American Holidays. Maymie R. Krythe. LC 61-6450. (Illus.). 1962. 9.95 o.p. (ISBN 0-06-003090-9, HarpT). Har-Row.

All About Angels. 1977. study guide 1.50 o.p. (ISBN 0-8307-0513-9, 61-002-01). Regal.

All About Angels. C. Leslie Miller. 1976. pap. 1.25 (ISBN 0-89129-233-0). Jove Pubns.

All About Aquariums. Earl Schneider. (Illus., Orig.). pap. 4.95 (ISBN 0-87666-003-0, PS601). TFH Pubns.

All About Aviation. Robert D. Loomis. (Allabout Ser, No. 51). (Illus.). (gr. 5-8). 1964. 4.39 o.p. (ISBN 0-394-90251-3, BYR). Random.

All About Bettas. Walt Maurus. (Orig.). 1976. pap. 5.95 (ISBN 0-87666-452-4, PS-654). TFH Pubns.

All About Bible Study. Herbert Lockyer. 1977. 9.95 (ISBN 0-310-28160-1). Zondervan.

All About Bikes & Bicycling. Max Alth. 1972. pap. 2.95 o.p. (ISBN 0-8015-0146-6). Dutton.

All About Boas & Other Snakes. Mervin F. Roberts. (Illus.). 96p. (Orig.). 1975. pap. 2.95 (ISBN 0-87666-904-6, PS-313). TFH Pubns.

All About Brook Trout. Elliot. 1980. Repr. 8.95 (ISBN 0-89272-090-5). Down East.

All About Cams. 2.95 o.p. (ISBN 0-934572-12-7). Johnson VA.

All About Canaries. rev ed. Irene Evans & Paul Paradise. (Illus.). 96p. 1976. pap. 2.50 (ISBN 0-87666-953-4, PS315). TFH Pubns.

All About Canaries. J. M. Neslan. (Illus.). 1979. 9.95 o.p. (ISBN 0-686-01017-5, 8051, Dist. by Arco). Barrie & Jenkins.

All About Caravan Holidays. Christine Fagg. 1975. 7.95 (ISBN 0-236-30931-5, Pub. by Paul Elek). Merrimack Bk Serv.

All About Cats As Pets. Marjorie Zaum. (Illus.). 64p. (gr. 3-5). 1981. PLB 6.97 (ISBN 0-686-69306-X). Messner.

All About CB Two-Way Radio. Editorial & Technical Staff of Radio Shack. (RL 9). 1976. pap. 1.25 o.p. (ISBN 0-451-82043-6, XY2043, Sig). NAL.

All About Chameleons & Anoles. Mervin F. Roberts. (Illus.). 1977. pap. 2.50 (ISBN 0-87666-902-X, PS-310). TFH Pubns.

All About Chess. I. A. Horowitz. 1971. pap. 2.95 o.s.i. (ISBN 0-02-028880-8, Collier). Macmillan.

All About Chess. I. A. Horowitz. 1971. 6.95 o.s.i. (ISBN 0-02-554110-2). Macmillan.

All About Christmas. Maymie R. Krythe. LC 54-8965. 1954. lib. bdg. 8.97 o.s.i. (ISBN 0-06-003151-4, HarpT). Har-Row.

All About Cichlids. Braz Walker. (Illus., Orig.). 1978. pap. 4.95 (ISBN 0-87666-472-9, PS-751). TFH Pubns.

All About Cockatiels. Gerald R. Allen & Connie J. Allen. (Illus.). 1977. 4.95 (ISBN 0-87666-955-0, PS746). TFH Pubns.

All About Coffee. William H. Ukers. LC 71-178659. (Illus.). 1975. Repr. of 1935 ed. 50.00 (ISBN 0-8103-4092-5). Gale.

All About Cribbage. Douglas Anderson. 1978. pap. 3.95 (ISBN 0-87691-262-5). Winchester Pr.

All About Cribbage. G. Douglas Anderson. 1971. 8.95 (ISBN 0-87691-041-X). Winchester Pr.

All About Crop Dusting. Miles E. Gibson. pap. 7.00 (ISBN 0-685-46364-8, Pub. by Diversified). Aviation.

All About Crossbreeds & Mongrels. Margaret Sheldon & Barbara Lockwood. 1971. 3.95 o.p. (ISBN 0-7207-0478-2, Pub. by Michael Joseph). Merrimack Bk Serv.

All About Cubical Quad Antennas. 2nd ed. William I. Orr & Stuart D. Cowan. LC 59-13141. (Illus.). 112p. 1959. 4.75 (ISBN 0-933616-03-1). Radio Pubns.

All About Dinosaurs. Roy C. Andrews. (Allabout Ser.: No. 1). (Illus.). (gr. 4-6). 1953. 3.95 (ISBN 0-394-80201-2, BYR); PLB 5.39 (ISBN 0-394-90201-7). Random.

All About Discus. (Illus.). pap. 6.95 (ISBN 0-87666-035-9, PS669). TFH Pubns.

All About Dogs. Barbara Joyce. (Illus.). 3.50x (ISBN 0-392-06370-0, SpS). Soccer.

All About Doll Houses. Barbara L. Farlie & Charlotte L. Clarke. LC 75-513. (Illus.). 272p. 1975. 16.95 (ISBN 0-672-51976-3). Bobbs.

All About Doll Houses. Barbara L. Farlie & Charlotte L. Clarke. LC 75-513. (Illus.). 1977. pap. 18.95 (ISBN 0-672-52367-1). Bobbs.

All About Elephants. Carl Burger. (Allabout Ser, No. 56). (Illus.). (gr. 5-10). 1965. 2.95 o.p. (ISBN 0-394-80256-X, BYR). Random.

All About Finches. Ian Harman & Matthew M. Vriends. (Illus.). 1978. 9.95 (ISBN 0-87666-965-8, PS-765). TFH Pubns.

All About Frames. Barbara Kulicke & Peter Wood. (Illus.). 1980. cancelled (ISBN 0-394-41461-6). Pantheon.

All About Ghosts. Christopher Maynard. LC 77-17613. (The World of the Unknown). (Illus.). (gr. 4-5). 1978. PLB 6.95 (ISBN 0-88436-469-0). EMC.

All About Ground Covers. Ed. by Ortho Books Editorial Staff. LC 77-89688. (Illus.). 1978. pap. 4.95 Midwest-Northeast ed. (ISBN 0-917102-55-X); pap. 4.95 South ed. (ISBN 0-917102-56-8); pap. 4.95 West ed. (ISBN 0-917102-57-6). Ortho.

All About Growing Fruits & Berries. Ed. by Prtho Books Editorial Staff. LC 76-29250. (Illus.). 1977. pap. 4.95; pap. midwest-northeast ed. (ISBN 0-917102-29-0); pap. west ed. (ISBN 0-917102-28-2); pap. south ed. (ISBN 0-917102-30-4). Ortho.

All About Guppies. Leon F. Whitney. (Orig.). pap. 5.95 (ISBN 0-87666-083-9, PS603). TFH Pubns.

All About H. Hatterr. rev. ed. G. V. Desani. LC 77-97137. 1970. 5.95 o.p. (ISBN 0-374-10280-5). FS&G.

All About Himalayan Cats. Joan M. Brearley. (Illus.). 96p. (Orig.). 1976. 3.95 (ISBN 0-87666-756-6, PS736). TFH Pubns.

All About Home Freezing. Audrey Ellis. 1971. pap. 2.95 (ISBN 0-600-31644-0). Transatlantic.

All About Horses & Ponies. E. Hartley Edwards. 1976. 7.95 (ISBN 0-491-01726-X). Transatlantic.

All About Houses. Bill Dugan. 72p. (gr. 4-8). 1975. 3.95 o.p. (ISBN 0-307-15789-X, Golden Pr); PLB 10.69 o.p. (ISBN 0-307-65789-2). Western Pub.

All About Iguanas. Mervin F. Roberts & Martha D. Roberts. (Orig.). 1976. pap. 2.50 (ISBN 0-87666-903-8, PS311). TFH Pubns.

All About Judo. Geoff Gleeson. (Sports Library). (Illus.). 1979. 12.95 (ISBN 0-8069-9100-3); pap. 6.95 (ISBN 0-8069-9102-X). Sterling.

All About Land Hermit Crabs. new ed. Mervin F. Roberts. (Illus.). 1978. pap. text ed. 2.00 (ISBN 0-87666-920-8, PS-767). TFH Pubns.

All About Landscaping. Lin Cottin. Ed. by Ortho Books Editorial Staff. LC 80-66347. (Illus.). 96p. (Orig.). 1981. pap. 4.95 (ISBN 0-917102-87-8). Ortho.

All About Locks & Locksmithing. Max Alth. (Illus.). 1972. pap. 4.50 (ISBN 0-8015-0151-2, Hawthorn). Dutton.

All About Me. Deborah Manley. LC 78-21097. (Ready, Set, Look Ser.). (Illus.). (gr. k-3). 1979. PLB 9.65 (ISBN 0-8172-1304-X). Raintree Pubs.

All About Mice. Howard Hirschhorn. (Illus.). 96p. (Orig.). 1974. pap. 2.50 (ISBN 0-87666-210-6, M-542). TFH Pubns.

All About Monsters. Carey Miller. LC 77-17933. (World of the Unknown). (Illus.). (gr. 4-5). 1978. PLB 6.95 (ISBN 0-88436-467-4). EMC.

All About Mopeds. Max Alth. LC 78-2348. (Concise Guides Ser.). (Illus.). (gr. 7 up). 1978. PLB 6.45 (ISBN 0-531-01496-7). Watts.

All About Moths & Butterflies. Robert S. Lemmon. (gr. 4-6). 1956. 2.95 o.p. (ISBN 0-394-80215-2, BYR). Random.

All About Obedience Training for Dogs. Mollie Mulvany. 1973. 9.95 (ISBN 0-7207-0616-5, Pub. by Michael Joseph). Merrimack Bk Serv.

All About Our Fifty States. rev. ed. Margaret Ronan. LC 78-16658. (gr. 5-9). 1978. 3.95 (ISBN 0-394-80244-6); PLB 4.99 (ISBN 0-394-90244-0). Random.

All About Pennsylvania. Lucille Wallower. Ed. by Ellen J. Wholey. (Illus.). (gr. 3-4). 1961. pap. 3.15 (ISBN 0-931992-05-2). Penns Valley.

All About Poodles. Margaret Sheldon & Barbara Lockwood. 1970. 8.95 (ISBN 0-7207-0320-4, Pub. by Michael Joseph). Merrimack Bk Serv.

All About Pruning. Ortho Books Editorial Staff. LC 78-57891. (Illus.). 1979. pap. 4.95 (ISBN 0-917102-73-8). Ortho.

All About Puppies-- Your Dog's First Year. Bob Bartos. (Illus.). 1980. pap. 1.95 (ISBN 0-451-09177-9, J9177, Sig). NAL.

All About Rabbits. Howard Hirschhorn. (Illus.). 96p. (Orig.). 1974. pap. 2.50 (ISBN 0-87666-214-9, M-543). TFH Pubns.

All About Raising Children, Nineteen Eighty-One. 1980. 10.95 (ISBN 0-911094-07-5). Pacific Santa Barbara.

All About Rats. Howard Hirschhorn. (Illus.). 96p. (Orig.). 1974. pap. 2.50 (ISBN 0-87666-217-3, M-544). TFH Pubns.

All About Repairing Major Household Appliances. Carl Bryant. (Illus.). 240p. (80 packages of sketches). 1974. pap. 4.95 (ISBN 0-8015-0158-X, Hawthorn). Dutton.

All About Rhoda. Peggy Herz. (Illus.). (gr. 7-12). 1975. pap. 1.25 o.p. (ISBN 0-590-10113-7, Schol Pap). Schol Bk Serv.

All About Rifle Hunting & Shooting in America. Ed. by Steve Ferber. 1977. 12.95 (ISBN 0-87691-244-7). Winchester Pr.

All About Rockets & Space Flight. Harold L. Goodwin. (Allabout Bk). (gr. 5-9). 1970. PLB 4.39 (ISBN 0-394-90259-9). Random.

All About Roses. Ed. by Staff of Ortho Books. LC 76-29248. 1977. pap. 4.95 (ISBN 0-917102-23-1). Ortho.

All About Sailing: A Handbook for Juniors. Mario Brunet. 1976. pap. 7.95 (ISBN 0-8120-0699-2). Barron.

All About Salamanders. Mervin F. Roberts. 96p. (Orig.). 1976. pap. 2.50 (ISBN 0-87666-901-1, PS-312). TFH Pubns.

All About Small Game Hunting in America. Ed. by Russell Tinsley. 1976. 11.95 (ISBN 0-87691-222-6). Winchester Pr.

All About Steam Cooking. Carol Truax. LC 79-6878. (Illus.). 272p. 1981. 12.95 (ISBN 0-385-15548-4). Doubleday.

All About Strange Beasts of the Past. Roy C. Andrews. (Allabout Ser.: No. 17). (Illus.). (gr. 4-6). 1956. PLB 5.39 (ISBN 0-394-90217-3, BYR). Random.

All About Suing & Being Sued. Arthur J. Sabin. LC 80-23991. (Illus.). 128p. (Orig.). 1981. pap. 12.95 (ISBN 0-89037-185-7); handbk. 15.00 (ISBN 0-89037-188-1). Anderson World.

All About Surf Fishing. Jack Fallon. (Illus.). 1975. 11.95 (ISBN 0-87691-201-3). Winchester Pr.

All About Swimming Pools. Gary Reed. LC 76-20375. (Illus.). 1976. 6.95 o.p. (ISBN 0-8306-6844-6); pap. 4.95 (ISBN 0-8306-5844-0, 844). TAB Bks.

All About Teaching: An Introduction to a Profession. Donald E. Schultze. 1977. pap. text ed. 7.50 (ISBN 0-8191-0205-9). U Pr of Amer.

All About the Atom. Ira M. Freeman. (gr. 4-6). 1956. 2.95 o.p. (ISBN 0-394-80210-1, BYR). Random.

All About the Beagle. Heather Priestley. 1973. 9.95 (ISBN 0-7207-0613-0, Pub. by Michael Joseph). Merrimack Bk Serv.

All About the Boxer. John F. Gordon. 1970. 9.95 (ISBN 0-7207-0317-4, Pub. by Michael Joseph). Merrimack Bk Serv.

All About the Bull Terrier. Tom Horner. 1973. 9.95 (ISBN 0-7207-0691-2, Pub. by Michael Joseph). Merrimack Bk Serv.

All About the Chihuahua. Mona Huxham. (Illus.). 1976. 9.95 (ISBN 0-7207-0891-5, Pub. by Michael Joseph). Merrimack Bk Serv.

All About the Cocker Spaniel. John F. Gordon. 1971. 8.95 (ISBN 0-7207-0424-3, Pub. by Michael Joseph). Merrimack Bk Serv.

All About the Collie. Ada L. Bishop. (All About Ser.). (Illus.). 1980. 16.95 (ISBN 0-7207-1215-7, Pub. by Michael Joseph). Merrimack Bk Serv.

All About the Collie. Ada L. Bishop. 1971. 8.95 o.p. (ISBN 0-7207-0450-2, Pub. by Michael Joseph). Merrimack Bk Serv.

All About the Dachshund. Katharine Raine. (All About Ser.). (Illus.). 1980. 16.95 (ISBN 0-7207-1178-9, Pub. by Michael Joseph). Merrimack Bk Serv.

All About the Dictionary. Alan W. Riese & Herbert J. LaSalle. (Orig.). (gr. 8-11). 1976. pap. text ed. 5.25 (ISBN 0-87720-330-X). AMSCO Sch.

All About the English Springer Spaniel. Olga M. Hampton. (All About Ser.). (Illus.). 1980. 16.95 (ISBN 0-7207-1274-2, Pub. by Michael Joseph). Merrimack Bk Serv.

All About the German Shepherd Dog. Madeleine Pickup. (All About Ser.). (Illus.). 170p. 1980. 16.95 (ISBN 0-7207-1219-X, Pub. by Michael Joseph). Merrimack Bk Serv.

All About the Golden Retriever. Lucille Sawtell. (All About Ser.). (Illus.). 1980. 16.95 (ISBN 0-7207-1217-3, Pub. by Michael Joseph). Merrimack Bk Serv.

All About the Golden Retriever. Lucille Sawtell. 1975. 14.95 o.p. (ISBN 0-7207-0449-9, Pub. by Michael Joseph). Merrimack Bk Serv.

All About the Human Mind: An Introduction to Psychology for Young People. Robert M. Goldenson. (Allabout Ser.: No. 47). (Illus.). (gr. 4 up). 1963. PLB 5.39 (ISBN 0-394-90247-5, BYR). Random.

All About the Jack Russell Terrier. Mona Huxham. 1975. 8.95 (ISBN 0-7207-0825-7, Pub. by Michael Joseph). Merrimack Bk Serv.

All About the Labrador. Mary Roslin-Williams. (All About Ser.). (Illus.). 1980. 16.95 (ISBN 0-7207-1218-1, Pub. by Michael Joseph). Merrimack Bk Serv.

All About the Labrador. Mary R. Williams. 1975. 8.95 o.p. (ISBN 0-7207-0842-7, Pub. by Michael Joseph). Merrimack Bk Serv.

All About the Old English Sheepdog. Jean Gould. 1973. 8.95 (ISBN 0-7207-0619-X, Pub. by Michael Joseph). Merrimack Bk Serv.

All About the St. Bernard. Richard Beaver & Rachel Beaver. (All About Ser.). 1980. 16.95 (ISBN 0-7207-1197-5, Pub. by Michael Joseph). Merrimack Bk Serv.

All About the Shetland Sheepdog. Felicity M. Rogers. (All About Ser.). (Illus.). 140p. 1980. 16.95 (ISBN 0-7207-1222-X, Pub. by Michael Joseph). Merrimack Bk Serv.

All About the Shetland Sheepdog. rev. ed. Felicity M. Rogers. 1980. 14.95 o.p. (ISBN 0-7207-0618-1, Pub. by Michael Joseph). Merrimack Bk Serv.

All About the Yorkshire Terrier. Mona Huxham. 1971. 9.95 (ISBN 0-7207-0333-6, Pub. by Michael Joseph). Merrimack Bk Serv.

All About Tomatoes. LC 76-29249. 1977. pap. 4.95 ea.; pap. west ed. (ISBN 0-917102-25-8); pap. midwest-northeast ed. (ISBN 0-917102-26-6); pap. south ed. (ISBN 0-917102-27-4). Ortho.

All About UFO's. Ted Wilding-White. LC 77-17599. (World of the Unknown Ser). (Illus.). (gr. 4-5). 1978. PLB 6.95 (ISBN 0-88436-468-2). EMC.

All About Upholstering. John Bergen. LC 77-85359. (Illus.). 1978. pap. 7.50 (ISBN 0-8015-0169-5, Hawthorn). Dutton.

All About Us. Eva K. Evans. (gr. 4-7). 1957. PLB 6.08 o.p. (ISBN 0-307-60180-3, Golden Pr). Western Pub.

All About Vegetables. rev. ed. Ken Burke & Walter Doty. Ed. by Ortho Books Editorial Staff. LC 80-66344. (Illus.). 112p. 1981. pap. 4.95 (ISBN 0-917102-90-8). Ortho.

All About Volcanoes & Earthquakes. Frederick H. Pough. (Allabout Ser: No. 4). (Illus.). (gr. 4-6). 1953. PLB 4.39 o.p. (ISBN 0-394-90204-1, BYR). Random.

All About Wildfowling in America. Ed. by Jerome Knap. 1976. 11.95 (ISBN 0-87691-177-7). Winchester Pr.

All About Wine. Blake Ozias. (Apollo Eds.). (Illus.). 144p. 1972. pap. 4.95 o.s.i. (ISBN 0-8152-0332-2, A332, TYC-T). T Y Crowell.

All About Words: An Adult Approach to Vocabulary Building. Maxwell Nurnberg & Morris Rosenblum. (RL 7). 1971. pap. 2.25 (ISBN 0-451-61681-2, ME1879, Ment). NAL.

All About Your Cat's Health. Geoffrey West. (All About Ser.). (Illus.). 176p. 1980. 16.50 (ISBN 0-7207-1277-7, Pub. by Michael Joseph). Merrimack Bk Serv.

All About Your Name Anne, Anna, Annie, Annette, Anita, Hannah, Nan. Tom Glazer. LC 77-82444. (gr. 1 up). 1978. 4.95a o.p. (ISBN 0-385-04279-5); PLB (ISBN 0-385-04299-X). Doubleday.

All About Your Name David, Dave, Davy, Davis, Davies, Davidson. Tom Glazer. LC 77-82443. (gr. 1 up). 1978. 4.95a o.p. (ISBN 0-385-06388-1); PLB (ISBN 0-385-06397-0). Doubleday.

All About Your Name Elizabeth, Eliza, Betsy, Beth, Bette, Betty, Lizzie, Liz. Tom Glazer. LC 77-82442. (gr. 1 up). 1978. 4.95a o.p. (ISBN 0-385-06399-7); PLB (ISBN 0-385-06404-7). Doubleday.

All About Your Name James, Jim, Jamie, Jimmy. Tom Glazer. LC 77-15153. (gr. 1 up). 1978. 4.95 o.p. (ISBN 0-385-06436-5); PLB (ISBN 0-385-06449-7). Doubleday.

All About Your Name John, Johnny, Jack, Jackie. Tom Glazer. LC 77-15154. (gr. 1 up). 1978. 4.95 o.p. (ISBN 0-385-06424-1); PLB (ISBN 0-385-06428-4). Doubleday.

All About Your Name Joseph, Joe, Joey, Jo-Jo. Tom Glazer. LC 77-15155. (gr. 1 up). 1978. 4.95a o.p. (ISBN 0-385-06554-X); PLB (ISBN 0-385-06558-2). Doubleday.

All About Your Name Katherine, Catherine, Cathy, Kate, Katie, Kathy. Tom Glazer. LC 77-15151. (gr. 1 up). 1978. 4.95a o.p. (ISBN 0-385-06476-4); PLB (ISBN 0-385-06536-1). Doubleday.

All About Your Name Mary, Marion, Maria, Marie, Miriam, Maureen, Molly. Tom Glazer. LC 77-82441. (gr. 1 up). 1978. 4.95a o.p. (ISBN 0-385-06405-5); PLB (ISBN 0-385-06406-3). Doubleday.

All About Your Name Susan, Susie, Susanna, Suzanne, Sue. Tom Glazer. LC 77-15156. (gr. 1 up). 1978. 4.95a o.p. (ISBN 0-385-06579-5); PLB (ISBN 0-385-06643-0). Doubleday.

All About Your Name William, Willie, Billy, Will, Bill, Willy. Tom Glazer. LC 76-23763. (gr. 1 up). 1978. 4.95a o.p. (ISBN 0-385-06419-5); PLB (ISBN 0-385-06420-9). Doubleday.

All About Your Pet Puppy. Joyce Stranger. (All About Ser.). (Illus.). 1980. 16.95 (ISBN 0-7207-1216-5, Pub. by Michael Joseph). Merrimack Bk Serv.

All-American Boy. Charles Eastman. (Illus.). 1973. pap. 2.75 o.p. (ISBN 0-374-50922-0, N406). FS&G.

All Around. Theodore L. Harris et al. (Keys to Independence in Reading Ser.). (Illus., Orig.). (gr. 1). 1973. text ed. 2.37 (ISBN 0-87892-012-9); 4.38 (ISBN 0-87892-013-7); wkbk. avail. (ISBN 0-87892-014-5). Economy Co.

All Because I'm Older. Phyllis Naylor. LC 80-18586. (Illus.). 32p. (ps-4). 1981. PLB 8.95 (ISBN 0-689-30824-8). Atheneum.

All Bisque & Half Bisque Dolls. Genevieve Angione. LC 76-77265. (Illus.). 357p. 1981. Repr. 25.00 (ISBN 0-916838-39-0). Schiffer.

All Breed Dog Grooming Guide. Sam Kohl & Catherine Goldstein. LC 72-86425. (Illus.). 288p. 1973. spiral bdg. 11.95 (ISBN 0-668-02729-0). Arco.

All but the People. G. Wolfskill & J. A. Hudson. 1969. 7.95 o.s.i. (ISBN 0-02-630900-9). Macmillan.

All Butterflies. Marcia Brown. (Illus.). 32p. (ps-2). pap. 2.95 (ISBN 0-689-70483-6, A-110, Aladdin). Atheneum.

All-by-Herself. Betty Baker. (Illus.). (gr. 1-3). 1980. 5.95 (ISBN 0-688-80242-7); lib. bdg. 5.71 (ISBN 0-688-84242-9). Morrow.

All by Myself. Jane B. Moncure. LC 76-5487. (Illus.). (ps-3). 1976. 5.95 (ISBN 0-913778-40-0). Childs World.

All Color World of Farm Animals. Burton. (Illus.). 1980. 5.95 (ISBN 0-7064-1008-4). Mayflower Bks.

All Compact Orientable Three Dimensional Manifolds Admit Total Foliations. Detlef Hardorp. LC 80-16612. (Memoirs: No. 233). 1980. 4.00 (ISBN 0-8218-2233-0). Am Math.

All Creatures Great & Small. James Herriot. LC 72-79632. 1972. 10.95 (ISBN 0-312-01960-2, A20000). St Martin.

All Day Long. Richard Scarry. (Golden Look-Look Book Ser). (Illus.). 1976. limp bdg. 0.95 (ISBN 0-307-11825-8, Golden Pr); PLB 5.38 (ISBN 0-307-61825-0). Western Pub.

All Deliberate Speed: Segregation & Exclusion in California Schools, 1855-1975. Charles M. Wollenberg. 1977. 14.95x (ISBN 0-520-03191-1); pap. 3.50 (ISBN 0-520-03728-6). U of Cal Pr.

All Drawn by Horses. James Arnold. LC 79-51087. (Illus.). 1979. 24.00 (ISBN 0-7153-7682-9). David & Charles.

All Dreams Never Die. James C. Conant. 1977. 4.50 o.p. (ISBN 0-682-48920-4). Exposition.

All Ends Up: Cartoons from American Scientist. Sid Harris. (Illus.). 128p. 1980. pap. 5.95 (ISBN 0-86576-000-4). W Kaufmann.

All Fall Down. Donald Goddard. 384p. 1980. 12.95 (ISBN 0-686-62157-3). Times Bks.

All Fall Down: One Man Against the Waterfront Mob. Donald Goddard. 320p. 1980. 14.95 (ISBN 0-8129-0938-0). Times Bks.

All Fools. George Chapman. Ed. by Frank Manley. LC 68-10664. (Regents Renaissance Drama Ser). 1968. 6.95x (ISBN 0-8032-0255-5); pap. 1.65x (ISBN 0-8032-5256-0, BB 229, Bison). U of Nebr Pr.

All for Art: The Ricketts & Shannon Collection. Fitzwilliam Museum. Ed. by J. Darracott. LC 79-51597. (Illus.). 1979. 36.00 (ISBN 0-521-22841-7); pap. 9.95 (ISBN 0-521-29674-9). Cambridge U Pr.

All for Fall. Ethel Kessler & Leonard Kessler. LC 74-2249. (Illus.). 40p. (ps-3). 1974. 5.95 o.s.i. (ISBN 0-8193-0735-1, Four Winds); PLB 5.41 o.s.i. (ISBN 0-8193-0736-X). Schol Bk Serv.

All for Love. John Dryden. Ed. by David Vieth. LC 72-128912. (Regents Restoration Drama Ser). 1972. 9.75x (ISBN 0-8032-0380-2); pap. 2.95x (ISBN 0-8032-5379-6, BB 276, Bison). U of Nebr Pr.

All for Nothing. Richard H. Adamson. Date not set. pap. price not set (ISBN 0-89126-075-7). Military Aff Aero.

All for Nothing. Larry Sturholm & John Howard. Ed. by Robert D. Shangle. (Illus.). 1976. 7.95 (ISBN 0-917630-01-7, Pub by Bls). Beautiful Am.

All Fur Flies & How to Dress Them. W. H. Lawrie. LC 68-14407. (Illus.). 1968. 7.95 o.p. (ISBN 0-498-06796-3). A S Barnes.

All G.O.D.'s Children. John Craig. LC 75-1256. 210p. 1975. 6.95 o.p. (ISBN 0-688-02913-2). Morrow.

All God's Chillun. J. Garfield Owens. LC 79-134251. 1971. 3.75 o.p. (ISBN 0-687-01020-9). Abingdon.

All God's Chillun Got Guns. Jed Cross. 192p. (Orig.). 1976. pap. 0.95 o.p. (ISBN 0-445-00691-9). Popular Lib.

All God's Creatures: The Autobiography of Sam Pryor. Sam Pryor & John Burnett. 1981. 10.00 (ISBN 0-533-04946-6). Vantage.

All Graduates & Gentlemen: Marsh's Library. Muriel McCarthy. (Illus.). 239p. 1980. 22.50x (ISBN 0-8476-3141-9). Rowman.

All Hail the Might State. June Welch. (Illus.). 1979. 14.95 (ISBN 0-87244-048-6). Texian.

All Hallows' Eve. Charles Williams. 274p. 1981. pap. 5.95 (ISBN 0-8028-1215-5). Eerdmans.

All I Need Is Love. Nancy A. Smith. LC 77-6036. (Orig.). 1977. pap. 2.75 (ISBN 0-87784-723-1). Inter-Varsity.

All in All. Anne S. White. 128p. (Orig.). 1980. pap. 2.50 (ISBN 0-9605178-0-4). Victorious Ministry.

All-in-One Calorie Counter. rev. ed. Jean Carper & Patricia A. Krause. 304p. (Orig.). 1980. pap. 2.50 (ISBN 0-553-13976-2). Bantam.

All-in-One Carbohydrate Gram Counter. rev. ed. Jean Carper & Patricia A. Krause. 304p. 1980. pap. 2.50 (ISBN 0-553-13977-0). Bantam.

All in the Family: A Critical Appraisal. Richard Adler. LC 79-89505. (Illus.). 384p. 1979. 25.95 (ISBN 0-03-053996-X). Praeger.

All in the Family: Animal Species Around the World. Gilda Berger. (Science Is What & Why Bk.). (Illus.). 48p. (gr. 7-10). 1981. PLB 5.99 (ISBN 0-698-30730-5). Coward.

All in the Name of the Lord. Bill Stringfellow. 176p. 1981. pap. 2.95 (ISBN 0-939286-00-9). Concerned Pubns.

All Is Well. Julius Lester. 1976. 9.95 o.p. (ISBN 0-688-03045-9). Morrow.

All Kinds of Codes. Walt Babson. LC 76-17529. (Illus.). 144p. (gr. 4 up). 1976. 8.95 (ISBN 0-590-07427-X, Four Winds). Schol Bk Serv.

All Kinds of Families. Norma Simon. Ed. by Caroline Rubin. LC 75-42283. (Concept Bks). (Illus.). 40p. (gr. k-2). 1975. 6.95 (ISBN 0-8075-0282-0). A Whitman.

All Kinds of Planes. Seymour Reit. (Golden Look-Look Bks.). (ps-3). 1978. PLB 5.38 (ISBN 0-307-61853-6, Golden Pr); pap. 0.95 (ISBN 0-307-11853-3). Western Pub.

All Kinds of Ships. Seymour Reit. (Golden Look-Look Bks.). (ps-3). 1978. PLB 5.38 (ISBN 0-307-61854-4, Golden Pr); pap. 0.95 (ISBN 0-307-11854-1). Western Pub.

All Kinds of Trains. Seymour Reit. (Golden Look-Look Bks.). (ps-3). 1978. PLB 5.38 (ISBN 0-307-61852-8, Golden Pr); pap. 0.95 (ISBN 0-307-11852-5). Western Pub.

All Kneeling. Anne Parrish. 1976. lib. bdg. 13.95 (ISBN 0-89968-154-9). Lightyear.

All Men Are Brothers. Mohandas K. Gandhi. LC 59-426. 1969. 15.00x (ISBN 0-231-02919-5). Columbia U Pr.

All Men Are Brothers - Shui Huchuan, Vol. I. Tr. by Pearl S. Buck. (John Day Bk.). 1968. Repr. of 1933 ed. 10.00 o.s.i. (ISBN 0-381-98017-0, A2000, TYC-T). T Y Crowell.

All Men Tall. Thomas G. Wheeler. LC 70-77313. (gr. 8 up). 1969. 9.95 (ISBN 0-87599-157-2). S G Phillips.

All Mirrors Are Magic Mirrors. Welleran Poctarnees. (Illus.). 1981. 16.95 (ISBN 0-914676-30-X, Star & Elephant Bk); pap. 9.95 (ISBN 0-914676-33-4). Green Tiger.

All My Children. Jacqui L. Schiff & Beth Day. LC 78-126389. 240p. 1970. 8.95 (ISBN 0-87131-036-8). M Evans.

All My Children. rev. ed. Jacqui L. Schiff & Betty Day. 1977. pap. 1.95 (ISBN 0-515-05422-4). Jove Pubns.

All My Eyes See. Gerard M. Hopkins. Ed. by R. K. Thornton. 148p. 1980. pap. 12.95x (ISBN 0-904461-06-8, Pub. by Geolfrith Pr England). Intl Schol Bk Serv.

All My Men. Bernard Ashley. LC 78-12683. (gr. 6 up). 1978. 9.95 (ISBN 0-87599-228-5). S G Phillips.

All My Patients Are Under the Bed. Louis J. Camuti. 1980. 10.95 (ISBN 0-671-24271-7). S&S.

All My Patients Under the Bed. Louis J. Camuti et al. 1980. lib. bdg. 14.50 (ISBN 0-8161-3170-8, Large Print Bks). G K Hall.

All My Yesterdays. Prem Bhatia. (Illus.). 179p. 1972. 6.75x (ISBN 0-685-30444-2). Intl Pubns Serv.

All My Yesterdays. Edward G. Robinson & Leonard Spigelgass. 1975. pap. 1.95 o.p. (ISBN 0-451-06428-3, J6428, Sig). NAL.

All New Complete Book of Bicycling. Eugene A. Sloane. (Illus.). 1981. 19.95 (ISBN 0-671-24967-3). S&S.

All New Mad Secret File on Spy Vs. Spy. Antonio Prohias. (Mad Ser). (Illus.). 192p. 1973. pap. 1.75 (ISBN 0-446-94421-1). Warner Bks.

All New Sophie Lavitt's Penny Pincher's Cookbook. Sophie Leavitt. 512p. 1980. pap. 2.95 (ISBN 0-553-13329-2). Bantam.

All Night L.A. John Pashdag & Jim Woller. Ed. by Susan Harper & Jane Vandenburgh. LC 78-3557. (Illus.). 1978. pap. 4.95 o.p. (ISBN 0-87701-112-5). Chronicle Bks.

All Night Long. Eileen Lottman. 192p. (Orig.). 1981. pap. 2.50 (ISBN 0-515-06000-3). Jove Pubns.

All Occasion Finger Plays for Young Children. Compiled by Patricia Shely. (Standard Ideas Ser.). (Illus.). 1978. pap. 1.75 (ISBN 0-87239-211-2, 2812). Standard Pub.

All-Occasion Game Book. Sally E. Stuart. (Illus.). 64p. (Orig.). 1981. pap. 2.95 (ISBN 0-87239-444-1, 2798). Standard Pub.

All-Of-A-Kind Family Downtown. Sydney Taylor. (gr. 3-6). 1973. pap. 1.50 (ISBN 0-440-42032-6, YB). Dell.

All-Of-A-Kind Family Uptown. Sydney Taylor. (Illus.). (gr. 4-7). 1968. pap. 1.50 (ISBN 0-440-40091-0, YB). Dell.

All of Grace. C. H. Spurgeon. 128p. 1981. pap. 2.50 (ISBN 0-88368-097-1). Whitaker Hse.

All of Grace. Charles H. Spurgeon. pap. 1.50 (ISBN 0-8024-0001-9). Moody.

All of Grace. Charles H. Spurgeon. (Summit Books). 1976. pap. text ed. 2.45 (ISBN 0-8010-8095-9). Baker Bk.

All of Micro Vol. 2: The 6502 Journal No. 7-12 Oct-Nov 78 - May 79. Computerist Inc. Ed. by Robert M. Tripp. (Illus.). 8.00 (ISBN 0-938222-01-5). Computerist.

All-of-Sudden Susan. Elizabeth Coatsworth. LC 74-6200. (Illus.). 80p. (gr. 3-5). 1974. 7.95g (ISBN 0-02-722610-7, 72261). Macmillan.

All Our Kin: Strategies for Survival in a Black Community. Carol B. Stack. 1975. pap. 3.95 (ISBN 0-06-090424-0, CN424, CN). Har-Row.

All Our Secrets. Mary Drayton. 384p. (Orig.). 1981. pap. 2.95 (ISBN 0-449-14391-0, GM). Fawcett.

All Out for Everest. Michael Montgomery. 1975. 12.95 (ISBN 0-236-40012-6, Pub. by Paul Elek). Merrimack Bk Serv.

All Over Again. Nathaniel Benchley. LC 80-1800. (Illus.). 240p. 1981. 11.95 (ISBN 0-385-15859-9). Doubleday.

All Paris. Ed. by Editore Bonechi. LC 76-23572. (Encore Edition). (Illus.). 1976. 4.95 o.p. (ISBN 0-684-15936-8, ScribT). Scribner.

All Paris. Giovanna Magi. LC 77-365195. (Illus.). 128p. (Orig.). 1975. pap. 15.00x (ISBN 88-7009-055-8). Intl Pubns Serv.

All Possible Worlds, a History of Geographical Ideas. 2nd ed. Preston E. James & Geoffrey J. Martin. LC 80-25021. 650p. 1981. text ed. 19.95 (ISBN 0-471-06121-2). Wiley.

All-Pro Baseball Stars 1980. Weber. (gr. 7-12). 1980. pap. 1.25 (ISBN 0-590-31537-4, Schol Pap). Schol Bk Serv.

All-Pro Basketball Stars 1979. rev. ed. Bruce Weber. (gr. 7-12). 1979. pap. 1.25 o.p. (ISBN 0-590-12064-6, Schol Pap). Schol Bk Serv.

All-Pro Basketball Stars 1980. (gr. 7-12). 1980. pap. 1.25 (ISBN 0-590-31238-3, Schol Pap). Schol Bk Serv.

All Purpose Guide to Paddling. 1976. pap. 5.95 (ISBN 0-8092-7259-8). Contemp Bks.

All-RN Nursing Staff. Genrose Alfano. LC 81-80201. (Nursing Dimensions Administration Ser.). 250p. 1981. pap. text ed. 11.95 (ISBN 0-913654-68-X). Nursing Res.

All Round Ministry. C. H. Spurgeon. 1978. pap. 5.45 (ISBN 0-85151-277-1). Banner of Truth.

All Said & Done. Simone De Beauvoir. 1975. pap. 2.50 o.s.i. (ISBN 0-446-81191-2). Warner Bks.

All Season Hunting. Bob Gilsvik. 1976. 11.95 (ISBN 0-87691-181-5). Winchester Pr.

All Series, Bks. 1-4. Herbert Lockyer. Incl. Bk. 1. All the Apostles of the Bible. 11.95 (ISBN 0-310-28010-9); Bk. 2. All the Books & Chapters of the Bible. 10.95 (ISBN 0-310-28020-6); Bk. 3. All the Doctrines of the Bible. 11.95 (ISBN 0-310-28050-8); Bks. 2 & 3 Set. 21.90 (ISBN 0-310-28168-7); Bk. 4. All the Children of the Bible. 12.95 (ISBN 0-310-28030-3); Bk. 5. All the Holy Days & Holidays. 11.95 (ISBN 0-310-28060-5); Bk. 6. All the Kings & Queens of the Bible. 10.95 (ISBN 0-310-28070-2); Bks. 5 & 6 Set. 21.90 (ISBN 0-310-28178-4); Bk. 7. All the Men of the Bible. 11.95 (ISBN 0-310-28080-X); Bk. 8. All the Women of the Bible. 9.95 (ISBN 0-310-28150-4); Bks. 7 & 8 Set. 20.90 (ISBN 0-310-28188-1); Bk. 9. All the Miracles of the Bible. 10.95 (ISBN 0-310-28100-8); Bk. 10. All the Parables of the Bible. 12.95 (ISBN 0-310-28110-5); Bks. 9 & 10 Set. 21.90 (ISBN 0-310-28198-9); Bk. 11. All the Prayers of the Bible. 11.95 (ISBN 0-310-28120-2); Bk. 12. All the Promises of the Bible. 11.95 (ISBN 0-310-28130-X); Bks. 11 & 12 Set. 24.90 (ISBN 0-310-28208-X); Bk. 13. All the Trades & Occupations of the Bible. 11.95 (ISBN 0-310-28140-7); Bk. 14. All the Messianic Prophecies of the Bible. 14.95 (ISBN 0-310-28090-7). Zondervan.

All Star Turn-About Quiz Book. Mark Tan. 1977. pap. 2.00 o.p. (ISBN 0-685-75811-7, 0416-3). Price Stern.

All-Sufficiency of the Gospel. Melvin J. Wise. 5.95 (ISBN 0-89315-000-2). Lambert Bk.

All-Terrain Adventure Vehicles. John W. Malo. LC 70-187074. (Illus.). 192p. 1972. 7.95 o.s.i. (ISBN 0-686-66685-2). Macmillan.

All-Terrain Adventure Vehicles. John W. Malo. LC 70-187074. 1972. pap. 3.95 o.s.i. (ISBN 0-02-029230-9, Collier). Macmillan.

All That Glittered: Selected Correspondence of Lionel Phillips, 1890-1924. Lionel Phillips. Ed. by Maryna Fraser & Alan Jeeves. (Illus.). 444p. 1977. text ed. 31.00x (ISBN 0-19-570100-3). Oxford U Pr.

All That Glitters. Jane McCarthy. 192p. (YA) 1976. 4.95 o.p. (ISBN 0-685-64242-9, Avalon). Bouregy.

All That Glitters. George Rose. 1980. pap. 5.95 (ISBN 0-9602462-6-6). Working Pr CA.

All That Jazz. H. B. Gilmour. (Orig.). pap. 2.25 (ISBN 0-515-05374-0). Jove Pubns.

All That Money & No Cash. Donald Clugston. 128p. 1981. 7.50 (ISBN 0-682-49678-2). Exposition.

All That You Need to Know About Camp Counseling. Evelyn C. Stutts. (Illus.). 1981. 4.95 (ISBN 0-8062-1708-1). Carlton.

All the Apostles of the Bible. Lockyer. 1972. 10.95 (ISBN 0-310-28010-9, 10052). Zondervan.

All the Best Card Games. David Parlett. 1979. 19.95 (ISBN 0-7134-0387-X, Pub. by Batsford England). David & Charles.

All the Best Rubbish. Ivor Noel-Hume. LC 73-4093. (Illus.). 320p. 1974. 10.00 o.p. (ISBN 0-06-011997-7, HarpT). Har-Row.

All the Buffalo Returning. Dorothy M. Johnson. LC 78-22425. 1979. 6.95 (ISBN 0-396-07668-8). Dodd.

All the Classroom Is a Stage: The Creative Classroom Environment. Shirley Heck & Jon P. Cobes. LC 78-7600. (Illus.). 1978. 18.25 (ISBN 0-08-022248-X); pap. 9.95 (ISBN 0-08-022247-1). Pergamon.

All the Colors of Darkness. Lloyd Biggle, Jr. 1975. pap. 1.25 o.p. (ISBN 0-685-54123-1, LB2956K, Leisure Bks). Nordon Pubns.

All the Days of My Life. Rebecca Lovato. LC 77-74003. 1977. 6.00 (ISBN 0-89430-014-8). Morgan-Pacific.

All the Days Were Summer. Jack Bickham. LC 80-2895. 240p. 1981. 10.95 (ISBN 0-385-17597-3). Doubleday.

All the Divine Names & Titles in the Bible. Herbert Lockyer. 352p. 1975. 12.95 (ISBN 0-310-28040-0). Zondervan.

All the Good People I've Left Behind. Joyce Carol Oates. 250p. 1978. 14.00 o.p. (ISBN 0-87685-394-7); pap. 5.00 (ISBN 0-87685-393-9). Black Sparrow.

All the King's Men. nd ed. James L. Johnson. LC 80-83842. 328p. 1981. pap. 3.25 (ISBN 0-89081-267-5). Harvest Hse.

All the King's Men Notes. Robert H. Lynn. (Orig.). pap. 1.95 (ISBN 0-8220-0146-2). Cliffs.

All the Naked Heroes. Alan Kapelner. LC 60-5611. 1960. 4.00 o.s.i. (ISBN 0-8076-0102-0). Braziller.

All the Pomises. Lockyer. Date not set. Set. 24.90 (ISBN 0-686-69347-7, 10089). Zondervan. Postponed.

All the President's Men. Carl Bernstein & Bob Woodward. (Illus.). 1976. pap. 3.50 (ISBN 0-446-96983-4). Warner Bks.

All the Pretty Horses. Susan Jeffers. LC 73-19053. (Illus.). 32p. (gr. k-3). 1974. 6.95g o.s.i. (ISBN 0-02-747680-4). Macmillan.

All the Promises of the Bible. Lockyer. 1962. 10.95 (ISBN 0-310-28130-X, 10074). Zondervan.

All the Queen's Men. Neville Williams. (Elizabeth & Her Courtiers). (Illus.). 272p. 1972. 12.95 o.s.i. (ISBN 0-02-629110-X). Macmillan.

All the Rivers Run. Nancy Cato. 1979. pap. 2.95 (ISBN 0-451-08693-7, E8693, Sig). NAL.

All the Silver Pennies. B. J. Thompson. (Illus.). (gr. 1-6). 1967. 7.95 o.s.i. (ISBN 0-02-789330-8). Macmillan.

All the Stars in Heaven: The Story of Louis B. Mayer & Metro-Goldwyn-Mayer. Gary Carey. (Illus.). 1980. 15.00 (ISBN 0-525-05245-3). Dutton.

All the Talents; a Satirical Poem, in Four Dialogues. to Which Is Added, a Pastoral Epilogue, Repr. of 1807. Eaton S. Barrett. Ed. by Donald H. Reiman. Bd. with Second Titan War Against Heaven; or, the Talents Buried Under Portland-Isle. Repr. of 1807 ed; Talents Run Mad; or, Eighteen Hundred & Sixteen. a Satirical Poem. Repr. of 1816 ed. LC 75-31150. (Romantic Context Ser.: Poetry 1789-1830). 1979. lib. bdg. 47.00 (ISBN 0-8240-2104-5). Garland Pub.

All the Things You Aren't...Yet. Jackie Humphries. LC 77-92468. 1980. cancelled (ISBN 0-8499-0071-9, 0071-9); pap. 5.95 (ISBN 0-8499-2891-5). Word Bks.

All the Things Your Mother Never Taught You. Charlotte Slater. (Illus.). 294p. 1975. pap. 4.95 o.p. (ISBN 0-8362-0625-8). Andrews & McMeel.

All the Times (The East-West Chronicles) Jim Doerter. (Illus.). 1980. pap. 7.00 (ISBN 0-913232-69-6). W Kaufmann.

All the Trees & Woody Plants of the Bible. D. A. Anderson. 1979. cloth 10.95 (ISBN 0-8499-0138-3). Word Bks.

All the Ways of Building. Louise Lamprey. (Illus.). (gr. 7 up). 1933. 5.95 o.s.i. (ISBN 0-02-751380-7). Macmillan.

All the World Is Kin. Bernice E. Hicks. (Illus.). 212p. 1981. lib. bdg. 9.95 (ISBN 0-87961-116-2); pap. 5.95 (ISBN 0-87961-117-0). Naturegraph.

All the World's Aircraft Nineteen Eighty to Nineteen Eighty-One. Taylor. 1980. 135.00 (ISBN 0-531-03953-6). Watts.

All the World's Aircraft Nineteen Seventy-Nine to Nineteen Eighty. Taylor. 1980. 99.50 (ISBN 0-531-03915-3). Watts.

All the World's Fighting Ships, Eighteen Ninety-Eight. Ed. by Fred T. Jane. LC 69-14519. (Illus.). Repr. of 1898 ed. 14.95x (ISBN 0-685-06494-8, Pub by Arco). Biblo.

All the World's Fighting Ships, 1922-1946. Ed. by Conway Maritime Press. (Illus.). 448p. 1980. 65.00 (ISBN 0-8317-0303-2). Mayflower Bks.

All Their Kingdoms. Madeleine A. Polland. 1981. 11.95 (ISBN 0-440-00019-X). Delacorte.

All These Condemned. John MacDonald. 1981. pap. 1.95 (ISBN 0-449-14239-6, GM). Fawcett.

All These Earths. F. M. Busby. 1978. pap. 1.75 o.p. (ISBN 0-425-03902-1, Medallion). Berkley Pub.

All Things Are Possible & Penultimate Words & Other Essays. Lev Shestov. LC 76-8303. xiii, 239p. 1977. 13.50x (ISBN 0-8214-0237-4). Ohio U Pr.

All Things Are Possible Through Prayer. Charles L. Allen. 1975. pap. 1.25 (ISBN 0-89129-072-9, PV072). Jove Pubns.

All Things Are Possible Through Prayer. Charles L. Allen. (Orig.). pap. 1.95 (ISBN 0-515-05982-X). Jove Pubns.

All Things Bright & Beautiful. James Herriot. LC 73-87407. 400p. 1974. 10.95 (ISBN 0-312-02030-9). St Martin.

All Things Bright & Beautiful? A Sociological Study of Infants' Classrooms. Ronald King. LC 78-4518. 1978. 25.25 (ISBN 0-471-99653-X, Pub. by Wiley-Interscience). Wiley.

All Things in Their Time. LaWant P. Jack. pap. 5.95 (ISBN 0-89036-145-2). Hawkes Pub Inc.

All Things Made New: A Comprehensive Outline of the Baha'i Faith. rev. ed. John Ferraby. 1975. 14.00 (ISBN 0-900125-23-3, 7-32-16); pap. 7.50 (ISBN 0-900125-24-1, 7-32-17). Baha'i.

All Things New. Arthur E. Bloomfield. LC 42-5300. 1959. pap. 5.95 (ISBN 0-87123-007-0); study guide .95 (ISBN 0-87123-520-X). Bethany Fell.

All Things to All Men. Godfrey Hodgson. 1980. 12.95 (ISBN 0-671-24782-4). S&S.

All Things Weird & Wonderful. Stuart Briscoe. 1977. pap. text ed. 3.50 (ISBN 0-88207-749-X). Victor Bks.

All Things Wise & Wonderful. James Herriot. LC 77-76640. 1977. 10.95 (ISBN 0-312-02031-7). St Martin.

All Things Wise & Wonderful. Pasadena Art Alliance. 1975. pap. 4.50 (ISBN 0-937042-00-5). Pasadena Art.

All This & Snoopy, Too: Selected Cartoons from "You Can't Win, Charlie Brown", Vol. 2. Charles M. Schulz. (Peanuts Ser.). (Illus.). (gr. 5 up). 1978. pap. 1.50 (ISBN 0-449-23824-5, Crest). Fawcett.

All Those Cessna 150's: Owners Manuals 1959-1977. National Flightshops. Date not set. pap. 12.95 (Pub. by National Flightshops). Aviation.

All Through the Day. Guy King. 128p. 1980. pap. 3.95 (ISBN 0-310-41831-3). Zondervan.

All Through the House: A Guide to Home Weatherization. Thomas Blandy & Denis Lamoureux. (Illus., Orig.). 1980. pap. 6.95 (ISBN 0-07-005871-7). McGraw.

All Through the Night. Grace L. Hill. 1980. pap. cancelled. Bantam.

All-Thumbs Color-Blind Book of Interior Decorating. Joan Lowenthal. (Illus.). 1977. 6.95 o.p. (ISBN 0-8092-7259-8). Contemp Bks.

All-Time Rosters of Major League Baseball Clubs. S. C. Thompson. LC 73-156. 800p. 1973. 12.00 o.p. (ISBN 0-498-01380-4). A S Barnes.

All Upon a Stone. Jean C. George. LC 75-101929. (Illus.). (gr. 2-5). 1971. PLB 7.49 o.p. (ISBN 0-690-05533-1, TYC-J). T Y Crowell.

All We Know of Heaven. Sandee Cohen. (Orig.). 1981. pap. 2.50 (ISBN 0-451-09891-9, E9891, Sig). NAL.

All We Know of Heaven. Dore Mullen. (Orig.). 1980. pap. 2.50 (ISBN 0-440-10178-6). Dell.

All Year Long. Richard Scarry. (Golden Look-Look Bks.). (Illus.). (ps-1). 1976. PLB 5.38 (ISBN 0-307-61826-9, Golden Pr); pap. 0.95 (ISBN 0-307-11826-6). Western Pub.

All You Must Know About Psychology in Order to Know Yourself. Douglas J. Pierce. (Illus.). 1980. 27.45 (ISBN 0-89920-008-7). Am Inst Psych.

All You Need to Know About Defined Benefit Keogh Plans. Howard M. Phillips. 120p. 1980. text ed. 20.00 looseleaf (ISBN 0-89529-130-4). Avery Pub.

All You Should Know About Arthritis. Ruth Adams & Frank Murray. 256p. (Orig.). 1979. pap. 2.25 (ISBN 0-915962-28-4). Larchmont Bks.

All You Should Know About Beverages for Your Health & Well Being. Ruth Adams & Frank Murray. 286p. 1976. pap. 1.75 (ISBN 0-915962-17-9). Larchmont Bks.

All You Should Know About Health Foods. Ruth Adams & Frank Murray. 352p. pap. 2.50 (ISBN 0-915962-01-2). Larchmont Bks.

Allagash. Lew Dietz. LC 78-8326. 1978. 11.50x o.p. (ISBN 0-89621-001-4); pap. 5.95x (ISBN 0-89621-000-6). Thorndike Pr.

Allah Conspiracy. Christopher Warren. LC 80-27097. 224p. 1981. 10.95 (ISBN 0-8253-0052-5). Beaufort Bks NY.

Allan Dwan. Peter Bogdanovich. (Belvedere Bk.). 220p. 1981. pap. 5.95 (ISBN 0-87754-320-8). Chelsea Hse.

Allan Pinkerton. Lavere Anderson. (gr. k-6). Date not set. pap. price not set (ISBN 0-440-40210-7, YB). Dell.

Allan Quatermain, Being an Account of His Further Adventures & Discoveries in Company with Sir Henry Curtis, Bart., Commander John Good, R.N., & One Umslopogaas. H. Rider Haggard. Ed. by R. Reginald & Douglas Menville. LC 80-19297. (Newcastle Forgotten Fantasy Library: Vol. 18). 278p. 1980. Repr. of 1978 ed. lib. bdg. 10.95x (ISBN 0-89370-517-9). Borgo Pr.

Allan Swenson's Big Fun to Grow Book. Allan A. Swenson. (gr. 4-6). 1980. pap. 3.50 o.p. (ISBN 0-679-20510-1). McKay.

Allan's Wife. H. Rider Haggard. Ed. by R. Reginald & Douglas Menville. LC 80-8671. (Newcastle Forgotten Fantasy Library: Vol. 24). 200p. 1980. lib. bdg. 11.95x (ISBN 0-89370-523-3). Borgo Pr.

Allart van Everdingen. Alice I. Davies. LC 77-94692. (Outstanding Dissertations in the Fine Arts Ser.). 1979. lib. bdg. 64.50 (ISBN 0-8240-3223-3). Garland Pub.

Allegoriae Poeticae, Repr. Of 1520 Ed. Albricus. Incl. Theologia Mythologica. Georg Pictorius. Repr. of 1532 ed; Apotheoseos Tam Exterarum Gentium Quam Romanorum Deorum. Georg Pictorius. Repr. of 1558 ed. LC 75-27845. (Renaissance & the Gods Ser.: Vol. 4). (Illus.). 1976. lib. bdg. 73.00 (ISBN 0-8240-2053-7). Garland Pub.

Allegory & Mirror: Tradition & Structure in Middle English Literature. James I. Wimsatt. LC 71-101376. 1970. 20.00x (ISBN 0-672-63502-X). Irvington.

Allegory of Love: A Study of Medieval Tradition. Clive S. Lewis. 1936. 22.00x (ISBN 0-19-811562-8); pap. 4.95x (ISBN 0-19-500343-8). Oxford U Pr.

Allegra. Clare Darcy. LC 74-82400. 1975. 7.95 o.s.i. (ISBN 0-8027-0475-1). Walker & Co.

Allen Bakke Vs. Regents of the University of California, 6 vols. 1978. 44.00 ea. Oceana.

Allen-Barker-Hines Peripheral Vascular Diseases. 5th ed. John L. Juergens et al. LC 78-65379. (Illus.). 981p. 1980. text ed. 60.00 (ISBN 0-7216-5229-8). Saunders.

Allen: The Biography of an Army Officer 1859-1930. Heath Twichell, Jr. 1974. 23.50 (ISBN 0-8135-0778-2). Rutgers U Pr.

Allende's Chile. Ed. by Kenneth Medhurst. LC 73-81735. 212p. 1973. 17.95 (ISBN 0-312-02100-3). St Martin.

Allen's Synonyms & Antonyms. rev. & enl. ed. F. Sturges Allen. Ed. by T. H. Motter. LC 38-12323. 1938. 12.50 o.p. (ISBN 0-06-010070-2, HarpT). Har-Row.

Allen's Synonyms & Antonyms. F. Sturges Allen. pap. 3.50 (ISBN 0-06-463328-4, EH 328, EH). Har-Row.

Allergic Contact Dermatitis in the Guinea Pig: Identification of Contact Allergens. Bertil Magnusson & Albert M. Kligman. (Illus.). 160p. 1970. 23.75 (ISBN 0-398-01200-8). C C Thomas.

Allergic Diseases: Diagnosis & Management. 2nd ed. Roy Patterson. (Illus.). 624p. 1980. text ed. 42.50 (ISBN 0-397-50468-3). Lippincott.

Allergies. Sarah Riedman. (First Books Ser.). (Illus.). (gr. 4-6). 1978. PLB 6.45 s&l (ISBN 0-531-01352-9). Watts.

Allergies. Alvin Silverstein & Virginia B. Silverstein. LC 77-1284. (gr. 4 up). 1977. 7.95 (ISBN 0-397-31758-1); pap. 2.95 (ISBN 0-397-31759-X). Lippincott.

Allergies & You. Shelia L. Burns. LC 79-26637. (Illus.). 64p. (gr. 3-7). 1980. PLB 6.97 (ISBN 0-671-33044-6). Messner.

Allergies & Your Child. Doris J. Rapp. LC 71-155528. 1972. 6.95 o.p. (ISBN 0-03-086578-6). HR&W.

Allergies & Your Family. Doris J. Rapp. LC 79-93250. (Illus.). 352p. 1980. 12.95 (ISBN 0-8069-5558-9); lib. bdg. 11.69 (ISBN 0-8069-5559-7); pap. 6.95 (ISBN 0-8069-8878-9). Sterling.

Allergies: How to Find & Conquer. John Barton & Margaret Barton. (Illus.). 280p. 1980. pap. 15.00 (ISBN 0-937216-01-1). J&M Barton.

Allergies: What They Are & What to Do About Them. Jack Rudolph. 1973. pap. 1.75 (ISBN 0-515-05142-X, V3101). Jove Pubns.

Allergy. John J. Condemi & Robert Schwartz. (Medical Examination Review Book Ser.: No. 26). 1973. spiral bdg. 16.50 (ISBN 0-87488-132-3). Med Exam.

Allergy. European Congress of Allergology & Clinical Immunology, 9th. Ed. by A. W. Frankland & M. A. Ganderton. (Illus.). 400p. (Orig.). 1975. pap. text ed. 32.00x o.p. (ISBN 0-8464-0125-8). Beekman Pubs.

Allergy & Clinical Immunology. Ed. by Richard F. Lockey. LC 78-62073. 1979. 42.50 (ISBN 0-87488-665-1). Med Exam.

Allergy & Immunology in Children. Frederic Speer & Robert J. Dockhorn. (Illus.). 780p. 1973. 54.50 (ISBN 0-398-02670-X). C C Thomas.

Allergy & Your Child. Emile Somekh. LC 73-14291. 288p. 1974. 9.95 o.s.i. (ISBN 0-06-013969-2, HarpT). Har-Row.

Allergy Book. Harsha V. Dehejia. 184p. 1981. 10.95 (ISBN 0-442-21887-7). Van Nos Reinhold.

Allergy, Brains, & Children Coping. new ed. Ray C. Wunderlich. LC 72-96304. (Illus.). 170p. 1973. 9.25 (ISBN 0-910812-12-8); pap. 6.90 (ISBN 0-910812-13-6). Johnny Reads.

Allergy Case Studies. Ed. by Irving H. Itkin. 1973. spiral bdg. 14.00 (ISBN 0-87488-027-0). Med Exam.

Allergy Cooking. Marion L. Conrad. (Orig.). pap. 2.25 (ISBN 0-515-05738-X). Jove Pubns.

Allergy Cures Your Allergist Never Mentioned. Sterling R. Booth, Jr. 1981. 12.95 (ISBN 0-87949-191-4). Ashley Bks.

Allergy Encyclopedia. Ed. by Asthma & Allergy Foundation of America & Craig T. Norback. (Orig.). 1981. pap. price not set (ISBN 0-452-25270-9, Z5270, Plume Bks). NAL.

Allergy of the Nervous System. Frederic Speer. (Illus.). 280p. 1970. text ed. 27.50 (ISBN 0-398-01822-7). C C Thomas.

Allergy: Principles & Practice. Elliott Middleton et al. LC 77-9311. (Illus.). 1978. 99.50 (ISBN 0-8016-3419-9). Mosby.

Allerton & Dreux; or, the War of Opinion, 1851. Jean Ingelow. Ed. by Robert L. Wolff. LC 75-475. (Victorian Fiction Ser.). 1975. lib. bdg. 66.00 (ISBN 0-8240-1553-3). Garland Pub.

Alleviating Economic Distress: Evaluating a Federal Effort. Raymond Milkman et al. LC 71-174597. (Illus.). 320p. 1972. 20.00 o.p. (ISBN 0-669-81216-1). Lexington Bks.

Alleys: A Novel. R. D. Taylor. LC 80-65066. 144p. 1980. 6.95 (ISBN 0-931604-06-0); pap. 3.95 (ISBN 0-931604-07-9). Curbstone Pub NY TX.

Allgemeine Enzyklopaedie der Wissenschaften und Kuste (Ersch-Gruber, 167 vols. (Ger.). 1969. Set. write for info. Pergamon.

Alliance Against Hitler: The Origins of the Franco-Soviet Pact. William E. Scott. LC 62-20214. 1962. 14.75 o.p. (ISBN 0-686-66403-5). Duke.

Alliance in Decline: A Study in Anglo-Japanese Relations 1908-23. Ian H. Nish. (University of London Historical Studies: No. 33). (Illus.). 472p. (Orig.). 1972. text ed. 47.00x (ISBN 0-485-13133-1, Athlone Pr). Humanities.

Alliance in Eskimo Society. Ed. by D. L. Guemple. LC 72-3423. 1972. 7.50 o.p. (ISBN 0-295-95236-9). U of Wash Pr.

Alliance Politics. Richard E. Neustadt. LC 77-120855. 1970. 15.00x (ISBN 0-231-03066-5); pap. 6.00x (ISBN 0-231-08307-6). Columbia U Pr.

Alliances & Balance of Power. M. V. Naidu. LC 74-82531. 256p. 1975. 17.95x (ISBN 0-312-02135-6). St Martin.

Alliances & Small Powers. Robert L. Rothstein. LC 68-28401. (Institute of War & Peace Studies). 1968. 20.00x (ISBN 0-231-03113-0). Columbia U Pr.

Allied Bayonets of World War Two. J. Anthony Carter. LC 69-13592. (Twentieth Century Arms Ser). (Illus.). 1969. 3.50 o.p. (ISBN 0-668-01862-3). Arco.

Allied Escort Ships of World War II. Peter R. Elliott. LC 77-85752. 1978. 19.50 (ISBN 0-87021-801-8). Naval Inst Pr.

Allied Health Manpower. Harry I. Greenfield. LC 75-76249. (Illus.). 1969. 20.00x (ISBN 0-231-03226-9). Columbia U Pr.

Allies on the Rhine, Nineteen Forty-Five to Nineteen-Fifty. Elena Skrjabina. Ed. & illus. by Norman Luxenburg. LC 79-28187. (Illus.). 176p. 1980. 12.95 (ISBN 0-8093-0939-4). S Ill U Pr.

Alligators. Ada Graham & Frank Graham. LC 79-50671. (Audubon Readers Ser.: No. 5). (Illus.). (gr. 5 up). 1979. 7.95 (ISBN 0-440-00390-3); PLB 7.45 (ISBN 0-440-00391-1). Delacorte.

Alligators & Crocodiles. rev. ed. Herbert S. Zim. LC 78-6615. (gr. 4-6). 1978. PLB 6.67 (ISBN 0-688-32170-4). Morrow.

Alligators & Other Crocodilians. Ruth B. Gross. LC 77-18310. (Illus.). 64p. (gr. 1-5). 1978. 7.95 (ISBN 0-590-07556-X, Four Winds). Schol Bk Serv.

Alligators Are Awful: And They Have Terrible Manners, Too. David McPhail. LC 79-7607. (Illus.). (gr. 1-3). 1980. 7.95a (ISBN 0-385-13582-3); PLB (ISBN 0-385-13583-1). Doubleday.

Alligators, Raccoons, & Other Survivors: The Wildlife of the Future. Barbara Ford. LC 80-28193. (Illus.). 96p. (gr. 4-6). 1981. 8.95 (ISBN 0-688-00369-9); PLB 8.59 (ISBN 0-688-00370-2). Morrow.

Alligator's Song. Robert Tallon. (Illus.). 48p. (ps-3). 4.95 (ISBN 0-8193-1043-3); PLB 5.95 (ISBN 0-8193-1044-1). Parents.

Alligator's Song. Robert Tallon. (Illus.). 48p. (ps-3). 1981. PLB 5.95 (ISBN 0-8193-1044-1); pap. 4.95 (ISBN 0-8193-1043-3). Parents.

Alliterative Morte Arthure, the Owl & the Nightingale, & Five Other Middle English Poems: In a Modernized Version with Comments on the Poems & Notes. John C. Gardner. LC 73-7728. (Arcturus Books Paperbacks). 310p. 1973. pap. 7.95 (ISBN 0-8093-0648-4). S Ill U Pr.

Alliterative Tradition in the Fourteenth Century. Ed. by Bernard Levy & Paul Szarmach. LC 80-84665. 230p. 1980. write for info. (ISBN 0-87338-255-2). Kent St U Pr.

Alloantigen Systems of Human Leucocytes & Platelets. Fulop. 1979. 32.00 (ISBN 0-9960015-2-2, Pub. by Kaido Hungary). Heyden.

Allocating Health Resources for the Aged & Disabled: Technology Versus Politics. Robert Morris. 1981. price not set (ISBN 0-669-04329-X). Lexington Bks.

Allocating the Home Help Services. Neil Howell. 110p. 1979. pap. text ed. 11.25x (ISBN 0-7199-1026-9, Pub. by Bedford England). Renouf.

Allocation of Responsibility. Ed. by Max Gluckman. 321p. 1972. text ed. 19.50x (ISBN 0-7190-0491-8). Humanities.

Allocation Under Uncertainty: Equilibrium & Optimality Proceedings. Jacques H. Dreze. (IEA Ser.). 1974. 29.95 (ISBN 0-470-22166-6). Halsted Pr.

Allos: 41 Writings by 41 Writers. Ed. by Kenneth Gaburo et al. LC 80-80809. (Illus.). 448p. 1980. softcover 20.95. Lingua Pr.

All's Well That Ends Well. William Shakespeare. Ed. by Arthur Quiller-Couch et al. (New Shakespeare Ser). 23.95 (ISBN 0-521-07525-4); pap. 4.50x (ISBN 0-521-09468-2). Cambridge U Pr.

Allumette. Tomi Ungerer. LC 73-23055. (Illus.). 40p. (gr. k-3). 1974. 5.95 o.s.i. (ISBN 0-8193-0730-0, Four Winds); PLB 5.41 o.s.i. (ISBN 0-8193-0731-9). Schol Bk Serv.

Allusions: Cultural, Literary, Biblical, & Historical: A Thematic Dictionary. Ed. by Laurance Urdang. 1980. 45.00 (ISBN 0-8103-1124-0). Gale.

Alma on the Mississippi, 1848-1932. Barbara Anderson-Sannes. Ed. by Michael Doyle et al. LC 80-68241. (Illus.). 198p. (Orig.). 1980. pap. 11.95 (ISBN 0-9604684-0-4). Alma Hist Soc.

Alma-Tadema. encore ed. Vern Swanson. (Illus.). 1977. 5.95 o.p. (ISBN 0-684-16366-7, ScribT). Scribner.

Almacen De Dios: Exodo, 16 Lecciones, Vol. 2. Bernice C. Jordan. (Pasos De Fe Ser.). (Span.). tchrs'. manual 2.25 (ISBN 0-86508-403-3); figuras 7.95 (ISBN 0-86508-404-1). BCM Inc.

Almages, a Survey. O. Pedersen. (Illus.). 1974. 60.00x (ISBN 87-7492-087-1, D-751). Vanous.

Almanac & Yearbook 1978. annual ed. (Illus.). 1978. 5.95 o.p. (ISBN 0-685-86501-0, Pub. by Reader's Digest). Norton.

Almanac & Yearbook 1981. Reader's Digest. (Illus.). 1981. 6.95 (ISBN 0-89577-090-3, Pub. by Reader's Digest). Norton.

Almanac for Americans. Willis Thornton. LC 70-175784. (Illus.). viii, 418p. 1973. Repr. of 1941 ed. 22.00 (ISBN 0-8103-3276-0). Gale.

Almanac for Music Lovers. Elizabeth C. Moore. LC 70-167078. (Tower Bks). xiv, 382p. 1972. Repr. of 1940 ed. 24.00 (ISBN 0-8103-3940-4). Gale.

Almanac of American Letters. Randy F. Nelson. 350p. (Orig.). 1981. 16.95 (ISBN 0-86576-018-7); pap. 9.95 (ISBN 0-86576-008-X). W Kaufmann.

Almanac of American Politics - 1972. Michael Barone et al. LC 70-160417. (Illus.). 1972. 15.00 (ISBN 0-87645-053-2); pap. 6.95 (ISBN 0-87645-056-7). Gambit.

Almanac of British & American Literature. John O. Stark. LC 78-24249. 1979. lib. bdg. 20.00x (ISBN 0-87287-188-6). Libs Unl.

Almanac of Rural Living. Harvey C. Neese. 1979. 14.95 (ISBN 0-688-03411-X); pap. 8.95 (ISBN 0-688-08411-7). Morrow.

Almanac of Words at Play. Willard R. Espy. (Illus.). 352p. 1975. 12.95 (ISBN 0-517-52090-7); pap. 7.95 (ISBN 0-517-52463-5). Potter.

Almanac of World Crime. Ed. by Jay R. Nash. LC 79-6871. (Illus.). 432p. 1981. 19.95 (ISBN 0-385-15003-2). Doubleday.

Almanachs Populaires Aux XVIIe et XVIIIe Siecles: Essai D'histoire Sociale. Genevieve Bolleme. (Livre et Societes: No. 3). 1969. pap. 16.50x (ISBN 90-2796-265-0). Mouton.

Almanacs of the United States, 2 Vols. Milton Drake. LC 62-10127. 1962. Set. 45.00 (ISBN 0-8108-0001-2). Scarecrow.

Almayer's Folly. Joseph Conrad. lib. bdg. 13.95x (ISBN 0-89966-056-8). Buccaneer Bks.

Almighty & the Dollar. Jim McKeever. 400p. 1980. 10.95 (ISBN 0-931608-09-0); pap. 5.95 (ISBN 0-931608-10-4). Omega Pubns OR.

Almonds & Raisins. Maisie Mosco. 384p. (Orig.). 1981. pap. cancelled (ISBN 0-553-13913-4). Bantam.

Almonds to Zoybeans: A Natural Foods Cookbook. Mothey Parsons. (Illus.). 192p. 1973. pap. 1.50. Larchmont Bks.

Almoran & Hamnet: An Oriental Tale 1761, 2 vols. in 1. John Hawkesworth. Ed. by Michael F. Shugrue. (Flowering of the Novel, 1740-1775 Ser: Vol. 57). 1974. lib. bdg. 50.00 (ISBN 0-8240-1156-2). Garland Pub.

Almost a Champion. Paul J. Deegan. LC 74-14517. (Dan Murphy Sports Ser). 40p. (gr. 3-6). 1975. PLB 5.95 (ISBN 0-87191-402-6); pap. 2.95 (ISBN 0-89812-151-5). Creative Ed.

Almost a Layman. Samuel L. Hoard. 1981. price not set. Drake's Ptg & Pub.

Almost a Rainbow: A Book of Poems. Joan W. Anglund. (Illus.). 64p. 1980. 4.95 (ISBN 0-394-50072-5). Random.

Almost All-White Rabbity Cat. Meindert DeJong. LC 72-178599. (Illus.). 128p. (gr. 3-6). 1972. 7.95 (ISBN 0-02-726560-9). Macmillan.

Almost an Englishman. Charles Hannam. (gr. 6 up). 1979. PLB 8.95 (ISBN 0-233-97119-X). Andre Deutsch.

Almost April. Zoa Sherburne. (gr. 7 up). 1956. PLB 7.44 (ISBN 0-688-31013-3). Morrow.

Almost Like Sisters. Betty Cavanna. (gr. 7 up). 1963. 8.75 (ISBN 0-688-21014-7). Morrow.

Almost Midnight: Reforming the Late Night News. Itzhak Roeh et al. LC 80-16991. (People & Communication: Vol. 11). (Illus.). 200p. 1980. 18.50 (ISBN 0-8039-1504-7). Sage.

Almost Midnight: Reforming the Late Night News. Itzhak Roeh et al. LC 80-16991. (People & Communication: Vol. 11). (Illus.). 200p. 1980. pap. 8.95 (ISBN 0-8039-1505-5). Sage.

Almost Periodic Functions. Harald Bohr. LC 47-5500. 1980. 8.50 (ISBN 0-8284-0027-X). Chelsea Pub.

Almost Transparent Blue. Ryu Murakami. Tr. by Nancy Andrew from Japanese. LC 77-75959. 126p. 1977. 9.95x (ISBN 0-87011-305-4). Kodansha.

Almost Whole Earth Catalog of Process Oriented Enrichment Materials. Emily Stewart & Martha H. Dean. 1980. pap. 12.95 (ISBN 0-936386-12-6). Creative Learning.

Alms Race: The Impact of American Voluntary Aid Abroad. Eugene Linden. 1976. 10.00 o.p. (ISBN 0-394-49607-8). Random.

Aloe Vera. Carol M. Kent. LC 78-74978. (Illus.). 1979. pap. 6.00 (ISBN 0-9604886-0-X). C M Kent.

Aloes of South Africa. G. W. Reynolds. 1975. Repr. 51.00 (ISBN 0-86961-064-3). Horticultural.

Aloes of Tropical Africa & Madagascar. G. W. Reynolds. (Illus.). 1966. 51.00 (ISBN 0-685-12174-7). Horticultural.

Aloha Love. Bella Jarrett. 1979. pap. 1.25 o.s.i. (ISBN 0-440-10697-4). Dell.

Aloineae: A Biosystematic Survey. Herbert P. Riley & Shyamal K. Majumdar. LC 77-92927. (Illus.). 192p. 1980. 28.75x (ISBN 0-8131-1376-8). U Pr of Ky.

Alone, Again! Hildreth Scott. (Uplook Ser.). 1976. pap. 0.75 (ISBN 0-8163-0251-0, 01496-9). Pacific Pr Pub Assn.

Alone Against the Atlantic: The Observer Single-Handed Transatlantic Race, 1960-1980. Frank Page. LC 80-69349. (Illus.). 128p. 1981. 27.00x (ISBN 0-7153-8116-4). David & Charles.

Alone, Alone, All, All Alone. David R. Belgum. (Crossroads Ser.). 80p. (Orig.). 1972. pap. 1.95 (ISBN 0-570-06764-2, 12-2391). Concordia.

Alone in the Caribbean. Frederic A. Fenger. (Illus.). 1958. 6.95 o.p. (ISBN 0-686-00951-7). Wellington.

Alone in Wolf Hollow. Dana Brookins. LC 77-13118. (gr. 3-6). 1978. 7.95 (ISBN 0-395-28849-5, Clarion). HM.

Alone: Surviving As a Widow. Elizabeth Mooney. 320p. 1981. 10.95 (ISBN 0-399-12601-5). Putnam.

Alone Through the Dark Sea. Thomas Whiteside. LC 64-12964. 1964. 5.00 o.s.i. (ISBN 0-8076-0275-2). Braziller.

Alone, Unarmed but Safe--the Woman's Judo Defense Book. Buddy Clark. (Illus.). 128p. 1981. 8.00 (ISBN 0-682-49712-6); pap. 6.00 (ISBN 0-682-49711-8). Exposition.

Alone with America. enlarged ed. Richard Howard. LC 79-64718. 1980. 25.00 (ISBN 0-689-11000-6); pap. 12.95 (ISBN 0-689-70594-8, 177). Atheneum.

Alone with God: A Manual of Biblical Meditation. Campbell McAlpine. 1981. pap. 3.95 (ISBN 0-87123-000-3, 210000). Bethany Fell.

Along a Highland Road. J. F. Grant. 208p. 1980. 25.00x (ISBN 0-85683-048-8, Pub. by Shepheard-Walwyn England). State Mutual Bk.

Along Came a Dog. Meindert DeJong. LC 57-9265. (Illus.). 192p. (gr. 4-7). 1980. pap. 1.95 (ISBN 0-06-440114-6, Trophy). Har-Row.

Along Came a Llama. Ruth J. Ruck. (Illus.). 1978. 13.95 (ISBN 0-571-11277-3, Pub. by Faber & Faber). Merrimack Bk Serv.

Along Came the Model T! How Henry Ford Put the World on Wheels. Robert Quackenbush. LC 77-10057. (Illus.). 40p. (gr. k-5). 1978. 6.50 (ISBN 0-590-07714-7, Four Winds); PLB 6.19 o.p. (ISBN 0-8193-0953-2). Schol Bk Serv.

Along Came the Witch: A Journal of the 1960's. Helen Bevington. LC 75-31653. 216p. 1976. 8.95 o.p. (ISBN 0-15-105080-5). HarBraceJ.

Along the Border: A History of Virgilina, Virginia & the Surrounding Area in Halifax & Mecklenburg Counties in Virginia & Person & Granville Counties in North Carolina. Harry R. Mathis. LC 64-7237. (Illus.). 344p. 1964. 9.00x (ISBN 0-685-65080-4). Va Bk.

Along the Color Line: Explorations in the Black Experience. August Meier & Elliott Rudwick. LC 76-27293. (Blacks in the New World Ser.). 1977. 17.50 (ISBN 0-252-00636-4). U of Ill Pr.

Along the Edges: Special Issue 19. Ray Boxer. pap. 1.00 o.p. (ISBN 0-685-78393-6). The Smith.

Along the Old York Road. James Cawley & Margaret Cawley. 1965. pap. 2.75 o.p. (ISBN 0-8135-0487-2). Rutgers U Pr.

Along the Pennine Way. J. H. Peel. LC 79-52376. (Illus.). 1979. 19.95 (ISBN 0-7153-7833-3). David & Charles.

Along the Seashore. Margaret W. Buck. (Illus., Orig.). (gr. 3-9). 1964. 5.95 (ISBN 0-687-01114-0). Abingdon.

Along the Susquehanna. Ellis W. Roberts. 128p. 1980. 7.95 (ISBN 0-686-28856-4). Colwyn-Tangno.

Along the Trail. Richard Hovey. LC 76-108772. 1970. Repr. of 1903 ed. 14.50 (ISBN 0-685-05680-5). AMS Pr.

Along This Way: The Autobiography of James Weldon Johnson. James W. Johnson. LC 72-8404. (Civil Liberties in American History). (Illus.). 450p. 1973. Repr. of 1933 ed. lib. bdg. 39.50 (ISBN 0-306-70539-7). Da Capo.

Alonso De Castillo Solorzano. Alan Soons. (World Author Ser.: No. 457). 1978. 12.95 (ISBN 0-8057-6294-9). Twayne.

Alonzo Purr: The Seagoing Cat. Mary Carey. (Tell-a-Tale Readers). (Illus.). (gr. k-3). 1978. PLB 4.77 (ISBN 0-307-68569-1, Whitman). Western Pub.

Alouette. Jean Anouilh. Ed. by Merlin Thomas & Simon Lee. (Orig., Fr.,). 1975. pap. text ed. 8.95x incl. exercises (ISBN 0-89197-005-3). Irvington.

Alpes et le Rhone. (Beautes de la France). (Illus.). 1978. 18.25 (ISBN 2-03-013923-8, 3154). Larousse.

Alph & Ralph. Annie Ingle. (Illus.). (gr. 1-4). 1980. 3.95 (ISBN 0-525-69304-1, Gingerbread); PLB 5.95 (ISBN 0-525-69305-X). Dutton.

Alpha Backgammon. Baron V. Ball. LC 80-19226. (Illus.). 1980. pap. 5.95 (ISBN 0-688-08714-0, Quill). Morrow.

Alpha Centauri. Robert Siegel. LC 80-68330. 256p. (gr. 4 up). 1980. 9.95 (ISBN 0-89107-180-6, Cornerstone Bks.). Good News.

Alpha Curse. Walter D. Lee. 1981. 8.95 (ISBN 0-8062-1578-X). Carlton.

Alpha-Getoprotein: Laboratory Procedures & Clinical Applications. Kirkpatrick. 1981. write for info. Masson Pub.

Alpha-II. Thomas Hubschman. (Orig.). 1979. pap. 1.95 (ISBN 0-532-23266-6). Manor Bks.

Alpha Moonbase Technical Notebook. David Hirsch. (Illus.). (gr. 4 up). 1977. 9.95 (ISBN 0-931064-02-3). Starlog.

Alpha Syllabus: A Handbook of Human EEG Alpha Activity. Ed. by Barbara B. Brown & Jay Klug. 368p. 1974. text ed. 34.50 (ISBN 0-398-03020-0); pap. text ed. 28.50 (ISBN 0-398-03021-9). C C Thomas.

Alpha the Myths of Creation. Charles H. Long. (Patterns of Myth Ser.). 6.00 o.s.i. (ISBN 0-8076-0238-8). Braziller.

Alphabet. Virginia Polish. (Starting off with Phonics Ser.: Bk. 2). (Illus.). (gr. k). 1980. pap. text ed. 2.21 (ISBN 0-87895-052-4); tchrs. manual 2.00 (ISBN 0-87895-062-1). Modern Curr.

Alphabet. Gillian Youldon. (All A-Board Bks). 16p. (ps-2). 1981. 3.50 (ISBN 0-686-69397-3). Watts.

Alphabet & Elements of Lettering. rev. ed. Frederic W. Goudy. 8.50 (ISBN 0-8446-2145-5). Peter Smith.

Alphabet Cat. Floyd Black. LC 79-1911. (Illus.). (ps-3). 1979. 1.95 (ISBN 0-525-69008-5, Gingerbread Bks); PLB 5.95 (ISBN 0-525-69009-3, Gingerbread Bks). Dutton.

Alphabet of Grace. Frederick Buechner. (Orig.). 1977. pap. 3.95 (ISBN 0-8164-2163-3). Crossroad NY.

Alphabet Soup. A. C. Collins. (Cornerstone Ser.). (gr. 1-6). 1970. pap. text ed. 4.12 o.p. (ISBN 0-201-41001-X, Sch Div); tchr's manual 5.04 o.p. (ISBN 0-201-41002-8). A-W.

Alphabet Soup. rev. ed. Alberta C. Collins & Mildred A. Dawson. (Cornerstone Ser.). (gr. 2-3). 1978. pap. text ed. 4.52 (ISBN 0-201-41022-2, Sch Div); tchr's. ed. 5.56 (ISBN 0-201-41023-0). A-W.

Alphabet Symphony. Bruce McMillan. LC 77-5491. (ps-3). 1977. 7.25 (ISBN 0-688-80112-9); PLB 6.96 (ISBN 0-688-84112-0). Greenwillow.

Alphabet World. Barry Miller. LC 77-127470. (Illus.). (gr. k-1). 1971. 6.95 o.s.i. (ISBN 0-02-766970-X). Macmillan.

Alphabetic & Phonetic Texts of Informal Speech with Statistical Analyses. Edward C. Carterette & Margaret H. Jones. 1975. 42.50x (ISBN 0-520-01476-6). U of Cal Pr.

Alphabetical List of Battles, 1754-1900. Ed. by Newton A. Strait. 1968. Repr. of 1905 ed. 15.00 (ISBN 0-8103-3339-2). Gale.

Alphabetischer Katalog der Bibliothek Des Johann Gottfried Herder - Instituts: Second Supplement. Johann Gottfried Herder Institute. (Library Catalogs-Supplements Ser.). 1981. lib. bdg. 350.00 (ISBN 0-8161-0277-5). G K Hall.

Alphabets & Ornaments. Ernst Lehner. (Pictorial Archive Series). (Illus.). 1968. pap. 6.50 (ISBN 0-486-21905-4). Dover.

Alphabets Old & New for the Use of Craftsmen. 3rd ed. Lewis F. Day. LC 68-23148. 1968. Repr. of 1910 ed. 15.00 (ISBN 0-8103-3301-5). Gale.

Alphagenics. Anthony A. Zaffuto. 1975. pap. 1.75 o.s.i. (ISBN 0-446-59899-2). Warner Bks.

Alphanumeric Filing Rules for Business Documents. Herbert H. Hoffman. 118p. 1977. pap. 4.00x (ISBN 0-89537-001-8). Headway Pubns.

Alphonse & the Stonehenge Mystery. Jim Smith. (Frog Band Ser.). (Illus.). 32p. (gr. 1-3). 1980. 7.95 (ISBN 0-316-80162-3). Little.

Alphonse Daudet. Alphonse Roche. LC 75-25549. (World Authors Ser.: France: No. 380). 1976. lib. bdg. 12.50 (ISBN 0-8057-6223-X). Twayne.

Alphonse Mucha. rev. & enl. ed. Jiri Mucha & Marina Henderson. LC 73-90408. (Illus.). 1974. 25.00 (ISBN 0-312-55160-6). St Martin.

Alphonse Mucha Photographs. Graham Ovenden. LC 73-89210. (Illus.). 1974. 15.95 o.p. (ISBN 0-685-48994-9). St Martin.

Alpine Christ & Other Poems. Robinson Jeffers. Ed. by William Everson. 1974. 15.00 (ISBN 0-9600372-4-1). Cayuco's.

Alpine Flora of New Giunea, 4 vols. P. Van Royan. Incl. Vol. 1. General Part. 1980. lib. bdg. 50.00; Vol. 2. Taxonomic Part II: Cupressaceae to Poaceae. 1980. lib. bdg. 150.00 (ISBN 3-7682-1244-0); Vol. 3. Taxonomic Part 2: Winteraceae to Polygonaceae. 1981. lib. bdg. 100.00 (ISBN 3-7682-1245-9); Vol. 4. Taxonomic Part 3: Fagaceae to Asteraceae. 1981. lib. bdg. 100.00 (ISBN 3-7682-1246-7). 400.00 set (ISBN 3-7682-1247-5). Lubrecht & Cramer.

Alpine Flower Designs for Artists & Craftsmen. Francois Gos & Karen Baldausky. (Illus.). 64p. (Orig.). 1980. pap. 4.00 (ISBN 0-486-23982-9). Dover.

Alpine Garden Plants in Color. Will Ingwersen. (Illus.). 168p. 1981. 12.95 (ISBN 0-7137-0968-5, Pub. by Blandford Pr England); pap. 6.95 (ISBN 0-7137-1143-4). Sterling.

Alpine Guide, 2 vols. Robin G. Collomb. LC 75-455891. (Illus.). 1969. Vol. 1, Chamonix & Mont Blanc. Vol. 2, Zermatt & District. 10.00x ea.; 10.00x (ISBN 0-686-66323-3). Set (ISBN 0-09-456670-4). Intl Pubns Serv.

Alpine, Texas: Then & Now. Clifford B. Casey. (Illus.). 446p. 1980. 20.00 (ISBN 0-933512-33-3). Pioneer Bk Tx.

Alps. Shiro Shirahata. LC 80-50658. (Illus.). 220p. 1980. 75.00 (ISBN 0-8478-0316-3). Rizzoli Intl.

Alsatian Cooking. Gaertner & Frederick. 1981. 16.95 (ISBN 0-8120-5403-2). Barron.

Alsatian Owner's Encyclopaedia. Madeleine Pickup. 1964. 8.95 (ISBN 0-7207-0001-9, Pub. by Michael Joseph). Merrimack Bk Serv.

ALSED Directory of Specialists & Research Institutions. (Educational Studies & Documents: No. 14). 54p. (Orig.). 1974. pap. 3.25 (ISBN 92-3-001134-7, U14, UNESCO). Unipub.

Alt-Kraeuterbuchlein. Ed. by Alexander Von Bernus. (Insel-Taschenbuecher: It 456). (Illus.). 153p. (Ger.). 1980. pap. text ed. 4.55 (ISBN 3-458-32156-X, Pub. by Insel Verlag Germany). Suhrkamp.

Altai-Iran und Voelkerwanderung. Josef Strzygowski. (Arbeiten des Kunsthistorischen Instituts der Universitat Wien: No. 5). (Illus., Ger.). 1981. Repr. of 1917 ed. lib. bdg. 100.00x (ISBN 0-89241-156-2). Caratzas Bros.

Altair Design. Ensor Holiday. (Illus.). (gr. 1 up). 1973. pap. 3.95 (ISBN 0-394-82548-9). Pantheon.

Altair Design 3. Ensor Holiday. (Illus.). 1976. pap. 3.95 (ISBN 0-394-83329-5). Pantheon.

Altair Design 4. Ensor Holiday. LC 77-17417. (gr. 1 up). 1978. pap. 3.95 (ISBN 0-394-83794-0). Pantheon.

Altar & the City. Mario Di Cesare. 240p. 1974. 17.50x (ISBN 0-231-03830-5); pap. 7.50x (ISBN 0-231-03831-3). Columbia U Pr.

Altar De Sacrificios Excavations: General Summary & Conclusions. Gordon R. Willey. LC 73-77202. (Peabody Museum Papers: Vol. 64, No. 3). 1973. pap. text ed. 10.00 (ISBN 0-87365-185-5). Peabody Harvard.

Altar Service of the Protestant Episcopal Church. write for info (ISBN 0-19-526784-2, 221). Oxford U Pr.

Altarmenisches Elementarbuch. Antoine Meillet. 1980. Repr. of 1913 ed. 25.00x (ISBN 0-88206-043-0). Caravan Bks.

Altas of Overdentures & Precision Attachments. Joseph Jumber. (Illus.). 256p. 1981. 60.00. Quint Pub Co.

Alten Uebersetzungen Des Neuen Testaments, Die Kirchenvaeterzitate und Lektionare: Der Gegenwaertige Stand Ihrer Erforschung und Ihre Bedeutung Fuer Die griechische Textgeschichte. Ed. by Kurt Aland. (Arbeiten zur neutestamentlichen Textforschung 5). xxiv, 590p. 1972. 89.40x (ISBN 3-11-004121-9). De Gruyter.

Alter Sonnets. Paul Jacob. 8.00 (ISBN 0-89253-481-8); flexible cloth 4.00 (ISBN 0-89253-482-6). Ind-US Inc.

Alterations of Personality. Alfred Binet. Tr. by Helen G. Baldwin from Fr. Bd. with On Double-Consciousness. Repr. of 1890 ed. (Contributions to the History of Psychology Ser., Vol. V, Pt. C: Medical Psychology). 1978. Repr. of 1896 ed. 30.00 (ISBN 0-89093-169-0). U Pubns Amer.

Altered Destinies. William Stockton. 1980. pap. 2.50 (ISBN 0-451-09460-3, E9460, Sig). NAL.

Altered Landscapes. Photos by John Pfhal. (Untitled 26 Ser.). (Illus.). 56p. (Orig.). 1981. pap. 10.95 (ISBN 0-933286-23-6). Friends Photography.

Altered States of Awareness: Readings from Scientific American. Intro. by Timothy J. Teyler. LC 76-190436. (Illus.). 1972. pap. text ed. 7.95x (ISBN 0-7167-0855-8). W H Freeman.

Altering Collective Bargaining: Citizen Participation in Educational Decision Making. Charles W. Cheng. LC 75-36415. (Special Studies). 192p. 1976. text ed. 22.95 (ISBN 0-275-56300-6). Praeger.

Altering Course. Richard J. Vogt. 1979. 10.95 (ISBN 0-393-03230-2). Norton.

Altering Medicaid Provider Reimbursement Methods. John Holahan et al. (Medicaid Cost Containment Ser.). 215p. 1977. pap. 8.50 (ISBN 0-685-99509-7, 17800). Urban Inst.

Altering: Ready-to-Wear Fashions. Ann Aletti & Jeanne Brinkley. (gr. 10-12). 1976. text ed. 13.28 (ISBN 0-87002-083-8); avail. tchr's guide 1.00 (ISBN 0-87002-110-9). Bennett IL.

Alternate Energy Sources. Ed. by Jamal T. Manassah. 1981. Pt. A. write for info. (ISBN 0-12-467101-2); Pt. B. write for info. (ISBN 0-12-467102-0). Acad Pr.

Alternate Energy Sources. Jane W. Watson. LC 78-10872. (First Bks.). (Illus.). (gr. 4 up). 1979. PLB 6.45 s&l (ISBN 0-531-02252-8). Watts.

Alternate Energy Sources, E-007: A Study. rev. ed. Business Communications Staff. 1977. 525.00 o.p. (ISBN 0-89336-009-0). BCC.

Alternate Realities. Lawrence LeShan. 252p. 1976. 8.95 (ISBN 0-87131-217-4). M Evans.

Alternate Services - Their Role in Mental Health: A Field Study of Free Clinics, Runaway Houses, Counseling Centers & the Like. Raymond M. Glasscote et al. 1975. pap. 10.00 (ISBN 0-685-63942-8, P209-0). Am Psychiatric.

Alternate Sources of Energy: A Bibliography of Solar, Geothermal, Wind & Tidal Energy, & Environmental Architecture. Barbara K. Harrah & David F. Harrah. LC 75-17853. 1975. 10.00 (ISBN 0-8108-0839-0). Scarecrow.

Alternate States of Consciousness. Ed. by Norman E. Zinberg. LC 76-46722. (Illus.). 1979. pap. text ed. 7.95 (ISBN 0-02-935930-9). Free Pr.

Alternate Test Items to Accompany West's Business Law: Text & Cases. Kenneth W. Clarkson et al. 169p. Date not set. price not set (ISBN 0-8299-0508-1). West Pub.

Alternate Worlds: An Illustrated History of Science Fiction. James Gunn. (Illus.). 224p. 1976. pap. 8.95 o.p. (ISBN 0-89104-049-8). A & W Pubs.

Alternating Basis Algorithm for Assignment Problems. R. S. Barr et al. 1977. 2.50 (ISBN 0-686-64191-4). U CO Busn Res Div.

Alternating Current Fundamentals. John R. Duff & Milton Kaufman. (Electrical Trades Ser.). (gr. 9-10). 1980. 16.00 (ISBN 0-8273-1133-8); pap. 14.20 (ISBN 0-8273-1142-7); instr's guide 1.75 (ISBN 0-8273-1142-7). Delmar.

Alternating Current Machines. 4th ed. M. G. Say. LC 76-15265. 1976. 19.95 (ISBN 0-470-15133-1). Halsted Pr.

Alternative Acquisitions Handbook. Ed. by James P. Danky. 250p. 1981. pap. text ed. 15.95 (ISBN 0-918212-44-8). Neal-Schuman.

Alternative Altars: Unconventional & Eastern Spirituality in America. Robert S. Ellwood, Jr. LC 78-15089. xvi, 192p. 1981. pap. 5.50 (ISBN 0-226-20620-3). U of Chicago Pr.

Alternative Approach to Allergies: The New Field of Clinical Ecology Unravels the Environmental Causes of Mental & Physical Ills. Theron G. Randolph & Ralph W. Moss. LC 80-7866. 264p. 1980. 11.95 (ISBN 0-690-01998-X). Lippincott & Crowell.

Alternative Approaches to Capital Gains Taxation. Martin David. LC 68-30592. (Studies of Government Finance). 1968. 9.95 (ISBN 0-8157-1742-3); pap. 3.95 (ISBN 0-8157-1741-5). Brookings.

Alternative Cooking. Greet Buchner. 1979. pap. 3.95 o.s.i. (ISBN 0-7225-0469-1). Newcastle Pub.

Alternative Development Strategies & Appropriate Technology: Science Policy for an Equitable World Order. Romesh K. Diwan & Dennis Livingston. (Pergamon Policy Studies). 1979. 28.00 (ISBN 0-08-023891-2). Pergamon.

Alternative Directions in Economic Policy. Ed. by Frank J. Bonello & Thomas R. Swartz. LC 77-17422. 1978. 3.95x (ISBN 0-268-00584-2); pap. 3.95 o.p. (ISBN 0-268-00585-0). U of Notre Dame Pr.

Alternative Draft of a Penal Code for the Federal Republic of Germany. Tr. by Joseph J. Darby from Ger. LC 76-43177. (American Ser. of Foreign Penal Codes: Vol. 21). 157p. 1977. text ed. 17.50x (ISBN 0-8377-0041-8). Rothman.

Alternative Education: A Sourcebook for Parents, Teachers, Students & Administrators. Ed. by Mario D. Fantini. LC 73-13104. 400p. 1976. pap. 4.50 o.p. (ISBN 0-385-06389-X, Anch). Doubleday.

Alternative Education: Programs & Research. Ed. by Anthony Pugliese. 1978. pap. 10.00 o.p. (ISBN 0-686-00901-0, D-117). Essence Pubns.

Alternative Educational Systems. Edward Ignas & Raymond J. Corsini. LC 78-61883. 1979. text ed. 10.95 (ISBN 0-87581-246-5); pap. text ed. 7.95 o.p. (ISBN 0-87581-242-2). Peacock Pubs.

Alternative Energy Demand Futures to 2010. Committee on Nuclear & Alternative Energy Sources. 1979. pap. 10.00 (ISBN 0-309-02939-2). Natl Acad Pr.

Alternative Energy Source Primer. (Illus.). 280p. 1980. Repr. of 1977 ed. 28.00 (ISBN 0-8103-1032-5). Gale.

Alternative Energy Sources: Proceedings, 9 vols. Miami International Conference on Alternative Energy Sources, 2nd. Ed. by T. Nejat Veziroglu. LC 80-25788. (Illus.). 4300p. 1981. Set. text ed. 595.00 (ISBN 0-89116-208-9). Hemisphere Pub.

Alternative Energy Strategies: Constraints & Opportunities. John Hagel, III. LC 75-23968. 1976. text ed. 27.95 (ISBN 0-275-56090-2). Praeger.

Alternative Fuels: Chemical Energy Resources. E. M. Goodger. LC 80-11796. 238p. 1980. 43.95x (ISBN 0-470-26952-9). Halsted Pr.

Alternative Future for America Two: Essays & Speeches. rev.& enl. ed. Robert Theobald. LC 71-97027. Orig. Title: Alternative Future for America. 199p. 1970. 8.95x o.p. (ISBN 0-8040-0002-6); pap. 3.95x (ISBN 0-8040-0003-4). Swallow.

Alternative Future for America's Third Century. Robert Theobald. LC 76-3135. 266p. 1976. pap. 4.95x (ISBN 0-8040-0725-X). Swallow.

Alternative Futures of Africa. Ed. by Timothy M. Shaw. (Westview Special Studies on Africa). (Illus.). 1981. lib. bdg. 26.50x (ISBN 0-89158-769-1). Westview.

Alternative Futures: Political Choices for Tomorrow. Ed. by Ralph E. Hamil & Mary E. Dillon. Date not set. pap. cancelled (ISBN 0-8120-0564-3). Barron.

Alternative in Eastern Europe. Rudolph Bahro. 464p. 1981. 19.50 (ISBN 0-8052-7056-6, Pub. by NLB England); pap. 9.50 (ISBN 0-8052-7098-1). Schocken.

Alternative, Innovative & Traditional Schools: Some Personal Views. Len Solo. LC 80-7950. 232p. 1980. lib. bdg. 17.25 (ISBN 0-8191-1087-6); pap. text ed. 9.50 (ISBN 0-8191-1088-4). U Pr of Amer.

Alternative Natural Energy Sources in Building Design. 2nd ed. Albert J. Davis & Robert P. Schubert. 256p. 1981. 17.95 (ISBN 0-442-23143-1); pap. 9.95 (ISBN 0-442-22008-1). Van Nos Reinhold.

Alternative Realities: A Study of Communes & Their Members. Andrew Rigby. (International Library of Sociology). 1974. 25.00 (ISBN 0-7100-7715-7). Routledge & Kegan.

Alternative Schools. Lyn Broad. 1977. pap. 7.95 o.p. (ISBN 0-87545-009-1). Natl Sch Pr.

Alternative Schools: Ideologies, Realities, Guidelines. Ed. by Terrence Deal & Robert Nolan. LC 78-18505. (Illus.). 1978. 18.95x (ISBN 0-88229-383-4); pap. 10.95x (ISBN 0-88229-613-2). Nelson-Hall.

Alternative Social Services for Women. Ed. by Naomi Gottlieb. LC 80-164. 1980. 22.50x (ISBN 0-231-04212-4). Columbia U Pr.

Alternative Society: Software for the Nineteen-Eighties. De Cronin Hastings. 160p. 1980. 17.95 (ISBN 0-7153-7880-5). David & Charles.

Alternative Sources of Event Data on Zambian Foreign Policy. Timothy M. Shaw & Douglas G. Anglin. (Foreign & Comparative Studies Program, African Ser.: No. XXXVI). 1981. pap. text ed. price not set (ISBN 0-915984-60-1). Syracuse U Foreign Comp.

Alternative Sources of Protein for Animal Production. Division of Biology & Agriculture. (Illus.). 184p. 1973. pap. 8.25 o.p. (ISBN 0-309-02114-6). Natl Acad Pr.

Alternative Strategies for Coping with Crime. Ed. by Norman Tutt. (Aspects of Social Policy Ser.). 1978. 29.50x (ISBN 0-631-16240-2, Pub. by Basil Blackwell); pap. 12.50x (ISBN 0-631-16250-X). Biblio Dist.

Alternative Style: Options in Compostition. Winston Weathers. 144p. 1980. text ed. 6.19x (ISBN 0-686-69598-4). Hayden.

Alternative Three. Miles A. Watkins et al. 1979. pap. 2.25 (ISBN 0-380-44677-4). Avon.

Alternative to Institutionalization: The Highland Heights Experiment. Sylvia Sherwood et al. Ed. by Robert Kastenbaum & Theodore Barber. (Cushing Hospital Ser. on Aging). 1981. write for info. (ISBN 0-88410-720-5). Ballinger Pub.

Alternative to Psychiatric Hospitalization. Harry Gottesfeld. LC 77-7318. 1979. 12.95 (ISBN 0-470-99188-7). Halsted Pr.

Alternative Tradition: A Study of Unbelief in the Ancient World. James A. Thrower. (Religon & Society Ser.). 1979. 35.25x (ISBN 90-279-7997-9). Mouton.

Alternative Treatments for Cancer. Steven Lehrer. LC 78-31430. (Illus.). 1979. 13.95 (ISBN 0-88229-473-3); pap. 7.95 (ISBN 0-88229-666-3). Nelson-Hall.

Alternative Views of the New International Economic Order: A Survey & Analysis of Major Academic Research Reports. Jorge Lozoya et al. (Pergamon Policy Studies). 1980. 20.00 (ISBN 0-08-024644-3). Pergamon.

Alternative Vision: The Socialist Party in the 1930's. Frank A. Warren. LC 74-181. 288p. 1974. 12.50x (ISBN 0-253-30520-9). Ind U Pr.

Alternative Work Schedules: Integrating Individual & Organizational Needs. Allan R. Cohen & Herman Gadon. LC 78-52506. 1978. pap. text ed. 6.50 (ISBN 0-201-01052-6). A-W.

Alternatives for Delivering Public Services: Toward Improved Performance. Ed. by E. S. Savas. LC 77-6335. 1977. lib. bdg. 18.50x (ISBN 0-89158-306-8). Westview.

Alternatives in Development: Is Europe Responding to Third World Needs? Ed. by J. West. 1974. text ed. 19.50 (ISBN 0-08-018169-4). Pergamon.

Alternatives in Energy Conservation: The Use of Earth Covered Buildings. National Science Foundation Research Applications Directorate. 1979. pap. cancelled (ISBN 0-930978-90-0). Solar Energy Info.

Alternatives in Print: An International Catalog of Books, Pamphlets, Periodicals & Audiovisual Materials. Task Force on Alternatives in Print of the Social Responsibilities Round Table of the American Library Association. LC 76-54384. 1980. 39.95x (ISBN 0-918212-20-0). Neal-Schuman.

Alternatives to College. Linda Atkinson. LC 78-5957. (Career Concise Guides Ser.). (Illus.). 1978. lib. bdg. 6.95 s&l (ISBN 0-531-01495-9). Watts.

Alternatives to Incorporation for Persons in Quest of Profit: Cases & Materials on Partnerships, Joint Ventures & Related Agency Concepts. Daniel W. Fessler. LC 80-18481. (American Casebook Ser.). 284p. 1980. pap. text ed. 8.95 (ISBN 0-8299-2102-8). West Pub.

Altfranzosische Liedersammlung, Deranonyme Teil der Liederhandschriften Knpx. Ed. by Hans Spanke. LC 80-2161. 1981. Repr. of 1925 ed. 54.50 (ISBN 0-404-19025-1). AMS Pr.

Althea. Madeleine Robins. (Orig.). 1977. pap. 1.50 o.p. (ISBN 0-449-23268-9, Crest). Fawcett.

Although...Those Who Overcame. Barbara G. Smith. 1981. pap. 9.95 (ISBN 0-914598-03-1). Padre Prods.

Altopascio: A Study in Tuscan Rural Society, 1587-1784. Frank McArdle. LC 76-53261. (Cambridge Studies in Early Modern History). (Illus.). 1978. 34.95 (ISBN 0-521-21619-2). Cambridge U Pr.

Altruism, Socialization, & Society. J. Philippe Rushton. (P-H Ser. in Social Learning Theory). (Illus.). 1980. text ed. 17.95 (ISBN 0-13-023408-7). P-H.

Aluminum Toxicology Symposium. Ed. by Leopold Liss. (Neurotoxicology Ser.: Vol. 1, No. 4). (Illus.). 1980. text ed. 29.00 (ISBN 0-930376-18-8). Pathotox Pubs.

Alumni College Movement. Linda Carl. 1977. pap. 9.50 (ISBN 0-89964-001-X). CASE.

Alun Lewis: Selected Poetry & Prose. Alun Lewis. 1966. text ed. 8.95x o.p. (ISBN 0-04-821011-0). Allen Unwin.

Alusiones Literarias En la Obra Narrativa De Francisco Ayala. Rosario Hiriart. 1972. 10.50 (ISBN 0-88303-016-0); pap. 7.50 (ISBN 0-685-73218-5). E Torres & Sons.

Alvar Aalto-Sketches. Alvar Aalto. Ed. by Goran Schildt. Tr. by Stuart Wrede from Swed. & Finn. (Illus.). 1978. 27.50 (ISBN 0-262-01053-4). MIT Pr.

Alvarez Journal. Rex Burns. LC 75-6365. (Harper Novel of Suspense). 208p. 1975. 8.95 o.p. (ISBN 0-06-010576-3, HarpT). Har-Row.

Alvin Fernald, Foreign Trader. Clifford B. Hicks. (gr. 4-6). 1979. pap. 1.50 (ISBN 0-671-29941-7). PB.

Alvin Fernald: Superweasel. Hicks. (gr. 4-6). pap. 1.25 o.s.i. (ISBN 0-686-68474-5, 29844). Archway.

Alvin Turner As Farmer. William Kloefkorn. 1977. pap. 4.00 (ISBN 0-931534-02-X). Windflower Pr.

Alvise Vivarini: His Art & Influence. . Steer. (Illus.). 200p. Date not set. price not set (ISBN 0-521-23363-1). Cambridge U Pr.

Always Movin' on: The Life of Langston Hughes. James S. Haskins. (Illus.). 128p. (gr. 7 up). 1976. PLB 6.90 o.p. (ISBN 0-531-01211-5). Watts.

Always on Sunday. Peggy Whedon. 1980. 12.95 (ISBN 0-393-01407-X). Norton.

Always on the Offense. Mike Schmidt & Barbara Walder. LC 80-69764. 1981. 12.95 (ISBN 0-689-11165-7). Atheneum.

Always the Poor: Mother Teresa, Her Life & Message. Jose Gonzalez-Balado. Tr. by Olimpia Diaz, Sr. from Span. 112p. (Orig.). 1980. pap. 2.50 (ISBN 0-89243-134-2). Liguori Pubns.

Always with Jesus. rev. ed. Daughters of St. Paul. (Illus.). 1973. 3.95 o.s.i. (ISBN 0-8198-0265-4). Dghtrs St Paul.

Always Young: A Biography. new ed. Frank Dolson. LC 75-20961. (Illus.). 206p. (Orig.). 1975. pap. 3.95 (ISBN 0-89037-072-9); handbk. 4.95 (ISBN 0-89037-073-7). Anderson World.

Alyx. Lolah Burford. LC 76-18883. 1977. 8.95 o.s.i. (ISBN 0-02-518100-9, 51810). Macmillan.

Alzheimer's Disease: Senile Dementia & Related Disorders. Ed. by Robert Katzman et al. LC 77-84132. (Aging Ser.: Vol. 7). 1978. 49.00 o.p. (ISBN 0-89004-225-X). Raven.

Am I Eligible? The Easy Way to Calculate the Beog Index, 1980-1981. Robert Leider. 16p. 1980. pap. 1.00 (ISBN 0-917760-20-4). Octameron Assocs.

Am I Greedy If I Want More? Beatrice Chernuchin Schuman. (Illus.). 179p. 1979. 9.95 (ISBN 0-8119-0329-X). Fell.

Am I Losing My Faith? William E. Hulme. LC 71-133035. (Pocket Counsel Bks.). 56p. (Orig.). 1971. pap. 1.75 (ISBN 0-8006-0154-8, 1-154). Fortress.

Am I Not a Man & a Brother: The Antislavery Crusade of Revolutionary America, 1688-1788. Ed. by Roger Bruns. LC 76-6118. (Illus.). 600p. 1981. pap. 11.95 (ISBN 0-87754-213-9). Chelsea Hse.

Am I OK - If I Feel the Way I Do? Vincenza Gagliostro. LC 80-2077. 128p. 1981. pap. 2.75 (ISBN 0-385-17437-3, Im). Doubleday.

Am I Ok--If I Feel the Way I Do? Sr. Vincenzia Gagliostro. (Illus.). 128p. (Orig.). (gr. 5-9). 1980. pap. 2.45 (ISBN 0-529-05779-4). Collins Pubs.

Am I Too Loud? Gerald Moore. (Illus.). 1979. 22.50 (ISBN 0-241-90019-0, Pub. by Hamish Hamilton England). David & Charles.

AMA Book of Skin & Hair Care. Ed. by Linda A. Schoen. (Illus.). 1976. 8.95 o.s.i. (ISBN 0-397-01157-1); pap. 4.95 (ISBN 0-397-01158-X). Lippincott.

AMA Drug Evaluations. 4th ed. AMA. LC 76-9254. 1470p. 1980. 58.00 (ISBN 0-471-08125-6, Pub. by Wiley Med). Wiley.

AMA Handbook of First Aid & Emergency Care. American Medical Association. (Illus.). 256p. 1980. 5.95 (ISBN 0-394-73668-0). Random.

Amadeus. Peter Shaffer. LC 79-3415. 128p. 1981. 10.95 (ISBN 0-06-014041-0, HarpT). Har-Row.

Amadis De Gaula. Frank Pierce. LC 75-25907. (World Authors Ser.: Spain: No. 372). 1976. lib. bdg. 12.50 (ISBN 0-8057-6220-5). Twayne.

Amadis De Gaule & Its Influence on Elizabethan Literature. John J. O'Connor. LC 76-96031. 1970. 21.00 (ISBN 0-8135-0622-0). Rutgers U Pr.

Amadu's Bundle. Tr. by Gulla Kell & Ronald Moody. (African Writers Ser.). 1972. pap. text ed. 1.95 (ISBN 0-435-90118-4). Heinemann Ed.

Amaeru: The Expression of Reciprocal Dependency in Japanese Politics & Law. new ed. Douglas D. Mitchell. LC 76-43354. 1977. 22.00 o.p. (ISBN 0-89158-710-1). Westview.

Amalfi: Aspects of the City & Her Ancient Territories. Robert Gathorne-Hardy. (Illus.). 1968. 8.95 (ISBN 0-571-08576-8, Pub. by Faber & Faber). Merrimack Bk Serv.

Amalia. Ed. by James C. Babcock et al. LC 49-8551. (Graded Spanish Readers, Bk. 1). (Span). (gr. 10-11). 1949. pap. text ed. 3.65 (ISBN 0-395-04124-4, 3-02245). HM.

Amana Grass. Jon Silkin. LC 71-153105. (Wesleyan Poetry Program: Vol. 59). 1971. 10.00x (ISBN 0-8195-2059-4, Pub. by Wesleyan U Pr); pap. 4.95 (ISBN 0-8195-1059-9). Columbia U Pr.

Amanda. Paula Christian. 144p. 1981. pap. 6.50 (ISBN 0-931328-07-1). Timely Bks.

Amanda. Pamela Conrad. (Orig.). 1980. pap. 2.25 (ISBN 0-505-51554-7). Tower Bks.

Amanda Fair. Dorothy Hamilton. LC 80-25073. (Illus.). 136p. (gr. 5-10). 1981. pap. 3.25 (ISBN 0-8361-1943-6). Herald Pr.

Amanda-Miranda. Richard Peck. 544p. 1981. pap. 2.95 (ISBN 0-380-53850-4). Avon.

Amanda's Choice. Isabelle Holland. LC 71-101901. (gr. 4-6). 1970. 9.95 (ISBN 0-397-31112-5). Lippincott.

Amant Rendu Cordelier a L'observance D'amours. Martial D'Auvergne. (Societe Des Anciens Textes Francais Ser: Vol. 15). (Fr). 1881. 20.00; pap. 15.50 (ISBN 0-384-56560-3). Johnson Repr.

Amapa Storytellers. Stanley L. Robe. (U. C. Publ. in Folklore Studies: Vol. 24). 1972. pap. 10.00x (ISBN 0-520-09391-7). U of Cal Pr.

Amaranth: From the Past for the Future. John N. Cole. (Illus.). 1979. 8.95 (ISBN 0-87857-240-6). Rodale Pr Inc.

Amaryllis at the Fair. Richard Jefferies. 192p. 1980. pap. 3.95 (ISBN 0-686-68572-5, Pub. by Quartet England). Horizon.

Amarynthus...with Other Poems. Horatio Smith. Ed. by Donald H. Reiman. LC 75-31255. (Romantic Context Ser.: Poetry 1789-1830). 1977. Repr. of 1821 ed. lib. bdg. 47.00 (ISBN 0-8240-2202-5). Garland Pub.

Amate Siquiera un Poco. LC 78-57808. 182p. (Orig., Span.). 1978. pap. 3.95 (ISBN 0-89922-120-3). Edit Caribe.

Amateur. Robert Littell. 1981. 12.95 (ISBN 0-671-41873-4). S&S.

Amateur Archaeologist's Handbook. rev. ed. Maurice Robbins & Mary B. Irving. (Illus.). 304p. 1973. 11.95 (ISBN 0-690-05569-2, TYC-T). T Y Crowell.

Amateur Archaeologist's Handbook. 3rd ed. Maurice Robbins & Mary B. Irving. LC 80-7901. (Illus.). 304p. 11.95 (ISBN 0-690-01976-9, HarpT). Har-Row.

Amateur Astronomer's Handbook. rev. ed. James Muirden. LC 74-5411. (Illus.). 384p. 1974. 12.95 (ISBN 0-690-00505-9, TYC-T). T Y Crowell.

Amateur Astronomer's Handbook. J. B. Sidgwick. (Illus.). 576p. 1981. pap. write for info. (ISBN 0-486-24034-7). Dover.

Amateur Astronomer's Handbook. 4th, rev. ed. J. B. Sidgwick. (Illus.). 568p. 1980. 24.95 (ISBN 0-89490-049-8). Enslow Pubs.

Amateur Athlete Yearbook 1978. (Illus.). 1978. softcover 3.00 (ISBN 0-685-59726-1). AAU Pubns.

Amateur Beekeeping. Edward L. Sechrist. LC 55-11865. (Illus.). 148p. 1981. pap. 4.95 (ISBN 0-8159-5001-2). Devin.

Amateur Cabinetmaking. Vernon M. Albers. LC 70-37801. (Illus.). 128p. 1972. 7.95 o.p. (ISBN 0-498-01012-0); large type 6.95 o.p. (ISBN 0-498-01855-5). A S Barnes.

Amateur Corpse. Simon Brett. 1978. 7.95 o.p. (ISBN 0-684-15571-0, ScribT). Scribner.

Amateur Drama: Production & Management. Martyn Hepworth. (Illus.). 120p. 1980. 16.95 (ISBN 0-7134-0937-1, Pub. by Batsford England). David & Charles.

Amateur FM Conversion & Construction Projects. Kenneth W. Sessions. LC 74-79584. (Illus.). 256p. 1974. 8.95 o.p. (ISBN 0-8306-4722-8); pap. 5.95 o.p. (ISBN 0-8306-3722-2, 722). TAB Bks.

Amateur Greenhouse Gardening. Kenneth A. Beckett. 1980. 14.95 (ISBN 0-8464-0991-7). Beekman Pubs.

Amateur Horse Breeder. 2nd ed. A. Leighton Hardman. (Illus.). 240p. 1980. 16.95 (ISBN 0-7207-1177-0). Transatlantic.

Amateur Magician's Handbook. 3rd, rev. ed. Henry Hay. LC 72-78265. (Illus.). 400p. 1972. 12.95 (ISBN 0-690-05711-3, TYC-T). T Y Crowell.

Amateur Naturalist's Handbook. Vinson Brown. (Illus.). 432p. 1980. 15.95 (Spec); pap. 6.95. P-H.

Amateur Navigator's Handbook. Sallie Townsend & Virginia Ericson. LC 73-15985. (Illus.). 256p. 1974. 11.95 (ISBN 0-690-00192-4, TYC-T). T Y Crowell.

Amateur Orchestra. Leonard Duck. (Student's Music Library Ser). 1949. 6.95 (ISBN 0-234-77312-X). Dufour.

Amateur Photographer's Handbook. 8th ed. Aaron Sussman. LC 72-2558. (Illus.). 420p. 1973. 12.50 (ISBN 0-690-05782-2, TYC-T). T Y Crowell.

Amateur Psychologist's Dictionary. Robert M. Diamond & John C. Woodward. LC 66-17176. (Illus.). 1966. 4.50 o.p. (ISBN 0-668-01454-7). Arco.

Amateur Radio: Super Hobby! Vince Luciani. LC 80-51260. (Illus.). 144p. 1981. 14.95x (ISBN 0-9602310-2-1); pap. 8.95x (ISBN 0-9602310-1-3). Cologne Pr.

Amateur Wind Instrument Maker, Revised Edition. Trevor Robinson. LC 80-5381. (Illus.). 136p. 1981. pap. 8.95 (ISBN 0-87023-312-2). U of Mass Pr.

Amateur Wine Making. 4th ed. S. M. Tritton. (Illus.). 1968. 7.95 o.p. (ISBN 0-571-04646-0, Pub. by Faber & Faber). Merrimack Bk Serv.

Amateur's Guide to Foaling. Lorch. (Illus.). 1978. 4.37 (ISBN 0-85131-302-7, Dist. by Sporting Book Center). J A Allen.

Amazing Adventures. Ed. by Mary Verdick. (Pal Paperbacks Ser., Kit A). (Illus., Orig.). (gr. 7-12). 1972. pap. text ed. 1.25 (ISBN 0-8374-3482-3). Xerox Ed Pubns.

Amazing Adventures of Flash Gordon, 6 vols. King Features. Incl. Vol. 1 (ISBN 0-448-17240-2); Vol. 2 (ISBN 0-448-17241-0); Vol. 3. 192p (ISBN 0-448-17242-9); Vol. 4 (ISBN 0-448-17155-4); Vol. 5 (ISBN 0-448-17208-9); Vol. 6 (ISBN 0-448-17245-3). (Flash Gordon Cartoon Ser.). 192p. 1980. pap. 1.75 ea. (Tempo). G&D.

Amazing Adventures of Lord Gore: A True Saga of the Old West. Jack Roberts. Ed. by Russ Collman. (Illus.). 1977. 27.00 (ISBN 0-913582-07-7). Sundance.

Amazing Bill Mazer's Baseball Trivia. Bill Mazer & Stan Fischler. 224p. (Orig.). 1981. pap. 2.50 (ISBN 0-446-91784-2). Warner Bks.

Amazing Dandelion. Millicent E. Selsam & Jerome Wexler. (Illus.). (gr. 2-5). 1977. 7.25 (ISBN 0-688-22129-7); PLB 6.96 (ISBN 0-688-32129-1). Morrow.

Amazing Diet Secret of a Desperate Housewife. Nancy Pryor. (Illus.). 180p. 1981. 9.95 (ISBN 0-8119-0420-2, Pegasus Rex). Fell.

Amazing Dope Tales. Stephen Gaskin. (Illus.). 1980. pap. 7.00 (ISBN 0-913990-29-9). Book Pub Co.

Amazing Earthworm. Lilo Hess. (Illus.). 48p. (gr. 2-7). 1979. 7.95 (ISBN 0-684-16079-X). Scribner.

Amazing Egg. Robert M. McClung. LC 79-23461. (Illus.). 128p. (gr. 4-6). 1980. 9.95 (ISBN 0-525-25480-3). Dutton.

Amazing Facts About Animals. Gyles Brandreth. (Amazing Facts Books Ser.). (Illus.). 32p. (gr. 5-8). pap. 2.95 (ISBN 0-385-17017-3). Doubleday.

Amazing Facts About Our Earth. Gyles Brandreth. LC 80-1087. (Amazing Facts Books Ser.). (Illus.). 32p. (gr. 5-8). 1981. pap. 2.95 (ISBN 0-385-17016-5). Doubleday.

Amazing Facts About Prehistoric Animals. Gyles Brandreth. LC 80-1085. (Amazing Facts Books Ser.). (Illus.). 32p. 1981. pap. 2.95 (ISBN 0-385-17019-X). Doubleday.

Amazing Facts About the Body. Gyles Brandreth. LC 80-1088. (Amazing Facts Books Ser.). (Illus.). 32p. (gr. 5-8). 1981. pap. 2.95. Doubleday.

Amazing Grace. Anita Bryant. 1971. 5.95 o.p. (ISBN 0-8007-0468-1). Revell.

Amazing Grace. Judith Davis. 1981. 12.95 (ISBN 0-453-00399-0, H399). NAL.

Amazing Grace: John Newton's Story. John Pollock. LC 78-3142. 192p. 1980. 9.95 (ISBN 0-06-066653-6). Har-Row.

Amazing Lost Money-Secret of the U. S. Government. J. Andrew Douglas. 228p. 1981. 9.95 (ISBN 0-8119-0417-2, Pegasus Rex). Fell.

Amazing Love. Corrie T. Boom. 1976. pap. 1.25 (ISBN 0-89129-183-0). Jove Pubns.

Amazing Love. Corrie T. Boom. (Orig.). pap. 1.50 (ISBN 0-515-04898-4). Jove Pubns.

Amazing Mail Order Business & How to Succeed in It. Howard Sparks. LC 66-17336. 1966. 9.95 (ISBN 0-8119-0005-3). Fell.

Amazing Memory of Harvey Bean. Molly Cone. (gr. 3-6). 1980. 5.95 (ISBN 0-395-29181-X). HM.

Amazing Miss Laura. Colman. (gr. 9-12). 1980. pap. 1.25 (ISBN 0-590-30006-7, Schol Pap). Schol Bk Serv.

Amazing Miss Laura. Hila Colman. LC 76-17316. 192p. (gr. 7 up). 1976. PLB 6.48 (ISBN 0-688-32079-1). Morrow.

Amazing Mrs. Pollifax. Dorothy Gilman. 1978. pap. 1.95 (ISBN 0-449-23447-9, Crest). Fawcett.

Amazing Mumford Forgets the Magic Words. Patricia Thackray. (Young Reader Ser.). (Illus.). 24p. (gr. k-3). 1979. PLB 5.00 (ISBN 0-307-60178-1, Golden Pr). Western Pub.

Amazing Mycroft Mysteries. H. F. Heard. LC 80-52557. 768p. 1980. 14.95 (ISBN 0-8149-0840-3). Vanguard.

Amazing Oversight: Total Participation for Productivity. Parvin S. Titus & Ben S. Graham, Jr. LC 79-10070. 1979. 13.95 (ISBN 0-8144-5510-7). Am Mgmt.

Amazing Pig. Paul Galdone. (Illus.). 32p. (ps-3). 1981. 8.95 (ISBN 0-395-29101-1, Clarion). HM.

Amazing Power of Solar-Kinetics. Madeleine C. Morris. 1977. 8.95 o.p. (ISBN 0-13-023697-7). P-H.

Amazing Saints: The Story of a Family of Christian Evangelists. Phil Saint. 224p. 1972. pap. 2.50 o.p. (ISBN 0-912106-40-9). Logos.

Amazing Sea Otter. Victor B. Scheffer. (Illus.). 192p. (gr. 7 up). 1981. 10.95 (ISBN 0-684-16878-2). Scribner.

Amazing Secrets of the Masters of the Far East. Robert Collier. 9.95 (ISBN 0-912576-02-2). R Collier.

Amazing Space Ship Adventures, 3 bks. Louis Slobodkin. Incl. Space Ship Under the Apple Tree; Space Ship Returns to the Apple Tree; Three-Seated Space Ship. (Young Science Fiction Ser.). (Illus.). (gr. 3-5). 1981. Boxed Set. pap. 7.95 (ISBN 0-02-045220-9). Macmillan.

Amazing Travels of Ingrid Our Turtle. Peter Lippman. (ps-3). 1973. PLB 7.15 o.p. (ISBN 0-307-62050-6, Golden Pr). Western Pub.

Amazing Visions of the Endtime. Michael X. 1970. pap. 5.95 (ISBN 0-685-00408-2). Saucerian.

Amazon. Rosemary McConnell. LC 78-62990. (Rivers of the World Ser.). (Illus.). 1978. lib. bdg. 7.95 (ISBN 0-686-51133-6). Silver.

Amazon. Tom Sterling. (World's Wild Places Ser). (Illus.). 1973. 12.95 (ISBN 0-8094-2003-1). Time-Life.

Amazon. Tom Sterling. (World's Wild Places Ser.). (Illus.). 1978. lib. bdg. 11.97 (ISBN 0-686-51015-1). Silver.

Amazon Adventure. Willard Price. (gr. 6-9). 1949. 7.95 o.p. (ISBN 0-381-99732-4, A02200, JD-J). John Day.

Amazon Forest & River. Ghillean T. Prance & Anne E. Prance. (Illus.). 1981. 14.95 (ISBN 0-8120-5330-3). Barron.

Amazon Poetry: An Anthology. Ed. by Joan Larkin & Elly Bulkin. 1975. pap. 3.50 (ISBN 0-918314-07-0). Out & Out.

Amazon Town: A Study of Man in the Tropics. Charles Wagley. (Illus.). 363p. 1976. pap. 6.95 (ISBN 0-19-519839-5, GB458, GB). Oxford U Pr.

Amazonia: Man & Culture in a Counterfeit Paradise. Betty J. Meggers. LC 74-141427. (Worlds of Man Ser). 1971. 11.00x (ISBN 0-88295-608-6); pap. 5.75x (ISBN 0-88295-609-4). AHM Pub.

Amazonian Indians. Stephens Hugh-Jones. (Civilization Library). (Illus.). (gr. 5-8). 1979. PLB 6.90 s&l (ISBN 0-531-01448-7). Watts.

Amazons. Cleo Birdwell. LC 80-80241. 400p. 1980. 12.95 (ISBN 0-03-055426-8). HR&W.

Amazzone Corsara, Overo L'avilda Regina De Goti. Carlo Pallavicino. LC 76-21006. (Italian Opera 1640-1770 Ser.). 1978. lib. bdg. 70.00 (ISBN 0-8240-2612-8). Garland Pub.

Ambassade De Talleyrand: A Londres. Ed. by G. Pallain. LC 72-12238. (Europe 1815-1945 Ser.). 464p. 1973. Repr. of 1891 ed. lib. bdg. 49.50 (ISBN 0-306-70575-3). Da Capo.

Ambassador: Twentieth Century Interpretations. Ed. by A. Stone, Jr. 1969. 8.95 (ISBN 0-13-023937-2, Spec); pap. 1.25 (ISBN 0-13-023929-1, Spec). P-H.

Ambassadors. Henry James. 1902. 11.95 o.s.i. (ISBN 0-06-012170-X, HarpT). Har-Row.

Ambassadors. Henry James. 1957. 12.95x (ISBN 0-460-00987-7, Evman); pap. 2.95 (ISBN 0-460-01987-2). Dutton.

Ambassador's Wife in Iran. Cynthia Helms. LC 80-25090. (Illus.). 284p. 1981. 9.95 (ISBN 0-396-07881-8). Dodd.

Amber Dreams: A Pictorial Roger Zelazny Bibliography. Compiled by Daniel J. Levack & Mark Owings. (Illus.). 128p. 1980. 17.50 (ISBN 0-934438-40-4); pap. 6.95 (ISBN 0-934438-39-0). Underwood-Miller.

Amber: The Golden Gem of the Ages. Patty C. Rice. 1980. 26.95 (ISBN 0-442-26138-1). Van Nos Reinhold.

Amber Wellington, Daredevil. Dianne Glaser. LC 74-78854. (Illus.). 128p. (gr. 3-7). 1975. 5.95 o.s.i. (ISBN 0-8027-6197-6). Walker & Co.

Amberleigh. Carole N. Douglas. 352p. (Orig.). 1980. pap. 2.50 (ISBN 0-515-05715-0). Jove Pubns.

Ambidextrous Universe: Mirror Asymmetry & Time-Reversed Worlds. rev. ed. Martin Gardner. (Illus.). 1979. 12.50 (ISBN 0-684-15789-6, ScribT). Scribner.

Ambientes Hispanicos One: No. 1. Leon Narvaez. LC 79-15478. (Illus.). 1979. 8.95 (ISBN 0-88436-544-1); pap. text ed. 5.95 (ISBN 0-88436-543-3). EMC.

Ambientes Hispanicos Two. Leon Narvaez. LC 80-12977. (Illus.). 1980. text ed. 9.50 (ISBN 0-88436-547-6); pap. text ed. 6.50 (ISBN 0-88436-546-8). EMC.

Ambiguity & Choice in Organizations. 2nd ed. James G. March & Johan P. Olsen. 420p. 1980. pap. 29.00x (ISBN 8-2000-1960-8). Universitet.

Ambiguity in Moral Choice. Richard A. McCormick. (Pere Marquette Theology Lectures). 1977. pap. 6.95 (ISBN 0-87462-505-X). Marquette.

Ambiguous Adventure. C. Kane. 1969. pap. 1.25 o.s.i. (ISBN 0-02-052410-2, Collier). Macmillan.

Ambiguous Image: Narrative Style in Modern European Cinema. Roy Armes. LC 75-37266. (Illus.). 256p. 1976. 15.00x (ISBN 0-253-30560-8). Ind U Pr.

Ambition: The Secret Passion. Joseph Epstein. 320p. 1980. 13.95 (ISBN 0-525-05280-1). Dutton.

Ambivalent America: A Psycho-Political Dialogue. June L. Tapp & Fred Krinsky. 1971. pap. text ed. 4.95x (ISBN 0-02-478870-8, 47887). Macmillan.

Ambrose Bierce. M. E. Grenander. (U. S. Authors Ser.: No. 180). lib. bdg. 8.50 o.p. (ISBN 0-8057-0056-0). Twayne.

Ambrose Bierce: A Braver Man Than Anybody Knew. Laurence I. Berkove. (Illus.). 1981. 16.00 (ISBN 0-88233-349-6). Ardis Pubs.

Ambrotype: Old & New. Thomas P. Feldvebel. LC 80-65216. (Illus.). 51p. 1980. pap. 9.95 (ISBN 0-89938-001-8). Graph Arts Res RIT.

Ambulance Calls: Review Problems in Emergency Care. Nancy L. Caroline. 1980. pap. text ed. 9.95 (ISBN 0-316-12871-6, Little Med Div). Little.

Ambulatory Care Systems, Vol. 1: Design of Ambulatory Care Systems for Improved Patient Flow. Edward Rising. LC 76-55865. 1977. 16.95 (ISBN 0-669-01323-4). Lexington Bks.

Ambulatory Care Systems, Vol. 2: Location, Layout, & Information Systems for Efficient Operations. Richard Giglio. LC 76-55865. 1977. 19.50 (ISBN 0-669-01324-2). Lexington Bks.

Ambulatory Care Systems, Vol. 3: Evaluation of Outpatient Facilities. Paula L. Stamps. LC 76-55865. (Illus.). 1978. 21.50 (ISBN 0-669-01325-0). Lexington Bks.

Ambulatory Care Systems, Vol. 4: Designing Medical Services for Health Maintenance Organizations. J. R. Coleman & F. C. Kaminsky. LC 76-55865. (Illus.). 1977. 27.95 (ISBN 0-669-01327-7). Lexington Bks.

Ambulatory Care Systems, Vol. 5: Financial Design & Administration of Health Maintenance Organizations. J. R. Coleman & F. C. Kaminsky. LC 76-55865. 1977. 26.95 (ISBN 0-669-01328-5). Lexington Bks.

Ambulatory Care: Theory & Practice. Seth B. Goldsmith. LC 77-10315. 1977. 21.50 (ISBN 0-912862-46-7). Aspen Systems.

Ambulatory Electrocardiography: Including Holter Recording Technology. Harold L. Kennedy. LC 80-26155. (Illus.). 300p. 1981. text ed. write for info. (ISBN 0-8121-0762-4). Lea & Febiger.

Ambulatory Health Care in the City of Boston. Deborah Jones et al. (Abt Health-Medical Reports). 1974. pap. 43.00x o.p. (ISBN 0-89011-472-2, HMD-101). Abt Assoc.

Ambulatory Obstetrics: A Clinical Guide. R. S. Gibbs & C. E. Gibbs. LC 79-18554. 1979. pap. text ed. 10.95 (ISBN 0-471-05227-2, Pub. by Wiley Medical). Wiley.

Ambulatory Pediatrics for Nurses. 2nd ed. Marie Brown & Mary A. Murphy. (Illus.). 624p. 1980. text ed. 17.95 (ISBN 0-07-008291-X, HP). McGraw.

Ambulatory Pediatrics for Nurses. Marie S. Brown & Mary A. Murphy. (Illus.). 480p. 1975. 15.95 o.p. (ISBN 0-07-008290-1, HP). McGraw.

Ambulatory Surgery & the Basics of Emergency Surgical Care. Ed. by Mark W. Wolcott. (Illus.). 640p. 1981. pap. text ed. 39.50 (ISBN 0-397-50480-2). Lippincott.

Ambulatory Surgical Centers: Development & Management. Ed. by Thomas R. O'Donovan. LC 76-15767. 1976. 27.00 (ISBN 0-912862-21-1). Aspen Systems.

Ambuscade. Frank O'Rourke. Bd. with Thunder on the Buckhorn. 1980. pap. 1.95 (ISBN 0-451-09490-5, Sig). NAL.

Ambush & Other Poems. Stewart Conn. LC 78-91030. 1970. 3.95 o.s.i. (ISBN 0-02-527300-0). Macmillan.

Ambush at Adams Crossing. Edwin Booth. 192p. (YA) 1976. 4.95 o.p. (ISBN 0-685-64243-7, Avalon). Bouregy.

Ambush at Derati Wells. Peter McCurtin. (Soldier of Fortune Ser). 1977. pap. 1.25 (ISBN 0-505-51153-3). Tower Bks.

Ambush at Jubilo Junction. Leslie Ernenwein. 1976. pap. 0.95 o.p. (ISBN 0-685-69142-X, LB361, Leisure Bks). Nordon Pubns.

Ambush at Torture Canyon. Max Brand. 1981. pap. write for info. (ISBN 0-671-41557-3). PB.

Ambush Murders: The True Account of the Killing of Two California Policemen. Ben Bradlee, Jr. LC 79-10418. (Illus.). 1979. 12.95 (ISBN 0-396-07624-6). Dodd.

Ambush Range. Don P. Jenison. 224p. (Orig.). 1980. pap. 1.95 (ISBN 0-89083-696-5). Zebra.

Ambushers. Donald Hamilton. 1978. pap. 1.95 (ISBN 0-449-14102-0, GM). Fawcett.

AMC Field Guide to Trail Building & Maintenance. Robert Proudman. (Illus.). 1977. pap. 5.95 o.p. (ISBN 0-910146-13-6). Appalach Mtn.

AMC Field Guide to Trail Building & Maintenance. 2nd ed. Robert Proudman & Reuben Rajala. (Illus.). 210p. 1981. pap. 5.95 (ISBN 0-910146-30-6). Appalach Mtn.

AMC Guide to Backcountry Facilities. Ray Leonard. (Illus.). 250p. (Orig.). 1980. pap. 6.95 (ISBN 0-910146-31-4): Appalach Mtn.

AMC Service-Repair Handbook: Pacer, Gremlin, Hornet-1971-1979. Ray Hoy. Ed. by Jeff Robinson. (Illus.). 1977. pap. 10.95 (ISBN 0-89287-139-3, A129). Clymer Pubns.

AMC White Water Handbook for Canoe & Kayak. John Urban & Walley Williams. (Illus.). 200p. 1981. pap. 4.95 (ISBN 0-910146-28-4). Appalach Mtn.

AMC White Water Handbook for Canoe & Kayak. John T. Urban. LC 66-86174. (Illus.). 1976. pap. 3.95 o.p. (ISBN 0-910146-00-4). Appalach Mtn.

Amcha: An Oral Testament of the Holocaust. Saul S. Friedman. LC 79-67054. 1979. pap. text ed. 14.25 (ISBN 0-8191-0867-7). U Pr of Amer.

Amebiasis in Man. Ed. by C. A. Padilla Y Padilla & G. M. Padilla. (Illus.). 198p. 1974. 19.75 (ISBN 0-398-03165-7). C C Thomas.

Amedeo Amedei. Lee A. Smith. (Greenbird Ser.). 1975. 12.00 (ISBN 0-88253-494-7); pap. text ed. 4.80 (ISBN 0-88253-493-9). Ind-US Inc.

Amelia. Megan Daniel. 1980. pap. 1.75 (ISBN 0-451-09487-5, E9487, Sig). NAL.

Amelia Bedelia. Peggy Parish. (Illus.). (gr. 2-3). 1970. pap. 1.25 (ISBN 0-590-09069-0, Schol Pap); pap. 3.50 bk. & record (ISBN 0-590-20642-7). Schol Bk Serv.

Amelia Bedelia & the Baby. Peggy Parish. LC 80-22263. (Read-Alone Bk.). (Illus.). 64p. (gr. 1-3). 1981. 5.95 (ISBN 0-688-00316-8); PLB 5.71 (ISBN 0-688-00321-4). Greenwillow.

Amelia Bedelia Helps Out. Peggy Parish. 64p. (gr. 1-3). 1981. pap. 1.95 (ISBN 0-380-53405-3, Camelot). Avon.

Amelia Earhart. (Explorers & Discoverers Ser.). (gr. 1). 1974. pap. text ed. 2.80 (ISBN 0-205-03899-9, 8038996); tchrs'. guide 12.00 (ISBN 0-205-03866-2, 803866X). Allyn.

Amelia Earhart - Charles Lindbergh. Naunerle C. Farr & John N. Fago. (Pendulum Illustrated Biography Ser.). (Illus.). (gr. 4-12). 1979. text ed. 4.50 (ISBN 0-88301-361-4); pap. text ed. 1.45 (ISBN 0-88301-349-5); wkbk. 0.95 (ISBN 0-88301-373-8). Pendulum Pr.

Amelia Quackenbush. Sharlya Gold. LC 73-7129. (gr. 3-6). 1973. 5.95 (ISBN 0-395-28856-8, Clarion). HM.

Amelia's Flying Machine. Barbara Hazen. LC 76-51861. (ps-3). 1977. PLB 6.95 (ISBN 0-385-08139-1). Doubleday.

Amelie Rives (Princess Troubetzkoy) Welford D. Taylor. (U. S. Authors Ser.: No. 217). 1971. lib. bdg. 10.95 (ISBN 0-8057-0625-9). Twayne.

Amen. Yehuda Amichai. LC 76-50164. 1977. 7.95 o.s.i. (ISBN 0-06-010090-7, HarpT); pap. 4.95 o.s.i. (ISBN 0-06-010089-3, TD-278, HarpT). Har-Row.

Amen-Worte Jesu: Eine Untersuchung zum Problem der Legitimation in apokalyptischer Rede. Klaus Berger. (Beiheft 39 Zur Zeitschrift fuer Die neutestamentliche Wissenschaft Ser.). (Ger). 1970. 26.00x (ISBN 3-11-006445-6). De Gruyter.

Amending of the Federal Constitution. Lester B. Orfield. LC 74-146151. (American Constitutional & Legal History Ser). (Illus.). 1971. Repr. of 1942 ed. lib. bdg. 25.00 (ISBN 0-306-70094-8). Da Capo.

Amendment Number One to the Fourth Edition of Ship's Routing. 36p. 1979. 11.00 (IMCO). Unipub.

Amendments of Mr. Collier's False & Imperfect Citations: From the Old Batchelour, Double Dealer, Love for Love, Mourning Bride, Vol. 23. William Congreve. LC 73-170439. (The English Stage Ser.). lib. bdg. 50.00 (ISBN 0-8240-0606-2). Garland Pub.

America, 2 vols. Charles M. Dollar. Incl. Vol. 1. Changing Times to 1877. 13.95 (ISBN 0-471-21767-0); study guide avail. (ISBN 0-471-05908-0); Vol. 2. Changing Times Since 1865. 13.95 (ISBN 0-471-04769-4); study guide avail. (ISBN 0-471-05907-2). LC 78-12242. 1979. Combined Ed. 19.95 (ISBN 0-471-05029-6); tchr's manual avail. (ISBN 0-471-04906-9). Wiley.

America. Ralph Steadman. LC 74-82705. 1977. pap. 6.95 o.p. (ISBN 0-394-73307-X). Random.

America Adopts the Automobile, 1895-1910. James J. Flink. 1970. 12.00 (ISBN 0-685-16770-4). MIT Pr.

America Against Poverty. Edward James. (Library of Social Policy & Administration). 1970. 10.00x (ISBN 0-7100-6760-7). Routledge & Kegan.

America: An Aerial View. Date not set. 5.95 (ISBN 0-517-25701-7). Aerial Photo.

America & England, 1558-1776. Ed. by Joseph E. Illick. LC 70-11183. 1970. pap. text ed. 5.95x (ISBN 0-89197-006-1). Irvington.

America & the Aftermath of the Jamoson Raid. C. Tsehloane Keto. LC 80-65851. (Transactions Ser.: Vol. 70, Pt. 8). 1980. 6.00 (ISBN 0-87169-708-4). Am Philos.

America & the Arab States: An Uneasy Encounter. Robert W. Stookey. LC 75-25874. (America & the World Ser). 298p. 1975. pap. text ed. 10.95x (ISBN 0-471-82976-5). Wiley.

America & the Holocaust. (American Jewish History Ser.: Vol. 68, Pt. 3). 1979. 6.00. Am Jewish Hist Soc.

America & the World Nineteen Seventy-Eight. Ed. by William P. Bundy. (Pergamon Policy Studies). 260p. 1979. 31.00 (ISBN 0-08-023896-3); pap. 5.50 (ISBN 0-08-023895-5). Pergamon.

America & the World Nineteen Seventy-Nine. Ed. by William P. Bundy. (Pergamon Policy Studies). 281p. 1980. 31.00 (ISBN 0-08-025952-9); pap. 5.95 (ISBN 0-08-025951-0). Pergamon.

America & the World 1980. (Pergamon Policy Studies on International Politics). 1981. 30.01 (ISBN 0-08-027515-X); pap. 6.95 (ISBN 0-08-027514-1). Pergamon.

America & Western Europe: Problems & Prospects of European-American Relations. Ed. by Karl Kaiser & Hans-Peter Schwartz. LC 78-19242. 1979. 14.95 (ISBN 0-669-02450-3). Lexington Bks.

America Arms for a New Century: The Making of a Great Military Power. James L. Abrahamson. LC 80-69716. (Illus.). 1981. 17.95 (ISBN 0-02-900190-0). Free Pr.

America As a Multicultural Society. Ed. by Milton M. Gordon & Richard D. Lambert. (Annals of the American Academy of Political & Social Science Ser.: No. 454). 250p. 1981. 7.50 (ISBN 0-87761-260-9); pap. 6.00 (ISBN 0-87761-261-7). Am Acad Pol Soc Sci.

America at Two Hundred. Richard B. Morris & Henry F. Graff. (Headline Ser.: 227). (Illus.). 1979. pap. 2.00 (ISBN 0-87124-032-7, 75-26057). Foreign Policy.

America Begins. rev. ed. Alice Dalgliesh. (Illus.). (gr. 2-5). 1958. reinforced bdg. 6.95 o.p. (ISBN 0-684-13455-1, ScribJ). Scribner.

America Bicentennial Queen. 5.00 o.p. (ISBN 0-685-83312-7). Chatham Pub CA.

America, Britain & Russia: Their Co-Operation & Conflict 1941-1946. William H. McNeill. Repr. of 1953 ed. 50.00 (ISBN 0-685-92793-8); text ed. 45.00 (ISBN 0-686-66463-9). Johnson Repr.

America by Design: Science, Technology, & the Rise of Corporate Capitalism. David F. Noble. (Galaxy Books). 410p. (Orig.). 1979. pap. 5.95 (ISBN 0-19-502618-7, GB 588, GB). Oxford U Pr.

America Changing Time: A Brief History. C. M. Dollar. LC 80-10684. 729p. 1980. 12.95 (ISBN 0-471-06087-9). Wiley.

America Comes of Age: A French Analysis. 2nd ed. Andre Siegfried. Tr. by Doris Hemming & H. H. Hemming. LC 68-16244. (American Scene Ser.). 368p. 1974. Repr. of 1927 ed. lib. bdg. 32.50 (ISBN 0-306-71025-0). Da Capo.

America Dances. Agnes De Mille. (Illus.). 1980. 24.95 (ISBN 0-02-530730-4). Macmillan.

America En el Horizonte: Una Perspectiva Cultural. Ernesto Ardura. LC 79-54965. (Coleccion De Estudios Hispanicos: Hispanic Studies Collection). (Illus.). 161p. (Orig., Span.). Date not set. pap. 9.95 (ISBN 0-89729-240-5). Ediciones.

America En Su Literatura. 2nd ed. Anita Arroyo. LC 77-3041. (Illus.). 1978. 15.00 (ISBN 0-8477-3175-8); pap. text ed. 12.00 (ISBN 0-8477-3182-0). U of PR Pr.

America Enters the Eighties: Some Social Indicators. Ed. by Conrad Taeuber & Richard D. Lambert. (Annals of the American Academy of Political & Social Science Ser.: No. 453). (Illus.). 350p. 1981. 10.00 (ISBN 0-87761-258-7); pap. 8.00 (ISBN 0-87761-259-5). Am Acad Pol Soc.
America Faces Russia. Thomas A. Bailey. 1964. 8.75 (ISBN 0-8446-1037-2). Peter Smith.
America: Framing of a Nation, 2 vols. Bailey. LC 74-15253. 1975. Vol. 1. pap. text ed. 11.95 (ISBN 0-675-08756-2); Vol. 2. pap. text ed. 11.95 (ISBN 0-675-08749-X). Merrill.
America Goes to War. Bruce Catton. LC 58-13602. (Illus.). 1971. pap. 5.00x (ISBN 0-8195-6016-2, Pub. by Wesleyan U Pr). Columbia U Pr.
America Grows. Authur F. Scitt. 1981. 10.95 (ISBN 0-533-04906-7). Vantage.
America Grows Up: A History for Peter. Gerald W. Johnson. (Illus.). (gr. 5 up). 1960. 8.75 (ISBN 0-688-21015-5). Morrow.
America II: Special Issue 21. Robin White et al. pap. 1.00 o.p. (ISBN 0-685-78394-4). The Smith.
America in an Interdependent World: Problems of United States Foreign Policy. Ed. by David A. Baldwin. LC 75-41909. (Illus.). 372p. 1976. pap. text ed. 8.50x (ISBN 0-87451-127-5). U Pr of New Eng.
America in Decline: Imperialism's Greatest Crisis, Developments Toward War & Revolution, in the U.S. & Worldwide in the 1980's. Raymond Lotta et al. (Illus.). 600p. (Orig.). 1981. 30.00 (ISBN 0-916650-12-X); pap. 9.95 (ISBN 0-916650-13-8). Banner Pr IL.
America in Depression & War. Richard Lowitt. LC 73-810600. (Orig.). 1979. pap. text ed. 5.95x (ISBN 0-88273-022-3). Forum Pr MO.
America in Eighteen Seventy-Six: The Way We Were. Lally Weymouth & Milton Glaser. 1976. pap. 7.95 (ISBN 0-394-71616-7, V-616, Vin); pap. 7.95 (ISBN 0-394-71616-7). Random.
America in Fiction: An Annotated List of Novels That Interpret Aspects of Life in the United States, Canada, & Mexico. 6th ed. Otis W. Coan & Richard G. Lillard. Date not set. price not set. Pacific Bks.
America in Her Centennial Year 1876. James W. Campbell. LC 79-6757. 272p. 1980. pap. text ed. 10.50 (ISBN 0-8191-0947-9). U Pr of Amer.
America in Literature. Incl. Midwest. Ed. by Ronald Szymanski. LC 79-4078 (ISBN 0-684-16137-0); Northeast. Ed. by James Lape. LC 78-25617 (ISBN 0-684-16063-3); Small Town. Ed. by Flory J. Schultheiss. LC 79-4209 (ISBN 0-684-16138-9); South. Ed. by Sara Marshall. LC 78-25615 (ISBN 0-684-16136-2); West. Ed. by Peter Monahan. LC 78-24512 (ISBN 0-684-16087-0). (gr. 9-12). 1979. pap. 6.50 ea. (ScribC). Scribner.
America in Literature, 2 vols. Theodore L. Gross et al. LC 76-49486. 1978. Vol. 1. pap. text ed. 13.95 (ISBN 0-471-32808-1); Vol. 2. pap. text ed. 13.95 (ISBN 0-471-32809-X); tchrs. manual 3.00 (ISBN 0-471-04050-9). Wiley.
America in Mid Passage. Charles A. Beard & Mary R. Beard. (Rise of American Civilization Ser. Vol. 3). 1966. 15.00 (ISBN 0-8446-1062-3). Peter Smith.
America in Modern Italian Literature. Donald Heiney. 278p. 1965. 15.50 (ISBN 0-8135-0471-6). Rutgers U Pr.
America in the Cold War: Twenty Years of Revolution & Response, 1947-1967. Walter La Feber. LC 70-38955. (Problems in American History Ser.). 232p. 1969. 9.95x (ISBN 0-471-51133-1). Wiley.
America in the Pacific. Foster R. Dulles. LC 73-86595. (American Scene Ser). 1969. Repr. of 1932 ed. 29.50 (ISBN 0-306-71431-0). Da Capo.
America in the Sixties. Ronald Berman. LC 68-10365. 1968. 9.95 o.s.i. (ISBN 0-02-902980-5). Free Pr.
America in the World Economy. Charles P. Kindleberger. (Headline Ser.: 237). (Illus.). 1977. pap. 3.00 (ISBN 0-87124-043-2, 77-86278). Foreign Policy.
America in the 1980's. Editorial Research Reports. Ed. by Editorial Research Reports. (Editorial Research Reports Ser.). 220p. Date not set. pap. 6.95 (ISBN 0-87187-194-7). Congr Quarterly.
America in Theological Perspective. Ed. by Thomas M. McFadden. 1976. 9.95 (ISBN 0-8164-0294-9). Crossroad NY.
America Is Born: A History for Peter. Gerald W. Johnson. (Illus.). (gr. 5 up). 1959. 8.75 (ISBN 0-688-21071-6). Morrow.
America, Land of Wonders. Frances Wood & Dorothy Wood. LC 72-3155. (Illus.). 192p. (gr. 5 up). 1973. 5.95 (ISBN 0-396-06529-5). Dodd.
America, Lost & Found. Anthony Bailey. 1981. 9.95 (ISBN 0-394-51088-7). Random.
America, My Wilderness. Frederic Prokosch. 256p. 1972. 6.95 o.p. (ISBN 0-374-10388-7). FS&G.
America, Okinawa, & Japan: Case Studies for Foreign Policy Theory. Frederick L. Shiels. LC 79-5496. 1980. text ed. 18.50 (ISBN 0-8191-0893-6); pap. text ed. 11.25 (ISBN 0-8191-0894-4). U Pr of Amer.
America on Eight to Sixteen Dollars a Night 1978-79. 6th ed. Bob Christopher & Ellen Christopher. LC 77-85277. 1978. pap. 5.95 o.p. (ISBN 0-688-08321-8). Morrow.
America on Stage: Ten Great Plays of American History. Ed. by Stanley Richards. LC 75-7255. 960p. 1976. 12.50 o.p. (ISBN 0-385-03005-3). Doubleday.
America; or, a General Survey of the Political Situation of the Several Powers of the Western Continent. Alexander Everett. Ed. by Michael Hudson. (Neglected American Economists Ser.). 1974. lib. bdg. 50.00 (ISBN 0-8240-1002-7). Garland Pub.
America Personified: Portraits from History, 2 vols. David Burner & Robert D. Marcus. LC 74-76210. 224p. (Orig.). 1974. pap. text ed. 6.95 ea. Vol. 1 (ISBN 0-312-03010-X). Vol. 2 (ISBN 0-312-03045-2). St Martin.
America Rebels: Personal Narratives of the American Revoulution. Richard M. Dorson. 354p. Date not set. pap. 3.95 (ISBN 0-394-73277-4). Pantheon.
America Revisited: One Hundred & Fifty Years After Tocqueville. Eugene J. McCarthy. LC 77-92222. 1978. 7.95 o.p. (ISBN 0-385-03106-8). Doubleday.
America, Scandinavia, & the Cold War, Nineteen Forty-Five to Nineteen Forty Nine. Geir Lundestad. LC 80-73048. 416p. 1980. 27.50x (ISBN 0-231-04974-9). Columbia U Pr.
America Since Nineteen Twenty. Daniel Snowman. LC 79-30076. (Studies in Modern History). 1978. 19.95x (ISBN 0-435-31775-X); pap. text ed. 7.95x (ISBN 0-435-31776-8). Heinemann Ed.
America Since 1945. 2nd ed. Ed. by Robert D. Marcus & David Burner. LC 76-52588. 1977. pap. text ed. 8.95 (ISBN 0-312-03115-7). St Martin.
America Spreads Her Sails: U. S. Seapower in the 19th Century. Ed. by Clayton R. Barrow, Jr. LC 73-76271. 1973. 11.00 o.s.i. (ISBN 0-87021-071-8). Naval Inst Pr.
America the Beautiful in the Words of Henry David Thoreau. Ed. by Country Beautiful Foundation. 1966. 7.95 o.p. (ISBN 0-688-01046-6). Morrow.
America the Land of Contrasts: A Briton's View of His American Kin. James F. Muirhead. LC 74-87430. (American Scene Ser). Orig. Title: Bodley Head. 1970. Repr. of 1902 ed. lib. bdg. 32.50 (ISBN 0-306-71576-7). Da Capo.
America: The New Imperialism. Vernon Kiernan. 306p. 1978. 19.00 (ISBN 0-905762-18-5, Pub. by Zed Pr). Lawrence Hill.
America, the True Church & the End of the Age: Where the United States Fits in Biblical Prophecy. James A. McCune. (Illus.). 227p. (Orig.). 1980. pap. 5.95 (ISBN 0-9604732-0-3). Yorkshire Pub.
America Through Baseball. David Q. Voigt. LC 75-20434. 232p. 1976. 13.95 (ISBN 0-88229-272-2). Nelson-Hall.
America Through the Eye of My Needle: Common Sense for the 80's. Josephine Alexander. 192p. 1981. 9.95 (ISBN 0-8037-0194-2). Dial.
America: Travel & Exploration. Steven Kagle. LC 78-71883. 1979. 11.95 (ISBN 0-87972-134-0); pap. 6.95 (ISBN 0-87972-171-5). Bowling Green Univ.
America U.S. Stamp Album. Ed. by Larry Grossman. (Illus.). 1980. 12.95 (ISBN 0-685-78366-9). Grossman Stamp.
America Votes: What You Should Know About Elections Today. Kevin V. Mulcahy & Richard S. Katz. LC 76-15592. 1976. pap. text ed. 4.95 (ISBN 0-13-023788-4, Spec). P-H.
America-Watching: Perspectives in the Course of an Incredible Century. Gerald W. Johnson. LC 76-12459. 368p. 1976. 12.95 (ISBN 0-916144-05-4). Stemmer Hse.
American. Henry James. (Norton Critical Edition). 1978. 14.95. Norton.
American Academics: Then & Now. Logan Wilson. (Illus.). 1979. pap. text ed. 15.95x (ISBN 0-19-502482-6). Oxford U Pr.
American Academy in Rome, 1894-1969. Alan Valentine & Lucia Valentine. LC 72-92663. 200p. 1973. 10.95x (ISBN 0-8139-0444-7). U Pr of Va.
American Academy of Orthopaedic Surgeons: Instructional Course Lectures, Vols. 21-29. American Academy of Orthopaedic Surgeons. Incl. Vol. 21. 1972. 37.50 (ISBN 0-8016-0010-3); Vol. 22. 1973. 37.50 (ISBN 0-8016-0011-1); Vol. 23. 1974. 34.50 (ISBN 0-8016-0012-X); Vol. 24. 328p. 1975. 38.50 (ISBN 0-8016-0013-8); Vol. 25. 1976. 38.50 (ISBN 0-8016-0014-6); Vol. 26. 1977. 38.50 (ISBN 0-8016-0022-7); Vol. 27. 1978. 34.50 (ISBN 0-8016-0023-5); Vol. 28. 1979. 44.50 (ISBN 0-8016-0032-4); Vol. 29. 184p. 1980. 38.00 (ISBN 0-8016-0047-2). LC 43-17054. Mosby.
American Addition: History of a Black Community. Felix James. LC 78-65427. (Illus.). 1979. pap. 8.25 (ISBN 0-8191-0663-1). U Pr of Amer.
American Adventure, 2 vols. The Educational Research Council. (Concepts & Inquiry Ser). (Orig.). (gr. 8). 1975. Vol. 1. text ed. 16.92 (ISBN 0-205-04623-1, 8046239); 12.00 (ISBN 0-205-04624-X, 8046247); Vol. 2. text ed. 16.92 (ISBN 0-205-04625-8, 8046255); 12.00 (ISBN 0-205-04626-6, 8046263). Allyn.
American Agriculture & U.S. Foreign Policy. Ed. by Richard Fraenkel et al. LC 78-19761. 1979. 19.95 (ISBN 0-03-043101-8). Praeger.
American Alcoholic: The Nature-Nurture Controversy in Alcoholic Research & Therapy. William Madsen. (Illus.). 272p. 1980. 15.50 (ISBN 0-398-02926-1). C C Thomas.
American Ambassador: Joseph C. Grew & the Development of the United States Diplomatic Tradition. Waldo H. Heinrichs, Jr. Ed. by Frank Freidel. LC 78-66536. (History of the United States Ser.: Vol. 7). 474p. 1979. lib. bdg. 35.00 (ISBN 0-8240-9705-X). Garland Pub.
American Ammunition & Ballistics. Edward Matunas. (Illus.). 1979. 13.95 (ISBN 0-87691-290-0). Winchester Pr.
American & British Literature Nineteen Forty Five to Nineteen Seventy Five: An Annotated Bibliography of Contemporary Scholarship. John L. Somer & Barbara E. Cooper. LC 79-19299. 1980. 20.00x (ISBN 0-7006-0195-3). Regents Pr KS.
American & British Technology in the Nineteenth Century. H. J. Habakkuk. 32.95 (ISBN 0-521-05162-2); pap. 8.95x (ISBN 0-521-09447-X). Cambridge U Pr.
American & British Theatrical Biography: A Directory. J. P. Wearing. LC 78-31162. 1013p. 1979. 40.00 (ISBN 0-8108-1201-0). Scarecrow.
American & English Popular Entertainment: A Guide to Information Sources. Ed. by Don B. Wilmeth. LC 79-22869. (Performing Arts Information Guide Ser.: Vol. 7). 1980. 30.00 (ISBN 0-8103-1454-1). Gale.
American & European Revolutions, 1776-1848: Sociopolitical & Ideological Aspects. Ed. by Jaroslaw Pelenski. LC 79-22599. (Illus.). 430p. 1980. text ed. 17.50x (ISBN 0-87745-097-8, 8294). U of Iowa Pr.
American & Japanese Coloring & Talking Books, Bk. 8. Sugimura et al. (gr. k-4). pap. 0.75 ea.; Bk. 6, Customs. o.s.i. (ISBN 0-8048-0012-X); Bk. 8, Riding. (ISBN 0-8048-0017-0); Bk. 9, Houses. o.s.i. (ISBN 0-8048-0016-2). Bk. 10, Story Book Heroes. o.s.i. (ISBN 0-8048-0019-7). C E Tuttle.
American & Soviet Military Trends: Since the Cuban Missile Crisis. John M. Collins. LC 78-58310. (Illus.). 1978. text ed. 14.95 (ISBN 0-89206-003-4); pap. 10.95 (ISBN 0-89206-002-6). CSI Studies.
American Animated Cartoon. Gerald Peary & Dannis Peary. (Illus.). 1980. pap. 10.95 (ISBN 0-525-47639-3). Dutton.
American Anthropology, the Early Years: Proceedings. American Ethnological Society, 1974. Ed. by John V. Murra. (AES Ser). (Illus.). 235p. 1976. pap. text ed. 12.95 (ISBN 0-8299-0097-7). West Pub.
American Anti-Imperialism: 1895-1901. Blanche Cooke & Gerald Markowitz. LC 78-147760. (Library of War & Peace; Documentary Anthologies). 1974. lib. bdg. 38.00 (ISBN 0-8240-0500-7). Garland Pub.
American Anti-War Movements. Joseph R. Conlin. (Insight Ser). 144p. (Orig.). 1968. 4.95x (ISBN 0-02-474030-6, 47403). Macmillan.
American Antique Furntire, 2 vols. Edgar G. Miller, Jr. (Illus.). Set. 32.50 (ISBN 0-8446-2589-2). Peter Smith.
American Antique Toys, Eighteen-Thirty to Nineteen-Hundred. Bernard Barenholtz & Inez McClintock. (Illus.). 264p. 1980. 45.00 (ISBN 0-686-62681-8, 0668-6). Abrams.
American Antiques. Ann K. Cole. (Golden Guide Ser.). 1967. PLB 9.15 (ISBN 0-307-63537-6, Golden Pr); pap. 1.95 o.p. (ISBN 0-307-24013-4). Western Pub.
American Appraisals of Soviet Russia: 1917-1977. Ed. by Eugene Anschel. LC 78-5920. 1978. 18.00 (ISBN 0-8108-1135-9). Scarecrow.
American-Arab Relations from Wilson to Nixon. Faiz S Abu-Jaber. LC 78-65853. 1979. pap. 10.50 (ISBN 0-8191-0680-1). U Pr of Amer.
American Architects from the Civil War to the First World War: A Guide to Information Sources. Ed. by Lawrence Wodehouse. LC 73-17525. (Art & Architecture Information Guide Ser.: Vol. 3). 380p. 1976. 30.00 (ISBN 0-8103-1269-7). Gale.
American Architects from the First World War to the Present: A Guide to Information Sources. Ed. by Lawrence Wodehouse. LC 74-10259. (Art & Architecture Information Guide Ser.: Vol. 4). 380p. 1977. 30.00 (ISBN 0-8103-1270-0). Gale.
American Architectural Books: A List of Books, Portfolios, and Pamphlets on Architecture and Related Subjects Published in America Before 1895. Henry R. Hitchcock. LC 75-25672. (Architectural and Decorative Arts Ser.). xii, 130p. 1975. Repr. of 1962 ed. lib. bdg. 19.50 (ISBN 0-306-70742-X). Da Capo.
American Architecture: A History, 1607-1976. Marcus Whiffen & Frederick Koeper. 600p. 1981. text ed. 20.00 (ISBN 0-262-23105-0). MIT Pr.
American Architecture & Art: A Guide to Information Sources. David M. Sokol. LC 73-17563. (American Studies Information Guide Ser.: Vol. 2). 480p. 1976. 30.00 (ISBN 0-8103-1255-7). Gale.
American Aristides: A Biography of George Wythe. Imogene E. Brown. LC 77-89776. 1980. 28.50 (ISBN 0-8386-2142-2). Fairleigh Dickinson.
American Aristocracy: The Lives & Times of James Russell, Amy, & Robert Lowell. C. David Heymann. LC 79-9351. (Illus.). 1980. 17.95 (ISBN 0-396-07608-4). Dodd.
American Arms Changing Europe. W. R. Schilling. 1973. 15.00x (ISBN 0-231-03704-X); pap. 7.50x (ISBN 0-231-03705-8). Columbia U Pr.
American Art. John Wilmerding. (Pelican History of Art Ser.: No. 40). 1976. 40.00 o.p. (ISBN 0-670-11678-5). Viking Pr.
American Art & American Art Collections, 2 vols. Ed. by Walter Montgomery. LC 75-28883. (Art Experience in Late 19th Century America Ser.: Vol. 17). (Illus.). 1976. Repr. of 1889 ed. Set. lib. bdg. 178.00 (ISBN 0-8240-2241-6). Garland Pub.
American Art Nouveau Glass. Albert C. Revi. LC 68-18778. (Illus.). 476p. 1981. Repr. 40.00 (ISBN 0-916838-40-4). Schiffer.
American Art of the Twentieth Century. Sam Hunter & John Jacobus. (Illus.). 580p. 1974. text ed. 20.95 (ISBN 0-13-024075-3). P-H.
American Art: Painting, Sculpture, Architecture, Decorative Arts, Photography. M. Brown et al. 1979. 21.95 (ISBN 0-13-024653-0). P-H.
American Art: Readings from the Colonial Era to the Present. Harold Spencer. LC 80-12325. (Illus.). 1980. pap. text ed. 10.95x (ISBN 0-684-16608-9, ScribC). Scribner.
American Art, Seventeen Hundred to Nineteen Sixty: Sources & Documents. Ed. by John W. McCoubrey. (Orig.). 1965. pap. 10.95x ref. ed. (ISBN 0-13-024521-6). P-H.
American Art Since Nineteen Hundred. Barbara Rose. LC 72-83563. (Illus.). 320p. 1975. text ed. 13.95x. Praeger.
American Artist Art School Directory: 1976-77. National Art Education Association. 1977. pap. 1.75 (ISBN 0-686-10436-6). Natl Art Ed.
American Artist Diary Nineteen Eighty. (Illus.). 1979. 9.95 o.p. (ISBN 0-8230-0207-1). Watson-Guptill.
American Artists Today in Black, Vol. I. Hobie L. Williams. Ed. by Mosezelle White & Bobby Roberts, II. 87p. (Orig.). 1981. pap. text ed. 7.95x (ISBN 0-936026-11-1). R&M Pub Co.
American Artists Today in Black, Vol. II. Hobie L. Williams. Ed. by Mosezelle White & Bobby Roberts, II. 103p. (Orig.). Date not set. pap. text ed. 8.95 (ISBN 0-936026-12-X). R&M Pub Co.
American Association of Architectural Bibliographers' Papers, Vol. 1. Ed. by William B. O'Neal. Incl. Henry-Russell Hitchcock. James H. Grady; Walter Gropius. Carol Shillaber; Philip C. Johnson. William O'Neal; Early Architecture of Virginia. Frederick D. Nichols. LC 65-14273. 128p. 1965. 10.00x (ISBN 0-8139-0003-4). U Pr of Va.
American Association of Architectural Bibliographers' Papers, Vol. 2. Ed. by William B. O'Neal. Incl. Sibyl Moholy-Nagy. Philip C. Johnson & William B. O'Neal; Holabird & Roche. William Rudd; Early Architecture of Virginia. Frederick D. Nichols. LC 65-14273. 113p. 1966. 10.00x (ISBN 0-8139-0004-2). U Pr of Va.
American Association of Architectural Bibliographers' Papers, Vol. 3. Ed. by William B. O'Neal. Incl. Walter Gropius. LC 65-14273. 138p. 1966. 10.00x (ISBN 0-8139-0005-0). U Pr of Va.

American Association of Architectural Bibliographers' Papers, Vol. 5. Ed. by William B. O'Neal. Incl. Henry-Russell Hitchcock. James H. Grady; Architectural Comment in American Magazines, 1783-1815. J. Meredith Neil; The Adam Style in America, 1770-1820. Sterling M. Boyd; Calvert Vaux. John D. Sigle; Alvar Aalto. Peter W. Beal. LC 65-14273. 106p. 1968. 10.00x (ISBN 0-8139-0007-7). U Pr of Va.

American Association of Architectural Bibliographers' Papers, Vol. 6. Ed. by William B. O'Neal. Incl. Jefferson As an Architect. William B. O'Neal. LC 65-14273. (Illus.). 150p. 1969. 10.00x (ISBN 0-8139-0281-9). U Pr of Va.

American Association of Architectural Bibliographers' Papers, Vol. 7. Ed. by William B. O'Neal. Incl. Sir Nikolaus Pevsner. John R. Barr. LC 65-14273. 124p. 1970. 10.00x (ISBN 0-8139-0299-1). U Pr of Va.

American Association of Architectural Bibliographers' Papers, Vol. 9. Ed. by William B. O'Neal. Incl. Supplement to the Bibliography of Walter Gropius. Ed. by Ise Gropius; Bibliography of Works About Sir Christopher Wren. Ed. by Gail G. Stringer; Benjamin Henry Latrobe. Ed. by Paul F. Norton; Frank Lloyd Wright in Print 1959-1970. Compiled by James Muggenberg. LC 65-14273. 1972. 10.00x (ISBN 0-8139-0391-2). U Pr of Va.

American Association of Architectural Bibliographers Papers, Vol. 10. Ed. by William B. O'Neal. Incl. A Bibliography of Antonio Gaudi & the Catalan Movement, 1870-1930. Compiled by George R. Collins & Maurice E. Farinas. LC 65-14273. 1973. 12.50x (ISBN 0-8139-0477-3). U Pr of Va.

American Association of Architectural Bibliographers Papers, Vol. 11: Index to Papers 1-10. Ed. by William B. O'Neal. LC 65-14273. 1975. 12.50x (ISBN 0-8139-0608-3). U Pr of Va.

American Association of University Women Archives 1881-1976. Ed. by Barbara A. Sokolosky. 115p. 1980. pap. write for info. (ISBN 0-667-00651-6). Microfilming Corp.

American Atheist Radio Series of Ingersoll the Magnificent. Madalyn M. O'Hair. 1977. pap. 3.00. Am Atheist.

American-Austrian Private International Law. Seidl-Hohenveldern. 1963. 9.00 (ISBN 0-379-11411-9). Oceana.

American Averages. Mike Feinsilber & William B. Mead. LC 79-8567. pap. 7.95 (Dolp). Doubleday.

American Averages: Amazing Facts of Everyday Life. Mike Feinsilber & William B. Mead. LC 79-8567. 432p. 1980. 14.95 (ISBN 0-385-15175-6). Doubleday.

American Ballad Operas. Ed. by Walter H. Rubsamen. LC 74-4466. (Ballad Opera Ser.). 1974. lib. bdg. 50.00 (ISBN 0-8240-0927-4). Garland Pub.

American Banks Abroad: Edge Act Companies & Multinational Banking. James C. Baker & M. Gerald Bradford. LC 73-18135. (Special Studies). 202p. 1974. text ed. 21.95 o.p. (ISBN 0-275-28819-6). Praeger.

American Baptists: Whence & Whither. Norman H. Maring. (Orig.). 1968. pap. 2.50 o.p. (ISBN 0-8170-0398-3). Judson.

American Bar - The Canadian Bar - The International Bar: 1981. 63rd ed. Ed. by Sarah Livermore et al. LC 18-21110. 3062p. 1981. 130.00 (ISBN 0-931398-06-1). R B Forster.

American Bar - the Canadian Bar - the International Bar, 1979. 61st ed. Ed. by Mary Reincke & Sylvia Stokes. LC 18-21110. 1979. 110.00 o.p. (ISBN 0-931398-04-5). R B Forster.

American Baroque. Lamar Herrin. 336p. 1981. pap. 3.50 (ISBN 0-380-77362-7, 77362, Bard). Avon.

American Baseball. David Q Voigt. Incl. Vol. 1. From Gentlemen's Sport to Commissioner System. 336p. 1966. 15.95 (ISBN 0-8061-0702-2); Vol. 2. From Comissioners to Continental Expansion. 350p. 1970. 15.95 (ISBN 0-8061-0904-1). (Illus.). Set. o.p. **24.95 set (ISBN 0-8061-0941-6). U of Okla Pr.**

American Basketry & Woodenware: A Collector's Guide. William C. Ketchum. LC 73-6486. (Illus.). 256p. 1974. 6.95 o.s.i. (ISBN 0-02-562970-0). Macmillan.

American Bastille. John A. Marshall. LC 71-121115. (Civil Liberties in American History Ser). 1970. Repr. of 1869 ed. lib. bdg. 69.50 (ISBN 0-306-71963-0). Da Capo.

American Battleships, Eighteen Eighty-Six to Nineteen Twenty-Three: Predreadnought Design & Construction. John C. Reilly & Robert L. Scheina. LC 79-91326. 236p. 1980. 29.95 (ISBN 0-87021-524-8). Naval Inst Pr.

American Beauty. Mary E. Barrett. 288p. 1980. 12.95 (ISBN 0-525-05285-2). Dutton.

American Beer Can Encyclopedia. Thomas Toepfer. (Illus.). 1979. pap. 7.95 (ISBN 0-89145-150-1). Collector Bks.

American Bibliography, 14 vols. Charles Evans. Incl. Vols 1-12. 200.00 (ISBN 0-8446-1173-5); Vol. 13. 1799-1800. 25.00 (ISBN 0-8446-1174-3); Vol. 14. Index. Compiled by R. P. Bristol. 25.00 (ISBN 0-8446-1175-1). Peter Smith.

American Bibliography, Eighteen Hundred & One to Eighteen -Nineteen, 22 vols. Ralph R. Shaw & R. H. Shoemaker. LC 58-7809. (Includes addenda, list of sources, library symbols, title index & author index). Set Vols. Prices For Separate Vols. On Request, 1958-1963. 225.50 (ISBN 0-8108-0192-2). Scarecrow.

American Bicycle Atlas. American Youth Hostels. 1981. pap. 5.95 (ISBN 0-525-93172-4). Dutton.

American Biographies. Wheeler Preston. LC 73-10407. x, 1147p. 1975. Repr. of 1940 ed. 48.00 (ISBN 0-8103-4054-2). Gale.

American Black Scientists & Inventors. Edward S. Jenkins et al. 1975. pap. 2.50 (ISBN 0-87355-003-X). Natl Sci Tchrs.

American Black Women in the Arts & Social Sciences: A Bibliographic Survey. rev. ed. Ora Williams. LC 77-17055. (Illus.). 1978. 10.00 (ISBN 0-8108-1096-4). Scarecrow.

American Book Auction Catalogues, 1713-1934. Ed. by George L. McKay. 1967. Repr. of 1937 ed. 20.00 (ISBN 0-8103-3311-2). Gale.

American Book of Medical Astrology. Eileen Nauman. (Illus.). 368p. (Orig.). 1981. pap. 14.95 (ISBN 0-917086-28-7). Astro Comp Serv.

American Book Prices Current, Vol. 86. Ed. by Katherine Leab & Daniel Leab. 1981. 79.75 (ISBN 0-914022-11-3). Am Book Prices.

American Book Prices Current Index: Nineteen Seventy Five to Nineteen Seventy-Nine, 2 vols. Ed. by Katharine K. Leab & Daniel J. Leab. 1980. Set. 250.00x (ISBN 0-914022-10-5, 314557). Vol. 1, 1020p. Vol. 2, 1030p. Bancroft Parkman.

American Book-Prices Current: 1968, Vol. 74. LC 3-14577. 1971. 50.00x (ISBN 0-231-03609-4). Columbia U Pr.

American Book-Prices Current: 1969, Vol. 75. LC 3-14577. 1972. 50.00x (ISBN 0-231-03637-X). Columbia U Pr.

American Book Prices Current: 1980, Vol. 86. Ed. by Katharine K. Leab & Daniel J. Leab. 1200p. 1981. 79.75 (ISBN 0-914022-10-5); prepub. 62.30 (ISBN 0-686-68816-3). Bancroft Parkman.

American Book Publishing Record Annual Cumulative 1980. 1260p. 1981. text ed. 59.00 (ISBN 0-8352-1245-9). Bowker.

American Book Publishing Record Cumulative 1980. 1260p. 1981. 59.00 (ISBN 0-8352-1245-9). Bowker.

American Book Publishing Record Cumulative 1975-1979. 1981. 125.00 (ISBN 0-8352-1371-4). Bowker.

American Book Publishing Record Cumulative 1876-1949, 14 vols. 20000p. 1980. 1500.00 (ISBN 0-686-64537-5); after Dec. 31st 1975.00. Bowker.

American Book Publishing Record Cumulative 1950-1977: An American National Bibliography. LC 66-19741. 1979. 1975.00 set (ISBN 0-8352-1094-4). Bowker.

American Book Publishing Record 1876-1949. 1980. 1975.00 (ISBN 0-8352-1245-9). Bowker.

American Book Trade Directory 1979. Ed. by Jaques Cattell Press. LC 15-23627. 1026p. 1979. 49.95 o.p. (ISBN 0-8352-1137-1). Bowker.

American Book Trade Directory 1980. 26th ed. Ed. by Jaques Cattell Press. LC 15-23627. 1090p. 1980. 54.95 o.p. (ISBN 0-8352-1252-1). Bowker.

American Bureaucracy. 2nd ed. Peter Woll. 1977. 12.50x (ISBN 0-393-05615-5); pap. 5.95x (ISBN 0-393-09141-4). Norton.

American Business. Boy Scouts Of America. LC 19-600. (Illus.). 48p. (gr. 6-12). 1975. pap. 0.70x (ISBN 0-8395-3325-X, 3325). BSA.

American Business Abroad: Six Lectures on Direct Investment. Charles P. Kindleberger. LC 69-12325. (Illus.). 1969. 16.00x o.p. (ISBN 0-300-01096-6); pap. 3.95 o.p. (ISBN 0-300-01085-0, Y213). Yale U Pr.

American Business & Public Policy: The Politics of Foreign Trade. 2nd ed. Raymond A. Bauer et al. LC 63-8171. (Illus.). 1972. 24.95x (ISBN 0-202-24128-9); pap. 13.95x (ISBN 0-202-24129-7). Aldine Pub.

American Business History. Herman E. Krooss & Charles Gilbert. 352p. 1972. pap. 11.95x ref ed. (ISBN 0-13-024083-4). P-H.

American Calendar Customs, Vol. I. Catherine H. Ainsworth. LC 79-52827. (Calendar Customs & Holidays Ser.). 104p. (Orig.). (gr. 5-12). 1979. pap. 5.00 (ISBN 0-933190-06-9). Clyde Pr.

American Calendar Customs, Vol. II. Catherine H. Ainsworth. LC 79-55784. (Calender Customs). 200p. (Orig.). 1980. pap. 10.00 (ISBN 0-933190-07-7). Clyde Pr.

American Car Since Seventeen Seventy-Five: An Encyclopedic Survey. Automobile Quarterly Editors. (Illus.). 1971. 17.95 o.p. (ISBN 0-525-05300-X). Dutton.

American Car Spotter's Guide: 1966-1980. Tad Burness. (Illus.). 432p. (Orig.). 1981. pap. 16.95 (ISBN 0-87938-102-7). Motorbooks Intl.

American Catholic Catechism. Ed. by George Dyer. LC 75-7786. 320p. 1975. 10.00 o.p. (ISBN 0-8164-1196-4); pap. 4.95 (ISBN 0-8164-2588-4). Crossroad NY.

American Catholic Family. John L. Thomas. LC 80-15221. (Illus.). xii, 471p. 1980. Repr. of 1956 ed. lib. bdg. 33.50x (ISBN 0-313-22473-0, THAC). Greenwood.

American Catholic Thought on Social Questions. Ed. by Aaron Abell. LC 66-30548. 1968. pap. 10.95 (ISBN 0-672-60090-0, AHS58). Bobbs.

American Catholicism: Where Do We Go from Here? George Devine. 144p. (Orig.). 1974. pap. 9.95 (ISBN 0-13-023986-0). P-H.

American Catholics & the Roosevelt Presidency, 1932-1936. George Q. Flynn. LC 68-12968. 288p. 1968. 11.00x (ISBN 0-8131-1165-X). U Pr of Ky.

American Challenge. J. J. Servan-Schreiber. 1976. pap. 1.65 (ISBN 0-380-01016-X, 11965, Discus). Avon.

American Challenge. R. R. Spitzer & Gregg Hoffman. (Illus.). 360p. 1980. 12.50 (ISBN 0-87319-019-X). C Hallberg.

American Chameleon. William White, Jr. LC 76-51162. (Nature Ser.). (Illus.). (gr. 7 up). 1977. 7.95 (ISBN 0-8069-3532-4); PLB 7.49 (ISBN 0-8069-3533-2). Sterling.

American Chess Masters from Morphy to Fischer. Arthur Bisquier & Andy Soltis. LC 73-18510. (Illus.). 260p. 1974. 9.95 o.s.i. (ISBN 0-02-511050-0). Macmillan.

American Children. Susan Kismaric. 1981. 14.95 (ISBN 0-87070-229-7, 037338); pap. 7.95 (ISBN 0-87070-232-7, 037346). NYGS.

American Children: Photographs in the Collection of the Museum of Modern Art. Susan Kismaric. (Springs Mills Series on the Art of Photography). (Illus.). 80p. 1981. 14.95 (ISBN 0-87070-232-7); pap. 7.95 (ISBN 0-87070-229-7). Museum Mod Art.

American Christianity: An Historical Interpretation with Representative Documents. lib. rep. ed. H. Shelton Smith et al. 1960. Vol. I. 30.00x (ISBN 0-684-15744-6, ScribT); Vol. II. 30.00x (ISBN 0-684-15745-4). Scribner.

American Cinema: Directors & Directions: 1929-1968. Andrew Sarris. 1969. pap. 5.50 (ISBN 0-525-47227-4). Dutton.

American Cinema: The Art, the Industry, the Audience, the Artists. Louis Giannetti. 255p. 1981. text ed. 17.95 (ISBN 0-13-024687-5); pap. text ed. 11.95 (ISBN 0-13-024679-4). P-H.

American City. Michael Weber & Anne Lloyd. (Illus.). 463p. 1975. pap. text ed. 11.95 (ISBN 0-8299-0036-5); instrs.' manual avail. (ISBN 0-8299-0580-4). West Pub.

American City Novel. Blanche H. Gelfant. 1970. Repr. of 1954 ed. 8.95 o.p. (ISBN 0-8061-0293-4). U of Okla Pr.

American City Planning Since 1890. Mel Scott. (California Studies in Urbanization & Environmental Design). 1969. 39.50x (ISBN 0-520-01382-4); pap. 12.95x (ISBN 0-520-02051-0, CAL235). U of Cal Pr.

American Civil Engineer, Eighteen Fifty-Two to Nineteen Seventy-Four. William H. Wisely. LC 74-17792. 464p. 1974. text ed. 20.00 (ISBN 0-87262-000-X). Am Soc Civil Eng.

American Civil War. Peter Parish. LC 74-84660. 750p. 1975. text ed. 29.50x (ISBN 0-8419-0176-7); pap. text ed. 17.50 o.p. (ISBN 0-8419-0197-X). Holmes & Meier.

American Civil War. G. Schomaekers. (Illus.). 1979. 14.95 (ISBN 0-7137-0872-7, Pub. by Blandford Pr England). Sterling.

American Civil War: An English View. Garnet Wolseley. Ed. by James A. Rawley. LC 64-22632. 1964. 9.95 (ISBN 0-8139-0242-8). U Pr of Va.

American Civil War Navies: A Bibliography. Myron J. Smith, Jr. LC 72-6063. (American Naval Bibliography Ser.: Vol. 3). 1972. 13.50 (ISBN 0-8108-0509-X). Scarecrow.

American Civilization: An Introduction. A. N. Hollander & Sigmund Skard. 1970. Repr. of 1968 ed. text ed. 13.25x (ISBN 0-582-48226-7). Humanities.

American Civilization: An Introduction to the Social Sciences. 3rd ed. Maurice Boyd & Donald B. Worcester. 800p. 1973. text ed. 10.95x o.p. (ISBN 0-205-03821-2, 8138214). Allyn.

American Clock: A Mural for Theatre. Arthur Miller. 144p. 1981. 10.95 (ISBN 0-670-11728-5). Viking Pr.

American Clock, 1725-1865: From the Mabel Brady Garvan & Other Collections at Yale University. Edward A. Battison & Patricia E. Kane. LC 72-93856. (Illus.). 208p. 1973. 19.95 (ISBN 0-8212-0493-9, 036706). NYGS.

American Codification Movement: A Study of Antebellum Legal Reform. Charles M. Cook. LC 80-662. (Contributions in Legal Studies: No. 14). 272p. 1981. lib. bdg. 35.00 (ISBN 0-313-21314-3, CAC/). Greenwood.

American College & American Culture. Carnegie Commission On Higher Education. Ed. by O. Handlin & M. F. Handlin. 1970. 8.95 o.p. (ISBN 0-07-010015-2, P&RB). McGraw.

American College & University. Frederick Rudolph. 1965. pap. 4.95 (ISBN 0-394-70288-3, Vin). Random.

American College Testing Preparation Guide. Jerry Bobrow et al. (Cliffs Test Preparation Ser.). (Illus.). (gr. 10-12). 1979. pap. 3.50 wkbk. (ISBN 0-8220-2004-1). Cliffs.

American College Testing Program Exams. 7th ed. David R. Turner. LC 77-7519. (gr. 11-12). 1977. lib. bdg. 6.00 o.p. (ISBN 0-668-04355-5); pap. 5.00 o.p. (ISBN 0-668-04363-6). Arco.

American Colleges: The Uncertain Future. Ed. by William P. Lineberry. (Reference Shelf Ser: Vol. 47, No. 3). 1975. 6.25 (ISBN 0-8242-0571-5). Wilson.

American Colonial Charter. L. P. Kellogg. LC 71-75291. (Era of the American Revolution Ser). 1971. Repr. of 1904 ed. lib. bdg. 14.50 (ISBN 0-306-71292-X). Da Capo.

American Colonies in the Seventeenth Century. Compiled by Alden T. Vaughan. LC 78-151118. (Goldentree Bibliographies in American History Ser.). (Orig.). 1971. 10.95x (ISBN 0-88295-529-2); pap. 6.95x (ISBN 0-88295-528-4). AHM Pub.

American Commentary on the New Testament, 7 vols. Ed. by Alvah Hovey. Incl. Matthew. Ed. by John A. Broadus (ISBN 0-8170-0002-X); Mark & Luke. Ed. by William N. Clark & George R. Bliss (ISBN 0-8170-0003-8); John. Ed. by Alvah Hovey (ISBN 0-8170-0004-6); Acts & Romans (ISBN 0-8170-0005-4); Corinthians-Thessalonians. Ed. by Ezra P. Gould (ISBN 0-8170-0006-2); Timothy-Peter (ISBN 0-8170-0007-0); John, Jude, & Revelation (ISBN 0-8170-0008-9). Set. 70.00 (ISBN 0-8170-0001-1); 10.95 ea. Judson.

American Commercial Policy: Three Historical Essays. Ugo Rabbeno. (Neglected American Economists Ser.). 1974. lib. bdg. 50.00 (ISBN 0-8240-1031-0). Garland Pub.

American Communist Party: A Critical History. Irving Howe & Lewis Coser. LC 73-22072. (FDR & the Era of the New Deal Ser.). x, 612p. 1974. Repr. of 1962 ed. lib. bdg. 39.50 (ISBN 0-306-70636-9). Da Capo.

American Compromise. Richard C. Vitzthum. 1978. pap. 5.95 (ISBN 0-8061-1477-0). U of Okla Pr.

American Compromise: Theme & Method in the Histories of Bancroft, Parkman, & Adams. Richard C. Vitzthum. LC 73-7429. 300p. 1974. 12.95x (ISBN 0-8061-1142-9). U of Okla Pr.

American Confidence Man. David W. Maurer. 316p. 1974. 16.75 (ISBN 0-398-02974-1); pap. 9.75 (ISBN 0-398-02976-8). C C Thomas.

American Conflicts Law. 3rd ed. Robert A. Leflar. 1977. 35.00 (ISBN 0-672-83415-4, Bobbs-Merrill Law). Michie.

American Conservative Thought in the Twentieth Century. Ed. by William F. Buckley, Jr. LC 76-99163. (American Heritage Ser. No. 82). 1970. pap. 7.95 (ISBN 0-672-51327-7, AHS82). Bobbs.

American Constitution, Cases-Comments-Questions. 5th ed. William B. Lockhart et al. LC 80-54210. 1181p. 1980. text ed. 20.95 (ISBN 0-8299-2132-X). West Pub.

American Constitutional Development. Ed. by Alpheus T. Mason & D. Grier Stephenson. LC 74-32555. (Goldentree Bibliographies in American History Ser.). 1977. o. p. 12.95x; pap. text ed. 12.95x (ISBN 0-88295-545-4). AHM Pub.

American Constitutional Law: Cases & Text. 2nd ed. Albert B. Saye. LC 78-20883. 597p. 1979. text ed. 12.95 (ISBN 0-8299-2028-5). West Pub.

American Constitutional Law: Introductory Essays & Selected Cases. 6th ed. A. T. Mason & Wiliam M. Beaney. 1978. text ed. 21.95 (ISBN 0-13-024778-2). P-H.

American Constitutional System. 5th ed. C. H. Pritchett. Ed. by Eric M. Munson. (American Government Ser.). 160p. 1981. pap. text ed. 6.95 (ISBN 0-07-050893-3). McGraw.

American Consumer: Issues & Decisions. 2nd ed. Herbert M. Jelley & Robert O. Herrmann. (gr. 11-12). 1978. pap. text ed. 12.20 (ISBN 0-07-032341-0, G); student activity guide 5.32 (ISBN 0-07-032342-9); tchrs. manual & key 6.00 (ISBN 0-07-032343-7). McGraw.

American Controversy: A Bibliographical Study of the British Pamphlets About the American Disputes, 1764-1783, 2 vols. Thomas R. Adams. LC 77-76348. 1980. Set. 60.00x (ISBN 0-87057-150-8, Pub. by Brown U Pr). Univ Pr of New England.

American Controversy: A Bibliographical Study of the British Pamphlets About the American Disputes, 1764-1783, 2 vols. Thomas R. Adams. LC 77-76348. 1140p. 1981. Set. text ed. 60.00 (ISBN 0-87057-150-8). U Pr of New Eng.

American Conveyance Patterns. D. Barlow Burke. LC 77-4628. (Real Estate & Urban Land Economics Ser.). 1978. 21.00 (ISBN 0-669-01731-0). Lexington Bks.

American Cooking. Dale Brown. LC 68-9172. (Foods of the World Ser). (Illus.). (gr. 6 up). 1968. PLB 14.94 (ISBN 0-8094-0060-X, Time-Life). Silver.

American Cooking. Dale Brown. (Foods of the World Ser). (Illus.). 1968. 14.95 (ISBN 0-8094-0033-2). Time-Life.

American Cooking: Creole & Acadian. Peter S. Feibleman. (Foods of the World Ser). (Illus.). 1971. 14.95 (ISBN 0-8094-0054-5). Time-Life.

American Cooking: Creole & Acadian. Peter S. Feibleman. LC 78-16778. (Foods of the World Ser.). (Illus.). (gr. 6 up). 1971. PLB 14.94 (ISBN 0-8094-0081-2, Pub. by Time-Life). Silver.

American Cooking: New England. Jonathan N. Leonard. (Foods of the World Ser). (Illus.). 1970. 14.95 (ISBN 0-8094-0049-9). Time-Life.

American Cooking: New England. Jonathan N. Leonard. LC 70-133841. (Foods of the World Ser.). (Illus.). (gr. 6 up). 1970. lib. bdg. 14.94 (ISBN 0-8094-0076-6, Pub. by Time-Life). Silver.

American Cooking: Southern Style. Eugene Walter. (Foods of the World Ser). (Illus.). 1971. 14.95 (ISBN 0-8094-0051-0). Time-Life.

American Cooking: Southern Style. Eugene Walter. LC 76-173191. (Foods of the World Ser.). (Illus.). (gr. 6 up). 1971. lib. bdg. 14.94 (ISBN 0-8094-0078-2, Pub. by Time-Life). Silver.

American Cooking: The Eastern Heartland. Jose Wilson. (Foods of the World Ser). (Illus.). 1971. 14.95 (ISBN 0-8094-0052-9). Time-Life.

American Cooking: The Eastern Heartland. Jose Wilson. LC 70-150960. (Foods of the World Ser.). (gr. 6 up). 1971. lib. bdg. 14.94 (ISBN 0-8094-0079-0, Pub. by Time-Life). Silver.

American Cooking: The Great West. Jonathan N. Leonard. (Foods of the World Ser). (Illus.). 1971. 14.95 (ISBN 0-8094-0053-7). Time-Life.

American Cooking: The Great West. Jonathan N. Leonard. LC 76-156273. (Foods of the World Ser.). (Illus.). (gr. 6 up). 1971. 14.94 (ISBN 0-8094-0080-4, Pub. by Time-Life). Silver.

American Cooking: The Melting Pot. Dale Brown et al. LC 76-173191. (Foods of the World Ser.). (Illus.). (gr. 6 up). 1971. lib. bdg. 14.94 (ISBN 0-8094-0082-0, Pub. by Time-Life). Silver.

American Cooking: The Melting Pot. James P. Shenton et al. (Foods of the World Ser). (Illus.). 1971. 14.95 (ISBN 0-8094-0055-3). Time-Life.

American Cooking: The Northwest. Dale Brown. LC 73-138262. (Foods of the World Ser.). (Illus.). (gr. 6 up). 1970. lib. bdg. 14.94 (ISBN 0-8094-0077-4, Pub. by Time-Life). Silver.

American Counties. 3rd ed. Joseph N. Kane. LC 70-186010. 1972. 20.50 (ISBN 0-8108-0502-2). Scarecrow.

American Country Pottery. Don Raycraft & Carol Raycraft. 1975. 6.95 o.p. (ISBN 0-87069-120-1). Wallace-Homestead.

American Court Systems: Readings in Judicial Process & Behavior. Ed. by Sheldon Goldman & Austin Sarat. LC 78-19160. (Illus.). 1978. text ed. 24.95x (ISBN 0-7167-0061-1); pap. text ed. 12.95x (ISBN 0-7167-0060-3). W H Freeman.

American Crewel Work. Mary T. Landon & Susan B. Swan. LC 79-104869. (Illus.). 1970. 9.95 o.s.i. (ISBN 0-02-567870-1). Macmillan.

American Crewel Work. Mary T. Landon & Susan B. Swan. (Illus.). 1976. pap. 5.95 o.s.i. (ISBN 0-02-011730-2, Collier). Macmillan.

American Crusade for Wildlife. James B. Trefethen. (Illus.). 384p. 1975. 13.95 (ISBN 0-87691-207-2). Winchester Pr.

American Cuisine Minceur Cookbook. Michele Evans. (Orig.). 1977. pap. 2.25 o.s.i. (ISBN 0-446-92167-X). Warner Bks.

American Cultural Patterns: A Cross-Cultural Perspective. Edward C. Stewart. LC 70-26361. 1971. pap. text ed. 6.50 (ISBN 0-933662-01-7). Intercult Pr.

American Culture & Religion. William W. Sweet. LC 72-78372. ix, 114p. 1972. Repr. of 1951 ed. lib. bdg. 12.50x (ISBN 0-8154-0421-2). Cooper Sq.

American Cultures. Boy Scouts, of America. LC 19-600. (Illus.). 32p. (gr. 6-12). 1980. pap. 0.70x (ISBN 0-8395-3388-8, 3388). BSA.

American Cut Glass. Edwin G. Warman. (Illus.). 5.95 o.p. (ISBN 0-685-21838-4). Warman.

American Dad. Tama Janowitz. 256p. 1981. 11.95 (ISBN 0-399-12585-X). Putnam.

American Daughter. rev. ed. Era B. Thompson. (Midway Reprint Ser). x, 302p. 1974. pap. 7.95x o.s.i. (ISBN 0-226-79784-8). U of Chicago Pr.

American Dawn: A New Model of American Prehistory. Louis A. Brennan. LC 71-93718. (Illus.). 1970. 14.95 (ISBN 0-02-514910-5). Macmillan.

American Decorative Wall Painting: 1700-1850. Nina F. Little. 1972. pap. 7.50 o.p. (ISBN 0-525-47335-1). Dutton.

American Defense Policy. 4th ed. John E. Endicott, Jr. & Roy W. Stafford, Jr. LC 77-23161. (Illus.). 1977. 25.00x o.p. (ISBN 0-8018-1960-1); pap. 9.50x (ISBN 0-8018-1961-X). Johns Hopkins.

American Defense Policy from Eisenhower to Kennedy: The Politics of Changing Military Requirements, 1957-1961. Richard A. Aliano. LC 74-27709. xi, 309p. 1975. 16.00 (ISBN 0-8214-0181-5). Ohio U Pr.

American Defense Policy from Eisenhower to Kennedy: The Politics of Changing Military Requirements, 1957-1961. Richard A. Aliano. LC 74-27709. xi, 309p. 1978. pap. 8.00x (ISBN 0-8214-0406-7). Ohio U Pr.

American Delinquency: Its Meaning & Construction. LaMar T. Empey. 1978. 17.95x (ISBN 0-256-01985-1). Dorsey.

American Democracy in English Politics, 1815-1850. David P. Crook. 1965. 7.25x o.p. (ISBN 0-19-821338-7). Oxford U Pr.

American Democracy on Trial. Ed. by Monroe Billington & Duane Leach. 1968. pap. text ed. 5.95x o.p. (ISBN 0-8211-0102-1). McCutchan.

American Democracy: The Third Century. Richard Kraemer et al. (Illus.). 1978. pap. text ed. 13.50 (ISBN 0-8299-0160-4); instrs.' manual avail. (ISBN 0-8299-0498-0). West Pub.

American Democrat. James F. Cooper. LC 80-83794. 280p. 1981. 9.00 (ISBN 0-913966-91-6); pap. 4.00 (ISBN 0-913966-92-4). Liberty Fund.

American Denominational Organization: A Sociological View. Ed. by Ross P. Scherer. LC 80-13859. 378p. 1980. pap. 14.95x (ISBN 0-87808-173-9, Ecclesia). William Carey Lib.

American Diabetes Association, American Dietetic Association Family Cookbook. The American Diabetes Association & The American Dietetic Association. LC 80-16722. 320p. 1980. 12.95 (ISBN 0-13-024901-7). P-H.

American Diary Literature. Stephen Kagle. (United States Author Ser.: No. 342). 1979. lib. bdg. 13.50 (ISBN 0-8057-7280-4). Twayne.

American Dictionaries of the English Language Before 1861. Eva M. Burkett. LC 78-11677. 1979. lib. bdg. 16.50 (ISBN 0-8108-1179-0). Scarecrow.

American Dictionary of Printing & Bookmaking. LC 66-27215. 1967. Repr. of 1894 ed. 24.00 (ISBN 0-8103-3345-7). Gale.

American Dimension. 2nd ed. Arens Montague. 1981. 8.95 (ISBN 0-88284-119-X). Alfred Pub.

American Dimension: Cultural Myths & Social Realities. 2nd ed. W. Arens & Susan Montague. LC 80-26355. 250p. 1976. pap. text ed. 8.95x (ISBN 0-88284-030-4). Alfred Pub.

American Diplomacy in the Great Depression: Hoover-Stimson Foreign Policy, 1929-1933. Robert H. Ferrell. (Illus.). 1969. Repr. of 1957 ed. 16.50 o.p. (ISBN 0-208-00749-0, Archon). Shoe String.

American Diplomacy in the Orient. John W. Foster. LC 74-112309. (Law, Politics, & History Ser). 1970. Repr. of 1903 ed. lib. bdg. 42.50 (ISBN 0-306-71915-0). Da Capo.

American Diplomacy: Nineteen Hundred to Nineteen Fifty. George F. Kennan. 1952. pap. 1.50 (ISBN 0-451-61168-3, MW1811, Ment). NAL.

American Diplomatic & Consular Practice. 2nd ed. Graham H. Stuart. LC 52-13689. 1952. 34.50x (ISBN 0-89197-008-8). Irvington.

American Diplomatic & Public Papers, the United States & China, Ser. 1: The Treaty System & the Taiping Rebellion, 1842-1860, 21 vols. Ed. by Jules Davids. LC 73-77510. 1974. Set. 1095.00 (ISBN 0-8420-1703-8). Scholarly Res Inc.

American Diplomatic Code, Embracing a Collection of Treaties & Conventions Between U.S. & Foreign Powers from 1778 to 1834, 2 Vols. Jonathan Elliot. LC 74-129032. (Research & Source Works Ser.: No. 605). 1971. Repr. lib. bdg. 63.00 (ISBN 0-8337-1036-2). B Franklin.

American Diplomatic Experience. Daniel M. Smith. LC 73-175171. (Illus., Orig.). 1972. pap. text ed. 10.95 (ISBN 0-395-12569-3). HM.

American Diplomatic History Before 1900. Compiled by Norman A. Graebner. LC 77-85991. (Goldentree Bibliographies in American History). 1978. text ed. 16.95x (ISBN 0-88295-573-X); pap. text ed. 12.95x (ISBN 0-88295-543-8). AHM Pub.

American Diplomatic Relations with the Middle East, 1784-1975: A Survey. Thomas A. Bryson. LC 76-44344. 1977. 21.00 (ISBN 0-8108-0988-5). Scarecrow.

American Diplomatic Revolution: A Documentary History of the Cold War, 1941-1947. Joseph M Siracusa. LC 76-54281. (National University Publications Ser. in American Studies). 1977. 12.50 (ISBN 0-8046-9174-6); pap. 6.95 (ISBN 0-8046-9180-0). Kennikat.

American Dissent from Thomas Jefferson to Cesar Chavez: The Rhetoric of Reform & Revolution. LC 80-12577. 180p. 1980. pap. text ed. 6.50 (ISBN 0-89874-083-5). Krieger.

American Dissent from Thomas Jefferson to Cesar Chavez: The Rhetoric of Reform & Revolution. Thomas E. Hachey & Ralph E. Weber. LC 80-12577. 1980. pap. 6.50. Krieger.

American Dissenter: The Life of Algie Martin Simons, 1870-1950. Kent Kreuter & Gretchen Kreuter. LC 68-55042. (Illus.). 248p. 1969. 12.00x (ISBN 0-8131-1177-3). U Pr of Ky.

American Dissertations on Foreign Education: Israel, Vol. XIII. Francis Parker & Betty J. Parker. 464p. 1980. 32.00x (ISBN 0-87875-152-1). Whitston Pub.

American Dissertations on Foreign Education: Iran & Iraq, Vol. XII. Francis Parker & Betty J. Parker. 425p. 1980. 28.50x (ISBN 0-87875-151-3). Whitston Pub.

American Doctrine of Judicial Supremacy. Charles G. Haines. LC 73-250. (American Constitutional & Legal History Ser.). 726p. 1973. Repr. of 1932 ed. lib. bdg. 69.50 (ISBN 0-306-70569-9). Da Capo.

American Dog Book. Kurt Unkelbach. 1976. 14.95 (ISBN 0-87690-201-8). Dutton.

American Drama from Its Beginnings to the Present. Compiled by E. Hudson Long. LC 79-79170. (Goldentree Bibliographies in Language & Literature). (Orig.). 1970. pap. 6.95x (ISBN 0-88295-522-5). AHM Pub.

American Drama to Nineteen Hundred: A Guide to Information Sources. Ed. by Walter J. Meserve. (American Literature, English Literature, & World Literature in English Information Guide Ser.: Vol. 28). 1980. 30.00 (ISBN 0-8103-1365-0). Gale.

American Drawing: A Guide to Information Sources. Ed. by Lamia Doumato. LC 79-63743. (Art & Architecture Information Guide Ser.: Vol. 11). 1979. 30.00 (ISBN 0-8103-1441-X). Gale.

American Dream in the Great Depression. Charles R. Hearn. LC 76-56623. (Contributions in American Studies Ser: No. 28). 1977. lib. bdg. 17.95 (ISBN 0-8371-9478-4, HAD/). Greenwood.

American Dreams, American Nightmares. Ed. by David Madden. LC 72-5512. (Arcturus Books Paperbacks). 271p. 1972. pap. 7.95 (ISBN 0-8093-0600-X). S Ill U Pr.

American Dreams: Meditations on Life in the United States. John K. Roth. LC 76-26877. 194p. 1976. pap. 6.95 (ISBN 0-88316-527-9). Chandler & Sharp.

American Dynasties Today. Wall Street Journal Editors. LC 80-68102. (Illus.). 330p. 1980. 12.95 (ISBN 0-87094-228-X). Dow Jones-Irwin.

American Eagle: The Story of a Navajo Vietnam Veteran. Larry Lee. 1977. pap. text ed. 3.50 (ISBN 0-686-12227-5). Packrat Pr.

American Economic & Business History Information Sources. Ed. by Robert W. Lovett. LC 78-137573. (Management Information Guide Ser.: No. 23). 1971. 30.00 (ISBN 0-8103-0823-1). Gale.

American Economic History. Harry N. Scheiber et al. (Illus.). 432p. 1976. text ed. 24.50 scp (ISBN 0-06-042001-4, HarpC). Har-Row.

American Economic History: A Guide to Information Sources. Ed. by William K. Hutchinson. LC 73-17577. (Economic Information Guide Ser.: Vol. 16). 250p. 1980. 30.00 (ISBN 0-8103-1287-5). Gale.

American Economic History Before 1860. Compiled by George R. Taylor. LC 70-79173. (Goldentree Bibliographies in American History Ser). (Orig.). 1969. pap. 6.95x (ISBN 0-88295-526-8). AHM Pub.

American Economics Ser. Attiyeh & Lumsden. (gr. 10-12). 1972. pap. text ed. 9.00 each incl. 7 texts, tchrs' manuals, test plus 1 suppl. (ISBN 0-8449-0700-6). Learning Line.

American Economy. R. J. Sampson et al. 1975. 15.36 (ISBN 0-395-19780-5); 7.16 (ISBN 0-395-20467-4). HM.

American Economy: An Historical Introduction to the Problem's of the 1970's. Ed. by Arthur M. Johnson. LC 74-2652. (Urgent Issues in American Society Ser). 1974. 10.00 o.s.i. (ISBN 0-02-916580-6). Free Pr.

American Economy: An Historical Introduction to the Problems of the 1970's. Ed. by Arthur M. Johnson. LC 74-2652. (Urgent Issues in American Society Ser). 1975. pap. text ed. 6.95 (ISBN 0-02-916590-3). Free Pr.

American Economy in a Historical Perspective. Richard Vedder. 1975. text ed. 18.95x (ISBN 0-534-00465-2). Wadsworth Pub.

American Economy in Perspective. Lloyd G. Reynolds. Ed. by Barbara Brooks & Bonnie Lieberman. (Illus.). 430p. 1981. pap. text ed. 14.95x (ISBN 0-07-052028-3, C); write for info instrs.' manual (ISBN 0-07-052030-5). McGraw.

American Education: A Problem-Centered Approach. 3rd ed. Lisa L. Schwartz. LC 78-62182. 1978. pap. text ed. 13.75 (ISBN 0-8191-0508-2). U Pr of Amer.

American Education: An Introduction to Social & Political Aspects. Joel Spring. LC 77-17608. (Educational Policy, Planning, & Theory Ser.). 1978. pap. text ed. 8.95x (ISBN 0-582-28020-6). Longman.

American Education & Vocationalism: A Documentary History 1870-1970. Ed. by Marvin Lazerson & W. Norton Grubb. LC 73-87511. 1974. text ed. 8.75 (ISBN 0-8077-2413-0); pap. text ed. 4.00x (ISBN 0-8077-2414-9). Tchrs Coll.

American Education in the Electric Age: New Perspectives on Media & Learning. Ed. by Peter L. Klinge. LC 74-1220. 224p. pap. 10.95 (ISBN 0-87778-069-2). Educ Tech Pubns.

American Education: Its Organization & Control. Robinson. 1968. pap. text ed. 10.95 (ISBN 0-675-09823-8). Merrill.

American Educational History: A Guide to Informational History. Ed. by Timothy Walch & Michael W. Sedlak. LC 80-19646. (American Government & History Information Guide Ser.: Vol. 10). 350p. 1981. 30.00 (ISBN 0-8103-1478-9). Gale.

American Electoral Behavior: Change & Stability. Ed. by Samuel A. Kirkpatrick. LC 75-32374. (Sage Contemporary Social Science Issues Ser.: Vol. 24). 1976. 4.95x (ISBN 0-8039-0582-3). Sage.

American Electoral Politics: Strategies for Renewal. Alan Clem. 1980. pap. text ed. 9.95 (ISBN 0-442-24475-4). D Van Nostrand.

American Electrician's Handbook. 10th ed. Terrell Croft et al. 1664p. 1980. 39.50 (ISBN 0-07-013931-8, P&RB). McGraw.

American Encyclopaedia of Printing. Ed. by J. Luther Ringwalt & John Bidwell. LC 78-74411. (Nineteenth-Century Book Arts & Printing History Ser.: Vol. 21). (Illus.). 1980. lib. bdg. 66.00 (ISBN 0-8240-3895-9). Garland Pub.

American Energy Choices Before the Year Two Thousand. Ed. by Elihu Bergman et al. LC 78-7122. (Illus.). 1978. 16.95 (ISBN 0-669-02398-1). Lexington Bks.

American Engineer in China. William B. Parsons. LC 78-74326. (Modern Chinese Economy Ser.). 315p. 1980. lib. bdg. 33.00 (ISBN 0-8240-4256-5). Garland Pub.

American English. Albert H. Marckwardt. 1958. pap. text ed. 4.95x o.p. (ISBN 0-19-500960-6). Oxford U Pr.

American English Dialects in Literature. Eva M. Burkett. LC 78-17742. 1978. 12.00 (ISBN 0-8108-1151-0). Scarecrow.

American English for International Businessmen. text ed. 6.95 (ISBN 0-88499-055-9, 2000); Set Of 12 Tapes. 225.00 (ISBN 0-88499-160-1); Set Of 6 Cassettes. 115.00 (ISBN 0-88499-161-X). Inst Mod Lang.

American Engravers. C. Roger Bleile. (Illus.). 191p. 1980. 29.95 (ISBN 0-917714-29-6). Beinfeld Pub.

American Enlightment: The Shaping of the American Experiment & a Free Society. Ed. by Adrienne Koch. LC 64-21765. (American Epochs Ser). 1965. 10.00 o.s.i. (ISBN 0-8076-0278-7); pap. 4.95 o.s.i. (ISBN 0-8076-0393-7). Braziller.

American Entomologists. Arnold Mallis. LC 78-132316. (Illus.). 1971. 35.00 (ISBN 0-8135-0686-7). Rutgers U Pr.

American Environment. Ed. by W. R. Mead. (Institute of U. S. Studies Monographs Ser: No. 1). (Illus.). 72p. (Orig.). 1974. pap. text ed. 7.00x (ISBN 0-485-12901-9, Athlone Pr). Humanities.

American Environment: Readings in the History of Conservation. 2nd ed. Roderick Nash. LC 75-10913. 384p. 1976. pap. text ed. 9.50 (ISBN 0-201-05239-3). A-W.

American Environmental History: The Exploitation & Conservation of Natural Resources. Joseph M. Petulla. LC 75-4870. (Illus.). 1977. 18.00x (ISBN 0-87835-058-6); pap. text ed. 10.95x (ISBN 0-87835-055-1). Boyd & Fraser.

American Ephemeris for the 20th Century: Noon. Neil F. Michelsen. (American Ephemeris Ser.). 620p. (Orig.). 1980. pap. 15.95 (ISBN 0-917086-20-1, Pub. by Astro Computing Serv). Para Res.

American Ephemeris for the 20th Century: Midnight. Neil F. Michelsen. (American Ephemeris Ser.). 620p. (Orig.). 1980. pap. 15.95 (ISBN 0-917086-19-8, Pub. by Astro Computing Serv). Para Res.

American Ephemeris: Nineteen Eighty-One. Neil F. Michelsen. 1980. pap. 1.00 (ISBN 0-917086-24-4). Para Res.

American Ephemeris 1901 to 1930. Neil F. Michelsen. (The American Ephemeris Ser). 17.50 o.p. (ISBN 0-917086-11-2, Pub. by Astro Computing Serv.); pap. 14.95 o.p. (ISBN 0-917086-12-0). Para Res.

American Ephemeris 1977. 1978. pap. 1.00 o.p. (ISBN 0-917086-09-0, Pub. by Astro Computing Serv.). Para Res.

American Ephemeris 1978. 1978. pap. 1.00 o.p. (ISBN 0-917086-13-9, Pub. by Astro Computing Serv.). Para Res.

American Ephemeris 1979. 1979. 1.00 o.p. (ISBN 0-917086-17-1, Pub. by Astro Comp Serv). Para Res.

American Ephemeris: 1991 to 2000. Neil F. Michelsen. 1980. pap. 5.00 (ISBN 0-917086-21-X). Para Res.

American Epic: Virgil - A Story of Love. Daniel M. Jones. 73p. 1981. 6.95 (ISBN 0-533-01646-0). Vantage.

American Epitaphs Grave & Humorous. Charles L. Wallis. (Illus.). 7.50 (ISBN 0-8446-4832-9). Peter Smith.

American Espionage: From Secret Service to C.I.A. Rhodri Jeffreys-Jones. LC 77-74854. (Illus.). 1977. 14.95 (ISBN 0-02-916360-9). Free Pr.

American Essay Serials from Franklin to Irving. Bruce I. Granger. LC 78-4120. 1978. 14.50x (ISBN 0-87049-221-7). U of Tenn Pr.

American Essays, 2 vols. T. William Youngs. (Orig.). 1981. Vol. 1. pap. text ed. 8.95 ea. (ISBN 0-316-97727-6). Vol. 2 (ISBN 0-316-97729-2). training manual free (ISBN 0-316-97728-4). Little.

American Establishment. Leonard Silk & Mark Silk. LC 80-50533. 351p. 1980. 13.95 (ISBN 0-465-00134-3). Basic.

American Establishment & Other Reports, Opinions, & Speculations. Richard H. Rovere. LC 80-22247. x, 308p. 1981. Repr. of 1962 ed. lib. bdg. 27.50x (ISBN 0-313-22646-6, ROAE). Greenwood.

American Etchings. S. R. Koehler. Bd. with American Art. LC 75-28876. (Art Experience in Late 19th Century America Ser.: Vol. 12). (Illus.). 1976. Repr. of 1886 ed. lib. bdg. 72.50 (ISBN 0-8240-2236-X). Garland Pub.

American Ethnic Groups. Ed. by Thomas Sowell. 254p. 1978. pap. 7.50 (ISBN 0-87766-210-X, 16100). Urban Inst.

American Ethnic Groups Sourcebook or Supplementary Text. 5th ed. J. Kinton. 1980. lib. bdg. 10.95 (ISBN 0-915574-16-0). Soc Sci & Soc Res.

American Ethnicity. Howard M. Bahr et al. 1979. text ed. 17.95x (ISBN 0-669-90399-X). Heath.

American Ethnicity. Joseph Hraba. LC 78-61877. 1979. text ed. 12.95 (ISBN 0-87581-236-8). Peacock Pubs.

American Evangelicals, 1800-1900: An Anthology. William G. McLoughlin. 8.00 (ISBN 0-8446-0793-2). Peter Smith.

American Expansion: A Book of Maps. Randall D. Sale & Edwin D. Karn. LC 78-24508. (Illus.). 1979. pap. 3.95x (ISBN 0-8032-9104-3, BB 698, Bison). U of Nebr Pr.

American Experience in Indonesia: The University of Kentucky Affiliation with the Agricultural University at Bogor. Howard W. Beers. LC 75-132824. (Illus.). 288p. 1971. 16.00x (ISBN 0-8131-1235-4). U Pr of Ky.

American Experiment: Japan 1945-1952. Toshio Nishi. (Publication Ser.: No. 244). 380p. 1981. 19.95 (ISBN 0-8179-7441-5). Hoover Inst Pr.

American Experiment: Japan 1945-1952, No. 244. Toshio Nishi. 380p. 1981. 19.95 (ISBN 0-8179-7441-5). Hoover Inst Pr.

American Extremes. Daniel Cosio Villegas. Tr. by Americo Paredes from Span. LC 64-11188. (Pan American Paperbacks Ser.: No. 1). Orig. Title: Extremos de America. 1964. pap. 4.95x (ISBN 0-292-70069-5). U of Tex Pr.

American Family: A Demographic History. Ed. by Rudy R. Seward. LC 78-19609. (Sage Library of Social Research: Vol. 70). 1978. 18.00x (ISBN 0-8039-1112-2); pap. 8.95x (ISBN 0-8039-1113-0). Sage.

American Family Christian Philosophy of Life. Anthony J. West. (Illus.). 1979. 37.75 (ISBN 0-89266-203-4). Am Classical Coll Pr.

American Family: Dying or Developing? Ed. by David Reiss & Howard Hoffman. LC 78-24447. 264p. 1979. 21.95 (ISBN 0-306-40117-7, Plenum Pr). Plenum Pub.

American Family in Social-Historical Perspective. 2nd ed. Michael Gordon. LC 77-86000. 1978. text ed. 16.95 (ISBN 0-312-02311-1); pap. text ed. 9.95 (ISBN 0-312-02312-X). St Martin.

American Family Life Films. Judith Trojan. LC 80-14748. 508p. 1981. 25.00 (ISBN 0-8108-1313-0). Scarecrow.

American Family: Past, Present, & Future. Michael Gordon. 1977. text ed. 1.95x (ISBN 0-394-31722-X). Random.

American Family Styles. Jack Kinton. 1981. pap. 2.95 (ISBN 0-915574-22-5). Soc Sci & So.

American Family Styles: Current Guide to the Literature. (Spcialized Bibliography Ser.: No. 4). 1981. 8.95 (ISBN 0-915574-11-X). Soc Sci & Soc Res.

American Fantasy & Science Fiction. Marshall Tymn. LC 80-19217. 224p. 1980. Repr. of 1979 ed. lib. bdg. 12.95x (ISBN 0-89370-029-0). Borgo Pr.

American Farmer & the New Deal. Theodore Saloutos. 312p. 1981. text ed. 17.50 (ISBN 0-8138-1760-9). Iowa St U Pr.

American Farmers in the World Crisis. Carl T. Schmidt. LC 79-1591. 1981. Repr. of 1941 ed. 23.50 (ISBN 0-88355-896-3). Hyperion Conn.

American Farming & Food. Finlay Dunn. 1980. lib. bdg. 75.00 (ISBN 0-8490-3185-0). Gordon Pr.

American Fashion Designs by Wilson Folmar. Montgomery Museum of Fine Arts. Ed. by Katherine Campbell. LC 78-61234. (Illus.). 48p. 1978. pap. 5.00 o.p. (ISBN 0-89280-011-9). Montgomery Mus.

American Federal Government. 14th ed. John Ferguson et al. 592p. 1981. text ed. 17.95 (ISBN 0-07-020527-2, C); instr's manual 4.95 (ISBN 0-07-020529-9). McGraw.

American Fiction: An Historical & Critical Survey. Arthur H. Quinn. (gr. 11 up). 1981. Repr. of 1947 ed. text ed. 23.50x (ISBN 0-8290-0032-1). Irvington.

American Fiction: Historical & Critical Essays. James Nagel. (United States Author Ser.). 1978. lib. bdg. 16.95 (ISBN 0-8057-9006-3). Twayne.

American Fiction, Nineteen Hundred to Nineteen-Fifty: A Guide to Information Sources. Ed. by James Woodress. LC 73-17501. (American Literature, English Literature, & World Literatures in English Information Guide Ser.: Vol. 1). 246p. 1974. 30.00 (ISBN 0-8103-1201-8). Gale.

American Fiction, Seventeen Seventy-Four to Nineteen Hundred: Cumulative Author Index to the Microfilm Collection. 416p. 1974. 45.00 (ISBN 0-89235-023-7). Res Pubns Conn.

American Fiction to Nineteen Hundred: A Guide to Information Sources. Ed. by David K. Kirby. LC 73-16982. (American Literature, English Literature, & World Literatures in English Information Guide Ser.: Vol. 4). 260p. 1975. 30.00 (ISBN 0-8103-1210-7). Gale.

American Film Industry. Ed. by Tino Balio. LC 75-32070. (Illus.). 1976. 25.00 (ISBN 0-299-07000-X); pap. 8.95 (ISBN 0-299-07004-2). U of Wis Pr.

American Fisherman's Fresh & Salt Water Guide. Ed. by Vin T. Sparano. 1976. 12.95 (ISBN 0-87691-214-5). Winchester Pr.

American Flower Painting. Dennis R. Anderson. (Illus.). 84p. 1980. text ed. 25.00 (ISBN 0-8230-0211-X). Watson-Guptill.

American Fly Tyer's Handbook. Ed. by Kenneth E. Bay. (Illus.). 1979. 14.95 (ISBN 0-87691-287-0). Winchester Pr.

American Folk Art: From the Traditional to the Naive. Lynette I. Rhodes. LC 77-9240. (Themes in Art Ser.). (Illus.). 120p. 1978. pap. 7.95x (ISBN 0-910386-42-0, Pub. by Cleveland Mus Art). Ind U Pr.

American Folk Legend: A Symposium. Ed. by Wayland D. Hand. (Library Reprint Ser.: No. 98). 1979. Repr. of 1971 ed. 18.50x (ISBN 0-520-03836-3). U of Cal Pr.

American Folk Painters. John Ebert & Katherine Ebert. LC 75-11914. (Encore Edition). (Illus.). 1975. 7.95 o.p. (ISBN 0-684-14966-4, ScribT). Scribner.

American Folk Portraits: Paintings & Drawings from the Abbey Aldrich Rockefeller Folk Art Center. Ed. by Beatrix T. Rumford. 1981. 35.00 (ISBN 0-686-69213-6). NYGS.

American Folklore: A Bibliography, 1950-1974. Cathleen C. Flanagan & John T. Flanagan. LC 77-23381. 1977. 19.50 (ISBN 0-8108-1073-5). Scarecrow.

American Folklore & Legend. (Illus.). 1978. 18.95 (ISBN 0-89577-045-8, Pub. by Reader's Digest). Norton.

American Folklore & the Historian. Richard M. Dorson. pap. write for info. (ISBN 0-226-15869-1). U of Chicago Pr.

American Ford. Lorin Sorensen. (Fordiana Ser.). (Illus.). 263p. 1975. 49.50 (ISBN 0-87938-079-9). Silverado.

American Foreign Policy. Valentine J. Belfiglio. LC 78-66047. (Illus.). 1979. pap. text ed. 8.00 (ISBN 0-8191-0681-X). U Pr of Amer.

American Foreign Policy: A Contemporary Introduction. Thomas L. Brewer. (Illus.). 1980. pap. text ed. 10.50 (ISBN 0-13-026740-6). P-H.

American Foreign Policy: A History. Thomas G. Paterson et al. 1977. text ed. 16.95x (ISBN 0-669-94698-2). Heath.

American Foreign Policy: An Analytical Approach. William C. Vocke. LC 74-19681. (Illus.). 1976. pap. text ed. 9.95 (ISBN 0-02-933420-9). Free Pr.

American Foreign Policy & American Business, 2 vols. new ed. Lawrence Deville. (Illus.). 1979. Set. 77.50 (ISBN 0-89266-143-7). Am Classical Coll Pr.

American Foreign Policy & American Business: The Two Worlds in Conflict. 1975. 59.45. Inst Econ Finan.

American Foreign Policy & American Business: The Two Worlds in Conflict. Lawrence Deville. (Illus.). 85p. 1975. 51.75 (ISBN 0-913314-46-3). Am Classical Coll Pr.

American Foreign Policy: Changing Perspectives on National Security. rev. ed. Henry T. Nash. 1978. pap. text ed. 12.95x (ISBN 0-256-02055-8). Dorsey.

American Foreign Policy: Opposing Viewpoints. Ed. by David L. Bender & Gary E. McCuen. (Opposing Viewpoints Ser.: Vol. 6). (Illus.). 88p. (gr. 9-12). 1972. lib. bdg. 8.95 (ISBN 0-912616-30-X); pap. 3.95 (ISBN 0-912616-05-9). Greenhaven.

American Foreign Policy: Pattern & Process. Charles W. Kegley, Jr. & Eugene R. Wittkopf. LC 78-65249. 1979. text ed. 16.95 (ISBN 0-312-02326-X); pap. text ed. 10.95x (ISBN 0-312-02327-8). St Martin.

American Foreign Policy, Present to Past: A Narrative with Readings & Documents. Ed. by Lloyd Gardner. LC 74-2651. (Urgent Issues in American Society Ser). 1975. pap. text ed. 7.95 (ISBN 0-02-911300-8). Free Pr.

American Foreign Relations: A Historiographical Review. Ed. by Gerald K. Haines & J. Samuel Walker. LC 80-545. (Contributions in American History: No. 90). (Illus.). xiii, 369p. 1981. lib. bdg. 35.00 (ISBN 0-313-21061-6, HAF/). Greenwood.

American Foreign Relations, 1971: A Documentary Record. Ed. by Richard P. Stebbins & Elaine P. Adam. LC 75-13518. 658p. 1976. 28.50x (ISBN 0-8147-7763-5). NYU Pr.

American Foreign Relations, 1972: A Documentary Record. Ed. by Richard P. Stebbins & Elaine P. Adam. LC 75-15127. 590p. 1976. 28.50x (ISBN 0-8147-7764-3). NYU Pr.

American Foreign Relations, 1973: A Documentary Record. Ed. by Richard P. Stebbins & Elaine P. Adams. LC 76-15891. 1976. 28.50x (ISBN 0-8147-7775-9). NYU Pr.

American Foreign Relations, 1974: A Documentary Record. Ed. by Richard P. Stebbins & Elaine P. Adam. LC 76-47172. 1977. 28.50x (ISBN 0-8147-7776-7). NYU Pr.

American Foreign Relations, 1975: A Documentary Record. Richard P. Stebbins & Elaine P. Adam. LC 77-6093. 1977. 28.50x (ISBN 0-8147-7783-X). NYU Pr.

American Founding: Politics, Statesmanship, & the Constitution. Ed. by Ralph A. Rossum & Gary L. McDowell. (National University Publications, Political Science Ser.). 1981. 17.50 (ISBN 0-8046-9283-1). Kennikat.

American Franciscan Missions in Central America. Leonard F. Bacigalupo. LC 80-68205. 480p. 1980. 14.50 (ISBN 0-933402-20-1); pap. 8.95 (ISBN 0-933402-21-X). Charisma Pr.

American Garland, Being a Collection of Ballads Relating to America, 1536-1759. Charles H. Firth. LC 68-20123. 1969. Repr. of 1915 ed. 15.00 (ISBN 0-8103-3411-9). Gale.

American Genealogist: Being a Catalogue of Family Histories, a Bibliography of American Genealogy or a List of the Title Pages of Books & Pamphlets on Family History. 5th ed. LC 74-34247. 406p. 1975. Repr. of 1900 ed. 30.00 (ISBN 0-8103-4151-4). Gale.

American Genesis: The American Indian & the Origins of Modern Man. Jeffrey Goodman. LC 80-18652. (Illus.). 288p. 1981. 11.95 (ISBN 0-671-25139-2). Summit Bks.

American Girl. Howard C. Christy. LC 76-4778. 1976. lib. bdg. 35.00 (ISBN 0-306-70854-X); pap. 9.95 (ISBN 0-306-80042-X). Da Capo.

American Girl Book of Horse Stories. American Girl Magazine Staff. (Illus.). (gr. 5-9). 1963. PLB 5.99 (ISBN 0-394-90899-6, BYR). Random.

American Girl Book of Teen-Age Questions. American Girl Magazine Staff. (Illus.). (gr. 5-9). 1963. PLB 3.99 o.p. (ISBN 0-394-91807-X, BYR). Random.

American Girl Cookbook. American Girl Magazine Staff. (Illus.). (gr. 5-9). 1966. PLB 5.99 (ISBN 0-394-91548-8). Random.

American Gold. Ernest Seeman. 1979. pap. 2.50 (ISBN 0-380-43679-5, 43679). Avon.

American Gothic: The Mind & Art of Ralph Adams Cram. Robert Muccigrosso. LC 79-5436. 1980. pap. text ed. 11.25 (ISBN 0-8191-0884-7). U Pr of Amer.

American Government. (Wiley Self-Teaching Guides Ser.). 200p. 1981. write for info. (ISBN 0-471-01351-X). Wiley.

American Government. S. B. Rosenhack. (gr. 10-12). 1972. pap. text ed. 9.00 each incl 2 texts, tchrs' manual, & tests (ISBN 0-8449-0800-2). Learning Line.

American Government. 2nd ed. Walter E. Volkomer. LC 78-13663. (Illus.). 1979. pap. text ed. 12.50 (ISBN 0-13-027300-7). P-H.

American Government: A Brief Introduction. 2nd ed. Max J. Skidmore & Marshall C. Wanke. LC 76-41545. (Illus.). 1977. pap. text ed. 7.50x (ISBN 0-312-02485-1). St Martin.

American Government: A Modular Approach. Robert L. Spurrier & James J. Lawler. 1978. pap. text ed. 12.95 (ISBN 0-8403-1903-7). Kendall-Hunt.

American Government & Politics. 2nd ed. Peter Fotheringham et al. 1978. 19.95 o.p. (ISBN 0-571-04973-7, Pub. by Faber & Faber); pap. 9.95 (ISBN 0-571-04889-7). Merrimack Bk Serv.

American Government & Politics. Ed. by B. K. Shrivastava & Thomas B. Casstevens. 1980. text ed. 20.00x (ISBN 0-391-01798-5). Humanities.

American Government & Politics Today. 3rd. ed. Charles P. Sohner & Helen P. Martin. 1979. text ed. 12.95x (ISBN 0-673-15241-3); study guide 4.95x (ISBN 0-673-15243-X). Scott F.

American Government: Conscious Self Sovereignty. John M. Dorsey. 1969. 4.95x (ISBN 0-8143-1637-9). Wayne St U Pr.

American Government: Continuity & Change. Allen Schick & Adrienne Pfister. (Illus.). 629p. (gr. 10-12). 1975. 17.44 (ISBN 0-395-18825-3); instrs' guide & key 6.72 (ISBN 0-395-18816-4); student's wk. guide 5.96 (ISBN 0-395-18824-5). HM.

American Government for Law Enforcement Training. Donald W. Berney. LC 75-8915. (Nelson Hall Law Enforcement Ser.). 1976. 20.95x (ISBN 0-88229-152-1). Nelson-Hall.

American Government: Ideals & Reality. Abraham Holtzman. (Illus.). 1980. pap. text ed. 12.50 (ISBN 0-13-027151-9). P-H.

American Government: Ideas & Issues. David R. Berman & John C. Bollens. LC 80-83670. 1981. pap. 6.95 (ISBN 0-913530-22-0). Palisades Pubs.

American Government: Institutions & Policies. James Q. Wilson. 1979. text ed. 16.95 (ISBN 0-669-01621-7); student handbk. 4.95 (ISBN 0-669-02521-6); inst. guide free to adopters (ISBN 0-669-02531-3); test item file free to adopters (ISBN 0-669-02522-4). Heath.

American Government: Past, Present, Future. Theodore L. Becker. 560p. 1976. pap. text ed. 12.95x o.p. (ISBN 0-205-04726-2); instr's manual free o.p. (ISBN 0-685-62607-5). Allyn.

American Government: Policy & Process. 3rd ed. Robert L. Morlan. LC 78-69574. (Illus.). 1979. pap. text ed. 12.50 (ISBN 0-395-26631-9); inst. manual 0.70 (ISBN 0-395-26632-7). HM.

American Government: Readings & Cases. 7th ed. Woll. 1981. pap. text ed. 8.95 (ISBN 0-316-95143-9); tchrs'. manual free (ISBN 0-316-95144-7). Little.

American Government: Strategy & Choice 1980. Peter H. Aranson. (Political Science Ser.). (Illus.). 600p. 1981. text ed. 18.95 (ISBN 0-87626-023-7). Winthrop.

American Graffiti. W. Huyck et al. LC 73-17640. 1979. pap. 1.95 (ISBN 0-345-28408-9). Ballantine.

American Graffiti. George Lucas. 1979. pap. 1.75 (ISBN 0-394-17072-5, B373, BC). Grove.

American Graphic Art. Frank Weitenkampf. LC 74-6198. 1974. Repr. of 1912 ed. 20.00 (ISBN 0-8103-4020-8). Gale.

American Guide to British Social Science Resources. Herbert M. Levine & Dolores B. Owen. LC 76-22690. 1976. 13.50 (ISBN 0-8108-0950-8). Scarecrow.

American Habitat: A Historical Perspective. Ed. by Barbara G. Rosenkrantz & William A. Koelsch. LC 72-90281. (Illus.). 1973. 10.00 o.s.i. (ISBN 0-02-927290-4). Free Pr.

American Handbook of Psychiatry: Advances & New Directions, Vol. VII. Silvano Arieti & Keith H. Brodie. LC 80-68960. (American Handbook of Psychiatry Ser.). 784p. 1981. 45.50x (ISBN 0-465-00157-2). Basic.

American Health & Safety Series. Igel & Calloway. (gr. 8-12). 1972. pap. text ed. 6.00 incl. 6 texts, tchrs' manuals, & tests (ISBN 0-8449-1100-3). Learning Line.

American Health Care System: Issues & Problems. Paul R. Torrens. LC 78-4666. (Issues & Problems in Health Care Ser.). 1978. pap. text ed. 8.95 (ISBN 0-8016-5012-7). Mosby.

American Heart Association Cookbook. Ruthe Eshelman & Mary Winston. 1977. pap. 6.95 (ISBN 0-345-28827-0). Ballantine.

American Hearth. Ed. by Richard I. Barons. (Illus.). 1976. pap. 6.00 (ISBN 0-89062-085-7, Pub. by Roberson Ctr). Pub Ctr Cult Res.

American Heritage. Boy Scouts of America. LC 19-600. 48p. 1976. pap. 0.70x (ISBN 0-8395-3398-5). BSA.

American Heritage Book of the Revolution. Bruce Lancaster. Ed. by Richard M. Ketchum. LC 58-10707. (Illus.). 384p. 1958. deluxe ed. 22.00 slipcased (ISBN 0-8281-0351-8, BO19D). Am Heritage.

American Heritage Cookbook. Ed. by American Heritage & Helen McCully. LC 80-12470. (Illus.). 272p. 1980. 14.50 (ISBN 0-8281-0403-4, Dist. by Scribner). Am Heritage.

American Heritage Dictionary. Ed. by Peter Davies. Date not set. pap. 2.50 (ISBN 0-440-10207-3). Dell.

American Heritage Dictionary of the English Language. 1970. pap. 2.25 (ISBN 0-8372-9992-6). Bowmar-Noble.

American Heritage History of American Business & Industry. Alex Groner et al. LC 72-80699. 384p. 1972. deluxe ed. 20.00 o.p. (ISBN 0-8281-0313-5, BO52DI-00). Am Heritage.

American Heritage History of Notable American Houses. Marshall B. Davidson. LC 75-149724. (Illus.). 384p. 1971. 19.95 (ISBN 0-8281-0258-9, Dist. by Scribner); deluxe ed. 22.50 slipcased (ISBN 0-8281-0259-7, Dist. by Scribner). Am Heritage.

American Heritage History of Seafaring America. Alexander Laing. Ed. by Joseph J. Thorndike. LC 74-5301. (Illus.). 352p. 1974. deluxe ed. 30.00 (ISBN 0-8281-0266-X, BO35D); 25.00 (ISBN 0-8281-0265-1, BO35R). Am Heritage.

American Heritage History of the Automobile in America. Stephen W. Sears. LC 77-23047. (Illus.). 352p. 1977. 12.95 (ISBN 0-8281-0200-7, Dist.by Scribner); deluxe ed. 39.95 slipcased (ISBN 0-8281-0201-5, Dist. by Scribner). Am Heritage.

American Heritage History of the Great West. David Lavender. Ed. by Alvin M. Josephy, Jr. LC 65-23041. (Illus.). 416p. 1973. Repr. of 1965 ed. 19.95 (ISBN 0-8281-0303-8, B037R). Am Heritage.

American Heritage History of the Indian Wars. Robert M. Utley & Wilcomb E. Washburn. LC 77-23044. (Illus.). 352p. 1977. 12.95 (ISBN 0-8281-0202-3, Dist. by Scribner); deluxe ed. 39.95 slipcased (ISBN 0-8281-0203-1, Dist. by Scribner). Am Heritage.

American Heritage History of the Law in America. Bernard Schwartz. LC 74-8264. (Illus.). 379p. 1981. pap. 12.95 (ISBN 0-8281-0426-3, Dist. by Scribner). Am Heritage.

American Heritage History of the Thirteen Colonies. Louis B. Wright. LC 67-23814. (Illus.). 384p. 1967. 27.50 (ISBN 0-8281-0299-6, Dist. by Scribner); Bo555d. deluxe ed. 32.50 slipcased (ISBN 0-8281-0304-6, Dist. by Scribner). Am Heritage.

American Heritage History of the Thirteen Colonies. Louis B. Wright. LC 67-23814. (Illus.). 384p. 1981. pap. 12.95 (ISBN 0-8281-0429-8, Dist. by Scribner). Am Heritage.

American Heritage History of the Twenties & Thirties. Edmund Stillman. LC 72-117350. 416p. 1970. deluxe ed. 25.00 slipcased (ISBN 0-8281-0093-4, Dist. by Scribner). Am Heritage.

American Heritage Pictorial History of the Presidents of the United States, 2 vols. American Heritage Editors. Ed. by Kenneth W. Leish. LC 68-15858. (Illus.). 1968. 9.98 o.p. (ISBN 0-8281-0320-8, B102R1-16). Am Heritage.

American Heritage Picture History of World War II. C. L. Sulzberger. Ed. by David G. McCullough. LC 66-24214. (Illus.). 640p. 1966. Set. 20.00 (ISBN 0-8281-0331-3, B011R). Am Heritage.

American Historical Explanations. rev. ed. Gene Wise. 415p. 1980. 20.00x (ISBN 0-8166-0954-3); pap. 8.95x (ISBN 0-8166-0957-8). U of Minn Pr.

American Historical Fiction. 3rd ed. A. T. Dickinson, Jr. LC 78-146503. 1971. 12.50 o.p. (ISBN 0-8108-0370-4). Scarecrow.

American Historical Fiction & Biography for Children & Young People. Jeanette K. Hotchkiss. LC 73-13715. 1973. 10.00 (ISBN 0-8108-0650-9). Scarecrow.

American Historical Prints: Early Views of American Cities, Etc., from the Phelps Stokes & Other Collections. I. N. Stokes & Daniel C. Haskell. LC 77-180284. (Illus.). 235p. 1974. Repr. of 1933 ed. 28.00 (ISBN 0-8103-3950-1). Gale.

American Historical Societies: 1790-1860. Leslie W. Dunlap. LC 73-16331. (Perspectives in American History Ser.: No. 7). 238p. Repr. of 1944 ed. lib. bdg. 15.00x (ISBN 0-87991-343-6). Porcupine Pr.

American History. 3rd ed. Rebecca B. Gruver. (Illus.). 1076p. 1981. One Vol. Ed. text ed. 17.95 (ISBN 0-201-05051-X); Vol. I. pap. 12.95 (ISBN 0-201-05052-8); Vol. II. pap. 12.95 (ISBN 0-201-05053-6). A-W.

American History. 3rd ed. Rebecca B. Gruver. LC 75-14794. 1981. text ed. write for info. (ISBN 0-201-05051-X); Vol. 1. pap. text ed. 12.95 (ISBN 0-201-05052-8); Vol. 2. pap. text ed. 12.95 (ISBN 0-201-05053-6); write for info. mstr's manual (ISBN 0-201-05054-4); Vol. 1. write for info. study guide (ISBN 0-201-05055-2); Vol. 2. write for info. study guide (ISBN 0-201-05056-0). A-W.

American History - British Historians: A Cross-Cultural Approach to the American Experience. David H. Burton. LC 76-8458. 328p. 1976. 17.95x (ISBN 0-88229-280-3); pap. 8.95x (ISBN 0-88229-584-5). Nelson-Hall.

American History & the Social Sciences. Edward N. Saveth. LC 64-20308. 1964. 15.95 (ISBN 0-02-927750-7). Free Pr.

American History at a Glance. 4th ed. Marshall Smelser & Joan R. Gundersen. (Illus.). 1979. pap. text ed. 3.95 (ISBN 0-06-463475-2, EH 475, EH). Har-Row.

American History: Brief Edition, 2 vols. Rebecca B. Gruver. 1978. Set. pap. text ed. 12.95 o.p. (ISBN 0-201-02699-6); Vol. 1. pap. text ed. 8.95 o.p. (ISBN 0-201-02697-X); Vol. 2. pap. text ed. 8.95 o.p. (ISBN 0-201-02698-8). A-W.

American History Made Simple. rev. ed. Jack C. Estrin. 1956. pap. 3.50 (ISBN 0-385-01214-4, Made). Doubleday.

American History: Pre-Colonial to the Present Day. rev. ed. David A. Midgley. LC 77-4648. (gr. 9-12). 1977. pap. text ed. 5.50 (ISBN 0-8120-0787-5). Barron.

American History: Retrospect & Prospect. G. A. Billias & G. N. Grob. LC 71-128471. 1971. 14.95 (ISBN 0-02-903490-6); pap. text ed. 7.95 (ISBN 0-02-903510-4). Free Pr.

American History Through Conflicting Interpretations. David F. Kellum. LC 68-54674. 1969. text ed. 6.00x (ISBN 0-8077-1604-9). Tchrs Coll.

American Home: Architecture & Society, 1815-1915. David Handlin. LC 79-14894. (Illus.). 1979. 20.00 (ISBN 0-316-34300-5); pap. 7.95 (ISBN 0-316-34299-8). Little.

American Home: Architecture & Society 1815-1915. David Handlin. 1980. 20.00 (ISBN 0-316-34300-5); pap. text ed. 8.95 (ISBN 0-316-34299-8). Little.

American Hospital Association Guide to the Health Care Field. American Hospital Association. 510p. 1980. pap. 50.00 (ISBN 0-87258-280-9, 2480). Am Hospital.

American Houses: Colonial, Classic, Contemporary. Edwin Hoag. LC 64-19042. (Illus.). (gr. 7-9). 1964. 12.95 (ISBN 0-397-30721-7). Lippincott.

American Humor: A Study of the National Character. Constance Rourke. LC 31-7953. 1971. pap. 3.95 o.p. (ISBN 0-15-605590-2, HB213, Harv). HarBraceJ.

American Hymns Old & New. Ed. by Albert Christ-Janer et al. LC 79-4630. (Illus.). 833p. 1980. 45.00 (ISBN 0-231-03458-X); pre-december 19.95 (ISBN 0-686-61142-X). Columbia U Pr.

American Ideal of Equality & Constitutional Change: From Jefferson's Declaration to the Burger Court. Charles Redenius. (National University Publications, Political Science Ser.). 1981. 17.50 (ISBN 0-8046-9282-3). Kennikat.

American Ideas About Adult Education Sevventeen Ten to Nineteen Fifty-One. Ed. by C. Hartley Grattan. LC 59-8042. (Classics in Education Ser.: No. 2). (Orig.). 1959. 7.90 o.p. (ISBN 0-8077-1461-5); pap. text ed. 3.75 o.p. (ISBN 0-8077-1458-5). Tchrs Coll.

American Ideology: Science, Technology & Organization As Modes of Rationality. H. T. Wilson. (International Library of Sociology Ser.). 1977. 28.00x (ISBN 0-7100-8501-X). Routledge & Kegan.

American Immigration Policy Nineteen Twenty Four to Nineteen Fifty Two. Robert A. Divine. LC 70-166323. (Civil Liberties in American History Ser). 200p. 1972. Repr. of 1957 ed. lib. bdg. 22.50 (ISBN 0-306-70244-4). Da Capo.

American in Polynesia. W. Patrick Strauss. (Illus.). vii, 187p. 1964. 5.00 (ISBN 0-87013-078-1). Mich St U Pr.

American in Saudi Arabia. 2nd ed. Eve Lee. LC 80-83093. (Country Orientation Ser.). (Illus.). 100p. 1980. pap. text ed. 7.50 (ISBN 0-933662-11-4). Intercult Pr.

American Indian: A Rising Ethnic Force. Ed. by Herbert L. Marx, Jr. (Reference Shelf Ser: Vol. 45, No. 5). 1973. 6.25 (ISBN 0-8242-0508-1). Wilson.

American Indian & Indo-European Studies: Papers in Honor of Madison S. Beeler. Ed. by Kathryn Klar et al. 1980. text ed. 79.50x (ISBN 90-279-7876-X). Mouton.

American Indian & the United States: A Documentary History, 4 vols. Compiled by E. Wilcomb. LC 72-10259. 1973. Set. lib. bdg. 175.00 (ISBN 0-313-20137-4). Greenwood.

American Indian Antiques. Virginia Vidler. LC 74-9302. (Illus.). 1976. 20.00 o.p. (ISBN 0-498-01495-9). A S Barnes.

American Indian Art: Form & Tradition. Walker Art Center & The Minneapolis Institute of Arts. Ed. by Ryan. (Illus.). 1973. pap. 8.00 o.p. (ISBN 0-525-47347-5). Dutton.

American Indian Beadwork. B. Hunt. 1971. pap. 4.95 (ISBN 0-02-011700-0, Collier). Macmillan.

American Indian Craft Book. Marz Minor & Nono Minor. LC 77-14075. (Illus.). 1978. 15.00 (ISBN 0-8032-0974-6); pap. 5.50 (ISBN 0-8032-5891-7, BB 661, Bison). U of Nebr Pr.

American Indian Environments: Ecological Issues in Native American History. Ed. by Christopher Vecsey & Robert W. Venables. LC 80-26458. (Illus.). 236p. 1980. text ed. 18.00x (ISBN 0-8156-2226-0); pap. text ed. 9.95x (ISBN 0-8156-2227-9). Syracuse U Pr.

American Indian: Essays from the Pacific Historical Review. Ed. by Norris Hundley, Jr. LC 74-76443. 151p. 1975. 11.80 (ISBN 0-87436-139-7); pap. text ed. 5.20 (ISBN 0-87436-140-0). ABC-Clio.

American Indian Ethnohistory, 118 vols. Ed. by David A. Horr. (Illus.). lib. bdg. 2400.00 set (ISBN 0-685-37527-7); lib. bdg. 42.00 ea. Garland Pub.

American Indian Food & Lore. Carolyn Neithammer. LC 73-7681. (Illus.). 256p. 1974. pap. 7.95 (ISBN 0-02-010000-0, Collier). Macmillan.

American Indian from Beginning to End. Jack Doyle. 6.95 o.p. (ISBN 0-685-58603-0). Vantage.

American Indian Frontier. W. C. MacLeod. 1968. Repr. of 1928 ed. 18.50 o.p. (ISBN 0-7129-0336-4, Dist by Shoe String). Dawson Pub.

American Indian in Graduate Studies: A Bibliolgrapy of Theses & Dissertations, 2 vols, Vol. 25. Fred J. Dockstader. 1973. Set. pap. 18.00 (ISBN 0-934490-06-6); Vol. 1. pap. 10.00 (ISBN 0-934490-07-4); Vol. 2. pap. 10.00 (ISBN 0-934490-08-2). Mus Am Ind.

American Indian in North Carolina. 2nd ed. Douglas L. Rights. LC 57-9277. (Illus.). 1981. Repr. of 1972 ed. 10.00 (ISBN 0-910244-09-X). Blair.

American Indian in Short Fiction: An Annotated Bibliography. Peter G. Beidler & Marion F. Egge. LC 79-20158. 1979. 11.00 (ISBN 0-8108-1256-8). Scarecrow.

American Indian: Language & Literature. Jack W. Marken. LC 76-4624. (Goldentree Bibliographies in Language & Literature). 1978. pap. text ed. 12.95x (ISBN 0-88295-553-5). AHM Pub.

American Indian Languages & American Linguistics. Ed. by Wallace Chafe. 1976. pap. text ed. 9.25x (ISBN 90-316-0086-5). Humanities.

American Indian Leaders: Studies in Diversity. Ed. by R. David Edmunds. LC 80-431. (Illus.). xiv, 260p. 1980. 19.50x (ISBN 0-8032-1800-1); pap. 5.95 (ISBN 0-8032-6705-3, BB 746, Bison). U of Nebr Pr.

American Indian Life. Ed. by Elsie C. Parsons. LC 22-16158. (Illus.). 1967. 15.00x (ISBN 0-8032-3651-4); pap. 4.50 (ISBN 0-8032-5148-3, BB 364, Bison). U of Nebr Pr.

American Indian Medicine. Virgil J. Vogel. LC 69-10626. (Civilization of the American Indian Ser.: Vol. 95). (Illus.). 1970. 19.95 (ISBN 0-8061-0863-0). U of Okla Pr.

American Indian Mythology. Alice Marriott & Carol K. Rachlin. LC 68-21613. (Apollo Eds.). (Illus.). 211p. 1972. pap. 4.95 (ISBN 0-8152-0335-7, A335, TYC-T). T Y Crowell.

American Indian Myths & Mysteries. Vincent H. Gaddis. (RL 10). 1978. pap. 1.95 o.p. (ISBN 0-451-08086-6, J8086, Sig). NAL.

American Indian Painting & Sculpture. Patricia J. Broder. LC 80-66526. (Illus.). 160p. 1981. 29.95 (ISBN 0-89659-147-6). Abbeville Pr.

American Indian: Past & Present. 2nd ed. Roger L. Nichols. LC 80-20436. 283p. 1980. text ed. 9.95 (ISBN 0-471-06321-5). Wiley.

American Indian: Perspectives for the Study of Social Change. Fred Eggan. LC 80-67926. (Lewis Henry Morgan Lectures). 192p. 1981. 22.50 (ISBN 0-521-23752-1); pap. 6.95 (ISBN 0-521-28210-1). Cambridge U Pr.

American Indian Poetry. Helen A. Howard. (United States Authors Ser.: No. 334). 1979. lib. bdg. 13.50 (ISBN 0-8057-7271-5). Twayne.

American Indian Poetry: An Anthology of Songs & Chants. new ed. Ed. by George W. Cronyn. LC 73-133483. 1970. pap. 5.95 (ISBN 0-87140-026-X). Liveright.

American Indian Policy in the Formative Years: The Indian Trade & Intercourse Acts, 1790-1834. Francis P. Prucha. LC 62-9428. 1970. pap. 3.25 (ISBN 0-8032-5706-6, BB 510, Bison). U of Nebr Pr.

American Indian Today. 2nd ed. Stuart Levine & Nancy Lurie. LC 67-24839. (Illus.). 1971. lib. bdg. 6.00 o.p. (ISBN 0-912112-13-1). Everett-Edwards.

American Indian Tomahawks: Contributions, Vol. 19. 2nd ed. Harold L. Peterson. LC 67-30973. (Illus.). 1971. 10.00 o.p. (ISBN 0-934490-24-4). Mus Am Ind.

American Indian Tools & Ornaments. 1981. 8.95 (ISBN 0-679-20509-8). McKay.

American Indians & Federal Aid. Alan L. Sorkin. (Studies in Social Economics). 231p. 1971. 10.95 (ISBN 0-8157-8044-3). Brookings.

American Indians: Their History, Condition & Prospects from Original Notes & Manuscripts... Together with an Appendix Containing Thrilling Narratives, Daring Exploits, Etc. Henry R. Schoolcraft. LC 75-7083. (Indian Captivities Ser.: Vol. 60). 1977. Repr. of 1851 ed. lib. bdg. 44.00 (ISBN 0-8240-1684-X). Garland Pub.

American Individualism. Clark H. Hoover. Ed. by Frank Freidel. LC 78-66528. (History of the United States 1876-1976 Ser.: Vol. 8). 1979. lib. bdg. 11.00 (ISBN 0-8240-9704-1). Garland Pub.

American Individualism & the Promise of Progress: Inaugural Lecture. J. R. Pole. (Inaugural Lecture Ser.). 30p. pap. 5.95 (ISBN 0-19-951526-3). Oxford U Pr.

American Inequality: A Macroeconomic History. Jeffrey G. Williamson & Peter H. Lindert. (Institute for Research on Poverty Monograph). 1980. 29.50 (ISBN 0-12-757160-4). Acad Pr.

American Influence on English Education. W. H. Armytage. (Students Library of Education). (Orig.). 1967. text ed. 5.50x (ISBN 0-7100-4201-9); pap. text ed. 3.25x (ISBN 0-7100-4206-X). Humanities.

American Interiors. Ed. by Architectural Digest Editors. (Illus.). 1978. 35.00 o.p. (ISBN 0-670-11972-5, Studio). Viking Pr.

American Interiors from Colonial Era to Nineteen Fifteen. Edgar D. Mayhew & Minor Myer, Jr. (Illus.). 304p. 1980. 45.00 (ISBN 0-684-16293-8). Scribner.

American International Law Cases, Vols. 21-22. F. Ruddy. 1980. 45.00 ea. (ISBN 0-379-20400-2). Vol. 21. Vol. 22 (ISBN 0-379-20401-0). Oceana.

American International Law Cases: 1971-1978, Vols. 1-20. Francis Deak. 45.00 ea. Oceana.

American Irish. rev. ed. William V. Shannon. 1966. 9.95 o.s.i. (ISBN 0-02-609950-0). Macmillan.

American Jazz Music. Wilder Hobson. LC 76-22565. (Roots of Jazz Ser.). 1976. Repr. of 1939 ed. lib. bdg. 19.50 (ISBN 0-306-70816-7). Da Capo.

American Jewish Bibliography. A. S. Rosenbach. 1926. 10.00 o.p. (ISBN 0-685-05623-6). Am Jewish Hist Soc.

American Jewish Landmarks: A Travel Guide and History, Vol. 1. Bernard Postal & Lionel Koppman. LC 76-27401. (Orig.). 1977. 18.50 (ISBN 0-8303-0151-8); pap. 10.50 (ISBN 0-8303-0152-6). Fleet.

American Jewish Year Book, 1979, Vol. 79. LC 99-4040. 1979. 15.00 o.p. (ISBN 0-87495-000-7). Am Jewish Comm.

American Jewish Year Book, 1981, Vol. 81. LC 99-4040. 1980. 20.00 (ISBN 0-8276-0185-9). Am Jewish Comm.

American Jewish Yearbook, Vol. 80. Ed. by Morris Fine et al. 650p. 1980. 15.00 (ISBN 0-8276-0173-5, 454). Jewish Pubn.

American Jewry & the Holocaust: The American Jewish Joint Distribution Committee, 1939-1945. Yehuda Bauer. 550p. 1981. 25.00 (ISBN 0-8143-1672-7). Wayne St U Pr.

American Jews: The Building of a Voluntary Community. Eli Ginzberg. (Texts & Studies Ser.). 1980. write for info. Am Jewish Hist Soc.

American Journal of Nursing: Five Year Cumulative Indexes. 1971. 1966-1970 6.00 (ISBN 0-937126-92-6); 1951-1955 3.90 (ISBN 0-937126-95-0). Am Journal Nurse.

American Justice: Is America a Just Society? Ed. by Gary E. McCuen. (Opposing Viewpoints Ser.: Vol. 9). (Illus.). 1975. lib. bdg. 8.95 (ISBN 0-912616-34-2); pap. text ed. 3.95 (ISBN 0-912616-15-6). Greenhaven.

American Kernel Lessons: Intermediate Student's Book. Robert O'Neill et al. (Illus.). 1978. pap. text ed. 4.50x (ISBN 0-582-79706-3); tchr's guide 4.50 (ISBN 0-582-79707-1); students tests 1.50x (ISBN 0-582-79708-X); Set 1. cassettes 11.95 (ISBN 0-582-79715-2); Set 2. cassette 19.95x (ISBN 0-582-79716-0); Set 3. cassettes 34.95x (ISBN 0-582-79710-1); tapescript 2.25x (ISBN 0-582-79709-8). Longman.

American Knives. Harold L. Perteron. 1980. 15.00 (ISBN 0-88227-016-8). Gun Room.

American Knives. Harold L. Peterson. LC 58-7523. 1975. pap. 4.95 (ISBN 0-684-16943-6, SL611, ScribT). Scribner.

American Labor and European Politics: The AFL As a Transnational Force. Roy Godson. LC 76-491. 1976. 17.50x (ISBN 0-8448-0919-5); pap. 9.95x (ISBN 0-8448-0920-9). Crane-Russak Co.

American Labor & the Multinational Corporation. Ed. by Duane Kujawa. LC 72-85977. (Special Studies in International Economics & Development). 1973. 28.50x (ISBN 0-275-28717-3); pap. text ed. 12.95x (ISBN 0-89197-657-4). Irvington.

American Labor in a Changing World Economy. Carnegie Endowment for International Peace. LC 78-15545. (Praeger Special Studies). 1978. 31.95 (ISBN 0-03-045281-3). Praeger.

American Labor: The Twentieth Century. Ed. by Jerold S. Auerbach. LC 69-14822. (American Heritage Ser). 1969. pap. 9.50 (ISBN 0-672-60128-1, 78). Bobbs.

American Labor Unions. 2nd, rev. ed. Florence Peterson. LC 63-10629. 1963. 12.50x o.p. (ISBN 0-06-034830-5, HarpT). Har-Row.

American Labor Unions: Political Values & Financial Structure. Dan C. Heldman. 1977. 10.00 (ISBN 0-685-85740-9). Coun Am Affairs.

American Laborer, Devoted to the Cause of Protection to Home Industry, Embracing the Arguments, Reports & Speeches of the Ablest Civilians of the United States in Favor of the Policy of Protection to American Labor. Ed. by Horace Greeley. (Neglected American Economists Ser.). 1974. lib. bdg. 50.00 (ISBN 0-8240-1005-1). Garland Pub.

American Land. Smithsonian Institution. 1979. 21.95. Smithsonian Expo Bks.

American Land: The Smithsonian Book of the American Environment. Smithsonian Institution. (Smithsonian Exposition Book). (Illus.). 1980. 21.95 (ISBN 0-89577-004-0). Norton.

American Landmarks: Properties of the National Trust for Historic Preservation. National Trust for Historic Preservation. (Illus.). 72p. (Orig.). 1980. pap. 5.95 (ISBN 0-89133-093-3). Preservation Pr.

American Landscape: A Critical Anthology of Prose & Poetry. Ed. by John Conron. (Illus.). 640p. 1974. pap. text ed. 14.95x (ISBN 0-19-501767-6). Oxford U Pr.

American Law Enforcement: A History. David Johnson. LC 80-68814. (Orig.). 1981. text ed. 15.95x (ISBN 0-88273-271-4). Forum Pr MO.

American Law of Landlords & Tenant, Vol. 1. Robert Schoshinski. LC 80-81653. 1980. 60.00. Lawyers Co-Op.

American Law of Medical Malpactice, 2 vols. Steven Pegalis & Harvey Wachsman. LC 79-90712. 1980. 95.00. Lawyers Co-Op.

American Law of Products Liability, 6 vols. 2nd ed. Robert D. Hursh & Henry J. Bailey. LC 73-88585. 1976. 255.00 (ISBN 0-686-14536-4). Lawyers Co-Op.

American Law of Property: 1977 Supplement. A. James Casner. 1977. pap. 65.00 (ISBN 0-316-13138-5). Little.

American Law of Slavery, Eighteen Ten-Eighteen Sixty: Considerations of Humanity & Interest. Mark V. Tushnet. LC 80-8582. 288p. 1981. 20.00x (ISBN 0-691-04681-6); pap. 9.50x (ISBN 0-691-10104-3). Princeton U Pr.

American Law of Zoning, 5 vols. Robert M. Anderson. LC 68-28408. 1976. 212.50 (ISBN 0-686-14539-9, 024A). Lawyers Co-Op.

American Legacy, 3 vols. 49.00 (ISBN 0-87827-221-6). Ency Brit Ed.

American Legal Culture, 1908-1940. John W. Johnson. LC 80-1027. (Contributions in Legal Studies: No. 16). 192p. 1981. lib. bdg. 23.95 (ISBN 0-313-22337-8, JAM/). Greenwood.

American Legal Processes. William P. McLauchlan. LC 76-26579. (Viewpoints on American Politics Ser.). 1977. pap. text ed. 9.95x (ISBN 0-471-58561-0). Wiley.

American Legal System. David E. Brody. 1978. text ed. 16.95x (ISBN 0-669-01439-7); instructor's manual free (ISBN 0-669-01840-6). Heath.

American Legislative Process. 5th ed. William J. Keefe & Morris S. Ogul. (Illus.). 544p. 1981. text ed. 17.95 (ISBN 0-13-028043-7). P-H.

American Legislative Process: Congress & the States. 4th ed. William J. Keefe & Morris Ogul. (Illus.). 1977. text ed. 17.95 (ISBN 0-13-028100-X). P-H.

American Liberalism. William Gerber. LC 74-32118. (World Leaders Ser.: No. 51). 1975. lib. bdg. 10.95 (ISBN 0-8057-3604-2). Twayne.

American Library Directory 1979. 32nd ed. Ed. by Jaques Cattell Press. LC 23-3581. 1979. 49.95 o.p. (ISBN 0-8352-1139-8). Bowker.

American Library Directory 1980. 33rd ed. Ed. by Jaques Cattell Press. LC 23-3581. 1700p. 1980. 54.95 (ISBN 0-8352-1251-3). Bowker.

American Life. Jeb S. Magruder. LC 74-78466. (Illus.). 352p. 1974. 10.00 o.p. (ISBN 0-689-10603-3). Atheneum.

American Limerick Book. Hugh Oliver & Keith MacMillan. LC 80-21813. (Illus.). 96p. 1981. 9.95 (ISBN 0-8253-0001-0). Beaufort Bks NY.

American Literary Criticism: Vol. I, 1800-1860. John Rathbun. (United States Authors Ser.: No. 339). 1979. lib. bdg. 12.50 (ISBN 0-8057-7263-4). Twayne.

American Literary Criticism: Vol. II, 1860-1905. Harry Clark & John Rathbun. (United States Authors Ser.: No. 340). 1979. lib. bdg. 12.50 (ISBN 0-8057-7264-2). Twayne.

American Literary Criticism: Vol. III, 1905-1965. Arnold L. Goldsmith. (United States Author Ser.: No. 341). 1979. lib. bdg. 12.50 (ISBN 0-8057-7265-0). Twayne.

American Literary Yearbook, Vol. 1. LC 68-21521. 1968. Repr. of 1919 ed. 18.00 (ISBN 0-8103-3149-7). Gale.

American Literature: A Brief History. rev. ed. Walter Blair et al. 1974. pap. 6.95x o.p. (ISBN 0-673-05931-6). Scott F.

American Literature: A Collection of Critical Essays. Michael T. Gilmore. (Twentieth Century Interpretations Ser.). 192p. 1980. text ed. 10.95 o.p. (ISBN 0-13-222513-1, Spec); pap. 3.95 o.p. (ISBN 0-13-222463-1). P-H.

American Literature, Eighteen Hundred Eighty to Nineteen Thirty. A. C. Ward. LC 74-14490. 273p. 1975. Repr. of 1932 ed. lib. bdg. 11.50x (ISBN 0-8154-0506-5). Cooper Sq.

American Literature: Poe Through Garland. Compiled by Harry H. Clark. LC 77-137641. (Goldentree Bibliographies in Language & Literature Ser). (Orig.). 1971. 10.95x (ISBN 0-88295-509-8); pap. 6.95x (ISBN 0-88295-508-X). AHM Pub.

American Literature, Seventeen Sixty-Four to Seventeen Eighty-Nine: The Revolutionary Years. Ed. by Everett Emerson. 1977. 20.00 (ISBN 0-299-07270-3). U of Wis Pr.

American Literature Survey. Ed. by Milton R. Stern & Seymour L Gross. Incl. Vol. 1. Colonial & Federal to 1800. 672p. pap. text ed. 5.25 (ISBN 0-14-015085-4); Vol. 2. The American Romantics 1800-1860. Pref. by Van W. Brooks. 720p. pap. text ed. 4.95 (ISBN 0-14-015086-2); Vol. 3. Nation & Region 1860-1900. Pref. by Howard M. Jones. 736p. pap. text ed. 4.95 (ISBN 0-14-015087-0); Vol. 4. The Twentieth Century. Pref. by Malcolm Cowley. 736p. pap. text ed. 5.95 (ISBN 0-14-015088-9). LC 74-3690. (Viking Portable Library). 1977. Penguin.

American Literature: The Makers & the Making, 2 vols. Cleanth Brooks et al. 1200p. 1973. Vol. 1. text ed. 16.95x (ISBN 0-312-02625-0); Vol. 2. text ed. 17.95x (ISBN 0-312-02695-1); Vol. 1. pap. text ed. 12.95 (ISBN 0-312-02590-4); Vol. 2. pap. text ed. 14.95 (ISBN 0-312-02660-9). St Martin.

American Literature, the Makers & the Making, 4 vols. Cleanth Brooks et al. Incl. Bk. A. The Beginnings to 1826. 364p. pap. text ed. 8.95x (ISBN 0-312-02765-6); Bk. B. 1826 to 1861. 920p. pap. text ed. 10.95x (ISBN 0-312-02800-8); Bk. C. 1861 to 1914. 656p. pap. text ed. 9.95x (ISBN 0-312-02835-0); Bk. D. 1914 to the Present. 1216p. pap. text ed. 11.95 (ISBN 0-312-02870-9). 1974. St Martin.

American Literature: The Makers & the Making. Cleanth Brooks et al. 1856p. (Shorter edition). 1974. text ed. 16.95 (ISBN 0-312-02730-3). St Martin.

American Literature: The New England Heritage. Ed. by James Nagel & Richard Astro. LC 80-8517. 250p. 1981. lib. bdg. 30.00 (ISBN 0-8240-9467-0). Garland Pub.

American Literature Through Bryant. Compiled by Richard B. Davis. LC 76-79172. (Goldentree Bibliographies in Language & Literature Ser.). 160p. (Orig.). 1969. pap. 6.95x (ISBN 0-88295-510-1). AHM Pub.

American Literature to Nineteen Hundred. Intro. by Lewis Leary. 1981. pap. 8.95 (ISBN 0-312-02876-8). St Martin.

American Literature: Tradition & Innovation, 4 vols. Harrison T. Meserole et al. Incl. Vol. 1. From the Beginnings to William Cullen Bryant. 12.95x o.p. (ISBN 0-669-95943-X); Vol. 2. Ralph Waldo Emerson to Sidney Lanier. 11.95x o.p. (ISBN 0-669-95950-2); Vol. 3. Walt Whitman to Stephen Crane. 11.95x o.p. (ISBN 0-669-95968-5); Vol. 4. Henry Adams to the Present. 11.95x o.p. (ISBN 0-669-95976-6). 1969. Heath.

American Lobster: The Biology of Homarus Americanus. Stanley J. Cobb. (Marine Technical Report Ser.: No. 49). 1976. pap. 2.00 (ISBN 0-938412-01-9). URI MAS.

American Loyalist Claims. Peter W. Coldham. LC 80-8609. 615p. 1980. 24.00 (ISBN 0-915156-45-8). Natl Genealogical.

American Made. Shylah Boyd. 384p. 1976. pap. 1.95 o.p. (ISBN 0-449-22861-4, C2861, Crest). Fawcett.

American Made: Men Who Shaped the American Economy. Harold C. Livesay. LC 79-15971. (Illus.). 1980. Repr. of 1979 ed. 11.95 (ISBN 0-316-52871-4); pap. text ed. 6.95 (ISBN 0-316-52874-9). Little.

American Mafia: Genesis of a Legend. Joseph L. Albini. LC 70-147120. (Orig.). 1979. Repr. of 1971 ed. 22.50x (ISBN 0-89197-013-4). Irvington.

American Mail: Enlarger of the Common Life. Wayne E. Fuller. LC 72-78254. (History of American Civilization Ser.). 390p. 1980. pap. 12.00x (ISBN 0-226-26885-3, Midway). U of Chicago Pr.

American Manual Alphabet. Valerie J. Sutton. (Illus.). 1976. pap. text ed. 3.00x (ISBN 0-914336-31-2). Move Short Soc.

American Marxist Literary Criticism: 1926-1941-a Bibliography. David R. Peck. (Bibliographical Ser.: No. 10). 1975. 1.00 (ISBN 0-89977-012-6). Am Inst Marxist.

American Masterpieces from the National Gallery of Art. John Wilmerding. LC 80-15192. (Illus.). 180p. 1980. 32.50 (ISBN 0-933920-10-5). Hudson Hills.

American Medical Association's Handbook of First Aid & Emergency Care. (Illus.). 1980. pap. 5.95 (ISBN 0-394-73668-0). Random.

American Medical Biography, 2 Vols. 2nd ed. James Thacher. LC 67-25447. (American Medicine Ser). 1967. Repr. of 1828 ed. lib. bdg. 55.00 (ISBN 0-306-70944-9). Da Capo.

American Medical Directory, 5 vols. American Medical Association. LC 7-10295. (Vol. 5 is the Directory of Women Physicians). 1979. Set. 225.00 (ISBN 0-88416-274-5). Vol. 1 (ISBN 0-88416-275-3). Vol. 2 (ISBN 0-88416-276-1). Vol. 3 (ISBN 0-88416-277-X). Vol. 4 (ISBN 0-88416-278-8). Vol. 5 (ISBN 0-88416-279-6). PSG Pub.

American Medicine in Transition, 1840-1910. John S. Haller, Jr. LC 80-14546. (Illus.). 334p. 1981. 27.95 (ISBN 0-252-00806-5). U of Ill Pr.

American Mediterranean. Marilyn Weigold. 1974. 12.95 o.p. (ISBN 0-8046-9064-2). Kennikat.

American Men & Women of Letters, 31 vols. Ed. by Daniel Aaron. 1981. Set. pap. 160.00 (ISBN 0-87754-149-3). Chelsea Hse.

American Merchant Seamans Manual. 6th ed. F. M. Cornell & A. C. Hoffman. Ed. by William B. Hayler. LC 56-12402. (Illus.). 1981. 25.00x (ISBN 0-87033-267-8). Cornell Maritime.

American Mesozoic Mammalia. George G. Simpson. (Illus.). 1929. 125.00x (ISBN 0-685-89733-8). Elliots Bks.

American Metropolitan Systems: Present & Future. Stanley D. Brunn & James O. Wheeler. 250p. 1980. 27.95 (ISBN 0-470-27018-7, Pub. by Halsted Pr). Wiley.

American-Mexican War: An Annotated Bibliography. Ed. by Norman E. Tutorow. LC 80-1789. (Illus.). 456p. 1981. lib. bdg. 39.95 (ISBN 0-313-22181-2, TMA/). Greenwood.

American Midwives: 1860 to the Present. Judy B. Litoff. LC 77-83893. (Contributions in Medical History: No. 1). 1978. lib. bdg. 17.50 (ISBN 0-8371-9824-0, LAM/). Greenwood.

American Military Commitments Abroad. Roland A. Paul. 1973. 16.50 (ISBN 0-8135-0739-1). Rutgers U Pr.

American Military Professionalism. Sam C. Sarkesian. LC 80-27027. (Pergamon Policy Studies on International Politics). 1981. 25.00 (ISBN 0-08-027178-2). Pergamon.

American Military: Readings in the History of the Military in American Society. Ed. by Russell F. Weigley. (Themes & Social Forces in American History Ser). (Orig.). 1969. pap. text ed. 6.95 (ISBN 0-201-08594-1). A-W.

American Military Uniforms, 1639-1968: A Coloring Book. Peter F. Copeland. (Coloring Book Ser.). 48p. (Orig.). 1976. pap. 1.75 (ISBN 0-486-23239-5). Dover.

American Militia, Decade of Decision, 1789-1800. John K. Mahon. LC 60-63132. (Social Science Monographs: No. 6). 1960. pap. 3.25 (ISBN 0-8130-0153-6). U Presses Fla.

American Minatures Seventeen Thirty to Eighteen Fifty: One Hundred & Seventy-Three Portraits. Harry B. Wehle. LC 71-87684. (Library of American Art Ser.). 1970. Repr. of 1927 ed. lib. bdg. 27.50 (ISBN 0-306-71708-5). Da Capo.

American Minorities: The Justice Issue. Elton Long et al. (Law Enforcement Ser.). (Illus.). 256p. 1975. pap. 9.95x (ISBN 0-13-028118-2). P-H.

American Minority Relations. 3rd ed. James W. Vander Zanden. 1972. 17.95x (ISBN 0-8260-8870-8). Wiley.

American Mirror: Social, Ethical & Religious Aspects of American Literature, 1930-1940. Halford E. Luccock. LC 75-156806. 1971. Repr. of 1940 ed. lib. bdg. 27.50x (ISBN 0-8154-0385-2). Cooper Sq.

American Missions in Bicentennial Perspective. Ed. by R. Pierce Beaver. LC 77-7569. 1977. pap. 10.95 (ISBN 0-87808-153-4). William Carey Lib.

American Moment: American Poetry in the Mid-Century. Geoffrey Thurley. LC 77-91071. 1978. 22.50 (ISBN 0-312-02884-9). St Martin.

American Montage. Celeste Loucks & Everett Hullum. Ed. by Elaine S. Furlow. (Human Touch: No. 3). (Illus.). 1976. 6.95 (ISBN 0-686-16312-5); lib. bdg. 6.95 (ISBN 0-937170-10-0). Home Mission.

American Multinationals & American Interests. C. Fred Bergsten. LC 77-91786. 1978. 21.95 (ISBN 0-8157-0920-X); pap. 13.95 (ISBN 0-8157-0919-6). Brookings.

American Music: A Panorama. Daniel Kingman. LC 78-22782. 1979. pap. text ed. 10.95 (ISBN 0-02-871260-9). Schirmer Bks.

American Musical Stage Before 1800. Julian Mates. 1962. 20.00 (ISBN 0-8135-0393-0). Rutgers U Pr.

American Musical Theater. rev. ed. Lehman Engel. 388p. 1975. 9.95 o.s.i. (ISBN 0-02-536080-9). Macmillan.

American Myth, American Reality. James O. Robertson. 1980. text ed. 16.95 (ISBN 0-8090-2504-3). Hill & Wang.

American Myth & the European Mind: American Studies in Europe, 1776-1960. Sigmund Skard. LC 61-15199. 1961. 7.00x o.p. (ISBN 0-8122-7323-0). U of Pa Pr.

American Myths & Legends, 2 vols. Charles M. Skinner. LC 78-175743. (Illus.). 697p. 1975. Repr. of 1903 ed. Set. 40.00 (ISBN 0-8103-4036-4). Gale.

American Nation: A History of the United States, 2 vols. 4th ed. John A. Garraty. LC 78-10712. 1979. pap. text ed. 13.50 ea. scp (ISBN 0-06-044711-7, HarpC); Vol. 1, To 1877. (ISBN 0-06-042267-X); Vol. 2, Since 1865. (ISBN 0-06-042268-8); inst. manual free (ISBN 0-06-362235-1); Set. scp student review manuals 6.50 (ISBN 0-686-67507-X). Vol. I (ISBN 0-06-044709-5). Vol. II. Har-Row.

American National Election Study, 1974. Warren E. Miller et al. LC 75-12906. 1975. codebook 24.00 (ISBN 0-89138-111-2). ICPSR.

American National Government & Public Policy. Randall B. Ripley. LC 73-10574. (Illus., Orig.). 1974. pap. text ed. 7.95 (ISBN 0-02-926540-1). Free Pr.

American National Standard Compiling U. S. Microform Publishing Statistics. American National Standards Institute, Standards Committee Z39 on Library Work, Documentation & Related Publishing Practices. 1979. 3.50 (ISBN 0-686-28241-8, Z39.40). ANSI.

American Naval Heritage in Brief. 2nd ed. Paolo E. Coletta. LC 79-6603. 689p. 1980. 22.50 (ISBN 0-8191-0927-4); pap. 11.00 (ISBN 0-8191-0928-2). U Pr of Amer.

American Navy, Seventeen Eighty-Nineteen to Eighteen-Sixty: A Bibliography. Myron J. Smith, Jr. LC 73-18464. (American Naval Bibliography Ser.: Vol. 2). 1974. 18.50 (ISBN 0-8108-0659-2). Scarecrow.

American Navy 1865-1918: A Bibliography. Myron J. Smith, Jr. LC 74-11077. (American Naval Bibliography Ser.: Vol. 4). 1974. 15.00 (ISBN 0-686-67008-6). Scarecrow.

American Navy, 1918-1941: A Bibliography. Myron J. Smith, Jr. LC 74-11077. (American Naval Bibliography Ser.: Vol. 5). 1974. 18.00 (ISBN 0-8108-0756-4). Scarecrow.

American Negro Academy. Alfred A. Moss, Jr. LC 80-18026. 400p. 1981. 30.00 (ISBN 0-8071-0699-2); pap. 12.95 (ISBN 0-8071-0782-4). La State U Pr.

American Negro Folktales. Ed. by Richard M. Dorson. 1976. pap. 1.50 o.p. (ISBN 0-449-30791-3, Prem). Fawcett.

American Negro Slavery. Ulrich B. Phillips. 12.50 (ISBN 0-8446-1348-7). Peter Smith.

American Negro Slavery: A Documentary History. Ed. by Michael Mullin. (Documentary History of the U.S. Ser.). (Orig.). 1975. pap. 5.95x o.p. (ISBN 0-06-131806-X, TB1806, Torch). Har-Row.

American Negro Slavery & Abolition. W. Moore. LC 73-148362. 1971. 10.00 (ISBN 0-89388-000-0); pap. 5.95. Okpaku Communications.

American Neo-Colonialism: Its Emergence in the Philippines & Asia. William J. Pomeroy. LC 71-10385. 1970. 7.50 o.p. (ISBN 0-7178-0251-5); pap. 2.85 (ISBN 0-7178-0252-3). Intl Pub Co.

American Neptune Pictorial Supplements: Instruments of Navigation, Vol. 17. (Illus.). 1975. pap. 3.25 (ISBN 0-87577-104-1). Peabody Mus Salem.

American Neptune Pictorial Supplements: Marine Paintings of John Faunce Leavitt, Vol. 18. 1976. pap. 3.50 (ISBN 0-87577-105-X). Peabody Mus Salem.

American Neptune Pictorial Supplements: Marine Paintings of William Henry Luscomb & Benjamin Franklin West of Salem, Vol. 20. 1978. pap. 3.75 (ISBN 0-87577-107-6). Peabody Mus Salem.

American Neptune Pictorial Supplements. Photographs of Shipbuilding in Bath, Maine, Vol. 9. pap. 2.50 (ISBN 0-87577-096-7). Peabody Mus Salem.

American Neptune Pictorial Supplements. Prints, Paintings, Photographs of American Clipper Ships, Vol. 1. 1959. pap. 2.50 (ISBN 0-87577-090-8). Peabody Mus Salem.

American Neptune Pictorial Supplements: The Art of the Shipcarvers at the Peabody Museum of Salem, Vol. 19. 1977. pap. 3.75 (ISBN 0-87577-106-8). Peabody Mus Salem.

American Neptune Pictorial Supplements, Vol. 2. Antoine Roux. 1960. pap. 2.50 (ISBN 0-87577-091-6). Peabody Mus Salem.

American Neptune Pictorial Supplements, Vol. 3. Civil War Blockade Runners. 1961. pap. 2.50 (ISBN 0-87577-092-4). Peabody Mus Salem.

American Neptune Pictorial Supplements, Vol. 6. Steamships. 1964. pap. 2.50 (ISBN 0-87577-093-2). Peabody Mus Salem.

American Neptune Pictorial Supplements, Vol. 7. Fitz Hugh Lane. 1965. pap. 2.50 (ISBN 0-87577-094-0). Peabody Mus Salem.

American Neptune Pictorial Supplements, Vol. 8. American & Canadian Fishing Schooners. 1966. pap. 2.50 (ISBN 0-87577-095-9). Peabody Mus Salem.

American Neptune Pictorial Supplements, Vol. 10. Penobscot Maine Museum Searsport, Maine. 1968. pap. 2.50 (ISBN 0-87577-097-5). Peabody Mus Salem.

American Neptune Pictorial Supplements, Vol. 11. Robert Salmon. 1969. pap. 2.50 (ISBN 0-87577-099-1). Peabody Mus Salem.

American Neptune Pictorial Supplements, Vol. 12. Yachting. 1970. pap. 2.50 (ISBN 0-87577-099-1). Peabody Mus Salem.

American Neptune Pictorial Supplements, Vol. 13. Life Between Decks Under Sail. 1971. pap. 2.50 (ISBN 0-87577-100-9). Peabody Mus Salem.

American Neptune Pictorial Supplements, Vol. 14. Michele F. Corne. pap. 2.50 (ISBN 0-87577-101-7). Peabody Mus Salem.

American Neptune Pictorial Supplements, Vol. 15 Whaling Vessels. 1973. pap. 2.50 (ISBN 0-87577-102-5). Peabody Mus Salem.

American Neptune Pictorial Supplements, Vol. 16 Antonio N. G. Jacobsen. 1974. pap. 2.50 (ISBN 0-87577-103-3). Peabody Mus Salem.

American Newspaperman. Bernard A. Weisberger. LC 61-8647. (Chicago History of American Civilization Ser.). (Illus.). 1961. lib. bdg. 10.00x o.s.i. (ISBN 0-226-89138-0). U of Chicago Pr.

American Newspapers in the Nineteen Seventies. Ernest C. Hynds. (Studies in Media Management). 1975. 13.50 o.p. (ISBN 0-8038-0375-3); pap. text ed. 7.95x o.p. (ISBN 0-8038-0383-4). Hastings.

American Newsreel, 1911-1967. Raymond Fielding. LC 73-177334. (Illus.). 392p. 1981. pap. 7.95 (ISBN 0-8061-1717-6). U of Okla Pr.

American Nightmare: The Success Ideal & Work Discrimination. Clarice Stasz. LC 80-6191. 192p. 1981. 14.95 (ISBN 0-8052-3765-8). Schocken.

American Nineteen Sixties: Imaginative Acts in a Decade of Change. Jerome Klinkowitz. 116p. (gr. 9-12). 1980. 10.95 (ISBN 0-8138-1380-8). Iowa St U Pr.

American Notes. Charles Dickens. 7.50 (ISBN 0-8446-1154-9). Peter Smith.

American Notes & Queries Supplement, First Person Female American: A Selected & Annotated Bibliography of the Autobiographies of American Women Living After 1950, Vol. II. Ed. by Carolyn H. Rhodes. LC 77-93778. 453p. 1980. 28.50 (ISBN 0-87875-140-8). Whitston Pub.

American Novel & the Nineteen Twenties. Ed. by Malcolm Bradbury & David Palmer. (Stratford-Upon-Avon Ser.: No. 13). 269p. 1971. pap. text ed. 13.50x (ISBN 0-8419-5819-X). Holmes & Meier.

American Novel: Background Readings & Criticism. C. Wegelin. LC 76-136274. 1972. pap. text ed. 6.95 o.s.i. (ISBN 0-02-934590-1). Free Pr.

American Novel, 1789 to 1959, 2 vols. Donna Gerstenberger & George Hendrick. LC 61-9356. 333p. 1961. Vol. 1. 12.50 o.p. (ISBN 0-8040-0007-7); Vol. 1. pap. 9.95x (ISBN 0-8040-0006-9). Swallow.

American Novelists Nineteen Ten to Nineteen Forty-Five, 2 vols. Ed. by James J. Martine. (Dictionary of Literary Biography Ser.). (Illus.). 800p. 1981. Set. 108.00 (ISBN 0-8103-0931-9). Gale.

American Novelists Since World War II: Second Series. Ed. by James Kipler. (Dictionary of Literary Biography Ser.: Vol. 6). (Illus.). 300p. 1980. 54.00 (ISBN 0-8103-0908-4). Gale.

American Novelists Since World War Two. Ed. by Jeffrey Helterman. LC 77-82804. (Dictionary of Literary Biography: Vol. 2). (Illus.). 1978. 54.00 (ISBN 0-8103-0914-9, Bruccoli Clark Book). Gale.

American Numismatic Society Museum Notes. Incl. Vol. 4. 1950. pap. 5.00 (ISBN 0-89722-018-8); Vol. 7. 1957. pap. 5.00 (ISBN 0-89722-020-X); Vol. 8. 1958. pap. 5.00 (ISBN 0-89722-021-8); Vol. 10. 1962. pap. 7.50 (ISBN 0-89722-023-4); Vol. 11. 1964. pap. 10.00 (ISBN 0-89722-024-2); Vol. 12. 1966. pap. 7.50 (ISBN 0-89722-025-0); Vol. 13. 1967. pap. 7.50 (ISBN 0-89722-026-9); Vol. 14. 1968. pap. 6.00 (ISBN 0-89722-027-7); Vol. 15. 1969. pap. 6.00 (ISBN 0-89722-028-5); Vol. 16. 1970. pap. 7.50 (ISBN 0-89722-029-3); Vol. 17. 1971. pap. 10.00 (ISBN 0-89722-030-7); Vol. 18. 1972. pap. 10.00 (ISBN 0-89722-031-5). Am Numismatic.

American Oblique: Writing About the American Experience. Joseph Trimmer & Robert Kettler. LC 75-31025. (Illus.). 416p. 1976. pap. text ed. 9.25 (ISBN 0-395-21917-5); inst. manual 1.45 (ISBN 0-395-21920-5). HM.

American Occupational Structure. Peter M. Blau & Otis D. Duncan. LC 78-50657. 1978. pap. text ed. 8.95 (ISBN 0-02-903670-4). Free Pr.

American Opera & Its Composers. Edward E. Hipsher. LC 77-25413. (Music Reprint Ser., 1978). (Illus.). 1978. Repr. of 1927 ed. lib. bdg. 35.00 (ISBN 0-306-77516-6). Da Capo.

American Opera Librettos. Andrew H. Drummond. LC 72-8111. 1973. 10.00 (ISBN 0-8108-0553-7). Scarecrow.

American Operetta: From H.M.S. Pinafore to Sweeney Todd. Gerald Bordman. (Illus.). 240p. 1981. 15.95 (ISBN 0-19-502869-4). Oxford U Pr.

American Opinion & the Irish Question: 1910-1923. Francis M. Carroll. LC 78-58897. 1978. 25.00x (ISBN 0-312-02890-3). St Martin.

American Original: The Story of Kwik-Kopy Printing. Ed. by Peggy Palmer. (Illus.). 139p. 1980. text ed. 8.95 (ISBN 0-918464-29-3); pap. text ed. 2.95 (ISBN 0-918464-30-7). D Armstrong.

American Overseas Library Technical Assistance, 1940-1970. Beverly J. Brewster. LC 75-23006. 1976. 21.00 (ISBN 0-8108-0827-7). Scarecrow.

American Pageant: A History of the Republic, 2 vols. 6th ed. Thomas A. Bailey & David M. Kennedy. 1979. complete ed. 19.95 (ISBN 0-669-00355-7); 12.95x ea. Vol. I (ISBN 0-669-00353-0). Vol. II (ISBN 0-669-00354-9). guidebk. 6.95x (ISBN 0-669-01697-7); quizbk. free (ISBN 0-669-01698-5). Heath.

American Pages. Bozhidar Bozhilov. Tr. by Cornelia Bozhilova. LC 80-83427. (International Poetry: Vol. 5). 40p. 1981. 10.95 (ISBN 0-8214-0596-9); pap. 6.95 (ISBN 0-8214-0597-7). Ohio U Pr.

American Painting: A Guide to Information Sources. Sydney S. Keaveney. LC 73-17522. (Art & Architecture Information Guide Ser.: Vol. 1). 296p. 1974. 30.00 (ISBN 0-8103-1200-X). Gale.

American Painting in the Metropolitan Museum of Art: A Catalogue of Works by Artists Born Between 1846 & 1864. Doreen B. Burke. LC 80-81074. 528p. 1980. 75.00x (ISBN 0-691-03961-5). Princeton U Pr.

American Painting, Nineteen Hundred to Nineteen Seventy. Time-Life Books Editors. (Library of Art). (Illus.). 1970. 15.95 (ISBN 0-8094-0258-0). Time-Life.

American Painting, Nineteen Hundred to Nineteen Seventy-Six. John I. Baur. LC 75-27361. (Illus.). 102p. 1975. pap. 6.00 (ISBN 0-89062-022-9, Pub. by Katonah). Pub Ctr Cult Res.

American Paintings in the Museum of Fine Arts, Boston, 2 vols. (Illus.). 1968. boxed 30.00 (ISBN 0-87846-005-5). Mus Fine Arts Boston.

American Paintings in the Museum of Fine Arts, Boston, 2 vols. LC 68-27634. (Illus.). 1968. Boxed Set. 40.00 (ISBN 0-87846-005-5, Pub. by Mus Fine Fine Arts Boston). C E Tuttle.

American Paintings in the Toledo Museum of Art. Toledo Museum of Art Staff. (Illus.). 276p. 1980. lib. bdg. cancelled (ISBN 0-935172-00-9); pap. cancelled (ISBN 0-935172-01-7). Toledo Mus Art.

American Paintings of the Sixties & Seventies: Selections from the Whitney Museum of American Art. Mitchell D. Kahan. LC 80-80977. (Illus.). 88p. 1980. pap. 8.00 (ISBN 0-89280-015-1). Montgomery Mus.

American Paradise: Four Hundred Years on the Monterey Coast. Fredric Hobbs & Deborah Hobbs. Ed. by Gail Larrick. LC 80-66581. (Illus.). 224p. (Orig.). Date not set. pap. 9.95 (ISBN 0-89395-044-0). Cal Living Bks.

American Parties & Elections. new ed. Harold F. Gosnell & Richard G. Smolka. (Political Science Ser.). 288p. 1976. pap. text ed. 15.95 (ISBN 0-675-08620-5). Merrill.

American Party System & the American People. 2nd ed. Fred L. Greenstein. LC 73-110080. (Foundations of Modern Political Science Ser). 1970. pap. 6.95 ref. ed. (ISBN 0-13-028415-7). P-H.

American Party Systems. rev. 2nd ed. Ed. by W. N. Chambers & Walter D. Burnham. (Illus.). 380p. 1975. pap. 5.95x (ISBN 0-19-501917-2). Oxford U Pr.

American Penmanship Eighteen Hundred to Eighteen Fifty: A History of Writing & a Bibliography of Copybooks from Jenkins to Spencer. Ray Nash. LC 78-106556. 303p. 1969. 15.95x (ISBN 0-912296-10-0, Dist. by U Pr of Va). Am Antiquarian.

American People, 2 vols. David Burner et al. Incl. Vol. I. To Eighteen Seventy-Seven. 342p (ISBN 0-9603726-2-8); Vol. II. From Eighteen Sixty. 440p (ISBN 0-9603726-3-6). (Illus., Orig.). 1980. Combined Edition. pap. text ed. 14.95 (ISBN 0-9603726-0-1); pap. text ed. 9.75 ea. Revisionary.

American People: A History. Arthur S. Link et al. (Illus.). 1008p. 1981. text ed. 16.95 (ISBN 0-88295-804-6); Vol. I. pap. text ed. 8.95 (ISBN 0-88295-805-4); Vol. II. pap. text ed. 8.95 (ISBN 0-88295-806-2). AHM Pub.

American People in the Depression. new ed. David Kennedy. LC 72-95873. (American People Ser.). (Illus.). 176p. (gr. 9-12). 1973. PLB 2.95 o.p. (ISBN 0-88301-091-7); pap. 2.50 (ISBN 0-88301-075-5). Pendulum Pr.

American People in the Twentieth Century: Nineteen Hundred to Nineteen Eighty. David Burner et al. (Illus., Orig.). 1980. pap. 7.95x o.p. (ISBN 0-686-26623-4). Revisionary.

American Petroleum Industry, 2 vols. Harold F. Williamson et al. Incl. Vol. 1. The Age of Illumination, 1859 to 1899; Vol. 2. The Age of Energy, 1899 to 1959. LC 80-22253. (Northwestern University Studies in Business History). (Illus.). 1981. lib. bdg. 125.00x set (ISBN 0-313-22788-8, WIAC). Greenwood.

American Petroleum Industry: The Age of Illumination, 1859-1899; the Age of Energy, 1899-1959, 2 vols. Harold F. Williamson et al. LC 80-22253. (Northwestern University Studies in Business History). (Illus.). 1981. Repr. of 1959 ed. Set. lib. bdg. 125.00x (ISBN 0-313-22788-8, WIAC). Greenwood.

American Pewter. John Barrett Kerfoot. LC 75-29215. (Illus.). xxii, 236p. 1976. Repr. of 1924 ed. 34.00 (ISBN 0-8103-4147-6). Gale.

American Pewter in the Museum of Fine Arts Boston. 1974. 15.00 o.p. (ISBN 0-87846-080-2); pap. 5.95 (ISBN 0-686-67134-1). Mus Fine Arts Boston.

American Philanthropy. Robert H. Bremner. LC 60-7246. (Chicago History of American Civilization Ser). (Illus.). 1960. 5.00x (ISBN 0-226-07326-2); pap. 2.25 o.s.i. (ISBN 0-226-07327-0, CHAC2). U. of Chicago Pr.

American Philanthropy Abroad: A History. Merle Curti. 1963. 35.00 (ISBN 0-8135-0422-8). Rutgers U Pr.

American Philanthropy in the Near East, 1820-1960. Robert L. Daniel. LC 74-81451. xii, 322p. 1970. 15.00x (ISBN 0-8214-0063-0). Ohio U Pr.

American Piety: The Nature of Religious Commitment. Rodney Stark & Charles Y. Glock. (Patterns of Religious Commitment: No. 1). 1968. 17.50x (ISBN 0-520-01210-0); pap. 2.65 (ISBN 0-520-01756-0, CAL197). U of Cal Pr.

American Pistol & Revolver Design & Performance. L. R. Wallack. 1978. 14.95 (ISBN 0-87691-255-2). Winchester Pr.

American Place Names. Alfred H. Holt. LC 68-26574. 1969. Repr. of 1938 ed. 15.00 (ISBN 0-8103-3235-3). Gale.

American Playwrights: A Critical Survey, Vol. 1. Bonnie Marranca & Gautam Dasgupta. LC 80-23745. 225p. 1981. text ed. 13.95x (ISBN 0-89676-047-2); pap. text ed. 10.00x (ISBN 0-89676-048-0). Drama Bk.

American Playwrights: A Critical Survey, Vol. 2. Bonnie Marranca & Gautam Dasgupta. Date not set. price not set (ISBN 0-89676-049-9); pap. price not set (ISBN 0-89676-050-2). Drama Bk. Postponed.

American Playwrights on Drama. 2nd ed. Eugene O'Neill et al. Ed. by Horst Frenz. 196p. Date not set. text ed. price not set (ISBN 0-89676-059-6); pap. text ed. price not set (ISBN 0-89676-060-X). Drama Bk. Postponed.

American Pocket Watch Production Totals & Dates, Plus Inventory Pages. Roy Ehrhardt. 56p. 1979. 3.00 (ISBN 0-913902-30-6). Heart Am Pr.

American Poems: A Contemporary Collection. Ed. by Jascha Kessler. LC 64-10627. (Crosscurrents-Modern Critiques Ser.). 1964. 7.95 o.p. (ISBN 0-8093-0119-9). S Ill U Pr.

American Poetry. Ed. by John R. Brown & Bernard Harris. (Stratford-Upon-Avon Studies: No. 7). 244p. 1973. pap. text ed. 9.75x (ISBN 0-8419-5814-9). Holmes & Meier.

American Poetry. Karl Shapiro. 1960. pap. 8.95 scp (ISBN 0-690-07664-9, HarpC). Har-Row.

American Poetry & Prose, 3 Vols. 5th ed. Ed. by Norman Foerster et al. LC 70-137981. 1970. pap. 13.25 ea.; Vol. 1. pap. (ISBN 0-395-04460-X); Vol. 2. pap. (ISBN 0-395-04461-8); Vol. 3. pap. (ISBN 0-395-04462-6). HM.

American Poetry & Prose, 2 pts. 5th ed. Ed. by Norman Foerster et al. LC 70-137981. 1970. pap. 15.50 ea. Pt. 1 (ISBN 0-395-04458-8). Pt. 2 (ISBN 0-395-04459-6). text ed. 18.50 2 pts in one vol. (ISBN 0-686-57582-2). HM.

American Poetry in the Eighteen Nineties: A Study of American Verse, 1890-1899. Carlin T. Kindilien. LC 56-12410. (Brown University Studies: No. 20). 223p. 1956. 8.50x (ISBN 0-87057-039-0, Pub. by Brown U Pr). Univ Pr of New England.

American Poetry in the Twentieth Century. Kenneth Rexroth. LC 73-17882. 400p. 1973. pap. 2.95 o.p. (ISBN 0-8164-9167-4). Continuum.

American Poets in Nineteen Seventy-Six. William Heyen. LC 75-37522. (Illus.). 517p. 1976. 12.05 (ISBN 0-672-52174-1); pap. 10.50 (ISBN 0-672-61349-2). Bobbs.

American Poets Since World War II, 2 vols. Ed. by Donald J. Greiner. (Dictionary of Literary Biography Ser.: Vol. 5). (Illus.). 1980. 108.00 set (ISBN 0-8103-0924-6, Bruccoli Clark). Gale.

American Police Handgun Training. Charles R. Skillen & Mason Williams. (Illus.). 216p. 1977. 14.75 (ISBN 0-398-03684-5). C C Thomas.

American Policy in Southern Africa: The Stakes & the Stance. 2nd ed. Ed. by Rene Lemarchand. LC 80-6222. 513p. 1981. lib. bdg. 22.75 (ISBN 0-8191-1436-7); pap. text ed. 12.50 (ISBN 0-8191-1437-5). U Pr of Amer.

American Policy Studies. Charles Press. 200p. 1981. pap. text ed. 7.95 (ISBN 0-471-07866-2). Wiley.

American Policy Toward Communist China, 1949-1969. Foster R. Dulles. LC 70-184974. 1972. pap. 8.95x (ISBN 0-88295-728-7). AHM Pub.

American Political Bosses & Machines. Fred J. Cook. LC 73-6777. (gr. 7 up). 1973. PLB 5.90 o.p. (ISBN 0-531-02646-9). Watts.

American Political Experience: An Introduction to Government. David V. Edwards. 1979. 17.95 (ISBN 0-13-028373-8); pap. 4.95 learning guide (ISBN 0-13-028340-1). P-H.

American Political History As Social Analysis: Essays by Samuel P. Hays. Samuel P. Hays. LC 79-17567. (Twentieth-Century America Ser.). 1980. 25.00x (ISBN 0-87049-276-4). U of Tenn Pr.

American Political Institutions in the 1970's: A Political Science Quarterly Reader. Ed. by Demetrios Caraley. LC 76-8494. 416p. 1976. 22.50x (ISBN 0-231-04106-3); pap. 10.00 (ISBN 0-231-04107-1). Columbia U Pr.

American Political Parties. Robert Huckshorn. LC 79-9328. 1980. text ed. 13.95 (ISBN 0-87872-235-1). Duxbury Pr.

American Political Parties: Potential & Performance. Judson L. James. LC 79-77133. (Studies in Contemporary American Politics Ser.). (Orig.). 1969. 7.65 o.p. (ISBN 0-672-53504-1); pap. 4.95 (ISBN 0-672-63504-6). Pegasus.

American Political Thought. Dolbeare. 300p. 1981. text ed. price not set (ISBN 0-87872-276-9). Duxbury Pr.

American Political Thought. Max J. Skidmore. LC 77-86296. 1978. text ed. 19.95 (ISBN 0-312-02894-6); pap. text ed. 7.95 (ISBN 0-312-02895-4). St Martin.

American Political Tradition. Richard Hofstadter. LC 73-20353. 1954. pap. 3.95 (ISBN 0-394-70009-0, Vin). Random.

American Political Women: Contemporary & Historical Profiles. Esther Stineman. LC 80-24478. 225p. 1980. lib. bdg. 19.50x (ISBN 0-87287-238-6). Libs Unl.

American Political Writers: 1588-1800. Richard E. Amacher. (United States Authors Ser.: No. 394). 1979. 13.50 (ISBN 0-8057-7217-0). Twayne.

American Politics & Public Policy. Ed. by Walter D. Burnham & Martha W. Weinberg. (MIT Studies in American Politics & Public Policy: 4th). 1978. text ed. 20.00 (ISBN 0-262-02132-3). MIT Pr.

American Politics & Public Policy. Ed. by Walter D. Burnham & Martha W. Weinberg. (MIT Studies in American Politics & Public Policy). 432p. (Orig.). 1980. pap. text ed. 8.95 (ISBN 0-262-52061-3). MIT Pr.

American Politics & Public Policy. Michael P. Smith. 1972. pap. text ed. 5.95 (ISBN 0-394-31650-9). Random.

American Politics: Changing Expectations. Ronald Pynn. 1981. text ed. write for info. (ISBN 0-442-25865-8). D Van Nostrand.

American Politics: Directions of Change, Dynamics of Choice. Richard E. Morgan et al. LC 78-18644. (Political Science Ser.). (Illus.). 1979. text ed. 15.95 (ISBN 0-201-01434-3); inst. manual avail. 4.00. A-W.

American Politics: Playing the Game. Susan Rouder. LC 76-13962. Orig. Title: Game of American Politics: How to Play. (Illus.). 1977. pap. text ed. 12.50 (ISBN 0-395-24971-6); inst. manual 1.00 (ISBN 0-395-24972-4). HM.

American Politics, Policies & Priorities. 3rd ed. Alan Shank. 350p. 1980. text ed. 13.60 (ISBN 0-205-07165-1, 767165-2). Allyn.

American Politics: Policies, Power, & Change. 3rd rev ed. Kenneth M. Dolbeare & Murray J. Edelman. 1979. pap. text ed. 12.95x o.p. (ISBN 0-669-01724-8); instr's manual o.p. (ISBN 0-669-00149-X). Heath.

American Politics: Policies, Power, & Change. 4th ed. Kenneth M. Dolbeare & Murray J. Edelman. 592p. 1981. pap. text ed. 12.95 (ISBN 0-669-03348-0); student guide 5.95 (ISBN 0-669-03957-8); instructor's guide (ISBN 0-669-03701-X). Heath.

American Popular Music: The Twentieth Century. Berenice R. Morris. LC 74-2461. (American Popular Music Ser). (Illus.). 72p. (gr. 4-6). 1974. PLB 4.33 o.p. (ISBN 0-531-02729-5). Watts.

American Porcelain. Lloyd Herman. (Illus.). 150p. 1980. pap. 14.95 (ISBN 0-917304-60-8, Pub. by Timber Pr). Intl Schol Bk Serv.

American Postcard Guide to Tuck. rev. ed. Sally S. Carver. (Illus.). 1980. pap. 7.95 (ISBN 0-686-18747-4). Carves.

American Potters: The Work of 20 Modern Masters. Garth Clark. 144p. 1981. 24.50 (ISBN 0-8230-0213-6). Watson-Guptill.

American Pragmatists. Ed. by Milton R. Konvitz & Gail Kennedy. (Orig.). 1960. pap. 4.95 o.p. (ISBN 0-452-00105-6, F105, Mer). NAL.

American Presidency. rev. ed. Clinton Rossiter. LC 60-5436. 1960. pap. 2.95 o.p. (ISBN 0-15-605598-8, HB35, Harv). HarBraceJ.

American President. Robert DiClerico. (Illus.). 1979. pap. 10.50 ref. ed. (ISBN 0-13-028555-2). P-H.

American Presidential Elections: Trust & the Rational Voter. Jeffrey A. Smith. 224p. 1980. 20.95 (ISBN 0-03-056143-4). Praeger.

American Primitive Painting. Jean Lipman. (Illus.). 11.00 (ISBN 0-8446-4574-5). Peter Smith.

American Profile. 2nd ed. Morton Borden & Otis Graham. 1978. pap. text ed. 11.95x (ISBN 0-669-84822-0); inst. manual free (ISBN 0-669-99994-6). Heath.

American Profiles. Ed. by Esmond Wright. LC 68-90664. (Selections from History Today Ser.: No. 7). (Illus.). 1969. pap. 3.95 (ISBN 0-05-001534-6). Dufour.

American Pronghorn Antelope. Compiled by James D. Yoakum. LC 79-89207. (Illus.). 244p. (Orig.). 1979. pap. 4.50 (ISBN 0-933564-05-8). Wildlife Soc.

American Prose to Eighteen Twenty: A Guide to Information Sources. Tr. by Donald Yannela & John Roch. LC 79-63741. (American Literature, English Literature, & World Literatures in English Information Guide Ser.: Vol. 21). 600p. 1979. 30.00 (ISBN 0-8103-1361-8). Gale.

American Prosody. Gay W. Allen. 1966. Repr. lib. bdg. 20.00x (ISBN 0-374-90133-3). Octagon.

American Protestant Women in World Mission. rev. ed. R. Pierce Beaver. LC 80-14366. Orig. Title: All Loves Excelling. 224p. 1980. pap. 7.95 (ISBN 0-8028-1846-3). Eerdmans.

American Protestantism & a Jewish State. Hertzel Fishman. LC 72-3746. (Schaver Publication Fund for Jewish Studies Ser). 254p. 1973. 12.95x (ISBN 0-8143-1481-3). Wayne St U Pr.

American Psalmody. 2nd ed. Frank J. Metcalf. LC 68-13274. (Music Reprint Ser). (Illus.). 1968. Repr. of 1917 ed. lib. bdg. 12.50 (ISBN 0-306-71132-X). Da Capo.

American Psychiatric Association Membership Directory. 1980. 13.00 (ISBN 0-685-37529-3, P151-0); non-members 8.00 (ISBN 0-685-37530-7, 151-1). Am Psychiatric.

American Psychiatric Association Membership Directory. 1975. 8.00 o.p. (ISBN 0-685-84697-0, 151-1). Am Psychiatric.

American Psychiatry: Past, Present, & Future. Ed. by George Kriegman et al. LC 75-8962. 200p. 1975. 9.95x (ISBN 0-8139-0571-0). U Pr of Va.

American Public Works Association Directory, 1977-1980. Ed. by Rodney R. Fleming et al. 1978. pap. 20.00 (ISBN 0-917084-26-8). Am Public Works.

American Puritan Imagination. S. Bercovitch. LC 73-94136. 256p. 1974. 36.00 (ISBN 0-521-20392-9); pap. 10.50x (ISBN 0-521-09841-6). Cambridge U Pr.

American Puritans. Ed. by Perry Miller. LC 56-7536. 1956. pap. 2.95 (ISBN 0-385-09204-0, A80, Anch). Doubleday.

American Quantity Cookbook: Tracing Our Food Traditions. Ed. by Jane Wallace. LC 76-3419. 1976. 24.95 (ISBN 0-8436-2096-X). CBI Pub.

American Quest. Clinton Rossiter. LC 76-142095. (Fund for the Republic Ser.). 1971. 9.50 o.p. (ISBN 0-15-106110-6). HarBraceJ.

American Quilts & How to Make Them. Carter Houck & Myron Miller. LC 75-5541. 1975. pap. 12.95 (ISBN 0-684-16272-5, ScribT). Scribner.

American Race Theorists. Byram Campbell. 1978. pap. 4.00x (ISBN 0-911038-33-7). Noontide.

American Racism: Exploration of the Nature of Prejudice. Roger Daniels & Harry H. Kitano. 1969. pap. text ed. 7.95 (ISBN 0-13-028993-0). P-H.

American Rape: A True Account of the Giles-Johnson Case. A. Robert Smith & James V. Giles. LC 75-17823. (Illus.). 300p. 1975. 10.00 o.p. (ISBN 0-915220-05-9); pap. 4.95 o.p. (ISBN 0-915220-32-6, 522967). New Republic.

American Red Cross--the First Century: A Pictorial History. Patrick F. Gilbo. LC 80-8204. (Illus.). 256p. 1981. 25.00 (ISBN 0-06-011461-4, HarpT). Har-Row.

American Reference Books Annual 1972. 3rd ed. Ed. by Bohdan S. Wynar. LC 75-120328. 1972. 30.00x o.p. (ISBN 0-87287-049-9). Libs Unl.

American Reference Books Annual 1975. 6th ed. Ed. by Bohdan S. Wynar. LC 75-120328. 904p. 1975. lib. bdg. 30.00x o.p. (ISBN 0-87287-114-2). Libs Unl.

American Reference Books Annual 1977, Vol. 8. Ed. by Bohdan S. Wynar. LC 75-120328. 1977. lib. bdg. 30.00x o.p. (ISBN 0-87287-144-4). Libs Unl.

American Reference Books Annual 1978, Vol. 9. Ed. by Bohdan S. Wynar. LC 75-120328. 1978. lib. bdg. 35.00x o.p. (ISBN 0-87287-185-1). Libs Unl.

American Reference Books Annual 1980, Vol. 11. Ed. by Bohdan S. Wynar et al. LC 75-120328. 1980. lib. bdg. 45.00x (ISBN 0-87287-217-3). Libs Unl.

American Reference Books Annual 1981, Vol. 12. Ed. by Bohdan S. Wynar et al. LC 75-12038. 800p. 1981. lib. bdg. 45.00x (ISBN 0-87287-250-5). Libs Unl.

American Regional Theatre History to 1900: A Bibliography. Compiled by Carl F. Larson. LC 79-11282. 1979. 11.00 (ISBN 0-8108-1216-9). Scarecrow.

American Register of Exporters & Importers. LC 46-15595. (Eng. & Span. & Fr. & Ger., Annual). 1979. 50.00 o.p. (ISBN 0-686-18951-5). Thomas Intl Pub.

American Religion & Philosophy: A Guide to Information Sources. Ed. by Ernest R. Sandeen & Frederick Hale. LC 73-17562. (American Studies Information Guide Ser.: Vol. 5). 1978. 30.00 (ISBN 0-8103-1262-X). Gale.

American Religion: Proceedings. American Academy of Religion, 1974. Ed. by Edwin S. Gaustad. LC 74-14211. (American Academy of Religion. Section Papers). 1974. pap. 4.50 (ISBN 0-88420-116-3, 010910). Scholars Pr Ca.

American Religious Experiment: Piety & Practicality. Ed. by Clyde L. Manschreck & Barbara B. Zikmund. LC 76-7199. (Studies in Ministry & Parish Life). 128p. 1976. 12.95x (ISBN 0-913552-06-2); pap. 5.50x (ISBN 0-913552-07-0). Exploration Pr.

American Renaissance. Jack Kemp. 1981. pap. 2.50 (ISBN 0-425-04848-9). Berkley Pub.

American Renaissance: Art & Expression in the Age of Emerson & Whitman. F. O. Matthiessen. 1968. pap. 10.95 (ISBN 0-19-500759-X, 230, GB). Oxford U Pr.

American Renaissance in New England. Ed. by Joel Myerson. LC 77-82803. (Dictionary of Literary Biography Ser.: Vol. 1). (Illus.). 1978. 54.00 (ISBN 0-8103-0913-0, Bruccoli Clark Bk). Gale.

American Republic. John A. Schutz & Richard S. Kirkendall. LC 77-9346. (Illus.). 1978. text ed. 16.95x (ISBN 0-88273-250-1). Forum Pr MO.

American Response to the Foreign Industrial Challenge in High Technology Industries. Ed. by Myra Hodgson. 175p. (Orig.). 1980. pap. 95.00 (ISBN 0-686-69372-8). W Fraser Pubs.

American Revolution. Bruce Bliven, Jr. LC 80-20813. (Landmark Bks.). (Illus.). 160p. (gr. 5-9). 1981. pap. 2.95 (ISBN 0-394-84696-6). Random.

American Revolution. John Guyatt. Ed. by Malcolm Yapp et al. (World History Ser.). (Illus.). 32p. (gr. 10). 1980. Repr. of 1977 ed. lib. bdg. 5.95 (ISBN 0-89908-135-5); pap. text ed. 1.95 (ISBN 0-89908-110-X). Greenhaven.

American Revolution. Eric Robson. LC 74-171392. (Era of the American Revolution Ser.). 254p. 1972. Repr. of 1955 ed. lib. bdg. 25.00 (ISBN 0-306-70417-X). Da Capo.

American Revolution. Compiled by John Shy. LC 72-178292. (Goldentree Bibliographies in American History Ser.). 152p. (Orig.). 1973. pap. 6.95x (ISBN 0-88295-532-2). AHM Pub.

American Revolution: A Constitutional Interpretation. Charles H. McIlwain. LC 74-166335. (Era of the American Revolution Ser.). 198p. 1973. Repr. of 1923 ed. lib. bdg. 22.50 (ISBN 0-306-70249-5). Da Capo.

American Revolution: A General History, 1763-1790. rev. ed. E. James Ferguson. 1979. pap. text ed. 10.50x (ISBN 0-256-02195-3). Dorsey.

American Revolution: A Heritage of Change. Ed. by John Parker & Carol Urness. LC 75-24503. 1975. 10.00 (ISBN 0-9601798-0-1). Assocs James Bell.

American Revolution & the West Indies. Charles W. Toth. 1975. 12.95 (ISBN 0-8046-9110-X, Natl U). Kennikat.

American Revolution: Changing Perspectives. 2nd ed. William Fowler & E. Wallace Coyle. LC 79-88424. (Illus.). 231p. 1981. pap. text ed. 9.95x (ISBN 0-930350-21-9). NE U Pr.

American Revolution in the West. George M. Waller. LC 75-44471. (Illus.). 155p. 1976. 18.95 (ISBN 0-88229-279-X). Nelson-Hall.

American Revolution, Seventeen Seventy Five to Seventeen Eighty-Three. John R. Alden. LC 53-11826. (New American Nation Ser). 1954. 19.95x (ISBN 0-06-010045-1, HarpT). Har-Row.

American Revolution: The Search for Meaning. Ed. by Richard J. Hooker. (Problems in American History Ser). 1970. pap. text ed. 8.95x (ISBN 0-471-40891-3). Wiley.

American Revolution Within America. Merrill Jensen. LC 74-11113. 224p. 1974. 12.00x (ISBN 0-8147-4154-1). NYU Pr.

American Revolutionaries in the Making. Charles S. Sydnor. Orig. Title: Gentlemen Freeholders. 1965. pap. text ed. 3.50 (ISBN 0-02-932390-8). Free Pr.

American Rights Policies. Jay A. Sigler. 1975. pap. text ed. 9.95x (ISBN 0-256-01700-X). Dorsey.

American Road to Nuremberg: The Documentary Record, 1944-1945. Bradley F. Smith. LC 80-83830. 234p. 1981. price not set (ISBN 0-8179-7481-4). Hoover Inst Pr.

American Robin. Len Eiserer. LC 76-25438. (Illus.). 1976. 16.95 (ISBN 0-88229-228-5). Nelson-Hall.

American Rose. Julia Markus. 320p. 1981. 12.95 (ISBN 0-395-30229-3). HM.

American Royal. Anne Rudeen. (Orig.). 1977. pap. 2.50 (ISBN 0-446-81827-5). Warner Bks.

American Rugs & Carpets: From the Seventeenth Century to Modern Times. Helene Von Rosenstiel. LC 78-50700. (Illus.). 1978. 25.00 o.p. (ISBN 0-688-03325-3). Morrow.

American Scene-Early Twentieth Century. Emily Wasserman. (Illus.). 1975. Repr. 5.95 o.p. (ISBN 0-88308-006-0). Lamplight Pub.

American Scene: Varieties of American History, 2 vols. Ed. by Robert D. Marcus & David Burner. LC 73-136426. (Orig.). 1971. Vol. 1 Colonial Period To 1877. pap. text ed. 5.95x (ISBN 0-89197-018-5); Vol. 2 Since 1865. pap. text ed. 5.95x (ISBN 0-685-03161-6); pap. text ed. 5.95x brief ed. (colonial period to present) (ISBN 0-89197-019-3); instructor's manual free (ISBN 0-89197-020-7). Irvington.

American Science in the Age of Jackson. George H. Daniels. LC 67-28710. 1968. 20.00x (ISBN 0-231-03073-8). Columbia U Pr.

American Science of Politics: Its Origins & Conditions. Bernard Crick. 1959. 6.75x o.p. (ISBN 0-520-00278-4). U of Cal Pr.

American Screenwriters One & Two, 2 vols. Ed. by Robert Morsberger & Tracy Thompson. (Dictionary of Literary Biography Ser.). (Illus.). 1981. Set. 108.00 (ISBN 0-8103-0917-3, Bruccoli Clark Book). Gale.

American Sculpture: A Guide to Information Sources. Ed. by Janis K. Ekdahl. LC 74-11544. (Art & Architecture Information Guide Ser.: Vol. 5). 1977. 30.00 (ISBN 0-8103-1271-9). Gale.

American Sea Power in the Old World: The United States Navy in European and Near Eastern Waters, 1865-1917. William N. Still, Jr. LC 79-6572. (Contributions in Military History: No. 24). (Illus.). xi, 291p. 1980. lib. bdg. 29.95 (ISBN 0-313-22120-0, STA/). Greenwood.

American Seances with Eusapia Palladino. Hereward Carrington. LC 54-7143. 1954. 3.75 o.p. (ISBN 0-912326-03-4). Garrett-Helix.

American Seasons. Edwin W. Teale. LC 76-11794. (Illus.). 1976. 17.50 (ISBN 0-396-07353-0). Dodd.

American Secondary School. L. O. Taylor et al. LC 60-6321. 1960. text ed. 24.00x (ISBN 0-89197-021-5); pap. text ed. 10.95x (ISBN 0-89197-022-3). Irvington.

American Secretaries of the Navy, 2 vols. Paolo Coletta. LC 78-70967. (Illus.). 1750p. 1980. Set. slipcased 59.95x (ISBN 0-87021-073-4). Naval Inst Pr.

American Self: Myth, Ideology, & Popular Culture. Ed. by Sam B. Girgus. 288p. 1980. 20.00x (ISBN 0-8263-0557-1). U of NM Pr.

American Short Fiction: Readings & Criticism. Ed. by James K. Bowen & Richard VanDerBeets. LC 74-115055. (Orig.). 1970. pap. 9.50 (ISBN 0-672-60648-8). Bobbs.

American Short Stories. 3rd ed. Eugene Current-Garcia & Walton R. Patrick. 1976. pap. 9.95x (ISBN 0-673-15008-9). Scott F.

American Short Stories of the Nineteenth Century. Ed. by John Cournos. 1955. 11.50x (ISBN 0-460-00840-4, Evman); pap. 3.95 (ISBN 0-460-01840-X). Dutton.

American Short Story. Arthur Voss. LC 72-9264. 300p. 1973. 12.95 o.p. (ISBN 0-8061-1070-8). U of Okla Pr.

American Shotgun Design & Performance. L. R. Wallack. 1977. 14.95 (ISBN 0-87691-236-6). Winchester Pr.

American Showcase, Vol.1. Ed. by Tennyson Schad & Ira Shapiro. (Illus.). 226p. pap. 19.95 (ISBN 0-931144-01-9). Am Showcase.

American Showcase, Vol. 2. Ed. by Tennyson Schad & Ira Shapiro. (Illus.). 266p. 35.00 (ISBN 0-931144-04-3); pap. 22.50 (ISBN 0-931144-03-5). Am Showcase.

American Showcase, Vol. 3. Ira Shapiro & Tennyson Schad. 336p. 1980. 37.50 o.p. (ISBN 0-931144-06-X); pap. 25.00 o.p. (ISBN 0-931144-05-1). Am Showcase.

American Showcase, Vol.4. Ed. by Tennyson Schad & Ira Shapiro. (Illus.). 40.00 (ISBN 0-931144-08-6); pap. 27.50 (ISBN 0-931144-07-8). Am Showcase.

American Shrines in England. Bernadine Bailey. LC 75-20586. 1977. 15.00 o.p. (ISBN 0-498-01727-3). A S Barnes.

American Sign Language Dictionary. Martin L. Sternberg. LC 75-25066. (Illus.). 1981. 30.00 (ISBN 0-06-014097-6, HarpT). Har-Row.

American Silver Sixteen Fifty-Five to Eighteen Twenty-Five. Kathryn C. Buhler. 1972. 45.00 (ISBN 0-87846-064-0); pap. 20.00 (ISBN 0-87846-148-5). Mus Fine Arts Boston.

American Singing Book. Simeon P. Cheney. (Earlier American Music Ser.). (Illus.). 1980. Repr. of 1879 ed. lib. bdg. 25.00 (ISBN 0-306-77322-8). Da Capo.

American Slave Code in Theory & Practice. William Goodell. LC 68-55888. Repr. of 1853 ed. 19.75x (ISBN 0-8371-0450-5). Negro U Pr.

American Slavery - American Freedom: The Ordeal of Colonial Virginia. Edmund S. Morgan. 454p. 1975. 11.95 (ISBN 0-393-05554-X); pap. text ed. 5.95x (ISBN 0-393-09156-2). Norton.

American Soaring Handbook. Soaring Society of America. (Illus.). 1972. ring binder 27.50x o.p. (ISBN 0-911720-65-0, Pub. by Soaring Soc). Aviation.

American Social History Before 1860. Compiled by Gerald N. Grob. LC 72-102037. (Goldentree Bibliographies in American History Ser). (Orig.). 1970. pap. 6.95x (ISBN 0-88295-515-2). AHM Pub.

American Social History Since 1860. Compiled by Robert H. Bremner. LC 70-146848. (Goldentree Bibliographies in American History Ser). (Orig.). 1971. 14.95x (ISBN 0-88295-504-7); pap. 10.95x (ISBN 0-88295-503-9). AHM Pub.

American Social Order. J. D. Douglas. LC 70-142360. 1971. 8.95 (ISBN 0-02-907510-6); pap. text ed. 8.95 (ISBN 0-02-907530-0). Free Pr.

American Social Problems: Challenges to Existence. William McCord & Arline McCord. LC 76-47622. 1977. pap. 9.95 (ISBN 0-8016-3221-8). Mosby.

American Social Psychology: Its Origins, Development, & European Background. Fay B. Karpf. (Reprints in Sociology Ser). 1971. lib. bdg. 24.00x (ISBN 0-697-00216-0); pap. 8.95x (ISBN 0-89197-658-2). Irvington.

American Social Thought: Sources & Interpretations, Vol. 2, Since the Civil War. Robert A. Skotheim & Michael McGiffert. LC 75-140946. (History Ser). 1972. pap. text ed. 8.50 (ISBN 0-201-07045-6). A-W.

American Socialism & Black Americans: From the Age of Jackson to World War II. Philip S. Foner. LC 77-71858. (Contributions in Afro-American & African Studies: No. 33). 1977. lib. bdg. 25.00 (ISBN 0-8371-9545-4, FAS/). Greenwood.

American Society in Wartime. Ed. by William F. Ogburn. LC 72-2380. (FDR & the Era of the New Deal Ser.). 237p. 1972. Repr. of 1943 ed. lib. bdg. 25.00 (ISBN 0-306-70484-6). Da Capo.

American Society of Composers, Authors & Publishers Biographical Dictionary. 4th ed. Ed. by Jaques Cattell Press. 560p. 1980. 43.95 (ISBN 0-8352-1283-1). Bowker.

American Society of Composers, Authors, & Publishers Copyright Law Symposium, No. 22. LC 40-8341. 1977. 16.00x (ISBN 0-231-04278-7). Columbia U Pr.

American Society of Composers, Authors & Publishers Copyright Law Symposium, No. 23. LC 40-8341. 1977. 13.50x (ISBN 0-231-04348-1). Columbia U Pr.

American Society of Composers, Authors, & Publishers Copyright Symposium, No. 25. Ed. by ASCAP. 1980. 17.50x (ISBN 0-231-04866-1). Columbia U Pr.

American Sociology & Pragmatism: Mead, Chicago Sociology, & Symbolic Interaction. J. David Lewis & Richard L. Smith. LC 80-15489. (Illus.). 1981. lib. bdg. 25.00 (ISBN 0-226-47697-9). U of Chicago Pr.

American South: Four Seasons of the Land. William A. Bake & James J. Kilpatrick. LC 80-80754. (Illus.). 224p. 1980. 29.95 (ISBN 0-8487-0495-9). Oxmoor Hse.

American Southwest: Its Peoples & Cultures. Lynn I. Perrigo. LC 76-146926. 1980. Repr. of 1971 ed. 14.95x (ISBN 0-8263-0403-6). U of NM Pr.

American Soviet Relations 1921-1933. Tarun C. Bose. 228p. 1967. 7.50 (ISBN 0-8002-2398-5). Intl Pubns Serv.

American Speech for Foreign Students. John W. Black. 272p. 1970. pap. 22.75 photocopy ed. spiral (ISBN 0-398-00161-8). C C Thomas.

American Sporting Collector's Handbook. Ed. by Allan J. Liu. 1976. 13.95 (ISBN 0-87691-217-X). Winchester Pr.

American Sportsmen & the Origins of Conservation. John F. Reiger. (Illus.). 352p. 1975. 11.95 (ISBN 0-87691-173-4). Winchester Pr.

American Stables: An Architectural Tour. Julius T. Sadler, Jr. & Jacqueline D. Sadler. 1981. 29.95 (ISBN 0-8212-1105-6). NYGS.

American Stage to World War I: A Guide to Information Sources. Ed. by Don B. Wilmeth. LC 78-53488. (Performing Arts Information Guide Ser.: Vol. 4). 1978. 30.00 (ISBN 0-8103-1392-8). Gale.

American State & Local Government. 2nd ed. John A. Straayer. (Political Science Ser.). 1977. pap. 11.50 (ISBN 0-675-08489-X). Merrill.

American State Papers Bearing on Sunday Legislation. Ed. by W. A. Blakely. LC 79-122165. (Civil Liberties in American History Ser). 1970. Repr. of 1911 ed. lib. bdg. 75.00 (ISBN 0-306-71973-8). Da Capo.

American State Political Parties & Elections. Malcolm E. Jewell & David M. Olson. 1978. pap. text ed. 11.50 (ISBN 0-256-02053-1). Dorsey.

American State Trials: 1659-1920, 17 vols. Ed. by John D. Lawson. LC 74-182150. 1972. Repr. of 1914 ed. Set. lib. bdg. 295.00 (ISBN 0-8420-0510-2). Scholarly Res Inc.

American Statesmen, 41 vols. Ed. by Arthur M. Schlesinger, Jr. 1981. Set. pap. 180.00 (ISBN 0-87754-199-X). Chelsea Hse.

American Steamships on the Atlantic, 3 vols. Cedric Ridgely-Nevitt. LC 78-66835. 550p. 1980. 75.00 (ISBN 0-87413-140-5). U Delaware Pr.

American Steel Industry Eighteen Fifty to Nineteen Seventy: A Geographical Interpretation. Kenneth Warren. (Oxford Research Studies in Geography). (Illus.). 354p. 1973. 36.00x (ISBN 0-19-823214-4). Oxford U Pr.

American Story. LC 75-16576. (Illus.). 1975. 9.95 (ISBN 0-89387-000-5). Sat Eve Post.

American Studies: A Conceptual Approach. Irving L. Gordon. (gr. 11). 1975. text ed. 15.34 (ISBN 0-87720-600-7); pap. text ed. 9.33 (ISBN 0-87720-603-1). AMSCO Sch.

American Studies in Transition. rev. ed. Ed. by Marshall W. Fishwick. LC 57-11986. 1968. Repr. of 1964 ed. 9.00x o.p. (ISBN 0-8122-7478-4). U of Pa Pr.

American Studies: Topics & Sources. Ed. by Robert H. Walker. LC 75-35675. (Illus.). 320p. (Orig.). 1976. lib. bdg. 22.50 (ISBN 0-8371-8559-9, WBE/). Greenwood.

American Stuff. Federal Writer's Project. (FDR & the Era of the New Deal Ser.). 1976. Repr. of 1937 ed. lib. bdg. 29.50 (ISBN 0-306-70806-X). Da Capo.

American Sublime: Landscape & Scenery of the Lower Hudson Valley. Raymond J. O'Brien. (Illus.). 336p. 1981. 19.95 (ISBN 0-686-69182-2). Columbia U Pr.

American Supreme Court. Robert G. McCloskey. LC 60-14235. (History of American Civilization Ser.). 1960. 12.00x (ISBN 0-226-55673-5); pap. 5.95 (ISBN 0-226-55675-1, CHAC13). U of Chicago Pr.

American Surrender. Michael Brady. 1979. 9.95 o.s.i. (ISBN 0-440-00469-1). Delacorte.

American Sword, Seventeen Seventy-Five to Nineteen Forty-Five. Harold L. Peterson. LC 65-25409. (Illus.). 1977. 22.50 (ISBN 0-686-15789-3). Ray Riling.

American System of Government. 14th ed. John H. Ferguson & Dean E. McHenry. Ed. by Eric M. Munson. (Illus.). 688p. Date not set. text ed. price not set (ISBN 0-07-020528-0, C); instr's manual 4.95 (ISBN 0-07-020529-9). McGraw. Postponed.

American System: Speeches on the Tariff Question, & on Internal Improvements. Andrew Stewart. (Neglected American Economists Ser.). 1974. lib. bdg. 50.00 (ISBN 0-8240-1019-1). Garland Pub.

American Tableaux, No. 1: Sketches of Aboriginal Life. V. V. Vide. LC 75-7085. (Indian Captivities Ser.: Vol. 62). 1976. Repr. of 1846 ed. lib. bdg. 44.00 (ISBN 0-8240-1686-6). Garland Pub.

American Tariff Controversies in the Nineteenth Century, 2 vols. Edward Stanwood. (Neglected American Economists Ser.). 1974. Set. lib. bdg. 76.00 (ISBN 0-8240-1033-7); lib. bdg. 50.00 ea. Garland Pub.

American Teenager. Myron Harris & Jane Norman. LC 80-51249. 300p. Date not set. 12.95 (ISBN 0-89256-141-6). Rawson Wade.

American Theatre. Ed. by M. Bradbury & D. Palmer. (Stratford-Upon-Avon Studies: No. 10). 228p. 1967. pap. text ed. 11.75x (ISBN 0-8419-5816-5). Holmes & Meier.

American Theatre. Victoria Wehrum. LC 73-9972. (First Bks.). (Illus.). 72p. (gr. 5-8). 1974. PLB 4.90 o.p. (ISBN 0-531-00792-8). Watts.

American Theatre Annual, 1978-1979. Ed. by Catharine R. Hughes. (Illus.). 1980. 35.00 (ISBN 0-8103-0418-X, Incorporates New York Theatre Annual). Gale.

American Themes. J. A. Krout. LC 63-17362. 1963. 20.00x (ISBN 0-231-02633-1). Columbia U Pr.

American Themes. Ed. by Esmond Wright. LC 68-88949. (Selections from History Today Ser.: No. 1). (Illus.). 1969. 5.00 (ISBN 0-05-001529-X); pap. 3.95 (ISBN 0-685-09156-2). Dufour.

American Thinking About Peace & War: New Essays on American Thought & Attitudes. Ed. by Ken Booth & Moorhead Wright. 1978. text ed. 18.50x (ISBN 0-06-490581-0). B&N.

American Thought & Religious Typology. Ursula Brumm. LC 76-97737. 1970. 18.00 (ISBN 0-8135-0621-2). Rutgers U Pr.

American Tongue & Cheek: A Populist Guide to Our Language. Jim Quinn. 1981. 11.95 (ISBN 0-394-50905-6). Pantheon.

American Tory. Ed. by Morton Borden & Penn Borden. LC 73-168739. (Great Lives Observed). 160p. 1972. 8.95 (ISBN 0-13-031393-9, Spec); pap. 2.45 o.p. (ISBN 0-13-031385-8, Spec). P-H.

American Touch in Micronesia. David Nevin. 1977. 9.95 o.p. (ISBN 0-393-05617-1). Norton.

American Trade Schools Directory, 1974. LC 53-8387. 45.00 (ISBN 0-87514-002-5). Croner.

American Tradition in Painting. John W. McCoubrey. LC 63-11371. (Illus.). (YA) (gr. 9 up). 1963. 7.95 o.p. (ISBN 0-8076-0215-9). Braziller.

American Tragedy. Theodore Dreiser. LC 78-55741. 1978. Repr. of 1948 ed. lib. bdg. 16.50x (ISBN 0-8376-0424-9). Bentley.

American Tramp & Underworld Slang. Godfrey Irwin. LC 75-149783. 1971. Repr. of 1931 ed. 18.00 (ISBN 0-8103-3748-7). Gale.

American Transcendentalists. Ed. by Perry Miller. LC 57-11433. 1957. pap. 3.50 (ISBN 0-385-09326-8, A119, Anch). Doubleday.

American Transplant: The Rockefeller Foundation & Peking Union Medical College. Mary B. Bullock. LC 77-83098. 280p. 1981. 17.50x (ISBN 0-520-03559-3). U of Cal Pr.

American Transplant: The Rockefeller Foundation & Peking Union Medical College. Mary Brown Bullock. 1980. 17.50 (ISBN 0-520-03559-3). U of Cal Pr.

American Trial Judges: Their Work Styles & Performance. John P. Ryan et al. LC 80-756. (Illus.). 1980. 19.95 (ISBN 0-02-927620-9). Free Pr.

American Universities & Colleges: A Dictionary of Name Changes. Alice H. Songe. LC 78-5497. 1978. lib. bdg. 12.00x (ISBN 0-8108-1137-5). Scarecrow.

American University As an Instrument of Republican Culture: Sir George Watson Lecture Delivered in the University of Leicester - March 1970. Oscar Handlin. (Sir George Watson Lectures). 1970. pap. text ed. 1.50x (ISBN 0-7185-1097-6, Leicester). Humanities.

American University in Summer. Clarence A. Schoenfeld & Donald N. Zillman. 1967. 20.00x (ISBN 0-299-04520-X). U of Wis Pr.

American Values. Ed. by David L. Bender. (Opposing Viewpoints Ser.: Vol. 10). (Illus.). 1975. lib. bdg. 10.95 (ISBN 0-912616-35-0); pap. text ed. 4.95 (ISBN 0-912616-16-4). Greenhaven.

American Values: Continuity & Change. Ralph H. Gabriel. LC 74-24. (Contributions in American Studies: No. 15). 230p. 1974. lib. bdg. 17.95 (ISBN 0-8371-7355-8, GAV/). Greenwood.

American Vaudeville: Its Life & Times. Douglas Gilbert. (Illus.). 10.00 (ISBN 0-8446-2128-5). Peter Smith.

American Victorian Architecture. Ed. by Arnold Lewis & Keith Morgan. LC 73-92261. Orig. Title: Architecture American. (Illus.). 160p. 1975. pap. 6.95 (ISBN 0-486-23177-1). Dover.

American Victorian Architecture: American Victorian Architecture: a Survey of the 70's & 80's in Contemporary Photographs. Arnold Lewis & Keith Morgan. 12.50 (ISBN 0-8446-5217-2). Peter Smith.

American Victoriana: Floor Plans & Renderings from the Gilded Age. Eugene Mitchell. LC 79-20404. (Illus., Orig.). 1979. 19.95 (ISBN 0-87701-147-8, Prism Editions). Chronicle Bks.

American Violence: A Documentary History. Ed. by Richard Hofstadter & Michael Wallace. LC 73-111238. 1971. pap. 4.95 (ISBN 0-394-71686-8, Vin). Random.

American Vision: Actual & Ideal Society in Nineteenth-Century Fiction. A. N. Kaul. LC 80-13606. (Yale Publications in American Studies: No. 7). xi, 340p. 1980. Repr. of 1963 ed. lib. bdg. 27.00x (ISBN 0-313-22427-7, KAAV). Greenwood.

American Vision: Essay on the Future of Democratic Capitalism. Michael Novak. 1978. pap. 4.25 (ISBN 0-8447-3324-5). Am Enterprise.

American Visionary Fiction: Mad Metaphysics As Salvation Psychology. Richard Finholt. (National University Publications Literary Criticism Ser.). 1977. 12.00 (ISBN 0-8046-9191-6). Kennikat.

American Voices: A Historical Reader, 2 vols. Robert Marcus & David Burner. 1979. pap. 8.95x ea. Vol. 1 (ISBN 0-673-15172-7). Vol. 2 (ISBN 0-673-15173-5). Scott F.

American Voter. Angus Campbell et al. LC 76-21115. 1976. Repr. of 1960 ed. lib. bdg. 15.00x o.s.i. (ISBN 0-226-09253-4). U of Chicago Pr.

American Voter. Angus Campbell et al. LC 76-21115. (Midway Reprint Ser.). 576p. 1980. lib. bdg. 18.00x (ISBN 0-226-09254-2). U of Chicago Pr.

American Voter: An Abridgement. Angus Campbell et al. LC 64-20076. (Illus.). 1964. pap. text ed. 11.95 (ISBN 0-471-13335-3). Wiley.

American War & Peace, Eighteen Sixty to Eighteen Seventy-Seven. Emory M. Thomas. (Illus.). 240p. 1973. pap. 10.95 (ISBN 0-13-032391-8). P-H.

American War Songs. National Society of the Colonial Dames of America. LC 73-156922. 1974. Repr. of 1925 ed. 18.00 (ISBN 0-8103-3722-3). Gale.

American Way of Divorce: Prescriptions for Change. Sheila Kessler. LC 74-28078. 192p. 1975. 12.95 (ISBN 0-88229-234-X). Nelson-Hall.

American Way of War: A History of United States Military Strategy & Policy. Russell F. Weigley. LC 72-91169. 708p. 1973. 14.95 (ISBN 0-02-625650-9). Macmillan.

American Way of War: A History of U. S. Military Strategy & Policy. Russell F. Weigley. LC 77-74434. (Wars of the United States Ser.). (Illus.). 602p. 1977. pap. 7.95x (ISBN 0-253-28029-X). Ind U Pr.

American Way of Working: A Collection of Writings from Henry David Thoreau to Joseph Heller. Ed. by Michael Spring. 272p. (Orig.). 1980. pap. 2.50 (ISBN 0-553-13925-8). Bantam.

American West in the Thirties: One Hundred Twenty-Two Photographs by Arthur Rothstein. Arthur Rothstein. (Illus.). 128p. (Orig.). 1981. pap. price not set (ISBN 0-486-24106-8). Dover.

American West: New Perspectives, New Dimensions. Ed. by Jerome O. Steffen. LC 78-58097. 238p. 1981. pap. 6.95 (ISBN 0-8061-1744-3). U of Okla Pr.

American Whaling in Hudson Bay, Eighteen Sixty-One to Nineteen Nineteen. Renny A. Stackpole. LC 79-110367. (Illus.). 68p. 1969. pap. 3.00 (ISBN 0-913372-01-3). Mystic Seaport.

American Wild Flowers Coloring Book. Paul E. Kennedy. (Illus.). 48p. 1971. pap. 1.75 (ISBN 0-486-20095-7). Dover.

American Woman. M. McBee & K. Blake. 1974. 7.95 (ISBN 0-02-476280-6, 47628); pap. 4.95x (ISBN 0-02-476270-9, 47627). Macmillan.

American Woman: Her Changing Social, Economic & Political Roles, 1920-1970. William H. Chafe. 336p. 1974. pap. 5.95 (ISBN 0-19-501785-4, GB406). Oxford U Pr.

American Woman: Her Role in the Revolutionary War. Esther Perica. LC 80-28294. (Cameo Series of Notable Women). 1981. pap. price not set (ISBN 0-912526-28-9). Lib Res.

American Woman in Sport. Ellen W. Gerber et al. 1974. text ed. 16.95 (ISBN 0-201-02353-9). A-W.

American Woman Playwright: A View of Criticism & Characterization. Judith Olauson. LC 80-51605. 190p. 1981. 12.50x (ISBN 0-87875-198-X). Whitston Pub.

American Woman's Cook Book. rev ed. Ed. by Ruth Berolzheimer. 960p. 1973. 10.95 (ISBN 0-385-00732-9). Doubleday.

American Women: American Women: Fifteen Hundred Biographies with Over Fourteen Hundred Portraits, 2 vols. Frances E. Willard & Mary A. Livermore. LC 73-7985. Orig. Title: Woman of the Century. 824p. 1974. Repr. of 1897 ed. Set. 68.00 (ISBN 0-8103-3225-6). Gale.

American Women & the Labor Movement, 1825-1974: An Annotated Bibliography. Martha J. Soltow & Mary K. Wery. LC 76-40169. 1976. 10.00 (ISBN 0-8108-0986-9). Scarecrow.

American Women Poets: Pioneers of Modern Poetry. Jean Gould. LC 79-25670. (Illus.). 352p. 1980. 10.95 (ISBN 0-396-07828-1). Dodd.

American Women Writers: A Critical Reference Guide, Vol. 2, F-Le. Ed. by Lina Mainiero. LC 78-20945. 1980. 45.00 (ISBN 0-8044-3152-3). Ungar.

American Wooden Bridges. Compiled By American Society of Civil Engineers. 184p. 1976. pap. text ed. 24.75 (ISBN 0-87262-002-6). Am Soc Civil Eng.

American Woodenware & Other Primitives. Ed. by Don Maust. (Illus.). 1974. 8.95 o.p. (ISBN 0-685-49052-1). Warman.

American Worker in the Twentieth Century. Eli Ginzberg & H. Berman. LC 63-10647. 1963. 14.95 (ISBN 0-02-911730-5). Free Pr.

American Writer & the Great Depression. Ed. by Harvey Swados. LC 65-23009. (Illus., Orig.). 1966. pap. 10.50 (ISBN 0-672-60098-6, AHS63). Bobbs.

American Writers: A Collection of Literary Biographies, 6 vols. Ed. by Leonard Unger. LC 73-1759. 1979. Set. lib. bdg. 275.00 (ISBN 0-684-16104-4). Scribner.

American Writers in Paris, Nineteen Twenty to Nineteen Thirty-Nine. Ed. by Karen L. Rood. LC 79-26101. (Dictionary of Literary Biography Ser.: Vol. 4). (Illus.). 1980. 54.00 (ISBN 0-8103-0916-5, Bruccoli Clark Book). Gale.

American Writers on Education After 1865. Abraham Blinderman. (World Leader Ser.: No. 54). 1976. lib. bdg. 10.95 (ISBN 0-8057-7654-0). Twayne.

American Writings on Popular Education: The 19th Century. Ed. by Rush Welter. LC 73-151611. (American Heritage Ser). 1971. 13.50 (ISBN 0-672-51508-3, AHS-81); pap. 7.95 (ISBN 0-672-60134-6). Bobbs.

American Yoga. Ed. by Deena Brown. LC 79-6156. (Illus.). 144p. (Orig.). 1981. pap. 9.95 (ISBN 0-394-17649-9, E751, Ever). Grove.

American Youth in a Changing Culture. Ed. by Grant S. McClellan. (Reference Shelf Ser.). 266p. 1972. 6.25 (ISBN 0-8242-0466-2). Wilson.

American 1890s: Life & Times of a Lost Generation. Larzer Ziff. LC 79-14754. 1979. 17.95x (ISBN 0-8032-4900-4); pap. 5.95x (ISBN 0-8032-9900-1, BB 711, Bison). U of Nebr Pr.

Americana Annual, 1980. Ed. by Edward Humphrey & James E. Churchill. LC 23-10041. (Illus.). 1980. write for info. o.p. (ISBN 0-7172-0211-9). Grolier Ed Corp.

Americana Annual, 1981. Ed. by Edward Humphrey & James E. Churchill. LC 23-10041. (Illus.). 1981. write for info. (ISBN 0-7172-0212-7). Grolier Ed Corp.

Americana Mazes. Susan Poe. 32p. (Orig.). (gr. 3 up). 1980. pap. 1.50 (ISBN 0-937518-07-7). Hartley Hse.

Americanisms: Old & New. John S. Farmer. LC 75-44079. 1976. Repr. of 1889 ed. 38.00 (ISBN 0-8103-3746-0). Gale.

Americanistes: New French Criticism on Modern American Fiction. Ed. by Ira D. Johnson & Christiane Johnson. LC 76-58512. (National University Publications Literary Criticism Ser.). (Illus.). 1977. 12.95 o.p. (ISBN 0-8046-9176-2). Kennikat.

Americanization of Canada. Samuel Moffett. LC 79-189601. (Social History of Canada Ser.). 128p. 1972. pap. 3.50 (ISBN 0-8020-6143-5). U of Toronto Pr.

Americanization of Micronesia: A Study of the Consolidation of the U. S. Role in the Pacific. Roger W. Gale. LC 78-68800. 1979. pap. text ed. 12.00 (ISBN 0-8191-0703-4). U Pr of Amer.

Americanization of the Synagogue, 1820-1870. Leon A. Jick. LC 75-18213. (Illus.). 260p. 1976. text ed. 15.00x (ISBN 0-87451-119-4). U Pr of New Eng.

Americanizing the American Indians: Writings by the "Friends of the Indian," 1880-1900. Ed. by Francis P. Prucha. LC 77-14102. 1978. pap. 4.95 (ISBN 0-8032-5881-X, BB 643, Bison). U of Nebr Pr.

Americano En el Teatro De Sor Juana Ines De la Cruz. Maria E. Perez. 1975. 14.00 (ISBN 0-88303-020-9); pap. 11.00 (ISBN 0-685-73221-5). E Torres & Sons.

Americans All, 2 vols. George Mannello. (Orig.). (gr. 11-12). 1973. Vol. 1. pap. text ed. 6.25 (ISBN 0-87720-611-2); Vol. 2. pap. text ed. 6.25 (ISBN 0-87720-613-9); self-study wkbk, 1974 4.92 (ISBN 0-87720-614-7). AMSCO Sch.
Americans & Chinese: A Historical Essay & a Bibliography. Ed. by Liu Kwang-Ching. LC 63-19141. 1963. 10.00x (ISBN 0-674-03000-1). Harvard U Pr.
Americans & Free Enterprise. Henry C. Dethloff. LC 78-15515. (Illus.). 1979. ref. ed. 16.95 (ISBN 0-13-032490-6). P-H.
Americans & the Arts. National Research Center of the Arts. LC 80-28923. (Illus., Orig.). Date not set. pap. 10.00 (ISBN 0-915400-27-8). Am Council Arts.
Americans & the Arts: A Survey of Public Opinion. National Research Center of the Arts. LC 74-33144. (Illus., Orig.). 1974. pap. text ed. 5.00 (ISBN 0-915400-00-6). Am Council Arts.
Americans & the Arts: Highlights. National Research Center of the Arts. (Orig.). pap. 3.00 (ISBN 0-915400-28-6). Am Council Arts.
Americans & the California Dream, 1850-1915. Kevin Starr. (Illus.). 512p. 1981. pap. 11.50 (ISBN 0-87905-083-7). Peregrine Smith.
American's Guide to Britain. Robin Winks. LC 77-23341. 1977. pap. 6.95 (ISBN 0-684-15189-8, ScribT). Scribner.
Americans Import Merit: Origins of the United States Civil Service System & the Influence of the British Model. Richard E. Titlow. LC 78-65352. 1978. pap. text ed. 12.50 (ISBN 0-8191-0655-0). U Pr of Amer.
Americans in Conflict: The Civil War & Reconstruction. David Lindsey. 208p. 1974. pap. text ed. 7.75 (ISBN 0-395-14068-4, 3-33320). HM.
Americans in Paris. George Wickes. (Illus.). xvi, 302p. 1980. pap. 6.95 (ISBN 0-306-80127-2). Da Capo.
Americans in Persia. Arthur Millspaugh. LC 76-9837. (Politics & Strategy of World War II Ser.). 1976. Repr. of 1946 ed. lib. bdg. 27.50 (ISBN 0-306-70764-0). Da Capo.
Americans Interpret Their Civil War. Thomas J. Pressly. LC 62-17572. 1965. pap. text ed. 6.95 (ISBN 0-02-925450-7). Free Pr.
Americans: Nineteen Seventy-Six. Commission on Critical Choices. Ed. by Irving Kristol. Paul H. Weaver. LC 75-44719. (Critical Choices for Americans Ser.: Vol. 2). 1976. 18.95 (ISBN 0-669-00415-4). Lexington Bks.
Americans of Dream & Deed. Robert J. Lowenherz & Lila Lowenherz. (Orig.). (gr. 7-8). 1981. pap. text ed. 7.08 (ISBN 0-87720-397-0). AMSCO Sch.
Americans: The National Experience. Daniel J. Boorstin. 1967. pap. 5.95 (ISBN 0-394-70358-8, V-358, Vin). Random.
Americans to the Moon: The Story of Project Apollo. Gene Gurney. LC 77-103405. (Landmark Giant Ser.: No. 20). (gr. 5-9). 1970. 4.95 (ISBN 0-394-81853-9); PLB 5.99 (ISBN 0-394-91853-3). Random.
Americans Together: Structured Diversity in a Midwestern Town. Herve Varenne. LC 77-10109. 1977. pap. text ed. 10.25x (ISBN 0-8077-2519-6). Tchrs Coll.
American's Tourist Manual for Peoples Republic of China. John E. Felber. LC 73-93210. 224p. 1980. pap. 7.95 (ISBN 0-686-64369-0). Intl Intertrade.
American's Tourist Manual for the U.S.S.R. John E. Felber. LC 72-78512. (Illus.). 1979. pap. 7.95 (ISBN 0-910794-02-2). Intl Intertrade.
America's Aging Population: Issues Facing Business & Society, Report No. 785. Shirley H. Rhine. (Illus.). viii, 60p. 1980. pap. 15.00 (ISBN 0-8237-0221-9). Conference Bd.
America's Backing Guide. rev. ed. Raymond Bridge. 448p. 1981. 14.95 (ISBN 0-684-16872-3, ScribT). Scribner.
America's Bad Men. Pat McCarthy. Ed. by Thomas Mooney. (Pal Paperbacks Ser., Kit A). (Illus., Orig.). (gr. 7-12). 1974. pap. text ed. 1.25 (ISBN 0-8374-3476-9). Xerox Ed Pubns.
America's Best Vegetable Recipes. Farm Journal Editors. LC 74-89068. (Illus.). 1970. 8.95 (ISBN 0-385-03155-6). Doubleday.
America's Capacity to Produce. Edwin G. Nourse et al. (Brookings Institution Reprint Ser.). (Illus.). Repr. of 1934 ed. lib. bdg. 29.00x (ISBN 0-697-00176-8). Irvington.
America's Changing Population. Ed. by Oliver Bell. (Reference Shelf Ser.). 1974. 6.25 (ISBN 0-8242-0522-7). Wilson.
America's Choice. James R. Evans. 150p. (Orig.). 1981. lib. bdg. 11.95 (ISBN 0-933028-17-2); pap. 6.95 (ISBN 0-933028-16-4). Fisher Inst.
America's Colonial Experiment. Julius W. Pratt. 1964. 7.50 o.p. (ISBN 0-8446-1362-2). Peter Smith.
America's Coming Bankruptcy: How the Government Is Wrecking Your Dollar. Harvey W. Peters. LC 72-91216. 1973. 7.95 o.p. (ISBN 0-87000-200-7). Arlington Hse.
America's Coming Nightmare Inflation, Economic Collapse & Crime Revolution. Fred Muller. 120p. 1980. 10.00 (ISBN 0-686-68648-9). State Ptg.
America's Community Police: An Evaluative Bibliography. 1977. 1.25 o.p. (ISBN 0-685-80770-3). Soc Sci & Soc Res.
America's Concentration Camps. Allan R. Bosworth. (Illus.). 1967. 12.95x (ISBN 0-393-05338-5). Norton.
America's Cup: An Informal History. Ian Dear. LC 80-65596. (Illus.). 192p. 1980. 19.95 (ISBN 0-396-07848-6). Dodd.
America's Dilemma in Asia: The Case of South Korea. Harold H. Sunoo. LC 78-24029. 1979. 15.95x (ISBN 0-88229-357-5). Nelson-Hall.
America's Dilemma: Jobs Vs. Prices. Alfred L. Malabre, Jr. LC 78-18809. 1978. 9.95 (ISBN 0-396-07586-X). Dodd.
America's Educational Tradition: An Interpretive History. William M. French. 1964. text ed. 8.95x o.p. (ISBN 0-669-20107-3). Heath.
America's Energy Famine: Its Cause & Cure. Ruth S. Knowles. LC 80-8040. 337p. 1980. 14.95 (ISBN 0-8061-1669-2). U of Okla Pr.
America's Energy: Reports from "the Nation" on 100 Years of Struggles for the Democratic Control of Our Resources. Ed. by Robert Engler. 1981. 17.95 (ISBN 0-394-51142-5); pap. 7.95 (ISBN 0-394-73909-4). Pantheon.
America's Fascinating Indian Heritage. (Illus.). 1979. 17.95 (ISBN 0-89577-019-9, Pub. by Reader's Digest). Norton.
America's Favorite Restaurants & Inns. 7th, rev. ed. Bob Christopher & Ellen Christopher. LC 79-2034. 1019p. (Orig.). 1980. pap. 6.95 (ISBN 0-688-08550-4). Morrow.
America's Favorite Songs. 256p. 1981. pap. 2.49 (ISBN 0-8256-3207-2, Quick Fox). Music Sales.
America's Favorite Sports Stars. Steve Gelman & Rita Gelman. (gr. 4-6). 1978. pap. 1.50 o.p. (ISBN 0-590-05355-8, Schol Pap). Schol Bk Serv.
America's Favorites. Kay Lee & Marshall Lee. (Illus.). 160p. 1980. 17.95 (ISBN 0-399-12514-0). Putnam.
America's First Football Game. Laurence Swinburne & Irene Swinburne. LC 78-14865. (Famous Firsts Ser.). (Illus.). 1978. lib. bdg. 7.35 (ISBN 0-686-51096-8). Silver.
America's Flying Book. Ed. by Flying Magazine. LC 72-1213. (Illus.). 320p. 1972. 14.95 o.p. (ISBN 0-684-12929-9, ScribT). Scribner.
America's Freedom Trail. Victor M. Alper. LC 75-44414. (Illus.). 672p. 1976. pap. 7.95 o.s.i. (ISBN 0-02-097150-8, 09715, Collier). Macmillan.
America's Future in Symbolic Prophecy. Dennis M. Battle. (Illus.). 52p. 1981. pap. 2.50 (ISBN 0-933464-10-X). D M Battle Pubns.
America's Garden Heritage. 1.95 o.p. (ISBN 0-686-21149-9). Bklyn Botanic.
America's Gauntlet: Manuscript 1 of the Humanist Papers. Robert Kneeter. pap. 5.00 (ISBN 0-938722-01-8). Word Ent.
America's Great Depression. rev. ed. Murray N. Rothbard. (Studies in Economic Theory). 361p. 1975. 12.00; pap. 4.95. NYU Pr.
America's Great Outdoors. 29.00 (ISBN 0-87827-250-X). Ency Brit Ed.
America's Health Care Crisis. William S. Hendricks. LC 80-66321. 1980. 9.95 (ISBN 0-686-28081-4). Ducky Ent.
America's Heritage Trail. Victor M. Alper. LC 75-45110. (Illus.). 351p. 1976. pap. 7.95 o.s.i. (ISBN 0-02-097160-5, 09716, Collier). Macmillan.
America's Heritage Trail. Victor M. Alper. (Illus.). 1976. 12.95 o.s.i. (ISBN 0-02-501690-3, 50169). Macmillan.
America's Historic Inns & Taverns. rev. ed. Irvin Haas. LC 76-45410. (Illus.). 1977. 8.95 o.p. (ISBN 0-668-04189-7). Arco.
America's Hive of Honey: Foreign Influences on American Fiction Through Henry James. David Kirby. LC 80-20672. 231p. 1980. 12.50 (ISBN 0-8108-1349-1). Scarecrow.
America's Immigrant Women. Cecyle S. Neidle. LC 75-12738. (Immigrant Heritage of America Ser.). 1975. lib. bdg. 10.95 (ISBN 0-8057-8400-4). Twayne.
America's Impact on the World: A Study of the Role of the U. S. in the World Economy 1750-1970. William Woodruff. LC 74-23474. 296p. 1975. 19.95 (ISBN 0-470-95963-0). Halsted Pr.
Americas in the Nineteen Eighties: An Agenda for the Decade Ahead. Alejandro Orfila. LC 80-5935. 166p. 1980. lib. bdg. 17.25 (ISBN 0-8191-1333-6); pap. text ed. 8.75 (ISBN 0-8191-1334-4). U Pr of Amer.
America's Italian Founding Fathers: 1770-1780. Adolph Caso. 285p. 1975. 10.00 (ISBN 0-8283-1667-8). Dante U Am.
America's Lighthouses. rev. ed. Francis R. Holland, Jr. (Illus.). 240p. 1981. pap. 19.95 (ISBN 0-8289-0441-3) Greene.
America's Lighthouses: Their Illustrated History Since 1716. Francis R. Holland, Jr. LC 74-170080. 1972. 17.50 o.p. (ISBN 0-8289-0148-1). Greene.
America's Longest War: The U. S. & Vietnam 1950 to 1975. George C. Herring. LC 79-16408. (America in Crisis Ser.). 1979. text ed. 14.95 o.p. (ISBN 0-471-01546-6); pap. text ed. 7.95 (ISBN 0-471-01547-4). Wiley.
America's Lost Plays, 21 Vols. in 11. Ed. by Barrett H. Clark. Incl. Vols. 1 & 2. 440p. 19.50x (ISBN 0-253-30650-7); Vols. 3 & 4. 500p. 15.00x (ISBN 0-253-30651-5); Vols. 9 & 10. 568p. 15.00x (ISBN 0-253-30654-X); Vols. 11 & 12. 480p. 15.00x (ISBN 0-253-30655-8); Vols. 13 & 14. 600p. 15.00x (ISBN 0-253-30656-6); Vols. 15 & 16. 492p. 15.00x (ISBN 0-253-30657-4); Vols. 17 & 18. 704p. 15.00x (ISBN 0-253-30658-2); Vols. 19 & 20. 768p. 15.00x (ISBN 0-253-30659-0); Vol. 21. 178p. 9.95x (ISBN 0-253-30660-4). LC 63-18068. 1963-69. Ind U Pr.
America's Military Past: A Guide to Information Sources. Ed. by Jack C. Lane. LC 74-11517. (American Government & History Information Guide Ser.: Vol. 7). 1980. 30.00 (ISBN 0-8103-1205-0). Gale.
America's Money: The Story of Our Coins & Currency. J. Earl Massey. LC 68-31772. (Illus.). 1968. 6.95 o.s.i. (ISBN 0-690-08656-3, TYC-T). T Y Crowell.
America's Most Bizarre Murderer: Edward Gein. Robert Gollmar. (Illus.). 254p. 1981. 9.95 (ISBN 0-87319-020-3). C Hallberg.
America's Most Successful Fund Raising Letters. Ed. by Joseph Dermer. 14.75 (ISBN 0-686-24210-6). Public Serv Materials.
America's Music: From the Pilgrims to the Present. rev. ed. G. Chase. (Music Ser.). 1966. text ed. 15.95 o.p. (ISBN 0-07-010672-X, C). McGraw.
America's Natural Resources. rev. ed. Ed. by C. H. Callison. 1967. 14.95 (ISBN 0-8260-1685-5, Pub. by Wiley-Interscience). Wiley.
America's New Railroads. Robert S. Carper. LC 77-84563. (Illus.). 256p. 1980. 25.00 (ISBN 0-498-02179-3). A S Barnes.
America's Past: A New World Archaeology. Thomas C. Patterson. 168p. 1973. pap. 5.95x (ISBN 0-673-05273-7). Scott F.
America's Place in the World Economy. Brenda Forman. LC 69-11494. (Curriculum Related Bks). (gr. 9-12). 1969. 5.50 o.p. (ISBN 0-15-203168-5, HJ). HarBraceJ.
America's Prisons: Correctional Institutions or Universities of Crime. rev. ed. Ed. by Gary E. McCuen. (Opposing Viewpoints Ser.: Vol. 5). (gr. 9 up). 1973. lib. bdg. 10.60 o.p. (ISBN 0-912616-29-6); pap. text ed. 4.60 o.p. (ISBN 0-912616-11-3). Greenhaven.
America's Prisons: Opposing Viewpoints. David L. Bender. (Opposing Viewpoints Ser.). 140p. (gr. 12). 1980. lib. bdg. 8.95 (ISBN 0-89908-330-7); pap. text ed. 3.95 (ISBN 0-89908-305-6). Greenhaven.
America's Response to China: An Interpretive History of Sino-American Relations. W. I. Cohen. (America & the World Ser.). 1971. pap. text ed. 8.95x o.p. (ISBN 0-471-16336-8). Wiley.
America's Response to China: An Interpretive History of Sino-American Relations. 2nd ed. Warren I. Cohen. LC 80-13383. (America & the World Ser.). 265p. 1980. pap. text ed. 8.95 (ISBN 0-471-06089-5). Wiley.
America's Retreat from Victory. Joseph R. McCarthy. (Americanist Classics Ser). 1965. pap. 1.00 pocketsize o.p. (ISBN 0-88279-002-1). Western Islands.
America's Road to Empire: The War with Spain & Overseas Expansion. Howard W. Morgan. LC 64-8714. (America in Crisis Ser.). 124p. 1965. pap. text ed. 7.95 (ISBN 0-471-61520-X). Wiley.
America's Soaring Book. Ed. by Flying Magazine. LC 74-32016. 1975. 12.95 o.p. (ISBN 0-684-14208-2, ScribT). Scribner.
America's Sporting Heritage: 1850-1950. John R. Betts. LC 73-10590. 1974. text ed. 16.95 (ISBN 0-201-00557-3). A-W.
America's Technology Slip. Simon Ramo. LC 80-21525. 350p. 1980. 14.95 (ISBN 0-471-05976-5, Pub. by Wiley-Interscience). Wiley.
America's Troubled Children. Melinda Maidens. (Editorials on File Ser.). 220p. 1980. lib. bdg. 19.95 (ISBN 0-87196-369-8). Facts on File.
America's Witness for Christ. Harold I. Hansen. LC 80-84565. 350p. 1981. 8.95 (ISBN 0-88290-174-5). Horizon Utah.
America's Witness for Jesus Christ. Compiled by Arthur Wallace. 70p. 1978. pap. 1.95 (ISBN 0-937892-04-1). LL Co.
America's Wonderful Little Hotels & Inns. Barbara Crossette. (Illus.). 400p. 1981. 14.95 (ISBN 0-312-92016-4); pap. 8.95 (ISBN 0-312-92016-4). St Martin.
America's Wonderful Little Hotels & Inns: New, Revised 1981-82 Edition. Ed. by Barbara Crossette. (Illus.). 400p. 1981. 14.95 (ISBN 0-312-92016-4); pap. 8.95 (ISBN 0-312-92017-2). Congdon & Lattes.
America's Yesterdays: Images of Our Lost Past Discovered in the Photographic Archives of the Library of Congress. Oliver Jensen. (Illus.). 352p. 1978. 12.95 (ISBN 0-8281-3074-4, Dist. by Scribner). Am Heritage.
America's Yesterdays: Images of Our Lost Past Discovered in the Photographic Archives of the Library of Congress. Oliver Jensen. LC 78-18426. (Illus.). 352p. 1978. deluxe ed. 39.95 slipcased (ISBN 0-8281-3073-6). Am Heritage.
Americo Castro & the Meaning of Spanish Civilization. Jose R. Barcia. 1977. 20.00x (ISBN 0-520-02920-8). U of Cal Pr.
Amerika: Bilderbuch Tines Architekten. Erich Mendelsohn. LC 76-40319. (Architecture & Decorative Art Ser.). (Ger.). 1977. Repr. of 1926 ed. lib. bdg. 45.00 (ISBN 0-306-70830-2). Da Capo.
Ameriki: Book One, & Selected Earlier Poems. George Economou. LC 77-3612. 1977. pap. 4.00 (ISBN 0-915342-20-0). SUN.
Amethyst Love. Rebecca Danton. (Regency Romance Ser.). 1977. pap. 1.50 o.p. (ISBN 0-449-23400-2, Crest). Fawcett.
Amethyst Quest. Lois A. Sunagel. (YA) 1975. 5.95 (ISBN 0-685-52991-6, Avalon). Bouregy.
Amgydalin (Laetrile) Therapy. Bruce W. Halstead. (Illus.). 1977. pap. 3.00 (ISBN 0-933904-06-1). Gold Quill Pubs CA.
Amiable Baltimoreans. Francis F. Beirne. LC 68-9401. xiv, 400p. 1968. Repr. 22.00 (ISBN 0-8103-5031-9). Gale.
Amigo. Byrd B. Schweitzer. (gr. 1-3). 1963. 5.95g o.s.i. (ISBN 0-02-781300-2). Macmillan.
Amigos De Dios. Sylvia Mandeville. Tr. by Edna L. Gutierrez from Eng. (Serie Apunta Contu Dedo). 1980. pap. 7.95 (ISBN 0-311-38532-X, Edit Mundo). Casa Bautista.
Amillenialism Today. William Cox. 1972. pap. 2.75 (ISBN 0-87552-151-7). Presby & Reformed.
Aminergic & Peptidergic Receptors: Satellite Symposium of the Third Congress of the Hungarian Pharmacological Society, Szeged, 1979. Ed. by E. S. Vizi & Marie Wollemann. LC 80-41281. (Advances in Pharmacological Research & Practice Ser.: Vol. VII). 220p. 1981. 41.00 (ISBN 0-08-026839-0). Pergamon.
Amino Acid Analysis. J. M. Rattenbury. 320p. 1981. 89.95 (ISBN 0-470-27141-8). Halsted Pr.
Amino Acid Metabolism & Its Disorders. Charles R. Scriver & Leon E. Rosenberg. LC 72-90726. (Major Problems in Clinical Pediatrics Ser.: Vol. 10). (Illus.). 510p. 1973. text ed. 22.00 (ISBN 0-7216-8044-5). Saunders.
Amino Acid Neurotransmitters, Vol. 29. Ed. by Francis V. DeFeudis & Paul Mandel. (Advances in Biochemical Psychopharmacology). 500p. 1981. 45.00 (ISBN 0-89004-595-X). Raven.
Amino Acids As Chemical Transmitters. Ed. by Frade Fonnum. LC 78-2362. (NATO Advanced Study Institutes Ser.: Series A, Life Sciences, Vol. 16). 759p. 1978. 49.50 (ISBN 0-306-35616-3, Plenum Pr). Plenum Pub.
Amino Acids, Peptides & Proteins: An Introduction. 1st English ed. H. D. Jakubke & H. Jeschkeit. Tr. by G. P. Cotterrell & J. H. Jones. LC 77-23945. 1978. 27.95 (ISBN 0-470-99279-4). Halsted Pr.
Aminocyclitol Antibiotics. Ed. by Kenneth L Rinehart & Tetsuo Suami. LC 80-10502. (ACS Symposium Ser.: No. 125). 1980. 39.50 (ISBN 0-8412-0554-X). Am Chemical.
Aminoglycosides: Microbiology, Use & Toxicology. Whelton. Date not set. price not set (ISBN 0-8247-1364-8). Dekker.
Amiri Baraka. Lloyd Brown. (United States Author Ser.: No. 383). 1980. lib. bdg. 9.95 (ISBN 0-8057-7137-9). Twayne.
Amiri Baraka - Leroi Jones. Werner Sollors. 1978. 17.50 (ISBN 0-231-04226-4). Columbia U Pr.
Amish Cooking. Ed. by Mark E. Miller. 320p. 1981. Repr. 14.95 (ISBN 0-8361-1958-4). Herald Pr.
Amistad Revolt, Eighteen Thirty-Nine: The Slave Uprising Aboard the Spanish Schooner. Helen Kromer. LC 72-5731. (Focus Bks.). (Illus.). 96p. 1973. PLB 4.90 o.p. (ISBN 0-531-02456-3). Watts.
Amitie Exemplaire: Villiers De L'isle-Adam et Stephane Mallarme. Georges Jean-Aubry. LC 80-205. (Symbolists Ser.). (Illus.). 228p. (Fr.). 1980. Repr. of 1942 ed. 18.50 (ISBN 0-404-16300-9). AMS Pr.
Ammianus & the Historia Augusta. Ronald Syme. 1968. 26.00x (ISBN 0-19-814344-3). Oxford U Pr.
Ammonia Absorption Refrigeration. Marcel J. Bogart. (Illus.). 320p. 1981. 32.95 (ISBN 0-87201-027-9). Gulf Pub.

Amnesia. 2nd ed. Whitty & Zangwill. 1977. 19.95 (ISBN 0-407-00056-9). Butterworths.

Amnesia-Analgesia Techniques in Dentistry. Stanley R. Spiro. (Amer. Lec. in Dentistry Ser.). (Illus.). 248p. 1973. 19.50 (ISBN 0-398-02638-6). C C Thomas.

Amniotic Fluid & Its Clinical Significance. Sandler. Date not set. price not set (ISBN 0-8247-1346-X). Dekker.

Amniotic Fluid: Physiology, Biochemistry, & Clinical Chemistry. Samuel Natelson et al. LC 74-4444. (Current Topics in Clinical Chemistry Ser.). 416p. 1974. 48.95 (ISBN 0-471-63063-2, Pub. by Wiley Medical). Wiley.

Amoco Cadiz Oil Spill. Ed. by M. F. Spooner. (Illus.). 1979. pap. text ed. 7.75 (ISBN 0-08-023830-0). Pergamon.

Amoco Motor Club Guide to Mini-Vacations in the Southeast. (Illus.). 1981. 14.95 (ISBN 0-8092-7122-2); pap. 6.95 (ISBN 0-8092-7121-4). Contemp Bks.

Among Cannibals. Carl Lumholtz. 1979. Repr. of 1888 ed. text ed. 26.00x (ISBN 0-904573-13-3). Humanities.

Among Friends: Personal Letters of Dean Acheson. Ed. by David S. McLellan & David C. Acheson. LC 79-24127. 1980. 17.95 (ISBN 0-396-07721-8). Dodd.

Among My Klediments. June C. Cash. 160p. 1981. pap. 4.95 (ISBN 0-310-38171-1). Zondervan.

Among the Dolls. William Sleator. 80p. (gr. 2-5). 1975. PLB 8.95 (ISBN 0-525-25563-X). Dutton.

Among the Indians: Four Years on the Upper Missouri, 1858-1862. Henry A. Boller. Ed. by Milo M. Quaife. LC 76-100810. (Illus.). 370p. 1972. pap. 4.50 (ISBN 0-8032-5714-7, BB 514, Bison). U of Nebr Pr.

Among the Innocent. Elizabeth B. De Trevino. 360p. 1981. 13.95 (ISBN 0-385-13397-9). Doubleday.

Among the Mescalero Apaches: The Story of Father Albert Braun, O. F. M. Dorothy Emerson. LC 73-76302. 1980. pap. 8.50 (ISBN 0-8165-0714-7). U of Ariz Pr.

Among the Mormons: Historic Accounts by Contemporary Observers. Ed. by William Mulder & A. Russell Mortensen. LC 58-5825. xiv, 496p. 1973. 8.50 (ISBN 0-8032-5778-3, BB 568, Bison). U of Nebr Pr.

Among the Mystics: The Development of Mysticism from Its Rise in the East. William Fairweather. 161p. Repr. of 1936 ed. 3.50 (ISBN 0-567-02104-1). Attic Pr.

Amongst the Shans. Archibald R. Colquhoun. (Illus.). 1968. Repr. of 1885 ed. 17.00 o.p. (ISBN 0-8188-0023-2). Paragon.

Amor & la Juventud. Joan Goetze. Tr. by Lidia D. Montero from Eng. Orig. Title: Let's Look at Love. (Illus.). 1979. Repr. of 1975 ed. 1.70 (ISBN 0-311-46058-5, Edit Mundo). Casa Bautista.

Amor, Asombroso Amor. Corrie T. Boom. Orig. Title: Amazing Love. 1980. pap. 1.80 (ISBN 0-311-40035-3, Edit Mundo). Casa Bautista.

Amor, Fe y Esperanza. Adolfo Robleto. (No. 2). 1980. 1.80 (ISBN 0-311-08757-4). Casa Bautista.

Amorelle. Grace L. Hill. 320p. Repr. of 1934 ed. lib. bdg. 13.30x (ISBN 0-89190-055-1). Am Repr-Rivercity Pr.

Amorelle, No. 4. Grace L. Hill. 224p. 1980. pap. 1.95 (ISBN 0-553-13726-3). Bantam.

Amores. Ovid. Ed. by E. J. Kenney. Incl. Medicamina Faciei Femineae; Ars Amatoria; Remedia Amoria. (Oxford Classical Texts Ser). 1961. 15.95x (ISBN 0-19-814642-6). Oxford U Pr.

Amorotica: A New Collection of Erotic Poetry. Ed. by Elliot Fried. (Illus.). 144p. 1981. 12.95 (ISBN 0-935232-05-2); pap. 8.95 (ISBN 0-935232-04-4). Deep River Pr. Postponed.

Amorphous & Liquid Semiconductors, 2 vols. Ed. by J. Stuke & W. Brenig. LC 74-12437. 1441p. 1974. Set. 124.95 (ISBN 0-470-83485-4). Halsted Pr.

Amorphous Solids. Ed. by W. A. Phillips. (Topics in Current Physics Ser.: Vol. 24). (Illus.). 190p. 1981. 32.00 (ISBN 0-387-10330-9). Springer-Verlag.

Amorum Emblemata....Emblemes of Love. Otho V. Vaenius. Ed. by Stephen Orgel. LC 78-68196. (Philosophy of Images Ser.: Vol. 9). (Illus.). 1980. lib. bdg. 66.00 (ISBN 0-8240-3683-2). Garland Pub.

Amos. Ray Beeley. pap. 1.45 o.p. (ISBN 0-686-12507-X). Banner of Truth.

Amos Among the Prophets: Composition & Theology. Robert B. Coote. 144p. 1981. pap. 5.50 (ISBN 0-8006-1400-3, 1-1400). Fortress.

Amos & Boris. William Steig. LC 72-165403. (Illus.). 32p. (ps-3). 1971. 7.95 (ISBN 0-374-30278-2). FS&G.

Amos & Hosea. W. R. Harper. LC 5-7893. (International Critical Commentary Ser.). 608p. Repr. of 1905 ed. text ed. 20.00x (ISBN 0-567-05018-1). Attic Pr.

Amos' Oracles Against the Nations. J. Barton. LC 78-67630. (Society for Old Testament Study Ser.). 1980. 17.50 (ISBN 0-521-22501-9). Cambridge U Pr.

Amount & Sharing of Aid. Jagdish N. Bhagwati. LC 73-123777. (Monographs: No. 2). 208p. 1970. 1.50 (ISBN 0-686-28693-6). Overseas Dev Council.

Amour, L'Amitie et Laa Fourberie: Une Etude Des Premieres Comedies De Corneille. Cynthia B. Kerr. (Stanford French & Italian Studies: Vol. 20). 152p. (Fr.). 1980. pap. 20.00 (ISBN 0-915838-19-2). Anma Libri.

Amours of Edward the Fourth: An Historical Novel. Bd. with Elysium: The State of Love & Honour in the Superior Regions of Bliss. LC 78-170503. (Foundations of the Novel Ser.: Vol. 1). lib. bdg. 50.00 (ISBN 0-8240-0513-9). Garland Pub.

Amours of Phillaris & Olinda: Or the Intrigues of Windsor, Repr. Of 1730. Bd. with Forced Virgin: or the Unnatural Mother. LC 70-170577; Narzanes: or the Injured Statesman. LC 70-170578; Unparallel'd Imposter: or the Whole Life Artifices & Forgeries of Japhet Cook, Alias Sir Peter Stranger. LC 70-170579. LC 70-170576. (Foundations of the Novel Ser.: Vol. 54). lib. bdg. 50.00 (ISBN 0-8240-0566-X). Garland Pub.

Ampharic Letters of Emperor Theodore of Ethiopia. Ed. by Girma-Selassie Asfaw et al. (Oriental Documents-British Academy Ser.). 1979. pap. 24.00x (ISBN 0-19-725988-X). Oxford U Pr.

Amphetamine Abuse. Ed. by J. Robert Russo. (Illus.). 176p. 1972. photocopy ed. spiral 17.50 (ISBN 0-398-01635-6). C C Thomas.

Amphetamines & Related Stimulants, Vol. 1. John Caldwell. 1980. 59.95 (ISBN 0-8493-5347-5). CRC Pr.

Amphibian in Transplantation Immunity. Ed. by E. P. Volpe. (Monographs in Developmental Biology: Vol. 14). (Illus.). x, 150p. 1980. pap. 74.25 (ISBN 3-8055-1087-X). S Karger.

Amphibians. J. F. Frazer & O. H. Frazer. (Wykeham Science Ser.: No. 25). 1972. 9.95x (ISBN 0-8448-1152-1). Crane Russak Co.

Amphibians & Reptiles of California. Robert C. Stebbins. LC 72-165229. (California Natural History Guides: No. 31). Orig. Title: Reptiles & Amphibians of the San Francisco Bay Area. (Illus.). 112p. 1972. pap. 5.95 (ISBN 0-520-02090-1). U of Cal Pr.

Amphibians: Guidelines for the Breeding, Care & Management of Laboratory Animals. Institute of Laboratory Animal Resources. (Illus.). 160p. 1974. pap. 10.75 (ISBN 0-309-02210-X). Natl Acad Pr.

Amphibians of North America. Hobart M. Smith. (Golden Field Guide Ser.). (Illus.). 1978. 7.95 (ISBN 0-307-47008-3, Golden Pr); PLB 10.00 (ISBN 0-307-63662-3); pap. 4.95 (ISBN 0-307-13662-0). Western Pub.

Amphibious Campaign for West Florida & Louisiana, 1814-1815: A Critical Review of Strategy & Tactics at New Orleans. Wilburt S. Brown. LC 68-10992. (Illus.). 253p. 1969. 15.95 o.p. (ISBN 0-8173-5100-0). U of Ala Pr.

Amphibious Weather. Sue Standing. (Orig.). 1981. pap. 2.25 (ISBN 0-939010-02-X). Zephyr.

Amphitryon. Moliere. (Documentation thematique). (Fr.). pap. 2.95 (ISBN 0-685-92173-5, 203). Larousse.

Amphitryon & Two Other Plays. Plautus. Ed. by Lionel Casson. 1971. pap. 4.95 (ISBN 0-393-00601-8, Norton Lib.). Norton.

Amphitryon: Three Plays in New Verse Translation. Tr. by Charles E. Passage & James H. Mantinband. (Studies in Comparative Literature: No. 57). 307p. 1974. 16.50x (ISBN 0-8078-7057-9); pap. 8.00 (ISBN 0-8078-7057-9). U of NC Pr.

Amphoras & the Ancient Wine Trade. Virginia R. Grace. (Excavations of the Athenian Agora Picture Bks.: No. 6). (Illus.). 1979. pap. 1.50x (ISBN 0-87661-619-8). Am Sch Athens.

Amphoteric Surfactants. Bluestein. Date not set. price not set (ISBN 0-8247-1277-3). Dekker.

Amphoto Guide to Special Effects. Lida Moser. (Illus.). 168p. 1980. 10.95 (ISBN 0-8174-3523-9); pap. 6.95 (ISBN 0-8174-3524-7). Amphoto.

Amphoto Pocket Companion: Konica TC & FS-I. Bob Mitchell. (Illus.). 128p. 1980. pap. 4.95 spiral bdg. (ISBN 0-8174-5525-6). Amphoto.

Amphoto Pocket Companion: Yashica FR, FR-I & FR-II. Milton Heiberg. (Illus.). 128p. 1980. spiral bdg. 4.95 (ISBN 0-8174-5534-5). Amphoto.

Amphoto Travel Guides. Al Moldvay & Erica Fabian. 1980. 5.95 ea. Watson-Guptill.

Amplified New Testament. 1968. pap. 2.25 o.s.i. (ISBN 0-515-04666-3). Jove Pubns.

Ampurias Exchange. Angus Ross. 1977. 6.95 o.s.i. (ISBN 0-8027-5364-7). Walker & Co.

Amputation Surgery & Rehabilitation: The Toronto Experience. Ed. by J. P. Kostuik & Robert Gillespie. (Illus.). 1981. text ed. price not set (ISBN 0-443-08024-0). Churchill. Postponed.

Amrita - Liber CCCXLIII. Alastor DeKerval, pseud. LC 77-8311. 1980. 45.00 (ISBN 0-913576-29-8); deluxe ed. (ISBN 0-913576-19-0). Thelema Pubns.

Amsterdam. Hans Konig. (Great Cities Ser.). (Illus.). 1977. lib. bdg. 14.94 (ISBN 0-686-51000-3). Silver.

Amsterdam. Hans Koning. Ed. by Time-Life Books. (Great Cities Ser.). (Illus.). 1977. 14.95 (ISBN 0-8094-2290-5). Time-Life.

Amsterdam: Capital City of the Netherlands. Jan Weggalaer. (Q Books: Famous Cities). (Illus.). (gr. 3-6). 1978. 3.95 (ISBN 0-8467-0446-3, Pub. by Two Continents). Hippocrene Bks.

Amsterdam in the Age of Rembrandt. John J. Murray. (Centers of Civilization Ser.: No. 21). 5.95x o.p. (ISBN 0-8061-0746-4). U of Okla Pr.

Amsterdam to Nairobi: The World Council of Churches & the Third World. Ernest Lefever. 126p. 1979. 10.00 (ISBN 0-89633-025-7); pap. 5.00 (ISBN 0-89633-024-9). Ethics & Public Policy.

Amtrak Story: A Pictorial History. Earl P. Williams, Jr. 1979. pap. 5.50 (ISBN 0-685-80663-4). Maryland Hist Pr.

Amulet. Michael McDowell. 352p. 1980. pap. 2.50 (ISBN 0-380-40584-9, 40584). Avon.

Amusemens De Spa; or, the Gallantries of the Spaw in Germany, Pt. 1. Karl L. Pollnitz. LC 78-170597. (Foundations of the Novel Ser.: Vol. 67). lib. bdg. 50.00 (ISBN 0-8240-0579-1). Garland Pub.

Amusemens De Spa; or, the Gallantries of the Spaw in Germany, Pt. 2. Karl L. Pollnitz. LC 78-170597. (Foundations of the Novel Ser.: Vol. 68). lib. bdg. 50.00 (ISBN 0-8240-0580-5). Garland Pub.

Amusement Park Machines. Christine Hahn. LC 78-26920. (Machine World Ser.). (Illus.). (gr. 2-4). 1979. PLB 9.95 (ISBN 0-8172-1330-9). Raintree Pubs.

Amusettes. Steckman & Sklarew. (Illus.). (gr. 7-9). 1973. pap. text ed. 3.50 (ISBN 0-88345-185-9, 18082). Regents Pub.

Amy. Paul Ricchiuti. (Uplook Ser.). 1976. pap. 0.75 (ISBN 0-8163-0252-9, 01550-3). Pacific Pr Pub Assn.

Amy & the Cloudbasket. Ellen Pratt. LC 75-25035. (Illus.). 38p. (Orig.). (ps-3). 1975. pap. 3.00 (ISBN 0-914996-08-8). Lollipop Power.

Amy Carmichael of Dohnavur. Frank Houghton. 7.95 (ISBN 0-87508-063-4); pap. 5.95 (ISBN 0-87508-084-7). Chr Lit.

Amy for Short. Laura J. Numeroff. LC 76-8842. (Ready to Read Ser.). (Illus.). 48p. (gr. 1-4). 1976. 7.95 (ISBN 0-02-768180-7, 76818). Macmillan.

Amy Jean. Lorinda Hagen. 1976. pap. 1.75 o.p. (ISBN 0-505-51151-7). Tower Bks.

Amy: The World of Amy Lowell & the Imagist Movement. Jean Gould. LC 75-11563. 350p. 1975. 12.50 (ISBN 0-396-07022-1). Dodd.

Amy Vanderbilt Complete Book of Etiquette: A Guide to Contemporary Living. Amy Vanderbilt. Rev. by Letitia Balderige. 272p. 1981. pap. 3.50 (ISBN 0-553-14582-7). Bantam.

Amy Vanderbilt Complete Book of Etiquette. rev. ed. Letitia Baldridge. LC 77-16896. 1978. 11.95 (ISBN 0-385-13375-8); thumb-indexed 12.95 (ISBN 0-385-14238-2). Doubleday.

Amy's Dinosaur. Syd Hoff. LC 80-14082. (Illus.). 48p. (ps-2). 1980. pap. 3.95 (ISBN 0-671-41338-4, Pub. by Windmill). S&S.

Ana. Gordon Stowell. Tr. by S. D. De Lerin from English. (Libros Pescaditos Sobre Personajes Biblicos). (Illus.). 1978. pap. 0.40 (ISBN 0-311-38512-5, Edit Mundo). Casa Bautista.

Anabantoids Gouramis & Related Species. Robert J. Goldstein. (Illus.). 7.95 (ISBN 0-87666-750-7, PS672). TFH Pubns.

Anabaptists & Thomas Muntzer. James M. Stayer & Werner O. Packull. 176p. 1980. pap. text ed. 9.95 (ISBN 0-8403-2235-6). Kendall-Hunt.

Anacoluthon. Tom Bridwell. (Orig.). 1980. limited signed ed. 20.00x (ISBN 0-915316-79-X); pap. 5.00x (ISBN 0-915316-78-1). Pentagram.

Anaerobic Bacteria: Selected Topics. Ed. by Dwight W. Lambe et al. 324p. 1980. 29.50 (ISBN 0-686-63458-6, Plenum Pr). Plenum Pub.

Anaerobic Bacteriology: Clinical & Laboratory Practice. 3rd ed. A. T. Willis. 1977. 24.95 (ISBN 0-407-00081-X). Butterworths.

Anaerobic Bacteriology for the Clinical Laboratory. Sylvia Silver. LC 79-23329. 1980. pap. 9.50 (ISBN 0-8016-4625-1). Mosby.

Anaerobic Digestion. Ed. by D. A. Stafford et al. (Illus.). xii, 528p. 1980. 95.00x (ISBN 0-85334-904-5). Burgess-Intl Ideas.

Anaerobic Fermentation of Agricultural Residue: Potential for Improvement & Implementation. U.S. Dept. of Energy. 455p. 1981. pap. 39.50 (ISBN 0-89934-099-7). Solar Energy Info.

Anaesthesia for Eye, Ear, Nose & Throat Surgery. D. F. Morrow & J. D. Morrison. (Illus.). 160p. 1975. text ed. 18.95 o.s.i. (ISBN 0-443-01187-7). Churchill.

Anaesthetics for Medical Students. 9th ed. Gordon Ostlere & Roger Bryce-Smith. 148p. 1981. text ed. 9.75 (ISBN 0-443-01863-4). Churchill.

Anagraphs: A Slew of Sight Puzzles. Helen E. Estes. LC 80-54813. 1981. pap. 2.95. Walker & Co.

Anais Nin. Bettina L. Knapp. LC 78-57692. (Modern Literature Ser.). 1978. 10.95 (ISBN 0-8044-2481-0); pap. 3.45 (ISBN 0-8044-6371-9). Ungar.

Anais Nin: An Introduction. Benjamin Franklin & Duane Schneider. LC 79-10635. 1980. 16.00x (ISBN 0-8214-0395-8). Ohio U Pr.

Anais Nin: An Introduction. Benjamin Franklin & Duane Schneider. LC 79-10635. 309p. 1980. pap. 8.50x (ISBN 0-8214-0432-6). Ohio U Pr.

Anais Nin Observed: Portrait of a Woman As Artist. Robert Snyder. LC 76-3123. (Illus.). 116p. 1976. pap. 9.95 (ISBN 0-8040-0708-X). Swallow.

Anais Nin Reader. Ed. by Philip K. Jason. LC 72-91913. 316p. 1972. 10.00 o.p. (ISBN 0-8040-0595-8); pap. 7.95 (ISBN 0-8040-0596-6). Swallow.

Analecta Dublinensia. Ed. by Marvin L. Colker. 1975. 22.00 o.p. (ISBN 0-910956-56-1). Medieval.

Analects of Confucius. Arthur D. Waley. 1938. 13.50 o.p. (ISBN 0-04-181002-3). Allen Unwin.

Analise. Lisa Gregory. 304p. (Orig.). 1981. pap. 2.75 (ISBN 0-515-05469-0). Jove Pubns.

Analiz, Stil' I Veyanie: O Romanakh Gr. L. N. Tolstogo. Konstantin Leontiev. LC 65-24667. (Slavic Reprint Ser.: No. 3). 158p. (Rus.). 1968. pap. 3.00 (ISBN 0-87057-090-0, Pub. by Brown U Pr). Univ Pr of New England.

Analog & Digital Communication Systems. Martin Roden. 1979. 25.95 (ISBN 0-13-032722-0). P-H.

Analog & Digital Communications: Concepts, Systems & Applications, & Services in Electrical Dissemination of Aural, Visual & Data Information. W. David Gregg. LC 76-58417. 1977. text ed. 30.95 (ISBN 0-471-32661-5). Wiley.

Analog & Hybrid Computing. D. E. Hyndman. LC 75-120691. 1970. 25.00 (ISBN 0-08-015573-1); pap. 13.25 (ISBN 0-08-015572-3). Pergamon.

Analog Bullet. Martin Smith. 1978. pap. 1.50 (ISBN 0-505-51220-3). Tower Bks.

Analog Computer Programming. Rekoff. 1967. text ed. 17.95 (ISBN 0-675-09735-5). Merrill.

Analog I-O Design: Acquisition, Conversion, Recovery. Patrick Garrett. (Illus.). 1981. text ed. 21.95 (ISBN 0-8359-0208-0); solutions manual avail. Reston.

Analog Integrated Circuits. A. B. Grebene. (IEEE Reprint Ser.). 1978. 28.95 (ISBN 0-471-05210-8, Pub. by Wiley-Interscience); pap. 19.00x (ISBN 0-686-67364-6). Wiley.

Analog Integrated Circuits: Operational Amplifiers & Analog Multipliers. Miklos Herpy. 479p. 1980. 58.95 (ISBN 0-471-99604-1, Pub. by Wiley-Interscience). Wiley.

Analog MOS Integrated Circuits. Ed. by P. R. Gray et al. LC 80-22116. 1980. 30.95 (ISBN 0-87942-141-X). Inst Electrical.

Analog MOS Integrated Circuits. Paul Gray. 400p. 1980. 28.00 (ISBN 0-471-08966-4, Pub. by Wiley-Interscience); pap. 18.00 (ISBN 0-471-08964-8). Wiley.

Analog Science Fact Reader. Ed. by Ben Bova. LC 73-87398. 1976. pap. 8.95 (ISBN 0-312-03220-X). St Martin.

Analog Signal Processing & Instrumentation. A. F. Arbel. LC 79-13461. (Illus.). 1980. 77.50 (ISBN 0-521-22469-1). Cambridge U Pr.

Analog Systems for Microprocessors & Minicomputers. Patrick H. Garrett. (Illus.). 1978. 21.95 (ISBN 0-87909-035-9); instructor's manual free. Reston.

Analogical Imagination: Christian Theology & the Culture of Pluralism. David Tracy. 288p. 1981. 17.50 (ISBN 0-8245-0122-5). Crossroad NY.

Analog's Golden Anniversary Anthology. Ed. by Stanley Schmidt. 384p. 1980. 10.95 (ISBN 0-8037-0217-5). Davis Pubns.

Analoguing: Theory & Model Construction. Leonard C. Hawes. LC 74-19706. 1975. pap. text ed. 7.50 (ISBN 0-201-02822-0). A-W.

Analogy. Anttila. (Trends in Linguistics: No. 10). 1977. 25.30 (ISBN 9-0279-7975-8). Mouton.

Analogy: A Basic Bibliography. Raimo Antilla & Warren Brewer. (Library & Information Sources in Linguistics: No. 1). 1977. text ed. 17.25x (ISBN 0-391-01677-6). Humanities.

Analogy & Talking About God: A Critique of the Thomistic Approach. John S. Morreall. LC 77-18494. 1978. pap. text ed. 7.75 (ISBN 0-8191-0423-X). U Pr of Amer.

Analutical & Combinational Generalizations of the Rogers-Ramanujan Identities. David M. Bressoud. LC 79-27622. (Memoirs Ser.). 1980. 6.00 (ISBN 0-8218-2227-6, MEMO-227). Am Math.

Analylitic Methods in Communicative Algebra. Draper. Date not set. price not set (ISBN 0-8247-1282-X). Dekker.

Analyse Empirique De la Causalite. 3rd ed. Ed. by Raymond Boudon & Paul Lazarsfeld. (Methodes De la Sociologie: No. 2). 1976. pap. 20.50x (ISBN 90-2796-158-1). Mouton.

Analyse Socio-Economique De L'environement: Problemes De Methode. (Environment & Social Sciences: No. 3). 1973. pap. 20.50 (ISBN 90-2797-259-1). Mouton.

Analyse und Bewertung Von Pflanzengesell-Schaften Im Noerdliche Frankenjura - ein Beitrag Zum Problem der Quantifizierung Unter-Schiedlich Anthropogen Beeinflusster Oekosystems. H. J. Schuster. (Dissertationes Botanicae: No. 53). (Illus.). 482p. (Ger.). 1981. pap. text ed. 40.00x (ISBN 3-7682-1264-5, Pub. by Cramer Germany). Lubrecht & Cramer.

Analyses for Soil Structure Interaction: Effects for Nuclear Power Plants. Compiled by American Society of Civil Engineers. 1979. pap. text ed. 13.50 (ISBN 0-87262-183-9). Am Soc Civil Eng.

Analysing Foreign Policy: An Introduction to Some Conceptual Problems. Roy E. Jones. 1970. 8.95x o.p. (ISBN 0-7100-6810-7). Routledge & Kegan.

Analysing Jobs. M. B. Youngman et al. 168p. 1978. text ed. 26.50x (ISBN 0-566-02089-0, Pub. by Gower Pub Co England). Renouf.

Analysis. 2nd ed. O. Forster. Incl. No. 1. Differential & Integralrechnung Einer Veranderlichen. 208p. 1976 (ISBN 3-528-07224-5); No. 2. Differentialrechnung im Rn Gewohnliche Differentialgleichungen. 1977. (Mathematik Grundkurs Ser.). (Ger.). pap. 9.00 ea. Birkhauser.

Analysis a Public Issues: Decision-Making in a Democracy. James P. Shaver & A. Guy Larkins. 232p. (gr. 9-12). 1973. pap. text ed. 10.88 (ISBN 0-395-13466-8); tchrs. guide & ans. key pap. 17.22 (ISBN 0-395-13467-6). HM.

Analysis & Adjustment of Survey Measurements. Edward M. Mikhail & Gordon Gracie. 368p. 1980. text ed. 28.50 (ISBN 0-442-25369-9). Van Nos Reinhold.

Analysis & Application of Rare Earth Materials. Odd B. Michelsen. 374p. 1973. 57.00x (ISBN 8-200-04780-6, Dist. by Columbia U Pr). Universitet.

Analysis & Control of Less-Desirable Flavors in Foods & Beverages. Ed. by George Charalambous. 1980. 24.50 (ISBN 0-12-169065-2). Acad Pr.

Analysis & Design in Geotechnical Engineering, 2 vols. Compiled By American Society of Civil Engineers. 1975. Set. pap. text ed. 26.00 (ISBN 0-87262-121-9). Am Soc Civil Eng.

Analysis & Design of Certain Quantitative Multiresponse Experiments. S. N. Roy et al. 314p. 1971. 25.00 (ISBN 0-08-006917-7). Pergamon.

Analysis & Design of Integrated Electronic Circuits. Paul M. Chirlian. (Illus.). 976p. 1981. text ed. 31.50 scp (ISBN 0-06-041266-6, HarpC); avail. Har-Row.

Analysis & Design of Sequential Digital Systems. L. F. Lind & J. C. Nelson. LC 76-49959. 1977. 25.95 (ISBN 0-470-99021-X). Halsted Pr.

Analysis & Design of Structural Sandwich Panels. H. G. Allen. 1969. text ed. 29.00 (ISBN 0-08-012870-X); pap. text ed. 17.00 (ISBN 0-08-012869-6). Pergamon.

Analysis & Forecasting of the British Economy. M. J. Surrey. LC 75-171683. (National Institute of Economic & Social Research, Occasional Papers: No. 25). (Illus.). 100p. 1972. 15.50x (ISBN 0-521-09675-8). Cambridge U Pr.

Analysis & Optimization of Systems: Proceedings. Ed. by A. Bensoussan & J. L. Lions. (Lecture Notes in Control & Information Sciences Ser.: Vol. 28). 999p. 1981. pap. 57.90 (ISBN 0-387-10472-0). Springer-Verlag.

Analysis & Presentation of Experimental Results. R. H. Leaver & T. R. And Thomas. LC 74-30111. 1974. text ed. 10.95 (ISBN 0-470-52027-2). Halsted Pr.

Analysis & Synthesis of Linear Time-Variable Systems. Allen R. Stubberud. 1965. 18.00x (ISBN 0-520-01230-5). U of Cal Pr.

Analysis & Synthesis of Time Delay Systems. Henryk Gorecki et al. LC 79-40508. 1980. write for info. (ISBN 0-471-27622-7, Pub by Wiley-Interscience). Wiley.

Analysis & Valuation of Retail Locations. Edwin Rams. 1976. 29.95 (ISBN 0-87909-033-2). Reston.

Analysis, Computation, Presentation of Engineering Information. Robert M. Barnett. 8.50 (ISBN 0-89741-000-9); pap. 5.00 (ISBN 0-89741-000-9). Roadrunner Tech.

Analysis, Design & Implementation of Information Systems. rev. ed. Henry C. Lucas. (Management Information Systems Ser.). (Illus.). 416p. 1980. text ed. 23.95 (ISBN 0-07-038927-6, C); instructor's manual 9.95 (ISBN 0-07-038928-4). McGraw.

Analysis for Action: Nursing Care of the Elderly. Shirley R. Good & Susan S. Rodgers. (Illus.). 1980. pap. text ed. 10.95 (ISBN 0-13-032623-2). P-H.

Analysis for Marketing Decisions. James H. Donnelly et al. 1970. text ed. 14.95x o.p. (ISBN 0-256-00139-1). Irwin.

Analysis Manual for Hospital Information Systems. Owen Doyle et al. (Illus.). 463p. (Orig.). 1980. pap. text ed. 42.50 (ISBN 0-914904-41-8). Health Admin Pr.

Analysis of Air Pollutants. Peter O. Warner. LC 75-26685. (Environmental Science & Technology Ser.). 329p. 1976. 33.00 (ISBN 0-471-92107-6, Pub. by Wiley-Interscience). Wiley.

Analysis of Binary Data. D. R. Cox. (Monographs on Applied Probability & Statistics). 142p. 1970. text ed. 14.50x o.p. (ISBN 0-412-15340-8, Pub. by Chapman & Hall). Methuen Inc.

Analysis of Binary Data. D. R. Cox. (Moonographs on Applied Probability & Statistics). 1970. 10.95 o.p. (ISBN 0-470-18125-7). Halsted Pr.

Analysis of Biological Materials: Proceedings of a Conference Held in Pretoria, South Africa, October 1977. Ed. by L. R. Butler. (Illus.). 1979. 37.00 (ISBN 0-08-022853-4). Pergamon.

Analysis of Capital Cost Recovery. (Statement of Tax Policy Ser.: No. 7). 1980. pap. 3.50. Am Inst CPA.

Analysis of Categorical Data: Dual Scaling & Its Applications. Shizuhiko Nishisato. (Mathematical Expositions Ser.). 148p. 1980. 25.00x (ISBN 0-8020-5489-7). U of Toronto Pr.

Analysis of Certain Major Classes of Upper Palaeolitic Tools. Hallam L. Movius, Jr. et al. LC 68-55995. (ASPR Bulletin: No. 26). 1969. pap. text ed. 10.00 (ISBN 0-87365-527-3). Peabody Harvard.

Analysis of Color Changes & Social Behavior of Tilapia Mossambica. E. H. Neil. (U. C. Publ. in Zoology: Vol. 75.1). 1964. pap. 5.50x (ISBN 0-520-09330-5). U of Cal Pr.

Analysis of Convariance & Alternatives. Bradley E. Huitema. LC 80-11319. 1980. 27.50 (ISBN 0-471-42044-1, Pub. by Wiley-Interscience). Wiley.

Analysis of Covariance. Albert R. Wildt & Olli Vahtola. LC 78-64331. (University Papers Ser.: Quantitative Applications in the Social Sciences No. 12). 1978. pap. 3.50x (ISBN 0-8039-1164-5). Sage.

Analysis of Cross-Classified Categorical Data. 2nd ed. Stephen Fienberg. 1980. text ed. 14.00x (ISBN 0-262-06071-X). MIT Pr.

Analysis of Design & Fabrication of Welded Structures. Masubuchi. 1980. 120.00 (ISBN 0-08-022714-7). Pergamon.

Analysis of Dietary Fiber in Food. Theander & James. 288p. 1981. 35.00 (ISBN 0-8247-1192-0). Dekker.

Analysis of Educational Costs & Expenditure. J. Hallak. (Fundamentals of Educational Planning Ser., No. 10). (Orig.). 1969. pap. 6.00 (ISBN 92-803-1029-1, U16, UNESCO). Unipub.

Analysis of Electric Circuits. 2nd ed. Egon Brenner & M. Javid. (Electrical & Electronic Engineering Ser.). 1967. text ed. 29.95 (ISBN 0-07-007630-8, C); instructor's manual 2.75 (ISBN 0-07-007636-7); answers bk. 2.50 (ISBN 0-07-007635-9). McGraw.

Analysis of Electric Circuits. Frederick Driscoll, Jr. LC 72-3691. (Illus.). 544p. 1973. text ed. 19.95 (ISBN 0-13-032912-6). P-H.

Analysis of Engineering Cycles. 2nd ed. R. W. Haywood. LC 74-7056. 1975. text ed. 21.00 o.p. (ISBN 0-08-017947-9); pap. text ed. 11.75 o.p. (ISBN 0-08-017948-7). Pergamon.

Analysis of Engineering Cycles. 3rd ed. R. W. Haywood. LC 79-41225. (Illus.). 320p. 1980. 45.00 (ISBN 0-08-025441-1); pap. text ed. 15.75 (ISBN 0-08-025440-3). Pergamon.

Analysis of Essential Oils by Gas Chromatography & Mass Spectrometry. Yoshiro Masada. LC 75-46590. 1976. 59.95 (ISBN 0-470-15019-X). Halsted Pr.

Analysis of Euclidian Space. K. Hoffman. 1975. text ed. 23.95 (ISBN 0-13-032656-9). P-H.

Analysis of Explosives. Jehuda Yinon & Shmuel Zitrin. (Pergamon Ser. in Analytic Chemistry: Vol. 3). (Illus.). 300p. 1981. 60.00 (ISBN 0-08-023846-7); pap. 25.00 (ISBN 0-08-023845-9). Pergamon.

Analysis of Financial Statements. Leopold A. Bernstein. LC 78-55533. 1978. 13.95 (ISBN 0-87094-164-X). Dow Jones-Irwin.

Analysis of Groundwater Flow. A. J. Raudkivi & R. A. Callander. LC 76-10776. 1976. 28.50 o.p. (ISBN 0-470-15117-X). Halsted Pr.

Analysis of Health Care Delivery. James M. Rosser & Howard E. Mossberg. LC 80-11611. 188p. 1980. Repr. of 1977 ed. lib. bdg. write for info. (ISBN 0-89874-158-0). Krieger.

Analysis of Indian Agro-Ecosystems. Rodger Mitchell. (Environmental Science Ser.). 180p. 1980. 6.50x (ISBN 0-89955-329-X, Pub. by Interprint India). Intl Schol Bk Serv.

Analysis of Information Systems. 2nd ed. Charles Meadow. LC 72-11518. (Information Sciences Ser.). 416p. 1973. 27.50 (ISBN 0-471-59002-9, Pub. by Wiley-Interscience). Wiley.

Analysis of International Politics. James Rosenau et al. LC 70-184005. 1972. 17.95 (ISBN 0-02-927030-8). Free Pr.

Analysis of International Relations. 2nd ed. K. Deutsch. (Foundations of Modern Political Science Ser.). 1978. pap. 9.95 (ISBN 0-13-033217-8). P-H.

Analysis of Inventory Systems. George Hadley & T. M. Whitin. (Illus.). 1963. ref. ed. 21.00 (ISBN 0-13-032953-3). P-H.

Analysis of John Barth's Weltanschauung: His View of Life & Literature. Evelyn Glaser-Wohrer. (Salzburg Studies in English Literature: No. 5). 1977. pap. text ed. 31.25x (ISBN 0-391-01385-8). Humanities.

Analysis of Leaf Development. R. Maksymowych. LC 72-83585. (Developmental & Cell Biology Monographs: No. 1). (Illus.). 112p. 1973. 35.50 (ISBN 0-521-20017-2). Cambridge U Pr.

Analysis of Linear Circuits: Passive & Active Components. Victor M. Rooney. 608p. 1975. text ed. 19.95 (ISBN 0-675-08886-0); instructor's manual 3.95 (ISBN 0-675-08886-0). Merrill.

Analysis of Linear Networks & Systems: A Matrix-Oriented Approach with Computer Applications. Shu-Park Chan et al. LC 70-156589. 1972. text ed. 25.95 (ISBN 0-201-00953-6). A-W.

Analysis of Linear Systems. D. G. Cheng. 1959. 22.95 (ISBN 0-201-01020-8). A-W.

Analysis of Marine Steam Indicator Diagrams. J. S. Mackay. 130p. 1949. 27.50x (ISBN 0-85264-019-6, Pub. by Griffin England). State Mutual Bk.

Analysis of Metallurgical Failures. Vito J. Colangelo & F. A. Heiser. LC 73-19773. (Science & Technology of Materials Ser). 384p. 1974. 33.00 (ISBN 0-471-16450-X, Pub. by Wiley-Interscience). Wiley.

Analysis of Mineral Number Four. Moses Goldberg. (Orig.). 1981. playscript 2.00 (ISBN 0-87602-234-4). Anchorage.

Analysis of Mississippi Industrial Location Factors. William F. Davidge & Kenneth W. Hollman. 1978. 4.00 (ISBN 0-938004-02-6). U MS Bus Econ.

Analysis of Motives: Early American Psychology & Fiction. Allan G. Smith. (Costerus Ser.). 189p. 1980. pap. text ed. 23.00x (ISBN 90-6203-861-1). Humanities.

Analysis of Music. John D. White. 1976. 15.50 (ISBN 0-13-033233-X). P-H.

Analysis of Nominal Data. H. T. Reynolds. LC 77-72851. (University Papers: Quantitative Applications in the Social Sciences, No. 7). 1977. 3.50x (ISBN 0-8039-0653-6). Sage.

Analysis of Numerical Methods. Eugene Isaacson & H. B. Keller. LC 66-17630. 1966. 30.95 (ISBN 0-471-42865-5). Wiley.

Analysis of Organizations. 2nd ed. Joseph A. Litterer. LC 72-8586. (Management & Administration Ser). (Illus.). 640p. 1973. text ed. 23.50x (ISBN 0-471-54106-0). Wiley.

Analysis of Organoaluminium & Organozinc Compounds. T. R. Crompton. 1968. text ed. 56.00 (ISBN 0-08-012578-6). Pergamon.

Analysis of Outdoor Recreation Demand: A Review & Annotated Bibliography of the Current State-of-the-Art. Richard H. Eathorne. (Public Administration Ser.: Bibliography P-563). 93p. 1980. pap. 10.00. Vance Biblios.

Analysis of Police Concepts & Programs. David A. Hansen. (Illus.). 144p. 1972. 12.75 (ISBN 0-398-02464-2). C C Thomas.

Analysis of Policy Arguments. Ralph S. Hambrick, Jr. & William P. Snyder. (Learning Packages in the Policy Sciences: No. 13). 72p. (Orig.). 1979. pap. text ed. 3.50 (ISBN 0-936826-02-9). Pol Stud Assocs.

Analysis of Policy Impact. Ed. by John Grumm & Stephen Wasby. 1980. pap. 5.00 (ISBN 0-918592-39-9). Policy Studies.

Analysis of Policy Impact. Ed. by John G. Grumm & Stephen L. Wasby. (Policy Studies Orgnization Bk.). 224p. 1981. 23.95x (ISBN 0-669-03951-9). Lexington Bks.

Analysis of Primary Medical Care. W. J. Stephen. LC 77-83999. (Illus.). 1979. 37.50 (ISBN 0-521-21860-8). Cambridge U Pr.

Analysis of Public Systems. Ed. by Alvin W. Drake et al. 480p. 1972. 24.00x (ISBN 0-262-04038-7). MIT Pr.

Analysis of Qualitative Data, Vol. I: Introductory Topics (TXX) Shelby Haberman. LC 77-25731. 1978. 24.50 (ISBN 0-12-312501-4). Acad Pr.

Analysis of Road Expenditures & Payments by Vehicle Class (1956-1975) Kiran U. Bhatt et al. (Institute Paper). 282p. 1977. pap. 7.00 (ISBN 0-87766-188-X, 18400). Urban Inst.

Analysis of Second Congress of Young Communist League (UJC) in Cuba. 1972. pap. 1.00 o.p. (ISBN 0-8270-2955-1). OAS.

Analysis of Social Skill. Ed. by W. T. Singleton et al. (NATO Conference Ser., Series III, Human Factors: Vol. II). 350p. 1980. 35.00 (ISBN 0-306-40337-4). Plenum Pub.

Analysis of Statically Indeterminate Structures. John I. Parcel & R. B. Moorman. 1955. 32.50 (ISBN 0-471-65868-5, Pub. by Wiley-Interscience). Wiley.

Analysis of Structural Member Systems. Jerome J. Connor, Jr. LC 74-22535. 1976. 33.95 o.p. (ISBN 0-8260-2098-4). Wiley.

Analysis of Structural Systems for Torsion. 1973. pap. 23.25 (ISBN 0-685-85112-5, SP-35) (ISBN 0-685-85113-3). ACI.

Analysis of Structures: Based on the Minimal Principles & the Principle of Virtual Displacement. Nicholas J. Hoff. LC 56-6503. 1956. 30.00 (ISBN 0-471-40590-6, Pub. by Wiley-Interscience). Wiley.

Analysis of Structures by the Force-Displacement Method. M. Smolira. xii, 389p. 1980. 62.50 (ISBN 0-85334-814-6, Pub. by Applied Science). Burgess-Intl Ideas.

Analysis of Subjective Culture. Ed. by Harry C. Triandis. LC 74-178910. (Comparative Studies in Behavioral Science Ser). 1972. 34.50 (ISBN 0-471-88905-9, Pub. by Wiley-Interscience). Wiley.

Analysis of Tall Buildings by the Force Displacement Method. M. Smolira. LC 74-19011. 299p. 1975. 49.95 (ISBN 0-470-80620-6). Halsted Pr.

Analysis of Teaching Physical Education. Anderson. LC 79-20074. 1979. pap. 8.95 (ISBN 0-8016-0179-7). Mosby.

Analysis of the Distribution of Pocket Gopher Species in Northeastern California (Genus Thomomys). C. S. Thaeler, Jr. (U. C. Publ. in Zoology: Vol. 86). 1968. pap. 6.50x (ISBN 0-520-09343-7). U of Cal Pr.

Analysis of the Energy Efficiency & Economic Viability of Expanded Magnesium Utilization. George B. Kenney. LC 78-75004. (Outstanding Dissertations on Energy Ser.). 1979. lib. bdg. 20.00 (ISBN 0-8240-3975-0). Garland Pub.

Analysis of "The Institute of the Christian Religion" of John Calvin. Ford L. Battles & John Walchenbach. 1980. pap. 10.95 (ISBN 0-8010-0766-6). Baker Bk.

Analysis of the Interchurch World Movement Report on the Steel Strike. Marshall Olds. LC 73-139199. (Civil Liberties in American History Ser). 1971. Repr. of 1923 ed. lib. bdg. 47.50 (ISBN 0-306-70082-4). Da Capo.

Analysis of the Labor-Intensive Continuous Rice Production System. (IRRI Research Paper Ser.: No. 29). 39p. 1979. pap. 5.00 (R069, IRRI). Unipub.

Analysis of the Law. Matthew Hale & Jacob Giles. Ed. by David S. Berkowitz & Samuel E. Thorne. LC 77-86566. (Classics of English Legal History in the Modern Era Ser.: Vol. 8). 435p. 1979. lib. bdg. 40.00 (ISBN 0-8240-3057-5). Garland Pub.

Analysis of the Lexicographic Resources Used by American Biblical Scholars Today. John E. Gates. LC 72-88670. (Society of Biblical Literature. Dissertation Ser.). (Illus.). 1972. pap. text ed. 7.50 (ISBN 0-89130-164-X, 060108). Scholars Pr Ca.

Analysis of the Poetic Text. Yury Lotman. 296p. 1981. pap. 6.50 (ISBN 0-88233-107-8). Ardis Pubs.

Analysis of the Tangut Script. Eric Grinstead. (Scandinavian Inst. of Asian Studies: No. 10). 376p. 1975. pap. text ed. 21.00x (ISBN 0-7007-0059-5). Humanities.

Analysis of the Textual Character of the Bohairic Deuteronomy. Melvin K. Peters. LC 78-12958. (Society of Biblical Literature, Septuagint & Cognate Studies: No. 9). 1980. pap. 10.50 (ISBN 0-89130-264-6, 060409). Scholars Pr Ca.

Analysis of Thermally Stimulated Processes. Reuven Chen & D. Y. Kirsh. Date not set. 60.00 (ISBN 0-08-022930-1). Pergamon.

Analysis of Transference. Merton M. Gill. LC 80-15652. (Psychological Issues, Monograph: No. 53). 1981. text ed. 25.00 (ISBN 0-8236-0144-7, 00-0144). Intl Univs Pr.

Analysis of Turbulent Boundary Layers. Tuncer Cebeci & A. M. Smith. 1974. 51.00 (ISBN 0-12-164650-5); lib. ed. 65.00 (ISBN 0-12-164651-3); microfiche 37.00 (ISBN 0-12-164652-1). Acad Pr.

Analysis of Variance. Gudmund R. Iversen & Helmut Norpoth. LC 76-25695. (University Papers: Quantitative Applications in the Social Sciences, No. 1). 1976. 3.50x (ISBN 0-8039-0650-1). Sage.

Analysis of Variance. Henry Scheffe. LC 59-14994. (Wiley Series in Probability & Mathematical Statistics). (Illus.). 1959. 31.95 (ISBN 0-471-75834-5). Wiley.

Analysis of Variance in Complex Experimental Designs. Harold R. Lindman. LC 74-11211. (Illus.). 1974. text ed. 24.95x (ISBN 0-7167-0774-8); answers to exercises avail. W H Freeman.

Analysis of Vertebrate Structure. Milton Hildebrand. LC 73-11486. (Illus.). 704p. 1974. text ed. 26.50x (ISBN 0-471-39580-3). Wiley.

Analysis One. Serge A. Lang. 1968. 20.95 (ISBN 0-201-04172-3). A-W.

Analysis, Treatment & Disposal of Ferricyanide in Photographic Effluents. Eastman Kodak Company. 65p. 1979. pap. 5.75 (ISBN 0-87985-244-5, J-54). Eastman Kodak.

Analysis Two. Serge A. Lang. 1969. text ed. 22.95 (ISBN 0-201-04179-0). A-W.

Analysis with Ion-Selective Electrodes. J. Vesely et al. 1978. 67.95 (ISBN 0-470-26296-6). Halsted Pr.

Analyst's Guide to TRIM: The Transfer Income Model. Margaret B. Sulvetta. (Institute Paper). 104p. 1976. pap. 4.50 (ISBN 0-87766-182-0, 16500). Urban Inst.

Analytic Chemistry of the Condensed Phosphates. S. Greenfield & S. Clift. LC 74-32261. 1975. text ed. 27.00 (ISBN 0-08-018174-0). Pergamon.

Analytic Essays in Folklore. Alan Dundes. (Studies in Folklore Ser.: No. 2). 1975. pap. text ed. 28.25x (ISBN 90-279-3231-X). Mouton.

Analytic Function Theory, 2 vols. 2nd ed. Einar Hille. LC 73-647. 308p. 1973. 12.95. Vol. 1 (ISBN 0-8284-0269-8). Vol. 2 (ISBN 0-8284-0270-1). Chelsea Pub.

Analytic Functions Kozubnik 1979: Proceedings. Ed. by J. Lawrynowicz. (Lecture Notes in Mathematics: Vol. 798). 476p. 1980. pap. 27.00 (ISBN 0-387-09985-9). Springer-Verlag.

Analytic Genitive in the Modern Arabic Dialects. Kerstin E. Harning. (Orientalia Gothoburgensia Ser.: No. 5). 1981. pap. text ed. 17.00 (ISBN 91-7346-087-7). Humanities.

Analytic Geometry. Charles C. Carico & Irving Drooyan. LC 79-21633. 1980. 16.95 (ISBN 0-471-06435-1); student supplement avail. (ISBN 0-471-06378-9). Wiley.

Analytic Geometry. Cletus O. Oakley. (Illus., Orig.). 1957. pap. 3.95 (ISBN 0-06-460068-8, CO 68, COS). Har-Row.

Analytic Geometry. 3rd ed. Frederick H. Steen & D. H. Ballou. 1963. text ed. 17.95x (ISBN 0-471-00570-3). Wiley.

Analytic Geometry & the Calculus: Student Study Guide, 2 vols. 4th ed. A. W. Goodman. (Illus.). 1980. pap. text ed. 6.95 ea. Vol. I (ISBN 0-02-344970-5). Vol. II (ISBN 0-02-344980-2). Macmillan.

Analytic Geometry with Vectors. 2nd ed. Douglas F. Riddle. 1978. 18.95x (ISBN 0-534-00485-7). Wadsworth Pub.

Analytic Number Theory: An Introduction. R. Bellman. 1980. 19.50 (ISBN 0-8053-0360-X). A-W.

Analytic Philosophy of Education As a Sub-Discipline of Educology: An Introduction to Its Techniques & Application. James E. Christensen & Jamer E. Fisher. LC 79-66235. 1979. pap. text ed. 9.00 (ISBN 0-8191-0802-2). U Pr of Amer.

Analytic Properties of Feynman Diagrams in Quantum Field Theory. I. T. Todorov. Tr. by Clifford Risk. 168p. 1971. 27.00 (ISBN 0-08-016544-3). Pergamon.

Analytic Reading Inventory. 2nd ed. Mary L. Woods & Alden J. Moe. (Illus.). 160p. 1981. spiral bdg. 7.95 (ISBN 0-675-08059-2). Merrill.

Analytic S-Matrix. Richard J. Eden et al. 1966. 44.50 (ISBN 0-521-04869-9). Cambridge U Pr.

Analytic Theory of Continued Fractions. H. S. Wall. LC 66-24296. 14.95 (ISBN 0-8284-0207-8). Chelsea Pub.

Analytic Topology. Gordon T. Whyburn. LC 63-21794. (Colloquium Pbns. Ser.: Vol. 28). 1980. Repr. of 1971 ed. 26.00 (ISBN 0-8218-1028-6, COLL-28). Am Math.

Analytic Trigonometry with Applications. 2nd ed. Raymond Barnett. 1980. text ed. 17.95x (ISBN 0-534-00728-7). Wadsworth Pub.

Analytical & Critical Bibliography of the Tribes of Tierra Del Fuego & Adjacent Territory. John M. Cooper. (Map). 1967. pap. text ed. 13.50x (ISBN 90-6234-005-9). Humanities.

Analytical & Quantitative Methods in Microscopy. Ed. by G. A. Meek & H. Y. Elder. LC 76-22983. (Society for Experimental Biology Seminar Ser: No. 3). (Illus.). 1977. 42.50 (ISBN 0-521-21404-1); pap. 15.95x (ISBN 0-521-29141-0). Cambridge U Pr.

Analytical Applications of Complex Equilibria. J. Inczedy. LC 75-25687. (Ser. in Analytical Chemistry). 415p. 1976. 78.95 (ISBN 0-470-42713-2). Halsted Pr.

Analytical Applications of NMR. D. E. Leyden & R. H. Cox. LC 77-1229. (Chemical Analysis Ser: Vol. 48). 1977. 40.00 (ISBN 0-471-53403-X, Pub. by Wiley-Interscience). Wiley.

Analytical Archaeology. 2nd ed. David L. Clarke. LC 78-16957. 1978. 27.50x (ISBN 0-231-04630-8). Columbia U Pr.

Analytical Archaeology. 2nd ed. David L. Clarke & Robert Chapman. 1981. pap. text ed. 12.50 (ISBN 0-231-04631-6). Columbia U Pr.

Analytical Atomic Absorption Spectroscopy: Selected Methods. Ed. by Jon C. Van Loon. LC 79-25448. 1980. 35.00 (ISBN 0-12-714050-6). Acad Pr.

Analytical Calculus, 4 vols. Edwin A. Maxwell. 1954. Vol. 1. 14.50x (ISBN 0-521-05696-9); Vol. 2. 21.50x (ISBN 0-521-05697-7); Vol. 3. 16.95x (ISBN 0-521-05698-5); Vol. 4. 21.95x (ISBN 0-521-05699-3). Cambridge U Pr.

Analytical Chemistry. 2nd ed. Donald J. Pietrzyk & Clyde Frank. 700p. 1979. 18.95 (ISBN 0-12-555160-6); pap. text ed. 3.00 instr's manual (ISBN 0-12-555162-2). Acad Pr.

Analytical Chemistry - Part 1. T. S. West. (Mtp International Review of Science-Physical Chemistry Ser. 1: Vol. 12). (Illus.). 1981. Set. 29.50, index vol. 12.50 (ISBN 0-685-02107-6). Univ Park.

Analytical Chemistry - Part 2. T. S. West. (Mtp International Review of Science-Physical Chemistry Ser. 1: Vol. 13). (Illus.). 1981. Set. 29.50, index vol. 12.50 (ISBN 0-685-02109-2). Univ Park.

Analytical Chemistry in Space. R. E. Wainerdi. 1970. text ed. 10.00 (ISBN 0-08-006887-1). Pergamon.

Analytical Chemistry of Aluminum. V. N. Tikhonov. LC 72-4102. (Analytical Chemistry of the Elements Ser.). 250p. 1973. 41.95 (ISBN 0-470-86787-6). Halsted Pr.

Analytical Chemistry of Boron. A. A. Nemodruk & Z. K. Karalova. (Analytical Chemistry of the Elements Ser.). 1971. 29.95 (ISBN 0-470-63168-6). Halsted Pr.

Analytical Chemistry of Fluorine. N. S. Nikolaev et al. LC 72-4101. (Analytical Chemistry of the Elements Ser.). 222p. 1973. 38.95 (ISBN 0-470-63860-5). Halsted Pr.

Analytical Chemistry of Gallium. A. M. Dymov & A. P. Savostin. (Analytical Chemistry of the Elements Ser.). 1971. 31.95 (ISBN 0-470-22932-2). Halsted Pr.

Analytical Chemistry of Molybdenum. A. I. Busev. (Analytical Chemistry of the Elements Ser.). 1971. 23.95 o.p. (ISBN 0-470-12601-9). Halsted Pr.

Analytical Chemistry of Molybdenum & Tungsten. W. T. Elwell & D. F. Wood. 292p. 1971. text ed. 55.00 (ISBN 0-08-016673-3). Pergamon.

Analytical Chemistry of Neptunium. V. A. Mikhailov. LC 72-4103. (Analytical Chemistry of the Elements Ser.). 235p. 1973. 39.95x (ISBN 0-470-60300-3). Halsted Pr.

Analytical Chemistry of Nuclear Materials. (Technical Reports Ser.: No. 18). 88p. (Orig.). 1963. pap. 3.25 (ISBN 92-0-145163-6, IAEA). Unipub.

Analytical Chemistry of Nuclear Materials: Second Panel Report. (Technical Reports Ser.: No. 62). (Orig.). 1966. pap. 6.50 (ISBN 92-0-145266-7, IAEA). Unipub.

Analytical Chemistry of Organic Halogen Compounds. L. Mazor. LC 75-5934. 400p. 1975. text ed. 50.00 (ISBN 0-08-017903-7). Pergamon.

Analytical Chemistry of Polycyclic Aromatic Compounds. Milton L. Lee et al. 1981. write for info. (ISBN 0-12-440840-0). Acad Pr.

Analytical Chemistry of Radium. V. M. Vdovenko & Yu V. Dubasov. Tr. by N. Mandel from Rus. LC 74-30131. (Analytical Chemistry of Elements Ser.). 198p. 1925. 45.95 (ISBN 0-470-90488-7). Halsted Pr.

Analytical Chemistry of Silicon. L. V. Myshlyaeva & V. V. Krasnoshchekov. Tr. by J. Schmorak from Rus. LC 73-20490. 230p. 1974. 37.50 o.p. (ISBN 0-470-62785-9). Halsted Pr.

Analytical Chemistry of Synthetic Dyes. K. Venkataraman. LC 76-39881. 1977. 63.00 (ISBN 0-471-90575-5, Pub. by Wiley-Interscience). Wiley.

Analytical Chemistry of the Platinum Metals. S. I. Ginzburg et al. Ed. by P. Shelnitz. Tr. by N. Kaner from Rus. LC 74-34394. (Analytical Chemistry of the Elements Ser.). 673p. 1975. 79.95 (ISBN 0-470-30220-8). Halsted Pr.

Analytical Chemistry of Transplutonium Elements. B. I. Myasoedov et al. Ed. by D. Slutzkin. Tr. by N. Kaner from Rus. LC 73-17086. (Analytical Chemistry of the Elements Ser.). 404p. 1974. 41.95 (ISBN 0-470-62715-8). Halsted Pr.

Analytical Chemistry of Yttrium & the Lanthanide Elements. D. I. Ryabchikov & V. A. Ryabukhin. (Analytical Chemistry of the Elements Ser.). 1971. 23.95 o.p. (ISBN 0-470-74786-2). Halsted Pr.

Analytical Chemistry of Zirconium & Hafnium. Elinson. (Analytical Chemistry of the Elements Ser.). 1972. 32.95 (ISBN 0-470-23780-5). Halsted Pr.

Analytical Chemistry of Zirconium & Hafnium. A. K. Mukherji. LC 71-109236. 1970. 49.00 (ISBN 0-08-006886-3). Pergamon.

Analytical Concordance of the Books of the Apocrypha. Lester T. Whitelocke. LC 78-61389. 1978. pap. text ed. 16.75 ea.; Vol. 1. (ISBN 0-8191-0603-8); Vol. 2. (ISBN 0-8191-0604-6). U Pr of Amer.

Analytical Congressional Directory. Jeffrey M. Elliot & R. Reginald. (Borgo Reference Library: Vol. 12). 256p. (Orig.). 1981. lib. bdg. 19.95 (ISBN 0-89370-141-6); pap. text ed. 9.95 (ISBN 0-89370-241-2). Borgo Pr.

Analytical Control of Radiopharmaceuticals. (Illus., Orig.). 1970. pap. 13.50 (ISBN 92-0-141070-0, IAEA). Unipub.

Analytical Decision Making in Engineering Design. James Siddall. (Illus.). 1972. ref. ed. 24.95 (ISBN 0-13-034538-5). P-H.

Analytical Emission Spectroscopy. J. Mika & T. Torok. LC 73-75866. 260p. 1974. 42.50x (ISBN 0-8448-0203-4). Crane-Russak Co.

Analytical Engine: Computers-Past, Present, & Future. rev. ed. Jeremy Bernstein. 128p. 1981. 8.95; pap. 4.95. Morrow.

Analytical Foundations of Marxian Economic Theory. John Roemer. LC 80-22646. (Illus.). 224p. Date not set. price not set (ISBN 0-521-23047-0). Cambridge U Pr.

Analytical Framework for Regional Development Policy. Charles L. Leven et al. 1970. 17.50x (ISBN 0-262-12036-4). MIT Pr.

Analytical Franco-Jewish Gazetteer, 1939-1945. Soza Szajkowski. 1966. 50.00 (ISBN 0-685-13733-3). Ktav.

Analytical Geometry & Calculus: With Technical Applications. Jerry D. Strange & Bernard J. Rice. 1970. text ed. 19.95 (ISBN 0-471-83190-5). Wiley.

Analytical Greek New Testament. Ed. by Timothy Friberg & Barbara Friberg. 1000p. 1981. 16.95 (ISBN 0-8010-3496-5). Baker Bk.

Analytical Heat Diffusion Theory. A. V. Luikov. 1969. 43.50 (ISBN 0-12-459756-4). Acad Pr.

Analytical Hebrew & Chaldee Lexicon. Benjamin Davidson. 16.95 (ISBN 0-310-20290-6, Pub. by Bagster). Zondervan.

Analytical Index to the Ballad-Entries (1557-1709) in the Registers of the Company of Stationers of London. London Stationers' Company. LC 67-1586. xviii, 324p. Repr. of 1967 ed. 15.00 (ISBN 0-8103-5019-X). Gale.

Analytical Instrumentation: Growth Markets, G-052. Ed. by Business Communications. 1980. 750.00 (ISBN 0-89336-218-2). BCC.

Analytical Interpretation of Martin Buber's 'I & Thou' Alexander Kohanski. LC 74-4349. 1975. pap. 2.75 (ISBN 0-8120-0505-8). Barron.

Analytical Laser Spectroscopy, Vol. 50. N. Omenetto. 550p. 1979. 47.50 (ISBN 0-471-65371-3, 1-075). Wiley.

Analytical Measurements & Instrumentation for Process & Pollution Control. Paul N. Cheremisinoff & Harlan J. Perlis. LC 80-70319. 450p. 1981. text ed. 49.95 (ISBN 0-250-40405-2). Ann Arbor Science.

Analytical Methods for Coal & Coal Products, 2 vols. Ed. by Clarence Karr, Jr. LC 78-4928. 58.00 ea. Vol. 1, 1978 (ISBN 0-12-399901-4). Vol. 2, 1979 (ISBN 0-12-399902-2). Set. 91.00. Acad Pr.

Analytical Methods for Organic Cyano Groups. M. F. Ashworth. 1971. text ed. 27.00 (ISBN 0-08-016191-X). Pergamon.

Analytical Methods for Pesticides, Plant Growth Regulators & Food Additives, 10 vols. Ed. by Gunter Zweig. Incl. Vol. 1. Principles, Methods & General Applications. 1963. 62.75 (ISBN 0-12-784301-9); Vol. 2. Insecticides. 1964. 62.75 (ISBN 0-12-784302-7); Vol. 3. Fungicides, Nematocides & Soil Fumigants, Rodenticides, & Food & Feed Additives. 1964. 36.50 (ISBN 0-12-784303-5); Vol. 4. Herbicides (Plant Growth Regulators) 1964. 36.50 (ISBN 0-12-784304-3); Vol. 5. 1967. 60.00 (ISBN 0-12-784305-1); Vol. 6. 68.50 (ISBN 0-12-784306-X); Vol. 7. Thin-Layer & Liquid Chromatography & Analysis of Pesticides of International Importance. 1974. o.s.i (ISBN 0-12-784307-8); Vol. 8. Government Regulations, Pheromone Analyses, Additional Pesticides. Ed. by Gunter Zweig & Joseph Sharma. 1976. 62.75 (ISBN 0-12-784308-6); Vol. 10. Newer & Updated Methods. Ed. by Gunter Zweig & Joseph Sharma. 1978. 48.00 (ISBN 0-12-784310-8); Vol. 11. 1980. 46.00 (ISBN 0-12-784311-6). Set. 514.00. Acad Pr.

Analytical Methods for Use in Geochemical Exploration. R. E. Stanton. LC 76-26050. 1976. pap. 6.95 o.p. (ISBN 0-470-98920-3). Halsted Pr.

Analytical Methods in Nuclear Fuel Cycle. (Illus.). 586p. (Orig.). 1973. pap. 37.50 (ISBN 92-0-050072-2, IAEA). Unipub.

Analytical Methods Used in Sugar Refining. Ed. by R. W. Plews. (Illus.). 1969. 37.30x (ISBN 0-444-20046-0, Pub. by Applied Science). Burgess-Intl Ideas.

Analytical Photogrammetry. Sanjib K. Ghosh. LC 79-1063. (Illus.). 1979. 28.00 (ISBN 0-08-023883-1). Pergamon.

Analytical Problems. Ed. by F. L. Boschke. (Topics in Current Chemistry Ser.: Vol. 95). (Illus.). 210p. 1981. 56.70 (ISBN 0-387-10402-X). Springer-Verlag.

Analytical Profiles of Drug Substances, Vols. 1-3 & 5-6. Ed. by Klaus Florey et al. Vol. 1, 1972. 41.00 (ISBN 0-12-260801-1); Vol. 2. 1973. 39.00 (ISBN 0-12-260802-X); Vol. 3, 1974. 36.00 (ISBN 0-12-260803-8); Vol. 4, 1975. 43.00 (ISBN 0-12-260804-6); Vol. 5, 1976. 37.50 (ISBN 0-12-260805-4); Vol. 6, 1977. 41.00 (ISBN 0-12-260806-2). Acad Pr.

Analytical Profiles of Drug Substances, Vol. 9. Ed. by Klaus Florey. 1981. 34.00 (ISBN 0-12-260809-7). Acad Pr.

Analytical Sourcebook of Concepts in Dramatic Theory. Oscar L. Brownstein & Darlene M. Daubert. LC 80-1200. 584p. 1981. lib. bdg. 45.00 (ISBN 0-313-21309-7, BRN/). Greenwood.

Analytical Techniques for Financial Management. Jerome S. Osteryoung & Daniel E. McCarty. LC 79-17196. (Finance Ser.). 1980. pap. text ed. 11.95 (ISBN 0-88244-196-5). Grid Pub.

Analytical Techniques in Environmental Chemistry. International Congress on Analytical Techniques in Environmental Chemistry, Barcelona, 27-30 November 1978. Ed. by J. Albaiges. LC 79-41670. 1980. 98.00 (ISBN 0-08-023809-2). Pergamon.

Analytical Techniques in Occupational Health Chemistry. Ed. by Donald D. Dollberg & Allen W. Verstuyft. LC 79-28460. (ACS Symposium Ser.: No. 120). 1980. 28.00 (ISBN 0-8412-0539-6). Am Chemical.

Analytical Transport Planning. Robert Lane et al. LC 72-11852. 283p. 1973. 26.95 (ISBN 0-470-51440-X). Halsted Pr.

Analyze Your Personality Through Color. Alfred W. Munzert. (Test Yourself Ser.). 1980. pap. 3.95 (ISBN 0-671-34036-0). Monarch Pr.

Analyzer of Medical-Biological Words: A Clarifying Dissection of Medical Terminology, Showing How It Works, for Medics, Paramedics, Students, & Visitors from Foreign Countries. J. E. Schmidt. 224p. 1973. 10.75 (ISBN 0-398-02682-3). C C Thomas.

Analyzing an Art Museum. William S. Hendon. LC 79-10753. 27.95 (ISBN 0-03-050386-8). Praeger.

Analyzing English: An Introduction to Descriptive Linguistics. Howard Jackson. (Pergamon Institute of English). (Illus.). 1980. pap. 11.95 (ISBN 0-08-024556-0). Pergamon.

Analyzing Multivariate Data. P. Green & Barban. 1978. 28.95 (ISBN 0-03-020786-X). Dryden Pr.

Analyzing Nigerian-Americans Under a New Economic Order. John E. Njoku. LC 80-5916. 128p. (Orig.). 1981. pap. text ed. 7.50 (ISBN 0-8191-1448-0). U Pr of Amer.

Analyzing Panel Data. Gregory B. Markus. LC 79-91899. (University Papers: No. 18). (Illus.). 1979. pap. 3.50x (ISBN 0-8039-1372-9). Sage.

Analyzing Performance Problems; or, You Really Oughta Wanna. Robert F. Mager & Peter Pipe. LC 73-140896. 1970. pap. text ed. 4.50 (ISBN 0-8224-0301-3); quick reference checklist, set of 25 3.95 (ISBN 0-8224-0302-1); performance analysis poster 3.50 (ISBN 0-8224-0303-X). Pitman Learning.

Analyzing Political Change in Africa. Ed. by James R. Scarritt. (Westview Replica Edition). 344p. 1980. lib. bdg. 26.50x (ISBN 0-89158-275-4). Westview.

Analyzing Psychological Variables. Joseph Thompson & William Buchanan. 1979. pap. text ed. 10.95x (ISBN 0-684-15981-3, ScribC). Scribner.

Analyzing Public Policy Issues. William D. Coplin & Michael K. O'Leary. (Learning Packages in the Policy Sciences: No. 17). (Illus.). 50p. 1980. pap. text ed. 3.00 (ISBN 0-936826-06-1). Pol Stud Assocs.

Analyzing Qualitative-Categorical Data: Log-Linear Models & Latentstructure Analysis. Leo A. Goodman. Ed. by Jay Magidson. 1978. text ed. 18.50 (ISBN 0-89011-513-3). Abt Assoc.

Analyzing Qualitative-Categorical Data. Leo A. Goodman. Ed. by Jay Magidson. 1978. text ed. 30.00 o.p. (ISBN 0-201-02505-1). A-W.

Analyzing Social Settings. John Lofland. 1971. pap. 7.95x (ISBN 0-534-00631-0). Wadsworth Pub.

Analyzing Teaching Behavior. Ned A. Flanders. (Education Ser). 1970. 19.95 (ISBN 0-201-02052-1). A-W.

Analyzing the Criminal Justice System. Jack LaPatra. LC 77-2678. (Illus.). 1978. 17.95 (ISBN 0-669-01625-X). Lexington Bks.

Analyzing the Stock Market: Statistical Evidence & Methodology. 2nd ed. H. Russell Fogler. LC 77-75801. (Finance & Real Estate Ser.). 1978. pap. text ed. 10.50 (ISBN 0-88244-138-8). Grid Pub.

Analyzing Informal Fallacies. S. Engel. 1980. pap. 7.50 (ISBN 0-13-032854-5). P-H.

Ananda K. Coomaraswamy. Vishwanath S. Naravane. (World Leaders Ser.: No. 75). 1978. 12.50 (ISBN 0-8057-7722-9). Twayne.

Ananda K. Coomaraswamy. P. S. Sastri. Ed. by C. D. Narasimhaiah. (Indian Writers Ser.). 203p. 1975. 6.50 (ISBN 0-88253-700-8). Ind-US Inc.

Ananse Tales: A Course in Controlled Composition. Gerald Dykstra et al. (Prog. Bk.). (gr. 9-12). 1966. pap. text ed. 2.95x (ISBN 0-8077-1269-8); tchr's. manual 1.15 (ISBN 0-8077-1272-8); wkbk. 3.95x (ISBN 0-8077-1273-6). Tchrs Coll.

Anansi the Spider: A Tale from the Ashanti. Gerald McDermott. (Illus.). (gr. k-3). 1977. pap. 1.95 o.p. (ISBN 0-14-050216-5, Puffin). Penguin.

Anansi, the Spider Man. Philip K. Sherlock. LC 54-5619. (Illus.). (gr. 3-7). 1954. 9.95 (ISBN 0-690-08905-8, TYC-J). T Y Crowell.

Anaphilosophia. Martino Oberto. Tr. by Rosa Maria Salamone from Ital. LC 78-58984. (Illus.). 1981. pap. 17.95 (ISBN 0-915570-10-6). Oolp Pr.

Anaphora in Generative Grammar. T. Wasow. (Studies in Generative Linguistic Analysis: No. 2). 1980. text ed. 44.25x (ISBN 90-6439-162-9). Humanities.

Anaphoric Options of Indefinite Noun Phrases in English. Jeanette S. DeCarrico. (Linguistics Research Monograph Ser.: Vol. 3). 1981. text ed. 32.00 (ISBN 0-932998-03-8). Noit Amrofer.

Anarchiad: A New England Poem 1786-1787. LC 67-18713. 1967. 18.00x (ISBN 0-8201-1027-2). Schol Facsimiles.

Anarchical Society. Hedley Bull. LC 76-21786. 1977. 22.50x (ISBN 0-231-04132-2). Columbia U Pr.

Anarchical Society: A Study of Order in World Politics. Hedley Bull. 1979. pap. 8.00 (ISBN 0-231-04133-0). Columbia U Pr.

Anarchism. Eltzbacher. 1970. 15.00 (ISBN 0-686-62261-8). Chips.

Anarchism. A. Ritter. LC 80-40589. 196p. 1981. 27.50 (ISBN 0-521-23324-0). Cambridge U Pr.

Anarchism & Socialism. Georgii V. Plekhanov. Tr. by Eleanor M. Aveling. LC 79-2921. 148p. 1981. Repr. of 1912 ed. 15.00 (ISBN 0-8305-0090-1). Hyperion Conn.

Anarchism for Beginners. Colin Ward. (Pantheon Documentary Comic Books). (Illus.). 1981. 8.95 (ISBN 0-394-50923-4); pap. 2.95 (ISBN 0-394-74822-0). Pantheon.

Anarchism in Germany, Vol. 1: The Early Movement. Andrew R. Carlson. LC 78-186946. 1972. 16.50 (ISBN 0-8108-0484-0). Scarecrow.

Anarchism: Political Innocence or Social Violence. James D. Forman. LC 74-13436. (Studies in Contemporary Politics Ser). 160p. (gr. 7 up). 1975. PLB 5.90 o.p. (ISBN 0-531-02790-2). Watts.

Anarchist Collectives: Workers' Self-Management in the Spanish Revolution (1936 to 1939) Ed. by Sam Dolgoff. LC 73-88239. (Illus.). 160p. (Orig.). 1974. 10.00 (ISBN 0-914156-03-9); pap. 4.95 o.p. (ISBN 0-914156-02-0). Free Life.

Anarchist Reader. Ed. by George Woodcock. 1977. text ed. 23.75x (ISBN 0-391-00709-2). Humanities.

Anarchist Women: 1870-1920. Margaret Marsh. Ed. by Allen F. Davis. (American Civilization Ser.). (Illus.). 250p. 1980. 19.50 (ISBN 0-87722-202-9). Temple U Pr.

Anarchy & Culture: The Problem of the Contemporary University. Ed. by David Martin. LC 74-80271. 1969. 20.00x (ISBN 0-231-03317-6). Columbia U Pr.

Anastasia Krupnik. Lois Lowry. (Skylark Ser.). 128p. 1981. pap. cancelled (ISBN 0-686-69197-0). Bantam.

Anathemata. David Jones. (Orig.). 1972. pap. 8.95 o.p. (ISBN 0-571-10127-5, Pub. by Faber & Faber). Merrimack Bk Serv.

Anatoly Karpov: Chess Is My Life. Anatoly Karpov & A. Roshal. (Pergamon Chess Ser.). (Illus.). 1980. text ed. 35.00 (ISBN 0-08-023118-7); pap. text ed. 15.00 (ISBN 0-08-023119-5). Pergamon.

Anatoly Karpov's Games As World Champion Nineteen Seventy-Five to Nineteen Seventy-Seven. K. J. O'Connell & David Levy. 1978. pap. 16.95 (ISBN 0-7134-0227-X, Pub. by Batsford England). David & Charles.

Anatomia Humana. W. Henry Hollinshead. 1000p. 1981. pap. text ed. 26.00 (ISBN 0-06-313375-X, Pub. by by HarlA Mexico). Har-Row.

Anatomia y Fisiologica. Gerald Tortora & Nicholos Anagnostakos. (Span.). 1977. pap. text ed. 12.50 (ISBN 0-06-317150-3, IntlDept). Har-Row.

Anatomic Guide for Electromyographer: The Limbs. 2nd ed. Edward F. Delagi & Aldo Perotto. (Illus.). 224p. 1980. 18.75 (ISBN 0-398-03951-8). C C Thomas.

Anatomical Atlas of the Neonate. Lassau. 1981. write for info. Masson Pub.

Anatomical Preparations. Milton Hildebrand. 1968. 15.75x (ISBN 0-520-00558-9); pap. 4.75 o.p. (ISBN 0-520-00559-7). U of Cal Pr.

Anatomical Studies Upon Brains of Criminals. Moriz Benedikt. Tr. by E. P. Fowler from Ger. (Historical Foundations of Forensic Psychiatry & Psychology Ser.). (Illus.). 185p. 1980. Repr. of 1881 ed. lib. bdg. 22.50 (ISBN 0-306-76071-1). Da Capo.

Anatomico-Roentgenographic Studies of the Spine. Lee A. Hadley. (Illus.). 560p. 1979. 26.75 (ISBN 0-398-02818-4). C C Thomas.

Anatomie of Abuses, Part One. Philip Stubbes. LC 71-170409. (English Stage Ser.: Vol. 7). lib. bdg. 50.00 (ISBN 0-8240-0590-2). Garland Pub.

Anatomie of Popish Tyrannie. Thomas Bell. LC 74-28833. (English Experience Ser.: No. 714). 1975. Repr. of 1603 ed. 16.00 (ISBN 90-221-0714-0). Walter J Johnson.

Anatomy. 2nd ed. Ed. by Ernest W. April. LC 79-83717. (Basic Sciences PreTest Self-Assessment & Review Ser.). (Illus.). 1980. 9.95 (ISBN 0-07-050961-1). McGraw-Pretest.

Anatomy. George W. Corner. (Illus.). 1964. Repr. of 1930 ed. pap. 6.50 o.s.i. (ISBN 0-02-843150-2). Hafner.

Anatomy - A Regional Atlas of the Human Body. 2nd ed. Carmine D. Clemente. (Illus.). 392p. 1981. text ed. price not set (ISBN 0-8067-0322-9). Urban & S.

Anatomy: A Regional Study of Human Structure. 4th ed. Ernest Gardner et al. LC 74-17753. (Illus.). 881p. 1975. text ed. 26.00 (ISBN 0-7216-4018-4). Saunders.

Anatomy & Ballet. 5th ed. Celia Sparger. LC 76-146051. (Illus.). 1970. 14.95 (ISBN 0-87830-006-6). Theatre Arts.

Anatomy & Physiology. 2nd ed. W. Evan. (Illus.). 480p. 1976. pap. 21.95 ref. ed. (ISBN 0-13-035196-2); lab. manual 8.95 (ISBN 0-13-035170-9). P-H.

Anatomy & Physiology. 3rd ed. Marguerite C. Holmes & Marvine I. Gottlieb. (Nursing Examination Review Bk: Vol. 5). 1975. pap. 6.00 (ISBN 0-87488-505-1). Med Exam.

Anatomy & Physiology, 4 bks. B. J. Melloni et al. 1971. 375.00 set o.p. (ISBN 0-07-076420-4, HP); 100.00 ea. o.p. Bk. 1 (ISBN 0-07-076421-2). Bk. 2 (ISBN 0-07-076422-0). Bk. 3 (ISBN 0-07-076423-9). Bk. 4 (ISBN 0-07-076424-7). McGraw.

Anatomy & Physiology. John Raynor. 1977. text ed. 19.50 scp (ISBN 0-06-045339-7, HarpC); instructor's manual free (ISBN 0-06-365350-8); scp study guide 6.50 (ISBN 0-06-045338-9). Har-Row.

Anatomy & Physiology. Jack Rudman. (College Proficiency Examination Ser.: CLEP-37). (Cloth bdg. avail. on request). pap. 9.95 (ISBN 0-8373-5437-4). Natl Learning.

Anatomy & Physiology, 2 vols. Edwin B. Steen & Ashley Montagu. Incl. Cells, Tissues, Integument, Skeletal, Muscular & Digestive Systems, Blood, Lymph, Circulatory System (ISBN 0-06-460098-X, 98); Urinary, Respiratory & Nervous Systems, Sensations & Sense Organs, Endocrine & Reproductive Systems (ISBN 0-06-460099-8, CO 99). 1959. 4.50 ea. (COS). Har-Row.

Anatomy & Physiology - a Dynamic Approach. Anthony N. Chee. (Illus.). 287p. (Orig.). 1979. pap. text ed. 13.95x (ISBN 0-89641-020-X). American Pr.

Anatomy & Physiology: A Laboratory Manual. James Crouch & Micheline Carr. LC 76-56507. (Illus.). 1977. pap. text ed. 11.95 (ISBN 0-87484-356-1). Mayfield Pub.

Anatomy & Physiology: A Programmed Approach to, 15 bks. R. J. Brady. Incl. Cell. 1972. pap. 6.95 (ISBN 0-87618-031-4); Cardiovascular System. 1970. pap. 6.95 (ISBN 0-87618-037-3); Digestive System. 1972. pap. 6.95 (ISBN 0-87618-040-3); Endocrine System. 1972. pap. 6.95 (ISBN 0-87618-042-X); Lymphatic & Reticuloendothelial System. 1973. pap. 6.95 (ISBN 0-87618-038-1); Muscular System. 1972. pap. 6.95 (ISBN 0-87618-034-9); Nervous System. 1972. pap. 6.95 (ISBN 0-87618-035-7); Nutrition, Metabolism, Fluid, & Electrolyte Balance. 1972. pap. 6.95 (ISBN 0-87618-043-8); Reproduction in Humans. 1973. pap. 6.95 (ISBN 0-87618-045-4); Reproductive System. 1972. pap. 6.95 (ISBN 0-87618-044-6); Respiratory System. 1972. pap. 6.95 (ISBN 0-87618-039-X); Skeletal System. 1972. pap. 6.95 (ISBN 0-87618-033-0); Skin. 1972. pap. 6.95 (ISBN 0-87618-032-2); Special Senses. 1972. pap. 6.95 (ISBN 0-87618-036-5); Urinary System. 1974. pap. 6.95 (ISBN 0-87618-041-1). (Illus.). Set. 89.95 (ISBN 0-87618-635-5). R J Brady.

Anatomy & Physiology Applied to Obstetrics. S. Verralls. (Illus.). 128p. 1969. pap. text ed. 5.00x o.p. (ISBN 0-8464-0132-0). Beekman Pubs.

Anatomy & Physiology for Nurses. 3rd ed. Ed. by T. W. Glenister & Jean R. Ross. (Illus.). 630p. 1980. pap. text ed. 27.00x (ISBN 0-433-12102-5). Intl Ideas.

Anatomy & Physiology for Nurses. new ed. Evelyn Pearce. 1975. pap. text ed. 4.95 (ISBN 0-571-04891-9, Pub. by Faber & Faber). Merrimack Bk Serv.

Anatomy & Physiology Laboratory Manual. 10th ed. Catherine P. Anthony & Gary A. Thibodeau. LC 78-11927. (Illus.). 1979. pap. text ed. 9.95 (ISBN 0-8016-0270-X). Mosby.

Anatomy & Physiology of Capillaries. August Krogh. 1929. 65.00x (ISBN 0-685-89734-6). Elliots Bks.

Anatomy & Physiology of Farm Animals. 3rd ed. R. D. Frandson. LC 80-25775. (Illus.). 494p. 1981. text ed. write for info. (ISBN 0-8121-0759-4). Lea & Febiger.

Anatomy & Physiology of Obstetrics. 6th ed. C. W. Burnett. Ed. by Mary Anderson. (Illus.). 1979. 9.95 (ISBN 0-571-04682-7, Pub. by Faber & Faber); pap. 5.95 (ISBN 0-571-04992-3). Merrimack Bk Serv.

Anatomy & Physiology of Obstetrics. C. W. Burnett. 1969. text ed. 8.95 o.p. (ISBN 0-571-04682-7, Pub. by Faber & Faber). Merrimack Bk Serv.

Anatomy & Physiology of Obstetrics. C. W. Burnett. 1970. pap. text ed. 5.95 o.p. (ISBN 0-571-09236-5, Pub. by Faber & Faber). Merrimack Bk Serv.

Anatomy & Physiology of Speech: Laboratory Textbook. Harold M. Kaplan. LC 80-82927. (Illus.). 180p. 1981. text ed. 21.50 (ISBN 0-932126-04-9); pap. text ed. 16.50 (ISBN 0-932126-05-7). Graceway.

Anatomy & Physiology of the Peripheral Hearing Mechanism. J. Donald Harris. LC 73-12474. (Studies in Communicative Disorders Ser). 1974. pap. text ed. 4.50 (ISBN 0-672-61304-2). Bobbs.

Anatomy & Physiology of the Speech Mechanism. Boyd Sheets. LC 72-81499. (Studies in Communicative Disorders Ser.). 1973. pap. text ed. 4.50 (ISBN 0-672-61275-5). Bobbs.

Anatomy for Children. Ilse Goldsmith. LC 64-15111. (Illus.). (gr. 3-8). 1964. 7.95 (ISBN 0-8069-3000-4); PLB 7.49 (ISBN 0-8069-3001-2). Sterling.

Anatomy Lessons from the Great Masters. Robert B. Hale & Terence Coyle. (Illus.). 1977. 21.50 (ISBN 0-8230-0222-5). Watson-Guptill.

Anatomy of a Friendship. John M. Reisman. 260p. 1981. pap. 6.95 (ISBN 0-86616-004-3). Lewis Pub Co.

Anatomy of a Hybrid. Leonard Verduin. 184p. 1976. pap. 4.95 o.p. (ISBN 0-8028-1615-0). Eerdmans.

Anatomy of a Murder. Robert Traver. 2.95 (ISBN 0-89559-009-3). Green Hill.

Anatomy of a Peasant Economy. 149p. 1978. pap. 12.50 (R040, IRRI). Unipub.

Anatomy of a Scientific Institution: The Paris Academy of Sciences, 1666-1803. Roger Hahn. LC 70-130795. (Illus.). 1971. 27.50x (ISBN 0-520-01818-4). U of Cal Pr.

Anatomy of a Successful Salesman. Arthur Mortell. LC 72-97792. 1973. 9.95 (ISBN 0-87863-041-4). Farnswth Pub.

Anatomy of a Theme. Robert H. Meyer. 128p. 1969. pap. text ed. 3.95x (ISBN 0-02-476430-2, 47643). Macmillan.

Anatomy of AFDC Errors. Marc Bendick, Jr. et al. (Institute Paper). 158p. 1978. pap. 4.00 (ISBN 0-87766-217-7, 20500). Urban Inst.

Anatomy of an Illness As Perceived by the Patient. Norman Cousins. 176p. 1981. pap. 4.95 (ISBN 0-553-01293-2). Bantam.

Anatomy of an International Year: Book Year 1972. (Reports & Papers on Mass Communication, No. 71). 37p. (Orig.). 1974. pap. 2.50 (ISBN 92-3-101186-3, U20, UNESCO). Unipub.

Anatomy of Anti-Communism: A Report Prepared for the Peace Education Division of the American Friends Service Committee. American Friends Service Committee. LC 68-30758. (Orig.). 1969. 2.25 o.p. (ISBN 0-8090-1346-0). Hill & Wang.

Anatomy of College English. Thomas W. Wilcox. LC 72-11970. (Higher Education Ser.). 1973. 10.95x o.p. (ISBN 0-87589-163-2). Jossey-Bass.

Anatomy of Criticism. Northrop Frye. 1957. 19.50x (ISBN 0-691-06004-5); pap. 4.95 (ISBN 0-691-01298-9). Princeton U Pr.

Anatomy of Drama. Marjorie Boulton. 1968. pap. 8.95 (ISBN 0-7100-6090-4). Routledge & Kegan.

Anatomy of Evil. Charles W. Conn. 1981. 7.95 (ISBN 0-8007-1177-7). Revell.

Anatomy of Film. Bernard F. Dick. LC 76-28140. 1978. pap. text ed. 7.95 (ISBN 0-312-03395-8). St Martin.

Anatomy of Food Service Design 1. Ed. by Jule Wilkinson. LC 75-5730. (Illus.). 224p. 1975. 21.50 (ISBN 0-8436-0569-3). CBI Pub.

Anatomy of Food Service Design 2. Ed. by Jule Wilkinson. LC 75-5730. (Illus.). 1978. 21.50 (ISBN 0-8436-2105-2). CBI Pub.

Anatomy of Hallucinations. Fred H. Johnson. LC 77-22711. 1978. 18.95x (ISBN 0-88229-155-6). Nelson-Hall.

Anatomy of Historical Knowledge. Maurice Mandelbaum. LC 76-46945. (Illus.). 256p. 1977. 15.00x (ISBN 0-8018-1929-6); pap. 4.95 (ISBN 0-8018-2180-0). Johns Hopkins.

Anatomy of Inquiry: Philosophical Studies in the Theory of Science. Israel Scheffler. 390p. 1982. lib. bdg. 19.50 (ISBN 0-915144-97-2); pap. text ed. 8.50 (ISBN 0-915144-98-0). Hackett Pub. Postponed.

Anatomy of Judgement: An Investigation into the Processes of Perception & Reasoning. M. L. Abercrombie. 1980. Repr. of 1960 ed. pap. text ed. write for info. o.p. (ISBN 0-391-01057-3). Humanities.

Anatomy of Language: Saying What We Mean. Marjorie Boulton. 1971. pap. 7.95 (ISBN 0-7100-6351-2). Routledge & Kegan.

Anatomy of Local Radio-TV Copy. 4th ed. William Peck. 1976. vinyl 5.95 o.p. (ISBN 0-8306-6890-X, 890). TAB Bks.

Anatomy of Love: A Study of the Tristan of Gottfried Von Strassburg. William T. Jackson. LC 70-154859. 1971. 16.00x (ISBN 0-231-03504-7). Columbia U Pr.

Anatomy of Mathematics. 2nd ed. R. B. Kershner & L. R. Wilcox. 480p. 1974. 21.50x o.p. (ISBN 0-8260-4970-2). Wiley.

Anatomy of Melancholy. Robert Burton. Ed. by Holbrook Jackson. (Rowman & Littlefield University Library). 547p. 1972. 23.50x (ISBN 0-87471-672-1). Rowman.

Anatomy of Orofacial Structures. Richard W. Brand & Donald E. Isselhard. LC 77-14586. 1977. pap. text ed. 19.95 (ISBN 0-8016-0740-X). Mosby.

Anatomy of Pattern. Lewis F. Day. Ed. by Peter Stansky & Rodney Shewan. LC 76-17764. (Aesthetic Movement & the Arts & Crafts Movement Ser.). (Illus.). 1977. Repr. of 1887 ed. lib. bdg. 44.00 (ISBN 0-8240-2469-9). Garland Pub.

Anatomy of Poetry. Marjorie Boulton. 1970. pap. 7.95 (ISBN 0-7100-6091-2). Routledge & Kegan.

Anatomy of Printing. John Lewis. 1970. 45.00 o.p. (ISBN 0-571-08768-X, Pub. by Faber & Faber). Merrimack Bk Serv.

Anatomy of Prose. Marjorie Boulton. 1968. pap. 7.95 (ISBN 0-7100-6089-0). Routledge & Kegan.

Anatomy of Regional Activity Rates. J. Bowers. Bd. with Regional Social Accounts for the U.K. V. H. Woodward. (Economic & Social Research Ser: No. 1). 1971. 13.95 (ISBN 0-521-07719-2). Cambridge U Pr.

Anatomy of Revolution. Crane Brinton. 7.75 (ISBN 0-8446-1740-7). Peter Smith.

Anatomy of Social Inequality. Charles Hurst. LC 78-31587. (Illus.). 1979. text ed. 16.95 (ISBN 0-8016-2314-6). Mosby.

Anatomy of Speech Notions. R. E. Longacre. (Pdr Press Publications in Tagmemics,: No. 3). 1976. pap. text ed. 20.00x (ISBN 90-316-0090-3). Humanities.

Anatomy of the Common Marmoset. J. Beattie. LC 78-72711. 1980. Repr. of 1927 ed. 27.50 (ISBN 0-404-18281-X). AMS Pr.

Anatomy of the Dicotyledons, 2 vols. 2nd ed. Ed. by C. R. Metcalfe & L. Chalk. (Illus.). 1979. Set. 55.00x (ISBN 0-19-854383-2). Oxford U Pr.

Anatomy of the Economic Forces Which Decide the Life & Death of Our Modern Societies. Alexander M. Remington. (Illus.). 148p. 1981. 49.75 (ISBN 0-918968-91-7). Inst Econ Finan.

Anatomy of the Head, Neck, Face, & Jaws. 2nd ed. Lawerence A. Fried. LC 80-16800. (Illus.). 299p. 1980. text ed. 17.50 (ISBN 0-8121-0717-9). Lea & Febiger.

Anatomy of the Human Body. R. D. Lockhart et al. (Illus.). 698p. 1981. pap. 35.00 (ISBN 0-571-07037-X, Pub. by Faber & Faber). Merrimack Bk Serv.

Anatomy of the Human Body. Robert D. Lockhart et al. (Illus.). 1969. text ed. 23.50 o.p. (ISBN 0-397-58090-8). Lippincott.

Anatomy of the Monocotyledons, 4 vols. Ed. by C. R. Metcalfe. Incl. Vol. 1. Gramineae. 1960. o.p. (ISBN 0-19-854339-5); Vol. 2. Palmae. P. B. Tomlinson. 1961. 49.00x (ISBN 0-19-854344-1); Vol. 3. Commelinales-Zingiberales. P. B. Tomlinson. 1969. 48.00x (ISBN 0-19-854365-4); Vol. 4. Juncales. D. F. Cutler. 1969. 42.00x (ISBN 0-19-854369-7); Vol. 5. Cyperaceae. C. R. Metcalfe. (Illus.). 610p. 1971. 62.00x (ISBN 0-19-854372-7); Vol. 6. Dioscoreales. E. S. Ayensu. (Illus.). 226p. 1972. 49.00x (ISBN 0-19-854376-X). Oxford U Pr.

Anatomy of the Nervous System. 10th rev. ed. Stephen W. Ranson. Ed. by Sam L. Clark. LC 59-5080. (Illus.). 1959. 18.00 (ISBN 0-7216-7455-0). Saunders.

Anatomy of the Nervous System of Octopus Vulgaris. John Z. Young. (Illus.). 1971. 69.00x (ISBN 0-19-857340-5). Oxford U Pr.

Anatomy of the Novel. Marjorie Boulton. 1975. pap. 7.95 (ISBN 0-7100-8136-7). Routledge & Kegan.

Anatomy of the Novella: The European Tale Collection from Boccaccio & Chaucer to Cervantes. Robert J. Clements & Joseph Gibaldi. LC 76-52548. 1977. 15.00x (ISBN 0-8147-1369-6); pap. 7.00x (ISBN 0-8147-1370-X). NYU Pr.

Anatomy of the Ocular Adnexa: Guide to Orbital Dissection. F. Mausolf. (Illus.). 66p. 1975. pap. 8.75 (ISBN 0-398-03172-X). C C Thomas.

Anatomy of the Rat. Eunice C. Greene. (Illus.). 1971. Repr. of 1935 ed. 65.00 (ISBN 0-02-845440-5). Hafner.

Anatomy of the Vertebrates: A Laboratory Guide. 3rd ed. George Kent. LC 77-16049. (Illus.). 1978. pap. 8.50 lab manual (ISBN 0-8016-2644-7). Mosby.

Anatomy of Wonder. 2nd ed. Neil Barron. 450p. 1981. 22.50 (ISBN 0-8352-1339-0). Bowker.

Anatomy Px: A Practical Introduction to Anatomical Correlates of the Physical Examination. Bryce L. Munger & Irwin L. Baird. (Illus.). 80p. 1980. pap. 6.95 (ISBN 0-683-06151-8). Williams & Wilkins.

Anatomy Review. 6th ed. Sidney A. Cohn & Marvin Gottlieb. LC 80-20349. (Basic Science Review Bks.). 1980. pap. 8.50 (ISBN 0-87488-201-X). Med Exam.

Ancestor Hunting. Lorraine Henriod. LC 79-10767. (Illus.). 64p. (gr. 3-5). 1979. PLB 7.29 (ISBN 0-671-32998-7). Messner.

Ancestors: Native Artisans of the Americas. Ed. by Anna C. Roosevelt & James Smith. LC 79-89536. (Illus.). 230p. (Orig.). 1980. pap. 17.50 (ISBN 0-295-95780-8, Pub. by Mus Am Ind). U of Wash Pr.

Ancestral Constitution. M. I. Finley. 1971. text ed. 3.25x (ISBN 0-521-08352-4). Cambridge U Pr.

Ancestral Lines Revised. Carl Boyer, 3rd. 1981. 40.00 (ISBN 0-936124-05-9). C Boyer.

Ancestral Voices. James Lees-Milne. 1978. 10.95 o.p. (ISBN 0-684-15647-4, ScribT). Scribner.

Anchor: A Handbook of Classroom Ideas to Motivate the Teaching of Intermediate Language Arts. (Spice Ser). 1970. 6.50 (ISBN 0-89273-109-5). Educ Serv.

Anchor Atlas of World History, Vol. 2. Herman Kinder & Werner Hilgemann. 1978. pap. 5.95 (ISBN 0-385-13355-3, Anch). Doubleday.

Anchor Dictionary of Astronomy. Valerie Illingworth. LC 79-6538. (Illus.). 448p. (Orig.). 1980. pap. 6.95 (ISBN 0-385-15936-6, Anch). Doubleday.

Anchor Duplicating Masters, 2 vols. (Spice Duplicating Masters Ser). 1974. Vol. 1, Grades 4-6. 5.95 (ISBN 0-89273-505-8); Vol. 2, Grades 6-8. 5.25 (ISBN 0-89273-506-6). Educ Serv.

Anchor in the Sea: An Anthology of Psychological Fiction. Ed. by Alan Swallow. LC 77-94406. 243p. 1947. pap. 4.95x (ISBN 0-8040-0010-7). Swallow.

Anchorage: A Pictorial History. Claus M. Naske & Ludwig J. Rowinski. Ed. by Donna R. Friedman. (Illus.). 208p. 1981. pap. price not set (ISBN 0-89865-106-9). Donning Co.

Anchored in Love. Michael Orgill. 1976. pap. 1.50 (ISBN 0-89129-152-0). Jove Pubns.

Anchoring Systems. Ed. by Michael E. McCormick. 1979. pap. text ed. 40.00 (ISBN 0-08-022694-9). Pergamon.

Ancien Francais. A. J. Greimas. 271p. (Orig.). 1974. bds. 27.50 (ISBN 2-03-070335-4, 3609). Larousse.

Ancient Adirondacks. Lincoln Barnett. (American Wilderness Ser.). (Illus.). 184p. 1974. 12.95 (ISBN 0-8094-1233-0). Time-Life.

Ancient Adirondacks. Lincoln Barnett. LC 74-75617. (American Wilderness). (Illus.). (gr. 6 up). 1974. PLB 11.97 (ISBN 0-8094-1234-9, Pub. by Time-Life). Silver.

Ancient Africa. John Addison. LC 74-104309. (Young Historians Ser). (Illus.). (gr. 8-10). 1971. PLB 6.89 o.p. (ISBN 0-381-99998-X, A02900, JD-J). John Day.

Ancient African Kingdoms. (Black History Illustrated: No. 15). 1972. pap. 0.59 o.p. (ISBN 0-685-78158-5). Guild Bks.

Ancient African Religion & the African American Church. Ulysses D. Jenkins. LC 78-65794. (Illus.). 1978. 10.00 (ISBN 0-933184-00-X); pap. 5.95 (ISBN 0-933184-10-7). Flame Intl.

Ancient America. John Guyatt. Ed. by Margaret Killingray et al. (World History Ser.). (Illus.). 32p. (gr. 10). 1980. Repr. of 1977 ed. lib. bdg. 5.95 (ISBN 0-89908-033-2); pap. text ed. 1.95 (ISBN 0-89908-008-1). Greenhaven.

Ancient America. Jonathan Leonard. LC 67-15619. (Great Ages of Man). (Illus.). (gr. 6 up). 1967. PLB 11.97 (ISBN 0-8094-0374-9, Pub. by Time-Life). Silver.

Ancient America. Jonathan N. Leonard. (Great Ages of Man Ser). (Illus.). 1967. 12.95 (ISBN 0-8094-0352-8). Time-Life.

Ancient Americans: The Archaeological Story of Two Continents. Emily C. Davis. LC 74-12555. (Illus.). 311p. 1975. Repr. of 1931 ed. lib. bdg. 15.00x (ISBN 0-8154-0497-2). Cooper Sq.

Ancient & Modern Medicine: A Preventive & Therapeutic Synthesis. Dennis Chernin et al. 200p. (Orig.). Date not set. pap. price not set (ISBN 0-89389-068-5). Himalayan Intl.

Ancient Andean Life. Edgar L. Hewett. LC 67-29547. (Illus.). 1968. Repr. of 1939 ed. 15.00x (ISBN 0-8196-0204-3). Biblo.

Ancient Architecture: Egypt, Mesopotamia, Crete, Greece. Seton Lloyd et al. LC 73-2843. (History of World Architecture Ser.). (Illus.). 418p. 1975. 45.00 (ISBN 0-8109-1020-9). Abrams.

Ancient Art & Ritual. Jane Harrison. 1978. Repr. of 1913 ed. text ed. 13.00x (ISBN 0-239-00180-X). Humanities.

Ancient Art: Pre-Greek & Greek Architecture. LC 76-14062. (Garland Library of the History of Art). 1977. lib. bdg. 50.00 (ISBN 0-8240-2411-7). Garland Pub.

Ancient Art: Pre-Greek & Greek Art. LC 76-14063. (Garland Library of the History of Art). 1977. lib. bdg. 50.00 (ISBN 0-8240-2412-5). Garland Pub.

Ancient Art: Roman Art & Architecture. LC 76-14064. (Garland Library of the History of Art). 1977. lib. bdg. 50.00 (ISBN 0-8240-2413-3). Garland Pub.

Ancient Arts of Central Asia. Tamara T. Rice. (World of Art Ser). (Illus.). 1965. pap. 9.95 (ISBN 0-19-520001-2). Oxford U Pr.

Ancient Astronomical Observations & the Accelerations of the Earth & Moon. Robert R. Newton. LC 70-122011. (Illus.). 309p. 1970. 19.50x o.p. (ISBN 0-8018-1180-5). Johns Hopkins.

Ancient Ballads & Legends of Hindustan. Toru Dutt. 1975. 15.00 (ISBN 0-88253-496-3); pap. text ed. 6.75 (ISBN 0-88253-495-5). Ind-US Inc.

Ancient Beliefs in the Immortality of the Soul. Clifford H. Moore. LC 63-10283. (Our Debt to Greece & Rome Ser). 183p. Repr. of 1930 ed. 18.50x (ISBN 0-8154-0154-X). Cooper Sq.

Ancient Carpenters' Tools. 5th ed. Henry C. Mercer. (Illus.). 339p. 1975. 12.95 (ISBN 0-8180-0818-0). Bucks Co Hist.

Ancient China. Edward Schafer. LC 67-30847. (Great Ages of Man). (Illus.). (gr. 6 up). 1967. PLB 11.97 (ISBN 0-8094-0379-X, Pub. by Time-Life). Silver.

Ancient China. Edward H. Schafer. (Great Ages of Man Ser). (Illus.). 1967. 12.95 (ISBN 0-8094-0357-9). Time-Life.

Ancient Chinese Bronzes. 2nd ed. William Watson. (Illus.). 1977. 39.00 (ISBN 0-571-04917-6, Pub. by Faber & Faber). Merrimack Bk Serv.

Ancient Chinese Ceramic Sculpture: From Han Through T'ang, 2 vols. Ezekiel Schloss. 1977. Set. 300.00 (ISBN 0-686-25749-9). Castle Pub Co.

Ancient Chinese Political Theories. Kuo-Cheng Wu. (Studies in Chinese Government & Law). 340p. 1977. Repr. of 1928 ed. 24.00 (ISBN 0-89093-068-6). U Pubns Amer.

Ancient Civilization. The Educational Research Council. (Human Adventure Concepts & Inquiry Ser). (gr. 5). 1975. pap. text ed. 6.30 (ISBN 0-205-04442-5, 8044422); tchrs'. guide 5.20 (ISBN 0-205-04443-3, 8044430). Allyn.

Ancient Civilizations. Emilie Kuhrt. (Visual World Ser.). 1978. s&l 7.90 (ISBN 0-531-09073-6); lib. bdg. 5.95 (ISBN 0-531-09091-4). Watts.

Ancient Civilizations of Mexico & Central America. 3rd rev. ed. Herbert J. Spinden. LC 67-29554. (Illus.). 1968. Repr. of 1928 ed. 10.50x (ISBN 0-8196-0215-9). Biblo.

Ancient Civilizations: 4000 B.C. to 400 A.D. 2nd ed. Ed. by Norman F. Cantor & Michael S. Werthman. LC 72-76355. (AHM Structure of European History Ser.: Vol. 1). 284p. 1972. pap. text ed. 5.95x (ISBN 0-88295-710-4). AHM Pub.

Ancient Cures, Charms & Usages of Ireland. Jane F. Wilde. LC 74-137347. 1970. Repr. of 1890 ed. 20.00 (ISBN 0-8103-3599-9). Gale.

Ancient Curious & Famous Wills. Virgil M. Harris. xiii, 472p. 1981. Repr. of 1911 ed. lib. bdg. 39.50x (ISBN 0-8377-0633-5). Rothman.

Ancient Double-Entry Bookkeeping. John B. Geijsbeek. 1975. Repr. text ed. 15.00 (ISBN 0-914348-16-7). Scholars Bk.

Ancient Economy. M. I. Finley. (Sather Classical Lectures: Vol. 43). 1973. 16.50x (ISBN 0-520-02436-2); pap. 3.95 (ISBN 0-520-02564-4). U of Cal Pr.

Ancient Ecuador: Culture, Clay & Creativity, 3000-300 B.C. Donald W. Lathrap et al. LC 74-25248. (Illus.). 110p. (Orig., Eng. & Span.). 1980. pap. 5.95 (ISBN 0-914868-07-1). Field Mus.

Ancient Egypt. Wendy Boase. (Civilization Library). (Illus.). (gr. 5-8). 1978. PLB 6.90 s&l (ISBN 0-531-01402-9). Watts.

Ancient Egypt. Lionel Casson. LC 65-28872. (Great Ages of Man). (Illus.). (gr. 6 up). 1965. PLB 11.97 (ISBN 0-8094-0367-6, Pub. by Time-Life). Silver.

Ancient Egypt. Lionel Casson. (Great Ages of Man Ser). (Illus.). 1965. 12.95 (ISBN 0-8094-0345-5). Time-Life.

Ancient Egypt: A Survey. Elfriede Preger. LC 78-54099. (Illus.). 1978. pap. 6.95 (ISBN 0-89708-001-7). And Bks.

Ancient Egypt As Represented in the Museum of Fine Arts, Boston. 6th rev ed. William S. Smith. LC 60-13944. (Illus.). 1968. Repr. of 1960 ed. 4.50 (ISBN 0-87846-004-7). Mus Fine Arts Boston.

Ancient Egypt to the Eighteenth Century. Liliane Funcken & Fred Funcken. (Arms & Uniforms: Vol. 1). (Illus.). 155p. (gr. 6-10). 1972. 11.95x (ISBN 0-7063-1814-5). Intl Pubns Serv.

Ancient Egyptian Book of Two Ways. Leonard H. Lesko. (California Library Reprint Ser.). 1978. 15.00x (ISBN 0-520-03514-3). U of Cal Pr.

Ancient Egyptian Cut & Use Stencils. Ed. by Theodore Menten. (Illus.). 1978. pap. 3.25 (ISBN 0-486-23626-9). Dover.

Ancient Egyptian Literature, Vol. 3: A Book of Readings. Miriam Lichtheim. 1980. 15.75x (ISBN 0-520-03882-7); pap. 3.95 (ISBN 0-520-04020-1). U of Cal Pr.

Ancient Egyptian Magic. Bob Brier. LC 80-15608. (Illus.). 320p. 1980. 14.95 (ISBN 0-688-03654-6). Morrow.

Ancient Egyptians & Chinese in America. R. A. Jairazbhoy. (Old World Origins of American Civilization Ser). (Illus.). 110p. 1974. 13.50x o.p. (ISBN 0-87471-571-7). Rowman.

Ancient Egyptians: How They Lived & Worked. Jill Kamil. 1977. 11.95 (ISBN 0-8023-1267-5). Dufour.

Ancient Energy: Key to the Universe. Maxine K. Asher. LC 78-19497. (Illus.). 1979. 8.95 (ISBN 0-06-060308-9, HarpR). Har-Row.

Ancient Engineers. L. Sprague De Camp. 1977. pap. 2.25 o.p. (ISBN 0-394-25777-4). Ballantine.

Ancient Europe: From the Beginnings of Agriculture to Classical Antiquity. Stuart Piggott. LC 64-21369. (Illus.). 1966. 22.95x (ISBN 0-202-33002-8). Aldine Pub.

Ancient Fathers of the Church: Translated Narratives from the Evertinos on Passions & Perfection in Christ. Archimandrite Chrysostomos. (Illus.). 118p. 1980. 7.95 (ISBN 0-916586-77-4); pap. 4.95. Hellenic Coll Pr.

Ancient Funerall Monuments Within the United Monarchie of Great Britaine, Ireland & the Islands Adjacent. John Weever. LC 79-84145. (English Experience Ser.). 910p. 1979. Repr. of 1631 ed. lib. bdg. 125.00 (ISBN 90-221-0961-5). Walter J Johnson.

Ancient Ghana & Mali. Nehemia Levtzion. LC 79-27281. 1980. text ed. 18.75x (ISBN 0-8419-0431-6, Africana); pap. text ed. 9.75x (ISBN 0-8419-0432-4). Holmes & Meier.

Ancient Glass in the Museum of Fine Arts, Boston. Axel Von Saldern. LC 67-31751. (Illus.). 1968. 8.50 o.p. (ISBN 0-87846-007-1); pap. 2.95 (ISBN 0-87846-157-4). Mus Fine Arts Boston.

Ancient Greece. Margaret Killingray. Ed. by Malcolm Yapp & Edmund O'Connor. (World History Ser.). Orig. Title: Mediterranean. (Illus.). 32p. (gr. 10). 1980. Repr. of 1977 ed. lib. bdg. 5.95 (ISBN 0-89908-026-X); pap. text ed. 1.95 (ISBN 0-89908-001-4). Greenhaven.

Ancient Greek Horsemanship. J. K. Anderson. (Illus.). 1961. 28.50x (ISBN 0-520-00023-4). U of Cal Pr.

Ancient Greek Literature. Kenneth Dover. 196p. 1980. 15.50 (ISBN 0-19-219137-3); pap. 6.95 (ISBN 0-19-289124-3). Oxford U Pr.

Ancient Greek Numerical Systems. M. N. Tod. 128p. 1979. 20.00 (ISBN 0-89005-290-5). Ares.

Ancient Greeks. Anton Powell & Patricia Vanags. LC 78-2646. (Civilization Library). (Illus.). (gr. 5 up). 1978. PLB 6.90 s&l (ISBN 0-531-01446-0). Watts.

Ancient Greeks: How They Lived & Worked. Maurice Pope. LC 75-41966. 192p. 1976. 11.95 (ISBN 0-8023-1264-0). Dufour.

Ancient Hindu Refugees: Badaga Social History 1550-1975. Ed. by Paul Hockings. (Studies in Anthropology). 1980. text ed. 23.50x (ISBN 90-279-7798-4). Mouton.

Ancient History Atlas. Micheal Grant. LC 73-654430. (Illus.). 112p. 1972. 6.95 o.s.i. (ISBN 0-02-545130-8). Macmillan.

Ancient History: From Its Beginnings to the Fall of Rome. Michael Cheilik. LC 79-76467. (Orig.). 1969. pap. 3.95 (ISBN 0-06-460001-7, CO 1, COS). Har-Row.

Ancient India. 2nd. ed. Romila Thapar. 1969. pap. 2.00 (ISBN 0-88253-275-8). Ind-US Inc.

Ancient India & Its Influence on Modern Times. Robert G. Wirsing & Nancy Wirsing. LC 73-6740. (First Bks.). (gr. 4-6). 1973. PLB 4.90 o.p. (ISBN 0-531-00806-1). Watts.

Ancient Indian Costume, Six Hundred B.C - A.D. Seven Hundred & Fifty. Roshan Alkazi. (Illus.). 1978. text ed. 35.00x o.p. (ISBN 0-7069-0732-9). Humanities.

Ancient Indian Magic & Folklore: An Introduction. Margaret Stutley. LC 79-13211. (Illus.). 1980. 18.50 (ISBN 0-87773-712-6). Great Eastern.

Ancient Indonesia: And Its Influence in Modern Times. Donald E. Weatherbee. LC 74-3004. (First Bks. Ser). (Illus.). 96p. (gr. 5-10). 1974. PLB 6.45 (ISBN 0-531-02732-5). Watts.

Ancient Iraq. rev. ed. Georges Roux. 480p. 1980. pap. 5.95 (ISBN 0-14-020828-3, Pelican). Penguin.

Ancient Israel. 2nd ed. Harry M. Orlinsky. (Development of Western Civilization Ser). (Illus., Orig.). (gr. 10 up). 1960. 9.50x o.p. (ISBN 0-8014-0324-3); pap. text ed. 2.95x o.p. (ISBN 0-8014-9849-X). Cornell U Pr.

Ancient Japan: And Its Influence in the Modern World. Richard L. Walker. LC 74-28238. (First Bks). (Illus.). 96p. (gr. 5 up). 1975. PLB 4.90 o.p. (ISBN 0-531-00827-4). Watts.

Ancient Japanese Nobility: The Kabane Ranking System. Richard J. Miller. (Publications in Occasional Papers, Vol. 7). 1974. pap. 14.50x (ISBN 0-520-09494-8). U of Cal Pr.

Ancient Judaism. M. Weber. LC 52-8156. 1967. pap. text ed. 7.95 (ISBN 0-02-934130-2). Free Pr.

Ancient Landscapes: Studies in Field Archaeology. John Bradford. LC 80-23204. (Illus.). xvii, 297p. 1980. Repr. of 1957 ed. lib. bdg. 49.75x (ISBN 0-313-22849-3, BRAL). Greenwood.

Ancient Law: The Connection with the Early History of Society & Its Relation to Modern Ideas. Henry S. Maine. 9.00 (ISBN 0-8446-0784-3). Peter Smith.

Ancient Life in Mexico & Central America. Edgar L. Hewett. LC 67-29546. (Illus.). 1968. Repr. of 1936 ed. 15.00x (ISBN 0-8196-0205-1). Biblo.

Ancient Life in the American Southwest. Edgar L. Hewett. LC 67-29548. (Illus.). 1968. Repr. of 1930 ed. 15.00x (ISBN 0-8196-0203-5). Biblo.

Ancient Malta & Its Antiquities. Harrison Lewis. 1977. pap. text ed. 10.50x (ISBN 0-901072-25-7). Humanities.

Ancient Mariners. Lionel Casson. 1959. 9.95 (ISBN 0-02-522830-7). Macmillan.

Ancient Mind & Its Heritage, 2 vols. Elmer G. Suhr. Incl. Vol. 1. Exploring the Primitive, Egyptian & Mesopotamian Cultures. 1959. text ed. 5.00 o.p. (ISBN 0-682-40097-1); Vol. 2. Exploring the Hebrew, Hindu, Greek & Chinese Cultures. 1960. text ed. 5.00 o.p. (ISBN 0-682-40098-X). University). Exposition.

Ancient Mirrors of Womanhood, 2 vols. Merlin Stone. 224p. Vol. I. pap. 6.95 (ISBN 0-9603352-0-X); Vol. II. pap. 7.95 (ISBN 0-9603352-1-8). New Sibylline.

Ancient Mirrors of Womanhood: Our Goddess & Heroine Heritage, Vol. 2. Merlin Stone. (Illus.). 224p. Date not set. pap. 7.95 (ISBN 0-9603352-1-8). New Sibylline.

Ancient Mysteries Described. William Hone. LC 67-23905. (Illus.). 1969. Repr. of 1823 ed. 15.00 (ISBN 0-8103-3444-5). Gale.

Ancient Mysteries Reader. Ed. by Peter Haining. LC 74-18802. 336p. 1975. 7.95 o.p. (ISBN 0-385-09867-7). Doubleday.

Ancient Mystical White Brotherhood. Frater Achad. pap. 4.50 (ISBN 0-87516-212-6). De Vorss.

Ancient Myth & Modern Man. Gerald A. Larue. LC 74-9527. 320p. (Orig.). 1975. 11.95 (ISBN 0-13-035493-7); pap. 10.50 (ISBN 0-13-035485-6). P-H.

Ancient Myths: The First Science Fiction. Laurence Swinburne & Irene Swinburne. LC 77-10915. (Myth, Magic & Superstition Ser.). (Illus.). (gr. 4-5). 1977. PLB 9.65 (ISBN 0-8172-1042-3). Raintree Pubs.

Ancient Native Americans. Ed. by Jesse D. Jennings. LC 78-7989. (Illus.). 1978. pap. text ed. 21.95x (ISBN 0-7167-0074-3). W H Freeman.

Ancient Near East. Cyrus H. Gordon. 1965. pap. 6.95 (ISBN 0-393-00275-6, Norton Lib). Norton.

Ancient Near East. Malcolm Yapp. Ed. by Margaret Killingray et al. (World History Ser.). (Illus.). 32p. (gr. 10). 1980. Repr. of 1977 ed. lib. bdg. 5.95 (ISBN 0-89908-025-1); pap. text ed. 1.95 (ISBN 0-89908-000-6). Greenhaven.

Ancient Near East in Pictures with Supplement. 2nd ed. Ed. by James B. Pritchard. Incl. Ancient Near Eastern Texts Relating to the Old Testament with Supplement. 3rd ed (ISBN 0-691-03502-4). 1969. deluxe ed. 46.50x ea. (ISBN 0-691-03502-4); Set. 82.50x (ISBN 0-686-66606-2). Princeton U Pr.

Ancient Ones. Janet Lewis. (Illus.). 1979. pap. 7.50 o.p. (ISBN 0-931832-12-8). No Dead Lines.

Ancient Orient & Old Testament. Kenneth A. Kitchen. LC 66-30697. 1966. 5.95 (ISBN 0-87784-907-2). Inter-Varsity.

Ancient Pagan Symbols. Elisabeth E. Goldsmith. LC 68-18025. (Illus.). xxxix, 220p. 1976. Repr. of 1929 ed. 15.00 (ISBN 0-8103-4140-9). Gale.

Ancient Persia & Iranian Civilization. Clement Huart. (History of Civilization Ser.). (Illus.). 1972. 25.00x (ISBN 0-7100-7242-2). Routledge & Kegan.

Ancient Persian Bronzes in the Adam Collection. P. R. Moorey. 1974. 36.00 (ISBN 0-571-10216-6, Pub. by Faber & Faber). Merrimack Bk Serv.

Ancient Persians: How They Lived & Worked. Brian Dicks. 1979. 14.95 (ISBN 0-7153-7711-6). David & Charles.

Ancient Plants & the World They Lived In. Henry N. Andrews. (Illus.). 288p. 1947. 19.50x o.p. (ISBN 0-8014-0015-5). Comstock.

Ancient Rain: Poems 1956-1978. Bob Kaufman. Ed. by Raymond Foye. 96p. 1981. 12.00 (ISBN 0-8112-0790-0); pap. 4.95 (ISBN 0-8112-0801-X). New Directions.

Ancient Roman Architecture. Unione Fototeca. 141p. 1979. binder 725.00 (ISBN 0-89664-008-6, Pub. by K G Saur); write for info. microfiche (Pub. by K G Saur). Gale.

Ancient Roman Religion. Ed. by Frederick C. Grant. 1957. 6.50 (ISBN 0-672-61171-6, LLA138). Bobbs.

Ancient Romances: A Literary-Historical Account of Their Origins. Ben E. Perry. (Sather Classical Lectures: No. 37). 1967. 20.00x (ISBN 0-520-01003-5). U of Cal Pr.

Ancient Romans. Chester G. Starr. (Illus.). 1971. 13.95x (ISBN 0-19-501455-3); pap. 8.95x (ISBN 0-19-501454-5). Oxford U Pr.

Ancient Romans: How They Lived & Worked. O. A. W. Dilke. 1975. 11.95 (ISBN 0-7153-6553-3). Dufour.

Ancient Rome. Michael Davison. LC 79-57555. (Abbeville Library of Art Ser.: No. 1). (Illus.). 112p. (Orig.). 1980. pap. 4.95 (ISBN 0-89659-124-7). Abbeville Pr.

Ancient Ruins of the Southwest: An Archaeological Guide. David Noble. LC 80-83016. (Illus.). 128p. 1981. pap. 8.95 (ISBN 0-87358-274-8). Northland.

Ancient Science & Modern Civilization. George Sarton. LC 54-10992. 1964. pap. 1.65x o.p. (ISBN 0-8032-5228-5, 302, Bison). U of Nebr Pr.

Ancient Skyscrapers: The Native American Pueblos. Sherry Paul. LC 78-23992. (Famous Firsts Ser.). (Illus.). 1978. lib. bdg. 7.35 (ISBN 0-686-51097-6). Silver.

Ancient Songs & Ballads, from the Reign of King Henry 2nd to the Revolution. Joseph Ritson. LC 67-23930. 1968. Repr. of 1877 ed. 20.00 (ISBN 0-8103-3417-8). Gale.

Ancient Spaniards. Gerard Nicolini. (Illus.). 312p. 1975. 15.95 o.p. (ISBN 0-347-00023-1). Saxon.

Ancient Spartans. J. T. Hooker. (Illus.). 254p. 1980. 29.50x (ISBN 0-460-04352-8, Pub. by J M Dent England). Biblio Dist.

Ancient State, Authorite & Proceedings of the Court of Requests by Julius Caesar. Ed. by L. M. Hill. LC 73-93399. (Studies in English Legal History). 308p. 1975. 49.00 (ISBN 0-521-20386-4). Cambridge U Pr.

Ancient Sun: Proceedings of the Conference on the Ancient Sun: Fossil Record in the Earth, Moon & Meteorites, Boulder Colorado, October 16-19, 1979. Ed. by Lunar & Planetary Institute. LC 80-20084. (Geochimica & Cosmochimica Acta: Suppl. 13). 500p. 1980. 56.00 (ISBN 0-08-026324-0). Pergamon.

Ancient Synagogues of the Iberian Peninsula. Don A. Halperin. LC 78-62577. (Social Sciences Monographs: No. 38). (Illus.). 1969. pap. 3.25 (ISBN 0-8130-0272-9). U Presses Fla.

Ancient Teaching of Yoga & the Spiritual Evolution of Man. Joan Cooper. 218p. 1980. 14.75x (ISBN 0-7050-0064-8, Pub. by Skilton & Shaw England). State Mutual Bk.

Ancient Tribes of the Klamath Country. Carrol B. Howe. LC 68-28922. (Illus.). 1972. 7.50 o.p. (ISBN 0-8323-0131-0); pap. 4.95 o.p. (ISBN 0-8323-0279-1). Binford.

Ancient Visions. James Cornell. (Illus.). 288p. 1980. cancelled o.p. (ISBN 0-686-61460-7, ScribT). Scribner.

Ancient Visitors. Daniel Cohen. LC 75-21220. 224p. (gr. 4-7). 1976. 7.95 (ISBN 0-385-09786-7). Doubleday.

Ancient Wisdom. 9th ed. Annie Besant. 1972. 5.95 (ISBN 0-8356-7038-4). Theos Pub Hse.

Ancient Wisdom Revived: A History of the Theosophical Movement. Bruce F. Campbell. 224p. 1980. 12.95 (ISBN 0-520-03968-8). U of Cal Pr.

Ancient World. Thomas W. Africa. (Illus., Orig.). 1969. pap. text ed. 12.50 (ISBN 0-395-04095-7, 3-00250). HM.

Ancient World. R. J. Cootes & L. E. Snellgrove. (Longman Secondary Histories). (Illus.). 1974. pap. text ed. 6.95x (ISBN 0-582-20503-4). Longman.

Ancient World. Paul Titley. (Let's Make History Ser.). (Orig.). 1980. pap. 3.50 (ISBN 0-263-06335-6). Transatlantic.

Ancient World: An Historical Perspective. Henry C. Boren. (Illus.). 384p. 1976. ref. ed. 16.95x (ISBN 0-13-036442-8). P-H.

Ancient Writing & Its Influence. Berthold L. Ullman. (Medieval Academy Reprints for Teaching Ser.). 260p. 1981. pap. 7.50x (ISBN 0-8020-6435-3). U of Toronto Pr.

Ancilla to Classical Reading. Moses Hadas. LC 54-6132. 1954. pap. 7.50x (ISBN 0-231-08517-6). Columbia U Pr.

Ancillary Ocular Studies. J. B. Rutstein. 1975. 12.95 (ISBN 0-407-00002-X). Butterworths.

Ancrene Wisse, Pts. 6 & 7. Ed. by Geoffrey Shepherd. (Old & Middle English Texts). 116p. 1972. pap. 6.95x (ISBN 0-06-496228-8). B&N.

And a Cast of Thousands. Celeste Loucks et al. Ed. by Elaine S. Furlow. (Human Touch Photo-Text Ser.). (Illus.). 1978. 6.95 (ISBN 0-937170-11-9). Home Mission.

And Always a Detective: Chapters on the History of Detective Fiction. R. F. Stewart. LC 79-56436. 352p. 1980. 36.00 (ISBN 0-7153-7922-4). David & Charles.

And Chaos Died. Joanna Russ. 1979. pap. 1.95 (ISBN 0-425-04135-2). Berkley Pub.

And Everywhere, Children! Association for Childhood Education International. LC 78-25932. (gr. 4-7). 1979. 9.50 (ISBN 0-688-80215-X). Greenwillow.

And Four to Go. Rex Stout. 208p. 1980. pap. 2.25 (ISBN 0-553-14452-9). Bantam.

And God Wants People. Mary L. Lacy. LC 62-11717. 1976. pap. 1.25 o.p. (ISBN 0-8042-3594-5). John Knox.

And Heaven & Nature Sings. James R. Bjorge. (Illus.). 1977. pap. 4.95 (ISBN 0-570-03047-1, 6-1172). Concordia.

And I Alone Survived. Lauren Elder & Shirley Streshinsky. 1979. pap. 1.95 o.p. (ISBN 0-449-23864-4, Crest). Fawcett.

And I Alone Survived. Lauren Elder & Shirley Streshinsky. 1978. 7.95 o.p. (ISBN 0-525-05481-2, Thomas Congdon Book). Dutton.

And I Remember Spain. Murray Sperber. 1974. pap. 3.95 o.s.i. (ISBN 0-02-054030-2, Collier). Macmillan.

And I Remember Spain: A Spanish Civil War Anthology. Ed. by Murray Sperber. 368p. 1974. 7.95 o.s.i. (ISBN 0-02-612960-4). Macmillan.

And I Thought I Was Crazy! Quirks, Idiosyncrasies & Meshugass That People Are into. Judy Reiser. LC 80-15360. (Illus.). 138p. (Orig.). 1980. pap. 4.95 (ISBN 0-671-25399-9, 91707-2, Fireside). S&S.

And It Came to Pass. Jean Slaughter. LC 70-127471. (Illus.). (gr. k-3). 1971. 4.95 o.s.i. (ISBN 0-02-782900-6). Macmillan.

And It Came to Pass - Not to Stay. R. Buckminster Fuller. 1976. 9.95 o.s.i. (ISBN 0-02-541810-6). Macmillan.

And Kill MIGs. Lou Drendel. pap. 6.95 (ISBN 0-89747-056-7). Squad Sig Pubns.

And Kyroot Said: Contemporary Work Commentaries from a Sanguinary Cosmic Sage. Jan. 315p. 1980. 9.00 (ISBN 0-936380-04-7). Chan Shal Imi.

And Merely Teach: Irreverent Essays on the Mythology of Education. 2nd ed. Arthur E. Lean. LC 75-42233. 164p. 1976. 8.95x (ISBN 0-8093-0744-8); pap. 4.95 (ISBN 0-8093-0745-6). S Ill U Pr.

And No Birds Sang. Farley Mowat. LC 79-23231. 1980. 10.95 (ISBN 0-316-58695-1, Pub. by Atlantic-Little Brown). Little.

And No Quarter: An Italian Partisan in World War II-Memoirs of Giovanni Pesce. Giovanni Pesce. Tr. by Frederick Shaine from It. LC 75-127826. 269p. 1972. 10.95x (ISBN 0-8214-0081-9). Ohio U Pr.

And Not to Yield: An Autobiography. Ella Winter. LC 63-15320. 5.95 o.p. (ISBN 0-15-106820-8). HarBraceJ.

And Now Miguel. Joseph Krumgold. LC 53-8415. (Illus.). (gr. 6 up). 1953. 9.95 (ISBN 0-690-09118-4, TYC-J). T Y Crowell.

And Now New Zealand. 3rd ed. Harry Morton. LC 77-353297. 1976. pap. 5.00x (ISBN 0-908565-07-0). Intl Pubns Serv.

And Now Tomorrow. Rachel Field. 1942. 10.95 (ISBN 0-02-537740-X). Macmillan.

And on the Eighth Day. Ellery Queen. 1976. pap. 1.75 (ISBN 0-345-28291-4). Ballantine.

And One for the Dead. Pierre Audemars. Date not set. 9.95 (ISBN 0-8027-5440-6). Walker & Co.

And One Was a Wooden Indian. Betty Baker. LC 77-117957. (gr. 5-9). 1970. 4.95g o.s.i. (ISBN 0-02-708310-1). Macmillan.

And Other Neighborly Names: Social Process & Cultural Image in Texas Folklore. Ed. by Richard Bauman & Roger D. Abrahams. (Illus.). 333p. 1981. text ed. 25.00x (ISBN 0-292-70352-X). U of Tex Pr.

And Perhaps: The Story of Ruth Dayan. Ruth Dayan & Helga Dudman. LC 72-79920. 1973. 6.95 o.p. (ISBN 0-15-106845-3). HarBraceJ.

And Say What He Is: The Life of a Special Child. J. B. Murray & Emily Murray. LC 75-5810. 304p. 1975. 12.00x (ISBN 0-262-13115-3); pap. 4.95 (ISBN 0-262-63069-9). MIT Pr.

And Send the Sun Tomorrow: A Journal of My Father's Last Days. Maura Bremer. 1979. pap. 2.95 (ISBN 0-03-049396-X). Winston Pr.

And Smoking Flax Shall He Not Quench: Reflections on New Testament Themes. Thomas A. Fay. LC 79-57202. 170p. 1979. 8.95 (ISBN 0-936100-00-1). Paraclete Bks.

And the Bands Played on: An Informal History of British Dance Bands. Sid Colin. (Illus.). 1978. 16.95 (ISBN 0-241-89589-8, Pub. by Hamish Hamilton England). David & Charles.

And the Desert Shall Rejoice: Conflict, Growth, & Justice in Arid Environments. Arthur Maass & Raymond L. Anderson. LC 77-17866. 1978. 22.50x (ISBN 0-262-13134-X). MIT Pr.

And the Envelopes Please. Richard Altman. LC 77-26775. 1978. 7.95 o.p. (ISBN 0-397-01279-9); pap. 3.95 (ISBN 0-397-01270-5). Lippincott.

And the Man Who Was Travelling Never Got Home. H. L. VanBrunt. LC 80-65698. (Poetry Ser.). 1980. 9.95 (ISBN 0-915604-35-3); pap. 4.95 (ISBN 0-915604-36-1). Carnegie-Mellon.

And the Poor Get Children: Radical Perspectives on Population Dynamics. LC 80-8932. 288p. 1981. 16.00 (ISBN 0-686-69511-9). Monthly Rev.

And the Two Shall Become One Flesh, a Study of Traditions in Ephesians 5: 1-33. J. Paul Sampley. LC 77-152644. (New Testament Studies: No. 16). 1971. 26.50 (ISBN 0-521-08131-9). Cambridge U Pr.

And the War Came: The North and the Secession Crisis, 1860-1861. Kenneth M. Stampp. LC 80-15742. (Illus.). xvii, 331p. 1980. Repr. of 1950 ed. lib. bdg. 27.25x (ISBN 0-313-22566-4, STAN). Greenwood.

And Their Eyes Were Opened. Michael Scanlan & Ann T. Shields. 1976. pap. 2.50 (ISBN 0-89283-035-2). Servant.

And Then I Wrote... Joan Baez. (Illus.). 352p. 1980. 14.95 (ISBN 0-671-44849-8). Summit Bks.

And Then Take Hands. Compiled by W. M. Von Heider. LC 79-55738. 1981. tchers & parents ed. 14.95 (ISBN 0-89742-012-8). Dawne-Leigh.

And Then the Sun. Pradip Sen. 8.00 (ISBN 0-89253-734-5); flexible cloth 4.80 (ISBN 0-89253-735-3). Ind-US Inc.

And Then There Was. Joanie Whitebird. LC 78-63429. (Illus., Orig.). Date not set. pap. cancelled o.p. (ISBN 0-930138-06-6). Harold Hse.

And Then There Were None. Agatha Christie. (Enriched Classics Ser.). (YA) pap. 2.25 (ISBN 0-671-82683-2). WSP.

And They All Sang Hallelujah: Plain-Folk Camp-Meeting Religion, 1800-1845. Dickson D. Bruce, Jr. LC 74-11344. (Illus.). 1974. 8.50x (ISBN 0-87049-157-1); pap. 4.75 (ISBN 0-87049-310-8). U of Tenn Pr.

And This Is Laura. Ellen Conford. (gr. 5-7). 1980. pap. 1.75 (ISBN 0-671-56077-8). PB.

And to Think That I Saw It on Mulberry Street. Dr. Seuss. LC 37-38873. (gr. k-3). 5.95 (ISBN 0-8149-0387-8). Vanguard.

And Tyler Too. Donald B. Chidsey. LC 78-807. 1978. 7.95 (ISBN 0-525-66585-4). Elsevier-Nelson.

And We Have to Live (y Tenemos Que Vivir) Argentina D. Lozano. Tr. by Lillian Sears from Span. LC 78-59598. 1978. softcover 6.00 (ISBN 0-89430-032-6). Morgan-Pacific.

And Would You Believe It! Thoughts About the Creed. Basset, Bernard, S.J. 1978. pap. 2.45 (ISBN 0-385-13367-7, Im). Doubleday.

And You Give Me a Pain, Elaine. Stella Pevsner. LC 78-5857. (gr. 6 up). 1978. 7.50 (ISBN 0-395-28877-0, Clarion). HM.

And You Give Me a Pain, Elaine. Stella Pevsner. (gr. 7-9). 1981. pap. 1.95 (ISBN 0-671-56020-4). Archway.

And You Shall Teach Them Diligently: A Study of the Current State of Religious Education in the Reform Movement. Stuart A. Gertman. 1977. pap. 5.00 (ISBN 0-8074-0052-1, 383760). UAHC.

And You Visited Me. Dennis Saylor. LC 79-88403. 1979. pap. 6.95 (ISBN 0-933350-21-X). Morse Pr.

And You Wonder, Herman, Why I Never Want to Go to Italian Restaurants? Jim Unger. (Alligator Books Ser.). 1977. pap. 2.50 (ISBN 0-8362-0702-5). Andrews & McMeel.

Andaman Islanders. Alfred R. Radcliffe-Brown. 1964. pap. text ed. 5.95 (ISBN 0-02-925580-5). Free Pr.

Andaman Story. N. Iqbal Singh. (Illus.). 321p. 1978. 20.00x (ISBN 0-7069-0632-2, Pub. by Croom Helm Ltd. England). Biblio Dist.

Andarilha Para O Senhor. Tr. by Corrie Ten Boom. (Portugese Bks.). (Port.). 1979. 1.50 (ISBN 0-8297-0638-0). Life Pubs Intl.

Andean Group: A Case Study in Economic Integration Among Developing Countries. David Morawetz. LC 74-3070. 216p. 1974. 23.00x (ISBN 0-262-13109-9). MIT Pr.

Andean Pact: A Political Analysis. Roger W. Fontaine. LC 76-54540. (Washington Papers Ser.: No. 45). 1977. 3.50x (ISBN 0-8039-0790-7). Sage.

Andele, or the Mexican - Kiowa Captive. a Story of Real Life Among the Indians, Repr. Of 1899 Ed. John J. Methvin. Bd. with Grandfather's Captivity & Escape. Mrs. L. G. Benton. Repr; Stirring Adventures of the Joseph R. Brown Family. Their Captivity During the Indian Uprising of 1862 & Description of Their Old Home Near Sacred Heart-Destroyed by the Indians. George G. Allanson. Repr. LC 75-7131. (Indian Captivities Ser.: Vol. 103). 1976. lib. bdg. 44.00 (ISBN 0-8240-1727-7). Garland Pub.

Andersen's Fairy Tales. Hans C. Andersen. (gr. 1-5). 1963. 4.95g o.s.i. (ISBN 0-02-700920-3). Macmillan.

Andersen's Fairy Tales. (Illustrated Junior Library). (Illus.). 352p. 1981. pap. 4.95 (ISBN 0-448-11022-9). G&D.

Anderson County. Katherine B. Hoskins. LC 79-126928. (Tennessee County History Ser.). (Illus.). 1979. 12.50x (ISBN 0-87870-061-7). Memphis St Univ.

Andersonville. MacKinley Kantor. 1971. pap. 2.95 (ISBN 0-451-09279-1, E9279, Sig). NAL.

Andersonville. MacKinley Kantor. LC 55-8257. 1955. 10.95 o.s.i. (ISBN 0-690-00329-3, TYC-T). T Y Crowell.

Andersonville: A Story of Rebel Military Prisons. abr. ed. John McElroy. 5.00 (ISBN 0-686-66276-8). Peter Smith.

Andersonville: A Story of Rebel Military Prisons. abr. ed. John McElroy. 1977. pap. 1.75 o.p. (ISBN 0-449-30764-6, X764, Prem). Fawcett.

Andes. Jack MacKinnon. (World's Wild Places Ser.). (Illus.). 1976. 12.95 (ISBN 0-8094-2050-3). Time-Life.

Ando Shoeki & the Anatomy of Japanese Feudalism. E. Herbert Norman. (Studies in Japanese History & Civilization). 254p. 1979. Repr. of 1949 ed. 26.25 (ISBN 0-89093-224-7). U Pubns Amer.

Andover in the American Revolution: A New England Town in a Period of Crisis, 1763-1790. Edward M. Harris. LC 76-13303. (Illus.). 1976. 9.50 (ISBN 0-9603160-0-0). Town of Andover.

Andre. Dietz. 1979. pap. 6.95 (ISBN 0-89272-052-2). Down East.

Andre Breton. J. F. Matthews. LC 67-16892. (Columbia Essays on Modern Writers Ser.: No. 26). (Orig.). 1967. pap. 2.00 (ISBN 0-231-02910-1, MW26). Columbia U Pr.

Andre Breton: L'Ecriture surrealiste. Gerard Durozoi & Bernard Lecherbonnier. (Collection themes et textes). 255p. (Orig., Fr.). 1974. pap. 6.50 (ISBN 2-03-035025-7, 2664). Larousse.

Andre Chenier. Richard Smernoff. (World Author Ser.: France: No. 418). 1977. lib. bdg. 12.50 (ISBN 0-8057-6258-2). Twayne.

Andre Chenier: Elegies & Camille. Bilingual ed. Tr. by L. R. Lind from Fr. LC 77-18578. 1978. pap. text ed. 7.75 (ISBN 0-8191-0412-4). U Pr of Amer.

Andre Chenier: His Life, Death & Glory. Vernon Loggins. LC 65-13701. xii, 292p. 1965. 12.95x (ISBN 0-8214-0009-6). Ohio U Pr.

Andre Gide. Thomas Cordle. (World Authors Ser.: France: No. 86). lib. bdg. 12.50 (ISBN 0-8057-2364-1). Twayne.
Andre Gide. Vinio Rossi. LC 68-54458. (Columbia Ser.: No. 35). (Orig.). 1968. pap. 2.00 (ISBN 0-231-02960-8, MW35). Columbia U Pr.
Andre Kertesz, No. 6. Carole Kismark. LC 77-70070. (Aperture History of Photography Ser.). 1977. pap. 8.95 (ISBN 0-912334-96-7). Aperture.
Andre Kertesz: Sixty Years of Photography. Andre Kertesz. Ed. by Nicolas Ducrot. (Large Format Ser). (Illus.). 1978. pap. 8.95 o.p. (ISBN 0-14-004744-1). Penguin.
Andre Malraux. Denis Boak. 1968. 12.95x o.p. (ISBN 0-19-815379-1). Oxford U Pr.
Andre Malraux. Wilbur Frohock. (Columbia Essays on Modern Writers Ser.: No. 71). 1974. pap. 2.00 (ISBN 0-231-03441-5). Columbia U Pr.
Andre Malraux. James R. Hewitt. LC 70-15661. (Modern Literature Ser.). 1978. 10.95 (ISBN 0-8044-2379-2). Ungar.
Andre Malraux & the Metamorphosis of Death. Thomas J. Kline. 250p. 1973. 15.00x (ISBN 0-231-03608-6). Columbia U Pr.
Andre Maurois. David G. Larg. 239p. 1980. Repr. of 1931 ed. lib. bdg. 25.00 (ISBN 0-8492-1633-8). R West.
Andre Previn: A Biography. Martin Bookspan & Ross Yockey. LC 80-2746. (Illus.). 384p. 1981. 14.95. Doubleday.
Andrea Costa & the Rise of Socialism in the Romagna. Manuel G. Gonzales. LC 79-6771. 419p. 1980. text ed. 21.75 (ISBN 0-8191-0952-5); pap. text ed. 13.75 (ISBN 0-8191-0953-3). U Pr of Amer.
Andrea Palladio. Lionello Puppi. LC 74-21496. (Illus.). 456p. 1975. 60.00 (ISBN 0-8212-0645-1, 039705). NYGS.
Andreae & the Formula of Concord. Robert Kolb. 1977. pap. 7.50 (ISBN 0-570-03741-7, 12-2645). Concordia.
Andres Bello. Rafael Caldera. 1977. text ed. 25.00x o.p. (ISBN 0-04-920049-6). Allen Unwin.
Andreuccio de Perugia. Boccaccio. (Easy Reader, A). pap. 2.90 (ISBN 0-88436-049-0, ITA110051). EMC.
Andrew Carnegie. George Swetnam. (United States Authors Ser.: No. 355). 1980. lib. bdg. 10.95 (ISBN 0-8057-7239-1). Twayne.
Andrew Furuseth, Emancipator of the Seamen. Hyman G. Weintraub. (Institute of Industrial Relations, UC Berkeley). 1959. 18.50x (ISBN 0-520-01322-0). U of Cal Pr.
Andrew Jackson. Robert V. Remini. (World Leaders Ser). 1966. lib. bdg. 8.95 o.p. (ISBN 0-8057-3048-6). Twayne.
Andrew Jackson. William G. Sumner. LC 80-18576. (American Statesmen Ser.). 405p. 1981. pap. 6.95 (ISBN 0-87754-176-0). Chelsea Hse.
Andrew Jackson: Symbol for an Age. John W. Ward. (YA) (gr. 9 up). 1962. pap. 4.95 (ISBN 0-19-500699-2, GB). Oxford U Pr.
Andrew Johnson & Reconstruction. Eric L. McKitrick. LC 60-5467. 1964. pap. 12.00x (ISBN 0-226-56046-5). U of Chicago Pr.
Andrew Johnson & the Uses of Constitutional Power. James E. Sefton. (Library of American Biography). 1980. 9.95 (ISBN 0-316-77990-3); pap. 4.95 (ISBN 0-316-77989-X). Little.
Andrew Lang. Eleanor Langstaff. (English Authors Ser.: No. 241). 1978. 12.50 (ISBN 0-8057-6719-3). Twayne.
Andrew Law: American Psalmodist. Richard A. Crawford. LC 68-15331. (Pi Kappa Lambda Studies in American Music). (Illus.). 1968. 16.75x o.s.i. (ISBN 0-8101-0070-3). Northwestern U Pr.
Andrew M. White, Educator, Historian, Diplomat. Glenn C. Altschuler. LC 78-58065. (Illus.). 1978. 17.50x (ISBN 0-8014-1156-4). Cornell U Pr.
Andrew Marvell: Essays on the Tercentenary of His Death. Ed. by R. I. Brett & G. F. Grant. 1979. 19.95x (ISBN 0-19-713435-1). Oxford U Pr.
Andrew Murray & His Message. W. M. Douglas. (Christian Biography Ser.). 336p. 1981. pap. 3.95 (ISBN 0-8010-2908-2). Baker Bk.
Andrew Young: A Biography. Carl Gardner. LC 77-88945. (Illus.). 1978. 10.95 o.p. (ISBN 0-8069-8118-0, 002700). Sterling.
Andrey Bely: A Critical Review. Ed. by Gerald Janecek. LC 77-75449. 232p. 1978. 16.00x (ISBN 0-8131-1368-7). U Pr of Ky.
Andro, the Star of Bethlehem. Anne Claire. (Illus.). 32p. (Orig.). (gr. k-6). 1981. pap. 1.95 (ISBN 0-87239-472-7, 2870). Standard Pub.
Androcles & the Lion. Gerald Rose & Elizabeth Rose. (Illus.). (ps-5). 1971. 6.50 (ISBN 0-571-09774-X, Pub. by Faber & Faber). Merrimack Bk Serv.
Androcles & the Lion. George B. Shaw. (Penguin Plays Ser.). (Orig.). (YA) (gr. 9 up). 1963. pap. 2.95 (ISBN 0-14-048010-2, PL5). Penguin.
Androgens & Antiandrogens. Ed. by Luciano Martini & Marcella Motta. LC 76-19853. 1977. 36.00 (ISBN 0-89004-141-5). Raven.
Androgynous Manager. Alice G. Sargent. 240p. 1981. 12.95 (ISBN 0-8144-5568-9). Am Mgmt.
Androgyny: Toward a New Theory of Sexuality. June Singer. LC 76-2825. 1977. pap. 3.95 (ISBN 0-385-11026-X, Anch). Doubleday.
Androids, Time Machines, & Blue Giraffes. Ed. by Roger Elwood & Vic Ghidalia. 384p. 1973. 6.95 o.s.i. (ISBN 0-695-80369-7). Follett.
Andromache. Euripides. Ed. by P. T. Stevens. (Plays of Euripides Ser.). 264p. 1971. 14.95x (ISBN 0-19-814183-1). Oxford U Pr.
Andromache. Jean B. Racine. Tr. by Herma Briffault from Fr. 1957. 4.75 (ISBN 0-8120-5006-1); pap. text ed. 1.95 (ISBN 0-8120-0028-5). Barron.
Andromache Oof Euripides: An Interpretation. David Kovacs. LC 80-11220. write for info. (ISBN 0-89130-389-8); lib. bdg. 10.00x (ISBN 0-89130-390-1). Scholars Pr CA.
Andrus Bindery: A History of the Shop 1831-1838, Hartford. 1940. 2.00 (ISBN 0-686-26774-5). Conn Hist Soc.
Andy Adams' Campfire Tales. Andy Adams. Ed. by Wilson M. Hudson. LC 75-29131. (Illus.). xxxii, 296p. 1976. 13.50x (ISBN 0-8032-0870-7); pap. 6.50 (ISBN 0-8032-5835-6, 615, Bison). U of Nebr Pr.
Andy & Mister Cunningham. Jane Thayer. (Illus.). (ps-3). 1969. PLB 6.48 o.p. (ISBN 0-688-31024-9). Morrow.
Andy & the School Bus. Jerrold Beim. (Illus.). (gr. k-3). 1947. PLB 7.44 (ISBN 0-688-31022-2). Morrow.
Andy Jessup. Winston M. Estes. 1977. pap. 1.75 o.s.i. (ISBN 0-380-01852-7, 36491). Avon.
Andy Says Bonjour. Pat Diska & Chris Jenkyns. LC 54-11522. (Illus.). (gr. 1-3). 1954. 5.95 (ISBN 0-8149-0297-9). Vanguard.
Andy: That's My Name. T. De Paola. (ps-3). 1973. 6.95 (ISBN 0-13-036731-1); pap. 2.50 (ISBN 0-13-036749-4). P-H.
Andy Warhol's Exposures. 1980. 12.50 (ISBN 0-448-12658-3). G&D.
Ane Breif Descriptioun of the Well of the Woman-Hill Besyde Abirdene. Gilbert Skeyne. LC 72-233. (English Experience Ser.: No. 104). 1969. Repr. of 1580 ed. 7.00 (ISBN 90-221-0104-5). Walter J Johnson.
Anecdotes of Destiny. Isak Dinesen. 1958. 8.95 o.p. (ISBN 0-394-41528-0). Random.
Anecdotes of Frederick Handel & John Christopher Smith. William Coxe. (Music Reprint Ser.). 1979. Repr. of 1799 ed. 22.50 (ISBN 0-306-79512-4). Da Capo.
Anecdotes of Public Men. J. W. Forney. LC 70-87540. (American Scene Ser). 1970. Repr. of 1873 ed. lib. bdg. 25.00 (ISBN 0-306-71456-6). Da Capo.
Anemone Fishes. new ed. Gerald Allen. 20.00 (ISBN 0-87666-001-4, H-942). TFH Pubns.
Anencephaly. Ronald J. Lemire et al. LC 77-83688. 1977. 28.00 (ISBN 0-89004-179-2). Raven.
American Theatre Annual, 1979-80. Ed. by Catharine R. Hughes. (Illus.). 200p. 1981. 35.00 (ISBN 0-8103-0419-8). Gale.
Anesthesia. Ed. by Ronald D. Miller. (Illus.). 1500p. 1981. lib. bdg. 65.00 (ISBN 0-443-08082-8). Churchill.
Anesthesia & Neurosurgery. James E. Cottrell & Herman Turndorf. LC 79-24676. (Illus.). 1979. text ed. 49.50 (ISBN 0-8016-1036-2). Mosby.
Anesthesia & the Obese Patient. Ed. by Burnell R. Brown, Jr. (Contemporary Anesthesia Practice Ser.: Vol. 6). 1981. write for info. (ISBN 0-8036-1273-7). Davis Co.
Anesthesia & the Patient with Endocrine Disease. Ed. by Burnell R. Brown, Jr. LC 80-13067. (Contemporary Anesthesia Practice Ser.: Vol. 3). (Illus.). 210p. 1980. text ed. 24.00 (ISBN 0-8036-1264-8). Davis Co.
Anesthesia & the Patient with Liver Disease. Ed. by Burnell R. Brown, Jr. LC 80-22088. (Contemporary Anesthesia Practice Ser.: Vol. 4). 190p. 1980. 25.00 (ISBN 0-8036-1268-0). Davis Co.
Anesthesia & Uncommon Diseases: Pathophysiologic & Clinical Correlations. 2nd ed. Jordan Katz et al. (Illus.). 600p. Date not set. text ed. price not set (ISBN 0-7216-5302-2). Saunders.
Anesthesia for Infants & Children. 4th ed. Betty J. Smith. LC 79-18284. (Illus.). 1979. text ed. 52.50 (ISBN 0-8016-4699-5). Mosby.
Anesthesia for Outpatient Surgery. David D. Cohen & John B. Dillon. (Illus.). 84p. 1970. 11.75 (ISBN 0-398-00324-6). C C Thomas.
Anesthesiology. 4th ed. Robert C. Brown. (Medical Examination Review Book Ser.: Vol. 12). 1980. spiral bdg. 8.50 o.p. (ISBN 0-87488-112-9). Med Exam.
Anesthesiology. 5th ed. Ed. by Thomas J. DeKornfeld & Michael W. Detmar. LC 61-66847. 1980. pap. 15.00. Med Exam.
Anesthesiology Continuing Education Review. Robert E. Johnstone. 1975. spiral bdg. 14.00 (ISBN 0-87488-353-9). Med Exam.
Anesthetic Implications of Congenital Anomalies in Children. Ed. by Linda C. Stehling & Howard L. Zauder. 224p. 1980. 18.50x (ISBN 0-8385-0102-8). ACC.
Aneurysmal Subarachnoid Hemorrhage: Report of the Cooperative Study. Adolph L. Sahs et al. (Illus.). write for info. (ISBN 0-8067-1861-7). Urban & S.
Anfange der Hebraischen Grammaik (1895) Together with Die Hebraische Sprachwissenschaft Vom 10, Bus Zum 16. Jahrhundert (1892) Wilhelm Bacher. (Studies in the History of Linguistics: No. 4). 1974. text ed. 42.75x (ISBN 0-391-01676-8). Humanities.
Anfibios y Reptils de Puerto Rico. Juan A. Rivero. LC 76-11798. (Illus.). 448p. (Orig.). 1976. pap. write for info. (ISBN 0-8477-2317-8). U. of PR Pr.
Angekommen. David Shotter. 1975. pap. text ed. 8.95x o.p. (ISBN 0-435-38843-6); two tapes 54.00 o.p. (ISBN 0-435-38846-0). Heinemann Ed.
Angel Book. Ann Cameron. (Illus.). 1977. pap. 6.95 o.p. (ISBN 0-345-27263-3). Ballantine.
Angel Dust Blues. Todd Strasser. (gr. 7-12). 1981. pap. 1.75 (ISBN 0-440-90956-2, LE). Dell.
Angel in Armor. Ernest Becker. LC 69-12803. 1969. 5.95 o.s.i. (ISBN 0-8076-0488-7). Braziller.
Angel in Armor: A Post-Freudian Perspective on the Nature of Man. Ernest Becker. LC 69-12803. 1975. pap. 3.95 (ISBN 0-02-902280-0). Free Pr.
Angel in Heavy Shoes: A Katie Rose Story. Lenora M. Weber. LC 68-13589. (gr. 7-11). 1968. 10.95 (ISBN 0-690-09189-3, TYC-J). T Y Crowell.
Angel in My House. Tobias Palmer. LC 75-22990. (Illus.). 64p. 1975. pap. 1.95 o.p. (ISBN 0-87793-103-8). Ave Maria.
Angel in My House. Tobias Palmer. 64p. 1981. pap. 1.95x (ISBN 0-912484-21-7). Joseph Nichols.
Angel in the Fire. Frances Roberts. 1979. pap. 2.50 (ISBN 0-932814-31-X). Kings Farspan.
Angel in the House. Pamela D'Arcy. (Orig.). 1980. pap. 1.75 (ISBN 0-515-05199-3). Jove Pubns.
Angel Inn. Comtesse De Segur. Tr. by Joan Aiken from Fr. LC 78-12784. (Illus.). (gr. 3 up). 1978. 9.95 (ISBN 0-916144-28-3); pap. 6.95 (ISBN 0-916144-29-1). Stemmer Hse.
Angel of Apocalypse: Blake's Idea of Milton. Joseph A. Wittreich, Jr. LC 74-27316. 328p. 1975. 30.00x (ISBN 0-299-06800-5). U of Wis Pr.
Angel of Bethesda. Cotton Mather. Ed. by Gordon W. Jones. LC 72-185323. 384p. 1972. 19.95x (ISBN 0-8271-7220-6, Dist. by U Pr of Va). Am Antiquarian.
Angel of Light. Joyce C. Oates. 480p. 1981. 14.95 (ISBN 0-525-05483-9). Dutton.
Angel Range. John Reese. 1976. pap. 0.95 o.p. (ISBN 0-685-72360-7, LB386NK, Leisure Bks). Nordon Pubns.
Angel Unaware. Dale E. Rogers. 1975. pap. 1.25 (ISBN 0-685-84180-4, PV091). Jove Pubns.
Angel Unaware. Dale E. Rogers. (Orig.). pap. 1.50 (ISBN 0-515-05325-2). Jove Pubns.
Angela Davis: An Autobiography. Angela Davis. LC 73-20580. 1974. 8.95 o.p. (ISBN 0-394-48978-0, Co-Pub. with Geis). Random.
Angela Preuss: Ten Million Dollar Lady. Angela Preuss & Sherrill Stevens. 125p. 1980. 10.95 (ISBN 0-931804-07-8). Skipworth Pr.
Angeles: Agentes Secretos de Dios. Billy Graham. Tr. by Juan Rojas from Eng. LC 76-20259. 168p. (Orig., Span.). 1976. pap. 2.75 (ISBN 0-89922-069-X). Edit Caribe.
Angelfish. Braz Walker. (Illus.). 1974. 4.95 (ISBN 0-87666-755-8, PS-711). TFH Pubns.
Angelfish: Its Life Cycle. William White, Jr. LC 75-14511. (Colorful Nature Ser.). (Illus.). 64p. (gr. 5 up). 1975. 9.95 (ISBN 0-8069-3482-4); PLB 9.29 (ISBN 0-8069-3483-2). Sterling.
Angell Fayre or Strumpet Lewd: Jane Shaw As an Example of Erring Beauty in 16th Century Literature, 2 vols. Esther Y. Beith-Halahmi. (Salzburg Studies in English Literature, Elizabethan & Renaissance Studies: Nos. 26-27). 361p. 1974. Set. pap. text ed. 50.25x (ISBN 0-391-01322-X). Humanities.
Angelo. Jean Giono. Tr. by Alma E. Murch. 1960. 10.95 o.p. (ISBN 0-7206-0440-0). Dufour.
Angels. Billy Graham. 1976. pap. 2.50 (ISBN 0-671-43281-8). PB.
Angels & Indians. Joan Hodgson. (Illus.). (gr. 2-7). 1974. 6.95 (ISBN 0-85487-033-4). De Vorss.
Angels & Men. Ladislaus Boros. 1976. 6.95 (ISBN 0-8164-0329-5). Crossroad NY.
Angels & Other Strangers. Katherine Paterson. (Illus.). 128p. (gr. 1-8). 1980. pap. 1.95 (ISBN 0-380-51144-4, 51144, Camelot). Avon.
Angels & Other Strangers: Family Christmas Stories. Katherine Paterson. LC 79-63797. (gr. 1 up). 1979. 8.95 (ISBN 0-690-03992-1, TYC-J). T Y Crowell.
Angels & Principalities. A. W. Carr. (Society for the New Testament Studies Monographs: No. 42). 240p. Date not set. price not set (ISBN 0-521-23429-8). Cambridge U Pr.
Angel's Laundromat. Ed. by Lucia Berlin. (New World Writing Ser). (Illus.). 96p. (Orig.). 1981. pap. 4.95 (ISBN 0-686-69426-0). Turtle Isl Foun.
Angels on Assignment. Charles Hunter & Frances Hunter. 1979. pap. 3.50 (ISBN 0-917726-33-2). Hunter Bks.
Angels: Secret Agents of God & Satan. H. M. Richards, Jr. LC 80-22223. (Flame Ser.). 64p. 1980. pap. 0.95 (ISBN 0-8127-0313-8). Southern Pub.
Anger & Assertiveness in Pastoral Care. David W. Augsburger. Ed. by Howard J. Clinebell & Howard W. Stone. LC 78-14660. (Creative Pastoral Care & Counseling Ser.). 96p. 1979. pap. 2.95 (ISBN 0-8006-0562-4, 1-562). Fortress.
Anger, & Beyond: The Negro Writer in the United States. Ed. by Herbert Hill. 1966. 10.00 o.p. (ISBN 0-06-011892-X, HarpT). Har-Row.
Anger in Young Children. Florence Goodenough. LC 77-141547. (University of Minnesota Institute of Child Welfare Monographs: No. 9). (Illus.). 278p. 1975. Repr. of 1931 ed. lib. bdg. 22.00x (ISBN 0-8371-5894-X, CWGA). Greenwood.
Anger: Psychology, Physiology, Pathology. Frederic R. Stearns. 84p. 1972. photocopy ed. spiral 10.75 (ISBN 0-398-02612-2). C C Thomas.
Angie's First Case. Donal J. Sobol. LC 80-70011. (Illus.). 128p. (gr. 3-7). 1981. 8.95 (ISBN 0-590-07564-0, Four Winds). Schol Bk Serv.
Angina Pectoris, Vol. 1. I. E. Katzeff & H. Edwards. (Annual Research Reviews). 1978. 26.40 (ISBN 0-88831-023-4). Eden Med Res.
Angiography in Trauma: A Work Atlas. Yoram Ben-Menachem. (Illus.). 350p. Date not set. text ed. 75.00 (ISBN 0-7216-1733-6). Saunders.
Angiography in Vascular Disease. Harvey L. Neiman & James S. Yao. (Illus.). 700p. 1981. text ed. write for info. (ISBN 0-443-08030-5). Churchill. Postponed.
Angiotensin Converting Enzyme Inhibitors: Mechanisms of Action & Clinical Implications. Z. P. Horowitz. 1981. text ed. price not set (ISBN 0-8067-0821-2). Urban & S.
Angle of Repose. Wallace Stegner. 1978. pap. 2.50 (ISBN 0-449-23796-6, Crest). Fawcett.
Angler's Encyclopaedia. Colin Willock. 1975. 14.95 (ISBN 0-7207-0639-4, Pub. by Michael Joseph). Merrimack Bk Serv.
Angler's Guide to Baja California. Tom Miller. Ed. by Shirley Miller. (Illus.). 1979. pap. 5.95x (ISBN 0-914622-04-8). Baja Trail.
Angler's Guide to the Salt Water Game Fishes: Atlantic & Pacific. Edward C. Migdalski. (Illus.). 1958. 12.95 o.p. (ISBN 0-8260-6080-3). Ronald Pr.
Angler's Workshop. Letcher Lambuth. 212p. 1979. 49.50x (ISBN 0-918400-01-5, Pub. by Champoeg Pr). Intl Schol Bk Serv.
Angles Are Easy As Pie. Robert Froman. LC 75-6608. (Young Math Ser). (Illus.). 40p. (gr. k-3). 1976. PLB 7.89 (ISBN 0-690-00916-X, TYC-J). T Y Crowell.
Anglia Libera. John Toland et al. Ed. by David S. Berkowitz & Samuel E. Thorne. LC 77-89231. (Classics of English Legal History in the Modern Era Ser.: Vol. 71). 400p. 1979. lib. bdg. 40.00 (ISBN 0-8240-3171-7). Garland Pub.
Anglican Hymn Book. 12.50x o.p. (ISBN 0-85190-073-9). Attic Pr.
Anglican Partners. James W. Kennedy. 1978. 2.00 (ISBN 0-686-28772-X). Forward Movement.
Anglicimos Profesionales De Puerto Rico. Elena Mellado De Hunter. LC 80-17935. (Coleccion Mente y Palabra). 241p. (Span.). 1980. 6.25 (ISBN 0-8477-0578-1); pap. 5.00 (ISBN 0-8477-0579-X). U of PR Pr.
Angling in Norway. E. Welle-Strand. (Illus.). 1972. pap. 5.00x (ISBN 0-89918-510-X, N-510). Vanous.
Angling Ways. Eric Marshall-Hardy. 1978. 10.95 o.p. (ISBN 0-214-66870-3, 8007, Dist. by Arco). Barrie & Jenkins.
Anglo-American & German Abbreviations in Environmental Protection. Peter Wennrich. 624p. 1979. 60.00 (ISBN 0-89664-096-5, Pub. by K G Saur). Gale.
Anglo-American & German Abbreviations in Science & Technology Supplement. 1981. 52.50 (ISBN 3-598-20512-0). Bowker.
Anglo-American Cataloguing Rules. 1967. pap. 11.00x (ISBN 0-85365-310-0, Pub. by Lib Assn England). Oryx Pr.

Anglo-American Legal Bibliographies. W. L. Friend. 1966. 15.00x (ISBN 0-8377-2128-8). Rothman.

Anglo-American Political Relations, Sixteen Seventy-Five to Seventeen Seventy-Five. Ed. by Alison G. Olson & Richard M. Brown. LC 73-108758. 1970. 20.00 (ISBN 0-8135-0624-7). Rutgers U Pr.

Anglo-American Steamship Rivalry in China, 1862-1874. Ed. by Liu Kwang-Ching. LC 62-9426. (East Asian Ser: No. 8). (Illus.). 1962. 10.00x (ISBN 0-674-03601-8). Harvard U Pr.

Anglo-Boer War. David Johnson. (Jackdaw Ser: No. 68). (Illus.). 1969. 5.95 o.p. (ISBN 0-670-12618-7, Grossman). Viking Pr.

Anglo-Indian Dictionary: A Glossary of Indian Terms Used in English and of Such English & Other Than Indian Terms As Have Obtained Special Meanings in India. George C. Whitworth. 1977. Repr. of 1885 ed. 13.50 o.p. (ISBN 0-8364-0380-0). South Asia Bks.

Anglo-Indians. V. R. Gaikwad. 1968. 10.00x (ISBN 0-210-27090-X). Asia.

Anglo-Irish of the Nineteenth Century, 3 vols. John Banim & Michael Banim. Ed. by Robert L. Wolff. (Ireland Nineteenth Century Fiction Ser. Two: Vol. 20). 934p. 1979. Set. lib. bdg. 96.00 (ISBN 0-8240-3469-4). Garland Pub.

Anglo-Maratha Relations & Malcolm Seventeen Ninety-Eight to Eighteen Thirty. U. N. Chakravorty. 1979. text ed. 15.00x (ISBN 0-210-40623-2). Asia.

Anglo-Norman England, Ten Sixty-Six to Eleven Fifty-Four. M. Altschul. LC 78-80816. (Bibliographical Handbooks of the Conference on British Studies). 1969. 17.50 (ISBN 0-521-07582-3). Cambridge U Pr.

Anglo-Norman Era in Scottish History. G. W. Barrow. 240p. 1980. 49.50x (ISBN 0-19-822473-7). Oxford U Pr.

Anglo-Norman Ulster: The History & Archaeology of an Irish Barony 1177-1400. T. E. McNeill. (Illus.). 166p. 1980. text ed. 32.50x (ISBN 0-686-64580-4). Humanities.

Anglo-Saxon Age. D. J. Fisher. LC 74-159804. (History of England Ser.). 350p. 1974. text ed. 22.00x (ISBN 0-582-48277-1); pap. text ed. 10.95x (ISBN 0-582-48084-1). Longman.

Anglo-Saxon & English Vocabularies, 2 Vols. T. Wright. Set. 125.00 (ISBN 0-685-05174-9). Adler.

Anglo-Saxon Animal Art & Its Germanic Background. George Speake. (Illus.). 164p. 1980. text ed. 50.00x (ISBN 0-19-813194-1). Oxford U Pr.

Anglo-Saxon Architecture. H. M. Taylor. LC 65-3244. (Illus.). 1978. Vol. 1, 1965. 90.00 (ISBN 0-521-22481-0); Vol. 2. 85.00 (ISBN 0-521-22482-9); Vol. 3. 105.00 (ISBN 0-521-21692-3); Set. 235.00 (ISBN 0-521-21693-1). Cambridge U Pr.

Anglo-Saxon Architecture, 2 vols. H. M. Taylor & Joan Taylor. LC 65-3244. (Illus.). 868p. 1981. pap. 39.50 (ISBN 0-521-29914-4). Cambridge U Pr.

Anglo-Saxon Chronicle. Garmonsway. 1975. pap. 4.50 (ISBN 0-460-11624-X, Evman). Dutton.

Anglo-Saxon Church: Its History, Revenues & General Character. 4th ed. Henry Soames. LC 80-2212. 1981. Repr. of 1856 ed. 39.50 (ISBN 0-404-18786-2). AMS Pr.

Anglo-Saxon Dictionary. Compiled by Joseph Bosworth et al. 2066p. 1972. Repr. of 1898 ed. 98.00x (ISBN 0-19-863101-4); 1921 supplement & addenda 79.00x (ISBN 0-19-863112-X); addenda 1972 pap. 14.50x (ISBN 0-19-863110-3). Oxford U Pr.

Anglo-Saxon England, 8 vols. Ed. by Peter A. Clemoes. Incl. Vol. 1. 320p. 1972. 47.50 (ISBN 0-521-08557-8); Vol. 2. 300p. 1973. 47.50 (ISBN 0-521-20218-3); Vol. 3. 320p. 1974. 47.50 (ISBN 0-521-20574-3); Vol. 4. 270p. 1975. 47.50 (ISBN 0-521-20868-8); Vol. 5. 1976. 47.50 (ISBN 0-521-21270-7); Vol. 6. 1977. 47.50 (ISBN 0-521-21701-6); Vol. 7. 1979. 47.50 (ISBN 0-521-22164-1); Vol. 8. 1980. 57.50 (ISBN 0-521-22788-7). LC 78-19043. (Illus.). Cambridge U Pr.

Anglo-Saxon England. 3rd ed. Frank Stenton. (Oxford History of England Ser.). 1971. 33.00x (ISBN 0-19-821716-1). Oxford U Pr.

Anglo-Saxon England, Vol. 9. P. Clemoes. LC 78-190423. (Anglo-Saxon England Ser.). (Illus.). 330p. Date not set. 56.00 (ISBN 0-521-23449-2). Cambridge U Pr.

Anglo-Saxon Poems. Francis P. Magoun, Jr. 49p. 1980. Repr. of 1965 ed. write for info. (ISBN 0-89984-334-4). Century Bookbindery.

Anglo-Saxon Prose. Ed. by Michael Swanton. (Rowman & Littlefield University Library). 188p. 1975. 11.00x (ISBN 0-87471-545-8); pap. 5.00x (ISBN 0-87471-544-X). Rowman.

Anglo-Saxon Sceattas in England: Their Origin, Chronology & Distribution. C. H. Sutherland. (Numismatic Chronicle Reprint Ser.). pap. 2.50 (ISBN 0-915018-30-6). Attic Bks.

Anglo-Saxon Writs. Florence E. Harmer. LC 80-2225. 1981. Repr. of 1952 ed. 69.50 (ISBN 0-404-18762-5). AMS Pr.

Anglo Saxons: How They Lived & Worked. G. A. Lester. LC 76-20156. 1976. 11.95 (ISBN 0-8023-1266-7). Dufour.

Anglo-Scandinavian Law Dictionary. R. Anderson. 1977. pap. 15.00x (ISBN 82-00-02365-6, Dist. by Columbia U Pr). Universitet.

Anglo-Scottish Literary Relations: Fourteen Thirty to Fifteen Fifty. G. Kratzmann. LC 78-74537. 1980. 36.00 (ISBN 0-521-22665-1). Cambridge U Pr.

Angola: Five Centuries of Conflict. Lawrence W. Henderson. LC 79-5089. (Africa in the Modern World Ser.). (Illus.). 1979. 17.50x (ISBN 0-8014-1247-1). Cornell U Pr.

Angola in Flames. Kavalam M. Panikkar. 1962. 5.00x (ISBN 0-210-26856-5). Asia.

Angola Under the Portuguese: The Myth & the Reality. Gerald J. Bender. (Perspectives on Southern Africa Ser.: No. 23). 1978. 19.50x (ISBN 0-520-03221-7); pap. 7.95x (ISBN 0-520-04274-3). U of Cal Pr.

Angola Under the Portuguese: The Myth & the Reality. Gerald J. Bender. (Illus.). 315p. 1981. pap. 6.95x (ISBN 0-520-04274-3, CAMPUS 269). U of Cal Pr.

Angolan Revolution Vol. 1: The Anatomy of an Explosion, 1950-1962. John A. Marcum. (Studies in Communism, Revisionism & Revolution). 1969. 30.00x (ISBN 0-262-13048-3). MIT Pr.

Angolan Revolution Volume II: Exile Politics & Guerrilla Warfare, 1962-1976. John A. Marcum. LC 69-11310. 1978. 30.00x (ISBN 0-262-13136-6). MIT Pr.

Angry Book. Theodore I. Rubin. 1969. pap. 3.95 (ISBN 0-02-077820-1). Macmillan.

Angry Candy, the American As Consumer. John Pauker. LC 76-24127. (Illus.). 1976. pap. 2.50 (ISBN 0-917530-01-2). Pig Iron Pr.

Angry Eye: A Comment on Life & Letters. Max Harris. 1974. text ed. 16.00 (ISBN 0-08-017373-X). Pergamon.

Angry Goddess. Jai Ratan. 8.00 (ISBN 0-89253-634-9). Ind-US Inc.

Angry Sea. rev. ed. Jean N. Dale & Willard D. Sheeler. (Reading & Exercise Ser.: No. 2). 1975. pap. 2.50 (ISBN 0-89285-051-5); cassette tapes 29.50 (ISBN 0-89285-069-8). ELS Intl.

Angry Sea. Ed. by Jean N. Dale & Willard D. Sheeler. (Reading & Exercise Ser.). (Illus.). (gr. k-6). 1973. pap. text ed. 2.50x (ISBN 0-19-433620-4). Oxford U Pr.

Angry Voices: Left-Of-Center Politics in the New Deal Era. Donald R. McCoy. LC 78-137975. (American History & Culture in the Twentieth Century Ser). 1971. Repr. of 1958 ed. 13.50 (ISBN 0-8046-1431-8). Kennikat.

Anguish of Change. Louis Harris. 1974. pap. text ed. 5.95x (ISBN 0-393-09315-8). Norton.

Anguish of the Jews: Twenty-Three Centuries of Anti-Semitism. Edward H. Flannery. (Orig.). 1965. 6.95 o.p. (ISBN 0-686-66479-5); pap. 2.95 (ISBN 0-02-032280-1). Macmillan.

Angular Momentum. 2nd ed. David M. Brink & George R. Satchler. (Oxford Library of the Physical Sciences). (Orig.). 1968. pap. 14.95x (ISBN 0-19-851419-0). Oxford U Pr.

Angus Lost. Marjorie Flack. (ps-k). 1941. 5.95a (ISBN 0-385-07214-7); PLB (ISBN 0-385-07601-0); pap. 1.49 (ISBN 0-385-08009-3). Doubleday.

Angus y el Gato. Marjorie Flack. LC 76-40263. (ps-k). 1977. PLB 4.95 (ISBN 0-385-11697-7). Doubleday.

Anhydrobiosis. Ed. by John H. Crowe & James S. Clegg. LC 73-12354. (Benchmark Papers in Biological Concepts Ser.). 496p. 1973. text ed. 43.50 (ISBN 0-12-786277-3). Acad Pr.

Ania V Strane Chudes. Lewis Carroll. Tr. by Vladimir Nabokov. 1981. 15.00 (ISBN 0-88233-658-4); pap. 6.50 (ISBN 0-88233-659-2). Ardis Pubs.

Animadversions on Mr. Congreve's Late Answer to Mr. Collier: In Dialogue Between Mr. Smith & Mr. Johnson. LC 78-170440. (English Stage Ser.: Vol. 24). lib. bdg. 50.00 (ISBN 0-8240-0607-0). Garland Pub.

Animal Acrobats. David Nockels. LC 80-25703. (Animal Pop-Up Ser.). (Illus.). 12p. (ps-3). 1981. 3.50 (ISBN 0-8037-0088-1). Dial.

Animal Agriculture: Human Needs in the 21st Century. Ed. by Wilson G. Pond et al. 600p. 1980. lib. bdg. 20.00x (ISBN 0-86531-032-7). Westview.

Animal Agriculture: The Biology, Husbandry, & Use of Domestic Animals. 2nd ed. Ed. by H. H. Cole & W. N. Garrett. LC 79-18984. (Animal Science Ser.). (Illus.). 1980. text ed. 21.95x (ISBN 0-7167-1099-4). W H Freeman.

Animal Alphabet from A to Z. Barbara S. Hazen. (Illus.). 24p. (gr. k-1). 1976. PLB 7.15 o.p. (ISBN 0-307-69050-4, Golden Pr). Western Pub.

Animal, Animal, Where Do You Live? Jane B. Moncure. LC 75-29237. (Illus.). (ps-3). 1975. 5.95 (ISBN 0-913778-14-1). Childs World.

Animal Appetites. George F. Mason. (Illus.). (gr. 3-7). 1966. 6.25 o.p. (ISBN 0-688-21030-9). Morrow.

Animal Architects. Russell Freedman. LC 79-141404. (Illus.). 126p. (gr. 4-7). 1971. 5.95 (ISBN 0-8234-0182-0). Holiday.

Animal Athletes. David Nockels. LC 80-25008. (Animal Pop-Up Ser.). (Illus.). 12p. (ps-3). 1981. 3.50 (ISBN 0-8037-0106-3). Dial.

Animal Babies. (Block Bk.). (ps). 1981. 2.50 (ISBN 0-686-69365-5, Golden Pr). Western Pub.

Animal Babies. Robert Broomfield. (Illus.). (ps). 1979. 1.25 (ISBN 0-370-02008-1, Pub. by Chatto Bodley Jonathan). Merrimack Bk Serv.

Animal Baggage. George F. Mason. (Illus.). (gr. 5-9). 1961. 6.75 (ISBN 0-688-21031-7); PLB 5.52 o.p. (ISBN 0-688-31031-1). Morrow.

Animal Behavior. 3rd ed. Vincent G. Dethier & Eliot Stellar. 1970. pap. 9.95 ref ed. (ISBN 0-13-037440-7). P-H.

Animal Behavior. Niko Tinbergen. LC 65-13829. (Life Nature Library). (Illus.). (gr. 5 up). 1965. PLB 8.97 o.p. (ISBN 0-8094-0634-9, Pub. by Time-Life). Silver.

Animal Behavior. Niko Tinbergen. (Young Readers Library). (Illus.). 1977. lib. bdg. 7.95 (ISBN 0-686-51084-4). Silver.

Animal Behavior in Laboratory & Field. 2nd ed. Edward O. Price & Allen W. Stokes. (Illus.). 1975. pap. text ed. 9.95x (ISBN 0-7167-0762-4); tchr's manual avail. W H Freeman.

Animal Behavior: Readings from Scientific American. Intro. by Thomas Eisner & Edward O. Wilson. LC 75-2383. (Illus.). 1975. text ed. 19.95x (ISBN 0-7167-0511-7); pap. text ed. 9.95x (ISBN 0-7167-0510-9). W H Freeman.

Animal Behaviour: A Systems Approach. Frederick M. Toates. LC 79-41405. 304p. 1980. 50.00 (ISBN 0-471-27724-X); pap. 19.00 (ISBN 0-471-27723-1). Wiley.

Animal Biochromes & Structural Colours. Denis Fox. 1976. 33.75x (ISBN 0-520-02347-1). U of Cal Pr.

Animal Builders. David Nockels. LC 80-26316. (Animal Pop-Up Ser.). (Illus.). 12p. (ps-3). 1981. 3.50 (ISBN 0-8037-0113-6). Dial.

Animal Cafe. John Stadler. LC 80-15072. (Illus.). 32p. (gr. k-2). 8.95 (ISBN 0-87888-166-2). Bradbury Pr.

Animal Castle. Tanith Lee. 40p. (gr. 2 up). 1972. 4.95 (ISBN 0-374-30337-1). FS&G.

Animal Communication. Hubert Frings & Mable Frings. LC 76-50562. 1977. 9.95 o.p. (ISBN 0-8061-1392-8); pap. 5.95 (ISBN 0-8061-1393-6). U of Okla Pr.

Animal Cooperation: A Look at Sociobiology. Hallie Black. (Illus.). 64p. (gr. 7-9). 1981. 7.95 (ISBN 0-688-00360-5); PLB 7.63 (ISBN 0-688-00361-3). Morrow.

Animal Cracks. Robert Quackenbush. LC 75-1199. (Fun-To-Read Bk.). (Illus.). 64p. (gr. 1-4). 1975. 6.95 o.p. (ISBN 0-688-41702-7); PLB 6.67 (ISBN 0-688-51702-1). Lothrop.

Animal Cytology & Evolution. 3rd ed. M. J. White. LC 79-190418. (Illus.). 1000p. 1973. 105.00 (ISBN 0-521-07071-6); pap. 29.95x (ISBN 0-521-29227-1). Cambridge U Pr.

Animal Daddies & My Daddy. Barbara S. Hazen. (Illus.). 24p. (gr. k-2). 1968. PLB 5.00 (ISBN 0-307-60756-9, Golden Pr). Western Pub.

Animal Dads Take Over. Jonathan M. Shebar & Sharon S. Shebar. (Illus.). 64p. (gr. 3-5). 1981. PLB 6.97 (ISBN 0-671-34003-4). Messner.

Animal Defenses. (Wild, Wild World of Animals Ser.). (Illus.). 1979. lib. bdg. 11.97 (ISBN 0-686-51177-8). Silver.

Animal Defenses. Time-Life Television Editors. (Wild, Wild World of Animals). (Illus.). 1979. 10.95 (ISBN 0-913948-23-3). Time-Life.

Animal Dictionary. Jane Watson. (Illus.). (ps-2). 1960. PLB 4.57 o.p. (ISBN 0-307-60533-7, Golden Pr). Western Pub.

Animal Disguises. Aileen Fisher. (Nature Ser.). (gr. k-6). 1973. PLB 6.96 (ISBN 0-8372-0860-2); filmstrip & 7 records 18.00 (ISBN 0-8372-0205-1); filmstrip & cassette 18.00 (ISBN 0-8372-0871-8). Bowmar-Noble.

Animal Diversity. 3rd ed. Earl D. Hanson. (Foundations of Modern Biology Ser). (Illus.). 192p. 1972. pap. 9.95 ref. ed. (ISBN 0-13-037150-5). P-H.

Animal Doctor. Lucas Younker & D. V. Fried. 1976. pap. 2.50 (ISBN 0-515-05888-2). Jove Pubns.

Animal Doctor: The Making of a Veterinarian. Lucas Younker & John J. Fried. 256p. 1981. pap. 2.50. Jove Pubns.

Animal Doctors: What It's Like to Be a Veterinarian. Patricia Curtis. LC 76-5593. (Illus.). (gr. 5 up). 1977. 7.95 o.s.i. (ISBN 0-440-00140-4). Delacorte.

Animal Drawing-Anatomy & Action for Artists. Charles R. Knight. (Orig.). 1959. pap. text ed. 4.50 (ISBN 0-486-20426-X). Dover.

Animal Drawing & Painting. Walter J. Wilwerding. (Illus.). 1966. pap. 4.50 (ISBN 0-486-21716-7). Dover.

Animal Drawing: Animal Anatomy & Psychology for Artists & Laymen. Charles R. Knight. (Illus.). 8.50 (ISBN 0-8446-0742-8). Peter Smith.

Animal Ecology in Tropical Africa. new ed. D. F. Owen. LC 75-46586. (Tropical Ecology Ser). (Illus.). 1976. text ed. 18.95x (ISBN 0-582-44363-6); pap. text ed. 8.50x (ISBN 0-582-44362-8). Longman.

Animal Engineering: Readings from Scientific American. Intro. by Donald R. Griffin. LC 74-12112. (Illus.). 1974. pap. text ed. 7.95x (ISBN 0-7167-0508-7). W H Freeman.

Animal Expressions. rev. ed. Animal Welfare Institute. (Illus.). 54p. 1974. pap. text ed. 2.00 (ISBN 0-938414-06-2). Animal Welfare.

Animal Facts & Feats. Ed. by Gerald L. Wood. LC 76-51163. (Guinness Family Ser.). 1977. 17.95 (ISBN 0-8069-0104-7); lib. bdg. 15.99 (ISBN 0-8069-0105-5). Sterling.

Animal Fair. Illus. by Janet Stevens. (Illus.). 32p. (ps-2). 1981. PLB 8.95 (ISBN 0-8234-0388-2). Holiday.

Animal Faith & Spiritual Life: Previously Unpublished & Uncollected Writings by George Santayana with Critical Essays on His Thought. Ed. by John Lachs. LC 67-20665. (Century Philosophy Ser.). 1967. 28.50x (ISBN 0-89197-607-8). Irvington.

Animal Families. Robert Kraus. LC 80-51360. (Windmill Board Bks.). (Illus.). 16p. (ps). 1980. board book 3.50 (ISBN 0-671-41532-8, Pub. by Windmill). S&S.

Animal Feeding & Nutrition. 4th ed. Marshall H. Jurgens. 1978. wire coil bdg. 11.95 (ISBN 0-8403-0600-8). Kendall Hunt.

Animal Friends. Judy Dunn. LC 73-125913. (Illus.). (gr. k-3). 1970. PLB 6.75 (ISBN 0-87191-044-6). Creative Ed.

Animal Friends. Allan L. Hulsizer. LC 79-66936. (Illus.). 63p. 1980. 5.95 (ISBN 0-533-04421-9). Vantage.

Animal Friends. Jane Werner. (ps-3). 1953. PLB 4.57 o.p. (ISBN 0-307-60560-4, Golden Pr). Western Pub.

Animal Friends & Neighbors. Jan Pfloog. (ps-2). 1973. PLB 10.69 o.p. (ISBN 0-307-65773-6, Golden Pr). Western Pub.

Animal Friends Everywhere! Illus. by Garth Williams. (Golden Storytime Bks.). (Illus.). (ps). 1980. pap. 4.50 boxed set (ISBN 0-307-15514-5, Golden Pr). Western Pub.

Animal Games. Brian Wildsmith. (Illus.). 24p. (ps-3). 1981. 5.95 (ISBN 0-19-279731-X). Oxford U Pr.

Animal Gametes, Vol. 1. Male. Vishwa Nath. (Illus.). 1966. 25.00x (ISBN 0-210-31158-4). Asia.

Animal Gametes, Vol. 2. Female. Vishwa Nath. (Illus.). 1971. 25.00x (ISBN 0-210-98197-0). Asia.

Animal Genetics. Frederick B. Hutt. (Illus.). 1964. 21.95 (ISBN 0-8260-4625-8). Wiley.

Animal Genetics & Evolution: Selected Papers. Ed. by J. M. Van Brink & N. N. Vorontsov. (Illus.). 393p. 1980. lib. bdg. 99.00 (ISBN 90-6193-602-0). Kluwer Boston.

Animal Geography. Wilma George. 1962. pap. text ed. 9.95 (ISBN 0-435-60345-0). Heinemann Ed.

Animal Habits. George F. Mason. (Illus.). (gr. 5-9). 1959. PLB 6.48 (ISBN 0-688-31034-6). Morrow.

Animal Hat Shop. Sara Murphey. (Beginning-to-Read Ser.). (Illus.). (gr. 1-3). 1964. 2.50 o.p. (ISBN 0-695-80425-1). Follett.

Animal Health. James K. Baker & William J. Greer. LC 78-62054. 1980. 24.65 (ISBN 0-8134-2053-9, 2053); text ed. 18.50x (ISBN 0-686-67467-7). Interstate.

Animal Health Products Design & Evaluation. Ed. by Donald C. Monkhouse. LC 78-69826. 1978. softcover 18.00 (ISBN 0-917330-23-4). Am Pharm Assn.

Animal Homes. Brian Wildsmith. (Illus.). 24p. (ps-3). 1981. 5.95 (ISBN 0-19-279732-8). Oxford U Pr.

Animal Hormones, Pt. 2: Control of Growth & Metamorphosis. P. M. Jenkin. LC 60-8977. 1970. 42.00 (ISBN 0-08-015648-7). Pergamon.

Animal House. Ivor Cutler. (Illus.). (gr. k-3). 1977. 8.25 (ISBN 0-688-22110-6); PLB 7.92 (ISBN 0-688-32110-0). Morrow.

Animal Houses. Aileen Fisher. (Nature Ser.). (gr. k-6). 1973. PLB 6.96 (ISBN 0-8372-0859-9); filmstrip & record 18.00 (ISBN 0-8372-0204-3); filmstrip & cassette 18.00 (ISBN 0-685-27357-1). Bowmar-Noble.

Animal Husbandry. 2nd ed. R. D. Park et al. (Illus.). 1970. pap. 16.95x (ISBN 0-19-859422-4). Oxford U Pr.

Animal Identification: A Reference Guide, 2 vols. R. W. Sims. Incl. Vol. 1. Marine & Brackish Water Animals. 108p (ISBN 0-471-27765-7); Vol. 2. Land & Freshwater Animals. 108p (ISBN 0-471-27766-5). 1980. 25.00 ea. Wiley.

Animal Intelligence: Experimental Studies. E. L. Thorndike. 1965. Repr. of 1911 ed. 11.95 (ISBN 0-02-853470-0). Hafner.

Animal Intelligenge. George J. Romanes. (Contributions to the History of Psychology Ser.: No. 7, Pt. a: Orientations). 1978. 30.00 (ISBN 0-89093-156-9). U Pubns Amer.

Animal Jackets. Aileen Fisher. (Nature Ser.). (gr. k-6). 1973. PLB 6.96 (ISBN 0-8372-0861-0); filmstrip & record 18.00 (ISBN 0-685-27352-0); filmstrip & cassette 18.00 (ISBN 0-8372-0872-6). Bowmar-Noble.

Animal Language. Robert Whiteside. LC 80-14822. (Illus.). 112p. 1981. 9.95 (ISBN 0-8119-0297-8, 111). Fell.

Animal Liberation. Peter Singer. 1977. pap. 3.50 (ISBN 0-380-01782-2, 35253, Discus). Avon.

Animal Magnetism. Francine Prose. 1979. pap. 1.95 o.p. (ISBN 0-425-04099-2). Berkley Pub.

Animal Manners. Barbara S. Hazen. 1974. PLB 9.15 o.p. (ISBN 0-307-63748-4, Golden Pr). Western Pub.

Animal Marvels. David Nockels. LC 80-25443. (Animal Pop-Up Ser.). (Illus.). 12p. (ps-3). 1981. 3.50 (ISBN 0-8037-0085-7). Dial.

Animal Memory. Ed. by Werner K. Honig & Henry James. 1971. 32.50 (ISBN 0-12-355050-5). Acad Pr.

Animal Migration. Thevenin. 3.95 o.s.i. (ISBN 0-8027-0015-2). Walker & Co.

Animal Migration & Navigation. Philip Street. LC 75-30276. (Illus.). 1976. 9.95 o.p. (ISBN 0-684-14516-2, ScribT). Scribner.

Animal Migration, Orientation & Navigation. Ed. by S. A. Gautheaux, Jr. 1981. 39.00 (ISBN 0-12-277750-6). Acad Pr.

Animal Models for Biochemical Research, No. 2. Institute of Laboratory Animal Resources. 1969. 4.00 o.p. (ISBN 0-309-01736-X). Natl Acad Pr.

Animal Models for Biomedical Research, No. 3. Institute of Laboratory Animal Resources. LC 76-607190. (Illus.). 1970. pap. 5.75 (ISBN 0-309-01854-4). Natl Acad Pr.

Animal Models for Biomedical Research, No. 4. Institute Of Laboratory Animal Resources. LC 76-607190. (Illus., Orig.). 1971. pap. text ed. 6.25 (ISBN 0-309-01918-4). Natl Acad Pr.

Animal Models in Human Reproduction. Ed. by Mario Serio & Luciano Martini. 499p. 1980. text ed. 45.00 (ISBN 0-89004-522-4). Raven.

Animal Models of Comparative & Developmental Aspects of Immunity & Disease: Proceedings. International Symposium of the American Society of Zoologists, Toronto, December 27-30, 1977. Ed. by M. Eric Gershwin & Edwin L. Cooper. LC 78-15022. 1978. text ed. 43.00 (ISBN 0-08-022648-5). Pergamon.

Animal Nutrition. J. W. Lassiter & Hardy M. Edwards. 1982. text ed. 17.95 (ISBN 0-8359-0222-6); instr's. manual free (ISBN 0-8359-0223-4). Reston.

Animal Nutrition. 2nd ed. P. McDonald & R. A. Edwards. (Illus.). 475p. 1976. pap. text ed. 18.95x (ISBN 0-582-44157-9). Longman.

Animal Nutrition & Feeding Practices in India. 2nd ed. S. K. Ranjhan. 350p. 1980. 13.50x (ISBN 0-7069-0509-1). Intl Pubns Serv.

Animal Physiology. Roger Eckert. LC 77-6648. (Biology Ser.). (Illus.). 1978. text ed. 26.95x (ISBN 0-7167-0570-2). W H Freeman.

Animal Physiology. 3rd ed. Knut Schmidt-Nielsen. (Biological Science & Foundations of Modern Biology Ser). 1970. ref. ed. 13.95x (ISBN 0-13-037390-7); pap. 9.95x ref. ed. (ISBN 0-13-037382-6). P-H.

Animal Physiology. 2nd ed. Knut Schmidt-Nielsen. LC 78-56822. (Illus.). 1978. 24.95x (ISBN 0-521-22178-1). Cambridge U Pr.

Animal Physiology: Adaptations in Function. F. Reed Hainsworth. (Life Sciences Ser.). (Illus.). 600p. 1981. text ed. 19.95 (ISBN 0-201-03401-8). A-W.

Animal Plant & Microbial Toxins. Ed. by Y. Sawai. 1976. pap. text ed. 16.25 (ISBN 0-08-019965-8). Pergamon.

Animal Play Behavior. Robert M. Fagen. (Illus.). 688p. 1981. text ed. 29.95x (ISBN 0-19-502760-4); pap. text ed. 12.95x (ISBN 0-19-502761-2). Oxford U Pr.

Animal Reproduction. Ed. by Harold W. Hawk. LC 78-65535. (Beltsville Symposia in Agricultural Research Ser.: No. 3). (Illus.). 434p. 1979. text ed. 27.50. Allanheld.

Animal Reproduction, No. 3. Ed. by Harold W. Hawk. LC 78-65535. (Illus.). 1979. text ed. 32.95 (ISBN 0-470-26672-4). Halsted Pr.

Animal Rights & Human Obligation. Tom Regan & P. Singer. 256p. 1976. pap. 8.50 (ISBN 0-13-037523-3). P-H.

Animal Rights: Stories of People Who Defend the Rights of Animals. Patricia Curtis. LC 79-22451. (Illus.). 160p. (gr. 7 up). 1980. 8.95 (ISBN 0-590-07650-7, Four Winds). Schol Bk Serv.

Animal Science. Boy Scouts of America. LC 19-600. (Illus.). 64p. (gr. 6-12). 1975. pap. 0.70x (ISBN 0-8395-3395-0, 3395). BSA.

Animal Science. C. C. Chamberlain et al. 1982. text ed. 17.95 (ISBN 0-8359-0224-2); instr's. manual free (ISBN 0-8359-0225-0). Reston.

Animal Science. 7th ed. M. Eugene Ensminger. LC 76-1512. (Illus.). 1977. 29.95 (ISBN 0-8134-1798-8, 1798); text ed. 29.95x (ISBN 0-685-03860-2). Interstate.

Animal Science & Industry. 2nd ed. D. Acker. 1971. text ed. 21.95 (ISBN 0-13-037655-8). P-H.

Animal Science: Reproduction, Climate, Meat & Wool. N. T. Yeates et al. 2296p. 1975. text ed. 32.00 (ISBN 0-08-018209-7). Pergamon.

Animal Shapes. Brian Wildsmith. (Illus.). 24p. (ps-3). 1981. 5.95 (ISBN 0-19-279733-6). Oxford U Pr.

Animal Social Behavior. Wittenberger. (Illus.). 748p. 1981. text ed. price not set (ISBN 0-87872-295-5). Duxbury Pr.

Animal Sounds. George F. Mason. (Illus.). (gr. 5-9). 1948. PLB 6.48 (ISBN 0-688-31036-2). Morrow.

Animal Stories. Walter De La Mare. (Encore Ser.). (Illus.). (gr. 3-7). 1940. 5.95 (ISBN 0-684-20797-4, ScribJ). Scribner.

Animal Sumi-E in Three Weeks. Sadami Yamada. LC 65-27100. (Illus.). 32p. pap. 3.50 (ISBN 0-87040-006-1). Japan Pubns.

Animal Tales. Warren Lyfick. LC 79-56339. (Illus.). 48p. (gr. 2-6). PLB 5.39g (ISBN 0-933258-01-1). Riverhouse Pubns.

Animal Tales. Ernest Nister. (Illus.). 7.95 (ISBN 0-529-05612-7). Philomel.

Animal Territories. Daniel Cohen. (Illus.). 96p. (gr. 4-8). 1975. 6.95g (ISBN 0-8038-0368-0). Hastings.

Animal Tissue Techniques. 4th ed. Gretchen L. Humason. LC 78-17459. (Illus.). 1979. text ed. 24.95x (ISBN 0-7167-0299-1). W H Freeman.

Animal Tracks. George F. Mason. (Illus.). (gr. 5-9). 1943. PLB 6.00 o.p. (ISBN 0-688-31041-9). Morrow.

Animal Tracks & Hunter Signs. Ernest Thompson Seton. LC 58-7366. 1958. 6.95 o.p. (ISBN 0-385-06862-X). Doubleday.

Animal Tracks of the Pacific Northwest. Karen Pandell & Chris Stall. (Illus.). 96p. (Orig.). 1981. pap. 3.95 (ISBN 0-89886-012-1). Mountaineers.

Animal Traps & Trapping. James A. Bateman. LC 70-144110. (Illus.). 228p. 1971. 10.95 (ISBN 0-8117-0103-4). Stackpole.

Animal Tricks. Brian Wildsmith. (Illus.). 24p. (ps-3). 1981. 5.95 (ISBN 0-19-279743-3). Oxford U Pr.

Animal Twilight, Man & Game in Eastern Africa. J. L. Cloudsley-Thompson. (Illus.). 1967. 10.50 (ISBN 0-85429-062-1). Dufour.

Animal Wastes. Ed. by E. Paul Taiganides. (Illus.). 1977. 86.90 (ISBN 0-85334-721-2, Pub. by Applied Science). Burgess-Intl Ideas.

Animal Worlds. Marston Bates. (Illus.). (YA) 1963. 20.00 o.p. (ISBN 0-394-41533-7). Random.

Animal Worlds. A. T. Rowland-Entwistle & Joan Cooke. LC 76-13655. (Modern Knowledge Library). (Illus.). 48p. (gr. 9 up). 1976. 3.95 o.p. (ISBN 0-531-02441-5); PLB 5.90 o.p. (ISBN 0-531-01196-8). Watts.

Animales Del Parque. Arcadia Lopez. (Illus.). 1973. pap. 2.00 (ISBN 0-913632-06-6). Am Univ Artforms.

Animales Que Ayudan. S. P. Russell. Orig. Title: Four Legged Helpers. 1979. 0.85 (ISBN 0-311-38510-9). Casa Bautista.

Animals. George S. Fichter. 1973. PLB 7.62 o.p. (ISBN 0-307-61453-0, Golden Pr). Western Pub.

Animals. Alice Mattison. LC 79-54884. 72p. 1979. pap. 4.95 (ISBN 0-914086-29-4). Alicejamesbooks.

Animals, Aging, & the Aged. Leo K. Bustad. (Wesley W. Spink Lectures in Comparative Medicine Ser.). (Illus.). 224p. 1981. 19.50x (ISBN 0-8166-0966-7). U of Minn Pr.

Animals All. Deborah Manley. LC 78-21029. (Ready, Set, Look Ser.). (Illus.). (gr. k-3). 1979. PLB 9.65 (ISBN 0-8172-1309-0). Raintree Pubs.

Animals Alone & Together. Margaret Cosgrove. LC 77-12625. (gr. 7 up). 1978. 5.95 (ISBN 0-396-07520-7). Dodd.

Animals & Environment Fitness; Physiological & Biochemical Aspects of Adaptations & Ecology: Proceedings, Vol. 1. First Conference of the European Society for Comparative Physiology & Biochemistry, 27-31 August, 1979, Liege, Belgium. Ed. by R. Gilles. (Illus.). 638p. 1980. 105.00 (ISBN 0-686-63496-9). Pergamon.

Animals & Ethics. Edward Carpenter. 48p. 1980. 6.00x (ISBN 0-7224-0180-9, Pub. by Watkins England). State Mutual Bk.

Animals & Maps. Wilma George. (Illus.). 1969. 25.00x (ISBN 0-520-01480-4). U of Cal Pr.

Animals & Men. Kenneth Clark. LC 76-52335. (Illus.). 1977. 19.95 o.p. (ISBN 0-688-03200-1). Morrow.

Animals & Their Ears. Olive L. Earle & Michael Kantor. LC 73-13047. (Illus.). 64p. (gr. 3-7). 1974. PLB 6.48 (ISBN 0-688-30106-1). Morrow.

Animals & Their Legal Rights, rev. ed. Emily S. Leavitt et al. Ed. by Christine Stevens. LC 77-70142. (Illus.). 215p. 1978. pap. text ed. 2.00 (ISBN 0-938414-00-3). Animal Welfare.

Animals & Their Niches: How Species Share Resources. Laurence Pringle. (Illus.). (gr. 3-7). 1977. 6.25 (ISBN 0-688-22127-0); PLB 6.00 (ISBN 0-688-32127-5). Morrow.

Animals & Things. Gus Gregory. (Illus.). 36p. (gr. k-3). 1979. 2.95 (ISBN 0-8059-2435-3). Dorrance.

Animals! Animals! Peter Lippman. (Illus.). (gr. k-4). 1976. 5.95 (ISBN 0-307-16808-5, Golden Pr); PLB 10.69 o.p. (ISBN 0-307-66808-8). Western Pub.

Animals, Animals, Animals. Ed. by George Booth et al. LC 79-1653. (Illus.). 256p. 1981. pap. 8.95 (ISBN 0-06-090853-X, C*N 853, CN). Har-Row.

Animals Are My Life. Eddie Straiton. (Illus.). 1979. pap. 15.75 (ISBN 0-85131-316-7, Dist. by Sporting Book Center). J A Allen.

Animals Around the Year. Marcelle Verite. (gr. 4-8). 1972. PLB 10.69 o.p. (ISBN 0-307-67848-2, Golden Pr). Western Pub.

Animals at My Doorstep. Helen Hoover. LC 66-13332. (Illus.). (gr. k-4). 1966. 5.95 o.s.i. (ISBN 0-8193-0125-6, Four Winds); PLB 5.41 o.s.i. (ISBN 0-8193-0126-4). Schol Bk Serv.

Animals at Peace. Alison Maddock. LC 71-185643. (Animal Life Ser.). (Illus.). 152p. (YA) 1972. 8.95 o.s.i. (ISBN 0-06-012728-7, HarpT). Har-Row.

Animals, Birds & Plants of the Bible. Hilda L. Rostron. (Ladybird Ser). (Illus.). (gr. 1-5). 1964. bds. 1.49 (ISBN 0-87508-830-9). Chr Lit.

Animals Build Amazing Homes. Hedda Nussbaum. LC 79-11326. (Step-up Bks.: No. 29). (Illus.). (gr. 2-5). 1979. 3.95 (ISBN 0-394-83850-5, BYR); PLB 4.99 (ISBN 0-394-93850-X). Random.

Animals Can Be Almost Human. Readers Digest. 1980. 16.95 (ISBN 0-89577-069-5, Pub. by Readers Digest Assoc). Norton.

Animals, Feed, Food & People: An Analysis of the Role of Animals in Food Production. Ed. by R. L. Baldwin. (AAAS Selected Symposium: No. 42). 150p. 1980. lib. bdg. 16.00x (ISBN 0-89158-779-9). Westview.

Animals for Research. 10th ed. Institute for Laboratory Animal Resources. 1979. pap. 6.25 (ISBN 0-309-02920-1). Natl Acad Pr.

Animals: Illustrations of Mammals, Birds, Fish, Insects, Etc. A Pictorial Archive from Nineteenth-Century Sources. Ed. by Jim Harter. LC 78-73302. (Pictorial Archive Ser.). (Illus.). 1979. pap. 7.95 (ISBN 0-486-23766-4). Dover.

Animals in Art. Ana M. Berry. LC 79-162506. (Tower Bks). (Illus.). 1971. Repr. of 1929 ed. 18.00 (ISBN 0-8103-3900-5). Gale.

Animals in Art. Jessica Rawson. (Illus.). 1978. 14.95 (ISBN 0-684-15650-4, ScribT); pap. 9.95 (ISBN 0-684-16920-7, SL791, ScribT). Scribner.

Animals in Art & Thought to the End of the Middle Ages. Francis D. Klingender. Ed. by Evelyn Antal & John Harthan. 1971. 50.00x (ISBN 0-262-11040-7). MIT Pr.

Animals in Folklore. Ed. by J. R. Porter & W. M. Russell. (Folklore Society Mistletoe Ser.). (Illus.). 1978. 22.50x o.p. (ISBN 0-8476-6065-6). Rowman.

Animals in Fur. Clarence J. Hylander. (Illus.). (gr. 7 up). 1956. 8.95g (ISBN 0-02-746200-5). Macmillan.

Animals in Peril: Man's War against Wildlife. Peter Verney. LC 79-2786. 190p. 1980. 12.95 (ISBN 0-8425-1714-6). Brigham.

Animals in Research: New Perspectives in Animal Experimentation. David Sperlinger. 384p. 1980. 49.50 (ISBN 0-471-27843-2, Pub. by Wiley-Interscience). Wiley.

Animals in the Service of Man. Edward Hyams. LC 78-147890. (Illus.). 1972. 7.75 o.p. (ISBN 0-397-00780-9). Lippincott.

Animals in Winter. Henrietta Bancroft & Richard G. Van Gelder. LC 63-17543. (Let's-Read-&-Find-Out Science Bk). (Illus.). (gr. k-3). 1963. 7.89 (ISBN 0-690-09261-X, TYC-J). T Y Crowell.

Animals' Merry Christmas. Kathryn Jackson. (Illus.). 72p. (ps-3). 1950. PLB 9.15 (ISBN 0-307-63773-5, Golden Pr); pap. 2.95 (ISBN 0-307-13773-2). Western Pub.

Animals Near & Far. Helen Hoover. LC 68-21089. (Illus.). (gr. k-3). 1970. 5.95 o.s.i. (ISBN 0-8193-0388-7, Four Winds); PLB 5.41 o.s.i. (ISBN 0-8193-0389-5). Schol Bk Serv.

Animals Next Door: A Guide to Zoos & Aquariums of the Americas. Harry Gersh. LC 71-104745. (Orig.). 1971. pap. 4.50x (ISBN 0-8303-0088-0, Acad Edns). Fleet.

Animals of East Africa. Paul Deegan. LC 72-140641. (World's People Ser.). (Illus.). (gr. 5-12). 1971. PLB 6.95 (ISBN 0-87191-050-0). Creative Ed.

Animals of Europe. Robert Wolff. LC 77-78379. (Illus.). (gr. 3-9). 1969. PLB 12.00 (ISBN 0-87460-092-8). Lion.

Animals of Farmer Jones. Leah Gale. (ps-1). 1970. PLB 5.00 (ISBN 0-307-60282-6, Golden Pr). Western Pub.

Animals of Long Ago. Judith Diment & Anthony Harvey. LC 78-64663. (Fact Finders Ser.). (Illus.). 1979. lib. bdg. 3.96 (ISBN 0-686-51123-9). Silver.

Animals of the Americas. Robert Wolff. LC 73-78378. (Illus.). (gr. 3-9). 1969. PLB 12.00 (ISBN 0-87460-093-6). Lion.

Animals of the Bible. Isaac Asimov. LC 77-16893. (gr. 2-5). 1978. 7.95a (ISBN 0-385-07195-7); PLB (ISBN 0-385-07215-5). Doubleday.

Animals of the Bible. Dorothy P. Lathrop. (Illus.). (ps-6). 1969. 9.79 (ISBN 0-397-31536-8). Lippincott.

Animals of the Fields & Meadows. Julie Becker. LC 77-8496. (Animals Around Us Ser.). (Illus.). (gr. 2-6). 1977. PLB 6.95 (ISBN 0-88436-394-5). EMC.

Animals of the Oceans: The Ecology of Marine Life. Martin V. Angel & Tegwyn Harris. LC 77-2490. (Illus.). 1977. 10.95 o.p. (ISBN 0-8467-0344-0, Pub. by Two Continents). Hippocrene Bks.

Animals of the Ponds & Streams. Julie Becker. LC 77-8497. (Animals Around Us Ser.). (Illus.). (gr. 2-6). 1977. PLB 6.95 (ISBN 0-88436-398-8). EMC.

Animals of the Sea. Millicent Selsam. LC 75-27447. (Illus.). 40p. (gr. k-3). 1976. 6.95 (ISBN 0-590-07458-X, Four Winds). Schol Bk Serv.

Animals of the Seashore. Julie Becker. LC 77-8106. (Animals Around Us Ser.). (Illus.). (gr. 2-6). 1977. PLB 6.95 (ISBN 0-88436-392-9). EMC.

Animals of the Seashore. 4th ed. Muriel L. Guberlet. LC 62-142921. (Illus.). 1981. 12.50 o.p. (ISBN 0-8323-0121-3); pap. 8.95 (ISBN 0-8323-0386-0). Binford.

Animals of the Woods & Forests. Julie Becker. LC 77-8253. (Animals Around Us Ser.). (Illus.). (gr. 2-6). 1977. PLB 6.95 (ISBN 0-88436-396-1). EMC.

Animals on the Farm. Jan Pfloog. (Illus.). 24p. (ps-4). 1968. PLB 5.00 (ISBN 0-307-60573-6, Golden Pr). Western Pub.

Animals One to Ten. Deborah Manley. LC 78-26648. (Ready, Set, Look Ser.). (Illus.). (gr. k-3). 1979. PLB 9.65 (ISBN 0-8172-1302-3). Raintree Pubs.

Animals Parasitic in Man. rev. ed. Geoffrey Lapage. (Illus.). 8.75 (ISBN 0-8446-2427-6). Peter Smith.

Animals' Rights: Considered in Relation to Social Progress. rev. ed. Henry S. Salt. LC 80-50160. 1980. 9.95 (ISBN 0-9602632-0-9). Soc Animal Rights.

Animals Should Definitely Not Act Like People. Judi Barrett. LC 80-13364. (Illus.). 32p. (ps-2). 1980. 9.95 (ISBN 0-689-30768-3). Atheneum.

Animals Sounds. Illus. by Aurelius Battaglia. (Golden Sturdy Bk.). (Illus.). 22p. 1981. 3.50 (ISBN 0-307-12122-4, Golden Pr). Western Pub.

Animals Tame & Wild. James Herriot et al. Ed. by Gilbert Phelps & John Phelps. LC 78-57781. (Illus.). 1979. 16.95 (ISBN 0-8069-3098-5); lib. bdg. 14.99 (ISBN 0-8069-3099-3). Sterling.

Animals That Burrow. Dean Morris. LC 77-8114. (Read About Animals Ser.). (Illus.). (gr. k-3). 1977. PLB 9.95 (ISBN 0-8393-0012-3). Raintree Child.

Animals That Live in Shells. Dean Morris. LC 77-7911. (Read About Animals Ser.). (Illus.). (gr. k-3). 1977. PLB 9.95 (ISBN 0-8393-0013-1). Raintree Child.

Animals Without Backbones. rev., 2nd ed. Ralph Buchsbaum. LC 48-9508. (Illus.). 405p. 1975. pap. 9.50 (ISBN 0-226-07870-1). U of Chicago Pr.

Animals Without Backbones. Robert Pfadt. (Beginning-to-Read Bks). (Illus.). (gr. 2-4). 1967. pap. 1.50 o.p. (ISBN 0-695-30428-3); PLB 3.39 o.p. (ISBN 0-695-80428-6). Follett.

Animals Without Backbones: An Introduction to the Invertebrates. rev. ed. Ralph Buchsbaum. LC 48-9508. (Illus.). (gr. 9 up). 1948. text ed. 16.00 (ISBN 0-226-07869-8). U of Chicago Pr.

Animals You Will Never Forget. Readers Digest Editorial Staff. (Illus.). 1969. 16.95 (ISBN 0-393-21422-2). Norton.

Animated Film. Ralph Stephenson. LC 72-1785. 208p. 1981. pap. 5.95 (ISBN 0-498-01202-6). A S Barnes.

Animated Scale Models Handbook. Adolph F. Frank. LC 80-22858. (Illus.). 160p. 1981. lib. bdg. 10.00 (ISBN 0-668-05118-3, 5118). Arco.

Animated Thumbtack Railroad, Dollhouse & All-Around Surprise Book: (Evening Edition) Louis Phillips. LC 75-12637. (Illus.). 96p. (gr. 3 up). 1975. 6.95 (ISBN 0-397-31646-1); pap. 2.95 o.p. (ISBN 0-397-31647-X, LSC-37). Lippincott.

Animating Films Without a Camera. Jacques Bourgeois. LC 74-82324. (Little Craft Bk.). (Illus.). 48p. (gr. 7-9). 1974. 5.95 (ISBN 0-8069-5304-7); PLB 6.69 (ISBN 0-8069-5305-5). Sterling.

Animus & Anima. Emma Jung. Tr. by Cary F. Baynes & Hildegard Nagel. 94p. 1969. pap. text ed. 6.50 (ISBN 0-88214-301-8). Spring Pubns.

Anion & Proton Transport, Vol. 341. new ed. Ed. by William A. Brodsky. LC 80-15917. 610p. 1980. 107.00 (ISBN 0-89766-070-6). NY Acad Sci.

Anionic Polymeric Drugs. L. Guy Donaruma et al. LC 80-11364. (Polymers in Biology & Medicine Ser.: Vol. 1). 1980. 39.50 (ISBN 0-471-05530-1, Pub. by Wiley-Interscience). Wiley.

Anionic Surfactants: Biology. C. Gloxhuber. (Surfactant Ser.: Vol. 9). 59.75 (ISBN 0-8247-6946-5). Dekker.

Anise. Patricia Phillips. (Orig.). 1978. pap. 1.95 o.s.i. (ISBN 0-515-04515-2). Jove Pubns.

Anishinabe: Six Studies of Modern Chippewa. Ed. by J. Anthony Paredes. LC 79-20091. (Illus.). xi, 436p. 1980. 27.50 (ISBN 0-8130-0625-2). U Presses Fla.

Anisotropic Mechanical Behavior of Zircalor-2. Ronald G. Ballinger. LC 78-74995. (Outstanding Dissertations on Energy Ser.). 1979. lib. bdg. 27.50 (ISBN 0-8240-3986-6). Garland Pub.

Anita Bryant, Dale Evans Rogers: Two Stars for God. William Peterson. 1974. pap. 1.25 o.s.i. (ISBN 0-446-76508-2). Warner Bks.

Anita Bryant Story. Anita Bryant. 1977. 6.95 o.p. (ISBN 0-8007-0897-0). Revell.

Anjea; Infanticide, Abortion & Contraception in Savage Society. Herbert Aptekar. LC 79-2929. 192p. 1981. Repr. of 1931 ed. 17.50 (ISBN 0-8305-0097-9). Hyperion Conn.

Ankle Fractures: Treatment Without Casts. Leo K. Cooper. (Illus.). 124p. 1974. 23.75 (ISBN 0-398-03155-X). C C Thomas.

Ankylosing Spondylitis. Andrei Calin & James F. Fries. (Discussions in Patient Management Ser.). 1978. spiral 10.00 (ISBN 0-87488-887-5). Med Exam.

Ankylosing Spondylitis. J. H. Moll. (Illus.). 320p. 1980. text ed. 75.00x (ISBN 0-443-01830-8). Churchill.

Ankylosing Spondylitis & Its Variants. Association of Bone & Joint Surgeons. Ed. by Marshall R. Urist. (Clinical Orthopaedics Ser., Vol. 74). 1971. 12.00 o.p. (ISBN 0-685-22852-5). Lippincott.

Ann Landers Encyclopedia A to Z. Ann Landers. Date not set. 7.95 (ISBN 0-345-28892-0). Ballantine.

Ann Landers Talks to Teenagers about Sex. Ann Landers. 1978. pap. 1.95 (ISBN 0-449-24208-0, Crest). Fawcett.

Ann Miller: Tops in Taps. Jim Connor. (Illus.). 224p. (Orig.). 1981. 19.95 (ISBN 0-531-09949-0); pap. 10.95 (ISBN 0-531-09950-4). Watts.

Ann Radcliffe & Her Influence on Later Writers. J. M. Tompkins. Ed. by Devendra P. Varma. LC 79-8485. (Gothic Studies & Dissertations Ser.). 1980. lib. bdg. 22.00x (ISBN 0-405-12681-6). Arno.

Ann Radcliffe & the Gothic Romance: A Psychoanalytic Approach. Leona F. Sherman. Ed. by Devendra P. Varma. LC 79-8480. (Gothic Studies & Dissertations Ser.). 1980. lib. bdg. 22.00x (ISBN 0-405-12679-4). Arno.

Ann Radcliffe: The Novel of Suspense & Terror. John A. Stoler. Ed. by Devendra P. Varmer. LC 79-8483. (Gothic Studies & Dissertations Ser.). 1980. lib. bdg. 25.00x (ISBN 0-405-12670-0). Arno.

Ann Radcliffe's Gothic Landscape of Fiction & the Various Influences Upon It. Lynne E. Heller. Ed. by Devendra P. Varma. LC 79-8452. (Gothic Studies & Dissertations Ser.). (Illus.). 1980. lib. bdg. 40.00x (ISBN 0-405-12666-2). Arno.

Ann Radcliffe's Novels: Experiments in Setting. David S. Durant. Ed. by Devendra P. Varma. LC 79-8450. (Gothic Studies & Dissertations Ser.). 1980. lib. bdg. 21.00x (ISBN 0-405-12665-4). Arno.

Ann Taylor Gilbert's Album. Intro. by Christina D. Stewart. LC 75-32206. 525p. 1977. lib. bdg. 38.00 (ISBN 0-8240-2316-1). Garland Pub.

Anna & Bent. Bent A. Larsen. (Destiny Ser.). 1979. pap. 4.95 (ISBN 0-8163-0330-4, 01617-0). Pacific Pr Pub Assn.

Anna & the Echo-Catcher. Adam Munthe. (Illus.). 32p. (gr. k-3). 1981. 9.95 (ISBN 0-7011-2498-9, Pub. by Chatto-Bodley-Jonathan). Merrimack Bk Serv.

Anna Comnena. Rae Dalven. LC 78-169634. (World Authors Ser.: Greece: No. 213). lib. bdg. 10.95 (ISBN 0-8057-2240-8). Twayne.

Anna Hastings: The Story of a Washington Newspaperperson. Allen Drury. LC 77-4151. 1977. 8.95 o.p. (ISBN 0-688-03221-4). Morrow.

Anna Held & Flo Ziegfeld. Liane Carrera. 1979. 10.00 o.p. (ISBN 0-682-49309-0). Exposition.

Anna Karenin. rev. ed. Leo Tolstoy. Tr. by Rosemary Edmonds from Rus. (Classics Ser). 1978. pap. 3.95 (ISBN 0-14-044041-0). Penguin.

Anna Olsson: A Child of the Prarie. Martha Winblad. (Illus.). 1978. pap. 10.00. W a Linder.

Anna Pavlova. (Profiles Ser.). (Illus.). 64p. (gr. 3-6). 1981. 7.95 (ISBN 0-241-10481-5, Pub. by Hamish Hamilton England). David & Charles.

Anna Pavlova. V. Svetloff. Tr. by A. Grey from Fr. (Illus.). 224p. 1974. pap. 6.95 (ISBN 0-486-23047-3). Dover.

Anna to the Infinite Power. Mildred Ames. 204p. (gr. 7 up). 1981. 9.95 (ISBN 0-684-16855-3). Scribner.

Annabelle. Ruth Bornstein. LC 77-20059. (Illus.). (gr. k-1). 1978. 5.89 (ISBN 0-690-03804-6, TYC-J); PLB 4.79 (ISBN 0-690-03810-0). T Y Crowell.

Annabelle. Ann Fairfax. 176p. (Orig.). 1980. pap. 1.75 (ISBN 0-515-05399-6). Jove Pubns.

Annales De Demographie Historique, 1974. 560p. (Orig.). 1976. pap. text ed. 37.00x (ISBN 0-686-22614-3). Mouton.

Annals of English Drama: Nine Seventy-Five to Seventeen Hundred. rev. ed. Alfred Harbage. Ed. by S. Schoenbaum. LC 64-57462. 1964. 18.00x o.p. (ISBN 0-8122-7483-0). U of Pa Pr.

Annals of Imperial Rome. Tacitus. Tr. by Michael Grant. (Classics Ser.). 1956. pap. 3.95 (ISBN 0-14-044060-7). Penguin.

Annals of Life Insurance Medicine: Proceedings, Vol. 6. International Congress of Life Insurance, 13th, Madrid 1979. Ed. by E. Tanner & M. L. Hefti. (Illus.). 270p. 1980. 37.80 (ISBN 0-387-10050-4). Springer-Verlag.

Annals of Progress: The Story of Lenoir County & Kinston, North Carolina. William S. Powell. 1963. pap. 2.00 (ISBN 0-86526-124-5). NC Archives.

Annals of Tacitus, Books One to Six, Vol. 2. (Cambridge Classical Texts & Commentaries: No. 23). 576p. Date not set. price not set (ISBN 0-521-20213-2). Cambridge U Pr.

Annals of the Association of American Geographers: 1971 & Later. pap. 30.00 (ISBN 0-685-72536-7). Assn Am Geographers.

Annals of the ICRP, Vol. 5, No. 1-6. Ed. by F. D. Sowby. (ICRP Publication: No. 30, Supplement to Part 2). 756p. 1980. 100.00. Pergamon.

Annals of the International Year of the Quiet Sun. Incl. Vol. 1. Geophysical Measurements: Techniques, Observational Schedules & Treatment of Data. 1968. 25.00x (ISBN 0-262-09005-8); Vol. 2. Solar & Geophysical Events 1960-1965 (Calendar Record) 1968. 20.00x (ISBN 0-262-09006-6); Vol. 3. Proton Flare Project. 1969. 25.00x (ISBN 0-262-09007-4); Vol. 4. Solar-Terrestrial Physics: Solar Aspects. 1969. 25.00x (ISBN 0-262-09008-2); Vol. 5. Solar-Terrestrial Physics: Terrestrial Aspects. 1969. 25.00x (ISBN 0-262-09009-0); Vol. 6. Survey of IQSY Observations & Bibliography. 1970. 30.00x (ISBN 0-262-09010-4); Vol. 7. Sources & Availability of IQSY Data. 1970. 25.00x (ISBN 0-262-09011-2). MIT Pr.

Annals of the Nyingma Lineage, Vol. 11. Ed. by Tarthang Tulku. (Illus.). 1977. pap. 15.00 (ISBN 0-913546-32-1). Dharma Pub.

Annapurna: A Woman's Place. Arlene Blum. LC 80-13288. (Illus.). 272p. 1980. 14.95 (ISBN 0-87156-236-7). Sierra.

Anna's Country. Elizabeth Lang. 320p. (Orig.). 1981. pap. 6.95 (ISBN 0-930044-19-3). Naiad Pr.

Anna's Song. Arthur Oberg. Ed. by Joan M. Webber & Richard Blessing. LC 79-4847. 112p. 1980. 8.95 (ISBN 0-295-95681-X). U of Wash Pr.

Anne & the Princesses Royal. 2nd ed. Helen Cathcart. 205p. 1975. 8.75 (ISBN 0-491-01321-3). Transatlantic.

Anne & the Sand Dobbies: A Story of Death for Children & Their Parents. John B. Coburn. 120p. 1980. pap. 3.95 (ISBN 0-686-60134-3). Crossroad NY.

Anne Bradstreet: The Tenth Muse. Elizabeth W. White. 1971. 17.95 (ISBN 0-19-501440-5). Oxford U Pr.

Anne Frank: A Portrait in Courage. Ernst Schnabel. LC 58-12702. (Illus.). 7.50 o.p. (ISBN 0-15-107527-1). HarBraceJ.

Anne Frank: The Diary of a Young Girl. rev. ed. Anne Frank. (YA) 1967. 9.95a (ISBN 0-385-04019-9); PLB (ISBN 0-385-09190-7). Doubleday.

Anne Frank: The Diary of a Young Girl. Anne Frank. pap. 2.50 (ISBN 0-671-80243-7); enriched classic edition 2.25 (ISBN 0-671-82748-0). PB.

Anne Royall's U. S. A. Bessie R. James. 1972. 27.50 (ISBN 0-8135-0732-4). Rutgers U Pr.

Anne's House of Dreams, No. 5. L. M. Montgomery. 240p. (gr. 7-9). 1981. pap. 2.25 (ISBN 0-553-14995-4). Bantam.

Annexation of Bosnia, Nineteen Eight to Nineteen Nine. Bernadotte E. Schmitt. LC 71-80588. 1971. Repr. of 1937 ed. 13.75 (ISBN 0-86527-002-3). Fertig.

Annie Hall. Woody Allen. 1978. 7.95 o.p. (ISBN 0-394-50071-7). Random.

Annie: Herald of Home Missions. Eva B. Lloyd. (Orig.). 1981. pap. 1.25 (ISBN 0-8054-9502-9). Broadman.

Annie Oakley. Harrison et al. (Illus.). 35p. (gr. 1-9). 1981. 2.95 (ISBN 0-86575-185-4). Dormac.

Annie Oakley & Buffalo Bill's Wild West: One Hundred & Two Illustrations. Isabelle S. Sayers. (Illus.). 96p. (Orig.). 1981. pap. price not set (ISBN 0-486-24120-3). Dover.

Annie O'Kay's Riddle Roundup. Ann Bishop. (Illus.). 40p. (gr. 2-5). 1981. 7.95 (ISBN 0-525-66727-X). Elsevier-Nelson.

Annie Pat & Eddie. Carolyn Haywood. (Illus.). (gr. 3-7). 1960. PLB 7.92 (ISBN 0-688-31045-1). Morrow.

Annihilation Factor. Barrington J. Bayley. 144p. 1980. 11.95 (ISBN 0-85031-311-2, Pub. by Allison & Busby England); pap. 4.95 (ISBN 0-85031-320-1, Pub. by Allison & Busby England). Schocken.

Anniversaries, Epithalamions & Epicedes. John Donne. Ed. by W. Milgate. (Elglish Texts Ser.). (Illus.). 1978. 45.00x (ISBN 0-19-812729-4). Oxford U Pr.

Anno Domini. George Steiner. LC 80-15345. 205p. 1980. Repr. of 1964 ed. 10.95 (ISBN 0-87951-113-3). Overlook Pr.

Anno's Magical ABC: An Anamorphic Alphabet. Anno Mitsumasa. (Illus.). 64p. 1981. 15.95 (ISBN 0-399-20788-0). Philomel.

Annotated Bibliography of American Indian & Eskimo Autobiographies. H. David Brumble, III. LC 80-23449. 190p. 1981. 10.95x (ISBN 0-8032-1175-9). U of Nebr Pr.

Annotated Bibliography of Canada's Major Authors: Margaret Atwood, Leonard Cohen, Archibald Lampman, E. J. Pratt, & Al Purdy, Vol.iI. Ed. by Robert Leeker. (Reference Book Ser.). 1981. 26.00 (ISBN 0-8161-8552-2). G K Hall.

Annotated Bibliography of Films in Automation, Data Processing, & Computer Science. Martin B. Solomon, Jr. & Nora G. Lovan. LC 67-23778. 1967. pap. 4.50x (ISBN 0-8131-1145-5). U Pr of Ky.

Annotated Bibliography of Health Economics. Ed. by A. J. Culyer et al. LC 77-79018. 1977. 29.95x (ISBN 0-312-03873-9). St Martin.

Annotated Bibliography of Korean Music. Bang-Song Song. LC 75-163013. (A (Bibliographies), No. 2). xiv, 251p. (Orig.). 1971. pap. text ed. 11.75x (ISBN 0-913360-04-X). Asian Music Pub.

Annotated Bibliography of Modern Anglo-Irish Drama. E. H. Mikhail. LC 80-51874. 306p. 1981. 20.00x (ISBN 0-87875-201-3). Whitston Pub.

Annotated Bibliography of the Published Writings of Roger Fry. Donald A. Laing. LC 78-68305. (Garland Reference Library of the Humanities Ser.). 200p. 1979. lib. bdg. 25.00 (ISBN 0-8240-9838-2). Garland Pub.

Annotated Bibliography of the Visual Arts of East Africa. Eugene C. Burt. LC 80-7805. (Traditional Arts of Africa Ser.). 392p. 1980. 20.00x (ISBN 0-253-17225-X). Ind U Pr.

Annotated Bibliography of Tree Growth & Growth Rings, 1950-62. Sharlene Agerter & Waldo S. Glock. LC 64-17274. 1965. 2.00 (ISBN 0-8165-0002-9). U of Ariz Pr.

Annotated Bibliography on Microwaves: Their Properties, Production, & Application to Food Processing. Samuel A. Goldblith & Robert V. Decareau. 1973. 21.50x (ISBN 0-262-07049-9). MIT Pr.

Annotated Bibliography on Taxation As an Instrument of Land Planning Policy. Ed. by Michael M. Bernard. (Lincoln Institute Monograph: No. 80-8). 90p. 1980. pap. text ed. 4.00. Lincoln Inst Land.

Annotated Civil Code of Japan, 4 vols. Tr. by Joseph E. De Becker from Japanese. (Studies in Japanese Law & Government). 1200p. 1979. 95.00 (ISBN 0-89093-215-8). U Pubns Amer.

Annotated Discography of Music in Spain Before 1650. Roger D. Tinnell. 146p. 1980. 12.00. Hispanic Seminary.

Annotated Guide to Robert E. Howard's Sword & Sorcery. Robert Weinberg. LC 80-19169. 160p. 1980. Repr. of 1976 ed. lib. bdg. 13.95x (ISBN 0-89370-030-4). Borgo Pr.

Annotated Gulliver's Travels. Ed. by Isaac Asimov. (Illus.). 1980. 19.95 (ISBN 0-517-53949-7). Potter.

Annotated Index to the Cantos of Ezra Pound. John H. Edwards & William W. Vasse. 1980. 20.00x (ISBN 0-520-01923-7). U of Cal Pr.

Annotated International Bibliography of Nutrition Education. Ed. by Clara M. Taylor & Katharine P. Riddle. LC 71-132937. 1971. pap. text ed. 5.75x (ISBN 0-8077-2255-3). Tchrs Coll.

Annotated Jules Verne: From the Earth to the Moon. Jules Verne. Tr. by Walter J. Miller from Fr. LC 78-3327. (Illus.). 1978. 16.95 o.p. (ISBN 0-690-01701-4, TYC-T). T Y Crowell.

Annotated Jules Verne: Twenty Thousand Leagues Under the Sea. Jules Verne. Ed. by Walter J. Miller. LC 76-10968. (Illus.). 1978. 16.95 o.s.i. (ISBN 0-690-01151-2, TYC-T). T Y Crowell.

Annotated Lolita. Vladimir Nabokov. Ed. by Alfred Appel, Jr. 1970. pap. 6.95 (ISBN 0-07-045730-1). McGraw.

Annotated Mahabharata Bibliography. P. Lal. 31p. 1973. 10.00 (ISBN 0-88253-306-1); pap. text ed. 5.00 (ISBN 0-89253-786-8). Ind-US Inc.

Annotated Oscar Wilde. Oscar Wilde. (Illus.). 320p. Date not set. 25.00 (ISBN 0-89835-052-2). Abaris Bks.

Annotated Pilgrim's Progress. Warren Wiersbe. 1980. 6.95 (ISBN 0-8024-0229-1). Moody.

Annotated Quotations from Chairman Mao. John DeFrancis. LC 74-20080. (Linguistic Ser). 336p. 1975. text ed. 22.50x (ISBN 0-300-01749-9); pap. text ed. 8.95x (ISBN 0-300-01870-3). Yale U Pr.

Annotated Social Contract. Jean J. Rousseau. Ed. by Charles M. Sheroner. pap. 3.95 (ISBN 0-452-00369-5, FM369, Mer). NAL.

Annotated Wizard of Oz. Michael P. Hearn. (Illus.). 384p. 1973. 20.00 (ISBN 0-517-50086-8). Potter.

Annotated World List of Selected Current Geographical Serials. rev., 4th ed. Chauncy D. Harris. LC 80-17561. (Research Papers: No. 194). 165p. 1980. pap. 8.00 (ISBN 0-89065-101-9). U Chicago Dept Geog.

Annoted Index to the Sermons of John Donne, 2 vols. Troy D. Reeves. Incl. Vol. 1 (ISBN 0-391-02146-X); Vol. 2 (ISBN 0-391-02147-8). (Elizabethan Studies: No. 95). 1980. pap. text ed. 25.00 ea. Humanities.

Annuaire Francais De Droit International, Vol. 25. Ed. by Centre National De la Recherche Scientifique. LC 57-28515. 1288p. 1979. 125.00x (ISBN 2-222-02737-3). Intl Pubns Serv.

Annuaire Statistique De la France 1979. 84th ed. Institut National De la Statistique et Des Etudes Economiques. LC 79-39079. (Illus.). 920p. (Fr.). 1979. 80.00x (ISBN 0-8002-2274-1). Intl Pubns Serv.

Annual Accounting Review: Vol. 1 1979. S. Weinstein & M. Walker. 265p. 1979. lib. bdg. 35.50 (ISBN 3-7186-0009-9). Harwood Academic.

Annual Bibliography of British & Irish History: Publications of 1979, Vol. 5. Ed. by G. Elton. 1981. text ed. 30.00x (ISBN 0-391-01774-8). Humanities.

Annual Bibliography of British & Irish History, 1975. Ed. by Geoffrey R. Elton. 1976. text ed. 31.25x (ISBN 0-391-00619-3). Humanities.

Annual Bulletin of Coal Statistics for Europe, Vol. XIII, 1978. 100p. 1979. pap. 8.00 (ISBN 0-686-61470-4, UN79-2E20, UN). Unipub.

Annual Bulletin of Gas Statistics, Vol. 24. 97p. 1979. pap. 8.00 (ISBN 0-686-68941-0, UN79/2E26, UN). Unipub.

Annual Bulletin of General Energy Statistics for Europe, Nineteen Seventy-Eight, Vol. XI. 157p. 1980. pap. 12.00 (UN80/2E8, UN). Unipub.

Annual Bulletin of Trade in Chemical Products, Vol. 5. 285p. 1980. pap. 19.00 (UN79-2E29, UN). Unipub.

Annual Conference: Proceedings, 1979. American Water Works Association. (AWWA Handbooks). (Illus.). 1200p. 1979. pap. text ed. 48.00 (ISBN 0-89867-229-5). Am Water Wks Assoc.

Annual Conference Proceedings, 1980. American Water Works Association. (AWWA Handbooks Ser.). (Illus.). 1452p. 1980. pap. text ed. 48.00 (ISBN 0-89867-238-4). Am Water Wks Assn.

Annual Cropping Systems in the Tropics. M. J. Norman. LC 79-10625. (Illus.). x, 276p. 1980. text ed. 20.00 (ISBN 0-8130-0632-5). U Presses Fla.

Annual Customs & Festivals in Peking. Tun Li-Ch'En. Tr. by Derk Bodde from Chinese. (Illus.). 175p. 1981. 10.00 (ISBN 0-85656-029-4). Great Eastern.

Annual Debate Resources, 3 vols. 1980. cancelled (ISBN 0-686-64871-4). Bowker.

Annual Diagram. Reinheld Ebestin. 160p. 1980. pap. 9.95 (ISBN 0-88231-122-0). ASI Pub Inc.

Annual Directory of Vegetarian Restaurants. 288p. 1980. 6.95 (ISBN 0-686-28725-8). Daystar Pub Co.

Annual Fund Ideas. Ed. by Virginia L. Carter. 48p. 1979. pap. 10.50 (ISBN 0-89964-016-8). CASE.

Annual Handbook for Group Facilitators, 1977. John E. Jones & J. William Pfeiffer. LC 73-92841. (Series in Human Relations Training). 288p. 1977. pap. 20.00 (ISBN 0-88390-091-2); looseleaf ntbk. 44.50 (ISBN 0-88390-090-4). Univ Assocs.

Annual Handbook for Group Facilitators, 1973. Ed. by John E. Jones & J. William Pfeiffer. LC 73-92841. (Series in Human Relations Training). 290p. 1973. pap. 20.00 (ISBN 0-88390-081-5); pap. 44.50 looseleaf ntbk. (ISBN 0-88390-073-4). Univ Assocs.

Annual Handbook for Group Facilitators, 1979. Ed. by John E. Jones & J. William Pfeiffer. LC 73-92841. (Human Relations Training Ser.). 296p. 1979. pap. 20.00 (ISBN 0-88390-095-5); looseleaf notebook 44.50 (ISBN 0-88390-093-9). Univ Assocs.

Annual Handbook for Group Facilitators 1981. Ed. by John E. Jones & J. William Pfeiffer. (Ser. in Human Relations Training). 290p. (Orig.). 1981. pap. 20.00 (ISBN 0-686-69076-1). Univ Assocs.

Annual Handbook for Group Facilitators, 1974. Ed. by J. William Pfeiffer & John E. Jones. LC 73-92841. (Series in Human Relations Training). 290p. 1974. pap. 20.00 (ISBN 0-88390-082-3); looseleaf 44.50 (ISBN 0-88390-074-2). Univ Assocs.

Annual Handbook for Group Facilitators, 1972. Ed. by J. William Pfeiffer & John E. Jones. LC 73-92841. (Series in Human Relations Training). 272p. 1972. pap. 20.00 (ISBN 0-88390-085-8); pap. 14.50 (ISBN 0-88390-072-6). Univ Assocs.

Annual Handbook for Group Facilitators, 1976. Ed. by J. William Pfeiffer & John E. Jones. LC 73-92841. (Series in Human Relations Training). 292p. 1976. pap. 20.00 (ISBN 0-88390-088-2); looseleaf notebk. 44.50 (ISBN 0-88390-087-4). Univ Assocs.

Annual Handbook for Group Facilitators, 1978. Ed. by J. William Pfeiffer & John E. Jones. LC 73-92841. (Series in Human Relations Training). 296p. 1978. pap. 20.00 (ISBN 0-88390-099-8); looseleaf notebook 44.50 (ISBN 0-88390-098-X). Univ Assocs.

Annual Handbook for Group Facilitators, 1980. Ed. by J. William Pfeiffer & John E. Jones. LC 73-92841. (Series in Human Relations Training). 296p. 1980. pap. 20.00 (ISBN 0-88390-097-1); looseleaf notebook 44.50 (ISBN 0-88390-096-3). Univ Assocs.

Annual Handbook for Group Facilitators,1975. Ed. by John E. Jones & J. William Pfeiffer. LC 73-92841. (Series in Human Relations Training). 290p. 1975. pap. 20.00 (ISBN 0-88390-079-3); looseleaf 44.50 (ISBN 0-88390-078-5). Univ Assocs.

Annual Index to Botanical Literature: 1979. Torrey Botanical Club, N.Y. 1980. lib. bdg. 130.00 (ISBN 0-8161-0369-0). G K Hall.

Annual Index to Motion Picture Credits, 1978. Academy of Motion Picture Arts & Sciences. Ed. by Verna Ramsey. LC 79-644761. 1979. lib. bdg. 150.00 (ISBN 0-313-20950-2, AN78). Greenwood.

Annual Index to Motion Picture Credits, 1979. Academy of Motion Picture Arts & Sciences. Ed. by Verna Ramsay. LC 79-644761. 430p. 1980. lib. bdg. 150.00 (ISBN 0-313-20951-0, AN79). Greenwood.

Annual Index to Motion Picture Credits, 1980: Nineteen Eighty. Academy of Motion Pictures Arts & Sciences. LC 79-644761. 450p. 1981. lib. bdg. 150.00 (ISBN 0-313-20952-9, AN80). Greenwood.

Annual Index to Popular Music Record Reviews 1972. Andrew D. Armitage & Dean Tudor. LC 73-8909. 1973. 16.50 (ISBN 0-8108-0636-3). Scarecrow.

Annual Index to Popular Music Record Reviews 1973. Andrew D. Armitage & Dean Tudor. LC 73-8909. 1974. 24.00 (ISBN 0-8108-0774-2). Scarecrow.

Annual Index to Popular Music Record Reviews 1974. Andrew D. Armitage & Dean Tudor. LC 73-8909. 1976. 24.00 (ISBN 0-8108-0865-X). Scarecrow.

Annual Index to Popular Music Record Reviews 1975. Andrew D. Armitage & Dean Tudor. LC 73-8909. 1976. 24.00 (ISBN 0-8108-0934-6). Scarecrow.

Annual Index to Popular Music Record Reviews 1977. Dean Tudor & Linda Biesenthal. LC 73-8909. 1979. 25.00 (ISBN 0-8108-1217-7). Scarecrow.

Annual Index to Popular Music Record Reviews 1976. Dean Tudor et al. LC 73-8909. 1977. 25.00 (ISBN 0-8108-1070-0). Scarecrow.

Annual Meeting Programs. Entomological Society of America. 5.00 ea. Entomol Soc.

Annual of Archetypal Psychology & Jungian Thought. annual Ed. by James Hillman. 304p. 1975. pap. 12.00 (ISBN 0-88214-010-8). Spring Pubns.

Annual of Industrial Property Law, 1975. Ed. by John Warden. 1975. text ed. 36.00x (ISBN 0-8377-0206-2). Rothman.

Annual of Power & Conflict Nineteen Seventy-Nine to Nineteen Eighty. Ed. by Institute for the Study of Conflict. 465p. 1980. 50.00x (ISBN 0-8448-1386-9). Crane-Russak Co.

Annual of Power & Conflict, 1978-1979: A Survey of Political Violence & International Influence. 8th ed. Ed. by Brian Crozier. 1979. 34.00 (ISBN 0-8103-1035-X, Pub. by Inst Study Conflict). Gale.

Annual of Power & Conflict, 1979-80: A Survey of Political Violence & International Influence. 9th ed. Ed. by Brian Crozier. LC 77-370326. 510p. 1980. 65.00x (ISBN 0-8002-2671-2). Intl Pubns Serv.

Annual of Psychoanalysis, Vol. 7. Ed. by Chicago Institute for Psychoanalysis. LC 72-91376. (Annual of Psychoanalysis Ser.). 490p. 1980. text ed. 22.50x (ISBN 0-8236-0368-7, 00-0368). Intl Univs Pr.

Annual Price Survey - Family Budget Costs. annual 1976. pap. 6.00 mimeo (ISBN 0-86671-030-2). Comm Coun Great NY.

Annual Price Survey of Family Living Costs in the Greater New York Area, 1979: Family Budget Costs. 1980. write for info. Comm Coun Great NY.

Annual Progress in Child Psychiatry & Child Development, 12 vols. Ed. by Stella Chess & Alexander Thomas. Incl. Vol. 1. 1968. o.p.; Vol. 2. 1969. (ISBN 0-685-57359-1); Vol. 3. 1970.; Vol. 4. 1971.; Vol. 5. 1972. o.p.; Vol. 6. 1973; Vol. 7. 1974; Vol. 8. 1975; Vol. 9. 1976; Vol. 10. 1977; Vol. 11. 1978; Vol. 12. 1979 (ISBN 0-87630-216-9). LC 68-23452. (Illus.). Vols. 2-4 & 6-12. 20.00 ea. Brunner-Mazel.

Annual Progress in Child Psychiatry & Child Development 1980. Ed. by Stella Chess & Alexander Thomas. LC 66-4030. 600p. 1980. 25.00 (ISBN 0-87630-248-7). Brunner-Mazel.

Annual Register of Grant Support: 1975-1976. LC 69-18307. 646p. 1975. 47.50 (ISBN 0-8379-1902-9). Marquis.

Annual Register of Grant Support: 1980-81. 14th ed. LC 69-18307. 750p. 1980. 57.50 (ISBN 0-8379-1907-X, 031096). Marquis.

Annual Report. Conference on Electrical Insulation & Dielectric Phenomena. Incl. 1952. 61p. 3.00 (ISBN 0-309-00020-3); 1957. 69p. 3.00 (ISBN 0-309-00570-1); 1958. 57p. 3.00 (ISBN 0-686-64608-8); 1963. 144p. 5.00 (ISBN 0-309-01141-8); 1964. 146p. 5.00 (ISBN 0-309-01238-4); 1965. 139p. 5.00 (ISBN 0-686-64609-6); 1966. 129p. 10.00 (ISBN 0-309-01484-0); 1967. 201p. 10.00 (ISBN 0-309-01578-2); 1968. 204p. 10.00 (ISBN 0-309-01705-X); 1969. 193p. 15.00 (ISBN 0-309-01764-5); 1970. 258p. 15.00 (ISBN 0-309-01870-6); 1971. 289p. 15.00 (ISBN 0-309-02032-8); 1972. 496p. 20.00 (ISBN 0-309-02112-X); 1973. 638p. 25.00 (ISBN 0-309-02229-0); 1974. 706p. 25.00 (ISBN 0-309-02416-1); 1975. 544p. 22.00 (ISBN 0-686-64610-X); 1976. 576p. 25.00 (ISBN 0-686-64611-8); 1977. 596p. 25.00 (ISBN 0-309-02866-3); 1978. 405p. 25.00 (ISBN 0-309-02861-2); 1979. 25.00 (ISBN 0-309-02933-3). Natl Acad Pr.

Annual Report: A Kentucky Energy Resource Utilization Program. Ed. by R. William De Vore. (Illus., Orig.). 1979. pap. 4.50 (ISBN 0-89779-026-X, IMMR45-PR8-79); microfiche 3.50 (ISBN 0-89779-027-8). OES Pubns.

Annual Report of the Board of Regents of the Smithsonian Institution Showing the Operation, Expenditures & Condition of the Institution for the Year Ending June 30, 1897: A Memorial of George Brown Goode Together with a Selection of His Papers on Museums & on the History of Science in America. U. S. House of Representatives, 55th Congress, 2nd Session, Doc. No. 575, Pt. 3. Ed. by I. Bernard Cohen. LC 79-7964. (Three Centuries of Science in America Ser.). (Illus.). 1980. Repr. of 1901 ed. lib. bdg. 55.00x (ISBN 0-405-12545-3). Arno.

Annual Report of the Museum of Anthropology, University of Missouri, Columbia, Mo., 1977-1978. Ed. by Lawrence Feldman. (Annual Report Ser.). (Illus.). 1978. pap. 6.30 o.p. (ISBN 0-913134-86-4). Mus Anthro Mo.

Annual Report of the Museum of Anthropology, University of Missouri, Columbia, Missouri, 1976-1977. Ed. by Lawrence H. Feldman & Richard Diehl. (Annual Report Ser.). (Illus.). 1977. pap. 6.75x o.p. (ISBN 0-913134-92-9). Mus Anthro Mo.

Annual Report of the Museum of Anthropology, University of Missouri, Columbia, Missouri, 1975-1976. Ed. by Elsebet S. Rowlett et al. (Illus.). 1977. pap. 2.50x o.p. (ISBN 0-913134-93-7). Mus Anthro Mo.

Annual Reports in Medicinal Chemistry, Vol. 15. Ed. by Hans-Jurgen Hess. 1980. 22.50 (ISBN 0-12-040515-6). Acad Pr.

Annual Reports in Organic Synthesis, Vols. 1-3. Ed. by John McMurry & R. Bryan Miller. Vol. 1. 1971. 26.00 (ISBN 0-12-040801-5); Vol. 2. 1972. 26.00 (ISBN 0-12-040802-3); Vol. 3, 1973. 26.00 (ISBN 0-12-040803-1). Acad Pr.

Annual Reports in Organic Synthesis 1976, Vol. 7. Ed. by R. Bryan Miller & L. G. Wade, Jr. 1977. 25.50 (ISBN 0-12-040807-4). Acad Pr.

Annual Reports in Organic Synthesis, 1979, Vol. 10. Ed. by L. G. Wade, Jr. & Martin J. O'Donnell. 1980. 23.50 (ISBN 0-12-040810-4). Acad Pr.

Annual Reports on Competition Policy in OECD Member Countries, 2 pts. Organization for Economic Cooperation & Development. Incl. No. 1. 94p. 6.25 o.p. (ISBN 0-686-14856-8); No. 2. 109p. 6.25 o.p. (ISBN 92-64-11575-7). 1976. OECD.

Annual Reports on Competition Policy in OECD Member Countries, Vol. 2. (Document Ser.). 134p. 1979. 9.50 (ISBN 92-64-12009-2). OECD.

Annual Reports on Consumer Policy in OECD Member Countries, 1976. 1976. 5.00 o.p. (ISBN 92-64-11577-3). OECD.

Annual Reports on Fermentation Processes. Ed. by D. Perlman & G. T. Tsao. 1978. 25.00 (ISBN 0-12-040302-1). Acad Pr.

Annual Reports on NMR Spectroscopy. Ed. by E. F. Mooney. Incl. Vol. 1. 1968. 49.00 (ISBN 0-12-505350-9); Vol. 5B. 1974. 62.00 (ISBN 0-12-505345-2); Vol. 6, 2 pts. 1976-78. Pt. B. 34.00 (ISBN 0-12-505346-0); Pt. C. 90.00 (ISBN 0-12-505347-9); Vol. 7. 1978. 43.50 (ISBN 0-12-505307-X); Vol. 8. 1978. 71.00 (ISBN 0-12-505308-8); Vol. 9. 1978. 57.50 (ISBN 0-12-505309-6). Acad Pr.

Annual Review in Automatic Programming. Ed. by M. I. Halpern. (Illus.). 222p. 1980. 55.00 (ISBN 0-08-020242-X). Pergamon.

Annual Review of Allergy 1977-1978. Claude A. Frazier. 1978. spiral bdg. 22.50 (ISBN 0-87488-329-6). Med Exam.

Annual Review of Anthropology, Vol. 9. Ed. by Bernard J. Siegel et al. LC 72-82136. (Illus.). 1980. text ed. 20.00 (ISBN 0-8243-1909-5). Annual Reviews.

Annual Review of Astronomy & Astrophysics, Vol. 18. Ed. by Geoffrey Burbidge et al. LC 63-8846. (Illus.). 1980. text ed. 20.00 (ISBN 0-8243-0918-9). Annual Reviews.

Annual Review of Biochemistry, Vol. 49. Ed. by Esmond E. Snell et al. LC 32-25093. (Illus.). 1980. text ed. 21.00 (ISBN 0-8243-0849-2). Annual Reviews.

Annual Review of Biochemistry, Vol 50. Ed. by Esmond E. Snell. LC 32-25093. (Illus.). 1218p. 1981. text ed. 21.00 (ISBN 0-8243-0850-6). Annual Reveiws.

Annual Review of Biophysics & Bioengineering, Vol. 10. Ed. by L. J. Mullins et al. LC 79-188446. (Illus.). 1981. text ed. 20.00 (ISBN 0-8243-1810-2). Annual Reviews.

Annual Review of Birth Defects, 1977: Proceedings, 3 vols. Birth Defects Annual Conference, 10th Memphis, Tenn., June, 1977. Ed. by Robert L. Summitt & Daniel Bergsma. Incl. No. 6A. Cell Surface Factors,Immune Deficiencies, Twin Studies. LC 78-17058. 240p. 28.00 (ISBN 0-8451-1020-9); No. 6B. Recent Advances & New Syndromes. LC 78-17056. 400p. 46.00 (ISBN 0-8451-1021-7); No. 6C. Sex Differentiation & Chromosomal Abnormalities. LC 78-17057. 51.00 (ISBN 0-8451-1022-5). (Birth Defects: Original Article Ser.: Vol. 14, No. 6). (Illus.). 1978. Set. 125.00 (ISBN 0-8451-0951-0). A R Liss.

Annual Review of Clinical Biochemistry, Vol. 1. Ed. by David M. Goldberg. LC 80-15463. 1980. 19.95 (ISBN 0-471-04036-3, Pub. by Wiley Med). Wiley.

Annual Review of Earth & Planetary Sciences, Vol. 9. Ed. by G. W. Wetherill et al. LC 72-82137. (Illus.). 1981. 20.00 (ISBN 0-8243-2009-3). Annual Reviews.

Annual Review of Ecology & Systematics, Vol. 11. Ed. by Richard F. Johnston et al. LC 71-135616. (Illus.). 1980. text ed. 20.00 (ISBN 0-8243-1411-5). Annual Reviews.

Annual Review of Energy, Vol. 5. Ed. by Jack M. Hollander et al. (Illus.). 1980. text ed. 20.00 (ISBN 0-8243-2305-X). Annual Reviews.

Annual Review of English Books on Asia 1978-79. Ed. by Anthony Ferguson. LC 74-4918. 256p. (Orig.). 1980. pap. 10.00 (ISBN 0-8425-1840-1). Brigham.

Annual Review of Entomology. 20.50 ea. Entomol Soc.

Annual Review of Entomology, Vol. 26. Ed. by T. E. Mittler et al. LC 56-5750. (Illus.). 1981. text ed. 20.00 (ISBN 0-8243-0126-9). Annual Reviews.

Annual Review of Fluid Mechanics, Vol. 13. Ed. by M. Van Dyke et al. LC 74-80866. (Illus.). 1981. text ed. 20.00 (ISBN 0-8243-0713-5). Annual Reviews.

Annual Review of Genetics, Vol. 14. Ed. by Herschel L. Roman et al. LC 67-29891. (Illus.). 1980. text ed. 20.00 (ISBN 0-8243-1214-7). Annual Reviews.

Annual Review of Gerontology & Geriatrics. Ed. by Carl Eisdorfer & Bernard Starr. (Illus.). 416p. 1980. text ed. 25.50 (ISBN 0-8261-3080-1). Springer Pub.

Annual Review of Information Science & Technology, Vol. 11, 1976. Ed. by Martha E. Williams. LC 66-25096. (Illus.). 1976. 42.50 (ISBN 0-87715-212-8). Knowledge Indus.

Annual Review of Information Science & Technology, Vol. 13. Ed. by Martha E. Williams. LC 66-25096. 1978. 42.50 (ISBN 0-914236-21-0). Knowledge Indus.

Annual Review of Information Science & Techology 1979, Vol. 14. Ed. by Martha E. Williams. LC 66-25096. 1979. 42.50 (ISBN 0-914236-44-X). Knowledge Indus.

Annual Review of Materials Science, Vol. 10. Ed. by Robert A. Huggins et al. LC 75-172108. (Illus.). 1980. text ed. 20.00 (ISBN 0-8243-1710-6). Annual Reviews.

Annual Review of Medicine: Selected Topics in the Clinical Sciences, Vol. 32. Ed. by W. P. Creger et al. LC 51-1659. (Illus.). 1981. 20.00 (ISBN 0-8243-0532-9). Annual Reviews.

Annual Review of Microbiology, Vol. 34. Ed. by Mortimer P. Starr et al. LC 49-432. (Illus.). 1980. text ed. 20.00 (ISBN 0-8243-1134-5). Annual Reviews.

Annual Review of Neuroscience, Vol. 4. Ed. by W. M. Cowan et al. (Illus.). 1981. 20.00 (ISBN 0-8243-2404-8). Annual Reviews.

Annual Review of Nuclear & Particle Science, Vol. 30. Ed. by J. D. Jackson et al. LC 53-995. (Annual Review of Nuclear Science Ser.: 1950-1977). (Illus.). 1980. text ed. 22.50 (ISBN 0-8243-1530-8). Annual Reviews.

Annual Review of Nuclear Science, Vol. 22. Ed. by E. Segre et al. LC 53-995. (Illus.). 1972. text ed. 19.50 (ISBN 0-8243-1522-7). Annual Reviews.

Annual Review of Nuclear Science, Vol. 23. Ed. by E. Segre et al. LC 53-995. (Illus.). 1973. text ed. 19.50 (ISBN 0-8243-1523-5). Annual Reviews.

Annual Review of Nuclear Science, Vol. 25. Ed. by Emilio Segre et al. LC 53-995. (Illus.). 1975. text ed. 19.50 (ISBN 0-8243-1525-1). Annual Reviews.

Annual Review of Nuclear Science, Vol. 26. Ed. by E. Segre et al. LC 53-995. (Illus.). 1976. text ed. 19.50 (ISBN 0-8243-1526-X). Annual Reviews.

Annual Review of Nuclear Science, Vol. 27. Ed. by Emilio Segre et al. LC 53-995. (Illus.). 1977. text ed. 19.50 (ISBN 0-8243-1527-8). Annual Reviews.

Annual Review of Nutrition, Vol. 1. Ed. by W. J. Darby et al. (Illus.). 1981. text ed. 20.00 (ISBN 0-8243-2801-9). Annual Reviews.

Annual Review of Pharmacology & Toxicology, Vol. 20. Ed. by Robert George & Ronald Okun. LC 61-5649. (Illus.). 1980. text ed. 17.00 (ISBN 0-8243-0420-9). Annual Reviews.

Annual Review of Pharmacology & Toxicology, Vol. 21. Ed. by R. George et al. LC 61-5649. (Illus.). 1981. 20.00 (ISBN 0-8243-0421-7). Annual Reviews.

Annual Review of Physical Chemistry, Vol. 31. Ed. by B. S. Rabinovitch et al. LC 51-1658. (Illus.). 1980. text ed. 20.00 (ISBN 0-8243-1031-4). Annual Reviews.

Annual Review of Physiology, Vol. 42. Ed. by I. S. Edelman et al. LC 39-15404. (Illus.). 1980. text ed. 17.00 (ISBN 0-8243-0342-3). Annual Reviews.

Annual Review of Physiology, Vol. 43. Ed. by I. S. Edelman et al. LC 39-15404. (Illus.). 1981. text ed. 20.00 (ISBN 0-8243-0343-1). Annual Reviews.

Annual Review of Phytopathology, Vol. 13. Ed. by Ken F. Baker et al. LC 63-8847. (Illus.). 1975. text ed. 17.00 (ISBN 0-8243-1313-5). Annual Reviews.

Annual Review of Phytopathology, Vol. 18. Ed. by Raymond G. Grogan et al. LC 63-8847. (Illus.). 1980. text ed. 20.00 (ISBN 0-8243-1318-6). Annual Reviews.

Annual Review of Plant Physiology, Vol 32. Ed. by W. R. Briggs et al. (Illus.). 1981. text ed. 20.00 (ISBN 0-8243-0632-5). Annual Reviews.

Annual Review of Psychology, Vol. 32. Ed. by Mark R. Rosenzweig & Lyman W. Porter. LC 50-13143. (Illus.). 1981. text ed. 20.00 (ISBN 0-8243-0232-X). Annual Reviews.

Annual Review of Public Health, Vol. 1. Ed. by Lester Breslow et al. (Illus.). 1980. text ed. 17.00 (ISBN 0-8243-2701-2). Annual Reviews.

Annual Review of Public Health, Vol 2. Ed. by Lester Breslow et al. 1981. text ed. 20.00 (ISBN 0-8243-2702-0). Annual Reviews.

Annual Review of Rehabilitation, Vol. 1, 1980. Elizabeth Pan et al. 1980. text ed. 27.50 (ISBN 0-8261-3090-9). Springer Pub.

Annual Review of Sociology, Vol. 1. Ed. by Alex Inkeles et al. LC 75-648500. (Illus.). 1975. text ed. 17.00 (ISBN 0-8243-2201-0). Annual Reviews.

Annual Review of Sociology, Vol. 6. Ed. by Alex Inkeles et al. LC 75-648500. (Illus.). 1980. text ed. 20.00 (ISBN 0-8243-2206-1). Annual Reviews.

Annual Statistical Bulletin, 1978. OPEC (Organization of Petroleum Exporting Companies) LC 74-640556. (Illus.). 179p. 1979. pap. 22.50x (ISBN 0-8002-2211-3). Intl Pubns Serv.

Annual Survey of American Law, 1979. 1980. 26.00 (ISBN 0-379-12238-3). Oceana.

Annual Survey of Corporate Contributions, 1977. Kathryn Troy. LC 76-24946. (Report Ser.: No. 759). (Illus.). 1979. pap. 15.00 o.p. (ISBN 0-8237-0195-6). Conference Bd.

Annual Survey of Psychoanalysis: A Comprehensive Survey of Current Psychoanalytic Practice & Theory, 10 vols. Ed. by John Frosch & Nathaniel Ross. Incl. Vol. 1. 1952 (ISBN 0-8236-0160-9); Vol.2. 1953 (ISBN 0-8236-0180-3); Vol. 3. 1956 (ISBN 0-8236-0200-1); Vol. 4. 1958 (ISBN 0-8236-0220-6); Vol. 5. 1959 (ISBN 0-8236-0240-0); Vol. 6. 1961 (ISBN 0-8236-0260-5); Vol. 7. 1963 (ISBN 0-8236-0280-X); Vol. 8. 1965 (ISBN 0-8236-0300-8); Vol. 9. 1967 (ISBN 0-8236-0320-2); Vol. 10 (ISBN 0-8236-0340-7). LC 52-12082. text ed. 25.00 ea. o.p. Intl Univs Pr.

Annual '79: Bologna Book Fair. 8.00. Boston Public Lib.

Annuals. James U. Crockett. (Encyclopedia of Gardening Ser). (Illus.). 1971. 11.95 (ISBN 0-8094-1081-8). Time-Life.

Annuals. James U. Crockett. LC 78-140420. (Time-Life Encyclopedia of Gardening). (Illus.). (gr. 6 up). 1971. lib. bdg. 11.97 (ISBN 0-8094-1082-6, Pub. by Time-Life). Silver.

Annulment. Ronald Rubin. 1978. pap. 1.50 o.s.i. (ISBN 0-515-04453-9). Jove Pubns.

Annulment or Divorce? William H. Marshner. 96p. (Orig.). 1978. pap. 2.95 (ISBN 0-931888-00-X, Chris. Coll. Pr.). Christendom Pubns.

Annus Mirabilis: A Bibliography of Medieval Times. Jill Phillips. (Bibliographies for Librarians Ser.). 1980. lib. bdg. 75.00 (ISBN 0-8490-1398-4). Gordon Pr.

Ano' Ano: The Seed. Kristin Zambucka. pap. 8.50. Mawa Pub.

Anointed for Burial. Todd Burke & DeAnn Burke. 1977. pap. 2.95 (ISBN 0-88270-485-0). Logos.

Anointed to Serve: The Story of the Assemblies of God. William W. Menzies. LC 79-146707. (Illus.). 1971. 10.95 (ISBN 0-88243-465-9, 02-0465). Gospel Pub.

Anomalistic Psychology. Leonard Zusne & Warren H. Jones. LC 80-17345. 502p. 1981. text ed. 29.95 (ISBN 0-89859-068-X). L Erlbaum Assocs.

Anomie & Deviant Behavior: A Discussion & Critique. Marshall B. Clinard. LC 64-20314. (Illus.). 1964. 9.95 (ISBN 0-02-905560-1); pap. text ed. 4.95 (ISBN 0-02-905550-4). Free Pr.

Anonymous & Pseudononymous Publications of Twentieth Century Authors. M. C. Dobelis. Date not set. 16.95x (ISBN 0-918230-06-3). Barnstable.

Anorexia Nervosa. R. L. Palmer. 160p. 1981. pap. 3.95 (ISBN 0-14-022065-8, Pelican). Penguin.

Anorexia Nervosa. Robert A. Vigersky. LC 76-57005. 1977. 31.50 (ISBN 0-89004-185-7). Raven.

Another Almanac of Words at Play. Willard R. Espy. (Illus.). 1980. 14.95 (ISBN 0-517-53187-9); pap. 8.95 (ISBN 0-517-53188-7). Potter.

Another Brown Bag. Jerry M. Jordan. LC 80-36849. (Illus.). 1980. pap. 5.95 (ISBN 0-8298-0406-4). Pilgrim NY.

Another Chance. Diane Carlson. Ed. by Mary Verdick. (Beginning Pal Paperbacks Ser.). (Illus., Orig.). (gr. 7-12). 1977. pap. text ed. 1.25 (ISBN 0-8374-3460-2). Xerox Ed Pubns.

Another Chance: Hope & Health for Alcoholic Families. Sharon Wegsheider. 1980. 12.95 (ISBN 0-8314-0059-5). Sci & Behavior.

Another Eden: a New Paradise: A Story of the Regeneration of Mankind, an Epic Poem. J. Hollis. LC 79-53813. (Illus.). 68p. 1980. pap. 10.00 (ISBN 0-933486-18-9). Am Poetry Pr.

Another I, Another You. Richard Shickel. 1979. pap. 2.25 o.p. (ISBN 0-345-28098-9). Ballantine.

Another Kind of Autumn. Loren Eiseley. LC 77-8130. (Encore Edition). (Illus.). 1977. 4.95 (ISBN 0-684-16352-7, ScribT). Scribner.

Another Kind of Love. Paula Christian. LC 79-92584. 144p. 1980. pap. 6.50 (ISBN 0-931328-06-3). Timely Bks.

Another Kind of Love: Homosexuality & Spirituality. Richard Woods. LC 77-27729. 1978. pap. 1.95 (ISBN 0-385-14312-5, Im). Doubleday.

Another Lonely Voice: The Urdu Short Stories of Saadat Hasan Manto. Leslie A. Flemming. 1979. 10.75. UC Ctr S&SE Asian.

Another Look, 3 levels. Mary Townley. (Townley Art Project Ser.). (gr. k-2). 1978. Level A. pap. text ed. 6.32 (ISBN 0-201-07646-2, Sch Div); Level B. pap. text ed. 6.32 (ISBN 0-201-07647-0); Level C. pap. text ed. 6.32 (ISBN 0-201-07648-9); 24.44 o.p. tchr's ed. (ISBN 0-201-07649-7). A-W.

Another Man Gone: The Black Runner in Contemporary Afro-American Literature. Phyllis R. Klotman. (Literary Criticism Ser). 1976. 12.00 (ISBN 0-8046-9149-5, Natl U). Kennikat.

Another Man O' War. Clarence W. Anderson. (Illus.). (gr. 4-6). 1966. 4.95g o.s.i. (ISBN 0-02-701610-2). Macmillan.

Another One Thousand & One Fishing Tips & Tricks. Vlad Evanoff. 1975. pap. 3.95 o.p. (ISBN 0-8015-0308-6). Dutton.

Another Part of the House. Winston Estes. 1978. pap. 1.75 o.s.i. (ISBN 0-380-01959-0, 38406). Avon.

Another Part of the Twenties. Paul A. Carter. LC 76-27679. 1977. 13.50x (ISBN 0-231-04134-9); pap. 7.50x (ISBN 0-231-04135-7). Columbia U Pr.

Another Part of the Wood. Beryl Bainbridge. 8.95 (ISBN 0-8076-0965-X). Braziller.

Another Part of the Wood: A Self Portrait. Kenneth Clark. 304p. 1976. pap. 2.25 o.p. (ISBN 0-345-24919-4). Ballantine.

Another Path. Gladys Taber. LC 63-17678. 1963. 8.95 (ISBN 0-397-00260-2). Lippincott.

Another Roadside Attraction. Tom Robbins. 1975. pap. 2.95 (ISBN 0-345-29245-6). Ballantine.

Another Roadside Attraction. Tom Robbins. 352p. 1981. pap. 6.95 (ISBN 0-345-29469-6). Ballantine.

Another Song, Another Season: Poems & Portrayals. Roger White. 1979. 8.50 (ISBN 0-85398-087-X, 7-32-36, Pub. by G Ronald England); pap. 3.95 (ISBN 0-85398-088-8, 7-32-37, Pub. by G Ronald England). Baha'i.

Another Song to Sing: An Illustrated Discography of Johnny Cash. John L. Smith. (Illus.). 1981. pap. 5.95 (ISBN 0-915608-06-5). Country Music Found.

Another Voice. Ed. by Marcia Millman & Rosabeth Moss Kanter. LC 75-8206. 400p. 1975. pap. 3.50 o.p. (ISBN 0-385-04032-6, Anch). Doubleday.

Another Way of Laughter: An Anthology of Sufi Humor. Massud Farzan. 1973. pap. 1.95 o.p. (ISBN 0-525-47357-2). Dutton.

Another Woman's House. Mignon G. Eberhart. 192p. 1973. pap. 0.95 o.p. (ISBN 0-445-00507-6). Popular Lib.

Another World. Eden, Anthony, Earl of Avon, K.G., P.C., M.C. LC 77-74298. 1977. 7.95 o.p. (ISBN 0-385-12719-7). Doubleday.

Another World: Adventures in Otherness. Ed. by Gardner Dozois. (gr. 7 up). 1977. 7.95 o.s.i. (ISBN 0-695-80695-5); lib. ed. 7.98 o.s.i. (ISBN 0-695-40695-7). Follett.

Anouilh: Five Plays, Vol. 1. Jean Anouilh. Incl. Romeo & Jeannette; Rehearsal; Ermine; Antigone; Eurydice. 340p. (Orig.). 1958. pap. 4.95 (ISBN 0-8090-0710-X, Mermaid). Hill & Wang.

Anowa. Ama A. Aidoo. (Sun-Lit Ser.). 64p. 1980. 9.00x (ISBN 0-89410-087-4); pap. 5.00x (ISBN 0-89410-088-2). Three Continents.

ANPAO: An American Indian Odyssey. Jamake Highwater. LC 77-9264. (gr. 5-9). 1977. 10.95 (ISBN 0-397-31750-6); pap. 3.95. Lippincott.

ANS COBOL Programming. 2nd ed. J. Saxon & W. Englander. 1978. pap. text ed. 12.95 (ISBN 0-13-037770-8). P-H.

Anselm & a New Generation. Rosemary G. Evans. 230p. 1980. 34.50x (ISBN 0-19-826651-0). Oxford U Pr.

Anselm & Talking About God. G. R. Evans. 1978. 28.50x (ISBN 0-19-826647-2). Oxford U Pr.

Anselm: Fides Quaerens Intellectum. Karl Barth. Tr. by Ian W. Robertson from Ger. LC 76-10795. (Pittsburgh Reprint Ser.: No. 2). 1976. text ed. 3.75 (ISBN 0-915138-09-3). Pickwick.

Anselm of Canterbury: Why God Became Man. Anselm Of Canterbury. Ed. by Jasper Hopkins & Herbert Richardson. 105p. 1980. cover 4.950soft (ISBN 0-88946-009-4). E Mellen.

Anselm's Doctrine of Freedom & The Will. G. Stanley Kane. (Texts & Studies in Religion, Vol. 10). 1981. soft cover 24.95x (ISBN 0-88946-914-8). E Mellen.

Anselm's Proslogion: An Introduction. R. A. Herrera. LC 79-66421. 1979. pap. text ed. 8.75 (ISBN 0-8191-0825-1). U Pr of Amer.

ANSI-X3-SPARC DBMS Framework Report of the Study Group on Database Management Systems. Ed. by Dennis Tsichritzis & Anthony Klug. (Illus.). xii, 19p. 1978. saddle-stitch 7.00 (ISBN 0-88283-013-9). AFIPS Pr.

Answer for Today, Vol. 1. Chuck Smith. 72p. (Orig.). 1980. pap. 1.95 (ISBN 0-936728-09-4). Word for Today.

Answer Is God. Elise M. Davis. 1975. pap. 1.25 (ISBN 0-685-84181-2, PV068). Jove Pubns.

Answer to Anxiety. Herman W. Gockel. 1965. pap. 4.95 (ISBN 0-570-03704-2, 12-2254). Concordia.

Answer to Humanistic Psychology. Nelson E. Hinmon. LC 80-81890. 144p. 1980. pap. text ed. 3.95 (ISBN 0-89081-259-4). Harvest Hse.

Answer to in-Law Relationships. Norman Wright. (Orig.). pap. 1.25 (ISBN 0-89081-076-1). Harvest Hse.

Answer to Loneliness. Norman Wright. (Orig.). pap. 1.25 (ISBN 0-89081-077-X). Harvest Hse.

Answer to Parent-Teen Relationships. Norman Wright. (Orig.). pap. 1.25 (ISBN 0-89081-075-3). Harvest Hse.

Answer to Submission & Decision Making. Norman Wright. pap. 1.25 (ISBN 0-89081-078-8). Harvest Hse.

Answer to the Cultist at Your Door. Robert Passantino et al. LC 80-83850. 1981. pap. 4.95 (ISBN 0-89081-275-6). Harvest Hse.

Answer to the First Part of a Certain Conference, Concerning Succession, Published...Under the Name of R. Dolman. Sir John Hayward. LC 74-28861. (English Experience Ser.: No. 741). 1975. Repr. of 1603 ed. 13.00 (ISBN 90-221-0741-8). Walter J Johnson.

Answer Unto the Catholiques Supplication, Presented Unto the Kings Maiestie, for a Tolleration of Popish Religion in England...Annexed the Supplication of the Papists. Christopher Muriell. LC 74-28874. (English Experience Ser.: No. 753). 1975. Repr. of 1603 ed. 3.50 (ISBN 90-221-0753-1). Walter J Johnson.

Answere to a Letter (Saint German, Christopher) LC 73-6097. (English Experience Ser.: No. 566). 1973. Repr. of 1535 ed. 8.00 (ISBN 90-221-0566-0). Walter J Johnson.

Answere to the Hollanders Declaration, Concerning the Occurrents of the East India. LC 72-168. (English Experience Ser.: No. 327). 1971. Repr. of 1622 ed. 7.00 (ISBN 90-221-0327-7). Walter J Johnson.

Answeres of Some Brethren of the Ministerie to the Replies Concerning the Late Covenant. LC 74-80155. (English Experience Ser.: No. 636). 1974. Repr. of 1638 ed. 18.50 (ISBN 90-221-0636-5). Walter J Johnson.

Answering the Tough Ones. David Dewitt. 160p. 1980. pap. 3.95 (ISBN 0-8024-8971-0). Moody.

Answers & Explanations to Commercial Pilot Written Test Guide. John King & Martha King. (Pilot Training Ser.). (Illus.). 68p. 1979. pap. 6.95 (ISBN 0-89100-153-0, E*A-61-71-B*G). Aviation Maintenance.

Answers & Explanations to Instrument Rating Written Test Guide. John King & Martha King. (Pilot Training Ser.). (Illus.). 90p. 1978. pap. 7.95 (ISBN 0-89100-091-7, E*A-61-8A*D*G). Aviation Maintenance.

Answers & Explanations to Private Pilot - Airplane Written Test Guide. John King & Martha King. (Pilot Training Ser.). 58p. 1979. pap. 6.95 (ISBN 0-89100-104-2, E*A-61-32C*G). Aviation Maintenance.

Answers: Decision-Making Techniques for Managers. rev. ed. Richard Taffler. (Illus.). 256p. 1981. 13.95 (ISBN 0-13-037861-5, Spectrum); pap. text ed. 6.95 (ISBN 0-13-037853-4). P-H.

Answers for New Parents: Adjusting to Your New Role. Howard J. Osofsky & Joy Osofsky. 212p. 1980. 11.95 (ISBN 0-8027-0666-5); 6.95 (ISBN 0-8027-7169-6). Walker & Co.

Answers from the Word. James A. Cross. 1974. pap. 2.25 (ISBN 0-87148-012-3). Pathway Pr.

Answers on Blueprint Reading. 3rd ed. Roland Palmquist. LC 77-71585. 1977. 9.95 (ISBN 0-672-23283-9). Audel.

Answers on the Way. Desmond Ford. LC 76-17704. (Dimension Ser). 1976. pap. 5.95 (ISBN 0-8163-0253-7, 01636-0). Pacific Pr Pub Assn.

Answers to Inequity. Joel S. Berke. LC 73-7237. 1974. 17.90 (ISBN 0-685-42625-4); text ed. 16.20 (ISBN 0-685-42626-2). McCutchan.

Answers to Questions. 2nd ed. F. F. Bruce. 1978. pap. 7.95 (ISBN 0-310-21991-4). Zondervan.

Answers to Questions on the Ocean. Robert Crosbie. 249p. 1933. 5.00 (ISBN 0-938998-12-9). Theosophy.

Answers to Selected Problems in Multi-Variable Calculus with Linear Algebra & Series. William F. Trench & Bernard Kolman. 1972. 3.00 (ISBN 0-12-699056-5). Acad Pr.

Answers to Tough Questions Skeptics Ask About the Christian Faith. Josh McDowell & Don Stewart. 190p. 1980. pap. 4.95 (ISBN 0-918956-65-X). Campus Crusade.

Answers to Your Mushroom Questions Plus Recipes. Donna Myer. LC 77-87780. (Illus.). 1977. pap. 3.95x (ISBN 0-9601516-1-3). Mushroom Cave.

Answers to Your People Problems. John G. Kerbs. LC 68-25949. (Harvest Ser.). 1978. pap. 3.95 (ISBN 0-8163-0192-1, 01634-5). Pacific Pr Pub Assn.

Answers to Your Questions About the Bible. Joseph C. Swaim. 15.00 o.s.i. (ISBN 0-8149-0217-0). Vanguard.

Ant & Bee. Angela Banner. LC 63-20113. (Ant & Bee Bks). (Illus.). (gr. k-3). 1958. 2.95 o.p. (ISBN 0-531-01155-0). Watts.

Ant & Bee & the ABC. Angela Banner. LC 66-16692. (Ant & Bee Bks). (Illus.). (gr. k-3). 1967. 2.95 o.p. (ISBN 0-531-01156-9). Watts.

Ant & Bee & the Doctor. Angela Banner. LC 77-152853. (Ant & Bee Ser). (Illus.). (gr. k-3). 1971. PLB 2.95 o.p. (ISBN 0-531-0167-4). Watts.

Ant & Bee & the Rainbow. Angela Banner. (Ant & Bee Bks). (Illus.). (gr. k-3). 1963. 2.95 o.p. (ISBN 0-531-01157-7). Watts.

Ant & Bee Go Shopping. Angela Banner. LC 74-185921. (Ant & Bee Bks.). (Illus.). 80p. (gr. k-3). 1972. 2.95 o.p. (ISBN 0-531-01168-2). Watts.

Ant & Bee Time. Angela Banner. LC 69-12354. (Ant & Bee Bks). (Illus.). (gr. k-3). 1969. 2.95 o.p. (ISBN 0-531-01163-1). Watts.

Ant & the Elephant. Bill Peet. LC 74-79918. (Illus.). 48p. (gr. k-3). 1972. reinforced bdg. 8.95 (ISBN 0-395-16963-1); pap. 2.95 (ISBN 0-395-29205-0). HM.

Antarctic: Bottom of the World. Julian May. Ed. by Publication Associates. LC 79-156054. (Investigating the Earth Ser). (Illus.). (gr. 4-6). 1972. PLB 5.95 o.p. (ISBN 0-8719-058-6). Creative Ed.

Antarctica: Exploring the Frozen Continent. Maggi Scarf. (Illus.). (gr. 3-6). 1970. PLB 4.39 o.p. (ISBN 0-394-90799-X). Random.

Antarctica: The Worst Place in the World. Allyn Z. Baum. (gr. 5-8). 1967. 4.95g o.s.i. (ISBN 0-02-708490-6). Macmillan.

Ante-Bellum South Carolina: A Society & Cultural History. Rosser H. Taylor. LC 79-98180. (American Scene Ser). 1970. Repr. of 1942 ed. lib. bdg. 25.00 (ISBN 0-306-71834-0). Da Capo.

Ante la Perdida De un Ser Querido. Granger Westberg. Tr. by Jorge A. Rodriguez. 1980. Repr. of 1978 ed. 0.95 (ISBN 0-311-46081-X). Casa Bautista.

Anteater Named Arthur. Bernard Waber. LC 67-20374. (Illus.). (gr. k-3). 1967. reinforced bdg. 9.95 (ISBN 0-395-20336-8). HM.

Anteater Named Arthur. Bernard Waber. (gr. k-3). 1977. pap. 3.95 (ISBN 0-395-25936-3). HM.

Antebellum American Culture: An Interpretive Anthology. David B. Davis. 1979. pap. text ed. 8.95 (ISBN 0-669-01476-1). Heath.

Antebellum Culture. Carl Bode. LC 59-8759. (Illus.). 1970. Repr. of 1959 ed. lib. bdg. 7.00x o.p. (ISBN 0-8093-0464-3). S Ill U Pr.

Antebellum Writers in New York & the South. Ed. by Joel Myerson. LC 79-1548. (Dictionary of Literary Biography Ser.: Vol 3.). (Illus.). 1979. 54.00 (ISBN 0-8103-0915-7, Bruccoli Clark Bk). Gale.

Antelope: The Ordeal of the Recaptured Africans in the Administrations of James Monroe & John Quincy Adams. John T. Noonan, Jr. 1977. 15.75 (ISBN 0-520-03319-1). U of Cal Pr.

Antenna Syndrome. Alan Marks. 1979. pap. 1.75 (ISBN 0-505-51343-9). Tower Bks.

Antenna Theory & Design. (Illus.). 608p. 1981. 38.00 (ISBN 0-13-038356-2). P-H.

Antenna Theory & Design. Warren L. Stutzman & Gary A. Thiele. 672p. 1981. text ed. 26.95 (ISBN 0-471-04458-X). Wiley.

Antenna Theory & Design. Paul H. Williams. 15.95x (ISBN 0-392-07549-0, SpS). Soccer.

Antennas. L. J. Blake. (Electronic Technlogy Ser.). 1966. pap. 15.95 (ISBN 0-471-07928-6). Wiley.

Antennas. F. R. Connor. (Introductory Topics in Electronics & Telecommiunication). 99p. 1972. pap. 11.00x (ISBN 0-7131-3279-5). Intl Ideas.

Antennas in Matter: Fundamentals, Theory & Applications. Ronald W. King et al. 784p. 1981. text ed. 75.00x (ISBN 0-262-11074-1). MIT Pr.

Anterior Restoration, Fixed Bridgework, & Esthetics. David S. Shelby. (Illus.). 416p. 1976. 38.75 (ISBN 0-398-03322-6). C C Thomas.

Antheil & the Treatise on Harmony. 2nd ed. Ezra Pound. LC 68-27463. (Music Ser). (gr. 9 up). 1968. Repr. of 1927 ed. lib. bdg. 17.50 (ISBN 0-306-70981-3). Da Capo.

Anthem in England & America. Elwyn A. Wienandt & Robert H. Young. LC 76-76225. 1970. 15.95 (ISBN 0-02-935230-4). Free Pr.

Anthem in New England Before Eighteen Hundred. Ralph T. Daniel. (Music Reprint Ser.). 1979. Repr. of 1966 ed. 27.50 (ISBN 0-306-79511-6). Da Capo.

Anthems & Anthem Composers. Myles B. Foster. LC 76-125047. (Music Ser). 1970. Repr. of 1901 ed. lib. bdg. 19.50 (ISBN 0-306-70012-3). Da Capo.

Anthems for Men's Voices, 2 vols. Peter Le Huray et al. Incl. Vol. 1. Altos, Tenors & Basses. 6.75x o.p. (ISBN 0-19-353234-4); Vol. 2. Tenors & Basses. 6.75x o.p. (ISBN 0-19-353235-2). 1965. Oxford U Pr.

Anthill: A Play. Obi B. Egbuna. (Three Crowns Book). 1965. pap. 1.95x o.p. (ISBN 0-19-911067-0). Oxford U Pr.

Anthologie. Ed. by Alexander D. Gibson. LC 66-28097. (Orig., Fr.). 1967. pap. 5.95 (ISBN 0-672-63008-7). Odyssey Pr.

Anthologie De la Litterature Francaise, 2 vols. 2nd ed. Ed. by Henri Clouard & Robert Leggewie. 860p. 1975. Vol. 1. pap. text ed. 12.95x (ISBN 0-19-501877-X); Vol. 2. pap. text ed. 12.95x (ISBN 0-19-501878-8). Oxford U Pr.

Anthologie de la Poesie Francaise du Seizieme Siecle. Ed. by Floyd Gray. LC 67-10343. (Fr.). 1977. 29.50x (ISBN 0-89197-026-6); pap. text ed. 18.95x (ISBN 0-89197-659-0). Irvington.

Anthologie d'humour Francais. Paul Mankin & Alex Szogyi. 1970. pap. 6.95x (ISBN 0-673-05111-0). Scott F.

Anthology of Atheism & Rationalism. Ed. by Gordon Stein. LC 80-81326. (Skeptic's Bookshelf Ser.). 354p. 1980. 16.95 (ISBN 0-87975-136-3). Prometheus Bks.

Anthology of Austrian Drama. Ed. & intro. by Douglas A. Russell. LC 76-19836. 400p. 1981. 22.50 (ISBN 0-8386-2003-5). Fairleigh Dickinson. Postponed.

Anthology of Brazilian Modernist Poetry. G. Pontiero. 1969. text ed. 18.75 (ISBN 0-08-013327-4); pap. text ed. 9.25 (ISBN 0-08-013326-6). Pergamon.

Anthology of Children's Literature. 5th ed. Edna Johnson et al. 1977. text ed. 21.95 (ISBN 0-395-24554-0). HM.

Anthology of Chinese Literature, Vol. 2. From the Fourteenth Century to the Present. Ed. by Cyril Birch & Donald Keene. Tr. by Cyril Birch from Chinese. (Illus.). 1972. pap. 4.95 (ISBN 0-394-17766-5, E584, Ever). Grove.

Anthology of Concrete Poetry. Emmett Williams. 10.00. Green Hill.

Anthology of Contemporary French Poetry. Ed. & tr. by G. D. Martin. (Edinburgh Bilingual Library: No. 5). 216p. 1972. 10.95x (ISBN 0-292-71006-2); pap. 5.50x (ISBN 0-292-71004-6). U of Tex Pr.

Anthology of Contemporary Romanian Poetry. Ed. by Roy MacGregor-Hastie. 1969. 13.95 (ISBN 0-7206-0280-7). Dufour.

Anthology of Danish Literature. new bilingual ed. Ed. by F. J. Billeskov-Jansen & P. M. Mitchell. LC 72-132475. 1971. Repr. of 1964 ed. 25.00x o.p. (ISBN 0-8093-0487-2). S Ill U Pr.

Anthology of Danish Literature: Middle Ages to Romanticism. bilingual ed. Ed. by F. J. Billeskov-Jansen & P. M. Mitchell. LC 72-5610. (Arcturus Books Paperbacks). 272p. 1972. pap. 6.95 (ISBN 0-8093-0596-8). S Ill U Pr.

Anthology of Danish Literature: Realism to the Present. bilingual ed. Ed. by F. J. Billeskov-Jansen & P. M. Mitchell. LC 72-5610. (Arcturus Books Paperbacks). 352p. 1972. pap. 7.95 (ISBN 0-8093-0597-6). S Ill U Pr.

Anthology of German Poetry from Holderlin to Rilke. Ed. by Angel Flores. 8.50 (ISBN 0-8446-1185-9). Peter Smith.

Anthology of Holocaust Literature. Jacob Glatstein et al. LC 68-19609. (Temple Bks). 1972. pap. text ed. 5.95x (ISBN 0-689-70343-0, T23). Atheneum.

Anthology of I Ching. W. A. Sherrill & W. K. Chu. 1978. 22.00 (ISBN 0-7100-8590-7). Routledge & Kegan.

Anthology of Indo-English Poetry. Gauri Deshpande. 162p. 1975. pap. text ed. 2.50 (ISBN 0-88253-455-6). Ind-US Inc.

Anthology of Islamic Literature: From the Rise of Islam to Modern Times. Ed. by James Kritzeck. 1975. pap. 5.95 (ISBN 0-452-00498-5, F498, Mer). NAL.

Anthology of Italian Poems, 13th-19th Century. Tr. by Lorna De Lucchi. LC 66-30496. (Eng. & Ital.). 1922. 14.00x (ISBN 0-8196-0198-5). Biblo.

Anthology of Japanese Literature: Earliest Era to Mid-Nineteenth Century. Ed. by Donald Keene. 1955. pap. 7.95 (ISBN 0-394-17221-3, E216, Ever). Grove.

Anthology of Jesus. James Marchant. Ed. by Warren W. Wiersbe. LC 80-25038. 1981. Repr. of 1926 ed. 8.95 (ISBN 0-8254-4015-7). Kregel.

Anthology of Kumarila Bhatt's Works. Kjmarila Bhatt. Ed. by P. S. Sharma. 96p. 1980. text ed. 9.00x (ISBN 0-8426-1647-0). Verry.

Anthology of Medieval Latin Love Poetry: No. 8. Joseph Szoverffy. 1976. 18.00 o.p. (ISBN 0-686-23384-0). Classical Folia.

Anthology of Mentor Poetry for the Sixties. Pref. by Ivan McShane. pap. 3.00 (ISBN 0-87423-015-2). Westburg.

Anthology of Mexican Modern Poetry. Ed. by Linda Scheer & Miguel Ramirez. 170p. Date not set. 13.50 (ISBN 0-931556-06-6); pap. 4.50 (ISBN 0-931556-07-4). Translation Pr. Postponed.

Anthology of Modern Arabic Poetry. Ed. by Mounah A. Khouri & Hamid Algar. Tr. by Mounah A. Khouri & Hamid Algar. 1974. 18.50x (ISBN 0-520-02234-3); pap. 3.95 (ISBN 0-520-02898-8). U of Cal Pr.

Anthology of Modern French Poetry. Ed. by P. Broome & G. Chesters. LC 75-40769. 224p. 1976. 36.00 (ISBN 0-521-20793-2); pap. 8.95x (ISBN 0-521-20929-3). Cambridge U Pr.

Anthology of Modern Kashmiri Verse 1930-1960. Ed. by Trilokinath Raina. Tr. by Trithokinath Raina from Kashmiri. 280p. 1974. lib. bdg. 12.50 (ISBN 0-88253-469-6). Ind-US Inc.

Anthology of Modern Writing from Sri Lanka. Ed. by Ranjini Obeyesekere & Chitra Fernando. (Monographs of the Association for Asian Studies: No. XXXVIII). 1981. text ed. 12.95x (ISBN 0-8165-0702-3); pap. text ed. 6.50x (ISBN 0-8165-0703-1). U of Ariz Pr.

Anthology of Modern Yiddish Poetry. Ruth Whitman. LC 66-25551. 141p. 1979. pap. 4.95. Workmen's Circle.

Anthology of Old Russian Literature. Ed. by Adolf Stender-Petersen. LC 55-14251. (Columbia Slavic Studies). (Illus.). 1955. 27.50x (ISBN 0-231-01897-5). Columbia U Pr.

Anthology of Russian Literature in the Soviet Period from Gorki to Pasternak. Ed. by Bernard G. Guerney. (Russian Library Ser). (Orig.). 1960. pap. 2.95 o.p. (ISBN 0-394-70717-6, Vin). Random.

Anthology of Spanish-American Literature, 2 vols. 2nd ed. Ed. by John E. Englekirk et al. (Span.). 1968. Vol. 1. pap. text ed. 11.50 (ISBN 0-13-038786-X); Vol. 2. pap. text ed. 12.50 (ISBN 0-13-038794-0). P-H.

Anthology of Spanish Poetry from the Beginnings to the Present Day, Including Both Spain & Spanish America. Ed. by John A. Crow. LC 79-4619. 1979. text ed. 8.95 (ISBN 0-8071-0482-5); pap. text ed. 7.95x (ISBN 0-8071-0483-3). La State U Pr.

Anthology of Twentieth-Century Brazilian Poetry. Ed. by Elizabeth Bishop & Emanuel Brasil. Tr. by Paul Blackburn et al from Port. LC 75-184359. 224p. (Orig.). 1972. pap. 7.50x (ISBN 0-8195-6023-5, Pub. by Wesleyan U Pr). Columbia U Pr.

Anthology of Twentieth Century French Theater. 7.95x o.p. (ISBN 0-685-92174-3, 3604). Larousse.

Anthology of Twentieth Century Music. Mary H. Wennerstrom. 1969. pap. 18.50 (ISBN 0-13-038489-5). P-H.

Anthology of Twentieth-Century New Zealand Poetry. Ed. by Vincent O'Sullivan. (Oxford Paperbacks Ser). 1970. pap. 6.50x o.p. (ISBN 0-19-281092-8). Oxford U Pr.

Anthomyiidae of California, Exclusive of Subfamily Scatophaginae (Diptera) H. C. Huckett. (Bulletin of the California Insect Survey: Vol. 12). 1971. pap. 8.00x (ISBN 0-520-09355-0). U of Cal Pr.

Anthony Adverse, Pt. 2: The Other Bronze Boy. Hervey Allen. 1978. pap. 2.50 o.s.i. (ISBN 0-446-81621-3). Warner Bks.

Anthony & Sabrina. Ray Prather. LC 73-3888. (Illus.). 32p. (gr. k-3). 1973. 4.95g o.s.i. (ISBN 0-02-775030-2). Macmillan.

Anthony Burgess. A. A. DeVitis. (English Authors Ser.: No. 132). lib. bdg. 10.95 (ISBN 0-8057-1068-X). Twayne.

Anthony Caro. William Rubin. LC 74-21725. (Illus.). 196p. 1975. 17.50 (ISBN 0-87070-275-0); pap. 7.95 (ISBN 0-87070-276-9). Museum Mod Art.

Anthony Comstock: His Career of Cruelty & Crime. De Robigne M. Bennett. LC 73-121102. (Civil Liberties in American History Ser). 1971. Repr. of 1878 ed. lib. bdg. 17.50 (ISBN 0-306-71968-1). Da Capo.

Anthony Mann. Jeanine Basinger. (Theatrical Arts Ser.). 1979. lib. bdg. 12.50 (ISBN 0-8057-9263-5). Twayne.

Anthony Merry Redivivus: A Reappraisal of the British Minister to the United States, 1803-6. Malcom Lester. LC 77-20910. 1978. 13.95x (ISBN 0-8139-0750-0). U Pr of Va.

Anthony Munday: The English Romayne Lyfe. Ed. by G. B. Harrison. 105p. 1980. Repr. of 1925 ed. lib. bdg. 22.50 (ISBN 0-89760-543-8). Telegraph Bks.

Anthony Powell. Neil Brennan. (English Authors Ser.: No. 158). 1974. lib. bdg. 10.95 (ISBN 0-8057-1454-5). Twayne.

Anthony Trollope. Ed. by Tony Bareham. (Barnes & Noble Critical Studies). 207p. 1980. 26.00x (ISBN 0-389-20027-1). B&N.

Anthony Trollope. Alice Fredman. LC 74-136496. (Columbia Essays on Modern Writers Ser.: No. 56). 48p. 1971, pap. 2.00 (ISBN 0-231-03081-9, MW56). Columbia U Pr.

Anthony Trollope. Arthur Pollard. 1978. 15.00x (ISBN 0-7100-8811-6). Routledge & Kegan.

Anthony Trollope: His Art & Scope. P. D. Edwards. LC 77-27915. 1978. 21.95x (ISBN 0-312-04271-X). St Martin.

Anthony Trollope: His Perception of Character & the Traumatic Experience. Janet Emmerich. LC 79-3734. 1980. text ed. 13.00 (ISBN 0-8191-0918-5); pap. text ed. 6.00 (ISBN 0-8191-0919-3). U Pr of Amer.

Anthony Trollope: The Critical Heritage. Ed. by Donald Smalley. 1969. 40.00x (ISBN 0-7100-6153-6). Routledge & Kegan.

Anthracyclines: Current Status & New Developments. Ed. by Stanley T. Crooke & Steven D. Reich. 1980. 27.50 (ISBN 0-12-197780-3). Acad Pr.

Anthrophysical Form: Two Families & Their Neighborhood Environments. Robert L. Vickery, Jr. LC 73-183896. 1973. 9.95x (ISBN 0-8139-0393-9). U Pr of Va.

Anthropogenic Compounds. (Handbook of Environmental Chemistry Ser.: Vol. 3 Pt, A). (Illus.). 290p. 1980. 57.90 (ISBN 0-387-09690-6). Springer-Verlag.

Anthropological Analysis of Food-Getting Technology. Wendell H. Oswalt et al. LC 76-17640. 1976. 27.50 (ISBN 0-471-65729-8, Pub. by Wiley-Interscience). Wiley.

Anthropological Papers in Memory of Earl H. Swanson, Jr. Ed. by Lucille B. Harten et al. (Special Publication of the Idaho Museum of Natural History). 200p. (Orig.). 1980. write for info. Idaho Mus Nat Hist.

Anthropological Perspectives on Latin American Urbanization. Ed. by Wayne A. Cornelius & Felicity M. Trueblood. LC 73-86706. (Latin American Urban Research: Vol. 4). 1974. 20.00x (ISBN 0-8039-0313-8); pap. 9.95x (ISBN 0-8039-0852-0). Sage.

Anthropological Research: The Structure of Inquiry. 2d ed. Pertti J Pelto & Gretel H. Pelto. LC 76-62583. 1978. 29.95 (ISBN 0-521-21673-7); pap. 10.95x (ISBN 0-521-29228-X). Cambridge U Pr.

Anthropological Romance of Bali 1597-1972. J. A. Boon. LC 76-19626. (Geertz Ser.). (Illus.). 1977. 29.95 (ISBN 0-521-21398-3); pap. 7.95x (ISBN 0-521-29226-3). Cambridge U Pr.

Anthropologie Du Conscrit Francais D'apres les Comptes Numeriques et Sommaires Du Recrutement De L'armee, 1819-1826: Presentation Cartographique. Jean P. Aron et al. (Civilisation et Societes: No. 28). 1972. 41.75 (ISBN 90-2797-167-6). Mouton.

Anthropologists' Cookbook. Ed. by Jessica Kuper. LC 77-80179. (Illus.). 1978. text ed. 12.50x (ISBN 0-87663-301-7); pap. 6.95 (ISBN 0-87663-971-6). Universe.

Anthropologists in the Field. D. G. Jongmans & Peter C. Gutkind. 1967. text ed. 25.50x (ISBN 90-232-0079-9). Humanities.

Anthropology. 3rd ed. Carol R. Ember & Melvin Ember. (Illus.). 592p. 1981. text ed. 17.95 (ISBN 0-13-037002-9). P-H.

Anthropology. 2nd ed. M. Ember & C. Ember. 1977. 17.95 (ISBN 0-13-036962-4); study guide & wkbk. 4.95 (ISBN 0-13-036970-5). P-H.

Anthropology. Eric A. Wolf. 113p. 1974. pap. 2.95x (ISBN 0-393-09290-9). Norton.

Anthropology: A General Introduction. Victor Barnouw. 1979. 18.50 (ISBN 0-256-02113-9); pap. text ed. 2.50 study guide (ISBN 0-256-02113-9). Dorsey.

Anthropology: Aborigines, 3 vols. (British Parliamentary Papers Ser.). 1971. Set. 198.00x (ISBN 0-7165-1493-1, Pub. by Irish Academic Pr Ireland). Biblio Dist.

Anthropology, an Introduction. 3rd ed. Lowell E. Holmes & Wayne Parris. LC 80-22138. 450p. 1981. text ed. 14.95 (ISBN 0-471-08107-8). Wiley.

Anthropology & Art: Readings in Cross-Cultural Aesthetics. Ed. by Charlotte M. Otten. LC 75-43853. (Texas Press Source Books in Anthropology: No. 10). 1976. pap. 9.95 (ISBN 0-292-70313-9). U of Tex Pr.

Anthropology & Change in Rural Areas. Ed. by Bernardo Berdichewsky. (World Anthropology Ser.). (Illus.). 564p. text ed. 52.65x (ISBN 90-279-7810-7). Mouton.

Anthropology & History. Edward E. Evans-Pritchard. 1961. pap. text ed. 1.25x o.p. (ISBN 0-7190-0254-0). Humanities.

Anthropology & Language Science in Educational Development. LC 73-75746. (Educational Studies & Documents, No. 11). 58p. (Orig.). 1973. pap. 2.50 (ISBN 92-3-101095-6, U32, UNESCO). Unipub.

Anthropology & Social Change. Lucy Mair. (Monographs on Social Anthropology Ser: No. 38). 1969. text ed. 7.00x (ISBN 0-485-19538-0, Athlone Pr); pap. text ed. 9.50x (ISBN 0-391-00210-4). Humanities.

Anthropology & the Classics. Clyde Kluckhohn. LC 61-11106. 76p. 1961. 5.00 (ISBN 0-87057-065-X, Pub. by Brown U Pr). Univ Pr of New England.

Anthropology: Culture, Society & Evolution. John J. Collins. (Illus.). 480p. 1975. text ed. 17.95 (ISBN 0-13-038596-4). P-H.

Anthropology Full Circle. I. Rossi et al. LC 74-33027. 444p. (Orig.). 1977. pap. text ed. 10.95 (ISBN 0-03-038926-7, HoltC); aval. instructor's manual (ISBN 0-03-036236-9). HR&W.

Anthropology in Use: The Bibliographic Chronology of the Development of Applied Anthropology. John Van Willigen. (Orig.). 1980. pap. 8.90 (ISBN 0-913178-66-7). Redgrave Pub Co.

Anthropology of Dance. Anya P. Royce. LC 77-74428. (Illus.). 256p. 1980. pap. 6.95 (ISBN 0-253-20235-3). Ind U Pr.

Anthropology of Health. Ed. by Eleanor E. Bauwens. LC 78-6776. 1978. pap. text ed. 11.95 (ISBN 0-8016-0516-4). Mosby.

Anthropology of Northern China. Sergei M. Shirokogoroff. (Orig.). 1966. Repr. of 1923 ed. text ed. 9.00x (ISBN 90-6234-039-3). Humanities.

Anthropology of Pre-Capitalist Societies. Ed. by Joel Kahn & Josep Llobera. 1980. text ed. write for info. (ISBN 0-391-01943-0); pap. text ed. price not set. Humanities.

Anthropology of Taiwanese Society. Ed. by Emily M. Ahern. Hill Gates. LC 79-64212. 480p. 1981. 30.00x (ISBN 0-8047-1043-0). Stanford U Pr.

Anthropology of the City: An Introduction to Urban Anthropology. Edwin Eames & Judith G. Goode. LC 76-57696. 1977. pap. text ed. 11.95 (ISBN 0-13-038414-3). P-H.

Anthropology on the Great Plains. Ed. by W. Raymond Wood & Margot Liberty. LC 79-28369. (Illus.). viii, 306p. 1980. 25.00x (ISBN 0-8032-4708-7). U of Nebr Pr.

Anthropology, Psychology, Education, Language & Philosophy. M. J. Clarke. 1966. pap. 6.00x o.p. (ISBN 0-19-437712-1). Oxford U Pr.

Anthropology, Relativism & Method: An Inquiry into the Methodological Principles of a Science of Culture. J. Tennekes. (Studies of Developing Countries: No. 10). 1971. text ed. 22.25x (ISBN 90-232-0855-2). Humanities.

Anthropology: The Exploration of Human Diversity. 2nd ed. Conrad P. Kottak. 1978. text ed. 16.95 (ISBN 0-394-31276-7); study guide 4.25 (ISBN 0-394-31836-6). Random.

Anthropology: The Humanizing Process. Evelyn S. Kessler. 192p. 1974. text ed. 10.25x o.p. (ISBN 0-205-04415-8); pap. text ed. 6.95x o.p. (ISBN 0-205-04420-4). Allyn.

Anthropology Through Science Fiction. Ed. by Martin H. Greenberg et al. 350p. (Orig.). 1974. 16.95 (ISBN 0-312-04305-8); pap. text ed. 8.95 (ISBN 0-312-04340-6). St Martin.

Anthropology Toward History: Culture & Work in a 19th-Century Maine Town. Richard Horwitz. LC 77-74560. (Illus.). 1978. lib. bdg. 17.50x (ISBN 0-8195-5014-0, Pub. by Wesleyan U Pr). Columbia U Pr.

Anthropometry for Designers. rev. ed. John Crooney. 144p. 1981. pap. 12.00 (ISBN 0-442-22013-8). Van Nos Reinhold.

Anthropos-Specter-Beast. Tadeusz Konwicki. Tr. by George Korwin-Rodziszewski & Audrey Korwin-Rodziszewski. LC 77-13500. 320p. (gr. 9 up). 1977. 9.95 (ISBN 0-87599-218-8). S G Phillips.

Anti-Apartheid: Transnational Conflict & Western Policy in the Liberation of South Africa. George W. Shepherd, Jr. LC 77-71868. (Studies in Human Rights: No. 3). 1977. lib. bdg. 17.50x (ISBN 0-8371-9537-3, SHA/). Greenwood.

Anti-Appeasers: Conservative Opposition to Appeasement in the 1930's. Neville Thompson. 1971. 28.50x (ISBN 0-19-821487-1). Oxford U Pr.

Anti-Capitalistic Mentality. Ludwig Von Mises. LC 56-12097. 140p. 1978. pap. 5.00 (ISBN 0-910884-06-4). Libertarian.

Anti-Coloring Book of Red-Letter Daus. Susan Striker. (Illus.). 64p. (Orig.). 1981. pap. 3.95 (ISBN 0-03-057873-6). HR&W.

Anti-Diuretic Hormone, Vol. 1. Mary L. Forsling. (Annual Research Reviews Ser.). 1977. 19.20 (ISBN 0-904406-51-2). Eden Med Res.

Anti-Diuretic Hormone, Vol. 2, 1977. Mary L. Forsling. LC 78-309279. (Annual Research Reviews). 1978. 24.00 (ISBN 0-88831-016-1). Eden Med Res.

Anti-Duhring. Frederick Engels. 1976. 4.95 (ISBN 0-8351-0473-7); pap. 3.25 (ISBN 0-8351-0010-3). China Bks.

Anti-Dumping Law in a Liberal Trade Order. Richard Dale. Date not set. price not set (ISBN 0-312-04373-2). St Martin.

Anti-Epileptic Drugs: Quantitative Analysis & Interpretation. Ed. by C. E. Pippenger et al. LC 76-58055. 1978. 36.50 (ISBN 0-89004-197-0). Raven.

Anti Fungal Chemotherapy. D. C. Speller. LC 79-40524. 1980. 96.25 (ISBN 0-471-27620-0, Pub. by Wiley-Interscience). Wiley.

Anti-Gravity Force. John L. Cooper. LC 80-83402. 160p. 1981. pap. text ed. 9.95 (ISBN 0-8403-2300-X). Kendall-Hunt.

Anti-Hegelianism & the Theory of the Infinite. Mark H. Laffleur. (Illus.). 131p. 1981. 31.45 (ISBN 0-89266-281-6). Am Classical Coll Pr.

Anti-Muffins. Madeleine L'Engle. (Education of the Public & the Public School Ser.). (Illus.). 48p. (gr. 3-6). 1981. 7.95 (ISBN 0-8298-0415-3). Pilgrim NY.

Anti-Oxidants & Corrosion Inhibitors. 1980. 850.00 (ISBN 0-89336-261-1, C-020). BCC.

Anti-Rationalists: Art Nouveau Architecture & Design. Ed. by Nikolaus Pevsner & J. M. Richards. LC 76-12192. (Icon Editions). (Illus.). 210p. 1976. pap. 7.95 o.s.i. (ISBN 0-06-430076-5, IN-76, HarpT). Har-Row.

Anti-Samuelson. Marc Linder. Incl. Vol. I. Macroeconomics: Basic Problems of Capitalist Economy (ISBN 0-916354-14-8) (ISBN 0-916354-15-6); Vol. II. Microeconomics: Money & Banking (ISBN 0-916354-16-4) (ISBN 0-916354-17-2). 1977. 20.00 ea.; pap. text ed. 6.95 ea. Urizen Bks.

Anti-Sartre: With an Essay on Camus. Colin Wilson. LC 80-24098. (Milford Series: Popular Writers of Today: Vol. 34). 64p. (Orig.). 1981. lib. bdg. 8.95x (ISBN 0-89370-149-1); pap. text ed. 2.95x (ISBN 0-89370-249-8). Borgo Pr.

Anti-Scepticism: Henry Lee. Ed. by Rene Wellek. LC 75-11231. (British Philosophers & Theologians of the 17th & 18th Centuries Ser.). 1977. lib. bdg. 42.00 (ISBN 0-8240-1784-6). Garland Pub.

Anti-Slavery, Religion & Reform. Christine Bolt & Seymour Dresher. 275p. 1980. 27.50 (ISBN 0-208-01783-6, Archon). Shoe String.

Anti-Story: An Anthology of Experimental Fiction. P. Stevick. LC 78-131596. 1971. pap. text ed. 6.95 (ISBN 0-02-931500-X). Free Pr.

Anti-Stress Workbook. Barbara North & Penelope Crittenden. (Illus.). 79p. (Orig.). 1980. pap. 4.95 (ISBN 0-938480-00-6). Healthworks.

Anti-Theatrical Tracts Seventeen Two-Seventeen Four: Stage Plays Arraigned & Condemned. William Ames. Bd. with Scourge for the Play-Houses. Richard Burridge; Humble Application to the Queen...to Suppress Playhouses. John Feild; Letter from Several Members of the Society for Reformation of Manners. LC 77-170480. (English Stage Ser.: Vol. 44). lib. bdg. 50.00 (ISBN 0-8240-0627-5). Garland Pub.

Anti-Trust: Guidelines for the Business Executive. Richard M. Calkins. 325p. 17.50 (ISBN 0-87094-231-X). Dow Jones-Irwin.

Anti-Trust Laws of the U. S. A. 2nd ed. Allan D. Neale. LC 73-92251. (National Institute of Economic & Social Research Economic & Social Studies: No. 19). 1970. 13.95x (ISBN 0-521-09528-X). Cambridge U Pr.

Anti-Tussive Agents, 3 vols. H. Salem & D. M. Aviado. 1970. Set. text ed. 130.00 (ISBN 0-08-013340-1). Pergamon.

Antiarrhythmic Agents. Arthur J. Moss & Robert D. Patton. (Illus.). 176p. 1973. 14.75 (ISBN 0-398-02622-X). C C Thomas.

Antibias Regulations of Universities: Faculty Problems & Their Solutions. Carnegie Commission on Higher Education. 1974. 5.95 o.p. (ISBN 0-07-010120-5, P&RB). McGraw.

Antibiotic & Chemotherapy. 5th ed. L. P. Garrod et al. (Illus.). 480p. (Orig.). 1981. text ed. write for info. (ISBN 0-443-02143-0). Churchill.

Antibiotic Resistance: Proceedings. Ed. by S. Mitsuhashi et al. (Illus.). 410p. 1981. 55.50 (ISBN 0-387-10322-8). Springer-Verlag.

Antibiotic Therapy. P. P. Toskes. (Clinical Monographs Ser.). (Illus.). 1974. pap. 7.95 (ISBN 0-87618-061-6). R J Brady.

Antibiotic Therapy in Obstetrics & Gynecology. Ronald S. Gibbs. 224p. 1981. 16.50 (ISBN 0-471-06003-8, Pub. by Wiley Med). Wiley.

Antibiotics & Antibiosis in Agriculture. Woodbine. LC 77-30021. (Nottingham Easter School Ser.). 1978. text ed. 64.95 (ISBN 0-408-70917-0). Butterworths.

Antibiotics & Hospitals: Proceedings. Symposium Milan, Italy, November 1978. Ed. by Carlo Grassi & Guiseppe Ostino. LC 79-5390. (Progress in Clinical & Biological Research Ser.: Vol. 35). 238p. 1979. 28.00x (ISBN 0-8451-0035-1). A R Liss.

Antibiotics: Origin, Nature & Properties, 3 vols. Ed. by T. Korzybski et al. 1979. 48.00 (ISBN 0-914826-14-X). Am Soc Microbio.

Antibodies in Human Diagnosis & Therapy. Ed. by Edgar Haber & Richard M. Krause. LC 75-32089. (Royal Society of Medicine Foundation Ser.). 1977. 34.50 (ISBN 0-89004-089-3). Raven.

Antibody Production. Ed. by L. E. Glynn & M. W. Steward. 1981. 15.00 (ISBN 0-471-27916-1, Pub. by Wiley-Interscience). Wiley.

Antic Fables: Patterns of Evasion in Shakespeare's Comedies. A. P. Riemer. LC 80-13330. 1980. 18.95 (ISBN 0-312-04369-4). St Martin.

Antic Spectre: Satire in Early Gothic Novels. Fredric Weiss. Ed. by Devendra P. Varma. LC 79-8489. (Gothic Studies & Dissertations Ser.). 1980. lib. bdg. 25.00x (ISBN 0-405-12664-6). Arno.

Anticancer Agents Based on Natural Product Models. Ed. by John M. Cassady & John D. Douros. LC 79-6802. (Medicinal Chemistry Ser.). 1980. 49.50 (ISBN 0-12-163150-8). Acad Pr.

Antichrist. Vincent B. Miceli. LC 80-66294. 1981. 12.95 (ISBN 0-8158-0395-8). Chris Mass.

Antichrist in Seventeenth Century England. Christopher Hill. 1971. 9.95x (ISBN 0-19-713911-6). Oxford U Pr.

Antichrist in the Middle Ages: A Study of Medieval Apocalypticism, Art, & Literature. Richard K. Emmerson. LC 79-3874. (Illus.). 320p. 1981. 19.50 (ISBN 0-295-95716-6). U of Wash Pr.

Anticipatory Grief. Bernard Schoenberg et al. (Thanatology Ser.). 336p. 1974. 20.00x (ISBN 0-231-03770-8). Columbia U Pr.

Anticoagulant & Thrombolytic Therapy in Surgery. Nikolai N. Malinovsky & Valery A. Kozlov. LC 78-21077. (Illus.). 1979. 37.50 (ISBN 0-8016-3079-7). Mosby.

Anticonvulsant Drugs, Vols. 1-2. Ed. by J. Mercier. LC 72-8044. 1974. Vol. 1. text ed. 64.00 (ISBN 0-08-016840-X); Vol. 2. text ed. 50.00 (ISBN 0-08-017245-8). Pergamon.

Anticonvulsant Therapy. 2nd ed. M. J. Eadie & J. H. Tyrer. (Illus.). 1980. text ed. 42.50 (ISBN 0-443-01917-7). Churchill.

Antidepressants. Medical Economics Company. 1972. 6.95 (ISBN 0-87489-026-8). Med Economics.

Antidepressants: Neurochemical, Behavioral, & Clinical Perspectives. Ed. by Salvatore J. Enna et al. 275p. 1981. 27.00 (ISBN 0-89004-534-8). Raven.

Antidumping Law: Policy & Implementation, Vol. I. (Michigan Yearbook of International Legal Studies). 332p. 1980. 24.00 o.p. (ISBN 0-686-65207-X). U of Mich Pr.

Antient & Modern Stages Survey'd. James Drake. LC 70-170446. (English Stage Ser.: Vol. 32). lib. bdg. 50.00 (ISBN 0-8240-0615-1). Garland Pub.

Antiepileptic Drugs. Ed. by D. M. Woodbury et al. LC 70-181310. (Illus.). 1972. 31.50 (ISBN 0-911216-29-4). Raven.

Antiepileptic Drugs: Mechanisms of Action. Ed. by G. H. Glaser et al. J. Kiffin Penry. 1980. text ed. 74.50 (ISBN 0-89004-251-9). Raven.

Antiepileptic Therapy: Advances in Drug Monitoring. Ed. by Svein Johannessen et al. 1980. text ed. 42.00 (ISBN 0-89004-407-4). Raven.

Antietam: The Photographic Legacy of America's Bloodiest Day. William A. Frassanito. LC 78-2336. (Encore Edition). (Illus.). 1978. 5.95 (ISBN 0-684-16835-9, ScribT). Scribner.

Antifederalists. Ed. by Cecelia M. Kenyon. LC 65-23008. (Orig.). 1966. pap. 9.10 o.p. (ISBN 0-672-60052-8, AHS38). Bobbs.

Antigens. Ed. by Michael Sela. 1974. Vol. 1. 52.50 (ISBN 0-12-635501-0). Acad Pr.

Antigens, Vol. 5. Ed. by Michael Sela. 1979. 38.00 (ISBN 0-12-635505-3); 32.75, by subscription. Acad Pr.

Antigone. smaller ed. Sophocles. Ed. by Jebb. (Gr., Gr). 1971. text ed. 9.95x (ISBN 0-521-06525-9). Cambridge U Pr.

Antigone. Sophocles. Tr. by Richard Braun. (Greek Tragedy in New Translations Ser). 96p. 1973. 10.95x (ISBN 0-19-501741-2). Oxford U Pr.

Antigone. Sophocles. Tr. by Gilbert Murray. 1924. pap. text ed. 3.95x (ISBN 0-04-882048-2). Allen Unwin.

Antigua, Guatemala: City & Area Guide. Mike Shawcross. (Illus.). 74p. 1979. pap. 4.95 (ISBN 0-933982-17-8). Bradt Ent.

Antike Berichte ueber die Essener. 2nd ed. Alfred Adam. Ed. by Christoph Burchard. (Kleine Texte fuer Vorlesungen und Uebungen, 182). 80p. 1972. pap. text ed. 11.65x (ISBN 3-11-004183-9). De Gruyter.

Antike und moderne Tragoedie: Neun Abhandlungen. Kurt Von Fritz. (Ger). 1962. 45.90x (ISBN 3-11-005039-0). De Gruyter.

Antimetabolites in Biochemistry, Biology & Medicine: Proceedings, Prague, 1978. Ed. by J. Skoda & P. Langen. (Federation of European Biochemical Societies Symposium: Vol. 57). (Illus.). 1979. text ed. 60.00 (ISBN 0-08-024384-3). Pergamon.

Antimicrobial Food Additives: Characteristics, Uses, Effects. E. Lueck. (Illus.). 280p. 1980. 39.80 (ISBN 0-387-10056-3). Springer-Verlag.

Antimicrobial Therapy. 3rd ed. Benjamin M. Kagan. LC 80-50252. (Illus.). 542p. 1980. text ed. 35.00 (ISBN 0-7216-5234-4). Saunders.

Antimony Deposits in the Murchison Range of the Northeastern Transvaal Republic of South Africa. Rolf Muff. LC 78-321157. (Monograph Series on Mineral Deposits: Vol. 16). (Illus.). 90p. (Orig.). 1978. pap. 40.00x (ISBN 3-443-12016-4). Intl Pubns Serv.

Antinomian Controversy. Chas F. Adams. LC 74-164507. 1976. Repr. of 1892 ed. lib. bdg. 19.50 (ISBN 0-306-70290-8). Da Capo.

Antioch: City & Imperial Administration in the Later Roman Empire. J. H. Liebeschuetz. 312p. 1972. 29.95x (ISBN 0-19-814295-1). Oxford U Pr.

Antioqueno Colonization in Western Colombia. rev. ed. James J. Parsons. LC 68-58002. (Illus.). 1968. 20.00x (ISBN 0-520-01464-2). U of Cal Pr.

Antioxidants & Stabilizers for Polymers. James R. Critser, Jr. (Ser. 3-75). 1976. 100.00 (ISBN 0-914428-34-9). Lexington Data.

Antiparasitic Chemotherapy. Ed. by H. Schoenfeld. (Antibiotics & Chemotherapy. Ser.: Vol. 30). (Illus.). 200p. 1981. 72.00 (ISBN 3-8055-2160-X). S Karger.

Antipodes. Richard Brome. Ed. by Ann Haaker. LC 66-13403. (Regents Renaissance Drama Ser.). 1966. 8.95x (ISBN 0-8032-0253-9); pap. 1.65x (ISBN 0-8032-5254-4, BB 219, Bison). U of Nebr Pr.

Antipsychotic Drugs: Pharmacodynamics & Pharmacokinetics. Ed. by G. Sedvall et al. 286p. 1976. text ed. 64.00 (ISBN 0-08-019688-8). Pergamon.

Antique Advertising Paper Dolls. Ed. by Barbara W. Jendrick. (Illus.). 64p. (Orig.). 1981. pap. write for info. (ISBN 0-486-24045-2). Dover.

Antique Airplanes. Chris Sorensen & Flying Magazine Editors. LC 78-11272. (Encore Edition). (Illus.). 1979. 8.95 (ISBN 0-684-16927-4, ScribT). Scribner.

Antique Automoblies. Clarence Hornung. (Illus.). 1978. pap. 1.75 (ISBN 0-486-22742-1). Dover.

Antique Bottles in Color. Edward Fletcher. (Color Ser.). (Illus.). 1976. 9.95 (ISBN 0-7137-0793-3, Pub by Blandford Pr England). Sterling.

Antique Chinese Rugs. Ed. by Tiffany Studios Editors. LC 69-16178. (Illus.). 1969. Repr. of 1908 ed. 11.00 (ISBN 0-8048-0025-1). C E Tuttle.

Antique Collector's Guide. David Benedictus. LC 80-69368. 1981. 14.95 (ISBN 0-689-11146-0). Atheneum.

Antique Country Furniture of North America, & Details of Its Construction. John G. Shea. 228p. 1980. pap. 9.95 (ISBN 0-442-25156-4). Van Nos Reinhold.

Antique Dealers Pocketbook. Lyle. LC 74-3739. 1974. 4.95 o.p. (ISBN 0-684-13828-X, ScribT). Scribner.

Antique Dolls Go to a Paper Doll Wedding. 8p. (gr. 8-12). 1978. pap. 3.50 (ISBN 0-914510-09-6). Evergreen.

Antique Firearms. Franklin Dennis. LC 77-86542. (Illus.). 1978. Repr. 14.95 o.p. (ISBN 0-89141-050-3). Presidio Pr.

Antique French Doll Coloring Books. Peggy J. Rosamond. 8p. (gr. 8-12). pap. 3.50 (ISBN 0-914510-06-1). Evergreen.

Antique French Doll Paper Dolls. Peggy J. Rosamond. 8p. (gr. 8-12). 1976. pap. 3.50. Evergreen.

Antique Furniture Guide. 160p. 5.00 o.p. (ISBN 0-685-26805-5). Warman.

Antique Houses: Their Construction & Restoration. Edward P. Friedland. Ed. by Cyril L. Nelson. (Illus.). 288p. 1981. 14.95 (ISBN 0-525-93076-0). Dutton.

Antique-Hunter's Handbook. Ronald Rawlings. LC 77-91720. (Leisure & Travel Ser.). (Illus.). 1978. 7.50 (ISBN 0-7153-7578-4). David & Charles.

Antique Jewelry & Trinkets. Frederick W. Burgess. LC 74-178622. (Illus.). xvi, 399p. 1972. Repr. of 1919 ed. 21.00 (ISBN 0-8103-3863-7). Gale.

Antique Maps for the Collector. Richard Van De Gohm. LC 72-91999. 160p. 1973. 7.95 o.s.i. (ISBN 0-02-621540-3). Macmillan.

Antique Metalware. Ed. by James R. Mitchell. LC 77-70771. (Antiques Magazine Library). (Illus.). 1977. 12.95x o.s.i. (ISBN 0-87663-298-3, Main Street); pap. 7.95 (ISBN 0-87663-970-8). Universe.

Antique Paper Dolls: Nineteen Fifteen to Nineteen Twenty. Ed. by Arnold Arnold. LC 75-3822. 1975. pap. 5.00 (ISBN 0-486-23176-3). Dover.

Antique Paper Dolls: The Edwardian Era. Epinal. LC 75-2935. (Illus.). 1975. pap. 2.95 (ISBN 0-486-23175-5). Dover.

Antique Sheffield Plate. G. Bernard Hughes. 1970. 40.50 o.p. (ISBN 0-686-63852-2, Pub. by Batsford England). David & Charles.

Antique Shopping in Southern California: Comprehensive Guide to Shops in Seven Counties. Joan Olson & Elaine Williams. (Illus.). 300p. (Orig.). 1980. pap. 8.95 (ISBN 0-9602924-0-3). Willows Pr.

Antique Valentines. Dan D'Immperio. LC 80-23002. (Illus.). 160p. 1981. write for info. (ISBN 0-498-02505-5). A S Barnes.

Antique Watches. (Illus.). 1978. pap. 3.95 o.p. (ISBN 0-89145-024-6). Collector Bks.

Antiquers. Elizabeth Stillinger. LC 80-7625. (Illus.). 320p. 1980. 16.95 (ISBN 0-394-40329-0). Knopf.

Antiques & Collectibles: A Bibliography of Works in English, 16th Century to 1976. Linda Franklin. LC 77-25026. (Illus.). 1978. 40.00 (ISBN 0-8108-1092-1). Scarecrow.

Antiques for Amateurs on a Shoestring Budget. Marguerite A. Brunner. 1977. pap. 3.95 o.p. (ISBN 0-89104-063-3). A & W Pubs.

Antiques from the Victorian Home. Bea Howe. 1973. 45.00 (ISBN 0-7134-0730-1, Pub. by Batsford England). David & Charles.

Antiques Guide to Decorative Arts in America 1600-1875. Elizabeth Stillinger. 1973. pap. 6.95 o.p. (ISBN 0-525-47334-3). Dutton.

Antiques Oddities & Curiosities. rev. ed. Edwin G. Warman. (Illus.). 1980. pap. cancelled o.p. (ISBN 0-685-21839-2). Warman.

Antiques, the Amateur's Questions. Hampden Gordon. (Illus.). 1951. pap. 3.95 (ISBN 0-7195-0511-9). Transatlantic.

Antiques Treasury, No. 1. (Illus.). 3.00 o.p. (ISBN 0-685-21845-7). Warman.

Antiques Treasury, No. 2. enl. ed. (Illus.). 4.00 o.p. (ISBN 0-685-21846-5). Warman.

Antiques Treasury, No. 3. enl. ed. (Illus.). 4.00 o.p. (ISBN 0-685-21842-2). Warman.

Antiques Treasury, No. 4. (Illus.). 4.00 o.p. (ISBN 0-685-21841-4). Warman.

Antiques Treasury, No. 5. (Illus.). 4.00 o.p. (ISBN 0-685-21840-6). Warman.

Antiques Treasury, No. 6. enl. ed. (Illus.). 4.00 o.p. (ISBN 0-685-00923-8). Warman.

Antiques Treasury, No. 7. 4.00 o.p. (ISBN 0-685-26802-0). Warman.

Antiques Treasury, No. 8. 4.00 o.p. (ISBN 0-685-26803-9). Warman.

Antiques Treasury Books, 8 bks. (Illus.). Set. 25.00 o.p. (ISBN 0-685-33344-2). Warman.

Antiqui und Moderni: Traditionsbewusstsein und Fortschrittsbewusstsein Im spaeten Mittelalter. LC 73-82432. (Miscellanea Mediaevalia Ser.: Vol. 9). 545p. 1974. 87.00x (ISBN 3-11-004538-9). De Gruyter.

Antiquities of Canterbury. William Somner. (Classical Town Histories Ser.). 1977. Repr. of 1703 ed. 57.50x (ISBN 0-8476-6120-2). Rowman.

Antiquities of Indian Tibet, 2 vols. A. H. Francke. 1972. Repr. Set. 35.00x (ISBN 0-8364-0382-7). South Asia Bks.

Antiquities of South Arabia. Al-Hamdani & Al-Hasan Ibn Ahmad. Tr. by Nabih A. Fairs from Arabic. LC 79-2864. (Illus.). 119p. 1981. Repr. of 1938 ed. 13.50 (ISBN 0-8305-0033-2). Hyperion Conn.

Antiquity Explained & Represented in Sculptures, 2 vols. Bernard de Montfaucon. Tr. by David Humphreys. LC 75-27881. (Renaissance & the Gods Ser.: Vol. 36). (Illus.). 1977. Repr. of 1722 ed. Set. lib. bdg. 146.00 (ISBN 0-8240-2085-5); lib. bdg. 73.00 ea. Garland Pub.

Antitheatrical Prejudice. Jonas Barish. 1981. 20.00 (ISBN 0-520-03735-9). U of Cal Pr.

Antitrust - Cases, Economic Notes, & Other Materials. 2nd ed. Richard A. Posner & Frank H. Easterbrook. LC 80-25590. (American Casebook Ser.). (Illus.). 1980. text ed. 22.95 (ISBN 0-8299-2115-X). West Pub.

Antitrust Action & Market Structure. Don E. Waldman. LC 78-8813. (Illus.). 1978. 19.95 (ISBN 0-669-02401-5). Lexington Bks.

Antitrust & the Health Care Provider. Martin Thompson. LC 79-9371. 1979. text ed. 30.00 (ISBN 0-89443-159-5). Aspen Systems.

Antitrust Consent Decrees, 2 vols. Talbot S. Lindstrom & Kevin P. Tighe. LC 74-76323. 1974. Set. 94.00 (ISBN 0-686-14482-1). Lawyers Co-Op.

Antitrust Economics & Legal Analysis. Eugene M. Singer. LC 80-19847. (Economics Ser.). 200p. 1981. pap. 12.95 (ISBN 0-88244-227-9). Grid Pub.

Antitrust Law. lawyers ed. Phillip E. Areeda & Donald F. Turner. 1980. Vol, I-V. text ed. 235.00 set (ISBN 0-316-05052-0). Little.

Antitrust Law & Economics in a Nutshell. 2nd ed. Ernest Gellhorn. (Nutshell Ser.). 426p. 1981. pap. text ed. write for info. (ISBN 0-8299-2117-6). West Pub.

Antitrust Laws of the U. S. A. 3rd ed. A. D. Neale & D. G. Goyder. (Economic & Social Research Ser.: No. 19). 525p. 1981. 42.50 (ISBN 0-521-23569-3); pap. 14.95 (ISBN 0-521-28044-3). Cambridge U Pr.

Antitumor Compounds of Natural Origin. Ed. by Adorjan Aszalos. 1981. Vol. 1. 64.95 (ISBN 0-8493-5520-6); Vol. 2. 67.95 (ISBN 0-8493-5521-4). CRC Pr.

Antivirals & Virus Diseases of Man. Ed. by George J. Galasso et al. LC 78-67025. 1979. 62.50 (ISBN 0-89004-222-5). Raven.

Antoine Bloye. Paul Nizan. Tr. by Edmund Stevens from Fr. LC 72-92034. 256p. (YA) 1973. 6.95 o.p. (ISBN 0-85345-277-6, CL2776). Monthly Rev.

Antoine's Restaurant Cookbook. Roy F. Guste, Jr. (Illus.). 1980. pap. 9.95 (ISBN 0-393-00027-3). Norton.

Antoinette Pope's New School Cookbook. Antoinette Pope. 1088p. 1973. 14.95 (ISBN 0-02-598060-2). Macmillan.

Antologia De Cuentos Hispanoamericanos. Alberto M. Vazquez. (gr. 12). 1976. pap. text ed. 6.95 (ISBN 0-88345-264-2). Regents Pub.

Antologia De la Literatura Hispano-Americana. Ed. by Arturo Torres-Rioseco. (Span.). (gr. 11-12). 1979. text ed. 26.50x o.p. (ISBN 0-8290-0022-4); pap. text ed. 14.95x o.p. (ISBN 0-89197-546-2). Irvington.

Antologia De Lecturas: Curso De Espanol, Primer Semestra, 2 tomes. Tome 1, 2nd Ed. Rev. 6.25 (ISBN 0-8477-3166-9); Tome 2, 2nd Ed., Rev. (ISBN 0-8477-3161-8). U of PR Pr.

Antologia Del Realismo Magico: Ocho Cuentos Hispanoamericanos. Ed. by E. Dale Carter, Jr. LC 73-114674. (Span). 1970. pap. 4.50 (ISBN 0-672-63009-5). Odyssey Pr.

Antologia Poetica De Miguel Yacenko. Miquel Yacenko. Date not set. pap. 1.65 (ISBN 0-311-08756-6). Casa Bautista.

Anton Chekhov: Four Plays. Anton Chekhov. Tr. by David Magarshack. Incl. Seagull; Uncle Vanya; Three Sisters; Cherry Orchard. 256p. (Orig.). 1969. pap. 5.95 (ISBN 0-8090-0743-6, Mermaid). Hill & Wang.

Anton Chekhov's Short Stories. Anton Chekhov. Ed. by Ralph E. Matlaw. Tr. by Constance Garnett et al. (Critical Edition). 1979. text ed. 24.95 (ISBN 0-393-04528-5); pap. text ed. 5.95x (ISBN 0-393-09002-7). Norton.

Anton Chekov's Plays. Ed. by Eugene K. Bristow. (Norton Critical Edition Ser.). 1978 12.95 (ISBN 0-393-04432-7); pap. 6.95 1977 (ISBN 0-393-09163-5). Norton.

Anton Dvorak. Paul Stefan. LC 79-146147. (Music Ser.). 1971. Repr. of 1941 ed. lib. bdg. 25.00 (ISBN 0-306-70105-7). Da Capo.

Anton Raphael Mengs & Neoclassicism. Thomas Pelzel. LC 78-74375. (Fine Arts Dissertations, Fourth Ser.). (Illus.). 1980. lib. bdg. 27.50 (ISBN 0-8240-3962-9). Garland Pub.

Anton Von Webern: Perspectives. Compiled by Hans Moldenhauer & Demar Irvine. LC 77-9523. (Music Reprint Ser., 1978). (Illus.). 1978. Repr. of 1966 ed. lib. bdg. 22.50 (ISBN 0-306-77518-2). Da Capo.

Anton Webern: An Introduction to His Works. Walter Kolneder. Tr. by Humphrey Searle. 1968. 18.50x o.p. (ISBN 0-520-00662-3). U of Cal Pr.

Antonfrancesco Grazzini: Poet, Dramatist, & Novelliere 1503-1584. Robert J. Rodini. 1970. 25.00 (ISBN 0-299-05590-6). U of Wis Pr.

Antoni Gaudi: Architecture in Barcelona. Gabriele Sterner. (Illus.). 1981. pap. 3.50 (ISBN 0-8120-2293-9). Barron.

Antonin Artaud. Julia F. Costich. (World Authors Ser.: No. 492). 1978. lib. bdg. 12.50 (ISBN 0-8057-6333-3). Twayne.

Antonin Artaud: Man of Vision. Bettina L. Knapp. LC 79-9637. 233p. 1980. pap. 5.95 (ISBN 0-8040-0809-4). Swallow.

Antoninus Bassianus Caracalla: An Edition & Translation. Ed. by William E. Mahaney & Walter K. Sherwin. Tr. by Walter K. Sherwin & Jay M. Freyman. (Salzburg Studies in English Literature, Elizabethan & Renaissance Studies: No. 52). 189p. (Orig.). 1976. pap. text ed. 25.00x (ISBN 0-391-01467-6). Humanities.

Antonio & Francesco Guardi: Their Life & Milieu: With a Catalogue of Their Figure Drawings. Alice Binion. LC 75-23782. (Outstanding Dissertations in the Fine Arts - 17th & 18th Century). (Illus.). 1976. lib. bdg. 48.00 (ISBN 0-8240-1979-2). Garland Pub.

Antonio Buero Vallejo. Martha T. Halsey. (World Authors Ser.: Spain: No. 260). 1971. lib. bdg. 10.95 (ISBN 0-8057-2925-9). Twayne.

Antonio Buero Vallejo: The First Fifteen Years. Joelyn Ruple. 1971. 12.95 (ISBN 0-88303-006-3); pap. 8.95 (ISBN 0-685-73210-X). E Torres & Sons.

Antonio De Guevara. Joseph R. Jones. LC 75-4572. (World Authors Ser.: Spain: No. 360). 1975. lib. bdg. 10.95 (ISBN 0-8057-2409-5). Twayne.

Antonio Fogazzaro. Robert A. Hall, Jr. (World Authors Ser.: No. 470). 1978. lib. bdg. 12.50 (ISBN 0-8057-6311-2). Twayne.

Antonio Gramsci & the Party: The Prison Years. Paolo Spriano. 1979. text ed. 18.25x (ISBN 0-85315-486-4). Humanities.

Antonio Gramsci & the Revolution That Failed. Martin Clark. LC 76-49754. 1977. 22.50x (ISBN 0-300-02077-5). Yale U Pr.

Antonio Gramsci: Conservative Schooling for Radical Politics. Harold Entwistle. (Routledge Education Bks.). 1979. 21.00 (ISBN 0-7100-0333-1); pap. 9.50 (ISBN 0-7100-0334-X). Routledge & Kegan.

Antonio Gramsci: Towards an Intellectual Bibliography. Alastair Davidson. (International Library of Social & Political Thought). 1977. text ed. 19.50x (ISBN 0-391-00671-1). Humanities.

Antonio Machado. Carl W. Cobb. (World Authors Ser.: Spain: No. 161). lib. bdg. 10.95 (ISBN 0-8057-2556-3). Twayne.

Antonio's Revenge: The Second Part of Antonio & Mellida. John Marston. Ed. by G. K. Hunter. LC 65-12161. (Regents Renaissance Drama Ser.). 1965. pap. 6.50x (ISBN 0-8032-0273-3). U of Nebr Pr.

Antony & Cleopatra. William Shakespeare. Ed. by John R. Brown. LC 77-127584. (Casebook Ser). 1970. pap. text ed. 2.50 o.s.i. (ISBN 0-87695-046-2). Aurora Pubs.

Antony & Cleopatra. William Shakespeare. Ed. by Arthur Quiller-Couch et al. (New Shakespeare Ser). 23.95 (ISBN 0-521-07526-2); pap. 4.50x (ISBN 0-521-09469-0). Cambridge U Pr.

Ants & Insects. (MacDonald Educational Ser.). (Illus., Arabic.). 3.50 (ISBN 0-686-53076-4). Intl Bk Ctr.

Ants of Colorado: Their Ecology, Taxonomy & Geographic Distribution. Robert E. Gregg. LC 62-63446. (Illus.). 1963. 19.50x (ISBN 0-87081-027-8). Colo Assoc.

Ants of God. W. T. Tyler. 288p. 1981. 10.95 (ISBN 0-8037-0270-1). Dial.

Ants: Their Structure, Development, & Behavior. rev. ed. William M. Wheeler. LC 10-8253. (Columbia Biological Ser.: No. 9). (Illus.). 1960. 35.00x (ISBN 0-231-00121-5). Columbia U Pr.

Antwerp: An Historical Descourse, or Rather a Teragicall Historie of Antwerpe Since the Departure of King Phillip of Spaine Out of Netherland. LC 79-84083. (English Experience Ser.: No. 903). 56p. 1979. Repr. of 1586 ed. lib. bdg. 7.00 (ISBN 90-221-0903-8). Walter J Johnson.

Anuario Estatistico Do Brazil. 40th ed. LC 73-642043. (Illus.). 853p. (Portuguese.). 1980. pap. 85.00x (ISBN 0-8002-2696-8). Intl Pubns Serv.

Anus Mundi: 1,500 Days in Auschwitz-Birkenau. Wieslaw Kielar. Tr. by Susanne Flatauer. 352p. 1980. 13.95 (ISBN 0-8129-0921-6). Times Bks.

Anuska's Complete Body Makeover Book. Celestina Wallis et al. (Illus.). 224p. 1981. 11.95 (ISBN 0-399-12579-5). Putnam.

Anxiety & Neurotic Disorders. Barclay Martin. LC 76-151033. (Approaches to Behavior Pathology Ser). 1971. pap. text ed. 10.95 (ISBN 0-471-57353-1). Wiley.

Anxiety, Depression, & Organic Disease. Jonathan O. Cole. (Illus.). 1976. pap. text ed. 18.50 (ISBN 0-89147-037-9). CAS.

Anxiety, Depression & Phobia. Denis Cronin. 1979. 9.95x o.s.i. (ISBN 0-8464-0054-5). Beekman Pubs.

Anxiety Free Statistics. Ann L. Egan. 1977. pap. text ed. 4.95 o.p. (ISBN 0-8403-0928-7). Kendall-Hunt.

Anxiety into Energy. Victor P. Pease. 1981. 12.95 (ISBN 0-8015-0335-3, Hawthorn). Dutton.

Anxiety: New Research & Changing Concepts. Ed. by Donald F. Klein & Judith G. Rabkin. 325p. 1981. 29.50 (ISBN 0-686-69136-9). Raven.

Anxiety, Resolution, Relaxation, & Systematic Flexible Hierachy, Tape Uses, Set-AH. Russell E. Mason. 1975. pap. 50.00x (ISBN 0-89533-009-1); incl. tape-1a, t-9, t-5a, t-10, t-8, t-11, Notes, Clinical Applications & Substitution Training. F I Comm.

Any Color So Long As It's Black: The First Fifty Years of Automobile Advertising. Peter Roberts. LC 76-6044. (Illus.). 1976. 14.95 o.p. (ISBN 0-688-03102-1). Morrow.

Any Day of Your Life. David Kherdian. LC 75-4381. 64p. 1975. 10.00 (ISBN 0-87951-034-X); ltd. ed. 15.00 (ISBN 0-685-53416-2). Overlook Pr.

Any Day of Your Life. David Kherdian. LC 75-4381. 1977. pap. 5.95 (ISBN 0-87951-062-5). Overlook Pr.

Any Love Notes Today? Wilma J. Jacobs. LC 76-48409. 143p. (Orig.). 1976. pap. 4.95 (ISBN 0-89146-002-0). Learn Pathways.

Any Love Notes Today? Wilma J. Jacobs. 1976. 4.95 (ISBN 0-89146-002-0). J&J Dist.

Any Miracle God Wants to Give. Danny E. Morris. (Prayer in My Life Ser.: Ser. I). 1974. pap. 1.00x (ISBN 0-8358-0314-7). Upper Room.

Any Number Can Play. Dennis Bloodworth. LC 72-79865. 1972. 6.95 o.p. (ISBN 0-374-10537-5). FS&G.

Any Other Song: A Plea for Holistic Communication. E. J. Daniel. LC 79-24892. 185p. 1980. pap. text ed. 9.95 (ISBN 0-87619-460-9). R J Brady.

Any Oven Cookbook. (Orig.). pap. 5.95 (ISBN 0-87502-083-6). Benjamin Co.

Any Person, Any Study: An Essay on Higher Education in the United States. Carnegie Commission On Higher Education. Ed. by E. Ashby. 1971. 8.50 o.p. (ISBN 0-07-010022-5, P&RB). McGraw.

Any Tow Can Play. Elizabeth Cadell. 224p. 1981. 9.95. Morrow.

Anya. Susan F. Schaeffer. LC 73-20990. 520p. 1974. 8.95 o.s.i. (ISBN 0-02-607020-0). Macmillan.

Anya. Susan F. Schaeffer. 1975. pap. 2.95 (ISBN 0-380-00573-5, 48645, Bard). Avon.

Anybody Home? Aileen Fisher. LC 78-22508. (Illus.). 32p. (ps-2). 1980. 6.95 (ISBN 0-690-04054-7, TYC-J); PLB 6.89 (ISBN 0-690-04055-5). T Y Crowell.

Anybody's Roller Skating Book. Tom Cuthbertson. (Illus.). (YA) 1981. 8.95 (ISBN 0-89815-042-6); pap. 4.95 (ISBN 0-89815-040-X). Ten Speed Pr.

Anybody's Spring. A. A. Murray. LC 60-9717. 1960. 3.95 (ISBN 0-8149-0165-4). Vanguard.

Anyhow, I'm Glad I Tried. Judith Vigna. Ed. by Caroline Rubin. LC 78-12883. (Concept Bks). (Illus.). 32p. (gr. k-2). 1978. 6.95g (ISBN 0-8075-0378-9). A Whitman.

Anyhow Stories, Repr. Of 1882 Ed. Lucy L. Clifford. Bd. with Wooden Tony - an Anyhow Story. Repr. of 1892 ed. LC 75-32186. (Classics of Children's Literature, 1621-1932: Vol. 49). (Illus.). 1976. lib. bdg. 38.00 (ISBN 0-8240-2298-X). Garland Pub.

Anyone Can Fly. rev. ed. Jules Bergman. LC 73-9141. 1977. 12.95 (ISBN 0-385-02830-X). Doubleday.

Anyone Can Make Big Money Buying Art. Morton Shulman. 1977. 7.95 o.s.i. (ISBN 0-02-610560-8). Macmillan.

Anyone Can Prophesy. Robert B. Hall. LC 77-8267. 1977. pap. 3.95 (ISBN 0-8164-2158-7). Crossroad NY.

Anyone Can Sing: How to Become the Singer You Always Wanted to Be. Joan Wall & Ricky Weatherspoon. LC 77-12892. 1978. pap. 5.95 (ISBN 0-385-13185-2, Dolp). Doubleday.

Anyone Here Know Right from Wrong? Bill Stearns. 1976. pap. 1.95 (ISBN 0-88207-724-4). Victor Bks.

Anyone's Son: A True Story. Roberta Roesch & Harry De La Roche. (Illus.). 1979. 9.95 o.p. (ISBN 0-8362-6608-0). Andrews & McMeel.

Anything Book. A. Link. 1981. 28.50 o.p. (ISBN 0-686-68301-3). Porter.

Anything Can Happen. George Papashvily & Helen Papashvily. LC 44-41894. 1945. lib. bdg. 8.29 o.s.i. (ISBN 0-06-013256-6, HarpT). Har-Row.

Anything Can Happen Book. Joe Wayman et al. (gr. k-8). 1976. 5.95 (ISBN 0-916456-06-4, GA55). Good Apple.

Anything for a Friend. Ellen Conford. 1981. pap. 1.95 (ISBN 0-671-56069-7). Archway.

Anything Goes, Bk. I. Ed. by Wendy Barish. 1981. 2.95 (ISBN 0-671-43051-3). Wanderer Bks.

Anything Goes, Bk. II. Ed. by Wendy Barish. 192p. 1981. price not set. Wanderer Bks.

Anything Out of Place Is Dirt. Michael C. Daniels. (Writers Workshop Ser.). 106p. 1975. 9.00 (ISBN 0-88253-498-X); pap. text ed. 4.80 (ISBN 0-88253-497-1). Ind-US Inc.

Anytime Book for Busy Families. Crystal Zinkiewicz. LC 79-67098. 1979. spiral bdg. 4.95x (ISBN 0-8358-0378-3). Upper Room.

Anywhere Else but Here. Bruce Clements. LC 77-10081. 208p. (gr. 4 up). 1980. 8.95 (ISBN 0-374-30371-1). FS&G.

Anzio, Nineteen Forty-Four: An Unexpected Fury. Peter Verney. (Illus.). 265p. 1980. 25.00 (ISBN 0-7134-1323-9, Pub. by Batsford England). David & Charles.

Ao Adao, Com Amor. Tr. by Douglas Roberts. (Portugese Bks.). (Port.). 1979. 1.55 (ISBN 0-8297-0857-X). Life Pubs Intl.

Aortic Andtricuspid Valvular Disease. Sr. Anna Barry. (Surgical Aspects of Cardiovascular Disease: Nursing Intervention Series). 100p. 1980. pap. 6.95 (ISBN 0-8385-0189-3). ACC.

Aortic Arch & Its Malformations: With Emphasis on the Angiographic Features. Wade H. Shuford & Robert G. Sybers. (Illus.). 288p. 1973. 26.50 (ISBN 0-398-02854-0). C C Thomas.

Aortic Arch Surgery. Mary Jo Aspinall. (Surgical Aspects of Cardiovasculardisease: Nursing Intervention Series). 100p. 1980. pap. 6.95 (ISBN 0-686-69603-4). ACC.

APA Guidelines for Psychiatric Services Covered Under Health Insurance Plans. 2nd ed. 1969. pap. 1.75 (ISBN 0-685-24844-5, P227-0). Am Psychiatric.

Apache. Will L. Comfort. (Western Fiction Ser.). 1980. lib. bdg. 11.95 (ISBN 0-8398-2678-8). Gregg.

Apache Agent: The Story of John P. Clum. Woodworth Clum. LC 77-14135. (Illus.). 1978. 13.95x (ISBN 0-8032-0967-3); pap. 4.25 (ISBN 0-8032-5886-0, BB 654, Bison). U of Nebr Pr.

Apache Devil. Edgar R. Burroughs. 224p. 1975. pap. 1.25 o.p. (ISBN 0-345-24605-5). Ballantine.

Apache Devil. Edgar R. Burroughs. 1976. Repr. of 1933 ed. lib. bdg. 14.20x (ISBN 0-89966-043-6). Buccaneer Bks.

Apache: Fast Living, No. 19. William M. James. 160p. (Orig.). 1981. pap. 1.50 (ISBN 0-523-40696-7). Pinnacle Bks.

Apache Indians, Vol. 2. Incl. The Ascarate Grant. Jocelyn J. Bowden; An Ethnological Study of Tortugas, New Mexico. Alan J. Oppenheimer. (American Indian Ethnohistory Ser: Indians of the Southwest). (Illus.). lib. bdg. 42.00 (ISBN 0-8240-0716-6). Garland Pub.

Apache Indians, Vol. 3. Incl. Aboriginal Use & Occupation of Certain Lands by Tigua, Manso & Suma Indians. Rex E. Gerald; History & Administration of the Tigua Indians of Ysleta Del Sur During the Spanish Colonial Period. Myra E. Jenkins; Apache Ethnohistory: Government, Land & Indian Policies Relative to Lipan, Mescalero & Tigua Indians. Kenneth F. Neighbours. (American Indian Ethnohistory Ser: Indians of the Southwest). (Illus.). lib. bdg. 42.00 (ISBN 0-8240-0717-4). Garland Pub.

Apache Indians I: A Study of the Apache Indians. Albert H. Schroeder. (American Indian Ethnohistory Ser: Indians of the Southwest). lib. bdg. 42.00 (ISBN 0-8240-0715-8). Garland Pub.

Apache Indians IV. Albert H. Schroeder. Ed. by David A. Horr. (American Indian Ethnohistory Ser.). 1978. lib. bdg. 42.00 (ISBN 0-8240-0719-0). Garland Pub.

Apache Indians IX. Averam B. Bender. Ed. by David A. Horr. (American Indian Ethnohistory Ser.). 1978. lib. bdg. 42.00 (ISBN 0-8240-0711-5). Garland Pub.

Apache Indians: Raiders of the Southwest. Gordon C. Baldwin. LC 77-21439. (Illus.). 240p. (gr. 7 up). 1978. 9.95 (ISBN 0-590-07321-4, Four Winds). Schol Bk Serv.

Apache Indians: Raiders of the Southwest. Sonia Bleeker. (Illus.). (gr. 4-7). 1951. PLB 6.48 (ISBN 0-688-31046-X). Morrow.

Apache Indians V. Averam B. Bender et al. Ed. by David A. Horr. (American Indian Ethnohistory Ser.). 1978. lib. bdg. 42.00 (ISBN 0-8240-0720-4). Garland Pub.

Apache Indians VI. B. L. Gordon et al. Ed. by David A. Horr. (American Indian Ethnohistory Ser.). 1978. lib. bdg. 42.00 (ISBN 0-8240-0708-5). Garland Pub.

Apache Indians VII. Jicarilla Apache Tribe. Ed. by David A. Horr. (American Indian Ethnohistory Ser.). 1978. lib. bdg. 42.00 (ISBN 0-8240-0709-3). Garland Pub.

Apache Indians VIII. Alfred B. Thomas et al. Ed. by David A. Horr. (American Indian Ethnohistory Ser.). 1978. lib. bdg. 42.00 (ISBN 0-8240-0710-7). Garland Pub.

Apache Indians X. Verne F. Ray et al. Ed. by David A. Horr. (American Indian Ethnohistory Ser.). 1978. lib. bdg. 42.00 (ISBN 0-8240-0718-2). Garland Pub.

Apache Indians XI. Alfred B. Thomas et al. Ed. by David A. Horr. (American Indian Ethnohistory Ser.). 1978. lib. bdg. 42.00 (ISBN 0-8240-0712-3). Garland Pub.

Apache Indians XII. Harry W. Basehart. Ed. by David A. Horr. (American Indian Ethnohistory Ser.). 1978. lib. bdg. 42.00 (ISBN 0-8240-0713-1). Garland Pub.

Apache Kill. William Hopson. 256p. (YA) 1974. 5.95 (ISBN 0-685-40095-6, Avalon). Bouregy.

Apache Land. Ross Santee. LC 47-11035. (Illus.). 1971. pap. 4.25 (ISBN 0-8032-5737-6, BB 534, Bison). U of Nebr Pr.

Apache War. Peter McCurtin. (Sundaance Ser.). 1980. pap. 1.75 (ISBN 0-8439-0780-0). Nordon Pubns.

Apache Wells. Robert Steelman. 160p. 1975. pap. 0.95 o.p. (ISBN 0-345-24755-8). Ballantine.

Apaches: A Critical Bibliography. Michael E. Melody. LC 77-6918. (Newberry Library Center for the History of the American Indian Bibliographical Ser.). 96p. 1977. pap. 3.95x (ISBN 0-253-30764-3). Ind U Pr.

Apart from a Little Dampness, Herman, How's Everything Else? Jim Unger. (Alligator Bks). (Illus.). 96p. 1975. pap. 2.50 (ISBN 0-8362-0622-3). Andrews & McMeel.

Apartamento de Soltero. new ed. Rodolfo David. (Pimienta Collection Ser). 160p. (Span.). 1974. pap. 1.00 o.p. (ISBN 0-88473-198-7). Fiesta Pub.

Apartheid. John Addison. (Today's World Ser.). (Illus.). 72p. (gr. 7-9). 1981. 15.95 (ISBN 0-7134-2485-0, Pub. by Batsford England). David & Charles.

Apartheid. Edgar Brookes. (World Studies Ser.). 1968. cased 13.00x o.s.i. (ISBN 0-7100-2994-2). Routledge & Kegan.

Apartheid: A Geographical Perspective. Anthony Lemon. 1977. 19.95 (ISBN 0-347-01106-3, 00313-1, Pub. by Saxon Hse). Lexington Bks.

Apartheid in America: An Historical & Legal Analysis of Contemporary Racial Residential Segregation in the United States. James A. Kushner. LC 80-67048. (Scholarly Monographs). 135p. 1980. pap. 12.00 (ISBN 0-8408-0509-8). Carrollton Pr.

Apartheid: Its Effects on Education, Science, Culture, and Information. rev. 2nd ed. LC 71-188870. 256p. (Orig.). 1972. pap. 9.25 (ISBN 92-3-100980-X, U33, UNESCO). Unipub.

Apartheid Power & Historical Falsification. (Insights Ser.). 144p. 1980. pap. 14.50 (ISBN 92-3-101769-1, U 970, UNESCO). Unipub.

Apartment Communities: The Next Big Market. C. Norcross & J. Hysom. LC 68-57114. 1968. pap. 4.75 (ISBN 0-87420-061-X, TB61). Urban Land.

Apartment Development: Strategy for Successful Decision Making. J. Ross McKeever. LC 74-79436. (Special Publications Ser.). (Illus.). 80p. 1974. pap. 9.75 (ISBN 0-87420-560-3). Urban Land.

Apartment House Close Up. Peter Schaaf. LC 80-11301. (Illus.). 32p. (ps-3). 1980. 7.95 (ISBN 0-590-07670-1, Four Winds). Schol Bk Serv.

Apartment House Incinerators: Flue-Fed. Federal Housing Administration - Building Research Advisory Board. 1965. pap. 3.00 (ISBN 0-309-01280-5). Natl Acad Pr.

Apartment Three. Ezra J. Keats. LC 78-123135. (Illus.). (gr. k-4). 1971. 8.95 o.s.i. (ISBN 0-02-749510-8). Macmillan.

Apartment Workshop. Kenn Oberrecht. 1980. 12.95 (ISBN 0-87691-313-3). Winchester Pr.

Apathy & Participation. Giuseppe DiPalma. LC 70-120924. 1970. 9.95 o.s.i. (ISBN 0-02-907470-3). Free Pr.

APB-FASB. 13th ed. LC 79-55006. 8.00 (ISBN 0-932788-12-2). Bradley CPA.

Ape & the Child. W. N. Kellogg & L. A. Kellogg. 1967. 17.50 (ISBN 0-02-847590-9). Hafner.

Ape into Human: A Study of Human Evolution. 2nd ed. S. L. Washburn & Ruth Moore. (Illus.). 194p. 1980. pap. text ed. 5.95 (ISBN 0-316-92374-5). Little.

Aperture Antennas & Diffraction Theory. E. V. Jull. 1981. pap. price not set. Inst Electrical.

Aperture History of Photography Series Giftpak. Incl. Henri Cartier Bresson. LC 76-21993 (ISBN 0-89381-000-2); Jacques Lartique. LC 76-22000 (ISBN 0-89381-001-0); Robert Frank. LC 76-22001 (ISBN 0-89381-002-9); Alfred Stieglitz. LC 76-25728 (ISBN 0-89381-004-5); Wynn Bullock. LC 76-25727 (ISBN 0-89381-003-7). (Illus.). 90p. 1976. Set. pap. 39.95 (ISBN 0-685-63920-7); pap. 8.95 ea. over boards; slipcased set avail. (ISBN 0-89381-038-X). Aperture.

Aperture Nineteen: Four, No. 76. Robert Coles & Alan Trachtenberg. (Illus.). 88p. 1975. pap. 9.50 (ISBN 0-912334-72-X). Aperture.

Aperture: No. 77. J. Williams et al. 1977. pap. 9.50 (ISBN 0-89381-013-4). Aperture.

Apes. Helen Kay. (Illus.). (gr. 5-8). 1970. 8.95g (ISBN 0-02-749490-X). Macmillan.

Apes & Angels: The Irishman in Victorian Caricature. L. Perry Curtis, Jr. LC 75-607991. (Illus.). 140p. 1971. 8.95x o.p. (ISBN 0-87474-107-6). Smithsonian.

Apes in Fact & Fiction. Gilda Berger. (gr. 5 up). 1980. PLB 7.90 (ISBN 0-531-04152-2). Watts.

Apes of God. Wyndham Lewis. (Illus.). 625p. (Orig.). 1981. 20.00 (ISBN 0-87685-513-3); deluxe ed. 30.00 (ISBN 0-87685-514-1); pap. price not set (ISBN 0-87685-512-5). Black Sparrow.

Apex of Power: The Prime Minister & Political Leadership in Canada. 2nd ed. T. Hockin. 1977. pap. 11.25 (ISBN 0-13-038653-7). P-H.

APhA Drug Names. Ed. by L. Luan Corrigan. Janet Shoff. LC 78-78275. 1979. softcover 18.00 (ISBN 0-917330-24-2). Am Pharm Assn.

Aphasia. Arnold Pick. (Illus.). 168p. 1973. text ed. 14.75 (ISBN 0-398-02658-0). C C Thomas.

Aphasia: Assessment & Treatment. Ed. by Martha T. Sarno & Olle Hook. LC 80-80488. (Illus.). 288p. 1980. 34.50 (ISBN 0-89352-086-1). Masson Pub.

Aphasia, My World Alone. rev. ed. Helen H. Wulf. 144p. 1979. 9.50x. Wayne St U Pr.

Aphasia Rehabilitation. D. F. Ross & S. H. Spencer. (Illus.). 272p. 1980. 19.50 (ISBN 0-398-04031-1); pap. 14.75 (ISBN 0-398-04024-9). C C Thomas.

Aphasia Therapy Manual. Joseph C. Aurelia. LC 73-90607. 1974. pap. text ed. 2.95x o.p. (ISBN 0-8134-1627-2, 1627). Interstate.

Aphasia Therapy Manual. 2nd ed. Joseph C. Aurelia. 1980. pap. text ed. 3.95x (ISBN 0-8134-2112-8, 2112). Interstate.

Aphasic Child: A Neurological Basis for His Education & Rehabilitation. Alice C. Roberts. 96p. 1970. 7.50 (ISBN 0-398-01595-3). C C Thomas.

Aphids. Rodger Blackman. (Invertebrate Types Ser.). (Illus.). 176p. 1981. pap. 12.00 (ISBN 0-08-025943-X). Pergamon.

Aphorismes of Christian Religion or a Verie Compendious Abridgement of M I Calvins Institutions Set Forth by M I Piscator. Jean Calvin. Tr. by H. Holland. LC 73-6107. (English Experience Ser.: No. 575). 1973. Repr. of 1596 ed. 26.00 (ISBN 90-221-0575-X). Walter J Johnson.

Aphorisms. Hazrat Inayat Khan. (Collected Works of Hazrat Inayat Khan). 128p. (Orig.). 1981. pap. 4.95 (ISBN 0-930872-22-3, 1008P). Sufi Order Pubns.

Aphorisms of Yoga. Bhagwan S. Patanjali. (Illus., Orig.). 1973. pap. 5.50 (ISBN 0-571-10320-0, Pub. by Faber & Faber). Merrimack Bk Serv.

Aphrodite's Cave. N. Richard Nash. LC 80-1069. 480p. 1980. 13.95 (ISBN 0-385-14294-3). Doubleday.

Apicoectomy. Herbert Harnisch. (Illus.). 151p. 1975. 42.00. Quint Pub Co.

Apinaye. Curt Nimuendaju. Tr. by Robert H. Lowie. (Illus.). 1967. pap. text ed. 9.50x (ISBN 9-0623-4032-6). Humanities.

APL: An Introduction. Howard Peelle. (gr. 10 up). 1978. pap. text ed. 10.50 (ISBN 0-8104-5122-0). Hayden.

APL in Practice. Allen J. Rose & Barbara A. Schick. LC 80-5351. 374p. 1980. 25.00 (ISBN 0-471-08275-9, Pub. by Wiley-Interscience). Wiley.

APL-STAT: A Do-It-Yourself Guide to Computational Statistics Using APL. James B. Ramsey & Gerald L. Musgrave. LC 80-15016. 340p. 1981. pap. 14.95 solutions manual (ISBN 0-534-97985-8). Lifetime Learn.

APL-360 with Statistical Examples. Keith W. Smillie. 1974. text ed. 11.95 (ISBN 0-201-07069-3). A-W.

Aplastic Anemia. Ed. by H. Heimpel et al. (Illus.). 290p. 1980. pap. 36.50 (ISBN 0-387-09772-4). Springer-Verlag.

Aplicacoes Da Teoria De Grupos Na Espectroscopia De Raman E Do Infravermelho. OAS General Secretariat. (Fisica Monografia: No. 14). 102p. 1980. pap. text ed. 2.00 (ISBN 0-8270-1126-1). OAS.

Apocalipsis de Juan: Un Comentario. George E. Ladd. Tr. by Arnoldo Canclini from Eng. LC 78-50625. 269p. (Orig., Span.). 1978. pap. 5.50 (ISBN 0-89922-111-4). Edit Caribe.

Apocalpyse. Joseph A. Seiss. 14.95 (ISBN 0-310-32760-1). Zondervan.

Apocalypse. Emil Bock. 1980. pap. 12.50 (ISBN 0-903540-42-8, Pub. by Floris Books). St George Bk Serv.

Apocalypse. Adela Y. Collins. Ed. by Wilfrid Harrington & Donald Senior. (New Testament Message Ser.: Vol. 22). 172p. 1979. 9.00 (ISBN 0-89453-145-X); pap. 4.95 (ISBN 0-89453-210-3). M Glazier.

Apocalypse: Nuclear Catastrophe in World Politics. Louis R. Beres. LC 80-13541. (Illus.). 1980. 20.00 (ISBN 0-226-04360-6). U of Chicago Pr.

Apocalypse of Adam: A Literary & Source Analysis. Charles W. Hedrick. LC 79-26013. (Society of Biblical Literature Dissertation Ser.: No. 46). Date not set. price not set (ISBN 0-89130-369-3, 060146); pap. price not set. Scholars Pr CA.

Apocalypse of Elijah. Albert Pietersma et al. LC 79-24788. 1981. price not set (ISBN 0-89130-371-5, 060219); pap. 7.50 (ISBN 0-89130-372-3). Scholars Pr CA.

Apocalypse of Our Time & Other Writings by Vasily Razanov. R. Payne. 1977. text ed. 10.95 (ISBN 0-03-028911-4, HoltC). HR&W.

Apocalypse: The Book of Revelation. Jacques Ellul. 1977. 10.95 (ISBN 0-8164-0330-9). Crossroad NY.

Apocalypse Unsealed. Robert F. Riggs. LC 80-81698. 1981. 18.95 (ISBN 0-8022-2367-2). Philos Lib.

Apocalypso. Ami Ray. 10.00 (ISBN 0-89253-637-3); flexible cloth 5.00 (ISBN 0-89253-638-1). Ind-US Inc.

Apocalyptic Tradition in Reformation Britain 1530-1645. Katherine R. Firth. (Historical Monographs). (Illus.). 1979. 37.50x (ISBN 0-19-821868-0). Oxford U Pr.

Apocalyptic Vision in the Poetry of Shelley. Ross G. Woodman. LC 64-5257. 1964. 15.00x o.p. (ISBN 0-8020-5136-7). U of Toronto Pr.

Apocalyptic Vision of the Book of Daniel. John J. Collins. LC 77-23124. (Harvard Semitic Monograph). 1977. text ed. 9.00 (ISBN 0-89130-133-X, 040016). Scholars Pr Ca.

Apocrypha & Pseudepigrapha of the Old Testament, 2 Vols. R. H. Charles et al. Vol. 1. 74.00x (ISBN 0-19-826155-1); Vol. 2. 69.00x (ISBN 0-19-826152-7). Oxford U Pr.

Apocrypha: Bridge of the Testaments. Robert C. Dentan. 1954. pap. 3.00 (ISBN 0-8164-2002-5, SP13). Crossroad NY.

Apocryphal New Testament. Tr. by Montague R. James. 1924. 27.00x (ISBN 0-19-826121-7). Oxford U Pr.

Apolistic Preaching & Its Developments: Three Lectures with an Appendix on Eschatology & History. C. H. Dodd. (Twin Brooks Ser.). 96p. 1980. pap. 4.95 (ISBN 0-8101-2404-1). Baker Bk.

Apollinaire: Poet Among the Painters. Francis Steegmuller. LC 80-67030. 392p. 1980. pap. 10.95 (ISBN 0-87923-352-4, Nonpareil Bks). Godine.

Apollo Fountain. Dorothy Daniels. 224p. 1976. pap. 1.75 o.s.i. (ISBN 0-446-84800-X). Warner Bks.

Apollo's Daughter. (Harlequin Romances Ser.). 192p. 1980. pap. 1.25 (ISBN 0-373-02356-1, Pub. by Harlequin). PB.

Apologetics. Paul J. Glenn. LC 80-51330. 298p. 1980. write for info. o.p. (ISBN 0-89555-157-8). Tan Bks Pubs.

Apologia & Two Folk Plays: The Great Highway, the Crownbride & Swanwhite. August Strindberg. Tr. by Walter Johnson from Swedish. LC 80-51072. (Illus.). 244p. 1981. 19.50 (ISBN 0-295-95760-3). U of Wash Pr.

Apologia of Robert Keane: The Self-Portrait of a Puritan Merchant. Bernard Bailyn. 6.50 (ISBN 0-8446-0470-4). Peter Smith.

Apologia Pro Vita Sua. John Henry Cardinal Newman. 1977. pap. 3.50 (ISBN 0-385-12646-8, Im). Doubleday.

Apologie for Women. William Heale & Henry Swinburne. Ed. by David S. Berkowitz & Samuel E. Thorne. LC 77-86658. (Classics of English Legal History in the Modern Era Ser.: Vol. 42). 322p. 1979. lib. bdg. 40.00 (ISBN 0-8240-3091-5). Garland Pub.

Apologie or Defence of Such True Christians As Are Commonly Called Brownists. Henry Ainsworth & Francis Johnson. LC 70-25742. (English Experience Ser.: No. 217). Repr. of 1604 ed. 16.00 (ISBN 90-221-0424-9). Walter J Johnson.

Apologies, Good Friends... An Interim Biography of Daniel Berrigan, S. J. Jack Deedy. 152p. 1981. pap. 6.95 (ISBN 0-8190-0641-6). Fides Claretian.

Apology. Plato. Ed. by A. M. Adam. (Gr). text ed. 5.50x (ISBN 0-521-05958-5). Cambridge U Pr.

Apology for Actors. Thomas Heywood. Bd. with Refutation of the 'Apology for Actors' Iohn Greene. LC 74-170415. (English Stage Ser.: Vol. 12). lib. bdg. 50.00 (ISBN 0-8240-0595-3). Garland Pub.

Apology for Christianity in a Series of Letters Addressed to Edward Gibbon. Richard Watson. Ed. by Rene Wellek. LC 75-25132. (British Philosophers & Theologians of the 17th & 18th Centuries Ser.). 1977. lib. bdg. 42.00 (ISBN 0-8240-1765-X). Garland Pub.

Apology for Heroism: A Brief Autobiography of Ideas. Mulk R. Anand. 143p. 1974. 3.60 (ISBN 0-88253-478-5). Ind-US Inc.

Apology for Poetry. Philip Sidney. Ed. by Forrest Robinson. LC 73-122682. 1970. pap. 3.95 (ISBN 0-672-60254-7). Bobbs.

Apology for Poetry or the Defence of Poesy. Philip Sidney. Ed. by Geoffrey Shepherd. (Old & Middle English Texts Ser.). 244p. 1979. pap. 8.95x (ISBN 0-686-63938-3). B&N.

Apology for the Life of Mrs. Shamela Andrews. Henry Fielding. 80p. 1980. Repr. of 1926 ed. lib. bdg. 12.50 (ISBN 0-8492-4616-4). R West.

Apology for Wonder. Sam Keen. LC 69-17017. 1969. pap. 4.95 (ISBN 0-06-064261-0, RD 158, HarpR). Har-Row.

Apology of Actors. Haywood Thomas. Bd. with Refutation of the Apology for Actors. 20.00x (ISBN 0-8201-1198-8). Schol Facsimiles.

Apostle. John Pollock. Orig. Title: Man Who Shook the World. 244p. 1972. pap. 3.95 (ISBN 0-88207-233-1). Victor Bks.

Apostle from Space. Gordon Harris. 1978. pap. 1.95 pocketsize o.p. (ISBN 0-88270-281-5). Logos.

Apostle of Sight: The Story of Victor Rambo. Dorothy C. Wilson. 255p. 1980. 7.95 (ISBN 0-915684-54-3). Christian Herald.

Apostles. Donald Guthrie. 432p. 1981. pap. 10.95 (ISBN 0-310-25421-3). Zondervan.

Apostles' Creed: Do You Really Believe It? D. Bruce Lockerbie. 1977. pap. 2.50 (ISBN 0-88207-748-1). Victor Bks.

Apostles of Revolution. rev. & enl. ed. Max Nomad. 1961. pap. 1.50 o.s.i. (ISBN 0-02-074560-5, Collier). Macmillan.

Apostolic Age. G. B. Caird. (Studies in Theology). 1974. pap. 13.50x (ISBN 0-7156-0010-9, Pub. by Duckworth England). Biblio Dist.

Apostolic Fathers. J. B. Lightfoot. (Twin Brooks Ser). pap. 5.95 (ISBN 0-8010-5514-8). Baker Bk.

Apostolic Fathers: New Translations of Early Christian Writings. Ed. by Jack Sparks. LC 78-14870. 1978. pap. 5.95 (ISBN 0-8407-5661-5). Nelson.

Apostolic Succession in the Liberal Catholic Church. 2nd ed. Allan W. Cockerham. (Illus.). 1980. pap. text ed. 2.80 (ISBN 0-918980-09-7). St Alban Pr.

Apostolos Makrakis--An Evaluation of Half A Century. Constantine Andronis. 369p. (Orig.). 1966. pap. 4.00x (ISBN 0-938366-33-5). Orthodox Chr.

Apothecary in Colonial Virginia. Harold Gill, Jr. LC 76-187597. (Williamsburg Research Studies Ser.). 1972. pap. 3.00 o.p. (ISBN 0-910412-99-5). Williamsburg.

Apothecary Jars: Pharmaceutical Pottery & Porcelain in Europe & the East 1150-1850. Rudolf E. Drey. (Illus.). 1978. 48.00 (ISBN 0-571-09965-3, Pub. by Faber & Faber). Merrimack Bk Serv.

Apotheosis in Ancient Portraiture. H. P. L'Orange. (Illus.). 156p. 1981. Repr. of 1947 ed. lib. bdg. 40.00x (ISBN 0-89241-149-X). Caratzas Bros.

Appalachia in the Sixties: Decade of Reawakening. Ed. by David S. Walls & John B. Stephenson. LC 78-160052. (Illus.). 1979. pap. 6.50x (ISBN 0-8131-0135-2). U Pr of Ky.

Appalachia: The Mountains, the Place, & the People. Betty L. Toone. LC 72-3119. (First Bks). (Illus.). 96p. (gr. 5-8). 1972. PLB 4.90 o.p. (ISBN 0-531-00769-3). Watts.

Appalachian Fertility Decline. Gordon F. De Jong. LC 68-12966. (Illus.). 154p. 1968. pap. 6.75x (ISBN 0-8131-1160-9). U Pr of Ky.

Appalachian Hill Country Cook Book. Delmer Robinson. LC 80-83183. (Illus.). 156p. 1980. 9.95 (ISBN 0-934750-04-1). Jalamap.

Appalachian Mountains. Photos by Clyde Smith. LC 80-65134. (Belding Imprint Ser.). (Illus.). 160p. (Text by Wilma Dykeman & Stokley Dykeman). 1980. 29.50 (ISBN 0-912856-59-9). Graphic Arts Ctr.

Appalachian Speech. Walt Wolfram & Donna Christian. LC 76-15079. 1976. pap. 8.75x (ISBN 0-87281-050-X). Ctr Appl Ling.

Appalachian Wilderness: The Great Smoky Mountains. rev. ed. Eliot Porter & Edward Abbey. (Illus.). 1973. 12.95 o.p. (ISBN 0-525-05686-6). Dutton.

Appalachian Winter. Betsy Sholl. LC 77-93267. 72p. 1978. pap. 4.95 (ISBN 0-914086-21-9). Alicejamesbooks.

Appalachian Women: An Annotated Bibliography. Sidney S. Farr. LC 80-5174. 224p. 1981. price not set (ISBN 0-8131-1431-4). U Pr of Ky.

Apparatus for F. Scott Fitzgerald's The Great Gatsby: Under the Red, White & Blue. Matthew J. Bruccoli. LC 74-4142. (S. C. Apparatus of Definitive Editions: No. 1). 1974. 14.95x (ISBN 0-87249-313-X); deluxe ed. 95.00x (ISBN 0-87249-323-7). U of SC Pr.

Apparel Manufacturing Handbook. Jacob Solinger. 800p. 1981. text ed. 60.00 (ISBN 0-442-21904-0). Van Nos Reinhold.

Apparent Restivity Observations & the Use of Square Array Techniques. G. M. Habberjam. (Geoexploration Monographs: No. 9). (Illus.). 1979. 55.00x (ISBN 3-443-13013-5). Intl Pubns Serv.

Apparition in April. K. N. Daruwalla. 8.00 (ISBN 0-89253-454-0); flexible cloth 4.80 (ISBN 0-89253-455-9). Ind-US Inc.

Apparitions. John Ashbery et al. 60p. ltd. signed ed. 50.00 (ISBN 0-935716-10-6). Lord John.

Apparitions. G. N. Tyrrell. 1962. pap. 0.95 o.s.i. (ISBN 0-02-078090-7, Collier). Macmillan.

Apparitions: An Archetypal Approach to Death, Dreams & Ghosts Jungian Classics. rev. ed. Aniela Jaffe. 1979. pap. text ed. 9.50 (ISBN 0-88214-500-2). Spring Pubns.

Apparitions & Haunted Houses: A Survey of Evidence. Ernest N. Bennett. LC 76-164100. Repr. of 1939 ed. 22.00 (ISBN 0-8103-3752-5). Gale.

Apparitions in Late Medieval & Renaissance Spain. William A. Christian, Jr. LC 80-8541. (Illus.). 304p. 1981. 20.00x (ISBN 0-691-05326-X). Princeton U Pr.

Appeal of Fascism. Alistair Hamilton. Ed. by A. Bartholomew. 1971. 7.95 o.s.i. (ISBN 0-02-547670-X). Macmillan.

Appeal to the Men of Great Britain on Behalf of Women. Mary Hays. Ed. by Gina Luria. LC 74-8547. (Feminist Controversy in England, 1788-1810 Ser.). 1974. lib. bdg. 50.00 (ISBN 0-8240-0868-5). Garland Pub.

Appearance & Reality in International Relations. Grant Hugo. LC 72-137420. 207p. 1970. 15.00x (ISBN 0-231-03468-7). Columbia U Pr.

Appearance & Reality in Politics. W. E. Connolly. 224p. Date not set. price not set (ISBN 0-521-23026-8). Cambridge U Pr.

Appearances & Realities: Misunderstanding in Human Relations. Gustav Ichheiser. LC 70-110631. (Social & Behavioral Science Ser.). 1970. 15.95x o.p. (ISBN 0-87589-060-1). Jossey-Bass.

Appearances of Death. Dell Shannon. 208p. 1980. pap. 1.95 (ISBN 0-553-13953-3). Bantam.

Appearing. Penney E. Wheeler. LC 79-16298. (Orion Ser.). 1979. pap. 2.95 (ISBN 0-8127-0231-X). Southern Pub.

Appel Des Etrangers Dans Nos Colonies. Turmeau De la Morandiere. (Principal French Demographic Works of the 18th Century Ser.). (Fr.). 1976. lib. bdg. 27.50x o.p. (ISBN 0-8287-0839-8); pap. text ed. 17.50x o.p. (ISBN 0-685-71507-8). Clearwater Pub.

Appelard & Liverwurst. Mercer Mayer. LC 77-21233. (Illus.). 40p. (gr. k-3). 1978. 8.95 (ISBN 0-590-07506-3, Four Winds). Schol Bk Serv.

Appelman's Outlines & Illustrations. Hyman Appelman. (Pocket Pulpit Library). 128p. 1981. pap. 2.95 (ISBN 0-8010-0072-6). Baker Bk.

Appendices to a Study of the Master Universe. William S. Sadler, Jr. LC 75-21657. 1975. 21.00 (ISBN 0-686-17215-9). Second Soc Foun.

Appetites. Linda Schor. 256p. 1975. pap. 1.50 o.s.i. (ISBN 0-446-78812-0). Warner Bks.

Appetites of Man: An Invitation to Better Nutrition from Nine Healthier Societies. Sally DeVore & Thelma White. LC 77-11231. 1978. pap. 4.95 o.p. (ISBN 0-385-13512-2, Anch). Doubleday.

Apple a Day. Joyce Hays. LC 74-30978. 1976. 9.95 o.p. (ISBN 0-498-01720-6). A S Barnes.

Apple a Day, in a Different Way: 365 Wholesome & Tasty Recipes. Ed. by Judith A. Spriggle. 1980. spiral bdg. 5.95 (ISBN 0-938686-02-X). H Spriggle.

Apple & the Ax. Barbara J. Crane. (Crane Reading System-English Ser.). (Illus.). (gr. k-2). 1977. pap. text ed. 2.95 (ISBN 0-89075-097-1). Crane Pub Co.

Apple & the Spectroscope. Thomas R. Henn. 1966. pap. 3.95x (ISBN 0-393-09703-X, NortonC). Norton.

Apple Basic for Business: For the Apple II. Alan Parker & John Stewart. 1981. text ed. 16.95 (ISBN 0-8359-0228-5); pap. text ed. 11.95 (ISBN 0-8359-0226-9); instrs'. manual avail. (ISBN 0-8359-0229-3). Reston.

Apple Book. Dick Martin. (Illus.). 24p. (ps-4). 1964. PLB 5.38 (ISBN 0-307-68904-2, Golden Pr). Western Pub.

Apple Cart. George B. Shaw. (Penguin Plays Ser.). 1956. pap. 2.50 (ISBN 0-14-048008-0). Penguin.

Apple Crunch. Fred Huber. 320p. 1981. 10.95 (ISBN 0-87223-687-0). Seaview Bks.

Apple-Growing Community: Yakima, Washington. (gr. 2). 1974. pap. text ed. 3.80 (ISBN 0-205-03887-5, 8038872); tchrs'. guide 12.00 (ISBN 0-205-03884-0, 8038848). Allyn.

Apple II User's Guide. Lon Poole. 500p. 1981. pap. 15.00 (ISBN 0-931988-46-2). Osborne-McGraw.

Apple Is My Sign. Mary Riskind. (gr. 5-8). 1981. 7.95 (ISBN 0-395-30852-6). HM.

Apple Kitchen Cookbook. Demetria Taylor. 1978. pap. 3.95 (ISBN 0-445-08525-8). Popular Lib.

Apple Picker's Manual. Arthur Harvey. 27p. 1968. pap. 1.00 (ISBN 0-934676-05-4). Greenlf Bks.

Apple Pie. A. Wellington. 1979. 5.95 (ISBN 0-13-038745-2). P-H.

Apple Pie Adventure of an Apple Pie. (ISBN 0-486-22413-9). pap. 1.75 (ISBN 0-486-21722-1). Dover.

Apple Tree: Christmas Music from the Cambridge Hymnal. D. Holbrook & E. Postan. LC 76-12916. 1976. 14.95 (ISBN 0-521-21479-3); pap. 5.75 (ISBN 0-521-29116-X). Cambridge U Pr.

Apple Tree, Lean Down. Mary Pearce. 1977. pap. 2.50 o.p. (ISBN 0-345-25655-7). Ballantine.

Apple Tree: Pre-Post Test Booklet. Boren et al. 52p. (gr. 1 up). 1972. 4.95 (ISBN 0-86575-026-2). Dormac.

Apple War. Bernice Myers. LC 72-8191. (Illus.). 48p. (gr. k-3). 1973. 5.95 o.s.i. (ISBN 0-8193-0650-9, Four Winds); PLB 5.41 o.s.i. (ISBN 0-8193-0651-7). Schol Bk Serv.

Applehood & Motherpie. Junior League of Rochester, Inc. Ed. by Tracy K. Kessler. 330p. 1981. 12.95 (ISBN 0-9605612-0-X). Jr League Rochester.

Apples. Nonny Hogrogian. LC 71-146626. (ps-2). 1972. 4.95 o.s.i. (ISBN 0-02-744010-9). Macmillan.

Apples: A Bushel of Fun & Facts. Bernice K. Hunt. LC 75-17911. (Finding-Out Books for Science & Social Studies, Grades 1-4). (Illus.). 64p. (gr. 2-4). 1976. PLB 6.95 (ISBN 0-8193-0838-2, Pub by Parents). Enslow Pubs.

Apples from Shinar. Hyam Plutzik. LC 59-12479. (Wesleyan Poetry Program: Vol. 2). (Orig.). 1959. 10.00x (ISBN 0-8195-2002-0, Pub. by Wesleyan U Pr); pap. 4.95x (ISBN 0-8195-1002-5). Columbia U Pr.

Appleton's Cyclopaedia of American Biography, 7 vols. LC 67-14061. Repr. of 1888 ed. 240.00 (ISBN 0-8103-3155-1). Gale.

Applicability of Organizational Sociology. C. Argyris. (Illus.). 138p. 1974. 24.50 (ISBN 0-521-08448-2); pap. 7.95x (ISBN 0-521-09894-7). Cambridge U Pr.

Applicable Finite Mathematics. David S. Moore & James W. Yackel. 432p. 1974. text ed. 20.50 (ISBN 0-395-17771-5); instructors' manual 2.15 (ISBN 0-395-17813-4). HM.

Application & Numberical Solution of Intergral Equations. Ed. by R. S. Anderson & F. R. De Hoog. (Mechanics Analysis Ser.: No. 6). 265p. 1980. 27.50x (ISBN 90-286-0450-2). Sijthoff & Noordhoff.

Application Design Handbook for Distributed Systems. Robert L. Patrick. LC 79-27205. (Illus.). 212p. 1980. text ed. 22.50 (ISBN 0-8436-1601-6). CBI Pub.

Application of Adsorption to Wastewater Treatment. (Illus.). 1981. text ed. 40.00 (ISBN 0-937976-03-2). Enviro Pr.

Application of Comparative Morphology in the Identification of Intestinal Parasites. J. W. Moose. (American Lectures in Clinical Microbiology Ser.). (Illus.). 56p. 1973. 10.75 (ISBN 0-398-02874-5). C C Thomas.

Application of Cybernetic Analysis to the Study of International Politics. Stephen D. Bryen. 147p. 1971. 27.50x (ISBN 90-247-5076-8). Intl Pubns Serv.

Application of Engineering in Microelectronic Industries. C. E. Jowett. 184p. 1975. text ed. 22.00x (ISBN 0-220-66278-9, Pub. by Busn Bks England). Renouf.

Application of Finite Difference Equations to Shell Analysis. M. Soare. 1968. 71.00 (ISBN 0-08-010214-X). Pergamon.

Application of Food Irradiation in Developing Countries. (Technical Reports Ser.: No. 54). (Orig.). 1966. pap. 8.25 (ISBN 92-0-115066-0, IAEA). Unipub.

Application of GPSS Five to Discrete System Simulation. Geoffrey Gordon. (Illus.). 336p. 1975. 23.95 (ISBN 0-13-039057-7). P-H.

Application of Induced Sterility for Control of Lepidopterous Populations. (Orig.). 1971. pap. 10.75 (ISBN 92-0-111271-8, IAEA). Unipub.

Application of Isotope Techniques in Hydrology. (Technical Reports Ser.: No. 11). (Orig.). 1962. pap. 2.75 (ISBN 92-0-145062-1, IAEA). Unipub.

Application of Learning Theory to ESP Performance. Charles T. Tart. LC 75-14709. (Parapsychological Monograph Ser.: No. 15). 1975. pap. 6.00 (ISBN 0-912328-25-8). Parapsych Foun.

Application of Mathematical Modelling to Process Development & Design. L. M. Rose. LC 74-14543. 364p. 1974. 49.95 (ISBN 0-470-73351-9). Halsted Pr.

Application of Measurement to Health & Physical Education. 5th ed. H. Harrison Clarke. (Illus.). 464p. 1976. 17.50x (ISBN 0-13-039024-0). P-H.

Application of Meteorology to Safety at Nuclear Plants. (Safety Ser.: No. 29). (Orig.). 1968. pap. 2.75 (ISBN 92-0-123368-X, ISP-211, IAEA). Unipub.

Application of Nuclear Techniques to Geothermal Studies: Proceedings. Ed. by E. Barbier. 1978. pap. text ed. 77.00 (ISBN 0-08-021670-6). Pergamon.

Application of Ornament. Lewis F. Day. Ed. by Peter Stansky & Rodney Shewan. LC 76-17767. (Aesthetic Movement & the Arts & Crafts Movement Ser.). 1977. Repr. of 1888 ed. lib. bdg. 44.00x (ISBN 0-8240-2471-0). Garland Pub.

Application of Plasmas to Chemical Processing. Ed. by Raymond F. Baddour & Robert S. Timmins. 1967. 23.00x (ISBN 0-262-02027-0). MIT Pr.

Application of Proteolytic Enzymes to Protein Structure Studies, Vol. 2. 2nd ed. Elemer Mihalyi. 1978. 59.95 (ISBN 0-8493-5190-1). CRC Pr.

Application of Psychiatric Insights to Cross-Cultural Communication, Vol. 4. Group for the Advancement of Psychiatry Conference. LC 62-2872. (Symposium No. 7). 1961. pap. 0.75 o.p. (ISBN 0-87318-065-8). Adv Psychiatry.

Application of Rock Mechanics: Proceedings. U. S. National Committee on Rock Mechanics, 15th, South Dakota School of Mines & Technology, Sept. 1973 & American Society of Civil Engineers. Ed. by Earl R. Haskins, Jr. 672p. 1976. text ed. 27.00 (ISBN 0-87262-154-5). Am Soc Civil Eng.

Application of Science & Medicine to Sport. Ed. by Albert W. Taylor. (Illus.). 352p. 1975. 32.75 (ISBN 0-398-02961-X). C C Thomas.

Application of Security Systems & Hardware. Richard B. Cole. 272p. 1970. pap. 27.95 photocopy ed. sprial (ISBN 0-398-00332-7). C C Thomas.

Application of Solar Technology to Today's Energy Needs: Executive Summary. Office of Technology Assessment. 1980. pap. 14.95 (ISBN 0-89934-004-0). Solar Energy Info.

Application of Systems Analysis to Problems of Irrigation, Drainage & Flood Control: A Manual for Engineers & Water Technologists. Ed. by International Commission on Irrigation & Drainage, New Delhi, India. (Water Development, Supply & Management Ser.: Vol. 11). (Illus.). 1980. text ed. 48.00 (ISBN 0-08-023425-9); pap. text ed. 18.00 (ISBN 0-08-023431-3). Pergamon.

Application of Technological Developments to Physically Disabled People. Joseph LaRocca & Jerry Turen. (Institute Paper). 113p. 1978. pap. 3.50 (ISBN 0-87766-225-8, 23200). Urban Inst.

Application of Technology to Improve Productivity in the Service Sector of the National Economy. National Academy of Engineering. LC 72-85833. Orig. Title: Productivity in the Service Sector of the Economy. (Illus.). 344p. 1973. pap. 10.50 (ISBN 0-309-02041-7). Natl Acad Pr.

Application of the Anglo-American Cataloguing Rules. 2nd ed. (Contributions to Librarianship Ser., No. 4). 1980. pap. 5.00 (ISBN 0-930214-06-4). U TX Austin Gen Libs.

Application of the Dose Limitation System for Radiation Protection: Practical Implications. (Proceedings Ser.). 674p. 1980. pap. 83.50 (ISBN 92-0-020379-5, ISP 521, IAEA). Unipub.

Application of the Myers-Briggs Type Indicator to Medicine & Other Health Professions, 2 vols. Mary H. McCaulley. Incl. Monograph I. 554p. 1978. pap. 20.00 (ISBN 0-935652-03-5); Monograph II. 288p. 1977. pap. 15.00 (ISBN 0-935652-04-3). (Illus.). 842p. (Orig.). Set. pap. 30.00 (ISBN 0-935652-05-1). Ctr Applications Psych.

Application of the Scriptures: A Refutation of Dispensationalism. A. W. Pink. pap. 1.25 (ISBN 0-685-88366-3). Reiner.

Application-Oriented Algebra: An Introduction to Discrete Mathematics. James L. Fisher. 1977. text ed. 21.50 scp (ISBN 0-7002-2504-8, HarpC). Har-Row.

Applications, Basics & Computing of Exploratory Data Analysis. Velleman & Hogalin. (Illus.). 228p. 1981. pap. text ed. 10.95 (ISBN 0-87872-273-4). Duxbury Pr.

Applications in Business Communication. John M. Penrose. 1981. pap. text ed. 7.95 (ISBN 0-03-058202-4). Dryden Pr.

Applications in School & Home. R. Vance Hall. (Managing Behavior Ser.: Part 3). 1974. 3.35 (ISBN 0-89079-003-5). H & H Ent.

Applications in School Mathematics. (National Council of Teachers of Mathematics Yearbook). 1979. 12.00 (ISBN 0-87353-139-6). NCTM.

Applications in Technology of Right Triangular Trigonometry: Unit 5. Rudolf A. Zimmer. 64p. 1980. pap. text ed. 4.95 (ISBN 0-8403-2278-X). Kendall-Hunt.

Applications of Absorption Spectroscopy of Organic Compounds. J. Dyer. 1965. pap. 10.95 (ISBN 0-13-038802-5). P-H.

Applications of Adaptive Control. Ed. by Kumpati Narendra & Richard Monopoli. 1980. 39.50 (ISBN 0-12-514060-6). Acad Pr.

Applications of Artificial Intelligence for Organic Chemistry: The Dendral Project. R. K. Lindsay et al. (Artificial Intelligence Ser.). (Illus.). 208p. 1980. text ed. 35.00 (ISBN 0-07-037895-9, C). McGraw.

Applications of College Mathematics. A. William Gray & Otis M. Ulm. 1970. text ed. 11.95x (ISBN 0-02-474540-5, 47454). Macmillan.

Applications of Economic Principles in Public Utility Industries. Ed. by Werner Sichel & Thomas G. Gies. (Michigan Business Studies: Vol. 2, No. 3). (Illus.). 180p. 1981. price not set (ISBN 0-87712-211-3). U Mich Busn Div Res.

Applications of Energy: Nineteenth Century. Ed. by B. R. Lindsay. (Benchmark Papers in Energy Ser.: Vol. 2). 1976. 47.00 (ISBN 0-12-786961-1). Acad Pr.

Applications of Fuzzy Sets to Systems Analysis. C. V. Negoita & D. A. Ralescu. LC 75-35789. 1976. 27.95 (ISBN 0-470-63105-8). Halsted Pr.

Applications of Glass Capilary Gas Chromatography. Jennings. Date not set. price not set (ISBN 0-8247-1223-4). Dekker.

Applications of Inductive Logic: Proceedings of a Conference at the Queen's College, Oxford, August 1978. Ed. by L. J. Cohen & M. B. Hesse. (Illus.). 410p. 1980. 65.00x (ISBN 0-19-824584-X). Oxford U Pr.

Applications of Inductively Coupled Plasmas to Emission Spectroscopy. Ed. by Ramon M. Barnes. LC 78-70143. (Eastern Analytical Symposium Ser). (Illus., Orig.). 1978. pap. 21.75 (ISBN 0-89168-020-9). Franklin Inst Pr.

Applications of Ion Selective Membrane Electrodes in Organic Analysis. G. E. Baiulescu & V. V. Cosofret. (Series in Analytical Chemistry). 1977. 59.95 (ISBN 0-470-99192-5). Halsted Pr.

Applications of Item Response Theory to Practical Testing Problems. Frederic M. Lord. LC 79-24186. (Illus.). 288p. 1980. text ed. 29.95 (ISBN 0-89859-006-X). L Erlbaum Assocs.

Applications of Lasers in Materials Processing. Ed. by Edward A. Metzbower. 1979. 32.00 (ISBN 0-87170-084-0). ASM.

Applications of Linear Algebra. 2nd ed. Howard Anton & Chris Rorres. 1979. pap. text ed. 8.95 (ISBN 0-471-05337-6). Wiley.

Applications of Linguistics: Selected Papers on the Second International Congress of Applied Linguistics, Cambridge. Ed. by G. E. Perren & J. L. Trim. (Illus.). 1972. 69.50 (ISBN 0-521-08088-6). Cambridge U Pr.

Applications of Lithium in Ceramics. J. H. Fishwick. (Illus.). 176p. 1974. 22.50 (ISBN 0-8436-0611-8). CBI Pub.

Applications of Mossbauer Spectroscopy, Vol. 2. Richard L. Cohen. 1980. write for info (ISBN 0-12-178402-9). Acad Pr.

Applications of Nuclear Magnetic Resonance Spectroscopy in Organic Chemistry. 2nd ed. L. M. Jackman & S. Sternhell. 1969. 50.00 (ISBN 0-08-012542-5). Pergamon.

Applications of Numerical Methods to Heat Transfer. E. F. Nogotov. (Illus.). 1978. pap. text ed. 28.50 (ISBN 0-07-046852-4, C). McGraw.

Applications of Operations Research Models to Libraries: A Case Study in the Use of Monographs in the Francis A. Countway Library of Medicine, Harvard University. Chen Ching-Chih. LC 75-28210. 192p. 1976. text ed. 20.00x (ISBN 0-262-03056-X). MIT Pr.

Applications of Personal Control. Ed. by Andrew Baum & Jerome E. Singer. LC 79-25025. (Advances in Environmental Psychology Ser.: Vol. 2). (Illus.). 208p. 1980. text ed. 19.95 (ISBN 0-89859-018-3). L Erlbaum Assocs.

Applications of Photochemistry in Probing Biological Targets. Ed. by Andrew M. Tometsko & Frederic M. Richard. LC 80-15368. (N.Y. Academy of Sciences Annals: Vol. 346). 1980. 88.00x (ISBN 0-89766-080-3); pap. write for info. (ISBN 0-89766-081-1). NY Acad Sci.

Applications of Sieve Methods to the Theory of Numbers. C. Hooley. LC 75-27796. (Cambridge Tracts in Mathematics Ser.: No. 70). 122p. 1976. 32.95 (ISBN 0-521-20915-3). Cambridge U Pr.

Applications of Soils Information in Forestry. 1.50 o.p. (ISBN 0-686-20726-2). SUNY Environ.

Applications of Statistical Sampling to Auditing. James K. Loebbecke & Alvin A. Arens. (Illus.). 400p. 1981. 23.95 (ISBN 0-13-039156-5). P-H.

Applications of Statistics to Industrial Experimentation. Cuthbert Daniel. LC 76-2012. (Applied Probability & Statistics Ser.). 294p. 1976. 25.95 (ISBN 0-471-19469-7, Pub. by Wiley-Interscience). Wiley.

Applications of Stochastic Processes to Sediment Transport: Sedimentation Process in Rivers & Coastal Environments. Ed. by H. W. Shen. H. Kikkawa. LC 79-67693. 1979. 27.50 (ISBN 0-686-64297-X). WRP.

Applications of the Electromagnetic Reciprocity Principle. C. D. Monteath. 1973. 27.00 (ISBN 0-08-016895-7). Pergamon.

Applications of the Mossbauer Effect in Chemistry & Solid-State Physics. (Technical Reports Ser.: No. 50). (Illus., Orig.). 1966. pap. 12.00 (ISBN 92-0-035066-6, IAEA). Unipub.

Applications of Thermodynamics. Bernard D. Wood. (Mechanical Engineering Ser). 1969. text ed. 21.95 o.p. (ISBN 0-201-08740-5). A-W.

Applications of Thermodynamics. 3rd ed. Bernard D. Wood. (Mechanical Engineering Ser.). 1981. text ed. write for info. A-W.

Applied Abstract Analysis. Jean-Pierre Aubin. LC 77-2382. (Pure & Applied Mathematics, a W-I Ser. of Texts, Monographs & Tracts). 1977. 33.95 (ISBN 0-471-02146-6, Pub. by Wiley-Interscience). Wiley.

Applied Accounting Theory: A Financial Reporting Perspective. Philip E. Meyer. 1980. 20.95x (ISBN 0-256-02360-3). Irwin.

Applied Acoustics. G. Porges. 1979. pap. 18.95 (ISBN 0-470-26748-8). Halsted Pr.

Applied Algebra for the Computer Sciences. Arthur Gill. (Illus.). 416p. 1976. 23.95 (ISBN 0-13-039222-7). P-H.

Applied Algebra II. Thomas J. McHale & Paul T. Witzke. 1980. pap. text ed. 12.95 (ISBN 0-201-04775-6). A-W.

Applied Analytical Mathematics for Physical Scientists. James T. Cushing. LC 75-9611. 672p. 1975. text ed. 28.95 (ISBN 0-471-18997-9). Wiley.

Applied & Computational Complex Analysis: Power Series, Integration-Conformal Mapping-Location of Zeroes. Henry Henrici. LC 73-19723. (Pure & Applied Mathematics Ser.: Vol. 1). 704p. 1974. 45.95 (ISBN 0-471-37244-7, Pub. by Wiley-Interscience). Wiley.

Applied & Computational Complex Analysis: Special Functions-Integral Transforms-Asymptotics-Continued Fractions, Vol. 2. Peter Henrici. LC 73-19723. 1977. 45.95 (ISBN 0-471-01525-3, Pub. by Wiley-Interscience). Wiley.

Applied & Decorative Arts: A Bibliographic Guide to Basic Reference Works, Histories, & Handbooks. Donald L. Ehresmann. LC 76-55416. 1977. lib. bdg. 22.50x (ISBN 0-87287-136-3). Libs Unl.

Applied Animal Nutrition: The Use of Feedstuffs in the Formulation of Livestock Rations. 2nd ed. E. W. Crampton & L. E. Harris. LC 68-10996. (Animal Science Ser.). (Illus.). 1969. text ed. 26.95x (ISBN 0-7167-0814-0). W H Freeman.

Applied Animal Reproduction. John W. Fuquay & H. Joe Bearden. (Illus.). 352p. 1980. text ed. 16.95 (ISBN 0-8359-0249-8); instr's. manual free. Reston.

Applied Anthropology in America. Ed. by Elizabeth M. Eddy & William L. Partridge. 1978. 25.00x (ISBN 0-231-04466-6); pap. 10.00x (ISBN 0-231-04467-4). Columbia U Pr.

Applied APL Programming. Wilbur R. LePage. LC 78-6619. (Illus.). 1978. pap. 15.95 ref. (ISBN 0-13-040063-7). P-H.

Applied Audiology for Children. 2nd 4th pt ed. D. C. Dale. (Illus.). 176p. 1979. 14.75 (ISBN 0-398-00387-4). C C Thomas.

Applied Automata Theory. Ed. by Julius T. Tou. LC 68-26634. (Electrical Science Ser). 1969. 48.50 (ISBN 0-12-696230-8). Acad Pr.

Applied Basic Programming. Roy Ageloff & Richard Mojena. 464p. 1980. pap. text ed. 14.95x (ISBN 0-534-00808-9). Wadsworth Pub.

Applied Behavior Modification. W. Doyle Gentry. LC 74-28290. (Illus.). 164p. 1975. pap. text ed. 9.50 (ISBN 0-8016-1803-7). Mosby.

Applied Biochemistry of Clinical Disorders. Ed. by Allan G. Gornall. (Illus.). 544p. 1981. pap. text ed. write for info. (ISBN 0-06-141010-1, Harper Medical). Har-Row.

Applied Biopharmaceutics & Pharmacokinetics. Leon Shargel & Andrew B. Yu. 288p. 1980. pap. text ed. 18.50x (ISBN 0-8385-0206-7). ACC.

Applied Business Communications. Feinberg. 1981. 15.95 (ISBN 0-88284-125-4). Alfred Pub.

Applied Business Mathematics. 2nd ed. Moran & Aubuchon. 368p. 1976. pap. text ed. 15.95 (ISBN 0-205-04889-7, 174889-0); instr's manual avail. (ISBN 0-205-04920-6, 174920-X); test manual avail. (ISBN 0-205-05548-6, 175548-X). Allyn.

Applied Business Statistics. Fadil H. Zuwaylif. 1974. text ed. 17.95 (ISBN 0-201-08906-8). A-W.

Applied Business Statistics: An Elementary Approach. 2nd ed. Elam E. McElroy. 1979. text ed. 18.95x (ISBN 0-8162-5535-0); inst. manual 4.95x (ISBN 0-8162-5537-7); wkbk. 6.95x (ISBN 0-8162-5536-9). Holden-Day.

Applied Calculus. 2nd ed. Coughlin. 480p. 1980. text ed. 20.95 (ISBN 0-205-06910-X, 5669103). Allyn.

Applied Calculus. Raymond F. Coughlin. 384p. 1976. text ed. 15.95x o.p. (ISBN 0-205-04890-0); instr. supplement free o.p. (ISBN 0-205-04891-9). Allyn.

Applied Calculus for Business & Economics. Jagdish C. Arya & Robin W. Lardner. (Illus.). 528p. 1981. text ed. 18.95 (ISBN 0-13-039255-3). P-H.

Applied Cardiovascular Physiology. 2nd ed. G. R. Kelman. 1977. 34.95 (ISBN 0-407-10881-5). Butterworths.

Applied Chiropractic in Distortion Analysis. William J. Kotheimer. (Illus.). 200p. 1976. 8.95 (ISBN 0-8059-2329-2). Dorrance.

Applied Circuit Theory: Matrix & Computer Methods. P. R. Adby. LC 79-41458. (Series in Electrical & Electronic Engineering). 1980. 94.95x (ISBN 0-470-26908-1). Halsted Pr.

Applied Climatology. John Hobbs. LC 79-5287. (Westview Studies in Physical Geography). (Illus.). 224p. 1980. lib. bdg. 30.00x (ISBN 0-89158-697-0). Westview.

Applied Coastal Geomorphology. 1st u.s. ed. Ed. by J. A. Steers. 1971. 17.50x (ISBN 0-262-19088-5). MIT Pr.

Applied Combinatorial Mathematics. Ed. by Edwin F. Beckenbach. 630p. 1981. lib. bdg. write for info. (ISBN 0-89874-172-6). Krieger.

Applied Communication Research: A Dramatistic Approach. John F. Cragan & Donald C. Shields. 432p. 1981. text ed. 17.95x (ISBN 0-917974-53-0). Waveland Pr.

Applied Cook-Freezing. Compiled by P. Glanfield. (Illus.). xii, 203p. 1980. 35.00x (ISBN 0-85334-888-X). Burgess-Intl Ideas.

Applied Cross-Cultural Psychology: Proceedings. International Conference of Selected Papers, 2nd, Kingston. Ont. August, 6-10, 1974. Ed. by J. W. Berry & W. Lonner. 340p. (Orig.). 1975. pap. text ed. 19.50 (ISBN 0-686-27809-7, Pub. by Swets Pub Serv Holland). Swets North Am.

Applied Decision Making for Nurses. Jo Ann G. Ford et al. LC 78-15713. (Illus.). 1979. pap. text ed. 9.50 (ISBN 0-8016-1624-7). Mosby.

Applied Differential Equations. 3rd ed. Murray R. Spiegal. 1980. text ed. 23.95 (ISBN 0-13-040097-1). P-H.

Applied Differential Equations. 2nd ed. Murray R. Spiegel. 1967. text ed. 21.95 (ISBN 0-13-040089-0). P-H.

Applied Discrete-Choice Modelling. David A. Hensher. Ed. by Lester W. Johnson. LC 80-23517. 468p. 1980. 29.95 (ISBN 0-470-27078-0). Halsted Pr.

Applied Dream Analysis: A Jungian Approach. Mary Ann Mattoon. 1978. 13.95x (ISBN 0-470-26418-7). Halsted Pr.

Applied Dynamic Programming. Richard E. Bellman & S. Dreyfus. (Rand Corporation Research Studies). 1962. 20.00 (ISBN 0-691-07913-7). Princeton U Pr.

Applied Econometrics. Potluri M. Rao & Roger L. Miller. 1971. 18.95x (ISBN 0-534-00031-2). Wadsworth Pub.

Applied Economics in Banking & Finance. H. Carter & I. Partington. 1979. 29.00x (ISBN 0-19-877108-8). Oxford U Pr.

Applied Electricity for Engineers. 2nd ed. L. Bessonov. Tr. by Boris Kuznetsov from Rus. (Illus.). 792p. 1973. 20.00x o.p. (ISBN 0-8464-0142-8). Beekman Pubs.

Applied Electromagnetism. P. Hammond. 396p. 1972. text ed. 25.00 (ISBN 0-08-016381-5); pap. text ed. 11.25 (ISBN 0-08-016382-3). Pergamon.

Applied Electronic Communication: Circuits, Systems, Transmission. Robert Kellejian. 608p. 1980. text ed. 23.95 (ISBN 0-574-21535-2, 13-4535); instr's. guide avail. (ISBN 0-574-21536-0, 13-4536). SRA.

Applied Electronics. 2nd ed. Truman S. Gray. (Illus.). 1954. 26.00x (ISBN 0-262-07002-2). MIT Pr.

Applied Electronics for Veterinary Medicine & Animal Physiology. W. R. Klemm. (Illus.). 484p. 1976. 41.50 (ISBN 0-398-03477-X). C C Thomas.

Applied Engineering Mechanics. 3rd ed. Alfred E. Jensen & H. Chenoweth. 1971. 16.95 (ISBN 0-07-032480-8, G); problem answers 1.50 (ISBN 0-07-032481-6). McGraw.

Applied Engineering Mechanics: Statistics & Dynamics. Boothroyd & Poli. 23.50 (ISBN 0-8247-6945-7). Dekker.

Applied Engineering Statistics for Practicing Engineers. Lawrence Mann, Jr. LC 76-129578. 1970. pap. 8.95 (ISBN 0-8436-0317-8). CBI Pub.

Applied Finite Mathematics. Howard Anton & Bernard Kalman. 1974. 13.95 o.p. (ISBN 0-12-059550-8). Acad Pr.

Applied Finite Mathematics. 2nd ed. Howard Anton & Bernard Kolman. 558p. 1978. 16.95 (ISBN 0-12-059565-6); instrs'. manual avail. (ISBN 0-12-059564-8). Acad Pr.

Applied Finite Mathematics. Brown & Brown. 1977. 18.95x o.p. (ISBN 0-534-00499-7). Wadsworth Pub.

Applied Finite Mathematics with Calculus. Howard Anton & Bernard Kolman. 760p. 1978. 17.95 (ISBN 0-12-059560-5); instrs'. manual 3.00 (ISBN 0-12-059567-2). Acad Pr.

Applied Fluid Mechanics. 2nd ed. Robert L Mott. (Mechanical Technology Ser.). 1979. text ed. 19.95 (ISBN 0-675-08305-2); instructor's manual 3.95 (ISBN 0-686-67359-X). Merrill.

Applied Foodservice Sanitation. 2nd ed. National Institute for Foodservice Industry. 1978. text ed. 12.95x (ISBN 0-669-00792-7); coursebook 4.25 (ISBN 0-669-02106-7); instructor's manual free (ISBN 0-669-02730-8). Heath.

Applied Fortran Four Programming. 2nd ed. John R. Sturgul & M. J. Merchant. 1977. pap. text ed. 15.95x (ISBN 0-534-00440-7). Wadsworth Pub.

Applied Fortran Program W Standard Fortan, Watfor, Watfiv & Structured Watfiv. Merchant & Sturgul. 1977. 15.95x (ISBN 0-534-00497-0). Wadsworth Pub.

Applied Functional Analysis. Jean-Pierre Aubin. LC 78-20896. (Pure & Applied Mathematics: Texts, Monographs & Tracts). 1979. 28.95 (ISBN 0-471-02149-0, Pub. by Wiley-Interscience). Wiley.

Applied Functional Analysis: A First Course for Students of Mechanics & Engineering Science. J. T. Ogden. LC 78-541. (Illus.). 1979. ref. 27.95 (ISBN 0-13-040162-5). P-H.

Applied Functions of a Complex Variable. A. Kyrala. LC 74-176285. 1972. 35.00 (ISBN 0-471-51129-3, Pub. by Wiley-Interscience). Wiley.

Applied Gamma-Ray Spectrometry. 2nd rev. ed. F. Adams & R. Dams. LC 79-114847. 1970. text ed. 92.00 (ISBN 0-08-006888-X). Pergamon.

Applied General Mathematics. Robert Smith. LC 79-51586. (General Mathematics Ser.). (Illus.). 480p. 1981. text ed. price not set (ISBN 0-8273-1674-7); price not set instr's. guide (ISBN 0-8273-1675-5). Delmar.

Applied Genetics: A Booming Industry C-032. 1981. 950.00 (ISBN 0-89336-285-9). BCC.

Applied Geometric Programming. Charles S. Beightler & Donald T. Phillips. LC 75-44391. 1976. 34.95 (ISBN 0-471-06390-8). Wiley.

Applied Geophysics. W. M. Telford et al. LC 74-16992. (Illus.). 700p. 1975. 95.50 (ISBN 0-521-20670-7); pap. 29.95x (ISBN 0-521-29146-1). Cambridge U Pr.

Applied Geophysics for Engineers & Geologists. D. H. Griffiths & R. F. King. 1965. 27.00 (ISBN 0-08-010750-8); pap. 9.50 (ISBN 0-08-010749-4). Pergamon.

Applied Geophysics for Geologists & Engineers: The Elements of Geophysical Prospecting. D. H. Griffiths & R. F. King. (Illus.). 224p. Date not set. 30.00 (ISBN 0-08-022071-1); pap. 14.50 (ISBN 0-08-022072-X). Pergamon.

Applied Geotechnology: A Text for Students & Engineers on Rock Excavation & Related Topics. A. Roberts. (Illus.). 416p. 1981. 50.00 (ISBN 0-08-024015-1); pap. 25.00 (ISBN 0-08-024014-3). Pergamon.

Applied Graph Theory. Clifford W. Marshall. 1971. 30.50 o.p. (ISBN 0-471-57300-0, Pub. by Wiley-Interscience). Wiley.

Applied Group Theory. A. P. Cracknell. 1968. 46.00 (ISBN 0-08-013328-2); pap. 12.75 (ISBN 0-08-012286-8). Pergamon.

Applied Health Services Research. John D. Thompson. LC 75-12482. (Illus.). 1977. 19.95 (ISBN 0-669-00028-0). Lexington Bks.

Applied Human Relations: An Organizational Approach. Jack Halloran. (Illus.). 1978. ref. ed. 17.95 (ISBN 0-13-040857-3); activity guide 6.95 (ISBN 0-13-040824-7). P-H.

Applied Hydraulics & Pneumatics in Industry. J. R. Fawcett. (Illus.). 1968. 35.00x (ISBN 0-85461-077-4). Intl Ideas.

Applied Hydro & Aeromechanics. Ludwig Prandtl & O. G. Tietjens. Ed. by Jacob P. Den Hartog. (Illus.). 1934. pap. text ed. 5.00 (ISBN 0-486-60375-X). Dover.

Applied Industrial Control--an Introduction. M. G. Singh et al. (International Ser. on Systems & Control: Vol. 1). (Illus.). 450p. 1980. 52.00 (ISBN 0-08-024764-4); pap. 21.00 (ISBN 0-08-024765-2). Pergamon.

Applied Instrumentation in the Process Industries: A Survey, Vol. 1. 2nd ed. William G. Andrew & H. B. Williams. 1979. 37.95 (ISBN 0-87201-382-0). Gulf Pub.

Applied Instrumentation in the Process Industries, Vol. 2. 2nd ed. William G. Andrews & H. B. Williams. (Practical Guidelines Ser.). (Illus.). 330p. 1980. 37.95 (ISBN 0-87201-383-9). Gulf Pub.

Applied Iterative Methods. L. A. Hageman & D. M. Young. (Computer Science & Applied Mathematics Ser.). 1981. price not set (ISBN 0-12-313340-8). Acad Pr.

Applied Linear Algebra. R. J. Goult. LC 78-40608. 1979. pap. text ed. 16.95x (ISBN 0-470-26864-6). Halsted Pr.

Applied Linear Algebra. 2nd ed. Ben Noble & James W. Daniel. (Illus.). 1977. ref. ed. 20.95 (ISBN 0-13-041343-7). P-H.

Applied Linear Algebra. Alden F. Pixley. LC 80-8241. 264p. 1980. lib. bdg. 18.50 (ISBN 0-8191-1169-4); pap. text ed. 10.50 (ISBN 0-8191-1170-8). U Pr of Amer.

Applied Linear Optimization. Paul H. Randolph & Howard D. Meeks. LC 78-50044. (Industrial Engineering Ser.). 1978. pap. text ed. 8.95 o.p. (ISBN 0-88244-144-2). Grid Pub.

Applied Linear Regression. S. Weisberg. LC 80-10378. (Probability & Mathematical Statistics: Applied Probability & Statistics Section). 1980. 24.95 (ISBN 0-471-04419-9, Pub. by Wiley-Interscience). Wiley.

Applied Linear Statistical Models. John Neter & William Wasserman. 1974. text ed. 21.95x (ISBN 0-256-01498-1). Irwin.

Applied Managerial Economics. Julian Simon. (Illus.). 560p. 1975. ref. ed. 20.95 (ISBN 0-13-041194-9). P-H.

Applied Mathematical Demography. Nathan Keyfitz. LC 77-1360. 1977. 28.95 (ISBN 0-471-47350-2, Pub. by Wiley-Interscience). Wiley.

Applied Mathematical Programming. Stephen P. Bradley et al. LC 76-10426. (Illus.). 1977. text ed. 23.95 (ISBN 0-201-00464-X). A-W.

Applied Mathematics for Business, Economics, & the Social Sciences. Frank S. Budnick. (Illus.). 1979. text ed. 18.50 (ISBN 0-07-008851-9, C); wkbk. 6.96 (ISBN 0-07-008854-3); instructor's manual 7.95 (ISBN 0-07-008852-7). McGraw.

Applied Mathematics for Physical Chemistry. James R. Barrante. (Illus.). 160p. 1974. pap. text ed. 10.95 (ISBN 0-13-041384-4). P-H.

Applied Mathematics for Technical Programs: Algebra. Robert G. Moon. LC 73-75638. 1973. pap. text ed. 16.95 (ISBN 0-675-08943-3); media: audiocassettes 140.00, 2-5 sets, 95.00 ea., 6 or more sets, 70.00 ea. (ISBN 0-675-08910-7); instructor's manual 3.95 (ISBN 0-686-66867-7); test 3.95 (ISBN 0-686-66868-5). Merrill.

Applied Mathematics for Technical Programs: Arithmetic & Geometry. Robert Moon. LC 72-96904. 1973. pap. text ed. 16.95 (ISBN 0-675-08983-2); media: audiocassettes 140.00, 2-5 sets, 95.00 ea., 6 or more sets, 70.00 ea. (ISBN 0-675-08918-2); instructor's manual 3.95 (ISBN 0-686-66869-3); test 3.95 (ISBN 0-686-66870-7). Merrill.

Applied Mathematics for Technical Programs: Trigonometry. Robert G. Moon. LC 73-77913. 1973. pap. text ed. 17.95 (ISBN 0-675-08923-9); media: audiocassettes 140.00, 2-5 sets, 95.00 ea., 6 or more sets, 70.00 ea. (ISBN 0-675-08900-X); instructor's manual 3.95 (ISBN 0-686-66871-5). Merrill.

Applied Mechanical Vibrations. David V. Hutton. (Mechanical Engineering Ser.). (Illus.). 416p. 1980. text ed. 23.95x (ISBN 0-07-031549-3, C); solutions manual avail. (ISBN 0-07-031550-7). McGraw.

Applied Mechanics. Charles E. Smith. Incl. Dynamics (ISBN 0-471-80178-X); Statics (ISBN 0-471-80460-6). 1976. text ed. 18.95x ea. Wiley.

Applied Mechanics - More Dynamics. Charles E. Smith. LC 75-44021. 1976. text ed. 23.95x (ISBN 0-471-79996-3). Wiley.

Applied Modeling of Hydrologic Time Series. 1981. 29.50 (ISBN 0-918334-37-3). WRP.

Applied Multivariate Analysis. John E. Overall & C. James Klett. 522p. 1981. Repr. of 1972 ed. lib. bdg. price not set (ISBN 0-89874-325-7). Krieger.

Applied Nonparametric Statistics. Wayne W. Daniel. LC 77-74515. (Illus.). 1978. text ed. 21.50 (ISBN 0-395-25795-6); sol. manual 1.15 (ISBN 0-395-25796-4). HM.

Applied Nonstandard Analysis. Martin Davis. LC 76-28484. (Pure & Applied Mathematics Ser.). 1977. text ed. 25.95 (ISBN 0-471-19897-8, Pub. by Wiley-Interscience). Wiley.

Applied Nuclear Power for Practicing Engineers. Knud Pedersen et al. LC 78-170128. 1972. 11.95 (ISBN 0-8436-0326-7). CBI Pub.

Applied Numerical Analysis. 2nd ed. Curtis F. Gerald. LC 77-79469. (Illus.). 1978. text ed. 21.95 (ISBN 0-201-02696-1). A-W.

Applied Numerical Modeling: Proceedings of the International Conference, University of Southampton, 11-15 July, 1977. Ed. by C. A. Brebbia. LC 77-11141. 1978. 49.95 (ISBN 0-470-99271-9). Halsted Pr.

Applied Operations Research: A Survey. Gary E. Whitehouse & Ben L. Wechsler. LC 76-16545. 1976. 22.95x (ISBN 0-471-02552-6); solutions manual avail. (ISBN 0-685-66900-9). Wiley.

Applied Optics: A Guide to Optical Systems Design, 2 vols. L. Levi. LC 67-29942. (Pure & Applied Optics Ser.). Vol. 1, 1968. 41.95 (ISBN 0-471-53110-3, Pub. by Wiley-Interscience); Vol. 2, 1980. 75.00 (ISBN 0-471-05054-7). Wiley.

Applied Optics & Optical Engineering: A Comprehensive Treatise, 5 vols. Ed. by R. Kingslake. Incl. Vol. 1. Light: Its Generation & Modification. 1965 (ISBN 0-12-408601-2); Vol. 2. The Detection of Light & Infrared Radiation. 1965 (ISBN 0-12-408602-0); Vol. 3. Optical Components. 1965 (ISBN 0-12-408603-9); Vol. 4. Optical Instruments, Part 1. 1967 (ISBN 0-12-408604-7); Vol. 5. Optical Instruments, Part 2. 1969 (ISBN 0-12-408605-5). 48.50 ea.; Set. 197.50. Acad Pr.

Applied Optimal Control. rev. ed. A. E. Bryson & Yu-Chi Ho. LC 75-16114. 1979. pap. text ed. 15.95 (ISBN 0-470-26774-7). Halsted Pr.

Applied Optimal Control: Optimization, Estimation, & Control. rev. ed. A. E. Bryson & Y. C. Ho. LC 75-16114. (Illus.). 481p. 1981. pap. 15.95 (ISBN 0-89116-228-3). Hemisphere Pub.

Applied Optimal Design: Mechanical & Structural Systems. Edward J. Haug & Jasbir S. Arora. LC 79-11437. 1979. 32.50 (ISBN 0-471-04170-X, Pub. by Wiley-Interscience). Wiley.

Applied Petroleum Reservoir Engineering. Benjamin C. Craft & M. F. Hawkins. 1959. 31.95 (ISBN 0-13-041285-6). P-H.

Applied Pharmacology. Walter Modell et al. LC 75-21148. (Illus.). 975p. 1976. 25.00 (ISBN 0-7216-6425-3). Saunders.

Applied Pharmacology. 12th ed. H. O. Schild. (Illus.). 500p. 1981. pap. text ed. 32.00 (ISBN 0-443-02199-6). Churchill.

Applied Pharmacology for the Dental Hygienists. Barbara Requa-Clark & Sam V. Holroyd. 427p. 1981. pap. 11.95 (ISBN 0-8016-2239-5). Mosby.

Applied Plant Anatomy. D. F. Cutler. LC 77-3290. (Illus.). 1978. pap. text ed. 14.95x (ISBN 0-582-44128-5). Longman.

Applied Police & Fire Photography. Raymond P. Siljander. (Illus.). 336p. 1976. 24.75 (ISBN 0-398-03566-0). C C Thomas.

Applied Practice Management: A Strategy for Stress Control. Thomas M. Cooper & John A. DiBiaggio. LC 79-15266. (Illus.). 1979. text ed. 26.50 (ISBN 0-8016-1082-6). Mosby.

Applied Probability Models with Optimization Applications. Sheldon M. Ross. LC 73-111376. 1970. text ed. 19.95x (ISBN 0-8162-7336-7). Holden-Day.

Applied Program Evaluation in Local Government. Theodore H. Poister et al. LC 78-20374. 240p. 1979. 23.95 (ISBN 0-669-02731-6). Lexington Bks.

Applied Psychology in Law Enforcement & Corrections. Ed. by Richard E. Hardy & John G. Cull. (American Lectures in Social & Rehabilitation Psychology Ser.). (Illus.). 248p. 1973. 14.50 (ISBN 0-398-02862-1). C C Thomas.

Applied Psychology of Work Behavior: A Book of Readings. Ed. by Dennis W. Organ. 1978. pap. 10.95x (ISBN 0-256-02080-9). Business Pubns.

Applied Readings in Personnel & Human Resource Management. Randall S. Schuler et al. (Management Ser.). (Illus.). 300p. 1981. pap. text ed. 6.36 (ISBN 0-8299-0408-5). West Pub.

Applied Real Estate Math. 2nd ed. Joseph Polley. (Illus.). 256p. 1980. pap. text ed. 10.95 (ISBN 0-8359-0252-8). Reston.

Applied Regression: An Introduction. Michael S. Lewis-Beck. LC 80-5821. (Quantitative Applications in the Social Sciences Ser.: No. 22). (Illus.). 79p. 1980. pap. 3.50 (ISBN 0-8039-1494-6). Sage.

Applied Regression Analysis. 2nd ed. N. R. Draper & H. Smith. LC 80-17951. (Wiley Ser. in Probability & Mathematical Statics - Applied Probability & Statistics). 720p. 1981. 22.50 (ISBN 0-471-02995-5, Pub. by Wiley-Interscience). Wiley.

Applied Reichian Therapy. Sean Haldane. 1981. text ed. 34.50x (ISBN 0-8290-0121-2); audiotape cassette avail. Irvington.

Applied Research & Statistics for Teachers. E. Burns. (Illus.). 264p. 1980. lexotone 12.00 (ISBN 0-398-03984-4). C C Thomas.

Applied Respiratory Physiology. 2nd ed. J. F. Nunn. 1977. 59.95 (ISBN 0-407-00060-7). Butterworths.

Applied Science in the Casting of Metals. K. Strauss. 1970. 50.00 (ISBN 0-08-015711-4). Pergamon.

Applied Sciences Research & Utilization of Lunar Resources. F. J. Malina. 1970. 50.00 (ISBN 0-08-015565-0). Pergamon.

Applied Solar Energy: An Introduction. Aden B. Meinel & Marjorie P. Meinel. 400p. 1976. text ed. 25.95 (ISBN 0-201-04719-5). A-W.

Applied Statistical Methods. Irving W. Burr. (Operations Research & Industrial Engineering Ser.). 1973. 21.95 (ISBN 0-12-146150-5). Acad Pr.

Applied Statistics. John Neter et al. 1978. text ed. 20.95 (ISBN 0-205-05982-1); instr's man. avail. (ISBN 0-205-05983-X); solutions man. avail. (ISBN 0-205-06038-2). Allyn.

Applied Statistics: Analysis of Variance & Regression. Olive J. Dunn & Virginia A. Clark. LC 73-13683. (Probability & Mathematical Statistics Ser.). 387p. 1974. 25.95 (ISBN 0-471-22700-5, Pub. by Wiley-Interscience). Wiley.

Applied Statistics & Analytic Techniques for Public Administrators. Meier & Brudney. 1981. 15.95. Duxbury Pr.

Applied Statistics for Business & Economics. Henrick J. Malik & Kenneth Mullen. LC 74-12800. (Illus.). 496p. 1975. text ed. 17.95 (ISBN 0-201-04410-2); instr's manual 4.00 (ISBN 0-201-04472-2). A-W.

Applied Statistics for Engineers. C. Wilson. (Illus.). 1972. pap. text ed. 22.30x (ISBN 0-85334-529-5, Pub. by Applied Science). Burgess-Intl Ideas.

Applied Statistics for Management Studies. 2nd ed. David Croft. (Illus.). 304p. (Orig.). 1976. pap. text ed. 15.95x (ISBN 0-7121-0136-5, Pub. by Macdonald & Evans England). Intl Ideas.

Applied Statistics for Science & Industry. Albert Romano. 1977. text ed. 20.95x o.p. (ISBN 0-205-05575-3, 5655757); instr's manual avail. o.p. (ISBN 0-205-05576-1, 5655765). Allyn.

Applied Stochastic Processes. Ed. by G. Adomian. 1980. 21.00 (ISBN 0-12-044380-5). Acad Pr.

Applied Stream Sanitation. Clarence J. Velz. LC 71-120710. (Environmental Science & Technology Ser). 1970. 55.00 (ISBN 0-471-90525-9, Pub. by Wiley-Interscience). Wiley.

Applied Superconductivity, 2 vols. Vernon New House. 1975. Vol. 1. 60.00 (ISBN 0-12-517701-1); Vol. 2. 48.50 (ISBN 0-12-517702-X); Set. 88.25. Acad Pr.

Applied Surveillance Photography. Raymond P. Siljander. (Illus.). 120p. 1975. 14.50 (ISBN 0-398-03376-5). C C Thomas.

Applied Techniques for Cold Environments, 2 vols. Compiled By American Society of Civil Engineers. 1176p. 1978. pap. text ed. 64.00 (ISBN 0-87262-182-0). Am Soc Civil Eng.

Applied Thermodynamics for Engineering Technologists. 3rd ed. T. D. Eastop & A. McConkey. (Illus.). 1978. pap. text ed. 18.50x (ISBN 0-582-44197-8). Longman.

Applied Thermodynamics for Engineers. V. Srinijasan. (Illus.). 400p. Date not set. text ed. 25.00 (ISBN 0-7069-1177-6, Pub. by Vikas India). Advent Bk.

Applied Time Series Analysis for Managerial Forecasting. Charles R. Nelson. LC 72-88942. 350p. 1973. text ed. 23.95x (ISBN 0-8162-6366-3). Holden-Day.

Applied Time Series Analysis for the Social Sciences. Richard McCleary et al. LC 79-27873. (Illus.). 331p. 1980. 19.95 (ISBN 0-8039-1205-6); pap. 12.50 (ISBN 0-8039-1206-4). Sage.

Applied Underwater Acoustics. D. G. Tucker & B. K. Gazey. 1966. 27.00 (ISBN 0-08-011817-8); pap. 15.00 (ISBN 0-08-011816-X). Pergamon.

Applied Veterinary Anatomy. 2nd ed. Robert E. Habel. (Illus.). 1978. pap. text ed. 7.00x (ISBN 0-9600444-4-2). Habel.

Applied Veterinary Histology. William J. Banks. (Illus.). 540p. 1981. write for info. (0410-7). Williams & Wilkins.

Applied Water Resource Systems Planning. David C. Major & Roberto L. Lenton. (Environmental Sciences Ser.). (Illus.). 1979. text ed. 24.95 (ISBN 0-13-043364-0). P-H.

Applying Data Structures. Theodore G. Lewis & Marilyn Z. Smith. LC 75-25004. (Illus.). 1976. text ed. 21.95 (ISBN 0-395-24060-3). HM.

Applying Educational Research: A Practical Guide for Teachers. Walter R. Borg. 368p. (Orig.). 1981. text ed. 14.50 (ISBN 0-582-28145-8). Longman.

Applying Microprocessors. Electronics Magazine. Ed. by Stephen E. Scrupski & Laurence Altman. LC 76-30685. (Illus.). 191p. 1977. pap. text ed. 9.95 (ISBN 0-07-099705-5, R-701). McGraw.

Applying Norm-Referenced & Criterion-Referenced Measurement in Education. Victor R. Martuza. 1977. text ed. 19.95x (ISBN 0-205-05871-X); test items avail. (ISBN 0-685-71780-1). Allyn.

Applying the Assessment Center Method. J. L. Moses & C. Byham. LC 76-30476. 1978. text ed. 24.00 (ISBN 0-08-019581-4). Pergamon.

Appointment at Bloodstar. E. E. Smith & Stephen Goldin. (Family D'Alembert Ser: No. 5). 1978. pap. 1.50 (ISBN 0-515-04005-3). Jove Pubns.

Appointment in Calcutta. Elliot Tokson. 1979. pap. 1.95 o.p. (ISBN 0-449-14131-4, GM). Fawcett.

Appointment in Jerusalem. Lydia Prince & Derek Prince. 1978. pap. 2.50 o.p. (ISBN 0-8499-4109-1, 4109-1, Dist. by Word Bks.). Chosen Bks Pub.

Appointment in Samarra. John O'Hara. 1934. 3.00 o.p. (ISBN 0-394-41542-6). Random.

Appollinaire Guillaume: Alcools. Ed. by A. E. Pilkington. (French Texts Ser.). 1970. pap. text ed. 10.00x (ISBN 0-631-00710-5, Pub. by Basil Blackwell). Biblio Dist.

Appomatax Commander. Bernard Cresap. (Illus.). 384p. 1981. 15.00 (ISBN 0-498-02432-6). A S Barnes.

Apportionment Cases. Richard C. Cortner. LC 75-100408. 296p. 1970. 15.50x (ISBN 0-87049-107-5). U of Tenn Pr.

Appraisal & Development Through Objectives & Results. George L. Morrisey. (Illus.). 1972. pap. text ed. 8.95 (ISBN 0-201-04834-5). A-W.

Appraisal & Diagnosis of Speech & Language Disorders. H. Peterson & J. Marquardt. 1981. 18.95 (ISBN 0-13-043505-8). P-H.

Appraisal & Valuation Manuals, 1955-1971, 8 vols, Vols. 1-5 & 7-9. LC 56-15500. 15.00 ea. Vol. 1. 1955-56 (ISBN 0-937828-01-7). Vol. 2, 1956-57 (ISBN 0-937828-02-5). Vol. 3, 1958 (ISBN 0-937828-03-3). Vol. 4, 1959 (ISBN 0-937828-04-1). Vol. 5, 1960 (ISBN 0-937828-05-X). Vol. 7, 1962-63 (ISBN 0-937828-07-6). Vol. 8, 1964-65 (ISBN 0-937828-08-4). Vol. 9, 1966-71 (ISBN 0-937828-09-2). Am Soc Appraisers.

Appraisal Interview: Three Basic Approaches. Norman R. F. Maier. LC 75-40984. 228p. 1976. pap. 15.00 (ISBN 0-88390-111-0). Univ Assocs.

Appraisal Manual, 1981. 2nd ed. Robert S. Godfrey. 320p. 1981. pap. 33.00 (ISBN 0-911950-35-4). Means.

Appraisal of Development Projects: A Practical Guide to Project Analysis with Case Studies & Solutions. Michael Roemer & Joseph J. Stern. LC 74-30710. (Special Studies). (Illus.). 252p. 1975. text ed. 24.95 (ISBN 0-275-05960-X). Praeger.

Appraisal of Farmland: Use-Value Assessment Laws & Property Taxation, No. 8. new ed. American Society of Appraisers. LC 78-74140. (Monograph). 1979. pap. 5.00 (ISBN 0-937828-17-3). Am Soc Appraisers.

Appraisal of Halogenated Fire Extinguishing Agents. Committee on Fire Research & Committee on Toxicology. (Illus.). 360p. 1972. pap. 7.75 (ISBN 0-309-02111-1). Natl Acad Pr.

Appraisal of Intelligence. A. W. Heim. 1970. pap. text ed. 12.50x (ISBN 0-901225-62-2, NFER). Humanities.

Appraisal of Interperiod Income Tax Allocation. James E. Wheeler & William F. Galliart. LC 74-84803. 1974. 10.00 o.p. (ISBN 0-910586-10-1). Finan Exec.

Appraisal of Machinery & Equipment. LC 73-97948. (ASA Monograph: No. 2). 1969. 5.00 (ISBN 0-937828-11-4). Am Soc Appraisers.

Appraisal of Real Estate. 7th ed. American Institute of Real Estate Appraisers. 1978. 22.50 (ISBN 0-911780-46-7). Am Inst Real Estate Appraisers.

Appraisal of Roadside Advertising Signs. Donald T. Sutte, Jr. 1972. 7.00 (ISBN 0-911780-28-9). Am Inst Real Estate Appraisers.

Appraisal of Speech Pathology & Audiology: A Symposium. Ed. by John W. Wingo & Gordon F. Holloway. (Illus.). 220p. 1973. 16.75 (ISBN 0-398-02771-4). C C Thomas.

Appraisal of Teaching: Concepts & Process. Gary D. Borich. LC 76-6007. (Illus.). 1977. text ed. 14.95 (ISBN 0-201-00841-6). A-W.

Appraisal of the Nineteen-Fifty Census Income Data. G. Garvy. (National Bureau of Economic Research: F.23). 1958. 23.50 (ISBN 0-691-04102-4). Princeton U Pr.

Appraisal Principles & Procedures. Henry Babcock. 289p. 1980. pap. text ed. 20.00 (ISBN 0-937828-19-X). Am Soc Appraisers.

Appraiser & Real Estate Feasibility Studies. Reaves C. Lukens, Jr. 1972. 5.00 (ISBN 0-911780-30-0). Am Inst Real Estate Appraisers.

Appraising Educational Research: A Case Study Approach. Jason Millman & D. Gowin. LC 73-18004. (Educational Movement, Research & Statistics Ser.). (Illus.). 224p. 1974. pap. 10.95 ref. ed. (ISBN 0-13-043638-0). P-H.

Appraising Employee Performance. (Study Units Ser.) 1978. pap. 9.00 (ISBN 0-89401-107-3). Didactic Syst.

Appraising the Single Family Residence. George F. Bloom & Henry S. Harrison. 1978. 20.00 (ISBN 0-911780-40-8). Am Inst Real Estate Appraisers.

Appreciating Costume. Lucy Barton. 1969. pap. 4.50 (ISBN 0-685-06786-6). Baker's Plays.

Appreciating Poetry. Richard P. Sugg. 1975. pap. text ed. 9.50 (ISBN 0-395-19375-3); instructor's manual pap. 1.50 (ISBN 0-395-19373-7). HM.

Appreciation of Architecture: Landscape & Buildings. K. Lindley. (Illus.). 58p. 1972. text ed. 4.65 o.p. (ISBN 0-08-015677-0). Pergamon.

Appreciation of Literary Forms: Advanced Level. James A. Giroux & Glenn R. Williston. Ed. by Edward Spargo. (Comprehension Skills Ser). (Illus.). 1974. pap. text ed. 2.40x (ISBN 0-89061-018-5). Jamestown Pubs.

Appreciation of Literary Forms: Middle Level. Glenn R. Williston. (Comprehension Skills Ser.). (Illus.). 64p. 1976. pap. text ed. 2.40x (ISBN 0-89061-070-3, CB7M). Jamestown Pubs.

Apprentice to Genius: Years with Frank Lloyd Wright. Edgar Tafel. 1980. 19.95 (ISBN 0-07-062815-7). McGraw.

Apprenticeship of Duddy Kravitz. Mordecai Richler. Ed. by George Young. (Illus.). 288p. (Orig.). 1974. pap. 1.50 o.p. (ISBN 0-345-24154-1). Ballantine.

Apprenticeship of Duddy Kravitz. Mordecai Richler. 304p. 1981. pap. 2.95 (ISBN 0-553-14584-3). Bantam.

Apprenticeship Research: Emerging Findings & Future Trends. Ed. by Vernon M. Briggs, Jr. & Felician F. Foltman. 1981. pap. price not set (ISBN 0-87546-085-2). NY Sch Indus Rel.

Approach Interview to Owners of a Closely Held Corp. S. Monroe. 1981. 24.95 (ISBN 0-87863-209-3). Farnswth Pub. Postponed.

Approach of Operational Research to Planning in India. P. C. Mahalanobis. 1964. 6.50x o.p. (ISBN 0-210-27055-1). Asia.

Approach of War, 1938-1939. Christopher Thorne. (gr. 11 up). 1969. 6.95 (ISBN 0-312-04655-3). St Martin.

Approach to Chemical Analysis, 2 vols. H. N. Wilson. 1966. Set. 25.00 (ISBN 0-08-011543-8); Set. pap. 12.75 (ISBN 0-08-011542-X). Pergamon.

Approach to Econometrics. R. J. Allard. 227p. 1974. 18.75 (ISBN 0-470-02311-2). Krieger.

Approach to Econometrics. R. J. Allard. 240p. 1974. 27.00x (ISBN 0-86003-003-2, Pub. by Allan Pubs England); pap. 13.50x (ISBN 0-86003-102-0). State Mutual Bk.

Approach to Economics. Ludwig H. Mai. (Quality Paperback: No. 83). (Orig.). 1970. pap. 2.95 (ISBN 0-8226-0083-8). Littlefield.

Approach to Engineering Mathematics. A. H. Douglas. 1971. pap. 10.75 (ISBN 0-08-016016-6). Pergamon.

Approach to Environmental Psychology. Albert Mehrabian & James A. Russell. 266p. 1980. pap. 8.95x o.p. (ISBN 0-262-63071-0). MIT Pr.

Approach to Environmental Psychology. Albert Mehrabian & James A. Russsell. 240p. 1974. 15.00x (ISBN 0-262-13090-4); pap. 8.95x (ISBN 0-262-63071-0). MIT Pr.

Approach to Latin. James Paterson & Edwin Macnaughton. (Illus.). Pt. 1 1938. text ed. 5.00x (ISBN 0-05-000292-9); Pt. 2 1969. text ed. 5.00x (ISBN 0-05-000293-7). Longman.

Approach to Literature. 5th ed. Cleanth Brooks et al. 832p. 1975. ref. ed. 18.95x (ISBN 0-13-043802-2). P-H.

Approach to Occupational Therapy. 3rd ed. Ed. by M. S. Jones. P. Jay. 1977. 44.95 (ISBN 0-407-00053-4). Butterworths.

Approach to Print: A Basic Guide to the Printing Process. Roy Brewer. (Illus.). 165p. 1972. 7.50 o.p. (ISBN 0-7137-0531-0). Transatlantic.

Approach to the Further Education of the Physically Handicapped. John Panckhurst & Arthur G. McAllister. (Illus.). 139p. 1980. pap. text ed. 13.75x (ISBN 0-85633-195-3, NFER). Humanities.

Approach to Urban Sociology. Peter H. Mann. (International Library of Sociology & Social Reconstruction). 1965. text ed. 8.00x (ISBN 0-7100-3453-9). Humanities.

Approach to Zen: The Reality of Zazen. Kosho Uchiyama. LC 73-83957. (Illus.). 128p. 1973. pap. 4.75 o.p. (ISBN 0-87040-252-8). Japan Pubns.

Approaches. Elizabeth Klein. Ed. by Robert Bensen. (Chapbook: No. 5). 1980. pap. 3.75. Red Herring.

Approaches in Linguistic Methodology. Ed. by Irmengard Rauch & Charles T. Scott. 1967. 17.50x (ISBN 0-299-04240-5). U of Wis Pr.

Approaches Ser., No. 2: Our World. Peter Abbs. 1974. pap. text ed. 2.95x (ISBN 0-435-10022-X). Heinemann Ed.

Approaches to Archaeology. Peter J. Fowler. LC 77-81910. (Illus.). 1977. 18.95x (ISBN 0-312-04665-0). St Martin.

Approaches to Asian Civilizations. Ed. by William T. De Bary & Ainslie T. Embree. LC 63-20226. (Companions to Asian Studies). 1964. 17.50x (ISBN 0-231-02648-X). Columbia U Pr.

Approaches to Beginning Reading. Robert C. Aukerman. LC 70-144330. (Illus.). 1971. pap. text ed. 14.95 (ISBN 0-471-03691-9). Wiley.

Approaches to Canadian Politics. J. Redekop. 1978. pap. 11.25 (ISBN 0-13-043729-8). P-H.

Approaches to Controlling Air Pollution. Ann F. Friedlaender. LC 77-25484. (MIT Bicentennial Ser.: Vol. 3). 1978. 27.50x (ISBN 0-262-06064-7). MIT Pr.

Approaches to Counseling & Psychotherapy: A Brief Overview of Issues, Systems, & Applications. Ed. by Michael Braswell et al. LC 79-6845. 154p. 1980. pap. text ed. 7.75 (ISBN 0-8191-0964-9). U Pr of Amer.

Approaches to Democracy: Philosophy of Government at the Close of the Twentieth Century. W. J. Stankiewicz. 1981. 25.00 (ISBN 0-312-04668-5). St Martin.

Approaches to Drama. David A. Male. (Unwin Education Books). 1973. text ed. 25.00x (ISBN 0-04-372007-2); pap. text ed. 7.95x (ISBN 0-04-372008-0). Allen Unwin.

Approaches to E. M. Forester. Vasant A. Shahane. 1981. 10.25 (ISBN 0-391-02200-8). Humanities.

Approaches to Education for Character: Strategies for Change in Higher Education. Ed. by Clarence H. Faust & Jessica Feingold. LC 70-83386. 1969. 22.50x (ISBN 0-231-03262-5). Columbia U Pr.

Approaches to English Historical Linguistics: An Anthology. Ed. by Roger Lass. LC 69-14526. 1969. pap. text ed. 12.95x (ISBN 0-03-074505-5). Irvington.

Approaches to Faunal Analysis in the Middle East. Ed. by Richard H. Meadow & Melinda A. Zeder. LC 78-50908. (Peabody Museum Bulletin). 1978. pap. text ed. 10.00 (ISBN 0-87365-951-1). Peabody Harvard.

Approaches to Individualized Education. Ed. by Jan Jeter. LC 80-67363. 83p. (Orig.). 1980. pap. 4.75 (ISBN 0-87120-101-1, 611-80204). Assn Supervision.

Approaches to Insanity: A Philosophical & Sociological Study. Jeff Coulter. 170p. 1973. 23.50x (ISBN 0-85520-049-9, Pub. by Martin Robertson, England); pap. 11.50x (ISBN 0-85520-048-0). Biblio Dist.

Approaches to Language Testing. Ed. by Bernard Spolsky. LC 78-62080. (Advances in Language Testing Ser.: No. 2). 1978. pap. text ed. 4.95x (ISBN 0-87281-075-5). Ctr Appl Ling.

Approaches to Learning: The Best of ACLD, Vol. 1. Ed. by William M. Cruickshank. (Illus.). 240p. 1980. pap. 11.95x (ISBN 0-8156-2203-1). Syracuse U Pr.

Approaches to Marvell: The York Tercentenary Lectures. Ed. by C. A. Patrides. (Illus.). 1978. 28.00x (ISBN 0-7100-8818-3). Routledge & Kegan.

Approaches to Poetics. Ed. by Seymour Chatman. (Studies of the English Institute Ser.). 208p. 1973. text ed. 12.50x (ISBN 0-231-03781-3). Columbia U Pr.

Approaches to Poetry. 2nd ed. Walter Blair & W. K. Chandler. LC 52-13690. 1953. 38.00x (ISBN 0-89197-027-4); pap. text ed. 18.95x. Irvington.

Approaches to Science Fiction. Donald L. Lawler. LC 77-77995. (Illus.). 1978. pap. text ed. 10.50 (ISBN 0-395-25496-5); inst. manual 0.50 (ISBN 0-395-25497-3). HM.

Approaches to Self-Assessment in Foreign Language Learning. Mats Oskarsson. (PIE Council of Europe Language Learning Ser.). 1980. pap. 4.95 (ISBN 0-08-024594-3). Pergamon.

Approaches to Sociology: An Introduction to the Major Trends in British Sociology. Ed. by John Rex. (International Library of Sociology Ser.). 1974. 23.50x (ISBN 0-7100-7824-2); pap. 10.00 (ISBN 0-7100-7825-0). Routledge & Kegan.

Approaches to Teaching Chaucer's Canterbury Tales. Ed. by Joseph Gibaldi. LC 80-22909. (Approaches to Teaching Masterpieces of World Literature Ser.: No. 1). xvi, 175p. (Orig.). 1980. 13.50x (ISBN 0-87352-476-4); pap. 6.50x (ISBN 0-87352-475-6). Modern Lang.

Approaches to the Care of Adolescents. Kalafatich. 1975. 15.50 o.p. (ISBN 0-8385-0289-X). ACC.

Approaches to the History of Spain. rev. ed. Jaime Vicens Vives. Tr. by Joan C. Ullman. 1970. 14.50x (ISBN 0-520-01784-6); pap. 6.95x (ISBN 0-520-01422-7, CAMPUS22). U of Cal Pr.

Approaches to the Study of International Relations. 2nd ed. C. Boasson. (Polemological Studies: No. 2). (Illus.). 112p. 1972. pap. text ed. 9.25x (ISBN 90-232-0923-0). Humanities.

Approaches to the Study of Social Structure. Ed. by Peter M. Blau. LC 75-2809. 1975. 14.95 (ISBN 0-02-903650-X). Free Pr.

Approaches to the Theory of Optimization. J. Ponstein. LC 79-41419. (Cambridge Tracts in Mathematics: No. 77). (Illus.). 140p. 1980. 36.50 (ISBN 0-521-23155-8). Cambridge U Pr.

Approaches to the Validation of Manipulation Therapy. Alfred A. Buerger & Jerome S. Tobis. (Illus.). 352p. 1977. 34.50 (ISBN 0-398-03565-2). C C Thomas.

Approaches to Training & Development. Dugan Laird. LC 77-81193. (Illus.). 1978. text ed. 14.95 (ISBN 0-201-04112-X). A-W.

Approaches to Translation: Aspects of Translation. Peter Newmark. LC 80-41008. (MFLP Ser.). 160p. 1980. 23.95 (ISBN 0-08-024603-6); pap. 11.95 (ISBN 0-08-024602-8). Pergamon.

Approaches to Vocal Rehabilitation. Morton Cooper & Marcia H. Cooper. (Illus.). 420p. 1977. 29.75 (ISBN 0-398-03517-2). C C Thomas.

Approaching Collapse of the International Banking System. Alfred E. Sydell. (Illus.). 127p. 1981. 67.85 (ISBN 0-930008-75-8). Inst Econ Pol.

Approaching Oblivion: Road Signs on the Treadmill Toward Tomorrow. Harlan Ellison. LC 73-147791. 1974. 8.95 o.s.i. (ISBN 0-8027-5541-0). Walker & Co.

Approaching Sociology: A Critical Introduction. Margaret A. Coulson & C. Riddell. (Students Library of Sociology). 1970. 12.95 (ISBN 0-7100-6877-8); pap. 5.00 (ISBN 0-7100-6878-6). Routledge & Kegan.

Approaching the Peculiarity of the Caribbean Plight Within the Paradox of the Representative State in the Contemporary World-System. 37p. 1980. pap. 5.00 (ISBN 92-808-0135-X, TUNU 063, UNU). Unipub.

Appropriate Community Technologies Sourcebook. Ken Bossong & Jan Simpson. (Illus.). 180p. (Orig.). 1981. pap. text ed. 7.50 (ISBN 0-89988-055-X). Citizens Energy.

Appropriate Community Technologies Sourcebook, Vol. I. Ken Bossong & Jan Simpson. (Illus., Orig.). 1980. pap. 3.00 (ISBN 0-89988-056-8). Citizens Energy.

Appropriate Form: An Essay on the Novel. Barbara Hardy. 1971. pap. 5.95x o.s.i. (ISBN 0-8101-0335-4). Northwestern U Pr.

Appropriate Technology. Ram Das. 1981. 11.95 (ISBN 0-533-04744-7). Vantage.

Appropriate Technology in Water Supply & Waste Disposal: Proceedings. Environmental Impact Analysis Research Council at the Chicago National Convention, Oct. 1978. Ed. by American Society of Civil Engineers. 288p. 1979. pap. text ed. 17.00 (ISBN 0-87262-148-0). Am Soc Civil Eng.

Appropriate Technology: Scope for Co-Operation Among the Countries of the West African Economic Community. M. J. Woillet. Ed. by International Labour Office, Geneva. ii, 104p. (Orig.). 1980. pap. 5.70 (ISBN 92-2-102359-1). Intl Labour Office.

Appropriateness Review of Health Services: Manual for Lawyers, Planners & Hospitals. American Hospital Association. LC 80-23209. 128p. 1980. pap. 18.75 (ISBN 0-87258-336-8, 1527). Am Hospital.

Appropriating Hegel. Crawford Elder. Ed. by Andrew Brennan & William Lyons. (Scots Philosophical Monographs: Vol. 3). 116p. 1980. 12.00 (ISBN 0-08-025729-1). Pergamon.

Approval Plans & Academic Libraries. Kathleen McCullough et al. LC 77-8514. (Neal-Schuman Professional Bk). 1977. lib. bdg. 13.95x (ISBN 0-912700-05-X). Oryx Pr.

Approved Practices in Beautifying the Home Grounds. 5th ed. Norman K. Hoover. (Illus.). (gr. 9-12). 1979. 14.00 (ISBN 0-8134-2042-3, 2042); text ed. 10.50x (ISBN 0-685-42158-9). Interstate.

Approved Practices in Beef Cattle Production. 5th ed. Ed. by Edward M. Juergenson. (Illus.). (gr. 9-12). 1980. 14.00 (ISBN 0-8134-2093-8, 2093); text ed. 10.50x (ISBN 0-686-60695-7). Interstate.

Approved Practices in Crop Production. Elwood A. Brickbauer & William P. Mortenson. LC 77-89853. (Illus.). (gr. 9-12). 1978. 14.00 (ISBN 0-8134-1975-1, 1975); text ed. 10.50x (ISBN 0-685-03864-5). Interstate.

Approved Practices in Dairying. 4th ed. Elwood M. Juergenson & William P. Mortenson. LC 77-74120. (Illus.). (gr. 9-12). 1977. 14.00 (ISBN 0-8134-1954-9, 1954); text ed. 10.50x (ISBN 0-685-03866-1). Interstate.

Approved Practices in Feeds & Feeding. 5th ed. Daniel W. Cassard & Elwood M. Juergenson. LC 76-62743. (Illus.). (gr. 9-12). 1977. 14.00 (ISBN 0-8134-1901-8, 1901); text ed. 10.50x (ISBN 0-685-03868-8). Interstate.

Approved Practices in Fruit & Vine Production. 2nd ed. Arnold H. Scheer & E. M. Juergenson. (Illus.). 550p. 1976. 14.00 (ISBN 0-8134-1704-X, 1704); text ed. 10.50x (ISBN 0-685-55573-9). Interstate.

Approved Practices in Pasture Management. 3rd ed. Malcolm H. McVickar. LC 72-97443. (Illus.). (gr. 9-12). 1974. 13.00 o.p. (ISBN 0-8134-1547-0, 1547); text ed. 9.75x o.p. (ISBN 0-685-42160-0). Interstate.

Approved Practices in Raising & Handling Horses. Donald E. Ulmer & E. M. Juergenson. LC 73-80303. 1974. 14.00 (ISBN 0-8134-1594-2, 1594); text ed. 10.50x (ISBN 0-685-42152-X). Interstate.

Approved Practices in Sheep Production. 3rd ed. Elwood M. Juergenson. (Illus.). (gr. 9-12). 1981. 14.00 o.p. (ISBN 0-8134-2163-2, 2163); text ed. 10.50x o.p. (ISBN 0-685-03870-X). Interstate.

Approved Practices in Sheep Production. 4th ed. Elwood M Juergenson. (Illus.). (gr. 9-12). 1981. 13.00 (ISBN 0-8134-2163-2, 2163); text ed. 9.75x. Interstate.

Approved Practices in Soil Conservation. 4th ed. Albert B. Foster. LC 72-81495. (Illus.). 1973. 14.00 o.p. (ISBN 0-8134-1486-5, 1486); text ed. 10.50x o.p. (ISBN 0-685-42162-7). Interstate.

Approved Practices in Soil Conservation. 5th ed. Albert B. Foster. (Illus.). 1981. 13.00 (ISBN 0-8134-2170-5, 2170); text ed. 9.75x. Interstate.

Approved Practices in Swine Production. 5th ed. J. K. Baker & E. M. Juergenson. LC 79-142330. 1979. 14.00 (ISBN 0-8134-2038-5, 2038); text ed. 10.50x (ISBN 0-685-41955-X). Interstate.

Approximate Analysis of Randomly Excited Non-Linear Controls. Harold W. Smith. (Press Research Monographs: No. 34). 1966. 13.00x (ISBN 0-262-19027-3). MIT Pr.

Approximate Calculation of Multiple Integrals. A. Stroud. LC 77-159121. (Automatic Computation Ser). (Illus.). 1972. ref. ed. 26.95 (ISBN 0-13-043893-6). P-H.

Approximation, 2 Vols. in 1. Serge Bernstein & Charles D. Poussin. LC 69-16996. (Fr). 13.95 (ISBN 0-8284-0198-5). Chelsea Pub.

Approximation by Polynomials with Integral Coefficients. LeBaron O. Ferguson. LC 79-20331. (Mathematical Surveys: Vol. 17). 1980. 25.60 (ISBN 0-8218-1517-2). Am Math.

Approximation of Elliptic Boundary-Value Problems. new ed. Jean-Pierre Aubin. LC 79-26276. 386p. 1980. Repr. of 1972 ed. lib. bdg. 26.00 (ISBN 0-89874-077-0). Krieger.

Approximation of Functions by Polynomials & Splines. Ed. by S. B. Steckin. (Trudy Steklov: No. 145). Date not set. price not set o.p. (ISBN 0-8218-3049-X). Am Math.

Approximation of Functions: Theory & Numerical Methods. Guenter Meinardus. Tr. by L. L. Schumaker. LC 67-21464. (Springer Tracts in Natural Philosophy: Vol. 13). (Illus.). 1967. 41.30 (ISBN 0-387-03985-6). Springer-Verlag.

Approximation Theorems of Mathematical Statistics. Robert J. Serfling. LC 80-13493. (Wiley Ser. in Probability & Statistics: Probability & Mathematical Statistics). 400p. 1980. 34.95 (ISBN 0-471-02403-1). Wiley.

Approximation Theory & Methods. M. J. Powell. (Illus.). 300p. Date not set. price not set (ISBN 0-521-22472-1); pap. price not set (ISBN 0-521-29514-9). Cambridge U Pr.

Approximation Theory III. Ed. by E. W. Cheney. 1980. 59.00 (ISBN 0-12-171050-5). Acad Pr.

Aprenda a Ser Lider. G. S. Dobbins. Tr. by S. P. Molina from Eng. Orig. Title: Learning to Lead. 126p. (Span.). Date not set. pap. price not set (ISBN 0-311-17013-7). Casa Bautista.

Aprendamos a Amar a Dios. Richard Peace. Tr. by Grace S. Roberts from Eng. LC 75-29951. (Orig., Span.). 1975. pap. 1.50 (ISBN 0-89922-056-8). Edit Caribe.

Aprendamos a Amar a Otros. Richard Peace. Tr. by Grace S. Roberts from Eng. LC 75-29980. 71p. (Orig., Span.). 1975. pap. 1.50 (ISBN 0-89922-057-6). Edit Caribe.

Aprendamos a Amarnos a Nosotros Mismos. Richard Peace. Tr. by Grace S. Roberts from Eng. LC 75-29987. 69p. (Orig., Span.). 1975. pap. 1.50 (ISBN 0-89922-058-4). Edit Caribe.

Aprende En Espanol y En Ingles: Level 1-Reader B. Alicia Castroleal & Diamantina V. Suarez. 1979. pap. text ed. 2.50 (ISBN 0-88345-389-4); 5.25 o.p. (ISBN 0-88345-391-6). Regents Pub.

Aprende En Espanol y En Ingles: Readiness Level. Suarez & Castroleal. (gr. k-1). 1978. tchr's manual (a) 5.25 (ISBN 0-88345-364-9); tchr's manual (b) 5.25 (ISBN 0-88345-365-7); cassettes, teacher's manuals & spirit masters 100.00 (ISBN 0-685-78815-6). Regents Pub.

Apricot ABC. Miska Miles. LC 68-22072. (Illus.). (gr. k-3). 1969. 8.95 (ISBN 0-316-57030-3, Pub. by Atlantic Monthly Pr). Little.

April Fool. Alice Schertle. LC 80-21435. (Illus.). 32p. (gr. k-3). 1981. 7.95 (ISBN 0-688-41990-9); PLB 7.63 (ISBN 0-688-51990-3). Morrow.

April Fool Mystery. Joan L. Nixon & Ann Fay. LC 80-18809. (First Read-Alone Mysteries Ser.). (Illus.). 32p. (gr. 1-3). 1980. 5.50g (ISBN 0-8075-0406-8). A Whitman.

April Fourth, Nineteen Eighty-One: Pivotal Day in a Critical Year. Jim Gross et al. (Illus.). 1980. pap. 7.00 (ISBN 0-933646-12-7). Aries Pr.

April Game. Diogenes. 224p. 1981. pap. 2.50 (ISBN 0-87216-784-4). Playboy Pbks.

April Girl, No. 4. Iris Bromige. 192p. 1974. pap. 0.95 o.p. (ISBN 0-345-26663-3). Ballantine.

April Gold, No. 27. Grace L. Hill. 224p. 1980. pap. 1.95 (ISBN 0-553-14170-8). Bantam.

April Lady. Georgette Heyer. 288p. 1981. pap. 2.50 (ISBN 0-515-06004-6). Jove Pubns.

April of Enchantment. Maxine Patrick. (Orig.). 1981. pap. 1.75 (ISBN 0-451-09579-0, Sig). NAL.

April Snow. Lillian Budd. 1979. pap. 1.95 (ISBN 0-380-45401-7, 45401). Avon.

April Twilights (1903) rev. ed. Willa Cather. Ed. by Bernice Slote. LC 76-14216. (Illus.). 1976. pap. 2.25 (ISBN 0-8032-5851-8, BB 629, Bison). U of Nebr Pr.

Aptian & Albian Tetragonitidae (Ammonoidea) from Northern California. M. A. Murphy. (U. C. Publ. in Geological Sciences: Vol. 70). 1967. pap. 5.50x (ISBN 0-520-09173-6). U of Cal Pr.

Aptian Cenomanian Members of the Ammonite Genus Tetragonites. M. A. Murphy. (U. C. Publ. in Geological Sciences: Vol. 69). 1967. pap. 7.00x (ISBN 0-520-09172-8). U of Cal Pr.

Aptitude, Learning, & Instruction: Cognitive Process Analyses, Vol. 1. Ed. by Richard E. Snow et al. LC 80-18040. 368p. 1980. text ed. 29.95 (ISBN 0-89859-043-4). L Erlbaum Assocs.

Aptitude, Learning, & Instruction: Cognitive Process Analyses, Vol. 2. Ed. by Richard E. Snow et al. LC 80-18039. 352p. 1980. text ed. 29.95 (ISBN 0-89859-046-9). L Erlbaum Assocs.

Aptitude Testing at Eighteen Plus. Bruce Choppin & Lea Orr. (NFER Research Reports). 160p. (Orig.). 1976. pap. text ed. 13.75x (ISBN 0-85633-109-0, NFER). Humanities.

Aptitudes & Instructional Methods: A Handbook for Research on Interactions. Lee J. Cronbach & Richard E. Snow. LC 76-5510. (Illus.). 1981. pap. text ed. 18.50x (ISBN 0-8290-0103-4). Irvington.

Aptoelectronics: Growth G-062. 1981. 850.00 (ISBN 0-89336-286-7). BCC.

Apuleius & His Influence. Elizabeth H. Haight. LC 63-10290. (Our Debt to Greece & Rome Ser). (Illus.). 190p. 1963. Repr. of 1930 ed. 17.50x (ISBN 0-8154-0108-6). Cooper Sq.

Apuleius & the Golden Ass. James Tatum. LC 78-74220. (Illus.). 1979. 15.00x (ISBN 0-8014-1163-7). Cornell U Pr.

Apuleius philosophus Platonicus: Untersuchungen zur Apologie (De magia) und zu De Mundo. Frank Regen. (Untersuchungen zur antiken Literatur und Geschichte, 10). 123p. 1971. 26.00x (ISBN 3-11-003678-9). De Gruyter.

Apu's Initiation. Rupendra G. Majumdar. (Redbird Bk.). 45p. 1976. lib. bdg. 9.00 (ISBN 0-89253-090-1); flexible bdg 4.80 (ISBN 0-89253-130-4). Ind-US Inc.

Aqquyunlu: Clan, Confederation, & Empire. John E. Woods. LC 74-27613. (Studies in Middle Eastern History: No. 3). 1976. 27.50x (ISBN 0-88297-011-9). Bibliotheca.

Aqua - Rhythmics: Exercises for the Swimmimg Pool. Ilse Nolte-Heuritsch. LC 78-57782. (Illus.). 1978. 7.95 (ISBN 0-8069-4130-8); lib. bdg. 7.49 (ISBN 0-8069-4131-6); pap. 4.95 o.p. (ISBN 0-8069-4132-4). Sterling.

Aqua-Vu: A Limnological Reconnaissance Study of Lago Di Braies ("Prager Wildsee) Dolomites, N. Italy. G. B. Engelen. (Communications of the Inst. of Earth Sciences, Ser. A.: No. 1). (Illus.). 63p. (Orig.). 1976. pap. text ed. 8.75x (ISBN 9-0620-3317-2). Humanities.

Aqua-Vu: Groundwater Hydraulics. J. J. De Vries. (Communications of the Inst. of Earth Sciences, Ser. A.: No. 6). 45p. 1975. pap. text ed. 8.75x (ISBN 0-685-66840-1). Humanities.

Aqua-Vu: Some Calculation Method for Determination of the Travel Time of Groundwater. J. J. DeVries & C. A. J. Appelo. (Communications of the Inst. of Earth Sciences, Ser. A: No. 5). pap. text ed. 8.75x (ISBN 0-685-78791-5). Humanities.

Aqua-Vua: A Catalogue of Hydrological Research Projects Over the Period 1966-1972 in the Hydrology Program of the Inst. of Earth Sciences, Amsterdam, No. 2. G. B. Engelen. (Communication of the Institute of Earth Sciences, Ser. A: No. 2). 35p. 1976. pap. text ed. 4.75x (ISBN 0-685-66839-8). Humanities.

Aquacultural Engineering. F. W. Wheaton. LC 77-22876. (Ocean Engineering Ser.). 1977. 47.50 (ISBN 0-471-93755-X, Pub by Wiley-Interscience). Wiley.

Aquaculture & Algae Culture-Processes & Products. A. Shaw Watson. LC 79-17067. (Food Technology Review: No. 53). (Illus.). 1980. 32.00 (ISBN 0-8155-0779-8). Noyes.

Aquaculture Development in China: Report on an FAO-UNEP Aquaculture Study Tour to the People's Republic of China. 73p. 1980. pap. 6.00 (ISBN 92-5-100811-6, F1861, FAO). Unipub.

Aquaculture Economics: Basic Concepts & Methods of Analysis. Yung C. Shang. (Westview Special Studies in Agricultural Sciences). 140p. 1981. lib. bdg. 17.50x (ISBN 0-86531-047-5). Westview.

Aquaculture in Alaska: A Resource Potential. write for info. (ISBN 0-914500-03-1). U of AK Inst Marine.

Aquaculture in the United States: Constraints & Opportunities. Board on Renewable Resources. 1978. pap. 7.50 (ISBN 0-309-02740-3). Natl Acad Pr.

Aquaculture of Grey Mullets. Ed. by O. H. Oren. LC 79-53405. (International Biological Programme: No. 26). (Illus.). 450p. Date not set. price not set (ISBN 0-521-22926-X). Cambridge U Pr.

Aquaculture Practices in Taiwan. T. P. Chen. (Illus.). 176p. 13.75 (ISBN 0-85238-080-1, FN). Unipub.

Aquametry: A Treatise on Methods for the Determination of Water, Part 1. 2nd ed. John Mitchell, Jr. & Donald M. Smith. LC 77-518. (Chemical Analysis Ser: Vol. 5). 1977. 46.50 (ISBN 0-471-02264-0). Wiley.

Aquametry: A Treatise on Methods for the Determination of Water, Pt. 3. 2nd ed. John Mitchell, Jr. & Donald M. Smith. LC 77-518. (Chemical Analysis Ser.). 1980. 80.00 (ISBN 0-471-02266-7, Pub. by Wiley-Interscience). Wiley.

Aquarelle & Watercolor Complete. J. Van Ingen. LC 78-180461. (Illus.). 80p. (YA) 1972. 12.95 o.p. (ISBN 0-8069-5210-5); PLB 11.69 o.p. (ISBN 0-8069-5211-3). Sterling.

Aquarian Anastasis. Lew P. Price. LC 65-9503. 1975. pap. 5.95 (ISBN 0-917578-01-5). Eternal Ent.

Aquarian Revelations. Brad Steiger. (Orig.). 1980. pap. cancelled o.p. (ISBN 0-89407-029-0). Strawberry Hill.

Aquarium. Stewart Conn. 1980. pap. 4.95 (ISBN 0-7145-3560-5). Riverrun NY.

Aquarium. David LeRoi. 5.50x (ISBN 0-392-06613-0, LTB). Soccer.

Aquarium Ecology. Hellmuth Wachtel. Tr. by Gwynne Vevers from Ger. (Illus.). 128p. 1973. pap. 4.95 (ISBN 0-87666-024-3, PS-964). TFH Pubns.

Aquarium Fish. U. Erich Friese. (Illus.). 96p. 1980. 2.95 (ISBN 0-87666-512-1, KW026). TFH Pubns.

Aquarium Fish Diseases. Rolf Geisler. (Illus., Orig.). 1963. pap. 2.00 (ISBN 0-87666-008-1, M516). TFH Pubns.

Aquarium Fishes. Dick Mills. LC 80-80742. (Arco Fact Guides in Color Ser.). (Illus.). 128p. 1980. 7.95 (ISBN 0-668-04944-8, 4944-8). Arco.

Aquarium Fishes in Color. J. M. Madsen. LC 74-31451. (Illus.). 224p. 1975. 6.95 o.s.i. (ISBN 0-02-579170-2, 57917). Macmillan.

Aquarium Guide. Jim Kelly. 6.98 o.p. (ISBN 0-385-01557-7). Doubleday.

Aquariums. Anthony Evans. (Foyle's Handbks). 1973. 3.95 (ISBN 0-685-55811-8). Palmetto Pub.

Aquarius. James A. Lely. (Sun Signs Ser.). (Illus.). (gr. 4-12). 1978. PLB 5.95 (ISBN 0-87191-651-7); pap. 2.95 (ISBN 0-89812-080-2). Creative Ed.

Aquarius. Julia Parker. (Pocket Guides to Astrology Ser.). (Orig.). 1980. pap. write for info. (ISBN 0-671-25555-X, Fireside). S&S.

Aquatic & Wetland Plants of Southeastern United States: Dicotyledons. Robert K. Godfrey & Jean W. Wooten. LC 80-16452. (Illus.). 864p. 1981. lib. bdg. 40.00x (ISBN 0-8203-0532-4). U of Ga Pr.

Aquatic Animal Health. Agricultural Board. LC 73-15707. 1973. pap. 3.00 (ISBN 0-309-02142-1). Natl Acad Pr.

Aquatic Buildings - Baederbauten: Vol. 2, Reference Book on Aquatic Buildings, Establishments & Facilities, Construction-Plant-Equipment-Operation-Economy. Dietrich Fabian. LC 72-595812. (Illus.). 560p. 1970. 62.50x (ISBN 3-7667-0185-1). Intl Pubns Serv.

Aquatic Chemistry: An Introduction Emphasizing Chemical Equilibria in Natural Waters. 2nd ed. Werner Stumm & James J. Morgan. 806p. 1981. 38.00 (ISBN 0-471-04831-3, Pub. by Wiley-Interscience). Wiley.

Aquatic Diptera. Oskar A. Johannsen. LC 78-7782. (Illus.). 370p. 1969. Repr. of 1937 ed. 17.50 (ISBN 0-911836-01-2); pap. 8.95 o.p. (ISBN 0-911836-03-9). Entomological Repr.

Aquatic Ecosystems: An Operational Research Approach. Jan Erik Beyer. LC 79-57217. (Illus.). 316p. 1981. 20.00 (ISBN 0-295-95719-0). U of Wash Pr.

Aquatic Insects of California, with Keys to North American Genera & California Species. Ed. by Robert L. Usinger. (Illus.). 1956. 22.75x (ISBN 0-520-01293-3). U of Cal Pr.

Aquatic Microbiology. 2nd ed. G. Rheinheimer. LC 79-40645. 240p. 1980. 28.00 (ISBN 0-471-27643-X, Pub. by Wiley-Interscience). Wiley.

Aquatic Microbiology. Gerhard Rheinheimer. LC 72-8615. 220p. 1974. 21.00 o.p. (ISBN 0-471-71803-3, Pub. by Wiley-Interscience). Wiley.

Aquatic Miniatures. (Wild, Wild World of Animals Ser.). (Illus.). 1979. lib. bdg. 11.97 (ISBN 0-686-51179-4). Silver.

Aquatic Oligochaete Biology. Ed. by Ralph O. Brinkhurst & David G. Cook. 530p. 1980. 55.00 (ISBN 0-306-40338-2). Plenum Pub.

Aquatic Pollution. Edward A. Laws. LC 80-23311. (Environmental Science & Technology Ser.). 600p. 1981. 35.00 (ISBN 0-471-05797-5, Pub. by Wiley-Interscience). Wiley.

Aqui Mismo. Kenneth R. Scholberg & Diana E. Scholberg. (Illus., Orig.). 1980. pap. text ed. 6.95 (ISBN 0-88377-148-9). Newbury Hse.

Aquinas. Anthony Kenney. 86p. 1980. 7.95 (ISBN 0-8090-2724-0); pap. 2.95 (ISBN 0-8090-1407-6). Hill & Wang.

Aquinas & Natural Law. Daniel J. O'Connor. (New Studies in Ethics Series). (Orig.). 1969. pap. 4.95 (ISBN 0-312-04690-1). St Martin.

Aquinas Reader. Ed. by Mary T. Clark. LC 72-76709. pap. 3.50 (ISBN 0-385-02505-X, Im). Doubleday.

Aquis Submersus. Theodor Storm. Ed. by Patricia M. Boswell. (Blackwell's German Text Ser.). 1974. pap. 9.95x (ISBN 0-631-01920-0, Pub. by Basil Blackwell). Biblio Dist.

Ar-Rafed: Arabic-Arabic Dictionary. Al-Amir Nasiruddin. 1971. 16.00x (ISBN 0-685-72028-4). Intl Bk Ctr.

ARA: A Brief Exposition of Arabic & Islamic Scientific Heritage. A. A. Al-Daffa. 1979. pap. text ed. 10.95 (ISBN 0-471-05348-1). Wiley.

ARA Engineering Mechanics, 2 vols. J. L. Heriman. Incl. Vol. 1. SI Statics (ISBN 0-471-06312-6); Vol. 2. SI Dynamics (ISBN 0-471-06311-8). 1980. 18.95 ea. Wiley.

ARA Principles of Refrigeration: SI Version. 2nd ed. R. J. Dossat. 1980. 14.95 (ISBN 0-471-06326-6). Wiley.

ARA University Calculus & Subjects of the Plane: Arabic Edition. C. Wade. 1981. pap. price not set (ISBN 0-471-06324-X). Wiley.

Arab-African Connection: Political & Economic Realities. Victor T. Levine & Timothy W. Luke. (Special Studies on Africa & the Middle East). 1979. lib. bdg. 18.00x (ISBN 0-89158-398-X). Westview.

Arab Americans Almanac. 3rd ed. (Illus.). 300p. 1981. pap. 12.00 (ISBN 0-685-65297-1). News Circle.

Arab & Persian Painting in the Fogg Art Museum, Vol. II. Marianna S. Simpson. Ed. by Peter Walsh & Andrea Kaliski. LC 80-10525. (Fogg Art Museum Handbooks). (Illus.). 125p. 1980. pap. 8.50 (ISBN 0-916724-10-7). Fogg Art.

Arab Awakening. George Antonius. 16.00x (ISBN 0-685-77089-3). Intl Bk Ctr.

Arab Border-Villages in Israel. Abner Cohen. 1965. text ed. 28.00x (ISBN 0-7190-0251-6). Humanities.

Arab Boycott of Israel: Economic Aggression and World Reaction. Dan S. Chill. LC 76-14431. 1976. text ed. 24.95 (ISBN 0-275-56810-5). Praeger.

Arab Business Yearbook Nineteen Eighty. Date not set. 39.50 (ISBN 0-531-03945-5). Watts.

Arab Civilization to A.D. 1500. Douglas Dunlop. (Arab Background Ser.). 1971. 25.00x (ISBN 0-685-77094-X). Intl Bk Ctr.

Arab Conquest of Egypt & the Last Thirty Years of the Roman Dominion. Alfred J. Butler. Ed. by P. M. Fraser. 1978. text ed. 52.00x (ISBN 0-19-821678-5). Oxford U Pr.

Arab Development Funds in the Middle East. Soliman Demir. LC 79-503. (Pergamon Policy Studies). 1979. 28.00 (ISBN 0-08-022489-X). Pergamon.

Arab Executive. MUNA. LC 80-13711. 1980. write for info. (ISBN 0-312-04697-9). St Martin.

Arab Heritage. Ed. by Nabih A. Faris. LC 79-2856. 279p. 1981. Repr. of 1944 ed. 23.50 (ISBN 0-8305-0030-8). Hyperion Conn.

Arab Historians of the Crusades. Ed. by Francesco Gabrieli. (Islamic World Ser.). 1978. 20.00x (ISBN 0-520-03616-6). U of Cal Pr.

Arab Industrialization & Economic Integration. Ed. by Roberto Aliboni. LC 78-10632. 1979. 23.95 (ISBN 0-312-04702-9). St Martin.

Arab-Islamic Bibliography: Based on Giuseppe Gabrieli's Manvale Di Bibliografia Muselmana. Ed. by Diana Grimwood-Jones et al. 1977. text ed. 52.00x (ISBN 0-391-00691-6). Humanities.

Arab-Israel Conflict & U N. Ed. by Avrahm G. Mezerik. 1962. pap. 25.00 (ISBN 0-685-13185-8, 73). Intl Review.

Arab-Israeli Conflict. Schools Council History 13-16 Project. (Modern World Problems Ser.). (Illus.). 1979. Repr. of 1977 ed. lib. bdg. 9.95 (ISBN 0-912616-68-7); pap. text ed. 4.45 (ISBN 0-912616-67-9). Greenhaven.

Arab-Israeli Conflict: A Historical, Political, Social, & Military Bibliography. Ronald M. DeVore. LC 76-17575. (War-Peace Bibliography Ser.: No. 4). 273p. 1976. text ed. 9.65 (ISBN 0-87436-229-6). ABC-Clio.

Arab-Israeli Conflict: Psychological Obstacles to Peace. Daniel Heradstveit. 1979. pap. 23.50x (ISBN 82-00-01822-9, Dist. by Columbia U Pr.). Universitet.

Arab-Israeli Dilemma. 2nd ed. Fred J. Khouri. LC 68-20483. 1976. pap. 6.95x (ISBN 0-8156-2178-7). Syracuse U Pr.

Arab-Israeli Military Political Relations: Arab Perceptions & the Politics of Escalation. John W. Amos. 1979. text ed. 39.50 (ISBN 0-08-023865-3). Pergamon.

Arab-Israeli War, Nineteen Forty-Eight. Edgar O'Ballance. LC 79-2877. (Illus.). 220p. 1981. Repr. of 1957 ed. 19.75 (ISBN 0-8305-0045-6). Hyperion Conn.

Arab Lands of Western Asia. Joseph J. Malone. LC 73-5948. (Illus.). 288p. 1973. ref. ed. 13.95x (ISBN 0-13-043968-1); pap. text ed. 9.95 (ISBN 0-13-043950-9). P-H.

Arab Marco Polo: Ibn Battuta. Lucile McDonald. LC 75-4651. (Illus.). 160p. (gr. 6 up). 1975. 7.95 (ISBN 0-525-66441-6). Elsevier-Nelson.

Arab Maritime Data Nineteen Eighty. (Benn Directories Ser.). 1980. 92.50 (ISBN 0-686-60662-0, Pub by Benn Pubns). Nichols Pub.

Arab Nation: Nationalism & Class Struggle. Samir Amin. 116p. 1978. 12.95 (Pub. by Zed Pr); pap. 4.95 (ISBN 0-905762-23-1). Lawrence Hill.

Arab Nationalism: A Critical Inquiry. Ed. by Bassam Tibi. 1980. 20.00 (ISBN 0-312-04716-9). St Martin.

Arab Nationalism: An Anthology. Ed. by Sylvia G. Haim. (California Library Reprint Ser.). 1974. 19.50x (ISBN 0-520-02645-4); pap. 3.85 (ISBN 0-520-03043-5). U of Cal Pr.

Arab of the Desert: A Glimpse into Badawin Life in Kuwait & Saudi Arabia. H. R. Dickson. 1952. 47.50 o.p. (ISBN 0-04-953001-1). Allen Unwin.

Arab Oil & Gas Directory 1979-80. 5th ed. The Arab Petroleum Research Center, Paris. LC 75-646597. (Illus.). 415p. 1979. 150.00x (ISBN 0-8002-2231-8). Intl Pubns Serv.

Arab Oil: Impact on Arab Countries & Global Implications. Naiem A. Sherbiny. Ed. by Mark A. Tessler. LC 75-19820. (Special Studies). (Illus.). 340p. 1976. text ed. 34.95 (ISBN 0-275-55810-X). Praeger.

Arab Politics: The Search for Legitimacy. Michael C. Hudson. LC 77-75379. 1977. 27.50x (ISBN 0-300-02043-0); pap. 8.95 (ISBN 0-300-02411-8). Yale U Pr.

Arab Predicament: Arab Political Thought & Practice Since 1967. Fouad Ajami. 250p. Date not set. price not set (ISBN 0-521-23914-1). Cambridge U Pr.

Arab Press: News Media & Political Process in the Arab World. William A. Rugh. (Illus.). 224p. 1979. 18.00x (ISBN 0-8156-2191-4); pap. 6.95s (ISBN 0-8156-0159-X). Syracuse U Pr.

Arab Response to Multinationals. Riad A. Ajami. 1979. 20.95 (ISBN 0-03-048436-7). Praeger.

Arab Strategies & Israel's Response. Yehoshafat Harkabi. LC 77-70273. 1977. 12.95 (ISBN 0-02-913760-8); pap. 4.95 (ISBN 0-02-913780-2). Free Pr.

Arab Tells His Story; a Study in Loyalties. Edward S. Atiyah. LC 79-3071. (Illus.). 229p. 1981. Repr. of 1946 ed. 19.75 (ISBN 0-8305-0023-5). Hyperion Conn.

Arab-Turkish Relations & the Emergence of Arab Nationalism. Zeine N. Zeine. LC 80-25080. 156p. 1981. Repr. of 1958 ed. lib. bdg. 19.75x (ISBN 0-313-22705-5, ZEAT). Greenwood.

Arab Village: A Social Structural Study of a Transjordanian Peasant Community. Richard T. Antoun. LC 70-633555. (Social Science Ser.: No. 29). (Illus.). 210p. 1972. pap. 15.00x (ISBN 0-253-38450-8). Ind U Pr.

Arab Women. Ed. by Ann Dearden. (Minority Rights Reports Ser.: No. 27). 20p. 1976. pap. 2.50 (ISBN 0-89192-037-4). Interbk Inc.

Arab World: A Guide to Business, Economics & Industrial Information Sources. Joseph O. Mekeirle. LC 79-91352. 1980. 75.00 (ISBN 0-916400-07-7). Inter Crescent.

Arab World: Fourth Edition of the United States & the Arab World. William R. Polk. LC 80-16995. (American Foreign Policy Library). 1981. text ed. 22.50x (ISBN 0-674-04316-2); pap. text ed. 8.95x (ISBN 0-674-04317-0). Harvard U Pr.

Arab World in the Twentieth Century. T. R. Little. LC 77-179782. (Young Historian Ser.). (Illus.). 112p. (gr. 8-10). 1972. 4.50 o.p. (ISBN 0-381-99763-4, A05300, JD-J). John Day.

Arab World Today. Richard Tames. (Today Ser.). (Illus.). 96p. 1980. text ed. 15.00x (ISBN 0-7182-0461-1, SpS). Soccer.

Arabe Francais Dictionnaire, 2 vols. Kazirmski. 70.00x (ISBN 0-686-63571-X). Intl Bk Ctr.

Arabel & Mortimer. Joan Aiken. LC 79-6577. (Illus.). 160p. (gr. 4 up). 1981. 9.95a (ISBN 0-385-15642-1); PLB (ISBN 0-385-15643-X). Doubleday.

Arabella, Lyrische Komodie in Drei Aufzugen. Hugo Von Hofmannsthal. Ed. by Hugo Schmidt. (Ger). 1963. pap. 2.95x (ISBN 0-393-09605-X, NortonC). Norton.

Arabesques. Nikolai Gogol. Tr. by Alexander Tulloch from Rus. 1981. 17.50 (ISBN 0-88233-435-2). Ardis Pubs.

Arabia. David G. Hogarth. LC 79-2862. 139p. 1981. Repr. of 1922 ed. 15.00 (ISBN 0-8305-0036-7). Hyperion Conn.

Arabia, the Gulf, & the West: A Critical View of Arabs & Their Oil Policy. John B. Kelly. LC 80-80787. 530p. 1980. 25.00 (ISBN 0-465-00415-6). Basic.

Arabian Gulf Government & Public Services Directory 1980-81. 1980. 175.00x (Pub. by Parrish-Rogers England). State Mutual Bk.

Arabian Highlands. J. B. Philby. LC 76-10643. (Middle East in the 20th Century). 1976. Repr. of 1952 ed. lib. bdg. 55.00 (ISBN 0-306-70765-9). Da Capo.

Arabian Medicine. Edward G. Browne. LC 79-2852. (Illus.). 138p. 1981. Repr. of 1962 ed. 16.00 (ISBN 0-8305-0028-6). Hyperion Conn.

Arabian Nights. Padraic Colum. (Illus.). (gr. 4-6). 1964. 4.95 o.s.i. (ISBN 0-02-722940-8). Macmillan.

Arabian Nights. Ed. by Kate Wiggins & Nora Smith. 1974. pap. 3.95 o.p. (ISBN 0-684-13809-3, SL523, ScribT). Scribner.

Arabian Peninsula, Red Sea, & Gulf: Strategic Considerations. Ed. by Enver M. Koury & Emile A. Nakhleh. LC 79-88430. 100p. 1979. pap. 6.00 (ISBN 0-934484-14-7). Inst Mid East & North Africa.

Arabian Studies-One. Ed. by R. B. Serjeant & R. L. Bidwell. (Illus.). 200p. 1974. 21.50x o.p. (ISBN 0-87471-482-6). Rowman.

Arabian Transport Directory 1980-81. 1980. 95.00x (Pub. by Parrish-Rogers England). State Mutual Bk.

Arabic-Arabic Dictionary. Muhit Al Muhit & Butrus Al-Bustani. 50.00 (ISBN 0-686-53117-5). Intl Bk Ctr.

Arabic-Arabic Dictionary of the Names of Towns & Villages in Lebanon. Annis Freyha. 1974. 15.00x (ISBN 0-685-72040-3). Intl Bk Ctr.

Arabic Conversation. Mounir Ghandour. pap. 5.00; book & cassettes 30.00. Intl Bk Ctr.

Arabic Dialogue, 4 vols. Hana Fakoury. pap. text ed. 25.00 (ISBN 0-686-63574-4). Intl Bk Ctr.

Arabic-English Advanced Learners Dictionary. Anthony Salmone. 30.00x (ISBN 0-685-89874-1). Intl Bk Ctr.

Arabic-English Dictionary. William Wortabet. 1968. 18.00x (ISBN 0-685-72027-6). Intl Bk Ctr.

Arabic-English Dictionary: Colloquial Arabic of Egypt. Socrates Spiro. 1973. 25.00 (ISBN 0-685-77125-3). Intl Bk Ctr.

Arabic-English Dictionary of Agricultural Terms. Ahmad Khatib. pap. 10.00x (ISBN 0-685-89876-8). Intl Bk Ctr.

Arabic-English; English-Arabic Dictionary. Wortabet & Porter. 1979. 15.00 (ISBN 0-685-96662-3). Intl Bk Ctr.

Arabic-English Learners Dictionary. F. Steingass. 1972. 30.00 (ISBN 0-685-77126-1). Intl Bk Ctr.

Arabic English Lexicon in 8 Volumes. Wm. Lane. 230.00x (ISBN 0-685-77121-0). Intl Bk Ctr.

Arabic-English Pocket Dictionary. John Wortabet. 1980. pap. 5.50x. Intl Bk Ctr.

Arabic-English Students Dictionary. Dar El Mashreq. 12.00x (ISBN 0-686-53116-7). Intl Bk Ctr.

Arabic External Sources for the History of Africa to the South of Sahara. Tadeusz Lewicki. (Illus.). 102p. (Orig.). 1974. pap. text ed. 6.50x (ISBN 0-7007-0020-X). Humanities.

Arabic for Beginners. Abu-Samayah. 1976. pap. 8.00x (ISBN 0-685-88940-8). Intl Bk Ctr.

Arabic Grammar. G. M. Wickens. LC 77-82523. 180p. 1980. write for info. (ISBN 0-521-21885-3); pap. 12.95 (ISBN 0-521-29301-4). Cambridge U Pr.

Arabic Handwriting Workbook. Lily Sayegh. 1979. 4.50x (ISBN 0-917062-03-5). Intl Bk Ctr.

Arabic in a Nutshell. Dilaver Berberi. (Funk & W Bk.). 256p. 1975. pap. 2.95 o.s.i. (ISBN 0-308-10145-6, F106, TYC-T). T Y Crowell.

Arabic Materials in English Translation: A Bibliography of Works from the Pre-Islamic Period to 1977 Arabic. Margaret Anderson. 1980. lib. bdg. 22.50 (ISBN 0-8161-7954-9). G K Hall.

Arabic Phonology: An Acoustical & Physiological Investigation. Salman H. Al-Ani. (Janua Linguarum, Ser. Practica: No. 61). 1970. pap. text ed. 31.75x (ISBN 90-2790-727-7). Mouton.

Arabic: Phonology & Script. Al-Ani & Shammas. 1980. 9.00x (ISBN 0-917062-04-3). Intl Bk Ctr.

Arabic Poetry: A Primer for Students. Arthur J. Arberry. (Orig.). 1965. 36.00 (ISBN 0-521-04037-X); pap. 13.50x (ISBN 0-521-09257-4). Cambridge U Pr.

Arabic Proverbs: Or the Manners & Customs of the Modern Egyptian Illustrated from Their Proverbial Sayings Current at Cairo. Tr. by J. K. Burckhardt. 1972. Repr. text ed. 12.50x (ISBN 0-7007-0019-6). Humanities.

Arabic Standard Atlas. Mohammed Nasr. (Arabic.). pap. 10.00x. Intl Bk Ctr.

Arabic Thought and Its Place in History. rev. ed. De Lacy O'Leary. LC 80-1917. 1981. Repr. of 1939 ed. 35.00 (ISBN 0-404-18982-2). AMS Pr.

Arabs. Edward Atiyah. (Arab Background Ser.). 1968. pap. 6.95x (ISBN 0-685-77090-7). Intl Bk Ctr.

Arabs. Maxime Rodinson. Tr. by Arthur Goldhammer. LC 80-25916. (Illus.). 140p. 1981. lib. bdg. price not set (ISBN 0-226-72355-0); pap. price not set (ISBN 0-226-72356-9). U of Chicago Pr.

Arabs & the English. 2nd ed. Sari J. Nasir. (Illus.). 1980. pap. 9.50 (ISBN 0-582-78306-2). Longman.

Arabs & the Islamic World. Frank Ross, Jr. LC 78-13219. (Illus.). (gr. 7 up). 1979. 10.95 (ISBN 0-87599-220-X). S G Phillips.

Arabs & Zionism Before World War One. Neville Mandel. LC 73-78545. 1977. 20.00 o.p. (ISBN 0-520-02466-4); pap. 4.95 (ISBN 0-520-03940-8). U of Cal Pr.

Arabs, Christians, Jews. James Hefley & Marti Hefley. 1978. 7.95 o.p. (ISBN 0-88270-290-4). Logos.

Arabs in the Jewish State: Israel's Control of a National Minority. Ian Lustick. (Modern Middle East Ser.: No. 6). 400p. 1980. text ed. 19.95x (ISBN 0-292-70347-3); pap. 10.95 (ISBN 0-292-70348-1). U of Tex Pr.

Arabs Today. Joel Carmichael. LC 76-41554. 240p. 1977. pap. 2.95 (ISBN 0-385-11351-X, Anch). Doubleday.
Arachidonic Acid Metabolism in Inflammation & Thrombosis: Proceedings of the First European Workshop on Inflammation, Basel, 1979. Ed. by K. Brune & M. Baggiolini. (Agents & Actions Supplements: No. 4). (Illus.). 1979. pap. 38.00 (ISBN 3-7643-1095-2). Birkhauser.
Arachnids. Keith R. Snow. LC 70-109151. 1970. 15.00x (ISBN 0-231-03419-9). Columbia U Pr.
Aragonese Version of the Libro De Marco Polo. John J. Nitti. 1980. write for info. Hispanic Seminary.
Arakawa. The Minneapolis Institute of Arts. (Illus.). 1979. 8.00. Minneapolis Inst Arts.
Arakawa, No. 223. (Maeght Gallery: Derriere le Miroir Ser.). 1977. pap. 19.95 (ISBN 0-8120-0893-6). Barron.
Aramaic Approach to the Gospels & Acts. 3rd ed. Matthew Black. 1967. 32.00x (ISBN 0-19-826157-8). Oxford U Pr.
Aramaic Documents of the Fifth Century B. C. abr. & rev. ed. G. R. Driver. 1957. 7.00x o.p. (ISBN 0-19-815404-6). Oxford U Pr.
Aramaic Handbook, 4 vols. Ed. by Franz Rosenthal. LC 67-111051. 377p. 1967. Set. 52.50x (ISBN 3-447-00693-5). Intl Pubns Serv.
Aramco, the United States, & Saudi Arabia: A Study of the Dynamics of Foreign Oil Policy, 1933-1950. Irvine H. Anderson. LC 80-8535. 288p. 1981. 15.00x (ISBN 0-691-04679-4). Princeton U Pr.
Aran Islands. Daphne Pochin-Mould. (Island Set). (Illus.). 171p. 1973. 16.95 (ISBN 0-7153-5782-4). David & Charles.
Aranea. Jenny Wagner. LC 78-55212. (Illus.). (gr. k-2). 1978. 7.95 (ISBN 0-87888-138-7). Bradbury Pr.
Arangetral. S. Santhi. (Indian Poetry Ser.). 66p. 1974. lib. bdg. 6.95 (ISBN 0-88253-463-7). Ind-US Inc.
Arapaho - Cheyenne Indians. Incl. Ethnological Report on Cheyenne & Arapaho: Aboriginal Occupation. Zachary Gussow; Historical Development of the Arapacho-Cheyenne Land Area. Leroy R. Hafen; Cheyenne & Arapaho Indians: Historical Background, Social & Economic Conditions. Arthur A. Ekirch, Jr; Findings of Fact, & Opinion. Indian Claims Commission. (American Indian Ethnohistory Ser: Plains Indians). (Illus.). lib. bdg. 42.00 (ISBN 0-8240-0732-8). Garland Pub.
Arapahoes, Our People. Virginia C. Trenholm. LC 76-108799. (Civilization of the American Indian Ser.: Vol. 105). (Illus.). 1970. 16.95 (ISBN 0-8061-0908-4). U of Okla Pr.
Aratus Ascribed to Germanicus Caesar. Ed. by D. B. Gain. (University of London Classical Studies Ser.: No. 8). (Illus.). 200p. 1976. text ed. 36.50x (ISBN 0-485-13708-9, Athlone Pr). Humanities.
Arbeitsdiagnose - Neve Wege der Chirusischen Diagnose und Therapie. M. Hobsley. Tr. by Caroline Seemann from Eng. Orig. Title: Pathways in Surgical Management. 480p. (Ger.). 1981. pap. 58.75 (ISBN 3-8055-0747-X). S Karger.
Arbitration & Collective Bargaining. 2nd ed. Paul Prasow & Edward Peters. 480p. 22.00x (ISBN 0-07-050674-4, C). McGraw.
Arbitration & Representation: Applications in Air & Rail Labor Relations. John W. Gohmann. LC 80-84183. 336p. 1981. text ed. 22.50 (ISBN 0-8403-2335-2). Kendall-Hunt.
Arbitration & the Hague Court. John W. Foster. 148p. 1980. Repr. of 1904 ed. lib. bdg. 18.50x (ISBN 0-8377-0535-5). Rothman.
Arbitration of Subcontracting & Wage Incentive Disputes: Proceedings. National Academy of Arbitrators, Annual Meeting. Ed. by James L. Stern & Barbara D. Dennis. LC 79-24133. 1980. 20.00 (ISBN 0-87179-318-0). BNA.
Arbol De la Violeta. Plenn. 1964. 6.95 (ISBN 0-87751-015-6, Pub by Troutman Press). E Torres & Sons.
Arbor Day. Bob Reese. Ed. by Alton Jordan. (Holidays Ser.). (Illus.). (gr. k-3). 1977. PLB 3.50 (ISBN 0-89868-031-X, Read Res); pap. text ed. 1.75 (ISBN 0-89868-064-6). ARO Pub.
Arbor House Treasury of Horror & the Supernatural. Ed. by Bill Pronzini et al. LC 80-70220. 512p. (Orig.). 1981. 19.95 (ISBN 0-87795-309-0); pap. 8.95 (ISBN 0-87795-319-8). Arbor Hse.
Arboreal Man. F. W. Jones. 1964. Repr. of 1917 ed. 10.75 o.s.i. (ISBN 0-02-847300-0). Hafner.
Arboriculturalist's Companion. N. D. James. 1972. 17.25x (ISBN 0-631-14110-3, Pub. by Basil Blackwell). Biblio Dist.
Arbuthnot Anthology of Children's Literature. 4th ed. Zena Sutherland. 1976. 18.95x (ISBN 0-673-15000-3). Scott F.
Arbuthnot Lectures Nineteen-Seventy to Nineteen Seventy-Nine. Association for the Library Service to Children. LC 79-26095. 214p. 1980. 12.50 (ISBN 0-8389-3240-1). ALA.
Arc Pair Grammar. David E. Johnson & Paul M. Postal. LC 80-7533. (Illus.). 700p. 1980. 35.00x (ISBN 0-691-08270-7). Princeton U Pr.
Arca de Noe. Jane Latourette. Tr. by Fernando Villalobos from Eng. (Libros Arco). Orig. Title: Story of Noah's Ark. (Illus.). 32p. (Orig., Span.). (gr. 1-3). 1975. pap. 0.95 o.s.i. (ISBN 0-89922-036-3). Edit Caribe.
Arcadia at Versailles: Noble Amateur Musicians & Their Musettes & Hurdy-Gurdies at the French Court (C. 1660-1789), a Visual Study. Richard D. Leppert. 138p. 1978. pap. text ed. 32.50 (ISBN 90-265-0246-X, Pub. by Swets Pub Serv Holland). Swets North Am.
Arcana of Astrology. W. J. Simmonite. LC 80-19739. 426p. 1980. Repr. of 1974 ed. lib. bdg. 11.95x (ISBN 0-89370-626-4). Borgo Pr.
Arcane. Carl Sherrell. (Orig.). 1978. pap. 1.95 o.s.i. (ISBN 0-515-04466-0). Jove Pubns.
Arch Books Aloud, Set 25. (Books Aloud Ser.). (Illus.). 32p. (gr. k-4). 1974. pap. 3.29 (ISBN 0-570-06828-2, 59-2025). Concordia.
Arch Books Aloud, Set 26. (Books Aloud Ser). (Illus.). 32p. (gr. k-4). 1974. pap. 3.29 (ISBN 0-570-06829-0, 59-2026). Concordia.
Arch Books Aloud, Set 27. (Books Aloud Ser.). (Illus.). 32p. (gr. k-4). 1974. pap. 3.29 (ISBN 0-570-06830-4, 59-2027). Concordia.
Arch Books Aloud, Set 28. (Books Aloud Ser). (Illus.). 32p. (gr. k-4). 1974. pap. 3.29 (ISBN 0-570-06831-2, 59-2028). Concordia.
Arch Books Aloud, Set 29. (Books Aloud Ser.). (Illus.). 32p. (gr. k-4). 1974. pap. 3.29 (ISBN 0-570-06832-0, 59-2029). Concordia.
Arch Books Aloud Set 30. (Books Aloud Ser). (Illus.). 32p. (gr. k-3). 1974. pap. 3.29 (ISBN 0-570-06833-9, 59-2030). Concordia.
Arch Bridges & Their Builders, 1735-1835. E. C. Ruddock. LC 77-82514. (Illus.). 1979. 82.50 (ISBN 0-521-21816-0). Cambridge U Pr.
Arch Dams: A Review of British Research & Development. Thomas Telford Editorial Staff, Ltd. 168p. 1980. 60.00x (ISBN 0-901948-14-4, Pub. by Telford England). State Mutual Bk.
Arch of a Circle. Doris Vidaver & Pearl A. Sherry. (Illus.). 144p. 1981. 7.95 (ISBN 0-8040-0807-8); pap. 3.95 (ISBN 0-8040-0808-6). Swallow.
Archaelogy in Bible Lands. Howard Vos. (Illus.). 1977. 12.95 (ISBN 0-8024-0293-3). Moody.
Archaeologica Graeca: Or, the Antiquities of Greece, 2 vols. John Potter. Ed. by Burton Feldman & Robert Richardson. LC 78-60893. (Myth & Romanticism Ser.: Vol. 19). (Illus.). 1980. Set. lib. bdg. 120.00 (ISBN 0-8240-3568-2); lib. bdg. 66.00 ea. Garland Pub.
Archaeological Atlas of the World. David Whitehouse & Ruth Whitehouse. (Illus.). 1975. text ed. 27.95x (ISBN 0-7167-0274-6); pap. 14.95x (ISBN 0-7167-0273-8). W H Freeman.
Archaeological Excavations in Thailand, 3 vols. Vol. 1. 23.50x (ISBN 0-685-12352-9); Vol. 2. 26.50x o.p. (ISBN 0-685-12353-7); Vol. 3. 17.50x (ISBN 0-685-12354-5). Humanities.
Archaeological Explorations in Caves of the Point of Pines Region, Arizona. James C. Gifford. LC 79-9180. (Anthropological Papers: No. 36). 1980. 8.95x (ISBN 0-8165-0360-5). U of Ariz Pr.
Archaeological History of the Ancient Middle East. Jack Finegan. (Illus.). 1979. lib. bdg. 35.00 (ISBN 0-89158-164-2, Dawson). Westview.
Archaeological Investigations at Molpa, San Diego County, California. D. L. True et al. (U. C. Publ. in Anthropology: Vol. 11). pap. 10.50x (ISBN 0-520-09490-5). U of Cal Pr.
Archaeological Investigations at the Ring Brothers Site Complex, Thousand Oaks, California. Ed. by C. William Clewlow, Jr. et al. (Institute of Archaeology Monographs: No. 13). (Illus.). 156p. 1979. pap. 7.00 (ISBN 0-917956-13-3). UCLA Arch.
Archaeological Investigations Near Tipasa, Algeria. L. Cabot Briggs. LC 63-5554. (ASPR Bulletin: No. 21). 1963. pap. text ed. 10.00 (ISBN 0-87365-522-2). Peabody Harvard.
Archaeological Sediments: A Survey of Analytical Methods. Myra L. Shackley. LC 75-1193. 159p. 1975. 27.95 (ISBN 0-470-77870-9). Halsted Pr.
Archaeological Studies in Szechwan. T-K. Cheng. 1957. 47.50 (ISBN 0-521-04635-1). Cambridge U Pr.
Archaeological Survey in the Lower Yazoo Basin, Mississippi: 1949-1955. Philip Phillips. LC 77-80028. (Peabody Museum Papers: Vol. 60). 1970. pap. text ed. 50.00 (ISBN 0-87365-173-1). Peabody Harvard.
Archaeology. Michael Carter. (Illus.). 176p. 1980. 12.95 (ISBN 0-7137-0861-1, Pub. by Blandford Pr England); pap. 6.95 (ISBN 0-7137-1067-5, Pub. by Blandford Pr England). Sterling.
Archaeology. Geoffrey Palmer. LC 68-112513. (Pegasus Books: No. 12). (Illus.). (gr. 9 up). 1968. 10.50x (ISBN 0-234-77996-9). Intl Pubns Serv.
Archaeology: A Bibliographical Guide to the Basic Literature. Robert F. Heizer et al. LC 77-83376. 400p. 1980. lib. bdg. 38.00 (ISBN 0-8240-9826-9). Garland Pub.
Archaeology & Old Testament Study. Ed. by D. Winton Thomas. 1967. 33.50x (ISBN 0-19-813150-X). Oxford U Pr.
Archaeology & the Landscape: Essays for L. V. Grinsell. Ed. by P. J. Fowler. (Illus.). 1972. text ed. 12.00x (ISBN 0-212-98398-9). Humanities.
Archaeology & the New Testament. Merrill F. Unger. (Illus.). 1962. 12.95 (ISBN 0-310-33380-6). Zondervan.
Archaeology by Experiment. John Coles. (Illus.). 1974. pap. 3.50 o.p. (ISBN 0-684-14078-0, SL562, ScribT). Scribner.
Archaeology: Field Methods. William S. Dancey. (Modern Physical Anthropology Ser.). 184p. (Orig.). 1981. pap. text ed. write for info. (ISBN 0-8087-0440-0). Burgess.
Archaeology in Sussex to AD1500. Ed. by P. L. Drewett. 110p. 1980. pap. 20.95x (ISBN 0-900312-67-X, Pub. by Council Brit Arch England). Intl Schol Bk Serv.
Archaeology in the Upper Delaware Valley: A Study of the Cultural Chronology of the Tocks Island Reservoir. Ed. by W. Fred Kinsey. LC 72-169104. (Pennsylvania Historical & Museum Commission Anthropological Ser.: No. 2). (Illus.). 499p. 1972. 13.00 (ISBN 0-911124-68-3). Pa Hist & Mus.
Archaeology of Anglo-Saxon England. David M. Wilson. (Illus.). 532p. Date not set. pap. price not set (ISBN 0-521-28390-6). Cambridge U Pr.
Archaeology of Beringia. Frederick Hadleigh-West. (Illus.). 320p. 1981. 30.00x (ISBN 0-231-05172-7). Columbia U Pr.
Archaeology of Central Asia & the Indian Border Lands, 3 vols. S. P. Gupta. 1979. text ed. 28.00 ea. (ISBN 0-391-02092-7). Humanities.
Archaeology of Crete. John D. Pendlebury. LC 63-18049. (Illus.). 12.00x (ISBN 0-8196-0121-7). Biblo.
Archaeology of India. D. P. Agrawal. (Scandinavian Institute of Asian Studies Monograph). (Illus.). 320p. 1981. pap. text ed. 23.50 (ISBN 0-7007-0140-0). Humanities.
Archaeology of Industry. Kenneth Hudson. LC 75-38404. (Encore Edition). 1976. 3:95 o.p. (ISBN 0-684-15719-5, ScribT). Scribner.
Archaeology of Knowledge: Includes the Discourse on Language. Michel Foucault. Tr. by A. M. Sheridan-Smith. LC 72-1135. 1972. 28.50x (ISBN 0-394-47118-0). Irvington.
Archaeology of Mesopotamia: From the Old Stone Age to the Persian Conquest. Seton Lloyd. 1980. pap. 8.95 (ISBN 0-500-79007-8). Thames Hudson.
Archaeology of New England. Dean R. Snow. LC 80-982. (New World Archaeological Record Ser.). 1980. 32.50 (ISBN 0-12-653950-2). Acad Pr.
Archaeology of New Testament Cities in Western Asia Minor. Edwin Yamauchi. LC 80-66991. (Baker Studies in Biblical Archaeology). 160p. 1980. pap. 7.95 (ISBN 0-8010-9915-3). Baker Bk.
Archaeology of North America: American Indians & Their Origins. Dean Snow. (Illus.). 272p. 1980. pap. 12.95 (ISBN 0-500-27183-6). Thames Hudson.
Archaeology of South India: Tamilnadu. K. S. Ramachandran. 1980. 40.00x (ISBN 0-8364-0669-9, Pub. by Sundeep). South Asia Bks.
Archaeology of the Anglo-Saxon Settlements. E. Thurlow Leeds. (Oxford Reprints Ser). (Illus.). 1913. 19.50x (ISBN 0-19-813161-5). Oxford U Pr.
Archaeology of the Autlan-Tuxcacuesco Area of Jalisco, II: The Tuxcacuesco-Zapotitlan Zone. Isabel Kelly. (U. C. Publ. in Ibero-Americana: Vol. 27). 1949. pap. 9.00x (ISBN 0-520-09194-9). U of Cal Pr.
Archaeology of the Frivolous: Reading Condillac. Jacques Derrida. Tr. by John P. Leavey, Jr. from Fr. (Duquesne Studies - Philosophical Ser.: Vol. 37). 130p. 1980. text ed. 10.95x (ISBN 0-391-01636-9). Duquesne.
Archaeology of the New Testament: The Mediterranean World of the Early Christian Apostles. Jack Finegan. (Illus.). 400p. 1981. 35.00x (ISBN 0-86531-064-5). Westview.
Archaeology of the Point St. George Site, & Tolowa Prehistory. Richard A. Gould. (U. C. Publ. in Anthropology: Vol. 4). 1966. pap. 7.00x (ISBN 0-520-09003-9). U of Cal Pr.
Archaeology of U. S. Ed. by Richard A. Gould & Michael Schiffer. LC 80-2332. (Studies in Archaeology). 1981. price not set (ISBN 0-12-293580-2). Acad Pr.
Archaeology: The Evaluation of Ancient Societies. T. Patterson. 1981. pap. 11.95 (ISBN 0-13-044040-X). P-H.
Archaeology, the Rabbis, & Early Christianity. Eric M. Meyers & James F. Strange. LC 80-24208. 208p. 1981. pap. 7.95 (ISBN 0-687-01680-0). Abingdon.
Archaeology Under Water: An Atlas of the World's Submerged Sites. Ed. by Keith Muckelroy. LC 79-18380. (Illus.). 1980. 24.95 (ISBN 0-07-043951-6). McGraw.
Archaic Dictionary. William R. Cooper. LC 73-76018. 1969. Repr. of 1876 ed. 40.00 (ISBN 0-8103-3885-8). Gale.
Archaic Greece. L. H. Jeffery. LC 75-10758. (Illus.). 300p. 1976. 22.50 (ISBN 0-312-04760-6). St Martin.
Archaic Greece: The Age of Experiment. Anthony Snodgrass. (Orig.). 1981. pap. price not set (ISBN 0-520-04373-1, CAL 505). U of Cal Pr.
Archaic Greek Gems: Schools & Artists in the Sixth & Early Fifth Centuries. John Boardman. LC 68-25581. (Illus.). 1968. 16.75x o.s.i. (ISBN 0-8101-0029-0). Northwestern U Pr.
Archaicon: A Collection of Unusual Archaic English. J. Ernest Barlough. LC 73-14926. 1974. 11.00 (ISBN 0-8108-0683-5). Scarecrow.
Archbishop Grindal, 1519-1589: The Struggle for a Reformed Church in England. Patrick Collinson. 1979. 30.00x (ISBN 0-520-03831-2). U of Cal Pr.
Archbishop Lefebvre & Religious Liberty. Michael Davies. 1980. 1.00. Tan Bks Pubs.
Archbishop Romero: Martyr of Salvador. Placido Erdozain. Tr. by John McFadden & Ruth Warner. (Illus.). 128p. (Orig.). 1981. pap. 4.95 (ISBN 0-88344-019-9). Orbis Bks.
Archbishop Thomas & King Henry Second. T. Corfe. LC 74-14442. (Introduction to the History of Mankind Ser). (Illus.). (gr. 6-11). 1975. pap. text ed. 3.95 (ISBN 0-521-20646-4). Cambridge U Pr.
Archeological History of the Hocking Valley. James L. Murphy. LC 73-92906. (Illus.). xi, 360p. 1975. 20.00 (ISBN 0-8214-0151-3). Ohio U Pr.
Archeological Investigations at the Red Willow Reservoir. Roger T. Grange, Jr. (Publications in Anthropology Ser.: No. 9). (Illus.). 238p. (Orig.). 1980. pap. 10.00 (ISBN 0-686-28124-1). Nebraska Hist.
Archeology & a Science of Man. Wilfred T. Neill. LC 77-11038. 1977. 28.50x (ISBN 0-231-03661-2). Columbia U Pr.
Archeology & Bible History. Joseph P. Free. LC 69-15256. (Illus.). 1950. pap. text ed. 5.95 o.p. (ISBN 0-88207-801-1). Victor Bks.
Archeology of Cape Denbigh. James L. Giddings. LC 63-10231. (Illus.). 331p. 1964. 25.00 (ISBN 0-87057-080-3, Pub. by Brown U Pr). Univ Pr of New England.
Archeology of the Death Valley Salt Pan. Alice Hunt. (Illus.). xvi, 313p. 1960. Repr. 25.50 (ISBN 0-384-24920-5). Johnson Repr.
Archer Method of Winning at 21. John Archer. LC 73-6449. 240p. 1973. 7.95 o.p. (ISBN 0-8092-9021-9). Contemp Bks.
Archery. Boy Scouts Of America. LC 19-600. (Illus.). 48p. (gr. 6-12). 1978. pap. 0.70x (ISBN 0-8395-3381-0, 3381). BSA.
Archery. Edmund Burke. LC 62-12117. (Illus., Orig.). 1963. pap. 1.75 o.p. (ISBN 0-668-00862-8). Arc Bks.
Archery. Donald W. Campbell. (Sports Ser). 1970. pap. 4.25x ref. ed. (ISBN 0-13-043992-4). P-H.
Archery at the Dark of the Moon: Poetic Problems in Homer's Odyssey. Norman Austin. LC 73-94442. 300p. 1975. 20.00x (ISBN 0-520-02713-2). U of Cal Pr.
Archery for Beginners. John Williams. LC 75-35000. (Illus.). 192p. 1976. pap. 5.95 o.p. (ISBN 0-8092-8288-7). Contemp Bks.
Archery Handbook. Edmund H. Burke. LC 54-9236. (Illus.). 1954. lib. bdg. 4.95 o.p. (ISBN 0-668-00336-7); pap. 2.95 o.p. (ISBN 0-668-04002-5). Arco.
Archery Is for Me. Art Thomas. LC 81-22. (Sports for Me Bks.). (Illus.). (gr. 2-5). 1981. PLB 5.95 (ISBN 0-8225-1091-X). Lerner Pubns.
Archery World's Complete Guide to Bow Hunting. G. Helgeland. 1975. 8.95 o.p. (ISBN 0-13-044024-8); pap. 3.95 (ISBN 0-13-044016-7). P-H.
Arches, Continuous Frames, Columns, & Conduits: Selected Papers. Hardy Cross. LC 63-17046. (Illus.). 1963. 14.00 (ISBN 0-252-72315-5). U of Ill Pr.
Archetypal Images in Greek Religion, 5 vols. Carl Kerenyi. Tr. by R. Manheim. Incl. Vol. 1. Prometheus: Archetypal Image of Human Existence. 1963. o.p. (ISBN 0-691-09705-4); Vol. 2. Dionysos: Archetypal Image of Industructible Life. 1976. 36.00x (ISBN 0-691-09863-8); Vol. 3. Asklepios: Archetypal Image of the Physician's Existence. 1959. 16.50 (ISBN 0-691-09703-8); Eleusis: Archetypal Image of Mother & Daughter. 1967. o.p. (ISBN 0-691-09704-6); Vol. 5. Zeus & Hera-Archetypal Image of Father, Husband & Wife. 1975. 18.00 (ISBN 0-691-09864-6). (Bollingen Ser.: Vol. 65). Princeton U Pr.

Archetypal Themes in Modern Story. Ed. by Jack Matthews. 256p. 1973. text ed. 7.95 (ISBN 0-312-04795-9). St Martin.

Archetypes & the Collective Unconscious: Bollingen Ser. C. G. Jung. Tr. by R. F. Hull from Ger. LC 75-156. (Xx: 9,I). (Illus.). 560p. 1980. 30.00x (ISBN 0-691-09761-5); pap. 9.95 (ISBN 0-691-01833-2). Princeton U Pr.

Archetypes of Carlos Fuentes: From Witch to Androgne. Gloria Duran. 240p. 1980. 22.50 (ISBN 0-208-01775-5, Archon). Shoe String.

Archie Griffen. Edward F. Dolan, Jr. & Richard B. Lyttle. (Illus.). (gr. 4 up). 1978. pap. 1.25 (ISBN 0-671-78694-6). PB.

Archie's Family Album. Allan Hartley. (Spire Comics Ser.). 1978. pap. 0.49 (ISBN 0-8007-8532-0). Revell.

Archigraphia. Ed. by Walter Herdeg. (Illus.). 1978. 39.50 (ISBN 0-8038-0470-9). Hastings.

Archimedes in the Middle Ages, Vol. 1. Arabo-Latin Tradition. Marshall Clagett. (Medieval Science Pubns., No. 6). (Illus.). 1964. 50.00x (ISBN 0-299-03360-0). U of Wis Pr.

Archimedes Russell: Upstate Architect. Evamaria Hardin. (Illus.). 108p. 1980. pap. 5.95 (ISBN 0-8156-0165-4). Syracuse U Pr.

Archimedes Takes a Bath. Joan Lexau. LC 69-11084. (Illus.). (gr. 2-5). 1969. PLB 6.89 o.p. (ISBN 0-690-09900-2, TYC-J). T Y Crowell.

Archipenko: A Study of the Early Works, 1908-1920. Katherine J. Michaelsen. LC 76-23644. (Outstanding Dissertations in the Fine Arts - 2nd Series - 20th Century). (Illus.). 1977. Repr. of 1975 ed. lib. bdg. 60.00 (ISBN 0-8240-2712-4). Garland Pub.

Archipenko: The Sculpture & Graphic Art. Donald Karshan. LC 75-19245. (Illus.). 164p. 1976. 45.00 o.p. (ISBN 0-89158-500-1). Westview.

Architect, 2 vols. William Ranlett. LC 76-21851. (Architecture & Decorative Art Ser.). (Illus.). 1976. Repr. of 1857 ed. lib. bdg. 85.00 (ISBN 0-306-70799-3). Da Capo.

Architect & Sculptor in Classical Greece. Bernard Ashmole. LC 72-76019. (The Wrightsman Lectures Ser.). (Illus.). 218p. 1972. 22.50 (ISBN 0-8147-0553-7). NYU Pr.

Architect: Chapters in the History of the Profession. Ed. by Spiro Kostof. LC 75-46368. (Illus.). 1976. 25.00x (ISBN 0-19-502067-7). Oxford U Pr.

Architect in History. Martin S. Briggs. LC 69-15613. (Architecture & Decorative Art Ser.). (Illus.). 400p. 1974. Repr. of 1927 ed. lib. bdg. 29.50 (ISBN 0-306-70584-2). Da Capo.

Architect in Practice. Arthur J. Willis & W. N. George. 333p. 1974. text ed. 26.50x (ISBN 0-258-96959-8, Pub. by Granada England). Renouf.

Architect: The First Ten Years. John Donaghey. LC 80-66726. (Illus.). 96p. (Orig.). (gr. 12). 1980. pap. text ed. 7.50 (ISBN 0-9604298-0-8). J Donaghey.

Architectonic Knowledge in the New Arcadia (1590) Sidney's Use of Heroic Journey. Josephine A. Roberts. (Salzburg Studies in English Literature: Elizabethan & Renaissance Ser.: No. 69). 1978. pap. text ed. 25.00x (ISBN 0-391-01510-9). Humanities.

Architectonics of the Cerebral Cortex. Ed. by Mary A. Brazier & Hellmuth Petsche. LC 77-83694. (International Brain Research Organization (IBRO) Monograph Ser.: Vol. 3). 1978. 47.00 (ISBN 0-89004-140-7). Raven.

Architectonics of the Human Telencephalic Cortex. H. Braak. (Studies of Brain Functions: Vol. 4). (Illus.). 147p. 1981. 27.50 (ISBN 0-387-10312-0). Springer-Verlag.

Architector, 2 vols. Francois Bucher. LC 77-86233. (Illus.). 1980. Set. 85.00 (ISBN 0-913870-47-1). Abaris Bks.

Architects. Leonard E. Fisher. LC 70-101748. (Colonial Americans Ser). (Illus.). (gr. 4-6). 1970. PLB 4.90 o.p. (ISBN 0-531-01041-4). Watts.

Architects' & Builders' Handbook. 18th ed. Frank E. Kidder & Harry Parker. 1931. 75.00 (ISBN 0-471-47421-5, Pub. by Wiley-Interscience). Wiley.

Architects' Data. Ernst Neufert. Ed. by Rudolf Herz. (Illus.). 1978. text ed. 34.95x o.s.i. (ISBN 0-8464-0145-2). Beekman Pubs.

Architect's Data: The Handbook of Building Types, 2nd (International) English Edition. E. Neufert. 420p. 1980. 69.95x (ISBN 0-470-26947-2). Halsted Pr.

Architects of Adjustment: The History of the Psychological Profession in America. Donald S. Napoli. (National University Publications, American Studies Ser.). 185p. 1981. 20.00 (ISBN 0-8046-9269-6). Kennikat.

Architects of Destruction. Leslie K. Campbell. 282p. (Orig.). 1980. pap. 4.95 (ISBN 0-9605164-4-1). Self.

Architects of London. Alastair Service. 1979. 22.95 (ISBN 0-8038-0017-7). Hastings.

Architect's Working Details, 15 vols. Ed. by D. A. Boyne & Lance Wright. Incl. Repr. of 1953 ed. Vol. 1 (ISBN 0-85139-022-6); Repr. of 1954 ed. Vol. 2 (ISBN 0-85139-023-4); Repr. of 1955 ed. Vol. 3 (ISBN 0-85139-024-2); Repr. of 1957 ed. Vol. 4 (ISBN 0-85139-025-0); Repr. of 1958 ed. Vol. 5 (ISBN 0-85139-026-9); Repr. of 1959 ed. Vol. 6; Repr. of 1960 ed. Vol. 7 (ISBN 0-85139-028-5); Vol. 8. Repr. of 1961 ed (ISBN 0-85139-029-3); Repr. of 1962 ed. Vol. 9 (ISBN 0-85139-030-7); Repr. of 1954 ed. Vol. 10 (ISBN 0-85139-031-5); Repr. of 1965 ed. Vol. 11 (ISBN 0-85139-032-3); Repr. of 1965 ed. Vol. 12 (ISBN 0-85139-033-1); Repr. of 1969 ed. Vol. 13 (ISBN 0-85139-034-X); Repr. of 1971 ed. Vol. 14 (ISBN 0-85139-035-8); Repr. of 1973 ed. Vol. 15. 17.50 (ISBN 0-85139-036-6). 1978. 275.00 set (ISBN 0-685-38821-2, Pub. by Architectural); 25.00 ea. Nichols Pub.

Architects Year Book 14: The Inner City. Ed. by D. Kennedy & M. I. Kennedy. LC 74-2429. 1974. 32.50 (ISBN 0-470-46904-8). Halsted Pr.

Architectural Aerodynamics. R. M. Aynsley et al. (Illus.). 1977. text ed. 49.70x (ISBN 0-85334-698-4, Pub. by Applied Science). Burgess-Intl Ideas.

Architectural & Engineering Concerns in Solar System Design, Installation & Operation. Prc Energy Analysis Company & Stephen Weinstein. 51p. 1980. pap. 10.95 (ISBN 0-89934-052-0, H044-PP). Solar Energy Info.

Architectural Digest American Interiors. Ed. by Paige Rense. LC 77-23652. (Illus.). 1978. 35.00x o.s.i. (ISBN 0-89535-002-5). Knapp Pr.

Architectural Drafting & Construction. Ernest H. Weidhass. 560p. 1981. text ed. 24.95; instr's hdbk. avail. Allyn.

Architectural Drafting & Construction. Ernest R. Weidhass. 560p. 1974. text ed. 18.50x o.p. (ISBN 0-205-04221-X); instr's hndbk avail. o.p. (ISBN 0-205-04222-8). Allyn.

Architectural Drafting & Design. 3rd ed. Ernest Weidhaas. 1977. text ed. 18.50x o.p. (ISBN 0-205-05624-5); tchr's manual avail. o.p. (ISBN 0-205-05625-3). Allyn.

Architectural Drafting Fundamentals. John E. Ball. (Illus.). 336p. 1980. text ed. 13.95 (ISBN 0-8359-0254-4). Reston.

Architectural Draftsman's Reference Handbook. S. Lewis. 1981. 25.00 (ISBN 0-13-044164-3). P-H.

Architectural Drawing. 3rd ed. Lawton M. Patten & Milton Rogness. (Illus.). 1977. pap. text ed. 9.95 (ISBN 0-8403-1809-X). Kendall-Hunt.

Architectural Drawing in the R. I. B. A. J. C. Palmes. pap. 2.50 (ISBN 0-685-20562-2). Transatlantic.

Architectural Drawings: Nineteen Sixty-Eight to Nineteen Seventy-Six. Helmut Jacoby. Date not set. 22.95 (ISBN 0-8038-0016-9). Hastings.

Architectural History of Venice. Deborah Howard. LC 80-24856. (Illus.). 260p. 1981. pap. text ed. 32.50x (ISBN 0-8419-0681-5). Holmes & Meier.

Architectural Illustration. L. Dudley. 1976. 29.95 (ISBN 0-13-044610-6). P-H.

Architectural Models. Rolf Janke. Date not set. 29.95 (ISBN 0-8038-0012-6). Hastings.

Architectural Photography. Joseph W. Molitor. LC 76-6537. 180p. 1976. 34.50 (ISBN 0-471-61312-6, Pub. by Wiley-Interscience). Wiley.

Architectural Polychromy of the Eighteen Thirty's. David Van Zanten. LC 76-23648. (Outstanding Dissertations in the Fine Arts - 2nd Ser. - Nineteenth Century). (Illus.). 1977. Repr. of 1970 ed. lib. bdg. 63.00 (ISBN 0-8240-2733-7). Garland Pub.

Architectural Practice: Architecture-Professional & Technical. John H. Turner. 1979. 33.00 (ISBN 0-7134-2799-X, Pub. by Batsford England). David & Charles.

Architectural Scale. Heath Licklider. LC 66-14230. (Illus.). 1966. 5.00 o.p. (ISBN 0-8076-0351-1). Braziller.

Architectural Sculpture in New York City. Stephen M. Jacoby. LC 74-15247. (Illus.). 128p. (Orig.). 1975. pap. text ed. 5.00 (ISBN 0-486-23120-8). Dover.

Architectural Sculpture in Romanesque Provence. Alan Borg. (Oxford Studies in the History of Art & Architecture). 210p. 1972. 37.50x (ISBN 0-19-817192-7). Oxford U Pr.

Architectural Supervision on Site. A. A. MacFarlane. (Illus.). 1973. text ed. 29.90x (ISBN 0-85334-574-0, Pub. by Applied Science). Burgess-Intl Ideas.

Architectural Working Drawings. Ralph W. Liebing & Mimi F. Paul. LC 76-48154. 1977. 22.50 (ISBN 0-471-53432-3, Pub. by Wiley-Interscience). Wiley.

Architecturally Speaking. Eugene Raskin. 1970. pap. 3.95x (ISBN 0-8197-0003-7). Bloch.

Architecture. 1980. text ed. 7.95 (ISBN 0-686-65125-1, 63893); pap. text ed. 5.95 (ISBN 0-686-65126-X, 63907). Natl Textbk.

Architecture. Boy Scouts Of America. LC 19-600. (Illus.). 48p. (gr. 6-12). 1966. pap. 0.70x (ISBN 0-8395-3321-7, 3321). BSA.

Architecture. Sinclair Gauldie. (Appreciation of the Arts Ser). (Illus., Orig.). 1969. pap. 6.95 o.p. (ISBN 0-19-211902-8). Oxford U Pr.

Architecture: A Performing Art. John Andrews & Jennifer Taylor. (Illus.). 208p. 1981. cancelled (ISBN 0-19-550557-3). Oxford U Pr.

Architecture, Ambition, & Americans: A Social History of American Architecture. rev. ed. Wayne Andrews. LC 78-50786. (Illus.). 1979. pap. text ed. 7.95 (ISBN 0-02-900750-X). Free Pr.

Architecture, Ambition, & Americans: A Social History of American Architecture. rev. ed. Wayne Andrews. LC 78-50786. (Illus.). 1978. 17.95 (ISBN 0-02-900770-4). Free Pr.

Architecture & Allied Design: An Environmental Design Perspective. Anthony C. Antoniades. (Illus.). 384p. (Orig.). 1980. pap. text ed. 17.95 (ISBN 0-8403-2154-6). Kendall-Hunt.

Architecture & Color. Waldron Faulkner. 142p. 1981. Repr. of 1972 ed. text ed. price not set. Krieger.

Architecture & Design of Treatment Environments. 1977. 2.00 o.p. (ISBN 0-685-83138-8, 124). Am Psychiatric.

Architecture & Interior Design: A Basic History of the Eighteenth Through Twentieth Centuries, 2 vol. set. V. K. Ball. 1980. Set. 80.00 (ISBN 0-471-08721-1, Pub. by Wiley-Interscience); Set. pap. 50.00 (ISBN 0-471-08720-3); pap. 27.50 (ISBN 0-471-08722-X). Wiley.

Architecture & Interior Design: A Basic History of the Eighteenth Through Twentieth Centuries. V. K. Ball. 464p. 1980. pap. 27.50 (ISBN 0-471-08722-X, Pub. by Wiley-Interscience). Wiley.

Architecture & Interior Design: A Basic History Through the Seventeenth Century. Victoria K. Ball. LC 79-21371. 1980. 45.00 (ISBN 0-471-05162-4, Pub. by Wiley-Interscience); pap. 27.50 (ISBN 0-471-08719-X). Wiley.

Architecture & Interior Design: Europe & America from the Colonial Era to Today. Victoria K. Ball. LC 79-24851. 1980. 45.00 (ISBN 0-471-05161-6, Pub. by Wiley-Interscience); pap. 27.50 (ISBN 0-471-08722-X). Wiley.

Architecture & People. Eugene Raskin. 192p. 1974. ref. ed. 16.95 (ISBN 0-13-044594-0). P-H.

Architecture & You: How to Experience & Enjoy Buildings. William W. Caudill et al. (Illus.). 1978. 18.50 (ISBN 0-8230-7040-9, Whitney Lib); pap. 12.95 (ISBN 0-8230-7041-7). Watson-Guptill.

Architecture As Art. SITE. (Illus.). 112p. 1981. pap. 14.95 (ISBN 0-312-04814-9). St Martin.

Architecture: Design-Engineering-Drawing. rev. ed. William P. Spence. (gr. 9-12). 1979. text ed. 18.60 (ISBN 0-87345-097-3); quizzes & problems 5.00 (ISBN 0-87345-098-1); ans. key avail. (ISBN 0-685-14523-9). McKnight.

Architecture Evolving: An Illinois Saga. William T. Brown. Ed. by Marilyn Hasbrouck. LC 76-45690. (Illus.). 1976. 25.00x (ISBN 0-931028-02-7); pap. 15.00x (ISBN 0-931028-01-9). Teach'em.

Architecture for Adult Education. Commission of Architecture of AEA. 74p. 1953. 2.30. Adult Ed.

Architecture for People. Ed. by Byron Mikellides. LC 79-48067. (Illus.). 196p. 1980. 18.95 (ISBN 0-03-057491-9); pap. 9.95 (ISBN 0-03-057489-7). HR&W.

Architecture in Australia: A History. J. M. Freeland. (Illus.). 1968. 15.00 o.p. (ISBN 0-8426-1262-9). Verry.

Architecture in Colonial Massachusetts: A Conference Held by the Colonial Society of Massachusetts, September 19 & 20, 1974. Ed. by Abbot L. Cummings. LC 79-51657. 1979. 25.00x (ISBN 0-8139-0855-8). U Pr of Va.

Architecture in Northern Ghana: A Study of Forms & Functions. Labelle Prussin. LC 75-84789. (Illus.). 1969. 18.50x (ISBN 0-520-01613-0). U of Cal Pr.

Architecture in Puerto Rico. Jose A. Fernandez. Date not set. 16.95 (ISBN 0-8038-0009-6). Hastings.

Architecture in Tennessee: Seventeen Sixty-Eight to Eighteen Ninety-Seven. James A. Patrick. (Illus.). 1981. 24.95 (ISBN 0-87049-223-3). U of Tenn Pr.

Architecture in the Seventies. Udo Kultermanh. (ABPC Ser.). (Illus.). 160p. 1980. 29.95 (ISBN 0-8038-0019-3). Hastings.

Architecture in the Shoin Style: Japanese Feudal Residences. Fumio Hashimoto. Tr. by H. Mack Horton. LC 79-91519. (Japanese Arts Library: Vol. 10). (Illus.). 220p. 1981. 16.95 (ISBN 0-87011-414-X). Kodansha.

Architecture in the United States: A Survey of Architectural Styles Since 1776. Ralph W. Hammett. LC 76-4917. 1976. 28.00 (ISBN 0-471-34721-3, Pub. by Wiley-Interscience). Wiley.

Architecture in Virginia: An Official Guide to Four Centuries of Building in the Old Dominion. Ed. by William B. O'Neal. LC 67-13230. (Illus., Orig.). 1968. 4.95 o.s.i. (ISBN 0-8027-0020-9); pap. 2.95 o.s.i. (ISBN 0-8027-7006-1). Walker & Co.

Architecture, Industry & Wealth: Collected Papers by William Morris. William Morris. Ed. by Sydney J. Freedberg. LC 77-25760. (Connoisseurship, Criticism & Art History Ser.: Vol. 13). 163p. 1979. lib. bdg. 21.00 (ISBN 0-8240-3271-3). Garland Pub.

Architecture Machine. Nicholas Negroponte. (Illus.). 164p. 1970. 7.95 o.p. (ISBN 0-262-14008-X); pap. 4.95 (ISBN 0-262-64010-4). MIT Pr.

Architecture of Ancient Greece. W. Bell Dinsmoor. LC 73-12401. 1973. 21.00x (ISBN 0-8196-0283-3). Biblo.

Architecture of Bruce Goff. Jeffrey Cook. LC 78-2135. (Icon Editions). (Illus.). 1978. 22.50 (ISBN 0-06-430950-9, HarpT). Har-Row.

Architecture of Bruce Goff Buildings & Projects, 1916-1974, 2 vols. David G. De Long. LC 76-23610. (Outstanding Dissertations in the Fine Arts - 2nd Series - American). (Illus.). 1977. Repr. Set. lib. bdg. 121.00 (ISBN 0-8240-2682-9). Garland Pub.

Architecture of Charles Bulfinch. Harold Kirker. (Illus.). 1977. 18.50x (ISBN 0-674-04390-1). Harvard U Pr.

Architecture of Concurrent Programs. P. Brinch-Hanson. 1977. 24.95 (ISBN 0-13-044628-9). P-H.

Architecture of Country Houses. Andrew J. Downing. LC 68-16230. (Architecture & Decorative Art Ser). (Illus.). 1968. Repr. of 1850 ed. 39.50 (ISBN 0-306-71034-X). Da Capo.

Architecture of Digital Computers. R. G. Garside. (Oxford Applied Mathematics & Computing Science Ser.). (Illus.). 376p. 1980. text ed. 74.00x (ISBN 0-19-859627-8); pap. text ed. 34.50x (ISBN 0-19-859638-3). Oxford U Pr.

Architecture of England. Bruce Allsop & Ursula Clark. (Illus.). 1964. 7.50 (ISBN 0-85362-006-7, Oriel); pap. 5.00. Routledge & Kegan.

Architecture of Experience. Graham Martin. 256p. 1981. 26.50x (ISBN 0-85224-409-6, Pub. by Edinburgh U Pr Scotland). Columbia U Pr.

Architecture of Form. Ed. by L. March. LC 74-80354. (Cambridge Urban & Architectural Studies: No. 4). (Illus.). 552p. 1976. 78.00 (ISBN 0-521-20528-X). Cambridge U Pr.

Architecture of Historic Lexington. Royster Lyle, Jr. & Pamela H. Simpson. LC 76-49890. 1980. Repr. of 1977 ed. 19.50x (ISBN 0-8139-0647-4). U Pr of Va.

Architecture of Honolulu. Geoffrey W. Fairfax. (Illus.). 1972. 6.95 (ISBN 0-89610-037-5); pap. 4.95 o.p. (ISBN 0-89610-036-7). Island Her.

Architecture of Humanism: A Study in the History of Taste. Geoffrey Scott. (Illus.). 224p. 1974. pap. 5.95 (ISBN 0-393-00734-0). Norton.

Architecture of Knowledge. George Towner. LC 80-5127. 220p. 1980. text ed. 17.75 (ISBN 0-8191-1049-3); pap. text ed. 9.50 (ISBN 0-8191-1050-7). U Pr of Amer.

Architecture of Los Angeles. Paul Gleve & Julius Shulman. LC 80-28988. 1981. 35.00 (ISBN 0-8310-7142-7). Howell-North.

Architecture of Ludwig Wittgenstein: A Documentation with Excerpts from the Family Recollections by Hermine Wittgenstein. Bernhard Leitner. LC 72-97706. (Nova Scotia Ser). (Illus.). 127p. 1976. 22.50x (ISBN 0-8147-4968-2); pap. 12.95 (ISBN 0-8147-4969-0). NYU Pr.

Architecture of Mexico: Yesterday & Today. Hans Beacham. 1969. 15.00 (ISBN 0-8038-0013-4). Architectural.

Architecture of Mexico: Yesterday & Today. Hans Beacham. Date not set. 15.00 o.p. (ISBN 0-8038-0013-4). Hastings.

Architecture of Minard Lafever. Jacob Landy. LC 69-19461. (Illus.). 1970. 22.50x (ISBN 0-231-03132-7). Columbia U Pr.

Architecture of Scotland. J. G. Dunbar. 1978. 30.00 (ISBN 0-7134-1142-2, Pub. by Batsford England). David & Charles.

Architecture of Scotland. George Hay. (Oriel Guides). (Illus.). 11.50 (ISBN 0-85362-038-5, Oriel). Routledge & Kegan.

Architecture of Self-Help Communities. Michael Seelig. LC 77-15116. (Illus.). 1978. 25.00 o.p. (ISBN 0-07-056045-5, P&RB). McGraw.

Architecture of the French Enlightenment. Allan Braham. 1980. 55.00 (ISBN 0-520-04117-8). U of Cal Pr.

Architecture of the Renaissance. Leonard Benevolo. Tr. by Judith Landry. LC 76-54186. 1978. Repr. lib. bdg. 75.00 o.p. (ISBN 0-89158-720-9). Westview.

Architecture of the Southwest: Indian, Spanish, American. 1st ed. Trent E. Sanford. LC 76-100242. (Illus.). 1971. Repr. of 1950 ed. lib. bdg. 28.25x (ISBN 0-8371-4012-9, SAAS). Greenwood.

Architecture of Ventura Rodriguez, 2 vols. Thomas Reese. LC 75-23810. (Outstanding Dissertations in the Fine Arts - 18th Century). (Illus.). 1976. Set. lib. bdg. 121.00 (ISBN 0-8240-2004-9). Garland Pub.

Architecture of Victorian London. John Summerson. LC 75-16130. (Illus.). 1976. 10.95x (ISBN 0-8139-0592-3). U Pr of Va.

Architecture: The World We Build. P. M. Bardi. LC 77-153826. (International Library). (Illus.). 128p. (gr. 7-12). 1972. PLB 6.90 o.p. (ISBN 0-531-02104-1). Watts.

Architecture Without Architects: A Short Introduction to Non-Pedigreed Architecture. Bernard Rudofsky. LC 64-8755. 1969. pap. 5.95 (ISBN 0-385-07487-5). Doubleday.

Architecture: 1949 to 1965. Philip C. Johnson. (Illus.). 1966. 15.00 o.p. (ISBN 0-03-057960-0). HR&W.

Architecture 1970-1980: A Decade of Change. Architectural Record Magazine. Ed. by Jeanne Davern & Architectural Record. (Architectural Record Book). (Illus.). 320p. 1980. 29.50 (ISBN 0-07-002352-2). McGraw.

Archival & Manuscript Materials at the Hoover Institution on War, Revolution & Peace: A Checklist of Major Collections. Hoover Institution Staff. LC 75-29805. 36p. 1978. 2.00x (ISBN 0-8179-4102-9). Hoover Inst Pr.

Archival Resources. Compiled by Steven A. Siegel. (Jewish Immigrants of the Nazi Period in the USA). 1979. 42.00 (ISBN 0-89664-027-2, Pub. by K G Saur). Gale.

Archive Buildings & Equipment. Michael Duchein. (ICA Handbook Ser.: Vol. 1). 201p. 1977. pap. text ed. 25.00 (ISBN 3-7940-3780-4, Pub. by K G Saur). Gale.

Archives & Local History. 2nd ed. F. G. Emmison. (Illus.). 111p. 1974. bds. 15.00x (ISBN 0-8476-1283-X). Rowman.

Archives & Manuscript Repositories in the USSR: Estonia, Latvia & Belorussia. Patricia K. Grimsted. LC 79-15427. (Studies of the Russian Institute, Columbia University). 1981. 60.00x (ISBN 0-691-05279-4). Princeton U Pr.

Archives & Manuscripts: Exhibits. Gail F. Casterline. LC 80-80072. (Saa Basic Manual Ser.). 72p. (Orig.). 1980. pap. 7.00 (ISBN 0-931828-18-X). Soc Am Archivists.

Archives & the Computer. Michael Cook. LC 80-41286. 152p. 1980. text ed. 27.00 (ISBN 0-408-10734-0). Butterworths.

Archives from Elephantine: The Life of an Ancient Jewish Military Colony. Bezalel Porten. (Illus.). 1968. 27.50x (ISBN 0-520-01028-0). U of Cal Pr.

Archives of Ebla: An Empire Inscribed in Clay. Giovanni Pettinato. LC 77-16939. (Illus.). 384p. 1981. 15.95 (ISBN 0-385-13152-6). Doubleday.

Archives of Family Practice 1980. Ed. by John P. Geyman. 416p. 1980. 34.50x (ISBN 0-8385-0324-1). ACC.

Archives of Family Practice, 1981. John P. Geyman. 448p. 1981. 36.00 (ISBN 0-8385-0325-X). ACC.

Archives of the Peat Bogs. Harry Godwin. (Illus.). Date not set. price not set (ISBN 0-521-23784-X). Cambridge U Pr.

Archives: The Light of Faith. John T. Corrigan. (Catholic Library Association Studies in Librarianship: No. 4). 1980. 4.00 (ISBN 0-87507-008-6). Cath Lib Assn.

Archivists & Machine-Readable Records. Carolyn L. Geda et al. Ed. by Erik W. Austin & Francis X. Blouin. 1980. pap. text ed. 10.00 (ISBN 0-931828-19-8). Soc Am Archivists.

Archivo Jose Marti: Repertorio Critico, Medio Siglo De Estudios Martianos. Carlos Ripoll. 1971. 14.50 (ISBN 0-88303-010-1); pap. 11.50 (ISBN 0-685-73214-2). E Torres & Sons.

Archy & Mehitabel. Don Marquis. LC 62-56573. 6.95 (ISBN 0-385-04572-7); pap. 1.95 (ISBN 0-385-09478-7). Doubleday.

Arcimboldo the Marvelous. Andre P. De Mandiargues. LC 77-25439. (Illus.). 1978. 28.50 o.p. (ISBN 0-8109-0689-9). Abrams.

Arco Foscari: the Building of a Triumphal Gateway in Fifteenth Century Venice. Debra Pincus. LC 75-23808. (Outstanding Dissertations in the Fine Arts - Fifteenth Century). (Illus.). 1976. lib. bdg. 53.00 (ISBN 0-8240-2002-2). Garland Pub.

Arco Motor Vehicle Dictionary: English & Spanish. Ed. by Robert F. Lima. LC 76-77605. 368p. 1980. pap. 7.95 (ISBN 0-668-04982-0, 4982-0). Arco.

Arcology: The City in the Image of Man. Paolo Soleri. 1970. reduced size o.p. 27.50x (ISBN 0-262-19060-5); pap. 14.95 (ISBN 0-262-69041-1). MIT Pr.

Arco's Complete Woodworking Handbook. rev. ed. Jeannette T. Adams. LC 80-18786. 768p. 1980. lib. bdg. 12.95 (ISBN 0-668-04829-8, 4829-8). Arco.

Arctic Animal Ecology. H. Remmert. (Illus.). 250p. 1981. pap. 24.80 (ISBN 0-387-10169-1). Springer-Verlag.

Arctic Art: Eskimo Ivory. James G. Smith. 127p. soft cover 19.95x (ISBN 0-934490-37-6). Mus Am Ind.

Arctic Cat: Snowmobile Service-Repair, 1974-1979. Mike Bishop. Ed. by Eric Jorgensen. (Illus.). 1977. pap. 8.95 (ISBN 0-89287-172-5, X951). Clymer Pubns.

Arctic Diary of Russell Williams Porter. Russell W. Porter. Ed. by Herman R. Friis. LC 75-45375. (Illus.). 160p. 1976. 12.95x (ISBN 0-8139-0649-0). U Pr of Va.

Arctic Mission. Jill Burrell & Maurice Burrell. 1976. 1.55 (ISBN 0-08-017621-6). Pergamon.

Arctic Prairies. Ernest T. Seton. (Nature Library Ser.). (Illus.). 320p. 1981. pap. 5.95 (ISBN 0-06-090841-6, CN 841, CN). Har-Row.

Arctic Summer: Birds in North Norway. Richard Vaughan. (Illus.). 152p. 1980. 17.50 (ISBN 0-904614-01-8, Pub. by Anthony Nelson Ltd England). Buteo.

Arctic: Top of the World. Julian May. Ed. by Publication Associates. LC 75-156053. (Investigating the Earth Ser). (Illus.). (gr. 4-6). 1971. PLB 5.95 o.p. (ISBN 0-87191-057-8). Creative Ed.

Arctouros: Hellenic Studies Presented to Bernard M. Knos on the Occasion of His 65th Birthday. Ed. by Glen W. Bowerstock et al. 462p. 1980. 99.00x (ISBN 3-1100-7798-1). De Gruyter.

Arcturus Adventure. William Beebe. (Nature Library Ser.). 450p. 1981. pap. 5.95 (ISBN 0-06-090846-7, CN 846, CN). Har-Row.

Ardent Love Poetry by Dante Alighieri. Dante Alighieri. Tr. by Elliott Norton. (Most Meaningful Classics in World Culture Ser.). (Illus.). 117p. 1981. 59.45. Am Classical Coll Pr.

Ardente No Espiritu. (Portuguese Bks.). 1979. write for info. (ISBN 0-8297-0787-5). Vida Pub.

Ardis Anthology of Recent Russian Literature. Ed. by Carl R. Proffer & Ellendea Proffer. 1976. pap. 6.95 o.p. (ISBN 0-394-73291-X). Random.

Ardis Anthology of Russian Futurism. Ed. by Carl Proffer & Ellendea Proffer. (Illus.). 413p. 1980. 22.50 (ISBN 0-88233-469-7); pap. 7.50. Ardis Pubs.

Ardizzone's Hans Anderson. Edward Ardizzone. 1979. 10.95 (ISBN 0-689-50128-5, Mcelderry Bk). Atheneum.

Ardizzone's Kilvert: Selections from the Diary of the Rev. Francis Kilvert 1870-79. abr. ed. Illus. by Edward Ardizzone. (Illus.). 176p. (gr. 5-7). 1980. 7.95 (ISBN 0-224-01276-2, Pub. by Chatto Bodley Jonathan). Merrimack Bk Serv.

Are Government Organizations Immortal? Herbert Kaufman. 1976. pap. 3.95 (ISBN 0-8157-4839-6). Brookings.

Are Pesticides Really Necessary? Keith C. Barons. 280p. 1981. pap. 6.95 (ISBN 0-89526-888-4). Regnery-Gateway.

Are Science & Technology Neutral? Joan Lipscombe & Bill Williams. (Science in a Social Context Ser.). 1979. pap. 3.95 (ISBN 0-408-71312-7). Butterworths.

Are the Stars Out Tonight? The Story of the Famous Ambassador & Cocoanut Grove... Hollywood's Hotel. Margaret T. Burk. (Illus.). 190p. 1980. text ed. 15.00 (ISBN 0-937806-00-5). M Burk.

Are There Alien Beings? The Story of UFOs. Gerald S. Snyder. LC 80-10453. (Illus.). 160p. (gr. 7 up). 1980. PLB 7.79 (ISBN 0-671-33077-2). Messner.

Are There Any Answers? Clark H. Pinnock. 48p. 1976. pap. 1.75 (ISBN 0-87123-009-7). Bethany Fell.

Are There Spooks in the Dark? Claudia Fregosi. LC 76-9789. (Illus.). 32p. (gr. k-3). 1977. 5.95 (ISBN 0-590-07451-2, Four Winds). Schol Bk Serv.

Are Those Your Good Pants? Parker et al. 128p. (Orig.). 1981. pap. 1.75 (ISBN 0-449-14390-2, GM). Fawcett.

Are We Alone? James Trefil & Robert Rood. (Illus.). 224p. 1981. 10.95 (ISBN 0-684-16826-X, ScribT). Scribner.

Are We Still Best Friends? Carol Barkin & Elizabeth James. LC 75-19482. (Moods & Emotions Ser.). (Illus.). 32p. (gr. k-3). 1975. PLB 8.95 (ISBN 0-8172-0032-0). Raintree Pubs.

Are You a Computer Literate? Karen Billings & David Moursund. LC 79-56396. 150p. 1979. pap. 8.95 (ISBN 0-686-61254-X). Dilithium Pr.

Are You Anybody? Marilyn Funt. 352p. 1981. pap. 2.75 (ISBN 0-523-41413-7). Pinnacle Bks.

Are You Confused? Paavo Airola. 4.95 o.p. (ISBN 0-685-90564-0). Bi World Indus.

Are You Mad? Glen J. Hatfield. 1963. pap. 0.75 (ISBN 0-9600216-1-2). Hatfield.

Are You My Mother? In English & Spanish. Tr. by Carlos Rivera & P. D. Eastman. (Spanish Beginner Bks: No. 4). (gr. 2-4). 1967. 3.95 (ISBN 0-394-81596-3); PLB 5.99 (ISBN 0-394-91596-8). Random.

Are You Nobody? Paul Tournier et al. LC 66-21649. (Orig.). 1966. pap. 2.45 (ISBN 0-8042-3356-X). John Knox.

Are You Paying Too Much for Your Car? Herman Douglas. Ed. by Peggy Sweitzer. 1979. write for info. Web Pub Hse.

Are You Ready to Mainstream: Helping Preschoolers with Learning & Behavior Problems. Samuel J. Braun & Miriam G. Lasher. 1978. pap. text ed. 7.95 (ISBN 0-675-08443-1). Merrill.

Are You Real, God? Muriel K. Larson. pap. 2.95 (ISBN 0-89728-020-2, 654470). Omega Pubns OR.

Are You Tense? The Benjamin System of Muscular Therapy. Ben E. Benjamin. LC 77-88778. 1978. 15.95 (ISBN 0-394-49511-X); pap. 7.95 (ISBN 0-394-73499-8). Pantheon.

Are Young Children Egocentric? Ed. by M. V. Cox. 1980. 20.00 (ISBN 0-312-04839-4). St Martin.

Area. Jane J. Srivastava. LC 73-18057. (Young Math Ser.). (Illus.). (gr. 1-5). 1974. 7.95 (ISBN 0-690-00404-4, TYC-J); PLB 7.89 (ISBN 0-690-00405-2). T Y Crowell.

Area Health Education Centers: The Pioneering Years, 1972-1978. Charles E. Odegaard. LC 79-56245. (Carnegie Council on Policy Studies in Higher Education). 124p. 1980. pap. 5.00 (ISBN 0-295-95787-5). U of Wash Pr.

Area of Suspicion. John D. MacDonald. 208p. 1978. pap. 1.75 o.p. (ISBN 0-449-14008-3, GM). Fawcett.

Arena. Harlan Wade. Tr. by Mamie M. Contreras from Eng. LC 78-26821. (Book About Ser.). Orig. Title: Sand. (Illus., Sp.). (gr. k-3). 1979. PLB 7.30 (ISBN 0-8172-1476-3). Raintree Pubs.

Arena of Ants: A Novel. James Schevill. (Illus., Orig.). 1977. pap. 7.50 (ISBN 0-914278-11-8). Copper Beech.

Arena of International Finance. C. A. Coombs. 1976. 22.95 (ISBN 0-471-01513-X, Pub. by Wiley-Interscience). Wiley.

Areopagitica. John Milton. 80p. 1972. Repr. of 1644 ed. 7.50x (ISBN 0-87556-219-1). Saifer.

Aretha Franklin. James T. Olsen. LC 74-14672. (Rock'n Pop Stars Ser.). (Illus.). 32p. (gr. 4-12). 1974. PLB 5.95 (ISBN 0-87191-390-9); pap. 2.75 o. p. (ISBN 0-89812-100-0). Creative Ed.

Argentina: A City & a Nation. 2nd ed. James R. Scobie. (Latin American Histories Ser). 1971. 14.95 (ISBN 0-19-501479-0); pap. text ed. 4.95x (ISBN 0-19-501480-4). Oxford U Pr.

Argentina & the Failure of Democracy: Conflict Among the Political Elites, 1904-1955. Peter H. Smith. LC 74-5907. 320p. 1974. 20.00 (ISBN 0-299-06600-2). U of Wis Pr.

Argentina's Foreign Policies. Edward S. Milenky. LC 77-90536. 1978. lib. bdg. 28.00x (ISBN 0-89158-427-7). Westview.

Argentine Art before the Hispanic Domination. Giancarlo Puppo. (Illus.). 276p. 1980. 50.00 (ISBN 0-295-95772-7, Pub. by Edicolor Argentina). U of Wash Pr.

Argentine Economy. Aldo Ferrer. 1967. 18.00x (ISBN 0-520-00404-3). U of Cal Pr.

Argentine Penal Code. (American Series of Foreign Penal Codes: No. 6). 1963. 15.00x (ISBN 0-8377-0026-4). Rothman.

Argentis. E. C. Tubb. 112p. 1980. Repr. lib. bdg. 9.95x cancelled (ISBN 0-89370-097-5). Borgo Pr.

Argia. Antonio Cesti. Ed. by Howard M. Brown. LC 76-21082. (Italian Opera 1640-1770 Ser.: Vol. 3). 1978. lib. bdg. 75.00 (ISBN 0-8240-2602-0). Garland Pub.

Argillite: Art of the Haida. Leslie Drew & Douglas Wilson. (Illus.). 350p. 1980. 40.00x (ISBN 0-87663-609-1). Universe.

Arguing with God: The Angry Prayers of Job. Dale Patrick. 1977. pap. 2.95 (ISBN 0-8272-0013-7). Bethany Pr.

Argument: A Guide to Formal & Informal Debate. 2nd ed. Abne M. Eisenberg & Joseph A. Ilardo. (Speech Communication Ser.). (Illus.). 1980. pap. 11.95 (ISBN 0-13-045989-5). P-H.

Argument: Brown vs. Board of Education of Topeka, 1925-55, 2 vols. 2nd ed. Ed. by Leon Friedman. LC 70-75118. (Oral Arguments Before the Supreme Court Ser.). 610p. 1981. Set. pap. 12.95 (ISBN 0-87754-210-4). Chelsea Hse.

Argument of Master Nicholas Fuller, in the Case of Thomas Lad, & Richard Maunsell...Proved That the Ecclesiasticall Commissioners Have No Power...to Imprison...His Maiesties Subjects. Nicholas Fuller. LC 74-28857. (English Experience Ser.: No. 738). 1975. Repr. of 1607 ed. 3.50 (ISBN 90-221-0738-8). Walter J Johnson.

Argument of the Book of Job Unfolded. William H. Green. 10.75 (ISBN 0-686-12967-9). Klock & Klock.

Argumentation & Debate. James E. Sayer. LC 79-24519. 1980. 13.50 (ISBN 0-88284-102-5). Alfred Pub.

Argumentation & Debate: A Classified Bibliography. 2nd ed. Arthur N. Kruger. LC 74-17198. 1975. 21.00 (ISBN 0-8108-0749-1). Scarecrow.

Argumentation & Debate: Rational Decision-Making. 4th ed. Austin J. Freeley. 1976. 15.95x (ISBN 0-534-00420-2). Wadsworth Pub.

Argumentation & the Decision Making Process. Richard D. Rieke & Malcolm O. Sillars. LC 74-20900. 288p. 1975. 13.95 (ISBN 0-471-72165-4). Wiley.

Argumentation: Approaches to Theory Formation: Proceedings. Symposium on Theory of Argumentation, Groningen, October 11-13, 1978. Ed. by Marten & Barth. (Studies in Language Companion Ser.: No. 8). 250p. 1980. text ed. 31.50x (ISBN 90-272-3007-2). Humanities.

Argumentation: Inquiry & Advocacy. George W. Ziegelmueller & Charles A. Dause. LC 74-7358. (Speech Communications Ser.). (Illus.). 336p. 1975. 14.95 (ISBN 0-13-046029-X). P-H.

Argumentation: Reasoning in Communication. Vernon Jensen. 1980. text ed. 15.95 (ISBN 0-442-25396-6); instr's. manual 2.00 (ISBN 0-442-24213-1). D Van Nostrand.

Arguments, Arrows, Trees, & Truth. 2nd ed. Harlan B. Miller. Ed. by Dwight Schumway. (Illus.). 242p. (Orig.). 1980. pap. text ed. 8.65x (ISBN 0-89894-036-2). Advocate Pub Group.

Arguments in History: Britain in the 19th Century. N. H. Brasher. LC 68-10753. (Illus.). 1969. 15.95 (ISBN 0-312-04900-5). St Martin.

Arguments of Idea. Peyton Houston. 1980. pap. 8.50 (ISBN 0-912330-45-7). Jargon Soc.

Ariadne. Batya Podos. LC 80-70233. 52p. (Orig.). 1980. pap. 3.00 (ISBN 0-9603628-2-7). Frog in Well.

Arias from a Love Opera: Other Poems. Robert Conquest. LC 71-79030. 1970. 4.95 o.s.i. (ISBN 0-02-527570-4). Macmillan.

Arid-Land Ecosystems: Structure, Functioning & Management, Vol. 2. Ed. by D. W. Goodall & R. A. Perry. LC 77-84810. (International Biological Programme Ser.: No. 17). 550p. Date not set. 110.00 (ISBN 0-521-22988-X). Cambridge U Pr.

Arid Land Irrigation in Developing Countries: Environmental Problems & Effects. Ed. by E. Barton Worthington. 1977. text ed. 105.00 (ISBN 0-08-021588-2). Pergamon.

Arid Zone Settlement Planning: The Israeli Experience. Ed. by Gideon Golany. (Pergamon Policy Studies). 1979. 53.00 (ISBN 0-08-023378-3). Pergamon.

Ariel Custer. Grace L. Hill. 192p. 1981. pap. 1.95 (ISBN 0-553-14520-7). Bantam.

Ariel: Essays on the Arts & the History & Philosophy of Medicine. Felix Marti-Ibanez. LC 62-8490. (Illus.). 1962. 6.50 o.p. (ISBN 0-910922-16-0). MD Pubns.

Ariel: The Book of Fantasy. 1977. 6.95 (ISBN 0-345-27319-2). Ballantine.

Aries. Kathleen Paul. (Sun Signs). (Illus.). (gr. 4-12). 1978. PLB 5.95 (ISBN 0-87191-641-X); pap. 2.95 (ISBN 0-89812-071-3). Creative Ed.

Aries I. Ed. by John Grant. LC 79-53731. 192p. 1979. 15.95 (ISBN 0-7153-7777-9). David & Charles.

Aries Press Journal: The New Age Anthology. Ed. by Cettie DeMaroo & Del O'Connor. (Illus.). 1980. pap. 3.00 quarterly (ISBN 0-933646-14-3); annual subscription 10.00. Aries Pr.

Arilla Sun Down. Virginia Hamilton. LC 76-13180. 256p. (gr. 7 up). 1976. 9.25 (ISBN 0-688-80058-0); PLB 8.88 (ISBN 0-688-84058-2). Greenwillow.

Ariodant. Etienne Mehul. Ed. by Philip Gossett & Charles Rosen. LC 76-49220. (Early Romantic Opera Ser.). 1979. lib. bdg. 82.00 (ISBN 0-8240-2938-0). Garland Pub.

Arise & Evangelize. Don J. Jennings. 1975. pap. 1.25 (ISBN 0-87398-024-7, Pub. by Bibl Evang Pr). Sword of Lord.

Arise, My Love. Solomon. LC 75-4077. (Illus.). 56p. (From King James Version - Song of Songs). 1975. 15.95 (ISBN 0-570-03253-9, 15-2161); pap. 6.95 (ISBN 0-570-03712-3, 12-2614). Concordia.

Aristocats. Walt Disney Productions. LC 73-15626. (Illus.). 48p. 1974. 3.95 o.p. (ISBN 0-394-82553-5, BYR); PLB 4.99 o.p. (ISBN 0-394-92553-X). Random.

Aristocracy of Labor. G. MacKenzie. LC 73-80484. (Studies in Sociology). (Illus.). 208p. 1973. pap. 9.95x (ISBN 0-521-09825-4). Cambridge U Pr.

Aristocrats & Traders: Sevillian Society in the Sixteenth Century. Ruth Pike. LC 76-37756. 256p. 1972. 17.50 (ISBN 0-8014-0699-4). Cornell U Pr.

Aristophanes. Lois S. Spatz. (World Authors Ser.: No. 482). 1978. lib. bdg. 10.95 (ISBN 0-8057-6323-6). Twayne.

Aristophanes: Clouds, Women in Power, Knights. Tr. by K. McLeish. LC 78-51680. (Translations from Greek & Roman Authors). 1980. 28.50 (ISBN 0-521-22009-2); pap. 7.95 (ISBN 0-521-29707-9). Cambridge U Pr.

Aristophanes: Essays in Interpretation. Ed. by J. Henderson. LC 80-40042. (Yale Classical Studies: No. 26). 248p. Date not set. 35.00 (ISBN 0-521-23120-5). Cambridge U Pr.

Aristophanic Comedy. K. J. Dover. 1972. 14.00 o.p. (ISBN 0-520-01976-8); pap. 7.95x (ISBN 0-520-02211-4, CAMPUS77). U of Cal Pr.

Aristote. D. Ross. (Publications Gramma Ser.). 1971. 26.50x (ISBN 0-685-33030-3). Gordon.

Aristotelianism. John L. Stocks. LC 63-10300. (Our Debt to Greece & Rome Ser). 1963. Repr. of 1930 ed. 16.50x (ISBN 0-8154-0220-1). Cooper Sq.

Aristotelis Valaoritis. Constantine Santas. LC 76-10673. (World Author Ser: No. 406). 1976. lib. bdg. 12.50 (ISBN 0-8057-6246-9). Twayne.

Aristotle. John Ferguson. (World Authors Ser.: Greece: No. 211). lib. bdg. 10.95 (ISBN 0-8057-2064-2). Twayne.

Aristotle. G. R. Mure. LC 75-17199. 282p. 1975. Repr. of 1932 ed. lib. bdg. 22.25x (ISBN 0-8371-8298-0, MUAR). Greenwood.

Aristotle. John H. Randall. LC 60-6030. 1960. 20.00x (ISBN 0-231-02359-6); pap. 6.00x (ISBN 0-231-08529-X). Columbia U Pr.

Aristotle & His World View. Franz Brentano. Tr. by Rolf George & Roderick Chisholm. 1978. 15.50x (ISBN 0-520-03390-6). U of Cal Pr.

Aristotle & the Arabs: The Aristotelian Tradition in Islam. F. E. Peters. LC 68-29431. (New York Studies in Near Eastern Civilization: No. 1). 1968. 15.00x (ISBN 0-8147-0342-9). NYU Pr.

Aristotle & Xenophon on Democracy & Oligarchy. John M. Moore. LC 74-16713. 1975. 19.50x (ISBN 0-520-02863-5); pap. 5.95x (ISBN 0-520-02909-7). U of Cal Pr.

Aristotle Detective. Margaret Doody. (Penguin Crime Monthly Ser.). 1981. pap. 2.95 (ISBN 0-14-005753-6). Penguin.

Aristotle for Everyone: Difficult Thought Made Easy. Mortimer J. Adler. 1978. 10.95 (ISBN 0-02-503100-7). Macmillan.

Aristotle: Growth & Structure of His Thought. Geoffrey E. Lloyd. LC 68-21195. (Orig.). 1968. 38.50 (ISBN 0-521-07049-X); pap. 9.95x (ISBN 0-521-09456-9). Cambridge U Pr.

Aristotle on Memory. Richard Sorabji. LC 72-79966. 122p. 1972. 6.50 (ISBN 0-87057-137-0, Pub. by Brown U Pr). Univ Pr of New England.

Aristotle on Mind & the Senses. Ed. by G. E. Lloyd & G. E. Owen. LC 77-9389. (Classical Studies). 1978. 38.50 (ISBN 0-521-21669-9). Cambridge U Pr.

Aristotle Onassis. Nicholas Fraser et al. LC 77-24417. (Illus.). 1977. 12.50 o.p. (ISBN 0-397-01218-7). Lippincott.

Aristotle, Rhetoric I: A Commentary. William M. Grimaldi. LC 79-53372. 1980. 45.00 (ISBN 0-8232-1048-0). Fordham.

Aristotle: Selections from Seven Books. enl. ed. Aristotle. Ed. by Philip Wheelwright. 1951. pap. 7.50 (ISBN 0-672-63010-9). Odyssey Pr.

Aristotle: The Classical Heritage of Rhetoric. Keith Erickson. LC 74-10775. 1974. 14.00 (ISBN 0-8108-0740-8). Scarecrow.

Aristotle's Categories & Propositions (De Interpretatione) H. G. Apostle. LC 80-80777. 157p. (Orig.). 1980. lib. bdg. 12.00 (ISBN 0-9602870-4-3); pap. text ed. 6.00 (ISBN 0-9602870-5-1). Peripatetic.

Aristotle's Concept of Dialectic. J. D. Evans. LC 76-22982. 1977. 22.95 (ISBN 0-521-21425-4). Cambridge U Pr.

Aristotle's De Partibus Animalium: Critical & Literary Commentaries. Ingemar During. LC 78-66548. (Ancient Philosophy Ser.). 223p. 1980. lib. bdg. 22.00 (ISBN 0-8240-9602-9). Garland Pub.

Aristotle's Ethical Theory. 2nd ed. W. F. Hardie. 472p. 1981. 49.95x (ISBN 0-19-824632-3); pap. 24.95x (ISBN 0-19-824633-1). Oxford U Pr.

Aristotle's Ethics. J. L. Ackrill. text ed. 15.00x (ISBN 0-391-00281-3). Humanities.

Aristotle's Nicomachean Ethics: Commentary & Analysis. Francis H. Eterovich. LC 80-5202. 331p. 1980. text ed. 19.75 (ISBN 0-8191-1056-6); pap. text ed. 11.50 (ISBN 0-8191-1057-4). U Pr of Amer.

Aristotle's Physics. Hippocrates G. Apostle. LC 80-80037. 386p. 1980. lib. bdg. 17.50 (ISBN 0-9602870-2-7); pap. text ed. 8.50 (ISBN 0-9602870-3-5). Peripatetic.

Aristotle's Physics. Aristotle. Tr. by Richard Hope. LC 61-5498. 1961. pap. 4.50x (ISBN 0-8032-5093-2, BB122, Bison). U of Nebr Pr.

Aristotle's Posterior Analytics. H. G. Apostle. LC 81-80233. (Apostle Translations of Aristotle's Works Ser.: Vol. 4). 350p. (Orig.). 1981. text ed. 19.20x (ISBN 0-9602870-6-X); pap. text ed. 9.60x (ISBN 0-9602870-7-8). Peripatetic.

Aristotle's Theology: A Commentary on the Book of Metaphysics. L. Elders. (Philosophical Texts & Studies). 336p. 1972. text ed. 43.50x (ISBN 90-232-0978-8). Humanities.

Arithma Games-Whole Numbers. (gr. 1-4). 1980. pap. 7.20 (ISBN 0-913688-48-7). Pawnee Pub.

Arithmetic. Dennis Bila et al. LC 76-19446. 1976. 5.95x (ISBN 0-87901-058-4). Worth.

Arithmetic. 3rd ed. Mervin L. Keedy & Marvin L. Bittinger. LC 78-18648. 1979. pap. text ed. 13.95 (ISBN 0-201-03791-2); avail. instructor's manual with tests (ISBN 0-201-03792-0); test book 9.95 (ISBN 0-201-03795-5); student's guide to margin exercises 3.95 (ISBN 0-201-03794-7). A-W.

Arithmetic. 2nd ed. S. Preis & G. Cocks. 1980. pap. 14.95 o.p. (ISBN 0-13-046201-2). P-H.

Arithmetic: A Practical Approach. G. J. Shugar & R. S. Bauman. 1977. pap. text ed. 10.95x (ISBN 0-02-478520-2). Macmillan.

Arithmetic: A Review. J. L. Nanney & R. D. Shaffer. text ed. 15.95x (ISBN 0-471-62990-1). Wiley.

Arithmetic: A Text-Workbook. Charles D. Miller & Stanley A. Salzman. 1981. pap. text ed. 13.95x (ISBN 0-673-15274-X). Scott F.

Arithmetic: An Applied Approach. Richard N. Aufmann & Vernon C. Barker. LC 77-77005. (Illus.). 1978. pap. text ed. 15.25 (ISBN 0-395-25791-3); inst. manual 0.50 (ISBN 0-395-25790-5). HM.

Arithmetic & Algebra. 2nd ed. Daniel D. Benice. (Illus.). 1979. pap. text ed. 14.95 (ISBN 0-13-046094-X). P-H.

Arithmetic & Calculators: How to Deal with Arithmetic in the Calculator Age. William G. Chinn et al. LC 77-11111. (Illus.). 1978. text ed. 22.95x (ISBN 0-7167-0016-6); pap. text ed. 12.95x (ISBN 0-7167-0015-8); solutions manual avail. W H Freeman.

Arithmetic & Learning Disabilities: Guidelines for Identification & Remediation. Stanley W. Johnson. 1979. pap. text ed. 10.95x (ISBN 0-205-06504-X). Allyn.

Arithmetic Applied Mathematics. Donald Greenspan. LC 80-40295. (Illus.). 172p. 1980. 29.00 (ISBN 0-08-025047-5); pap. 12.00 (ISBN 0-08-025046-7). Pergamon.

Arithmetic Clear & Simple. Julio A. Mira. (Orig.). 1965. pap. 2.95 (ISBN 0-06-463270-9, EH 270, EH). Har-Row.

Arithmetic, Complete Course. Charlene Pappin. Ed. by Eugene Maier. 1970. pap. text ed. 10.95x (ISBN 0-02-476650-X, 47665); progress tests 9.95x (ISBN 0-02-476640-2, 47664). Macmillan.

Arithmetic for Careers. Curriculum Committee of St. Paul Technical Vocational Institute. LC 78-52661. (Mathematics Ser.). 1980. pap. text ed. 15.00 (ISBN 0-8273-1676-3); instructor's guide 1.75 (ISBN 0-8273-1677-1). Delmar.

Arithmetic for College Students. Karl J. Smith. 400p. 1981. text ed. 16.95 (ISBN 0-8185-0422-6). Brooks-Cole.

Arithmetic for Self-Study. 2nd ed. Frances S. Mangan. 1975. text ed. 15.95x (ISBN 0-534-00380-X). Wadsworth Pub.

Arithmetic for the Trades: A Guided Approach. Robert A. Carman & Hal M. Saunders. 1980. pap. text ed. write for info. (ISBN 0-471-05968-4). Wiley.

Arithmetic Fundamentals. new ed. Jack G. Pease & Robert Russell. 240p. 1975. pap. text ed. 11.95x (ISBN 0-675-08767-8). Merrill.

Arithmetic Made Simple. A. P. Sperling. pap. 3.50 (ISBN 0-385-00983-6, Made). Doubleday.

Arithmetic Modules. T. J. McHale & P. T. Witzke. 125p. 1975. module 1 4.95 (ISBN 0-201-04751-9); module 2 4.95 (ISBN 0-201-04752-7); module 3 4.95 (ISBN 0-201-04753-5); module 4 4.95 (ISBN 0-201-04754-3); module 5 4.95 (ISBN 0-201-04756-X); test bklt 4.95 (ISBN 0-201-04758-6); ans. keys avail. (ISBN 0-685-52163-X). A-W.

Arithmetic of Dosages & Solutions. 5th ed. Laura K. Hart. (Illus.). 100p. 1981. spiral bdg. 7.95 (ISBN 0-8016-2076-7). Mosby.

Arithmetic Primer. Paul Shoecraft. (gr. 4 up). 1979. pap. text ed. 11.50 (ISBN 0-201-07321-8, Sch Div); tchrs'. materials 4.90 (ISBN 0-201-07143-6, Sch Div). A-W.

Arithmetic Review for Electronics. Nelson M. Cooke & Herbert F. Adams. 1968. 11.95 (ISBN 0-07-012516-3, G); answers to review problems 1.00 (ISBN 0-07-012517-1). McGraw.

Arithmetic Series, 10 bks. Francis H. Wise & Joyce M. Wise. Incl. Bk. 3. An Adding XV. 1979 (ISBN 0-915766-45-0); Vol. 2. Arithmetic Books 6-10. 1979; Bk. 4. Subtraction. 1980; Bk. 5. Column. 1980; Bk. 6. Multiply. 1980; Bk. 7. Division. 1980; Bk. 8. Fractions. 1980; Bk. 9. Carry. 1980; Bk. 10. Borrow. 1980. (Illus.). 105p. (gr. k-2). pap. 1.50 ea. Wise Pub.

Arithmetic Skills. Calman Goozner. (gr. 7-12). 1973. text ed. 11.17 (ISBN 0-87720-238-9); pap. text ed. 5.83 (ISBN 0-87720-237-0); wkbk 7.08 (ISBN 0-87720-236-2). AMSCO Sch.

Arithmetic Skills in Everyday Life: A Self-Correcting Competency Assessment. David Spangler. 112p. 1980. pap. text ed. 2.95x (ISBN 0-534-00917-4). Wadsworth Pub.

Arithmetic: The Essentials. Richard C. Spangler. 576p. (Orig.). 1981. pap. text ed. 15.95 (ISBN 0-675-08066-5); tchr's. ed. 5.95 (ISBN 0-675-09971-4). Merrill.

Arithmetic with Pushbutton Accuracy. Herman R. Hyatt et al. LC 76-4558. 1977. text ed. 17.95 (ISBN 0-471-22308-5); tchrs. manual 5.00 (ISBN 0-471-02395-7). Wiley.

Arithmetic Without Trumpets or Drums. Martin Zuckerman. 1978. pap. text ed. 16.95 (ISBN 0-205-06163-X); instr's man. avail. (ISBN 0-205-05916-3). Allyn.

Arithmetical Abstractions: The Movement Toward Conceptual Maturity Under Differing Systems of Instructions. William A. Brownell. (U. C. Publ. in Education: Vol. 17). 1967. pap. 10.00x (ISBN 0-520-09063-2). U of Cal Pr.

Arithmetical Disabilities in Cerebral Palsied Children: Programmed Instruction - a Remedial Approach. Simon H. Haskell. 132p. 1973. 10.75 (ISBN 0-398-02537-1). C C Thomas.

Arithmetics Groups. J. E. Humphreys. (Lecture Notes in Mathematics: Vol. 789). 158p. 1980. pap. 11.80 (ISBN 0-387-09972-7). Springer-Verlag.

Arizona. 23.00 (ISBN 0-89770-079-1). Curriculum Info Ctr.

Arizona. Lawrence C. Powell. (States & the Nation Ser.). (Illus.). 1976. 12.95 (ISBN 0-393-05575-2, Co-Pub by AASLH). Norton.

Arizona! Jay J. Wagoner. (Illus.). (gr. 4). 1979. text ed. 11.95x (ISBN 0-87905-105-1). Peregrine Smith.

Arizona: A Short History. Odie B. Faulk. (Illus.). 1970. 7.95 (ISBN 0-8061-0917-3); pap. 4.95 (ISBN 0-8061-1222-0). U of Okla Pr.

Arizona Cavalcade. Ed. by Joseph Miller. (Illus.). 1962. 7.95 (ISBN 0-8038-0320-6). Hastings.

Arizona Flora. 2nd rev. ed. Thomas H. Kearney et al. (Illus.). 1960. 26.50 (ISBN 0-520-00637-2). U of Cal Pr.

Arizona Gold Placers & Placering. Eldred D. Wilson. (Illus.). 148p. 1980. pap. 5.95 (ISBN 0-89632-003-0). Del Oeste.

Arizona in Literature. Mary G. Boyer. LC 74-145714. 1971. Repr. of 1935 ed. 32.00 (ISBN 0-8103-3703-7). Gale.

Arizona Industrial Minerals. 1975. 15.80. Minobras.

Arizona: Its Constitution & Government. Gerald Hansen. LC 78-65846. (Illus.). 1979. text ed. 7.50 (ISBN 0-8191-0673-9). U Pr of Amer.

Arizona Justice. Gordon D. Shirreffs. 1977. pap. 1.50 (ISBN 0-505-51195-9). Tower Bks.

Arizona Life & Disability. 1980. 13.50 (ISBN 0-930868-07-2). Merritt Co.

Arizona Longhorn Adventure. Sandy Dengler. 128p. (gr. 5-8). 1980. pap. 1.95 (ISBN 0-8024-0299-2). Moody.

Arizona Nights. Stewart E. White. 1976. lib. bdg. 15.75x (ISBN 0-89968-124-7). Lightyear.

Arizona Odyssey: Bibliographic Adventures in Nineteenth Century Magazines. David M. Goodman. LC 73-94875. 1969. 20.00 (ISBN 0-685-67969-1). AZ Hist Foun.

Arizona Pageant: A Short History of the 48th State. Madeline F. Pare & Bert M. Fireman. LC 65-65080. 1978. text ed. 7.00 (ISBN 0-685-67966-7). AZ Hist Foun.

Arizona Project: How a Team of Investigative Reporters Got Revenge on Deadline. Michael F. Wendland. 1978. 9.95 o.p. (ISBN 0-8362-0728-9). Andrews & McMeel.

Arizona Property & Casualty. 1978. 13.00 (ISBN 0-930868-08-0). Merritt Co.

Arizona Real Estate Laws. LC 74-180200. 1979. looseleaf 29.50 (ISBN 0-918356-00-8). MSC Inc.

Arizona School Law. Emil Larson. LC 64-17272. 1964. 2.00 (ISBN 0-8165-0277-3). U of Ariz Pr.

Arizona State Industrial Directory, 1980. State Industrial Directories Corp. 1980. pap. 35.00 (ISBN 0-89910-025-2). State Indus Dir.

Arizona Supplement to Modern Real Estate Practice. 3rd ed. Charles E. Myler, Jr. 200p. (Orig.). 1980. pap. 7.95 (ISBN 0-88462-295-9). Real Estate Ed Co.

Arizona Territory 1863-1912: A Political History. Jay J. Wagoner. LC 69-16331. (Illus.). 512p. 1970. pap. 12.95x (ISBN 0-8165-0176-9). U of Ariz Pr.

Arizona Trails. David Mazel. Ed. by Thomas Winnett. LC 80-53682. (Wilderness Press Trail Guide Ser.). (Illus.). 192p. (Orig.). 1981. pap. 7.95 (ISBN 0-89997-003-6). Wilderness Pr.

Arizona: Travel Guide. 5th ed. Sunset Editors. LC 78-53677. (Illus.). 112p. 1978. pap. 4.95 (ISBN 0-376-06056-5, Sunset Bks.). Sunset-Lane.

Arizona's Heritage. Jay Wagoner. LC 77-10778. (Illus.). (gr. 8-12). 1977. text ed. 15.00x (ISBN 0-87905-028-4). Peregrine Smith.

Arizona's Natural Environment: Landscapes & Habitats. Charles H. Lowe, Jr. 136p. 1972. pap. 3.95x (ISBN 0-8165-0349-4). U of Ariz Pr.

Arizona's Story: A Short History. Frank Love. (Illus.). 1979. pap. 7.95x (ISBN 0-87108-218-7); tchr's ed. 3.95 (ISBN 0-87108-234-9). Pruett.

Arjuna in Meditation. Tr. by Harry Aveling. 1976. 14.00 (ISBN 0-89253-799-X); flexible cloth 8.00 (ISBN 0-89253-800-7). Ind-US Inc.

Ark & the Dove: The Beginnings of Civil & Religious Liberties in America. J. Moss Ives. LC 76-79200. (Illus.). 1969. Repr. of 1936 ed. 32.50x (ISBN 0-8154-0293-7). Cooper Sq.

Ark II: Social Response to Environmental Imperatives. Dennis C. Pirages & Paul R. Ehrlich. (Illus.). 1974. pap. text ed. 9.95x (ISBN 0-7167-0847-7). W H Freeman.

Ark Narrative. Antony F. Campbell. LC 75-2361. (Society of Biblical Literature. Dissertation Ser.). vii, 282p. 1975. pap. 6.00 (ISBN 0-89130-218-2, 060116). Scholars Pr Ca.

Ark of Bones: And Other Stories. Henry Dumas. Ed. by Eugene Redmond. LC 74-4143. 1974. pap. 2.95 o.p. (ISBN 0-394-70947-0). Random.

Ark of Doom. Richard Woodley. 1978. pap. 1.50 o.s.i. (ISBN 0-440-15927-X). Dell.

Ark Royal: A Pictorial History of the Royal Navy's Last Conventional Aircraft Carrier. Paul Beaver. (Illus.). 96p. 1980. 19.95 (ISBN 0-85059-381-6). Aztex.

Ark: The Foundations One to Thirty Three. Ronald Johnson. 88p. 1980. 12.50 (ISBN 0-86547-011-1); pap. 6.00 (ISBN 0-86547-012-X). N Point Pr.

Arkadii Averchenko. Nechistaia Sila. (Panteon Sovietov Molodym Liugiam, Deti). 1979. 7.95 (ISBN 0-89830-010-X). Russica Pubs.

Arkansas. 28.00 (ISBN 0-89770-078-3). Curriculum Info Ctr.

Arkansas. Harry S. Ashmore. (States & the Nation Ser.). (Illus.). 1978. 12.95 (ISBN 0-393-05669-4, Co-Pub by AASLH). Norton.

Arkansas: A Guide to the State. LC 72-84459. 1941. 40.00 (ISBN 0-403-03309-8). Somerset Pub.

Arkansas Property & Casualty. 1980. 14.00 (ISBN 0-930868-09-9). Merritt Co.

Arkansas State Industrial Directory, 1980. State Industrial Directories Corp. 1980. pap. 40.00 (ISBN 0-89910-000-7). State Indus Dir.

Arkansas Statutes Annotated, 25 vols. write for info (ISBN 0-672-84050-2, Bobbs-Merrill Law); write for info. 1979 suppl. (ISBN 0-672-82483-3). Michie.

Arkansas Supplement for Modern Real Estate Practice. Donald R. Epley. 1978. pap. 7.95 o.p. (ISBN 0-88462-345-9). Real Estate Ed Co.

Arkansas Supplement for Modern Real Estate Practice. nd ed. Donald R. Epley. 160p. (Orig.). 1980. pap. 7.95 (ISBN 0-88462-344-0). Real Estate Ed Co.

Arkansas Valley Interurban. M. D. Isely. (Special Ser.: No. 19). (Illus.). 1977. pap. 6.00 (ISBN 0-916374-29-7). Interurban.

Arkansas...Its Land & People. Matt Bradley. LC 80-81993. (Illus.). 112p. 1980. 25.00 (ISBN 0-9604642-0-4); limited gift edition 55.00 (ISBN 0-9604642-1-2). Mus Sci & Hist.

Arkansaw Bear. Aurand Harris. (Orig.). 1980. playscript 2.00 (ISBN 0-87602-226-3). Anchorage.

Arlene Alda's ABC Book. Arlene Alda. LC 80-66261. (Illus.). 64p. (ps-2). 1981. 12.95 (ISBN 0-89742-043-8). Dawne-Leigh. Postponed.

Arlette. Nicolas Freeling. 1981. 10.95 (ISBN 0-394-51454-8). Pantheon.

Arli. James W. Burke. LC 78-66393. 1978. 8.95 o.p. (ISBN 0-916054-80-2). Caroline Hse.

Arlington: Child of the Columbia. Marion T. Weatherford. LC 77-80362. (Illus.). 280p. 1977. pap. 6.95 (ISBN 0-87595-056-6). Oreg Hist Soc.

Arlo Guthrie Book. Arlo Guthrie. 1969. pap. 2.95 o.s.i. (ISBN 0-02-060680-X, Collier). Macmillan.

Arm in Arm. Remy Charlip. LC 80-18091. (Illus.). 48p. (gr. 1-5). 1980. Repr. of 1969 ed. 9.95 (ISBN 0-590-07758-9, Four Winds). Schol Bk Serv.

Arm of the Starfish. Madeline L'Engle. (YA) (gr. 7-12). 1979. pap. 1.75 (ISBN 0-440-90183-9, LFL). Dell.

Armada. Michael Jahn. 224p. (Orig.). 1981. pap. 2.25 (ISBN 0-449-14388-0, GM). Fawcett.

Armada. Bryce Walker. Ed. by Time-Life Bks. Eds. (Seafarers Ser.). (Illus.). 176p. 1981. 14.95 (ISBN 0-8094-2697-8). Time-Life.

Armadale. Wilkie Collins. (Zodiac Press Ser.). 1978. 9.95 (ISBN 0-7011-1375-8, Pub. by Chatto Bodley Jonathan). Merrimack Bk Serv.

Armageddon. Leon Uris. pap. 3.50 (ISBN 0-440-10290-1). Dell.

Armageddon: Heaven's Holy War on Earth. Dennis M. Battle. LC 80-65197. 56p. 1980. pap. 2.50 (ISBN 0-933464-07-X). D M Battle Pubns.

Armagedom. Tr. by John F. Walwoord & John E. Walwoord. (Portuguese Bks.). 1979. 1.40 (ISBN 0-8297-0639-9). Life Pubs Intl.

Armagedon. Tr. by John F. Walwoord & John E. Walwoord. (Spanish Bks.). (Span.). 1979. 1.90 (ISBN 0-8297-0495-7). Life Pubs Intl.

Armament of British Aircraft Nineteen Hundred & Nine to Nineteen Thirty-Nine. H. F. King. (Putnam Aeronautical Ser.). (Illus.). 1980. 17.95 (ISBN 0-370-00057-9, Pub. by Chatto Bodley Jonathan). Merrimack Bk Serv.

Armance. Marie H. Beyle. Tr. by Gilbert Sale & Suzanne Sale. 7.25 o.p. (ISBN 0-85036-090-0). Dufour.

Armand Hammer Collection: Five Centuries of Masterpieces. Ed. by John Walker. (Illus.). 296p. 1980. 85.00 o.p. (ISBN 0-686-62685-0, 1069-1). Abrams.

Armand-Jean De Rance, Abbot of la Trappe: His Influence in the Cloister & the World. A. J. Krailsheimer. (Illus.). 384p. 1974. text ed. 34.50x (ISBN 0-19-815744-4). Oxford U Pr.

Armchair Engineer. Hall C. Roland. 120p. (Orig.). 1981. pap. 4.95 (ISBN 0-918398-51-7). Dilithium Pr.

Armchair Millionaire. Fred H. Vice. 120p. (Orig.). pap. 7.95 (ISBN 0-87364-204-X). Paladin Ent.

Armed America: Its Face in Fiction: A History of the American Military Novel. Wayne Charles Miller. LC 75-111521. 294p. 1970. 12.00x (ISBN 0-8147-0473-5). NYU Pr.

Armed Forces of the United Kingdom. Chris Chant. LC 80-66428. (Illus.). 80p. 1980. 14.95 (ISBN 0-7153-8024-9). David & Charles.

Armed Forces of the USSR. Harriet Scott & William Scott. (Illus.). 1979. lib. bdg. 30.00 (ISBN 0-89158-276-2); pap. 12.50 (ISBN 0-86531-087-4). Westview.

Armed Forces of the USSR. rev. ed. Harriet F. Scott & William F. Scott. 440p. 1981. lib. bdg. 27.50x (ISBN 0-86531-194-3); pap. text ed. 12.50x (ISBN 0-86531-087-4). Westview.

Armed Forces of the World: A Reference Handbook. 4th ed. Ed. by Robert C. Sellers. LC 76-12874. (Special Studies). 1977. text ed. 32.50 (ISBN 0-275-23200-X). Praeger.

Armed Love. Eleanor Lerman. (Wesleyan Poetry Program: Vol. 68). 1973. pap. 4.95 (ISBN 0-8195-1068-8, Pub. by Wesleyan U Pr). Columbia U Pr.

Armed Robbery: Offenders & Their Victims. John M. Macdonald. 456p. 1975. 24.75 (ISBN 0-398-03350-1). C C Thomas.

Armed Struggle in Palestine: A Political - Military Analysis. Bard O'Neill. LC 78-2285. (Westview Special Studies on the Middle East Ser.). 1978. lib. bdg. 26.50x (ISBN 0-89158-333-5). Westview.

Armed with the Spirit: Missionary Experiences in Samoa. W. Karl Brewer. LC 75-15553. (Illus.). 237p. 1975. pap. 4.95 o.p. (ISBN 0-8425-0817-1). Brigham.

Armenia & the Near East. Fridtjof Nansen. LC 76-25120. (Middle East in the Twentieth Century Ser.). 1977. Repr. of 1928 ed. lib. bdg. 29.50 (ISBN 0-306-70760-8). Da Capo.

Armenia: Cradle of Civilisation. 3rd ed. D. M. Lang. (Illus.). 330p. 1980. 35.00 (ISBN 0-04-956009-3, 2619). Allen Unwin.

Armenia on the Road to Independence, 1918. Richard G. Hovannisian. (Near Eastern Center, UCLA). 1967. 18.75x (ISBN 0-520-00574-0). U of Cal Pr.

Armenia: The Survival of a Nation. Christopher J. Walker. LC 80-10461. 1980. 30.00 (ISBN 0-312-04944-7). St Martin.

Armenian Arm of Theology. Howard A. Slaatte. 1977. 7.50 (ISBN 0-8191-0252-0). U Pr of Amer.

Armenian Cookbook. Rachel Hogrogian. LC 76-139312. (Illus.). 1975. pap. 4.95 (ISBN 0-689-70518-2, 208). Atheneum.

Armenian-English - English-Armenian Dictionary. 2nd, rev. ed. Mardiros Koushakdjian & Dicran Khantrouni. 1372p. 1976. 35.00 (ISBN 0-686-68934-8). Heinman.

Armenian-English Dictionary. Mathias Bedrossian. 30.00x (ISBN 0-685-85420-5). Intl Bk Ctr.

Armenian Mythology & African Mythology. Mardiros H. Ananikian. (Mythology of All Races Ser.: Vol. VII). Repr. of 1932 ed. 23.50 (ISBN 0-8154-0011-X). Cooper Sq.

Armenian Poetry Old & New: A Bilingual Anthology. Tr. by Aram Tolegian. LC 79-971. (Eng. & Armenian.). 1979. 18.95x (ISBN 0-8143-1608-5). Wayne St U Pr.

Armenian Revolutionary Movement: The Development of Armenian Political Parties Through the Nineteenth Century. Louise Z. Nalbandian. (Near Eastern Center, UCLA). 1963. 15.75 (ISBN 0-520-00914-2). U of Cal Pr.

Armenian Version of IV Ezra. Ed. by Michael E. Stone. LC 78-17084. 1979. 15.00 (ISBN 0-89130-287-5); pap. 10.50 (ISBN 0-89130-255-7, 210201). Scholars Pr Ca.

Armenians. David M. Lang & Christopher Walker. (MRG Reports Ser.: No. 32). 1976. pap. 2.50 (ISBN 0-89192-170-2). Interbk Inc.

Armenians: History of a Genocide. Yves Ternon. LC 80-19499. 1980. write for info. (ISBN 0-88206-038-4). Caravan Bks.

Armenians in the Service of the Ottoman Empire, 1860-1908. Mesrob K. Krikorian. (Direct Editions Ser.). (Orig.). 1978. pap. 10.50 (ISBN 0-7100-8564-8). Routledge & Kegan.

Armies & Societies in Europe: 1494-1789. Andre Corvisier. Tr. by Abigail T. Siddall from Fr. LC 78-62419. 224p. 1979. 12.95x (ISBN 0-253-12985-0). Ind U Pr.

Armies Encamped in the Fields Beyond the Unfinished Avenues. Morton Marcus. (Illus.). 56p. 1977. pap. 2.50 (ISBN 0-937310-07-7). Jazz Pr.

Armies in the Sand: The Struggle for Mecca & Medina. John Sabini. (Illus.). 224p. 1981. 16.95 (ISBN 0-500-01246-6). Thames Hudson.

Armies of the Night. Norman Mailer. 1971. pap. 2.50 (ISBN 0-451-09053-5, E9053, Sig). NAL.

Armies of the Streets: The New York City Draft Riots of 1863. Adrian Cook. LC 73-80463. (Illus.). 336p. 1974. 17.50x (ISBN 0-8131-1298-2). U Pr of Ky.

Armonia De los Cuatro Evangelios. A. T. Robertson. Tr. by F. W. Patterson & Arturo Parajon. 1979. pap. 4.55 (ISBN 0-311-04302-X). Casa Bautista.

Armonia Familiar. Al Compton. 1980. pap. 0.85 (ISBN 0-311-46078-X). Casa Bautista.

Armonias Corales, Vol. 1. Tr. by Tony Arango. 144p. (Orig., Span.). 1977. pap. 4.75 (ISBN 0-89922-082-7). Edit Caribe.

Armor. Hugh Gregor. LC 78-64662. (Fact Finders Ser.). (Illus.). 1979. lib. bdg. 3.96 (ISBN 0-686-51124-7). Silver.

Armor: Yesterday & Today. Karin Mango. LC 80-18103. (Illus.). 128p. (gr. 4 up). 1980. PLB 8.29 (ISBN 0-671-34015-8). Messner.

Armored Gisant Before Fourteen Hundred. Judith W. Hurtig. LC 78-74368. (Outstanding Dissertations in the Fine Arts, Fourth Ser.). 1979. lib. bdg. 52.00 (ISBN 0-8240-3956-4). Garland Pub.

Armorial Families: A Directory of Gentlemen of Coat-Armour, Vol. 1 & 2. Ed. by Arthur C. Fox-Davies. LC 76-94029. (Illus.). 1970. Repr. Set. 38.50 (ISBN 0-8048-0721-3). C E Tuttle.

Armour & Artillery Nineteen Seventy-Nine to Nineteen Eighty. Foss. 1980. 99.50 (ISBN 0-531-03916-1). Watts.

Armour Book in Honcho-Gunkiko. Arai Hakuseki. 35.00 (ISBN 0-87556-164-0). Saifer.

Armour of Imperial Rome. H. Russell Robinson. LC 74-11777. (Illus.). 112p. 1974. 17.50 o.p. (ISBN 0-684-13956-1, ScribT). Scribner.

Armoured Fighting Vehicles of the World. 3rd ed. Date not set. price not set (ScribT). Scribner.

Armoured Fighting Vehicles of the World. rev. ed. Christopher F. Foss. LC 77-74717. (Illus.). 1978. 8.95 o.p. (ISBN 0-684-15225-8, ScribT). Scribner.

Armoured Train. John Balfour. (Illus.). 168p. 1981. 25.50 (ISBN 0-7134-2547-4, Pub. by Batsford England). David & Charles.

Armour's Almanac: Around the Year in 365 Days. Richard Armour. (Illus.). 1962. 4.95 o.p. (ISBN 0-07-002253-4, GB). McGraw.

Arms Across the Sea. Philip J. Farley et al. LC 77-91804. 1978. 9.95 (ISBN 0-8157-2746-1); pap. 3.95 (ISBN 0-8157-2745-3). Brookings.

Arms, Alliances & Stability. Partha Chatterjee. LC 73-20977. (Illus.). 1975. 24.95 (ISBN 0-470-14935-3). Halsted Pr.

Arms & Armor Annual, Vol. I. Ed. by Robert Held. 320p. 1973. pap. 9.95 (ISBN 0-695-80407-3). Arma Pr.

Arms & Influence. Thomas C. Schelling. (Henry L. Stimson Lectures Ser.). 1967. pap. 5.45x (ISBN 0-300-00221-1, Y190). Yale U Pr.

Arms & Politics in the Dominican Republic. G. Pope Atkins. (Special Studies on Latin America & the Caribbean). 158p. 1981. lib. bdg. 20.00x (ISBN 0-86531-112-9). Westview.

Arms & the Man. George B. Shaw. (Penguin Plays Ser.). (YA) (gr. 9 up). 1950. pap. 2.75 (ISBN 0-14-048102-8). Penguin.

Arms & the Man. George B. Shaw. Ed. by Louis Crompton. LC 68-22306. 1969. pap. 5.50 (ISBN 0-672-61087-6). Bobbs.

Arms & the Man. George B. Shaw. Ed. by Norma Jenckes. LC 79-56802. (Bernard Shaw Early Texts: Play Manuscripts in Facsimile). 1981. lib. bdg. 45.00 (ISBN 0-8240-4578-5). Garland Pub.

Arms & the Men: The Arms Trade & Governments. Basil Collier. (Illus.). 320p. 1980. 37.00 (ISBN 0-241-10308-8, Pub. by Hamish Hamilton England). David & Charles.

Arms & Women. Boris Uxkull. 1966. 5.95 o.s.i. (ISBN 0-02-621270-6). Macmillan.

Arms, Autarky, & Agression. William Carr. (Foundations of Modern History Ser.). 136p. 1973. 7.00 (ISBN 0-393-05486-1); pap. 3.95x (ISBN 0-393-09361-1). Norton.

Arms Control & Defense Postures in the Nineteen-Eighties. Ed. by Richard Burt. (Special Studies in National Security & Defense Policy Ser.). 220p. 1981. lib. bdg. 24.00x (ISBN 0-86531-162-5). Westview.

Arms Control & Disarmament. Robert Lawrence. LC 72-88750. (Burgess Critical Issues in Political Science Ser.). 1973. pap. text ed. 2.95 o.p. (ISBN 0-8087-1222-5). Burgess.

Arms Control & European Security: A Guide to East-West Negotiations. Joseph I. Coffey. LC 76-29615. (Praeger Special Studies). 1977. text ed. 29.95 (ISBN 0-275-24340-0). Praeger.

Arms Control & Military Force. Ed. by Christoph Bertram. LC 80-67836. (Adelphi Library: Vol. 3). 272p. 1981. text ed. 32.50 (ISBN 0-916672-70-0). Allanheld.

Arms Control & Salt II. W. K. Panofsky. LC 79-5182. (Jessie & John Danz Lecture Ser.). 88p. 1979. pap. 2.95 (ISBN 0-295-95700-X). U of Wash Pr.

Arms Control & Security: Current Issues. Ed. by Wolfram F. Hanrieder. 1979. lib. bdg. 28.50x (ISBN 0-89158-382-3); pap. text ed. 11.00x (ISBN 0-89158-385-8). Westview.

Arms Control & Technological Innovation. David Carlton & Carlo Schaerf. LC 77-8790. 1977. 28.95 (ISBN 0-470-99274-3). Halsted Pr.

Arms Control Arrangements for the Far East. Ed. by Yuan-li Wu. LC 67-20822. (Publications Ser.: No. 54). 1967. pap. 5.00 (ISBN 0-8179-1542-7). Hoover Inst Pr.

Arms Control II: A New Approach to International Security. Ed. by Ryukichi Imai & John Barton. LC 80-22700. 352p. 1981. lib. bdg. 25.00 (ISBN 0-89946-069-0). Oelgeschlager.

Arms Control: Readings from Scientific American. Intro. by Herbert F. York. LC 73-4963. (Illus.). 1973. text ed. 19.95x (ISBN 0-7167-0880-9); pap. text ed. 9.95x (ISBN 0-7167-0879-5). W H Freeman.

Arms Control: The Interwar Naval Limitation Agreements. Robert A. Hoover. (Monograph Series in World Affairs). 124p. (Orig.). 1980. pap. 4.00 (ISBN 0-87940-062-5). U of Denver Intl.

Arms, Defense Policy & Arms Control. Ed. by Franklin A. Long & George W. Rathjens. 1976. 8.95x (ISBN 0-393-05573-6); pap. text ed. 6.95x (ISBN 0-393-09188-0). Norton.

Arms for the Poor: President Carter's Polocies on Arms Transfers to the Third World. Graham Kearns. 136p. (Orig.). 1980. pap. text ed. 10.95 (ISBN 0-908160-57-7). Bks Australia.

Arms, Industry & America. Ed. by Kenneth S. Davis. (Reference Shelf Ser.). 1971. 5.75 (ISBN 0-8242-0446-8). Wilson.

Arms of Kiangnan: Modernization in the Chinese Ordnance Industry 1860-1895. Thomas L. Kennedy. 1978. lib. bdg. 24.50x (ISBN 0-89158-258-4). Westview.

Arms of Time: A Memoir. Rupert Hart-Davis. (Illus.). 176p. 1979. 19.95 (ISBN 0-241-10305-3, Pub. by Hamish Hamilton England). David & Charles.

Arms Race & Sino Soviet Relations. Walter C. Clemens, Jr. LC 68-21253. (Publication Ser.: No. 72). 1968. 7.50 (ISBN 0-8179-1722-5); pap. 3.95 (ISBN 0-8179-1722-5). Hoover Inst Pr.

Arms Transfer to the Third World: Problems & Policies. Uri Ra'Anan et al. LC 77-17949. (Westview Special Studies in International Relations & U.S. Foreign Policy). 1978. lib. bdg. 37.50x (ISBN 0-89158-092-1). Westview.

Arms Transfers & U. S. Foreign & Military Policy, Vol. I. Alvin Cottrell et al. LC 80-50062. (Significant Issues Ser.: No. 7). 63p. 1980. 5.95 (ISBN 0-89206-013-1). CSI Studies.

Arms Transfers in the Modern World. Ed. by Stephanie G. Neuman & Robert E. Harkavy. LC 78-19778. (Praeger Special Studies Ser.). 400p. 1980. 31.95 (ISBN 0-03-045361-5); student ed. 11.95 (ISBN 0-03-051171-2). Praeger.

Armsmear. Henry Barnard & J. D. Butler. (Illus.). 399p. 1976. 16.95 (ISBN 0-686-68856-2). Beinfeld Pub.

Armstrong Error: A Reporter Exposes Herbert W. Armstrong. Charles DeLoach. 124p. 1971. pap. 1.25 o.p. (ISBN 0-912106-13-1). Logos.

Armstrongism: The Worldwide Church of God Examined in the Searching Light of Scripture. Robert L. Sumner. 424p. 1974. 7.95 (ISBN 0-87398-025-5, Pub. by Bibl Evang Pr). Sword of Lord.

Army & Politics in Argentina, 1945-1962: Peron to Frondizi. Robert A. Potash. LC 79-64220. (Illus.). xiv, 418p. 1980. 25.00x (ISBN 0-8047-1056-2). Stanford U Pr.

Army Ants: A Study in Social Organization. T. C. Schneirla. Ed. by Howard R. Topoff. LC 70-149408. (Illus.). 1971. text ed. 19.95x (ISBN 0-7167-0933-3). W H Freeman.

Army Badges & Insignia of World War II: Great Britain, Poland, Belgium, Italy, USSR, Germany. Guido Rosignoli. (Illus.). 228p. 1980. 10.95 (ISBN 0-7137-0697-X, Pub. by Blandford Pr England). Sterling.

Army Badges & Insignia of World War 2, Book 2. Guido Rosignoli. LC 72-85765. (Illus.). 208p. 1976. 8.95 (ISBN 0-02-605080-3, 60508). Macmillan.

Army Badges & Insignia Since 1945. Guido Rosignoli. (Illus.). 218p. 1980. 9.95 (ISBN 0-7137-0648-1, Pub. by Blandford Pr England). Sterling.

Army, James II & the Glorious Revolution. John Childs. 25.00 (ISBN 0-312-04949-8). St Martin.

Army Life in a Black Regiment. Thomas W. Higginson. 1962. pap. 0.95 o.s.i. (ISBN 0-02-033260-2, Collier). Macmillan.

Army of Flanders & the Spanish Road: 1567-1659. Geoffrey Parker. LC 76-180021. (Cambridge Studies in Early Modern History). (Illus.). 288p. 1972. 43.95 (ISBN 0-521-08462-8); pap. 11.95x (ISBN 0-521-09907-2). Cambridge U Pr.

Army of the Aged. Richard L. Neuberger & Kelley Loe. LC 72-2379. (FDR & the New Deal Ser). 332p. 1973. Repr. of 1936 ed. lib. bdg. 32.50 (ISBN 0-306-70518-4). Da Capo.

Army of the Indian Moghuls: Its Organization & Administration. William Irvine. 1962. 7.75x o.p. (ISBN 0-8426-0249-6). Verry.

Army of the Potomac: Part 1. LC 76-41427. (Civil War Monographs). 1977. lib. bdg. 41.00 (ISBN 0-527-17550-1); pap. 35.00 (ISBN 0-527-17548-X). Kraus Repr.

Army Officer's Guide. 41st, rev. ed. Lawrence P. Crocker. (Illus.). 560p. (Orig.). 1981. pap. 12.95 (ISBN 0-8117-2040-3). Stackpole.

Army Politics in Cuba, 1898-1958. Louis A. Perez, Jr. LC 75-35440. (Pitt Latin American Ser.). 1976. 12.95x (ISBN 0-8229-3303-9). U of Pittsburgh Pr.

Army Uniforms of World War II. Andrew Mollo & Malcolm McGregor. (Illus.). 183p. 1980. 9.95 (ISBN 0-7137-0611-2, Pub. by Blandford Pr England). Sterling.

Army Vehicle Manuals. Ed. by Dennis R. Spence. (Military Vehicle Reference Ser.: No. 1). 121p. 1980. pap. 15.00x (ISBN 0-938242-00-8). Portrayal.

Arna Bontemps-Langston Hughes Letters (1925-1967) Ed. by Charles H. Nichols. LC 79-17341. 1980. 17.95 (ISBN 0-396-07687-4). Dodd.

Arnheim 1944. Janusz Piekalkiewicz. Tr. by H. A. Barker & A. J. Barker. (Illus.). 1977. 17.50x (ISBN 0-7110-0826-4). Intl Pubns Serv.

Arnhem Nineteen Hundred & Forty-Four: Germany's Last Victory. Janusz Piekalkiewicz. (Encore Edition). (Illus.). 1978. 4.95 (ISBN 0-684-16551-1, ScribT). Scribner.

Arnica the Wonder Herb. Phyllis Speight. 1977. text ed. 3.00x (ISBN 0-686-68090-1). Beekman Pubs.

Arnold Bennett. Harvey Darton. 127p. 1980. Repr. lib. bdg. 17.50 (ISBN 0-89760-131-9). Telegraph Bks.

Arnold Bennett. John Wain. LC 67-16889. (Columbia Essays on Modern Writers Ser.: No. 23). (Orig.). 1967. pap. 2.00 (ISBN 0-231-02724-9, MW23). Columbia U Pr.

Arnold Bennett: A Last Word. Frank Swinnerton. LC 78-8204. 1978. 7.95 o.p. (ISBN 0-385-14545-4). Doubleday.

Arnold Bennett: The Critical Heritage. James Hepburn. (Critical Heritage Ser.). 576p. 1981. pap. 48.50 (ISBN 0-7100-0512-1). Routledge & Kegan.

Arnold J. Toynbee. Kenneth Winetrout. (World Leaders Ser.: No. 47). 1975. lib. bdg. 10.95 (ISBN 0-8057-3725-1). Twayne.

Arnold Schoenberg Letters. Arnold Schoenberg. Ed. by E. Stein. (Illus.). 1958. 8.75 o.p. (ISBN 0-685-20371-9). St Martin.

Arnold Schonberg. Egon Wellesz. Tr. by W. H. Kerridge. LC 69-12698. (Music Ser). (Ger). 1969. Repr. of 1925 ed. lib. bdg. 19.50 (ISBN 0-306-71226-1). Da Capo.

Arnold Shoenberg. Charles Rosen. LC 80-8773. 113p. (Orig.). 1981. pap. 4.95 (ISBN 0-691-02706-4). Princeton U Pr.

Arnold Wesker Als Gesellschaftskritiker. Valeska Lindemann. (Poetic Drama Ser.: No.60). (Ger.). 1980. pap. text ed. 25.00 (ISBN 0-391-02204-0). Humanities.

Arnold Zweig. George Salamon. LC 75-12736. (World Author Ser.: Germany: No. 361). 1975. lib. bdg. 12.50 (ISBN 0-8057-6212-4). Twayne.

Arnold's Bodybuilding for Men. Arnold Schwarsenneger. 1981. 14.95 (ISBN 0-671-25613-0). S&S.

Arnoldwesker Als Gesellschaftskritiker. Lindemann. (Poetic Drama & Poetic Theory Ser.). 1980. pap. text ed. 25.00x. Humanities.

Aroma & Flavour in Wine Making. J. G. Carr. (Illus.). 88p. 1975. 5.50 o.p. (ISBN 0-263-05594-9). Transatlantic.

Aromatic Amino Acid Hydroxylases & Mental Disease. M. B. Youdim. LC 79-40642. 1980. 79.50 (ISBN 0-471-27606-5, Pub. by Wiley-Interscience). Wiley.

Aromatic Character & Aromaticity. Geoffrey M. Badger. LC 68-29650. (Chemistry Texts Ser). (Illus., Orig.). 1969. 26.95 (ISBN 0-521-07339-1). Cambridge U Pr.

Aromatic Hydrocarbons: Vol. I, Pt. 7, Vapor-Liquid Equilibrium Data Collection. J. Gmehling et al. Ed. by D. Behrens & R. Eckermann. (Dechema Chemistry Data Ser.). 564p. 1980. text ed. 106.00x (ISBN 3-9215-6723-8, Pub. by Dechema Germany). Scholium Intl.

Aromatic Nitration. K. Schofield. (Illus.). 350p. Date not set. 67.50 (ISBN 0-521-23362-3). Cambridge U Pr.

Around Old Bethany. R. L. Berry. 83p. pap. 0.75. Faith Pub Hse.

Around the House. Deborah Manley. LC 78-31854. (Ready, Set, Look Ser.). (Illus.). (gr. k-3). 1979. PLB 9.65 (ISBN 0-8172-1307-4). Raintree Pubs.

Around the House That Jack Built: A Tale of Ecology. Roz Abisch. LC 70-174606. (Illus.). (gr. k-3). 1972. 5.95 o.s.i. (ISBN 0-8193-0553-7, Four Winds); PLB 5.41 o.s.i. (ISBN 0-8193-0554-5). Schol Bk Serv.

Around the Lord's Table. A. B. Lipscomb. 1.75 (ISBN 0-89225-020-8). Gospel Advocate.

Around the Moon. Jules Verne. (Childrens Illustrated Classics Ser). (Illus.). 1970. 9.00x o.p. (ISBN 0-460-05087-7, Pub. by J. M. Dent England). Biblio Dist.

Around the Wicket Gate. C. H. Spurgeon. pap. 2.25 (ISBN 0-686-09098-5). Pilgrim Pubns.

Around the World in Eighty Days. John Burningham. (Illus.). (ps up). 1979. 14.95 (ISBN 0-224-00659-2, Pub. by Chatto Bodley Jonathan). Merrimack Bk Serv.

Around the World in Eighty Days: Student Activity Book. Marcia Sohl & Gerald Dackerman. (Now Age Illustrated Ser.). (Illus.). (gr. 4-12). 1976. wkbk. 0.95 (ISBN 0-88301-285-5). Pendulum Pr.

Around the World in Eighty Ways. Hans G. Guggenheim. 64p. (Orig.). 1981. pap. 6.00 (ISBN 0-682-49683-9). Exposition.

Around the World with Koa Koala. Kathryn Jackson. (Illus.). 144p. (ps-3). 1974. PLB 12.23 o.p. (ISBN 0-307-66817-7, Golden Pr). Western Pub.

Around the World with My Red Balloon. Gilbert V. Beers. (ps-3). 1973. 4.95 (ISBN 0-8024-0303-4). Moody.

Arpa Sagrada. Ruiz V. Agustin. 1979. pap. 1.95 (ISBN 0-311-08751-5). Casa Bautista.

Arqueologia de la Costa Norte De Honduras. Doris Stone. (Peabody Museum Memoirs: Vol. 9, No. 1). 1975. pap. 12.00 (ISBN 0-87365-678-4). Peabody Harvard.

Arquitectura En San Juan De Puerto Rico (Siglo XIX) Maria D. Castro De Davila. LC 78-21582. (Illus.). 1979. 15.00 (ISBN 0-8477-2110-8). U of PR Pr.

Arrainment of the Whole Societie of Jesuites in Fraunce: Holden-the Twelfth & Thirteenth of July, 1594. Antoine Arnauld. LC 79-84084. (English Experience Ser.: No. 904). 68p. 1979. Repr. of 1594 ed. lib. bdg. 8.00. Walter J Johnson.

Arranged Marriage. Inge Trachtenberg. 272p. 1975. 6.95 o.p. (ISBN 0-393-08705-0). Norton.

Arrangement for Life. Sheila Tagliavia. LC 79-3418. 1980. 12.95 (ISBN 0-06-014214-6, HarpT). Har-Row.

Arrangement Regarding Bovine Meat. (Illus.). 11p. 1980. pap. 2.00 (ISBN 0-686-63035-1, G138, GATT). Unipub.

Arrangements & Spreads. B. Grunbaum. LC 71-38926. (CBMS Regional Conference Series in Mathematics: No. 10). 1980. Repr. of 1974 ed. 7.60 (ISBN 0-8218-1659-4, CBMS-10). Am Math.

Arrays of Cylindrical Dipoles. R. W. King et al. LC 67-26069. (Illus.). 1968. 68.50 (ISBN 0-521-05887-2, 2). Cambridge U Pr.

Arrest, Search & Seizure. Lawrence C. Waddington. LC 73-7366. (Criminal Justice Ser). 320p. 1974. text ed. 12.95x (ISBN 0-02-478940-2). Macmillan.

Arrest Sitting Bull. Douglas Jones. 1978. pap. 2.50 o.s.i. (ISBN 0-446-81474-1). Warner Bks.

Arrhythmia Analysis by Intracardiac Electrocardiography. John W. Lister et al. (Illus.). 360p. 1976. 44.75 (ISBN 0-398-03423-0). C C Thomas.

Arrival of B. B. King: The Authorized Biography. Charles Sawyer. LC 79-6085. (Illus.). 288p. 1980. 14.95 (ISBN 0-385-15929-3). Doubleday.

Arrivals & Departures. William D. Sheldon et al. (gr. 6). 1973. text ed. 11.20 (ISBN 0-205-03562-0, 5235626); tchrs'. guide 11.20 (ISBN 0-205-03563-9, 5235634); activity bk. 3.96 (ISBN 0-205-03564-7, 5235642); tchrs'. ed. 3.96 (ISBN 0-205-03565-5, 5235650); activities' masters 28.00 (ISBN 0-205-03566-3, 5235669). Allyn.

Arriving at a Place You Never Left. Lois Ruby. (YA) (gr. 7-12). 1980. pap. 1.50 (ISBN 0-440-90254-1, LFL). Dell.

Arriving at the Nadir. Thomas Johnson. (Illus., Orig.). 1975. pap. 2.50 (ISBN 0-914278-06-1). Copper Beech.

Arrogance of Humanism. David Ehrenfeld. (Galaxy Bk.: No. 637). 304p. 1981. pap. 5.95 (ISBN 0-19-502890-2). Oxford U Pr.

Arrogance of Power. J. William Fulbright. 1967. pap. 1.95 o.p. (ISBN 0-394-70378-2, V378, Vin). Random.

Arrogance on Campus. Lewis B. Mayhew. LC 71-128699. (Higher Education Ser.). 1970. 11.95x o.p. (ISBN 0-87589-074-1). Jossey-Bass.

Arrow & D-Fifty Pick-Ups 1979-81. LC 80-70343. (Illus.). 192p. pap. 8.95. Chilton.

Arrow Book of Good "N" Easy Cooking. Sanders. (gr. 3-5). 1980. pap. 1.25 (ISBN 0-590-30066-0, Schol Pap). Schol Bk Serv.

Arrow in the Blue. Arthur Koestler. LC 77-85781. (Danube Edition Ser). 1970. 12.95 (ISBN 0-02-565020-3). Macmillan.

Arrow in the Sun. Theodore V. Olson. 1980. pap. write for info. (ISBN 0-671-83541-6). PB.

Arrow of God. Robert Cassilis. 184p. 1980. 16.95 (ISBN 0-241-10187-5, Pub. by Hamish Hamilton England). David & Charles.

Arrow to the Sun: A Pueblo Indian Tale. Gerald McDermott. (Illus.). 48p. (gr. 1 up). 1974. PLB 10.95 (ISBN 0-670-13369-8). Viking Pr.

Arrow Word Puzzles. Murray Rockowitz. 64p. (gr. 3-7). 1980. pap. 1.25 (ISBN 0-590-30914-5, Schol Pap). Schol Bk Serv.

Arrows to the Heart. Jackie Larsen. LC 77-91631. 1977. softcover 4.95 (ISBN 0-9602474-1-6). J Larsen.

Arrowsmith. Sinclair Lewis. pap. 1.95 (ISBN 0-451-51371-1, CJ1371, Sig Classics). NAL.

Arroyos & Environmental Change in the American South-West. Ronald U. Cooke & Richard W. Reeves. (Oxford Research Studies in Geography Ser.). (Illus.). 1976. 36.00x (ISBN 0-19-823213-6). Oxford U Pr.

ARS Guide to Finding Servicing Information. 1.00 (ISBN 0-686-27837-2). Antique Radio.

Ars Moriendi, That Is to Saye the Craft for to Deye for the Helthe of Mannes Sowle. LC 74-80159. (English Experience Ser.: No. 639). 1974. Repr. of 1491 ed. 3.50 (ISBN 90-221-0639-X). Walter J Johnson.

Ars Orientalis: The Arts of Islam & the East, Vols. 3-11. Incl. Vol. 2. 1959. 31.00 o.p. (ISBN 0-934686-17-3); Vol. 3. 1959. 25.00 (ISBN 0-934686-18-1); Vol. 4. 1961. o.p. (ISBN 0-686-24514-8); Vol. 5. 1963. 32.00 (ISBN 0-934686-19-X); Vol. 6. 1968. 18.00 (ISBN 0-934686-20-3); Vol. 7. 1968. 11.00 (ISBN 0-934686-21-1); Vol. 8. 1970. 30.00 (ISBN 0-934686-22-X); Vol. 9, 1973. 15.00 (ISBN 0-934686-23-8); Vol.10, 1975. 20.00 (ISBN 0-934686-24-6); Vol.11, 1979. 30.00 (ISBN 0-934686-25-4). (Illus., Co-Pub. by University of Michigan). Freer.

Ars Semiotica, Vol. 2, No. 3. Romeo. 1979. pap. text ed. 20.50x. Humanities.

Arsenal of Democracy: American Weapons Available for Export. rev. ed. Tom Gervasi. LC 80-993. (Illus.). 1981. pap. 9.95 (ISBN 0-394-17662-6, E760, Ever). Grove.

Arsenal of Democracy: The Story of American War Production. Donald M. Nelson. LC 72-2378. (FDR & the Era of the New Deal Ser.). 439p. 1973. Repr. of 1946 ed. lib. bdg. 39.50 (ISBN 0-685-27840-9). Da Capo.

Arsenic: Medical & Biological Effects of Environmental Pollutants. 1977. pap. 13.75 (ISBN 0-309-02604-0). Natl Acad Pr.

Arshile Gorky: The Implication of Symbols. Harry Rand. LC 77-25046. (Illus.). 256p. 1981. 40.00 (ISBN 0-8390-0209-2). Allanheld.

Arshile Gorky: The Implication of Symbols. Harry Rand. LC 77-25046. (Illus.). 256p. 1981. text ed. 40.00 (ISBN 0-8390-0209-2). Allanheld & Schram.

Arson! Arnold Madison. LC 78-6877. (Illus.). (gr. 5 up). 1978. PLB 6.90 s&l (ISBN 0-531-02243-9). Watts.

Arson Investigation. Robert E. Carter. 1978. text ed. 13.95x (ISBN 0-02-472400-9). Macmillan.

Art. Boy Scouts Of America. LC 19-600. (Illus.). 48p. (gr. 6-12). 1968. pap. 0.70x (ISBN 0-8395-3320-9, 3320). BSA.

Art Activities Almanac. 1962. 4.95x (ISBN 0-8143-1066-4). Wayne St U Pr.

Art Activities for the Very Young. F. L. Hoover. LC 61-11263. (Illus.). (gr. k-3). 1961. pap. 5.25 (ISBN 0-87192-000-X). Davis Mass.

Art Against Ideology. Ernst Fischer. LC 70-77506. Orig. Title: Kunst und Koexistence. (Ger). 1969. 6.95 o.s.i. (ISBN 0-8076-0510-7). Braziller.

Art Anatomy. William Rimmer. pap. 5.00 (ISBN 0-486-20908-3). Dover.

Art & Adventure of Beekeeping. Ormond Aebi & Harry Aebi. LC 74-14661. (Illus.). 224p. 1975. 9.95 (ISBN 0-913300-39-X); pap. 5.95 (ISBN 0-913300-38-1). Unity Pr.

Art & Adventure of Traveling Cheaply. Rick Berg. 1981. pap. 2.95 (ISBN 0-451-09729-7, E9729, Sig). NAL.

Art & Animation: The Story of the Halas & Batchelor Animation Studio. Roger Manwell. (Illus.). 128p. 1980. 26.50 (ISBN 0-8038-0494-6, Visual Communications). Hastings.

Art & Antique Restorers Handbook. George Savage. 1978. 8.50 o.p. (ISBN 0-214-20268-2, 8008, Dist. by Arco). Barrie & Jenkins.

Art & Architecture in Belgium: 1600 to 1800. Gerson & Ter Kuile. (Pelican History of Art Ser.: No. 18). 1978. 40.00 (ISBN 0-670-13380-9). Viking Pr.

Art & Architecture in Italy Sixteen Hundred to Seventeen Fifty. Rudolf Wittkower. (Pelican History of Art). (Illus.). 664p. 1980. pap. 19.95 (ISBN 0-14-056116-1). Penguin.

Art & Architecture in the Service of Politics. Ed. by Henry A. Millon & Linda Nochlin. 1978. 37.50x (ISBN 0-262-13137-4). MIT Pr.

Art & Architecture of Ancient Egypt. rev ed. W. Stevenson Smith. 360p. 1981. pap. 19.95 (ISBN 0-14-056114-5). Penguin.

Art & Architecture of Medieval Russia. Arthur Voyce. (Illus.). 1967. pap. 9.95 (ISBN 0-8061-1096-1). U of Okla Pr.

Art & Artists in Connecticut. H. W. French. LC 70-87543. (Library of American Art Ser). 1970. Repr. of 1879 ed. lib. bdg. 19.50 (ISBN 0-306-71459-0). Da Capo.

Art & Artists of Our Time: With Many Illustrations, 3 vols. Clarence Cook. Ed. by H. Barbara Weinberg. LC 75-28881. (Art Experience in Late 19th Century America Ser.: Vol. 15). (Illus.). 1976. Repr. of 1888 ed. Set. lib. bdg. 250.00 (ISBN 0-8240-2239-4). Garland Pub.

Art & Background of Old English Poetry. Barbara C. Raw. LC 78-390. 1978. 19.95x (ISBN 0-312-04984-6). St Martin.

Art & Ceremony in Late Antiquity. Sabine MacCormack. (Transformation of the Classical Heritage Ser.). (Illus.). 450p. 1981. 35.00x (ISBN 0-520-03779-0). U of Cal Pr.

Art & Commerce: American Prints of the Nineteenth Century. 1979. 15.00x (ISBN 0-87846-130-2). U Pr of Va.

Art & Commerce: American Prints of the Nineteenth Century. Ed. by Museum of Fine Arts, Boston. LC 78-13848. (Illus.). 1978. 15.00 (ISBN 0-87846-130-2). Mus Fine Arts Boston.

Art & Craft of Ceramic Sculpture. Thelma F. Winter. LC 73-20150. (Illus.). 269p. 1973. 28.95 (ISBN 0-470-95475-2). Halsted Pr.

Art & Craft of Poetry. Daisy Aldan. 96p. 1981. 7.95 (ISBN 0-88427-047-5, Dist. by Caroline Hse). North River.

Art & Craft of Poetry: A Guide for Students & Teachers. Daisy Aldan. 7.95 (ISBN 0-88427-050-5). Green Hill.

Art & Craft of Wall Stenciling. Richard M. Bacon. LC 76-41361. (Funk & W Bk.). 1977. 9.95 (ISBN 0-308-10274-6, TYC-T). T Y Crowell.

Art & Environment in Native America. Ed. by Mary E. King & Idris R. Traylor, Jr. (Special Publications: No. 7). (Illus., Orig.). 1974. pap. 8.00 (ISBN 0-89672-032-2). Tex Tech Pr.

Art & Experience in Classical Greece. J. J. Pollitt. LC 74-160094. (Illus.). 1972. 32.50 (ISBN 0-521-08065-7); pap. 8.95x (ISBN 0-521-09662-6). Cambridge U Pr.

Art & Handicraft. John Sedding. Ed. by Peter Stansky & Rodney Shewan. LC 76-17777. (Aesthetic Movement & the Arts & Crafts Movement Ser.). 1977. Repr. of 1893 ed. lib. bdg. 44.00x (ISBN 0-8240-2482-6). Garland Pub.

Art & Human Emotions. Egon Weiner. (Illus.). 104p. 1975. 9.75 (ISBN 0-398-03265-3). C C Thomas.

Art & Imagination of W. E. B. Dubois. Arnold Rampersad. 1976. 15.00x (ISBN 0-674-04711-7). Harvard U Pr.

Art & Industry of Sandcastles. Jan Adkins. LC 76-141615. (gr. k up). 1971. 7.95 (ISBN 0-8027-0336-4). Walker & Co.

Art & Its Objects. 2nd ed. Richard Wollheim. LC 79-20790. 1980. 29.50 (ISBN 0-521-22898-0); pap. 8.95 (ISBN 0-521-29706-0). Cambridge U Pr.

Art & Life of Jean-Francois Millet. Marc H. Langlois. (Illus.). 121p. 1980. 33.45 (ISBN 0-930582-76-4). Gloucester Art.

Art & Life: The Building & Decoration of Cities. Cobden-Sanderson et al. Ed. by Peter Stansky & Rodney Shewan. LC 76-17778. (Aesthetic Movement & the Arts & Crafts Movement). 1978. Repr. of 1897 ed. lib. bdg. 44.00x (ISBN 0-8240-2484-2). Garland Pub.

Art & Meaning of Magic. Israel Regardie. 3.00 o.p. (ISBN 0-685-22166-0). Weiser.

Art & Money: An Irreverent History. Aubrey Menen. LC 79-18359. 226p. 1980. 11.95 (ISBN 0-07-041483-1). McGraw.

Art & Mysteries in Tombs, Mummies & Catacombs. Emmett D. Davisson. (Illus.). 1980. deluxe ed. 41.50 deluxe binding (ISBN 0-930582-63-2). Gloucester Art.

Art & Philosophy: Readings in Aesthetics. 2nd ed. Ed. by W. E. Kennick. LC 78-65213. 1979. text ed. 14.95x (ISBN 0-312-05391-6). St Martin.

Art & Politics of Thomas Nast. Morton Keller. LC 68-19762. (Illus.). 365p. 1975. pap. 9.95 (ISBN 0-19-501929-6, GB437, GB). Oxford U Pr.

Art & Practice of Talismanic Magic. Ophiel. pap. 5.00 (ISBN 0-87728-445-8). Weiser.

Art & Religion. Von O. Vogt. 1921. 37.50x o.p. (ISBN 0-685-69881-5). Elliots Bks.

Art & Science of Book Publishing. Herbert S. Bailey, Jr. LC 73-95935. (Illus.). 1970. 10.00 o.p. (ISBN 0-06-010192-X, HarpT). Har-Row.

Art & Science of Breeding Dogs. Ernest R. Garrison. 1979. 29.75 (ISBN 0-89266-163-1). Am Classical Coll Pr.

Art & Science of Clairvoyance. C. W. Leadbeater. (Illus.). 1979. 47.50 (ISBN 0-89266-182-8). Am Classical Coll Pr.

Art & Science of Effective Thinking. George R. Lyman. (Illus.). 1979. 37.45 (ISBN 0-89266-208-5). Am Classical Coll Pr.

Art & Science of Fly Fishing. 2nd ed. Lenox Dick. (Illus.). 1972. 7.95 o.p. (ISBN 0-87691-053-3). Winchester Pr.

Art & Science of Fly Fishing. Lenox Dick. 1977. pap. 3.95 (ISBN 0-8065-0587-7). Citadel Pr.

Art & Science of Growing Crystals. John J. Gilman. LC 63-11432. (Wiley Science & Technology of Materials Ser.). 1963. 49.95 (ISBN 0-471-30177-9, Pub. by Wiley-Interscience). Wiley.

Art & Science of Managing Hotels-Restaurants-Institutions. J. Vallen et al. Orig. Title: Art & Science of Modern Innkeeping. 1978. 14.25x (ISBN 0-8104-9470-1). Hayden.

Art & Science of Psychomancy with Concrete & Practical Applications. August V. Littleton. (Library of Scientific Psychology Bk.). (Illus.). 107p. 1981. 29.45 (ISBN 0-89920-022-2). Am Inst Psych.

Art & Science of Real Estate Investment Analysis. Edward J. Golden. 300p. 1980. pap. text ed. 15.00 (ISBN 0-9604532-0-2). Adv Prof Seminars.

Art & Science of the Polygraph Technique. James A. Matte. (Illus.). 296p. 1980. 29.50 (ISBN 0-398-04044-3). C C Thomas.

Art & Science of Wall Street Scalping for the Gaining of Superlative Profits. John F. Rinaldi. 1980. 37.55 (ISBN 0-918968-50-X). Inst Econ Finan.

Art & Sexual Politics. T. B. Hess & E.. C. Baker. 1973. 5.95 o.s.i. (ISBN 0-02-551260-9). Macmillan.

Art & Skill of Delegation. Lawrence L. Steinmetz. LC 75-28727. (Illus.). 220p. 1976. pap. text ed. 8.95 (ISBN 0-201-07269-6). A-W.

Art & Society: Essays in Marxist Aesthetics. Adolfo S. Vazquez. Tr. by Maro Riofrancos. LC 72-92025. 288p. 1974. 13.50 o.p. (ISBN 0-85345-269-5, CL2695). Monthly Rev.

Art & Stained Glass. Claude Lips. LC 72-92255. 96p. 1973. pap. 5.95 (ISBN 0-385-08286-X). Doubleday.

Art & Substance in George Meredith: A Study in Narrative. Walter F. Wright. LC 80-14417. vii, 211p. 1980. Repr. of 1953 ed. lib. bdg. 19.00x (ISBN 0-313-22514-1, WRAS). Greenwood.

Art & Technics. Lewis Mumford. LC 52-1930. (Bampton Lecture Ser. in American: No. 4). 1952. 12.50x (ISBN 0-231-01903-3); pap. 2.45 (ISBN 0-231-08509-5, 9). Columbia U Pr.

Art & Technique of Analytic Group Therapy. Martin Grotjahn. LC 76-22916. 1977. 25.00x (ISBN 0-87668-252-2). Aronson.

Art & Technology: A Symposium on Classical Bronzes. Ed. by Suzannah Doeringer et al. 1970. 15.00 (ISBN 0-262-04030-1). MIT Pr.

Art & the Bible. Francis A. Schaeffer. LC 73-75891. 64p. 1973. pap. 1.95 (ISBN 0-87784-443-7). Inter-Varsity.

Art & the Creative Consciousness. Graham Collier. (Illus.). 208p. 1973. pap. text ed. 7.95 (ISBN 0-13-046706-5). P-H.

Art & the Formation of Taste. Lucy Crane. LC 76-17755. (Aesthetic Movement Ser.: Vol. 9). (Illus.). 1977. Repr. of 1882 ed. lib. bdg. 44.00x (ISBN 0-8240-2458-3). Garland Pub.

Art & the Question of Meaning. Hans Kung. 96p. (Ger.). 1981. 7.95 (ISBN 0-8245-0016-4). Crossroad NY.

Art & Theological Imagination. John W. Dixon, Jr. (Illus.). 1978. 12.95 (ISBN 0-8164-0397-X). Crossroad NY.

Art & Times of the Guitar: From the Hittites to the Hippies. Frederick V. Grunfeld. 1969. 9.95 o.s.i. (ISBN 0-02-546290-3). Macmillan.

Art Anti-Art: Anartism Explored. Helene Parmelin. Tr. by J. A. Underwood from Fr. 1980. pap. 5.95 (ISBN 0-7145-2571-5, Pub. by M Boyars). Merrimack Bk Serv.

Art Anti-Art: Anartism Explored. Helene Parmelin. 1977. text ed. 9.25x (ISBN 0-7145-2570-7). Humanities.

Art Appreciation Made Simple. John P. Sedgwick, Jr. pap. 3.95 (ISBN 0-385-01222-5, Made). Doubleday.

Art As You See It: Wiley Self Teaching Guide. I. Bell et al. 326p. 1979. write for info. (ISBN 0-471-03326-1). Wiley.

Art at Auction Nineteen Seventy-Eight to Nineteen Seventy-Nine: Two Hundred & Forty-Fifth Season. Diana De Froment. (Illus.). 496p. 1979. 40.00 (ISBN 0-85667-063-4, Pub. by Sotheby Parke Bernet England). Biblio Dist.

Art at Auction, 1969-70. 35.00x o.p. (ISBN 0-670-13401-5, Pub. by Sotheby Parke Bernet England). Biblio Dist.

Art at Auction 1979-80: The Year at Sotheby Parke Bernet. Ed. by Joan A. Speers. (Illus.). 496p. 1980. 45.00 (ISBN 0-85667-010-3, Pub. by Sotheby Parke Bernet England). Biblio Dist.

Art at Educational Institutions in the United States: A Handbook of Permanent, Semi-Permanent & Temporary Works of Art at Elementary & Secondary Schools, Colleges & Universities. Emma L. Fundaburk & Thomas Davenport. LC 74-3187. (Illus.). 1974. 45.00 (ISBN 0-8108-0715-7). Scarecrow.

Art: Basic for Young Children. Lila Lasky & Rose Mukerji. (Illus.). 148p. (Orig.). 1980. pap. text ed. write for info. (ISBN 0-912674-73-3). Natl Assn Child Ed.

Art Book of Spanish, Italian, French & Egyptian Pottery. M. S. Lockwood. 1979. deluxe ed. 37.45 (ISBN 0-930582-41-1). Gloucester Art.

Art Careers. Ed. by Louise Horton. LC 75-12785. (Career Concise Guide Ser). (Illus.). 72p. (gr. 5 up). 1975. PLB 6.45 (ISBN 0-531-02841-0). Watts.

Art Censorship: A Chronology of Proscribed & Prescribed Art. Jane Clapp. LC 76-172789. (Illus.). 1972. 22.50 (ISBN 0-8108-0455-7). Scarecrow.

Art Chretien, son Developement Iconographique des Origines a nos Jours. 2nd ed. L. Brehier. (Illus.). 480p. (Fr.). 1981. Repr. of 1928 ed. lib. bdg. 125.00 (ISBN 0-89241-138-4). Caratzas Bros.

Art Critics & the Avant-Garde: New York, 1900-1913. Arlene R. Olson. Ed. by Donald B. Kuspit. (Studies in Fine Arts - Criticism: No. 18). 118p. 1980. 21.95 (ISBN 0-8357-1093-9, Pub. by UMI Res Pr). Univ Microfilms.

Art, Culture, & Environment: A Catalyst for Teaching. June K. McFee & Rogena M. Degge. 416p. 1980. pap. text ed. 13.95 (ISBN 0-8403-2330-1). Kendall-Hunt.

Art De Conjuguer: Huit Milles Verses. Bescherelle. (Fr). 7.00 (ISBN 0-685-20225-9). Schoenhof.

Art Deco. Victor Arwas. (Illus.). 304p. 1980. 45.00 (ISBN 0-686-62692-3, 0691-0). Abrams.

Art Deco Architecture in New York, 1920-1940. Don Vlack. LC 74-6577. (Icon Editions). (Illus.). 190p. 1975. 17.50x o.s.i. (ISBN 0-06-438850-6, HarpT). Har-Row.

Art Deco Interiors in Color. Charles R. Fry. LC 77-75887. (Illus.). 1977. pap. 5.00 (ISBN 0-486-23527-0). Dover.

Art Deco Los Angeles. Photos by Ave Pildas. LC 77-4581. (Illus.). 1977. pap. 4.95 o.s.i. (ISBN 0-06-013338-4, TD-295, HarpT). Har-Row.

Art Deco Stained Glass Pattern Book. Ed Sibbett, Jr. LC 77-77051. (Illus.). 1977. pap. 2.50 (ISBN 0-486-23550-5). Dover.

Art Deco Style in Household Objects, Architecture, Sculpture, Graphics, Jewelry. Ed. by Theodore Menten. (Illus.). 192p. (Orig.). 1972. pap. 6.00 (ISBN 0-486-22824-X). Dover.

Art Des Emblemes. Claude F. Menestrier. Ed. by Stephen Orgel. LC 78-68185. (Philosophy of Images Ser.: Vol. 15). (Illus.). 1979. lib. bdg. 66.00 (ISBN 0-8240-3689-1). Garland Pub.

Art Des Emblemes, Ou S'enseigne la Morale Par les Figures De la Fable, De L'Histoire et De la Nature. Claude Menestrier. Ed. by Stephen Orgel. LC 78-68190. (Philosophy of Images Ser.: Vol. 18). (Illus.). 1980. lib. bdg. 66.00 (ISBN 0-8240-3692-1). Garland Pub.

Art Directors Annual. 54th ed. (Illus.). 800p. 1975. 29.95 o.p. (ISBN 0-8230-1907-1). Watson-Guptill.

Art Director's Index to Photographer: American Section, No. 7. Roto-Vision Editors. (Illus., Orig.). 1981. pap. 17.50 (ISBN 2-88046-010-7, Pub. by Roto-Vision Switzerland). Norton.

Art Directors' Index to Photographers. 6th ed. LC 74-16143. (Illus.). 1979. 70.00x (ISBN 0-902337-02-5). Intl Pubns Serv.

Art Director's Index to Photographers. Roto-Vision Editors. (Art Directors Index Ser.: No. 7). (Illus.). 1981. 80.00 (ISBN 2-88046-005-0, Pub. by Roto-Vision Switzerland); pap. 17.50. Norton.

Art, Economics & Change: The Kulebele of Northern Ivory Coast. Dolores Richter. (Illus.). 165p. (Orig.). 1980. pap. 8.95 (ISBN 0-932382-01-0). Psych Graphic.

Art Education: A Guide to Information Sources. Ed. by Clarence Bunch. LC 73-17518. (Art & Architecture Information Guide Ser: Vol. 6). 1977. 30.00 (ISBN 0-8103-1272-7). Gale.

Art Education & the World of Work. Ed. by Ronald H. Silverman. 208p. 1980. 9.75 (ISBN 0-686-27490-3). Natl Art Ed.

Art Embroidery. M. S. Lockwood & E. Glaister. LC 76-17758. (Aesthetic Movement Ser.: Vol. 13). (Illus.). 1977. Repr. of 1878 ed. lib. bdg. 44.00x (ISBN 0-8240-2462-1). Garland Pub.

Art Experience: Oil Painting. Leonard E. Fisher. LC 72-5406. (Illus.). 64p. 1973. PLB 6.90 (ISBN 0-531-02609-4). Watts.

Art Fabric. Mildred Constantine & Jack L. Larsen. 240p. 1981. 39.95 (ISBN 0-442-21638-6). Van Nos Reinhold.

Art, Feat & Mystery: The Story of Thomas Webb & Sons, Glassmakers. H. W. Woodward. 61p. 1978. 25.00x (ISBN 0-9506439-0-4, Pub. by Mark & Moody England). State Mutual Bk.

Art for Commerce. Michael Turner & David Vaisey. Date not set. cancelled o.p. (ISBN 0-8038-0382-6). Hastings.

Art for Elementary Classrooms. G. Hubbard. Date not set. 14.95 (ISBN 0-13-047274-3). P-H.

Art for Teachers of Children. 2nd ed. Chandler Montgomery. LC 72-97008. 1973. text ed. 17.95 (ISBN 0-675-08962-X). Merrill.

Art for the Fun of It: A Guide for Teaching Young Children. Peggy D. Jenkins. (Illus.). 224p. 1980. 13.95 (Spec); pap. 6.95. P-H.

Art for the Fun of It: A Guide for Teaching Young Children. Peggy D. Jenkins. (Illus.). 208p. 1980. 13.95 (ISBN 0-13-047241-7, Spec); pap. 6.95 (ISBN 0-13-047233-6). P-H.

Art for Young America. Heyne & Van Winkle. 1979. text ed. 15.96 (ISBN 0-87002-294-6). Bennett IL.

Art Forgeries & How to Examine Paintings Scientifically. O. Kurtz. (Illus.). 1979. deluxe ed. 57.45 (ISBN 0-930582-32-2). Gloucester Art.

Art Forms from Plant Life. William M. Harlow. LC 75-25002. Orig. Title: Patterns of Life: the Unseen World of Plants. (Illus.). 1974. pap. 4.50 (ISBN 0-486-23262-X). Dover.

Art from Many Hands: Multicultural Art Projects for Home & School. Jo M. Schuman. (Illus.). 320p. 1980. 22.95 (ISBN 0-13-047217-4, Spec); pap. 10.95 (ISBN 0-13-047217-4). P-H.

Art Fundamentals. Morton Garchik. LC 78-10336. (Illus.). 1979. 14.95 (ISBN 0-87396-082-3). Stravon.

Art Fundamentals: Theory & Practice. 4th ed. Otto G. Ocvirk & Robert O. Bone. 225p. 1981. pap. text ed. write for info. (ISBN 0-697-03232-9). Wm C Brown.

Art Furniture. E. W. Godwin. Ed. by Peter Stansky & Rodney Shewan. Incl. Artistic Conservatories. Maurice Adams. LC 76-18322. (Aesthetic Movement & the Arts & Crafts Movement Ser.: Vol. 14). 1978. Repr. of 1880 ed. lib. bdg. 44.00x (ISBN 0-8240-2463-X). Garland Pub.

Art Galleries of Britain & Ireland: A Guide to Their Collections. Joan Abse. LC 75-24944. (Illus.). 231p. 1975. 15.00 (ISBN 0-8386-1850-2). Fairleigh Dickinson.

Art Glass Handbook & Price Guide. J. Hotchkiss. 1972. pap. 3.95 (ISBN 0-8015-0360-4, Hawthorn). Dutton.

Art Glass Sampler. John Shuman. (Illus.). 1978. softbound 12.95 o.p. (ISBN 0-87069-171-6). Wallace-Homestead.

Art Has Many Faces. Katharine Kuh. LC 51-13484. (Illus.). 1951. 10.95 o.s.i. (ISBN 0-06-003180-8, HarpT). Har-Row.

Art Historical Problems of a Roman Land. James N. Carder. LC 77-94730. (Outstanding Dissertations in the Fine Arts Ser.). 1979. lib. bdg. 33.00x (ISBN 0-8240-3218-7). Garland Pub.

Art History. Jack Rudman. (Undergraduate Program Field Test Ser.: UPFT-1). (Cloth bdg. avail. on request). pap. 9.95 (ISBN 0-8373-6001-3). Natl Learning.

Art History & Class Struggle. rev. ed. Nicos Hadjinicolaou. Tr. by Louise Asmal from Fr. (Illus.). 1978. text ed. 19.50x (ISBN 0-904383-32-6); pap. text ed. 9.50x (ISBN 0-904383-27-X). Humanities.

Art in America: A Critical & Historical Sketch. S. G. Benjamin. Ed. by H. Barbara Weinberg. LC 75-28872. (Art Experience in Late 19th Century America Ser.: Vol. 8). (Illus.). 1976. Repr. of 1880 ed. lib. bdg. 58.00x (ISBN 0-8240-2232-7). Garland Pub.

Art in America: From Colonial Days Through the Nineteenth Century. Robert Myron & Abner Sundell. LC 69-10347. (Illus.). (gr. 7-10). 1969. 4.95g o.s.i. (ISBN 0-02-767770-2, CCPr). Macmillan.

Art in Cartooning. Cartoonists' Guild. (Illus.). 1979. pap. 9.95 o.p. (ISBN 0-684-16398-5, ScribT). Scribner.

Art in Context. 2nd ed. Jack A. Hobbs. 320p. 1980. text ed. 12.95 (ISBN 0-686-64964-8, HC). HarBraceJ.

Art in Detroit Public Places. Dennis A. Nawrocki & Thomas J. Holleman. (Illus.). 160p. 1980. 9.95 (ISBN 0-8143-1653-0); pap. 4.95 (ISBN 0-8143-1649-2). Wayne St U Pr.

Art in Education. Howard Conant & Arne Randall. (YA) (gr. 9 up). 1963. 9.28 (ISBN 0-87002-064-1). Bennett IL.

Art in Great Britain & Ireland. Walter Armstrong. 332p. 1980. Repr. of 1913 ed. lib. bdg. 65.00 (ISBN 0-8492-3206-6). R West.

Art in Judaism: A Course Syllabus. 1976. includes filmslip & viewer 5.50 (ISBN 0-8074-0188-9, 244330). UAHC.

Art in Needlework. Lewis F. Day & Mary Buckle. Ed. by Peter Stansky & Rodney Shewan. LC 76-17769. (Aesthetic Movement & the Arts & Crafts Movement Ser.). 1977. Repr. of 1900 ed. lib. bdg. 44.00x (ISBN 0-8240-2473-7). Garland Pub.

Art in Needlework: A Book About Embroidery. Lewis F. Day & Mary Buckle. LC 74-159927. Repr. of 1900 ed. 18.00 (ISBN 0-8103-3062-8). Gale.

Art in Ornament & Dress. Charles Blanc. LC 77-156923. (Tower Bks). (Illus.). 1971. Repr. of 1876 ed. 20.00 (ISBN 0-8103-3922-6). Gale.

Art in Primitive Societies. Richard L. Anderson. (Illus.). 1979. pap. 10.95 ref. ed. (ISBN 0-13-048108-4). P-H.

Art in Revolution. John Berger. LC 68-26045. 1969. pap. 4.95 (ISBN 0-394-41562-0). Pantheon.

Art in Society. Ken Baynes. LC 74-21587. (Illus.). 288p. 1975. 45.00 (ISBN 0-87951-027-7). Overlook Pr.

Art in Society: Studies in Style, Culture & Aesthetics. Ed. by Michael Greenhalgh & Vincent Megaw. LC 78-69954. 1978. 29.95 (ISBN 0-312-05267-7). St Martin.

Art in the Early Church. rev. ed. Walter Lowrie. 11.00 (ISBN 0-8446-2492-6). Peter Smith.

Art in the Education of Subnormal Children. Pauline Tilley. (Illus.). 128p. (Orig.). 1975. 10.00x o.s.i. (ISBN 0-8464-0151-7). Beekman Pubs.

Art in the Humanities. 2nd ed. Patrick D. De Long. 1970. pap. text ed. 8.50 (ISBN 0-13-046979-3). P-H.

Art in the Primary School. Kay Melzi. 1967. text ed. 7.50x (ISBN 0-631-11880-2). Humanities.

Art in the Seventies. Edward Lucie-Smith. (Illus.). 128p. 1980. 29.95 (ISBN 0-8014-1328-1); pap. 14.95 (ISBN 0-8014-9194-0). Cornell U Pr.

Art in Time. Patricia P. Havlice. LC 76-14885. 1970. 9.50 o.p. (ISBN 0-8108-0333-X). Scarecrow.

Art Index, Vols. 1-26. 1929-1953. Vols. 1-8. 1929-1953 50.00 ea. (ISBN 0-685-22229-2); Vols. 9-18. 1953-1970 95.00 ea. (ISBN 0-685-22230-6); Vols. 19-27. 11/1970-10/1978 set sold on service basis (ISBN 0-685-22231-4). Wilson.

Art Institute of Chicago: 100 Masterpieces. LC 78-56322. 1978. 35.00 o.s.i. (ISBN 0-528-81033-2). Rand.

Art Life of William Rimmer: Sculptor, Painter, & Physician. Truman H. Bartlett. LC 68-27718. (Library of American Art Ser.). (Illus.). 1970. Repr. of 1890 ed. lib. bdg. 27.50 (ISBN 0-306-71166-4). Da Capo.

Art: Magic, Impulse & Control-a Guide to Viewing. William Bradley. (Illus.). 208p. 1973. 12.95 (ISBN 0-13-046664-6); pap. text ed. 7.50 (ISBN 0-13-046656-5). P-H.

Art Metal & Enameling. Leslie V. Hawkins. 234p. (gr. 9-12). 1974. text ed. 11.60 (ISBN 0-87002-157-5). Bennett IL.

Art Militaire et les Armees Au Moyen Age En Europe et Dans le Proche Orient, 2 vols. Ferdinand Lot. LC 80-2017. 1981. Repr. of 1946 ed. 90.00 (ISBN 0-686-28932-3). AMS Pr.

Art Museum As Educator. Ed. by Barbara Newsom. 1978. 40.00x (ISBN 0-520-03248-9); pap. 14.95 (ISBN 0-520-03249-7). U of Cal Pr.

Art Museum: Power, Money & Ethics. Karl E. Meyer. (Illus.). 352p. 1981. pap. 8.95. Morrow.

Art Museums of New England. S. Lane Faison, Jr. 548p. 1981. 20.00 (ISBN 0-87923-372-9); pap. 10.00 (ISBN 0-87923-373-7). Godine.

Art Nouveau. Gabriele Sterner. (Pocket Art Ser.). (Illus.). 1981. pap. 3.50 (ISBN 0-8120-2105-3). Barron.

Art Nouveau Decorative Ironwork: One Hundred & Fifty Photographic Illustrations. Theodore Menten. (Illus.). 144p. 1981. pap. write for info. (ISBN 0-486-23986-1). Dover.

Art Nouveau Stained Glass Pattern Book. Ed Sibbett, Jr. LC 77-87497. (Pictorial Archives Ser.). (Illus.). 1978. pap. 2.75 (ISBN 0-486-23577-7). Dover.

Art Nouveau Style Book of Alphonse Mucha. Alphonse Mucha. (Illus.). 80p. 1980. pap. 7.95 (ISBN 0-486-24044-4). Dover.

Art Noveau Album. Kathy Torrence. (Illus.). 80p. 1981. 19.95 (ISBN 0-525-06980-1); pap. 10.95 (ISBN 0-525-47635-0). Dutton.

Art Observations. Charles B. Rogers. (Illus.). 64p. 1980. pap. 5.95 (ISBN 0-686-64396-8). Rogers Hse Mus.

Art of A. Henry Nordhausen. Laurence E. Schmeckebier. LC 80-20077. (Illus.). 168p. 1980. 45.00 (ISBN 0-914016-73-3). Phoenix Pub.

Art of Accompanying & Coaching. K. Adler. LC 79-147128. (Music Ser.). 260p. 1971. lib. bdg. 27.50 (ISBN 0-306-70360-2); pap. 7.95 (ISBN 0-306-80027-6). Da Capo.

Art of Advertising. Ernestine Miller. (Illus.). 64p. 1980. pap. 10.95 (ISBN 0-312-05416-5). St Martin.

Art of Advocacy. Lloyd P. Stryker. 284p. 1979. pap. 5.95 (ISBN 0-89062-069-5, Pub. by Hughes Press). Pub Ctr Cult Res.

Art of Aging. Evelyn Mandel. Ed. by Miriam Frost. Orig. Title: The Gray Matter. (Illus.). 176p. (Orig.). 1981. 14.95 (ISBN 0-03-059063-9); pap. 8.95 (ISBN 0-03-059063-9). Winston Pr.

Art of Alexander Pope. Ed. by Howard Erskine-Hill. LC 78-62593. (Critical Studies Ser.). 1979. text ed. 19.75x (ISBN 0-685-62564-8). B&N.

Art of Alfred Hitchcock. Donald Spoto. LC 79-7672. (Illus.). 1979. pap. 9.95 (ISBN 0-385-15569-7, Dolp). Doubleday.

Art of All Nations, 1850-1873: A Continuation of the Triumph of Art for the Public. Elizabeth G. Holt. LC 80-1666. (Illus.). 640p. (Orig.). 1981. pap. 8.95 (ISBN 0-385-14879-8, Anch). Doubleday.

Art of America from Jackson to Lincoln. Shirley Glubok. LC 72-81066. (Illus.). 48p. (gr. 4-8). 1973. 9.95 (ISBN 0-02-736250-7). Macmillan.

Art of America in the Early Twentieth Century. Shirley Glubok. LC 74-6329. (Illus.). 48p. (gr. 4 up). 1974. 9.95 (ISBN 0-02-736180-2). Macmillan.

Art of America in the Gilded Age. Shirley Glubok. LC 73-6048. (Art of America Ser). (Illus.). 48p. (gr. 4 up). 1974. 9.95 (ISBN 0-02-736100-4). Macmillan.

Art of America Since World War II. Shirley Glubok. LC 75-34453. (Art History Ser.: Vol. 6). (Illus.). 48p. (gr. 3 up). 1976. 10.95 (ISBN 0-02-736310-4, 73631). Macmillan.

Art of Ancient Cyprus. Department of Classical Art. 1972. pap. 2.95 (ISBN 0-87846-068-3). Mus Fine Arts Boston.

Art of Andrew Wyeth. Ed. by Wanda Corn. LC 73-93900. (Illus.). 1975. pap. 12.95 (ISBN 0-8212-0685-0, 052280). NYGS.

Art of Anthony Trollope. Geoffrey Harvey. LC 80-5088. x, 177p. 1980. 22.50 (ISBN 0-312-04998-6). St Martin.

Art of Argument. Carlos L. Hunsinger. LC 79-15660. Date not set. 10.95 (ISBN 0-87949-154-X). Ashley Bks.

Art of Argument. Vernon L. Taylor. LC 71-150111. 1971. 10.00 (ISBN 0-8108-0376-3). Scarecrow.

Art of Aromatheraphy: The Beautifying & Healing Properties of the Essential Oils of Flowers & Herbs. Robert B. Tisserand. (Illus.). 1978. pap. 7.95 (ISBN 0-89281-001-7). Inner Tradit.

Art of Aromatherapy. R. B. Tisserand. 320p. 1977. 18.00x (ISBN 0-8464-0993-3). Beekman Pubs.

Art of Aromatherapy. Robert Tisserand. 1978. pap. 7.95 (ISBN 0-685-62088-3). Weiser.

Art of Asking Questions. 1980 ed. Stanley L. Payne. LC 80-7824. 264p. 1980. 22.50x (ISBN 0-691-08104-2); pap. 6.95 (ISBN 0-691-02367-0). Princeton U Pr.

Art of Attack in Chess. V. Vukovic. 1965. 24.00 (ISBN 0-08-011197-1); pap. text ed. 11.90 (ISBN 0-08-011196-3). Pergamon.

Art of Beauty, Repr. Of 1878. E. Haweis. Ed. by Peter Stansky & Rodney Shewan. Incl. Art of Dress. Repr. of 1879 ed. LC 76-17760. (Aesthetic Movement & the Arts & Crafts Movement Ser.). 1978. lib. bdg. 44.00x (ISBN 0-8240-2465-6). Garland Pub.

Art of Being a Boss: Inside Intelligence from Top-Level Business Leaders & Young Executives on the Move. Robert J. Schoenberg. 1978. 11.95 (ISBN 0-397-01291-8). Lippincott.

Art of Being Human. McNamara, William, O.C.D. pap. 1.95 (ISBN 0-385-08323-8, E45, Echo). Doubleday.

Art of Benin. Paula Ben-Amos. (Tribal Art Ser.). (Illus.). 96p. 1980. pap. 9.95 (ISBN 0-500-06009-6). Thames Hudson.

Art of Bernard Leach. Ed. by Carol Hogben. (Illus.). 1978. 32.50 o.p. (ISBN 0-8230-0263-2). Watson-Guptill.

Art of Biblical Narrative. Robert Alter. LC 80-68958. 208p. 1981. 13.95 (ISBN 0-465-04420-4). Basic.

Art of Blacksmithing. Alex W. Bealer, 3rd. LC 76-4546. (Funk & W Bk.). (Illus.). 448p. 1976. 16.95 (ISBN 0-308-10254-1, TYC-T). T Y Crowell.

Art of Brachygraphie: That Is, to Write As Fast As a Man Speaketh Treatably, Writing but One Letter for a Word. Peter Bales. LC 70-38146. (English Experience Ser.: No. 426). 120p. 1972. Repr. of 1597 ed. 11.50 (ISBN 90-221-0426-5). Walter J Johnson.

Art of Bricklaying. J. Edgar Ray. Ed. by Harold V. Johnson. (Illus.). (gr. 9-12). 1971. pap. text ed. 11.00 (ISBN 0-87002-271-7). Bennett IL.

Art of Byzantium & the Medieval West: Selected Studies. Ernst Kitzinger. Ed. by W. Eugene Kleinbauer. LC 75-34728. (Illus.). 448p. 1976. 22.50x (ISBN 0-253-31055-5). Ind U Pr.

Art of Calligraphy: A Practical Guide. Marie Angel. (Illus.). 1978. pap. 7.95 (ISBN 0-684-15518-4, ScribT). Scribner.

Art of Cartooning. Syd Hoff. LC 72-12659. (Illus.). 224p. 1973. 11.95 (ISBN 0-87396-072-6). Stravon.

Art of Central Banking. 2nd ed. Ralph G. Hawtrey. Repr. of 1932 ed. 25.00x (ISBN 0-678-05174-7). Kelley.

Art of Charles Prendergast. Richard J. Wattenmaker. LC 68-9480. (Illus.). 1968. pap. 3.00 (ISBN 0-87846-141-8, Pub. by Mus Fine Arts Boston). C E Tuttle.

Art of Charlotte Bronte. Earl A. Knies. LC 69-15917. x, 234p. 1969. 11.95x (ISBN 0-8214-0059-2). Ohio U Pr.

Art of Chess Combination: A Guide for All Players of the Game. Eugene Znosko-Borovsky. Tr. by Philip W. Sergeant. (Illus.). 1936. pap. 3.50 (ISBN 0-486-20583-5). Dover.

Art of China. Shirley Glubok. LC 72-81059. (Illus.). 48p. (gr. 4 up). 1973. 9.95 (ISBN 0-02-736170-5). Macmillan.

Art of Chinese Cooking. Benedictine Sisters Of Peking Editors. LC 56-11125. (Illus., Orig.). 1956. pap. 5.95 (ISBN 0-8048-0035-9). C E Tuttle.

Art of Christian Listening. Thomas N. Hart. 128p. (Orig.). 1981. pap. 4.95 (ISBN 0-8091-2345-2). Paulist Pr.

Art of Church Canvass. Allan D. Weenink. LC 78-69998. 1978. pap. 4.95 (ISBN 0-87983-172-3). Keats.

Art of Claud Lovat Fraser. Clive E. Driver. 1971. pap. 6.50 (ISBN 0-686-28309-0). Rosenbach Mus and Lib.

Art of Clear Thinking. Rudolf Flesch. (Illus.). 212p. 1973. pap. 2.95 (ISBN 0-06-463369-1, EH 369, EH). Har-Row.

Art of Coarse Acting. rev. ed. Michael Green. LC 80-20310. (Illus.). 136p. 1981. tchrs' ed. 10.00 (ISBN 0-89676-041-3). Drama Bk.

Art of Colonial America. Shirley Glubok. LC 77-102964. (Art of Bks). (Illus.). (gr. 4 up). 1970. 10.95 (ISBN 0-02-736070-9). Macmillan.

Art of Community. Spencer H. Maccallum. LC 78-112866. 1976. 8.95x o.p. (ISBN 0-916054-12-8); pap. text ed. 3.95x o.p. (ISBN 0-916054-13-6). Green Hill.

Art of Computer Programming: Semi-Numerical Algorithms, Vol. 2. 2nd ed. Donald E. Knuth. 1981. text ed. 25.95 (ISBN 0-201-03822-6). A-W. Postponed.

Art of Computer Programming, Vol. 1: Fundamental Algorithms. 2nd ed. Donald E. Knuth. LC 73-1830. 640p. 1974. 25.95 (ISBN 0-201-03809-9). A-W.

Art of Computer Programming, Vol. 3: Sorting & Searching. Donald E. Knuth. 1973. 25.995 (ISBN 0-201-03803-X). A-W.

Art of Conducting. Michael Bowles. LC 74-23419. (Music Ser.). 210p. 1975. Repr. of 1959 ed. lib. bdg. 19.50 (ISBN 0-306-70718-7). Da Capo.

Art of Cooking for the Diabetic. Katherine Middleton & Mary A. Hess. 1979. pap. 2.75 (ISBN 0-451-08719-4, E8719, Sig). NAL.

Art of Cooking with Love & Wheatgerm. Jane Kindelehrer. Ed. by Charlie Gerras. LC 76-49579. 1977. 9.95 (ISBN 0-87857-148-5); pap. 7.95 (ISBN 0-87857-280-5). Rodale Pr Inc.

Art of Counseling. Rollo May. (Series B). 1978. pap. 4.50 (ISBN 0-687-01766-1). Abingdon.

Art of Counterpoint. Charles H. Kitson. LC 75-4973. (Music Reprint Ser.). 344p. 1975. Repr. of 1924 ed. lib. bdg. 32.50 (ISBN 0-306-70668-7). Da Capo.

Art of Courtly Love. Andreas Capellanus. Tr. by John J. Perry. 1969. pap. text ed. 4.95x (ISBN 0-393-09848-6, NortonC). Norton.

Art of Courtly Love. abr ed. Andreas Capellanus. Ed. by F. W. Locke. Tr. by John J. Parry. LC 56-12400. (Milestones of Thought Ser.). 3.75 (ISBN 0-8044-2108-0); pap. 1.95 (ISBN 0-8044-6075-2). Ungar.

Art of Crewel Embroidery. Mildred Davis. 13.95 o.p. (ISBN 0-87245-074-0). Textile Bk.

Art of Criticism. Dominique Bouhours. Repr. of 1705 ed. write for info. Schol Facsimil.

Art of Cyprus. Tony P. Spiteris. Tr. by Thomas Burton from Fr. LC 75-128117. (Illus.). 1970. 29.95 o.p. (ISBN 0-688-61003-X). Reynal.

Art of D. H. Lawrence. K. Sagar. 279p. 1976. 42.00 (ISBN 0-521-06181-4); pap. 10.95 (ISBN 0-521-09387-2). Cambridge U Pr.

Art of Deception. 2nd ed. Nicholas Capaldi. LC 75-21077. 200p. 1979. pap. text ed. 5.95 (ISBN 0-87975-058-8). Prometheus Bks.

Art of Decoration. Mrs. E. Haweis. LC 76-17761. (Aesthetic Movement Ser.: Vol. 17). 1977. Repr. of 1889 ed. lib. bdg. 44.00x (ISBN 0-8240-2466-4). Garland Pub.

Art of Decorative Design. Christopher Dresser. LC 76-17751. (Aesthetic Movement Ser.: Vol. 4). (Illus.). 1977. Repr. of 1862 ed. lib. bdg. 44.00x (ISBN 0-8240-2453-2). Garland Pub.

Art of Defense in Chess. Andrew Soltis. LC 74-25728. 1975. 9.95 o.p. (ISBN 0-679-13043-8). McKay.

Art of Developing a Career. Theodore W. Friel & Robert R. Carkhuff. LC 74-75375. (Career Skills Ser.). (Illus.). 229p. 1974. pap. text ed. 8.95x student's guide o.p. (ISBN 0-914234-40-4). Human Res Dev Pr.

Art of Developing a Career: A Helper's Guide. Theodore W. Friel & Robert R. Carkhuff. LC 74-75375. (Illus., Prog. Bk.). 1974. teachers' ed. 11.95x (ISBN 0-914234-41-2). Human Res Dev Pr.

Art of Digital Design: An Introduction to Top-Down Design. David E. Winkel & Franklin P. Prosser. (Illus.). 1980. text ed. 25.95 (ISBN 0-13-046607-7). P-H.

Art of Diplomacy: The American Experience. Thomas A. Bailey. LC 68-11680. 1968. 18.95x (ISBN 0-89197-032-0); pap. text ed. 6.95x (ISBN 0-89197-033-9). Irvington.

Art of Djuna Barnes: Duality & Damnation. Louis F. Kannenstine. LC 76-55152. 1977. 12.00x (ISBN 0-8147-4564-4); pap. 5.00x (ISBN 0-8147-4565-2). NYU Pr.

Art of Drama. Ronald Peacock. LC 73-3026. 263p. 1974. Repr. of 1957 ed. lib. bdg. 18.75x (ISBN 0-8371-6825-2, PEAD). Greenwood.

Art of Drawing on Stone, Giving a Full Explanation of the Various Styles of the Different Methods to Be Employed to Ensure Success, & of the Modes of Correcting, As Well As of the Several Causes of Failure. Charles J. Hullmandel. LC 78-74392. (Nineteenth-Century Book Arts & Printing History Ser.: Vol. 7). 1980. lib. bdg. 22.00 (ISBN 0-8240-3881-9). Garland Pub.

Art of Dura-Europos. Ann Perkins. (Illus.). 140p. 1973. 45.00x (ISBN 0-19-813164-X). Oxford U Pr.

Art of Dying. Ian Crichton. 166p. 1976. text ed. 17.00x (ISBN 0-7206-0353-6). Humanities.

Art of Dying. Robert E. Neale. LC 72-11361. 160p. 1973. 5.95 (ISBN 0-06-066087-2, HarpR); pap. 4.95 (ISBN 0-06-066085-6, RD-200). Har-Row.

Art of Electronics. Paul Horowitz & Winfield Hill. LC 79-27170. (Illus.). 544p. 1980. 24.95 (ISBN 0-521-23151-5). Cambridge U Pr.

Art of Electrostatic Precipitation. Jacob Katz. (Illus.). 350p. 1980. text ed. 45.00x (ISBN 0-9603986-1-9). Scholium Intl.

Art of Embattailing an Army, or the Second Part of Aelian's Tacticks. Tacitus Aelianus. Tr. by J. Bingham. LC 68-54605. (English Experience Ser.: No. 70). Repr. of 1629 ed. 21.00 (ISBN 90-221-0070-7). Walter J Johnson.

Art of Emily Bronte. Ed. by Anne Smith. LC 76-19859. (Barnes & Noble Critical Studies). 1976. text ed. 23.50x (ISBN 0-06-496376-4); pap. text ed. 9.95x (ISBN 0-389-20054-9). B&N.

Art of Empathy: A Manual for Improving Accuracy of Interpersonal Perception. Kenneth Bullmer. LC 74-11280. 140p. 1975. pap. text ed. 7.95 (ISBN 0-87705-228-X). Human Sci Pr.

Art of England: Lectures Given in Oxford by John Ruskin During His Second Tenure of the Slade Professorship. John Ruskin. Ed. by Sydney J. Freedberg. LC 77-25769. (Connoisseurship, Criticism, & Art History Ser.: Vol. 23). 292p. 1979. lib. bdg. 21.00 (ISBN 0-8240-3281-0). Garland Pub.

Art of Etching. E. S. Lumsden. (Illus.). 8.50 (ISBN 0-8446-2497-7). Peter Smith.

Art of Faulkner's Novels. Peter Swiggart. 1962. 12.95x o.p. (ISBN 0-292-73166-3). U of Tex Pr.

Art of Flower Arranging. Zibby Tozer. (Orig.). 1981. pap. 7.95 (ISBN 0-446-97760-8). Warner Bks.

Art of Flower Painting. William Duffield. (Library of the Arts). (Illus.). 1977. 37.50 (ISBN 0-89266-070-8). Am Classical Coll Pr.

Art of Followership (What Happened to the Indians?) Berlie J. Fallon. LC 73-90397. (Fastback Ser.: No. 33). (Illus., Orig.). 1974. pap. 0.75 (ISBN 0-87367-033-7). Phi Delta Kappa.

Art of Freefall Relative Work. rev. ed. Pat Works. LC 75-21405. 1979. 14.95 (ISBN 0-930438-04-3); pap. 7.95 (ISBN 0-930438-01-9). RWU Parachuting.

Art of Friendship. Christine Leefeldt & Ernest Callenbach. 1980. pap. 2.75 (ISBN 0-425-04674-5). Berkley Pub.

Art of Gardening. Thomas Hill. LC 79-84117. (English Experience Ser.: No. 936). 276p. 1979. Repr. of 1608 ed. lib. bdg. 26.00. Walter J Johnson.

Art of German Cooking. Betty Wason. LC 67-11151. 1967. 8.95 (ISBN 0-385-06362-8). Doubleday.

Art of Getting Your Own Sweet Way. Philip B. Crosby. 1975. pap. 3.95 o.p. (ISBN 0-8015-0358-2). Dutton.

Art of Getting Your Own Sweet Way. 2nd ed. Philip B. Crosby. (Illus.). 224p. 1981. 12.95 (ISBN 0-07-014515-6). McGraw.

Art of God Incarnate: Theology & Image in Christian Tradition. Aidan Nichols. LC 80-81443. 192p. 1980. pap. 7.95 (ISBN 0-8091-2300-2). Paulist Pr.

Art of Good Shooting. J. E. Ruffer. (Illus.). 125p. 1976. 6.95 o.p. (ISBN 0-7153-5521-X). David & Charles.

Art of Gothic: Ann Radcliffe's Major Novels, Nelson C. Smith. Ed. by Devendra P. Varma. LC 79-8481. (Gothic Studies & Dissertations Ser.). 1980. lib. bdg. 22.00x (ISBN 0-405-12680-8). Arno.

Art of Greece - 1400-31 B.C. Sources & Documents. Jerry J. Pollitt. 1965. pap. text ed. 10.95 (ISBN 0-13-047183-6). P-H.

Art of Greek Cookery. St. Paul's Greek Orthodox Church Women. LC 63-18214. 8.95 (ISBN 0-385-03793-7). Doubleday.

Art of Guido Mazzoni. Timothy Verdon. LC 77-94719. (Outstanding Dissertations in the Fine Arts Ser.). 1978. lib. bdg. 43.00x (ISBN 0-8240-3253-5). Garland Pub.

Art of Gun Collecting. Gene E. Miller. 1981. 8.95 (ISBN 0-8062-1599-2). Carlton.

Art of Handmade Flowers. Miyuki Iida & Tomoko Iida. LC 77-128687. (Illus.). 124p. 1971. 14.95 (ISBN 0-87011-136-1). Kodansha.

Art of Handmade Flowers. Miyuki Iida & Tomoko Iida. LC 77-128687. (Illus.). 124p. 1980. pap. 9.95 (ISBN 0-87011-419-0). Kodansha.

Art of Hanging Loose in an Uptight World. Ken Olson. 208p. 1978. pap. 2.25 (ISBN 0-449-23613-7, Crest). Fawcett.

Art of Health Care. William A. Anthony. LC 75-40867. 104p. 1976. pap. text ed. 8.95x (ISBN 0-914234-25-0). Human Res Dev Pr.

Art of Helping, IV. 4th ed. Robert Carkhuff et al. LC 79-91075. (Life Skills). 243p. pap. text ed. 9.95x (ISBN 0-914234-10-2, CAH4); tchrs. guide 12.95 (ISBN 0-914234-11-0); wkbk. 6.95 (ISBN 0-914234-12-9). Human Res Dev Pr.

Art of Hokusai in Book-Illustration. Jack Hillier. 1980. 95.00 (ISBN 0-520-04137-2). U of Cal Pr.

Art of Holding the Violin & Bow As Exemplified by Ole Bull. Crosby. Repr. lib. bdg. 19.00 (ISBN 0-403-03869-3). Scholarly.

Art of Illustrating Sermons. Ian Macpherson. (Minister's Paperback Library). 220p. 1976. pap. 3.95 o.p. (ISBN 0-8010-5987-9). Baker Bk.

Art of India. Shirley Glubok. LC 72-78087. (Illus.). (gr. 5-8). 1969. 5.95g o.s.i. (ISBN 0-02-736040-7). Macmillan.

Art of Indian Cuisine: Everday Menus, Feasts, & Holiday Banquets. Pranati Sen Gupta. Ed. by Beth Backman. 240p. 1980. pap. 5.95 o.p. (ISBN 0-8015-0367-1, Hawthorn). Dutton.

Art of Indoor Gardening: Green Magic for Blooming Miracles. Jan Aaron. LC 74-21357. 208p. 1981. 13.95 (ISBN 0-8303-0146-1). Fleet.

Art of Inner Listning. J. K. Crum. 1975. pap. 1.25 (ISBN 0-89129-092-3, PV092). Jove Pubns.

Art of Instructing the Infant Deaf & Dumb: Including De L'Epee's Method of Educating Mutes. John P. Arrowsmith. (Contributions to the History of Psychology B, Psychometrics & Educational Psychology Ser.). 1980. Repr. of 1819 ed. 30.00 (ISBN 0-89093-319-7). U Pubns Amer.

Art of Intercession. Kenneth E. Hagin. 1980. pap. 3.25 (ISBN 0-89276-503-8). Hagin Ministries.

Art of International Negotiation. F. Posses. 195p. 1978. text ed. 23.50x (ISBN 0-220-66315-7, Pub. by Busn Bks England). Renouf.

Art of Italian Cooking. Maria LoPinto & Milo Miloradovich. 1948. 7.95 o.p. (ISBN 0-385-06603-1). Doubleday.

Art of James Joyce: Method & Design in Ulysses & Finnegans Wake. A. Walton Litz. 1964. pap. 3.95 (ISBN 0-19-500258-X, GB). Oxford U Pr.

Art of James Thurber. Richard C. Tobias. LC 68-20938. vi, 196p. 1969. 13.50x (ISBN 0-8214-0058-4). Ohio U Pr.

Art of Japan. Shirley Glubok. LC 75-89584. (Art of Bks). (Illus.). (gr. 4 up). 1970. 5.95g o.s.i. (ISBN 0-02-736080-6). Macmillan.

Art of Jazz: Ragtime to Bebop. Ed. by Martin Williams. (Da Capo Quality Paperbacks Ser.). 248p. 1981. pap. 6.95 (ISBN 0-306-80134-5). Da Capo.

Art of John Dryden. Paul Ramsey. LC 70-80088. 224p. 1969. 10.00x (ISBN 0-8131-1184-6). U Pr of Ky.

Art of John Martin. William Feaver. (Illus.). 360p. 1975. 36.00x (ISBN 0-19-817334-2). Oxford U Pr.

Art of Khajuraho. R. Nath. 1980. 90.00x (ISBN 0-8364-0608-7, Pub. by Abhina India). South Asia Bks.

Art of Kissing. Hugh Morris. LC 76-40626. 1977. pap. 1.95 (ISBN 0-385-12630-1, Dolp). Doubleday.

Art of Landscape Painting with a Detailed Analysis of the Colours to Use in Watercolouring. Theodore Rowbotham. 1979. deluxe ed. 39.35 (ISBN 0-930582-21-7). Gloucester Art.

Art of Latin America Since Independence. rev. ed. Ed. by Stanton L. Catlin & Terence Grieder. (Illus.). 246p. 1966. pap. 5.00 (ISBN 0-913456-01-2). Interbk Inc.

Art of Leadership in War: The Royal Navy from the Age of Nelson to the End of World War II. John Horsfield. LC 79-54059. (Contributions in Military History: No. 21). (Illus.). xiv, 240p. 1980. lib. bdg. 25.00 (ISBN 0-313-20919-7, HLE/). Greenwood.

Art of Learning. Z. Pietrasiński. 1969. 21.00 (ISBN 0-08-012019-9). Pergamon.

Art of Learning to Love Yourself. Cecil Osborne. 1976. 2.50 (ISBN 0-310-30572-1). Zondervan.

Art of Lebanese Cooking. George Rayess. 14.00 (ISBN 0-685-77131-8). Intl Bk Ctr.

Art of Listening: Developing Musical Perception. 4th ed. Jeanne S. Bamberger & Howard Brofsky. LC 78-20837. 1979. pap. text ed. 15.50 scp (ISBN 0-06-040943-6, HarpC); inst. manual free (ISBN 0-06-360966-5); Set Of 5 Records. scp 26.50 (ISBN 0-06-040981-9). Har-Row.

Art of Literary Research. 2nd. rev. ed. Richard D. Altick. 11.95x (ISBN 0-393-09227-5, NortonC); text ed. 5.95x (ISBN 0-393-09590-8). Norton.

Art of Living. Ed. by Reader's Digest Editors. (Orig.). 1980. pap. 2.50 (ISBN 0-425-04549-8). Berkley Pub.

Art of Living. John C. Swayze. LC 78-78054. 1979. pap. 2.25 o.p. (ISBN 0-87216-545-0). Playboy Pbks.

Art of Living, Vol. 1. Robert R. Leichtman & Carl Japikse. 242p. Date not set. pap. 5.00 (ISBN 0-89804-032-9). Ariel Pr.

Art of Living, Vol. 2. Robert R. Leichtman & Carl Japikse. (Illus.). 249p. (Orig.). 1980. pap. 5.00 (ISBN 0-89804-033-7). Ariel Pr.

Art of Living & Other Stories. John Gardner. LC 80-20988. (Illus.). 320p. 12.95 (ISBN 0-394-51674-5). Knopf.

Art of Loving. Erich Fromm. 128p. 1974. pap. 1.95 (ISBN 0-06-080291-X, P291, PL). Har-Row.

Art of Loving: An Enquiry into the Nature of Love. Erich Fromm. pap. 3.50 (ISBN 0-06-090001-6, CN 1, CN). Har-Row.

Art of Magic. Adrion. 1981. pap. 8.95 (ISBN 0-8120-2248-3). Barron.

Art of Magic. T. Nelson Downs. Ed. by John N. Hilliard. 352p. 1980. pap. 4.50 (ISBN 0-486-24005-3). Dover.

Art of Making Beer. Stanley F. Anderson & Raymond Hull. 1971. pap. 3.50 (ISBN 0-8015-0380-9, Hawthorn). Dutton.

Art of Making Furniture. John Makepeace et al. LC 80-52623. (Illus.). 192p. 1981. 21.95 (ISBN 0-8069-5426-4); lib. bdg. 18.39 (ISBN 0-8069-5427-2). Sterling.

Art of Making Wax Flowers & Fruit As an Interesting & Profitable Career. Charles M. Pfeiffer. (Illus.). 117p. 1981. 39.85 (ISBN 0-930582-87-X). Gloucester Art.

Art of Making Wine. Stanley F. Anderson & Raymond Hull. 1971. pap. 2.95 (ISBN 0-8015-0390-6, Hawthorn). Dutton.

Art of Managing Managers. Neil R. Sweeney. 120p. 1981. text ed. price not set (ISBN 0-201-07644-6). A-W.

Art of Managing People. Philip Hunsacker & Anthony Alessandra. (Illus.). 1980. 15.95 (ISBN 0-13-047472-X, Spec); pap. 7.95 (ISBN 0-13-047464-9, Spec). P-H.

Art of Margaret Atwood: Essays in Criticism. Ed. by A. E. Davidson & C. N. Davidson. 250p. 1981. 18.95 (ISBN 0-88784-080-9, Pub. by Hse Anansi Pr Canada). U of Toronto Pr.

Art of Mark Twain. William M. Gibson. LC 75-25455. 225p. 1976. 14.95x (ISBN 0-19-501993-8). Oxford U Pr.

Art of Maurice Sendak. Selma G. Lanes. (Illus.). 264p. 1980. 45.00 (ISBN 0-8109-1600-2, 1600-2). Abrams.

Art of Maya Hieroglyphic Writing. Ian Graham. 1971. pap. 2.50 (ISBN 0-87365-998-8). Peabody Harvard.

Art of Mixing Drinks. C. Carter Smith. (Orig.). 1981. pap. 7.95 (ISBN 0-446-97759-4). Warner Bks.

Art of Narration in Wolfram's "Parzival" & Albrecht's "Jungerer Titurel". Linda B. Parshall. LC 79-21146. (Anglica Germanica Ser.: No. 2). 380p. Date not set. price not set (ISBN 0-521-22237-0). Cambridge U Pr.

Art of Negotiating. Gerard I. Nierenberg. (Illus.). 1971. pap. 3.95 (ISBN 0-346-12272-4). Cornerstone.

Art of Negotiating. Gerard I. Nierenberg. LC 68-30720. 1968. 9.95 (ISBN 0-8015-0408-2, Hawthorn). Dutton.

Art of Officiating Sports. 3rd ed. John W. Bunn. 1967. text ed. 16.50 (ISBN 0-13-047803-2). P-H.

Art of Painting & Drawing with Colored Crayons. Henry Murray. (Illus.). Repr. of 1865 ed. deluxe ed. 27.45 (ISBN 0-930582-35-7). Gloucester Art.

Art of Painting on Glass. Albinas Elskus. (Illus.). 152p. 1980. 17.95 (ISBN 0-684-16465-5, ScribT). Scribner.

Art of Paper Tearing. Eric Hawkesworth. 1970. 6.50 (ISBN 0-571-09189-X, Pub. by Faber & Faber). Merrimack Bk Serv.

Art of Parisian Cooking. Colette Black. (Orig.). 1962. pap. 0.95 o.s.i. (ISBN 0-02-009160-5, Collier). Macmillan.

Art of Paul Sawyier. Arthur F. Jones. LC 75-41988. (Illus.). 208p. Date not set. pap. cancelled (ISBN 0-8131-0145-X). U Pr of Ky. Postponed.

Art of Personality. Inayat Khan. (Sufi Message of Hazrat Inayat Khan Ser.: Vol. 3). 1979. 6.95 (ISBN 90-6077-570-8, Pub. by Servire BV Netherlands). Hunter Hse.

Art of Persuasion: How to Write Effectively About Almost Anything. Terry Balanger & Steward La Casce. LC 78-38278. 1972. pap. 3.95x (ISBN 0-684-15053-0, ScribT). Scribner.

Art of Philosophy: An Introductory Reader. F. Westphal. LC 78-38042. (Illus.). 352p. 1972. pap. text ed. 11.95 (ISBN 0-13-048025-8). P-H.

Art of Photography. (Life Library of Photography). (Illus.). 1971. 14.95 (ISBN 0-8094-1042-7). Time-Life.

Art of Photography. Shirley Glubok. LC 77-4985. (Art of...Ser.). (Illus.). (gr. 4 up). 1977. 10.95 (ISBN 0-02-736680-4, 73668). Macmillan.

Art of Physical Investigation & the Scientific Use of Man's Imagination. John Tyndall. (Illus.). 1979. Repr. of 1898 ed. 47.75 (ISBN 0-89901-001-6). Found Class Reprints.

Art of Piano Playing. Heinrich Neuhaus. Tr. by D. A. Leibovitch. 1978. 10.95 o.p. (ISBN 0-214-65364-1, 8020, Dist. by Arco). Barrie & Jenkins.

Art of Picture Research: A Guide to Current Practice, Procedure, Techniques & Resources. Hilary Evans. (Illus.). 33.00 (ISBN 0-7153-7763-9). David & Charles.

Art of Pipewelding. Ralph H. Kimbro. 1981. 10.00 (ISBN 0-8062-1633-6). Carlton.

Art of Playing Safe in Wall Street: Wall Street Discoveries Capable of Maximizing Your Stock Market Profits & of Practically Eliminating Your Stock Market Potential Losses. Arthur F. Osgood. (Illus.). 99p. 1981. 23.75 (ISBN 0-918968-88-7). Inst Econ Finan.

Art of Playing the Flute: Breath Control. Roger Mather. LC 80-52140. (A Series of Workbooks: Vol. 1). (Illus.). 88p. (Orig.). 1980. pap. 6.95 (ISBN 0-9604640-0-X). Romney Pr.

Art of Poetry: A Greek View of Poetry & Drama. Aristotle. Ed. by W. Hamilton Fyfe. 1940. 6.95x (ISBN 0-19-814106-8). Oxford U Pr.

Art of Politics: Electoral Strategies & Campaign Management. James Brown & Philip M. Seib. LC 76-1872. (Illus.). 225p. 1976. pap. 7.95x (ISBN 0-88284-036-3). Alfred Pub.

Art of Positional Play. Reshevsky. 1976. 14.95 o.p. (ISBN 0-679-13051-9). McKay.

Art of Prayer. Igumen Chariton. Tr. by Palmer Kadloubovsky. 1966. 21.95 (ISBN 0-571-06899-5, Pub. by Faber & Faber). Merrimack Bk Serv.

Art of Preaching. Alan Of Lille. Tr. by Gillian R. Evans. (Cistercian Fathers Ser.: No. 23). (Orig., Lat.). 1981. pap. price not set (ISBN 0-87907-923-1). Cistercian Pubns.

Art of Presence: The Poet & Paradise Lost. Arnold Stein. 1976. 16.75x (ISBN 0-520-03167-9). U of Cal Pr.

Art of Problem Solving. Robert R. Carkhuff. LC 72-91238. (Life Skills Ser.). (Illus.). 143p. 1973. pap. text ed. 8.50x (ISBN 0-914234-01-3). Human Res Dev Pr.

Art of Problem Solving: Accompanied by Ackoff's Fables. Russell L. Ackoff. LC 78-5627. 1978. 15.50 (ISBN 0-471-04289-7, Pub. by Wiley-Interscience). Wiley.

Art of Psychotherapy. Anthony Storr. 204p. 1980. 13.95 (ISBN 0-686-68763-9). S&S.

Art of Ragtime Guitar. Straw Dog. LC 73-94403. (Green Note Musical Publications Ser.). (Illus.). 1975. Repr. of 1974 ed. 10.95 (ISBN 0-02-871300-1); pap. 6.95 (ISBN 0-02-870990-X). Schirmer Bks.

Art of Ragtime Guitar. Straw Dog & Richard Saslow. LC 73-94403. (Guitar Heritage Ser.). 96p. 1974. pap. 8.95 (ISBN 0-912910-04-6). Green Note Music.

Art of Responsive Drawing. 2nd ed. Nathan Goldstein. LC 76-25001. (Illus.). 1977. 18.95 (ISBN 0-13-048629-9). P-H.

Art of Riding: Set Forthe in a Breefe Treatise. John Astley. LC 68-54610. (English Experience Ser.: No. 10). 80p. 1968. Repr. of 1584 ed. 13.00 (ISBN 90-221-0010-3). Walter J Johnson.

Art of Royal Icing. Audrey Holding. (Illus.). xviii, 176p. 1980. pap. 16.25x (ISBN 0-85334-860-X, Pub. by Applied Science). Burgess-Intl Ideas.

Art of Rudyard Kipling. J. M. Tompkins. LC 65-26135. 1965. pap. 3.95x (ISBN 0-8032-5200-5, BB 332, Bison). U of Nebr Pr.

Art of Screen Printing. Anthony Kinsey. 1979. 24.00 (ISBN 0-7134-1544-4, Pub. by Batsford England). David & Charles.

Art of Seeing. Aldous Huxley. (Illus.). 1975. pap. 4.95 (ISBN 0-685-52953-3, Pub. by Montana Bks). Madrona Pubs.

Art of Selfishness. David Seabury. 1979. pap. 3.95 (ISBN 0-346-12258-9). Cornerstone.

Art of Silhouette. Desmond Coke. LC 73-110809. (Illus.). 1970. Repr. of 1913 ed. 18.00 (ISBN 0-8103-3549-2). Gale.

Art of Sinclair Lewis. D. J. Dooley. LC 65-17173. 1967. pap. 4.25x (ISBN 0-8032-5051-7, BB 199, Bison). U of Nebr Pr.

Art of Singing. W. J. Henderson. LC 78-4953. (Music Reprint 1978 Ser.). 1978. Repr. of 1938 ed. lib. bdg. 35.00 (ISBN 0-306-77593-X). Da Capo.

Art of Singing: A Compendium of Thoughts on Singing Published Between 1777 & 1927. Brent J. Monahan. LC 78-16630. 1978. 15.00 (ISBN 0-8108-1155-3). Scarecrow.

Art of Software Testing. Glenford J. Myers. LC 78-12923. (Business Data Processing Ser.). 1979. 18.95 (ISBN 0-471-04328-1, Pub. by Wiley-Interscience). Wiley.

Art of Southeast Asia: Cambodia, Vietnam, Thailand, Loas, Burma, Java & Bali. Phillip Rawson. (World of Art Ser.). (Illus.). 1967. pap. 9.95 (ISBN 0-19-520005-5). Oxford U Pr.

Art of Spanish Cooking. Betty Wason. LC 62-15903. 1963. 7.95 o.p. (ISBN 0-385-03191-2). Doubleday.

Art of Speaking Made Simple. William R. Gondin & Edward W. Mammen. 1954. pap. 3.50 (ISBN 0-385-01201-2, Made). Doubleday.

Art of Srivijaya. 68p. 1980. pap. 36.00 (ISBN 92-3-101656-3, U 1043, UNESCO). Unipub.

Art of Stage Dancing. Ned Wayburn. LC 80-69259. (Belvedere Bk.). (Illus.). 382p. 1980. pap. 9.95 (ISBN 0-87754-250-3). Chelsea Hse.

Art of Stage Lighting. rev. ed. Frederick Bentham. (Illus.). 1976. 16.95 (ISBN 0-87830-009-0). Theatre Arts.

Art of Styling Sentences: Twenty Patterns to Success. Marie L. Waddell et al. LC 70-184892. (gr. 9-12). 1972. pap. text ed. 2.95 (ISBN 0-8120-0440-X). Barron.

Art of Successful Deer Hunting. Francis E. Sell. 1980. pap. 5.95 (ISBN 0-932558-13-5). Willow Creek.

Art of Successful Entrepreneurship & How to Get It. Vance A. Schieffermann. (Illus.). 1981. 49.95 (ISBN 0-918968-82-8). Inst Econ Pol.

Art of Successful Praying. Gordon Lindsay. (School of Prayer Ser.). 1.25 (ISBN 0-89985-079-0). Christ Nations.

Art of Sukhothai. Miriam M. Scott & Carol Stratton. (Illus.). 200p. 1980. 35.95x (ISBN 0-19-580434-1). Oxford U Pr.

Art of Survival. Cord Christian Troebst. LC 74-10030. 288p. 1975. pap. 3.50 o.p. (ISBN 0-385-01129-6, Dolp). Doubleday.

Art of Synthesis. Alan Leo. (Astrologer's Library). 1979. pap. 6.95 (ISBN 0-89281-178-1). Inner Tradit.

Art of Table Setting & Flower Arrangement. rev. ed. Sylvia Hirsch. (Illus.). 1967. 9.95 (ISBN 0-690-10325-5, TYC-T). T Y Crowell.

Art of Tantra. Philip Rawson. LC 77-18400. (World of Art Ser.). (Illus.). 1978. pap. 9.95 (ISBN 0-19-520055-1). Oxford U Pr.

Art of Teaching Christianity. Wayne R. Rood. (Illus., Orig.). 1968. pap. 5.95 (ISBN 0-687-01924-9). Abingdon.

Art of Technical Writing: A Manual for Scientists, Engineers, & Students. Eugene H. Ehrlich & Daniel Murphy. LC 64-12081. (Apollo Eds.). 1969. pap. 3.95 o.s.i. (ISBN 0-8152-0226-1, A226, TYC-T). T Y Crowell.

Art of Ted Hughes. 2nd ed. K. Sagar. LC 77-90217. 1978. 44.00 (ISBN 0-521-21954-X); pap. 10.95 (ISBN 0-521-29321-9). Cambridge U Pr.

Art of the Actor. Charles Coquelin. 1932. pap. 2.95 o.p. (ISBN 0-04-792005-X). Allen Unwin.

Art of the Amateur Nineteen Sixteen to Nineteen Twenty: The Modern Irish Drama V. Robert Hogan & R. Burnham. (Irish Theatre Ser.: No. 11). 400p. 1980. text ed. 35.50x (ISBN 0-391-02153-2). Humanities.

Art of the American Folk Preacher. Bruce A. Rosenberg. LC 77-111649. 1970. 15.95 (ISBN 0-19-500092-7). Oxford U Pr.

Art of the Ancient Near East. Pierre Amiet. (Illus.). 604p. 1980. 95.00 (ISBN 0-686-62712-1, 0638-4). Abrams.

Art of the Ancient Near East. Seton Lloyd. (World of Art Ser.). (Illus.). 1961. pap. 9.95 (ISBN 0-19-519919-7). Oxford U Pr.

Art of the Ancient World. Mrs. H. Groenewegen Frankfort & Bernard Ashmole. (Janson Art History Ser). (Illus.). 512p. 1972. text ed. 21.95x (ISBN 0-13-047001-5). P-H.

Art of the Book in Central Asia. 314p. 1980. 130.00 (ISBN 92-3-101677-6, U 968, UNESCO). Unipub.

Art of the Brothers Hildebrandt. Ian Summers. (Illus.). 1979. 8.95 (ISBN 0-345-27396-6); pap. 15.00 (ISBN 0-345-27830-5). Ballantine.

Art of the Byzantine Era. David T. Rice. (World of Art Ser.). (Illus.). 1963. pap. 9.95x (ISBN 0-19-519925-1). Oxford U Pr.

Art of the Comic Strip. Shirley Glubok. LC 78-24342. (Illus.). (gr. 4 up). 1979. 10.95 (ISBN 0-02-736500-X). Macmillan.

Art of the Dance. Isadora Duncan. LC 71-85671. (Illus.). 14.95 (ISBN 0-87830-005-8); pap. 8.95 (ISBN 0-87830-555-6). Theatre Arts.

Art of the Dance in French Literature from Theophile Gautier to Paul Valery. Deirdre Priddin. 1952. text ed. 4.00x (ISBN 0-391-01947-3). Humanities.

Art of the Drama. Fred B. Millett & Gerald E. Bentley. (Illus.). 1947. 29.00x (ISBN 0-89197-034-7). Irvington.

Art of the Engineer. Ken Baynes & Francis Pugh. LC 80-29190. (Illus.). 240p. 1981. 60.00 (ISBN 0-87951-128-1). Overlook Pr.

Art of the Fantastic. Ed. by Gerry De La Ree. (Illus.). 1978. 15.50 (ISBN 0-938192-00-0). De La Ree.

Art of the Film. 2nd ed. Ernest Lindgren. (Illus.). 1970. pap. 2.95 o.s.i. (ISBN 0-02-061190-0, Collier). Macmillan.

Art of the Gawain-Poet. W. A. Davenport. 1978. text ed. 28.50x (ISBN 0-485-11173-X, Athlone Pr). Humanities.

Art of the Illuminated Manuscript. David M. Robb. LC 78-37830. (Illus.). 356p. 1973. 50.00 o.p. (ISBN 0-498-01118-6). A S Barnes.

Art of the Medieval World: Architecture, Sculpture, Painting, the Sacred Arts. G. Zarnecki. 1976. 21.95 (ISBN 0-13-047514-9). P-H.

Art of the Muppets. (Illus.). 1980. pap. 5.95 (ISBN 0-553-01313-0). Bantam.

Art of the Mystery Story. Howard Haycraft. LC 75-28263. 1975. Repr. of 1946 ed. 16.00x (ISBN 0-8196-0289-2). Biblo.

Art of the New American Nation. Shirley Glubok. LC 76-160073. (Art of Ser). (Illus.). (gr. 4 up). 1972. 9.95 (ISBN 0-02-736140-3). Macmillan.

Art of the Northwest Coast Indians. Shirley Glubok. LC 74-22384. (Illus.). 48p. (gr. 4 up). 1975. 9.95 (ISBN 0-02-736150-0). Macmillan.

Art of the Novel. Henry James. 1934. lib. rep. ed. 6.95x (ISBN 0-684-15531-1, ScribC); pap. text ed. 5.95x (ISBN 0-684-15050-6, SL10, ScribC). Scribner.

Art of the October Revolution. Compiled by Mikhail Guerman. (Illus.). 1979. 30.00 o.p. (ISBN 0-8109-0675-9). Abrams.

Art of the Old West. Shirley Glubok. LC 79-123138. (Illus.). (gr. 4 up). 1971. 5.95g o.s.i. (ISBN 0-02-736090-3). Macmillan.

Art of the Pacific: Conversations by James Neneish. Commentary by David Immone. (Illus.). 1980. 29.95 (ISBN 0-8109-0686-4). Abrams.

Art of the Pacific Islands. Peter Gathercole et al. LC 79-3637. (Illus.). 368p. 1980. 45.00x (ISBN 0-253-10145-X). Ind U Pr.

Art of the Paperweight: Saint Louis. Gerard Ingold. Ed. by L. H. Selman Ltd. (Illus.). 1981. price not set (ISBN 0-933756-01-1). Paperweight Pr.

Art of the Photogram: Photography Without a Camera. Norman S. Weinberger. LC 78-20702. (Illus.). 1981. 19.95 (ISBN 0-8008-0371-X, Pentalic). Taplinger.

Art of the Plains Indians. Shirley Glubok. LC 75-14064. (Illus.). 48p. (gr. 4 up). 1975. 9.95 (ISBN 0-02-736360-0, 73636). Macmillan.

Art of the Primitives. Oto Bihalji-Merin. (Pocket Art Ser.). (Illus.). 1981. pap. 5.50 (ISBN 0-8120-2185-1). Barron.

Art of the Real World. Ed. by Eleanor M. Lang. (Masterworks of Literature Ser.). 1979. pap. 5.50x (ISBN 0-686-68076-6, M50). Coll & U Pr.

Art of the Renaissance. Peter Murray & Linda Murray. (World of Art Ser.). (Illus.). 1963. pap. 9.95 (ISBN 0-19-519928-6). Oxford U Pr.

Art of the Renaissance. Manfred Wundram. LC 73-175861. (History of Art Ser.). (Illus.). 196p. 1972. 8.95x o.s.i. (ISBN 0-87663-170-7). Universe.

Art of the Southeastern Indians. Shirley Glubok. LC 77-20850. (Illus.). (gr. 4 up). 1978. 9.95 (ISBN 0-02-736480-1, 73648). Macmillan.

Art of the Southwest Indians. Shirley Glubok. LC 78-133558. (Art of Ser). (Illus.). (gr. 4 up). 1971. 9.95 (ISBN 0-02-736120-9). Macmillan.

Art of the Spanish in the United States & Puerto Rico. Shirley Glubok. LC 75-185218. (Illus.). (gr. 4up). 1972. 9.95 (ISBN 0-02-736130-6). Macmillan.

Art of the Theatre. Michael O'Donovan. 50p. 1980. Repr. of 1947 ed. lib. bdg. 10.00 (ISBN 0-8492-7308-0). R West.

Art of the Twenties. William S. Lieberman. LC 79-62957. (Illus.). 144p. 1979. pap. 8.95 (ISBN 0-87070-216-5). Museum Mod Art.

Art of the Vikings. Shirley Glubok. LC 78-6849. (Illus.). (gr. 4 up). 1978. 10.95 (ISBN 0-02-736460-7, 73646). Macmillan.

Art of the Woodland Indians. Shirley Glubok. LC 76-12434. (Illus.). (gr. 4 up). 1976. 10.95 (ISBN 0-02-736440-2, 73644). Macmillan.

Art of Thinking: Port-Royal Logic. Antoine Arnauld. Tr. by James Dickoff & Patricia James. LC 63-16933. (Orig.). 1964. pap. 10.95 (ISBN 0-672-60358-6, LLA144). Bobbs.

Art of Thornton Wilder. Malcolm L. Goldstein. LC 65-10239. 1965. 9.95x (ISBN 0-8032-0057-9); pap. 2.95x (ISBN 0-8032-5074-6, BB 308, Bison). U of Nebr Pr.

Art of Transition in Plato. Grace H. Billings. Ed. by Leonardo Taran. LC 78-66578. (Ancient Philosophy Ser.: Vol. 2). 110p. 1979. lib. bdg. 13.00 (ISBN 0-8240-9609-6). Garland Pub.

Art of Trumpet Playing. Keith Johnson. 168p. 1981. 11.95. Iowa St U Pr.

Art of Understanding Yourself. Cecil Osborne. LC 67-11612. (Orig.). 1968. pap. 3.50 (ISBN 0-310-30592-6); 1.50 (ISBN 0-310-30593-4). Zondervan.

Art of Valuation. Arlo Woolery. LC 78-5471. 1978. 15.95 (ISBN 0-669-02340-X). Lexington Bks.

Art of Versification: Matthew of Vendome. Aubrey E. Galyon. 135p. 1980. pap. 8.50 (ISBN 0-8138-1370-0). Iowa St U Pr.

Art of Victorian Prose. George Levine & William Madden. 1968. pap. 6.95x (ISBN 0-19-500953-3). Oxford U Pr.

Art of War. Christian Feest. (Tribal Art Ser.). (Illus.). 96p. 1980. pap. 9.95 (ISBN 0-500-06010-X). Thames Hudson.

Art of War. Henri Jomini. Repr. of 1862 ed. lib. bdg. 28.50x (ISBN 0-8371-5014-0, JOAW). Greenwood.

Art of War. rev. ed. Niccolo Machiavelli. Tr. by Ellis Farneworth. LC 64-66078. (Orig.). 1965. pap. 6.95 (ISBN 0-672-60434-5, LLA196). Bobbs.

Art of War. Sun Tzu. Tr. & intro. by Samuel B. Griffith. 1971. pap. 4.95 (ISBN 0-19-501476-6, 361, GB). Oxford U Pr.

Art of War: Waterloo to Mons. William McElwee. LC 74-17459. (Midland Bks.: No. 214). 352p. 1975. pap. 4.95x (ISBN 0-253-20214-0). Ind U Pr.

Art of Warfare in the Age of Napoleon. Gunther E. Rothenberg. LC 77-86495. (Illus.). 288p. 1978. 15.00 (ISBN 0-253-31076-8). Ind U Pr.

Art of Watching Films: Film Analysis. Joseph M. Boggs. LC 77-87343. 1978. 9.95 (ISBN 0-8053-0970-5). Benjamin-Cummings.

Art of Wilhelm Lehmbruck. Reinhold Heller. (Illus.). 200p. 1972. 17.50 o.s.i. (ISBN 0-02-550800-8). Macmillan.

Art of William Blake. Anthony Blunt. (Icon Editions). (Illus.). 208p. 1974. pap. 5.95x o.s.i. (ISBN 0-06-430045-5, IN-45, HarpT). Har-Row.

Art of William Blake. Anthony F. Blunt. LC 75-173034. (Illus.). 1959. 22.50x (ISBN 0-231-02364-2). Columbia U Pr.

Art of Winning Corporate Grants. Howard Hillman. LC 79-64398. (Art of Winning Grants Ser.). 1980. 8.95 (ISBN 0-8149-0822-5). Vanguard.

Art of Winning Foundation Grants. Howard Hillman & Karin Abarbanel. LC 75-387. 192p. 1975. 8.95 (ISBN 0-8149-0759-8). Vanguard.

Art of Winning Government Grants. Howard Hillman. LC 77-75582. 1977. 8.95 (ISBN 0-8149-0784-9). Vanguard.

Art: Of Wonder & a World. rev. ed. Jean M. Morman. (Illus.). 1978. text ed. 11.90x (ISBN 0-912242-12-4); pap. 8.15x o.p. (ISBN 0-912242-11-6); tchr's manual 3.15 (ISBN 0-685-62930-9). Art Educ.

Art of Wood Carving. Colletti. 160p. 1977. 10.95 o.p. (ISBN 0-13-049247-7, Spec); pap. 4.95 o.p. (ISBN 0-13-049239-6). P-H.

Art of Wood Turning. William W. Klenke. (gr. 7-12). 1954. 11.60 (ISBN 0-87002-104-4). Bennett IL.

Art of Woodworking & Furniture Appreciation. 2nd ed. Laszlo Katz. (Illus.). 1980. 37.50 (ISBN 0-686-00808-1). PFC.

Art of Working. R. B. Lal. 5.00 o.p. (ISBN 0-210-34038-X). Asia.

Art of Writing. Ruggiero. 1981. 11.95 (ISBN 0-88284-118-1); manuel free (ISBN 0-88284-129-7). Alfred Pub.

Art of Writing Business Reports & Proposals. Howard Hillman. (Illus.). 256p. 1981. 12.50 (ISBN 0-8149-0850-0). Vanguard.

Art of Writing Successful R & D Proposals. Donald C. Orlich & Patricia R. Orlich. 1979. pap. 9.40 (ISBN 0-913178-51-9, Pub. by Two Continents). Hippocrene Bks.

Art of Writing Successful R & D Proposals. Donald C. Orlich & Patricia R. Orlich. 1977. 9.40 (ISBN 0-913178-51-9). Redgrave Pub Co.

Art of Wrought Metalwork for House & Garden. Otto Schmirler. Date not set. 60.00 (ISBN 0-8038-0018-5). Hastings.

Art of Zaire: 100 Works from the National Collection. Joseph Cornet. (Illus.). 150p. 1975. 10.75 (ISBN 0-89192-061-7). Interbk Inc.

Art on the Edge. Harold Rosenberg. (Illus.). 288p. 1975. 14.95 (ISBN 0-02-604900-7). Macmillan.

Art Perfected: Portraiture from the Cronise Studio. Susan Seyl. LC 80-83177. (Illus.). 160p. 1980. pap. text ed. 10.95 (ISBN 0-87595-070-1). Oreg Hist Soc.

Art Prices Current: A Record of Sale Prices at the Principal London, Continental, & American Auction Rooms 1972-73. LC 9-23300. (Vol. 50). 1976. 80.00x (ISBN 0-7129-0693-2). Intl Pubns Serv.

Art Projects for the Mentally Retarded Child. Ellen J. Sussman. (Illus.). 108p. 1976. 10.75 (ISBN 0-398-03535-0); pap. 7.00 (ISBN 0-398-03534-2). C C Thomas.

Art Quaderno of Nineteenth Century Steel Engravings of Ancient Landscapes. Eddy D. Moya. (Illus.). 1979. 179.80 (ISBN 0-930582-49-7). Gloucester Art.

Art Search & Self Discovery. James A. Schinnelen. LC 67-12110. (Illus.). (gr. 7-12). 1975. 18.95 (ISBN 0-87192-070-0). Davis Mass.

Art Secrets Artists Follow in Their Search for Greatness. Nathaniel Lamballe. (Illus.). 90p. 1975. 37.50 (ISBN 0-913314-48-X). Am Classical College Pr.

Art, Sex & Symbol: The Mystery of Tatooing. R. W. B. Scutt & Christopher Gotch. LC 73-10526. (Illus.). 320p. 1974. 20.00 o.p. (ISBN 0-498-01343-X). A S Barnes.

Art Since Pop. J. Walker. LC 77-76780. (Modern Movements in Art Ser.). 1978. pap. 1.95 (ISBN 0-8120-0876-6). Barron.

Art, Society, Revolution: Russia 1917-1921. Nils A. Nilsson. 272p. 1980. text ed. 25.00x (ISBN 0-391-01939-2). Humanities.

Art Song. James H. Hall. 1953. pap. 6.95 (ISBN 0-8061-1197-6). U of Okla Pr.

Art Spirit. Robert Henri. Ed. by Margery A. Ryerson. LC 39-4273. (Illus.). 1960. pap. 4.95 (ISBN 0-397-00121-5, KB18, Key). Lippincott.

Art, Style & History: A Selective History of Art. Jon D. Longaker. 1970. pap. 8.95x (ISBN 0-673-05998-7). Scott F.

Art Teacher's Resource Book. Leslie A. Baker. (Illus.). 1978. ref. 16.95 (ISBN 0-87909-022-7). Reston.

Art: The Way It Is. J. Richardson. 1974. pap. 10.95 (ISBN 0-13-049221-3). P-H.

Art Theft: Its Scope, Its Impact, & Its Control. Bonnie Burnham. LC 78-71095. 192p. 1978. pap. 8.00x (ISBN 0-89062-067-9, Pub. by Intl Found Art Res). Pub Ctr Cult Res.

Art Thoughts: the Experiences & Observations of an American Amateur in Europe. James J. Jarves. Ed. by H. Barbara Weinberg. LC 75-28866. (Art Experience in Late 19th Century America Ser.: Vol. 2). (Illus.). 1976. Repr. of 1869 ed. lib. bdg. 37.50x (ISBN 0-8240-2226-2). Garland Pub.

Art Through the Ages, 2 vol. ed. 7th ed. Horst De la Croix & Richard G. Tansey. Incl. Vol. 1. Ancient Medieval & Non-European Art. 481p. pap. text ed. 11.95 (ISBN 0-686-65008-5); Vol. 2. Renaissance & Modern Art. 489p. pap. text ed. 4.95 (ISBN 0-686-65009-3). 1980. write for info. study guide (HC). HarBraceJ.

Art Treasures of America, 3 vols. Edward Strahan. LC 75-28871. (Art Experience in Late 19th Century America Ser.: Vol. 7). (Illus.). 1976. Set. lib. bdg. 290.00 (ISBN 0-8240-2231-9). Garland Pub.

Artaud at Rodez. Charles Marowitz. 112p. 1981. pap. 5.95 (ISBN 0-7145-2632-0, Pub. by M. Boyars). Merrimack Bk Serv.

Artaud: Four Texts. Antonin Artaud. Tr. by Clayton Eshleman from Fr. (Illus.). 80p. 1981. 9.95 (ISBN 0-915572-57-5); pap. 4.50 (ISBN 0-915572-56-7). Panjandrum.

Artaud's Theatre of Cruelty. Albert Bermel. LC 77-76510. 1977. 3.95 (ISBN 0-8008-0395-7). Taplinger.

Arte De Ensenar. C. H. Benson. Tr. by Fernando P. Villalobos from Eng. (Curso Para Maestros Cristianos: No. 5). Orig. Title: Teaching Techniques. 128p. (Span.). 1971. pap. 2.50 (ISBN 0-89922-016-9); instructor's manual 1.50 (ISBN 0-89922-017-7). Edit Caribe.

Arte de la Conversacion, el Arte de la Composicion. 2nd ed. Jose L. Ponce De Leon. 264p. (Span.). 1975. pap. text ed. 12.95x scp (ISBN 0-06-045249-8, HarpC); tapes 195.00 (ISBN 0-685-54221-1). Har-Row.

Arte of English Poesie. G. Puttenham. Ed. by G. D. Willcock & A. Walker. 1970. 65.00 (ISBN 0-521-07782-6). Cambridge U Pr.

Arte of Warre, (Certain Waies of the Orderyng of Souldiours) Niccolo Macchiavelli. Tr. by P. Whitehorne. LC 79-26097. (English Experience Ser.: No. 135). 1969. Repr. of 1562 ed. 42.00 (ISBN 90-221-0135-5). Walter J Johnson.

Arte y Sensualidad: Cincuenta Imagenes Del Hombre y De la Tierra. Esteban Tollinchi. LC 79-19403. (Illus.). 710p. 1980. write for info. (ISBN 0-8477-2111-6); pap. write for info. (ISBN 0-8477-2112-4). U of PR Pr.

Artemus Ward: Charles Farrar Browne. Don C. Seitz. 338p. 1980. Repr. of 1919 ed. lib. bdg. 40.00 (ISBN 0-89760-824-0). Telegraph Bks.

Arterial Baroreceptors & Hypertension. Ed. by Peter Sleight. (Illus.). 380p. 1981. text ed. 67.50x (ISBN 0-19-261259-X). Oxford U Pr.

Arterial Pole of the Embryonic Heart. Henk-Maarten Laane. 160p. 1978. pap. text ed. 26.50 (ISBN 90-265-0297-4, Pub. by Swets Pub Serv Holland). Swets North Am.

Arteries & Veins of the Human Brain. Roger B. Stephens & Donald L. Stilwell. (Illus.). 196p. 1969. 27.75 (ISBN 0-398-01857-X). C C Thomas.

Artes E Ideas, Vol. 2. rev. ed. William Flemming. 8.75 o.p. (ISBN 0-8477-2103-5). U of PR Pr.

Artes Populares in America. (Span.). 1973. pap. 1.00 (ISBN 0-8270-4300-7). OAS.

Artful Balance: The Parallel Structures of Style. Mary P. Hiatt. LC 75-11673. 192p. 1975. text ed. 13.60x (ISBN 0-8077-2487-4); pap. text ed. 7.50x (ISBN 0-8077-2486-6). Tchrs Coll.

Artful Lady. Sabina Clark. (Second Chance at Love, Regency Ser.: No. 6). (Orig.). 1981. pap. 1.75 (ISBN 0-515-05863-7). Jove Pubns.

Arthritis & Rheumatism: The Facts. J. T. Scott. (Facts Ser.). (Illus.). 126p. 1980. 11.95x (ISBN 0-19-261168-2). Oxford U Pr.

Arthritis & You. Martha Robinson. 88p. 1980. 15.00x (ISBN 0-86025-847-5, Pub. by Ian Henry Pubns England). State Mutual Bk.

Arthritis: Diseases & Treatment, 3 vols. 3rd ed. John A. Mills. Incl. Bk. 1. Inflammation (ISBN 0-89147-049-2); Bk. 2. Arthritis (ISBN 0-89147-050-6); Bk. 3. Anti-Inflammatory Therapy. (Illus.) (ISBN 0-89147-051-4). 1977. Set. pap. text ed. 45.00 (ISBN 0-89147-048-4). pap. text ed. 16.50 ea. CAS.

Arthritis: End the Agony. Shideler Harpe. Date not set. 9.95 (ISBN 0-88280-057-4). ETC Pubns. Postponed.

Arthritis Exercise Book. Semyon E. Krewer. 256p. (Orig.). 1981. pap. 7.95 (ISBN 0-346-12497-2). Cornerstone.

Arthritis Helpbook: What You Can Do for Your Arthritis. Kate Loring & James F. Fries. (Illus.). 160p. 1980. 11.95 (ISBN 0-201-03796-3); pap. 6.95 (ISBN 0-201-03797-1). A-W.

Arthritis of the Knee. Ed. by M. A. Freeman. (Clinical Features & Surgical Management Ser.). (Illus.). 320p. 1980. 110.00 (ISBN 0-387-09699-X). Springer-Verlag.

Arthritis Self-Help Program. The G-Jo Institute. 1980. pap. 4.50 (ISBN 0-916878-10-4). Falkynor Bks.

Arthritis: The New Treatments. rev. ed. Julian Freeman. (Illus.). 1981. pap. 5.95 (ISBN 0-8092-5960-5). Contemp Bks.

Arthrography. Robert H. Freiberger & Jeremy J. Kaye. 1979. 48.50x (ISBN 0-8385-0423-X). ACC.

Arthropod Phylogeny with Special Reference to Insects. H. Bruce Boudreaux. LC 78-16638. 1979. 24.95 (ISBN 0-471-04290-0, Pub. by Wiley-Interscience). Wiley.

Arthur Adamov. John H. Reilly. LC 74-2162. (World Authors Ser.: France: No. 318). 1974. lib. bdg. 10.95 (ISBN 0-8057-2005-7). Twayne.

Arthur Ashe. Charles Morse & Ann Morse. LC 74-954. (Creative's Superstars Ser). 32p. 1974. 5.50 o.p. (ISBN 0-87191-340-2). Creative Ed.

Arthur Ashe: World Tennis Champion. Julian May. LC 75-28932. (Sports Close-up Ser.). (gr. 3-9). 1975. PLB 5.95 o.p. (ISBN 0-913940-31-3); pap. 2.95 o.p. (ISBN 0-913940-98-4). Crestwood Hse.

Arthur Ashe's Tennis Clinic. Arthur Ashe. LC 80-84951. (Illus.). 144p. 1981. 12.95 (ISBN 0-914178-44-X, 42904-3). Golf Digest Bks.

Arthur Baker's Historic Calligraphic Alphabets. Arthur Baker. (Pictorial Archive Ser.). (Illus.). 96p. (Orig.). 1980. pap. 3.50 (ISBN 0-486-24054-1). Dover.

Arthur C. Clarke. Eric S. Rabkin. LC 80-25922. (Starmont Reader's Guide: No. 1). 80p. 1980. Repr. of 1979 ed. lib. bdg. 9.95x (ISBN 0-89370-032-0). Borgo Pr.

Arthur Fiedler & the Boston Pops. Harry E. Dickson. 276p. 1981. 12.95 (ISBN 0-686-69044-3). HM.

Arthur Foote, 1853-1937: An Autobiography. Arthur Foote. LC 78-2021. (Music Reprint Ser.,1978). (Illus.). 1978. Repr. of 1946 ed. lib. bdg. 25.00 (ISBN 0-306-77531-X). Da Capo.

Arthur Frommer's Guide to Amsterdam - Holland, 1981-82. 224p. Date not set. pap. 2.95 (ISBN 0-671-41427-5). Frommer-Pasmantier.

Arthur Frommer's Guide to Athens, 1981-82. 224p. 1981. pap. 2.95 (ISBN 0-671-41428-3). Frommer-Pasmantier.

Arthur Frommer's Guide to Boston, 1981-82. 224p. 1981. pap. 2.95 (ISBN 0-671-41429-1). Frommer-Pasmantier.

Arthur Frommer's Guide to China, 1981-82. 464p. Date not set. pap. 8.95 (ISBN 0-671-43030-0). Frommer-Pasmantier.

Arthur Frommer's Guide to Dublin, Ireland: 1981-82. pap. 2.95 (ISBN 0-671-41431-3). Frommer-Pasmantier.

Arthur Frommer's Guide to Hawaii, 1981-82. 224p. 1981. pap. 2.95 (ISBN 0-671-41430-5). Frommer-Pasmantier.

Arthur Frommer's Guide to Las Vegas, 1981-82. 224p. 1981. pap. 2.95 (ISBN 0-671-24909-6). Frommer Pasmantier.

Arthur Frommer's Guide to Lisbon-Madrid, 1981-82. 224p. 1981. pap. 2.95 (ISBN 0-671-41433-X). Frommer-Pasmantier.

Arthur Frommer's Guide to London, 1981-82. 224p. 1981. pap. 2.95 (ISBN 0-671-41434-8). Frommer-Pasmantier.

Arthur Frommer's Guide to Los Angeles, 1981-82. 224p. 1981. pap. 2.95 (ISBN 0-671-41435-6). Frommer-Pasmantier.

Arthur Frommer's Guide to Mexico City, Acapulco: 1981-82. pap. 2.95 (ISBN 0-671-41436-4). Frommer-Pasmantier.

Arthur Frommer's Guide to New Orleans, 1981-82. 224p. Date not set. pap. 2.95 (ISBN 0-671-41437-2). Frommer-Pasmantier.

Arthur Frommer's Guide to New York, 1981-82. 224p. 1981. pap. 2.95 (ISBN 0-671-41438-0). Frommer-Pasmantier.

Arthur Frommer's Guide to Paris, 1981-82. 224p. 1981. pap. 2.95 (ISBN 0-671-41439-9). Frommer-Pasmantier.

Arthur Frommer's Guide to Philadelphia, 1981-82. 224p. Date not set. pap. 2.95 (ISBN 0-671-41440-2). Frommer-Pasmantier.

Arthur Frommer's Guide to Rome, 1981-82. 224p. 1981. pap. 2.95 (ISBN 0-671-24917-7). Frommer-Pasmantier.

Arthur Frommer's Guide to San Francisco, 1981-82. 224p. 1981. pap. 2.95 (ISBN 0-671-41442-9). Frommer-Pasmantier.

Arthur Frommer's Guide to Washington, D. C., 1981-82. 224p. 1981. pap. 2.95 (ISBN 0-671-41443-7). Frommer-Pasmantier.

Arthur Gets What He Spills. Louise Armstrong. LC 78-32029. (Let Me Read Ser.). (Illus.). (gr. 6-10). 1979. 4.95 (ISBN 0-685-94651-7, HJ); pap. 1.95 o.p. (ISBN 0-15-607945-3). HarBraceJ.

Arthur, King of Britain: History, Romance, Chronicle & Criticism. Ed. by Richard L. Brengle. (Orig.). 1964. pap. 9.50 (ISBN 0-13-049270-1). P-H.

Arthur Koestler. Sidney A. Pearson, Jr. (English Authors Ser.: No. 228). 1978. lib. bdg. 12.50 (ISBN 0-8057-6699-5). Twayne.

Arthur Lee: A Virtuous Revolutionary. Louis W. Potts. LC 80-21831. (Southern Biography Ser.). 320p. 1981. 25.00x (ISBN 0-8071-0785-9). La State U Pr.

Arthur Machen: A Bibliography. Henry Danielson. LC 79-149784. 1971. Repr. of 1923 ed. 15.00 (ISBN 0-8103-3682-0). Gale.

Arthur Mervyn, or Memoirs of the Year Seventeen Ninety-Three. Charles B. Brown. Ed. by Sydney J. Krause & S. W. Reid. LC 79-92808. (Novels & Related Works of Charles Brockden Brown Ser.: Vol. 3). 590p. 1980. 27.50x (ISBN 0-87338-241-2). Kent St U Pr.

Arthur Miller. rev. ed. Leonard Moss. (United States Author Ser.: No. 115). (gr. 10-12). 1980. lib. bdg. 8.95 (ISBN 0-8057-7311-8). Twayne.

Arthur Miller's Collected Plays, Vol. II. Arthur Miller. LC 80-52008. 704p. 1981. 17.95 (ISBN 0-670-13598-4). Viking Pr.

Arthur Mitchell. Tobi Tobias. LC 74-13730. (Biography Ser.). (Illus.). (gr. 1-5). 1975. PLB 7.89 (ISBN 0-690-00662-4, TYC-J). T Y Crowell.

Arthur Murphy. Robert D. Spector. (English Authors Ser.: No. 258). 1979. lib. bdg. 13.50 (ISBN 0-8057-6751-7). Twayne.

Arthur O. Lovejoy & the Quest for Intelligibility. Daniel J. Wilson. LC 79-25902. xvii, 248p. 1980. 18.00x (ISBN 0-8078-1431-8). U of NC Pr.

Arthur Rackham. Fred Gettings. LC 75-21767. (Illus.). 192p. 1976. 20.00 o.s.i. (ISBN 0-02-543080-7). Macmillan.

Arthur Rex. Thomas Berger. 1980. pap. 3.25 (ISBN 0-440-10362-2). Dell.

Arthur Rimbaud. Charles Chadwick. (French Poets Ser.). 1978. text ed. 26.00x (ISBN 0-485-14610-X, Athlone Pr); pap. text ed. 13.00x (ISBN 0-485-12210-3). Humanities.

Arthur Rimbaud. F. C. St. Aubyn. (Twayne's World Authors Ser.: France: No. 369). 1975. lib. bdg. 12.50 (ISBN 0-8057-6192-6). Twayne.

Arthur Rimbaud: A Season in Hell & Illuminations. Arthur Rimbaud. Tr. by Enid R. Peschel. (Illus.). 200p. 1973. 13.95 (ISBN 0-19-501727-7). Oxford U Pr.

Arthur Rimbaud: Complete Works. Tr. by Paul Schmidt from Fr. LC 74-1853. 336p. 1975. 15.00 o.s.i. (ISBN 0-06-013834-3, HarpT). Har-Row.

Arthur Schnitzler: Professor Bernhardi. Ed. by Martin Swales. LC 73-183731. 153p. 1972. 6.70 (ISBN 0-08-016801-9); pap. 5.15 (ISBN 0-08-016806-X). Pergamon.

Arthur Shearly Cripps. John R. Doyle, Jr. (World Authors Ser.: No. 365). 1975. lib. bdg. 12.50 (ISBN 0-8057-6216-7). Twayne.

Arthur Wing Pinero. Walter Lazenby. (English Authors Ser.: No. 150). lib. bdg. 10.95 (ISBN 0-8057-1444-8). Twayne.

Arthurian Literature in the Middle Ages: A Collaborative History. Ed. by Roger S. Loomis. 1959. 59.00x (ISBN 0-19-811588-1). Oxford U Pr.

Arthurian Romances. Chretien De Troyes. Tr. by W. W. Comfort. 1955. 6.00x (ISBN 0-460-00698-3, Evman); pap. 3.95 (ISBN 0-460-01698-9). Dutton.

Arthur's Adventure in the Abandoned House. Fernando Krahn. LC 80-22249. (Illus.). (ps-1). 1981. PLB 7.95 (ISBN 0-525-25945-7). Dutton.

Arthur's Britain: History & Archaeology AD 367-634. L. Alcock. 1972. 19.95 (ISBN 0-312-05530-7). St Martin.

Arthur's Eyes. Marc Brown. 32p. (gr. 1-3). 1981. pap. 1.95 (ISBN 0-380-53389-8, Camelot). Avon.

Arthur's New Power. Russell Hoban. LC 77-11550. (Illus.). (gr. 1-5). 1978. 6.95 (ISBN 0-690-01370-1, TYC-J); PLB 7.89 (ISBN 0-690-01371-X). T Y Crowell.

Arthur's New Power. Russell Hoban. (gr. k-6). 1980. pap. 1.50 (ISBN 0-440-40183-6, YB). Dell.

Arthur's Nose. Marc Brown. 32p. (gr. 1-3). 1981. pap. 1.95 (ISBN 0-380-53397-9, Camelot). Avon.

Arthur's Valentine. Marc Brown. (Illus.). (gr. 1-3). 1980. 7.95g (ISBN 0-316-11062-0, Pub. by Atlantic-Little Brown). Little.

Artic Summer & Other Fiction. E. M. Forster. (The Abinger Edition of E. M. Forster: Vol. 9). 342p. 1981. 35.00x (ISBN 0-8419-0670-X). Holmes & Meier.

Article Five Convention Process: A Symposium. P. G. Kauper et al. LC 70-150510. (Symposia on Law & Society Ser). 1971. Repr. lib. bdg. 25.00 (ISBN 0-306-70185-5). Da Capo.

Articles & Features. Roy P. Nelson. LC 77-85340. (Illus.). 1978. text ed. 14.95 (ISBN 0-395-25517-1). HM.

Articles of Confederation: An Interpretation of the Social Constitutional History of the American Revolution, 1774-1781. Merill Jensen. 1940. pap. 7.95x (ISBN 0-299-00204-7). U of Wis Pr.

Articles of Peace: In a Treatie. LC 71-171753. (English Experience Ser.: No. 378). 1971. Repr. of 1605 ed. 7.00 (ISBN 90-221-0378-1). Walter J Johnson.

Articles on American & British Literature: An Index to Selected Periodicals, 1950-1977. Larry B. Corse & Sandra B. Corse. 450p. 1981. 30.00x (ISBN 0-8040-0408-0). Swallow.

Articles on Aristotle: Ethics & Politics, Vol. 2. Ed. by Jonathan Barnes et al. LC 77-2064. 1979. 25.00 (ISBN 0-312-05478-5). St Martin.

Articles on Aristotle: Vol. I: Metaphysics. Ed. by Jonathan Barnes et al. LC 77-20604. 1979. 25.00 (ISBN 0-312-05479-3). St Martin.

Articles on Aristotle: Vol. IV: Psychology & Aesthetics. Ed. by Jonathan Barnes et al. LC 77-20604. 25.00 (ISBN 0-312-05480-7). St Martin.

Articles on Women Writers, 1960-1975: A Bibliography. Narda Lacey Schwartz. LC 77-9071. 236p. 1977. text ed. 24.95 (ISBN 0-87436-252-0). ABC-Clio.

Articles to Be Inquired of, in the First Metropoliticall Visitation of the Most Reverend Father, Richarde...Archbishop of Canterbury. Church of England. LC 74-28851. (English Experience Ser.: No. 732). 1975. Repr. of 1605 ed. 3.50 (ISBN 90-221-0732-9). Walter J Johnson.

Articular Cartilage in Health & Disease. Association of Bone & Joint Surgeons. Ed. by Marshall R. Urist. (Clinical Orthopaedics Ser., Vol. 64). 1969. 15.00 (ISBN 0-685-22845-2). Lippincott.

Articulate Body. Pavel Machotka & John P. Spiegel. (Illus.). 250p. 1980. 18.50 (ISBN 0-8290-0229-4). Irvington.

Articulate Energy. Donald Davie. 1976. 17.50x (ISBN 0-7100-8155-3). Routledge & Kegan.

Articulate Intervention: The Interface of Science, Mathematics & Administration. Hylton Boothroyd. LC 78-13026. (ORASA Text Ser.: No. 1). 1978. pap. 19.95 (ISBN 0-470-26536-1). Halsted Pr.

Articulate Silences. Shiv K. Kumar. (Writers Workshop Redbird Ser). 34p. 1975. 6.75 (ISBN 0-88253-500-5); pap. text ed. 4.00 (ISBN 0-88253-499-8). Ind-US Inc.

Articulated Locomotives of North America. 45.00. Chatham Pub CA.

Articulated Steam Locomotives of North America: A Catalogue of "Giant Steam". Robert A. LeMassena. (Illus.). 416p. 45.00 (ISBN 0-913582-26-3). Sundance.

Articulation & Learning: New Dimensions in Research, Diagnostics, & Therapy. 2nd ed. Ed. by W. Dean Wolfe & Daniel J. Goulding. (Illus.). 350p. 1980. text ed. 23.75 (ISBN 0-398-04007-9). C C Thomas.

Articulation & Voice: Effective Communication. Joseph A. DeVito et al. LC 74-14615. (No. 20). 127p. 1975. 3.95 (ISBN 0-672-61350-6, SC20). Bobbs.

Articulation Curriculum for the S Sound. Nancy Polow. (Illus.). 108p. 1975. pap. 9.75 spiral bdg. (ISBN 0-685-57027-4). C C Thomas.

Articulation Learning. William M. Diedrich & Jeff Bangert. 416p. text ed. 24.50 (ISBN 0-933014-59-7). College-Hill.

Artifact in Behavioral Research. Ed. by R. Rosenthal & R. L. Rosnow. (Social Psychology Ser). 1969. 15.50 (ISBN 0-12-597750-6). Acad Pr.

Artifacts: An Introduction to Early Materials & Technology. rev. ed. Henry Hodges. (Illus., Orig.). 1976. pap. text ed. 11.75x (ISBN 0-212-35918-5). Humanities.

Artifacts & the American Past: Techniques for the Teaching Historian. Thomas J. Schlereth. 300p. 1981. pap. 13.95 (ISBN 0-910050-47-3). AASLH.

Artifacts of Altar De Sacrificios. Gordon R. Willey. LC 72-93407. (Peabody Museum Papers: Vol. 64, No. 1). pap. text ed. 25.00 (ISBN 0-87365-183-9). Peabody Harvard.

Artificial Cells. Thomas Ming Swi Chang. (Illus.). 224p. 1972. pap. 24.50 photocopy ed. spiral (ISBN 0-398-02257-7). C C Thomas.

Artificial Curiosities: An Exposition of Native Manufactures Collected on the Three Pacific Voyages of Captain James Cook, R.N. Adrienne L. Kaeppler. LC 77-91442. (Bernia P. Bishop Museum Special Publications: No. 65). (Illus.). 310p. 1980. pap. 27.50 (ISBN 0-295-95727-1). U of Wash Pr.

Artificial Insemination of Dairy & Beef Cattle. 6th ed. H. A. Herman & F. A. Madden. 1980. 13.95x (ISBN 0-87543-109-7). Lucas.

Artificial Insemination of Dairy Goat. Harry A. Herman. Date not set. 2.50 (ISBN 0-686-26684-6). Dairy Goat.

Artificial Insemination of Farm Animals. Enos J. Perry. 473p. 1968. 20.00 (ISBN 0-8135-0577-1). Rutgers U Pr.

Artificial Insemination with Husband Sperm. Wilfred J. Finegold. 112p. 1980. 14.75 (ISBN 0-398-04094-X). C C Thomas.

Artificial Intelligence & Natural Man. Margaret Boden. LC 76-8117. (Illus.). 537p. 1981. pap. 8.95 (ISBN 0-465-00453-9). Basic.

Artificial Intelligence in Medicine. Ed. by Peter Szolovits. (AAAS Selected Symposium: No. 51). 130p. 1981. lib. bdg. 15.00x (ISBN 0-89158-900-7). Westview.

Artificial Larynx. Yvan Lebrun et al. (Neurolinguistics Ser.: Vol. 1). 90p. 1973. pap. text ed. 15.75 (ISBN 90-265-0173-0, Pub. by Swets Pub Serv Holland). Swets North Am.

Artificial Paranoia: A Computer Simulation of Paranoid Processes. K. M. Colby. 1976. text ed. 17.25 (ISBN 0-08-018162-7); pap. text ed. 9.00 (ISBN 0-08-018161-9). Pergamon.

Artificial Satellites. G. V. Thompson. (gr. 4 up). 1962. 4.25 o.p. (ISBN 0-298-78953-1). Dufour.

Artificial Substrates: Proceedings. American Microscopical Society Symposium, 1980. Ed. by John Cairns, Jr. 1981. text ed. price not set. Ann Arbor Science.

Artificial World Around Us. Lucy Kavaler. LC 63-10233. (Illus.). (gr. 6-9). 1963. 7.95 (ISBN 0-381-99774-X, A05800, JD-J). John Day.

Artillery in Color: Nineteen Twenty to Nineteen Sixty-Three. Ian Hogg. LC 80-379. (Illus.). 192p. 1980. 11.95 (ISBN 0-668-04939-1); pap. 7.95 (ISBN 0-668-04941-3). Arco.

Artillery of the Press. James Reston. LC 67-11330. 1967. 10.00 o.p. (ISBN 0-06-013542-5, HarpT). Har-Row.

Artillery of the World. 3rd ed. Foss. 1981. 12.95 (ScribT). Scribner.

Artillery of the World. 2nd, rev. ed. Foss. 1980. 12.95 o.p. (ISBN 0-684-16722-0, ScribT). Scribner.

Artillery of the World. 2nd ed. Christopher Foss. LC 76-6642. (Illus.). 192p. 1976. 8.95 o.p. (ISBN 0-684-14787-4, ScribT). Scribner.

Artisan to Graduate Essays Presented to Commemorate the Foundation in 1824 of the Manchester Mechanics Institution, Now the University of Manchester Institute of Science & Technology. Ed. by D. S. Cardwell. 288p. 1974. 33.00x (ISBN 0-7190-1272-4, Pub. by Manchester U Pr England). State Mutual Bk.

Artisans & Sans-Culottes. Gwyn A. Williams. LC 69-14476. (Foundations of Modern History Ser). 1969. pap. text ed. 3.95x (ISBN 0-393-09832-X, NortonC). Norton.

Artisans-Appalachia-USA. David Gaynes. 1977. pap. 4.95 (ISBN 0-686-27863-1). Appalach Consortium.

Artist. M. B. Goffstein. LC 79-2663. (Illus.). 32p. 1980. 7.95 (ISBN 0-06-022012-0, HarpJ); PLB 7.89 (ISBN 0-06-022013-9). Har-Row.

Artist & Audience. African Literature Association. 1979. 22.00 (ISBN 0-89410-122-6); pap. 15.00 (ISBN 0-89410-123-4). Three Continents.

Artist & His Money. Aubrey Menen. LC 79-18359. (Illus.). 1980. 12.95 (ISBN 0-07-041483-1). McGraw.

Artist & Political Vision. Ed. by Benjamin Barber & Michael J. McGrath. 300p. 1981. 19.95 (ISBN 0-87855-380-0). Transaction Bks.

Artist & the Built Environment. Donald Stoltenberg. LC 79-53779. (Illus.). 160p. 1980. 18.95 (ISBN 0-87192-118-9). Davis Mass.

Artist & the Country House: A History of Country House & Garden View Painting. John Harris. (Illus.). 376p. 1979. 100.00 (ISBN 0-85667-053-7, Pub. by Sotheby Parke Bernet England). Biblio Dist.

Artist... & the Legend: A Visit to China Is Remembered & the Legends Unfold... Ed. by Judith G. Werley. LC 74-81927. (Illus.). (gr. 7 up). 1974. 20.00x (ISBN 0-933652-09-7). Domjan Studio.

Artist & the Studio: In the Eighteenth & Nineteenth Centuries. Ronnie L. Zakon. LC 78-51885. (Themes in Art Ser.). (Illus.). 68p. 1978. pap. 4.95x (ISBN 0-910386-40-4, Pub. by Cleveland Mus Art). Ind U Pr.

Artist & the Unicorn. Brooks Wright. 1978. 16.95 (ISBN 0-89062-058-X). Rockland County Hist.

Artist & the Writer in France: Essays in Honour of Jean Seznec. Ed. by Francis Haskell et al. (Illus.). 200p. 1974. 36.00x (ISBN 0-19-817187-0). Oxford U Pr.

Artist As Critic: Critical Writings of Oscar Wilde. Ed. by Richard Ellmann. LC 69-16431. 1969. 10.00 o.p. (ISBN 0-394-41553-1). Random.

Artist Gallery Partnership: A Practical Guide to Consignment. Tad Crawford & Susan Mellon. LC 80-28108. (Orig.). 1981. pap. 4.50 (ISBN 0-915400-26-X). Am Council Arts.

Artist in America. 3rd rev. ed. Thomas H. Benton. LC 68-20096. (Illus.). 1968. 15.00 o.p. (ISBN 0-8262-0071-0). U of Mo Pr.

Artist in American Society. Neil Harris. LC 66-25399. 1966. 7.50 o.s.i. (ISBN 0-8076-0382-1). Braziller.

Artist in Nineteenth Century Fiction. Bo Jeffares. 195p. 1979. text ed. 23.75x (ISBN 0-391-00976-1). Humanities.

Artistic America, Tiffany Glass & Art Nouveau. Samuel Bing. (Illus.). 288p. (Orig.). 1980. pap. 9.95 (ISBN 0-262-52025-7). MIT Pr.

Artistic Anatomy of a Human Figure. Henry Warren. (Art Appreciation Books Ser.). (Illus.). 1978. Repr. of 1868 ed. deluxe ed. 39.50 (ISBN 0-930582-12-8). Gloucester Art.

Artistic & Psychological Analysis of Beauty. William Hogarth. (Illus.). 127p. 1981. 31.45 (ISBN 0-930582-90-X). Gloucester Art.

Artistic Country Seats, 2 vols, Vols. I & II. Ed. by George W. Sheldon. LC 78-17476. (Architecture & Decorative Arts: 1978). (Illus.). 1978. Repr. of 1887 ed. Set. lib. bdg. 125.00 (ISBN 0-306-70829-9); lib. bdg. 70.00 ea. Vol. I (ISBN 0-306-77598-0). Vol. II (ISBN 0-306-77599-9). Da Capo.

Artistic Expression. Ed. by John Hospers. LC 71-142225. (Century Philosophy Ser). (Illus., Orig.). 1971. 28.50x (ISBN 0-89197-035-5); pap. text ed. 9.50x (ISBN 0-89197-036-3). Irvington.

Artistic Homes; or, How to Furnish with Taste. Sylvia's Home Help Series. Ed. by Peter Stansky & Rodney Shewan. LC 76-17759. (Aesthetic Movement & the Arts & Crafts Movement Ser.). 1978. Repr. of 1881 ed. lib. bdg. 44.00x (ISBN 0-8240-2464-8). Garland Pub.

Artistic Reproduction of the Personality of the Human Figure. Frederick H. Sidwell. (Illus.). 1980. deluxe ed. 37.25 (ISBN 0-930582-62-4). Gloucester Art.

Artistic Theory in Italy, 1450-1600. Anthony Blunt. 1956. 22.50x (ISBN 0-19-817106-4); pap. 4.95x (ISBN 0-19-881050-4, OPB). Oxford U Pr.

Artistic Woodturning. Dale L. Nish. LC 80-21302. (Illus.). 288p. 1980. 17.95 (ISBN 0-8425-1842-8); pap. 12.95 (ISBN 0-8425-1826-6). Brigham.

Artist's Airbrush Manual. Clement Marten. (Illus.). 72p. 1980. 25.00 (ISBN 0-7153-7997-6). David & Charles.

Artists Compared by Age, Sex, & Earnings in 1970 & 1976. (Report Ser.: No. 12). 56p. 1980. pap. 2.50 (ISBN 0-89062-077-6, Pub. by Ctr for Arts Info). Pub Ctr Cult Res.

Artist's Contracts of the Early Renaissance. Hannelore Glasser. LC 76-23624. (Outstanding Dissertations in the Fine Arts - 2nd Series - 15th Century). (Illus.). 1977. Repr. of 1965 ed. lib. bdg. 56.00 (ISBN 0-8240-2694-2). Garland Pub.

Artists in Crime. Ngaio Marsh. (Ngaio Marsh Mystery Ser.). pap. 1.95 (ISBN 0-515-05414-3). Jove Pubns.

Artist's Letters from Japan. John La Farge. LC 74-130311. (Library of American Art Ser.). (Illus.). 1970. Repr. of 1897 ed. lib. bdg. 35.00 (ISBN 0-306-70064-6). Da Capo.

Artist's Market Nineteen Eighty. Ed. by Lynne Lapin. (Illus.). 480p. 1980. 11.95 (ISBN 0-89879-029-8). Writers Digest.

Artists of America: S. T.,A Series of Biographical Sketches of American Artists. Charles E. Lester. LC 68-8689. (American Art Ser). (Illus.). 1970. Repr. of 1846 ed. lib. bdg. 29.50 (ISBN 0-306-71169-9). Da Capo.

Artists of the American West: A Biographical Dictionary, Vol. II. Doris Dawdy. LC 72-91919. 300p. 1981. 22.95x (ISBN 0-8040-0352-1). Swallow.

Artists of the Old West. John C. Ewers. LC 73-79662. 240p. 1973. 14.95 o.p. (ISBN 0-385-04474-7). Doubleday.

Artists of the Western Hemisphere: Précursors of Modernism, 1860-1930. Stanton L. Catlin. LC 67-29739. (Illus.). 60p. 1968. pap. 2.00 (ISBN 0-913456-02-0). Interbk Inc.

Artists: Portraits from Four Decades. Arnold Newman. 180p. 1980. 49.95 (ISBN 0-8212-1099-8, 052779). NYGS.

Artist's Reminiscences. Walter Crane. LC 68-21763. (Illus.). 1968. Repr. of 1907 ed. 18.00 (ISBN 0-8103-3522-0). Gale.

Artists USA Nineteen Eighty One to Nineteen Eighty Two. 7th ed. Foundation for the Advancement of Artists. LC 78-134303. (Illus.). 1981. 30.00 (ISBN 0-912916-07-9). Foun Adv Artists.

Artists' Vehicles & Metaphorical Machinery. Kay Larson. (Illus.). 1980. pap. 8.00 (ISBN 0-904540-26-X). U of Pa Contemp Art.

Artist's Voice. Katharine Kuh. LC 62-9893. (Illus.). 1962. 10.95 o.p. (ISBN 0-06-012465-2, HarpT). Har-Row.

Arts & Artists. Jeremy Kingston. (Horizons of Knowledge Ser.). (Illus.). 1980. lib. bdg. 19.95 (ISBN 0-87196-404-X). Facts on File.

Arts & City Planning. Ed. by Robert Porter. LC 80-14076. 1980. pap. text ed. 9.95 (ISBN 0-915400-20-0). Am Council Arts.

Arts & Crafts As Root Technologies. J. Ben Lieberman. (Root Technologies Ser.: Bk. I). Date not set. write for info (ISBN 0-918142-14-8); pap. write for info (ISBN 0-918142-15-6). Myriade. Postponed.

Arts & Crafts Discovery Units: Arts & Crafts Discovery Units. Incl. Crayon (ISBN 0-87628-523-X); Mobiles (ISBN 0-87628-524-8); Paper (ISBN 0-87628-525-6); Papier Mache (ISBN 0-87628-526-4); Printing (ISBN 0-87628-527-2); Puppets (ISBN 0-87628-528-0); Tempera (ISBN 0-87628-529-9); Tissue (ISBN 0-87628-530-2); Watercolor (ISBN 0-87628-531-0); Weaving (ISBN 0-87628-532-9). (ps-2). 1974. 5.95x ea. Ctr Appl Res.

Arts & Crafts Essays. William Morris et al. LC 76-17783. (Arts & Crafts Movement Ser.: Vol. 34). 1977. Repr. of 1893 ed. lib. bdg. 44.00x (ISBN 0-8240-2483-4). Garland Pub.

Arts & Crafts for Physically & Mentally Disabled: The How, What & Why of It. Elaine Gould & Loren Gould. (Illus.). 368p. 1978. 38.00 (ISBN 0-398-03783-3). C C Thomas.

Arts & Crafts in New England. 1704-1775. George F. Dow. LC 67-2035. (Architecture & Decorative Art Ser). (Illus.). 1967. Repr. of 1927 ed. 29.50 (ISBN 0-306-70955-4). Da Capo.

Arts & Crafts in New York, Seventeen Twenty-Six to Seventeen Seventy-Six. Rita S. Gottesman. LC 70-127254. (Architecture & Decorative Art Ser.: Vol. 35). 1970. Repr. of 1938 ed. lib. bdg. 39.50 (ISBN 0-306-71129-X). Da Capo.

Arts & Crafts in Philadelphia, Maryland, & South Carolina, 1721-1785, 2 Vols. Ed. by Alfred C. Prime. LC 79-75356. (Architecture & Decorative Art Ser). 1969. Repr. of 1929 ed. Set. lib. bdg. 45.00 (ISBN 0-306-71320-9). Da Capo.

Arts & Crafts Movement: A Study of Its Sources, Ideals & Influence on Design Theory. Gillian Naylor. 1980. pap. 10.95 (ISBN 0-262-64018-X). MIT Pr.

Arts & Crafts of Chester County, Pa. Margaret B. Schiffer. (Illus.). 356p. Date not set. cancelled (ISBN 0-916838-35-8). Schiffer.

Arts & Cultural Programs on Radio & Television, Report No. 4. (National Endowment for the Arts Research Division Reports). 92p. (Orig.). 1977. pap. 3.50x (ISBN 0-89062-091-1, Pub. by Natl Endow Arts). Pub Ctr Cultures.

Arts & Ideas. 6th ed. William Fleming. LC 79-20123. 502p. 1980. pap. text ed. 14.95 (ISBN 0-03-046531-1, HoltC). HR&W.

Arts & Inspiration: Mormon Perspectives. Ed. by Steven P. Sondrup. LC 80-21927. (Illus.). 240p. 1980. pap. 8.95 (ISBN 0-8425-1845-2). Brigham.

Arts & Personal Growth. Ed. by Malcolm Ross. LC 80-40260. (Curriculum Issues in Arts Education Ser.: Vol. 1). (Illus.). 136p. 1980. 14.75 (ISBN 0-08-024714-8). Pergamon.

Arts & Psychotherapy. Shaun McNiff. (Illus.). 280p. 19.75. C C Thomas.

Arts & Society in England Under William & Mary. Mary Ede. (Illus.). 218p. 1979. 23.50x (ISBN 0-8476-6261-6). Rowman.

Arts & the People. 242p. 1973. pap. 5.00x perfect bound (ISBN 0-89062-000-8, Pub. by National Research Center for the Arts). Pub Ctr Cult Res.

Arts & the Soviet Child: The Esthetic Education of Children in the U.S.S.R. Miriam Morton. LC 72-156840. 1972. 10.95 o.s.i. (ISBN 0-02-921990-6). Free Pr.

Arts & the World of Business. 2nd ed. Charlotte Georgi. LC 78-12103. 1979. lib. bdg. 10.00 (ISBN 0-8108-1174-X). Scarecrow.

Arts & Their Interrelations: Bucknell Review, Fall 1978. Ed. by Harry R. Garvin. LC 78-62038. 192p. 1979. 12.00 (ISBN 0-8387-2355-1). Bucknell U Pr.

Arts & Tourism: A Profitable Partnership. (Orig.). 1981. pap. cacelled (ISBN 0-915400-30-8). Am Council Arts.

Arts in America: A Bibliography, 4 vols. Ed. by Bernard Karpel. LC 79-15321. 2800p. 1979-1980. Set. 190.00x (ISBN 0-87474-578-0). Smithsonian.

Arts in Britain in World War One. John Ferguson. (Illus.). 131p. 1980. 26.50x (ISBN 0-8476-6262-4). Rowman.

Arts in Canada: The Last Fifty Years. Ed. by W. J. Keith & B. Z. Shek. 192p. 1980. 20.00x (ISBN 0-8020-2401-7); pap. 6.95 (ISBN 0-8020-6425-6). U of Toronto Pr.

Arts in Cultural Diversity. International Society for Education Through Art. 292p. (Orig.). 1980. 21.95. Praeger.

Arts in the Economic Life of the City. The Urban Innovations Group, Inc. LC 79-29764. (Illus.). 150p. (Orig.). 1980. text ed. 14.95 (ISBN 0-915400-16-2); pap. text ed. 9.95 (ISBN 0-915400-17-0). Am Council Arts.

Arts in Therapy. Bob Fleshman & Jerry L. Fryrear. LC 80-20334. 240p. 1981. text ed. 19.95 (ISBN 0-88229-520-9); pap. text ed. 9.95 (ISBN 0-88229-762-7). Nelson-Hall.

Arts Management: An Annotated Bibliography. rev. ed. Compiled by Stephen Benedict. LC 80-25918. 48p. 1980. pap. 5.00 (ISBN 0-89062-046-6, Pub. by Ctr for Arts Info). Pub Ctr Cult Res.

Arts Management: An Annotated Bibliography. Compiled by Linda Coe. 1978. pap. 3.00x o.p. (ISBN 0-89062-062-8, Pub. by Natl Endow Arts). Pub Ctr Cultures.

Arts of a Vanished Era. Whatcom Museum of History & Art. LC 68-9204. (Whatcom Museum Ser.). (Illus.). 64p. 1968. pap. 5.00 (ISBN 0-295-95576-7). U of Wash Pr.

Arts of China. Hugo Munsterberg. LC 70-188012. 1972. 29.50 (ISBN 0-8048-0039-1). C E Tuttle.

Arts of China. rev. ed. Michael Sullivan. LC 76-44639. (Cal Ser.: No. 350). (Illus.). 1978. 20.00 o.p. (ISBN 0-520-03366-3); pap. 9.95 (ISBN 0-520-03367-1). U of Cal Pr.

Arts of China: Neolithic Cultures to the T'ang Dynasty, Vol. 1. Terukazu Akiyama et al. LC 68-17454. (Arts of China Ser: Vol. 1). (Illus.). 1968. 85.00 (ISBN 0-87011-064-0). Kodansha.

Arts of China: Paintings in Chinese Museums. Yoshio Yonezawa et al. LC 68-17454. (Arts of China Ser: Vol. 3). (Illus.). 1970. 75.00 (ISBN 0-87011-128-0). Kodansha.

Arts of China, Vol. 2: Buddhist Cave Temples. Terukazu Akiyama & Saburo Matsubara. Tr. by Alexander Soper. LC 68-17454. (Arts of China Ser: Vol. 2). (Illus.). 248p. 1969. 85.00 (ISBN 0-87011-089-6). Kodansha.

Arts of Japan, 2 vols. Seiroku Noma. Tr. by John Rosenfield. LC 65-19186. Orig. Title: Nihon Bijutsu. (Illus.). 1978. 22.50 ea. Vol. I (ISBN 0-87011-335-6). Vol. II (ISBN 0-87011-336-4). Kodansha.

Arts of Japan Vol. 1: Ancient & Medieval. Seiroku Noma. LC 65-19186. (Arts of Japan Ser.: Vol. 1). (Illus.). 1967. 85.00 (ISBN 0-87011-018-7). Kodansha.

Arts of Japan Vol. 2: Late Medieval to Modern. Seiroku Noma. LC 65-19186. (Arts of Japan Ser.: Vol. 2). (Illus.). 1967. 85.00 (ISBN 0-87011-050-0). Kodansha.

Arts of Korea. Chewon Kim & L. Kim Lee. LC 73-79768. (Illus.). 364p. 1974. 85.00 (ISBN 0-87011-206-6). Kodansha.

Arts of the Alchemists. Cottie A. Burland. LC 79-8598. Repr. of 1968 ed. 27.50 (ISBN 0-404-18451-0). AMS Pr.

Arts of the Environment. Ed. by Gyorgy Keppes. (Vision & Value Ser). (Illus.). 244p. 1972. 17.50 (ISBN 0-8076-0620-0). Braziller.

Arts of the Italian Renaissance: The Painting, Sculpture, Architecture. Walter Paatz. (Illus.). 264p. 1974. text ed. 14.95 (ISBN 0-13-047316-2). P-H.

Arts of the Japanese Sword. B. W. Robinson. (Illus.). 1979. 38.00 (ISBN 0-571-04723-8, Pub. by Faber & Faber). Merrimack Bk Serv.

Arts of the Raven: Masterworks by the Northwest Coast Indian. Wilson Duff. (Illus.). 112p. 1967. pap. 11.50 (ISBN 0-295-95583-X, Pub. by Vancouver Art Canada). U of Wash Pr.

Arts of the South Pacific. Jean Guiart. LC 63-7331. (Arts of Mankind Ser). 30.00 o.s.i. (ISBN 0-8076-0500-X). Braziller.

Arts on the Level: The Fall of the Elite Object. Murray Krieger. LC 80-25401. (Hodges Lectures). (Illus.). 112p. 1981. text ed. 7.50x (ISBN 0-87049-308-6). U of Tenn Pr.

Arts Play: Creative Activities in Art, Music, Dance & Drama for Young Children. L. Burton & K. Kuroda. (ps-3). 1981. write for info. spiral bdg. (ISBN 0-201-00201-9, Sch Div). A-W.

Arts Yellow Pages. 1977. pap. 7.50 o.p. (ISBN 0-89192-184-2). Interbk Inc.

Arundel. Kenneth Roberts. LC 33-19961. 1944. 12.95 (ISBN 0-385-04024-5). Doubleday.

Arundel. Kenneth Roberts. 1976. pap. 1.95 o.p. (ISBN 0-449-30690-9, C690, Prem). Fawcett.

Arya Dharm: Hindu Consciousness in Nineteenth-Century Punjab. Kenneth W. Jones. LC 74-27290. 350p. 1976. 21.50x (ISBN 0-520-02919-4). U of Cal Pr.

Aryan & Non-Aryan in India. Ed. by Madhav M. Deshpande & Peter E. Hook. LC 78-60016. (Michigan Papers on South & Southeast Asia: No. 14). 350p. 1979. 16.50x (ISBN 0-89720-012-8); pap. 12.50x (ISBN 0-89148-014-5). Ctr S&SE Asian.

Aryatarangini: The Saga of the Indo-Aryans, Vol. 2. A. Kalyanaraman. 1970. 20.00x (ISBN 0-210-22305-7). Asia.

As a Man Thinketh. James Allen. (Inspiration Classics Ser.). 4.95 (ISBN 0-8007-1076-2). Revell.

As a Wild Bird Returning. William E. Bard. 4.50 o.p. (ISBN 0-685-48826-8). Nortex Pr.

A's & B's of Academic Scholarships: A Guide to Current Programs, 1980-1982. 3rd ed. Robert Leider. LC 78-52571. 52p. 1980. pap. 2.00 (ISBN 0-917760-18-2). Octameron Assocs.

As Battles Raged. Elizabeth Aspril. (Illus., Orig.). 12.95 (ISBN 0-9604750-1-X); pap. 7.95 (ISBN 0-9604750-0-1). E Keys.

As Bill Sees It: Selected Writings of the A. A.'s Co-Founder. 333p. 1967. 5.00 (ISBN 0-916856-03-8). AAWS.

As Built with Second Thoughts, Reforming What Was Old. David McCord. pap. 3.00. Boston Public Lib.

As Close As Possible. Bruce L. Baker et al. LC 77-81502. 1977. text ed. 13.95 (ISBN 0-316-07827-1); pap. text ed. 9.95 (ISBN 0-316-07829-8). Little.

As Days Go By. Theodore L. Harris et al. (Keys to Independence in Reading Ser.). (Illus., Orig.). (gr. 2). 1973. text ed. 2.70 (ISBN 0-87892-026-9); tchrs' manual 3.96 (ISBN 0-87892-027-7); wkbk. avail. (ISBN 0-87892-028-5). Economy Co.

As Driven Sands: The Arab Refugees 1948-1969. Balfour Brickner & Marc Saperstein. (Issues of Conscience Ser). (Orig.). 1969. pap. 0.50 (ISBN 0-8074-0090-4, 707925). UAHC.

As for Me & My House. Louis A. Priolo. (Orig.). 1976. pap. 1.75 o.p. (ISBN 0-88368-077-7). Whitaker Hse.

As I Feel It. Tim Reid. Ed. by Daphne Maxwell. LC 80-54670. (Illus.). 62p. 1981. 8.95 (ISBN 0-931748-19-4). Lincoln Pub.

As I Passed by. Beatrice C. Harris. 1977. 3.00 (ISBN 0-686-28895-5). Klassen.

As I Remember. Blanche W. Davis. 1981. 7.95 (ISBN 0-8062-1660-3). Carlton.

As I Walked Out One Evening: A Book of Ballads. Helen Plotz. LC 76-10306. 288p. (gr. 5-9). 1976. 9.25 (ISBN 0-688-80054-8); PLB 8.88 (ISBN 0-688-84054-X). Greenwillow.

As If It Will Matter. Jody Aliesan. LC 78-63399. 60p. (Orig.). 1978. 15.00 (ISBN 0-931188-04-0); pap. 4.00 (ISBN 0-931188-03-2). Seal Pr WA.

As It Was & World Without End. Helen Thomas. (Orig.). 1972. pap. 7.95 (ISBN 0-571-10135-6, Pub. by Faber & Faber). Merrimack Bk Serv.

As It Was Told: A Play for Christmas. Ed Irsch. 16p. (Orig.). 1980. pap. text ed. 1.55 (ISBN 0-89536-439-5). CSS Pub.

As Never Before. Avery Brooke. 1976. 5.95 (ISBN 0-8164-0905-6). Crossroad NY.

As of a Trumphet. Aumra. 1968. 4.95 (ISBN 0-686-27649-3). Cole-Outreach.

AS One Skill Booklet. Barbara J. Crane. (Crane Reading System - English Ser.). (Illus.). (gr. k-2). 1977. pap. text ed. 12.20 per 10 (ISBN 0-89075-026-2). Crane Pub Co.

As Orange Goes: Twelve California Families & the Future of American Politics. Karl A. Lamb. 1974. 8.95x (ISBN 0-393-05520-5); pap. 6.95x (ISBN 0-393-09235-6). Norton.

As Peking Sees Us: People's War in the United States & Communist China's America Policy. Wu Yuan-li. LC 70-88765. (Studies: No. 25). (Illus.). 1969. pap. 3.00 (ISBN 0-8179-3252-6). Hoover Inst Pr.

As Serious As Your Life. Valerie Wilmer. (Illus.). 296p. (Orig.). 1980. 14.95 (ISBN 0-88208-112-8); pap. 7.95 (ISBN 0-88208-113-6). Lawrence Hill.

As Summers Die. Winston Groom. LC 80-17451. 319p. 1980. 12.95 (ISBN 0-671-40072-X). Summit Bks.

As the Snow on the High Hills. Louise H. McCraw. 198p. (Orig.). 1979. pap. 2.00 (ISBN 0-89323-001-4). BMA Pr.

As the Twig Is Bent: Readings in Early Childhood Education. Ed. by Robert H. Anderson & Harold G. Shane. LC 71-135675. 1971. pap. text ed. 11.50 (ISBN 0-395-11218-4, 3-01135). HM.

As Tomorrow Becomes Today. Charles W. Sullivan, 3rd. 480p. 1974. pap. text ed. 8.95 (ISBN 0-13-050021-6). P-H.

As Touching the Holy. Albert Wells. (Direction Bks.). (Orig.). 1980. pap. 2.45 (ISBN 0-8010-9637-5). Baker Bk.

AS Two Skill Booklet. Barbara J. Crane. (Crane Reading System - English Ser.). (Illus.). (gr. k-2). 1977. pap. text ed. 12.20 per 10 (ISBN 0-89075-028-9). Crane Pub Co.

As Wide As the River. Dean Hughes. LC 80-14646. 150p. 1980. 6.95 (ISBN 0-87747-820-1). Deseret Bk.

As You Like It. Ron Chaddock. LC 80-82091. (Understand Ye Shakespeare Ser.). 1980. pap. 8.95 deluxe ed. (ISBN 0-933350-34-1). Morse Pr.

As You Like It. William Shakespeare. Ed. by Arthur Quiller-Couch et al. (New Shakespeare Ser). 1968. 23.95 (ISBN 0-521-07527-0); pap. 4.50x (ISBN 0-521-07527-0). Cambridge U Pr.

As You Like It. William Shakespeare. Ed. by Ralph Sargeant. (Shakespeare Ser.). 1959. pap. 2.25 (ISBN 0-14-071417-0, Pelican). Penguin.

As You Think. Gerald B. Nash. (Uplook Ser.). 1978. pap. 0.75 (ISBN 0-8163-0193-X, 0176507). Pacific Pr Pub Assn.

As Your Child Grows: The First 18 Months. rev. ed. Katherine M. Wolf & Aline B. Auerbach. 27p. 1976. pap. 1.50 (ISBN 0-686-12269-0). Jewish Bd Family.

ASA Refresher Courses in Anesthesiology. American Society of Anesthesiologists. 170p. (Annual). 1975. Vol. 2 (1974) 8.00 (ISBN 0-685-59107-7); Vol. 3 (1975) 10.00 (ISBN 0-685-59108-5). Lippincott.

Asami Library: A Descriptive Catalogue. Chaoying Fang. Ed. by Elizabeth Huff. LC 69-16505. (Illus.). 1969. 34.50x (ISBN 0-520-01521-5). U of Cal Pr.

Asante in the Nineteenth Century. I. Wilks. LC 74-77834. (African Studies: No. 13). (Illus.). 872p. 1975. 69.50 (ISBN 0-521-20463-1). Cambridge U Pr.

Asbestos Sampling & Analysis. Gyan S. Rajhans & John Sullivan. 1981. text ed. 37.50 (ISBN 0-686-69577-1). Ann Arbor Science.

Asbestosis: A Comprehensive Bibliography. Compiled by Alberta D. Berton. (Biomedical Information Guides Ser.: Vol. 1). 395p. 1980. 85.00 (ISBN 0-306-65176-9, IFI). Plenum Pub.

Ascanius; or, the Young Adventurer, 1746. John Burton. Ed. by Michael F. Shugrue. (Flowering of the Novel, 1740-1775 Ser: Vol. 17). 1974. lib. bdg. 50.00 (ISBN 0-8240-1116-3). Garland Pub.

ASCE-ICE-CSCE: Joint Conference on Predicting & Designing for Natural & Man Made Hazards, 1978. Compiled By American Society of Civil Engineers. 300p. 1979. pap. text ed. 30.00 (ISBN 0-87262-187-1). Am Soc Civil Eng.

Ascendancies. D. G. Compton. LC 80-7823. 1980. 12.95 o.p. (ISBN 0-399-12484-5). Berkley Pub.

Ascendancy of Europe: Aspects of European History 1815-1914. M. S. Anderson. 1972. pap. text ed. 11.50 (ISBN 0-582-48348-4). Longman.

Ascendant: Your Karmic Doorway. Martin Schulman. 1981. pap. 6.95 (ISBN 0-87728-507-1). Weiser.

Ascent of Life: A Philosophical Study of the Theory of Evolution. Thomas A. Goudge. LC 61-65468. 1961. 12.50x o.p. (ISBN 0-8020-1152-7). U of Toronto Pr.

Ascent of Mount Carmel. St. John Of The Cross. 480p. 1973. pap. 2.95 o.p. (ISBN 0-385-01111-3, Im). Doubleday.

Ascent of the Mountain, Flight of the Dove: An Invitation to Religious Studies. rev. ed. Michael Novak. LC 77-20463. 1978. pap. 5.95 (ISBN 0-06-066322-7, RD 232, HarpR). Har-Row.

Ascent: The Mountaineering Experience in Word & Image. Ed. by Allen Steck & Steve Roper. LC 80-13855. (Illus.). 272p. (Orig.). 1980. pap. 14.95 (ISBN 0-87156-240-5). Sierra.

Ascent to Excellence in Catholic Education: A Guide to Effective Decision-Making. Mary-Angela Harper. 7.95. Natl Cath Educ.

Ascent to God. Jeffrey Sobosan. 1981. 9.95 (ISBN 0-88347-128-0). Thomas More.

Ascent to Truth. Thomas Merton. 1981. 5.95 (ISBN 0-15-608682-4, Harv). HarBraceJ.

Ascent 1975-76: The Mountaineering Experience in Word & Image. Ed. by Allen Steck & Steve Roper. (Illus.). 128p. 1976. pap. 8.95 (ISBN 0-87156-189-1). Sierra.

Ascents of Wonder. Ed. by David Gerrold. 1977. pap. 1.50 o.p. (ISBN 0-445-04128-5). Popular Lib.

Ascetic Works of Saint Basil. Basilius. Tr. & intro. by W. K. Clarke. LC 80-2352. 1981. Repr. of 1925 ed. 47.50 (ISBN 0-404-18902-4). AMS Pr.

Asceticism & Eroticism in the Mythology of Siva. Wendy D. O'Flaherty. (Illus.). 401p. 1973. 36.00x (ISBN 0-19-713573-0). Oxford U Pr.

Ascetics, Authority, & the Church in the Age of Jerome & Cassian. Phillip Rousseau. (Historical Monographs). 1978. 36.00x (ISBN 0-19-821870-2). Oxford U Pr.

Aschehougs Konversasjonsleksikon, 20 vols. new, rev. ed. (Norwegian.). 1972-1975. 860.00 (ISBN 0-8277-3000-4). Maxwell Sci Intl.

Ascomycete Systematics: The Luttrellian Concept. R. D. Reynolds. (Springer Series in Microbiology). (Illus.). 272p. 1981. 42.80 (ISBN 0-387-90488-3). Springer-Verlag.

Ascorbinsaeure in der Pflanzenzelle. H. Metzner. Bd. with Vitamin C in the Animal Cell. G. H. Bourne. (Protoplasmatologia: Vol. 2B, Pt. 2b). (Illus.). iv, 159p. (Eng., Ger.). 1957. pap. 44.30 o.p. (ISBN 0-387-80453-6). Springer-Verlag.

Ascott Quebec Canada Eighteen Twenty Five Census. Jay M. Holbrook. LC 80-117991. 1976. pap. 7.50 (ISBN 0-931248-06-X). Holbrook Res.

ASEAN Report, 2 vols. Thomas W. Allen. Ed. by Barry Wain. Incl. Vol. 1. Comparative Assessment of the ASEAN Countries; Vol. 2. Evolution & Programs of ASEAN. (Illus.). 414p. 1980. Set. pap. 125.00 (ISBN 0-295-95740-9, 80-110683). U of Wash Pr.

Ash Deposits & Corrosion Due to Impurities in Combustion Gases: Proceedings. new ed. Ash Deposit & Corrosion from Impurities in Combustion Gases Symposium, June 26-July 1, 1977, New England College, Henniker, New Hampshire. Ed. by R. W. Bryers. LC 78-7001. 1978. text ed. 57.50 (ISBN 0-89116-074-4, Co-Pub by McGraw Intl). Hemisphere Pub.

Ash Road. Ivan Southall. LC 77-15063. (gr. 5-9). 1978. 7.95 (ISBN 0-688-80135-8); PLB 7.63 (ISBN 0-688-84135-X). Greenwillow.

Ash Wednesday Supper. Giordano Bruno. Tr. by Stanley L. Jaki. (Illus.). 174p. 1975. text ed. 28.90x (ISBN 90-2797-581-7). Mouton.

Ashanti. R. S. Rattray. (Illus.). 1981. Repr. of 1923 ed. 27.00 (ISBN 0-19-823149-0). Oxford U Pr.

Ashanti of Ghana. Sonia Bleeker. (Illus.). (gr. 4-7). 1966. PLB 6.67 (ISBN 0-688-31052-4). Morrow.

Ashanti Proverbs: The Primitive Ethics of a Savage People. R. S. Rattray. 1981. 14.95x (ISBN 0-19-823147-4). Oxford U Pr.

Asher Brown Durand: His Art & Art Theory in Relations to His Times. David B. Lawall. LC 76-23635. (Outstanding Dissertations in the Fine Arts Ser.). 1978. lib. bdg. 97.00x (ISBN 0-8240-2704-3). Garland Pub.

Ashes: A Collection of Poems. Reid W. Stafford. 1977. 4.50 o.p. (ISBN 0-533-02977-5). Vantage.

Ashes & Blood. Charles R. Pike. LC 80-70093. (Jubal Cade Westerns Ser.). 160p. 1981. pap. 2.95 (ISBN 0-87754-242-2). Chelsea Hse.

Ashes of Gold. Kshitij Mohan. (Writers Workshop Redbird Ser.). 39p. 1975. 8.00 (ISBN 0-88253-502-1); pap. text ed. 4.80 (ISBN 0-88253-501-3). Ind-US Inc.

Ashes of Windrow. Juanita T. Osborne. 192p. (YA) 1976. 5.95 (ISBN 0-685-59251-0, Avalon). Bouregy.

Asheville: A Pictorial History. Mitzi Tessier. Ed. by Donna R. Fredman. (Illus.). 208p. 1981. pap. price not set (ISBN 0-89865-116-6). Donning Co.

Ashley Book of Knots. Clifford W. Ashley. 1944. 19.95 (ISBN 0-385-04025-3). Doubleday.

Asia: A Natural History. Pierre Pfeffer. LC 68-28330. (The Continents We Live On, Ser, Vol. 6). (Illus.). 1968. 20.00 o.p. (ISBN 0-394-41570-1). Random.

Asia & Pacific Annual Review, 1981. rev. ed. (Annual Review Ser.). (Illus.). 1981. pap. 24.95 (ISBN 0-528-84516-0). Rand.

Asia & the Road Ahead: Issues for the Major Powers. Robert A. Scalapino. LC 75-15219. 1975. 15.95 (ISBN 0-520-03066-4); pap. 4.95 (ISBN 0-520-03173-3). U of Cal Pr.

Asia in the Modern World. Ed. by Helen G. Matthew. (Illus.). 1963. pap. 1.25 o.p. (ISBN 0-451-61215-9, MY1215, Ment). NAL.

Asia Pacific Stories. Murtagh Murphy. (Oxford Progressive English Readers Ser.). (Illus.). 1974. pap. text ed. 2.95x (ISBN 0-19-580718-9). Oxford U Pr.

Asia: Teaching About, Learning From. Seymour Fersh. LC 77-16458. (Illus.). 1978. pap. text ed. 8.25x (ISBN 0-8077-2539-0). Tchrs Coll.

Asia Yearbook 1980. Ed. by Far Eastern Economic Review. (Illus.). 320p. 1980. 12.50x (ISBN 962-7010-06-5). Intl Pubns Serv.

Asian-American Authors. Ed. by William Adams et al. (Multi-Ethnic Literature Ser.). pap. 5.32 (ISBN 0-395-24039-5); inst. guide 4.80 (ISBN 0-395-24042-5). HM.

Asian-American Periodicals & Newspapers: A Union List of Holdings in the Library of the State Historical Society of Wisconsin & the Libraries of the University of Wisconsin-Madison. Maureen E. Hady & James P. Danky. LC 79-22630. 1979. pap. 2.00x (ISBN 0-87020-191-3). State Hist Soc Wis.

Asian Americans: Identity, Adaptation & Survival. Ed. by Proshanta Nandi & Elena Yu. (Monograph Ser.). (Orig.). 1981. cancelled (ISBN 0-934584-13-3). Pacific-Asian. Postponed.

Asian & African Studies, Vol. 12. Ivan Dolezal. 1977. text ed. 11.75x (ISBN 0-7007-0101-X). Humanities.

Asian & African Studies, Vol. 15. Ed. by Ivan Dolezal. 1980. text ed. 13.00x (ISBN 0-7007-0130-3). Humanities.

Asian & African Studies, Vol. 16. Ed. by Ivan Dolezal. 360p. 1980. text ed. 13.00x (ISBN 0-7007-0137-0). Humanities.

Asian & African Studies, Vol. 14, No. 14. Ed. by Ivan Dolezal. 1978. text ed. 13.00x (ISBN 0-7007-0121-4). Humanities.

Asian & African Studies: 1972, Vol. 8. Ed. by Ivan Dolezal. 360p. 1972. text ed. 9.00x (ISBN 0-7007-0040-4). Humanities.

Asian & African Systems of Slavery. James L. Watson. 1980. 22.75 (ISBN 0-520-04031-7). U of Cal Pr.

Asian Art: Selections from the Collection of Mr. and Mrs. John D. Rockefeller, 3rd. Sherman E. Lee. (Illus.). 1970. pap. text ed. 35.00 (ISBN 0-89192-278-4). Interbk Inc.

Asian Business Directory 1978. (Illus.). 2655p. 1980. 100.00 (ISBN 0-8002-2732-8). Intl Pubns Serv.

Asian Christian Theology: Emerging Themes. rev. ed. Ed. by Douglas J. Elwood. 1980. pap. write for info. (ISBN 0-664-24354-1). Westminster.

Asian Development: Problems & Prognosis. John Badgley. LC 78-142354. 1971. pap. text ed. 4.50 o.s.i. (ISBN 0-02-901140-X). Free Pr.

Asian Dollar Market: International Offshore Financing. Anindya K. Bhattacharya. LC 76-2900. (Praeger Special Studies). 1977. 17.95 o.p. (ISBN 0-275-56610-2). Praeger.

Asian Electrical & Electronics Trades Directory 1979-80. Nobutaka Yashiro. Ed. by T. Hirayama & Y. Takalashi. (Illus.). 1979. pap. 140.00x (ISBN 0-8002-0350-X). Intl Pubns Serv.

Asian Fighting Arts. Donn F. Draeger & Robert W. Smith. 1974. pap. 1.95 o.p. (ISBN 0-425-02501-2, Medallion). Berkley Pub.

Asian Fighting Arts. Robert W. Smith & Donn F. Draeger. LC 69-16366. (Illus.). 1969. 16.50 o.p. (ISBN 0-87011-079-9). Kodansha.

Asian Figures. Tr. by W. S. Merwin. LC 72-92617. 64p. 1973. pap. 6.95 (ISBN 0-689-10557-6). Atheneum.

Asian Flavors. Kay Shimizu. LC 70-164869. 1971. 7.00 o.p. (ISBN 0-682-47305-7, Banner). Exposition.

Asian Ideas of East & West: Tagore & His Critics in Japan, China, & India. Stephen N. Hay. LC 73-89972. (East Asian Ser.: No. 40). 1970. text ed. 20.00x (ISBN 0-674-04975-6). Harvard U Pr.

Asian in North America. Stanford M. Lyman. LC 77-9095. 299p. 1977. text ed. 15.00 (ISBN 0-87436-254-7). ABC-Clio.

Asian Journal of Thomas Merton. Thomas Merton. Ed. by Naomi B. Stone et al. LC 71-103370. (Illus.). 448p. 1973. 12.50 (ISBN 0-8112-0464-2); pap. 6.95 (ISBN 0-8112-0570-3, NDP394). New Directions.

Asian Journalism: A Selected Bibliography of Sources on Journalism in China & Southeast Asia. Elliott S. Parker & Emelia M. Parker. LC 79-22785. 484p. 1979. 25.00 (ISBN 0-8108-1269-X). Scarecrow.

Asian Libraries & Librarianship: An Annotated Bibliography of Selected Books & Periodicals & a Draft Syllabus. G. Raymond Nunn. LC 73-6629. 1973. 10.00 (ISBN 0-8108-0633-9). Scarecrow.

Asian Literature in English: A Guide to Information Sources. Ed. by G. L. Anderson. (American, English Literature & World Literatures in English Information Guide Ser.: Vol. 31). 300p. 1981. 30.00 (ISBN 0-8103-1362-6). Gale.

Asian Medical Systems: A Comparative Study. Ed. by Charles Leslie. LC 73-91674. 1976. 23.75x (ISBN 0-520-02680-2); pap. 7.95x (ISBN 0-520-03511-9). U of Cal Pr.

Asian Minor: The True Story of Ganymede. Felice Picano. (Illus.). 80p. 1981. 19.95 (ISBN 0-933322-07-0); pap. 5.95 (ISBN 0-933322-06-2). Sea Horse.

Asian Philosophy Today. Ed. by Dan Riepe. 300p. 1980. write for info. (ISBN 0-677-05530-7). Gordon.

Asian Regional Conference, Manila, December 1980, 9th Session: Problems of Rural Workers in Asia & the Pacific, Report III. International Labour Office. ii, 104p. (Orig.). 1980. pap. 10.00 (ISBN 92-2-102500-4). Intl Labour Office.

Asian Religions-History of Religion: Proceedings. American Academy of Religion, 1974. Ed. by Harry Partin. LC 74-14213. (American Academy of Religion. Section Papers). 1974. pap. 4.50 (ISBN 0-88420-114-7, 010912). Scholars Pr Ca.

Asian Socioeconomic Development: A National Accounts Approach. Ed. by Kazushi Ohkawa & Bernard Key. 326p. 1980. text ed. 27.50x (ISBN 0-8248-0743-X). U Pr of Hawaii.

Asian Socioeconomical Development: A National Accounts Approach. Kazushi Ohkawa & Bernard Key. 326p. 1980. text ed. 27.50. U Pr of Hawaii.

Asian Women. (Illus.). 1971. pap. 3.50x o.p. (ISBN 0-934052-02-6). Asian Am Stud.

Asian Women in Transition. Ed. by Sylvia A. Chipp & Justin J. Green. LC 79-20517. (Illus.). 256p. 1980. text ed. 16.00x (ISBN 0-271-00251-4); pap. text ed. 8.95x (ISBN 0-271-00257-3). Pa St U Pr.

Asians in America. H. Brett Melendy. (American Immigrant Ser.). 340p. 1981. pap. 6.95 (ISBN 0-88254-513-2). Hippocrene Bks.

Asians in America: Filipinos, Koreans, & East Indians. H. Brett Melendy. (Immigrant Heritage of America Ser.). 1977. lib. bdg. 10.95 (ISBN 0-8057-8414-4). Twayne.

Asians in East Africa: Jayhind & Uhuru. Agehananda Bharati. LC 72-85882. 416p. 1972. 19.95x (ISBN 0-911012-49-4). Nelson-Hall.

Asians: Their Heritage & Their Destiny. 5th ed. Paul T. Welty. LC 76-27357. 1976. pap. text ed. 6.50 scp (ISBN 0-397-47359-1, HarpC). Har-Row.

Asia's New Giant: How the Japanese Economy Works. Ed. by Hugh Patrick & Henry Rosovsky. 1976. 24.95 (ISBN 0-8157-6934-2); pap. 14.95 (ISBN 0-8157-6933-4). Brookings.

Asia's Nuclear Future. W. H. Overholt. LC 77-778. 1977. lib. bdg. 26.50x (ISBN 0-89158-217-7). Westview.

Asiatic Mode of Production: Science & Politics. Ed. by Anne M. Bailey. (Illus.). 352p. 1981. price not set (ISBN 0-7100-0737-X) (ISBN 0-7100-0738-8). Routledge & Kegan.

Asiatic Mode of Production: Sources Development & Critique in the Writings of Karl Marx. Lawrence Krader. 454p. 1975. text ed. 58.25x (ISBN 90-232-1289-4). Humanities.

Asimov on Astronomy. Isaac Asimov. LC 73-80946. 288p. 1975. pap. 4.50 (ISBN 0-385-06881-6, Anch). Doubleday.

Asimov on Physics. Isaac Asimov. 1978. pap. 2.50 (ISBN 0-380-41848-7, 41848). Avon.

Asimov on Science Fiction. Isaac Asimov. LC 80-2246. 288p. 1981. 13.95 (ISBN 0-385-17443-8). Doubleday.

Asimov's Guide to the Bible, Vol. 1. Isaac Asimov. LC 68-23566. 12.50 (ISBN 0-385-07399-2). Doubleday.

Asimov's Guide to the Bible: The New Testament. Isaac Asimov. 1971. pap. 5.95 (ISBN 0-380-01031-3, 46862). Avon.

Asimov's Mysteries. Isaac Asimov. 1979. pap. 1.95 (ISBN 0-449-24011-8, Crest). Fawcett.

Ask for Me Tomorrow. Margaret Millar. 1977. pap. 1.50 (ISBN 0-380-01805-5, 35618). Avon.

Ask Me for Tomorrow. Margaret Millar. 1976. 6.95 o.p. (ISBN 0-394-40883-7). Random.

Ask Me No Questions. Margaret Storey. (gr. 5 up). 1975. PLB 7.95 o.p. (ISBN 0-525-25972-4). Dutton.

Ask Me Now. Al Young. 1980. 11.95 (ISBN 0-07-072360-5). McGraw.

Ask Mister Bear. Marjorie Flack. (gr. k-3). 1958. 6.95 (ISBN 0-02-735390-7). Macmillan.

Ask That Mountain. Dick Scott. 1977. text ed. 19.95x o.p. (ISBN 0-435-32803-4). Heinemann Ed.

Ask the Fellows Who Cut the Hay. George E. Evans. (Illus., Orig.). 1965. pap. 6.95 (ISBN 0-571-06353-5, Pub. by Faber & Faber). Merrimack Bk Serv.

Ask the Right Question. Michael Z. Lewin. 1979. pap. 1.95 o.p. (ISBN 0-425-04027-5). Berkley Pub.

Asking & Giving: A Report on Hospital Philanthropy. Robert M. Cunningham, Jr. LC 79-28315. 148p. (Orig.). 1980. pap. 12.50 (ISBN 0-87258-300-7, 1030). Am Hospital.

Asking for It. Joan Taylor. 258p. 1980. 9.95 (ISBN 0-312-92027-X). Congdon & Lattes.

Asking for It. Joan Taylor. 258p. 1980. 10.95 (ISBN 0-312-92027-X). St Martin.

Asking for Trouble. Donald Woods. LC 80-69643. 1981. 11.95 (ISBN 0-689-11159-2). Atheneum.

Asking Questions. Peter Abbs. (Approaches Ser.: No. 3). 1974. pap. text ed. 2.95x o.p. (ISBN 0-435-10023-8). Heinemann Ed.

Asking Questions: A Classroom Model for Teaching the Bible. D. Bruce Lockerbie. Ed. by Diane Zimmerman. LC 80-18198. (Orig.). 1980. pap. text ed. 4.95 (ISBN 0-915134-75-6). Mott Media.

Asking Questions About Behavior: An Introduction to What Psychologists Do. 2nd ed. Michael E. Doherty & Kenneth M. Shemberg. 1978. pap. 6.95x (ISBN 0-673-15043-7). Scott F.

Asking the Right Questions. M. Neil Browne & Stuart M. Keely. 224p. 1981. pap. text ed. 6.95 (ISBN 0-13-049395-3). P-H.

Askins on Pistols & Revolvers. Charles Askins. Ed. by Ted Bryant & Bill Askins. 144p. 1980. text ed. 25.00 (ISBN 0-935998-22-5); pap. 8.95 (ISBN 0-935998-21-7). Natl Rifle Assn.

Asleep in Another Country. Melinda Mueller. 1979. 4.00 (ISBN 0-918116-17-1). Jawbone Pr.

Asma'ul-Husna: The 99 Beautiful Names of Allah. M. R. Bawa Muhaiyaddeen. (Illus.). 211p. 1979. pap. 4.95 (ISBN 0-914390-13-9). Fellowship Pr PA.

A.S.M.D. Multi-Graded Arithmetic Practice & Drill Sheets. Valerie E. Mock. (Makemaster Bk.). (gr. 1-8). 1977. pap. 14.95 (ISBN 0-8224-0462-1). Pitman Learning.

ASME Guide for Gas Transmission & Distribution Piping System (Includes Addenda Through December 1978: 1976. 1976. pap. 100.00 o.p. (ISBN 0-685-67491-6, A00030). ASME.

ASME Guide for Gas Transmission & Distribution Piping System: Includes All Addenda Through December 1982. 1980. pap. 125.00 (ISBN 0-685-67491-6, AX3080). ASME.

ASME Orientation & Guide for Use of Si (Metric) Units. 8th ed. 1978. pap. text ed. 2.00 (ISBN 0-685-41936-3, E00058). ASME.

ASME Steam Tables. 4th ed. C. A. Meyer et al. 1979. pap. text ed. 22.50 (G00038). ASME.

Asoka & Indian Civilization. Helen Kanitkar & Hemant Kanitkar. Ed. by Malcolm Yapp et al. (World History Ser.). (Illus.). 32p. (gr. 10). 1980. Repr. lib. bdg. 5.95 (ISBN 0-89908-035-9); pap. text ed. 1.95 (ISBN 0-89908-010-3). Greenhaven.

Asoka the Great: India's Royal Missionary. Emil Lengyel. LC 71-83650. (Biography Ser). (gr. 7 up). 1969. PLB 6.90 (ISBN 0-531-00947-5). Watts.

Asokan Inscriptions. R. Basak. (Illus.). 1959. 5.50x o.p. (ISBN 0-8426-1147-9). Verry.

Asot Mishpat. Abraham Shumsky & Adaia Shumsky. (Mah Tov Hebrew Teaching Ser.: Bk. 1). (Illus.). (gr. 4-8). 1969. text ed. 5.00 (ISBN 0-8074-0178-1, 405301); tchrs'. guide 3.50 (ISBN 0-8074-0179-X, 205302); wkbk. 3.50 (ISBN 0-8074-0180-3, 405300). UAHC.

Asparagus. A. W. Kidner. (Illus.). 1959. 6.95 (ISBN 0-571-06771-9, Pub. by Faber & Faber). Merrimack Bk Serv.

Aspect. B. Comrie. (Textbooks in Linguistics). 180p. 1976. 34.95 (ISBN 0-521-21109-3); pap. 9.95x (ISBN 0-521-29045-7). Cambridge U Pr.

Aspect Anthology. Intro. by Edward J. Hogan et al. (Illus.). 250p. (Orig.). 1981. pap. 3.95 (ISBN 0-939010-01-1). Zephyr.

Aspects De la Reforme De L'enseignement En Chine Au Debut Du XXe Siecle D'apres Des Ecrits De Zhang Jian. Marianne Bastide. (Recherches: No. 64). (Illus.). 1971. pap. 28.80 (ISBN 0-686-22139-7). Mouton.

Aspects of Air Law & Civil Air Policy in the Seventies. H. A. Wassenbergh. LC 79-538221. 1970. 30.00x (ISBN 90-247-5003-2). Intl Pubns Serv.

Aspects of Alice: Lewis Carroll's Dreamchild As Seen Through the Critics' Looking Glasses. Ed. by Robert Phillips. LC 70-178822. (Illus.). 15.00 (ISBN 0-8149-0700-8). Vanguard.

Aspects of Altaic Civilization II: Proceedings. Permanent International Altaistic Conference, 18th Meeting, Bloomington, June 29-July 5, 1975. Ed. by Paul A. Draghi & Larry V. Clark. (Indiana University Uralic & Altaic Ser.: Vol. 134). 212p. 1978. 34.00 (ISBN 0-933070-02-0). Ind U Res Inst.

Aspects of Altaic Civilization: Proceedings. Permanent International Altaistic Conference, Indiana University, 1962. Ed. by David Francis & Denis Sinor. LC 80-28299. (Uralic & Altaic Ser.: Vol. 23). ix, 263p. 1981. Repr. of 1962 ed. lib. bdg. 25.00x (ISBN 0-313-22945-7, PIAA). Greenwood.

Aspects of American Film History Prior to 1920. Anthony Slide. LC 78-2912. 1978. 10.00 (ISBN 0-8108-1130-8). Scarecrow.

Aspects of Animal Movement. Ed. by H. Y. Elder & E. R. Trueman. LC 79-8520. (Society for Experimental Biology Seminar Ser.: No. 5). (Illus.). 250p. 1980. 44.50 (ISBN 0-521-23086-1); pap. 16.50 (ISBN 0-521-29795-8). Cambridge U Pr.

Aspects of Anxiety. 2nd ed. Pref. by C. Hardin Branch. LC 68-27538. 1968. 4.50 o.p. (ISBN 0-397-59024-5). Lippincott.

Aspects of Auditory Perception: Non-Verbal Sounds & Speech. Richard M. Warren. (Pergamon General Psychology Ser.). 225p. 1981. price not set (ISBN 0-08-025957-X). Pergamon.

Aspects of Biophysics. William Hughes. LC 78-8992. 1979. text ed. 25.95 (ISBN 0-471-01990-9). Wiley.

Aspects of Brackish Water Fish & Crustacean Culture in the Mediterranean. 135p. 1981. pap. 7.25 (ISBN 92-5-000964-X, F2103, FAO). Unipub.

Aspects of British Politics, 1904-1919. D. Collins. 1965. 25.00 (ISBN 0-08-010987-X); pap. 12.75 (ISBN 0-08-010986-1). Pergamon.

Aspects of Chemistry for Health-Related Sciences: Concepts & Correlations. Conrad L. Stanitski, Jr. & C. Sears. 1979. 19.95 (ISBN 0-13-049262-0); study guide 6.95 (ISBN 0-13-049254-X). P-H.

Aspects of Chinese Education. Ed. by C. T. Hu. LC 73-95245. 1969. pap. 5.00x (ISBN 0-8077-1528-X). Tchrs Coll.

Aspects of Classical Chinese Syntax. Christoph Harbsmeier. (Sias Monograph: No. 45). 328p. 1980. pap. text ed. 17.00x (ISBN 0-7007-0139-7). Humanities.

Aspects of Death in Early Greek Art & Poetry. Emily Vermeule. LC 76-55573. (Sather Classical Lectures: Vol. 46). 1979. 24.95x (ISBN 0-520-03405-8). U of Cal Pr.

Aspects of Death in Early Greek Art & Poetry. Emily Vermeule. (Sather Classical Lectures Ser.: No. 46). 1981. pap. 7.95 (ISBN 0-520-04404-5, CAL 504). U of Cal Pr.

Aspects of Development & Underdevelopment. Joan Robinson. LC 78-25610. (Modern Economics Ser.). 1979. 22.95 (ISBN 0-521-22637-6); pap. 5.95 (ISBN 0-521-29589-0). Cambridge U Pr.

Aspects of Developmental & Paediatric Ophthalmology. Ed. by Peter Gardiner et al. (Clinics in Developmental Medicine Ser. No. 32). 126p. 1969. 10.75 o.p. (ISBN 0-685-24727-9). Lippincott.

Aspects of Deviance. E. Vaz. 1976. pap. 7.95 (ISBN 0-13-049304-X). P-H.

Aspects of Distributed Computer Systems. Harold Lorin. LC 80-16689. 450p. 1980. 27.50 (ISBN 0-471-08114-0, Pub. by Wiley-Interscience). Wiley.

Aspects of Educational Technology: Educational Technology to the Year 2000, Vol. 14. Association for Educational & Training Technology. Ed. by Leo Evans & Roy Winterburn. 450p. 1980. 37.50x (ISBN 0-85038-383-8). Nichols Pub.

Aspects of Educational Technology VIII: Findings of the 1974 Conference for Programmed Learning & Educational Technology. J. P. Baggaley et al. 384p. 1975. 21.00x o.p. (ISBN 0-8464-0156-8). Beekman Pubs.

Aspects of Educational Technology XII: Educational Technology in a Changing World. Association for Programmed Learning & Educational Technology. 1978. 32.50x (ISBN 0-85038-137-1, Pub by Kogan Pg). Nichols Pub.

Aspects of Educational Technology XIII: Educational Technology 20 Years on. Association for Programmed Learning & Educational Technology Conference, 1979. Ed. by G. Terry Page & Quentin Whitlock. 1979. 35.00x (ISBN 0-85038-247-5). Nichols Pub.

Aspects of Educational Technology XI: The Spread of Educational Technology. Ed. by P. J. Hills. J. Gilbert. 1977. 32.50x (ISBN 0-85038-093-6, Pub by Kogan Pg). Nichols Pub.

Aspects of Ethnicity: Understanding Differences in Pluralistic Classrooms. Wilma Longstreet. LC 78-16631. (Orig.). 1978. pap. text ed. 10.50x (ISBN 0-8077-2529-3). Tchrs Coll.

Aspects of French Literature. Ed. by Robert J. Nelson & Neal Oxenhandler. LC 61-5992. (Fr.). 1961. 29.50x (ISBN 0-89197-037-1); pap. text ed. 12.95x (ISBN 0-89197-038-X). Irvington.

Aspects of Gongora's Soledades. John Beverley. (Purdue University Monograhs in Romance Languages: No. 1). 1981. text ed. 23.00x (ISBN 90-272-1711-4). Humanities.

Aspects of Hamlet. Ed. by K. Muir & S. Wells. LC 78-18100. (Illus.). 1979. 26.50 (ISBN 0-521-22228-1); pap. 8.95x (ISBN 0-521-29400-2). Cambridge U Pr.

Aspects of Hindi Grammar. Ed. by Yamuna Kachru. 1980. 12.50x (ISBN 0-8364-0666-4, Pub. by Manohar India). South Asia Bks.

Aspects of Human Biology: Theory Relevant to Medical Laboratory Sciences. Frank Spencer. (Illus.). 352p. 1972. 22.95 o.p. (ISBN 0-407-70400-0). Butterworths.

Aspects of Human Settlement Planning. United Nations Conference on Human Settlements. LC 77-9877. (Habitat Ser.). 350p. 1978. 52.00 (ISBN 0-08-022011-8). Pergamon.

Aspects of Hydrocarbon Radiolysis. Ed. by T. Gaumann & J. Hoigne. LC 68-19261. 1968. 38.00 (ISBN 0-12-277650-X). Acad Pr.

Aspects of Indian History & Civilization. B. Prakash. 1965. 8.50 (ISBN 0-8426-1681-0). Verry.

Aspects of Indian Writing in English. M. K. Naik. 319p. (Orig.). 1979. pap. text ed. 4.50x (ISBN 0-333-90301-3). Humanities.

Aspects of Indian Writing in English. Ed. by M. K. Naik. 319p. (Orig.). 1980. pap. text ed. 5.50x (ISBN 0-333-90301-3). Humanities.

Aspects of Language & Culture. Carol M. Eastman. LC 74-28741. (Publications in Anthropology Ser.). (Illus.). 168p. 1975. pap. text ed. 5.95x (ISBN 0-88316-514-7). Chandler & Sharp.

Aspects of Language & Language Teaching. W. A. Bennett. (Illus., Orig.). 1968. 24.95 (ISBN 0-521-04164-3); pap. 6.95x (ISBN 0-521-09512-3, 512). Cambridge U Pr.

Aspects of Late Silurian Conodonts. Lennart Jepsson. (Fossils & Strata Ser: No. 6). 1975. pap. text ed. 13.00x (ISBN 8-200-09373-5, Dist. by Columbia U Pr). Universitet.

Aspects of Macbeth: Articles Reprinted from Shakespeare Survey. Ed. by K. Muir & P. Edwards. LC 76-56239. (Reprint Offshoot Ser. from Shakespeare Survey). (Illus.). 1977. 26.50 (ISBN 0-521-21500-5); pap. 8.95x (ISBN 0-521-29176-3). Cambridge U Pr.

Aspects of Management. 2nd ed. Samuel Eilon. 1979. text ed. 26.00 (ISBN 0-08-022480-6); pap. text ed. 11.25 (ISBN 0-08-022479-2). Pergamon.

Aspects of Motion Perception. Paul A. Kolers. LC 73-188746. 232p. 1972. text ed. 32.00 (ISBN 0-08-016843-4). Pergamon.

Aspects of Nuclear Reactor Safety: Proceedings. International Colloquium on Irradiation Tests for Reactor Safety Programmes, Petten, Holland, June 1979 & Joint Research Center, Petten Establishment of the Commission of the European Communities. (European Applied Research Reports Special Topics Ser.). 600p. 1980. lib. bdg. 46.00 (ISBN 3-7186-0016-1). Harwood Academic.

Aspects of "Official" Painting & Philosophic Art, 1789-1799. Diane Kelder. LC 75-23797. (Outstanding Dissertations in the Fine Arts - 18th Century). (Illus.). 1976. lib. bdg. 37.50 (ISBN 0-8240-1992-X). Garland Pub.

Aspects of Othello. Ed. by K. Muir & P. Edwards. LC 76-57095. (Articles Reprinted from Shakespeare Survey Ser.). (Illus.). 1977. 26.50 (ISBN 0-521-21499-8); pap. 7.95x (ISBN 0-521-29175-5). Cambridge U Pr.

Aspects of Pacific Ethnohistory. Alan Tippett. LC 73-8820. (Illus.). 216p. (Orig.). 1973. pap. 5.95 (ISBN 0-87808-132-1). William Carey Lib.

Aspects of Political Ideas & Institutions in Ancient India. 2nd ed. rev. ed. & enl. ed. R. S. Sharma. 1968. 6.75x o.p. (ISBN 0-8426-1523-7). Verry.

Aspects of Political Mobilization in South Asia. Ed. by Robert I. Crane. LC 76-5434. (Foreign & Comparative Studies-South Asia Ser.: No. 1). 1976. pap. text ed. 4.50x (ISBN 0-915984-75-X). Syracuse U Foreign Comp.

Aspects of Preventive Psychiatry. Ed. by G. N. Christodoulou. (Bibliotheca Psychiatrica: No. 160). (Illus.). vi, 142p. 1980. soft cover 42.00 (ISBN 3-8055-1218-X). S Karger.

Aspects of Quantum Theory. Ed. by A. Salam & E. P. Wigner. LC 72-75298. (Illus.). 300p. 1972. 40.95 (ISBN 0-521-08600-0). Cambridge U Pr.

Aspects of Reading Education. Ed. by Susanna Pflaum-Connor. LC 77-95250. (National Society for the Study of Educ., Series on Contemp Educ. Issues). 1978. 16.00 (ISBN 0-8211-1517-0); text ed. 14.50 (ISBN 0-685-04964-7). McCutchan.

Aspects of Roman Life: Folder 1. Peter Hodge. (Illus.). 1977. folder 12.85x (ISBN 0-582-31416-X). Longman.

Aspects of Science Fiction. Ed. by G. D. Doherty. (gr. 9 up). 1959. pap. 4.95 (ISBN 0-7195-2215-3). Transatlantic.

Aspects of Scientific Explanation. Carl G. Hempel. LC 65-15441. 1970. pap. text ed. 9.95 (ISBN 0-02-914340-3). Free Pr.

Aspects of Slow & Persistent Virus Infections. Ed. by David A. Tyrrell. (New Perspectives in Clinical Microbiology Ser.: Vol. 2). 286p. 1980. lib. bdg. 42.10 (ISBN 90-247-2281-0, Pub. by Martinus Nijhoff). Kluwer Boston.

Aspects of the Development of Competence. Ed. by W. Andrew Collins. LC 80-20568. (Minnesota Symposia on Child Psychology: Vol. 14). 288p. 1981. 19.95 (ISBN 0-89859-070-1). L Erlbaum Assocs.

Aspects of the French Revolution. Alfred Cobban. LC 68-24195. 1968. 6.95 o.p. (ISBN 0-8076-0454-2). Braziller.

Aspects of the Grammar of Focus in English. Adrian Akmajian. Ed. by Jorge Hankamer. LC 78-66534. (Outstanding Dissertations in Linguistics Ser.). 1979. lib. bdg. 37.50 (ISBN 0-8240-9691-6). Garland Pub.

Aspects of the History of English. John C. McLaughlin. LC 75-94889. (Illus.). 1970. 29.00x (ISBN 0-89197-666-3). Irvington.

Aspects of the Introduction of Food Irradiation in Developing Countries. (Illus.). 113p. (Orig.). 1974. pap. 8.25 (ISBN 92-0-111673-X, IAEA). Unipub.

Aspects of the Iranian Revolution. 35p. 1980. pap. 5.00 (ISBN 92-808-0038-8, TUNU 064, UNU). Unipub.

Aspects of the Kinetics & Dynamics of Surface Reactions. Ed. by Uzi Landman. LC 80-68004. (AIP Conference Proceedings: No. 61). 343p. 1980. lib. bdg. 22.25 (ISBN 0-88318-160-6). Am Inst Physics.

Aspects of the Lappish Minority Situation. Harald Eidheim. 86p. 1971. 10.50x (ISBN 8-200-02328-1, Dist. by Columbia U Pr). Universitet.

Aspects of the Physiology of Crustacea. A. P. Lockwood. (Illus.). 1968. 21.95x (ISBN 0-7167-0667-9). W H Freeman.

Aspects of the Present. Margaret Mead & Rhoda Metraux. 288p. 1981. pap. 6.95. Morrow.

Aspects of Twentieth-Century Music. Richard Delone et al. (Illus.). 541p. 1974. 20.95x (ISBN 0-13-049346-5). P-H.

Aspects of Upper Great Lakes Anthropology: Papers in Honor of Lloyd A. Wilford. Ed. by Elden Johnson. LC 74-17003. (Prehistoric Archaeology Ser: No. 11). (Illus.). 190p. 1974. pap. 9.50 (ISBN 0-87351-087-9). Minn Hist.

Aspects of Verification in Sanskrit Lyric Poetry. Sheldon Pollock. (American Oriental Ser.: Vol. 61). 1977. 11.00. Am Orient Soc.

Aspekte der kontrastiven Syntax am Beispiel des Niederlaendischen und Deutschen. Jelle Stegemann. (Studia Linguistica Germanica). 201p. 1979. text ed. 34.25x (ISBN 3-11-008017-6). De Gruyter.

Aspen Design Conference Visitor. C. R. Goeldner & Gwen Gortmaker. 56p. 1976. 10.00 (ISBN 0-89478-029-8). U CO Busn Res Div.

Aspen Epicure. Ed. by Michael Whitcomb. (Epicure Library). (Orig.). 1979. pap. 2.50 (ISBN 0-89716-050-9). Peanut Butter.

Aspen Handbook on the Media: 1977-1979 Edition, a Selective Guide to Research, Organizations, & Publications in Communications. Ed. by William L. Rivers et al. LC 77-14556. (Praeger Special Studies). 1977. 32.50 (ISBN 0-03-023141-8). Praeger.

Aspen Manual of Transfusion Therapy. Ed. by Roanne Rutman. 250p. 1981. text ed. write for info. (ISBN 0-89443-281-8). Aspen Systems.

Aspen on the Roaring Fork. Frank L. Wentworth. Ed. by Russ Collman & Stanna Meyers. (Illus.). 1976. 30.00 o.p. (ISBN 0-913582-15-8). Sundance.

Aspen Skier: (1977-78) C. R. Goeldner. 80p. 1978. 15.00 (ISBN 0-89478-043-3). U CO Busn Res Div.

Aspen Summer Visitor. C. R. Goeldner & Cheryl Fellhauer. 97p. 1976. 10.00 (ISBN 0-89478-028-X). U CO Busn Res Div.

Aspen: The One Hundred Year High. The Living Art Company. LC 79-55797. (Illus.). 1980. 34.95 (ISBN 0-916728-30-7). Bks in Focus.

Aspinall Era. H. A. Bullied. 17.95x (ISBN 0-392-07597-0, SpS). Soccer.

Aspiration Cytology of the Breast. Hubert Schondorf. Tr. by Volker Schneider. LC 77-24004. (Illus.). 1978. text ed. 32.00 (ISBN 0-7216-8013-5). Saunders.

Aspiration-Glow & Dedication-Flow, 2 pts. Sri Chinmoy. (Orig.). 1977. Pt. 1, 60p. pap. text ed. 2.00 (ISBN 0-88497-386-7); Pt. 2, 70p. pap. 2.00 (ISBN 0-686-68529-6). Aum Pubns.

Aspirations of Young Migrant Workers in Western Europe. (Educational Studies & Documents Ser: No. 21). 38p. 1976. pap. 2.50 (ISBN 92-3-101333-5, U42, UNESCO). Unipub.

Assassin. Evelyn Anthony. 1978. pap. 1.50 o.p. (ISBN 0-425-03678-2, Medallion). Berkley Pub.

Assassination American Style. John Hurley. 209p. (Orig.). 1980. pap. cancelled (ISBN 0-933990-03-0). Canterbury Pr.

Assassination! Kennedy, King, Kennedy. Stephen Goode. LC 78-10227. (Illus.). (gr. 6 up). 1979. PLB 7.90 s&l (ISBN 0-531-02213-7). Watts.

Assassination of John F. Kennedy: A Comprehensive Historical & Legal Bibliography, 1963-1979. Compiled By DeLloyd J. Guth & David R. Wrone. LC 79-6184. (Illus.). lvi, 442p. 1980. lib. bdg. 37.50 (ISBN 0-313-21274-0, GJK/). Greenwood.

Assassination of Mahatma Gandhi. K. L. Gauba. 1969. pap. 3.50 (ISBN 0-88253-140-9). Ind-US Inc.

Assassination of Martin Luther King, Jr. Doris Faber & Howard Faber. LC 78-1726. (Focus Bks.). (Illus.). 1978. lib. bdg. 6.45 s&l (ISBN 0-531-02465-2). Watts.

Assassination on Embassy Row. John Dinges & Saul Landau. 432p. 1981. pap. 5.95 (ISBN 0-07-016998-5). McGraw.

Assassination Please Almanac. Tom Miller. LC 76-55654. (Illus.). 1977. pap. 5.95 o.p. (ISBN 0-8092-7903-7). Contemp Bks.

Assassination Tapes. George O'Toole. LC 74-21057. 1975. 8.95 o.p. (ISBN 0-89110-000-8). Penthouse Pr.

Assassinations: Dallas & Beyond - a Guide to Coverups & Investigations. Peter D. Scott et al. 1976. 15.00 (ISBN 0-394-40107-7). Random.

Assassins. Elia Kazan. LC 70-16484. 312p. 1981. pap. 7.95 (ISBN 0-8128-6076-4). Stein & Day.

Assassins. Joyce C. Oates. LC 75-25141. 576p. 1975. 10.95 (ISBN 0-8149-0767-9). Vanguard.

Assassins Play-off. Warren Murphy. (Destroyer Ser.: No. 20). 192p. (Orig.). 1975. pap. 1.50 (ISBN 0-523-40294-5). Pinnacle Bks.

Assateague. William H. Wroten. LC 72-79769. (Illus.). 1972. pap. 2.00 (ISBN 0-87033-168-X, Pub. by Tidewater). Cornell Maritime.

Assault. Allen R. Matthews. LC 80-14926. (Great Classic Stories of World War II Ser.). 1980. 8.95 (ISBN 0-396-07874-5); pap. 5.95 (ISBN 0-396-07875-3). Dodd.

Assault of Indian Tribalism: The General Allotment Law (Dawes Act) of 1887. Wilcomb E. Washburn. LC 74-23141. (America's Alternatives Ser.). 79p. 1975. pap. 2.75 o.p. (ISBN 0-397-47337-0). Lippincott.

Assault on Authority: Dialogue or Dilemma? William W. Meissner. LC 70-152878. 1971. 7.95x o.p. (ISBN 0-88344-018-0). Orbis Bks.

Assault on Eternity. R. E. Byrd. 352p. 1980. 9.95 (ISBN 0-87021-085-8). Naval Inst Pr.

Assault on Eternity: Richard E. Byrd & the Exploration of Antarctica, 1946-47. Lisle A. Rose. LC 79-93232. (Illus.). 352p. 1980. 19.95 (ISBN 0-87021-085-8). Naval Inst Pr.

Assay of Protein & Polypeptide Hormones. H. Van Cauwenberge & P. Franchimont. LC 76-108930. 1970. 34.00 (ISBN 0-08-015685-1). Pergamon.

Assays: Critical Approaches to Medieval & Renaissance Texts, Vol. 1. Ed. by Peggy A. Knapp & Michael A. Stugrin. LC 80-54059. 200p. 1981. 15.95x (ISBN 0-8229-3439-6). U of Pittsburgh Pr.

Assembler Language for Fortran, Cobol & PL-1 Programmers. new ed. Shan S. Kuo. LC 73-2138. 1974. text ed. 20.95 (ISBN 0-201-03954-0). A-W.

Assembler Language Programming: Systems-360 & 370. Sharon Tuggle. LC 74-84276. 400p. 1975. pap. text ed. 15.95 (ISBN 0-574-19160-7, 13-4015); instr's guide avail. (ISBN 0-574-19161-5, 13-4016). SRA.

Assembler Language Programming: The IBM System 360. 2nd ed. George W. Struble. 496p. 1975. text ed. 20.95 (ISBN 0-201-07322-6). A-W.

Assembly Language Fundamentals, 360-370. Rina Yarmish & Joshua Yarmish. LC 79-64125. 1979. text ed. 18.95 (ISBN 0-201-08798-7). A-W.

Assembly Language Programming & the IBM 360 & 370 Computers. Walter G. Rudd. 1976. 21.95 (ISBN 0-13-049536-0); wkbk. 6.95 (ISBN 0-13-049510-7). P-H.

Assembly Language Programming: Z8000. Lance Leventhal et al. (Assembly Language Programming: No. 6). (Orig.). 1980. pap. 19.99 (ISBN 0-931988-36-5). Osborne-McGraw.

Assembly Language Programming: 6502. Lance Leventhal. (Assembly Language Programming: No. 4). (Orig.). 1979. pap. text ed. 16.99 (ISBN 0-931988-27-6). Osborne-McGraw.

Assembly Language Programming: 6809. Lance Leventhal. (Assembly Language Programming: No. 5). (Orig.). 1980. pap. text ed. 16.99 (ISBN 0-931988-35-7). Osborne-McGraw.

Assembly Level Programming for Small Computers. Walter J. Weller. LC 75-13436. (Illus.). 256p. 1975. 18.95 (ISBN 0-669-00049-3). Lexington Bks.

Assembly of the Gods: The Divine Council in Canaanite & Hebrew Literature. E. Theodore Mullen, Jr. LC 80-10128. (Harvard Semitic Museum Monographs: No. 24). 10.50x (ISBN 0-89130-380-4, 04 00 24). Scholars Pr CA.

Assertion Training: A Facilitator's Guide. Colleen Kelley. LC 78-69787. 382p. 1979. 18.50 (ISBN 0-88390-146-3). Univ Assocs.

Assertion Training: A Humanistic-Behavioral Guide to Self-Dignity. Sherwin B. Cotler & Julio J. Guerra. LC 76-1704. (Illus., Orig.). 1976. pap. text ed. 8.95 (ISBN 0-87822-173-5). Res Press.

Assertive Christian. Michael Emmons & David Richardson. Ed. by Miriam Frost. 156p. (Orig.). 1981. pap. 5.95 (ISBN 0-03-059057-4). Winston Pr.

Assess Your Chess Fast. Alberic De Galway. 1978. 17.95 (ISBN 0-7134-1055-8, Pub. by Batsford England); pap. 10.95 (ISBN 0-7134-1056-6). David & Charles.

Assessing Children's Language: Guidelines for Teachers. Andrew Stibbs. 1980. pap. text ed. 4.25x (ISBN 0-7062-3853-2, Pub. by Ward Lock Educational England). Hayden.

Assessing Comprehension in a School Setting. T. Dieterich et al. Ed. by Peg Griffin. LC 78-59785. (Linguistics & Reading Ser.: No. 3). 1978. pap. text ed. 6.95x (ISBN 0-87281-072-0). Ctr Appl Ling.

Assessing Corporate Talent: A Key to Managerial Manpower Planning. Robert B. Finkle & William S. Jones. LC 71-120702. 1970. 23.95 (ISBN 0-471-25896-2, Pub. by Wiley-Interscience). Wiley.

Assessing International Disaster Needs. Committee on International Disaster Assistance. 1979. pap. 6.00 (ISBN 0-309-02893-0). Natl Acad Pr.

Assessing Life Skills Competence: The New York State External High School Diploma Program. Ruth S. Nickse. LC 80-82712. (CBE Forum Ser.: Bk. 3). 1980. pap. 8.95 (ISBN 0-8224-0515-6). Pitman Learning.

Assessing Minority Group Children. Ed. by Thomas Oakland & Beeman N. Phillips. LC 68-52341. 128p. 1973. text ed. 12.95 (ISBN 0-87705-154-2). Human Sci Pr.

Assessing Organizational Change: Rushton Quality of Work Experiment. Paul S. Goodman. LC 78-31857. (Organizational Behavior Assessment & Change Ser.). 1979. 27.95 (ISBN 0-471-04782-1, Pub. by Wiley-Interscience). Wiley.

Assessing Potential Ocean Pollutants. Ocean Affairs Board. 1975. pap. 9.25 (ISBN 0-309-02325-4). Natl Acad Pr.

Assessing Quality in Health Care. Institute of Medicine. LC 77-74650. 1977. pap. 6.50 o.p. (ISBN 0-309-02611-3). Natl Acad Pr.

Assessing Special Students. James McLoughlin & Rena Lewis. (Special Education Ser.). (Illus.). 640p. 1981. text ed. 17.95 (ISBN 0-675-08151-3). Merrill.

Assessing Students Appraising Teaching. J. C. Clift & B. W. Imrie. 160p. 1981. 24.95 (ISBN 0-470-27098-5). Halsted Pr.

Assessing Study Abroad Programs for Secondary School Students. H. Loew. (Language in Education Ser.: No. 29). 1980. pap. text ed. 2.95 (ISBN 0-87281-128-X). Ctr Appl Ling.

Assessing Teacher Performance: Task Analysis & Clinical Evaluation. Robert C. Hawley. LC 80-67945. 112p. (Orig.). 1981. pap. 9.95 (ISBN 0-913636-12-6). Educ Res MA.

Assessing the Effectiveness of Advertising. Jack Potter & Mark Lowell. 281p. 1975. text ed. 24.50x (ISBN 0-220-69730-2, Pub. by Busn Bks England). Renouf.

Assessing the Patient Representative Program in Hospitals. National Society of Patient Representatives of the American Hospital Association. LC 80-28949. (Illus., Orig.). 1981. pap. 8.00 (ISBN 0-87258-334-1, 1082). Am Hospital.

Assessing Vocational Education Research & Development. Committee on Vocational Education Research & Development, National Research Council. LC 76-46196. 1976. pap. 8.00 (ISBN 0-309-02526-5). Natl Acad Pr.

Assessing Your Patients. LC 80-36819. (Nursing Photobook Ser.). (Illus.). 160p. 1980. text ed. 12.95 (ISBN 0-916730-24-7). InterMed Comm.

Assessment & Collection of Data on Post-Harvest Foodgrain Losses. (FAO Economic & Social Development Paper: No. 13). 71p. 1981. pap. 6.00 (ISBN 92-5-100934-1, F2072, FAO). Unipub.

Assessment & Management of Developmental Changes & Problems in Children. Marcene L. Powell. (Illus.). 350p. 1981. pap. 12.95 (ISBN 0-8016-1520-8). Mosby.

Assessment & Modification of Emotional Behavior. Ed. by Kirk R. Blankstein et al. (Studies of Communication & Effect Ser.: Vol. 6). (Illus.). 235p. 1980. 25.00 (ISBN 0-306-40502-4, Plenum Pr). Plenum Pub.

Assessment & Performance of Implanted Cardiac Pacemakers. Ed. by G. D. Green. 1975. 35.95 (ISBN 0-407-00015-1). Butterworths.

Assessment & Treatment of Test Anxiety. Ed. by Charles D. Spielberger & Peter R. Vagg. (Clinical & Community Psychology Ser.). 352p. 1981. text ed. 25.00 (ISBN 0-89116-212-7). Hemisphere Pub. Postponed.

Assessment Centers. Terry Maris. 1981. text ed. cancelled (ISBN 0-89832-014-3). Brighton Pub Co.

Assessment for Transition: A Study of New Procedure. R. Sumner & K. Bradley. (Illus.). 1977. pap. text ed. 9.75 (ISBN 0-85633-132-5, NFER). Humanities.

Assessment in Education. D. G. Lewis. 198p. 1975. 17.95 (ISBN 0-470-53197-5). Halsted Pr.

Assessment in Higher Education. John Heywood. LC 76-12786. 1977. 39.75 (ISBN 0-471-99404-9, Pub. by Wiley-Interscience). Wiley.

Assessment in Schools. David Satterly. (Theory & Practice in Education Ser.: Vol. 1). 320p. 1981. 40.00x (ISBN 0-631-11151-4, Pub. by Basil Blackwell England); pap. 19.95x (ISBN 0-631-12564-7). Biblio Dist.

Assessment in Special & Remedial Education. John Salvia & James Ysseldyke. LC 77-72891. (Illus.). 1977. pap. text ed. 18.95 (ISBN 0-395-25073-0); inst. manual 0.50 (ISBN 0-395-25072-2). HM.

Assessment in Special & Remedial Education. 2nd ed. John Salvia & James E. Ysseldyke. (Illus.). 576p. 1981. text ed. write for info. (ISBN 0-395-29694-3). HM.

Assessment Intervention in Emergency Nursing. Lanros. LC 78-9832. 19.95 (ISBN 0-87618-990-7). R J Brady.

Assessment of Airborne Radioactivity. (Illus., Orig.). 1967. pap. 37.50 (ISBN 92-0-020367-1, IAEA). Unipub.

Assessment of Brain Damage: A Neuropsychological Key Approach. Elbert W. Russell et al. LC 73-121914. (Personality Disorders Ser). 1970. 25.95 (ISBN 0-471-74550-2, Pub. by Wiley-Interscience). Wiley.

Assessment of Erosion. M. DeBoodt & D. Gabriels. 400p. 1981. 67.50 (ISBN 0-471-27899-8, Pub. by Wiley-Interscience). Wiley.

Assessment of Erosion. Ed. by M. De Boodt. D. Gabriels. 400p. 1981. 79.00 o.p. (ISBN 0-8260-7790-0, Pub. by Wiley-Interscience). Wiley.

Assessment of Industrial Activity in the Field of Biomedical Engineering. Committee On Interplay Of Engineering With Biology And Medicine. LC 79-171609. 1971. pap. text ed. 6.00 (ISBN 0-309-01925-7). Natl Acad Pr.

Assessment of Land Value: Proceedings. Ed. by Daniel M. Holland. (Publication No. 5 of the Committee on Taxation Resources & Economic Development). 1970. 25.00 (ISBN 0-299-05621-X). U of Wis Pr.

Assessment of Lives: Personality Evaluation in a Bureaucratic Society. Charles A. Dailey. LC 70-168860. (Behavioral Science Ser.). 1971. 14.95x o.p. (ISBN 0-87589-108-X). Jossey-Bass.

Assessment of Local Drug Abuse Problems. Leon G. Hunt. LC 76-42694. 1977. 19.95 (ISBN 0-669-01053-7). Lexington Bks.

Assessment of Managers: An International Comparison. Bernard M. Bass et al. LC 78-24670. (Illus.). 1979. 17.95 (ISBN 0-02-901960-5). Free Pr.
Assessment of Medical Care for Children. Institute of Medicine. (Contrasts in Health Status Ser.). (Illus.). 224p. 1974. 12.00 (ISBN 0-309-02145-6); pap. 8.50 (ISBN 0-686-66904-5). Natl Acad Pr.
Assessment of Mercury in the Environment. Environmental Studies Board. 1978. pap. 8.00 (ISBN 0-309-02736-5). Natl Acad Pr.
Assessment of Morality. J. Wilson. (General Ser.). 1973. pap. text ed. 10.00x (ISBN 0-85633-012-4, NFER). Humanities.
Assessment of Persons. Norman D. Sundberg. (Illus.). 1977. 18.95 (ISBN 0-13-049585-9). P-H.
Assessment of Population Affinities in Man. Ed. by J. S. Weiner & J. Huizinga. 192p. 1972. 28.00x (ISBN 0-19-857352-9). Oxford U Pr.
Assessment of Radioactive Contamination in Man. (Illus.). 698p. (Orig.). 1972. pap. 51.00 (ISBN 92-0-020072-9, ISP290, IAEA). Unipub.
Assessment of Resources & Needs in Highway Technology Education. Compiled By American Society of Civil Engineers. 232p. 1975. pap. text ed. 10.00 (ISBN 0-87262-117-0). Am Soc Civil Eng.
Assessment of Sexual & Marital Function: Special Issue of Journal of Sex & Marital Therapy. Raul C. Schiavi. 1979. pap. 7.95x (ISBN 0-87705-468-1). Human Sci Pr.
Assessment of Sexual Function: A Guide to Interviewing, Vol. 8. GAP Committee on Medical Education. LC 74-158143. (Report No. 88). 1973. pap. 4.00 (ISBN 0-87318-122-0). Adv Psychiatry.
Assessment of Social Research: Guidelines for the Use of Research in Social Work & Social Science. Tony Tripodi et al. LC 69-20179. 1969. pap. text ed. 9.95 (ISBN 0-87581-033-0). Peacock Pubs.
Assessment of Sublethal Effects of Pollutants in the Sea. Royal Society. Ed. by H. A. Cole. (Illus.). 1979. text ed. 53.60 (ISBN 0-85403-112-X, Pub. by Royal Soc. London). Scholium Intl.
Assessment of Technological Decisions: Case Studies. E. Braun et al. (Science in a Social Context Ser.). 1979. pap. text ed. 3.95 (ISBN 0-408-71313-5). Butterworths.
Assessment of the Child in Primary Health Care. John H. Gundy. (Illus.). 208p. 1981. pap. text ed. 7.95 (ISBN 0-07-025197-5). McGraw.
Assessment of the Community Mental Health Movement. Ed. by Walter E. Barton & Charlotte J. Sanborn. LC 76-54610. (Illus.). 1977. 22.95 (ISBN 0-669-01309-9). Lexington Bks.
Assessment Questions for Integrated Science: Questions 9 to 15, Bk. 2. Stuart Kellington. 1979. pap. text ed. 3.95x o.p. (ISBN 0-435-57503-1); tchr's. ed. 9.95x o.p. (ISBN 0-435-57501-5). Heinemann Ed.
Assessment Strategies for Cognitive-Behavioral Intervention. Ed. by P. C. Kendall & S. D. Hollon. 1980. 29.50 (ISBN 0-12-404460-3). Acad Pr.
Assessment with Projective Techniques: A Concise Introduction. Albert Rabin. 1981. text ed. 22.95 (ISBN 0-8261-3550-1); pap. text ed. cancelled (ISBN 0-8261-3551-X). Springer Pub.
Asset Markets, Exchange Rates, & Economic Integration. Polly R. Allen & Peter B. Kenen. LC 79-16874. (Illus.). 1980. 55.00 (ISBN 0-521-22982-0). Cambridge U Pr.
Asset Prices in Economic Analysis. Samuel Chase, Jr. (California Library Reprint Series: No. 22). 1971. 18.50x (ISBN 0-520-01928-8). U of Cal Pr.
Asset Valuation & Income Determination: A Consideration of the Alternatives. Ed. by Robert R. Sterling. LC 73-160580. 1971. text ed. 10.00 (ISBN 0-914348-11-6). Scholars Bk.
Assignment. Laurence Leamer. 256p. 1981. 10.95 (ISBN 0-8037-0266-3). Dial.
Assignment--Afghan Dragon. Edward S. Aarons. (Assignment Ser.). 1978. pap. 1.95 (ISBN 0-449-14085-7, GM). Fawcett.
Assignment--Amazon Queen. Edward S. Aarons. (Assignment Ser.). 1977. pap. 1.25 o.p. (ISBN 0-449-13544-6, GM). Fawcett.
Assignment--Angelina. Edward S. Aarons. 1974. pap. 0.95 o.p. (ISBN 0-449-12989-6, M2989, GM). Fawcett.
Assignment--Ankara. Edward S. Aarons. 176p. 1975. pap. 1.25 o.p. (ISBN 0-449-13377-X, P3377, Gm). Fawcett.
Assignment--Bangkok. Edward S. Aarons. 192p. 1975. pap. 1.25 o.p. (ISBN 0-449-13343-5, P3343-125, GM). Fawcett.
Assignment--Black Viking. Edward S. Aarons. (Assignment Ser.). 1978. pap. 1.75 o.p. (ISBN 0-449-14017-2, GM). Fawcett.
Assignment--Budapest. Edward S. Aarons. 1977. pap. 1.25 o.p. (ISBN 0-449-13785-6, GM). Fawcett.
Assignment--Ceylon. Edward S. Aarons. 208p. 1981. pap. 1.95 (ISBN 0-449-13583-7, 0-449-13583-7, GM). Fawcett.
Assignment--Golden Girl. Edward S. Aarons. (Assignment Ser.). 1979. pap. 1.95 (ISBN 0-449-14140-3, GM). Fawcett.
Assignment--Helene. Edward S. Aarons. (Sam Durrell Ser.). 1978. pap. 1.50 o.p. (ISBN 0-449-13955-7, GM). Fawcett.
Assignment--Lili Lamaris. Edward S. Aarons. 1978. pap. 1.50 o.p. (ISBN 0-449-13934-4, GM). Fawcett.
Assignment--Moon Girl. Edward S Aarons. 1977. pap. 1.50 o.p. (ISBN 0-449-13856-9, GM). Fawcett.
Assignment--Nuclear Nude. Edward S. Aarons. 192p. 1974. pap. 0.95 o.p. (ISBN 0-449-12815-6, M2815, GM). Fawcett.
Assignment--Peking. Edward S. Aarons. 192p. 1975. pap. 1.25 o.p. (ISBN 0-449-13293-5, P3293, GM). Fawcett.
Assignment--Quayle Question. Edward S. Aarons. 1979. pap. 1.75 o.p. (ISBN 0-449-14226-4, GM). Fawcett.
Assignment--Sheba. Will B. Aarons. 192p. 1977. pap. 1.50 o.p. (ISBN 0-449-13696-5, GM). Fawcett.
Assignment--Silver Scorpion. Edward S. Aarons. 1976. pap. 1.95 o.p. (ISBN 0-449-14294-9, GM). Fawcett.
Assignment--Star Stealers. Edward S. Aarons. 1978. pap. 1.50 o.p. (ISBN 0-449-13944-1, GM). Fawcett.
Assignment--Sulu Sea. Edward S. Aarons. 160p. 1981. pap. 1.95 (ISBN 0-449-13875-5, GM). Fawcett.
Assignment--Tiger Devil. Will B. Aarons. 1978. pap. 1.75 o.p. (ISBN 0-449-14052-0, GM). Fawcett.
Assignment--Treason. Edward S. Aarons. 1977. pap. 1.50 o.p. (ISBN 0-449-13913-1, GM). Fawcett.
Assignment--Unicorn. Edward S. Aarons. 1978. pap. 1.50 o.p. (ISBN 0-449-13998-0, GM). Fawcett.
Assignment & Matching Problems: Solution Methods with FORTRAN-Programs. R. E. Burkhard & U. Derigs. (Lecture Notes in Economics & Mathematical Systems Ser.: Vol. 184). 148p. 1981. pap. 15.00 (ISBN 0-387-10267-1). Springer-Verlag.
Assignment: Burma. Lee O. Miller. (Orig.). 1980. pap. 1.75 (ISBN 0-505-51498-2). Tower Bks.
Assignment Ceylon. Edward S. Aarons. 208p. 1981. pap. 1.95 (ISBN 0-449-13583-7, GM). Fawcett.
Assignment in Eternity. Robert A. Heinlein. (RL 7). 1970. pap. 1.95 (ISBN 0-451-09360-7, J9360, Sig). NAL.
Assignment: Tokyo. Gladys H. Hunter. 234p. (Orig.). 1980. 9.95 (ISBN 0-931290-33-3). Nettleton Hse.
Assignment Wildlife. Anne LaBastille. (Illus.). 1980. 11.95 (ISBN 0-525-05910-5). Dutton.
Assignments. Photos by Snowdon. (Illus.). 136p. 1972. 12.50 o.p. (ISBN 0-688-00027-4). Morrow.
Assignments for Vibrational Spectra of 700 Benzene Derivatives, 2 vols. G. Varsanyi. LC 74-8113. 1974. Set. 79.95 (ISBN 0-470-90330-9). Halsted Pr.
Assimilation of Ethnic Groups: The Italian Case. James A. Crispino. 175p. Date not set. 9.95x (ISBN 0-913256-39-0). Ctr Migration.
Assimilation Patterns of Immigrants in the United States: A Case Study of Korean Immigrants in the Chicago Area. Won M. Hurh & Hei C. Kim. LC 78-59860. (Illus.). 1978. pap. text ed. 7.75 (ISBN 0-8191-0553-8). U Pr of Amer.
Assissi Embroidery. Pamela M. Ness. (Illus.). 1978. pap. 1.75 (ISBN 0-486-23743-5). Dover.
Assist Three: For Consonant Blends of L, R, & S. Octavia Milton. 50p. 1981. pap. text ed. 13.00 (ISBN 0-88450-729-7). Communication Skill.
Assistance to Racist Regimes in Southern Africa: Impact on the Enjoyment of Human Rights. 41p. 1979. pap. 4.00 (ISBN 0-686-68943-7, UN79/14/3, UN). Unipub.
Assistant Secretaries: Problems & Processes of Appointment. Dean E. Mann & Jameson W. Doig. 1965. 12.95 (ISBN 0-8157-5452-3). Brookings.
Assistantships & Fellowships in Mathematics in 1980-1981. 1.00 (ISBN 0-685-47853-X, ASST). Am Math.
Assize of Novel Disseisin. Donald W. Sutherland. 1973. 29.95x (ISBN 0-19-822410-9). Oxford U Pr.
Associate Medical Examiner. Jack Rudman. (Career Examination Ser.: C-2722). (Cloth bdg. avail on request). 1980. pap. 14.00 (ISBN 0-8373-2722-9). Natl Learning.
Associated Congenital Anomalies. M. El'Shafie & C. H. Klippel. (Illus.). 200p. 1980. 35.00 (ISBN 0-683-02800-6). Williams & Wilkins.
Associated Ground Subjects, Vol. 4. N. H. Birch & A. E. Bramson. (Flight Briefing for Pilots Ser.). (Illus.). 1978. 6.95 o.p. (ISBN 0-685-59598-6, Flying-Zd). Ziff-Davis Pub.
Association Football (Soccer) Laws Illustrated. Stanley Lover. 1977. 12.95 (ISBN 0-7207-0879-6). Transatlantic.
Association Internationale Des Travailleurs, Vol. 1. French Government Public. 1976. lib. bdg. 12.00x o.p. (ISBN 0-8287-1329-4); pap. text ed. 5.00x o.p. (ISBN 0-685-71492-6). Clearwater Pub.
Association Internationale Des Travailleurs, Vol. 2. French Government Public. 1976. lib. bdg. 15.00x o.p. (ISBN 0-8287-1330-8); pap. text ed. 7.50x o.p. (ISBN 0-685-71490-X). Clearwater Pub.
Association of American Library Schools, 1915-1968: An Analytical History. Donald G. Davis, Jr. LC 73-16014. 1974. 15.00 (ISBN 0-8108-0642-8). Scarecrow.
Association of Executive Recruiting Consultants. 2nd ed. Ed. by Jaques Cattell Press. 300p. 1981. 38.50 (ISBN 0-8352-1355-2). Bowker.
Association of Executive Recruiting Consultants. Ed. by Jaques Cattell Press. 256p. 1980. 38.50 (ISBN 0-8352-1256-4). Bowker.
Association System of the European Community. Jacqueline D. Matthews. LC 76-12865. 1977. text ed. 22.95 (ISBN 0-275-23270-0). Praeger.
Association Theory Today: An Essay in Systematic Psychology. E. S. Robinson. 1964. pap. 7.95 o.s.i. (ISBN 0-02-851010-0). Hafner.
Associations & Consultants. Stanley Hyman. 1970. 15.00x o.p. (ISBN 0-8464-0158-4). Beekman Pubs.
Associative Learning: A Cognitive Analysis. James G. Greeno et al. LC 77-17096. (Century Psychology Ser.). (Illus.). 1978. 18.95 (ISBN 0-13-049650-2). P-H.
Associative Memory: A System-Theoretical Approach. T. Kohonen. (Communication & Cybernetics Ser.: Vol. 17). 1977. 27.70 (ISBN 0-387-08017-1). Springer-Verlag.
Assommoir De Zola. J. Dubois. (Collection Themes & Textes Ser.). 224p. (Orig., Fr.). 1973. pap. 6.50 (ISBN 2-03-035018-4, 2647). Larousse.
Asssembly Line. Robert Linhart. Tr. by Margaret Rosland from Fr. Orig. Title: L'Etabli. 144p. (Orig.). 1981. pap. text ed. 6.95x (ISBN 0-87023-322-X). U of Mass Pr.
Assumption & Myth in Physical Theory. H. Bondi. 1967. 10.95 (ISBN 0-521-04282-8). Cambridge U Pr.
Assur 114446: La Famiglia "a". C. Saporetti. Ed. by G. Bucellati. (Cybernetica Mesopotamia Ser.). 139p. 1979. pap. 9.50 soft only (ISBN 0-89003-036-7). Undena Pubns.
Assuring Learning With Self-Instructional Packages, or Up the Up Staircase. Rita B. Johnson & Stuart R. Johnson. 1973. pap. text ed. 9.95 (ISBN 0-201-03327-5). A-W.
Assuring Product Integrity. Eugene R. Carrubba et al. 160p. 1975. 21.95 (ISBN 0-669-00088-4). Lexington Bks.
Assuring Quality Ambulatory Health Care: The Martin Luther King, Jr. Health Center. Ed. by Donald A. Smith & Gitanjali Mukerjee. (Westview Special Studies in Health Care Ser.). 1978. lib. bdg. 24.50x (ISBN 0-89158-409-9). Westview.
Assuring Structural Integrity of Steel Reactor Pressure Vessels. Ed. by L. E. Steele & K. E. Stahlkopf. (Illus.). xii, 220p. 1980. 40.00x (ISBN 0-85334-906-1). Burgess-Intl Ideas.
Assuring the Confidentiality of Social Research Data. Robert F. Boruch & Joe S. Cecil. LC 78-65113. (Illus.). 1979. 19.95x (ISBN 0-8122-7761-9). U of Pa Pr.
Assuring the Legal Rights of Older Citizens. Ed. by Angela O'Rand & Wayne Vasey. (Center for Gerontological Studies & Programs Ser.: Vol.27). Date not set. price not set. U Presses Fla.
Assyrian & Bablyonian Literature. Intro. by Robert F. Harper. 462p. 1980. Repr. of 1904 ed. lib. bdg. 50.00 (ISBN 0-89984-292-5). Century Bookbindery.
Assyrian Dictionary of the Oriental Institute of the University of Chicago. Ed. by A. Leo Oppenheim & Erica Reiner. Incl. Vol. 1, A, Pt. 2. 1976. Repr. of 1968 ed. 42.00x (ISBN 0-918986-07-9); Vol. 3, D. 1977. Repr. of 1959 ed. 17.00x (ISBN 0-918986-09-5); Vol. 4, E. 1974. Repr. of 1958 ed. 31.00x (ISBN 0-918986-10-9); Vol. 7, I-J. 1974. Repr. of 1960 ed. 25.00x (ISBN 0-918986-13-3); Vol. 9, L. 1978. Repr. of 1973 ed. 35.00x (ISBN 0-918986-15-X); Vol. 10, M, Pts 1 & 2. LC 56-58292. 1978. 110.00x (ISBN 0-918986-16-8); Vol. 16, S. 1977. Repr. of 1962 ed. 22.00x (ISBN 0-918986-18-4). LC 56-58292. Oriental Inst.
Assyrian Dictionary of the Oriental Institute of the University of Chicago, 2 pts, Vol. 11, N. Ed. by Erica Reiner et al LC 56-58292. 1981. Pt. 1 & 2. lib. bdg. 110.00x (ISBN 0-918986-17-6). Oriental Inst.
Astaire & Rogers. Suzanne Topper. (Illus.). 1976. pap. 1.50 o.p. (ISBN 0-8439-0380-5, LB380DK, Leisure Bks). Nordon Pubns.
Asterix & Caesar's Gift. Goscinny & Uderzo. Tr. by Anthea Bell & Derek Hockridge. (Illus.). 1979. pap. 4.95 (ISBN 2-205-06920-9, Pub. by Dargaud Canada). C Berke.
Asterix & Cleopatra. Goscinny & Uderzo. Tr. by Anthea Bell & Derek Hockridge. (Illus.). 1979. pap. 4.95 (ISBN 0-340-17220-7, Pub. by Dargaud Canada). C Berke.
Asterix & the Big Fight. Goscinny & Uderzo. Tr. by Anthea Bell & Derek Hockridge. (Illus.). 1979. pap. 4.95 (ISBN 0-340-19167-8, Pub. by Dargaud Canada). C Berke.
Asterix & the Cauldron. Goscinny & Uderzo. Tr. by Anthea Bell & Derek Hockridge. (Illus.). 1979. pap. 4.95 (ISBN 2-205-06912-8, Pub. by Dargaud Canada). C Berke.
Asterix & the Chieftain's Shield. Goscinny & Uderzo. Tr. by Anthea Bell & Derek Hockridge. (Illus.). 1979. pap. 4.95 (ISBN 2-205-06910-1, Pub. by Dargaud Canada). C Berke.
Asterix & the Golden Sickle. Goscinny & Uderzo. Tr. by Anthea Bell & Derek Hockridge. (Illus.). 1979. pap. 4.95 (ISBN 0-685-92306-1, Pub. by Dargaud Canada). C Berke.
Asterix & the Great Crossing. Goscinny & Uderzo. Tr. by Anthea Bell & Derek Hockridge. (Illus.). 1979. pap. 4.95 (ISBN 2-205-06921-7, Pub. by Dargaud Canada). C Berke.
Asterix & the Laurel Wreath. Goscinny & Uderzo. Tr. by Anthea Bell & Derek Hockridge. (Illus.). 1979. pap. 4.95 (ISBN 2-205-06917-9, Pub. by Dargaud Canada). C Berke.
Asterix & the Mansions of the Gods. Goscinny & Uderzo. Tr. by Anthea Bell & Derek Hockridge. (Illus.). 1979. pap. 4.95 (ISBN 2-205-06916-0, Pub. by Dargaud Canada). C Berke.
Asterix & the Normans. Goscinny & Uderzo. Tr. by Anthea Bell & Derek Hockridge. (Illus.). 1979. pap. 4.95 (ISBN 2-205-06908-X, Pub. by Dargaud Canada). C Berke.
Asterix & the Roman Agent. Goscinny & Uderzo. Tr. by Anthea Bell & Derek Hockridge. (Illus.). 1979. pap. 4.95 (ISBN 0-340-19168-6, Pub. by Dargaud Canada). C Berke.
Asterix & the Soothsayer. Goscinny & Uderzo. Tr. by Anthea Bell & Derek Hockridge. (Illus.). 1979. pap. 4.95 (ISBN 2-205-06918-7, Pub. by Dargaud Canada). C Berke.
Asterix at the Olympic Games. Goscinny & Uderzo. Tr. by Anthea Bell & Derek Hockridge. (Illus.). 1979. pap. 4.95 (ISBN 2-205-06911-X, Pub. by Dargaud Canada). C Berke.
Asterix in Britain. Goscinny & Uderzo. Tr. by Anthea Bell & Derek Hockridge. (Illus.). 1979. pap. 4.95 (ISBN 2-205-06907-1, Pub. by Dargaud Canada). C Berke.
Asterix in Spain. Goscinny & Uderzo. Tr. by Anthea Bell & Derek Hockridge. (Illus.). 1979. pap. 4.95 (ISBN 0-340-18326-8, Pub. by Dargaud Canada). C Berke.
Asterix in Switzerland. Goscinny & Uderzo. Tr. by Anthea Bell & Derek Hockridge. (Illus.). 1979. pap. 4.95 (ISBN 2-205-06915-2, Pub. by Dargaud Canada). C Berke.
Asterix the Gaul. Goscinny & Uderzo. Tr. by Anthea Bell & Derek Hockridge. (Illus.). 1979. pap. 4.95 (ISBN 0-340-17210-X, Pub. by Dargaud Canada). C Berke.
Asterix the Gladiator. Goscinny & Uderzo. Tr. by Anthea Bell & Derek Hockridge. (Illus.). 1979. pap. 4.95 (ISBN 0-340-18320-9, Pub. by Dargaud Canada). C Berke.
Asterix the Goths. Goscinny & Uderzo. Tr. by Anthea Bell & Derek Hockridge. (Illus.). 1979. pap. 4.95 (ISBN 2-205-06902-0, Pub. by Dargaud Canada). C Berke.
Asterix the Legionary. Goscinny & Uderzo. Tr. by Anthea Bell & Derek Hockridge. (Illus.). 1979. pap. 4.95 (ISBN 0-340-18321-7, Pub. by Dargaud Canada). C Berke.
Asteroids. Alan E. Nourse. LC 74-12020. (Illus.). (gr. 4-8). 1975. PLB 6.45 (ISBN 0-531-00822-3). Watts.
Asteroids, Comets, Meteoric Matter: Proceedings. Ed. by Cornelia Cristescu & W. J. Klepczynski. (Illus.). 333p. 1975. text ed. 50.00x (ISBN 0-87936-008-9). Scholium Intl.
Asthma. Ed. by T. J. Clark & S. Godfrey. LC 76-57835. (Illus.). 1977. text ed. 24.00 (ISBN 0-7216-2596-7). Saunders.
Asthma. Ed. by H. Herzog. (Progress in Respiration Research Ser.: Vol. 14). (Illus.). x, 314p. 1980. pap. 54.00 (ISBN 3-8055-0991-X). S Karger.
Asthma - Discussions in Patient Management. Henry M. Williams, Jr. & Chang Shim. 1976. spiral bdg. 8.00 o.p. (ISBN 0-87488-876-X). Med Exam.

Asthma & Hay Fever. Oscar Swineford, Jr. (Amer. Lec. Allergy & Immunology Ser.). (Illus.). 508p. 1971. 26.75 (ISBN 0-398-02390-5). C C Thomas.

Asthma & Hay Fever & Other Allergic Diseases for Victims & Their Families. Oscar Swineford, Jr. (Illus.). 186p. 1973. pap. 18.75 photocopy ed. (ISBN 0-398-02767-6). C C Thomas.

Asthma, Hay Fever & Other Allergies. Allan Knight. LC 80-22839. (Positive Health Guides Ser.). (Illus.). 112p. 1981. 9.95 (ISBN 0-668-04675-9); pap. 5.95 (ISBN 0-668-04681-3). Arco.

Asthma Is Curable. Jacob J. Robbins. 1965. 6.00 o.p. (ISBN 0-682-43045-5, University). Exposition.

Asthma-Physiology, Immunopharmacology & Treatment. Ed. by L. M. Lichtenstein & K. F. Austen. 1974. 37.00 (ISBN 0-12-068450-0). Acad Pr.

Asthma: Physiology, Immunopharmacology & Treatment, Vol. 2. Ed. by L. M. Lichtenstein et al. 1977. 37.00 (ISBN 0-12-448502-2). Acad Pr.

Astonish Us in the Morning: Tyrone Guthrie Remembered. Alfred Rossi. 1981. 13.95 (ISBN 0-8143-1669-7); pap. 5.95 (ISBN 0-8143-1670-0). Wayne St U Pr.

Astonished Man. Blaise Cendrars. LC 80-9056. 260p. 1981. 12.95 (ISBN 0-8128-2814-3). Stein & Day.

Astonished Muse. rev. ed. Reuel Denney. LC 57-6985. (Midway Reprint Ser). xx, 282p. 1975. pap. text ed. 9.00x o.s.i. (ISBN 0-226-14303-1). U of Chicago Pr.

Astor Family: A Unique Exploration of One of America's First Families. John D. Gates. LC 79-6580. 288p. 1981. 12.95 (ISBN 0-385-14909-3). Doubleday.

Astounding Science Fiction, July, Nineteen Thirty-Nine. Ed. by Martin H. Greenberg. 184p. 1981. Repr. of 1939 ed. write for info. (ISBN 0-8093-0991-2). S Ill U Pr.

Astra, No. 59. Grace L. Hill. 240p. 1980. pap. 1.95 (ISBN 0-553-13819-7). Bantam.

Astral Plane. Charles W. Leadbeater. 1973. 3.75 (ISBN 0-8356-7093-7). Theos Pub Hse.

Astro-Psychology. Karen Zondag-Hamaker. 1980. pap. 7.95 (ISBN 0-87728-465-2). Weiser.

Astrodynamics, 1975. new ed. Ed. by William F. Powers & Herbert E. Rauch. LC 57-43769. (Advances in the Astronautical Science Ser: Vol. 33). (Illus.). 1976. lib. bdg. 35.00x (ISBN 0-87703-079-0); microfiche supplement 35.00 (ISBN 0-87703-142-8). Am Astronaut.

Astrodynamics, 1979, 2 pts. Ed. by P. A. Penzo et al. (Advances in the Astronautical Sciences Ser.: Vol. 40). 1980. lib. bdg. 45.00 ea. Pt. 1 (ISBN 0-87703-107-X). Pt. 2 (ISBN 0-87703-109-6). Pt. 1. pap. 35.00 ea. (ISBN 0-87703-108-8). Pt. 2 (ISBN 0-87703-110-X). fiche suppl. 20.00 (ISBN 0-87703-139-8). Univelt Inc.

Astrologer in the Underground. Andrzej Busza. Tr. by Jagna Boraks & Micheal Bullock. LC 70-108331. 61p. 1970. 6.95 (ISBN 0-8214-0073-8). Ohio U Pr.

Astrologer's Handbook. Frances Sakoian & Louis S. Acker. LC 78-160647. (Illus.). 480p. (YA) 1973. 13.95 (ISBN 0-06-013734-7, HarpT). Har-Row.

Astrologer's Note Book. Donna Van Toen. 128p. 1981. pap. 6.95 (ISBN 0-87728-521-7). Weiser.

Astrologia: Que Dice la Biblia? I. D. Thomas et al. Tr. by Jose Luis Martinez Diaz from Eng. (Coleccion Doctrinas Modernas Ser.: No. 7). Orig. Title: Astrology & the Bible. 1980. pap. 0.55 (ISBN 0-311-05031-X, Edit Mundo). Casa Bautista.

Astrological Aspects. Leyla Rael & Dane Rudhyar. 1980. pap. 9.95 (ISBN 0-88231-112-3). ASI Pubs Inc.

Astrological Books in Print, 1981-82. Para Research, Inc. 144p. (Orig.). 1981. pap. 4.95 (ISBN 0-686-69331-0). Para Res.

Astrological Guide to Self-Awareness. Donna Cunningham. LC 78-57820. 1978. pap. 5.95 (ISBN 0-916360-09-1). CRCS Pubns NV.

Astrological Houses: The Spectrum of Individual Experience. Dane Rudhyar. LC 74-180105. pap. 3.95 (ISBN 0-385-03827-5). Doubleday.

Astrological Insights into Personality. Betty Lundsted. 384p. (Orig.). 1980. pap. 9.95 (ISBN 0-917086-22-8, Pub. by Astro Computing Serv.). Para Res.

Astrological Keys to Self Realization & Self Actualization. Clara Weiss. 1980. pap. 4.95 (ISBN 0-87728-509-8). Weiser.

Astrological Self-Publishing. Ed. by C. J. Puotinen. 1977. pap. 5.95 o.p. (ISBN 0-930840-04-6). Ninth Sign.

Astrology. Christopher McIntosh. 128p. 1973. pap. 1.25 o.p. (ISBN 0-06-087041-9, HW). Har-Row.

Astrology: An Illustrated Manual for Teachers & Students. Pat Bemis. 1978. pap. 6.00 (ISBN 0-686-68269-6). Macoy Pub.

Astrology & Alcoholism: Genetic Key to the Horoscope. Ann E. Parker. 1981. pap. 7.95 (ISBN 0-87728-519-5). Weiser.

Astrology & Biochemistry. Vanda Sawtell. 1980. lib. bdg. 15.95 (ISBN 0-85032-174-3, Pub. by Daniel Co England). State Mutual Bk.

Astrology & Foretelling the Future: A Concise Guide. Thomas Aylesworth. LC 72-8797. (Illus.). 96p. (gr. 5 up). 1973. PLB 4.90 o.p. (ISBN 0-531-02606-X). Watts.

Astrology & Its Practical Application. Else Parker. LC 80-20026. 202p. 1980. Repr. of 1977 ed. lib. bdg. 11.95x (ISBN 0-89370-639-6). Borgo Pr.

Astrology & Sexual Analysis. Morris C. Goodman. 1973. pap. 1.95 o.s.i. (ISBN 0-446-89501-6). Warner Bks.

Astrology & the Edgar Cayce Readings. rev. ed. Margaret H. Gammon. 1973. pap. 2.95 (ISBN 0-87604-067-9). ARE Pr.

Astrology & the Modern Psyche: An Astrologer Looks at Depth Psychology. Dane Rudhyar. LC 76-21583. 1976. pap. 5.95 (ISBN 0-916360-05-9). CRCS Pubns NV.

Astrology & the Tarot. A. E. Thierens. LC 80-53344. 159p. 1980. Repr. of 1975 ed. lib. bdg. 10.95x (ISBN 0-89370-631-0). Borgo Pr.

Astrology for All. Alan Leo. (Astrologer's Library). 1979. pap. 6.95 (ISBN 0-89281-175-7). Inner Tradit.

Astrology for All. Bhawani Mishra. (Illus.). 200p. (Orig.). 1974. pap. 2.95 (ISBN 0-88253-299-5). Ind-US Inc.

Astrology for & About Young People. Sue Ann. LC 80-65881. (Illus.). 177p. 1980. pap. 9.95 perfect bdg. (ISBN 0-9604172-0-6). Sue Ann.

Astrology for Dogs (& Owners) William Fairchild. (Illus.). 95p. 1981. 8.95 (ISBN 0-241-10380-0, Pub. by Hamish Hamilton England). David & Charles.

Astrology for Everyone. rev. ed. Edward Lyndoe. (Illus.). 1970. 7.95 o.p. (ISBN 0-525-05919-9). Dutton.

Astrology for the Working Girl. McKenzie-Paige. 1980. pap. 1.75 (ISBN 0-505-51467-2). Tower Bks.

Astrology Game. Malcolm Dean. 256p. 1981. 11.95 (ISBN 0-8253-0002-9). Beaufort Bks NY.

Astrology Guide to Your Sex Life. Vivian E. Robson. LC 67-16883. (Illus., Orig.). 1963. pap. 0.95 (ISBN 0-668-01628-0). Arc Bks.

Astrology: How & Why It Works. Marc E. Jones. LC 76-84580. 1974. 13.50 o.p. (ISBN 0-87878-005-X, Sabian). Great Eastern.

Astrology Inside Out. Bruce E. Nevin. (Illus.). 288p. (Orig.). 1981. pap. 9.95 (ISBN 0-914918-19-2). Para Res.

Astrology: Its Techniques & Ethics. C. Aq Libra. LC 80-23764. 259p. 1980. Repr. of 1976 ed. lib. bdg. 10.95x (ISBN 0-89370-635-3). Borgo Pr.

Astrology, Karma & Transformation: The Inner Dimensions of the Birthchart. Stephen Arroyo. LC 76-21588. (Illus.). 1978. 10.95 (ISBN 0-916360-04-0); pap. 7.95 (ISBN 0-916360-03-2). CRCS Pubns NV.

Astrology Love Book. Ann Mathers. 1969. pap. 1.50 (ISBN 0-451-08908-1, W8908, Sig). NAL.

Astrology, Mysticism & the Occult: A Critical Bibliography of Debunking Books & Articles. Laird M. Wilcox. 1980. pap. 9.95 (ISBN 0-933592-09-4). Edit Res Serv.

Astrology of Relationship: A Humanistic Approach to the Practice of Synastry. Michael R. Meyer. LC 75-44528. 280p. 1976. pap. 3.95 (ISBN 0-385-11556-3, Anch). Doubleday.

Astrology of Sexuality. Martin Schulman. 1981. pap. 7.95 (ISBN 0-87728-481-4). Weiser.

Astrology, Psychology & the Four Elements. Stephen Arroyo. LC 75-27828. 208p. (Orig.). 1975. 9.95 (ISBN 0-916360-02-4); pap. 6.95 (ISBN 0-916360-01-6). CRCS Pubns NV.

Astrology: Sense or Nonsense? Roy A. Gallant. LC 73-15340. (Illus.). 256p. (gr. 7-9). 1974. PLB 6.95 (ISBN 0-385-08673-3). Doubleday.

Astrology-the Cosmic Stradivarius. Lew P. Price. LC 51-6501. 1974. pap. 12.00 (ISBN 0-685-46895-X). Eternal Ent.

Astrology, the Divine Science. rev. ed. Marcia Moore & Mark Douglas. LC 77-82609. (Illus.). 1978. 20.00 (ISBN 0-912240-04-0). Arcane Pubns.

Astrology, Wisdom of the Stars. Larry Kettelkamp. (Illus.). 128p. (gr. 5-9). 1973. PLB 7.44 (ISBN 0-688-30085-5). Morrow.

Astrology: Your Personal Sun Sign Guide. Beatrice Ryder. 1970. pap. 1.25 o.s.i. (ISBN 0-446-76700-X). Warner Bks.

Astronauta y la Lumbrera De la Noche. James B. Irwin, Jr. & W. A. Emerson. Date not set. Repr. of 1978 ed. 3.75 (ISBN 0-311-01066-0). Casa Bautista.

Astronautics for Peace & Human Progress: Proceedings. International Astronautical Congress, 29th, Dubrovnik, 1-8 October 1978. Ed. by L. G. Napolitano. LC 79-40049. (Illus.). 1979. 82.00 (ISBN 0-685-97183-X). Pergamon.

Astronomical Calendar: 1981. Guy Ottewell. (Illus.). 1980. pap. 8.00 (ISBN 0-934546-04-5). Astron Cal.

Astronomical Companion. Guy Ottewell. (Illus.). 1979. pap. 12.00 (ISBN 0-934546-01-0). Astron Cal.

Astronomical Description of the Late Comet from the 18. of Novemb. 1618 to the 16. of December Following. John Bainbridge. LC 74-28828. (English Experience Ser.: No. 710). 1975. Repr. of 1619 ed. 6.00 (ISBN 90-221-0710-8). Walter J Johnson.

Astronomical Telescope. B. V. Barlow & A. S. Everest. (Wykeham Science Ser.: No. 31). 1975. 9.95x (ISBN 0-8448-1158-0). Crane Russak Co.

Astronomy. Frank N. Bash. (Illus.). 1977. pap. 16.95 (ISBN 0-06-043853-3, HarpC). Har-Row.

Astronomy. Boy Scouts Of America. LC 19-600. (Illus.). 80p. (gr. 6-12). 1971. pap. 0.70x (ISBN 0-8395-3303-9, 3303). BSA.

Astronomy. Roger B. Culver. (Illus.). 1979. pap. 4.95 (ISBN 0-06-460158-7, CO 158, COS). Har-Row.

Astronomy. Dinah L. Moche. LC 77-27367. (Self-Teaching Guides Ser.). 1978. pap. text ed. 7.95 (ISBN 0-471-01764-7). Wiley.

Astronomy. new ed. L. W. Page. (Orig.). (gr. 7-12). 1973. pap. text ed. 6.44 (ISBN 0-201-05651-8, Sch Div); tchr's manual 2.84 (ISBN 0-201-05652-6). A-W.

Astronomy, 2 vols. Royal Institution Library of Science. LC 75-132808. 1970. Set. 45.95 (ISBN 0-470-74388-3). Halsted Pr.

Astronomy. Walter A. Thurber et al. (Exploring Earth Science Program Ser.). (gr. 7-12). 1976. pap. text ed. 4.96 (ISBN 0-205-04743-2, 6947433). Allyn.

Astronomy & Astrophysics Abstracts: Literature 1979, Pt. 2, Vol. 26. Ed. by S. Boehme et al. 794p. 1980. 69.70 (ISBN 0-387-10134-9). Springer-Verlag.

Astronomy & Astrophysics Abstracts, Vol. 27: Literature 1980, Pt. 1. Ed. by S Boehme et al. 939p. 1981. 69.70 (ISBN 0-387-10479-8). Springer-Verlag.

Astronomy & Cosmology: A Modern Course. Fred Hoyle. LC 74-28441. (Illus.). 1975. text ed. 24.95x (ISBN 0-7167-0351-3). W H Freeman.

Astronomy & Space Exploration. Russell K. Rickert. 1974. text ed. 9.50 (ISBN 0-201-06431-6). A-W.

Astronomy Data Book. 2nd ed. J. Hedley Robinson & James Muirden. LC 78-21698. 1979. 14.95 (ISBN 0-470-26594-9). Halsted Pr.

Astronomy Data Book. new ed. J. Hedley Robinson & James Muirden. (Illus.). 1979. 21.50 (ISBN 0-7153-7743-4). David & Charles.

Astronomy: Fundamentals & Frontiers. 3rd ed. Robert Jastrow & Malcolm H. Thompson. LC 76-46622. 1977. text ed. 22.95x (ISBN 0-471-01845-7); tchr's manual avail. (ISBN 0-471-02728-6); study guide 8.95 (ISBN 0-471-03035-X). Wiley.

Astronomy: How Man Learned About the Universe. L. W. Page. (gr. 9-12). 1969. pap. 6.95 (ISBN 0-201-05650-X). A-W.

Astronomy Illustrated. 3rd ed. Ed. by B. Lee Bonneau & Billy A. Smith. 1980. pap. text ed. 13.95 (ISBN 0-8403-2168-6). Kendall-Hunt.

Astronomy in China. Commission on International Relations. 1979. pap. 6.25 (ISBN 0-309-02867-1). Natl Acad Pr.

Astronomy Made Simple. rev. ed. Meir H. Degani. LC 76-2836. 224p. 1976. pap. 3.95 (ISBN 0-385-08854-X). Doubleday.

Astronomy: Principles & Practice. A. E. Roy & D. Clarke. LC 76-51875. 1977. 34.50x (ISBN 0-8448-1071-1); pap. 19.50x (ISBN 0-8448-1073-8). Crane-Russak Co.

Astronomy: The Cosmic Journey. William K. Hartmann. 1978. text ed. 21.95x (ISBN 0-534-00546-2); study guide 1979 7.95x (ISBN 0-534-00711-2). Wadsworth Pub.

Astronomy: The Structure of the Universe. Archie E. Roy & David Clarke. LC 76-51877. 1977. 24.50x. Crane-Russak Co.

Astronomy with Binoculars. James Muirden. LC 77-11568. (Illus.). 1979. 9.95 (ISBN 0-690-01723-5, TYC-T). T Y Crowell.

Astrophysical Concepts. Martin Harwit. LC 73-3135. 561p. 1973. text ed. 28.95 (ISBN 0-471-35820-7). Wiley.

Astrophysical Formulae: A Compendium for the Physicist & Astrophysicist. K. R. Lang. LC 73-20809. 800p. 1974. 95.20 o.p. (ISBN 0-387-06605-5). Springer-Verlag.

Astrophysical Formulae: A Compendium for the Physicist & Astrophysicist. K. R. Lang. (Springer Study Edition). (Illus.). 1979. pap. 31.00 o.p. (ISBN 0-387-09064-9). Springer-Verlag.

Astrophysical Formulae: A Compendium for the Physicist & Astrophysicist. K. R. Lang. (Illus.). 735p. 1980. pap. 49.50 (ISBN 0-387-09933-6). Springer-Verlag.

Astrophysical Quantities. 3rd ed. C. W. Allen. (Illus.). 320p. 1973. text ed. 37.50x (ISBN 0-485-11150-0, Athlone Pr). Humanities.

Astrophysics. William K. Rose. LC 72-89470. 1973. 24.50x (ISBN 0-03-079155-3); pap. text ed. 12.50x (ISBN 0-89197-667-1). Irvington.

Astrophysics & Stellar Astronomy. Thomas L. Swihart. LC 73-603. (Space Science Text Ser.). 1968. 20.95 (ISBN 0-471-83990-6, Pub. by Wiley-Interscience). Wiley.

Astrophysics of Gaseous Nebulae. Donald E. Osterbrock. LC 74-11264. (Astronomy & Astrophysics Ser.). (Illus.). 1974. text ed. 29.95x (ISBN 0-7167-0348-3). W H Freeman.

Astrorhythms. Mary Orser et al. LC 78-22160. (Orig.). 1979. pap. 4.95 (ISBN 0-06-090632-4, CN 632, CN). Har-Row.

Asundered: Biblical Teachings on Divorce & Remarriage. Robert Kysar & Myrna Kaysar. LC 77-79591. 1978. 6.95 (ISBN 0-8042-1096-9). John Knox.

Asya Vamasya Hymn (The Riddle of the Universe) Tr. by C. Kunhan Raja from Sanskrit. 6.50 (ISBN 0-89744-120-6, Pub. by Ganesh & Co. India). Auromere.

Asylum. Aidan Higgins. 1980. 12.95 (ISBN 0-7145-0229-4); pap. 5.95 (ISBN 0-7145-0230-8). Riverrun NY.

Asylum Picnic. Robert Matte, Jr. Ed. by Kirk Robertson. LC 77-73205. 1980. pap. 3.00 (ISBN 0-916918-07-6). Duck Down.

Asylum Piece. Anna Kavan. LC 79-28536. 1980. Repr. 11.95 (ISBN 0-935576-02-9). Unity Pr.

Asylum World. John Jakes. 1969. pap. 1.95 o.s.i. (ISBN 0-446-89720-5). Warner Bks.

Asylums: Essays on the Social Situation of Mental Patients & Other Inmates. Erving Goffman. LC 61-13812. 1961. 22.95x o.p. (ISBN 0-202-30000-5). Aldine Pub.

Asylums: Essays on the Social Situation of Mental Patients & Other Inmates. Erving Goffman. LC 61-13812. pap. 4.50 (ISBN 0-385-00016-2, A277, Anch). Doubleday.

Asymmetrical Function of the Brain. Ed. by M. Kinsbourne. LC 77-8633. (Illus.). 1978. 39.50 (ISBN 0-521-21481-5). Cambridge U Pr.

Asymmetries 1-260. Mac Low. pap. write for info. (ISBN 0-914162-38-1). Knowles.

Asymptotic Analysis. J. D. Murray. Orig. Title: Introduction to Asymptotic Analysis. 160p. 1974. 17.95x (ISBN 0-19-853153-2). Oxford U Pr.

Asymptotic Expansions. Edward T. Copson. (Cambridge Tracts in Mathematics & Mathematical Physics). 1965. 21.50 (ISBN 0-521-04721-8). Cambridge U Pr.

Asymptotic Theory of Extreme Order Statistics. Janos Galambos. LC 78-1916. (Series in Probability & Mathematical Staistics: Applied Probability & Statistics). 1978. 33.50 (ISBN 0-471-02148-2, Pub. by Wiley-Interscience). Wiley.

At a Foreign University: An International Study of Adaptation & Coping. Otto Klineberg & W. Frank Hull, IV. 22.95 (ISBN 0-03-052486-5). Praeger.

At a Journal Workshop: The Basic Text & Guide for Using the Intensive Journal. Ira Progoff. LC 75-13932. 1975. 12.50 (ISBN 0-87941-003-5); pap. 6.95, 1977 (ISBN 0-87941-006-X). Dialogue Hse.

At Button's. Garry Wills. 1979. 8.95 o.p. (ISBN 0-8362-6108-9). Andrews & McMeel.

At Camp Kee Tov: Ethics for Jewish Juniors. Helen Fine. (Illus.). text ed. 5.00 (ISBN 0-8074-0128-5, 121711). UAHC.

At Every Turn! It's Ballet. D. Sorine. LC 80-19232. (Illus.). 49p. (ps-3). 1981. 8.95 (ISBN 0-394-84473-4); pap. 1.95 (ISBN 0-394-94473-9). Knopf.

At High Risk. Palma Harcourt. LC 77-91361. 1978. 7.95 o.s.i. (ISBN 0-8027-5382-5). Walker & Co.

At Highest Risk: Protecting Children from Environmental Pollution. Christopher Norwood. 1981. pap. 4.95 (ISBN 0-14-005830-3). Penguin.

At Home. Naomi May. 1980. pap. 4.95. Riverrun NY.

At Home. new ed. William D. Sheldon et al. (preprimer 1). 1973. pap. text ed. 3.92 (ISBN 0-205-03515-9, 5235154). Allyn.

At Home: A Visit in Four Languages. Esther Hautzig. LC 68-23063. (Illus., Eng, Fr, Span & Rus.). (gr. k-2). 1968. 8.95 (ISBN 0-02-743470-2). Macmillan.

At Home in the Wild. Frances Wood & Dorothy Wood. LC 76-534619. (gr. 6-9). 1977. 5.95 (ISBN 0-396-07429-4). Dodd.

At Home in the World. Patricia K. Helman. 120p. (Orig.). 1980. pap. 4.95 (ISBN 0-87178-065-8). Brethren.
At Home in the World: Views & Reviews. Sam Hamill. 125p. 1981. 15.00 (ISBN 0-918116-23-6); pap. 6.00 (ISBN 0-918116-22-8). Jawbone Pr.
At Home with Alternative Energy: A Comprehensive Guide to Creating Your Own Systems. Michael Hackleman. LC 79-48056. (Illus.). 152p. (Orig.). 1980. pap. 8.95 (ISBN 0-915238-38-1). Peace Pr.
At Home with Japanese Cooking. Elizabeth Andoh. LC 79-3501. (Illus.). 228p. 1980. 15.00 (ISBN 0-394-41219-2). Knopf.
At Home with Science. O. F. Kilgour. 1976. pap. text ed. 5.95x o.p. (ISBN 0-435-42231-6). Heinemann Ed.
At Home with Sex. Rex Johnson. 1979. pap. 3.95 (ISBN 0-88207-639-6). Victor Bks.
At Lady Molly's. Anthony Powell. (A Dance to the Music of Time: Vol. 2). 1976. pap. 2.50 (ISBN 0-445-08446-4). Popular Lib.
At Last to the Ocean: The Story of the Endless Cycle of Water. Joel Rothman. LC 70-129753. (Illus.). (gr. k-3). 1971. 7.95 (ISBN 0-02-777800-2, CCPr). Macmillan.
At Least I'm Getting Better: Poems for Kids & Other People. Judi Lalli. (Orig.). 1981. pap. 4.95t (ISBN 0-915166-49-6). Impact Pubs CA.
At Mary Bloom's. Aliki. LC 75-45482. (Illus.). 32p. (gr. k-3). 1976. PLB 7.92 (ISBN 0-688-84048-5). Greenwillow.
At Odds: Women & the Family in America from the Revolution to the Present. Carl N. Degler. 544p. 1981. pap. 8.95 (ISBN 0-19-502934-8, GB 645, GB). Oxford U Pr.
At Passion's Tide. Pamela Windsor. 240p. (Orig.). 1980. pap. 2.25 (ISBN 0-515-05639-1). Jove Pubns.
At Summer's End: Southpoems. Percival A. Miller. 66p. 1980. pap. 4.95 (ISBN 0-8059-2739-5). Dorrance.
At the Back of the North Wind. George MacDonald. (Illus.). (gr. 4-6). 1964. 4.95g o.s.i. (ISBN 0-02-761540-5). Macmillan.
At the Back of the North Wind. George MacDonald. (Childrens Illustrated Classics Ser). (Illus.). 1973. Repr. of 1956 ed. 9.00x o.p. (ISBN 0-460-05036-2, Pub. by J. M. Dent England). Biblio Dist.
At the Back of the North Wind. George MacDonald. LC 75-32174. (Classics of Children's Literature, 1621-1932: Vol. 37). (Illus.). 1976. Repr. of 1871 ed. PLB 38.00 (ISBN 0-8240-2286-6). Garland Pub.
At the Battle of Jericho! Ho! Ho! Norman Habel. LC 56-1219. (Purple Puzzle Tree Bk). (Illus.). (ps-5). 1971. pap. 0.85 (ISBN 0-570-06515-1). Concordia.
At the Beach. Eugene Booth. LC 77-7659. (Raintree Spotlight Book). (Illus.). (gr. k-3). 1977. PLB 8.25 (ISBN 0-8393-0111-1). Raintree Child.
At the Center of the World. Betty Baker. LC 72-88820. (Illus.). 64p. (gr. 3-6). 1973. PLB 4.95g o.s.i. (ISBN 0-02-708290-3). Macmillan.
At the Circus. Eugene Booth. LC 77-7946. (Raintree Spotlight Book). (Illus.). (gr. k-3). 1977. PLB 8.25 (ISBN 0-8393-0112-X). Raintree Child.
At the Cross. Charles Ludwig. 1975. pap. 1.25 (ISBN 0-515-03578-5). Jove Pubns.
At the Crossroads. Daniel E. Lewis. 64p. 1980. 6.50 (ISBN 0-682-49631-6). Exposition.
At the Crossroads of Knowledge. V. Axel Firsoff. 146p. 8.95 (ISBN 0-86025-812-2). Ross-Erikson.
At the Earth's Core: Pellucidar, Tamar of Pelluicidar. Edgar R. Burroughs. (Illus.). 9.00 (ISBN 0-8446-1778-4). Peter Smith.
At the Edge of History: Speculations on the Transformation of Culture. William I. Thompson. LC 70-138769. (Illus.). 1971. 9.95 o.s.i. (ISBN 0-06-014316-9, HarpT). Har-Row.
At the Edge of Psychology: Essays on Politics & Culture. Ashis Nandy. 152p. 1981. 9.95 (ISBN 0-19-561205-1). Oxford U Pr.
At the Fair. Eugene Booth. LC 77-7961. (Raintree Spotlight Book). (Illus.). (gr. k-3). 1977. PLB 8.25 (ISBN 0-8393-0114-6). Raintree Child.
At the Fallow's Edge. Astrid Ivask. Tr. by Inara Cedrins. LC 79-114869. (Inklings Ser.: No. 3). (Latvian & Eng.). Date not set. 5.00 (ISBN 0-930012-33-X). Mudborn. Postponed.
At the Feet of the Master. Alcyone. 1970. pap. 1.95 (ISBN 0-8356-0196-X, Quest). Theos Pub Hse.
At the Front Door of the Atlantic. Anthony Kerrigan. 1969. 6.95 o.p. (ISBN 0-85105-008-5). Dufour.
At the Going Down of the Sun: Hong Kong & South East Asia, 1914-45. Oliver Lindsay. (Illus.). 250p. 1981. 25.00 (ISBN 0-241-10542-0, Pub. by Hamish Hamilton England). David & Charles.
At the Heart of the Whirlwind. John P. Adams. LC 75-9343. 160p. 1976. 6.95 o.p. (ISBN 0-06-060080-2, HarpR). Har-Row.
At the Homeopath's. Margaret Chatterjee. (Writers Workshop Greenbird Ser.). 87p. 1975. 12.00 (ISBN 0-88253-504-8); pap. text ed. 5.00 (ISBN 0-88253-503-X). Ind-US Inc.
At the Hour of Death. Karlis Osis & Erlendur Haraldsson. 1980. pap. 3.95 (ISBN 0-686-69250-0, 49486, Discus). Avon.
At the Last Moment. J. C. Layman. LC 78-63646. 1979. 6.95 (ISBN 0-533-03994-0). Vantage.
At the Mind's Limits: Contemplations by a Survivor on Auschwitz & Its Realities. Jean Amery. Tr. by Sidney Rosenfeld & Stella P. Rosenfeld. LC 80-7682. 160p. 1980. 12.50 (ISBN 0-253-17724-3). Ind U Pr.
At the Mouth of the Luckiest River. Arnold Griese. LC 72-7548. (Illus.). 80p. (gr. 2-5). 1973. 8.95 o.p. (ISBN 0-690-10786-2, TYC-J); PLB 8.79 (ISBN 0-690-10787-0). T Y Crowell.
At the Piano with Faure. Marguerite Long. LC 79-63623. (Illus.). 1981. 11.75 (ISBN 0-8008-0505-4, Crescendo). Taplinger.
At the Pleasure of the Board. Joseph F. Kauffman. 132p. 1980. 15.00 (ISBN 0-8268-1440-9). ACE.
At the Pleasure of the Mayor. Theodore J. Lowi. LC 64-11216. 1964. 12.95 (ISBN 0-02-919420-2). Free Pr.
At the Point of Production: The Local History of the I.W.W. Ed. by Joseph R. Conlin. LC 80-1708. (Contributions in Labor History Ser.: No. 10). 328p. 1981. lib. bdg. 29.95 (ISBN 0-313-22046-8, CPP/). Greenwood.
At the Red Summit: Interpreter Behind the Iron Curtain. Erwin Weit. 256p. 1973. 6.95 o.s.i. (ISBN 0-02-625780-7). Macmillan.
At the Seven Stars. John Beatty & Patricia Beatty. (Illus.). (gr. 7-10). 1967. 4.95g o.s.i. (ISBN 0-02-708550-3). Macmillan.
At the Sign of the Barber's Pole. William Andrews. LC 74-77164. 1969. Repr. of 1904 ed. 15.00 (ISBN 0-8103-3846-7). Gale.
At the Temple Church. H. G. Woods. (Scholar As Preacher Ser.). 252p. Repr. of 1911 ed. 7.75 (ISBN 0-567-04406-8). Attic Pr.
At the White House: Assignments to Six Presidents. Robert C. Pierpoint. (Illus.). 192p. 1981. 10.95 (ISBN 0-399-12281-8). Putnam.
At the Zoo. Eugene Booth. LC 77-7627. (Raintree Spotlight Book). (Illus.). (gr. k-3). 1977. PLB 8.25 (ISBN 0-8393-0107-3). Raintree Child.
At Willy Tucker's Place. Alison Morgan. LC 76-41183. (Illus.). (gr. 4-12). 1976. 5.95 o.p. (ISBN 0-525-66515-3). Elsevier-Nelson.
At Wit's End. Erma Bombeck. 1979. pap. 2.25 (ISBN 0-449-23784-2, Crest). Fawcett.
At Wit's End Corner. Garver. (Illus.). pap. 0.50 o.p. (ISBN 0-686-12326-3). Christs Mission.
At Work. Richard Scarry. (Golden Look-Look Ser.). (Illus.). 24p. 1976. limp bdg. 0.95 (ISBN 0-307-11824-X, Golden Pr); PLB 5.38 (ISBN 0-307-61824-2). Western Pub.
ATA Annual Directory. annual 269p. pap. 7.00 (ISBN 0-686-13198-3). Am Theatre Assoc.
Atget's Gardens. William H. Adams. LC 79-7037. (Illus.). 1979. 19.95 o.p. (ISBN 0-385-15319-8); pap. 9.95 o.p. (ISBN 0-385-15320-1). Doubleday.
Athabasca. Alistair MacLean. 1981. lib. bdg. 13.95 (ISBN 0-8161-3147-3, Large Print Bks). G K Hall.
Athabasca. Alistair Maclean. LC 80-1067. 336p. 1980. 11.95 (ISBN 0-385-17204-4). Doubleday.
Athapaskan Adaptations: Hunters & Fishermen of the Subarctic Forests. James W. Van Stone. LC 73-89518. (Worlds of Man Ser.). 176p. 1974. text ed. 11.00x (ISBN 0-88295-610-8); pap. text ed. 5.75x (ISBN 0-88295-611-6). AHM Pub.
Atheism & the Rejection of God: Contemporary Philosophy & "The Brothers Karamazov". Stewart R. Sutherland. 1977. 24.50x (ISBN 0-631-17500-8, Pub. by Basil Blackwell). Biblio Dist.
Atheism in Christianity. E. Bloch. 12.50 (ISBN 0-8164-9102-X). Continuum.
Atheism: The Case Against God. George H. Smith. LC 79-2726. (Skeptic's Bookshelf Ser.). 355p. 1979. pap. 6.95 (ISBN 0-87975-124-X). Prometheus Bks.
Atheist Debater's Handbook: The/Skeptics Bookshelf. B. C. Johnson. 100p. 1981. 15.95 (ISBN 0-87975-152-5); pap. 9.95 (ISBN 0-87975-154-1). Prometheus Bks.
Atheist Primer. Madalyn M. O'Hair. 1980. pap. 3.00. Am Atheist.
Atheist Truth Vs. Religion's Ghosts. Robert G. Ingersoll. 1980. pap. 3.29. Am Atheist.
Atheist's Bertrand Russell. Jon G. Murray. 1980. pap. 3.29 (ISBN 0-911826-14-9). Am Atheist.
Atheist's Values. Richard Robinson. 1975. pap. 12.75x (ISBN 0-631-15970-3, Pub. by Basil Blackwell). Biblio Dist.
Athena's Airs. Zabrina Faire. (Orig.). 1980. pap. 1.75 (ISBN 0-446-94463-7). Warner Bks.
Athene. Karl Kerenyi. Tr. by Murray Stein from Ger. (Orig.). 1978. pap. text ed. 7.00 (ISBN 0-88214-209-7). Spring Pubns.
Athenian Agora, a Short Guide. rev. ed. Homer A. Thompson. (Excavations of the Athenian Agora Picture Bks.: No. 16). (Illus.). 1980. pap. 1.50x (ISBN 0-87661-622-8). Am Sch Athens.
Athenian Black Figure Vases. John Boardman. LC 73-89034. (World of Art Ser.). (Illus.). 253p. 1975. pap. 9.95 (ISBN 0-19-519760-7). Oxford U Pr.
Athenian Odyssey. William Taylor. 4.95 (ISBN 0-89353-025-5). Green Hill.
Athenian Odyssey. William M. Taylor. 1977. 4.95 (ISBN 0-89353-025-5). W M Taylor.
Athenian Red Figure Vases: The Archaic Period, a Handbook. John Boardman. (World of Art Ser.). (Illus.). 1979. pap. 9.95x (ISBN 0-19-520155-8). Oxford U Pr.
Athenian Year. Benjamin D. Meritt. (Sather Classical Lectures: No. 32). 1961. 12.50x o.p. (ISBN 0-520-00851-0). U of Cal Pr.
Athens. W. Davenport. (Great Cities Ser.). (Illus.). 1978. lib. bdg. 14.94 (ISBN 0-686-51001-1). Silver.
Athens. new ed. William Davenport. Ed. by Time-Life Books. (Great Cities Ser.). (Illus.). 1978. 14.95 (ISBN 0-8094-2298-0). Time-Life.
Athens. Gladys Nicol. 1978. 24.00 (ISBN 0-7134-0627-5). David & Charles.
Athens: A Pictorial History. James Reap. Ed. by Donna R. Friedman. (Illus.). 208p. 1981. pap. price not set (ISBN 0-89865-110-7). Donning Co.
Athens & Jerusalem. Lev Shestov. Tr. by Bernard Martin. LC 66-18480. 447p. 1966. 16.00x o.s.i. (ISBN 0-8214-0022-3). Ohio U Pr.
Athens in Decline 404-86 B. C. Claude Mosse. Tr. by Jean Stewart. (Illus.). 1973. 21.50 (ISBN 0-7100-7649-5). Routledge & Kegan.
Athens in the Age of Pericles. Charles A. Robinson, Jr. (Centers of Civilization Ser.: No. 1). (Illus.). 1959. pap. 3.95x (ISBN 0-8061-0935-1). U of Okla Pr.
Athens in the Middle Ages. Kenneth M. Setton. 270p. 1980. 60.00x (ISBN 0-902089-84-6, Pub. by Variorum England). State Mutual Bk.
Athens of the Panhandle: A History of Clarendon College. Ethel Harvey. 10.95 (ISBN 0-685-48816-0). Nortex Pr.
Athens World Conference, 1963: Proceedings. World Peace Through Law Centre. 890p. 1964. 12.50x o.p. (ISBN 0-8002-0674-6). Intl Pubns Serv.
Atherosclerosis Drug Discovery. Ed. by Charles E. Day. LC 76-5395. (Advances in Experimental Medicine & Biology: Vol. 67). 468p. 1976. 42.50 (ISBN 0-306-39067-1, Plenum Pr). Plenum Pub.
Atherosclerosis Reviews, Vol. 1. Ed. by Rodolfo Paoletti & Antonio M. Gotto, Jr. LC 75-14582. 1976. 24.50 (ISBN 0-89004-038-9). Raven.
Atherosclerosis Reviews, Vol. 2. Ed. by Rodolfo Paoletti & Antonio M. Gotto. LC 75-14582. 1977. 25.00 (ISBN 0-89004-061-3). Raven.
Atherosclerosis Reviews, Vol. 3. Ed. by Rodolfo Paoletti & Antonio M. Gotto, Jr. LC 75-14582. 1978. 27.00 (ISBN 0-89004-217-9). Raven.
Atherosclerosis Reviews, Vol. 4. Ed. by Rodolfo Paoletti & Antonio M. Gotto. LC 75-14582. 1978. 28.00 (ISBN 0-89004-218-7). Raven.
Atherosclerosis Reviews, Vol. 5. Ed. by Rodolfo Paoletti & Antonio M. Gotto. LC 75-14582. 1979. text ed. 28.00 (ISBN 0-89004-275-6). Raven.
Atherosclerosis Reviews, Vol. 6. Ed. by Antonio Gotto & Rodolfo Panoletti. LC 75-14582. 1979. text ed. 28.00 (ISBN 0-89004-276-4). Raven.
Athlete: Writings, Drawings, Photographs & Television Sports; an Original Collection of 25 Years of Work. Robert Riger. 1980. 24.95 (ISBN 0-671-24940-1). S&S.
Athlete's Body. Ken Sprague. 1981. 10.95 (ISBN 0-87477-140-4); pap. 7.95 (ISBN 0-87477-151-X). J P Tarcher.
Athlete's Guide to Sports Medicine. Ellington Darden. (Illus.). 1981. 14.95 (ISBN 0-8092-7160-5); pap. 6.95 (ISBN 0-8092-7159-1). Contemp Bks.
Athletes in the School: A Psychological & Sociological Perspective. Ed. by Fred Streit & Donald L. Halsted. 27p. 1977. pap. 8.50 o.p. (ISBN 0-686-00902-9, D-104). Essence Pubns.
Athlete's Kitchen: A Nutrition Guide & Cookbook. Nancy Clark. (Illus.). 276p. 1981. pap. 9.95 (ISBN 0-8436-2212-1). CBI Pub.
Athletic Revolution. Jack Scott. LC 71-155098. 1971. 12.95 (ISBN 0-02-928330-2). Free Pr.
Athletic Trainers Guide: Prevention, Care - Treatment of Sports Injuries to Young Athletes. Michael R. Schiavi. (Illus.). 1981. 11.95 (ISBN 0-87460-317-X). Lion.
Athletic Trainers Guide to Injuries of Young Athletes. Michael Schiari. (Illus.). 224p. 1981. 12.00 (ISBN 0-87460-317-X). Lion.
Athletic Training: A Study & Laboratory Guide. Daniel D. Arnheim & Carl E. Klafs. LC 78-145. 1978. pap. text ed. 9.95 (ISBN 0-8016-0329-3). Mosby.
Athletic Training & Conditioning. rev. ed. O. W. Dayton. (Illus.). 1965. 16.50 (ISBN 0-8260-2555-2). Wiley.
Athletic Training & Physical Fitness: Physiological Principles & Practices of the Conditioning Process. new ed. Jack H. Wilmore. 1977. text ed. 19.95 (ISBN 0-205-05630-X). Allyn.
Athleticism in the Victorian & Edwardian Public School. J. A. Mangan. (Illus.). 336p. Date not set. price not set (ISBN 0-521-23388-7). Cambridge U Pr.
Athletics. Boy Scouts Of America. LC 19-600. (Illus.). 24p. (gr. 6-12). 1964. pap. 0.70x (ISBN 0-8395-3324-1, 3324). BSA.
Athletics for Student & Coach. Ian Ward & Denis Watts. (Illus.). 180p. 1976. 14.00 (ISBN 0-7207-0881-8). Transatlantic.
Athletics: Jumping & Vaulting. Denis Watts. (Pelham Pictorial Sports Instruction Ser.). (Illus.). 1979. 9.95 (ISBN 0-7207-0919-9). Transatlantic.
Athletics, Sports & Games. John Murrell. (Greek & Roman Topics Ser.). 1975. pap. text ed. 3.95x (ISBN 0-04-930006-7). Allen Unwin.
Athletics: Throwing. Howard Payne & Rosemary Payne. (Pelham Pictorial Sports Instruction Ser.). (Illus.). 1979. 9.95 (ISBN 0-7207-0925-3). Transatlantic.
Athletics: Track Events. John LeMasurier & Denis Watts. (Pelham Pictorial Sports Instruction Ser.). (Illus.). 1979. 9.95 (ISBN 0-7207-0970-9). Transatlantic.
Atlanta. Milt Machlin. 1978. pap. 2.50 (ISBN 0-380-43539-X, 43539). Avon.
Atlanta: A City of the Modern South. LC 72-84460. 1942. 45.00 (ISBN 0-403-02200-2). Somerset Pub.
Atlantic Beaches. Jonathan Leonard. LC 72-79775. (American Wilderness Ser). (Illus.). (gr. 6 up). 1972. lib. bdg. 11.97 (ISBN 0-8094-1157-1, Pub. by Time-Life). Silver.
Atlantic Beaches. Jonathan N. Leonard. LC 72-79775. (American Wilderness Ser.). (Illus.). 1972. 12.95 (ISBN 0-8094-1156-3). Time-Life.
Atlantic Community in Crisis: A Redefinition of the Transatlantic Relationship. Ed. by Walter F. Hahn & Robert L. Pflatzgraff, Jr. (Pergamon Policy Studies). 386p. 1979. 42.00 (ISBN 0-08-023003-2). Pergamon.
Atlantic Conference. Intro. by Frank Church. LC 70-150596. 1971. pap. 1.25 o.p. (ISBN 0-913456-82-9). Interbk Inc.
Atlantic Connection. Philip H. Trezise. 200p. 1975. pap. 3.95 (ISBN 0-8157-8527-5). Brookings.
Atlantic Crisis. Robert Kleiman. (Orig.). 1964. pap. 2.95x (ISBN 0-393-09753-6). Norton.
Atlantic Crossing. Melvin Maddocks. Ed. by Time-Life Books. (Seafarers Ser.). (Illus.). 176p. 1981. 14.95 (ISBN 0-8094-2726-5). Time Life.
Atlantic Flyway. Robert Elman. (Illus.). 280p. 1980. 24.95 (ISBN 0-87691-329-X). Winchester Pr.
Atlantic Pact. Halford Hoskins. 5.00 (ISBN 0-8183-0229-1). Pub Aff Pr.
Atlantic Salmon: Its Future. A. E. Went. 272p. 1980. 52.50x (ISBN 0-85238-103-4, Pub. by Fishing News England). State Mutual Bk.
Atlantic Shore. John Hay & P. Farb. (Illus.). 1966. 10.00 o.s.i. (ISBN 0-06-070743-7, HarpT). Har-Row.
Atlantic Slave Trade: A Census. Philip D. Curtin. 1969. 25.00x (ISBN 0-299-05400-4); pap. 8.50x (ISBN 0-299-05404-7). U of Wis Pr.
Atlantis. Helen O'Clery. (Pegasus Books: No. 29). (Illus.). 192p. 1971. 10.50x (ISBN 0-234-77358-8). Intl Pubns Serv.
Atlantis: Antediluvian World. Ignatius Donnelly. LC 80-8340. (Harper's Library of Spiritual Wisdom). (Illus.). 512p. 1981. pap. 6.95 (ISBN 0-06-061960-0, HarpR). Har-Row.
Atlantis Discovered. Lewis Spence. 1973. Repr. of 1924 ed. 18.00 (ISBN 0-685-70656-7). Gale.
Atlantis, Fact or Fiction: From the Edgar Cayce Readings. Edgar E. Cayce. 1962. pap. 1.50 (ISBN 0-87604-018-0). ARE Pr.
Atlantis in Ireland: Round Towers of Ireland. Henry O'Brian. (Illus.). 544p. 1977. pap. 9.50 (ISBN 0-8334-1758-4, Steinerbooks). Multimedia.
Atlantis: The Making of Myth. Phyllis Y. Forsyth. (Illus.). 256p. 1980. 19.50x (ISBN 0-7735-0355-2). McGill-Queens U Pr.
Atlantis: The Missing Continent. David McMullen. LC 77-22138. (Great Unsolved Mysteries Ser.). (Illus.). (gr. 4-5). 1977. PLB 9.65 (ISBN 0-8172-1047-4). Raintree Pubs.
Atlantis to the Latter Days. 3rd ed. H. C. Randall-Stevens. (Illus.). 1966. 12.50 (ISBN 0-685-22167-9). Weiser.
Atlas a Color De Oirugia. Lick F. Rainer. 600p. 1981. pap. text ed. write for info. (ISBN 0-06-315030-1, Pub. by HarlA Mexico). Har-Row.

Atlas & Dissection Guide for Comparative Anatomy: Lab Manual. 3rd ed. Saul Wischnitzer. (Illus.). 1979. pap. 9.95x (ISBN 0-7167-0197-9); individual exercises 0.50 ea. W H Freeman.

Atlas der chirurgischen Schnitt--und Nahttechnik. 2nd ed. J. Zoltan. (Illus.). 176p. 1980. 69.00 (ISBN 3-8055-0439-X). S Karger.

Atlas general Larousse. Harold Fullard & H. C. Darby. Ed. by Georges Reynaud-Dulaurier. (Illus.). 312p. (Fr.). 1973. 85.50 (ISBN 2-03-000922-9, 997). Larousse.

Atlas Historico Westminster De la Biblia. 134p. pap. 14.95 (ISBN 0-311-15030-6). Casa Bautista.

Atlas Linguarum Europae-Ale. Ed. by A. Weijnen. 216p. 1980. text ed. 22.50 (ISBN 90-232-1697-0). Humanities.

Atlas Mundial, No. 9555. rev. ed. American Map Company. (Illus.). (gr. 7-12). 1979. pap. 1.10 (ISBN 0-8416-9555-5). Am Map.

Atlas of Acute Hand Injuries. S. C. Sandzen, Jr. LC 79-21848. (Illus.). 456p. 1980. 95.00 (ISBN 0-88416-030-0, Dist. by McGraw). PSG Pub.

Atlas of Africa. Ed. by Regine Van Chi-Bonnardel. LC 73-17932. 1974. 100.00 (ISBN 0-02-901070-5). Free Pr.

Atlas of African History. Colin McEvedy. (Orig.). 1980. pap. 8.95 (ISBN 0-14-051083-4). Penguin.

Atlas of African Military Strategy. Candler. 102p. Date not set. 29.95 (ISBN 0-02-905750-7). Macmillan.

Atlas of Anatomy & Surgical Approaches in Orthopaedic Surgery, Vol. 1: Upper Extremity. Rodolfo Cosentino. (Illus.). 208p. 1960. 19.75 (ISBN 0-398-00349-1). C C Thomas.

Atlas of Anatomy & Surgical Approaches in Orthopaedic Surgery, Vol. 2: Lower Extremity. Rodolfo Cosentino. (Illus.). 276p. 1973. pap. 24.50 spiral bd. (ISBN 0-398-00350-5). C C Thomas.

Atlas of Ancient Civilizations. Keith Branigan. LC 75-22115. (John Day Bk.). (Illus.). 1976. 12.95 o.s.i. (ISBN 0-381-98284-X, TYC-T). T Y Crowell.

Atlas of Ancient Egypt. John Baines & Jaromir Malek. (Illus.). 240p. 1980. 29.95 (ISBN 0-87196-334-5). Facts on File.

Atlas of Animal Anatomy for Artists. rev. ed. W. Ellenberger et al. Ed. by Lewis S. Brown. Tr. by Helen Weinbaum. (Illus.). 192p. (YA) (gr. 9-12). 1956. pap. 6.00 (ISBN 0-486-20082-5). Dover.

Atlas of Artifacts: Encountered in the Preparation of Microscopic Tissue Sections. Samuel W. Thompson, 2nd & Lee G. Luna. (Illus.). 208p. 1978. 27.75 (ISBN 0-398-03624-1). C C Thomas.

Atlas of Autoimmune Diseases. Sharad Deodhar & Robert M. Nakamura. (Atlas Ser.). 1976. 95.00 (ISBN 0-685-78052-X, 15-A-002-00). Am Soc Clinical.

Atlas of Bedside Procedures. Thomas J. Vander Salm et al. LC 79-65313. 1979. pap. text ed. 18.95 (ISBN 0-316-89605-5). Little.

Atlas of Benthic Shelf Foraminfera of the Southwest Atlantic. Ed. by E. Boltovskoy et al. (Illus.). v, 153p. 1980. lib. bdg. 57.90 (ISBN 90-6193-604-7). Kluwer Boston.

Atlas of Black Dermatology. Theodore Rosen & Sandy Martin. 1981. text ed. price not set (ISBN 0-316-75709-8). Little.

Atlas of Breeding Birds: London. David Montier. 1977. 60.00 (ISBN 0-7134-0876-6, Pub. by Batsford England). David & Charles.

Atlas of Cat Anatomy. 3rd ed. David B. Horsburgh & James P. Heath. (Illus.). 1950. pap. 2.00x o.p. (ISBN 0-8047-0357-4). Stanford U Pr.

Atlas of Children's Surgery. Robert E. Gross. LC 70-108366. (Illus.). 1970. 24.00 (ISBN 0-7216-4287-X). Saunders.

Atlas of Clinical Cytology. Paul L. Cardozo. (Illus.). 1979. text ed. 99.00 (ISBN 0-397-50456-X). Lippincott.

Atlas of Clinical Haematology. 2nd ed. H. Begemann & J. Rastetter. Ed. by L. Heilmeyer. Tr. by H. J. Hirsch from Ger. LC 72-86892. (Illus.). xv, 324p. 1972. 118.50 o.p. (ISBN 0-387-05949-0). Springer-Verlag.

Atlas of Colposcopy. Mestwerdt. Ed. by A. Meier. 1981. text ed. price not set (ISBN 0-7216-6268-4). Saunders.

Atlas of Comparative Embryology: A Laboratory Guide to Invertebrate & Vertebrate Embryos. Victor B. Eichler. LC 77-16023. (Illus.). 1978. pap. text ed. 11.50 (ISBN 0-8016-1492-9). Mosby.

Atlas of Comparative Primate Hematology. H. J. Huser. 1970. 54.00 (ISBN 0-12-362750-8). Acad Pr.

Atlas of Complete Dentures. Gino Passamonti. (Illus.). 140p. 1979. 48.00 (ISBN 0-931386-08-X). Quint Pub Co.

Atlas of Computer Tomography: Volume Two, Abdominal Computer Tomography. A. L. Baert. (Illus.). 210p. 1980. 116.90 (ISBN 0-387-10093-8). Springer-Verlag.

Atlas of Computerized Emission Tomography. Peter J. Ell et al. (Illus.). 288p. 1980. text ed. 115.00x (ISBN 0-443-02228-3). Churchill.

Atlas of Computerized Tomography Scans in Pediatric Neurology. J. T. Jabbour et al. 1977. 36.00 o.p. (ISBN 0-87488-979-0). Med Exam.

Atlas of Deep Mycoses. Karlhanns Salfelder. LC 79-67221. (Illus.). 140p. 1980. text ed. 47.50 (ISBN 0-7216-7898-X). Saunders.

Atlas of Deep Sky Splendors. 4th ed. Hans Vehrenberg. (Illus.). 1978. 39.95 (ISBN 0-933346-03-4). Sky Pub.

Atlas of Dermatology. Gernot Rassner. Ed. by Guinter Kahn. LC 78-5704. (Illus.). 1978. text ed. 27.50 (ISBN 0-8067-1601-0). Urban & S.

Atlas of Descriptive Histology. 3rd ed. Edward J. Reith & Michael H. Ross. 1977. text ed. 17.95 scp (ISBN 0-06-045368-0, HarpC). Har-Row.

Atlas of Detailed Normal Pneumoencephalographic Anatomy. 2nd ed. Giovanni Di Chiro. (Illus.). 360p. 1971. 35.50 (ISBN 0-398-00447-1). C C Thomas.

Atlas of Diagnostic Cytology. Claude Gompel. LC 77-27068. 1978. text ed. 58.95 (ISBN 0-471-02278-0, Pub. by Wiley Medical). Wiley.

Atlas of Diseases of the Oral Mucosa. 3rd ed. Pindborg. LC 78-54520. 1980. 75.00 (ISBN 0-7216-7277-9). Saunders.

Atlas of Ear Surgery. 3rd ed. William H. Saunders et al. LC 79-5235. (Illus.). 1979. text ed. 52.50 (ISBN 0-8016-4318-X). Mosby.

Atlas of Early American History: The Revolutionary Era, 1769-1790. Ed. by Lester Cappon. 1976. 150.00 (ISBN 0-686-53820-X). Newberry.

Atlas of Economic Structure & Policies, Vol. 2. P. S. Florence. LC 68-30840. 1970. 14.50 (ISBN 0-08-013218-9). Pergamon.

Atlas of Electroencephalography in Coma & Cerebral Death: EEG at the Bedside or in the Intensive Care Unit. Ed. by D. R. Bennett et al. LC 74-14470. 254p. 1976. 92.00 (ISBN 0-911216-91-X). Raven.

Atlas of Electron Scanning Microscopy in Microbiology. Zensaku Yoshii et al. (Illus.). 240p. 1976. 55.00 o.p. (ISBN 0-683-09325-8). Williams & Wilkins.

Atlas of Electronic Spectra of Five-Nitrofuran Compounds. J. Eidus et al. 1972. 22.95 (ISBN 0-470-23430-X). Halsted Pr.

Atlas of Endoscopic Retrograde Cholangiopancreatography. Edward T. Stewart et al. LC 77-11169. (Illus.). 1977. text ed. 53.50 (ISBN 0-8016-4803-3). Mosby.

Atlas of Energy Budgets of Plant Leaves. D. M. Gates & U. N. Papian. 1971. 38.00 (ISBN 0-12-277250-4). Acad Pr.

Atlas of External Disease of the Eye: The Crystalline Lens, Vol. 5. David D. Donaldson. LC 66-26959. (Illus.). 1976. 58.50 o.p. (ISBN 0-8016-1428-7). Mosby.

Atlas of External Diseases of the Eye: The Cornea & Sclera, Vol. 3. 2nd ed. David D. Donaldson. LC 79-20605. 1979. text ed. 89.50 (ISBN 0-8016-1434-1). Mosby.

Atlas of Five-Day Normal Sea-Level Pressure Charts for the Northern Hemisphere. James F. Lahey et al. 1958. wired bdg. 50.00x (ISBN 0-299-01663-3). U of Wis Pr.

Atlas of Five Hundred Mb Wind Characteristics for the Northern Hemisphere. James F. Lahey et al. 1958. wired bdg. 50.00x (ISBN 0-299-01703-6). U of Wis Pr.

Atlas of Foot Radiology. Montagne. 1981. price not set (ISBN 0-89352-097-7). Masson Pub.

Atlas of Freshwater Testate Amoebae. C. G. Ogden. (Illus.). 228p. 1980. text ed. 49.50x (ISBN 0-19-858502-0). Oxford U Pr.

Atlas of General Surgery. Ed. by Charles Rob & Rodney Smith. LC 80-41016. (Operative Surgery Ser.). (Illus.). 786p. 1980. text ed. 59.95 (ISBN 0-407-00206-5). Butterworths.

Atlas of Greek World. Peter Levi. 239p. 1981. 29.95 (ISBN 0-87196-448-1). Facts on File.

Atlas of Gross Neuropathology. Robert E. Slemmer. (Illus.). 236p. (Orig.). 1981. 42.50 (ISBN 0-87527-239-8). Green.

Atlas of Human Anatomy. 6th rev. & enl. ed. Franz Frohse et al. LC 61-15471. (Illus.). 180p. 1961. pap. text ed. 9.00x (ISBN 0-06-480289-2). B&N.

Atlas of Human Anatomy. Luis Lopez-Antunez. Tr. by Harry Monsen. LC 69-17808. (Illus.). 1971. 29.00 (ISBN 0-7216-5790-7). Saunders.

Atlas of Human Anatomy. Johannes Sobotta. Ed. by Frank H. Figge & Walter J. Hild. Incl. Vol. 1. Regions, Bones, Ligaments & Muscles. text ed. 39.50 (ISBN 0-8067-1719-X); Vol. 2. Visceral Anatomy (Cardiovascular, Lymphatic, Digestive, Respiratory & Urogenital Systems) text ed. 39.50 (ISBN 0-8067-1729-7); Vol. 3. Central Nervous System, Autonomic Nervous System, Sense Organs & Skin, Peripheral Nerves & Vessels. text ed. 45.00 (ISBN 0-8067-1739-4). (Illus.). 1978. Repr. of 1974 ed. complete set 112.00 (ISBN 0-686-67832-X); Set. 112.00 (ISBN 0-686-67833-8). Urban & S.

Atlas of Human Limb Joints. J. Guyot. (Illus.). 252p. 1981. 146.30 (ISBN 0-387-10380-5). Springer-Verlag.

Atlas of Human Parasitology. Lawrence R. Ash & Thomas C. Orihel. LC 80-25291. (Illus.). 176p. 1980. text ed. 45.00 (ISBN 0-89189-081-5, 16-7-001-00). Am Soc Clinical.

Atlas of Illinois. Ed. by Charles W. Collins. (State Atlas Ser). (Illus.). 1976. lib. bdg. 26.95x o.p. (ISBN 0-89534-003-8). Am Pub Co WI.

Atlas of Improved Surgical Procedures for Common Foot Disorders: Ingrown Toenail & Hammertoe. George C. Wee. (Illus.). 80p. 1972. 8.75 (ISBN 0-398-02498-7). C C Thomas.

Atlas of Infant Behavior, Vol. 2. Arnold Gesell. (Illus.). 1934. 125.00x (ISBN 0-685-69821-1). Elliots Bks.

Atlas of Iowa, State Atlas Ser. Ed. by Charles W. Collins. (Illus.). 1974. lib. bdg. 19.95x o.p. (ISBN 0-89534-007-0). Am Pub Co WI.

Atlas of Ireland. (Illus.). 112p. 1980. lib. bdg. 99.50. St Martin.

Atlas of Landforms. 2nd ed. LC 73-14921. (Illus.). 144p. 1974. text ed. 19.95 (ISBN 0-471-03628-5). Wiley.

Atlas of Limb Prosthetics: Surgical & Prosthetic Principles. American Academy of Orthopaedic Surgeons. (Illus.). 668p. 1980. 74.50 (ISBN 0-8016-0058-8). Mosby.

Atlas of London. E. Jones & D. J. Sinclair. 1969. 205.00 (ISBN 0-08-013255-3). Pergamon.

Atlas of Man & Religion. Gordon Hawes & Stanley Knight. 1970. 6.00 (ISBN 0-08-006999-1, Religious Educ Pr). Pergamon.

Atlas of Medicinal Plants of Middle America: Bahamas to Yucatan. Julia Morton. (Illus.). 1400p. 1981. 147.50 (ISBN 0-398-04036-2). C C Thomas.

Atlas of Metal-Ligand Equilibria in Aqueous Solution. J. Kragten. LC 77-12168. 1978. 149.95 (ISBN 0-470-99309-X). Halsted Pr.

Atlas of Military Strategy. David G. Chandler. (Illus.). 1980. Repr. 29.95 (ISBN 0-02-905750-7). Free Pr.

Atlas of Montana Elections: Eighteen Eighty-Nine to Nineteen Seventy-Six. Ellis Waldron & Paul Wilson. 1979. 33.00 (ISBN 0-686-23488-X); pap. 19.95. U of MT Pubns Hist.

Atlas of Neonatal Electroencephalography. Sarah Werner et al. LC 77-83692. 1977. 81.00 (ISBN 0-89004-080-X). Raven.

Atlas of Neuroanatomy for Radiologists: Surface & Sectional-with CT Scanning Correlation. William B. Dublin & Arthur B. Dublin. (Illus.). 320p. 1981. 37.50 (ISBN 0-87527-204-5). Green.

Atlas of Neuropathology. Nathan Malamud & Asao Hirano. (Illus.). 1975. 57.50x (ISBN 0-520-02221-1). U of Cal Pr.

Atlas of New York. Ed. by Charles W. Collins. (State Atlas Ser). (Illus.). lib. bdg. 29.95x o.p. (ISBN 0-89534-002-X). Am Pub Co WI.

Atlas of Non-Invasive Techniques: Sound & Pulse Tracings-Echograms. Aldo A. Luisada et al. (Illus.). 568p. 1976. vinyl 45.75 (ISBN 0-398-03555-5). C C Thomas.

Atlas of Normal Vertebral Angiograms. Ed. by G. H. Boulay. 144p. 1976. 54.95 (ISBN 0-407-00042-9). Butterworths.

Atlas of Nuclear Medicine Imaging. Sheldon Baum et al. 432p. 1980. 78.00x (ISBN 0-8385-0447-7). ACC.

Atlas of Nutritional Data on United States & Canadian Feeds. Committee on Animal Nutrition, Agricultural Board. LC 76-612077. 1972. 15.50 (ISBN 0-309-01919-2). Natl Acad Pr.

Atlas of Ohio, State Atlas Ser. Ed. by Charles W. Collins. (Illus.). 1975. lib. bdg. 26.95x o.p. (ISBN 0-89534-008-9). Am Pub Co WI.

Atlas of Operative Dentistry. 3rd ed. William W. Howard. (Illus.). 295p. 1981. spiral bdg. 19.95 (ISBN 0-8016-2282-4). Mosby.

Atlas of Oral Pathology. Roy M. Smith et al. (Illus.). 204p. 1981. text ed. 24.95 (ISBN 0-8016-4684-7). Mosby.

Atlas of Oral Pathology. William G. Young & Heddie O. Sedano. LC 80-29439. (Illus.). 256p. 1981. 25.00x (ISBN 0-8166-1040-1). U of Minn Pr.

Atlas of Oral Surgery. Benjamin J. Gans. LC 73-187485. (Illus.). 232p. 1972. 34.50 o.p. (ISBN 0-8016-1723-5). Mosby.

Atlas of Orthodontic Principles. 2nd ed. Raymond C. Thurow. LC 77-7096. (Illus.). 1977. text ed. 38.50 (ISBN 0-8016-4951-X). Mosby.

Atlas of Orthopaedic Surgery. 2nd ed. Loius A. Goldstein. LC 80-23987. (Illus.). 1000p. 1981. text ed. 90.00 (ISBN 0-8016-1884-3). Mosby.

Atlas of Paediatric Endoscopy: Upper Respiratory Tract & Oesophagus. Bruce Benjamin. (Illus.). 1981. text ed. 37.50x (ISBN 0-19-261179-8). Oxford U Pr.

Atlas of Pathologic Pneumoencephalographic Anatomy. Giovanni Di Chiro et al. (Illus.). 594p. 1967. 74.50 (ISBN 0-398-00448-X). C C Thomas.

Atlas of Pathological Computer Tomography, Vol. 1: Cranio-Cerebral Computed Tomography. Ed. by A. Wackenheim et al. (Illus.). 150p. 1980. Set. 116.90 (ISBN 0-387-09879-8). Springer-Verlag.

Atlas of Pediatric Nuclear Medicine, Nineteen Seventy-Eight. Philip O. Alderson. LC 78-24369. (Illus.). 1978. text ed. 46.50 (ISBN 0-8016-0107-X). Mosby.

Atlas of Pedodontics. 2nd ed. John M. Davis et al. (Illus.). 425p. 1980. 32.50 (ISBN 0-7216-2977-6). Saunders.

Atlas of Pelvic Surgery. Clifford R. Wheeless, Jr. LC 80-27140. (Illus.). 400p. 1981. text ed. write for info. (ISBN 0-8121-0727-6). Lea & Febiger.

Atlas of Physical & Chemical Properties of Puget Sound & Its Approaches. Eugene E. Collias et al. LC 74-10057. (Washoington Sea Grant). (Illus.). 248p. 1974. pap. 18.50 (ISBN 0-295-95345-4). U of Wash Pr.

Atlas of Plant Life. Herbert L. Edlin & Anthony Huxley. LC 73-734361. (John Day Bk.). (Illus.). 128p. 1973. 11.95 (ISBN 0-381-98245-9, TYC-T). T Y Crowell.

Atlas of Primitive Man in China. Institute of Vertebrate Paleontology & Paleoanthropology of the Chinese Academy of Sciences. (Illus.). 200p. 1980. text ed. 52.50 (ISBN 0-442-20013-7, Pub. by Sci Pr China). Van Nos Reinhold.

Atlas of Radiation Dose Distributions. Incl. Vol. 1. Single-Field Isodose Charts. Compiled by E. W. Webster & K. C. Tsien. 50p. 1965. 31.75 (ISBN 92-0-112065-6, ISP96); Vol. 2. Multiple-Field Isodose Charts. Compiled by M. Cohen & Susan J. Martin. 132p. 1966. 31.75 (ISBN 92-0-112066-4); Vol. 3. Moving-Field Isodose Charts. Compiled by K. C. Tsien et al. 57p. 1967. 33.25 (ISBN 92-0-112067-2); Vol. 4. Brachytherapy Isodose Charts - Sealed Radium Sources. Compiled by Marilyn Stovall et al. 56p. 1972. 45.00 (ISBN 92-0-112072-9). (Technical Directory Ser.). (Illus., Loose-leaf ring-binder, IAEA). Unipub.

Atlas of Reconstructive Burn Surgery. Roger E. Salisbury & A. Griswold Bevin. 1981. text ed. price not set (ISBN 0-7216-7903-X). Saunders.

Atlas of Renal & Urinary Tract Cytology & Its Histopathologic Bases. G. Berry Schumann & Mark Weiss. (Illus.). 240p. 1980. text ed. 55.00 (ISBN 0-397-50443-8). Lippincott.

Atlas of Representative Stellar Spectra. Yasumasa Yamashita et al. LC 78-535. 1978. 69.95 (ISBN 0-470-26315-6). Halsted Pr.

Atlas of Rock-Forming Minerals in Thin Section. W. S. Mackenzie & C. Guilford. 98p. 1980. pap. 22.50x (ISBN 0-470-26921-9). Halsted Pr.

Atlas of Spectral Data & Physical Constants for Organic Compounds, 6 vols. 2nd ed. Ed. by J. Grasselli & W. Ritchey. LC 72-2452. 1975. Set. 700.00 (ISBN 0-87819-317-0). CRC Pr.

Atlas of Stereochemistry: Absolute Configurations of Organic Molecules, 2 vols. 2nd ed. Klyne & J. Buckingham. (Illus.). 1978. 49.95 ea. Vol. I (ISBN 0-19-520058-6). Vol. II (ISBN 0-19-520059-4). Oxford U Pr.

Atlas of Stereoscopic Aerial Photographs & Landsat Imagery of North America. W. Kenneth Hamblin. LC 79-91239. (Illus.). 208p. (Orig.). 15.95 (ISBN 0-935698-00-0). Tasa Pub Co.

Atlas of Strabismus Surgery. 2nd ed. Eugene M. Helveston. LC 77-3542. (Illus.). 1977. text ed. 41.50 (ISBN 0-8016-2138-0). Mosby.

Atlas of Sulphur Deficiency in Commercial Plants. 18p. 1978. pap. 5.00 (ISBN 0-643-00210-3, CO03, CSIRO). Unipub.

Atlas of Surgery, Vol 1. 2nd ed. Horst-Eberhard Grewe & Karl Kremer. Tr. by H. J. Hirsch from Ger. LC 77-84671. 1980. write for info. (ISBN 0-7216-4273-X). Saunders.

Atlas of Surgical Approaches to the Bones of the Dog & Cat. 2nd ed. D. L. Piermattei & R. G. Greeley. LC 77-27755. (Illus.). 1979. text ed. 25.00 (ISBN 0-7216-7241-8). Saunders.

Atlas of Surgical Exposures of the Extremities. Sam W. Banks & Harold Laufman. LC 52-12872. (Illus.). 1973. 32.00 (ISBN 0-7216-1530-9). Saunders.

Atlas of the Andromeda Galaxy. Paul W. Hodge. (Illus.). 80p. 1981. 50.00 (ISBN 0-295-95795-6). U of Wash Pr.

Atlas of the Biologic Resources of the Hudson Estuary. Estuarine Study Group. (Illus.). 104p. (Orig.). 1977. pap. 5.50 (ISBN 0-89062-096-2, Pub. by Boyce Thompson Inst Plant Res). Pub Ctr Cult Res.

Atlas of the Blood & Bone Marrow. 2nd ed. Ed. by R. Philip Custer. LC 78-165276. (Illus.). 562p. 1974. text ed. 45.00 (ISBN 0-7216-2815-X). Saunders.

Atlas of the Body & Mind. Ed. by Paul Tiddens. LC 75-41710. (Illus.). 208p. 1976. 19.95 (ISBN 0-528-83095-3). Rand.

Atlas of the Human Brain & the Orbit for Computed Tomography. 2nd ed. William R. Scott et al. (Illus.). 124p. 1980. 32.50 (ISBN 0-87527-155-3). Green.

Atlas of the Human Brain for Computerized Tomography. Takayoshi Matsui & Asao Hirano. LC 77-95453. (Illus.). 1978. 66.00 (ISBN 0-89640-027-1). Igaku-Shoin.

Atlas of the Middle-Earth. Karen W. Fonstad. 224p. 1981. 14.95 (ISBN 0-686-69045-1). HM.

Atlas of the Mughal Empire: Political & Economic Maps with Detailed Notes, Bibliography, & Index. Irfan Habib. (Illus.). 120p. 1980. 69.00x (ISBN 0-19-560379-6). Oxford U Pr.

Atlas of the Newborn. Neil O'Doherty. LC 78-70614. (Illus.). 1979. text ed. 34.00 (ISBN 0-685-99716-2). Lippincott.

Atlas of the Oscular Fundus. O. Marchesani & H. Sautter. 1959. 80.00 (ISBN 0-02-848820-2). Hafner.

Atlas of the Osteochondhoses. Louis W. Breck. (Illus.). 192p. 1971. pap. 16.00 photocopy ed. spiral (ISBN 0-398-00218-5). C C Thomas.

Atlas of the Planets. Paul Doherty. LC 80-12347. (Illus.). 144p. 1980. 16.95 (ISBN 0-07-017341-9, GB). McGraw.

Atlas of the Textural Patterns of Basic & Ultrabasic Rocks & Their Genetic Significance. S. S. Augustithis. 1979. 150.00x (ISBN 3-11-006571-1). De Gruyter.

Atlas of Thoracic Surgery, 2 vols. Ed. by Boris V. Petrovsky. LC 78-23699. (Illus.). 1979. Set. 150.00 (ISBN 0-8016-3832-1). Mosby.

Atlas of Three Hundred Mb Wind Characteristics for the Northern Hemisphere. James F. Lahey et al. 1960. wired bdg. 50.00x (ISBN 0-299-01963-2). U of Wis Pr.

Atlas of Tooth Form. 4th ed. Russell C. Wheeler. LC 69-17806. (Illus.). 1969. 16.00 (ISBN 0-7216-9276-1). Saunders.

Atlas of Topograhical & Applied Human Anatomy Index, Vol. 3, Index. 2nd ed. Eduard Pernkopf. Ed. by Helmut Ferner. LC 79-25264. 100p. 1980. text ed. 12.00 (ISBN 0-8067-1572-3). Urban & S.

Atlas of Topographical & Applied Human Anatomy: Head & Neck, Vol. 1. 2nd ed. Eduard Pernkopf. Ed. by Helmut Ferner. Tr. by Harry Monsen from Ger. LC 79-25264. (Illus.). 1980. text ed. 98.00 (ISBN 0-8067-1552-9). Urban & S.

Atlas of Topographical & Applied Human Anatomy: Head & Neck, Vol. 1. rev. 2nd ed. Eduard Pernkoph. Ed. by Helmut Ferner. Tr. by Harry Monsen from Ger. LC 79-25264. Orig. Title: Atlas der Topographischen und Angewamdten Anatomie Des Menschen. (Illus.). 308p. 1980. Repr. of 1963 ed. text ed. 98.00 (ISBN 0-7216-7198-5). Saunders.

Atlas of Topographical & Applied Human Anatomy: Thorax, Abdomen & Extremities, Vol. 2. 2nd ed. Eduard Pernkopf. Ed. by Helmut Ferner. Tr. by Harry Monsen from Ger. LC 79-25264. (Illus.). 1980. text ed. 98.00 (ISBN 0-8067-1562-6). Urban & S.

Atlas of Tumors of the Skin. new ed. Alfred W. Kopf et al. 1978. text ed. 80.00 (ISBN 0-7216-5487-8). Saunders.

Atlas of Ultrastructure: Ultrastructural Features in Pathology. Ed. by C. Howard Tseng. 224p. 1980. 32.50x (ISBN 0-8385-0462-0). ACC.

Atlas of Utah. Ed. by Wayne L. Wahlquist et al. (Illus.). 298p. 1981. lib. bdg. 29.95 (ISBN 0-8425-1831-2). Brigham.

Atlas of Vaginal Surgery. Guelfo Sani & Leon Kos. LC 76-55407. 1977. 66.50 (ISBN 0-471-02275-6, Pub. by Wiley Medical). Wiley.

Atlas of Vascular Surgery. Robert R. Linton. LC 72-80791. (Illus.). 504p. 1973. text ed. 80.00 (ISBN 0-7216-5783-4). Saunders.

Atlas of Vertebrate Cells in Tissue Culture. Ed. by George G. Rose. 1971. 53.50 (ISBN 0-12-596856-6). Acad Pr.

Atlas of Weapons & War. John Williams. LC 76-3515. (John Day Bk.). 1976. 12.95 o.s.i. (ISBN 0-381-98291-2, TYC-T). T Y Crowell.

Atlas of Wisconsin. Ed. by Charles W. Collins. (State Atlas Ser). (Illus.). 1972. lib. bdg. 15.95x o.p. (ISBN 0-89534-009-7). Am Pub Co WI.

Atlas of Wisconsin. Arthur H. Robinson et al. LC 73-15262. 124p. 1974. 22.50 (ISBN 0-299-06530-8); pap. 8.95 (ISBN 0-299-06534-0). U of Wis Pr.

Atlas of World Cultures. George P. Murdock. LC 80-53030. (Illus.). 152p. 1981. 9.95x (ISBN 0-8229-3432-9). U of Pittsburgh Pr.

Atlas of World Wildlife. Mitchell Beazley. LC 73-3724. (Illus.). 208p. 1973. 16.95 (ISBN 0-528-83039-2). Rand.

Atlas Shrugged. Ayn Rand. 1957. 15.00 (ISBN 0-394-41576-0). Random.

Atma-Bodhi, Self Knowledge. Sankaracharya. Tr. by T. M. Mahadevan. lib. bdg. 8.50 (ISBN 0-89253-043-X); pap. text ed. 2.00 (ISBN 0-89253-044-8). Ind-US Inc.

Atmosphere. 3rd ed. Richard Anthes et al. (Illus.). 384p. 1981. text ed. 17.95 (ISBN 0-675-08043-6); instr's. manual 3.95 (ISBN 0-686-69485-6). Merrill.

Atmosphere. 2nd ed. Richard A. Anthes et al. (Physical Science Ser.). 1978. text ed. 18.95 (ISBN 0-675-08423-7). Merrill.

Atmosphere. Walter A. Turber et al. (Exploring Earth Science Program Ser.). (gr. 7-12). 1976. pap. text ed. 4.96 (ISBN 0-205-04744-0, 6947441). Allyn.

Atmosphere: An Introduction to Meteorology. F. Lutgens & E. Tarbuck. 1979. 17.95 (ISBN 0-13-050104-2). P-H.

Atmosphere & Ocean: Our Fluid Environments. J. G. Harvey. LC 77-377903. 1978. pap. 9.95x (ISBN 0-8448-1293-5). Crane-Russak Co.

Atmospheres. Barbato & Ayer. 250p. Date not set. text ed. price not set (ISBN 0-08-025583-3); pap. text ed. price not set (ISBN 0-08-025582-5). Pergamon.

Atmospheric Diffusion. 2nd ed. Frank Pasquill. LC 74-7054. 429p. 1974. 79.95 (ISBN 0-470-66892-X). Halsted Pr.

Atmospheric Motion & Air Pollution: An Introduction for Students of Engineering & Science. Richard A. Dobbins. LC 79-952. (Environmental Science & Technology: Texts & Monographs). 1979. 32.50 (ISBN 0-471-21675-5, Pub. by Wiley-Interscience). Wiley.

Atmospheric Pollutants in Natural Waters. Steven J. Eisenreich. 1981. text ed. 40.00 (ISBN 0-250-40369-2, Dist. by Butterworths). Ann Arbor Science.

Atmospheric Pollution. 3rd rev. ed. A. R. Meetham. 1964. 15.15 (ISBN 0-08-010143-7). Pergamon.

Atmospheric Pollution: Its History, Origins & Prevention. 4th ed. A. R. Meetham et al. (Illus.). 288p. 1980. 38.00 (ISBN 0-08-024003-8); pap. 15.00 (ISBN 0-08-024002-X). Pergamon.

Atmospheric Sciences: An Introductory Survey. John M. Wallace & Peter Hobbs. 467p. 1977. 22.95 (ISBN 0-12-732950-1). Acad Pr.

Atmospheric Sciences & Man's Needs: Priorities for the Future. Committee On Atmospheric Sciences. LC 70-611003. (Orig.). 1971. pap. text ed. 4.00 (ISBN 0-309-01912-5). Natl Acad Pr.

Atmospheric Sciences: Problems & Applications. Committee on Atmospheric Sciences. 1977. pap. 7.75 (ISBN 0-309-02626-1). Natl Acad Pr.

Atmospheric Sulfur Deposition: Environmental Impact & Health Effects. Ed. by D. S. Shriner et al. 586p. 1980. 29.50 (ISBN 0-250-40380-3). Ann Arbor Science.

Atmospheric Waves. Tom Beer. LC 74-13429. 300p. 1974. 59.95 (ISBN 0-470-06185-5). Halsted Pr.

Atom Besieged: Nuclear Dissent in France & Germany. Dorothy Nelkin & Michael Pollack. 352p. 1980. text ed. 17.50 (ISBN 0-262-14034-9). MIT Pr.

Atom Bomb. David Killingray. Ed. by Malcolm Yapp et al. (World History Ser.). (Illus.). 32p. (gr. 10). 1980. Repr. of 1977 ed. lib. bdg. 5.95 (ISBN 0-89908-235-1); pap. text ed. 1.95 (ISBN 0-89908-210-6). Greenhaven.

Atom Bomb Spies. H. Montgomery Hyde. LC 80-65998. (Illus.). 1980. 14.95 (ISBN 0-689-11075-8). Atheneum.

Atom, Man, & the Universe: The Long Chain of Complications. Hannes Alfven. Tr. by John Hoberman. LC 69-15872. 1969. text ed. 10.95x (ISBN 0-7167-0327-0). W H Freeman.

Atomic Absorption & Atomic Florescence Spectroscopy. LC 74-26513. 923p. 1973. 108.95 o.p. (ISBN 0-470-68998-6). Halsted Pr.

Atomic Absorption & Atomic Fluorescence Spectometry: Proceedings. Ed. by Maurice Pinta. LC 73-3959. 1973. 49.95 (ISBN 0-470-68995-1). Halsted Pr.

Atomic Absorption Fluoresence & Flame Emission Spectroscopy: A Practical Approach. 2nd ed. K. C. Thompson & R. J. Reynolds. 1979. 47.95 (ISBN 0-470-26478-0). Halsted Pr.

Atomic Absorption Spectrophotometry. 2nd ed. W. T. Elwell & J. A. Gidley. 1966. 18.00 (ISBN 0-08-012063-6). Pergamon.

Atomic Absorption Spectroscopy-Past, Present & Future: To Commemorate the 25th Anniversary of Alan Walsh's Landmark Paper in Spectrochimica Acta. P. W. Boumans. 248p. 1981. pap. 32.50 (ISBN 0-08-026267-8). Pergamon.

Atomic Age & the Philosophy of the Far East. George Ohsawa. (Illus.). 1977. 7.95 o.s.i. (ISBN 0-918860-28-8). G Ohsawa.

Atomic & Molecular Collisions. Harrie Massey. LC 79-11716. 1979. 39.95x (ISBN 0-470-26742-9). Halsted Pr.

Atomic & Molecular Processes. Ed. by David R. Bates. (Pure & Applied Physics Ser.: Vol. 13). 1962. 52.50 (ISBN 0-12-081450-1). Acad Pr.

Atomic & Molecular Structure: The Development of Our Concepts. Walter J. Lehmann. LC 70-37434. 1972. text ed. 21.50x o.p. (ISBN 0-471-52440-9). Wiley.

Atomic Artillery & the Atomic Bomb. John K. Robertson. 1979. Repr. of 1945 ed. lib. bdg. 10.00 (ISBN 0-8492-7712-4). R West.

Atomic Bomb. Margaret Gowing & Lorna Arnold. (Science in a Social Context Ser.). 1979. pap. text ed. 3.95 (ISBN 0-408-71311-9). Butterworths.

Atomic Dynamics in Liquids. N. H. March & M. P. Tosi. LC 76-16040. 1977. 59.95 (ISBN 0-470-15145-5). Halsted Pr.

Atomic Energy. Irving Adler. LC 75-132946. (Illus.). (gr. 3-6). 1971. PLB 7.89 (ISBN 0-381-99613-1, AO6100, JD-J). John Day.

Atomic Energy. Boy Scouts Of America. LC 19-600. (Illus.). 72p. (gr. 6-12). 1965. pap. 0.70x (ISBN 0-8395-3275-X, 3275). BSA.

Atomic Energy for Military Purposes: The Official Report on the Development of the Atomic Bomb Under the Auspices of the United States Government, 1940-1945. Henry D. Smyth. (Politics & Strategy of World War II Ser: No. 2). 1976. Repr. of 1945 ed. lib. bdg. 25.00 (ISBN 0-306-70767-5). Da Capo.

Atomic Energy Review-Molybdenum: Physico-Chemical Properties of Its Compounds & Alloys. (Special Issue Ser.: No. 7). 714p. 1980. pap. 85.75 (ISBN 92-0-149080-1, IAER 75, IAEA). Unipub.

Atomic Energy Review; Thorium: Physico-Chemical Properties of Its Compounds & Alloys. (Special Issue Ser.: No. 5). (Illus.). 241p. 1975. pap. 18.25 (ISBN 92-0-149075-5, IAEA5, IAEA). Unipub.

Atomic Energy: The Story of Nuclear Science. Irene D. Jaworski & Alexander Joseph. LC 60-13702. (Illus.). (gr. 9 up). 1961. 4.95 o.p. (ISBN 0-15-204438-8, HJ). HarBraceJ.

Atomic Masses & Fundamental Constants 6. Ed. by Jerry A. Nolen & Walter Benenson. 585p. 1980. 59.50 (ISBN 0-306-40441-9, Plenum Pr). Plenum Pub.

Atomic Nuclei & Their Particles. E. J. Burge. (Oxford Physics Ser.). (Illus.). 1977. pap. text ed. 14.95x (ISBN 0-19-851835-8). Oxford U Pr.

Atomic Spectra & Atomic Structure. 2nd ed. Gerhard Herzberg. Tr. by J. W. Spinks. (Illus.). 1944. pap. text ed. 3.50 (ISBN 0-486-60115-3). Dover.

Atomic Structure. E. U. Condon & H. Odabasi. LC 77-88673. (Illus.). 1980. 83.50 (ISBN 0-521-21859-4); pap. 26.00x (ISBN 0-521-29893-8). Cambridge U Pr.

Atomic Transmutation: Memoirs of Fred Soddy. Muriel Howorth. 1953. 7.50 o.p. (ISBN 0-911268-01-4). Rogers Bk.

Atomica. Steve Karpf & Elinor Karpf. (Orig.). 1981. pap. write for info. (ISBN 0-440-10384-3). Dell.

Atomospheric Dispersion in Nuclear Power Plant Siting. (Safety Ser.: No. 50-SG-S3). 1981. pap. 14.75 (ISBN 92-0-623180-4, ISP 549, IAEA). Unipub.

Atoms & Information Theory: An Introduction to Statistical Mechanics. Ralph Baierlein. LC 71-116369. (Illus.). 1971. text ed. 24.95x (ISBN 0-7167-0332-7). W H Freeman.

Atoms & Molecules: Student Edition. Mitchel Weissbluth. 1980. lib ed 24.50 (ISBN 0-12-744452-1). Acad Pr.

Atoms and Quanta, Book 7. W. Bolton. LC 80-41395. (Study Topics in Physics Ser.). 96p. 1980. pap. text ed. write for info. (ISBN 0-408-10658-1). Butterworths.

Atoms & Waves: Physics, Bk.2. L. J. Campbell & R. J. Carlton. (Secondary Science Ser.). (Illus., Orig.). (gr. 8-11). 1975. pap. text ed. 6.95 (ISBN 0-7100-7740-8). Routledge & Kegan.

Atoms at Work. George P. Bischof. LC 51-100007. (Illus.). (gr. 5-8). 1951. 4.50 o.p. (ISBN 0-15-204617-8, HJ). HarBraceJ.

Atoms, Energy & Machines. Jack McCormick. LC 66-30642. (Creative Science Ser). (Illus.). (gr. 4-9). 1967. PLB 7.95 (ISBN 0-87191-010-1). Creative Ed.

Atom's Eve: Ending the Nuclear Age, an Anthology. Ed. by Mark Reader et al. (McGraw-Hill Paperbacks Ser.). 288p. (Orig.). 1980. pap. 5.95 (ISBN 0-07-051287-6, SB). McGraw.

Atoms in Contact. B. R. Jennings & V. J. Morris. (Oxford Paperbacks Ser). (Illus.). 112p. 1974. text ed. 16.95x (ISBN 0-19-851809-9); pap. text ed. 4.95x o.p. (ISBN 0-19-851804-8). Oxford U Pr.

Atoms, Molecules & Lasers. Lectures, International Winter College, Trieste, 1973. (Illus.). 710p. 1975. pap. 50.50 (ISBN 92-0-130374-2, IAEA). Unipub.

Atoms, Peace & Vitamin C: Linus Pauling. White. 1980. PLB 9.95 (ISBN 0-8027-6390-1); 8.95 (ISBN 0-8027-6389-8). Walker & Co.

Atoms Within Us. Ernest Borek. LC 61-6159. (Illus.). (gr. 9 up). 1961. 17.00x (ISBN 0-231-02391-X); pap. 5.00x (ISBN 0-231-08535-4). Columbia U Pr.

Atoms Within Us. rev. ed. Ernest Borek. LC 80-19010. 272p. 1980. text ed. 20.00x (ISBN 0-231-04386-4); pap. text ed. 6.00x (ISBN 0-231-04387-2). Columbia U Pr.

Atonememt: The Origins of the Doctrine in the New Testament. Martin Hengel. Tr. by John Bowden from Ger. LC 80-2384. 128p. 1981. pap. 6.95 (ISBN 0-8006-1446-1, 1-1446). Fortress.

Atopic Dermatitis. George Rajka. LC 74-14868. (Major Problems in Dermatology Ser: No. 3). (Illus.). 165p. 1975. 25.00 (ISBN 0-7216-7448-8). Saunders.

ATP-GA. K. T Boyd. (Illus.). 96p. 1981. pap. 9.25 (ISBN 0-8138-0510-4). Iowa St U Pr.

Atraves Da Biblia. Tr. by Myer Pearlman. (Portugese Bks.). (Port.). 1979. 3.95 (ISBN 0-8297-0641-0). Life Pubs Intl.

Atrevete a Disciplinar. Tr. by James Dobson. (Spanish Bks.). (Span.). 1978. 1.90 (ISBN 0-8297-0499-X). Life Pubs Intl.

Atrocity Week. Andrew McCoy. 1979. pap. 2.25 o.s.i. (ISBN 0-446-82534-4). Warner Bks.

Attached Solar Greenhouse. W. F. Yanda & Susan Yanda. (Sp. & Eng.). 1976. pap. 2.00 (ISBN 0-89016-028-7). Lightning Tree.

Attack. Collis Ehrlich. 160p. (Orig.). 1981. pap. 2.25 (ISBN 0-345-28476-3). Ballantine.

Attack & Counterattack in Chess. Fred Reinfeld. 1970. pap. 1.95 (ISBN 0-06-463204-0, EH 204, EH). Har-Row.

Attack at Michilimackinac, 1763: Alexander Henry's Travels & Adventures in Canada & the Indian Territories Between the Years 1760 & 1764. Ed. by David A. Armour. (Illus.). 1971. pap. 2.50 (ISBN 0-911872-37-X). Mackinac Island.

Attack of the Cat. Peter G. Timm. LC 80-27359. (Prime Time Adventures Ser.). (Illus.). 64p. (gr. 4 up). 1981. PLB 7.95 (ISBN 0-516-02101-X). Childrens.

Attack on Privacy. John C. Raines. LC 73-16691. 160p. 1974. 4.95 o.p. (ISBN 0-8170-0621-4). Judson.

Attacking Faulty Reasoning. T. Edward Damer. 1979. pap. text ed. 6.95x (ISBN 0-534-00750-3). Wadsworth Pub.

Attacking Hay Fever & Winning. Catherine J. Frompovich. Ed. by April M. Koppenhaver. (Orig.). 1981. pap. 2.00. C J Frompovich.

Attacking Rural Poverty: How Non-Formal Education Can Help. Philip H. Coombs & Manzoor Ahmed. LC 73-19350. (World Bank Ser). (Illus.). 308p. 1974. 18.50x (ISBN 0-8018-1600-9); pap. 6.95x (ISBN 0-8018-1601-7). Johns Hopkins.

Attaining Financial Peace of Mind: A Practical Guide for the Thinking Person. Jack Johnstad & Lois Johnstad. LC 80-67104. (Illus.). 320p. 1980. pap. 8.95 (ISBN 0-937346-00-4). Bright Spirit.

Attar of the Ice Valley. Leonard Wibberley. LC 68-13683. 176p. (gr. 7 up). 1968. 3.95 (ISBN 0-374-30451-3). FS&G.

Attempted Evocation of the Civil War. Agnes Yarnall. 93p. 1980. 8.95 (ISBN 0-8059-2749-2). Dorrance.

Attempted Whig Revolution of Sixteen Seventy-Eight to Sixteen Eighty-One. Francis S. Ronalds. 202p. 1974. Repr. of 1937 ed. 12.50x o.p. (ISBN 0-87471-467-2). Rowman.

Attendant's Confession, the Fortune Teller, & Life. Joaquim M. Assis. Ed. & tr. by Isaac Goldberg. (International Pocket Library). pap. 2.00 (ISBN 0-8283-1426-8). Branden.

Attention & Achievement. Anne M. Bober. 32p. 1977. pap. 8.00 o.p. (ISBN 0-686-00903-7, D-102). Essence Pubns.

Attention & Information Processing in Schizophrenia: Proceedings. Scottish Rite Schizophrenia Research Program, Conference, Rochester, 2-6 May 1976. Ed. by S. Matthyse. 1979. text ed. 99.50 (ISBN 0-08-023126-8). Pergamon.

Attention & Memory. G. Underwood. LC 75-17614. 231p. 1975. text ed. 34.00 (ISBN 0-08-019615-2); pap. text ed. 14.00 (ISBN 0-08-018754-4). Pergamon.

Attention & Performance, Vol. 7. Ed. by Jean Requin. LC 78-13662. (International Symposium on Attention & Performance). 1978. 29.95 (ISBN 0-470-26521-3). Halsted Pr.

Attention & Performance VIII. Ed. by Raymond S. Nickerson. LC 80-23850. 864p. 1980. 49.95 (ISBN 0-89859-038-8). L Erlbaum Assocs.

Attention, Arousal & the Orientation Reaction. R. Lynn. 1966. text ed. 19.50 (ISBN 0-08-011524-1); pap. text ed. 9.50 (ISBN 0-08-013840-3). Pergamon.

Attestation of Many Learned, Godly, & Famous Divines...Justifying...That the Church Government Ought to Bee Always with the Peoples Free Consent. Henry Jacob. LC 74-28868. (English Experience Ser.: No. 747). 1975. Repr. of 1613 ed. 16.00 (ISBN 90-221-0747-7). Walter J Johnson.

Attic Bilingual Vases & Their Painters. Beth Cohen. LC 77-94689. (Outstanding Dissertations in the Fine Arts Ser.). 1978. lib. bdg. 80.00 (ISBN 0-8240-3220-9). Garland Pub.

Attic Red-Figure Vase-Painters, 3 Vols. 2nd ed. John D. Beazley. 1963. Set. 175.00x (ISBN 0-19-813146-1). Oxford U Pr.

Attic Term. Antonia Forest. (gr. 5 up). 1976. 10.95 (ISBN 0-571-10970-5, Pub. by Faber & Faber). Merrimack Bk Serv.

Attic White-Ground: Its Development on Shapes Other Than Lekythoi. John R. Mertens. LC 76-23641. (Outstanding Dissertations in the Fine Arts - 2nd Series - Ancient). (Illus.). 1977. Repr. of 1972 ed. lib. bdg. 48.00x (ISBN 0-8240-2711-6). Garland Pub.

Attica: My Story. Russell G. Oswald. LC 72-77002. 1972. 7.95 o.p. (ISBN 0-385-08199-5). Doubleday.

Attitude & Attitude Change. Harry C. Triandis. LC 76-140555. (Foundations of Social Psychology Ser). (Illus.). 1971. pap. text ed. 9.50 (ISBN 0-471-88831-1). Wiley.

Attitude & Opinion Research: Why You Need It, How to Do It. Walter K. Lindenmann. 1977. 9.50 (ISBN 0-89964-028-1). CASE.

Attitude Change: A Critical Analysis of Theoretical Approaches. Charles A. Kiesler et al. LC 68-56162. (Psychology Ser). 1969. 24.95 (ISBN 0-471-47465-7). Wiley.

Attitude of Tennesseans Toward the Union, Eighteen Forty-Seven to Eighteen Sixty-One. Mary E. Campbell. LC 60-53338. 1961. 7.50 (ISBN 0-910294-15-1). Brown Bk.

Attitude Organization & Change: An Analysis of Consistency Among Attitude Components. Milton J. Rosenberg et al. LC 80-14704. (Yale Studies in Attitude & Communication: Vol. 3). (Illus.). x, 239p. 1980. Repr. of 1960 ed. lib. bdg. 22.25x (ISBN 0-313-22435-8, ROAT). Greenwood.

Attitude Research at Bay: Proceedings. Attitude Research Conference, October, 1974, San Francisco. Ed. by Deborah K. Johnson & William D. Wells. LC 76-24880. 1976. pap. 12.00 o.p. (ISBN 0-87757-078-7). Am Mktg.

Attitude Research Enters the Eighties. Richard W. Olshavsky. LC 80-20621. (Proceedings Ser.). 196p. 1980. pap. 12.00 (ISBN 0-87757-145-7). Am Mktg.

Attitude Research Enters the Eighties. Ed. by Richard W. Olshavsky. LC 80-20621. (Proceedings Ser.). 196p. 1980. 12.00 (ISBN 0-87757-145-7). Am Mktg.

Attitudes & Anticipated Behavior of Dentists Under Various Reimbursement Arrangements. Robert D. Eilers & Robert C. Jones. 1972. pap. text ed. 2.75x o.p. (ISBN 0-256-00265-7). Irwin.

Attitudes & Interests in Education. K. M. Evans. 1965. pap. 6.50 (ISBN 0-7100-7166-3). Routledge & Kegan.

Attitudes & Opinions. S. Oskamp. LC 76-52999. 1977. 19.95 (ISBN 0-13-050393-2). P-H.

Attitudes & Their Measurement. Nigel Lemon. 1973. 38.00 (ISBN 0-7134-0983-5, Pub. by Batsford England). David & Charles.

Attitudes I. Virgil Leach. Date not set. pap. 2.95 (ISBN 0-89137-803-0). Quality Pubns.

Attitudes II. Virgil Leach. 1981. pap. 2.95 (ISBN 0-89137-804-9). Quality Pubns.

Attitudes, Interaction & Personality. Ed. by Lajos Kardos. Tr. by B. Dajka et al. (Illus.). 149p. 1980. 10.50x (ISBN 963-05-2088-5). Intl Pubns Serv.

Attitudes of the Dutch Population on Alternative Life Styles & Environmental Deterioration. 40p. pap. 5.00 (ISBN 9-28080-138-4, TUNU 065, UNU). Unipub.

Attitudes Toward English Usage: A History of the War of Words. Edward Finegan. 1980. pap. 9.95x (ISBN 0-8077-2581-1). Tchrs Coll.

Attitudes Toward the Handicapped: A Comparison Between Europe & the United States. Leopold Lippman. (American Lecture in Special Education Ser.). 136p. 1972. text ed. 10.50 (ISBN 0-398-02341-7). C C Thomas.

Attitudes Towards Mental Patients. Alexander Askenasy. (New Babylon, Studies in the Social Sciences). 1974. text ed. 34.10x (ISBN 90-2797-891-3). Mouton.

Attorney for the Situation. Leland Hazard. LC 74-83549. 325p. 1975. 12.50x (ISBN 0-231-03898-4). Columbia U Pr.

Attorney Malpractice: Law & Procedure, Vol.1. David J. Meisel. LC 79-89562. 1980. 47.50. Lawyers Co-Op.

Attorneys As Activists: Evaluating the American Bar Association's BASICS Program. Ross F. Conner & C. Ronald Huff. LC 79-19830. (Contemporary Evaluation Research: Vol. 1). (Illus.). 263p. 1979. 18.95x (ISBN 0-8039-1363-X); pap. 9.95x (ISBN 0-8039-1364-8). Sage.

Attorney's Fees, 2 vols. Stuart M. Speiser. LC 72-91431. 1973. 100.00 (ISBN 0-686-05453-9). Lawyers Co-Op.

Attorney's Malpractice Prevention Manual. 4th ed. Laurie H. Hutzler. (Illus.). 1979. 29.95x (ISBN 0-937542-00-8); pap. 15.00x (ISBN 0-937542-01-6). Legal Mgmt Serv.

Attorneys Medical Deskbook. Dan J. Tennenhouse. LC 75-15123. 1975. 50.00 (ISBN 0-686-20645-2). Lawyers Co-Op.

Attractive & Easy-to-Build Wood Projects. Robert B. Russell. (Illus.). 64p. (Orig.). 1980. pap. 3.00 (ISBN 0-486-23965-9). Dover.

Attributes of God. Arthur W. Pink. 1961. pap. 2.95 (ISBN 0-685-19823-5). Reiner.

Attributos De Dios. A. W. Pink. 2.50 (ISBN 0-686-12561-4). Banner of Truth.

Au Jour le Jour: A French Review. 2nd ed. Jean Sareil & William Ryding. LC 73-18083. 240p. 1974. text ed. 12.95 (ISBN 0-13-052977-X). P-H.

Au Pays De la Magie. Henri Michaux. Ed. by Peter Broome. (Athlone French Poets Ser). 1977. text ed. 20.75x (ISBN 0-485-14711-4, Athlone Pr); pap. text ed. 10.75x (ISBN 0-485-12711-3). Humanities.

AUBER Membership Directory 1980. Association for University Business & Economic Research-AUBER. (Orig.). 1980. pap. 10.00. Bureau Busn Res U Wis.

Auburn: A Pictorial History. H. E. Logue & John D. Simms. (Illus.). 192p. 1980. ltd. ed. 29.95 (ISBN 0-89865-048-8); pap. 12.95 (ISBN 0-89865-049-6). Donning Co.

Aucassin & Nicolette: Kritischer Text Mit Paradigmen & Glossar. Ed. by Hermann Suchier & Walther Suchier. LC 80-2239. 1981. Repr. of 1932 ed. 31.00 (ISBN 0-404-19035-9). AMS Pr.

Aucassin et Nicolete. F. W. Bourdillon. 128p. 1919. 9.00x (ISBN 0-7190-0387-3, Pub. by Manchester U Pr England). State Mutual Bk.

Auckland Classical Essays: Presented to E. M. Blaiklock. Ed. by B. F. Harris. 234p. 1970. 10.25x o.p. (ISBN 0-19-647597-X). Oxford U Pr.

Auckland Through a Victorian Lens. William Main. LC 78-670050. (Illus.). 1977. 22.50x (ISBN 0-908582-05-6). Intl Pubns Serv.

Auction. Tom Murphy. (Orig.). 1980. pap. 2.95 (ISBN 0-451-09478-6, Sig). NAL.

Auction: A Modern Novel, 1760, 2 vols. in 1. Mrs. A. Woodfin. Ed. by Michael F. Shugrue. (Flowering of the Novel, 1740-1775 Ser: Vol. 54). 1974. lib. bdg. 50.00x (ISBN 0-8240-1153-8). Garland Pub.

Auction Companion. Daniel J. Leab & Katherine K. Leab. LC 80-8208. 224p. 1981. 12.95 (ISBN 0-06-012556-X, HarpT); pap. 5.95 (ISBN 0-06-090850-5, CN 850). Har-Row.

Auction Yearlings of 1978. pap. 10.00 (ISBN 0-936032-02-2). Thoroughbred Own and Breed.

Auctioneering. Philip A. Engelmeier. Ed. by Richard Paulaha & Darlette Engelmeier. Orig. Title: Be a Journeyman Auctioneer. (Illus.). 70p. (Orig.). 1980. pap. 10.00. Engelmeier.

Auctions & Auctioneering. Ralph Cassady, Jr. 1967. 22.75x (ISBN 0-520-00216-4). U of Cal Pr.

Auctions of Nineteen Seventy-Nine. Date not set. pap. 10.00 (ISBN 0-936032-03-0). Thoroughbred Own & Breed.

Auctions of 1980. Blood-Horse Editors. (Annual Supplement of the Blood-Horse). (Illus.). 190p. (Orig.). 1981. pap. 10.00 (ISBN 0-936032-36-7). Thoroughbred Own & Breed.

Auden. B. Everett. 1980. 17.50 (ISBN 0-685-99622-0). Chips.

Auden's Poetry. Justin Replogle. LC 68-8508. (Washington Paperback Ser.: No. 60). 271p. 1971. 9.95 (ISBN 0-295-78563-2); pap. 2.95 (ISBN 0-295-95141-9, WP-60). U of Wash Pr.

Audi Four Thousand-Five Thousand 1977-81. LC 80-70341. (Illus.). 208p. 1980. pap. 8.95. Chilton.

Audi Fox Service Manual, 1973, 1974, 1975, 1976, 1977, 1978, 1979. Robert Bentley, Inc. LC 79-53187. (Illus.). 1979. pap. 24.95 (ISBN 0-8376-0097-9). Bentley.

Audi Service-Repair Handbook: Fox--1973-1977. Eric Jorgensen. Ed. by Jeff Robinson. (Illus.). 1977. pap. 10.95 (ISBN 0-89287-155-5, A132). Clymer Pubns.

Audi Service-Repair Handbook: 100 LS Series, 1970-1977. 2nd ed. Brick Price. Ed. by Jeff Robinson. (Illus.). 1976. pap. 10.95 (ISBN 0-89287-096-6, A131). Clymer Pubns.

Audience Analysis: A Programmed Approach to Receiver Behavior. James W. Gibson & Michael Hanna. (Illus.). 1976. pap. 10.95 (ISBN 0-13-050724-5). P-H.

Audience Analysis for Technical Writing. Thomas E. Pearsall. (Illus., Orig.). 1969. pap. text ed. 5.95x (ISBN 0-02-476490-6, 47649). Macmillan.

Audience Participation: Theatre for Young People. Brian Way. 1980. pap. 7.95 (ISBN 0-87440-000-7). Bakers Plays.

Audience Studies of the Performing Arts & Museums: A Critical Review Report No.9, No. 9. (National Endowment for the Arts Research Division Reports). 106p. (Orig.). 1978. pap. 3.00x (ISBN 0-89062-092-X, Pub. by Natl Endow Arts). Pub Ctr Cultures.

Audience, the Message, the Speaker. 2nd ed. Hasling. 1975. 9.955 (ISBN 0-07-026990-4, C); instructor's manual 3.95 (ISBN 0-07-026991-2). McGraw.

Audio & Video Interference Cures. Larry Kahaner. 128p. 1979. pap. 6.10 (ISBN 0-8104-0895-3). Hayden.

Audio Biographies. G. A. Briggs. LC 65-1434. 1963. 12.50 o.p. (ISBN 0-89046-020-5). Herman Pub.

Audio Equipment Tests. Gordon J. King. (Illus.). 1979. text ed. 18.00 (ISBN 0-408-00336-7). Butterworths.

Audio Service in Public Libraries. Edward Boverie. (Illus.). 175p. (Orig.). Date not set. spiral 7.50 (ISBN 0-913578-21-5). Inglewood CA. Postponed.

Audio Servicing: Text/Lab Manual. 1st ed. Andy J. Wells. (Illus.). 144p. 9.95 (ISBN 0-07-069247-5). McGraw.

Audio Servicing: Theory & Practice. 1st ed. Andy J. Wells. (Illus.). 240p. (Orig.). pap. text ed. 13.95 (ISBN 0-07-069246-7, G); lab manual 9.95 (ISBN 0-07-069247-5). McGraw.

Audio Systems. Clyde N. Herrick. LC 74-9696. 1974. 17.95 (ISBN 0-87909-049-9). Reston.

Audio Technology Systems: Principles, Applications & Troubleshooting. Derek Cameron. (Illus.). 1978. text ed. 17.95 (ISBN 0-87909-050-2). Reston.

Audio-Tutorial Approach to Learning: Through Independent Study & Integrated Experiences. 3rd ed. S. N. Postlethwait et al. LC 70-187724. 1972. pap. text ed. 8.95 o.p. (ISBN 0-8087-6002-5). Burgess.

Audio-Tutorial Introductory Biology: Principles. rev. ed. Marvin R. Barnum et al. (Illus., Orig.). 1969. text ed. 6.95x (ISBN 0-02-473600-7, 47360); tapes 375.00 (ISBN 0-02-473580-9, 47358); tape script 6.95 (ISBN 0-02-473610-4, 47361). Macmillan.

Audio Visual Aids: Uses & Resources in Gerontology. Ira S. Hirschfield & Theresa N. Lambert. LC 78-59262. 1978. pap. 4.50 (ISBN 0-88474-047-1). USC Andrus Geron.

Audio-Visual Guide to American Holidays. Ed. by Carol A. Emmens & Harry Maglione. LC 78-6230. 1978. lib. bdg. 13.50 (ISBN 0-8108-1140-5). Scarecrow.

Audio-Visual Instruction: Technology, Media & Methods. 5th ed. Ed. by James W. Brown & Richard B. Lewis. (Illus.). 1976. text ed. 19.95 (ISBN 0-07-008165-4, C); instructor's manual 5.95 (ISBN 0-07-008171-9); transparencies 25.00 (ISBN 0-07-008172-7). McGraw.

Audio-Visual Program, No. 5. Anthony B. Colletti. (Keystone Publications' Audio-Visual Program Ser.). 1979. 215.00 (ISBN 0-912126-39-6); instrs's. guide 7.07 (ISBN 0-912126-37-X); student wkbk. 1.79 (ISBN 0-912126-38-8). Keystone Pubns.

Audiological Assessment. 2nd ed. Darrell E. Rose. 1978. 20.95 (ISBN 0-13-050815-2). P-H.

Audiological Evaluation of the Pediatric Patient. Maurice H. Miller & Ira A. Polisar. (Amer. Lec. in Speech & Hearing Ser.). (Illus.). 132p. 1971. 9.50 (ISBN 0-398-02160-0). C C Thomas.

Audiology. 4th ed. Hayes A. Newby. LC 78-14797. (Illus.). 1979. ref. 19.95 (ISBN 0-13-050856-X). P-H.

Audiology, Education & the Hearing Impaired Child. Fred H. Bess & Freeman E. McConnell. (Illus.). 325p. 1981. pap. text ed. 15.95 (ISBN 0-8016-0671-3). Mosby.

Audiology for the Physician. Robert W. Keith. (Illus.). 352p. 1980. 30.00 (ISBN 0-683-04551-2). Williams & Wilkins.

Audiology for the School Speech-Language Clinician. J. G. Clark. (Illus.). 208p. 1980. 14.75 (ISBN 0-398-04004-4). C C Thomas.

Audiometric Interpretation: A Manual of Basic Audiometry. Lyle L. Lloyd & Harriet Kaplan. 1978. pap. 19.95 (ISBN 0-8391-0759-5). Univ Park.

Audiovisual, Draughting, Office, Reproduction & Other Ancillary Equipment & Supplies: Equipment Planning Guide for Vocational & Technical Trading & Education Programmes. International Labour Office, Geneva. (No. 15). (Illus.). 279p. (Orig.). 1979. pap. 22.80 (ISBN 9-22-102112-2). Intl Labour Office.

Audiovisual Equipment & Materials: A Basic Repair & Maintenance Manual. Don Schroeder & Gary Lare. LC 79-384. 172p. 1979. pap. text ed. 10.00 (ISBN 0-8108-1206-1). Scarecrow.

Audiovisual Market Place A Multimedia Guide 1981: A Multimedia Guide. 11th ed. Ed. by O. Weber. LC 69-18201. 1981. pap. 32.50 (ISBN 0-8352-1333-1). Bowker.

Audiovisual Media & Libraries: Selected Readings. Emanuel T. Prostano. LC 72-89111. 276p. 1972. lib. bdg. 18.50x (ISBN 0-87287-053-7). Libs Unl.

Audiovisual Primer. rev. ed. Michael Goudket. LC 72-93755. (Illus.). 77p. 1974. pap. text ed. 3.25x (ISBN 0-8077-2437-8). Tchrs Coll.

Audiovisual Script Writing. Norton S. Parker. 1974. pap. 7.00 (ISBN 0-8135-0797-9). Rutgers U Pr.

Audiovisuals for Women. Joan Nordquist. LC 80-14691. 153p. 1980. lib. bdg. 10.95x (ISBN 0-89950-011-0); pap. 8.95x (ISBN 0-89950-012-9). McFarland & Co.

Audit Committee. 1978. pap. 1.50. Am Inst CPA.

Audit Decisions in Accounting Practice. Ed. by Richard S. Woods. 350p. 1973. 11.50 (ISBN 0-8260-9575-5, 98631, Pub. by Wiley-Hamilton). Wiley.

Audit Director's Guide: How to Serve Effectively on the Corporate Audit Committee. Louis Braiott, Jr. LC 80-23989. 250p. 1980. 24.95 (ISBN 0-471-05866-1, Pub. by Ronald Pr). Wiley.

Audit Practice Case: Midwestern Products, Inc. Robert L. Grinaker & Ben B. Barr. 1967. text ed. 13.50x (ISBN 0-256-00172-3). Irwin.

Audit Problem: Crafters, Inc. Arthur W. Holmes & David C. Burns. 1980. pap. 12.95x (ISBN 0-256-02162-7). Irwin.

Auditing. 6th ed. Leslie R. Howard. 320p. (Orig.). 1978. pap. text ed. 11.95x (ISBN 0-7121-0169-1, Pub. by Macdonald & Evans England). Intl Ideas.

Auditing. rev. ed. Jack C. Robertson. 1979. text ed. 19.95x (ISBN 0-256-02212-7). Business Pubns.

Auditing: An Integrated Approach. A. Arens & J. Loebbecke. (Illus.). 1976. 19.95 o.p. (ISBN 0-13-051698-8). P-H.

Auditing: An Integrated Approach. 2nd ed. A. Arens & J Loebbecke. 1980. 21.00 (ISBN 0-13-051656-2). P-H.

Auditing Corporate Data-Processing Activities, No. 776. Paul R. Macchiaverna. (Illus.). 85p. (Orig.). 1980. pap. 5.00 (ISBN 0-8237-0212-X); pap. text ed. 15.00 (ISBN 0-686-64787-4). Conference Bd.

Auditing in the Electronic Environment: Theory, Practice & Literature. Delroy L. Cornick. LC 80-81813. 300p. 1980. 19.75 (ISBN 0-912338-23-7); microfiche 14.75. Lomond.

Auditing: Integrated Concepts & Procedures. Donald H. Taylor & G. William Glezen. LC 78-16264. 1979. text ed. 24.95 (ISBN 0-471-84654-6); solutions manual avail. (ISBN 0-471-04565-9); tchrs. manual (ISBN 0-471-05296-5). Wiley.

Auditing Judgement: A Book of Cases. Alan P. Johnson. 1980. 19.95x (ISBN 0-256-02382-4). Irwin.

Auditing Manual. 9th ed. 15.00 (ISBN 0-932788-00-9). Bradley CPA.

Auditing Manual. Frederick Staples. 181p. 1980. pap. 9.50. Counting Hse.

Auditing: Philosophy & Technique. John W. Cook & Gary M. Winkle. LC 75-31033. (Illus.). 512p. 1976. text ed. 18.50 o.p. (ISBN 0-395-20660-X); inst. manual 3.25 o.p. (ISBN 0-395-20662-6). HM.

Auditing: Philosophy & Technique. 2nd ed. John W. Cook & Gary M. Winkle. LC 79-88718. (Illus.). 1980. text ed. 19.75 (ISBN 0-395-28660-3); instructor's manual 3.25 (ISBN 0-395-28661-1). HM.

Auditing Principles. 4th ed. H. Stettler. 1977. text ed. 19.95 (ISBN 0-13-051706-2); practice case 10.95 (ISBN 0-13-694521-X); audit workpapers, 3rd ed. 7.95 (ISBN 0-13-052712-2). P-H.

Auditing: Standards & Procedures. 9th ed. Arthur W. Holmes & David C. Burns. 1979. text ed. 19.95 (ISBN 0-256-02161-9). Irwin.

Auditing the Data Processing Function. Richard W. Lott. (Illus.). 1980. 17.95 (ISBN 0-8144-5527-1). Am Mgmt.

Auditing the Modern Hospital. B. T. Hall. 256p. 1977. 32.95 (ISBN 0-686-68587-3, 14920). Hospital Finan.

Auditing Theory & Practice. Roger H. Hermanson et al. 1976. text ed. 16.95x o.p. (ISBN 0-256-01445-0). Irwin.

Auditing Theory & Practice. rev. ed. Roger H. Hermanson et al. 1980. 19.95x (ISBN 0-256-02330-1). Irwin.

Auditions & Scenes: American & British Theatre. Richard O. Bell & Joan K. Bell. LC 80-80119. 200p. Date not set. pap. 9.95 (ISBN 0-9603626-1-4). Armado & Moth.

Auditions & Scenes from Shakespeare. Richard O. Bell & Joan K. Bell. LC 79-54914. 161p. (Orig.). 1979. pap. 7.95 (ISBN 0-9603626-0-6). Armado & Moth.

Auditorium Acoustics. Ed. by Robin MacKenzie. LC 75-16445. 231p. 1975. 42.95 (ISBN 0-470-56284-6). Halsted Pr.

Auditory Analysis Skillsbook. Jerome Rosner. (gr. k-3). 1981. 17.50 (ISBN 0-8027-9127-1). Walker & Co.

Auditory & Hearing Prosthetic Research. Ed. by Vernon D. Larson et al. 1979. 21.50 (ISBN 0-685-67602-1). Grune.

Auditory & Motor Skills. Virginia Polish. (Starting off with Phonics Ser.: Bk. 1). (gr. k). 1980. pap. text ed. 2.21 (ISBN 0-87895-051-6); tchr's manual 2.00 (ISBN 0-87895-061-3). Modern Curr.

Auditory & Visual Pattern Recognition. David J. Getty & James H. Howard, Jr. 240p. 1981. professional ref. text 16.50 (ISBN 0-89859-087-6). L Erlbaum Assocs.

Auditory Discrimination Practice Exercises. Carol Smith. 1981. pap. 3.95 (ISBN 0-8134-2168-3, 2168). Interstate.

Auditory Dysfunction. Sanford E. Gerber & George T. Mencher. (Illus.). 256p. 1980. text ed. 19.95 (ISBN 0-933014-60-0). College-Hill.

Auditory Perception of Speech: An Introduction to Principles & Problems. Derek A. Sanders. LC 76-27320. (Illus.). 1977. text ed. 16.95 (ISBN 0-13-052787-4). P-H.

Auditory Processing Disorders & Remediation. 2nd ed. Bernice E. Heasley. (Illus.). 168p. 1980. pap. 16.50 spiral bdg. (ISBN 0-398-04047-8). C C Thomas.

Auditory, Reading & Dialogue Comprehension Exercises in Spanish. Susanne Vasi & Joseph Tomasino. (gr. 9-12). 1973. pap. text ed. 2.95 cancelled (ISBN 0-88345-025-9, 18113); tchr's manual 3.50 (ISBN 0-88345-026-7, 18135); cassettes 40.00 (ISBN 0-685-48110-7). Regents Pub.

Auditory Regiona of Primates & Eutherian Insectivores. R. D. MacPhee. (Contributions to Primatology Ser.: Vol. 18). (Illus.). 280p. 1981. pap. 35.00 (ISBN 3-8055-1963-X). S Karger.

Auditory Techniques. C. Griffiths. (Illus.). 232p. 1974. 22.75 (ISBN 0-398-03047-2). C C Thomas.

Audrey. Mary Johnston. 1976. lib. bdg. 11.95 (ISBN 0-89968-150-6). Lightyear.

Audrey Rose. Frank De Felitta. 1977. pap. 3.25 (ISBN 0-446-82472-0). Warner Bks.

Audubon. John Chancellor. (Illus.). 1978. 17.95 o.p. (ISBN 0-670-14053-8, Studio). Viking Pr.

Audubon & His Journal, 2 vols. Maria R. Aududon. Ed. by Daniel Aaron. (American Men & Women of Letters Audubon & His Journals Ser.). (Illus.). 1100p. 1981. pap. 14.95 (ISBN 0-87754-174-4). Chelsea Hse.

Audubon & Other Capers: Confessions of a Texas Bookmaker. John H. Jenkins. LC 76-2347. (Illus.). 1976. 12.50 (ISBN 0-8363-0139-0). Jenkins.

Audubon Birds. Roger T. Peterson. LC 79-57407. (Abbeville Library of Art: No. 4). (Illus.). 112p. 1980. pap. 4.95 (ISBN 0-89659-091-7). Abbeville Pr.

Audubon Cat. Mary Calhoun. LC 80-16278. (Illus.). 32p. (gr. k-3). 1981. 7.95 (ISBN 0-688-22253-6); PLB 7.63 (ISBN 0-688-32253-0). Morrow.

Audubon Field Guide to North American Mammals. John O. Whitaker, Jr. LC 79-3525. (Illus.). 752p. 1980. 9.95 (ISBN 0-394-50762-2). Knopf.

Audubon Field Guide to North American Trees. western ed. Elbert L. Little, Jr. 1980. 9.95 o.p. (ISBN 0-394-50761-4). Knopf.

Audubon, Homer, Whistler, & the 19th Century America. John Wilmerding. (Illus.). 1975. Repr. 5.95 o.p. (ISBN 0-88308-011-7). Lamplight Pub.

Audubon Illustrated Handbook of American Birds. Edgar M. Reilly, Jr. (Illus.). 544p. 1968. 20.00 o.p. (ISBN 0-685-48741-5, Pub by National Audubon Society). Interbk Inc.

Audubon in Florida: With Selections from the Writings of John James Audubon. Kathryn H. Proby. LC 72-85114. (Illus.). 384p. 1974. pap. 14.95 (ISBN 0-87024-301-2). U of Miami Pr.

Audubon Society Encyclopedia of North American Birds. John K. Terres. LC 80-7616. (Illus.). 1280p. 1980. 60.00 (ISBN 0-394-46651-9). Knopf.

Audubon Society Field Guide to North American Butterflies. Robert Pyle. LC 80-84240. (Illus.). 864p. 1981. 11.95 (ISBN 0-394-51914-0). Knopf.

Audubon Society Field Guide to North American Insects & Spiders. Lorus Milne & Margery Milne. LC 80-7620. (Illus.). 1008p. 1980. 9.95 (ISBN 0-394-50763-0). Knopf.

Audubon Society Field Guide to North American Seashells. Herald A. Rehder. LC 80-84239. 864p. 1981. 9.95 (ISBN 0-394-51913-2). Knopf.

Audubon Society Handbook for Birders. Stephen W. Kress. (Illus.). 320p. 1981. 14.95 (ISBN 0-684-16336-5, ScribT). Scribner.

Auf Deutsch, Bitte. Vols. 1-3. text ed. 7.95 ea.; tapebks. vols. 1 & 2 5.95 ea.; readers vols. 1 & 2 6.95 ea.; teachers's manual o.p. (ISBN 0-88499-080-X); cassette sets vols. 1 & 2 115.00 ea.; tape sets vols. 1 & 2 225.00 ea. Inst Mod Lang.

Aufstieg und Niedergang der Roemischen Welt, Vol. 9, Pt. 2. 1979. 211.80x (ISBN 3-11007-175-4). De Gruyter.

Aufstieg und Niedergang der Roemischen Welf: Tiel II, Vol. 19, Pt. 1. 1979. 223.50x (ISBN 3-11007-968-2). De Gruyter.

Auge y Decadencia De la Trata Negrera En Puerto Rico (1820-1860) Arturo Morales-Carrione. LC 77-11193. (Illus.). 1978. pap. cancelled o.p. (ISBN 0-8477-0850-0). U of PR Pr.

Augers. Paula Rankin. LC 80-70565. (Poetry Ser.). 1980. 9.95 (ISBN 0-915604-45-0); pap. 4.95 (ISBN 0-915604-46-9). Carnegie-Mellon.

Augmenting Agents in Cancer Therapy. Ed. by Evan M. Hersh et al. (Progress in Cancer Research & Therapy Ser.). 585p. 1981. text ed. 49.00 (ISBN 0-89004-525-9). Raven.

Augsburg Confession: Anniversity Edition. Tr. by Theodore G. Tappert. 64p. 1980. pap. 1.25 (ISBN 0-8006-1385-6, 1-1385). Fortress.

August Bebels Briefwechsel Mit Friedrich Engels. Werner Blumenberg. (Quellen und Untersuchungen Zur Geschichte der Deutschenund Osterreichischen Arbeiterbewegung: No. 6). 1965. 123.50x (ISBN 90-2790-155-4). Mouton.

August Belmont: A Political Biography. Irving Katz. LC 68-19751. (Illus.). 1968. 16.00x (ISBN 0-231-03112-2). Columbia U Pr.

August Sander. Illus. by August Sander. LC 77-70069. (The Aperture Historie of Photography Ser.). (Illus.). 1978. bds. 8.95 (ISBN 0-89381-007-X). Aperture.

August Strindberg. Walter Johnson. LC 76-17910. (World Authors Ser: No. 410). 1976. lib. bdg. 12.50 (ISBN 0-8057-6250-7). Twayne.

August: 1939. Nicholas Fleming. (Illus.). 242p. 1980. 19.50x (ISBN 0-8419-7200-1). Holmes & Meier.

Augusta Tabor: Her Side of the Scandal. Caroline Bancroft. 1955. pap. 1.50 (ISBN 0-933472-14-5). Johnson Colo.

Augustan Lyric. Ed. by Donald Davie. (Poetry Bookshelf). 1974. pap. text ed. 3.95x (ISBN 0-435-15701-9). Heinemann Ed.

Auguste Comte: Correspondance Generale et Confessions, Tome 1, 1814-1840. Ed. by Paulo E. Berredo Carneiro & Pierre Arnaud. (Archives Positivistes). 1973. pap. 40.00x (ISBN 90-2797-192-7). Mouton.

Auguste Comte: Ecrits De Jeunesse 1816-1828. Ed. by Paulo E. Berredo Carneiro & Pierre Arnaud. (Archives Positivistes). 1971. pap. 52.35x (ISBN 90-2796-767-9). Mouton.

Auguste Comte: The Foundation of Sociology. Kenneth Thompson. LC 75-12566. 1975. 19.95 (ISBN 0-470-85988-1). Halsted Pr.

Auguste Forel & the Baha'i Faith. Peter Muhlschlegel. Tr. by Helene Neri from Ger. 1979. pap. 1.85 (ISBN 0-85398-076-4, 7-32-35, Pub by G Ronald England). Baha'i.

Augustine: His Life & Thought. W. Thomas Smith. LC 79-92071. (Illus.). 190p. (Orig.). 1980. pap. 8.50 (ISBN 0-8042-0871-9). John Knox.

Augustine: Later Works. Ed. by John Burnaby. (Library of Christian Classics Ichthus Edition). 1980. pap. 9.95 (ISBN 0-664-24165-4). Westminster.

Augustine Laure, S.J., Missionary to the Yakimas. Victor Garrand. 1977. 6.95 (ISBN 0-87770-176-8); pap. 4.95 (ISBN 0-87770-187-3). Ye Galleon.

Augustine of Hippo: A Biography. Peter Brown. 1967. 15.00 o.p. (ISBN 0-520-00186-9); pap. 4.95 o.p. (ISBN 0-520-01411-1, CAL179). U of Cal Pr.

Augustine on the Body. Margaret R. Miles. LC 79-14226. (American Academy of Religion, Dissertation Ser.: No. 31). 1979. 12.00x (ISBN 0-89130-288-3, 010131); pap. 7.50 (ISBN 0-89130-289-1). Scholars Pr Ca.

Augustinian Humanism: Studies in Human Bondage & Earthly Grace. James W. Woelfel. LC 79-5376. 1979. pap. text ed. 7.50 (ISBN 0-8191-0874-X). U Pr of Amer.

Augusto Roa Bastos. David W. Foster. (World Authors Ser.: No. 507 (Paraguay)). 1978. 12.50 (ISBN 0-8057-6348-1). Twayne.

Augustus Earle: Travel Artist: Paintings & Drawings in the Rex Nan Kivell Collection National Library of Australia. Jocelyn Hackforth-Jones. 157p. 1980. 50.00x (ISBN 0-85967-631-5, Pub. by Scolar Pr England). Biblio Dist.

Auk, the Dodo, & the Oryx: Vanished & Vanishing Creatures. Robert Silverberg. LC 67-10476. (Illus.). (gr. 7 up). 1967. 10.95 (ISBN 0-690-11106-1, TYC-J). T Y Crowell.

Auks of the World. (Illus.). 250p. 1981. 30.00 (ISBN 0-88839-084-X). Hancock Hse.

Auld Acquaintance: An Autobiography. Guy Lombardo & Jack Altshul. 1976. pap. 1.95 o.p. (ISBN 0-345-25244-6). Ballantine.

Aum. (Agni Yoga Ser.). 1959. flexible cover 9.00x (ISBN 0-933574-12-6). Agni Yoga Soc.

Aunt Blanche's Memory Book. Bernice Dittmer. LC 79-92334. 1980. 50.00 o.p. (ISBN 0-930208-08-0). Mangan Bks.

Aunt Ellen's Crochet Handbook: A Treasury of Techniques & Projects. Staff of Workbasket Magazine. LC 80-85484. (Illus., Orig.). 1981. pap. 2.95 (ISBN 0-86675-325-7, 3257). Mod Handicraft.

Aunt Erma's Cope Book. Erma Bombeck. 1980. pap. 2.75 (ISBN 0-449-24334-6, Crest). Fawcett.

Aunt Ethel: An Ending. Nancy Holt. LC 79-92752. 1980. pap. 5.00 (ISBN 0-930378-11-3). Printed Matter.

Aunt Hack's Rock House Kitchen: A Cookbook with a Story. Georgia Ericson. 1977. write for info. Crosby County.

Aunt Matilda's Ghost. Mignon F. Ballard. (gr. 11 up). 1978. 5.95 o.s.i. (ISBN 0-87695-210-4); pap. 3.95 (ISBN 0-87695-211-2). Aurora Pubs.

Aunt Maude & the Faisan D'or. Barbara Devor. 1980. 6.00 (ISBN 0-682-49563-8). Exposition.

Aunt Vinnie's Invasion. Karin Anckarsvard. LC 62-17039. (Illus.). 128p. (gr. 5-9). 1962. 4.50 o.p. (ISBN 0-15-204621-6, HJ). HarBraceJ.

Auntie Mame. Patrick Dennis. LC 54-11512. 1954. 8.95 (ISBN 0-8149-0085-2). Vanguard.

Aunty. Vic Volk. LC 75-30964. (Illus.). (ps-3). 1975. 3.95 (ISBN 0-916144-01-1). Stemmer Hse.

Aural Habilitation: The Foundations of Verbal Learning in Hearing-Impaired Children. Daniel Ling & Agnes H. Ling. 1978. 12.50 (ISBN 0-88200-121-3). Bell Assn Deaf.

Auraria: Where Denver Began. Don D. Etter. LC 72-85656. (Illus.). 100p. 1980. pap. 8.95 (ISBN 0-87081-093-6). Colo Assoc.

Auras: An Essay on the Meaning of Colors. Edgar Cayce. 1973. pap. 1.25 (ISBN 0-87604-012-1). ARE Pr.

Aureng-Zebe. John Dryden. Ed. by Frederick M. Link. LC 78-123119. (Regents Restoration Drama Series). 1971. 8.75x (ISBN 0-8032-0377-2); pap. 2.35x (ISBN 0-8032-5376-1, BB 275, Bison). U of Nebr Pr.

Auriculas & Primroses. W. R. Hecker. 1971. 10.50 o.p. (ISBN 0-8231-6033-5). Branford.

Aurora. Joan Smith. 224p. 1980. 10.95 o.s.i. (ISBN 0-8027-0651-7). Walker & Co.

Aurora: Canadian Writing in 1978. Ed. by Morris Wolfe. LC 78-1227. 1979. pap. 7.95 (ISBN 0-385-13646-3). Doubleday.

Aurora Floyd, 3 vols. Ed. by Robert L. Wolff. LC 79-50468. (Mary Elizabeth Braddon Ser.: Vol. 1). 1979. Set. lib. bdg. 96.00 (ISBN 0-8240-4350-2); lib. bdg. 38.00 ea. Garland Pub.

Aurora: New Canadian Writing Nineteen Eighty. Morris Wolfe. LC 80-719. 312p. 1981. pap. 9.95 (ISBN 0-385-15771-1). Doubleday.

Aus Nah und Fern. 2nd ed. L. B. Foltin. 1963. pap. text ed. 7.70 (ISBN 0-395-04464-2). HM.

Aus Schleiermachers Leben, in Briefen, 4 vols. xxxvi, 2006p. (Ger.). 1974. Repr. of 1863 ed. 223.53x (ISBN 3-11-002261-3). De Gruyter.

Auschwitz: Nazi Extermination Camp. Danuta Czech et al. Tr. by Iain W. Taylor from Pol. (Illus.). 192p. (Orig.). 1978. pap. 7.50x (ISBN 0-8002-2294-6). Intl Pubns Serv.

Auseinandersetzungen an der Pariser Universitaet im Xiii Jahrhundert. (Miscellanea Mediaevalia Ser, Vol. 10). 1976. 78.00x (ISBN 3-11-005986-X). De Gruyter.

Auspices. Cid Corman. (Orig.). 1978. limited signed ed. 20.00x (ISBN 0-915316-59-5); pap. 5.00x (ISBN 0-915316-58-7). Pentagram.

Austalian Literature: A Reference Guide. 2nd ed. Fred Lock & Alan Lawson. (Australian Bibliographies Ser.). 134p. 1980. pap. text ed. 10.95x (ISBN 0-19-554214-2). Oxford U Pr.

Austin. R. J. Wyatt. LC 80-68896. (Illus.). 256p. 1981. 38.00 (ISBN 0-7153-7948-8). David & Charles.

Austin: A Pictorial History. Larry Willoughby. Ed. by Donna R. Friedman. (Illus.). 208p. 1981. pap. write for info. (ISBN 0-89865-078-X). Donning Co.

Austin Clarke: A Study of His Writing. G. Craig Tapping. 368p. 1980. lib. bdg. 29.00x (ISBN 0-389-20041-7). B&N.

Austin Colony Pioneers. Worth S. Ray. LC 77-144991. (Illus.). 17.50 (ISBN 0-8363-0007-6). Jenkins.

Austin-Healy 3000 1959-1967. R. M. Clarke. (Brookland Bks). (Illus.). 100p. 1979. pap. text ed. 11.95 (ISBN 0-906589-64-9, Pub. by Enthusias England). Motorbooks Intl.

Austrailian Books in Print. 1980. 39.50 (ISBN 0-8352-1316-1). Bowker.

Austral English. Edward E. Morris. LC 68-18003. 1968. Repr. of 1898 ed. 34.00 (ISBN 0-8103-3287-6). Gale.

Australia. Elizabeth Cornelia. LC 78-56592. (Countries Ser.). (Illus.). 1978. lib. bdg. 7.95 (ISBN 0-686-51148-4). Silver.

Australia. 3rd. rev. ed. R. M. Crawford. 1970. text ed. 5.00x (ISBN 0-09-105110-X, Hutchinson U Lib). Humanities.

Australia. R. L. Heathcote. (World's Lanscapes Ser.). (Illus.). 240p. 1976. text ed. 19.50x o.p. (ISBN 0-582-48166-X); pap. text ed. 12.95x (ISBN 0-582-48179-1). Longman.

Australia. Paul Ritchie. (Illus.). 1968. 3.95g o.s.i. (ISBN 0-02-776140-1). Macmillan.

Australia. 4th ed. Sunset Editors. LC 80-80853. (Illus.). 128p. 1980. pap. 5.95 (ISBN 0-376-06064-6, Sunset Bks). Sunset-Lane.

Australia & Britain: Studies in a Changing Relationship. Ed. by A. F. Madden & W. H. Morris-Jones. 191p. 1980. 25.00x (ISBN 0-7146-3149-3, F Cass Co). Biblio Dist.

Australia & Japan: Issues in the Economic Relationship. Pref. by John Crawford & Saburo Okita. (Australia-Japan Economic Relations Research Project Monograph: No. 2). (Illus.). 140p. 1980. pap. text ed. 5.95 (ISBN 0-9596197-1-2). Bks Australia.

Australia & Japan: Nuclear Energy Issues in the Pacific. Ed. by Stuart Harris & Keichi Oshima. (Australia-Japan Economic Relations Research Project Monograph: No. 3). (Illus.). 245p. 1980. pap. text ed. 9.95 (ISBN 0-9596197-2-0). Bks Australia.

Australia & New Zealand. A. Trollope. (Colonial History Ser.). 1968. Repr. of 1873 ed. 35.00 o.p. (ISBN 0-7129-0729-7, Dist by Shoe String). Dawson Pub.

Australia & New Zealand: Pacific Community. Lyn Harrington. LC 70-82914. (World Neighbors Ser). (Illus.). (gr. 6 up). 1969. PLB 6.80 o.p. (ISBN 0-525-67007-6). Elsevier-Nelson.

Australia & the Aborigines. (gr. 2). 1974. pap. text ed. 5.80 (ISBN 0-205-03882-4, 8038821); tchrs'. guide 5.80 (ISBN 0-205-04228-7, 8042284). Allyn.

Australia & the League of Nations. Ed. by W. J. Hudson. 224p. 1980. 20.00x (ISBN 0-424-00084-9, Pub. by Sydney U Pr Australia). Intl Schol Bk Serv.

Australia Bombshell. Margaret Hundley. 1981. 5.75 (ISBN 0-8062-1645-X). Carlton.

Australia Handbook 1978. 18th ed. (Illus.). 1979. pap. 7.50x (ISBN 0-642-03908-9). Intl Pubns Serv.

Australia: History & Horizons. Roderick Cameron. LC 76-155154. (Illus.). 286p. 1971. 25.00x (ISBN 0-231-03559-4). Columbia U Pr.

Australia in Pictures. Sterling Publishing Company Editors. LC 66-16198. (Visual Geography Ser.). (Orig.). (gr. 4-12). PLB 4.99 o.p. (ISBN 0-8069-1041-0); pap. 2.95 (ISBN 0-8069-1040-2). Sterling.

Australia in World Affairs: Nineteen Seventy to Seventy Five. Ed. by W. J. Hudson. 466p. 1981. text ed. 29.50x (ISBN 0-86861-369-X, 2565). Allen Unwin.

Australia on Fifteen & Twenty Dollars a Day. 287p. 1981. pap. 4.95 (ISBN 0-671-25491-X). Frommer-Pasmantier.

Australia: The Quiet Continent. 2nd ed. D. Pike. (Illus.). 1970. 29.95 (ISBN 0-521-07745-1); pap. 9.95x (ISBN 0-521-09604-9, 365). Cambridge U Pr.

Australia, Travel Survival Kit. Tony Wheeler. (Illus.). 1979. pap. 3.95 (ISBN 0-908086-04-0). Hippocrene Bks.

Australian Adventure: Letters from an Ambassador's Wife. Anne Clark. (Illus.). 1969. 12.95 (ISBN 0-292-70001-6). U of Tex Pr.

Australian Agricultural Plants. D. L. Jackson. Date not set. write for info. (ISBN 0-686-15350-2, Pub. by Sydney U Pr). Intl Schol Bk Serv. Postponed.

Australian & New Zealand Fishing. Ed. by Jack Pollard. LC 73-473961. (Illus.). 960p. 1977. 15.00x (ISBN 0-7271-0168-4). Intl Pubns Serv.

Australian Architecture, 1901 to 1951: Sources of Modernism. Ed. by Donald L. Johnson. 240p. 1980. 35.00x (ISBN 0-424-00071-7, Pub. by Sydney U Pr Australia). Intl Schol Bk Serv.

Australian Barley. R. W. Fitzsimmons & C. W. Wrigley. 1980. 20.00x (ISBN 0-643-00344-4, Pub. by CSJRO Australia). State Mutual Bk.

Australian Barleys. 64p. 1979. pap. 13.50 (ISBN 0-643-00344-4, CO02, CSIRO). Unipub.

Australian Barleys. R. W. Fitzsimmons & C. W. Wrigley. 86p. 1980. 9.95x (ISBN 0-643-00344-4, Pub. by CSIRO Australia). Intl Schol Bk Serv.

Australian Book of Cake Decorating. Bernice Vercoe & Dorothy Evans. 1973. 8.95x o.p. (ISBN 0-600-07190-1). Exposition.

Australian Book of Flower Arrangements. Beryl Guertner. (Illus.). 12.50x (ISBN 0-392-06790-0, ABC). Soccer.

Australian Bushflowers. Jean Langley. (Illus.). 19.50x (ISBN 0-7018-0330-4, ABC). Soccer.

Australian Christmas. Helen Gibson. (Illus.). 32p. (ps-1). 1980. Repr. of 1961 ed. cancelled o.s.i. (ISBN 0-934680-01-9). Cobbers.

Australian Composition in the Twentieth Century. Ed. by Frank Callaway. David Tunley. 1979. 42.00x (ISBN 0-19-550522-0). Oxford U Pr.

Australian Conference on Electrochemistry, 1st. Ed. by J. A. Friend. 1964. 44.00 o.p. (ISBN 0-08-010501-7). Pergamon.

Australian Democracy in Crisis: A New Theoretical Introduction to Australian Politics. Andrew Theophanpous. 224p. 1980. 27.00 (ISBN 0-19-554200-2). Oxford U Pr.

Australian Desert Life. Keith Davey. 6.50x (ISBN 0-392-07552-0, SpS). Soccer.

Australian Economic Framework. 4th ed. N. T. Drohan & J. H. Day. (Illus.). 1975. 12.50x (ISBN 0-686-60736-8). Intl Pubns Serv.

Australian Federal System. Jean Holmes & Campbell Sharman. LC 77-78552. 1978. pap. text ed. 8.50x (ISBN 0-86861-080-1). Allen Unwin.

Australian Finches. Curt A. Enehjelm. Tr. by U. Erich Friese from Ger. Orig. Title: Australische Prachtfinken. (Illus.). 1979. 2.95 (ISBN 0-87666-987-9, KW-027). TFH Pubns.

Australian Great Barrier Reef in Colour. rev. ed. Keith Gillett. (Illus.). 96p. 1980. Repr. of 1968 ed. 11.95 (ISBN 0-589-50199-2, Pub. by Reed Books Australia). C E Tuttle.

Australian House & Garden Book of Chrysanthemums. Margaret Masters. pap. 6.50x (ISBN 0-392-06885-0, ABC). Soccer.

Australian in the First World War. B. Gammage. (Cambridge Introduction to the History of Mankind Ser.). (Illus.). 1976. pap. text ed. 3.95 (ISBN 0-521-21018-6). Cambridge U Pr.

Australian Labor Movement: Eighteen Fifty to Nineteen Seven. R. N. Ebbels. 15.00x (ISBN 0-392-07633-0, SpS). Soccer.

Australian Literature to Nineteen Hundred: A Guide to Information Sources. Ed. by Barry G. Andrews & William H. Wilde. LC 74-11521. (American Literature, English Literature & World Literatures in English Information Guide Ser.: Vol. 22). 472p. 1980. 30.00 (ISBN 0-8103-1215-8). Gale.

Australian Local Government: Organizational & Social Planning. M. Jones. 1978. pap. text ed. 14.95x (ISBN 0-686-65324-6, 00512). Heinemann Ed.

Australian Monetary Policy. David Rowan. (Illus.). 313p. 1981. text ed. 22.50x (ISBN 0-86861-360-6, 2318); pap. text ed. 13.95x (ISBN 0-86861-368-1, 2319). Allen Unwin.

Australian National Bibliography, 1976. 16th ed. National Library of Australia. LC 63-33739. 1464p. 1977. 67.50x (ISBN 0-8002-1048-4). Intl Pubns Serv.

Australian National Bibliography 1979, 2 vols. 19th ed. Canberra Nat'l. Library of Australia. LC 63-33739. 1980. Set. 67.50x (ISBN 0-8002-1860-4). Intl Pubns Serv.

Australian National Elections of 1977. Ed. by Howard R. Penniman. 1980. pap. 8.25 (ISBN 0-8447-3357-1). Am Enterprise.

Australian Native Orchids in Colour. Leo Cady & E. R. Rotherham. (Reed Colourbook Ser.). (Illus.). 112p. 1970. 11.75 (ISBN 0-589-07011-8, Pub. by Reed Bks Australia). C E Tuttle.

Australian Native Plants for Home Gardens. 6th rev. ed. A. E. Brooks. (Illus.). 1979. 13.95x (ISBN 0-85091-091-9, Pub. by Lothian). Intl Schol Bk Serv.

Australian Official Publications. Howard Coxon. LC 80-40046. (Guides to Official Publications Ser.: Vol. 5). (Illus.). 227p. 1980. 36.00 (ISBN 0-08-023131-4). Pergamon.

Australian Outback. Ian Moffit. (World's Wild Places Ser.). (Illus.). 1976. lib. bdg. 11.97 (ISBN 0-686-51016-X). Silver.

Australian Outback. Ian Moffitt. (World's Wild Places Ser.). (Illus.). 1976. 12.95 (ISBN 0-8094-2059-7). Time-Life.

Australian Paintings of the Heidelberg School: The Jack Manton Collection. Ed. by Patrick McCaughey. (Illus.). 160p. 1979. text ed. 65.00x (ISBN 0-19-550592-1). Oxford U Pr.

Australian Parrots. 2nd ed. Joseph M. Forshaw. (Illus.). 224p. 1980. 75.00 (ISBN 0-686-62188-3); write for ltd. ed. Eastview.

Australian Political Parties. G. Starr. 1978. pap. text ed. 12.95x (ISBN 0-686-65414-5, 00513). Heinemann Ed.

Australian Renewable Energy Resources Index: Issue No. 1. Ed. by Robert D. Clark. 1979. pap. 7.00x (ISBN 0-686-24273-4, Pub. by CSIRO). Intl Schol Bk Serv.

Australian Schools & the Law. 2nd ed. A. E. Knott et al. (Educational Organization & Administration Ser.). 180p. (Orig.). 1981. pap. text ed. 10.25 (ISBN 0-7022-1549-X). U of Queensland Pr.

Australian Social Security Today. Ed. by T. H. Kewley. 248p. 1980. 22.50x (ISBN 0-424-00067-9, Pub. by Sydney U Pr Australia). Intl Schol Bk Serv.

Australian Spider. John Child. pap. 6.50x (ISBN 0-392-07647-0, SpS). Soccer.

Australian Tertiary Deposits Containing Terrestrial Mammals. R. A. Stirton et al. (U. C. Publ. in Geological Sciences: Vol. 77). 1968. pap. 6.00x (ISBN 0-520-09180-9). U of Cal Pr.

Australian Vegetation. Ed. by R. H. Groves. LC 80-40421. (Illus.). 350p. Date not set. price not set (ISBN 0-521-23436-0); pap. price not set (ISBN 0-521-29950-0). Cambridge U Pr.

Australian Wheat Varieties. 126p. 1975. pap. 15.50 (ISBN 0-643-00143-3, CO08, CSIRO). Unipub.

Australian Wheat Varieties. G. K. Ferns. 1980. 25.00x (ISBN 0-643-00143-3, Pub. by CSJRO Australia). State Mutual Bk.

Australian Wheat Varieties, Suppl. 1. 30p. 1978. pap. 13.50 (ISBN 0-643-00325-8, CO01, CSIRO). Unipub.

Australian Yearbook of International Law 1970-1973, Vol. 1. 1975. 30.00 (ISBN 0-379-00482-8). Oceana.

Australians: How They Live & Work. Nancy Learmonth. LC 72-89452. 166p. 1973. text ed. 8.95 (ISBN 0-03-029571-8, HoltC). HR&W.

Australia's Animals Discovered. Peter Stanbury & Graeme Phipps. (Illus.). 120p. 1980. 23.40 (ISBN 0-08-024796-2). Pergamon.

Australia's Immigrants. Geoffrey Sherington. (Australian Experience Ser.). 216p. 1981. text ed. 16.95x (ISBN 0-86861-010-0, 2511); pap. text ed. 9.95x (ISBN 0-86861-018-6, 2512). Allen Unwin.

Australia's Last Explorer: Ernest Giles. Geoffrey Dutton. (Great Travellers Ser.). (Illus.). 1970. 7.50 (ISBN 0-571-09325-6, Pub. by Faber & Faber). Merrimack Bk Serv.

Australia's North. Stanley Breeden & Kay Breeden. (Natural History of Australia Ser.: No. 3). 208p. 1980. 34.95x (ISBN 0-00-211441-0, Pub. by W Collins Australia). Intl Schol Bk Serv.

Austria. Carol Rothkopf. (First Bk. Ser). (Illus.). 72p. (gr. 5 up). 1976. PLB 4.90 o.p. (ISBN 0-531-00842-8). Watts.

Austria. Virginia Waite. (Batsford Countries of Europe Ser.). 1970. 8.95 o.p. (ISBN 0-8038-0343-5). Hastings.

Austria from Habsburg to Hitler, 2 vols. Charles A. Gulick. Incl. Vol. I. Labor's Workshop of Democracy; Vol. II. Facism's Subversion of Democracy (ISBN 92-0159-280-9). (California Library Reprint Ser.: No. 109). 1980. Repr. of 1948 ed. Set. 85.00x o.p. (ISBN 0-520-04211-5). U. of Cal Pr.

Austria from Habsburg to Hitler, 2 vols. Charles A. Gulick. Incl. Vol. I. Labor's Workshop of Democracy; Vol. II. Fascism's Subversion of Democracy. (California Library Reprint Ser.: No. 109). 1936p. 1981. Repr. of 1948 ed. Set. 85.00x (ISBN 0-520-04211-5). U. of Cal Pr.

Austria in Pictures. Sterling Publishing Company Editors. LC 64-15115. (Visual Geography Ser). (Orig.). (gr. 5 up). PLB 4.99 (ISBN 0-8069-1063-1); pap. 2.95 (ISBN 0-8069-1062-3). Sterling.

Austria in the Year Nineteen Seventy-Nine: How Austria Weathered the Economic Storm of the Seventies. 24p. 1980. pap. 5.00 (ISBN 92-808-0141-4, TUNU 066, UNU). Unipub.

Austrian Example. Kurt Waldheim. 224p. 1973. 6.95 o.s.i. (ISBN 0-02-622490-9). Macmillan.

Austrian-German Arbitral Tribunal, Vol. 11. Ignaz Seidl-Hohenveldern. 1972. 10.00x (ISBN 0-8156-2159-0). U Pr of Va.

Austrian Mind: An Intellectual & Social History. William M. Johnston. (California Library Reprint Ser.). 1976. 35.00x (ISBN 0-520-03182-2). U of Cal Pr.

Austrian Penal Act, 1852 & 1945 As Amended to 1965. (American Series of Foreign Penal Codes: No. 12). 1966. 15.00x (ISBN 0-8377-0032-9). Rothman.

Austrian Social Democracy, Eighteen Eighty-Nine to Nineteen Fourteen. Vincent J. Knapp. LC 79-5509. 1980. text ed. 19.50 (ISBN 0-8191-0906-1); pap. text ed. 11.25 (ISBN 0-8191-0907-X). U Pr of Amer.

Austrian War Government. Josef Redlich. (Economic & Social History of the World War Ser.). 1929. 47.50x (ISBN 0-685-69855-6). Elliots Bks.

Austria...the Inn Way. Margaret Zellers. 162p. 1981. 4.95 (ISBN 0-937334-01-4). Berkshire Traveller.

Austro-Marxism. Ed. by Tom Bottomore & Patrick Goode. 1978. text ed. 29.95x (ISBN 0-19-827229-4); pap. text ed. 8.50x (ISBN 0-19-827230-8). Oxford U Pr.

Austronesian Studies: Papers from the Second Eastern Conference on Austronesian Languages. Ed. by Paz B. Naylor. LC 79-87814. (Michigan Papers on South & Southeast Asia: No. 15). 314p. (Orig.). 1980. pap. 8.00x (ISBN 0-89148-015-3). Ctr S&SE Asian.

Auswertung und Deutung Des EKG. 12th ed. A. H. Lemmerz & R. R. Schmidt. (Illus.). xii, 260p. 1981. pap. 29.50 (ISBN 3-8055-1932-X). S Karger.

Authentic Christianity. Ray C. Stedman. (Orig.). pap. 1.75 (ISBN 0-89129-249-7). Jove Pubns.

Authentic Indian Designs. Ed. by Maria Naylor. LC 74-17711. (Illus.). 256p. 1975. pap. 6.50 (ISBN 0-486-23170-4). Dover.

Authentic Love: An Existential Vision. 2nd ed. James Park. LC 76-5602. 232p. 1978. pap. 6.00x (ISBN 0-89231-510-5). Existential Bks.

Authentic Teacher. Clark Moustakas. LC 80-67902. 1981. pap. 8.95 (ISBN 0-89615-031-3). Guild of Tutors.

Authenticity in Art: The Scientific Detection of Forgery. S. J. Fleming. LC 75-27303. (Illus.). 150p. 1976. 16.50x (ISBN 0-8448-0752-4). Crane-Russak Co.

Authenticity of Prometheus Bound. Mark Griffith. LC 76-14031. (Cambridge Classical Studies). 1977. 44.00 (ISBN 0-521-21099-2). Cambridge U Pr.

Authentick Memoirs of...Sally Salisbury, Vol. 41. Charles Walker. Ed. by Michael Shugrve. Incl. Agreeable Caledonian. Eliza Haywood. LC 79-170557. (Foundations of the Novel Ser.). 1973. Repr. of 1723 ed. lib. bdg. 50.00 (ISBN 0-8240-0553-8). Garland Pub.

Author & Subject Catalogues of the Library of the Peabody Museum of Archaeology & Ethnology: Fourth Supplement, 7 vols. Peabody Museum of Archaeology & Ethnology. (Bib Guides). 1979. lib. bdg. 980.00 set (ISBN 0-8161-0253-8). G K Hall.

Author Biographies Master Index, 2 vols. Ed. by Dennis La Beau. LC 76-27212. (Gale Biographical Index: No. 3). 1978. Set. 98.00 (ISBN 0-8103-1085-6). Gale.

Author Biographies Master Index - Supplement. Barbara McNeil & Miranda Herbert. 1980. pap. 65.00 (ISBN 0-8103-1088-0). Gale.

Author Catalog of the Library of the New York Academy of Medicine, Second Supplement. New York Academy of Medicine. 1979. lib. bdg. 500.00 (ISBN 0-8161-1181-2). G K Hall.

Author Index of Zentralblatt fuer Mathematik, und Ihre Grenzgebiete, 1931-1939, 2 pts. 70.00 (ISBN 0-685-64497-9, MREVIN 131-40). Am Math.

Author Index to Esquire 1933-1973. Herman Baron. LC 76-10625. 299p. 1976. 13.50 (ISBN 0-8108-0935-4). Scarecrow.

Author Index to the Handbook of Latin American Studies: No. 1-28, 1936-1966. Compiled by Francisco Jose & Maria E. Cardona. LC 36-32633. 1968. 32.50x (ISBN 0-8130-0265-6). U Presses Fla.

Author Newsletters & Journals. Ed. by Margaret C. Patterson. LC 79-63742. (American Literature, English Literature, & World Literature in English Information Guide Ser.: Vol. 19). 1979. 30.00 (ISBN 0-8103-1432-0). Gale.

Author of Waverley. D. D. Devlin. LC 71-146129. 142p. 1971. 12.00 (ISBN 0-8387-7925-5). Bucknell U Pr.

Author-Title Index to Joseph Sabin's Dictionary of Books Relating to America, 3 vols. John E. Molnar. LC 74-6291. 1974. Set. 135.00 (ISBN 0-8108-0652-5). Scarecrow.

Authoritarian Brazil: Origins, Policies, & Future. Ed. by Alfred Stepan. LC 73-77167. (Illus.). 1973. 15.00x (ISBN 0-300-01622-0); pap. 5.95x (ISBN 0-300-01991-2). Yale U Pr.

Authoritarian Personality. T. W. Adorno et al. 1969. pap. 9.95 o.p. (ISBN 0-393-00492-9, N492, Norton Lib). Norton.

Authority & Challenge: A Portrait of Europe 1300-1600. Donald Lindsay & Mary R. Price. (Portrait of Europe Ser). (Illus.). 360p. 1975. 16.00x (ISBN 0-19-913118-X); pap. 9.95x (ISBN 0-19-913220-8). Oxford U Pr.

Authority & Power. Ed. by Brian Tierney & Peter Linehan. 274p. 1981. 59.50. Cambridge U Pr.

Authority & the Individual. Bertrand Russell. (Unwin Paperbacks). 1949. pap. 3.95 (ISBN 0-04-170030-9). Allen Unwin.

Authority Control: Proceedings of the LITA Institute. Ed. by D. Kaye Gapen & Library & Information Technology Association. 1981. price not set (ISBN 0-912700-85-8). Oryx Pr.

Authority in Social Casework. R. Foren & R. Bailey. 1968. 11.25 (ISBN 0-08-012962-5). Pergamon.

Authority in the Church: A Study in Changing Paradigms. T. Howland Sanks. LC 74-16565. (American Academy of Religion. Dissertation Ser.). 1974. pap. 7.50 (ISBN 0-88420-119-8, 010102). Scholars Pr Ca.

Authority of Scripture: A Study of the Reformation & Post-Reformation Understanding of the Bible. John K. Reid. LC 79-8716. 286p. 1981. Repr. of 1962 ed. lib. bdg. 25.00x (ISBN 0-313-22191-X, REAS). Greenwood.

Authority of the Bible. Jack Cottrell. (Direction Bks.). 1979. pap. 1.95 (ISBN 0-8010-2436-6). Baker Bk.

Authority of the Past. Sheila McDonough. LC 76-141690. (American Academy of Religion. Studies in Religion). 46p. 1970. pap. 4.50 (ISBN 0-89130-153-4, 010001). Scholars Pr Ca.

Authority, Participation & Cultural Change in China. Ed. by S. T. Schram. (Contemporary China Institute Publications). (Illus.). 260p. 1973. 47.50 (ISBN 0-521-20296-5); pap. 14.50x (ISBN 0-521-09820-3). Cambridge U Pr.

Authority, Responsibility & Education. 3rd ed. R. S. Peters. 1973. pap. text ed. 7.95x (ISBN 0-04-170028-7). Allen Unwin.

Authority to Teach: A Study in the Ecclesiology of Henry Edward Manning. Charles H. Drexler. LC 77-18567. 1978. pap. text ed. 9.00 (ISBN 0-8191-0410-8). U Pr of Amer.

Authorized Daily Prayer Book. Joseph H. Hertz. (Eng. & Heb.). 1948. 17.50x (ISBN 0-8197-0094-0). Bloch.

Authors & Audiences in Traditional Malay Literature. Amin Sweeney. (Monograph: No. 20). 86p. 1981. pap. 7.00x (Pub by Northern Ill Univ Ctr S E Asian Stud). Cellar.

Authors & Their Works, with Dates. E. Cobham Brewer. LC 71-134907. 1970. Repr. of 1898 ed. 36.00 (ISBN 0-8103-3025-3). Gale.

Authors by Profession, Vol. 1. Victor Bonham-Carter. 1979. 12.95 (ISBN 0-913232-59-9). W Kaufmann.

Authors' Choice. Gillian Avery et al. LC 76-126978. (Illus.). (gr. 7 up). 1971. 8.95 o.p. (ISBN 0-690-11141-X, TYC-J). T Y Crowell.

Author's Craft & Other Critical Writings of Arnold Bennett. Arnold Bennett. Ed. by Samuel Hynes. LC 68-12706. (Regents Critics Ser). 1968. 11.95x (ISBN 0-8032-0451-5); pap. 3.95x (ISBN 0-8032-5451-2, BB 410, Bison). U of Nebr Pr.

Authors: Critical & Biographical References. Richard E. Combs. LC 73-16744. (A guide to 4,700 critical & biographical passages in books). 1971. 10.00 (ISBN 0-8108-0448-4). Scarecrow.

Author's Farce. Henry Fielding. Ed. by Charles Woods. LC 65-27454. (Regents Restoration Drama Ser). 1966. 9.50x (ISBN 0-8032-0359-4); pap. 1.65x (ISBN 0-8032-5358-3, BB 255, Bison). U of Nebr Pr.

Author's Guide to Journals in Administration, Business & Management. Ed. by Richard J. Vargo. LC 80-16956. (Author's Guide to Journals Ser.). 432p. 1981. 24.95 (ISBN 0-917724-12-7). Haworth Pr.

Author's Guide to Journals in Library & Information Science. Ed. by Norman Stevens. Nora Stevens. (Author's Guide to Journals Ser.). 1981. 16.95 (ISBN 0-917724-13-5). Haworth Pr.

Author's Guide to Journals in Nursing & Related Fields. Steven D. Warner & Kathryn D. Schweer. (Author's Guide to Journals Ser.). 1981. 19.95 (ISBN 0-917724-11-9). Haworth Pr.

Authors in the News, 2 vols. Ed. by Barbara Nykoruk. LC 75-13541. (Illus.). 502p. 42.00 ea.; Vol. 1 1975. (ISBN 0-8103-0043-5); Vol. 2 1976. (ISBN 0-8103-0045-1). Gale.

Author's Names 1981. 1981. 125.00 (ISBN 0-8352-1095-2). Bowker.

Authors of Books for Young People. 2nd ed. Martha E. Ward & Dorothy A. Marquardt. LC 70-157057. 1971. 20.50 (ISBN 0-8108-0404-2). Scarecrow.

Authors of Books for Young People: Supplement to the 2nd Edition. Martha E. Ward & Dorothy A. Marquardt. LC 78-16001. 1979. lib. bdg. 13.00 (ISBN 0-8108-1159-6). Scarecrow.

Autism: A Practical Guide for Parents & Professionals. Maria J. Paluszny. 200p. 1980. pap. 9.95x (ISBN 0-8156-2225-2). Syracuse U Pr.

Autism: A Reappraisal of Concepts & Treatment. Ed. by Michael Rutter & Eric Schopler. LC 77-26910. (Illus.). 562p. 1978. 24.50 (ISBN 0-306-31096-1, Plenum Pr). Plenum Pub.

Autism & Childhood Psychosis. Frances Tustin. LC 72-85216. 1973. 20.00x (ISBN 0-87668-055-4). Aronson.

Autism: Diagnosis, Instruction, Management, & Research. James E. Gillium. write for info. (ISBN 0-398-04072-9). C C Thomas.

Autism: New Directions in Research & Education. Ed. by Christopher D. Webster et al. LC 79-19732. (Pergamon Policy Studies). 1980. 24.50 (ISBN 0-08-025083-1). Pergamon.

Autism: Nightmare Without End. Dorothy J. Beavers. Ed. by Debbie Hammond. 1980. 14.95 (ISBN 0-87949-167-1). Ashley Bks.

Autistic Child. I. Newton Kugelmass. (Illus.). 382p. 1974. 22.75 (ISBN 0-398-01059-5). C C Thomas.

Autistic Child. Ole I. Lovaas. LC 76-5890. 256p. 1977. text ed. 16.95 (ISBN 0-8290-0253-7). Irvington.

Autistic Children. Ed. by Brian Roberts & Barbara Furneaux. (Special Needs in Education Ser.). 1979. pap. 7.95 (ISBN 0-7100-0348-X). Routledge & Kegan.

Autistic Children: Teaching, Community & Research Approaches. Ed. by Brian Roberts & Barbara Furneaux. (Special Needs in Education Ser.). 1977. 17.00x (ISBN 0-7100-8704-7). Routledge & Kegan.

Auto Ads. Jane Stern & Michael Stern. 1978. 12.95 (ISBN 0-394-50094-6). Random.

Auto Audio: How to Select & Install Stereo Equipment. Walter G. Salm. 144p. 1980. pap. 7.70 (ISBN 0-8104-0759-0). Hayden.

Auto Body Repair for the Do-It-Yourselfer. Advanced Learning Inc. LC 76-1132. 1976. pap. 6.95 (ISBN 0-672-23238-3). Audel.

Auto-Carto IV, 2 vols. 1979. member 17.50; non-member 30.00. ASP.

Auto Electronics Simplified. Clayton Hallmark. LC 74-25566. (Illus.). 256p. 1975. pap. 5.95 (ISBN 0-8306-3749-4, 749). TAB Bks.

Auto Fleet Management. Hermann S. Botzow. LC 67-30632. 1968. 23.95 (ISBN 0-471-09100-6, Pub. by Wiley-Interscience). Wiley.

Auto Mechanics for the Complete Dummy. 2nd ed. Philip R. Martin. Ed. by John Ritums & Dennis Guido. LC 74-14655. (Illus.). 1981. pap. write for info. (ISBN 0-930968-01-8). Motormatics.

Auto Racing. Charles Coombs. LC 73-153770. (Illus.). (gr. 5-9). 1971. 7.25 (ISBN 0-688-21053-8); PLB 6.96 (ISBN 0-688-31053-2). Morrow.

Auto Repair Book. John Doyle. 1977. 9.95 (ISBN 0-385-12193-8); school & library ed. 12.95 (ISBN 0-385-13306-5). Doubleday.

Auto Work & Its Discontents. Ed. by B. J. Widick. LC 76-16095. (Policy Studies in Employment & Welfare: No. 25). (Illus.). 128p. 1976. 8.00x o.p. (ISBN 0-8018-1856-7); pap. 3.95x (ISBN 0-8018-1857-5). Johns Hopkins.

Autoantibodies to Nuclear Antigens: Immunochemical Specificities & Significance in Systemic Rheumatic Diseases. Robert M. Nakamura et al. LC 78-18282. (Illus.). 1978. pap. text ed. 18.00 (ISBN 0-89189-061-0, 45-A-004-00). Am Soc Clinical.

Autobiographical Notes of Charles Evans Hughes. Charles E. Hughes. Ed. by David J. Danelski & Joseph S. Tulchin. LC 72-88130. (Studies in Legal History). 1973. 17.50x (ISBN 0-674-05325-7). Harvard U Pr.

Autobiographical Novel. Kenneth Rexroth. LC 78-8823. 382p. 1978. pap. 6.95 (ISBN 0-915520-15-X). Ross-Erikson.

Autobiographical Reminiscences: With Family Letters & Notes on Music. Charles Gounod. LC 68-16235. (Music Ser). 1970. Repr. of 1896 ed. lib. bdg. 25.00 (ISBN 0-306-71081-1). Da Capo.

Autobiographical Sketch by John Marshall. John Marshall. Ed. by John S. Adams. LC 71-160849. (American Constitutional Legal History Ser.). (Illus.). 74p. 1973. Repr. of 1937 ed. lib. bdg. 15.00 (ISBN 0-306-70216-9). Da Capo.

Autobiographies. Charles Darwin & Thomas H. Huxley. Ed. by Gavin De Beer. (Oxford English Memoirs & Travels Ser.). (Illus.). 190p. 1974. 14.95x o.p. (ISBN 0-19-255410-7). Oxford U Pr.

Autobiographies. Richard Kostelanetz. LC 79-87601. (Rockbottom Prosework Ser.). 288p. (Orig.). 1980. pap. 8.00 (ISBN 0-930012-42-9); 15.00 o.p. (ISBN 0-930012-41-0). Mudborn.

Autobiography. Maurianne Adams. LC 67-23041. 1968. pap. 2.50 (ISBN 0-672-60898-7, CR12). Bobbs.

Autobiography. Cellini. (Classic Ser). 1956. pap. 4.50 (ISBN 0-14-044049-6). Penguin.

Autobiography. Yukichi Fukuzawa. Tr. by E. Kiyooka. LC 66-15468. (Illus.). 1966. 122.50 (ISBN 0-231-02884-9); pap. 10.00x (ISBN 0-231-08373-4). Columbia U Pr.

Autobiography. Edward Gibbon. (World's Classics, No. 139). 14.95 (ISBN 0-19-250139-9). Oxford U Pr.

Autobiography. John S. Mill. LC 57-14630. 1957. pap. 5.50 (ISBN 0-672-60281-4, LLA91). Bobbs.

Autobiography. Margaret Sanger. 10.00 (ISBN 0-8446-0241-8). Peter Smith.

Autobiography, 2 vols. Louis Spohr. LC 69-12693. (Music Ser). (Ger). 1969. Repr. of 1878 ed. lib. bdg. 39.50 (ISBN 0-306-71222-9). Da Capo.

Autobiography. Rudolf Steiner. (Spiritual Science Library). (Illus.). 560p. 1980. 18.00x (ISBN 0-8334-0757-0). Multimedia.

Autobiography & Deliverance. 2nd ed. Mark Rutherford. (Victorian Library). 1970. Repr. of 1888 ed. text ed. 10.00x (ISBN 0-7185-5000-5, Leicester). Humanities.

Autobiography & Imagination: Studies in Self-Scrutiny. John Pilling. 200p. 1981. price not set (ISBN 0-7100-0730-2). Routledge & Kegan.

Autobiography & Letters of Mrs. Margaret Oliphant. Ed. by Mrs. H. Coghill. (Victorian Library). 520p. 1974. Repr. of 1899 ed. text ed. 15.75x (ISBN 0-7185-5019-6, Leicester). Humanities.

Autobiography & Other Poems. Tony Towle. LC 77-3591. 1977. pap. 4.00 (ISBN 0-915342-18-9). SUN.

Autobiography & Selected Writings. Benjamin Franklin. Ed. & intro. by Jesse Lemisch. Date not set. pap. 2.50 (ISBN 0-451-51463-7, CJ1332, Sig Classics). NAL.

Autobiography: Memoirs, & Experiences of Moncure Daniel Conway, 2 Vols. Moncure Conway. LC 76-87495. (American Public Figures Ser). (Illus.). 1970. Repr. of 1904 ed. lib. bdg. 85.00 (ISBN 0-306-71402-7). Da Capo.

Autobiography of a Boy. G. S. Street. LC 76-19978. (Decadent Consciousness Ser.: Vol. 23). 1977. Repr. of 1894 ed. lib. bdg. 38.00 (ISBN 0-8240-2772-8). Garland Pub.

Autobiography of a Chinese Woman, Buwei Yang Chao. Chao Pu-Wei. Tr. by Chao Yuen-Ren. LC 72-100225. Repr. of 1947 ed. lib. bdg. 22.50x (ISBN 0-8371-3712-8, CHCW). Greenwood.

Autobiography of a Female Slave. Martha G. Browne. LC 71-92745. Repr. 22.50x (ISBN 0-8371-2194-9). Negro U Pr.

Autobiography of a Thief. Andrew K. Munro. 155p. 1973. 8.50 (ISBN 0-7181-0944-9). Transatlantic.

Autobiography of a Working Woman. Adelheid D. Popp. Tr. by E. C. Harvey. LC 79-2950. (Illus.). 135p. 1981. Repr. of 1912 ed. 14.50 (ISBN 0-8305-0113-4). Hyperion Conn.

Autobiography of Alice B. Toklas. Gertrude Stein. 7.25 (ISBN 0-8446-3003-9). Peter Smith.

Autobiography of an Unknown Indian. Nirad C. Chaudhuri. 1968. 18.00x (ISBN 0-520-00224-5). U of Cal Pr.

Autobiography of Archibald H. Rowan, Esq. Archibald H. Rowan. 476p. 1972. Repr. of 1840 ed. 19.00x (ISBN 0-7165-0011-6, Pub. by Irish Academic Pr Ireland). Biblio Dist.

Autobiography of Benjamin Franklin. (Literature Ser). (gr. 10-12). 1970. pap. text ed. 3.58 (ISBN 0-87720-721-6). AMSCO Sch.

Autobiography of Benjamin Franklin. Benjamin Franklin. 1962. pap. 2.95 (ISBN 0-02-002910-1, Collier). Macmillan.

Autobiography of Benjamin Franklin. Benjamin Franklin. (Keith Jennison Large Type Bks). (gr. 6 up). PLB 7.95 o.p. (ISBN 0-531-00159-8). Watts.

Autobiography of Benjamin Franklin: A Genetic Text. Benjamin Franklin. Ed. by J. A. Lemay & P. M. Zall. 328p. 1981. 23.50x (ISBN 0-87049-256-X). U of Tenn Pr.

Autobiography of Big Bill Haywood. William D. Haywood. LC 74-2407. 1966. 5.95 o.p. (ISBN 0-7178-0012-1); pap. 2.95 (ISBN 0-7178-0011-3). Intl Pub Co.

Autobiography of Charles Caldwell, M. D. Charles Caldwell. LC 67-27450. (Science & Medicine Ser.). 1968. Repr. of 1855 ed. 45.00 (ISBN 0-306-70978-3). Da Capo.

Autobiography of Christopher Kirkland, 1885. Eliza L. Linton. Ed. by Robert L. Wolff. LC 75-1532. (Victorian Fiction Ser.). 1975. lib. bdg. 66.00 (ISBN 0-8240-1604-1). Garland Pub.

Autobiography of Colonel John Trumbull. John Trumbull. Ed. by T. Sizer. LC 79-116912. (Library of American Art Ser). (Illus.). 1970. Repr. of 1953 ed. lib. bdg. 39.50 (ISBN 0-306-71242-3). Da Capo.

Autobiography of Emperor Haile Sellasis I: My Life & Ethiopia's Progress 1892-1937. Haile Sellasie I. Ed. & tr. by Edward Ullendorff. (Illus.). 1976. 24.50x (ISBN 0-19-713589-7). Oxford U Pr.

Autobiography of Francis Place 1771-1854. Mary Thale. LC 78-174265. (Illus.). 344p. 1972. 42.00 (ISBN 0-521-08399-0). Cambridge U Pr.

Autobiography of G. Lowes Dickinson. Ed. by Dennis Proctor. (Illus.). 287p. 1973. 12.50x (ISBN 0-7156-0647-6, Pub. by Duckworth England). Biblio Dist.

Autobiography of George Muller. George Muller. Ed. by H. Lincoln Wayland. (Giant Summit Books Ser.). 490p. 1981. pap. 8.95 (ISBN 0-8010-6105-9). Baker Bk.

Autobiography of James Clarence Mangan. James C. Mangan. Ed. by James Kilroy. (New Dolmen Chapbooks: No. 9). 40p. 1968. pap. text ed. 2.50x (ISBN 0-85105-138-3, Dolmen Pr). Humanities.

Autobiography of James Gallier, Architect. James Gallier. LC 69-13715. (Architecture & Decorative Art Ser.). 1973. Repr. of 1864 ed. lib. bdg. 25.00 (ISBN 0-306-71247-4). Da Capo.

Autobiography of Jeanette Li. Jeanette Li. Tr. by Rose A. Huston. 1971. pap. 3.95 (ISBN 0-686-12522-3). Banner of Truth.

Autobiography of John Ludlow, Christian Socialist. Ed. by A. D. Murray. 1980. 30.00x (ISBN 0-7146-3085-3, F Cass Co). Biblio Dist.

Autobiography of Karl Von Dittersdorf. Karl D. Von Dittersdorf. Tr. by A. D. Coleridge. LC 77-100655. (Music Ser). (Ger). 1970. Repr. of 1896 ed. lib. bdg. 22.50 (ISBN 0-306-71864-2). Da Capo.

Autobiography of Malcolm X. Malcolm X. 1977. pap. 2.75 (ISBN 0-345-29420-3). Ballantine.

Autobiography of Mark Rutherford, Dissenting Minister, 1881. William H. White. Ed. by Robert L. Wolff. Bd. with Mark Rutherford's Deliverance, 1885. LC 75-1514. (Victorian Fiction Ser.). 1975. lib. bdg. 66.00 (ISBN 0-8240-1587-8). Garland Pub.

Autobiography of Mark Twain. Mark Twain. Ed. by Charles Neider. (Illus.). 1959. 20.00 o.s.i. (ISBN 0-06-014368-1, HarpT). Har-Row.

Autobiography of Martin Van Buren, 2 vols. Martin Van Buren. Ed. by John Fitzpatrick. LC 72-75314. 820p. 1973. Repr. of 1920 ed. Set. lib. bdg. 69.50 (ISBN 0-306-71275-X). Da Capo.

Autobiography of Maxim Gorky, 3 vols. in 1. Maxim Gorky. Tr. by Isidore Schneider. Incl. My Childhood; In the World; My Universities. 10.00 (ISBN 0-8446-2143-9). Peter Smith.

Autobiography of My Mother. Rosellen Brown. LC 75-36581. 288p. 1976. 7.95 o.p. (ISBN 0-385-09896-0). Doubleday.

Autobiography of No One. (Illus.). 128p. 1981. 7.95 (ISBN 0-89962-048-5). Todd & Honeywell.

Autobiography of Rudolf Jordan. Rudolf Jordan. LC 80-70948. (Illus.). 227p. 1981. 10.95 (ISBN 0-8119-0415-6). Fell.

Autobiography of Saint Therese of Lisieux: The Story of a Soul. St. Therese of Lisieux. 1957. pap. 2.45 (ISBN 0-385-02903-9, D56, Im). Doubleday.

Autobiography of Sam Houston. Samuel Houston. Ed. by Donald Day & Harry H. Ullom. LC 80-18864. (Illus.). xviii, 298p. 1980. Repr. of 1954 ed. lib. bdg. 29.95x (ISBN 0-313-22704-7, HOAUS). Greenwood.

Autobiography of Samuel Bamford, 2 vols. Samuel Bamford. Ed. & intro. by W. H. Chaloner. Incl. Vol. 1. Early Days. Repr. of 1849 ed; Vol. 2. Passages in the Life of a Radical. Repr. of 1844 ed. LC 67-23461. 30.00x (ISBN 0-678-05025-2). Kelley.

Autobiography of Samuel Johnson. Samuel Johnson. 1956. 4.50 o.p. (ISBN 0-8040-0078-6). Swallow.

Autobiography of Science. Ed. by Forest R. Moulton & Justus J. Schifferes. 748p. 1980. 25.00x (ISBN 0-7195-0979-3, Pub. by Murray Pubs England). State Mutual Bk.

Autobiography of W. E. Burghardt Du Bois: A Soliloquy on Viewing My Life from the Last Decade of Its First Century. William E. Du Bois. Ed. by Herbert Aptheker. LC 68-14103. (Illus.). 1968. 15.00 (ISBN 0-7178-0235-3); pap. 3.95 (ISBN 0-7178-0234-5). Intl Pub Co.

Autobiography of William Allen White. William A. White. 1946. 6.95 o.s.i. (ISBN 0-02-627100-1). Macmillan.

Autobiography of William Jay. William Jay. 1974. 10.95 (ISBN 0-85151-177-5). Banner of Truth.

Autobiography of Yukichi Fukuzawa. Tr. by Eiichi Kiyooka. 407p. (Japanese.). 1980. pap. text ed. 10.00x (ISBN 0-231-08373-4). Columbia U Pr.

Autobiography: Volume I, Journey East, Journey West 1907-1937. Mircea Eliade. LC 80-8357. 352p. 1981. 17.50 (ISBN 0-06-065227-6, HarpR). Har-Row.

Autobody Repair. Lester G. Duenk et al. 1977. 15.84 (ISBN 0-87002-164-8); student's guide 3.96 (ISBN 0-685-73828-0); student's guide 3.24 (ISBN 0-87002-243-1). Bennett IL.

Autobody Repair & Refinishing. Robert P. Schmidt. 350p. 1981. text ed. 18.95 (ISBN 0-8359-0247-1); instr's. manual free (ISBN 0-8359-0248-X). Reston.

Autocourse, Nineteen Eighty to Nineteen Eighty-One, No. 29. Maurice Hamilton. (Illus.). 240p. 1981. 39.95 (ISBN 0-905138-12-0, Pub. by Hazelton England). Motorbooks Intl.

Autocourse 1977-1978. Ed. by Mike Kettlewell. (Ser. No.26). (Illus.). 1978. 26.95 o.p. (ISBN 0-905138-03-1). Motorbooks Intl.

Autofact West Proceedings, Vol. 1. Intro. by William Beebe. LC 80-53423. (Illus.). 939p. 1980. pap. 55.00 (ISBN 0-87263-065-X). SME.

Autofact West Proceedings, Vol. 2. Intro. by Frank McCarty. LC 80-53423. (Illus.). 842p. 1980. pap. 55.00 (ISBN 0-87263-066-8). SME.

Automata, Languages, & Machines. Samuel Eilenberg. (Pure & Applied Mathematics: A Series of Monographs & Textbooks, Vol. 58). Vol. A 1974. 44.50 (ISBN 0-12-234001-9); Vol. B 1976. 40.00 (ISBN 0-12-234002-7). Acad Pr.

Automata, Languages & Programming: Seventh Colloquim. Ed. by J. W. Bakker & J. Van Leeuwen. (Lecture Notes in Computer Sciences: Vol. 85). 671p. 1980. pap. 31.90 (ISBN 0-387-10003-2). Springer-Verlag.

Automata Theory: An Engineering Approach. Igor Aleksander. LC 74-32509. (Computer Systems Engineering Ser.). 1975. 19.50x (ISBN 0-8448-0657-9). Crane-Russak Co.

Automata Theory: Machines & Languages. Richard Kain. (Computer Science Ser). (Illus.). 320p. 1972. text ed. 24.95 o.p. (ISBN 0-07-033195-2, C). McGraw.

Automated Instrumentation for Radioimmunoassay. Lemuel J. Bowie. 240p. 1980. 59.95 (ISBN 0-8493-5747-0). CRC Pr.

Automated Inventory Management for the Distributor. Gordon Graham. LC 80-17655. 350p. 1980. 19.95 (ISBN 0-8436-0794-7). CBI Pub.

Automated Library Circulation Systems, 1979-1980. Alice H. Bahr. LC 79-16189. (Professional Librarian Ser.). (Illus.). 1979. softcover 24.50x (ISBN 0-914236-34-2). Knowledge Indus.

Automated Medical Records & the Law. Ed. by Eric W. Springer. LC 70-110587. 1971. 25.00 (ISBN 0-912862-02-5). Aspen Systems.

Automated Structural Analysis: An Introduction. W. R. Spillers. 1972. 21.00 (ISBN 0-08-016782-9). Pergamon.

Automatic Chemical Analysis. J. K. Foreman & P. B. Stockwell. LC 74-14671. (Series in Analytical Chemistry). 346p. 1974. 54.95 (ISBN 0-470-26619-8). Halsted Pr.

Automatic Continuity of Linear Operators. A. M. Sinclair. LC 74-31804. (London Mathematical Society Lecture Note Ser.: No. 21). 120p. 1976. 14.50x (ISBN 0-521-20830-0). Cambridge U Pr.

Automatic Control in Power Generation, Distribution & Protection: Proceedings. IFAC Symposium, Pretoria, Republic of South Africa 15-19 September 1980. Ed. by J. F. Herbst. LC 80-40912. 550p. Date not set. 105.00 (ISBN 0-686-63497-7). Pergamon.

Automatic Control in Space: Proceedings. IFAC Symposium, 8th, Oxford, England, 2-6 July 1979. Ed. by C. W. Munday. (IFAC Proceedings Ser.). 492p. 1980. 105.00 (ISBN 0-08-024449-1). Pergamon.

Automatic Control System Technology. Daniel P. Sante. (Illus.). 1980. text ed. 19.95 (ISBN 0-13-054627-5). P-H.

Automatic Control Systems. 3rd ed. Benjamin C. Kuo. (Illus.). 640p. 1975. ref. ed. 27.95 (ISBN 0-13-054973-8). P-H.

Automatic Control Theory. Benjamin E. DeRoy. (Electronic Technology Ser.). (Illus.). 1966. pap. 11.95 (ISBN 0-471-20371-8). Wiley.

Automatic Controls for Heating & Airconditioning: Principles & Applications. K. M. Letherman. (International Series on Heating, Ventilation & Refrigeration: Vol. 15). (Illus.). 220p. 1981. 30.00 (ISBN 0-08-023222-1). Pergamon.

Automatic Data Processing, System 360 Edition. Frederick P. Brooks & Kenneth E. Iverson. LC 68-31293. 1969. 30.00 (ISBN 0-471-10605-4, Pub. by Wiley-Interscience). Wiley.

Automatic Dishwasher, Disposer, Trash Masher Compactor. Ed. by A. Ross Sabin. (Illus.). 168p. (gr. 11). 1978. 20.00 (ISBN 0-938336-07-X). Whirlpool.

Automatic Dryers. Ed. by A. Ross Sabin. (Illus.). 160p. (gr. 11). 20.00 (ISBN 0-938336-05-3). Whirlpool.

Automatic Generation of Assemblers. John D. Wick. LC 79-50822. (Outstanding Dissertations in the Computer Sciences). 1980. lib. bdg. 25.00 (ISBN 0-8240-4418-5). Garland Pub.

Automatic Information Organization & Retrieval. Gerald Salton. LC 68-25664. (Illus.). 1968. text ed. 25.95 o.p. (ISBN 0-07-054485-9, C). McGraw.

Automatic Neuromuscular Transmission. M. R. Bennett. LC 76-182026. (Physiological Society Monographs: No. 30). (Illus.). 400p. 1973. 54.00 (ISBN 0-521-08463-6). Cambridge U Pr.

Automatic Potentiometric Titrations. Gyula Svehla. 1977. text ed. 50.00 (ISBN 0-08-021590-4). Pergamon.

Automatic Poverty: The Ricardo Phenomenon. Bill Jordan. 208p. 1981. price not set (ISBN 0-7100-0824-4); pap. price not set (ISBN 0-7100-0825-2). Routledge & Kegan.

Automatic Process Control. Ed. by Paul N. Cheremisinoff & Harlan J. Perlis. 150p. 1981. text ed. write for info. (ISBN 0-250-40400-1). Ann Arbor Science.

Automatic Test Equipment: Hardware, Software, & Management. Ed. by F. Liguori. LC 74-18892. (IEEE Press Selected Reprint Ser). 253p. 1974. 17.95 (ISBN 0-471-53536-2, Pub. by Wiley-Interscience); pap. 8.95x o.p. (ISBN 0-471-53537-0). Wiley.

Automatic Transmission Fundamentals. William K. Husselbee. (Illus.). 1980. text ed. 17.95 (ISBN 0-8359-0257-9). Reston.

Automatic Transmission Service: A Text-Workbook. William Husselbee. (Orig.). 1981. pap. 9.95 (ISBN 0-8359-0266-8). Reston.

Automatic Transmissions. 2nd ed. M. Brycha. 1981. 16.95 (ISBN 0-13-054577-5). P-H.

Automatic Transmissions. Walter B. Larew. LC 66-27600. (Illus.). 1966. 11.50 o.p. (ISBN 0-8019-5184-4). Chilton.
Automatic Transmissions. Howard F. Tucker. LC 78-62623. (gr. 7-12). 1980. pap. text ed. 13.20 (ISBN 0-8273-1648-8); instructor's guide 1.25 (ISBN 0-8273-1649-6). Delmar.
Automatic Transmissions Workbook on Service & Repair. Howard Tucker. LC 80-67593. (Automotive Technology Ser.). (Illus.). 64p. (Orig.). 1981. pap. text ed. 6.00 (ISBN 0-8273-1894-4). Delmar.
Automatic Turning Machines. 2nd ed. Ed. by J. E. Matthews et al. (Engineering Craftsmen: No. H30/3). (Illus.). 1978. spiral bdg. 21.00x (ISBN 0-85083-405-8). Intl Ideas.
Automatic Washers. Ed. by A. Ross Sabin. (Illus.). 200p. (gr. 11). 1975. 20.00 (ISBN 0-938336-04-5). Whirlpool.
Automatic Writing. Anita M. Muhl. (Illus.). 1964. 4.50 o.p. (ISBN 0-912326-08-5). Garrett-Helix.
Automation & Control in Transport. F. T. Barwell. 1972. 42.00 (ISBN 0-08-016962-7). Pergamon.
Automation & Data Processing in Psychiatry. (Task Force Report: No. 3). 1971. pap. 3.00 o.p. (ISBN 0-685-24865-8, 234). Am Psychiatric.
Automation & Industrial Workers: A Fifteen Nation Study--Vol. 1, Pt. 1. Jan Forslin et al. (Illus.). 1979. 61.00 (ISBN 0-08-023339-2). Pergamon.
Automation, Education, & Human Values. Ed. by William Brickman & Stanley Lehrer. (Illus.). 7.00 (ISBN 0-8446-0037-7). Peter Smith.
Automation in Hematology: What to Measure & Why. Ed. by D. W. Ross et al. (Illus.). 730p. 1981. pap. 46.00 (ISBN 0-387-10225-6). Springer-Verlag.
Automation in Libraries. 2nd ed. Richard T. Kimber & A. Boyd. 1974. text ed. 28.00 (ISBN 0-08-017969-X). Pergamon.
Automation in Mining, Mineral & Metal Processing: Proceedings. Third IFAC Symposium, Montreal, Canada, 18-20 August 1980. Ed. by J. O'Shea & M. Polis. LC 80-40809. (Illus.). 712p. 1981. 145.00 (ISBN 0-08-026164-7); pap. 90.00 (ISBN 0-08-026143-4). Pergamon.
Automation in the Office. L. Day. 1981. text ed. price not set (ISBN 0-86103-044-3, Westbury Hse). Butterworth.
Automation, Machine-Readable Records & Archival Administration: An Annotated Bibliography. Richard M. Kesner. LC 79-92994. 72p. 1980. pap. 6.00 (ISBN 0-931828-22-8). Soc Am Archivists.
Automation of Clinical Electroencephalography. Ed. by P. Kellaway & I. Petersen. LC 72-96334. (Illus.). 326p. 1973. 34.50 (ISBN 0-911216-45-6). Raven.
Automation on Shipboard. G. Bonwick. 1967. 25.00 (ISBN 0-312-06195-1). St Martin.
Automechanics. rev. ed. Harold Glenn. (gr. 9-12). 1976. text ed. 14.64 (ISBN 0-87002-169-9); wkbk & ans. sheets 3.96 (ISBN 0-87002-180-X); avail. tchr's guide. Bennett IL.
Automechanics: An Introduction & Guide. Edward A. Little. LC 73-14689. (Illus.). 128p. (gr. 7 up). 1974. PLB 5.88 o.p. (ISBN 0-531-02670-1). Watts.
Automobile. Byron J. Alpers & Mitchell L. Afrow. (Shoptalk - Vocational Reading Skills). (gr. 9-12). 1978. pap. text ed. 5.12 (ISBN 0-205-05819-1, 4958195); 5.40 (ISBN 0-205-05824-8). Allyn.
Automobile Ads List: Life Magazine Nineteen Forty to Nineteen Forty-Nine. Phillip K. Cottrill. 100p. (Orig.). 1980. pap. 9.95 (ISBN 0-937234-40-0). Rigel.
Automobile Ads List: Life Magazine Nineteen-Fifty to Nineteen Fifty-Nine. Phillip K. Cottrill. 100p. (Orig.). 1980. pap. 9.95 (ISBN 0-937234-50-8). Rigel.
Automobile Ads List Life Magazine Nineteen Sixty to Nineteen Sixty-Nine. Phillip K. Cottrill. LC 80-52108. 91p. (Orig.). 1980. pap. 9.95 (ISBN 0-937234-60-5). Rigel.
Automobile Almanac-Annual. 1980. 6.95 (ISBN 0-686-51337-1); pap. 2.95 (ISBN 0-686-51338-X). Am Sports Sales.
Automobile Archaeology. David B. Wise. (Illus.). 160p. 1981. 35.95 (ISBN 0-85059-455-3). Aztex.
Automobile Design Liability. Richard M. Goodman. LC 78-94828. 1970. 85.00 (ISBN 0-686-14535-6, 052A). Lawyers Co-Op.
Automobile Electrical & Electronic Equipment. 9th ed. A. P. Young & L. Griffiths. Ed. by G. E. Fardon. (Illus.). 1980. 24.95 (ISBN 0-408-00463-0). Butterworths.
Automobile Engine Lubrication. A. Schilling. (Illus.). 480p. 1972. text ed. 45.00x (ISBN 0-900645-00-8). Scholium Intl.
Automobile Gasoline Conservation. Robert G. McGillivray. (Institute Paper). 67p. 1976. pap. 3.00 (ISBN 0-87766-162-6, 14100). Urban Inst.
Automobile Insurance & No-Fault Law. M. G. Woodroof, 3rd & John R. Fonseca. LC 74-76324. 1974. 47.50 (ISBN 0-686-14511-9). Lawyers Co-Op.
Automobile Liability Insurance. Irwin E. Schermer. LC 73-82715. 1979. looseleaf with 1978 rev. pages 110.00 (ISBN 0-87632-102-3). Boardman.
Automobile Repair Guide. 4th ed. Boyce Dwiggins. LC 78-50206. 1978. 14.95 (ISBN 0-672-23291-X). Audel.
Automobile Year, No. 28. (Illus.). 1981. 39.95 (ISBN 0-393-01450-9). Norton.
Automobile Year, No. 18: 1970-1971. Ami Guichard. (Illus.). 1970. 19.95 o.p. (ISBN 0-8019-6389-3). Chilton.
Automobile Year, No. 21: 1973-1974. Ami Guichard. (Illus.). 1973. 25.00 o.p. (ISBN 0-8019-6392-3). Chilton.
Automobiles. rev. ed. James Bendick. LC 78-6252. (First Bks.). (Illus.). (gr. 4-6). 1978. PLB 6.45 s&l (ISBN 0-531-02227-7). Watts.
Automobiles, Past & Present. Walter Buehr. LC 68-12323. (Illus.). (gr. 5-9). 1968. PLB 6.96 (ISBN 0-688-31054-0). Morrow.
Automorphic Forms, Representations & L-Functions, 2 vols. Ed. by A. Borel. LC 78-21184. (Proceedings of Symposia in Pure Mathematics: Vol. 33). 1980. 34.00 set (ISBN 0-686-52415-2, PSPUM-33); Pt. 1. 20.00 (ISBN 0-8218-1435-4); Pt. 2. 20.00 (ISBN 0-685-99018-4). Am Math.
Automorphic Functions. Lester R. Ford. LC 52-8647. 14.95 (ISBN 0-8284-0085-7). Chelsea Pub.
Automotive Aerodynamics. Society of Automotive Engineers. 1978. 22.00 (ISBN 0-89883-104-0). Soc Auto Engineers.
Automotive Air Conditioning. B. Dwiggins. LC 76-14093. (gr. 9-12). 1978. pap. 11.00 (ISBN 0-8273-1007-2); instructor's guide 3.00 (ISBN 0-8273-1008-0). Delmar.
Automotive Air Conditioning. K. L. MacDonald. LC 78-57176. 1978. pap. 7.95 (ISBN 0-672-23318-5). Audel.
Automotive Air Conditioning. Clifford L. Samuels. (Illus.). 288p. 1981. text ed. 17.95 o.p. (ISBN 0-13-054213-X); pap. text ed. 13.95 (ISBN 0-13-054205-9). P-H.
Automotive Air Conditioning. Paul Weissler. (Illus.). 1981. text ed. 13.95 (ISBN 0-8359-0261-7); pap. 12.95 (ISBN 0-8359-0260-9); solutions manual free. Reston.
Automotive Air Conditioning & Climate Control. James M. Kirkpatrick & Michael K. Weaver. LC 78-994. 1978. pap. 14.85 (ISBN 0-672-97098-8); wkbk. 4.95 (ISBN 0-672-97099-6); tchr's manual 3.33 (ISBN 0-672-97100-3). Bobbs.
Automotive Brake System. David A. Coghlan. 1980. pap. text ed. 10.95 (ISBN 0-534-00822-4, Breton Pubs). Wadsworth Pub.
Automotive Chassis & Accessory Circuits. M. F. Brejcha & C. L. Samuels. LC 76-14835. (Illus.). 1977. 17.95 (ISBN 0-13-055475-8). P-H.
Automotive Cooling System Training & Reference Manual. Richard Armento. (Illus.). 1979. text ed. 16.95 (ISBN 0-8359-0265-X); pap. text ed. 10.95 (ISBN 0-8359-0264-1). Reston.
Automotive Diagnosis & Tune-up. new ed. Guy F. Wetzel. (gr. 9-12). 1974. text ed. 17.16 (ISBN 0-87345-100-7). McKnight.
Automotive Electricity. Boyce H. Dwiggins. (Illus.). 352p. 1981. text ed. 18.95 (ISBN 0-8359-0268-4); pap. text ed. 12.95 (ISBN 0-8359-0267-6). Reston.
Automotive Electronic Instrumentation: Displays & Sensors. Society of Automotive Engineers. 1980. 24.95 (ISBN 0-89883-228-4). Soc Auto Engineers.
Automotive Electronic Systems. Society of Automotive Engineers. 1979. 24.95 (ISBN 0-89883-212-8). Soc Auto Engineers.
Automotive Electronics & Electrical Equipment. 9th ed. William H. Crouse. (Illus.). 1980. pap. text ed. 14.50 (ISBN 0-07-014831-7); instructor's planning guide 2.50 (ISBN 0-07-014833-3); wkbk. 6.95 (ISBN 0-07-014832-5). McGraw.
Automotive Emission Control & Tune-Up Procedures,1976. Ignition Manufacturers Institute. pap. 11.95 (ISBN 0-13-054809-X). P-H.
Automotive Emission Control & Tune-up Procedures. 3rd ed. Ignition Manufacturers Institute. (Illus.). 1980. text ed. 17.95 (ISBN 0-13-054791-3); pap. text ed. 13.95 (ISBN 0-13-054783-2). P-H.
Automotive Encyclopedia. William K. Toboldt & Larry Johnson. LC 78-27798. (Illus.). 792p. 1981. text ed. 16.00 (ISBN 0-87006-314-6). Goodheart.
Automotive Encyclopedia. rev. ed. William K. Toboldt & Larry Johnson. (Illus.). 792p. 1981. text ed. 16.00 (ISBN 0-87006-314-6). Goodheart.
Automotive Engine. M. J. Nunny. (Illus.). 280p. 1976. 20.00 (ISBN 0-408-00178-X). Transatlantic.
Automotive Engine Repair & Overhaul. Frederick Peacock & Thomas Gaston. (Illus.). 480p. 1980. text ed. 17.95 (ISBN 0-8359-0276-5). Reston.
Automotive Engine Tuning. Richard Day. 1981. pap. text ed. 14.95 (ISBN 0-8359-0270-6). Reston.
Automotive Engines. 6th ed. William H. Crouse & Donald L. Anglin. (Illus.). 96p. 1980. 14.50 (ISBN 0-07-014825-2, G); instructor's planning guide 2.50 (ISBN 0-07-014827-9). McGraw.
Automotive Engines & Related Systems: Principles & Service. Frank Thiessen & D. N. Dales. (Illus.). 1981. text ed. 18.95 (ISBN 0-8359-0280-3); pap. 14.95 (ISBN 0-8359-0279-X); instr's manual free. Reston.
Automotive Fuel Economy, No. 2. Society of Automotive Engineers. 1979. 18.95 (ISBN 0-89883-106-7). Soc Auto Engineers.
Automotive Fuel, Ignition, & Emission Control Systems. Glen E. Ireland. 1980. pap. 10.95 (ISBN 0-534-00866-6, Breton Pubs). Wadsworth Pub.
Automotive Fuel, Lubricating & Cooling Systems. 6th ed. William H. Crouse & Donald L. Anglin. Ed. by D. E. Gilmore. (Illus.). 352p. 1980. pap. text ed. 17.95 (ISBN 0-07-014862-7, G); wkbk. avail. (ISBN 0-07-014863-5). McGraw.
Automotive Handbook. Robert Bosch & Society of Automotive Engineers. 1979. 10.95 (ISBN 0-89883-510-0). Soc Auto Engineers.
Automotive Mechanics. Richard Day. (Illus.). 1980. text ed. 15.95 (ISBN 0-8359-0272-2). Reston.
Automotive Oscilloscope. N. W. Whited. LC 76-3937. (Illus.). 88p. (gr. 10-12). 1977. pap. 5.40 (ISBN 0-8273-1033-1). Delmar.
Automotive Principles & Service. Frank J. Thiessen & Davis Dales. (Illus.). 1980. text ed. 19.95 (ISBN 0-8359-0287-0); free instrs'. manual (ISBN 0-8359-0288-9). Reston.
Automotive Repair & Maintenance. Robert G. Schipf. LC 73-84413. (Spare Times Guides: No. 1). 1973. lib. bdg. 7.50 o.p. (ISBN 0-87287-066-9). Libs Unl.
Automotive Science. L. E. Jensen et al. LC 76-3940. 1977. pap. 6.60 (ISBN 0-8273-1302-0); instructor's guide 1.60 (ISBN 0-8273-1303-9). Delmar.
Automotive Sensors. Society of Automotive Engineers. 1979. 16.95 (ISBN 0-89883-213-6). Soc Auto Engineers.
Automotive Service & Repair Tools. Harry G. Hill. LC 73-907400. 288p. 1975. pap. 10.36 (ISBN 0-8273-1035-8); instructor's guide 1.60 (ISBN 0-8273-1036-6). Delmar.
Automotrix: Manual De Reparaciones Automotrices. William K. Toboldt. Ed. & tr. by George Loinaz. LC 76-22993. (Illus.). (gr. 11 up). 1977. 35.00 o.p. (ISBN 0-916628-01-9). Lineal Cleworth.
Automotrix Two: Manual De Reparaciones Automotrices. rev. ed. William K. Toboldt. LC 80-81966. (Illus., Span.). 1980. 45.00 (ISBN 0-916628-02-7). Lineal Cleworth.
Autonomic Nervous System: Morphological, Comparative, Clinical & Surgical Aspects. Joseph Pick. LC 68-20600. (Illus.). 1970. 69.00 o.p. (ISBN 0-397-50257-5). Lippincott.
Autonomous Categories. M. Barr. (Lecture Notes in Mathematics: Vol. 752). 1979. pap. 9.00 (ISBN 0-387-09563-2). Springer-Verlag.
Autonomous House. Nicholson. 4.25 (ISBN 0-915248-31-X). Vermont Crossroads.
Autonomous House: Design & Planning for Self-Sufficiency. Brenda Vale & Robert Vale. LC 75-15354. (Illus.). 1977. pap. 5.95 (ISBN 0-87663-979-1). Universe.
Autonomous Image: Cinematic Narration & Humanism. A. J. Prats. xvi, 171p. 1981. price not set (ISBN 0-8131-1406-3). U Pr of Ky.
Autonomy & Rigid Character. David Shapiro. LC 80-68953. 167p. 1981. 12.95x (ISBN 0-465-00567-5). Basic.
Autonomy at Work: A Sociotechnical Analysis. Gerald I. Susman. LC 75-23997. (Praeger Special Studies Ser). 256p. 1976. text ed. 26.50 (ISBN 0-275-56140-2). Praeger.
Autonomy in Nursing. Mary O. Mundinger. LC 79-25630. (Illus.). 222p. 1980. text ed. 22.00 (ISBN 0-89443-171-4). Aspen Systems.
Autopoiesis, Dissipative Structures & Spontaneous Social Orders. Ed. by Milan Zeleny. (AAAS Selected Symposium Ser.: No. 55). 150p. 1980. lib. bdg. 20.00x (ISBN 0-86531-035-1). Westview.
Autopsy on People's War. Chalmers Johnson. (Quantum Book). 1974. 11.50x (ISBN 0-520-02516-4); pap. 2.85 (ISBN 0-520-02518-0). U of Cal Pr.
Autopsy Pathology Procedure & Protocol. Dudley L Weber et al. (Illus.). 136p. 1973. 21.75 (ISBN 0-398-02625-4). C C Thomas.
Autoradiography. Helmut A. Fischer & Gottfried Werner. Tr. by M. R. Ashworth from Ger. LC 70-164842. (Working Methods in Modern Science Ser). 1971. 39.50x (ISBN 3-1100-3523-5). De Gruyter.
Autoridad Espiritual. Tr. by Watchman Nee. (Spanish Bks.). (Span.). 1978. 1.75 (ISBN 0-8297-0805-7). Life Pubs Intl.
Autoridade Espirituale. 1980. pap. 1.85 (ISBN 0-686-69356-6). Vida Pubs.
Autoridade Espirituale. T. S. Nee. Ed. by Vera Balthazar. Tr. by Luiz A. Caruso from Eng. 240p. (Portuguese.). 1979. pap. 1.85 (ISBN 0-8297-0922-3). Vida Pubs.
Autorite Spirituelle. Tr. by Watchman Nee. (French Bks.). (Fr.). 1979. 1.75 (ISBN 0-686-28817-3). Life Pubs Intl.
Autos, 1981: Ratings, Specifications & Best Buys. rev. ed. 96p. (Orig.). Date not set. pap. 2.50 (ISBN 0-89552-071-0). DMR Pubns.
Autosegmental Phonology. John A. Goldsmith. Ed. by Jorge Hankamer. LC 78-67735. (Outstanding Dissertations in Linguistics Ser.). 1979. lib. bdg. 22.00 (ISBN 0-8240-9673-8). Garland Pub.
Autoshaping & Conditioning Theory. Ed. by C. M. Locurto et al. 1980. 30.00 (ISBN 0-12-454480-0). Acad Pr.
Autoxidation of Hydrocarbons & Polyolefins: Kinetics & Mechanisms. L. Reich & S. S. Stivala. 1969. 59.50 o.p. (ISBN 0-8247-1580-2). Dekker.
Autumn. Richard L. Allington & Kathleen Krull. LC 80-25190. (Beginning to Learn About Ser.). (Illus.). 32p. (ps-2). 1981. PLB 9.65 (ISBN 0-8172-1343-0). Raintree Child.
Autumn Hawk Flights: The Migrations in Eastern North America. Donald S. Heintzelman. (Illus.). 500p. 1975. 20.00 o.p. (ISBN 0-8135-0777-4). Rutgers U Pr.
Autumn Heroes. Oliver Jacks. 1979. pap. 1.95 o.p. (ISBN 0-425-04037-2). Berkley Pub.
Autumn Lace. Eileen Jackson. 1976. 7.95 o.s.i. (ISBN 0-8027-0538-3). Walker & Co.
Autumn Lace. Eileen Jackson. 1977. pap. 1.50 o.p. (ISBN 0-449-23297-2, Crest). Fawcett.
Autumn Leaves. Ruth H. Miller. LC 80-82931. 54p. 1981. 9.95 (ISBN 0-686-28764-9). R J Pub.
Autumn of the Eagle. George Laycock. LC 73-1368. (Illus.). 256p. 1973. 6.95 o.p. (ISBN 0-684-13413-6, ScribT). Scribner.
Autumn of the Patriarch. Gabriel G. Marquez. 1977. pap. 2.95 (ISBN 0-380-01774-1, 51300, Bard). Avon.
Autumn Rose. Fiona Hill. 1979. pap. 2.25 o.p. (ISBN 0-425-04224-3). Berkley Pub.
Autumn Rose. Fiona Hill. LC 78-7615. 1978. 9.95 o.p. (ISBN 0-399-12280-X). Berkley Pub.
Autumn Song. Margaret Pargeter. (Harlequin Romances Ser.). 192p. 1980. pap. 1.25 o.p. (ISBN 0-373-02350-2, Pub. by Harlequin). PB.
Autumnal Equinox. Sibnarayan Ray. (Redbird Ser). 1975. 10.00 (ISBN 0-89253-601-2); pap. text ed. 4.80 (ISBN 0-88253-711-3). Ind-US Inc.
Auxiliares Basicos Para el Estudio Biblico. Tomas De La Fuente. (Illus.). 424p. (Span.). 1980. pap. 4.80 (ISBN 0-311-42067-2). Casa Bautista.
Auxiliary Gift & Coffee Shop Management. American Hospital Association. LC 76-26604. (Orig.). 1976. pap. 18.25 (ISBN 0-87258-155-1, 1122). Am Hospital.
Auxiliary Gift & Coffee Shop Management. 2nd ed. 136p. 1976. 16.25 (ISBN 0-686-68589-X, 1122). Hospital Finan.
Auxiliary: New Concepts, New Directions. American Hospital Association. LC 74-22174. 244p. (Orig.). 1974. pap. 16.25 (ISBN 0-87258-160-8, 1075). Am Hospital.
Auyana. Sterling Robbins. Date not set. price not set o.p. (ISBN 0-295-95788-3). U of Wash Pr. Postponed.
Availability: Gabriel Marcel & the Phenomenology of Human Openness. Joe McCown. LC 77-22358. (American Academy of Religion. Studies in Religion: No. 14). 1978. pap. 5.00 (ISBN 0-89130-144-5, 010014). Scholars Pr Ca.
Available Light. Ken Buckner. Ed. by Mike Stensvold. LC 76-15435. (Petersen's How.to Photographic Library). (Illus.). 80p. 1976. pap. 3.95 o.p. (ISBN 0-8227-4003-6). Petersen Pub.
Available Light. Ed. by Mike Stensvold. LC 80-83130. (Petersen's Photographic Library). (Illus.). 160p. (Orig.). (gr. 8-12). 1980. pap. 8.95 (ISBN 0-8227-4042-7). Petersen Pub.
Available Pay Survey Reports: An Annotated Bibliography. 2nd ed. Ed. by Steven Langer. 1980. Pt. I. pap. 89.50 (ISBN 0-916506-21-5). Abbott Langer Assocs.
Available Pay Survey Reports: An Annotated Bibliography, Pts. 2 & 3. 2nd ed. Ed. by Steven Langer. 1980. Pt. 1. pap. 39.50 (ISBN 0-916506-45-2); Pt. 2. pap. 19.50 (ISBN 0-916506-46-0). Abbott Langer Assocs.
Availing Prayer. Fay C. Martin. 120p. pap. 1.00. Faith Pub Hse.

Avalanche! Steve Cohen. 1980. pap. 2.50 (ISBN 0-89083-672-8, Kable News Co). Zebra.

Avalanche. A. Rutgers Van Der Loef. (Illus.). (gr. 7 up). 1958. 7.75 (ISBN 0-688-21055-4). Morrow.

Avalanche Patrol. Montgomery M. Atwater. (gr. 7-9). 1963. PLB 5.69 o.p. (ISBN 0-394-90923-2, BYR). Random.

Avalanches & Snow Safety. Colin Fraser. (Illus.). 1978. 14.95 o.p. (ISBN 0-684-14794-7, ScribT). Scribner.

Avant-Garde Choral Music: An Annotated Selected Bibliography. James D. May. LC 76-30577. 1977. 12.00 (ISBN 0-8108-1015-8). Scarecrow.

Avant-Garde Drama: A Casebook. Bernard F. Dukore & Daniel C. Gerould. 1976. scp 7.50 (ISBN 0-690-00848-1, HarpC). Har-Row.

Avant-Garde in Russia: New Perspectives. Ed. by Stephanie Barron & Maurice Tuchman. (Illus.). 250p. 1980. 27.50 (ISBN 0-262-20040-6). MIT Pr.

Avant-Garde in Russia, 1910-1930: New Perspectives. Stephanie Barron et al. Tr. by Jack Hirshman & Andrzej Wojciechowski. (Illus.). 288p. (Orig., Rus. Ger. Fr. Pol.). 1980. pap. 11.95 o.p. (ISBN 0-87587-095-3). La Co Art Mus.

Avant-Garde Theatrale: French Theatre Since 1950. Ed. by Tom Bishop. LC 74-29373. 1975. 15.00x (ISBN 0-8147-0985-0); pap. 7.00x (ISBN 0-8147-0986-9). NYU Pr.

Avanzando: Gramatica espanola y lectura. Sara L. De La Vega & Carmen S. Parr. LC 77-18537. 1978. text ed. 12.95 (ISBN 0-471-02731-6); wkbk. a 6.95x (ISBN 0-471-02732-4); wkbk. b 6.95x (ISBN 0-471-02733-2). Wiley.

Avatar. Poul Anderson. 1979. pap. 2.50 (ISBN 0-425-04861-6). Berkley Pub.

Avatars & the Masters. Sri Chinmoy. 60p. (Orig.). 1979. pap. 2.00 o.p. (ISBN 0-88497-370-0). Aum Pubns.

Avatars of Thrice Great Hermes: An Approach to Romanticism. Ernest L. Tuveson. LC 78-75206. 280p. 1981. 17.50 (ISBN 0-8387-2264-4). Bucknell U Pr.

Avengers: Marvel Novel. (YA) 1980. pap. 1.95 (ISBN 0-671-82093-1). PB.

Avenging Angels. Linwood Carson. 1976. pap. 1.50 o.p. (ISBN 0-685-72575-8, LB408, Leisure Bks). Nordon Pubns.

Avenging Gun. J. L. Bouma. 1978. pap. 1.50 (ISBN 0-505-51327-7). Tower Bks.

Avenging Maid. Janis S. May. (Orig.). 1980. pap. 1.50 o.s.i. (ISBN 0-440-10329-0). Dell.

Avenida Alabanza. Tr. by Don Gossett. (Spanish Bks.). (Span.). 1978. 1.60 (ISBN 0-8297-0902-9). Life Pubs Intl.

Aventura de Morir. Nancy Karo & Alvera Mickelson. Tr. by Jose Flores from Eng. LC 77-15812. 197p. (Orig., Span.). 1977. pap. 3.50 (ISBN 0-89922-098-3). Edit Caribe.

Aventura de Yolanda; Yolanda's Hike. (ps-3). 1.50. New Seed.

Aventuras De Bartolillo. Efren Quintanilla. (Span.). 7.95 (ISBN 84-241-5634-X). E Torres & Sons.

Aventuras de Don Quijote: Relatos Ilustrados. Miguel De Cervantes. (Span.). 9.00 (ISBN 84-241-5412-6). E Torres & Sons.

Aventuras de Tom Sawyer. Mark Twain. (Span.). 9.00 (ISBN 84-241-5630-7). E Torres & Sons.

Aventures D'Alice au Pays des Merveilles. Lewis Carroll. Tr. by Henri Bue from Eng. (Illus.). 196p. (Fr.). (gr. 4-8). 1972. pap. 3.25 (ISBN 0-486-22836-3). Dover.

Avenue of the Righteous. Peter Hellman. (Illus.). 1980. 11.95 (ISBN 0-689-11109-6). Atheneum.

Avenues of Salt Lake City. Karl T. Haglund & Philip F. Notarianni. LC 80-54105. (Illus.). 176p. 1980. pap. 7.50 (ISBN 0-913738-31-X). Utah St Hist Soc.

Avenues to Antiquity: Readings from Scientific American. Intro. by Brian M. Fagan. LC 75-42293. (Illus.). 1976. text ed. 19.95x (ISBN 0-7167-0542-7); pap. text ed. 9.95x (ISBN 0-7167-0541-9). W H Freeman.

Avenues to Understanding: Dynamics of Therapeutic Interactions. W. Mueller. 1973. text ed. 12.95 (ISBN 0-13-055012-4). P-H.

Average American Book. Barry Tarshis. 1981. pap. 2.50 (ISBN 0-451-09486-7, E9486, Sig). NAL.

Average Length of Stay on Short-Stay Hospitals United States, 1977. Frank Lewis. Ed. by Audrey Shipp. (Ser. 13-50). 50p. 1980. pap. text ed. 1.75 (ISBN 0-8406-0198-0). Natl Ctr Health Stats.

Average Purse Tables. Huey Mahl. (Gambler's Book Shelf). 64p. 1976. pap. 2.95 (ISBN 0-89650-564-2). Gamblers.

Averages. Jane J. Srivastava. LC 75-5927. (Young Math Ser.). (Illus.). 40p. (gr. 1-5). 1975. 7.95 (ISBN 0-690-00742-6, TYC-J); PLB 7.89 (ISBN 0-690-00743-4). T Y Crowell.

Averroe's Commentary on Plato's Republic. Ed. by Edwin I. Rosenthal. (University of Cambridge Oriental Pubns.: No. 1). 1966. 51.00 (ISBN 0-521-06130-X). Cambridge U Pr.

Averrois Cordubensis Commentarium Medium in Porphyrii Isagogen et Aristoelis Categorias, Eng. Ed. Averrois. Ed. by Herbert A. Davidson. 1969. 7.50 (ISBN 0-910956-53-7). Medieval Acad.

Avery Index to Architectural Periodicals: Third Supplement. Columbia University. (Library Catalogs-Bib. Guides). 1979. lib. bdg. 120.00 (ISBN 0-8161-0282-1). G K Hall.

Avery's Knot. Mary Cable. 248p. 1981. 11.95 (ISBN 0-399-12569-8). Putnam.

Avian Biology, 5 vols. Donald S. Farner & James R. King. Vol. 1, 1971. 62.50, by subscription 52.50 (ISBN 0-12-249401-6); Vol. 2, 1972. 55.50, by subscription 47.75 (ISBN 0-12-249402-4); Vol. 3, 1973. 61.25, by subscription 52.50 (ISBN 0-12-249403-2); Vol. 4, 1974. 53.75 (ISBN 0-12-249040-1); Vol. 5, 1975. 68.50, subscription 58.50 (ISBN 0-12-249405-9). Acad Pr.

Avian Endocrinology. August Epple & Milton Stetson. 1980. lib ed 34.00 (ISBN 0-12-240250-2). Acad Pr.

Avian Myology. J. C. George & Andrew J. Berger. 1966. 49.00 (ISBN 0-12-280150-4). Acad Pr.

Aviary Birds in Color. Frank Woolham et al. (Illus.). 1974. 11.95 (ISBN 0-7137-0707-0, Pub by Blandford Pr England). Sterling.

Aviation. Boy Scouts Of America. LC 19-600. (Illus.). 72p. (gr. 6-12). 1968. pap. 0.70x (ISBN 0-8395-3293-8, 3293). BSA.

Aviation - Space Dictionary. 6th ed. E. J. Gentle & L. W. Reithmaier. LC 80-67567. (Illus.). 1980. 18.95 (ISBN 0-8168-3002-9). Aero.

Aviation-Aerospace Fundamentals Instructors Guide. Jeppesen Sanderson. (Illus.). 1979. text ed. 31.80 3-ring binder ed. (ISBN 0-88487-031-6, SA418077). Jeppesen Sanderson.

Aviation-Aerospace Fundamentals Student Exercise Book. Jeppesen Sanderson. (Illus.). 1979. pap. text ed. 4.85 (ISBN 0-88487-041-3, SA325952). Jeppesen Sanderson.

Aviation Careers. Arnold Madison. (Career Concise Guides Ser.). (Illus.). 1977. lib. bdg. 6.45 (ISBN 0-531-01300-6). Watts.

Aviation Consumer Used Aircraft Guide. Aviation Consumer. Ed. by Richard Weeghman. (McGraw-Hill Series in Aviation). (Illus.). 224p. 1981. 18.95 (ISBN 0-07-002543-6). McGraw.

Aviation Electronics Handbook. Ed Safford. LC 72-97217. (Illus.). 406p. 1975. pap. 8.95 (ISBN 0-8306-4631-0, 631). TAB Bks.

Aviation, Environment & World Order. S. Bhatt. 196p. 1980. text ed. 15.00x (ISBN 0-391-01809-4). Humanities.

Aviation Europe Nineteen Eighty-One. 34th ed. Intro. by R. E. Williams. (Illus.). 170p. 1980. pap. 27.50x (ISBN 0-85499-888-8). Intl Pubns Serv.

Aviation Fundamentals. 6th ed. (Illus.). 1980. pap. text ed. 8.95 (ISBN 0-88487-059-6, SA315335); student exercise bk. 4.85 (ISBN 0-88487-060-X, SA325760). Jeppesen Sanderson.

Aviation Fundamentals Instructor's Guide. 5th ed. 1980. 10.00 (ISBN 0-88487-061-8, SA418068). Jeppesen Sanderson.

Aviation Industry: Current Perspectives & Problems. (Commercial Law & Practice Course Handbook Series 1978-79: Vol. 195). 1978. pap. 20.00 (ISBN 0-685-90306-0, A4 3027). PLI.

Aviation Instructor's Handbook. Federal Aviation Administration. (Pilot Training Ser.). 170p. 1977. pap. 3.75 (ISBN 0-89100-170-0, E*A-A*C60-14). Aviation Maintenance.

Aviation Law for Pilots. 3rd ed. S. E. Taylor & H. A. Parmar. 137p. 1978. text ed. 19.95x (ISBN 0-258-97114-2, Pub. by Granada England). Renouf.

Aviation Maintenance Handbook & Standard Hardware Digest. Dale Crane. (Illus.). 1976. pap. 4.95 (ISBN 0-89100-060-7). Aviation Maint.

Aviation Maintenance Handbook & Standard Hardware Digest. 2nd ed. Ed. by David Jones & Dale Crane. 1981. pap. write for info. (ISBN 0-89100-151-4). Aviation Maintenance.

Aviation Mechanics Certification Guide. Ed. by Larry Reithmaior. LC 80-11630. (Illus.). 1980. 6.95 (ISBN 0-932882-01-3). Palomar Bks.

Aviation Psychology. Stanley N. Roscoe et al. 1980. text ed. 16.50 (ISBN 0-8138-1925-3). Iowa St U Pr.

Aviation Quarterly. Richard B. Bierman. (Illus.). Date not set. 12.00 (Pub. by Avn Quarterly). Aviation.

Aviation Safety Bibliography & Source Book. Frank H. King & Viola W. King. LC 80-21946. (Aviation Management Ser.). 80p. (Orig.). 1980. pap. write for info. (ISBN 0-89100-138-7). Aviation Maintenance.

Aviation Technician Training Ser. Incl. Aircraft Corrosion Control. 3.00 o.p. (ISBN 0-685-79350-8); Aircraft Oxygen Systems. 3.00 o.p. (ISBN 0-685-79351-6); Aircraft Painting & Finishing. 4.00 o.p. (ISBN 0-685-79352-4); Fuel Metering Systems for Aircraft. 4.00 o.p. (ISBN 0-685-79353-2); Basic Electricity for A&P Mechanics. 4.00 o.p. (ISBN 0-685-79354-0). (Illus.). 1975. Aviation.

Aviation Tort Law, 3 vols. Stuart Speiser & Charles Krause. LC 78-55326. 1980. 180.00. Lawyers Co-Op.

Aviation Weather. Arco Editorial Board. LC 78-23251. (Illus.). 1979. pap. text ed. 8.00 o.p. (ISBN 0-668-04413-6, 4413). Arco.

Aviation Weather. 2nd ed. Federal Aviation Administration. (Pilot Training Ser.). (Illus.). 219p. 1975. pap. 7.00 (ISBN 0-89100-160-3, E*A*A*C61-006A). Aviation Maintenance.

Aviation Weather: Ac 00-6A. Federal Aviation Administration. pap. 7.00 (ISBN 0-685-46352-4, Pub. by Cooper). Aviation.

Aviation Weather Services. 3rd ed. Federal Aviation Administration. (Pilot Training Ser.). (Illus.). 123p. 1979. pap. 4.50 (ISBN 0-89100-161-1, E*A-A*C61-0045B). Aviation Maintenance.

Aviator. Ernest K. Gann. LC 80-68543. 1981. 10.95 (ISBN 0-87795-299-X). Arbor Hse.

Aviator's Catalog: A Source Book of Aeronautica. Timothy R. Foster. 288p. 1980. 24.95 (ISBN 0-442-21201-1); pap. 16.95 (ISBN 0-442-22465-6). Van Nos Reinhold.

Aviatrix. Elinor Smith. (Illus.). 32p. 1981. 12.95 (ISBN 0-15-110372-0). HarBraceJ.

Avicenna & the Visionary Recital. Henri Corbin. Tr. by Willard R. Task from French. 320p. 1980. pap. text ed. 12.50 (ISBN 0-88214-213-5). Spring Pubns.

Avicenna'a Psychology. Avicenna. Ed. by F. Rahman. LC 79-2848. 127p. 1981. Repr. of 1952 ed. 14.50 (ISBN 0-8305-0024-3). Hyperion Conn.

Aviones. Bob Ottun. Tr. by Rene Sanchez. (ps-3). 1977. PLB 5.92 o.p. (ISBN 0-307-68836-4, Golden Pr). Western Pub.

Avocational Activities for the Handicapped: A Handbook for Avocational Counseling. Robert P. Overs et al. (American Lectures in Social & Rehabilitation Psychology Ser.). 208p. 1974. 13.75 (ISBN 0-398-02975-X). C C Thomas.

Avoid the One-Way Trip to Washington. Venita VanCaspel. 1980. pap. 1.50 (ISBN 0-8359-0297-8). Reston.

Avoiding Burnout: Time Management for D. R.E.'s. Clarice Flagel. 60p. (Orig.). 1981. pap. 4.95 (ISBN 0-697-01782-6). Wm C Brown.

Avoiding Teacher Malpractice. Rennard Strickland. 1976. 8.95 (ISBN 0-8015-7457-9, Hawthorn). Dutton.

Avon Five: Avons Collectors Handbook & Price Guide. LC 77-89478. (Illus.). 1977. pap. 14.95 (ISBN 0-686-64373-9). Avons Res.

Avon Four: Avons Collectors Handbook & Price Guide. LC 75-21080. (Illus.). 1975. pap. 12.95 (ISBN 0-686-64372-0). Avons Res.

Avon Six: Avons Collectors Handbook & Price Guide. (Illus.). 1979. pap. 19.95 (ISBN 0-931864-06-2). Avons Res.

Avon Two: Western Collector Handbook & Price Guide. (Illus.). 1971. pap. 4.95 o.p. (ISBN 0-685-87874-0). Avons Res.

Avoth. Yitzchak Magriso. Tr. by David N. Barocas. Intro. by & Aryeh Kaplan. 400p. 14.95 (ISBN 0-686-27542-X). Maznaim.

Avyakta Upanisad. Tr. by P. Lal from Sanskrit. 25p. 1973. 8.00 (ISBN 0-88253-272-3). Ind-US Inc.

Awake in a Nightmare. Ethan Feinsod. 1981. 14.95 (ISBN 0-393-01431-2). Norton.

Awaken the Heart. Dorothy Vernon. 192p. (Orig.). 1980. pap. 1.50 (ISBN 0-671-57011-0). S&S.

Awakening. new ed. Kate Chopin. Ed. by Margaret Culley. (Critical Edition Ser.). 256p. 1977. 10.00 (ISBN 0-393-04434-3); pap. text ed. 4.95x (ISBN 0-393-09172-4). Norton.

Awakening. Fay Young. 64p. 1981. 5.00 (ISBN 0-682-49701-0). Exposition.

Awakening Electromagnetic Spectrum. new ed. Robert J. Bearns. LC 74-76050. (Illus.). 128p. (Orig.). 1974. pap. 7.98 (ISBN 0-914706-00-4). Awakening Prods.

Awakening Giant: Britain in the Industrial Revolution. E. R. Chamberlin. 1976. 30.00 (ISBN 0-7134-3053-2, Pub. by Batsford England). David & Charles.

Awakening Grace, Poems at the Feet of the Silent Master. Jeanne R. Foster. Ed. by Jeanne Shaw & Darwin Shaw. (Illus.). 1977. 4.95 (ISBN 0-913078-28-X). Sheriar Pr.

Awakening Intuition. Frances E. Vaughan. LC 77-27685. 1979. pap. 3.95 (ISBN 0-385-13371-5, Anch). Doubleday.

Awakening Nightmare: A Breakthrough in Treating the Mentally Ill. 1972. 9.95 o.p. (ISBN 0-686-67702-1). Exposition.

Awakening of a Sleeping Giant: Third World Leaders & National Liberation. Thomas Hachey & Ralph E. Weber. LC 80-12517. 160p. 1981. pap. text ed. 6.50 (ISBN 0-89874-081-9). Krieger.

Awakening of a Sleeping Giant: Third World Leaders National Liberation. Thomas E. Hachey & Ralph E. Weber. 1980. pap. 6.50 (ISBN 0-89874-081-9). Krieger.

Awakening of Faith. Tr. by Yoshito Hakeda. LC 67-13778. 1967. 17.50x (ISBN 0-231-03025-8). Columbia U Pr.

Awakening of Faith, Attributed to Asvaghosha. Tr. by Yoshito S. Hakeda. 128p. 1974. pap. 5.00 (ISBN 0-231-08336-X). Columbia U Pr.

Awakening of Nationalistic Drives & the Tragic Dilemma of the Soviet Leadership. Mark H. Saviter. (The Major Currents in Contemporary World History Library). (Illus.). 113p. 1981. 67.75 (ISBN 0-930008-83-9). Inst Econ Pol.

Awakening of Western Legal Thought. Max Hamburger. LC 76-79515. 1969. Repr. of 1942 ed. 12.00x (ISBN 0-8196-0246-9). Biblo.

Awakening of Western Legal Thought. Max Hamburger. Tr. by Bernard Miall. Repr. of 1942 ed. lib. bdg. 12.50x (ISBN 0-8371-3103-0, HALT). Greenwood.

Awakening of Zen. D. T. Suzuki. Ed. by Christmas Humphreys. LC 79-17444. 1980. pap. 5.95 (ISBN 0-87773-715-0, Prajna). Great Eastern.

Awakening the Slower Mind. V. Bruce. 1969. 22.00 (ISBN 0-08-006387-X); pap. 10.75 (ISBN 0-08-006386-1). Pergamon.

Award. Lawrence Bantleman. 9.00 (ISBN 0-89253-648-9); flexible cloth 4.80 (ISBN 0-89253-649-7). Ind-US Inc.

Award Movies: A Complete Guide from A to Z. Roy Pickard. LC 80-54142. (Illus.). 354p. 1981. 14.95 (ISBN 0-8052-3767-4); pap. 6.95 (ISBN 0-8052-0677-9). Schocken.

Award Winning ASCE Papers in Geotechnical Engineering. Compiled By American Society of Civil Engineers. 824p. 1977. pap. text ed. 32.00 (ISBN 0-87262-092-1). Am Soc Civil Eng.

Awards, Honors & Prizes: United States & Canada, Vol. 1. 4th ed. Ed. by Paul Wasserman. LC 78-16691. 1978. 62.00 (ISBN 0-8103-0378-7). Gale.

Awareness. Eileen J. Garrett. LC 60-53468. 1947. 5.00 o.p. (ISBN 0-912326-01-8). Garrett-Helix.

Awareness & Flexibility: The Keys to Successful Credit Judgment. Donald E. Miller. 32p. 1974. pap. 1.50 (ISBN 0-934914-14-1). NACM.

Awareness: Exercises in Basic Composition Skills. 2nd ed. Suanne Maca-Roueche & Dorothy Patterson. LC 77-20918. 1978. pap. text ed. 10.50 (ISBN 0-471-03460-6). Wiley.

Awareness Games: Personal Growth Through Group Interaction. Claus-Juergen Hoeper et al. Tr. by Hilary Davies. 160p. 1976. pap. 4.95 (ISBN 0-312-06300-8). St Martin.

Awareness of Dying. Barney G. Glaser & Anselm L. Strauss. LC 65-12454. 1965. 15.95x (ISBN 0-202-30001-3). Aldine Pub.

Awareness of Self Discovery. William Samuel. 1981. pap. write for info. (ISBN 0-916108-13-9). Seed Center.

Awareness of Self Discovery. William Samuel. 1970. 7.00 o.p. (ISBN 0-916108-52-X). Seed Center.

Awareness Techniques: Waldara Answers, 2 vols. in one. 1975. pap. 2.95 (ISBN 0-934258-05-8). W a Reilly.

Away & Beyond. A. E. Van Vogt. 1977. pap. 1.75 o.s.i. (ISBN 0-515-04426-1). Jove Pubns.

Away from Home. Lee Berkson. 36p. 1980. pap. 2.50 (ISBN 0-933180-19-5). Spoon Riv Poetry.

Away Goes Sally. Elizabeth Coatsworth. (Illus.). (gr. 4-6). 1934. 6.95g o.s.i. (ISBN 0-02-719300-4). Macmillan.

Away We Go! A Guidebook of Family Trips to Places of Interest in New Jersey, Nearby Pennsylvania & New York. 4th ed. Ed. by Michaela M. Mole. 1976. pap. 3.50 o.p. (ISBN 0-8135-0817-7). Rutgers U Pr.

Away Went the Balloons. Carolyn Haywood. (Illus.). (gr. 3-7). 1973. 6.95 o.p. (ISBN 0-688-20095-8); PLB 7.92 (ISBN 0-688-30095-2). Morrow.

Awful Evelina. Susan B. Pfeffer. Ed. by Kathy Pacini. LC 79-108. (Concept Bk.: Level I). (Illus.). (gr. k-3). 1979. 6.95g (ISBN 0-8075-0494-7). A Whitman.

Awful Mess. Anne Rockwell. LC 80-16779. (Illus.). 40p. (ps-2). 1980. Repr. of 1973 ed. 7.95 (ISBN 0-590-07784-8, Four Winds). Schol Bk Serv.

Awful Thursday. Ron Roy. LC 78-14049. (I Am Reading Bk.). (Illus.). (gr. 1-4). 1979. 3.95 (ISBN 0-394-84003-8); PLB 5.99 (ISBN 0-394-94003-2). Pantheon.

Awinning Combination. Nick Bollitier & Julie Anthony. (Illus.). 224p. 1980. 12.50 o.p. (ISBN 0-684-16710-7, ScribT). Scribner.

Awkward Song. Allan Kornblum. LC 80-18370. 54p. 1980. 20.00 (ISBN 0-915124-33-5, Bookslinger); pap. 5.00 (ISBN 0-915124-32-7). Toothpaste.

Awl-Birds. J. K. Stanford. (Illus.). 1949. 4.95 (ISBN 0-8159-5016-0). Devin.

Awntyrs off Arthure at the Terne Wathelyne: A Critical Edition. Robert J. Gates. LC 69-16539. (Haney Foundation Ser). 1969. 12.00x (ISBN 0-8122-7587-X). U of Pa Pr.

AWP Catalogue of Writing Programs. 3rd. ed. Ed. by Kathy Walton. LC 80-67017. 120p. 1980. pap. 5.00 (ISBN 0-936266-01-5). Assoc Writing.

AWWA Distribution System Symposium Nineteen Eighty: Proceedings: 1980. American Water Works Association. (AWWA Handbooks Proceedings Ser.). (Illus.). 179p. 1980. pap. text ed. 9.50 (ISBN 0-89867-235-X). Am Water Wks Assn.

Axel. DeL'Isle A. Villiers. 1970. 10.95 (ISBN 0-19-647518-X). Dufour.

Axiological Ethics. J. N. Findlay. LC 79-115982. (New Studies in Ethics). 1970. pap. 4.95 (ISBN 0-312-06335-0). St Martin.

Axiomatic Analysis. Robert Katz. 1978. 25.00 (ISBN 0-685-60304-0). Mathco.

Axiomatic Method in Phonology. Tadeusz Batog. 1968. text ed. 8.50x (ISBN 0-7100-2980-2). Humanities.

Axiomatic Proof Techniques for Parallel Programs. Susan S. Owicki. LC 79-50560. (Outstanding Dissertations in the Computer Sciences Ser.: Vol. 14). 203p. 1980. lib. bdg. 22.00 (ISBN 0-8240-4413-4). Garland Pub.

Axiomatic Semantics: A Linguistic Theory. Sandor G. Hervey. 320p. 1980. 20.00x (ISBN 0-7073-0222-6, Pub. by Scottish Academic Pr). Columbia U Pr.

Axiomatic Set Theory, 2 Vols, Vol. 13. Symposia in Pure Mathematics-Los Angeles-July, 1967. LC 78-125172. Vol. 1 Ed. By Dana Scott. 24.00 (ISBN 0-8218-0245-3, PSPUM-13.1); Vol. 2 Ed. By T. J. Jech. 26.80 (ISBN 0-8218-0246-1, PSPUM-13.2). Am Math.

Axiomatic Theory of Language with Applications to English. Ty Pak. LC 80-12010. (Edward Sapir Monograph Ser. in Language, Culture & Cognition: No. 6). vi, 129p. (Orig.). 1979. pap. 6.00x (ISBN 0-933104-08-1). Jupiter Pr.

Axiomatics. R. Blanche. Tr. by G. B. Keene. (Monographs in Modern Logic). 1967. pap. 5.00 (ISBN 0-7100-3802-X). Routledge & Kegan.

Axiomatization of the Theory of Relativity. Hans Reichenbach. Ed. & tr. by Maria Reichenbach. LC 68-21540. 1968. 18.50x (ISBN 0-520-01525-8). U of Cal Pr.

Axioms & Quotations of Yosef Ben-Jochannan. E. Curtis Alexander. LC 80-70287. (Illus.). 118p. (gr. 8-12). 1980. pap. 6.95 (ISBN 0-938818-01-5). ECA Pub.

Axioms & Quotations of Yosef ben-Jochannan. E. Curtis Alexander. LC 80-70287. (Illus.). 118p. (Orig.). 1980. pap. 6.95 (ISBN 0-938818-01-5). ECA Assoc.

Axion Esti. Odysseus Elytis. Tr. by Edmund Keeley & George Savidis. LC 79-49274. (Pitt Poetry Ser.). 1979. pap. 4.95 (ISBN 0-8229-5318-8). U of Pittsburgh Pr.

Axis. Clive Irving. 1981. pap. 2.95 (ISBN 0-553-14590-8). Bantam.

Axis Mundi Poems. Deena Metzger. (Illus.). 52p. (Orig.). 1981. pap. 4.95 (ISBN 0-937310-09-3). Jazz Pr.

Axmann Agenda. Michael Pettit. (Orig.). 1980. pap. 2.50 o.s.i. (ISBN 0-440-10152-2). Dell.

Axonal Transport, Degeneration, & Regeneration in the Visual System of the Goldfish. H. Wolburg. (Advances in Anatomy, Embryology & Cell Biology Ser.: Vol. 67). (Illus.). 100p. 1981. pap. 28.50 (ISBN 0-387-10336-8). Springer-Verlag.

Axones & Kyrbeis of Drakon & Solon. Ronald Stroud. LC 77-20329. (Publications in Classical Studies: Vol. 19). 1979. 8.00x (ISBN 0-520-09590-1). U of Cal Pr.

Aya. Eleanor Wilner. LC 79-4753. 1979. lib. bdg. 8.00x (ISBN 0-87023-277-0); pap. 3.95 (ISBN 0-87023-278-9). U of Mass Pr.

Ayer a las Siete. Tr. by Jeanne Hale. (Spanish Bks.). (Span.). 1977. 1.80 (ISBN 0-8297-0812-X). Life Pubs Intl.

Ayer Directory of Publications: 1981. rev. ed. LC 80-70115. 1981. 66.00 (ISBN 0-910190-20-8). Ayer Pr.

Ayesha: The Return of She. H. Rider Haggard. (Illus.). 1978. pap. 3.50 (ISBN 0-486-23649-8). Dover.

Ayesha: The Return of She. H. Rider Haggard. Ed. by R. Reginald & Douglas Menville. LC 80-19298. (Newcastle Forgotten Fantasy Library: Vol. 14). 359p. 1980. Repr. of 1977 ed. lib. bdg. 10.95x (ISBN 0-89370-513-6). Borgo Pr.

AYH Bike Hike Book. LC 75-35656. (Packit Ser.). (Illus.). 128p. 1976. pap. 2.95 (ISBN 0-8117-2005-5). Stackpole.

Azande: History & Political Institutions. Edward E. Evans-Pritchard. 1971. 36.00x (ISBN 0-19-823170-9). Oxford U Pr.

Azasulfones: Versatile Precursors for Aryl Free Radicals & Aryl Cations. M. Kobayashi. (Sulfur Reports Ser.). 28p. flexicover 7.50 (ISBN 3-7186-0040-4). Harwood Academic.

Azemia: A Descriptive & Sentimental Novel, Interspersed with Pieces of Poetry, by Jaquetta Agneta Mariana Jenks, 2 vols. William Beckford. Ed. by Gina Luria. LC 74-8006. (Feminist Controversy in England, 1788-1810 Ser.). 1974. Set. lib. bdg. 76.00 (ISBN 0-8240-0850-2); lib. bdg. 50.00 ea. Garland Pub.

Azerbaijan: Mosques, Turrets, Palaces. Ilona Turanszky. Tr. by Laszlo Boros. (Illus.). 184p. 1979. 22.50x (ISBN 963-13-0321-7). Intl Pubns Serv.

Azolla As an Aquatic Green Manure: Use & Management in Crop Production. Thomas A. Lumpkin & Donald L. Plucknett. (Tropical Agriculture Ser.: No. 15). 1981. lib. bdg. 22.50x (ISBN 0-89158-451-X). Westview.

Azorin. Kathleen M. Glenn. (World Authors Ser: No. 604). 1981. lib. bdg. 14.95 (ISBN 0-8057-6446-1). Twayne.

Aztec. Gary Jennings. (Illus.). 1980. 15.95 (ISBN 0-689-11045-6). Atheneum.

Aztec Image in Western Thought. Benjamin Keen. LC 74-163952. 1971. 40.00 (ISBN 0-8135-0698-0). Rutgers U Pr.

Aztec Skull. Anthea Goddard. LC 76-56606. 1977. 5.95 o.s.i. (ISBN 0-8027-6285-9). Walker & Co.

Aztecs. Judith Crosher et al. LC 77-86189. (Peoples of the Past Ser.). (Illus.). 1977. lib. bdg. 7.95 (ISBN 0-686-51154-9). Silver.

Aztecs. Nigel Davies. LC 80-12141. (Illus.). 419p. 1980. 15.95 (ISBN 0-8061-1686-2); pap. 7.95 (ISBN 0-8061-1691-9). U of Okla Pr.

Aztecs. Jill Hughes. (Gloucester Press Ser.). (gr. 4-8). 1980. PLB 6.90 (ISBN 0-531-03414-3). Watts.

Aztecs, & Their Presecessors: Archaeology of Mesoamerica. 2nd ed. Muriel P. Weaver. (Studies in Archaeology). 1981. write for info. (ISBN 0-12-785936-5). Acad Pr.

Aztecs, People of the Sun. Alfonso Caso. Tr. by Lowell Dunham. (Civilization of the American Indian Ser.: No. 50). (Illus.). 1978. Repr. of 1958 ed. 16.95 (ISBN 0-8061-0414-7). U of Okla Pr.

Aztlan: An Anthology of Mexican-American Literature. Ed. by Stan Steiner & Luis Valdez. 416p. Date not set. pap. 3.45 (ISBN 0-394-71770-8, Vin). Random.

Azuela & the Mexican Underdogs. Stanley L. Robe. LC 76-20031. 1979. 20.00x (ISBN 0-520-03293-4). U of Cal Pr.

Azul... Otras Poemas. Ruben Dario. (Span). 3.75x o.s.i. (ISBN 0-686-00843-X). Colton Bk.

Azusa Street. Frank Bartleman. 1980. pap. 4.95 (ISBN 0-88270-439-7). Logos.

B

B & C: Mycological Association of M. J. Berkeley & M. A. Curtis. Ronald H. Petersen. (Bibliotheca Mycologica: 72). (Illus.). 120p. 1980. pap. text ed. 15.00 (ISBN 3-7682-1258-0). Lubrecht & Cramer.

B B C Hymn Book. British Broadcasting Corporation. 1951. words only 3.75x (ISBN 0-19-231302-9); words & music 9.95x (ISBN 0-19-231301-0). Oxford U Pr.

B Book. Phyllis McGinley. LC 68-19821. (Illus.). (gr. 1-3). 1968. 2.95g o.s.i. (ISBN 0-02-765370-6, CCPr). Macmillan.

B Lymphocytes in the Immune Response. Ed. by M. Cooper et al. (Developments in Immunology: Vol. 3). 1979. 45.00 (ISBN 0-444-00319-3, North Holland). Elsevier.

B. M. Fraeijs De Veubeke Memorial Volume of Selected Papers. M. Geradin. 79p. 1980. 57.50x (ISBN 90-286-0900-8). Sijthoff & Noordhoff.

B-Seventeen Flying Fortress. Steve Birdsall. LC 65-16862. (Famous Aircraft Ser.). (Illus.). 1979. pap. 4.95 (ISBN 0-8168-5646-X). Aero.

B-Seventeen Fortress at War. Roger A. Freeman. LC 76-39858. (Illus.). 1977. 20.00 (ISBN 0-684-14872-2, ScribT). Scribner.

B-Thirty-Six in Action. 1980. pap. 4.95 (ISBN 0-89747-101-6). Squad Sig Pubns.

B-Twenty-Four Liberator. Martin Bowman. LC 80-50342. (Illus.). 128p. 1980. 14.95 (ISBN 0-528-81538-5). Rand.

B-Twenty-Nine Book. Frederick Johnsen. (Illus.). 1978. pap. 3.95 (ISBN 0-911721-40-1, Pub. by Bomber). Aviation.

B: Twenty-Nine Letters from Coconut Grove. Sandy Campbell. 1974. wrappers, ltd. ed. 20.00x (ISBN 0-917366-03-4). S Campbell.

B-Twenty Six Marauder at War. Roger Freeman. LC 78-7161. (Illus.). 1979. 17.95 (ISBN 0-684-15998-8, ScribT). Scribner.

Baal. Robert McCammon. 1980. pap. 2.25 (ISBN 0-686-69249-7, 36319). Avon.

Baalbeck Caravans. Charis Waddy. (Arab Background Ser.). 1967. 8.95x (ISBN 0-685-77106-7). Intl Bk Ctr.

Baalbek. Friedrich Ragette. LC 80-19626. (Illus.). 128p. 1981. 18.00 (ISBN 0-8155-5059-6). Noyes.

Bab Ballads. W. S. Gilbert. Ed. by James Ellis. LC 77-102668. 1970. 17.50x (ISBN 0-674-05800-3, Belknap Pr); pap. 8.95 (ISBN 0-674-05801-1). Harvard U Pr.

Bab: The Herald of the Day of Days. H. M. Balyuzi. (Illus.). 1973. 9.95 (ISBN 0-85398-048-9, 7-31-50, Pub. by G Ronald England); pap. 3.65 (ISBN 0-85398-054-3, 7-31-51, Pub. by G Ronald England). Baha'i.

Baba Yaga's Geese & Other Russian Stories. Tr. by Bonnie Carey from Rus. LC 73-77852. (Midland Bks.: No. 222). (Illus.). 128p. (gr. 1-6). 1973. 10.00x o.s.i. (ISBN 0-253-10500-5); pap. 5.95x (ISBN 0-253-20222-1). Ind U Pr.

Babaji. Leonard Orr. 1980. pap. 10.00 (ISBN 0-686-27683-3). L Orr.

Babar & the Ghost. Laurent De Brunhoff. LC 80-5753. (Illus.). 32p. 1981. PLB 6.99 (ISBN 0-394-94660-X); pap. 4.95 boards (ISBN 0-394-84660-5). Random.

Babar & the Wully-Wully. DeBrunhoff. (Illus.). (gr. 3). Date not set. pap. cancelled o.p. (ISBN 0-590-30046-6, Schol Pap). Schol Bk Serv.

Babar & Zephir. Jean De Brunhoff. Tr. by Merle Haas. (Illus.). (ps). 1942. 4.95 (ISBN 0-394-80579-8, BYR); PLB 5.99 (ISBN 0-394-90579-2). Random.

Babar Comes to America. Laurent De Brunhoff. (Illus.). (gr. k-2). 1965. 4.95 (ISBN 0-394-80588-7, BYR); PLB 5.99 (ISBN 0-394-90588-1). Random.

Babar Learns to Cook. Laurent De Brunhoff. LC 78-11769. (Picturebacks Ser.). (Illus.). (ps-1). 1979. PLB 4.99 (ISBN 0-394-94108-X, BYR); pap. 1.25 (ISBN 0-394-84108-5). Random.

Babar Saves the Day. Laurent De Brunoff. LC 76-11684. (Picturebacks Ser.). (Illus.). (gr. 3-6). 1976. pap. 1.25 (ISBN 0-394-83341-4, BYR). Random.

Babar's Birthday Surprise. Laurent De Brunhoff. (ps-2). 1970. 4.95 (ISBN 0-394-80591-7, BYR); PLB 5.99 (ISBN 0-394-90591-1). Random.

Babar's French Lessons. Laurent De Brunhoff. (Illus.). (ps). 1963. 5.95 (ISBN 0-394-80587-9, BYR); PLB 5.99 (ISBN 0-394-90587-3). Random.

Babar's Little Library: Stories About Earth, About Fire, About Air, About Water, 4 bks. (Illus.). (ps-2). 1980. Set. 4.95 (ISBN 0-394-84365-7). Random.

Babar's Mystery. Laurent De Brunhoff. LC 78-55912. (Illus.). (gr. 1-3). 1978. 4.95 (ISBN 0-394-83920-X, BYR); PLB 5.99 (ISBN 0-394-93920-4). Random.

Babar's Spanish Lessons. Laurent De Brunhoff. (Illus.). (gr. k-3). 1965. 5.95 (ISBN 0-394-80589-5, BYR); PLB 5.99 (ISBN 0-394-90589-X). Random.

Babe Didrikson: The World's Greatest Woman Athlete. Gene Schoor. LC 77-16944. (gr. 4-7). 1978. 7.95a (ISBN 0-385-13031-7); PLB (ISBN 0-385-13032-5). Doubleday.

Babe! Mildred Didrickson Zaharias. James Hahn & Lynn Hahn. Ed. by Howard Schroeder. (Sports Legends Ser.). (Illus.). 48p. (Orig.). (gr. 3-5). 1981. PLB 5.95 (ISBN 0-89686-122-8); pap. text ed. 2.95 (ISBN 0-89686-137-6). Crestwood Hse.

Babe: Mildred Didriksen Zaharias. Beatrice S. Smith. LC 75-42046. (Sport Profiles Ser.). (Illus.). 49p. (gr. 4-11). 1976. PLB 8.50 (ISBN 0-8172-0136-X). Raintree Pubs.

Babe Ruth & Hank Aaron: The Home Run Kings. James Haskins. LC 74-11018. (Illus.). 96p. (gr. 5 up). 1975. pap. 1.75 o.p. (ISBN 0-688-46654-0). Lothrop.

Babel. Alan Burns. 1980. pap. cancelled (ISBN 0-7145-0011-9). Riverrun NY.

Babel. Patti Smith. 1979. pap. text ed. 2.75 (ISBN 0-425-04230-8). Berkley Pub.

Babes in Arms: Youth in the Army. David Gottlieb. LC 80-15830. (Illus.). 173p. 1980. 14.95 (ISBN 0-8039-1499-7). Sage.

Babies Need Books. Dorothy Butler. LC 80-14027. 1980. 9.95 (ISBN 0-689-11112-6). Atheneum.

Babits & Psychoanalysis Christiana. Anton N. Nyerges. 100p. (Orig.). 1981. pap. price not set (ISBN 0-9600954-2-X). Nyerges.

Baboon Mothers & Infants. Jeanne Altmann. LC 79-21568. (Illus.). 1980. text ed. 17.50x (ISBN 0-674-05856-9). Harvard U Pr.

Babur the Tiger. Harold Lamb. 1979. pap. 1.95 o.p. (ISBN 0-523-40473-5). Pinnacle Bks.

Babus, Brahmans & Bureaucrats: A Critique of the Administrative System in Pakistan. Nazim. LC 73-936432. 144p. 1973. 5.75x o.p. (ISBN 0-88386-281-6). South Asia Bks.

Baby. John Burningham. LC 75-4564. (Illus.). (ps-1). 1975. 3.95 (ISBN 0-690-00900-3, TYC-J); PLB 4.89 (ISBN 0-690-00901-1). T Y Crowell.

Baby: A Novel. Kirsten Thorup. Tr. by Nadia Christensen from Danish. LC 80-17844. (Pegasus Prize for Literature Ser.). 208p. 1980. 9.95 (ISBN 0-8071-0772-7). La State U Pr.

Baby Animal ABC. Robert Broomfield. (Picture Ser). (Orig.). 1968. pap. 1.95 (ISBN 0-14-050006-5, Puffin). Penguin.

Baby Animal Book. Daphne Davis. 24p. (ps-1). 1964. PLB 5.38 (ISBN 0-307-68902-6, Golden Pr). Western Pub.

Baby Animals. Incl. Puppies & Dogs (ISBN 0-528-87070-X); Kittens & Cats (ISBN 0-528-87071-8); Ponies & Horses (ISBN 0-528-87072-6); Zoo Animals (ISBN 0-528-87073-4); Farm Animals (ISBN 0-528-87074-2); Animal Friends (ISBN 0-528-87075-0). (Illus.). (ps-1). 1979. pap. 1.25 ea. Rand.

Baby Animals. (Ladybird Stories Ser.). (Illus., Arabic.). 2.50 (ISBN 0-686-53063-2). Intl Bk Ctr.

Baby Animals. Lisa Bonfort. (Illus.). (ps-1). 1980. 2.95 (ISBN 0-525-69409-9, Gingerbread). Dutton.

Baby Animals. Garth Williams. (ps-1). 1956. PLB 4.57 o.p. (ISBN 0-307-60517-5, Golden Pr). Western Pub.

Baby Animals. Zokeisha. (Puppet Story Board Bks.). (Illus.). 12p. (ps-k). Date not set. boards 2.95 (ISBN 0-671-42645-1, Little Simon). S&S.

Baby Animals & Their Mothers. Ed. by Hanns Reich. (Illus.). (gr. 3 up). 1965. 7.95 o.p. (ISBN 0-8090-2010-6, Terra Magica). Hill & Wang.

Baby Book. Rosemary Sturgess. LC 77-76097. 1977. 13.50 (ISBN 0-7153-7438-9). David & Charles.

Baby Brokers: The Marketing of White Babies in America. Lynn McTaggart. 1980. 10.95 (ISBN 0-8037-0354-6). Dial.

Baby Farm Animals. Garth Williams. (Big Picture Bk.). 24p. (gr. 1-3). 1953. 1.95 (ISBN 0-307-10545-8, Golden Pr); PLB 7.62 (ISBN 0-307-60545-0). Western Pub.

Baby Farm Animals. Garth Williams. (Big Picture Bk.). (Illus.). 24p. (ps-3). 1977. Repr. of 1958 ed. PLB 5.00 (ISBN 0-307-60545-0, Golden Pr). Western Pub.

Baby in a Basket. Ruth S. Odor. LC 79-12092. (Bible Story Books). (Illus.). (ps-3). 1979. PLB 5.50 (ISBN 0-89565-086-X). Childs World.

Baby Jesus. Hilda L. Rostron. (Ladybird Ser). (Illus.). 1961. bds. 1.49 (ISBN 0-87508-832-5). Chr Lit.

Baby Just Now? 6th ed. Walter Trobisch. LC 80-17213. 56p. 1980. pap. 2.25 (ISBN 0-87784-849-1). Inter-Varsity.

Baby Listens. Illus. by Eloise Wilkin. (Baby's First Golden Bks.). (Illus.). 8p. (ps). Date not set. 1.25 (ISBN 0-307-10754-X, Golden Pr). Western Pub.

Baby Looks. Illus. by Eloise Wilkin. (Baby's First Golden Bks.). (Illus.). 8p. (ps). Date not set. 1.25 (ISBN 0-307-10753-1, Golden Pr). Western Pub.

Baby Love. Joyce Maynard. LC 80-2707. 288p. 1981. 10.95 (ISBN 0-394-51802-0). Knopf.

Baby Moses in a Basket. (Tell-a-Bible Story Ser.). (Illus.). 28p. bds. 0.69 (ISBN 0-686-68638-1, 3682). Standard Pub.

Baby-Sitter. Linda Duczman. LC 76-44229. (Moods & Emotions Ser.). (Illus.). (gr. k-3). 1977. PLB 8.95 (ISBN 0-8172-0065-7, Raintree Editions). Raintree Pubs.

Baby-Sitting: A Concise Guide. Rubie Saunders. (YA) (gr. 7-9). 1979. pap. 1.50 (ISBN 0-671-56012-3). PB.

Baby Starts to Grow. Paul Showers. LC 69-11827. (Let's-Read-&-Find-Out Science Bk). (Illus.). (gr. k-3). 1969. PLB 7.89 (ISBN 0-690-11320-X, TYC-J); (ISBN 0-685-20467-7); filmstrip with record 11.95 (ISBN 0-690-11321-8); film with cassette 14.95 (ISBN 0-690-11323-4). T Y Crowell.

Baby Talk. D. Leb Tannenbaum. (Illus.). 32p. (gr. 1-3). 1981. pap. 1.95 (ISBN 0-380-76935-2, Camelot). Avon.

Baby Talk & Infant Speech. Ed. by Walburga Von Raffler-Engel & Yvan Lebrun. (Neurolinguistics Ser.: Vol. 5). 362p. 1976. text ed. 46.00 (ISBN 90-265-0229-X, Pub. by Swets Pub Serv Holland). Swets North Am.

Baby, That Was Rock & Roll: The Legendary Leiber & Stoller. Robert Palmer. 1978. pap. 8.95 (ISBN 0-89396-037-3). Urizen Bks.

Babylon. Anthony Esler. 320p. 1981. pap. 2.75 (ISBN 0-449-24375-3, Crest). Fawcett.

Babylon Cookbook. Julie Najors. (Arabic.). pap. 12.00x (ISBN 0-686-63556-3). Intl Bk Ctr.

Babylon Mystery Religion: Ancient & Modern. Ralph Woodrow. (Illus.). 1966. 3.00 (ISBN 0-916938-00-X). R Woodrow.

Babylon Revisited & Other Stories. F. Scott Fitzgerald. 1960. pap. 4.95 (ISBN 0-684-71757-3, ScribT). Scribner.

Babylonian Cuisine: Chaldean Cookbook from the Middle East. Julia Najor. 1981. 10.00 (ISBN 0-533-04628-9). Vantage.

Babylonian Wisdom Literature. Wilfred G. Lambert. (Illus.). 1960. 37.50x (ISBN 0-19-815424-0). Oxford U Pr.

Baby?...Maybe: A Guide to Making the Most Fateful Decision of Your Life. rev. ed. Elizabeth M. Whelan. LC 79-55437. 256p. 1980. 11.95 (ISBN 0-672-52628-X); pap. 8.95 (ISBN 0-672-52629-8). Bobbs.

Baby's Early Years: A Record Book. Lenora Moragne & Rudolph Moragne. (Illus.). 1975. spiral bdg. 4.45 o.p. (ISBN 0-917230-02-7). LenChamps Pubs.

Baby's First Christmas. Illus. by Eloise Wilkin. LC 80-80710. (Board Bks). (Illus.). 14p. (ps). 1980. 2.95 (ISBN 0-394-84575-7). Random.

Baby's House. Geolo McHugh. (Illus.). 24p. (gr. k-1). 1976. PLB 7.15 o.p. (ISBN 0-307-69051-2, Golden Pr). Western Pub.

Baby's Journal. Illus. by Marie Madeleine. (Illus.). 1978. 11.95 (ISBN 0-684-15979-1, ScribT). Scribner.

Baby's Opera. Illus. by Walter Crane. (Illus.). 56p. (gr. k up). 1981. 4.95 (ISBN 0-671-42551-X, Pub. by Windmill). S&S.

Babyselling: The Scandal of Black-Market Adoption. Nancy C. Baker. LC 77-93231. 1978. 8.95 (ISBN 0-8149-0798-9). Vanguard.

Babysitter's & Parents Babysitting Instruction Manual. Date not set. 1.95 (ISBN 0-686-64614-2). Johnson VA. Postponed.

Babysitter's Guide. Sherman. (Illus.). (gr. 7-12). 1980. pap. 1.25 (ISBN 0-590-31342-8, Schol Pap). Schol Bk Serv.

Baccarat Decisions. Huey Mahl. (System Check Ser.). 1978. pap. 2.95 (ISBN 0-89650-614-2). Gamblers.

Baccarat: Fair & Foul. Hoffman. (Gambler's Book Shelf Ser.). 1977. pap. 2.95 (ISBN 0-89650-578-2). Gamblers.

Bacchae of Euripides. G. S. Kirk. LC 78-31827. 1979. 21.95 (ISBN 0-521-22675-9); pap. 5.50x (ISBN 0-521-29613-7). Cambridge U Pr.

Bacchae of Euripides: A New Translation with a Critical Essay. Euripides. Tr. by Donald Sutherland. LC 68-11566. 1968. pap. 3.50x (ISBN 0-8032-5194-7, BB 377, Bison). U of Nebr Pr.

Bacchus. Myron Tassin. LC 74-20526. (Illus.). 96p. 1975. 15.00 (ISBN 0-88289-061-1). Pelican.

Bach. Eva M. Grew & Sydney Grew. (Master Musicians Ser.: No. M113). (Illus.). 1979. pap. 4.50 (ISBN 0-8226-0703-4). Littlefield.

Bach & the Dance of God. Wilfrid Mellers. 1981. 39.95 (ISBN 0-19-520232-5). Oxford U Pr.

Bach Cantatas. J. A. Westrup. LC 70-80507. (BBC Music Guides: No. 3). (Illus.). 60p. (Orig.). 1969. pap. 2.95 (ISBN 0-295-95017-X). U of Wash Pr.

Bach Family: Seven Generations of Creative Genius. Karl Geiringer. (Music Reprint 1980 Ser.). (Illus.). 1980. Repr. of 1954 ed. lib. bdg. 35.00 (ISBN 0-306-79596-5). Da Capo.

Bach Organ Book. Homer D. Blanchard. (The Little Organ Books Ser.: No. 3). (Illus.). Date not set. pap. price not set. Praestant.

Bach: The Conflict Between the Sacred & the Secular. Leo Schrade. LC 73-4331. 1974. Repr. of 1955 ed. lib. bdg. 16.50 (ISBN 0-306-70581-8). Da Capo.

Bachelor of Arts. R. K. Narayan. 1980. pap. 3.95 (ISBN 0-686-69041-9). U of Chicago Pr.

Bachelor of Salamanca, 2 vols. in 1. Alain R. Le Sage. Tr. by John Lockman. LC 80-2488. 1981. Repr. of 1767 ed. 98.50 (ISBN 0-404-19122-3). AMS Pr.

Bachelor Party. Hal Hickman. 1978. pap. 1.75 o.p. (ISBN 0-685-54625-X, 04767-8). Jove Pubns.

Bachelor Party. Hal Hickman. LC 77-4842. 1977. 7.95 o.p. (ISBN 0-397-01236-5). Lippincott.

Bachelor's Fare. Gail Clark. (Orig.). 1981. pap. price not set (ISBN 0-671-41276-0). PB.

Bachelor's Japan. Boye DeMente. LC 67-11428. (Orig.). 1967. pap. 5.95 (ISBN 0-8048-0052-9). C E Tuttle.

Bachelor's Pad Cookbook. Joey Williams. LC 80-69572. (Illus.). 183p. 1980. pap. 7.95 (ISBN 0-938280-00-7). Corinth Hse.

Bachman's Law: A Novel. Richard Thorman. 1981. 12.95 (ISBN 0-393-01443-6). Norton.

Bacillariophyta: Diatomeae. Friedrich Hustedt. (Suesswasserflora Mitteleuropas Ser.: Vol. 10). (Illus.). 466p. (Ger.). 1976. 71.75x (ISBN 3-87429-111-1). Lubrecht & Cramer.

Back. Henry Green. 256p. 1981. pap. 5.95 (ISBN 0-8112-0798-6, NDP517). New Directions.

Back Bay. William Martin. 1981. pap. 3.50 (ISBN 0-671-41504-2). PB.

Back from the Dead. Harry Hone. (Illus.). 1978. pap. text ed. write for info o.p. (ISBN 0-9601168-2-6); pap. text ed. write for info o.p. (ISBN 0-9601168-3-4). Am Biog Ctr.

Back from the Edge. Norman Shockley. LC 79-56163. (Illus.). 96p. (Orig.). 1979. pap. 3.75x (ISBN 0-8358-0392-9). Upper Room.

Back in Circulation. J. L. Block. 1969. 5.95 o.s.i. (ISBN 0-02-511580-4). Macmillan.

Back in the World: An Annotated Bibliography of American Imaginative Responses to the War in Viet Nam, 1960-1980. John Nemo. 208p. 1981. 29.95x (ISBN 0-933180-15-2). Ellis Pr.

Back in Town. Ed. by Susan Bent. LC 80-23860. (Illus.). 1980. pap. text ed. 7.95 (ISBN 0-918606-02-0). Heidelberg Graph.

Back on the Street: The Diversion of Juvenile Offenders. Robert M. Carter & Malcolm Klein. (Illus.). 400p. 1976. pap. 12.95 (ISBN 0-13-055319-0). P-H.

Back Pains. Howard Kurland. (Illus.). 1981. 12.95 (ISBN 0-671-41379-1). S&S.

Back-Relief from Pain. Alan Stoddard. LC 78-24488. (Positive Health Guides Ser.). (Illus.). 1979. 8.95 (ISBN 0-668-04677-5, 4677-5); pap. 4.95 (ISBN 0-668-04684-8, 4684-8). Arco.

Back Roads of Arizona. Earl Thollander & Edward Abbey. LC 78-51122. (Illus.). 1978. 17.95 o.p. (ISBN 0-87358-170-9); pap. 12.50 o.p. (ISBN 0-87358-177-6). Northland.

Back Roads of Washington. Earl Thollander. (Illus.). 208p. 1981. 15.95 (ISBN 0-517-54269-2); pap. 9.95 (ISBN 0-517-54270-6). Potter.

Back Side of God. Bill Austin. 1980. pap. 3.95 (ISBN 0-8423-0115-1). Tyndale.

Back to Back. Edith Campion. (Orig.). 1981. pap. 7.95 (ISBN 0-89407-041-X). Strawberry Hill. Postponed.

Back to Basics. Reader's Digest. (Illus.). 1981. 19.95 (ISBN 0-89577-086-5, Pub. by Reader's Digest). Norton.

Back to Basics, 3 bks. Rockowitz. Incl. Bk. 1. English (ISBN 0-8120-2086-3); Bk. 2. Grammar (ISBN 0-8120-2087-1); Bk. 3. Reading (ISBN 0-8120-2103-7). 1981. pap. 3.95 ea. Barron.

Back to Basics Mathematics, 3 vols. Edward Williams. Incl. Vol. 1. From Addition to Division. LC 78-21490 (ISBN 0-8120-0691-7); Vol. 2. Improving Skills with Fractions (ISBN 0-8120-0692-5); Vol. 3. Decimals, Percents & Other Matter (ISBN 0-8120-0693-3). LC 78-21490. (Math Ser.). 1979. pap. text ed. 4.75 ea. Barron.

Back to Basics Natural Beauty Handbook. Alexander York. 1978. pap. text ed. 1.95 (ISBN 0-515-04536-5). Jove Pubns.

Back to Basics with Basile. Frank M. Basile. Ed. by Marianne Glick. 305p. (Orig.). 1979. pap. 13.00 (ISBN 0-937008-01-X). Charisma Pubns.

Back to B.C. Johnny Hart. (B.C. Ser.). (Illus.). 1978. pap. 1.50 (ISBN 0-449-13626-4, GM). Fawcett.

Back to Methuselah. Bernard Shaw. (Plays Ser.). 1972. pap. 2.95 (ISBN 0-14-048011-0). Penguin.

Back to Methuselah. rev. ed. George B. Shaw. 1947. 4.95x (ISBN 0-19-500181-8). Oxford U Pr.

Back to School: A College Guide for Adults. William C. Haponski & Charles McCabe. Ed. by Linnea Leedham. (Illus.). 256p. cancelled (ISBN 0-88421-095-2); pap. cancelled (ISBN 0-88421-172-X). Butterick Pub.

Back to Texas. Owen G. Irons. (YA) 1978. 5.95 (ISBN 0-685-85776-X, Avalon). Bouregy.

Back to the Beanstalk: Enchantment & Reality for Couples. Judith R. Brown. LC 79-89476. 1980. 6.95 (ISBN 0-930626-03-6); pap. 3.95 (ISBN 0-930626-04-4). Psych & Consul Assocs.

Back to the City: The Making of a Movement? Shirley Laska & Daphne Spain. (Pergamon Policy Studies). 1980. 42.00 (ISBN 0-08-024641-9); pap. 9.95 (ISBN 0-08-024640-0). Pergamon.

Back to the Drawing Board: Planning for Livable Cities. Wolf Von Eckardt. LC 78-12257. (Illus.). 1978. 10.00 o.p. (ISBN 0-915220-45-8). New Republic.

Back to the Stone Age. Edgar R. Burroughs. 192p. 1976. pap. 1.95 (ISBN 0-441-04636-3). Ace Bks.

Back to the Top of the World. Hans Ruesch. 1974. pap. 1.50 o.p. (ISBN 0-345-23884-2). Ballantine.

Back to Work. Harold L. Ickes. LC 72-7426. (FDR & the Era of the New Deal Ser.). (Illus.). 276p. Repr. of 1935 ed. lib. bdg. 29.50 (ISBN 0-306-70527-3). Da Capo.

Backbench Diaries of Richard Crossman. Ed. by Janet Morgan. 1072p. 1981. text ed. 35.00 (ISBN 0-8419-0686-6). Holmes & Meier.

Backbench Opinion in the House of Commons, 1945-1955. Hugh B. Berrington. 1974. text ed. 32.00 (ISBN 0-08-016748-9). Pergamon.

Backbencher & Parliament. Ed. by Dick Leonard & Herman Valentine. LC 78-185906. 1972. 18.95 (ISBN 0-312-06475-6). St Martin.

Backcountry. Calvin Rutstrum. LC 80-22052. (Illus.). 200p. 1981. pap. 10.00 (ISBN 0-934802-07-6). Ind Camp Supply.

Backdoor Guide to Entering a Profession. Allen Michaels. 60p. (Orig.). 1981. pap. 10.00. Sunrise PA.

Backgammon. A. Obolensky & T. James. 1969. pap. 4.95 (ISBN 0-02-081030-X, Collier). Macmillan.

Backgammon. Don Stern. 1977. PLB 6.45 (ISBN 0-531-01298-0). Watts.

Backgammon for Blood. Bruce Becker. 1974. 8.95 (ISBN 0-87690-123-2). Dutton.

Backgammon Games & Strategies. Nicolaos Tzannes & Basil Tzannes. LC 74-9300. (Illus.). 256p. 1976. 9.95 o.p. (ISBN 0-498-01497-5). A S Barnes.

Backgammon, the Cruelest Game: The Art of Winning. Barclay Cooke & Jon Bradshaw. LC 74-8725. (Illus.). 1974. 15.00 (ISBN 0-394-48812-1); pap. 5.95 (ISBN 0-394-73243-X). Random.

Backgammon: The Modern Game. Terence Reese & Robert Brinig. LC 76-19770. (Illus.). 1976. 9.95 (ISBN 0-8069-4930-9); PLB 9.29 (ISBN 0-8069-4931-7). Sterling.

Background for Architecture. Seward H. Rathburn. 1926. 42.50x (ISBN 0-685-69854-8). Elliots Bks.

Background for Calculus. Ada Peluso. 1978. pap. text ed. 15.95 (ISBN 0-8403-2295-X, 40229501). Kendall-Hunt.

Background in Tennessee. facsimile ed. Evelyn Scott. LC 80-15703. (Tennesseana Editions). 324p. 1980. Repr. of 1937 ed. 11.50 (ISBN 0-87049-297-7). U of Tenn Pr.

Background of African Art. lim. ed. Melville J. Herskovits. LC 67-18433. (Cooke-Daniels Lecture Ser., Denver Art Museum). (Illus.). 1945. 10.50x (ISBN 0-8196-0201-9). Biblo.

Background of Immigrant Children. Ivor Morrish. (Unwin Education Books). 1971. text ed. 18.95x o.p. (ISBN 0-04-301034-2). Allen Unwin.

Background of the Epistles. William Fairweather. 1977. 14.50 (ISBN 0-686-12966-0). Klock & Klock.

Background of the Gospels. William Fairweather. 1977. 15.00 (ISBN 0-686-12965-2). Klock & Klock.

Background Patterns, Textures & Tints. Clarence Hornung. (Pictorial Archive Ser.). (Illus.). 112p. (Orig.). 1976. pap. 5.00 (ISBN 0-486-23260-3). Dover.

Background Readings in Building Library Collections. 2nd ed. Ed. by Phyllis Van Orden & Edith B. Phillips. LC 78-31263. 1979. 13.50 (ISBN 0-8108-1200-2). Scarecrow.

Background to Buckling. H. G. Allen & P. S. Bulson. (Illus.). 1980. text ed. 32.95x (ISBN 0-07-084100-4). McGraw.

Background to Crisis: Policy & Politics in Gierek's Poland. Roger E. Kanet & Maurice D. Simon. (Westview Replica Edition). 1980. lib. bdg. 27.50x (ISBN 0-89158-393-9). Westview.

Background to Migraine: Proceedings. Migraine Symposium, 5th, London, 1972. Ed. by J. N. Cumings. 1973. 23.00 (ISBN 0-387-91115-4). Springer Verlag.

Background to Racing. Kenneth Stewart. (Illus.). 12.25 (ISBN 0-85131-221-7, Dist. by Sporting Book Center). J A Allen.

Background to the English Renaissance: Introductory Lectures, (Dickens, Gombrich, Hale, Pattison, & Trapp) Ed. by J. B. Trapp. 1974. 13.00x o.p. (ISBN 0-85641-022-5, Pub. by Basil Blackwell England); pap. 5.00x o.p. (ISBN 0-85641-023-3). Biblio Dist.

Background to the Gospel of St. Mark. Rudolf Steiner. 1968. 9.75 o.p. (ISBN 0-85440-191-1). Anthroposophic.

Background to the New Testament. Harry Hollinson. 4.00x (ISBN 0-392-07650-0, SpS). Soccer.

Background with Chorus. Frank Swinnerton. 236p. 1980. Repr. of 1956 ed. lib. bdg. 30.00 (ISBN 0-8492-8124-5). R West.

Backgrounding the News: The Newspaper & the Social Sciences. Sidney Kobre. LC 70-137063. (Illus.). 271p. 1974. Repr. of 1939 ed. lib. bdg. 23.00x (ISBN 0-8371-5526-6, KOBN). Greenwood.

Backgrounds in Music Theory. Maurice Whitney. 1954. pap. 5.95 (ISBN 0-02-872870-X). Schirmer Bks.

Backgrounds of American Literary Thought. 3rd ed. Rod W. Horton & Herbert W. Edwards. 1974. pap. 12.95 (ISBN 0-13-056291-2). P-H.

Backgrounds to Augustan Poetry, Gallus, Elegy & Rome. D. O. Ross. LC 74-31782. 260p. 1975. 32.00 (ISBN 0-521-20704-5). Cambridge U Pr.

Backgrounds to Medieval English Literature. Robert W. Ackerman. (Orig.). 1966. 4.50x o.p. (ISBN 0-394-30627-9, RanC). Random.

Backhoe Gothic. Jean DeWeese. LC 80-1670. (Romantic Suspense Ser.). 192p. 1981. 9.95 (ISBN 0-385-12099-0). Doubleday.

Backpacker's Africa: Seventeen Walks of the Cape to Cairo Route. (Backbacker Guide Ser.). (Illus.). 98p. 1977. pap. 4.95 (ISBN 0-9505797-1-8). Bradt Ent.

Backpacker's Digest. 3rd ed. Cheri Elliott. (Illus.). 1981. pap. 8.95 (ISBN 0-910676-21-6, 6536). DBI.

Backpacker's Digest. 2nd. rev. ed. Ed. by C. R. Learn & Jack Lewis. (DBI Bks). 288p. (Orig.). 1976. pap. 7.95 o.p. (ISBN 0-695-80645-9). Follett.

Backpacking. Tony Gibbs. LC 74-11326. (Career Concise Guide Ser.). (Illus.). 72p. (gr. 7 up). 1975. PLB 4.90 o.p. (ISBN 0-531-02786-4). Watts.

Backpacking. Jamie Peters. LC 79-56581. (Illus.). 128p. 1980. 13.50 (ISBN 0-7153-7966-6). David & Charles.

Backpacking. Don Robinson. (Illus.). 112p. 1981. 12.95 (ISBN 0-8069-9180-1, Pub. by EP Publishing England); pap. 6.95 (ISBN 0-8069-9182-8). Sterling.

Backpacking. Shirley Zelaznak. Ed. by Howard Schroeder. LC 79-27800. (Back to Nature). (Illus.). (gr. 3-5). 1980. lib. bdg. 5.95 (ISBN 0-89686-069-8). Crestwood Hse.

Backpacking: a Comprehensive Guide. Showell Styles. 1977. 7.95 o.p. (ISBN 0-679-50722-1); pap. 4.95 o.p. (ISBN 0-679-50723-X). McKay.

Backpacking & Trekking in Chile & Argentina Plus the Falkland Islands. Hilary Bradt & John Pilkington. LC 80-68116. (Backpacker Guide Ser.). (Illus.). 144p. 1980. pap. 7.95 (ISBN 0-9505797-7-7). Bradt Ent.

Backpacking & Trekking in Peru & Bolivia. 3 rd rev. & enl ed. Hilary Bradt & George Bradt. LC 80-115. (Backpacker Guide Ser.). (Illus.). 1980. pap. 7.95 (ISBN 0-9505797-6-9). Bradt Ent.

Backpacking for Trout. Bill Cairns. (Illus.). 160p. 1980. 14.00 (ISBN 0-913276-32-4). Greene.

Backpacking Guide to the Southern Mountains. rev. ed. Samuel M. Blankenship. (Orig.). 1975. pap. 1.95 o.p. (ISBN 0-89176-472-0, 6472). Mockingbird Bks.

Backpacking in Mexico & Central America, Including the Darien Gap. Hilary Bradt & George Bradt. (Backpacker Guide Ser.). (Illus.). 1978. pap. 6.95 (ISBN 0-9505797-3-4). Bradt Ent.

Backpacking in Venezuela, Colombia & Equador. George Bradt & Hilary Bradt. (Backpacking Ser). (Illus.). 1979. pap. 6.95 (ISBN 0-9505797-6-9). Bradt Ent.

Backpacking Is for Me. Art Thomas. LC 80-12847. (Sports for Me Books Ser.). (Illus.). 48p. (gr. 2-5). 1980. PLB 5.95g (ISBN 0-8225-1095-2). Lerner Pubns.

Backpacking with Small Children. James H. Stout & Ann M. Stout. LC 74-23854. (Funk & W Bk.). (Illus.). 224p. 1975. 7.95 (ISBN 0-308-10182-0, TYC-T). T Y Crowell.

Backpacking Woman. Lynn Thomas. LC 79-6890. 288p. (Orig.). 1980. pap. 6.95 (ISBN 0-385-15303-1, Anch). Doubleday.

Backroads of Southern Europe. David Yeadon. LC 80-8222. (Illus.). 256p. 1981. 15.00 (ISBN 0-06-014779-2, CN 838, HarpT); pap. 6.95 (ISBN 0-06-090838-6). Har-Row.

Backroads of Texas. W. E. Syers. LC 79-50253. 1979. pap. 6.95 (ISBN 0-88415-053-4). Pacesetter Pr.

Backslider. Max Crawford. 1978. pap. 1.75 o.s.i. (ISBN 0-380-01921-3, 37663). Avon.

Backstage Broadway: Careers in the Theater. William E. Thomas. LC 80-10393. (Career Bks.). (Illus.). 160p. (gr. 7 up). 1980. PLB 7.79 (ISBN 0-671-33002-0). Messner.

Backstage: With the Ballet. Pierre Petitjean. Tr. by Richard Seaver & Jeannette Seaver. (Large Format Ser.). 1979. pap. 9.95 o.p. (ISBN 0-14-005185-6). Penguin.

Backward Beasts. Albert G. Miller. (ABC Serendipity Ser). (gr. 2-6). 1973. pap. 4.35 o.p. (ISBN 0-8372-0819-X). Bowmar-Noble.

Backward in Time. Leo P. Kelley. LC 79-51079. (Space Police Bks.). (Illus.). 64p. (gr. 4 up). 1980. PLB 7.95 (ISBN 0-516-02231-8). Childrens.

Backward Look: Germans Remember. Daniel Lang. (Illus.). 144p. (Orig.). 1981. pap. 4.95 (ISBN 0-07-036241-6). McGraw.

Backward Prayer. Robert J. Wieland. (Uplook Ser.). 32p. 1971. pap. 0.75 (ISBN 0-8163-0064-X, 02042-0). Pacific Pr Pub Assn.

Backward Toward Revolution: The Chinese Revolutionary Party. Edward Friedman. 1974. pap. 5.95x (ISBN 0-520-03279-9). U of Cal Pr.

Backwoods Utopias: The Sectarian Origins & the Owenite Phase of Communitarian Socialism in America: 1663-1829. 2nd ed. Arthur Bestor. LC 76-92852. 1971. 15.00x (ISBN 0-8122-7193-9); pap. 8.50x (ISBN 0-8122-1004-2, Pa Paperbks). U of Pa Pr.

Backyard Birddom. Mary J. Ericson. LC 66-19146. (Illus.). 1974. 2.95 (ISBN 0-87208-079-X); pap. 1.50 (ISBN 0-87208-010-2). Island Pr.

Backyard Birds of the East & Middle West. Vinson Brown. (Illus.). 1971. pap. 2.50 (ISBN 0-87666-412-5, M-540). TFH Pubns.

Backyard Farming. Lee Foster. (Urban Life Practical Solutions to the Challenges of the 80's Ser.). 96p. (Orig.). pap. 4.95 (ISBN 0-87701-224-5). Chronicle Bks.

Backyard Pony: Selecting & Owning a Horse. Frederick L. Devereux, Jr. LC 75-5544. 96p. (gr. 6 up). 1975. 5.88 o.p. (ISBN 0-531-02833-X). Watts.

Backyard Revolution: Understanding the New Citizen Movement. Harry C. Boyte. 264p. 1980. 14.95 (ISBN 0-87722-192-8). Temple U Pr.

Backyard Roughing It Easy. Dian Thomas. 1980. pap. 5.95 (ISBN 0-449-90018-5, Columbine). Fawcett.

Backyard Vacation: Outdoor Fun in Your Own Neighborhood. Carolyn Haas et al. (Illus.). 116p. (gr. 3-6). 1980. 9.95 (ISBN 0-316-33686-6); pap. 5.95 (ISBN 0-316-33685-8). Little.

Backyard Vegetable Gardening for the Beginner. Hugh Wiberg. LC 70-171918. 1971. 5.00 o.p. (ISBN 0-682-47329-4, Banner). Exposition.

Backyard Wild Birds of the Pacific Northwest & California. V. Brown. pap. 2.50 (ISBN 0-87666-411-7, M521). TFH Pubns.

Backyards & Tiny Gardens. Judith Berrisford. 1977. 8.95 o.p. (ISBN 0-571-11034-7, Pub. by Faber & Faber); pap. 5.95 (ISBN 0-571-10837-7). Merrimack Bk Serv.

Bacon. Anthony Quinton. (Past Masters Ser.). 1981. 7.95 (ISBN 0-8090-2790-9); pap. 2.95 (ISBN 0-8090-1414-9). Hill & Wang.

Bacteremia: Laboratory & Clinical Aspects. A. C. Sonnenwirth. (Amer. Lec. in Clinical Microbiology Ser.). (Illus.). 120p. 1973. 11.75 (ISBN 0-398-02829-X). C C Thomas.

Bacteria: How They Affect Other Living Things. Dorothy H. Patent. LC 79-21567. (Illus.). 128p. (gr. 9 up). 1980. 8.95 (ISBN 0-8234-0401-3). Holiday.

Bacterial Chemotaxis As a Model Behavioral System. Daniel E. Koshland, Jr. (Distinguished Lecture Ser. of the General Physiologists: Vol. 2). 210p. 1980. text ed. 19.50 (ISBN 0-89004-468-6). Raven.

Bacterial Genetics. 2nd ed. Werner Braun. LC 65-12318. (Illus.). 1965. 10.95 o.p. (ISBN 0-7216-1921-5). Saunders.

Bacterial Outer Membranes: Biogenesis & Functions. Masayori Inouye. LC 79-13999. 1980. 57.50 (ISBN 0-471-04676-0, Pub. by Wiley-Interscience). Wiley.

Bacteriology. William W. Ford. (Illus.). 1964. pap. 8.25 o.s.i. (ISBN 0-02-844800-6). Hafner.

Bacteriology: Principles & Practice. 6th rev ed. Arthur H. Bryan et al. (Orig.). 1962. pap. 3.95 (ISBN 0-06-460003-3, CO 3, COS). Har-Row.

Bacteriophage Biochemistry. Christopher K. Mathews. LC 70-143542. (ACS Monograph: No. 166). 1971. 31.75 (ISBN 0-8412-0288-5). Am Chemical.

Bacterium. Raymond Biel. 320p. 1980. pap. 9.95 (ISBN 0-934444-07-2). Aazunna.

Baculoviruses for Insect Pest Control: Safety Considerations. Ed. by Max Summers et al. LC 75-36871. 1975. 9.00 (ISBN 0-914826-07-7). Am Soc Microbio.

Bad Bear. Rudolf Neumann. Tr. by Jack Prelutsky. (Illus.). (gr. k-3). 1967. 3.95g o.s.i. (ISBN 0-02-768090-8). Macmillan.

Bad Bell of San Salvador. Patricia Beatty. (Illus.). 256p. (gr. 5-9). 1973. PLB 7.25 o.p. (ISBN 0-688-20081-8); PLB 7.92 (ISBN 0-688-30081-2). Morrow.

Bad Blood. Barbara Petty. 1980. pap. 2.25 o.s.i. (ISBN 0-440-10438-6). Dell.

Bad Blood: The Tuskegee Syphilis Experiment. James H. Jones. LC 80-69281. (Illus.). 1981. 12.95 (ISBN 0-02-916670-5). Free Pr.

Bad Child's Book of Beasts. Hilaire Belloc. (Illus.). 6.50 (ISBN 0-8446-1627-3). Peter Smith.

Bad Company: The Story of California's Legendary & Actual Stage-Robbers, Bandits, Highwaymen & Outlaws from the Fifties to the Eighties. Joseph H. Jackson. LC 77-7300. (Illus.). 1977. 17.50x (ISBN 0-8032-0930-4); pap. 5.95 (ISBN 0-8032-5866-6, BB 649, Bison). U of Nebr Pr.

Bad Guy. Nicholas Brady. 1977. pap. 1.50 (ISBN 0-505-51202-5). Tower Bks.

Bad Jack & the Lincoln Boys. Anne Colver. LC 76-17629. (Read to Myself Ser.). (Illus.). 48p. (gr. k-3). 1976. PLB 7.75 (ISBN 0-8172-0155-6). Raintree Pubs.

Bad Luck Stars of Sports. Gordon Carlson. Ed. by Thomas J. Mooney. (Pal Paperbacks Ser., Kit A). (Illus., Orig.). (gr. 7-12). 1976. pap. text ed. 1.25 (ISBN 0-8374-3499-8). Xerox Ed Pubns.

Bad Medicine & Good: Tales of the Kiowas. Wilbur S. Nye. (Illus.). 1969. Repr. of 1962 ed. 13.95 o.p. (ISBN 0-8061-0521-6). U of Okla Pr.

Bad Mouth Christopher. Christopher Sharp. (gr. 1-4). 1980. pap. 3.50 (ISBN 0-570-03482-5, 56-1703). Concordia.

Bad Mouth: Fugitive Papers on the Dark Side. Robert M. Adams. (Quantum Ser.). 1977. 11.50x (ISBN 0-520-03381-7); pap. 2.65 (ISBN 0-520-03530-5). U of Cal Pr.

Bad News, Vol.1. Glasgow University Media Group. 326p. 1981. price not set (ISBN 0-7100-0792-2). Routledge & Kegan.

Bad Nigger! The National Impact of Jack Johnson. Al-Tony Gilmore. LC 74-80590. 1975. 12.95 (ISBN 0-8046-9061-8, Natl U). Kennikat.

Bad Night at Dry Creek. Cameron Judd. 1981. pap. 1.75 (ISBN 0-8439-0894-7, Leisure Bks). Nordon Pubns.

Bad Spellers Dictionary. Joseph Kreivsky & Jordon L. Linfield. 1967. 2.50 (ISBN 0-394-49199-8). Random.

Bad Thad. Judy Malloy. LC 80-11349. (Illus.). 32p. (ps-k). 1980. PLB 7.95 (ISBN 0-525-26148-6). Dutton.

Bad Times of Irma Baumlein. Carol R. Brink. LC 76-182018. (Illus.). (gr. 4-6). 1972. 8.95 (ISBN 0-02-714220-5). Macmillan.

Bad Times of Irma Baumlein. Carol R. Brink. LC 76-182018. (Illus.). 144p. (gr. 4-6). 1974. pap. 2.95 (ISBN 0-02-041900-7, Collier). Macmillan.

Bad Willie. Judith Wolman. LC 78-74876. (Illus.). (gr. k-3). Date not set. 3.50 (ISBN 0-89799-175-3); pap. price not set (ISBN 0-89799-176-1). Dandelion Pr. Postponed.

Baddeck & Other Poems. Anne Hussey. LC 78-9337. (Wesleyan Poetry Program: Vol. 92). 1978. pap. 10.00x (ISBN 0-8195-2092-6, Pub. by Wesleyan U Pr); pap. 4.95 (ISBN 0-8195-1092-0). Columbia U Pr.

Badge of Madness. James Willwerth. 1978. pap. 1.75 o.p. (ISBN 0-449-23487-8, Crest). Fawcett.

Badgers. Ernest Neal. (Illus.). 1978. 19.95 (ISBN 0-7137-0816-6, Pub. by Blandford Pr England). Sterling.

Badlanders. Jack Slade. (Lassiter Ser.). 1978. pap. 1.50 (ISBN 0-505-50597-5). Tower Bks.

Badlands. Champ Clark. (American Wilderness Ser.). (Illus.). 1975. 12.95 (ISBN 0-8094-1208-X). Time-Life.

Badlands. Champ Clark. LC 74-18063. (American Wilderness). (Illus.). (gr. 6 up). 1974. PLB 11.97 (ISBN 0-8094-1209-8, Pub. by Time-Life). Silver.

Badminton. E. Brown. (Illus., Orig.). 1975. pap. 5.50 (ISBN 0-571-10659-5, Pub. by Faber & Faber). Merrimack Bk Serv.

Badminton. Barbara J. Burris & Arne L. Olson. 96p. 1974. pap. text ed. 2.95x o.p. (ISBN 0-205-04388-7). Allyn.

Badminton. 2nd ed. Tony Grice. (Illus.). 71p. 1980. pap. text ed. 3.95x (ISBN 0-89641-053-6). American Pr.

Badminton. Roger Mills. (Sports Library). (Illus.). 1979. 12.95 (ISBN 0-8069-9104-6); pap. 6.95 (ISBN 0-8069-9106-2). Sterling.

Badminton. Barry C. Pelton. (Prentice-Hall Sports Ser.). (Illus.). 1971. pap. text ed. 4.25x (ISBN 0-13-055327-1). P-H.

Badminton at Great Barrington; or, Gustave Mahler & the Chattanooga Choo-Choo. Michael Benedikt. LC 80-5258. (Pitt Poetry Ser.). xii, 81p. 1980. 9.95 (ISBN 0-8229-3423-X); pap. 4.50 (ISBN 0-8229-5322-6). U of Pittsburgh Pr.

Badminton Complete. rev. ed. Pat Davis. LC 75-5170. (Illus.). 192p. 1976. 7.95 o.p. (ISBN 0-498-01696-X). A S Barnes.

Baedeker's Great Britain, Vol. 3. Karl Baedeker. (Illus.). 1971. 7.95 o.s.i. (ISBN 0-02-504970-4). Macmillan.

Baedeker's United States. Ed. by Karl Baedeker. LC 76-77703. (American Scene Ser.). Orig. Title: United States with an Excursion into Mexico. (Illus.). 520p. 1971. Repr. of 1893 ed. lib. bdg. 17.50 (ISBN 0-306-71341-1). Da Capo.

Bag Full of Nothing. Jay Williams. LC 73-22186. (Illus.). 40p. (ps-3). 1974. 5.95 o.s.i. (ISBN 0-8193-0774-2, Four Winds); PLB 5.41 o.s.i. (ISBN 0-8193-0725-4). Schol Bk Serv.

Bag Lady. Jean-Claude Van Itallie. 1980. pap. 1.25 (ISBN 0-686-68847-3). Dramatists Play.

Bag O' Tales. Effie Power. LC 68-26598. 1968. Repr. of 1934 ed. 19.00 (ISBN 0-8103-3486-0). Gale.

Bag of Marbles. Joseph Joffo. LC 74-11132. 304p. 1974. 6.95 o.p. (ISBN 0-395-19392-3). HM.

Bag of Noodles. Wally Armbruster. (Illus.). (YA) 1973. pap. 2.50 (ISBN 0-570-03158-3, 12-2543). Concordia.

Bag of Tricks: Fun Things to Make & Do with the Groceries. James Razzi. LC 75-136996. (Illus.). (gr. k-3). 1971. 5.95 o.s.i. (ISBN 0-8193-0449-2, Four Winds); PLB 5.41 o.s.i. (ISBN 0-8193-0450-6). Schol Bk Serv.

Bag Without Holes: How to Prepare for Your Family, Your Finances, Your Future. Fred Eggerichs & Bernard Palmer. LC 74-23435. 96p. 1975. pap. 2.25 o.p. (ISBN 0-87123-028-3). Bethany Fell.

Bagatelle. Maurice Denuziere. LC 78-655. 1978. 9.95 o.p. (ISBN 0-688-03316-4). Morrow.

Bagdad Ate It. Phyllis Green. (gr. k-3). 1980. 3.95 (ISBN 0-531-03429-1); PLB 6.45 (ISBN 0-531-02855-0). Watts.

Bagels! Bagels! & More Bagels! A Saga of Good Eating with Recipes, Legend & Lore. (Illus.). 1979. 6.95 o.s.i. (ISBN 0-528-81099-5). Rand.

Baghdad in Bygone Days: From the Journals and Correspondence of Claudius Rich, Traveler, Artist, Linguist, Antiquary, and British Resident of Baghdad, 1808-1821. Constance Alexander. LC 80-1939. 1981. Repr. of 1928 ed. 41.50 (ISBN 0-404-18951-2). AMS Pr.

Bagpipe: The History of a Musical Instrument. Francis Collinson. (Illus.). 278p. 1975. 25.00 (ISBN 0-7100-7913-3). Routledge & Kegan.

Bagthorpes Unlimited. Helen Cresswell. 1980. pap. 1.75 (ISBN 0-380-49296-2, 49296, Camelot). Avon.

Bagthorpes vs the World. Helen Cresswell. (Illus.). (gr. 1 up). 1980. pap. 1.95 (ISBN 0-380-51102-9, 51102, Camelot). Avon.

Bagthorpes vs the World: Being the Fourth Part of the Bagthorpe Saga. Helen Cresswell. LC 79-13260. (gr. 5 up). 1979. 7.95 (ISBN 0-02-725420-8, 72542). Macmillan.

Baha'i Education: A Compilation. Extracts from the Writings of Baha'u'llah, 'Abdu'l-Baha, & Shoghi Effendi. Research Department of the Universal House of Justice. 1977. pap. 3.00 (ISBN 0-87743-117-5, 7-15-59). Baha'i.

Baha'i Faith: A Summary Reprinted from the Encyclopedia Britannica. Firuz Kazemzadeh. 1977. large type 0.60 (ISBN 0-87743-121-3, 7-40-79); 1976 ed. 0.50 (ISBN 0-87743-152-3, 7-40-80). Baha'i.

Baha'i: Follower of the Light. rev ed. Ray Meyer. (Illus.). 1979. pap. 3.00 (ISBN 0-909991-01-4, 7-31-96). Baha'i.

Baha'i Holy Places at the World Centre. The Universal House of Justice Staff. LC 78-15959. 1968. 2.00 (ISBN 0-87743-066-7, 7-15-02). Baha'i.

Baha'i Prayers. Baha'u'llah, the Bab & Abdu'l-Baha. LC 54-10901. 4.00 (ISBN 0-87743-012-8, 7-15-05). Baha'i.

Baha'i Prayers & Tablets for the Young. Baha'u'llah & Abdu'L-Baha. LC 77-2228. (Illus.). 1978. 4.00 (ISBN 0-87743-115-9, 7-15-54). Baha'i.

Baha'i World: An International Record 1954-1963, Vol. XIII. The Universal House of Justice. LC 27-5882. (Illus.). 1970. 17.50x o.s.i. (ISBN 0-87743-042-X, 7-33-13). Baha'i.

Baha'i World: An International Record 1963-1968, Vol. XIV. The Universal House of Justice. LC 27-5882. (Illus.). 1974. 16.00 (ISBN 0-87743-099-3, 7-33-14). Baha'i.

Baha'i World: An International Record 1968-1973, Vol. XV. The Universal House of Justice. (Illus.). 1976. 17.50x o.s.i. (ISBN 0-85398-059-4, 7-33-15). Baha'i.

Baha'i World: An International Record 1973-1976, Vol. XVI. Universal House of Justice. (Illus.). 1979. 20.00 (ISBN 0-85398-075-6, 7-33-16). Baha'i.

Baha'i World Faith. 2nd ed. Baha'u'llah & Abdu'l-Baha. LC 56-8259. 1956. 10.00 (ISBN 0-87743-013-6, 7-15-20). Baha'i.

Bahamas. F. C. Evans & N. Young. LC 76-16133. (Illus.). 1977. 4.75x (ISBN 0-521-21292-8). Cambridge U Pr.

Bahamas. George Hunte. 1974. 24.00 (ISBN 0-7134-2992-5, Pub. by Batsford England). David & Charles.

Bahamas Handbook & Businessman's Annual 1980-81. 18th ed. Ed. by S. P. Dupuch. LC 61-45647. (Illus.). 1980. pap. 15.00x (ISBN 0-8002-2694-1). Intl Pubns Serv.

Bahamas Handbook & Businessman's Annual, 1980 to 1981. 18th ed. Ed. by S. P. Dupuch. (Illus.). 478p. (Orig.). 1980. pap. 15.00x (ISBN 0-8002-2694-1). Intl Pubns Serv.

Baha'u'llah & the New Era: An Introduction to the Baha'i Faith. 5th rev. ed. J. E. Esslemont. 1980. pap. 1.50 (ISBN 0-87743-160-4, 7-31-05). Baha'i.

Baha'u'llah: The King of Glory. H. M. Balyuzi. (Illus.). 1980. 22.50 (ISBN 0-85398-090-X, 7-32-47, Pub. by G Ronald England). Baha'i.

Bahnwarter Theil und Fasching. Gerhart Hauptmann. Ed. by S. D. Stirk. (Blackwell's German Texts Ser.). 1975. pap. 9.95x (ISBN 0-631-01540-X, Pub. by Basil Blackwell). Biblio Dist.

Bahrain: Political Development in a Modernizing Society. Emile A. Nakhleh. LC 75-37274. (Illus.). 208p. 1976. 18.95 (ISBN 0-669-00454-5). Lexington Bks.

Bail Reform in America. Wayne Thomas. 1977. 15.95 (ISBN 0-520-03131-8). U of Cal Pr.

Bailes a Colores, 3 units. Irma Vela. (Illus.). 1972-74. Unit I. basic dance kit o.p. 10.50 (ISBN 0-913632-04-X); Unit II. pap. 20.50 teacher's kit (ISBN 0-913632-10-4); Unit III. social studies system o.p. 83.50 (ISBN 0-913632-11-2). Am Univ Artforms.

Bailey & Love's Short Practice of Surgery. 17th ed. Ed. by A. J. Harding Rains & H. David Ritchie. Orig. Title: Short Practice of Surgery. (Illus.). 1977. text ed. 64.00 (ISBN 0-87488-900-6). Med Exam.

Bailey's Industrial Oil & Fat Products, Vol. II. 4th ed. Daniel Swern. 675p. 1981. 50.00 (ISBN 0-471-83958-2, Pub. by Wiley-Interscience). Wiley.

Bailey's Industrial Oil & Fat Products, Vol. 1. 4th ed. Daniel Swern. LC 78-31275. 1979. 55.00 (ISBN 0-471-83957-4, Pub. by Wiley-Interscience). Wiley.

Bailout: America's Billion Dollar Gamble on the "New" Chrysler Corporation. Reginald Stuart. LC 80-70279. (Illus.). 210p. (Orig.). 1981. pap. write for info. (ISBN 0-89708-050-5). And Bks.

Bailout: The Story of Parachuting & Skydiving. Don Dwiggins. LC 69-10892. (America in the Making Ser). (Illus.). (gr. 5 up). 1969. 5.95g o.s.i. (ISBN 0-02-732890-2, CCPr). Macmillan.

Baily's Hunting Directory 78-79. (Illus.). 1978. 36.00 (ISBN 0-85131-272-1, Dist. by Sporting Book Center). J A Allen.

Bait. Arati Nagarwalla. (Writers Workshop Bluebird Ser.). 33p. 1975. 5.00 (ISBN 0-88253-506-4); pap. text ed. 4.00 (ISBN 0-88253-505-6). Ind-US Inc.

Baja California. William Johnson. LC 72-85157. (American Wilderness Ser). (Illus.). (gr. 6 up). 1972. lib. bdg. 11.97 (ISBN 0-8094-1161-X, Pub. by Time-Life). Silver.

Baja California. William W. Johnson. (American Wilderness Ser.). (Illus.). 1972. 12.95 (ISBN 0-8094-1160-1). Time-Life.

Baja California. Eliot Porter. 1969. pap. 3.95 o.p. (ISBN 0-345-21640-7). Ballantine.

Baja Chart. Arnold D. Senterfitt. 1980. plastic coated 9.50 (Pub. by Senterfitt). Aviation.

Bajazet. Jean Racine. Ed. by Cuthbert Girdlestone. (French Texts Ser.). 1964. pap. text ed. 4.50x o.p. (ISBN 0-631-00560-9, Pub. by Basil Blackwell). Biblio Dist.

Bajun & the Sea. Ross-Larson. LC 77-190183. (Illus.). (gr. 4-8). 1972. PLB 6.95 (ISBN 0-87191-208-2). Creative Ed.

Bake Bread. Hannah Solomon. LC 76-18807. (Illus.). (gr. 5-12). 1976. 7.95 (ISBN 0-397-31670-4); pap. 3.95 o.p. (ISBN 0-397-31671-2). Lippincott.

Bake Breads from Frozen Dough. 2nd ed. Sylvia Ogren. LC 76-25064. (Illus.). 1979. pap. 6.95 (ISBN 0-87518-137-6). Dillon.

Bake Your Own Bread. Stanley Dworkin & Florence Dworkin. (Illus.). 224p. 1973. pap. 1.95 (ISBN 0-451-09424-7, J9424, Sig). NAL.

Baked Potatoes in My Pockets. Dorothy Bodwell. 1977. 6.95 o.p. (ISBN 0-685-81417-3). Vantage.

Baker Street Irregulars in the Case of the Cinema Swindle. Terrance Dicks. 128p. (gr. 4 up). 1981. 8.95 (ISBN 0-525-66728-8). Elsevier-Nelson.

Baker Street Irregulars in the Case of the Ghost Grabbers. Terrance Dicks. 128p. (gr. 4 up). 1981. 8.95 (ISBN 0-525-66729-6). Elsevier-Nelson.

Baker's Bible Atlas. rev. ed. Charles F. Pfeiffer. (Illus.). 1961. Repr. 14.95 (ISBN 0-8010-6930-0). Baker Bk.

Baker's Clinical Neurology, 3 vols. Loose Leaf Reference Services. Ed. by Abe B. Baker et al. loose leaf bdg. 250.00 (ISBN 0-06-148006-1, Harper Medical); revision pages 30.00 (ISBN 0-685-57884-4). Har-Row.

Baker's Dozen. rev. ed. Georgiana C. Newman & Mildred A. Dawson. (Cornerstone Ser.). (gr. 2-3). 1978. pap. text ed. 4.52 (ISBN 0-201-41024-9, Sch Div); tchr's ed. 5.56 (ISBN 0-201-41025-7). A-W.

Baker's Handbook of Bible Lists. Compiled by Andrew E. Hill. 288p. (Orig.). 1981. pap. 6.95 (ISBN 0-8010-4242-9). Baker Bk.

Baker's Hawk. Jack M. Bickham. LC 73-79644. 240p. 1974. 6.95 o.p. (ISBN 0-385-01852-5). Doubleday.

Baker's Manual for Quantity Baking & Pastry Making. rev., 3rd ed. Joseph Amendola. (Illus.). 220p. 1972. 13.25x (ISBN 0-8104-9458-2). Hayden.

Bakery Factory. Aylette Jenness. LC 77-8094. (Illus.). (gr. 3-7). 1978. 5.95 (ISBN 0-690-03805-4, TYC-J); PLB 7.89 (ISBN 0-690-01338-8). T Y Crowell.

Bakery Lane Soup Bowl. Marge Mitchell & Joan Sedgwick. 1977. pap. 6.95 (ISBN 0-394-73375-4). Random.

Bakery Restaurant Cookbook. Louis Szathmary. LC 80-36675. 1980. 12.95 (ISBN 0-8436-2195-8). CBI Pub.

Bakery Technology & Engineering. 2nd ed. Samuel A. Matz. (Illus.). 1972. text ed. 41.50 (ISBN 0-87055-109-4). AVI.

Baking Breads. Rosemary Wadey. LC 77-85021. (Penny Pinchers Ser.). (Illus.). 1978. 2.95 (ISBN 0-7153-7535-0). David & Charles.

Baking in a Box, Cooking on a Can. Gail K. Haines. LC 80-26678. (Illus.). 128p. (gr. 4-6). 1981. PLB 6.67 (ISBN 0-688-00376-1); pap. 4.95 (ISBN 0-688-00373-7). Morrow.

Bakke, DeFunis & Minority Admissions: The Quest for Equal Opportunity. Allan P. Sindler. 1978. pap. text ed. 10.95 (ISBN 0-582-28053-2). Longman.

Baku Commune, 1917-1918: Class & Nationality in the Russian Revolution. Roger G. Suny. LC 76-155966. (Studies of the Russian Institute Ser.). (Illus.). 1972. 22.00x (ISBN 0-691-05193-3). Princeton U Pr.

Balaam's Apocalyptic Prophecies: A Study in Reading Scripture. Calvin Seerveld. pap. 3.95 (ISBN 0-88906-110-6). Wedge Pub.

Balance in Management. Clark Caskey. LC 68-57174. 1968. 9.95 (ISBN 0-685-79073-8). Masterco Pr.

Balance of Births & Deaths, 2 vols. Robert R. Kuczynski. Incl. Vol. I. Western & Northern Europe. Repr. of 1928 ed (ISBN 0-697-00159-8); Vol. 2. Eastern & Southern Europe. Repr. of 1931 ed (ISBN 0-697-00160-1). (Brookings Institution Reprint Ser). lib. bdg. 22.50x ea. Irvington.

Balance of Economic Power: North-South Confrontation on Raw Materials. Enver M. Koury. LC 76-23819. 125p. 1977. pap. 6.00 (ISBN 0-934484-09-0). Inst Mid East & North Africa.

Balance of Military Power: The Arab-Israeli Conflict. Enver M. Koury. LC 76-57912. 111p. 1977. pap. 5.00 (ISBN 0-934484-10-4). Inst Mid East & North Africa.

Balance of Payments Adjustment Process in Developing Countries. Sidney Dell & Roger Lawrence. LC 79-22818. (Pergamon Policy Studies Ser.). 120p. 1980. 18.25 (ISBN 0-08-025577-9). Pergamon.

Balance of Payments Adjustment Process. Working Party No. 3, Economic Policy Committee. 32p. 1966. 0.80 o.p. (ISBN 0-686-14785-5). OECD.

Balance of Payments: Theory & Economic Policy. Robert M. Stern. LC 72-78222. 488p. 1973. 27.95x (ISBN 0-202-06059-4). Aldine Pub.

Balance of Payments Theory & the United Kingdom Experience. A. P. Thirlwall. (Illus.). 323p. 1980. text ed. 35.00x (ISBN 0-8419-5077-6). Holmes & Meier.

Balance of Power or Hegemony: The Interwar Monetary System. Ed. by Benjamin M. Rowland. LC 75-27423. 266p. 1976. 15.00x (ISBN 0-8147-7368-0). NYU Pr.

Balance Wheel. Taylor Caldwell. 512p. 1980. pap. 2.75 (ISBN 0-515-05412-7). Jove Pubns.

Balanced Involvement: Safety, Production Motivation. John P. Gausch. (Monographs: No.3). cancelled (ISBN 0-686-21671-7); cancelled (ISBN 0-686-21672-5). ASSE.

Balanced National Growth. Ed. by Kevin Allen. LC 78-13820. 352p. 1979. 23.95 (ISBN 0-669-02668-9). Lexington Bks.

Balanced Science of Renewable Resources with Particular Reference to Fisheries. Henry A. Regier. LC 78-4979. (Washington Sea Grant Ser.). 110p. 1978. pap. 10.50 (ISBN 0-295-95602-X). U of Wash Pr.

Balanchine's Complete Stories of the Great Ballets. George Balanchine & Francis Mason. LC 76-55684. 1977. 19.95 (ISBN 0-385-11381-1). Doubleday.

Balancing Act: A Congruence of Symbols. Seymour Hakim. 55p. (Orig.). 1981. pap. 6.00x (ISBN 0-913054-12-7). Poet Gal Pr.

Balancing Acts. Lynne S. Schwartz. LC 80-8366. 224p. 1981. 9.95 (ISBN 0-06-013702-9, HarpT). Har-Row.

Balancing Jobs & Family Life: Do Flexible Work Schedules Help? Halcyone H. Bohen & Anamaria Viveros-Long. (Illus.). 328p. 1981. 19.50 (ISBN 0-87722-199-5). Temple U Pr.

Balboa. (Explorers & Discoverers - Concepts & Inquiry Ser: The Educational Research Council Social Science Program). (gr. 1). 1974. pap. text ed. 2.80 (ISBN 0-205-03868-9, 8038686); tchrs'. guide 12.00 (ISBN 0-205-03866-2, 803866X). Allyn.

Balcony of Europe. Aidan Higgins. LC 72-10772. 1973. 8.95 o.p. (ISBN 0-440-00654-6, Sey Lawr). Delacorte.

Balcony of Evil. Georgia M. Shewmake. 192p. (YA) 1976. 5.95 (ISBN 0-685-62023-9, Avalon). Bouregy.

Balder & the Mistletoe: A Story for the Winter Holidays. Edna Barth. LC 78-4523. (Illus.). (gr. 2-5). 1979. 7.95 (ISBN 0-395-28956-4, Clarion). HM.

Baldness Be My Friend. Richard Boston. 1978. 14.95 (ISBN 0-241-89732-7, Pub. by Hamish Hamilton England). David & Charles.

Baldwin. Keith Middlemas & John Barnes. LC 70-87902. 1970. 14.95 o.s.i. (ISBN 0-02-507370-2). Macmillan.

Baldwin Locomotive Works (BALDWIN) General Catalogue 1915. (Illus.). 1972. 9.00 (ISBN 0-913556-02-5); pap. 6.00 (ISBN 0-913556-03-3). Spec Pr NJ.

Baldwin Thwarts the Opposition: The British General Election of 1935. Tom Stannage. 320p. 1980. 50.00x (ISBN 0-7099-0341-3, Pub. by Croom Helm Ltd England). Biblio Dist.

Balearic Islands: Majorca, Minorca, Ibiza & Formentera. Hazel Thurson. 1977. 24.00 (ISBN 0-7134-0882-0). David & Charles.

Balfour Conspiracy. Ian St. James. LC 80-69378. 1981. 10.95 (ISBN 0-689-11140-1). Atheneum.

Bali: Behind the Mask. Ana Daniel. LC 79-3481. (Illus.). 224p. 1981. 30.00 (ISBN 0-394-50264-7); pap. 15.00 (ISBN 0-394-73844-6). Knopf.

Balkan Cultural Studies. Stavro Skendi. (East European Monograph: No. 72). 256p. 1980. 20.00x (ISBN 0-914710-66-4). East Eur Quarterly.

Balkan Revolutionary Tradition. Dmitrije Djordjevic & Stephen Fischer-Galati. LC 80-24039. 272p. 1981. 17.50x (ISBN 0-231-05098-4). Columbia U Pr.

Balkan Society in the Age of Greek Independence. Ed. by Richard Clogg. (Studies in Russian & East European History). 1981. 29.00x (ISBN 0-389-20024-7). B&N.

Balkans in Our Time. rev. ed. Robert L. Wolff. 1978. pap. text ed. 8.95x (ISBN 0-393-09010-8). Norton.

Balkans: 1815-1914. L. S. Stavrianos. (Berkshire Ser.). 144p. 1963. pap. 5.50 o.p. (ISBN 0-685-72303-8, Pub. by HR&W). Krieger.

Ball & Roller Bearings. P. S. Houghton. (Illus.). 1976. 104.40x (ISBN 0-85334-598-8, Pub. by Applied Science). Burgess-Intl Ideas.

Ball, Bat & Bishop: The Origin of Ball Games. Robert W. Henderson. LC 73-10389. (Illus.). 221p. 1974. Repr. of 1947 ed. 18.00 (ISBN 0-8103-3877-7). Gale.

Ball Book. Margaret Hillert. (Just Beginning-to-Read Ser.). (Illus.). 32p. (gr. 1-6). 1981. PLB 4.39 (ISBN 0-695-41553-0); pap. 1.50 (ISBN 0-695-31553-6). Follett.

Ball Book. Lynn Rothman. (Golden Bk. for Early Childhood). (Illus.). 24p. (gr. k-1). 1979. PLB 5.38 (ISBN 0-307-68887-9, Golden Pr). Western Pub.

Ball Four, Plus Ball Five. rev. ed. Jim Bouton. LC 80-6165. 432p. 1981. 12.95 (ISBN 0-8128-2771-6). Stein & Day.

Ball of Clay. John Hawkinson. LC 72-13350. (Illus.). 48p. (gr. 3-7). 1974. 6.50g (ISBN 0-8075-0557-9). A Whitman.

Ball That Wouldn't Bounce. Mel Cebulash. (Illus.). (gr. k-3). 1972. pap. 1.25 (ISBN 0-590-09297-9, Schol Pap); pap. 3.50 bk. & record (ISBN 0-686-68502-4). Schol Bk Serv.

Ballad & the Folk. David Buchan. 1972. 23.00 (ISBN 0-7100-7322-4). Routledge & Kegan.

Ballad as Song. Bertrand H. Bronson. LC 74-84045. (Illus.). 1969. 22.50x (ISBN 0-520-01399-9). U of Cal Pr.

Ballad of Lucy Lum. Don Mitchell & Joe Wayman. (gr. k-8). 1977. 5.95 (ISBN 0-916456-10-2, GA56). Good Apple.

Ballad of Mich-o-Tta-Wa. Raymond R. Gallagher. 64p. 1979. 2.95 (ISBN 0-8059-2595-3). Dorrance.

Ballad of Reading Gaol. Oscar Wilde. (Illus.). 1978. pap. 3.50 o.p. (ISBN 0-904526-26-7, Journeyman Press). Carrier Pigeon.

Ballad of T. Rantula. Kit Reed. 224p. 1981. pap. 1.95 (ISBN 0-449-70003-8, Juniper). Fawcett.

Ballad of the Long-Tailed Rat. Charlotte Pomerantz. LC 74-13611. (Illus.). 32p. (ps-2). 1975. 6.95g (ISBN 0-02-774890-1, 77489). Macmillan.

Ballade of the Scottysshe Kynge. John Skelton. LC 67-23927. 1969. Repr. of 1882 ed. 15.00 (ISBN 0-8103-3461-5). Gale.

Ballads & Sea Songs of Newfoundland. Ed. by Elisabeth Greenleaf. LC 68-20767. (Illus.). xix, 395p. 1968. Repr. of 1933 ed. 15.00 (ISBN 0-8103-5013-0). Gale.

Ballads & Songs Collected by the Missouri Folk-Lore Society. 2nd ed. Ed. by Henry M. Belden. LC 55-7519. 1955. 15.00x (ISBN 0-8262-0142-3). U of Mo Pr.

Ballads, Blues, & the Big Beat. Donald Myrus. (gr. 7 up). 1966. 5.95g o.s.i. (ISBN 0-02-768060-6). Macmillan.

Ballads of Books. Ed. by Brander Matthews. LC 70-141032. 1971. Repr. of 1887 ed. 15.00 (ISBN 0-8103-3384-8). Gale.

Ballads of the Kentucky Highlands. Henry H. Fuson. 219p. 1980. Repr. of 1931 ed. text ed. 25.00 (ISBN 0-8492-4706-3). R West.

Ballantine Diagramless Puzzle Book. Ed. by Newspaper Enterprise Assn. 128p. (Orig.). 1975. pap. 1.95 o.p. (ISBN 0-345-24542-3). Ballantine.

Ballantine Find-a-Quote Puzzle Book. Newspaper Enterprise Ass'n. 128p. (Orig.). 1975. pap. 1.95 o.p. (ISBN 0-345-24543-1). Ballantine.

Ballantine Teachers' Guide to Science Fiction. L. David Allen. (Orig.). 1975. pap. 2.50 (ISBN 0-345-27989-1). Ballantine.

Ballantine's Law Dictionary with Pronunciations. 3rd ed. Ed. by William S. Anderson. LC 68-30931. 1969. 17.00x o.p. (ISBN 0-686-14540-2). Lawyers Co-Op.

Ballantyne's Textbook of the Fundus of the Eye. 3rd ed. Ed. by Isaac C. Michaelson. (Illus.). 912p. 1981. text ed. 1.62 (ISBN 0-443-01782-4). Churchill.

Ballet As Body Language: The Anatomy of Ballet for Student & Dance Lover. Joan McConnell & Teena McConnell. 1977. 13.95 (ISBN 0-06-012957-3, HarpT); pap. 7.95 o.p. (ISBN 0-06-012964-6, TD-289, HarpT). Har-Row.

Ballet Basics. Sandra N. Hammond. LC 73-91991. 1974. 11.95 (ISBN 0-87484-259-X); pap. text ed. 6.95 (ISBN 0-87484-258-1). Mayfield Pub.

Ballet for Drina. Jean Estoril. LC 58-9223. (gr. 5-10). 5.95 (ISBN 0-8149-0299-5). Vanguard.

Ballet Guide. Walter Terry. LC 75-20240. (Illus.). 400p. 1976. 15.00 (ISBN 0-396-07024-8). Dodd.

Ballet of the Second Empire. Ivor Guest. LC 73-15010. (Illus.). 332p. 1974. 20.00x (ISBN 0-8195-4067-6, Pub. by Wesleyan U Pr). Columbia U Pr.

Ballet Shoes. Noel Streatfeild. (gr. 4-6). 1979. pap. 1.75 (ISBN 0-440-41508-X, YB). Dell.

Ballet Technique. Tamara Karsavina. LC 68-28084. (Illus.). 1956. 10.45 (ISBN 0-87830-011-2). Theatre Arts.

Ballistic Science for the Law Enforcement Officer. Charles G. Wilber. (Illus.). 324p. 1977. 30.75 (ISBN 0-398-03579-2). C C Thomas.

Balloon Affair. Marion M. Layne. 202p. 1981. 8.95 (ISBN 0-396-07951-2). Dodd.

Balloon Book: How to Launch, Navigate, & Land a Balloon. Paul Fillingham. (Illus.). 1979. pap. 8.95 o.p. (ISBN 0-679-50928-3). McKay.

Ballooning: The Complete Guide to Riding the Winds. Dick Wirth & Jerry Young. LC 80-5281. (Illus.). 168p. 1980. 20.00 (ISBN 0-394-51338-X). Random.

Balloons & Airships. Lennart Ege. LC 73-18513. (Color Ser.). (Illus.). 230p. 1974. 9.95 (ISBN 0-02-535050-1). Macmillan.

Balloons: From Paperbags to Skyhooks. Peter Burchard. (Illus.). (gr. 3-5). 1960. 5.95g o.s.i. (ISBN 0-02-715600-1). Macmillan.

Ballou-Wright Automobile Supplies Catalog, 1906. Pref. by Ron Brentano. LC 74-635336. (Illus.). 90p. 1971. pap. 2.95 (ISBN 0-87595-028-0). Oreg Hist Soc.

Ballpoint Bananas & Other Jokes for Kids. Charles Keller. (Illus.). (gr. 3-7). 1973. pap. 1.95 (ISBN 0-13-055517-7). P-H.

Ballroom Dancing. 8th ed. Alex Moore. (Illus.). 324p. (gr. 9 up). 1980. Repr. of 1974 ed. text ed. 17.95x (ISBN 0-273-00381-X, LTB). Soccer.

Ballroom Dancing. Mayphine V. Zant. (Illus.). 1978. 12.95 o.p. (ISBN 0-679-50796-5); pap. 6.95 o.p. (ISBN 0-679-50797-3). McKay.

Ballroom of the Skies. John D. MacDonald. 1979. pap. 1.95 (ISBN 0-449-14143-8, GM). Fawcett.

Balls! Richard Rohmer. 352p. 1980. 12.95 (ISBN 0-8253-0003-7). Beaufort Bks NY.

Balm in Gilead & Other Plays. Lanford Wilson. Incl. Balm in Gilead; Home Free; Ludlow Fair. 116p. (Orig.). 1965. pap. 4.50 (ISBN 0-8090-1208-1, New Mermaid). Hill & Wang.

Balsa Wood & Its Properties. Dreisbach. 3.00 o.p. (ISBN 0-686-00166-4). Columbia Graphs.

Baltasar Gracian. Virginia R. Foster. (World Authors Ser.: Spain: No. 337). 176p. 1975. lib. bdg. 12.50 (ISBN 0-8057-2398-6). Twayne.

Balthazar. Lawrence Durrell. 1961. pap. 2.50 o.p. (ISBN 0-525-47081-6). Dutton.

Baltic States: Estonia, Latvia, Lithuania the Years of Independence, 1917-1940. George Von Rauch. 1974. 20.00x (ISBN 0-520-02600-4). U of Cal Pr.

Baltimore Colts. Julian May. (NFL Today Ser.). (gr. 4-8). 1980. lib. bdg. 6.45 (ISBN 0-87191-728-9); pap. 2.95 (ISBN 0-89812-231-7). Creative Ed.

Baltimore Colts. Julian May. LC 74-988. (Superbowl Champions Ser). 48p. 1974. PLB 6.45 (ISBN 0-87191-331-3); pap. 2.95 (ISBN 0-89812-084-5). Creative Ed.

Baltimore Renaissance: Poetry. Ed. by Stephen D. Ciesielski & Nancy Edison. (New Poets Ser.: Vol. 8). 50p. 1980. pap. 4.00 (ISBN 0-932616-06-2). New Poets.

Baltimore: The Building of an American City. Sherry H. Olson. LC 79-21950. 289p. 1980. text ed. 22.95x (ISBN 0-8018-2224-6). Johns Hopkins.

Baltramiejus Vilentas' Lithuanian Translation of the Gospels & Epistles (1579, 2 vols. Ed. by Gordon B. Ford, Jr. LC 66-1610. 1966. 100.00 ea. o.p. Vol. 1 (ISBN 0-910198-18-7). Vol. 2 (ISBN 0-910198-19-5). Baltica Pr.

Balzac Criticism in France, 1850-1900: The Making of a Reputation. David Bellos. 1976. 37.50x (ISBN 0-19-815530-1). Oxford U Pr.

Balzac's Comedie Humaine. Herbert J. Hunt. 1959. pap. text ed. 13.00x (ISBN 0-485-12008-9, Athlone Pr). Humanities.

Bambi. Mel Crawford. Tr. by Rene Sanchez. (Illus.). 24p. (Span.). (ps-3). 1977. PLB 5.92 o.p. (ISBN 0-307-68830-5, Golden Pr). Western Pub.

Bambi Book. Walt Disney. (ps-1). 1966. PLB 5.38 (ISBN 0-307-68930-1, Golden Pr). Western Pub.

Bambi, Friends of the Forest. Walt Disney Studio. (Illus.). (gr. k-3). 1976. PLB 5.00 (ISBN 0-307-60132-3, Golden Pr). Western Pub.

Bamboo Dancers. N. V. Gonzales. 276p. 1961. 8.95 (ISBN 0-8040-0018-2). Swallow.

Bamboo Grove: An Introduction to Sijo. Richard Rutt. LC 70-84785. (Center for Japanese & Korean Studies, UC Berkeley). 1971. 14.50x (ISBN 0-520-01611-4). U of Cal Pr.

Bamboo Horses: Wooden Dragons - .22 Hornet. Steven D. Lakey. LC 80-69812. 60p. (Orig.). 1980. text ed. 4.95 (ISBN 0-936748-03-6, 0003); pap. text ed. 3.25 (ISBN 0-936748-04-4). Fade In.

Bamboo Research in Asia. 228p. 1981. pap. 15.00 (ISBN 0-88936-267-X, I*O*R*C 159, IDRC). Unipub.

Bamboula at Kourion: The Necropolis & the Finds, Excavated by J. F. Daniel. J. L. Benson. LC 72-133204. (Haney Foundation Ser). (Illus.). 192p. 1973. 60.00x (ISBN 0-8122-7635-3). U of Pa Pr.

Ban on Aerosols? 1977. pap. 15.00 o.p. (ISBN 0-89192-196-6). Interbk Inc.

Banach Algebra Techniques in the Theory of Toeplitz Operators. R. G. Douglas. LC 73-1021. (CBMS Regional Conference Ser. in Mathematics: No. 15). 1980. Repr. of 1973 ed. 11.20 (ISBN 0-8218-1665-9, CBMS-15). Am Math.

Banach Spaces of Analytic Functions & Absolutely Summing Operators. Aleksander Pelczynski. LC 77-9884. (Conference Board of the Mathematical Sciences Ser.: No. 30). 1980. Repr. of 1977 ed. 7.00 (ISBN 0-8218-1680-2, CBMS30). Am Math.

Banalata Sen. Jibanananda Das. Tr. by P. Lal from Bengali. 20p. 1975. 8.00 (ISBN 0-88253-512-9); pap. text ed. 4.00 (ISBN 0-88253-511-0). Ind-US Inc.

Banana: A Novel. Bonnie Bluh. LC 75-28030. 288p. 1976. 8.95 o.s.i. (ISBN 0-02-511900-1, 51190). Macmillan.

Banana Bottom. Claude McKay. LC 73-14676. 317p. 1974. pap. 5.95 (ISBN 0-15-610650-7, HB273, Harv). HarBraceJ.

Bananas. Woody Allen. 1978. 7.95 o.p. (ISBN 0-394-50049-0). Random.

Bananas B- Guide to School Survival. Pat Arthur & Joe Arthur. 96p. (Orig.). (gr. 7 up). 1980. pap. 1.25 (ISBN 0-590-30028-8, Schol Pap). Schol Bk Serv.

Bananas Don't Grow on Trees: A Guide to Popular Misconceptions. Joseph Rosenbloom. LC 78-57783. (Illus.). (gr. 6 up). 1978. 6.95 (ISBN 0-8069-3100-0); PLB 7.49 (ISBN 0-8069-3101-9). Sterling.

Bananas in Pyjamas. Carey Blyton. 28p. 1973. 7.50 (ISBN 0-571-10138-0). Transatlantic.

Bananas in Pyjamas: A Book of Nonsense. Carey Blyton. (Orig.). (ps-5). 1976. pap. 3.95 (ISBN 0-571-10671-4, Pub. by Faber & Faber). Merrimack Bk Serv.

Bananas Yearbook 1979. Teen. pap. 2.25 o.p. (ISBN 0-590-12078-6, Schol Pap). Schol Bk Serv.

Bananas Yearbook 1980. (gr. 7-12). 1980. pap. 2.25 (ISBN 0-590-31471-8, Schol Pap). Schol Bk Serv.

Banaras, 1974 Poems. Vimala Rao. 1976. 8.00 (ISBN 0-89253-827-9); flexible cloth 4.80 (ISBN 0-89253-828-7). Ind-US Inc.

Banbury Bog. Phoebe A. Taylor. 1978. Repr. of 1938 ed. lib. bdg. 9.00x (ISBN 0-89966-247-1). Buccaneer Bks.

Banbury Report Four: Cancer Incidence in Defined Populations. Ed. by John Cairns et al. LC 80-7676. (Banbury Report Ser.: Vol. 4). (Illus.). 458p. 1980. 45.00x (ISBN 0-87969-203-0). Cold Spring Harbor.

Banbury Report 7-the Carcinogen & Mutagen Formation in the Gastrointestinal Tract. Ed. by W. Robert Bruce et al. (Banbury Report Ser.). (Illus.). 1981. 60.00x (ISBN 0-87969-206-5). Cold Spring Harbor.

Banbury Tale. Maggie MacKeever. 1977. pap. 1.50 o.p. (ISBN 0-449-23174-7, Crest). Fawcett.

Bancroft Library, University of California, Berkeley: Catalog of Printed Books, Third Supplement. University of California. (Library Catalogs-Bib. Guides). 1979. lib. bdg. 795.00 (ISBN 0-8161-1163-4). G K Hall.

Band Director's Brain Bank. R. Jack Mercer. pap. 9.50 (ISBN 0-686-15897-0). Instrumentalist Co.

Band Holding Company Performance Controversy. Duane B Graddy. LC 78-65842. 1979. pap. text ed. 24.50 (ISBN 0-8191-0678-X). U Pr of Amer.

Band Music Guide. 17.50. Instrumental Co.

Band Theory of Metals. S. L. Altmann. 1970. text ed. 32.00 (ISBN 0-08-015602-9); pap. text ed. 12.75 (ISBN 0-08-015601-0). Pergamon.

Banda. Philip Short. 358p. 1974. 20.00 (ISBN 0-7100-7631-2). Routledge & Kegan.

Bandages of Soft Illusion. Phillip J. Wingate. LC 79-65281. (Illus.). 98p. 1979. 11.75 (ISBN 0-935968-06-7); pap. 8.75 o.s.i. (ISBN 0-935968-10-5). Holly Pr.

Bandit in Black. Paul E. Lehman. 1979. pap. 1.25 (ISBN 0-505-51368-4). Tower Bks.

Bandits. E. J. Hobsbawm. (Illus.). 1981. pap. 3.95 (ISBN 0-394-74850-6). Pantheon.

Bandits. Eric J. Hobsbawn. (Pageant of History Ser). (Illus.). 1969. 4.50 o.s.i. (ISBN 0-440-00420-9). Delacorte.

Bandolero. John Benteen. (Fargo). 1977. pap. 1.25 (ISBN 0-505-51144-4). Tower Bks.

Bands of America. Harry W. Schwartz. LC 74-23385. (Illus.). 320p. 1975. Repr. of 1957 ed. lib. bdg. 29.00 (ISBN 0-306-70672-5). Da Capo.

Bands of the World. Al G. Wright & Stanley Newcomb. 14.00 (ISBN 0-686-15894-6). Instrumentalist Co.

Banff Purchase: An Exhibition of Photography in Canada. The Banff Centre. 112p. 1980. 19.95 (ISBN 0-471-99829-X). Wiley.

Bangalee. Steve Cosgrove. (Serendipity Bks). (Illus.). (gr. k-4). 1978. PLB 6.95 (ISBN 0-87191-666-5). Creative Ed.

Bangkok. J. Blofeld. (Great Cities Ser.). (Illus.). 1979. lib. bdg. 11.97 (ISBN 0-8094-3101-7); kivar bdg. 11.49 (ISBN 0-8094-3102-5). Silver.

Bangladesh Documents, 2 vols. Ed. by Sheelendra Singh. 1972. Set. pap. 33.00 set (ISBN 0-8002-0445-X). Intl Pubns Serv.

Bangladesh: Equitable Growth? Joseph F. Stepanek. LC 78-16797. 1979. text ed. 22.00 (ISBN 0-08-023335-X). Pergamon.

Bangladesh: Principles & Perspectives. A. K. Pavithran. LC 70-183008. viii, 109p. 1971. pap. text ed. 6.25x (ISBN 0-912004-02-9). W W Gaunt.

Bangladesh: The Test Case for Development. Just Faaland & John R. Parkinson. LC 76-851. 1976. 26.50x (ISBN 0-89158-546-X). Westview.

Banished Angel. Luisa Pasamanik. Tr. by Carter Aldridge. LC 75-516551. 1978. 12.00 o.p. (ISBN 0-686-18968-X). Green River.

Banji's Magic Wheel. Letta Schatz. (Picture Bk). (Illus.). 32p. (gr. k-3). 1974. 5.95 o.p. (ISBN 0-695-80441-3); PLB 5.97 o.p. (ISBN 0-695-40441-5). Follett.

Bank Control of Large Corporations in the United States. David M. Kotz. 1978. 14.50x (ISBN 0-520-03321-3); pap. 3.95 (ISBN 0-520-03937-8). U of Cal Pr.

Bank Credits & Acceptances. 5th ed. Henry Harfield. (Illus.). 363p. 1974. 24.95 (ISBN 0-8260-3835-2). Ronald Pr.

Bank Director's Handbook. Edwin B. Cox et al. (Illus.). 200p. 1981. 19.95 (ISBN 0-86569-056-1). Auburn Hse.

Bank Frauds: Their Detection & Prevention. 2nd ed. 276p. 1965. 19.95 (ISBN 0-471-06574-9). Wiley.

Bank Holding Companies & the Public Interest. Michael A. Jessee & Steven A. Seelig. LC 76-8744. 1977. 21.50- (ISBN 0-669-00689-0). Lexington Bks.

Bank Loans Secured by Field-Warehouse Receipts. Albert G. Sweetser. LC 57-7980. 112p. (Orig.). 1957. pap. 5.00 (ISBN 0-9605500-1-1). A G Sweetser.

Bank of England, 2 Vols. John H. Clapham. 1945. Set. 71.50 set (ISBN 0-521-04662-9). Cambridge U Pr.

Bank of England: 1891-1944. R. S. Sayers. LC 75-46116. 1976. 165.00 set (ISBN 0-521-21475-0); Vol. 1. (ISBN 0-521-21067-4); Vol. 2. (ISBN 0-521-21068-2); Vol. 3 (appendixes) (ISBN 0-521-21066-6). Cambridge U Pr.

Bank Reconciliation Projects. Robert J. McCullough & Kenneth Everard. 1959. pap. text ed. 1.48 o.p. (ISBN 0-8224-0165-7); key 0.72 o.p. (ISBN 0-8224-0233-5). Pitman Learning.

Bank Reconciliation Projects. 2nd ed. Robert J. McCullough & Kenneth Everard. 1979. pap. 2.40 (ISBN 0-8224-0634-9); key 1.00 (ISBN 0-8224-0635-7). Pitman Learning.

Bankers. Martin Mayer. 608p. 1976. pap. text ed. 3.50 (ISBN 0-345-29569-2). Ballantine.

Banker's Almanac & Year Book 1978-79. 134th ed. LC 20-372. 1979. 90.00x o.p. (ISBN 0-611-00636-7). Intl Pubns Serv.

Banker's Almanac & Year Book 1979-80. 135th ed. LC 20-372. 2441p. 1980. 100.00x (ISBN 0-686-65039-5). Intl Pubns Serv.

Bankers & Diplomats in China Nineteen Seventeen to Nineteen Twenty-Five: The Anglo-American Relationship. Roberta A. Dayer. 324p. 1980. 25.00x (ISBN 0-7146-3118-3, F Cass Co). Biblio Dist.

Bankers' Diplomacy: Monetary Stabilization in the Twenties. Richard H. Meyer. LC 79-111120. (Columbia Studies in Economics Ser.: No. 4). 1970. 20.00x (ISBN 0-231-03325-7). Columbia U Pr.

Bankers in West Africa: The Story of the Bank of British West Africa Limited. Richard Fry. (Illus.). 1976. text ed. 14.50x (ISBN 0-09-126910-5). Humanities.

Bankers of the Rich & the Bankers of the Poor: The Role of Export Credit in Development Finance. Nathaniel McKitterick & Jenkins B. Middleton. LC 72-76253. (Monographs: No. 6). 70p. 1972. 2.00 (ISBN 0-686-28689-8). Overseas Dev Council.

Banking & Currency in Hong Kong: A Study of Postwar Financial Development. Y. C. Jao. 350p. 1975. 37.50x (ISBN 0-8419-5002-4). Holmes & Meier.

Banking & Finance. E. Mary Cooper. (Australian Life Ser.: No. 6). 1980. pap. 6.95x (ISBN 0-686-26706-0, Pub. by Lothian). Intl Schol Bk Serv.

Banking & Finance Careers. Jo Ann Whatley. (Career Concise Guides Ser.). (Illus.). (gr. 7 up). 1978. PLB 6.45 s&l o.s.i. (ISBN 0-531-01346-4). Watts.

Banking & Sales: A Consultative Guide to Cross Selling Financial Products & Services. Linda Richardson. 165p. 1981. 19.95 (ISBN 0-471-09010-7, Pub. by Wiley-Interscience). Wiley.

Banking & the Global System. William Curran. 184p. 1980. 19.95 (ISBN 0-85941-030-7). Herman Pub.

Banking Automation, 1970-71, 2 Vols. Ed. by Geoffrey W. Dummer et al. 1971. 300.00 set (ISBN 0-08-016120-0). Pergamon.

Banking Crisis & Recovery Under the Roosevelt Administration. J. F. O'Connor. LC 73-171696. (FDR & the Era of the New Deal Ser.). 168p. 1971. Repr. of 1938 ed. lib. bdg. 20.00 (ISBN 0-306-70366-1). Da Capo.

Banking Crisis of 1933. Susan E. Kennedy. LC 72-91666. 280p. 1973. 16.00x (ISBN 0-8131-1285-0). U Pr of Ky.

Banking in Canada. Jurgen Ebel. Ed. by L. N. Blythe. 80p. (Orig.). 1978. pap. text ed. 10.95x (ISBN 0-7121-0259-0, Pub. by Macdonald & Evans England). Intl Ideas.

Banking in India. Khaja S. Hasan. Ed. by L. N. Blythe. 112p. (Orig.). 1979. pap. text ed. 10.95x (ISBN 0-7121-0260-4, Pub. by Macdonald & Evans England). Intl Ideas.

Banking in Western Europe. Ed. by Richard S. Sayers. 1962. 22.500 (ISBN 0-19-828143-9). Oxford U Pr.

Banking Language. Jim Richey. (Spiritual Vocabulary Ser.). (Illus.). 48p. (gr. 7-12). 1980. pap. text ed. 2.45 (ISBN 0-915510-37-5). Janus Bks.

Banking Law Anthology, Vol.1. Philip A. Garon. 1981. 59.95. Intl Lib.

Banking Laws of Kuwait. Tr. by N. H. Karam. 275p. 1979. 22.00x (ISBN 0-86010-139-8, Pub.by Graham & Trotman England). State Mutual Bk.

Banking on the Biosphere? Robert E. Stein & Brian Johnson. 1979. 22.95 (ISBN 0-669-02734-0). Lexington Bks.

Banking on the Poor: The World Bank's Antipoverty Work in Developing Countries. Robert Ayres. 384p. 1981. write for info. Overseas Dev Council.

Banknote Collector's Guide & Companion. Ervin J. Felix. Ed. by Marcus F. DeLenc. (Illus.). 144p. (Orig.). 1981. pap. 1.50 (ISBN 0-937458-03-1). Harris & Co.

Bankruptcy. 1981 ed. 200p. 1981. 6.00 (ISBN 0-87526-194-9). Gould.

Bankruptcy & Insolvency Accounting. 2nd ed. Grant W. Newton. 500p. 1981. 29.95 (ISBN 0-471-07992-8). Ronald Pr.

Bankruptcy & Insolvency Accounting: Practice & Procedure. G. W. Newton. 1975. 29.95 (ISBN 0-8260-6715-8). Ronald Pr.

Bankruptcy: Do It Yourself. Janice Kosel. (Illus.). 192p. 1980. write for info (ISBN 0-201-08305-1). A-W.

Bankruptcy: Do It Yourself in California. Janice Kosel. 1980. 12.00 (ISBN 0-917316-29-0). Nolo Pr.

Bankruptcy in United States History. Charles Warren. LC 75-172175. (American Constitutional & Legal History Ser). 196p. 1972. Repr. of 1935 ed. lib. bdg. 19.50 (ISBN 0-306-70214-2). Da Capo.

Bankruptcy Practice & Procedure 1978. (Commercial Law & Practice Course Handbook Ser. 1977-78: Vol. 194). 1978. pap. 20.00 o.p. (ISBN 0-685-63703-4, A4-3023). PLI.

Bankruptcy: Problem, Process, Reform. David T. Stanley et al. LC 79-161592. 1971. 11.95 (ISBN 0-8157-8098-2). Brookings.

Bankruptcy Reform Act of 1978. (Commercial Law & Practice Course Handbook Series 1978-79: Vol. 198). 1978. pap. 20.00 o.p. (ISBN 0-685-90318-4, A4-3029). PLI.

Bankruptcy Risk in Financial Depository Intermediaries: Assessing Regulatory Effects. Michael F. Koehn. LC 79-2411. (Arthur D. Little Bk.). (Illus.). 176p. 1979. 20.95- (ISBN 0-669-03169-0). Lexington Bks.

Banks & Bankruptcy: Strategies for Dealing with Troubled Situations, Vol. 275. (Corporate Law & Practice Course Handbook Ser. 1977-78). 1978. pap. 20.00 o.p. (ISBN 0-685-47598-0, B4-5566). PLI.

Banks & Their Competitors. Institute of Bankers, UK. 108p. 1980. 12.00x (ISBN 0-85297-057-9, Pub. by Woodhead-Faulkner England). State Mutual Bk.

Banks Letters: A Calendar of the Manuscript Correspondence of Sir Joseph Banks Preserved in the British Museum, the British Museum (Natural History) & Other Collections in Great Britain. Ed. by Warren R. Dawson. 965p. 1958. 78.00x (ISBN 0-565-00085-3, Pub. by Brit Mus Nat Hist England). Sabbot-Natural Hist Bks.

Bankson Language Screening Test. N. Bankson. 1977. 18.95 (ISBN 0-8391-1126-6). Univ Park.

Bannatyne Manuscript: National Library of Scotland Advocates' Ms 1.1.6. facsim. ed. 826p. 1981. Repr. of 1568 ed. 340.00x (ISBN 0-85967-540-8, Pub. by Scolar Pr England). Biblio Dist.

Banned: Controversial Literature & Political Control in British India, 1907-1947. N. Gerald Barrier. LC 73-92241. 1974. 17.50x o.p. (ISBN 0-8262-0159-8). U of Mo Pr.

Banner Bold & Beautiful. Ann F. Barron. 1978. pap. 1.95 o.p. (ISBN 0-449-13877-1, GM). Fawcett.

Banner Book. Betty Wolfe. LC 74-80378. (Illus.). 96p. 1974. 6.95 (ISBN 0-8192-1173-7). Morehouse.

Banner in the Sky. James R. Ullman. (gr. 7-9). 1980. pap. 1.75 (ISBN 0-671-56081-6). Archway.

Banner in the Sky. James R. Vilman. (YA) (gr. 7-9). 1980. pap. 1.75 (ISBN 0-671-56081-6). PB.

Banner Red & Gold. Annelise Kamada. 1980. pap. 2.75 (ISBN 0-446-95082-3). Warner Bks.

Bannerman. Jay Flynn. 1976. pap. 1.25 o.p. (ISBN 0-685-72574-X, LB389, Leisure Bks). Nordon Pubns.

Bannerman Border Incident. Jay Flynn. 1976. pap. 1.25 o.p. (ISBN 0-685-72573-1, LB401, Leisure Bks). Nordon Pubns.

Bannermans Catalogue of Military Goods 1927. facsimile ed. LC 80-68006. (Illus.). 384p. 1981. pap. 12.95 (ISBN 0-910676-20-8). DBI.

Banners. Joanne Marxhausen. (A Nice Place to Live Ser.). 1978. pap. 2.25 (ISBN 0-570-07750-8, 12-2709). Concordia.

Banners at Shenandoah. Bruce Catton. 254p. 1976. Repr. of 1955 ed. lib. bdg. 13.95x (ISBN 0-89244-019-8). Queens Hse.

Banners of Silk. Rosalind Laker. LC 80-1453. 480p. 1981. 13.95 (ISBN 0-385-15902-1). Doubleday.

Banners of the Sa'yen. B. R. Stateham. (Science Fiction Ser.). 1981. pap. 2.25 (ISBN 0-87997-636-5, UE1636). DAW Bks.

Bannerstone House: A Frank Lloyd Wright House, Springfield, Illinois. 5th ed. Tom R. Cavanaugh & Payne E. Thomas. 48p. 1977. pap. 3.75 (ISBN 0-398-00299-1). C C Thomas.

Banquet Book. Arno B. Schmidt. 256p. 1980. 19.95 (ISBN 0-8436-2147-8). CBI Pub.

Banquet: 5 Short Stories. Rosellen Brown et al. LC 78-56621. (Illus.). 1978. 12.00x (ISBN 0-915778-24-6); pap. 4.00 (ISBN 0-915778-25-4); deluxe ed. 85.00x deluxe ed (ISBN 0-915778-23-8). Penmaen Pr.

Bantam New College German & English Dictionary. Ed. by John C. Traupman. 768p. (Orig.). (gr. 7-12). 1981. pap. 2.50 (ISBN 0-553-14155-4). Bantam.

Bantam Step by Step Book of Needlecraft. 512p. 1980. pap. 14.95 (ISBN 0-553-01221-5). Bantam.

Bantam Story. rev. ed. (Orig.). 1980. pap. write for info. (ISBN 0-553-13256-3). Bantam.

Bantu Civilization of Southern Africa. E. Jefferson Murphy. LC 73-17194. (Illus.). 256p. (gr. 7 up). 1974. 12.95 (ISBN 0-690-00399-4, TYC-J). T Y Crowell.

Bantu Education to 1968. Ed. by Muriel Horrell. LC 76-484665. 176p. 1968. 5.00x (ISBN 0-8002-0521-9). Intl Pubns Serv.

Bantu Myths & Other Tales. Jan Knappert. (Nisaba Ser.: No. VII). 1977. text ed. 20.50x (ISBN 90-04-05423-5). Humanities.

Bantu-Speaking Peoples of South Africa. Ed. by W. D. Hammond-Tooke. (Illus.). 1974. 35.00x (ISBN 0-7100-7748-3). Routledge & Kegan.

Bantu-Speaking Peoples of Southern Africa. Ed. by W. D. Hammond-Tooke. (Illus.). 298p. 1980. pap. 35.00 (ISBN 0-7100-0708-6). Routledge & Kegan.

Bapteme Dans le Saint-Sprit. Tr. by Willard Cantelon. (French Bks.). (Fr.). 1979. 0.95 (ISBN 0-8297-0929-0). Life Pubs Intl.

Baptism. Ed. by Richard E. Todd. (Grace Bible Ser.). (Illus.). 16p. (Orig.). (gr. 1-6). 1980. pap. 0.50 (ISBN 0-9605324-0-4). R E Todd.

Baptism. Johannes Warns. Date not set. 11.50 (ISBN 0-86524-063-9). Klock & Klock.

Baptism in the Holy Spirit. Derek Prince. 1966. pap. 1.25 (ISBN 0-934920-07-9, B-19). Derek Prince.

Baptism in the Spirit According to Scripture: The Report of a Reformed Church Theologian. J. A. Schep. pap. 2.50 o.p. (ISBN 0-912106-78-6). Logos.

Baptism: It's Mode & Subjects. Alexander Carson. Ed. by John Young. LC 80-8067. 1981. 12.95 (ISBN 0-8254-2324-4). Kregel.

Baptism, Penance, Eucharist, & Confirmation. 7.95 (ISBN 0-685-61631-2, PL306). Pflaum Pr.

Baptism with the Holy Spirit. R. A. Torrey. 96p. 1972. pap. 1.95 (ISBN 0-87123-029-1); pap. 0.95 (ISBN 0-87123-030-5). Bethany Fell.

Baptismal Names. 4th ed. Joseph L. Weidenhan. LC 68-26618. 1968. Repr. of 1931 ed. 24.00 (ISBN 0-8103-3136-5). Gale.

Baptist Bibliography: A Compilation of Leading Baptist Authors Back Through the Years, 25 vols. Set. 250.00 o.p. (ISBN 0-686-12409-X). Church History.

Baptist Convictions. Winthrop S. Hudson. pap. 0.85 ea. (ISBN 0-8170-0295-2). pap. 8.50 doz. Judson.

Baptistery of Pisa. Christine Smith. LC 77-94715. (Outstanding Dissertations in the Fine Arts Ser.). 1978. lib. bdg. 44.00 (ISBN 0-8240-3249-7). Garland Pub.

Baptists & the Bible. Russ Bush & Tom Nettles. 1980. 10.95 (ISBN 0-8024-0466-9). Moody.

Baptists in Upper & Lower Canada before 1820. Stuart Ivison & Fred Rosser. LC 57-2798. (Illus.). 1956. 15.00x (ISBN 0-8020-5046-8). U of Toronto Pr.

Baptized in the Spirit & Spiritual Gifts. new ed. Steve B. Clark. 1967. pap. 1.50 (ISBN 0-89283-033-6). Servant.

Bar Bizarre. Dakin Williams. 270p. 1980. write for info. (ISBN 0-86629-009-5). Sunrise MO.

Bar Games, Bets & Challenges. Alan Erickson. (Orig.). 1981. pap. 1.95 (ISBN 0-446-90648-4). Warner Bks.

Bar Joint Denture. Eugene J. Dolder & Gustav T. Durrer. (Illus.). 150p. 1978. 42.00 (ISBN 0-931386-02-0). Quint Pub Co.

Bar Mitzvah Illustrated. 7th ed. Ed. by Abraham I. Katsh. LC 76-23713. (Illus.). 1976. 10.95 (ISBN 0-88400-048-6). Shengold.

Barabudur: History & Significance of a Buddhist Monument. Ed. by Hiram W. Woodward. Luis O. Gomez. 1981. 20.00 (ISBN 0-89581-151-0). Lancaster-Miller.

Baralong Affair. Alan Coles. 1981. write for info. Sheridan. Postponed.

Barba the Slaver. 1979. pap. 1.75 o.p. (ISBN 0-345-25670-0). Ballantine.

Barbados. George Hunte. (Batsford Countries Ser). Date not set. 9.95 (ISBN 0-8038-0755-4). Hastings.

Barbados: A Smiling Island. Bruce G. Lynn. LC 78-113993. 1975. 6.50 (ISBN 0-910294-16-X). Brown Bk.

Barbados & America. David L. Kent. LC 80-80184. 1980. 25.00 (ISBN 0-9604886-1-8). C M Kent.

Barbara Kraus Calories & Carbohydrates. Barbara Kraus. 1979. pap. 4.95 o.p. (ISBN 0-452-25207-5, Z5207, Plume). NAL.

Barbara Kraus Guide to Calories: 1981 Edition. Barbara Kraus. (Orig.). 1981. pap. 1.75 (ISBN 0-451-09580-4, E9580, Sig). NAL.

Barbara Kraus Guide to Carbohydrates: 1981 Edition. Barbara Kraus. (Orig.). 1981. pap. 1.75 (ISBN 0-451-09581-2, E9581, Sig). NAL.

Barbara Kraus Guide to Fibers in Foods. Barbara Kraus. 1980. 7.95 (ISBN 0-453-00368-0, H368). NAL.

Barbara Kraus 1980 Calorie Guide to Brand Names & Basic Foods. Barbara Kraus. (Orig.). 1980. pap. 1.50 (ISBN 0-451-09032-2, W9032, Sig). NAL.

Barbara Kraus 1980 Carbohydrate Guide to Brand Names & Basic Foods. Barbara Kraus. (Orig.). 1980. pap. 1.50 (ISBN 0-451-09033-0, W9033, Sig). NAL.

Barbara Pearlman's Dance Exercises. Barbara Pearlman. LC 76-52009. 1978. 6.95 (ISBN 0-385-12665-4, Dolp). Doubleday.

Barbara Walker's Learn to Knit Afghan Book. Barbara Walker. LC 73-10906. (Encore Edition). (Illus.). 1976. pap. 1.95 (ISBN 0-684-16929-0, SL666, ScribT). Scribner.

Barbara Walters: Today's Woman. Jason Bonderoff. 1975. pap. 1.50 o.p. (ISBN 0-8439-0306-6, Leisure Bks). Nordon Pubns.

Barbara's Pony, Buttercup. Jane B. Moncure. LC 76-52921. (Illus.). (ps-3). 1977. 5.50 (ISBN 0-913778-74-5). Childs World.

Barbarian Europe. Gerald Simons. LC 68-54209. (Great Ages of Man). (Illus.). (gr. 6 up). 1968. PLB 11.97 (ISBN 0-8094-0380-3, Pub. by Time-Life). Silver.

Barbarian Within, & Other Fugitive Essays & Studies. Walter J. Ong. 1962. 9.95 (ISBN 0-02-593260-8). Macmillan.

Barbarians. Malcolm Todd. 1981. 27.00 (ISBN 0-7134-1669-6, Pub. by Batsford England). David & Charles.

Barbarians & Romans, A. D. Four Hundred Eighteen to Five Hundred Eighty-Four: The Techniques of Accomodation. Walter Goffart. LC 80-7522. 240p. 1980. 25.00 (ISBN 0-691-05303-0). Princeton U Pr.

Barbarians in Greek Tragedy. Helen H. Bacon. 1961. 22.50x o.p. (ISBN 0-685-69787-8). Elliots Bks.

Barbarous Mexico. new ed. John K. Turner. (Texas Pan American Series). (Illus.). 1969. 12.95 (ISBN 0-292-78418-X). U of Tex Pr.

Barbary Bride. Melissa Masters. 1980. pap. 2.50 o.s.i. (ISBN 0-440-14645-3). Dell.

Barbary Shore. Norman Mailer. LC 79-26233. 312p. 1980. Repr. of 1951 ed. 15.95 (ISBN 0-86527-218-2). Fertig.

Barbecue with Beard. James Beard. 1976. pap. 2.25 o.s.i. (ISBN 0-446-82975-7). Warner Bks.

Barbed Arrows. Charles H. Spurgeon. (Charles H. Spurgeon Library). 280p. 1980. pap. 3.95 (ISBN 0-8010-8185-8). Baker Bk.

Barbed Wire on the Isle of Man. Alexander Ramati. LC 79-3361. 252p. 1980. 10.95 (ISBN 0-15-256039-4). HarBraceJ.

Barbell Way to Physical Fitness. Bruce Randall. (Illus.). 1970. 9.95 (ISBN 0-385-09053-6). Doubleday.

Barber, Barber, Shave a Pig. Nina Howard. 16p. (ps-k). 1981. tchr's ed. 4.95 (ISBN 0-917206-13-4). Children Learn Ctr.

Barber of Seville. Pierre De Beaumarchais. Tr. by Vincent Luciani from Fr. Bd. with Marriage of Figaro. (World Classics in Tr.). (Eng.). 1965. 6.50 (ISBN 0-8120-5007-X); pap. 3.25 (ISBN 0-8120-0029-3). Barron.

Barber's Shop. rev. & enl. ed. Richard W. Proctor. LC 74-79753. (Illus.). 1971. Repr. of 1883 ed. 15.00 (ISBN 0-8103-3036-9). Gale.

Barbey D'Aurevilly. Armand B. Chartier. (World Authors Ser.: France: No. 468). 1977. lib. bdg. 12.50 (ISBN 0-8057-6305-8). Twayne.

Barbier de Seville. Pierre Beaumarchais. Ed. by E. J. Arnould. (French Texts Ser.). 1977. pap. text ed. 10.00x (ISBN 0-631-00620-6, Pub. by Basil Blackwell). Biblio Dist.

Barbiturates: Their Use, Misuse & Abuse. Donald R. Wesson & David E. Smith. LC 76-41079. 224p. 1977. text ed. 16.95 (ISBN 0-87705-249-2); pap. 8.95 (ISBN 0-87705-314-6). Human Sci Pr.

Barboza Credentials. Peter Driscoll. LC 76-10483. 1976. 8.95 o.p. (ISBN 0-397-01145-8). Lippincott.

Barbra Streisand. Patricia M. Eldred. (Rock 'n Pop Stars Ser.). (Illus.). (gr. 4-12). 1975. PLB 5.95 o. p. (ISBN 0-87191-459-X); pap. 2.95 (ISBN 0-89812-118-3). Creative Ed.

Barbs, Prongs, Points, Prickers, & Stickers: Complete & Illustrated Catalogue of Antique Barbed Wire. Robert T. Clifton. LC 78-88140. (Illus.). 1970. 13.95 (ISBN 0-8061-0875-4); pap. 7.95 (ISBN 0-8061-0876-2). U of Okla Pr.

Barchester Towers. Anthony Trollope. 1956. 12.95x (ISBN 0-460-00030-6, Evman); pap. 4.50 (ISBN 0-460-01030-1). Dutton.

Barchester Towers. Anthony Trollope. pap. 2.95 (ISBN 0-451-51380-0, CE1380, Sig Classics). NAL.

Barchester Towers. Anthony Trollope. (Zodiac Press Ser.). 1978. 9.95 (ISBN 0-7011-1250-6, Pub. by Chatto Bodley Jonathan). Merrimack Bk Serv.

Barclay's Bridge Teacher's Manual for Five-Card Majors. rev ed. Shirley Silverman. 250p. 1980. loose leaf 28.95x (ISBN 0-87643-017-5). Barclay Bridge.

Bard's Theme. Robert Emmert Gray. 1977. 5.00 o.p. (ISBN 0-682-48961-1). Exposition.

Bare Bones Camera Course for Film & Video. 2nd ed. Tom Schroeppel. LC 79-92048. (Illus.). 89p. (Orig.). 1980. pap. 5.95 (ISBN 0-9603718-0-X). Schroeppel.

Bare Essence. Meredith Rich. 320p. (Orig.). 1981. pap. 2.95 (ISBN 0-449-14386-4, GM). Fawcett.

Bare Nell. Leslie Thomas. LC 78-3960. 1978. 8.95 o.p. (ISBN 0-312-06641-4). St Martin.

Barefoot Boy with Cheek. Max Shulman. 1.95 o.p. (ISBN 0-686-67648-3). Doubleday.

Barefoot Bride. Dorothy Cork. (Harlequin Romances). 192p. 1981. pap. 1.25 (ISBN 0-373-02390-1, Pub. by Harlequin). P-H.

Barefoot Days of the Soul. Maxie D. Dunnam. LC 75-19910. 1976. 4.95 o.p. (ISBN 0-87680-432-6, 80432). Word Bks.

Barefoot Doctor's Manual. rev. ed. Revolutionary Health Committee of Hunan Province. (Illus.). 1977. lib. bdg. 17.50 (ISBN 0-88930-037-2, Pub. by Cloudburst Canada); pap. 8.95 (ISBN 0-88930-012-7). Madrona Pubs.

Barefoot in the Grass: The Story of Grandma Moses. William H. Armstrong. LC 74-122338. (gr. 5 up). 1970. PLB 4.95 (ISBN 0-385-00454-0). Doubleday.

Barefoot in the Head. Brian Aldiss. 224p. 1981. pap. 2.25 (ISBN 0-380-53561-0, 53561). Avon.

Barefoot in the Sky. Sheila Scott. LC 73-8350. (Illus.). 324p. 1974. 7.95 o.s.i. (ISBN 0-02-608660-3). Macmillan.

Barford Abbey, 1768, 2 vols. in 1. Susannah Minnifie Guunning. Ed. by Michael F. Shugrue. (Flowering of the Novel, 1740-1775 Ser: Vol. 83). 1974. lib. bdg. 50.00 (ISBN 0-8240-1182-1). Garland Pub.

Bargain Bride. Evelyn S. Lampman. (gr. 7 up). pap. 2.95 (ISBN 0-689-70493-3, A-120, Aladdin). Atheneum.

Bargain Price Offers & Similar Marketing Practices. OECD. (Illus., Orig.). 1980. pap. text ed. 6.00 (ISBN 92-64-12033-5, 24-80-01-1). OECD.

Bargain Shopper's Guide to Europe. Marjorie Michaels. (Illus., Orig.). 1980. pap. 5.95 (ISBN 0-8037-0502-6). Dial.

Bargaining Equilibrium in Games & Social Situations. J. C. Harsanyi. LC 75-39370. (Illus.). 352p. 1977. 47.50 (ISBN 0-521-20886-6). Cambridge U Pr.

Bargaining for Cities, Municipalities & Intergovernmental Relations: An Assessment. Lionel D. Feldman & Katherine A. Graham. 143p. 1979. pap. text ed. 10.95x (ISBN 0-920380-21-2, Pub. by Inst Res Pub Canada). Renouf.

Bargaining for Health: Labor Unions, Health Insurance, & Medical Care. Raymond Munts. 1967. 25.00 (ISBN 0-299-04320-7). U of Wis Pr.

Bargaining for Justice: Case Disposition & Reform in the Criminal Courts. Suzann R. Buckle & Leonard G. Buckle. LC 75-19769. (Special Studies). 1977. text ed. 20.95 (ISBN 0-275-22830-4). Praeger.

Bargaining in International Conflicts. Charles Lockhart. 1979. 15.00x (ISBN 0-231-04560-3). Columbia U Pr.

Bargaining Tactics: A Reference Manual for Public Sector Labor Negotiations. Richard G. Neal & Frances I. Felts. LC 80-83023. 275p. 1981. 30.00 (ISBN 0-686-28742-8); pap. 25.00 (ISBN 0-686-28743-6). Neal Assoc.

Bargello: A Golden Hands Pattern Book. (Illus.). 1973. 4.95 o.p. (ISBN 0-394-48795-8). Random.

Bargello Antics. Dorothy Kaestner. (Illus.). 1980. 14.95 o.p. (ISBN 0-684-15995-3, ScribT); pap. 8.95 (ISBN 0-684-15996-1, ScribT). Scribner.

Bargello Borders. Nancy Hall & Jean Riley. (Illus.). 1977. pap. 9.95 o.p. (ISBN 0-684-15287-8, SL745, ScribT). Scribner.

Bargello Magic: How to Design Your Own. Pauline Fischer & Anabel Lasker. LC 79-182757. 1972. 12.95 o.p. (ISBN 0-03-088259-1). HR&W.

Bargello, Step by Step. Geraldine Cosentino. (Step by Step Craft Ser). 1974. PLB 9.15 o.p. (ISBN 0-307-62011-5, Golden Pr); pap. 2.95 (ISBN 0-307-42011-6, Golden Pr). Western Pub.

Barham Downs, 2 vols. Robert Bage. Ed. by Ronald Paulson. LC 78-60850. (Novel 1720-1805 Ser.: Vol. 9). 1979. Set. lib. bdg. 62.00 (ISBN 0-8240-3659-X). Garland Pub.

Barkal Temples. Dows Dunham. 1970. 40.00 (ISBN 0-87846-108-6). Mus Fine Arts Boston.

Barkerville, Quesnel, & the Cariboo Gold Rush. Gordon R. Elliot. LC 79-301801. (Illus.). 216p. 1980. pap. 7.95 (ISBN 0-295-95775-1, Pub. by Douglas & McIntyre Canada). U of Wash Pr.

Barking Deer. Jonathan Rubin. LC 73-88042. 1974. 7.95 o.s.i. (ISBN 0-8076-0727-4). Braziller.

Barley & Malt: Biology, Biochemistry, Technology. Ed. by Arthur H. Cook. 1962. 68.00 o.s.i. (ISBN 0-12-186550-9). Acad Pr.

Barlow Exposed. Elwyn Jones. LC 76-28040. 1977. 7.95 o.p. (ISBN 0-312-06685-6). St Martin.

Barn Blind. Jane Smiley. LC 79-3417. 1980. 9.95 o.s.i. (ISBN 0-06-014016-X, HarpT). Har-Row.

Barn Fever & Other Poems. Peter Davison. 64p. 1981. 10.00 (ISBN 0-689-11126-6); pap. 5.95 (ISBN 0-689-11163-0). Atheneum.

Barnaby Frost Plants a Seed. Laurel Lee. (ps-3). 1980. 5.95 (ISBN 0-8423-0118-6). Tyndale.

Barnaby Rudge. Charles Dickens. 1966. 17.95x (ISBN 0-460-00076-4, Evman); pap. 2.95 o.p. (ISBN 0-460-01076-X, Evman). Dutton.

Barnaby Shrew, Black Dan & the Mighty Wedgwood. Steve Augarde. (Illus.). (ps-3). 1980. 7.95 (ISBN 0-233-97104-1). Andre Deutsch.

Barnaby Shrew Goes to Sea. Steve Augarde. (Illus.). (ps-3). 1979. PLB 8.95 (ISBN 0-233-96957-8). Andre Deutsch.

Barnacle & His Friends. Alex Monroe. (Illus.). 42p. (Orig.). (gr. 1-6). 1980. pap. 2.75 (ISBN 0-933614-07-1). Peregrine Pr.

Barnet & Stubbs's Practical Guide to Writing. 3rd ed. Sylvan Barnet & Marcia Stubbs. 424p. 1980. pap. text ed. 7.95 (ISBN 0-316-08155-8); instructor's manual free (ISBN 0-316-08156-6). Little.

Barney the Beard. Eve Bunting. LC 73-23111. (Illus.). 48p. (ps-3). 1975. 5.95 o.s.i. (ISBN 0-8193-0728-9, Four Winds); PLB 5.41 o.s.i. (ISBN 0-8193-0729-7). Schol Bk Serv.

Barney's Picnic. Leslie Max. (Play & Learn Shape Board Bks). 14p. (gr. k-3). 1981. bds. 2.95 comb bdg. (ISBN 0-89828-101-6, 6002, Ottenheimer Pubs Inc). Tuffy Bks.

Barnhart Dictionary of New English Since 1963. Ed. by Clarence L. Barnhart et al. LC 73-712. 512p. (YA) 1973. 14.95 o.s.i. (ISBN 0-06-010223-3, HarpT). Har-Row.

Barnstormers & Speed Kings. Paul O'Neil. Ed. by Time-Life Bks. Eds. (Epic of Flight Ser.). (Illus.). 176p. 1981. 12.95 (ISBN 0-8094-3275-7). Time-Life.

Baron & Feme. Ed. by David S. Berkowitz & Samuel E. Thorne. LC 77-86664. (Classics of English Legal History in the Modern Era Ser.: Vol. 43). 445p. 1979. lib. bdg. 40.00 (ISBN 0-8240-3092-3). Garland Pub.

Baron Friedrich Von Hugel & the Modernist Crisis in England. Lawrence F. Barmann. LC 77-153014. 1972. 39.00 (ISBN 0-521-08178-5). Cambridge U Pr.

Baron in the Trees. Italo Calvino. Tr. by Archibald Colquhoun. 1977. pap. 3.50 (ISBN 0-15-610680-9, HPL). HarBraceJ.

Baron Von Kodak, Shirley Temple & Me. Ann Valery. 14.95x (ISBN 0-8464-0168-1). Beekman Pubs.

Baroness Pontalba's Buildings. Leonard Huber & Samuel Wilson, Jr. 1973. pap. 3.95 (ISBN 0-911116-40-0). Pelican.

Baronial Household of the Thirteenth Century. Margaret W. Labarge. (Illus.). 235p. 1980. 22.50x (ISBN 0-389-20068-9); pap. 9.95x (ISBN 0-389-20034-4). B&N.

Barons of the Welsh Frontier: The Corbet, Pantulf, & Fitz Warin Families, 1066 - 1272. Janet Meisel. LC 80-10273. xx, 231p. 1980. 19.95x (ISBN 0-8032-3064-8). U of Nebr Pr.

Baroque Age of England. Judith Hook. (Illus.). 207p. 1976. 30.00 (ISBN 0-500-23229-6). Transatlantic.

Baroque & Rococo Art. Germain Bazin. (World of Art Ser.). (Illus.). 1964. pap. 9.95 (ISBN 0-19-519927-8). Oxford U Pr.

Baroque & Rococo Art. Erich Hubala. LC 73-88459. (History of Art Ser). (Illus.). 196p. 1976. 8.95x (ISBN 0-87663-195-2). Universe.

Baroque & Rococo Silks. Peter Thornton. 1965. 33.00 o.p. (ISBN 0-571-06315-2, Pub. by Faber & Faber). Merrimack Bk Serv.

Baroque Architecture. Martin S. Briggs. LC 67-23634. (Architecture & Decorative Art Ser). 1967. Repr. of 1913 ed. 29.50 (ISBN 0-306-70960-0). Da Capo.

Baroque Architecture. Christian Norberg-Schulz. LC 74-149851. (History of World Architecture Ser). (Illus.). 1971. 45.00 (ISBN 0-8109-1002-0). Abrams.

Baroque Churches of Central Europe. John Bourke. (Illus.). 1978. pap. 10.95 (ISBN 0-571-10689-7, Pub. by Faber & Faber). Merrimack Bk Serv.

Baroque Music. 2nd ed. Claude Palisca. (P-H History of Music Ser.). (Illus.). 1980. text ed. 13.95 (ISBN 0-13-055954-7); pap. text ed. 8.45 (ISBN 0-13-055947-4). P-H.

Baroque Music. Claude V. Palisca. (Prentice-Hall History of Music Series). (Orig.). 1968. pap. 10.95 ref. ed. (ISBN 0-13-055962-8). P-H.

Baroque Music: A Practical Guide for the Performer. Victor Rangel-Ribeiro. LC 80-5222. (Illus.). 260p. 1981. 15.00 (ISBN 0-02-871980-8). Schirmer Bks.

Baroque Operatic Arias, Bk.1. Denis Arnold. Ed. by Anthony Ford. 1971. 13.10x o.p. (ISBN 0-19-713412-2). Oxford U Pr.

Baroque Sculpture. H. Busch & B. Lohse. 1965. 14.95 o.s.i. (ISBN 0-02-518760-0). Macmillan.

Baroque Times in Old Mexico: Seventeenth-Century Persons, Places, & Practices. Irving A. Leonard. (Illus.). 1959. pap. 4.95 (ISBN 0-472-06110-0, 110, AA). U of Mich Pr.

Baroque Times in Old Mexico: Seventeenth-Century Persons, Places, & Practices. Irving A. Leonard. LC 80-29256. (Illus.). xi, 260p. 1981. Repr. of 1978 ed. lib. bdg. 25.50x (ISBN 0-313-22826-4, LEBT). Greenwood.

Baroreceptors & Hypertension. Ed. by P. Kezdi. 1967. 67.00 (ISBN 0-08-012488-7). Pergamon.

Barquilla que Casi Se Hundio. Mary Warren. Tr. by Fernando Villalobos from Eng. (Libros Arco Ser.). (Illus.). 32p. (Orig., Span.). (gr. 1-3). 1978. pap. 0.95 (ISBN 0-89922-125-4). Edit Caribe.

Barracuda: Tiger of the Sea. Francine Jacobs. (Illus.). 48p. (gr. 1-4). 1981. 8.95 (ISBN 0-8027-6413-4); lib. bdg. 9.85 (ISBN 0-8027-6414-2). Walker & Co.

Barranca Del Cobre De Mexico. Joseph Wampler. Tr. by Lucy Ann Neblett from Eng. LC 78-657149. (Illus., Span.). 1978. pap. 6.00 (ISBN 0-935080-00-7). J Wampler.

Barred from School: Two Million Children. Thomas J. Cottle. LC 76-20607. 1976. 7.95 o.p. (ISBN 0-915220-12-1); pap. 3.95 o.p. (ISBN 0-915220-40-7, 24165). New Republic.

Barred Road. Adele De Leeuw. (gr. 7-10). 1964. 5.95g o.s.i. (ISBN 0-02-726760-1). Macmillan.

Barren Corn. Georgette Heyer. 1976. Repr. of 1930 ed. lib. bdg. 13.35x (ISBN 0-89966-123-8). Buccaneer Bks.

Barren Land Showdown. Luke Short. 1981. pap. 1.75 (ISBN 0-449-14138-1, GM). Fawcett.

Barrett Wendell. Robert T. Self. LC 75-12735. (U. S. Authors Ser.: No. 261). 1975. lib. bdg. 12.50 (ISBN 0-8057-7160-3). Twayne.

Barrier Contraception & Breast Cancer. A. N. Gjorgov. (Contributions to Gynecology & Obstetrics Ser.: Vol. 8). (Illus.). 1980. soft cover 49.75 (ISBN 3-8055-0330-X). S Karger.

Barriers & Hazards in Counseling. Dorothy E. Johnson & Mary J. Vestermark. LC 73-14990. (Orig.). 1970. pap. text ed. 9.50 (ISBN 0-395-04694-7, 3-28202). HM.

Barriers Between Women. Paula Caplan. 167p. 1981. 15.00 (ISBN 0-89335-103-2). Spectrum Pub.

Barriers to Corporate Growth. Barry D. Baysinger et al. LC 80-8603. 1981. price not set (ISBN 0-669-04323-0). Lexington Bks.

Barriers to Efficient Capital Investment in Asian Agriculture. (IRRI Research Paper Ser.: No. 24). 20p. 1979. pap. 5.00 (R064, IRRI). Unipub.

Barriers to Entry: A Theoretical Treatment. C. C. Weizsaecker. (Lecture Notes in Economics & Mathematical Systems Ser.: Vol. 185). (Illus.). 220p. 1981. pap. 19.00 (ISBN 0-387-10272-8). Springer-Verlag.

Barriers to Higher Education in the Federal Republic of Germany. Willi Becker. (Access to Higher Education). 1977. pap. 2.50 (ISBN 0-89192-216-4). Interbk Inc.

Barriers to Increased Rice Production in Eastern India. (IRRI Research Search Paper Ser.: No. 25). 23p. 1979. pap. 5.00 (R065, IRRI). Unipub.

Barrington-Bernard Correspondence, & Illustrative Matter, 1760-1770. Edward Channing & Archibald C. Coolidge. LC 75-109612. (Era of the American Revolution Ser). 1970. Repr. of 1912 ed. lib. bdg. 32.50 (ISBN 0-306-71909-6). Da Capo.

Barrio Boy. Ernesto Galarza. 1971. pap. 4.95x (ISBN 0-268-00441-2); 8.95x o.p. (ISBN 0-268-00440-4). U of Notre Dame Pr.

Barron's Compact Guide to Colleges. 2nd ed. College Division of Barron's Educational Ser., Inc. LC 80-26124. (Illus.). 352p. (gr. 11-12). 1980. pap. 2.75 (ISBN 0-8120-2288-2). Barron.

Barron's Guide to Graduate Business Schools: Eastern Edition. rev. ed. Eugene Miller. LC 80-12843. 1980. pap. text ed. 5.95 (ISBN 0-8120-2068-5). Barron.

Barron's Guide to Graduate Schools. Incl. Vol. 1. Social Sciences, Psychology (ISBN 0-8120-0549-X). 1975. pap. 6.95 (ISBN 0-8120-0549-X). Barron.

Barron's Guide to Graduate Schools. Incl. Vol. 2. Natural Sciences, Health Agriculture (ISBN 0-8120-0581-3); Vol. 3. English Communications, Foreign Languages (ISBN 0-8120-0580-5); Vol. 4. Math, Physical Sciences, Computer Science (ISBN 0-8120-0582-1); Vol. 5. Education (ISBN 0-8120-0583-X); Vol. 6. Engineering (ISBN 0-8120-0584-8). Date not set. pap. price not set. Barron.

Barron's Guide to Law Schools. Elliot Epstein et al. LC 77-13268. 1978. pap. 5.50 o.p. (ISBN 0-8120-0737-9). Barron.

Barron's Guide to Medical, Dental & Allied Health Science Careers. rev. ed. Saul Wischnitzer. LC 76-41772. (gr. 12). 1977. pap. 6.50 (ISBN 0-8120-0719-0). Barron.

Barron's Guide to Medical, Dental & Allied Health Science Careers. rev. ed. Saul Wischnitzer. 286p. 1981. pap. text ed. 6.50 (ISBN 0-8120-2281-5). Barron.

Barron's Handbook of College Transfer Information. Nicholas C. Proia. (Barron's Educational Ser.). 304p. 1980. pap. 5.95 (ISBN 0-8120-2166-5). Barron.

Barron's How to Prepare for Advanced Placement in Mathematics. rev. ed. Shirley Hockett. (gr. 10-12). 1981. pap. text ed. 8.50 (ISBN 0-8120-2071-5). Barron.

Barron's How to Prepare for Civil Service Examinations: Clerks, Stenographers, Typists. 4th ed. Edwin Riemer & Louis Leibling. (Barron's Educational Ser.). 405p. 1981. pap. text ed. 5.95 (ISBN 0-8120-2033-2). Barron.

Barron's How to Prepare for College Entrance Examinations. Brownstein & Weiner. LC 80-330. 1980. 15.00 (ISBN 0-8120-5323-0); pap. 5.95 (ISBN 0-8120-2191-6). Barron.

Barron's How to Prepare for College Entrance Examinations. 9th rev ed. Samuel C. Brownstein & Mitchel Weiner. LC 78-9661. (gr. 11-12). 1978. 15.00 o.p. (ISBN 0-8120-5323-0); pap. 5.95 o.p. (ISBN 0-8120-2025-1). Barron.

Barron's How to Prepare for the CLEP Examinations - General Examination. rev. ed. Ed. by W. Doster. LC 78-32129. 1979. pap. 6.50 (ISBN 0-8120-2011-1). Barron.

Barron's How to Prepare for the College Entrance Examinations (SAT) 10th ed. Samuel C. Brownstein & Mitchel Weiner. 704p. (gr. 11-12). 1980. text ed. 19.00 (ISBN 0-8120-5402-4); pap. text ed. 5.95 (ISBN 0-8120-2191-6). Barron.

Barron's How to Prepare for the Competency Examination in Mathematics. Angelo Wieland. (gr. 7-12). 1981. pap. text ed. 5.95 (ISBN 0-8120-2246-7). Barron.
Barron's How to Prepare for the Dental Admission Test (DAT) Herman Hu. 256p. 1981. pap. text ed. 4.95 (ISBN 0-8120-2162-2). Barron.
Barron's How to Prepare for the Graduate Record Examination. rev. ed. Samuel C. Brownstein & Mitchel Weiner. LC 78-15175. 1979. 12.95 (ISBN 0-8120-5164-5); pap. 6.95 (ISBN 0-8120-2032-4). Barron.
Barron's How to Prepare for the Graduate Record Examination in Literature: With 3 Model Examinations & a Complete Survey of the Elements of Literature. Benjamin W. Griffith, Jr. Date not set. pap. text ed. 3.95 (ISBN 0-686-62943-4). Barron.
Barron's How to Prepare for the High School Equivalency Exam (GED) rev. ed. Rockowitz et al. (gr. 10-12). 1978. pap. text ed. 6.95 (ISBN 0-8120-0645-3). Barron.
Barron's How to Prepare for the High School Equavalency Examination(GED) Science. Eugene J. Farley & Alice R. Farley. (gr. 11-12). 1981. pap. text ed. 4.25 (ISBN 0-8120-2055-3). Barron.
Barron's How to Prepare for the High School Equivalency Examination: The Social Studies Test. Eugene J. Farley. 1980. pap. text ed. 3.95 (ISBN 0-8120-2056-1). Barron.
Barron's How to Prepare for the High School Equivalency Examination: The Reading Skills Test. Eugene J. Farley. 1980. pap. text ed. 3.95 (ISBN 0-8120-2057-X). Barron.
Barron's How to Prepare for the New Medical College Admission Test MCAT. Hugo Seibel & Kenneth E. Guyer. LC 77-24613. 1977. pap. text ed. 6.50 o.p. (ISBN 0-8120-0821-9). Barron.
Barron's How to Prepare for the New Medical College Admission Test (MCAT) Hugo Seibel & Kenneth E. Guyer. LC 80-15470. 1981. pap. text ed. 6.50 (ISBN 0-8120-2190-8). Barron.
Barron's How to Prepare for the Test of Standard Written English. Weiner & Green. 1981. pap. 4.95 (ISBN 0-8120-2095-2). Barron.
Barron's Practice Exercises for the TOEFL (Test of English As a Foreign Language) Sharpe. LC 79-65306. 1980. pap. 7.95 (ISBN 0-8120-2164-9). Barron.
Barron's Preview Examination to Prepare for High School Equivalency Tests. 2nd, rev. ed. Eugene J. Farley. 1979. pap. text ed. 18.00 (ISBN 0-8120-0992-4). Barron.
Barron's Profile of Barnard College. (College Profiles Ser.). 1977. pap. text ed. 2.50 o.p. (ISBN 0-8120-1006-X). Barron.
Barron's Profile of Boston University. (College Profiles Ser.). 1976. pap. text ed. 2.50 o.p. (ISBN 0-8120-1010-8). Barron.
Barron's Profile of Brown University. (College Profiles Ser.). 1978. pap. text ed. 2.50 (ISBN 0-8120-1014-0). Barron.
Barron's Profile of Bucknell University. (College Profiles Ser.). 1977. pap. text ed. 2.50 o.p. (ISBN 0-8120-1015-9). Barron.
Barron's Profile of Clark University. (College Profiles Ser.). 1977. pap. text ed. 2.50 o.p. (ISBN 0-8120-1177-5). Barron.
Barron's Profile of Colby College. (College Profiles Ser.). 1976. pap. text ed. 2.50 o.p. (ISBN 0-8120-1024-8). Barron.
Barron's Profile of Colgate University. (College Profiles Ser.). 1976. pap. text ed. 2.50 o.p. (ISBN 0-8120-1025-6). Barron.
Barron's Profile of College of William & Mary. (College Profiles Ser.). 1976. pap. text ed. 2.50 o.p. (ISBN 0-8120-1026-4). Barron.
Barron's Profile of Dartmouth College. (College Profiles Ser.). 1976. pap. text ed. 2.50 o.p. (ISBN 0-8120-1031-0). Barron.
Barron's Profile of Drew University. (College Profiles Ser.). 1977. pap. text ed. 2.50 o.p. (ISBN 0-8120-1227-5). Barron.
Barron's Profile of George Washington University. (College Profiles Ser.). 1977. pap. text ed. 2.50 o.p. (ISBN 0-8120-1043-4). Barron.
Barron's Profile of Howard University. (College Profiles Ser.). 1977. pap. text ed. 2.50 o.p. (ISBN 0-8120-1061-2). Barron.
Barron's Profile of Middlebury College. (College Profiles Ser.). 1976. pap. text ed. 2.50 o.p. (ISBN 0-8120-1076-0). Barron.
Barron's Profile of Montclair State College. (College Profiles Ser.). 1976. pap. text ed. 2.50 o.p. (ISBN 0-8120-1288-7). Barron.
Barron's Profile of Muskigum College. (College Profiles Ser.). 1976. pap. 2.50 o.p. (ISBN 0-8120-1302-6). Barron.
Barron's Profile of Northeastern University. (College Profiles Ser.). 1976. pap. text ed. 2.50 o.p. (ISBN 0-8120-1184-8). Barron.
Barron's Profile of Ohio University. (College Profiles Ser.). 1976. pap. text ed. 2.50 o.p. (ISBN 0-8120-1255-0). Barron.
Barron's Profile of Princeton University. (College Profiles Ser.). 1976. pap. text ed. 2.50 o.p. (ISBN 0-8120-1091-4). Barron.
Barron's Profile of Purdue University. (College Profiles Ser.). 1977. pap. text ed. 2.50 o.p. (ISBN 0-8120-1093-0). Barron.
Barron's Profile of Seton Hall University. (College Profiles Ser.). 1977. pap. text ed. 2.50 o.p. (ISBN 0-8120-1106-6). Barron.
Barron's Profile of Smith College. (College Profiles Ser.). 1977. pap. text ed. 2.50 o.p. (ISBN 0-8120-1109-0). Barron.
Barron's Profile of SUC at Brockport. (College Profiles Ser.). 1976. pap. text ed. 2.50 o.p. (ISBN 0-8120-1277-1). Barron.
Barron's Profile of SUC at Cortland. (College Profiles Ser.). 1977. pap. text ed. 2.50 o.p. (ISBN 0-8120-1278-X). Barron.
Barron's Profile of SUC at Geneseo. (College Profiles Ser.). 1977. pap. text ed. 2.50 o.p. (ISBN 0-8120-1280-1). Barron.
Barron's Profile of SUC at New Paltz. (College Profiles Ser.). 1977. pap. text ed. 2.50 o.p. (ISBN 0-8120-1281-X). Barron.
Barron's Profile of SUC at Potsdam. (College Profiles Ser.). 1977. pap. text ed. 2.50 o.p. (ISBN 0-8120-1286-0). Barron.
Barron's Profile of Swarthmore College. (College Profiles Ser.). 1976. pap. text ed. 2.50 o.p. (ISBN 0-8120-1113-9). Barron.
Barron's Profile of Syracuse University. (College Profiles Ser.). 1976. pap. text ed. 2.50 o.p. (ISBN 0-8120-1114-7). Barron.
Barron's Profile of Tufts University. (College Profiles Ser). 1976. pap. text ed. 2.50 o.p. (ISBN 0-8120-1119-8). Barron.
Barron's Profile of University of Bridgeport. (College Profiles Ser.). 1977. pap. text ed. 2.50 o.p. (ISBN 0-8120-1125-2). Barron.
Barron's Profile of University of Cincinnati. (College Profiles Ser.). 1977. pap. text ed. 2.50 o.p. (ISBN 0-8120-1128-7). Barron.
Barron's Profile of University of Connecticut. (College Profile Ser.). 1976. pap. text ed. 2.50 o.p. (ISBN 0-8120-1129-5). Barron.
Barron's Profile of University of Miami. (College Profiles Ser.). 1977. pap. text ed. 2.50 o.p. (ISBN 0-8120-1138-4). Barron.
Barron's Profile of University of Michigan. (College Profiles Ser.). 1977. pap. text ed. 2.50 o.p. (ISBN 0-8120-1139-2). Barron.
Barron's Profile of Vassar College. (College Profiles Ser.). 1976. pap. text ed. 2.50 o.p. (ISBN 0-8120-1148-1). Barron.
Barron's Profile of Villanova University. (College Profiles Ser.). 1976. pap. text ed. 2.50 o.p. (ISBN 0-8120-1149-X). Barron.
Barron's Profile of Washington & Lee University. (College Profiles Ser.). 1976. pap. text ed. 2.50 o.p. (ISBN 0-8120-1150-3). Barron.
Barron's Profile of Wheaton College, Mass. (College Profiles Ser.). 1977. pap. text ed. 2.50 o.p. (ISBN 0-8120-1299-2). Barron.
Barron's Profile of Yale College. (College Profiles Ser.). 1977. pap. 2.50 o.p. (ISBN 0-8120-1159-7). Barron.
Barron's Profiles of American Colleges: Descriptions of the Colleges, Vol. 1. 1980. 23.95 (ISBN 0-8120-5407-5); pap. 9.95 (ISBN 0-8120-2201-7). Barron.
Barron's Profiles of American Colleges: Regional Editions. College & Education Division. (gr. 10-12). 1981. Northeast. pap. text ed. 5.75 (ISBN 0-8120-2271-8); West. pap. text ed. 4.95 (ISBN 0-8120-2272-6); South. pap. text ed. 5.75 (ISBN 0-8120-2273-4); Midwest. pap. text ed. 5.75 (ISBN 0-8120-2274-2). Barron.
Barron's Simplified Approach to Goethe's Faust 1 & 2. Vincent F. Hopper. (YA) 1964. pap. text ed. 1.50 o.p. (ISBN 0-8120-0173-7). Barron.
Barron's Verbal Aptitude Workbook for College Entrance Examinations. rev. ed. Mitchel Weiner. (gr. 10-12). 1979. pap. text ed. 3.75 (ISBN 0-8120-2074-X). Barron.
Barron's Vocabulary Builder: A Systematic Plan for Building a Vocabulary, Testing Progress & Applying Knowledge. rev. ed. Samuel C. Brownstein & Mitchel Weiner. LC 75-14340. (Orig.). (gr. 9-12). 1975. pap. 3.25 (ISBN 0-8120-0964-9). Barron.
Barry Manilow. Ann Morse. (Rock 'n Pop Stars Ser.). (Illus.). (gr. 4-12). 1978. PLB 5.95 (ISBN 0-87191-617-7); pap. 2.95 (ISBN 0-89812-122-1). Creative Ed.
Barry Richards Story. Barry Richards. (Illus.). 1978. 10.95 o.p. (ISBN 0-571-11187-4, Pub. by Faber & Faber). Merrimack Bk Serv.
Bars of Iron. Ethel M. Dell. (Barbara Cartland's Library of Love: Vol. 9). 278p. 1979. 12.95x (ISBN 0-7156-1384-7, Pub. by Duckworth England). Biblio Dist.
Bart Starr: A Biography. Gene Schoor. LC 76-56332. (gr. 4-7). 1977. PLB 6.95 (ISBN 0-385-11695-0). Doubleday.
Bart Starr: Professional Quarterback. Tex Maule. LC 72-7355. (Illus.). 128p. (gr. 5 up). 1973. PLB 5.90 o.p. (ISBN 0-531-02610-8). Watts.
Bartender's Guide to Baseball. Richard Lally. 304p. (Orig.). 1981. pap. 2.50 (ISBN 0-446-91736-2). Warner Bks.
Barter Book. Dyanne Simon. 1979. 8.95 o.p. (ISBN 0-87690-352-9); pap. 4.50 o.p. (ISBN 0-87690-290-5). Dutton.
Barter: How to Get Almost Anything Without Money. Constance Stapleton & Phyllis Richman. LC 77-21624. 1978. 9.95 o.p. (ISBN 0-684-15193-6, ScribT); pap. 4.95 (ISBN 0-684-15320-3, ScribT). Scribner.
Barthes Reader. Roland Barthes. Ed. by Susan Sontag. 1981. 17.95 (ISBN 0-8090-2815-8); pap. 8.95 (ISBN 0-8090-1394-0). Hill & Wang.
Bartholomew Fair. Ben Jonson. Ed. by Edward Partridge. LC 63-14700. (Regents Renaissance Drama Ser). xx, 187p. 1964. 2.95x (ISBN 0-8032-5264-1, BB 202, Bison). U of Nebr Pr.
Bartlett's Familiar Quotations: Fifteenth & 125th Anniversary Edition. rev. & enl. ed. John Bartlett. LC 68-15664. 1980. 24.95 (ISBN 0-316-08275-9). Little.
Bartok's String Quartets. Janos Karpati. 1978. 19.95 o.p. (ISBN 0-214-20469-3, 8060, Dist. by Arco). Barrie & Jenkins.
Bartolome Arzans de Orsua y Vela's History of Potosi. Lewis Hanke. LC 65-24779. (Illus.). 81p. 1965. 8.00x (ISBN 0-87057-093-5, Pub. by Brown U Pr). Univ Pr of New England.
Bartolome Bermejo. Eric Young. 1975. 42.00 (ISBN 0-236-31041-0, Pub. by Paul Elek). Merrimack Bk Serv.
Bartolome De Torres Naharro. John Lihani. (World Authors Ser.: No. 522). 1979. lib. bdg. 14.50 (ISBN 0-8057-6363-5). Twayne.
Barwick. David Marr. (Illus.). 336p. 1981. 19.50 (ISBN 0-86861-058-5, 2566). Allen Unwin.
Baryshnikov. Mikhail Baryshnikov. Ed. by Charles E. France. (Illus.). 64p. 1980. 12.95 (ISBN 0-686-62682-6, 2225-8). Abrams.
Baryshnikov: From Russia to the West. Gennady Smakov. (Illus.). 1981. 17.50 (ISBN 0-374-10908-7). FS&G.
Basal Ganglia. Ed. by Melvin D. Yahr. LC 75-25114. (Association for Research in Nervous & Mental Disease Research Publications: Vol. 55). 1976. 48.00 (ISBN 0-89004-099-0). Raven.
Basal Reader Approach to Reading. Robert C. Aukerman. 400p. 1981. text ed. 14.95 (ISBN 0-471-03082-1); pap. text ed. 8.95 (ISBN 0-471-09066-2). Wiley.
Basalts & Phase Diagrams: An Introduction to the Quantitative Use of Phase Diagrams in Igneous Petrology. S. A. Morse. (Illus.). 400p. 1980. 29.80 o.p. (ISBN 0-387-90477-8). Springer-Verlag.
BASE. Ellis et al. (gr. 4 up). 1974. pap. text ed. 2.58 (ISBN 0-87892-840-5); tchr's handbook 2.58 (ISBN 0-87892-844-8); tapes 129.15 (ISBN 0-87892-845-6). Economy Co.
Base Case. Julian Rathbone. 1981. 9.95 (ISBN 0-394-50911-0). Pantheon.
Base Change for GL (2) R. Langlands. LC 79-28820. (Annals of Mathematics Studies: No. 96). 225p. 1980. 17.50x (ISBN 0-691-08263-4); pap. 7.00x (ISBN 0-691-08272-3). Princeton U Pr.
Base Five. David A. Adler. LC 74-18325. (Young Math Ser.). (Illus.). (gr. k-3). 1975. 7.95 (ISBN 0-690-00668-3, TYC-J); PLB 7.89 (ISBN 0-690-00669-1). T Y Crowell.
Baseball. 6th rev. ed. Benjamin Brewster. Ed. by Bill Gutman. (First Bks.). (Illus.). (gr. 4-6). 1979. PLB 6.45 s&l (ISBN 0-531-00479-1). Watts.
Baseball. Dick Siebert & Otto Vogel. LC 68-18803. (Athletic Institute Ser). (Illus.). (gr. 7 up). 1968. 6.95 (ISBN 0-8069-4300-9); PLB 7.49 (ISBN 0-8069-4301-7). Sterling.
Baseball Album. Gerald S. Couzens. LC 79-25044. (Illus.). 256p. 1980. 14.00 (ISBN 0-690-01864-9). Lippincott & Crowell.
Baseball Book. Joe Kaufman. (Golden Bk. for Early Childhood). (Illus.). 24p. (gr. k-2). 1976. PLB 5.38 (ISBN 0-307-68975-1, Golden Pr). Western Pub.
Baseball Century: The First 100 Years of the National League. Henry Berry & Bob Cook. (Illus.). 256p. 1976. 19.95 o.s.i. (ISBN 0-02-510380-6). Macmillan.
Baseball Economics & Public Policy. Jesse W. Markham & Paul V. Teplitz. LC 79-6032. 1981. write for info. (ISBN 0-669-03607-2). Lexington Bks.
Baseball Handbook for Coaches & Players. Jim Depel. LC 75-19308. (Illus.). 96p. 1976. 7.95 o.p. (ISBN 0-684-14264-3, ScribT); pap. 4.95 (ISBN 0-684-14265-1, SL 593, ScribT). Scribner.
Baseball Handbook: Strategies & Techniques for Winning. abr ed. Walter Alston & Don Weiskopf. 504p. 1974. pap. 17.95x (ISBN 0-205-04317-8). Allyn.
Baseball Language: A Running Press Glossary. Richard Scholl. LC 77-410. (Orig.). 1977. lib. bdg. 12.90 o.p. (ISBN 0-914294-79-2); pap. 2.95 o.p. (ISBN 0-914294-80-6). Running Pr.
Baseball Pals. Matt Christopher. (Illus.). (gr. 4-6). 1956. 6.95 (ISBN 0-316-13950-5). Little.
Baseball Picture Quiz Book. Bert Sugar & John Grafton. (Illus.). 128p. (Orig.). 1980. pap. 5.00 (ISBN 0-486-23987-X). Dover.
Baseball Play & Strategy. 2nd ed. Ethan Allen. LC 69-14668. (Illus.). 350p. 1969. 14.95 (ISBN 0-8260-0305-2). Wiley.
Baseball Quiz Book, No. 2. Ted Misa. 1975. pap. 3.50 o.p. (ISBN 0-8015-0523-2). Dutton.
Baseball Quiz Book (or Who's on First?, No. 1. Ted Misa. 128p. 1974. pap. 3.50 (ISBN 0-8015-0524-0, Hawthorn). Dutton.
Baseball Reader: Favorites from the Fireside Books of Baseball. Ed. by Charles Einstein. 1980. 12.95 (ISBN 0-690-01898-3). Lippincott.
Baseball Rules Illustrated. George Sullivan. 96p. (Orig.). 1981. pap. 3.95 (ISBN 0-346-12524-3). Cornerstone.
Baseball: The Early Years. Harold Seymour. 1960. 17.95 (ISBN 0-19-500100-1). Oxford U Pr.
Baseball: The Golden Age. Harold Seymour. 1971. 18.95 (ISBN 0-19-501403-0). Oxford U Pr.
Baseball Three Thousand. Charles G. Waugh & Martin H. Greenberg. 240p. (gr. 7 up). 1981. 9.95 (ISBN 0-525-66732-6). Elsevier-Nelson.
Baseball Transition Nineteen Fifty to Nineteen Seventy-Nine. Richard S. Kubik. (Illus.). 124p. 1981. 10.00 (ISBN 0-682-49676-6). Exposition.
Baseball Trivia Book. Burt R. Sugar. LC 75-44566. Orig. Title: Who Was Harry Steinfeldt? & Other Baseball Trivia Questions. 176p. 1981. pap. 1.95 (ISBN 0-87216-824-7). Playboy Pbks.
Baseball Trivia Puzzler, No. 1. Robert Kelly. (Orig.). 1981. pap. 1.95 (ISBN 0-440-00393-8). Dell.
Baseball's Finest Pitchers. Nathan Aaseng. LC 80-12275. (Sports Heroes Library). (Illus.). 72p. (gr. 4 up). 1980. PLB 5.95g (ISBN 0-8225-1061-8). Lerner Pubns.
Baseball's Golden Dozen. Joseph Bruno. 1976. 8.50 o.p. (ISBN 0-682-48564-0, Banner). Exposition.
Baseball's Great Moments. Herb Gluck. LC 74-23539. (Major League Library Ser.: No. 23). (Illus.). 160p. (gr. 5 up). 1975. 2.50 o.p. (ISBN 0-394-83030-X, BYR); PLB 3.69 (ISBN 0-394-93030-4). Random.
Baseball's Greatest Catcher: Johnny Bench. Jay H. Smith. (Allstars Ser.). (Illus.). (gr. 2-6). 1977. PLB 5.95 o.p. (ISBN 0-87191-589-8). Creative Ed.
Baseball's Greatest Sluggers. Bill Libby. (Major League Baseball Library: No. 19). (Illus.). (gr. 5 up). 1973. 2.50 o.p. (ISBN 0-394-82538-1, BYR); PLB 3.69 (ISBN 0-394-92538-6). Random.
Baseball's Most Valuable Players. George Vecsey. (Major League Baseball Library: No. 5). (Illus.). (gr. 5-9). 1966. 2.50 o.p. (ISBN 0-394-80185-7, BYR); PLB 3.69 (ISBN 0-394-90185-1). Random.
Baseball's One Hundred: A Personal Ranking of the Best Players in Baseball History. Maury Allen. (Illus.). 352p. 1981. 14.95 (ISBN 0-89104-208-3); pap. 6.95 (ISBN 0-89104-200-8). A & W Pubs.
Baseball's Pennant Races: A Graphic View. John W. Davenport. 1981. 19.95 (ISBN 0-934794-02-2); pap. 12.95 (ISBN 0-934794-03-0). First Impressions.
Baseball's Ten Greatest Games. John Thorn. LC 80-66251. (Illus.). 208p. (gr. 5 up). 1981. 9.95 (ISBN 0-590-07665-5, Four Winds). Schol Bk Serv.
Baseball's Zaniest Stars. Howard Liss. LC 71-146650. (Major League Baseball Library: No. 15). (Illus.). (gr. 5-9). 1971. 2.50 o.p. (ISBN 0-394-82142-4, BYR); PLB 3.69 (ISBN 0-394-92142-9). Random.
Basel. W. Schweizer. 1975. bds. 7.50 (ISBN 0-911268-27-8). Rogers Bk.
Baseline Study of U.S. Industry Solar Exports for Nineteen Seventy-Nine. Bereny et al. 73p. 1981. Repr. of 1980 ed. 35.00 (ISBN 0-89934-080-6). Solar Energy Info.
Basement Nukes: The Consequences of Cheap Weapons of Mass Destruction. Erwin S. Strauss. 1980. pap. 6.95. Loompanics.
Bases of Argument: Ideas in Conflict. Craig R. Smith & David M. Hunsaker. LC 72-173978. (Speech Communication Ser.: No. 17). 1972. pap. 4.50 (ISBN 0-672-61156-2). Bobbs.
Bases of Design. Walter Crane. Ed. by Peter Stansky & Rodney Shewan. LC 76-17756. (Aesthetic Movement & the Arts & Crafts Movement Ser.: Vol. 10). 1977. Repr. of 1898 ed. lib. bdg. 44.00 (ISBN 0-8240-2459-1). Garland Pub.
Bases of Modern Librarianship. C. M. White. 1964. 22.00 (ISBN 0-08-010627-7). Pergamon.
Bases of Tantra Sadhana. Parasurama. Tr. by M. P. Pandit. 52p. (Sanskrit.). 1980. 2.00 (ISBN 0-89744-983-5, Pub. by Dipti Pubns India). Auromere.
Bases of Yoga. Sri Aurobindo. 168p. 1979. pap. 1.75 (ISBN 0-89071-288-3, Pub. by Sri Aurobindo Ashram India). Matagiri.

Basic. 2nd ed. Robert L. Albrecht et al. LC 77-14998. (Self-Teaching Guide Ser.). 1978. pap. text ed. 8.95x (ISBN 0-471-03500-9). Wiley.
BASIC. Steven Lawlor. 1979. pap. text ed. 11.95x (ISBN 0-534-00694-9). Wadsworth Pub.
BASIC. Samuel Maratek. 1975. 13.95 (ISBN 0-12-470450-6); answer bk. 3.00 (ISBN 0-12-470452-2). Acad Pr.
BASIC: A Computer Programming Language with Business & Management Applications. 3rd ed. C. Carl Pegels & R. C. Verkler. 1978. pap. text ed. 12.95 (ISBN 0-8162-6684-0); instr'. manual 1.95 (ISBN 0-8162-6683-2). Holden-Day.
BASIC: A First Course. Robert G. Thompson. (Data Processing Ser.). (Illus.). 352p. 1981. text ed. 13.95 (ISBN 0-675-08057-6); tchr's. manual avail. Merrill.
BASIC: A Hands-on Method. 2nd ed. Herbert C. Peckham. (Illus.). 320p. 1980. pap. text ed. 12.95 (ISBN 0-07-049160-7). McGraw.
BASIC: A Programmed Text. Seymour Hirsch. LC 75-6806. 496p. 1975. text ed. 15.95 (ISBN 0-471-40045-9). Wiley.
BASIC: A Simplified Structural Approach. Nelson et al. 1980. pap. text ed. 12.95 (ISBN 0-8359-0338-9); soln. manual avail. (ISBN 0-8359-0339-7). Reston.
Basic Abstract Algebra. Otto F. Schilling & W. Stephen Piper. 416p. 1975. text ed. 20.95x o.p. (ISBN 0-205-04273-2, 5642736). Allyn.
Basic Accounting. 2nd ed. Calvin Engler. 1969. 8.25 o.p. (ISBN 0-672-96016-8); pap. text ed. 8.95 (ISBN 0-672-96017-6); tchr's manual 5.00 (ISBN 0-672-96018-4); wkbk. 6.60 (ISBN 0-672-96019-2); practice set 6.95 (ISBN 0-672-96020-6). Bobbs.
Basic Accounting, 2 vols. Jeffrey Madura. (Illus.). 1981. pap. text ed. 8.50 (ISBN 0-686-66062-5). Bk. 1 (ISBN 0-916780-16-3). Bk. 2 (ISBN 0-916780-17-1). Set. pap. text ed. 17.00 (ISBN 0-916780-19-8). CES.
Basic Accounting. 2nd ed. J. O. Magee. 352p. 1979. pap. text ed. 11.95x (ISBN 0-7121-0284-1, Pub. by Macdonald & Evans England). Intl Ideas.
Basic Accounting. 3rd ed. Albert Slavin & Isaac Reynolds. LC 74-20045. 1975. text ed. 18.95 (ISBN 0-03-089468-9). Dryden Pr.
Basic Accounting & Budgeting for Nursing Homes. Jerry L. Rhoads. 460p. 1981. 24.95 (ISBN 0-8436-0795-5). CBI Pub.
Basic, Advanced Systematic Substitution Training, Set-AS. Russell E. Mason. 1975. pap. 25.00 (ISBN 0-89533-017-2); incl. tape 12 (ISBN 0-89533-042-3); t-13 (ISBN 0-89533-043-1); t-14 (ISBN 0-89533-044-X); notes (ISBN 0-89533-025-3); tran-ascendance forms H.E.S.T-a set avail. F I Comm.
Basic Advertising. Donald W. Jugenheimer & Gordon E. White. LC 79-12108. (Grid Series in Advertising & Journalism). 1980. text ed. 20.50 (ISBN 0-88244-181-7). Grid Pub.
Basic Advertising Layout Designs. Kenwood Spriggle. wire-o bdg. 50.00 (ISBN 0-938686-05-4). H Spriggle.
Basic Algebra. Marvin Schlichting. 400p. 1980. text ed. 14.95 (ISBN 0-442-25765-1); instr's. manual 2.95 (ISBN 0-442-25767-8). Van Nos Reinhold.
Basic Algebra. new ed. M. Wilcox. (gr. 9-10). 1977. pap. text ed. 12.12 (ISBN 0-201-08573-9, Sch Div); tchr's ed. 15.36 (ISBN 0-201-08574-7). A-W.
Basic Algebra for College Students. Corrinne P. Brase & Charles H. Brase. LC 75-26093. (Illus.). 480p. 1976. text ed. 14.25 (ISBN 0-395-20656-1); options guide & solutions manual 1.75 (ISBN 0-395-20655-3). HM.
Basic Algebra One. Nathan Jacobson. LC 73-22316. (Illus.). 1974. text ed. 23.95x (ISBN 0-7167-0453-6); solutions 2.50x (ISBN 0-7167-1030-7). W H Freeman.
Basic Algebra Two. Nathan Jacobson. LC 73-22316. 1980. 29.95x (ISBN 0-7167-1079-X); answer bk. avail. W H Freeman.
BASIC: An Introduction to Computer Programming Using the BASIC Language. 3rd ed. William F. Sharpe & Nancy L. Jacob. LC 78-72148. (Illus.). 1979. 14.95 (ISBN 0-02-928380-9); pap. text ed. 7.95 (ISBN 0-02-928390-6). Free Pr.
Basic Analytical Chemistry. L. Pataki & E. Zapp. (Analytical Chemistry Ser.: Vol. 2). (Illus.). 1980. 38.00 (ISBN 0-08-023850-5). Pergamon.
Basic Anatomy: A Laboratory Manual: the Human Skeleton, the Cat. 2nd ed. B. L. Allen. (Illus.). 1980. 9.95x (ISBN 0-7167-1091-9). W H Freeman.
Basic Anatomy & Physiology for Radiographers. 2nd ed. M. R. Dean. (Illus.). 1976. 21.00 (ISBN 0-632-00287-5, Blackwell). Mosby.
Basic Anatomy for the Allied Health Professions. Royce L. Montgomery. LC 79-19131. (Illus.). 1980. text ed. 22.75 (ISBN 0-8067-1231-7). Urban & S.
BASIC & Chemistry. Len Soltzberg et al. 1975. pap. text ed. 9.75 (ISBN 0-395-21720-2). HM.
Basic & Clinical Pharmacology of Digitalis. Bernard H. Marks. (Illus.). 344p. 1972. 27.75 (ISBN 0-398-02350-6). C C Thomas.
Basic & Therapeutic Aspects of Perinatal Pharmacology. Ed. by P. L. Morselli et al. LC 74-21981. (Monograph of the Mario Negri Institute of Pharmacological Research). 1975. 37.50 (ISBN 0-89004-016-8). Raven.
Basic Animal Husbandry. John M. Kays. 1958. text ed. 18.95x ref. ed. (ISBN 0-13-056598-9). P-H.
Basic Animal Science. W. T. Berry, Jr. et al. (Illus.). 187p. Repr. wire coil lab. manual 6.95 (ISBN 0-89641-052-8). American Pr.
Basic Animation Stand Techniques. Brian G. Salt. LC 76-40298. 1977. text ed. 26.00 (ISBN 0-08-021368-5). Pergamon.
Basic Appliance Repair, Vol. 1: Dishwashers, Garbage Disposers, Electric Ranges & Ovens. Cliff Porter. (Illus.). 1971. 5.95 o.p. (ISBN 0-8104-0785-X); Set. transparencies 151.15s.p. o.p. (ISBN 0-685-03715-0, C001); transparencies 2.15 ea. o.p. Hayden.
Basic Appliance Repair, Vol. 2: Laundry Equipment - Washers & Dryers. Cliff Porter. (Illus.). 1975. pap. 5.98 o.p. (ISBN 0-8104-5846-2). Hayden.
Basic Approach to Executive Decision Making. Alfred R. Oxenfeldt et al. (Illus.). 1978. 14.95 (ISBN 0-8144-5467-4). Am Mgmt.
Basic Approaches to Group Psychotherapy & Group Counseling. 2nd ed. Ed. by George M. Gazda. (Illus.). 560p. 1979. 21.50 (ISBN 0-398-03212-2). C C Thomas.
Basic Arc Welding. Ivan H. Griffin et al. LC 76-4309. 1977. pap. text ed. 5.00 (ISBN 0-8273-1250-4); instructor's guide 1.00 (ISBN 0-8273-1251-2). Delmar.
Basic Architectural Drawing. Clarence F. Hillary. (Promotion of the Arts Library Bk.). (Illus.). 141p. 1981. 37.45 (ISBN 0-930582-98-5). Gloucester Art.
Basic Arithmetic. Michael Gallo & Charles Kiehl. 1981. write for info. (ISBN 0-8302-0756-2). Goodyear.
Basic Arithmetic. 2nd ed. Robert Moon. (Mathematics Ser.). 1977. pap. text ed. 15.95 (ISBN 0-675-08627-2); cassettes 160.00 (ISBN 0-675-08515-2); 2-6 sets 100.00, 7 or more sets 75.00 (ISBN 0-686-57848-1); instructor's manual 3.95 (ISBN 0-686-67518-5); tests 1 & 2 3.95 ea. Merrill.
Basic Arithmetic. Robert Moon et al. LC 78-144087. 1971. pap. text ed. 14.95 (ISBN 0-675-09230-2); instructor's manual 3.95 (ISBN 0-686-66280-6); test 3.95 (ISBN 0-686-66281-4). Merrill.
Basic Arrythmias. new ed. Gail Walraven. (Illus.). 510p. (Orig.). 1980. pap. text ed. 14.95 (ISBN 0-87619-627-X). R J Brady.
Basic Arts of Financial Management. 2nd ed. Leon Simons. 249p. 1978. text ed. 25.75x (ISBN 0-220-66370-X, Pub. by Busn Bks England). Renouf.
Basic Arts of Management. W. J. Taylor & T. F. Watling. 207p. 1977. text ed. 22.00x (ISBN 0-220-66812-4, Pub. by Busn Bks England). Renouf.
Basic Arts of Marketing. Ray L. Willsmer. 230p. 1976. text ed. 22.00x (ISBN 0-220-66307-6, Pub. by Busn Bks England). Renouf.
Basic Aspects of the Glaucomas. Adnan H. Halasa. (Illus.). 244p. 1972. 19.75 (ISBN 0-398-02529-0). C C Thomas.
Basic Astronavigation. Conrad Dixon. (Illus.). 1979. 8.95 (ISBN 0-229-98579-3, ScribT). Scribner.
Basic Auditing Principles. 5th ed. Arthur W. Holmes & Wayne S. Overmyer. (Illus.). 1976. text ed. 17.95x (ISBN 0-256-01778-6). Irwin.
Basic Background for Test Interpretation. Harley D. Christiansen. (Illus.). 96p. (Orig.). 1981. pap. text ed. 8.95 (ISBN 0-915456-04-4). P Juul Pr.
Basic Bacteriology. 4th ed. Carl Lamanna et al. (Illus.). 1973. 26.50 o.p. (ISBN 0-683-04854-6). Williams & Wilkins.
Basic Band Repertory: British Band Classics from the Conductor's Point of View. Frederick Fennell. 1980. pap. 6.00. Instrumental Co.
Basic BASIC: An Introduction to Computer Programming in BASIC Language. 2nd ed. James S. Coan. (gr. 10 up). 1978. text ed. 13.95x (ISBN 0-8104-5107-7); pap. text ed. 10.50x (ISBN 0-8104-5106-9); tchrs. guide 1.40 (ISBN 0-8104-5108-5). Hayden.
Basic BASIC Programming: Self-Instructional Manual & Text. Anthony P. Peluso et al. (Computer Science Ser). 1971. pap. 13.95 (ISBN 0-201-05845-6). A-W.
Basic Beekeeping. Owen Meyer. 1979. pap. 3.95 o.s.i. (ISBN 0-7225-0477-2). Newcastle Pub.
Basic Beekeeping & Honey Book. Louise G. Hanson & Lily A. Davis. 1977. 10.95 o.p. (ISBN 0-679-50746-9); pap. 6.95 (ISBN 0-679-50817-1). McKay.
Basic Beginner Book. Corley & Steurer. (Speak English! Ser.). (Illus.). 80p. 1980. pap. text ed. 3.95 (ISBN 0-88499-652-2). Inst Mod Lang.
Basic Behavior Modification. Albert Mehrabian. LC 77-85582. (New Vistas in Counseling Ser.: Vol. 9). 1978. 10.95 (ISBN 0-87705-322-7). Human Sci Pr.
Basic Behavioral Statistics. Robert E. Gehring. LC 77-78447. (Illus.). 1978. text ed. 19.95 (ISBN 0-395-24684-9); study guide 6.95 (ISBN 0-395-24683-0); inst. manual 0.65 (ISBN 0-395-25511-2). HM.
Basic Beliefs. (Aglow Bible Study: Bk. 5). 64p. 1974. pap. 1.95 (ISBN 0-930756-09-6, 4220-5). Women's Aglow.
Basic Beliefs of Christmas. Douglas Beyer. 64p. 1981. pap. 3.50 (ISBN 0-8170-0896-9). Judson.
Basic Bible Dictionary: Simplified Descriptions of Bible People. Velda Matthews. (Illus.). (gr. 4 up). 1978. pap. 1.95 (ISBN 0-87239-250-3, 2781). Standard Pub.
Basic Bible Dictionary: Simplified Descriptions of Bible Places. Velda Matthews. (Illus.). (gr. 4 up). 1978. pap. 1.95 (ISBN 0-87239-254-6, 2782). Standard Pub.
Basic Bible Dictionary: Simplified Definitions of Bible Words. Velda Matthews & Ray Beard. (Illus.). (gr. 4 up). 1977. pap. 1.95 (ISBN 0-87239-249-X, 2780). Standard Pub.
Basic Bible Doctrine. Millard F. Day. 1953. pap. 1.50 (ISBN 0-8024-0239-9). Moody.
Basic Bible Study for New Christians. Keith L. Brooks. (Teach Yourself the Bible Ser). 1961. pap. 1.75 (ISBN 0-8024-0478-2). Moody.
Basic Bibliography on Experimental Design in Marketing. David M. Gardner & Russell W. Belk. LC 80-19563. (Bibliography Ser.: No. 37). 59p. 1980. pap. 6.00 (ISBN 0-87757-142-2). Am Mktg.
Basic Biogeography. Nigel V. Pears. LC 77-8108. (Illus.). 1977. pap. text ed. 12.95x (ISBN 0-582-48401-4). Longman.
Basic Biology for the Tropics, 2 vols. R. H. Stone. (Illus.). (gr. 9). 1973. text ed. 6.95 ea. Vol. 1 (ISBN 0-521-08233-1). Vol. 2 (ISBN 0-521-08612-4). Cambridge U Pr.
Basic Biomechanics of the Skeletal System. Ed. by Victor H. Frankel & Margareta Nordin. LC 79-24593. (Illus.). 303p. 1980. text ed. 20.00 (ISBN 0-8121-0708-X). Lea & Febiger.
Basic Biostatistics in Medicine & Epidemiology. Alfred A. Rimm et al. 352p. 1980. pap. text ed. 16.50x (ISBN 0-8385-0528-7). ACC.
Basic Black with Pearls. Helen Weinzweig. (Anansi Fiction Ser.: No. 41). 136p. (Orig.). 1980. pap. 7.95 (ISBN 0-88784-079-5, Pub. by Hse Anansi Pr Canada). U of Toronto Pr.
Basic Black with Pearls. Helen Weinzweig. LC 80-22304. 135p. 1981. 7.95 (ISBN 0-688-00397-4). Morrow.
Basic Blackjack Betting. Charles Einstein. (Gambler's Book Shelf). (Orig.). 1980. pap. 2.95 (ISBN 0-89650-619-3). Gamblers.
Basic Blueprint Reading & Sketching. C. Thomas et al. LC 76-56490. 1978. 6.60 (ISBN 0-8273-2050-7); instructor's guide 1.60 (ISBN 0-8273-2051-5). Delmar.
Basic Boat Building. Richard Frisbee. LC 74-6890. (Illus.). 288p. 1975. 6.95 (ISBN 0-8092-8390-5); pap. 6.95 o.p. (ISBN 0-8092-8342-5). Contemp Bks.
Basic Bodywork & Painting. 5th, rev. ed. Ed. by Jay Storer. LC 73-79967. (Illus.). 192p. (Orig.). 1981. pap. 4.95 (ISBN 0-8227-5057-0). Petersen Pub.
Basic Bone Radiology. Harry Griffiths. 182p. 1980. text ed. 15.50x (ISBN 0-8385-0535-X). ACC.
Basic Book of Antiques. George Michael. LC 74-77072. (Illus.). 1979. pap. 5.95 (ISBN 0-668-04712-7). Arco.
Basic Book of Business. John R. Klug. 350p. 1980. Repr. of 1977 ed. 50.00 (ISBN 0-932648-16-9). Boardroom.
Basic Book of Drafting. Paul I. Wallach. (Illus.). 1979. 5.95 (ISBN 0-8269-1170-6). Am Technical.
Basic Book of Greenhouse Growing. W. E. Shewell-Cooper. (Illus.). 1978. 15.00 (ISBN 0-214-20499-5). Transatlantic.
Basic Bookeeping. J. O. Magee. 256p. (Orig.). 1979. pap. text ed. 10.00x (ISBN 0-7121-0274-4, Pub. by Macdonald & Evans England). Intl Ideas.
Basic Botany. Claire Skellern & Paul Rogers. (Illus.). 208p. (Orig.). 1977. pap. text ed. 9.95x (ISBN 0-7121-0255-8, Pub. by Macdonald & Evans England). Intl Ideas.
Basic Bridge. (Purse Books). pap. 0.49 o.s.i. (ISBN 0-440-60814-7). Dell.
Basic Business & Professional Speech Communication. Ted Frank & David Ray. (Speech Communication Ser.). (Illus.). 1979. pap. text ed. 14.95 (ISBN 0-13-057273-X). P-H.
Basic Business Communication. Raymond V. Lesikar. 1979. 16.95x (ISBN 0-256-02141-4). Irwin.
Basic Business Communications. Robert M. Archer & R. Ames. 1971. text ed. 16.95 (ISBN 0-13-057299-3). P-H.
Basic Business Facts: Evaluating Money Resources. William G. Moore, Sr. 1980. pap. text ed. 1.99 (ISBN 0-934488-02-9). Williams Ent.
Basic Business Finance: Text. Pearson Hunt et al. 1974. text ed. 17.95x (ISBN 0-256-01553-8). Irwin.
Basic Business Finance: Text & Cases. 4th ed. Pearson Hunt et al. 1971. text ed. 19.95x (ISBN 0-256-00209-6). Irwin.
Basic Business Logistics. Ronald H. Ballou. (Illus.). 1978. ref. ed. 19.95 (ISBN 0-13-057364-7). P-H.
Basic Business Mathematics. John Ernest & Charlotte Ernest. 1977. text ed. 13.95 (ISBN 0-02-472610-9). Macmillan.
Basic Business Statistics: Concepts & Applications. M. Berenson & D. Levine. 1979. 21.00 (ISBN 0-13-057596-8); studyguide & wkbk. 7.50 (ISBN 0-13-057588-7). P-H.
Basic Calculus. Darel W. Hardy. LC 74-83957. (Contemporary Undergraduate Mathematics Ser.). (Illus.). 1975. text ed. 14.95 o.p. (ISBN 0-8185-0138-3); instructor's manual avail. o.p. (ISBN 0-685-52375-6). Brooks-Cole.
Basic Calculus with Applications. Donald Williams & Thomas J. Woods. 1979. text ed. 19.95x (ISBN 0-534-00685-X). Wadsworth Pub.
Basic Carburetion & Fuel Systems. 6th, rev. ed. Ed. by Spence Murray. LC 68-6315. (Petersen's Basic Repair & Maintenance Manuals Ser.). (Illus.). (gr. 9-12). 1977. pap. 6.95 (ISBN 0-8227-5013-9). Petersen Pub.
Basic Carpentry. John Capotosto. (Illus.). 544p. 1975. 15.95 o.p. (ISBN 0-87909-064-2). Reston.
Basic Carpentry Illustrated. Sunset Editors. LC 72-77140. (Illus.). 88p. 1972. pap. 4.95 (ISBN 0-376-01014-2, Sunset Bks). Sunset-Lane.
Basic Carrier Telephony. 3rd, rev. ed. David Talley. (Illus.). (gr. 10 up). 1977. pap. 8.95 (ISBN 0-8104-5848-9); exam 0.50 (ISBN 0-8104-0727-2); final exam 0.50 (ISBN 0-8104-0728-0). Hayden.
Basic Characteristics Typical of Women Criminals. Cesare Lombroso. (Library of Scientific Psychology). (Illus.). 1981. 74.95 (ISBN 0-89901-032-6). Found Class Reprints.
Basic Chassis, Suspension & Brakes. 4th rev. ed. Ed. by Spencer Murray. LC 74-78893. (Petersen's Basic Repair & Maintenance Manuals Ser.). 1978. pap. 6.95 (ISBN 0-8227-5021-X). Petersen Pub.
Basic Chemical Research in Government Laboratories. Committee For The Survey Of Chemistry. 1966. pap. 3.75 (ISBN 0-685-17304-6). Natl Acad Pr.
Basic Chemical Thermodynamics. 2nd ed. E. Brian Smith. (Oxford Chemistry Ser.). (Illus.). 1977. 13.95x (ISBN 0-19-855507-5); pap. 7.95x (ISBN 0-19-855508-3). Oxford U Pr.
Basic Chemistry. Roger D. Barry. LC 74-79831. (Allied Health Ser). 1975. pap. text ed. 9.65 (ISBN 0-672-61376-X); lab manual 6.35 (ISBN 0-672-61377-8); answer key 3.33 (ISBN 0-672-61432-4). Bobbs.
Basic Chemistry. 3rd ed. Stewart Brooks & Cynthia Norton. LC 75-37515. (Illus.). 102p. 1976. pap. 8.50 (ISBN 0-8016-0797-3). Mosby.
Basic Chemistry. 2nd ed. William S. Seese & Grudo H. Daub. (Illus.). 1977. text ed. 18.95 (ISBN 0-13-057513-5); students guide 6.95 (ISBN 0-13-057539-9); lab. experiments 8.95 (ISBN 0-13-057547-X). P-H.
Basic Chemistry. 3rd ed. William S. Seese & Guido H. Daub. 608p. 1981. text ed. 19.95 (ISBN 0-13-057679-4). P-H.
Basic Chemistry Experiments for the Life Sciences. Edward H. Frieden. 1977. spiral bdg. o.p. 3.95 o.p. (ISBN 0-88252-066-0). Paladin Hse.
Basic Chemistry of Life. Milton Toporek. LC 80-11980. (Illus.). 522p. 1980. pap. text ed. 16.95 (ISBN 0-8016-5002-X). Mosby.
Basic Chess Openings. Raymond Edwards. (Chess Handbooks). 144p. 1976. pap. 4.95 (ISBN 0-7100-8296-7). Routledge & Kegan.
Basic Chess Openings. rev. ed. Raymond Edwards. (Routledge Chess Handbooks Ser.: No. 4). (Illus., Orig.). 1981. pap. price not set (ISBN 0-7100-0853-8). Routledge & Kegan.
Basic Christian Ethics. Paul Ramsey. LC 78-56925. 424p. 1980. pap. text ed. 9.50x (ISBN 0-226-70383-5). U of Chicago Pr.
Basic Christian Maturity Leaders Guide. 1975. pap. 2.50 (ISBN 0-89283-025-5). Servant.
Basic Circuit Analysis. Gerald J. Kirwin & Stephen Grodzinsky. LC 79-88449. (Illus.). 1980. text ed. 26.50 (ISBN 0-395-28488-0); solutions manual 0.75 (ISBN 0-395-28489-9). HM.
Basic Circuit Theory with Digital Computations. L. P. Huelsman. (Illus.). 1972. ref. ed. 27.95 (ISBN 0-13-057430-9). P-H.
Basic Circulatory Physiology. Daniel Richardson. 1976. text ed. 13.95 (ISBN 0-316-74422-0, Little Med Div). Little.

Basic Civil Procedure: Cases & Materials. Jonathan M. Landers & James A. Martin. 1196p. 1981. price not set. Little.

Basic Classroom Skills Through Games. Irene W. Bell & Jeanne E. Wieckert. LC 80-351. 1980. 17.50 (ISBN 0-87287-207-6). Libs Unl.

Basic Clinical Physiology. 3rd ed. J. H. Green. (Illus.). 1979. pap. text ed. 10.95x (ISBN 0-19-263331-7). Oxford U Pr.

Basic Clinical Surgery for Nurses & Medical Students. 2nd ed. Ed. by John McFarland. LC 80-40150. (Illus.). 1980. 31.95 (ISBN 0-407-80101-4). Butterworths.

Basic Coastal Engineering. Robert M. Sorensen. LC 77-29256. (Ocean Engineering Ser.). 1978. 27.50 (ISBN 0-471-81370-2, Pub. by Wiley-Interscience). Wiley.

Basic COBOL Programming: Self-Instructional Manual & Text. L. M. Spitzbarth. 1970. pap. 13.95 (ISBN 0-201-07133-9). A-W.

Basic College Issues. Alan Kraus. (Orig.). 1968. pap. text ed. 3.95 o.p. (ISBN 0-394-30339-3, RanC). Random.

Basic Color Terms: Their Universality & Evolution. Brent Berlin & Paul Kay. LC 70-76541. (Illus.). 1969. 15.75x (ISBN 0-520-01442-1). U of Cal Pr.

Basic Community in the African Churches. Marie-France P. Jassy. Tr. by Sr. Jeanne M. Lyons from Fr. LC 72-93342. Orig. Title: Communaute De Base Dans les Eglises Africaines. 195p. 1973. pap. 4.95x o.p. (ISBN 0-88344-025-3). Orbis Bks.

Basic Complex Analysis. Jerrold E. Marsden. LC 72-89894. (Illus.). 1973. text ed. 22.95x (ISBN 0-7167-0451-X). W H Freeman.

Basic Computer Logic. John Scott. LC 80-5074. (The Lexington Books Series in Computer Science). 1981. write for info. (ISBN 0-669-03706-0). Lexington Bks.

Basic Computer Programming for Statistics: A Manual. Richard G. Fegan & Susan L. Brosche. 1979. pap. 5.95 o.p. (ISBN 0-13-057950-5). P-H.

Basic Computer Programs for the Home. Charles Sternberg. 336p. 1979. pap. 9.95 (ISBN 0-8104-5154-9). Hayden.

Basic Computer Programs in Science & Engineering. Jules H. Gilder. 256p. 1980. pap. 9.95 (ISBN 0-8104-0761-2). Hayden.

Basic Concepts for Parents: Parenthood in a Free Nation, Vol. 1. Ethel Kawin. (Illus.). 1969. pap. 2.00 (ISBN 0-931682-05-3). Purdue Univ Bks.

Basic Concepts in Anatomy & Physiology: A Programmed Presentation. 4th ed. Catherine P. Anthony & Gary A. Thibodeau. LC 79-19392. (Illus.). 1979. pap. text ed. 10.50 (ISBN 0-8016-0260-2). Mosby.

Basic Concepts in Music. 2nd ed. Gary M. Martin. 288p. 1980. pap. text ed. 12.95x (ISBN 0-534-00761-9). Wadsworth Pub.

Basic Concepts in Reading Instruction. 2nd ed. Arnold Burron & Amos L. Claybaugh. (Elementary Education Ser.). 1977. pap. text ed. 8.95 (ISBN 0-675-08539-X). Merrill.

Basic Concepts in Relativity & Early Quantum Theory. R. Resnick. 1972. pap. 11.95 (ISBN 0-471-71703-7). Wiley.

Basic Concepts in Sociology. Max Weber. 1980. pap. 3.95 (ISBN 0-8065-0304-1). Lyle Stuart.

Basic Concepts of Chemistry. Leo J. Malone. LC 80-19501. 480p. 1981. text ed. 16.95 (ISBN 0-471-06381-9). Wiley.

Basic Concepts of Chemistry. 2nd ed. Alan Sherman et al. LC 79-88447. (Illus.). 1980. text ed. 13.25 (ISBN 0-395-28153-9); instrs' manual 1.00 (ISBN 0-395-28154-7); study guide 6.25 (ISBN 0-395-28702-2); lab experiments 9.50 (ISBN 0-395-28155-5). HM.

Basic Concepts of Geometry. Walter Prenowitz & M. Jordan. (Illus.). 1965. text ed. 24.95x (ISBN 0-471-00451-0). Wiley.

Basic Concepts of Helping: A Wholistic Approach. Carolyn C. Hames & Dayle Joseph. 260p. 1980. pap. text ed. 9.50x (ISBN 0-8385-0558-9). ACC.

Basic Concepts of Mathematics for Elementary Teachers. Roy Dubisch. LC 76-1742. 1977. text ed. 16.95 o.p. (ISBN 0-201-01167-0); instr's manual 2.50 o.p. (ISBN 0-201-01168-9). A-W.

Basic Concepts of Mathematics for Elementary Teachers. 2nd ed. Roy Dubisch. LC 80-19446. (Mathematics Ser.). (Illus.). 483p. 1981. write for info. (ISBN 0-201-03170-1). A-W.

Basic Concepts of Measurement. Brian D. Ellis. LC 65-19150. 1968. 42.50 (ISBN 0-521-04889-3); pap. 14.95x (ISBN 0-521-09556-5). Cambridge U Pr.

Basic Concepts of Physics. 2nd ed. Arthur Beiser. LC 70-163762. 1972. text ed. 18.95 (ISBN 0-201-00491-7). A-W.

Basic Concepts of Structural Analysis. F. Beaufait. 1977. text ed. 27.95 (ISBN 0-13-058347-2). P-H.

Basic Concepts of Structural Analysis. A. Hall & A. P. Kabailo. LC 77-8289. 1977. 21.95 (ISBN 0-470-99213-1). Halsted Pr.

Basic Concrete Construction Practices. Portland Cement Association. LC 74-28253. (National Concrete Technology Curriculum Project Ser). 480p. 1975. text ed. 29.95 (ISBN 0-471-67430-3); instructor's guide avail. (ISBN 0-471-67436-2). Wiley.

Basic Considerations in Mental Retardation: A Preliminary Report, Vol. 4. GAP Committee on Mental Retardation. LC 62-2872. (Report No. 43). 1959. pap. 2.00 (ISBN 0-87318-056-9). Adv Psychiatry.

Basic Construction Blueprint Reading. Mark W. Huth. 144p. 1980. 9.95 (ISBN 0-442-23874-6). Van Nos Reinhold.

Basic Construction Blueprint Reading. Mark W. Huth. LC 79-50919. (gr. 9). 1980. pap. text ed. 7.20 (ISBN 0-8273-1865-0); instructor's guide 1.45 (ISBN 0-8273-1866-9). Delmar.

Basic Construction Materials. 2nd ed. Charles Herubin & Theodore Marotta. 1981. text ed. 17.50 (ISBN 0-8359-0362-1); solutions manual avail. (ISBN 0-8359-0363-X). Reston.

Basic Corporate Taxation. 3rd ed. Douglas A. Kahn. LC 80-27245. 531p. 1980. pap. text ed. 18.95 (ISBN 0-8299-2114-1). West Pub.

Basic Correlative Echocardiography Technique & Interpretation. S. Kra. 1977. spiral bdg. 16.00 o.p. (ISBN 0-87488-978-2). Med Exam.

Basic Corrosion & Oxidation. J. M. West. 247p. 1981. 69.95 (ISBN 0-470-27080-2). Halsted Pr.

Basic Cost Accounting Concepts. Henry R. Anderson & Mitchell H. Raiborn. LC 76-12017. (Illus.). 720p. 1977. text ed. 19.95 (ISBN 0-395-20646-4); instructor's manual with solutions 7.25 (ISBN 0-395-20648-0); test bank 3.25 (ISBN 0-395-20649-9). HM.

Basic Course in Gulf Arabic. Hamdi Qafisheh. 16.00x (ISBN 0-686-63543-4). Intl Bk Ctr.

Basic Course in Statistics. G. M. Clarke & D. Cooke. LC 78-10749. 1979. pap. text ed. 19.95 (ISBN 0-470-26527-2). Halsted Pr.

Basic Course of Practical Metalwork. John R. Bedford. (gr. 9-12). pap. text ed. 8.95 (ISBN 0-7195-0079-6). Transatlantic.

Basic Crafts. Lindbeck et al. (gr. 7-12). 1979. text ed. 11.00 (ISBN 0-87002-275-X); student guide 2.60 (ISBN 0-87002-296-2). Bennett IL.

Basic Criminal Investigations. U.S. Army. (Illus.). 1977. pap. 4.00 o.p. (ISBN 0-87364-086-1). Paladin Ent.

Basic Criminal Law, Cases & Materials. 2nd ed. George E. Dix & M. Michael Sharlot. 650p. 1980. text ed. 17.95 (ISBN 0-8299-0318-6); instrs.' manual avail. (ISBN 0-8299-0588-X). West Pub.

Basic Criminal Procedure, Cases, Comments & Questions. 5th ed. Yale Kamisar et al. LC 52-52950. (American Casebook Ser.). 920p. 1980. pap. text ed. 13.95 (ISBN 0-8299-2109-5). West Pub.

Basic Data on Health Care Needs of Adults 25-74 Years of Age: United States, 1971-75. Wilbur C. Hadden. Ed. by Klaudia Cox. (Ser. 11, No. 218). 50p. 1980. pap. text ed. 1.75 (ISBN 0-8406-0197-2). Natl Ctr Health Stats.

Basic Data on Spirometry in Adults Twenty-Five to Seventy-Four Years of Age: United States 1971-75. Richard J. O'Brien & Terence A. Drizd. Ed. by Klaudia Cox. (Ser. 11, No. 222). 50p. Date not set. pap. text ed. 1.75 (ISBN 0-8406-0205-7). Natl Ctr Health Stats.

Basic Data Processing. Janet K. Budzik & Clarence A. Sims. 1972. text ed. 16.95 (ISBN 0-201-00775-4). A-W.

Basic Decoding Skillsbook. Jerome Rosner. (gr. k-3). 1981. 10.80 (ISBN 0-8027-9128-X). Walker & Co.

Basic Design & Utilization of Instructional Television. 2nd ed. Kenneth Coffelt & Bob Combs. (Bridges for Ideas Ser.). 1981. pap. text ed. 14.95 (ISBN 0-913648-13-2). U Tex Austin Film Lib.

Basic Design: Principles & Practice. Kenneth F. Bates. LC 74-25356. (Funk & W Bk.). (Illus.). 176p. 1975. pap. 3.95 o.p. (ISBN 0-308-10151-0, F-110, TYC-T). T Y Crowell.

Basic Developments in Fluid Dynamics, 2 Vols. Ed. by Maurice Holt. Vol. 1. 1965. 55.25 (ISBN 0-12-354001-1); Vol. 2, 1968. 36.50 (ISBN 0-12-354002-X). Acad Pr.

Basic Digital Electronics: Understanding Number Systems, Boolean Algebra & Logical Circuits. Ray Ryan. LC 74-14326. (Illus.). 1975. pap. 7.95 (ISBN 0-8306-3728-1, 728). TAB Bks.

Basic Digital Electronics with MSI Applications. John A. Dempsey. LC 75-9009. 320p. 1976. text ed. 20.95 (ISBN 0-201-01478-5). A-W.

Basic Doctrines of the Bible. A. Schuetze. 1969. pap. 2.50 (ISBN 0-8100-0016-4). Northwest Pub.

Basic Documents, Vol. 1. 92p. 1979. 16.50 (IMCO). Unipub.

Basic Documents of Human Rights. 2nd ed. Ed. by Ian Brownlie. 450p. 1981. 67.50 (ISBN 0-19-876124-4); pap. 24.95 (ISBN 0-19-876125-2). Oxford U Pr.

Basic Dog Training. Miller Watson. (Illus.). 1979. 2.95 (ISBN 0-87666-673-X, KW-022). TFH Pubns.

Basic Double Weave Theory. Sara Farrar. 1980. 4.95 (ISBN 0-686-27271-4). Robin & Russ.

Basic Drafting. Feirer & Lindbeck. (gr. 9-12). 1978. 6.00 (ISBN 0-87002-287-3); pap. 4.32 (ISBN 0-87002-273-3); activities for basic drafting 2.64 (ISBN 0-87002-306-3). Bennett IL.

Basic Drafting Problems. Lawrence E. Gerevas. 1972. pap. 7.30 o.p. (ISBN 0-672-97612-9); pap. 5.00 answer bk o.p. (ISBN 0-672-97613-7). Bobbs.

Basic Drafting Technology. 2nd ed. Elmer A. Rotmans et al. LC 78-50424. (gr. 8). 1980. pap. text ed. 18.00 (ISBN 0-8273-1293-8); instr's. guide 2.25 (ISBN 0-8273-1294-6). Delmar.

Basic Drama Projects. rev. ed. Fran A. Tanner. 1977. lib. bdg. 6.60 (ISBN 0-931054-00-1). Clark Pub.

Basic Drawing for Biology Students. Emil G. Bethke. (Illus.). 100p. 1969. 10.75 (ISBN 0-398-00148-0). C C Thomas.

Basic Driver Education. James S. Bonner et al. (gr. 7-12). 1966. pap. text ed. 3.25x o.p. (ISBN 0-8134-1125-4, 1125); tchrs' manual 3.25x o.p. (ISBN 0-8134-1126-2, 1126); study cards 6.95x o.p. (ISBN 0-8134-1339-7, 1339). Interstate.

Basic Drug Calculations for Nurses. Meta Brown. LC 79-10785. 1979. pap. 9.50 (ISBN 0-8016-4488-7). Mosby.

Basic Earth Science. John Tomikel. LC 80-66211. (Earth Science Ser.: No. 1). (Illus.). 166p. (Orig.). (gr. 9-12). 1981. pap. 6.00x (ISBN 0-910042-38-1). Allegheny.

Basic Econometrics: An Introductory Text for Economists. M. S. Common. LC 76-7466. (Modern Economics Ser.). (Illus.). 1976. pap. text ed. 16.95x (ISBN 0-582-44670-8). Longman.

Basic Economics. 2nd ed. Edwin G. Dolan. 736p. 1980. text ed. 20.95 (ISBN 0-03-050356-6). Dryden Pr.

Basic Economics. 4th ed. Rudolph W. Trenton. 1978. pap. text ed. 14.95 (ISBN 0-13-059139-4). P-H.

Basic Economics for Conservative Democrats. Lyndon H. LaRouche, Jr. LC 80-5684. (Illus.). 172p. (Orig.). 1980. pap. 3.95 (ISBN 0-933488-04-1). New Benjamin.

Basic Electric Circuit Analysis. David E. Johnson et al. LC 77-24210. (Illus.). 1978. ref. 27.95x (ISBN 0-13-060137-3). P-H.

Basic Electric Circuits. 2nd ed. A. M. Brookes. LC 75-8774. 368p. 1975. text ed. 27.00 (ISBN 0-08-018310-7); pap. text ed. 13.25 (ISBN 0-08-018309-3). Pergamon.

Basic Electric Power Engineering. Olle I. Elgerd. LC 76-1751. (Electrical Engineering Ser.). 1977. text ed. 24.95 (ISBN 0-201-01717-2); sol. man. avail. (ISBN 0-201-01918-3). A-W.

Basic Electrical Engineering. 5th ed. A. E. Fitzgerald et al. (Electrical Engineering Ser.). (Illus.). 832p. 1981. text ed. 28.95x (ISBN 0-07-021154-X); write for info solutions manual (ISBN 0-07-021155-8). McGraw.

Basic Electrical Engineering. Robert H. Nau. LC 58-5633. 1958. 16.95 (ISBN 0-471-07212-5); instr's manual avail. (ISBN 0-471-07582-5). Wiley.

Basic Electrical Power Distribution, 2 Vols. rev. 2nd ed. Anthony J. Pansini. (Illus.). 1971. pap. 6.75 ea.; Vol. 1. pap. (ISBN 0-8104-0818-X); Vol. 2. pap. (ISBN 0-8104-0819-8); exam set vol. 1 0.30 (ISBN 0-8104-0821-X); exam set vol. 2 0.30 (ISBN 0-8104-0822-8). Hayden.

Basic Electrical Power Transformers. Anthony J. Pansini. 1976. pap. 6.75 (ISBN 0-8104-0020-0); final exam 0.30 (ISBN 0-8104-0600-4). Hayden.

Basic Electrical Power Transmission. Anthony J. Pansini. (Illus.). 128p. 1975. pap. 7.50 (ISBN 0-8104-0598-0); final exam 0.30 (ISBN 0-8104-0599-7). Hayden.

Basic Electricity. Luis E. Figueredo. 1980. pap. text ed. 14.95 (ISBN 0-89669-053-9). Collegium Bk Pubs.

Basic Electricity. 2nd ed. W. M. Gibson. LC 76-7398. 1976. pap. text ed. 11.50x (ISBN 0-582-44181-1). Longman.

Basic Electricity. 4th ed. A. Marcus & W. Marcus. 1973. 19.96 (ISBN 0-13-060152-7). P-H.

Basic Electricity. Miller. (gr. 9-12). 1978. 6.00 (ISBN 0-87002-288-1); pap. 4.32 (ISBN 0-87002-276-8). Bennett IL.

Basic Electricity. Charles W. Ryan. LC 76-4031. (Self-Teaching Guides Ser.). 1976. pap. text ed. 7.95 (ISBN 0-471-74787-4). Wiley.

Basic Electricity. U. S. Navy (Bureau of Naval Personnel) 1960. pap. 6.50 (ISBN 0-486-20973-3). Dover.

Basic Electricity, 5 Vols. rev. ed. Van Valkenburgh et al. (Illus.). 1978. combined ed. 25.15 (ISBN 0-8104-0881-3); Set. pap. 29.25 (ISBN 0-8104-0875-9); pap. 5.85 ea.; Vol. 1, Rev. Ed. pap. (ISBN 0-8104-0876-7); Vol. 2, Rev. Ed. pap. (ISBN 0-8104-0877-5); Vol. 3, Rev. Ed. pap. (ISBN 0-8104-0878-3). Vol. 5,rev. pap. (ISBN 0-8104-0880-5). Hayden.

Basic Electricity, Vol. 4. rev. ed. Van Valkenburgh, Nooger & Neville, Inc. (Illus.). 1978. pap. 5.85 (ISBN 0-8104-0879-1). Hayden.

Basic Electricity - Electronics. Training & Retraining Inc. LC 63-23001. 1968. Bk 1. 12.10 o.p. (ISBN 0-672-20711-7); Bk 2. 12.10 o.p. (ISBN 0-672-20712-5); tchr's guide 6.67 o.p. (ISBN 0-672-20174-7). Bobbs.

Basic Electricity- Electronics, Vol. 1: Basic Principles. 2nd ed. Training & Retraining, Inc. LC 80-5004. 1980. pap. 6.95 o.p. (ISBN 0-672-21501-2). Bobbs.

Basic Electricity & DC Circuits. 2nd ed. Ralph A. Oliva & Charles W. Dale. LC 79-92192. (Basic Electricity Ser.). (Illus.). 924p. 1980. text ed. 19.95 (ISBN 0-89512-034-8). Tex Instr Inc.

Basic Electricity Electronics, 5 vols. 2nd ed. Training & Retraining Inc. Incl. Vol. 1. Basic Principles. LC 80-50045. 6.95 (ISBN 0-672-21501-2); Vol. 2. How AC & DC Circuits Work. LC 63-23002 (ISBN 0-672-20168-2, 20168); Vol. 3. Understanding Tube & Transistor Circuits. LC 64-14336 (ISBN 0-672-20169-0, 20169); Vol. 4. Understanding & Using Test Instruments. LC 64-14337 (ISBN 0-672-20170-4, 20170); Vol. 5. Motors & Generators - How They Work. LC 64-14338. pap. (ISBN 0-672-20171-2, 20171). (YA) 1966. pap. 5.50 ea.; pap. 26.95 set (ISBN 0-672-21740-6, 21740). Sams.

Basic Electricity for Appliances. Ed. by A. Ross Sabin. (Illus.). 255p. (gr. 11). 1973. 20.00 (ISBN 0-938336-00-2). Whirlpool.

Basic Electricity for Electronics. Richard Blitzer. LC 73-20102. 727p. 1974. text ed. 21.95 (ISBN 0-471-08160-4). Wiley.

Basic Electromagnetic Fields. Herbert P. Neff, Jr. (Illus.). 608p. Date not set. text ed. 28.50 scp (ISBN 0-06-044785-0, HarpC). Har-Row.

Basic Electronic & Electrical Drafting. James D. Bethune. (Illus.). 1980. text ed. 17.95 (ISBN 0-13-060301-5). P-H.

Basic Electronic Switching for Telephone Systems. David Tally. 1975. pap. 8.35 (ISBN 0-8104-5808-X); exam set 0.80 (ISBN 0-8104-0591-1); final exam 0.30 (ISBN 0-8104-0594-6). Hayden.

Basic Electronics. new ed. Don Carper. (Technology Ser). (Illus.). 576p. 1975. text ed. 21.95x (ISBN 0-675-08779-1); instructor's manual 3.95 (ISBN 0-686-67095-7). Merrill.

Basic Electronics. Glade Wilcox. LC 60-7871. 412p. 1960. 12.50 o.p. (ISBN 0-685-72304-6, Pub. by HR&W). Krieger.

Basic Electronics Course. Norman H. Crowhurst. LC 75-178692. 1972. 11.95 (ISBN 0-8306-2588-7); pap. 9.95 (ISBN 0-8306-1588-1, 588). TAB Bks.

Basic, Elementary Systematic Substitution Training, Set-ES. Russell E. Mason. 1973. pap. 25.00 (ISBN 0-89533-015-6); Relaxation Training, Substitution Training incl.; tape-1 (ISBN 0-89533-030-X); t-4 (ISBN 0-686-67261-5); t-5 (ISBN 0-89533-035-0). F I Comm.

Basic Engine Hot Rodding. 2nd ed. Ed. by Spence Murray. LC 75-181330. (Petersen's Enthusiasts Ser.). (Illus.). 1975. pap. 4.95 o.p. (ISBN 0-8227-0097-2). Petersen Pub.

Basic Engineering Craft Activities. Savage. 1980. pap. text ed. write for info. (ISBN 0-408-00568-8). Butterworths.

Basic Engineering Elements, 14 vols. Incl. Vol. 1. Reading Engineering Drawings; Vol. 2. Limits & Fits; Vol. 3. Calculations; Vol. 4. Micrometers; Vol. 5. Linear, Bore, Slip & Vernier Gauges; Vol. 6. Ferrous & Non-Ferrous Metals; Vol. 7. Drills, Reamers & Contebores; Vol. 8. Boring Bars & Heads; Vol. 9. Turning Tools; Vol. 10. Thread Cutting; Vol. 11. Screwed Joints; Vol. 12. Speeds & Feeds; Vol. 13. Coolant Equipment; Vol. 14. Safety. (Illus.). 1978. Set. 31.50x (ISBN 0-685-91099-7). Intl Ideas.

Basic Engineering Principles. James A. Merkel. (Illus.). 1974. pap. 15.00 (ISBN 0-87055-301-1). AVI.

Basic Engineering Sciences & Structural Engineering for Engineer-in-Training Examinations. H. Jack Apfelbaum & Walter O. Ottesen. Ed. by Lawrence J. Hollander. (Professional Engineering Examinations Ser.). (Illus.). 1970. 23.95 (ISBN 0-8104-5712-1). Hayden.

Basic English Revisited: A Student Handbook. 4th ed. Patrick Sebranek & Verne Meyer. (Illus.). (gr. 7-12). 1980. pap. text ed. 3.00 (ISBN 0-686-27693-0). Basic Eng Rev.

Basic English Usage: The Parts of Speech. Frank V. Mooney & Cleveland A. Thomas. (Illus.). (gr. 7-12). 1962. pap. text ed. 37.80 (ISBN 0-89290-116-0, A133-SA). Soc for Visual.

Basic English Usage: The Sentence. Frank V. Mooney & Cleveland A. Thomas. (Illus.). (gr. 7-12). 1964. pap. text ed. 49.50 (ISBN 0-89290-117-9, A133SB). Soc for Visual.

Basic Equitation. Jean Licart. (Illus.). pap. 6.10 (ISBN 0-85131-202-0, Dist. by Sporting Book Center). J A Allen.

Basic Exercises in Algebra & Trigonometry. J. Richard Lux & Richard S. Pieters. (Illus.). 365p. (Orig.). (gr. 10-12). 1979. pap. text ed. 5.50x (ISBN 0-88334-122-0). Ind Sch Pr.

Basic Exercises in Immunochemistry: A Laboratory Manual. A. Nowotny. (Illus.). 1969. 22.60 o.p. (ISBN 0-387-04666-6). Springer-Verlag.

Basic Experimental Chemistry: A Laboratory Manual for Beginning Students. rev. ed. Christian Anderson & J. L. Hawes. 1971. pap. 9.95 (ISBN 0-8053-0222-0). Benjamin-Cummings.

Basic Facts About Colitis. S. J. Goulston & V. J. McGovern. (Illus.). 144p. 1981. 25.00 (ISBN 0-08-026862-5); pap. 11.20 (ISBN 0-08-026861-7). Pergamon.

Basic Facts About the United Nations. 133p. 1980. pap. 1.95 (ISBN 0-686-68944-5, UN80/1/5, UN). Unipub.

Basic Farm Machinery. 3rd ed. J. M. Shippen et al. (Illus.). 1980. 52.00 (ISBN 0-08-024912-4); pap. 16.00 (ISBN 0-08-024911-6). Pergamon.

Basic Film Technique. Ken Daley. (Media Manual Series). (Illus.). 160p. 1980. pap. 9.95 (ISBN 0-240-51016-X). Focal Pr.

Basic Finance. Mayo. 1978. 19.95 (ISBN 0-7216-6209-9). Dryden Pr.

Basic Financial Management. John D. Martin et al. (Illus.). 1979. ref. 20.95 (ISBN 0-13-060541-7); study guide 8.95 (ISBN 0-13-060558-1). P-H.

Basic Financial Management. rev. ed. Curtis W. Symonds. (Illus.). 1978. 13.95 (ISBN 0-8144-5481-X). Am Mgmt.

Basic First Aid, 4 vols. American National Red Cross. (Illus.). Set. pap. 5.25 slipcased (ISBN 0-385-17211-7). Doubleday.

Basic Fitness. E. G. Bartlett. LC 76-1402. (Illus.). 128p. 1976. 10.50 (ISBN 0-7153-7172-X). David & Charles.

Basic Food Chemistry. Frank A. Lee. (Illus.). 1975. pap. text ed. 19.50 (ISBN 0-87055-289-9). AVI.

Basic Food Microbiology. George J. Banwart. (Illus.). 1979. pap. text ed. 31.50 (ISBN 0-87055-322-4). AVI.

Basic Football Strategy: An Introduction for Young Players. Edward F. Dolan, Jr. LC 76-3438. 144p. (gr. 5-9). 1976. 7.95a (ISBN 0-385-03998-0); PLB (ISBN 0-385-04184-5). Doubleday.

BASIC for Business. Parker & Silbey. (Illus.). 1980. 15.95 (ISBN 0-8359-0351-6); pap. text ed. 10.95 (ISBN 0-8359-0349-4); solutions manual free (ISBN 0-8359-0350-8). Reston.

Basic for Business Students. Michael Trombetta. LC 80-15605. 320p. 1981. pap. text ed. 9.95 (ISBN 0-201-07611-X). A-W.

Basic for Everyone. Thomas Worth. (Illus.). 368p. 1976. 13.95 (ISBN 0-13-061481-5); pap. write for info. P-H.

Basic Formal Structures in Music. P. Fontaine. 1967. text ed. 17.95 (ISBN 0-13-061416-5). P-H.

Basic Forms in Music. Charles W. Walton. LC 73-81046. 1974. text ed. 9.95x (ISBN 0-88284-010-X). Alfred Pub.

Basic Formulas of Fiction. rev. ed. William Foster-Harris. 1977. Repr. of 1960 ed. 7.95x (ISBN 0-8061-0135-0). U of Okla Pr.

Basic FORTRAN IV Programming. rev. ed. J. J. Healy & D. J. DeBruzzi. 1975. pap. 13.95 (ISBN 0-201-02827-1). A-W.

Basic FORTRAN IV with WATFOR & WATFIV. C. R. Bauer & A. P. Peluso. 1974. 13.95 (ISBN 0-201-00411-9) (ISBN 0-686-67380-8). A-W.

Basic Framework for Economics. Richard H. Leftwich. 1980. pap. 9.95x (ISBN 0-256-02309-3); student wkbk. avail. (ISBN 0-256-02358-1). Business Pubns.

BASIC from the Ground up. David Simon. (Computer Programming Ser.). 1978. pap. 10.75 (ISBN 0-8104-5760-1); pap. text ed. 7.95x (ISBN 0-8104-5117-4). Hayden.

Basic Gardening Illustrated. Sunset Editors. LC 74-20013. (Illus.). 128p. 1975. pap. 3.95 o.p. (ISBN 0-376-03074-7, Sunset Bks). Sunset-Lane.

Basic Gardening: Introduction to. 3rd ed. Sunset Editors. LC 80-53478. (Illus.). 160p. 1981. pap. 5.95 (ISBN 0-376-03075-5, Sunset Bks). Sunset-Lane.

Basic General Metals. Joseph W. Giachino. (gr. 9-12). 1969. text ed. 6.96 (ISBN 0-02-817070-9). Macmillan.

Basic Geographic Techniques in the Analysis of Public Policy. Girma Kebbede. (Learning Packages in the Policy Sciences Ser.: No. 18). (Illus.). 46p. (Orig.). 1978. pap. text ed. 3.00 (ISBN 0-936826-07-X). Pol Stud Assocs.

Basic Geometry. 3rd ed. George D. Birkhoff & R. Beatley. LC 59-7308. (gr. 9-12). 1959. text ed. 12.00 (ISBN 0-8284-0120-9); tchr's manual 2.50 (ISBN 0-8284-0034-2); answer bk. 1.50 (ISBN 0-8284-0162-4). Chelsea Pub.

BASIC: Getting Started. William S. Davis. 69p. 1981. pap. text ed. 5.95 (ISBN 0-201-03258-9). A-W.

Basic Grammar of Modern English. B. Liles. 1979. 14.95 (ISBN 0-13-061853-5). P-H.

Basic Greek Vocabulary. John R. Cheadle. 1939. text ed. 4.50 (ISBN 0-312-06790-9). St Martin.

Basic Guide to Flying. Paul Fillingham. 1977. pap. 5.95 (ISBN 0-8015-0526-7, Hawthorn). Dutton.

Basic Guide to Photography. 2nd ed. Lou Jacobs, Jr. Ed. by Mike Stensvold. LC 73-79969. (Photography How-to Ser.). (Illus.). (gr. 8-12). 1980. pap. 5.95 (ISBN 0-8227-4038-9). Petersen Pub.

Basic Guide to Pictorial Perspective. Benjamin Green. (A Promotion of the Arts Library Book). (Illus.). 97p. 1981. 27.75 (ISBN 0-86650-001-4). Gloucester Art.

Basic Guide to Plastics in Packaging. Stanley Sacharow & Roger C. Griffin, Jr. LC 72-91986. 1973. 21.95 (ISBN 0-8436-1208-8). CBI Pub.

Basic Guidebook for Industrial Designers. Randolph J. Haddon. (Illus.). 129p. 1981. 47.45 (ISBN 0-930582-92-6). Gloucester Art.

BASIC Handbook: An Encyclopedia of the BASIC Computer Language. 2nd ed. David A. Lien. Ed. by Dave Gunzel. LC 78-64886. (CompuSoft Learning Ser.). 1981. pap. 19.95 (ISBN 0-932760-00-7). CompuSoft.

Basic Handbook of Mental Illness. rev. ed. Harry Milt. LC 73-19278. 128p. 1974. 5.95 o.p. (ISBN 0-684-13738-0, ScribT); pap. 2.95 o.p. (ISBN 0-684-13753-4, SL513, ScribT). Scribner.

Basic Handtools for the Aviation Technician. Bruce C. Johnson. (Aviation Technician Training Ser.). (Orig.). 1980. pap. write for info. (ISBN 0-89100-204-9). Aviation Maintenance.

Basic Health Education. Vincent Irwin & Michael Spira. (Illus.). 1978. pap. text ed. 10.95x (ISBN 0-582-48829-X). Longman.

Basic Health Planning Methods. Allen D. Spiegel & Herbert Harvey Hyman. LC 78-10780. 1978. 37.95 (ISBN 0-89443-077-7). Aspen Systems.

Basic Heat Transfer. M. Necati Ozisik. (Illus.). 1976. text ed. 23.95 (ISBN 0-07-047980-1, C); student manual 4.95 (ISBN 0-07-047981-X). McGraw.

Basic Hebrew: A Textbook of Contemporary Hebrew. Marnin Feinstein. LC 73-77286. 1973. 6.75x (ISBN 0-8197-0287-0). Bloch.

Basic Helicopter Handbook. 3rd ed. Federal Aviation Administration. (Pilot Training Ser.). (Illus.). 111p. 1978. pap. 3.75 (ISBN 0-89100-162-X, E*A-A*C61-13B). Aviation Maintenance.

Basic Hematology: An Introduction for Student Medical Technologists & Medical Assistants. Arthur Simmons. (Illus.). 296p. 1973. text ed. 24.75 photocopy ed. spiral (ISBN 0-398-02536-3). C C Thomas.

Basic Histology. 3rd rev. ed. Luis C. Junqueira & Jose Carneiro. LC 80-81941. (Illus.). 504p. 1980. lexotone cover 15.50 (ISBN 0-87041-202-7). Lange.

Basic History of Art. 2nd ed. H. W. Janson et al. (Illus.). 444p. 1981. pap. text ed. 15.95 (ISBN 0-686-69326-4). P-H.

Basic Home Repairs Illustrated. Sunset Editors. LC 73-115166. (Illus.). 96p. 1971. pap. 4.95 (ISBN 0-376-01025-8, Sunset Bks). Sunset-Lane.

Basic Horsemanship-English & Western: A Complete Guide for Riders & Instructors. Illus. by Eleanor F. Prince. LC 71-144289. 384p. 1974. 12.95 (ISBN 0-385-06587-6). Doubleday.

Basic Hospital Financial Management. Donald R. Beck. 350p. 1980. text ed. 24.00 (ISBN 0-89443-329-6). Aspen Systems.

Basic Hotel Front Office Procedures: A Basic Guide. Peter F. Renner. LC 80-17905. 295p. 1980. pap. text ed. 12.95 (ISBN 0-8436-2190-7). CBI Pub.

Basic Human Anatomy & Physiology. 3rd ed. Charlotte M. Dienhart. LC 78-64706. (Illus.). 1979. pap. text ed. 11.95 (ISBN 0-7216-3082-0). Saunders.

Basic Human Needs Approach to Development: Some Policy Issues. Ed. by Danny M. Leipziger. LC 80-19938. 256p. 1981. lib. bdg. 20.00 (ISBN 0-89946-021-6). Oelgeschlager.

Basic Human Physiology: Normal Function & Mechanisms of Disease. 2nd ed. Arthur C. Guyton. LC 76-4248. (Illus.). 1977. text ed. 22.50 (ISBN 0-7216-4383-3). Saunders.

Basic Hydraulics. Andrew L. Simon. LC 80-15341. 256p. 1981. text ed. 18.95 (ISBN 0-471-07965-0). Wiley.

Basic Ice Skating Skills. Robert S. Ogilvie. LC 68-54414. (Illus.). (gr. 7-9). 1968. 10.95 (ISBN 0-397-00518-0); pap. 7.95 (ISBN 0-397-00519-9, LP10). Lippincott.

Basic Ideas About Singing: The Teaching of Theodore Harrison, an American Maestro. Roger D. Fee. LC 78-63254. pap. text ed. 5.75 (ISBN 0-8191-0614-3). U Pr of Amer.

Basic Ideas of Science of Mind. Ernest Holmes. 1957. pap. 3.50 (ISBN 0-911336-23-0). Sci of Mind.

Basic Ignition & Electrical Systems. 5th rev. ed. Ed. by Jon C. Jay. LC 73-79968. (Basic Repair & Maintenance Manuals Ser.). (Illus.). (gr. 9-12). 1977. pap. 6.95 (ISBN 0-8227-5014-7). Petersen Pub.

Basic Imaging Procedures in Nuclear Medicine. Nancy A. Clifton & Pamela J. Simmons. 192p. 1981. pap. 13.50 (ISBN 0-8385-0578-3). ACC.

Basic Immunology & Its Medical Application. 2nd ed. James T. Barrett. LC 80-14328. (Illus.). 304p. 1980. pap. text ed. 14.95 (ISBN 0-8016-0495-8). Mosby.

Basic Industrial Drafting. Spence. 1979. pap. text ed. 9.28 (ISBN 0-87002-297-0); worksheets 6.08 (ISBN 0-87002-142-7). Bennett IL.

Basic Industrial Resources of the USSR. Theodore Shabad. LC 75-101133. 1969. 27.50x (ISBN 0-231-03077-0). Columbia U Pr.

Basic Inorganic Chemistry. Albert F. Cotton & Geoffrey Wilkinson. LC 75-26832. 579p. (Arabic Translation available). 1976. 23.95 (ISBN 0-471-17557-9). Wiley.

Basic Instrumentation for Engineers & Physicists. A. M. Brookes. 1968. text ed. 15.00 (ISBN 0-08-012538-7); pap. 6.50 (ISBN 0-08-012537-9). Pergamon.

Basic Instruments & Selected Documents: Protocols, Decisions, Reports, 1978 to 1979 & Thirty-Fifth Session. 26th supl. ed. 393p. 1981. pap. 25.00 (G141, GATT). Unipub.

Basic International Bibliography of Archive Administration. Compiled by Michel Duchein. (Archivum Ser.: Vol. 25). 1978. pap. 35.00 (ISBN 0-89664-005-1, Pub. by K G Saur). Gale.

Basic Investments. Herbert B. Mayo. 544p. 1980. text ed. 19.95 (ISBN 0-03-054691-5). Dryden Pr.

Basic Issues of American Democracy. 8th ed. Samuel Hendel & Hillman Bishop. 1975. pap. 9.95 (ISBN 0-13-062521-3). P-H.

Basic Judaism. Milton Steinberg. LC 47-30768. (Modern Classic Ser.). 5.95 o.p. (ISBN 0-15-110697-5). HarBraceJ.

Basic Judo. E. G. Bartlett. LC 75-2707. (Illus.). 1975. pap. 2.95 o.p. (ISBN 0-668-03790-3). Arco.

Basic Keyboard Skills: An Introduction to Accompaniment Improvisation, Transposition & Modulation, with an Appendix on Sight Reading. William Pelz. LC 80-22820. vii, 173p. 1981. Repr. of 1963 ed. PLB 23.50x (ISBN 0-313-22882-5, PEBK). Greenwood.

Basic Labor Relations 1977 Course Handbook, Vol. 104. (Litigation & Administration Practice Course Handbook Ser., 1977-78: Vol. 104). 1977. pap. 20.00 o.p. (ISBN 0-685-86089-2, H4-3854). PLI.

Basic Lacrosse Strategy: An Introduction for Young Players. Henry E. Flanagan, Jr. & Robert Gardner. (Illus.). 1979. 7.95 (ISBN 0-385-14001-0). Doubleday.

Basic Language: Messages & Meanings, Level 3. Norma W. Biedenharn et al. (gr. 9). 1978. 11.96 (ISBN 0-06-530108-0, SchDept); tchr's guide 11.16 (ISBN 0-06-530208-7). Har-Row.

Basic Language: Messages & Meanings Level 5. Norma W Biedenharn et al. (gr. 11). 1973. 11.96 (ISBN 0-06-530104-8, SchDept); tchrs manual 10.00 (ISBN 0-06-530204-4); wkbk. 5.88 (ISBN 0-06-530304-0); tchr's. wkbk. 11.16 (ISBN 0-06-530404-7). Har-Row.

Basic Language: Messages & Meanings 1973, Level 1. Norma W. Biedenharn et al. (gr. 7). 11.32 (ISBN 0-06-530100-5, SchDept); tchrs. manual 10.00 (ISBN 0-06-530200-1); wkbk. 5.16 (ISBN 0-06-530300-8); tchr's wkbk. 10.24 (ISBN 0-06-530400-4). Har-Row.

Basic Language: Messages & Meanings 1973, Level 2. Norma W. Biedenharn & Pauline C. Davis. (gr. 8). 11.32 (ISBN 0-06-530101-3, SchDept); tchr's manual 10.00 (ISBN 0-06-530201-X); wkbk. 5.16 (ISBN 0-06-530301-6); tchr's. wkbk. 10.24 (ISBN 0-06-530401-2). Har-Row.

Basic Language: Messages & Meanings 1973, Level 3. Norma W. Biedenharn et al. (gr. 9). 11.96 (ISBN 0-06-530102-1, SchDept); tchrs manual 10.00 (ISBN 0-06-530202-8); wkbk. 5.64 (ISBN 0-06-530302-4); tchr's. wkbk. 11.16 (ISBN 0-06-530402-0). Har-Row.

Basic Language: Messages & Meanings 1978, Level 4. Norma W. Biedenharn. (gr. 10). 1978. 11.96 (ISBN 0-06-530109-9, SchDept); tchr's guide 11.16 (ISBN 0-06-530209-5). Har-Row.

Basic Language: Messages & Meanings 1973, Level 4. Norma W. Biedenharn et al. (gr. 10). 11.96 (ISBN 0-06-530103-X, SchDept); tchr's. manual 10.00 (ISBN 0-06-530203-6); wkbk. 5.64 (ISBN 0-06-530303-2); tchr's wkbk. 11.16 (ISBN 0-06-530403-9). Har-Row.

Basic Language: Messages & Meanings 1973, Level 6. Norma W. Biedenharn et al. (gr. 12). 11.96 (ISBN 0-06-530105-6, SchDept); tchr's manual 10.00 (ISBN 0-06-530205-2); wkbk. 5.88 (ISBN 0-06-530305-9); tchr's. wkbk. 11.16 (ISBN 0-06-530405-5). Har-Row.

Basic Languages: Messages & Meanings 1978, Level 5. Norma W. Biedenharn et al. (gr. 11). 1978. 11.96 (ISBN 0-06-530110-2, SchDept); tchr's guide 11.16 (ISBN 0-06-530210-9). Har-Row.

Basic Languages: Messages & Meanings 1978, Level 6. Norma W. Biedenharn et al. (gr. 12). 1978. 11.96 (ISBN 0-06-530111-0, SchDept); tchr's guide 11.16 (ISBN 0-06-530211-7). Har-Row.

Basic Latin American Legal Materials 1970-1975. Ed. by Juan Aguilar & Armando E. Gonzalez. LC 77-78814. (American Association of Law Libraries Publication Ser: No. 13). 1977. pap. 12.50x (ISBN 0-8377-0111-2). Rothman.

Basic Latin Vocabulary. John Wilson & C. Parsons. 1960. text ed. 5.95 (ISBN 0-312-06825-5). St Martin.

Basic Law of Color Theory. Harald Kuppers. (Illus.). 224p. 1981. pap. text ed. 2.95 (ISBN 0-8120-2173-8). Barron.

Basic Laws of Arithmetic: Exposition of the System. Gottlob Frege. Ed. & tr. by Montgomery Furth. (gr. 9-12). 1965. 12.00x o.p. (ISBN 0-520-00432-9). U of Cal Pr.

Basic Leader Skills: Handbook for Church Leaders. Richard E. Rusbuldt. 64p. 1981. pap. 4.95 (ISBN 0-8170-0920-5). Judson.

Basic Learning Skills: Base Words & Word Parts Learning Module. Robert Burleigh. (gr. 2-3). 1978. pap. text ed. 215.00 (ISBN 0-89290-108-X, CM-38D). Soc for Visual.

Basic Learning Skills: Consonant Sounds Learning Module. Robert Burleigh. (gr. k-2). 1978. pap. text ed. 290.00 (ISBN 0-89290-106-3, CM-38B). Soc for Visual.

Basic Learning Skills: Vowel Sounds Learning Module. Robert Burleigh. (gr. 1-3). 1978. pap. text ed. 290.00 (ISBN 0-89290-107-1, CM-38C). Soc for Visual.

Basic Library for Bible Students. Warren W. Wiersbe. (Orig.). 1981. pap. 2.95 (ISBN 0-8010-9641-3). Baker Bk.

Basic Library Skills: A Short Course. Carolyn Wolf & Richard Wolf. 110p. 1981. lib. bdg. write for info (ISBN 0-89950-018-8). McFarland & Co.

Basic Life Support: Skills Manual. Phillips. LC 77-8351. 1977. pap. 11.95 (ISBN 0-87618-883-8). R J Brady.

Basic Linear Algebra with Applications. Garfield C. Schmidt. LC 79-16225. (Applied Mathematics Ser.). 536p. 1980. text ed. 34.50 (ISBN 0-89874-000-2). Krieger.

Basic Literature of American Public Administration, 1787-1950. Ed. by Frederick C. Mosher. LC 79-28553. 1980. text ed. 18.00x (ISBN 0-8419-0574-6); pap. text ed. 9.50x (ISBN 0-8419-0575-4). Holmes & Meier.

Basic Logic: The Fundamental Principles of Formal Deductive Reasoning. 2nd ed. Raymond J. McCall. 1962. pap. 3.95 (ISBN 0-06-460052-1, CO 52, COS). Har-Row.

Basic Lubrication Theory. 2nd ed. Alastair Cameron. LC 76-48204. 1977. 34.95 (ISBN 0-470-99020-1). Halsted Pr.

Basic Machine Technology. Thomas C. Olivo. 1980. 19.95 (ISBN 0-672-97171-2); pap. 4.95 student's manual o.p. (ISBN 0-672-97172-0); instructor's guide 6.67 (ISBN 0-672-97173-9). Bobbs.

Basic Macroeconomics: Understanding National Income, Inflation & Unemployment. Edwin G. Dolan. 400p. 1980. pap. text ed. 12.95 (ISBN 0-03-051276-X). Dryden Pr.

Basic Made Easy: A Guide to Programming Microcomputers & Minicomputers. Cassel & Swanson. (Illus.). 272p. 1980. text ed. 14.95 (ISBN 0-8359-0399-0); pap. text ed. 10.95 (ISBN 0-8359-0398-2). Reston.

Basic Management: An Experience Based Approach. Hyler J. Bracey & Aubrey Sanford. 1977. pap. 11.95x (ISBN 0-256-01933-9). Business Pubns.

Basic Managerial Finance. 2nd ed. Erwin E. Nemmers & Alan E. Grunewald. LC 74-17164. 750p. 1975. text ed. 19.95 (ISBN 0-8299-0025-X); 7.95 (ISBN 0-8299-0027-6); study guide avail. (ISBN 0-8299-0564-2); instrs.' manual avail. West Pub.

Basic Manual of Fly Tying. Paul N. Fling & Donald L. Puterbaugh. LC 77-80194. (Illus.). 1979. pap. 7.95 (ISBN 0-8069-8146-6). Sterling.

Basic Manx, Irish & Scottish Gaelic. Timothy Healy. 1977. pap. text ed. 9.25x (ISBN 90-6296-021-9). Humanities.

Basic Maps of the U.S. Economy, Nineteen Hundred Sixty-Seven to Nineteen Hundred Ninety. NPA Center for Economic & Demographic Projections Staff. 304p. 1979. 25.00 (ISBN 0-686-28102-0). Natl Planning.

Basic Marketing. George D. Downing. LC 79-142984. 448p. 1971. 17.95x (ISBN 0-675-09233-7); instructor's manual 3.95 (ISBN 0-686-66708-5). Merrill.

Basic Marketing: A Managerial Approach. 6th ed. E. Jerome McCarthy. 1978. text ed. 19.95 (ISBN 0-256-02048-5). Irwin.

Basic Marketing: A Managerial Approach. 2nd ed. E. Jerome McCarthy & Stanley J. Shapiro. 1979. text ed. 19.95 (ISBN 0-256-02138-4). Irwin.

Basic Marketing: Concepts, Decisions & Strategies. 2nd ed. Edward W. Cundiff & Richard R. Still. LC 79-138478. 1971. ref. ed. 18.95 (ISBN 0-13-062638-4); study guide 4.95 (ISBN 0-13-062620-1). P-H.

Basic Masonry Illustrated. Sunset Editors. LC 80-53484. (Illus.). 96p. (Orig.). 1981. pap. 4.95 (ISBN 0-376-01360-5, Sunset Bks.). Sunset-Lane.

Basic Materials for the Piano Student. 2nd. ed. Marcelle Vernazza et al. 1972. plastic comb 7.95x o.p. (ISBN 0-697-03628-6). Wm C Brown.

Basic Materials in Music Theory: A Programmed Course. 4th ed. Paul Harder. 1978. pap. text ed. 14.50 (ISBN 0-205-06045-5). Allyn.

Basic Maternity Nursing. 4th ed. Persis M. Hamilton. LC 78-26998. (Illus.). 1979. pap. 10.95 (ISBN 0-8016-2031-7). Mosby.

Basic Math, 9 bks. Gibbons. Incl. Gr. K. pap. text ed. 2.92 (ISBN 0-8009-1401-5); tchr's. ed. 4.40 (ISBN 0-8009-1403-1); Gr. 1 & 2. pap. text ed. 4.64 ea.; Gr. 1. pap. text ed. (ISBN 0-8009-1406-6); Gr. 2. pap. text ed. (ISBN 0-8009-1410-4); tchr's. eds, 6.16 ea. Gr. 1 (ISBN 0-8009-1408-2). Gr. 2 (ISBN 0-8009-1412-0); Gr. 3-6. Gr. 3. pap. text ed. 4.64 (ISBN 0-8009-1414-7); Gr. 4. pap. text ed. 4.64 (ISBN 0-8009-1425-2); Gr. 5. 4.64 (ISBN 0-8009-1433-3); Gr. 6. tchr's. eds. 6.16 ea. (ISBN 0-8009-1443-0); tchr's. ed. gr. 3 6.16 (ISBN 0-8009-1416-3); tchr's. ed. gr. 4 6.16 (ISBN 0-8009-1427-9); tchr's. ed. gr. 5 6.16 (ISBN 0-8009-1437-6); tchr's. ed. gr. 6 6.16 (ISBN 0-8009-1445-7); tests for gr. 3-6 1.12 ea.; Gr. 7 & 8. pap. text ed. 5.08 ea.; Gr. 7. pap. text ed. (ISBN 0-8009-1462-7); Gr. 8. pap. text ed. (ISBN 0-8009-1472-4); tchr's. eds. 6.60 ea. Gr. 7 (ISBN 0-8009-1464-3). Gr. 8 (ISBN 0-8009-1474-0). tests for gr. 7-8 1.12 ea. Gr. 7 (ISBN 0-8009-1468-6). Gr. 8 (ISBN 0-8009-1476-7). (gr. k-8). 1977-78. McCormick-Mathers.

Basic Math for Calculus. Dennis G. Zill et al. 1978. text ed. 18.95x (ISBN 0-534-00568-3). Wadsworth Pub.

Basic Mathematical Skills: A Guided Approach. R. A. Carman & M. J. Carman. 1975. 17.95 (ISBN 0-471-13495-3). Wiley.

Basic Mathematical Skills: A Guided Approach. 2nd ed. Robert A. Carman & Marilyn J. Carman. LC 80-19121. 560p. 1981. pap. text ed. 16.95 (ISBN 0-471-03608-0). Wiley.

Basic Mathematical Statistics for Behavioral Sciences & Techniques for Data Compilation in Ecological Studies. Hattye H. Liston et al. 1976. text ed. 13.50x (ISBN 0-8191-0093-5). U Pr of Amer.

Basic Mathematics. Frank A. Bailey. 1977. pap. 10.95x (ISBN 0-673-15064-X). Scott F.

Basic Mathematics. Walter C. Brown. 96p. (Combination text & workbook). 1980. pap. 4.80 (ISBN 0-87006-315-4). Goodheart.

Basic Mathematics. rev. ed. Walter C. Brown. 128p. 1981. pap. text ed. 4.80 (ISBN 0-87006-317-0). Goodheart.

Basic Mathematics, 2 vols. Norman Crowhurst. (Illus., Orig.). (gr. 9 up). 1961. Vol. 1 Arithmetic. pap. 7.65 (ISBN 0-8104-0447-8); Vol. 2 Integrated Algebra, Geometry & Calculus. pap. 7.65 (ISBN 0-8104-0448-6); Vol. 1. exam set 0.50 (ISBN 0-8104-0567-9); Vol. 2. exam set 0.50 (ISBN 0-8104-0568-7). Hayden.

Basic Mathematics. 3rd ed. M. Wiles Keller & James H. Zant. LC 78-69602. (Illus.). 1979. pap. text ed. 14.95 (ISBN 0-395-27050-2); inst. annot. ed. 15.95 (ISBN 0-395-27051-0). HM.

Basic Mathematics, 12 bks. 2nd ed. James A. Smith. Incl. Bk. 1. Numbers & Numerals. 1.50 (ISBN 0-916780-00-7); Bk. 2. Addition of Whole Numbers & Subtraction of Whole Numbers. 3.95 (ISBN 0-916780-01-5); Bk. 3. Multiplication of Whole Numbers. 3.00 (ISBN 0-916780-02-3); Bk. 4. Division of Whole Numbers. 3.55 (ISBN 0-916780-03-1); Bk. 5. Fractions & Fractional Numbers. 1.80 (ISBN 0-916780-04-X); Bk. 6. Addition & Subtraction of Fractional Numbers & Multiplication & Division of Fractional Numbers. 3.55 (ISBN 0-916780-05-8); Bk. 7. Decimal Numerals: Addition & Subtraction with Decimals & Multiplication & Division with Decimals. 3.95 (ISBN 0-916780-06-6); Bk. 8. Percents & Applications. 2.45 (ISBN 0-916780-07-4); Bk. 9. Formulas & Applications. 3.30 (ISBN 0-916780-08-2); Bk. 10. Measurement & Applications. 3.70 (ISBN 0-916780-09-0); Bk. 11. Measurement in Geometry. 3.75 (ISBN 0-916780-10-4); Bk. 12. Units of Measure & the Metric System. 3.00 (ISBN 0-916780-11-2). (Illus.). 1974. pap. text ed. 30.00 set (ISBN 0-916780-12-0); tchr's. manual 3.20 (ISBN 0-916780-14-7); student test booklet 3.30 (ISBN 0-916780-13-9). CES.

Basic Mathematics. Gabriella Wepner. 1981. write for info. Franklin Inst Pr.

Basic Mathematics. Martin M. Zuckerman. 520p. 1980. text ed. 14.95 (ISBN 0-442-21911-3); instr's. manual 2.50 (ISBN 0-442-23264-0). Van Nos Reinhold.

Basic Mathematics: A Program for Semi-Independent Study. John D. Baley et al. 1978. pap. text ed. 13.95x (ISBN 0-669-01019-7); inst. resource bk. free (ISBN 0-669-01020-0); Set. cassette 125.00 (ISBN 0-669-01165-7); free tapescript (ISBN 0-669-01022-7). Heath.

Basic Mathematics: Algebra with Arithmetic. Harold S. Engelsohn. LC 79-21287. 1980. text ed. 18.95 (ISBN 0-471-24145-8). Wiley.

Basic Mathematics for Administration. Frank P. Fowler & E. W. Sandberg. LC 62-15189. 1962. text ed. 19.95 (ISBN 0-471-26976-X). Wiley.

Basic Mathematics for Allied Health. G. Shugar et al. 1975. pap. 9.95x (ISBN 0-02-478500-8, 47850). Macmillan.

Basic Mathematics for Business Analysis. rev. ed. O. J. Curry & John E Pearson. 1970. text ed. 10.95x o.p. (ISBN 0-256-00087-5). Irwin.

Basic Mathematics for College Students. Karl J. Smith. LC 80-20492. 400p. (Orig.). 1981. pap. text ed. 15.95 (ISBN 0-8185-0419-6). Brooks-Cole.

Basic Mathematics for College Students. 6th ed. Stein. 1980. text ed. 17.80 (ISBN 0-205-06814-6). Allyn.

Basic Mathematics for Electronics. 4th ed. Nelson M. Cooke & Herbert F. Adams. (Illus.). 1976. text ed. 17.25 (ISBN 0-07-012512-0, G); answers to even-numbered problems 2.95 (ISBN 0-07-012511-2); study guide 4.25 (ISBN 0-07-000305-X). McGraw.

Basic Mathematics for Science & Engineering. P. G. Andres et al. LC 55-8369. 1955. text ed. 27.95 (ISBN 0-471-02970-X). Wiley.

Basic Mathematics for Technicians. C. W. Schofield. (Illus.). 1977. pap. text ed. 11.00x (ISBN 0-7131-3379-1). Intl Ideas.

Basic Mathematics for the Biological & Social Sciences. F. H. Marriott. LC 73-99863. 1970. text ed. 17.25 (ISBN 0-08-006663-1); pap. 9.25 (ISBN 0-08-006664-X). Pergamon.

Basic Mathematics Simplified. 4th ed. LC 76-3941. (Illus.). 368p. 1977. 15.00 (ISBN 0-8273-1270-9); pap. 11.20 (ISBN 0-8273-1269-5); instructor's guide 3.00 (ISBN 0-8273-1271-7). Delmar.

Basic Mathematics: Skills & Structure. John F. Haldi. (Illus., LC 77-073943). 1978. pap. text ed. 14.25 (ISBN 0-395-25117-6); inst. manual 2.00 (ISBN 0-395-25114-1). HM.

Basic Mathematics: What Every College Student Should Know. Shirley Hockett. (Illus.). 1977. pap. 14.95 (ISBN 0-13-063446-8). P-H.

Basic Measurement & Evaluation of Science Instruction. Rodney L. Doran. (Illus.). 144p. (Orig.). 1980. pap. 3.00 (ISBN 0-87355-016-1). Natl Sci Tchrs.

Basic Mechanisms of Ocular Motility & Their Clinical Implications. Ed. by G. Lennerstrand & P. Bach-Y-Rita. 1975. text ed. 115.00 (ISBN 0-08-018885-0). Pergamon.

Basic Media Skills Through Games. Irene W. Bell & Jeanne E. Wieckert. LC 79-941. 1979. 17.50 (ISBN 0-87287-194-0). Libs Unl.

Basic Medical Laboratory Subjects. Patrick Cuviella & Hugh Woosley. LC 74-18675. (Allied Health Ser). 1975. pap. 5.10 (ISBN 0-672-61383-2). Bobbs.

Basic Medical Laboratory Technology. C. J. Kirk. (Illus.). 1975. 21.00x o.s.i. (ISBN 0-8464-0179-7). Beekman Pubs.

Basic Medical Laboratory Technology. C. J. Kirk et al. LC 76-3314. 1975. 26.50 o.p. (ISBN 0-471-01799-X, Pub. by Wiley Medical). Wiley.

Basic Medical Microbiology. 2nd ed. Robert R. Boyd & Bryan G. Hoerl. 1981. text ed. write for info (ISBN 0-316-10433-7). Little.

Basic Medical Terminology. Patrick J. Fisher. LC 74-77820. (Allied Health Ser). 1975. pap. text ed. 12.20 (ISBN 0-672-61385-9); tchr's manual 5.00 (ISBN 0-672-61386-7); tape cassette 96.45 (ISBN 0-672-61387-5). Bobbs.

Basic Medical Virology. Prier. LC 66-22708. 724p. 1966. 18.50 o.p. (ISBN 0-685-54436-2, Pub. by Williams & Wilkins). Krieger.

Basic Metallurgy. Donald Brown. LC 80-68584. (Mechanical Ser.). (Illus.). 272p. (Orig.). 1981. pap. text ed. 10.40 (ISBN 0-8273-1769-7); price not set instr's. guide (ISBN 0-8273-1770-0). Delmar.

Basic Metallurgy. Foss. Date not set. text ed. price not set (ISBN 0-685-67274-3). Bennett IL. Postponed.

Basic Metalwork. Feirer & Lindbeck. (gr. 9-12). 1978. 6.00 (ISBN 0-87002-289-X); pap. 4.32 (ISBN 0-87002-240-7). Bennett IL.

Basic Meteorology Exercise Manual. rev. ed. Carl R. Chelius & Henry J. Frentz. (Illus.). 1978. 8.50 (ISBN 0-8403-1623-2). Kendall-Hunt.

Basic Methods for Mental Health Practitioners. Marvin W. Kahn. 350p. Date not set. ref. ed. 15.95. Winthrop.

Basic Methods of Linear Functional Analysis. J. D. Pryce. 1973. text ed. 12.00x (ISBN 0-09-113411-0, Hutchinson). Humanities.

Basic Metric Style Manual for Secretaries. new ed. Ed. by John Corbett. 1976. pap. 2.95x (ISBN 0-912702-04-4). Global Eng.

Basic Metric Surveying. 2nd ed. W. S. Whyte. (Illus.). 312p. 1976. pap. 18.50 (ISBN 0-408-00197-6). Transatlantic.

Basic Microbiology. Orten C. Skinner. LC 74-78590. (Allied Health Ser). 1975. pap. 7.65 (ISBN 0-672-61390-5). Bobbs.

Basic Microbiology. 4th ed. Wesley A. Volk & Margaret F. Wheeler. LC 79-25907. 611p. 1980. text ed. 19.50x (ISBN 0-397-54313-1). Lippincott.

Basic Microbiology with Applications. 2nd ed. Thomas D. Brock & Katherine M. Brock. (Illus.). 1978. 20.95 (ISBN 0-13-065284-9). P-H.

Basic Microeconomics: Understanding Prices & Markets. 2nd ed. Edwin G. Dolan. 400p. 1980. pap. text ed. 12.95 (ISBN 0-03-051281-6). Dryden Pr.

Basic Microprocessors & Sixty-Eight Hundred. Ron Bishop. 1979. pap. 13.95 (ISBN 0-8104-0758-2). Hayden.

Basic Molecular Biology. F. W. Price. 497p. 1979. 25.95 (ISBN 0-471-69729-X). Wiley.

Basic Music: Functional Musicianship for the Non-Music Major. 5th ed. Robert E. Nye & Bjorner Bergethon. (Illus.) 240p. 1981. pap. text ed. 11.95 (ISBN 0-13-065672-0). P-H.

Basic Musicianship for Classroom Teachers. Charles Hoffer & Marjorie Hoffer. 1976. pap. text ed. 12.95x (ISBN 0-534-00394-X). Wadsworth Pub.

Basic Network Theory. Paul M. Chirlian. LC 68-25648. (Electrical & Electronic Eng. Ser). (Illus.). 1968. 24.50 (ISBN 0-07-010788-2, C); ans. bk. 1.50 (ISBN 0-07-010789-0); solutions manual 3.00 (ISBN 0-07-010792-0). McGraw.

Basic Neurochemistry. 3rd ed. George J. Siegel et al. 1981. write for info (ISBN 0-316-79002-8). Little.

Basic Neuroradiology. Mohammad Sarwar et al. (Illus.). 500p. 1981. 47.50 (ISBN 0-87527-230-4). Green.

Basic Nuclear Engineering. 3rd ed. Arthur R. Foster & Robert L. Wright, Jr. 1977. text ed. 26.95x (ISBN 0-205-05697-0); sol. manual free (ISBN 0-205-05698-9). Allyn.

Basic Nuclear Engineering. K. S. Ram. LC 77-795. 1977. 12.95 (ISBN 0-470-99105-4). Halsted Pr.

Basic Nuclear Medicine. Baum. 1975. 17.50 o.p. (ISBN 0-8385-0613-5). ACC.

Basic Nuclear Physics for Medical Personnel. Herbert L. Jackson. (Illus.). 164p. 1973. 13.75 (ISBN 0-398-02663-7). C C Thomas.

Basic Numerical Analysis with FORTRAN. A. Balfour & W. T. Beveridge. 1977. text ed. 12.25 o.p. (ISBN 0-686-67891-5); pap. text ed. 9.95x (ISBN 0-435-77484-0). Heinemann Ed.

Basic Nursing Procedures. Grace V. Hornemann. LC 77-94835. (Illus.). 272p. 1980. pap. 9.80 (ISBN 0-8273-1320-9); instructors's guide 1.50 (ISBN 0-8273-1321-7). Delmar.

Basic Nursing Skills. Frances Britton. (Illus.). 224p. 1981. pap. text ed. 7.95 (ISBN 0-87619-921-X). R J Brady.

Basic Nutrition in Health & Disease: Including Selection & Care of Food. 7th ed. Phyllis Howe. 450p. 1981. pap. text ed. price not set (ISBN 0-7216-4796-0). Saunders.

Basic Oral Communication. 3rd ed. Glenn R. Capp et al. (Illus.). 416p. 1981. pap. text ed. 12.95 (ISBN 0-13-065979-7). P-H.

Basic Oral Spanish. Joseph W. Barlow. (Illus.). 1947. text ed. 16.95x o.p. (ISBN 0-89197-042-8); pap. text ed. 9.95x o.p. (ISBN 0-89197-043-6). Irvington.

Basic Organic Chemistry: Arabic Translation, Pt. 1. 256p. 1978. 6.95 (ISBN 0-471-04526-8). Wiley.

Basic-Pack Statistics Programs. Dennie Van Tassel. (Ser. in Personal Computing). (Illus.). 240p. 1981. pap. text ed. 16.95 (ISBN 0-13-066381-6). P-H.

Basic Pathophysiology: A Conceptual Approach. Maureen E. Groer & Maureen E. Shekleton. LC 78-21170. (Illus.). 1979. pap. 18.95 (ISBN 0-8016-1983-1). Mosby.

Basic Pattern Making: An Individualized Approach. Connie Littman. LC 76-14097. (gr. 9-12). 1977. pap. text ed. 7.20 (ISBN 0-8273-0581-8); instructor's guide 1.50 (ISBN 0-8273-0582-6). Delmar.

Basic Patterns of Historical Action in the Chematized Analysis of the Philosophy of History. Ray A. Langley. (Major Currents in Contemporary World History Library). (Illus.). 129p. 1981. 49.25 (ISBN 0-930008-84-7). Inst Econ Pol.

Basic Pediatric Nursing. 3rd ed. Persis M. Hamilton. LC 77-20662. (Illus.). 1978. pap. text ed. 13.95 (ISBN 0-8016-2039-2). Mosby.

Basic Pharmacology. R. W. Foster & Barry Cox. LC 80-49873. (Illus.). 296p. 1980. text ed. 18.95 (ISBN 0-407-00170-0). Butterworths.

Basic Pharmacology for Health Occupations. Henry Hitner & Barbara T. Nagle. (Health Occupations Ser.). 1980. pap. 12.95 (ISBN 0-672-61437-5); tchrs. manual 6.67 (ISBN 0-672-61438-3). Bobbs.

Basic Pharmacology for Nurses. 7th ed. Jessie Squire & Bruce D. Clayton. 400p. 1981. pap. text ed. 13.95 (ISBN 0-8016-4743-6). Mosby.

Basic Pharmacology in Medicine. 2nd ed. Joseph R. DiPalma. (Illus.). 640p. 1981. text ed. 25.00 (ISBN 0-07-017011-8, HP). McGraw.

Basic Physical Chemistry for the Life Sciences. 3rd ed. Virginia R. Williams et al. LC 77-13374. (Illus.). 1978. text ed. 23.95x (ISBN 0-7167-0027-1); answer bk. avail. (ISBN 0-685-87690-X). W H Freeman.

Basic Physical Disabilities Procedures: A Manual in Occupational Therapy. Amy Killingsworth. (Illus.). 1976. pap. 15.00 (ISBN 0-930638-00-X). Cal-Syl Pr.

Basic Physical Science for Technicians. A. B. Pollard & C. W. Schofield. (Illus.). 1977. pap. 11.00x (ISBN 0-7131-3384-8). Intl Ideas.

Basic Physics in Diagnostic Ultrasound. Joseph L. Rose et al. LC 79-14932. 1979. 29.95 (ISBN 0-471-05735-5, Pub. by Wiley Medical). Wiley.

Basic Physics of Radiation Therapy. 2nd ed. Joseph Selman. (Illus.). 768p. 1976. 34.75 (ISBN 0-398-03247-5). C C Thomas.

Basic Physics of the Solar System. V. M. Blanco & S. W. McCuskey. 1961. 17.95 (ISBN 0-201-00615-4). A-W.

Basic Physiology. Fred E. D'Amour. LC 61-5603. (Illus.). 1961. text ed. 17.50x (ISBN 0-226-13517-9). U of Chicago Pr.

Basic Physiology. Ed. by P. D. Sturkie. (Illus.). 350p. 1981. 19.80 (ISBN 0-387-90485-9). Springer-Verlag.

Basic Pipe Estimating. Lloyd Burkholder, Sr. 224p. (Orig.). 1981. pap. 15.50 (ISBN 0-910460-84-1). Craftsman.

Basic Plane Surveying. Arthur Siegle. LC 77-87883. 1979. pap. text ed. 7.20 (ISBN 0-8273-1698-4); instructor's guide 1.60 (ISBN 0-8273-1699-2). Delmar.

Basic Plumbing. Tom Philbin. (Illus.). 1977. 14.50 (ISBN 0-87909-065-0). Reston.

Basic Plumbing. Slater & Smith. LC 77-85751. 1979. pap. text ed. 6.40 (ISBN 0-8273-1204-0); instructor's guide 1.60 (ISBN 0-8273-1205-9). Delmar.

Basic Police Report Writing. 2nd ed. Allen Z. Gammage. (Police Science Ser.). (Illus.). 344p. 1978. 15.75 (ISBN 0-398-03204-1). C C Thomas.

Basic Popultaion Genetics. Bruce Wallace. LC 80-39504. (Illus.). 736p. 1981. 25.00x (ISBN 0-231-05042-9). Columbia U Pr.

Basic Practice of Chemical Engineering. Esber I. Shaheen. 1975. text ed. 27.50 (ISBN 0-395-17645-X); solutions manual 4.05 (ISBN 0-395-18791-5). HM.

Basic Principles. R. Vance Hall. (Managing Behavior Ser.: Part 2). 1975. 3.35 (ISBN 0-89079-002-7). H & H Ent.

Basic Principles & Calculations in Chemical Engineering. 3rd ed. David M. Himmelblau. (P-H Int'l Series in Physical & Chemical Engineering Sciences). (Illus.). 544p. 1974. ref. ed. 27.95 (ISBN 0-13-066472-3). P-H.

Basic Principles of American Government. William R. Sanford & Carl R. Green. (gr. 10-12). 1977. text ed. 14.92 (ISBN 0-87720-622-8); pap. text ed. 8.50 (ISBN 0-87720-619-8). AMSCO Sch.

Basic Principles of Ayurveda. Bhagan Dash & Lalitesh Kashyap. 655p. 1980. 37.00x (ISBN 0-391-02208-3). Humanities.

Basic Principles of Classical Ballet. rev. ed. Agrippina Vaganova. Tr. by Anatole Chujoy et al. LC 68-17402. (Illus.). 1969. pap. 2.50 (ISBN 0-486-22036-2). Dover.

Basic Principles of Classical Ballet: Russian Ballet Technique. Agrippina Vaganova. (Illus.). 7.50 (ISBN 0-8446-0949-8). Peter Smith.

Basic Principles of Computerized Tomography. David O. Davis. 1981. write for info. (ISBN 0-87527-200-2). Green.

Basic Principles of Design. Manfred Maier. 392p. 1981. pap. 35.00 (ISBN 0-442-21206-2). Van Nos Reinhold.

Basic Principles of Electricity. Vester Robinson. LC 72-91115. 464p. 1973. ref. ed. 14.95 (ISBN 0-87909-062-6). Reston.

Basic Principles of Long-Term Patient Care: Developing a Therapeutic Community. Charles H. Kramer & Jeannette R. Kramer. (Illus.). 380p. 1976. 26.75 (ISBN 0-398-03453-2). C C Thomas.

Basic Principles of Music Theory. Joseph Brye. (Illus.). 1965. 18.95 (ISBN 0-8260-1460-7). Wiley.

Basic Principles of Nucleic Chemistry. Ts'o. 1974. Vol. 1. 55.50, subscription 45.00 (ISBN 0-12-701901-4); Vol. 2, 1974. 52.50, subscription 42.50 (ISBN 0-12-701902-2). Acad Pr.

Basic Principles of Oral Radiography. Myron J. Kasle & Robert Langlais. (Exercises in Dental Radiology Ser.: Vol. 4). (Illus.). 200p. 1981. text ed. price not set (ISBN 0-7216-5291-3). Saunders.

Basic Principles of Otometry. John A. Victoreen. (Illus.). 232p. 1973. 16.75 (ISBN 0-398-02616-5). C C Thomas.

Basic Principles of Spectroscopy. Raymond Chang. LC 77-10971. 314p. 1978. lib. bdg. 19.50 (ISBN 0-88275-613-3). Krieger.

Basic Probability Theory. Robert B. Ash. LC 76-109394. 1970. 25.95 (ISBN 0-471-03450-9). Wiley.

Basic Problems, Concepts & Techniques. rev. ed. A. R. Dooley et al. 738p. 1968. 28.95 (ISBN 0-471-21829-4). Wiley.

Basic Problems in Cross-Cultural Psychology: Selected Papers from the 3rd International Conference of the International Association for Cross-Cultural Psychology, Tilburg, July 12-16, 1976. Ed. by Ype H. Poortinga. 380p. 1977. pap. text ed. 27.75 (ISBN 90-265-0247-8, Pub. by Swets Pub Serv Holland). Swets North Am.

Basic Problems of Marx's Philosophy. Nathan Rotenstreich. 1965. pap. 5.55 o.p. (ISBN 0-672-61210-0, LLA164). Bobbs.

Basic Problems of Philosophy. 4th ed. Daniel J. Bronstein et al. LC 79-179449. 656p. 1972. text ed. 17.95 (ISBN 0-13-067637-3). P-H.

Basic Production Management. 2nd ed. Elwood S. Buffa. LC 74-28396. (Management & Administration Ser.). 683p. 1975. text ed. 22.95x (ISBN 0-471-11801-X); instructor's guide avail. (ISBN 0-471-11804-4). Wiley.

Basic Production Management, 2 vols. Elwood S. Buffa. Incl. Vol. 1. Short Course in Managing Day-to-Day Operations. LC 75-27388 (ISBN 0-471-11830-3); Vol. 2. Short Course in Planning & Designing Productive Systems. LC 75-27389 (ISBN 0-471-11831-1). (Business Administration Ser.). 1975. Set. text ed. 37.90 (ISBN 0-471-11832-X, Pub. by Wiley-Interscience); text ed. 18.95 ea. Wiley.

Basic Production Techniques for Motion Pictures. 2nd ed. Ed. by Eastman Kodak Company. LC 76-16716. (Illus.). 64p. (Orig.). 1976. pap. 5.00 (ISBN 0-87985-004-3, P18). Eastman Kodak.

BASIC Programming & Applications. C. Joseph Sass. 368p. 1976. pap. text ed. 15.95x (ISBN 0-205-05422-6); ans. bk. 2.50 (ISBN 0-205-05423-4). Allyn.

Basic Programming for Business. Irvine F. Forkner. (Illus.). 288p. 1978. pap. text ed. 13.95x (ISBN 0-13-066423-5). P-H.

Basic Programming for Scientists & Engineers. Wilbert N. Hubin. LC 77-21343. (Illus.). 1978. pap. 13.95 ref. ed. (ISBN 0-13-066480-4). P-H.

Basic Programming for the Financial Executive. Thomas J. Humphrey. LC 78-5670. 1978. 29.95 (ISBN 0-471-03020-1, Pub. by Wiley-Interscience). Wiley.

BASIC Programming Primer. Mitchell Waite & Michael Pardee. LC 78-64987. 1979. pap. 10.95 (ISBN 0-672-21586-1). Sams.

BASIC Programming: Self-Taught. Seymour C. Hirsch. (Illus.). 1980. pap. text ed. 11.95 (ISBN 0-8359-0432-6). Reston.

Basic Property Law. 3rd ed. Olin L. Browder et al. LC 79-11898. (American Casebook Ser.). 1979. text ed. 24.95 (ISBN 0-8299-2037-4). West Pub.

Basic Psychiatric Concepts in Nursing. 4th ed. Joan J. Kyes & Charles K. Hofling. LC 79-23254. 736p. 1980. text ed. 17.75 (ISBN 0-397-54246-1). Lippincott.

Basic Psychiatry: A Primer of Concepts & Terminology. 2nd ed. James L. Mathis et al. 1972. pap. 10.75 o.p. (ISBN 0-8385-0623-2). ACC.

Basic Psychiatry for Corrections Workers. Henry L. Hartman. 488p. 1978. 23.75 (ISBN 0-398-03663-2). C C Thomas.

Basic Psychoanalytic Concepts, 4 vols. Ed. by Humberto Nagera. (Hampstead Clinic Psychoanalytic Library). 1977. pap. text ed. 4.95x ea.; Vol. 1. o.p. (ISBN 0-04-150059-8); Vol. 2. o.p. (ISBN 0-04-150060-1); Vol. 3. o.p. (ISBN 0-04-150061-X); Vol. 4. (ISBN 0-04-150062-8). Allen Unwin.

Basic Psychology. 4th ed. L. Dodge Fernald & Peter S. Fernald. LC 77-78910. (Illus.). 1979. pap. text ed. 15.75 (ISBN 0-395-25826-X); inst. manual 0.95 (ISBN 0-395-25827-8); student guidebk. 6.95 (ISBN 0-395-25828-6); test bank 2.95 (ISBN 0-395-25829-4). HM.

Basic Psychology: Brief Version. 3rd ed. Howard H. Kendler. LC 76-20875. (Illus.). 1977. pap. text ed. 16.95 (ISBN 0-8053-5195-7); instr's guide 2.95 (ISBN 0-8053-5196-5). Benjamin-Cummings.

Basic Psychotherapeutics: A Programmed Text. C. W. Johnson et al. 605p. 1980. soft bound 14.95 (ISBN 0-89335-128-8). Spectrum Pub.

Basic Radio, Vols. 1-6. rev. 2nd ed. Marvin Tepper. (Illus.). 888p. 1974. combined ed. o.p. 24.95 (ISBN 0-8104-5927-2); Vol. 1. pap. 6.50 (ISBN 0-8104-5921-3); Vol. 2. pap. 6.95 (ISBN 0-8104-5922-1); Vol. 3. pap. 6.20 (ISBN 0-8104-5923-X); Vol. 4. pap. 5.75 o.p. (ISBN 0-8104-5924-8); Vol. 5. pap. 5.75 o.p. (ISBN 0-8104-5925-6); Vol. 6. pap. 5.75 o.p. (ISBN 0-8104-5926-4); Set Of 6 Vols. pap. 29.55 o.p. (ISBN 0-8104-5920-5); transparencies. 106.20, 0.50 ea. exams for vols., 1, 2, or 3 (ISBN 0-8104-0576-8). Hayden.

Basic Radio Course. John T. Frye. LC 61-16513. (Illus.). 1961. 8.95 o.p. (ISBN 0-8306-1104-5); pap. 5.95 (ISBN 0-8306-0104-X, 104). TAB Bks.

Basic Reading Inventory. Jerry L. Johns. (Kendall-Hunt Reading Ser.). (pre-primer-8). 1978. pap. text ed. 5.95 (ISBN 0-8403-2315-8). Kendall-Hunt.

Basic Reading Patterns: Words & Sentences. Marvyl Doyle & Marie Mittwer. (gr. 10 up). 1969. pap. text ed. 8.95 (ISBN 0-13-068031-1). P-H.

Basic Reading Skills: Reading Readiness Learning Module. Robert Burleigh. (gr. k-1). 1977. pap. text ed. 215.00 (ISBN 0-89290-105-5, CM-38A). Soc for Visual.

Basic Readings in Drug Therapy. J. DiPalma & M. Rodman. 1972. pap. 6.95 (ISBN 0-87489-084-5). Med Economics.

Basic Readings in Social Security. U. S. Department of Health, Education & Welfare Library. LC 68-55120. (Illus.). 1968. Repr. of 1960 ed. lib. bdg. 15.00x (ISBN 0-8371-0705-9, RESS). Greenwood.

Basic Real Estate Finance & Investments. Donald R. Eply & James A. Millar. LC 79-19530. 1980. text ed. 21.95 (ISBN 0-471-03635-8); tchrs'. manual avail. (ISBN 0-471-03878-4). Wiley.

Basic Reference Sources: A Self-Study Manual. 2nd ed. Margaret Taylor. LC 73-14500. 1981. 12.50 (ISBN 0-8108-0662-2). Scarecrow.

Basic Rehabilitation Techniques: A Self-Instructional Guide. 2nd. ed. Robert D. Sine et al. 250p. 1981. text ed. write for info. (ISBN 0-89443-342-3). Aspen Systems.

Basic Requirements for Personnel Monitoring. (Safety Ser.: No. 14). 40p. 1980. pap. 6.00 (ISBN 92-0-123980-7, ISP 559, IAEA). Unipub.

Basic Retailing. 2nd ed. C. Larson. 1981. 20.95 (ISBN 0-13-068072-9). P-H.

Basic Riding Techniques. (Illus.). 96p. 1979. pap. 2.95 (ISBN 0-87857-284-8). Rodale Pr Inc.

Basic Rockcraft. Royal Robbins. (Illus.). 1970. wrappers 2.95 (ISBN 0-910856-34-6). La Siesta.

Basic Science & Diagnosis, Vol. I. Richard J. Kones. LC 79-89752. (New Horizons in Cardiovascular Disease Ser.). 288p. 1980. 32.50 (ISBN 0-87993-101-9). Futura Pub.

Basic Science & Diagnosis, Vol. 2. Richard J. Kones. LC 79-89752. (New Horizons in Cardiovascular Disease Ser.). 272p. 1980. 29.50 (ISBN 0-87993-144-2). Futura Pub.

Basic Science for Dental Auxiliaries. Clarinda E. Olson. (Illus.). 1980. pap. 12.95 ref. ed. (ISBN 0-13-069245-X). P-H.

Basic Science Nursing Review. R. Carole Kine et al. LC 80-22950. 208p. (Orig.). 1981. pap. text ed. 8.00 (ISBN 0-668-05133-7, 5133). Arco.

Basic Science Principles of Nuclear Medicine. Ed. by Charles M. Boyd & Glenn V. Dalrymple. LC 74-664. (Illus.). 1974. text ed. 26.50 o.p. (ISBN 0-8016-0729-9). Mosby.

Basic Sciences. 3rd ed. E. Jeff Burkes & Matthew T. Wood. (Dental Assisting Manuals: No. 2). 120p. 1980. 7.00 (ISBN 0-8078-1376-1). U of NC Pr.

Basic Scientific Subroutines, Vol. I. Fred Ruckdeschel. Ed. by T. J. Deubofsky. 1980. 19.95 (ISBN 0-07-054201-5, BYTE Bks). McGraw.

Basic Security Training Manual. Thomas J. Wagner et al. 136p. 1979. text ed. 10.75 (ISBN 0-398-03949-6). C C Thomas.

Basic Sexual Medicine. Eric Trimmer. 1978. 24.00x (ISBN 0-433-32660-3). Intl Ideas.

Basic Shapes...Plus. Kenneth Holmes. (Illus.). 24p. (gr. k-3). 1980. pap. 3.95 (ISBN 0-933358-63-6). Enrich.

Basic Sheet Metal Skills. P. M. Johnston & M. Liebowitz. LC 76-14085. 1977. pap. text ed. 10.40 (ISBN 0-8273-1237-7); instructor's guide 3.00 (ISBN 0-8273-1238-5). Delmar.

Basic Ship Theory, Vols. 1 & 2. 2nd ed. K. J. Rawson & E. C. Tupper. (Illus.). 352p. 1976. Vol. 1. pap. text ed. 19.95x (ISBN 0-582-44523-X); Vol. 2. pap. text ed. 21.00x (ISBN 0-582-44524-8). Longman.

Basic Shiphandling for Masters, Mates & Pilots. P. F. Willerton. 152p. 1981. 17.50x (ISBN 0-540-07333-4). Sheridan.

Basic Skills for Nursing Assistants. Linda L. Young. 128p. 1980. wire coil & shrink wrap 9.95 (ISBN 0-8403-2219-4). Kendall-Hunt.

Basic Skills in Kindergarten: Foundations for Formal Learning. Walter B. Barbe et al. 1980. 10.00 (ISBN 0-88309-104-6). Zaner-Bloser.

Basic Skills in Sports for Men & Women. 6th ed. David A. Armbruster, Sr. & Frank F. Musker. LC 74-14684. 1975. pap. text ed. 8.50 o.p. (ISBN 0-8016-0285-8). Mosby.

Basic Skills in Technical Mathematics, Vols. 1-4. Robert M. Barr. 1977. Vol. 1. pap. 5.50 o.p. (ISBN 0-205-05831-0); Vol. 2. 5.00x o.p. (ISBN 0-205-05833-7); Vol. 3. 6.00x o.p. (ISBN 0-205-05834-5); Vol. 4. 6.25x o.p. (ISBN 0-205-05835-3). Allyn.

Basic Skills with Decimals & Percents. J. Howett. 128p. 1980. pap. text ed. 3.00 (ISBN 0-8428-2118-X). Cambridge Bk.

Basic Skills with Fractions. J. Howett. 128p. 1980. pap. text ed. 3.00 (ISBN 0-8428-2117-1). Cambridge Bk.

Basic Skills with Whole Numbers. J. Howett. 128p. 1980. pap. text ed. 3.00 (ISBN 0-8428-2116-3). Cambridge Bk.

Basic Skills Word List. 1980. pap. 14.95 (ISBN 0-932166-02-4). Instruct Object.

Basic Sleep Mechanisms. Ed. by Olga Petre-Quadens & John D. Schlag. (NATO Advanced Study Institute Ser.). 1974. 43.50 (ISBN 0-12-552950-3). Acad Pr.

Basic Sociological Research Design. Grant Bogue. 1981. pap. text ed. 8.95x (ISBN 0-673-15349-5). Scott F.

Basic Soils Engineering. 2nd ed. B. K. Hough. LC 69-14671. (Illus.). 635p. 1969. 23.95 (ISBN 0-8260-4445-X); tchrs. manual avail. (ISBN 0-471-07502-7). Wiley.

Basic Spanish Grammar. Ana C. Jarvis & Raquel Lebredo. (Orig.). Date not set. pap. text ed. 8.95 (ISBN 0-669-03086-4); Business & Finance wkbk. 6.95 (ISBN 0-669-03089-9); spanish for communication wkbk. 6.95 (ISBN 0-669-03592-0); wkbk. for Medical Personnel 6.95 (ISBN 0-669-03090-2); wkbk. for Law Enforcement Personnel 6.95 (ISBN 0-669-03593-9); Social Sciences wkbk. (ISBN 0-699-03593-9) 6.95, inst. guide free to adopters (ISBN 0-686-65955-4); business cassettes 35.00 (ISBN 0-669-03465-7); medical cassettes 35.00 (ISBN 0-669-03466-5); social sciences cassettes (isbn 0-669-03464 9) 35.00, spanish for communications cassettes, 35.00 (ISBN 0-669-03634-X). Heath.

Basic Spanish One, 6 vols. Francisco Gaona. 1971. Set. 12.75 (ISBN 0-86589-032-3). Vol. 1, Units 1,2 (ISBN 0-86589-033-1). Vol. 2, Units 3-4 (ISBN 0-86589-034-X). Vol. 3, Units 5-6 (ISBN 0-86589-035-8). Vol. 4, Units 7-8 (ISBN 0-86589-036-6). Vol. 5, Units 9-10 (ISBN 0-86589-037-4). Vol. 6, Unit 11-12 (ISBN 0-86589-038-2). Student Guide I (ISBN 0-86589-039-0). Individual Learn.

Basic Spanish Pronunciation. Ralph S. Boggs. (Orig., Span.). (gr. 9-11). 1969. pap. 2.95 (ISBN 0-88345-012-7, 17442); tapes o.p. 40.00 (ISBN 0-685-19784-0); cassettes 60.00 (ISBN 0-685-19785-9). Regents Pub.

Basic Spelling Skills. 2nd ed. Learning Technology Incorporated. Ed. by Alton L. Raygor. (Basic Skills Ser.). 1979. pap. text ed. 7.95x (ISBN 0-07-044415-3); cassette tapes & transcripts 25.00 (ISBN 0-07-044416-1). McGraw.

Basic Spoken German Grammar. J. Pfeffer et al. LC 73-8875. (Illus.). 384p. 1974. text ed. 13.95 (ISBN 0-13-061994-9); tapes o.p. 150.00 (ISBN 0-13-062182-X); wkbk. & guide to tapes 6.95 (ISBN 0-13-062000-9). P-H.

Basic Statistical Concepts. 2nd ed. Albert E. Bartz. 438p. 1981. 15.95 (ISBN 0-8087-4041-5); write for info. wkbk by george g. seifert (ISBN 0-8087-4201-9). Burgess.

Basic Statistical Concepts: A Self-Instructional Text. 2nd ed. Jack I. Bradley & James N. McClelland. 1978. pap. 7.95x (ISBN 0-673-15075-5). Scott F.

Basic Statistics. David Blackwell. LC 69-16250. 1969. text ed. 12.95 o.p. (ISBN 0-07-005531-9, C); instructors' commentary 1.50 o.p. (ISBN 0-07-005544-0). McGraw.

Basic Statistics. William L. Hays. LC 67-21786. (Basic Concepts in Psychology Ser). (Orig.). 1967. pap. text ed. 5.95 o.p. (ISBN 0-8185-0294-0). Brooks-Cole.

Basic Statistics. 5th ed. Dick A. Leabo. (Illus.). 1976. text ed. 18.95x (ISBN 0-256-01835-9). Irwin.

Basic Statistics: A Modern Approach. 2nd ed. Morris Hamburg. 496p. 1979. text ed. 18.95 (ISBN 0-15-505109-1, HC); study guide. pap. 6.95 (ISBN 0-15-505111-3); solutions manual avail. (ISBN 0-15-505110-5). HarBraceJ.

Basic Statistics: A Primer for the Biomedical Sciences. 2nd ed. Olive J. Dunn. LC 77-9328. (Probability & Mathematical Statistics: Applied Probability & Statistics Section). 1977. 19.95 (ISBN 0-471-22744-7, Pub. by Wiley-Interscience). Wiley.

Basic Statistics: A Real World Approach. 2nd ed. Vincent E. Cangelosi et al. (Illus.). 1979. text ed. 17.95 (ISBN 0-8299-0194-9); pap. study guide 6.95 (ISBN 0-8299-0245-7); wkbk avail. (ISBN 0-8299-0464-6). West Pub.

Basic Statistics: A Real World Approach. 2nd ed. Vincent E. Cangelosi et al. (Illus.). 1979. pap. text ed. 15.95 (ISBN 0-8299-0268-6); international ed. avail. (ISBN 0-8299-0464-6). West Pub.

Basic Statistics: An Introduction. George W. Summers & William S. Peters. 1977. text ed. 18.95x (ISBN 0-534-00471-7); wkbk. 8.95x (ISBN 0-534-00498-9). Wadsworth Pub.

Basic Statistics for Business & Economics. Howard L. Balsley. LC 76-24237. 1978. text ed. 19.95 o.p. (ISBN 0-88244-086-1); student problem manual 8.25 o.p. (ISBN 0-88244-154-X). Grid Pub.

Basic Statistics for Business & Economics. 2nd ed. Paul G. Hoel & Raymond J. Jessen. LC 76-54504. (Management & Administration Ser.). 1977. 22.95x (ISBN 0-471-40268-0); study guide 6.95 (ISBN 0-471-01697-7). Wiley.

Basic Statistics for Business & Economics. Leonard J. Kazmier. (Illus.). 1979. text ed. 16.95 (ISBN 0-07-033445-5, C); wkbk. 6.50 (ISBN 0-07-033446-3); instructor's manual 4.95 (ISBN 0-07-033447-1). McGraw.

Basic Statistics for Education & the Behavioral Sciences. Sharon L. Weinberg & Kenneth P. Goldberg. LC 78-56433. (Illus.). 1979. text ed. 18.75 (ISBN 0-395-26853-2); inst. manual 0.80 (ISBN 0-395-26854-0). HM.

Basic Statistics for Health Science Students. David S. Phillips. LC 77-13865. (Psychology Ser.). (Illus.). 1978. text ed. 14.95x (ISBN 0-7167-0051-4); pap. text ed. 7.95x (ISBN 0-7167-0050-6). W H Freeman.

Basic Statistics for Nurses. Rebecca G. Knapp. LC 77-26950. 1978. pap. 10.95 (ISBN 0-471-03545-9, Wiley Medical). Wiley.

Basic Statistics for the Behavioral Sciences. Kenneth D. Hopkins & Gene V. Glass. LC 77-10877. (Educational, Measurement, Research & Statistics Ser.). (Illus.). 1978. pap. text ed. 18.95 (ISBN 0-13-069377-4). P-H.

Basic Statistics in Business & Economics. 2nd ed. George W. Summers & William S. Peters. 1977. 20.95x (ISBN 0-534-00479-2); wkbk 9.95x (ISBN 0-534-00512-8). Wadsworth Pub.

Basic Statistics of the Community: Comparison with Some European Countries. 16th ed. 1978. pap. 7.50x (ISBN 9-2825-0323-2). Intl Pubns Serv.

Basic Statistics: Tales of Distributions. 2nd ed. Chris Spatz & James O. Johnston. 1980. text ed. 16.95 (ISBN 0-8185-0384-X). Brooks-Cole.

Basic Steel Design. 2nd ed. Bruce G. Johnson et al. 1980. text ed. 24.95 (ISBN 0-13-069344-8). P-H.

Basic Steps in Astronomy. John Boulton. (Illus.). 100p. 1980. 9.95 (ISBN 0-7137-1012-8, Pub. by Blandford Pr England). Sterling.

Basic Story Techniques. Helen R. Smith. 1964. pap. 5.95x (ISBN 0-8061-1170-4). U of Okla Pr.

Basic Strokes. Paul J. Deegan. LC 75-41383. (Sports Instruction Ser.). (Illus.). (gr. 3-9). 1976. PLB 5.95 (ISBN 0-87191-502-2); pap. 2.95 (ISBN 0-686-67434-0). Creative Ed.

Basic Structural Analysis. Kurt H. Gerstle. (Civil Engineering & Engineering Mechanics Ser). (Illus.). 560p. 1973. ref. ed. 27.95 (ISBN 0-13-069393-6). P-H.

Basic Structure of Swahili. James L. Brain. (African Special Publications: No. 1). 151p. (Orig.). 1977. pap. text ed. 4.50x (ISBN 0-915984-58-X). Syracuse U Foreign Comp.

Basic Surgery. Ed. by John A. McCredie. (Illus.). 1977. pap. text ed. 18.50 (ISBN 0-02-378740-6). Macmillan Info.

Basic Surgical Care. 2nd ed. R. Roaf & L. J. Hodkinson. (Illus.). 280p. 1977. 20.95x (ISBN 0-8464-0183-5); pap. text ed. 14.00x (ISBN 0-686-60819-4). Beekman Pubs.

Basic Synoptic Networks of Observing Stations. (Illus.). 492p. 1980. pap. 45.00 (ISBN 0-686-60293-5, WMO450, WMO). Unipub.

Basic Tailoring. Ed. by Time Life Books. LC 74-80076. (Art of Sewing Ser.). (gr. 6 up). 1974. lib. bdg. 11.97 (ISBN 0-8094-1719-7, Pub. by Time-Life). Silver.

Basic Teacher Skills: Handbook for Church School Teachers. Richard E. Rusbuldt. 144p. 1981. pap. 4.95 (ISBN 0-8170-0919-1). Judson.

Basic Teachings of the Great Philosophers. Frost, S. E., Jr., B.D., Ph.D. LC 62-15320. pap. 2.95 (ISBN 0-385-03007-X, C398, Dolp). Doubleday.

Basic Teachings of the Great Psychologists. rev. ed. S. Stansfeld Sargent & Kenneth R. Stafford. LC 62-15320. pap. 3.50 (ISBN 0-385-03006-1, C397, Dolp). Doubleday.

Basic Teachings of the Philosophers. S. E. Frost, Jr. 314p. 1980. Repr. of 1942 ed. lib. bdg. 25.00 (ISBN 0-89987-256-5). Darby Bks.

Basic Technical Mathematics. 3rd ed. Allyn J. Washington. LC 77-71469. 1978. pap. text ed. 21.95 (ISBN 0-8053-9520-2); instr's guide 8.95 (ISBN 0-8053-9522-9). Benjamin-Cummings.

Basic Technical Mathematics with Calculus. 3rd ed. Allyn J. Washington. LC 77-71470. 1978. pap. text ed. 22.95 (ISBN 0-8053-9521-0); instr's guide 8.95 (ISBN 0-8053-9522-9). Benjamin-Cummings.

Basic Technical Mathematics with Calculus: Metric Version. 3rd ed. Allyn J. Washington. LC 77-71471. 1978. pap. text ed. 22.95 (ISBN 0-8053-9523-7); instr's guide 8.95 (ISBN 0-8053-9524-5). Benjamin-Cummings.

Basic Techniques of Preparative Organic Chemistry. W. Sabel. 1967. pap. 7.00 (ISBN 0-08-012307-4). Pergamon.

Basic Teeline. James Hill & I. C. Hill. 1969. pap. text ed. 4.95x o.p. (ISBN 0-435-45331-9); tchr's ed 1.75x o.p. (ISBN 0-435-45335-1). Heinemann Ed.

Basic Telephone Switching Systems. 2nd ed. David Talley. 1979. pap. 9.60 (ISBN 0-8104-5687-7). Hayden.

Basic Tennis Illustrated. Merritt Cutler. (Illus.). 111p. 1980. pap. 4.95 0 (ISBN 0-486-24006-1). Dover.

Basic Textiles: A Learning Package. Carol H. Siewert et al. 228p. 1973. 11.50 (ISBN 0-395-14220-2). HM.

Basic Theory & Application of Transistors. U. S. Army. (Illus.). 1962. pap. text ed. 3.50 (ISBN 0-486-20380-8). Dover.

Basic Theory of Corporate Finance. Kenneth J. Bourdeaux & Hugh W. Long. LC 76-27895. (Illus.). 1977. pap. text ed. 19.95 (ISBN 0-13-069435-5). P-H.

Basic Theory of Structures. J. S. Browne. 1966. 25.00 (ISBN 0-08-011654-X); pap. 12.75 (ISBN 0-08-011653-1). Pergamon.

Basic Theory of Waveguide Junctions & Introductory Microwave Network Analysis. D. M. Kerns & R. W. Beatty. 1967. text ed. 17.25 (ISBN 0-08-012064-4). Pergamon.

Basic Thirty-Five mm Photo Guide. Craig Alesse. LC 79-54311. (Illus.). 110p. (Orig.). 1979. pap. 10.95 (ISBN 0-936262-00-1). Amherst Media.

Basic Tig & Mig Welding. 2nd ed. I. H. Griffin et al. LC 76-14085. 1977. pap. text ed. 5.20 (ISBN 0-8273-1260-1); instructor's guide 1.00 (ISBN 0-8273-1262-8). Delmar.

Basic Tools of Research. 3rd ed. Philip Vitale. LC 74-8827. (gr. 9-12). 1975. pap. text ed. 3.50 (ISBN 0-8120-0627-5). Barron.

Basic Training: A Portrait of Today's Army. Burnham Holmes. LC 78-22128. (Illus.). 128p. (gr. 7 up). 1979. 8.95 (ISBN 0-590-07528-4, Four Winds). Schol Bk Serv.

Basic Training for Horses--English & Western. Illus. by Eleanor F. Prince. LC 76-42383. (Illus.). 1979. 12.95 (ISBN 0-385-03244-7). Doubleday.

Basic Training for the Second Half of Life. Robert Linn. 1980. pap. write for info. PB.

Basic Training for Young Horses & Ponies. British Horse Society & Pony Club. LC 76-54933. 1977. pap. 1.95 (ISBN 0-8120-0757-3). Barron.

Basic Transistors. rev.,2nd ed. Alexander Schure. 152p. 1976. pap. text ed. 8.95 (ISBN 0-8104-0860-0); exam 0.50 (ISBN 0-8104-0597-0); final exam 0.20 (ISBN 0-8104-0598-9). Hayden.

Basic Trigonometry with Applications in Technology. Rudolph A. Zimmer. LC 80-82834. 256p. 1980. pap. text ed. 10.95 (ISBN 0-8403-2273-9). Kendall-Hunt.

Basic TV Staging. Gerald Millerson. Date not set. pap. 7.95 o.p. (ISBN 0-8038-0747-3). Hastings.

Basic Verbal Skills. rev. ed. Philip Burnham & Richard Lederer. 245p. (gr. 9-12). 1975. pap. text ed. 4.75x (ISBN 0-88334-067-4); wkbk. 2.50x (ISBN 0-88334-130-1). Ind Sch Pr.

Basic Verbal Skills. 2nd ed. Philip Burnham & Richard Lederer. 243p. (gr. 9-12). 1980. pap. text ed. 4.95x (ISBN 0-88334-134-4). Ind Sch Pr.

Basic Verbal Skills for the Middle School. Philip Burnham & Richard Lederer. (gr. 6-9). 1976. pap. text ed. 5.25x (ISBN 0-88334-098-4); wkbk. 2.50x (ISBN 0-88334-074-7). Ind Sch Pr.

Basic Visual Processes & Learning Disability. Gerald Leisman. (Illus.). 456p. 1976. 35.75 (ISBN 0-398-03454-0). C C Thomas.

Basic Water Treatment -- for Application Worldwide. George Smethurst. 228p. 1980. 40.00x (ISBN 0-7277-0071-5, Pub. by Telford England). State Mutual Bk.

Basic Wiring. (Home Repair & Improvement Ser.). (Illus.). 1976. 10.95 (ISBN 0-8094-2358-8). Time-Life.

Basic Wiring. LC 76-12151. (Home Repair & Improvement). (Illus.). (gr. 7 up). 1976. pap. 11.97 (ISBN 0-8094-2359-6, Pub. by Time-Life). Silver.

BASIC with Style: Programming Proverbs. Paul Nagin & Henry F. Ledgard. (gr. 10 up). 1978. pap. text ed. 7.15 (ISBN 0-8104-5115-8). Hayden.

Basic Woodworking. Feirer. (gr. 9-12). 1978. 6.00 (ISBN 0-87002-290-3); pap. 4.32 (ISBN 0-87002-274-1). Bennett IL.

Basic Woodworking Projects. Harry McGinnis & M. J. Ruley. (gr. 7-9). 1959. text ed. 13.28 (ISBN 0-87345-043-4). McKnight.

Basic Word List. Brownstein & Weiner. 1981. pap. 2.50 (ISBN 0-8120-0709-3). Barron.

BASIC Workbook: Creative Techniques for Beginning Programmers. Kenneth E. Schoman, Jr. (gr. 10 up). 1977. pap. text ed. 7.15x (ISBN 0-8104-5104-2). Hayden.

Basic World Place Location. Milton D. Rafferty & Scott Harris. (Illus.). 1977. pap. text ed. 2.95 (ISBN 0-8403-1791-3). Kendall-Hunt.

Basic Writer's Book. Anne Agee & Gary Kline. (Illus.). 384p. 1981. text ed. 11.95 (ISBN 0-13-069476-2). P-H.

Basic Writing: A Practical Approach. Sue Lorch. 300p. 1981. pap. text ed. 8.95. Winthrop.

Basic Writing: Essays for Teachers, Researchers, & Administrators. Daniel R. Hoeber & Lawrence N. Kasden. LC 80-14634. 185p. (Orig.). 1980. pap. 9.50 (ISBN 0-8141-0268-9). NCTE.

Basic Writing Skills. Robert Burleigh & Mary Jane Gray. LC 77-730072. (Illus.). (gr. 6-8). 1976. pap. text ed. 225.00 (ISBN 0-89290-115-2, CM-39). Soc for Visual.

Basic Writing Skills with Activities & Tests. Joyce Gardner. (gr. k-6). 1978. spiral bdg. 6.50x (ISBN 0-933892-00-4). Child Focus Co.

Basic Writings, Vol. 1. Saint Thomas Aquinas. Ed. by Anton C. Pegis. 1945. 15.00 o.p. (ISBN 0-394-41617-1). Random.

Basic Writings of Mo Tzu, Hsun Tzu, & Han Fei Tzu. Ed. & tr. by Burton Watson. LC 67-16170. (Records of Civilization, Sources & Studies: No. 74). 1967. 16.00x (ISBN 0-231-02515-7). Columbia U Pr.

Basic Writings on Politics & Philosophy. Friedrich Engels & Karl Marx. LC 59-12053. pap. 4.95 (ISBN 0-385-09420-5, A185, Anch). Doubleday.

Basics & Beyond. Berman & Shevitz. 1981. pap. text ed. write for info. (ISBN 0-8302-0992-1). Goodyear.

Basics for Buyers: A Practical Guide to Better Purchasing. Somerby R. Dowst. LC 74-156479. (Illus.). 1971. 15.95 (ISBN 0-8436-1301-7). CBI Pub.

Basics for Municipal Bond Lawyers: Course Handbook. Ed. by Robert S. Amdursky. LC 80-82474. (Nineteen Seventy-Nine to Nineteen Eighty Corporate Law & Practice Course Handbook Ser.). 887p. 1980. pap. 25.00 (ISBN 0-686-69164-4, B4-6551). PLI.

Basics: For Peace, Democracy & Social Progress. Gus Hall. 348p. (Orig.). 1980. 14.00 (ISBN 0-7178-0580-8); pap. 4.50 (ISBN 0-7178-0578-6). Intl Pub Co.

Basics of Astrology, 3 vols. Ove H. Sehested. LC 73-90440. 1973. Set. 3 vols. bound in 1 14.95 (ISBN 0-9601080-4-1). Vol. 1. pap. 4.95 (ISBN 0-9601080-1-7); Vol. 2. pap. 4.95 (ISBN 0-9601080-2-5); Vol. 3. pap. 3.95 (ISBN 0-9601080-3-3). Uranus Pub.

Basics of Circuit Analysis for Practicing Engineers. Gordon E. Johnson. LC 71-150505. 1971. 10.95 (ISBN 0-8436-0320-8); pap. 4.95 o.p. (ISBN 0-8436-0321-6). CBI Pub.

Basics of Consequentialism. David L. Cale. LC 80-82228. (Illus.). 160p. 1980. 12.95 (ISBN 0-87012-393-9); pap. 7.95 (ISBN 0-87012-389-0). Laurel Inst.

Basics of Data Communications. Electronics Magazine. Ed. by Harry R. Karp. LC 76-16475. (Illus.). 303p. 1976. pap. text ed. 12.95 (ISBN 0-07-019159-X, R-603). McGraw.

Basics of Digital Computers, 3 Vols. rev. 2nd ed. John S. Murphy. (Illus.). (gr. 10-12). 1970. Set. pap. 15.95x o.p. (ISBN 0-8104-0737-X). Vol. 1. pap. 5.35 (ISBN 0-8104-0738-8); Vol. 2. pap. 6.45 o.p. (ISBN 0-8104-0739-6); Vol. 3. pap. 6.45 (ISBN 0-8104-0740-X); transparencies 255.30 (ISBN 0-685-03720-7); exam set, vol. 1 0.40 (ISBN 0-8104-0742-6); exam set vol. 2 0.40 (ISBN 0-8104-0743-4); exam set vol. 3 0.40 (ISBN 0-8104-0744-2). Hayden.

Basics of Electroorganic Synthesis. Demetrios Kyriacou. 230p. 1980. 24.50 (ISBN 0-471-07975-8, Pub. by Wiley-Interscience). Wiley.

Basics of Food Allergy. James C. Breneman. (Illus.). 296p. 1978. 35.75 (ISBN 0-398-03670-5). C C Thomas.

Basics of Fractional Horsepower Motors & Repair. Gerald Schweitzer. (Illus.). 1960. pap. 7.65 (ISBN 0-8104-0418-4). Hayden.

Basics of Investing. Benton E. Gup. LC 78-17521. (Ser. in Finance). 1979. text ed. 21.50 (ISBN 0-471-33620-3); tchrs. manual avail. (ISBN 0-471-04813-5); tests avail. (ISBN 0-471-05663-4); study guide avail. (ISBN 0-471-05573-5). Wiley.

Basics of Librarianship. C. Harrison & R. Oakes. 1980. pap. 12.50x (Pub. by Lib Assn England). Oryx Pr.

Basics of Model Rocketry. Douglas R. Pratt. Ed. by Burr Angle. LC 80-84580. (Illus., Orig.). 1981. pap. 2.50 (ISBN 0-89024-557-6). Kalmbach.

Basics of Online Searching. Charles T. Meadow & Pauline Atherton. (Information Science Ser.). 200p. 1981. 14.95 (ISBN 0-471-05283-3, Pub. by Wiley-Interscience). Wiley.

Basics of Private & Public Management. Stahrl W. Edmunds. LC 77-9147. 1978. 22.95 (ISBN 0-669-01679-9). Lexington Bks.

Basics of Radiopharmacy. Buck A. Rhodes & Barbara Y. Croft. LC 77-26557. 1978. pap. text ed. 17.95 (ISBN 0-8016-4127-6). Mosby.

Basics of Reprography. Arthur Tyrell. (Reprographic Library). Date not set. 12.50 o.p. (ISBN 0-8038-0733-3). Hastings.

Basics of Structural Steel Design. Samuel H. Marcus. (Illus.). 464p. 1977. text ed. 20.95 (ISBN 0-87909-069-3); student manual avail. Reston.

Basidiomycetes That Decay Aspen in North America. J. P. Lindsey & R. L. Gilbertson. (Bibliotheca Mycologica Ser.: No. 63). 1978. lib. bdg. 60.00 (ISBN 3-7682-1193-2). Lubrecht & Cramer.

Basil. Wilkie Collins. 352p. 1980. pap. 4.50 (ISBN 0-486-24015-0). Dover.

Basil & Boris in London. Ron Van Der Meer & Atie Van Der Meer. 1979. pap. 1.45 available in 5 pk. (ISBN 0-85122-169-6, Pub. by Dinosaur Pubns). Merrimack Bk Serv.

Basil & the Lost Colony. Eve Titus. (gr. 3-6). 1981. pap. 1.50 (ISBN 0-671-41602-2). Archway.

Basil & the Pygmy Cats. Eve Titus. (Illus.). 178p. (gr. 3-6). 1980. pap. 1.75 (ISBN 0-671-41478-X). Archway.

Basil Brush Goes Flying. Peter Firmin. 1977. 4.95 (ISBN 0-13-066639-4). P-H.

Basil of Baker Street. Eve Titus. (gr. 3-6). 1958. pap. 1.75 (ISBN 0-671-41729-0). Archway.

Basil Rathbone: His Life & His Films. Michael B. Druxman. LC 74-3611. (Illus.). 256p. 1975. 12.00 o.p. (ISBN 0-498-01471-1). A S Barnes.

Basin & Range. John McPhee. 1981. 10.95 (ISBN 0-374-10914-1). FS&G.

Basin-Plateau Aboriginal Sociopolitical Groups. 2nd ed. Julian H. Steward. (Smithsonian Institution Bureau of Ethnology Ser.: Bulletin 120). 1975. pap. 8.00x (ISBN 0-87480-014-5). U of Utah Pr.

Basis for Cancer Therapy One, No. 1. International Cancer Congress, 12th, Buenos Aires, 5-11 October 1978. LC 79-40485. (Advances in Medical Oncology, Research & Education: Vol. V). 1979. 68.00 (ISBN 0-08-024388-6). Pergamon.

Basis for Cancer Therapy Two. International Cancer Congress, 12th, Buenos Aires, 5-11 October 1979. LC 79-40064. (Advances in Medical Oncology Research & Education: Vol. VI). (Illus.). 1979. 68.00 (ISBN 0-08-024389-4). Pergamon.

Basis for Music Education. Keith Swanwick. (Orig.). 1979. pap. text ed. 13.25x (ISBN 0-85633-180-5). Humanities.

Basis for Sensorimotor Development-Normal & Abnormal: The Influence of Primitive, Postural Reflexes on the Development & Distribution of Tone. Mary R. Fiorentino. (Illus.). 184p. 1981. text ed. 14.75 (ISBN 0-398-04179-2). C C Thomas.

Basis Jahrbuch: Jahrbuch Fuer Deutsche Gegenwartsliteratur, Bd. 10. (Suhrkamp Taschenbuecher: Bd. 589). 263p. (Orig., Ger.). 1980. pap. text ed. 6.50 (ISBN 3-518-37089-8, Pub. by Insel Verlag Germany). Suhrkamp.

Basis of Accounting. Eugene J. Laughlin. LC 76-15721. (Accounting Ser.). 1977. text ed. 17.50 o.p. (ISBN 0-88244-137-X). Grid Pub.

Basis of Organic Chemistry. 2nd ed. Ralph J. Fessenden & Joan S. Fessenden. 1978. text ed. 17.95 (ISBN 0-205-05740-3); ans. bk. avail. (ISBN 0-205-05741-1). Allyn.

Basis of Sex Education. Peter J. Fitzgerald. 1981. 7.95 (ISBN 0-533-04636-X). Vantage.

Basket Case. Robert Newton Peck. LC 78-60298. (gr. 10 up). 1979. 5.95 (ISBN 0-385-14362-1). Doubleday.

Basket Counts. Matt Christopher. (Illus.). (gr. 4-6). 5.95 o.p. (ISBN 0-316-14014-7). Little.

Basket Maker Artists. Don M. Chase. (Illus.). 1978. pap. 2.50 (ISBN 0-918634-34-2). D M Chase.

Basketball. rev. ed. Phog Allen et al. LC 65-20875. (Athletic Institute Ser). (Illus.). (gr. 5 up). 1968. 6.95 o.p. (ISBN 0-8069-4302-5); PLB 7.49 o.p. (ISBN 0-8069-4303-3). Sterling.

Basketball. Brian Naysmith & Terry Hill. 1978. 10.50 (ISBN 0-7153-7509-1). David & Charles.

Basketball--Hockey Trivia Puzzle, No. 1. 1981. pap. 1.95 (ISBN 0-440-00738-0). Dell.

Basketball Basics. Greggory Morris. LC 75-34142. (Illus.). (gr. 2-6). 1976. 6.95 (ISBN 0-13-072256-1); pap. 1.50 (ISBN 0-13-072223-5). P-H.

Basketball Coaching & Playing. Ed. by B. Jagger. 1971. 12.75 (ISBN 0-571-04743-2). Transatlantic.

Basketball: Concepts & Techniques. Robert J. Cousy & Frank Power, Jr. 1970. 19.95 (ISBN 0-205-02749-0, 622749X). Allyn.

Basketball: How to Improve Your Technique. Arthur Kaplan. LC 73-14538. (Career Concise Guide Ser.). (Illus.). 72p. 1974. PLB 4.90 o.p. (ISBN 0-531-02674-4). Watts.

Basketball Methods. Pete Newell & John Benington. (Illus.). 1962. 14.95 (ISBN 0-8260-6710-7). Wiley.

Basketball: Picking Winners Against the Spread. A. J. Friedman. (Orig.). 1978. pap. 2.95 (ISBN 0-89650-620-7, Gambler's Book Shelf). Gamblers.

Basketball Schedules Book. 4.00 (ISBN 0-686-22333-0). NAIA Pubns.

Basketball Techniques for Women. Patsy E. Neal. (Illus.). 1966. 15.50 (ISBN 0-8260-6620-8). Wiley.

Basketball: Techniques, Teaching & Training. 2nd rev. ed. Brian Coleman. LC 78-54017. (Illus.). 1978. 9.95 o.p. (ISBN 0-498-02275-7). A S Barnes.

Basketball Toss up. Alex B. Allen. LC 73-7317. (Springboard Ser.). (Illus.). 64p. (Remedial Reader). (gr. 3-8). 1972. 5.75g (ISBN 0-8075-0578-1). A Whitman.

Basketball's Finest Center: Kareem Abdul-Jabbar. Paula Taylor. (Allstars Ser.). (Illus.). (gr. 2-6). 1977. PLB 5.95 o.p. (ISBN 0-87191-584-7). Creative Ed.

Basketballs for Breakfast. Alice Sankey. LC 63-20350. (Pilot Book Ser). (Illus.). (gr. 3-5). 1963. 6.95g (ISBN 0-8075-0583-8). A Whitman.

Basketmaking from the Beginning. Lura La Barge. LC 75-38908. (Funk & W Bk.). (Illus.). 112p. 1976. 7.95 o.s.i. (ISBN 0-308-10243-6, TYC-T); pap. 4.95 o.s.i. (ISBN 0-308-10244-4, TYC-T). T Y Crowell.

Basketry. Boy Scouts Of America. LC 19-600. (Illus.). 32p. (gr. 6-12). 1968. pap. 0.70x (ISBN 0-8395-3313-6, 3313). BSA.

Basketry. Rachel Gilman & Nancy Bess. (Step-by-Step Crafts Ser.). (Illus.). 1977. PLB 9.15 o.p. (ISBN 0-307-62021-2, Golden Pr); pap. 2.95 (ISBN 0-307-42021-3). Western Pub.

Basketry. Glen Pownall. (New Craft Bk.). 80p. 1980. 7.50 (ISBN 0-85467-023-8, Pub. by Viking Sevenseas New Zealand). Intl Schol Bk Serv.

Basketry Book. Sherry De Leon. LC 77-2777. (Illus.). 1978. 12.95 o.p. (ISBN 0-03-017866-5); pap. 7.95 o.p. (ISBN 0-03-042851-3). HR&W.

Basketry of the Papago & Pima Indians: Anthropological Papers of the Am. Museum of Natural History, Vol. 17, Pt. 4. Mary L. Kissell. LC 72-8827. (Beautiful Rio Grande Classics Ser). lib. bdg. 10.00 o.s.i. (ISBN 0-87380-095-8); pap. 8.00 o.p. (ISBN 0-87380-133-4). Rio Grande.

Basketry of the San Carlos Apache Indians: Anthropological Papers of the Am. Museum of Natural History, Vol. 31, Pt. 2. Helen H. Roberts. LC 72-10331. (Beautiful Rio Grande Classics Ser). lib. bdg. 10.00 o.s.i. (ISBN 0-87380-096-6); pap. 8.00 o.p. (ISBN 0-87380-134-2). Rio Grande.

Basketry Technology: A Guide to Identification & Analysis. James M. Adovasio. (Manuals on Archeology Ser.: No. 1). (Illus.). x, 182p. 1977. 18.00x (ISBN 0-202-33035-4). Taraxacum.

Baskets of Rural America. Gloria A. Teleki. (Illus.). 1975. pap. 7.50 (ISBN 0-525-47409-9). Dutton.

Basketwork Through the Ages. Henry H. Bobart. LC 72-171354. 188p. 1971. Repr. of 1936 ed. 15.00 (ISBN 0-8103-3400-3). Gale.

Basque & the Boy. John A. Croner. 1981. 10.95 (ISBN 0-87949-176-0). Ashley Bks.

Basques. Kenneth Medhurst. (Minority Rights Group: No. 9). 1972. pap. 2.50 (ISBN 0-89192-098-6). Interbk Inc.

Basques: The Franco Years & Beyond. Robert P. Clark. LC 79-24926. (Basque Bk.). xvii, 434p. 1980. 17.50 (ISBN 0-87417-057-5). U of Nev Pr.

Bass. Robert H. Boyle & Elgin Ciampi. (Illus.). 144p. 1980. 27.50 (ISBN 0-393-01379-0). Norton.

Bass Myths Exploded: Newest Ways to Catch Largemouths. Jerry Gibbs. (Illus.). 1978. 10.95 o.p. (ISBN 0-679-50859-7). McKay.

Bass Viol in French Baroque Chamber Music. Julie A. Sadie. Ed. by George Buelow. (Studies in Musicology). 250p. 1981. 29.95 (ISBN 0-8357-1116-1, Pub. by UMI Res Pr). Univ Microfilms.

Basset Hound. E. Fitch Daglish. (Foyle's Handbks). 1973. 3.95 (ISBN 0-685-55818-5). Palmetto Pub.

Basset Hounds. Diane McCarty & Mrs. Travis Look. (Illus.). 125p. 1979. 2.95 (ISBN 0-87666-679-9, KW-069). TFH Pubns.

Bassoon Technique. Archie Camden. 1962. 7.75 (ISBN 0-19-318606-3). Oxford U Pr.

Bassumtyte Treasure. Jane L. Curry. LC 77-14381. (gr. 4-7). 1978. 8.95 (ISBN 0-689-50100-5, McElderry Bk). Atheneum.

Bastard. John Wainwright. 1976. 7.95 o.p. (ISBN 0-312-06930-8). St Martin.

Bastard, No. 1. John Jakes. (Kent Family Chronicles). 1978. pap. 2.95 (ISBN 0-515-05862-9). Jove Pubns.

Bastard Photostory. Photos by John Jakes. (Orig.). 1980. pap. 2.75 (ISBN 0-515-05433-X). Jove Pubns.

Bastard Roses. Alma Villanueva. 1981. pap. 4.00 (ISBN 0-915016-31-1). Second Coming.

Bastardy. John Brydall. Ed. by David Berkowitz & Samuel Thorne. LC 77-86581. (Classics of English Legal History in the Modern Era Ser.). 1979. lib. bdg. 55.00 (ISBN 0-8240-3064-8). Garland Pub.

Bat Is Born. Randall Jarrell. LC 76-52725. (ps-3). 1978. 5.95a o.p. (ISBN 0-385-12223-3); PLB (ISBN 0-385-12224-1). Doubleday.

Bat-Poet. Randall Jarrell. (Illus.). (gr. 4-6). 1964. 8.95g (ISBN 0-02-747640-5). Macmillan.

BAT-Twenty-One: Based on the True Story of Lt. Col. Iceal E. Hambleton, USAF. William C. Anderson. LC 80-20648. 1980. 9.95 (ISBN 0-13-069500-9). P-H.

Batal Al Abtal. Abed Al-Esmani. pap. 5.95x. Intl Bk Ctr.

Batarde. Violette Leduc. Tr. by Derek Coltman. 488p. 1965. 12.95 o.p. (ISBN 0-374-18232-9); pap. 7.95 (ISBN 0-374-51371-6). FS&G.

Batek Negrito Religion: The World-View & Rituals of a Hunting & Gathering People of Peninsular Malaysia. Kirk Endicott. (Illus.). 1979. 34.95x (ISBN 0-19-823197-0). Oxford U Pr.

Bates Family. Reginald Ottley. LC 69-18627. (gr. 4-6). 1969. 4.50 o.p. (ISBN 0-15-205726-9, HJ). HarBraceJ.

Batfish: The Champion "Submarine-Killer" Submarine of World War Ii. Hughston E. Lowder & Jack Scott. LC 80-12155. (Illus.). 300p. 1980. 10.95 (ISBN 0-13-066563-0). P-H.

Bath. Edith Sitwell. LC 78-14145. (Illus.). 1981. Repr. of 1932 ed. 26.00 (ISBN 0-88355-818-1). Hyperion Conn.

Bath: An Architectural Guide. Charles Robertson. 1975. 33.00 (ISBN 0-571-10750-8, Pub. by Faber & Faber); pap. 9.95 (ISBN 0-571-10805-9). Merrimack Bk Serv.

Bath Book. Linda Presto. (Illus.). (gr. k-2). 1978. PLB 5.38 (ISBN 0-307-68935-2, Golden Pr). Western Pub.

Ba'th Party: A History from Its Origins to 1966. John F. Devlin. LC 75-41903. (Publications Ser.: No. 156). 372p. 1976. 11.95 (ISBN 0-8179-6561-0). Hoover Inst Pr.

Bath Sixteen Eighty to Eighteen Fifty: A Social History. R. S. Neale. (Illus.). 400p. 1981. price not set (ISBN 0-7100-0639-X). Routledge & Kegan.

Bath Tangle. Georgette Heyer. (Regency Romance Ser.). 320p. 1981. pap. 1.95 (ISBN 0-515-05760-6). Jove Pubns.

Bathing Girl. Ludovic Janvier. Tr. by John Mathew. 1980. 8.95 (ISBN 0-7145-3519-2). Riverrun NY.

Bathroom Remodeling. Charles Self. (Illus.). 224p. 1980. 12.95 (ISBN 0-8359-0436-9); pap. 4.95 (ISBN 0-8359-0435-0). Reston.

Bathrooms. Sunset Editors. LC 80-80856. (Illus.). 80p. 1980. pap. 3.95 (ISBN 0-376-01326-5, Sunset Bks). Sunset-Lane.

Bathsheba to Rehoboam - Man & Sin. E. M. Blaiklock & A. S. Wood. (Bible Characters & Doctrines). 1972. pap. 1.75 o.p. (ISBN 0-8028-1461-1). Eerdmans.

Batik As a Hobby. Vivian Stein. LC 69-19491. (Illus.). (gr. 9 up). 1969. 6.95 o.p. (ISBN 0-8069-5132-X); PLB 6.69 o.p. (ISBN 0-8069-5133-8). Sterling.

Batik in Many Forms. Laura Adasko & Alice Huberman. LC 74-16376. (Illus.). 176p. 1975. 12.95 o.p. (ISBN 0-688-00340-0). Morrow.

Batiment: Enquete D'histoire Economidue XIVe-XIXe Siecles, Tome 1. Ed. by Jean-Pierre Bardet et al. (Maisons Rurales et Urbaines Dans la France Traditionnello Industrite et Artisanat: No. 6). 1971. pap. 51.20x (ISBN 90-2796-880-2). Mouton.

Baton Techniques & Training. Takayuki Kubota & Paul F. McCaul. (Illus.). 320p. 1974. 14.75 (ISBN 0-398-02338-7). C C Thomas.

Baton Twirling. Nancy L. Robison. LC 78-73746. (Free Time Fun Ser.). (Illus.). 56p. (gr. 3 up). 1980. PLB 6.79 (ISBN 0-8178-5999-3). Harvey.

Bats. Richard Mandell. LC 80-83027. 170p. (Orig.). 1981. pap. 4.50 (ISBN 0-9605008-0-4). Hermes Hse.

Bats. Valerie Pitt. LC 76-12535. (First Bks.). (Illus.). 72p. (gr. 5-8). 1976. PLB 4.90 o.p. (ISBN 0-531-00335-3). Watts.

Bats, Cats, & Sacred Cows. Tamara Wilcox. LC 77-10834. (Myth, Magic & Superstition Ser.). (Illus.). (gr. 4-5). 1977. PLB 9.65 (ISBN 0-8172-1026-1). Raintree Pubs.

Bats in the Dark. John Kaufmann. LC 72-158695. (Let's Read & Find-Out Science Bk). (gr. k-3). 1972. 6.95 (ISBN 0-690-11780-9, TYC-J); PLB 7.89 (ISBN 0-690-11781-7). T Y Crowell.

Bats in the Night. George Laycock. LC 80-25834. (Illus.). 64p. (gr. 1-5). 1981. 9.95 (ISBN 0-590-07653-1, Four Winds). Schol Bk Serv.

Bats of Jalisco, Mexico. Larry C. Watkins et al. (Special Publications: No. 1). (Illus., Orig.). 1972. pap. 2.00 (ISBN 0-89672-026-8). Tex Tech Pr.

Bats: Wings in the Night. Patricia Lauber. LC 68-23672. (Gateway Ser.: No. 47). (Illus.). (gr. 3-6). 1968. PLB 5.39 (ISBN 0-394-90147-9, BYR). Random.

Batsford Book of Country Verse. Samuel Carr. 1979. 17.95 (ISBN 0-7134-2019-7, Pub. by Batsford England). David & Charles.

Batsford Book of Light Verse for Children. Ed. by Gavin Ewart. 1978. 17.95 (ISBN 0-7134-0916-9). David & Charles.

Batsford Book of Sewing. Ann Ladbury. 1978. pap. 13.50 (ISBN 0-7134-0199-0, Pub. by Batsford England). David & Charles.

Batsford Book of Sporting Verse. Ed. by Peter Verney. (Illus.). 131p. 1980. 17.95 (ISBN 0-7134-2009-X, Pub. by Batsford England). David & Charles.

Batsford Book of Stories in Verse for Children. Charles Causley. 1979. 17.95 (ISBN 0-7134-1529-0). David & Charles.

Batsford Book of the Cotswolds. Gary Hogg. 1979. pap. 11.95 (ISBN 0-7134-2449-4, Pub. by Batsford England). David & Charles.

Batsford Book of the Siamese Cat. Phyllis Lauder. 1974. 14.95 (ISBN 0-7134-2828-7, Pub. by Batsford England). David & Charles.

Batsford Colour Book of Ireland. Kenneth McNally. 1975. 10.50 (ISBN 0-7134-2904-6, Pub. by Batsford England). David & Charles.

Batsford Colour Book of Kent. Judith Glover. 1976. 11.95 (ISBN 0-7134-3153-9, Pub. by Batsford England). David & Charles.

Batsford Colour Book of Shakespeare's Country. Gary Hogg. 1976. 10.50 (ISBN 0-7134-3151-2, Pub. by Batsford England). David & Charles.

Batsford Colour Book of Sussex. Judith Glover. (Illus.). 64p. 1980. pap. 8.95 (ISBN 0-7134-3275-6, Pub. by Batsford England). David & Charles.

Batsford Colour Book of Wales. Cledwyn Hughes. 1975. 8.95 (ISBN 0-7134-3003-6, Pub. by Batsford England). David & Charles.

Batsford Fide Chess Yearbook, 1975-1976. F. J. O'Connell. 159p. 1976. 16.95 (ISBN 0-7134-1223-2). David & Charles.

Batsford Fide Chess Yearbook, 1976-1977. K. J. O'Connell. 1977. 16.95 (ISBN 0-7134-0675-5). David & Charles.

Batsford Fide Chess Yearbook, 1977-1978. K. J. O'Connell. 1978. 16.95 (ISBN 0-7134-1223-2). David & Charles.

Batsford Guide to Racing Cars. Dennis Jenkinson. 1979. 14.95 (ISBN 0-7134-1273-9, Pub. by Batsford England). David & Charles.

Batsford Guide to the Industrial Archaeology of Central Southern England. C. A. Buchanon & R. A. Buchanon. (Illus.). 192p. 1980. 45.00 (ISBN 0-7134-1364-6, Pub. by Batsford England). David & Charles.

Batsford Guide to the Industrial Archaeology of East Anglia. David Alderton & John Booker. LC 79-56490. (Illus.). 150p. 1980. 40.00 (ISBN 0-7134-2233-5, Pub. by Batsford England). David & Charles.

Batsford Guide to Veteran Cars. Francis Sutton-Scott & D. G. Shapland. 1979. 14.95 (ISBN 0-7134-1182-1, Pub. by Batsford England). David & Charles.

Batsford Guide to Vintage Cars. Cecil Clutton et al. 1976. 14.95 o.p. (ISBN 0-686-63854-9, Pub. by Batsford England). David & Charles.

Battenberg & Point Lace: Techniques, Stitches & Designs from Victorian Needlework. Ed. by Jules Kliot & Kaethe Kliot. (Illus.). 1978. pap. text ed. 3.50 o.p. (ISBN 0-916896-12-9). Lacis Pubns.

Batter My Heart. Robb Murray. (Orion Ser.). 192p. 1980. pap. write for info. (ISBN 0-8127-0301-4). Southern Pub.

Battered Child. 3rd rev. ed. C. Henry Kempe & Ray E. Helfer. LC 80-14329. (Illus.). 1980. 25.00 (ISBN 0-226-43038-3). U of Chicago Pr.

Battered Child Syndrome. S. M. Smith. 1976. 29.95 (ISBN 0-407-00046-1). Butterworths.

Battered Rich. Steve Bassett. Ed. by Sylvia Ashton. 1980. 11.95 (ISBN 0-87949-159-0). Ashley Bks.

Battered Spouses. Nick Miller. 69p. 1975. pap. text ed. 5.00x (ISBN 0-7135-1936-3, Pub. by Bedford England). Renouf.

Battered Women. Donna M. Moore. LC 79-982. (Focus Editions Ser.: Vol. 9). (Illus.). 232p. 1979. 18.95 (ISBN 0-8039-1162-9); pap. 9.95 (ISBN 0-8039-1163-7). Sage.

Battered Women's Directory. 8th ed. Betsy Warrior et al. 1981. pap. 5.00 (ISBN 0-9601544-5-0). B Warrior.

Battery Chargers & Testers: Operation, Repair, & Maintenance. Charles R. Cantonwine. LC 73-153135. (Illus.). 1971. 12.50 o.p. (ISBN 0-8019-5621-8). Chilton.

Battery Mates. William R. Cox. LC 77-16871. (gr. 5 up). 1978. 5.95 (ISBN 0-396-07525-8). Dodd.

Batting Machine. Mel Knopf. 192p. 1981. 9.95 (ISBN 0-89962-205-4). Todd & Honeywell.

Batting Secrets of the Major Leaguers. (Illus.). 112p. 1981. write for info. (ISBN 0-671-41315-5). Messner.

Battle Against Bacteria: A Fresh Look. P. E. Baldry. LC 76-639. (Illus.). 140p. 1976. 18.95 (ISBN 0-521-21268-5). Cambridge U Pr.

Battle Against Isolation. Walter Johnson. LC 72-3376. (FDR & the Era of the New Deal Ser.). 270p. 1974. Repr. of 1944 ed. lib. bdg. 29.50 (ISBN 0-306-70480-3). Da Capo.

Battle & the Books: Some Aspects of Henry James. Edward Stone. LC 64-22886. xi, 234p. 1964. 12.95x (ISBN 0-8214-0002-9). Ohio U Pr.

Battle Coast: An Illustrated History of D-Day. R. H. Hunter & T. C. Brown. (Illus.). 142p. 1974. 14.50 (ISBN 0-902875-24-8). Transatlantic.

Battle Drums & Geysers, 3 vols. Ed. by Orrin H. Bonney & Lorraine G. Bonney. Incl. Vol. I. Lt. Gustavus C. Doane: His Life & Remarkable Military Career; Vol. II. Exploration of Yellowstone Park, Lt. Doane's Yellowstone Journal; Vol. III. Lt. G. C. Doane's Snake River Journal of 1876. (Illus.). 1978. Vols. I & III. pap. 3.95; pap. 4.95. Bonney.

Battle for Britain. Harry T. Sutton. 1979. pap. 3.50 o.p. (ISBN 0-7134-2119-3, Pub. by Batsford England). David & Charles.

Battle for Burma. E. D. Smith. 1979. 27.00 (ISBN 0-7134-0737-9, Pub. by Batsford England). David & Charles.

Battle for Europe: Nineteen Eighteen. H. Essame. 1972. 22.50 o.p. (ISBN 0-7134-1173-2, Pub. by Batsford England). David & Charles.

Battle for Guadalcanal. Samuel B. Griffith, 2nd. (Bantam War Book Ser.). 352p. 1980. pap. 2.50 (ISBN 0-553-13643-7). Bantam.

Battle for Iwo Jima. Robert Leckie. (gr. 5-9). 1967. 2.95 o.p. (ISBN 0-394-80418-X, BYR). Random.

Battle for North Africa. John Strawson. LC 73-93216. (Illus.). 1970. 7.95 o.p. (ISBN 0-684-10582-9, ScribT). Scribner.

Battle for Sales. Robert J. Houlehen & Elvajean Hall. LC 73-6962. (Illus.). 160p. (gr. 7 up). 1973. 5.95 o.p. (ISBN 0-397-31249-0). Lippincott.

Battle for the American Church. George A. Kelly. LC 80-22348. 528p. 1981. pap. 8.95 (ISBN 0-385-17433-0, Im). Doubleday.

Battle for the Bundu: The First World War in East Africa. Charles Miller. LC 73-14013. (Illus.). 380p. 1974. 9.95 o.s.i. (ISBN 0-02-584930-1). Macmillan.

Battle for the Mind. Tim LaHoye. 1980. 8.95 (ISBN 0-8007-5043-8); pap. 4.95 (ISBN 0-8007-1121-1). Revell.

Battle for the Rock: The Story of Wolfe & Montcalm. Joseph Schull. (Illus.). (gr. 4-6). 1960. 4.95 o.p. (ISBN 0-685-20372-7). St Martin.

Battle for Trafalgar. Geoffry Bennett. 1977. 27.00 (ISBN 0-7134-3269-1, Pub. by Batsford England). David & Charles.

Battle for Yanga. Bv. Ben Kendrick. LC 80-20643. 127p. 1980. pap. 3.95 (ISBN 0-87227-074-2). Reg Baptist.

Battle Horse. Harry Kullman. Tr. by George Blecher & Lone T. Blecher. Orig. Title: Stridshasten. 192p. (gr. 6 up). 1981. 8.95 (ISBN 0-87888-175-1). Bradbury Pr.

Battle Hymn of China. Agnes Smedley. LC 74-32113. (China in the 20th Century Ser). xxiii, 528p. 1975. Repr. of 1943 ed. lib. bdg. 45.00 (ISBN 0-306-70693-8). Da Capo.

Battle in the Arctic Seas: The Story of Convoy Pq 17. Theodore Taylor. LC 75-33655. (Illus.). (gr. 5 up). 1976. 8.95 (ISBN 0-690-01084-2, TYC-J). T Y Crowell.

Battle Lines. Hans-Georg Rauch. (Illus.). 1977. 6.95 o.p. (ISBN 0-684-15139-1, ScribT). Scribner.

Battle of Aughrim & the God Who Eats Corn. Richard Murphy. 1968. 4.95 o.p. (ISBN 0-571-08724-8, Pub. by Faber & Faber). Merrimack Bk Serv.

Battle of Bataan: America's Greatest Defeat. Robert Conroy. LC 69-11294. (Battle Books Ser). (Illus.). (gr. 5-8). 1969. 4.95g o.s.i. (ISBN 0-02-724290-0). Macmillan.

Battle of Belleau Wood: The Marines Stand Fast. Richard Suskind. LC 69-12747. (Battle Books Ser). (Illus.). (gr. 5-8). 1969. 4.50 o.s.i. (ISBN 0-685-14701-0). Macmillan.

Battle of Britain. L. Mosley. LC 76-45540. (World War II Ser.). (Illus.). (gr. 6 up). 1977. PLB 14.94 (ISBN 0-8094-2459-2, Pub. by Time-Life). Silver.

Battle of Britain. Ed. by Leonard Mosley. (World War II Ser.). 1977. 12.95 (ISBN 0-8094-2458-4). Time-Life.

Battle of Britain. Bruce Robertson. (Caler Illustrated Ser.). (Illus.). 60p. 1970. pap. text ed. 4.95 o.p. (ISBN 0-87059-000-6, Pub. by Caler). Aviation.

Battle of Britain: The Triumph of R.A.F. Fighter Pilots. Richard Hough. LC 73-138029. (Battle Bks). (Illus.). (gr. 5-8). 1971. 5.95 o.s.i. (ISBN 0-02-744590-9). Macmillan.

Battle of Bubble & Sqeak. Philippa Pearce. (Illus.). (gr. 2-7). 1979. PLB 7.95 (ISBN 0-233-96986-1). Andre Deutsch.

Battle of Dienbienphu. Jules Roy. LC 64-25121. (Illus.). 1965. 15.00 o.p. (ISBN 0-06-013715-0, HarpT). Har-Row.

Battle of Fallen Timbers, August 20, 1794: President Washington Secures the Ohio Valley. John Tebbel. LC 76-188480. (Focus Bks). (Illus.). 96p. (gr. 6-9). 1972. PLB 6.45 (ISBN 0-531-02457-1). Watts.

Battle of Hastings, England & Europe, 1035-1066. Sten Korner. LC 80-2221. 1981. Repr. of 1964 ed. 38.00 (ISBN 0-404-18765-X). AMS Pr.

Battle of Jerusalem: The Six-Day War of June, 1967. Clifford Irving. LC 69-11302. (Battle Bks). (Illus.). (gr. 5-8). 1970. 8.95g (ISBN 0-02-747340-6). Macmillan.

Battle of Leyte Gulf. G. C. Skipper. LC 80-27265. (World at War Ser.). (Illus.). 48p. (gr. 3-8). 1981. PLB 7.95 (ISBN 0-516-04788-4). Childrens.

Battle of Maldon & Other Old English Poems. Kevin Crossley-Holland & Bruce Mitchell. LC 65-13048. 138p. 1975. pap. 3.95 o.p. (ISBN 0-312-07000-4). St Martin.

Battle of Maldon, with a Supplement. Ed. by E. V. Gordon. D. G. Scragg. LC 76-28820. (Old and Middle English Texts Ser.). 1976. pap. text ed. 5.25x (ISBN 0-06-492494-7). B&N.

Battle of Midway: Victory in the Pacific. Richard Hough. LC 70-89588. (Battle Bks). (gr. 5-8). 1970. 4.50g o.s.i. (ISBN 0-02-744600-X). Macmillan.

Battle of Pavia. Jean Giono. 15.00 (ISBN 0-7206-0780-9). Dufour.

Battle of Pharsalus. Claude Simon. Tr. by Richard Howard from Fr. LC 72-138436. Orig. Title: Bataille De Pharsale. 1971. 5.95 o.p. (ISBN 0-8076-0579-4). Braziller.

Battle of Reuben Robin & Kite Uncle John. Mary Calhoun. LC 72-12949. (Illus.). 32p. (gr. k-3). 1973. PLB 7.92 (ISBN 0-688-30075-8). Morrow.

Battle of Saint Street. Roy Brown. LC 74-152287. (gr. 5-8). 1971. 4.95 o.s.i. (ISBN 0-02-714920-X). Macmillan.

Battle of San Jacinto. Sam Houston. wrappers 4.50 (ISBN 0-8363-0010-6). Jenkins.

Battle of Saratoga. Rupert Furneaux. LC 69-17940. 320p. 1981. pap. 7.95 (ISBN 0-8128-6125-6). Stein & Day.

Battle of Sirte. S. W. C. Pack. LC 74-31677. (Sea Battles in Close-up Ser.: No. 14). 1975. 7.50 (ISBN 0-87021-813-1). Naval Inst Pr.

Battle of Springfield: June, 1780. Springfield Historical Society. LC 80-15765. (Illus.). 1980. 3.95x (ISBN 0-89490-041-2). Enslow Pubs.

Battle of the Alamo. Keith Murphy. LC 78-26292. (Raintree Great Adventures). (Illus.). (gr. 3-6). 1979. PLB 8.95 (ISBN 0-8393-0154-5). Raintree Child.

Battle of the Atlantic. Barrie Pitt. LC 79-74822. (World War II Ser.). (Illus.). (gr. 6 up). 1977. PLB 14.94 (ISBN 0-8094-2467-3, Pub. by Time-Life). Silver.

Battle of the Atlantic. Barrie Pitt. Ed. by Time-Life Books. (World War II). 1977. 12.95 (ISBN 0-8094-2466-5). Time-Life.

Battle of the Books in Its Historical Setting. Anne E. Burlingame. LC 68-54230. 1969. Repr. of 1920 ed. 9.00x (ISBN 0-8196-0224-8). Biblo.

Battle of the Bulge. Stephen W. Sears & S. L. A. Marshall. LC 74-78441. (American Heritage Junior Library). (Illus.). 154p. (gr. 5 up). 1969. 9.95 (ISBN 0-06-025252-9, Dist. by Har-Row); PLB 6.89 o.p. (ISBN 0-06-025253-7). Am Heritage.

Battle of the Bulge. Ogden Tanner. (World War II Ser.). (Illus.). 1979. lib. bdg. 14.94 (ISBN 0-8094-2531-9); kivar bdg. 9.93 (ISBN 0-8094-2532-7). Silver.

Battle of the Coral Sea. LC 80-25088. (World at War Ser.). (Illus.). 48p. (gr. 3-8). 1981. PLB 7.95 (ISBN 0-516-04787-6). Childrens.

Battle of the Queens. Jean Plaidy. 320p. 1981. 10.95 (ISBN 0-399-12604-X). Putnam.

Battle of the Strong. Gilbert Parker. 1976. lib. bdg. 18.50x (ISBN 0-89968-078-X). Lightyear.

Battle of the Washita: The Sheridan-Custer Indian Campaign of 1867-1869. Stan Hoig. LC 79-14844. 1979. 15.75x (ISBN 0-8032-2307-2); pap. 4.95 (ISBN 0-8032-7204-9, BB 720, Bison). U of Nebr Pr.

Battle of Trafalgar. Alan Villiers. (gr. 5-9). 1965. 4.50g o.s.i. (ISBN 0-02-791830-0). Macmillan.

Battle of Waterloo. J. Christopher Herold & Gordon Wright. LC 67-15416. (Horizon Caravel Bks). (Illus.). 153p. (gr. 6 up). 1967. 9.95 (ISBN 0-06-022307-3, Dist. by Har-Row); PLB 6.89 o.p. (ISBN 0-06-022308-1). Am Heritage.

Battle of Waterloo: The End of an Empire. Manuel Komroff. (gr. 5-9). 1964. 8.95g (ISBN 0-02-750920-6). Macmillan.

Battle of Wounded Knee: The Ghost Dance Uprising. Barbara Bonham. LC 71-125374. (gr. 6-8). 1970. 6.95 o.p. (ISBN 0-8092-8761-7); PLB avail o.p. (ISBN 0-685-04779-2). Contemp Bks.

Battle of Yorktown. Thomas J. Fleming & Francis S. Ronalds. LC 68-28247. (American Heritage Junior Library). (Illus.). 154p. (gr. 5 up). 1968. 9.95 (ISBN 0-8281-0357-7, JO20-0); PLB 6.89 o.p. (ISBN 0-06-020130-4). Am Heritage.

Battle Pay. Peter McCurtin. (Soldier of Fortune Ser.). 1978. pap. 1.50 (ISBN 0-505-51233-5). Tower Bks.

Battle Report. Harvey Shapiro. LC 66-23924. (Wesleyan Poetry Program: Vol. 32). (Orig.). 1966. pap. 10.00x (ISBN 0-8195-2032-2, Pub. by Wesleyan U Pr); pap. 4.95 (ISBN 0-8195-1032-7). Columbia U Pr.

Battle Songs of the Second American Revolution. James E. Norwood & David Angerman. LC 79-50654. 1979. pap. 12.00 (ISBN 0-915854-20-1). Friend Freedom.

Battle to Breathe. Louis J. Klingbeil & Reinhold L. Klingbeil. LC 76-170374. (Better Living Ser). (Illus.). 64p. 1971. pap. 0.95 (ISBN 0-8127-0059-7). Southern Pub.

Battledores: Friendship. 0.70 (ISBN 0-87675-089-7). Horn Bk.

Battledores: The Horse. 0.70 (ISBN 0-87675-088-9). Horn Bk.

Battleground. Curry Vaughan & Bob Slosser. pap. 3.95 o.p. (ISBN 0-88270-301-3, P301-2). Logos.

Battleground of Freedom: South Carolina in the Revolution. Nat Hilborn & Sam Hilborn. LC 70-143042. (Illus.). 256p. 1970. 12.95 o.s.i. (ISBN 0-87844-000-3). Sandlapper Store.

Battles & Leaders of the Civil War, 4 vols. Ed. by Roy F. Nichols. Incl. Vol. 1. From Sumter to Shiloh; Vol. 2. North to Antientam. 5.95 o.p. (ISBN 0-686-66596-1); Vol. 3. Retreat from Gettysburg; Vol. 4. Way to Appomatox. 1957. boxed set 50.00 o.p. (ISBN 0-498-07014-X, Yoseloff). A S Barnes.

Battles for Cassino. E. D. Smith. LC 75-12057. (Encore Edition). (Illus.). 1975. 3.95 o.p. (ISBN 0-684-15456-0, ScribT). Scribner.

Battles of Coxinga. Donald Keene. (Cambridge Oriental Ser). 1951. 38.50 (ISBN 0-521-05469-9). Cambridge U Pr.

Battles of the Constitution: Old Ironsides & the Freedom of the Sea. Robert Goldston. LC 71-78084. (Battle Books Ser). (Illus.). (gr. 5-9). 1969. 7.95 (ISBN 0-02-736330-9). Macmillan.

Battles of the Forty-Five. Katherine Tomasson & Francis Buist. 1978. 27.00 (ISBN 0-7134-0769-7, Pub. by Batsford England). David & Charles.

Battles with Model Tanks. Donald Featherstone & Keith Robinson. (Illus.). 160p. 1980. pap. 8.95 (ISBN 0-88254-541-8, Pub. by MacDonald & Jane's England). Hippocrene Bks.

Battleship Bismark: A Survivor's Story. Burkhard Baron Von Mullenheim-Rechberg. LC 80-81093. 284p. 1980. 15.95 (ISBN 0-87021-096-3). Naval Inst Pr.

Battleships: Allied Battleships of World War Two. Robert O. Dulin, Jr. & William H. Garzke, Jr. LC 79-90551. (Battleships Ser.: Vol. 2). (Illus.). 352p. 1980. 38.95 (ISBN 0-87021-100-5). Naval Inst Pr.

Battleships of the World. Siegfried Breyer. (Illus.). 570p. 1980. 50.00 (ISBN 0-686-65674-1). Mayflower Bks.

Battlestar Galactica. James A. Lely. (T. V. & Movie Tie-Ins Ser.). 32p. (gr. 4-12). 1979. PLB 5.95 (ISBN 0-87191-701-7); pap. 2.95 (ISBN 0-89812-033-0). Creative Ed.

Battlestar Galactica: Flight to Kobal, No. 3. Glen A. Larson & Robert Thurston. 1979. pap. 2.25 (ISBN 0-425-04992-2). Berkley Pub.

Battlestar Galactica Four: the Young Warriors. Glen A. Larson & Robert Thurston. 288p. 1980. pap. 2.25 (ISBN 0-425-04997-3). Berkley Pub.

Battlewagon. Wallace L. Exum. 1981. pap. write for info. (ISBN 0-89865-093-3). Donning Co.

Batuvus Moped Owner Service-Repair. Ed Scott. Ed. by Eric Jorgensen. (Illus.). 104p. (Orig.). 1978. pap. 6.00 (ISBN 0-89287-199-7, M438). Clymer Pubns.

Bau und Entwicklung der Flechtenpycnidien und Ihrer Goniedien. G. Vobis. (Bibliotheca Lichenologica: No. 14). 200p. (Ger.). 1981. pap. text ed. 25.00x (ISBN 3-7682-1270-X, Pub. by Cramer Germany). Lubrecht & Cramer.

Baudelaire: A Fire to Conquer Darkness. Nicole W. Jouve. LC 79-14978. 1980. 22.50 (ISBN 0-312-07005-5). St Martin.

Baudelaire: A Self-Portrait. Charles P. Baudelaire. Ed. by Lois B. Hyslop & Francis E. Hyslop. LC 78-20447. 1981. Repr. of 1957 ed. 22.00 (ISBN 0-88355-827-0). Hyperion Conn.

Baudelaire & Freud. Leo Bersani. (Quantum Ser.). 1978. 11.95x (ISBN 0-520-03402-3); pap. 2.65 (ISBN 0-520-03535-6). U of Cal Pr.

Baudelaire et Hoffmann. Rosemary H. Lloyd. LC 78-58796. (Fr.). 1979. 38.00 (ISBN 0-521-22459-4). Cambridge U Pr.

Baudelaire et le Grotesque. Yvonne B. Rollins. LC 78-54094. (Fr.). 1978. pap. text ed. 9.75 (ISBN 0-8191-0498-1). U Pr of Amer.

Baudelaire Revisited: Forty-One Poems. Kendall E. Lappin. Ed. by Susan G. Pheiffer. (Illus.). 196p. 1981. 11.95 (ISBN 0-9605710-1-9); pap. 7.95 (ISBN 0-9605710-0-0). KEL Pubns.

Baudelaire, Sartre & Camus: Lectures & Commentaries. Garnet Rees. 86p. 1976. pap. text ed. 10.00x (ISBN 0-7083-0601-2). Verry.

Baudouin de Courtenay Anthology: The Beginnings of Structural Linguistics. Jan Baudouin de Courtenay. Tr. by Edward Stankiewicz. LC 78-135012. (History & Theory of Linguistics Ser.). 412p. 1972. 21.95x (ISBN 0-253-31120-9). Ind U Pr.

Bauhaus Nineteen Ninteen to Nineteen Twenty-Eight. Ed. by Herbert Bayer et al. LC 77-169299. (Illus.). 1976. pap. 8.95 (ISBN 0-87070-240-8). Museum Mod Art.

Baukunst der Armenier und Europa, 2 vols. Josef Strzygowski. (Arbeiten des Kunsthistorischen Instituts der Universitat Wien: Nos. 9-10). (Illus.). xii, 888p. (Ger.). 1981. Repr. of 1918 ed. Set. lib. bdg. 200.00x (ISBN 0-89241-157-0). Caratzas Bros.

Baule Statuary Art: Meaning & Modernization. Philip L. Ravenhill. Bd. with Beauty in the Eyes of the Baule: Aesthetics & Cultural Values. Susan M. Vogel. LC 79-24004. (Working Papers in the Traditional Arts: Nos. 5 & 6). (Illus.). 1980. pap. text ed. 4.95x (ISBN 0-89727-006-1). Inst Study Human.

Bauliche Massmalmen Zum Energie-Sparen in der Gemeinde. (Ger.). 1976. pap. 8.00 o.p. (ISBN 0-89192-130-3). Interbk Inc.

Baumback's Guide to Entrepreneurship. C. Baumback. 1981. 13.95 (ISBN 0-13-066761-7). P-H.

Baumgartner's Canned Foods. 7th ed. A. C. Hersom & E. D. Hulland. (Illus.). 400p. 1980. text ed. 35.00 (ISBN 0-443-02122-8). Churchill.

Bauxite & Aluminum: An Introduction to the Economics of Non-Fuel Minerals. Ferdinand E. Banks. LC 78-24632. 208p. 1979. 21.00 (ISBN 0-669-02771-5). Lexington Bks.

Bavaria. 3rd ed. (Panorama in Color Ser.). (Illus.). 93p. 1970. 30.00x (ISBN 3-524-00023-1). Intl Pubns Serv.

Bavaria. James Bunting. (Batsford Countries of Europe Ser). 216p. 1972. 8.95 o.p. (ISBN 0-8038-0740-6). Hastings.

Bawds & Lodgings: A History of the London Bankside Brothels, 100-1675. E. J. Burford. (Illus.). 208p. 1976. text ed. 14.75x (ISBN 0-7206-0144-4). Humanities.

Baxter's Alaska. Robert Baxter. 1981. 9.95 (ISBN 0-913384-47-X). Rail Europe-Baxter.

Baxter's Britrail Guide. Robert Baxter. LC 72-83184. 1979. 8.95 (ISBN 0-913384-28-3). Rail-Europe-Baxter.

Baxter's Eurailpass Travel Guide. Robert Baxter. LC 74-169913. 1980-81. 9.95 (ISBN 0-913384-33-X). Rail-Europe-Baxter.

Baxter's Florida. Robert Baxter. 1981. 9.95 (ISBN 0-913384-34-8). Rail-Europe-Baxter.

Baxter's Mexico. Robert Baxter. 1981. 9.95 (ISBN 0-913384-42-9). Rail-Europe-Baxter.

Baxter's U. S. A. (the U. S. A. by Car, Bus, Train & Plane) Robert Baxter. LC 77-92700. 1980-81. perfect bdg. 12.95 (ISBN 0-913384-44-5). Rail-Europe-Baxter.

Baxter's Western Canada. Robert Baxter. 1981. 9.95 (ISBN 0-913384-41-0). Rail-Europe-Baxter.

Bay Area at Your Feet: Walks with San Francisco's Margot Patterson Doss. rev. ed. Margot P. Doss. (Illus.). 288p. (Orig.). 1981. pap. 7.95 (ISBN 0-89141-097-X). Presidio Pr.

Bay Area Houses. Ed. by Sally Woodbridge. (Illus.). 1979. pap. 13.95 (ISBN 0-19-502527-X, GB568, GB). Oxford U Pr.

Bay Area Houses. Sally Woodbridge et al. LC 76-9261. (Illus.). 1976. 39.95 (ISBN 0-19-502084-7). Oxford U Pr.

Bay Area Sports & Recreation Directory. Martin Ilian. 224p. (Orig.). 1981. pap. 7.95 (ISBN 0-87701-164-8). Chronicle Bks.

Bay Bib: Rhode Island Marine Bibliography, 2 vols. (Marine Technical Report: Nos 70 & 71). 5.00 ea.; keyword in context index 2.00 (ISBN 0-938412-02-7). URI MAS.

Bay City Rollers. Tam Paton & Michael Wale. pap. 0.95 o.p. (ISBN 0-425-03044-X). Berkley Pub.

Bay of Pigs. Haynes Johnson. (Illus.). 1964. 10.50 o.p. (ISBN 0-393-04263-4). Norton.

Bay of Stars. Robyn Donald. (Harlequin Romances). 192p. 1981. pap. 1.25 (ISBN 0-373-02391-X, Pub. by Harlequin). PB.

Bayard Taylor. Paul G. Wermuth. (U. S. Authors Ser.: No. 228). 1973. lib. bdg. 10.95 (ISBN 0-8057-0718-2). Twayne.

Bayesian Full Information Structural Analysis. Juan-Antonio Morales. LC 70-155592. (Lecture Notes in Operation Research: Vol. 43). 1971. pap. 10.70 o.p. (ISBN 0-387-05417-0). Springer-Verlag.

Bayesian Inference in Statistical Analysis. George E. Box & George C. Tiao. LC 78-172804. 1973. text ed. 24.95 (ISBN 0-201-00622-7). A-W.

Bayeux in the Late Eighteenth Century. Olwen H. Hufton. 1967. 33.00x (ISBN 0-19-821462-6). Oxford U Pr.

Bayonet: The History & Development of the Sword, Sabre, & Knife Bayonet. Anthony Carter. LC 74-5449. (Encore Edition). 1974. 3.95 o.p. (ISBN 0-684-15394-7, ScribT). Scribner.

Bayonets in the Sun. William Moore. LC 77-76645. 1978. 7.95 o.p. (ISBN 0-312-07016-0). St Martin.

Bayou Belle. George H. Smith. LC 67-1512. (Illus.). (gr. 6-8). 1967. PLB 7.89 (ISBN 0-381-99704-9, A07200, JD-J). John Day.

Bayou Passions. Maggie Lyons. (Orig.). 1979. pap. 1.95 (ISBN 0-515-04740-6, 04740-6). Jove Pubns.

Bayous. Peter Feibleman. LC 73-84544. (American Wilderness Ser). (Illus.). (gr. 6 up). 1973. lib. bdg. 11.97 (ISBN 0-8094-1189-X, Pub. by Time-Life). Silver.

Bayous. Peter S. Feibleman. (American Wilderness Ser.). (Illus.). 240p. 1973. 12.95 (ISBN 0-8094-1188-1). Time-Life.

Bayreuth: The Early Years; an Account of the Wagner Festival, 1876-1914 As Seen by Celebrated Visitors & Participants. Ed. by Robert Hartford. (Illus.). 288p. 1981. 19.95 (ISBN 0-521-23822-6). Cambridge U Pr.

Bazaar. Susan Wood. LC 80-14985. 64p. 1981. 10.95 (ISBN 0-03-057856-6, Owl Bk); pap. 5.95 (ISBN 0-03-057709-8). HR&W.

Bazaar Stall. Monica Stuart & Gill Soper. 1979. 11.95 o.p. (ISBN 0-571-11280-3, Pub. by Faber & Faber); pap. 5.95 (ISBN 0-571-11289-7). Merrimack Bk Serv.

Bazak Guide to Israel 1980-1981. Bazak Guidebook Publishers, Ltd. (Illus.). 1980. pap. 7.95 o.p. (ISBN 0-06-090758-4, CN 758, CN). Har-Row.

Bazak Guide to Israel 1981-1982. LC 66-1422. (Illus.). 500p. (Orig.). 1981. pap. 7.95 (ISBN 0-06-090847-5, CN 847, CN). Har-Row.

B.C. Great Zot, I'm Beautiful. Johnny Hart. (B.C. Ser.). (Illus.). 1978. pap. 1.50 (ISBN 0-449-13614-0, GM). Fawcett.

B.C. Is Alive & Well. Johnny Hart. (B.C. Ser.). (Illus.). 1978. pap. 1.50 (ISBN 0-449-13651-5, GM). Fawcett.

B.C. One More Time. Johnny Hart. (B.C. Ser.). (Illus.). 1978. pap. 1.50 (ISBN 0-449-13646-9, GM). Fawcett.

B.C. Where the Hell Is Heck? Johnny Hart. 1978. pap. 1.50 (ISBN 0-449-14022-9, GM). Fawcett.

BCPL-The Language & Its Compiler. M. Richards & C. Whitby-Strevens. LC 77-71098. (Illus.). 1980. 26.50 (ISBN 0-521-21965-5). Cambridge U Pr.

Be a Better Pilot. Alan Bramson. LC 80-13401. (Illus.). 256p. 1980. 14.95 (ISBN 0-668-04901-4, 4901-4). Arco.

Be a Guest at Your Own Party. Ruth Macpherson. (Illus., Orig.). 1981. pap. 6.95 (ISBN 0-8437-3377-2). Hammond Inc.

Be a Magician! How to Put on a Magic Show & Mystify Your Friends. Jay Boyar. (Illus.). 160p. (gr. 7 up). 1981. PLB price not set (ISBN 0-671-42273-1). Messner.

Be a Mother & More. Joyce S. Mitchell. 224p. (Orig.). 1980. pap. 2.95 (ISBN 0-553-13926-6). Bantam.

Be a Motivation Leader. Leroy Eims. 144p. 1981. pap. 3.95 (ISBN 0-89693-008-4). Victor Bks.

Be a Real Teen. Warren W. Wiersbe. 128p. (Orig.). (YA) 1971. pap. 1.50 (ISBN 0-8024-6047-X). Moody.

Be a Winner. Edward Lewis. (Gamblers Book Shelf). 160p. 1979. pap. 2.95 (ISBN 0-89650-530-8). Gamblers.

Be a Winner in Baseball. Charles Coombs. (Illus.). 128p. (gr. 5-9). 1973. PLB 7.44 (ISBN 0-688-30093-6). Morrow.

Be a Winner in Basketball. Charles Coombs. LC 75-17778. (Illus.). 128p. (gr. 5-9). 1975. PLB 7.44 (ISBN 0-688-32039-2); pap. 2.45 (ISBN 0-688-27039-5). Morrow.

Be a Winner in Football. Charles Coombs. LC 74-5932. 128p. (gr. 5-9). 1974. 7.44 (ISBN 0-688-30119-3); pap. 2.45 (ISBN 0-688-25119-6). Morrow.

Be a Winner in Horsemanship. Charles Coombs. LC 76-17118. (Illus.). 128p. (gr. 5-9). 1976. 7.25 (ISBN 0-688-22080-0); PLB 6.96 (ISBN 0-688-32080-5). Morrow.

Be a Winner in Ice Hockey. Charles Coombs. LC 73-10769. (Illus.). 128p. (gr. 5-9). 1974. PLB 6.50 (ISBN 0-688-30099-5); pap. 2.45 (ISBN 0-688-25099-8). Morrow.

Be a Winner in Skiing. Charles I. Coombs. LC 77-2621. (gr. 5-9). 1977. 7.25 (ISBN 0-688-22131-9); PLB 6.96 (ISBN 0-688-32131-3). Morrow.

Be a Winner in Soccer. Charles Coombs. (gr. 5-9). 1977. 7.25 (ISBN 0-688-22099-1); PLB 6.96 (ISBN 0-688-32099-6). Morrow.

Be a Winner in Soccer. Charles Coombs. (Illus.). (gr. 5-7). 1980. pap. write for info. (ISBN 0-671-41104-7). PB.

Be a Winner in Tennis. Charles Coombs. LC 74-23262. (Illus.). 128p. (gr. 5-9). 1975. PLB 7.44 (ISBN 0-688-32020-1); pap. 2.45 (ISBN 0-688-27022-0). Morrow.

Be a Winner in Track & Field. Charles Coombs. LC 75-33077. (Illus.). 128p. (gr. 5-9). 1976. 7.75 (ISBN 0-688-22064-9); PLB 7.44 (ISBN 0-688-32064-3). Morrow.

Be Alive As Long As You Live: The Older Person's Guide to Exercise for Joyful Living. Frankel & Richard. 1981. 11.95 (ISBN 0-690-01892-4). Lippincott & Crowell.

Be Assertive: A Practical Guide for Human Service Workers. Sandra S. Sundel & Martin Sundel. LC 79-20431. (Sage Human Service Guides: Vol. 11). (Illus.). 1980. pap. 8.00x (ISBN 0-8039-1289-7). Sage.

Be Complete. Warren Wiersbe. 160p. 1981. pap. 3.50 (ISBN 0-88207-257-9). Victor Bks.

Be Expert with Map & Compass: The Orienteering Handbook. rev. ed. Bjorn Kjellstrom. LC 76-12550. (Illus.). 176p. 1976. pap. 7.95 (ISBN 0-684-14270-8, SL595, ScribT). Scribner.

Be Filled with the Spirit. Lehman Strauss. 1976. pap. 1.95 o.p. (ISBN 0-310-33072-6). Zondervan.

Be Free. Warren W. Wiersbe. 160p. 1975. pap. 2.95 (ISBN 0-88207-716-3). Victor Bks.

Be Free: Happiness Is Owning Your Own Business. Robert Haisman. 1980. cancelled (ISBN 0-346-12464-6). Cornerstone.

Be Good, Sweet Maid: An Anthology of Women & Literature. Ed. by Janet Todd. 175p. 1981. text ed. 22.00x (ISBN 0-8419-0692-0). Holmes & Meier.

Be Good to Each Other-An Open Letter on Marriage. Lowell Erdahl & Carol Erdahl. 1976. 3.95 (ISBN 0-8015-0584-4, Hawthorn). Dutton.

Be Good to Each Other: An Open Letter on Marriage. Lowell Erdahl & Carol Erdahl. LC 80-8893. 96p. 1981. pap. 3.95 (ISBN 0-06-062248-2, HarpR). Har-Row.

Be Good to Yourself. Thomas A. Whiting. LC 80-27304. 128p. 1981. 6.95 (ISBN 0-687-02800-0). Abingdon.

Be Happier, Be Healthier. Gayelord Hauser. 1976. pap. 1.50 o.p. (ISBN 0-449-22715-4, Q2715, Crest). Fawcett.

Be Honest with Yourself. Doreen Croft. 1976. pap. text ed. 8.95x (ISBN 0-534-00452-0). Wadsworth Pub.
Be Joyful. Warren W. Wiersbe. LC 74-76328. 1974. pap. 2.95 (ISBN 0-88207-705-8). Victor Bks.
Be Mature. Warren W. Wiersbe. 1978. pap. 2.95 (ISBN 0-88207-771-6). Victor Bks.
Be Merry & Wise: John Locke & Eighteenth-Century English Children's Books. Samuel F. Pickering. Date not set. 16.50 (ISBN 0-87049-290-X). U of Tenn Pr. Postponed.
Be More Than You Are. (Orig.). pap. 3.95 (ISBN 0-89081-071-0). Harvest Hse.
Be of Good Courage. E. J. Saleska. 1948. 0.85 (ISBN 0-570-03678-X, 74-1004). Concordia.
Be Ready. Warren W. Wiersbe. 1979. pap. 2.95 (ISBN 0-88207-782-1). Victor Bks.
Be Ready at Eight. Peggy Parish. LC 78-11847. (Ready-to-Read Ser.). (Illus.). (gr. 1-4). 1979. 7.95 (ISBN 0-02-769830-0). Macmillan.
Be Real. Warren W. Wiersbe. LC 72-77014. 190p. 1972. pap. 2.95 (ISBN 0-88207-046-0). Victor Bks.
Be Rich. Robert Collier. pap. 1.50 (ISBN 0-912576-05-7). R Collier.
Be Rich. Warren W. Wiersbe. 176p. 1976. pap. 2.95 (ISBN 0-88207-730-9). Victor Bks.
Be Right. Warren W. Wiersbe. 1977. pap. 2.95 (ISBN 0-88207-729-5). Victor Bks.
Be Somebody! A Practical Philosophy for All Times. Warren F. Hannas. LC 80-81396. (Illus.). 165p. 1980. 11.95 (ISBN 0-936888-01-6). Pr Vision Studios.
Be the Leader You Were Meant to Be. Leroy Eims. 132p. 1975. pap. 2.95 (ISBN 0-88207-723-6). Victor Bks.
Be the Woman You Want to Be. Ruthe White. LC 77-88190. 1978. pap. 3.95 (ISBN 0-89081-114-8, 1148). Harvest Hse.
Be Young with Yoga. Richard L. Hittleman. 240p. 1973. pap. 1.95 o.s.i. (ISBN 0-446-89432-X). Warner Bks.
Be Your Own Caterer: Recipes & Suggestions for Dinners, Buffets & Cocktail Parties. Trudy Cannon. 216p. 1975. 9.95 o.s.i. (ISBN 0-02-521150-1). Macmillan.
Be Your Own Chiropractor: Through Biokinetic Exercises. rev. 2nd ed. John E. Barton & Margaret Barton. Orig. Title: Biokinetic Exercises. (Illus.). 210p. 1979. pap. 8.00 (ISBN 0-937216-03-8). J&M Barton.
Be Your Own Doctor: Let Living Food Be Your Medicine. Ann Wigmore. 176p. pap. text ed. 1.95. Hippocrates.
Be Your Own Gardening Expert. D. G. Hessayon. 36p. 1977. pap. 1.95 (ISBN 0-8119-0355-9). Fell.
Be Your Own House Plant Expert. D. G. Hessayon. 1976. pap. 1.95 (ISBN 0-8119-0356-7). Fell.
Be Your Own House Plant Spotter. D. G. Hessayon. 1977. 1.95 (ISBN 0-8119-0357-5). Fell.
Be Your Own Rose Expert. D. G. Hessayon & Harry Wheatcroft. 36p. 1977. pap. 1.95 (ISBN 0-8119-0358-3). Fell.
Be Your Own Sex Therapist. Carole Altman. (Illus.). 1976. pap. 7.95 o.p. (ISBN 0-399-11678-8). Berkley Pub.
Be Your Own Television Repairman. new ed. Bernard Guth. LC 65-1629. (Illus.). 1965. pap. 1.95 o.p. (ISBN 0-8019-0370-X). Chilton.
Beach Buddies of Bygone Days. Corrie Thompson. (gr. 1-3). 4.95 o.p. (ISBN 0-685-48835-7). Nortex Pr.
Beach Club. Claire Howard. (Orig.). 1980. pap. 2.50 (ISBN 0-446-91616-1). Warner Bks.
Beach Colors & Beach Creatures. Elizabeth Gregory. (Illus.). 1981. 6.95 (ISBN 0-933184-17-4); pap. 5.50 (ISBN 0-933184-18-2). Flame Intl.
Beach Girls. John D. MacDonald. 1978. pap. 1.75 o.p. (ISBN 0-449-14081-4, GM). Fawcett.
Beach in My Bedroom. Jane B. Moncure. LC 77-12960. (Creative Dramatics Ser.). (Illus.). (ps-3). 1978. PLB 5.50 (ISBN 0-89565-005-3); pap. 2.50 (ISBN 0-89565-038-X). Childs World.
Beach Processes & Coastal Hydrodynamics. Ed. by John S. Fisher & Robert Dolan. (Benchmark Papers in Geology Ser.: Vol. 39). 1977. 37.50 (ISBN 0-12-786471-7). Acad Pr.
Beach Troop of the Gombe. Timothy W. Ransom. LC 77-92573. 1979. 18.00 (ISBN 0-8387-1704-7). Bucknell U Pr.
Beachcomber. Patti Beckman. 192p. (Orig.). 1980. pap. 1.50 (ISBN 0-671-57037-4). S&S.
Beachcomber. Mary L. Blackstock. 3.95 o.p. (ISBN 0-685-48829-2). Nortex Pr.
Beachcombers. Helen Cresswell. 144p. (gr. 5up). 1972. 7.95 (ISBN 0-02-725470-4). Macmillan.
Beachcomber's Botany. Loren C. Petry. LC 68-26716. (Illus.). 160p. 1975. 5.95 (ISBN 0-85699-119-8). Chatham Pr.
Beachcomber's Guide to Gulf Coast Marine Life. Nick Fotheringham. LC 80-10607. (Illus.). 1980. pap. 6.95 (ISBN 0-88415-496-3). Pacesetter Pr.
Beachcomber's Guide to Gulf Coast Marine Life. rev. ed. Nick Fotheringham & Susan L. Brunenmeister. Orig. Title: Common Marine Invertebrates of the Northwestern Gulf Coast. (Illus.). 176p. (Orig.). 1980. pap. 6.95 (ISBN 0-88415-062-3). Gulf Pub.
Beaches of Baja. Walt Wheelock. (Illus.). 1972. 2.50 (ISBN 0-910856-28-1). La Siesta.
Beachview Tower: A High-Rise Saga. Arthur Bienenfeld. LC 78-61219. 1978. 10.00 (ISBN 0-89430-029-6). Morgan-Pacific.
Beadcraft, Step by Step. Judith Glassman. (Step by Step Craft Ser). 1974. PLB 9.15 o.p. (ISBN 0-307-62012-3, Golden Pr); pap. 2.95 (ISBN 0-307-42012-4). Western Pub.
Beads Plus Macrame: Applying Knotting Techniques to Beadcraft. Grethe La Croix. LC 78-151710. (Little Craft Book Ser). (Illus.). (gr. 8 up). 1971. 5.95 (ISBN 0-8069-5168-0); PLB 6.69 (ISBN 0-8069-5169-9). Sterling.
Beads to Boxes. Time-Life Books Editors. LC 78-50707. (Encyclopedia of Collectibles Ser.). (Illus.). 1978. lib. bdg. 10.95 (ISBN 0-686-50973-0). Silver.
Beady Bear. Don Freeman. (Illus.). (gr. 3-6). 1977. pap. 1.95 o.p. (Puffin); cassette o.p. 17.95 o.p. (ISBN 0-670-15058-4). Penguin.
Beagle Guide. John F. Gordon. 6.98 o.p. (ISBN 0-385-01558-5). Doubleday.
Beagle Has Landed, Vol. II. Charles Schulz. 128p. 1981. pap. 1.75 (ISBN 0-449-24373-7, Crest). Fawcett.
Beagle Has Landed. Charles M. Schulz. LC 78-53776. (New Peanuts Parade Ser). 1978. pap. 2.95 (ISBN 0-03-044781-X). HR&W.
Beagle Record. Ed. by Darwin R. Keynes. LC 77-82500. (Illus.). 1979. 79.00 (ISBN 0-521-21822-5). Cambridge U Pr.
Beagles. E. Fitch Daglish. Ed. by Christina Foyle. (Foyle's Handbks). 1973. 3.95 (ISBN 0-685-55802-9). Palmetto Pub.
Beagles. Beverly Pisano & A. D. Holcombe. (Illus.). 125p. 1979. 2.95 (ISBN 0-87666-686-1, KW-080). TFH Pubns.
Beaker Folk: Copper Age Archaeology in Western Europe. R. J. Harrison. (Ancient People & Places Ser.). (Illus.). 180p. 1981. 19.95 (ISBN 0-500-02098-1). Thames Hudson.
Beaker Pottery of Great Britain & Ireland, 2 vols. David L. Clarke. LC 69-11269. (Illus.). 1969. Set. 160.00 set (ISBN 0-521-07249-2). Cambridge U Pr.
Beam Antenna Handbook. 5th ed. William I. Orr & Stuart D. Cowan. LC 55-11982. 200p. 1958. 5.95 (ISBN 0-933616-04-X). Radio Pubns.
Beam Ends. Errol Flynn. 1976. Repr. of 1937 ed. lib. bdg. 13.35x (ISBN 0-89966-092-4). Buccaneer Bks.
Beams & Framed Structures. 2nd ed. J. Heyman. LC 74-2234. 160p. 1974. text ed. 18.75 (ISBN 0-08-017945-2); pap. text ed. 9.25 (ISBN 0-08-017946-0). Pergamon.
Bean Boy. Joan C. Bowden. LC 78-12150. (Ready-to-Read Ser.). (Illus.). (gr. 1-4). 1979. 7.95 (ISBN 0-02-711800-2). Macmillan.
Bean Cookery. Sue Deeming. (Orig.). 1980. pap. 5.95 (ISBN 0-89586-037-6). H P Bks.
Beany & the Beckoning Road. Lenora M. Weber. LC 52-7645. (gr. 5 up). 1952. 10.95 (ISBN 0-690-12313-2, TYC-J). T Y Crowell.
Beany Has a Secret Life. Lenora M. Weber. LC 55-5839. (gr. 5 up). 1955. 10.95 (ISBN 0-690-12384-1, TYC-J). T Y Crowell.
Beany Malone. Lenora M. Weber. LC 48-1943. (gr. 5 up). 1948. 10.95 (ISBN 0-690-12455-4, TYC-J). T Y Crowell.
Bear, a Bobcat & Three Ghosts. Anne Rockwell. LC 77-5084. (Ready-to-Read Ser.). (Illus.). (gr. 1-4). 1977. 7.95 (ISBN 0-02-777460-0, 77746). Macmillan.
Bear & the Fly. Paula Winter. (Illus.). (ps-k). Date not set. pap. 1.50 (ISBN 0-590-31568-4). Schol Bk Serv.
Bear Book. Jan Pfloog. (Illus.). 24p. (gr. k-1). 1976. PLB 5.38 (ISBN 0-307-68977-8, Golden Pr). Western Pub.
Bear Called Paddington. Michael Bond. LC 60-9096. (Illus.). (gr. 3-7). 1968. pap. 1.50 (ISBN 0-440-40483-5, YB). Dell.
Bear Circus. William Pene Du Bois. (Viking Seafarer Ser). (Illus.). (gr. k-2). 1973. pap. 1.50 o.s.i. (ISBN 0-670-05085-7, Puffin). Penguin.
Bear Cub Scout Book. rev. ed. Boy Scouts Of America. LC 67-14538. (Illus.). 192p. (gr. 4). 1973. flexible bdg. 1.75x (ISBN 0-8395-3231-8, 3231). BSA.
Bear in the Air. Leslie Williams. LC 80-10290. (Illus.). 28p. (gr. k up). 1980. 7.95 (ISBN 0-916144-54-2). Stemmer Hse.
Bear in the Bathtub. Ellen Jackson. LC 80-26535. (Illus.). 32p. (ps-3). 1981. PLB 6.95 (ISBN 0-201-04701-2, A-W Childrens). A-W.
Bear in the Boat. Ilse-Margret Vogel. (Little Golden Reader). (Illus.). (gr. k-3). 1979. PLB 5.38 (ISBN 0-307-60397-0, Golden Pr). Western Pub.
Bear Island. Alistair MacLean. LC 77-163654. 1971. 5.95 o.p. (ISBN 0-385-07192-2). Doubleday.
Bear Island. Alistair MacLean. 1979. pap. 2.25 (ISBN 0-449-23560-2, Crest). Fawcett.
Bear, Man & God: Eight Approaches to Faulkner's the Bear. 2nd ed. Francis L. Utley et al. (Orig.). 1971. pap. text ed. 5.95x (ISBN 0-394-31546-4, RanC). Random.
Bear Market Investment Strategies. Harry Schultz. LC 80-70618. 235p. 1981. 13.95 (ISBN 0-87094-224-7). Dow Jones-Irwin.
Bear Paw Horses. Will Henry. 224p. 1980. pap. 1.75 (ISBN 0-553-14236-4). Bantam.
Bear Weather. Lillie D. Chaffin. LC 69-10498. (Illus.). (gr. k-2). 1969. 4.95g o.s.i. (ISBN 0-02-717890-0). Macmillan.
Bear Went Over the Mountain: Tall Tales of American Animals. Ed. by Robert B. Downs. LC 73-148835. 1971. Repr. of 1964 ed. 18.00 (ISBN 0-8103-3279-5). Gale.
Bear Who Slept Through Christmas. John Barrett. 32p. (gr. k-6). 2.95 (ISBN 0-89542-943-8); pap. 2.25 o.p. (ISBN 0-89542-942-X). Ideals.
Bearded Collie. G. O. Willison. (Foyle's Handbks). 1971. 3.95 (ISBN 0-685-55805-3). Palmetto Pub.
Beardmore: The History of a Scottish Industrial Giant. John R. Hume & Michael S. Moss. 1980. text ed. 34.95 o.p. (ISBN 0-435-32589-2). Heinemann Ed.
Beard's Massage. Paul Becker & Elizabeth C. Wood. 1981. pap. price not set (ISBN 0-7216-9592-2). Saunders.
Bearknife Gold. Alan Marks. 1980. pap. 1.75 (ISBN 0-505-51453-2). Tower Bks.
Bears. George Shea. LC 80-20367. (Creatures Wild & Free Ser.). (gr. 1-6). 1981. 5.95 (ISBN 0-88436-772-X). EMC.
Bears Almanac. Stanley Berenstain & Janice Berenstain. (gr. 1-4). 1973. 3.95 (ISBN 0-394-82693-0, BYR); PLB 5.99 (ISBN 0-394-92693-5). Random.
Bears & Other Carnivores. LC 76-26830. (Wild, Wild World of Animals Ser.). (Illus.). (gr. 5 up). 1977. PLB 11.97 (ISBN 0-913948-08-X, Pub. by Time-Life). Silver.
Bears & Other Carnivores. Time-Life Television. (Wild, Wild World of Animals Ser.). (Illus.). 1976. 10.95 (ISBN 0-913948-08-X). Time-Life.
Bears' House. Marilyn Sachs. LC 76-157621. (gr. 4-7). 1971. 6.95a (ISBN 0-385-03363-X); PLB (ISBN 0-385-06632-5). Doubleday.
Bears in the Wild. Ada Graham & Frank Graham. LC 80-68732. (Audubon Reader: No. 6). (Illus.). 128p. (gr. 4-7). 1981. 8.95 (ISBN 0-440-00532-9); PLB 8.44 (ISBN 0-440-00538-8). Delacorte.
Bear's Magic & Other Stories. Carla Stevens. (gr. k-3). 1977. pap. 1.50 (ISBN 0-590-01506-0, Schol Pap); pap. 3.50 bk. & record (ISBN 0-590-20800-4). Schol Bk Serv.
Bears of Blue River. Charles Major. (Illus.). (gr. 5-7). 1963. 4.75g o.s.i. (ISBN 0-02-762200-2). Macmillan.
Bears of Yellowstone. Paul D. Schullery. LC 79-65734. (Illus.). 180p. (Orig.). 1980. 10.95 (ISBN 0-934948-01-1); pap. 5.95 (ISBN 0-934948-00-3). Yellowstone Lib.
Bear's Surprise Party. Joan Bowden. (Eager Readers Ser). (gr. k-3). 1975. PLB 5.00 (ISBN 0-307-60809-3, Golden Pr). Western Pub.
Bear's Toothache. David McPhail. (gr. 2-8). 1978. pap. 2.50 (ISBN 0-14-050263-7, Puffin). Penguin.
Bears Upstairs. Dorothy Haas. LC 78-54683. (gr. 5-9). 1978. 7.95 (ISBN 0-688-80169-2); PLB 7.63 (ISBN 0-688-84169-4). Greenwillow.
Bears Upstairs. Dorothy Haas. (gr. k-6). 1981. pap. 1.75 (ISBN 0-440-40448-7, YB). Dell.
Bear's Water Picnic. John Yeoman. LC 70-116757. (Illus.). (gr. k-3). 1971. 4.95g o.s.i. (ISBN 0-02-793640-6). Macmillan.
Bears Who Went to the Seaside. Susanna Gretz. LC 72-86763. (Picture Bk). (Illus.). 32p. (gr. k-2). 1973. 4.95 o.p. (ISBN 0-695-80375-1); PLB 5.97 lib. ed. o.p. (ISBN 0-695-40375-3). Follett.
Beast. Susan Meddaugh. (gr. k-3). 1981. 8.95 (ISBN 0-395-30349-4). HM.
Beast in Man. Emile Zola. 1956. 13.95 (ISBN 0-236-31007-0, Pub. by Paul Elek). Merrimack Bk Serv.
Beast in the Bed. Barbara Dillon. LC 80-15069. (Illus.). 32p. (gr. k-3). 1981. 7.95 (ISBN 0-688-22254-4); PLB 7.63 (ISBN 0-688-32254-9). Morrow.
Beast Master. Andre Norton. 1978. pap. 1.95 (ISBN 0-449-23637-4, Crest). Fawcett.
Beast of Lor. Clyde R. Bulla. LC 77-6751. (Illus.). (gr. 3-7). 1977. 7.95 (ISBN 0-690-01377-9, TYC-J). T Y Crowell.
Beast on the Brink. Betty Levin. (Illus.). (gr. 5-7). 1980. pap. 1.95 (ISBN 0-380-76141-6, 76141, Camelot). Avon.
Beast Within. Edward Levy. LC 78-73871. 1981. 10.95 (ISBN 0-87795-225-6). Arbor Hse.
Beastly Folklore. Joseph D. Clark. LC 68-12617. 1968. 11.00 (ISBN 0-8108-0009-8). Scarecrow.
Beastly Neighbors: Or Why Earwigs Make Good Mothers. Mollie Rights & Tim Solga. (Brown Paper School Ser.). (Illus.). 128p. (Orig.). (gr. 3 up). 1981. 9.95 (ISBN 0-316-74576-6); pap. 5.95 (ISBN 0-316-74577-4). Little.
Beast's Mark & Number: 666. Dennis M. Battle. (Illus.). 52p. 1981. pap. 2.50 (ISBN 0-933464-11-8). D M Battle Pubns.
Beasts of Hades. Graham Diamond. LC 80-84370. (Adventures of the Empire Princess Ser: No. 4). 256p. (Orig.). 1981. pap. 2.25 (ISBN 0-87216-821-2). Playboy Pbks.
Beasts of the Field Puzzles. Sandy Dengler. 1979. pap. 1.95 (ISBN 0-8024-0680-7). Moody.
Beasts of the Southern Wild & Other Stories. Doris Betts. LC 73-4138. 202p. 1973. 7.95 o.s.i. (ISBN 0-06-010321-3, HarpT). Har-Row.
Beat Heart Disease! Risteard Mulcahy. LC 78-24490. (Positive Health Guide Ser.). (Illus.). 1979. 8.95 (ISBN 0-668-04678-3, 4678-3); pap. 4.95 (ISBN 0-668-04685-6, 4685-6). Arco.
Beat the Odds: Microcomputer Simulations of Casino Games. Hans Sagan. 192p. 1980. pap. 7.95 (ISBN 0-8104-5181-6). Hayden.
Beat the Races. Thomas Flanagan. LC 72-650. 1973. pap. 1.45 o.p. (ISBN 0-668-02644-8). Arc Bks.
Beat the Story-Drum, Pum-Pum. Ashley Bryan. LC 80-12045. (Illus.). 80p. (gr. 4-6). 1980. 10.95 (ISBN 0-689-30769-1). Atheneum.
Beat the System. Robert F. Allen & Charlotte Kraft. (Illus.). 1980. 9.95 (ISBN 0-07-001080-3). McGraw.
Beat the System! A Way to Create More Human Environments. Robert F. Allen & Carlotte Kraft. (Illus.). 1980. 15.95 (ISBN 0-07-001080-3). McGraw.
Beat the Turtle Drum. Constance C. Greene. (gr. 4 up). 1979. pap. 1.75 (ISBN 0-440-40875-X, YB). Dell.
Beating Around the Bush. Clara L. Brown. (Illus.). 1967. 3.95 o.p. (ISBN 0-8158-0060-6). Chris Mass.
Beating Inflation with Real Estate. Kenneth R. Harney. (Illus.). 1979. 12.95 (ISBN 0-394-50342-2). Random.
Beating the Adoption Game. Cynthia Martin. LC 80-16883. 1980. 9.95 (ISBN 0-916392-60-0). Oak Tree Pubns.
Beating the Bookie. Huey Mahl. (Gambler's Book Shelf Ser.). 1975. pap. 2.95 (ISBN 0-89650-547-2). Gamblers.
Beating the Insanity Defense: Denying the License to Kill. David M. Nissman et al. LC 80-8028. 1980. 18.95 (ISBN 0-669-03943-8). Lexington Bks.
Beating the Used Car Hustle. Robert Levering. LC 79-18647. 1980. pap. 5.95 (ISBN 0-87701-150-8). Chronicle Bks.
Beatitudes. Maureen Curley. (Children of the Kingdom Activities Ser.). (gr. 4-7). 1977. 7.95 (ISBN 0-686-13692-6). Pflaum Pr.
Beatitudes. Thomas Watson. 7.95 o.p. (ISBN 0-686-12491-X). Banner of Truth.
Beatitudes & the Lord's Prayer for Everyman. William Barclay. LC 75-9309. 256p. 1975. pap. 4.95 (ISBN 0-06-060393-3, RD112, HarpR). Har-Row.
Beatitudes: Jesus' Pattern for a Happy Life. Marilyn Norquist. 112p. 1981. pap. 2.95 (ISBN 0-89243-136-9). Liguori Pubns.
Beatles. Patricia Pirmanten. LC 74-14656. (Rock'n Pop Stars Ser.). (Illus.). 32p. (gr. 4-12). 1974. PLB 5.95 (ISBN 0-87191-398-4); pap. 2.95 (ISBN 0-89812-106-X). Creative Ed.
Beatles. Geoffrey Stokes. 256p. 1980. 29.95 (ISBN 0-8129-0928-3). Times Bks.
Beatles Illustrated Lyrics. Ed. by Alan Aldridge. (Illus.). 1969. 5.95 o.s.i. (ISBN 0-440-00472-1, Sey Lawr). Delacorte.
Beatles in Their Own Words. Compiled by Miles. 1979. pap. 5.95 (ISBN 0-8256-3925-5, Quick Fox). Music Sales.
Beatrice & Vanessa. John Yeoman. LC 74-13122. (Illus.). 32p. (gr. k-2). 1975. 5.95 o.s.i. (ISBN 0-02-793660-0). Macmillan.
Beatrice Di Tenda, 2 vols. Vincenzio Bellini. Ed. by Charles Rosen & Philip Gosset. LC 76-49178. (Early Romantic Opera Ser.: Vol. 5). 567p. 1980. lib. bdg. 82.00 (ISBN 0-8240-2904-6). Garland Pub.
Beatrice; or, the Unknown Relatives, 1852. Catherine Sinclair. Ed. by Robert L. Wolff. LC 75-453. (Victorian Fiction Ser.). 1975. lib. bdg. 66.00 (ISBN 0-8240-1532-0). Garland Pub.
Beatrice Trum Hunter's Whole-Grain Baking Sampler. Beatrice T. Hunter. LC 74-190457. 320p. 1974. pap. 2.25 (ISBN 0-87983-078-6). Keats.
Beatrice Webb's American Diary, Eighteen Ninety-Eight. Beatrice Webb. Ed. by David Shannon. (Illus.). 1963. 17.50 (ISBN 0-299-02851-8). U of Wis Pr.

Beatrix Farrand's Plant Book for Dumbarton Oaks. Ed. by Diane K. McGuire. LC 80-12169. (Illus.). 1980. 20.00x (ISBN 0-88402-095-9, Ctr Landscape Arch); pap. 10.00x. Dumbarton Oaks.

Beatrix Potter. Ann M. Mayer. LC 74-2082. (People to Remember Ser.). 40p. 1974. 5.95 (ISBN 0-87191-324-0). Creative Ed.

Beatrix Potter, Children's Storyteller. Patricia D. Frevert. Ed. by Ann Redpath. (People to Remember Ser.). (Illus.). 32p. (gr. 5-9). 1981. PLB 5.95 (ISBN 0-87191-801-3). Creative Ed.

Beatrix Potter's Birthday Book. Beatrix Potter. Ed. by Enid Linder. LC 73-89833. (Illus.). 160p. (gr. 3 up). 1974. 6.95 (ISBN 0-7232-1758-0); leather bdg. 11.95 (ISBN 0-7232-1815-3). Warne.

Beats: Essays in Criticism. Lee Bartlett. LC 80-28179. 250p. 1981. lib. bdg. write for info (ISBN 0-89950-026-9). McFarland & Co.

Beatty's Cabin: Adventures in Pecos High Country. Elliott S. Barker. LC 77-88836. 1977. Repr. of 1953 ed. 17.50 (ISBN 0-88307-537-7); pap. 6.95 o.p. (ISBN 0-88307-536-9). Gannon.

Beau Barron's Lady. Helen Ashfield. 192p. 1981. 9.95 (ISBN 0-312-07057-8). St Martin.

Beau Brocade. Emmuska Orczy. 275p. 1980. Repr. of 1905 ed. lib. bdg. 13.95x (ISBN 0-89968-194-8). Lightyear.

Beau Geste. Percival C. Wren. 1976. lib. bdg. 17.75x (ISBN 0-89968-135-2). Lightyear.

Beau Ideal. Percival C. Wren. 1976. lib. bdg. 16.75x (ISBN 0-89968-136-0). Lightyear.

Beau Sabreur. Percival C. Wren. 1976. lib. bdg. 16.75x (ISBN 0-89968-136-0). Lightyear.

Beaufort Sisters. Jon Cleary. 1980. pap. 2.50 (ISBN 0-445-04578-7). Popular Lib.

Beaumarchais. Joseph Sungolowsky. LC 74-10580. (World Authors Ser.: France: No. 334). 1974. lib. bdg. 10.95 (ISBN 0-8057-2122-3). Twayne.

Beaumarchais: A Biography. Frederick Grendel. Tr. by Roger Greaves. (Illus.). 344p. 1977. 14.95 o.s.i. (ISBN 0-690-01210-1, TYC-T). T Y Crowell.

Beaumont Tradition. Dorothy Daniels. 192p. (Orig.). 1976. pap. 1.25 o.s.i. (ISBN 0-446-86254-1). Warner Bks.

Beaute: From Head to Toe-a la Francais. Nadine Corbasson & Gisele De Bruchard. Tr. by Katherine Turley from Fr. (Illus.). 64p. 1974. pap. 3.95 o.s.i. (ISBN 0-02-046100-3, Collier). Macmillan.

Beauties of Modern Architecture. 2nd ed. Minard Lafever. LC 68-29602. (Architecture & Decorative Art Ser.: Vol. 18). (Illus.). 1968. Repr. of 1835 ed. lib. bdg. 25.00 (ISBN 0-306-71040-4). Da Capo.

Beauties of the Rose. facsimile ed. Henry Curtis. (Illus.). 120p. 65.00x (ISBN 0-936736-00-3). Sweetbrier.

Beautifood: Looking Better Through Nutrition. Karen Rall. LC 80-83615. (Illus.). 160p. (Orig.). 1981. pap. 6.95 (ISBN 0-89087-307-0). Celestial Arts.

Beautiful Alaska. Paul M. Lewis. Ed. by Robert D. Shangle. LC 78-102338. (Illus.). 72p. 1976. 14.95 (ISBN 0-915796-14-7); pap. 7.95 (ISBN 0-915796-13-9). Beautiful Am.

Beautiful America. Paul M. Lewis. Ed. by Robert D. Shangle. LC 79-22245. (Illus.). 1979. 27.50 (ISBN 0-89802-000-X). Beautiful Am.

Beautiful & Damned. F. Scott Fitzgerald. 1920. lib. rep. ed. 17.50x (ISBN 0-684-15153-7, ScribT); pap. 4.95 (ISBN 0-684-71758-1, SL90, ScribT). Scribner.

Beautiful Arizona. Paul M. Lewis. Ed. by Robert D. Shangle. LC 78-8732. (Illus.). 72p. 1978. 14.95 (ISBN 0-915796-40-6); pap. 7.95 (ISBN 0-915796-39-2). Beautiful Am.

Beautiful Atlanta. Paul M. Lewis. Ed. by Robert D. Shangle. LC 80-25850. (Illus.). 72p. 1980. 14.95 (ISBN 0-89802-121-9); pap. 7.95 (ISBN 0-89802-120-0). Beautiful Am.

Beautiful Boston. Paul M. Lewis. Ed. by Robert D. Shangle. LC 80-15184. (Illus.). 72p. 1980. 14.95 (ISBN 0-89802-172-3); pap. 7.95 (ISBN 0-89802-171-5). Beautiful Am.

Beautiful California. 3rd ed. Sunset Editors. LC 76-29190. (Illus.). 224p. 1977. pap. 8.95 (ISBN 0-376-05035-7, Sunset Bks). Sunset-Lane.

Beautiful California Coast. Paul M. Lewis. Ed. by Robert D. Shangle. LC 79-13134. 72p. 1979. 14.95 (ISBN 0-915796-97-X); pap. 7.95 (ISBN 0-915796-96-1). Beautiful Am.

Beautiful California Desert. Paul M. Lewis. Ed. by Robert D. Shangle. LC 78-14890. (Illus.). 72p. 1979. 14.95 (ISBN 0-89802-067-0); pap. 7.95 (ISBN 0-89802-066-2). Beautiful Am.

Beautiful California Missions. Lee Foster. Ed. by Robert D. Shangle. LC 78-102341. (Illus.). 72p. 1977. 14.95 (ISBN 0-915796-23-6); pap. 7.95 (ISBN 0-915796-22-8). Beautiful Am.

Beautiful California Mountains. Paul M. Lewis. Ed. by Robert D. Shangle. LC 80-11107. (Illus.). 72p. 1980. 14.95 (ISBN 0-89802-127-8); pap. 7.95 (ISBN 0-89802-126-X). Beautiful Am.

Beautiful Chicago. Brian Berger. Ed. by Robert D. Shangle. LC 80-13116. (Illus.). 72p. 1980. 14.95 (ISBN 0-89802-117-0); pap. 7.95 (ISBN 0-89802-116-2). Beautiful Am.

Beautiful Colorado. Paul M. Lewis. Ed. by Robert D. Shangle. LC 75-27463. 72p. 1979. 14.95 (ISBN 0-915796-08-2); pap. 6.95 (ISBN 0-915796-07-4). Beautiful Am.

Beautiful Colorado Country. Paul M. Lewis. Ed. by Robert D. Shangle. LC 80-18366. (Illus.). 72p. 1980. 14.95 (ISBN 0-89802-058-1); pap. 6.95 (ISBN 0-89802-057-3). Beautiful Am.

Beautiful Crafts Book. Ed. by Editorial Staff. LC 76-21846. (Illus.). (YA) 1976. 16.95 (ISBN 0-8069-5366-7); PLB 14.99 (ISBN 0-8069-5367-5). Sterling.

Beautiful Dallas. Robin Will. Ed. by Robert D. Shangle. LC 80-18361. (Illus.). 72p. 1980. 14.95 (ISBN 0-89802-098-0); pap. 7.95 (ISBN 0-89802-097-2). Beautiful Am.

Beautiful Delaware. Michael Fagan. Ed. by Robert D. Shangle. LC 80-21494. (Illus.). 72p. 1980. 14.95 (ISBN 0-89802-207-X); pap. 7.95 (ISBN 0-89802-208-8). Beautiful Am.

Beautiful Denver. Paul M. Lewis. Ed. by Robert D. Shangle. (Illus.). 72p. 1981. 14.95 (ISBN 0-89802-119-7); pap. 7.95 (ISBN 0-89802-118-9). Beautiful Am.

Beautiful Film Stories. Anna Bakacs. 1978. 7.95 o.p. (ISBN 0-533-03297-0). Vantage.

Beautiful Florida. Paul M. Lewis. Ed. by Robert D. Shangle. LC 79-1428. (Illus.). 72p. 1979. 14.95 (ISBN 0-915796-71-6); pap. 7.95 (ISBN 0-915796-70-8). Beautiful Am.

Beautiful Georgia. Paul M. Lewis. Ed. by Robert D. Shangle. LC 78-7895. 72p. 1978. 14.95 (ISBN 0-915796-42-2); pap. 7.95 (ISBN 0-915796-41-4). Beautiful Am.

Beautiful Girl. Alice Adams. 1980. pap. write for info. (ISBN 0-671-83218-2). PB.

Beautiful Girl. Ogilvie. (gr. 7-12). 1980. pap. 1.50 (ISBN 0-590-31277-4, Schol Pap). Schol Bk Serv.

Beautiful Hawaii. rev. ed. Paul M. Lewis. (Illus.). 72p. 1980. 14.95 (ISBN 0-89802-109-X); pap. 7.95 (ISBN 0-89802-108-1). Beautiful Am.

Beautiful Hawaii. Sunset Editors. LC 77-72508. (Illus.). 208p. 1977. pap. 8.95 (ISBN 0-376-05373-9, Sunset Bks). Sunset-Lane.

Beautiful Idaho. Paul M. Lewis. Ed. by Robert D. Shangle. LC 79-779. 72p. 1979. 14.95 (ISBN 0-915796-93-7); pap. 7.95 (ISBN 0-915796-92-9). Beautiful Am.

Beautiful Illinois. Andrea Kennet. Ed. by Robert D. Shangle. LC 80-18774. (Illus.). 72p. 1980. 14.95 (ISBN 0-915796-73-2); pap. 7.95 (ISBN 0-915796-72-4). Beautiful Am.

Beautiful in Music. Edward Hanslick. Tr. by Gustav Cohen & Morris Weitz. LC 57-14627. 1957. pap. 3.95 (ISBN 0-672-60211-3, LLA45). Bobbs.

Beautiful in Music: A Contribution to the Revisal of Musical Aesthetics. rev. ed. Eduard Hanslick. Tr. by Gustav Cohen. LC 74-1362. (Music Ser.). 174p. 1974. Repr. of 1891 ed. lib. bdg. 19.50 (ISBN 0-306-70649-0). Da Capo.

Beautiful Indiana. Sheryl White. Ed. by Robert D. Shangle. LC 80-26310. (Illus.). 72p. 1980. 14.95 (ISBN 0-89802-160-X); pap. 7.95 (ISBN 0-89802-159-6). Beautiful Am.

Beautiful Iowa. Brian Berger. Ed. by Robert D. Shangle. LC 79-28596. (Illus.). 72p. 1980. 14.95 (ISBN 0-89802-107-3); pap. 7.95 (ISBN 0-89802-106-5). Beautiful Am.

Beautiful Kentucky. Sheryl White. Ed. by Robert D. Shangle. LC 80-25924. (Illus.). 72p. 1980. 14.95 (ISBN 0-915796-67-8); pap. 7.95 (ISBN 0-915796-66-X). Beautiful Am.

Beautiful Kweilin. 1978. pap. 10.95 (ISBN 0-8351-0570-9). China Bks.

Beautiful Las Vegas. Duke London. Ed. by Robert D. Shangle. LC 79-18837. (Illus.). 72p. 1980. 14.95 (ISBN 0-89802-079-4); pap. 7.95 (ISBN 0-89802-078-6). Beautiful Am.

Beautiful Legs: You Can Have Them. Jeffrey Weber. LC 80-67533. 1980. cancelled (ISBN 0-9604892-2-3). Five Arms Corp.

Beautiful Los Angeles. William C. Curran. Ed. by Robert D. Shangle. LC 79-12045. 72p. 1979. 14.95 (ISBN 0-89802-056-5); pap. 7.95 (ISBN 0-89802-055-7). Beautiful Am.

Beautiful Louisiana. Brian Berger. Ed. by Robert D. Shangle. (Illus.). 72p. 1981. 14.95 (ISBN 0-89802-111-1); pap. 7.95 (ISBN 0-89802-110-3). Beautiful Am.

Beautiful Machine. Maggie Lettvin. 448p. 1975. pap. 2.95 o.p. (ISBN 0-345-27350-8). Ballantine.

Beautiful Maryland. James F. Waesche. Ed. by Robert D. Shangle. LC 79-22530. (Illus.). 72p. 1980. 14.95 (ISBN 0-915796-65-1); pap. 7.95 (ISBN 0-915796-64-3). Beautiful Am.

Beautiful Massachusetts. Paul M. Lewis. 72p. 1980. 14.95 (ISBN 0-915796-57-0); pap. 7.95 (ISBN 0-915796-56-2). Beautiful Am.

Beautiful Michigan, Vol. II. Louis Cook. Ed. by Robert D. Shangle. LC 78-105527. (Illus.). 72p. 14.95 (ISBN 0-915796-89-9); pap. 7.95 (ISBN 0-915796-88-0). Beautiful Am.

Beautiful Michigan. Stanley Radhuber. Ed. by Robert D. Shangle. LC 78-52648. (Illus.). 72p. 1978. 14.95 (ISBN 0-915796-10-4); pap. 7.95 (ISBN 0-915796-09-0). Beautiful Am.

Beautiful: Michigan Country. Louis Cook & Robert D. Shangle. (Illus.). 72p. 1980. 14.95 (ISBN 0-89802-203-7); pap. 7.95 (ISBN 0-89802-204-5). Beautiful Am.

Beautiful Minnesota. Robin Will. 72p. 1978. write for info. (ISBN 0-915796-61-9); pap. write for info. (ISBN 0-915796-60-0). Beautiful Am.

Beautiful Missouri. Paul M. Lewis. LC 80-14717. (Illus.). 72p. 1980. 14.95 (ISBN 0-89802-123-5); pap. 7.95 (ISBN 0-89802-122-7). Beautiful Am.

Beautiful Montana, Vol. II. Rick Graetz. LC 78-102354. 72p. 1979. text ed. 14.95 (ISBN 0-89802-006-9); pap. 7.95 (ISBN 0-89802-005-0). Beautiful Am.

Beautiful Montana. Rick Graetz. Ed. by Robert D. Shangle. LC 78-102354. (Illus.). 1977. 14.95 (ISBN 0-915796-25-2); pap. 7.95 (ISBN 0-915796-24-4). Beautiful Am.

Beautiful Montana Country. Lewis Cook. Ed. by Robert D. Shangle. (Illus.). 72p. 1980. 12.95 (ISBN 0-89802-205-3); pap. 6.95 (ISBN 0-89802-206-1). Beautiful Am.

Beautiful Monterey Peninsula & Big Sur. Ed. by Robert D. Shangle. LC 80-20374. (Illus.). 72p. 1980. 14.95 (ISBN 0-89802-164-2); pap. 7.95 (ISBN 0-89802-163-4). Beautiful Am.

Beautiful Mt. Hood. Robin Carey. Ed. by Robert D. Shangle. LC 78-102323. (Illus.). 1977. 14.95 (ISBN 0-915796-27-9); pap. 7.95 (ISBN 0-915796-26-0). Beautiful Am.

Beautiful Naturecraft Book. (Illus.). 1979. 16.95 (ISBN 0-8069-5388-8); lib. bdg. 13.99 (ISBN 0-8069-5389-6). Sterling.

Beautiful Nevada. Robin Will. Ed. by Robert D. Shangle. (Illus.). 72p. 1981. 14.95 (ISBN 0-89802-101-4); pap. 7.95 (ISBN 0-89802-100-6). Beautiful Am.

Beautiful New Jersey. Paul M. Lewis. Ed. by Robert D. Shangle. LC 80-23325. (Illus.). 72p. 1980. 14.95 (ISBN 0-89802-113-8); pap. 7.95 (ISBN 0-89802-112-X). Beautiful Am.

Beautiful New Mexico. Craig A. Ryan. Ed. by Robert D. Shangle. LC 79-16748. (Illus.). 80p. 1979. 14.95 (ISBN 0-89802-073-5); pap. 7.95 (ISBN 0-89802-072-7). Beautiful Am.

Beautiful New Orleans. Brian Berger. Ed. by Robert D. Shangle. (Illus.). 72p. 1981. 14.95 (ISBN 0-89802-123-5); pap. 7.95 (ISBN 0-89802-122-7). Beautiful Am.

Beautiful New York. William Curran. LC 79-90287. 80p. 1979. 14.95 (ISBN 0-89802-004-2); pap. 7.95 (ISBN 0-89802-003-4). Beautiful Am.

Beautiful New York City. Ed. by Robert D. Shangle & Robert D. Shngle. LC 79-27008. (Illus.). 72p. 1980. 14.95 (ISBN 0-89802-096-4); pap. 7.95 (ISBN 0-89802-095-6). Beautiful Am.

Beautiful North Carolina. John M. Fagan. Ed. by Robert D. Shangle. LC 79-18081. (Illus.). 72p. 1980. 14.95 (ISBN 0-89802-075-1); pap. 7.95 (ISBN 0-89802-074-3). Beautiful Am.

Beautiful North Idaho. Paul M. Lewis. LC 79-4546. 72p. 1979. 14.95 (ISBN 0-915796-95-3); pap. 7.95 (ISBN 0-915796-94-5). Beautiful Am.

Beautiful Northern California, Vol. II. William Curran. Ed. by Robert D. Shangle. LC 78-9901. 72p. 1978. 14.95 (ISBN 0-915796-87-2); pap. 7.95 (ISBN 0-915796-86-4). Beautiful Am.

Beautiful Northwest. Sunset Editors. LC 77-78147. (Illus.). 224p. 1977. pap. 8.95 (ISBN 0-376-05053-5, Sunset Bks). Sunset-Lane.

Beautiful Ohio. Robin Will. LC 78-9935. 72p. 1980. 14.95 (ISBN 0-915796-77-5); pap. 7.95 (ISBN 0-915796-76-7). Beautiful Am.

Beautiful Oklahoma. Brian Berger. LC 80-10968. (Illus.). 72p. 1980. 14.95 (ISBN 0-89802-008-5); pap. 7.95 (ISBN 0-89802-007-7). Beautiful Am.

Beautiful Orange County. Paul M. Lewis. Ed. by Robert D. Shangle. LC 80-25846. (Illus.). 72p. 1980. 14.95 (ISBN 0-89802-174-X); pap. 7.95 (ISBN 0-89802-173-1). Beautiful Am.

Beautiful Oregon. Paul M. Lewis. Ed. by Robert D. Shangle. LC 75-314222. (Illus.). 72p. 1974. 14.95 (ISBN 0-915796-04-X); pap. 7.95 (ISBN 0-915796-00-7). Beautiful Am.

Beautiful Oregon, Vol. II. Paul M. Lewis. Ed. by Robert D. Shangle. LC 78-13762. (Illus.). 72p. 1978. 14.95 (ISBN 0-915796-79-1); pap. 7.95 (ISBN 0-915796-78-3). Beautiful Am.

Beautiful Oregon Coast. Paul M. Lewis. Ed. by Robert D. Shangle. LC 78-102344. (Illus.). 72p. 1977. 14.95 (ISBN 0-915796-21-X); pap. 7.95 (ISBN 0-915796-20-1). Beautiful Am.

Beautiful Oregon Country. Brian Berger. Ed. by Robert D. Shangle. LC 79-1107. (Illus.). 72p. 1979. 14.95 (ISBN 0-89802-092-1); pap. 7.95 (ISBN 0-89802-091-3). Beautiful Am.

Beautiful Oregon Mountains. Paul M. Lewis. (Illus.). Date not set. 14.95 (ISBN 0-915796-99-6); pap. 7.95 (ISBN 0-915796-98-8). Beautiful Am. Postponed.

Beautiful Pacific Coast. Paul M. Lewis. Ed. by Robert D. Shangle. (Illus.). 72p. 1980. 14.95 (ISBN 0-89802-125-1); pap. 7.95 (ISBN 0-89802-124-3). Beautiful Am.

Beautiful Pennsylvania. Paul M. Lewis. LC 79-26331. (Illus.). 72p. 1980. 14.95 (ISBN 0-915796-59-7); pap. 7.95 (ISBN 0-915796-58-9). Beautiful Am.

Beautiful Phantoms. Barry Gifford. 1981. pap. 5.00 (ISBN 0-686-28912-9). Tombouctou.

Beautiful Philadelphia. Paul M. Lewis. Ed. by Robert D. Shangle. (Illus.). 72p. 1980. 14.95 (ISBN 0-89802-115-4); pap. 7.95 (ISBN 0-89802-114-6). Beautiful Am.

Beautiful Pittsburgh. Andrea Kennet. Ed. by Robert D. Shangle. LC 79-20481. (Illus.). 80p. 1980. 14.95 (ISBN 0-89802-088-3); pap. 7.95 (ISBN 0-89802-087-5). Beautiful Am.

Beautiful Portland. Robin Will. Ed. by Robert D. Shangle. LC 79-778. 72p. 1979. 14.95 (ISBN 0-915796-91-0); pap. 7.95 (ISBN 0-915796-90-2). Beautiful Am.

Beautiful San Diego. Loren Mitchell. Ed. by Robert D. Shangle. LC 79-17663. (Illus.). 80p. 1979. 14.95 (ISBN 0-89802-060-3); pap. 7.95 (ISBN 0-89802-059-X). Beautiful Am.

Beautiful San Francisco. Lee Foster. Ed. by Robert D. Shangle. LC 78-102340. (Illus.). 72p. 1977. 14.95 (ISBN 0-915796-19-8); pap. 7.95 (ISBN 0-915796-18-X). Beautiful Am.

Beautiful San Juans Island & Puget Sound. Ann Rule. Ed. by Robert D. Shangle. LC 79-1204. (Illus.). 80p. 1980. 14.95 (ISBN 0-89802-081-6); pap. 7.95 (ISBN 0-89802-080-8). Beautiful Am.

Beautiful Scotland. W. H. Murray. 1978. pap. 5.95 (ISBN 0-7134-3217-9, Pub. by Batsford England). David & Charles.

Beautiful Seattle. Ann Rule. Ed. by Robert D. Shangle. LC 79-23392. (Illus.). 80p. 1979. 14.95 (ISBN 0-89802-071-9); pap. 7.95 (ISBN 0-89802-070-0). Beautiful Am.

Beautiful Southern California. Lee Foster. Ed. by Robert D. Shangle. LC 78-8532. (Illus.). 72p. 1978. 14.95 (ISBN 0-915796-38-4); pap. 7.95 (ISBN 0-915796-37-6). Beautiful Am.

Beautiful String Art Book. Raymond Gautard. LC 78-58375. (Illus.). 1978. 19.95 (ISBN 0-8069-5386-1); lib. bdg. 16.79 (ISBN 0-8069-5387-X). Sterling.

Beautiful Swimmers: Watermen, Crabs & the Chesapeake Bay. William W. Warner. 1977. pap. 3.50 (ISBN 0-14-004405-1). Penguin.

Beautiful Tennessee. Robin Will. (Illus.). 72p. 1981. 14.95 (ISBN 0-89802-103-0); pap. 7.95 (ISBN 0-89802-102-2). Beautiful Am.

Beautiful Texas. Robin Will. Ed. by Robert D. Shangle. LC 78-23422. (Illus.). 72p. 1978. 14.95 (ISBN 0-915796-75-9); pap. 7.95 (ISBN 0-915796-74-0). Beautiful Am.

Beautiful Things. Thomas McGrath & Chris Jenkyns. LC 60-15076. (Illus.). (gr. k-3). 1960. 3.50 (ISBN 0-8149-0364-9). Vanguard.

Beautiful Utah. Paul M. Lewis. Ed. by Robert D. Shangle. LC 78-102331. (Illus.). 72p. 1976. 14.95 (ISBN 0-915796-30-9); pap. 7.95 (ISBN 0-915796-29-5). Beautiful Am.

Beautiful Utah Country. Paul M. Lewis. Ed. by Robert D. Shangle. LC 80-11826. (Illus.). 72p. 1980. 14.95 (ISBN 0-89802-162-6); pap. 7.95 (ISBN 0-89802-161-8). Beautiful Am.

Beautiful Vancouver U. S. A. Brian Berger. Ed. by Robert D. Shangle. LC 79-19900. (Illus.). 72p. 1980. 14.95 (ISBN 0-89802-090-5); pap. 7.95 (ISBN 0-89802-089-1). Beautiful Am.

Beautiful Vermont. Michael Fagan. LC 80-14775. (Illus.). 72p. 1980. 14.95 (ISBN 0-89802-105-7); pap. 7.95 (ISBN 0-89802-104-9). Beautiful Am.

Beautiful Virginia. Parke Rouse, Jr. Ed. by Robert D. Shangle. LC 80-11162. (Illus.). 72p. 1980. 14.95 (ISBN 0-89802-077-8); pap. 7.95 (ISBN 0-89802-076-X). Beautiful Am.

Beautiful Washington. Paul M. Lewis. LC 75-314223. (Illus.). 72p. 1974. 14.95 (ISBN 0-915796-05-8); pap. 7.95 (ISBN 0-915796-02-3). Beautiful Am.

Beautiful Washington, Vol. II. Paul M. Lewis. LC 75-31422. (Illus.). 72p. 1978. 14.95 (ISBN 0-915796-81-3); pap. 7.95 (ISBN 0-915796-80-5). Beautiful Am.

Beautiful Washington D. C. William C. Curran. Ed. by Robert D. Shangle. LC 79-17658. (Illus.). 80p. 1979. 14.95 (ISBN 0-89802-010-7); pap. 7.95 (ISBN 0-89802-009-3). Beautiful Am.

Beautiful Ways Songs. pap. 0.30. Faith Pub Hse.

Beautiful Wisconsin. William Curran. Ed. by Robert D. Shangle. LC 79-777. 80p. 1979. 14.95 (ISBN 0-915796-63-5); pap. 7.95 (ISBN 0-915796-62-7). Beautiful Am.

Beautiful Women in Art & Poetry. Wellington De Sackerville. (Illus.). 1979. deluxe ed. 31.75 (ISBN 0-930582-39-X). Gloucester Art.

Beautiful Wyoming. Brian Berger. Ed. by Robert D. Shangle. LC 79-25372. (Illus.). 72p. 1980. 14.95 (ISBN 0-89802-094-8); pap. 7.95 (ISBN 0-89802-093-X). Beautiful Am.
Beautiful Yosemite National Park. Robin Will. LC 79-15850. (Illus.). 80p. 14.95 (ISBN 0-89802-069-7); pap. 7.95 (ISBN 0-89802-068-9). Beautiful Am.
Beauty. Manoje Basu. Tr. by Sachindra L. Ghosh. 103p. 1969. pap. 1.80 (ISBN 0-88253-011-9). Ind-US Inc.
Beauty & Sadness. Yasunari Kawabata. Tr. by Howard Hibbett from Jap. 1975. 7.95 o.p. (ISBN 0-394-46055-3). Knopf.
Beauty & Sadness. Yasunari Kawabata. Tr. by Howard Hibbet from Jap. (Perigee Japanese Library). 224p. pap. 4.95 (ISBN 0-399-50529-6, Perigee). Putnam.
Beauty & the Beast. (Illus.). Arabic 2.50x (ISBN 0-685-82810-7). Intl Bk Ctr.
Beauty & the Beast. Caren Caraway. (Stemmer House Story-to-Color Book). (Illus.). (ps up). 1980. 2.95 (ISBN 0-916144-46-1). Stemmer Hse.
Beauty & the Beast. Madame De Beaumont. LC 76-57884. (Illus.). (ps-2). 1978. 8.95 (ISBN 0-87888-119-0). Bradbury Pr.
Beauty & the Beasts: The Art of Hannes Bok. Ed. by Gerry De La Ree. 1978. 15.50 o.p. (ISBN 0-686-12087-6). De La Ree.
Beauty Care for the Eyes. LeRoy Koopman. 96p. 1975. pap. 2.50 (ISBN 0-310-26832-X). Zondervan.
Beauty Care for the Tongue. LeRoy Koopman. (Illus.). 96p. (Orig.). 1974. pap. 2.25 (ISBN 0-310-26842-7). Zondervan.
Beauty Lost - Then Found. Virginia Stephens. 1981. 6.95 (ISBN 0-8062-1574-7). Carlton.
Beauty Makeover Guide. Judith Ross & Susan Acton. LC 78-19956. 190p. 1981. pap. 6.95 (ISBN 0-8128-6113-2). Stein & Day.
Beauty Mature Woman. Dorothy Seiffert. (Illus.). 1977. 8.95 o.p. (ISBN 0-8015-3100-4). Dutton.
Beauty of California. Paul M. Lewis. Ed. by Robert D. Shangle. LC 79-9212. (Illus.). 1979. 27.50 (ISBN 0-89802-002-6). Beautiful Am.
Beauty of Caring. Lloyd J. Ogilvie. LC 80-80464. 1981. pap. 4.95 (ISBN 0-89081-244-6). Harvest Hse.
Beauty of Friendship. Lloyd J. Ogilvie. LC 80-80463. 1980. pap. 4.95 (ISBN 0-89081-243-8). Harvest Hse.
Beauty of God's Whisper. Randy Becton. 1980. pap. 3.95 (ISBN 0-89137-310-1). Quality Pubns.
Beauty of Love. Lloyd J. Ogilvie. LC 80-80465. (Orig.). 1980. pap. 4.95 (ISBN 0-89081-245-4). Harvest Hse.
Beauty of Oregon. Brian Berger. Ed. by Robert D. Shangle. (Illus.). 160p. 1980. 27.50 (ISBN 0-89802-128-6). Beautiful Am.
Beauty of Sharing. Lloyd J. Ogilvie. LC 80-8880. (Orig.). 1981. pap. 4.95 (ISBN 0-89081-246-2). Harvest Hse.
Beauty of Sport: A Cross-Disciplinary Inquiry. Benjamin Lowe. (Illus.). 1977. 14.95 (ISBN 0-13-066589-4). P-H.
Beauty of Washington. Paul M. Lewis. Ed. by Robert D. Shangle. (Illus.). 160p. 1980. 27.50 (ISBN 0-89802-129-4). Beautiful Am.
Beauty of Wholeness: Program Resource for Women 1981. Ed. by Imogene Goodyear. 1980. pap. 4.00 (ISBN 0-8309-0294-5). Herald Hse.
Beauty Questions & Answers. Linda Clark & Kay Lee. 1977. pap. 2.25 (ISBN 0-515-05647-2). Jove Pubns.
Beauty Unknown Color Lithographs. Ed. by Daphne & Nelson. (New Age Ser.: No. 502). 1976. 12.00 (ISBN 0-89007-502-6). C Stark.
Beauty's Daughter. Mollie Hardwick. 1978. pap. 1.95 o.p. (ISBN 0-425-03866-1). Berkley Pub.
Beaux-Arts Tradition in French Architecture. Donald D. Egbert. Ed. by David Van Zanten. LC 79-23798. (Illus.). 220p. 1980. 22.50x (ISBN 0-691-03943-7); pap. 12.50 (ISBN 0-691-10106-X). Princeton U Pr.
Beaux Gestes: A Guide to French Body Talk. Laurence Wylie & Rick Stafford. (Illus.). 1977. 8.95 o.p.; pap. 3.95 (ISBN 0-525-03025-5). Dutton.
Beaux' Stratagem. George Farquhar. Ed. by Vincent F. Hopper & Gerald B. Lahey. LC 62-1307. (Illus.). 1964. pap. text ed. 1.95 (ISBN 0-8120-0031-5). Barron.
Beaux' Stratagem. George Farquhar. Ed. by Charles N. Fifer. LC 77-89834. (Regents Restoration Drama Ser.). 1977. 9.95x (ISBN 0-8032-0384-5); pap. 2.75x (ISBN 0-8032-5384-2, BB 279, Bison). U of Nebr Pr.
Beaver Men. Mari Sandoz. (American Procession Ser). (Illus.). 1975. Repr. of 1964 ed. 9.95 (ISBN 0-8038-0674-4). Hastings.
Beaver Men: Spearheads of Empire. Mari Sandoz. LC 77-14081. (Illus.). 1978. pap. 5.95 (ISBN 0-8032-5884-4, BB 658, Bison). U of Nebr Pr.
Beaver of Weeping Water. Marian Rumsey. LC 69-11542. (Illus.). (gr. 3-7). 1969. PLB 6.00 o.p. (ISBN 0-688-31074-5). Morrow.
Beaver Who Wouldn't Die. Monica G. De Bruyn. LC 75-2968. (Picture Bk). (Illus.). 32p. (gr. 2-4). 1975. 5.95 o.p. (ISBN 0-695-80586-X); lib. ed. 5.97 o.p. (ISBN 0-695-40586-1). Follett.
Beavers & Other Pond Dwellers. Time Life Books Editors. (Wild, Wild World of Animals). (Illus.). 1978. 10.95 (ISBN 0-913948-16-0). Time-Life.
Beavers & Pond Dwellers. LC 77-82678. (Wild, Wild World of Animals Ser.). (Illus.). 1978. lib. bdg. 11.97 (ISBN 0-686-51168-9). Silver.
Beaver's Way. Keith Hay et al. Ed. by Russell Bourne & Bonnie S. Lawrence. (Ranger Rick's Best Friends Ser.: No. 1). (gr. 1-6). 1973. 2.50 o.p. (ISBN 0-912186-06-2). Natl Wildlife.
Because It Is Absurd. Pierre Boulle. LC 74-164984. 8.95 (ISBN 0-8149-0697-4). Vanguard.
Because of the Sand Witches There. Mary Q. Steele. LC 75-5932. (Illus.). 192p. (gr. 3-7). 1975. 8.25 (ISBN 0-688-80001-7); PLB 7.92 (ISBN 0-688-84001-9). Greenwillow.
Because We Have Good News: A Layman's Guide for Person-to-Person Evangelism in Community. Wallace E. Fisher. LC 73-12233. 128p. (Orig.). 1973. pap. 2.95 (ISBN 0-687-02532-X). Abingdon.
Becker the Counterfeiter. G. F. Hill. 111p. 1979. 20.00 (ISBN 0-916710-52-1). Obol Intl.
Beckett the Shape Changer. Ed. by Katharine Worth. 1975. 15.00 (ISBN 0-7100-8123-5). Routledge & Kegan.
Becketts of Punch. Arthur W. A Beckett. LC 69-17341. 1969. Repr. of 1903 ed. 18.00 (ISBN 0-8103-3518-2). Gale.
Beckoning. Josh Webster. (Orig.). 1980. pap. 2.95 (ISBN 0-440-10943-4). Dell.
Beckoning Heart. Alyssa Morgan. 1981. pap. 1.50 o.s.i. (ISBN 0-440-10749-0). Dell.
Becky. Karen Hirsch. LC 80-27619. (Illus.). 40p. (gr. k-3). 1981. PLB 4.95 (ISBN 0-87614-144-0). Carolrhoda Bks.
Becky. John Wilson. LC 66-10507. (Illus.). (gr. k-3). 1967. 6.79 (ISBN 0-690-12669-7, TYC-J). T Y Crowell.
Becky & Her Brave Cat, Bluegrass. Miriam E. Mason. (Illus.). (gr. 3-5). 1960. 3.95 o.s.i. (ISBN 0-02-762950-3). Macmillan.
Becky & the Bookworm. Joan M. Lexau. LC 78-73526. (Illus.). (gr. 2-5). Date not set. 3.50 (ISBN 0-89799-150-8); pap. price not set (ISBN 0-89799-068-4). Dandelion Pr. Postponed.
Becky Landers Frontier Warrior. Constance L. Skinner. (gr. 4-6). 1967. 3.95g o.s.i. (ISBN 0-02-782810-7); pap. 0.79 o.s.i. (ISBN 0-686-66480-9). Macmillan.
Become an Ex-Smoker. Brian G. Danaher & Edward Lichtenstein. LC 78-1679. (Self-Management Psychology Ser.). (Illus.). 1978. 11.95 (ISBN 0-13-072249-9, Spec); pap. 5.95 (ISBN 0-13-072231-6, Spec). P-H.
Becoming a Better Elementary Science Teacher: A Reader. Robert B. Sund & Rodger W. Bybee. LC 72-90162. 1973. pap. text ed. 15.95x (ISBN 0-675-09059-8). Merrill.
Becoming a Dentist: A Longitudinal Study of Dental Students. Basil J. Sherlock & Richard T. Morris. (Illus.). 152p. 1972. text ed. 12.75 (ISBN 0-398-02411-1). C C Thomas.
Becoming a Driver. new ed. Rosemary Grebel & Phyllis Pogrund. Ed. by Elaine Katz. (Survival Guides Ser.). (Illus.). 64p. (Orig.). (gr. 7 up). 1980. pap. text ed. 2.85 (ISBN 0-915510-43-X). Janus Bks.
Becoming a Family Therapist: Developing an Integrated Approach to Working with Families. Charles H. Kramer. LC 80-11322. 256p. 1980. text ed. 19.95 (ISBN 0-87705-470-3). Human Sci Pr.
Becoming a Father: A Handbook for Expectant Fathers. Sean Gresh. Ed. by L. Leedham. 160p. 1980. 12.95 (ISBN 0-88421-099-5). Butterick Pub.
Becoming a Grandmaster. R. D. Keene. 1977. 13.95 (ISBN 0-7134-0830-8, Pub. by Batsford England). David & Charles.
Becoming a Lawyer: A Humanistic Perspective on Legal Education, Professionalism. Elizabeth Dvorkin & Jack Himmelstein. 200p. 1981. pap. text ed. 17.95 (ISBN 0-8299-2126-5). West Pub.
Becoming a Mother. Theodore R. Seidman & Marvin H. Albert. 240p. 1980. pap. 1.95 (ISBN 0-686-69184-9, Crest). Fawcett.
Becoming a Prophetic Community. J. Elliott Corbett & Elizabeth S. Smith. LC 80-17618. 201p. (Orig.). 1980. pap. 7.95 (ISBN 0-8042-0784-4). John Knox.
Becoming a Psychotherapist. Jacquelin Goldman. (Amer. Lec. Psychology Ser.). (Illus.). 140p. 1976. 12.75- (ISBN 0-398-03497-4). C C Thomas.
Becoming a Secondary School Science Teacher. 3rd ed. Leslie Trowbridge et al. 352p. 1981. pap. text ed. 15.95 (ISBN 0-675-08030-4). Merrill.
Becoming a Teacher of Young Children. Margaret Z. Lay & John E. Dopyera. 1977. text ed. 15.95x (ISBN 0-669-99796-X). Heath.
Becoming a Teacher: The Passage to Professional Status. Elizabeth M. Eddy. LC 71-90069. 1969. pap. 6.00x (ISBN 0-8077-1274-4). Tchrs Coll.
Becoming a Woman. B. Lott. 1980. pap. cancelled (ISBN 0-398-04053-2); pap. write for info. (ISBN 0-398-04067-2). C C Thomas.
Becoming a Woman: The Socialization of Gender. Bernice Lott. (Illus.). 464p. 1980. 24.75 (ISBN 0-398-04053-2); pap. 18.50 (ISBN 0-398-04067-2). C C Thomas.
Becoming a Writer. Dorothea Brande. LC 80-53146. 256p. 1981. pap. 5.95 (ISBN 0-87477-164-1). J P Tarcher.
Becoming an Effective Counselor: Skills for Interpersonal Problem Solving. Dennis C. Kinlaw. LC 79-92072. (Illus.). 144p. (Orig.). 1981. pap. 6.50 (ISBN 0-8042-1108-6). John Knox.
Becoming Bilingual: A Guide to Language Learning. Donald N. Larson & William A. Smalley. LC 74-8839. (Applied Cultural Anthropology Ser.). 425p. (Orig.). 1974. pap. 6.95x (ISBN 0-87808-718-4). William Carey Lib.
Becoming Christian: A Theology of Baptism As the Sacrament of Human History. Alexander Ganoczy. Tr. by John G. Lynch from Fr. LC 76-23530. 1976. pap. 2.95 (ISBN 0-8091-1980-3). Paulist Pr.
Becoming Comprehensive: Case Histories. Ed. by E. Halsall. 1970. 18.00 (ISBN 0-08-015820-X); pap. 12.75 (ISBN 0-08-015819-6). Pergamon.
Becoming Delinquent: Young Offenders & the Correctional Process. Ed. by Peter G. Garabedian & Don C. Gibbons. LC 73-91727. (Illus.). 1970. text ed. 16.95x (ISBN 0-202-30103-6). Aldine Pub.
Becoming Deviant. David Matza. 1969. pap. text ed. 10.95 (ISBN 0-13-073171-4). P-H.
Becoming Human Through Art: Aesthetic Experience in the School. Edmund B. Feldman. 1970. ref. ed. 19.95 (ISBN 0-13-072363-0). P-H.
Becoming Involved in Teaching. Kenneth T. Henson & Marvin A. Henry. LC 75-46377. 1976. 8.95 o.p. (ISBN 0-916768-01-5); pap. 5.95 o.p. (ISBN 0-685-89710-9). Sycamore Pr.
Becoming Modern: Individual Change in Six Developing Countries. Alex Inkeles & David H. Smith. LC 73-92534. 416p. 1974. text ed. 18.50x (ISBN 0-674-06375-9); pap. 7.95 (ISBN 0-674-06376-7). Harvard U Pr.
Becoming Orgasmic: A Sexual Growth Program for Women. J. Heiman et al. 1976. text ed. 11.95 (ISBN 0-13-072652-4, Spec); pap. text ed. 5.95 (ISBN 0-13-072645-1). P-H.
Becoming Visible. Philip Lamantia. (Pocket Poet Ser.: No. 39). 72p. 1981. pap. 3.00 (ISBN 0-686-69340-X). City Lights.
Becoming Visible: Women in European History. Renate Bridenthal & Claudia Koonz. LC 76-11978. 1977. pap. text ed. 9.50 (ISBN 0-395-24477-3). HM.
Bed & Board: The Economics of Love, Marriage, & Dependency. Anne S. Beller. 1981. 10.95 (ISBN 0-686-68238-6). FS&G.
Bed & Breakfast Stops Nineteen Eighty-One. British Tourist Authority. (Illus.). 96p. 1981. pap. write for info. (Pub. by Auto Assn-British Tourist Authority England). Merrimack Bk Serv.
Bed Exercises for Convalescent Patients. Nila K. Covalt. 244p. 1968. pap. 19.75 photocopy ed. spiral (ISBN 0-398-00352-1). C C Thomas.
Bed-Stuy Beat. Rose Blue. LC 75-117178. (Illus.). (gr. 4-6). 1970. PLB 5.90 (ISBN 0-531-01940-3). Watts.
Bed-Time-Story. Jill Robinson. LC 74-8578. 1974. 7.95 o.p. (ISBN 0-394-48803-2, BYR). Random.
Bed-Wetting: Origins & Treatment. rev. ed. Warren B. Baller. 300p. 1976. 21.00 (ISBN 0-08-017859-6). Pergamon.
Bedbug & Selected Poetry. Vladimir Mayakovsky. Ed. by Patricia Blake. Tr. by Max Hayward & George Reavey. LC 75-10805. (Midland Bks.: No. 189). 320p. 1975. 10.50x (ISBN 0-253-31130-6); pap. 3.95x (ISBN 0-253-20189-6). Ind U Pr.
Bedding & Furniture Materials, Vol. 14. Ed. by Carlos J. Hilado. LC 73-82115. (Fire & Flammability Ser.). (Illus.). 1976. pap. 20.00x (ISBN 0-87762-174-8). Technomic.
Bedeviled. Cary Hidalgo-Gato. LC 79-66162. 446p. 1980. 11.95 (ISBN 0-533-04364-6). Vantage.
Bedford Village: The City in the Dawn, Part 2. Hervey Allen. 1978. pap. 2.50 o.s.i. (ISBN 0-446-81436-9). Warner Bks.
Bedlam Patterns: Love & the Idea of Madness in Poe's Fiction. Richard Benton. 1979. pap. 2.75 (ISBN 0-910556-13-X). Enoch Pratt.
Bedouin. Shirley Kay. LC 77-88174. (This Changing World Ser.). 1978. 14.50x (ISBN 0-8448-1228-5). Crane-Russak Co.
Bedouin. Fidelity Lancaster. LC 78-2679. (Civilization Library). (Illus.). (gr. 5 up). 1978. PLB 6.90 s&l (ISBN 0-531-01447-9). Watts.
Bedouins, Wealth, & Change: A Study of Rural Development in the United Arab Emirates & the Sultanate of Oman. 64p. 1980. pap. 11.75 (TUNU 086, UNU). Unipub.
Bedrock: Images from the Wayside. Del Smith & Michael Cauthron. LC 75-16938. (Illus.). 128p. 1975. 10.50 (ISBN 0-89052-015-1). Madrona Pr.
Bedroom Set. David Rogers. 1979. pap. 1.75 o.p. (ISBN 0-449-14188-8, GM). Fawcett.
Bedrooms. Sunset Editors. LC 80-80857. (Illus.). 80p. (Orig.). 1980. pap. 3.95 (ISBN 0-376-01111-4, Sunset Bks). Sunset-Lane.
Bedside Diagnostic Examination. 3rd ed. Elmer L. DeGowin & Richard L. DeGowin. (Illus.). 1976. pap. text ed. 16.95 (ISBN 0-02-328050-6). Macmillan.
Bedside Mad. Ed. by Mad Magazine Editors. (Mad Ser.). (Illus.). 192p. 1973. pap. 1.75 (ISBN 0-446-94358-4). Warner Bks.
Bedside Nursing: An Introduction. 3rd ed. Joan Darwin et al. (Illus.). 236p. 1976. pap. 12.95x (ISBN 0-433-07133-8). Intl Ideas.
Bedside Nursing Techniques in Medicine & Surgery. 2nd ed. Audrey L. Sutton. LC 69-12891. 1969. pap. 11.95 (ISBN 0-7216-8666-4). Saunders.
Bedtime Mother Goose. Ed. by Evelyn Stone. (Look-Look Ser.). (Illus.). 24p. (ps). 1980. pap. 0.95 (ISBN 0-307-11855-X, Golden Pr). Western Pub.
Bedtime Stories. Zokeisha. (Puppet Story Board Bks.). (Illus.). 12p. (ps-k). Date not set. boards 2.95 (ISBN 0-671-42644-3, Little Simon). S&S.
Bee. Nancy Reese. Ed. by Alton Jordan. (I Can Read Underwater Books). (Illus.). (gr. k-3). 1974. PLB 3.50 (ISBN 0-89868-005-0, Read Res); pap. text ed. 1.75 (ISBN 0-89868-038-7). ARO Pub.
Bee Book. Barbara J. Crane. (Crane Reading System-English Ser.). (Illus.). (gr. k-2). 1977. pap. text ed. 2.80 (ISBN 0-89075-094-7). Crane Pub Co.
Bee Gees. Larry Pryce. LC 80-68161. (Illus.). 144p. 1981. pap. 2.95 (ISBN 0-87754-251-1). Chelsea Hse.
Bee Gees. Craig Schumacher. (Rock'n Roll Stars Ser.). 32p. (gr. 4-12). 1979. PLB 5.95 (ISBN 0-87191-697-5); pap. 2.95. Creative Ed.
Bee Gees: A Photo-Bio. Kim Stevens. 1979. pap. 1.95 (ISBN 0-515-05158-6). Jove Pubns.
Bee Keepers Encyclopedia. Alexander S. Deans. LC 75-23248. (Illus.). 1979. Repr. of 1949 ed. 18.00 (ISBN 0-8103-4176-X). Gale.
Bee My Valentine. Miriam Cohen. LC 77-21950. (Illus.). (gr. k-3). 1978. 7.95 (ISBN 0-688-80129-3); PLB 7.63 (ISBN 0-688-84129-5). Greenwillow.
Bee Tree & Other Stuff. Robert N. Peck. LC 75-10054. (Illus.). 128p. (gr. 3 up). 1975. 6.95 o.s.i. (ISBN 0-8027-6227-1); PLB 6.85 o.s.i. (ISBN 0-8027-6232-8). Walker & Co.
Beebi, the Little Blue Bell. Kal Gezi & Ann Bradford. LC 75-34179. (Illus.). (ps-3). 1976. 5.50 (ISBN 0-913778-29-X). Childs World.
Beef & Veal. (Good Cook Ser.). (Illus.). 1979. lib. bdg. 11.97 (ISBN 0-686-50996-X). Silver.
Beef Cattle. 7th ed. A. L. Neumann. LC 76-46616. 1977. 28.95 (ISBN 0-471-63236-8). Wiley.
Beef Cattle Science. 5th ed. M. E. Ensminger. LC 74-29763. (Illus.). 1976. 29.95 (ISBN 0-8134-1752-X, 1752); text ed. 22.95x (ISBN 0-685-76907-0). Interstate.
Beef, Leather & Grass. Edmund Randolph. LC 80-18818. (Illus.). 304p. 1981. 14.95 (ISBN 0-8061-1517-3). U of Okla Pr.
Beef Production. T. L. Dodsworth. 100p. 1972. text ed. 18.75 (ISBN 0-08-017016-1); pap. text ed. 7.75 (ISBN 0-08-017017-X). Pergamon.
Beef Production & Management. Gary L. Minish & Danny G. Fox. (Illus.). 1979. text ed. 16.95 (ISBN 0-8359-0445-8); instrs'. manual avail. Reston.
Beef Production in the South. Stewart H. Fowler. LC 78-55815. (Illus.). (gr. 9-12). 1979. 29.95 (ISBN 0-8134-2035-0); text ed. 22.95x (ISBN 0-685-12569-6, 2035). Interstate.
Beekeeping. Boy Scouts Of America. LC 19-600. (Illus.). 48p. (gr. 6-12). 1975. pap. 0.70x (ISBN 0-8395-3362-4, 3362). BSA.
Beekeeping. John E. Eckert & Frank R. Shaw. (Illus.). 1960. 15.95 (ISBN 0-02-534910-4). Macmillan.
Beekeeping. Lillee Zireau. LC 77-185674. (Handicraft Ser.: Bk. 6). (Illus.). 32p. (Orig.). (gr. 7-12). 1971. lib. bdg. 2.45 incl. catalog cards (ISBN 0-87157-906-5); pap. 1.25 vinyl laminated covers (ISBN 0-87157-406-3). SamHar Pr.
Beelzebub's Tales to His Grandson, 3 vols. G. I. Gurdjieff. 1973. Set. pap. 13.95 (ISBN 0-525-47351-3); pap. 3.95 ea. o.p.; Vol. 1. o.p. (ISBN 0-525-47348-3); Vol. 2. o.p. (ISBN 0-525-47349-1); Vol. 3. o.p. (ISBN 0-525-47350-5). Dutton.
Been Down So Long It Looks Like Up to Me. Richard Farina. 1966. 8.95 o.p. (ISBN 0-394-41683-X). Random.

Been There: Post Office Poems & Other Poems. Margaret La Pice. pap. 3.95 (ISBN 0-9604508-0-7). M La Pice.

Beer, Bubbles & Bucks. Lou Dersch. 225p. 1981. 9.95 (ISBN 0-86629-008-7). Sunrise MO.

Beer Can Collectors Bible. Jack Martells. Date not set. pap. 5.95 (ISBN 0-394-28918-8). Ballantine.

Beer Drinker's Guide to Early Retirement. Downs Canaday. (Illus.). 96p. 1981. pap. 5.95 (ISBN 0-931896-03-7). Cove View.

Beer Making for All. James MacGregor. (Orig.). 1973. pap. 3.95 (ISBN 0-571-10252-2, Pub. by Faber & Faber). Merrimack Bk Serv.

Beer Naturally. Michael Hardman. (Illus., Orig.). 1978. pap. 4.50 (ISBN 0-8467-0430-7, Pub. by Two Continents). Hippocrene Bks.

Bees. (MacDonald Educational Ser.). (Illus., Arabic.). 3.50 (ISBN 0-686-53077-2). Intl Bk Ctr.

Bees & Beekeeping. Roger A. Morse. LC 74-14082. (Illus.). 320p. 1975. 17.50x (ISBN 0-8014-0920-9). Comstock.

Bees & Beelines. Judy Hawes. LC 64-10864. (Let's-Read-&-Find-Out Science Bk). (Illus.). (gr. k-3). 1964. bds. 6.95 (ISBN 0-690-12739-1, TYC-J); PLB 7.89 (ISBN 0-690-12740-5); filmstrip & record 11.95 (ISBN 0-690-12741-3); filmstrip with cassette 14.95 (ISBN 0-690-12743-X). T Y Crowell.

Bees & the Law. Murray Loring. LC 80-66362. 128p. 1981. 6.95 (ISBN 0-915698-07-2). Dadant & Sons.

Bees, Bee Keeping, Honey & Pollination. Walter L. Gojmerac. (Illus.). 1980. lib. bdg. 19.50 (ISBN 0-87055-342-9). AVI.

Bees Can't Fly, but They Do: Things That Are Still a Mystery to Science. David C. Knight. LC 76-8491. 48p. (gr. 3 up). 1976. 7.95 (ISBN 0-02-750860-9, 75086). Macmillan.

Bees of the Genus Ceratina in America North of Mexico (Hymenoptera: Apidea) Howell V. Daly, Jr. (U. C. Publ. in Entomology: Vol. 74). 1973. pap. 11.25x (ISBN 0-520-09484-0). U of Cal Pr.

Bees, Wasps, & Hornets. Robert M. McClung. LC 73-151942. (Illus.). (gr. 3-7). 7.95 (ISBN 0-688-21075-9); PLB 7.63 (ISBN 0-688-31075-3). Morrow.

Beethoven. David Jacobs & Elliot Forbes. (Horizon Caravel Bks). (Illus.). 152p. (gr. 6 up). 1970. 9.95 (ISBN 0-8281-5026-5, J039-0); PLB 12.89 (ISBN 0-06-022797-4, Dist. by Har-Row). Am Heritage.

Beethoven. Stanley Sadie. (Great Composers Ser.). (Illus.). 1967. 7.95 o.p. (ISBN 0-571-08094-4, Pub. by Faber & Faber). Merrimack Bk Serv.

Beethoven - Opus Sixty-Nine First Movement: Pianaforte & Violoncello. W. J. Mitchell. LC 74-120289. 6.00x (ISBN 0-231-03417-2). Columbia U Pr.

Beethoven: A Critical Biography. Vincent D'Indy. LC 72-125054. (Music Ser). (Illus.). 1970. Repr. of 1913 ed. lib. bdg. 14.50 (ISBN 0-306-70019-0). Da Capo.

Beethoven: Biography of a Genius. George R. Marek. LC 72-85745. (Funk & W Bk.). (Illus.). 1969. 17.50 o.s.i. (ISBN 0-308-70104-6, TYC-T). T Y Crowell.

Beethoven: His Life & Times. Ates Orga. LC 78-53221. (Life & Time of the Composer Ser.). (Illus.). 1978. 16.95 (ISBN 0-8467-0487-0, Pub. by Two Continents); pap. 5.95 (ISBN 0-8467-0460-9). Hippocrene Bks.

Beethoven in France. Leo Schrade. LC 77-16533. (Music Reprint Ser.: 1978). 1978. lib. bdg. 35.00 (ISBN 0-306-77538-7). Da Capo.

Beethoven Medal. K. M. Peyton. LC 71-175109. (Illus.). (gr. 6-9). 1972. 8.95 (ISBN 0-690-12846-0, TYC-J). T Y Crowell.

Beethoven, Performers & Critics: The International Beethoven Congress Detroit, 1977. Ed. by Robert Winter & Bruce Carr. (Illus.). 228p. 1981. 16.95 (ISBN 0-8143-1658-1). Wayne St U Pr.

Beethoven, Sibelius & "the Profound Logic". Lionel Pike. (Studies in Symphonic Analysis). (Illus.). 1978. text ed. 44.25x (ISBN 0-485-11178-0, Athlone Pr). Humanities.

Beethoven String Quartets, 2 vols. Basil Lam. Incl. Vol. 1. (BBC Music Guides Ser.: No. 32). 64p. pap. (ISBN 0-295-95423-X); Vol. 2. (BBC Music Guides Ser.: No. 33). 64p. pap. (ISBN 0-295-95424-8). LC 75-5008. (Illus.). 1975. pap. 1.95 ea. U of Wash Pr.

Beethoven's Early Sketches in the 'fischhof Miscellany' Berlin Autograph 28, 2 vols. Douglas P. Johnson. Ed. by George Buelow. (Studies in Musicology). 887p. 1980. Set. 59.95 (ISBN 0-8357-1137-4, Pub. by UMI Res Pr); Vol. 1. (ISBN 0-8357-1138-2); Vol. 2. (ISBN 0-8357-1139-0). Univ Microfilms.

Beethoven's Nine Symphonies, & the Nine Lesser Mysteries. Corinne Heline. 4.50 (ISBN 0-87613-000-7). New Age.

Beethoven's Piano-Playing: With an Essay on the Execution of the Trill. Franz Kullak. LC 72-14059. 110p. 1973. Repr. of 1901 ed. lib. bdg. 14.95 (ISBN 0-306-70564-8). Da Capo.

Beethoven's Pianoforte Sonatas Discussed. Eric Blom. LC 68-21092. (Music Ser). 1968. Repr. of 1938 ed. 22.50 (ISBN 0-306-71059-5). Da Capo.

Beethoven's String Quartets. P. Radcliffe. LC 77-26271. (Illus.). 1978. 22.50 (ISBN 0-521-21963-9); pap. 5.95 (ISBN 0-521-29326-X). Cambridge U Pr.

Beetle Bailey: On Parade. Mort Walker. (Beetle Bailey Ser.: No. 6). 128p. (gr. 5 up). pap. 1.50 (ISBN 0-448-12258-8, Tempo). G&D.

Beetle Bailey Shape up or Ship Out. (Beetle Bailey Cartoon Ser.). 128p. 1981. pap. 1.50 (ISBN 0-448-12659-1, Tempo). G&D.

Beetle Bailey We're All in the Same Boat, No.7. Mort Walker. 128p. (gr. 8-12). 1981. pap. 1.50 (ISBN 0-448-12259-6, Tempo). G&D.

Beetle in the Anthill. Arkady Strugatsky & Boris Strugatsky. Tr. by Antonina W. Bouis. (Best of Soviet Science Fiction Ser.). 256p. 1980. 11.95 (ISBN 0-02-615120-0). Macmillan.

Beetle Leg. John Hawkes. LC 51-14554. 1967. pap. 4.95 (ISBN 0-8112-0062-0). New Directions.

Beetles of the Pacific Northwest, 5 pts. Melville H. Hatch et al. Incl. Pt. 1. Introduction & Adephaga. 348p. 1953. o.p. (ISBN 0-295-73715-8); Pt. 2. Staphyliniformia. 384p. 1957. o.p. (ISBN 0-295-73716-6); Pt. 3. Pselaphidae & Diversicornia 1. 503p. 1962. 25.00 (ISBN 0-295-73717-4); Pt. 4. Macrodactyles, Palpicornes, & Heteromera. 268p. 1965. o.p. (ISBN 0-295-73718-2); Pt. 5. Rhipiceroidea, Sternoxi, Phytophaga, Rhynchophora, & Lamellicornia. 650p. 1971. 25.00 (ISBN 0-295-73719-0). LC 53-9444. (Publications in Biology Ser.: No. 16). (Illus.). U of Wash Pr.

Beetles of the United States. 2nd ed. Ross H. Arnett. 1980. write for info. o.p. (ISBN 0-916846-08-3). World Natural Hist.

Beezus & Ramona. Beverly Cleary. (Illus.). (gr. 3-7). 1955. 7.75 (ISBN 0-688-21076-7); PLB 7.44 (ISBN 0-688-31076-1); pap. 1.50 (ISBN 0-688-25078-5). Morrow.

Befo'de War Spirituals: Words & Melodies. Ed. by Edward A. McIlhenny. LC 72-1724. Repr. of 1933 ed. 21.50 (ISBN 0-685-02341-9). AMS Pr.

Before-After All Alone. new ed. Newton T. Hess. 80p. 1980. looseleaf bdg. 7.50x (ISBN 0-9605232-0-0). Bala Pub Div.

Before & After Socrates. Francis M. Cornford. 23.95 (ISBN 0-521-04726-9); pap. 5.95x (ISBN 0-521-09113-6). Cambridge U Pr.

Before Calling the Doctor. Phyllis Speight. 1976. pap. 3.00x (ISBN 0-8464-0994-1). Beekman Pubs.

Before Civilization. Colin Renfrew. 1979. pap. 5.95 (ISBN 0-521-29643-9). Cambridge U Pr.

Before Columbus. Muriel Batherman. (gr. k-3). 1981. 8.95 (ISBN 0-395-30088-6). HM.

Before Death Comes. Maurice Rawlings. 224p. 1980. 7.95 (ISBN 0-8407-5191-5). Nelson.

Before Divorce. John M. Vayhinger. Ed. by William E. Hulme. LC 72-171512. (Pocket Counsel Bks). 56p. 1972. pap. 1.75 (ISBN 0-8006-1106-3, 1-1106). Fortress.

Before First Grade: Training Project for Culturally Disadvantaged Children. Susan W. Gray et al. LC 66-24872. (Orig.). 1966. pap. text ed. 4.95x (ISBN 0-8077-1464-X). Tchrs Coll.

Before Sleep. Philip Booth. 1980. pap. 5.95 (ISBN 0-14-042286-2). Penguin.

Before Sleep. Philip Booth. 96p. 1980. 11.95 (ISBN 0-670-15529-2). Viking Pr.

Before Speech. Ed. by Margaret Bullowa. LC 78-51671. (Illus.). 1979. 42.50 (ISBN 0-521-22031-9); pap. 9.95 (ISBN 0-521-29522-X). Cambridge U Pr.

Before the Colors Fade. Otha Wearin. 5.95 o.p. (ISBN 0-87069-007-8). Wallace-Homestead.

Before the Dawn. Joseph Altsheler. 1976. lib. bdg. 16.70x (ISBN 0-89968-000-3). Lightyear.

Before the Economy Dips: Planning Protective Action. Eugene H. Fram & Herbert J. Mossien. (Presidents Association Special Studies: No. 66). 1977. 20.00 o.p. (ISBN 0-8144-4066-5). Am Mgmt.

Before the Golden Age, Bk. 2. Isaac Asimov. 320p. 1975. pap. 1.50 o.p. (ISBN 0-449-22715-4, Q2452, Crest). Fawcett.

Before the Golden Age: Book 3. Isaac Asimov. 1978. pap. 1.95 o.p. (ISBN 0-449-23593-9, Crest). Fawcett.

Before the Industrial Revolution: European Economy & Society, 1000-1700. 2nd ed. Carlo M. Cipolla. (Illus.). 1980. pap. text ed. 6.95x (ISBN 0-393-95115-4). Norton.

Before the Law: An Introduction to the Legal Process. 2nd ed. John J. Bonsignore et al. LC 78-69606. (Illus.). 1979. pap. text ed. 12.50 (ISBN 0-395-27514-8). HM.

Before the Rebel Flag Fell. F. Roy Johnson. 1968. 4.95 (ISBN 0-930230-03-5). Johnson NC.

Before the Times. Rebecca Patten & Priscilla Patten. LC 80-36848. (Illus.). 1980. pap. 6.95 (ISBN 0-89407-038-X); casebound 9.95 (ISBN 0-89407-047-9). Strawberry Hill.

Before the Universe. Frederik Pohl & C. M. Kornbluth. 224p. (Orig.). 1980. pap. 1.95 (ISBN 0-553-11042-X). Bantam.

Before They Were Men. Charles Wertenbaker. Repr. of 1931 ed. 8.00x o.p. (ISBN 0-685-84015-8). Va Bk.

Before Watergate. Ed. by Abraham S. Eisenstadt et al. (Brooklyn College Studies on Society in Change Ser.: No. 4). 1979. 17.50x (ISBN 0-930888-01-4). Brooklyn Coll Pr.

Before You Invest: Questions & Answers on Real Estate. Earl Snyder. 1981. text ed. 12.95 (ISBN 0-8359-0453-9). Reston.

Before You Love Again. Ralph I. Hyatt. (Paperbacks Ser.). 192p. 1980. pap. 3.95 (ISBN 0-07-031555-8, GB). McGraw.

Before You Were a Baby. Paul Showers & Kay S. Showers. LC 68-13588. (Let's-Read-&-Find-Out Science Bk). (Illus.). (gr. k-3). 1968. PLB 7.89 (ISBN 0-690-12882-7, TYC-J). T Y Crowell.

Before You Were Born. Joan L. Nixon. LC 79-91741. (Illus.). 32p. (ps up). 1980. 5.95 (ISBN 0-87973-353-5); pap. 3.95 (ISBN 0-87973-343-8). Our Sunday Visitor.

Beggar. Fereidoun M. Esfandiary. 1965. 7.95 (ISBN 0-8392-1154-6). Astor-Honor.

Beggar. Nagib Mahfouz. (Arabic.). pap. 5.50 (ISBN 0-685-82811-5). Intl Bk Ctr.

Beggar's Gulch. Cameron Judd. (Orig.). 1980. pap. 1.75 (ISBN 0-8439-0733-9, Leisure Bks). Nordon Pubns.

Beggar's Opera. John Gay. Ed. by Benjamin W. Griffith, Jr. LC 61-18353. 1962. pap. text ed. 3.25 (ISBN 0-8120-0032-3). Barron.

Beggar's Opera. John Gay. Ed. by Edgar V. Roberts. LC 68-21878. (Regents Restoration Drama Ser). 1969. 11.50x (ISBN 0-8032-0362-4); pap. 3.65x (ISBN 0-8032-5361-3, BB 269, Bison). U of Nebr Pr.

Beggar's Opera, Imitated & Parodied. Ed. by Walter H. Rubsamen. (Ballad Opera Ser.). 1974. lib. bdg. 50.00 (ISBN 0-8240-0900-2). Garland Pub.

Begin Bridge with Reese. Terence Reese. LC 77-79501. (Illus.). (gr. 6 up). 1977. 6.95 o.p. (ISBN 0-8069-4932-5); PLB 6.69 o.p. (ISBN 0-8069-4933-3). Sterling.

Begin Two A. William Caxton. LC 72-5980. (English Experience Ser.: No. 508). 1973. Repr. of 1480 ed. 61.00 (ISBN 90-221-0508-3). Walter J Johnson.

Beginner's Bible. Ed. by Margherita Fanchiotti & Nathaniel Micklem. (Illus.). 1958. 9.75x o.p. (ISBN 0-19-234104-9). Oxford U Pr.

Beginner's Book of Geometry. Grace C. Young & William H. Young. LC 76-114211. Orig. Title: First Book of Geometry. (gr. 1-5). 1970. Repr. of 1905 ed. text ed. 9.50 (ISBN 0-8284-0231-0). Chelsea Pub.

Beginner's Book of off-Loom Weaving. Xenia L. Parker. LC 77-16880. (gr. 5 up). 1978. 6.95 (ISBN 0-396-07558-4). Dodd.

Beginner's Book of Sewing. Lydia P. Encinas. LC 76-53438. (gr. 7 up). 1977. 5.95 (ISBN 0-396-07424-3). Dodd.

Beginner's Book of Vegetable Gardening. Sigmund A. Lavine. LC 76-53439. (gr. 7 up). 1977. 5.95 (ISBN 0-396-07410-3). Dodd.

Beginner's CB & Two-Way Radio Repairing. Newt Smelser. LC 80-23818. (Illus.). 232p. 1981. text ed. 29.95 (ISBN 0-88229-573-X); pap. text ed. 14.95 (ISBN 0-88229-763-5). Nelson-Hall.

Beginners Coin Collecting Kit: For U. S. Coins. (gr. 4 up). 1980. 5.95 (ISBN 0-307-09394-8). Western Pubs OH.

Beginner's Cookbook. Girl Scouts of the USA. (gr. 1-6). 1972. pap. 0.95 (ISBN 0-88441-442-6, 26-114, Pub. by Dell). GS.

Beginner's Grammar of the Greek New Testament. William H. Davis. 1923. 8.95x (ISBN 0-06-061710-1, HarpR). Har-Row.

Beginner's Guide to American Bonsai. Jerald P. Stowell. LC 77-15372. 1978. 14.95 (ISBN 0-87011-326-7). Kodansha.

Beginner's Guide to Birdkeeping. Rosemary Low. (Illus.). 217p. 1975. 14.95 (ISBN 0-7207-0673-4). Transatlantic.

Beginner's Guide to Botany. C. L. Duddington. 1970. 6.95 (ISBN 0-7207-0365-4, Pub. by Michael Joseph). Merrimack Bk Serv.

Beginner's Guide to Bridge. Norman Squire. (Beginner's Guide Ser.). 6.95 (ISBN 0-7207-0468-5, Pub. by Michael Joseph). Merrimack Bk Serv.

Beginner's Guide to Coin Collecting. Howard Linecar. 9.95 (ISBN 0-7207-0015-9). Transatlantic.

Beginner's Guide to Computer Logic. Gerald Stapleton. LC 70-155978. (Illus.). 1971. pap. 5.95 (ISBN 0-8306-0548-7, 548). TAB Bks.

Beginner's Guide to Computers & Microprocessors--with Projects. C. K. Adams. (Illus.). (gr. 10 up). 1978. 10.95 (ISBN 0-8306-9890-6); pap. 7.95 (ISBN 0-8306-1015-4, 1015). TAB Bks.

Beginner's Guide to Gemmology. Read. 9.95 (ISBN 0-686-27953-0). Butterworths.

Beginners Guide to Good Gardening. David Carr. (Illus.). 243p. 1980. 14.95 (ISBN 0-7137-0934-0, Pub. by Blandford Pr England). Sterling.

Beginner's Guide to Ham Radio. Len Buckwalter. LC 77-82931. 1978. pap. 4.95 (ISBN 0-385-11514-8, Dolp). Doubleday.

Beginner's Guide to Home Coarse Tacklemaking. Leonard F. Burrell. (Illus.). 134p. 1973. 12.95 (ISBN 0-7207-0548-7). Transatlantic.

Beginners Guide to Home Computers. Marvin Grosswirth. LC 77-16918. 1978. pap. 4.50 (ISBN 0-385-13572-6, Dolp). Doubleday.

Beginner's Guide to Home Freezing. Mary Norwak. (Beginners Guide Ser.). 1973. 12.95 (ISBN 0-7207-0660-2, Pub. by Michael Joseph). Merrimack Bk Serv.

Beginner's Guide to Hydroponics (Soilless Gardening) James S. Douglas. 1972. 8.50 (ISBN 0-7207-0572-X, Pub. by Michael Joseph). Merrimack Bk Serv.

Beginner's Guide to Lightweight Camping. P. F. Williams. (Beginners Guide Ser.). 1975. 8.95 o.p. (ISBN 0-7207-0818-4, Pub. by Michael Joseph). Merrimack Bk Serv.

Beginner's Guide to Making Electronic Gadgets. R. H. Warring. 1977. 9.95 o.p. (ISBN 0-8306-7958-8); pap. 5.95 (ISBN 0-8306-6958-2, 958). TAB Bks.

Beginner's Guide to Photographing People. Ralph Hattersley. LC 77-12860. 1978. pap. 4.95 (ISBN 0-385-12689-1, Dolp). Doubleday.

Beginner's Guide to Photography. John Wasley. 1974. 20.00 (ISBN 0-7207-0696-3). Transatlantic.

Beginner's Guide to Riding. Veronica Heath. 1971. 8.50 (ISBN 0-7207-0440-5). Transatlantic.

Beginner's Guide to Shorecasting. Foy Forsberg. (Illus.). 183p. 1975. 10.95 (ISBN 0-7207-0753-6). Transatlantic.

Beginner's Guide to Sightsinging & Musical Rudiments. M. Friedman. 1981. pap. 12.95 (ISBN 0-13-074088-8). P-H.

Beginner's Guide to Squash. Richard Hawkey. 141p. 1973. 14.50 (ISBN 0-7207-0682-3). Transatlantic.

Beginner's Guide to Super Eight Film Making. Arnold Eagle. (Illus.). 1980. cancelled (ISBN 0-679-50925-9); pap. cancelled (ISBN 0-679-50926-7). McKay.

Beginner's Guide to the Fungi. C. L. Duddington. 1972. 6.95 (ISBN 0-7207-0448-0, Pub. by Michael Joseph). Merrimack Bk Serv.

Beginner's Guide to the Skies. Clarence H. Cleminshaw. LC 76-28317. 1977. 9.95 (ISBN 0-690-01214-4, TYC-T). T Y Crowell.

Beginner's Guide to Tropical Fish: Fish Tanks, Aquarium Fish, Pond Fish, Ponds & Marines. Reginald Dutta. 1977. 14.00 (ISBN 0-7207-0832-X). Transatlantic.

Beginner's Guide to TV Repair. 2nd ed. George Zwick. (Illus.). 1979. 10.95 (ISBN 0-8306-9758-6); pap. 5.95 (ISBN 0-8306-1013-8, 1013). TAB Bks.

Beginner's Guide to Weather Forecasting. Lawrence Beitman. (Beginners Guide Ser.). 1975. 10.95 o.p. (ISBN 0-7207-0819-2, Pub. by Michael Joseph). Merrimack Bk Serv.

Beginner's Guide to Woodturning. Gordon Stokes. (Illus.). 124p. 1975. 18.00 (ISBN 0-7207-0637-8). Transatlantic.

Beginner's Handbook of Biological Transmission Electron Microscopy. Brenda Weakley. (Illus.). 272p. (Orig.). 1981. pap. 16.50 (ISBN 0-443-02091-4). Churchill.

Beginner's Handbook of Electronics. George H. Olsen. 1980. text ed. 19.95 (ISBN 0-13-074211-2, Spec); pap. text ed. 7.95 (ISBN 0-13-074203-1). P-H.

Beginner's Handbook of IC Projects. David L. Heiserman. (Illus.). 272p. 1981. 18.95 (ISBN 0-13-074229-5). P-H.

Beginner's Manual for the Pascal System. Ken Bowles. (Orig.). 1980. pap. 11.95 (ISBN 0-07-006745-7, BYTE Bks). Macgraw.

Beginner's New Testament Greek Grammar. Sakae Kubo. LC 79-64247. 1979. pap. text ed. 9.50 (ISBN 0-8191-0761-1). U Pr of Amer.

Beginner's Photography Simplified. Stuart Nordheimer. 1975. 10.95 o.p. (ISBN 0-13-074070-5, Spec). P-H.

Beginner's Running Guide. Hal Higdon. LC 78-369. (Illus.). 340p. 1978. 10.00 (ISBN 0-89037-130-X). Anderson World.

Beginners's Guide to Quilting. Caren Caraway. (gr. 7 up). 1980. 8.95 (ISBN 0-679-20532-2). McKay.

Beginning a Community Museum. Howard Levy & Lynn Ross-Molloy. LC 75-27098. 84p. 1975. pap. 3.00 (ISBN 0-89062-009-1, Pub. by NYSCA.). Pub Ctr Cult Res.

Beginning Algebra. 3rd ed. Margaret L. Lial & Charles D. Miller. 1980. text ed. 16.95x (ISBN 0-673-15330-4). Scott F.

Beginning Algebra. Charles P. McKeague. 1980. pap. 13.95 (ISBN 0-12-484765-X). Acad Pr.

Beginning Algebra. 2nd ed. John Minnick & Raymond Strauss. (Illus.). 288p. 1976. text ed. 15.95 (ISBN 0-13-073791-7). P-H.

Beginning Algebra. 2nd ed. Mustafa Munem & William Tschirhart. LC 76-27110. (Illus.). 1977. 15.95x (ISBN 0-87901-063-0); study guide 6.95x (ISBN 0-685-34683-8). Worth.
Beginning Algebra: An Individualized Approach. Irving Drooyan & William Wooton. LC 78-625. 1978. 18.50 (ISBN 0-471-03877-6). Wiley.
Beginning Algebra for College Students. Karl J. Smith & Patrick J. Boyle. LC 76-46476. (Contemporary Undergraduate Mathematics Seri Es). (Illus.). 1976. text ed. 15.95 (ISBN 0-8185-0184-7); study guide 5.95 (ISBN 0-8185-0219-3). Brooks-Cole.
Beginning Algebra for College Students. 2nd ed. Karl J. Smith & Patrick J. Boyle. LC 80-12572. 1980. text ed. 15.95 (ISBN 0-8185-0365-3). Brooks-Cole.
Beginning Algebra for Mature Students. James Meadowcroft, II. 1971. pap. text ed. 13.95 (ISBN 0-13-073726-7). P-H.
Beginning & the End. Nagib Mahfouz. (Arabic.). pap. 5.50x (ISBN 0-685-82812-3). Intl Bk Ctr.
Beginning Basic. D. Keith Carver. LC 79-20457. 1980. pap. text ed. 12.95 (ISBN 0-8185-0368-8). Brooks-Cole.
Beginning BASIC. Paul M. Chirlian. 1978. pap. 10.95 (ISBN 0-918398-06-1). Dilithium Pr.
Beginning BASIC. P. E. Gosling. 104p. 1977. pap. 10.95 (ISBN 0-333-22304-7). Robotics Pr.
Beginning: Berkeley, 1964. Max Heirich. LC 77-125074. (Illus.). 1971. 17.50x (ISBN 0-231-03467-9). Columbia U Pr.
Beginning Chinese for Intermediate Schools, 2 vols. Juliet Choi & John Defrancis. viii, 145p. (Orig.). 1980. Set. pap. text ed. 15.45 (ISBN 0-89644-639-5). Chinese Materials.
Beginning College Spanish: From Sounds to Structures. John B. Dalbor. 672p. 1972. text ed. 15.95 (ISBN 0-394-31175-2, RanC); wkbk. 5.50 (ISBN 0-394-31182-5); tapes 200.00x (ISBN 0-686-66665-8). Random.
Beginning Composition Through Pictures. J. B. Heaton. (Illus.). 1975. pap. text ed. 3.25x (ISBN 0-582-55519-1). Longman.
Beginning Course in Computer Science Using UBASIC. Marvin A. Griffin et al. 1978. pap. text ed. 11.95 (ISBN 0-8403-1965-7, 40196502). Kendall-Hunt.
Beginning Crafts for Beginning Readers. Alice Gilbreath. LC 71-184461. (Picture Bk). (Illus.). 32p. (gr. 1-4). 1972. 2.95 o.p. (ISBN 0-695-80317-4); PLB 5.97 o.p. (ISBN 0-695-40317-6). Follett.
Beginning: Creation & Me. (Children of the Kindgom Activities Ser.). (gr. k-4). 1973. 7.95 (ISBN 0-686-13682-9). Pflaum Pr.
Beginning Dressage Book: A Guide to the Basics for Horse & Rider. Joan Fry & Kathryn Denby-Wrightson. LC 80-16950. (Illus.). 224p. 1981. 10.95 (ISBN 0-668-04969-3, 4969). Arco.
Beginning Field Hockey. Helen Spencer. 1970. pap. 3.95x o.p. (ISBN 0-534-00640-X). Wadsworth Pub.
Beginning French. 5th ed. William Hendrix. LC 77-93107. (Illus.). 1978. pap. text ed. 15.75 (ISBN 0-395-25739-5); wkbk. 6.60 (ISBN 0-395-25740-9); tapes 207.28 (ISBN 0-395-25741-7). HM.
Beginning French with Preschoolers: A Montessori Handbook. Rachel Adler-Golden & Debbie Gordon. LC 80-83136. (Illus.). 85p. 1980. pap. text ed. 6.00 (ISBN 0-915676-04-4). Montessori Wkshps.
Beginning German: A Practical Approach. Terrence L. Hansen et al. LC 73-180137. (Ger). 1972. text ed. 17.95 (ISBN 0-471-00671-8); tchr's manual avail. (ISBN 0-471-00766-8); wkbk. 6.95 (ISBN 0-471-00672-6). Wiley.
Beginning Gliding: The Fundamentals of Soaring Flight. Derek Piggott. (Illus.). 1977. 20.00x (ISBN 0-06-495569-9). B&N.
Beginning Gymnastics. Bill Sands. (Illus.). 1981. 14.95 (ISBN 0-8092-5948-6); pap. 6.95 (ISBN 0-8092-5947-8). Contemp Bks.
Beginning Gymnastics for College Women. H. Davis. (Illus.). pap. 4.50 wrappers (ISBN 0-8363-0011-4). Jenkins.
Beginning Hydroponics. Richard Nicholls. 224p. 1979. pap. 1.95 o.p. (ISBN 0-441-05340-8). Charter Bks.
Beginning in Bookselling: Grafton Books on Library Science. I. Babbidge. 1977. PLB 9.00x (ISBN 0-233-96019-8). Westview.
Beginning-Intermediate Grammar of Hellenistic Greek, 3 vols. 2nd, rev. ed. Robert W. Funk. Incl. Vol. 1. Morphology; Vol. 2. Syntax; Vol. 3. Appendices. LC 72-88769. (Society of Biblical Literature. Sources for Biblical Studies). (Orig.). 1977. Set. pap. text ed. 18.00 (ISBN 0-89130-148-8). Scholars Pr Ca.
Beginning Italian. 3rd ed. Vincenzo Cioffari. 1979. text ed. 15.95x (ISBN 0-669-00580-0); wkbk. & lab manual 5.95x (ISBN 0-669-00581-9); tapes-reels 60.00 (ISBN 0-669-00582-7); cassettes 60.00 (ISBN 0-669-00583-5). Heath.
Beginning Japanese, Pt. 1. Eleanor H. Jorden & Hamako I. Chaplin. (Illus.). 1962. 27.50x o.p. (ISBN 0-300-00609-8); pap. text ed. 7.95x (ISBN 0-300-00135-5). Yale U Pr.
Beginning Japanese, Pt. 2. Eleanor H. Jorden & Hamako I. Chaplin. (Linguistic Ser). (Illus.). 1963. text ed. 27.50x (ISBN 0-300-00610-1); pap. text ed. 7.95x (ISBN 0-300-00136-3). Yale U Pr.
Beginning Karate. Tonny Tulleners. Ed. by John Corcoran. LC 74-78904. (Ser. 206s). (Illus.). 1974. pap. text ed. 6.95 (ISBN 0-89750-027-X). Ohara Pubns.
Beginning Korean. Samuel E. Martin & Young-Sook C. Lee. LC 69-15452. (Linguistic Ser.). 1969. pap. text ed. 17.50x (ISBN 0-300-00285-8). Yale U Pr.
Beginning Metric Measurement Learning Module. Daniel Quinn & Emilie C. Cook. 1974. pap. text ed. 124.00 (ISBN 0-89290-132-2, CM-53). Soc for Visual.
Beginning Mobiles. Peggy Parish. LC 79-9950. (Ready-to-Read Handbook). (Illus.). (gr. 1-4). 1979. 7.95 (ISBN 0-02-770030-5). Macmillan.
Beginning Model Theory: The Completeness Theorem & Some Consequences. Jane Bridge. (Oxford Logic Guides Ser.). 1977. 19.50x (ISBN 0-19-853157-5). Oxford U Pr.
Beginning News Writing. William E. Francois. LC 74-16752. (Journalism & Advertising Ser.). 1975. pap. text ed. 9.50 (ISBN 0-88244-065-9). Grid Pub.
Beginning of Christian Philosophy. E. F. Osborn. LC 79-8911. 256p. Date not set. price not set; pap. price not set (ISBN 0-521-29855-5). Cambridge U Pr.
Beginning of Ideology. D. R. Kelly. 358p. Date not set. price not set (ISBN 0-521-23504-9). Cambridge U Pr.
Beginning of Life. Eva K. Evans. LC 69-10462. (Illus.). (gr. k-4). 1969. 3.95g o.s.i. (ISBN 0-02-733710-3, CCPr). Macmillan.
Beginning of the Earth. Franklyn M. Branley. LC 79-184979. (Let's-Read-&-Find-Out Science Book). (Illus.). (gr. k-3). 1972. 6.95 o.p. (ISBN 0-690-12987-4, TYC-J); PLB 7.89 (ISBN 0-690-12988-2). T Y Crowell.
Beginning of the Future: A Historical Approach to Graduation in the Arts & Sciences. Carnegie Commission on Higher Education. Ed. by Richard J. Storr. 128p. 1973. 8.95 o.p. (ISBN 0-07-010056-X, P&RB). McGraw.
Beginning of the Great Game in Asia 1828-1834. Edward Ingram. (Illus.). 1979. 39.50x (ISBN 0-19-822470-2). Oxford U Pr.
Beginning of the Long Dash: A History of Timekeeping in Canada. Malcolm M. Thomson. 1978. 17.50x (ISBN 0-8020-5383-1). U of Toronto Pr.
Beginning of the West: Annals of the Kansas Gateway to the American West 1540-1854. Louise Barry. LC 78-172225. (Illus.). 1972. 14.75 (ISBN 0-87726-001-X). Kansas St Hist.
Beginning Phonics for Parents. new ed. Emma G. Felder. LC 77-135316. (Illus.). 1974. pap. 1.55 (ISBN 0-910812-05-5). Johnny Reads.
Beginning Piano for Adults. Allan Miller. 1970. 5.95 o.s.i. (ISBN 0-02-584810-0). Macmillan.
Beginning Place. Ursula LeGuin. 192p. 1981. pap. 2.25 (ISBN 0-553-14259-3). Bantam.
Beginning Polish, 2 vols. rev ed. Alexander M. Schenker. LC 72-91305. 1973. Vol. 1. text ed. o.p. (ISBN 0-685-29210-X); Vol. 2. text ed. 22.50 (ISBN 0-300-01670-0); Vol. 1. pap. text ed. 8.00 (ISBN 0-300-01653-0); Vol. 2. pap. text ed. 10.00 (ISBN 0-300-01671-9). Yale U Pr.
Beginning Psychology. rev. ed. Perry London. 1978. text ed. 18.95x (ISBN 0-256-02057-4). Dorsey.
Beginning Racquetball Drills. Jean Sauser & Arthur Shay. (Illus., Orig.). 1981. pap. 3.95 (ISBN 0-8092-5928-1). Contemp Bks.
Beginning Reading Bookshelf. (Classroom Libraries). (gr. k-3). 127.11 o.p. (ISBN 0-531-00730-8). Watts.
Beginning Science Bookshelf. (Classroom Libraries). (gr. k-3). 107.94 o.p. (ISBN 0-531-00732-4). Watts.
Beginning Social Studies Library. (Classroom Libraries). (gr. k-3). 111.99 o.p. (ISBN 0-531-00728-6). Watts.
Beginning Spanish: A Concept Approach. 4th ed. Zenia S. Da Silva. (Illus.). 1978. text ed. 19.50 scp (ISBN 0-06-047488-2, HarpC); scp tape manual 7.50 (ISBN 0-06-041507-X); scp tapes 275.00 (ISBN 0-686-68024-3). Har-Row.
Beginning Spanish: A Cultural Approach. 4th ed. Richard Armitage et al. (Illus.). 1979. text ed. 15.00 (ISBN 0-395-27507-5); wkbk. 6.25 (ISBN 0-395-27508-3). HM.
Beginning Spanish by Easy Steps. Emily B. Leal & Susan Hamilton. (Orig.). (gr. 7-10). 1975. wkbk. 7.58 (ISBN 0-87720-507-8). AMSCO Sch.
Beginning Spanish Course. 3rd ed. Donald K. Barton et al. 1976. text ed. 16.95x (ISBN 0-669-96776-9); wkbk. 5.95x (ISBN 0-669-96784-X); tape set 8 reels 40.00 (ISBN 0-669-96792-0); 8 cassettes 40.00 (ISBN 0-669-00082-5). Heath.
Beginning Stained Glass Patterns, Bk. 1. Joel L. Wallach. (Illus.). 48p. (Orig.). 1980. pap. 4.95x (ISBN 0-934280-04-5). Glass Works.
Beginning Stained Glass Patterns, Bk. 2. Joel L. Wallach. (Illus.). 48p. (Orig.). 1980. pap. 4.95x (ISBN 0-934280-05-3). Glass Works.
Beginning Tagalog: A Course for Speakers of English. Ed. by J. Donald Bowen. (Orig.). 1965. pap. 17.75x (ISBN 0-520-00156-7). U of Cal Pr.
Beginning Teacher: A Practical Guide to Problem Solving. Robert J. Krejewski & R. Baird Shuman. 128p. 1979. pap. 5.75 (ISBN 0-686-63677-5, 1489-8-06). NEA.
Beginning Teaching in Professional Partnership. Norman Evans. LC 78-13675. 1978. pap. text ed. 6.50x (ISBN 0-8419-6215-4). Holmes & Meier.
Beginning the Rest of Your Life: A Guide to an Active Retirement. Harry Disston. LC 78-75301. Date not set. cancelled (ISBN 0-498-02356-7). A S Barnes.
Beginning the Rest of Your Life: A Guide to an Active Retirement. Harry Disston. 160p. (Orig.). 1981. pap. 4.95 (ISBN 0-87000-518-9). Arlington Hse.
Beginning the Third Century: The Liberal-Led March to Communism. R. Dean Pine. 1977. 4.95 o.p. (ISBN 0-533-02844-2). Vantage.
Beginning to Feel the Magic. Linda Weltner. 168p. (gr. 6 up). 1981. 8.95 (ISBN 0-316-93052-0). Little.
Beginning to See. rev., enl. ed. Sujata. 1980. pap. 4.50 (ISBN 0-913300-06-3). Unity Pr.
Beginning to See the Light: Pieces of a Decade. Ellen Willis. LC 80-22890. 320p. 1981. 12.95 (ISBN 0-394-51137-9). Knopf.
Beginning to Write in French: A Workbook in French Composition. Christopher Kendris. LC 65-25685. (gr. 7-12). 1971. pap. text ed. 3.50 (ISBN 0-8120-0234-2). Barron.
Beginning to Write in French: A Workbook in French Composition. rev. ed. Christopher Kendris. 1981. pap. text ed. 3.50 (ISBN 0-8120-2261-0). Barron.
Beginning to Write in Spanish: A Workbook in Spanish Composition. Christopher Kendris. LC 66-25379. (gr. 7-12). 1971. pap. text ed. 3.50 (ISBN 0-8120-0235-0). Barron.
Beginning to Write in Spanish: A Workbook in Spanish Composition. rev ed. Christopher Kendris. 1981. pap. text ed. 3.50 (ISBN 0-686-59969-1). Barron.
Beginning with Mrs. McBee. Cecil Maiden & Hilary Knight. LC 60-15411. (Illus.). (gr. k-3). 1959. 5.95 (ISBN 0-8149-0356-8). Vanguard.
Beginning with Poems. Ed. by Reuben A. Brower et al. (Orig.). 1966. 10.95x (ISBN 0-393-09685-8); pap. 8.95x (ISBN 0-393-09509-6). Norton.
Beginning with Tropicals. Diane Schofield. pap. 2.00 (ISBN 0-87666-165-7, M523). TFH Pubns.
Beginning Your Marriage, 2 vols. John L. Thomas. 1980. pap. 1.95 standard ed., LC 80-65486 (ISBN 0-915388-06-5); pap. 1.95 interfaith ed., LC 80-65487 (ISBN 0-915388-07-3). Buckley Pubns.
Beginning Your Ministry. C. W. Brister et al. LC 80-25763. 160p. (Orig.). 1981. pap. 6.95 (ISBN 0-687-02780-2). Abingdon.
Beginnings. Prabhu Guptara. 8.00 (ISBN 0-89253-689-6); flexible cloth 4.80 (ISBN 0-89253-690-X). Ind-US Inc.
Beginnings, Egypt & Assyria. Warren R. Dawson. (Illus.). 1964. pap. 8.25 o.s.i. (ISBN 0-02-843800-0). Hafner.
Beginnings in Poetry. 2nd ed. William J. Martz. 320p. 1973. pap. 7.95x (ISBN 0-673-07713-6). Scott F.
Beginnings in Relational Communication. Kenneth L. Villard & Leland Whipple. LC 75-33845. 275p. 1976. pap. text ed. 14.95x (ISBN 0-471-90812-6); instructor's manual avail. (ISBN 0-471-01479-6). Wiley.
Beginnings in the Old Testament. Howard F. Vos. pap. 3.50 (ISBN 0-8024-0610-6). Moody.
Beginnings of Architecture: The Eternal Present, a Contribution on Constancy & Change, Vol. 2. Sigfried Giedon. LC 80-8733. (A. W. Mellon Lectures in the Fine Arts, 1957, Bolligen Ser.: XXXV: 6,11). (Illus.). 604p. 1981. 42.50x (ISBN 0-691-09945-6); pap. 15.00 (ISBN 0-691-09945-6). Princeton U Pr.
Beginnings of Christology, together with The Lord's Supper. Willi Marxsen. Tr. by Paul J. Achtemeier & Lorenz Nieting. LC 79-7384. 128p. 1979. pap. 4.95 (ISBN 0-8006-1372-4, 1-1372). Fortress.
Beginnings of Communist Rule in Poland, December 1943-June 1945. A. Polonsky & Boleslaw Drukier. 400p. 1980. 37.50x (ISBN 0-7100-0540-7). Routledge & Kegan.
Beginnings of Imperial Rome: Rome in the Mid-Republic. Chester G. Starr. 86p. 1980. 10.00x (ISBN 0-472-09317-7). U of Mich Pr.
Beginnings of Solid State Physics. Ed. by Nevill Mott. (Royal Society Ser.). 177p. 1980. lib. bdg. 30.00x (ISBN 0-85403-143-X, Pub. by Royal Soc London). Scholium Intl.
Beginnings of the Teaching of Modern Subjects in England. Foster Watson. 1978. Repr. of 1909 ed. 19.00x o.p. (ISBN 0-85409-704-X). Charles River Bks.
Beginnings of Visual Photochemistry: Translations & Biographies in Honor of F. Boll & F. W. Kuhne. Ed. by T. Shipley. 1978. text ed. 30.00 (ISBN 0-08-021534-3). Pergamon.
Beginnings: The Psychology of Early Childhood. Barbara S. McClinton & Blanche G. Meier. LC 77-17619. (Illus.). 1978. text ed. 16.95 (ISBN 0-8016-3217-X). Mosby.
Beginnings to Fifteen Fifty-Eight. Intro. by Allan MacLaine. 96p. 1981. pap. 4.95 (ISBN 0-312-07190-6). St Martin.
Begleitumstaende: Frankfurter Vorlesungen. Uwe Johnson. (Edition Suhrkamp. Neue Folge: No. 19). 300p. (Orig., Ger.). 1980. pap. 7.80 (ISBN 3-518-11019-5, Pub. by Insel Verlag Germany). Suhrkamp.
Begonias: The Complete Reference Guide. Mildred L. Thompson & Edward J. Thompson. 352p. 1981. 35.00 (ISBN 0-8129-0932-1). Times Bks.
Begraebnis Eines Schirmflicker. Meinrad Inglin. 260p. (Ger.). 1980. text ed. 16.25 (ISBN 3-288-03326-7, Pub. by Insel Verlag Germany). Suhrkamp.
Begriff des Empirismus: Erkenntnistheoretische Studien am Beispiel John Lockes. Lorenz Krueger. (Quellen und Studien zur Philosophie, Vol. 6). xii, 283p. 1973. 41.75x (ISBN 3-11-004133-2). De Gruyter.
Behavior: A Guide for Managers. C. Charron et al. 1977. 14.95 (ISBN 0-87909-078-2). Reston.
Behavior Analysis & Behavior Modification: An Introduction. Richard Malott et al. LC 78-380. (Illus.). 442p. (Orig.). 1978. pap. 11.00 (ISBN 0-914474-20-0); tests avail. F Fournies.
Behavior Analysis: Areas of Research & Application. Eugene Ramp & George Semb. LC 74-340095. (Illus.). 432p. 1975. ref. ed. 19.95 (ISBN 0-13-074195-7). P-H.
Behavior Analysis in Business & Industry: A Total Performance System. Dale M. Brethower. (Illus.). 130p. (Orig.). 1972. pap. 10.00 (ISBN 0-914474-06-5); instr's. manual avail. F Fournies.
Behavior Analysis of Child Development. Sidney W. Bijou & Donald M. Baer. (Child Psychology Ser.). 1978. pap. 9.50 ref. ed. (ISBN 0-13-066712-9). P-H.
Behavior & Conscious Experience: A Conceptual Analysis. Kendon R. Smith. LC 69-15918. 139p. 1969. 9.00x (ISBN 0-8214-0052-5). Ohio U Pr.
Behavior & Ecology of Nocturnal Prosimians: Field Studies in Gabon & Madagascar. P. Charles-Dominique & R. D. Martin. (Advances in Ethology Ser.: Vol. 9). (Illus.). 91p. (Orig.). 1972. pap. text ed. 23.50. Parey Sci Pubs.
Behavior & Ecology of Wolves. new ed. Erich Klinghammer. LC 77-89306. (Illus.). 1980. lib. bdg. 37.50 (ISBN 0-8240-7019-4, Garland STPM Pr). Garland Pub.
Behavior & Existence: An Introduction to Empirical Humanistic Psychology. Howard Pollio. 512p. 1981. text ed. 18.95 (ISBN 0-8185-0425-0). Brooks-Cole.
Behavior & Health Care: A Humanistic Helping Process. Jane E. Chapman & Harry H. Chapman. LC 75-15579. 194p. 1975. pap. 8.50 o.p. (ISBN 0-8016-0947-X). Mosby.
Behavior & Illness. Ruth Wu. (Scientific Foundations of Nursing Practice Ser.). (Illus.). 224p. 1973. pap. 11.95 ref. ed. (ISBN 0-13-074138-8). P-H.
Behavior & Learning. Howard Rachlin. LC 76-2068. (Psychology Ser.). (Illus.). 1976. text ed. 21.95x (ISBN 0-7167-0568-0). W H Freeman.
Behavior & Life: An Introduction to Psychology. Frank J. Bruno. 1980. text ed. 18.95 (ISBN 0-471-02191-1); study guide 5.50 (ISBN 0-471-06340-1); tests avail. (ISBN 0-471-06342-8). Wiley.
Behavior & Morphology in the Glandulocaudine Fishes (Ostariophysi, Characidae) Keith Nelson. (U. C. Publ. in Zoology: Vol. 75.2). 1964. pap. 6.50x (ISBN 0-520-09331-3). U of Cal Pr.
Behavior & Taxonomy of the Epicauta Maculata Group (Coleoptera: Meloidae) J. D. Pinto. (U. C. Publications in Entomology Ser.: Vol. 89). 1980. pap. 12.00 (ISBN 0-520-09616-9). U of Cal Pr.
Behavior As an Ecological Factor. Ed. by David E. Davis. LC 74-3006. (Benchmark Papers in Ecology Ser: Vol. 2). 408p. 1974. text ed. 37.50 (ISBN 0-12-786322-2). Acad Pr.

Behavior Change. John Lutzker & Jerry Martin. LC 80-20798. 400p. 1980. text ed. 18.95 (ISBN 0-8185-0420-X). Brooks-Cole.

Behavior Contracting: Arranging Contingencies of Reinforcement. Daniel O'Banion & Donald L. Whaley. LC 80-20231. 1980. text ed. 18.95 (ISBN 0-8261-3150-6); pap. 11.95 (ISBN 0-8261-3151-4). Springer Pub.

Behavior Control & Modification of Physiological Activity. D. Mostofsky. 1976. text ed. 25.95 (ISBN 0-13-073908-1). P-H.

Behavior, Development, & Training of the Dog: A Primer of Canine Psychology. Frederic J. Sautter & John A. Glover. LC 77-7582. 1978. lib. bdg. 8.95 o.p. (ISBN 0-668-04336-9); pap. 4.95 o.p. (ISBN 0-668-04491-8). Arco.

Behavior, Development & Training of the Horse: A Primer of Equine Psychology. Frederic J. Sautter & John A. Glover. LC 80-23654. 176p. 1980. lib. bdg. 9.95 (ISBN 0-668-04809-3, 4809). Arco.

Behavior Disorders in Children. 4th ed. Harry Bakwin & Ruth M. Bakwin. LC 75-173330. (Illus.). 690p. 1972. 29.00 (ISBN 0-7216-1502-3). Saunders.

Behavior Disorders of Childhood & Adolescence. Richard L. Jenkins. (Illus.). 148p. 1973. text ed. 9.75 (ISBN 0-398-02786-2). C C Thomas.

Behavior Genetics & Evolution. Lee Ehrman & Peter Parsons. (Illus.). 496p. 1981. text ed. 22.95 (ISBN 0-07-019276-6, C). McGraw.

Behavior in Infancy & Early Childhood. Yvonne Brackbill & G. G. Thompson. LC 67-15056. 1967. text ed. 14.95 (ISBN 0-02-904530-4). Free Pr.

Behavior in Organizations. rev. ed. James B. Lau. 1979. pap. text ed. 13.50x (ISBN 0-256-02122-8). Irwin.

Behavior in Organizations. rev. ed. H. Joseph Reitz. 1980. 19.95x (ISBN 0-256-01792-1). Irwin.

Behavior in Organizations: A Multi-Dimensional View. 2nd ed. Robert E. Coffey et al. LC 74-12372. (Illus.). 608p. 1975. 21.95 (ISBN 0-13-073148-X). P-H.

Behavior in Organizations: A Systems Approach to Managing. 2nd ed. Edgar F. Huse & James L. Bowditch. LC 76-9329. (Illus.). 1977. text ed. 18.95 (ISBN 0-201-02965-0). A-W.

Behavior in Public Places: Notes on Social Organization of Gatherings. Erving Goffman. LC 80-19005. viii, 248p. 1980. Repr. of 1963 ed. lib. bdg. 22.25x (ISBN 0-313-22390-4, GOBP). Greenwood.

Behavior in Public Places: Notes on the Social Organization of Gatherings. Erving Goffman. LC 62-11850. 1963. 15.95 (ISBN 0-02-911930-8); pap. 4.50 (ISBN 0-02-911940-5). Free Pr.

Behavior in Small Groups. Alfred Benjamin. LC 77-73213. 1977. pap. text ed. 6.25 (ISBN 0-395-25447-7). HM.

Behavior in the Insect World. Lorus J. Milne & Margery Milne. (Illus.). 192p. 1980. cancelled o.p. (ISBN 0-684-16627-5, ScribT). Scribner.

Behavior Management in Dentistry for Children. Gerald Z. Wright. LC 74-31840. (Illus.). 266p. 1975. text ed. 25.00 o.p. (ISBN 0-7216-9608-2). Saunders.

Behavior Management: The New Science of Managing People at Work. Lawrence M. Miller. LC 77-28602. 1978. 19.95 (ISBN 0-471-02947-5, Pub. by Wiley-Interscience). Wiley.

Behavior Modification. 2nd ed. W. Edward Craighead et al. LC 80-83115. 576p. 1981. text ed. 18.50 (ISBN 0-395-29721-4). HM.

Behavior Modification: A Practical Approach for Educators. 2nd ed. James E. Walker. LC 79-21107. 1980. pap. text ed. 12.95 (ISBN 0-8016-5338-X). Mosby.

Behavior Modification & "Punishment" of the Innocent: Towards a Justification of the Institution of Legal Punishment. George Schedler. 1977. pap. text ed. 17.25x (ISBN 90-6032-084-0). Humanities.

Behavior Modification & the Nursing Process. 2nd ed. Rosemarian Berni & Wilbert E. Fordyce. LC 76-57775. (Illus.). 1977. pap. text ed. 9.00 (ISBN 0-8016-0656-X). Mosby.

Behavior Modification Comes to Camelot. Lucien P. Leduc. (Scholarly Monograph Ser.). 140p. 1980. pap. 9.00 (ISBN 0-686-64783-1). Carrollton Pr.

Behavior Modification in Educational Settings. Ed. by Roger D. Klein et al. (Illus.). 568p. 1973. 21.75 (ISBN 0-398-02538-X). C C Thomas.

Behavior Modification in Mental Retardation: The Education & Rehabilitation of the Mentally Retarded Adolescent & Adult. William I. Gardner. LC 79-149839. 1971. 21.95x (ISBN 0-202-25000-8). Aldine Pub.

Behavior Modification in Rehabilitation Medicine. Laurence P. Ince. (Illus.). 316p. 1976. 29.50 (ISBN 0-398-03532-6). C C Thomas.

Behavior Modification in Rehabilitation Settings: Applied Principles. Ed. by John G. Cull & Richard E. Hardy. (American Lectures in Social & Rehabilitation Psychology Ser.). (Illus.). 272p. 1974. text ed. 19.75 (ISBN 0-398-03131-2). C C Thomas.

Behavior Modification in Residential Treatment for Children: Model of a Program. Frank Pizzat. LC 72-11554. 98p. 1973. text ed. 12.95 (ISBN 0-87705-097-X). Human Sci Pr.

Behavior Modification in the Human Services: Introduction to Concepts & Applications. Martin Sundel & Sandra S. Sundel. LC 74-23342. 283p. 1975. pap. text ed. 11.50x o.p. (ISBN 0-471-83567-6). Wiley.

Behavior Modification in the Natural Environment. Roland Tharp & Ralph Wetzel. LC 75-91418. 1969. 17.95 (ISBN 0-12-686050-5). Acad Pr.

Behavior Modification Procedure: A Sourcebook. Ed. by Edwin J. Thomas. LC 73-89513. 368p. 1974. text ed. 21.95x (ISBN 0-202-36018-0); pap. text ed. 10.95x (ISBN 0-202-36019-9). Aldine Pub.

Behavior Modification: What Is It & How to Do It. Joseph Pear & Gary Martin. LC 77-10849. (Illus.). 1978. pap. text ed. 14.95 (ISBN 0-13-066787-0). P-H.

Behavior Modification with Children: A Clinical Training Manual. Alexander J. Tymchuk. (Illus.). 149p. 1974. pap. text ed. 8.00 o.p. (ISBN 0-398-03125-8). C C Thomas.

Behavior of Captive Wild Animals. Ed. by Hal Markowitz. LC 77-18156. (Illus.). 1978. text ed. 18.95x (ISBN 0-88229-385-0). Nelson-Hall.

Behavior of Marine Animals, Vols. 1-3. H. E. Winn & B. L. Olla. Incl. Vol. 1. Invertebres. 244p. 1972. 27.50 (ISBN 0-306-37571-0); Vol. 2. Vertebrates. 259p. 1972. 27.50 (ISBN 0-306-37572-9); Vol. 3. Cetaceans. 460p. 1978. 37.50 (ISBN 0-306-37573-7). LC 79-16775 (Plenum Pr). Plenum Pub.

Behavior of Marine Animals: Marine Birds, Vol. 4. Ed. by Joanna Burger & Bori L. Olla. (Behavior of Marine Animals: Current Perspectives in Research). (Illus.). 498p. 1980. 45.00 (ISBN 0-306-37574-5, Plenum Pr). Plenum Pub.

Behavior of Marine Animals: Marine Birds, Vol. 4. Ed. by Joanna Burger et al. 545p. 1980. 45.00 (ISBN 0-306-37574-5, Plenum Pr). Plenum Pub.

Behavior of Minor Elements in Paddy Soils. (IRRI Research Paper Ser.: No. 8). 15p. 1977. pap. 5.00 (R048, IRRI). Unipub.

Behavior of Non-Human Primates: Modern Research Trends. Ed. by Allan M. Schrier et al. 1965-74. Vol. 1. 35.00 (ISBN 0-12-629101-2); Vol. 2. 32.50 (ISBN 0-12-629102-0); Vol. 3. 32.50 (ISBN 0-12-629103-9); Vol. 4. 32.50 (ISBN 0-12-629104-7). Acad Pr.

Behavior of Organisms: Experimental Analysis. B. Skinner. 1966. 18.95 (ISBN 0-13-073213-3). P-H.

Behavior Principles. 2nd ed. Charles B. Ferster et al. LC 74-19287. (Illus.). 674p. 1975. Repr. text ed. 20.95 (ISBN 0-13-072611-7). P-H.

Behavior Principles in Everyday Life. John D. Baldwin & Janice I. Baldwin. (Illus.). 336p. 1981. text ed. 14.95 (ISBN 0-13-072751-2). P-H.

Behavior Rating Scale. Veralee Hardin. 1975. saddle stitched 1.50x (ISBN 0-87543-123-2); 0.75x (ISBN 0-686-65583-4). Lucas.

Behavior Research & Technology in Higher Education. James M. Johnston. (Illus.). 536p. 1975. 27.50 (ISBN 0-398-03315-3). C C Thomas.

Behavior: The Control of Perception. William T. Powers. LC 73-75697. 320p. 1973. text ed. 16.95x (ISBN 0-202-25113-6). Aldine Pub.

Behavior Theraphy: Techniques & Empirical Findings. 2nd ed. David C. Rimm & John C. Masters. 538p. 1979. 18.95 (ISBN 0-12-588860-0). Acad Pr.

Behavior Therapist. Carl E. Thoresen. LC 80-11725. 120p. (Orig.). 1980. pap. text ed. 5.95 (ISBN 0-8185-0408-0). Brooks-Cole.

Behavior Therapy & Health Care. Ed. by Roger C. Katz & Steven Zlutnik. LC 74-7331. 1975. 23.00; text ed. 19.80 o.p. (ISBN 0-08-017829-4); pap. text ed. 14.50 (ISBN 0-08-017828-6). Pergamon.

Behavior Therapy: Application & Outcome. K. Daniel O'Leary & G. Terence Wilson. (Social Learning Theory Ser.). (Illus.). 480p. 1975. ref. ed. 19.95 (ISBN 0-13-073890-5). P-H.

Behavior Therapy for Depression: Present Status & Future Directions. Ed. by Lynn P. Rehm. 1980. 29.50 (ISBN 0-12-585880-9). Acad Pr.

Behavior Therapy in Clinical Psychiatry. Victor C. Meyer & Edward S. Chesser. LC 71-159480. 1971. 20.00x (ISBN 0-87668-043-0). Aronson.

Behavior Therapy in Psychiatry. American Psychiatric Association. LC 74-3227. 182p. 1974. Repr. 17.50x (ISBN 0-87668-139-9). Aronson.

Behavior Therapy in Psychiatry. (Task Force Report: No. 5). 75p. 1973. 5.00 (ISBN 0-685-38357-1, P191-0). Am Psychiatric.

Behavior Therapy: Philosophical & Empirical Foundations. Edward Erwin. 1981. price not set (ISBN 0-12-242150-7). Acad Pr.

Behavior Therapy: Scientific, Philosophical & Moral Foundations. E. Erwin. 1978. 29.95 (ISBN 0-521-22293-1); pap. 8.95x (ISBN 0-521-29439-8). Cambridge U Pr.

Behavior Therapy: Toward an Applied Clinical Science. W. Stewart Agras et al. LC 78-32069. (Psychology Ser.). (Illus.). 1979. text ed. 14.95x (ISBN 0-7167-1086-2); pap. text ed. 7.95x (ISBN 0-7167-1087-0). W H Freeman.

Behavior Therapy with Children, Vol. 1. Ed. by Anthony M. Graziano. LC 79-80906. 1971. text ed. 27.95x (ISBN 0-202-26046-1). Aldine Pub.

Behavior Therapy with Children, Vol. 2. Ed. by Anthony M. Graziano. LC 74-29461. 1975. lib. bdg. 28.95 (ISBN 0-202-26082-8). Aldine Pub.

Behavior Therapy with Children, Vol. 3. Anthony M. Graziano. 1981. write for info. (ISBN 0-202-26087-9). Aldine Pub.

Behavior Therapy with Hyperactive & Learning Disabled Children. Ed. by Benjamin B. Lahey. (Illus.). 1979. text ed. 16.95x (ISBN 0-19-502478-8); pap. text ed. 8.95x (ISBN 0-19-502479-6). Oxford U Pr.

Behavioral & Management Science in Marketing. Harry L. Davis & Alvin J. Silk. LC 77-18878. 1978. 29.95 (ISBN 0-471-07179-X). Ronald Pr.

Behavioral & Quantitative Perspectives on Terrorism. Ed. by Yonah Alexander. John M. Gleason. LC 80-39752. (Pergamon Press Series on International Politics). 300p. 1981. 32.50 (ISBN 0-08-025989-8). Pergamon.

Behavioral & Social Science Research in the Department of Defense: A Framework for Management. 1971. 3.00 (ISBN 0-309-01913-3). Natl Acad Pr.

Behavioral Applications in Public Management: A Reader. Harvey J. Wolf & George W. Frangia. LC 79-63852. (Illus.). 1979. pap. text ed. 7.75 (ISBN 0-8191-0744-1). U Pr of Amer.

Behavioral Approach to Historical Analysis. Robert F. Berkhofer, Jr. LC 69-11485. (Illus.). 1971. pap. text ed. 6.95 (ISBN 0-02-902960-0). Free Pr.

Behavioral Approach to the Care of Adolescents. Marilyn J. Aten & Elizabeth R. McAnarney. 200p. 1981. pap. text ed. 10.50 (ISBN 0-8016-3201-3). Mosby.

Behavioral Approaches to Children with Developmental Delays. Sally M. O'Neil et al. (Illus.). 1977. pap. 9.50 (ISBN 0-8016-3709-0). Mosby.

Behavioral Assessment: A Practical Handbook. 2nd ed. Ed. by Michel Hersen & Alan Bellack. (Pergamon General Psychology Ser.: No. 98). (Illus.). 500p. 1981. 42.50 (ISBN 0-08-025956-1); pap. 19.50 (ISBN 0-08-025955-3). Pergamon.

Behavioral Assessment: A Practical Handbook. 2nd ed. Ed. by Michel Hersen & Alan S. Bellack. (Pergamon General Psychology Ser.). 500p. Date not set. price not set (ISBN 0-08-025956-1); pap. price not set (ISBN 0-08-020531-3). Pergamon.

Behavioral Assessment Childhood Disorders. Ed. by Eric Nash. Leif Terdal. (Behavioral Assessment Ser.). 750p. 1981. 27.50 (ISBN 0-89862-141-0). Guilford Pr.

Behavioral Assessment of Adult Disorders. Ed. by David H. Barlow. (Guilford Behavioral Assessment Ser.). 500p. 1981. 25.00 (ISBN 0-89862-140-2). Guilford Pr.

Behavioral Biology of Aplysia. Eric R. Kandel. LC 78-18226. (Psychology Ser.). (Illus.). 1979. text ed. 48.00x (ISBN 0-7167-0021-2); pap. text ed. 24.95 (ISBN 0-7167-1070-6). W H Freeman.

Behavioral Concepts & Nursing Throughout the Lifespan. Sharon L. Roberts. 1978. ref. 14.95x (ISBN 0-13-074559-6); pap. text ed. 11.95x (ISBN 0-13-074567-7). P-H.

Behavioral Concepts & the Critically Ill Patient. S. Roberts. 1976. 15.95 (ISBN 0-13-074476-X). P-H.

Behavioral Concepts & the Nursing Process. Sylvia Jasmin & Louise Trygstad-Durland. LC 78-26960. (Illus.). 1979. pap. text ed. 8.50 (ISBN 0-8016-2435-5). Mosby.

Behavioral Concepts in Management. 3rd ed. David Hampton. (Contemporary Thought in Mngt. Ser.). 1978. pap. text ed. 8.95x (ISBN 0-534-00576-4). Wadsworth Pub.

Behavioral Decisions in Organizations. 2nd ed. Alvar Elbing. 1978. 18.95x (ISBN 0-673-15225-9). Scott F.

Behavioral Development of Nonhuman Primates: An Abstracted Bibliography. Faren R. Akins et al. LC 79-26700. 314p. 1980. 75.00 (ISBN 0-306-65189-0). IFI Plenum.

Behavioral Foundations of System Development. David Meister. LC 76-1834. (Human Factors Ser.). 464p. 1976. 37.50 (ISBN 0-471-59195-5). Wiley.

Behavioral Group Therapy 1980: An Annual Review. Ed. by Dennis Upper & Steven M. Ross. (Illus., Orig.). 1980. text ed. 24.95 (ISBN 0-87822-210-3). Res Press.

Behavioral Insights for Supervision. new ed. Ralph W. Reber & Gloria B. Terry. (Illus.). 320p. 1975. pap. 11.95 ref. ed. (ISBN 0-13-073163-3). P-H.

Behavioral Intervention: Contemporary Strategies. W. Robert Nay. LC 76-7510. 384p. 1976. 19.95 (ISBN 0-470-15088-2). Halsted Pr.

Behavioral Intervention in Health Care. Laura B. Gordon. (Behavioral Sciences for Health Care Professionals Ser.). 128p. 1981. lib. bdg. 15.00x (ISBN 0-86531-018-1); pap. text ed. 6.00x (ISBN 0-86531-019-X). Westview.

Behavioral Intervention in Human Problems. Ed. by Henry C. Rickard. LC 76-112398. 434p. 1971. 31.00 (ISBN 0-08-016327-0); pap. 11.55 (ISBN 0-08-017737-9). Pergamon.

Behavioral Mechanisms in Ecology. Douglas H. Morse. LC 80-12130. 1980. text ed. 25.00x (ISBN 0-674-06460-7). Harvard U Pr.

Behavioral Medicine: Practical Applications in Health Care. Barbara G. Melamed & Lawrence J. Siegel. LC 80-13418. (Springer Series on Behavior Therapy & Behavioral Medicine: Vol. 6). (Illus.). 1980. text ed. 22.95 (ISBN 0-8261-2170-5). Springer Pub.

Behavioral Methods for Control of Chronic Pain & Illness. Wilbert E. Fordyce. LC 75-31782. (Illus.). 256p. 1976. 12.95 (ISBN 0-8016-1621-2). Mosby.

Behavioral Methods in Social Work: Helping Children, Adults, & Families in Community Settings. Ed. by Steven P. Schinke. (Modern Applications of Social Work Ser.). 448p. 1980. 24.95 (ISBN 0-202-36026-1). Aldine Pub.

Behavioral Neuroscience: An Introduction. Carl W. Cotman & James L. McGaugh. LC 79-50214. 1979. 21.95 (ISBN 0-12-191650-2). Acad Pr.

Behavioral Objectives-Evaluation in Nursing. 2nd ed. Dorothy Reilly. 200p. 1980. pap. text ed. 11.95 (ISBN 0-8385-0634-8). ACC.

Behavioral Pediatrics & Child Development: A Clinial Handbook. 2nd ed. Thomas J. Kenny & Raymond L. Clemmens. (Illus.). 225p. 1980. lib. bdg. 23.95 (ISBN 0-683-04595-4). Williams & Wilkins.

Behavioral Pediatrics & Child Development. Kenny & Clemmens. 240p. 1975. 16.95 o.p. (ISBN 0-683-04592-X). Williams & Wilkins.

Behavioral Pediatrics: Psychological Aspects of Child Health Care. Stanford Friedman & Robert Hoekelman. (Illus.). 448p. 1980. text ed. 19.95 (ISBN 0-07-022426-9, HP). McGraw.

Behavioral Pharmacology. 1st ed. Stanley D. Glick & Joseph Goldfarb. 1977. text ed. 19.50 o.p. (ISBN 0-8016-1851-7). Mosby.

Behavioral Pharmacology. Susan D. Iversen & Leslie L. Iversen. (Illus.). 275p. 1975. text ed. 19.95x (ISBN 0-19-501860-5). Oxford U Pr.

Behavioral Pharmacology. 2nd ed. Susan D. Iversen & Leslie L. Iversen. (Illus.). 288p. 1981. text ed. 17.95 (ISBN 0-19-502778-7); pap. text ed. 10.95 (ISBN 0-19-502779-5). Oxford U Pr.

Behavioral Problems & the Disabled: Assessment & Management. Duane S. Bishop. (Rehabilitation Medicine Library Ser.). (Illus.). 480p. 1980. lib. bdg. 39.00 (ISBN 0-683-00751-3). Williams & Wilkins.

Behavioral Problems in Organizations. C. Cooper. 1979. 15.95 (ISBN 0-13-073080-7). P-H.

Behavioral Problems of Childhood. Ed. by Stewart Gabel. 1981. price not set (ISBN 0-8089-1336-0). Grune.

Behavioral Problems of Farm Animals. M. Kiley-Worthington. (Illus.). 1977. pap. 15.00 (ISBN 0-85362-163-2, Oriel). Routledge & Kegan.

Behavioral Research: Theory, Procedure, & Design. 2nd ed. Lawrence S. Meyers & Neal E. Grossen. LC 78-2212. (Psychology Ser.). (Illus.). 1978. text ed. 17.95x (ISBN 0-7167-0049-2). W H Freeman.

Behavioral Revolution & Communist Studies: Applications of Behaviorally-Oriented Political Research on the Soviet Union & Eastern Europe. Roger E. Kanet. LC 73-116810. 1971. 10.95 o.s.i. (ISBN 0-02-916990-9). Free Pr.

Behavioral Science & Dental Practice. new ed. Samuel F. Dworkin et al. LC 77-26634. (Illus.). 1978. text ed. 16.95 (ISBN 0-8016-1484-8). Mosby.

Behavioral Science & Modern Penology: A Book of Readings. William H. Lyle, Jr. & Thetus W. Horner. (Illus.). 376p. 1973. 16.50 (ISBN 0-398-02677-7). C C Thomas.

Behavioral Science & the Manager's Role. rev. & enl. 2nd ed. Ed. by William B. Eddy & W. Warner Burke. LC 79-67692. 375p. 1980. pap. 18.50 (ISBN 0-88390-123-4). Univ Assocs.

Behavioral Science Foundations of Consumer Behavior. Joel B. Cohen. LC 79-142357. 1972. 15.95 (ISBN 0-02-905860-0). Free Pr.

Behavioral Science in Clinical Medicine. Stewart Wolf & Helen Goodell. (Illus.). 256p. 1976. 19.75 (ISBN 0-398-03444-3). C C Thomas.

Behavioral Science in Family Practice. Ed. by Gerald M. Rosen et al. 300p. 1980. 19.50x (ISBN 0-8385-0638-0). ACC.

Behavioral Science: Research & Public Policy. David Meister. (Pergamon Policy Studies). 350p. Date not set. price not set (ISBN 0-08-024659-1). Pergamon.

Behavioral Science Research in New Guinea. Division Of Behavioral Sciences. 1967. pap. 8.75 (ISBN 0-309-01493-X). Natl Acad Pr.

Behavioral Science Techniques: An Annotated Bibliography for Health Professionals. Monique K. Tichy. LC 75-3628. 132p. 1975. text ed. 16.50 o.p. (ISBN 0-275-05250-8). Praeger.

Behavioral Sciences: PreTest Self-Assessment & Review. Ed. by Timothy Teyler. LC 78-50594. (Basic Sciences: Pretest Self Assessment & Review Ser.). (Illus.). 1979. pap. 9.95 (ISBN 0-07-051606-5). McGraw-Pretest.

Behavioral Significance of Color: Proceedings. new ed. Animal Behavior Society Symposium, 1977. Ed. by Edward H. Burtt, Jr. LC 77-14618. 1979. lib. bdg. 42.00x (ISBN 0-8240-7016-X, Garland STPM Pr). Garland Pub.

Behavioral Social Aspects of Contraceptive Sterilization. Ed. by Sidney H. Newman & Zanvel E. Klein. LC 77-94. 1978. 18.95 (ISBN 0-669-01442-7). Lexington Bks.

Behavioral Social Work: An Introduction. John S. Wodarski. LC 78-26356. 1979. text ed. 24.95x (ISBN 0-87705-375-8); pap. text ed. 9.95x (ISBN 0-87705-395-2). Human Sci Pr.

Behavioral Sociology: The Experimental Analysis of Social Process. Robert L. Burgess. LC 79-90821. (Illus.). 1969. 22.50x (ISBN 0-231-03203-X); pap. 10.00x (ISBN 0-231-08673-3). Columbia U Pr.

Behavioral Studies of the Hypothalmus. Panksepp Morgane. 480p. Date not set. 93.50. Dekker.

Behavioral Study of Rural Modernization: Social & Economic Change in Thai Villages. Charles A. Murray. LC 77-7827. (Praeger Special Studies). 1977. 21.95 (ISBN 0-03-022856-5). Praeger.

Behavioral Theory of the Firm. Richard M. Cyert & J. G. March. 1963. ref. ed. 19.95 (ISBN 0-13-073304-0). P-H.

Behavioral Travel-Demand Models. Ed. by Peter R. Stopher & Arnim H. Mevburg. LC 76-14666. 1976. 27.95 (ISBN 0-669-00734-X). Lexington Bks.

Behavioral Treatment of Alcoholism. P. M. Miller. 1976. 27.00 (ISBN 0-08-019519-9); pap. 10.75 (ISBN 0-08-019518-0). Pergamon.

Behavioral Treatments of Obesity: A Practical Handbook. Ed. by John P. Foreyt. 1977. text ed. 21.00 (ISBN 0-08-019902-X). Pergamon.

Behaviorism & Schooling. Ira Steinberg. 1980. 20.00 (ISBN 0-312-07253-8). St Martin.

Behaviorism & the Limits of Scientific Method. Brian Mackenzie. Ed. by D. Mackay. (International Library of Philosophy & Scientific Method Ser.). 1977. text ed. 13.00x (ISBN 0-391-00620-7). Humanities.

Behaviour & Chemical State of Irradiated Ceramic Fuels. (Illus.). 437p. (Orig.). 1974. pap. 26.75 (ISBN 92-0-051074-4, IAEA). Unipub.

Behaviour Assessment Battery. Chris Kiernan & Malcolm Jones. (General Ser.). 1977. pap. text ed. 19.25x (ISBN 0-685-05810-7, NFER). Humanities.

Behaviour Modification for the Mentally Handicapped. Ed. by W. Yule & J. Carr. 304p. 1980. 30.00x (ISBN 0-85664-841-8, Pub. by Croom Helm England). State Mutual Bk.

Behaviour Modification in Social Work. Derek Jehu et al. LC 70-37111. 192p. 1972. 20.25 (ISBN 0-471-44140-6, Pub. by Wiley-Interscience). Wiley.

Behaviour of Centrioles & the Structure & Formation of the Achromatic Figure. H. A. Went. (Protoplasmatologia: Vol. 6, Pt. G1). (Illus.). 1966. pap. 30.70 o.p. (ISBN 0-387-80783-7). Springer-Verlag.

Behaviour of Piles. Institute of Civil Engineers. 244p. 1980. 75.00x (ISBN 0-901948-07-1, Pub. by Telford England). State Mutual Bk.

Behaviour of Tritium in the Environment. 1979. pap. 59.00 (ISBN 92-0-020079-6, ISP498, IAEA). Unipub.

Behaviour of Wood Products in Fire: Proceedings, Oxford, 1977. United Nations Economic Commission for Europe, Timber Committee. 1977. pap. text ed. 30.00 (ISBN 0-08-021990-X). Pergamon.

Behaviour Studies in Psychiatry. S. J. Hutt & C. Hutt. 1970. 17.25 (ISBN 0-08-015780-7). Pergamon.

Behavioural & Ecological Genetics: A Study in Drosophila. P. A. Parsons. (Illus.). 231p. 1973. 37.50x (ISBN 0-19-857354-5). Oxford U Pr.

Behavioural Ecology. Ed. by John R. Krebs & Nicholas B. Davies. LC 78-8414. (Illus.). 1978. text ed. 34.00x (ISBN 0-87893-433-2); pap. text ed. 19.50x (ISBN 0-87893-434-0). Sinauer Assoc.

Behavioural Strategy of Teachers. H. Alan Paisey. (General Ser). 192p. (Orig.). 1975. pap. text ed. 17.50x (ISBN 0-85633-054-X, NFER). Humanities.

Behaviourial Science in Medicine. Helen Winefield & Marilyn Peay. 357p. 1980. 40.00x (Pub. by Beaconsfield England). State Mutual Bk.

Behavorial Community Psychology: Progress & Prospects. Ed. by David Glenwick & Leonard Jason. LC 79-21457. 1979. 23.95 (ISBN 0-03-052111-4). Praeger.

Behind Barres: The Mystique of Masterly Teaching. Joseph Gale. LC 79-56900. (Illus.). 96p. 12.95 (ISBN 0-87127-115-X). Dance Horiz.

Behind Closed Doors. Robert Woolf. (RL 7). 1977. pap. 1.95 o.p. (ISBN 0-451-07423-8, J7423, Sig). NAL.

Behind Closed Doors: Secret Papers on the Failure of Romanian-Soviet Negotiations 1931-1932. Ed. by Walter M. Bacon, Jr. LC 77-78050. (Archival Documentation Publications Ser.: No. 180). (Illus.). 228p. 1979. 17.50 (ISBN 0-8179-6801-6). Hoover Inst Pr.

Behind Communism. Frank L. Britton. 97p. (Orig.). 1979. pap. 1.75x (ISBN 0-911038-82-5). Noontide.

Behind Ghetto Walls: Black Family Life in a Federal Slum. Lee Rainwater. LC 77-113083. 1970. text ed. 20.95x (ISBN 0-202-30113-3); pap. text ed. 9.95x (ISBN 0-202-30114-1). Aldine Pub.

Behind Mud Walls, Nineteen Thirty to Nineteen Sixty: With a Sequel: the Village in 1970. rev. ed. William Wiser & Charlotte Wiser. 1972. 15.75x (ISBN 0-520-02093-6); pap. 3.95 (ISBN 0-520-02101-0, CAL91). U of Cal Pr.

Behind That Door Lies Your Fortune. Eva Thomas. 4.50 o.p. (ISBN 0-685-33191-1). Vantage.

Behind the Ballots. James A. Farley. LC 72-2370. (FDR & the Era of the New Deal Ser). (Illus.). 402p. 1973. Repr. of 1938 ed. lib. bdg. 35.00 (ISBN 0-306-70475-7). Da Capo.

Behind the Big Top. David L. Hammarstrom. LC 78-69647. (Illus.). 1980. 19.95 (ISBN 0-498-02205-6). A S Barnes.

Behind the Circus Scene. Don Fenton & Barb Fenton. Ed. by Howard Schroeder. LC 80-14521. (Behind the Scenes Ser.). (Illus.). (gr. 4). 1980. PLB 5.95 (ISBN 0-89686-059-0); pap. 2.95 (ISBN 0-89686-064-7). Crestwood Hse.

Behind the Cloud. Emilie Loring. 208p. 1981. pap. 1.95 (ISBN 0-553-14295-X). Bantam.

Behind the Death Ball. Alfred Hitchcock. 1979. pap. 1.50 o.s.i. (ISBN 0-440-13497-8). Dell.

Behind the Newspaper Scene. Don Fenton & Barb Fenton. Ed. by Howard Schroeder. LC 80-14593. (Behind the Scenes Ser.). (Illus.). (gr. 4). 1980. PLB 5.95 (ISBN 0-89686-058-2); pap. 2.95 (ISBN 0-89686-063-9). Crestwood Hse.

Behind the Radio Scene. Don Fenton & Barb Fenton. Ed. by Howard Schroeder. LC 80-14594. (Behind the Scenes Ser.). (Illus.). (gr. 4). 1980. PLB 5.95 (ISBN 0-89686-061-2); pap. 2.95 (ISBN 0-89686-066-3). Crestwood Hse.

Behind the Ranges. Mrs. Howard Taylor. 1980. pap. 3.95 (ISBN 0-85363-003-8). OMF Bks.

Behind the Scene. Douglas Reed. (Pt. 2 of Far & Wide). 1976. pap. 3.50x (ISBN 0-911038-41-8). Noontide.

Behind the Scenes at the Horse Hospital. Fern Brown. Ed. by Kathleen Tucker. (Behind the Scenes Ser.). (Illus.). 48p. (gr. 3-9). 1981. 7.50 (ISBN 0-8075-0610-9). A Whitman.

Behind the Scenes at the Zoo. Georg Zappler. LC 76-42418. 1977. PLB 5.95 (ISBN 0-385-09514-7). Doubleday.

Behind the Scenes in American Government. 3rd ed. Woll. 1981. pap. text ed. 7.95 (ISBN 0-316-95137-4); tchrs'. manual free. Little.

Behind the Shield: The Police in Urban Society. Arthur Niederhoffer. LC 67-16896. 1969. pap. 2.95 (ISBN 0-385-06128-5, A653, Anch). Doubleday.

Behind the Sports Scene. Don Fenton & Barb Fenton. Ed. by Howard Schroeder. LC 80-14070. (Behind the Scenes Ser.). (Illus.). (gr. 4). 1980. PLB 5.95 (ISBN 0-89686-060-4); pap. 2.95 (ISBN 0-89686-065-5). Crestwood Hse.

Behind the Television Scene. Don Fenton & Barb Fenton. Ed. by Howard Schroeder. LC 80-14151. (Behind the Scenes Ser.). (Illus.). (gr. 4). 1980. PLB 5.95 (ISBN 0-89686-062-0); pap. 2.95 (ISBN 0-89686-067-1). Crestwood Hse.

Behind the Urals: An American Worker in Russia's City of Steel. John Scott. LC 72-88916. (Classics in Russian Studies: No. 3). 288p. 1973. pap. 3.95x (ISBN 0-253-10600-1). Ind U Pr.

Behind the War in Eritrea. Ed. by Basil Davidson et al. 150p. 1980. pap. text ed. 8.95. Barber Pr.

Behold Our Land. Russell Lord. LC 74-2395. (FDR & the Era of the New Deal Ser.). 309p. 1974. Repr. of 1938 ed. lib. bdg. 27.50 (ISBN 0-306-70593-1). Da Capo.

Behold, the Land: Ayin Letzion. rev. ed. Helen Fine. LC 67-21069. (gr. 5-8). 1977. text ed. 6.50 (ISBN 0-8074-0129-3, 127270); teachers guide 1971 o.p. 5.00 (ISBN 0-685-20726-9, 207271). UAHC.

Behold the Man, Jesus. Alma T. Knight. 3.95 o.p. (ISBN 0-685-48827-6). Nortex Pr.

Behold the Mighty Dinosaur. Ed. by David Jablonski. 1981. 10.95 (ISBN 0-525-66704-0). Elsevier-Nelson.

Behold These Hills. Nan T. Hunt. (Illus.). Date not set. cancelled (ISBN 0-89482-050-8). pap. 6.50 (ISBN 0-89482-045-1). Stevenson Pr.

Behold Thy Mother. Thomas S. Monson. 1976. pap. 0.50 o.p. (ISBN 0-87747-586-5). Deseret Bk.

Behold Your God: A Woman's Workshop on the Attributes of God. Myrna Alexander. pap. 2.50 (ISBN 0-310-37131-7). Zondervan.

Beijing Street Voices. David S. Goodman. (Illus.). 192p. 1981. 20.00 (ISBN 0-7145-2703-3, Pub. by M Boyars). Merrimack Bk Serv.

Being a Christian Today. Ladislaus Boros. Tr. by M. Benedict Davies. LC 79-13607. 124p. 1979. 7.95 (ISBN 0-8164-0440-2). Crossroad NY.

Being a Food Service Worker. Hospital Research & Educational Trust of the AHA. (Illus.). 1967. pap. 9.95 (ISBN 0-87618-046-2). R J Brady.

Being a Lunar Type in a Solar World. Donna Cunningham. 1981. pap. 6.95 (ISBN 0-87728-521-7). Weiser.

Being a Parent: Unchanging Values in a Changing World. Karl S. Bernhardt. Ed. by David K. Bernhardt. LC 74-484635. 1970. pap. 4.00 (ISBN 0-8020-6106-0). U of Toronto Pr.

Being Alone, Being Together. Terry Berger. LC 75-20302. (Moods & Emotions Ser.). (Illus.). 32p. (gr. k-3). 1976. Repr. of 1974 ed. PLB 8.95 (ISBN 0-8172-0047-9). Raintree Pubs.

Being an Authorized English Version of Das Leben Richard Wagner, 6 vols. William A. Ellis & C. F. Glassenapp. LC 77-2022. (Music Reprint Ser., 1977). 1977. Repr. of 1902 ed. lib. bdg. 37.50 ea.; 195.00 (ISBN 0-306-70887-6). Da Capo.

Being & Alienation. Rostam Keyon. LC 78-61109. 350p. 1981. 10.00 (ISBN 0-686-69333-7). Philos Lib.

Being & Breakfast. Marti Duncan. 1975. 1.00. Windless Orchard.

Being & Caring: A Journey to Self. Victor Daniels & Laurence J. Horowitz. 1976. pap. text ed. 9.95 (ISBN 0-87484-374-X). Mayfield Pub.

Being & Death: An Outline of Integrationist Philosophy. Jose Ferrater Mora. 1965. 18.00x (ISBN 0-520-00402-7). U of Cal Pr.

Being & Existence in Kierkegaard's Pseudonymous Works. J. W. Elrod. 1975. 16.50 (ISBN 0-691-07204-3). Princeton U Pr.

Being & God: Introduction to the Philosophy of Being & to Natural Theology. George P. Klubertanz & Maurice R. Holloway. LC 63-15359. 1963. 29.00x (ISBN 0-89197-045-2); pap. text ed. 16.50x (ISBN 0-89197-674-4). Irvington.

Being & Nothingness. Jean-Paul Sartre. Tr. by Hazel E. Barnes. pap. 4.95 (ISBN 0-671-41890-4). WSP.

Being & Time. Martin Heidegger. LC 72-78334. 1962. 19.95 (ISBN 0-06-063850-8, HarpR). Har-Row.

Being Beautiful: The Story of Cosmetics from Ancient Art to Modern Science. Carolyn Meyer. 1977. 7.25 (ISBN 0-688-22125-4); lib. bdg. 6.96 (ISBN 0-688-32125-9). Morrow.

Being Bernard Berenson. Meryle Secrest. (Illus.). 1980. pap. 7.95 (ISBN 0-14-005697-1). Penguin.

Being Fat (Has Nothing to Do with Food) A Handbook for the Yo-Yo-Dieter. Pat TerHuen & Lynda Smith. LC 80-80247. (Illus.). 80p. 1981. pap. 3.95 (ISBN 0-89087-314-3). Celestial Arts.

Being Free: Reflections on America's Cultural Revolution. Gibson Winter. 1970. 4.95 o.p. (ISBN 0-02-630500-3); pap. 1.95 (ISBN 0-685-04267-7). Macmillan.

Being Here: Poetry Nineteen Seventy-Seven to Nineteen Eighty. Robert P. Warren. 108p. 1980. 8.95 (ISBN 0-394-51304-5). Random.

Being in God's Family. Marian Baden. (Concordia Weekday Ser. - Gr. 3-4. Bk. 4, 2-V). 1967. pap. text ed. 2.15 (ISBN 0-570-06658-1, 22-2028); manual 4.85 (ISBN 0-685-08548-1, 22-2029). Concordia.

Being Indian in Hueyapan: A Study of Forced Identity in Contemporary Mexico. Judith N. Friedlander. LC 74-23047. (Illus.). 224p. (Orig.). 1975. text ed. 14.95 (ISBN 0-312-07280-5); pap. text ed. 6.95 (ISBN 0-312-07315-1). St Martin.

Being Jewish, Being Human: A Gift Book of Poems & Readings. Ed. by Dov P. Elkins. LC 79-88298. Date not set. softbound 16.50 (ISBN 0-918834-07-4). Growth Assoc. Postponed.

Being Joyous. Larry Yarborough. LC 72-96151. pap. 0.50 tchr's guide (ISBN 0-8054-5318-0). Broadman.

Being Lucky: Reminiscences & Reflections. Herman B. Wells. LC 80-7493. 512p. 1980. 17.50x (ISBN 0-253-11556-6). Ind U Pr.

Being Married. Evelyn M. Duvall & Reuben L. Hill. 1960. text ed. 9.95x o.p. (ISBN 0-669-22780-3). Heath.

Being Me. Grady Nutt. LC 71-145984. (gr. 7 up). 1971. pap. 2.75 (ISBN 0-8054-6909-5). Broadman.

Being Mentally Ill: A Sociological Theory. Thomas J. Scheff. LC 66-15207. 210p. 1966. pap. text ed. 5.95x (ISBN 0-202-30252-0). Aldine Pub.

Being, Nothing & God. George Seidel. 1970. text ed. 15.00x (ISBN 90-232-0061-6). Humanities.

Being Number One: Rebuilding the U. S. Economy. Gail G. Schwartz & Pat Choate. 1980. 14.95 (ISBN 0-669-04308-7). Lexington Bks.

Being of Sound Mind: A Book of Eccentric Wills. Gerald Warner. (Illus.). 112p. 1981. 14.50 (ISBN 0-241-10471-8, Pub. by Hamish Hamilton England). David & Charles.

Being Urban: A Social Psychological View of City Life. David A. Karp et al. 1976. pap. text ed. 7.95x (ISBN 0-669-95703-8). Heath.

Being Where You Are. Martin Cecil. 1974. 2.95 (ISBN 0-686-27650-7). Cole-Outreach.

Beirut Incident. Nick Carter. (Nick Carter Ser.). 192p. (Orig.). 1981. pap. 1.95 (ISBN 0-441-05381-5). Charter Bks.

Beitraege zum Verstaendnis der Odyssee. Hartmut Erbse. (Untersuchungen zur Antiken Literatur und Geschichte 13). 1972. 48.25x (ISBN 3-11-004045-X). De Gruyter.

Beitraege zur Kenntnis der Meeresalgen von Neapel, zugleich mikrophotographischer Atlas. Georg Funk. (Pubbl. d. Stazione Zool. di Napoli). (Illus., Ger.). 1978. Repr. of 1935 ed. lib. bdg. 48.60 (ISBN 3-87429-146-4). Lubrecht & Cramer.

Beitraege zur Orchideenkunde von Colombia. R. Schlechter. (Feddes Repertorium: Beiheft 27). 183p. (Ger.). 1980. Repr. of 1924 ed. lib. bdg. 40.55x (ISBN 3-87429-182-0, Pub. by Koeltz Germany). Lubrecht & Cramer.

Beitraege zur Orchideenkunde von Zentralamerika, 2 vols. in one. R. Schelchter. (Feddes Repertorium: Beiheft 17 & 18). 402p. (Ger.). 1980. Repr. of 1922 ed. lib. bdg. 70.20x (ISBN 3-87429-181-2, Pub. by Koeltz Germany). Lubrecht & Cramer.

Beitrage Zur Geschicte der Deutschen Romantischen Oper Zwischen Spohrs "Faust" und Wagner's "Lohengrin". Siegfried Goslich. LC 80-2281. 1981. Repr. of 1937 ed. 31.50 (ISBN 0-404-18846-X). AMS Pr.

Bel-Air. Mary McClusky. 256p. (Orig.). 1981. pap. 2.50 (ISBN 0-523-41158-8). Pinnacle Bks.

Bel Canto. Elster Kay. (Student's Music Library Ser). 1962. 6.95 (ISBN 0-234-77547-5). Dufour.

Bel Canto & Its Golden Age. Phillip A. Duey. (Music Reprint Ser.: 1980). 1980. Repr. of 1951 ed. lib. bdg. 22.50 (ISBN 0-306-76021-5). Da Capo.

Bel Canto: Theoretical & Practical Vocal Method. Mathilde Marchesi. 1970. pap. text ed. 5.00 (ISBN 0-486-22315-9). Dover.

Bel-Heirs. Victor Fitzmaurice. 1981. 9.95 (ISBN 0-533-04875-3). Vantage.

Bela Bartok: An Analysis of His Music. Emo Lendvai. (Illus.). 115p. 1971. text ed. 10.50x (ISBN 0-900707-04-6). Humanities.

B'ela Bart'ok: Essays. Ed. by Benjamin Suchoff. LC 76-5202. (Illus.). 1976. 75.00 (ISBN 0-312-07350-X). St Martin.

Belarmino & Apolonio. Ramon Perez de Ayala. Tr. by Gabriel Berns & Murray Baumgarten. 1971. 16.95x (ISBN 0-520-01786-2). U of Cal Pr.

Belchamber. Howard O. Sturgis. LC 76-15624. 1976. Repr. of 1905 ed. 14.50 (ISBN 0-86527-219-0). Fertig.

Belden, the White Chief: Or, Twelve Years Among the Wild Indians of the Plains from the Diaries & Manuscripts of George P. Belden. facsimile ed. Ed. by James S. Brisbin. LC 73-92900. (Illus.). xxvi, 513p. 1974. Repr. of 1870 ed. 15.00 (ISBN 0-8214-0150-5). Ohio U Pr.

Beleaguered City: Richmond, 1861-1865. Alfred H. Bill. LC 80-16702. (Illus.). xiv, 313p. 1980. Repr. of 1946 ed. lib. bdg. 29.75x (ISBN 0-313-22568-0, BIBE). Greenwood.

Beleaguered Minorities: Cultural Politics in America. S. J. Makielski, Jr. LC 73-12290. (Illus.). 1973. text ed. 18.95x (ISBN 0-7167-0789-6); pap. text ed. 9.95x (ISBN 0-7167-0788-8). W H Freeman.

Belehrung und Verkuendigung: Schriften zur deutschen Literatur vom Mittelalter bis zur Neuzeit. Friedrich-Wilhelm Wentzlaff-Eggebert. Ed. by Manfred Dick & Gerhard Kaiser. 344p. 1975. 85.30x (ISBN 3-11-005714-X). De Gruyter.

Belerion: Ancient Sites of Land's End. Craig Weatherhill. 96p. 1980. 15.00x (ISBN 0-906720-01-X, Pub. by Hodge England). State Mutual Bk.

Belfast: Approach to Crisis. Ian Budge & Cornelius O'Leary. LC 72-85194. 1973. 18.95 (ISBN 0-312-07420-4). St Martin.

Belfast Cookery Book. Margaret Bates. 222p. 1975. pap. 10.00 (ISBN 0-08-018952-0). Pergamon.

Belgium. new ed. Raymond C. Riley. LC 76-18938. (Westview Special Studies in Industrial Geography). (Illus.). 1976. lib. bdg. 26.00x (ISBN 0-89158-625-3). Westview.

Belgium & Luxembourg in Pictures. Sterling Publishing Company Editors. (Visual Geography Ser). (Illus.). (gr. 5 up). 1966. PLB 4.99 o.p. (ISBN 0-8069-1065-8); pap. 2.95 o.p. (ISBN 0-8069-1064-X). Sterling.

Belgium's Return to Neutrality: An Essay in the Frustrations of Small Power Diplomacy. David O Kieft. 200p. 1972. 16.50x (ISBN 0-19-821497-9). Oxford U Pr.

Belgrade & Beyond: The CSCE Process in Perspective. Nils Andren & Karl E. Birnbaum. (East West Perspectives: No. 5). 27.50x (ISBN 90-286-0250-X). Sijthoff & Noordhoff.

Belgravia. David Linzee. 1981. pap. 2.25 o.s.i. (ISBN 0-440-10472-6). Dell.

Belief & History. Wilfred C. Smith. LC 75-50587. 1977. 12.95x (ISBN 0-8139-0670-9). U Pr of Va.

Belief & Life: Studies in the Thought of the Fourth Gospel. W. B. Selbie. (Short Course Ser.). 151p. 1916. text ed. 2.95 (ISBN 0-567-08314-4). Attic Pr.

Belief & Unbelief. Michael Novak. 1965. 4.95 o.s.i. (ISBN 0-02-590750-6). Macmillan.

Belief, Attitude, Intention, & Behavior: An Introduction to Theory & Research. Martin Fishbein & Icek Ajzen. 544p. 1975. 20.95 (ISBN 0-201-02089-0). A-W.

Belief Factor. Richard V. Riccio. 1980. 8.95 (ISBN 0-89962-009-4). Todd & Honeywell.

Belief in a Just World: A Fundamental Delusion. Melvin J. Lerner. (Perspectives in Social Psychology Ser.). (Illus.). 200p. 1980. 22.50 (ISBN 0-306-40495-8, Plenum Pr). Plenum Pub.

Belief in Redemption: Explorations in Doctrine from the New Testament to Today. Dietrich Wiedekehr. Tr. by Jeremy Moiser from Ger. LC 78-24088. Orig. Title: Glaube an Erlosung. 120p. 1981. pap. 5.95 (ISBN 0-8042-0476-4). John Knox.

Belief in Science & in Christian Life. Ed. by Thomas F. Torrance. 160p. 1981. pap. 11.00x (ISBN 0-905312-11-2, Pub. by Sottish Academic Pr Scotland). Columbia U Pr.

Belief, Truth & Knowledge. Allen Armstrong. LC 72-83586. 240p. 1973. 35.50 (ISBN 0-521-08706-6); pap. 10.50x (ISBN 0-521-09737-1). Cambridge U Pr.

Beliefs, Attitudes & Values: A Theory of Organization & Change. Milton Rokeach. LC 68-21322. (Social & Behavioral Science Ser.). 1968. 14.95x (ISBN 0-87589-013-X). Jossey-Bass.

Believe! Richard De Vos. 1981. pap. price not set (ISBN 0-671-41757-6). PB.

Believe! Richard M. DeVos & Charles P. Conn. 1975. 5.95 (ISBN 0-8007-0732-X); pap. 2.50 (ISBN 0-8007-8267-4, Spire Bks). Revell.

Believe & Make-Believe. new ed. William D. Sheldon et al. (gr. 4). 1973. text ed. 10.80 (ISBN 0-205-03552-3, 5235529); tchrs' guide 10.80 (ISBN 0-205-03553-1, 5235537); activity bk. 3.96 (ISBN 0-205-03554-X, 5235545); activities' masters 28.00 (ISBN 0-205-03556-6, 5235561); tchrs'. ed. activity bk. 3.96 (ISBN 0-205-03555-8, 5235553). Allyn.

Believe in Spring. Sybil Conrad. LC 67-29446. (gr. 7 up). 1968. 5.95 (ISBN 0-8149-0290-1). Vanguard.

Believe It or Not: An Anthology of Ancient Tales Retold. Florence C. Chang. LC 80-68258. (Chinese Can Be Fun Ser.: Bk. 3). (Illus.). 80p. (gr. 10-12). 1980. pap. text ed. 3.75 (ISBN 0-936620-02-1). Ginkgo Hut.

Believer's Daily Renewal. Andrew Murray. 144p. 1981. pap. 2.95 (ISBN 0-87123-147-6, 210147). Bethany Fell.

Believing. Michele McCarty. 160p. 1980. pap. text ed. 4.25 (ISBN 0-697-01753-2); tchr's manual 5.00. Wm C Brown.

Believing. Michele McCarty. 160p. 1980. pap. 4.25 (ISBN 0-697-01753-2); tchrs'. manual 5.00 (ISBN 0-697-01754-0). Wm C Brown.

Believing: Myron Floren & His Friends' Scrapbook. Roger Elwood & Myron Floren. LC 80-50525. (Illus.). 208p. 1981. 14.95 (ISBN 0-87239-420-4, 5003). Standard Pub.

Belinda, or, the Rivals. A. S. Holmes. (Found Books: No. 2). 122p. (Orig.). 1975. pap. 3.95 (ISBN 0-88784-333-6, Pub. by Hse Anansi Pr Canada). U of Toronto Pr.

Belinskii & Russian Literary Criticism: The Heritage of Organic Aesthetics. Victor Terras. LC 73-2050. 384p. 1973. 32.50x (ISBN 0-299-06350-X). U of Wis Pr.

Belinsky, Chernyshevsky, & Dobrolyubov: Selected Criticism. Ed. by Ralph E. Matlaw. LC 75-34729. (Midland Books: No. 200). 256p. 1976. 9.50x (ISBN 0-253-31155-1); pap. 2.95x (ISBN 0-253-20200-0). Ind U Pr.

Belisarius, 1767. Jean Francois Marmontel. Ed. by Michael F. Shugrue. (Flowering of the Novel, 1740-1775 Ser: Vol. 81). 1974. lib. bdg. 50.00 (ISBN 0-8240-1180-5). Garland Pub.

Belize. Ralph L. Woodward, Jr. (World Bibliographical Ser.: No. 21). 1980. write for info. (ISBN 0-903450-41-0). Abc-Clio.

Bell. Dorothy Daniels. (Orig.). 1971. pap. 1.75 o.s.i. (ISBN 0-446-84964-2). Warner Bks.

Bell & Cohn's Handbook of Grammar, Style & Usage. 2nd ed. James K. Bell & Adrian Cohn. 1976. pap. text ed. 3.95x (ISBN 0-02-470630-2, 470630). Macmillan.

Bell & the Drum: A Study of Shih Ching As Formulaic Poetry. C. H. Wang. (Illus.). 1975. 17.50x (ISBN 0-520-02441-9). U of Cal Pr.

Bell Beaker Cultures of Spain & Portugal. new ed. Richard J. Harrison. Ed. by Lorna Condon. LC 76-52631. (American School of Prehistoric Research Bulletins Ser.: No. 35). (Illus.). 1977. pap. 30.00 (ISBN 0-87365-538-9). Peabody Harvard.

Bell for Adano. John Hersey. (Literature Ser). (gr. 9-12). 1970. pap. text ed. 3.92 (ISBN 0-87720-749-6). AMSCO Sch.

Bell Is Phony. R. Bryan Sloan. 1976. pap. 4.00 (ISBN 0-916378-08-X). Oasis Pr.

Bell Tower of Wyndspelle. Aola Vandergriff. (Orig.). 1975. pap. 1.95 o.s.i. (ISBN 0-446-89716-7). Warner Bks.

Bella Figura. Trina Mascott. LC 76-28045. 1977. 8.95 o.p. (ISBN 0-312-07455-7). St Martin.

Belle Catherine. Juliette Benzoni. 1973. pap. 1.95 (ISBN 0-380-01855-1, 36525). Avon.

Belle Epoque: Masterworks by Combaz, Leo Jo & Livemont. Yolande Oostens-Wittamer. LC 79-92749. (Illus.). 64p. (Orig.). 1980. pap. 8.95 (ISBN 0-88397-027-9). Intl Exhibit Foun.

Belle Etoile. David G. Speer & Marilene B. Speer. (Illus.). 1970. text ed. 11.95 o.p. (ISBN 0-07-060031-7, C); pap. text ed. 8.95 o.p. (ISBN 0-07-060032-5). McGraw.

Belle Methode Ou l'Art De Bien Chanter. Jean Millet. LC 71-126600. (Music Ser). 76p. 1973. Repr. of 1666 ed. lib. bdg. 18.50 (ISBN 0-306-70044-1). Da Capo.

Belle of Bath. Dorothy Mack. (Candelight Romance Ser.). (Orig.). Date not set. pap. 1.50 (ISBN 0-440-10617-6). Dell.

Belle of the Fifties: Memoirs of Mrs. Virginia Clay of Alabama. Ed. by Ada Sterling. LC 79-84187. (American Scene Ser). 1969. Repr. of 1905 ed. lib. bdg. 39.50 (ISBN 0-306-71395-0). Da Capo.

Belle Starr. Speer Morgan. 1980. pap. write for info. (ISBN 0-671-83227-1). PB.

Bellefleur. Joyce C. Oates. 1980. 13.95 (ISBN 0-525-06302-1, Henry Robbins Book). Dutton.

Bellefleur. Sondra Stanford. (Harlequin Romances Ser.). 192p. 1980. pap. 1.25 o.p. (ISBN 0-373-02354-5, Pub. by Harlequin). PB.

Belles & Beaux on Their Toes: Dancing Stars in Young America. Mary G. Swift. LC 79-6661. 1980. text ed. 19.75 (ISBN 0-8191-0922-3); pap. text ed. 12.00 (ISBN 0-8191-0923-1). U Pr of Amer.

Belles Heures of Jean, Duke of Berry. Commentaries by Millard Meiss & Elizabeth H. Beatson. LC 74-75688. (Illus.). 268p. 1974. slip-cased ed. 70.00 (ISBN 0-8076-0750-9); leatherbound 150.00 (ISBN 0-685-49198-6). Braziller.

Belles Letters Series, the English Drama. Oliver Goldsmith. 283p. 1980. Repr. of 1905 ed. lib. bdg. 30.00 (ISBN 0-89987-324-3). Century Bookbindery.

Belles Lettres. Kathleen Chandler. (Illus.). 160p. 1981. 7.95 (ISBN 0-89962-204-6). Todd & Honeywell.

Belles on Their Toes. Frank B. Gilbreth, Jr. & Ernestine G. Carey. LC 50-13907. (Illus.). 1950. 8.95 (ISBN 0-690-13023-6, TYC-T). T Y Crowell.

Bellet's Essentials of Cardiac Arrhythmias. 2nd ed. Richard H. Helfant. (Illus.). 450p. 1980. text ed. 24.50 (ISBN 0-7216-4626-3). Saunders.

Belleza Radiante. Tr. by Joyce Landorf. (Spanish Bks.). (Span.). 1978. 1.90 (ISBN 0-8297-0807-3). Life Pubs Intl.

Bellievre & Villeroy: Power in France Under Henry Third & Henry Fourth. Edmund H. Dickerman. LC 70-127365. (Illus.). 200p. 1971. 10.00x (ISBN 0-87057-131-1, Pub. by Brown U Pr). Univ Pr of New England.

Bellringer. Ruth Laurene. LC 74-75851. (Illus.). 1974. 20.00x (ISBN 0-933652-08-9). Domjan Studio.

Bell's Acrostic Dictionary. W. M. Baker. LC 77-141772. 1971. Repr. of 1927 ed. 15.00 (ISBN 0-8103-3379-1). Gale.

Bells, Bells, Bells. Bernadine Bailey. LC 77-16859. (Illus.). (gr. 4 up). 1978. 5.95 (ISBN 0-396-07551-7). Dodd.

Bell's British Theatre, Consisting of the Most Esteemed English Plays, 41 vols. 1776-1802. John Bell. Set. 1127.50 (ISBN 0-404-00800-3); 27.50 ea.; write for info. listing (ISBN 0-685-05697-X). AMS Pr.

Bells in Winter. Czeslaw Milosz. Tr. by Czeslaw Milosz & Lillian Vallee. LC 78-5617. (gr. 10-12). 1978. 9.95 (ISBN 0-912946-56-3). Ecco Pr.

Bell's Miniature Series of Great Writers: Shakespeare. Alfred Ewen. 128p. 1980. Repr. of 1904 ed. lib. bdg. 20.00 (ISBN 0-89984-178-3). Century Bookbindery.

Bell's New Pantheon, 2 vols. John Bell. Ed. by Burton Feldman & Robert D. Richardson. LC 78-60919. (Myth & Romanticism Ser.: Vol. 4). 809p. 1979. Set. lib. bdg. 120.00 (ISBN 0-8240-3553-4). Garland Pub.

Bells: Their History, Legends, Making, & Uses. Satis N. Coleman. LC 74-159919. (Illus.). 1971. Repr. of 1928 ed. 28.00 (ISBN 0-8103-3906-4). Gale.

Belly Dance Costume Book. rev. ed. Zarifa Aradoon. Ed. by David Bain. LC 77-88919. (Illus.). 1981. pap. 15.00 (ISBN 0-930486-04-8). Dream Place.

Belonging: An Introduction to the Christian Church. Sherman E. Johnson. 1978. 1.65 (ISBN 0-686-28773-8). Forward Movement.

Belorussia Under Soviet Rule, Nineteen Seventeen to Nineteen Fifty-Seven. Ivan S. Lubachko. LC 79-160047. (Illus.). 240p. 1972. 13.00x (ISBN 0-8131-1263-X). U Pr of Ky.

Beloved. P. C. Kuttykrishnan. Tr. by R. R. Menon from Malayalam. 194p. 1975. pap. 2.80 (ISBN 0-88253-696-6). Ind-US Inc.

Beloved Benjamin Is Waiting. Jean E. Karl. (gr. 7-12). 1980. pap. 1.50 (ISBN 0-440-90836-1, LFL). Dell.

Beloved Enemy. Barbara Corcoran. 160p. (Orig.). 1981. pap. 1.95 (ISBN 0-345-28667-7). Ballantine.

Beloved Friend: The Story of Tchaikowsky & Nadejda Von Meck. Catherine Bowen & Barbara Von Meck. LC 73-3923. 1976. Repr. of 1961 ed. lib. bdg. 32.00x (ISBN 0-8371-6861-9, BOBF). Greenwood.

Beloved Invader. Eugenia Price. LC 65-20589. 1965. 10.95 (ISBN 0-397-10013-2). Lippincott.

Beloved Scoundrel. Clarissa Ross. 1980. pap. 1.95 (ISBN 0-8439-0710-X, Leisure Bks). Nordon Pubns.

Beloved Was Bahamas. Harriett Weaver. LC 74-76442. 184p. (gr. 4-6). 1974. 6.95 (ISBN 0-8149-0740-7). Vanguard.

Below the Sahara. Ed. by E. F. Bleiler. (Frank Reade Library: Vol. 9). 1980. lib. bdg. 44.00 (ISBN 0-8240-3547-X). Garland Pub.

Belt Conveyors for Bulk Materials. 2nd ed. Conveyor Equipment Manufacturers Assoc. LC 78-31987. 1979. 32.50 (ISBN 0-8436-1008-5). CBI Pub.

Beltran: Basque Sheepman of the American West. Beltran Paris. As told to William A. Douglass. LC 79-20311. (Basque Book Ser.). (Illus.). 186p. 1979. 10.00 (ISBN 0-87417-054-0). U of Nev Pr.

Belts for All Occasions. Sarah Hobson. (Illus.). 64p. (Orig.). 1976. 6.95 (ISBN 0-263-05599-X). Transatlantic.

Belvidere Apollo: A Prize Poem, Repr. Of 1812 Ed. Henry H. Milman. Bd. with Fazio: A Tragedy. Repr. of 1815 ed; Samor, Lord of the Bright City: An Heroic Poem. Repr. of 1818 ed. LC 75-31232. (Romantic Context: Poetry 1789-1830 Ser.: Vol. 83). 1977. lib. bdg. 47.00 (ISBN 0-8240-2182-7). Garland Pub.

Bembelman's Bakery. Melinda Green. LC 77-22858. (Illus.). 40p. (ps-3). 1978. 6.95 (ISBN 0-590-07719-8, Four Winds); PLB 5.41 o.p. (ISBN 0-8193-0914-1). Schol Bk Serv.

Ben & Me. Robert Lawson. (gr. 3-6). 1973. pap. 1.50 (ISBN 0-440-42038-5, YB). Dell.

Ben & the Porcupine. (Illus.). 32p. (ps-3). 1981. 8.95 (ISBN 0-395-30171-8, Clarion). HM.

Ben Asher's Creed. Aron Dotan. LC 76-27649. (Society of Biblical Literature. Masoretic Studies). 1977. pap. 7.50 (ISBN 0-89130-084-8, 060503). Scholars Pr Ca.

Ben Franklin Laughing: Anecdotes from Original Sources by & About Benjamin Franklin. Ed. by P. M. Zall. 1980. 9.95 (ISBN 0-520-04026-0). U of Cal Pr.

Ben Franklin Laughing: Anecdotes from Original Sources by & About Benjamin Franklin. Ed. by Paul M. Zall. 216p. 1981. 12.95 (ISBN 0-520-04026-0). U of Cal Pr.

Ben Hunt's Big Book of Whittling. W. Ben Hunt. 1970. 11.95 (ISBN 0-02-557430-2). Macmillan.

Ben Hur. Lew Wallace. (Classics Ser). (YA) (gr. 9 up). pap. 1.95 (ISBN 0-8049-0074-4, CL-74). Airmont.

Ben Hur. Lew Wallace. Tr. by Ginette D. De Reedy. (Biblioteca de Libros Condensados). Date not set. pap. 1.50 (ISBN 0-311-37012-8). Casa Bautista.

Ben Jonson. J. B. Bamborough. (English Literature Ser.). 1970. pap. text ed. 4.75x (ISBN 0-09-101691-6, Hutchinson U Lib). Humanities.

Ben Jonson. Claude J. Summers & Ted-Larry Pebworth. (English Authors Ser.: No. 268). 1979. 12.50 (ISBN 0-8057-6764-9). Twayne.

Ben Jonson: A Quadricentennial Bibliography, 1947-1972. D. Heyward Brock & James M. Welsh. LC 74-2424. (Author Bibliography Ser.: No. 16). 1974. 10.00 (ISBN 0-8108-0710-6). Scarecrow.

Ben Jonson & Elizabethan Music. 2nd ed. Willa M. Evans. LC 65-18503. (Music Ser). 1965. Repr. of 1929 ed. 14.50 (ISBN 0-306-70907-4). Da Capo.

Ben Jonson & the Cavalier Poets. new ed. Hugh MacLean. (Critical Editions Ser.). 1975. 12.50 (ISBN 0-393-04387-8); pap. 6.95x (ISBN 0-393-09308-5). Norton.

Ben Jonson & the Lucianic Tradition. D. Duncan. LC 78-18093. 1979. 29.95 (ISBN 0-521-22359-8). Cambridge U Pr.

Ben Jonson's Art. Esther C. Dunn. 159p. 1980. Repr. of 1925 ed. lib. bdg. 30.00 (ISBN 0-8495-1122-4). Arden Lib.

Ben Jonson's "Dotages" A Reconsideration of the Late Plays. Larry S. Champion. LC 67-29338. 168p. 1967. 10.00x (ISBN 0-8131-1143-9). U Pr of Ky.

Ben Lilly Legend. J. Frank Dobie. (Illus.). 253p. 1981. pap. 6.95x (ISBN 0-292-70728-2). U of Tex Pr.

Ben Nicholson. LC 74-91553. (Tate Gallery Ser.). (Illus.). 1977. 5.75 (ISBN 0-8120-5174-2). Barron.

Ben on the Ski Trail. Leonard Shortall. (Illus.). (ps-3). 1965. 7.25 o.p. (ISBN 0-688-31081-8). Morrow.

Ben Retallick. E. V. Thompson. 406p. 1981. 12.95 (ISBN 0-312-07517-0). St Martin.

Ben Shahn: His Graphic Art. James T. Soby. LC 57-12840. 1957. 25.00 o.s.i. (ISBN 0-8076-0053-9). Braziller.

Ben Shahn: Paintings. James T. Soby. LC 63-18187. 1963. 35.00 o.p. (ISBN 0-8076-0241-8). Braziller.

Benares: The Sacred City of the Hindus. M. A. Sherring. LC 75-906423. 1975. Repr. 17.00x o.p. (ISBN 0-88386-668-4). South Asia Bks.

Bench & Bar of the Commonwealth of Massachusetts, 2 vols. William Davis. (American Constitutional & Legal History Ser). 1299p. 1974. Repr. of 1895 ed. Set. lib. bdg. 115.00 (ISBN 0-306-70612-1). Da Capo.

Bench Woodwork. Feirer. (gr. 7-9). 1978. text ed. 11.16 (ISBN 0-87002-201-6); student guide 3.00 (ISBN 0-87002-203-2). Bennett IL.

Benchley Lost & Found: Thirty-Nine. Robert Benchley. (Illus.). 6.75 o.p. (ISBN 0-8446-0484-4). Peter Smith.

Benchmark & Blaze: The Emergence of William Everson. Ed. by Lee Bartlett. LC 78-2137. 1979. lib. bdg. 13.50 (ISBN 0-8108-1198-7). Scarecrow.

Benchwarmers: The Private World of the Powerful Federal Judges. Joseph C. Goulden. 416p. 1976. pap. 1.95 o.p. (ISBN 0-345-24852-X). Ballantine.

Benchwork. 2nd ed. Robert G. Dixon. LC 80-66607. (Machine Trades - Machine Shop Ser.). (Illus.). 208p. 1981. pap. text ed. 7.40 (ISBN 0-8273-1743-3); instr's. guide 1.10 (ISBN 0-8273-1744-1). Delmar.

Bend, the Lip, the Kid: Real Life Stories. Jaimy Gordon. LC 78-15579. 1978. pap. 4.00 (ISBN 0-915342-25-1). SUN.

Bend with the Wind. Elisabeth Moore. LC 78-31664. Date not set. 12.95 (ISBN 0-87949-142-6). Ashley Bks.

Bendigo Pottery. Paul A. Scholes. (Illus.). 281p. 1980. 34.95 (4040, Pub. by Lowden Pub Co Australia). Bks Australia.

Bendigo Shafter. Louis L'Amour. 1980. lib. bdg. 15.95 (ISBN 0-8161-3144-9, Large Print Bks). G K Hall.

Beneath the Eagle's Wings: Americans in Occupied Japan. John C. Perry. LC 80-15331. (Illus.). 256p. 1980. 12.95 (ISBN 0-396-07876-1). Dodd.

Beneath the Singing Pines. Louise J. Walker. (Illus.). (gr. 6-10). 1967. 7.95 (ISBN 0-910726-80-9). Hillsdale Educ.

Beneath the Underdog. Charles Mingus. 1980. pap. 3.95 (ISBN 0-14-003880-9). Penguin.

Beneath the Wheel. Hermann Hesse. Tr. by Michael Roloff from Ger. 192p. 1968. pap. 3.95 (ISBN 0-374-50748-1, N360). FS&G.

Beneath Your Feet. Seymour Simon. LC 76-57066. (Illus.). (gr. 2-4). 1977. 5.95 o.s.i. (ISBN 0-8027-6293-X); PLB 5.85 (ISBN 0-8027-6294-8). Walker & Co.

Benedetto Croce's Poetry & Literature: An Introduction to the Criticism & History of Poetry & Literature. Benedetto Croce. Tr. & intro. by Giovanni Gullace. LC 80-19511. 1981. 24.95x (ISBN 0-8093-0982-3). S Ill U Pr.

Benedict Arnold: Traitor of the Revolution. Ronald Syme. (Illus.). (gr. 5-9). 1970. PLB 6.24 (ISBN 0-688-31083-4). Morrow.

Benedict De Spinoza. Henry E. Allison. LC 75-2059. (World Authors Ser.: No. 351). 1975. lib. bdg. 12.50 (ISBN 0-8057-2853-8). Twayne.

Benedict Kiely. Grace Eckley. LC 72-187616. (English Authors Ser.: No. 145). lib. bdg. 10.95 (ISBN 0-8057-1304-2). Twayne.

Benedictines in Britain. Turner & Rogers. Date not set. 12.95 (ISBN 0-8076-0992-7). Braziller.

Benedictus' Art Deco Designs in Color. Edouard Benedictus. (Illus.). 1980. pap. 6.00 (ISBN 0-486-23971-3). Dover.

Benedikt. (Profile Edition Ser.). (Illus.). 1978. pap. 4.00 o.p. (ISBN 0-931238-02-1); pap. 8.00 signed ed. o.p. (ISBN 0-931238-03-X). Grilled Flowers Pr.

Benefaction or Bondage? Social Policy & the Aged. M. Leigh Rooke & C. Ray Wingrove. LC 79-5437. 1980. pap. text ed. 7.50 (ISBN 0-8191-0885-5); text ed. 15.25 (ISBN 0-8191-1037-X). U Pr of Amer.

Beneficial Modifications of the Marine Environment. National Academy of Sciences, Division of Earth Sciences. (Illus.). 128p. 1972. pap. 4.75 (ISBN 0-309-02034-4). Natl Acad Pr.

Beneficiation of Mineral Fines. Ed. by P. Somasundaran & N. Arbiter. LC 79-91945. (Illus.). 406p. (Orig.). 1979. pap. text ed. 21.00x (ISBN 0-89520-259-X). Soc Mining Eng.

Benefit-Cost Analysis. Lee G. Anderson & Russell F. Settle. LC 77-3108. (Illus.). 1977. 16.95 (ISBN 0-669-01465-6). Lexington Bks.

Benefit-Cost Analysis for Program Evaluation. Mark S. Thompson. LC 80-13110. (Illus.). 310p. 1980. 20.00 (ISBN 0-8039-1483-0); pap. 9.95 (ISBN 0-8039-1484-9). Sage.

Benefit-Cost Analysis of Data Used to Allocate Funds. B. P. Spencer. (Lecture Notes in Statistics: Vol. 3). 296p. 1980. pap. 16.80 (ISBN 0-387-90511-1). Springer-Verlag.

Benefit-Cost Analysis of Government Programs. Edward M. Gramlich. (Illus.). 304p. 1981. text ed. 15.95 (ISBN 0-13-074757-2). P-H.

Benefit Plans in American Colleges. William C. Greenough & Francis P. King. LC 77-79995. 1969. 22.50x (ISBN 0-231-03287-0); pap. 9.00x (ISBN 0-231-08632-6). Columbia U Pr.

Benefits in Development for Less Developed Countries Under the EEC's Generalized Scheme of Preferences & Yaounde Agreement. Delsie Gandia. LC 79-91005. 160p. 1980. text ed. 20.00 (ISBN 0-916672-47-6). Allanheld.

Benefits of Health & Safety Regulation. Public Interest Economics Foundation. Ed. by Allen R. Ferguson & Judith Behn. 1981. write for info. (ISBN 0-88410-721-3). Ballinger Pub.

Benefits of Old Age: Social Welfare Policies for the Elderly. Elizabeth A. Kutza. LC 80-24241. 192p. 1981. lib. bdg. 18.00 (ISBN 0-226-46565-9); pap. 5.95 (ISBN 0-226-46566-7). U of Chicago Pr.

Benefits of Psychotherapy. Mary L. Smith et al. LC 80-11610. 320p. 1981. text ed. 22.50x (ISBN 0-8018-2352-8). Johns Hopkins.

Benevolent Man; or, the History of Mr. Belville, 1775, 2 vols. in 1. Alexander Bicknell. Ed. by Michael F. Shugrue. (Flowering of the Novel, 1740-1775 Ser: Vol. 108). 1974. lib. bdg. 50.00 (ISBN 0-8240-1207-0). Garland Pub.

Bengal: The Nationalist Movement, 1876-1940. Leonard Gordon. 1974. 20.00x (ISBN 0-231-03753-8). Columbia U Pr.

Bengali Poems on Calcutta. Samir Dasgupta. 1973. 15.00 (ISBN 0-88253-324-X); pap. text ed. 6.75 (ISBN 0-88253-795-4). Ind-US Inc.

Benign Enlargement of the Prostate. K. E. Shuttleworth et al. (Illus.). 1974. 16.95x (ISBN 0-433-30270-4). Intl Ideas.

Benin. K. Elliott. (Cambridge Introduction to the History of Mankind Ser.). 1973. 3.95 (ISBN 0-521-08028-2). Cambridge U Pr.

Benin & the Europeans, Fourteen Eighty-Five to Eighteen Ninety-Seven. Alan Ryder. LC 68-54523. (Ibadan History Ser). 1969. text ed. 11.25x (ISBN 0-582-64514-X). Humanities.

Benin Under British Administration,1897-1938: The Impact of Colonial Rule on an African Kingdom. Philip A. Igfabe. (Ibadan History Ser.). 1978. text ed. 36.50x (ISBN 0-391-00564-2). Humanities.

Beningfield's Countryside. Gordon Beningfield. LC 80-5366. 144p. 1980. 19.95 (ISBN 0-670-15815-1, Studio). Viking Pr.

Benito Mussolini: A Dictator Dies. G. C. Skipper. LC 80-25345. (World at War Ser.). (Illus.). 48p. (gr. 3-8). 1981. PLB 7.95 (ISBN 0-516-04790-6). Childrens.

Benito Perez Galdos. Walter T. Pattison. (World Authors Ser.: Spain: No. 341). 184p. 1975. lib. bdg. 12.50 (ISBN 0-8057-2689-6). Twayne.

Benito Perez Galdos: A Selective Annotated Bibliography. Compiled by Hensley C. Woodbridge. LC 75-2045. 333p. 1975. 15.00 (ISBN 0-8108-0800-5). Scarecrow.

Benito Perez Galdos: Tormento. Ed. by Eamon J. Rodgers. 1976. text ed. 27.00 (ISBN 0-08-018089-2); pap. text ed. 14.00 (ISBN 0-08-018088-4). Pergamon.

Benito Perez Galdos: Torquemada en la Hoguera. Ed. by J. L. Brooks. 100p. 1973. text ed. 5.90 (ISBN 0-08-016917-1); pap. text ed. 4.10 (ISBN 0-08-016918-X). Pergamon.

Benjamin & the Bible Donkies. Beverly Amstutz. (Illus.). 1981. pap. 2.50 (ISBN 0-937836-03-6). Precious Res.

Benjamin Banneker. (Black History Illustrated: No. 4). (Illus.). 1968. pap. 0.59 o.p. (ISBN 0-685-78149-6). Guild Bks.

Benjamin Britten, Nineteen Thirteen to Nineteen Seventy-Six: Pictures from A Life. Donald Mitchell. (Encore Edition). (Illus.). 1979. 8.95 (ISBN 0-684-16550-3, ScribT). Scribner.

Benjamin Budge & Barnaby Ball. Florence P. Heide. (Illus.). (gr. k-3). 1970. pap. 1.25 (ISBN 0-590-02353-5, Schol Pap); pap. 3.50 bk. & record (ISBN 0-590-04397-8). Schol Bk Serv.

Benjamin Constant. John Cruickshank. (World Authors Ser.: France: No. 297). 1974. lib. bdg. 12.50 (ISBN 0-8057-2242-4). Twayne.

Benjamin Disraeli. Paul Bloomfield. Ed. by Bonamy Dobree et al. Bd. with William Makepeace Thackeray. Laurence A. Brander; Charles Dickens. K. J. Fielding; Anthony Trollope. Hugh S. Davies. LC 63-63096. (British Writers & Their Work Ser: Vol. 9). 1965. pap. 3.25x (ISBN 0-8032-5659-0, BB 452, Bison). U of Nebr Pr.

Benjamin Disraeli: A List of Writings by & About Him. R. W. Stewart. LC 72-3906. (Author Bibliographies Ser.: No. 7). 1972. 10.00 (ISBN 0-8108-0489-1). Scarecrow.

Benjamin Disraeli in Spain & Malta. Donald Sultana. (Salzburg Studies in English Literature, Romantic Reassessment Ser.: No. 51). (Illus.). 102p. 1975. pap. text ed. 25.00x (ISBN 0-391-01541-9). Humanities.

Benjamin Disraeli: Prime Minister Extraordinary. Neil Grant. LC 69-11143. (Biography Ser.). (Illus.). (gr. 7 up). 1969. PLB 5.90 o.p. (ISBN 0-531-00867-3). Watts.

Benjamin Franklin. John B. McMaster. LC 80-23681. (American Men & Women of Letters Ser.). 300p. 1980. pap. 4.95 (ISBN 0-87754-161-2). Chelsea Hse.

Benjamin Franklin. Raymond J. Seeger. LC 73-7981. 200p. 1973. 16.50 (ISBN 0-08-017648-8). Pergamon.

Benjamin Franklin. Carl C. Van Doren. LC 73-8566. (Illus.). 845p. 1973. Repr. of 1938 ed. lib. bdg. 47.25x (ISBN 0-8371-6964-X, VABF). Greenwood.

Benjamin Franklin: A Biography in His Own Words. Benjamin T. Fleming. (Founding Fathers Ser.). (Illus.). 416p. (YA) 1972. 16.95 o.s.i. (ISBN 0-06-011286-7, HarpT). Har-Row.

Benjamin Franklin: A Profile. Esmond Wright. 227p. 1970. pap. 6.95 o.p. (ISBN 0-8090-4657-1). Hill & Wang.

Benjamin Franklin: An Autobiographical Portrait. Ed. by Alfred Tamarin. LC 78-78091. (Illus.). (gr. 7 up). 1969. 6.50g o.s.i. (ISBN 0-02-788790-1). Macmillan.

Benjamin Franklin & Jonathan Edwards. Carl Van Doren. 1979. Repr. of 1920 ed. lib. bdg. 20.00 (ISBN 0-8495-5525-6). Arden Lib.

Benjamin Franklin Autobiography & Selections from his Other Writings. Benjamin Franklin. Ed. by Herbert W. Schneider. LC 52-14644. pap. 5.50 (ISBN 0-672-60003-X, AHS2). Bobbs.

Benjamin Franklin on Education. Ed. by John H. Best. LC 62-20697. (Orig.). 1962. text ed. 8.75 (ISBN 0-8077-1080-6); pap. text ed. 4.00x (ISBN 0-8077-1077-6). Tchrs Coll.

Benjamin Franklin, Printer. John C. Oswald. LC 74-3020. 1974. Repr. of 1917 ed. 24.00 (ISBN 0-8103-3642-1). Gale.

Benjamin Helm Bristow: Border State Politician. Ross A. Webb. LC 74-80089. (Illus.). 384p. 1969. 14.50x (ISBN 0-8131-1182-X). U Pr of Ky.

Benjamin of Nazareth. Mary Ranger. (Starlight Ser.). (Illus.). (gr. 5-8). 1981. pap. 1.95 (ISBN 0-570-03615-1, 39-1103). Concordia.

Benjamin Penhallow Shillaber. John Q. Reed. (U. S. Authors Ser.: No. 209). lib. bdg. 10.95 (ISBN 0-8057-0664-X). Twayne.

Benjamin Peret. J. H. Matthews. LC 74-30229. (World Authors Ser.: France: No. 359). 1975. lib. bdg. 12.50 (ISBN 0-8057-2691-8). Twayne.

Benjamin the Waggoner by William Wordsworth. William Wordsworth. Ed. by Paul Betz. (Illus.). 336p. 1981. 35.00 (ISBN 0-8014-1270-6). Cornell U Pr.

Benjamin Tompson, Colonial Bard: A Critical Edition. Ed. by Peter White. LC 79-21367. (Illus.). 230p. 1980. text ed. 16.75x (ISBN 0-271-00250-6). Pa St U Pr.

Benjamin Wisner Bacon: Pioneer in American Biblical Criticism. Roy A. Harrisville. LC 76-16178. (Society of Biblical Literature. Studies in Biblical Scholarship). 1976. pap. 7.50 (ISBN 0-89130-110-0, 061102). Scholars Pr Ca.

Benjamin's Open Day. Jane White. 192p. 1979. 16.95 (ISBN 0-241-89978-8, Pub. by Hamish Hamilton England). David & Charles.

Benji. Allison Thomas. (Orig.). (gr. 5-9). 1975. pap. 1.75 (ISBN 0-515-05749-5). Jove Pubns.

Benji, Fastest Dog in the West. Gina Ingoglie. (Big Picture Book Ser.). (Illus.). (gr. k-3). 1979. PLB 7.62 (ISBN 0-307-10826-0, Golden Pr). Western Pub.

Benji the Detective. Jean Lewis. (Tell-a-Tale Readers). (Illus.). (gr. k-3). PLB 4.77 (ISBN 0-307-68640-X, Whitman). Western Pub.

Benmussa Directs. Helene Cixous & Simone Benmussa. 1981. pap. 4.75 (ISBN 0-7145-3764-0). Riverrun NY.

Bennett Cerf's Houseful of Laughter. Bennett Cerf. (Illus.). (gr. 6-9). 1963. 4.95 (ISBN 0-394-80956-4, BYR); PLB 6.99 (ISBN 0-394-90956-9). Random.

Bennett, Number Three: People in Glass Houses. Elliott Lewis. 192p. (Orig.). Date not set. pap. 1.95 (ISBN 0-523-41437-4). Pinnacle Bks.

Bennett's Welcome. Inglis Fletcher. 480p. 1980. pap. 2.75 (ISBN 0-553-13448-5). Bantam.

Benn's Press Directory 1979, 2 vols. Incl. United Kingdom: Annual. 1979. Vol. 1. 50.00 (ISBN 0-686-57722-1); Overseas: Annual. Vol. 2. 40.00 (ISBN 0-686-57723-X). 75.00 set (ISBN 0-686-57721-3, Pub. by Benn Pubns). Nichols Pub.

Benny Uncovers a Mystery. Gertrude C. Warner. Ed. by Caroline Rubin. LC 76-15222. (Boxcar Children Mysteries-Pilot Bk.). (Illus.). 128p. (gr. 3-8). 1976. PLB 6.95 (ISBN 0-8075-0644-3). A Whitman.

Benny's Nose. Mel Cebulash. (Illus.). (gr. k-3). 1972. pap. 1.25 (ISBN 0-590-09298-7, Schol Pap); pap. 3.50 bk. & record (ISBN 0-590-04352-8). Schol Bk Serv.

Benoni. William R. Hartson. 1977. 15.95 (ISBN 0-7134-0246-6, Pub. by Batsford England); pap. 12.50 (ISBN 0-7134-0247-4). David & Charles.

Ben's Trumpet. Rachel Isadora. LC 78-12885. (Illus.). (gr. k-3). 1979. 7.50 (ISBN 0-688-80194-3). Greenwillow.

Bent World. Ronald Elsdon. 200p. (Orig.). 1981. pap. 5.95 (ISBN 0-87784-834-3). Inter-Varsity.

Bentivoglio of Bologna: A Study in Despotism. Cecilia M. Ady. 1937. 11.00x o.p. (ISBN 0-19-821481-2). Oxford U Pr.

Bent's Fort. David Lavender. LC 54-7322. (Illus.). 1972. pap. 4.95 (ISBN 0-8032-5753-8, BB 545, Bison). U of Nebr Pr.

Benvenuto Cellini. 1979. 6.00 o.p. (ISBN 0-460-00051-9, Evman). Dutton.

Benzene & Its Industrial Derivatives. Ed. by Eric Hancock. LC 74-28074. 597p. 1975. 84.95 (ISBN 0-470-34780-5). Halsted Pr.

Benzene, Xylene, & Toluene in Aquatic Systems: A Review. Arthur L. Buikema, Jr. & Albert C. Hendricks. LC 80-67170. (Illus.). 69p. (Orig.). pap. 3.75 (ISBN 0-89364-038-7, API 847-86250). Am Petroleum.

Benzimidazoles & Congeneric Tricyclic Compounds, Pt. 1, Vol. 40. P. N. Preston. (Chemistry of Heterocyclic Compounds Ser.). 848p. 1981. write for info. (ISBN 0-471-03792-3, Pub. by Wiley-Interscience). Wiley.

Benzimidazoles & Congeneric Tricyclic Compounds, Vol. 40, Pt. 2. P. N. Preston. LC 80-17383. (Chemistry of Heterocyclic Compounds Ser.). 1200p. 1980. 120.00 (ISBN 0-471-03792-3, Pub. by Wiley-Interscience). Wiley.

Benzodiazepines. Ed. by S. Garattini et al. LC 78-181304. (Monograph of the Mario Negri Institute for Pharmacological Research). (Illus.). 707p. 1973. 60.00 (ISBN 0-911216-25-1). Raven.

Beobachtung und Beurteilung von Kindern und Jugendlichen. 13th ed. H. Thomae. (Psychologische Praxis: Band 15). (Illus.). vi, 90p. 1980. soft cover 7.25 (ISBN 3-8055-1526-X). S Karger.

Beowulf: A Dual Language Edition. Ed. by Howell D. Chickering, Jr. LC 75-21250. pap. 4.95 (ISBN 0-385-06213-3). Doubleday.

Beowulf: A Norton Critical Edition. new ed. Ed. by Joseph F. Tuso. Tr. by E. Talbot Donaldson. 224p. 1976. 10.00 (ISBN 0-393-04413-0); pap. text ed. 3.95x (ISBN 0-393-09225-9). Norton.

Beowulf: An Introduction. Ed. by Raymond W. Chambers. 1959. 55.00 (ISBN 0-521-04615-7). Cambridge U Pr.

Beowulf & Finnesburg Fragment: A Translation into Modern English Prose. John R. Clark-Hall. 1950. text ed. 10.50x o.p. (ISBN 0-04-829001-7). Allen Unwin.

Beowulf & Other Old English Poems. Tr. by Constance B. Hieatt. LC 67-25645. (Orig.). (gr. 9-12). 1967. pap. 3.95 (ISBN 0-672-63012-5). Odyssey Pr.

Beowulf & Sir Gawain & the Green Knight. rev ed. Tr. by G. H. Gerould. 1935. 11.95 (ISBN 0-8260-3380-6). Wiley.

Beowulf Scholarship: An Annotated Bibliography. Douglas D. Short. LC 79-7924. 353p. 1980. lib. bdg. 38.00 (ISBN 0-8240-9530-8). Garland Pub.

Beowulf, the Oldest English Epic. Beowulf. Tr. by Charles W. Kennedy. 1940. 11.95x (ISBN 0-19-500929-0). Oxford U Pr.

Bereavement: It's Psychological Aspects. new ed. Ed. by Bernard Schoenberg & Irwin Gerber. 368p. 1975. 20.00x (ISBN 0-231-03974-3). Columbia U Pr.

Bereishis-Genesis, Vol. 5. Meir Zlotowitz. (Art Scroll Tanach Ser.). 1980. 14.95 (ISBN 0-89906-358-6); pap. 11.95 (ISBN 0-89906-359-4). Mesorah Pubns.

Bereishis-Genesis: Vol. 4, Vayeitzei-Vayishlach. Meir Zlotowitz. (Art Scroll Tanach Ser.). 400p. 1979. 13.95 (ISBN 0-89906-356-X); pap. 11.25 (ISBN 0-89906-357-8). Mesorah Pubns.

Berenstain Bears Go to School. Stan Berenstain & Janice Berenstain. LC 77-79853. (Picturebacks Ser.). (Illus.). (ps-2). 1978. PLB 4.99 (ISBN 0-394-93736-8, BYR); pap. 1.25 (ISBN 0-394-83736-3). Random.

Beresheet: A Kindergarten Guide. Helen Bessler. LC 68-30816. (Orig.). 1969. pap. text ed. 4.50 (ISBN 0-8074-0130-7, 244310). UAHC.

Berger Building Cost File Unit Prices Central Edition, 1980. Building Cost File. 1980. pap., text ed. 27.95 (ISBN 0-686-63069-6). Van Nos Reinhold.

Berger Building Cost File Unit Prices Eastern Edition, 1980. Building Cost File. 1980. pap. text ed. 27.95 (ISBN 0-686-63070-X). Van Nos Reinhold.

Berger Building Cost File Unit Prices Southern Edition, 1980. Building Cost File. 1980. pap. text ed. 27.95 (ISBN 0-686-63071-8). Van Nos Reinhold.

Berger Building Cost File Unit Prices Western Edition, 1980. Building Cost File. 1980. pap. text ed. 27.95 (ISBN 0-686-63072-6). Van Nos Reinhold.

Berger Building Cost File 1981: General Construction Trades with Comparative Building Systems & Costs, 4 editions, Vol. 1. Compiled by Building Cost File. Incl. Eastern Edition (ISBN 0-442-21240-2); Western Edition (ISBN 0-442-21238-0); Central Edition (ISBN 0-442-21237-2); Southern Edition (ISBN 0-442-21236-4). 210p. 1980. pap. text ed. 34.95 ea. Van Nos Reinhold.

Berger Building Cost File 1981: Mechanical & Electrical Trades with Comparative Building Systems Costs, 4 editions, Vol. II. Compiled by Building Cost File. Incl. Eastern Edition (ISBN 0-442-21235-6); Western Edition (ISBN 0-442-21234-8); Central Edition (ISBN 0-442-21232-1); Southern Edition (ISBN 0-442-21231-3). 105p. 1980. pap. text ed. 24.95 ea. Van Nos Reinhold.

Berggasse Nineteen: Sigmund Freud's Home & Offices, Vienna, 1938; the Photographs of Edmund Engelman. Edmund Engelman. LC 80-23056. 1981. pap. 15.00 (ISBN 0-226-20847-8). U of Chicago Pr.

Bergkristall und Andere Erzaehlungen. Adalbert Stifter. (Insel Taschenbuecher: It 438). 325p. (Ger.). 1980. pap. text ed. 5.85 (ISBN 3-458-32138-1, Pub. by Insel Verlag Germany). Suhrkamp.

Bergschrund. Robert Bringhurst. (Sono Nis Ser.). 104p. 1975. 10.95 o.s.i. (ISBN 0-913600-40-7). Kanchenjunga Pr.

Bergschrund. Robert Bringhurst. (Sono Nis Ser). (Illus.). 104p. 1975. pap. 5.95 (ISBN 0-913600-50-4). Kanchenjunga Pr.

Bergson and His Influence. A. E. Pilkington. LC 75-22555. 300p. 1976. 45.00 (ISBN 0-521-20971-4). Cambridge U Pr.

Bergson & the Evolution of Physics. Ed. & tr. by P. A. Gunter. LC 77-77844. 1969. 19.50x (ISBN 0-87049-092-3). U of Tenn Pr.

Bergsteigen: Basic Rock Climbing. R. C. Aleith. LC 75-5853. (Illus.). 192p. 1975 (ISBN 0-684-15389-0, ScribT). pap. 6.95 (ISBN 0-684-14203-1, SL578, ScribT). Scribner.

Bering Sea Oceanography: An Update Nineteen Seventy-Two to Nineteen Seventy-Four. Ed. by Y. Takenouti & D. W. Hood. 12.00 (ISBN 0-914500-06-6). U of AK Inst Marine.
Berkeley. Harry M. Bracken. LC 74-15569. 176p. 1975. 15.95 (ISBN 0-312-07595-2). St Martin.
Berkeley. George Pitcher. (Arguments of the Philosophers Ser.). 1977. 22.50 (ISBN 0-7100-8685-7). Routledge & Kegan.
Berkeley & Malebranche: A Study in the Origins of Berkeley's Thought. A. A. Luce. 1934. 24.50x (ISBN 0-19-824319-7). Oxford U Pr.
Berkeley Co-Op Food Book. Ed. by Helen Black. (Orig.). 1980. pap. 7.95 (ISBN 0-915950-43-X). Bull Pub.
Berkeley-Philosophical Works: Including the Works on Vision. George Berkeley. (Rowman & Littlefield University Library). 1980. pap. 8.75x (ISBN 0-8476-6231-4). Rowman.
Berkeley Poets Cooperative Anthology, 1970-1980. Ed. by Berkeley Poets Cooperative. 300p. 1980. pap. 6.95 (ISBN 0-917658-12-4). Berkeley Poets.
Berkeley Police Story. Alfred E. Parker. (Illus.). 308p. 1972. 29.50 (ISBN 0-398-02373-5). C C Thomas.
Berkley Showcase, Vol. 4. Ed. by Victoria Schochet & John Silbersack. 1981. pap. 2.25 (ISBN 0-425-04804-7). Berkley Pub.
Berkley Showcase: New Writings in Science Fiction, Vol. II. Ed. by Victoria Schochet & John Silbersack. (Orig.). 1980. pap. 2.25 (ISBN 0-425-04553-6). Berkley Pub.
Berkshire. Ed. by Philip Morgan. (Domesday Bk.: Vol. 5). (Illus.). 160p. 1979. 15.00x (ISBN 0-8476-3143-5). Rowman.
Berkshire Trails for Walking & Ski Touring. Whit Griswold. LC 79-4901. (Illus.). 224p. 1978. lib. bdg. 10.25 o.p. (ISBN 0-914788-13-2). East Woods.
Berlese, Acari Myriopoda et Scorpiones Eighteen Hundred Eighty-Two - Nineteen Hundred Three, 12 vols. L. Van Der Hammen. 4616p. 1980. Set. 315.00 (ISBN 90-6193-603-9). Kluwer Boston.
Berlin. Karl Baedeker. 1966. 6.95 o.s.i. (ISBN 0-02-504750-7). Macmillan.
Berlin. new ed. Frederic V. Grunfeld & Time-Life Editors. (Great Cities Ser.). (Illus.). 1977. 14.95 (ISBN 0-8094-2282-4). Time-Life.
Berlin. Frederick V. Grunfeld. (The Great Cities Ser.). (Illus.). (gr. 6 up). 1977. PLB 14.94 (ISBN 0-8094-2283-2, Pub by Time-Life). Silver.
Berlin: Contemporary Writing from Berlin. Ed. by Mitch Cohen. LC 77-642342. (Rockbottom Specials Ser.). (Illus., Eng. & Ger.). Date not set. 15.00 o.p. (ISBN 0-930012-23-2); pap. 6.00 o.p. (ISBN 0-930012-22-4). Mudborn. Postponed.
Berlin-Frage Nineteen Forty-Nine to Nineteen Fifty-Five: Verhandlungsgrundlagen und Eindaemmungspolitik. Dennis L. Bark. (Veroeffentlichungen der Historischen Kommission Zu Berlin Ser.: Vol. 36). xiv, 544p. 1972. 72.80x (ISBN 3-11-003639-8). De Gruyter.
Berlin in der Weltpolitik 1945-1970. Hans Herzfeld. (Veroeffentlichungen der Historischen Kommission zu Berlin, Vol. 38). xxii, 666p. (Ger.). 1973. 72.95 (ISBN 3-11-003890-0). De Gruyter.
Berlin Novels of Theodor Fontane. Henry Garland. 296p. 1980. 42.00 (ISBN 0-19-815765-7). Oxford U Pr.
Berlin Olympics, Nineteen Thirty-Six: Black American Athletes Counter Nazi Propaganda. James P. Barry. LC 74-20173. (World Focus Bks). (Illus.). 88p. (gr. 7 up). 1975. PLB 4.90 o.p. (ISBN 0-531-01090-2). Watts.
Berlin Philharmonic from Bulow to Karajan: Home & History of a World-Famous Orchestra. Wolfgang Stresemann. (Illus., Orig.). pap. 15.00x (ISBN 3-8777-6518-1). Heinman.
Berlin Police Force in the Weimar Republic, 1918-1933. Liang, Hsi-huey. LC 74-85452. (Illus.). 1970. 20.00x (ISBN 0-520-01603-3). U of Cal Pr.
Berlin Stories. Christopher Isherwood. LC 79-17316. 1979. Repr. of 1946 ed. lib. bdg. 12.50x (ISBN 0-8376-0449-4). Bentley.
Berliner Unternehmer waehrend der fruehen Industrialisierung: Herkunft, sozialer Status und politischer Einfluss. Hartmut Kaelble. (Veroeffentlichungen der Historischen Kommission zu Berlin 40). xii, 302p. (Ger.). 1972. 42.00x (ISBN 3-11-003873-0). De Gruyter.
Berlioz & the Romantic Century, 2 vols. 3rd ed. Jacques Barzun. LC 77-97504. (Illus.). 1969. Set. 50.00x (ISBN 0-231-03135-1). Columbia U Pr.
Berlioz Style. Brian Primmer. 1973. 16.50x (ISBN 0-19-713136-0). Oxford U Pr.
Berlioz Symphonie Fantastique. Hector Berlioz. Ed. by Edward T. Cone. (Critical Scores Ser). 1971. pap. 5.95x (ISBN 0-393-09926-1). Norton.
Bermuda Petrel: The Bird That Would Not Die. Francine Jacobs. LC 80-20466. (Illus.). 40p. (gr. k-3). 1981. 7.95 (ISBN 0-688-00240-4); PLB 7.63 (ISBN 0-688-00244-7). Morrow.
Bermuda Triangle. Jim Collins. LC 77-21808. (Great Unsolved Mysteries Ser.). (Illus.). (gr. 4-5). 1977. PLB 9.65 (ISBN 0-8172-1050-4). Raintree Pubs.
Bermuda Triangle & Other Mysteries of Nature. Dolan. (Triumph Bks.). 1980. PLB 6.90 (ISBN 0-531-04113-1, A23). Watts.
Bermuda Triangle Mystery Solved. Lawrence D. Kusche. 1975. pap. 2.50 (ISBN 0-446-91489-4). Warner Bks.
Bermuda's Antique Furniture & Silver. Bryden B. Hyde. LC 76-157116. (Illus.). 1971. 15.00x (ISBN 0-938420-03-8). Md Hist.
Bernard-Lazare. Nelly Wilson. LC 77-82524. 1979. 42.00 (ISBN 0-521-21802-0). Cambridge U Pr.
Bernard Leach: A Potter's Work. LC 73-92991. 305p. 1967. 14.75 (ISBN 0-87011-226-0). Kodansha.
Bernard Malamud. Sheldon J. Hershinow. LC 79-4877. (Modern Literature Ser.). 160p. 1980. 10.95 (ISBN 0-8044-2377-6). Ungar.
Bernard Malamud. Sidney Richman. (U. S. Authors Ser.: No. 109). 1966. lib. bdg. 9.95 (ISBN 0-8057-0472-8). Twayne.
Bernard Mandeville. Richard I. Cook. (English Authors Ser.: No. 170). 1974. lib. bdg. 12.50 (ISBN 0-8057-1371-9). Twayne.
Bernard of Clairvaux on the Song of Songs, Vol. I. Tr. by Kilian Walsh. (Cistercian Fathers Er.: No. 4). pap. 4.00 (ISBN 0-87907-104-4). Cistercian Pubns.
Bernard of Clairvaux: Sermons I on Conversations; Lenten Sermons on the Psalm "He Who Dwells". Bernard Of Clairvaux. Tr. by Marie-Bernard Said. (Cistercian Fathers Ser.: No. 25). (Lat.). 1981. price not set (ISBN 0-87907-125-7); pap. price not set (ISBN 0-87907-925-8). Cistercian Pubns.
Bernard of Clairvaux: Sermons on the Song of Songs, Vol. III. Tr. by Kilian Walsh & Irene Edmonds. (Cistercian Fathers Ser.: No. 31). 1979. 15.95; pap. 5.00 (ISBN 0-87907-931-2). Cistercian Pubns.
Bernard of Clairvaux: The Irishman. Tr. by Robert T. Mayer. LC 78-768. (Cistercian Fathers Ser.). 1978. 7.95 (ISBN 0-685-87078-2); pap. 4.00 (ISBN 0-87907-910-X). Cistercian Pubns.
Bernard of Clairvaux, Treatises III: On Grace & Free Choice, in Praise of the New Knighthood. Tr. by Daniel O'Donovan. (Cistercian Studies Ser.: No. 3). 1977. 10.95 (ISBN 0-87907-119-2); pap. 4.95 (ISBN 0-87907-719-0). Cistercian Pubns.
Bernard Shaw Companion. Michael Hardwick & Mollie Hardwick. LC 73-86599. 193p. 1974. 6.50 o.p. (ISBN 0-312-07665-7). St Martin.
Bernard Shaw, Director. Bernard F. Dukore. LC 79-11727. (Illus.). 199p. 1971. 9.50 o.p. (ISBN 0-295-95083-8). U of Wash Pr.
Bernard Shaw: Platform & Pulpit. Ed. by Dan-Laurence. 1979. 9.95x (ISBN 0-8464-0088-X). Beekman Pubs.
Bernard Shaw: The Darker Side. Arnold Silver. LC 79-92454. (Illus.). 384p. 1981. text ed. 25.00x (ISBN 0-8047-1091-0). Stanford U Pr.
Bernard Shaw: The Matter with Ireland. Ed. by Dan Laurence. 1979. 9.95x (ISBN 0-8464-0087-1). Beekman Pubs.
Bernard Shaw's Marxian Romance. Paul A. Hummert. LC 75-144815. 1973. 13.95x (ISBN 0-8032-0774-3). U of Nebr Pr.
Bernard Shaw's Nondramatic Literary Criticism. Bernard Shaw. Ed. by Stanley Weintraub. LC 70-149739. (Regents Critics Ser). xxviii, 246p. 1972. 12.50x (ISBN 0-8032-0466-3); pap. 3.95x (ISBN 0-8032-5466-0, BB 414, Bison). U of Nebr Pr.
Bernard Shaw's Plays: Major Barbara, Heartbreak House, Saint Joan, Too Good to Be True. George B. Shaw. Ed. by Warren S. Smith. (Critical Editions Ser). 1970-71. pap. text ed. 5.95x (ISBN 0-393-09942-3). Norton.
Bernard Wolfe. Carolyn Geduld. LC 78-187612. (U. S. Authors Ser.: No. 211). lib. bdg. 10.95 (ISBN 0-8057-0832-4). Twayne.
Bernardo Bertolucci's Last Tango in Paris. Bernardo Bertolucci & Franco Arcalli. (Illus.). 256p. 1974. 7.95 o.p. (ISBN 0-440-02041-7). Delacorte.
Bernart Von Ventadorn. Bernart De Ventadorn. LC 80-2176. 1981. Repr. of 1915 ed. 49.50 (ISBN 0-404-19004-9). AMS Pr.
Bernhard Eduard Fernow: A Story of North American Forestry. Andrew D. Rodgers, 3rd. 1969. Repr. of 1951 ed. 13.95 o.s.i. (ISBN 0-02-851090-9). Hafner.
Bernheim's New Studies in Hypnotism. Tr. by Richard S. Sandor. 1980. 27.50 (ISBN 0-8236-0496-9). Intl Univs Pr.
Bernice Myers' Book of Giggles. Myers. (ps-3). 1980. pap. 1.25 (ISBN 0-590-30067-9, Schol Pap). Schol Bk Serv.
Bernini. Howard Hibbard. (Illus., Orig.). 1966. pap. 5.95 (ISBN 0-14-020701-5, Pelican). Penguin.
Bernini & the Unity of the Visual Arts, 2 vols. Irving Lavin. (Illus.). 498p. 1980. text ed. 89.00x (ISBN 0-19-520184-1). Oxford U Pr.
Bernzomatic Torch Tips. Robert Brightman. 6.95 (ISBN 0-916752-16-X). Green Hill.
Berry Book: The Illustrated Home Gardener's Guide to Growing & Using Over 50 Kinds & 300 Varieties of Berries from Strawberries, Blueberries & Raspberries to Currants, Dewberries, & Gooseberries. Robert Hendrickson. LC 78-22326. (Illus.). 192p. 1981. 9.95 (ISBN 0-385-13589-0). Doubleday.
Berry Cookbook. Kyle D. Fulwiler. 120p. 1981. pap. 5.95 (ISBN 0-914718-59-2). Pacific Search.
Berryhill. Barbara C. Bennett. (Orig.). 1979. pap. 1.95 (ISBN 0-686-68907-0). Manor Bks.
Berry's Book of How It Works. Roland Berry. 1976. 5.95 (ISBN 0-7136-1585-0). Transatlantic.
Berserker. Frank Spiering. 256p. 1981. pap. 2.75 (ISBN 0-515-05401-1). Jove Pubns.
Bersognian Philosophy & Thomism. Jacques Maritain. 1955. 6.00 o.p. (ISBN 0-8022-1057-0). Philos Lib.
Berta Hart Nance: A Brand of Innocence. 1st ed. Elsa M. Turner. (Illus.). 248p. 1974. 15.00 o.p. (ISBN 0-89015-059-1). Nortex Pr.
Bertelsmann Lexikon, 10 vols. (Ger.). 1972-1976. Set. 720.00 (ISBN 0-8277-3001-2). Maxwell Sci Intl.
Berthold Wolpe. Paul Atterbury. (Illus.). 96p. 1981. 22.00 (ISBN 0-571-11655-8, Pub. by Faber & Faber). Merrimack Bk Serv.
Bertolt Brecht. Martin Esslin. LC 74-76246. (Columbia Essays on Modern Writers Ser.: No. 42). 48p. 1969. pap. 2.00 (ISBN 0-231-02962-4, MW42). Columbia U Pr.
Bertolt Brecht. Willy Haas. LC 68-31450. (Modern Literature Ser.). 1970. 10.95 (ISBN 0-8044-2323-7); pap. 3.45 (ISBN 0-8044-6237-2). Ungar.
Bertolt Brecht. Claude Hill. (World Authors Ser.: Germany: No. 331). 1975. lib. bdg. 12.50 (ISBN 0-8057-2179-7). Twayne.
Bertolt Brecht Gesammelte Prosa in Vier Baenden: Dreigroschenroman, Vol. 3. Bertolt Brecht. (Edition Suhrkamp: Bd. 184). (Ger.). 1980. pap. text ed. 4.55 (ISBN 3-518-10184-6, Pub. by Insel Verlag Germany). Suhrkamp.
Bertolt Brecht, Gesammelte Prosa in Vier Baenden: Die Geschafte Des Herrn Julius Caesar, Fluechtlingsgesprache, Register. Bertolt Brecht. (Edition Suhrkamp: 185). (Ger.). 1980. pap. text ed. 4.55 (ISBN 3-518-10185-4, Pub. by Insel Verlag Germany). Suhrkamp.
Bertolt Brecht, Gesammelte Prosa in Vier Baenden: Geschichten Vom Herrn Keuner Me-Ti - Buch der Wendungen der Tui-Roman, Vol. 2. Bertolt Brecht. (Edition Suhrkamp: 183). (Ger.). 1980. pap. text ed. 4.55 (ISBN 3-518-10183-8, Pub. by Insel Verlag Germany). Suhrkamp.
Bertolt Brecht: Gesammelte Prosa in Vier Baenden, Vol. 1. Bertolt Brecht. (Edition Suhrkamp: 182). (Ger.). 1980. pap. text ed. 4.55 (ISBN 3-518-10182-X, Pub. by Insel Verlag Germany). Suhrkamp.
Bertolt Brecht in America. James K. Lyon. LC 80-7543. (Illus.). 428p. 1980. 19.75 (ISBN 0-691-06443-1). Princeton U Pr.
Bertolt Brecht's Berlin: A Scrapbook of the Twenties. Wolf Von Eckardt & Sander Gilman. LC 73-9153. 1977. pap. 5.95 (ISBN 0-385-12363-9, Anch). Doubleday.
Bertram, a Poetical Tale, Repr. Of 1814. Samuel E. Brydges & Edward Quillinan. Bd. with Occasional Poems, Written in the Year 1811. Repr. of 1814 ed; Select Poems. Repr. of 1814 ed; Five Sonnets Addressed to Wootton, the Spot of the Author's Nativity. Repr. of 1819 ed; Edward Quillian: Dunluce Castle, a Poem, 4 pts. Repr. of 1814 ed. LC 75-31171. (Romantic Context Ser.: Poetry 1789-1830: Vol. 25). 1978. lib. bdg. 47.00 (ISBN 0-8240-2124-X). Garland Pub.
Bertram Family. Elizabeth Charles. Ed. by Robert L. Wolff. LC 75-494. (Victorian Fiction Ser.). 1975. Repr. of 1876 ed. lib. bdg. 66.00 (ISBN 0-8240-1570-3). Garland Pub.
Bertrand Barere: A Reluctant Terrorist. Leo Gershoy. 1962. 25.00 o.p. (ISBN 0-691-05105-4). Princeton U Pr.
Bertrand Russell: An Introduction: Edited Selections from His Writings. Bertrand Russell. Ed. by E. H. Carr. 1975. text ed. 12.50x (ISBN 0-04-192032-5); pap. text ed. 6.50x (ISBN 0-04-192033-3). Allen Unwin.
Bertrand Russell Case. John Dewey & Horace M. Kallen. LC 78-37289. (Civil Liberties in American History Ser). 228p. 1972. Repr. of 1941 ed. lib. bdg. 25.00 (ISBN 0-306-70426-9). Da Capo.
Bertrand Russell Speaks His Mind. Bertrand Russell. LC 74-3626. (Illus.). 173p. 1974. Repr. of 1960 ed. lib. bdg. 17.50x (ISBN 0-8371-7445-7, RUBR). Greenwood.
Bert's Hall of Great Inventions. Revena Dwight. (Sesame Street Bks.). (Illus.). 1972. PLB 5.00 (ISBN 0-307-60321-0, Golden Pr). Western Pub.
Beruehrungsfreie Nierensteinzertruemmerung Durch Extrakorporal Erzeugte, Fokussierte Stosswellen. Charles Chaussy et al. (Beitraege Zur Urology Ser.: Vol. 2). vi, 94p. 1980. pap. 36.00 (ISBN 3-8055-1901-X). S Karger.
Beryllium--A Potential Environmental Contaminant. Charles G. Wilber. (Illus.). 128p. 1980. 14.75. (ISBN 0-398-04118-0). C C Thomas.
Beryllium: Its Metallurgy & Properties. Henry H. Hausner. 1965. 25.00x (ISBN 0-520-00541-4). U of Cal Pr.
Beryllium: Physico-Chemical Properties of Its Compounds & Alloys. (Atomic Energy Review Ser.: Special Issue No. 4). (Illus.). 175p. (Orig.). 1974. pap. 12.00 (ISBN 92-0-149073-9, IAEA). Unipub.
Beside the Fire. Douglas Hyde. 254p. Date not set. Repr. of 1910 ed. 11.00x (ISBN 0-7165-2073-7, Pub by Irish Academic Pr). Biblio Dist.
Beside the Sea of Glass: The Song of the Lamb. Daniel Berrigan. (Classic Prayer Ser.). (Illus.). 1978. pap. 4.95 (ISBN 0-8164-2174-9). Crossroad NY.
Besieged. Thomas Cullinan. 1970. 6.95 o.p. (ISBN 0-8180-0607-2). Horizon.
Besieged by Love. Maryann Young. (Candelight Romance Ser.). (Orig.). Date not set. pap. 1.50 (ISBN 0-440-10581-1). Dell.
Bess & Harry. large print ed. Jhan Robbins. LC 80-27985. 1981. Repr. of 1980 ed. 9.95 (ISBN 0-89621-263-7). Thorndike Pr.
Bess & the Sphinx. Elizabeth Coatsworth. (Illus.). (gr. 3-5). 1967. 6.95 (ISBN 0-02-719420-5). Macmillan.
Bessemer & Lake Erie Railroad, 1869-1969. Roy C. Beaver. LC 73-97230. 1969. 17.95 (ISBN 0-87095-033-9). Golden West.
Bessie. Chris Albertson. LC 79-163353. 253p. 1981. pap. 6.95. Stein & Day.
Best About Backpacking. Ed. by Denise Van Lear. LC 74-76312. (Totebook). (Illus.). 382p. 1974. pap. 7.95 (ISBN 0-87156-099-2). Sierra.
Best American Short Stories Nineteen Eighty. Ed. by Stanley Elkin & Shannon Ravenel. 496p. 1980. 12.95 (ISBN 0-395-29446-0). HM.
Best Baths. Jane Cary. LC 80-67154. (Illus., Orig.). 1980. 12.95 (ISBN 0-932944-19-1); pap. 5.95 (ISBN 0-932944-20-5). Creative Homeowner.
Best Bets for Babies. Brooke Beebe. (Orig.). pap. 4.95 (ISBN 0-440-50453-8, Dell Trade Pbks). Dell.
Best Bicycle Tours, Vol. 2. Editors of Bicycling. Ed. by Kathy Fones. (Bicycling Magazine Book Ser.). (Illus.). 96p. (Orig.). 1981. pap. 2.95 (ISBN 0-87857-324-0). Rodale Pr Inc.
Best Book on CB Radio. Walheim L. Ray. LC 76-41094. (Illus.). 1976. pap. cancelled o.p. (ISBN 0-685-71227-3). H P Bks.
Best Books, 6 Vols. 3rd. ed. William S. Sonnenschein. LC 68-58760. 1969. Repr. of 1935 ed. Set. 220.00 (ISBN 0-8103-3362-7). Gale.
BEST: Building Essential Skills Together. Grant Von Harrison. 1976. complete set 38.85 (ISBN 0-87892-261-X). Economy Co.
Best Burglar Alarm. Brenda Seabrooke. LC 78-7455. (Illus.). (gr. k-3). 1978. 7.95 (ISBN 0-688-22165-3); PLB 7.63 (ISBN 0-688-32165-8). Morrow.
Best Christmas Pageant Ever. Barbara Robinson. (Illus.). (gr. 3-5). 1973. pap. 1.75 (ISBN 0-380-00769-X, 51441, Camelot). Avon.
Best Christmas Pageant Ever. Barbara Robinson. 96p. 1979. pap. 1.75 (ISBN 0-380-48066-2, 48066). Avon.
Best Cookin' in the Country. Tom Wiecks. LC 79-91262. (Illus., Orig.). 1979. pap. 6.95 (ISBN 0-935566-00-7). Barleycorn.
Best Critical Chart Studies Issued by the Stock Market Chartists Club of America. Ed. by Carlo M. Flumiani. (Illus.). 1978. 47.50 (ISBN 0-89266-104-6). Am Classical Coll Pr.
Best Critical Studies Issued by the American Institute for Management & Inventiveness, 2 vols. Ed. by Robert M. Montgomery. 1979. Set. deluxe ed. 67.45 (ISBN 0-918968-25-9). Inst Econ Finan.
Best Days. Julius Horwitz. LC 80-12649. 216p. 1980. 10.95 (ISBN 0-03-056051-9). HR&W.
Best Days of Your Life. Rosemarie Stewart. 1977. pap. 1.95 (ISBN 0-515-03660-9). Jove Pubns.
Best Defense. Joel Moldovsky & Rose DeWolf. 288p. 1975. 8.95 o.s.i. (ISBN 0-02-585590-5). Macmillan.
Best Detective Fiction: A Guide from Godwin to the Present. Melvyn P. Barnes. (Guides to Subject Literature Ser.). 121p. (Orig.). 1975. 10.00 (ISBN 0-208-01376-8, Linnet). Shoe String.

Best Detective Stories of the Year: Thirty-Fifth Annual Collection. Edward D. Hoch. 224p. 1981. 10.95 (ISBN 0-525-06440-0). Dutton.

Best Dishes from Europe & the Orient: A New Collection of Recipes. Netta Parker. 1970. 10.00 (ISBN 0-571-08442-7). Transatlantic.

Best Editorial Cartoons of the Year: Nineteen Eighty-One Edition. Ed. by Charles Brooks. (Best Editorial Cartoons of the Year Ser.: Vol. 9). (Illus.). 160p. 1981. pap. 7.95 (ISBN 0-88289-280-0); pap. 5.95 (ISBN 0-88289-281-9). Pelican.

Best Editorial Cartoons of the Year: 1978 Edition. Ed. by Charles Brooks. LC 73-643645. (Best Editorial Cartoon Ser.). (Illus.). 1978. 11.95 o.p. (ISBN 0-88289-192-8); pap. 5.95 (ISBN 0-88289-193-6). Pelican.

Best Editorial Cartoons of the Year: 1979 Edition. Ed. by Charles Brooks. (Best Editorial Cartoon Ser.). (Illus.). 1979. 11.95 (ISBN 0-88289-229-0); pap. 5.95 o.p. (ISBN 0-88289-230-4). Pelican.

Best Electronics Projects. Electronics Illustrated Editors. (Illus.). 112p. (YA) 1973. lib. bdg. 3.95 o.p. (ISBN 0-668-01724-4). Arco.

Best Ever Fantasy Mazes. Susan Poe. (Illus.). 32p. (Orig.). (gr. 3 up). 1980. pap. 1.50 (ISBN 0-937518-04-2). Hartley Hse.

Best Ever How-to-Get-a-Job Book. Richard H. Stansfield. LC 80-967. 176p. Date not set. 10.95 (ISBN 0-8019-6974-3); pap. 6.95 (ISBN 0-8019-6975-1). Chilton.

Best Evidence: Deception & Disguise in the Assassination of John F. Kennedy. David S. Lifton. 1981. 16.95 (ISBN 0-02-571870-3). Macmillan.

Best Free Attractions in the East. John Whitman. Ed. by Kathe Grooms. (Best Free Attractions Ser.). (Illus., Orig.). 1981. pap. 3.95 (ISBN 0-915658-35-6). Meadowbrook Pr.

Best Free Attractions in the Midwest. John Whitman. Ed. by Kathe Grooms. (Best Free Attractions Ser.). (Illus.). 200p. 1981. pap. 3.95 (ISBN 0-915658-37-2). Meadowbrook Pr.

Best Free Attractions in the South. John Whitman. Ed. by Kathe Grooms. (Best Free Attractions Ser.). (Illus.). 200p. 1981. pap. 3.95 (ISBN 0-915658-38-0). Meadowbrook Pr.

Best Free Attractions in the West. John Whitman. Ed. by Kathe Grooms. (Best Free Attractions Ser.). (Illus.). 200p. 1981. pap. 3.95 (ISBN 0-915658-36-4). Meadowbrook Pr.

Best Friend. Shirley Simon. (gr. 4-6). 1979. pap. 1.75 (ISBN 0-671-56013-1). PB.

Best Friends. Consuelo Baehr. 1980. 11.95 (ISBN 0-440-00841-7). Delacorte.

Best Friends. Miriam Cohen. LC 70-146620. (Illus.). (ps-1). 1971. 6.95 (ISBN 0-02-722800-2). Macmillan.

Best Friends. James A. Warner & Margaret J. White. (Illus.). 176p. 1980. 27.50 (ISBN 0-89479-045-5). A & W Pubs.

Best from American Canals. American Canal Society. (Illus.). 84p. 1980. 6.00 (ISBN 0-933788-32-0). Am Canal & Transport.

Best from Orbit One to Ten. Ed. by Damon Knight. pap. 1.95 o.p. (ISBN 0-425-03161-6). Berkley Pub.

Best Games of Chess. Siegbert Tarrasch. Ed. by Fred Reinfeld. 1947. pap. 6.00 (ISBN 0-486-20644-0). Dover.

Best Games People Play. Richard Sharp. (Illus.). 12.95x (ISBN 0-8464-0188-6); pap. 5.95x (ISBN 0-8464-0194-0). Beekman Pubs.

Best Guide to Allergy. Allan V. Giannini. (Appleton Consumer Health Guides). 160p. 1981. 12.95 (ISBN 0-8385-0645-3); pap. 5.95 (ISBN 0-8385-0644-5). ACC.

Best in Camp. Mike Neigoff. LC 78-79545. (Pilot Book Ser). (Illus.). (gr. 4-7). 1969. 6.95g (ISBN 0-8075-0660-5). A Whitman.

Best in Children's Literature. Ed. by Walter Loban & Lillian Watkins. Incl. Sense & Nonsense. record ed. o.p. (ISBN 0-8372-1936-1); cassette o.p. (ISBN 0-8372-1942-6); Ocean Capers. record ed. (ISBN 0-8372-1933-7); cassette (ISBN 0-8372-1939-6); Never Never Land. record ed. (ISBN 0-8372-1934-5); cassette; Myths & Legends Around the World. record ed. (ISBN 0-8372-1932-9); cassette (ISBN 0-8372-1938-8). (Ser. 4). (gr. k-4). set 54.75 ea. Bowmar-Noble.

Best in Children's Literature. Ed. by Walter Loban & Lillian Watkins. Incl. Funny Bones. record ed. (ISBN 0-8372-0932-3); cassette; Friendly Dragons. record ed. (ISBN 0-8372-0937-4); cassette; Ecology. record ed. (ISBN 0-8372-0941-2); cassette (ISBN 0-8372-1056-9); Folktales from Other Lands. record ed (ISBN 0-8372-1011-9); cassette. (Ser. 3). (gr. k-4). set 54.75 ea. Bowmar-Noble.

Best in OffBeat Humor. Paul B. Lowrey. 1968. 2.95 (ISBN 0-442-82144-1). Peter Pauper.

Best in Show: Breeding & Exhibiting Budgerigars. Gerald S. Binks. 1976. 11.95 (ISBN 0-85223-064-8, Pub. by Michael Joseph). Merrimack Bk Serv.

Best Is Yet to Come. Charles C. Ryrie. 128p. 1981. pap. 2.95 (ISBN 0-8024-4938-7). Moody.

Best Jewish Sermons 5733-34. Ed. by Saul Teplitz. LC 58-3698. (Best Jewish Sermons Ser: No. 12). 1974. 10.00x o.p. (ISBN 0-685-47974-9). Jonathan David.

Best Joke Book for Kids. J. Eckstein & J. Gleit. (Illus.). (gr. 7-12). 1977. pap. 1.50 (ISBN 0-380-01734-2, 43385, Camelot). Avon.

Best Karate: Seven Kata: 7 Katta: Jutte, Hangstsu, Empi. Masatoshi Nakayama. LC 77-74829. (Best Karate Ser.: Vol. 7). (Illus.). 144p. 1980. pap. 6.95 (ISBN 0-87011-390-9). Kodansha.

Best Karate: 8 Kata: Gankaku, Jion. Masatoshi Nakayama. LC 77-74829. (Best Karate Ser.: Vol. 8). (Illus.). 144p. (Orig.). 1981. pap. 6.95 (ISBN 0-87011-402-6). Kodansha.

Best Kept Secret: Sexual Abuse of Children. Florence Rush. LC 80-19525. 296p. 1980. 11.95 (ISBN 0-13-074781-5). P-H.

Best-Kept Secret: The Story of the Atomic Bomb. John Purcell. LC 63-13795. (Illus.). (gr. 7 up). 1963. 6.95 (ISBN 0-8149-0378-9). Vanguard.

Best Kept Woman in the World. Cynthia Halstead. 1976. pap. 1.50 (ISBN 0-505-50998-9). Tower Bks.

Best Laid Plans. Gail Parent. 300p. 1981. 10.95 (ISBN 0-399-12510-8). Putnam.

Best-Laid Plans: America's Juvenile Court Experiment. Ellen Ryerson. 1978. 8.95 o.p. (ISBN 0-8090-2905-7); pap. 4.95 (ISBN 0-8090-0135-7). Hill & Wang.

Best Laid Plans: Student Development in an Experimental College Program. Robert F. Suczek. LC 72-5891. (Higher Education Ser.). 1972. 11.95x o.p. (ISBN 0-87589-149-7). Jossey-Bass.

Best Little Boy in the World. John Reid. 1977. pap. 2.25 (ISBN 0-345-28872-6). Ballantine.

Best Little Girl in the World. Steven Levenkron. 1979. pap. 2.50 (ISBN 0-446-91836-9). Warner Bks.

Best Local-Retail Ads. Ed. by Arnold Fochs. 248p. 1975. pap. 14.92 (ISBN 0-685-99089-3). A J Pub.

Best-Loved Bible Stories: Old Testament & New Testament, 2 vols. World Book Childcraft International, Inc. LC 79-55309. (Illus.). 90p. (gr. 4-8). 1980. write for info. (ISBN 0-7166-2059-6). World Bk-Childcraft.

Best Loved Poems of the American People. Ed. by Hazel Felleman. 1936. 8.95 (ISBN 0-385-00019-7). Doubleday.

Best Loved Songs of the American People. Denes Agay. LC 74-4502. 416p. 1975. 14.95 (ISBN 0-385-00004-9); pap. 7.95 (ISBN 0-385-14006-1). Doubleday.

Best Man No. 7. Grace L. Hill. 176p. 1981. pap. 1.95 (ISBN 0-553-14505-3). Bantam.

Best Man to Die. Routh Rendell. 1981. pap. 1.95 (ISBN 0-345-29693-1). Ballantine.

Best Methods of Study. 4th ed. Samuel Smith et al. (Illus.). 1970. pap. 2.95 (ISBN 0-06-460028-9, CO 28, COS). Har-Row.

Best Mom in the World. Judy Delton & Elaine Knox-Wagner. Ed. by Kathy Pacini. LC 78-27238. (Concept Bk.: Level I). (Illus.). (gr. k-2). 1979. 6.50g (ISBN 0-8075-0665-6). A Whitman.

Best Mystery & Suspense Plays of the Modern Theatre. Ed. by Stanley Richards. 1979. pap. 7.95 (ISBN 0-380-46466-7). Avon.

Best Newspaper Writing. 1979: Winners of the American Society of Newspaper Editors Competition. Ed. by Roy P. Clark. (Illus.). 176p. (Orig.). 1980. pap. 3.95 o.p. (ISBN 0-935742-01-8). Mod Media Inst.

Best of A. W. Tozer. A. W. Tozer. (Best Ser). 1978. pap. 2.50 (ISBN 0-8010-8845-3). Baker Bk.

Best of Alan Coren. Alan Coren. 424p. 1981. 15.95 (ISBN 0-312-07711-4). St Martin.

Best of All! Cecily Hogan. (Young Reader Ser.). (Illus.). (gr. k-3). 1979. PLB 5.00 (ISBN 0-307-60170-6, Golden Pr). Western Pub.

Best of Aubrey Beardsley. Clark, Kenneth, Sir. 1979. 16.95 o.p. (ISBN 0-385-14543-8). Doubleday.

Best of Ben, 5 vols. B. Feldman. 1981. Set. 8.95 (ISBN 0-87863-205-0). Farnswth Pub.

Best of Bishop: Light Verse from the New Yorker & Elsewhere. Morris Bishop. Ed. by Charlotte P. Reppert. LC 80-66902. (Illus.). 224p. 1980. 12.95 (ISBN 0-8014-1310-9). Cornell U Pr.

Best of C. L. Moore. C. L. Moore. 384p. (Orig.). 1976. pap. 2.25 (ISBN 0-345-28952-8). Ballantine.

Best of Children's Literature. Nila B. Smith et al. Incl. Sunny & Gay. (gr. 1). text ed. 3.12 (ISBN 0-672-70530-3); Foolish & Wise. (gr. 2). text ed. 3.32 (ISBN 0-672-70534-6); Fun All Around. (gr. 3). text ed. 3.56 (ISBN 0-672-70538-9); Shining Hours. (gr. 4). text ed. 3.76 (ISBN 0-672-70542-7); Time for Adventure. (gr. 5). text ed. 4.04 (ISBN 0-672-70546-X); Beyond the Horizon. (gr. 6). text ed. 4.16 (ISBN 0-672-70550-8). (gr. 1-6). 1968. tchrs' manuals o.p. 1.40. Bobbs.

Best of Corvette News. Ed. by Karl Ludvigsen. LC 76-20955. 1976. 42.50 (ISBN 0-915038-07-2); leather bdg. 57.95 (ISBN 0-915038-20-X). Princeton Pub.

Best of David Hamilton. Photos by David Hamilton. LC 80-83280. (Illus.). 144p. 1980. pap. 10.95 (ISBN 0-688-00403-2, Quill). Morrow.

Best of Dryden. Ed. by L. I. Bredvold. 1933. 14.95 (ISBN 0-8260-1265-5). Wiley.

Best of E. E. "Doc" Smith. E. E. Smith. (Family D'alembert Ser.). (Orig.). pap. 1.75. Jove Pubns.

Best of Edmond Hamilton. Ed. by Leigh Brackett. LC 77-574. 1977. pap. 1.95 o.p. (ISBN 0-345-25900-9). Ballantine.

Best of Ethnic Home Style Cooking. Mary P. Wilde. LC 80-50406. 240p. 1981. 10.95 (ISBN 0-87477-138-2). J P Tarcher.

Best of Everything. William Davis. 224p. 1981. 9.95 (ISBN 0-312-07713-0). St Martin.

Best of Everything. Rona Jaffe. 1976. pap. 2.75 (ISBN 0-380-00581-6, 54221). Avon.

Best of Everything. Rona Jaffe. 1976. Repr. of 1958 ed. lib. bdg. 18.95x (ISBN 0-89966-130-0). Buccaneer Bks.

Best of Families. Ellin Berlin. 1978. pap. 1.95 o.p. (ISBN 0-449-23541-6, Crest). Fawcett.

Best of Ford. Mary Moline. (Illus.). 1973. 10.00 (ISBN 0-913444-01-4, Pub. by Rumbleseat Press). Motorbooks Intl.

Best of French Cooking. LC 78-56244. (Illus.). 1978. 19.95 (ISBN 0-88332-088-6, 8134). Larousse.

Best of Friends. John Aspinall. LC 76-26211. (Illus.). 1977. 15.00 o.s.i. (ISBN 0-06-010153-9, HarpT). Har-Row.

Best of Fritz Leiber. Ed. by Judy Lynn Del Rey. 352p. (Orig.). 1974. pap. 2.25 (ISBN 0-345-28351-1). Ballantine.

Best of Grimm's Fairy Tales. Grimm Brothers. LC 79-63439. (Illus.). (gr. k-3). 1980. 9.95 (ISBN 0-88332-150-5); PLB 10.95 (ISBN 0-88332-122-X). Larousse.

Best of H. A. Ironside. H. A. Ironside. (Best Ser.). 296p. (Orig.). 1981. pap. 4.95 (ISBN 0-8010-5033-2). Baker Bk.

Best of Henry Kuttner. Intro. by Ray Bradbury. 416p. 1975. pap. 1.95 o.p. (ISBN 0-345-24415-X). Ballantine.

Best of Henry Longhurst. Ed. by Mark Wilson. LC 78-69793. 208p. 1978. 8.50 (ISBN 0-914178-22-9, 24574). Golf Digest.

Best of Instauration 1976. Ed. by Wilmot Robertson. 117p. 1980. pap. 10.00 (ISBN 0-914576-11-9). Howard Allen.

Best of Jewish Cooking. Ed. by Phyllis Frucht et al. 1981. pap. 9.95 (ISBN 0-686-69080-X). Dial.

Best of Joe Weider's Muscle & Fitness Bodybuilding Nutrition & Training Programs. Joe Weider. (Illus.). 1981. 12.95 (ISBN 0-8092-5917-6); pap. 5.95 (ISBN 0-8092-5916-8). Contemp Bks.

Best of Joe Weider's Muscle & Fitness Training Tips & Routines. Joe Weider. (Illus.). 1981. 12.95 (ISBN 0-8092-5911-7); pap. 5.95 (ISBN 0-8092-5910-9). Contemp Bks.

Best of Joe Weider's Muscle & Fitness: The Worlds's Leading Bodybuilders Answer Your Questions. Joe Weider. (Illus.). 1981. 12.95 (ISBN 0-8092-5914-1); pap. 5.95 (ISBN 0-8092-5912-5). Contemp Bks.

Best of John Fahey. John Fahey. Ed. by John Lescroat. LC 77-82830. (Illus.). 176p. 1978. pap. 7.95 (ISBN 0-8256-9515-5). Guitar Player.

Best of John H. Jowett. John H. Jowett. (Best Ser.). 256p. (Orig.). 1981. pap. 3.95 (ISBN 0-8010-5142-8). Baker Bk.

Best of Judith Merril. Judith Merril. 1976. pap. 1.25 o.s.i. (ISBN 0-446-86058-1). Warner Bks.

Best of Life. 1973. 24.95 (ISBN 0-8094-1700-6). Time-Life.

Best of Life. Ed. by Time-Life Bks. Editors. (Illus.). 1973. kivar 19.92 o.p. (ISBN 0-685-72981-8, Pub. by Time-Life). Silver.

Best of Literature. Nila B. Smith et al. Incl. Voyages in Reading. (gr. 7). text ed. 6.00 (ISBN 0-672-70565-6); tchrs' ed 6.00 (ISBN 0-685-23133-X); Challenges in Reading. (gr. 8). text ed. 6.40 (ISBN 0-672-70569-9); tchrs' ed 6.40 (ISBN 0-685-23134-8); Riches in Reading. (gr. 9). text ed. 6.76 (ISBN 0-672-70562-1). (Reading Literature Ser.). (gr. 7-9). 1969. tchrs' manuals o.p. 1.40. Bobbs.

Best of Micro, Vol. 1. Computerist Inc. Ed. by Robert M. Tripp et al. (Illus.). 176p. (Orig.). 1978. pap. 6.00 (ISBN 0-938222-00-7). Computerist.

Best of Micro: June 1979 to May 1980, Vol. 3. Micro Ink, Inc. Ed. by Robert M. Tripp. (The Best of Micro Ser.). (Illus.). 320p. (Orig.). 1980. pap. 10.00 (ISBN 0-938222-03-1). Computerist.

Best of Micro: June 1980 to May 1981, Vol.4. Micro Ink, Inc. Ed. by Robert M. Tripp. (The Best of Micro Ser.). (Illus.). Date not set. pap. price not set (ISBN 0-938222-04-X). Computerist.

Best of Micro: Vol. 2, Oct-Nov 78 to May 79. Micro Ink, Inc. Ed. by Robert M. Tripp. (Illus.). 224p. (Orig.). pap. 8.00 (ISBN 0-938222-02-3). Computerist.

Best of Mr. Punch: The Humorous Writings of Douglas Jerrold. Ed. by Richard M. Kelly. LC 73-111045. (Illus.). 1970. 18.50x (ISBN 0-87049-116-4). U of Tenn Pr.

Best of Neighbors. Glyn Hughes. 64p. 1980. signed ed. 14.95x (ISBN 0-686-68860-0, Pub. by Geolfrith Pr England); pap. 7.50x (ISBN 0-904461-57-2). Intl Schol Bk Serv.

Best of O. Henry. O. Henry. LC 78-14841. 1978. lib. bdg. 12.90 (ISBN 0-89471-047-8); pap. 4.95 (ISBN 0-89471-046-X). Running Pr.

Best of O. Henry: Student Activity Book. Marcia Sohl & Gerald Dackerman. (Now Age Illustrated Ser.). (Illus.). (gr. 4-12). 1976. wkbk. 0.95 (ISBN 0-88301-292-8). Pendulum Pr.

Best of on the Run. Ed. by Bob Anderson. pap. cancelled o.s.i. (ISBN 0-89037-208-X). Anderson World.

Best of Origami. Samuel Randlett. (Illus.). 185p. 1981. 12.95 (ISBN 0-571-10275-1, Pub. by Faber & Faber). Merrimack Bk Serv.

Best of Pandora. new ed. Alaine Joseph et al. Ed. by Lois Wickstrom. (Illus., Orig.). Date not set. pap. price not set (ISBN 0-916176-09-6). Sproing.

Best of Photojournalism, Vol. 5. National Press Photographers Association. LC 77-81586. (National Press Photographers Association, University of Missouri Journalism School Ser.). (Illus.). 256p. 1980. 24.95 (ISBN 0-8262-0321-3). U of Mo Pr.

Best of Photojournalism: Three. National Press Photographers Association & the University of Missouri School of Journalism & Edwin Bayrd. LC 77-8156. (Illus.). 1979. 16.95 o.p. (ISBN 0-88225-263-1). Newsweek.

Best of Photojournalism Two. National Press Photographers & the University of Missouri, School of Journalism. LC 77-81586. (Illus.). 1978. 16.95 o.p. (ISBN 0-88225-253-4); pap. 9.95 o.p. (ISBN 0-88225-252-6). Newsweek.

Best of Poe: Student Activity Book. Marcia Sohl & Gerald Dackerman. (Now Age Illustrated Ser.). (Illus.). (gr. 4-12). 1976. wkbk. 0.95 (ISBN 0-88301-293-6). Pendulum Pr.

Best of Popular Photography. Ed. by Harvey V. Fondiller. (Illus.). 1979. 29.95 (ISBN 0-87165-037-1); deluxe ed. 35.00 (ISBN 0-87165-037-1); deluxe ed. 100.00 signed (ISBN 0-685-96576-7). Ziff-Davis Pub.

Best of Quincy Scott. Hugh Scott. LC 80-83078. (Illus.). 216p. 1980. pap. 7.95 (ISBN 0-87595-087-6). Oreg Hist Soc.

Best of Rhys Davies. Rhys Davies. 16.95 (ISBN 0-7153-7756-6). David & Charles.

Best of Robert Silverberg. Robert Silverberg. 1980. pap. write for info. (ISBN 0-671-83497-5). PB.

Best of Sail Navigation. Ed. by Anne Madden. (Illus.). 1980. 13.95 (ISBN 0-914814-27-3). Sail Bks.

Best of Sail Navigation. Ed. by Sail Magazine. (Illus.). 1981. 13.95 (ISBN 0-393-03261-2). Norton.

Best of Shaker Cooking. Amy B. Miller & Persis Fuller. (Illus.). 1970. 10.00 o.s.i. (ISBN 0-02-584820-8). Macmillan.

Best of Shaker Cooking. Amy B. Miller & Persis Fuller. (Illus.). 480p. 1976. pap. 9.95 (ISBN 0-02-009810-3, Collier). Macmillan.

Best of Sholem Aleichem. Ed. by Irving Howe & Ruth Wisse. 1980. pap. 5.95 (ISBN 0-671-41092-X, Touchstone). S&S.

Best of Teacher's Arts & Crafts Workshop. Ruth L. Peck. 1974. 12.95 o.p. (ISBN 0-13-073668-6). P-H.

Best of Texas Monthly. limited ed. Ed. by William Broyles. (Illus.). 379p. 1978. 50.00 (ISBN 0-932012-01-9). Texas Month Pr.

Best of the Bargain. Janina Domanska. LC 76-13010. (Illus.). (gr. k-3). 1977. 8.95 (ISBN 0-688-80062-9); PLB 8.59 (ISBN 0-688-84062-0). Greenwillow.

Best of the Italian & Wall Street High Class Cuisine, 3 vols. Chef Alexander. Incl. Vol. 1. Soups, Fish, Meat (ISBN 0-89266-165-8); Vol. 2. Chicken, Eggs, Pasta & Rice, Vegetables (ISBN 0-89266-166-6); Vol. 3. Salads, Desserts, Coffees & Wines (ISBN 0-89266-167-4). (Essential Knowledge Library Bk.). (Illus.). 1979. plastic spiral bdg. 4.00 ea. o.p. Am Classical Coll Pr.

Best of the Left Bank: A Very Special Cookbook. Luc Meyer. 1980. pap. write for info. (ISBN 0-89716-064-9). Peanut Butter.

Best of the Old Northwest. Marge Davenport. LC 80-83780. (Illus., Orig.). 1981. pap. 6.95 (ISBN 0-938274-00-7). Paddlewheel.

Best of the Poetry Year: Poetry Dimension Annual 7. Ed. by Dannie Abse. 160p. 1980. 15.00x (ISBN 0-8476-3255-5). Rowman.

Best of the Poetry Year: Poetry Dimension Annual, 5. Ed. by Dannie Abse. 171p. 1978. 11.50x (ISBN 0-8476-3139-7). Rowman.

Best of the Rip off Press: More Fabulous Furry Freak Brothers, Vol. 4. Gilbert Shelton & Dave Sheridan. (Best of the Rip off Press Ser.). (Illus.). 96p. (Orig.). (YA) 1980. pap. 5.95 (ISBN 0-89620-086-8). Rip off.

Best of the Worst. Stan Lee. LC 79-1671. (Illus.). 1979. pap. 4.95 (ISBN 0-06-090728-2, CN 728, CN). Har-Row.

Best of Thomas M. Scortia. George Zebrowski. LC 80-2349. 288p. 1981. 11.95 (ISBN 0-385-14695-7). Doubleday.

Best of Thoreau's Journals. Ed. by Carl Bode. LC 67-15321. 1971. Repr. of 1967 ed. 8.95x o.p. (ISBN 0-8093-0475-9). S Ill U Pr.

Best of Times, the Worst of Times: Andrew Greeley & American Catholicism, 1950-1975. John N. Kotre. LC 78-14224. 1978. 14.95 (ISBN 0-88229-380-X); pap. 7.95 (ISBN 0-88229-597-7). Nelson-Hall.

Best of Trek No. 3. Ed. by Walter Irwin & G. B. Love. 1981. pap. 1.95 (ISBN 0-451-09582-0, J9582, Sig). NAL.

Best of Uffa: Fifty Great Yacht Designs from the Uffa Fox Books. Ed. by Guy Cole. LC 78-55781. (Illus.). 1979. 20.00 (ISBN 0-87742-102-1). Intl Marine.

Best of Walter A. Maier. Paul L. Maier. 1980. pap. 7.95 (ISBN 0-570-03823-5, 12-2786). Concordia.

Best Photos of the Civil War. Hirst D. Milhollen & James R. Johnson. LC 61-16881. (Illus.). 1961. lib. bdg. 3.95 o.p. (ISBN 0-668-00782-6). Arco.

Best Picture: The Academy Awards, 1927 to 1980. Hal Marienthal. LC 80-67901. 1981. 19.95 (ISBN 0-89615-029-1); pap. 11.95 (ISBN 0-89615-030-5). Guild of Tutors.

Best Plays of the Seventies. Stanley Richard. LC 79-6634. 816p. 1980. 17.95 (ISBN 0-385-14739-2). Doubleday.

Best Plays of 1963-1964, Vol. 3. Ed. by Henry Hewes. (Burns Mantle Yearbook of the Theater Ser.). 15.00 o.p. (ISBN 0-396-05074-3). Dodd.

Best Plays of 1964-1969, 5 Vols. Ed. by Otis L. Guernsey, Jr. (Burns Mantle Yearbook of the Theater Ser.). Set. 20.00 (ISBN 0-686-66398-5). Vol. 1 (ISBN 0-396-05211-8). Vol. 2 (ISBN 0-396-05435-8). Vol. 3. o.p. (ISBN 0-396-05634-2). Vol. 4 (ISBN 0-396-05843-4). Vol. 5 (ISBN 0-396-06028-5). Dodd.

Best Plays of 1969-1970. Ed. by Otis L. Guernsey, Jr. (Burns Mantle Yearbook of the Theater Ser.). (Illus.). 1970. 20.00 (ISBN 0-396-06249-0). Dodd.

Best Plays of 1971-1972. Ed. by Otis L. Guernsey, Jr. LC 20-21432. (Burns Mantle Yearbook of the Theater Ser.). (Illus.). 492p. 1972. 20.00 (ISBN 0-396-06698-4). Dodd.

Best Plays of 1972-1973. Ed. by Otis L. Guernsey, Jr. (Burns Mantle Yearbook of the Theater Ser.). (Illus.). 492p. 1973. 20.00 (ISBN 0-396-06878-2). Dodd.

Best Plays of 1973-1974. Ed. by Otis L. Guernsey, Jr. (Burns Mantle Yearbook of the Theater Ser.). (Illus.). 492p. 1974. 20.00 (ISBN 0-396-07017-5). Dodd.

Best Plays of 1974-1975. Ed. by Otis L. Guernsey, Jr. (Burns Mantle Yearbook of the Theater Ser.). (Illus.). 492p. 1975. 20.00 (ISBN 0-396-07220-8). Dodd.

Best Plays of 1975-1976. Otis L. Guernsey, Jr. (Burns Mantle Yearbook of the Theater Ser.). (Illus.). 1976. 20.00 (ISBN 0-396-07380-8). Dodd.

Best Plays of 1976-1977. Ed. by Otis L. Guernsey, Jr. (Burns Mantle Yearbook of Theater Ser.). (Illus.). 1977. 20.00 (ISBN 0-396-07501-0). Dodd.

Best Plays of 1977-1978. Ed. by Otis L. Guernsey, Jr. (Burns Mantle Yearbook of the Theater Ser.). (Illus.). 1979. 20.00 (ISBN 0-396-07637-8). Dodd.

Best Plays of 1978-1979. Ed. by Otis L. Guernsey, Jr. LC 20-21432. (Burns Mantle Yearbook of the Theater Ser.). (Illus.). 1980. 20.00 (ISBN 0-396-07723-4). Dodd.

Best Plays of 1979-1980. Ed. by Otis L. Guernsey, Jr. (Burns Mantle Yearbook of the Theatre Ser.). (Illus.). 550p. 1981. 20.00 (ISBN 0-396-07907-5). Dodd.

Best Poems of 1925. Ed. by Thomas Moult. LC 79-51986. (Granger Poetry Library). (Illus.). 1981. Repr. of 1926 ed. 15.00x (ISBN 0-89609-180-5). Granger Bk.

Best Poems of 1927. Ed. by Thomas Moult. LC 79-51986. (Granger Poetry Library). 1981. Repr. of 1928 ed. 15.00x (ISBN 0-89609-185-6). Granger Bk.

Best Poems of 1928. Ed. by Thomas Moult. LC 79-51986. (Granger Poetry Library). (Illus.). 1981. Repr. of 1929 ed. 15.00x (ISBN 0-89609-192-9). Granger Bk.

Best Poems of 1929. Ed. by Thomas Moult. LC 79-51986. (Granger Poetry Library). (Illus.). 1981. Repr. of 1929 ed. 15.00x (ISBN 0-89609-194-5). Granger Bk.

Best Poems of 1933. Ed. by Thomas Moult. LC 79-51986. (Granger Poetry Library). (Illus.). 1981. Repr. of 1933 ed. 15.00x (ISBN 0-89609-187-2). Granger Bk.

Best Poems of 1934. Ed. by Thomas Moult. LC 79-51986. (Granger Poetry Library). (Illus.). 1981. Repr. of 1934 ed. 15.00x (ISBN 0-89609-188-0). Granger Bk.

Best Poems of 1935. Ed. by Thomas Moult. LC 79-51986. (Granger Poetry Library). (Illus.). 1981. Repr. of 1935 ed. 15.00x (ISBN 0-89609-189-9). Granger Bk.

Best Poems of 1936. Ed. by Thomas Moult. LC 79-51986. (Granger Poetry Library). (Illus.). 1981. Repr. of 1936 ed. 15.00x (ISBN 0-89609-190-2). Granger Bk.

Best Poems of 1937. Ed. by Thomas Moult. LC 79-51986. (Granger Poetry Library). (Illus.). 1981. Repr. of 1937 ed. 15.00x (ISBN 0-89609-191-0). Granger Bk.

Best Quotations for All Occasions. rev ed. Ed. by Lewis C. Henry. 1977. pap. 2.25 (ISBN 0-449-30824-3, Prem). Fawcett.

Best Reference Books: Titles of Lasting Value Selected from American Reference Books Annual 1970-1976. Bohdan S. Wynar. LC 76-45781. 448p. 1976. lib. bdg. 22.50 (ISBN 0-87287-163-0). Libs Unl.

Best Reference Books, 1970-1980: Titles of Lasting Value Selected from American Reference Books Annual. Ed. by Susan Holte & Bohdan S. Wynar. 450p. 1981. lib. bdg. 30.00x (ISBN 0-87287-255-6). Libs Unl.

Best Restaurants New England. Patricia Brooks. LC 80-16277. 211p. (Orig.). 1980. pap. 3.95 (ISBN 0-89286-178-9). One Hund One Prods.

Best Restaurants New York. rev. ed. Stendahl. LC 80-18846. 225p. 1980. pap. 3.95 (ISBN 0-89286-167-3). One Hund One Prods.

Best Restaurants of San Francisco & Northern California. rev. ed. Jacqueline Killeen. LC 80-18764. (Illus.). 220p. 1980. pap. 3.95 (ISBN 0-89286-160-6). One Hund One Prods.

Best Restaurants Philadelphia & Environs. rev. ed. Elaine Tait. (Best Restaurants Ser.). (Illus.). 225p. 1981. pap. 3.95 (ISBN 0-89286-189-4). One Hurd One Prods.

Best Sales Promotions, Vol. 4. William A. Robinson. LC 80-66061. 1980. 24.95 (ISBN 0-87251-047-6). Crain Bks.

Best Science Fiction of the Year, No. 3. Ed. by Terry Carr. (Orig.). 1976. pap. 1.95 o.p. (ISBN 0-345-25015-X). Ballantine.

Best Science Fiction of the Year, No. 6. Ed. by Terry Carr. 1977. 9.95 o.p. (ISBN 0-03-020716-9). HR&W.

Best Science Fiction of the Year, No. 9. Ed. by Terry Carr. (Orig.). 1980. pap. 2.50 (ISBN 0-345-28601-4). Ballantine.

Best Science Fiction Stories. H. G. Wells. 7.50 (ISBN 0-8446-3149-3). Peter Smith.

Best Science Fiction Stories of the Year: Tenth Annual Collection. Gardner Dozois. 256p. 1981. 11.95 (ISBN 0-525-06499-0). Dutton.

Best-Seller: A Nostalgic Celebration of the Less Than Great Books You Have Always Been Afraid to Admit You Loved. Geoffrey Bocca. 1981. 12.95 (Wyndham Bks). S&S.

Best Sellers: Popular Fiction of the 1970s. John Sutherland. 272p. 1981. 18.95 (ISBN 0-7100-0750-7). Routledge & Kegan.

Best-Selling Chapters. Raymond Harris. (Illus.). 496p. (gr. 9 up). 1978. pap. text ed. 8.00x (ISBN 0-89061-151-3, 791). Jamestown Pubs.

Best-Selling Children's Books. Jean S. Kujoth. LC 72-11692. 1973. 10.00 (ISBN 0-8108-0571-5). Scarecrow.

Best SF: 1973. Ed. by Harry Harrison & Brian W. Aldiss. (Fic). (YA) 1974. 6.95 o.p. (ISBN 0-399-11301-0). Berkley Pub.

Best Short Plays, 1971. Ed. by Stanley Richards. LC 38-8006. (Best Short Plays Ser). 1971. 12.95 (ISBN 0-8019-5587-4). Chilton.

Best Short Plays 1972. Ed. by Stanley Richards. LC 38-8006. (Best Short Plays Ser). 479p. 1972. 12.95 (ISBN 0-8019-5588-2). Chilton.

Best Short Plays, 1973. Ed. by Stanley Richards. (Best Short Plays Ser.). 400p. 1973. 12.95 (ISBN 0-8019-5589-0). Chilton.

Best Short Plays, 1975. Ed. by Stanley Richards. 352p. 1975. 12.95 (ISBN 0-8019-6082-7). Chilton.

Best Short Plays 1977. Ed. by Stanley Richards. LC 38-8006. (Best Short Plays Ser.). (Illus.). 1977. 12.95 (ISBN 0-8019-6515-2, 6515). Chilton.

Best Short Plays, 1978. Ed. by Stanley Richards. LC 38-8006. (Best Short Plays Ser.). 1978. 12.95 (ISBN 0-8019-6642-6). Chilton.

Best Short Stories. Raymond Harris. (Illus.). 560p. (Orig.). (gr. 9 up). 1980. pap. text ed. 8.00x (ISBN 0-89061-234-X, 792). Jamestown Pubs.

Best Short Stories of Jack London. Jack London. LC 45-3830. 1953. 8.95 (ISBN 0-385-00021-9). Doubleday.

Best Short Stories of Ring Lardner. Ring Lardner. LC 57-13394. 346p. 1957. lib. rep. ed. 17.50x (ISBN 0-684-14743-2, ScribT); pap. 4.95 (ISBN 0-684-13648-1, SL494 ScribT). Scribner.

Best Shotguns Ever Made. Michael McIntosh. (Illus.). 192p. 1981. 12.95 (ISBN 0-684-16825-1, ScribT). Scribner.

Best Singing Games for Children of All Ages. rev. ed. Edgar S. Bley. LC 57-1014. (Illus.). (gr. k-6). 1959. 8.95 (ISBN 0-8069-4450-1); PLB 8.29 (ISBN 0-8069-4451-X). Sterling.

Best Stories for Girls. Ed. by N. Gretchen Greiner. (gr. 9 up). 1980. Box Set. pap. 3.75 (ISBN 0-307-13620-5, Golden Pr) Western Pub.

Best Tales of Hoffman. E. T. Hoffman. Ed. & intro. by E. F. Bleiler. 8.00 (ISBN 0-8446-2262-1). Peter Smith.

Best Tennis Humor: It Only Hurts When I Serve. Ed. by David Wiltse. (Illus.). 1980. 9.95 (ISBN 0-914178-37-7, Pub. by Tennis Mag). Golf Digest.

Best Test Design. Benjamin D. Wright & Mark H. Stone. LC 79-88489. 1979. 19.00. Mesa Pr IL.

Best Time of Day. Valerie Flournoy. LC 77-91641. (Picturebacks Ser.). (Illus.) (ps-2). 1979. PLB 4.99 (ISBN 0-394-93799-6, BYR); pap. 1.25 (ISBN 0-394-83799-1). Random.

Best Way in the World for a Woman to Make Money. David King & Karen Levine. 1980. pap. 4.95 (ISBN 0-446-97515-X). Warner Bks.

Best Way to Destroy a Ship: The Evidence of European Naval Operations in World War II. Tweed W. Ross, Jr. 1980. pap. 23.00 (ISBN 0-89126-069-2). Military Aff Aero.

Best, Worst & Most Unusual in Sports. Stan Fischler & Shirley Fischler. LC 77-4099. (Illus.). 1977. 10.95 (ISBN 0-690-01457-0, TYC-T). T Y Crowell.

Best, Worst, & Most Unusual in Sports. Stan Fischler & Shirley Fischler. 1979. pap. 2.25 (ISBN 0-449-23816-4, Crest). Fawcett.

Best Years. Pierre Gascar. LC 66-25398. 1966. 5.00 o.p. (ISBN 0-8076-0378-3). Braziller.

Best Years of My Life. Harold Russell & Dan Ferullo. (Illus.). 224p. 1981. 12.95 (ISBN 0-8397-1026-7). Eriksson.

Bestaire ou Cortege d'Orphee. Guillaume Apollinaire. Tr. by Lauren Shakely from Fr. LC 77-23500. (Illus.). 1977. 20.00 (ISBN 0-87099-165-5). Metro Mus Art.

Bestiary. Boynton Merrill, Jr. LC 75-3549. (Illus.). 72p. 1976. 8.00x (ISBN 0-8131-1329-6). U Pr of Ky.

Bestiary for St. Jerome: A Study of Animal Symbolism in European Religious Art. Herbert Friedmann. LC 79-607804. (Illus.). 378p. 1980. 35.00 (ISBN 0-87474-446-6). Smithsonian.

Bestiary, or the Parade of Orpheus. Guillaume Apollinaire. Tr. by Pepe Karmel from Fr. LC 80-66191. (Illus.). 80p. 1980. 10.00 (ISBN 0-87923-319-2); pap. 5.95 (ISBN 0-87923-359-1). Godine.

Bestseller. Joan Kretschmer. 1980. pap. write for info. (ISBN 0-671-83277-8). PB.

Besuch der Alten Dame. Friedrich Durrenmatt. Ed. by Paul K. Ackermann. LC 60-3863. (Ger). (gr. 11-12). 1960. pap. text ed. 7.20 (ISBN 0-395-04089-2). HM.

Bet on Yourself. Charles McGinn. (Illus.). 153p. (Orig.). 1980. pap. 3.95 (ISBN 0-89260-193-0). Hwong Pub.

Beta-Adrenergic Blocking Agents in the Management of Hypertension & Angina Pectoris. Ed. by Bruno Magnani. LC 74-15629. 1974. 19.50 (ISBN 0-89004-013-3). Raven.

Beta Hemolytic Streptococcal Diseases. Burtis B. Breese & Caroline Hall. (Illus.). 1978. 29.00x (ISBN 0-89289-400-8). HM Prof Med Div.

Beta Two-Microglobulin: Its Significance in Clinical Medicine. Ed. by M. D. Poulik. (Journal: Vox Sanguinis: Vol. 38, No. 6). (Illus.). 1980. soft cover 19.75 (ISBN 3-8055-1560-X). S Karger.

Beth Book. Sarah Grand. (Virago Modern Classics Ser.). 1981. pap. 6.95. Dial.

Bethesda, an Historical Sketch of Whitefield's House of Mercy in Georgia, & of the Union Society, His Associate & Successor in Philanthropy. Thomas Gamble, Jr. LC 78-187383. (Illus.). 150p. 1972. Repr. of 1902 ed. 13.50 (ISBN 0-87152-078-8). Reprint.

Bething's Folly. Barbara Metzger. LC 80-54483. 192p. 1981. 9.95 (ISBN 0-8027-0677-0). Walker & Co.

Betrayal in Vietnam. Louis Fanning. 1976. 8.95 o.s.i. (ISBN 0-87000-341-0). Arlington Hse.

Betrayal of Richard III. V. B. Lamb. 128p. 1980. 9.75x (ISBN 0-7050-0066-4, Pub. by Skilton & Shaw England). State Mutual Bk.

Betrayal of the Body. Alexander Lowen. 1969. pap. 2.95 (ISBN 0-02-077300-5, Collier). Macmillan.

Betrayal of the Negro: From Rutherford B. Hayes to Woodrow Wilson. R. W. Logan. Orig. Title: Negro in American Life & Thought. 1965. pap. 1.50 o.s.i. (ISBN 0-02-034490-2, Collier). Macmillan.

Betrayal of the State of Israel & the Foreign Policy of the United States: A Blueprint for Peace in the Middle East. new ed. Victor Marx. (Illus.). 1977. 47.50 (ISBN 0-89266-059-7). Am Classical Coll Pr.

Betrayal of Youth: Secondary Education Must Be Changed. James Hemming. LC 79-56484. (Ideas in Progress Ser.). 160p. 1980. 12.00 (ISBN 0-7145-2692-4, Pub. by M Boyars); pap. 6.95 (ISBN 0-7145-2693-2). Merrimack Bk Serv.

Betrayed Skies. Rudolf Braunberg & John M. Brownjohn. LC 79-7860. 384p. 1980. 12.95 (ISBN 0-385-15183-7). Doubleday.

Betrayers. Donald Hamilton. 1978. pap. 1.95 (ISBN 0-449-14060-1, GM). Fawcett.

Betrothed. Alessandro Manzoni. Tr. by Archibald Cloquhoun. 1956. 5.00x o.p. (ISBN 0-460-00999-0, Everyman). Dutton.

Betsey's Bbee Ree. Margaret Knox. (Illus.). 32p. (gr. k-4). 1980. 7.95 (ISBN 0-88319-055-9). Shoal Creek Pub.

Betsy & Joe. Maud H. Lovelace. LC 48-8096. (Illus.). (gr. 5-11). 1948. 9.95 (ISBN 0-690-13378-2, TYC-J). T Y Crowell.

Betsy & Mr. Kilpatrick. Carolyn Haywood. (Illus.). (gr. 3-7). 1967. 7.25 o.p. (ISBN 0-688-21085-6); PLB 7.92 (ISBN 0-688-31085-0). Morrow.

Betsy & Tacy Go Downtown. Maud H. Lovelace. LC 43-51264. (Illus.). (gr. 3-6). 1943. PLB 8.79 (ISBN 0-690-13450-9, TYC-J). T Y Crowell.

Betsy & Tacy Go Over the Big Hill. Maud H. Lovelace. LC 42-23557. (Illus.). (gr. 3-7). 1942. 9.95 (ISBN 0-690-13521-1, TYC-J); PLB 8.79 (ISBN 0-690-13521-1). T Y Crowell.

Betsy & the Circus. Carolyn Haywood. (Illus.). (gr. 4-6). 1954. PLB 7.92 (ISBN 0-688-31086-9). Morrow.

Betsy & the Great World. Maud H. Lovelace. LC 52-8657. (Illus.). (gr. 5-11). 1952. 9.95 (ISBN 0-690-13591-2, TYC-J). T Y Crowell.

Betsy in Spite of Herself. Maud H. Lovelace. LC 46-11995. (Illus.). (gr. 5-11). 1946. 9.95 (ISBN 0-690-13662-5, TYC-J). T Y Crowell.

Betsy-Tacy. Maud H. Lovelace. LC 40-30965. (Illus.). (gr. 1-5). 1940. PLB 8.79- (ISBN 0-690-13805-9, TYC-J). T Y Crowell.

Betsy-Tacy & Tib. Maud H. Lovelace. LC 41-18714. (Illus.). (gr. 3-7). 1941. PLB 8.79 (ISBN 0-690-13876-8, TYC-J). T Y Crowell.

Betsy Was a Junior: A Betsy-Tacy High School Story. Maud H. Lovelace. LC 46-11995. (Illus.). (gr. 5-11). 1947. 9.95 (ISBN 0-690-13946-2, TYC-J). T Y Crowell.

Betsy's Busy Summer. Carolyn Haywood. (Illus.). (gr. 3-7). 1956. PLB 8.40 (ISBN 0-688-31087-7). Morrow.

Betsy's Busy Summer. Carolyn Haywood. (Illus.). (gr. 3-5). 1980. pap. 1.75 (ISBN 0-671-56047-6). PB.

Betsy's Little Star. Carolyn Haywood. (Illus.). (gr. k-3). 1950. PLB 7.92 (ISBN 0-688-31088-5). Morrow.

Betsy's Play School. Carolyn Haywood. LC 77-1615. (Illus.). (gr. 4-6). 1977. 8.25 (ISBN 0-688-22115-7); PLB 7.92 (ISBN 0-688-32115-1). Morrow.

Betsy's Wedding. Maud H. Lovelace. LC 55-11108. (Illus.). (gr. 5-11). 1955. 9.95 (ISBN 0-690-13733-8, TYC-J). T Y Crowell.

Betsy's Winterhouse. Carolyn Haywood. (Illus.). (gr. 3-7). 1958. PLB 7.92 (ISBN 0-688-31090-7). Morrow.

Bettas. Marshall Ostrow. (Illus.). 96p. 1980. 2.95 (ISBN 0-87666-522-9, KW052). TFH Pubns.

Bettel und Garteteuffel. Ambrosius Pape. Ed. by Oliver F. Graves. LC 80-23210. liv, 440p. (Orig.). 1981. pap. 25.00 (ISBN 0-8173-0059-7). U of Ala Pr.

Better Angling with Simple Science. Mary M. Pratt. (Illus.). 144p. 9.50 (ISBN 0-85238-069-0, FN). Unipub.

Better Athletics-Field. new ed. John Heaton. (Better Books). (Illus.). 96p. (gr. 7 up). 1974. 14.50x o.p. (ISBN 0-7182-0496-4, SpS). Soccer.

Better Athletics: Field, (With Cross Country & Race Walking) rev. ed. John Heaton. (Better Bks.). (Illus.). 96p. 1980. text ed. 14.50x (ISBN 0-7182-1469-2, SpS). Soccer.

Better Baby Food Cookbook. Barbara Helmer. LC 80-22314. (Orig.). 1980. pap. 4.95 spiral bdg. (ISBN 0-87123-018-6, 210018). Bethany Fell.

Better Ballet. Richard Glasstone. LC 78-55577. (Better Sport Ser.). (Illus.). 95p. 1977. 8.50x (ISBN 0-7182-1453-6). Intl Pubns Serv.

Better Baseball for Boys. rev. ed. George Sullivan. LC 80-22022. (Better Sports Ser.). (Illus.). 64p. (gr. 5 up). 1981. PLB 6.95 (ISBN 0-396-07912-1). Dodd.

Better Basketball for Boys. new ed. George Sullivan. LC 80-1011. (Better Sports Ser.). (Illus.). 64p. (gr. 5 up). 1980. PLB 5.95 (ISBN 0-396-07857-5). Dodd.

Better Basketball for Girls. George Sullivan. LC 78-7732. (Better Sports Ser.). (Illus.). (gr. 5 up). 1978. PLB 5.95 (ISBN 0-396-07580-0). Dodd.

Better Bikes: A Manual for an Alternative Mode of Transportation. Tom Cuthbertson. LC 80-5101. (Illus.). 1980. 7.95 (ISBN 0-89815-025-6); pap. 4.95 (ISBN 0-89815-024-8). Ten Speed Pr.

Better Billiards & Snooker. new ed. Clive Everton. (Better Sports Ser). (Illus.). 90p. (gr. 7 up). 1976. text ed. 14.50x (ISBN 0-7182-1441-2, SpS). Soccer.

Better Brochures, Catalogs & Mailing Pieces. Janet Mas. (Illus.). 128p. 1981. 9.95 (ISBN 0-312-07730-0). St Martin.

Better Business Bureau Guide to Wise Buying. The Better Business Bureau. (Illus.). 1980. pap. 6.95 (ISBN 0-448-22075-X). Paddington.

Better Business Bureau Wise Buying Guide. The Better Business Bureau. 1980. lib. bdg. 17.50 (ISBN 0-87196-419-8). Facts on File.

Better Business Letters: A Programmed Book to Develop Skill in Writing. 2nd ed. James M. Reid & Anne Silleck. LC 77-88056. 1978. pap. text ed. 8.95 (ISBN 0-201-06327-1). A-W.

Better Camping. Alan Ryalls & Roger Marchant. (Better Ser.). (Illus.). 96p. (gr. 7 up). 1979. 14.50x (ISBN 0-7182-0494-8, SpS). Soccer.

Better Communications for Better Health. Helen Neal. LC 62-15058. 1962. 20.00x (ISBN 0-231-02584-X). Columbia U Pr.

Better Concrete Pavement Serviceability. Edwin A. Finney. (Monograph: No. 7). 1973. 16.75 (ISBN 0-685-85140-0, M-7). ACI.

Better Dancing. Courtney Castle. (Better Ser.). (Illus.). (gr. 7 up). 1976. 14.50x o.p. (ISBN 0-7182-0482-4, SpS). Soccer.

Better Days. Edward Hannibal. 1979. pap. 2.25 o.p. (ISBN 0-345-27979-4). Ballantine.

Better Discipline. S. O. Johnson. 142p. 1980. 11.50 (ISBN 0-398-03985-2). C C Thomas.

Better Dressmaking. Margaret McCrirrick. 1979. 18.95 (ISBN 0-7134-1092-2). David & Charles.

Better Eating Habits - A Step by Step Approach. Gloria K. Winber. (Illus.). 170p. (Orig.). pap. 5.95. Winfoto.

Better English. G. H. Vallins. (Andre Deutsch Language Library). 1977. lib. bdg. 11.50x (ISBN 0-233-95526-7). Westview.

Better English Made Easy. Henry Thomas. (YA) (gr. 7-12). 1975. pap. 1.95 (ISBN 0-445-08401-4). Popular Lib.

Better Eyesight Without Glasses. Bates. 1970. pap. 2.95 (ISBN 0-515-05897-1, A2332). Jove Pubns.

Better Eyesight Without Glasses. W. H. Bates. 208p. (Orig.). 1981. pap. 2.95 (ISBN 0-03-058012-9). HR&W.

Better Fishing: Freshwater. rev. ed. John Mitchell. LC 68-108518. (Illus.). 1978. 8.50x (ISBN 0-7182-1455-2). Intl Pubns Serv.

Better Football for Boys. new ed. George Sullivan. LC 80-12597. (Better Sports Ser.). (Illus.). 64p. (gr. 5 up). 1980. 5.95 (ISBN 0-396-07843-5). Dodd.

Better Guide Than Reason. Bradford. 12.95 (ISBN 0-89385-006-3); pap. 4.95. Green Hill.

Better Handwriting for You. rev. ed. Handwriting Institute. (gr. 1-8). 1972-75. Bk. 1. nonconsumable 2.25 (ISBN 0-8372-9509-2); Bks. 2 & 3. ea nonconsumable. 2.25 (ISBN 0-8372-9511-4); Bks. 1-3. text ed. 2.25 ea. alternate nonconsumable (ISBN 0-8372-9513-0); Bks. 2-3. text ed. 1.65 ea. transition eds.; Bks. 4-6. text ed. 2.25 ea. nonconsumable eds.; tchrs' eds. 3.90 ea.; handwriting aids avail. (ISBN 0-8372-9530-0); duplicating masters avail., wall charts. Bowmar-Noble.

Better Hockey for Girls. Brenda Read. (Better Ser.). (Illus.). text ed. 14.50x (ISBN 0-7182-1445-5, SpS). Soccer.

Better Homes & Gardens After-40 Health & Medical Guide. Better Homes & Gardens Books Editors. (Illus.). 480p. 1980. 24.95 (ISBN 0-696-00810-6). Meredith Corp.

Better Homes & Gardens All-Time Favorite Barbecue Recipes. Better Homes & Gardens Editors. 176p. 1980. pap. 2.25 (ISBN 0-553-13659-3). Bantam.

Better Homes & Gardens All-Time Favorite Cake & Cookie Recipes. Better Homes & Gardens Books Editors. (All-Time Favorite Recipes Ser.). (Illus.). 96p. 1980. 4.95 (ISBN 0-696-00620-0). Meredith Corp.

Better Homes & Gardens All-Time Favorite Fish & Seafood Recipes. Better Homes & Gardens Books Editors. (All-Time Favorite Recipes Ser.). (Illus.). 96p. 1980. 4.95 (ISBN 0-696-00495-X). Meredith Corp.

Better Homes & Gardens All-Time Favorite Fruit Recipes. Better Homes & Gardens Editors. (All Time Favorite Ser.). (Illus.). 1980. 4.95 (ISBN 0-696-00515-8). Meredith Corp.

Better Homes & Gardens All-Time Favorite Hamburger & Ground Meats Recipes. Ed. by Better Homes & Gardens Books. (All-Time Favorite Ser.). (Illus.). 1980. 4.95 (ISBN 0-696-00505-0). Meredith Corp.

Better Homes & Gardens All-Time Favorite Pies. Ed. by Better Homes & Gardens Books Editors. (Illus.). 1978. 4.95 (ISBN 0-696-00455-0). Meredith Corp.

Better Homes & Gardens Calorie Counter's Cookbook. Better Homes & Gardens Editors. 176p. 1981. pap. 2.50 (ISBN 0-553-14267-4). Bantam.

Better Homes & Gardens Calorie-Trimmed Recipes. Better Homes & Gardens Books Editors. (Illus.). 96p. 1980. 4.95 (ISBN 0-696-00605-7). Meredith Corp.

Better Homes & Gardens Complete Guide to Home Repair, Maintenance & Improvement. Ed. by Better Homes & Gardens Books. (Illus.). 1980. 19.95 (ISBN 0-696-00545-X). Meredith Corp.

Better Homes & Gardens Complete Step-by-Step Cook Book. Ed. by Better Homes & Gardens Books Editors. (Illus.). 1978. 19.95 (ISBN 0-696-00125-X). Meredith Corp.

Better Homes & Gardens Decorating Book. Ed. by Better Homes & Gardens Editors. LC 74-25586. (Illus.). 400p. 1975. 15.95 o.p. (ISBN 0-696-00091-1). Meredith Corp.

Better Homes & Gardens Family Medical Guide. rev. ed. Ed. by Better Homes & Gardens Editors. (Illus.). 1084p. 1973. 22.95 (ISBN 0-696-00342-2); prepub. 26.95 deluxe (ISBN 0-696-00343-0). Meredith Corp.

Better Homes & Gardens Gourmet Recipes Made Easy. Better Homes & Gardens Book Editors. (Illus.). 96p. 1980. 4.95 (ISBN 0-696-00525-5). Meredith Corp.

Better Homes & Gardens Low-Cost Cooking. Ed. by Better Homes & Gardens Books. (Illus.). 1980. 4.95 (ISBN 0-696-00541-7). Meredith Corp.

Better Homes & Gardens More from Your Microwave. Better Homes & Gardens Books Editors. (Illus.). 96p. 1980. 4.95 (ISBN 0-696-00615-4). Meredith Corp.

Better Homes & Gardens New Baby Book. Ed. by Better Homes & Gardens. 416p. 1980. pap. 2.75 (ISBN 0-553-13941-X). Bantam.

Better Homes & Gardens New Cook Book. rev. ed. LC 75-29783. 1976. 12.95 (ISBN 0-696-00010-5). Meredith Corp.

Better Homes & Gardens New Cookbook. Better Homes & Gardens. 832p. 1981. pap. 3.95 (ISBN 0-553-14866-4). Bantam.

Better Homes & Gardens Step-by-Step Basic Wiring. Better Homes & Gardens Books Editors. (Illus.). 96p. 1980. 4.95 (ISBN 0-696-00555-7). Meredith Corp.

Better Homes & Gardens Treasury of Christmas Crafts & Foods. Better Homes & Gardens Books Editors. (Illus.). 384p. 1980. 18.95 (ISBN 0-696-00025-3). Meredith Corp.

Better Homes & Gardens Woodworking Projects You Can Build. Better Homes & Gardens Editors. (You Can Build Ser.). (Illus.). 1980. 4.95 (ISBN 0-696-00325-2). Meredith Corp.

Better Ice Skating for Boys & Girls. George Sullivan. LC 76-12425. (Better Sports Ser.). (gr. 4-6). 1976. 5.95 (ISBN 0-396-07339-5). Dodd.

Better Jobs & Income Plan: A Guide to President Carter's Welfare Reform Proposal & Major Issues. James R. Storey et al. (Welfare Reform Policy Analysis Sr.: No. 1). 97p. 1978. pap. 4.00 (ISBN 0-87766-213-4, 21100). Urban Inst.

Better Karate: The Key to Better Technique. Steve Arneil & Bryan Dowler. (Better Bks.). (Illus.). 98p. 1980. text ed. 14.50 (ISBN 0-7182-1444-7, SpS). Soccer.

Better Kitchens. Cecile Shapiro et al. Ed. by Shirley M. Horowitz. LC 80-67151. (Illus.). 160p. (Orig.). 1980. 12.95 (ISBN 0-932944-23-X); pap. 6.95 (ISBN 0-932944-24-8). Creative Homeowner.

Better Late Than Never: How Men Can Avoid a Midlife Fitness Crisis. Daniel A. Girdano. (Illus.). 256p. 1981. 12.95t (ISBN 0-13-074773-4, Spec); pap. 5.95b (ISBN 0-13-074765-3). P-H.

Better Letters: A Handbook of Business & Personal Correspondence for Secretaries & Their Bosses. Jan Venolia. LC 80-82634. (Illus.). 175p. (Orig.). Date not set. write for info. (ISBN 0-9602584-3-4); pap. write for info. (ISBN 0-9602584-4-2); plastic spiral avail. Periwinkle Pr. Postponed.

Better Listening Skills. J. Sims & P. Peterson. (Illus.). 128p. 1981. pap. 6.95 (ISBN 0-13-074815-3). P-H.

Better Living & Breathing: A Manual for Patients. 2nd ed. Moser et al. LC 80-17943. (Illus.). 94p. 1980. pap. text ed. 4.95 (ISBN 0-8016-3565-9). Mosby.

Better Mousetrap: A Miscellany of Gadgets, Labor-Saving Devices, & Inventions That Intrigue. Aaron E. Klein & Cynthia L. Klein. (Illus.). 192p. (gr. 6 up). 1981. 10.95 (ISBN 0-8253-0030-4). Beaufort Bks NY.

Better Physical Fitness. Vaughan Thomas. LC 76-501663. (Better Sports Ser.). (Illus.). 93p. 1979. 8.50x (ISBN 0-7182-1461-7). Intl Pubns Serv.

Better Physical Fitness for Boys. David C. Cooke. LC 61-8310. (Illus.). (gr. 7-9). 1961. PLB 5.95 o.p. (ISBN 0-396-06586-4). Dodd.

Better Place I Know. Helen Cannon. 1979. pap. 2.25 (ISBN 0-380-75009-0, 75009). Avon.

Better Place to Live: New Designs for Tomorrow's Communities. Michael N. Corbett. Ed. by Carol Stoner. (Illus.). 256p. (Orig.). 1981. pap. 14.95 (ISBN 0-87857-348-8). Rodale Pr Inc.

Better Preaching. Lowell Erdall. (Preacher's Workshop Ser.). 1981. pap. text ed. 1.95 (ISBN 0-570-07408-8, 12-2680). Concordia.

Better Reading One: Factual Prose. 5th ed. Walter Blair et al. 1963. 7.95x o.p. (ISBN 0-673-05209-5). Scott F.

Better Roller Skating: The Key to Improved Performance. Richard Arnold. (Illus.). (gr. 7 up). 1977. 8.95 (ISBN 0-8069-4106-5); PLB 8.29 (ISBN 0-8069-4107-3). Sterling.

Better Science Through Safety. Ed. by Jack A. Gerlovich. 160p. 1981. text ed. 6.00 (ISBN 0-8138-1780-3). Iowa St U Pr.

Better Settlements Through Leverage. Philip Hermann. 1965. 19.50x o.p. (ISBN 0-686-00450-7). Lawyers Co-Op.

Better Shortwave Reception. 4th ed. William I. Orr & Stuart D. Cowan. LC 57-14916. (Illus.). 156p. 1957. 4.95 (ISBN 0-933616-05-8). Radio Pubns.

Better Soccer for Boys & Girls. George Sullivan. LC 77-16869. (Better Sports Ser.). (gr. 4 up). 1978. 5.95 (ISBN 0-396-07533-9). Dodd.

Better Telephoning: A Plan to Improve Your Telephone Technique. Vera Gough & B. R. Grier. 1970. pap. text ed. 3.90 o.p. (ISBN 0-08-006822-7). Pergamon.

Better Tennis. Harry Hopman. (Better Ser.). (Illus.). (gr. 7 up). 1976. 14.50x (ISBN 0-7182-0486-7, SpS). Soccer.

Better Than Divorce. Ruthe Spinnanger. 1978. pap. 3.95 o.p. (ISBN 0-88270-271-8). Logos.

Better Than Ever. Brothers. Date not set. 2.98 (ISBN 0-686-69201-2). Bonanza.

Better Than Gold. Ed. by Clinton T. Howell. LC 70-131117. (Illus.). 1970. 9.95 (ISBN 0-8407-5000-5); deluxe ed. 14.95 (ISBN 0-8407-5001-3). Nelson.

Better Than Gold & Silver. Sandra Mackey. 1975. pap. 3.75 (ISBN 0-89137-407-8). Quality Pubns.

Better Times Than These. Winston Groom. 1979. pap. 2.75 (ISBN 0-425-04098-4). Berkley Pub.

Better Track for Girls. George Sullivan. LC 80-21399. (Better Sports Ser.). (Illus.). 64p. (gr. 5 up). 1981. PLB 6.95 (ISBN 0-396-07911-3). Dodd.

Better Use of. Michael Hackleman. LC 80-9000. (Illus.). 144p. 1981. pap. 9.95 (ISBN 0-915238-50-0). Peace Pr.

Better Winemaking & Brewing for Beginners. B. C. A. Turner. 1972. 10.00 (ISBN 0-7207-0518-5). Transatlantic.

Betti: Corruzione Al Palazzo di Giustizia. Ed. by Vincent Luciani. 1980. pap. 4.95 (ISBN 0-913298-20-4). S F Vanni.

Bettina Von Arnims Briefromane. Waldemar Oehlke. 29.00 (ISBN 0-384-42980-7); pap. 26.00 (ISBN 0-685-02117-3). Johnson Repr.

Betty Crocker's Breads. Betty Crocker. (Illus.). 1974. PLB 7.62 o.p. (ISBN 0-307-69574-3, Golden Pr); pap. 2.95 (ISBN 0-307-09919-9). Western Pub.

Betty Crocker's Cookbook. 816p. 1980. pap. 2.95. Bantam.

Betty Crocker's Cooking American Style. (Illus.). 1976. wire-o 5.95 (ISBN 0-307-09648-3, Golden Pr); PLB 9.15 o.p. (ISBN 0-307-69618-9); pap. 2.95 (ISBN 0-307-09918-0). Western Pub.

Betty Crocker's Cooky Book. (Illus.). (gr. 7 up). 1963. PLB 9.15 (ISBN 0-307-69601-4, Golden Pr); pap. 2.95 o.p. (ISBN 0-307-09901-6). Western Pub.

Betty Crocker's Desserts Cookbook. 1974. pap. 2.95 o.p. (ISBN 0-307-09916-4, Golden Pr). Western Pub.

Betty Crocker's Dinner for Two. (Illus.). 1973. wire-o 5.95 (ISBN 0-307-09646-7, Golden Pr); PLB 9.15 o.p. (ISBN 0-307-69602-2); pap. 2.95 (ISBN 0-307-09915-6). Western Pub.

Betty Crocker's Dinner in a Dish. (Illus.). (gr. 9 up). 1965. PLB 9.15 o.p. (ISBN 0-307-69605-7, Golden Pr). Western Pub.

Betty Crocker's Dinner Parties. (Illus.). 1970. 5.95 (ISBN 0-307-09649-1, Golden Pr); pap. 2.95 o.p. (ISBN 0-307-09911-3). Western Pub.

Betty Crocker's Do-Ahead Cookbook. (Illus.). 160p. 1972. PLB 9.15 o.p. (ISBN 0-307-69614-6, Golden Pr); pap. 2.95 (ISBN 0-307-09914-8). Western Pub.

Betty Crocker's Easy Oven Meals. 1974. PLB 7.62 o.p. (ISBN 0-307-69570-0, Golden Pr). Western Pub.

Betty Crocker's Family Dinners in a Hurry. 1970. PLB 9.15 o.p. (ISBN 0-307-69610-3, Golden Pr); pap. 2.95 (ISBN 0-307-09910-5). Western Pub.

Betty Crocker's Growing Your Own Houseplants. (Betty Crocker Ser.). 1977. PLB 9.15 o.p. (ISBN 0-307-69904-8, Golden Pr); pap. 2.95 (ISBN 0-307-09904-0). Western Pub.

Betty Crocker's Hamburger Cookbook. 1973. PLB 9.15 o.p. (ISBN 0-307-69920-X, Golden Pr); pap. 2.95 (ISBN 0-307-09920-2). Western Pub.

Betty Crocker's Hostess Cookbook. (Illus.). (gr. 9 up). 1966. PLB 9.15 (ISBN 0-307-69606-5, Golden Pr). Western Pub.

Betty Crocker's International Cookbook. General Mills. (Illus.). 1980. 12.95 (ISBN 0-394-50453-4). Random.

Betty Crocker's Low Calorie Cookbook. 1973. PLB 7.62 o.p. (ISBN 0-307-69572-7, Golden Pr); pap. 2.95 (ISBN 0-307-09922-9). Western Pub.

Betty Crocker's Microwave Cooking. (Betty Crocker Ser.). 1977. PLB 9.15 o.p. (ISBN 0-307-69921-8, Golden Pr); pap. 2.95 (ISBN 0-307-09921-0). Western Pub.

Betty Crocker's Pie & Pastry Cookbook. (Illus.). 1968. PLB 9.15 o.p. (ISBN 0-307-69609-X, Golden Pr). Western Pub.

Betty Crocker's Salads. Betty Crocker. (Illus.). 1977. PLB 9.15 o.p. (ISBN 0-307-69900-5, Golden Pr); pap. 2.95 (ISBN 0-307-09900-8). Western Pub.

Betty Crocker's Starting Out. Western Publishing Editors. 512p. 1980. pap. 2.95 (ISBN 0-553-10528-0). Bantam.

Betty Groff's Country Goodness Cookbook. Betty Groff & Jose Wilson. LC 80-1093. (Illus.). 336p. 1981. 17.95 (ISBN 0-385-12120-2). Doubleday.

Betty Page: Private Peeks, Vol. 4. pap. 7.00 (ISBN 0-914646-33-8). Belier Pr.

Between Alchemy & Technology: The Chemical Laboratory. Frank Walmsley & Judith A. Walmsley. (Illus.). 272p. 1975. pap. text ed. 11.95 (ISBN 0-13-075945-7). P-H.

Between Births. Gauri Deshpande. 1975. 8.00 (ISBN 0-88253-508-0); pap. text ed. 4.00 (ISBN 0-88253-507-2). Ind-US Inc.

Between Black & White: Race, Politics, & the Free Coloreds in Jamaica, 1792-1865. Gad J. Heuman. LC 80-661. (Contributions in Comparative Colonial Studies: No. 5). (Illus.). 240p. 1981. lib. bdg. 35.00 (ISBN 0-313-20984-7, HBW/). Greenwood.

Between Concord & Plymouth: The Transcendentalists & the Watsons. L. D. Geller. (Illus.). 255p. 1973. 10.00 (ISBN 0-87451-999-3). U Pr of New Eng.

Between Consenting Adults. Cathrina Bauby. 252p. 1973. 7.95 o.s.i. (ISBN 0-02-507700-7). Macmillan.

Between Faith & Reason: An Approach to Individual & Social Psychology. Francisco Jose Moreno. LC 76-56926. 1977. 10.00x (ISBN 0-8147-5416-3). NYU Pr.

Between Faith & Tears. Kenneth E. Schemmer. 1981. pap. 3.95 (ISBN 0-8407-5770-0). Nelson.

Between Friends. Dorothea Bennett. 1980. pap. 2.25 (ISBN 0-446-92604-3). Warner Bks.

Between Friends. Sheila Garrigue. LC 77-90952. (gr. 5-7). 1978. 8.95 (ISBN 0-87888-133-6). Bradbury Pr.

Between Generations: The Six Stages of Parenthood. Ellen Galinsky. 320p. 1981. 14.95 (ISBN 0-8129-0924-0). Times Bks.

Between God & Man: A Judgment on War Crimes; a Play in Two Parts. Kinoshita Junji. Tr. & intro. by Eric J. Gangloff. LC 79-84890. (Illus.). 180p. (Japanese., Pt. 1, The Judgement; Pt. 2, Summer, a Romance of the South Seas). 1979. 15.00 (ISBN 0-295-95670-4). U of Wash Pr.

Between Heaven & Earth: Recipes for Living & Loving. Laura Archera Huxley. 1975. 8.95 o.p. (ISBN 0-374-11234-7). FS&G.

Between Hell & Charing Cross. Pamela Wilcox. 1978. 13.50 (ISBN 0-04-920051-8). Allen Unwin.

Between High Tides. Daisy Alden. 6.95. Green Hill.

Between Husband & Wife. Victor Salz. LC 72-83634. 282p. (Orig.). 1972. pap. 2.95 o.p. (ISBN 0-8091-1727-4, Deus). Paulist Pr.

Between Life & Death. R. Hammer. 1969. 6.95 o.s.i. (ISBN 0-02-547720-X). Macmillan.

Between Life & Death. Nathalie Sarraute. Tr. by Maria Jolas from Fr. 1980. pap. 11.95 (ISBN 0-7145-0122-0); pap. 4.95 (ISBN 0-7145-0123-9). Riverrun NY.

Between Love & Money: The Dialectics of Women, Work, & the Family. Natalie J. Sokoloff. LC 80-17101. 300p. 1980. 26.95 (ISBN 0-03-055296-6). Praeger.

Between Night & Morn. Kahlil Gibran. 1972. 3.75 o.p. (ISBN 0-8022-2081-9). Philos Lib.

Between Parent & Child. Haim G. Ginott. 1965. 10.95 (ISBN 0-02-543300-8). Macmillan.

Between Past & Present: French, English, & American Etching 1850-1950. Gabriel P. Weisberg & Ronnie L. Zakon. LC 76-53113. (Themes in Art Ser.). (Illus.). 78p. pap. 4.95x (ISBN 0-910386-33-1, Pub. by Cleveland Mus Art). Ind U Pr.

Between Planets. Robert A. Heinlein. (Del Rey Bk.). 1978. pap. 1.75 (ISBN 0-345-27796-1). Ballantine.

Between Power & Plenty: Foreign Economic Policies of Advanced Industrial States. Ed. by Peter J. Katzenstein. LC 77-91053. 1978. 25.00 (ISBN 0-299-07560-5); pap. 8.95 (ISBN 0-299-07564-8). U of Wis Pr.

Between Ring & Temple: A Book for Engaged L.D.S. Couples. Victor Cline et al. 1981. price not set (ISBN 0-913420-87-5). Olympus Pub Co.

Between Romanticism & Modernism: Four Studies in the Music of the Later Nineteenth Century. Carl Dahlhaus. Ed. by Joseph Kerman. Tr. by Mary Whittall from Ger. LC 78-54793. (California Studies in 19th Century Music). 100p. 1980. 10.00x (ISBN 0-520-03679-4). U of Cal Pr.

Between Silence & Light: Spirit in the Architecture of Louis I. Kahn. John Lobell. LC 78-65437. (Illus.). 1979. pap. 7.95 (ISBN 0-394-73687-7). Shambhala Pubns.

Between Sovereignty & Integration. Ed. by G. Ionescu. LC 73-19586. 192p. 1973. text ed. 17.95 (ISBN 0-470-42800-7). Halsted Pr.

Between Tears & Laughter. Mulk R. Anand. 171p. 1974. pap. 2.75 (ISBN 0-88253-311-8). Ind-US Inc.

Between the Bays: Somerset, Wicomico & Worcester Counties Maryland. Janice M. Caper. LC 78-71245. (Illus.). 86p. 1979. pap. 13.00 (ISBN 0-935968-05-9). Holly Pr.

Between the Hammer & the Anvil? Chinese & Russian Policies in Outer Mongolia, 1911-1921. Thomas E. Ewing. (Indiana University Uralic & Altaic Ser.). iv, 300p. 1980. text ed. 19.50 (ISBN 0-933070-06-3). Ind U Res Inst.

Between the Hammer & the Anvil? Chinese & Russian Policies in Outer Mongolia, 1911-1921. Thomas E. Ewing. (Indiana University Uralic & Altaic Ser.: Vol. 138). 300p. 1980. 20.00 (ISBN 0-933070-06-3). Ind U Res Inst.

Between the Lines. Benny Andrews. LC 78-60633. (Illus.). 111p. 1978. 19.95 (ISBN 0-918618-13-4); lib. bdg. 9.95 (ISBN 0-918618-12-6). Pella Pub.

Between the Testaments. D. S. Russell. LC 77-74742. 176p. 1960. pap. 3.95 (ISBN 0-8006-1856-4, 1-1856). Fortress.

Between the Thunder & the Sun. Alfred Coppel. LC 77-147228. 1971. 7.95 o.p. (ISBN 0-15-111950-3). HarBraceJ.

Between the Wars: America, Nineteen Nineteen to Nineteen Forty-One. 2nd ed. David A. Shannon. LC 78-69558. (Illus.). 1978. pap. text ed. 8.25 (ISBN 0-395-26535-5). HM.

Between Time & Eternity: The Essentials of Judaism. Jacob Neusner. 1975. pap. 7.95x (ISBN 0-8221-0160-2). Dickenson.

Between Tradition & Modernity: Wang T'ao & Reform in Late Ch'ing China. Paul A. Cohen. LC 74-75109. (East Asian Ser.: No. 77). 336p. 1974. text ed. 17.50x (ISBN 0-674-06875-0). Harvard U Pr.

Between Two Cultures: Migrants & Minorities in Britain. Ed. by James L. Watson. 1977. 36.00x (ISBN 0-631-18300-0, Pub. by Basil Blackwell); pap. 14.00x (ISBN 0-631-18710-3). Biblio Dist.

Between Two Cultures: The Vietnamese in America. Alan B. Henkin & Liem Thanh Nguyen. LC 80-69333. 125p. 1981. perfect bdg. 7.95 (ISBN 0-86548-039-7). Century Twenty One.

Between Two Moons. Raymond Mungo. 1972. 3.95 (ISBN 0-8070-6402-5, Pub. by Montana Bks); pap. 1.95 (ISBN 0-8070-6405-X). Madrona Pubs.

Between Two Rivers: Poems by Ten North Jersey Poets. Ed. by William J. Higginson & Penny Harter. 48p. (Orig.). 1981. pap. 3.95 (ISBN 0-89120-015-0). From Here.

Between Two Rivers: Union County Literature Today. Ed. by Penny Harter & William J. Higginson. 112p. (Orig.). 1980. pap. 4.95 (ISBN 0-89120-017-7). From Here.

Between Two Worlds: A Profile of Negro Higher Education. Carnegie Commission On Higher Education. Ed. by F. Bowles & DeCosta. 1971. 10.95 o.p. (ISBN 0-07-010024-1, P&RB). McGraw.

Between Two Worlds: An Introduction to Geography. 2nd ed. Robert A. Harper & Theodore H. Schmudde. LC 77-76418. (Illus.). 1977. text ed. 21.50 (ISBN 0-395-25164-8); inst. manual 0.90 (ISBN 0-395-25165-6). HM.

Between Two Worlds: The American Novel in the Nineteen Sixties. Sanford Pinsker. LC 79-64168. 139p. 1980. 7.50 (ISBN 0-87875-169-6). Whitston Pub.

Between Two Worlds: True Ghost Stories of the British Isles. D. A. MacManus. 1977. text ed. 11.25x (ISBN 0-900675-83-7). Humanities.

Between War & Peace: The Nature of International Crisis. Richard N. Lebow. LC 80-21982. 410p. 1981. text ed. 24.50 (ISBN 0-8018-2311-0). Johns Hopkins.

Between Wars & Other Poems. Anne Halley. 1965. pap. 3.50 o.p. (ISBN 0-87023-016-6). U of Mass Pr.

Between You & You: The Art of Listening to Yourself. J. J. McMahon. LC 79-89628. 1980. 9.95 (ISBN 0-8091-0300-1). Paulist Pr.

Between Your Status & Your Quo. Fay Angus. LC 74-15512. (Orig.). 1975. pap. 1.65 o.p. (ISBN 0-8307-0321-7, 50-131-00). Regal.

Beverage Management & Bartending. Peter E. Van Kleek. 144p. 1981. pap. text ed. 7.95 (ISBN 0-8436-2209-1). CBI Pub.

Beverages: Carbonated & Noncarbonated. rev. ed. J. G. Woodroof & G. Frank Phillips. (Illus.). 1981. text ed. 45.00 (ISBN 0-87055-381-X). AVI.

Beverages: Carbonated & Noncarbonated. rev. ed. J. G. Woodroof & G. Frank Phillips. (Illus.). 1981. lib. bdg. 45.00 (ISBN 0-87055-381-X). AVI.

Beverly Hills Diet: Get As Slim As You Like for the Rest of Your Life. Judy Mazel. 192p. 1981. 9.95 (ISBN 0-02-582600-X). Macmillan.

Beverly Johnson's Guide to a Life of Beauty. Beverly Johnson. 1980. 12.50 o.p. (ISBN 0-8129-0911-9). Times Bks.

Beverly of Graustark. George B. McCutcheon. 1976. lib. bdg. 16.25x (ISBN 0-89968-057-7). Lightyear.

Beware of Older Men. Merrit Malloy. LC 79-6886. 168p. 1980. 10.95 (ISBN 0-385-15941-2, Dolp); pap. 4.95 (ISBN 0-385-15942-0). Doubleday.

Beware of the Cat. Ian Pollock. LC 77-82688. (Illus.). 1977. pap. 2.95 (ISBN 0-8467-0385-8, Pub. by Two Continents). Hippocrene Bks.

Beware of the Trains. Edmund Crispin. 1981. pap. 2.95 (ISBN 0-14-005834-6). Penguin.

Beware the Greeks. Lyn Stimer. 256p. (Orig.). 1981. pap. 2.50 (ISBN 0-523-41115-4). Pinnacle Bks.

Bewick Collector, 2 Vols. Thomas Hugo. LC 67-24353. (Illus.). 1968. Repr. of 1866 ed. Set Incl. Suppl. 34.00 (ISBN 0-8103-3491-7). Gale.

Bewitching Grace. Paula Edwars. 192p. (Orig.). 1980. pap. 1.50 (ISBN 0-671-57023-4). S&S.

Bewitching Jewelry. Carl H. Giles & Barbara A. Williams. LC 74-30726. (Illus.). 1976. 12.00 o.p. (ISBN 0-498-01654-4). A S Barnes.

Beyond. Theodore Sturgeon. 1980. pap. 1.95 o.s.i. (ISBN 0-440-10740-7). Dell.

Beyond a Reasonable Doubt: Understanding the American Jury System. Melvyn B. Zerman. 9.95 (ISBN 0-690-04094-6). T y Crowell.

Beyond Academic Departments: The Story of Institutes & Centers. Stanley O. Ikenberry & Renee C. Friedman. LC 72-6045. (Higher Education Ser.). 1972. 10.95x o.p. (ISBN 0-87589-144-6). Jossey-Bass.

Beyond Alcoholism: Alcohol & Public Health Policy. Dan E. Beauchamp. 250p. 1980. 17.50 (ISBN 0-87722-189-8). Temple U Pr.

Beyond All Appearances. Paul Weiss. LC 74-5484. 413p. 1974. 18.95x (ISBN 0-8093-0617-4). S Ill U Pr.

Beyond All This. Mildred Anderson. 1979. pap. 4.95 o.p. (ISBN 0-8010-0128-5). Baker Bk.

Beyond All This Fiddle. A. Alvarez. LC 69-16460. 1969. 10.00 o.p. (ISBN 0-394-41674-0). Random.

Beyond Androcentrism: New Essays on Women & Religion. Ed. by Rita M. Gross. LC 77-13312. (AAR Aids for the Study of Religion: No. 6). 1977. pap. 7.50 (ISBN 0-89130-196-8, 010306). Scholars Pr Ca.

Beyond Belief: Essays on Religion in a Post-Traditional World. Robert N. Bellah. LC 77-109058. 1970. 8.95 o.p. (ISBN 0-06-060774-2, RD-129, HarpR). Har-Row.

Beyond Birth & Death. Swami A. C. Bhaktivedanta. LC 72-84844. (Illus.). 1972. pap. 1.50 (ISBN 0-912776-41-2). Bhaktivedanta.

Beyond Boom & Crash. Robert L. Heilbroner. 1978. 6.95 (ISBN 0-393-05707-0); pap. 2.95x (ISBN 0-393-95003-4). Norton.

Beyond Brokeness. Louis A. Smith & Joseph R. Barndt. (Orig.). 1980. pap. 2.95 (ISBN 0-377-00100-7). Friend Pr.

Beyond Camp David: Emerging Alignments & Leaders in the Middle East. Paul Jureidini & R. D. McLaurin. LC 80-27406. (Contemporary Issues in the Middle East Ser.). 232p. 1981. text ed. 18.00x (ISBN 0-8156-2235-X); pap. text ed. 8.95x (ISBN 0-8156-2236-8). Syracuse U Pr.

Beyond Cape Horn: Travels in the Antarctic. Charles Neider. LC 80-13220. (Illus.). 400p. 1980. 16.95 (ISBN 0-87156-233-2). Sierra.

Beyond Cape Horn: Travels in the Antarctic. Charles Neider. (Illus.). 424p. 1980. 18.95 o.p. (ISBN 0-87156-233-2). Sierra.

Beyond Capitalist Planning. Ed. by Stuart Holland. LC 78-19586. 1979. 19.95 (ISBN 0-312-07778-5). St Martin.

Beyond Charity: U. S. Voluntary Aid for a Changing Third World. John G. Sommer. LC 77-89276. 192p. 1977. pap. 3.95 (ISBN 0-686-28706-1). Overseas Dev Council.

Beyond Cholesterol. Edward Gruberg & Stephen Raymond. 208p. 1981. 9.95 (ISBN 0-312-07779-3). St Martin.

Beyond Cobol: Survival in Business Applications Programming. Gary D. Brown. 225p. 1981. 17.50 (ISBN 0-471-09030-1, Pub. by Wiley-Interscience). Wiley.

Beyond Contract. Alan Fox. (Society Today and Tomorrow Ser.). 1974. 16.95 o.p. (ISBN 0-571-10469-X, Pub. by Faber & Faber). Merrimack Bk Serv.

Beyond Control. George Leonard. LC 75-17505. 200p. 1975. 7.95 o.s.i. (ISBN 0-02-570350-1, 57035). Macmillan.

Beyond Control? A Study of Discipline in the Comprehensive School. Paul Francis. (Unwin Education Books). 1975. text ed. 16.50x o.p. (ISBN 0-04-371033-6); pap. text ed. 8.95x o.p. (ISBN 0-04-371034-4). Allen Unwin.

Beyond Cuba: Latin America Takes Charge of Its Future. Ed. by Luigi R. Einaudi. LC 73-8644. 250p. 1973. pap. 14.00x (ISBN 0-8448-0266-2). Crane-Russak Co.

Beyond Defeat. James E. Johnson & David W. Balsiger. 224p. 1980. pap. cancelled (ISBN 0-553-12651-2). Bantam.

Beyond Dependency: The Developing World Speaks Out. Ed. by Guy F. Erb & Valeriana Kallab. LC 75-23960. (Special Studies). 254p. 1975. text ed. 19.95 o.p. (ISBN 0-275-55580-1). Praeger.

Beyond Dependency: The Developing World Speaks Out. Ed. by Guy F. Erb & Valeriana Kallab. LC 75-23960. 268p. 1975. pap. 3.95 (ISBN 0-686-28707-X). Overseas Dev Council.

Beyond Despair: Directions for America's Third Century. rev. ed. Robert Theobald. 208p. 1981. 11.95 (ISBN 0-932020-04-6); pap. 7.95 (ISBN 0-932020-05-4). Seven Locks Pr.

Beyond Detente: Toward an American Foreign Policy. Paul Eidelberg. 12.95 (ISBN 0-89385-000-4). Green Hill.

Beyond Dogma & Despair: Toward a Critical Phenomenology of Politics. Fred A. Dallmayr. LC 80-53179. 256p. 1981. text ed. 19.95 (ISBN 0-268-00661-X). U of Notre Dame Pr.

Beyond Doubt: A Devotional Response to Questions of Faith. Cornelius Plantinga, Jr. LC 80-10647. (Illus.). 256p. (Orig.). 1980. pap. text ed. 4.95 (ISBN 0-933140-12-6). Bd of Pubns CRC.

Beyond Drugs. Stanley Einstein. LC 73-7940. 1974. text ed. 21.00 (ISBN 0-08-017767-0); pap. text ed. 12.00 (ISBN 0-08-017768-9). Pergamon.

Beyond Economic Man: A New Approach to Micro-Economic Theory. Harvey Leibenstein. (Illus.). 288p. 1976. 16.50x (ISBN 0-674-06891-2); pap. 6.95 (ISBN 0-674-06892-0). Harvard U Pr.

Beyond Ego. Roger Walsh & Frances Vaughn. 272p. 1981. pap. 6.95 (ISBN 0-87477-175-7). J P Tarcher.

Beyond Equality. David Montgomery. 544p. 1972. pap. 2.95 o.p. (ISBN 0-394-71744-9, V744, Vin). Random.

Beyond Equality: Labor & the Radical Republicans, 1862-1872. David Montgomery. LC 80-24434. 550p. 1981. pap. 9.95 (ISBN 0-252-00869-3). U of Ill Pr.

Beyond Existentialism & Zen: Religion in a Pluralistic World. George Rupp. 1979. 10.95x (ISBN 0-19-502462-1). Oxford U Pr.

Beyond Feelings: A Guide to Critical Thinking. Vincent R. Ruggiero. LC 74-34569. 191p. 1975. pap. text ed. 7.95x (ISBN 0-88284-020-7). Alfred Pub.

Beyond Forever. J. Bradford Olesker. (Orig.). 1981. pap. 1.95 (ISBN 0-451-09565-0, J9565, Sig). NAL.

Beyond Games & Scripts. Eric Berne & C. Steiner. 1978. pap. 2.50 (ISBN 0-345-28471-2). Ballantine.

Beyond Games: System Software for Your 6502 Personal Computer. Kenneth Skier. 200p. 1981. pap. 14.95 (ISBN 0-07-057860-5, BYTE Bks). McGraw.

Beyond Genre: New Directions in Literary Classification. Paul Hernadi. (Illus.). 224p. 1972. 19.50x o.p. (ISBN 0-8014-0732-X). Cornell U Pr.

Beyond Graustark: George Barr McCutcheon - Playwright Discovered. A. L. Lazarus & Victor H. Jones. (National University Publications, Literary Criticism Ser.). 1981. 15.00 (ISBN 0-8046-9280-7). Kennikat.

Beyond Her Sphere: Women & the Professions in American History. Barbara J. Harris. LC 78-4017. (Contributions in Women's Studies: No. 4). 1978. lib. bdg. 17.95x (ISBN 0-313-20415-2, HBS/). Greenwood.

Beyond Ideas into Information: A Writing Workbook. Dave Shaw & Greg Eisman. 192p. 1980. pap. text ed. 6.95 (ISBN 0-8403-2218-6). Kendall-Hunt.

Beyond Ideology: A Christian Response to Sociopolitical Conflict in Asia. Won Sul Lee. 1979. pap. 4.95 o.p. (ISBN 0-89107-163-6, Cornerstone Bks). Good News.

Beyond Industrial Growth. Ed. by Abraham Rotstein. LC 76-7440. 1976. pap. 4.95 (ISBN 0-8020-6286-5). U of Toronto Pr.

Beyond IR Eight IRRI's Second Decade. 27p. 1980. pap. 20.25 (ISBN 0-686-69538-0, R 113, IRRI). Unipub.

Beyond Liberalism. Henry S. Kariel. LC 76-48302. 160p. 1977. 8.00 (ISBN 0-88316-526-0). Chandler & Sharp.

Beyond Malpractice: Compensation for Medical Injuries. Institute of Medicine. LC 78-58382. 1978. pap. text ed. 6.50 (ISBN 0-309-02765-9). Natl Acad Pr.

Beyond Marx & Tito. S. Zukin. LC 74-12978. (Illus.). 272p. 1975. 29.95 (ISBN 0-521-20630-8). Cambridge U Pr.

Beyond Media: New Approaches to Mass Communication. Richard W. Budd & Brent D. Ruben. (gr. 10 up). 1978. pap. text ed. 13.25x (ISBN 0-685-38877-8). Hayden.

Beyond Medicine. Hans Holzer. 192p. 1974. pap. 1.95 (ISBN 0-345-28001-6). Ballantine.

Beyond Melancholy: John Webster & the Tragedy of Darkness. Robert F. Whitman. (Salzburg Studies in English Literature, Jacobean Drama Studies: No. 4). 1973. pap. text ed. 25.00x (ISBN 0-391-01565-6). Humanities.

Beyond Necessity: Art in the Folk Tradition. Kenneth L. Ames. (Illus.). 1978. 14.95x (ISBN 0-393-04499-8). Norton.

Beyond Normality: The Predictive Value & Efficiency of Medical Diagnosis. P. S. Galen & S. R. Gambino. LC 75-25915. 1975. 23.95 (ISBN 0-471-29047-5, Pub. by Wiley Medical). Wiley.

Beyond Orange & Green: The Political Eonomy of the Northern Ireland Crisis. 176p. 1978. 12.95 (ISBN 0-905762-16-9, Pub. by Zed Pr); pap. 6.95 (ISBN 0-905762-17-7). Lawrence Hill.

Beyond Our Selves. Catherine Marshall. (Spire Bk). 1968. pap. 1.95 o.p. (ISBN 0-8007-8003-5). Revell.

Beyond Probation: Juvenile Corrections & the Chronic Delinquent. Charles A. Murray & Louis A. Cox, Jr. LC 79-17859. (Sage Library of Social Research: Vol. 94). (Illus.). 1979. 18.00x (ISBN 0-8039-1336-2); pap. 8.95x (ISBN 0-8039-1337-0). Sage.

Beyond Psychology. Otto Rank. pap. text ed. 4.00 (ISBN 0-486-20485-5). Dover.

Beyond Punjab: A Sequel to Punjabi Century. Prakash Tandon. LC 73-123620. (Center for South & Southeast Asia Studies, Uc Berkeley). 1971. 18.50x (ISBN 0-520-01759-5). U of Cal Pr.

Beyond Relevancy: A Book for Teachers of the Future. Michael C. Giammatteo. (Illus.). 1973. pap. 10.00 (ISBN 0-918428-09-2). Sylvan Inst.

Beyond Schenkerism: The Need for Alternatives in Music Analysis. Eugene Narmour. LC 76-25632. xii, 238p. 1980. pap. 7.50 (ISBN 0-226-56848-2, P893, Phoen). U of Chicago Pr.

Beyond Security: Private Perceptions Among Arabs & Israelis. John E. Mroz. (Illus.). 230p. 1981. 20.00 (ISBN 0-08-027517-6); pap. 9.95 (ISBN 0-08-027516-8). Pergamon.

Beyond Separation: Further Studies of Children in Hospital. Ed. by David Hall & Margaret Stacey. (Medicine, Illness & Society Ser.). 1979. 18.00x (ISBN 0-7100-0163-0). Routledge & Kegan.

Beyond Sex Therapy. Martin Shepard. LC 75-162. 1975. 7.95 o.p. (ISBN 0-89110-001-6). Penthouse Pr.

Beyond Silence. Eleanor Cameron. LC 80-10350. (gr. 5-9). 1980. PLB 9.95 (ISBN 0-525-26463-9). Dutton.

Beyond "Spoon River" The Legacy of Edgar Lee Masters. Ronald Primeau. 208p. 1981. text ed. 22.50x (ISBN 0-292-70731-2). U of Tex Pr.

Beyond Stonehenge. Gerald S. Hawkins. LC 72-79671. (Illus.). 336p. (YA) 1973. 15.95 o.p. (ISBN 0-06-011786-9, HarpT). Har-Row.

Beyond Suffrage: Women in the New Deal. Susan Ware. (Illus.). 224p. 1981. text ed. 18.50 (ISBN 0-674-06921-8). Harvard U Pr.

Beyond Survival: A Guide for the Business Owner & His Family. Leon A. Danco. LC 74-29583. (Illus.). Date not set. Repr. of 1975 ed. 19.95 (ISBN 0-9603614-0-5). Univ Pr OH.

Beyond the Adirondacks: The Story of St. Regis Paper Company. Eleanor Amigo & Mark Neuffer. LC 80-1798. (Contributions in Economics & Economic History: No. 35). (Illus.). xi, 219p. 1980. lib. bdg. 22.95 (ISBN 0-313-22735-7, AFN/). Greenwood.

Beyond the Age of Waste. D. Gabor et al. LC 77-30309. 1978. text ed. 37.00 (ISBN 0-08-021835-0); pap. text ed. 17.00 (ISBN 0-08-021834-2). Pergamon.

Beyond the Age of Waste: A Report to the Club of Rome. 2nd ed. D. Gabor et al. LC 80-41614. (Illus.). 265p. 1981. lib. bdg. 42.00 (ISBN 0-08-027303-3); pap. 19.00 (ISBN 0-08-027304-1). Pergamon.
Beyond the Arab-Israeli Settlement: New Directions for U. S. Policy in the Middle East. R. K. Ramazani. LC 77-87564. (Foreign Policy Reports Ser.). 69p. 1977. 5.00 (ISBN 0-89549-006-4). Inst Foreign Policy Anal.
Beyond the Arctic Circle. George Laycock. LC 77-15844. (Illus.). 128p. (gr. 5-9). 1978. 7.95 (ISBN 0-590-07481-4, Four Winds). Schol Bk Serv.
Beyond the Aspen Grove. Ann Zwinger. (Nature Library). (Illus.). 384p. (Orig.). 1981. pap. 5.95 (ISBN 0-06-090842-4, CN 842, CN). Har-Row.
Beyond the Automobile: Reshaping the Transportation Environment. Tabor R. Stone. (Illus.). 1971. 5.95 o.p. (ISBN 0-13-076026-9, Spec). P-H.
Beyond the Balance Sheet: Evaluating Profit Potential. James Lines. LC 74-5512. 1974. 18.95 (ISBN 0-470-53906-2). Halsted Pr.
Beyond the Battle for the Bible. J. I. Packer. LC 80-68331. 160p. 1980. text ed. 7.95 (ISBN 0-89107-195-4, Cornerstone Bks). Good News.
Beyond the Bedroom Wall. Larry Woiwode. 1976. pap. 2.95 (ISBN 0-380-00684-7, 47670, Bard). Avon.
Beyond the Blue Event Horizon. Frederik Pohl. 1980. pap. 2.50 (ISBN 0-345-27535-7). Ballantine.
Beyond the Blue Mountains. Jean Plaidy. 480p. 1976. pap. 1.95 o.p. (ISBN 0-449-22773-1, Crest). Fawcett.
Beyond the Body. Sandra Gibson. 1979. pap. 2.25 (ISBN 0-505-51340-4). Tower Bks.
Beyond the Burning Lands. John Christopher. LC 78-152288. (gr. 5-9). 1971. 8.95 (ISBN 0-02-718420-X). Macmillan.
Beyond the Church. Frederick W. Robinson. Ed. by Robert L. Wolff. LC 75-1501. (Victorian Fiction Ser.). 1975. Repr. of 1866 ed. lib. bdg. 66.00 (ISBN 0-8240-1576-2). Garland Pub.
Beyond the City. A. Conan Doyle. LC 80-67703. (Conan Doyle Centennial Ser.). (Illus.). 150p. 1981. 11.95 (ISBN 0-934468-44-3). Gaslight.
Beyond the Classroom. Ruth Cathcart & Michael Strong. (Gateway to English Program). (Illus.). 208p. (Orig.). 1981. pap. text ed. 4.95 (ISBN 0-88377-170-5). Newbury Hse.
Beyond the Codices: The Nahua View of Colonial Mexico. Arthur J. Anderson et al. LC 74-29801. 225p. 1976. 21.50x (ISBN 0-520-02974-7). U of Cal Pr.
Beyond the Cotter. A. J. Mortlock & K. Hueneke. LC 79-53837. (Canberra Companions Ser.). (Illus.). 66p. (Orig.). 1980. pap. 3.95 (ISBN 0-7081-1581-0, 0541). Bks Australia.
Beyond the Couch: Dialogues in Teaching & Learning Psychoanalysis in Groups. Alexander Wolf et al. LC 70-11256. 1970. 25.00x (ISBN 0-87668-029-5). Aronson.
Beyond the Courtroom: Community Justice & Programs in Conflict Resolution. Benedict S. Alper & Lawrence T. Nichols. LC 78-20376. write for info. (ISBN 0-669-02724-3). Lexington Bks.
Beyond the Cross & the Switchblade. David Wilkerson. 1974. 5.95 o.p. (ISBN 0-912376-08-2). Chosen Bks Pub.
Beyond the Cross & the Switchblade. David Wilkerson. (Orig.). pap. 1.75 (ISBN 0-89129-151-2). Jove Pubns.
Beyond the Dark River. Monica Hughes. LC 80-36726. 168p. (gr. 5-8). 1981. PLB 7.95 (ISBN 0-689-30811-6). Atheneum.
Beyond the EAST Wind: Legends & Folktales of Vietnam. Quyen Van Duong & Jewell R. Coburn. LC 76-50345. (Illus.). 100p. 1976. 8.95 (ISBN 0-918060-01-X). Burn-Hart.
Beyond the Glass. Antonia White. (Virago Modern Classic). 286p. 1981. pap. 5.95 (ISBN 0-686-69081-8). Dial.
Beyond the Goal. Kyle Rote. 1976. pap. 1.25 o.p. (ISBN 0-425-03261-2). Berkley Pub.
Beyond the Gods: Taoist & Buddhist Mysticism. John Blofeld. 1974. 9.25 (ISBN 0-04-294084-2); pap. 6.95 (ISBN 0-04-294085-0). Allen Unwin.
Beyond the Great Glen. James R. Nicolson. LC 74-81071. (British Topographical Ser). (Illus.). 1975. 7.50 (ISBN 0-7153-6778-1). David & Charles.
Beyond the Inhabited World: Roman Britain. Anthony Thwaite. LC 76-17526. (Illus.). (gr. 6 up). 1977. 8.95 (ISBN 0-395-28926-2, Clarion). HM.
Beyond the Law. James A. Pike. LC 73-10754. 102p. 1974. Repr. of 1963 ed. lib. bdg. 11.75x (ISBN 0-8371-7021-4, PIBL). Greenwood.
Beyond the Letter. Israel Scheffler. (International Library of Philosophy & Scientific Method). (Illus.). 1979. 18.00x (ISBN 0-7100-0315-3). Routledge & Kegan.
Beyond the Melting Pot: The Negroes, Puerto Ricans, Jews, Italians, & Irish of New York City. 2nd rev ed. Nathan Glazer & Daniel P. Moynihan. 1970. 17.00x (ISBN 0-262-07039-1); pap. 4.95 (ISBN 0-262-57022-X). MIT Pr.
Beyond the Mind: Conversations on the Deeper Significance of Living. Dada. LC 77-85723. (Illus.). 1978. pap. 4.95 (ISBN 0-930608-01-1). Dada Ctr.
Beyond the Moon. Paolo Maffei. 1980. pap. 7.95 (ISBN 0-380-48744-6, 48744). Avon.
Beyond the Myths of Culture: Essays in Cultural Materialism. Ed. by Eric B. Ross. LC 79-6772. (Studies in Anthropology Ser.). 1980. 31.00 (ISBN 0-12-598180-5). Acad Pr.
Beyond the New Deal: Harry S. Truman & American Liberalism. Alonzo L. Hamby. (Contemporary American History Ser.). 655p. 1973. 22.50x (ISBN 0-231-03335-4); pap. 10.00x (ISBN 0-231-08344-0). Columbia U Pr.
Beyond the New Morality: The Responsibilities of Freedom. rev. ed. Germain Grisez & Russell Shaw. LC 80-18293. 240p. 1980. text ed. 10.95 (ISBN 0-268-00663-6); pap. 4.95 (ISBN 0-268-00665-2). U of Notre Damepr.
Beyond the North-South Stalemate. Roger D. Hansen. LC 78-10607. 348p. 1979. pap. 5.95 (ISBN 0-07-026049-4). Overseas Dev Council.
Beyond the Numbers Game: A Reader in Educational Evaluation. Ed. by David Hamilton et al. (Education Ser.). 1977. 17.20 (ISBN 0-8211-0416-0); text ed. 15.50x (ISBN 0-685-04966-3). McCutchan.
Beyond the Open Classroom: Toward Informal Education. Lorraine L. Morgan et al. LC 80-69235. 140p. 1981. perfect bdg. 9.50 (ISBN 0-86548-050-8). Century Twenty One.
Beyond the Paw-Paw Trees. Palmer Brown. (gr. 3-5). 1973. pap. 0.95 o.s.i. (ISBN 0-380-01055-0, 14605, Camelot). Avon.
Beyond the Presidency: The Residues of Power. Marie B. Hecht. (Illus.). 1976. 15.95 o.s.i. (ISBN 0-02-550190-9). Macmillan.
Beyond the Prize. Mark Denning. 1978. pap. 1.25 o.s.i. (ISBN 0-515-04473-3). Jove Pubns.
Beyond the Punitive Society: Operant Conditioning, Social & Political Aspects. Ed. by Harvey Wheeler. LC 73-1269. (Illus.). 1973. pap. text ed. 9.95x (ISBN 0-7167-0775-6). W H Freeman.
Beyond the Rainbow Mists: A Journey That Takes You Out of This World. Lane D. Endicott. 1981. 6.50 (ISBN 0-8062-1614-X). Carlton.
Beyond the Reach of Sense. Rosalind Heywood. 1974. pap. 3.45 o.p. (ISBN 0-525-47381-5). Dutton.
Beyond the River & the Bay: The Canadian Northwest in 1811. Eric Ross. LC 71-486954. (Illus.). 1970. pap. 4.50 (ISBN 0-8020-6188-5). U of Toronto Pr.
Beyond the Shadow of a Doubt. Wilbur Alexander. LC 74-181389. (Stories That Win Ser.). 1971. pap. 0.95 o.p. (ISBN 0-8163-0131-X, 02168-3). Pacific Pr Pub Assn.
Beyond the Sociology of Development. Ed. by Ivar Oxaal et al. (International Library of Sociology). 1975. 25.00 (ISBN 0-7100-8049-2); pap. 12.00 (ISBN 0-7100-8050-6). Routledge & Kegan.
Beyond the Tenth. T. Lobsang Rampa. pap. 2.50 (ISBN 0-685-22168-7). Weiser.
Beyond the Tetons. Ralph Maughan. (Illus.). 135p. (Orig.). 1981. pap. 5.95 (ISBN 0-87108-580-1). Pruett.
Beyond the Tomb. H. M. Riggle. 288p. 4.00. Faith Pub Hse.
Beyond the Valley of the Dollar. Craig R. Hover. (Illus.). 224p. Date not set. 10.95 (ISBN 0-89913-004-6). Entity Pub Co. Postponed.
Beyond the Veil: Male-Female Dynamics in a Modern Muslim Society. 2nd ed. Fatima Mernissi. 132p. 1981. pap. text ed. 6.95x (ISBN 0-87073-267-6). Schenkman.
Beyond the Vicarage. Noel Streatfield. LC 77-169824. 214p. (gr. 9 up). 1972. PLB 5.90 (ISBN 0-531-02018-5). Watts.
Beyond the "Vietnam Syndrome" U. S. Interventionism in the 1980's. Michael T. Klare. 80p. (Orig.). 1981. pap. 4.95 (ISBN 0-89758-027-3). Inst Policy Stud.
Beyond the Village: Local Politics in Madang, Papua New Guinea. Louise Morauta. (Monographs on Social Anthropology: No. 49). 208p. 1974. text ed. 19.50x (ISBN 0-391-00327-5, Athlone Pr). Humanities.
Beyond the Wall. Ann Boyle. 192p. (YA) 1976. 4.95 o.p. (ISBN 0-685-57547-0, Avalon). Bouregy.
Beyond the Weir Bridge. Hester Burton. LC 77-109906. (Illus.). (gr. 6 up). 1970. 4.95 o.p. (ISBN 0-690-14052-5, TYC-J). T Y Crowell.
Beyond the Zone System. Phil Davis. (Illus.). 256p. 1981. 19.95 (ISBN 0-930764-23-4); wkbk 8.95 (ISBN 0-930764-28-5). Curtin & London.
Beyond Their Sex: Learned Women of the European Past. Ed. by Patricial H. Labalme. LC 79-56638. 208p. 1980. 17.50x (ISBN 0-8147-4998-4). NYU Pr.
Beyond This Colored Glass. Jackie Larsen. LC 79-83904. (Illus.). 1970. softcover 4.95 (ISBN 0-9602474-2-4). J Larsen.
Beyond This Horizon. Robert A. Heinlein. (Science Fiction Ser.). 1981. PLB 14.95 (ISBN 0-8398-2672-9). Gregg.
Beyond Time & Matter. Aaron E. Klein. LC 73-79684. 120p. (gr. 7-9). 1973. 4.95 o.p. (ISBN 0-385-06106-4). Doubleday.
Beyond T.M. A Practical Guide to the Lost Tradition of Christian Meditation. Marilyn Helleberg. LC 80-82811. 144p. (Orig.). 1981. pap. 6.95 (ISBN 0-8091-2325-8). Paulist Pr.
Beyond Tradition & Modernity: Changing Religions in a Changing World. Zui Werblowsky. (Jordan Lectures in Comparative Religion, 11th Ser.). 146p. 1976. text ed. 16.25x (ISBN 0-485-17411-1, Athlone Pr). Humanities.
Beyond Tragedy: Essays on the Christian Interpretation of History. Reinhold Niebuhr. 1937. pap. 4.95 o.p. (ISBN 0-684-71853-7, SL38, ScribT). Scribner.
Beyond Ujamaa in Tanzania: Underdevelopment & an Uncaptured Peasantry. Goran Hyden. 1980. 20.00 (ISBN 0-520-03997-1); pap. 7.95 (ISBN 0-520-04017-1). U of Cal Pr.
Beyond Valium: The Brave New World of Psychochemistry. Seymour Rosenblatt & Reynolds Dodson. 316p. 1981. 13.95 (ISBN 0-399-12577-9). Putnam.
Beyond Violence. Jiddu Krishnamurti. LC 72-9875. 176p. 1973. pap. 3.95 (ISBN 0-06-064839-2, RD 61, HarpR). Har-Row.
Beyond Words. Ed. by Lester Alexander. LC 76-29896. (Illus.). 1977. 8.95 o.p. (ISBN 0-03-020871-8); pap. 5.95 (ISBN 0-03-016911-9). HR&W.
Beyond Words: An Introduction to Nonverbal Communication. Randall P. Harrison. LC 73-17202. (Speech Communication Ser). (Illus.). 208p. 1974. ref. ed. 14.95 (ISBN 0-13-076141-9); pap. 10.95 (ISBN 0-13-076133-8). P-H.
Beyond Words: Exciting New Word Games. Sid Sackson. LC 76-54201. (Illus.). 1977. pap. 2.95 o.p. (ISBN 0-394-83444-5). Pantheon.
Beyond Words: Mystical Fancy in Children's Literature. James E. Higgins. LC 71-96760. 1970. pap. 4.25x (ISBN 0-8077-1517-4). Tchrs Coll.
Beyond Yoga. Goldie Lipson. 1977. pap. 1.50 o.s.i. (ISBN 0-515-04419-9). Jove Pubns.
Beyonders. Manly W. Wellman. (Orig.). 1977. pap. 1.50 o.s.i. (ISBN 0-446-88202-X). Warner Bks.
Bezeichnungen fuer Gross-Klein, "Lang-Kurz" im Altschwedischen. Ingela Josefson. (Nordistica Gothoburgensia: 9). (Ger.). 1976. pap. text ed. 10.00x (ISBN 91-7346-025-7). Humanities.
B.F. Skinner. John A. Weigel. (World Leaders Ser.: No. 64). 1977. lib. bdg. 9.95 (ISBN 0-8057-7713-X). Twayne.
Bhabani Bhattacharya. K. R. Chandrasekharan. (Indian Writers Ser.). 1976. 8.50 (ISBN 0-89253-505-9). Ind-US Inc.
Bhabani Bhattacharya. Dorothy B. Shimer. (World Authors Ser.: India: No. 343). 1975. lib. bdg. 12.50 (ISBN 0-8057-2151-7). Twayne.
Bhagavad Gita, 8th prts. Tr. by Annie Besant. 1974. 1.75 (ISBN 0-8356-7001-5). Theos Pub Hse.
Bhagavad Gita. Tr. by P. Lal from Sanskrit. 71p. 1973. 8.00 (ISBN 0-88253-304-5); flexible bdg. 4.80 (ISBN 0-89253-542-3). Ind-US Inc.
Bhagavad Gita. Tr. by Swami Nikhilananda. LC 44-33674. 404p. with notes 7.00 (ISBN 0-911206-09-4); without notes, 256p. 3.00 (ISBN 0-911206-10-8). Ramakrishna.
Bhagavad Gita. Tr. by Swami S. Purhoit. (Illus.). 1977. 10.00 o.p. (ISBN 0-394-40671-0); pap. 5.95 (ISBN 0-394-72394-5). Knopf.
Bhagavad Gita. Swami Chidbhavananda. 1979. 8.50 (ISBN 0-89744-968-1). Auromere.
Bhagavad Gita: A Critical Rendering. Tr. by G. Feuerstein. 170p. 1980. text ed. cancelled (ISBN 0-8426-1666-7). Verry.
Bhagavad Gita: A Critical Rendering. G. Feurstein. 1981. text ed. write for info. (ISBN 0-391-02191-5). Humanities.
Bhagavad Gita, a Revelation: Mahabharata Bhagavad Gita. Dilipkumar Roy. 190p. 1975. 12.50 (ISBN 0-88253-698-2). Ind-US Inc.
Bhagavad Gita: A Translation & Critical Commentary. A. L. Herman. (Illus.). 200p. 1973. 11.75 (ISBN 0-398-02772-2). C C Thomas.
Bhagavad-Gita As It Is. abr. ed. Swami A. C. Bhaktivedanta. LC 75-34536. (Illus.). 330p. 1976. 6.95 (ISBN 0-912776-80-3); text ed. 3.95 (ISBN 0-685-65672-1); pap. write for info. (ISBN 0-685-65673-X); pap. text ed. 2.95 (ISBN 0-685-65674-8). Bhaktivedanta.
Bhagavad-Gita: Recension with Essays. Ed. by William Q. Judge. LC 70-92964. 1969. 6.00 (ISBN 0-911500-27-8); softcover 3.50 (ISBN 0-911500-28-6). Theos U Pr.
Bhagavad-Gita: Song of God. 3rd ed. Tr. by Swami Prabhavananda & Christopher Isherwood. LC 46-1825. 1972. 6.95 (ISBN 0-87481-008-6). Vedanta Pr.
Bhagavad-Gita: The Book of Devotion Dialogue Between Krishna, Lord of Devotion, & Arjuna, Prince of India. Tr. & intro. by William Q. Judge. xviii, 133p. 1930. Repr. of 1891 ed. 3.50 (ISBN 0-938998-09-9). Theosophy.
Bhagavad Gita: The Divine Message, 2 vols. Swami Abhedananda. 30.00 set o.s.i. (ISBN 0-87481-625-4). Vedanta Pr.
Bhagavadgita. (Sanskrit-Eng). 7.50x o.s.i. (ISBN 0-686-00844-8). Colton Bk.
Bhagavadgita. Tr. by P. Lal. 107p. 1971. pap. 2.00 (ISBN 0-88253-054-2). Ind-US Inc.
Bhagavadgita. 2nd ed. S. Radhakrishnan. 1949. 12.50 (ISBN 0-04-891028-7); pap. 10.95 (ISBN 0-04-891029-5). Allen Unwin.
Bhagavadgita. 2nd ed. S. Radhakrishnan. 388p. 1949. 12.50 (ISBN 0-04-891029-5). Allen Unwin.
Bhagavadgita in the Mahabharata: A Bilingual Edition. Ed. by J. A. Van Buitenen. LC 79-13021. 1981. lib. bdg. price not set (ISBN 0-226-84660-1, P880, Phoen); pap. price not set (ISBN 0-226-84662-8). U of Chicago Pr.
Bhagavadita, Vol. 8. Ed. by F. Max Mueller. Tr. by K. T. Telang. (Sacred Books of the East Ser.). 15.00x (ISBN 0-8426-1394-3). Verry.
Bhagavata Purana. Ed. by J. L. Shastri. Tr. by G. V. Tagare. (Ancient Indian Tradition & Mythology Ser.: Vols. 7, 8 & 9). 1976. 18.00x ea. Pt. 1 (ISBN 0-8426-0855-9). Pt. 2 (ISBN 0-8426-0882-6). Pt. 3 (ISBN 0-8426-0911-3). Verry.
Bhagavata Purana: Part 4. Ed. by J. L. Shastri. (Ancient Indian Tradition & Mythology Ser.: Vol. 10). 1978. text ed. 18.00 (ISBN 0-8426-1079-0). Verry.
Bhagavata Purana: Part 5. Ed. by J. L. Shastri. (Ancient Indian Tradition & Mythology Ser.: Vol. 11). (Contains index for vols. 1-5). 1979. text ed. 18.00x (ISBN 0-8426-1105-3). Verry.
Bhakti Ratnavali: An Anthology from the Bhagavata. Vishnu Puri. Tr. by Swami Tapasyananda from Sanskrit. 256p. 1980. pap. 5.95 (ISBN 0-87481-499-5). Vedanta Pr.
Bharata Natyam Dancer. 2nd ed. G. S. Sharat Chandra. (Redbird Bk.). 1976. 8.00 (ISBN 0-89253-129-0); flexible bdg. 4.80 (ISBN 0-89253-140-1). Ind-US Inc.
Bharata Natyam: Indian Classical Dance Art. Ed. by Sunil Kothari. LC 80-901925. (Illus.). 212p. 1979. 37.50x (ISBN 0-8002-2441-8). Intl Pubns Serv.
Bhartrhari. Harold G. Coward. (World Authors Ser.: India: No. 403). 1976. lib. bdg. 12.50 (ISBN 0-8057-6243-4). Twayne.
Bhartrihari: Poems. Tr. by Barbara S. Miller. (Bilingual, Orig). 1967. 15.00x (ISBN 0-231-02999-3). Columbia U Pr.
Bhojpuri Grammar. Shaligram Shukla. (Bhojpuri.). 1981. text ed. 10.00x (ISBN 0-87840-189-X). Georgetown U Pr.
Bhutan: A Physical & Cultural Geography. Pradyumna P. Karan. LC 67-17842. (Illus.). 112p. 1967. 21.50x (ISBN 0-8131-1137-4). U Pr of Ky.
Bhutto: A Political Biography. Salmaan Taseer. 208p. text ed. cancelled o.s.i. (ISBN 0-7069-1085-0, Pub. by Vikas India). Advent Bk.
Bias in Indian Historiography. Devahuti. 1980. text ed. write for info. (ISBN 0-391-02174-5). Humanities.
Bias of Communication. 2nd ed. Harold A. Innis. LC 65-97355. 1964. 12.50x o.p. (ISBN 0-8020-1040-7); pap. 6.50 (ISBN 0-8020-6027-7). U of Toronto Pr.
Biberswald. David Shotter. 1973. pap. text ed. 5.95x o.p. (ISBN 0-435-38835-5); tchr's ed. 3.95x o.p. (ISBN 0-435-38836-3); four tapes 80.00 o.p. (ISBN 0-435-38837-1). Heinemann Ed.
Bible: A Literary Survey. Charles W. Harwell & Daniel McDonald. LC 74-13465. 307p. 1975. pap. 11.95 (ISBN 0-672-63278-0). Bobbs.
Bible: A Pictorial History. Claus Westerman & Erich Lessing. (Illus.). 1976. 14.95 (ISBN 0-8164-1216-2); pap. 8.95 (ISBN 0-8164-1220-0). Crossroad NY.
Bible ABC Book. Solveig P. Russell. LC 67-27153. (Illus.). 1981. laminated bdg. 5.50 (ISBN 0-570-03418-3, 56-1065). Concordia.
Bible Activities for Kids, No. 1. Donna L. Pape & Virginia Mueller. (Illus.). 64p. (Orig.). (gr. 3-7). 1980. pap. 1.95 (ISBN 0-87123-148-4, 21048). Bethany Fell.
Bible Adventures. Carol Ferntheil. (Basic Bible Readers Ser.). (Illus.). (gr. 3). 1963. pap. 4.50 (ISBN 0-87239-260-0, 2757). Standard Pub.
Bible & Archaeology. wnd, rev. ed. J. A. Thompson. 512p. 1981. 13.95 (ISBN 0-8028-3545-7). Eerdmans.
Bible & Archaeology. John A. Thompson. (Illus.). 1962. 13.95 (ISBN 0-8028-3268-7). Eerdmans.
Bible & Christ: The Unity of the Two Testaments. Leopold Sabourin. LC 80-14892. 208p. (Orig.). 1980. pap. 6.95 (ISBN 0-8189-0405-4). Alba.
Bible & Modern Science. Henry Morris. 1956. pap. 1.50 (ISBN 0-8024-0572-X). Moody.

Bible & the Bermuda Triangle. George Johnson & Don Tanner. 1977. pap. 2.95 (ISBN 0-88270-321-8). Logos.

Bible & the Common Reader. rev. ed. Mary E. Chase. 1962. pap. 2.95 (ISBN 0-02-084390-9, Collier). Macmillan.

Bible & the World & Triluminal Science. Apostolos Makrakis. Ed. by Orthodox Christian Educational Society. Tr. by Denver Cummings from Hellenic. 531p. 1950. 6.00x (ISBN 0-938366-18-1). Orthodox Chr.

Bible & Tomorrow's News. Charles C. Ryrie. LC 69-17068. 190p. 1969. pap. 1.95 o.p. (ISBN 0-88207-017-7). Victor Bks.

Bible Answers. S. I. Emery. 1.95 o.p. (ISBN 0-686-12850-8). Schmul Pub Co.

Bible As History. 2nd, rev. ed. Werner Keller. Ed. by Joachim Rehork. Tr. by William Neil & B. H. Rasmussen. LC 80-22218. Orig. Title: Und Die Bibel Hat Docht Recht. (Illus.). 448p. 1981. 16.95 (ISBN 0-688-03724-0). Morrow.

Bible As Literature: Old Testament & the Apocrypha. 2nd ed. Buckner B. Trawick. 1970. pap. 4.50 (ISBN 0-06-460056-4, CO 56, COS). Har-Row.

Bible As Literature: The New Testament. 2nd ed. Buckner B. Trawick. (Orig.). 1968. pap. 2.95 (ISBN 0-06-460057-2, CO 57, COS). Har-Row.

Bible As Read & Preached in the Old Synagogue, Vol. 2. Jacob Mann. 1968. 39.50 (ISBN 0-685-22512-7). Ktav.

Bible Atlas. Charles F. Pfeiffer. LC 60-15536. 1975. 14.95 (ISBN 0-8054-1129-1). Broadman.

Bible Beasts. John Livesay. LC 74-84764. 1976. 3.00 (ISBN 0-8309-0130-2). Herald Hse.

Bible Between Fundamentalism & Philosophy. Henry P. Hamann. LC 80-65558. 80p. 1980. pap. 3.50 (ISBN 0-8066-1803-5, 10-0701). Augsburg.

Bible Bibliography, Nineteen Sixty-Seven to Nineteen Seventy-Three: Old Testament. Ed. by P. R. Ackroyd. 1975. 46.50x (ISBN 0-631-16070-1, Pub. by Basil Blackwell). Biblio Dist.

Bible: Breathed from God. Robert L. Saucy. 1978. pap. 3.95 (ISBN 0-88207-778-3). Victor Bks.

Bible: Chain of Truth. A. Marie Miles. 168p. pap. 1.25. Faith Pub Hse.

Bible Difficulties. William F. Arndt. 1981. 3.75 (ISBN 0-570-03120-6, 12-2357). Concordia.

Bible Doctrine of Final Things. Robert R. Taylor, Jr. 1977. 7.50 (ISBN 0-89315-019-3). Lambert Bk.

Bible Finger Plays for Young Children. Compiled by Patricia Shely. (Standard Ideas Ser.). (Illus.). 1978. pap. 1.75 (ISBN 0-87239-212-0, 2813). Standard Pub.

Bible for Students of Literature & Art. Ed. by G. B. Harrison. LC 64-13820. 1964. pap. 3.50 (ISBN 0-385-04475-5, A394, Anch). Doubleday.

Bible for Today's Church. Robert A. Bennett & O. C. Edwards. (Church's Teaching Ser.: Vol. 2). 1979. 9.50 (ISBN 0-8164-0419-4); pap. 3.95 (ISBN 0-8164-2215-X). Crossroad NY.

Bible Fun Book, No. 7. Steve Crain. 32p. (Orig.). (gr. k-4). 1981. oversized saddle stitched .89 (ISBN 0-87123-766-0, 220766). Bethany Fell.

Bible Game Ideas. Shirley Beegle. (Ideas Ser.). (Illus.). 1977. pap. text ed. 1.75 (ISBN 0-87239-118-3, 7958). Standard Pub.

Bible Handbook: A Guide for Basic Bible Learning. Michael Weed & Libby Weed. LC 73-91023. 1978. student's ed. 2.95 (ISBN 0-8344-0101-0); pocket ed. 2.95 (ISBN 0-686-65381-5); gift ed. o.s.i. 2.95 (ISBN 0-8344-0103-7). Sweet.

Bible Handbook for Young Learners. Michael Weed & Libby Weed. LC 73-91023. (Illus.). 236p. (gr. 3-8). 1974. kivar 5.95 o.p. (ISBN 0-8344-0082-0). Sweet.

Bible Heroes. A. C. Mueller. LC 56-1128. (Bible Story Booklet Ser). (Illus.). (gr. 3-5). 1981. pap. 0.69 (ISBN 0-570-06700-6, 56-1128). Concordia.

Bible Heroes. Ruth S. Odor. (Basic Bible Readers Ser.). (Illus.). (gr. 4). 1963. pap. 4.50 (ISBN 0-87239-261-9, 2758). Standard Pub.

Bible Heroes & Heroines. Maureen Curley. (Children of the Kingdom Activities Ser.). (gr. 4-7). 1975. 7.95 (ISBN 0-686-13688-8). Pflaum Pr.

Bible History Commentary: Old Testament. Werner H. Franzmann. LC 80-53145. (Illus.). 616p. 1981. 15.95 (ISBN 0-938272-04-7). Wis Ev Luth.

Bible in German: Old & New Testament. rev. ed. Tr. by Martin Luther. 15.00 o.p. (ISBN 3-4380-1221-9). Adler.

Bible in Its Literary Milieu. Ed. by John Maier & Vincent Tollers. (Orig.). 1980. pap. 12.95 (ISBN 0-8028-1799-8). Eerdmans.

Bible in Its World: The Bible & Archaeology Today. K. A. Kitchen. (Illus.). 1978. pap. 4.95 (ISBN 0-87784-797-5). Inter-Varsity.

Bible in Order. Ed. by Joseph Rhymer. LC 75-11363. 1950p. 1976. 35.00 o.p. (ISBN 0-385-11062-6). Doubleday.

Bible in Pictures. Ed. by Catholic Polls Inc. (Illus.). 12.95 o.p. (ISBN 0-685-74102-8). Guild Bks.

Bible in Pictures for Little Eyes. Kenneth N. Taylor. (Illus.). (gr. 3-6). 1956. 7.95 (ISBN 0-8024-0595-9). Moody.

Bible in Pocket, Gun in Hand: The Story of Frontier Religion. Ross Phares. LC 64-11375. 1971. pap. 3.95 (ISBN 0-8032-5725-2, BB 524, Bison). U of Nebr Pr.

Bible in Public Schools. 2nd ed. Johann B. Stallo et al. LC 67-27464. (Law, Politics & History Ser). 1967. Repr. of 1870 ed. lib. bdg. 35.00 (ISBN 0-306-70963-5). Da Capo.

Bible in the Light of Our Redemption. E. W. Kenyon. 320p. 1974. pap. 5.50 o.p. (ISBN 0-8007-0673-0). Revell.

Bible in the Wesleyan Heritage. Mack B. Stokes. LC 80-23636. 96p. (Orig.). 1981. pap. 3.95 (ISBN 0-687-03100-1). Abingdon.

Bible Index. Ed. by R. G. Bratcher & J. A. Thompson. 1970. pap. 1.00 (ISBN 0-8267-0005-5, 08511). United Bible.

Bible Inerrancy Primer. John Gerstner. Date not set. pap. 1.95 (ISBN 0-88469-144-6). BMH Bks.

Bible Jumble Word Puzzles. William Hendricks. 1978. pap. 2.50 (ISBN 0-310-37192-9). Zondervan.

Bible Key Word Quizzes. J. G. Malphurs. (Quiz & Puzzle Bks.). 1971. pap. 1.95 (ISBN 0-8010-5924-0). Baker Bk.

Bible Learning Activities: Youth - Grades Seven to Twelve. Bobbie Reed & Rex E. Johnson. LC 73-87520. (Illus.). 155p. (Orig.). (gr. 7-12). 1974. pap. 2.95 o.p. (ISBN 0-8307-0239-3, 97-013-03). Regal.

Bible Lessons for Juniors, 4 bks. Andrew Van Der Veer. Incl. Bk. 1. Creation Through Moses. 1.95 (ISBN 0-8010-9253-1); Bk. 2. Kings & Prophets. 1.95 (ISBN 0-8010-9251-5); Bk. 3. Life of Christ. 1.95 (ISBN 0-8010-9257-4); Bk. 4. Early Church. 1.50 (ISBN 0-8010-9255-8). Baker Bk.

Bible Lessons for Little People: Revised with Learning Centers. rev. ed. Evelyn Grogg. Rev. by Sarah Eberle. LC 80-53878. 144p. 1981. pap. 6.95 (ISBN 0-87239-430-1, 3368). Standard Pub.

Bible Manhunt. J. Curtis Manor. (Quiz & Puzzle Book Ser.). 128p. (Orig.). 1980. pap. 2.45 (ISBN 0-8010-6097-4). Baker Bk.

Bible Object Talks with Paper & Scissors. Francis Brown et al. Ed. by Patricia Shely. (Illus.). 1976. pap. 2.25 (ISBN 0-87239-116-7, 2747). Standard Pub.

Bible on the Life Hereafter. William Hendriksen. (Direction Books). 1971. pap. 3.45 (ISBN 0-8010-4189-9). Baker Bk.

Bible One, Two, Three's. Dana Eynon. (gr. k-1). 1977. pap. 1.00 o.p. (ISBN 0-87239-264-3, 2011). Standard Pub.

Bible Places Quiz Book. Erma Reynolds. (Quiz & Puzzle Books Ser.). 112p. (Orig.). 1981. pap. 2.45 (ISBN 0-8010-7703-6). Baker Bk.

Bible Plants for American Gardens. Eleanor A. King. LC 75-3646. (Illus.). 224p. 1975. pap. 3.50 (ISBN 0-486-23188-7). Dover.

Bible Prayerbook. Ed. by Eugene S. Geissler. LC 80-71052. 528p. (Orig.). 1981. pap. 4.95 (ISBN 0-87793-218-2). Ave Maria.

Bible Puppet Plays. Ewart A. Autry & Lola M. Autry. (Paperback Program Ser.). pap. 3.95 (ISBN 0-8010-0032-7). Baker Bk.

Bible Quiz Book. Barbara Burrage. (gr. 5 up). 1979. pap. 2.50 (ISBN 0-8192-1256-3). Morehouse.

Bible Quiz Book Nos. 1 & 2. 1.25 ea. (Pub. by Collins Pubs). No. 1 (ISBN 0-00-411721-2, BQ-1). No. 2 (ISBN 0-00-411723-9, BQ-2). World Bible.

Bible Quizzerama Puzzle Book. Barbara Burrage. 48p. (Orig.). (gr. 6 up). 1981. pap. 1.25 (ISBN 0-87239-446-8, 2836). Standard Pub.

Bible Quizzes for Everybody. Frederick Hall. (Quiz & Puzzle Bks.). 150p. 1980. pap. 2.95 (ISBN 0-8010-4032-9). Baker Bk.

Bible Quizzes for Everyone. Compiled by Susan Craig. (Fountain Bks). 96p. 1975. pap. 1.95 o.p. (ISBN 0-87239-039-X, 2294). Standard Pub.

Bible Reader's Encyclopedia & Concordance. W. Clow. (Illus.). 6.95 (ISBN 0-00-512008-X, RT1, Pub. by Collins Pubs). World Bible.

Bible Readings for Bible Students & for the Home & Fireside. Compiled by S. L. Speck & H. M. Riggle. 432p. 1902. 5.00. Faith Pub Hse.

Bible Readings for Couples. Margaret Wold & Erling Wold. LC 80-65541. 112p. (Orig.). 1980. pap. 2.95 (ISBN 0-686-61283-3, 10-0676). Augsburg.

Bible Speaks, 3 vols. Hella Taubes. Tr. by Lolla Bloch. (Illus.). (gr. 4-6). 1974. 7.50x ea.; Set. 20.00x. Bloch.

Bible Stories. Norman V. Peale. pap. 2.25 (ISBN 0-89129-049-4). Jove Pubns.

Bible Stories for Children. Retold by Geoffrey Horn & Arthur Cavanaugh. (Illus.). 1980. 12.95 (ISBN 0-686-64566-9). Macmillan.

Bible Stories for Everyone. Ed. by Daughters Of St. Paul. 1956. 6.00 o.s.i. (ISBN 0-8198-0008-2); pap. 5.00 o.s.i. (ISBN 0-8198-0009-0). Dghtrs St Paul.

Bible Stories for Little Children, 3 bks. Betty R. Hollender. (Illus.). (gr. k-3). text ed. 4.00 ea. o.p. UAHC.

Bible Stories to Grow by. Mary Batchelor. LC 80-65436. (Illus.). 96p. 1980. 8.95 (ISBN 0-915684-68-3). Christian Herald.

Bible Story. William Neil. (Fount Religious Paperbacks Ser). 1977. pap. 1.95 (ISBN 0-00-623184-5, FA3184, Pub. by Collins Pubs). World Bible.

Bible Story Book. Bethann Van Ness. LC 63-9758. 1963. 11.95 (ISBN 0-8054-4402-5). Broadman.

Bible Story Picture Book. Ed. by Eleanor Doan. LC 73-152801. (ps-3). 1972. 5.95 o.s.i. (ISBN 0-8307-0093-5, 5103509). Regal.

Bible Students Classic Library, 3 vols. Incl. Cruden's Complete Concordance. Alexander Cruden; Peloubet's Bible Dictionary. F. N. Peloubet; Ellicott's Bible Commentary. Charles J. Ellicott. Ed. by Donald Bowdle. Set. 43.85 (ISBN 0-310-35238-X). Zondervan.

Bible Studies. G. Adolf Deissmann. 385p. 1979. 14.95 (ISBN 0-88469-146-2). BMH Bks.

Bible Studies for Children. Illus. by Arvis Stewart. LC 79-27811. (Illus.). 336p. (gr. 1-5). 1980. 12.95 (ISBN 0-02-554060-2). Macmillan.

Bible Studies for the Preparation of the Bride. Rose E. Weiner & Robert T. Weiner, Jr. 195p. 1980. 4.95 (ISBN 0-686-68911-9). Maranatha Hse.

Bible Studies on the Overcoming Life. Robert T. Weiner & Rose E. Weiner. 110p. 1976. 3.95 (ISBN 0-686-68913-5). Maranatha Hse.

Bible Studies on the Overcoming Life II. Robert T. Weiner & Rose Ellen, Jr. 134p. 1976. 3.95 (ISBN 0-686-68912-7). Maranatha Hse.

Bible Study Can Be Exciting! Mary H. Garvin. 192p. 1976. pap. 3.95 o.p. (ISBN 0-310-24911-2). Zondervan.

Bible Study in My House? David Burnham & Sue Burnham. 1975. pap. 1.50 (ISBN 0-8024-0689-0). Moody.

Bible Study Puzzle Book. Thomas J. Marks. (gr. 9 up). 1981. pap. 2.50 saddlewire (ISBN 0-8054-9106-6). Broadman.

Bible Study Source Book: New Testament. Ed. by Robert C. Walton. LC 80-82195. 240p. 1981. pap. 9.95 (ISBN 0-8042-0009-2). John Knox.

Bible Study Source Book: Old Testament. Ed. by Robert C. Walton. LC 80-82194. 216p. 1981. pap. 9.95 (ISBN 0-8042-0008-4). John Knox.

Bible Study Sourcebook. Donald E. Demaray. (Illus.). kivar 8.95 (ISBN 0-310-23621-5). Zondervan.

Bible Tells Us So: Twelve Short Chapters on Major Themes of the Bible. R. B. Kuiper. 1978. pap. 2.95 (ISBN 0-85151-001-9). Banner of Truth.

Bible, the Supernatural & the Jews. McCandlish Phillips. LC 77-92532. 1970. pap. 6.95 (ISBN 0-87123-036-4, 210036). Bethany Fell.

Bible Today. Charles H. Dodd. 1946-1960. 19.95 (ISBN 0-521-04844-3); pap. 7.50 (ISBN 0-521-09118-7, 118). Cambridge U Pr.

Bible Translating. 2nd ed. E. A. Nida. 1961. 1.75 (ISBN 0-8267-0016-0, 08628). United Bible.

Bible Translations for Popular Use. William L. Wonderly. 1968. 1.50 (ISBN 0-8267-0004-7, 08509). United Bible.

Bible Truths. Alva J. McClain. 1981. pap. 1.00 (ISBN 0-88469-013-X). BMH Bks.

Bible Verses in Verse. Boris Randolph. LC 80-67992. 144p. 1980. pap. 3.95 (ISBN 0-87516-424-2). De Vorss.

Bible When You Want It. Ed. by Lewis G. Leary. 1951. 1.95 o.p. (ISBN 0-8096-1023-X). Follett.

Bible: Why Trust It? Mac Perry. (Orig.). 1981. pap. 4.95 (ISBN 0-88270-493-1). Logos.

Bible Word Chain Puzzles. William Hendricks & Glenn Van Noord. (Quiz & Puzzle Bks.). 96p. (Orig.). 1981. pap. 2.95 (ISBN 0-8010-4238-0). Baker Bk.

Bible Word Puzzles. Alice C. Botrom. (Illus.). 30p. (Orig.). 1980. pap. 1.50 (ISBN 0-89323-005-7). BMA Pr.

Bible Word Quest. new ed. Helen Pettigrew. 96p. 1975. pap. 1.95 (ISBN 0-8010-6965-3). Baker Bk.

Bible Word Search Puzzles, No. 2. Eleanor Doan. (Fun-to-Learn Ser.). 96p. (Orig.). 1980. pap. 1.75 (ISBN 0-310-23812-9). Zondervan.

Bible Workbook: New Testament. Catherine B. Walker. 1951. pap. 2.95 (ISBN 0-8024-0752-8). Moody.

Bible Workbook: Old Testament. Catherine B. Walker. 1943. pap. 2.95 (ISBN 0-8024-0751-X). Moody.

Bible's Legacy for Womanhood. Edith Deen. 1976. pap. 1.50 (ISBN 0-89129-100-8). Jove Pubns.

Bible's Teachings for the Happy Life. Ed. by David W. Graham. (Illus.). 1980. deluxe ed. 37.75 (ISBN 0-930582-57-8). Gloucester Art.

Biblia a Su Alcance, 8 bks. Incl. Bk. 1. Genesis a Nehemias. write for info. (ISBN 0-8297-0736-0); Bk. 2. Job a Jeremias. 3.25 (ISBN 0-8297-0737-9); Bk. 3. Lamentaciones a Malaquias. 3.25 (ISBN 0-8297-0738-7); Bk. 4. Mateo a 11 Corintios. 3.25 (ISBN 0-8297-0739-5); Bk. 5. Galatas-Romanos-Filipenses-Colosenses. 3.25 (ISBN 0-686-28838-6); Bk. 6. Filomeno 1-11 Timothy-Tito-Hebreos. 3.25 (ISBN 0-8297-0741-7); Bk. 7. Santiago 1-11 Pedro-Judas 1-11-11 John. 3.25 (ISBN 0-8297-0742-5); Bk. 8. Apocalipsis. 2.25 (ISBN 0-8297-0743-3). 1977. Life Pubs Intl.

Biblia con Notas. Ed. by Mervin Breneman. 1696p. (Span.). 1981. 14.95 (ISBN 0-89922-164-5); imitation leather 18.95 (ISBN 0-686-69098-2). Edit Caribe.

Biblia Hebraica Stuttgartensia. K. Ellinger. 1977. 19.25 (ISBN 3-438-05218-0, 60555). United Bible.

Biblia Pauperum. Ed. by Avril Henry. (Illus.). 112p. 1981. 55.00x (ISBN 0-85967-542-4, Pub. by Scolar Pr England). Biblio Dist.

Biblia Sacra Iuxta Vulgatam Versionem. 2nd ed. Ed. by R. Weber et al. 1975. 32.00 (ISBN 3-438-05302-0, 71686). United Bible.

Biblia Y Su Interpretation. Weldon Viertel. Orig. Title: Bible & Its Interpretation. 208p. Date not set. pap. write for info. (ISBN 0-311-03670-8). Casa Bautista.

Biblias Castellanas del Exilio. Enrique F. Fernandez. LC 76-5154. (Illus.). 190p. (Span.). 1976. pap. 3.50 (ISBN 0-89922-067-3). Edit Caribe.

Biblical & Near Eastern Studies. Ed. by Gary Tuttle. 1978. 15.00 o.p. (ISBN 0-8028-3500-7). Eerdmans.

Biblical Archaeologist Reader, Vol. 3. David Noel Freedman & Edward F. Campbell, Jr. LC 61-7649. 1970. pap. 2.45 o.p. (ISBN 0-385-05178-6, A250C, Anch). Doubleday.

Biblical Basis for Ministry. Ed. by Earl E. Shelp & Ronald Sunderlan. Paul J. Achtmeier et al. (Orig.). 1981. pap. price not set (ISBN 0-664-24371-1). Westminster.

Biblical-Caatechetical Homilies for Sundays & Holy Days (A, B & C) Based on the Lectionary & Reflecting the Syllabus of the Pastoral Homiletic Plan. David Q. Liptak. LC 79-27895. 370p. (Orig.). 1980. pap. 10.95 (ISBN 0-8189-0400-3). Alba.

Biblical Cosmology & Modern Science. Henry M. Morris. pap. 3.95 (ISBN 0-87552-349-8). Presby & Reformed.

Biblical Doctrine of Heaven. Wilbur M. Smith. 1980. text ed. 5.95 (ISBN 0-8024-0705-6). Moody.

Biblical Doctrine of the Reign of God. John Gray. 414p. Repr. of 1979 ed. text ed. 21.50x (ISBN 0-567-09300-X). Attic Pr.

Biblical Errancy. Norman Geisler. 1981. pap. cancelled (ISBN 0-310-39291-8, 18158P). Zondervan.

Biblical Faith & Social Ethics. E. Clinton Gardner. 1960. text ed. 19.50 scp (ISBN 0-06-042240-8, HarpC). Har-Row.

Biblical Family. V. Paul Marston. LC 80-68332. 208p. 1980. pap. 4.95 (ISBN 0-89107-192-X, Cornerstone Bks.). Good News.

Biblical Flood & the Ice Epoch. Donald W. Patten. 1966. 9.00; pap. 7.50. Pacific Mer.

Biblical Hebrew Step by Step: A Significant Breakthrough for Learning Biblical Hebrew. Menahem Mansoor. 1978. pap. 9.95 (ISBN 0-8010-6041-9). Baker Bk.

Biblical Interpretation in Religious Education. Mary C. Boys. LC 80-10249. 367p. (Orig.). 1980. pap. 10.95 (ISBN 0-89135-022-5). Religious Educ.

Biblical Interpreter: An Agrarian Bible in an Industrial Age. Richard L. Rohrbaugh. LC 78-54560. 132p. 1978. pap. 4.95 (ISBN 0-8006-1346-5, 1-1346). Fortress.

Biblical Law. H. B. Clark. 1980. pap. cancelled (ISBN 0-8323-0326-7). Binford.

Biblical Literature: Proceedings. American Academy of Religion, 1974. Ed. by Fred O. Francis. LC 74-14214. (American Academy of Religion. Section Papers). 1974. pap. 4.50 (ISBN 0-88420-112-0, 010914). Scholars Pr Ca.

Biblical Meditations for Advent & the Christmas Season. Carroll Stuhlmueller. LC 80-82083. (Biblical Meditations Ser.: Vol. 3). 288p. (Orig.). 1980. pap. 3.95 (ISBN 0-8091-2318-5). Paulist Pr.

Biblical Meditations for the Easter Season. Carroll C. Stuhmueller. LC 80-81030. 1980. pap. 2.95 (ISBN 0-8091-2283-9). Paulist Pr.

Biblical Period from Abraham to Ezra: A Historical Survey. William F. Albright. pap. 3.50x (ISBN 0-06-130102-7, TB102, Torch). Har-Row.

Biblical Preaching for Today's World. Lloyd M. Perry. 256p. 1973. 9.95 (ISBN 0-8024-0707-2). Moody.

Biblical Prophets in Outlined Notes. Leon Stancliff. 1976. 8.50 (ISBN 0-89225-176-X); pap. 7.00 (ISBN 0-89225-190-5). Gospel Advocate.

Biblical Reflections on Crises Facing the Church. Raymond E. Brown. LC 75-18961. 1975. pap. 3.45 (ISBN 0-8091-1891-2). Paulist Pr.

Biblical Studies in Final Things. William E. Cox. 1967. 3.95 (ISBN 0-87552-152-5). Presby & Reformed.

Biblical Studies: Meeting Ground of Jews & Christians. Ed. by Lawrence Boadt et al. LC 80-82812. (Stimulus Bk). 220p. (Orig.). 1981. pap. 7.95 (ISBN 0-8091-2344-4). Paulist Pr.

Biblical Systematics. Leroy Forlines. 1975. 7.95 (ISBN 0-89265-025-7); pap. 4.95 (ISBN 0-89265-038-9). Randall Hse.

Biblical Texts with Palestinian Pointing. E. J. Revell. LC 77-8893. (Society of Biblical Literature. Masoretic Studies). 1977. pap. 9.00 (ISBN 0-89130-141-0, 060504). Scholars Pr Ca.

Biblical Trace of the Church. William G. Schell. 173p. pap. 1.50. Faith Pub Hse.

Biblico-Theological Lexicon of New Testament Greek. 4th ed. Hermann Cremer. 960p. Repr. of 1895 ed. text ed. 32.00x (ISBN 0-567-01004-X). Attic Pr.

Biblio File: An Index of Prose Passages. Colin Swatridge & Susan Swatridge. 354p. 1980. 19.50x (ISBN 0-631-92640-2, Pub. by Basil Blackwell); pap. 10.50x (ISBN 0-631-92620-8). Biblio Dist.

Bibliografia Chicana: A Guide to Information Sources. Ed. by Arnulfo D. Trejo. LC 74-11562. (Ethnic Studies Information Guide: Vol. 1). 240p. 1975. 30.00 (ISBN 0-8103-1311-1). Gale.

Bibliografia De las Plantaciones. (Bibliography & Library Science Ser). 1964. pap. 1.50 Span ed. o.p. (ISBN 0-8270-3025-8). OAS.

Bibliografia Siciliana, Ovvero Gran Dizionario Bibliografico Delle Opere Editi E Inedite, Antiche E Moderne Di Autori Siciliani O Di Argomento Siciliano Stampate in Sicilia, 3 vols. Giuseppe M. Mira. 1873-1881. 82.50 (ISBN 0-8337-2400-2); inc. supplement by giuseppe salvo-cozzo (ISBN 0-685-06732-7). B Franklin.

Bibliographer's Manual of American History, 5 Vols. Thomas L. Bradford. Ed. by Stan V. Henkels. LC 67-14023. 1968. Repr. of 1907 ed. 92.00 (ISBN 0-8103-3319-8). Gale.

Bibliographer's Manual of English Literature, 8 Vols. William T. Lowndes. LC 66-28042. 1967. Repr. of 1864 ed. 135.00 (ISBN 0-8103-3217-5). Gale.

Bibliographia Araneorum: Analyse Methodique De Toute la Litterature Araneologique Jusqu'en 1939. Pierre Bonnet. LC 57-58745. 832p. 1968. Repr. 40.00 (ISBN 0-686-09299-6). Entomol Soc.

Bibliographia Augustiniana Seu Operum Collectio Quae, Divi Augustini Vitam et Doctrinam Quadantenus exponunt. E. Nebreda. (Classical Studies Ser.). (Lat.). Repr. of 1928 ed. lib. bdg. 28.00x (ISBN 0-697-00013-3). Irvington.

Bibliographia Philosophica, 1934-45, 2 vols. Ed. by G. A. De Brie. LC 51-5942. 1569p. 1954. Set. 92.50x (ISBN 0-8002-1231-2). Intl Pubns Serv.

Bibliographic Control of American Literature: Nineteen Twenty to Nineteen Seventy-Five. Vito J. Brenni. LC 79-12542. 484p. 1979. 11.00 (ISBN 0-8108-1221-5). Scarecrow.

Bibliographic Guide to Art & Architecture: 1980. The Research Libraries of the New York Public Library & the Library of Congress. (Library Catalogs-Bib. Guides Ser.). 1981. lib. bdg. 135.00 (ISBN 0-8161-6881-4). G K Hall.

Bibliographic Guide to Black Studies. New York Public Library Research Library & Library of Congress Research Library. 1979. lib. bdg. 60.00 (ISBN 0-8161-6864-4). G K Hall.

Bibliographic Guide to Black Studies: 1980. The Research Libraries of the New York Public Library, the Schomburg Collection & the Library of Congress. (Library Catalogs-Bib. Guides Ser.). 1981. lib. bdg. 70.00 (ISBN 0-8161-6882-2). G K Hall.

Bibliographic Guide to Business & Economics. New York Public Library Research Library & Library of Congress Research Library. 1979. lib. bdg. 205.00 (ISBN 0-8161-6865-2). G K Hall.

Bibliographic Guide to Business & Economics: Nineteen Seventy-Eight. The Research Libraris of the New York Public Library & the Library of Congress. (Library Catalogs-Bib. Guides). 1979. lib. bdg. 195.00 (ISBN 0-8161-6849-0). G K Hall.

Bibliographic Guide to Business & Economics: 1980. The Research Libraries of the New York Public Library & the Library of Congress. (Library Catalogs-Bib. Guides). 1981. lib. bdg. 225.00 (ISBN 0-8161-6883-0). G K Hall.

Bibliographic Guide to Conference Publications. New York Public Library Research Library & Library of Congress Research Library. 1979. lib. bdg. 130.00 (ISBN 0-8161-6866-0). G K Hall.

Bibliographic Guide to Conference Publication: 1980. The Research Libraries of the New York Public Library & the Library of Congress. (Library Catalogs-Bib. Guides Ser.). 1981. lib. bdg. 130.00 (ISBN 0-8161-6884-9). G K Hall.

Bibliographic Guide to Dance: Nineteen Seventy-Nine. The Research Libraries of the New York Public Library. (Library Catalogs-Bib. Guides). 1980. lib. bdg. 170.00 (ISBN 0-8161-6867-9). G K Hall.

Bibliographic Guide to Dance: 1978. Ed. by Research Libraries of the New York Public Library. (Bib.Guides). 1979. lib. bdg. 100.00 (ISBN 0-8161-6851-2). G K Hall.

Bibliographic Guide to Education: Nineteen Seventy-Eight. Teachers College Library. (Library Catalogs-Bibliographic Guides). 1979. lib. bdg. 75.00 (ISBN 0-8161-6852-0). G K Hall.

Bibliographic Guide to Education: 1980. The Research Libraries of the New York Public Library & Columbia University, Teachers College Library. (Library Catalog-Bib.Guides Ser.). 1981. lib. bdg. 85.00 (ISBN 0-8161-6880-6). G K Hall.

Bibliographic Guide to Educational Research. Dorothea M. Berry. LC 75-20134. 1975. 8.00 o.p. (ISBN 0-8108-0825-0). Scarecrow.

Bibliographic Guide to Educational Research. 2nd ed. Dorothea M. Berry. LC 80-20191. 224p. 1980. 11.00 (ISBN 0-8108-1351-3). Scarecrow.

Bibliographic Guide to Government Publications - Foreign: 1980. The Research Libraries of the New York Public Library & the Library of Congress. (Library Catalogs-Bib. Guides Ser.). 1981. lib. bdg. 195.00 (ISBN 0-8161-6886-5). G K Hall.

Bibliographic Guide to Government Publications - U. S. 1980. The Research Libraries of the New York Public Library & the Library of Congress. (Library Catalogs-Bib. Guides Ser.). 1981. lib. bdg. 195.00 (ISBN 0-8161-6887-3). G K Hall.

Bibliographic Guide to Government Publications. New York Public Library Research Library & Library of Congress Research Library. 1979. 180.00 (ISBN 0-8161-6870-9). G K Hall.

Bibliographic Guide to Latin American Studies: 1979. The Library of Congress & University of Texas Library (Austin) (Library Catalogs-Bib. Guides). 1980. lib. bdg. 245.00 (ISBN 0-8161-6872-5). G K Hall.

Bibliographic Guide to Latin American Studies: 1980. The Library of Congress & the University of Texas Library (Austin) (Bib. Guides). 1981. lib. bdg. 275.00 (ISBN 0-686-69556-9). G K Hall.

Bibliographic Guide to Law. Library of Congress. 1979. lib. bdg. 99.50 (ISBN 0-8161-6873-3). G K Hall.

Bibliographic Guide to Law: Nineteen Seventy-Eight. The Library of Congress. (Library Catalogs-Bib. Guides). 1979. lib. bdg. 95.00 (ISBN 0-8161-6856-3). G K Hall.

Bibliographic Guide to Law: 1980. The Research Libraries of He New York Public Library & the Library of Congress. (Bib. Guides Ser.). 1981. lib. bdg. 125.00 (ISBN 0-8161-6889-X). G K Hall.

Bibliographic Guide to Maps & Atlases: 1980. The Research Libraries of the New York Public Library & the Library of Congress. (Library Catalogs-Bib. Guides Ser.). 1981. lib. bdg. 95.00 (ISBN 0-8161-6890-3). G K Hall.

Bibliographic Guide to Music. New York Public Library Research Library & Library of Congress Research Library. 1979. lib. bdg. 85.00 (ISBN 0-8161-6875-X). G K Hall.

Bibliographic Guide to Music: 1980. The Research Libraries of the New York Public Library & the Library of Congress. (Libraries Catalogs-Bib. Guides Sew.). 1981. lib. bdg. 90.00 (ISBN 0-8161-6891-1). G K Hall.

Bibliographic Guide to North American History: 1980. The Research Library of the New York Public Library & the Library of Congress. (Bib.Guides Ser.). 1981. lib. bdg. 85.00 (ISBN 0-8161-6892-X). G K Hall.

Bibliographic Guide to Psychology: Nineteen Seventy-Eight. The Library of Congress & the Research Libraries of the New York Public Library. (Library Catalogs-Bib. Guides). 1979. lib. bdg. 60.00 (ISBN 0-8161-6859-8). G K Hall.

Bibliographic Guide to Psychology: 1980. The Research Libraries Fo the New York Public Library & the Library of Congress. (Library Catalogs-Guides Ser.). 1981. lib. bdg. 70.00 (ISBN -08161-6893-8). G K Hall.

Bibliographic Guide to Soviet & East European Studies, 1980. New York Public Library, Research Libraries & Library of Congress. (Library Catalogs - Bibliographic Guides Ser.). 1981. lib. bdg. 195.00 (ISBN 0-8161-6894-6). G K Hall.

Bibliographic Guide to Technology. New York Public Library Research Library. Ed. by Library of Congress. 1979. lib. bdg. 125.00 (ISBN 0-8161-6861-X). G K Hall.

Bibliographic Guide to Technology: 1979. The Research Libraries of the New York Public Library & the Library of Congress. (Library Catalogs-Bib. Guides). 1980. lib. bdg. 145.00 (ISBN 0-8161-6878-4). G K Hall.

Bibliographic Guide to Technology: 1980. The Research Libraries of the New York Public Library & the Library of Congress. (Bib. Guides). 1981. lib. bdg. 175.00 (ISBN 0-8161-6895-4). G K Hall.

Bibliographic Guide to the Literature of Contemporary American Poetry, 1970-1975. Phillis Gershator. LC 76-41812. 1976. 10.00 (ISBN 0-8108-0987-7). Scarecrow.

Bibliographic Guide to Theatre Arts: Nineteen Seventy-Nine. The Research Libraries of the New York Public Library & the Library of Congress. (Library Catalogs-Bib. Guides). 1980. lib. bdg. 70.00 (ISBN 0-8161-6862-8). G K Hall.

Bibliographic Guide to Theatre Arts: 1980. The Research Libraries of the New York Pubic Library & the Library of Congress. (Library Catalogs-Bib. Guides Ser.). 1981 (ISBN 0-8161-6896-2). lib. bdg. 75.00 (ISBN 0-686-69557-7). G K Hall.

Bibliographic Index, Vols. 5-8. (Sold on service basis). Ea. 125.00 ea. (ISBN 0-685-22233-0). Wilson.

Bibliographic Index to Romance Philology, Vols. 1-25. Mark G. Littlefield. 1974. 34.50x (ISBN 0-520-02455-9). U of Cal Pr.

Bibliographic Instruction: A Handbook. Beverly Renford & Linnea Hendrickson. LC 80-12300. 1980. pap. 14.95x (ISBN 0-918212-24-3). Neal-Schuman.

Bibliographic Notes on Xochioalco, Mexico. Marshall H. Saville. (INM Ser.: Vol. 11, No.6). 1928. pap. 1.00 (ISBN 0-934490-28-7). Mus Am Ind.

Bibliographical Account of English Theatrical Literature. Robert W. Lowe. LC 66-27665. 1966. Repr. of 1888 ed. 22.00 (ISBN 0-8103-3216-7). Gale.

Bibliographical Catalogue of Seventeenth-Century German Books Published in Holland. J. Bruckner. (Anglica Germanica: No. 13). 1971. text ed. 95.30x (ISBN 0-686-20922-2). Mouton.

Bibliographical Dictionary Plus the Bibliographical Miscellany. Adam Clarke. 1971. Repr. of 1802 ed. 55.00 o.p. (ISBN 0-8108-0399-2). Scarecrow.

Bibliographical Essay on the Collection of Voyages & Travels: Nuremburg, 1598-1660. A. Asher. Ed. by Levinus Hulsius. 1962. pap. text ed. 11.50x (ISBN 90-6041-001-7). Humanities.

Bibliographical Guide to the History of Indian-White Relations in the United States. Francis P. Prucha. LC 76-16045. 1977. lib. bdg. 25.00x (ISBN 0-226-68476-8); pap. 11.00x (ISBN 0-226-68477-6). U of Chicago Pr.

Bibliographical Handbook on Tudor England, Fourteen Eighty-Five to Sixteen Hundred Three. Ed. by Mortimer Levine. (Bibliographical Handbooks of the Conference on British Studies). 1968. 17.50 (ISBN 0-521-05543-1). Cambridge U Pr.

Bibliographical Society of America, Nineteen Hundred Four to Nineteen Seventy-Nine: A Retrospective Collection. LC 80-14334. 1980. 20.00x (ISBN 0-8139-0863-9). U Pr of Va.

Bibliographical Survey for a Foundation in Philosophy. Francis E. Jordak. LC 78-64564. 1978. pap. text ed. 14.50 (ISBN 0-8191-0635-6). U Pr of Amer.

Bibliographie Courante D'Articles de Periodiques Posterieurs a 1944 Sur les Problems Politiques, Economiques et Sociaux: Dixieme Supplement, 2 vols. Fondation des Sciences Politiques, Paris, France. (Bib.Guides). Orig. Title: Index to Post-1944 Periodical Articles on Political Economic & Social Problems - Tenth Supplement. 1979. Set. lib. bdg. 275.00 (ISBN 0-8161-0298-8). G K Hall.

Bibliographie Critique Sur les Relations Entre le Viet-Nam et l'Occident: Ouvrages et Articles En Langues Occidentales. Nguyen-The-Ank. (Illus.). 310p. 1970. 18.00x o.p. (ISBN 0-8002-0693-2). Intl Pubns Serv.

Bibliographie d'edtions Originales & Rares d'auteurs Francais des XVe, XVIe, XVIIe, XVIIIe Siecles Contenant Environ 6,000 Fac-Similes de Titres & Gravures. Avenir Tchemerzine. LC 73-87061. (Illus.). 420p. (Fr., Originally published in 10 vols. & reprinted in reduced format in 1 vol.). 1973. Repr. of 1927 ed. 105.00x (ISBN 0-914146-03-3). Somerset Hse.

Bibliographie des Francais dans l'Inde. Henry Scholberg & Emmanuel Divien. 216p. 1975. lib. bdg. 12.50 (ISBN 0-88253-738-5). Ind-US Inc.

Bibliographie Des Mazarinades, 4 vols. Celestin Moreau. (Societe De L'histoire De France: Nos. 61, 63, & 67). Repr. of 1850 ed. Set. 79.50 (ISBN 0-8337-2454-1); 4 supplements in 1 vol. incl. (ISBN 0-685-06734-3). B Franklin.

Bibliographie Du Laos. 2nd ed. Ed. by Pierre-Bernard Lafont. Incl. Vol. 1. 1666-1961. 269p; Vol. 2. 1962-1975. 413p. LC 65-53527. (Orig., Fr.). 1978. pap. 55.00x. Intl Pubns Serv.

Bibliographie Geographique Internationale, 1977: International Geographical Bibliography, 1977, Vol. 82. Ed. by Roger Brunet. 752p. (Fr.). 1979. Set, 5 Fasciculae. pap. 67.50x (ISBN 0-8002-2218-0). Intl Pubns Serv.

Bibliographie zur alteuropaeischen Religionsgeschichte II, 1965-1969: Eine interdisziplinaere Auswahl von Literatur zu den Rand-und Nachfolgekulturen der Antike in Europa unter besonderer Beruecksichtigung der nichtchristlichen Religionen. Ed. by Juergen Ahrendts. LC 68-86477. (Arbeiten Zur Fruehmittelalterforschung: Vol. 5). xxvi, 591p. 1974. 87.05x (ISBN 3-11-003398-4). De Gruyter.

Bibliography. 2nd rev. ed. Asghar Ali & Krishan Kumar. 1980. text ed. 12.50x (ISBN 0-7069-0738-8, Pub. by Vikas India). Advent Bk.

Bibliography & Footnotes: A Style Manual for Students & Writers. 3rd ed. Peyton Hurt. (Illus., Rev. & enl. ed.). 1968. pap. 5.75x (ISBN 0-520-00589-9, CAL150). U of Cal Pr.

Bibliography & Index of Experimental Range & Stopping Power Data. Ed. by Hans H. Andersen. LC 77-22415. 1978. text ed. 48.00 (ISBN 0-08-021604-8). Pergamon.

Bibliography & Index of Paleozoic Crinoids, Nineteen Forty-Two to Nineteen Sixty-Eight. Gary D. Webster. LC 73-76885. (Memoir: No. 137). 180p. 1973. 19.75x (ISBN 0-8137-1137-1). Geol Soc.

Bibliography for Beginners. 2nd ed. D. Gore. 1973. pap. text ed. 7.95 (ISBN 0-13-076109-5). P-H.

Bibliography for Teachers of Social Studies. Raymond A. Ducharme et al. LC 68-18106. 1968. pap. text ed. 3.50x (ISBN 0-8077-1255-8). Tchrs Coll.

Bibliography of ab initio Molecular Wave Functions: Supplement for 1970-1973. W. G. Richards et al. 376p. 1974. pap. 33.50x (ISBN 0-19-855356-0). Oxford U Pr.

Bibliography of Aeronautics. Paul Brockett. LC 66-25692. 1966. Repr. of 1910 ed. 50.00 (ISBN 0-8103-3320-1). Gale.

Bibliography of African Ecology: A Geographically & Topically Classified List of Books & Articles. Ed. by Dilwyn J. Rogers. LC 78-19935. (Special Bibliographic Ser: No. 6). 1979. lib. bdg. 37.50 (ISBN 0-313-20552-3, RAE/). Greenwood.

Bibliography of African International Relations. Mark W. DeLancey. (Westview Special Studies on Africa). 1980. lib. bdg. 26.50x (ISBN 0-89158-680-6). Westview.

Bibliography of Africana. Hans E. Panofsky. LC 72-823. (Contributions in Librarianship & Information Science Ser.: No. 11). 1975. lib. bdg. 18.95 (ISBN 0-8371-6391-9, PAA/). Greenwood.

Bibliography of Afro-American & Other American Minorities Represented in Library & Library Related Listings. Clara O. Jackson. (Bibliographical Ser.: No. 9). 1972. 1.50 (ISBN 0-89977-013-4). Am Inst Marxist.

Bibliography of Aggressive Behavior: A Reader's Guide to the Research Literature. Ed. by J. Michael Crabtree & Kenneth E. Moyer. LC 77-12900. 442p. 1977. 41.00x (ISBN 0-8451-0200-1). A R Liss.

Bibliography of Agricultural Meteorology. Ed. by Wang Jen-Yu & Gerald L. Barger. 1962. 45.00x (ISBN 0-299-02510-1). U of Wis Pr.

Bibliography of Agriculture Annual Cumulative, Vol. 43, 1979. 1980. lib. bdg. 199.75 (ISBN 0-912700-35-1). Oryx Pr.

Bibliography of American Historical Societies. 2nd ed. rev. ed. Appleton P. Griffin. LC 67-480. 1966. Repr. of 1907 ed. 42.00 (ISBN 0-8103-3080-6). Gale.

Bibliography of American Naval History. Ed. by Paolo E. Coletta. 453p. 1981. 14.95 (ISBN 0-87021-105-6). Naval Inst Pr.

Bibliography of Appraisal Literature. American Society of Appraisers. LC 73-92529. 769p. 1974. 30.00 (ISBN 0-937828-18-1). Am Soc Appraisers.

Bibliography of Arizona Ornithology. Anders H. Anderson. LC 76-163008. 27p. (Orig.). 1972. pap. 2.00 (ISBN 0-8165-0313-3). U of Ariz Pr.

Bibliography of Arnold J. Toynbee. Ed. by S. Fiona Morton. 300p. 1980. 74.00 (ISBN 0-19-215261-0). Oxford U Pr.

Bibliography of Arthur Waley. Francis A. Johns. LC 67-20388. 1968. 12.50 (ISBN 0-910294-17-8). Brown Bk.

Bibliography of Black Music: Reference Materials, Vol. 1. Dominique-Rene De Larma. LC 80-24681. (Greenwood Encyclopedia of Black Music). 144p. 1981. lib. bdg. 25.00 (ISBN 0-313-21340-2, DBI/01). Greenwood.

Bibliography of Bolted & Riveted Joints. Compiled By American Society of Civil Engineers. (Manual & Report on Engineering Practice Ser.: No. 48). 200p. 1967. text ed. 14.75 (ISBN 0-87262-222-3). Am Soc Civil Eng.

Bibliography of Bookplate Literature. Ed. by George W. Fuller. LC 72-178635. 151p. 1971. Repr. of 1926 ed. 24.00 (ISBN 0-8103-3190-X). Gale.

Bibliography of British & Irish Municipal History, Vol. 2. Ed. by G. H. Martin & Sylvia Macintyre. 1980. text ed. 20.00x (ISBN 0-391-01198-7, Leicester). Humanities.

Bibliography of British & Irish Municipal History: Vol. 1. General Works. Ed. by G. H. Martin & Sylvia Macintyre. 750p. 1972. text ed. 38.00x (ISBN 0-391-00265-1, Leicester). Humanities.

Bibliography of British History Eighteen Fifty-One to Nineteen Fourteen. Ed. by H. J. Hanham. 1976. 125.00x (ISBN 0-19-822389-7). Oxford U Pr.

Bibliography of British History Seventeen Eighty-Nine to Eighteen Fifty-One. Lucy M. Brown & Ian R. Christie. 1977. 89.00x (ISBN 0-19-822390-0). Oxford U Pr.

Bibliography of British History: Stuart Period, Sixteen Hundred to Seventeen-Fourteen. 2nd ed. Mary F. Keeler. (Bibliography of British History Ser). 1970. 49.00x (ISBN 0-19-821371-9). Oxford U Pr.

Bibliography of British History to Fourteen Eighty-Five, 2 vols. 2nd ed. Ed. by Edgar B. Graves. 1080p. 1974. Set. 98.00x (ISBN 0-19-822391-9). Oxford U Pr.

Bibliography of Canadian Folklore in English. Edith Fowke & Carole H. Carpenter. 232p. 1981. 15.00x (ISBN 0-8020-2394-0). U of Toronto Pr.

Bibliography of Canadian Urban History: Part V: Western Canada. Frederick H. Armstrong et al. (Public Adminstration Ser.: Bibliography P-541). 72p. 1980. pap. 7.50. Vance Biblios.

Bibliography of Cartography, First Supplement. Library of Congress, Geography & Map Division (Washington, D. C.) 1979. lib. bdg. 250.00 (ISBN 0-8161-0259-7). G K Hall.

Bibliography of Ceylon, 3 vols. 2nd ed. H. A. Goonetileke. LC 77-851302. 954p. 1973. Set. 140.00x (ISBN 3-85750-015-8). Intl Pubns Serv.

Bibliography of Chaucer, 1954-1963. William R. Crawford. LC 66-29836. (Publications in Language & Literature: No. 17). 188p. 1967. 11.50 (ISBN 0-295-74027-2). U of Wash Pr.

Bibliography of Child Psychiatry with a Selected List of Films. Ed. by Irving N. Berlin. LC 74-11813. 528p. 1976. 29.95 (ISBN 0-87705-244-1); pap. text ed. 14.95 (ISBN 0-87705-277-8). Human Sci Pr.

Bibliography of Chinese Government Serials: 1880-1949. Compiled by Julia Tung. LC 79-2456. 136p. (Orig.). 1979. pap. 5.00 (ISBN 0-8179-4242-4). Hoover Inst Pr.

Bibliography of Creative Dramatics. Ed. by Mary E. Klock. 40p. 1975. pap. 2.00 ATA members 1.00 (ISBN 0-686-13201-7). Am Theatre Assoc.

Bibliography of Discographies: Jazz, Vol. II. Daniel Allen. 200p. 1981. 35.00 (ISBN 0-8352-1342-0). Bowker.

Bibliography of Drug Abuse: A Supplement, 1977 to 1980. Theodora Andrews. 200p. 1981. lib. bdg. price not set (ISBN 0-87287-252-1). Libs Unl.

Bibliography of Early Secular American Music: Eighteenth Century. 3rd ed. Oscar G. Sonneck. LC 64-18992. (Music Ser). 1964. Repr. of 1945 ed. lib. bdg. 45.00 (ISBN 0-306-70902-3). Da Capo.

Bibliography of Education. Will S. Monroe. LC 68-30661. 1968. Repr. of 1897 ed. 15.00 (ISBN 0-8103-3337-6). Gale.

Bibliography of Educational Administration in the United Kingdom. D. A. Howell. (General Ser.). 1980. pap. text ed. 11.00x (ISBN 0-85633-151-1, NFER). Humanities.

Bibliography of Educational Publications for Alaska Native Languages. Jane McGary. 168p. (Orig.). 1979. pap. 5.00 (ISBN 0-89763-018-1). Natl Clearinghse Bilingual Ed.

Bibliography of English Translations from Medieval Sources, Nineteen Forty-Four to Nineteen Sixty-Eight. Compiled by Mary A. Ferguson. (Records of Civilization, Sources & Studies: No. 88). 256p. 1974. 20.00x (ISBN 0-231-03435-0). Columbia U Pr.

Bibliography of Epictetus. W. A. Oldfather. 177p. 1952. octavo 7.00. Holmes.

Bibliography of European Publications on Japan: Fifteen Forty-Two to Eighteen Fifty-Three. 418p. 1977. Repr. of 1940 ed. 70.00 (ISBN 3-7940-3173-3, Dist. by Gale Research Co). K G Saur.

Bibliography of Fishes, 3 vols. Bashford Dean. 1973. 169.50 (ISBN 3-87429-036-0). Lubrecht & Cramer.

Bibliography of Forest Botany in Japan: 1940 to 1963. Satoru Kurata. 160p. 1966. 12.50x o.p. (ISBN 0-8002-0695-9). Intl Pubns Serv.

Bibliography of Fossil Vertebrates, 1978. Joseph L. Gregory et al. 384p. (Orig.). 1981. 50.00 (ISBN 0-913312-52-5). Am Geol.

Bibliography of George Berkeley, Bishop of Cloyne: His Work & His Critics in the Eighteenth Century. Geoffrey Keynes. (Soho Bibliography Ser.). 1976. 25.00x (ISBN 0-19-818161-2). U of Pittsburgh Pr.

Bibliography of German. Kurt Schwerin. (Language Legal Monograph Ser.). 383p. 1977. text ed. 58.00 (ISBN 3-7940-7037-2, Pub. by K G Saur). Gale.

Bibliography of International Geographical Congresses, Eighteen Seventy-One to Nineteen Seventy-Six. George Kish. (Reference Bks.). 1979. lib. bdg. 32.50 (ISBN 0-8161-8226-4). G K Hall.

Bibliography of Japanese Education. Ulrich Teichler & Friederich Voss. 294p. 1974. pap. 19.50 (ISBN 3-598-03183-1, Pub. by K G Saur). Shoe String.

Bibliography of Jazz. Alan P. Merriam. LC 75-127282. (Roots of Jazz). 1970. Repr. of 1954 ed. lib. bdg. 18.50 (ISBN 0-306-70036-0). Da Capo.

Bibliography of Latin American Bibliographies. Arthur E. Gropp. LC 68-9330. 1968. 40.00 (ISBN 0-8108-0011-X). Scarecrow.

Bibliography of Latin American Bibliographies Published in Periodicals, 2 vols. Arthur E. Gropp. LC 75-32552. 1976. Set. 40.00 o.p. (ISBN 0-8108-0838-2). Scarecrow.

Bibliography of Latin American Bibliographies: Social Sciences & Humanities, Vol. 1. Ed. by Daniel R. Cordeiro. LC 78-11935. 1979. lib. bdg. 13.00 (ISBN 0-8108-1170-7). Scarecrow.

Bibliography of Latin American Bibliographies: Supplement 1965-1969. Arthur E. Gropp. LC 68-9330. 1971. 10.00 (ISBN 0-8108-0350-X). Scarecrow.

Bibliography of Literature Concerning Yemenite-Jewish Music. Paul F. Marks. LC 72-90431. (Detroit Studies in Music Bibliography Ser.: No. 27). 1973. pap. 5.00 (ISBN 0-911772-57-X). Info Coord.

Bibliography of Loyalist Source Material in the United States, Canada & Great Britain. Ed. by Greg Palmer. 700p. 1981. Set. lib. bdg. 85.00x (ISBN 0-930466-26-8). Meckler Bks.

Bibliography of Malawi. Edward F. Brown et al. (Foreign & Comparative Studies-Eastern African Bibliographic Ser.: No. 1). 161p. 1965. pap. 3.50x. Syracuse U Foreign Comp.

Bibliography of Malay & Arabic Periodicals Eighteen Seventy-Six to Nineteen Forty-One. William R. Roff. (London Oriental Bibliographies Ser: No. 3). 80p. 1972. 9.75x o.p. (ISBN 0-19-713572-2). Oxford U Pr.

Bibliography of Master's Theses & Doctoral Dissertations on Milwaukee Topics, 1911-1977. Byron Anderson. LC 80-27261. 136p. (Orig.). 1981. pap. 3.95x (ISBN 0-87020-202-2). State Hist Soc Wis.

Bibliography of Mathematics Published in Communist China During the Period of Nineteen Forty-Nine to Nineteen Sixty. C. K. Tsao. 1961. 1.00 o.p. (ISBN 0-686-67534-7, CCBIB). Am Math.

Bibliography of Middle Scots Poets. William Geddie. (Scottish Text Society Publications Ser: No. 61). 1969. Repr. of 1912 ed. 35.50 (ISBN 0-384-17975-4). Johnson Repr.

Bibliography of Minnesota Territorial Documents. Compiled by Esther A. Jerabek. LC 36-28069. 157p. 1936. pap. 3.00 (ISBN 0-87351-005-4). Minn Hist.

Bibliography of Modern Irish Drama, 1899-1970. E. H. Mikhail. LC 72-1373. 63p. 1972. 10.50 (ISBN 0-295-95229-6). U of Wash Pr.

Bibliography of Nepal. Basil C. Hedrick et al. LC 73-10075. 1973. 11.50 (ISBN 0-8108-0649-5). Scarecrow.

Bibliography of Noise for Nineteen Seventy-Five. Compiled by Judith Kramer-Greene. LC 72-87107. 171p. 1977. 10.00x (ISBN 0-87875-099-1). Whitston Pub.

Bibliography of Noise for Nineteen Seventy-Six. Ed. by Irving E. Stephens & Dorothy L. Barnes. LC 72-87107. 202p. 1978. 12.50 (ISBN 0-87875-128-9). Whitston Pub.

Bibliography of Non-Euclidean Geometry. 2nd ed. Duncan Y. Sommerville. LC 72-113150. 1960. text ed. 18.50 (ISBN 0-8284-0175-6). Chelsea Pub.

Bibliography of North American Gasteromycetes I: Phalales. W. R. Burk. 200p. 1981. pap. text ed. 20.00x (ISBN 3-7682-1262-9, Pub. by Cramer Germany). Lubrecht & Cramer.

Bibliography of Numerical Models for Tidal Rivers, Estuaries & Coastal Waters. Robert Gordon & Malcolm Spaulding. (Marine Technical Report Ser.: No. 32). 1974. pap. 2.00 (ISBN 0-938412-03-5). URI MAS.

Bibliography of Nursing Literature: Eighteen Fifty-Nine to Nineteen Sixty. A. M. Thompson. 1969. 27.95x (ISBN 0-85365-470-0, Pub. by Lib Assn England). Oryx Pr.

Bibliography of Nursing Literature: Nineteen Sixty-One to Nineteen Seventy. Ed. by A. M. Thompson. 1974. lib. bdg. 43.50x (ISBN 0-85365-316-X, Pub. by Lib Assn England). Oryx Pr.

Bibliography of Ontario History, 1867-1976: Cultural, Economic, Political, Social, 2 vols. Olga B. Bishop. 1980. 75.00 (ISBN 0-8020-2359-2). U of Toronto Pr.

Bibliography of Parliamentary Papers: General Alphabetical Indexes 1696-1899, 8 vols. Incl. Vol. 1. Hansard's Catalogue & Breviate of Parliamentary Papers: 1696-1834. 89.00x (ISBN 0-686-27258-7); Vol. 2. Report of Selected Committees, 1801-1852. 103.00x (ISBN 0-686-27259-5); Vol. 3. Accounts & Papers, Reports of Commissioners, Etc., 1801-1852. 141.00x (ISBN 0-686-27260-9); Vol. 4. Bills, Reports, Estimates, Accounts & Papers, 1852-1869. 111.00x (ISBN 0-686-27261-7); Vol. 5. Bills, 1801-1852. 107.00x (ISBN 0-686-27262-5); Vol. 6. Bills, Reports, Estimates & Accounts & Papers, 1870-1879. 93.00x (ISBN 0-686-27263-3); Vol. 7. Bills, Reports, Estimates & Accounts & Papers, 1880-1889. 93.00x (ISBN 0-686-27264-1); Vol. 8. Bills, Reports, Estimates, Accounts & Papers, 1890-1899. 103.00x (ISBN 0-686-27265-X). Pub. by Irish Academic Pr). Biblio Dist.

Bibliography of Pennsylvania History. Norman B. Wilkinson. LC 58-9079. 1957. 10.00 (ISBN 0-911124-07-1). Pa Hist & Mus.

Bibliography of Pennsylvania History: A Supplement. Carol Wall. 1977. 8.50 (ISBN 0-911124-90-X). Pa Hist & Mus.

Bibliography of Periodical Literature in Musicology & Allied Fields, No. 1 & 2. D. H. Daugherty et al. LC 71-177974. 148p. 1971. Repr. of 1940 ed. lib. bdg. 29.50 (ISBN 0-306-70413-7). Da Capo.

Bibliography of Photographic Processes in Use Before 1880: Their Materials, Processing, & Conservation. M. Susan Barger. LC 80-84390. 160p. 1980. pap. 37.50 (ISBN 0-89938-003-4). Graph Arts Res RIT.

Bibliography of Plant Viruses. Helen P. Beale. 1700p. 1976. 80.00x (ISBN 0-231-03763-5). Columbia U Pr.

Bibliography of Printing in America. George T. Watkins. Ed. by Irving Lew. (Bibliographical Reprint Ser.). 1962. pap. 15.00 ltd. ed. (ISBN 0-89782-002-9). Battery Pk.

Bibliography of Publications Designed to Raise the Standard of Scientific Literature. 1963. pap. 2.50 (ISBN 92-3-100540-5, U49, UNESCO). Unipub.

Bibliography of Publications on Old English Literature to the End of Nineteen Seventy-Two. Stanley B. Greenfield & Fred C. Robinson. LC 78-4989. 1980. 75.00x (ISBN 0-8020-2292-8). U of Toronto Pr.

Bibliography of Research Studies in Education, Nineteen Twenty-Six to Nineteen Forty, 4 vols. U. S. Office of Education. LC 74-1124. 4801p. 1974. Repr. of 1928 ed. Set. 195.00 (ISBN 0-8103-0975-0). Gale.

Bibliography of Resources in Bilingual Education: Curricular Materials. 322p. (Orig.). 1980. pap. 4.00 (ISBN 0-89763-016-5). Natl Clearinghse Bilingual Ed.

Bibliography of Rice Literature Translations Available in the International Rice Institute Library & Documentation Center. 191p. 1976. pap. 36.00 (R108, IRRI). Unipub.

Bibliography of Robert Watt. Robert Watt. LC 68-28119. 1968. Repr. of 1950 ed. 15.00 (ISBN 0-8103-3323-6). Gale.

Bibliography of Russian Word-Formation. Dean S. Worth. 1977. soft cover 14.95 (ISBN 0-89357-041-9). Slavica.

Bibliography of Samuel Taylor Coleridge. John L. Haney. 144p. 1980. Repr. of 1903 ed. lib. bdg. 20.00 (ISBN 0-8495-2299-4). Arden Lib.

Bibliography of Ship Passenger Lists (1538-1900) Being a Guide to Published Lists of Immigrants to the United States & Canada. Ed. by P. William Filby. 160p. 1981. 44.00 (ISBN 0-8103-1098-8). Gale.

Bibliography of Sir James George Frazer, O. M. T. Besterman. (Illus.). 1968. 11.00 o.p. (ISBN 0-7129-0245-7, Dist. by Shoe String). Dawson Pub.

Bibliography of Skiing Studies. 5th ed. C. R. Goeldner & Karen Dicke. 1980. 10.00 (ISBN 0-89478-050-6). U CO Busn Res Div.

Bibliography of Skiing Studies. C. R. Goeldner & Karen Dicke. 1978. 10.00 (ISBN 0-89478-039-5). U CO Busn Res Div.

Bibliography of Songsters Printed in America Before Eighteen Twenty-One. Irving Lowens. LC 75-5021. 1976. 19.95x (ISBN 0-912296-05-4, Dist. by U Pr of Va). Am Antiquarian.

Bibliography of Statistical Bibliographies. H. O. Lancaster. 1968. 11.75 (ISBN 0-934454-12-4). Lubrecht & Cramer.

Bibliography of Studies in Metaphysical Poetry, Nineteen Thirty-Nine to Nineteen Sixty. Ed. by Lloyd E. Berry. 1964. 12.50x (ISBN 0-299-03120-9). U of Wis Pr.

Bibliography of the Black Sparrow Press Nineteen Sixty-Six to Nineteen Seventy-Eight. Bradford Morrow & Seamus Cooney. (Illus.). 375p. 1980. 40.00 (ISBN 0-87685-465-X); ltd. ed. 75.00 (ISBN 0-87685-466-8). Black Sparrow.

Bibliography of the First Editions of Books by George Eliot (Mary Ann Evans) (1819-1880) Percival N. Muir. 52p. 1980. Repr. of 1927 ed. lib. bdg. 10.00 (ISBN 0-8492-6833-8). R West.

Bibliography of the First Letter of Christopher Columbus: Describing His Discovery of the New World. R. H. Major. 1971. Repr. of 1872 ed. text ed. 13.00x (ISBN 90-6041-083-1). Humanities.

Bibliography of the Harvard Chiapas Project: the First Twenty Years, Nineteen Fifty-Seven to Nineteen Seventy-Seven: The First Twenty Years, 1957 to 1977. Evon Vogt. Ed. by Lorna Condon. LC 78-51959. 1978. pap. text ed. 3.00 (ISBN 0-87365-794-2). Peabody Harvard.

Bibliography of the History of Agriculture in the U. S. Everett E. Edwards. LC 66-27834. 1967. Repr. of 1930 ed. 18.00 (ISBN 0-8103-3102-0). Gale.

Bibliography of the History of Electronics. George Shiers. LC 72-3740. 1972. 11.50 (ISBN 0-8108-0499-9). Scarecrow.

Bibliography of the Reform, Fourteen Fifty to Sixteen Forty-Eight: Relating to the United Kingdom & Ireland for the Years 1955-70. Ed. by Derek Baker. 1975. 25.00x (ISBN 0-631-15960-6, Pub. by Basil Blackwell). Biblio Dist.

Bibliography of the Sioux. Jack W. Marken & Herbert T. Hoover. LC 80-20106. (Native American Bibliography Ser.: No. 1). 388p. 1980. 17.50 (ISBN 0-8108-1356-4). Scarecrow.

Bibliography of the Socioeconomic Aspects of Medicine. Theodora Andrews. LC 74-34054. 1975. lib. bdg. 13.50x o.p. (ISBN 0-87287-104-5). Libs Unl.

Bibliography of the Waverly Novels. Greville Worthington. 143p. 1980. Repr. of 1931 ed. lib. bdg. 30.00 (ISBN 0-8495-5655-4). Arden Lib.

Bibliography of the Writings of Jonathan Swift. 2nd ed. H. Teerink. Ed. by Arthur H. Scouten. LC 62-11270. 1963. 25.00x o.p. (ISBN 0-8122-7373-7). U of Pa Pr.

Bibliography of Tourism & Travel Research Studies, Reports, & Articles, 9 vols. Karen Dicke & C. R. Goeldner. 1980. Set. 60.00 (ISBN 0-89478-052-2). U CO Busn Res Div.

Bibliography of Unfinished Books in the English Language. Albert R. Corns. Ed. by Archibald Sparke. LC 67-28093. 1968. Repr. of 1915 ed. 18.00 (ISBN 0-8103-3208-6). Gale.

Bibliography of United States - Latin American Relations Since 1810: A Selected List of Eleven Thousand Published References. Ed. by David F. Trask et al. LC 67-14421. 1968. 19.75x (ISBN 0-8032-0185-0). U of Nebr Pr.

Bibliography of William Carlos Williams. Emily M. Wallace. LC 68-27541. (Illus.). 1968. 27.50x (ISBN 0-8195-3091-3, Pub. by Wesleyan U Pr). Columbia U Pr.

Bibliography of William James. R. B. Perry. 1979. 28.50 o.p. (ISBN 0-685-94326-7). Porter.

Bibliography of William James. R. B. Perry. 1977. 34.50 o.p. (ISBN 0-685-81151-4). Porter.

Bibliography of Women & Literature. Ed. by Janet Todd. 150p. 1981. text ed. 22.00x (ISBN 0-8419-0693-9). Holmes & Meier.

Bibliography on Animal Rights & Related Matters. Charles R. Magel. LC 80-5636. 622p. 1981. lib. bdg. 28.50 (ISBN 0-8191-1488-X). U Pr of Amer.

Bibliography on Divorce. Kenneth D. Sell. 1981. price not set (ISBN 0-912700-81-5). Oryx Pr.

Bibliography on Espionage, Subversion, Destabilization & Problems of Counterintelligence & Internal Security. Laird M. Wilcox. 1980. pap. text ed. 9.95 (ISBN 0-933592-14-0). Edit Res Serv.

Bibliography on German Settlements in Colonial North America. Emil Meynen. LC 66-25870. 1966. Repr. of 1937 ed. 36.00 (ISBN 0-8103-3336-8). Gale.

Bibliography on Israel & Zionism. Ed. by Yona Alexander & Mordecai Chertoff. 1980. write for info. Herzl Pr.

Bibliography on Kenya. Shirin Kassam et al. (Foreign & Comparative Studies-Eastern African Bibliographic Ser.: No. 2). 461p. 1967. pap. 8.00x. Syracuse U Foreign Comp.

Bibliography on Land-Locked States. Martin I. Glassner. LC 80-51737. 60p. 1980. 20.00x (ISBN 90-286-0290-9). Sijthoff & Noordhodf.

Bibliography on Methods of Social & Business Research. W. A. Belson & B. A. Thompson. LC 72-11488. 300p. 1973. 24.95 (ISBN 0-470-06420-X). Halsted Pr.

Bibliography on Organizational Change in Schools, Selected & Annotated. Philip J. Runkel & Ann M. Burr. 1977. 4.00 (ISBN 0-936276-10-X). Ctr Educ Policy Mgmt.
Bibliography on Political Psychology: Ideological Belief Systems, Propaganda, Persuasion & Forms of Resistance Against Them. Laird M. Wilcox. 1980. pap. text ed. 9.95 (ISBN 0-933592-15-9). Edit Res Serv.
Bibliography on Socio-Economic Aspects of Asian Irrigation. 80p. 1976. pap. 6.00 (R039, IRRI). Unipub.
Bibliography on Taxation in Underdeveloped Countries. Richard M. Bird. LC 62-17751. 85p. (Orig.). 1962. pap. 2.00x o.p. (ISBN 0-915506-03-3). Harvard Law Intl Tax.
Bibliography on Terriorism, Assassination, Kidnapping, Bombing, Guerilla Warfare & Countermeasures Against Them. Laird M. Wilcox. 1980. pap. text ed. 8.95 (ISBN 0-933592-13-2). Edit Res Serv.
Bibliography on the American Left. Laird M. Wilcox. 1980. pap. 9.95 (ISBN 0-933592-05-1). Edit Res Serv.
Bibliography on the American Right. Laird M. Wilcox. 1980. pap. 9.95 (ISBN 0-933592-04-3). Edit Res Serv.
Bibliography on the Communist Problem in the United States. LC 71-169651. (Civil Liberties in American History Ser.). 474p. 1971. Repr. of 1955 ed. lib. bdg. 47.50 (ISBN 0-306-70234-7). Da Capo.
Bibliography on World Conflict & Peace. Elise Boulding et al. (Special Studies in Peace, Conflict & Conflict Resolution). 1979. lib. bdg. 19.50x (ISBN 0-89158-374-2). Westview.
Bibliography with Abstracts on Pump Sumps & Intakes. Prosser. 1978. pap. 21.00 (ISBN 0-900983-70-1, Dist. by Air Science Co). BHRA Fluid.
Bibliography Without Footnotes. 2nd. ed. Herbert H. Hoffman. 93p. 1978. pap. 4.00x (ISBN 0-89537-013-1). Headway Pubns.
Bibliogrpahy of Agriculture Annual Cumulative, Vol. 44, 1980. Date not set. lib. bdg. 245.00 (ISBN 0-912700-61-0). Oryx Pr.
Bibliopegia; or, the Art of Bookbinding in All Its Branches. John A. Arnett. Ed. by John Bidwell. LC 78-74390. (Nineteenth-Century Book Arts & Printing History Ser.: Vol. 5). (Illus.). 1980. lib. bdg. 27.50 (ISBN 0-8240-3879-7). Garland Pub.
Bibliophile Dictionary: A Biographical Record of the Great Authors, with Bibliographical Notices of Their Principal Works from the Beginning of History. LC 66-15269. 1966. Repr. of 1904 ed. 32.00 (ISBN 0-8103-3020-2). Gale.
Biblioteca Andina: Essays on the Lives & Works of the Chroniclers. Philip A. Means. LC 72-97615. (Illus.). 257p. 1973. Repr. of 1928 ed. 14.50x o.p. (ISBN 0-87917-025-5). Blaine Ethridge.
Bibliotheca Americana: Catalogue of the John Carter Brown Library in Brown University, Short-Title List of Additions, Books Printed 1471-1700. John Carter Brown Library. 67p. 1973. 10.00x (ISBN 0-87057-141-9). Univ Pr of New England.
Bibliotheca Americana: Catalogue of the John Carter Brown Library in Brown University, Books Printed 1675-1700. John Carter Brown Library. 484p. 1973. 50.00x (ISBN 0-87057-140-0, Pub. by Brown U Pr). Univ Pr of New England.
Bibliotheca Bolduaniana: A Renaissance Music Bibliography. Donald W. Krummel. LC 71-175176. (Detroit Studies in Music Bibliography Ser.: No. 22). 1972. 8.00 (ISBN 0-685-24023-1); pap. 6.50 (ISBN 0-685-24023-1). Info Coord.
Bibliotheca Canadensis: A Bio-Bibliographical Manual of Canadian Literature. Henry J. Morgan. LC 68-27177. 1968. Repr. of 1867 ed. 30.00 (ISBN 0-8103-3151-9). Gale.
Bibliotheca Chemica: A Catalogue of the Alchemical, Chemical & Pharmaceutical Books in the Collection of the Late James Young of Kelly & Furris, 2 vols. John Ferguson. LC 79-8610. Repr. of 1906 ed. 98.50 set (ISBN 0-404-18472-3). AMS Pr.
Bibliotheca Politica, 2 vols. Sir James Tyrrell. Ed. by David S. Berkowitz & Samuel E. Thorne. (English Legal History Ser.: Vol. 80). 1094p. 1979. 55.00 ea. (ISBN 0-8240-3067-2). Garland Pub.
Bibliotheca Washingtoniana. William S. Baker. LC 67-14022. 1967. Repr. of 1889 ed. 15.00 (ISBN 0-8103-3318-X). Gale.
Bibliothecae Alexandrinae Icones Symbolicae. Christophoro Giarda. Ed. by Stephen Orgel. LC 78-68230. (Philosophy of Images Ser.: Vol. 14). (Illus.). 1980. lib. bdg. 66.00 (ISBN 0-8240-3688-3). Garland Pub.
Bibliotheksbauten Des 19 Jahrhunderts in Deutschland. Hans M. Crass. (Illus.). 291p. (Ger.). 1976. text ed. 84.00 (ISBN 3-7940-3177-6, Pub. by K G Saur). Shoe String.
Bibliotheque Dramatique de Monsieur de Soleinne, 9 vols. in 8. Paul Lacroix. Incl. Bibliotheque Dramatique de Pont de Vesle, vii, 279p; Essai d'une Bibliographie General du Theatre, Ou Catalogue Raisonne de la Bibliotheque d'un Amateur. Joseph De Filippi. xiii, 224p; Table des Pieces de Theatre Descrites dans le Catalogue de la Bibliotheque de M. de Soleinne, par Charles Brunet. iv, 491p. Repr. 32.50 (ISBN 0-8337-1817-7). B Franklin.
Bibliotherapy & Its Widening Applications. Eleanor F. Brown. LC 74-28187. 1975. 14.50 (ISBN 0-8108-0782-3). Scarecrow.
Bibliotherapy: The Right Book at the Right Time. Claudia E. Cornett & Charles F. Cornett. LC 80-82684. (Fastback Ser.: No. 151). (Orig.). 1980. pap 0.75 (ISBN 0-87367-151-1). Phi Delta Kappa.
Biblohrafiia Ukrains'koi Presy, 1816-1916. Varfolomii Adrianovych Ihnatiienko. LC 74-220297. (Bibliohrafiia I Bibliotekonznavstvo). (Ukra.). 1968. 25.00 o.p. (ISBN 0-685-89029-5). Slavia Lib.
Bicentennial Conference on the United States Constitution. Frwd. by Warren E. Burger. Incl. Vol. I. Conference Papers; Vol. II. Conference Discussions. LC 78-65110. (Illus.). 1979. 20.00 o.p. (ISBN 0-8122-7763-5). U of Pa Pr.
Bicentennial Images. Robert Baxter. 1976. perfect bdg. 14.95 (ISBN 0-913384-19-4). Rail-Europe-Baxter.
Bickie's Cow College. Bert Rhoads. 1980. pap. 2.95 (ISBN 0-8280-0042-5). Review & Herald.
Bickie's Thunder Egg. Bert Rhoads. 1980. pap. 2.95 (ISBN 0-8280-0043-3, 02362-2). Review & Herald.
Bicultural Heritage: Themes for the Exploration of Mexican & Mexican-American Culture in Books for Children & Adolescents. Isabel Schon. LC 78-4332. 1978. 10.00 (ISBN 0-8108-1128-6). Scarecrow.
Bicycle Book for You. John Allis & Steve Lehrman. LC 78-2430. 1981. 8.95 (ISBN 0-689-10790-0). Atheneum.
Bicycle Book: The Total Illustrated Guide to Bicycles & Bicycling. John Wilcockson. Ed. by E. Holzer. (Illus.). 184p. 1980. 14.95 (ISBN 0-88421-156-8). Butterick Pub.
Bicycle Camping. Diana Armstrong. (Illus., Orig.). 1981. pap. 8.95. Dial.
Bicycle Commuting. Ed. by Bicycling Magazine. 1980. pap. 2.95 (ISBN 0-87857-301-1). Rodale Pr Inc.
Bicycle Mystery. Gertrude C. Warner. LC 79-126428. (Boxcar Children Mysteries-Pilot Bk.). (Illus.). 128p. (gr. 3-7). 1970. 6.95g (ISBN 0-8075-0708-3). A Whitman.
Bicycle-Pedestrian Planning & Design. Compiled By American Society of Civil Engineers. 712p. 1974. pap. text ed. 22.50 (ISBN 0-87262-065-4). Am Soc Civil Eng.
Bicycle Repair. Irene Kleeberg. LC 73-4798. (Career Concise Guide Ser.). (gr. 5 up). 1973. PLB 4.90 o.p. (ISBN 0-531-02636-1). Watts.
Bicycle Repair & Maintenance. Ben Burstyn. LC 72-86242. (Illus.). 224p. 1974. o. p. 6.95 (ISBN 0-668-02706-1); pap. 2.95 (ISBN 0-668-02708-8). Arco.
Bicycle Rider's Bible. Jeff Marshall. LC 79-6868. (Outdoor Bible Ser.). (Illus.). 176p. 1981. pap. 4.50 (ISBN 0-385-15134-9). Doubleday.
Bicycle Touring. Irene C. Kleeberg. LC 75-8999. (Career Concise Guide Ser.). (Illus.). 72p. (gr. 5 up). 1975. PLB 4.90 o.p. (ISBN 0-531-02838-0). Watts.
Bicycle Touring Book. Glenda Wilhelm & Tim Wilhelm. (Illus.). 228p. 1980. 12.95 (ISBN 0-87857-295-3); pap. 9.95 (ISBN 0-87857-307-0). Rodale Pr Inc.
Bicycle Transit: Its Planning & Design. Bruce L. Balshone et al. LC 75-55. (Special Studies). (Illus.). 186p. 1975. text ed. 21.95 (ISBN 0-275-05410-1). Praeger.
Bicycle Transportation: A Civil Engineer's Notebook. Compiled by American Society of Civil Engineers. LC 80-70171. 189p. pap. text ed. 15.50 (ISBN 0-87262-260-6). Am Soc Civil Eng.
Bicycles. Frederick Alderson. (Junior Reference Ser.). (Illus.). 64p. (gr. 7 up). 1974. 7.95 (ISBN 0-7136-1464-1). Dufour.
Bicycles. Alan Dahnsen. LC 78-7346. (Easy-Read Fact Bks.). (Illus.). (gr. 2-4). 1978. PLB 6.45 s&l (ISBN 0-531-01372-3). Watts.
Bicycles & Bicycling. George Fichter. (First Books Ser.). (Illus.). (gr. 4-6). 1978. PLB 6.45 s&l (ISBN 0-531-01403-7). Watts.
Bicycles & Bicycling: A Guide to Information Sources. Ed. by Mark Schultz & Barbara Schultz. LC 79-22839. (Sports, Games, & Pastimes Information Guide Ser.: Vol. 6). 1979. 30.00 (ISBN 0-8103-1448-7). Gale.
Bicycling. Charles Coombs. (Illus.). (gr. 5-9). 1972. PLB 6.96 o.p. (ISBN 0-688-20032-X); PLB 6.96 (ISBN 0-688-30032-4). Morrow.
Bicycling. Jean Durry. Ed. by J. B. Wadley. (Illus.). 220p. 1980. 19.95 (ISBN 0-8069-9226-3, Pub by Guinness Superlatives England). Sterling.
Bicycling. George S. Fichter & Keith Kingbay. (Golden Leisure Library). (Illus.). 120p. 1972. PLB 9.15 (ISBN 0-307-64351-4, Golden Pr). Western Pub.
Bicycling Book. John Krausz. (Illus.). 1980. 10.00 (ISBN 0-686-65922-8). Times Bks.
Bicycling California's Spine: Touring the Length of the Sierra Nevada. Bil Paul. LC 80-70010. (Bikeroots Ser.). (Illus.). 64p. (Orig.). 1981. pap. 3.95 (ISBN 0-9600650-3-2). Alchemist-Light.
Bicycling the Backroads of Southwest Washington. Erin Woods & Bill Woods. LC 80-14682. (Illus., Orig.). 1980. pap. 6.95 (ISBN 0-916890-91-0). Mountaineers.
Bid Better, Play Better. Dorothy A. Truscott. 1976. pap. 1.95 o.p. (ISBN 0-523-00997-6). Pinnacle Bks.
Bidding a Bridge Hand. Terence Reese. Orig. Title: Develop Your Bidding Judgment. 254p. 1972. pap. 3.50 (ISBN 0-486-22830-4). Dover.
Bidding & Oil Leases, Vol. 25. Ed. by Edward I. Altman. Ingo I. Walter. LC 79-3169. (Contemporary Studies in Economic & Financial Analysis Monographs). 320p. (Orig.). 1980. lib. bdg. 28.50 (ISBN 0-89232-148-2). Jai Pr.
Biddle's Bank: The Crucial Years. Jean A. Wilburn. 1967. 15.00x (ISBN 0-231-02981-0). Columbia U Pr.
Biedermann und Die Brandstifter. Max Frisch. Ed. by Paul K. Ackermann. (gr. 10-12). 1963. pap. text ed. 7.20 (ISBN 0-395-04090-6). HM.
Biedermeier Furniture. Georg Himmelheber. LC 74-29024. 1975. 30.00 o.p. (ISBN 0-684-14132-9, ScribT). Scribner.
Biedermeier Furniture. Georg Himmelheber. 1974. 48.00 (ISBN 0-571-08719-1, Pub. by Faber & Faber). Merrimack Bk Serv.
Big & Little. Joe Kaufman. (ps-1). 1967. PLB 7.62 (ISBN 0-307-60475-6, Golden Pr). Western Pub.
Big & Little. J. P. Miller. LC 75-36464. (Illus.). 14p. (ps-1). 1975. 2.50 (ISBN 0-394-83239-6, BYR). Random.
Big & Little Are Not the Same. Bob Ottum. (Tell-a-Tale Reader). 32p. (ps-3). 1980. PLB 4.77 (ISBN 0-307-68422-9, Golden Pr). Western Pub.
Big Anthony & the Magic Ring. Tomie De Paola. LC 78-23631. (gr. k-3). 1979. 7.95 (ISBN 0-15-207124-5, HJ). HarBraceJ.
Big Bag Book: How to Make All Kinds of Carry-Alls. Carter Houck & Myron Miller. (Encore Edition). (Illus.). 1977. pap. 2.95 (ISBN 0-684-16903-7). Scribner.
Big Band. Haskel Frankel. LC 65-19867. (gr. 7-9). 1965. 5.95 o.p. (ISBN 0-385-05863-2). Doubleday.
Big Bands. George T. Simon. 1974. 14.95 (ISBN 0-02-610980-8). Macmillan.
Big Bands Songbook. George T. Simon. LC 75-14419. (Illus.). 1976. pap. 8.95 o.s.i. (ISBN 0-690-01189-X, TYC-T). T Y Crowell.
Big Bang: The Creation & Evolution of the Universe. Joseph Silk. LC 79-19340. (Illus.). 1980. text ed. 18.00x (ISBN 0-7167-1084-6); pap. text ed. 9.95x (ISBN 0-7167-1085-4). W H Freeman.
Big Bears. Fred Johnson. Ed. by Russell Bourne & Bonnie S. Lawrence. LC 73-83783. (Ranger Rick's Best Friends Ser.). (Illus.). 32p. (gr. 1-6). 1973. 2.50 o.p. (ISBN 0-912186-05-4). Natl Wildlife.
Big Bend of the Rio Grande: A Guide to the Rocks, Landscape, Geologic History & Settlers of the Area of Big Bend National Park. R. A. Maxwell. (Illus.). 138p. 1968. Repr. 3.00 (GB 7). Bur Econ Geology.
Big Bird & Little Bird's Big & Little Book. Emily P. Kingsley. (Sesame Street Shape Bks.). (Illus.). (ps-3). 1977. PLB 5.38 (ISBN 0-307-68875-5, Golden Pr). Western Pub.
Big Birds B Book. (Wipe off Bks.). 9p. (ps). Date not set. 2.39 (ISBN 0-307-01842-3, Golden Pr). Western Pub.
Big Bird's Red Book. Roseanne Cerf & Jonathon Cerf. (Illus.). (gr. k-3). 1977. PLB 5.00 (ISBN 0-307-60157-9, Golden Pr). Western Pub.
Big Book of Auto Repair, 1981. Ed. by Kalton C. Lahue. LC 76-18639. 896p. 1980. pap. 14.95 (ISBN 0-8227-5054-6). Petersen Pub.
Big Book of Family Games. Jerome Meyer. (Illus.). 208p. 1980. pap. 4.95 (ISBN 0-8015-0624-7, Hawthorn). Dutton.
Big Book of Gleeb. Paul B. Lowney. (Illus.). 160p. 1975. 4.95 o.p. (ISBN 0-396-07223-2). Dodd.
Big Book of Jokes. Helen Hoke. LC 78-161837. (Big Bks). (Illus.). (gr. 4-6). 1971. PLB 6.90 (ISBN 0-531-01990-X). Watts.
Big Book of Kit Cars. Hot Rod Magazine Editorial Staff. (Illus.). 192p. (Orig.). 1980. pap. 8.95 (ISBN 0-8227-5062-7). Petersen Pub.
Big Book of Language Through Sounds. 2nd ed. Ann M. Flowers. LC 79-92515. 1980. pap. text ed. 6.95x (ISBN 0-8134-2114-4, 2114). Interstate.
Big Book of Mountaineering. Bruno Moravetz. (Illus.). 1980. 49.95 (ISBN 0-8120-5332-X). Barron.
Big Book of Recipes for Fun: Creative Learning Activities for Home and School. Carolyn B. Haas. (Illus.). 288p. (Orig.). 1980. pap. 10.95 (ISBN 0-914090-95-X). Chicago Review.
Big Book of Sounds. 3rd ed. Ann M. Flowers. LC 80-81413. 1980. pap. text ed. 6.95x (ISBN 0-8134-2142-X, 2142). Interstate.
Big Book of Tricks & Magic. James R. Blackman. (gr. 2 up). 1966. 3.95 (ISBN 0-394-80632-8, BYR). Random.
Big Boss. Anne Rockwell. LC 74-13660. (Ready-to-Read Ser.). (Illus.). 64p. (gr. 1-3). 1975. 7.95g (ISBN 0-02-777570-4). Macmillan.
Big Boy. 10.00 (ISBN 0-685-83313-5). Chatham Pub CA.
Big Boys. Max Ehrlich. 288p. 1981. 11.95 (ISBN 0-395-30525-X). HM.
Big Brown Bear. Georges Duplaix. (Illus.). (gr. k-3). 1946. PLB 5.00 (ISBN 0-307-60335-0, Golden Pr). Western Pub.
Big Business & the Mass Media. Bernard Rubin. LC 77-2516. 1977. 17.95 o.p. (ISBN 0-669-01517-2). Lexington Bks.
Big Business Reader. Ed. by Mark Green & Robert K Massie, Jr. LC 80-13542. 640p. (Orig.). 1980. pap. 4.95 (ISBN 0-8298-0398-X). Pilgrim NY.
Big Cats. George Shea. LC 80-23227. (Creatures Wild & Free). (gr. 1-6). 1981. text ed. 5.95 (ISBN 0-88436-774-6). EMC.
Big Cats. new rev. ed. Herbert S. Zim. LC 76-819. (Illus.). 64p. (gr. 3-7). 1976. PLB 6.48 (ISBN 0-688-32072-4). Morrow.
Big Cheese. Eve Bunting. LC 76-45381. (gr. 2-5). 1977. 7.95 (ISBN 0-02-715370-3, 71537). Macmillan.
Big Dallas Kill. Davis R. Baxter. 1980. 4.95 o.p. (ISBN 0-8062-1539-9). Carlton.
Big Dell Book of Crosswords & Pencil Puzzles. Ed. by Kathleen Rafferty. (Orig.). 1981. pap. 6.95 (ISBN 0-440-50970-X, Dell Trade Pbks). Dell.
Big Dipper. Franklyn M. Branley. LC 62-10999. (Let's-Read-&-Find-Out Science Bk). (Illus.). (gr. k-3). 1962. PLB 7.89 (ISBN 0-690-01116-4, TYC-J). T Y Crowell.
Big Dipper. June Epstein et al. (Illus.). 112p. (Orig.). (ps-3). 1981. pap. 9.95 (ISBN 0-19-554289-4). Oxford U Pr.
Big Drive. Wade Everett. 128p. 1981. pap. 1.75 (ISBN 0-345-29142-5). Ballantine.
Big Dummy's Guide to CB Radio. Albert Houston. Ed. by William Hershfield. (Illus.). 1976. 4.00 (ISBN 0-913990-04-3). Book Pub Co.
Big E. Edward P. Stafford. 1976. pap. 2.75 (ISBN 0-345-28795-9). Ballantine.
Big E: Learning Package One. Mary H. Garcia & Janet Gonzalez-Mena. Ed. by Lise B. Ragan. LC 75-27579. (Prog. Bk.). (gr. 1-2). 1976. tchr's ed. 9.95 (ISBN 0-88499-228-4); workbook 1.95 (ISBN 0-88499-230-6); pkg. of 10 tests 9.95 (ISBN 0-88499-229-2); program package 35.00 (ISBN 0-88499-231-4). Inst Mod Lang.
Big Eight Football: The Story, the Stars, the Stats of America's Toughest Conference. John McCallum. (Encore Edition). (Illus.). 1979. 5.95 (ISBN 0-684-16750-6). Scribner.
Big Elephant. Kathryn Jackson & Byron Jackson. (Illus.). 32p. (ps-1). 1974. PLB 7.15 o.p. (ISBN 0-307-62064-6, Golden Pr). Western Pub.
Big Enough Helper. Nancy Hall. (Illus.). (gr. k-3). 1978. PLB 5.00 (ISBN 0-307-60152-8, Golden Pr). Western Pub.
Big Fire in Baltimore. Rosa K. Eichelberger. LC 78-31311. (gr. 3 up). 1979. 10.95 (ISBN 0-916144-36-4); pap. 6.95 (ISBN 0-916144-37-2). Stemmer Hse.
Big Fish. Aileen Olsen. LC 75-116335. (Illus.). (gr. k-3). 1970. 6.75 (ISBN 0-688-41271-8); PLB 6.48 o.p. (ISBN 0-688-51271-2). Lothrop.
Big Foot, Little Foot. Kathleen M. Kimball. LC 78-68822. (Illus.). (ps-3). 1979. 5.00 (ISBN 0-933308-00-0). West Village.
Big Foot: Man, Monster, or Myth? Carrie Carmichael. LC 77-21317. (Great Unsolved Mysteries Ser.). (Illus.). (gr. 4-5). 1977. PLB 9.65 (ISBN 0-8172-1052-0). Raintree Pubs.
Big Foot: The Yeti & Sasquatch in Myth & Reality. John Napier. 1973. 9.95 o.p. (ISBN 0-525-06658-6). Dutton.
Big Foot's Range. Jack Slade. (Lassiter Ser.). 1979. pap. 1.75 (ISBN 0-505-51428-1). Tower Bks.
Big Foundations. Waldemar Nielsen. LC 72-3676. (Twentieth Century Fund Study). 475p. 1972. 17.50x (ISBN 0-231-03665-5); pap. 9.00x (ISBN 0-231-03666-3). Columbia U Pr.
Big Freeze. Ed. by Thomas J. Mooney. (Pal Paperbacks Ser., Kit A). (Illus., Orig.). (gr. 7-12). 1976. pap. text ed. 1.25 (ISBN 0-8374-3493-9). Xerox Ed Pubns.

Big Fun to Grow Book. Allan Swenson. 1980. pap. 3.50 (ISBN 0-679-20510-1). McKay.

Big Game of North America. rev. ed. Wildlife Management Institute. Ed. by Douglas L. Gilbert. LC 78-14005. (Illus.). 512p. 1979. 24.95 (ISBN 0-8117-0244-8). Stackpole.

Big Golden Animal ABC. Garth Williams. (gr. k-2). 1957. 1.95 (ISBN 0-307-10457-5, Golden Pr); PLB 7.62 (ISBN 0-307-60457-8). Western Pub.

Big Green Book: A Four-Season Guide to Vermont. Madeleine Kunin & Marilyn Stout. (Illus.). 352p. 1976. pap. 6.95 (ISBN 0-517-52517-8). Crown.

Big Gun Monitors: The History of the Design, Construction & Operation of the Royal Navy's Monitors. Ian Buxton. LC 80-81901. (Illus.). 215p. 1980. 19.95 (ISBN 0-87021-104-8). Naval Inst Pr.

Big Harold & Tiny Enid. Barbara Fisher. (Illus.). 26p. (Orig.). (gr. 1-3). 1975. pap. 2.00 (ISBN 0-934830-01-0). Ten Penny.

Big Hassle: Getting Along with Authority. Jack Canario. (Read on! - Write on! Ser.). (Illus.). 64p. (gr. 6-12). 1980. 2.85 (ISBN 0-915510-38-3). Janus Bks.

Big Hello. Janet Schulman. (gr. k-6). 1980. pap. 0.95 (ISBN 0-440-40484-3, YB). Dell.

Big Illusion. Mel Wood. Ed. by John E. Wood. (Illus.). 73p. 1981. 20.00 (ISBN 0-9604644-0-9). Sheephead Bks.

Big It & Other Stories. A. B. Guthrie, Jr. (Western Fiction Ser.). 1980. lib. bdg. 9.95 (ISBN 0-8398-2680-X). Gregg.

Big Joke Game. Scott Corbett. LC 78-179052. (Illus.). 128p. (gr. 3-6). 1972. 7.50 (ISBN 0-525-26515-5, Anytime Bks); PLB 7.50 o.p. (ISBN 0-525-45013-0, Anytime Bks). Dutton.

Big Little School. 2nd rev. & enl. ed. Robert W. Lynn & Elliott Wright. LC 79-27864. 178p. 1980. pap. 6.95 (ISBN 0-89135-021-7). Religious Educ.

Big Lonely. Lou Cameron. 1978. pap. 2.25 (ISBN 0-445-04200-1). Popular Lib.

Big Media, Little Media: Tools & Technologies for Instruction. Wilbur Schramm. LC 76-30522. (People & Communication: Vol. 2). 1977. 20.00x (ISBN 0-8039-0740-0); pap. 9.95x (ISBN 0-8039-0745-1). Sage.

Big-Men & Business: Entrepreneurship & Economic Growth in the New Guinea Highlands. Ben R. Finney. LC 72-93151. (Illus.). 250p. 1973. 12.00x (ISBN 0-8248-0262-4, Eastwest Ctr). U Pr of Hawaii.

Big Money. John Dos Passos. 1969. pap. 2.50 (ISBN 0-451-51353-3, CE1353, Sig Classics). NAL.

Big Mutt. John Reese. (Illus.). (gr. 5-7). 1969. pap. 1.75 (ISBN 0-671-29987-5). PB.

Big Ones, Little Ones. Tana Hoban. LC 75-34440. (Illus.). 32p. (gr. k-3). 1976. 7.25 (ISBN 0-688-80040-8); PLB 6.67 (ISBN 0-688-84040-X). Greenwillow.

Big Picnic & Other Meals in the New Testament. Lee H. Bristol. LC 75-13455. (Illus.). 96p. 1975. 4.95 o.p. (ISBN 0-8042-2286-X). John Knox.

Big Pig. D. Nolan. 1976. 5.95 (ISBN 0-13-076158-3). P-H.

Big Player: How a Team of Blackjack Players Made a Million Dollars. Ken Uston & Roger Rapoport. LC 76-29919. 1977. 7.95 o.p. (ISBN 0-03-016921-6). HR&W.

Big Potential for Rigid Oriented Containers: P-037. BCC Staff. (Illus.). 1976. 625.00 o.p. (ISBN 0-89336-051-1). BCC.

Big Primer on New England's Colonial Architecture. Isabella Hagelstein. (Regional & Recreational Guides Ser.). (Illus.). 1981. pap. 5.95 (ISBN 0-89046-074-4). Herman Pub.

Big Radio Comedy Program. Ed. by Ross Firestone. 1978. 14.95 o.p. (ISBN 0-8092-7909-6); pap. 8.95 o.p. (ISBN 0-8092-7908-8). Contemp Bks.

Big Ranch Country. J. W. Williams. 10.95 (ISBN 0-685-48783-0). Nortex Pr.

Big Red Bus. Ethel Kessler & Leonard Kessler. LC 57-8090. (gr. k up). 1964. PLB 7.95 (ISBN 0-385-07713-0). Doubleday.

Big Red Machine. Bob Hertzel. LC 75-45010. (Illus.). 1976. 7.95 o.p. (ISBN 0-13-076190-7). P-H.

Big Red Puzzle Book. Amy Wordsworth. 1980. pap. 7.95 o.p. (ISBN 0-89903-002-5). Caroline Hse.

Big Rock Candy Mountain. Wallace Stegner. 1973. Repr. of 1943 ed. 8.95 o.p. (ISBN 0-385-07905-2). Doubleday.

Big Rock Candy Mountain: A Paradigm of the Values of the Mass Consumption Society. 20p. 1981. pap. 10.00 (ISBN 92-808-0154-6, TUNU 106, UNU). Unipub.

Big Shots: Edwardian Shooting Parties. Jonathan G. Ruffier. (Illus.). 1978. 17.50 o.p. (ISBN 0-670-16376-7, Debrett's Peerage, Ltd.). Viking Pr.

Big Sister Little Brother. Terry Berger. LC 75-19467. (Identity II Ser.). (Illus.). 32p. (gr. k-3). 1975. Repr. of 1974 ed. PLB 7.95 o.p. (ISBN 0-8172-0049-5). Raintree Pubs.

Big Sister Tells Me That I'm Black. Arnold Adoff. LC 75-32249. 32p. (gr. k-4). 1976. reinforced bdg. 5.95 (ISBN 0-03-014546-5). HR&W.

Big Sisters Are Bad Witches. Morse Hamilton. LC 79-24907. (Illus.). 32p. (gr. k-3). 1981. 7.95 (ISBN 0-688-80268-0); PLB 7.63 (ISBN 0-688-84268-2). Greenwillow.

Big Sleep. Raymond Chandler. 224p. 1975. pap. 1.50 o.p. (ISBN 0-345-24565-2). Ballantine.

Big Snow. Berta Hader & Elmer Hader. (Illus.). (gr. k-3). 1948. 8.95 (ISBN 0-02-737910-8). Macmillan.

Big Snowy. Jim Slater. LC 80-53066. (A. Mazing Monsters Ser.). (Illus.). 1981. pap. 1.25 (ISBN 0-394-84736-9). Random.

Big Story. William Peil. (Illus.). 62p. (gr. 2-4). 1973. pap. 0.95 (ISBN 0-87793-124-0). Ave Maria.

Big Strawberry Book of the Earth: Our Ever-Changing Planet. Bendick. 110p. Date not set. 6.95 (ISBN 0-07-004514-3). McGraw.

Big Sur. Donald Pike & David Muench. Ed. by Gweneth R. DenDooven. LC 78-51408. (Illus.). 1979. 8.95 (ISBN 0-916122-68-9); pap. 3.75 (ISBN 0-916122-67-0). K C Pubns.

Big Susan. Elizabeth O. Jones. (Illus.). (gr. k-3). 1967. 3.95g o.s.i. (ISBN 0-02-747740-1). Macmillan.

Big Ten Football: Its Life & Times, Great Coaches, Players & Games. Mervin D. Hymen & Gordon S. White, Jr. (Illus.). 1977. 12.95 o.s.i. (ISBN 0-02-558070-1). Macmillan.

Big Thicket: A Challenge for Conservation. A. Y. Gunter. LC 73-184310. 1972. 14.95 (ISBN 0-8363-0120-X); pap. 8.50 (ISBN 0-685-02984-0). Jenkins.

Big Thompson: Profile of a Natural Disaster. David McComb. (Illus.). 1980. 19.95 (ISBN 0-87108-558-5). Pruett.

Big Tidy-up. Norah Smaridge. (Big Picture Bks.). (ps-3). 1970. PLB 7.62 (ISBN 0-307-60877-8, Golden Pr). Western Pub.

Big Time. Hal Morgan. (Illus.). 80p. 1981. pap. 6.95 (ISBN 0-312-07852-8). St Martin.

Big Trail. Max Brand. 1974. pap. 1.75 (ISBN 0-446-94333-9). Warner Bks.

Big Trouble. Jacquie Hann. LC 78-1712. (Illus.). 40p. (gr. k-3). 1978. 5.95 (ISBN 0-590-07557-8, Four Winds). Schol Bk Serv.

Big Two: Soviet-American Perceptions of Foreign Policy. Anatol Rapoport. LC 72-124676. 1972. 28.50x (ISBN 0-672-53507-6). Irvington.

Big V. Anthony Slide. LC 76-21247. 1976. 10.00 (ISBN 0-8108-0967-2). Scarecrow.

Big War. Anton Myrer. 1981. pap. 3.25 (ISBN 0-425-04672-9). Berkley Pub.

Big Welfare Mess: Public Assistance and Rehabilitation Approaches. Ed. by John G. Cull & Richard E. Hardy. (Amer. Lec. Social & Rehabilitation Psychology). 368p. 1973. 32.50 (ISBN 0-398-02796-X). C C Thomas.

Big White Puzzle Book. Ned Webster. 1980. pap. 7.95 o.p. (ISBN 0-89903-001-7). Caroline Hse.

Big Wilderness Canoe Manual. Bob Cary. (Illus.). 1978. 12.95 o.p. (ISBN 0-679-50862-7); pap. 6.95 o.p. (ISBN 0-679-50864-3). McKay.

Big Winds, Glass Mornings, Shadows Cast by Stars. Morton Marcus. 64p. (Orig.). 1980. pap. 4.95 (ISBN 0-937310-06-9). Jazz Pr.

Big Words for Little People. Donna L. Pape. 1973. pap. 1.49 o.p. (ISBN 0-87239-280-5, 2741). Standard Pub.

Big Yellow Bus Is a Good Friend of Mine. William S. Bradshaw, Jr. LC 80-54535. (Illus.). 24p. (gr. k-5). 1981. pap. 6.95 (ISBN 0-935054-03-0). Webb-Newcomb.

Bigallo: The Oratory & Residence of the Compagnia Del Bigallo Della Misericordia in Florence. Howard Saalman. LC 69-18285. (College Art Association Monographs: Vol. 19). (Illus.). 1969. 18.50x (ISBN 0-8147-0370-4). NYU Pr.

Bigfoot. Hal G. Evarts. 190p. (gr. k-3). pap. 2.95 (ISBN 0-689-70487-9, A-114, Aladdin). Atheneum.

Bigfoot. John Napier. pap. 1.50 o.p. (ISBN 0-425-03381-3). Berkley Pub.

Bigfoot All Over the Country. Marian T. Place. LC 78-7728. (Illus.). 1978. 6.50 (ISBN 0-396-07610-6). Dodd.

Bigfoot: America's Abominable Snowman. Elwood Baumann. LC 74-11407. (Illus.). 128p. (gr. 5 up). 1975. PLB 7.90 (ISBN 0-531-02793-7). Watts.

Bigger Giant. pap. 3.50 incl. record (ISBN 0-590-04390-0, Schol Pap). Schol Bk Serv.

Bigger Profits for the Smaller Firm. 2nd ed. E. G. Wood. 211p. 1978. pap. text ed. 12.25x (ISBN 0-220-66350-5, Pub. by Busn Bks England). Renouf.

Biggest & the Littlest Animals. Tony Palazzo. LC 77-112374. (Illus.). 40p. (gr. k-3). 1973. PLB 7.21 (ISBN 0-87460-225-4). Lion.

Biggest Bear. Lynd Ward. (Illus.). (gr. k-3). 1952. reinforced bdg. 8.95 (ISBN 0-395-14806-5). HM.

Biggest Bear. Lynd Ward. LC 52-8730. (Illus.). 80p. (gr. k-3). 1973. pap. 2.50 (ISBN 0-395-15024-8, Sandpiper). HM.

Biggest Company on Earth: A Profile of AT&T. Sonny Kleinfield. LC 80-13095. 352p. 1981. 14.95 (ISBN 0-03-045326-7). HR&W.

Biggest Giraffe. Mike Peterson & Robert Gadbois. LC 77-1981. (Books by Children for Children). (Illus.). (gr. 2-6). 1977. PLB 6.45 (ISBN 0-87191-609-6). Creative Ed.

Biggest Riddle Book in the World. Joseph Rosenbloom. LC 76-1165. (Illus.). 320p. (gr. 2 up). 1976. 7.95 (ISBN 0-8069-4532-X); PLB 8.29 (ISBN 0-8069-4533-8). Sterling.

Biggest Tongue-Twister Book in the World. Gyles Brandreth. LC 78-57784. (Illus.). (gr. 2 up). 1978. 5.95 (ISBN 0-8069-4594-X); PLB 6.69 (ISBN 0-8069-4595-8). Sterling.

Biggest Tongue Twister Book in the World. Gyles Brandreth. LC 78-7784. (Illus.). 123p. (gr. 3 up). 1980. pap. 2.95 (ISBN 0-8069-8972-6). Sterling.

Biggest Victory. Alfred Slote. (gr. 3-7). 1977. pap. 1.95 (ISBN 0-380-00907-2, 31732, Camelot). Avon.

Bigg's Cost Accounts. J. Wald. (Illus.). 400p. (Orig.). 1978. pap. text ed. 15.95x (ISBN 0-7121-0263-9, Pub. by Macdonald & Evans England). Intl Ideas.

Bignoniaceae: Crescentieae & Tourretieae, Pt. 1. Alwyn H. Gentry. LC 80-10846. (Flora Neotropica Monograph: No. 25). (Illus.). 132p. 1980. pap. 15.75 (ISBN 0-89327-222-1). NY Botanical.

Bignose. Jim Slater. LC 80-53065. (A. Mazing Monsters Ser.). (Illus.). 1981. pap. 1.25 (ISBN 0-394-84739-3). Random.

Bigotry & Blood: Documents on the Ulster Crisis. Charles Carlton. LC 76-17018. 1977. 12.95 (ISBN 0-88229-278-1); pap. 7.95 (ISBN 0-88229-469-5). Nelson-Hall.

Biharis in Bangladesh. Ben Whitaker. (Minority Rights Group: No. 11). 1972. pap. 2.50 (ISBN 0-89192-100-1). Interbk Inc.

Bijou Dream. Jack Warner, Jr. Ed. by Carole Baron. 1981. 12.95 (ISBN 0-517-54333-8). Crown.

Bike & Hike. J. S. Jones. (Illus.). 225p. 1977. pap. 5.95 o.p. (ISBN 0-902280-45-7). Bradt Ent.

Bike & Hike: Sixty Tours Around Great Britain & Ireland. J. Sydney Jones. (Illus., Orig.). 1978. pap. 3.95 (ISBN 0-8467-0439-0, Pub. by Two Continents). Hippocrene Bks.

Bike & Superbike. Mike Woollett. (Illus.). 64p. 1980. pap. 5.95 (ISBN 0-7134-0540-6, Pub. by Batsford England). David & Charles.

Bike Bag Book. Tom Cuthbertson. (Illus.). 128p. (Orig.). 1981. pap. 2.95 (ISBN 0-89815-039-6). Ten Speed Pr.

Bike! Motorcycles & the People Who Ride Them. Thierry Sagnier. LC 72-9151. (Illus.). 208p. 1974. 10.95 o.p. (ISBN 0-06-013736-3, HarpT); pap. 3.95 o.s.i. (ISBN 0-06-013743-6, TD-199, HarpT). Har-Row.

Bike, Skate & Skateboard Games. (Kids Paperback Ser.). (Illus.). 1977. PLB 7.62 (ISBN 0-307-62353-X, Golden Pr); pap. 1.95 (ISBN 0-307-12353-7). Western Pub.

Bikes & Riders. James Wagenvoord. pap. 3.95 Special Format o.s.i. (ISBN 0-380-01060-7, 13128). Avon.

Bikeways: One Hundred One Things to Do with a Bike. rev. ed. Lillian Frankel & Godfrey Frankel. LC 61-15857. (Illus.). 128p. (gr. 8 up). 1972. 6.95 (ISBN 0-8069-4004-2); PLB 7.49 (ISBN 0-8069-4005-0). Sterling.

Bikinians: A Study in Forced Migration. R. C. Kiste. LC 79-224. 1974. pap. 5.95 (ISBN 0-8465-3752-4). Benjamin-Cummings.

Bilateral Network of Social Relations in Konkama Lapp District. 3rd ed. Robert N. Pehrson. 1971. pap. text ed. 10.00x (ISBN 8-200-04133-6, Dist. by Columbia U Pr). Universitet.

Bildniszeichnungen Von J.A.D. Ingres, 5 vols. only vols. 1-4 are available. Hans Naef. (Illus.). 1980. 175.00x ea. (Pub. by Sotheby Parke Bernet England). Vol. 1 (ISBN 3-7165-0087-9). Vol. 2 (ISBN 3-7165-0249-9). Vol. 3.1979 (ISBN 3-7165-0250-2). Vol. 4 (ISBN 3-7165-0122-0). Biblio Dist.

Bilgewater. Jane Gardam. LC 77-2890. (gr. 7 up). 1977. 8.25 (ISBN 0-688-80108-0); PLB 7.92 (ISBN 0-688-84108-2). Greenwillow.

Bilingual Education Act: A Legislative Analysis. Arnold H. Leibowitz. LC 80-80121. 70p. (Orig.). 1980. pap. 4.20 (ISBN 0-89763-022-X). Natl Clearinghse Bilingual Ed.

Bilingual Education, Current Perspectives No.5: Synthesis. Center for Applied Linguistics. LC 77-80381. (Orig.). 1978. pap. 7.95 (ISBN 0-87281-076-3). Ctr Appl Ling.

Bilingual Education, Current Perspectives: Synthesis. Center for Applied Linguistics. LC 77-80381. 1978. pap. text ed. 7.95x o.p. (ISBN 0-87281-076-3). Ctr Appl Ling.

Bilingual Education for Hispanic Students in the United States. Ed. by Joshua A. Fishman & Gary D. Keller. (Orig.). 1981. pap. 17.95 (ISBN 0-8077-2603-6). Tchrs Coll.

Bilingual Education in American Schools: A Guide to Information Sources. Ed. by Francesco Cordasco. George Bernstein. LC 79-15787. (Education Information Guide Ser.: Vol. 3). 1979. 30.00 (ISBN 0-8103-1447-9). Gale.

Bilingual Education: Theories & Issues. Christina B. Paulston. 90p. 1980. pap. 8.95 (ISBN 0-88377-146-2). Newbury Hse.

Bilingual Guide to Business & Professional Correspondence: English-French. J. Harvard. 1976. 21.00 (ISBN 0-08-015973-7); pap. 10.75 (ISBN 0-08-015594-4). Pergamon.

Bilingual Guide to Business & Professional Correspondence, English-German, German-English. J. Harvard. 1975. 15.00 (ISBN 0-08-017654-2); pap. 7.75 (ISBN 0-08-017655-0). Pergamon.

Bilingual Guide to Business & Professional Correspondence: Spanish-English, English-Spanish. J. Harvard. 1970. 23.00 (ISBN 0-08-015793-9); pap. 7.75 (ISBN 0-08-015792-0). Pergamon.

Bilingualism in the Americas: A Research & Bibliographical Guide. Einar Haugen. (Publications of the American Dialect Society: No. 26). 159p. 1956. pap. 4.95 (ISBN 0-8173-0626-9). U of Ala Pr.

Bilingualism in the Southwest. 2nd, rev. ed. Ed. by Paul Turner. 1982. pap. text ed. write for info. (ISBN 0-8165-0729-5). U of Ariz Pr.

Bill. Joan Tate. (Joan Tate Ser.). pap. text ed. 1.95x o.p. (ISBN 0-435-11883-8). Heinemann Ed.

Bill Cosby. James T. Olsen. LC 74-6454. (Personal Closeups Ser). 32p. 1974. 5.75 o.p. (ISBN 0-87191-356-9). Creative Ed.

Bill Joel: A Photo Biography. Peter Gambaccini. 192p. (Orig.). 1980. pap. 2.50 (ISBN 0-515-05317-1). Jove Pubns.

Bill Martin Freedom Book Series, 10 bks. Bill Martin, Jr. Incl. Adam's Balm. Illus. by Michael Foreman (ISBN 0-8372-2052-1); America, I Know You. Illus. by Ted Rand (ISBN 0-8372-2048-3); Freedom's Apple Tree. Illus. by John Rambola (ISBN 0-8372-2047-5); Gentle, Gentle Thursday. Illus. by Samuel Maitin (ISBN 0-8372-2055-6); I Am Freedom's Child. Illus. by Symeon Shimin (ISBN 0-8372-2046-7); I Reach Out to the Morning. Illus. by Henry Markowitz (ISBN 0-8372-2054-8); It's America for Me. Illus. by Lou Glanzman (ISBN 0-8372-2049-1); Once There Were Bluebirds. Illus. by Bernard Martin. o.p. (ISBN 0-8372-0652-9); Poor Old Uncle Sam. Illus. by Sal Murdocca (ISBN 0-8372-2051-3); Spoiled Tomatoes. Illus. by Jay Ells (ISBN 0-8372-2050-5). (gr. 5-12). pap. 11.70 pkg. of 6 copies (ISBN 0-685-29088-3); tchrs' guide 4.35 (ISBN 0-8372-0708-8). 10 records 84.90 (ISBN 0-8372-0230-2). complete lab: 60 s-c, 50 activity cards & teacherhs guide 198.00 set (ISBN 0-8372-2449-7); bks., guide, activitycards, & cassettes 198.00 set (ISBN 0-8372-2044-0); book pack, 6 copies of one title avail.; activity cards 21.36 (ISBN 0-8372-1949-3). Bowmar-Noble.

Bill Monroe & His Blue Grass Boys: An Illustrated Discography. Neil V. Rosenberg. (Illus.). 122p. 1974. pap. 4.50 (ISBN 0-915608-02-2). Country Music Found.

Bill Nye. David B. Kesterson. (United States Authors Ser: No. 403). 1981. lib. bdg. 11.95 (ISBN 0-8057-7332-0). Twayne.

Bill Nye's Western Humor. Bill Nye. Ed. by T. A. Larson. LC 67-20599. (Illus.). 1968. 12.95x (ISBN 0-8032-0133-8); pap. 3.95 (ISBN 0-8032-5821-6, BB 605, Bison). U of Nebr Pr.

Bill of Rights. E. B. Fincher. (First Books Ser.). (Illus.). (gr. 4-6). 1978. PLB 6.45 s&l (ISBN 0-531-01347-2). Watts.

Bill of Rights for Children. H. H. Foster, Jr. (Amer. Lec Behavioral Science & Law Ser.). 96p. 1974. pap. 7.75 (ISBN 0-398-02986-5). C C Thomas.

Bill of Rites, a Bill of Wrongs, a Bill of Goods. Wright Morris. LC 80-389. x, 177p. 1980. 13.50x (ISBN 0-8032-3065-6); pap. 4.25 (ISBN 0-8032-8107-2, BB 738, Bison). U of Nebr Pr.

Bill of Roghts for Future Generations. Jacques-Yves Cousteau. (Illus.). 33p. (Orig.). 1980. pap. 1.50 (ISBN 0-913098-31-0). Myrin Institute.

Bill Russell. Paul J. Deegan. LC 73-13749. (Creative Superstars Ser.). 1974. PLB 5.95 o.p. (ISBN 0-87191-281-3). Creative Ed.

Bill Severn's Big Book of Magic. Bill Severn. 160p. (gr. 7 up). 1973. 8.95 o.p. (ISBN 0-679-20022-3). McKay.

Bill Sublette, Mountain Man. John E. Sunder. (Illus.). 1978. pap. 5.95 (ISBN 0-8061-1111-9). U of Okla Pr.

Bill W. Robert Thomsen. LC 74-1861. (Illus.). 382p. 1975. 15.95 (ISBN 0-06-014267-7, HarpT). Har-Row.

Bill Wallace of China. Jesse C. Fletcher. LC 63-17522. (Illus.). (gr. 7-10). 1963. pap. 1.25 (ISBN 0-8054-1113-5). Broadman.

Bill Walton. Larry Batson. LC 74-16498. (Sports Superstars Ser.). (Illus.). 32p. (gr. 3-9). 1974. PLB 5.50 o.p. (ISBN 0-87191-379-8). Creative Ed.

Bill Walton: On the Road with the Portland Trail Blazers. Jack Scott. LC 77-11569. (Illus.). 1978. 10.95 o.p. (ISBN 0-690-01694-8, TYC-T). T Y Crowell.

Billards As It Should Be Played. Willie Hoppe. 7.95 o.p. (ISBN 0-8092-8837-0). Contemp Bks.

Billboard Art. Sally Henderson & Robert Landau. LC 79-24115. (Illus.). 112p. (Orig.). 1980. pap. 9.95 (ISBN 0-87701-167-2, Prism Edns). Chronicle Bks.

Billet Circulaire. Alice Langellier & Paul Langellier. LC 66-12110. 1966. pap. text ed. 3.95x (ISBN 0-89197-516-0). Irvington.

Billetdoux: Two Plays. Francois Billetdoux. Tr. by Mark Rudkin. Incl. Tchin-Tchin; Chez Torpe. 1964. 3.50 o.p. (ISBN 0-8090-3010-1, Mermaid). Hill & Wang.

Billiards at Half-Past Nine. Heinrich Boll. 1975. pap. 2.95 (ISBN 0-380-00280-9, 51383, Bard). Avon.

Billie Jean King. James T. Olsen. LC 76-12090. (Creative Superstars Ser.). 1974. PLB 5.95 (ISBN 0-87191-275-9); pap. 2.95 (ISBN 0-89812-177-9). Creative Ed.

Billie Jean King: Queen of the Courts. Carol B. Church. Ed. by David L. Bender & Gary E. Mc Cuen. (Focus on Famous Women Ser). (Illus.). (gr. 3-9). 1976. 6.95 (ISBN 0-912616-41-5); read-along cassette 9.95 (ISBN 0-89908-240-8). Greenhaven.

Billie Jean King: Tennis Champion. Julian May. LC 74-82744. (Sports Close-up Ser.). (gr. 3-5). 1974. PLB 5.95 o.p. (ISBN 0-913940-09-7); pap. 2.50 o.p. (ISBN 0-913940-97-6). Crestwood Hse.

Billion Dollar Baby. Bob Greene. 1975. pap. 1.95 o.p. (ISBN 0-451-06713-4, J6713, Sig). NAL.

Billion Dollar Brain. Len Deighton. 1980. pap. 2.25 (ISBN 0-425-04470-X). Berkley Pub.

Billions of Bugs. Haris Petie. (Illus.). (ps-2). 1975. 5.95 (ISBN 0-13-076240-7); pap. 2.50 (ISBN 0-13-076174-5). P-H.

Bills & Acts: Legislative Procedure in Eighteenth Century England. Sheila Lambert. 1971. 39.00 (ISBN 0-521-08119-X). Cambridge U Pr.

Billy & Blaze. Clarence W. Anderson. (Illus.). (gr. k-3). 1962. 6.95 (ISBN 0-02-701880-6). Macmillan.

Billy Bedamned, Long Gone by. Patricia Beatty. (gr. 5-9). 1977. 8.25 (ISBN 0-688-22101-7); PLB 7.92 (ISBN 0-688-32101-1). Morrow.

Billy Bitzer, His Story. G. W. Bitzer. (Illus.). 1973. 10.00 o.p. (ISBN 0-374-11294-0). FS&G.

Billy Bowlegs War. James W. Covington. (Illus.). Date not set. write for info (ISBN 0-913122-06-8). Mickler Hse. Postponed.

Billy Budd. Herman Melville. (Literature Ser). (gr. 7-12). 1969. pap. text ed. 3.25 (ISBN 0-87720-703-8). AMSCO Sch.

Billy Budd. Herman Melville. Ed. by Milton Stern. LC 73-8967. (LL Ser: No. 43). 244p. 1975. 10.50 (ISBN 0-672-51466-4); pap. 6.50 (ISBN 0-672-61040-X). Bobbs.

Billy Budd. Herman Melville. (Now Age Illustrated V Ser.). (Illus.). 64p. (gr. 4-12). 1979. text ed. 4.50 (ISBN 0-88301-397-5); pap. text ed. 1.45 (ISBN 0-88301-385-1); student activity bk. 0.95 (ISBN 0-88301-409-2). Pendulum Pr.

Billy Budd & Other Stories. Herman Melville. pap. 1.75. Bantam.

Billy Budd with Reader's Guide. Herman Melville. (Amsco Literature Program). (gr. 10-12). 1971. pap. text ed. 3.92 (ISBN 0-87720-810-7); tchr's ed. 2.60 (ISBN 0-87720-910-3). AMSCO Sch.

Billy Durant: Creator of General Motors. Lawrence R. Gustin. 1973. 8.95 o.p. (ISBN 0-8028-3435-3). Eerdmans.

Billy Graham Talks to Teenagers. Billy Graham. (Orig.). (YA) pap. 1.25 (ISBN 0-89129-153-9). Jove Pubns.

Billy Jo Jive & the Case of the Missing Pigeons. John Shearer. (gr. k-6). 1980. pap. 1.50 (ISBN 0-440-40669-2, YB). Dell.

Billy Jo Jive & the Walkie-Talkie Caper: A Mystery. John Shearer. LC 80-17780. (Illus.). 48p. (gr. k-3). 1981. 7.95 (ISBN 0-440-00791-7); PLB 7.45 (ISBN 0-440-00792-5). Delacorte.

Billy Joe Tatum's Wild Foods Cookbook & Field Guide. Billy Joe Tatum. LC 75-8909. (Illus.). 256p. 1976. 8.95 (ISBN 0-911104-76-3); pap. 5.95 (ISBN 0-911104-77-1). Workman Pub.

Billy Lanes Encyclopaedia of Float Fishing. Billy Lane & Colin Graham. (Illus.). 1971. 9.50 (ISBN 0-7207-0514-2). Transatlantic.

Billy Sunday Speaks. Billy Sunday. Ed. by Karen Gullen. LC 76-127017. (Illus.). 220p. 1981. pap. 6.95 (ISBN 0-87754-141-8). Chelsea Hse.

Billy, the Condominium Cat. Esphyr Slobodkina. LC 79-23402. (Illus.). 1980. 6.95 (ISBN 0-201-09204-2, 9204). A-W.

Billy the Kid. Shuntaro Tanikawa. Tr. by Harold Wright from Japanese. lmtd. ed. 5.00 (ISBN 0-931460-21-2, Broadside). Bieler.

Billy Wilder. Bernard F. Dick. (Theater Arts Ser.). 1980. lib. bdg. 10.95 (ISBN 0-8057-9274-0). Twayne.

Billy's Basketball. Sylvia R. Tester. LC 76-15632. (Kids in Sports Ser.). (Illus.). (gr. 1-3). 1976. PLB 4.95 (ISBN 0-913778-57-5); pap. 2.75 (ISBN 0-89565-124-6). Childs World.

Bilmece: A Corpus of Turkish Riddles. Ihlan Basgoz & Andreas Tietze. (Publications in Folklore Studies Vol. 22). 1974. pap. 34.50x (ISBN 0-520-09145-0). U of Cal Pr.

Bimal in Bog, 2 vols. Baldev K. Vaid. 1972. Set. 28.00 (ISBN 0-88253-818-7); Set. pap. text ed. 9.60 (ISBN 0-88253-819-5). Ind-US Inc.

Binary & Multiple Systems of Stars. A. H. Batten. LC 72-88026. 288p. 1973. 32.00 (ISBN 0-08-016986-4). Pergamon.

Binary Numbers. Clyde Watson. LC 75-29161. (Young Math Ser.). (Illus.). (gr. 1-4). 1977. PLB 7.89 (ISBN 0-690-00993-3, TYC-J). T Y Crowell.

Binding of Leviathan: Conservatism & the Future. William Waldegrove. 1979. 17.95 (ISBN 0-241-89866-8, Pub. by Hamish Hamilton England). David & Charles.

Bing Crosby. Donald Shepherd & Robert Slatzer. (Illus.). 320p. 1981. 13.95 (ISBN 0-312-07866-8). St Martin.

Bingara Fauna: A Pleistocene Vertebrate Fauna from Murchison County, New South Wales, Australia. Leslie F. Marcus. (Publications in Geological Sciences: Vol. 114). 1976. pap. 12.50x (ISBN 0-520-09538-3). U of Cal Pr.

Bintel Brief. Isaac Metzker & Harry Golden. 1977. pap. 1.25 (ISBN 0-345-22903-7). Ballantine.

Bio-Adventures: The Drama of Medical Research. Desmond Zwar. LC 80-6168. 288p. 1981. 14.95 (ISBN 0-8128-2807-0). Stein & Day.

Bio-Biographical Index of Musicians in the United States of America Since Colonial Times. L. Ellinwood & K. Porter. LC 76-159677. (Music Ser). 1971. Repr. of 1956 ed. lib. bdg. 35.00 (ISBN 0-306-70183-9). Da Capo.

Bio-Energy - Bio-Energie. (Illus., Eng. & Ger.). 1978. pap. text ed. 12.00 o.p. (ISBN 0-89192-156-7, Pub. by Gottlieb Duttweiler Inst). Interbk Inc.

Bioactive Peptides Produced by Microorganisms. Ed. by Hamad Umezawa et al. LC 78-11402. 1979. 49.95x (ISBN 0-470-26562-0). Halsted Pr.

Bioavailability of Drug Products. Bioavailability of Drug Products Project. LC 77-94131. 1978. 18.00 (ISBN 0-917330-18-8). Am Pharm Assn.

Biochemical Actions of Hormones, 7 vols. Ed. by Gerald Litwack. Incl. Vol. 1. 1970. 52.75 (ISBN 0-12-452801-5); Vol. 2. 1972. 52.75 (ISBN 0-12-452802-3); Vol. 3. 1975. 51.50 (ISBN 0-12-452803-1); Vol. 4. 1977. 47.00 (ISBN 0-12-452804-X); Vol. 5. 1978. 42.50 (ISBN 0-12-452805-8); Vol. 6. 1979. 42.50 (ISBN 0-12-452806-6); Vol. 7. 1980. 45.00 (ISBN 0-12-452807-4). LC 70-107567. Acad Pr.

Biochemical Actions of Hormones, Vol. 8. Ed. by G. Litwack. 1981. write for info. (ISBN 0-12-452808-2). Acad Pr.

Biochemical Analysis in Crop Service. Simon R. Draper. (Illus.). 1976. 22.50x (ISBN 0-19-854128-7). Oxford U Pr.

Biochemical & Biophysical Perspectives in Marine Biology. D. C. Malins & J. R. Sargent. Vol. 1 1975. 47.00 (ISBN 0-12-466601-9); Vol. 2 1975. 49.50 (ISBN 0-12-466602-7); Vol. 3 1976. 63.50 (ISBN 0-12-466603-5). Acad Pr.

Biochemical & Pharmacological Roles of Adenosylmethionine & the Central Nervous System: Proceedings of an International Round Table on Adenosylmethionine & the Central Nervous System, Naples, Italy, May 1978. Ed. by V Zappia et al. (Illus.). 1979. 35.00 (ISBN 0-08-024929-9). Pergamon.

Biochemical Aspects of Renal Function: Proceedings of a Symposium Held in Honour of Professor Sir Hans Krebs FRS, at Merton College, Oxford, 16-19 September 1979. Ed. by D. B. Ross & W. G. Guder. (Illus.). 340p. pap. 55.00 (ISBN 0-08-025517-5). Pergamon.

Biochemical Characterization of Lymphokines: Proceedings of the Second International Lymphokine Workshop. Ed. by Alain L. De Weck et al. LC 80-289. 1980. 39.50 (ISBN 0-12-213950-X). Acad Pr.

Biochemical Coevolution: Proceedings. Biology Coloquium, 29th, Oregon State Univ. Ed. by Kenton L. Chambers. LC 52-19235. 128p. 1970. text ed. 6.00 (ISBN 0-87071-168-7). Oreg St U Pr.

Biochemical Differentiation in Insect Glands. Ed. by W. Beermann. LC 77-23423. (Results & Problems in Cell Differentiation: Vol. 8). (Illus.). 1977. 41.50 (ISBN 0-387-08286-7). Springer-Verlag.

Biochemical Disorders of the Skeleton. Roger Smith & Alan Apley. (Postgraduate Orthopedic Ser.). (Illus.). 1979. text ed. 59.95 (ISBN 0-407-00122-0). Butterworths.

Biochemical Education. Ed. by Charles Bryce. 208p. 1981. 33.00x (ISBN 0-7099-0600-5, Pub. by Croom Helm LTD England). Biblio Dist.

Biochemical Evolution. H. Gutfreund. 320p. Date not set. text ed. price not set (ISBN 0-521-23549-9); pap. text ed. price not set (ISBN 0-521-28025-7). Cambridge U Pr.

Biochemical Factors Concerned in the Functional Activity of the Nervous System. Ed. by D. Richter. 1969. pap. 27.00 (ISBN 0-08-013311-8). Pergamon.

Biochemical Genetics. 2nd ed. R. A. Woods. LC 79-41695. 80p. 1980. pap. 5.95 (ISBN 0-412-13160-9, 6340). Methuen Inc.

Biochemical Indicators of Radiation Injury in Man. (Orig.). 1971. pap. 24.25 (ISBN 92-0-021071-6, ISP280, IAEA). Unipub.

Biochemical Mechanisms in Hearing & Deafness. Ed. by Paparella. (Illus.). 416p. 1970. 27.50 (ISBN 0-398-01445-0). C C Thomas.

Biochemical Preparations, Vols. 3-12. Incl. Vol. 3. Ed. by E. E. Snell. 128p. 1953. o.p. (ISBN 0-471-80949-7); Vol. 5. Ed. by D. Shemin. 115p. 1957. o.p. (ISBN 0-471-78309-9); Vol. 6. Ed. by C. S. Vestling. 105p. 1960. 11.50 o.p. (ISBN 0-471-90684-0); Vol. 7. Ed. by H. A. Lardy. 102p. 1960. o.p. (ISBN 0-471-51744-5); Vol. 8. Ed. by A. Meister. 146p. 1961. o.p. (ISBN 0-471-59169-6); Vol. 9. Ed. by M. Coon. 149p. 1962. o.p. (ISBN 0-471-17109-3); Vol. 10. Ed. by G. B. Brown. 197p. 1963. o.p. (ISBN 0-471-10650-X); Vol. 11. Ed. by A. C. Maehly. 147p. 1966. o.p. (ISBN 0-471-56332-3); Vol. 12. Ed. by W. E. Lands. 152p. 1968. o.p. (ISBN 0-471-51378-4). LC 49-8306 (Pub by Wiley-Interscience). Wiley.

Biochemical Regulation of Blood Pressure. Richard L. Soffer. 425p. 1981. 35.00 (ISBN 0-471-05600-6, Pub. by Wiley-Interscience). Wiley.

Biochemical Screening in Relation to Mental Retardation. D. C. Cusworth. LC 73-129632. 1971. pap. 7.00 (ISBN 0-08-016416-1). Pergamon.

Biochemical Systematics & Evolution. Andrew Ferguson. LC 79-20298. 1980. 44.95x (ISBN 0-470-26856-5). Halsted Pr.

Biochemical Tests for Identification of Medical Bacteria. 2nd ed. Jean F. MacFaddin. (Illus.). 416p. 1980. softcover 26.50 (ISBN 0-683-05315-9). Williams & Wilkins.

Biochemistry. 2nd ed. Ed. by Ian Halkerston. LC 79-83718. (Basic Sciences PreTest Self-Assessment & Review Ser.). (Illus.). 1979. 9.95 (ISBN 0-07-050963-8). McGraw-Pretest.

Biochemistry. P. H. Jellinck. (Teach Yourself Ser.). 1973. pap. 2.95 o.p. (ISBN 0-679-10387-2). McKay.

Biochemistry. 2nd ed. Lubert Stryer. LC 80-24699. (Illus.). 1981. text ed. 29.95 (ISBN 0-7167-1226-1). W H Freeman.

Biochemistry. Michael Yudkin & Robin Offord. 1975. text ed. 22.95 (ISBN 0-395-17199-7); instructors manual 1.00 (ISBN 0-395-18266-2); slides (set of 20 35-mm) 11.25 (ISBN 0-395-18189-5). HM.

Biochemistry: A Case Oriented Approach. 3rd ed. Rex Montgomery et al. (Illus.). 1980. pap. text ed. 19.95 (ISBN 0-8016-3470-9). Mosby.

Biochemistry: A Problems Approach. 2nd ed. W. B. Wood. 1981. 12.95; solutions manual 3.95. Benjamin-Cummings.

Biochemistry: A Problems Approach. W. B. Wood et al. 1974. 12.95 o.p. (ISBN 0-8053-9850-3); tchr's suppl. 2.50 o.p. (ISBN 0-8053-9853-8); research games suppl. 1.75 o.p. (ISBN 0-8053-9854-6). Benjamin-Cummings.

Biochemistry & Morphogenesis. Joseph Needham. 1942. 99.50 (ISBN 0-521-05797-3). Cambridge U Pr.

Biochemistry & Pharmacology of the Basal Ganglia: Proceedings. Symposium of the Parkinson's Disease Information & Research Center, 2nd, Columbia University, 1965. Ed. by E. Costa et al. LC 66-21554. 1966. 13.50 o.p. (ISBN 0-911216-03-0). Raven.

Biochemistry & Physiology of Nitrogen & Sulfur Metabolism. Ed. by H. Bothe & A. Trebst. (Proceedings in Life Sciences Ser.). (Illus.). 370p. 1981. 49.80 (ISBN 0-387-10486-0). Springer-Verlag.

Biochemistry & Physiology of Protozoa, 3 vols. Ed. by S. H. Hutner & Andre Lwoff. Incl. Vol. 1. 1951. 36.00 o.p. (ISBN 0-12-363001-0); Vol. 2. 1955. 36.00 o.p. (ISBN 0-12-363002-9); Vol. 3. 1964. 48.00 o.p. (ISBN 0-12-363003-7). Acad Pr.

Biochemistry & Physiology of Protozoa, Vol. 1. 2nd ed. Ed. by Michael Levandowsky. LC 78-20045. 1979. 48.00, by subscription 41.50 (ISBN 0-12-444601-9). Acad Pr.

Biochemistry & Physiology of Protozoa, Vol. 2. 2nd ed. Ed. by Michael Levandowsky & S. H. Hutner. 1979. 51.00 (ISBN 0-12-444602-7); subscription 44.00 (ISBN 0-12-444602-7). Acad Pr.

Biochemistry & Physiology of Protozoa, Vol. 3. 2nd ed. Ed. by Michael Levandowsky & S. H. Hutner. LC 79-2045. 1980. 42.00 (ISBN 0-12-444603-5); subscription 35.50 (ISBN 0-12-444603-5). Acad Pr.

Biochemistry & Physiology of Protozoa, Vol. 4. 2nd ed. Ed. by M. Levandowsky & S. H. Hunter. 1980. write for info. (ISBN 0-12-444604-3). Acad Pr.

Biochemistry & Structure of Cell Organelles. Robert A. Reid & Rachel M. Leech. (Tertiary Level Biology Series). 176p. 1980. 34.95x (ISBN 0-470-26980-4); pap. text ed. 18.95x (ISBN 0-470-26981-2). Halsted Pr.

Biochemistry at Depth. Ed. by P. W. Hochachka. 203p. 1976. text ed. 37.00 (ISBN 0-08-019960-7). Pergamon.

Biochemistry Laboratory Manual. 3rd ed. F. M. Strong & H. Gilbert Koch. 260p. 1981. write for info. wire coil (ISBN 0-697-04705-9). Wm C Brown.

Biochemistry: Level Three. P. L. Davies. (Illus.). 224p. (Orig.). 1980. pap. text ed. 19.95x (ISBN 0-7121-0276-0). Intl Ideas.

Biochemistry of Adenosylmethionine. Ed. by Francesco Salvatore et al. LC 76-25565. 1977. 38.50x (ISBN 0-231-03895-X). Columbia U Pr.

Biochemistry of Alcohol & Alcoholism. L. J. Kricka & P. M. Clark. LC 79-40252. 1979. 59.95 (ISBN 0-470-26712-7). Halsted Pr.

Biochemistry of Animal Development, 3 vols. Ed. by Rudolf Weber. Incl. Vol. 1. Descriptive Biochemistry of Early Development. 1965. 52.50 (ISBN 0-12-740601-8); Vol. 2. Biochemical Control Mechanisms & Adaptations in Development. 1967. 48.75 (ISBN 0-12-740602-6); Vol. 3. 1975. 39.50 (ISBN 0-12-740603-4). Set. 118.75 (ISBN 0-685-23207-7). Acad Pr.

Biochemistry of Bacterial Growth. 2nd ed. Ed. by J. Mandelstam & K. McQuillen. LC 72-12036. 1973. pap. text ed. 24.95 (ISBN 0-470-56655-8). Halsted Pr.

Biochemistry of Characterized Neurons. Ed. by Neville N. Osborne. LC 76-55379. 1978. text ed. 50.00 (ISBN 0-08-021503-3). Pergamon.

Biochemistry of Cytodifferentiation. D. E. Truman. LC 73-21785. 122p. 1974. text ed. 13.95 (ISBN 0-470-89190-4). Halsted Pr.

Biochemistry of Development. Philip F. Benson. (Clinics in Developmental Medicine Ser. No. 37). 273p. 1971. 19.50 (ISBN 0-685-24729-5). Lippincott.

Biochemistry of Foreign Compounds. D. V. Parke. 1968. 27.00 (ISBN 0-08-012202-7). Pergamon.

Biochemistry of Functional & Experimental Psychoses. Hans Weil-Malherbe & Stephen I. Szara. (Amer. Lec. in Living Chemistry Ser.). (Illus.). 424p. 1971. 26.75 (ISBN 0-398-02435-9). C C Thomas.

Biochemistry of Glycoproteins & Proteoglycans. Ed. by William J. Lennarz. (Illus.). 395p. 1980. 35.00 (ISBN 0-306-40243-2, Plenum Pr). Plenum Pub.

Biochemistry of Green Plants. David W. Krogman. LC 73-7637. (Foundatons of Modern Biochemistry Ser). (Illus.). 224p. 1973. pap. 12.95 ref. ed. (ISBN 0-13-076455-8). P-H.

Biochemistry of Inorganic Compounds of Sulphur. A. B. Roy & P. Trudinger. LC 78-79056. (Illus.). 1970. 57.50 (ISBN 0-521-07581-5). Cambridge U Pr.

Biochemistry of Inorganic Polyphosphates. I. S. Kulaev. LC 78-31627. 1980. 61.50 (ISBN 0-471-27574-3, Pub. by Wiley-Interscience). Wiley.

Biochemistry of Insects. D. Gilmour. 1961. 36.50 (ISBN 0-12-284050-X). Acad Pr.

Biochemistry of Neural Disease. Ed. by Maynard M. Cohen. (Illus.). 1975. text ed. 27.50x (ISBN 0-06-140646-5, Harper Medical). Harper Row.

Biochemistry of Nonheme Iron. Anatoly Bezkorovainy. (Biochemistry of the Elments Ser.: Vol. 1). 430p. 1981. 45.00 (ISBN 0-306-40501-6, Plenum Pr). Plenum Pub.

Biochemistry of Normal & Pathological Connective Tissues. 412p. 1979. 41.50 (ISBN 2-222-02337-8). Masson Pub.

Biochemistry of Photosynthesis. 2nd ed. R. P. Gregory. 1977. 29.75 (ISBN 0-471-32676-3). Wiley.

Biochemistry of Plants: A Comprehensive Treatise, Photosynthesis, Vol. 8. Ed. by P. K. Stumpf & M. D. Hatch. 1981. write for info. Acad Pr.

Biochemistry of Psychiatric Disturbances. Ed. by G. Curzon. LC 80-40498. 1981. write for info. (ISBN 0-471-27814-9, Pub. by Wiley-Interscience). Wiley.

Biochemistry of Taste & Olfaction. Ed. by Robert H. Cagan & Morley R. Kare. (Nutrition Foundation Ser.). 1981. write for info. (ISBN 0-12-154450-8). Acad Pr.

Biochemistry of the Poliomyelitis Viruses. E. Kovacs. 1964. 18.75 (ISBN 0-08-010111-9). Pergamon.

Biochemistry of the Retina. Ed. by Clive N. Graymore. (Illus.). 1966. 23.50 (ISBN 0-12-297150-7). Acad Pr.

Biochemistry of Viruses. S. J. Martin. LC 77-8231. (Texts in Chemistry & Biochemistry Ser.). (Illus.). 1978. 38.50 (ISBN 0-521-21678-8); pap. 11.50x (ISBN 0-521-29229-8). Cambridge U Pr.

Biochemistry Review. David M. Glick. LC 80-19927. (Basic Science Review Bks.). 1980. pap. 8.50. Med Exam.

Biochemistry Review. 6th ed. Ed. by David M. Glick. (Basic Science Review Bks.). 1975. spiral bdg. 8.00 o.p. (ISBN 0-87488-202-8). Med Exam.

Biochemistry: The Chemical Reactions of Living Cells. David Metzler. 1129p. 1977. 29.50 (ISBN 0-12-492550-2); instr's manual 3.00 (ISBN 0-12-492552-9). Acad Pr.

Biochemistry: The Molecular Bases of All Structure & Function. 2nd ed. Albert L. Lehninger. LC 75-11082. 1975. text ed. 33.95x (ISBN 0-87901-047-9). Worth.

Biochemistry up to Date. Eric F. Powell. 1980. 25.00 (ISBN 0-85032-175-1, Pub. by Daniel Co England). State Mutual Bk.

Biochemistry Up to Date. Eric F. Powell. 66p. 1963. pap. 5.00x (ISBN 0-8464-0995-X). Beekman Pubs.

Biochromy: Natural Coloration of Living Things. Denis L. Fox. (Illus.). 1979. 26.75x (ISBN 0-520-03699-9). U of Cal Pr.

Biochronometry. Biology & Agriculture Division. LC 79-610527. (Illus.). 1971. text ed. 16.75 (ISBN 0-309-01866-8). Natl Acad Pr.

Biocolloids & Their Interactions with Special Reference to Coacervates & Related Systems. H. L. Booij & H. G. Bungenberg De Jong. (Protoplasmatologia: Vol. 1, Pt. 2). (Illus.). 1956. 46.70 o.p. (ISBN 0-387-80421-8). Springer-Verlag.

Bioconversion Sourcebook: (Abstracts) Paul N. Cheremisinoff. 1981. text ed. 29.95 (ISBN 0-250-40424-9). Ann Arbor Science.

Biocultural Adaptation in Prehistoric America. Ed. by Robert L. Blakely. LC 76-49155. (Southern Anthropological Society Ser: No. 11). 144p. 1977. pap. 6.50x (ISBN 0-8203-0417-4). U of Ga Pr.

Biocultural Basis of Health: Expanding Views of Medical Anthropology. Lorna G. Moore et al. LC 80-11554. (Illus.). 1980. pap. text ed. 11.95 (ISBN 0-8016-3481-4). Mosby.

Biodegradation of Polymers & Synthetic Polymers: Sessions of the 3rd International Biodegradation Symposium. Ed. by Applied Science Publishers Ltd. London. (Illus.). 1976. 26.00x (ISBN 0-85334-708-5, Pub. by Applied Science). Burgess-Intl Ideas.

Biodegradation Techniques for Industrial Organic Wastes. Ed. by D. J. De Renzo. LC 80-12834. (Pollution Technology Review Ser. 65; Chemical Technology Review Ser. 158). (Illus.). 358p. 1980. 28.00 (ISBN 0-8155-0800-X). Noyes.

Biodevelopmental Approach to Clinical Child Psychology: Cognitive Controls & Cognitive Control Therapy. Sebastiano Santostefano. LC 78-18485. (Wiley Ser. on Personality Processes). 1978. 45.00 (ISBN 0-471-75380-7, Pub. by Wiley-Interscience). Wiley.

Biodynamics of Hair Growth. John Savage. 1980. 17.50x (ISBN 0-686-64691-6, Pub. by Daniel Co England). State Mutual Bk.

Biodynamics of Hair Growth. John Savage. 88p. 1977. pap. 6.50x (ISBN 0-8464-0996-8). Beekman Pubs.

Bioelectric Recording Techniques, 3 pts. Ed. by Richard F. Thompson & Michael Patterson. Incl. Pt. A. Cellular Processes & Brain Potentials. 1973. 46.00 (ISBN 0-12-689401-9); Pt. B. 1974. 32.50 (ISBN 0-12-689402-7); Pt. C. Receptor & Effector Processes. 1974. 32.50 (ISBN 0-12-689403-5). 89.00 set (ISBN 0-686-66929-0). Acad Pr.

Bioelectrochemistry: Ions, Surfaces, Membranes. Ed. by Martin Blank. LC 80-18001. (Advances in Chemistry Ser.: No. 188). 1980. 58.00 (ISBN 0-8412-0473-X). Am Chemical.

Bioengineering: Proceedings of the Ninth Northeast Conference, March, 1981, Rutgers University, Piscataway, New Jersey. Ed. by Walter Welkowitz. (Illus.). 432p. 1981. pap. 60.00 (ISBN 0-08-027207-X). Pergamon.

Bioethics. rev. ed. Thomas Shannon. LC 76-18054. 640p. 1980. pap. 11.95 (ISBN 0-8091-2326-6). Paulist Pr.

Bioethics & the Limits of Science. Sean O'Reilly. 176p. (Orig.). 1980. pap. 5.95 (ISBN 0-931888-02-6, Chris. Coll. Pr.). Christendom Pubns.

Bioethics: Bridge to the Future. Van R. Potter. (Illus.). 1971. pap. 10.95 ref. ed. (ISBN 0-13-076505-8). P-H.

Biofeedback, Vol. II. Wilfred I. Hume. Ed. by D. F. Horrobin. (Biofeedback Research Review Ser.). 75p. 1980. Repr. of 1977 ed. 9.95x (ISBN 0-87705-966-7). Human Sci Pr.

Biofeedback, Vol. 1. Wilfrid I. Hume. Ed. by D. F. Horrobin. (Biofeedback Research Review Ser.). 126p. 1980. Repr. of 1977 ed. 9.95 (ISBN 0-87705-965-9). Human Sci Pr.

Biofeedback: A Survey of the Literature. Francine Butler. LC 78-6159. 352p. 1978. 45.50 (ISBN 0-306-65173-4). IFI Plenum.

Biofeedback: An Introduction & Guide. David G. Danskin & Mark A. Crow. 150p. (Orig.). 1981. pap. text ed. price not set (ISBN 0-87484-530-0). Mayfield Pub.

Biofeedback & Behavioral Medicine: Therapeutic Applications & Experimental Foundations, 1979 to 1980. Ed. by David Shapiro et al. 1981. text ed. 39.95 (ISBN 0-202-25129-2). Aldine Pub.

Biofeedback & Self-Control: An Aldine Reader on the Regulation of Bodily Processes & Consciousness. Ed. by Theodore X. Barber et al. LC 71-167858. 1971. 34.95x (ISBN 0-202-25048-2). Aldine Pub.

Biofeedback & Self-Control: Nineteen Seventy-Seven to Nineteen Seventy-Eight. Ed. by Johann Stoyva et al. 1979. text ed. 34.95 (ISBN 0-202-25128-4). Aldine Pub.

Biofeedback & Self-Control, 1971: An Aldine Annual on the Regulation of Bodily Processes & Consciousness. Ed. by Johann Stoyva et al. LC 74-151109. 350p. 1972. 34.95x (ISBN 0-202-25085-7). Aldine Pub.

Biofeedback & Self-Control, 1972: An Aldine Annual on the Regulation of Bodily Processes & Consciousness. Ed. by David Shapiro et al. LC 73-75702. 513p. 1973. 34.95x (ISBN 0-202-25107-1). Aldine Pub.

Biofeedback & Self Control, 1973: An Aldine Annual on the Regulation of Bodily Processes & Consciousness. Ed. by Neal E. Miller et al. LC 74-151109. 512p. 1974. text ed. 34.95 (ISBN 0-202-25108-X). Aldine Pub.

Biofeedback & Self-Control, 1974: An Aldine Annual on the Regulation of Bodily Processes & Consciousness. Ed. by L. V. DiCara et al. LC 74-151109. 530p. 1975. 34.95x (ISBN 0-202-25109-8). Aldine Pub.

Biofeedback & Self-Control 1975-76: An Aldine Annual on the Regulation of Bodily Processes & Consciousness. Ed. by Theodore X. Barber et al. LC 74-151109. 225p. 1976. 34.95x (ISBN 0-202-25110-1). Aldine Pub.

Biofeedback & Self-Control 1976-1977: An Aldine Annual on the Regulation of Bodily Processes & Consciousness. new ed. Ed. by Joe Kamiya et al. LC 77-81650. 1977. 34.95x (ISBN 0-202-25127-6). Aldine Pub.

Biofeedback & the Modification of Behavior. Aubrey J. Yates. LC 79-400. (Illus.). 524p. 1980. 24.50 (ISBN 0-306-40226-2, Plenum Pr). Plenum Pub.

Biofeedback, Behavior Therapy, & Hypnosis: Potentiating the Verbal Control of Behavior for Clinicians. Ed. by Ian Wickramasekera. LC 76-18294. 384p. 1976. 24.95x (ISBN 0-88229-193-9); pap. 13.95x (ISBN 0-88229-579-9). Nelson-Hall.

Biofeedback: Clinical Applications in Behavioral Medicine. D. Olton & A. Noonberg. 1980. 21.00 (ISBN 0-13-076315-2). P-H.

Biofeedback, Fasting & Meditation. Gary Null. (Orig.). 1974. pap. 1.50 o.s.i. (ISBN 0-515-03400-2, A3400). Jove Pubns.

Biofeedback Primer. Edward B. Blanchard & Leonard H. Epstein. LC 76-74321. (Clinical & Professional Psychology Ser.). 1978. pap. text ed. 7.50 (ISBN 0-201-00338-4). A-W.

Biofeedback Strategies for Interpersonal Relationships. Dorelle Heisel. 1981. write for info. Gordon.

Biofeedback Syllabus: A Handbook for the Psychophysiologic Study of Biofeedback. Barbara B. Brown. 516p. 1975. 45.50 (ISBN 0-398-03268-8); pap. 31.75 (ISBN 0-685-57029-0). C C Thomas.

Biofeedback Therapy, Vol. 1. Wilfrid I. Hume. 1976. 10.00 o.p. (ISBN 0-904406-46-6). Human Sci Pr.

Biofeedback: Turning on the Power of Your Mind. Marvin Karlins & Lewis M. Andrews. LC 79-39759. (YA) 1972. 8.95 (ISBN 0-397-00855-4). Lippincott.

Biofeedfack: Potential & Limits. Robert M. Stern & William J. Ray. LC 79-18700. (Illus.). viii, 197p. 1980. pap. 3.95 (ISBN 0-8032-9114-0, BB721, Bison). U of Nebr Pr.

Biofluid Mechanics, Vol. 2. Ed. by D. J. Schneck. 530p. 1980. 59.50 (ISBN 0-306-40426-5, Plenum Pr). Plenum Pub.

Biogas Handbook. David House. LC 80-8998. Orig. Title: Compleat Biogas Handbook. (Illus.). 224p. 1981. pap. 10.95 (ISBN 0-915238-47-0). Peace Pr.

Biogas Production & Utilization. Elizabeth C. Price & Paul N. Cheremisinoff. LC 79-56113. (Illus.). 1981. 29.95 (ISBN 0-250-40334-X). Ann Arbor Science.

Biogenesis & Turnover of Membrane Macromolecules. Ed. by John S. Cook. LC 75-25111. (Society of General Physiologists Ser: Vol. 31). 1976. 27.00 (ISBN 0-89004-092-3). Raven.

Biogenetic Stucturalism. Charles D. Laughlin & Eugene G. D'Aquili. (Illus.). 1974. text ed. 12.00x (ISBN 0-231-03817-8). Columbia U Pr.

Biogeochemistry of Ancient & Modern Environments. P. A. Trudinger. 723p. 1981. 52.00 (ISBN 0-387-10303-1). Springer-Verlag.

Biogeography. E. C. Pielou. LC 79-13306. 1979. 23.50 (ISBN 0-471-05845-9, Pub. by Wiley-Interscience). Wiley.

Biogeography: A Study of Plants in the Ecosphere. Joy Tivy. (Illus.). 1977. pap. text ed. 8.00x (ISBN 0-05-003122-8). Longman.

Biogeography: An Ecological & Evolutionary Approach. 3rd ed. Barry C. Cox et al. LC 79-22636. 1980. pap. text ed. 19.95x (ISBN 0-470-26893-X). Halsted Pr.

Biogeography: An Ecological & Evolutionary Approach. 2nd ed. C. B. Cox et al. LC 75-33270. 1976. text ed. 12.95 o.p. (ISBN 0-470-18131-1). Halsted Pr.

Biogeography: An Ecological Perspective. P. Dansereau. (Illus.). 1957. 22.50 (ISBN 0-8260-2330-4, Pub. by Wiley-Interscience). Wiley.

Biogeography, & Numerical Taxonomy of the Oegopsid Squid Family: Ommastrephidae in the Pacific Ocean. John H. Wormuth. (Bulletin of the Scipps Institution of Oceanography Ser.: Vol. 23). 1977. pap. 9.00x (ISBN 0-520-09540-5). U of Cal Pr.

Biograffiti: A Natural Selection. John M. Burns. 1980. pap. 3.95 (ISBN 0-393-00031-1). Norton.

Biografia De Goya. (Span.). 7.95 (ISBN 84-241-5416-9). E Torres & Sons.

Biografias Puertorriquenas. Rosa-Nieves & Melon. 1970. 18.95 (ISBN 0-685-73206-1, Pub by Troutman Press). E Torres & Sons.

Biograph Bulletins, 1896-1908. LC 76-148466. 1971. 25.00 (ISBN 0-913986-03-8). Locare.

Biographia Britannica Literaria, 2 vols. Thomas Wright. LC 68-22061. 1968. Repr. of 1842 ed. Set. 40.00 (ISBN 0-8103-3154-3). Gale.

Biographia Literaria. Samuel T. Coleridge. Ed. by George Watson. 1978. 6.50x (ISBN 0-460-10011-4, Evman); pap. 3.95 o.p. (ISBN 0-460-11011-X). Dutton.

Biographical Annals of the Civil Government of the United States. Charles Lanman. LC 68-30626. 1976. Repr. of 1876 ed. 42.00 (ISBN 0-8103-4300-2). Gale.

Biographical Books 1950-1980. 1557p. 1980. 75.00 (ISBN 0-8352-1315-3). Bowker.

Biographical Cyclopaedia of American Women, 2 vols. Ed. by Mabel W. Cameron. LC 24-7615. 408p. 1975. Repr. of 1924 ed. 64.00 (ISBN 0-8103-3990-0). Gale.

Biographical Dictionaries & Related Works: An International Bibliography. Ed. by Robert B. Slocum. LC 67-27789. 1967. 52.00 (ISBN 0-8103-0972-6); supplement no. 1 52.00 (ISBN 0-8103-0973-4); supplement no. 2 52.00 (ISBN 0-8103-0974-2). Gale.

Biographical Dictionaries Master Index - 1975-76: A Guide to More Than 800,000 Listings in Over 50 Current Who's Whos & Other Works of Collective Biography, 3 vols. Ed. by Dennis LaBeau & Gary Tarbert. LC 75-19059. (Gale Biographical Index: No. 1). 1975. 140.00 (ISBN 0-8103-1077-5). Gale.

Biographical Dictionaries Master Index: First & Second Supplements 1979-80. Ed. by Miranda C. Herbert & Barbara McNeil. LC 79-22270. 1979. Set. pap. 90.00 (ISBN 0-8103-1082-1). Gale.

Biographical Dictionary & Synopsis of Books, Ancient & Modern. Ed. by Charles D. Warner et al. LC 66-4326. Repr. of 1902 ed. 26.00 (ISBN 0-8103-3023-7). Gale.

Biographical Dictionary of Actors, Actresses, Musicians, Dancers, Managers, & Other Stage Personnel in London, 1660-1800, 6 vols. Philip H. Highfill, Jr. et al. Incl. Vol. 1. Abago to Belfille. 462p. 1973 (ISBN 0-8093-0517-8); Vol. 2. Belfort to Byzand. 494p. 1973 (ISBN 0-8093-0518-6); Vol. 3. Cabanel to Cory. 544p. 1975 (ISBN 0-8093-0692-1); Vol. 4. Coryne to Dvnion. 576p. 1975 (ISBN 0-8093-0693-X); Vol. 5. Eagan to Garrett. 504p. 1978 (ISBN 0-8093-0832-0); Vol. 6. Garrick to Gyngell. 512p. 1978 (ISBN 0-8093-0833-9). LC 71-157068. (Biographical Dictionary of Actors Ser.). (Illus.). 40.00x ea. S Ill U Pr.

Biographical Dictionary of American Civil Engineers. Compiled By American Society of Civil Engineers. 176p. 1972. pap. text ed. 13.75 (ISBN 0-87262-034-4). Am Soc Civil Eng.

Biographical Dictionary of American Educators, 3 vols. Ed. by John F. Ohles. LC 77-84750. 1978. lib. bdg. 115.00 (ISBN 0-8371-9893-3, OHB/). Greenwood.

Biographical Dictionary of Black Musicians & Music Educators, Vol. II. Lemuel Berry, Jr. (Illus.). 389p. (gr. 5-12). 1981. 20.00 (ISBN 0-932188-02-8). Ed Bk Pubs OK.

Biographical Dictionary of Black Musicians & Music Educators, Vol. I. Lemuel Berry, Jr. LC 78-62404. (gr. 5-12). 1978. 16.95 (ISBN 0-932188-00-1); pap. 12.95 (ISBN 0-932188-01-X). Ed Bk Pubs OK.

Biographical Dictionary of British Architects, 1600-1840. Howard Colvin. 1978. write for info. (ISBN 0-7195-3328-7). Intl Pubns Serv.

Biographical Dictionary of English Music. Jeffery Pulver. LC 69-16666. (Music Ser). 538p. 1972. Repr. of 1927 ed. lib. bdg. 42.50 (ISBN 0-306-71103-6). Da Capo.

Biographical Dictionary of Film. David Thomson. LC 75-20044. 1976. pap. 10.95 (ISBN 0-688-07974-1). Morrow.

Biographical Dictionary of Film. 2nd, rev. ed. David Thomson. LC 80-20500. 700p. 1981. 15.95 (ISBN 0-688-00132-7); pap. 10.95 (ISBN 0-688-00131-9). Morrow.

Biographical Dictionary of Japanese Literature. Sen'Ichi Hisamatsu. LC 75-14730. (Illus.). 437p. 1976. 35.00x (ISBN 0-87011-253-8). Kodansha.

Biographical Dictionary of Modern British Radicals Since 1770: 1833-1914, Vol.2. J. O. Baylen & N. J. Grossman. 1980. text ed. write for info. (ISBN 0-391-01058-1). Humanities.

Biographical Dictionary of Modern British Radicals Since 1770: 1915-1970, Vol. 3. Ed. by J. O. Baylen & N. J. Gossman. 1980. text ed. write for info. (ISBN 0-391-01059-X). Humanities.

Biographical Dictionary of Parapsychology. 1964. 9.00x o.p. (ISBN 0-912326-09-3). Garrett-Helix.

Biographical Dictionary of Railway Engineers. John Marshall. 1978. 15.95 (ISBN 0-7153-7489-3). David & Charles.

Biographical Dictionary of Republican China: A Personal Name Index, Vol. 5. Ed. by Janet Krompart. 1979. 27.50 (ISBN 0-231-04558-1). Columbia U Pr.

Biographical Dictionary of Republican China, 4 vols. Ed. by Howard L. Boorman & Richard C. Howard. Incl. Vol. 1. Ai-Ch'u. 1967. 35.00x (ISBN 0-231-08955-4); Vol. 2. Dalai-Ma. 1968. 35.00x (ISBN 0-231-08956-2); Vol. 3. Mao-Wu. 1970. 35.00x (ISBN 0-231-08957-0); Vol. 4. Yang-Bibliography. 1971. 40.00x (ISBN 0-231-08958-9). LC 67-12006. 1967. Columbia U Pr.

Biographical Dictionary of Scottish Graduates to A. D. 1410. D. E. Watt. 1977. 98.00x (ISBN 0-19-822447-8). Oxford U Pr.

Biographical Dictionary of Southern Authors. Ed. by Lucian L. Knight. LC 75-26631. (Library of Southern Literature). (Illus.). 1978. Repr. of 1929 ed. 38.00 (ISBN 0-8103-4269-3). Gale.

Biographical Dictionary of the British Colonial Governor: Volume I, Africa. Anthony Kirk-Greene. LC 80-81949. 256p. 1980. 31.95 (ISBN 0-8179-2611-9). Hoover Inst Pr.

Biographical Dictionary of the Confederacy. Jon L. Wakelyn. Ed. by Frank E. Vandiver. LC 72-13870. 1976. lib. bdg. 32.50x (ISBN 0-8371-6124-X, WCL). Greenwood.

Biographical Dictionary of the Left, 4 vols. Francis X. Gannon. Incl. Vol. 1. LC 78-113035. 624p. 1969. 8.00 (ISBN 0-88279-216-4); Vol. 2. 632p. 1971. 9.00 (ISBN 0-88279-223-7); Vol. 3. LC 76-12821. 1972. 9.00 (ISBN 0-88279-224-5); Vol. 4. LC 72-12821. 1973. 11.95 (ISBN 0-88279-226-1). Set. 32.95. Western Islands.

Biographical Dictionary of the Living Authors of Great Britain & Ireland. LC 66-16419. 1966. Repr. of 1816 ed. 28.00 (ISBN 0-8103-3019-9). Gale.

Biographical Dictionary of the Saints. Frederick G. Holweck. LC 68-30625. 1969. Repr. of 1924 ed. 40.00 (ISBN 0-8103-3158-6). Gale.

Biographical Dictionary of World War Two. Christopher Tunney. LC 72-90763. 216p. 1973. 8.95 o.p. (ISBN 0-685-31230-5). St Martin.

Biographical Directory of the American Academy of Pediatrics. Ed. by Jaques Cattell Press. 1604p. 1980. 95.00 (ISBN 0-8352-1282-3). Bowker.

Biographical Directory of the Fellows & Members of the APA As of October, 1977. 1977. 45.00 (ISBN 0-685-94001-2, 151-1). Bowker.

Biographical Directory of the South Carolina House of Representatives: Seventeen-Seventy-Five to Seventeen-Ninty, Vol. 3. Ed. by N. Louise Bailey & Elizabeth I. Cooper. 780p. 1981. text ed. 14.95 (ISBN 0-87249-406-3). U of SC Pr.

Biographical Encyclopedia of Scientists, 2 vols. Ed. by Urdang Assoc. 1981. lib. bdg. 80.00 (ISBN 0-87196-396-5). Vol. 1, 600p. Vol. 2, 600p. Facts on File.
Biographical Index of American Artists. Ralph C. Smith. LC 79-167186. 1976. Repr. of 1930 ed. 18.00 (ISBN 0-8103-4251-0). Gale.
Biographical Memoirs, Vol. 44. National Academy of Sciences. xii, 370p. 1974. 10.00 (ISBN 0-309-02238-X). Natl Acad Pr.
Biographical Memoirs, Vol. 45. National Academy of Sciences. vii, 465p. 1974. 10.00 (ISBN 0-309-02239-8). Natl Acad Pr.
Biographical Memoirs, Vol. 46, 47. National Academy of Sciences. 1975. Vol. 46. 10.00 (ISBN 0-309-02240-1); Vol. 47. 10.00 (ISBN 0-309-02245-2). Natl Acad Pr.
Biographical Memoirs, Vol. 48. (Biographical Memoirs Ser.). 1976. 10.00 (ISBN 0-309-02349-1). Natl Acad Pr.
Biographical Memoirs, Vol. 49. National Academy of Sciences. 1978. Vol. 49. 10.00 (ISBN 0-309-02449-8). Natl Acad Pr.
Biographical Register of the New South Wales Parliament 1901-70. Heather Radi et al. (Australian Parliaments, Biographical Notes: No. 6). 302p. 1979. text ed. 37.95 (ISBN 0-7081-1756-2, 0575, Pub. by ANUP Australia); pap. text ed. 18.95 (ISBN 0-7081-1757-0, 0574). Bks Australia.
Biographical Sketch: Writings of Benjamin Franklin. Rowe. 6.95 (ISBN 0-89315-003-7). Lambert Bk.
Biographical Sketches of the Graduates of Yale College, with Annals of the College History, Seventeen Hundred One to Eighteen Fifteen, 6 vols. Franklin B. Dexter. (Two vols. are unbound). 1912. Set. 350.00x (ISBN 0-686-51346-0). Elliots Bks.
Biography & Geneology Master Index, 8 vols. 2nd ed. Ed. by Miranda C. Herbert & Barbara McNeil. (Gale Biographical Index Ser.: No. 1). 1980. Set. 575.00 (ISBN 0-8103-1094-5). Gale.
Biography & Other Poems. Claire N. White. LC 80-2069. 96p. 1981. 9.95 (ISBN 0-385-15799-1). Doubleday.
Biography & Truth. Stanley Weintraub. LC 67-28300. (Composition & Rhetoric Ser.). 1967. pap. 2.50 (ISBN 0-672-60901-0, CR15). Bobbs.
Biography As Theology: How Life Stories Can Remake Today's Theology. James W. McClendon, Jr. LC 74-9715. 224p. 1974. 13.95 (ISBN 0-687-03540-6); pap. 6.50 (ISBN 0-687-03539-2). Abingdon.
Biography in the Eighteenth Century: Publications of the McMaster University Association for 18th Century Studies. J. D. Browning. LC 80-14652. (Vol. 8). 207p. 1980. 27.50 (ISBN 0-8240-4007-4). Garland Pub.
Biography of a Komodo Dragon. Alice L. Hopf. (Nature Biography Book). (Illus.). 64p. (gr. 7-11). 1981. PLB 6.99 (ISBN 0-399-61140-1). Putnam.
Biography of a Small Town. Elvin Hatch. LC 79-313. 1979. 22.50x (ISBN 0-231-04694-4). Columbia U Pr.
Biography of Alfonzo Love. Tresa Rivers. 1981. 6.95 (ISBN 0-533-03330-6). Vantage.
Biography of Archibald Rutledge. Idella F. Bodie. Ed. by Del Roberts. LC 80-50789. (gr. 5-12). 1981. 9.95 (ISBN 0-87844-046-1). Sandlapper Store.
Biography of Dorothy L. Sayers. James Brabazon. (Illus.). 320p. 1981. 15.95 (ISBN 0-684-16864-2, ScribT). Scribner.
Biography of Ezra Thompson Clark. Annie C. Tanner. (Utah, the Mormons, & the West: No. 5). 1975. 8.50 (ISBN 0-87480-156-7, Tanner). U of Utah Pr.
Biography of N. B. Hardeman. James M. Powell & Mary Nelle H. Powers. 9.00 o.p. (ISBN 0-89225-045-3). Gospel Advocate.
Biography of the Gods. A. Eustace Haydon. LC 67-13617. 1967. pap. 4.25 (ISBN 0-8044-6257-7). Ungar.
Biography of the Unborn. 2nd ed. M. S. Gilbert. 1963. 12.95 (ISBN 0-02-845260-7). Hafner.
Bioinorganic Chemistry: An Introduction. Ei-Ichiro Ochia. 1977. text ed. 25.95x o.p. (ISBN 0-205-05508-7). Allyn.
Biokinesiology: Vol II Neurovasculars. 3rd ed. John Barton & Margaret Barton. (Encyclopedia of Mind & Body). (Illus.). 110p. (Orig.). 1980. pap. 10.00 (ISBN 0-937216-05-4). J&M Barton.
Biologic & Clinical Basis of Infectious Diseases. 2nd ed. Guy P. Youmans et al. LC 78-65974. (Illus.). 849p. 1980. pap. text ed. 22.50 (ISBN 0-7216-9647-3). Saunders.
Biologic & Clinical Effects of Low-Frequency Magnetic & Electric Fields. Ed. by J. G. Llaurado et al. (Illus.). 384p. 1974. 44.75 (ISBN 0-398-03024-3). C C Thomas.
Biological Accumulators of Aluminum. G. Evelyn Hutchinson & Anne Wollack. 1943. pap. 24.50x (ISBN 0-686-50040-7). Elliots Bks.
Biological Activated Carbon for Drinking Water. Rip G. Rice. 1981. text ed. 69.90 2 vol. set (ISBN 0-250-40429-X); text ed. 39.95 vol. 1 (ISBN 0-250-40427-3); text ed. 39.95 vol. 2 (ISBN 0-250-40428-1). Ann Arbor Science.
Biological Activity of Thymic Hormones. Ed. by D. W. VanBekkum. LC 75-17617. 1975. 39.95 (ISBN 0-470-89835-6). Halsted Pr.
Biological & Agricultural Index, Vols. 19-24. 1964-70. Vols. 25-33 08/1970-07/1979. 75.00 ea. (ISBN 0-685-22239-X). Wilson.
Biological & Environmental Determinants of Early Development. Ed. by John I. Nurnberger. (ARNMD Research Publications Ser: Vol. 51). 1973. 34.50 (ISBN 0-683-00245-7). Raven.
Biological & Environmental Effects of Low-Level Radiation: Proceedings, Vol. 1. Symposium on Biological Effects of Low-Level Ionizing Radiation. (Illus.). 1976. pap. 36.50 (ISBN 92-0-010076-7, ISP409-1, IAEA). Unipub.
Biological & Environmental Effects of Low-Level Radiation: Proceedings, Vol. 2. Symposium on Biological Effects of Low-Level Ionizing Radiation. (Illus.). 1976. pap. 45.00 (ISBN 92-0-010176-3, ISP409-2, IAEA). Unipub.
Biological & Ethical Deviations in Human Beings. Ralph A. Carleton. (Illus.). 1980. 37.75 (ISBN 0-89920-007-9). Am Inst Psych.
Biological & Psychological Background to Education. C. G. Hussell & A. F. Laing. 1967. 14.50 (ISBN 0-08-012195-0); pap. 9.75 (ISBN 0-08-012194-2). Pergamon.
Biological & Social Meaning of Race. Ed. by Richard H. Osborne. LC 75-150652. (Psychology Ser). (Illus.). 1971. text ed. 16.95x (ISBN 0-7167-0935-X); pap. text ed. 8.95x (ISBN 0-7167-0934-1). W H Freeman.
Biological & Taxonomic Studies on Tortricine Moths, with Reference to the Species in California. J. A. Powell. (U. C. Publ. in Entomology: Vol. 32). 1964. pap. 10.00x (ISBN 0-520-09100-0). U of Cal Pr.
Biological Applications of Electron Spin Resonance. Ed. by Harold M. Swartz et al. LC 72-39768. 1972. 57.95 (ISBN 0-471-83870-5, Pub. by Wiley-Interscience). Wiley.
Biological Aspects of Freshwater Pollution: Proceedings of the Course Held at the Joint Research Centre, Ispra, Italy, 5-9 June 1978. Ed. by O. Ravera. (Illus.). 1979. 36.00 (ISBN 0-08-023442-9). Pergamon.
Biological Aspects of Mental Disorder. Solomon H. Snyder. (Illus.). 272p. 1981. pap. 8.95x (ISBN 0-19-502888-0). Oxford U Pr.
Biological Aspects of Water Pollution. Charles G. Wilber. (Illus.). 308p. 1971. text ed. 31.75 (ISBN 0-398-02062-0). C C Thomas.
Biological Awareness: Statements for Self-Discovery. Lee N. Cunningham & D. W. Edington. (Illus.). 224p. 1975. 14.95x (ISBN 0-13-077180-5). P-H.
Biological Balance & Thermal Modification. Ed. by Maurice Marois. (Towards a Plan of Actions for Mankind Ser: Vol. 3). 1977. text ed. 99.00 (ISBN 0-08-021447-9). Pergamon.
Biological Basis for Cancer Diagnosis, Vol. 4. Ed. by Margaret Fox. (Illus.). 1979. 68.00 (ISBN 0-08-024387-8). Pergamon.
Biological Basis of Dental Caries: An Oral Biology Textbook. Lewis Menaker. (Illus.). 532p. 1980. 45.00 (ISBN 0-06-141726-2, Harper Medical). Har-Row.
Biological Basis of Immunodeficiency. Ed. by Erwin W. Gelfand & Hans-Michael Dosch. 1979. text ed. 35.00 (ISBN 0-89004-361-2). Raven.
Biological Basis of Mental Activity. John I. Hubbard. 224p. 1975. text ed. 8.95 (ISBN 0-201-03086-1). A-W.
Biological Basis of Personality. H. J. Eysenck. (Amer. Lec. in Living Chemistry Ser). (Illus.). 420p. 1977. 27.75 (ISBN 0-398-00538-9). C C Thomas.
Biological Calcification: Cellular & Molecular Aspects. Ed. by Harald Schraer. LC 69-12161. 462p. 1970. 35.00 (ISBN 0-306-50073-6, Plenum Pr). Plenum Pub.
Biological Chemistry. Colin J. Suckling & Keith E. Suckling. LC 79-51830. (Cambridge Texts in Chemistry & Biochemistry Ser.). (Illus.). 350p. 1980. 59.50 (ISBN 0-521-22852-2); pap. 19.95 (ISBN 0-521-29678-1). Cambridge U Pr.
Biological Chemistry of Organelle Formation: Proceedings. Ed. by T. Buechel et al. (Colloquium Mosbach Ser.: Vol. 31). (Illus.). 290p. 1981. 44.00 (ISBN 0-387-10458-5). Springer-Verlag.
Biological Constraints to Farmers' Rice Yields in Three Philippine Provinces. (IRRI Research Paper Ser.: No. 30). 69p. 1979. pap. 5.00 (R070, IRRI). Unipub.
Biological Control by Natural Enemies. P. DeBach. LC 73-90812. (Illus.). 325p. 1974. 39.50 (ISBN 0-521-20380-5); pap. 11.95x (ISBN 0-521-09835-1). Cambridge U Pr.
Biological Control in Crop Production. Ed. by George C. Papavizas. (Beltsville Symposia in Agricultural Research Ser.: No. 5). 1981. text ed. 35.00 (ISBN 0-86598-037-3). Allanheld.
Biological Control of Plant Pests. 1.95 (ISBN 0-686-21131-6). Bklyn Botanic.
Biological Determinants of Sexual Behavior. Ed. by J. B. Hutchison. LC 76-57753. 1978. 88.95 (ISBN 0-471-99490-1, Pub by Wiley-Interscience). Wiley.
Biological Diversification in the Tropics. Ghillean T. Prance. 752p. 1981. 40.00x (ISBN 0-231-04876-9). Columbia U Pr.
Biological Effects of External Radiation. Ed. by H. A. Blair. (Illus.). 1967. Repr. of 1954 ed. 21.75 o.s.i. (ISBN 0-02-841430-6). Hafner.
Biological Effects of Neutron & Proton Irradiation, 2 vols. (Illus., Orig.). 1964. 17.75 ea. (IAEA). Vol. 1 (ISBN 92-0-010064-3). Vol. 2 (ISBN 92-0-010164-X). Unipub.
Biological Effects of Neutron Irradiation. (Illus.). 484p. (Orig.). 1974. pap. 37.00 (ISBN 92-0-010474-6, ISP52, IAEA). Unipub.
Biological Effects of Transmutation & Decay of Incorporated Radioisotopes. (Illus., Orig.). 1968. pap. 12.50 (ISBN 92-0-011268-4, IAEA). Unipub.
Biological Effects of Ultraviolet Radiation. Walter Harm. LC 77-88677. (IUPAB Biophysics Ser.: No. 1). (Illus.). 1980. 29.95 (ISBN 0-521-22121-8); pap. 9.95x (ISBN 0-521-29362-6). Cambridge U Pr.
Biological Efficiency of Protein Production. Ed. by J. G. Jones. LC 72-93672. (Illus.). 400p. 1973. 57.50 (ISBN 0-521-20179-9). Cambridge U Pr.
Biological Energy Interrelationships & Glossary of Energy Tables. National Research Council - Committee On Animal Nutrition. (Illus.). 1966. pap. 3.00 o.p. (ISBN 0-309-01411-5). Natl Acad Pr.
Biological Energy Resources. Malcolm Slesser & Chris Lewis. LC 79-10255. (Energy Ser.). 250p. 1979. text ed. 23.50x (ISBN 0-419-11340-1, Pub. by E & FN Spon). Methuen Inc.
Biological Factors in Temporal Lobe Epilepsy. C. Ounsted et al. (Clinics in Developmental Medicine Ser. No. 22). 135p. 1966. 9.00 (ISBN 0-685-24721-X). Lippincott.
Biological Foundations of Biomedical Engineering. Jacob Kline. LC 74-20221. 1976. text ed. 42.50 (ISBN 0-316-49857-2). Little.
Biological Foundations of Individuality & Culture. Eliot D. Chapple. LC 79-23284. 388p. (Orig.). 1980. lib. bdg. 17.50 (ISBN 0-89874-041-X). Krieger.
Biological Foundations of Language. Eric H. Lenneberg. LC 66-28746. 1967. 32.95 (ISBN 0-471-52626-6). Wiley.
Biological Foundations of Psychiatry, 2 vols. Ed. by Robert Grenell & Sabit Gabay. LC 74-15664. 690p. 1976. 43.50 ea.; Vol. 1. (ISBN 0-911216-96-0); Vol. 2. (ISBN 0-89004-126-1). Raven.
Biological Functions of Carbohydrates. David S. Candy. LC 80-18668. (Tertiary Level Biology Ser.). 197p. 1980. 34.95 (ISBN 0-470-27038-1). Halsted Pr.
Biological Functions of Proteinases. Ed. by H. Holzer & J. Tschesche. (Colloquium Mosbach: Vol. 30). (Illus.). 1980. 42.90 (ISBN 0-387-09683-3). Springer-Verlag.
Biological Growth & Spread: Proceedings. Ed. by W. Jaeger. (Lecture Notes in Biomathematics: Vol. 38). 511p. 1981. pap. 34.00 (ISBN 0-387-10257-4). Springer-Verlag.
Biological Ideas in Politics: An Essay in Political Adaptivity. W. J. Mackenzie. LC 78-20278. 1979. 10.95x (ISBN 0-312-07869-2). St Martin.
Biological Implications of Radionuclides Released from Nuclear Industries, Vols. 1 & 2. (Proceedings Ser.). 1980. Vol. I, 481 Pgs. 60.00 (ISBN 92-0-010479-7, ISP 522-1-2, IAEA); Vol. II, 442 Pgs. pap. 55.25 (ISBN 92-0-010579-3). Unipub.
Biological Macromolecules & Polyelectrolytes in Solution. Henryk Eisenberg. (Monographs on Physical Biochemistry). (Illus.). 1976. 39.95x (ISBN 0-19-854612-2). Oxford U Pr.
Biological Membranes: Their Structure & Function. R. Harrison & G. Lunt. LC 75-43543. (Tertiary Level Biology Ser). 264p. 1976. pap. text ed. 18.95 (ISBN 0-470-15220-6). Halsted Pr.
Biological Membranes: Thier Structure & Function. 2nd ed. Roger Harrison & George G. Lunt. LC 80-14062. (Tertiary Level Biology Ser). 288p. 1980. pap. text ed. 21.95x (ISBN 0-470-26971-5). Halsted Pr.
Biological Monitoring of Fish. Ed. by Charles H. Hocutt & Jay R. Stauffer, Jr. LC 79-3049. 432p. 1980. 31.95x (ISBN 0-669-03309-X). Lexington Bks.
Biological Nitrogen Fixation by Epiphytic Microoganisms in Rice Fields. (IRRI Research Paper Ser.: No. 47). 14p. 1981. pap. 5.00 (ISBN 0-686-69532-1, R 117, IRRI). Unipub.
Biological Nitrogen Fixation in Paddy Field Studies by SITU Acetylene-Reduction Assays: In Paddy Field Studies by SITU Acetylene-Reduction Assays. (IRRI Research Paper Ser.: No. 3). 16p. 1977. pap. 5.00 (R043, IRRI). Unipub.
Biological Oceanographic Processes. Timothy R. Parsons & M. Takahashi. LC 73-7758. 196p. 1974. text ed. 19.80 o.p. (ISBN 0-08-017603-8); pap. text ed. 12.10 o.p. (ISBN 0-08-017604-6). Pergamon.
Biological Oceanographic Processes. 2nd ed. Timothy R. Parsons et al. 1978. text ed. 38.00 (ISBN 0-08-021502-5); pap. text ed. 19.75 (ISBN 0-08-021501-7). Pergamon.
Biological Processes Design for Wastewater Treatment. Clifford W. Randall & Larry D. Benefield. (Environmental Sciences Ser.). (Illus.). 1980. text ed. 27.95 (ISBN 0-13-076406-X). P-H.
Biological Recognition & Assembly: Proceedings. ICN-UCLA Symposium, Keystone, Colo., February 1979. Ed. by J. Lake & C. Fred Fox. LC 80-7797. (Progress in Clinical & Biological Research Ser.: Vol. 40). 362p. 1980. 52.00x (ISBN 0-8451-0040-8). A R Liss.
Biological Rhythms in Birds: Neural & Endocrine Aspects. Ed. by Y. Tanabe et al. 373p. 1980. 49.60 (ISBN 0-387-10311-2). Springer-Verlag.
Biological Rhythms in Human & Animal Physiology. Gay G. Luce. Orig. Title: Biological Rhythms in Psychiatry & Medicine. 1971. Repr. of 1970 ed. pap. text ed. 4.00 (ISBN 0-486-22586-0). Dover.
Biological Science. 3rd ed. William T. Keeton. (Illus.). 1980. text ed. 21.95x (ISBN 0-393-95021-2); pap. tchr's manual free (ISBN 0-393-95031-X); study guide 4.95x (ISBN 0-393-95028-X). Norton.
Biological Separations in Iodinated Density-Gradient Media. 205p. 12.00 (ISBN 0-904147-02-9). Info Retrieval.
Biological Structure & Function: Proceedings, 2 Vols. I U B - I U B S Joint Symposium - 1st - Stockholm - 1960. Ed. by T. W. Goodwin & Olov Lindberg. 1961. Vol. 1. 50.00 (ISBN 0-12-289851-6). Acad Pr.
Biological Systematics. Hebert H. Ross. LC 73-2141. 1974. text ed. 17.95 (ISBN 0-201-06531-2). A-W.
Biological Tissue in Heart Valve Replacement. Ed. by M. I. Ionescu et al. (Illus.). 956p. 1971. 94.95 (ISBN 0-407-11730-X). Butterworths.
Biological Transmutations. C. L. Kervran. (Illus.). 180p. 1980. text ed. 14.95 (ISBN 0-8464-1069-9). Beekman Pubs.
Biological Wastewater Treatment: Theory & Applications. Grady & Lim. 984p. 1980. 75.00 (ISBN 0-8247-1000-2). Dekker.
Biological World. Alvin Nason & Robert L. DeHaan. LC 72-8573. 672p. 1973. text ed. 21.95x o.p. (ISBN 0-471-63045-4). Wiley.
Biologists Handbook of Pronunciations. Edmund Jaeger. 336p. 1960. pap. 29.75 photocopy ed., spiral (ISBN 0-398-00915-5). C C Thomas.
Biologist's Mathematics. Donald R. Causton. (Contemporary Biology Ser). 1978. pap. 18.95 (ISBN 0-7131-2605-1). Univ Park.
Biologlical Psychiatry Today, Vols. A & B. Ed. by J. Obiols et al. (Developments in Psychiatry: Vol. 2). 1979. 151.25 (ISBN 0-444-80117-0, North Holland). Elsevier.
Biology. 9th ed. Gordon Alexander & Douglas G. Alexander. (Illus.). 1970. pap. 3.95 (ISBN 0-06-460004-1, CO 4, COS). Har-Row.
Biology. 3rd ed. Helena Curtis. LC 78-68582. (Illus.). 1979. text ed. 21.95x (ISBN 0-87901-100-9); study guide 6.95x (ISBN 0-87901-101-7). Worth.
Biology. Gabrielle Edwards & Maurice Bleifeld. LC 58-19074. (High School Regents Exams & Answer Ser.). 1977. pap. 3.50 (ISBN 0-8120-0191-5). Barron.
Biology. 2nd ed. Richard A. Goldsby. (Illus.). 1979. text ed. 21.50 scp (ISBN 0-06-162409-8, HarpC); instr. manual avail. (ISBN 0-06-162402-0); scp study guide 6.50 (ISBN 0-685-63467-1). Har-Row.
Biology. Clyde F. Herreid. (Illus.). 1977. text ed. 20.95 (ISBN 0-686-65372-6). Macmillan.
Biology. William A. Jensen et al. 1979. text ed. 21.95x (ISBN 0-534-00621-3); study guide 5.95x (ISBN 0-534-00721-X). Wadsworth Pub.
Biology. 4th ed. John Kimball. LC 77-74322. (Life Sciences Ser.). 1978. text ed. 21.95 (ISBN 0-201-03761-0); lab manual 8.50 (ISBN 0-201-03692-4); study guide 6.95 (ISBN 0-201-03764-5). A-W.
Biology. Donald Ritchie & Robert Carola. LC 78-67450. (Life Sciences Ser.). 1979. text ed. 20.95 (ISBN 0-201-06335-2); inst. manual avail. (ISBN 0-201-06336-0); study guide avail. (ISBN 0-201-06337-9). A-W.
Biology. Jack Rudman. (Undergraduate Program Field Test Ser.: UPFT-2). (Cloth bdg. avail. on request) (ISBN 0-8373-6002-1). pap. 9.95 (ISBN 0-686-68259-9). Natl Learning.

Biology. 2nd ed. Aaron O. Wasserman. 832p. 1975. text ed. 19.95 (ISBN 0-201-08431-7); instr's manual 6.95 (ISBN 0-201-08434-1); study guide & wkbk. 4.95 (ISBN 0-686-67101-5); lab. manual 5.95 (ISBN 0-201-08403-1). A-W.

Biology: A Human Approach. 2nd ed. Irwin W. Sherman & Vilia G. Sherman. (Illus.). 636p. 1979. text ed. 18.95 o.p. (ISBN 0-19-502439-7). Oxford U Pr.

Biology: An Inquiry into the Nature of Life. rev. ed. Stanley L. Weinberg. 644p. 1974. text ed. 14.80x o.p. (ISBN 0-205-04487-5); instr's manual avail. o.p. (ISBN 0-205-04488-3). Allyn.

Biology & Adaptability of Natural Populations. James T. Giesel. LC 73-18288. 1974. pap. text ed. 7.95 o.p. (ISBN 0-8016-1812-6). Mosby.

Biology & Behavior of the Reedbuck (Redunca arundium Boddaert 1785) in the Kruger National Park. Harmut Jungius. (Illus.). 106p. (Orig.). 1971. pap. text ed. 20.00 (ISBN 3-490-02818-X). Parey Sci Pubs.

Biology & Conservation of the Callitrichidae. Ed. by Devra G. Kleiman. LC 78-2428. (Illus.). 1978. text ed. 25.00x (ISBN 0-87474-586-1); pap. text ed. 12.50x (ISBN 0-87474-587-X). Smithsonian.

Biology & Culture in Modern Perspective: Readings from Scientific American. Intro. by Joseph G. Jorgensen. LC 72-4237. (Illus.). 1972. text ed. 20.95x (ISBN 0-7167-0862-0); pap. text ed. 10.95x (ISBN 0-7167-0861-2). W H Freeman.

Biology & Geology of Coral Reefs, 4 vols. Ed. by O. A. Jones & R. Endean. Incl. Vol. 1. Geology. 1973. 48.50 (ISBN 0-12-389601-0); Vol. 2. Biology - One. 1974. 59.00 (ISBN 0-12-389602-9); Vol. 3. Biology - Two. 1975. 67.00 (ISBN 0-12-389603-7); Vol. 4. 1977. 51.50 (ISBN 0-12-389604-5). Set. 194.50. Acad Pr.

Biology & Man Laboratory Guide. Janet L. Schultz. 80p. 1980. pap. text ed. 5.95 (ISBN 0-8403-2351-4). Kendall-Hunt.

Biology & Management of Lobsters: Vol. 1, Physiology & Behavior. Ed. by J. Stanley Cobb & Bruce F. Phillips. LC 79-6803. 1980. 55.00 (ISBN 0-12-177401-5). Acad Pr.

Biology & Management of Lobsters: Vol. 2, Ecology & Management. Ed. by J. Stanley Cobb & Bruce F. Phillips. LC 79-6803. 1980. 45.00 (ISBN 0-12-177402-3) (ISBN 0-686-65861-2). Acad Pr.

Biology & Neurophysiology of the Conditioned Reflex & Its Role in Adaptive Behavior. Peter K. Anokhin. Tr. by Samuel A. Corson. LC 73-744. 592p. 1974. 94.00 (ISBN 0-08-017160-5); pap. text ed. 21.00 (ISBN 0-08-021516-5). Pergamon.

Biology & Pathology of Elastic Tissues. Ed. by A. M. Robert & L. Robert. (Frontiers of Matrix Biology Ser.: Vol. 8). (Illus.). viii, 232p. 1980. 74.25 (ISBN 3-8055-3078-1). S Karger.

Biology & Social Behavior. Allan Mazur & Leon S. Robertson. LC 72-169236. 1972. 12.95 (ISBN 0-02-920450-X); pap. text ed. 3.00 (ISBN 0-02-920410-0). Free Pr.

Biology & Taxonomy of the Bark Beetle Species in the Genus Pseudohylesinus Swaine (Coleoptera: Scolytidae). Donald E. Bright. (U. C. Publ. in Entomology: Vol. 54). 1969. pap. 6.50x (ISBN 0-520-09127-2). U of Cal Pr.

Biology & the Exploration of Mars. Space Science Board. 1965. 8.75 (ISBN 0-309-01296-1). Natl Acad Pr.

Biology & the Human Sciences. Ed. by J. W. Pringle. 1972. pap. 3.50x (ISBN 0-19-857122-4). Oxford U Pr.

Biology & the Physical Sciences. Ed. by Samuel Devons. LC 78-80272. 1969. 23.50x (ISBN 0-231-03134-3). Columbia U Pr.

Biology, Behavior & Emergence Rhythm of Two Species of Fannia (Diptera: Muscidae) M. J. Tauber. (U. C. Publ. in Entomology: Vol. 50). 1968. pap. 8.00x (ISBN 0-520-09122-1). U of Cal Pr.

Biology by Inquiry, 3 bks. Robert A. Clarke et al. Bk. 1. text ed. 6.95x o.p. (ISBN 0-435-59169-X); Bk. 2. text ed. 9.50x o.p. (ISBN 0-435-59171-1); Bk. 3. text ed. 7.95x o.p. (ISBN 0-435-59173-8); Bk. 3. tchr's guide 4.50 o.p. (ISBN 0-435-59174-6). Heinemann Ed.

Biology, Ecology & Host Specificity of Microlepidoptera Associated with Quercus Agrifolia (Fagaceae) Paul A. Opler. (U. C. Publications in Entomology Vol. 1). 1974. pap. 9.25x (ISBN 0-520-09500-6). U of Cal Pr.

Biology Experiments. Jack D. Bloom. LC 78-19643. (Pegasus Books: No. 14). 1968. 7.50x (ISBN 0-234-77998-5). Intl Pubns Serv.

Biology: Food & People. Robert Barrass. LC 74-21791. 224p. 1975. 18.95 (ISBN 0-312-08050-6). St Martin.

Biology for a Modern Society. Louis Levine. LC 76-46318. (Illus.). 1977. pap. 11.95 (ISBN 0-8016-2990-X). Mosby.

Biology for Survival: Text & Readings. Rosalyn Kane & George Wistreich. LC 73-7358. (Illus.). 480p. 1974. pap. text ed. 8.95x (ISBN 0-02-475270-3). Macmillan.

Biology for the Individual. Donald Reid & Philip Booth. Incl. Introduction to the Series. 1971. pap. text ed. o.p. (ISBN 0-435-59766-3); Bk. 1. Sorting Animals & Plants into Groups. 1971. pap. text ed. 4.50x o.p. (ISBN 0-435-59750-7); tchrs guide 5.95 o.p. (ISBN 0-435-59751-5); Bk 2. How Life Begins (Human Reproduction) 1971. pap. text ed. 4.50x o.p. (ISBN 0-435-59752-3); tchrs guide 8.25x o.p. (ISBN 0-435-59753-1); Bk 3. Movement in Animals. 1971. pap. text ed. 2.95x o.p. (ISBN 0-435-59754-X); tchrs guide 5.95 o.p. (ISBN 0-435-59755-8); Bk 4. Support in Animals & Plants. 1972. pap. text ed. 2.95x o.p. (ISBN 0-435-59756-6); Bk 5. Problems of Life in Hot, Cold, & Dry Climates. 1972. pap. text ed. 4.50x o.p. (ISBN 0-435-59758-2); tchrs guide 5.00x o.p. (ISBN 0-435-59759-0); Bk 6. Working with Very Small Things. 1974. pap. text ed. 4.50x o.p. (ISBN 0-435-59760-4); Bk 7. War Against Diseases. 1974. pap. text ed. 2.95x o.p. (ISBN 0-435-59762-0); Bks. 6 & 7. tchrs guide 5.50x o.p. (ISBN 0-435-59761-2); Bk 8. Plant Reproduction. 1973. pap. text ed. 4.50x o.p. (ISBN 0-435-59764-7); Bk. 9. Skeletons & Muscles. 1973. pap. text ed. 4.50x o.p. (ISBN 0-435-59764-7). Heinemann Ed.

Biology: Functional Man. J. Early & M. Marshall. (Illus.). 1978. text ed. 15.00x o.p. (ISBN 0-8464-0196-7). Beekman Pubs.

Biology in Human Affairs. Ed. by Edward M. East. 399p. 1980. Repr. of 1931 ed. lib. bdg. 30.00 (ISBN 0-8495-1348-0). Arden Lib.

Biology in Pest & Disease Control: Symposium of the British Ecological Society, 13th Oxford, 4-7 Jan. 72. Ed. by D. Price-Jones & M. E. Solomon. LC 73-12466. (British Ecological Society Symposia Ser.). 1974. 34.95 (ISBN 0-470-69727-X). Halsted Pr.

Biology in the Nineteenth Century. W. Coleman. LC 77-83989. (History of Science Ser.). (Illus.). 1978. 22.50 (ISBN 0-521-21861-6); pap. 7.50x (ISBN 0-521-29293-X). Cambridge U Pr.

Biology in the World of the Future. Hal Hellman. LC 70-12218. (World of the Future Ser.). (Illus.). 192p. (gr. 7 up). 1971. 6.95 (ISBN 0-87131-104-6). M Evans.

Biology: Introduction to Life. Alvin Nason & Philip Goldstein. 337p. (gr. 10-12). 1969. text ed. 17.56 o.p. (ISBN 0-201-05240-7, Sch Div). lab. manual 5.36 o.p. (ISBN 0-201-05242-3). A-W.

Biology Investigations. Sebastian Haskel & David Sygoda. (gr. 10-12). 1973. lab manual 7.08 (ISBN 0-87720-056-4). AMSCO Sch.

Biology-Its People & Its Papers. Howard B. Baumel & J. Joel Berger. 1973. pap. 3.50 (ISBN 0-87355-002-1, 471-14652). Natl Sci Tchrs.

Biology: Its Principles & Implications. 3rd ed. Garrett Hardin & Carl Bajema. LC 77-28507. (Illus.). 1978. 21.95x (ISBN 0-7167-0028-X). W H Freeman.

Biology Laboratory Manual. Leroy Scott & Starr Weih. 1980. coil binding 8.95 (ISBN 0-88252-106-3). Paladin Hse.

Biology Made Simple. Ethel R. Hanauer. LC 72-76229. pap. 3.95 (ISBN 0-385-01972-6, Made). Doubleday.

Biology of Adolescence. Herant Katchadourian. LC 76-44282. (Illus.). 1977. text ed. 18.95x (ISBN 0-7167-0376-9); pap. text ed. 10.95x (ISBN 0-7167-0375-0). W H Freeman.

Biology of Aging. M. J. Lamb. LC 77-9528. (Tertiary Level Biology Ser.). 1977. 24.95 (ISBN 0-470-99221-2). Halsted Pr.

Biology of Aging. Morris Rockstein & Marvin Sussman. 1979. pap. text ed. 8.95x (ISBN 0-534-00687-6). Wadsworth Pub.

Biology of Animal Viruses. 2nd ed. F. Fenner et al. 1974. 62.50 (ISBN 0-12-253040-3). Acad Pr.

Biology of Animals. 2nd ed. Cleveland P. Hickman et al. LC 77-10766. (Illus.). 1978. text ed. 19.50 (ISBN 0-8016-2166-6). Mosby.

Biology of Bats. Ed. by William A. Wimsatt. Vol. 1, 1970. 48.50, by subscription 41.75 (ISBN 0-12-758001-8). Vol. 2, 1971. 49.50, by subscription 42.50 (ISBN 0-12-758002-6). Acad Pr.

Biology of Bats of the New World Family Phyllostomatidae, Pt. I. Ed. by Robert J. Baker et al. (Special Publications: No. 10). (Illus., Orig.). 1976. pap. 8.00 (ISBN 0-89672-036-5). Tex Tech Pr.

Biology of Benthic Organisms: 11th European Symposium on Marine Biology, Galway, Ireland. Ed. by B. F. Keegan & P. O. Ceidigh. 1977. pap. text ed. 75.00 (ISBN 0-08-021378-2). Pergamon.

Biology of Bone. N. M. Hancox. LC 73-169578. (Biological Structure & Function Ser). (Illus.). 1972. 57.50 (ISBN 0-521-08342-7). Cambridge U Pr.

Biology of Bone Marrow Transplantation. Ed. by Robert P. Gale & C. Fred Fox. (ICN-UCLA Symposia on Molecular & Cellular Biology Ser.: Vol. 17). 1980. 40.00 (ISBN 0-12-273960-4). Acad Pr.

Biology of Brains. Ed. by W. B. Broughton. LC 74-178. 1974. 28.95 (ISBN 0-470-10630-1). Halsted Pr.

Biology of Cancer. 2nd rev. ed. Ed. by E. J. Ambrose & F. J. Roe. LC 74-26860. 315p. 1975. 57.95 (ISBN 0-470-02527-1). Halsted Pr.

Biology of Carbohydrates, Vol. 1. Victor Ginsburg. LC 80-20758. 336p. 1981. 35.00 (ISBN 0-471-03905-5, Pub. by Wiley-Interscience). Wiley.

Biology of Cartilage Cells. R. A. Stockwell. LC 78-67433. (Biological Structure & Function Ser.: No. 7). (Illus.). 1979. 63.50 (ISBN 0-521-22410-1). Cambridge U Pr.

Biology of Centipedes. J. G. Lewis. (Illus.). 350p. Date not set. price not set (ISBN 0-521-23413-1). Cambridge U Pr.

Biology of Cholinergic Function. Ed. by Alan M. Goldberg & Israel Hanin. LC 74-14473. 730p. 1976. 48.00 (ISBN 0-911216-98-7). Raven.

Biology of Communication. D. B. Lewis & D. M. Gower. LC 79-20920. (Tertiary Level Biology Ser.). 1980. 29.95x (ISBN 0-470-26859-X). Halsted Pr.

Biology of Conidial Fungi, 2 vols. G. T. Cole & B. Kendrick. 1981. Vol. 1. write for info. (ISBN 0-12-179501-2); Vol. 2. write for info. (ISBN 0-12-179502-0). Acad Pr.

Biology of Desmids. Alan J. Brook. LC 80-26374. (Botanical Monographs Ser.: Vol. 16). (Illus.). 1981. 36.50x (ISBN 0-520-04281-6). U of Cal Pr.

Biology of Diatoms. Ed. by Dietrich Werner. LC 76-55574. (Botanical Monographs: Vol. 13). 1977. 48.50x (ISBN 0-520-03400-7). U of Cal Pr.

Biology of Emotions: New Understanding Derived from Biological Multidisciplinary Investigation; First Electrophysiological Measurements. Edmund Jacobson. (Illus.). 232p. 1967. pap. 9.75 spiral (ISBN 0-398-00909-0). C C Thomas.

Biology of Fibroblast. Ed. by E. Kulonen & E. Kulonen. 1974. 97.00 (ISBN 0-12-428950-9). Acad Pr.

Biology of Free-Living Nematodes. Warwick L. Nicholas. (Illus.). 224p. 1975. 42.00x (ISBN 0-19-854379-4). Oxford U Pr.

Biology of Fresh Waters. Peter S. Maitland. (Tertiary Level Biology Ser.). 244p. 1980. pap. text ed. 24.95x (ISBN 0-470-26986-3). Halsted Pr.

Biology of Fungi. 3rd rev. ed. Cecil T. Ingold. (Hutchinson Biology Monographs). (Illus., Orig.). 1973. pap. text ed. 10.50x (ISBN 0-09-105120-7, Hutchinson U Lib). Humanities.

Biology of High-Altitude Peoples. Ed. by P. T. Baker. LC 76-50311. (International Biological Programme Ser.: No. 14). (Illus.). 1978. 68.00 (ISBN 0-521-21523-4). Cambridge U Pr.

Biology of Human Action. 2nd ed. Vernon Reynolds. LC 80-11856. (Illus.). 1981. text ed. 19.95x (ISBN 0-7167-1239-3); pap. text ed. 10.95x (ISBN 0-7167-1240-7). W H Freeman.

Biology of Insect Eggs, 3 vols. H. E. Hinton. LC 77-30390. (Illus.). 1500p. 1980. Set. 350.00 (ISBN 0-08-021539-4). Pergamon.

Biology of Mammalian Fertilization & Implantation. Ed. by Kamran S. Moghissi & E. S. Hafez. (Illus.). 520p. 1972. 42.50 (ISBN 0-398-02362-X). C C Thomas.

Biology of Nematodes. Neil A. Croll & B. E. Matthews. LC 75-505520. (Tertiary Level Biology Ser.). 1977. 18.95 (ISBN 0-470-99028-7). Halsted Pr.

Biology of Normal Human Growth. Ed. by Martin Ritzen et al. Date not set. price not set. Raven.

Biology of Nutrition, Pts. 1-2. Ed. by R. N. Fiennes. Incl. Pt. 1. The Evolution & Nature of Living Systems; Pt. 2. The Organizations & Nutritional Methods of Life Forms. 688p. 1972. Set. text ed. 125.00 (ISBN 0-08-016470-6). Pergamon.

Biology of Ophisthobranch Molluscs, Vol. 1. T. E. Thompson. (Illus.). 1976. 36.00x (ISBN 0-903874-04-0, Pub. by Brit Mus Nat Hist). Sabbot-Natural Hist Bks.

Biology of People. Sam Singer & Henry R. Hilgard. LC 77-17893. (Biology Ser.). (Illus.). 1978. text ed. 21.95x (ISBN 0-7167-0026-3); tchr's resource bk. 2.75x. W H Freeman.

Biology of Physical Activity. Dee Edington & V. Reggie Edgerton. LC 75-26095. (Illus.). 352p. 1976. text ed. 16.75 (ISBN 0-395-18579-3); inst. manual 1.75 (ISBN 0-395-18801-6). HM.

Biology of Plants. 2nd ed. Peter Raven & Ray Evert. LC 75-42980. (Illus.). 1976. 18.95x o.p. (ISBN 0-87901-054-1). Worth.

Biology of Plants. 3rd ed. Peter H. Raven et al. 1981. text ed. write for info. (ISBN 0-87901-132-7); write for info. lab manual (ISBN 0-87901-142-4); prep guide avail. (ISBN 0-87901-143-2). Worth.

Biology of Population Growth. Robert Snyder. 300p. 1980. 30.00x (Pub. by Croom Helm England). State Mutual Bk.

Biology of Populations. Robert H. MacArthur & J. H. Connell. LC 66-21070. 1966. text ed. 16.95x o.p. (ISBN 0-471-55974-1). Wiley.

Biology of Radiation Carcinogenesis. Ed. by John M. Yuhas et al. LC 74-14486. 1976. 34.50 (ISBN 0-89004-010-9). Raven.

Biology of Reinforcement: Facet of Brain Stimulation Reward. Ed. by Aryeh Routtenberg. (Behavioral Biology Ser.). 1980. 16.00 (ISBN 0-12-599350-1). Acad Pr.

Biology of Reproduction. P. J. Hogarth. LC 78-4620. (Tertiary Level Biology Ser.). 1978. text ed. 18.95 (ISBN 0-470-26314-8). Halsted Pr.

Biology of Termites, 2 Vols. Ed. by Kumar Krishna & Frances M. Weesner. 1969-70. Vol. 1. 69.00 (ISBN 0-12-426301-1); Vol. 2. 72.75 (ISBN 0-12-426302-X); Set. 115.00 (ISBN 0-685-05123-4). Acad Pr.

Biology of the Algae. 2nd ed. F. E. Round. LC 73-89991. 288p. 1974. 19.95 (ISBN 0-312-07875-7); pap. 14.95 (ISBN 0-312-07910-9). St Martin.

Biology of the Arthropoda. Kenneth U. Clarke. LC 73-2309. (Contemporary Biology Ser.). 270p. 1975. 24.50 (ISBN 0-444-19559-9). Univ Park.

Biology of the Bromeliads. David H. Benzing. 300p. (Orig.). 1980. pap. write for info (ISBN 0-916422-21-6). Mad River.

Biology of the Cell. Stephen Wolfe. 1972. 24.95x (ISBN 0-534-00106-8). Wadsworth Pub.

Biology of the Cell Cycle. J. M. Mitchinson. LC 72-160100. (Illus.). 1972. 49.50 (ISBN 0-521-08251-X); pap. 14.50x (ISBN 0-521-09671-5). Cambridge U Pr.

Biology of the Fluids of the Female Genital Tract. Ed. by S. Baba et al. 456p. 1979. 80.50 (ISBN 0-444-90069-1, Excerpta Medica). Elsevier.

Biology of the Future. Eckehard Munck. LC 73-15300. (International Library). (Illus.). 128p. (gr. 7 up). 1974. PLB 6.90 o.p. (ISBN 0-531-02118-1). Watts.

Biology of the Gene. 2nd ed. Louis Levine. LC 72-89495. (Illus.). 400p. 1973. text ed. 13.95 o.p. (ISBN 0-8016-2987-X). Mosby.

Biology of the Gene. 3rd ed. Louis Levine. LC 80-10730. (Illus.). 1980. pap. text ed. 17.95 (ISBN 0-8016-2988-8). Mosby.

Biology of the Invertebrates. 2nd ed. Cleveland P. Hickman. LC 72-83970. (Illus.). 720p. 1973. text ed. 18.95 (ISBN 0-8016-2170-4). Mosby.

Biology of the Living Primates. Elizabeth S. Watts. (Elements of Anthropology Ser). 80p. 1975. pap. text ed. 3.50x o.p. (ISBN 0-697-07538-9). Wm C Brown.

Biology of the Major Psychoses: A Comparative Analysis. Association for Research in Nervous & Mental Disease. Ed. by D. X. Freedman. LC 75-14571. (Research Publications: Vol. 54). 384p. 1975. 31.50 (ISBN 0-89004-034-6). Raven.

Biology of the Ovary. Ed. by P. M. Motta & E. S. Hafez. (Developments in Obstetrics & Gynecology Ser.: No. 2). 345p. 1980. lib. bdg. 86.85 (ISBN 90-247-2316-7). Kluwer Boston.

Biology of the Pig. Wilson G. Pond & Katherine A. Houpt. LC 77-90909. (Illus.). 352p. 1978. 25.00x (ISBN 0-8014-1137-8). Comstock.

Biology of the Plant Rusts: An Introduction. Larry J. Littlefield. (Illus.). 112p. 1981. text ed. 9.00. Iowa St U Pr.

Biology of the Race Problem. Wesley C. George. 72p. 1979. pap. 2.00x (ISBN 0-911038-76-0, 132). Noontide.

Biology of the Tapeworm Hymenolepis Diminuta. Ed. by Hisao Arai. 1980. 45.00 (ISBN 0-12-058980-X). Acad Pr.

Biology of Tribolium with Special Emphasis on Genetic Aspects, Vol. 2. Alexander Sokoloff. (Illus.). 628p. 1975. 75.00x (ISBN 0-19-857381-2). Oxford U Pr.

Biology of Tribolium: With Special Emphasis on Genetic Aspects, Vol. 3. A. Sokoloff. 1978. 98.00x (ISBN 0-19-857512-2). Oxford U Pr.

Biology of Tribolium with Special Emphasis on Genetic Effects, Vol. 1. A. Sokoloff. (Illus.). 1972. 45.00x (ISBN 0-19-857353-7). Oxford U Pr.

Biology of Tumor Viruses: Proceedings. Biology Colloquium, 34th, Oregon State University, 1973. Ed. by George S. Beaudreau. LC 52-19235. (Illus.). 144p. 1976. pap. text ed. 7.00 (ISBN 0-87071-173-3). Oreg St U Pr.

Biology of Women. Ethel Sloane. LC 79-15256. 1980. 16.95 (ISBN 0-471-02165-2, Pub. by Wiley-Medical). Wiley.

Biology One Hundred & Twenty: Laboratory Manual for Man & His Environment. Jack S. Griffith et al. 128p. 1980. pap. text ed. 7.95 (ISBN 0-8403-2228-3). Kendall-Hunt.

Biology: Principles & Issues. William C. Schefler. LC 75-28725. (Life Sciences Ser.). (Illus.). 384p. 1976. text ed. 17.95 (ISBN 0-201-06764-1); instructor's manual 2.00 (ISBN 0-201-06763-3). A-W.

Biology Teacher's Handbook: Biological Sciences Curriculum Study. 3rd ed. LC 77-27548. 1978. text ed. 24.95 (ISBN 0-471-01945-3). Wiley.

Biology: The Foundations. Stephen Wolfe. 1977. 18.95x (ISBN 0-534-00490-3). Wadsworth Pub.

Biology: The Human Perspective. Donald J. Farish. (Illus.). 1978. text ed. 19.50 scp (ISBN 0-06-041995-4, HarpC); inst. manual avail. (ISBN 0-685-86375-1); scp study guide 7.50 (ISBN 0-06-041992-X). Har-Row.

Biology: The Science of Life. Victor A. Greulach & Vincent J. Chiappetta. 1977. text ed. 17.95x (ISBN 0-673-15301-0); study guide 5.95x (ISBN 0-673-15302-9). Scott F.

Biology: The Unity & the Diversity of Life. David Kirk et al. 1978. text ed. 18.95x (ISBN 0-534-00540-3); wkbk. 6.95x (ISBN 0-534-00584-5). Wadsworth Pub.

Biology: Today & Tomorrow. Jack A. Ward & Howard R. Hetzel. (Illus.). 1980. text ed. 18.95 (ISBN 0-8299-0310-0); study guide 7.95 (ISBN 0-8299-0335-6); instrs.' manual avail. (ISBN 0-8299-0579-0). West Pub.

Bioluminescience & Chemiluminescence: Basic Chemistry & Analytical Applications. Ed. by Marlene Deluca & William McElroy. 1981. price not set (ISBN 0-12-208820-4). Acad Pr.

Biomass Alcohol for California: a Potential for the 1980's: Proceedings. Ed. by University of California, Davis. 52p. 1980. Repr. pap. 11.95 (ISBN 0-89934-059-8, B002-PP). Solar Energy Info.

Biomass As a Nonfossil Fuel Source. Ed. by Donald L. Klass. LC 80-26044. (ACS Symposium Ser.: No. 144). 1981. 42.00 (ISBN 0-8412-0599-X). Am Chemical.

Biomass As an Alternative Fuel. Carl Hall. LC 80-84729. 350p. 1981. 35.00 (ISBN 0-86587-087-X). Gov Insts.

Biomass Energy Projects: Planning & Management. Ed. by Louis J. Goodman & Ralph N. Love. (Pergamon Policy Studies). 300p. Date not set. price not set (ISBN 0-08-025564-7). Pergamon.

Biomass Energy Systems Program Summary Nineteen Eighty. OAO Corp. 220p. 1981. pap. 24.50 (ISBN 0-89934-103-9). Solar Energy Info.

Biomass: How? What? Where, E-039. Ed. by Business Communications. 1980. 850.00 (ISBN 0-89336-215-8). BCC.

Biomechanical Studies of the Musculo-Skeletal System. F. Gaynor Evans. 232p. 1961. pap. 22.50 photocopy ed. spiral (ISBN 0-398-04102-4). C C Thomas.

Biomechanics II. Ed. by J. Vredenbregt & J. Wartenweiler. (Medicine & Sport Ser.: Vol. 6). (Illus.). 1971. 29.50 (ISBN 0-8391-0530-4, Pub by Karger). Univ Park.

Biomechanics: Mechanical Properties of Living Tissues. Y. C. Fung. (Illus.). 400p. 1980. 29.80 (ISBN 0-387-90472-7). Springer-Verlag.

Biomechanics of Human Movement. David A. Winter. LC 79-12660. (Biomedical Engineering & Health Systems Ser.). 1979. 22.95 (ISBN 0-471-03476-2, Pub. by Wiley-Interscience). Wiley.

Biomechanics of Medical Devices. D. Ghista. 1981. 95.00 (ISBN 0-8247-6848-5). Dekker.

Biomechanics of Sports Techniques. 2nd ed. J. Hay. 1978. 18.95 (ISBN 0-13-077164-3). P-H.

Biomechanics of the Locomotor Apparatus. F. Pauwels. (Illus.). 520p. 1980. 175.90 (ISBN 0-387-09131-9). Springer-Verlag.

Biomechanics of Women's Gymnastics. Gerald S. George. 1980. text ed. 15.95 (ISBN 0-13-077461-8). P-H.

Biomechanics V. Ed. by P. V. Komi. (International Series on Biomechanics: Vol. Va & Vb). (Illus.). 700p. 1976. 39.50 ea. Vol. VA (ISBN 0-8391-0947-4). Vol. VB (ISBN 0-8391-0946-6). Univ Park.

Biomedical & Social Bases of Pediatrics. Kretchmer & Brasel. 1981. write for info. (ISBN 0-89352-093-4). Masson Pub.

Biomedical Applications of Gas Chromatography, 2 vols. Ed. by Herman A. Szymanski. Incl. Vol. 1. 324p. 1964. 37.50 (ISBN 0-306-37581-8); Vol. 2. 198p. 1968. 32.50 (ISBN 0-306-37582-6). LC 64-13147 (Plenum Pr). Plenum Pub.

Biomedical Applications of the Horseshoe Crab (Limulidae) Symposium, Woods Hole, Mass., October, 1978. Ed. by Elias Cohen. LC 79-1748. (Progress in Clinical & Biological Research Ser.: Vol. 29). 720p. 1978. 52.00x (ISBN 0-8451-0029-7). A R Liss.

Biomedical Aspects of Lactation. Stuart Patton & Robert G. Jensen. 1976. pap. text ed. 13.25 (ISBN 0-08-020192-X). Pergamon.

Biomedical Instrumentation & Measurements. 2nd ed. Leslie Cromwell et al. (Illus.). 1980. text ed. 22.95 (ISBN 0-13-076448-5). P-H.

Biomedical Polymers: Polymeric Materials & Pharmaceuticals for Biomedical Use. E. P. Goldberg & A. Nakajima. LC 80-17691. 1980. 32.00 (ISBN 0-12-287580-X). Acad Pr.

Biomedical Scientific & Technical Book Reviewing. Ching-Chih Chen. LC 76-20480. 1976. 10.00 (ISBN 0-8108-0939-7). Scarecrow.

Biometeorological Methods. R. E. Munn. LC 71-97488. (Environmental Science Ser). 1970. 15.50 (ISBN 0-12-510250-X); pap. 8.95 (ISBN 0-12-510256-9). Acad Pr.

Biometeorology: Proceedings, Vol. 6. International Biometeorological Congress, 7th, College Park, MD 1975. Ed. by H. E. Landsberg. 380p. (Supplements to vol. 19 & 20 of the international journal of biometeorology). 1976. pap. text ed. 77.50 (ISBN 90-265-0241-9, Pub. by Swets Pub Serv Holland). Swets North Am.

Biometeorology: Proceedings of the Eighth International Biometeorological Congress 9-15 September 1979.Supplement to Volume 24 of the International Journal of Biometeorology, No.7, Pt.1. Ed. by Z. Zemel & N. St. G. Hyslop. vi, 150p. 1980. pap. text ed. 44.75 (ISBN 90-265-0349-0). Swets North Am.

Biometeorology Seven: Proceedings, Supplement to Volume 24, of the International Journal of Biometeorology, Pts. 1 & 2. Eighth International Biometeorological Congress 9-15 September 1979. Ed. by Z. Zemel & N. Hyslop. 1981. pap. text ed. 78.95 (ISBN 90-265-0354-7). Swets North Am.

Biometeorology Seven: Proceedings, Supplement to Volume 24 of the International Journal of Biometeorology, Pt. 2. Eighth International Biometeorological Congress 9-15 September 1979. Ed. by Z. Zemel & N. Hyslop. 1981. pap. text ed. 44.75 (ISBN 90-265-0350-4). Swets North Am.

Biometerology-2: Proceedings, International Bioclimatological Congress - 3rd, Pts. 1 & 2. Ed. by S. W. Tromp & W. H. Weihe. 1967. 54.45 o.p. (ISBN 0-08-011045-2). Pergamon.

Biometrical Interpretation. Neil Gilbert. (Illus.). 130p. 1973. text ed. 11.50x o.p. (ISBN 0-19-854122-8). Oxford U Pr.

Biometrika Tables for Statisticians, Vol. 1. 3rd ed. Ed. by E. S. Pearson & H. O. Hartley. 270p. 1976. lib. bdg. 25.95x. Lubrecht & Cramer.

Biometrika Tables for Statisticians, Vol. 1. Ed. by E. S. Pearson & H. O. Hartley. 270p. 1976. 25.00x (ISBN 0-85264-700-X, Pub. by Griffin England). State Mutual Bk.

Biometrika Tables for Statisticians, Vol. 2. Ed. by E. S. Pearson & H. O. Hartley. 1976. 30.00x (ISBN 0-85264-701-8, Pub. by Griffin England). State Mutual Bk.

Biometrika Tables for Statisticians: Reprint with Corrections, Vol. 2. Ed. by E. S. Pearson & H. O. Hartley. 385p. 1976. Repr. lib. bdg. 30.50x. Lubrecht & Cramer.

Biometry, the Principles & Practice of Statistics in Biological Research. Robert R. Sokal & F. James Rohlf. LC 68-16819. (Biology Ser.). (Illus.). 1969. text ed. 28.95x (ISBN 0-7167-0663-6). W H Freeman.

Biometry: The Principles & Practices of Statistics in Biological Research. 2nd ed. Robert R. Sokal & F. James Rohlf. LC 81-4. 1981. text ed. price not set (ISBN 0-7167-1254-7). W H Freeman.

Biomonitoring Air Pollutants with Plants. William J. Manning & William A. Feder. (Illus.). x, 142p. 1981. 26.00x (ISBN 0-85334-916-9). Burgess-Intl Ideas.

Biomycin: Chemistry & Clinical Applications. Glickson. Date not set. price not set (ISBN 0-8247-1289-7). Dekker.

Bion Experiments: On the Origin of Life. Wilhelm Reich. Tr. by Derek Jordan & Inge Jordan. (Octagon edition). 1979. 22.50 (ISBN 0-374-96768-7); pap. 8.95 (ISBN 0-374-51446-1). FS&G.

Bionic Banana. Linda R. Churchill & E. Richard. LC 78-17512. (Illus.). (gr. 3 up). 1979. PLB 6.45 s&l (ISBN 0-531-02920-4). Watts.

Bionic Banana. E. Richard & Linda R. Churchill. (YA) (gr. 7-12). pap. 1.50 (ISBN 0-440-90852-3, LE). Dell.

Bionic Joke Book. Jim Simon. 1976. pap. 1.25 o.p. (ISBN 0-685-72572-3, LB406, Leisure Bks). Nordon Pubns.

Bionic Parts for People: The Real Story of Artificial Organs & Replacement Parts. Gloria Skurzynski. LC 78-54678. (Illus.). 160p. (gr. 7 up). 1978. 8.95 (ISBN 0-590-07490-3, Four Winds). Schol Bk Serv.

Bionic Woman: Extracurricular Activities, No. 2. Eileen Lottman. 1977. pap. 1.25 o.p. (ISBN 0-425-03326-0). Berkley Pub.

Bionic Woman: Welcome Home Jamie. Maud Willis. 1976. pap. 1.25 o.p. (ISBN 0-425-03230-2). Berkley Pub.

Bionics. Melvin Berger. (Impact Books Ser.). (Illus.). (gr. 7 up). 1978. PLB 6.90 s&l (ISBN 0-531-01354-5). Watts.

Bioorganic Chemistry, 2 vols. Ed. by E. E. Van Tamelen. Incl. Vol. 1. Enzyme Action. 1977. 49.75 (ISBN 0-12-714301-7); Vol. 2. 1978. 52.50, by subscription 83.00 (ISBN 0-12-714302-5). Acad Pr.

Bioorganic Chemistry: A Chemical Approach to Enzyme Action. H. Dugas & C. Penney. (Springer Advanced Texts in Chemistry Ser.). (Illus.). 416p. 1981. 29.80 (ISBN 0-387-90491-3). Springer-Verlag.

Biopharmaceutics & Relevant Pharmacokinetics. John G. Wagner. LC 75-160736. (Illus.). 375p. 1971. 16.50 (ISBN 0-914768-18-2). Drug Intl Pubns.

Biophilosophy. Bernhard Rensch. Tr. by Cecilia Sym from Ger. LC 72-132692. 1971. 20.00x (ISBN 0-231-03299-4). Columbia U Pr.

Biophysical Aspects of Cerebral Circulation. Ed. by Yu E. Moskalenko. LC 78-41243. (Illus.). 174p. 1980. 48.00 (ISBN 0-08-022672-8). Pergamon.

Biophysical Aspects of Radiation Quality - Second Panel Report. (Illus., Orig.). 1968. pap. 9.75 (ISBN 92-0-011068-1, IAEA). Unipub.

Biophysical Aspects of Radiation Quality - 1971. (Illus.). 561p. (Orig.). 1971. pap. 39.75 (ISBN 92-0-010271-9, ISP286, IAEA). Unipub.

Biophysical Aspects of Radiation Quality - 1965. (Technical Reports Ser.: No. 58). (Illus., Orig.). 1966. pap. 8.25 (ISBN 92-0-015066-7, IAEA). Unipub.

Biophysical Chemistry, Part I: The Conformation of Biological Macromolecules. Charles R. Cantor & Paul R. Schimmel. LC 79-22043. (Illus.). 1980. 31.95x (ISBN 0-7167-1042-0); pap. text ed. 16.95x (ISBN 0-7167-1188-5). W H Freeman.

Biophysical Chemistry, Part II: Techniques for the Study of Biological Structure & Function. Charles R. Cantor & Paul R. Schimmel. LC 79-24854. (Illus.). 1980. text ed. 37.95x (ISBN 0-7167-1189-3); pap. text ed. 19.95x (ISBN 0-7167-1190-7). W H Freeman.

Biophysical Chemistry, Part III: The Behavior of Biological Macromolecules. Charles R. Cantor & Paul R. Schimmel. LC 79-27860. (Illus.). 1980. 39.95x (ISBN 0-7167-1191-5); pap. text ed. 21.95x (ISBN 0-7167-1192-3). W H Freeman.

Biophysical Chemistry: Physical Chemistry in the Biological Sciences, Readings from Scientific American. Intro. by Victor A. Bloomfield & Rodney E. Harrington. LC 75-8748. (Illus.). 1975. text ed. 19.95x (ISBN 0-7167-0513-3); pap. text ed. 9.95x (ISBN 0-7167-0512-5). W H Freeman.

Biophysical Chemistry: Principles, Techniques & Applications. Alan G. Marshall. LC 77-19136. 1978. text ed. 28.95 (ISBN 0-471-02718-9); students manual avail. (ISBN 0-471-03674-9). Wiley.

Biophysical Chemistry, Vol. 1: Thermodynamics, Electrostatics & the Biological Significance of the Properties of Matter. John T. Edsall & Jeffries Wyman. 1958. 49.50 (ISBN 0-12-232201-0). Acad Pr.

Biophysical Lab Manual. John Bauldree et al. 1976. spiral bdg. 16.95 (ISBN 0-88252-057-1). Paladin Hse.

Biophysical Science. 2nd ed. Eugene Ackerman et al. (Illus.). 1979. ref. ed. 26.95 (ISBN 0-13-076901-0). P-H.

Biophysics Handbook I. University of Guelph. 208p. 1980. pap. text ed. 8.95 (ISBN 0-8403-2280-1). Kendall-Hunt.

Biophysics Handbook II. Guelph. 208p. 1980. pap. text ed. 8.95 (ISBN 0-8403-2281-X). Kendall-Hunt.

Biopolitics of International Relations. Ralph Pettman. LC 80-22926. (Pergamon Policy Studies on Biopolitics). 200p. 1981. 20.00 (ISBN 0-08-026329-1); pap. 9.95 (ISBN 0-08-026328-3). Pergamon.

Biopolitics: Search for a More Human Political Science. Wiegele. LC 79-16252. (Westview Special Studies). 1979. lib. bdg. 18.50x (ISBN 0-89158-691-1); pap. text ed. 8.00x (ISBN 0-89158-751-9). Westview.

Biopsy Diagnosis of the Digestive Tract. Heidrun Z. Rotterdam & Sheldon C. Sommers. (Biopsy Interpretation Ser.). 1981. text ed. price not set (ISBN 0-89004-541-0). Raven.

Biopsychosocial Approach to the Patient. Chase P. Kimball. (Illus.). 382p. 1981. softcover 24.00 (ISBN 0-686-69562-3, 9400-9). Williams & Wilkins.

Biopsychosocial Health. Stacey B. Day et al. 225p. 1980. pap. 10.50 (ISBN 0-934314-02-0). Intl Found Biosocial Dev.

Bioregulators of Reproduction. Ed. by Georgiana Jagiello & Henry J. Vogel. (P&S Biomedical Sciences Ser.). 1981. price not set. Acad Pr.

Bioresources for Development: The Renewable Way of Life. Ed. by Alexander King et al. LC 79-28229. (Pergamon Policy Studies). (Illus.). 368p. 1980. 39.50 (ISBN 0-08-025581-7). Pergamon.

Biorheology: Abstracts of the Second International Congress, No. 2. Ed. by A. Copley. 1976. pap. text ed. 23.50 (ISBN 0-08-019962-3). Pergamon.

Biorheology: Physics of Biological Tissues. Ed. by N. H. Hwang & D. R. Gross. (NATO Advanced Study Institute Ser.: Applied Science). 382p. 1980. 42.50x (ISBN 90-286-0950-4). Sijthoff & Noordhoff.

Biorheology: Proceedings of the Second International Congress. Ed. by A. Copley. 1976. pap. text ed. 47.00 (ISBN 0-08-019963-1). Pergamon.

Biorhythm: A Personal Science. rev. ed. Bernard Gittelson. 1978. pap. 2.95 (ISBN 0-446-93469-0). Warner Bks.

Biorhythm: Discovering Your Natural Ups & Downs. Pauline Bartel. (Impact Books Ser.). (Illus.). 1978. lib. bdg. 6.90 (ISBN 0-531-01355-3). Watts.

Biorhythm for Health Design. Kichinosuke Tatai. LC 76-29337. (Illus.). 152p. 1977. pap. 8.95 (ISBN 0-87040-393-1). Japan Pubns.

Biorhythm Sports Forecasting. Bernard Gittelson. 1978. pap. 2.95 o.s.i. (ISBN 0-446-83799-7). Warner Bks.

Bios Theoretikos. Trona Eriksen. 1977. pap. 19.00x (ISBN 82-00-05031-9, Dist. by Columbia U Pr). Universitet.

Biosocial Anthropology. Ed. by Robin Fox. LC 75-4110. (Association of Social Anthropologists, Ser. No. 1). 1975. 22.95 (ISBN 0-470-27033-0). Halsted Pr.

Biospeology, the Biology of Cavernicolous Animals. A. Vandel. 1965. 56.00 (ISBN 0-08-010242-5). Pergamon.

Biosphere: A Scientific American Book. Scientific American Editors. LC 78-140849. (Illus.). 1970. pap. text ed. 8.95x (ISBN 0-7167-0945-7). W H Freeman.

Biostatistical Analysis. Jerrold H. Zar. (Illus.). 608p. 1974. ref. ed. 23.95 (ISBN 0-13-076984-3). P-H.

Biostatistical Opinion of Parentage, Based on the Results of Blood Group Tests, 2 vols. Konrad Hummel. LC 72-175560. 1973. Set. 135.00x (ISBN 0-8002-1284-3). Vol. 1 (ISBN 3-437-10246-X). Vol. 2 (ISBN 3-437-10310-5). Intl Pubns Serv.

Biostatistics. Auram Goldstein. (Illus.). 1964. text ed. 18.95 (ISBN 0-02-344440-1). Macmillan.

Biostatistics: A Foundation for Analysis in the Health Sciences. 2nd ed. Wayne W. Daniel. LC 77-28253. (Probability & Mathematical Statistics Ser.). 1978. text ed. 23.95 (ISBN 0-471-02591-7); tchrs. ed. avail. (ISBN 0-471-03364-2). Wiley.

Biostatistics for the Health Professions. Lombard. 1975. 12.95 o.p. (ISBN 0-8385-0664-X). ACC.

Biostatistics in Pharmacology. new ed. Ed. by A. L. Delaunois. LC 78-40220. (International Encyclopedia of Pharmacology & Therapeutics: Section 7, Vol. 3). (Illus.). 1979. text ed. 75.00 (ISBN 0-08-021514-9). Pergamon.

Biostatistics in Pharmacology, Vol. 1-2. Ed. by A. L. Delaunois. 1128p. 1973. Set. text ed. 125.00 (ISBN 0-08-016556-7). Pergamon.

Biostatistics: 1064 Answers. J. J. Hubert & Carter. 64p. 1980. pap. text ed. 3.95 saddle stitched (ISBN 0-8403-2288-7). Kendall-Hunt.

Biostatistics: 1064 Questions. J. J. Hubert & Carter. LC 80-82899. 160p. 1980. pap. text ed. 6.95 (ISBN 0-8403-2287-9). Kendall-Hunt.

Biosynthesis. Ed. by J. W. Corcoran. (Antibiotics Ser.: Vol. 4). (Illus.). 500p. 1981. 97.00 (ISBN 0-387-10186-1). Springer-Verlag.

Biosynthesis, Modification & Processing of Cellular & Viral Polyproteins. Gebhard Koch & Dietmar Richter. 1980. 29.00 (ISBN 0-12-417560-0). Acad Pr.

Biosynthesis of Aromatic Compounds. Ulrich Weiss & John Edwards. LC 78-1496. 1980. 35.00 (ISBN 0-471-92690-6, Pub by Wiley-Interscience). Wiley.

Biosynthesis of Isoprenoid Compounds. John W. Porter & Sandra L. Spurgeon. 350p. 1981. 35.00 (ISBN 0-471-04807-0, Pub. by Wiley-Interscience). Wiley.

Biosynthesis of Mycotoxins: A Study in Secondary Metabolism. Ed. by P. S. Steyn. LC 80-12013. 1980. 44.00 (ISBN 0-12-670650-6). Acad Pr.

Biosynthesis of Natural Products Polyketides Terpenoids Steroids & Phnylpropano Ds. P. Manitto. 550p. 1981. 117.95 (ISBN 0-470-27100-0). Halsted Pr.

Biosystematic Monograph of the Genus Lophocolea (Dum.) Dum. (Hepaticopsida) in Europe. D. A. Vogelpoel. (Bryophytorum Bibliotheca Ser.: No. 15). (Illus.). 1981. pap. text ed. 30.00 (ISBN 3-7682-1177-0). Lubrecht & Cramer. Postponed.

Biosystematic Study of the Genus Brodiaea (Amaryllidaceae) Theodore F. Niehaus. (U. C. Publ. in Botany: Vol. 60). 1971. 7.00x (ISBN 0-520-09390-9). U of Cal Pr.

Biosystematic Survey of the Goldfield Genus Lasthenia (Compositae: Helenieae) Robert Ornduff. (U. C. Publ. in Botany: Vol. 40). 1966. pap. 6.50x (ISBN 0-520-09013-6). U of Cal Pr.

Biosystematics, Genetics, & Physiological Ecology of the Erythranthe Section of Mimulus. William M. Hiesey et al. LC 40-14859. (Experimental Studies on the Nature of Species: Vol. 5). (Illus.). 219p. 1971. 13.75 (ISBN 0-87279-639-6, 628). Carnegie Inst.

Biosystematics in Agriculture. Beltsville Symposia in Agricultural Research. Ed. by John A. Romberger. LC 77-84408. 1978. 29.95x (ISBN 0-470-26416-0). Halsted Pr.

Biosystematics in Agriculture. Ed. by John A. Romberger. LC 77-84408. (Beltsville Symposia in Agricultural Research Ser.: No. 2). 352p. 1978. text ed. 24.00. Allanheld.

Biosystematics of the Arizona, California & Oregon Species of the Genus Acanthoscelides Schilsky (Coleoptera: Bruchidae) Clarence D. Johnson. (U. C. Publ. in Entomology: Vol. 59). 1970. pap. 8.50x (ISBN 0-520-09132-9). U of Cal Pr.

Biotaxonomische Untersuchungen an Einigen Hefen der Gattung Saccharomyces. I. Neumann. 1972. 20.00 (ISBN 3-7682-5440-2). Lubrecht & Cramer.

Biotechnology: A Review & Annotated Bibliography. Ed. by Harry Rothman et al. 1980. 25.00 (ISBN 0-08-027177-4). Pergamon.

Biotechnology: Proceedings of the First European Congress on Biotechnology. Ed. by DECHEMA, Deutsche Gesellschaft Fuer Chemisches Apparatewesen E. V. (Dechema Monographs: Vol. 82). 304p. 1979. pap. text ed. 37.50 (ISBN 3-527-10765-7). Verlag Chemie.

Biotic Crises in Ecological & Evolutionary Time. Matthew H. Nitecki. LC 80-70597. 1981. 25.00 (ISBN 0-12-519640-7). Acad Pr.

Biotransformation & Fate of Chemicals in the Aquatic Environment. Ed. by A. W. Maki et al. (Illus.). 1980. write for info. (ISBN 0-914826-28-X). Am Soc Microbio.

Biotyping in the Clinical Microbiology Laboratory. Albert Balows & Henry Isenberg. (Amer. Lec. Clinical Microbiology). (Illus.). 128p. 1978. 12.00 (ISBN 0-398-03806-6). C C Thomas.

Biproportional Matrices & Input Output Change. M. Bacharach. LC 77-75823. (Department of Applied Economics Monographs: No. 16). (Illus.). 1970. 29.50 (ISBN 0-521-07594-7). Cambridge U Pr.

Bircher-Benner Health Guide. Ruth Kunz-Bircher. Tr. by Rosemarie Shed from Fr. LC 80-93644. Orig. Title: Guide De Sante Bircher. 160p. 1980. pap. 3.95 (ISBN 0-912800-87-9). Woodbridge Pr.

Bird & Flower Emblems of the United States. Hilda Simon. LC 78-7324. (gr. 5). 1978. 7.95 (ISBN 0-396-07581-9). Dodd.

Bird & I. Fazil Husnu Daglarca. Ed. by Stanley H. Barkan. Tr. by Talat Sait Halman. (Cross-Cultural Review Chapbook 4). 16p. (Turkish & Eng.). 1980. pap. 2.00 (ISBN 0-89304-803-8). Cross Cult.

Bird Atlas of Natal. D. Cyrus & N. Robson. (Illus.). 320p. 1980. text ed. 37.50 (ISBN 0-86980-215-1). Verry.

Bird Book. Ed. by Richard Shaw. LC 74-81672. (Animal Art Anthology Ser). (Illus.). 48p. (gr. 3-6). 1974. PLB 4.95 o.p. (ISBN 0-7232-6107-5). Warne.

Bird Companions. Lilo Hess. (Illus.). 32p. (gr. 4-7). 1981. 9.95 (ISBN 0-684-16874-X). Scribner.

Bird Faunas of Africa & Its Islands. R. E. Moreau. 1967. 58.50 (ISBN 0-12-506650-3). Acad Pr.

Bird Guide: Land Birds East of the Rockies. Chester A. Reed. 5.95 (ISBN 0-385-04809-2). Doubleday.

Bird Has No Wings: The Letters of Peter Schwiefert. Ed. by Claude Lanzmann. Tr. by Barbara Lucas. (Illus.). 224p. 1976. 8.95 o.p. (ISBN 0-312-08085-9). St Martin.

Bird Identification Engagement Book, 1981. Mass. Audubon Society. (Desk Date Bk.). (Illus.). 1981. 9.95 (ISBN 0-8289-0384-0). Greene.

Bird in a Box. Mary Milo. 335p. (Orig.). 1980. pap. 2.50 (ISBN 0-345-28673-1). Ballantine.

Bird in a Cage: Edited from the Quarto of 1633 with Introduction and Notes. James Shirley. Ed. by Stephen Orgel. LC 79-3121. (Renaissance Drama Second Ser.). 220p. 1980. lib. bdg. 24.00 (ISBN 0-8240-4486-X). Garland Pub.

Bird Keeping. Jurgen Nicolai. Tr. by Petra Bleher from Ger. (Illus.). 96p. 1980. 2.95 (ISBN 0-87666-997-6, KW034). TFH Pubns.

Bird Man. Ian Strange. (Illus.). 1976. 12.95 o.p. (ISBN 0-86033-015-X). Gordon-Cremonesi.

Bird Mania. Ruth Radlauer & Ed Radlauer. LC 80-21833. (Mania Bks). (Illus.). 32p. (gr. k-4). 1981. PLB 7.95g (ISBN 0-516-07782-1, Elk Grove Bks). Childrens.

Bird Migration. Donald R. Griffin. LC 74-76321. (Illus.). 192p. 1974. pap. 3.00 (ISBN 0-486-20529-0). Dover.

Bird Migrations: Ecological & Physiological Factors. Ed. by B. E. Bykhovskii. Tr. by E. D. Gordon from Rus. 298p. 1974. 42.95 (ISBN 0-470-12890-9). Halsted Pr.

Bird Navigation. 3rd ed. G. V. Matthews. LC 68-23181. (Cambridge Monographs in Experimental Biology). (Illus.). 1968. 27.50 (ISBN 0-521-07271-9); pap. 10.50x (ISBN 0-521-09541-7). Cambridge U Pr.

Bird of Dawning. John Masefield. 1943. 4.95 o.s.i. (ISBN 0-02-580760-9). Macmillan.

Bird of Passage. Mai Zetterling. LC 76-13050. 1976. 7.95 o.p. (ISBN 0-312-08120-0). St Martin.

Bird Seed & Lightning. Norman Borisoff. LC 72-75125. (Mystery & Adventure Ser.). (gr. 2-4). 1973. PLB 6.75 (ISBN 0-87191-206-6). Creative Ed.

Bird Song & Bird Behavior. Donald J. Borror. 1971. pap. 4.50 booklet with record (ISBN 0-486-22779-0). Dover.

Bird Song: Biology of Vocal Communication & Expression Inbirds. W. H. Thorpe. (Cambridge Monographs in Experimental Biology Ser: No. 12). 25.95 (ISBN 0-521-06628-X). Cambridge U Pr.

Bird Sounds. Gerhard Thielcke. Tr. by John Drury from Ger. LC 73-80579. (Ann Arbor Science Library). (Illus.). 176p. 1976. 6.95 o.p. (ISBN 0-472-00121-3). U of Mich Pr.

Bird Spotting. John Holland. (Illus.). 292p. 1981. pap. 6.95 (ISBN 0-7137-1148-5, Pub. by Blandford Pr England). Sterling.

Bird Study. Boy Scouts Of America. LC 19-600. (Illus.). 64p. (gr. 6-12). 1967. pap. 0.70x (ISBN 0-8395-3282-2, 3282). BSA.

Bird Table Book in Colour. Tony Soper. LC 77-89367. (Illus.). 1978. 11.95 (ISBN 0-7153-7404-4). David & Charles.

Bird Talk. Roma Gans. LC 71-132298. (Let's-Read- and- Find-Out Science Bk). (Illus.). (gr. k-3). 1971. PLB 7.89 (ISBN 0-690-14593-4, TYC-J). T Y Crowell.

Bird Taxidermy. James M. Harrison. LC 76-50731. (Illus.). 1977. 11.95 (ISBN 0-7153-7372-2). David & Charles.

Bird: The Legend of Charlie Parker. Ed. by Robert G. Reisner. LC 74-30084. (Roots of Jazz Ser). (Illus.). 256p. 1975. lib. bdg. 22.50 (ISBN 0-306-70677-6); pap. 6.95 (ISBN 0-306-80069-1). Da Capo.

Bird Vocalizations: Their Relation to Current Problems in Biology & Psychology. Ed. by R. A. Hinde. (Illus.). 1969. 72.00 (ISBN 0-521-07409-6). Cambridge U Pr.

Bird Who Saved the Jungle. Jeremy Kingston. (Illus.). 1977. 7.95 (ISBN 0-571-10303-0, Pub. by Faber & Faber); pap. 2.45 (ISBN 0-571-11130-0). Merrimack Bk Serv.

Bird You Care for. Felicia Ames. Date not set. pap. 1.75 (ISBN 0-451-07527-7, E7527, Sig). NAL.

Birdicide of Cock Robin, & Other Murderous Words Ending in Cide. Sam Goldstein. (Illus.). 68p. (Orig.). 1981. pap. 3.95 (ISBN 0-938338-04-8). Winds World Pr.

Birdlife at Chincoteague & the Virginia Barrier Islands. 1981. 7.50x (ISBN 0-87033-257-0, Pub by Tidewater). Cornell Maritime.

Birds. John Andrews. (Hamlyn Nature Guide Ser.). (Illus.). 1978. 8.95 (ISBN 0-600-31413-8). Transatlantic.

Birds. Aristophanes. Ed. & tr. by Peter D. Arnott. Bd. with Brothers Menaechmus. Plautus. LC 58-12716. (Crofts Classics Ser.). 1958. pap. text ed. 2.95x (ISBN 0-88295-004-5). AHM Pub.

Birds. Aristophanes. Tr. by Gilbert Murray. 1950. pap. text ed. 3.95x (ISBN 0-04-882019-9). Allen Unwin.

Birds. Aristophanes. pap. 1.50 (ISBN 0-451-61671-5, M*W1671, Ment). NAL.

Birds. Dean Morris. LC 77-8302. (Read About Animals Ser.). (Illus.). (gr. k-3). 1977. PLB 9.95 (ISBN 0-8393-0006-9). Raintree Child.

Birds. Roger T. Peterson. LC 63-16281. (Life Nature Library). (Illus.). (gr. 5 up). 1968. PLB 8.97 o.p. (ISBN 0-8094-0624-1, Pub. by Time-Life). Silver.

Birds. Roger T. Peterson. (Young Readers Library). (Illus.). 1977. lib. bdg. 7.95 (ISBN 0-686-51085-2). Silver.

Birds. Jane Watson. (Illus.). 24p. (ps-4). 1958. PLB 5.00 (ISBN 0-307-60184-6, Golden Pr). Western Pub.

Birds. Herbert S. Zim & Ira N. Gabrielson. (Golden Guide Ser). (Illus.). 1956. PLB 9.15 (ISBN 0-307-63505-8, Golden Pr); pap. 1.95 (ISBN 0-307-24490-3). Western Pub.

Birds: A Picture Source Book. Don Rice. 160p. 1980. pap. 8.95 (ISBN 0-442-20395-0). Van Nos Reinhold.

Birds & Fools Fly. John Urmston. 13.50x (ISBN 0-392-06708-0, SpS). Soccer.

Birds & Marshes of the Chesapeake Bay Country: Including the Chincoteague Salt Marshes. Brooke Meanley. LC 75-17558. (Illus.). 168p. 1975. pap. 6.50 (ISBN 0-87033-207-4, Pub. by Tidewater). Cornell Maritime.

Birds & the Beasts Were There. Margaret Millar. LC 66-12002. (Illus.). 1971. 10.00 o.p. (ISBN 0-394-42289-9). Random.

Birds & Their Nests. Olive L. Earle. (Illus.). (gr. 5 up). 1952. PLB 6.00 o.p. (ISBN 0-688-31098-2). Morrow.

Birds & Trees of North America, 2 vols. Rex Brasher. Ed. by Lisa McGaw. (Illus.). 1962. Set. 115.00x o.p. (ISBN 0-87471-299-8). Rowman.

Birds Are in Your Hands. Paula Hendrich. (Illus.). 160p. (gr. 5 up). Date not set. 8.95 (ISBN 0-688-00417-2); PLB 8.59 (ISBN 0-688-00418-0). Morrow. Postponed.

Birds As Pets. Paul Villiard. LC 73-20722. 224p. (gr. 5-9). 1974. PLB 6.95 o.p. (ISBN 0-385-04337-6). Doubleday.

Birds, Baboons, & Barefoot Bears. Jane B. Monroe. LC 77-13025. (Creative Dramatics Ser.). (Illus.). (ps-3). 1978. PLB 5.50 (ISBN 0-89565-006-1); pap. 2.50 (ISBN 0-89565-039-8). Childs World.

Birds: Brain & Behavior. Ed. by Irving Goodman & Martin Schein. 1974. 31.00 o.s.i. (ISBN 0-12-290350-1). Acad Pr.

Bird's Bright Ring. Meena Alexander. 1976. 8.00 (ISBN 0-89253-811-2); flexible cloth 4.80 (ISBN 0-89253-812-0). Ind-US Inc.

Bird's Defense to the Ruy Lopez. Gene H. McCormick & Andy Soltis. LC 80-28210. (Illus.). 220p. 1981. lib. bdg. write for info. McFarland & Co.

Birds: East Coast Edition. Ed. by Little, Brown Editors. (Explorer's Notebooks). (Illus.). 32p. (Orig.). (gr. 5 up). 1981. pap. 1.95 (ISBN 0-316-52775-0). Little.

Birds Eat & Eat & Eat. Roma Gans. LC 63-9213. (Let's-Read-&-Find-Out Science Bk). (Illus.). (gr. k-3). 1963. bds. 7.95 (ISBN 0-690-14514-4, TYC-J); PLB 6.89 o.p. (ISBN 0-690-14515-2); filmstrip with record 11.95 (ISBN 0-690-14516-0); filmstrip with cassette 14.95 (ISBN 0-690-14518-7). T Y Crowell.

Birds' Eggs & Nesting Habits. Siegfried Hoeher. (Color Ser.). (Illus.). 1974. 9.95 (ISBN 0-7137-0609-0, Pub by Blandford Pr England). Sterling.

Birds Fall Down. Rebecca West. 1980. pap. 2.50 (ISBN 0-446-91189-5). Warner Bks.

Birds for Pets & Pleasure. Neale Haley. LC 80-68740. (Illus.). 224p. (gr. 8). 1981. PLB 8.44 (ISBN 0-440-00476-4); pap. 4.95 (ISBN 0-440-00475-6). Delacorte.

Birds: In Fact & Legend. Walter Harter. LC 79-65065. (Illus.). 1979. 6.95 (ISBN 0-8069-3740-8); lib. bdg. 6.69 (ISBN 0-8069-3741-6). Sterling.

Birds in Flight. John Kaufmann. (Illus.). (gr. 5-9). 1970. PLB 6.96 (ISBN 0-688-31100-8). Morrow.

Birds in Legend, Fable & Folklore. Ernest Ingersoll. LC 68-26576. 1968. Repr. of 1923 ed. 18.00 (ISBN 0-8103-3548-4). Gale.

Birds in the Sun. Malcolm MacDonald. (Illus.). 1962. 22.50 (ISBN 0-85493-077-9). Dufour.

Birds of Africa. John Karmali. LC 80-5359. (Illus.). 192p. 1980. 25.00 (ISBN 0-670-16810-6, Studio). Viking Pr.

Birds of America, 7 vols. John J. Audubon. (Illus.). Repr. of 1840 ed. Set. 56.00 (ISBN 0-8446-1567-6); 8.00 ea. Peter Smith.

Birds of America. John J. Audubon. (Illus.). (gr. 5 up). 1947. 24.95 (ISBN 0-02-504440-0). Macmillan.

Birds of America. T. Gilbert Pearson. 1936. 17.95 (ISBN 0-385-00024-3). Doubleday.

Birds of Australia. Michael Morcombe. (Encore Editions). (Illus.). 1977. 3.95 o.p. (ISBN 0-684-14991-5, ScribT). Scribner.

Birds of Britain & Europe. Dennis Avon & Tony Tilford. (Illus.). 1975. 11.95 (ISBN 0-7137-0762-3, Pub by Blandford Pr England). Sterling.

Birds of California. Arnold Small. 1974. 13.95 (ISBN 0-87691-119-X). Winchester Pr.

Birds of Canada. W. Earl Godfrey. Tr. by John A. Crosby. (Illus.). 1966. 27.50 (ISBN 0-660-00126-8, 56282-4, Pub. by Natl Mus Canada). U of Chicago Pr.

Birds of Denver & Mountain Parks. 2nd rev. ed. Robert J. Niedrach & Robert B. Rockwell. (Popular Ser.: No. 5). 1959. 3.95 (ISBN 0-916278-13-1); pap. 2.20 o.p. (ISBN 0-916278-12-3). Denver Mus Natl Hist.

Birds of Derbyshire. R. A. Frost. 182p. 1980. 30.00x (ISBN 0-903485-46-X, Pub. by Moorland England). State Mutual Bk.

Birds of Eastern North America: 1981. Mass. Audubon Society. (Wallcalendars Ser.). (Illus.). 1980. pap. 6.95 (ISBN 0-8289-0381-6). Greene.

Birds of Field & Forest. new ed. Time-Life Editors. (Wild, Wild World of Animals Ser.). (Illus.). 1977. 10.95 (ISBN 0-913948-13-6). Time-Life.

Birds of Field & Forest. Time-Life Television. LC 77-5596. (Wild World of Animals Ser.). (gr. 5 up). 1977. lib. bdg. 11.98 (ISBN 0-685-80980-3). Silver.

Birds of Man's World. Derek Goodwin. LC 77-74922. (Illus.). 190p. 1978. 12.50 (ISBN 0-8014-1167-X). Comstock.

Birds of North America: A Personal Selection. Eliot Porter. 1972. 19.95 o.p. (ISBN 0-525-06698-5). Dutton.

Birds of Passage. M. J. Piore. LC 78-12067. 1979. 21.50 (ISBN 0-521-22452-7). Cambridge U Pr.

Birds of Passage: Migrant Labor & Industrial Societies. Michael J. Piore. LC 78-12067. (Illus.). 192p. 1980. pap. 6.95 (ISBN 0-521-28058-3). Cambridge U Pr.

Birds of Prey. Wildlife Education, Ltd. (Zoobooks). (Illus.). 20p. (Orig.). 1980. pap. 1.00 (ISBN 0-937934-01-1). Wildlife Educ.

Birds of Prey of the World. Mary L. Grossman & John Hamlet. (Illus.). 500p. 1964. 25.00 (ISBN 0-517-52181-4). Crown.

Birds of Prey of the World: A Coloured Guide to Identification of All the Diurnal Species Order Falconiformes. Friedhelm Weick & Leslie Brown. (Illus.). 159p. (Orig.). 1980. 48.00 (ISBN 3-490-08518-3). Parey Sci Pubs.

Birds of Sea, Shore, & Stream. LC 76-15576. (Wild, Wild World of Animals). (Illus.). (gr. 5 up). 1976. lib. bdg. 11.97 (ISBN 0-685-77624-7, Pub by Time-Life). Silver.

Birds of the Air. Sandy Dengler. 1979. pap. 1.95 (ISBN 0-8024-0681-5). Moody.

Birds of the Carolinas. Eloise F. Potter et al. LC 79-14201. (Illus.). viii, 408p. 1980. 14.95 (ISBN 0-8078-1399-0). U of NC Pr.

Birds of the Labrador Peninsula. W. E. Clyde Todd. LC 80-66715. (Illus.). 1980. 70.00x (ISBN 0-931130-06-9). Buteo.

Birds of the Northern Seas. Ada Graham & Frank Graham. (Illus.). 96p. 1981. 8.95a (ISBN 0-385-12565-8); PLB (ISBN 0-385-12566-6). Doubleday.

Birds of the Republic of Panama, 3 pts. Alexander Wetmore. Incl. Part 1. Tinamidae (Tinamous) to Rynchopidae (Skimmers) (Illus.). 483p. 1965. 17.50x (ISBN 0-87474-063-0); Part 2. Columbidae (Pigeons) to Picidae (Woodpeckers) (Illus.). 605p. 20.00x (ISBN 0-87474-064-9); Part 3. Passeriformes: Dendrocolaptidae (Woodcreepers) to Oxyruncidae (Sharpbills) 631p. 1965. 20.00x (ISBN 0-87474-122-X). LC 66-61061. (Illus.). 1968. Smithsonian.

Birds of the Sea, Shore & Stream. (Wild, Wild World of Animals Ser). 1976. 10.95 (ISBN 0-913948-07-1). Time-Life.

Birds of the Southwest Pacific. Ernst Mayr. (Illus.). 1968. pap. 16.80 (ISBN 3-7682-0533-9). Lubrecht & Cramer.

Birds of the Southwestern Desert. Gusse T. Smith. LC 56-2505. (Illus.). Date not set. pap. 5.95 (ISBN 0-9603270-0-2). Doubleshoe.

Birds of the West African Town & Garden. John H. Elgood. Ed. by H. Savory. LC 62-4439. (West African Nature Handbooks Ser). (Illus.). 1968. 5.00x (ISBN 0-582-60850-3). Intl Pubns Serv.

Birds of the West Coast, Vol. 2. J. F. Lansdowne. 1980. 40.00 (ISBN 0-395-29546-7). HM.

Birds of the World: A Checklist. rev. ed. James F. Clements. LC 75-29874. 1978. Repr. of 1975 ed. 15.00 (ISBN 0-8467-0123-5, Pub. by Two Continents). Hippocrene Bks.

Birds of Western North America: 1981. Mass. Audubon Society. (Wallcalendars Ser.). (Illus.). 1980. pap. 6.95 (ISBN 0-8289-0382-4). Greene.

Birds of Wisconsin. Owen J. Gromme. (Illus.). 1963. 37.50 (ISBN 0-299-03001-6). U of Wis Pr.

Birds-Poems, Prints & Projects. Victoria S. Morris. (Orig.). 1980. pap. 4.50 (ISBN 0-914318-13-6). V S Morris.

Birds: Readings from Scientific American. Intro. by Barry W. Wilson. LC 79-26134. (Illus.). 1980. text ed. 19.95x (ISBN 0-7167-1206-7); pap. 9.95x (ISBN 0-7167-1207-5). W H Freeman.

Birds: West Coast Edition. Ed. by Little, Brown Editors. (Explorer's Notebooks). (Illus.). 32p. (Orig.). (gr. 5 up). 1981. pap. 1.95 (ISBN 0-316-52776-9). Little.

Birds with Human Souls: A Guide to Bird Symbolism. Beryl Rowland. LC 77-4230. (Illus.). 1978. 15.00x (ISBN 0-87049-215-2). U of Tenn Pr.

Birdseye View of Language Arts: Worksheets in Spelling & Phonics, Word Structure, Word Meaning, Grammar & Usage. Beverly Cory. (Makemaster Bk.). (gr. 6-9). 1977. pap. 12.95 (ISBN 0-8224-0701-9). Pitman Learning.

Birdwatcher's Guide to Wildlife Sanctuaries. Jessie Kitching. LC 76-5388. 1976. 8.95 (ISBN 0-668-03949-3). Arco.

Birdwatching in Canada. David Stirling & Jim Woodford. 127p. 1975. pap. text ed. write for info. (ISBN 0-919654-28-2). Hancock Hse.

Birdy. William Wharton. 1979. pap. 2.50 (ISBN 0-380-47282-1, 47282). Avon.

Birmingham Counterfeit; or, Invisible Spectator, 1772, 2 vols. in 1. Ed. by Michael F. Shugrue. LC 74-16027. (Flowering of the Novel, 1740-1775 Ser: Vol. 98). 1974. lib. bdg. 50.00 (ISBN 0-8240-1197-X). Garland Pub.

Birth. Uwe Ahrens et al. LC 77-2603. (Illus.). 176p. 1981. pap. 9.95 (ISBN 0-06-090867-X, CN 867, CN). Har-Row.

Birth. Jean C. Lipke. LC 71-104891. (Being Together Books). (Illus.). (gr. 5-11). 1971. PLB 4.95 o.p. (ISBN 0-8225-0596-7). Lerner Pubns.

Birth & Death of Meaning. 2nd ed. Ernest Becker. LC 62-15359. 1971. 9.95 (ISBN 0-02-902170-7); pap. 5.95 (ISBN 0-02-902190-1). Free Pr.

Birth & Development of Ornament. F. Edward Hulme. LC 79-78173. (Illus.). xii, 340p. 1974. Repr. of 1893 ed. 21.00 (ISBN 0-8103-4026-7). Gale.

Birth & Fortune: The Impact of Numbers on Personal Welfare. Richard A. Easterlin. LC 79-56369. 205p. 1980. 11.95 (ISBN 0-465-00688-4). Basic.

Birth & Growth of Religion. George F. Moore. 188p. Repr. of 1927 ed. 2.95 (ISBN 0-567-02199-8). Attic Pr.

Birth Control. Tarvez Tucker. 1981. pap. 2.50 (ISBN 0-440-00566-3). Dell.

Birth Control & Controlling Birth: Women-Centered Perspectives. Helen B. Holmes et al. LC 80-82173. (Contempory Issues in Biomedicine, Ethics, & Society Ser.). 352p. 1980. 14.95 (ISBN 0-89603-022-9); pap. 7.95 (ISBN 0-89603-023-7). Humana.

Birth Control Book. Howard Shapiro. 1977. 10.00 o.p. (ISBN 0-312-08172-3). St Martin.

Birth Control Laws. M. W. Dennett. LC 70-119053. (Civil Liberties in American History Ser). 29.50 (ISBN 0-306-71942-8). Da Capo.

Birth Control Today: A Practical Approach to Intelligent Family Planning. Leon F. Whitney. (Illus.). 1962. pap. 0.95 o.s.i. (ISBN 0-02-078350-7, Collier). Macmillan.

Birth Defects & Fetal Development: Endocrine & Metabolic Factors. Kamran S. Moghissi. (Illus.). 352p. 1974. text ed. 32.75 (ISBN 0-398-02784-6). C C Thomas.

Birth Defects Compendium. 2nd ed. Ed. by Daniel Bergsma. LC 78-20651. 1222p. 1979. 50.00x (ISBN 0-8451-0203-6). A R Liss.

Birth in Four Cultures: A Cross-Cultural Investigation of Childbirth in Yucatan, Holland, Sweden & the United States. Brigitte Jordan. (Illus.). 1978. 14.95 o.p. (ISBN 0-88831-024-2). EPWP.

Birth in Four Cultures: A Cross-Cultural Investigation of Childbirth in Yucatan, Holland, Sweden & the United States. 2nd ed. Brigitte Jordan. (Illus.). 128p. 1980. pap. 6.95 (ISBN 0-920792-05-7). EPWP.

Birth of a Dilettante. Conda L. McConnaughhay. 1980. 7.95 (ISBN 0-533-04546-0). Vantage.

Birth of a Family. Clair Isbister. LC 78-52878. (Illus.). 1978. 8.95 o.p. (ISBN 0-8015-0653-0). Dutton.

Birth of a Kingdom: Studies in I & II Samuel & I Kings I-II. John J. Davis. pap. 4.95 (ISBN 0-88469-053-9). BMH Bks.

Birth of a Kingdom: Studies in One & Two Samuel & One Kings. John J. Davis. 1970. pap. 3.95 o.p. (ISBN 0-8010-2803-5). Baker Bk.

Birth of a New Physics. I. Bernard Cohen. LC 60-5918. 1960. pap. 2.50 (ISBN 0-385-09447-7, S10, Anch). Doubleday.

Birth of a New Physics. I. Bernard Cohen. LC 78-25792. (Illus.). 200p. 1981. Repr. of 1960 ed. lib. bdg. 19.75x (ISBN 0-313-20773-9, COBN). Greenwood.

Birth of a Plural Society: The Development of Northern Rhodesia Under the British South African Company. Lewis H. Gann. 1958. text ed. 18.00x (ISBN 0-685-12359-6). Humanities.

Birth of a Reformation: Life & Labours of D. S. Warner. A. L. Byers. (Illus.). 496p. Repr. 5.50. Faith Pub Hse.

Birth of a Transfer Society. Terry L. Anderson & Peter J. Hill. 130p. (Orig.). 1980. pap. 6.95 (ISBN 0-8179-7292-7). Hoover Inst Pr.

Birth of Christ. H. P. Lidden & J. Orr. Date not set. 13.95 (ISBN 0-86524-058-2). Klock & Klock.

Birth of Communist China. C. P. Fitzgerald. 1978. pap. 2.95 o.p. (ISBN 0-14-020694-9, Pelican). Penguin.

Birth of Forestry in America. Carl A. Schenck. LC 74-84457. 1974. 10.95 (ISBN 0-89030-001-1); pap. 4.50 (ISBN 0-89030-002-X). Appalach Consortium.

Birth of Greek Art. Pierre Demargne. LC 64-21312. (Arts of Mankind Ser). 30.00 o.s.i. (ISBN 0-8076-0502-6). Braziller.

Birth of Israel: The Drama As I Saw It. Jorge Garcia-Granados. (Return to Zion Ser.). viii, 291p. 1980. Repr. of 1948 ed. lib. bdg. 20.00x (ISBN 0-87991-141-7). Porcupine Pr.

Birth of Modern America, 1820-1850. Douglas T. Miller. LC 79-114173. (Illus.). 1970. pap. 7.50 (ISBN 0-672-63509-7). Pegasus.

Birth of Moses. Ed. by Catherine Chase. LC 78-73540. (Illus.). (gr. k-5). Date not set. price not set (ISBN 0-89799-151-6); pap. price not set (ISBN 0-89799-069-2). Dandelion Pr. Postponed.

Birth of Nations. Phillip C. Jessup. LC 73-15515. (Illus.). 1974. 17.50x (ISBN 0-231-03721-X). Columbia U Pr.

Birth of Popular Heresy. Ed. by R. I. Moore. LC 75-32934. (Documents of Medieval History Ser.). 176p. 1976. text ed. 22.95 (ISBN 0-312-08190-1). St Martin.

Birth of Sunset's Kittens. Carla Stevens. LC 69-14569. (Illus.). (gr. k-5). 1969. PLB 7.95 (ISBN 0-685-21698-5, A-W Childrens). A-W.

Birth of the Baha'i Faith. Debbie D. Wittman. (Illus., Orig.). (gr. 5-9). 1980. pap. 1.00 (ISBN 0-87743-146-9, 7-52-55). Baha'i.

Birth of the Body. Ray Stedman. 1975. pap. 2.95 o.p. (ISBN 0-88449-013-0). Vision Hse.

Birth of the English Common Law. R. C. Van Caenegem. LC 72-89812. 150p. 1973. 26.95 (ISBN 0-521-20097-0). Cambridge U Pr.

Birth of the King. Alice Schrage. LC 80-53874. 128p. 1981. pap. 1.95 (ISBN 0-8307-0765-4). Regal.

Birth of the Living God: A Psychoanalytic Study. Ana-Maria Rizzuto. LC 78-10475. (Illus.). 1979. 15.00x (ISBN 0-226-72100-0); pap. 6.50 (ISBN 0-226-72102-7). U of Chicago Pr.

Birth of the Living God: A Psychoanalytic Study. Ana-Maria Rizzuto. LC 78-10475. x, 246p. 1981. pap. 6.50 (ISBN 0-226-72102-7). U of Chicago Pr.

Birth of the Middle Ages, Three Ninety-Five to Eight Fourteen. Henry S. Moss. LC 80-24038. (Illus.). xvi, 291p. 1980. Repr. of 1964 ed. lib. bdg. 29.75x (ISBN 0-313-22708-X, MOBM). Greenwood.

Birth of the New Physics. I. Bernard Cohen. LC 78-25792. (Illus.). 200p. 1981. Repr. of 1960 ed. lib. bdg. 19.75x (ISBN 0-313-20773-9, COBN). Greenwood.

Birth of Writing. Robert Clarborne. LC 74-83646. (Emergence of Man Ser.). (gr. 6 up). 1974. PLB 11.49 o.p. (ISBN 0-8094-1282-9, Pub. by Time-Life). Silver.

Birth Order & Life Roles. Lucille K. Forer. 184p. 1969. pap. 14.75 photocopy ed. spiral (ISBN 0-398-00596-6). C C Thomas.

Birth Report. Sylvia Close. 356p. 1980. pap. text ed. 16.50x (ISBN 0-85633-191-0, NFER). Humanities.

Birthday Book. Jane Ike. (ps-1). 1975. PLB 4.60 o.p. (ISBN 0-307-68963-8, Golden Pr). Western Pub.

Birthday Book for Children. Kate Greenaway. (Illus.). (gr. 3-6). 1880. 6.95 (ISBN 0-7232-0216-8); lea. 9.95 (ISBN 0-7232-0217-6). Warne.

Birthday Box of Dreams. Monika Beisner. LC 74-18130. (Picture Bk). (Illus.). 32p. (ps-1). 1975. 4.95 o.s.i. (ISBN 0-695-80532-0); PLB 4.98 o.s.i. (ISBN 0-695-40532-2). Follett.

Birthday Candles Burning Bright. Sara Brewton & John E. Brewton. (Illus.). (gr. 4-6). 1960. 4.95g o.s.i. (ISBN 0-02-712560-2). Macmillan.

Birthday Goat. Nancy D. Watson. LC 73-3389. (Illus.). 40p. (ps-3). 1974. 6.95 (ISBN 0-690-00145-2, TYC-J); PLB 6.79 (ISBN 0-690-00146-0). T Y Crowell.

Birthday in Texas. C. Richard King. LC 80-11751. (Illus.). 64p. (gr. 3-6). 1980. 6.95 (ISBN 0-88319-051-6). Shoal Creek Pub.

Birthday Murderer. Jay Bennett. (YA) 1980. pap. 1.50 (ISBN 0-440-90576-1, LFL). Dell.

Birthday Murderer. Jay Bennett. LC 76-47239. (YA) 1977. 7.95 (ISBN 0-440-00584-1). Delacorte.

Birthday of the Infanta. Janet Lewis. 1980. s & l, wrappers 25.00 (ISBN 0-936576-03-0). Symposium Pr.

Birthday Trombone. Margaret A. Hartelius. (ps-1). 1977. PLB 5.95 (ISBN 0-385-12293-4). Doubleday.

Birthmark. Inez Wright. 7.50 o.p. (ISBN 0-8062-1231-4). Carlton.

Birthplace of an Army: A Study of the Valley Forge Encampment. John B. Trussell, Jr. LC 77-621150. 1976. 6.50 (ISBN 0-911124-88-8); pap. 4.00 (ISBN 0-911124-87-X). Pa Hist & Mus.

Birthplace Tables of Houses. Walter A. Koch & Elisabeth Schaeck. LC 75-22416. 1975. 12.00 (ISBN 0-88231-020-8); pap. text ed. 8.95 (ISBN 0-88231-021-6). ASI Pubs Inc.

Birthpyre. Larry Brand. 288p. (Orig.). 1980. pap. 2.25 (ISBN 0-380-76539-X, 76539). Avon.

Birthright. Phillip Finch. 1981. pap. 2.75 (ISBN 0-425-04590-0). Berkley Pub.

Birthrights. Richard Farson. LC 73-6487. 228p. 1974. 6.95 o.s.i. (ISBN 0-02-537170-3). Macmillan.

Bisbee Anthology Nineteen Eighty: Poetry. Ed. by Bisbee Press Collective. 62p. (Orig.). 1980. pap. 5.00 (ISBN 0-938196-00-6). Bisbee Pr.

Bisected Brain. Michael S. Gazzaniga. LC 77-105426. 172p. 1970. 18.50 (ISBN 0-306-50040-X, Plenum Pr). Plenum Pub.

Bisexual Female. (Illus.). 4.95 (ISBN 0-910550-29-8). Centurion Pr.

Bisexual Male. (Illus.). 4.95 (ISBN 0-910550-30-1). Centurion Pr.

Bisha of Burundi. Mary L. Clifford. LC 72-83780. (Illus.). 160p. (gr. 5 up). 1973. 7.95 o.p. (ISBN 0-690-14596-9, TYC-J). T Y Crowell.

Bishop & Chapter: The Governance of the Bishopric of Speyer to 1552. Lawrence G. Duggan. 1978. 22.00 (ISBN 0-8135-0857-6). Rutgers U Pr.

Bishop As Pawn: A Father Dowling Mystery. Ralph McInerny. LC 78-54978. (Father Dowling Ser.). 1978. 8.95 (ISBN 0-8149-0806-3). Vanguard.

Bishop Butler's Three Sermons Upon Human Nature. T. B. Kilpatrick. (Handbooks for Bible Classes Ser.). 123p. 1949. text ed. 3.50 (ISBN 0-567-08142-7). Attic Pr.

Bishop Endings. Yuri Averbakh. 1977. 18.95 (ISBN 0-7134-0096-X). David & Charles.

Bishop Percy's Folio Manuscript Ballards & Romances, 3 vols. Bishop Percy. Ed. by John W. Hales et al. LC 67-23962. 1866p. 1968. Repr. of 1868 ed. 110.00 (ISBN 0-8103-3409-7). Gale.

Bishop V. Knight Endings. Yuri Averbakh. 1977. 18.95 (ISBN 0-7134-3179-2). David & Charles.

Bishop Whipple's Southern Diary. Bishop Whipple. Ed. by Lester B. Shippee. LC 68-13637. (American Scene Ser). (Illus.). 1969. lib. bdg. 25.00 (ISBN 0-306-70987-2). Da Capo.

Bishops by Ballot: An Eighteenth-Century Ecclesiastical Revolution. Frederick V. Mills, Sr. 1978. 16.95 (ISBN 0-19-502411-7). Oxford U Pr.

Bishop's Confession. Jim Bishop. 448p. 1981. 14.95 (ISBN 0-316-09669-5). Little.

Bishop's Pawn, No. 4. Ritchie Perry. 192p. 1981. pap. 2.25 (ISBN 0-345-28971-4). Ballantine.

Bismarck. Martin Booth et al. Ed. by Martin Yapp & Margaret Killingray. (Greenhaven World History Ser.). (Illus.). 32p. (gr. 10). 1980. lib. bdg. 5.95 (ISBN 0-89908-048-0); pap. text ed. 1.95 (ISBN 0-89908-023-5). Greenhaven.

Bismarck. C. Grant Robertson. LC 68-9604. 1969. Repr. of 1918 ed. 21.00 (ISBN 0-86527-008-2). Fertig.

Bismarck & Europe. W. N. Medlicott & D. Coveney. 1972. 18.95 (ISBN 0-312-08225-8). St Martin.

Bismarck & His Times. George O. Kent. LC 78-2547. 192p. 1978. 12.50x (ISBN 0-8093-0858-4); pap. 5.95 (ISBN 0-8093-0859-2). S Ill U Pr.

Bismarck & Mangan: A Pictorial History. Nancy E. Hanson. (Illus.). 205p. 1981. pap. price not set (ISBN 0-89865-094-1). Donning Co.

Bismarck & State Socialism. William H. Dawson. 8.50 (ISBN 0-86527-009-0). Fertig.

Bismarck & the French Nation: 1848-1890. Allan Mitchell. LC 72-167692. 1971. 24.50x (ISBN 0-672-53510-6). Irvington.

Bismarck at the Crossroads: The Reorientation of German Foreign Policy After the Congress of Berlin 1878-1880. Bruce Waller. (University of London Historical Studies: No. 35). 273p. 1974. text ed. 32.50x (ISBN 0-485-13135-8, Athlone Pr). Humanities.

Bismarck's Diplomacy at Its Zenith. Joseph V. Fuller. 1922. 19.50 (ISBN 0-86527-011-2). Fertig.

Bisto Book of Meat Cookery. Sonia Allison. LC 80-66429. (Illus.). 128p. 1980. 14.95 (ISBN 0-7153-7893-7). David & Charles.

Bistro Style Cookery. Michael Raffael. 1978. 14.95 (ISBN 0-7198-2634-9, Northwood Pub.). CBI Pub.

Bit by Bit. Diana R. Tuke. (Illus.). 13.85 (ISBN 0-85131-033-8). J A Allen.

Bit of Christmas Whimsy. David Edman. LC 74-6474. (Illus.). 160p. 1971. 6.95 (ISBN 0-570-03234-2, 15-2128). Concordia.

Bit of Wit. Laurel Speer. (Gusto Press Poetry Discovery Ser.). (Orig.). 1979. pap. 4.95 (ISBN 0-933906-04-8). Gusto Pr.

Bit O'writin' & Other Tales. John Banim & Michael Banim. Ed. by Robert L. Wolff. (Ireland Nineteenth Century Fiction Ser. Two: Vol. 24). 928p. 1979. lib. bdg. 32.00 (ISBN 0-8240-3473-2). Garland Pub.

Bite of the Apple. Molly Perkins. 1981. 10.95. Riverrun NY.

Biting off the Bracelet: A Study of Children in Hospitals. Ann H. Beuf. LC 79-5047. 1979. 10.95 (ISBN 0-8122-7766-X). U of Pa Pr.

Bits & Bitting. British Horse Society & Pony Club. LC 76-55354. 1976. pap. 1.50 (ISBN 0-8120-0759-X). Barron.

Bits & Pieces. Frances L. Brandon. 4.00 o.p. (ISBN 0-8062-0545-8). Carlton.

Bits & Pieces. Blaise W. Liffick. (Orig.). 1980. pap. 8.95 (ISBN 0-07-037828-2, BYTE Bks). McGraw.

Bits of Faith & Love & Fun. Mary Jane Meyer. 1977. 4.50 o.p. (ISBN 0-682-48975-1). Exposition.

Bitter Cry of Outcast London. Andrew Mearns et al. Ed. by Anthony S. Wohl. (Victorian Library). 1970. Repr. of 1883 ed. text ed. 8.00x (ISBN 0-7185-5003-X, Leicester). Humanities.

Bitter Grass. Theodore V. Olson. 1980. pap. write for info. (ISBN 0-671-83541-6). PB.

Bitter Harvest: A History of California Farmworkers, 1879-1941. Cletus E. Daniel. LC 80-25664. 368p. 1981. 19.50x (ISBN 0-8014-1284-6). Cornell U Pr.

Bitter Harvest: The Odyssey of a Teacher. Constance Melaro. 1965. 8.95 (ISBN 0-8392-1148-1). Astor-Honor.

Bitter Pill: Doctors, Patients & Failed Expectations. Martin R. Lipp. LC 79-1673. 288p. 1980. 10.95 (ISBN 0-06-012649-3, HarpT). Har-Row.

Bitter Pills. David Mason & Fran Dyller. 224p. 1977. 10.00 (ISBN 0-8065-0531-1). Citadel Pr.

Bitter Root: The Pursuit of Freedom by a Man. Oliver M. Salisbury. (Illus.). 275p. 1980. pap. 8.95 (ISBN 0-87564-825-8). Superior Pub.

Bitter Victory: A History of Black Soldiers in World War I. Florette Henri & Richard Stillman. 1970. 4.95 o.p. (ISBN 0-385-05193-X); pap. 2.50 o.p. (ISBN 0-385-05194-8). Doubleday.

Bitter Winds of Love, No. 76. Barbara Cartland. 1978. pap. 1.50 o.s.i. (ISBN 0-515-04544-6). Jove Pubns.

Bittersweet. Susan Strasberg. (Illus.). 1981. pap. 3.50 (ISBN 0-451-09760-2, E9760, Sig). NAL.

Bittersweet: Surviving & Growing from Loneliness. Terri Schultz. LC 76-9797. 1976. 8.95 o.p. (ISBN 0-690-01180-6, TYC-T). T Y Crowell.

Bituminization of Radioactive Wastes. (Technical Reports Ser.: No. 116). (Illus., Orig.). 1970. pap. 8.25 (ISBN 92-0-125370-2, IAEA). Unipub.

Bituminous Coal in Texas. T. J. Evans. (Illus.). 65p. 1974. 2.00 (HB 4). Bur Econ Geology.

Bix: Man & Legend. Richard M. Sudhalter & Philip R. Evans. (Illus.). 1975. pap. 5.95 (ISBN 0-02-872500-X). Schirmer Bks.

Bizarre & Ornamental Alphabets. Carol B. Grafton. (Illus.). 128p. (Orig.). 1981. pap. price not set (ISBN 0-486-24105-X). Dover.

Bizarre Classix, Vol. 3. LC 76-41610. (Illus.). pap. 6.50 (ISBN 0-914646-21-4). Belier Pr.

Bizarre Comix. Incl. Vol. 2. LC 75-21507. pap. o.p. (ISBN 0-914646-03-6); Vol. 3. LC 75-45829. pap. 5.00 o.p. (ISBN 0-914646-04-4); Vol. 4. LC 75-45822. pap. 5.00 o.p. (ISBN 0-914646-05-2); Vol. 5. LC 76-22873. pap. 6.00 o.p. (ISBN 0-914646-07-9); Vol. 6. LC 76-22874. pap. 6.00 o.p. (ISBN 0-914646-08-7). (Illus.). 1976. Belier Pr.

Bizarre Imagery of Yoshitoshi: The Herbert R. Cole Collection. Roger Keyes & George Kuwayama. LC 80-15938. (Illus.). 112p. (Orig.). 1980. pap. 10.00 (ISBN 0-87587-096-1). La Co Art Mus.

Bizarre Photos, Vol. 4. pap. 7.00 (ISBN 0-914646-34-6). Belier Pr.

Bizarre Plants: Magical, Monstrous, Mythical. William A. Emboden. LC 73-2749. (Illus.). 160p. 1974. 10.95 o.s.i. (ISBN 0-02-535460-4). Macmillan.

Bjorn Borg. Gary Libman. (Sports Superstars Ser.). (Illus.). (gr. 3-9). 1979. PLB 5.95 (ISBN 0-87191-721-1); pap. 2.95 (ISBN 0-89812-161-2). Creative Ed.

Black Academic Libraries & Research Collections: An Historical Survey. Jessie C. Smith. LC 77-71857. (Contributions in Afro-American & African Studies: No. 34). 1977. lib. bdg. 16.95 (ISBN 0-8371-9546-2, SBA/). Greenwood.

Black Administrators in Higher Education: Conditions & Perceptions. Robert L. Hoskins. LC 78-19740. 1978. 24.95 (ISBN 0-03-046611-3). Praeger.

Black Aesthetic. Ed. by Addison Gayle, Jr. LC 71-123692. 1972. pap. 3.50 o.p. (ISBN 0-385-06951-0, Anch). Doubleday.

Black Africa. Donald G. Morrison et al. LC 72-143505. 1972. 45.00 (ISBN 0-02-921450-5). Free Pr.

Black African Empires. Joan Joseph. LC 73-14555. (First Bks). (Illus.). 72p. (gr. 5-7). 1974. PLB 4.90 o.p. (ISBN 0-531-00811-8). Watts.

Black African Literature in English: A Guide to Information Sources. Ed. by Bernth Lindfors. LC 73-16983. (American Literature, English Literature, & World Literatures in English Information Guide Ser.: Vol. 23). 1979. 30.00 (ISBN 0-8103-1206-9). Gale.

Black Aged in the United States: An Annotated Bibliography. Lenwood G. Davis. LC 80-1193. xviii, 200p. 1980. lib. bdg. 22.50 (ISBN 0-313-22560-5, DAB/). Greenwood.

Black America & International Issues. Ronald Walters. 1981. 12.95 (ISBN 0-933184-04-2); pap. 6.95 (ISBN 0-933184-05-0). Flame Intl.

Black American Fiction: A Bibliography. Carol Fairbanks & Eugene A. Engeldinger. LC 78-1351. 1978. 18.00 (ISBN 0-8108-1120-0). Scarecrow.

Black American in Books for Children: Readings in Racism. Donnarae MacCann & Gloria Woodard. LC 72-4490. 1972. 10.00 (ISBN 0-8108-0526-X). Scarecrow.

Black American in United States History. new ed. Edgar A. Toppin. (gr. 9-12). 1973. text ed. 12.20 (ISBN 0-205-03303-2, 7833032); tchrs.' guide 4.12 (ISBN 0-205-03304-0, 7833040). Allyn.

Black American Literature: A Critical History. Roger Whitlow. LC 73-75525. 1973. 14.95x (ISBN 0-88229-100-9). Nelson-Hall.

Black American Literature & Humanism. Ed. by Ronald B. Miller. LC 80-5179. 122p. 1981. price not set (ISBN 0-8131-1436-5). U Pr of Ky.

Black American Literature: Essays, Poetry, Fiction, Drama. Darwin T. Turner. 1970. pap. text ed. 12.95x (ISBN 0-675-09278-7). Merrill.

Black American Literature: 1760 to the Present. Ruth Miller. 1971. pap. text ed. 12.95x (ISBN 0-02-476420-5, 47642). Macmillan.

Black American Playwrights, Eighteen Hundred to the Present: A Bibliography. Esther S. Arata & Nicholas J. Rotoli. LC 76-2376. 302p. 1976. 14.50 (ISBN 0-8108-0912-5). Scarecrow.

Black American Short Story in the 20th Century: A Collection of Critical Essays. Ed. by Peter Bruck. 1977. pap. text ed. 25.25x (ISBN 90-6032-085-9). Humanities.

Black American Writers: Bibliographic Essays, 2 vols. Ed. by M. Thomas Inge et al. LC 75-38033. 200p. 1978. text ed. 15.95 ea.; Vol. 1. text ed. (ISBN 0-312-08260-6); Vol. 2. (ISBN 0-312-08295-9). St Martin.

Black American Writers Past & Present: A Biographical & Bibliographical Dictionary, 2 vols. Theressa G. Rush et al. LC 74-28400. 1975. Set. 35.00 (ISBN 0-8108-0785-8). Scarecrow.

Black Americans. 2nd ed. Alphonse Pinkney. (Ethnic Groups in American Life Ser.). (Illus.). 272p. 1975. text ed. 8.95 o.p. (ISBN 0-13-077537-1); pap. text ed. 7.95x (ISBN 0-13-077529-0). P-H.

Black Americans in the Roosevelt Era: Liberalism & Race. John B. Kirby. LC 79-10315. (Twentieth Century America Ser.). 1980. 14.50x (ISBN 0-87049-279-9). U of Tenn Pr.

Black Americans in World War II. A. Russell Buchanan. LC 76-53577. 149p. 1977. pap. 6.95 (ISBN 0-87436-277-6). ABC-Clio.

Black & White & Said All Over: Riddles. Catherine H. Ainsworth. LC 78-54873. (Folklore Bks.). 36p. 1980. 2.00 (ISBN 0-933190-02-6). Clyde Pr.

Black & White Identity Formation. rev. ed. Stuart T. Hauser & E. Kasendorf. 1981. write for info. (ISBN 0-89874-055-X). Krieger.

Black & White Mixed Marriages. Ernest Porterfield. LC 77-87996. 1978. 15.95 (ISBN 0-88229-131-9); pap. 7.95 (ISBN 0-88229-484-9). Nelson-Hall.

Black Armed Forces Officers, 1736-1971: A Documented Pictorial History. Jesse J. Johnson. LC 75-178014. (Illus.). 170p. 8.95 (ISBN 0-915044-10-2). Carver Pub.

Black Arrow. Robert L. Stevenson. (Childrens Illustrated Classics Ser). (Illus.). 1967. Repr. of 1957 ed. 9.00x o.p. (ISBN 0-460-05040-0, Pub. by J. M. Dent England). Biblio Dist.

Black Art: A Bibliography. National Art Education Association. 1970. pap. 1.00 (ISBN 0-686-00140-0, 061-02180). Natl Art Ed.

Black Artists of the New Generation. Elton C. Fax. LC 77-7053. (Illus.). 1977. 9.95 (ISBN 0-396-07434-0). Dodd.

Black As He's Painted. Ngaio Marsh. (Mystery Ser.). 224p. 1981. pap. 2.25 (ISBN 0-515-05871-8). Jove Pubns.

Black As I Am. Z. Mandela. LC 77-87417. (Illus.). 1978. pap. 5.95 (ISBN 0-89615-001-1). Guild of Tutors.

Black Athlete: His Story in American History. Jack Orr. (gr. 6 up). 1969. PLB 8.95 (ISBN 0-87460-104-5). Lion.

Black Authors & Education: An Annotated Bibliography of Books. James E. Newby. LC 79-9677. 113p. 1980. text ed. 15.00 (ISBN 0-8191-0974-6); pap. text ed. 7.50 (ISBN 0-8191-0975-4). U Pr of Amer.

Black Awakening in Capitalist America: An Analytic History. Robert L. Allen. LC 69-20059. pap. 3.50 (ISBN 0-385-07718-1, Anch). Doubleday.

Black Awareness: A Theology of Hope. Major J. Jones. (Orig.). 1971. pap. 5,95 o.p. (ISBN 0-687-03585-6). Abingdon.

Black B C's. Lucille Clifton. (Illus.). (ps-4). 1970. 5.95 o.p. (ISBN 0-525-26596-1). Dutton.

Black Ballots: Voting Rights in the South 1944-1969. Steven F. Lawson. LC 76-18886. (Contemporary American History Ser.). 1976. 25.00x (ISBN 0-231-03978-6); pap. 10.00x (ISBN 0-231-08352-1). Columbia U Pr.

Black Baptist Secondary Schools in Virginia, 1887-1957: A Study in Black History. Lester F. Russell. LC 80-22414. 218p. 1981. 12.50 (ISBN 0-8108-1373-4). Scarecrow.

Black Battlefleet. G. A. Ballard. 264p. 1980. 66.00x (ISBN 0-245-53030-4, Pub. by Nautical England). State Mutual Bk.

Black Battlefleet: Early Ironclads of the Royal Navy. G. A. Ballard. LC 79-49435. (Illus.). 245p. 1980. 38.95 (ISBN 0-87021-924-3). Naval Inst Pr.

Black Bear. Barbara Ford. (gr. 7 up). 1981. 8.95 (ISBN 0-395-30444-X). HM.

Black Bear. Voight. Orig. Title: Red Blade & the Black Bear. (gr. 5-6). 1979. pap. 1.25 (ISBN 0-590-31259-6, Schol Pap). Schol Bk Serv.

Black Bear Baby. Berniece Freschet. (See & Read Book). (Illus.). 48p. (gr. 6-9). 1981. PLB 6.99 (ISBN 0-399-61151-7). Putnam.

Black Beauty. (Illustrated Junior Library). (Illus.). 304p. 1981. pap. 4.95 (ISBN 0-448-11007-5). G&D.

Black Beauty. Anna Sewell. (Illus.). (gr. 3-6). 1962. 3.95g o.s.i. (ISBN 0-02-782070-X). Macmillan.

Black Beauty. Anna Sewell. Ed. by Eleanor G. Vance. (Illus.). (gr. k-3). 1949. 3.95 (ISBN 0-394-80637-9, BYR); PLB 4.99 (ISBN 0-394-90637-3). Random.

Black Beauty. Anna Sewell. LC 78-3823. (Raintree's Illustrated Classics). (Illus.). (gr. 5-8). 1978. PLB 9.65 (ISBN 0-8393-6209-9). Raintree Child.

Black Beauty's Clan. Josephine Pullein-Thompson et al. (Illus.). 288p. (gr. 7-9). 1980. 7.95 (ISBN 0-07-050913-1). McGraw.

Black Beauty's Family. Josephine Pullein-Thompson et al. (Illus.). 288p. (gr. 7-9). 1980. 7.95 (ISBN 0-07-050914-X). McGraw.

Black Belt Judo, Karate & Jujitsu: Advanced Techniques. 2nd, rev. ed. Bruce Tegner. LC 80-11673. (Illus., Orig.). 1980. pap. 3.95 (ISBN 0-87407-033-3, T-33). Thor.

Black Blood. Jon Hart. LC 80-71036. (Mercenaries Ser.). 128p. 1981. pap. 2.95 (ISBN 0-87754-227-9). Chelsea Hse.

Black Book. Middleton Harris et al. 1973. 15.00 (ISBN 0-394-48388-X); pap. 8.95 (ISBN 0-394-70622-6). Random.

Black Bourgeoisie. E. Franklin Frazier. 1965. pap. text ed. 6.95 (ISBN 0-02-910580-3). Free Pr.

Black British, White British. Dilip Hiro. LC 72-92026. 384p. 1973. 8.95 o.p. (ISBN 0-85345-270-9, CL2709); pap. 3.95 (ISBN 0-85345-304-7, PB3047). Monthly Rev.

Black Caesar, Pirate. Clifford L. Gardner. (Illus.). 96p. (gr. 9 up). 1980. 7.95 (ISBN 0-931948-09-6). Peachtree Pubs.

Black Capitalism: A Quantitative Analysis. Timothy M. Bates. LC 73-9060. (Special Studies in U.S. Economic,Social & Political Issues). 1973. 27.50x (ISBN 0-89197-680-9). Irvington.

Black Castle. Les Daniels. 1979. pap. 2.25 o.p. (ISBN 0-425-04198-0). Berkley Pub.

Black Cats & Other Superstitions. Shirley Blumenthal. LC 77-10623. (Myth, Magic & Superstition Ser.). (Illus.). (gr. 4-5). 1977. PLB 9.65 (ISBN 0-8172-1036-9). Raintree Pubs.

Black Cauldron. Lloyd Alexander. (gr. 7-12). 1980. pap. 1.75 (ISBN 0-440-90649-0, LFL). Dell.

Black Children-White Children: Competence, Socialization & Social Structure. Zena S. Blau. LC 80-1643. 1981. 19.95 (ISBN 0-02-903640-2). Free Pr.

Black Christian Nationalism: New Directions for the Black Church. Albert B. Cleage, Jr. 1972. pap. 5.95 (ISBN 0-688-06019-6). Morrow.

Black Church in the Sixties. Hart M. Nelsen & Anne K. Nelsen. LC 74-18937. 184p. 1976. pap. 5.50x (ISBN 0-8131-0137-9). U Pr of Ky.

Black Civilization: A Social Study of an Australian Tribe. rev. ed. W. Lloyd Warner. (Illus.). 8.75 (ISBN 0-8446-0954-4). Peter Smith.

Black Colleges in America. Ed. by Charles V. Willie & Ronald R. Edmonds. LC 78-17147. 1978. pap. text ed. 8.95x (ISBN 0-8077-2528-5). Tchrs Coll.

Black Community Control: A Study of Transition in a Texas Ghetto. Joyce E. Williams. LC 72-85984. (Special Studies in U.S. Economic, Social & Political Issues). 1973. 29.50x (ISBN 0-89197-681-7). Irvington.

Black Composer Speaks. David N. Baker et al. LC 77-24146. 1978. 24.00 (ISBN 0-8108-1045-X). Scarecrow.

Black Congressional Reconstruction Orators & Their Orations 1869-1879. Annjennette S. McFarlin. LC 75-45194. 343p. 1976. 15.00 (ISBN 0-8108-0902-8). Scarecrow.

Black Consciousness, Identity & Achievement: A Study of Students in Historically Black Colleges. Patricia Gurin & Edgar G. Epps. LC 75-5847. 545p. 1975. text ed. 25.50 (ISBN 0-471-33670-X). Wiley.

Black Consciousness in South Africa. Steve Biko. Ed. by Millard Arnold. LC 78-65570. 1979. pap. 5.95 (ISBN 0-394-72739-8, V-739, Vin). Random.

Black Consumer Profiles: Food Purchasing in the Inner City. Marcus Alexis et al. (Illus.). 106p. 1980. pap. 4.00 (ISBN 0-87712-195-8). U Mich Busn Div Res.

Black Corridor. Michael Moorcock. Bd. with Adventures of una Persson & Catherine Cornelius in the Twentieth Century. 52p. 1980. pap. 4.95 (ISBN 0-8037-1343-6). Dial.

Black Council. Panteleimon Kulish. Tr. by George S. Luckyj & Moira Luckyj. LC 72-97984. (Ukrainian Classics in Translation Ser.: No. 2). 1973. lib. bdg. 11.50x (ISBN 0-87287-063-4). Ukrainian Acad.

Black Cow Summer. Richard Graber. LC 80-7767. 224p. (YA) (gr. 7 up). 1980. 8.95 (ISBN 0-06-022118-6, HarpJ); PLB 8.79 (ISBN 0-06-022119-4). Har-Row.

Black Culture & Black Consciousness: Afro-American Folk Thought from Slavery to Freedom. Lawrence W. Levine. LC 76-9223. 1978. pap. 7.95 (ISBN 0-19-502374-9, GB530, GB). Oxford U Pr.

Black Dawn. Christopher Nicole. LC 77-76648. 1977. 10.95 o.p. (ISBN 0-312-08307-6). St Martin.

Black Death: A Chronicle of the Plague Compiled from Contemporary Sources. Johannes Nohl. (Unwin Bks.). (Illus.). 248p. 1961. pap. 3.95 o.p. (ISBN 0-04-942058-5, 9023). Allen Unwin.

Black Death: A Chronicle of the Plague Compiled from Contemporary Sources. Ed. by Johannes Nohl. 1961. pap. text ed. 3.25x (ISBN 0-04-942058-5). Humanities.

Black Destiny. Stanley J. Goodwin. 60p. 1981. pap. 1.95 (ISBN 0-686-28004-0). Northland Pubns WA.

Black Detroit & the Rise of the UAW. August Meier & Elliott Rudwick. (Illus.). 1979. 17.95 (ISBN 0-19-502561-X). Oxford U Pr.

Black Detroit & the Rise of the Uaw. August Meier & Elliott Rudwick. (Illus.). 304p. 1981. pap. 6.95 (ISBN 0-19-502895-3, GB 632, OPB). Oxford U Pr.

Black Drama Anthology. Ed. by Woodie King & Ron Milner. LC 77-181833. 675p. 1972. 25.00x (ISBN 0-231-03644-2). Columbia U Pr.

Black Easter - the Day After Judgment. James Blish. (Science Fiction Ser.). 1980. lib. bdg. 16.95 (ISBN 0-8398-2644-3). Gregg.

Black Economic Development. Flournoy A. Coles, Jr. LC 74-30495. 232p. 1975. 15.95 (ISBN 0-88229-176-9). Nelson-Hall.

Black Elite: The New Market for Highly Educated Black Americans. Carnagie Commission on Higher Education. LC 76-28702. (Carnegie Commission on Higher Education). (Illus.). 1977. 15.95 o.p. (ISBN 0-07-010116-7, P&RB). McGraw.

Black Elk Speaks. John C. Neihardt. (gr. 10-12). pap. 2.95 (ISBN 0-671-43268-0). PB.

Black Employment & the Law. Alfred W. Blumrosen. 1971. 30.00 (ISBN 0-8135-0682-4). Rutgers U Pr.

Black Empowerment. Barbara Solomon. LC 76-36972. 1976. 17.50x (ISBN 0-231-04086-5). Columbia U Pr.

Black Eros. Boris De Rachewiltz. Tr. by Longanesi & Co. 1964. 10.50 o.p. (ISBN 0-04-390001-1). Allen Unwin.

Black Executives in White Businesses. Jaslin U. Salmon. LC 79-66859. 1979. pap. text ed. 7.75 (ISBN 0-8191-0860-X). U Pr of Amer.

Black Experience: A Manual for Students in the Helping Professions. Ed. by Susan Reid. 1976. pap. text ed. 6.75x (ISBN 0-8191-0001-3). U Pr of Amer.

Black Experience in America. Norman Coombs. LC 73-186717. (Immigrant Heritage of America Ser.). 1972. lib. bdg. 10.95 (ISBN 0-8057-3208-X). Twayne.

Black Experience in Children's Audiovisual Materials. 32p. 1973. pap. 1.00 o.p. (ISBN 0-87104-610-5, Branch Lib). NY Pub Lib.

Black Experience in Children's Books. Barbara Rollock. 1974. pap. 2.50 o.p. (ISBN 0-87104-614-8, Branch Lib). NY Pub Lib.

Black Experience in Maryland. V. Foster Rollo. LC 79-64802. 92p. 1980. perfect bound 7.00 (ISBN 0-917882-09-1). Maryland Hist.

Black Experience in Religion: A Collection of Readings. Ed. by C. Eric Lincoln. LC 73-16508. 384p. 1974. pap. 4.50 (ISBN 0-385-01884-3, Anch). Doubleday.

Black Extended Family. Elmer P. Martin & Joanne M. Martin. LC 77-17058. 1980. pap. 4.50 (ISBN 0-226-50797-1, P872, Phoen). U of Chicago Pr.

Black-Eyed Susans: Classic Stories by & About Black Women. Ed. by Mary Helen Washington. LC 75-6169. 200p. 1975. pap. 2.95 (ISBN 0-385-09043-9, Anch). Doubleday.

Black Family. 2nd ed. Robert Staples. 1978. pap. 9.95x (ISBN 0-534-00557-8). Wadsworth Pub.

Black Family in Modern Society: Patterns of Stability & Security. John H. Scanzoni. 1977. pap. 9.00x (ISBN 0-226-73341-6, Phoen). U of Chicago Pr.

Black Family in the United States: A Selected Bibliography of Annotated Books, Articles, & Dissertations on Black Families in America. Lenwood G. Davis. LC 77-89109. 1978. lib. bdg. 12.95 (ISBN 0-8371-9851-8, DBF/). Greenwood.

Black Female Ph.D. Education & Career Development. McLean Tobin. LC 80-5578. 133p. 1980. lib. bdg. 15.25 (ISBN 0-8191-1312-3); pap. text ed. 7.25 (ISBN 0-8191-1313-1). U Pr of Amer.

Black Films & Film-Makers: A Comprehensive Anthology from Stereotype to Superhero. Compiled by Lindsay Patterson. LC 73-11545. 1975. 12.50 o.p. (ISBN 0-396-06843-X). Dodd.

Black Folks' Guide to Making Big Money in America. George Trower-Subira. 184p. 1980. 11.00 (ISBN 0-9605304-0-1). VSBE.

Black Foremothers: Three Lives. Feminist Press. (Women's Lives-Women's Work). (Illus.). (gr. 10-12). 1979. pap. text ed. 4.92 (ISBN 0-07-020433-0, W); tchr's. ed. 4.56 (ISBN 0-07-020434-9). McGraw.

Black Forest Clocks. John E. Tyler. (Illus.). 1977. 17.95x (ISBN 0-7198-0100-1). Intl Ideas.

Black Freedom: The Nonviolent Abolitionists from 1830 to the Civil War. Carleton Mabee. 1969. 12.95 (ISBN 0-02-577170-1). Macmillan.

Black Genesis. Devere. (Illus.). 120p. 1980. 13.95 (ISBN 0-312-08313-0). St Martin.

Black Genesis: An Annotated Bibliography for Black Genealogical Research. Ed. by James M. Rose & Alice Eichholz. LC 77-74819. (Genealogy & Local History Ser.: Vol. 1). (Illus.). 1978. 30.00 (ISBN 0-8103-1400-2). Gale.

Black Georgia in the Progressive Era, 1900-1920. John Dittmer. LC 77-24249. (Blacks in the New World Ser.). 251p. 1980. pap. 5.95 (ISBN 0-252-00813-8). U of Ill Pr.

Black Glove. Geoffrey Miller. LC 80-54087. 276p. 1981. 12.95 (ISBN 0-670-17166-2). Viking Pr.

Black Gods of the Metropolis: Negro Religious Cults of the Urban North. Arthur H. Fauset. LC 75-133446. 1971. pap. 4.50x (ISBN 0-8122-1001-8, Pa Paperbks). U of Pa Pr.

Black Hats. David Case. (Orig.). 1981. pap. 1.95 (ISBN 0-440-10648-6). Dell.

Black Heart: Gore-Browne & the Politics of Multiracial Zambia. Robert I. Rotberg. (Perspectives on Southern Africa Ser: Vol. 20). 1978. 20.00x (ISBN 0-520-03164-4). U of Cal Pr.

Black Heather. Virginia Coffman. Bd. with Night at Sea Abbey. 1980. pap. 1.95 (ISBN 0-451-09468-9, J9468, Sig). NAL.

Black Heritage in Social Welfare: 1860-1930. Ed. by Edyth L. Ross. LC 78-8403. 1978. 24.00 (ISBN 0-8108-1145-6). Scarecrow.

Black Heroes in Our Nation's History. Phillip T. Drotning. 1970. pap. 0.95 o.s.i. (ISBN 0-671-47834-6). WSP.

Black Hills Ghost Towns. Watson Parker & Hugh Lambert. LC 73-1501. (Illus.). 215p. 1974. 21.95 (ISBN 0-8040-0637-7, SB); pap. 11.95 (ISBN 0-8040-0638-5). Swallow.

Black Hills; or, the Last Hunting Ground of the Dakotahs. Annie D. Tallent. LC 74-76330. 594p. 1974. Repr. of 1899 ed. 14.95 (ISBN 0-88498-017-0); lim. leath. ed. 50.00 (ISBN 0-685-50457-3). Brevet Pr.

Black History: A Reappraisal. Ed. by Melvin Drimmer. LC 67-19105. 1969. pap. 5.95 o.p. (ISBN 0-385-08869-8, A08, Anch). Doubleday.

Black Hole. Alan D. Foster. LC 79-53894. (Illus., Orig.). 1979. pap. 1.95 (ISBN 0-345-28538-7). Ballantine.

Black Hole. Walt Disney Productions. Ed. by Edith Davis. (Illus.). 48p. (gr. 1-7). 1979. pap. 2.50 o.p. (ISBN 0-307-13505-5, Golden Pr). Western Pub.

Black Hole. Walt Disney Productions. (Young Reader). 24p. (ps-3). 1980. PLB 5.00 (ISBN 0-307-60105-6, Golden Pr). Western Pub.

Black Hole. Walt Disney Productions. (Illus.). (gr. 6-12). 1979. PLB 9.15 o.p. (ISBN 0-307-65305-6, Golden Pr). Western Pub.

Black Hole. Walt Disney Productions. (gr. 4-8). 1979. PLB 7.62 (ISBN 0-307-65306-4, Golden Pr). Western Pub.

Black Hole. Walt Disney Productions. Ed. by Edith Davis. (Illus.). 24p. (ps-3). 1979. 2.50 o.p. (ISBN 0-307-13506-3, Golden Pr). Western Pub.

Black Hole: Or the Makings of a Legend. Iris Macfarlane. 1975. text ed. 25.00x (ISBN 0-04-954019-X). Allen Unwin.

Black Holes & Other Secrets of the Universe. Lampton. (gr. 7 up). 1980. PLB 6.90 (ISBN 0-531-02284-6). Watts.

Black Holes & Warped Spacetime. William J. Kaufmann, 3rd. LC 79-18059. (Illus.). 1979. text ed. 14.00x o.p. (ISBN 0-7167-1152-4); pap. text ed. 8.95x (ISBN 0-7167-1153-2). W H Freeman.
Black Holes, Quasars, & the Universe. 2nd ed. Harry L. Shipman. (Illus.). 1980. 14.95 o.p. (ISBN 0-395-24374-2); pap. text ed. 8.95 (ISBN 0-395-28499-6). HM.
Black Holes: The End of the Universe? John Taylor. 1975. pap. 2.25 (ISBN 0-380-00327-9, 46805). Avon.
Black Home Ownership: A Sociological Case Study of Metropolitan Jacksonville. William A. Stacey. LC 73-186201. (Special Studies in U.S. Economic, Social & Political Issues). 1972. 28.50x (ISBN 0-275-04810-1). Irvington.
Black Homeland - Black Diaspora: Cross Currents of the African Relationship. Ed. by Jacob Drachler. LC 74-80066. 1975. 15.00 (ISBN 0-8046-9077-4, Natl U). Kennikat.
Black Horse Running. James Wood. LC 74-30874. 1977. 7.95 (ISBN 0-8149-0757-1). Vanguard.
Black Humor Fiction of the Sixties: A Pluralistic Definition of Man & His World. Max F. Schulz. LC 72-85538. xi, 156p. 1973. 12.00x (ISBN 0-8214-0125-4). Ohio U Pr.
Black Humor Fiction of the Sixties: A Pluralistic Definition of Man & His World. Max F. Schulz. LC 72-85538. 156p. 1980. pap. 5.95x (ISBN 0-8214-0574-8). Ohio U Pr.
Black Image in the White Mind: The Debate on Afro-American Character & Destiny, 1817-1914. George M. Fredrickson. 1977. pap. text ed. 8.50x (ISBN 0-06-131688-1, TB 1688, Torch). Har-Row.
Black Images. Wilfred Cartey. LC 75-113096. 1970. text ed. 9.40x o.p. (ISBN 0-8077-1145-4); pap. 7.75x (ISBN 0-8077-1144-6). Tchrs Coll.
Black Images of America, 1784-1870. Leonard I. Sweet. (Essays in American History Ser). 1976. pap. text ed. 4.95x (ISBN 0-393-09195-3). Norton.
Black Index: Afro-Americana in Selected Periodicals. Richard Newman. LC 80-835. (Garland Reference Library of Social Science; Critical Studies in Black Life & Culture). 280p. 1981. 35.00 (ISBN 0-8240-9513-8). Garland Pub.
Black Insights: Significant Literature by Black-Americans, 1760 to the Present. Ed. by Nick A. Ford. LC 77-127525. (Orig.). 1971. pap. text ed. 13.50 (ISBN 0-471-00168-6). Wiley.
Black Inventors of America. McKinley Burt, Jr. 1969. pap. 6.85 (ISBN 0-89420-095-X, 296959). Natl Book.
Black Is the Color of My TV Tube. Gil Noble. (Illus.). 1981. 10.00 (ISBN 0-8184-0297-0). Lyle Stuart.
Black Jack, John A. Logan & Southern Illinois in the Civil War Era. James P. Jones. LC 67-64456. 1967. 8.95 o.p. (ISBN 0-8130-0485-3). U Presses Fla.
Black Jack: Last of the Big Alligators. Robert M. McClung. (Illus.). (gr. 3-7). 1967. PLB 6.96 (ISBN 0-688-31103-2). Morrow.
Black Justice. David Umobuarie. (Three Crown Books Ser.). 204p. (Orig.). 1976. pap. 8.95 (ISBN 0-19-575232-5). Oxford U Pr.
Black Labor in America. Ed. by Milton Cantor. LC 74-111265. (Contributions in Afro-American & African Studies, No. 2). 1969. 16.95x (ISBN 0-8371-4667-4). Negro U Pr.
Black Language Reader. Robert H. Bentley & Samuel D. Crawford. 200p. 1973. pap. 5.95x o.p. (ISBN 0-673-07683-0). Scott F.
Black Letter Primer: An Introduction to Gothic Alphabets. Paul Shaw. LC 78-20699. (Illus.). 1981. pap. 4.95 (ISBN 0-8008-0808-8, Pentalic). Taplinger.
Black Librarian in America. Ed. & intro. by E. J. Josey. LC 79-17850. 1970. 10.00 (ISBN 0-8108-0362-3). Scarecrow.
Black Light. rev. ed. Galway Kinnell. 128p. 1980. pap. 5.00 (ISBN 0-86547-016-2). N Point Pr.
Black Lion. Patricia Fanthorpe & Lionel Fanthorpe. LC 80-19214. 160p. 1980. Repr. of 1979 ed. lib. bdg. 8.95 (ISBN 0-89370-094-0). Borgo Pr.
Black Lion. Patricia Fanthorpe & Lionel Fanthorpe. 1980. pap. 1.95 o.s.i. (ISBN 0-906901-00-6). Newcastle Pub.
Black Literature for High School Students. Barnara D. Stanford & Karima Amin. LC 78-16890. 1978. pap. text ed. 6.25x (ISBN 0-8077-2562-5, Pub. by Natl Coun Teach English). Tchrs Coll.
Black Lyon. Jude Deveraux. 1980. pap. 2.50 (ISBN 0-686-69258-6, 75911). Avon.
Black Macho & the Myth of the Superwoman. 1980. pap. 2.50 (ISBN 0-446-91262-X). Warner Bks.
Black Magic at Brillstone. Florence P. Heide & Roxanne Heide. Ed. by Ann Fay. (Pilot Bks.). 128p. (gr. 4-9). 1981. 6.95 (ISBN 0-8075-0782-2). A Whitman.
Black Majority: Negroes in Colonial South Carolina from 1670 Through the Stono Rebellion. Peter H. Wood. 384p. 1975. pap. 4.95 (ISBN 0-393-00777-4, Norton Lib). Norton.
Black Male in America: Perspectives on His Status in Contemporary Society. Ed. by Doris Y. Wilkinson & Ronald L. Taylor. LC 76-44310. 1977. 18.95 (ISBN 0-88229-227-7); pap. 9.95 (ISBN 0-88229-409-1). Nelson-Hall.
Black Man Comes to the City: A Documentary Account from the Great Migration to the Great Depression, 1915-1930. Robert B. Grant. LC 72-83821. 1972. 17.95 (ISBN 0-911012-45-1). Nelson-Hall.
Black Man in America, 1619-1790. Florence Jackson & J. B. Jackson. LC 73-101749. (Black Man in America Ser: Vol. 1). (Illus.). (gr. 7 up). PLB 4.90 o.p. (ISBN 0-531-01839-3). Watts.
Black Man in America, 1791-1861. Florence Jackson. LC 72-136833. (Black Man in America Ser: Vol. 2). (Illus.). (gr. 7 up). 1971. PLB 4.90 o.p. (ISBN 0-531-01965-9). Watts.
Black Man in America, 1861-1877. Florence Jackson. LC 71-183578. (Black Man in America Ser: Vol. 3). (Illus.). 96p. (gr. 4-6). 1971. PLB 4.90 o.p. (ISBN 0-531-02022-3). Watts.
Black Man in America, 1877-1905. Florence Jackson. LC 72-10406. (Black Man in America Ser: Vol. 4). (Illus.). 96p. (gr. 5 up). 1973. PLB 4.90 o.p. (ISBN 0-531-02611-6). Watts.
Black Man in America, 1905-1932. Florence Jackson. LC 73-12931. (Black Man in America Ser: Vol. 5). (Illus.). 96p. (gr. 7 up). 1974. PLB 4.90 o.p. (ISBN 0-531-02667-1). Watts.
Black Man in America 1932-1954. Florence Jackson. LC 74-13440. (Black Man in America Ser: Vol. 6). (Illus.). (gr. 4-6). 1975. PLB 4.90 o.p. (ISBN 0-531-02799-6). Watts.
Black Managers in White Corporations. John P. Fernandez. LC 75-6820. 308p. 1975. 29.95 (ISBN 0-471-25764-8, Pub. by Wiley-Interscience). Wiley.
Black Manhood: The Building of Civilization by the Black Man of the Nile. rev. ed. Tarharka. LC 79-65009. 1979. pap. text ed. 11.25 (ISBN 0-8191-0780-8). U Pr of Amer.
Black Manifesto in Jazz Poetry & Prose. Ted Joans. LC 79-869997. 1979. 9.95 (ISBN 0-7145-0713-X, Pub. by M Boyars); pap. 5.95 (ISBN 0-7145-0714-8). Merrimack Bk Serv.
Black Man's Burden Revisited. Michael Wolfers. LC 74-82176. 192p. 1975. 18.95 (ISBN 0-312-08330-0). St Martin.
Black Marble. Joseph Wambaugh. 1978. 9.95 o.s.i. (ISBN 0-440-00523-X). Delacorte.
Black Marsden. Wilson Harris. 1972. 4.95 o.p. (ISBN 0-571-10104-6, Pub. by Faber & Faber). Merrimack Bk Serv.
Black Men & Businessman: The Growing Awareness of a Social Responsibility. Steven M. Gelber. LC 74-77654. 320p. 1974. 17.50 (ISBN 0-8046-9062-6, Natl U). Kennikat.
Black Men of the Sea. Michael Cohn & Michael Platzer. LC 78-4873. (Illus.). 1978. 8.95 (ISBN 0-396-07546-0). Dodd.
Black Midas. 2nd ed. Jan Carew. 184p. 1981. 9.00x (ISBN 0-89410-124-2); pap. 5.00x (ISBN 0-89410-125-0). Three Continents.
Black Minute. James H. Artzner. 170p. (Orig.). 1980. 10.95 (ISBN 0-938936-00-X); pap. 4.95 (ISBN 0-938936-01-8). Daring Pr.
Black Moon. Winston Graham. (Poldark Ser.: No.5). 1977. pap. 2.25 (ISBN 0-345-27735-X). Ballantine.
Black Moses: The Story of Marcus Garvey & the Universal Negro Improvement Association. 2nd ed. E. David Cronon. (Illus.). 1969. pap. 7.95 (ISBN 0-299-01214-X). U of Wis Pr.
Black Music. Dean Tudor & Nancy Tudor. LC 78-15563. (American Popular Music on Elpee Ser). 1979. lib. bdg. 22.50x (ISBN 0-87287-147-9). Libs Unl.
Black Music in Our Culture: Curricular Ideas on the Subjects, Materials & Problems. Dominique-Rene De Lerma. LC 70-131429. 1970. 12.00x o.p. (ISBN 0-87338-110-6). Kent St U Pr.
Black Music of Two Worlds. John S. Roberts. 1974. pap. 3.95 (ISBN 0-688-24344-4). Morrow.
Black Mustanger. Richard Wormser. (Illus.). (gr. 5-9). 1971. 7.25 (ISBN 0-688-21104-6); PLB 6.96 (ISBN 0-688-31104-0). Morrow.
Black Nationalism. E. U. Essien-Udom. LC 62-12632. 368p. 1972. pap. 4.95 o.s.i. (ISBN 0-226-21853-8, P451, Phoen). U of Chicago Pr.
Black Nationalism in America. John H. Bracey et al. LC 79-99161. 1969. 10.00 o.p. (ISBN 0-672-51241-6, AHS89); pap. 10.95 (ISBN 0-672-60150-8, AHS89). Bobbs.
Black Nations in Action. Edward LaCoste. 3.75 o.p. (ISBN 0-685-26056-9). Vantage.
Black Neighbors: Negroes in a Northern Rural Community. 2nd ed. G. K. Hesslink. LC 73-8915. 345p. 1974. 8.95 (ISBN 0-672-51522-9); pap. text ed. 5.25 o.p. (ISBN 0-672-61237-2). Bobbs.
Black Night, White Snow: Russia's Revolutions 1905-1917. Harrison E. Salisbury. LC 74-18830. 1978. 14.95 o.p. (ISBN 0-385-00844-9). Doubleday.
Black, No Sugar. Namus Mothudi. 1981. 5.95 (ISBN 0-533-04824-9). Vantage.
Black Novelists & the Southern Literary Tradition. Ladell Payne. LC 80-21747. 144p. 1981. 11.00x (ISBN 0-8203-0536-7). U of Ga Pr.
Black Odyssey: John Lewis Waller & the Promise of American Life, 1878-1900. Randall B. Woods. LC 80-18965. (Illus.). 272p. 1981. 20.00x (ISBN 0-7006-0207-0). Regents Pr KS.
Black on Black: Commentaries by Negro Americans. Ed. by Arnold Adoff. LC 68-24101. (YA) (gr. 8 up). 1968. 5.95g o.s.i. (ISBN 0-02-700070-2). Macmillan.
Black Orchids. Rex Stout. 1976. pap. 1.75 (ISBN 0-515-05085-7). Jove Pubns.
Black Organizations: Issues on Survival Techniques. Ed. by Lennox S. Yearwood. LC 79-5500. 286p. 1980. pap. 9.50 (ISBN 0-8191-0898-7); 18.50 (ISBN 0-8191-0897-9). U Pr of Amer.
Black Out Loud: An Anthology of Modern Poems by Black Americans. Ed. by Arnold Adoff. LC 74-99117. (Illus.). (gr. 4 up). 1970. 5.95g o.s.i. (ISBN 0-02-700100-8). Macmillan.
Black Panther Leaders Speak. Ed. by G. Louis Heath. LC 76-3585. 177p. 1976. 10.00 (ISBN 0-8108-0915-X). Scarecrow.
Black Panthers Speak. Ed. by Philip S. Foner. LC 76-134927. 1970. pap. 2.95 o.s.i. (ISBN 0-397-00636-5). Lippincott.
Black Pearl & the Ghost. Walter D. Myers. LC 79-20268. (Illus.). (gr. 1-5). 1980. 6.95 (ISBN 0-670-17284-7). Viking Pr.
Black People & the Nineteen Eighty Census: Proceedings from a Conference on the Poplation Undercount, Vol. 1. Ed. by Chicago Center for Afro-American Studies & Research. LC 80-68927. (Black People & the Nineteen Eighty Census Ser.). (Illus.). 702p. 1980. pap. 20.00 (ISBN 0-937954-01-2); pap. 15.00. Chr Ctr Afro-Am Stud.
Black People & Their Culture: Selected Writings from the African Diaspora. Rosie L. Hooks et al. (Illus.). 141p. 1976. pap. 4.95 (ISBN 0-87474-531-4). Smithsonian.
Black People & Whence They Came: A Zulu View. M. M. Fuze. Ed. by A. T. Cope. Tr. by H. C. Lugg from Zulu. (Killie Campbell Africana Library Translation Ser.: No. 1). 206p. 1979. text ed. 21.00 (ISBN 0-86980-167-8). Verry.
Black Poets & Prophets. Ed. by Woodie King & Earl Anthony. pap. 1.50 o.p. (ISBN 0-451-61126-8, MW1126, Ment). NAL.
Black Political Parties: An Historical & Political Analysis. Hanes Walton, Jr. LC 76-143514. 1972. 10.95 (ISBN 0-02-933870-0). Free Pr.
Black Powder Handgun. Sam Fadala. LC 81-65102. 288p. (Orig.). 1981. pap. 8.95 (ISBN 0-910676-22-4, 9266). DBI.
Black Power & Christian Responsibility. C. Freeman Sleeper. 1969. 4.50 o.p. (ISBN 0-687-03596-1). Abingdon.
Black Power in South Africa: The Evolution of an Ideology. Gail M. Gerhart. LC 75-13149. (Perspectives on Southern Africa Ser.: Vol. 19). 1978. 16.50x (ISBN 0-520-03022-2, CAL 423); pap. 5.95 (ISBN 0-520-03933-5). U of Cal Pr.
Black Preacher in America. Charles V. Hamilton. 256p. 1972. pap. 3.45 o.p. (ISBN 0-688-05006-9). Morrow.
Black Preaching: Truth & Soul. Mervyn A. Warren. 1977. pap. text ed. 7.75x (ISBN 0-8191-0173-7). U Pr of Amer.
Black Presence in American Foreign Affairs. Jake C. Miller. LC 78-69860. 1978. pap. text ed. 11.00 (ISBN 0-8191-0584-8). U Pr of Amer.
Black Princess & Other Stories. A. V. Bharath. (Illus.). 96p. 1967. 1.00 (ISBN 0-88253-413-0). Ind-US Inc.
Black Prophet. William Carleton. 408p. 1972. Repr. of 1899 ed. 7.00x (ISBN 0-7165-1798-1, Pub by Irish Academic Pr). Biblio Dist.
Black Prophet: A Tale of the Irish Famine. William Carleton. Ed. by Robert L. Wolff. (Ireland Nineteenth Century Fiction Ser. Two: Vol. 41). 324p. 1979. lib. bdg. 32.00 (ISBN 0-8240-3490-2). Garland Pub.
Black Protest Thought in the Twentieth Century. 2nd ed. Ed. by Francis Broderick et al. LC 79-119007. (American Heritage Ser). 1971. pap. 10.95 (ISBN 0-672-61178-3, AHS-56R). Bobbs.
Black Psychology: Compelling Issues & Views. Louis N. Williams. LC 78-60627. 1978. pap. text ed. 7.50 (ISBN 0-8191-0562-7). U Pr of Amer.
Black Religion & American Evangelicalism: White Protestants, Plantation Missions, & the Flowering of Negro Christianity, 1787-1865. Milton C. Sernett. LC 75-4754. (ATLA Monograph: No. 7). (Illus.). 320p. 1975. 15.00 (ISBN 0-8108-0803-X). Scarecrow.
Black Religions in the New World. George E. Simpson. (Illus.). 1978. 27.50x (ISBN 0-231-04540-9). Columbia U Pr.
Black Representation & Urban Policy. Albert Karnig & Susan Welch. LC 80-16714. 1981. 20.00x (ISBN 0-226-42534-7). U of Chicago Pr.
Black Republicans: The Politics of the Black & Tans. Hanes Walton, Jr. LC 75-6718. 217p. 1975. 10.00 (ISBN 0-8108-0811-0). Scarecrow.
Black Resistance - White Law: A History of Institutional Racism in America. M. Berry. 1971. pap. text ed. 11.95 (ISBN 0-13-077735-8). P-H.
Black Resistance Before the Civil War. William F. Cheek. 1970. pap. text ed. 4.95x (ISBN 0-02-473550-7, 47355). Macmillan.
Black Rhetoric: A Guide to Afro-American Communication. Robert W. Glenn. LC 75-38912. 1976. 16.50 o.p. (ISBN 0-8108-0889-7). Scarecrow.
Black Rider. Burt Arthur. 1978. pap. 1.25 (ISBN 0-505-51258-0). Tower Bks.
Black Rider. Al Cody. (YA) 1977. 5.95 (ISBN 0-685-81421-1, Avalon). Bouregy.
Black Robes in Lower California. Peter M. Dunne. (California Library Reprint Series: No. 3). (Illus.). 1968. Repr. 22.50x (ISBN 0-520-00362-4). U of Cal Pr.
Black Rock: A Tale of the Selkirks. Ralph Connor. 1976. lib. bdg. 12.95x (ISBN 0-89968-014-3). Lightyear.
Black Roots in Southeastern Connecticut 1650-1900: A Guide to Information Sources. Ed. by James M. Rose & Barbara Brown. (Gale Genealogy & Local History Ser.: Vol. 8). 1980. 30.00 (ISBN 0-8103-1411-8). Gale.
Black Rose: A Story About 'Abdu'l-Baha in America. Anthony A. Lee. (Stories About 'abdu'l-Baha in America Ser.). (Illus.). 24p. (gr. k-5). 1979. pap. 2.50 (ISBN 0-933770-00-6). Kalimat.
Black Sabbath. Robert Wilkens. 4.95 o.p. (ISBN 0-685-46130-0). Vantage.
Black Scare: The Racist Response to Emancipation & Reconstruction. Forrest G. Wood. 1968. 19.50x (ISBN 0-520-01361-1); pap. 2.45 (ISBN 0-520-01664-5, CAL190). U of Cal Pr.
Black Scenes: Collection of Scenes from Plays Written by Black People About Black Experience. Ed. by Alice Childress. LC 70-150881. 4.95 o.p. (ISBN 0-385-01146-6). Doubleday.
Black Secretary's Horror. Mary B. Bush. 1981. 8.95 (ISBN 0-533-04698-X). Vantage.
Black Sects & Cults. Joseph R. Washington, Jr. LC 72-86649. 192p. 1972. pap. 2.95 o.p. (ISBN 0-385-00252-1, Anchor Pr). Doubleday.
Black Separatism & Social Reality. Raymond L. Hall. LC 75-34419. 1977. text ed. 35.00 (ISBN 0-08-019510-5); pap. text ed. 15.00 (ISBN 0-08-019509-1). Pergamon.
Black Separatism in the United States. Raymond L. Hall. LC 77-75515. 318p. 1978. text ed. 17.50x (ISBN 0-87451-146-1). U Pr of New Eng.
Black September: Its Short, Violent History. Christopher Dobson. Ed. by H. W. Griffin. (Illus.). 160p. 1974. 11.95 (ISBN 0-02-531900-0). Macmillan.
Black Sheep. Honore de Balzac. Tr. by Donald Adamson. (Classics Ser.). 352p. 1976. pap. 2.95 (ISBN 0-14-044237-5). Penguin.
Black Short Story Anthology. Ed. by Woodie King. LC 72-6773. 600p. 1972. text ed. 20.00x (ISBN 0-231-03711-2). Columbia U Pr.
Black Soldier. Jesse J. Johnson. 1976. 3.95 (ISBN 0-915044-04-8); pap. 1.50 rev. ed. (ISBN 0-915044-05-6); pap. 1.10 pocketbook (ISBN 0-915044-06-4). Carver Pub.
Black Song: The Forge & the Flame. John Lovell, Jr. (Illus.). 1972. 15.00 o.s.i. (ISBN 0-02-575700-8). Macmillan.
Black Spider. Jeremias Gotthelf. Tr. by H. M. Waidson. 1980. pap. 5.95 (ISBN 0-7145-0125-5). Riverrun NY.
Black Spirituality. Walter A. McCray. 150p. (Orig.). 1981. pap. 6.95 (ISBN 0-933176-04-X). Black Light Fellow.
Black Spring. Henry Miller. 1964. pap. 2.95 (ISBN 0-394-17471-2, B61, BC). Grove.
Black Stallion. Walter Farley. LC 41-21882. (Illus.). (gr. 3-7). 1944. 3.95 (ISBN 0-394-80601-8, BYR); PLB 5.99 (ISBN 0-394-90601-2); pap. 1.95 (ISBN 0-394-83609-X). Random.
Black Stallion & Flame. Walter Farley. (Illus.). (gr. 5 up). 1960. 3.95 (ISBN 0-394-80615-8, BYR); PLB 5.99 (ISBN 0-394-90615-2); pap. 1.95 (ISBN 0-394-84372-X). Random.
Black Stallion & the Girl. Walter Farley. (gr. 4 up). 1971. 3.95 (ISBN 0-394-82145-9, BYR); PLB 5.99 (ISBN 0-394-92145-3); pap. 1.95 (ISBN 0-394-83614-6). Random.

Black Stallion Challenged. Walter Farley. (Illus.). (gr. 5-9). 1964. 3.95 (ISBN 0-394-80617-4, BYR); PLB 5.99 (ISBN 0-394-90617-9); pap. 1.95 (ISBN 0-394-84371-1). Random.
Black Stallion Mystery. Walter Farley. (gr. 4-6). 1957. 3.95 (ISBN 0-394-80613-1, BYR); PLB 5.99 (ISBN 0-394-90613-6); pap. 1.95 (ISBN 0-394-83611-1). Random.
Black Stallion Returns. Walter Farley. LC 45-8763. (gr. 4-9). 1977. 3.95 (ISBN 0-394-80602-6, BYR); PLB 5.99 (ISBN 0-394-90602-0); pap. 1.95 (ISBN 0-394-83610-3). Random.
Black Stallion Revolts. Walter Farley. LC 49-6117. (gr. 4-9). 1977. 3.95 (ISBN 0-394-80609-3, BYR); PLB 5.99 (ISBN 0-394-90609-8); pap. 1.95 (ISBN 0-394-83613-8). Random.
Black Stallion's Courage. Walter Farley. (Illus.). (gr. 4-6). 1956. 3.95 (ISBN 0-394-80612-3, BYR); PLB 5.99 (ISBN 0-394-90612-8); pap. 1.95 (ISBN 0-394-83918-8). Random.
Black Stallion's Filly. Walter Farley. (Illus.). (gr. 4-6). 1952. 3.95 (ISBN 0-394-80608-5, BYR); PLB 5.99 (ISBN 0-394-90608-X); pap. 1.95 (ISBN 0-394-83916-1). Random.
Black Stallion's Ghost. Walter Farley. (Illus.). (gr. 5-9). 1969. 3.95 (ISBN 0-394-80618-2, BYR); PLB 5.99 (ISBN 0-394-90618-7); pap. 1.95 (ISBN 0-394-83919-6). Random.
Black Stallion's Sulky Colt. Walter Farley. (Illus.). (gr. 4-6). 1954. 3.95 (ISBN 0-394-80610-7, BYR); PLB 5.99 (ISBN 0-394-90610-1); pap. 1.95 (ISBN 0-394-83917-X). Random.
Black Star Over Japan: Rising Forces of Militarism. Albert Axelbank. 1972. 7.95 o.p. (ISBN 0-8090-3045-4). Hill & Wang.
Black Struggle: A History of the Negro in America. Bryan Fulks. LC 77-107211. (Illus.). (gr. 7 up). 1970. Repr. of 1970 ed. 5.95 o.s.i. (ISBN 0-440-00678-3). Delacorte.
Black Students in Higher Education: Conditions & Experiences in the 1970's. Ed. by Gail E. Thomas. LC 80-1702. (Contributions to the Study of Education: No. 1). 424p. 1981. lib. bdg. 29.95 (ISBN 0-313-22477-3, TBS/). Greenwood.
Black Students in Interracial Schools: A Guide for Students, Teachers & Schools. Ed Smith. LC 80-81701. 134p. (Orig.). 1980. pap. 7.95 (ISBN 0-686-69010-9). Garrett Pk.
Black Studies: Pitfalls & Potential. William E. Sims. LC 77-18563. 1978. pap. text ed. 7.75 (ISBN 0-8191-0316-0). U Pr of Amer.
Black Sun. Edward Abbey. 160p. 1981. pap. 5.95 (ISBN 0-88496-192-3). Capra Pr.
Black Swallow of Death. P. J. Carisella & James W. Ryan. 1972. 8.95 (Pub. by Carisella). Aviation.
Black Swallow of Death. P. J. Carisella & James W. Ryan. LC 72-75762. (Illus.). 271p. 1972. 8.95 (ISBN 0-911721-87-8). Aviation.
Black Swan. Paula Z. Hogan. LC 78-27416. (Life Cycles Ser.). (Illus.). (gr. k-3). 1979. PLB 9.95 (ISBN 0-8172-1254-X). Raintree Pubs.
Black Swan. Rafael Sabatini. 224p. 1976. pap. 1.50 o.p. (ISBN 0-345-24864-3). Ballantine.
Black Talk: Roots of Jazz. Ben Sidran. xvii, 201p. 1981. Repr. of 1971 ed. lib. bdg. 19.50 (ISBN 0-306-76056-8). Da Capo.
Black Teachers in Urban Schools: The Case of Washington D.C. Catherine B. Silver. LC 72-92467. (Special Studies in U.S. Economic, Social, & Political Issues). 1973. 24.00x (ISBN 0-8290-0456-4); pap. text ed. 12.50x (ISBN 0-89197-682-5). Irvington.
Black Texans: A History of Negroes in Texas 1528-1971. Alwyn Barr. LC 72-97935. (Negro Heritage Ser., No. 12). (Illus.). 259p. 1973. 12.50 (ISBN 0-8363-0016-5). Jenkins.
Black Theology & Black Power. James H. Cone. LC 70-76462. (Orig.). 1969. pap. 3.95 (ISBN 0-8164-2003-3, SP59). Crossroad NY.
Black Theology of Liberation. James H. Cone. LC 74-120333. 1970. pap. 4.50 (ISBN 0-397-10098-1). Lippincott.
Black Thursday. Martin Caidin. 272p. 1981. pap. 2.50 (ISBN 0-553-13582-1). Bantam.
Black Tide: The Santa Barbara Oil Spill & Its Consequences. Robert Easton. 1972. 10.00 o.s.i. (ISBN 0-440-00858-1). Delacorte.
Black Tiger at Le Mans. Patrick O'Connor. (gr. 5-8). 1967. pap. 0.95 o.p. (ISBN 0-425-03513-1, Highland). Berkley Pub.
Black Time: Fiction of Africa, the Caribbean, & the United States. Bonnie J. Barthold. LC 80-24336. (Illus.). 224p. 1981. 17.50x (ISBN 0-300-02573-4). Yale U Pr.
Black Torrent. Leopold Buczkowski. Tr. by David Welsh. 1970. 15.00x o.p. (ISBN 0-262-02064-5). MIT Pr.
Black Tower. P. D. James. 1980. pap. 2.25 (ISBN 0-445-08499-5). Popular Lib.
Black Viking. Bill Downey. 320p. (Orig.). 1981. pap. 2.50 (ISBN 0-449-14393-7, GM). Fawcett.
Black Walnut for Profit. Bruce Thompson. 285p. 1978. pap. 7.95x (ISBN 0-917304-40-3, Pub. by Timber Pr). Intl Schol Bk Serv.
Black Walnut for Profit: A Guide to Risks & Rewards. Bruce Thompson. (Illus.). 285p. Date not set. 9.95 o.p. (ISBN 0-686-69373-6); pap. 7.95 (ISBN 0-917304-40-3). Walnut AZ.
Black Watch: The History of the Royal Highland Regiment. Eric Linklater & Andro Linklater. (Illus.). 1979. 19.95 o.p. (ISBN 0-214-20083-3, 8087-6, Dist by Arco). Barrie & Jenkins.
Black, White & Red: The Problem of Shawnee College. George A. Dunlap. 64p. 1979. 3.95 (ISBN 0-8059-2622-4). Dorrance.
Black-White Relations in the Nineteen Eighties: Towards a Long-Term Policy. Hubert M. Blalock, Jr. LC 79-10224. 1979. 22.95 (ISBN 0-03-050461-9). Praeger.
Black Wings: The Unbeatable Crow. Joseph W. Lippincott. (Illus.). (gr. 7-9). 1947. 5.95 o.p. (ISBN 0-397-30123-5). Lippincott.
Black Woman. Ed. by La Frances Rodgers-Rose. LC 79-28712. (Sage Focus Editions: Vol. 21). (Illus.). 316p. 1980. 18.95 (ISBN 0-8039-1311-7); pap. 9.95x (ISBN 0-8039-1312-5). Sage.
Black Woman: An Anthology. Ed. by Toni Cade. 256p. 1974. pap. 1.95 (ISBN 0-451-61868-8, MJ1868, Ment). NAL.
Black Woman Cross-Culturally. Ed. by Filomina C. Steady. 400p. 1980. text ed. 24.95x (ISBN 0-87073-345-1); pap. text ed. 12.50x (ISBN 0-87073-346-X). Schenkman.
Black Woman in America: Sex, Marriage & the Family. Robert Staples. LC 72-95280. 1973. 15.95x (ISBN 0-911012-55-9); pap. 8.95x (ISBN 0-685-99065-6). Nelson-Hall.
Black Women in American Bands & Orchestras. D. Antoinette Handy. LC 80-19380. 394p. 1981. 17.50 (ISBN 0-8108-1346-7). Scarecrow.
Black Women in the Armed Forces: A Pictoral History. LC 74-24961. 125p. 1975. 10.00 (ISBN 0-915044-11-0); pap. 4.00 (ISBN 0-915044-12-9). Carver Pub.
Black Women Novelists: The Development of a Tradition, 1892-1976. Barbara Christian. LC 79-8953. (Contributions in Afro-American & African Studies: No. 52). xiv, 275p. 1980. lib. bdg. 25.00 (ISBN 0-313-20750-X, CBW/). Greenwood.
Black Worker: From Nineteen Hundred to Nineteen Nineteen, Vol. V. Philip S. Foner & Ronald L. Lewis. 1980. 17.50x (ISBN 0-87722-184-7). Temple U Pr.
Black Worker: The Era of Post-War Prosperity & the Great Depression, 1920 to 1936, Vol. VI. Ed. by Philip S. Foner. Ronald L. Lewis. 400p. 1981. 17.50x (ISBN 0-87722-196-0). Temple U Pr.
Black Writers in Latin America. Richard L. Jackson. LC 78-21431. 1979. 12.50x (ISBN 0-8263-0501-6). U of NM Pr.
Blackberry Named Patty. Irene Halick. 1977. pap. 1.50 o.p. (ISBN 0-917726-12-X). Hunter Bks.
Blackberry's Kitten. Lettice Cooper. LC 63-13798. (Illus.). (gr. 1-4). 1963. 3.00 (ISBN 0-8149-0291-X). Vanguard.
Blackboard Jungle. Evan Hunter. LC 73-183139. 320p. 1971. Repr. of 1954 ed. lib. bdg. 12.50x (ISBN 0-8376-0404-4). Bentley.
Blackfeet & Buffalo. James W. Schultz. Ed. by Keith C. Seele. 384p. pap. 7.95 (ISBN 0-8061-1700-1). U of Okla Pr.
Blackfeet Indians. Incl. Ethnological Report on the Blackfeet & Gros Ventre Tribes. John C. Ewers; Findings of Fact, & Opinion. Indian Claims Commission. (American Indian Ethnohistory Ser: Plains Indians). (Illus.). lib. bdg. 42.00 (ISBN 0-8240-0755-7). Garland Pub.
Blackfoot Lodge Tales: The Story of a Prairie People. George B. Grinnell. LC 62-4146. 1962. pap. 3.50 (ISBN 0-8032-5079-7, BB 129, Bison). U of Nebr Pr.
Blackie & Marie. Marta Koci. Tr. by Elizabeth D. Crawford from Ger. (Junior Bks.). Orig. Title: Schwarzack. (Illus.). 32p. (gr. k-3). 1980. 8.95 (ISBN 0-688-00217-X); PLB 8.59 (ISBN 0-688-00236-6). Morrow.
Blackie: The Biography of Blackbird. Anne Britton. 6.95 (ISBN 0-392-07664-0, SpS). Soccer.
Blacking up: The Minstrel Show in Nineteenth-Century America. Robert C. Toll. LC 74-83992. (Illus.). 1977. pap. 5.95 (ISBN 0-19-502172-X, 489, GB). Oxford U Pr.
Blackjack Hijack. Charles Einstein. 1976. 6.95 o.p. (ISBN 0-394-49459-8). Random.
Blackjack's Winning Formula. Jerry L. Patterson. 91p. 1980. write for info. (ISBN 0-9605112-0-2). Casino Gaming.
Blacklines Scrawl. Stanley H. Barkan. (Poetry Ser.). 1976. 8.95 o.p. (ISBN 0-89304-017-7, CCC108); signed ltd. ed. 10.00 (ISBN 0-89304-017-7); pap. 3.00x (ISBN 0-89304-010-X); pap. 3.00 signed ltd. ed. (ISBN 0-89304-018-5). Cross Cult.
Blackmail Machine. Felice Holman. LC 68-11002. (gr. 3-7). 1968. 8.95g (ISBN 0-02-744140-7). Macmillan.
Blackmail: Publicity & Secrecy in Everyday Life. Mike Hepworth. 192p. 1975. 14.95x (ISBN 0-7100-8235-5); pap. 6.95 (ISBN 0-7100-8236-3). Routledge & Kegan.
Blackout. Anne Rockwell & Harlow Rockwell. LC 78-12185. (Ready-to-Read Ser.). (Illus.). (gr. 1-4). 1979. 7.95 (ISBN 0-02-777610-7). Macmillan.
Blacks & Criminal Justice. Ed. by Charles E. Owens & Jimmy Bell. LC 76-43639. 1977. 16.95 (ISBN 0-669-01101-0). Lexington Bks.
Blacks in America. Earl Spangler. LC 71-150773. (In America Bks.). (Illus.). (gr. 5-11). 1980. PLB 5.95. Lerner Pubns.
Blacks in American Films: Today & Yesterday. Edward Mapp. LC 72-172946. (Illus.). 1972. 10.00 (ISBN 0-8108-0458-1). Scarecrow.
Blacks in American Movies: A Selected Bibliography. Anne Powers. LC 74-1925. 1974. 10.00 (ISBN 0-8108-0753-X). Scarecrow.
Blacks in Black & White: A Source Book on Black Films. Henry T. Sampson. LC 77-637. 1977. 15.50 (ISBN 0-8108-1023-9). Scarecrow.
Blacks in Classical Music: A Personal History. Raoul Abdul. LC 77-11645. 1978. 8.95 (ISBN 0-396-07394-8). Dodd.
Blacks in Hispanic Literature: A Collection of Critical Essays. Ed. by Miriam DeCosta. (Literary Criticism Ser). 1976. 12.00 (ISBN 0-8046-9140-1, Natl U). Kennikat.
Blacks in Mississippi Politics 1865-1900. Buford Satcher. LC 78-53792. 1978. pap. text ed. 9.50x (ISBN 0-8191-0513-9). U Pr of Amer.
Blacks in the Industrial World: Issues for the Manager. Theodore Purcell & Gerald Cavanagh. LC 74-184530. 1972. 15.95 (ISBN 0-02-925520-1); pap. text ed. 5.95 (ISBN 0-02-925480-9). Free Pr.
Blacks in the Performing Arts. William Cunningham & Marilyn Mahanand. 1981. 25.00 (ISBN 0-208-01849-2, Lib. Prof Pubns). Shoe String.
Blacks in the U. S. Armed Forces: Basic Documents, 13 vols. Ed. by Morris J. MacGregor & Bernard C. Nalty. LC 76-5603. 1977. Set. 750.00 (ISBN 0-8420-2098-5). Scholarly Res Inc.
Blacks in the West. W. Sherman Savage. LC 75-44657. (Contributions in Afro-American & African Studies: No.23). 288p. (Orig.). 1976. lib. bdg. 17.50 (ISBN 0-8371-8775-3, SBW/). Greenwood.
Blacks in White Colleges. George L. Cross. 1975. 8.95x o.p. (ISBN 0-8061-1266-2); pap. 3.95 (ISBN 0-8061-1267-0). U of Okla Pr.
Black's Law Dictionary. 5th ed. Henry C. Black. Ed. by Joseph R. Nolan & Michael J. Connolly. LC 79-12547. 1511p. 1979. text ed. 17.95 (ISBN 0-8299-2041-2); deluxe ed. 35.00 (ISBN 0-8299-2045-5). West Pub.
Blacks' Survival for the Nineteen Eighties & Beyond. Dorothy York. LC 80-50646. 63p. (Orig.). 1980. pap. 3.95 o.p. (ISBN 0-934616-07-8). Valkyrie Pr.
Black's Veterinary Dictionary. 13th ed. Ed. by Geoffrey West. (Illus.). 906p. 1979. 27.50x (ISBN 0-389-20125-1). B&N.
Blacksmiths. Leonard E. Fisher. LC 75-26684. (Colonial Americans Ser). (Illus.). 49p. (gr. 4-6). 1976. PLB 6.45 (ISBN 0-531-02901-8). Watts.
Blacksmith's Source Book: An Annotated Bibliography. James E. Fleming. 120p. 1981. write for info. (ISBN 0-8093-0989-0). S Ill U Pr.
Blackspirits. Ed. by Woodie King. 1972. pap. 1.95 o.p. (ISBN 0-394-71701-5, V701, Vin). Random.
Blackstone's Modern Card Tricks. rev. ed. Harry Blackstone. LC 58-5566. 1958. 5.95 o.p. (ISBN 0-385-00305-6). Doubleday.
Blacktower. Miriam Lynch. (Orig.). 1974. pap. 0.95 o.p. (ISBN 0-345-26595-5). Ballantine.
Bladder Cancer: Principles of Combination Therapy. Ed. by R. T. Oliver et al. (Illus.). 272p. 1981. text ed. 69.00 (ISBN 0-407-00187-5). Butterworth.
Bladder Control & Enuresis. I. Kolvin. Ed. by R. C. MacKeith. (Clinics in Developmental Medicine Ser.: Vols. 48 & 49). 328p. 1973. 32.00 (ISBN 0-685-59043-7). Lippincott.
Blade Coating Technology. Joseph H. Bigl et al. Ed. by C. Wells Clark. (TAPPI Press Reports). (Illus., Orig.). 1978. pap. 33.95 (ISBN 0-89852-373-7, 01 01 R073). TAPPI.
Blade of Grass. Gordon De Pree & Gladis De Pree. LC 65-19504. 1971. pap. 3.95 (ISBN 0-310-23641-X). Zondervan.
Blades of Passion. Claudette Williams. 1978. pap. 1.95 o.p. (ISBN 0-449-23481-9, Crest). Fawcett.
Blades' Surgical Diseases of the Chest. 4th ed. Ed. by Donald B. Effler. LC 78-7047. 1978. 67.50 (ISBN 0-8016-0697-7). Mosby.
Blaedud the Birdman. Vera Chapman. 1980. pap. 1.95 (ISBN 0-380-45070-4, 45070). Avon.
Blah. Jack Kent. LC 73-93851. (Illus.). (gr. k-2). 1970. 5.95 o.s.i. (ISBN 0-8193-0394-1, Four Winds); PLB 5.41 o.s.i. (ISBN 0-8193-0395-X). Schol Bk Serv.
Blaiklock's Handbook to the Bible. E. M. Blaiklock. 1981. pap. 5.95 (ISBN 0-8007-5055-1). Revell.
Blaise Cendrars: Pathe Baby. Julian Beck. (Pocket Poets Ser.). 112p. 1980. pap. 3.50 o.p. (ISBN 0-87286-108-2). City Lights.
Blaize. Anne Melville. 528p. 1981. 15.95 (ISBN 0-385-14832-1). Doubleday.
Blake & Antiquity. K. Raine. (A. W. Mellon Lecture: No. 11). 1978. 16.50x (ISBN 0-691-09943-X, 330); pap. 5.95 (ISBN 0-691-01802-2). Princeton U Pr.
Blake Dictionary: The Ideas & Symbols of William Blake. S. Foster Damon. LC 65-18187. (Illus.). 460p. 1973. Repr. of 1965 ed. 25.00 (ISBN 0-87057-088-9, Pub. by Brown U Pr). Univ Pr of New England.
Blake: Selected Poems & Letters. William Blake. Ed. by J. Bronowski. (Poets Ser.). 1958. pap. 2.95 (ISBN 0-14-042042-8). Penguin.
Blakely's Ark. Ian Macmillan. 1981. pap. 2.25 (ISBN 0-425-04928-0). Berkley Pub.
Blake's Human Form Divine. Anne K. Mellor. LC 72-161995. (Illus.). 1974. 31.50x (ISBN 0-520-02065-0). U of Cal Pr.
Blake's Illustrations to the Grave. William Blake. 1978. pap. 7.50 o.s.i. (ISBN 0-913668-22-2). Ten Speed Pr.
Blake's Job: William Blake's Illustrations of the Book of Job. William Blake. Ed. by S. Foster Damon. LC 66-13155. (Illus.). 66p. 1972. Repr. of 1966 ed. 10.00 (ISBN 0-87057-096-X, Pub. by Brown U Pr). Univ Pr of New England.
Blake's Sublime Allegory: Essays on the Four Zoas, Milton, & Jerusalem. Ed. by Stuart Curran & Joseph A. Wittreich, Jr. LC 72-1377. (Illus.). 504p. 1973. 29.50 (ISBN 0-299-06180-9). U of Wis Pr.
Blame the Teacher? Mildred Jackson. LC 79-54107. 180p. 1979. 5.95 (ISBN 0-8059-2672-0). Dorrance.
Blandford Book of Traditional Handicrafts. Ed. by John Rome. (Illus.). 240p. 1981. 22.50 (ISBN 0-7137-0951-0, Pub. by Blandford Pr England). Sterling.
Blanket. John Burningham. LC 76-17630. (Illus.). (ps-1). 1976. 3.95 (ISBN 0-690-01269-1, TYC-J); PLB 4.89 (ISBN 0-690-01270-5). T Y Crowell.
Blanket That Had to Go. Nancy E. Cooney. (Illus.). 32p. (gr. 4-8). 1981. 7.95 (ISBN 0-399-20716-3). Putnam.
Blankwaffen, 2 vols. Heribert Seitz. (Illus.). 1976. Set. 90.00 o.p. (ISBN 0-686-14976-9). Arma Pr.
Blasphemy in Massachusetts. Leonard Levy. LC 70-16634. 592p. 1974. lib. bdg. 55.00 (ISBN 0-306-70221-5). Da Capo.
Blast Cleaning & Allied Processes. H. J. Plaster. LC 73-155194. (Illus.). 374p. 1972. 57.50x (ISBN 0-901994-03-0). Intl Pubns Serv.
Blast Furnaces & Steel Slag: Production, Properties & Uses. A. R. Lee. LC 74-521. 119p. 1974. 16.95 (ISBN 0-470-52151-1). Halsted Pr.
Blast of War 1939-1945. Harold Macmillan. LC 67-28810. 1968. 20.00 o.p. (ISBN 0-06-012748-1, HarpT). Har-Row.
Blast Vibration Analysis. G. A. Bollinger. LC 79-22421. 149p. 1980. pap. 6.95 (ISBN 0-8093-0951-3). S Ill U Pr.
Blasting & Bombardiering. 2nd rev. ed. Wyndham Lewis. 1967. 21.50c (ISBN 0-520-00742-5). U of Cal Pr.
Blasting Operations. Gary B. Hemphill. (Illus.). 1980. 21.50 (ISBN 0-07-028093-2). McGraw.
Blastocyst-Endometrium Relationships. Ed. by F. Leroy. (Progress in Reproductive Biology Ser.: Vol. 7). (Illus.). 338p. 1980. 118.75 (ISBN 3-8055-0988-X). S Karger.
Blatherskite. Marian Potter. LC 80-18450. 192p. (gr. 4-6). 1980. 6.95 (ISBN 0-688-22249-8); PLB 6.67 (ISBN 0-688-32249-2). Morrow.
Blathwayt Atlas, Vol. 1, The Maps. Ed. by Jeannette D. Black. LC 78-654217. (Illus.). 1970. Set. unbound boxed 500.00x (ISBN 0-87057-125-7, Pub. by Brown U Pr). Univ Pr of New England.
Blathwayt Atlas: Vol. 2, Commentary. Jeannette D. Black. LC 78-654217. 235p. 1975. 25.00x (ISBN 0-87057-139-7, Pub. by Brown U Pr). Univ Pr of New England.
Blaue Kammerherr. Wolf Von Niebelschuetz. 1070p. (Ger.). 1980. Repr. 20.80 (ISBN 3-518-03736-6, Pub. by Insel Verlag Germany). Suhrkamp.
Blaue Reiter, No. 133-134. (Maeght Gallery: Derriere le Miroir Ser.). 1977. pap. 19.95 (ISBN 0-8120-0899-5). Barron.
Blaze & the Forest Fire. Clarence W. Anderson. (Illus.). (gr. k-3). 1962. 8.95 (ISBN 0-02-702080-0). Macmillan.

Blaze & the Gray Spotted Pony. C. W. Anderson. LC 68-10997. (Illus.). 48p. (gr. k-3). 1974. pap. 2.95 (ISBN 0-02-041480-3, 04148, Collier). Macmillan.

Blaze & the Gray Spotted Pony. Clarence W. Anderson. LC 68-10997. (Illus.). (ps-2). 1968. 6.95 (ISBN 0-02-701150-X). Macmillan.

Blaze & the Lost Quarry. Clarence W. Anderson. (Illus.). (gr. 1-3). 1966. 4.95g o.s.i. (ISBN 0-02-702490-3). Macmillan.

Blaze & the Mountain Lion. Clarence W. Anderson. (gr. 1-3). 1959. 8.95 (ISBN 0-02-702630-2). Macmillan.

Blaze & Thunderbolt. Clarence W. Anderson. (Illus.). (gr. 1-3). 1962. 8.95 (ISBN 0-02-702870-4). Macmillan.

Blaze Finds Forgotten Roads. Clarence W. Anderson. LC 76-117970. (Illus.). (gr. k-3). 1970. 6.95 (ISBN 0-02-701340-5). Macmillan.

Blaze Finds the Trail. Clarence W. Anderson. (Illus.). (gr. 1-3). 1962. 4.50g o.s.i. (ISBN 0-02-703130-6). Macmillan.

Blaze of Embers. Andre P. De Mandiargues. Tr. by April FitzLyon. 1980. 10.95 (ISBN 0-7145-0131-X). Riverrun NY.

Blaze of Noon: A Reading of Samson Agonistes. Anthony Low. 224p. 1974. 15.00x (ISBN 0-231-03842-9). Columbia U Pr.

Blaze Shows the Way. Clarence W. Anderson. LC 74-78090. (Illus.). (gr. 1-3). 1969. 6.95 (ISBN 0-02-701990-X). Macmillan.

Blazer & Ashland Oil: A Study in Management. Joseph L. Massie. LC 60-8519. (Illus.). 272p. 1960. 11.00x (ISBN 0-8131-1051-3). U Pr of Ky.

Blazing Star. C. Malcolm Gilman. LC 72-5188. (Illus.). 240p. 1973. 7.95 o.p. (ISBN 0-498-01220-4). A S Barnes.

Blazing Story of Washington County. Wilfred O. Dietrich. 10.95 (ISBN 0-685-48809-8). Nortex Pr.

Bleaching Earths. M. K. Hasruddin Siddiqui. 1968. 19.50 (ISBN 0-08-012738-X). Pergamon.

Bleaching of Pulp. 3rd ed. Rudra P. Singh et al. LC 78-78362. (TAPPI PRESS Bks). (Illus.). 1979. 69.95 (ISBN 0-89852-043-6, 01-02-B043). TAPPI.

Bleak House. Charles Dickens. Ed. by A. E. Dyson. LC 73-127567. (Casebook Ser). 1970. pap. text ed. 2.50 o.s.i. (ISBN 0-87695-038-1). Aurora Pubs.

Bleak House. Charles Dickens. (Critical Edition Ser.). 1978 17.50 (ISBN 0-393-04374-6); pap. 6.95x 1977 (ISBN 0-393-09332-8). Norton.

Bledding Sorrow. Harris. 408p. 1977. pap. 1.95 (ISBN 0-380-00936-6, 31971). Avon.

Blednii Ogon' Vladimir Nabokov. Tr. by Alexei Tsvetkov. (Rus.). 1981. 19.00 (ISBN 0-88233-602-9); pap. 12.50 (ISBN 0-88233-603-7). Ardis Pubs.

Bleeding Heart. Marilyn French. 416p. 1981. pap. 3.50 (ISBN 0-345-28896-3). Ballantine.

Bleeding Man & Other Science Fiction Stories. Craig Strete. LC 77-4505. (gr. 7 up). 1977. 8.25 (ISBN 0-688-80118-8); PLB 7.92 (ISBN 0-688-84118-X). Greenwillow.

Bleepers! Go to High School. (Illus., Orig.). 1981. pap. 1.95 (ISBN 0-446-97867-1). Warner Bks.

Bleepers in Love. (Illus., Orig.). 1980. pap. 1.95 (ISBN 0-446-97568-0). Warner Bks.

Bleepers in Space. (Illus., Orig.). 1980. pap. 1.95 (ISBN 0-446-97569-9). Warner Bks.

Bleepers! Meets the Monsters. (Illus., Orig.). 1981. pap. 1.95 (ISBN 0-446-97865-5). Warner Bks.

Blender Cookbook. Ann Seranne & Eileen Gaden. LC 61-11228. 7.95 o.p. (ISBN 0-385-07978-8). Doubleday.

Bless Me, Father. Neil Boyd. LC 77-9169. 1978. 8.95 o.p. (ISBN 0-312-08379-3). St Martin.

Bless the Nightingale: Ama Al ruisenor. Nellie P. Cartwright. LC 77-85799. 1977. 3.00 (ISBN 0-9601482-1-3). N P Cartwright.

Bless This Food. Anita Bryant. 1976. pap. 1.95 o.p. (ISBN 0-345-24900-3). Ballantine.

Bless This Mess. Jo Carr & Imogene Sorley. 1976. pap. 1.50 (ISBN 0-89129-130-X). Jove Pubns.

Blessed Are the Brood Mares. M. Phyllis Lose. (Illus.). 1978. 14.95 (ISBN 0-02-575250-2). Macmillan.

Blessed Are the Pure in Heart: The Beatitudes. Bernard Haring. (Illus.). 1977. pap. 4.95 (ISBN 0-8164-2125-0). Crossroad NY.

Blessed Is the Daughter. 7th ed. Meyer Waxman et al. LC 65-12053. (Illus.). 1980. 10.95 (ISBN 0-88400-064-8). Shengold.

Blessed Is the Ordinary. Gerhard E. Frost. (Illus.). 96p. pap. 4.95 (ISBN 0-03-056662-2). Winston Pr.

Blessed Is the Spot. Baha'u'llah. LC 58-8815. (Illus.). (gr. k-2). 1958. 4.50 (ISBN 0-87743-014-4, 7-52-40). Baha'i.

Blessed Kateri Takakwitha: Mohawk Maiden. Daughters of St Paul. 1980. 3.75 (ISBN 0-8198-1100-9); pap. 2.25 (ISBN 0-8198-1101-7). Dghtrs St Paul.

Blessed Rage for Order: The New Pluralism in Theology. David Tracy. 1975. 14.95 (ISBN 0-8164-4707-1). Crossroad NY.

Blessed Rage for Order: The New Pluralism in Theology. David Tracy. (Library of Contemporary Theology Ser.). 1979. pap. 8.95 (ISBN 0-8164-2202-8). Crossroad NY.

Blessed to Be a Blessing. James K. Wagner. LC 80-52615. 144p. (Orig.). 1980. pap. 4.50 (ISBN 0-8358-0410-0). Upper Room.

Blessing in Mosque & Mission. Larry G. Lenning. LC 80-25110. 176p. (Orig.). 1980. pap. write for info. (ISBN 0-87808-433-9). William Carey Lib.

Blessing: In the Bible & the Life of the Church, No. 3. Claus Westermann. Ed. by Walter Brueggeman & John R. Donahue. Tr. by Keith Crim from Ger. LC 78-54564. (Overtures to Biblical Theology Ser.). 144p. 1978. pap. 5.95 (ISBN 0-8006-1529-8, 1-1529). Fortress.

Blessing Way. Tony Hillerman. LC 73-96009. (Harper Novel of Suspense). 1970. 10.00 o.p. (ISBN 0-06-011896-2, HarpT). Har-Row.

Blessings: A Reappraisal of Their Nature, Purpose, & Celebration. Thomas G. Simons. 1981. pap. 12.95 (ISBN 0-686-69223-3). Resource Pubns.

Blessings from the Kitchen. Santa Barbara Third Ward Relief Society, Church of Jesus Christ of Latter Day Saints. 1972. 6.00 (ISBN 0-686-17209-4). Sandollar Pr.

Blessings of Illness. M. Basilea Schlink. LC 76-51103. 1977. pap. 1.95 (ISBN 0-88419-023-4). Creation Hse.

Blessman Approach. Lyle Blessman. LC 78-64483. 1978. 9.95 (ISBN 0-87863-175-5). Farnswth Pub.

Blickpunkt Deutschland. Jack R. Moeller et al. LC 76-190308. 416p. 1973. text ed. 16.76 (ISBN 0-395-13690-3, 2-37474); instr. ed. 16.52 (ISBN 0-395-14218-0, 2-37475); workbook 4.24 (ISBN 0-395-14212-1). HM.

Blight or Bloom. Fernando L. Dasbach. 198p. 1981. 12.50. Regenbogen-Verlag.

Blind Child in the Regular Kindergarten. Josephine Stratton. 64p. 1977. 9.75 (ISBN 0-398-03623-3). C C Thomas.

Blind Children Learn to Read. Berthold Lowenfeld et al. 196p. 1974. pap. 9.75 (ISBN 0-398-03205-X). C C Thomas.

Blind Connemara. Clarence W Anderson. (Illus.). (gr. 4-6). 1971. 4.95g o.s.i. (ISBN 0-02-705000-9). Macmillan.

Blind Cross: A Novel of Children's Crusade. Michael Mott. LC 68-27739. (gr. 7 up). 1970. 3.95 o.s.i. (ISBN 0-440-00646-5). Delacorte.

Blind Guards of Easter Island. Miriam W. Meyer. LC 77-14529. (Great Unsolved Mysteries Ser.). (Illus.). (gr. 4-5). 1977. PLB 9.65 (ISBN 0-8172-1048-2). Raintree Pubs.

Blind Love. Patrick Cauvin. 1978. pap. 1.75 o.p. (ISBN 0-449-23483-5, Crest). Fawcett.

Blind Love & Other Stories. V. S. Pritchett. Ed. by Jason Epstein. LC 70-85570. 1969. 7.95 o.p. (ISBN 0-394-41714-3). Random.

Blind Man & the Elephant. Lillian Quigley. LC 59-7209. (Illus.). (gr. k-4). 1959. reinforced bdg. 6.95 o.p. (ISBN 0-684-13276-1, ScribJ); pap. 0.95 o.p. (ISBN 0-684-12780-6, SBF19, ScribJ). Scribner.

Blind White Fish in Persia. Anthony Smith. (Unwin Bks). 1953. pap. 2.95 o.p. (ISBN 0-04-915010-3). Allen Unwin.

Blindness. Malcolm E. Weiss. (gr. 4 up). 1980. PLB 6.45 (ISBN 0-531-02939-5). Watts.

Blink, the Patchwork Bunny. Matthew V. Howard. (Kindergarten Read-to Bks.). (Illus.). (gr. k-2). PLB 5.95 o.p. (ISBN 0-513-00302-9). Denison.

Blinking Eye: Ralph Waldo Ellison & His American, French, German & Italian Critics, 1952-1971; Bibliographic Essays & a Checklist. Jacqueline Covo. LC 74-13042. (Author Bibliographies Ser.: No. 18). 1974. 10.00 (ISBN 0-8108-0736-X). Scarecrow.

Blinky & the Blends. Elizabeth Gregory. (Illus.). 1981. 6.95 (ISBN 0-933184-11-5); pap. 4.95 (ISBN 0-933184-12-3). Flame Intl.

Bliss. Elizabeth Gundy. 1978. pap. 1.95 (ISBN 0-515-04706-6). Jove Pubns.

Bliss Bibliographic Classification: Part T: Economics, Enterprise, Management. 2nd ed. Ed. by J. Mills & V. Broughton. Date not set. text ed. price not set (ISBN 0-408-70834-4). Butterworths.

Bliss Bibliography, Second Class H: Anthropology, Human Biology & Health Sciences. Bliss. 1981. price not set (ISBN 0-408-70828-X). Butterworth.

Bliss Carman. Donald Stephens. (World Authors Ser.: Canada: No. 8). 1966. lib. bdg. 10.95 (ISBN 0-8057-2200-9). Twayne.

Bliss Toys & Dollhouses: Eighty Nine Illustrations, Including the Complete 1911 Catalog. Ed. by Blair Whitton. (Illus.). 1979. pap. 2.75 (ISBN 0-486-23790-7). Dover.

Blissymbolics: Speaking Without Speech. Elizabeth Helfman. (Illus.). 144p. 1981. 10.95 (ISBN 0-525-66678-8). Elsevier-Nelson.

Blitzkreig. Robert Wernick. LC 76-25750. (World War II). (Illus.). (gr. 6 up). 1976. PLB 14.94 (ISBN 0-8094-2455-X, Pub by Time-Life). Silver.

Blitzkrieg. Robert Wernick. Ed. by Time-Life Books. (World War II Ser.). 1976. 12.95 (ISBN 0-8094-2454-1). Time-Life.

Blitzkrieg Story. Charles Messenger. LC 76-18633. (Encore Edition). (Illus.). 272p. 1976. 3.95 o.p. (ISBN 0-684-15712-8, ScribT). Scribner.

Blizzard. Robert Bahr. LC 80-14956. 1980. 9.95 (ISBN 0-13-077842-7). P-H.

Blizzard Voices. Ted Kooser. 1981. price not set (ISBN 0-931460-17-4). Bieler.

Block Copolymers. Ed. by D. C. Allport & W. H. Janes. LC 72-10339. 620p. 1973. 57.95 (ISBN 0-470-02517-4). Halsted Pr.

Block Copolymers. Ed. by D. Meier. (Mmi Press Symposium Ser.: Vol. 2). 350p. 1981. lib. bdg. 44.00 lib. bdg. (ISBN 0-686-65733-0). Harwood Academic.

Block-Level Planning. Association of Voluntary Agency for Rural Development, India. 128p. 1980. text ed. 18.95x (ISBN 0-7069-1063-X, Pub by Vikas India). Advent Bk.

Block or Day Release? A Comparative Study of Engineering Apprentices. B. M. Moore. (Research Reports Ser.). (Illus.). 198p. 1972. Repr. of 1969 ed. text ed. 13.75x (ISBN 0-901225-01-0, NFER). Humanities.

Block Polymers. Allen Noshay & James E. McGrath. 1977. 61.00 (ISBN 0-12-521750-1). Acad Pr.

Block Printing on Textiles. Janet Erickson. (Illus.). 168p. 1974. 12.95 o.p. (ISBN 0-8230-0501-1); pap. 9.95 o.p. (ISBN 0-8230-0502-X). Watson-Guptill.

Blockade of Germany After the Armistice, 1918-1919: Selected Documents of the Supreme Economic Council, Superior Blockade Council, American Relief Administration, & Other Wartime Organizations. Ed. by Suda L. Bane & Ralph Lutz. LC 79-80520. 874p. 1973. Repr. of 1942 ed. 28.00 o.p. (ISBN 0-86527-012-0). Fertig.

Blocking & Unblocking Plays in Bridge. Terence Reese & Roger Trezel. LC 76-13614. 64p. 1976. pap. 3.95 (ISBN 0-8119-0359-1). Fell.

Blocks for Transplants. 89p. 1980. pap. 9.95x (ISBN 0-901361-37-2, Pub. by Grower Bks England). Intl Schol Bk Serv.

Blonde Chicana Bride's Mexican Cookbook. Helen C. De Duran. (Wild & Woolly West Ser.: No. 40). (Illus., Orig.). 1980. 7.00 (ISBN 0-910584-95-8); pap. 2.00 (ISBN 0-910584-96-6). Filter.

Blonde Eckbert & Geschichte Vom Braven Kasperl und Dem Schonen Annerl. 7th ed. Ludwig Tiek & Brentano. Ed. by Margaret E. Atkinson. (Blackwell's German Text Ser.). 1972. pap. 5.50x (ISBN 0-631-01560-4, Pub. by Basil Blackwell). Biblio Dist.

Blondes Prefer Gentlemen-Brunettes, Too-Redheads Included. Sheila J. Daly. LC 49-10484. (Illus.). (gr. 9 up). 1949. 3.95 (ISBN 0-396-03061-0). Dodd.

Blondie, No. 2. Dean Young & Jim Raymond. (Blondie Cartoon Ser.). 128p. (Orig.). (gr. 3 up). 1981. pap. 1.50 (Tempo). G&D.

Blood. Herbert S. Zim. (Illus.). (gr. 3-7). 1968. PLB 6.48 (ISBN 0-688-31109-1). Morrow.

Blood & Burning. Algis Budrys. 1978. pap. 1.75 o.p. (ISBN 0-425-03861-0, Medallion). Berkley Pub.

Blood & Dreams. Leslie Waller. 1980. 12.95 (ISBN 0-686-68359-5). Putnam.

Blood & Flesh: Black American & African Identifications. Josephine Moikobu. LC 80-1706. (Contributions in African American Studies: No. 59). (Illus.). 224p. 1981. lib. bdg. 25.00 (ISBN 0-313-22549-4, MBF/). Greenwood.

Blood & Its Diseases. 2nd ed. Israel Chanarin et al. (Illus.). 320p. 1980. text ed. 18.00x (ISBN 0-443-02191-0). Churchill.

Blood & Knavery: A Collection of English Renaissance Pamphlets & Ballads of Crime & Sin. Joseph H. Marshburn & Alan R. Velie. LC 72-3523. (Illus.). 239p. 1973. 14.50 (ISBN 0-8386-1010-2). Fairleigh Dickinson.

Blood & Money. Thomas Thompson. 1981. pap. 3.25 (ISBN 0-440-10679-6). Dell.

Blood & Passion. Jefferey M. Wallman. (Orig.). 1980. pap. 2.25 (ISBN 0-505-51514-8). Tower Bks.

Blood & Semen: Kinship Systems of Highland New Guinea. Ed. by Edwin A. Cook & Denise O'Brien. LC 80-21559. (Anthropology Ser.: Studies in Pacific Anthropology). (Illus.). 532p. (Orig.). 1980. pap. 38.50 (ISBN 0-472-02710-7, IS-00117, Pub. by U of Mich Pr). Univ Microfilms.

Blood & Tissue Parasites. Ed. by James W. Smith. (Atlases of Diagnostic Medical Parasitology: 1). (Illus.). 1976. 76.50 (ISBN 0-89189-065-3, 15-7-006-00); microfiche ed. 22.00 (ISBN 0-89189-046-7, 17-7-006-00). Am Soc Clinical.

Blood & Water. Peter De Polnay. LC 75-40784. 199p. 1976. 7.95 o.p. (ISBN 0-312-08435-8). St Martin.

Blood Bank Policies & Procedures. Robert M. Greendyke & Jane C. Banzhaf. 1976. spiral bdg. 12.00 o.p. (ISBN 0-87488-652-X). Med Exam.

Blood Banking Principles Review Book: Essay Questions & Answers. Bernard Pirofsky et al. 1973. spiral bdg. 12.00 (ISBN 0-87488-339-3). Med Exam.

Blood Bay Colt. Walter Farley. (Illus.). (gr. 4-6). 1950. 3.95 (ISBN 0-394-80606-9, BYR); PLB 5.99 (ISBN 0-394-90606-3); pap. 1.95 (ISBN 0-394-83915-3). Random.

Blood Biochemistry. N. J. Russell et al. 128p. 1980. 24.00x (Pub. by Croom Helm England). State Mutual Bk.

Blood Bond. Emma Cave. 192p. 1981. pap. 2.50 (ISBN 0-449-24402-4, Crest). Fawcett.

Blood-Brain Barrier in Physiology & Medicine. Stanley I. Rapoport. LC 75-26280. 1976. 33.50 (ISBN 0-89004-079-6). Raven.

Blood Brothers. D. Anderson. LC 67-17800. (Illus.). 1969. 5.95 o.p. (ISBN 0-312-08400-5). St Martin.

Blood Brothers. Ann Ruffell. (gr. 7 up). 1980. PLB 7.90 (ISBN 0-531-04177-8). Watts.

Blood Compatible Synthetic Polymers: An Introduction. Stephen D. Bruck. (Illus.). 144p. 1974. 14.75 (ISBN 0-398-02931-8). C C Thomas.

Blood County. Curt Selby. 1981. pap. 2.25 (ISBN 0-87997-622-5, UE1622, Daw Bks). NAL.

Blood Donor Characteristics & Types of Blood Donations, U. S., 1973. Abigail J. Moss. LC 75-35546. (Ser. 10: No.106). 51p. 1976. pap. text ed. 1.50 (ISBN 0-8406-0056-9). Natl Ctr Health Stats.

Blood Drugs & Other Analytical Challenges. Ed. by E. Reid. LC 78-40411. (Methodological Surveys in Biology Ser.). 1978. 54.95 (ISBN 0-470-26445-4). Halsted Pr.

Blood Flow in Arteries. D. A. McDonald. 450p. 1974. 48.00 o.p. (ISBN 0-683-05760-X). Williams & Wilkins.

Blood Gases in Clinical Practice. Leopoldo Lapuerta. (Illus.). 132p. 1976. 16.75 (ISBN 0-398-03527-X). C C Thomas.

Blood in My Eye. George Jackson. (YA) 1972. 8.95 o.p. (ISBN 0-394-47981-5). Random.

Blood Is Not Enough: Stories of One Sq. Mile. Alex Blair. (Illus.). 172p. (Orig.). 1981. pap. 3.50 (ISBN 0-938918-00-1). Chong-Donnie.

Blood Island. James Fritzhand. 1981. pap. 2.75 (ISBN 0-671-83012-0). PB.

Blood Justice. Jory Sherman. (Gunn Ser.: No. 4). 256p. (Orig.). 1980. pap. 1.95 (ISBN 0-89083-670-1). Zebra.

Blood Money. Aaron Fletcher. (Bounty Hunter: No. 2). 1977. pap. 1.25 (ISBN 0-8439-0471-2, Leisure Bks). Nordon Pubns.

Blood of an Englishman. James McClure. LC 80-7607. 288p. 1981. 9.95 (ISBN 0-06-013046-6, HarpT). Har-Row.

Blood of Freedom. Earl J. Miers. LC 58-13521. (Williamsburg in America Ser.: Vol. 3). (Illus.). 4.95 o.p. (ISBN 0-910412-49-9). Williamsburg.

Blood of My Blood: The Dilemma of the Italian Americans. Richard Gambino. LC 73-11705. 360p. 1974. 4.50. Doubleday.

Blood of My Blood, the Dilemma of the Italian-Americans. Richard Gambino. 400p. 1975. pap. 4.50 (ISBN 0-385-07564-2, Anch). Doubleday.

Blood of Paradise. Stephen Goodwin. 1979. 8.95 o.p. (ISBN 0-525-06846-5). Dutton.

Blood of the Cross. Andrew Murray. 128p. 1981. pap. 2.50 (ISBN 0-88368-103-X). Whitaker Hse.

Blood of the People: Revolution & the End of Traditional Rule in Northern Sumatra. Anthony Reid. (Illus.). 308p. 1979. text ed. 34.50x (ISBN 0-19-580399-X). Oxford U Pr.

Blood of the West. Paul E. Lehman. 1979. pap. 1.50 (ISBN 0-505-51410-9). Tower Bks.

Blood on Frisco Bay. Jay Flynn. 1976. pap. 1.25 o.p. (ISBN 0-685-69143-8, LB36OZK, Leisure Bks). Nordon Pubns.

Blood on the Border. C. C. Clendenen. 1969. 12.50 o.s.i. (ISBN 0-02-526110-X). Macmillan.

Blood on the Land. Frank Bonham. 1978. pap. 1.75 o.p. (ISBN 0-425-04809-8). Berkley Pub.

Blood on the Range. Owen G. Irons. 1980. pap. 1.95 (ISBN 0-89083-686-8, Kable News Co). Zebra.

Blood on the Sand. Andrew Quiller. (Gladiator Ser.: No. 4). 1978. pap. 1.25 o.p. (ISBN 0-523-40094-2). Pinnacle Bks.

Blood on the Snow. John Elliott. LC 76-29859. 1977. 8.95 o.p. (ISBN 0-312-08452-8). St Martin.

Blood Oranges. John Hawkes. LC 74-152516. 1971 ed 6.95 (ISBN 0-8112-0285-2); pap. 4.95 1972 ed. (ISBN 0-8112-0061-2, NDP338). New Directions.

Blood Over Texas: The Unpopular Truth About Mexico's War with the United States. Sanford H. Montaigne. 1976. 8.95 o.p. (ISBN 0-87000-342-9). Arlington Hse.

Blood Platelets in Man & Animals, 2 Vols. B. Maupin. 1969. Set. 150.00 (ISBN 0-08-006405-1). Pergamon.
Blood Pressure Control, Vol. 1. Thomas G. Coleman. 248p. 1980. 32.50 (ISBN 0-88831-088-9). Eden Med Res.
Blood Pressure, Edema & Proteinuria in Pregnancy. Ed. by Emanuel A. Friedman. LC 76-10262. (Progress in Clinical & Biological Research: Vol. 7). 296p. 1976. 29.00x (ISBN 0-8451-0007-6). A R Liss.
Blood Red Dream. Michael Collins. LC 80-83589. (Dan Fortune Detective Mystery Ser.). 192p. 1981. pap. 2.25 (ISBN 0-87216-812-3). Playboy Pbks.
Blood Red Rose. Arthur Wise & Nicola Wise. LC 80-84375. 272p. 1981. pap. 2.50 (ISBN 0-87216-815-8). Playboy Pbks.
Blood Red Roses. Elizabeth B. Coker. LC 77-1366. 1977. 9.95 o.p. (ISBN 0-525-06860-0). Dutton.
Blood Red, Sister Rose. Thomas Keneally. 400p. 1976. pap. 1.95 o.p. (ISBN 0-345-24816-3). Ballantine.
Blood Red Wine. Laurence Delaney. (Orig.). Date not set. pap. 3.25 (ISBN 0-440-10714-8). Dell.
Blood Relations. Leonard Mosley. LC 79-55584. (Illus.). 1980. 17.50 (ISBN 0-689-11055-3). Atheneum.
Blood Relatives. Ed McBain. 1977. pap. 1.50 o.p. (ISBN 0-394-25462-7). Ballantine.
Blood-Retinal Barriers. Ed. by Jose G. Cunha-Vaz. (NATO Advanced Study Institutes Ser., Ser. A: Life Sciences: Vol. 32). 405p. 1980. 39.50 (ISBN 0-306-40430-3, Plenum Pr). Plenum Pub.
Blood Rites. Barry Nazarian. (Orig.). 1980. pap. 2.25 (ISBN 0-451-09203-1, E9203, Sig). NAL.
Blood Secrets. Craig Jones. LC 78-4743. 1978. 8.95 o.s.i. (ISBN 0-06-012264-1, HarpT). Har-Row.
Blood Sports. Paul R. Rothweiler. (Orig.). pap. 2.25 (ISBN 0-515-05410-0). Jove Pubns.
Blood Suckers. Ed. by Mary Verdick. (Pal Paperbacks Ser., Kit A). (Illus., Orig.). (gr. 7-12). 1976. pap. text ed. 1.25 (ISBN 0-8374-3500-5). Xerox Ed Pubns.
Blood Summer. Don Asher. 1979. pap. 1.95 o.p. (ISBN 0-425-03949-8). Berkley Pub.
Blood Supply of Bone. M. Brookes. 1971. 29.95x (ISBN 0-407-11900-0). Butterworths.
Blood, Sweat, Toil & Tears. Gerald C. Ellis. (Orig.). 1980. pap. 2.95 (ISBN 0-89260-171-X). Hwong Pub.
Blood Technology. James R. Critser, Jr. (Series 10BT-79). 101p. 1980. 80.00 (ISBN 0-914428-75-6). Lexington Data.
Blood Ties. Warren Adler. 1980. pap. write for info. (ISBN 0-671-83055-4). PB.
Blood Ties. Alexandra Roudybush. LC 80-1852. (Crime Club Ser.). 192p. 1981. 9.95 (ISBN 0-385-17339-3). Doubleday.
Blood Ties: A Woman's Autobiography. Anica V. Mander. 1976. 10.00 o.p. (ISBN 0-394-40766-0). Random.
Blood Trail. Gardner Fox. 1979. pap. 1.50 (ISBN 0-505-51367-6). Tower Bks.
Blood Vessels. W. J. Cliff. LC 74-31789. (Biological Structure & Functions Ser.: No. 6). (Illus.). 224p. 1976. 50.00 (ISBN 0-521-20753-3). Cambridge U Pr.
Blood Volume & Extracellular Fluid Volume. 2nd ed. Solomon N. Albert. (Amer. Lec. Anesthesiology Ser.). (Illus.). 336p. 1971. 27.50 (ISBN 0-398-02193-7). C C Thomas.
Blood Will Tell. Miles Napier. pap. 8.75 (ISBN 0-85131-254-3, Dist. by Sporting Book Center). J A Allen.
Blood Wrath. Chester Krone. LC 80-82852. 272p. (Orig.). 1981. pap. 2.50 (ISBN 0-87216-778-X). Playboy Pbks.
Bloodbath. William Wingate. 240p. 1981. pap. 2.50 (ISBN 0-553-14707-2). Bantam.
Bloodbath Hill. Pat Nobel. (Orig.). 1980. pap. 2.25 (ISBN 0-532-23187-2). Manor Bks.
Bloodborn. Robert Leckie. (Americans at War Ser.: No. 1). (Orig.). 1981. pap. 2.95 (ISBN 0-451-09801-3, E9801, Signet Bks). NAL.
Bloodhype. Alan D. Foster. 1977. pap. 2.25 (ISBN 0-345-29476-9). Ballantine.
Bloodletters & Badmen, Vol. 1. J. Robert Nash. (Illus.). 1975. pap. 2.75 (ISBN 0-446-95531-0). Warner Bks.
Bloodletters & Badmen, Vol. 2. J. Robert Nash. (Illus.). 1975. pap. 2.75 (ISBN 0-446-95532-9). Warner Bks.
Bloodletters & Badmen, Vol. 3. J. Robert Nash. (Illus.). 1975. pap. 2.75 (ISBN 0-446-95533-7). Warner Bks.
Bloodletters & Badmen: A Narrative Encyclopedia of American Criminals from the Pilgrims to the Present. Jay R. Nash. LC 72-95977. (Illus.). 640p. 1973. 16.95 o.p. (ISBN 0-87131-113-5); pap. 9.95 (ISBN 0-87131-200-X). M Evans.
Bloodlines. Charles Wright. LC 74-2196. (Wesleyan Poetry Program: Vol. 77). 80p. 1975. pap. 4.95 (ISBN 0-8195-1077-7, Pub. by Wesleyan U Pr). Columbia U Pr.
Bloodrush. Hugh Zachary. 1981. pap. 1.95 (ISBN 0-8439-0857-2, Leisure Bks). Nordon Pubns.
Bloodshed & Vengence in the Papuan Mountains: The Generation of Conflict in Tauade Society. C. R. Hallpike. (Illus.). 1977. 48.00x (ISBN 0-19-823192-X). Oxford U Pr.
Bloodstock Sales Analysis, 1962. Compiled by Bernard J. O'Sullivan. 1.75 (ISBN 0-85131-058-3, Dist. by Sporting Book Center). J A Allen.
Bloodstone. Kenneth L. Bjorgum. 256p. (Orig.). 1980. pap. 2.25 (ISBN 0-515-05475-5). Jove Pubns.
Bloodstones: Lines from a Marriage. Lucile Bogue. 1980. 5.50 (ISBN 0-8233-0324-1). Golden Quill.
Bloody Border. J. T. Edson. (J.T. Edson Ser.). 1978. pap. 1.50 o.p. (ISBN 0-425-03844-0, Medallion). Berkley Pub.
Bloody Bush. Gordon Davis. (Sergeant Ser.: No. 3). 288p. (Orig.). 1980. pap. 2.25 (ISBN 0-89083-647-7). Zebra.
Bloody Chamber. Angela Carter. LC 79-2645. 176p. 1981. pap. 3.95 (ISBN 0-06-090836-X, C*N 836, CN). Har-Row.
Bloody Country. James L. Collier & Christopher Collier. LC 75-34461. 192p. (gr. 7 up). 1977. 7.95 (ISBN 0-590-07411-3, Four Winds). Schol Bk Serv.
Bloody Gold. Chet Cunningham. 1980. pap. 1.75 (ISBN 0-505-51492-3). Tower Bks.
Bloody Provost: An Account of the Provost Service of the British Army & the Early Years of the Corps of Royal Military Police. R. A. Tyler. (Illus.). 246p. 1980. 23.75x (ISBN 0-8476-3166-4). Rowman.
Bloody Sands. J. D. Hardin. LC 80-80989. (Pinkerton Ser.: No. 8). 208p. (Orig.). 1980. pap. 1.75 (ISBN 0-87216-718-6). Playboy Pbks.
Bloody Sun. Marion Z. Bradley. 192p. (Orig.). 1975. pap. 2.50 (ISBN 0-441-06855-3). Ace Bks.
Bloody Trail to Texas. Jake Logan. LC 76-1706. (John Slocum Ser.: No. 7). 192p. 1976. pap. 1.75 (ISBN 0-87216-736-4). Playboy Pbks.
Blooming: A Small-Town Girlhood. Susan A. Toth. 244p. 1981. 10.95 (ISBN 0-316-85076-4). Little.
Blooming Success. Deborah Johnson. (Illus.). 1978. pap. 7.95 (ISBN 0-88453-019-1). Barrington.
Bloomsbury: A House of Lions. Leon Edel. 1979. pap. 2.75 (ISBN 0-380-50005-1, 50005). Avon.
Blossom on the Bough: A Book of Trees. Anne O. Dowden. LC 74-6192. (Illus.). (gr. 5 up). 1975. 10.95 (ISBN 0-690-00384-6, TYC-J). T Y Crowell.
Blossom Where You Are Planted. Ohla E. Nickerson. (Orig.). 1980. pap. 1.95 (ISBN 0-532-23200-3). Manor Bks.
Blow Away. Dean Selmier & Mark Kram. 1979. 9.95 o.p. (ISBN 0-670-17447-5). Viking Pr.
Blow Away the Black Clouds. Florence Littauer. LC 80-85334. 1981. pap. 3.95 (ISBN 0-89081-285-3). Harvest Hse.
Blow Molding Markets, P-029. rev. ed. BCC Staff. 1976. 500.00 o.p. (ISBN 0-89336-042-2). BCC.
Blow Molding P-029R: Markets, Technologies. 1979. 850.00 (ISBN 0-89336-198-4). BCC.
Blow Wind of God: Spirited Messages from the Writings of Billy Graham. Donald E. Demaray. 1977. pap. 1.50 o.p. (ISBN 0-451-07380-0, W7380, Sig). NAL.
Blowing on the Wind: The Nuclear Test Ban Debate, 1954-1960. Robert A. Divine. LC 77-25057. 1978. 15.95x (ISBN 0-19-502390-0). Oxford U Pr.
Blowing Rock: North Carolina. Aerial Photo. Date not set. 1.50 (ISBN 0-936672-08-0). Aerial Photo.
Blowing the Whistle on Intercollegiate Sports. J. Robert Evans. LC 74-78842. 1974. 11.95 (ISBN 0-911012-94-X). Nelson-Hall.
Blowout. Robert DeMaria. (Orig.). 1979. pap. 2.25 (ISBN 0-515-04527-6). Jove Pubns.
Blowout Prevention. 2nd ed. W. C. Goins & Riley Sheffield. 300p. 1981. 19.95 (ISBN 0-87201-073-2). Gulf Pub.
Blubber. Judy Blume. LC 73-94116. 160p. (gr. 4-6). 1974. 8.95 (ISBN 0-87888-072-0). Bradbury Pr.
Blue. Tom Clark. (Illus.). 80p. (Orig.). 1974. ltd. signed o.p. 15.00 (ISBN 0-87685-184-7); pap. 3.00 (ISBN 0-87685-183-9). Black Sparrow.
Blue & Brown Books. Ludwig Wittgenstein. pap. 3.95 (ISBN 0-06-090451-8, CN451, CN). Har-Row.
Blue Angels: An Illustrated History. Rosario Rausa. (Illus.). 1979. 14.50 (ISBN 0-911721-82-7, Pub. by Moran). Aviation.
Blue Annals. 2nd ed. A. N. Roerich. 1976. 37.50 (ISBN 0-89684-179-0). Orient Bk Dist.
Blue Apple. Nina Cassian. Tr. by Eve Feiler. (Cross-Cultural Review Chapbook 13). 16p. (Romanian & Eng.). 1980. pap. 2.00 (ISBN 0-89304-812-7). Cross Cult.
Blue Aspic. Edward Gorey. (Illus.). 1969. 4.95 (ISBN 0-8015-0738-3, Hawthorn). Dutton.
Blue Barns. Helen Sewell. (Illus.). (gr. k-3). 1933. 3.95g o.s.i. (ISBN 0-02-782150-1). Macmillan.
Blue Bay Mystery. Gertrude C. Warner. LC 61-15230. (Boxcar Children Mysteries-Pilot Bk.). (Illus.). (gr. 3-7). 6.95g (ISBN 0-8075-0793-8). A Whitman.
Blue Blood Will Out. Tim Heald. 192p. 1980. pap. 2.25 (ISBN 0-345-28904-8). Ballantine.
Blue Book Illustrated Price Guide to Collectable Cameras, 1839-1981: 2nd Silver Issue. 2nd ed. Myron Wolf. (Illus.). 224p. 1980. pap. 14.95 (ISBN 0-9604352-0-4). Photo Memorabilia.
Blue Book Nineteen Seventy-Six: Leaders of the English-Speaking World, 2 vols. LC 73-13918. 1979. Set. 78.00 (ISBN 0-8103-0216-0). Gale.
Blue Book of Broadminded Business Behavior. Auren Uris. LC 76-54769. 1977. 14.95 o.p. (ISBN 0-690-01422-8, TYC-T). T Y Crowell.
Blue Book of Questions & Answers for Second Mate, Chief Mate & Master. W. A. McEwen. LC 62-15957. (Illus.). 320p. 1969. pap. 8.50x (ISBN 0-87033-007-1). Cornell Maritime.
Blue Book of Questions & Answers for Third Mates. 2nd ed. W. A. McEwen. LC 65-25384. (Illus.). 1965. pap. 6.00x (ISBN 0-87033-008-X). Cornell Maritime.
Blue Book of the John Birch Society. Robert Welch. LC 74-29425. 1961. 4.00 (ISBN 0-88279-215-6); pap. 2.00 pocketsize (ISBN 0-88279-106-0). Western Islands.
Blue Bug's Book of Colors. Virginia Poulet. LC 80-23229. (Blue Bug Bks). (Illus.). 32p. (ps-3). 1981. PLB 7.95 (ISBN 0-516-03442-1). Childrens.
Blue Cat. F. D. Reeve. 1973. 6.95 o.p. (ISBN 0-374-11474-9); pap. 2.95 o.p. (ISBN 0-374-51048-2). FS&G.
Blue Cliff Record. Thomas Cleary & J. C. Cleary. LC 76-14202. 1978. 25.00 (ISBN 0-87773-706-1, Prajna). Great Eastern.
Blue-Coated Worker. R. Reiner. LC 77-85695. (Cambridge Studies in Sociology: No. 10). (Illus.). 1978. 38.50 (ISBN 0-521-21889-6); pap. 11.95 (ISBN 0-521-29482-7). Cambridge U Pr.
Blue Collar Aristocrats: Life Styles at a Working Class Tavern. E. E. LeMasters. LC 74-27309. 233p. 1975. 17.50 (ISBN 0-299-06550-2); pap. 5.95 (ISBN 0-299-06554-5). U of Wis Pr.
Blue Collar Community. William Kornblum. LC 74-5733. (Studies of Urban Society Ser). 1976. pap. 6.50 (ISBN 0-226-45038-4, P699, Phoen). U of Chicago Pr.
Blue-Collar Jobs for Women. Muriel Lederer. 1979. 12.95 o.p.; pap. 7.95 (ISBN 0-87690-319-7). Dutton.
Blue-Collar Journal: A College President's Sabbatical. John R. Coleman. LC 73-21902. 1974. 8.95 (ISBN 0-397-01030-3). Lippincott.
Blue Evenings in Berlin: Nabokov's Short Stories of the 1920s. Marina Turkevich Naumann. LC 77-82751. (New York University Studies in Comparative Literature: Vol. 9). 254p. 1978. 15.00x (ISBN 0-8147-5753-7). NYU Pr.
Blue Eyes & Gray. Emmuska Orczy. 1976. lib. bdg. 14.75x (ISBN 0-89968-014-3). Lightyear.
Blue Fairy Book. Ed. by Andrew Lang. (Illus.). (gr. 1-6). 1965. pap. 3.95 (ISBN 0-486-21437-0). Dover.
Blue Falcon. Robyn Carr. 1981. 12.95 (ISBN 0-316-12972-0). Little.
Blue Fire. Phyllis A. Whitney. 1981. pap. 2.25 (ISBN 0-449-24083-5, Crest). Fawcett.
Blue Frogs. Jeffrey Helterman. (Orig.). 1980. pap. 1.95 (ISBN 0-532-23197-X). Manor Bks.
Blue Garden. Barbara Howes. LC 72-3697. (Wesleyan Poetry Program: Vol. 62). (Orig.). 1972. 10.00x (ISBN 0-8195-2062-4, Pub. by Wesleyan U Pr); pap. 4.95 (ISBN 0-8195-1062-9). Columbia U Pr.
Blue Guide - Athens. 1981. pap. 19.95 (ISBN 0-528-84623-X). Rand.
Blue Guide - Belgium. 1977. 29.95 (ISBN 0-528-84662-0); pap. 19.95 (ISBN 0-528-84661-2). Rand.
Blue Guide - Channel Islands. 24.95 (ISBN 0-528-84620-5); pap. 15.95 (ISBN 0-528-84619-1). Rand.
Blue Guide - Crete. 1980. 19.95 (ISBN 0-528-84616-7); pap. 11.95 (ISBN 0-528-84615-9). Rand.
Blue Guide - Cyprus. 1980. pap. 22.95 (ISBN 0-528-84617-5). Rand.
Blue Guide - England. 1980. 24.95 (ISBN 0-528-84625-6); pap. 16.95 (ISBN 0-528-84728-7). Rand.
Blue Guide - Greece. 1981. pap. 24.95 (ISBN 0-528-87428-4). Rand.
Blue Guide - Italy, Northern. 1977. 29.95 (ISBN 0-528-84599-3); pap. 19.95 (ISBN 0-528-84600-0). Rand.
Blue Guide - London. 1978. 19.95 (ISBN 0-528-84638-8); pap. 12.95 (ISBN 0-528-84637-X). Rand.
Blue Guide - Moscow & Leningrad. 1980. 29.95 (ISBN 0-528-84611-6); pap. 24.95 (ISBN 0-528-84607-8). Rand.
Blue Guide - Normandy, Brittany, Loire Valley. 1977. 28.95 (ISBN 0-528-84597-7); pap. 19.95 (ISBN 0-528-84598-5). Rand.
Blue Guide - Paris. 1977. 24.95 (ISBN 0-528-84605-1); pap. 16.95 (ISBN 0-528-84659-0). Rand.
Blue Guide - Rome. 1979. 29.95 (ISBN 0-528-84629-9); pap. 16.95 (ISBN 0-528-84628-0). Rand.
Blue Guide - Scotland. 1980. 29.95 (ISBN 0-528-84612-4); pap. 19.95 (ISBN 0-528-84608-6). Rand.
Blue Guide - Sicily. 1981. 19.95 (ISBN 0-528-84621-3). Rand.
Blue Guide - Spain. 1980. 29.95 (ISBN 0-528-84614-0); pap. 19.95 (ISBN 0-528-84610-8). Rand.
Blue Guide - Venice. 1980. pap. 19.95 (ISBN 0-528-84609-4). Rand.
Blue Harbor. Phyllis Luxem. (YA) 1966. 5.95 (ISBN 0-685-07425-0, Avalon). Bouregy.
Blue Hawk. Peter Dickinson. 1977. pap. 1.95 o.p. (ISBN 0-345-25759-6). Ballantine.
Blue Haze. Netta Muskett. (Orig.). 1978. pap. 1.75 o.s.i. (ISBN 0-515-04539-X). Jove Pubns.
Blue Horse & Other Night Poems. Cedering-Siv Fox. LC 78-12793. (Illus.). (gr. 1-4). 1979. 8.95 (ISBN 0-395-28952-1, Clarion). HM.
Blue Hurricane. F. Van Wyck Mason. pap. 1.95 o.p. (ISBN 0-425-03182-9). Berkley Pub.
Blue Key. Kathalyn Krause. (Orig.). 1980. pap. 2.25 (ISBN 0-505-51536-9). Tower Bks.
Blue Lagoon Omnibus. Henry D. Stacpoole. 210p. (Orig.). 1981. Repr. of 1908 ed. 3.95x (ISBN 0-9605338-0-X). Blue Lagoon.
Blue Leader. Walter Wager. 336p. 1981. pap. 2.25 (ISBN 0-425-04628-1). Berkley Pub.
Blue Locket. Frances S. Moore. (YA) 1972. 5.95 (ISBN 0-685-28625-8, Avalon). Bouregy.
Blue Lotus. Margaret Way. (Harlequin Romances Ser.). (Orig.). 1980. pap. 1.25 o.p. (ISBN 0-373-02328-6, Pub. by Harlequin). PB.
Blue Magic. P. K. Saha. 80p. 1975. 14.00 (ISBN 0-88253-825-X); pap. 8.00 (ISBN 0-88253-826-8). Ind-US Inc.
Blue Man. Thomas Atkins. LC 77-77116. 1978. 7.95 o.p. (ISBN 0-385-12844-4). Doubleday.
Blue Monday. Calvin Forbes. LC 73-15011. (Wesleyan Poetry Program: Vol. 70). 1974. pap. 4.95 (ISBN 0-8195-1070-X, Pub. by Wesleyan U Pr). Columbia U Pr.
Blue Moon. Walter Wager. 1981. pap. 2.50 (ISBN 0-425-04929-9). Berkley Pub.
Blue Moon Ruby Tuesday. Elizabeth Marraffino. (Illus.). 60p. (Orig.). 1981. pap. 3.00 (ISBN 0-936556-02-1). Contact Two.
Blue Murder. Walter Wager. LC 80-67622. 1981. 10.95 (ISBN 0-87795-286-8). Arbor Hse.
Blue Mutiny. Blair Kling. LC 64-24507. 1966. 9.00x o.p. (ISBN 0-8122-7475-X). U of Pa Pr.
Blue Parka Man: Alaskan Gold Rush Bandit. H. C. Landru. LC 79-25575. (Illus.). 208p. 1980. 8.95 (ISBN 0-396-07821-4). Dodd.
Blue Print. George Otis. pap. 1.95 (ISBN 0-89728-021-0, 564816). Omega Pubns OR.
Blue Ribbon Breads. Ed. by Margie C. Jensen. (Blue Ribbon Cookbks: No. 6). (Illus.). 1978. pap. 3.95 o.p. (ISBN 0-695-80896-6). Follett.
Blue Ribbon Cakes. Ed. by Margie C. Jensen. (Blue Ribbon Cookbks: No. 6). (Illus.). 1978. pap. 3.95 o.p. (ISBN 0-695-80947-4). Follett.
Blue Ribbon Candies. Ed. by Margie C. Jensen. (Blue Ribbon Cookbks: No. 6). (Illus.). 1978. pap. 3.95 o.p. (ISBN 0-695-80950-4). Follett.
Blue Ribbon Cookies. Ed. by Margie C. Jensen. (Blue Ribbon Cookbks: No. 6). (Illus.). 1978. pap. 3.95 o.p. (ISBN 0-695-80948-2). Follett.
Blue Ribbon Jams & Jellies, Pickles & Relishes. Ed. by Margie C. Jensen. (Blue Ribbon Cookbks: No. 6). (Illus.). 1978. pap. 3.95 o.p. (ISBN 0-695-80894-X). Follett.
Blue Ribbon Pies. Ed. by Margie C. Jensen. (Blue Ribbon Cookbks: No. 6). (Illus.). 1978. pap. 3.95 o.p. (ISBN 0-695-80949-0). Follett.
Blue Rider. Paul Vogt. (Illus.). 1980. pap. 2.95 (ISBN 0-8120-2100-2). Barron.
Blue Ridge Billy. Lois Lenski. (Regional Stories Ser). (Illus.). (gr. 4-6). 1946. PLB 9.79 (ISBN 0-397-30120-0). Lippincott.
Blue Ridge Dinnerware. Bill Newbound & Betty Newbound. (Illus.). 1980. pap. 8.95 (ISBN 0-89145-129-3). Collector Bks.
Blue Ridge Trolly: The Hagerstown & Frederick Railway. Herbert Harwood. LC 73-97231. 13.95 o.p. (ISBN 0-87095-034-7). Golden West.
Blue Roses. Joyce Selznick. 336p. 1980. pap. 2.50 (ISBN 0-553-13463-9). Bantam.
Blue Ruin, No. 41. Grace L. Hill. 288p. 1981. pap. 1.95 (ISBN 0-553-14533-9). Bantam.
Blue Russell. Will Bryant. 1979. pap. 1.95 o.p. (ISBN 0-449-23840-7, Crest). Fawcett.
Blue Sea. Robert Kalan. LC 78-18396. (Illus.). (gr. k-3). 1979. 7.50 (ISBN 0-688-80184-6); PLB 7.20 (ISBN 0-688-84184-8). Greenwillow.
Blue Seed. Rieko Nakagawa. (Illus.). Date not set. 4.95 (ISBN 0-8038-0690-6). Hastings.
Blue Sloop at Dawn. Richard Bode. LC 79-1439. 1979. 8.95 (ISBN 0-396-07658-0). Dodd.
Blue Springs: Poems. Michael O'Brien. LC 74-34538. 1976. pap. 4.00 (ISBN 0-915342-06-5). SUN.

Blue Spruce. Dave Smith. (Illus.). 24p. 1980. 15.00 (ISBN 0-918092-17-5); pap. 4.00 (ISBN 0-918092-19-1); signed paper 8.00 (ISBN 0-918092-18-3). Tamarack Edns.

Blue Steel & Gunleather. John Bianchi. Ed. by James D. Mason. (Illus.). 213p. 1978. 9.95 (ISBN 0-917714-15-6). Beinfeld Pub.

Blue Thumb Guide to Working on Your House. Bill Schultz. LC 78-1992. (Illus.). 1978. pap. 5.95 o.p. (ISBN 0-87701-111-7, Prism Editions). Chronicle Bks.

Blue Turtle Moon Queen. Elihu Blotnick. (Illus.). 120p. (gr. 8-12). 1980. pap. 4.95 (ISBN 0-915090-20-1). Calif Street.

Blue Valentine. Owen Schultz. LC 78-12184. (Illus.). (gr. k-3). 1979. Repr. of 1965 ed. 6.50 (ISBN 0-688-22176-9); lib. bdg. 6.24 (ISBN 0-688-32176-3). Morrow.

Blue Water Dream. D. H. Clarke. 1980. 14.95 (ISBN 0-679-51004-4). McKay.

Blue Water Men & Women. Fred Humiston. 4.95 (ISBN 0-686-15976-4). G Gannett.

Blue Whale. Kazue Mizumura. LC 70-139107. (Let's-Read-and-Find-Out Science Bk). (Illus.). (gr. k-3). 1971. PLB 7.89 (ISBN 0-690-14994-8, TYC-J). T Y Crowell.

Blue Whale. George L. Small. LC 76-134986. (Illus.). 1973. 17.50x (ISBN 0-231-03288-9); pap. 4.95 (ISBN 0-231-08322-X). Columbia U Pr.

Blue Willow. Doris Gates. LC 40-32435. (gr. 4-6). 1976. pap. 2.50 (ISBN 0-14-030924-1, VS30, Puffin). Penguin.

Blueberry Connection: Blueberry Cookery. Beatrice R. Buszek. LC 80-14623. (Illus.). 1980. pap. 7.95 (ISBN 0-8289-0394-8). Greene.

Blueberry Culture. Ed. by Paul Eck & N. F. Childers. 1967. 25.00 (ISBN 0-8135-0535-6). Rutgers U Pr.

Blueberry God: The Education of a Finnish-American. Reino N. Hannula. LC 80-54183. 1981. 12.00 (ISBN 0-9605044-0-0). Quality Hill.

Bluebird: How You Can Help Its Fight for Survival. Lawrence Zeleny. LC 74-22832. (Midland Bks.: No. 212). (Illus.). 192p. 1976. pap. 4.95x (ISBN 0-253-20212-4). Ind U Pr.

Bluebird of Happiness: The Memoirs of Jan Peerce. Alan Levy. LC 75-25055. (Illus.). 1976. 12.50 o.p. (ISBN 0-06-013311-2, HarpT). Har-Row.

Bluebirds. David W. Frasure. 1981. 3.95 (ISBN 0-932298-08-7). Green Hill.

Bluebury Collection. Ann Waldron. LC 80-21846. (gr. 4-7). 1981. PLB 9.95 (ISBN 0-525-26739-5). Dutton.

Bluegrass Frontier. Dean Lipton. 368p. (Orig.). 1980. pap. 2.50 (ISBN 0-89083-667-1). Zebra.

Bluegrass Iggy. Mary W. Sullivan. LC 75-15912. 150p. (YA) (gr. 5 up). 1975. 6.95 o.p. (ISBN 0-525-66475-0). Elsevier-Nelson.

Bluegreen Tree. Agnes Smith. LC 76-50105. (Illus.). 108p. (Orig.). 1977. 9.00 (ISBN 0-686-28762-2). Westwind Pr.

Blueprint. Phillipe Van Rjndt. 1979. Repr. of 1977 ed. pap. 2.25 o.p. (ISBN 0-425-03876-9). Berkley Pub.

Blueprint for Humanity: Paul Tillich's Theology of Culture. Raymond F. Bulman. LC 78-75208. 248p. 1981. 18.50 (ISBN 0-8387-5000-1). Bucknell U Pr.

Blueprint for MBO: Setting Goals, Objectives & Action Plans That Work. Bonnie MacLean Abney. (Packaged books & materials). 1979. pap. 125.00 participant's material (ISBN 0-8224-7540-5); manager's material 195.00 (ISBN 0-8224-7558-8). Pitman Learning.

Blueprint for Medical Care. David Rutstein. 245p. 1974. 12.00x (ISBN 0-262-18065-0); pap. 5.95 (ISBN 0-262-68033-5). MIT Pr.

Blueprint for Raising a Child. Mike Phillips. 1978. pap. 3.95 (ISBN 0-88270-280-7). Logos.

Blueprint for Restaurant Success. George Wenzel. 1973. 21.50 (ISBN 0-8436-2001-3). CBI Pub.

Blueprint of Revolution: The Rebel, the Party, the Techniques of Revolt. Raymond M. Momboisse. 360p. 1970. 14.75 (ISBN 0-398-01323-3). C C Thomas.

Blueprint of the Plant. 3rd rev. ed. Winifred Trakimas et al. 178p. 1980. pap. text ed. 10.95 (ISBN 0-8087-3614-0). Burgess.

Blueprint Reading & Sketching for Carpenters: Residential. 3rd ed. Leo McDonnell & John Ball. LC 80-66027. (Blueprint Reading Ser.). (Illus.). 160p. 1981. pap. text ed. 9.80 (ISBN 0-8273-1354-3); price not set instr's guide (ISBN 0-8273-1355-1). Delmar.

Blueprint Reading, Checking & Testing, 2 Pts. 3rd ed. Otto A. Steinike. (Illus.). (gr. 9-10). 1956. Pt. 1. pap. text ed. 4.60 (ISBN 0-87345-080-9); Pt. 2. text ed. 3.96 s.p. (ISBN 0-87345-082-5). McKnight.

Blueprint Reading for Commercial Construction. Charles D. Willis. LC 77-87887. 1979. pap. 10.40 (ISBN 0-8273-1654-2); instructor's guide 2.25 (ISBN 0-8273-1655-0). Delmar.

Blueprint Reading for Construction. Walter C. Brown. LC 79-23958. 1980. pap. text ed. 13.92 spiral. Goodheart.

Blueprint Reading for Construction. Walter C. Brown. LC 79-23958. (Illus.). 338p. (Orig.). 1980. pap. text ed. 13.92 (ISBN 0-87006-286-7). Good Heart.

Blueprint Reading for Machinists-Advanced. LC 75-138355. 86p. 1972. 8.60 (ISBN 0-8273-0087-5); instructor's guide 1.60 (ISBN 0-8273-0088-3). Delmar.

Blueprint Reading for Plumbers: Residential & Commercial. rev. ed. Bartholomew D'Arcangelo et al. LC 78-24844. (Blueprint Reading Ser.). (gr. 7). 1980. pap. text ed. 9.68 (ISBN 0-8273-1367-5); instr's guide 1.60 (ISBN 0-8273-1368-3). Delmar.

Blueprint Reading for the Machine Trades. Russel R. Schultz. (Illus.). 304p. 1981. text ed. 16.95 (ISBN 0-13-077727-7). P-H.

Blueprint Reading for Welders. Bennett & Siy. LC 76-29579. (Illus.). 180p. 1978. pap. 8.40 (ISBN 0-8273-1059-5); instructor's guide 1.60 (ISBN 0-8273-1060-9); wall charts 4.00 (ISBN 0-8273-1063-3); transparencies 85.00 (ISBN 0-8273-1889-8). Delmar.

Blueprint Series, Vol. 2. Ed. by Mike Stensvold. LC 73-82543. (Photography How-to Ser.). (Illus.). 1978. pap. 3.95 (ISBN 0-8227-4017-6). Petersen Pub.

Blueprinting Reading & Sketching for Carpenters. McDonnell & Ball. LC 73-2165. 208p. 1975. 9.20 (ISBN 0-8273-1067-6); instructor's guide 1.60 (ISBN 0-8273-1068-4). Delmar.

Blueprinting Reading for Machinists-Intermediate. LC 75-138355. 132p. 1971. 8.60 (ISBN 0-8273-0085-9); instructor's guide 1.60 (ISBN 0-8273-0086-7). Delmar.

Blueprints for Living: Perspectives for Latter-day Saint Women, 2 vols. Ed. by Maren Mouritsen. 128p. 1980. pap. 5.95 ea. Vol. 1 (ISBN 0-8425-1812-6). Vol. 2 (ISBN 0-8425-1814-2). Brigham.

Blues: An Anthology. Ed. by W. C. Handy. 1972. 7.95 o.s.i. (ISBN 0-02-547760-9). Macmillan.

Blues: An Anthology. Ed. by W. C. Handy & Jerry Silverman. (Illus.). 1972. pap. 4.95 o.s.i. (ISBN 0-02-060710-5, Collier). Macmillan.

Blues & the Poetic Spirit. Paul Garon. LC 78-2025. (Roots of Jazz Ser.). (Illus.). 1978. Repr. of 1975 ed. lib. bdg. 19.50 (ISBN 0-306-77542-5). Da Capo.

Blues Anthology. Ed. by Edward Germain. 1981. 15.00x (ISBN 0-916156-50-8); pap. 6.50x (ISBN 0-916156-49-4). Cherry Valley.

Blues Brothers. Miami Mitch. (Orig.). 1980. pap. 2.50 (ISBN 0-515-05630-8). Jove Pubns.

Blues Guitarists. Guitar Player Editors. (Illus.). 3.95 o.p. (ISBN 0-8256-9518-X). Guitar Player.

Blues People: Negro Music in White America. Imamu A. Baraka. LC 80-15648. 244p. 1980. Repr. of 1963 ed. lib. bdg. 19.75x (ISBN 0-313-22519-2, JOBP). Greenwood.

Blues Revival. Bob Groom. (Paul Oliver Blues Ser.). pap. 2.95 (ISBN 0-913714-28-3). Legacy Bks.

Bluetezeit der deutsche Hanse: Hansische Geschichte Von der Zweiten Haelfte des Xiv Bis Zum Letzten Viertel Des Xv Jahrhunderts, 2 vols. E. Daenell. 1035p. 1973. Repr. of 1906 ed. Set. 135.30x (ISBN 3-11-004562-1). De Gruyter.

Blume in der Dichtung der Englischen Romantik. August W. Hoffmeister. (Salzburg Studies in English Literature Romantic Reassessment Ser.: No. 76). 1978. pap. text ed. 25.00x (ISBN 0-391-01412-9). Humanities.

Blumenfeld: My 100 Best Photos. Handel Teicher. LC 80-51502. (Illus.). 139p. 1981. 30.00 (ISBN 0-8478-0340-6). Rizzoli Intl.

Blunderbuss. Rupendra G. Majumdar. (Writers Workshop Redbird Ser.). 1975. 8.00 (ISBN 0-88253-510-2); pap. text ed. 4.80 (ISBN 0-88253-509-9). Ind-US Inc.

Bluntstone & the Wildkeepers. Nigel Grimshaw. (gr. 5-7). 1978. 7.95 (ISBN 0-571-10533-5, Pub. by Faber & Faber). Merrimack Bk Serv.

BMD: Biomedical Computer Programs. new ed. Ed. by W. J. Dixon. Orig. Title: BMD & BMD: X-Series Supplement (2 Books) (Orig.). 1973. pap. 12.95x (ISBN 0-520-02426-5). U of Cal Pr.

BMDP User's Digest. Ed. by Mary Ann Hill. (BMDP Statistical Software Ser.). 115p. 1979. text ed. 5.00 (ISBN 0-935386-00-9). UCLA Dept Biomath.

BMDP 1981. Ed. by W. J. Dixon & M. B. Brown. (Orig.). 1981. pap. 20.00x (ISBN 0-520-04408-8). U of Cal Pr.

BMW. Richard L. Busenkell. (Modern Automobile Ser.). (Illus.). Date not set. 12.95 (ISBN 0-393-01342-1). Norton.

BMW: A History. Halwart Schrader. Tr. by Ron Wakefield from Ger. LC 78-71792. (Illus.). 1979. 69.95 (ISBN 0-915038-15-3); leather edition 6.95 (ISBN 0-915038-21-8). Princeton Pub.

BMW Five Hundred & Six Hundred cc Twins, Nineteen Fifty-Five to Nineteen Sixty-Nine: Service-Repair-Performance. Mike Bishop. Ed. by Eric Jorgenson. (Illus.). 1978. pap. 9.95 (ISBN 0-89287-224-1, M308). Clymer Pubns.

BMW Service, Repair, Performance: 500-1000cc Twins, 1970-79. Mike Bishop. Ed. by Eric Jorgensen. (Illus.). 1978. pap. 9.95 (ISBN 0-89287-225-X, M309). Clymer Pubns.

BMW: Sixteen Hundred-Two Thousand & Two Series, 3rd ed. Jim Combs. Ed. by Jeff Robinson. (Illus.). 1978. pap. 10.95 (ISBN 0-89287-286-1, A138). Clymer Pubns.

BMW Three Hundred Twenty i: Nineteen Seventy-Seven to Nineteen Eighty Shop Manual. Jim Combs. Ed. by Eric Jorgensen. (Illus.). 248p. (Orig.). 1980. pap. text ed. 10.95 (ISBN 0-89287-326-4, A139). Clymer Pubns.

Bo Karate Weapon of Self-Defense. Funio Demura. Ed. by Gil Johnson & Geraldine Adachi. LC 76-13757. (Ser. 124). (Illus.). 1976. pap. text ed. 6.95 (ISBN 0-89750-019-9). Ohara Pubns.

Bo Rabbit Smart for True: Folktales from the Gullah. Priscilla Jaquith. (Illus.). 64p. (gr. 6-12). 1981. 8.95 (ISBN 0-399-20793-7); PLB 8.99 (ISBN 0-686-28869-6). Philomel.

Board & Administrative Management: Management for the Board. Peter W. Betts. 192p. 1977. text ed. 23.50x (ISBN 0-220-66338-6, Pub. by Busn Bks England). Renouf.

Board & Computer Management. J. N. Galley. 185p. 1978. text ed. 23.50x (ISBN 0-220-67000-5, Pub. by Busn Bks England). Renouf.

Board & Financial Management. B. Prodham. 175p. 1979. text ed. 24.50 (ISBN 0-220-66354-8, Pub. by Business Books England). Renouf.

Board & Management Audit. H. Washbrook. 262p. 1978. text ed. 30.75x (ISBN 0-220-66334-3, Pub. by Busn Bks England). Renouf.

Board & Management Development. David Frean. 188p. 1980. text ed. 30.75x (ISBN 0-220-66304-1, Pub. by Busn Bks England). Renouf.

Board & the Presentation of Financial Information to Management. J. Batty. 340p. 1978. text ed. 36.75x (ISBN 0-220-66352-1, Pub. by Busn Bks England). Renouf.

Board Compass: What It Means to Be a Director in a Changing World. Robert K. Mueller. (Arthur D. Little Books). (Illus.). 1979. 21.95 (ISBN 0-669-02903-3). Lexington Bks.

Board Games to Color & Play. Laura Palmer. (Illus.). 32p. (gr. 1-12). 1979. pap. 3.50 (ISBN 0-89844-002-5). Troubador Pr.

Board Members Are Child Advocates. Alan S. Gratch. (Orig.). 1980. pap. text ed. 4.95 (ISBN 0-87868-198-1). Child Welfare.

Board of Directors & Business Management. Melvin T. Copeland & Andrew R. Towl. LC 69-10079. 1969. Repr. lib. bdg. 20.25x (ISBN 0-8371-0052-6, COBD). Greenwood.

Board of Directors & Effective Management. 2nd ed. Harold Koontz. 286p. 1981. Repr. lib. bdg. write for info. (ISBN 0-89874-188-2). Krieger.

Boardman's Estate Management & Accounting, 2 Vols. rev. ed. Ed. by Elliott L. Biskind. LC 64-8482. 1969. looseleaf with 1980 suppl. 85.00 (ISBN 0-87632-056-6). Boardman.

Boardman's New York Family Law. rev. ed. Ed. by Elliott L. Biskind. LC 64-17549. 1972. looseleaf with 1980 suppl. 60.00 (ISBN 0-87632-058-2). Boardman.

Boards of Education-a Primer. Ed. by Olin J. Murdick & Jack F. Meyers. 78p. 1972. 2.00. Natl Cath Educ.

Boar's Head Theatre: An Inn-Yard Theatre of the Elizabethan Age. C. J. Sisson. (Illus.). 1972. 15.00x (ISBN 0-7100-7252-X). Routledge & Kegan.

Boast. Donald Miles. 256p. 1980. 11.95 (ISBN 0-312-08722-5). St Martin.

Boat. (Library of Boating Ser). (Illus.). 176p. 1975. 14.95 (ISBN 0-8094-2100-3). Time-Life.

Boat. Time Life Bks Editors. LC 74-19438. (Time Life Library of Boating Ser.). (Illus.). (gr. 6 up). 1975. PLB 13.95 (ISBN 0-8094-2101-1). Silver.

Boat Buff's Book of Embroidery: Needlepoint, Crewel, Applique. Carter Houck & Myron Miller. (Encore Edition). (Illus.). 1979. pap. 8.95 (ISBN 0-684-16052-8); pap. 4.95 (ISBN 0-684-16904-5). Scribner.

Boat Building with Plywood. 2nd ed. Glen L Witt & Ken Hankinson. 1978. text ed. 14.95 (ISBN 0-686-08738-0). Glen-L Marine.

Boat Electrics. John Watney. LC 80-68680. (Illus.). 160p. 1981. 24.50 (ISBN 0-7153-7957-7). David & Charles.

Boat Engines: A Manual for Work & Pleasure Boats. P. J. Bowyer. LC 79-5369. (Illus.). 1979. 22.50 (ISBN 0-7153-7776-0). David & Charles.

Boat for Peppe. Leo Politi. (Encore Ed.). (Illus.). 1950. pap. 1.49 o.p. (ISBN 0-684-15845-0, ScribJ). Scribner.

Boat Handling. (Library of Boating Ser.). (Illus.). 176p. 1975. 14.95 (ISBN 0-8094-2104-6). Time-Life.

Boat Handling. Time Life Bks Editors. LC 74-29194. (Time Life Library of Boating Ser.). (Illus.). (gr. 6 up). 1975. PLB 13.95 (ISBN 0-8094-2105-4). Silver.

Boat Living. Jack Wiley. LC 76-5201. (Illus.). 1976. 9.95 (ISBN 0-87742-078-5). Intl Marine.

Boat Maintenance: Ideas & Practice. Charles Jones. 192p. 1980. 12.00x (ISBN 0-245-52347-2, Pub. by Nautical England). State Mutual Bk.

Boat Owner's Fitting-Out Manual. Jeff Toghill. 224p. 22.95 (ISBN 0-442-26199-3). Van Nos Reinhold.

Boat Owner's Maintenance Manual. Jeff Toghill. (Illus.). 308p. 1976. Repr. of 1970 ed. 16.95 (ISBN 0-589-07057-6, Pub. by Reed Books Australia). C E Tuttle.

Boat Owner's Maintenance Manual. Jeff Toghill. (Illus.). 308p. 1970. Repr. 16.95 (ISBN 0-589-07057-6, Dist. by C E Tuttle). Reed.

Boat-Owner's Practical Dictionary. Denny Desoutter. (Practical Handbooks for the Yachtsman Ser.). (Illus.). 1978. 13.50 (ISBN 0-370-30041-6); pap. 7.95 (ISBN 0-370-30042-4). Transatlantic.

Boat Repairs & Conversions. 2nd ed. Michael Verney. LC 72-97994. 304p. 1977. 9.95 o.p. (ISBN 0-87742-031-9). Intl Marine.

Boat That Mooed. C. Fry. (Illus.). (ps-2). 1965. 4.75g o.s.i. (ISBN 0-02-735720-1). Macmillan.

Boat to Nowhere. Maureen C. Wartshi. 1981. pap. 1.50 (ISBN 0-686-68722-1, W9678, Sig). NAL.

Boat Who Wouldn't Float. Farley Mowat. 1970. 10.95 (ISBN 0-316-58650-1, Pub. by Atlantic Monthly Pr). Little.

Boat Who Wouldn't Float. Farley Mowat. 208p. 1981. pap. 2.50 (ISBN 0-553-14355-7). Bantam.

Boatbuilding & Repairing with Fiberglass. Melvin D. Willis. LC 74-176120. (Illus.). 1972. 12.50 (ISBN 0-87742-018-1). Intl Marine.

Boatbuilding Down East: How to Build the Maine Lobsterboat. Royal Lowell. LC 76-52309. (Illus.). 1977. 20.00 (ISBN 0-87742-088-2). Intl Marine.

Boatbuilding in Alluminum Alloy. E. H. Sims. 124p. 1980. 18.00x (ISBN 0-245-53128-9, Pub. by Nautical England). State Mutual Bk.

Boatbuilding in Your Own Backyard. 2nd ed. S. S. Rabl. LC 57-11361. (Illus.). 1958. 12.75 (ISBN 0-87033-009-8). Cornell Maritime.

Boatbuilding Manual. 2nd ed. Robert M. Steward. LC 79-90479. (Illus.). 228p. 1980. 18.50 (ISBN 0-87742-130-7). Intl Marine.

Boatbuilding with Steel (Including Boatbuilding with Aluminum) Gilbert Klingel & Thomas Colvin. LC 72-97402. 260p. 1973. 17.50 (ISBN 0-87742-029-7). Intl Marine.

Boatcook. Donna M. Doherty. (Illus.). 1979. pap. 4.50 o.p. (ISBN 0-915160-05-6). McKay.

Boater's Guide to Biscayne Bay: Miami to Jewfish Creek. George L. Sites. LC 75-173322. (Illus.). 1971. spiral bdg. 3.95 (ISBN 0-87024-233-4). U of Miami Pr.

Boating Dictionary: Sail & Power. John V. Noel. 304p. 1981. text ed. 16.95 (ISBN 0-442-26048-2). Van Nos Reinhold.

Boating Facts & Feats. Peter Johnson. LC 76-1163. (Illus.). 1979. pap. 7.95 (ISBN 0-8069-8860-6). Sterling.

Boating Facts & Feats. Peter Johnson. LC 76-1163. (Illus.). 256p. (YA) 1976. 17.95 (ISBN 0-8069-0094-6); PLB 15.99 (ISBN 0-8069-0095-4). Sterling.

Boating in Canada: Practical Piloting & Seamanship. 2nd ed. Garth Griffiths. LC 77-163820. (Illus.). 1971. 16.95 o.p. (ISBN 0-8020-1817-3). U of Toronto Pr.

Boating Skills & Seamanship. 8th ed. United States Coast Guard Auxiliary. LC 74-164688. (Illus.). 1979. pap. text ed. 7.00 (ISBN 0-930028-00-7). US Coast Guard.

Boatowner's Sheet Anchor. Carl D. Lane. 1973. pap. 3.50 o.p. (ISBN 0-8015-0774-X). Dutton.

Boats. Ruth Lachman. (ps-1). 1951. PLB 4.57 o.p. (ISBN 0-307-61501-4, Golden Pr). Western Pub.

Boats & Ships. Susan Harris. (Easy-Read Fact Bks.). (Illus.). (gr. 2-4). 1979. PLB 6.45 s&l (ISBN 0-531-02270-6). Watts.

Boat's Gonna Leave: A Study of Children Learning a Second Language from Conversations with Other Children. Anca M. Nemoianu. (Pragmatics & Beyond: No.13). 122p. 1980. pap. text ed. 17.25x (ISBN 90-272-2507-9). Humanities.

Boats of the Longshoremen. John Glasspool. 136p. 1980. 18.00x (ISBN 0-245-53111-4, Pub. by Nautical England). State Mutual Bk.

Bob & Bob: The First Five Years. Linda F. Burnham. LC 80-67655. (Illus.). 100p. (Orig.). 1980. pap. 12.00 (ISBN 0-937122-00-9). Astro Artz.

Bob Crosby: World Champion Cowboy. Thelma Crosby & Eve Ball. 6.00 o.p. (ISBN 0-685-48824-1). Nortex Pr.

Bob Dylan. Kathleen Beal. LC 74-13936. (Rock'n Pop Stars Ser.). (Illus.). 32p. (gr. 4-12). 1974. PLB 5.95 (ISBN 0-87191-399-2); pap. 2.95 (ISBN 0-89812-107-8). Creative Ed.

Bob Dylan. Anthony Scaduto. 320p. (RL 7). 1973. pap. 2.50 (ISBN 0-451-09289-9, E9289, Sig). NAL.

Bob Dylan: A Retrospective. Ed. by Craig McGregor. (Illus.). 1972. 10.95 (ISBN 0-688-01175-6); pap. 6.95 (ISBN 0-688-06025-0). Morrow.

Bob Griese. Charles Morse & Ann Morse. LC 74-4426. (Creative's Superstars Ser). 32p. 1974. 5.50 o.p. (ISBN 0-87191-345-3). Creative Ed.

Bob Hampton of Placer. Randall Parrish. 1976. lib. bdg. 16.70x (ISBN 0-89968-084-4). Lightyear.

Bob Hope. Paula Taylor. LC 74-19116. (Illus.). 40p. (gr. 4-8). 1974. PLB 5.95 (ISBN 0-87191-408-5). Creative Ed.

Bob Newhart. David Paige. (Stars of Stage & Screen Ser.). (Illus.). (gr. 3-8). 1977. PLB 5.95 (ISBN 0-87191-561-8). Creative Ed.

Bob Toski's Complete Guide to Better Golf. Bob Toski & Dick Aultman. LC 75-39958. (Illus.). 1980. pap. 7.95 (ISBN 0-689-70592-1). Atheneum.

Bob Vila's This Old House. Robert Vila & George Stephen. 1981. 20.00 (ISBN 0-525-93192-9); pap. 13.95 (ISBN 0-525-47670-9). Dutton.

Bobbin Lace. Brigita Fuhrmann. (Illus.). 1979. pap. cancelled o.p. (ISBN 0-8230-0521-6). Watson-Guptill.

Bobbin Lace. Brigita Fuhrmann. (Illus., Orig.). 1976. 15.95 o.p. (ISBN 0-8230-0520-8). Watson-Guptill.

Bobbin Lace, First Series: Les Dentelles Aux Fuseaux, 3 pts. rev. ed. Tr. & intro. by Mary McPeek. LC 73-18373. (Illus.). 255p. 1974. Repr. Set. 42.00 (ISBN 0-8103-3955-2); 25 corner patterns incl. (ISBN 0-685-49538-8). Gale.

Bobbin Lacemaking. Doris Southard. LC 77-2240. (Encore Edition). (Illus.). 1977. 4.95 (ISBN 0-684-16555-4, ScribT). Scribner.

Bobbin Lacemaking for Beginners. Amy Dawson. (Illus.). 1978. 6.95 (ISBN 0-7137-0817-4, Pub by Blandford Pr England). Sterling.

Bobbsey Twins: Secret in the Pirate's Cave. Laura L. Hope. (Bobbsey Twins Ser.). (gr. 2-5). 1980. PLB 7.95 (ISBN 0-671-41118-7); pap. 1.25 (ISBN 0-671-41113-6). Wanderer Bks.

Bobby Bagley POW. Rod Gragg. 1978. pap. 2.95 (ISBN 0-89728-022-9, 678434). Omega Pubns OR.

Bobby Bear & the Bees. M. O. Helmrath & J. L. Bartlett. LC 68-56806. (Bobby Bear Ser). (Illus.). (ps-1). 1970. PLB 7.99 prebound (ISBN 0-87783-003-7); pap. 2.75 deluxe ed (ISBN 0-87783-080-0); cassette 5.95 (ISBN 0-685-04642-7). Oddo.

Bobby Bear Finds Maple Sugar. M. O. Helmrath & J. L. Bartlett. LC 68-56805. (Bobby Bear Ser). (ps-1). 1970. PLB 7.99 prebound (ISBN 0-87783-005-3); pap. 2.75 deluxe ed (ISBN 0-87783-081-9); cassette 5.95 (ISBN 0-685-04643-5). Oddo.

Bobby Bear Goes Fishing. M. O. Helmrath & J. L. Bartlett. LC 68-56807. (Bobby Bear Ser). (Illus.). (ps-1). 1970. PLB 7.99 prebound (ISBN 0-87783-006-1); pap. 2.75 deluxe ed. (ISBN 0-87783-082-7); cassette 5.95 (ISBN 0-685-04644-3). Oddo.

Bobby Bear in the Spring. M. O. Helmrath & J. L. Bartlett. LC 68-56810. (Bobby Bear Ser). (Illus.). (ps-1). 1970. PLB 7.99 prebound (ISBN 0-87783-007-X); pap. 2.75 (ISBN 0-87783-083-5); cassette 5.95 (ISBN 0-685-04645-1). Oddo.

Bobby Bear Series, 10 bks. M. O. Helmrath & J. L. Bartlett. (Two titles by Marilue). (ps-1). Set. lib. bdg. 81.90 (ISBN 0-685-28655-X); Set. pap. 27.50 deluxe ed (ISBN 0-685-28656-8); (10) cassettes 59.50 (ISBN 0-685-28657-6). Oddo.

Bobby Bear's Halloween. M. O. Helmrath & J. L. Bartlett. LC 68-56808. (Bobby Bear Ser). (Illus.). (ps-1). 1970. PLB 7.99 prebound (ISBN 0-87783-004-5); pap. 2.75 deluxe ed (ISBN 0-87783-084-3); cassettes 5.95 (ISBN 0-685-04646-X). Oddo.

Bobby Bear's Rocket Ride. M. O. Helmrath & J. L. Bartlett. LC 68-56809. (Bobby Bear Ser). (Illus.). (ps-1). 1970. PLB 7.99 prebound (ISBN 0-87783-008-8); pap. 2.75 deluxe ed (ISBN 0-87783-087-8); cassette 5.95 (ISBN 0-685-04647-8). Oddo.

Bobby Fischer - the Greatest? Max Euwe. LC 78-66270. (Illus.). 1979. 9.95 (ISBN 0-8069-4950-3); lib. bdg. 9.29 (ISBN 0-8069-4951-1). Sterling.

Bobby Keeps Watch. Hester Monsma. (Voyager Ser.). 128p. (Orig.). (gr. 6-10). 1981. pap. 2.45 (ISBN 0-8010-6088-5). Baker Bk.

Bobby Orr. Jay H. Smith. LC 74-8848. (Sports Superstars Ser.). (Illus.). 32p. (gr. 3-9). 1974. PLB 5.95 (ISBN 0-87191-368-2); pap. 2.95 (ISBN 0-686-67087-6). Creative Ed.

Bobby Orr Story. John Devaney. (Pro Hockey Library: No. 6). (Illus.). (gr. 5 up). 1973. 2.50 o.p. (ISBN 0-394-82612-4, BYR); PLB 3.69 (ISBN 0-394-92612-9). Random.

Bobcat. Virginia F. Voight. LC 77-16876. (gr. 3-5). 1978. 5.95 (ISBN 0-396-07538-X). Dodd.

Bobcat of North America: Its History, Life Habits, Economic Status & Control, with List of Currently Recognized Subspecies. Stanley P. Young. LC 77-14021. (Illus.). 1978. 12.95x (ISBN 0-8032-0977-0); pap. 3.50 (ISBN 0-8032-5894-1, BB 663, Bison). U of Nebr Pr.

Boccaccio's Two Venuses. Robert Hollander. LC 77-5144. 1977. 20.00x (ISBN 0-231-04224-8). Columbia U Pr.

Bodega-Miwok Dictionary. Catherine A. Callaghan. (U. C. Publ. in Linguistics: Vol. 60). 1970. pap. 6.00x (ISBN 0-520-09257-0). U of Cal Pr.

Bodeoa of Palenque, Chiapas Mexico. Linda Schele & Peter Mat. LC 79-63728. (Illus.). 166p. 1978. pap. 20.00 (ISBN 0-88402-085-1, Ctr Pre-Columbian). Dumbarton Oaks.

Bodhisattva. Subhoranjan Dasgupta. 8.00 (ISBN 0-89253-465-6); flexible cloth 4.00 (ISBN 0-89253-466-4). Ind-US Inc.

Bodie 1859-1900. Wedertz. LC 72-96763. pap. 8.95 (ISBN 0-912494-20-4). Chalfant Pr.

Bodleian Manuscript of George Herbert's "the Temple". George Herbert. Date not set. write for info. Schol Facsimiles.

Bodley Head Henry James, 11 vols. Ed. by Leon Edel. Incl. Vol. 1. Europeans, Washington Square. 392p (ISBN 0-370-00616-X); Vol. 2. Awkward Age. 430p (ISBN 0-370-00617-8); Vol. 3. Bostonians. 448p (ISBN 0-370-00625-9); Vol. 4. Spoils of Poynton. 208p (ISBN 0-370-00626-7); Vol. 5. Portrait of a Lady. 626p (ISBN 0-370-00640-2); Vol. 6. What Maisie Knew. 284p (ISBN 0-370-00586-4); Vol. 7. Wings of the Dove. 540p (ISBN 0-370-01423-5); Vol. 8. Ambassadors. 468p (ISBN 0-370-01432-4); Vol. 9. Golden Bowl. 604p (ISBN 0-370-01456-1); Vol. 10. Princess Casamassima. 618p (ISBN 0-370-10237-1); Vol. 11. Daisy Miller, the Turn of the Screw. 198p (ISBN 0-370-10532-X). 1980. 12.95 ea. (Pub. by Chatto Bodley Jonathan); 130.00 set. Merrimack Bk Serv.

Bodley Head Henry James, 11 vols. Henry James. Incl. Vol. 1. The Europeans & Washington Square. 392p. 1967. 10.50x (ISBN 0-87471-341-2); Vol. 2. The Awkward Age. 432p. 1967. 14.50x (ISBN 0-87471-342-0); Vol. 3. The Bostonians. 448p. 1967. o.p. (ISBN 0-87471-343-9); Vol. 4. The Spoils of Poynton. 208p. 1967. 10.00x (ISBN 0-87471-344-7); Vol. 5. The Portrait of a Lady. 640p. 1968. 16.50x (ISBN 0-87471-345-5); Vol. 6. What Mazie Knew. 288p. 1969. 12.50x (ISBN 0-87471-346-3); Vol. 7. The Wings of the Dove. 544p. 1969. 11.00x (ISBN 0-87471-347-1); Vol. 8. The Ambassadors. 468p. 1970. 11.00x (ISBN 0-87471-348-X); Vol. 9. The Golden Bowl. 608p. 1971. 11.50x (ISBN 0-87471-349-8); Vol. 10. Princess Casamassima. 600p. 1972. 14.50x (ISBN 0-87471-350-1); Vol. 11. Daisy Miller & the Turn of the Screw. 208p. 1974. 10.00x (ISBN 0-87471-573-3). Rowman.

Body. Michael Benedikt. LC 68-27539. (Wesleyan Poetry Program: Vol. 40). 1968. pap. 10.00x (ISBN 0-8195-2040-3, Pub. by Wesleyan U Pr); pap. 4.95 (ISBN 0-8195-1040-8). Columbia U Pr.

Body Alive! Toward an Education in Movement. Yvonne Berge. LC 76-62748. (Illus.). 160p. 1977. 7.95 o.p. (ISBN 0-312-08723-3). St Martin.

Body & Mind. Keith Campbell. LC 79-123714. 1970. pap. 2.50 o.p. (ISBN 0-385-03022-3, Anch). Doubleday.

Body & Mind: Readings in Philosophy. Ed. by G. N. Vesey. 1964. text ed. 27.50x o.p. (ISBN 0-04-130010-6); pap. text ed. 11.50x o.p. (ISBN 0-04-130014-9). Allen Unwin.

Body As Property. Russell Scott. 1981. 14.95 (ISBN 0-670-17743-1). Viking Pr.

Body As Spirit: The Nature of Religious Feeling. Charles Davis. 160p. 1976. 8.95 (ISBN 0-8164-0288-4). Crossroad NY.

Body Book. Claire Rayner. LC 79-23363. (Illus.). (gr. k-7). 1980. 6.95 (ISBN 0-8120-5325-7). Barron.

Body Building: An Illustrated History. David Webster. (Illus.). 1981. Repr. lib. bdg. 10.95 (ISBN 0-668-04898-0). Arco.

Body-Building & Self-Defense. Myles Callum. 1962. pap. 2.95 (ISBN 0-06-463258-X, EH 258, EH). Har-Row.

Body-Building & Self-Defense. Myles Callum. LC 61-15729. (Illus.). (gr. 8-12). 1967. 7.95 (ISBN 0-8069-4031-X); PLB 6.69 (ISBN 0-8069-4007-7). Sterling.

Body-Building: Erzaehlung, Schauspiel, Essay. Bodo Kirchhoff. (Edition Suhrkamp. Neue Folge: Es. NF 5). 130p. (Orig., Ger.). 1980. pap. text ed. 4.55 (ISBN 3-518-11005-5, Pub. by Insel Verlag Germany). Suhrkamp.

Body Code: The Meaning in Movement. Warren Lamb & Elizabeth Watson. (Illus.). 1979. 16.00 (ISBN 0-7100-0017-0). Routledge & Kegan.

Body Compass. David Steingass. LC 76-78534. (Pitt Poetry Ser). 1969. 7.95 o.p. (ISBN 0-8229-3180-X); pap. 3.95 o.p. (ISBN 0-8229-5209-2). U of Pittsburgh Pr.

Body Composition in Animals & Man. Agricultural Board. 1968. pap. 14.25 (ISBN 0-309-01598-7). Natl Acad Pr.

Body Consciousness. Seymour Fisher. LC 74-9264. 176p. 1974. Repr. 17.50x (ISBN 0-87668-181-X). Aronson.

Body Consciousness: You Are What You Feel. Seymour Fisher. 192p. 1973. 12.95 (ISBN 0-13-078527-X, Spec). P-H.

Body Contouring & Conditioning Through Movement. 2nd ed. Christine M. MacIntyre & Janet A. Wessel. (Series in Basic Concepts & Skills of Physical Activity). 1977. pap. 4.95x o.p. (ISBN 0-205-05584-2). Allyn.

Body Count. Peter McCurtin. (Soldier of Fortune Ser.). 1977. pap. 1.50 (ISBN 0-505-51172-X). Tower Bks.

Body Ego Technique: An Educational & Therapeutic Approach to Body Image & Self Identity. J. Salkin. (Amer. Lec. in Special Education Ser.). (Illus.). 224p. 1973. 16.50 (ISBN 0-398-02826-5). C C Thomas.

Body Electric. Thelma Moss. 1979. 10.00 o.p. (ISBN 0-312-90437-1). St Martin.

Body Energy. James S. Skinner. LC 80-24094. (Illus.). 120p. (Orig.). 1981. pap. 5.95 (ISBN 0-89037-174-1). Anderson World.

Body Experience in Fantasy & Behavior. Seymour Fisher. LC 71-111878. (Century Psychology Ser). 1970. 29.50x (ISBN 0-89197-046-0); pap. text ed. 10.95x (ISBN 0-89197-683-3). Irvington.

Body Fluids & Electrolytes: A Programmed Presentation. 3rd ed. Norma J. Weldy. (Illus.). 1980. pap. 8.50 (ISBN 0-8016-5383-5). Mosby.

Body for a Buddy. Aaron M. Stein. LC 80-2897. (Crime Club Ser.). 192p. 1981. 9.95 (ISBN 0-385-17583-3). Doubleday.

Body Has a Head. Gustav Eckstein. LC 62-14529. 1970. 15.95 o.s.i. (ISBN 0-06-011153-4, HarpT). Har-Row.

Body Image: A Surgical Perspective. Frederick M. Grazer & Jerome R. Klingbeil. LC 79-23858. 1979. text ed. 74.50 (ISBN 0-8016-1965-3). Mosby.

Body Image, Self-Esteem, & Sexuality in Cancer Patients. Ed. by J. M. Vaeth. (Frontiers of Radiation Therapy & Oncology: Vol. 14). (Illus.). x, 134p. 1980. 49.25 (ISBN 3-8055-0036-X). S Karger.

Body Impolitic: A Reading of Four Novels by Herman Melville. Richard M. Blau. 219p. 1979. pap. text ed. 42.75x (ISBN 90-6203-571-X). Humanities.

Body in Question. Jonathan Miller. (Illus.). 1979. 15.95 (ISBN 0-394-50280-9). Random.

Body in the Brillstone Garage. Florence P. Heide & Roxanne Heide. Ed. by Fay Anne. LC 79-18368. (Pilot Bks.). (gr. 4-9). 1980. 6.95g (ISBN 0-8075-0825-X). A Whitman.

Body Language. Julius Fast. LC 72-106592. (Illus.). 192p. 1970. 8.95 (ISBN 0-87131-039-2). M Evans.

Body Language & the Social Order. Albert E. Scheflen. (Illus.). 192p. 1973. 13.95 (ISBN 0-13-079590-9, Spec); pap. 4.25 (ISBN 0-13-079582-8, Spec). P-H.

Body Language of Sex, Power & Aggression. Julius Fast. 1978. pap. 2.25 o.p. (ISBN 0-515-05670-7). Jove Pubns.

Body Magic. John Fisher. LC 78-6387. (Illus.). 158p. 1980. pap. 6.95 (ISBN 0-8128-6088-8). Stein & Day.

Body Manual: A Complete Family Guide. The Diagram Group. LC 79-21673. (Illus.). 1980. 16.95 (ISBN 0-448-22214-0). Paddington.

Body Mechanics & Patient Positioning: A Programmed Unit of Study for Nurses. Marie M. Seedor. LC 73-85804. 1977. pap. 8.75x (ISBN 0-8077-2524-2). Tchrs Coll.

Body, Mind & Spirit: The Journey Toward Wholeness. 2nd ed. Peter Albright & Bets P. Albright. (Illus.). 320p. 1981. pap. 9.95 (ISBN 0-8289-0386-7). Greene.

Body, Mind & Sugar. E. M. Abrahamson & A. W. Pezet. 1977. pap. 3.95 (ISBN 0-380-00903-X, 47415). Avon.

Body, Mind, & the B Vitamins. rev. ed. Ruth Adams & Frank Murray. 317p. 1972. pap. 1.95x (ISBN 0-915962-02-0). Larchmont Bks.

Body Movement: Coping with the Environment. D. Lewis & I. Bartenieff. 1980. 42.50 (ISBN 0-677-05500-5). Gordon.

Body of Divinity. Thomas Watson. 1978. 9.95 (ISBN 0-85151-145-7). Banner of Truth.

Body Politics. Julius Fast. (Orig.). 1980. pap. 2.25 (ISBN 0-505-51513-X). Tower Bks.

Body Politics: Power, Sex, & Nonverbal Communication. Nancy M. Henley. (Patterns of Social Behavior Ser.). (Illus.). 1977. 12.95 (ISBN 0-13-079640-9, Spec); pap. 3.95 (ISBN 0-13-079632-8). P-H.

Body Rub. Mark Andrews. 1976. pap. 1.50 o.p. (ISBN 0-685-74567-8, LB419DK, Leisure Bks). Nordon Pubns.

Body Sculpture: Plastic Surgery from Head to Toe. Simona Morini. 1972. 10.00 o.s.i. (ISBN 0-440-00740-2). Delacorte.

Body Snatchers. Jack Finney. (Science Fiction Ser.). (Illus.). 224p. 1976. Repr. of 1955 ed. lib. bdg. 12.50 (ISBN 0-8398-2332-0). Gregg.

Body, Soul & Blood: Recovering the Human in Medicine. William T. Sayers. LC 79-56194. 112p. 1980. pap. 4.95 (ISBN 0-935718-00-1). Asclepiad.

Body Structure & Function: An Individualized Course Guide & Work Book for Nursing & Health Related Occupations. Sondra Von Arb. LC 79-83909. 1979. pap. text ed. 8.95 (ISBN 0-933474-06-7). Minn Scholarly.

Body Structures & Functions. Elvira Ferris & Esther G. Skelley. LC 77-83347. 160p. 1979. pap. 7.20 (ISBN 0-8273-1322-5); instructor's guide 1.60 (ISBN 0-8273-1323-3); slide pocket 29.50 (ISBN 0-8273-1821-9). Delmar.

Body Temperature Control: In Relation to Anaesthesia, Surgery & Intensive Care. Anita Holdcroft. 1980. text ed. 29.95 (ISBN 0-02-858050-8). Macmillan.

Body Tensor Fields in Continuum Mechanics. Arthur S. Lodge. 1975. 48.00 (ISBN 0-12-454950-0). Acad Pr.

Body Vanishes. Yves Jacquemard & Jean-Michel Senecal. Tr. by Gordon Latta from Fr. LC 80-17077. 224p. 1980. 8.95 (ISBN 0-396-07884-2). Dodd.

Body Weather. Bruce Palmer. 1977. pap. 1.75 o.s.i. (ISBN 0-515-04386-9). Jove Pubns.

Bodyguard of Lies. Anthony Cave Brown. LC 72-9749. (Illus.). 962p. (YA) 1975. 19.95 o.s.i. (ISBN 0-06-010551-8, HarpT). Har-Row.

Bodymind. Ken Dychtwald. 1978. pap. 2.25 (ISBN 0-515-05561-1). Jove Pubns.

Bodymind Liberation: Achieving Holistic Health. Robert H. Woody. 172p. 1980. 15.50 (ISBN 0-398-04055-9). C C Thomas.

Body's Symmetry: Poems. Verandah Porche. pap. 2.95 o.p. (ISBN 0-06-090370-8, CN370, CN). Har-Row.

Bodyscapes. Martin H. Schreiber. LC 79-92484. (Illus.). 1980. pap. 14.95 (ISBN 0-89659-105-0). Abbeville Pr.

Bodysculpture. Ralph Carnes & Valerie Carnes. (Illus.). 192p. 1981. pap. 5.95 (ISBN 0-312-08735-7). St Martin.

Bodyworks: The Kids' Guide to Food & Physical Fitness. Carol Bershad & Deborah Bernick. (Illus.). 240p. (gr. 5-9). 1981. PLB 8.99 (ISBN 0-394-94752-5); pap. 5.95 (ISBN 0-394-84752-0). Random.

Boer War. Thomas Pakenham. LC 79-4779. 1979. 19.95 (ISBN 0-394-42742-4). Random.

Boffo: The Great Motorcycle Race. Frank Dickens. LC 77-22087. (Illus.). 40p. (ps-3). 1978. 6.95 (ISBN 0-590-07715-5, Four Winds); PLB 5.41 o.p. (ISBN 0-8193-0957-5). Schol Bk Serv.

Bogard-Warlick Debate (Total Depravity, Baptism, Apostasy) pap. 3.50 (ISBN 0-89315-004-5). Lambert Bk.

Bogart. David Hanna. (Orig.). 1976. pap. 1.50 o.p. (ISBN 0-685-62586-9, LB322, Leisure Bks). Nordon Pubns.

Bogart & Bacall. Joe Hyams. (Illus.). 1976. pap. 2.50 (ISBN 0-446-91228-X). Warner Bks.

Bogey Man. George Plimpton. LC 68-28213. (Illus.). 1968. 10.95 o.p. (ISBN 0-06-013362-7, HarpT). Har-Row.

Bogey's Baby. Howard Greenberger. LC 77-9178. (Illus.). 1978. 8.95 o.p. (ISBN 0-312-08740-3). St Martin.

Bogmail. Patrick McGinley. LC 80-26135. 264p. 1981. 9.95 (ISBN 0-89919-031-6). Ticknor & Fields.

Bohemia: The Protoculture Then & Now. Richard Miller. LC 77-14073. (Illus.). 1978. 17.95 (ISBN 0-88229-293-5); pap. 9.95 (ISBN 0-88229-518-7). Nelson-Hall.

Bohemian Girl: Blanche Yurka's Theatrical Life. Blanche Yurka. LC 79-81449. xii, 306p. 1970. 11.95 (ISBN 0-8214-0071-1). Ohio U Pr.

Bohemians & Critics: American Theatre Criticism in the Nineteenth Century. Tice L. Miller. LC 80-24430. x, 190p. 1981. 12.00 (ISBN 0-8108-1377-7). Scarecrow.

Boiarynia. Lesia Ukrainka. 56p. 1970. pap. 2.00. Slavia Lib.

Boileau & the Nature of Neo-Classism. Gordon Pocock. LC 79-50885. (Major European Authors Ser.). 1980. 34.00 (ISBN 0-521-22772-0). Cambridge U Pr.

Boiler & Pressure Vessel Code Ser. (Boiler & Pressure Code Ser.: See X). 1980. 55.00 (P00100); pap. 65.00 loose-leaf (V00100). ASME.

Boiling Coffee. Richard Nonas. 168p. 1980. 15.95 (ISBN 0-934378-12-6); pap. 8.95 (ISBN 0-934378-11-8). Tanam Pr.

Boiling Mad. Mad Magazine Editors. (Mad Ser). (Illus.). 192p. 1973. pap. 1.50 (ISBN 0-446-88740-4). Warner Bks.

Bois. Harlan Wade. Tr. by Claude Potvin & Rose-Ella Potvin. (Book About Ser.). Orig. Title: Wood. (Illus., Fr.). (gr. k-3). 1979. PLB 7.30 (ISBN 0-8172-1458-5). Raintree Pubs.

Boke of Iustices of Peas, the Charge with All the Processe of the Cessions. LC 76-57391. (English Experience Ser.: No. 808). 1977. Repr. of 1506 ed. lib. bdg. 11.50 (ISBN 90-221-0808-2). Walter J Johnson.

Boke of Secretes. Albertus Magnus. LC 76-28227. (English Experience Ser: No. 116). 168p. 1969. Repr. of 1525 ed. 15.00 (ISBN 90-221-0116-9). Walter J Johnson.

Bokhara Burnes. James Lunt. (Great Travellers Ser.). (Illus.). 1969. 7.50 (ISBN 0-571-08935-6, Pub. by Faber & Faber). Merrimack Bk Serv.

Bold Approach & Tested Advice of Benefit to Artists Valiantly Struggling for Artistic Success. Nathaniel Lamballe. (Institute for Human Development Ser.). (Illus.). 1978. deluxe bdg. 37.50 (ISBN 0-930582-03-9). Gloucester Art.

Bold Experiment: The Story of Educational Television in American Samoa. Wilbur Schramm et al. LC 79-67777. (Illus.). 264p. 1981. text ed. 17.50x (ISBN 0-8047-1090-2). Stanford U Pr.

Bold Ones. Gardner Fox. 1976. pap. 1.25 o.p. (ISBN 0-685-72571-5, LB398, Leisure Bks). Nordon Pubns.

Bold Ones on Campus. Donald L. Deffner. LC 73-78104. 1973. pap. 2.50 o.p. (ISBN 0-570-03162-1, 12-2566). Concordia.

Bold Pursuit. Zabrina Faire. 192p. (Orig.). 1980. pap. 1.75 (ISBN 0-446-94464-5). Warner Bks.

Bold Rider. Luke Short. 1978. pap. 1.25 o.s.i. (ISBN 0-440-10683-4). Dell.

Bold Stroke for a Wife. Susannah Centlivre. Ed. by Thalia Stathas. LC 67-12640. (Regents Restoration Drama Ser). 1968. 7.95x (ISBN 0-8032-0351-9); pap. 1.65x (ISBN 0-8032-5351-6, BB 267, Bison). U of Nebr Pr.

Boldest Dream: The Story of Twelve Who Climbed Mount Everest. Rick Ridgeway. LC 78-14080. (Illus.). 1979. 10.95 (ISBN 0-15-113432-4). HarBraceJ.

Boldness Be My Friend. Richard Pape. 1955. 12.95 (ISBN 0-236-30836-X, Pub. by Paul Elek). Merrimack Bk Serv.

Boldt. Ted Lewis. (Orig.). pap. 2.25 (ISBN 0-515-05640-5). Jove Pubns.

Boldt. Ted Lewis. 1976. 9.95 o.p. (ISBN 0-7181-1460-4, Pub. by Michael Joseph). Merrimack Bk Serv.

Boleslaw Lesmian: The Poet & His Poetry. Rochelle Stone. LC 73-84382. 1976. 22.75x (ISBN 0-520-02549-0). U of Cal Pr.

Boletin Estadistico De la OEA. Ed. by OAS General Secretariat Department of Publications. (Periodical-Quarterly Ser.). 207p. 4.00 (ISBN 0-686-68291-2). OAS.

Boletin Estadistico de la OEA: Enero-Junio 1980, Vol. 2, Nos. 1-2. Ed. by OAS General Secretariat. 221p. 1980. pap. text ed. 4.00. OAS.

Bolingbroke & Harley. Sheila Biddle. LC 73-20749. 1974. 10.00 o.p. (ISBN 0-394-46974-7). Knopf.

Bolivar. John Guyatt. Ed. by Malcolm Yapp et al. (World History Ser.). (Illus.). 32p. (gr. 10). 1980. lib. bdg. 5.95 (ISBN 0-89908-045-6); pap. text ed. 1.95 (ISBN 0-89908-020-0). Greenhaven.

Bolivar: Un Continente y un Destino. (Span.). 1972. 5.00 o.p. (ISBN 0-685-65419-2). OAS.

Bolivia in Pictures. Sterling Editors. LC 73-93603. (Visual Geography Ser). (Illus.). 64p. (gr. 5 up). 1974. PLB 4.99 (ISBN 0-8069-1177-8); pap. 2.95 (ISBN 0-8069-1176-X). Sterling.

Bolivian Indian Textiles: Traditional Designs & Costumes. Tamara E. Wasserman & Jonathan S. Hill. (Pictorial Archive Ser.). (Illus.). 64p. (Orig.). 1981. pap. price not set (ISBN 0-486-24118-1). Dover.

Boll Weevil & the Triple Play. Louis D. Rubin. 1979. 5.00 (ISBN 0-937684-00-7). Tradd St Pr.

Bolo. Keith Laumer. 1978. pap. 1.50 o.p. (ISBN 0-425-03450-X). Berkley Pub.

Bolo: The Annals of the Dinochrome Brigade. Keith Laumer. LC 76-9769. (YA) 1976. 6.95 o.p. (ISBN 0-399-11794-6, Dist. by Putnam). Berkley Pub.

Bol'shaia Sovetskaia Entsiklopediia, 51 Vols. & Annuals. 2nd ed. (Rus.). 1950. 825.00 (ISBN 0-8277-3002-0). Maxwell Sci Intl.

Bol'shaia Sovetskaia Entsiklopediia, Vols.1-21. 3rd ed. (Rus.). 1970-1974. 720.00 (ISBN 0-8277-3003-9). Maxwell Sci Intl.

Bolshevik Tradition: Lenin, Stalin, Khrushchev, Brezhnev. rev. ed. Robert H. McNeal. 224p. 1975. 8.95 o.p. (ISBN 0-13-079772-3, Spec); pap. 3.95 (ISBN 0-13-079764-2, Spec). P-H.

Bolsheviks. Adam B. Ulam. 1968. pap. 7.95 (ISBN 0-02-038100-X, Collier). Macmillan.

Bolsheviks & the National & Colonial Question, 1917-1928. Demetrio Boersner. LC 79-2894. 285p. 1981. Repr. of 1957 ed. write for info. (ISBN 0-8305-0062-6). Hyperion Conn.

Bolsheviks in the Tsarist Duma. A. Badayev. 1973. 16.50 (ISBN 0-86527-013-9). Fertig.

Bolshevism: An International Danger; Its Doctrine & Its Practice Through War & Revolution. Pavel N. Miliukov. LC 79-2915. 303p. 1981. Repr. of 1920 ed. 23.75 (ISBN 0-8305-0084-7). Hyperion Conn.

Bolshevism in Art & Other Expository Writings. Christopher Middleton. 1978. pap. text ed. 15.75x (ISBN 0-85635-155-5). Humanities.

Bolshoi Ballet. Judy Cameron. LC 74-25152. (Icon Editions, Helene Obolensky Enterprises Bk). (Illus.). 184p. 1975. 17.50 o.s.i. (ISBN 0-06-430600-3, HarpT). Har-Row.

Bolt-on Performance. Ed. by Hot Rod Magazine Editors. (Hot Rod Shop Ser.). (Illus.). 1981. pap. 8.95 (ISBN 0-8227-6013-4). Petersen Pub.

Bolt Upright: The Life of Thomas Moore, 2 vols. Hoover H. Jordan. (Salzburg Studies in English Literature, Romantic Reassessment Ser.: No. 38). (Illus.). 666p. 1975. Set. pap. text ed. 50.25x (ISBN 0-391-01440-4). Humanities.

Bolton & the Spanish Borderlands. Herbert E. Bolton. Ed. by John F. Bannon. 1964. 12.95 (ISBN 0-8061-0612-3); pap. 5.95 (ISBN 0-8061-1150-X). U of Okla Pr.

Bolts of Melody: New Poems of Emily Dickinson. Emily Dickinson. Ed. by Millicent T. Bingham & Mabel L. Todd. (Illus.). 1945. 8.95 o.s.i. (ISBN 0-06-011035-X, HarpT). Har-Row.

Bomba de Incendios. Philip Mann. Tr. by Georgian Kreps from Eng. (Shape Board Play Book). Orig. Title: Fire Engines. (Illus., Span.). (ps-3). 1981. bds. 3.50 plastic comb bdg (ISBN 0-89828-202-0, 5006SP). Tuffy Bks.

Bombay. R. Sundaram. (Illus.). 1966. 4.10 (ISBN 0-88253-412-2). Ind-US Inc.

Bomber Aircraft of the United States. T. L. Morgan. LC 66-28699. (Illus., Orig.). 1967. lib. bdg. 5.95 o.p. (ISBN 0-668-01596-9); pap. 2.95 (ISBN 0-668-01597-7). Arco.

Bomber Raid. James Campbell. 1978. pap. 1.75 (ISBN 0-505-51272-6). Tower Bks.

Bombers & Firesetters. John M. Macdonald. 264p. 1977. 18.50 (ISBN 0-398-03687-X). C C Thomas.

Bombers in Blue: PB4Y-2 Privateers & PB4Y-1 Liberators. Frederick A. Johnsen. (Illus.). 1979. pap. 3.95 (ISBN 0-911721-53-3, Pub. by Bomber). Aviation.

Bombers in Service: Patrol & Transport Aircraft Since 1960. rev. ed. Kenneth Munson. LC 75-14214. (Illus.). 156p. 1976. 6.95 o.s.i. (ISBN 0-02-587940-5, 58794). Macmillan.

Bombers: Patrol & Reconnaissance Aircraft 1914-1919. Kenneth Munson. LC 68-20156. (Illus.). (YA) 1968. 8.95 (ISBN 0-02-588060-8). Macmillan.

Bombers: World War Two. Kenneth Munson. 1969. 8.95 (ISBN 0-02-588020-9). Macmillan.

Bombyliidae of Chile (Diptera: Bombyliidae) J. C. Hall. (Publications in Entomology: Vol. 76). 1975. pap. 15.00x (ISBN 0-520-09510-3). U of Cal Pr.

Bon Usage. M. Grevisse. (Fr). 59.95 (ISBN 0-685-20226-7). Schoenhof.

Bon Voyage: The Cruise Guide to the Caribbean. James W. Morrison. LC 80-26848. 192p. 1980. 9.95 (ISBN 0-668-04865-4); pap. 6.95 (ISBN 0-668-04851-4). Arco.

Bonanza at Wishbone. Lee Floren. 1977. pap. 1.50 (ISBN 0-505-51183-5). Tower Bks.

Bonanza Trail: Ghost Towns & Mining Camps of the West. Muriel S. Wolle. (Illus.). 510p. 1953. Repr. pap. 14.95 (ISBN 0-8040-0685-7, SB). Swallow.

Bonanza West: The Story of the Western Mining Rushes 1848-1900. William S. Greever. 1963. 18.95 (ISBN 0-8061-0556-9). U of Okla Pr.

Bonaparte: Governor of Egypt. Francois Charles-Roux. Tr. by E. W. Dickes. LC 80-1932. (Illus., Fr.). 1981. Repr. of 1937 ed. 47.50 (ISBN 0-404-18958-X). AMS Pr.

Bonaparte Kiss. Sara Cardiff. (Orig.). 1979. pap. 1.75 o.p. (ISBN 0-449-24156-4, Crest). Fawcett.

Bonaventure Des Periers's Novel Pastimes & Merry Tales. Tr. by Raymond C. La Charite & Raymond La Charite. LC 70-190532. (Studies in Romance Languages: No. 6). 264p. 1972. 13.00x (ISBN 0-8131-1279-6). U Pr of Ky.

Bond Graph Techniques for Dynamic Systems in Engineering & Biology. Dean Karnopp et al. 1979. pap. text ed. 28.00 (ISBN 0-08-025056-4). Pergamon.

Bond Graphs: Introduction & Application. J. Thoma. LC 75-9763. 192p. 1975. text ed. 27.00 (ISBN 0-08-018882-6); pap. text ed. 16.00 (ISBN 0-08-018881-8). Pergamon.

Bond of Power. Joseph C. Pearce. 1981. 10.95 (ISBN 0-525-06950-X). Dutton.

Bond Slave. Sallie L. Bell. 1978. pap. 2.50 (ISBN 0-310-21092-5). Zondervan.

Bond Switch at Hypervalent Sulfur in Thiathiophtene Analogous Systems. K. Akiba. (Sulfur Reports Ser.). 29p. 1980. flexicover 7.50 (ISBN 3-7186-0037-4). Harwood Academic.

Bond Yield Tables, Four Percent to Fourteen Percent Nos. 154, 254, 2 vols. Financial Publishing Co. 6.00 ea. Finan Pub.

Bondage Freedom & Beyond: The Prose of Black Americans. Ed. by Addison Gayle, Jr. (Illus.). 1971. 4.95 (ISBN 0-385-08951-1, Zenith); pap. 2.50 (ISBN 0-385-08960-0). Doubleday.

Bondage of the Free. Kent H. Steffgen. 380p. (Orig.). 1966. pap. 1.00 (ISBN 0-911038-74-4, Vanguard). Noontide.

Bondage of the Will. Martin Luther. Tr. by J. I. Packer & O. R. Johnston. 323p. Repr. of 1957 ed. text ed. 14.95x (ISBN 0-227-67417-0). Attic Pr.

Bonding Problems. J. D. Dunitz et al. (Structure & Bonding Ser.: Vol.43). (Illus.). 240p. 1981. 58.00 (ISBN 0-387-10407-0). Springer-Verlag.

Bonds Between Atoms. Alan Holden. (Illus.). 1971. pap. text ed. 3.95x (ISBN 0-19-501498-7). Oxford U Pr.

Bonds: How to Double Your Money Quickly & Safely. Robert L. Holt. LC 80-66576. 1980. 10.00x (ISBN 0-930926-03-X). Calif Health.

Bonds of Love. Lisa Gregory. (Orig.). 1978. pap. text ed. 1.95 (ISBN 0-515-04646-9). Jove Pubns.

Bonds on Public Works. Ed. by NACM. 1981. pap. 4.75 (ISBN 0-934914-38-9). NACM.

Bonds on Public Works. NACM Publications Editors. 130p. 1980. pap. 4.50 o.p. (ISBN 0-934914-34-6). NACM.

Bone Grafts & Inplants, Vol. 87. Association of Bone & Joint Surgeons. Ed. by Marshall Urist. (Clinical Orthopaedics & Related Research Ser.). 1972. 12.00 o.p. (ISBN 0-685-34608-0). Lippincott.

Bone Hunters. Url N. Lanham. LC 73-5596. (Illus.). 336p. 1973. 20.00x (ISBN 0-231-03152-1). Columbia U Pr.

Bone Infarction in Sickle Cell Disease. Ed. by Stanley P. Bohrer. (Illus.). 400p. 1981. 39.50 (ISBN 0-87527-188-X). Green.

Bone-Marrow Conservation, Culture & Transplantation. (Illus., Orig.). 1969. pap. 10.75 (ISBN 92-0-111269-6, IAEA). Unipub.

Bone Marrow Morphology & Mechanics of Biopsy. E. M. Schleicher. (Illus.). 210p. 1974. 22.75 (ISBN 0-398-02838-9). C C Thomas.

Bone Mass. Association of Bone & Joint Surgeons. Ed. by Marshall R. Urist. (Clinical Orthopaedics Ser., Vol. 65). 1969. 15.00 (ISBN 0-685-22846-0). Lippincott.

Bone Modeling & Skeletal Modeling Errors: Orthopaedic Lectures, Vol. 4. Harold M. Frost. (Illus.). 224p. 1973. 19.75 (ISBN 0-398-02667-X). C C Thomas.

Bone of His Bone. F. J. Huegel. (Christian Classic Ser.). 96p. 1980. pap. 2.95 (ISBN 0-310-26321-2). Zondervan.

Bone Remodeling & Its Relationship to Metabolic Bone Diseases: Orthopaedic Lectures, Vol. 3. Harold M. Frost. (Illus.). 225p. 1973. 22.50 (ISBN 0-398-02588-6). C C Thomas.

Bone Repair & Fracture Healing in Man. Simon Sevitt. (Current Problems in Orthopaedics Ser.). (Illus.). 300p. 1981. lib. bdg. 62.00 (ISBN 0-443-01806-5). Churchill.

Bone-Sculpture. Agha S. Ali. (Writers Workshop Redbird Ser.). 32p. 1975. text ed. 8.00 (ISBN 0-89253-535-0); pap. text ed. 3.00 (ISBN 0-88253-727-X). Ind-US Inc.

Bone Tumors. 5th ed. Louis Lichtenstein. LC 77-22264. (Illus.). 1977. 47.50 (ISBN 0-8016-3005-3). Mosby.

Bone Tumors: Diagnosis & Treatment. Joseph M. Mirra. (Illus.). 1980. text ed. 69.50 (ISBN 0-397-50428-4). Lippincott.

Bone Tumors: General Aspects & Data on 6,221 Cases. 3rd ed. David C. Dahlin. (Illus.). 464p. 1978. 44.75 (ISBN 0-398-03692-6). C C Thomas.

Bonecrack. Dick Francis. LC 79-181670. (Harper Novel of Suspense). 208p. 1972. 8.95 o.s.i. (ISBN 0-06-011319-7, HarpT). Har-Row.

Bones. Pat Wagner. 1976. pap. 2.00 (ISBN 0-935060-00-6). Eggplant Pr.

Bones. Herbert S. Zim. (Illus.). (gr. 3-7). 1969. PLB 6.48 (ISBN 0-688-31115-6). Morrow.

Bones: Ancient Men & Modern Myths. Lewis R. Binford. LC 80-2327. (Studies in Archaeology Ser.). 1981. price not set (ISBN 0-12-100035-4). Acad Pr.

Bones & Distances. 2nd ed. Srinivas Rayaprol. (Redbird Bk.). 1976. 8.00 (ISBN 0-89253-117-7); flexible bdg. 4.00 (ISBN 0-89253-135-5). Ind-US Inc.

Bones & Kim. Lynn Strongin. LC 80-5311. 100p. 1980. pap. 5.50 (ISBN 0-933216-02-5). Spinsters Ink.

Bones & Muscles of the Human Form. Diane Murray & William Conte. (Illus.). 1980. pap. 2.95 (ISBN 0-88284-107-6). Alfred Pub.

Boney Fuller: Soldier, Strategist & Writer, 1878-1966. Anthony J. Trythall. 1977. 20.00 (ISBN 0-8135-0844-4). Rutgers U Pr.

Bonfire. Pamela H. Johnson. 192p. 1981. 10.95 (ISBN 0-684-16853-7, ScribT). Scribner.

Bong! How to Make & Use Waterpipes. Jackson Peters. (Illus.). 96p. (Orig.). 1980. pap. 5.95 (ISBN 0-935232-00-1). Deep River Pr.

Bong Nam & the Pheasants. Yushin Yoo. LC 79-15749. (Illus.). (ps-2). 1979. 6.95 (ISBN 0-13-079665-4); PLB 7.95 (ISBN 0-13-079657-3). P-H.

Bongleweed. Helen Cresswell. LC 73-4057. 128p. (gr. 5-9). 1973. 7.95 (ISBN 0-02-725500-X). Macmillan.

Bonhoeffer: Exile & Martyr. Eberhard Bethge. 192p. 1976. 7.95 (ISBN 0-8164-1211-1). Crossroad NY.

Bonhoeffer Legacy: Essays in Understanding. A. J. Klassen. 186p. (Orig.). 1981. pap. 13.95 (ISBN 0-8028-1744-0). Eerdmans.

Bonhoeffer: Worldly Preaching. Clyde E. Fant. LC 74-26806. 192p. 1975. 6.95 o.p. (ISBN 0-8407-5087-0); pap. 3.50 o.p. (ISBN 0-8407-5586-4). Nelson.

Bonn. Photos by P. Swiridoff. (Illus.). 1971. 20.00 (ISBN 0-911268-19-7). Rogers Bk.

Bonnaire. Delphine Marlowe. 688p. (Orig.). 1980. pap. 2.75 (ISBN 0-515-04764-3). Jove Pubns.

Bonnard. Andre Fermigier. Tr. by Althea Schlanoff. LC 69-12442. (Library of Great Painters). (Illus.). 1969. 35.00 (ISBN 0-8109-0041-6). Abrams.

Bonner's Stallion. T. V. Olsen. 1978. pap. 1.95 (ISBN 0-449-13925-5, GM). Fawcett.

Bonnes Vacances. A. Topping. (Illus., Fr.). (gr. 4-9). 1965. pap. text ed. 4.95 (ISBN 0-312-08785-3). St Martin.

Bonneville Cars. E. Radlauer & R. S. Radlauer. LC 73-3076. (Sports Action Bks). (gr. 3 up). 1973. PLB 5.90 o.p. (ISBN 0-531-02092-4). Watts.

Bonnie. Lee Wyndham. LC 60-50701. 5.95 o.p. (ISBN 0-385-07919-2). Doubleday.

Bonnie Prudden's Fitness Book: A Picture Guide with Exercises & Reducing Plans. Bonnie Prudden. 1959. 14.95 (ISBN 0-8260-7235-6). Ronald Pr.

Bonniers Trebandlexikon, 3 vols. (Swedish.). 1970. 145.00 (ISBN 0-8277-3004-7). Maxwell Sci Intl.

Bonny Squirrel & Mrs. Boyette. Bernice D. Smith. (Illus.). 1980. 4.50 (ISBN 0-533-03079-X). Vantage.

Bono Homini Donum: Essays in Historical Linguistics, in Memory of J. Alexander Kerns. Ed. by Arbeitman & Bomhard. (Current Issues in Linguistic Theory: No. 16). 700p. 1980. text ed. 80.00x (ISBN 90-272-3507-4). Humanities.

Bonsai. rev. 2nd ed. Sunset Editors. LC 75-26495. (Illus.). 80p. 1976. pap. 3.95 (ISBN 0-376-03044-5, Sunset Bks). Sunset-Lane.

Bonsai: Miniature Potted Trees. Kyuzo Murata. 116p. 1980. pap. 7.50 (ISBN 0-87040-241-2, Pub. by Shufunotomo Japan). Intl Schol Bk Serv.

Bonsai: Miniatures. Zeko Nakmura. (Illus.). 60p. 1980. pap. 4.50 (ISBN 0-87040-244-7, Pub. by Shufunotomo Japan). Intl Schol Bk Serv.

Bonsai: The Art of Dwarfing Trees. Ann K. Pipe. (Illus.). 1964. pap. 3.95 (ISBN 0-8015-0796-0, Hawthorn). Dutton.

Bonsai Your Pet. Hideo Takeda. (Illus., Orig.). 1980. pap. 5.95 (ISBN 0-8037-0678-2). Dial.

Bonus Years. Thomas B. Robb. LC 68-28076. 1968. 5.95 o.p. (ISBN 0-8170-0410-6). Judson.

Boo & the Flying Flews. Joan C. Bacon. (Eager Readers Ser). (gr. k-3). 1975. PLB 5.00 (ISBN 0-307-60803-4, Golden Pr). Western Pub.

Boo to a Goose. Joseph Low. LC 74-18188. 1975. 5.95 (ISBN 0-689-50009-2, Mcelderry Bk). Atheneum.

Boobies on My Bowsprit. Christa Lewis. 1981. 8.75 (ISBN 0-8062-1598-4). Carlton.

Book. Gloria Earl. 1981. 6.75 (ISBN 0-8062-1572-0). Carlton.

Book. Michael Rawley. (Illus.). 128p. 1981. 19.95 (ISBN 0-938580-00-0). Please Pr.

Book About Anna: For Children & Their Parents. Aline D. Wolf. (Illus.). 56p. (Orig.). 1981. pap. write for info. (ISBN 0-9601016-4-0). Parent-Child Pr.

Book About Chapbooks: The People's Literature of Bygone Times. Harry B. Weiss. LC 69-20399. (Illus.). x, 149p. Repr. of 1969 ed. 18.00 (ISBN 0-8103-5028-9). Gale.

Book About Fans: The History of Fans & Fan-Painting. M. A. Flory. LC 72-174940. (Illus.). xiv, 141p. 1975. Repr. of 1895 ed. 20.00 (ISBN 0-8103-4049-6). Gale.

Book About My Mother. Toby Talbot. 192p. 1980. 10.95 (ISBN 0-374-11542-7). FS&G.

Book About Us. (ps-5). 1.50. New Seed.

Book About Your Skeleton. Ruth B. Gross. (Illus.). (gr. k-4). 1979. 6.95g (ISBN 0-8038-0794-5). Hastings.

Book Auction Records. annual Incl. Vol. 61-67. 1965-71. 40.00x ea. Vol. 61, 1963-64 (ISBN 0-7129-0468-9). Vol. 62, 1964-65 (ISBN 0-7129-0466-2). Vol. 63, 1965-66. Vol. 64, 1966-67 (ISBN 0-7129-0467-0). Vol. 65, 1967-68 (ISBN 0-7129-0469-7). Vol. 66, 1968-69 (ISBN 0-7129-0457-3). Vol. 67, 1969-70 (ISBN 0-7129-0464-6); Vol. 68. 1970-71. 1200p. 1972. 45.00x (ISBN 0-7129-0525-1); Vol. 69. 1972-73. 1200p. 1973. 45.00x (ISBN 0-7129-0574-X); Index to Vols. 66-69 (1968-72) 1129p. 280.00x (ISBN 0-7129-0829-3); Vol. 70. 1972-73. 1974. 47.00x (ISBN 0-7129-0622-3); Vol. 71. 1973-74. 1975. 55.00x (ISBN 0-7129-0663-0); Vol. 72. 1974-75. 1976. 75.00x (ISBN 0-7129-0691-6); 1977-78. Ed. by Wendy Y. Heath. (Illus.). 727p. 1979. 125.00x (ISBN 0-7129-0926-5); Vol. 74. 1976-77. 519p. 1978. 75.00x (ISBN 0-7129-0822-6); Vol. 75. 1977-1978. 727p. 125.00x (ISBN 0-7129-0926-5). LC 5-18641. Intl Pubns Serv.

Book Auction Records: Vol. 76, Aug. 1978-July 1979. Ed. by Wendy Y. Heath. LC 5-18641. 518p. 1980. 162.50x (ISBN 0-7129-1012-3). Intl Pubns Serv.

Book Auctions in England in the Seventeenth Century. John Lawler. LC 68-30614. 1968. Repr. of 1898 ed. 15.00 (ISBN 0-8103-3310-4). Gale.

Book Availability & the Library User. Michael K. Buckland. LC 74-8682. 220p. 1975. text ed. 21.00 (ISBN 0-08-017709-3); pap. text ed. 11.50 (ISBN 0-08-018160-0). Pergamon.

Book Book. Steven Gilbar. 224p. 1981. 10.95 (ISBN 0-312-08803-5). St Martin.

Book Book. Charles Hunter. 1979. wire coil bdg. 4.50 (ISBN 0-88252-082-2). Paladin Hse.

Book Browser's Guide: Britain's Secondhand & Antiquarian Bookshops. Roy H. Lewis. LC 75-10562. 224p. 1975. 14.95 (ISBN 0-7153-7038-3). David & Charles.

Book Clubs & Printing Societies of Great Britain & Ireland. Harold H. Williams. LC 68-26622. 1971. Repr. of 1929 ed. 22.00 (ISBN 0-8103-3749-5). Gale.

Book Development in Africa. 1969. pap. 2.50 (ISBN 92-3-100777-7, U53, UNESCO). Unipub.

Book Development in Asia. 1967. pap. 2.50 (ISBN 92-3-100681-9, U54, UNESCO). Unipub.

Book for Ab. Alberta F. Owens. 1981. 4.75 (ISBN 0-8062-1677-8). Carlton.

Book for Boys & Girls: Or Country Rhymes for Children. John Bunyan. Ed. by Alison Lurie & Justin G. Sciller. Incl. Divine Songs. Isaac Watts; Moral Songs Composed for the Use of Children. Thomas Foxton. LC 75-32136. (Classics of Children's Literature Ser., 1621-1932). 1978. PLB 38.00 (ISBN 0-8240-2253-X). Garland Pub.

Book for Grandmothers. Ruth Goode. 1976. 7.95 o.s.i. (ISBN 0-02-544620-7). Macmillan.

Book for Normal Neurotics. Allan Fromme. 1981. 10.95 (ISBN 0-374-11544-3). FS&G.

Book for the Mind. Swami Muktananda. (Illus., Orig.). 1976. pap. 1.25 (ISBN 0-685-99448-1). SYDA Found.

Book Four. Aleister Crowley. pap. 4.95 (ISBN 0-87728-513-6). Weiser.

Book Hunter. John H. Burton. Ed. by Herbert J. Slater. LC 79-78122. 1971. Repr. of 1895 ed. 20.00 (ISBN 0-8103-3607-3). Gale.

Book Illustration & Decoration: A Guide to Research. Compiled by Vito J. Brenni. LC 80-1701. (Art Reference Collection Ser.: No. 1). viii, 191p. 1980. lib. bdg. 27.50 (ISBN 0-313-22340-8, BBI/). Greenwood.

Book Indexing. Mrs. M. D. Anderson. (Authors' & Printers' Guides Ser.: No. 8). 1971. 4.50 (ISBN 0-521-08202-1). Cambridge U Pr.

Book: Its History & Development. Cyril Davenport. LC 79-164212. (Tower Bks). (Illus.). viii, 258p. 1971. Repr. of 1930 ed. 20.00 (ISBN 0-8103-3944-7). Gale.

Book: Its Printers, Illustrators, & Binders, from Gutenberg to the Present Time. Henri Bouchot. Ed. by H. Grevel. LC 77-155741. (Illus.). 1971. Repr. of 1890 ed. 26.00 (ISBN 0-8103-3392-9). Gale.

Book-Lover's Enchiridion. Alexander Ireland. LC 78-76113. 1969. Repr. of 1888 ed. 18.00 (ISBN 0-8103-3895-5). Gale.

Book Lover's Southwest: A Guide to Good Reading. Walter S. Campbell. 1955. 14.95x o.p. (ISBN 0-8061-0320-5). U of Okla Pr.

Book Market: How to Write, Publish & Market Your Book. Aron Mathieu. LC 80-71059. 512p. 1981. 14.95 (ISBN 0-939014-00-9). Andover Pr.

Book Marketing Handbook: Tips & Techniques for the Sale & Promotion of Scientific, Technical, Professional, & Scholarly Books & Journals. Nat G. Bodian. 482p. 1980. 45.00 (ISBN 0-8352-1286-6). Bowker.

Book Numbers: A Historical Study & Practical Guide to Their Use. John P. Comaromi. 250p. 1981. lib. bdg. price not set (ISBN 0-87287-251-3). Libs Unl.

Book Numbers: Their History, Principles, and Application. Donald J. Lehnus. LC 80-23100. 158p. 1980. pap. 7.50 (ISBN 0-8389-0316-9). ALA.

Book of a Thousand Nights & One Night, 4 vols. Tr. by Powys Mathers from Fr. LC 77-188396. 1972. 60.00 o.p. (ISBN 0-312-09030-7, B50020). Vol. 1 (ISBN 0-312-09065-X). Vol. 2 (ISBN 0-312-09100-1). Vol. 3 (ISBN 0-312-09135-4). Vol. 4 (ISBN 0-312-09170-2). St Martin.

Book of a Thousand Tongues. Eric M. North. LC 73-174087. (Tower Bks). 386p. 1972. Repr. of 1938 ed. 22.00 (ISBN 0-8103-3948-X). Gale.

Book of Acts: A Radiant Commentary on the New Testament. Stanley M. Horton. LC 80-65892. 304p. 1981. 10.95 (ISBN 0-88243-317-2, 02-0317). Gospel Pub.

Book of Afternoon Tea. Marika H. Tenison. LC 79-56046. (Illus.). 96p. 1980. 11.95 (ISBN 0-7153-7929-1). David & Charles.

Book of American Clocks. Brooks Palmer. (Illus.). 1950. 19.95 (ISBN 0-02-594590-4). Macmillan.

Book of American Figure Painters. Mariana G. Van Rensselaer. Ed. by H. Barbara Weinberg. LC 75-28875. (Art Experience in Late 19th Century America Ser.: Vol. 11). (Illus.). 1976. Repr. of 1886 ed. lib. bdg. 72.50 (ISBN 0-8240-2235-1). Garland Pub.

Book of Aphrodisiacs. Raymond Stark. LC 80-6206. 212p. 1981. 11.95 (ISBN 0-8128-2798-8). Stein & Day.

Book of Baruch. Emanuel Tov. LC 75-30775. (Society of Biblical Literature. Texts & Translation-Pseudepigrapha Ser). 1975. pap. 4.50 (ISBN 0-89130-043-0, 060208). Scholars Pr Ca.

Book of Basic Sewing. Rhonda Popko. (Illus.). 104p. (Orig.). 1981. pap. 4.95 (ISBN 0-8326-2248-6, 7445). Delair.

Book of Beautiful Homes with Building Instructions. Clarence Montgomery. (Promotion of the Arts Library Bk.). (Illus.). 1979. 39.75 (ISBN 0-89266-194-1). Am Classical Coll Pr.

Book of Beer. Bob Abel. LC 76-6254. (Illus.). 1976. pap. 6.95 o.p. (ISBN 0-8092-9126-6). Contemp Bks.

Book of Boats. William Atkin & John Atkin. LC 76-25311. (Illus.). 1976. Repr. of 1948 ed. 9.95 (ISBN 0-87742-081-5). Intl Marine.

Book of Bobbin Lace Stitches. Bridget M. Cook & Geraldine Stott. (Illus.). 144p. 1980. 18.50 (ISBN 0-8231-5057-7). Branford.

Book of Bran. Carlson Wade. (Orig.). 1976. pap. 2.25 o.p. (ISBN 0-515-05687-1, Jove). BJ Pub Group.

Book of Bread. Ed. by Phyllis Noble. (Orig.). 1975. pap. 3.95 (ISBN 0-8164-1175-1). Crossroad NY.

Book of Breeething. 2nd ed. William S. Burroughs. LC 75-33858. (Illus.). 1980. 14.95 (ISBN 0-912652-72-1); signed 25.00 (ISBN 0-912652-73-X); pap. 4.95 (ISBN 0-912652-71-3). Blue Wind.

Book of Business Answers. John R. Klug. 1981. 50.00 (ISBN 0-932648-16-9). Boardroom.

Book of Calendars. Jerryl Keane. 700p. 1981. lib. bdg. 22.50 (ISBN 0-87196-467-8). Facts on File.

Book of Cats. Ed. by George Macbeth & Martin Booth. LC 76-43568. (Illus.). 1977. 25.00 o.p. (ISBN 0-688-03159-5). Morrow.

Book of Cats & Creatures. Ruth M. Sanders. LC 80-70012. (gr. 2-6). 1981. PLB 8.95 (ISBN 0-525-26773-5). Dutton.

Book of Characters from Theophrastus Joseph Hall, Sir Thomas Overbury, Nicolas Breton, John Earle, Thomas Fuller, & Other English Authors; Jean De la Bruyere, Vauvenargues, & Other French Authors. Richard Aldington. 559p. 1980. Repr. of 1924 ed. lib. bdg. 50.00 (ISBN 0-8482-0049-7). Norwood Edns.

Book of Christmas. Reader's Digest Editors. (Illus.). 304p. 1973. 15.95 o.p. (ISBN 0-393-21418-4). Norton.

Book of Coffee & Tea: A Guide to the Appreciation of Fine Coffees, Teas & Herbal Beverages. David Joel & Karl Schapira. LC 73-90585. (Illus.). 1977. pap. 6.95 (ISBN 0-312-08821-3). St Martin.

Book of Colt Engraving. 2nd ed. Robert L. Wilson. (Illus.). 560p. 1980. 50.00 (ISBN 0-917714-30-X). Beinfeld Pub.

Book of Comfort. P. B. Power. 1974. pap. 2.25 (ISBN 0-85151-203-8). Banner of Truth.

Book of Comfort & Joy. Editors of Ideals. LC 80-1192. 96p. 1981. 9.95 (ISBN 0-385-17289-3, Galilee). Doubleday.

Book of Common Prayer. 1928 ed. write for info. Oxford U Pr.

Book of Common Prayer. fac: ed. 1976. 15.00 (ISBN 0-8164-5088-9). Crossroad NY.

Book of Common Prayer & Administration of the Sacraments: According to the Use of the Church of England. 7.95x (ISBN 0-19-130601-0). Oxford U Pr.

Book of Common Prayer with the Additions & Deviations Proposed in 1928. 7.95 (ISBN 0-19-141202-3). Oxford U Pr.

Book of Common Worship. Church Of South India. 1962. 4.95x (ISBN 0-19-149906-4). Oxford U Pr.

Book of Conquests. Jim Fitzpatrick. 1978. pap. 8.95 o.p. (ISBN 0-525-47511-7). Dutton.

Book of Cons. Emil Krause. LC 80-68663. (Illus.). 96p. (Orig.). 1980. pap. 4.95 (ISBN 0-89708-029-7). And Bks.

Book of Counsel for Kings. Ghazali. Ed. by Jalal Huma I & H. D. Isaacs. Tr. by F. R. Bagley. 1964. 24.95x (ISBN 0-19-713129-8). Oxford U Pr.

Book of Count Lucanor & Patronio: A Translation of Don Juan Manuel's "el Conde Lucanor". Ed. by John E. Keller & L. Clark Keating. LC 76-24342. (Studies in Romance Languages: No. 16). 208p. 1977. 17.00x (ISBN 0-8131-1350-4). U Pr of Ky.

Book of Craftsmen: The Story of Man's Handiwork Through the Ages. Marjory Bruce. LC 70-185352. (Illus.). 283p. 1974. Repr. of 1937 ed. 18.00 (ISBN 0-8103-3960-9). Gale.

Book of Curves. Edward H. Lockwood & A. Prag. 1961. 32.95 (ISBN 0-521-05585-7). Cambridge U Pr.

Book of Daniel. W. C. Stevens. 190p. 1915. pap. 2.50 (ISBN 0-87509-061-3). Chr Pubns.

Book of Daniel Drew. Bouck White. 1980. pap. 6.95 (ISBN 0-8065-0745-4). Lyle Stuart.

Book of Danish Stiitchery. Danish Handcraft Guild. 136p. 1980. pap. 9.95 (ISBN 0-442-20179-6). Van Nos Reinhold.

Book of Days: A Miscellany of Popular Antiquities in Connection with the Calendar, Including Anecdote, Biography & History, Curiosities of Literature, & Oddities of Human Life & Character, 2 Vols. Ed. by Robert Chambers. LC 67-13009. (Illus.). 1967. Repr. of 1862 ed. 64.00 (ISBN 0-8103-3002-4). Gale.

Book of Decorative Details for Artists, Upholsterers, Architects, Builders, Cabinet & Furniture Makers. Herbert E. Binstead. (Illus.). 1979. deluxe ed. 49.75x (ISBN 0-930582-40-3). Gloucester Art.

Book of Dede Korkut: A Turkish Epic. Tr. by Faruk Sumer et.al from Turkish. LC 72-3214. (Illus.). 236p. 1972. 12.00 (ISBN 0-292-71501-3). U of Tex Pr.

Book of Desire. Stanley J. Goodwin. 1979. pap. 2.40 (ISBN 0-686-10271-1). Northland Pubns WA.

Book of Devotions. new ed. Elizabeth I. 1977. pap. text ed. 4.00x (ISBN 0-901072-57-5). Humanities.

Book of Do-In: Exercise for Physical & Spiritual Development. Michio Kushi. (Illus.). 176p. (Orig.). 1979. pap. 10.95 (ISBN 0-87040-382-6). Japan Pubns.

Book of Dogs. Barbara Woodhouse. 7.50x (ISBN 0-392-06367-0, SpS). Soccer.

Book of Dragons. Ruth Manning-Sanders. (Illus.). (gr. 2-6). 1965. PLB 7.95 o.p. (ISBN 0-525-26824-3). Dutton.

Book of Dreams. Jack Vance. (Science Fiction Ser). 1981. pap. 1.95 (ISBN 0-87997-587-3, UJ1587). Daw Bks.

Book of Dreams & Ghosts. Andrew Lang. LC 80-19690. 301p. 1980. Repr. of 1972 ed. lib. bdg. 9.95x (ISBN 0-89370-610-8). Borgo Pr.

Book of Easter. LC 76-159894. Repr. of 1911 ed. 26.00 (ISBN 0-8103-3401-1). Gale.

Book of Ebenezer le Page. G. B. Edwards. LC 80-2719. 416p. 1981. 13.95 (ISBN 0-394-51651-6). Knopf.

Book of Elephants. Compiled by Katie Wales. LC 76-23139. (Illus.). 64p. (ps-5). 1977. 6.95 (ISBN 0-590-07723-6, Four Winds); PLB 5.41 o.p. (ISBN 0-8193-0892-7). Schol Bk Serv.

Book of Elizathan Magic: Thomas Hill's Naturall & Artificial Conclusions. Thomas Ross. 84p. 1974. 15.00 (ISBN 3-4180-0204-8). Adler.

Book of English Essays. Ed. by W. E. Williams. 1981. pap. 3.95 (ISBN 0-14-043153-5). Penguin.

Book of English Lyrics. Ed. by Cecil D. Lewis. 1979. 5.95 (ISBN 0-7011-0909-2, Pub. by Chatto Bodley Jonathan). Merrimack Bk Serv.

Book of Enoch. Tr. by Richard Lawrence. LC 80-65736. 96p. 1980. pap. 3.00 (ISBN 0-934666-06-7). Artisan Sales.

Book of Essays. Ed. by Robert Chambers & Carlyle King. 1963. pap. text ed. 5.50 (ISBN 0-312-08855-8). St Martin.

Book of Esther. Tr. by Aryeh Kaplan. 268p. 7.95 (ISBN 0-686-27543-8); pap. 5.95 (ISBN 0-686-27544-6). Maznaim.

Book of Esther. Alexander Raleigh. Date not set. 9.00 (ISBN 0-86524-037-X). Klock & Klock.

Book of Esther: Motifs, Themes & Structure. Sandra B. Berg. LC 78-32035. (SBL Dissertation Ser.). 1979. 12.00 (ISBN 0-89130-306-5); pap. 7.50 (ISBN 0-89130-279-4, 060144). Scholars Pr Ca.

Book of Eve. Catherine De Vinck. 1979. text ed. 6.00 (ISBN 0-911726-40-3); stero record incl. Alleluia Pr.

Book of Executive Health: A Guide for Men & Women Executives Who Want to Live Longer. Times Bks. & British Medical Association. (Illus.). 224p. 1981. 12.95 (ISBN 0-13-080010-4, Spec); pap. 5.95 (ISBN 0-13-080002-3). P-H.

Book of Experiments. Leonard De Vries. (Illus.). (gr. 4-6). 1959. 4.95g o.s.i. (ISBN 0-02-730000-5). Macmillan.

Book of Ezekiel: A Commentary. Solomon B. Freehof. Ed. by Daniel B. Syme. (Jewish Commentary for Bible Readers Ser.). 1979. 15.00 (ISBN 0-8074-0033-5, 380010). UAHC.

Book of Fairies. Beatrice Phillpotts. (Illus.). 1979. 15.00 (ISBN 0-345-28091-1). Ballantine.

Book of Fairs. Helen Augur. LC 75-159875. (Tower Bks). (Illus.). xviii, 308p. 1972. Repr. of 1939 ed. 20.00 (ISBN 0-8103-3927-7). Gale.

Book of Faith. Elizabeth Goudge. 336p. 1980. pap. 2.50 (ISBN 0-553-11052-7). Bantam.

Book of Family Medical Questions. John G. Deaton & Elizabeth J. Pascoe. Ed. by Philip R. Alper. LC 79-4804. 1979. 15.95 (ISBN 0-394-41468-3). Random.

Book of Family Prayer. Gabe Huck. 1979. 12.50 (ISBN 0-8164-0415-1). Crossroad NY.

Book of Famous Wits. Walter C. Jerrold. LC 77-155086. 1971. Repr. of 1912 ed. 22.00 (ISBN 0-8103-3757-6). Gale.

Book of Favorite Games. Bryan Holme & Jeffery Simpson. (Illus.). 1979. cancelled (ISBN 0-670-17942-6, Studio). Viking Pr.

Book of Five Rings: A Guide to Strategy. Miyamoto Musashi. Tr. by Victor Harris from Japanese. LC 73-83986. (Illus.). 96p. 1974. 10.95 (ISBN 0-87951-018-8). Overlook Pr.

Book of Folklore. Sabine Baring-Gould. LC 69-16807. Repr. of 1913 ed. 18.00 (ISBN 0-8103-3603-0). Gale.

Book of Ford Books. David L. Lewis. (Illus.). 200p. 1981. price not set (ISBN 0-934780-04-8); pap. price not set (ISBN 0-934780-05-6). Bookman Dan.

Book of Fritz Leiber, Vols. I & II. Fritz Lieber. (Science Fiction Ser.). 1980. lib. bdg. 19.95 (ISBN 0-8398-2638-9). Gregg.

Book of Games: A Course in Spiritual Play. Hugh Prather. LC 80-2840. (Illus.). 176p. 1981. pap. 5.95 (ISBN 0-385-14779-1, Dolp). Doubleday.

Book of Ghosts & Goblins. Ruth Manning-Sanders. (Illus.). (gr. 2-5). 1973. pap. 1.25 o.p. (ISBN 0-525-45014-9, Anytime Bks). Dutton.

Book of Giggles. William Cole. (gr. k-6). 1980. pap. 1.25 (ISBN 0-440-40723-0, YB). Dell.

Book of Ginseng. Sarah Harriman. (Health Ser.). (Orig.). 1973. pap. 1.75 (ISBN 0-515-05438-0, A2988). Jove Pubns.

Book of Goddesses & Heroines. Patricia Monaghan. 1981. pap. 9.95 (ISBN 0-525-47664-4). Dutton.

Book of God's Love. M. R. Bawa Muhaiyaddeen. Ed. by Sharon Marcus & Karin Marcus. Tr. by Ajwad Macan-Markar et al from Tamil. (Illus.). 126p. 1981. 7.95 (ISBN 0-914390-19-8). Fellowship Pr.

Book of Golden Discs. Joseph Murrells. (Illus.). 1979. 21.95 o.p. (ISBN 0-214-20480-4, ADON 8086-8, Dist by Arco); pap. 11.95 o.p. (ISBN 0-214-20512-6, ADON 8081-7). Barrie & Jenkins.

Book of Grass Crafts. Mary H. Kahlenberg. (Illus.). 1981. 18.95 (ISBN 0-525-06983-6); pap. 12.95 (ISBN 0-525-47630-X). Dutton.

Book of Hawking, Hunting & Blasing of Arms. Juliana Berners. LC 74-25849. (English Experience Ser.: No. 151). 180p. 1969. Repr. of 1486 ed. 42.00 (ISBN 90-221-0151-7). Walter J Johnson.

Book of Hearts. (Illus.). 1977. pap. 4.95 o.s.i. (ISBN 0-446-87495-7). Warner Bks.

Book of Herbs. Edith F. Farwell. 1980. 5.95 (ISBN 0-935720-01-4). Green Hill.

Book of Herbs. Dorothy Hall. LC 74-3666. 1974. 7.95 o.p. (ISBN 0-684-13822-0, ScribT). Scribner.

Book of Hope: How Women Can Overcome Depression. Helen DeRosis & Victoria Y. Pellegrino. 1976. 9.95 o.s.i. (ISBN 0-02-531040-2). Macmillan.

Book of Horses. Glenn Balch. (Illus.). 96p. (gr. 3-7). 1967. 8.95 (ISBN 0-590-07048-7, Four Winds). Schol Bk Serv.

Book of Horses. Dorian Williams. LC 70-164017. (Illus.). 1971. 8.95 (ISBN 0-397-00888-0). Lippincott.

Book of Hours. Elizabeth Yates. 1976. 5.95 (ISBN 0-685-89238-7); pap. 2.95 (ISBN 0-8164-0900-5). Crossroad NY.

Book of Houses. Robert Cole. LC 80-16931. 132p. 1980. 8.95 (ISBN 0-934558-04-3); pap. 4.95 (ISBN 0-934558-01-9). Entwhistle Bks.

Book of Indian Beauty. Mulk Raj Anand & Krishina N. Hutheesing. LC 80-52066. (Illus.). 1981. 12.95 (ISBN 0-8048-1180-6). C E Tuttle.

Book of Indian Crafts & Costumes. Bernard S. Mason. (Illus.). 1946. 15.95 (ISBN 0-8260-5720-9). Wiley.

Book of Insults & Irreverent Quotations. D. C. Hook & L. Kahn. 1980. 9.95 (ISBN 0-8246-0250-1). Jonathan David.

Book of Insults II. Nancy McPhee. 144p. 1981. 7.95 (ISBN 0-312-08930-9). St Martin.

Book of Irish Curses. Patrick C. Power. 1975. pap. 4.95 (ISBN 0-87243-060-X). Templegate.

Book of Irish Verse. Ed. by John Montague. 400p. 1977. 14.95 (ISBN 0-02-585630-8, 58563). Macmillan.

Book of Isaiah: A Commentary. Soloman B. Freehof. Ed. by Daniel B. Syme. LC 72-2156. (Jewish Commentary for Bible Readers Ser.). 1972. 15.00 (ISBN 0-8074-0042-4, 383015). UAHC.

Book of Jazz. Leonard Feather. 1976. pap. 1.95 (ISBN 0-440-30680-9, LE). Dell.

Book of Jeremiah. John A. Thompson. LC 79-16510. (New International Commentary on the Old Testament Ser.). 1980. 22.50 (ISBN 0-8028-2369-6). Eerdmans.

Book of Job. Edgar Gibson. 1978. 9.75 (ISBN 0-686-12949-0). Klock & Klock.

Book of Job: A New Translation According to the Traditional Hebrew Text. 88p. 1980. 6.50 (ISBN 0-8276-0172-7). Jewish Pubn.

Book of Joshua. William G. Blaikie. 1978. 14.00 (ISBN 0-686-12943-1). Klock & Klock.

Book of Joshua. Marten H. Woudstra. LC 80-23413. (New International Commentary on the Old Testament). 400p. 1981. 16.95 (ISBN 0-8028-2356-4). Eerdmans.

Book of Jubilees. Tr. by Schodde. LC 80-53467. 96p. 1980. pap. 3.00 (ISBN 0-934666-08-3). Artisan Sales.

Book of Judith. Ed. by S. Zeitlin. 15.00 (ISBN 0-685-55556-9, Pub. by Dropsie U Pr). Ktav.

Book of Kells: A Selection from the Irish Medieval Manuscripts. Peter Brown. LC 80-7973. (Illus.). 96p. 1980. pap. 10.95 (ISBN 0-394-73960-4). Knopf.

Book of Kells: A Selection of Pages Reproduced with a Description & Notes. G. O. Simms. 1976. Repr. of 1961 ed. pap. text ed. 3.25x (ISBN 0-391-00608-8, Dolmen Pr). Humanities.

Book of Khalid. Ameen Rahani. (Arab Background Ser.). 12.00x (ISBN 0-685-77103-2). Intl Bk Ctr.

Book of "Ki" Co-Ordinating Body and Mind in Daily Life. Koichi Tohei. LC 76-29340. (Illus.). 128p. 1976. pap. 7.95 (ISBN 0-87040-379-6). Japan Pubns.

Book of Kings & Queens. Ruth Manning-Sanders. (Illus.). (gr. 2-6). 1978. PLB 7.95 o.p. (ISBN 0-525-26925-8). Dutton.

Book of Knitting & Crochet. Schachenmayr. Ed. by Nye. 300p. 1973. 11.25 (ISBN 0-8231-5031-3). Branford.

Book of Knowledge. Bernard Gunther et al. (Essence Books Ser). (YA) 1973. pap. 0.50 o.s.i. (ISBN 0-02-080190-4, Collier). Macmillan.

Book of Landscape Design. H. Stuart Ortloff & Henry B. Raymore. LC 59-12871. (Illus.). 320p. 1975. pap. 3.25 o.p. (ISBN 0-685-52306-3). Morrow.

Book of Laughter & Forgetting. Milan Kundera. LC 80-7657. 224p. 1980. 10.95 (ISBN 0-394-50896-3). Knopf.

Book of Leviticus. Samuel H. Kellogg. 1978. 19.00 (ISBN 0-686-12941-5). Klock & Klock.

Book of Leviticus: A Study Manual. Charles F. Pfeiffer. (Shield Bible Study Ser). (Orig.). pap. 2.95 (ISBN 0-8010-6889-4). Baker Bk.

Book of Life. Marsilio Ficino. Tr. by Charles Boer from Latin. 217p. 1980. pap. 12.50 (ISBN 0-88214-212-7). Spring Pubns.

Book of Life. Sinsheimer. 1976. 1.50 (ISBN 0-201-07026-X). A-W.

Book of Lists. David Wallechinsky & Irving Wallace. LC 77-1521. (Illus.). 1977. 12.95 (ISBN 0-688-03183-8). Morrow.

Book of Lists Number Two. Irving Wallace et al. LC 79-3732. (Illus.). 1980. 12.95 (ISBN 0-688-03574-4). Morrow.

Book of Lists Two. Irving Wallace et al. 1981. pap. 3.50 (ISBN 0-553-13101-X). Bantam.

Book of Love. David Delvin. 1977. pap. 1.95 o.s.i. (ISBN 0-515-04305-2). Jove Pubns.

Book of Love Poetry. Ed. by Jon Stallworthy. 385p. 1974. 17.95 (ISBN 0-19-519774-7). Oxford U Pr.

Book of Macrobiotics: The Universal Way of Health & Happiness. Michio Kushi. LC 76-29341. (Illus.). 176p. (Orig.). 1977. pap. 10.95 (ISBN 0-87040-381-8). Japan Pubns.

Book of Magic. John Mulholland. LC 63-9766. (Encore Edition). 1963. pap. 1.95 (ISBN 0-684-16914-2, SL379, ScribT). Scribner.

Book of Maine Fishing Maps. Harry Vanderweide. (Illus.). 96p. (Orig.). 1980. pap. 6.95 (ISBN 0-89933-007-X). DeLorme Pub.

Book of Margery Kempe. Margery B. Kempe. Ed. by Sanford B. Meech. (Early English Text Society Ser.). 1940. 24.95x (ISBN 0-19-722212-9). Oxford U Pr.

Book of Mars for You. Franklyn M. Branley. LC 68-11058. (Illus.). (gr. 3-6). 1968. 8.95 o.p. (ISBN 0-690-15295-7, TYC-J); PLB 8.79 (ISBN 0-690-15296-5). T Y Crowell.

Book of Masques. Jonson et al. 1967. 68.00 (ISBN 0-521-05455-9). Cambridge U Pr.

Book of Masques. Ed. by T. J. Spencer & S. Wells. (Illus.). 448p. 1981. pap. 19.95 (ISBN 0-521-29758-3). Cambridge U Pr.

Book of Medieval Latin for Schools. 3rd ed. Ed. by Helen Waddell. 1979. pap. 7.50x (ISBN 0-06-497276-3). B&N.

Book of Melvin. William Parham. LC 80-53663. (Illus.). 64p. (Orig.). 1981. pap. 3.95 (ISBN 0-938264-00-1). Veritas Pubns.

Book of Middle Eastern Food. Claudia Roden. 1974. pap. 4.95 (ISBN 0-394-71948-4, Vin). Random.

Book of Miniatures: Furniture & Accessories. Helen Ruthberg. LC 76-451. (Creative Crafts Ser.). 1976. 13.95 (ISBN 0-8019-6366-4); pap. 7.95 (ISBN 0-8019-6365-6). Chilton.

Book of Miso. William Shurtleff & Akiko Aoyagi. 768p. 1981. pap. 3.50 (ISBN 0-345-29107-7). Ballantine.

Book of Modern Jewish Etiquette: A Guide to All Occasions. Helen Latner. LC 80-22537. (Illus.). 416p. 19.95 (ISBN 0-8052-3757-7). Schocken.

Book of Mordechai: A Study of the Jews of Libya - Selections from the Highid Mordekhai of Mordechai Hakohen. Ed. & tr. by Harvey E. Goldberg. LC 80-11470. 1980. text ed. 19.50x (ISBN 0-89727-005-3). Inst Study Human.

Book of Mormon. large print flex bdg. 5.95 o.p. (ISBN 0-87747-623-3); lib. bdg. 6.00 o.p. (ISBN 0-87747-321-8). Deseret Bk.

Book of Mormon Charts. Ed. by M. Ross Richards & Marie C. Richards. pap. 1.95 o.p. (ISBN 0-87747-444-3). Deseret Bk.

Book of Mormon Lands & Times. J. Nile Washburn. LC 73-75395. 1975. 6.50 (ISBN 0-88290-020-X). Horizon Utah.

Book of Mormon Story. Mary P. Parrish. LC 66-10962. pap. 1.50 o.p. (ISBN 0-87747-024-3). Deseret Bk.

Book of Mourning. Margaret Newlin. 1981. 10.00 (ISBN 0-88233-677-0); pap. 4.00 (ISBN 0-88233-678-9). Ardis Pubs.

Book of Music: A Visual Guide to Musical Appreciation. Gill Rowley. LC 78-53427. 1978. 19.95 o.p. (ISBN 0-13-079988-2). P-H.

Book of Myths. Roger L. Green. (Childrens Illustrated Classics Ser). (Illus.). 1976. Repr. of 1965 ed. 9.00x o.p. (ISBN 0-460-05066-4, Pub. by J. M. Dent England). Biblio Dist.

Book of Myths. H. Sewell & T. Bulfinch. 1969. 9.95 (ISBN 0-02-782280-X). Macmillan.

Book of Nahum. Walter A. Maier. (Thornapple Commentaries). 392p. 1980. pap. 6.95 (ISBN 0-8010-6098-2). Baker Bk.

Book of New England Legends & Folk Lore. Samuel A. Drake. LC 69-19881. 1969. Repr. of 1901 ed. 20.00 (ISBN 0-8103-3829-7). Gale.

Book of Nonsense. Edward Lear. LC 80-5355. (Illus.). 56p. (gr. 4 up). 1980. 8.95 (ISBN 0-87099-241-4). Metro Mus Art.

Book of Nonsense. Mervin Peake. LC 75-4108. 1975. 7.95 (ISBN 0-7206-0412-5). Dufour.

Book of Nonsense, Repr. Of 1846 Ed. Edward Lear. Bd. with English Struwwelpeter. Heinrich Hoffman. Repr. of 1848 ed; Fairy Library Series. George Cruikshank. Repr. of 1864 ed. LC 75-32161. (Classics of Children's Literature, 1621-1932: Vol. 26). 1976. PLB 38.00 (ISBN 0-8240-2275-0). Garland Pub.

Book of Noodles: Stories of Simpletons. William A. Clouston. LC 67-24351. 1969. Repr. of 1888 ed. 15.00 (ISBN 0-8103-3519-0). Gale.

Book of Nursery & Mother Goose Rhymes. Marguerite De Angeli. (Illus.). (gr. k-3). 1954. 9.95a (ISBN 0-385-07232-5); PLB (ISBN 0-385-06246-X). Doubleday.

Book of Operas, Their Histories, Their Plots & Their Music. Henry E. Krehbiel. LC 80-2279. 1981. Repr. of 1919 ed. 42.50 (ISBN 0-404-18851-6). AMS Pr.

Book of Ornamental Knots. John Hensel. (Encore Edition). (Illus.). 1978. pap. 2.95 (ISBN 0-684-16900-2, ScribT); 12.50 (ISBN 0-684-13409-8). Scribner.

Book of Parables. Daniel Berrigan. 1977. 7.95 (ISBN 0-8164-0328-7). Crossroad NY.

Book of People. Christopher P. Andersen. (Illus.). 500p. 1981. 19.95 (ISBN 0-399-12617-1, Perigee); pap. 9.95 (ISBN 0-399-50530-X). Putnam.

Book of Pets. Stanley Leinwoll. LC 80-17598. (Illus.). 128p. (gr. 7 up). 1980. PLB 8.79 (ISBN 0-671-33071-3). Messner.

Book of Planet Earth for You. Franklyn M. Branley. LC 74-30408. (Illus.). 96p. (gr. 3-6). 1975. 8.79 (ISBN 0-690-00754-X, TYC-J). T Y Crowell.

Book of Poetry. Tr. by James Legge. (Eng. & Chinese.). 1967. Repr. of 1923 ed. 11.00 o.p. (ISBN 0-8188-0061-5). Paragon.

Book of Praises. Joyce Blackburn. 128p. (Orig.). (YA) 1980. pap. 3.95 (ISBN 0-310-42061-X). Zondervan.

Book of Prayers. Hilda L. Rostron. (Ladybird Ser). (Illus.). (gr. 1-3). 1964. bds. 1.49 (ISBN 0-87508-834-1). Chr Lit.

Book of Predictions. David Wallechinsky et al. (Illus.). 576p. 1980. 12.95 (ISBN 0-688-00024-X). Morrow.

Book of Presents: Easy-to-Make Gifts for Every Occasion. Ed. by Sonya Mills. LC 79-2187. 1979. 14.95 o.p. (ISBN 0-394-50782-7). Pantheon.

Book of Private Prayer. Hubert Van Zeller. 1973. pap. 3.95 (ISBN 0-87243-045-6). Templegate.

Book of Proverbs. Ralph Wardlaw. Date not set. 27.50 (ISBN 0-86524-042-6). Klock & Klock.

Book of Proverbs in Rhyme from the Holy Bible. Lotus H. Chandler. LC 79-56329. 1981. 6.95 (ISBN 0-533-04528-2). Vantage.

Book of Psalms. J. J. Stewart Perowne. 1976. 22.95 (ISBN 0-310-31040-7). Zondervan.

Book of Questions, Vol. 1. Edmond Jabes. Tr. by Rosmarie Waldrop from Fr. LC 75-34058. 1976. text ed. 12.00 o.p. (ISBN 0-8195-4091-9, Pub. by Wesleyan U Pr); pap. 7.95 (ISBN 0-8195-6043-X). Columbia U Pr.

Book of Questions: The Book of Yukel & Return to the Book, Vols. 2 & 3. Edmond Jabes. Tr. by Rosmarie Waldrop from Fr. LC 77-74561. 1977. 17.50 (ISBN 0-8195-5011-6, Pub. by Wesleyan U Pr); pap. 8.95 (ISBN 0-8195-6049-9). Columbia U Pr.

Book of Railway Journeys. Compiled by Ludovic Kennedy. (Illus.). 1980. 12.95 (ISBN 0-89256-135-1). Rawson Wade.

Book of Readings in Diagnostic & Corrective Reading. Veralee Hardin. 1974. pap. text ed. 5.00x (ISBN 0-87543-118-6). Lucas.

Book of Rejects. Ganell Taylor. 1980. 6.95 (ISBN 0-533-04796-X). Vantage.

Book of Reptiles & Amphibians. Michael H. Bevans. LC 55-9715. (gr. 4-9). 5.95 (ISBN 0-385-02196-8). Doubleday.

Book of Revelation. Alfred Heidenreich. 1977. 12.50 (ISBN 0-903540-03-7, Pub. by Floris Books); pap. 7.50 (ISBN 0-903540-04-5). St George Bk Serv.

Book of Revelations for the Aquarian Age. Lord Easu. Compiled by Gladys K. Rodehaver. (Illus., Orig.). 1980. pap. 6.95 (ISBN 0-930208-19-6). Mangan Bks.

Book of Rounds. Mary Taylor & Carol Dyk. 1977. pap. 14.95 (ISBN 0-87690-182-8). Dutton.

Book of Russian Idioms Illustrated. M. I. Dubrovin. LC 79-40433. (Illus.). 328p. 1981. 8.00 (ISBN 0-08-023594-8). Pergamon.

Book of Ruth. Syrell R. Leahy. 384p. 1978. pap. 1.95 o.p. (ISBN 0-449-22689-1, Crest). Fawcett.

Book of Sabbath. Charles Wengrov. (Illus.). 1962. 3.00 (ISBN 0-914080-43-1). Shulsinger Sales.

Book of Samplers. Marguerite Fawdry & Deborah Brown. (Illus.). 160p. 1980. 20.00 (ISBN 0-312-09006-4). St Martin.

Book of Science Verse. W. Eastwood. 279p. 1980. Repr. of 1961 ed. lib. bdg. 30.00 (ISBN 0-89984-177-5). Century Bookbindery.

Book of Scottish Verse. Ed. by Robert L. Mackie. (World's Classics Ser.). 1934. 7.95 (ISBN 0-19-250897-0). Oxford U Pr.

Book of Scripts. 2nd ed. Alfred Fairbank. (Illus.). 1977. 9.95 o.p. (ISBN 0-571-10876-8, Pub. by Faber & Faber); pap. 6.50 (ISBN 0-571-11080-0). Merrimack Bk Serv.

Book of Signs. Rudolf Koch. (Illus.). 8.50 (ISBN 0-8446-0744-4). Peter Smith.

Book of Snobs. William M. Thackeray. Ed. by J. Sutherland. LC 78-54067. 1978. 18.95x (ISBN 0-312-09011-0). St Martin.

Book of Soccer. Brian Glanville. (Illus.). 1979. 14.95 (ISBN 0-19-502585-7). Oxford U Pr.

Book of Sounds: A, B, C. Anne E. Hughes. LC 78-62981. (Learn-a-Sound). (Illus.). (gr. 1-3). 1979. PLB 9.95 (ISBN 0-8393-0188-X). Raintree Child.

Book of Sounds: Blends & Ends. Anne E. Hughes. LC 79-62984. (Learn-a-Sound). (Illus.). (gr. 1-3). 1979. PLB 9.95 (ISBN 0-8393-0191-X). Raintree Child.

Book of Sounds: ee, oo, ai. Anne E. Hughes. LC 79-62983. (Learn-a-Sound). (Illus.). (gr. 1-3). 1979. PLB 9.95 (ISBN 0-8393-0190-1). Raintree Child.

Book of Sounds: sl, ch, pr. Anne E. Hughes. LC 79-62982. (Learn-a-Sound). (Illus.). (gr. 1-3). 1979. PLB 9.95 (ISBN 0-8393-0189-8). Raintree Child.

Book of Space Brothers. Ed. by Timothy G. Beckley. (Illus., Orig.). 1968. pap. 6.95 o.p. (ISBN 0-685-20194-5). Saucerian.

Book of Spices. rev. ed. Frederick Rosengarten. 1973. pap. 1.95 (ISBN 0-515-03220-4, Y3220). Jove Pubns.

Book of Strange Facts & Useless Information. Scot Morris. LC 73-9040. 1979. pap. 5.95 (ISBN 0-385-00618-7, Dolp). Doubleday.

Book of Studies in Plant Form: With Some Suggestions for Their Application to Design. A. E. Lilley & W. Midgley. LC 70-89276. (Tower Bks). (Illus.). xvi, 131p. 1972. Repr. of 1896 ed. 15.00 (ISBN 0-8103-3947-1). Gale.

Book of Subtyl Histories & Fables of Esope. Aesopus. Bd. with Siege of Rhodes. Guillaume Caoursin. LC 76-14086. 1975. Repr. of 1484 ed. 34.00x (ISBN 0-8201-1154-6). Schol Facsimilies.

Book of Successful Bathrooms. Joseph F. Schram. LC 75-31489. (Illus.). 160p. 1975. 12.00 o.p. (ISBN 0-912336-16-1); pap. 5.95 o.p. (ISBN 0-912336-17-X). Structures Pub.

Book of Successful Fireplaces: How to Build, Decorate, & Use Them. 20th ed. R. J. Lytle & Marie-Jeanne Lytle. LC 77-9166. (Successful Book). (Illus.). 1977. 13.95 (ISBN 0-912336-52-8); pap. 6.95 (ISBN 0-912336-53-6). Structures Pub.

Book of Successful Kitchens. 2nd ed. Patrick J. Galvin. LC 77-25375. (Illus.). 136p. 1978. 13.95 (ISBN 0-912336-58-7); pap. 6.95 (ISBN 0-912336-59-5). Structures Pub.

Book of Successful Swimming Pools. Ronald Derven & Carol Nichols. LC 75-40520. (Illus.). 1976. 13.95 (ISBN 0-912336-20-X); pap. 6.95 (ISBN 0-912336-21-8). Structures Pub.

Book of Survival. Anthony Greenbank. (Illus.). 1968. 12.95 o.s.i. (ISBN 0-06-070873-5, HarpT). Har-Row.

Book of Takes. Paul Zelevansky. 1976. 15.00 (ISBN 0-9605610-0-5). Zartscorp.

Book of Talismans, Amulets & Zodiacal Gems. William T. Pavitt & Kate Pavitt. LC 72-157497. (Tower Bks). (Illus.). 1971. Repr. of 1914 ed. 26.00 (ISBN 0-8103-3901-3). Gale.

Book of Tall Tales: Featuring "The Shaggy Dog". Walt Disney Productions. LC 77-74466. (Disney's World of Adventure). (Illus.). (gr. 2-6). 1978. 3.95 (ISBN 0-394-83596-4, BYR); PLB 4.99 (ISBN 0-394-93596-9). Random.

Book of Tarot. Susan Gerulskis-Estes. 96p. 1981. pap. 5.95 (ISBN 0-87100-162-4). Morgan.

Book of Tests: The Ultimate Collection of Quizzes to Help You Find Out What You're Really Like. Bruce M. Nash & Randolph B. Monchick. LC 79-6611. 384p. 1980. pap. 8.95 (ISBN 0-385-15471-2, Dolp). Doubleday.

Book of the Afghan Hound. Joan M. Brearley. (Illus.). 1978. 20.00 (ISBN 0-87666-665-9, H-991). TFH Pubns.

Book of the Bible. Eunice Riedel et al. 560p. 1981. pap. 3.95 (ISBN 0-553-14649-1). Bantam.

Book of the Bounty' William Bligh & Others. Ed. by George Mackaness. Gavin Kennedy. (Everyman's Reference Library). 1981. 14.50x (ISBN 0-460-00950-8, Pub. by J. M. Dent England). Biblio Dist.

Book of the Cat. Ed. by Michael Wright & Sally Walters. LC 80-23570. (Illus.). 256p. 1981. 24.95 (ISBN 0-671-44753-X); pap. 9.95 (ISBN 0-671-41624-3). Summit Bks.

Book of the Courtier. Baldesar Castiglione. Tr. by George Bull. (Classics Ser.). 368p. 1976. pap. 2.95 (ISBN 0-14-044192-1). Penguin.

Book of the Cranberry Islands. Richard Grossinger. 1975. pap. 5.95 o.p. (ISBN 0-06-090373-2, CN373, CN). Har-Row.

Book of the Dead: An English Translation of the Chapters, Hymns, Etc., of the Theban Recension. 2nd ed. E. A. Budge. (Illus.). 1969. 35.00 (ISBN 0-7100-1128-8). Routledge & Kegan.

Book of the Dead: Based on the Ani, Hunefer & Anhai Papyri in the British Museum. Albert Champdor. Tr. by Faubion Bowers. LC 66-17862. (Illus.). 1966. 10.00 o.p. (ISBN 0-912326-17-4). Garrett-Helix.

Book of the Duke of True Lovers. Christine De Pisan. Tr. by Alice Kemp-Welch et al. LC 66-23313. (Illus.). Repr. of 1926 ed. 7.50x (ISBN 0-8154-0177-9). Cooper Sq.

Book of the Eskimos. Peter Freuchen. 1977. pap. 1.75 o.p. (ISBN 0-449-30802-2, Prem). Fawcett.

Book of the Foxhound. Daphne Moore. (Illus.). 17.50 (ISBN 0-85131-209-8, Dist. by Sporting Book Center). J A Allen.

Book of the Garand. Hatcher. 15.00 (ISBN 0-88227-014-1). Gun Room.

Book of the Goat. H. S. Pegler. Date not set. 6.00 (ISBN 0-686-26688-9). Dairy Goat.

Book of the Gods & Rites & the Ancient Calendar. Fr. Diego Duran. Tr. by Fernando Horcasitas & Doris Heyden. LC 73-88147. (Civilization of the American Indian Ser.: No. 102). (Illus.). 1971. 19.95 (ISBN 0-8061-0889-4); pap. 9.95 (ISBN 0-8061-1201-8). U of Okla Pr.

Book of the Hopi. Frank Waters. (Illus.). 1974. pap. 2.50 (ISBN 0-345-27573-X). Ballantine.

Book of the Lover & the Beloved. Ramon Lull. Ed. by Kenneth Leech. Tr. by J. Allison Peers. LC 78-61666. (Spiritual Masters Ser.). 1978. pap. 2.95 (ISBN 0-8091-2135-2). Paulist Pr.

Book of the Master Jesus, 3 vols. complete set. Incl. Vol. 1. Jesus of Nazareth. 1974 (ISBN 0-916700-04-6); Vol. 2. Jesus of Galilee. 227p. 1974 (ISBN 0-916700-05-4); Vol. 3. Christ the Lord. 1974 (ISBN 0-916700-06-2). (Illus.). perfect bdg. 3.50 ea. o.p. (ISBN 0-916700-12-7). Epiphany Pr.

Book of the Opera & the Ballet & the History of the Opera. Frederick H. Martens. LC 80-2289. 1981. Repr. of 1925 ed. 22.50 (ISBN 0-404-18857-5). AMS Pr.

Book of the Pekingese. Anna K. Nicholas & Joan M. Brearley. (Illus.). 352p. 1975. 12.95 (ISBN 0-87666-348-X, H-953). TFH Pubns.

Book of the Pig. Jack D. Scott. (Illus.). 64p. (ps up). 1981. 8.95 (ISBN 0-399-20718-X). Putnam.

Book of the Pug. Joan M. Brearley. (Illus.). 320p. 1980. 20.00 (ISBN 0-87666-683-7, H-1021). TFH Pubns.

Book of the Reasons Behind Astronomical Tables (Kitab Fi 'ilal Al-Zijat) Ali Ibn Sulayman al Hashimi. Ed. by E. S. Kennedy & David Pingree. Tr. by Fuad I. Haddad from Arabic. LC 77-14160. 400p. Date not set. 50.00x (ISBN 0-8201-1298-4). Schol Facsimiles. Postponed.

Book of the Rhymer's Club, Repr. Of 1892 Ed. Ed. by Ian Fletcher & John Stokes. Bd. with Second Book of the Rhymer's Club. Repr. of 1894 ed. LC 76-20022. (Decadent Consciousness Ser.: Vol. 26). 1977. lib. bdg. 38.00 (ISBN 0-8240-2775-2). Garland Pub.

Book of the Rover. Staten Abbey. pap. 4.50x (ISBN 0-392-05798-0, SpS). Soccer.

Book of the Royal Enfield. W. C. Haycroft. pap. 4.50x (ISBN 0-392-02349-0, SpS). Soccer.

Book of the Shih Tzu. Joan M. Brearley & Allen Easton. (Illus.). 304p. 1980. 30.00 (ISBN 0-87666-664-0, H-996). TFH Pubns.

Book of the Sonnet: Poems & Criticism. Ed. by Martin Kallich et al. LC 72-125263. 214p. 1972. text ed. 18.95x (ISBN 0-8290-0156-5); pap. text ed. 9.95x (ISBN 0-8290-0157-3). Irvington.

Book of the Subtyl Historyes & Fables of Esope. Aesop. LC 76-177403. (English Experience Ser.: No. 439). 288p. Repr. of 1484 ed. 49.00 (ISBN 90-221-0439-7). Walter J Johnson.

Book of the Triumph Two Thousand. Staten Abbey. pap. 4.50x (ISBN 0-392-05803-0, SpS). Soccer.

Book of the Unimat. D. J. Laidlaw-Dickson. LC 79-300391. (Illus.). 128p. (Orig.). 1977. pap. 9.50x (ISBN 0-85242-591-0). Intl Pubns Serv.

Book of the Vision Quest. Steven Foster & Meredith Little. (Illus.). 192p. (Orig.). 1981. pap. 10.00 (ISBN 0-933280-03-3). Island CA.

Book of the Wood Stove. Keith Williams. (Illus.). 152p. 1980. 14.95 (ISBN 0-7153-7926-7). David & Charles.

Book of Thel: A Facsimile & a Critical Text. William Blake. Ed. by Nancy Bogen. LC 74-155857. (Illus.). 82p. 1971. 15.00 (ISBN 0-87057-127-3, Pub. by Brown U Pr). Univ Pr of New England.

Book of Time. Ed. by John Grant & Colin Wilson. (Illus.). 320p. 1980. 32.00 (ISBN 0-7153-7764-7). David & Charles.

Book of Tokens - Tarot Meditations. rev. ed. enl. ed. Paul F. Case. (Illus.). 1974. 6.50 (ISBN 0-938002-00-7). Builders of Adytum.

Book of Trees. William C. Grimm. 1974. pap. 6.95 (ISBN 0-8015-0812-6, Hawthorn). Dutton.

Book of Tziril: A Family Chronicle. Bess Waldman. 270p. 1981. pap. 6.00x (ISBN 0-916288-09-9). Micah Pubns.

Book of Unicorns. Intro. by Welleran Poltarnees. (Illus.). 1978. 18.95 (ISBN 0-914676-08-3, Star & Elephant); pap. 10.95 (ISBN 0-914676-16-4). Green Tiger.

Book of Vampires. James W. Hinkley. (Easy-Read Fact Bks.). (Illus.). (gr. 2-4). 1979. PLB 6.45 s&l (ISBN 0-531-02276-5). Watts.

Book of Vampires. Dudley Wright. 1973. Repr. of 1924 ed. 15.00 (ISBN 0-685-32597-0). Gale.

Book of Venus for You. Franklyn M. Branley. LC 73-78256. (Illus.). (gr. 3-6). 1969. 8.95 (ISBN 0-690-15792-4, TYC-J); PLB 8.79 o.p. (ISBN 0-690-15793-2). T Y Crowell.

Book of Voices. Brian Swann. 1980. write for info.; pap. write for info. Latitudes Pr.

Book of Weird. Barbara Ninde Byfield. LC 73-79733. 160p. 1973. pap. 3.95 o.p. (ISBN 0-385-06591-4). Doubleday.

Book of Werewolves: Being an Account of Terrible Superstition. Sabine Baring-Gould. Repr. of 1865 ed. 15.00 (ISBN 0-685-32595-4). Gale.

Book of Whales. Richard Ellis. LC 80-7640. (Illus.). 224p. 1980. 25.00 (ISBN 0-394-50966-8). Knopf.

Book of What & How: An Illustrated Catalog of the Products & Inventions of the Modern World. Antonio Malipiero. LC 78-3965. (Illus.). 1978. 10.00 o.p. (ISBN 0-312-09198-2). St Martin.

Book of Wines. William Turner. LC 41-26942. 1980. Repr. of 1568 ed. 22.00x (ISBN 0-8201-1200-3). Schol Facsimiles.

Book of Witches. Ruth Manning-Sanders. (gr. 2-6). 1966. PLB 7.95 o.p. (ISBN 0-525-27054-X). Dutton.

Book on Casino Craps, Other Dice Games & Gambling Systems. C. I. Tulcea. 160p. 1980. 12.95 (ISBN 0-442-26713-4); pap. 8.95 (ISBN 0-442-25725-2). Van Nos Reinhold.

Book Production. Peter G. New. (Outlines of Modern Librarianship Ser.). 152p. 1979. text ed. 12.00 (ISBN 0-89664-411-1, Pub. by K G Saur). Shoe String.

Book Production, Fiction, & the German Reading Public. Albert Ward. 215p. (Eng. & Ger.). 1974. text ed. 26.00x (ISBN 0-19-818157-4). Oxford U Pr.

Book Publishers Directory. 3rd ed. Elizabeth Geiser & Annie Brewer. 500p. 1981. 160.00 (ISBN 0-8103-0191-1). Gale.

Book Publishers Directory. 2nd ed. Ed. by Elizabeth A. Geiser & Annie M. Brewer. LC 77-74820. 1979. 124.00 (ISBN 0-8103-0189-X). Gale.

Book Publishers Directory: Supplement to Second Edition. Ed. by Annie Brewer & Elizabeth Geiser. 200p. 1980. 45.00 (ISBN 0-8103-0190-3). Gale.

Book Publishing & Selling. B. Bliven. 1981. 28.50 o.p. (ISBN 0-686-68302-1). Porter.

Book Publishing: Inside Views. Ed. by Jean S. Kujoth. LC 76-155284. 1971. 15.50 (ISBN 0-8108-0420-4). Scarecrow.

Book Review Index: Annual Cumulation Covering 1980. Ed. by Gary C. Tarbert. LC 65-9908. (Book Review Index Ser.). 1981. 78.00 (ISBN 0-8103-0571-2). Gale.

Book Review Index Nineteen Sixty-Nine to Nineteen Seventy-Nine: A Master Cumulation, 6 vols. Ed. by Gary C. Tarbert. 3500p. 1981. Set. 375.00 (ISBN 0-8103-0570-4). Gale.

Book Scouting: How to Turn Your Love for Books in Print. Barbara L. Johnson. (Illus.). 192p. 1981. 10.95 (Spec); pap. 4.95. P-H.

Book Selection & Censorship: A Study of School & Public Libraries in California. Majorie Fiske. (California Library Reprint Series: No. 1). 1968. 15.75x (ISBN 0-520-00418-3). U of Cal Pr.

Book Selection: Principles & Practice. Rinaldo Lunati. Tr. by Luciana Marulli. 1975. 10.00 (ISBN 0-8108-0846-3). Scarecrow.

Book That Lives. Ernest Lloyd. (Uplook Ser.). 31p. 1954. pap. 0.75 (ISBN 0-8163-0065-8, 02435-6). Pacific Pr Pub Assn.

Book Theft & Library Security Systems: 1981-82. 2nd ed. Alice H. Bahr. LC 77-25284. (Illus.). 120p. 1980. pap. 24.50 (ISBN 0-914236-71-7). Knowledge Indus.

Book Where Michael Meets the Royal Street Elves & Learns About Whales & Whale Oil, the Electric Light, the Ostrich, & the Two-Headed Sea Serpent. R. D. Taylor. Ed. by Eje Wray. LC 78-55985. (Illus.). 80p. 1978. 6.95 o.p. (ISBN 0-931604-00-1); pap. 3.95 o.p. (ISBN 0-686-27762-7). Curbstone Pub NYTX.

Bookbinding. Boy Scouts Of America. LC 19-600. (Illus.). 24p. (gr. 6-12). 1969. pap. 0.70x (ISBN 0-8395-3378-0, 3378). BSA.

Bookbinding at Home: The Basics of Bookbinding Simply Explained in Words & Diagrams. K. Riberholt & A. Drastrup. (Illus.). 96p. (Orig.). 1981. pap. 5.95 (ISBN 0-8069-9270-0). Sterling.

Bookbinding: Its Background & Technique. Edith Diehl. (Illus.). 748p. 1980. pap. 12.00 (ISBN 0-486-24020-7). Dover.

Booke Called the Foundacion of Rhetorike. Richard Rainolde. LC 78-6210. (English Experience Ser.: No. 91). 1969. Repr. of 1563 ed. 16.00 (ISBN 90-221-0091-X). Walter J Johnson.

Booke Called the Treasure for Travellers. William Bourne. LC 77-25950. (English Experience Ser.: No. 911). 276p. 1979. Repr. of 1578 ed. lib. bdg. 26.00. Walter J Johnson.

Booke of Christian Ethicks or Moral Philosophie. William Fulbecke. LC 74-28856. (English Experience Ser.: No. 737). 1975. Repr. of 1587 ed. 6.00 (ISBN 90-221-0737-X). Walter J Johnson.

Booker Quiz. Christopher Booker. (Illus., Orig.). 1976. pap. 6.95 (ISBN 0-7100-8504-4). Routledge & Kegan.

Booker T. Washington. Shirley Graham. LC 55-9855. (Biography Ser.). (gr. 7 up). 1955. PLB 5.29 o.p. (ISBN 0-671-32562-0). Messner.

Booker T. Washington. Susan Poole. LC 78-64423. (Illus.). (gr. 1-4). Date not set. price not set (ISBN 0-89799-091-9); pap. price not set (ISBN 0-89799-060-9). Dandelion Pr. Postponed.

Booker T. Washington Papers, Vol. 10: 1909-11. Ed. by Louis R. Harlan & Raymond W. Smock. LC 75-186345. 525p. 1981. 20.00 (ISBN 0-252-00800-6). U of Ill Pr.

Bookfinder: A Guide to Children's Literature About the Needs & Problems of Youth Aged 2 to 15, 2 vols. Sharon S. Dreyer. 1981. Set. text ed. 69.50 (ISBN 0-913476-44-7); Vol. 1. text ed. 32.00 (ISBN 0-686-69405-8); Vol. 2. text ed. 37.50 (ISBN 0-913476-46-3). Am Guidance.

Bookfinder: A Guide to Children's Literature About the Needs & Problems of Youth, Vol. 1. Sharon S. Dreyer. (ps up). 1977. text ed. 37.50 (ISBN 0-913476-45-5). Am Guidance.

Bookhunter's Guide to the Northeast: 1979-80 Edition. Ed. by Ray P. Reynolds. 1979. pap. 5.60 (ISBN 0-934792-00-3). Ephemera.

Bookhunter's Guide to the West & Southwest, 1980-1982. Ed. by Ray P. Reynolds. (Bookhunter's Guides Ser.). 130p. (Orig.). 1980. pap. 6.60 (ISBN 0-934792-01-1). Ephemera.

Bookkeeping. Murray Neinstein & Elaine Kornbluh. LC 58-32560. (High School Exams & Answer Ser). (gr. 9-12). 1977. pap. 3.95 (ISBN 0-8120-0107-9). Barron.

Bookkeeping Made Easy. Alexander L. Sheff. (Orig.). 1971. pap. 3.50 (ISBN 0-06-463235-0, EH 235, EH). Har-Row.

Bookkeeping Made Simple. Louis W. Fields. 1956. pap. 3.50 (ISBN 0-385-01205-5, Made). Doubleday.

Bookmaking: The Illustrated Guide to Design, Production, Editing. rev & enlarged ed. Ed. by Marshall Lee. LC 79-65014. 1980. 29.50 (ISBN 0-8352-1097-9). Bowker.

Bookman's Guide to Americana. 7th ed. J. Norman Heard et al. LC 76-51257. 1977. 19.50 (ISBN 0-8108-1007-7). Scarecrow.

Bookman's London. Frank Swinnerton. (Illus.). 161p. 1980. Repr. of 1951 ed. lib. bdg. 30.00 (ISBN 0-8492-8129-6). R West.

Bookman's Price Index: A Guide to the Values of Rare & Other Out-of-Print Books. Ed. by Daniel F. McGrath. LC 64-8723. (Bookman's Price Index Ser.: Vol. 21). 900p. 1981. 78.00 (ISBN 0-8103-0621-2). Gale.

Bookmarks. Ed. by Frederic Raphael. 1978. 7.95 (ISBN 0-224-01074-3, Pub. by Chatto Bodley Jonathan). Merrimack Bk Serv.

Books About Books. Winslow L. Webber. LC 73-18456. 1974. Repr. of 1937 ed. 22.00 (ISBN 0-8103-3690-1). Gale.

Books & Bookcollecting. G. L. Brook. (Grafton Books on Library & Information Science). 175p. 1980. lib. bdg. 25.00x (ISBN 0-233-97154-8, Pub. by Andre Deutsch). Westview.

Books & Documents: Dating, Permanence & Preservation. Julius Grant. 1980. lib. bdg. 59.95 (ISBN 0-8490-3157-5). Gordon Pr.

Books & Other Printed Materials. Ed. by Cathleen C. Flanagan & James E. Duane. LC 80-23053. (Instructional Media Library: Vol. 1). 112p. 1981. 13.95 (ISBN 0-87778-161-3). Educ Tech Pubns.

Books & Periodicals for Medical Libraries in Hospitals. 5th ed. (Library Association Bk.). 80p. 1978. 4.50x (ISBN 0-85365-500-6, Pub. by Assn England). Oryx Pr.

Books & Their Makers During the Middle Ages, 2 Vols. George H. Putnam. 1962. Set. text ed. 42.50x (ISBN 0-391-01060-3). Humanities.

Books Are Fun. Geri Schobert. (Golden Books for Early Childhood). (Illus.). (ps-1). 1975. PLB 5.38 (ISBN 0-307-68956-5, Golden Pr). Western Pub.

Books at the Wake: A Study of Literary Allusions in James Joyce's "Finnegans Wake". James S. Atherton. LC 74-5407. (Arcturus Books Paperbacks). 308p. 1974. pap. 7.95 (ISBN 0-8093-0687-5). S Ill U Pr.

Books by Balzac: A Checklist of Books by Honore De Balzac, Compiled from the Papers of William Hobart Royce Presently in the Syracuse University Collection. Albert George. 1960. text ed. 10.50x (ISBN 0-391-01606-7). Humanities.

Books by Mail: A Handbook for Libraries. Choong H. Kim. LC 76-15335. (Illus.). 1977. lib. bdg. 22.50 (ISBN 0-8371-9029-0, KBM/). Greenwood.

Books, Children & Men. Paul Hazard. 1960. 9.00 (ISBN 0-87675-050-1); pap. 6.50 (ISBN 0-87675-051-X). Horn Bk.

Books for Sammies: The American Library Association During World War I. Arthur P. Young. (Beta Phi Mu Chapbook Ser.: No. 15). (Illus.). 175p. 1981. write for info. (ISBN 0-910230-15-3). Beta Phi Mu.

Books for the Developing Countries: Asia, Africa. Om Prakash & Clifford M. Fyle. 1965. pap. 2.50 (ISBN 92-3-100605-3, U58, UNESCO). Unipub.

Books for the Retarded Reader. 6th ed. J. A. Richardson et al. 1977. pap. text ed. 12.00x (ISBN 0-85563-152-X). Verry.

Books for Today's Children. Ed. by Jeanne Bracken & Sharon Wigutoff. 1979. pap. 3.00x (ISBN 0-912670-53-3). Feminist Pr.

Books for You to Make. Susan Purdy. LC 73-4568. (gr. 6 up). 1973. 8.79 (ISBN 0-397-31318-7). Lippincott.

Books in Bottles: The Curious in Literature. William G. Clifford. LC 70-78125. 1971. Repr. of 1926 ed. 15.00 (ISBN 0-8103-3791-6). Gale.

Books in Chains & Other Bibliographical Papers. William Blades. LC 68-30610. 1968. Repr. of 1892 ed. 15.00 (ISBN 0-8103-3298-1). Gale.

Books in Other Languages. 4th ed. Leonard Wertheimer. 1979. pap. 40.00 (ISBN 0-89664-147-3, Pub. by K G Saur). Gale.

Books in Print Supplement 1980-1981. 2700p. 1981. 58.00 (ISBN 0-8352-1328-5). Bowker.

Books in Search of Children: Essays & Speeches. Louise S. Bechtel. Ed. by Virginia Haviland. LC 79-78078. 1969. 6.95 o.s.i. (ISBN 0-02-508290-6). Macmillan.

Books in Series: Original Reprinted, in-Print, & Out-of-Print Books, Published or Distributed in the United States in Popular, Scholarly, & Professional Series, 3 vols. 3rd ed. 8560p. 1980. 150.00 (ISBN 0-8352-1314-5). Bowker.

Books in Spanish for Children & Young Adults: An Annotated Guide. Isabel Schon. LC 78-10299. (Libros Infantiles y Juveniles en Espanol: Una Guia Anotada). 1978. 10.00 (ISBN 0-8108-1176-6). Scarecrow.

Books in Stir: A Bibliographic Essay About Prison Libraries & About Books Written by Prisoners & Prison Employees. Rudolf Engelbarts. LC 70-180625. 1972. 10.00 (ISBN 0-8108-0450-6). Scarecrow.

Books in the Victorian Elementary School. A. Ellis. 1971. pap. 5.50x (ISBN 0-85365-025-X, Pub. by Lib Assn England). Oryx Pr.

Books, Libraries, & Research. Mary Hauer et al. 1978. pap. text ed. 5.95 (ISBN 0-8403-1953-3, 40195301). Kendall-Hunt.

Books, Libraries & You. 3rd ed. Jessie Boyd et al. (Illus.). (gr. 7-12). 1965. text ed. 3.96 o.p. (ISBN 0-684-51501-6, ScribC). Scribner.

Books of Elijah, Pts. 1 & 2. Michael E. Stone & John Strugnell. LC 79-15153. (Pseudepigrapha Ser.: No. 8). 1979. 10.50 (ISBN 0-89130-315-4, 060218); pap. 6.00 (ISBN 0-89130-316-2). Scholars Pr Ca.

Books of Ezra & Nehemiah. Walter D. Adeney. Date not set. 11.50 (ISBN 0-86524-050-7). Klock & Klock.

Books of Rachel. Joel Gross. 1981. 3.50 (ISBN 0-451-09561-8, E9561, Sig). NAL.

Books of the New Testament. Julianne Booth. (Arch Book Supplement Ser.). 1981. pap. 0.79 (ISBN 0-570-06150-4, 59-1305). Concordia.

Books of the New Testament. Herbert Mayer. LC 69-12766. 1981. pap. 3.95 (ISBN 0-570-03755-7, 12-2310). Concordia.

Books of the Old Testament. Julianne Booth. (Arch Book Supplement Ser.). 1981. pap. 0.79 (ISBN 0-570-06151-2, 59-1306). Concordia.

Books of the Old Testament. Walter E. Stuenkel. 1981. pap. 3.50 (ISBN 0-570-03749-2, 12-2653). Concordia.

Books of the Times: The New York Times Daily Book Reviews, 1980. (Illus.). 648p. 1981. 20.00 (ISBN 0-405-14021-5). Arno.

Books on Buddhism: An Annotated Subject Guide. Yushin Yoo. LC 76-2706. 263p. 1976. 11.00 o.p. (ISBN 0-8108-0913-3). Scarecrow.

Books, Puppets & the Mentally Retarded Student. John Champlin & Connie Champlin. (Illus.). 162p. (Orig.). 1981. pap. 9.95 (ISBN 0-938594-00-1). Spec Lit Pr.

Books Speaking to Books: A Contextual Approach to American Fiction. William T. Stafford. LC 80-25892. 224p. 1981. 16.50x (ISBN 0-686-69544-5). U of NC Pr.

Bookseller of the Last Century. Charles Welsh. LC 79-179343. (English Book Trade). Repr. of 1885 ed. lib. bdg. 17.50x (ISBN 0-678-00883-3). Kelley.

Bookshelves & Cabinets. Sunset Editors. LC 74-76541. (Illus.). 96p. (Orig.). 1974. pap. 3.95 (ISBN 0-376-01083-5, Sunset Bks). Sunset-Lane.

Bookstore Planning & Design. Ken White. (Illus.). 192p. 1982. 34.50 (ISBN 0-07-069851-1). McGraw.

Boolean Algebra & Its Applications. J. Eldon Whitesitt. 1961. 14.95 (ISBN 0-201-08660-3). A-W.

Boolean-Valued Models & Independence Proofs in Set Theory. John L. Bell. (Oxford Logic Guides Ser.). 1978. 23.50x (ISBN 0-19-853168-0). Oxford U Pr.

Boom & Bust, 1917-1932. Ernest R. May. LC 63-8572. (Life History of the United States). (Illus.). (gr. 5 up). 1974. PLB 9.96 (ISBN 0-8094-0559-8, Pub. by Time-Life). Silver.

Boom-De-Boom. Elaine Edelman. (Illus.). (ps-2). 1980. 4.95 (ISBN 0-394-84341-X); PLB 5.99 (ISBN 0-394-94341-4). Pantheon.

Boom or Busted: Family Dollars & Sense. Ed F. Hutka. 1979. 2.95 (ISBN 0-88270-452-4). Logos.

Boom Town Growth Management: A Case Study of Rock Springs, Green River, Wyoming. John S. Gilmore & Mary K. Duff. LC 75-25905. 200p. 1975. 26.25x (ISBN 0-89158-010-7). Westview.

Boomerang Hunter. Jim Kjelgaard. 1978. pap. 1.25 (ISBN 0-686-68376-5, 37408, Camelot). Avon.

Boomers. Joan Hurling. LC 78-63640. 1979. 8.95 (ISBN 0-8149-0814-4). Vanguard.

Boomtown: A Portrait of Burkburnett. Minnie M. Benton. 7.95 (ISBN 0-685-48792-X). Nortex Pr.

Boomtown Lawyer in the Osage. Charles L. Roff. (Illus.). 180p. 1975. 6.00 o.p. (ISBN 0-89015-101-6). Nortex Pr.

Boon Island. Kenneth Roberts. 192p. 1981. pap. 2.50 (ISBN 0-449-24408-3, Crest). Fawcett.

Boosters & Businessmen: Popular Economic Thought & Urban Growth in the Antebellum Middle West. Carl Abbott. LC 80-1795. (Contributions in American Studies: No. 53). (Illus.). 1981. lib. bdg. 27.50 (ISBN 0-313-22562-1, ABB/). Greenwood.

Boot Hill Brother. Morgan Hill. (Orig.). 1981. pap. 1.95 (ISBN 0-440-10794-6). Dell.

Booth Interstate. Thomas Rabbitt. LC 80-7975. 96p. 1981. 9.95 (ISBN 0-394-51382-7); pap. 4.95 (ISBN 0-394-73962-0). Knopf.

Booth Tarkington. Keith J. Fennimore. (U. S. Authors Ser.: No. 238). 1974. lib. bdg. 10.95 (ISBN 0-8057-0715-8). Twayne.

Boots. Alana Willoughby. Ed. by Alton Jordan. (I Can Read Underwater Bks). (Illus.). (gr. k-3). 1974. PLB 3.50 (ISBN 0-89868-006-9, Read Res); pap. text ed. 1.75 (ISBN 0-89868-039-5, Read Rest). ARO Pub.

Boots & Saddles at the Little Big Horn. James S. Hutchins. LC 76-17375. (Source Custeriana Ser.: No. 7). (Illus.). pap. 4.50 o.p. (ISBN 0-88342-237-9). Old Army.

Boots, Two. LaRue Selman. Ed. by Alton Jordan. (Buppet Series). (Illus.). (gr. k-3). 1981. PLB 4.50 (ISBN 0-89868-094-8, Read Res); pap. text ed. 1.95 (ISBN 0-89868-105-7). ARO Pub.

Bordas Encyclopedie, 23 vols. (Fr.). 1971-1975. Set. 545.00 (ISBN 0-8277-3053-5). Maxwell Sci Intl.

Bordeaux & Aquitane. Lynn Macdonald. 1976. 24.00 (ISBN 0-7134-3183-0). David & Charles.

Border Ballads. James Reed. (Illus.). 232p. 1973. text ed. 18.75x (ISBN 0-485-11144-6, Athlone Pr). Humanities.

Border Bandit. Max Brand. 192p. 1973. pap. 0.75 o.p. (ISBN 0-446-74218-X). Warner Bks.

Border Collies. Iris Combe. (Illus.). 1978. 15.95 (ISBN 0-571-11173-4, Pub. by Faber & Faber). Merrimack Bk Serv.

Border Crossings: International Fiction in Translation. Ed. by Robert Bonazzi & Brian Swann. (New Departures in Fiction: Vol. 3). 1980. pap. write for info. Latitudes Pr.

Border Economy: Regional Development in the Southwest. Niles Hansen. (Illus.). 208p. 1981. text ed. 17.95x (ISBN 0-292-75061-7); pap. text ed. 8.95x (ISBN 0-292-75063-3). U of Tex Pr.

Border Guns. Max Brand. 1975. pap. 1.95 (ISBN 0-446-90888-6). Warner Bks.

Border Healing Woman: The Story of Jewel Babb. Jewel Babb. 152p. 1981. text ed. 14.95 (ISBN 0-292-70729-0); pap. 5.95 (ISBN 0-292-70730-4). U of Tex Pr.

Border Kidnap. J. M. Marks. LC 77-12725. (gr. 6 up). 1977. 6.95 (ISBN 0-525-66551-X). Elsevier-Nelson.

Border Lion. L. D. Henry. (Orig.). 1980. pap. 1.95 (ISBN 0-532-23207-0). Manor Bks.

Border Raider. William Hopson. 1979. pap. 1.25 (ISBN 0-505-51420-6). Tower Bks.

Border Terriers. Frank Jackson & W. Ronald Irving. (Foyle's Handbks). 1969. 3.95 (ISBN 0-685-55815-0). Palmetto Pub.

Border Vengeance. B. M. Bower. (YA) 1971. 5.95 (ISBN 0-685-03333-3, Avalon). Bouregy.

Border War. A. A. Baker. 192p. (YA) 1976. 5.95 (ISBN 0-685-61051-9, Avalon). Bouregy.

Border Watch. Joseph Altsheler. 1976. lib. bdg. 16.70x (ISBN 0-89968-001-1). Lightyear.

Borderland. Neil Claremon. 1975. 6.95 o.p. (ISBN 0-394-49619-1, 49619). Knopf.

Borderland: A Historical & Geographical Study of Burgenland, Austria. Andrew F. Burghardt. (Illus.). 1962. 25.00x (ISBN 0-299-02680-9). U of Wis Pr.

Borderlands Beyond Science: Skeptical Inquiries into the Paranormal. Ed. by Kendrick Frazier. LC 80-84403. (Critiques of the Paranormal Ser.). 400p. 1981. 19.95 (ISBN 0-87975-147-9); pap. 9.95 (ISBN 0-87975-148-7). Prometheus Bks.

Borderlands of Western Civilization: A History of East Central Europe. O. Halecki. 1952. 18.95 (ISBN 0-8260-3740-2). Wiley.

Borderline Case. Hugh McLeave. 1979. 7.95 o.p. (ISBN 0-684-15803-5, ScribT). Scribner.

Borderline Conditions & Pathological Narcissism. Otto Kernberg. LC 75-5606. 368p. 1975. 25.00x (ISBN 0-87668-205-0). Aronson.

Borderline Patient. Roy R. Grinker, Sr. & Beatrice Werble. LC 77-44789. 1977. 25.00x (ISBN 0-87668-315-4). Aronson.

Borderline Phenomena & the Rorschach Test. Ed. by Jay S. Kwawer & Howard D. Lerner. 515p. 1980. text ed. 30.00 (ISBN 0-8236-0577-9, 00-0577). Intl Univs Pr.

Borderlines. Axel Madsen. 228p. 1975. 6.95 o.s.i. (ISBN 0-02-579180-X). Macmillan.

Borders-Grenzen. Peter P. Wiplinger. Tr. by Herbert Kuhner. LC 77-18422. (Bilingual Poetry Ser.: No. 1). (Ger.). 1977. 10.00x (ISBN 0-89304-022-3, CCC112); signed o.p. 10.50x (ISBN 0-89804-038-8); special signed ed. o.p. 25.00 (ISBN 0-89304-024-X); pap. 4.50x (ISBN 0-89304-023-1); pap. 6.50x signed ltd. ed. o.p. (ISBN 0-89304-039-8). Cross Cult.

Bordertown Blues. Allen Taylor. 1981. pap. 1.95 (ISBN 0-8439-0854-8, Leisure Bks). Nordon Pubns.

Bordertown Revisited. Frank J. Mangan. LC 73-86307. (Illus.). 1973. 6.00 (ISBN 0-930208-03-X, Pub by Guynes Pr). Mangan Bks.

Boreal Lower Cretaceous Geological Journal Special Issue, No. 5. R. Casey & P. F. Rawson. (Liverpool Geological Society & the Manchester Geological Association). 448p. 1973. 48.75 (ISBN 0-471-27752-5, Pub. by Wiley-Interscience). Wiley.

Bored of the Rings or Tolkien Revisited. Harvard Lampoon et Al. 1971. pap. 1.75 (ISBN 0-451-09441-7, E9441, Sig). NAL.

Borges & His Fiction: A Guide to His Mind & Art. Gene H. Bell-Villada. LC 80-17426. 352p. 1981. 19.00x (ISBN 0-8078-1458-X); pap. 10.00x (ISBN 0-8078-4075-0). U of NC Pr.

Borges on Writing. Jorge L. Borges. Ed. by Norman T. Di Giovanni et al. 1973. pap. 2.95 o.p. (ISBN 0-525-47352-1). Dutton.

Borges Reader: Luis Borges. Emir Monegal & Alistair Reid. 320p. 1980. 12.95 (ISBN 0-525-06998-4); pap. 7.95 (ISBN 0-525-47654-7). Dutton.

Borinquen: An Anthology of Puerto Rican Literature. Ed. by Maria T. Babin & Stan Steiner. 1974. 10.00 o.p. (ISBN 0-394-47462-7). Knopf.

Boris Karloff & His Films. Paul M. Jensen. LC 72-9940. (International Film Guide Ser.). (Illus.). 208p. 1975. 10.00 o.p. (ISBN 0-498-01324-3). A S Barnes.

Boris Pasternak. J. W. Dyck. (World Authors Ser.: Russia: No. 225). lib. bdg. 10.95 (ISBN 0-8057-2678-0). Twayne.

Boris Pasternak. H. Gifford. LC 76-9735. (Illus.). 1977. 38.50 (ISBN 0-521-21288-X). Cambridge U Pr.

Boris Pasternak: Stikhotvoreniia I Poemy. Boris Pasternak. 731p. (Rus.). 1981. pap. write for info. (ISBN 0-89830-038-X). Russica Pubs.

Boris Pasternak's Translations of Shakespeare. Anna K. France. LC 76-52027. 1978. 18.50x (ISBN 0-520-03432-5). U of Cal Pr.

Boris, the Lop-Sided Bear. Gladys Schmitt. (Illus.). (gr. 1-3). 1966. 2.95 o.s.i. (ISBN 0-02-781250-2, CCPr); PLB 3.95 o.s.i. (ISBN 0-02-781240-5, CCPr). Macmillan.

Boris Vian. Alfred Cismaru. (World Authors Ser.: France: No. 293). 1974. lib. bdg. 10.95 (ISBN 0-8057-2951-8). Twayne.

Born. Michael Poage. 1975. pap. 15.00 (ISBN 0-685-82994-4). Black Stone.

Born After Midnight. Aiden W. Tozer. 3.95 (ISBN 0-87509-258-6); pap. 2.75 (ISBN 0-87509-167-9); pap. 1.95 mass mkt (ISBN 0-87509-258-6). Chr Pubns.

Born Again. Allan Hartley. (Spire Christian Comic). 1978. pap. 0.49 (ISBN 0-8007-8535-5). Revell.

Born & Bred Unequal. George Taylor & N. Ayres. (Sociology of Education Ser). 1969. text ed. 6.00x (ISBN 0-582-32441-6); pap. text ed. 3.50x (ISBN 0-582-32442-4). Humanities.

Born at Risk. B. D. Colen. (Illus.). 240p. 1981. 9.95 (ISBN 0-312-09291-1). St Martin.

Born Curious: New Perspectives in Educational Theory. Robin Hodgkin. LC 75-16340. 1976. 22.95 (ISBN 0-471-40220-6, Pub. by Wiley-Interscience). Wiley.

Born in April. Natalja Wendel. LC 74-31096. 1975. 7.95 (ISBN 0-8119-0245-5). Fell.

Born in Fire: A Geological History of Hawaii. John Rublowsky. LC 79-2001. (Illus.). 96p. (gr. 5 up). 1981. 9.95 (ISBN 0-06-025088-7, HarpJ); PLB 9.89g (ISBN 0-06-025089-5). Har-Row.

Born in the Gardens. Peter Nichols. 1980. pap. 6.95 (ISBN 0-571-11476-8, Pub. by Faber & Faber). Merrimack Bk Serv.

Born in the Spirit of Jesus. Richard Reichert. 84p. (Orig.). 1980. pap. text ed. 2.75 (ISBN 0-697-01725-7); tchr's manual 3.50 (ISBN 0-697-01726-5); spirit masters 10.95 (ISBN 0-697-01727-3). Wm C Brown.

Born in Tibet. Chogyam Trungpa. LC 76-53358. (Clear Light Ser.). (Illus.). 1981. pap. 8.95 (ISBN 0-87773-718-5). Great Eastern.

Born Innocent. Hurwood & Dipego. 1975. pap. 1.95 (ISBN 0-441-07122-8). Ace Bks.

Born Loser. Tim Doyle. Ed. by Thomas J. Mooney. (Beginning Pal Paperbacks Ser.). (Illus., Orig.). (gr. 7-12). 1977. pap. text ed. 1.25 (ISBN 0-8374-3465-3). Xerox Ed Pubns.

Born of Love. Arleen Lorrance. (Illus., Orig.). 1981. pap. write for info. L P Pubns.

Born Out of Season. Melvin T. Chambers. 1978. 5.50 o.p. (ISBN 0-682-49063-6). Exposition.

Born to Be Hurt. Mariell O'Connor. Date not set. 6.95 (ISBN 0-8062-1685-9). Carlton.

Born to Be King. Constance Gluyas. 1977. pap. 1.95 o.s.i. (ISBN 0-515-04297-8). Jove Pubns.

Born to Grow. Larry Richards. LC 74-92603. 1974. pap. 2.50 (ISBN 0-88207-708-2). Victor Bks.

Born to Heal. Ruth Montgomery. 224p. 1976. pap. 2.25 (ISBN 0-445-08450-2). Popular Lib.

Born to Loose, Bound to Win. Lorry Lutz. LC 80-83877. 192p. (Orig.). 1981. pap. 5.95 (ISBN 0-89081-274-8). Harvest Hse.

Born to Rebel. Benjamin Mays. LC 77-123857. (Illus.). 1972. pap. 3.95 o.p. (ISBN 0-684-12971-X, SL378, ScribT). Scribner.

Born to the Sun. Margaret Caldwell. 1980. pap. 2.50 (ISBN 0-446-91236-0). Warner Bks.

Born Today, Born Yesterday: Reincarnation. Gwen Risedorf. LC 77-21406. (Myth, Magic & Superstition Ser.). (Illus.). (gr. 4-5). 1977. PLB 9.65 (ISBN 0-8172-1045-8). Raintree Pubs.

Born with a Golden Spoon. Gilbert Parker. 1976. lib. bdg. 13.85x (ISBN 0-89968-081-X). Lightyear.

Borneo. John MacKinnon. (World's Wild Places Ser.). (Illus.). 184p. 1975. 12.95 (ISBN 0-8094-2018-X). Time-Life.

Borneo. John MacKinnon. (World's Wild Places Ser.). (Illus.). 1978. lib. bdg. 11.97 (ISBN 0-686-51017-8). Silver.

Borobudur: The Buddhist Legend in Tone. Bedrich Forman. (Illus.). 1980. 16.95. Mayflower Bks.

Borobudur: The Buddhist Monument of Java (1971) D. Chihara. (Illus.). 1977. 75.00 (ISBN 0-685-79813-5). Heinman.

Borodin. Sergei A. Dianin. Tr. by Robert Lord from Rus. (Illus.). xi, 356p. 1980. Repr. of 1963 ed. lib. bdg. 29.75x (ISBN 0-313-22529-X, DIBO). Greenwood.

Boron Chemistry Four: Fourth International Meeting on Boron Chemistry, Salt Lake City & Snowbird, Utah, USA, 8-13 July 1979. Robert W. Parry & Goji Kodama. (IUPAC Symposium Ser.). 150p. 1980. 57.00 (ISBN 0-08-025256-7). Pergamon.

Boroughs Of Medieval Wales. Ed. by R. A. Griffiths. (Illus.). 1979. text ed. 50.00x (ISBN 0-7083-0681-0). Verry.

Borrasca de Pasiones. new ed. Rogelio Jaimes. (Pimienta Collection Ser). 160p. 1974. pap. 1.00 o.p. (ISBN 0-88473-193-6). Fiesta Pub.

Borribles. Michael De Larrabeiti. LC 77-12743. (gr. 5 up). 1978. 8.95 (ISBN 0-02-726700-8, 72670). Macmillan.

Borromini & the Roman Oratory: Style & Society. Joseph Connors. (Illus.). 528p. 1980. text ed. 45.00x (ISBN 0-262-03071-3). MIT Pr.

Borromini's San Carlo Alle Quattro Fontane: A Study in Multiple Form & Architectural Symbolism. Leo Steinberg. LC 75-23815. (Outstanding Dissertations in the Fine Arts - 17th Century). (Illus.). 1976. lib. bdg. 41.00 (ISBN 0-8240-2008-1). Garland Pub.

Borrowed Feathers & Other Fables. Freire Wright & Michael Foreman. LC 77-79844. (ps-3). 1978. 3.95 (ISBN 0-394-83730-4, BYR); PLB 4.99 (ISBN 0-394-93730-9). Random.

Borrowed Plumes. Elizabeth Ashton. (Harlequin Romances). 192p. 1981. pap. 1.25 (ISBN 0-373-02395-2, Pub. by Harlequin). PB.

Borrowed Time: The Thirty-Seven Years of Bobby Darin. Al DiOrio, Jr. (Illus.). 1980. 9.95 (ISBN 0-89471-111-3); lib. bdg. 12.90 (ISBN 0-89471-110-5). Running Pr.

Borrowing Time: Growing up with Juvenile Diabetes. Pasquale Covelli. LC 79-7083. 1979. 9.95 (ISBN 0-690-01841-X, TYC-T). T Y Crowell.

Bosch. Carl Linfert. LC 71-149853. (Library Great Painters Ser). (Illus.). 136p. 1971. 35.00 (ISBN 0-8109-0043-2). Abrams.

Bosch Book of the Motor Car: Its Evolution & Engineering Development. John Day. LC 75-39516. (Illus.). 256p. 1976. 15.00 o.p. (ISBN 0-312-09310-1). St Martin.

Bosquefos Utiles Para Laicos. Roy B. Lyon. (Illus.). 96p. (Span.). Date not set. pap. price not set (ISBN 0-311-42401-5). Casa Bautista.

Bosquejos Biblicos, Tomo 3. Daniel Campderros. 96p. 1980. pap. 1.85 (ISBN 0-311-43033-3). Casa Bautista.

Bosquejos Homileticos. Tr. by Elsie Blattner & Luisa Walker. (Spanish Bks.). 1979. 1.75 (ISBN 0-8297-0511-2). Life Pubs Intl.

Boss Came to Dinner & Other Stories. Bhisham Sahni. Tr. by Jai Ratan et al from Hindi. (Greenbird Book). 95p. 1975. 14.00 (ISBN 0-88253-264-2); pap. 6.75 (ISBN 0-88253-720-2). Ind-US Inc.

Boss Cowman: The Recollections of Ed Lemmon, 1857-1946. Ed Lemmon. Ed. by Nellie S. Yost. LC 69-10313. (Pioneer Heritage Ser: Vol. 6). (Illus.). xiv, 321p. 1969. 14.50x (ISBN 0-8032-0102-8); pap. 4.25 (ISBN 0-8032-5810-0, BB 5595, Bison). U of Nebr Pr.

Boss Lady: An Executive Woman Talks About Making It. Jo Foxworth. LC 77-2514. 1978. 9.95 o.s.i. (ISBN 0-690-01398-1, TYC-T). T Y Crowell.

Boss Nineteen Seventy-Six: Proceedings of an International Conference on the Behavior of off-Shore Structures, Norwegian Institute of Technology, Trondheim, 2-5 August 1976. Ed. by J. Kuvas. LC 77-75338. 1977. text ed. 110.00 o.p. (ISBN 0-08-021739-7). Pergamon.

Boss of Panamint. Leslie Ernenwein. 1975. pap. 0.95 o.p. (ISBN 0-685-59189-1, LB313, Leisure Bks). Nordon Pubns.

Boss Rule in the Gilded Age: Matt Quay of Pennsylvania. James A. Kehl. LC 80-5254. (Illus.). 315p. 1981. 24.95 (ISBN 0-8229-3426-4). U of Pittsburgh Pr.

Boss Seventy-Nine: Proceedings, 3 vols. Behavior of Offshore Structures, 2nd International Conference. 1500p. Set. pap. 169.00 (ISBN 0-906085-34-9, Dist. by Air Science Co). BHRA Fluid.

Bosses. rev. ed. John Haeger & Michael Weber. LC 78-73266. 1979. pap. text ed. 4.50 (ISBN 0-88273-103-3). Forum Pr MO.

Bosses. Alfred Steinberg. 384p. 1974. pap. 1.95 o.p. (ISBN 0-451-61293-0, MJ1293, Ment). NAL.

Bosses & Reformers: Urban Politics in America, 1880-1920. Ed. by Blaine A. Brownell & Warren E. Stickle. LC 72-4798. (New Perspectives in History Ser.). 250p. (Orig.). 1973. pap. text ed. 7.25 (ISBN 0-395-14050-1, 3-41025). HM.

Bosses in British Business. F. R. Jervis. 1974. 16.00 (ISBN 0-7100-7803-X). Routledge & Kegan.

Bossmen: Bill Monroe & Muddy Waters. James Rooney. (Illus.). 160p. 1972. Repr. of 1971 ed. pap. 0.99 o.p. (ISBN 0-8104-6106-4). Hayden.

Boston: A Documentary Novel of the Sacco-Vanzetti Case. Upton Sinclair. LC 77-86279. 1978. Repr. of 1928 ed. 16.50x (ISBN 0-8376-0420-6). Bentley.

Boston Athenaeum Art Exhibition Index: 1827-1874. Ed. by Robert F. Perkins et al. (Illus.). 1980. 50.00x (ISBN 0-262-16075-7). MIT Pr.

Boston Bay Mysteries & Other Tales. Edward R. Snow. LC 77-10901. (Illus.). 1977. bds. 8.95 (ISBN 0-396-07505-3). Dodd.

Boston English. Dana L. Wilson. (Illus.). 1976. pap. 1.95 (ISBN 0-8220-1633-8). Centennial.

Boston English Illustrated. Dana L. Wilson. (Illus.). 1976. pap. 1.95 o.p. (ISBN 0-686-65384-X). Cliffs.

Boston Furniture of the Eighteenth Century. Ed. by Walter M. Whitehill et al. LC 74-8139. 1975. 25.00x o.p. (ISBN 0-685-56093-7, Colonial Soc. of Massachusetts). U Pr of Va.

Boston Gazette & the Country Journal... No. 1986; Oct. 22, 1792, Repr. Of 1792 Ed. Bd. with Affecting History of the Dreadful Distresses of Frederic Manheim's Family. Repr. of 1793 ed; Horrid Indian Cruelties. Repr. of 1799 ed; True Narrative of the Sufferings of Mary Kinnan, Who Was Taken Prisoner by the Shawnee Nation of Indians. Repr. of 1794 ed; Narrative of the Sufferings of James Derkinderen, Who Was Taken Prisoner by the Halifax Indians. Repr. of 1796 ed; Journal of the Adventures of Matthew Bunn. Repr. of 1796 ed; Narrative of the Life & Adventures of Matthew Bunn. Repr. of 1827 ed. LC 75-7042. (Indian Captivities Ser.: Vol. 21). 1977. lib. bdg. 44.00 (ISBN 0-8240-1645-9). Garland Pub.

Boston Glee Book. Lowell Mason & George J. Webb. LC 76-52481. (Music Reprint Ser., 1977). 1977. Repr. of 1844 ed. lib. bdg. 27.50 (ISBN 0-306-70860-4). Da Capo.

Boston Handel & Haydn Society Collection of Church Music. Ed. by Lowell Mason. LC 77-171078. (Earlier American Music Ser.: Vol. 15). 324p. 1973. Repr. of 1822 ed. lib. bdg. 25.00 (ISBN 0-306-77315-5). Da Capo.

Boston in the Age of John Fitzgerald Kennedy. Walter M. Whitehill. (Centers of Civilization Ser.: No. 19). xvi, 208p. 1966. 4.95 o.p. (ISBN 0-8061-0681-6). U of Okla Pr.

Boston Job Bank. expanded ed. Robert L. Adams. 168p. 1980. pap. 5.95 (ISBN 0-937860-01-8). Adams Inc MA.

Boston Marathon. Joe Falls. 1977. 12.95 (ISBN 0-02-537100-2). Macmillan.

Boston Money Tree. Russell B. Adams, Jr. LC 76-27388. 1977. 11.95 o.s.i. (ISBN 0-690-01209-8, TYC-T). T Y Crowell.

Boston Opera Company. Quaintance Eaton. (Music Reprint Ser.). 1980. Repr. of 1965 ed. 25.00 (ISBN 0-306-79619-8). Da Capo.

Boston Postmaks to Eighteen Ninety. Maurice C. Blake & Wilbur W. Davis. LC 72-85120. (Illus.). 392p. 1974. Repr. of 1949 ed. 35.00x (ISBN 0-88000-040-6). Quarterman.

Boston Public Library: A Centennial History. Walter M. Whitehill. (Published by Harvard University). 1956. 4.75. Boston Public Lib.

Boston Public Library of the City of Boston: A History. Horace G. Wadlin. (Published by the Trustees of the Boston Public Library). 1911. 35.00. Boston Public Lib.

Boston Symphony Orchestra: 1881-1931. rev. ed. M. De Wolfe Howe. Ed. by John N. Burk. LC 77-16532. (Music Reprint Ser.: 1978). (Illus.). 1978. Repr. of 1931 ed. lib. bdg. 29.50 (ISBN 0-306-77533-6). Da Capo.

Boston Tea Party. Carole Charles. LC 75-33156. (Stories of the Revolution Ser.). (Illus.). (gr. 2-6). 1975. PLB 5.50 (ISBN 0-913778-18-4). Childs World.

Boston Tea Party. 2nd ed. Benjamin W. Labaree. (Illus.). 347p. 1981. Repr. of 1966 ed. price not set (ISBN 0-930350-16-2). NE U Pr.

Boston Tradition: American Paintings from the Museum of Fine Arts, Boston. Carol Troyen. LC 80-69210. (Illus.). 216p. (Orig.). 1980. pap. 15.95 (ISBN 0-917418-66-2). Am Fed Arts.

Boston Under Military Rule 1768-1769. Ed. by Oliver M. Dickerson. LC 70-118029. (Era of the American Revolution Ser). 1970. Repr. of 1936 ed. 17.50 (ISBN 0-306-71943-6). Da Capo.

Boston University Papers in African History, 2 vols. Ed. by Jeffrey Butler. LC 64-15197. (Pub. by Boston U Pr). Vol. 1. 1964. 12.50x (ISBN 0-8419-8709-2, Africana); Vol. 2. 1966. 15.00x (ISBN 0-8419-8710-6). Holmes & Meier.

Boston Ways: High, by, & Folk. rev. ed. George F. Weston, Jr. Ed. by Charlotte C. Raymond. LC 74-213. (Illus.). 352p. 1974. 10.00 o.p. (ISBN 0-8070-5180-2); pap. 3.95 (ISBN 0-8070-5181-0, BP520). Beacon Pr.

Boswell & Son. Donald McDougall. LC 77-17765. 1978. 10.00 o.p. (ISBN 0-312-09324-1). St Martin.

Boswell the Biographer. George Mallory. LC 73-18423. 1971. Repr. of 1912 ed. 20.00 (ISBN 0-8103-3675-8). Gale.

Boswell's Clap & Other Essays: Medical Analyses of Literary Men's Afflictions. William B. Ober. LC 78-16018. (Illus.). 320p. 1979. 19.95 (ISBN 0-8093-0889-4). S Ill U Pr.

Boswell's Creative Gloom: A Study of Imagery & Melancholy in the Writings of James Boswell. Allan Ingram. 1981. 28.50x (ISBN 0-389-20157-X). B&N.

Botanic Garden; a Poem in Two Parts. Erasmus Darwin. Ed. by Donald H. Reiman. Bd. with Pt. 1. Containing the Economy of Vegetation; Pt. 2. Loves of the Plants. with Philosophical Notes. LC 75-31194. (Romantic Context Ser.: Poetry 1789-1830). 1979. Repr. of 1791 ed. lib. bdg. 47.00 (ISBN 0-8240-2145-2). Garland Pub.

Botanical Names for English Readers. Randal H. Alcock. LC 73-174935. xviii, 236p. 1971. Repr. of 1876 ed. 18.00 (ISBN 0-8103-3823-8). Gale.

Botanical Prints: With Excerpts from the Artist's Notebooks. Henry Evans. LC 77-24323. (Illus.). 1977. pap. 14.95x (ISBN 0-7167-1118-4). W H Freeman.

Botanical Systematics, Vol. 1. Ed. by V. H. Heywood. 1976. 61.00 (ISBN 0-12-346901-5). Acad Pr.

Botanists of the Eucalypts. 160p. 1978. pap. 13.50 (ISBN 0-643-00271-5, CO07, CSIRO). Unipub.

Botany. Taylor Alexander et al. (Golden Guide Ser.). (Illus.). (gr. 7 up). 1970. PLB 9.15 (ISBN 0-307-63545-7, Golden Pr); pap. 1.95 o.p. (ISBN 0-307-24025-8). Western Pub.

Botany. Boy Scouts Of America. LC 19-600. (Illus.). 64p. (gr. 6-12). 1964. pap. 0.70x (ISBN 0-8395-3379-9, 3379). BSA.

Botany. J. H. Elliott. (Teach Yourself Ser.). 1973. pap. 3.50 o.p. (ISBN 0-679-10390-2). McKay.

Botany: A Brief Introduction to Plant Biology. Thomas L. Rost et al. LC 78-5433. 1979. text ed. 20.95 (ISBN 0-471-02114-8); tchrs. manual avail. (ISBN 0-471-03758-3). Wiley.

Botany: A Laboratory Manual for Weier. 5th ed. Michael Barbour et al. 1975. 10.95 (ISBN 0-471-04800-3). Wiley.

Botany: An Introductory of the Plant Kingdom. James D. Haynes. LC 74-7084. 514p. 1975. text ed. 23.95x (ISBN 0-471-36550-5). Wiley.

Botany & Chemistry of Hallucinogens. 2nd ed. Richard E. Schultes & Albert Hofmann. (Amer. Lec Living Chemistry). (Illus.). 464p. 1980. text ed. 29.75 (ISBN 0-398-03863-5). C C Thomas.

Botany Made Simple. Greulach, Victor A., Ph.D. LC 68-11764. 1968. pap. 2.50 o.p. (ISBN 0-385-01188-1, Made). Doubleday.

Botany of the Living Plant. 4th ed. Frederick O. Bower. (Illus.). 1969. Repr. of 1947 ed. 21.25 (ISBN 0-02-841800-X). Hafner.

Botany of the Voyage of H. M. S. Sulphur: Under the Command of Captain Sir Edward Belcher 1836-42. G. Bentham. (Illus.). 1968. 100.00 (ISBN 3-7682-0542-8). Lubrecht & Cramer.

Botchan. Natsume Soseki. Tr. by Alan Turney from Japanese. LC 71-174215. 173p. 1980. pap. 3.95 (ISBN 0-87011-367-4). Kodansha.

Both Ends of the Leash: Selecting & Training Your Dog. Kurt Unkelbach. (Illus.). (gr. 3-7). 1968. PLB 4.95 (ISBN 0-13-080275-1); pap. 1.50 (ISBN 0-13-080903-9). P-H.

Both of Me. Mary Stuart. LC 79-8038. (Illus.). 480p. 1980. 13.95 (ISBN 0-385-14494-6). Doubleday.

Both Sides of the Hill: Britain & the Palestine War. Jon Kimche & David Kimche. (Return to Zion Ser.). (Illus.). 287p. 1981. Repr. of 1960 ed. lib. bdg. 20.00x (ISBN 0-87991-145-X). Porcupine Pr.

Both Sides of the Mirror: The Science & Art of Ballet. Anna Paskevska. LC 79-51362. (Illus.). 200p. 1981. 22.50 (ISBN 0-87127-112-5). Dance Horiz.

Bothy Songs & Ballads of Aberdeen. Banff & Moray, Angus & the Mearns. John Ord. 493p. 1980. Repr. of 1930 ed. lib. bdg. 25.00 (ISBN 0-8492-7307-2). R West.

Botswana: An African Growth Economy. Penelope Hartland-Thunberg. LC 78-3477. (Westview Special Studies on Africa). (Illus.). 1978. lib. bdg. 18.00x (ISBN 0-89158-171-5). Westview.

Botticelli. Leopold Ettlinger & Helen Ettlinger. LC 76-26747. (World of Art Ser.). (Illus.). 1977. 17.95 (ISBN 0-19-519900-6); pap. 9.95 (ISBN 0-19-519907-3). Oxford U Pr.

Botticelli. Susan Legouix. LC 77-10355. (Oresko Art Book). (Illus.). 1977. 15.95 (ISBN 0-8467-0376-9, Pub. by Two Continents); pap. 9.95 (ISBN 0-8467-0379-3). Hippocrene Bks.

Bottin Auto Cycle Moto, 1979. LC 76-647308. 2197p. 1979. 37.00x (ISBN 2-7039-0452-5). Intl Pubns Serv.

Bottin International: International Business Register 1980, 2 vols. 183rd ed. LC 48-24844. 1916p. 1980. Set. 90.00 (ISBN 2-7039-0467-3). Intl Pubns Serv.

Bottin Mondain Nineteen Seventy-Nine. 1754p. 1978. 65.00x o.p. (ISBN 2-7039-0466-5). Intl Pubns Serv.

Bottin Mondain 1980. 1754p. 1980. 72.50x (ISBN 2-7039-0466-5). Intl Pubns Serv.

Bottin Professions 1979, 6 vols. LC 76-647504. 1979. Set. 275.00x (ISBN 0-8002-2365-9). Intl Pubns Serv.

Bottle & Glass Handbook. Don Maust. (Illus.). 5.95 o.p. (ISBN 0-685-21843-0). Warman.

Bottle Collecting in America. John P. Adams. LC 70-151175. (Illus.). 1971. pap. 5.95 o.p. (ISBN 0-912274-06-9). NH Pub Co.

Bottle Collector's Treasury. (Illus.). 5.00 o.p. (ISBN 0-685-26806-3). Warman.

Bottle of Psychology. Donall Nagreine. (Illus.). 64p. 1981. 5.00 (ISBN 0-682-49679-0). Exposition.

Bottle Price Manual. pap. 3.50 o.p. (ISBN 0-8015-0846-0). Dutton.

Bottlenecks of Business. Thurman W. Arnold. LC 72-2363. (FDR & the Era of the New Deal Ser.). 352p. 1973. Repr. of 1940 ed. lib. bdg. 35.00 (ISBN 0-306-70470-6). Da Capo.

Bottles. Regina Stewart & Geraldine Cosentino. (Golden Handbook of Collectibles Ser.). (Illus.). 1977. pap. 3.95 o.p. (ISBN 0-307-43176-2, Golden Pr). Western Pub.

Bottles on the Western Frontier. Rex L. Wilson. (Illus.). 1981. price not set (ISBN 0-8165-0414-8). U of Ariz Pr.

Bottom Deal. Zeke Masters. (Orig.). 1981. pap. price not set (ISBN 0-671-42618-4). PB.

Bottom Line: Communicating in the Organization. T. Harrell Allen. LC 78-24521. (Illus.). 1979. text ed. 16.95 (ISBN 0-88229-405-9). Nelson-Hall.

Bottom of the Sea. Augusta Goldin. LC 66-10194. (Let's-Read-&-Find-Out Science Bk). (Illus.). (ps-3). 1967. bds. 7.95 (ISBN 0-690-15863-7, TYC-J); PLB 7.89 (ISBN 0-690-15864-5). T Y Crowell.

Bottom, Thou Art Translated: Political Allegory in a Midsummer Night's Dream & Related Literature. Marion A. Taylor. LC 72-83545. 253p. (Orig.). 1973. pap. text ed. 20.00x (ISBN 90-6203-038-6). Humanities.

Botulism: The Organism, Its Toxins, the Disease. Louis Smith. (Illus.). 256p. 1977. 25.75 (ISBN 0-398-03543-1). C C Thomas.

Bouche Creole. Leon Soniat. LC 80-23178. (Illus.). 1981. spiral bdg. 8.95 (ISBN 0-88289-242-8). Pelican.

Boucher's Prosthodontic Treatment for Edentulous Patients. Judson C. Hickey & George A. Zarb. LC 80-11234. (Illus.). 1980. text ed. 34.50 (ISBN 0-8016-0725-6). Mosby.

Boudica: The British Revolt Against Rome A.D. 60. Graham Webster. 1978. 33.00 (ISBN 0-7134-1064-7, Pub. by Batsford England). David & Charles.

Boudicca's Revolt. Ian Andrews. (Introduction to the History of Mankind Ser.). 1972. 3.95 (ISBN 0-521-08031-2). Cambridge U Pr.

Boudoir: A Journal of Voluptuous Victorian Reading. LC 70-151439. 256p. (Orig.). 1980. pap. 3.50 (ISBN 0-394-17781-9, B 445, BC). Grove.

Boulders & Pebbles of Poetry & Prose. Anthony Caponi. (Illus.). 96p. 1972. 2.50 o.p. (ISBN 0-8309-0085-3). Independence Pr.

Boulevard Nights. Dewey Gram. (Orig.). 1979. pap. 1.95 o.s.i. (ISBN 0-446-90106-7). Warner Bks.

Boulez. Paul Griffiths. (Oxford Studies of Composers). (Illus.). 1979. pap. 10.50x (ISBN 0-19-315442-0). Oxford U Pr.

Bouncing Betsy. D. P. Lathrop. 1964. 3.95 o.s.i. (ISBN 0-02-753150-3). Macmillan.

Bouncy Baby Bunny Finds His Bed. Joan Bowden. (Illus.). (gr. k-3). 1977. PLB 5.00 (ISBN 0-307-60029-7, Golden Pr). Western Pub.

Bound for Glory. Woody Guthrie. LC 68-28884. 441p. 1976. 10.95 o.p. (ISBN 0-525-07025-7). Dutton.

Bound for the Stars: An Enthusiastic Look at the Opportunities & Challenges Space Exploration Offers. Benjamin Adelman & Saul J. Adelman. (Illus.). 368p. 1980. text ed. 17.95 (ISBN 0-13-080390-1, Spec); pap. text ed. 8.95 (ISBN 0-13-080382-0). P-H.

Bound to Be Free. Don Deffner. LC 80-81841. 1980. pap. 6.95 (ISBN 0-933350-38-4). Morse Pr.

Bound to the Soil: A Social History of Dorset, 1750-1918. Barbara Kerr. LC 67-30789. 1968. text ed. 11.50x (ISBN 0-391-01959-7). Humanities.

Boundaries & Landmarks. A. C. Mulford. 1977. pap. 8.50 (ISBN 0-686-18920-5, 611). CARBEN Survey.

Boundaries of Change in Community Work. Ed. by Paul Henderson et al. (National Institute Social Services Library: No. 37). (Illus.). 256p. 1980. text ed. 27.50x (ISBN 0-04-361038-2); pap. text ed. 12.50x (ISBN 0-04-361039-0). Allen Unwin.

Boundaries of Genre: Dostoevsky's "Diary of a Writer" & the Traditions of Literary Utopia. Gary S. Morson. 272p. 1981. text ed. 25.00x (ISBN 0-292-70732-0). U of Tex Pr.

Boundary & Space: An Introduction to the Work of D. W. Winnicott. Madeleine Davis & David Wallbridge. 212p. 1981. 17.50 (ISBN 0-87630-251-7). Brunner-Mazel.

Boundary Conditions & Global Management. Guido Loero. 1975. 25.50 (ISBN 0-12-455050-9). Acad Pr.

Boundary Control & Legal Principles. 2nd ed. Curtis M. Brown. LC 68-8712. 1969. 27.50 (ISBN 0-471-10660-7, Pub. by Wiley-Interscience). Wiley.

Boundary Element Method for Engineers. C. A. Brebbia. LC 78-9625. 1978. 39.95x (ISBN 0-470-26438-1). Halsted Pr.

Boundary-Interior Layer Interactions in Nonlinear Singular Perturbation Theory. F. A. Howes. LC 78-8693. 1978. 7.60 (ISBN 0-8218-2203-9, MEMO-203). Am Math.

Boundary Value Problems. 2nd ed. David L. Powers. 351p. 1979. 19.95 (ISBN 0-12-563760-8); instr'. manual 3.00 (ISBN 0-12-563762-4). Acad Pr.

Boundary Value Problems for Differential Equations III: Proceedings. Steklov Institute of Mathematics, No. 126. Ed. by V. P. Mihailhov. LC 70-9052. 1975. 34.80 (ISBN 0-8218-3026-0, STEKLO-126). Am Math.

Boundary Value Problems for Elliptic Pseudodifferential Equations. G. I. Eskin. (Mathematical Monographs: Vol. 52). 1981. price not set o.p. (ISBN 0-8218-4503-9). Am Math.

Boundary Value Problems of Mathematical Physics. Ed. by O. A. Ladyzenskaja. (Trudy Steklov: No. 147). Date not set. cancelled (ISBN 0-8218-3068-6). Am Math.

Boundary Value Problems of Mathematical Physics V: Proceedings. Steklov Institute of Mathematics, Academy of Sciences, U S S R, No. 102. Ed. by O. A. Ladyzenskaja. 1979. Repr. of 1970 ed. 28.40 (ISBN 0-8218-3002-3, STEKLO-102). Am Math.

Bounded Analytic Functions. John B. Garnett. (Pure & Applied Mathematics Ser.). 1981. price not set (ISBN 0-12-276150-2). Acad Pr.

Boundless Resource: A Prospectus for an Education-Work Policy. Willard Wirtz. LC 75-30556. 1975. 8.95 o.p. (ISBN 0-915220-07-5); pap. 3.95 o.p. (ISBN 0-915220-10-5). New Republic.

Bounds on Transfer Principles for Algebraically Closed & Complete Discretely Valued Fields. Scott S. Brown. LC 78-9121. 1978. 7.60 (ISBN 0-8218-2204-7, MEMO-204). Am Math.

Bounds Out of Bounds: A Compass for Recent American & British Poetry. Roberta Berke. 192p. 1981. 14.95 (ISBN 0-19-502872-4). Oxford U Pr.

Bountiful: A Poetry Digest. Ed. by Nan E. Chase. (First Annual Ser.). (Illus.). 53p. pap. 4.25 (ISBN 0-938512-00-5). Brigadoon.

Bounty Killer. John Benteen. (Sundance: No. 15). 1979. pap. 1.25 (ISBN 0-8439-0704-5, Leisure Bks). Nordon Pubns.

Bounty Road. Charles R. Pike. LC 80-70092. (Jubal Cade Westerns Ser.). 142p. 1981. pap. 2.95 (ISBN 0-87754-241-4). Chelsea Hse.

Bouquet of Laughter. Hettie M. Cook. LC 79-54023. 164p. 1980. 6.95 (ISBN 0-8059-2665-8). Dorrance.

Bourbon for Breakfast. Wendy Perriam. LC 80-1865. 288p. 1981. 11.95 (ISBN 0-385-17374-1). Doubleday.

Bourbon Restoration. Guillaume De Bertier De Sauvigny. Tr. by Lynn M. Case. LC 67-20654. 1967. 12.50 o.p. (ISBN 0-8122-7552-7). U of Pa Pr.

Bourbon Street Black: The New Orleans Black Jazzman. Jack V. Buerkle & Danny Barker. LC 73-77926. (Illus.). 254p. 1974. pap. 4.95 (ISBN 0-19-501832-X, GB415, GB). Oxford U Pr.

Bourgeois Century: A History of Europe 1780-1870. K. R. Perry. (Evolution of Western Society Ser.). 1972. text ed. 8.50x (ISBN 0-391-00225-2). Humanities.

Bourges Cathedral: the West Portals. Tania Bayard. LC 75-23780. (Outstanding Dissertations in the Fine Arts - Medieval). (Illus.). 1976. lib. bdg. 45.00 (ISBN 0-8240-1977-6). Garland Pub.

Bourne Identity. Robert Ludlum. 544p. 1981. pap. 3.75 (ISBN 0-553-14300-X). Bantam.

Boutell's Heraldry. rev. ed. Charles Boutell. LC 73-75030. (Illus.). 368p. 1978. 30.00 (ISBN 0-7232-2096-4). Warne.

Boutique Attire. Editors of Time-Life Books. LC 75-7826. (Art of Sewing). (Illus.). (gr. 6 up). 1975. PLB 11.97 (ISBN 0-8094-1751-0, Pub. by Time Life). Silver.

Bouvier Des Flandres. Claire McLean. 19.95 (ISBN 0-87714-077-4). Green Hill.

Bouvier Des Flandres. 2nd ed. Claire McLean. 1980. 19.95 (ISBN 0-87714-077-4). Caroline Hse.

Bouyancy Effects in Fluids. J. S. Turner. LC 72-76085. (Cambridge Monographs on Mechanics & Applied Mathematics). (Illus.). 350p. 1973. 47.95 (ISBN 0-521-08623-X). Cambridge U Pr.

Bovine Hematology. O. C. Straub. (Illus.). 64p. (Orig.). 1981. pap. text ed. 18.00. Parey Sci Pub.

Bow in the Cloud: And the First Bereavement. John R. MacDuff. (Summit Bks.). 148p. 1980. pap. 2.45 (ISBN 0-8010-6108-3). Baker Bk.

Bow Street Brangle. Margaret SeBastian. 1977. pap. 1.50 (ISBN 0-445-04040-8). Popular Lib.

Bow Wow! Meow! A First Book of Sounds. Melanie Bellah. (Illus.). (ps-3). 1963. PLB 5.00 (ISBN 0-307-60523-X, Golden Pr). Western Pub.

Bowditch for Yachtsmen: Piloting. Nathaniel Bowditch. 1980. pap. 7.95 (ISBN 0-679-50930-5). McKay.

Bowel Book: A Practical Guide to Good Health. David Ehrlich & George Wolf. LC 80-54140. 192p. 1981. 12.95x (ISBN 0-8052-3763-1); pap. 5.95 (ISBN 0-8052-0673-6). Schocken.

Bowen Family Theory & Its Uses. C. Margaret Hall. LC 79-64456. 1981. 20.00 (ISBN 0-87668-373-1). Aronson.

Bowhunting the White Deer. Dean Conatser. (Illus.). 1977. 12.95 (ISBN 0-87691-192-0). Winchester Pr.

Bowker Annual of Library & Book Trade Information 1981. 26th ed. LC 55-12434. (Illus.). 600p. 1981. 32.50 (ISBN 0-8352-1343-9). Bowker.

Bowl of Quince. Ward Ritchie. (Santa Susana Press Ser.). 1977. 30.00 (ISBN 0-937048-15-1). CSUN.

Bowl of Remembering. Alice S. Newton. (Illus.). 1980. 5.50 (ISBN 0-8233-0312-8). Golden Quill.

Bowl of Saki. Hazrat Inayat Khan. (Collected Works of Hazrat Inayat Khan). 144p. (Orig.). 1981. pap. 4.95 (ISBN 0-930872-20-7, 1007P). Sufi Order Pubns.

Bowler's Manual. 3rd ed. Lou Bellisimo. (Illus.). 128p. 1975. pap. text ed. 6.50 (ISBN 0-13-080432-0). P-H.

Bowling. 2nd ed. Richard T. Mackey. LC 74-75228. (Illus.). 71p. 1974. pap. 4.95 o.p. (ISBN 0-87484-305-7). Mayfield Pub.

Bowling. 3rd, rev. ed. Richard T. Mackey. LC 80-82563. 89p. 1980. pap. text ed. 4.95 (ISBN 0-87484-513-0). Mayfield Pub.

Bowling for All. 3rd ed. Joe Falcaro & M. Goodman. (Illus.). 1966. 11.50 (ISBN 0-8260-2975-2). Wiley.

Bowling for Everyone. Gene Berger. (Illus.). 1974. 5.50 o.p. (ISBN 0-312-09380-2). St Martin.

Bowling: Individualized Instructional Program. A. Annarino. 1973. pap. 4.25 (ISBN 0-13-080440-1). P-H.

Bowling Now. Don Russell. LC 78-75333. (Illus.). 1980. 9.95 (ISBN 0-498-02311-7). A S Barnes.

Bowling Talk. Howard Liss. (gr. 4-6). 1974. pap. 0.75 o.s.i. (ISBN 0-671-29619-1). Archway.

Bowling Talk. Howard Liss. (gr. 4-6). 1974. pap. 0.75 (ISBN 0-671-29619-1). PB.

Bowls: How to Become a Champion. C. M. Jones. (Illus., Orig.). 1976. pap. 3.95 (ISBN 0-571-10708-7, Pub. by Faber & Faber). Merrimack Bk Serv.

Bowls: The American Lawn Bowler's Guide. 4th rev. enl. ed. Harvey C. Maxwell. (Illus.). 1976. lib. bdg. 5.95 imitation leather (ISBN 0-685-64304-2). Am Lawn Bowlers.

Bowman Hendry McCalla: A Fighting Sailor. Paolo E. Coletta. LC 79-66975. (Illus.). 1979. pap. text ed. 10.50 (ISBN 0-8191-0863-4). U Pr of Amer.

Bowmar-Noble Handwriting, 9 bks. J. K. Noble. Incl. Bk. A (ISBN 0-8372-3752-1). tchr's ed. (ISBN 0-8372-3761-0); Bk. B (ISBN 0-8372-3753-X). tchr's ed. (ISBN 0-8372-3761-0); Bk. C (ISBN 0-8372-3754-8). tchr's ed. (ISBN 0-8372-3761-0); Bk. D (ISBN 0-8372-3755-6). tchr's ed. (ISBN 0-8372-3761-0); Bk. E (ISBN 0-8372-3756-4). tchr's ed. (ISBN 0-8372-3762-9); Bk. F (ISBN 0-8372-3757-2). tchr's ed. (ISBN 0-8372-3762-9); Bk. G (ISBN 0-8372-3758-0). tchr's ed. (ISBN 0-8372-3762-9); Bk. H (ISBN 0-8372-3759-9). tchr's ed. (ISBN 0-8372-3762-9); Bk. I (ISBN 0-8372-3760-2). tchr's ed. (ISBN 0-8372-3762-9). (80p. ea.). (gr. k-8). Date not set. pap. 1.95 ea.; tchr's eds. 2.52 ea. Bowmar-Noble.

Bows & Arrows. Saxton T. Pope. (California Library Reprint Ser.). 1974. Repr. 13.75x (ISBN 0-520-02641-1). U of Cal Pr.

Box Book. Cecelia Maloney. (Illus.). (gr. k-2). 1978. PLB 5.38 (ISBN 0-307-68910-7, Golden Pr). Western Pub.

Box Hill. Geoff Chapman & Bob Young. (Illus., Orig.). 1979. pap. 7.95 (ISBN 0-9504143-1-X). Bradt Ent.

Box of Brownies, 4 bks. Robert Kraus & Pam Kraus. Incl. Brownie's ABC. 32p; Brownie's Joke Book. 32p; Brownie's Song & Dance Book. 32p; You Can Count on Brownies. 32p. LC 80-50808. (Illus.). Date not set. Set. 7.95 (ISBN 0-671-41193-4, Pub. by Windmill). S&S.

Box-Office Clowns: Bob Hope, Jerry Lewis, Mel Brooks, Woody Allen. Frank Manchel. (Illus.). (gr. 7 up). 1979. PLB 7.90 s&l (ISBN 0-531-02881-X). Watts.

Box Poems & Old Sheets. Willa Schneberg & Larkin Warren. LC 78-74231. 88p. 1979. pap. 4.95 (ISBN 0-914086-25-1). Alicejamesbooks.

Box with Red Wheels. Maud Petersham & Miska Petersham. (gr. k-3). 1949. 8.95 (ISBN 0-02-771340-7). Macmillan.

Boxcar Children. Gertrude Warner. LC 42-1418. (Boxcar Children Mysteries Ser.). (gr. 3-7). 6.95g (ISBN 0-8075-0851-9, Pilot Bks). A Whitman.

Boxer Rebellion: Anti-Foreign Terror Seizes China. Irving Werstein. LC 79-172448. (World Focus Bks). (Illus.). (gr. 7 up). 1971. PLB 4.90 o.p. (ISBN 0-531-02150-5). Watts.

Boxers. Constance Wiley & Wilson Wiley. Ed. by Christina Foyle. (Foyle's Handbks). (Illus.). 1973. 3.95 (ISBN 0-685-55794-4). Palmetto Pub.

Boxes. (MacDonald Educational Ser.). (Illus., Arabic.). 3.50 (ISBN 0-686-53103-5). Intl Bk Ctr.

Boxing. Henry Cooper. (Pelham Pictorial Sports Instruction Ser). (Illus.). 1977. 10.95 (ISBN 0-7207-0790-0). Transatlantic.

Boxing Is for Me. Art Thomas. LC 80-20086. (Sports for Me Bks.). (Illus.). (gr. 2-5). 1981. PLB 5.95 (ISBN 0-8225-1133-9). Lerner Pubns.

Boxing: The Great Ones. Reg Gutterridge. 1975. 8.95 o.p. (ISBN 0-686-26632-3, Pub. by Michael Joseph). Merrimack Bk Serv.

Boxing's Heavyweight Championship. Julian May. LC 76-4861. (Sports Classics Ser.). (Illus.). (gr. 4-12). 1976. PLB 8.95 o.p. (ISBN 0-87191-503-0). Creative Ed.

Boy & a Boa. Abby Israel. LC 80-25812. 64p. (gr. 3-6). 1981. 8.95 (ISBN 0-8037-0708-8); PLB 8.44 (ISBN 0-8037-0716-9). Dial.

Boy & a Deer. Darrell A. Rolerson. LC 79-81623. (Illus.). (gr. 3 up). 1970. 4.50 o.p. (ISBN 0-396-07172-4). Dodd.

Boy & Girl Tramps of America. Thomas Minehan. LC 76-7792. (Americana Library: No.29). 280p. 1976. Repr. of 1934 ed. 16.00 (ISBN 0-295-95450-7). U of Wash Pr.

Boy & His Gang. S. Adams Puffer. 188p. 1980. Repr. of 1912 ed. lib. bdg. 25.00 (ISBN 0-89987-657-9). Darby Bks.

Boy & the Donkey. Diana Pullein-Thompson. LC 58-11463. (Illus.). (gr. 2-6). 1958. 7.95 (ISBN 0-87599-089-4). S G Phillips.

Boy & the Goats. Margaret Hillert. (Just Beginning-to-Read Ser.). (Illus.). 32p. (gr. 1-6). 1981. PLB 4.39 (ISBN 0-695-41545-X). Follett.

Boy & the Taniwha. R. L. Bacon. 1976. 4.55x o.p. (ISBN 0-8002-0767-X). Intl Pubns Serv.

Boy Called Plum. Darrell A. Rolerson. LC 73-11987. (gr. 4 up). 1974. 5.95 (ISBN 0-396-06871-5). Dodd.

Boy Captives, Being the True Story of the Experiences & Hardships of Clinton L. Smith & Jeff D. Smith, Among the Comanche & Apache Indians During the Early Days. Clinton L. Smith. LC 75-7138. (Indian Captivities Ser.: Vol. 110). 1976. Repr. of 1927 ed. lib. bdg. 44.00 (ISBN 0-8240-1734-X). Garland Pub.

Boy, Girl, & Garden. Stanley Waldrop. LC 76-20983. 1976. 7.95 (ISBN 0-9603364-1-9). Waldrop Pubns.

Boy in the Bush. D. H. Lawrence. 1981. pap. 3.95 (ISBN 0-14-001935-9). Penguin.

Boy in the Moon. Ib S. Olsen. Tr. by Virginia A. Jensen. LC 74-1418. (Illus.). 40p. (ps-3). 1977. 6.95 (ISBN 0-590-17713-3, Four Winds); lib. bdg. 6.95 (ISBN 0-590-07713-9). Schol Bk Serv.

Boy King & the Witch. Dellanna Gordon. (Illus.). 124p. (Orig.). 1980. pap. 3.95 (ISBN 0-89260-180-9). Hwong Pub.

Boy Labour & Apprenticeship, London Nineteen Eleven. Reginald A. Bray. LC 79-56952. (English Working Class Ser.). 1980. lib. bdg. 22.00 (ISBN 0-8240-0106-0). Garland Pub.

Boy Life & Labour: The Manufacture of Inefficiency, London Nineteen Fourteen. Arnold Freeman. LC 79-56956. (English Working Class Ser.). 1980. lib. bdg. 25.00 (ISBN 0-8240-0110-9). Garland Pub.

Boy Life on the Prairie. Hamlin Garland. LC 61-16185. (Illus.). 1961. pap. 5.50 (ISBN 0-8032-5070-3, BB 120, Bison). U of Nebr Pr.

Boy Named Charlie Brown. Charles M. Schulz. (Illus.). 144p. (gr. 5-7). 1981. pap. 2.25 (ISBN 0-449-23217-4, Crest). Fawcett.

Boy Named Manuel, ESL Reader. Curriculum Adaptation Network for Bilingual Bicultural Education. Ed. by Nathan Quinones. LC 76-5999. (Illus.). (gr. 1-3). 1976. pap. text ed. 2.50 o.p. (ISBN 0-8120-0676-3). Barron.

Boy Named Mary Jane & Other Silly Verse. William Cole. (Illus.). (gr. 4-6). 1977. 6.45 (ISBN 0-531-00394-9). Watts.

Boy Next Door. Betty Cavanna. (gr. 7 up). 1956. PLB 8.40 (ISBN 0-688-31116-4). Morrow.

Boy of Old Prague. S. Ish-Kishor. (gr. 3-5). 1980. pap. 1.50 (ISBN 0-590-30381-3, Schol Pap). Schol Bk Serv.

Boy on the Run. Bianca Bradbury. LC 74-22486. 160p. (gr. 4-7). 1975. 5.95 (ISBN 0-395-28848-7, Clarion). HM.

Boy or Girl? Elizabeth Whelan. LC 76-44667. (Illus.). 1977. 7.95 o.p. (ISBN 0-672-52276-4). Bobbs.

Boy Pharaoh. Noel Streatfeild. (Illus.). (gr. 2-7). 1972. 7.95 (ISBN 0-7181-0986-4, Pub. by Michael Joseph). Merrimack Bk Serv.

Boy Through the Ages. Dorothy M. Stuart. LC 77-89291. (Illus.). 1970. Repr. of 1926 ed. 15.00 (ISBN 0-8103-3578-6). Gale.

Boy Under the Bed. Philip Dacey. LC 80-8858. (Johns Hopkins Poetry & Fiction). 1981. text ed. 10.95x (ISBN 0-8018-2601-2); pap. text ed. 5.95x (ISBN 0-8018-2602-0). Johns Hopkins.

Boy Who Could Fly. Robert Newman. 1976. pap. 1.75 (ISBN 0-686-68377-3, 53306, Camelot). Avon.

Boy Who Cried Wolf. Ed. by Denise W. Guynn. (Aesop's Fable Bk). (Illus.). 16p. (ps). 1980. pap. 22.00 ten bks & one cass. (ISBN 0-89290-076-8, BC14-4). Soc for Visual.

Boy Who Dared to Rock: The Definitive Elvis. Paul Lichter. LC 76-52006. 1978. pap. 8.95 (ISBN 0-385-12636-0, Dolp). Doubleday.

Boy Who Drank Too Much. Shep Greene. (YA) 1980. pap. 1.50 (ISBN 0-440-91066-8, LFL). Dell.

Boy Who Dreamed of Rockets. Robert Quackenbush. LC 78-21882. (Illus.). 32p. (gr. k-5). 1978. lib. bdg. 6.95 (ISBN 0-590-07724-4, Four Winds); lib. bdg. 5.41 o.p. (ISBN 0-8193-0996-6). Schol Bk Serv.

Boy Who Drew Cats & Other Tales. Lafcadio Hearn. (gr. 1-3). 1963. 4.50g o.s.i. (ISBN 0-02-743480-X). Macmillan.

Boy Who Followed Ripley. Patricia Highsmith. 1980. 10.95 (ISBN 0-690-01911-4). Lippincott & Crowell.

Boy Who Had Wings. Jane Yolen. LC 73-17010. (Illus.). (ps-4). 1974. PLB 9.89 (ISBN 0-690-15900-5, TYC-J). T Y Crowell.

Boy Who Invented the Bubble Gun. Paul Gallico. 272p. 1974. 6.95 o.s.i. (ISBN 0-440-01789-0). Delacorte.

Boy Who Listened to Everyone. Mabel Watts. LC 63-8178. (Illus.). (gr. k-3). 1963. 5.95 o.s.i. (ISBN 0-8193-0030-6, Four Winds). Schol Bk Serv.

Boy Who Looked Like Shirley Temple. Bill Mahan. 1981. lib. bdg. 14.95 (ISBN 0-8161-3155-4, Large Print Bks). G K Hall.

Boy Who Sailed Around the World Alone. Robin L. Graham & Derek Gill. (Illus.). 144p. (gr. 6 up). 1973. 6.95 o.p. (ISBN 0-307-16510-8, Golden Pr); PLB 12.23 o.p. (ISBN 0-307-66510-0). Western Pub.

Boy Who Saved Earth. Jim Slater. LC 80-1662. (Illus.). 128p. (gr. 6-9). 1981. 8.95a (ISBN 0-385-17115-3); PLB (ISBN 0-385-17116-1). Doubleday.

Boy Who Saved the Stars. Doris Vallejo. Ed. by Robin Snelson. (Illus.). (gr. 3 up). 1978. 5.95 (ISBN 0-931064-05-8). Starlog.

Boy Who Saw Bigfoot. Marian T. Place. LC 78-23199. (gr. 4-6). 1979. 5.95 (ISBN 0-396-07644-0). Dodd.

Boy Who Shared. Scripture Union. 1978. pap. 0.49 (ISBN 0-87508-930-5). Chr Lit.

Boy Who Snuck in. Pat E. Dexter. (Apple Bks.). (Illus.). (gr. 5 up). 1981. pap. 3.50 (ISBN 0-570-07902-0, 56-1602). Concordia.

Boy Who Spoke Chimp. Jane Yolen. LC 79-27259. (Capers Ser.). (Illus.). 128p. (gr. 3-6). 1981. pap. 4.99 (ISBN 0-394-94467-4); PLB 8.99 (ISBN 0-394-84467-X). Knopf.

Boy Who Talked to Whales. Webster Smalley. (Orig.). 1981. playscript 2.00 (ISBN 0-87602-232-8). Anchorage.

Boy Who Was Afraid of the Dark. John Koenig. (Illus.). (ps-3). 0.35 o.s.i. (ISBN 0-8198-0208-5). Dghtrs St Paul.

Boy Who Was Followed Home. Margaret Mahy. LC 75-4866. 32p. (gr. k-3). 1975. PLB 5.90 o.p. (ISBN 0-531-02834-8). Watts.

Boy Who Would Not Say His Name. Elizabeth Vreeken. (Beginning-to-Read Bks). (gr. 2-4). 2.50 o.p. (ISBN 0-695-80814-1); PLB 2.97 o.p. (ISBN 0-695-40814-3); pap. 1.50 o.p. (ISBN 0-695-30814-9). Follett.

Boy with a Drum. David Harrison. (ps-1). 1971. PLB 7.15 o.p. (ISBN 0-307-63044-7, Golden Pr). Western Pub.

Boy with a Mission. (Encounter Ser.). (gr. 3-7). 2.25 o.s.i. (ISBN 0-8198-0229-8). Dghtrs St Paul.

Boy with Many Houses. Inger Sandberg. LC 76-84907. (Illus.). (ps-3). 1970. 4.95 o.s.i. (ISBN 0-440-00772-0, Sey Lawr). Delacorte.

Boy with the Parrot. Elizabeth Coatsworth. (Illus.). (gr. 4-6). 1964. 3.95g o.s.i. (ISBN 0-02-721640-3). Macmillan.

Boyd Cruise. Boyd Cruise. LC 76-24712. (Illus.). 72p. 1976. 20.00x (ISBN 0-917860-01-2). Historic New Orleans.

Boydell's Shakespeare Gallery. Winnifred H. Friedman. LC 75-23791. (Outstanding Dissertations in the Fine Arts - 17th & 18th Century). (Illus.). 1976. lib. bdg. 45.00 (ISBN 0-8240-1987-3). Garland Pub.

Boyd's Book of Odd Facts. L. M. Boyd. LC 78-66296. (Illus.). 1979. 9.95 (ISBN 0-8069-0166-7); lib. bdg. 9.89 (ISBN 0-8069-0167-5). Sterling.

Boyd's Book of Odd Facts. L. M. Boyd. 1980. pap. 1.75 (ISBN 0-451-09415-8, E9415, Sig). NAL.

Boyhood with Gurdjieff. Fritz Peters. 192p. 1980. pap. 4.95 (ISBN 0-88496-146-X). Capra Pr.

Boyne Valley Vision. Martin Brennan. 1981. text ed. 26.00x (ISBN 0-85105-362-9, Dolmen Pr). Humanities.

Boyne Water: A Tale of the O'Hara Family, 3 vols. John Banim & Michael Banim. Ed. by Robert L. Wolff. (Ireland Nineteenth Century Fiction Ser. Two: Vol. 17). 1329p. 1979. Set. lib. bdg. 96.00 (ISBN 0-8240-3466-X). Garland Pub.

Boyne Water: The Battle of the Boyne, 1690. Peter B. Ellis. LC 76-6753. 175p. 1976. text ed. 18.95x (ISBN 0-312-09415-9). St Martin.

Boys. Paul Burrow. LC 80-50129. 1980. 6.95 (ISBN 0-533-04598-3). Vantage.

Boy's Albuquerque, 1898-1912. Kenneth C. Balcomb. LC 79-2774. (Illus.). 1980. 8.95 (ISBN 0-8263-0525-3). U of NM Pr.

Boy's Book of Biking. Allan A. MacFarlan. (Illus.). 1970. pap. 1.25 (ISBN 0-671-29739-2). PB.

Boy's Book of Snakes: How to Recognize & Understand Them. Percy A. Morris. (Illus.). (gr. 6-12). 1948. 12.95 (ISBN 0-8260-6335-7). Ronald Pr.

Boy's Book of Verse: An Anthology. rev. ed. Helen D. Fish. (gr. 7-9). 1951. 8.95 o.p. (ISBN 0-397-30183-9). Lippincott.

Boy's Brigade. Austin Birch. 7.50 (ISBN 0-392-07678-0, SpS). Soccer.

Boys Have Feelings Too. Dale Carlson. LC 80-12895. (Illus.). 160p. (gr. 6 up). 1980. 8.95 (ISBN 0-689-30770-5). Atheneum.

Boys' Life Book of Baseball Stories. Boys' Life Magazine Editors. (Boys' Life Library, No. 6). (gr. 5-9). 1964. PLB 3.99 o.p. (ISBN 0-394-91017-6, BYR). Random.

Boys' Life Book of Basketball Stories. Ed. by Boys' Life Magazine Editors. (Boys' Life Library, No. 11). (Illus.). (gr. 5-9). 1966. 2.95 o.p. (ISBN 0-394-81546-7, BYR). Random.

Boys' Life Book of Wild Animal Stories. Ed. by Boys' Life Magazine Editors. (Boys' Life Library, No. 9). (gr. 5-9). 1965. 2.95 o.p. (ISBN 0-394-81067-8, BYR). Random.

Boys No More: A Black Psychologist's View of Community. Charles W. Thomas. 1971. pap. text ed. 4.95x (ISBN 0-02-478890-2, 47889). Macmillan.

Boys of Indy. Phil Berger & Larry Bortstein. 1978. pap. 1.95 o.p. (ISBN 0-523-40327-5). Pinnacle Bks.

Boys of Summer. Roger Kahn. LC 76-144179. 13.95 o.s.i. (ISBN 0-06-012239-0, HarpT). Har-Row.

Boys on the Bus: Riding with the Campaign Press Corps. Timothy Crouse. 1976. pap. 2.95 (ISBN 0-345-29338-X). Ballantine.

Boy's Second Book of Radio & Electronics. Alfred Morgan. LC 57-6078. (Illus.). 288p. (gr. 7-9). 1977. 6.95 (ISBN 0-684-13154-4). Scribner.

Boys Will Be Boys. E. S. Turner. 1979. 8.95 o.p. (ISBN 0-7181-1282-2, Pub. by Michael Joseph). Merrimack Bk Serv.

Boys Will Be Boys. Ernest S. Turner. LC 76-175338. (Illus.). 1977. Repr. of 1948 ed. 21.00 (ISBN 0-8103-4091-7). Gale.

Bozland: Dickens' Places & People. Percy Fitzgerald. LC 70-141754. 1971. Repr. of 1895 ed. 20.00 (ISBN 0-8103-3616-2). Gale.

BP Book of Industrial Archaeology. Neil Cossons. LC 74-20468. (Illus.). 1975. 19.95 (ISBN 0-7153-6250-X). David & Charles.

Bra Bockers Lexikon, Vols. 1-19. (Swedish.). 1973. 1085.00 (ISBN 0-8277-3063-2). Maxwell Sci Intl.

Braced Frameworks: An Introduction to the Theory of Structures. 2nd ed. E. W. Parkes. LC 74-10556. 1974. text ed. 23.00 (ISBN 0-08-018078-7); pap. text ed. 11.25 (ISBN 0-08-018077-9). Pergamon.

Bracton on the Laws & Customs of England, Vols. 1-4. Henry Bracton. Ed. by Samuel E. Thorne. LC 68-28697. Orig. Title: Legibus et Consuetudinibus Angliae. 1400p. 1968. Vols. 1 & 2. 60.00x (ISBN 0-674-08035-1, Belknap Pr); Vols. 3 & 4. 70.00 (ISBN 0-674-08038-6, Belknap Pr). Harvard U Pr.

Bradford Book of Collector's Plates: Nineteen Seventy-Eight. (Illus.). pap. 8.95 o.p. (ISBN 0-686-51572-2). Wallace-Homestead.

Bradford's History of Plymouth Plantation 1606-1646. Ed. by W. T. Davis. (Original Narratives Ser.). 436p. 1959. Repr. of 1908 ed. 18.50x (ISBN 0-686-63939-1). B&N.

Bradley: A Soldier's Story. Omar N. Bradley. (Illus.). 1978. pap. 6.95 (ISBN 0-528-88133-7). Rand.

Bradley Bibliography: A Guide to the Literature of the Woody Plants of the World, Published Before the Beginning of the 20th Century, 5 vols. A. Rehder. Ed. by C. S. Sargent. 3895p. 1976. Repr. Set. lib. bdg. 745.20x (ISBN 0-686-27682-5). Vol. I. Vol. II (ISBN 3-87429-107-3). Vol. III (ISBN 3-87429-108-1). Vol. IV (ISBN 3-87429-109-X). Vol. V (ISBN 3-87429-110-3). Lubrecht & Cramer.

Bradley CPA Review - A Practice. James C. Warner & Frank F. Weinberg. LC 79-83860. 1979. pap. 16.00 (ISBN 0-932788-06-8). Bradley CPA.

Bradley CPA Review Auditing. 9th ed. CPA Study Aids Inc. LC 77-93927. 1979. pap. 15.00 (ISBN 0-932788-00-9). Bradley CPA.

Bradley CPA Review Law. 9th ed. CPA Study Aids Inc. LC 77-94481. 1979. pap. 15.00 (ISBN 0-932788-01-7). Bradley CPA.

Bradley CPA Review Practice & Theory. 10th, rev. ed. A. M. Partington & Arthur C. Nieminsky. LC 79-89147. 1979. pap. 19.50 (ISBN 0-932788-11-4). Bradley CPA.

Bradley CPA Review Q & A Auditing. CPA Study Aids Inc. LC 79-83863. pap. 12.00 (ISBN 0-932788-07-6). Bradley CPA.

Bradley CPA Review Q & A Law. Gary A. Laursen. LC 79-83862. 1979. pap. 12.00 (ISBN 0-932788-09-2). Bradley CPA.

Bradley CPA Review Q & A Theory. A. M. Partington. LC 79-83865. 1979. pap. 12.00 (ISBN 0-932788-08-4). Bradley CPA.

Bradley CPA Review Quantitative Methods. 6th ed. Stanley Gurnick & Robert M. Dias. LC 78-50970. 1978. pap. 8.00 (ISBN 0-932788-03-3). Bradley CPA.

Bradley CPA Review Summary of Apb Opinions & Fasb Statements. 12th ed. CPA Study Aids Inc. LC 78-54096. 1974. pap. 7.95 o.p. (ISBN 0-932788-05-X). Bradley CPA.

Bradley CPA Review Taxation. 8th ed. James C. Warner. LC 78-65093. 1978. pap. 8.95 o.p. (ISBN 0-932788-04-1). Bradley CPA.

Bradley CPA Review Taxation. rev ed. Ed. by James C. Warner. LC 78-65093. 1980. pap. 9.00 (ISBN 0-932788-04-1). Bradley CPA.

Bradley Summary of Statements on Auditing Standards. LC 79-83865. 1979. pap. 7.00 (ISBN 0-932788-10-6). Bradley CPA.

Bradmoor Murder. Melville D. Post. 297p. 1980. Repr. of 1929 ed. lib. bdg. 14.25x (ISBN 0-89968-197-2). Lightyear.

Brady & Lawless's Favorite Bookstores. Frank Brady & Joann Lawless. (Illus.). 1978. 12.95 o.p. (ISBN 0-8362-7902-6). Andrews & McMeel.
Brady's Programmed Introduction to Respiratory Therapy. 2nd ed. Thomas A. Barnes & Jacob S. Israel. LC 79-27753. (Illus.). 365p. 1980. pap. text ed. 14.95 (ISBN 0-87619-624-5). R J Brady.
Brae Houe. Millie Sutherland. 1980. 12.95 (ISBN 0-7145-3646-6). Riverrun NY.
Brae House. Millie Sutherland. 1981. 11.95 (ISBN 0-7145-3646-6). Riverrun NY.
Bragon the Dragon Calendar Capers. Dunaway et al. (gr. 1-5). 1978. 9.95 (ISBN 0-916456-36-6, GA93). Good Apple.
Bragon the Dragon Tells Time. Dunaway et al. 1978. 9.95 (ISBN 0-916456-37-4, GA94). Good Apple.
Brahma Sutra: The Philosophy of Spiritual Life. S. Radhakrishnan. 1959. 16.95 (ISBN 0-04-294043-5). Allen Unwin.
Brahmanical Culture & Modernity. A. D. Moddie. 6.50x (ISBN 0-210-98130-X). Asia.
Brahmasutras & Their Principal Commentaries. B. Krishnamurti Sharma. LC 72-901912. 275p. 1974. Vol. 2. 15.00x (ISBN 0-8002-0447-6). Intl Pubns Serv.
Brahmin Priest of Tamil Nadu. K. Subramaniam. LC 74-13072. 183p. 1974. 13.95 (ISBN 0-470-83535-4). Halsted Pr.
Brahms & His Four Symphonies. Julius Harrison. LC 76-127285. (Music Ser). (Illus.). 1971. Repr. of 1939 ed. lib. bdg. 22.50 (ISBN 0-306-70033-6). Da Capo.
Brahms: His Life & Work. 2nd ed. Karl Geiringer. (Illus.). 400p. 1948. 19.95 (ISBN 0-04-780006-2). Allen Unwin.
Brahms Piano Music. Denis Matthews. LC 75-27955. (BBC Music Guides: No. 37). (Illus.). 64p. (Orig.). 1978. pap. 2.95 (ISBN 0-295-95480-9). U of Wash Pr.
Braided Cord Animals You Can Make. Claude Morin. LC 76-19816. (Easy Craft Ser.). (Illus.). (gr. 4 up). 1976. 5.95 o.p. (ISBN 0-8069-5400-0); PLB 5.89 o.p. (ISBN 0-8069-5401-9). Sterling.
Brain. Robin Cook. 320p. 1981. 11.95 (ISBN 0-399-12563-9). Putnam.
Brain: A Scientific American Book. Scientific American Editors. LC 79-21012. (Illus.). 1979. text ed. 15.95x (ISBN 0-7167-1150-8); pap. text ed. 7.95x (ISBN 0-7167-1151-6). W H Freeman.
Brain Acetylcholine & Neuropsychiatric Disease. Ed. by Kenneth L. Davis & Philip A. Berger. LC 79-862. 614p. 1979. 39.50 (ISBN 0-306-40157-6, Plenum Pr). Plenum Pub.
Brain Allergies: The Psycho-Nutrient Connection. William H. Philpott & Dwight K. Kalita. LC 79-93429. (Illus.). 260p. 1980. 15.00 (ISBN 0-87983-224-X). Keats.
Brain & Activation. Khomskaia. (National Library of Medicine Ser.). 380p. Date not set. text ed. 18.50 (ISBN 0-08-025993-6). Pergamon.
Brain & Behavior: Brain & Gonadal Function, Vol. 3. Ed. by Roger A. Gorski & Richard E. Whalen. (UCLA Forum in Medical Sciences). 1966. 50.00x (ISBN 0-520-00506-6). U of Cal Pr.
Brain & Behavior: Proceedings, 2 vols. Conferences on Brain & Behavior, los Angeles. Ed. by M. A. Brazier. Incl. Vol. 1. Brain & Behavior. First Conference, 1961; Vol. 2. The Internal Environment & Alimentary Behavior. Second Conference, 1962. 7.75 ea. Lubrecht & Cramer.
Brain & Behaviour: Psychobiology of Everyday Life. Frank Campbell & George Sinaer. (Illus.). 168p. 1980. 22.50 (ISBN 0-08-024788-1); pap. 11.25 (ISBN 0-08-024787-3). Pergamon.
Brain & Human Behavior. Association for Research in Nervous Mental Disease. 1966. 30.25 o.s.i. (ISBN 0-02-846390-0). Hafner.
Brain & Its Mind. 2nd ed. H. Kuhlenbeck & J. Gerlach. (Human Brain & Its Universe: Vol. 2). (Illus.). x, 398p. 1981. 118.75 (ISBN 3-8055-2403-X). S Karger.
Brain & Its Physiology. Daniel Noble. (Contributions to the History of Psychology E, V, Physiological Psychology Ser.). 1980. Repr. of 1846 ed. 30.00 (ISBN 0-89093-324-3). U Pubns Amer.
Brain & Its Role in the Phylogenetic Transformation of the Human Skull. Franz Weidenreich. LC 78-72707. Repr. of 1941 ed. 19.50 (ISBN 0-404-18278-X). AMS Pr.
Brain & Learning: Directions in Early Childhood Education. Marlin Languis et al. LC 80-81273. (Illus.). 72p. (Orig.). 1980. pap. text ed. 2.75 (ISBN 0-912674-72-5, NAEYC 111). Natl Assn Child Ed.
Brain & Mind. (CIBA Foundation Sympoium: No.69). 436p. 1979. 51.25 (ISBN 0-444-90095-0, Excerpta Medica). Elsevier.
Brain & Mind. Ed. by John R. Smythies. (International Library of Philosophy & Scientific Method Ser.). 1965. text ed. 23.50x (ISBN 0-7100-3624-8). Humanities.
Brain & Personality. Powell. LC 79-87638. (Illus.). 122p. 1979. 21.95 (ISBN 0-03-052701-5). Praeger.
Brain & Reward. E. T. Rolls. LC 74-32290. 124p. 1975. pap. text ed. 12.75 (ISBN 0-08-018225-9). Pergamon.
Brain, Behavior, & Bodily Disease. Ed. by Herbert Weiner et al. (Association of Research in Nervous & Mental Disease (ARNMD) Research Publications Ser.: Vol. 59). 388p. 1980. text ed. 37.00 (ISBN 0-89004-480-5). Raven.
Brain-Behavior Relationships. James R. Merikangas. LC 79-2075. 240p. 1981. 23.95x (ISBN 0-669-03082-1). Lexington Bks.
Brain Book. Peter Russell. 1979. 12.95 (ISBN 0-8015-0886-X, Hawthorn). Dutton.
Brain Changers: Scientists & the New Mind Control. Maya Pines. LC 73-8721. (Illus.). 1973. 10.00 o.p. (ISBN 0-15-113700-5). HarBraceJ.
Brain Child: A Mother's Diary. Peggy Napear. LC 72-9141. (Illus.). 576p. 1974. 10.00 o.p. (ISBN 0-06-013156-X, HarpT). Har-Row.
Brain Control: A Critical Examination of Brain Stimulation & Psychosurgery. Elliot S. Valenstein. LC 73-13687. (Illus.). 407p. 1973. 20.95 (ISBN 0-471-89784-1, Pub. by Wiley-Interscience); pap. 13.50x (ISBN 0-471-03328-6). Wiley.
Brain Damage & Mental Retardation: A Psychological Evaluation. 2nd ed. J. L. Khanna. (Illus.). 232p. 1973. 12.75 (ISBN 0-398-02631-9). C C Thomas.
Brain Death Criterion of Human Death. D. L. Stickel. (Illus.). 73p. 1981. 19.00 (ISBN 0-08-025814-X). Pergamon.
Brain Drain. Charles H. Kao. 178p. 1980. 10.50x (ISBN 0-89955-157-2, Pub. by Mei Ya Pub Taiwan); pap. 5.95x (ISBN 0-89955-188-2). Intl Schol Bk Serv.
Brain Drain. Warren Murphy. (Destroyer Ser.: No. 22). 192p. (Orig.). 1976. pap. 1.75 (ISBN 0-523-40898-6). Pinnacle Bks.
Brain Drain & Foreign Students. G. Lakshmana Rao. LC 78-10903. (Illus.). 1979. 25.00x (ISBN 0-312-09437-X). St Martin.
Brain Drain: Emigration & Return-A UNITAR Study. William A. Glaser. LC 77-30576. 1978. text ed. 22.00 (ISBN 0-08-022415-6); pap. text ed. 50.00 (ISBN 0-08-022419-9). Pergamon.
Brain Dysfunction in Aggressive Criminals. Russell R. Monroe. LC 78-4402. (Illus.). 1978. 19.95 (ISBN 0-669-02349-3). Lexington Bks.
Brain Dysfunction in Children: Etiology, Diagnosis & Management. Perry Black. 200p. 1980. text ed. 19.00 (ISBN 0-89004-022-2). Raven.
Brain Dysfunction in Infantile Febrile Convulsions. Mary A. Brazier & Flavio Coceani. LC 75-14564. (International Brain Research Organization Monograph: Vol. 2). 1976. 37.50 (ISBN 0-89004-068-0). Raven.
Brain Dysfunction in Metabolic Disorders, Vol. 53. Association for Research in Nervous & Mental Disease. Ed. by Fred Plum. LC 74-79190. 1974. 34.50 (ISBN 0-911216-81-2). Raven.
Brain Edema. M. De Vlieger. 185p. 1981. 27.50 (ISBN 0-471-04477-6, Pub. by Wiley-Med). Wiley.
Brain Energy Metabolism. B. K. Siesjo. 607p. 1978. 79.50 (ISBN 0-471-99515-0). Wiley.
Brain Failure: An Introduction to Current Concepts of Senility. Barry Reisberg. LC 80-69717. (Illus.). 1981. 19.95 (ISBN 0-02-926260-7). Free Pr.
Brain Failure & Resuscitation. Peter Safar & Ake Grenvik. (Clinics in Critical Care Medicine). (Illus.). 256p. 1981. lib. bdg. 22.50 (ISBN 0-443-08143-3). Churchill.
Brain Hypoxia. Ed. by J. B. Brierly & B. S. Meldrum. (Clinics in Developmental Medicine, Vol. 39-40). 1971. 25.50 (ISBN 0-685-27035-1). Lippincott.
Brain in Hominid Evolution. Phillip V. Tobias. LC 78-158458. (Illus.). 1971. 27.50x (ISBN 0-231-03518-7). Columbia U Pr.
Brain-Injured Children: With Special Reference to Doman-Delacato Methods of Treatment. Evan W. Thomas. (Illus.). 196p. 1974. text ed. 19.75 photocopy ed. spiral (ISBN 0-398-01915-0). C C Thomas.
Brain Mechanisms & Perceptual Awareness. Ed. by O. Pompeiano & C. Ajmone-Marsan. (IBRO Ser.: No. 8). 1981. text ed. price not set (ISBN 0-89004-603-4). Raven.
Brain Mechanisms & the Control of Behaviour. W. Ross Adey. LC 75-311367. 1975. 19.50x (ISBN 0-8448-0611-0). Crane-Russak Co.
Brain Mechanisms in Memory & Learning: From the Single Neuron to Man. Ed. by Mary A. Brazier. LC 78-67019. (International Brain Research Organization Monograph Ser.: Vol. 4). 1978. 34.50 (ISBN 0-89004-160-1). Raven.
Brain Mechanisms of Sensation. Yasuji Katsuki & Masayasu Sato. 320p. 1981. 28.50 (ISBN 0-471-08148-5, Pub. by Wiley Med). Wiley.
Brain-Mind & Parapsychology: Proceedings. International Conference, Montreal Canada, Aug. 24-25, 1978. Ed. by Betty Shapin & Lisette Coly. LC 79-84820. 1979. 14.00 (ISBN 0-912328-31-2). Parapsych Foun.
Brain Neurotransmitters & Receptors in Aging & Age-Related Disorders. Ed. by S. J. Enna et al. (Aging Ser.). 1981. text ed. price not set (ISBN 0-89004-643-3). Raven.
Brain of the Common Marmoset (Callithrix Jacchus) H. Stephan et al. (Illus.). 1980. 92.40 (ISBN 0-387-09782-1). Springer-Verlag.
Brain of the Firm. 2nd ed. Stafford Beer. LC 80-49979. 448p. 1981. 29.50 (ISBN 0-471-27687-1, Pub. by Wiley-Interscience). Wiley.
Brain Power: What Does It Mean to Be Smart? Gail K. Haines. (Impact Ser.). (Illus.). (gr. 7 up). 1979. PLB 6.90 s&l (ISBN 0-531-02287-0). Watts.
Brain Research & Personhood: A Philosophical Theological Inquiry. Eugene P. Wratchford. LC 79-51466. 1979. pap. text ed. 8.60 o.p. (ISBN 0-8191-0749-2). U Pr of Amer.
Brain Stem of the Cat: A Cytoarchitectonic Atlas with Stereotaxic Coordinates. Alvin L. Berman. (Illus.). 1968. 175.00 (ISBN 0-299-04860-8). U of Wis Pr.
Brain Surgeon: An Intimate View of His World. Lawrence Shainberg. 1979. 10.95 (ISBN 0-397-01310-8). Lippincott.
Brain Systems & Psychological Concepts. John Boddy. LC 77-21203. 1978. 39.75 (ISBN 0-471-99601-7); pap. 18.95 (ISBN 0-471-99600-9, Pub. by Wiley-Interscience). Wiley.
Brain-Teasers & Mind-Benders. Gyles Brandreth. LC 78-66297. (Illus.). (gr. 3 up). 1979. 5.95 (ISBN 0-8069-4596-6); PLB 6.69 (ISBN 0-8069-4597-4). Sterling.
Brain: The Last Frontier. Richard M. Restak. 1980. pap. 3.50 (ISBN 0-446-96975-3). Warner Bks.
Brain: The Last Frontier. Restak, Richard M., M.D. LC 78-68353. 1979. 12.95 (ISBN 0-385-13405-3). Doubleday.
Brain Tumors. D. Thomas & D. Graham. LC 80-49930. 1980. 74.95 (ISBN 0-407-00157-3). Butterworths.
Brain Unit Activity During Behavior. M. Ian Phillips. (Illus.). 376p. 1973. text ed. 22.50 (ISBN 0-398-02769-2). C C Thomas.
Brainbox. W. C. Chalk. (Instant Readers Ser.). 1971. pap. text ed. 2.50x o.p. (ISBN 0-435-11193-0). Heinemann Ed.
Brainchild. J. M. Johnston. (Orig.). 1979. pap. 1.95 (ISBN 0-532-23141-4). Manor Bks.
Brainfire. Campbell Black. 1980. pap. 2.50 (ISBN 0-451-09481-6, E9481, Sig). NAL.
Brains, Behavior, & Robotics. James S. Albus. 400p. 1981. 16.95 (ISBN 0-07-000975-9, BYTE Bks). McGraw.
Brain's Diseases of the Nervous System. 8th ed. Brain. Ed. by John N. Walton. (Illus.). 1977. text ed. 35.00x (ISBN 0-19-261309-X). Oxford U Pr.
Brains, Machines, & Persons. Donald MacKay. 112p. 1980. pap. 4.95 (ISBN 0-8028-1817-X). Eerdmans.
Brains of Animals & Man. Russell Freedman & James E. Morriss. LC 71-151754. (Illus.). 160p. (gr. 4-6). 1972. 8.95 (ISBN 0-8234-0205-3). Holiday.
Brains of Men & Machines. Ernest W. Kent. 1980. 15.95 (ISBN 0-07-034123-0, BYTE Bks); pap. 8.95 (ISBN 0-07-034122-2). McGraw.
Brainstorm. Walter D. Myers. (Triumph Books Ser.). (Illus.). 1977. PLB 6.90 (ISBN 0-531-01325-1). Watts.
Brainstorms: Philosophical Essays on Mind & Psychology. Daniel C. Dennett. LC 78-13723. (Higher Mental Processes Ser.). (Illus.). 384p. 1978. text ed. 21.50 (ISBN 0-89706-001-6); pap. 10.00 (ISBN 0-89706-002-4). Bradford Bks.
Brainteasers & Mindbenders. B. Hamilton. 1981. pap. 4.95 (ISBN 0-13-080945-4); 10.95 (ISBN 0-13-080952-7). P-H.
Braithwaite's Original Brass Band. Peter Stevenson. LC 80-18065. (Illus.). 32p. (gr. 6-9). 1981. 8.95 (ISBN 0-7232-6193-8). Warne.
Brakes. John Remling. LC 77-7262. (Automotive Mechanics Ser.). 1978. text ed. 14.95 (ISBN 0-471-71645-6). Wiley.
Branch Library Service. LC 77-17557. 66p. 1977. 5.00 (ISBN 0-913578-17-7). Inglewood Ca.
Branch Lines into the Eighties. H. I. Quayle & S. C. Jenkins. LC 79-56065. (Illus.). 96p. 1980. 16.95 (ISBN 0-7153-7980-1). David & Charles.
Branch Manager's Workbook. Albert J. Brown, Jr. LC 75-36011. 1975. plastic comb 10.00 (ISBN 0-87267-023-6); wkbk, 3 ring bdg. o.p. 15.00 (ISBN 0-87267-032-5). Bankers.
Branch Will Not Break. James Wright. LC 63-8858. (Wesleyan Poetry Program: Vol. 18). (Orig.). 1963. pap. 4.95 (ISBN 0-8195-1018-1, Pub. by Wesleyan U Pr). Columbia U Pr.
Branching Processes with Biological Applications. D. P. Jagers. LC 74-32296. (Wiley Series in Probability & Mathematical Statistics). 276p. 1975. 52.50 (ISBN 0-471-43652-6). Wiley.
Brancusi Photographer. Ed. by Marielle Tabart & Isabelle Monod-Fontaine. Tr. by Kim Sichel from Fr. LC 79-23563. (Illus.). 124p. 1980. 30.00 (ISBN 0-9601068-4-7); pap. 17.50 (ISBN 0-9601068-2-0). Agrinde Bks.
Brancusi: the Sculpture & Drawings. Sidney Geist. (Contemporary Artists Ser.). 1975. 65.00 o.p. (ISBN 0-8109-0124-2). Abrams.
Brand. Hendrik Ibsen. 1961. 5.00x o.p. (ISBN 0-460-00716-5, Evman). Dutton.
Brand Name & Trademark Guide: 1896, 1904, 1915, 1922, 1943, 1950, 1965, 1969. 10th ed. Ed. by Helena Matlack. (Illus.). 300p. 1978. 19.95 (ISBN 0-931744-03-2). Jewelers Circular.
Brand Name Calorie Counter. Corinne T. Netzer. (Orig.). 1981. pap. 2.75 (ISBN 0-440-10676-1). Dell.
Brand Name Carbohydrate Gram Counter. Corinne T. Netzer. (Orig.). 1981. pap. 2.75 (ISBN 0-440-10658-3). Dell.
Brand Name Guide to Calories & Carbohydrates. William I. Kaufman. (Orig.). 1973. pap. 2.25 o.p. (ISBN 0-515-05688-X, P3126). Jove Pubns.
Brand Name Guide to Sugar: Sucrose Content of Over 1,000 Common Foods & Beverages. Ira L. Shannon. LC 77-10902. (Illus.). 1977. 9.95 (ISBN 0-88229-454-7); pap. 1.95 (ISBN 0-88229-542-X). Nelson-Hall.
Brand Names: Who Owns What. George Frankenstein & Diane Frankenstein. 384p. 1981. lib. bdg. 45.00 (ISBN 0-87196-420-1). Facts on File.
Brand New Kitten. Sally Scott. LC 56-8355. (Illus.). (gr. 1-5). 1956. 4.95 o.p. (ISBN 0-15-211419-X, HJ). HarBraceJ.
Brand-New Monty Python Papperbok. (Illus.). 90p. 1976. pap. 6.95 o.s.i. (ISBN 0-446-87078-1). Warner Bks.
Brand New Old House Catalogue. Ed. by Lawrence Grow. (Illus.). 224p. 1980. 17.95 (ISBN 0-446-51214-1); pap. 9.95 (ISBN 0-446-97557-5). Warner Bks.
Brand of Empire. Luke Short. 1977. pap. 1.25 o.s.i. (ISBN 0-440-10770-9). Dell.
Brand of Possession. Carole Mortimer. (Harlequin Presents Ser.). 192p. (Orig.). 1981. pap. 1.50 (ISBN 0-373-10406-5, Pub. by Harlequin). PB.
Brand of Vengeance. Charles R. Pike. LC 80-70091. (Jubal Cade Westerns Ser.). 142p. 1981. pap. 2.95 (ISBN 0-87754-240-6). Chelsea Hse.
Branded. Rosalie Cates. Date not set. 10.95 (ISBN 0-87949-147-7). Ashley Bks.
Brandopfer. Goes. (Easy Readers, C). pap. 3.75 (ISBN 0-88436-057-1, GEA301051). EMC.
Brannigan. Ed Newsom. 208p. (Orig.). 1981. pap. 1.95 (ISBN 0-89083-713-9). Zebra.
Brann's Guide to Home Improvement. Donald R. Brann. LC 63-9605. (Illus.). 1963. 8.95 (ISBN 0-8303-0053-8). Fleet.
Braque, One Hundred Sixty Six, No. 166. (Maeght Gallery: Derriere le Miroir Ser.). 1977. pap. 19.95 (ISBN 0-8120-0896-0). Barron.
Brash American. Lester Samantha. (Orig.). 1981. pap. 1.50 (ISBN 0-440-10945-0). Dell.
Brashki: A Gypsy Fantasy. Barbara Housh. 1980. pap. 6.95 o.p. (ISBN 0-8362-6109-7). Andrews & McMeel.
Brasi! Contemporary Brazilian Writing. Ed. by Sasha Newborn. LC 77-642342. (Rockbottom Specials Ser.). (Illus., Eng. & Port.). Date not set. 12.00 o.p. (ISBN 0-930012-21-6); pap. 5.00 o.p. (ISBN 0-930012-20-8). Mudborn. Postponed.
Brasilia-Plan & Reality: A Study of Planned & Spontaneous Urban Settlement. David G. Epstein. LC 72-186103. 1973. 20.00x (ISBN 0-520-02203-3). U of Cal Pr.
Brass Anthology. 1980. 33.00 (ISBN 0-686-15890-3). Instrumentalist Co.
Brass Bands. Arthur R. Taylor. 1979. 29.95x (ISBN 0-8464-0057-X). Beekman Pubs.
Brass Butterfly. William Golding. 1969. pap. 4.95 (ISBN 0-571-09073-7, Pub. by Faber & Faber). Merrimack Bk Serv.
Brass Cupcake. John D. MacDonald. 1981. pap. 1.95 (ISBN 0-449-14141-1, GM). Fawcett.
Brass Diamonds. Berent Sandberg. 1980. 8.95 (ISBN 0-453-00383-4, H383). NAL.
Brass Diamonds. Berent Sandberg. 1981. pap. 2.50 (ISBN 0-451-09665-7, E9665, Sig). NAL.
Brass Ensemble Methods for Music Educators. J. D. Zorn. 1977. pap. text ed. 13.95x (ISBN 0-534-00503-9). Wadsworth Pub.
Brass: Jane Byrne & the Pursuit of Power. Kathleen W. FitzGerald. 1981. 11.95 (ISBN 0-8092-7006-4). Contemp Bks.
Brass Rainbow. Michael Collins. LC 79-57533. (Dan Fortune Detective Mystery). 176p. 1980. pap. 1.95 (ISBN 0-87216-672-4). Playboy Pbks.

Brass Solo & Study Guide. Paul G. Anderson. 15.00 (ISBN 0-686-15889-X). Instrumentalist Co.

Brass Target. Frederick Nolan. 1979. pap. 1.75 o.s.i. (ISBN 0-685-54627-6, 04849-6). Jove Pubns.

Brasses & Brass Rubbings. Clare Gittings. (Illus.). 1979. 6.95 (ISBN 0-7137-0520-5, Pub. by Blandford Pr England). Sterling.

Brassey's Warsaw Pact Infantry & Its Weapons: Defense Publications. Ed. by J. I. Owen. LC 76-6841. 1976. 17.00x (ISBN 0-89158-531-1). Westview.

Brassica Crops & Wild Allies. Ed. by S. Tsunoda et al. 360p. 1980. 38.00x (ISBN 0-89955-211-0, Pub. by JSSP Japan). Intl Schol Bk Serv.

Brasspounder. D. G. Sanders. LC 77-72820. (Illus.). 1978. 8.95 o.p. (ISBN 0-8015-0881-9). Dutton.

Brat Farrar. Josephine Tey. LC 79-19666. 1981. Repr. of 1949 ed. lib. bdg. 10.00x (ISBN 0-8376-0445-1). Bentley.

Brat Race. Norman Thelwell. LC 78-9766. (Illus.). 1978. 6.95 o.p. (ISBN 0-684-15638-5, ScribT). Scribner.

Brats & Mr. Jack. Hilary Milton. LC 80-23144. 160p. (gr. 5 up). 1980. 8.95 (ISBN 0-8253-0004-5). Beaufort Bks NY.

Brave & Bold. Charlotte Huber et al. (Wonder-Story Books Ser). Orig. Title: They Were Brave & Bold. (gr. 5). text ed. 11.84 (ISBN 0-06-517505-0, SchDept). Har-Row.

Brave Baby Elephant. Sesyle Joslin & Leonard Weisgard. LC 60-10245. (Illus.). (ps-1). 1960. 4.95 o.p. (ISBN 0-15-211598-6, HJ). HarBraceJ.

Brave Buffalo Fighter (Waditaka Tatahka Kisisohitika) John D. Fitzgerald. LC 73-80213. (Illus.). 192p. (gr. 5-7). 1973. PLB 7.50 o.p. (ISBN 0-8309-0100-0). Independence Pr.

Brave Horse. Manly Wellman. LC 68-24439. (Young Readers Ser.). (Illus., Orig.). (gr. 4-7). 1968. 3.95 o.p. (ISBN 0-910412-81-2). Williamsburg.

Brave Johnny O'Hare. Eleanor B. Heady. LC 74-77791. (Illus.). (gr. k-3). 1969. 5.95 o.p. (ISBN 0-8193-0275-9, Four Winds); PLB 5.41 o.p. (ISBN 0-8193-0276-7). Schol Bk Serv.

Brave Little Tailor. Grimm Brothers. LC 78-74631. (Illus.). (gr. k-3). 1980. PLB 6.95 (ISBN 0-88332-124-6). Larousse.

Brave Men. Ernie Pyle. LC 74-70. 474p. 1974. Repr. of 1944 ed. lib. bdg. 35.00x (ISBN 0-8371-7368-X, PYBM). Greenwood.

Brave New World of the Enlightenment. Louis I. Bredvold. 1961. 3.95 o.p. (ISBN 0-472-17755-9). U of Mich Pr.

Brave New World Revisited. Aldous Huxley. 1965. pap. 1.95 (ISBN 0-06-080023-2, P23, PL). Har-Row.

Bravely, Bravely in Business. Richard R. Conarroe. LC 72-78297. (Illus.). 1972. 10.95 (ISBN 0-8144-5304-X). Am Mgmt.

Bravely, Bravely...in Business. Richard R. Conarroe. (AMACOM Executive Bks). 1978. pap. 4.95 (ISBN 0-8144-7509-4). Am Mgmt.

Bravo Blow-Out. 287p. 1980. 100.00x (ISBN 8-272-70011-5, Pub. by Norwegian Info Norway). State Mutual Bk.

Bravo Maurice. Tr. by Mary Fitton. 10.00x o.p. (ISBN 0-8464-0206-8). Beekman Pubs.

Bravo Romeo. Ralph Peters. 320p. 1981. 11.95 (ISBN 0-399-90097-7). Marek.

Braxton Bragg & Confederate Defeat: Field Command, Vol. 1. Grady McWhiney. LC 69-19856. (Illus.). 1969. 20.00x (ISBN 0-231-02881-4). Columbia U Pr.

Brazen. Carter Brown. Bd. with Stripper. Date not set. pap. 1.95 (ISBN 0-451-09575-8, J575, Sig). NAL.

Brazen Horn. Denis Johnston. (Dolmen Editions: No. 22). (Illus.). 272p. 1976. text ed. 43.75x (ISBN 0-85105-259-2, Dolmen Pr). Humanities.

Brazer's Handbook. Charles R. Self, Jr. LC 78-56960. (Home Craftsman Ser.). (Illus.). 1978. pap. 5.95 (ISBN 0-8069-8178-4). Sterling.

Brazil. (Nagel Encyclopedia Guide). (Illus.). 448p. 1979. 38.00 (ISBN 0-686-60389-3, Pub. by Nagel Switzerland). Hippocrene Bks.

Brazil. John P. Dickenson. (Westview Special Studies in Industrial Geography). 1978. lib. bdg. 24.50x (ISBN 0-89158-832-9, Dawson). Westview.

Brazil. Ritchie Perry. LC 78-56598. (Countries Ser.). (Illus.). 1978. lib. bdg. 7.95 (ISBN 0-686-51149-2). Silver.

Brazil: A Political Analysis. Peter Flynn. LC 77-16243. (Nations of the Modern World Ser.). 1978. lib. bdg. 40.00x (ISBN 0-89158-747-0). Westview.

Brazil: A Political Analysis. Peter Flynn. (Nations of the Modern World Ser.). (Illus.). 1979. pap. text ed. 12.50x (ISBN 0-89158-694-6). Westview.

Brazil: A Study of Economic Types. Joao F. Normano. LC 67-29551. 1935. 12.00x (ISBN 0-8196-0208-6). Biblo.

Brazil & Africa. Jose H. Rodrigues. Tr. by Richard A. Mazzara & Sam Hileman. 1965. 23.75x (ISBN 0-520-01076-0). U of Cal Pr.

Brazil & Its Radical Left: An Annotated Bibliography on the Communist Movement & the Rise of Marxism, 1922-1972. Ed. by Ronald H. Chilcote. LC 80-12617. 1981. lib. bdg. 60.00 (ISBN 0-527-16821-1). Kraus Intl.

Brazil & the Great Powers, 1930-1939: The Politics of Trade Rivalry. Stanley E. Hilton. (Latin American Monographs Ser.: No. 38). 304p. 1975. 12.95x (ISBN 0-292-70713-4). U of Tex Pr.

Brazil: Anthropological Perspectives. Ed. by Maxine L. Margolis & William E. Carter. LC 79-11843. Orig. Title: Anthropology of Brazil. (Illus.). 1979. 21.50x (ISBN 0-231-04714-2). Columbia U Pr.

Brazil Books. Compiled by Anthony Knopp. 20p. 1970. pap. 1.00 (ISBN 0-913456-76-4, Pub by Ctr Inter-Am Rel). Interbk Inc.

Brazil: Foreign Relations of a Future World Power. new ed. Ronald Schneider. LC 76-28345. 1977. lib. bdg. 21.00 o.p. (ISBN 0-89158-200-2). Westview.

Brazil: From Colony to World Power. Donald E. Worcester. LC 73-1328. (Illus.). 1977. encore edition 3.95 (ISBN 0-684-15011-5, ScribC); pap. text ed. 3.95x (ISBN 0-684-13391-1, ScribC). Scribner.

Brazil in Pictures. Sterling Publishing Company Editors. LC 67-16015. (Visual Geography Ser). (gr. 6 up). PLB 4.99 (ISBN 0-8069-1081-X); pap. 2.95 (ISBN 0-8069-1080-1). Sterling.

Brazil in the International System. Ed. by Wayne A. Selcher. (Special Studies on Latin America & the Caribbean). 300p. 1981. lib. bdg. 26.50x (ISBN 0-89158-907-4). Westview.

Brazil: Politics in a Patrimonial Society. rev ed. Riordan Roett. LC 77-7825. (Praeger Special Studies). 1978. 23.95 (ISBN 0-03-022861-1); pap. 8.95 student ed (ISBN 0-03-022866-2). Praeger.

Brazil Since Nineteen Sixty Four: Modernization Under a Military Regime. Georges-Andre Fiechter. LC 75-16325. 296p. 1975. 36.95 o.p. (ISBN 0-470-26332-6). Halsted Pr.

Brazil 1969. Ed. by David Bronheim. LC 71-113454. 1970. pap. 1.50 o.p. (ISBN 0-913456-77-2). Interbk Inc.

Brazil 1980: The Protestant Handbook. William R. Read & Frank A. Ineson. 1973. pap. 4.95 (ISBN 0-912552-04-2). MARC.

Brazilian Cinema. Randal Johnson & Robert Stam. LC 80-66323. (Illus.). 260p. 1981. 20.00 (ISBN 0-8386-3078-2). Fairleigh Dickinson.

Brazilian Corporative State & Working-Class Politics. Kenneth P. Erickson. 1978. 19.50x (ISBN 0-520-03162-8). U of Cal Pr.

Brazilian Industrial Economy. William G. Tyler. LC 79-5440. 1981. price not set (ISBN 0-669-03448-7). Lexington Bks.

Brazilian Odyssey: Memoirs of a United Nations' Specialist. Cleveland J. Allen. 160p. 1981. pap. 7.50 (ISBN 0-8059-2746-8). Dorrance.

Brazilian Peasantry. Shepard Forman. LC 75-16156. 336p. 1975. 20.00x (ISBN 0-231-03106-8); pap. 10.00x (ISBN 0-231-08366-1). Columbia U Pr.

Brazilian Revolution of Nineteen Thirty & the Aftermath. Jordan M. Young. 1967. 11.00 (ISBN 0-8135-0545-3). Rutgers U Pr.

Brazilian Stone Meteorites. Klaus Keil & Celso P. Gomes. LC 80-5333. (Illus.). 192p. 1981. 20.00x (ISBN 0-8263-0543-1). U of NM Pr.

Brazilian Tenement. Aluisio Azevedo. Tr. by Harry W. Brown. 320p. 1977. Repr. of 1926 ed. 15.75 (ISBN 0-86527-222-0). Fertig.

Brazill - Journey in the Light of the Eucharist. Pope John Paul. 1980. write for info. (ISBN 0-8198-1102-5); pap. write for info. (ISBN 0-8198-1103-3). Dghtrs St Paul.

Brazil's Multilateral Relations Between First & Third Worlds. Wayne A. Selcher. LC 77-25273. (Westview Replica Edition Ser.). 1978. lib. bdg. 23.50 o.p. (ISBN 0-89158-088-3). Westview.

Breacadh. T. O'Maille. 146p. 1973. 10.00x (ISBN 0-7165-2237-3, Pub. by Irish Academic Pr Ireland). Biblio Dist.

Breach in the Wall: A Memoir of the Old China. Enid S. Candlin. 306p. 1973. 8.95 o.s.i. (ISBN 0-02-521100-5). Macmillan.

Bread-&-Butter Indian. Anne Colver. (gr. 3-6). 1972. pap. 1.75 (ISBN 0-380-00699-5, 52092, Camelot). Avon.

Bread & Butter Journey. Anne Colver. 1971. pap. 1.25 (ISBN 0-380-00708-8, 43802, Camelot). Avon.

Bread & Jam for Frances. Russell Hoban. (Illus.). (gr. k-3). 1969. pap. 1.50 (ISBN 0-590-02566-X, Schol Pap); pap. 3.50 bk. & record (ISBN 0-590-04414-1). Schol Bk Serv.

Bread & Roses. Richard Gambino. LC 79-67598. 480p. 1981. 13.95 (ISBN 0-87223-651-X). Seaview Bks.

Bread & Roses Too. Jack Newfield. 1971. pap. 3.95 o.p. (ISBN 0-525-03100-6). Dutton.

Bread & the Liturgy: The Symbolism of Early Christian & Byzantine Bread Stamps. George Galavaris. LC 75-98120. 1970. 21.50x (ISBN 0-299-05310-5). U of Wis Pr.

Bread Blessed & Broken. John Mossi. LC 74-16844. 1975. pap. 7.95 (ISBN 0-8091-1855-6). Paulist Pr.

Bread Book. Carlson Wade. 170p. 1974. pap. 1.95 (ISBN 0-06-463383-7, EH 383, EH). Har-Row.

Bread for Each Day. large print ed. M. R. DeHaan & H. G. Bosch. 1979. 8.95 (ISBN 0-310-23267-8); 7.95 (ISBN 0-310-23260-0). Zondervan.

Bread for the Journey. Ruth C. Duck. 96p. 1981. pap. 3.95 (ISBN 0-8298-0423-4). Pilgrim NY.

Bread, Hashish & Moon: Four Modern Arab Poets. Tr. by B. Bennani from Arabic. (Keepsake Ser.: Vol. 10). (Illus.). 1981. 10.00 (ISBN 0-87775-134-X); pap. 5.00 (ISBN 0-87775-135-8). Unicorn Pr.

Bread, Meat & Raisins After the Dance. James A. Gittings. LC 77-83883. 1977. 7.00 (ISBN 0-89430-006-7). Morgan-Pacific.

Bread of Christmas. Richard Andersen. 32p. 1981. pap. 1.50 (ISBN 0-570-06983-1, 12-2605). Concordia.

Bread Ovens of Quebec. Lise Boily & Jean-Francois Blanchette. (Illus.). 1979. pap. 8.95 (ISBN 0-660-00120-9, 56284-0, Pub. by Natl Mus Canada). U of Chicago Pr.

Bread Science & Technology. Y. Pomeranz & J. A. Shellenberger. (Illus.). 1971. 29.50 (ISBN 0-87055-104-3). AVI.

Bread Sculpture: The Edible Art. Ann Wiseman. LC 75-26909. (Illus.). 96p. (Orig.). 1975. 3.95 (ISBN 0-912238-74-7); pap. 2.95 (ISBN 0-912238-72-0). One Hund One Prods.

Bread: Social, Nutritional, & Agricultural Aspects of Wheaten Bread. Ed. by Arnold Spicer. (Illus.). 1975. 67.20x (ISBN 0-85334-637-2, Pub. by Applied Science). Burgess-Intl Ideas.

Bread Tray: Nearly 600 Recipes for Homemade Breads, Rolls, Muffins, & Biscuits. Louis P. De Gouy. LC 73-88329. vii, 463p. 1974. pap. 4.50 (ISBN 0-486-23000-7). Dover.

Bread Upon the Waters. Harry Fornari. LC 73-76524. (Illus.). 1973. 10.00 o.s.i. (ISBN 0-87695-166-3). Aurora Pubs.

Bread Upon the Waters: Federal Aids to the Maritime Industries. Gerald R. Jantscher. (Studies in the Regulation of Economic Activity). 164p. 1975. 10.95 (ISBN 0-8157-4574-5). Brookings.

Bread Winners. Mel London. (Illus.). 1979. 14.95 (ISBN 0-87857-269-4). Rodale Pr Inc.

Breads. Time-Life Books. (Good Cook Ser.). (Illus.). 176p. 1981. 12.95 (ISBN 0-8094-2900-4). Time Life.

Bread's Biological Transmutations. L. C. Kervan. Ed. by Jacques De Langre. LC 78-56122. 1979. pap. 3.00 (ISBN 0-916508-06-4). Happiness Pr.

Breads of the World: An Easy-to-Bake Collection from 46 Countries. Mariana Honig. LC 77-7208. (Illus.). 352p. pap. cancelled o.s.i. (ISBN 0-87754-254-6). Chelsea Hse.

Breadth & Depth in Economics. Ed. by Jacob S. Dreyer. LC 77-238. 1978. 18.95 (ISBN 0-669-01430-3). Lexington Bks.

Break a Leg Betsy Maybe. Lee Kingman. (YA) 1979. pap. 1.50 (ISBN 0-440-90794-2, LFL). Dell.

Break-Even Charts: Their Interpretation & Construction. Learning Systems Ltd. 1968. pap. text ed. 6.00 o.p. (ISBN 0-08-014050-5). Pergamon.

Break-Even Point: A Guide to the Process of Management for the Medical Office. Elizabeth P. Klein. LC 79-90728. (Illus.). 237p. 1979. wkbk. 30.00 (ISBN 0-9604250-0-4). E P Klein.

Break Him Down! Bill Powers. (Target Books). (Illus.). (gr. 3 up). 1977. PLB 6.45 s&l (ISBN 0-531-01273-5). Watts.

Break in the Sun. Bernard Ashley. (Illus.). 186p. (gr. 6 up). 1980. 9.95 (ISBN 0-87599-230-7). S G Phillips.

Break-Out from the Crystal Palace: The Anarcho-Psychological Critique-Stirner, Nietzsche, Dostoevsky. John Carroll. (International Library of Sociology). 1974. 18.00x (ISBN 0-7100-7750-5). Routledge & Kegan.

Break-up of Our Camp, Stories 1932-1935: The Collected Stories, Vol. 1. Paul Goodman. Ed. by Taylor Stoehr. 300p. 1978. 14.00 (ISBN 0-87685-330-0); deluxe ed. 25.00 (ISBN 0-87685-331-9); pap. 7.50 (ISBN 0-87685-329-7). Black Sparrow.

Breakaway. Ruth Hallman. LC 80-24977. (Highway Bk) (gr. 7 up). 1981. 8.95 (ISBN 0-664-32677-3). Westminster.

Breakfast & Brunch. Sunset Editors. LC 79-90335. (Illus.) 96p. 1980. pap. 4.95 (ISBN 0-376-02104-7, Sunset Bks). Sunset-Lane.

Breakfast & Brunch Dishes for Food Service Menu Planning. Eulalia Blair. LC 74-34100. (Foodservice Menu Planning Ser.). 256p. 1975. 16.50 (ISBN 0-8436-2057-9). CBI Pub.

Breakfast at Tiffany's. Truman Capote. 1959. pap. 1.25 (ISBN 0-451-07483-1, Y7483, Sig). NAL.

Breakfast Book. David St. John Thomas. LC 80-69350. (Illus.). 96p. 1981. 11.95x (ISBN 0-7153-8094-X). David & Charles.

Breakfast, Books & Dreams: A Day in Verse. Ed. by Michael P. Hearn. LC 80-13498. (Illus.). 48p. (gr. 7-10). 1981. 9.95g (ISBN 0-7232-6189-X). Warne.

Breakfast Cookery. Bruce H. Axler. 1974. pap. 3.55 (ISBN 0-672-96120-2). Bobbs.

Breakfast for Sammy. Cynthia Weissman. LC 77-13869. (Illus.). 32p. (gr. k-3). 1978. 6.95 (ISBN 0-590-07503-9, Four Winds). Schol Bk Serv.

Breakfast in Miami. Reinhard Lettau. Tr. by Julie Pradi & Reinhard Lettau. 1981. lib. bdg. 14.95 (ISBN 0-7145-3831-0); pap. 5.95 (ISBN 0-7145-3834-5). Riverrun NY. Postponed.

Breakfast in the Afternoon. Cynthia Basil. LC 78-10366. (Illus.). (gr. k-3). 1979. 7.50 (ISBN 0-688-22175-0); PLB 7.20 (ISBN 0-688-32175-5). Morrow.

Breakfast in the Ruins. Michael Moorcock. 1980. pap. 1.95 (ISBN 0-380-49148-6, 49148). Avon.

Breakfast of Champions. Kurt Vonnegut, Jr. 320p. pap. 2.75 (ISBN 0-440-13148-0). Dell.

Breakfast Preparation. Ser-Vol-Tel Institute. (Foodservice Career Education Ser.). 1974. pap. 4.95 (ISBN 0-8436-2030-7). CBI Pub.

Breakfast with a Stranger. Peter Kortner. LC 76-28043. 1977. 7.95 o.p. (ISBN 0-312-09520-1). St Martin.

Breakfast with Washington. Duncan Thomas. 160p. 1978. 6.95 (ISBN 0-8059-2475-2). Dorrance.

Breakheart Pass. Alistair MacLean. 224p. 1978. pap. 2.25 (ISBN 0-449-24092-4, Crest). Fawcett.

Breaking & Riding. James Fillis. Tr. by M. H. Hayes. (Illus.). 15.75 (ISBN 0-85131-044-3, Dist. by Sporting Book Center). J A Allen.

Breaking & Schooling. H. Faudel-Phillips. pap. 6.85 (ISBN 0-85131-185-7, Dist. by Sporting Book Center). J A Allen.

Breaking Barriers: the Report of the Fifth Assembly of World Council of Churches, Nairobi, 1975. David Paton. 384p. 1976. pap. 4.95 o.p. (ISBN 0-8028-1639-8). Eerdmans.

Breaking Camp. Marge Piercy. LC 68-16007. (Wesleyan Poetry Program: Vol. 39). 1968. 10.00x (ISBN 0-8195-2039-X, Pub. by Wesleyan U Pr); pap. 4.95 (ISBN 0-8195-1039-4). Columbia U Pr.

Breaking Communication Barriers with Roleplay. Todd Pinkerton. LC 75-32944. 1976. pap. 4.95 (ISBN 0-8042-1097-7). John Knox.

Breaking Down Barriers. Association of Teachers of Management. Ed. by Bob Garratt & John Stopford. 333p. text ed. 41.00x (ISBN 0-566-02122-6, Pub. by Gower Pub Co England). Renouf.

Breaking In. Donald Honig. LC 73-9547. (Illus.). 48p. (gr. 3 up). 1974. PLB 5.90 o.p. (ISBN 0-531-02658-2). Watts.

Breaking in. Ed. by Lawrence T. Lorimer. LC 74-18743. (Illus.). 224p. (gr. 7 up). 1974. PLB 4.69 (ISBN 0-394-92653-6). Random.

Breaking in Book Two: Real Life Stories on the Career Trail. Michael Edelhart. LC 80-2047. 240p. 1981. pap. 6.95 (ISBN 0-385-15581-6, Anch). Doubleday.

Breaking into Print: How to Get Your Work Published. P. Gearing & E. Brunson. 1977. 11.95 (ISBN 0-13-081687-6, Spec); pap. 3.45 (ISBN 0-13-081679-5, Spec). P-H.

Breaking of Northwall. Paul O. Williams. 288p. 1981. pap. 2.25 (ISBN 0-345-29259-6, Del Rey). Ballantine.

Breaking Out of the Middle-Age Trap. Leslie A. Westoff. 1980. 11.95 (ISBN 0-453-00378-8, H378). NAL.

Breaking Point. LaVada Weir. LC 74-641. (Laurie Newman Adventures Ser). 32p. (gr. 3-9). 1974. 5.95 (ISBN 0-87191-337-2). Creative Ed.

Breaking the Age Barrier. Elaine Partnow. 288p. (Orig.). 1981. pap. 2.95 (ISBN 0-523-40845-5). Pinnacle Bks.

Breaking the Cycle of Child Abuse. Christine Herbruck. 1979. 8.95 o.p. (ISBN 0-03-052691-4); pap. 5.95 (ISBN 0-03-045691-6). Winston Pr.

Breaking the Language Barrier with Spanish. Janice L. Logan. 1977. pap. text ed. 8.95 (ISBN 0-89420-035-6, 176040); cassette recordings 237.60 (ISBN 0-89420-127-1, 176000). Natl Book.

Breaking the Reading Barrier. Doris W. Gilbert. 1959. text ed. 9.50 (ISBN 0-13-081471-7). P-H.

Breaking the Sex Role Barrier. Robert L. Loeb & Vidal S. Clay. (gr. 6 up). 1977. lib. bdg. 7.45 (ISBN 0-531-00120-2). Watts.

Breaking the Sound Barrier: A Critical Anthology of the New Music. Gregory Battcock. (Thomas Congdon Bk.). (Illus.). 1981. pap. 9.95 (ISBN 0-525-47640-7). Dutton.

Breaking the Stained-Glass Barrier. David Womack. LC 72-11366. 1973. 5.95 o.p. (ISBN 0-06-069680-X, HarpR). Har-Row.

Breaking the Word Barrier. Doris W. Gilbert. LC 77-173596. (Illus.). 240p. 1972. pap. text ed. 8.95 (ISBN 0-13-081661-2). P-H.

Breaking Through. Harry C. Cordellos. LC 78-23270. (Illus.). 240p. (Orig.). 1981. pap. 6.95 (ISBN 0-89037-168-7). Anderson World.

Breaking Through: Freeing Yourself from Fear, Helplessness & Depression - Before It's Too Late. Julian A. Miller. LC 78-3310. 1979. 9.95 o.s.i. (ISBN 0-690-01771-5, TYC-T). T Y Crowell.

Breaking Through: Photography & Poetry Celebrating the Many Shades of Earthly Joys. Richard H. Heinzen & Neil L. Clemons. (Illus.). 80p. (Orig.). 1980. pap. 10.95 (ISBN 0-686-28881-5, 880). Sunshine Arts WA.

Breaking Through to Each Other: Creative Persuasion on the Job & in the Home. Jesse S. Nirenberg. LC 74-1841. 192p. 1976. 9.95 o.s.i. (ISBN 0-06-013207-8, HarpT). Har-Row.

Breaking up. Wayne Judd. (Uplook Ser.). 1978. pap. 0.75 (ISBN 0-8163-0194-8, 12466). Pacific Pr Pub Assn.

Breaking up. Loring Mandel & Jane Seskin. (Orig.). 1977. pap. 1.95 o.s.i. (ISBN 0-515-04361-3). Jove Pubns.

Breaking Wave. Nevil Shute. LC 80-83020. (Great War Stories Ser.). 310p. 1980. Repr. of 1955 ed. 16.95 (ISBN 0-933852-16-9). Nautical & Aviation.

Breaking with Orthodoxy in Public Administration. Gilbert B. Siegel. LC 80-5081. 706p. 1980. text ed. 25.00 (ISBN 0-8191-1042-6). U Pr of Amer.

Breakout. Kathryn Anger. LC 79-55871. (Feminist Novels Ser.). 128p. (Orig.). 1980. pap. 4.95 (ISBN 0-935772-01-4). Diotima Bks.

Breakout: In Search of New Theatrical Environments. James Schevill. LC 77-189192. (Illus.). 411p. 1972. 15.00x (ISBN 0-8040-0574-5); pap. 4.95x o.s.i. (ISBN 0-8040-0640-7). Swallow.

Breakthrough. Daisy Aldan. 6.95 (ISBN 0-913152-02-1). Green Hill.

Breakthrough. Ken Grimwood. 1977. pap. 2.25 o.p. (ISBN 0-345-25470-8). Ballantine.

Breakthrough in Teacher Education. James C. Stone. LC 68-54945. (Higher Education Ser.). 1968. 11.95x o.p. (ISBN 0-87589-024-5). Jossey-Bass.

Breakthrough: Meister Eckhart's Creation Spirituality. Intro. By Matthew Fox. LC 80-909. 600p. 1980. 15.95 (ISBN 0-385-17045-9). Doubleday.

Breakthrough: Meister Eckhart's Creation Spirituality in New Translation. Intro. By Matthew Fox. LC 80-909. 600p. 1980. pap. 7.95 (ISBN 0-385-17034-3, Im). Doubleday.

Breakthrough! Questions for Youth About God. Jay Kesler & Tim Stafford. (Campus Life Bk.). 176p. (Orig.). 1981. pap. 4.95 (ISBN 0-310-43371-1). Zondervan.

Breakthrough Rapid Reading. Peter Kump. 256p. 1980. 5.95 (ISBN 0-13-081554-3, Reward). P-H.

Breakthrough to Fluency: English As a Second Language for Young Children. Edie M. Garvie. 1977. pap. 8.50x (ISBN 0-631-93970-9, Pub. by Basil Blackwell). Biblio Dist.

Breakthrough to Literacy, 45 bks. David Mackay et al. Incl. Animals; Birds; Birthday Party; Cat, the Bird & the Tree; Christmastime; Crocodiles Are Dangerous; Cup of Tea; Day We Went to the Beach; Doctors & Nurses; Dressing up; Fish Book; Getting Married; I Fell Down; In Bed; Loose Tooth; My Mom; My Story; My Teacher; Old Houses; Our Baby; People; People in Stories; Playhouse; Rainy Day; Shopping; Soccer Book; Students' Sentence Maker; Students' Word Maker; Things I Can Do; Weather; At School. (gr. k-3). 1973. 1 copy ea. of 45 titles 39.30 (ISBN 0-8372-2159-5); complete breakthrough to literary prog. 270.00 (ISBN 0-8372-0858-0). Bowmar-Noble.

Breakthrough: Women in Archaeology. Barbara Williams. LC 80-7687. (Breakthrough Ser.). (Illus.). 190p. (gr. 5 up). 1981. 9.95 (ISBN 0-8027-6406-1). Walker & Co.

Breakthrough: Women in Television. Betsy Smith. LC 80-54704. (Illus.). 192p. 1981. 9.95 (ISBN 0-8027-6420-7). Walker & Co.

Breakthroughs. Charles Panati. 1981. pap. 3.25 (ISBN 0-425-04925-6). Berkley Pub.

Breakthroughs: Action Techniques for Strategic Change. James R. Emshoff. (Illus.). 1980. 15.95 (ISBN 0-8144-5612-X). Am Mgmt.

Breakthroughs in Geography. William Warntz & Peter Wolff. 3.95 o.p. (ISBN 0-452-25040-4, Z5040, Plume). NAL.

Breakthroughs in Mathematics. Peter Wolff. 2.75 o.p. (ISBN 0-452-25010-2, Z5010, Plume). NAL.

Breast. Ed. by H. Stephen Gallager et al. LC 78-14811. (Illus.). 1978. text ed. 69.50 (ISBN 0-8016-1727-8). Mosby.

Breast Cancer - Experimental & Clinical Aspects: Proceedings of the Second E.O.R.T.C. (European Organization for Research on Treatment of Cancer) Breast Cancer Working Conference, Held in Copenhagen, May 30 to June 2, 1979. Ed. by H. T. Mouridsen & T. Palshof. LC 79-41496. (Illus.). 475p. 1980. 78.00 (ISBN 0-08-025886-7). Pergamon.

Breast Cancer: Trends in Research & Treatment. Ed. by John C. Heuson et al. LC 76-22910. (European Organization for Research on Treatment of Cancer Monograph: Vol. 2). 1976. 32.00 (ISBN 0-89004-096-6). Raven.

Breast Carcinoma: The Radiologist's Expanded Role. Wende W. Logan. LC 77-13047. 1977. 53.50 (ISBN 0-471-03023-6, Pub. by Wiley Medical). Wiley.

Breast Feeding: A Practical Guide for the Medical Profession. Ruth A. Lawrence. LC 79-17277. (Illus.). 1979. pap. text ed. 17.50 (ISBN 0-8016-2897-0). Mosby.

Breast-Feeding & Natural Child Spacing: The Ecology of Natural Mothering. Sheila Kippley. 1975. pap. 3.50 (ISBN 0-14-003992-9). Penguin.

Breast Reconstruction Following Mastectomy. Nicholas G. Georgiade. LC 79-15679. (Illus.). 1979. text ed. 44.50 (ISBN 0-8016-1807-X). Mosby.

Breast Self-Examination. Albert R. Milan. LC 79-56529. (Illus.). 128p. 1980. pap. 3.50 (ISBN 0-89480-124-4). Liberty Pub.

Breastfeeding Handbook: A Practical Reference for Physicians, Nurses & Other Health Professionals. Johanna Goldfarb & Edith Tibbetts. LC 72-29691. (Illus.). 256p. 1980. pap. text ed. 14.95x (ISBN 0-89490-030-7). Enslow Pubs.

Breastfeeding Together. Ingrid Mitchell. (Illus.). 1978. 7.95 (ISBN 0-8164-9351-0). Continuum.

Breath of Air & a Breath of Smoke. John S. Marr. LC 70-161362. (Illus.). 48p. (gr. 3 up). 1971. 4.95 (ISBN 0-87131-038-4). M Evans.

Breath of Life: A Simple Way to Pray. Ron Delbene & Herb Montgomery. 128p. (Orig.). 1981. pap. 3.95 (ISBN 0-03-059059-0). Winston Pr.

Breath of Spring. Dallas A. Sall. (Illus.). 72p. (Orig.). 1980. pap. 4.95 (ISBN 0-9604344-1-0). Sunrise Pub OR.

Breathe Deeply & Avoid Colds. Emanuel Josephson. (Natural Health Ser.). 127p. (Orig.). 1957. pap. 5.00 (Pub. by Chedney). Alpine Ent.

Breathing Exercises for Asthma. Karen R. Butts. (Illus.). 66p. 1980. pap. 11.75 spiral (ISBN 0-398-04104-0). C C Thomas.

Breathing Space. John Bruce. LC 74-76302. (Anansi Fiction Ser.: No. 31). 120p. 1974. 10.95 (ISBN 0-88784-432-4, Pub. by Hse Anansi Pr Canada); pap. 5.95 (ISBN 0-88784-330-1). U of Toronto Pr.

Breathing, Speech, & Song. D. F. Proctor. (Illus.). 180p. 1980. 19.80 (ISBN 0-387-81580-5). Springer-Verlag.

Brecht As Thinker: Studies in Literary Marxism & Existentialism. Ralph Ley. Ed. by David J. Parent. LC 79-14407. (Illinois Language & Culture Ser.: No. 6). 604p. 1979. 37.75 (ISBN 0-8357-0413-0, IS-00077, Pub. by Applied Lit Pr). Univ Microfilms.

Brecht Commentaries. Eric Bentley. LC 80-998. 320p. (Orig.). 1981. 17.50 (ISBN 0-394-51994-9, GP838, Ever); pap. text ed. 9.50 (ISBN 0-394-17734-7, E743, Ever). Grove.

Brecht, Gesammelte Prosa in Vier Baenden. Bertolt Brecht. (Edition Suhrkamp: 182 to 185). 1600p. (Ger.). 1980. pap. text ed. 15.60 (ISBN 3-518-09519-6, Pub. by Insel Verlag Germany). Suhrkamp.

Brecht in Perspective. Ed. by Graham Bartram & Anthony Waine. (German Literature & Society: Vol. 2). 1980. text ed. write for info. (ISBN 0-85496-076-7). Humanities.

Brecht: Mutter Courage und Ihre Kinder. Bertold Brecht. Ed. by Volkmar Sander. (Illus., Ger.). (gr. 9-12). 1964. pap. text ed. 4.95x (ISBN 0-19-500835-9). Oxford U Pr.

Brecht the Dramatist. R. Gray. LC 75-19575. 240p. 1976. 36.50 (ISBN 0-521-20937-4); pap. 10.50 (ISBN 0-521-29003-1). Cambridge U Pr.

Breckenridge Skier. C. R. Goeldner & Yvonne Sletta. 97p. 1975. 10.00 (ISBN 0-89478-021-2). U CO Busn Res Div.

Breed of Horses. Moyra Williams. LC 75-134731. 1971. text ed. 15.00 (ISBN 0-08-007123-6). Pergamon.

Breed Your Dog. Leon F. Whitney. (Orig.). 1962. pap. 2.00 (ISBN 0-87666-255-6, DS1021). TFH Pubns.

Breeder's Guide for 1979. Ed. by Blood-Horse-Thoroughbred Owners & Breeders Assn. (Bound Supplements of the Blood-Horse). 1980. 51.75 (ISBN 0-936032-01-4). Thoroughbred Own & Breed.

Breeder's Guide for 1980. Thoroughbred Owners & Breeders Association. 1981. 57.50 (ISBN 0-936032-41-3). Thoroughbred O.

Breeders Guide, 1978. 46.75 (ISBN 0-936032-00-6). Thoroughbred Own and Breed.

Breeding Aquarium Fishes, Bk.6. Herbert R. Axelrod. (Illus.). 288p. 1980. 12.95 (ISBN 0-87666-536-9, H-995). TFH Pubns.

Breeding Biology of Birds. 1973. 21.50 (ISBN 0-309-02109-X). Natl Acad Pr.

Breeding Biology of the Egyptian Plover, Pluvianus aegyptius. Thoams R. Howell. (U. C. Publications in Zoology Ser.: Vol. 113). 1980. pap. 11.50 (ISBN 0-520-09603-7). U of Cal Pr.

Breeding Biology of the Gray Gull, Larus Modestus. Thomas R. Howell et al. (Publications in Zoology: Vol. 104). 1975. pap. 6.50x (ISBN 0-520-09516-2). U of Cal Pr.

Breeding Cockatiels. Julie Sturman & Dorothy Schults. (Illus.). 93p. 1980. 2.95 (ISBN 0-87666-889-9, KW-099). TFH Pubns.

Breeding Cockatoos. Anne Nothaft. (Illus.). 96p. 1979. 2.95 (ISBN 0-87666-877-5, KW-059). TFH Pubns.

Breeding Endangered Species in Captivity. R. D. Martin. 1975. 57.50 (ISBN 0-12-474850-3). Acad Pr.

Breeding Field Crops. J. M. Poehlman. (Illus.). 1977. text ed. 19.50 o.p. (ISBN 0-87055-251-1). AVI.

Breeding Field Crops. 2nd ed. John M. Poehlman. (Illus.). 1979. text ed. 26.50 (ISBN 0-87055-328-3). AVI.

Breeding for Improved Herbage & Seed Yield in Setaria Sphacelata (Schumach) Stapf & Hubbard Ex Moss. (Agricultural Research Reports: No. 900). 146p. 1981. pap. 29.00 (ISBN 90-220-0738-3, PDC 213, Pudoc). Unipub.

Breeding for Seed Protein Improvement Using Nuclear Techniques. (Illus.). 229p. 1976. pap. 18.25 (ISBN 92-0-111475-3, IAEA). Unipub.

Breeding of Pest Resistant Trees. Ed. by H. D. Gerhold et al. 1966. 64.00 (ISBN 0-08-011764-3). Pergamon.

Breeding Plants for Home & Garden. 1.95 (ISBN 0-686-21167-7). Bklyn Botanic.

Breeding the Racehorse. Frederico Tesio. Ed. & tr. by Edward Spinola. (Illus.). 13.10 (ISBN 0-85131-028-1, Dist. by Sporting Book Center). J A Allen.

Breeding Variegata Oncidiums. W. W. Moir & May A. Moir. LC 80-15946. (Illus.). 136p. 1980. pap. text ed. 12.00x (ISBN 0-8248-0712-X). U Pr of Hawaii.

Breeding Zebra Finches. Mervin F. Roberts. (Illus.). 96p. 1980. 2.95 (ISBN 0-87666-883-X, KW-056). TFH Pubns.

Breefe Declaration of That Which Is Happened As Well Within As Without Oastend. LC 70-171781. (English Experience Ser.: No. 406). 8p. Repr. of 1602 ed. 11.50 (ISBN 90-221-0406-0). Walter J Johnson.

Breeze of the Spirit: Sam Shoemaker & the Story of Faith-at-Work. Irving Harris. (Illus.). 1978. 8.95 (ISBN 0-8164-0399-6). Crossroad NY.

Brefe Collection of the Lawes of the Forest. John Manwood. Ed. by David Berkowitz & Samuel Thorne. LC 77-86654. (Classics of English Legal History in the Modern Era Ser.: Vol. 100). 1979. Repr. of 1598 ed. lib. bdg. 55.00 (ISBN 0-8240-3087-7). Garland Pub.

Bremen Town Musicians. Brothers Grimm. LC 79-16944. (Illus.). 32p. (gr. k-3). 1980. 7.95 (ISBN 0-688-80233-8); PLB 7.63 (ISBN 0-688-84233-X). Greenwillow.

Bremen-Town Musicians. Retold by Ruth B. Gross. (Illus.). (gr. k-3). 1975. pap. 1.95 (ISBN 0-590-09894-2, Schol Pap); pap. 3.50 bk. & record (ISBN 0-590-20713-X). Schol Bk Serv.

Bremen Town Musicians. Ilse Plume. LC 79-6622. (Illus.). 32p. (ps-3). 1980. 8.95a (ISBN 0-385-15161-6); PLB (ISBN 0-385-15162-4). Doubleday.

Bremen Town Musicians: A Grimms' Fairytale. Adapted by & illus. by Donna Diamond. LC 80-36838. (Illus.). 32p. (gr. k-2). 1981. 8.95 (ISBN 0-440-00826-3); PLB 8.44 (ISBN 0-440-00827-1). Delacorte.

Brenda the Brat. Annie Ingle. (Illus.). (gr. 1-4). 1980. 3.95 (ISBN 0-525-69306-8, Gingerbread); PLB 5.95 (ISBN 0-525-69307-6). Dutton.

Brendan Behan. Ted E. Boyle. (English Authors Ser.: No. 91). lib. bdg. 10.95 (ISBN 0-8057-1036-1). Twayne.

Brendan Behan: An Annotated Bibliography of Criticism. E. H. Mikhail. 1980. text ed. 23.50x (ISBN 0-06-494826-9). B&N.

Brereton Diaries. Lewis Brereton. (Politics & Strategy of World War II Ser.). 1976. Repr. of 1946 ed. lib. bdg. 35.00 (ISBN 0-306-70766-7). Da Capo.

Brethren. Bob Woodward & Scott Armstrong. 1980. pap. 3.50 (ISBN 0-380-52183-0, 52183). Avon.

Brethren, Hang Together. Robert C. Girard. 1980. pap. 6.95 (ISBN 0-310-39071-0). Zondervan.

Brethren in Colonial America. Donald F. Durnbaugh. (Illus.). 659p. (YA) 1967. 13.95 (ISBN 0-87178-110-7). Brethren.

Brethren in the New Nation. Roger Sappington. (Illus.). 1976. 13.95 (ISBN 0-87178-113-1). Brethren.

Brett Weston: Photographs from Five Decades. (Monograph). (Illus.). 168p. 1980. 39.50 (ISBN 0-89381-068-1); after Dec. 31, 1981 50.00 (ISBN 0-686-65239-8); ltd. ed. 400 copies 400.00 (ISBN 0-686-65240-1). Aperture.

Breve Diccionario Etimologico De la Lengua Castellana. Corominas. 25.00x o.s.i. (ISBN 0-686-00845-6). Colton Bk.

Brevet's Illinois Historical Markers & Sites. Ed. by Lina S. Plucker & Kaye L. Roerick. LC 75-253. (Historical Markers-Sites Ser). (Illus.). 300p. (Orig.). 1976. 10.95 o.p. (ISBN 0-88498-028-6); text ed. 6.95 o.p. (ISBN 0-685-52607-0); pap. 6.95 (ISBN 0-88498-029-4); pap. text ed. 4.95 o.p. (ISBN 0-685-52608-9). Brevet Pr.

Brevet's Nebraska Historical Markers- Sites. Ed. by N. Jane Hunt. LC 74-79979. (Historical Markers-Sites Ser). (Illus.). 228p. (Orig.). 1974. 10.95 o.p. (ISBN 0-88498-020-0); text ed. 8.06 o.p. (ISBN 0-685-50458-1); pap. 6.95 (ISBN 0-88498-021-9); pap. text ed. 4.46 o.p. (ISBN 0-685-50459-X). Brevet Pr.

Brevet's North Dakota Historical Markers & Sites. Ed. by Kaye L. Roehrick. LC 74-79978. (Historical Markers-Sites Ser). (Illus.). 176p. 1975. 10.95 (ISBN 0-88498-024-3); text ed. 6.95 o.p. (ISBN 0-685-52609-7); pap. 6.95 (ISBN 0-88498-025-1); pap. text ed. 4.46 o.p. (ISBN 0-685-52610-0). Brevet Pr.

Brevet's South Dakota Historical Markers. Ed. by N. Jane Hunt. LC 73-86007. (Historical Markers-Sites Ser). (Illus.). 285p. 1974. 10.95 (ISBN 0-88498-013-8); pap. 6.95 (ISBN 0-88498-014-6); text ed. 4.45 o.p. (ISBN 0-685-46502-0); map 1.95 (ISBN 0-685-46503-9). Brevet Pr.

Brevet's Wisconsin Historical Markers & Sites. Ed. by N. Jane Hunt. LC 74-79980. (Historical Markers-Sites Ser). (Illus.). 254p. 1974. 10.95 (ISBN 0-88498-015-4); text ed. 8.05 o.p. (ISBN 0-685-46505-5); pap. 6.95 (ISBN 0-88498-016-2); pap. text ed. 4.45 o.p. (ISBN 0-685-46506-3). Brevet Pr.

Breviate of Parliamentary Papers 1900-1916. P. Ford & G. A. Ford. 520p. 1970. Repr. of 1957 ed. 36.00x (ISBN 0-7165-0575-4, Pub. by Irish Academic Pr Ireland). Biblio Dist.

Breviate of Parliamentary Papers 1917-1939. P. Ford & G. A. Ford. 624p. 1970. Repr. of 1951 ed. 36.00x (ISBN 0-7165-0576-2, Pub. by Irish Academic Pr Ireland). Biblio Dist.

Breweries & Malsters in Europe, 1980. 69th ed. LC 46-33153. Orig. Title: Brauereien und Malzereien in Europa 1980. 610p. (Orig., Eng, Fr. & Ger.). 1980. 92.50x (ISBN 3-8203-0034-1). Intl Pubns Serv.

Brewing in Developing Countries. James Keddie & William Cleghorn. 200p. 1980. pap. 11.50x (ISBN 0-7073-0250-1, Pub. by Scottish Academic Pr Scotland). Columbia U Pr.

Brewing Industry in England, Seventeen Hundred to Eighteen Thirty. Peter Mathias. 1959. 71.95 (ISBN 0-521-05691-8). Cambridge U Pr.

Brewing Theory & Practice. E. J. Jeffrey. 25.00x (ISBN 0-392-05817-0, LTB). Soccer.

Brewing: Twenty Milwaukee Poets. Ed. & frwd. by Martin J. Rosenblum. LC 72-89435. 6.95 (ISBN 0-89018-008-3); soft 6.00x (ISBN 0-89018-007-5). Pentagram.

Brewster's Millions. George B. McCutcheon. 1976. lib. bdg. 15.25x (ISBN 0-89968-058-5). Lightyear.

Brewster's Millions. George B. McCutcheon. Ed. by David A. Jasen. (Continuum Classic of Humor Ser.). 224p. 1980. 11.95 (ISBN 0-8264-0019-1). Continuum.

Brezhia. Terri Belmar. 128p. 1981. 7.00 (ISBN 0-682-49721-5). Exposition.

Brezhnev: Soviet Politician. Paul J. Murphy. LC 80-15901. (Illus.). 371p. 1981. lib. bdg. 24.95x (ISBN 0-89950-002-1). McFarland & Co.

Brhadaranyaka Upanisad. Tr. by P. Lal from Sanskirt. (Saffronbird Book). 117p. (Eng.). 1975. text ed. 15.00 (ISBN 0-88253-827-6); pap. text ed. 6.75 (ISBN 0-88253-828-4). Ind-US Inc.

Brian Rust's Guide to Discography. Brian Rust. LC 79-6827. (Discographies: No. 4). (Illus.). x, 133p. 1980. lib. bdg. 19.95 (ISBN 0-313-22086-7, RGD/). Greenwood.

Brian Wildsmith's ABC. Brian Wildsmith. (Illus.). (gr. k-3). 1963. PLB 5.95 (ISBN 0-531-01525-4). Watts.

Brian Wildsmith's Fishes. Brian Wildsmith. LC 68-12046. (Illus.). (gr. k-3). 1968. PLB 5.95 o.p. (ISBN 0-531-01528-9). Watts.

Briar Rose & the Golden Eggs. Diane R. Massie. LC 73-1249. (Illus.). 48p. (gr. k-3). 1973. 5.95 o.s.i. (ISBN 0-8193-0684-3, Four Winds). Schol Bk Serv.

Briarwood Summer. Kay Richardson. 192p. (YA) 1976. 4.95 o.p. (ISBN 0-685-67080-5, Avalon). Bouregy.

Brick Book. Robert Hayward. LC 77-22. (Illus.). 1977. 12.95 o.s.i. (ISBN 0-690-01448-1, TYC-T). T Y Crowell.

Bricker's International Directory of University Executive Development Programs: 1981. 12th ed. Ed. by Samuel A. Pond & George W. Bricker. LC 73-110249. 1980. 85.00 (ISBN 0-9604804-0-4). Bricker's Intl.

Bricker's International Directory of University-Sponsored Executive Development Programs: 1979. George W. Bricker. LC 73-110249. 1978. 65.00 o.p. (ISBN 0-916404-04-8). Bricker's Intl.

Bricker's International Directory of University Sponsored Executive Development Programs: 1980. 11th ed. George W. Bricker & Samuel A. Pond. LC 73-110249. 1979. 75.00x o.p. (ISBN 0-916404-05-6). Bricker's Intl.

Bricker's International Directory: University Executive Development Programs. 12th ed. Ed. by Samuel A. Pond & George W. Bricker. LC 73-110249. 600p. 1980. 85.00x (ISBN 0-9604804-0-4). S A Pond.

Brickfield & Betrayal. Leslie P. Hartley. 15.00 (ISBN 0-241-02383-1). Dufour.

Bricklaying Simplified. Donald R. Brann. LC 77-140968. 1979. pap. 5.95 (ISBN 0-87733-668-7). Easi-Bild.

Bricks: Their Properties & Use. Brick Development Association. 1974. pap. text ed. 25.00x (ISBN 0-904406-04-0). Longman.

Bricks: To Build a House with. John Woodforde. (Illus.). 240p. 1975. 15.00 (ISBN 0-7100-8105-7). Routledge & Kegan.

Brickwork for Apprentices. 3rd ed. J. C. Hodge. (Illus.). 1971. pap. 13.95x (ISBN 0-7131-3250-7). Intl Ideas.

Brickworker's Bible. Charles R. Self. (Illus.). 378p. (Orig.). 1980. 15.95 (ISBN 0-8306-9942-2, 1204); pap. 8.95 (ISBN 0-8306-1204-1). Tab Bks.

Bridal Trap. Rena McKay. 192p. (Orig.). 1980. pap. 1.50 (ISBN 0-671-57036-6). S&S.

Bride & Bear. Margaret Savides. 1980. pap. 2.00. Quixote.

Bride & the Bachelors. Calvin Tomkins. (Illus.). 1976. pap. 4.95 (ISBN 0-14-004313-6). Penguin.

Bride at Eighteen. Hila Colman. (gr. 7 up). 1966. PLB 6.96 (ISBN 0-688-31122-9). Morrow.

Bride-Bush, or a Wedding Sermon. William Whately. LC 74-28893. (English Experience Ser.: No. 769). 1975. Repr. of 1617 ed. 5.00 (ISBN 90-221-0769-8). Walter J Johnson.

Bride for the Sahib & Other Stories. Khushwant Singh. 168p. 1967. pap. 2.00 (ISBN 0-88253-087-9). Ind-US Inc.

Bride Goes West. Nannie T. Alderson & Helena H. Smith. 5.00 o.p. (ISBN 0-8446-0452-6). Peter Smith.

Bride of a Stranger. Patricia Maxwell. 1978. pap. 1.50 o.p. (ISBN 0-449-13818-6, GM). Fawcett.

Bride of Dreams. 2nd ed. Frederik Van Eeden. LC 79-89934. 1980. cancelled (ISBN 0-89793-011-8). Hunter Hse.

Bride of Frankenstein. (Orig.). 1977. pap. 1.25 o.p. (ISBN 0-425-03414-3, Medallion). Berkley Pub.

Bride of Fu Manchu. Sax Rohmer. 1976. Repr. of 1933 ed. lib. bdg. 9.70 (ISBN 0-89190-801-3). Am Repr-Rivercity Pr.

Bride of Lammermoor. Walter Scott. 1955. 6.00x (ISBN 0-460-00129-9, Evman); pap. 3.50 (ISBN 0-460-01129-4, Evman). Dutton.

Bride of Lowther Fell. Margaret Forster. LC 80-69370. 1981. 11.95 (ISBN 0-689-11129-0). Atheneum.

Bride of Moat House. Norah Lofts. 208p. 1976. pap. 1.50 o.p. (ISBN 0-449-22527-5, Crest). Fawcett.

Bride of Pendorric. Victoria Holt. LC 63-12964. 10.95 (ISBN 0-385-01523-2). Doubleday.

Bride of Pendorric. Victoria Holt. 1978. pap. 1.95 (ISBN 0-449-23280-8, Crest). Fawcett.

Bride of Pendorric. Victoria Holt. 272p. 1981. pap. 2.50 (ISBN 0-449-23280-8, Crest). Fawcett.

Bride of the Innisfallen & Other Stories. Eudora Welty. LC 55-5248. 1972. pap. 3.95 (ISBN 0-15-614075-6, HB227, Harv). HarBraceJ.

Bride of the Machugh. Jan C. Speas. 1977. pap. 1.95 (ISBN 0-380-01825-X, 36152). Avon.

Bride of the Revolution: Krupskaya & Lenin. Robert H. McNeal. (Illus.). 320p. 1972. 10.00 o.p. (ISBN 0-472-61600-5). U of Mich Pr.

Bride of the Sun. Elizabeth Hunter. 192p. (Orig.). 1980. pap. 1.50 (ISBN 0-671-57051-X). S&S.

Bride of Vengeance. Rose Marie Abbot. (Candlelight Romance Ser.). (Orig.). 1981. pap. 1.50 (ISBN 0-440-10819-5). Dell.

Brides from Bridewell: Female Felons Sent to Colonial America. Walter H. Blumenthal. LC 73-7307. (Illus.). 139p. 1973. Repr. of 1962 ed. lib. bdg. 15.00x (ISBN 0-8371-6924-0, BLBB). Greenwood.

Bridewealth & Dowry. J. R. Goody & S. J. Tambiah. LC 72-95407. (Papers in Social Anthropology Ser.: No. 7). (Illus.). 128p. 1973. 19.95 (ISBN 0-521-20169-1); pap. 7.95x (ISBN 0-521-09805-X). Cambridge U Pr.

Bridge Across Jordan. A. P. Bounton. 6.95 o.p. (ISBN 0-8062-1202-0). Carlton.

Bridge Analysis. Boris Schapiro. LC 76-1167. (Illus.). 192p. (YA) 1976. 6.95 o.p. (ISBN 0-8069-4928-7); PLB 6.69 o.p. (ISBN 0-8069-4929-5). Sterling.

Bridge at the Top. Terence Reese. 1977. 14.95 (ISBN 0-571-11123-8, Pub. by Faber & Faber). Merrimack Bk Serv.

Bridge Between Matter & Spirit Is Matter Becoming Spirit. Paolo Soleri. LC 72-87501. 280p. 1973. pap. 2.95 (ISBN 0-385-02361-8, Anch). Doubleday.

Bridge Between the Testaments: Reappraisal of Judaism from the Exile to the Birth of Christianity. 2nd ed. Donald E. Gowan. LC 76-49996. (Pittsburgh Theological Monographs: No. 14). 1980. text ed. 12.95 (ISBN 0-915138-47-6). Pickwick.

Bridge Bidding: Lessons & Quizzes on Goren's Point Count Method. John Mallon. 1963. pap. 2.95 (ISBN 0-02-029200-7, Collier). Macmillan.

Bridge: Bidding Naturally. Amsbury. 1979. 17.95 (ISBN 0-7134-1619-X, Pub. by Batsford England). David & Charles.

Bridge: From Average to Expert. Seabrook. 1979. 17.95 (ISBN 0-7134-1623-8, Pub. by Batsford England). David & Charles.

Bridge: Improve Your Defence. Sowter. 1979. 17.95 (ISBN 0-7134-1621-1, Pub. by Batsford England). David & Charles.

Bridge in the Fourth Dimension. Victor Mollo. 1974. 11.95 (ISBN 0-571-10634-X, Pub. by Faber & Faber). Merrimack Bk Serv.

Bridge in the Fourth Dimension: Further Adventures of the Hideous Hog. Victor Mollo. 192p. 1981. pap. 6.95 (ISBN 0-571-11675-2, Pub. by Faber & Faber). Merrimack Bd Serv.

Bridge Inspection & Structural Analysis: Handbook of Bridge Inspection. Sung H. Park. LC 80-81421. (Illus.). 312p. (Orig.). 1980. pap. text ed. 15.00 (ISBN 0-9604440-0-9). S H Park.

Bridge Magic. Hugh Darwen. (Illus.). 1973. 13.50 (ISBN 0-686-24597-0, Pub. by Faber & Faber). Merrimack Bk Serv.

Bridge Maintenance: Inspection & Evaluation. White et al. 272p. 1981. 32.75 (ISBN 0-8247-1086-X). Dekker.

Bridge Match. J. W. Tait. 1976. 12.95 (ISBN 0-571-10949-7, Pub. by Faber & Faber). Merrimack Bk Serv.

Bridge of Catzad-Dum & Other Stories. Mark E. Rogers. (Illus.). 62p. (Orig.). 1980. pap. 6.00 ltd. digest-sized (ISBN 0-937528-00-5). Burning Bush.

Bridge of Friendship. Mabel E. Allan. LC 76-53432. (gr. 5 up). 1977. 5.95 (ISBN 0-396-07431-6). Dodd.

Bridge of Love. Leslie Caine. 192p. (Orig.). 1980. pap. 1.50 (ISBN 0-671-57010-2). S&S.

Bridge of Movie Producer Louis King. Jacques Carrie. LC 80-67977. 204p. (Orig.). 1981. pap. 6.95 (ISBN 0-937578-00-2). Fablewaves.

Bridge on Ice. Szymon Szechter. Tr. by Frances Carroll & Nina Karsov. 1978. 8.95 (ISBN 0-7145-2596-0, Pub. by M Boyars). Merrimack Bk Serv.

Bridge Over the River Kwai. Pierre Boulle. LC 54-11508. 8.95 (ISBN 0-8149-0072-0). Vanguard.

Bridge Play for Beginners. Alfred Sheinwold. (Orig.). 1970. 4.95 o.p. (ISBN 0-571-09528-3, Pub. by Faber & Faber). Merrimack Bk Serv.

Bridge Player's Alphabetical Handbook. Terence Reese & Albert Dormer. 224p. 1981. 19.95 (ISBN 0-571-11599-3, Pub. by Faber & Faber). Merrimack Bk Serv.

Bridge Table Tales. Rixi Markus. LC 80-67582. (Illus.). 64p. 1980. 11.95 (ISBN 0-7153-7947-X). David & Charles.

Bridge to Independence: The Kent Family Placement Project. Nancy Hazel. (Practice of Social Work Ser.). 208p. 1981. 25.00x (ISBN 0-631-12943-X, Pub. by Basil Blackwell England); pap. 12.50x (ISBN 0-631-12596-5). Biblio Dist.

Bridge to Terabithia. Katherine Paterson. (gr. 10 up). 1979. pap. 1.75 (ISBN 0-380-43281-1, 52365, Camelot). Avon.

Bridgeport Bus. 1980. pap. 4.50 (ISBN 0-14-005566-5). Penguin.

Bridgeport: First Hundred Years, 1873-1973. D. C. Sipes. 8.95 (ISBN 0-685-48791-1). Nortex Pr.

Bridges. Scott Corbett. LC 77-13871. (Illus.). 128p. (gr. 3-7). 1978. 10.95 (ISBN 0-590-07464-4, Four Winds). Schol Bk Serv.

Bridges. Anne MacGregor & Scott MacGregor. LC 80-23305. (Illus.). 56p. (gr. 4 up). 1981. PLB 9.55 (ISBN 0-688-51997-0); pap. 5.95 (ISBN 0-688-41997-6). Morrow.

Bridges Across the South: Technical Cooperation Among Developing Countries. B. P. Menon. (Pergamon Policy Studies). 1980. 21.00 (ISBN 0-08-024645-1); pap. 6.95 (ISBN 0-08-024646-X). Pergamon.

Bridges Between Clouds. Nonna Osipova. (Illus.). 61p. (Rus.). 1980. pap. 3.00 (ISBN 0-935500-03-0, TXU 9-644). Am Samizdat.

Bridges Between Clouds. Nonna Osipova. (Illus.). 100p. (Orig.). 1981. pap. 4.00 (ISBN 0-935500-07-3). Am Samizdat.

Bridges Not Walls. 2nd ed. John Stewart. LC 76-46606. (Speech Communication Ser.). 1977. pap. 8.95 (ISBN 0-201-07227-0). A-W.

Bridges of God. Donald A. McGavran. (Orig.). 1980. pap. 5.95 o.p. (ISBN 0-377-45071-5). Friend Pr.

Bridges of the Bodymind. Jeanne Achterberg & Frank Lawlis. LC 80-16596. (Illus.). 1980. text ed. 19.50 (ISBN 0-918296-14-5). Inst Personality & Ability.

Bridges to English, Bk. 1. Protase E. Woodford & Doris Kernan. Ed. by J. Rebisz. LC 80-21012. (Illus.). 144p. 1980. pap. text ed. 5.64 (ISBN 0-07-034481-7, W); write for info. tchrs. ed. (ISBN 0-07-034482-5); wkbk. 3.52 (ISBN 0-07-034483-3); cassettes avail. (ISBN 0-07-034484-1); cue cards avail. (ISBN 0-07-034485-X); tests avail. (ISBN 0-07-034486-8). McGraw.

Bridges to Understanding: International Programs of American Colleges & Universities. Carnegie Commission On Higher Education. 1970. 9.95 o.p. (ISBN 0-07-010016-0, P&RB). McGraw.

Bridges to Work: International Comparisons of Transitional Services. Beatrice G. Reubens. LC 76-28562. (Conservation of Human Resources Ser.: No. 3). 288p. 1977. text ed. 18.00 (ISBN 0-916672-05-0). Allanheld.

Bridging the Gap: College Reading. Brenda Smith. 1981. pap. text ed. 6.95x (ISBN 0-673-15364-9). Scott F.

Bridgman's Complete Guide to Drawing from Life. George B. Bridgman. (Illus.). 1970. 20.00 o.p. (ISBN 0-8069-5000-5); lib. bdg. 17.59 o.p. (ISBN 0-8069-5001-3). Sterling.

Bridled with Rainbows. Sara Brewton & John E. Brewton. (Illus.). (gr. 4-6). 1949. 4.95g o.s.i. (ISBN 0-02-712680-3). Macmillan.

Bridlewise & Otherwise. Rusty Bradley. 4.95 o.p. (ISBN 0-685-48789-X). Nortex Pr.

Brief American Lives: Four Studies in Collective Biography. Donald C. Yelton. LC 77-29102. 1978. 12.00 (ISBN 0-8108-1114-6). Scarecrow.

Brief & Extended Casework. William J. Reid & Ann W. Shyne. LC 70-79192. 1969. 13.00x (ISBN 0-231-03219-6). Columbia U Pr.

Brief Bibliography for Young Atheists. pap. 0.50 o.p. (ISBN 0-87784-135-7). Inter-Varsity.

Brief Casework with a Marital Problem. Lorna Guthrie & Janet Mattinson. 64p. 1971. 5.00x (ISBN 0-901882-03-8, CBO-901-I). Natl Assn Soc Wkrs.

Brief Chronicles, 3 pts. in 1. William Winter. LC 72-130085. (Dunlap Society Ser.: Nos. 7, 8, 10). 1971. Repr. of 1889 ed. 33.50 (ISBN 0-8337-3826-7). B Franklin.

Brief History of Chinese Fiction. Lu Hsun. 8.95 (ISBN 0-8351-0510-5). China Bks.

Brief History of Engineering. G. Martin Guest. (Illus.). 1974. pap. text ed. 11.00x (ISBN 0-245-52337-5). Intl Ideas.

Brief History of Norway. 7th ed. John Midgaard. LC 67-7814. (Norwegian Guides Ser). (Illus., Orig.). 1979. pap. 9.50x (ISBN 82-518-0053-6). Intl Pubns Serv.

Brief History of Physical Education. 5th ed. Emmett A. Rice et al. (Illus.). 1969. 17.95 (ISBN 0-8260-7430-8). Wiley.

Brief History of Russia to 1689. Alexander C. Niven. LC 78-54603. 1978. pap. text ed. 6.75x (ISBN 0-8191-0511-2). U Pr of Amer.

Brief History of the United States Since 1945. Robert D. Marcus. LC 74-24978. 224p. (Orig.). 1975. 15.95x (ISBN 0-312-09555-4); pap. text ed. 8.95 (ISBN 0-312-09590-2). St Martin.

Brief History of the Western World. Thomas Katsaros & George J. Schiro. LC 78-62178. 1978. pap. text ed. 13.25 (ISBN 0-8191-0466-3). U Pr of Amer.

Brief History of the World. George W. Botsford. (Illus.). 518p 1980. Repr. of 1917 ed. lib. bdg. 35.00 (ISBN 0-8492-3591-X). R West.

Brief Infinity: A Love Story in Haiku. Jayne M. Murdock. Ed. by Dick Murdock. LC 80-83998. (Illus.). 64p. (Orig.). 1981. pap. 6.00 (ISBN 0-932916-06-6). May Murdock.

Brief Memoir of Christina G. Rossetti. Ellen A. Proctor. 84p. 1980. Repr. of 1895 ed. lib. bdg. 10.00 (ISBN 0-8495-4391-6). Arden Lib.

Brief Numerical Methods. Wendell E. Grove. 1966. text ed. 17.95x (ISBN 0-13-082917-X). P-H.

Brief Outline on the Study of Theology. Friedrich Schleiermacher. Tr. by Terrence N. Tice. LC 66-10301. (Orig.). 1966. pap. 3.95 (ISBN 0-8042-0485-3). John Knox.

Brief Reviews from Circulation Research, 1978. Brian F. Hoffman. (AHA Monograph: No. 62). pap. 6.00 (ISBN 0-686-59599-8, 73-048-A). Am Heart.

Brief Reviews from Circulation Research, 1978. Brian F. Hoffman. (AHA Monograph: No. 64). pap. 6.00 (ISBN 0-686-59600-5, 73-049A). Am Heart.

Brief Sketch of the History of Political Parties in Japan. Arthur H. Lay. Bd. with Political Ideas of Modern Japan: An Interpretation Studies in Japanese Law & Government. Kiyoshi K. Kowakami. 461p. 1979. Repr. of 1902 ed. 22.00 (ISBN 0-89093-222-0). U Pubns Amer.

Brief Textbook of Surgery. Curtis P. Artz et al. LC 75-19839. (Illus.). 1976. text ed. 19.95 o.p. (ISBN 0-7216-1415-9). Saunders.

Brief Treatise of Testaments & Last Wills. Henry Swinburne. Ed. by David S. Berkowitz & Samuel E. Thorne. LC 77-89255. (Classics of English Legal History in the Modern Era Ser.: Vol. 80). 342p. 1979. lib. bdg. 40.00 (ISBN 0-8240-3179-2). Garland Pub.

Brief View of the Constitution of the United States. Peter S. Du Ponceau. LC 72-124893. (American Constitutional & Legal History Ser.). 1974. Repr. of 1834 ed. lib. bdg. 14.95 (ISBN 0-306-71986-X). Da Capo.

Brief Writing & Oral Argument. 4th rev. ed. Edward D. Re. LC 73-11059. 1977. 15.00 (ISBN 0-913338-22-2). Trans-Media Pub.

Briefe Conference of Divers Laws: Divided into Certain Regiments. Lloyd Lodowick. Ed. by David Berkowitz & Samuel Thorne. LC 77-86562. (Classics of English Legal History in the Modern Era Ser.: Vol. 64). 1979. Repr. of 1602 ed. lib. bdg. 55.00 (ISBN 0-8240-3051-6). Garland Pub.

Briefe Declaration for What Manner of Speciall Nusance Man May Have His Remedy by Assise. LC 76-38169. (English Experience Ser.: No. 446). 1972. Repr. of 1636 ed. 7.00 (ISBN 90-221-0446-X). Walter J Johnson.

Briefe Description of Hierusalem, Also a Mappe. Christianus van Adrichem. Tr. by T. Tymme. LC 70-29008. (English Experience Ser.: No. 125). 1969. Repr. of 1595 ed. 21.00 (ISBN 90-221-0125-8). Walter J Johnson.

Briefe Description of the Whole Worlde. George Abbot. LC 78-25701. (English Experience Ser.: No. 213). 68p. Repr. of 1599 ed. 9.50 (ISBN 90-221-0213-0). Walter J Johnson.

Briefe Discovery of the Idle Animadversions of Mark Ridley, Doctor of Phisicke. William Barlow. LC 71-38149. (English Experience Ser.: No. 429). 16p. 1972. Repr. of 1618 ed. 7.00 (ISBN 90-221-0429-X). Walter J Johnson.

Briefe Relation of the Discovery & Plantation of New England. LC 74-28876. (English Experience Ser.: No. 754). 1975. Repr. of 1622 ed. 3.50 (ISBN 90-221-0754-X). Walter J Johnson.

Briefe Relation of the Persecution Lately Made Against the Catholike Christians in Japonia. Taken Out of the Annuall Letters of the Soc. of Jesus. Tr. by William Wright. LC 75-26238. (English Experience Ser.: No. 159). 1969. Repr. of 1619 ed. 35.00 (ISBN 90-221-0159-2). Walter J Johnson.

Briefe Treatise of Testaments & Last Wils, Newly Corrected & Augmented. Henry Swinburne. LC 79-84140. (English Experience Ser.: No. 957). 620p. 1979. Repr. of 1635 ed. lib. bdg. 58.00 (ISBN 90-221-0957-7). Walter J Johnson.

Briefs of the American Revolution. Ed. by John P. Reid. (NYU School of Law Ser. in Anglo-American Legal History). 176p. 1981. text ed. 22.50x (ISBN 0-8147-7384-2). NYU Pr.

Briefwechsel Zwischen Carl Friedrich Gauss und W. Bolyai. Karl Gauss. 1971. Repr. of 1899 ed. 18.50 (ISBN 0-384-17765-4); 12.00 (ISBN 0-686-66286-5). Johnson Repr.

Brigade. John Shirley. 256p. 1981. pap. 2.25 (ISBN 0-380-77156-X, 77156). Avon.

Brigadier Gerard. Arthur C. Doyle. 192p. (Orig.). 1981. pap. 1.95 (ISBN 0-515-05530-1). Jove Pubns.

Brigance's Speech Communication. 3rd ed. Ed. by J. Jeffery Auer. Orig. Title: Speech Communication. 1967. pap. 11.95 (ISBN 0-13-082933-1). P-H.

Brigham Young. Harrison et al. (Illus.). 35p. (gr. 1-9). 1981. 2.95 (ISBN 0-86575-188-9). Dormac.

Brigham Young: The New York Years. (Charles Redd Monographs in Western History: No. 12). (Illus.). 1981. pap. text ed. 6.95 (ISBN 0-8425-1942-4). Brigham.

Bright & Morning Star. Rosemary Harris. LC 73-171566. 264p. (gr. 7 up). 1972. 4.95 o.s.i. (ISBN 0-02-742660-2). Macmillan.

Bright & Shining Breadboard. Rosalys Hall. LC 69-14329. (Illus.). (gr. k-3). 1969. 8.25 (ISBN 0-688-41121-5); PLB 7.92 o.p. (ISBN 0-688-51121-X). Lothrop.

Bright April. Marguerite De Angeli. (gr. 2-5). 1946. 5.95 o.p. (ISBN 0-385-07238-4). Doubleday.

Bright Blue Death. (Nick Carter Ser.). 1979. pap. cancelled (ISBN 0-441-08015-4). Charter Bks.

Bright Blue Plymouth Station Wagon. Robert Moore. 192p. 1972. pap. text ed. 5.95x (ISBN 0-87835-034-9). Boyd & Fraser.

Bright Book of Life: American Novelists & Storytellers from Hemingway to Mailer. Alfred Kazin. LC 80-24576. 334p. 1980. pap. text ed. 6.95 (ISBN 0-268-00664-4). U of Notre Dame Pr.

Bright Constellation: Documents of American Democracy. rev. ed. Henry W. Bragdon & Thomas H. Eliot. (Illus.). 277p. (gr. 10-12). 1980. pap. text ed. 4.95x (ISBN 0-88334-129-8). Ind Sch Pr.

Bright Days. Madye L. Chastain. LC 52-10063. (Illus.). (gr. 4-7). 4.50 o.p. (ISBN 0-15-212135-8, HJ). HarBraceJ.

Bright Delinquents: The Story of a Unique School. Robert Brooks. (General Ser.). 184p. (Orig.). 1972. pap. text ed. 11.50x (ISBN 0-901225-97-5, NFER). Humanities.

Bright Eyes: The Life of a Baby Jack Rabbit. John Unruh. LC 80-18667. (Illus.). 112p. (Orig.). (gr. 4 up). 1980. pap. 4.95 (ISBN 0-914598-02-3). Padre Prods.

Bright Lightu. John Wilson. 6.95 o.p. (ISBN 0-8062-1232-2). Carlton.

Bright Moments: Jazzpoems & Poetry About Jazz. Jim Stephens & Warren Woessner. 1980. pap. 4.00 (ISBN 0-932868-03-7). Abraxas.

Bright Orange for the Shroud. John D. Macdonald. LC 72-396. 1972. 7.95 o.s.i. (ISBN 0-397-00793-0). Lippincott.

Bright Orange for the Shroud. John D. MacDonald. (Travis McGee Ser.). 1978. pap. 2.25 (ISBN 0-449-14243-4, GM). Fawcett.

Bright Side of Death. Austin Crouch. (Illus.). 1951. pap. 1.25 o.p. (ISBN 0-8054-9201-1). Broadman.

Bright Star Falls. Lenora M. Weber. LC 59-11398. (gr. 5 up). 1959. 10.95 (ISBN 0-690-16005-4, TYC-J). T Y Crowell.

Bright Star of Exile: Jacob Adler & the Yiddish Theater. Lulla Rosenfeld. 1977. 12.95 o.p. (ISBN 0-690-01446-5, TYC-T). T Y Crowell.

Bright Underachievers. Jane B. Raph et al. LC 66-25459. 1966. text ed. 11.50x (ISBN 0-8077-2021-6). Tchrs Coll.

Bright Waters, Bright Fish. Roderick Haig-Brown. (Illus.). 160p. 1980. 19.95 (ISBN 0-917304-59-4, Timber Pr). Intl Schol Bk.

Bright Waters, Bright Fish. Roderick Haig-Brown. 1980. ltd. ed. 75.00 (ISBN 0-918400-05-8, Champoeg Pr). Intl Schol Bk.

Bright Wind of the Spirit. Steve Durasoff. LC 72-6536. 1976. pap. 2.95 o.p. (ISBN 0-88270-168-1). Logos.

Brighten the Corner. Monroe City County Fine Arts Council. Ed. by Elsie Little & Catherine Gibson. (Illus.). 188p. 1977. pap. 7.00x (ISBN 0-686-28490-9). Monroe County Lib.

Brightening Shadow. John Gay. LC 80-81852. (Illus., Orig.). (gr. 10-12). 1980. pap. text ed. write for info. (ISBN 0-933662-09-2). Intercult Pr.

Brighter Sun. Samuel Selvon. 215p. 1979. 9.00 (ISBN 0-89410-111-0); pap. 5.00 (ISBN 0-89410-110-2). Three Continents.

Brightest Stars. Ed. by C. De Jager. (Geophysics & Astrophysics Monographs: No. 19). 472p. 1981. PLB 73.50 (ISBN 90-277-1109-7, Pub. by D. Reidel); pap. 1.50 (ISBN 90-277-1109-7). Kluwer Boston.

Brighteyes. Donna K. Johnson. LC 78-4353. (Illus.). (gr. 1 up). 1978. 5.95 o.p. (ISBN 0-03-044651-1). HR&W.

Brighton Rock. Graham Greene. LC 38-15724. 316p. 1981. 14.95 (ISBN 0-670-19153-1). Viking Pr.

Brigitte Bardot: Woman from 30 to 40. Francoise Sagan. Tr. by Judith Sachs from Fr. 1977. pap. 6.95 o.s.i. (ISBN 0-440-00609-0, E Friede). Delacorte.

Brilliant Kids. Herbert Lieberman. 384p. 1975. 8.95 o.s.i. (ISBN 0-02-571810-X). Macmillan.

Brilliant Stars: The Baha'i Faith & the Education of Children. H. T. Rost. 1979. 8.95 (ISBN 0-85398-082-9, 7-32-45, Pub. by G Ronald England); pap. 3.95 (ISBN 0-85398-083-7, 7-32-46, Pub. by G Ronald England). Baha'i.

Brillstone Break-in. Florence P. Heide & Roxanne Heide. Ed. by Caroline Rubin. LC 77-2220. (Pilot Bks). (Illus.). (gr. 4-8). 1977. 6.95g (ISBN 0-8075-0888-8). A Whitman.

Bring a Bigger Basket. C. L. Paddock. (Uplook Ser.). 32p. 1962. pap. 0.75 (ISBN 0-8163-0066-6, 02605-4). Pacific Pr Pub Assn.

Bring Back Romance. Natalie Willner. 1979. pap. 1.95 o.p. (ISBN 0-425-04023-2). Berkley Pub.

Bring Down the Sun. Betty Lambert. 300p. 1980. 10.95 (ISBN 0-670-24857-6). Viking Pr.

Bring Forth Justice. Waldron Scott. LC 80-15992. 304p. 1980. pap. 11.95 (ISBN 0-8028-1848-X). Eerdmans.

Bring Forth the Body. Simon Raven. LC 75-31244. 1974. 12.50x (ISBN 0-85634-017-0). Intl Pubns Serv.

Bring Home the Ghost. K. Follis Cheatham. LC 80-7981. 325p. (gr. 7 up). 1980. 8.95 (ISBN 0-15-212485-3, HJ). HarBraceJ.

Bring Me a Unicorn: Diaries & Letters of Anne Morrow Lindbergh, 1922-1928. Anne M. Lindbergh. LC 71-182329. (Helen & Kurt Wolff Bk). 288p. 1972. 7.95 o.p. (ISBN 0-15-114180-0). HarBraceJ.

Bring Me All of Your Dreams. Ed. by Nancy Larrick. LC 79-26892. (Illus.). 128p. (gr. 5 up). 1980. 7.95 (ISBN 0-87131-313-8). M Evans.

Bring Me Men & Women: Mandated Changes at the U. S. Air Force Academy. Judith H. Stiehm. 1981. 19.95 (ISBN 0-520-04045-7). U of Cal Pr.

Bring Out Your Own Book. Barbara McFadyen & Marilyn G. Hoff. LC 80-67280. (Illus.). 96p. 1980. pap. 6.00 (ISBN 0-938018-00-0). Godiva Pub.

Bring the Book. G. W. Lane. 158p. 1968. 2.95 (ISBN 0-87148-104-9); pap. 2.25 (ISBN 0-87148-105-7). Pathway Pr.

Bringing Down the House. Richard P. Brickner. 1977. pap. 1.75 (ISBN 0-505-51139-8). Tower Bks.

Bringing Learning Home: How Parents Can Play a More Active & Effective Role in Their Children's Education. Mary S. Miller. LC 80-7856. 256p. 1981. 9.95 (ISBN 0-690-01952-1). Har-Row.

Bringing Opera to Life: Operatic Acting & Stage Direction. B. Goldovsky. 1968. 19.95 (ISBN 0-13-083105-0). P-H.

Bringing the Rain to Kapiti Plain. Verna Aardema. LC 80-25886. (Illus.). 32p. (ps). 1981. 9.95 (ISBN 0-8037-0809-2); PLB 9.43 (ISBN 0-8037-0807-6). Dial.

Bringing up Children in the Christian Faith. John H. Westerhoff, 3rd. 108p. (Orig.). 1980. pap. 4.95 (ISBN 0-03-056203-1). Winston Pr.

Brink. Rick Setlowe. 1977. pap. 1.50 o.s.i. (ISBN 0-515-04307-9). Jove Pubns.

Brink: The Cuban Missile Crisis, 1962. David Detzer. LC 78-4758. (Illus.). 1979. 11.95 o.s.i. (ISBN 0-690-01682-4, TYC-T). T Y Crowell.

Brinks Job. Noel Behn. (Illus.). 1978. pap. 2.50 o.s.i. (ISBN 0-446-91108-9). Warner Bks.

Brionne. Louis L'Amour. 160p. (Orig.). 1981. pap. 2.25 (ISBN 0-553-14754-4). Bantam.

Brisburial. Edward Pomerantz. 1981. 14.95x (ISBN 0-913660-13-2); pap. 7.95x (ISBN 0-913660-14-0). Magic Circle Pr.

Bristle Face. Zachary Ball. (Illus.). 206p. (gr. 5 up). 1962. 8.95 (ISBN 0-8234-0013-1). Holiday.

Britain. Reginald Hammond. LC 77-437537. (Red Guide Ser.). (Illus.). 256p. 1969. 7.50x (ISBN 0-7063-1082-9). Intl Pubns Serv.

Britain & America: An Interpretation of Their Culture 1945-1975. Daniel Snowman. LC 76-56927. 1977. usa 17.50x (ISBN 0-8147-7778-3). NYU Pr.

Britain & European Resistance, Nineteen Forty to Nineteen Forty-Five: A Survey of the Special Operations Executive, with Documents. David Stafford. LC 79-19224. 1980. 25.00 (ISBN 0-8020-2361-4). U of Toronto Pr.

Britain & France in the Middle East & North Africa. A. Williams. 1969. 6.95 (ISBN 0-312-09765-4). St Martin.

Britain & France: Ten Centuries. Ed. by Douglas Johnson & Francois Bedarida. 250p. 1980. cancelled (ISBN 0-87480-189-3). U of Utah Pr.

Britain & Ireland in Early Christian Times. Charles Thomas. LC 75-138860. (Illus., Orig.). 1971. pap. 3.95 o.p. (ISBN 0-07-064239-7, SP). McGraw.

Britain & Nuclear Weapons. Lawrence Freedman. 1981. text ed. 27.50x (ISBN 0-333-30494-2). Humanities.

Britain & Palestine, Nieneteen Seventy-Four to Nineteen Forty-Eight: Archival Sources for the History of the British Mandate. Compiled by Philip Jones. (British Academy Ser.). 256p. 1979. text ed. 55.00x (ISBN 0-19-725985-5). Oxford U Pr.

Britain & the Arab States: A Survey of Anglo-Arab Relations, 1920-1948. M. V. Seton-Williams. LC 79-2881. (Illus.). 330p. 1981. Repr. of 1948 ed. 26.50 (ISBN 0-8305-0049-9). Hyperion Conn.

Britain & the Balance of Power in North America, 1815-1908. Kenneth Bourne. 1967. 26.00x (ISBN 0-520-00153-2). U of Cal Pr.

Britain & the Casus Belli 1822-1902: A Study of Britain's International Position from Canning to Salisbury. Christopher Howard. 204p. 1974. text ed. 21.00x (ISBN 0-485-11149-7, Athlone Pr). Humanities.

Britain & the Commonwealth Alliance 1918-1939. Holland. 1979. text ed. 52.00x (ISBN 0-333-27295-1). Humanities.

Britain & the Congo Question, 1885-1913. S. J. Cookey. (Ibadan History Ser). (Illus.). 1968. text ed. 8.00x (ISBN 0-582-64511-5, 67-16973). Humanities.

Britain & the Dictators. R. W. Seton-Watson. 1968. Repr. of 1938 ed. 19.75 (ISBN 0-86527-015-5). Fertig.

Britain & the Eastern Question 1875-1878. Richard Millman. (Illus.). 1979. 65.00x (ISBN 0-19-822379-X). Oxford U Pr.

Britain & the Jews of Europe 1939-1945. Bernard Wasserstein. 1979. 19.95 (ISBN 0-19-822600-4). Oxford U Pr.

Britain & the Making of Europe. Ian D. Davidson. LC 74-182185. 1972. text ed. 18.95 (ISBN 0-312-09800-6). St Martin.

Britain & the Modern World. John Ray. 1974. pap. text ed. 7.95x o.p. (ISBN 0-435-31751-2). Heinemann Ed.

Britain & the Netherlands in Europe & Asia. Ed. by J. S. Bromley & E. H. Kossma. LC 68-17096. (Illus.). 1968. text ed. 18.95x (ISBN 0-312-10395-6). St Martin.

Britain & the Onset of Modernization in Brazil, 1850-1914. R. Graham. LC 68-21393. (Latin American Studies: No. 4). (Illus.). 1972. 42.50 (ISBN 0-521-07078-3); pap. 10.95x (ISBN 0-521-09681-2). Cambridge U Pr.

Britain & the Origins of the First World War. Zara Steiner. LC 76-55861. (Making of the Twentieth Century Ser). 160p. 1978. 16.95x (ISBN 0-312-09818-9); pap. 6.95 (ISBN 0-312-09819-7). St Martin.

Britain & the Persian Gulf, 1894-1914. Briton C. Busch. 1967. 20.00x (ISBN 0-520-00200-8). U of Cal Pr.

Britain & the Second World War. H. Pelling. 1970. pap. 1.95 o.p. (ISBN 0-531-06001-2, Fontana Pap). Watts.

Britain & the War for the Union, Vol. 2. Brian Jenkins. 480p. 1980. 26.50 (ISBN 0-7735-0354-4). McGill-Queens U Pr.

Britain & the War for Yugoslavia, Nineteen Forty to Nineteen Forty-Three. Mark C. Wheeler. (East European Monographs: No. 64). 1980. 18.50x (ISBN 0-914710-57-5). East Eur Quarterly.

Britain & the World, Sixteen Forty-Nine to Eighteen Fifteen. J. R. Jones. (Fontana History of England Ser.: No. 6). 1980. text ed. 31.50x (ISBN 0-391-01776-4). Humanities.

Britain & Vichy: The Dilemma of Anglo-French Relations, 1940-42. R. T. Thomas. (Making of the Twentieth Century Ser.). 1979. 19.95 (ISBN 0-312-09822-7). St Martin.

Britain: Continuity & Change. Roger Bivand & Ewa S. Bivand. LC 80-40778. (Illus.). 196p. 1981. 7.95 (ISBN 0-08-025312-1). Pergamon.

Britain, Egypt & the Middle East. John Darwin. LC 80-14718. 1980. write for info. (ISBN 0-312-09736-0). St Martin.

Britain, Europe & the World, 4 bks. Incl. Bk 2. 1485-1713. Dennis Witcombe. 1971. pap. text ed. 8.95x (ISBN 0-435-31101-8); Bk 3. 1714-1848. Roger Symonds. 1975. pap. text ed. 8.95x (ISBN 0-435-31102-6); Bk 4. 1848-1918. Tony Edwards & Graham Bearman. 1971. pap. text ed. 9.95x (ISBN 0-435-31103-4); Bk 5. 1918-1977. Paul Richardson. 1977. pap. text ed. 10.50x (ISBN 0-435-31105-0). Heinemann Ed.

Britain Faces Europe: 1957 to 1967. Robert L. Pfaltzgraff, Jr. LC 69-17748. 1969. 7.50 o.p. (ISBN 0-8122-7590-X). U of Pa Pr.

Britain: Four Countries, One Kingdom. Automobile Association & British Tourist Authority. (Illus.). 64p. Date not set. pap. price not set (ISBN 0-85122-188-2, Pub. by Auto Assn-British Tourist Authority England). Merrimack Bk Serv.

Britain, France & the Arab Middle East 1914-1920. Jukka Nevakivi. (Univ. of London Historical Studies: No. 23). 1969. text ed. 25.00x (ISBN 0-485-13123-4, Athlone Pr). Humanities.

Britain from Waterloo to the Great Exhibition. Michael Moss & Andrew Forrester. (History Broadsheets Ser.). 1976. pap. text ed. 6.95x o.p. (ISBN 0-435-31640-0). Heinemann Ed.

Britain in Colour. R. M. Lockley. 1976. 11.95 (ISBN 0-7134-0016-1, Pub. by Batsford England). David & Charles.

Britain in the Early Nineteenth Century. A. D. Harvey. LC 77-15016. 1978. 25.00x (ISBN 0-312-09747-6). St Martin.

Britain in Tomorrow's World. Grant Hugo. LC 78-84062. 1969. 20.00x (ISBN 0-231-03330-3). Columbia U Pr.

Britain in Transition: The Twentieth-Century. Alfred F. Havighurst. LC 78-16052. 1979. 25.00x (ISBN 0-226-31968-7); pap. text ed. 9.95 (ISBN 0-226-31969-5, P815, Phoen). U of Chicago Pr.

Britain, India, & the Arabs, 1914-1921. Briton C. Busch. LC 71-132421. 1971. 25.75x (ISBN 0-520-01821-4). U of Cal Pr.

Britain Observed: A Russian's View. V. V. Ovchinnikov. LC 80-40657. 224p. 1981. 22.50 (ISBN 0-08-023603-0); pap. 8.50 (ISBN 0-08-023608-1). Pergamon.

Britain Pre-Eminent: Studies in British World Influence in the Nineteenth Century. Ed. by C. J. Bartlett. LC 75-93447. (Problems in Focus Ser). 1969. 18.95 (ISBN 0-312-09835-9). St Martin.

Britain: Progress & Decline, Vol. 17. A. H. Birch et al. 154p. 1980. lib. bdg. 17.50 (ISBN 0-930598-18-0). Tulane Stud Pol.

Britain, Roosevelt & the New Deal: British Opinion, 1932-1938. John Dizikes. Ed. by Frank Friedel. LC 78-63282. (Modern American History Ser.: Vol. 7). 200p. 1979. lib. bdg. 30.00 (ISBN 0-8240-3631-X). Garland Pub.

Britain: Sixteen Eighty-Eight to Eighteen Fifteen. Jarrett. 1976. pap. 9.95 (ISBN 0-312-09695-X). St Martin.

Britain's Canal & River Craft. E. Paget-Tomlinson. 144p. 1980. 37.50x (ISBN 0-903485-90-7, Pub. by Moorland England). State Mutual Bk.

Britain's Developing Constitution. Peter Bromhead. LC 74-82270. 227p. 1974. 20.00 (ISBN 0-312-09905-3). St Martin.

Britain's Economic Performance. Ed. by Richard E. Caves & Lawrence B. Krause. 1980. 18.95 (ISBN 0-8157-1320-7); pap. 7.95 (ISBN 0-8157-1319-3). Brookings.

Britain's Green Mantle. A. G. Tansley. 1968. text ed. 25.00x (ISBN 0-04-580004-9). Allen Unwin.

Britain's Inner Cities. P. Lawless. 1981. text ed. 25.85 (ISBN 0-06-318184-3, Pub. by Har-Row Ltd England); pap. text ed. 13.10 (ISBN 0-06-318185-1). Har-Row.

Britain's Master Spy: The Adventures of Sidney Reilly. Sidney Reilly. 296p. 1980. Repr. of 1933 ed. lib. bdg. 35.00 (ISBN 0-89984-449-9). Century Bookbindery.

Britain's National Parks. Ed. by Mervyn Bell. LC 74-20450. (Illus.). 160p. 1975. 17.95 (ISBN 0-7153-6792-7). David & Charles.

Britain's Oil. Guy Arnold. (Illus.). 1979. 27.00 (ISBN 0-241-89995-8, Pub. by Hamish Hamilton England). David & Charles.

Britain's Prime Ministers from Walpole to Wilson. Royston E. Pike. (Illus.). 1970. 8.95 (ISBN 0-600-72032-2). Transatlantic.

Britain's Search for Health. Paul F. Gemmill. LC 60-11500. 1961. 9.00x o.p. (ISBN 0-8122-7286-2). U of Pa Pr.

Britain's Wild Larder. Claire Loewenfeld et al. LC 80-66426. (Illus.). 192p. 1980. 19.95 o.p. (ISBN 0-7153-7971-2). David & Charles.

Britannia: A History of Roman Britain. rev. ed. Sheppard Frere. (Illus.). 1978. 32.00x (ISBN 0-7100-8916-3). Routledge & Kegan.

Britannia Triumphans: Inigo Jones, Rubens & Whitehall Palace. Roy Strong. (Lectures Ser.). (Illus.). 72p. 1981. 10.95 (ISBN 0-500-55012-3). Thames Hudson.

Britannica Atlas. William A. Cleveland. (YA) (gr. 9 up). 1980. write for info. (ISBN 0-85229-390-9). Ency Brit Ed.

Britannica Book of English Usage. Ed. by Christine Timmons & Frank Gibney. LC 79-7706. (Encyclopedia Britannica Ser.). (Illus.). 504p. 1980. 17.95 (ISBN 0-385-14193-9). Doubleday.

Britannica Book of Music. Encyclopedia Britannica. Ed. by Benjamin Hadley et al. LC 79-7195. (Illus.). 1980. 24.95 (ISBN 0-385-14191-2). Doubleday.

Britannica Discovery Library, 12. 55.00 (ISBN 0-85229-298-8); spanish ed. 48.45 (ISBN 0-87827-223-2). Ency Brit Ed.

Britannica Junior Encyclopaedia, 15 vols. Marvin Martin. (Illus.). 1980. Set. write for info. (ISBN 0-85229-379-8). Ency Brit Ed.

Britannicus. Jean B. Racine. Ed. by Philip F. Butler. LC 68-10026. (Illus.). 1967. text ed. 9.95x (ISBN 0-521-29197-6). Cambridge U Pr.

British Academy: Proceedings, Vol. LXIII, 1977. (Illus.). 1979. 89.00 (ISBN 0-19-725983-9). Oxford U Pr.

British Accounting Standards: The First Ten Years. Ronald Leach & Edward Stamp. 160p. 1980. 40.00x (ISBN 0-85941-149-4, Pub. by Woodhead-Faulkner England). State Mutual Bk.

British Aircraft Guns of World War Two. (R.A.F. Museum Ser.: Vol. 9). (Illus.). 208p. 1980. 29.95 (ISBN 0-88254-495-0). Hippocrene Bks.

British Airports. John Taylor. pap. 3.00x (ISBN 0-392-07261-0, SpS). Soccer.

British Alternative Theatre Directory 1979. Ed. by Catherine Itzin. (Orig.). 1979. pap. text ed. cancelled o.s.i. (ISBN 0-903931-19-2, Pub. by John Offord Pubns England). Drama Bk.

British American Business Terms. Rudolf Sachs. 144p. (Orig.). 1975. pap. text ed. 10.00x (ISBN 0-7121-0242-6, Pub. by Macdonald & Evans England). Intl Ideas.

British-American Chamber of Commerce Yearbook & Directory Annual. 1981. 10.00 (ISBN 0-686-50038-5). Am Sports Sales.

British-American Relations, 1917-1918: The Role of Sir William Wiseman. Wilton B. Fowler. 1969. 18.50 (ISBN 0-691-04594-1). Princeton U Pr.

British & American Flintlocks. Frederick Wilkerson. (Country Life Collectors Guides Ser). 1972. 4.95 (ISBN 0-600-43590-3). Transatlantic.

British & American Poetry. Herbert Church, Jr. (gr. 9-11). 1970. pap. text ed. 4.25x (ISBN 0-88334-027-5). Ind Sch Pr.

British & Their Successors. Richard Symonds. 1966. 7.95 o.p. (ISBN 0-571-06677-1, Pub. by Faber & Faber). Merrimack Bk Serv.

British Approach to Politics. Michael Stewart. 1966. pap. text ed. 14.95x (ISBN 0-04-320038-9). Allen Unwin.

British Architect. 2nd ed. Abraham Swan. LC 67-25995. (Architecture & Decorative Art Ser). (Illus.). 1967. Repr. of 1758 ed. lib. bdg. 75.00 (ISBN 0-306-70961-9). Da Capo.

British Architects, Eighteen Forty-Nineteen Seventy-Six: A Guide to Information Sources. Ed. by Lawrence Wodehouse. LC 78-54116. (Art & Architecture Information Guide Ser.: Vol. 8). 1978. 30.00 (ISBN 0-8103-1393-6). Gale.

British Art & Antiques Yearbook Nineteen Seventy-Nine. Ed. by Marcelle d'Argy Smith. (Illus.). 1979. 36.00 (ISBN 0-900305-20-7, Natinal Magazine Co.). Gale.

British Art: From Holbein to the Present Day. Simon Wilson. LC 79-89630. (Illus.). 1980. 10.00 (ISBN 0-8120-5373-7). Barron.

British Attack on Unemployment. Arthur C. Hill & Isador Lubin. xiv, 325p. 1980. Repr. of 1934 ed. lib. bdg. 19.50x (ISBN 0-87991-087-9). Porcupine Pr.

British Authors Before Eighteen Hundred. Ed. by Stanley J. Kunitz & Howard Haycraft. (Illus.). 1952. 15.00 (ISBN 0-8242-0006-3). Wilson.

British Authors of the Nineteenth Century. Ed. by Stanley J. Kunitz & Howard Haycraft. (Illus.). 1936. 18.00 (ISBN 0-8242-0007-1). Wilson.

British Autobiography in the Seventeenth Century. Paul Delany. LC 69-19285. 1969. 17.50x (ISBN 0-231-03273-0). Columbia U Pr.

British Aviation Colours of World War Two. Intro. by J. M. Bruce. LC 76-13821. (R.A.F. Museum Ser.: Vol. 3). (Illus.). 1977. 11.95 o.p. (ISBN 0-88254-407-1). Hippocrene Bks.

British Barbarians. Grant Allen. Ed. by Ian Fletcher & John Stokes. LC 76-20062. (Decadent Consciousness Ser). 1977. lib. bdg. 38.00 (ISBN 0-8240-2751-5). Garland Pub.

British Bibliography & Textual Criticism: A Bibliography. T. H. Howard-Hall. (Index to British Literary Bibliography Ser.: Vols. IV & V). 1254p. 1979. Set. 115.00x (ISBN 0-19-818163-9). Oxford U Pr.

British Birds: A Field Guide. Alan J. Richards. LC 79-52375. (Illus.). 1979. 14.95 (ISBN 0-7153-7834-1). David & Charles.

British Bomber Since 1914. Peter Lewis. LC 67-15743. 1967. 9.95 (ISBN 0-370-00121-4). Aero.

British Book Illustration Yesterday & Today, with Commentary. Malcolm C. Salaman. Ed. by Geoffrey Holme. LC 73-175758. (Illus.). viii, 175p. 1974. Repr. of 1923 ed. 26.00 (ISBN 0-8103-3977-3). Gale.

British Bookplates: A Pictorial History. Brian N. Lee. LC 79-53732. (Illus.). 1979. 45.00 (ISBN 0-7153-7785-X). David & Charles.

British Books in Print, 1979, 2 vols. 1979. 115.00 o.p. (ISBN 0-85021-113-1). Bowker.

British Books in Print 1980. 5000p. 1980. 130.00 (ISBN 0-85021-119-0). Bowker.

British Borough Charters,1042-1216. Ed. by Adolphus Ballard. LC 80-2236. 1981. Repr. of 1913 ed. 49.50 (ISBN 0-404-18750-1). AMS Pr.

British Building Industry. M. E. Bowley. 1966. 59.50 (ISBN 0-521-04292-5). Cambridge U Pr.

British Business Elite: Its Attitudes to Class, Status & Power. John Fidler. 384p. 1981. price not set (ISBN 0-7100-0770-1). Routledge & Kegan.

British Butterflies: A Field Guide. Robert Goodden. 13.50 (ISBN 0-7153-7594-6, Pub. by Batsford England). David & Charles.

British Butterflies & Moths. J. D. Bradley & D. S. Fletcher. 1980. 6.00x (ISBN 0-902068-08-3, Pub. by Curwen England). State Mutual Bk.

British Canals: An Illustrated History. 5th ed. Charles Hadfield. (Canals of the British Isles Ser.). (Illus.). 1975. 19.95 (ISBN 0-7153-6700-5). David & Charles.

British Canals: An Illustrated History. 4th ed. Charles Hadfield. (Canals of the British Isles Ser.). (Illus.). 8.95. David & Charles.

British Canals: An Illustrated History. 6th ed. Charles Hadfield. LC 79-52377. (Illus.). 1979. 22.50 (ISBN 0-7153-7852-X). David & Charles.

British Castles. R. J. Unstead. LC 74-94224. (Illus.). (gr. 5-8). 1970. 9.95 (ISBN 0-690-16029-1, TYC-J). T Y Crowell.

British Columbia. Ed. by J. Lewis Robinson. (Studies in Canadian Geography). 1972. 10.00 o.p. (ISBN 0-8020-1922-6); pap. 5.50x o.p. (ISBN 0-8020-6162-1). U of Toronto Pr.

British Columbia. Ted Wrinkle. Ed. by Robert D. Shangle. LC 78-10233. (Illus.). 72p. 1977. 14.95 (ISBN 0-915796-44-9); pap. 7.95 (ISBN 0-915796-43-0). Beautiful Am.

British Commercial Computer Digest. 11th ed. Computer Consultants Ltd. 1970. 79.00 (ISBN 0-08-016279-7). Pergamon.

British Commercial Policy & Trade Expansion, 1750-1850. Judith B. Williams. Ed. by Ralph Davis & David Williams. 512p. 1972. 39.50x (ISBN 0-19-822360-9). Oxford U Pr.

British Constitution. Gerald P. Dartford. 1978. pap. text ed. 2.75x (ISBN 0-88334-107-7). Ind Sch Pr.

British Crossword Dictionary. Ed. by J. M. Bailie. LC 77-84889. 1978. 8.95 o.p. (ISBN 0-385-13625-0). Doubleday.

British Diplomacy & Swedish Politics, 1758-1773. Michael Roberts. LC 80-11499. 1980. 29.50x (ISBN 0-8166-0910-1). U of Minn Pr.

British Doctors at Home & Abroad. Brian Abel-Smith. 63p. 1964. pap. text ed. 3.75x (Pub. by Bedford England). Renouf.

British Drama: A Handbook & Brief Chronicle. Alan S. Downer. (Illus.). 1950. 29.50x (ISBN 0-89197-047-9); pap. text ed. 16.95x (ISBN 0-89197-048-7). Irvington.

British Economic & Social History. 2nd ed. J. Walker. 448p. (Orig.). 1979. pap. text ed. 18.95x (ISBN 0-7121-0266-3, Pub. by Macdonald & Evans England). Intl Ideas.

British Economic Fluctuations: Seventeen-Ninety to Nineteen Thirty-Nine. Ed. by Derek H. Aldcroft & Peter Fearon. LC 77-178900. 1972. text ed. 19.95 (ISBN 0-312-10045-0). St Martin.

British Economic Growth, Sixteen Eighty-Eight - Nineteen Fifty-Nine: Trends & Structure. 2nd ed. Phyllis Deane & W. A. Cole. LC 67-21956. (Cambridge Department of Applied Economics Monographs). (Illus.). 1969. 47.50 (ISBN 0-521-04801-X); pap. 14.95x (ISBN 0-521-09569-7). Cambridge U Pr.

British Economic History, Eighteen Seventy - Nineteen Fourteen. William H. Court. (Orig.). 1966. 53.95 (ISBN 0-521-04731-5); pap. 19.50x (ISBN 0-521-09362-7). Cambridge U Pr.

British Economic Policy: Nineteen Sixty to Nineteen Seventy-Four. F. T. Blackaby. LC 77-28282. (NIESR Economic & Social Policy Studies: No. 31). (Illus.). 1979. 67.50 (ISBN 0-521-22042-4); pap. 19.95x (ISBN 0-521-29597-1). Cambridge U Pr.

British Economic Thought & India Sixteen Hundred to Eighteen Fifty-Eight: A Study in the History of Development Economics. William J. Barber. 264p. 1975. 29.95x (ISBN 0-19-828265-6). Oxford U Pr.

British Economy. William Mennell. 64p. 1964. pap. 2.95x o.p. (ISBN 0-8464-0211-4). Beekman Pubs.

British Economy. M. H. Peston. 224p. 1980. 30.00x (ISBN 0-86003-014-8, Pub. by Allan Pubs England); pap. 19.95x (ISBN 0-86003-115-2). State Mutual Bk.

British Economy in Theory & Practice. James V. Livingstone. LC 74-13513. 240p. 1975. 18.95 (ISBN 0-312-10080-9). St Martin.

British Economy: Toward a Decent Society. Walter C. Neale. LC 79-16553. (Economics Ser.). 1980. pap. text ed. 7.95 (ISBN 0-88244-194-9); 12.95 (ISBN 0-686-65968-6). Grid Pub.

British Elections. Geoffrey Alderman. 1978. 30.00 (ISBN 0-7134-0195-8, Pub. by Batsford England); pap. 11.50 (ISBN 0-7134-0196-6). David & Charles.

British Electric Tramways. E. Jackson-Stevens. (Illus.). 112p. 1971. 16.95 (ISBN 0-7153-5105-2). David & Charles.

British Electrical Industry Eighteen Seventy-Five to Nineteen Fourteen. I. C. Byatt. 1979. 29.95x (ISBN 0-19-828270-2). Oxford U Pr.

British Empire & Commonwealth, Fifteen Hundred - Nineteen Sixty-One. W. D. Hussey. 1963. text ed. 11.95x (ISBN 0-521-05351-X). Cambridge U Pr.

British Empire, Eighteen Fifteen to Nineteen Thirty. Paul Knaplund. LC 68-9617. (Illus.). 1970. Repr. 27.50 (ISBN 0-86527-017-1). Fertig.

British Employment Statistics: A Guide to Sources & Methods. N. K. Buxton & D. I. MacKay. 1977. 46.50x (ISBN 0-631-17240-8, Pub. by Basil Blackwell). Biblio Dist.

British Escort Ships. Trevor Lenton. (Fact Files on World War 2 Ser). (Illus.). 64p. 1975. 5.95 o.p. (ISBN 0-668-03507-2); pap. 3.95 o.p. (ISBN 0-668-03609-5). Arco.

British Examinations: Techniques of Analysis. D. L. Nuttall & A. S. Willmott. (General Ser.). 1972. text ed. 13.25x (ISBN 0-901225-79-7, NFER). Humanities.

British Factory - Japanese Factory: The Origins of National Diversity in Employment Relations. Ronald P. Dore. LC 72-78948. 1973. 18.50x (ISBN 0-520-02268-8); pap. 7.95x (ISBN 0-520-02495-8, CAMPUS96). U of Cal Pr.

British Family Names. 2nd ed. Henry Barber. LC 68-17914. 1968. Repr. of 1903 ed. 18.00 (ISBN 0-8103-3109-8). Gale.

British Fighter Since 1912. Peter Lewis. LC 65-19381. (Illus.). 1965. 12.95 (ISBN 0-370-00063-3). Aero.

British Flying Boats & Amphibians, 1909-1952. Godfrey R. Duval. LC 66-19522. (Illus.). 1966. 8.75 o.p. (ISBN 0-370-00031-5). Aero.

British Folktales. Katharine M. Briggs. LC 77-2384. 1977. 10.00 (ISBN 0-394-41589-2). Pantheon.

British Folktales. Katherine M. Briggs. (Fairy Tale & Folklore Library). 1980. pap. 5.95 (ISBN 0-394-73993-0). Pantheon.

British Foreign Policy: Sixteen Sixty to Sixteen Seventy-Two. Keith Feiling. 1968. Repr. of 1930 ed. text ed. 11.50x (ISBN 0-7146-1473-4). Humanities.

British Foreign Policy Under Sir Edward Grey. Ed. by F. H. Hinsley. LC 76-19631. 1977. 93.00 (ISBN 0-521-21347-9). Cambridge U Pr.

British Freshwater Fishes: Factors Affecting Their Distribution. Margaret Varley. (Illus.). 148p. 15.00 (ISBN 0-85238-107-7, FN). Unipub.

British Furniture Today. Erno Goldfinger. (Illus.). 1951. 2.75 o.p. (ISBN 0-85458-899-X). Transatlantic.

British Further Education. A. J. Peters. 1967. 26.00 (ISBN 0-08-011893-3). Pergamon.

British General Election of 1959. David E. Butler. Ed. by Richard Rose. (Illus.). 293p. Repr. of 1970 ed. 27.50x (ISBN 0-7156-1549-1, F Cass Co). Biblio Dist.

British General Elections Nineteen Seventy-Nine. David Butler & Dennis Kavanagh. 416p. 1980. text ed. 50.00x (ISBN 0-8419-5081-4). Holmes & Meier.

British Government & Its Discontents. Nelson W. Polsby & Geoffrey Smith. LC 79-56372. 208p. 1981. 12.95 (ISBN 0-465-00765-1). Basic.

British Government & Politics. F. Randall. (Illus.). 288p. (Orig.). 1979. pap. text ed. 12.95x (ISBN 0-7121-0247-7, Pub. by Macdonald & Evans England). Intl Ideas.

British Government 1966 to 1975: Years of Reform. Frank Stacey. 254p. 1975. 24.95x (ISBN 0-19-876035-3). Oxford U Pr.

British Harvestment: Arachniad: Opilidnes: Keip and Notes for the Indentification of the Species. J. P. Sankey & T. H. Savory. 1974. 9.50 (ISBN 0-12-619050-X). Acad Pr.

British Historians & the West Indies. Eric E. Williams. LC 72-76470. 238p. 1972. text ed. 19.50x (ISBN 0-8419-0088-4, Africana). Holmes & Meier.

British Historical Facts Seventeen Sixty to Eighteen Thirty. Chris Cook et al. ix, 197p. 1980. 32.50 (ISBN 0-208-01868-9, Archon). Shoe String.

British History Atlas. Martin Gilbert. 1969. 4.95 o.s.i. (ISBN 0-02-543270-2). Macmillan.

British History, Eighteen Fifteen to Nineteen Thirty-Nine. W. D. Hussey. LC 79-149429. (Illus.). 1972. 11.50 (ISBN 0-521-07985-3). Cambridge U Pr.

British History Nineteen Two - Nineteen Fifty-Five. Elizabeth Eccleshare & Valerie St. Johnston. 1974. pap. text ed. 3.95x o.p. (ISBN 0-435-31170-0). Heinemann Ed.

British History, Seventeen Fourteen - Present Day. H. L. Peacock. 1968. pap. text ed. 10.50x o.p. (ISBN 0-435-31705-9). Heinemann Ed.

British Humanities Index 1978. Ed. by Library Association (London) LC 63-24940. 802p. 1979. 175.00x (ISBN 0-85365-901-X). Intl Pubns Serv.

British Humanities Index 1979. Library Asssociation (London) LC 63-24940. 744p. 1980. 190.00x (ISBN 0-85365-583-9). Intl Pubns Serv.

British Imperialism & Commercial Supremacy. Victor Berard. LC 70-80613. 298p. 1973. Repr. of 1906 ed. 16.50 (ISBN 0-86527-018-X). Fertig.

British in Malaya, Eighteen Eighty to Nineteen Forty-One: The Social History of a European Community in Colonial South-East Asia. John G. Butcher. (Illus.). 314p. 1979. 34.95x (ISBN 0-19-580419-8). Oxford U Pr.

British Independent Light Railways. John S. Morgan. LC 79-56060. 96p. 1980. 17.95 (ISBN 0-7153-7933-X). David & Charles.

British Indians in the Transvaal: Trade, Politics & Imperial Relations, 1885-1906. Bala Pillay. 1977. text ed. 11.00x (ISBN 0-582-64201-9). Longman.

British Industrial Investment in Malaysia, Nineteen Sixty-Three to Nineteen Seventy-One. Junid Saham. (East Asian Social Science Monographs). 366p. 1981. 37.00 (ISBN 0-19-580418-X). Oxford U Pr.

British Industry Between the Wars: Instability & Industrial Development 1919-1939. Ed. by Neil K. Buxton & Derek H. Aldcroft. 308p. 1979. 40.00x (ISBN 0-85967-383-9, Pub. by Scolar Pr England). Biblio Dist.

British Insurance. G. Clayton. 1971. 39.95 o.p. (ISBN 0-236-17618-8, Pub. by Faber & Faber). Merrimack Bk Serv.

British Intelligence in the Second World War: Its Influence on Strategy & Operations, Vol. I. F. H. Hinsley et al. LC 79-87703. 1979. 29.95 (ISBN 0-521-22940-5). Cambridge U Pr.

British Interparty Conferences: A Study of the Procedure of Conciliation in British Politics, Eighteen Sixty-Seven to Nineteen Twenty-One. John D. Fair. 366p. 1980. text ed. 49.00x (ISBN 0-19-822601-2). Oxford U Pr.

British "Intervention" in Transcaspia, 1918-1919. C. H. Ellis. 1963. 18.50x (ISBN 0-520-00381-0). U of Cal Pr.

British Invasion of Maryland, Eighteen Twelve to Eighteen Fifteen. William M. Marine. Ed. by Louis H. Dielman. LC 66-128. (Illus.). xx, 519p. Repr. of 1913 ed. 18.00 (ISBN 0-8103-5036-X). Gale.

British Islands & Their Vegetation, 2 Vols. Arthur G. Tansley. 1949. Set. 125.00 (ISBN 0-521-06600-X). Cambridge U Pr.

British Isles. 2nd ed. A. V. Hardy. (Geography of the British Isles Ser.). (Illus.). 160p. Date not set. pap. price not set (ISBN 0-521-22258-3). Cambridge U Pr.

British Isles. rev. ed. Vincent Malmstrom & Ruth Malmstrom. LC 77-83908. (World Cultures Ser). (Illus.). 164p. (gr. 6 up). 1978. text ed. 9.95 ea. 1-4 copies (ISBN 0-88296-173-X); text ed. 7.96 ea. 5 or more copies; tchrs'. guide 8.94 (ISBN 0-88296-369-4). Fideler.

British Isles. 6th ed. L. Dudley Stamp & S. H. Beaver. LC 70-17425. (Geographies for Advanced Studies). 1972. 35.00 (ISBN 0-312-10325-5). St Martin.

British Isles: A Regional Geography. 2nd ed. Henry Rees. (Illus.). 1972. text ed. 19.95x (ISBN 0-245-50745-0). Intl Ideas.

British Isles & Germany. rev. ed. Vincent H. Malmstrom et al. LC 77-83891. (World Cultures Ser.). (Illus.). 320p. (gr. 6 up). 1978. text ed. 12.43 ea. 1-4 copies (ISBN 0-88296-148-9); text ed. 9.94 ea. 5 or more copies; tchrs'. guide 8.94 (ISBN 0-88296-369-4). Fideler.

British Isles in Colour. Walter Allen. 1965. 27.00 (ISBN 0-7134-0002-1, Pub. by Batsford England). David & Charles.

British Isles Through Geological Time: A Northward Drift. J. P. Lovell. (Illus.). 1977. pap. text ed. 6.95x (ISBN 0-04-554003-9). Allen Unwin.

British Kitchen. Doreen Yarwood. (Illus.). 192p. 1981. 28.95 (ISBN 0-7134-1430-8, Pub. by Batsford England). David & Charles.

British Labour & Hitler's War. T. D. Burridge. 1977. 15.00 (ISBN 0-233-96714-1). Transatlantic.

British Labour Party: A Functioning Participatory Democracy. Harry B. Cole. 1977. pap. text ed. 5.75 (ISBN 0-08-021811-3). Pergamon.

British Landscape Drawings & Watercolors, Nineteen-Fifty to Eighteen-Fifty: Twenty-Four Examples from the Huntington Collection. Robert R. Wark. (Illus.). 64p. write for info. (ISBN 0-87328-116-0). Huntington Lib.

British Liberties. Ed. by David S. Berkowitz & Samuel E. Thorne. LC 77-89201. (Classics of English Legal History in the Modern Era Ser.: Vol. 57). 486p. 1979. lib. bdg. 40.00 (ISBN 0-8240-3156-3). Garland Pub.

British Library & AACR, Nineteen Sixty-Seven: A Study. Ed. by A. H. Chaplin. 1973. pap. 11.00x (ISBN 0-85365-286-4, Pub. by Lib Assn England). Oryx Pr.

British Library General Catalogue of Printed Books: 1979 to 1985, 360 vols. new ed. 1980. 23040.00 (ISBN 3-5983-0200-2, Pub. by K G Saur). Gale.

British Library History, Nineteen Seventy-Three to Nineteen Seventy-Six. Ed. by D. F. Keeling. (Bibliographic Ser.). pap. 15.50x (ISBN 0-85365-781-5, Pub. by Lib Assn England). Oryx Pr.

British Library History, Nineteen Sixty-Nine to Nineteen Seventy-Two. D. F. Keeling. (Bibliographic Ser.). 1975. pap. 13.50x (ISBN 0-85365-417-4, Pub. by Lib Assn England). Oryx Pr.

British Library History, Nineteen Sixty-Two to Nineteen Sixty-Eight. Ed. by D. F. Keeling. (Bibliographic Ser.). 1971. pap. 13.50x (ISBN 0-85365-345-3, Pub. by Lib Assn England). Oryx Pr.

British Literature, 2 vols. 3rd ed. Hazelton Spencer et al. 1974. text ed. 16.95x ea.; Vol. 1. text ed. (ISBN 0-669-84129-3); Vol. 2. text ed. (ISBN 0-669-84137-4). Heath.
British Locomotive Names of the 20th Century. 15.95x (ISBN 0-392-07681-0, SpS). Soccer.
British Machine-Tool Industry, 1850-1914. R. Floud. LC 75-46205. (Illus.). 180p. 1976. 29.95 (ISBN 0-521-21203-0). Cambridge U Pr.
British Management German Management. Jean A. Millar. text ed. 15.75x (ISBN 0-566-00289-2, Pub. by Gower Pub Co England). Renouf.
British Members of Parliament: A Self Portrait. Anthony King. 128p. 1975. 12.50 (ISBN 0-333-17170-5). Transatlantic.
British Military Policy Between the Two World Wars. Brian Bond. 480p. 1980. 48.00x (ISBN 0-19-822464-8). Oxford U Pr.
British Monarchy in Color. John Brooke-Little. (Color Ser.). (Illus.). 1976. 9.95 (ISBN 0-7137-0774-7, Pub by Blandford Pr England). Sterling.
British Monetary Policy, Nineteen Twenty-Four to Nineteen Thirty-One. D. E. Moggridge. LC 76-169576. (Department of Applied Economics Monographs: No. 21). 1972. 42.50 (ISBN 0-521-08225-0). Cambridge U Pr.
British Moralists, Sixteen Fifty to Eighteen Hundred, 2 Vols. Ed. by D. D. Raphael. 1969. Set. pap. 14.95x (ISBN 0-19-875010-2). Oxford U Pr.
British Mosses & Liverworts. 2nd ed. E. Vernon Watson. LC 68-22665. (Illus.). 1968. 50.00 (ISBN 0-521-06741-3). Cambridge U Pr.
British MP: A Socio-Economic Study of the House of Commons. Colin Mellors. (Illus.). 1978. 18.95 (ISBN 0-566-00138-1, 00708-0, Pub. by Saxon Hse England). Lexington Bks.
British Museum - Library. General Catalogue of Printed Books: Compact Edition. Basic Catalogue (to 1955, 27 vols. compact ed. 1967. Set. 750.00 (ISBN 0-918414-04-0). Readex Bks.
British Museum - Library. General Catalogue of Printed Books: Compact Edition. First Supplement (1956-1965, 5 vols. compact ed. 1974. Set. 150.00 (ISBN 0-918414-05-9). Readex Bks.
British Museum - Library. General Catalogue of Printed Books: Compact Edition. Second Supplement (1966-1970, 3 vols. compact ed. 1974. Set. 120.00 (ISBN 0-918414-06-7). Readex Bks.
British Museum - Library. General Catalogue of Printed Books: Compact Edition. Third Supplement (1971-1975, 2 vols. compact ed. 1980. Set. 150.00 (ISBN 0-918414-07-5). Readex Bks.
British Music Hall. Roy Busby. (Illus.). 1977. 28.00 o.p. (ISBN 0-236-40053-3, Pub. by Paul Elek). Merrimack Bk Serv.
British Music Hall 1840-1923: A Bibliography & Guide to Sources with a Supplement on European Music-Hall. Laurence Senelick et al. (Archon Books on Popular Entertainments Ser.). 1981. 37.50 (ISBN 0-208-01840-9, Archon). Shoe String.
British Music Yearbook, 1980. 6th ed. Ed. by Arthur Jacobs. 637p. 1980. pap. 24.50x (ISBN 0-8476-6255-1). Rowman.
British Musical Biography: A Dictionary of Musical Artists, Authors & Composers, Born in Britain & Its Colonies. James D. Brown & Stephen S. Stratton. LC 76-139197. (Music Ser). 1971. Repr. of 1897 ed. lib. bdg. 42.50 (ISBN 0-306-70076-X). Da Capo.
British Natural History Books from the Beginning to 1900: A Handlist. R. B. Freeman. 350p. 1980. 39.50 (ISBN 0-686-62545-5, Archon). Shoe String.
British Naval Aircraft Since Nineteen Hundred & Twelve. 4th ed. Owen Thetford. (Putnam Aeronautical Ser.). (Illus.). 1980. 23.95 (ISBN 0-370-30021-1, Pub. by Chatto Bodley Jonathan). Merrimack Bk Serv.
British Nitrates & Chilean Politics, 1886-1896: Balmaceda & North. Harold Blakemore. (Institute of Latin American Studies Monograph Ser: No. 4). (Illus.). 256p. 1974. text ed. 25.75x (ISBN 0-485-17704-8, Athlone Pr). Humanities.
British Novel: Conrad to the Present. Compiled by Paul L. Wiley. LC 79-178291. (Goldentree Bibliographies in Language & Literature Ser.). (Orig.). 1973. pap. 6.95x (ISBN 0-88295-530-6). AHM Pub.
British Novel: Scott Through Hardy. Ed. by Ian Watt. LC 72-96559. (Goldentree Bibliographies in Language & Literature Ser.). (Orig.). 1973. pap. 6.95x (ISBN 0-88295-533-0). AHM Pub.
British Official Films in the Second World War: A Descriptive Catalog. Frances Thorpe & Nicholas Pronay. 321p. 1980. 45.00 (ISBN 0-903450-27-5). ABC Clio.
British Official Publications. 2nd ed. J. E. Pemberton. LC 73-16231. 328p. 1974. text ed. 13.80 (ISBN 0-08-017797-2). Pergamon.
British Oil Policy: A Radical Alternative. Peter R. Odell. 75p. 1980. 35.00x (ISBN 0-85038-316-1). Nichols Pub.
British Orientalism & the Bengal Renaissance: The Dynamics of Indian Modernization, 1773-1835. David Kopf. 1969. 20.00x (ISBN 0-520-00665-8). U of Cal Pr.
British Ornithologist's Guide to Bird Life. Jim Flagg. (Illus.). 284p. 1980. 32.50 (ISBN 0-7137-0996-0, Pub. by Blandford Pr England). Sterling.
British Overseas. 2nd ed. Charles E. Carrington. LC 68-23176. (Illus.). 1968. 53.50 (ISBN 0-521-07174-7). Cambridge U Pr.
British-Owned Railways in Argentina: Their Effect on the Growth of Economic Nationalism, 1854-1948. Winthrop R. Wright. (Latin American Monographs: No. 34). 358p. 1974. 15.00 (ISBN 0-292-70710-X). U of Tex Pr.
British Pamphlet Press & the American Controversy, 1764 to 1783. Thomas R. Adams. 1979. pap. 4.50 o.p. (ISBN 0-912296-37-2, Dist. by U Pr of Va). Am Antiquarian.
British Parasitic Fungi. W. C. Moore. 1959. 68.50 (ISBN 0-521-05758-2). Cambridge U Pr.
British Parliament. Roland Young. 1962. 11.95x o.s.i. (ISBN 0-8101-0246-3). Northwestern U Pr.
British Parliamentary Democracy. Herbert S. Morrison. pap. 3.50x (ISBN 0-210-34064-9). Asia.
British Patent System. K. H. Boehm & A. Silberston. (Cambridge Dept. of Applied Economics Monographs: No. 13). 1967. 32.50 (ISBN 0-521-04274-7). Cambridge U Pr.
British People Nineteen Two - Nineteen Seventy-Five. Peter Mauger. 1976. pap. text ed. 13.95x (ISBN 0-435-31570-6). Heinemann Ed.
British People: Their Voice in Europe. Hansard Society for Parliamentary Government. (Illus.). 1977. 22.50 (ISBN 0-566-00174-8, 01609-8, Pub. by Saxon Hse England). Lexington Bks.
British Pharmacopoeia, 2 vols. 2nd ed. Ed. by Pharmaceutical Society of Great Britain. 1980. 150.00 (ISBN 0-11-320688-7, Pub. by Pharmaceutical). Vol. 1, 552 Pg. Vol. 2, 688 Pg. Rittenhouse.
British Philosophy of Administration: A Comparison of British & American Ideas 1900-1939. Rosamund Thomas. LC 77-5938. (Illus.). 1978. text ed. 24.00x (ISBN 0-582-50124-5). Longman.
British Poetry, Eighteen Eighty to Nineteen Twenty: Edwardian Voices. Ed. by Paul L. Wiley & Harold Orel. LC 73-79174. 1969. 29.50x (ISBN 0-89197-049-5); pap. text ed. 16.95x (ISBN 0-89197-050-9). Irvington.
British Police. Ed. by Simon Holdaway. LC 80-7573. (Illus.). 188p. 1980. 18.50 (ISBN 0-8039-1464-4); pap. 8.95 (ISBN 0-8039-1465-2). Sage.
British Policy & the Turkish Reform Movement: A Study in Anglo-Turkish Relations, 1826-1853. Frank E. Bailey. LC 74-80519. 1970. Repr. of 1942 ed. 17.50 (ISBN 0-86527-019-8). Fertig.
British Policy Towards the Amerindians in British Guiana, 1803-1973. M. N. Menezes. (Illus.). 1977. 39.50x (ISBN 0-19-821567-3). Oxford U Pr.
British Policy Towards the Ottoman Empire Nineteen Hundred Eight - Nineteen Fourteen. Joseph Heller. 1980. 26.00x (ISBN 0-7146-3127-2, F Cass Co). Biblio Dist.
British Politics & European Unity: Parties, Elites & Pressure Groups. Robert J. Lieber. LC 70-104104. 1970. 20.00x (ISBN 0-520-01675-0). U of Cal Pr.
British Politics & the Stamp Act Crisis: The First Phase of the American Revolution 1763-1767. P. D. Thomas. 395p. 1975. 37.50x (ISBN 0-19-822431-1). Oxford U Pr.
British Politics Today. Ed. by Bill Jones & Dennis Kavanagh. LC 78-21048. 1979. text ed. 13.50x (ISBN 0-8419-0473-1); pap. text ed. 6.00 o.p. (ISBN 0-8419-0475-8). Holmes & Meier.
British Popular Customs, Present & Past. Thomas F. Thiselton-Dyer. LC 67-23908. (Social History Reference Ser.). (Illus.). 1968. Repr. of 1876 ed. 18.00 (ISBN 0-8103-3261-2). Gale.
British Population Change Since 1860. Rosiland Mitchison. (Studies in Economic & Social History). 1977. pap. text ed. 4.75x (ISBN 0-333-13585-7). Humanities.
British Press & Germany, 1936-1939. Franklin R. Gannon. 1971. 16.50x o.p. (ISBN 0-19-821490-1). Oxford U Pr.
British Prime Ministers in the Twentieth Century, Vol. 1. Ed. by John J. Mackintosh. LC 77-76542. 1977. 19.95x (ISBN 0-312-10517-7). St Martin.
British Prime Ministers in the Twentieth Century, Vol. 2. Ed. by John P. Mackintosh. LC 77-76542. 1978. 19.95 (ISBN 0-312-10518-5). St Martin.
British Prisons. Mike Fitzgerald & Joe Sim. 1979. 16.00x o.p. (ISBN 0-631-11211-1, Pub. by Basil Blackwell England); pap. 6.95x o.p. (ISBN 0-631-11221-9, Pub. by Basil Blackwell England). Biblio Dist.
British Prosobranch & Other Operculate Gastropod Molluscs. Alistair Graham. (Synopses of the British Fauna: No. 2). 1972. 7.50 (ISBN 0-12-294850-5). Acad Pr.
British Publishers' Catalog Annual: 1980. 1980. catalog collection 275.00 (ISBN 0-930466-33-0). Meckler Bks.
British Qualifications. 10th ed. Ed. by Barbara Priestley. 1979. 40.00x (ISBN 0-85038-222-X, Pub by Kogan Pg). Nichols Pub.
British Racing Cars. R. L. Maiden. pap. 2.00x (ISBN 0-392-07213-0, SpS). Soccer.
British Radical Left Nineteen Thirty One - Nineteen Forty One. James Jupp. 423p. 1981. 27.50x (ISBN 0-7146-3123-X, F Cass Co). Biblio Dist.
British Radio Drama. John Drakakis. 300p. Date not set. 47.50 (ISBN 0-521-22183-8); pap. 15.95 (ISBN 0-521-29383-9). Cambridge U Pr.
British Rail in Action. Geoffrey Kichenside. 1977. 8.95 (ISBN 0-7153-7427-3). David & Charles.
British Rail Problem: A Case Study in Economic Disaster. Richard Pryke & John Dodgson. LC 75-30589. 288p. 1975. 28.75x (ISBN 0-89158-521-4). Westview.
British Rail: The First Twenty-Five Years. Michael R. Bonavia. LC 80-68687. (Illus.). 208p. 1981. 18.50 (ISBN 0-7153-8002-8). David & Charles.
British Railway Station. Gordon Biddle & Geoffrey Spence. LC 77-89382. 1977. 13.50 (ISBN 0-7153-7467-2). David & Charles.
British Raj & Indian Nationalism. Malcolm Yapp. Ed. by Margaret Killingray & Edmund O'Connor. (World History Ser.). (Illus.). 32p. (gr. 10). 1980. Repr. of 1977 ed. lib. bdg. 5.95 (ISBN 0-89908-228-9); pap. text ed. 1.95 (ISBN 0-89908-203-3). Greenhaven.
British Ranchero in Old California: The Life & Times of Henry Dalton & the Rancho Azusa. Sheldon G. Jackson. LC 77-79745. (Western Frontiersmen Ser.: Vol. 17). (Illus.). 1977. 22.50 o.p. (ISBN 0-87062-122-X). A H Clark.
British Regime in Wisconsin & the Northwest. Louise T. Kellogg. LC 74-124927. (American Scene Ser). (Illus.). 1970. Repr. of 1935 ed. lib. bdg. 35.00 (ISBN 0-306-71047-1). Da Capo.
British Regional Development Since World War I. Christopher M. Law. LC 80-66425. 176p. 1980. 38.00 (ISBN 0-7153-7974-7). David & Charles.
British Regional Employment Statistics: 1841-1971. C. H. Lee. LC 78-25698. 1980. 52.50 (ISBN 0-521-22666-X). Cambridge U Pr.
British Regulars in Montreal: An Imperial Garrison, 1832-1854. Elinor K. Senior. (Illus.). 300p. 1981. 29.95 (ISBN 0-7735-0372-2). McGill-Queens U Pr.
British Right: Conservative & Right-Wing Politics in Britian. Ed. by N. Nugent & R. King. (Illus.). 1977. 23.95 (ISBN 0-566-00156-X, 00989-X, Pub by Saxon Hse England). Lexington Bks.
British Rule in Malaya: The Malayan Civil Service & Its Predecessors, Eighteen Sixty-Seven to Nineteen Forty-Two. Robert Heussler. LC 80-658. (Contributions in Comparative Colonial Studies: No. 6). (Illus.). xx, 356p. 1981. lib. bdg. 37.50 (ISBN 0-313-22243-6, HBM/). Greenwood.
British Rule in Palestine. Bernard Joseph. (Return to Zion Ser.). vii, 279p. 1980. Repr. of 1949 ed. lib. bdg. 20.00x (ISBN 0-87991-136-0). Porcupine Pr.
British Rust Fungi. Malcolm Wilson & M. D. Henderson. 68.00 (ISBN 0-521-06839-8). Cambridge U Pr.
British Sail. Robert Simper. LC 76-58784. 1977. 24.00 (ISBN 0-7153-7263-7). David & Charles.
British Seagull Outboards. 152p. 8.00 o.p. (ISBN 0-89287-153-9, B660). Western Marine Ent.
British Secret Reports: India's Major Non-Violent Movements, 1919-1934. P. N. Chopra. 1980. 12.50x o.p. (ISBN 0-8364-0515-3). South Asia Bks.
British Shipping. 2nd ed. R. H. Thornton. (English Institution Ser). 1959. 29.95 (ISBN 0-521-06626-3). Cambridge U Pr.
British Ships & Seamen. Richard Cooper & Grant Uden. (Illus.). 591p. 1981. lib. bdg. 40.00x (ISBN 0-312-20028-5). St Martin.
British Silhouette Artists & Their Work: 1760-1860. Sue McKechnie. (Illus.). 798p. 1978. 180.00x (ISBN 0-85667-036-7, Pub. by Sotheby Parke Bernet England). Biblio Dist.
British Slave Emancipation: The Sugar Colonies & the Great Experiment, 1830-1865. William A. Green. (Illus.). 1976. 49.50x (ISBN 0-19-822436-2). Oxford U Pr.
British Social Democracy: A Study in Development & Decay. 2nd ed. David Howell. 340p. 1980. 28.50 (ISBN 0-312-10536-3). St Martin.
British Social Life in India 1608-1937. 2nd ed. Dennis Kincaid. (Illus.). 1973. 20.00 (ISBN 0-7100-7284-8). Routledge & Kegan.
British Soldier in America: A Social History of Military Life in the Revolutionary Period. Sylvia R. Frey. 240p. 1981. text ed. 25.00x (ISBN 0-292-78040-0). U of Tex Pr.
British Sporting & Animal Drawings & Paintings. Judy Egerton & Dudley Snelgrove. (From the Paul Mellon Collection Ser.). 1980. combined ed. 225.00 (ISBN 0-8120-5390-7). Barron.
British Statutes in American Law. Elizabeth G. Brown. LC 73-21605. (American Constitutional & Legal History Ser). 1974. Repr. of 1964 ed. lib. bdg. 35.00 (ISBN 0-306-70610-5). Da Capo.
British Steam Railway Locomotive: Volume I, 1825-1925. E. L. Ahron. 29.50x (ISBN 0-392-07695-0, SpS). Soccer.
British Steam Railway Locomotive: Volume 2, 1925-1965. O. S. Nock. 31.50x (ISBN 0-392-07700-0, SpS). Soccer.
British Stratigraphy. F. A. Middlemiss. (Introducing Geology Ser.). 1975. pap. text ed. 5.95x (ISBN 0-04-550023-1). Allen Unwin.
British Submarine. F. W. Lipscomb. 298p. 1980. 29.95x (ISBN 0-85177-086-X, Pub. by Cornell England.). State Mutual Bk.
British System of Government. 3rd ed. A. H. Birch. (Minerva Ser. of Students' Handbooks). 1973. text ed. 16.50x o.p. (ISBN 0-04-320091-5); pap. text ed. 8.95x o.p. (ISBN 0-04-320092-3). Allen Unwin.
British System of Government. 4th ed. Anthony H. Birch. (Minerva Series of Students Handbooks). (Illus.). 320p. 1980. text ed. 19.95x (ISBN 0-04-320142-3, 2485); pap. text ed. 7.95x (ISBN 0-04-320143-1, 2486). Allen Unwin.
British Tar in Fact & Fiction. Charles N. Robinson. LC 68-26601. (Illus.). 1968. Repr. of 1909 ed. 20.00 (ISBN 0-8103-3514-X). Gale.
British Technology Index: Annual Volume 1978. Ed. by Library Association, London. LC 63-23735. 828p. 1979. 285.00x (ISBN 0-85365-911-7). Intl Pubns Serv.
British Television Drama. Ed. by George Brandt. LC 80-41031. (Illus.). 300p. Date not set. price not set (ISBN 0-521-22186-2); pap. price not set (ISBN 0-521-29384-7). Cambridge U Pr.
British Theatre Directory 1979. Ed. by John Offord Pubns & British Theatre Institute. 1979. text ed. cancelled o.s.i. (ISBN 0-903931-20-6, Pub. by John Offord Pubns England). Drama Bk.
British Theatre Since Nineteen Fifty Five: A Reassessment. Ronald Hayman. 1979. 12.95 (ISBN 0-19-219127-6). Oxford U Pr.
British Tortricoid Moths. J. D. Bradley et al. Incl. Vol.1. Cochylidae & Tortricidae: Tortricinae. viii, 251p. 1973. 50.00x (ISBN 0-903874-01-6); Vol. 2. Tortrkidae: Olethreutinae. viii, 336p. 1979. 100.00x (ISBN 0-903874-06-7). (Illus., Pub. by Brit Mus Nat Hist England). Sabbot-Natural Hist Bks.
British Tourist Authority Guide to the North of England. Ed. by Jenny Willis. (Illus.). 158p. 1980. bds. 20.00x (ISBN 0-7099-0384-7, Pub. by Croom Helm Ltd England). Biblio Dist.
British Trade Unions, Eighteen Seventy-Five to Nineteen Thirty-Three. John Lovell. (Studies in Economic & Social History). 1977. pap. text ed. 5.00x (ISBN 0-333-17926-9). Humanities.
British Trade Unions Today. C. Jenkins & J. E. Mortimer. 1965. 13.75 (ISBN 0-08-011169-6); pap. 6.25 (ISBN 0-08-011168-8). Pergamon.
British Tyroglyphidae, 2 Vols. Albert D. Michael. Repr. of 1903 ed. Set. 69.50 (ISBN 0-384-38875-2). Johnson Repr.
British Union Catalogue of Periodicals 1979. Ed. by Gascoigne. 1980. text ed. 31.50 (ISBN 0-408-70857-3). Butterworths.
British War Aims & Peace Diplomacy Nineteen-Fourteen to Nineteen-Eighteen. V. H. Rothwell. 1971. 33.00x (ISBN 0-19-822349-8). Oxford U Pr.
British War Poetry in the Age of Romanticism: 1793-1815. Ed. by Betty T. Bennett. LC 75-31144. (Romantic Context: Poetry 1789-1830 Ser.: Vol. 1). 1977. lib. bdg. 47.00 (ISBN 0-8240-2100-2). Garland Pub.
British Watercolors, Seventeen Fifty to Eighteen Fifty. Pierpont Morgan Library. (Illus.). 1966. 5.00 (ISBN 0-685-19430-2). Pierpont Morgan.
British Watercolours in the Victoria & Albert Museum: An Illustrated Summary Catalogue of the National Collection. Lionel Lambourne. (Illus.). 455p. 1980. 125.00x (ISBN 0-85667-067-7, Pub. by Sotheby Parke Bernet England). Biblio Dist.
British Weights & Measures: A History from Antiquity to the Seventeenth Century. Ronald E. Zupko. 1977. 21.50 (ISBN 0-299-07340-8, 734). U of Wis Pr.

British Working Class Reader Seventeen-Ninety to Eighteen Forty-Eight: Literacy & Social Tension. Robert K. Webb. LC 55-27828. Repr. of 1955 ed. lib. bdg. 13.50x (ISBN 0-678-00578-8). Kelley.

British Writers, Vol. IV. Ed. by Ian Scott-Kilvert. LC 78-23483. 1981. lib. bdg. 55.00 (ISBN 0-684-16635-6). Scribner.

British Writers, Vol. V. Ed. by Ian Scott-Kilvert. LC 78-23483. 1981. lib. bdg. 55.00 (ISBN 0-684-16636-4). Scribner.

British Writers, Vol. III. Ed. by Ian Scott-Kilvert. LC 78-23483. 1980. lib. bdg. 55.00 (ISBN 0-684-16408-6). Scribner.

British Writers, Vol. II. Ed. by Ian Scott-Kilvert & British Council. LC 78-23483. (British Council Pamphlet Ser.). 1979. lib. bdg. 55.00 (ISBN 0-684-16407-8). Scribner.

British Writing on Disarmament Nineteen Fourteen - Nineteen Seventy Eight: A Bibliography. Lorna Lloyd & Nicholas Sims. 1979. 37.25x (ISBN 0-89397-052-2). Nichols Pub.

British Year Book of International Law 1978, Vol. XLIX. Ed. by R. Y. Jennings & Ian Brownlie. (British Year Book of International Law). (Illus.). 1980. 89.00x (ISBN 0-19-818178-7). Oxford U Pr.

British Year Book of International Law 1979, Vol. 50. R. Y. Jennings & Ian Brownlie. 464p. 1981. 98.00 (ISBN 0-19-825360-5). Oxford U Pr.

British Yearbook of Internaional Law. Royal Institute of International Affairs. Incl. Vol. 3. 1965. 15.95x (ISBN 0-19-214625-4); Vol. 7. 1965. 15.95x (ISBN 0-19-214629-7); Vol. 39, 1963. Ed. by H. Waldock & R. Y. Jennings. 1965. 24.95x (ISBN 0-19-214622-X); Vol. 40, 1964. Ed. by H. Waldock & R. Y. Jennings. 1966. 24.95x (ISBN 0-19-214623-8); Vol. 41, 1965-66. Ed. by H. Waldock & R. Y. Jennings. 1968. 24.95x (ISBN 0-19-214657-2); Ed. by H. Waldock & R. Y. Jennings. 1969. 24.95x (ISBN 0-19-214658-0); Vol. 44. Ed. by H. Waldcock & R. Y. Jennings. 1970. 24.95x (ISBN 0-19-214660-2); Vol. 45. Ed. by H. Waldock & R. Y. Jennings. 1973. 59.50x (ISBN 0-19-214661-0). (Royal Institute of International Affairs Ser.). Oxford U Pr.

Brittany Spaniels. Ed. by Beverly Pisano & Evelyn Monte. (Illus.). 128p. 1980. lib. bdg. 2.95 (ISBN 0-87666-708-6, KW092). TFH Pubns.

Britten. Imogen Holst. (Great Composer Ser.). (gr. 9 up). 1980. 10.95 (ISBN 0-571-18000-0, Pub. by Faber & Faber). Merrimack Bk Serv.

Britten. Michael Kennedy. (Master Musicians Ser.). (Illus.). 364p. 1981. 22.50x (ISBN 0-460-03175-9, Pub. by J. M. Dent England). Biblio Dist.

Britten & Auden in the Thirties: The Year 1936. Donald Mitchell. LC 80-25980. (Illus.). 174p. 1981. 15.00 (ISBN 0-295-95814-6). U of Wash Pr.

Britten's Old Clocks & Watches & Their Makers. 8th ed. Ed. by Cecil Clutten. (Illus.). 1973. 50.00 (ISBN 0-525-93140-6). Dutton.

Brittle Glass. Norah Lofts. 1977. pap. 1.75 o.p. (ISBN 0-449-23037-6, Crest). Fawcett.

Broad & Alien Is the World. Ciro Alegria. Tr. by Harriet de Onis from Span. 434p. 1973. 12.95 (ISBN 0-85036-176-1). Dufour.

Broad Church. Charles M. Davies. Ed. by Robert L. Wolff. LC 75-1505. (Victorian Fiction Ser.). 1975. Repr. of 1875 ed. lib. bdg. 66.00 (ISBN 0-8240-1579-7). Garland Pub.

Broad Grins: Comprising, with New Additional Tales in Verse, Those Formerly Published Under the Title of "My Nightgown & Slippers", Repr. Of 1802 Ed. George Colman. Bd. with Eccentricities for Edinburgh. Repr. of 1816 ed. LC 75-31180. (Romantic Context: Poetry 1789-1830 Ser.: Vol. 33). 1977. lib. bdg. 47.00 (ISBN 0-8240-2132-0). Garland Pub.

Broad Highway. Jeffrey Farnol. (Barbara Cartland's Library of Love: Vol. 16). 213p. 1980. 12.95x (ISBN 0-7156-1476-2, Pub. by Duckworth England). Biblio Dist.

Broad Street Bullies: The Incredible Story of the Philadelphia Flyers. Jack Chevalier. (Illus.). 192p. 1974. pap. 5.95 o.s.i. (ISBN 0-02-028180-3, Collier). Macmillan.

Broad Terms for United Nations Programmes & Activities, 1979. 186p. 1980. pap. 13.00 (ISBN 0-686-68945-3, UN79/0/1, UN). Unipub.

Broadax & Bayonet: The Role of the United States Army in the Development of the Northwest, Seventeen Ninety to Eighteen Thirty-Four. Francis P. Prucha. LC 53-6511. 279p. 1967. pap. 1.95 o.p. (ISBN 0-8032-5151-3, BB 360, Bison). U of Nebr Pr.

Broadcast Advertising: A Comprehensive Working Textbook. Sherilyn K. Zeigler & Herbert H. Howard. LC 78-50048. (Advertising & Journalism Ser.). 1978. pap. text ed. 10.50 (ISBN 0-88244-167-1). Grid Pub.

Broadcast & Two-Way Radio Operators Permit Handbook. 5th ed. Edward M. Noll. LC 79-65743. 1979. pap. 6.50 (ISBN 0-672-21627-2). Sams.

Broadcast Announcer's License Manual: A Guide to FCC Third Class Exam. P. Anthony Zeiss & Noel T. Smith. (Illus.). (gr. 10 up). 1976. pap. 7.15 (ISBN 0-8104-0826-0). Hayden.

Broadcast News Deskbook. Clark Edwards. 1972. text ed. 2.00x spiral bdg. (ISBN 0-87543-082-1). Lucas.

Broadcast News: The Inside Out. Julius Hunter & Lynne S. Gross. LC 79-2441. (Illus.). 1980. 14.95 (ISBN 0-8016-2319-7). Mosby.

Broadcast Programming. 5th ed. Ed. by Charles Clift, III & Archie Greer. LC 79-66407. (III). 1979. pap. text ed. 7.75 (ISBN 0-8191-0820-0). U Pr of Amer.

Broadcast Programming: Strategies for Winning Television & Radio Audiences. Susan T. Eastman & Sidney W. Head. 400p. 1980. text ed. 15.95x (ISBN 0-534-00882-8). Wadsworth Pub.

Broadcast Programming: The Current Perspective. 6th ed. Ed. by Charles Clift, III & Archie Greer. LC 80-8127. 249p. 1981. text ed. 8.50 (ISBN 0-8191-1429-4). U Pr of Amer.

Broadcasting & Bargaining: Labor Relations in Radio & Television. Ed. by Allen E. Koenig. 1970. 25.00 (ISBN 0-299-05521-3). U of Wis Pr.

Broadcasting & Detente. Gerhard Wettig. LC 77-72285. 1977. 14.95x (ISBN 0-312-10588-6). St Martin.

Broadcasting from the High Seas: The History of Offshore Radio in Europe 1958-76. Paul Harris. (Illus.). 1977. 20.00x (ISBN 0-904505-07-3, P Harris). Nichols Pub.

Broadcasting in a Free Society. Windlesham. (Mainstream Ser.). 172p. 1980. 19.50x (ISBN 0-631-11371-1, Pub. by Basil Blackwell). Biblio Dist.

Broadcasting in America. 3rd. ed. Sydney W. Head. LC 75-19534. (Illus.). 704p. 1976. text ed. 18.95 (ISBN 0-395-20644-8); inst. manual 1.75 (ISBN 0-395-20645-6). HM.

Broadcasting in Canada. E. S. Hallman. (Case Studies on Broadcasting Systems). (Orig.). 1977. pap. 14.00 (ISBN 0-7100-8528-1). Routledge & Kegan.

Broadcasting in Guyana. Ron Sanders. (Case Studies on Broadcasting Systems). (Orig.). 1978. pap. 14.00 (ISBN 0-7100-0025-1). Routledge & Kegan.

Broadcasting in Japan. Masami Ito et al. (Case Studies on Broadcasting Systems). (Orig.). 1978. pap. 14.00 (ISBN 0-7100-0043-X). Routledge & Kegan.

Broadcasting in Mexico. L. A. De Noriega & F. Leach. (Case Studies on Broadcasting Systems). (Orig.). 1979. pap. 12.50 (ISBN 0-7100-0416-8). Routledge & Kegan.

Broadcasting in Peninsular Malaysia. R. Adhikarya. (Case Studies on Broadcasting Systems). 1977. pap. 14.00 (ISBN 0-7100-8530-3). Routledge & Kegan.

Broadcasting in Sweden. Edward W. Ploman. (Case Studies on Broadcasting Systems). (Orig.). 1976. pap. 14.00 (ISBN 0-685-76681-0). Routledge & Kegan.

Broadcasting to the Soviet Union: International Politics & Radio. Maury Lisann. LC 74-14046. (Illus.). 224p. 1975. text ed. 23.95 (ISBN 0-275-05590-6). Praeger.

Broadcasting-Vision & Sound. D. Wilson. 1968. 4.50 (ISBN 0-08-012849-1). Pergamon.

Broadening Church. Lefferts A. Loetscher. LC 54-7110. 1957. 9.00x o.p. (ISBN 0-8122-7018-5). U of Pa Pr.

Broadman Comments: April-June, 1981. Donald F. Ackland. (Orig.). 1981. pap. 2.15 (ISBN 0-8054-1462-2). Broadman.

Broadman Comments, July-September, 1981. Dojnald F. Ackland. 1981. pap. 2.15 (ISBN 0-8054-1463-0). Broadman.

Broadman Comments, Nineteen Eighty-One-Eighty-Two. Donald F. Ackland et al. 1981. pap. 4.75 (ISBN 0-8054-1465-7). Broadman.

Broadman Comments, October-December, Nineteen Eighty. Donald F. Ackland et al. 1980. pap. 2.00 o.p. (ISBN 0-8054-1458-4). Broadman.

Broadway. rev. ed. Brooks Atkinson. LC 74-12077. (Illus.). 640p. 1974. 12.95 o.s.i. (ISBN 0-02-504180-0). Macmillan.

Broadway Musical: A Complete LP Discography. Gordon W. Hodgins. LC 80-18911. 188p. 1980. 10.00 (ISBN 0-8108-1343-2). Scarecrow.

Broca's Brain. Carl Sagan. 384p. 1980. pap. 2.95 (ISBN 0-345-28823-8). Ballantine.

Broch, Dramen: Kommentierte Werkausgabe, Bd. 7. Hermann Broch. (Suhrkamp Taschenbuecher: No. 538). 448p. (Ger.). 1980. pap. text ed. 6.50 (ISBN 3-518-37038-3, Pub. by Insel Verlag Germany). Suhrkamp.

Brockhaus, 2 vols. (Ger.). 1977. Set. 115.00. Pergamon.

Brockhaus Enzyklopaedie, 24 vols. 17th ed. 1966. Set. 1845.00 (ISBN 0-8277-3005-5). Maxwell Sci Intl.

Brockhaus Riemann Musiklexikon, Vol. 1, A-K. Carl Dahlhaus & Hans H. Eggebrecht. (Ger.). 1978. 99.50 (ISBN 3-7653-0303-8). Eur-Am Music.

Brogeen & the Bronze Lizard. Patricia Lynch. LC 77-99123. (Illus.). (gr. 4-6). 1970. 4.95g o.s.i. (ISBN 0-02-761490-5). Macmillan.

Brogeen Follows the Magic Tune. Patricia Lynch. LC 68-24105. (Illus.). (gr. 4-6). 1968. 4.95g o.s.i. (ISBN 0-02-761480-8). Macmillan.

Broke Down Engine. Ron Goulart. 1971. 10.95 (ISBN 0-02-544880-3). Macmillan.

Broken Boundaries-Broken Lives. Joy P. Gage. 1981. pap. 3.95 (ISBN 0-89636-068-7). Accent Bks.

Broken Chains. Benjamin C. Horrell. 1972. pap. 2.25 (ISBN 0-87148-106-5). Pathway Pr.

Broken Connection. Robert Lifton. 1980. pap. 7.95 (ISBN 0-671-41386-4, Touchstone). S&S.

Broken Covenant: American Civil Religion in Time of Trail. Robert N. Bellah. 1976. pap. 4.95 (ISBN 0-8164-2123-4). Crossroad NY.

Broken Family. Elizabeth Christman. 256p. 1981. 10.95 (ISBN 0-688-00473-3). Morrow.

Broken Fountain. Thomas Belmonte. LC 78-32167. 1979. 12.50 (ISBN 0-231-04542-5). Columbia U Pr.

Broken Hand: The Life of Thomas Fitzpatrick, Mountain Man, Guide & Indian Agent. Leroy R. Hafen. LC 80-23451. (Illus.). xiv, 359p. 1981. pap. 6.50 (ISBN 0-8032-7208-1, BB 753, Bison). U of Nebr Pr.

Broken Heart. John Ford. Ed. by Donald K. Anderson, Jr. LC 68-10354. (Regents Renaissance Drama Ser.). 1968. 7.95x (ISBN 0-8032-0259-8); pap. 1.65x (ISBN 0-8032-5259-5, BB 227, Bison). U of Nebr Pr.

Broken Icon: Intuitive Existentialism in Classical Russian Fiction. Geoffrey Clive. LC 70-182019. 228p. 1972. 7.95 o.s.i. (ISBN 0-02-526170-3). Macmillan.

Broken Image. Floyd W. Matson. 1964. 6.95 o.s.i. (ISBN 0-8076-0256-6). Braziller.

Broken Images. Simon Leys. (Allison & Busby's Motive Ser.). 160p. 1981. pap. 8.95 (ISBN 0-8052-8069-3, Pub. by Allison & Busby England). Schocken.

Broken Patterns. Pat Jordan. LC 76-48056. 1977. 7.95 (ISBN 0-396-07387-5). Dodd.

Broken Peace Pipes: A Four-Hundred Year History of the American Indian. Irvin M. Peithmann. 320p. 1964. 11.75 (ISBN 0-398-01468-X). C C Thomas.

Broken Shore: The Marin Peninsula, a Perspective on California History. Arthur Quinn. (Illus.). 288p. 1981. 14.95 (ISBN 0-87905-085-3). Peregrine Smith.

Broken Taboo: Sex in the Family. Blair Justice & Rita Justice. LC 78-23720. 1979. 14.95 (ISBN 0-87705-389-8). Human Sci Pr.

Broken Taboo: Sex in the Family. Blair Justice & Rita Justice. 304p. 1981. pap. 6.95 (ISBN 0-87705-482-7). Human Sci Pr.

Broken Vase. Rex Stout. 1976. pap. 1.25 o.s.i. (ISBN 0-515-04065-7). Jove Pubns.

Broken Vows: A Novel of Betrayal. Robert J. Charles. LC 80-25321. 1981. 10.95 (ISBN 0-934878-00-5). Dembner Bks.

Broken World, 1919-1939. Raymond J. Sontag. LC 77-156572. (Rise of Modern Europe Ser). (Illus.). 1971. 15.00x o.s.i. (ISBN 0-06-013954-4, HarpT). Har-Row.

Broker, Mediator, Patron, & Kinsman: An Historical Analysis of Key Leadership Roles in a Rural Malaysian District. Conner Bailey. LC 75-620140. (Papers in International Studies, Southeast Asia Ser.). 89p. 1980. pap. 9.00 (ISBN 0-89680-024-5). Ohio U Ctr Intl.

Brokers Beware: Selling Real Estate Within the Law. Fred Fisher. 220p. 1981. text ed. 15.95 (ISBN 0-8359-0569-1). Reston.

Broker's Wife. Max Collins. (Quarry Ser.). pap. 1.50 o.p. (ISBN 0-425-03187-X). Berkley Pub.

Bromeliaceae of Ecuador. Jean Gilmartin. (Monographiae Phanerogamarum Ser.: No. 5). (Illus.). 1972. 60.00 (ISBN 3-7682-0725-0). Lubrecht & Cramer.

Bromocriptine: A Clinical & Pharmacologica Review. Michael O. Thorner et al. 189p. 1980. text ed. 24.00 (ISBN 0-89004-419-8). Raven.

Broncbuster. Mike Clumpner. 220p. (Orig.). 1980. pap. 1.95 (ISBN 0-89083-671-X). Zebra.

Bronchial Asthma: Principles of Diagnosis & Treatment. M. Eric Gershwin. 1981. write for info. (ISBN 0-8089-1331-X). Grune.

Bronchial Carcinoma. Thomas W. Shields. (American Lectures in Surgery Ser.). (Illus.). 200p. 1974. text ed. 17.50 (ISBN 0-398-03095-2). C C Thomas.

Bronchology. Genrikh I. Lukomsky. LC 78-31431. (Illus.). 1979. 57.50 (ISBN 0-8016-3041-X). Mosby.

Bronte Sisters. 1200p. Date not set. 9.98 (ISBN 0-7064-1348-2). Mayflower Bks.

Brontes in Ireland. William Wright. LC 76-29146. (Illus.). 1981. Repr. of 1894 ed. 10.00 (ISBN 0-916620-12-3). Portals Pr.

Brontes: The Critical Heritage. Ed. by Miriam Allott. (Critical Heritage Ser). 1974. 39.00x (ISBN 0-7100-7701-7). Routledge & Kegan.

Brontosaurus Principle: A Manual for Corporate Survival. Thomas K. Connellan. 1976. 12.95 o.p. (ISBN 0-685-67122-4). P-H.

Bronx Art Deco Architecture: An Exposition. Donald Sullivan & Brian Danforth. (Illus.). 32p. 1976. pap. 3.50 (ISBN 0-89062-024-5, Pub. by W Bronx Rest). Pub Ctr Cult Res.

Bronx Zoo. Sparky Lyle & Peter Golenbeck. 1980. pap. 2.50 o.s.i. (ISBN 0-440-10764-4). Dell.

Bronze Age. Vere G. Childe. LC 63-18050. 1930. 10.00x (ISBN 0-8196-0123-3). Biblo.

Bronze Age Goldwork of the British Isles. Joan J. Taylor. LC 75-12160. (Gulbenkian Archaeological Ser.). (Illus.). 188p. 1981. 95.00 (ISBN 0-521-20802-5). Cambridge U Pr.

Bronze Age in Barbarian Europe. Jacques Briard. (Illus.). 1979. 25.00 (ISBN 0-7100-0086-3). Routledge & Kegan.

Bronze & Iron: Old Latin Poetry from Its Beginning to 100 B. C. Janet Lembke. 1973. 16.75x (ISBN 0-520-02164-9). U of Cal Pr.

Bronzes of West Africa. Leon Underwood. (gr. 10 up). 1968. 6.50 o.p. (ISBN 0-85458-090-5). Transatlantic.

Brook. Carol Carrick. (gr. k-2). 1967. 4.95g o.s.i. (ISBN 0-02-717330-5). Macmillan.

Brook Kerith. new ed. George Moore. LC 74-92700. 1969. 7.95 o.p. (ISBN 0-87140-507-5). Liveright.

Brookie & Her Lamb. rev. ed. M. B. Goffstein. 32p. (ps up). 1981. 6.95 (ISBN 0-374-30990-6). FS&G.

Brookings Papers on Economic Activity. Ed. by William C. Brainard & George L. Perry. 1981. pap. subscription on 2 issues (ISBN 0-8157-1110-7). Brookings.

Brooklyn Dodgers. Donald Honig. (Illus.). 192p. 1981. 16.95 (ISBN 0-312-10600-9). St Martin.

Brooklyn, U. S. A. Ed. by Rita S. Miller. (Brooklyn College Studies on Society in Change Ser.). (Illus.). 1979. 20.00 (ISBN 0-930888-02-2). Brooklyn Coll Pr.

Brooklyn: Where Else. Harry Bedell. 1981. 8.50 (ISBN 0-8062-1621-2). Carlton.

Brooks Range: Environmental Watershed. Ed. by Alaska Geographic Staff. LC 72-92087. (Alaska Geographic: Vol. 4, No. 2). (Illus.). 1977. pap. 9.95 o.p. (ISBN 0-88240-091-6). Alaska Northwest.

Broomtail, Brother of Lightning. Miriam E. Mason. (Illus.). (gr. 3-5). 1952. 3.75 o.s.i. (ISBN 0-02-763180-X); PLB 3.64 o.s.i. (ISBN 0-02-763200-8). Macmillan.

Brothel to Boomtown: Yuma's Lively Past. Frank Love & Leland Feitz. (Illus., Orig.). 1981. pap. 2.95 (ISBN 0-936564-19-9). Little London.

Brother. F. D. Reeve. 1971. 6.95 o.p. (ISBN 0-374-11697-0). FS&G.

Brother Beloved. Francena H. Arnold. 1967. pap. 2.25 (ISBN 0-8024-0050-7). Moody.

Brother Can You Spare a Dime? The Great Depression, 1929-1933. Milton Meltzer. (Sundial Paperbks.). 1972. pap. 1.95 (ISBN 0-394-70806-7, VS-6, Vin). Random.

Brother Carl. Susan Sontag. LC 72-82949. (Illus.). 192p. 1974. pap. 4.95 o.p. (ISBN 0-374-11700-4); pap. 4.95 (ISBN 0-374-51026-1). FS&G.

Brother Dusty-Feet. Rosemary Sutcliff. (Illus.). 240p. (gr. 6 up). 1980. Repr. of 1952 ed. 10.95 (ISBN 0-19-271444-9). Oxford U Pr.

Brother Enemy. Elisabeth Mace. LC 80-29258. 128p. (gr. 6 up). 1981. 7.95 (ISBN 0-8253-0031-2). Beaufort Bks NY.

Brother Jesus. write for info o.p. (ISBN 0-685-61386-0). Aum Pubns.

Brother Man. Roger Mais. (Caribbean Writers Ser.). 1974. pap. text ed. 3.95x (ISBN 0-435-98585-X). Heinemann Ed.

Brother Mann. Nigel Hamilton. LC 78-15114. 1979. 30.00 (ISBN 0-300-02348-0). Yale U Pr.

Brother Mouky & the Falling Sun. Karen Whiteside. LC 79-2014. (Illus.). 32p. (gr. k-3). 1980. 7.95 (ISBN 0-06-026407-1, HarpJ); PLB 7.89 (ISBN 0-06-026408-X). Har-Row.

Brother of the Wolves. Jean Thompson. LC 78-18014. (gr. 4-6). 1978. 7.95 (ISBN 0-688-22168-8); PLB 7.63 (ISBN 0-688-32168-2). Morrow.

Brother to Dragons. Robert P. Warren. 1953. 10.95 o.p. (ISBN 0-394-40312-6). Random.

Brother Whale. Roy Nickerson. LC 76-30828. (Illus.). 1977. pap. 5.95 (ISBN 0-87701-087-0). Chronicle Bks.

Brother, Which Drummer. Robert M. Brown. LC 60-7426. 1960. 4.50 o.p. (ISBN 0-15-114423-0). HarBraceJ.

Brother Wolf. Mildred T. Johnstone. LC 79-20422. (Illus.). 1980. 6.95 o.p. (ISBN 0-916820-13-0). Center Pubns.

Brotherhood. (Agni Yoga Ser.). 1962. 9.00x (ISBN 0-933574-13-4). Agni Yoga Soc.

Brotherhood of Mr. Shasta. Eugene E. Thomas. 307p. 1981. pap. 10.00 (ISBN 0-89540-067-7). Sun Pub.

Brotherhood of Mt. Shasta. Minoru Tanaka. 88p. 1981. pap. 4.50 (ISBN 0-89540-009-X). Sun Pub.

Brotherhood of Oil: Energy Policy & the Public Interest. Robert Engler. 1978. pap. 2.95 (ISBN 0-451-61892-0, ME1892, Ment). NAL.

Brotherly Love. William D. Blankenship. LC 80-70212. 1981. 11.95 (ISBN 0-87795-301-5). Arbor Hse.

Brothers. Bobby J. Nelson. LC 74-30378. 223p. 1975. 7.95 o.s.i. (ISBN 0-02-588590-1, 58859). Macmillan.

Brothers & Friends: An Intimate Portrait of C. S. Lewis; the Diaries of Major Warren Hamilton Lewis. Ed. by Clyde Kilby & Marj Mead. LC 80-7756. (Illus.). 1981. 14.95 (ISBN 0-06-065244-6, HarpR). Har-Row.

Brothers & Sisters. Ed. by Arnold Adoff. LC 76-102961. (Modern Stories by Black Americans Ser). (gr. 7 up). 1970. 6.95g o.s.i. (ISBN 0-02-700130-X). Macmillan.

Brothers & Sisters. Karl Koenig. 1980. pap. 6.95 (ISBN 0-903540-38-X, Pub. by Floris Books). St George Bk Serv.

Brothers & Sisters Are Like That: Stories to Read Yourself. Child Study Association. LC 78-158703. (Illus.). (gr. 1-4). 1971. 6.95 (ISBN 0-690-16041-0, TYC-J); PLB 7.89 (ISBN 0-690-16042-9). T Y Crowell.

Brothers & Sisters of the January Moon. Jack Libert. (Illus., Orig.). 1971. pap. 2.00 (ISBN 0-911732-58-6). Irego.

Brothers Ashkenazi. I. J. Singer. LC 80-66017. 1980. 14.95 (ISBN 0-689-11102-9). Atheneum.

Brothers Duchamp: Jacques Villon, Raymond Duchamp-Villon, Marcel Duchamp. Pierre Cabanne. LC 75-37285. (Illus.). 1976. 60.00 (ISBN 0-8212-0666-4, 109800). NYGS.

Brothers Mann. Nigel Hamilton. LC 78-15114. 431p. pap. 9.95 (ISBN 0-300-02668-4). Yale U Pr.

Brothers of Light: The Penitentes of the Southwest. A. Corbin Henderson. LC 77-88835. 1977. Repr. of 1937 ed. 13.50 (ISBN 0-88307-534-2); pap. 3.95 o.p. (ISBN 0-88307-535-0). Gannon.

Brothers of the Head. Brian Aldiss. (Illus.). 1977. pap. 7.95 (ISBN 0-8467-0386-6, Pub. by Two Continents). Hippocrene Bks.

Brothers of the Wind. Jane Yolen. (Illus.). 1981. 10.955 (ISBN 0-399-20787-2). Philomel.

Brothers on the Trail. Max Brand. 1972. pap. 1.95 (ISBN 0-446-86392-0). Warner Bks.

Brothers; or, Treachery Punish'd. Bd. with Memoirs of Capt. John Creichton. John Creichton; Perjur'd Citizen; or, Female Revenge. LC 79-170581. (Foundations of the Novel Ser.: Vol. 55). lib. bdg. 50.00 (ISBN 0-685-41749-2). Garland Pub.

Brothers to Demons, Brothers to Gods. Jack Willianson. 1981. pap. 2.25 (ISBN 0-425-04529-3). Berkley Pub.

Brown. Orville Schell. 1978. 10.00 (ISBN 0-394-41043-2). Random.

Brown Bag: A Bag Full of Sermons for Children. Jerry M. Jordan. (Illus.). 117p. 1981. pap. 5.95 (ISBN 0-8298-0411-0). Pilgrim NY.

Brown Bagging It: The Lunch Box Idea Book. Adeline G. Shell & Kay Reynolds. LC 78-10945. 1979. 8.95 (ISBN 0-671-18414-8); pap. 3.95 (ISBN 0-671-18342-7). Sovereign Bks.

Brown Buck. A. L. Buck. (Illus.). 1976. 7.95 (ISBN 0-7181-1456-6, Pub. by Michael Joseph). Merrimack Bk Serv.

Brown Families of Bristol Counties, Massachusetts & Rhode Island & Descendants of Jared Talbot. Carl Boyer, 3rd et al. LC 80-68755. (New England Colonial Families: Vol. 1). 219p. 1980. 18.35 (ISBN 0-936124-04-0). C Boyer.

Brown on Resolution. C. S. Forester. 1978. 6.95 (ISBN 0-370-00680-1, Pub. by Chatto Bodley Jonathan). Merrimack Bk Serv.

Brown Palace in Denver. Caroline Bancroft. 1955. pap. 1.50 (ISBN 0-933472-15-3). Johnson Colo.

Brown Planthopper: Threat to Rice Production in Asia. 369p. 1979. pap. 21.50 (R038, IRRI). Unipub.

Brown Rot Fungi of Fruit: Their Biology & Control. R. J. Byrde & H. J. Willetts. 1977. text ed. 19.50 (ISBN 0-08-019740-X). Pergamon.

Brown Trout Fisherman's Guide. David Richey. LC 78-53428. 1978. 10.95 o.p. (ISBN 0-8015-0952-1). Dutton.

Brownian Motion, Hardy Spaces & Bounded Mean Oscillation. K. E. Petersen. LC 76-46860. (London Mathematical Society Lecture Notes: No. 28). (Illus.). 1977. limp bdg. 14.50x (ISBN 0-521-21512-9). Cambridge U Pr.

Brownies. P. Cox. (Peter Possum Paperbacks Ser). 1967. pap. 0.95 o.p. (ISBN 0-531-05105-6). Watts.

Brownies at Home. Palmer Cox. LC 68-28403. (Illus.). (ps-3). 1968. pap. 2.00 o.p. (ISBN 0-486-21969-0). Dover.

Browning. Roy E. Gridley. (Routledge Author Guides). 1972. 16.00x (ISBN 0-7100-7368-2); pap. 7.95 (ISBN 0-7100-7369-0). Routledge & Kegan.

Browning Critics. Ed. by Boyd Litzinger & K. L. Knickerbocker. LC 65-27008. 448p. 1965. pap. 7.50x (ISBN 0-8131-0113-1). U Pr of Ky.

Browning Institute Studies. William S. Peterson. Incl. Vol. 1. 1973; Vol. 2. 1974; Vol. 3. 1975; Vol. 4. 1976; Vol. 5. 1977; Vol. 6. 1978; Vol. 7. 1979. 21.50x (ISBN 0-686-67542-8); Vol. 8. 1980. 23.50x (ISBN 0-686-67543-6). LC 73-80684. (Illus.). 23.00x (ISBN 0-685-92147-6, Pub. by Browning Inst). Pub. Ctr Cult Res.

Browning: The Poems. Robert Browning. (Penguin Poets Ser.). 1981. Vol. 1. pap. 4.95 (ISBN 0-14-042259-5); Vol. 2. pap. 4.95 (ISBN 0-14-042260-9). Penguin.

Browning's Beginnings: The Art of Disclosure. Herbert F. Tucker. 350p. 1980. 22.50x (ISBN 0-8166-0946-2). U of Minn Pr.

Browning's Clerical Characters. Charles T. Phipps. (Salzburg Studies in English Literature: Romantic Reassessment: No. 62). 336p. 1976. pap. text ed. 25.00x (ISBN 0-391-01497-8). Humanities.

Brownings Correspondence: A Checklist. Ed. by Philip Kelley & Ronald Hudson. LC 77-93932. (Illus.). 1978. 125.00x (ISBN 0-685-27179-X, Pub. by Browning Inst). Pub Ctr Cult Res.

Browning's Later Poetry, 1881-1889. Clyde de L. Ryals. LC 75-16927. 288p. 1975. 18.50x (ISBN 0-8014-0964-0). Cornell U Pr.

Brownings of Casa Guidi. Edward C. McAleer. (Illus.). 15.00x (ISBN 0-685-99384-1, Pub. by Browning Inst); pap. 6.95x (ISBN 0-930252-03-9). Pub Ctr Cult Res.

Brownlow North: His Life & Work. K. Moody-Stuart. 1961. 1.95 (ISBN 0-686-12509-6). Banner of Truth.

Brown's Book of Carburetors. 154p. 1980. 9.95. Madison Pub.

Browns of Providence Plantations: The Colonial Years. James B. Hedges. LC 52-5032. (Illus.). 379p. 1968. Repr. of 1952 ed. 15.00 (ISBN 0-87057-109-5, Pub. by Brown U Pr). Univ Pr of New England.

Browns of Providence Plantations: The Nineteenth Century. James B. Hedges. LC 68-23790. (Illus.). 325p. 1968. 15.00 (ISBN 0-87057-110-9, Pub. by Brown U Pr). Univ Pr of New England.

Brownstone. Ken Eulo. (Orig.). 1980. pap. write for info. PB.

Brownstone Cavalry. Howard Crook. 1981. 13.95 (ISBN 0-671-44776-9). Summit Bks.

Brownstone House. Rae Foley. 1978. Repr. 1.75 o.s.i. (ISBN 0-515-04491-1). Jove Pubns.

Brownsville Affair: National Crisis & Black Reaction. Ann J. Lane. LC 73-139357. 1973. 13.50 (ISBN 0-8046-9008-1); pap. 6.50 (ISBN 0-8046-9045-6). Kennikat.

Browser's Dictionary. John Ciardi. LC 79-1658. 464p. 1980. 16.95 (ISBN 0-06-010766-9, HarpT). Har-Row.

Bruce Catton's America. Bruce Catton. Ed. by Oliver Jensen. LC 79-17534. (Illus.). 224p. 1979. deluxe ed. 17.50 (ISBN 0-8281-0310-0, Dist. by Doubleday). Am Heritage.

Bruce Jay Friedman. Max F. Schulz. (U. S. Authors Ser.: No. 219). 1974. lib. bdg. 10.95 (ISBN 0-8057-0290-3). Twayne.

Bruce Jenner. Joe Soucheray. (Sports Superstars Ser.). (Illus.). (gr. 3-9). 1979. PLB 5.95 (ISBN 0-87191-723-8); pap. 2.95 (ISBN 0-89812-158-2). Creative Ed.

Bruce Jenner's Guide to the Olympics. Bruce Jenner & Marc Abraham. (Illus.). 1979. 12.95 o.p. (ISBN 0-8362-6702-8); pap. 6.95 o.p. (ISBN 0-8362-6700-1). Andrews & McMeel.

Bruce Learns About Life Insurance. Michael Braude. (Career Guidance Ser.). (Illus.). (gr. 3-6). PLB 2.00 o.p. (ISBN 0-513-00312-6). Denison.

Bruce Lee: The Man Only I Knew. Linda Lee. 1975. pap. 1.95 o.s.i. (ISBN 0-446-89407-9). Warner Bks.

Bruce Olson: Missionary of American Colonizer? Andres Kung. LC 80-69309. 1981. pap. 5.95 (ISBN 0-915684-83-7). Christian Herald.

Bruce Springsteen: A Photo Bio. Peter Gambaccini. 1979. pap. 2.25 (ISBN 0-515-05220-5). Jove Pubns.

Bruce Tegner's Complete Book of Jukado Self Defense: Jiu Jitsu Modernized. Bruce Tegner. LC 67-21359. (Illus.). 1968. 6.95 o.s.i. (ISBN 0-87407-504-1). Thor.

Bruchko. Olson. LC 73-81494. 1977. pap. 2.45 (ISBN 0-88419-133-8). Creation Hse.

Bruckner. rev ed. Hans-Hubert Schonzeler. (Illus.). 1978. pap. 7.95 (ISBN 0-7145-0145-X, Pub. by M Boyars). Merrimack Bk Serv.

Bruegel. Walter S. Gibson. (Illus.). 1977. 17.95 (ISBN 0-19-519952-9); pap. 9.95 (ISBN 0-19-519953-7). Oxford U Pr.

Bruin Country: A Pictorial Grand Tour of the Famed UCLA Campus. Fred E. Basten. LC 80-83610. (Illus.). 128p. (Orig.). 1980. pap. 9.95 (ISBN 0-937536-02-4). Graphics Calif.

Bruised Fight. Martin W. Teigland. 1981. 4.95 (ISBN 0-533-04386-7). Vantage.

Brujula Para el Ministro. Tr. by Alberto Scataglini et al. (Spanish Bks.). 1979. 3.75 (ISBN 0-8297-0877-4). Life Pubs Intl.

Brumaire. Mark Logan. LC 77-15864. 1978. 8.95 o.p. (ISBN 0-312-10677-7). St Martin.

Brunch: Great Ideas for Planning, Cooking & Serving. Pauline Durand & Yolande Languirand. LC 77-21616. 1978. pap. text ed. 2.95 (ISBN 0-8120-0726-3). Barron.

Brunel & His World. John Pudney. (Illus.). 128p. 1974. 8.75 o.p. (ISBN 0-500-13047-7). Transatlantic.

Brunelliaceae. J. Cuatrecasas. 1970. pap. 12.95 o.s.i. (ISBN 0-02-843320-3). Hafner.

Brunels Britain. Derrick Beckett. LC 80-66092. (Illus.). 256p. 1980. 25.00 (ISBN 0-7153-7973-9). David & Charles.

Bruno. Achim Broger. Tr. by Hilda Van Stockum from Ger. LC 75-15800. (Illus.). 160p. (gr. 3-6). 1975. 6.25 (ISBN 0-688-22051-7); PLB 6.00 (ISBN 0-688-32051-1). Morrow.

Bruno Lier: Ad Topica Carminum Amatorium Symbolae, Repr. Of 1914 Ed. Bruno Lier et al. Ed. by Steele Commager. Bd. with Keith Preston: Studies in the Diction of the Sermo Amatorius in Roman Comedy. Repr. of 1916 ed; Alfons Spies: Militat Omnis Amons. Repr. of 1930 ed. LC 77-70837. (Latin Poetry Ser.). 1979. lib. bdg. 25.00 (ISBN 0-8240-2973-9). Garland Pub.

Bruno Takes a Trip. Achim Broger. Tr. by Caroline Gueritz from Ger. LC 78-3878. (Illus.). (gr. k-3). 1978. 7.50 (ISBN 0-688-22138-6); PLB 7.20 (ISBN 0-688-32138-0). Morrow.

Bruno Taut & Paul Scheerbart's Vision: Utopian Aspects of German Expressionist Architecture. Rosemarie H. Bletter. LC 78-74362. (Outstanding Dissertations in the Fine Arts Ser.). (Illus.). 660p. 1979. lib. bdg. 55.00 (ISBN 0-8240-3951-3). Garland Pub.

Brush & Ink. Ed. by Gisela Armbruster & Helmut Brinker. (Illus.). 1979. pap. 17.50 (ISBN 0-87773-714-2). Great Eastern.

Brush Decoration for Ceramics. Marc Bellaire. 3.95 (ISBN 0-934706-02-6). Prof Pubns Ohio.

Brush up Your Basics: Clear Thinking, Clear Writing. Elizabeth Waterston. 112p. 1981. pap. text ed. 5.95 (ISBN 0-8403-2387-5). Kendall-Hunt.

Brush with the West. Dale A. Burk. (Illus.). 256p. 1980. 19.95 (ISBN 0-87842-133-5); limited ed. 60.00 (ISBN 0-87842-134-3). Mountain Pr.

Brut, Vol. 1. Layamon. Ed. by George L. Brook & R. F. Leslie. (Early English Text Society Ser.). 1963. 36.00x (ISBN 0-19-722250-1). Oxford U Pr.

Brutal Justice: The Ordeal of an American City. Henry Cohen. 248p. 1980. lib. bdg. 10.00x (ISBN 0-89444-027-6). John Jay Pr.

Bryce Canyon National Park. Ruth Radlauer. LC 79-22722. (Parks for People Ser.). (Illus.). 48p. (gr. 3 up). 1980. PLB 9.25 (ISBN 0-516-07484-9, Elk Grove Bks.). Childrens.

Bryce Canyon: The Story Behind the Scenery. John Bezy. Ed. by Gweneth R. Dendooven. LC 79-93079. (Illus.). 1980. 7.95 (ISBN 0-916122-70-0); pap. 3.00 (ISBN 0-916122-69-7). K C Pubns.

Bryophytes of the Pleistocene: The British Record & Its Chorological & Ecological Implications. J. H. Dickson. 1973. 79.00 (ISBN 0-521-08576-4). Cambridge U Pr.

B's & B's. Dale J. Schwartz. (Illus.). 116p. (Orig.). 1980. 2.95 (ISBN 0-935854-00-2). Baskin Pubs.

BSA Service-Repair Handbook: All 500 & 650cc Unit Construction Twins. Brick Price. Ed. by Eric Jorgensen. (Illus.). 1977. pap. 9.95 (ISBN 0-89287-182-2, M302). Clymer Pubns.

Bubble Bubble. Mercer Mayer. LC 80-16777. (Illus.). 40p. (ps-2). 1980. Repr. of 1973 ed. 7.95 (ISBN 0-590-07759-7, Four Winds). Schol Bk Serv.

Bubble Reputation. George Pottinger. 256p. 1981. 15.00x (ISBN 0-7073-0286-2, Pub. by Scottish Academic Pr Scotland). Columbia U Pr.

Bubbles. Beverly Sills. (Illus.). 1978. pap. 2.50 o.s.i. (ISBN 0-446-81520-9). Warner Bks.

Bubbles, Rainbows & Worms: Science Experiments for Pre-School Children. Sam E. Brown. LC 80-84598. (Illus.). 1981. pap. 5.95 (ISBN 0-87659-100-4). Gryphon Hse.

Buber on God & the Perfect Man. Pamela Vermes. Ed. by J. Neusner et al. LC 80-23406. (Brown Judaic Studies). 1981. 15.00 (ISBN 0-89130-426-6); pap. 10.50 (ISBN 0-89130-427-4). Scholars Pr CA.

Buccaneer King: The Biography of the Notorious Sir Henry Morgan, 1635-1688. Dudley Pope. LC 76-12156. (Illus.). 1978. 11.95 (ISBN 0-396-07566-5). Dodd.

Buccaneer Surgeon. Frank Slaughter. 1976. Repr. of 1954 ed. lib. bdg. 13.20 (ISBN 0-89190-533-2). Am Repr-Rivercity Pr.

Buccaneers & Marooners of America. Alexandre O. Exquemelin. Ed. by Howard Pyle. LC 78-142007. 1971. Repr. of 1891 ed. 21.00 (ISBN 0-8103-3620-0). Gale.

Buccaneers & Pirates of Our Coasts. new ed. Frank R. Stockton. (Illus.). (gr. 5 up). 1967. 9.95 (ISBN 0-02-788520-8). Macmillan.

Buccaneers & Pirates of Our Coasts. new ed. Frank R. Stockton. (Illus.). (gr. 5 up). 1967. pap. 0.79 o.s.i. (ISBN 0-02-045310-8, Collier). Macmillan.

Bucchero Pottery from Southern Etruria. T. B. Rasmussen. LC 78-13464. (Cambridge Classical Studies). (Illus.). 1979. 42.50 (ISBN 0-521-22316-4). Cambridge U Pr.

Buchanan's Texas Treasure. Jonas Ward. (Buchanan Ser.). 1978. pap. 1.75 (ISBN 0-449-14175-6, GM). Fawcett.

Buck. Bill Burchardt. LC 78-1188. 1978. 7.95 o.p. (ISBN 0-385-13439-8). Doubleday.

Buck Rogers. Carole Pierce & Robert Pierce. (Golden Storybook). (Illus.). (gr. 4-6). 1979. PLB 9.15 o.p. (ISBN 0-307-62083-2, Golden Pr); pap. 1.25 o.p. (ISBN 0-307-12083-X, Golden Pr). Western Pub.

Buck Rogers & the Children of Hopetown. Ravena Dwight. (Young Reader Ser.). (Illus.). (gr. k-3). 1979. PLB 5.00 (ISBN 0-307-60500-0, Golden Pr). Western Pub.

Buckboard Days. Sophie A. Poe. Ed. by Eugene Cunningham. (Illus.). 304p. 1981. write for info. (ISBN 0-8263-0572-5); pap. price not set (ISBN 0-8263-0573-3). U of NM Pr.

Buckboard Stranger. Stephen W. Meader. LC 54-8574. (Illus.). (gr. 7 up). 1954. 4.95 o.p. (ISBN 0-15-212851-4, HJ). HarBraceJ.

Buckdancer's Choice. James Dickey. LC 65-21079. (Wesleyan Poetry Program: Vol. 28). (Orig.). 1965. 7.50x o.p. (ISBN 0-8195-2028-4, Pub. by Wesleyan U Pr); pap. 4.95 (ISBN 0-8195-1028-9). Columbia U Pr.

Buckelew, the Indian Captive: Or the Life Story of F. M. Buckelew While a Captive Among the Lipan Indians in the Western Wilds of Frontier Texas As Related by Himself, Repr. Of 1911 Ed. Bd. with Life of M. Buckelew, the Indian Captive, As Related by Himself. Repr. of 1925 ed; In the Bosom of the Comanches: A Thrilling Tale of Savage Life, Massacre & Captivity Truthfully Told by a Surviving Captive. Theodore A. Babb. Repr. of 1912 ed. LC 75-7135. (Indian Captivities Ser.: Vol. 107). 1977. lib. bdg. 44.00 (ISBN 0-8240-1731-5). Garland Pub.

Buckeyes: Politics & Abolitionism in an Ohio Town, 1836-1845. Brand Whitlock. Ed. by Paul W. Miller. LC 76-8306. (Illus.). 273p. 1977. 12.95 (ISBN 0-8214-0222-6). Ohio U Pr.

Buckling Strength of Metal Structures. Friedrich Bleich. (Engineering Societies Monographs Ser). 1952. 37.50 o.p. (ISBN 0-07-005890-3, P&RB). McGraw.

Buckskin & Blanket Days: Memoirs of a Friend of the Indians. Thomas H. Tibbles. LC 57-7289. 1969. pap. 3.95 (ISBN 0-8032-5199-8, BB 503, Bison). U of Nebr Pr.

Buckskin Rider. W. F. Bragg. 1981. pap. 1.75 (ISBN 0-8439-0881-5, Leisure Bks). Nordon Pubns.

Bucky: A Guided Tour of Buckminster Fuller. Hugh Kenner. LC 79-182966. (Illus.). 352p. 1973. pap. 3.25 o.p. (ISBN 0-688-05141-3). Morrow.

Bucolici Graeci. Ed. by Andrew S. Gow. (Oxford Classical Texts). 1952. 14.95x (ISBN 0-19-814517-9). Oxford U Pr.

Bucolics. Virgil. Ed. by T. E. Page. Incl. Georgics. (Classic Ser). 396p. (Lat.). 1898. 9.95 o.p. (ISBN 0-312-84910-9). St Martin.

Bucomco: A Business Communication Simulation. John Melrose. LC 76-30752. 1977. text ed. 6.95 (ISBN 0-574-20025-8, 13-3025); instr's guide avail. (ISBN 0-574-20026-6, 13-3026). SRA.

BUC's Older Boat Price Guide 1980. 38.00 (ISBN 0-911778-83-7). Buc Intl.

BUC's Used Boat Price Guide 1980, Vol. II. 37th ed. LC 63-35604. (Orig.). 1980. 52.00 (ISBN 0-911778-43-8). BUC Intl.

Bucyrus. John Matthias. LC 75-132579. (New Poetry Ser.: No. 42). 102p. 1971. 7.95 (ISBN 0-8040-0522-2); pap. 3.95 (ISBN 0-8040-0523-0). Swallow.

Bud and Lou: The Abbott & Costello Story. Bob Thomas. LC 76-54743. 1977. 10.00 o.p. (ISBN 0-397-01195-4). Lippincott.

Bud Hastin's Avon Bottle Encyclopedia. 8th ed. Bud Hastin. (Illus.). 530p. 1981. 18.95. Avons Res.

Bud Hastin's Bottle Encyclopedia. 1979. 14.95 o.p. (ISBN 0-89145-098-X). Avons Res.

Buddha. F. W. Rawding. LC 74-14436. (Introduction to the History of Mankind Ser). (Illus.). 48p. (YA) 1975. pap. 3.95 (ISBN 0-521-20368-6). Cambridge U Pr.

Buddha & Jesus: Conversations. Carrin Dunne. 1975. pap. 3.95 (ISBN 0-87243-057-X). Templegate.

Buddha Maitrya-Amitabha Has Appeared. Jamshed Fozdar. LC 75-6131. (Illus.). 1976. 24.00 (ISBN 0-87743-119-1, 7-32-25); pap. 12.50 (ISBN 0-87743-120-5, 7-32-26). Baha'i.

Buddha, Marx & God: Some Aspects of Religion in the Modern World. 2nd ed. Trevor Ling. 1979. 25.00 (ISBN 0-685-62341-6). St Martin.

Buddha Way. William Corlett & John Moore. LC 79-15685. (Questions Ser.). 1980. 8.95 (ISBN 0-87888-153-0). Bradbury Pr.

Buddha's Kisses. Richard Ronan. 96p. 1980. pap. 4.95 (ISBN 0-917342-73-9, Pub. by Gay Sunshine). Bookpeople.

Buddha's Lions. Abhayadatta. Tr. by James Robinson from Tibean. (Tibetan Translation Ser.). (Illus.). 1979. 16.95 (ISBN 0-913546-60-7). Dharma Pub.

Buddhism. Thomas Berry. 1967. pap. 5.95 (ISBN 0-89012-017-X). Anima Pubns.

Buddhism. Alexandra David-Neel. pap. 2.75 (ISBN 0-380-46185-4, 46185, Discus). Avon.

Buddhism. I. G. Edmonds. (First Books Ser.). (Illus.). (gr. 5-8). 1978. PLB 6.45 s&l (ISBN 0-531-01349-9). Watts.

Buddhism. Ed. by Richard A. Gard. LC 61-15499. (Great Religions of Modern Man Ser). 8.95 (ISBN 0-8076-0166-7). Braziller.

Buddhism. Trevor Ling. (Living Religions Series). (Illus.). 1976. pap. 3.50x (ISBN 0-7062-3594-0). Intl Pubns Serv.

Buddhism. Michael Ridley. (Illus.). 1979. 14.95 (ISBN 0-7137-0886-7, Pub. by Blandford Pr England). Sterling.

Buddhism: A Brief Account. P. Pardue. 1971. pap. 1.95 o.s.i. (ISBN 0-02-088260-2, Collier). Macmillan.

Buddhism: A Religion of Infinite Compassion. Ed. by Clarence H. Hamilton. LC 52-1623. 1952. pap. 5.50 (ISBN 0-672-60340-3, LLA133). Bobbs.

Buddhism: A Subject Index to Periodical Articles in English, 1728-1971. Yushin Yoo. LC 73-8679. 1973. 10.00 (ISBN 0-8108-0557-X). Scarecrow.

Buddhism & Christianity. Ed. by M. Dhavamony. (Concilium Ser.: Vol. 116). pap. 4.95 (ISBN 0-8164-2612-0). Crossroad NY.

Buddhism & Its Place in the Mental Life of Mankind. Paul Dahlke. LC 78-72403. Repr. of 1927 ed. 29.00 (ISBN 0-404-17265-2). AMS Pr.

Buddhism & the Spirit Cults in Northeast Thailand. S. J. Tambiah. LC 73-108112. (Cambridge Studies in Social Anthropology: No. 2). (Illus.). 1970. 36.00 (ISBN 0-521-07825-3); pap. 14.95x (ISBN 0-521-09958-7). Cambridge U Pr.

Buddhism for Today. Nikkyo Niwano. 476p. 1980. pap. 10.95 (ISBN 0-8348-0147-7, Pub. by John Weathehill Inc Japan). C E Tuttle.

Buddhism in America. Emma M. Layman. LC 76-4566. (Illus.). 344p. 1976. 19.95x (ISBN 0-88229-166-1); pap. 10.95 (ISBN 0-88229-436-9). Nelson-Hall.

Buddhism in America: The Social Organization of an Ethnic Religious Institution. Tetsuden Kashima. LC 76-57837. (Contributions in Sociology: No. 26). (Illus.). 1977. lib. bdg. 18.95 (ISBN 0-8371-9534-9, KSO/). Greenwood.

Buddhism in Japan: With an Outline of Its Origins in India. E. Dale Saunders. LC 64-10900. (Illus.). 1964. 9.00x o.p. (ISBN 0-8122-7411-3); pap. 4.95x (ISBN 0-8122-1006-9, Pa Paperbks). U of Pa Pr.

Buddhism in Sinhalese Society, 1750-1900: A Study of Religious Revival & Change. Kirsiri Malagoda. LC 74-22966. 1976. 28.50x (ISBN 0-520-02873-2). U of Cal Pr.

Buddhism in the Modern World. Ed. by Heinrich Dumoulin & John C. Maraldo. LC 75-42342. 400p. 1976. 12.95 o.s.i. (ISBN 0-02-533790-4). Macmillan.

Buddhism: Its Essence & Development. Edward Conze. 8.25 (ISBN 0-8446-1889-6). Peter Smith.

Buddhism of Tibet & the Key to the Middle Way. Tenzin Gyatso. (Wisdom of Tibet Ser.). 1975. pap. 6.95 (ISBN 0-04-294087-7). Allen Unwin.

Buddhism: The First Millennium. Daisaku Ikeda. Tr. by Burton Watson. LC 77-84915. 1978. cancelled (ISBN 0-87011-321-6). Kodansha.

Buddhism: The Light of Asia. Kenneth K. Ch'en. LC 67-30496. 1968. 7.95 (ISBN 0-8120-6012-1); pap. text ed. 3.75 (ISBN 0-8120-0272-5). Barron.

Buddhism: The Religion & Its Culture. Ananda W. P. Guruge. (Cultural & Religious Patterns in India: No. 2). 248p. 1976. pap. text ed. 5.00 (ISBN 0-89253-050-2). Ind-US Inc.

Buddhism: The Religion of Analysis. Nolan P. Jacobson. LC 66-71124. (Arcturus Books Paperbacks). 202p. 1970. pap. 5.95 (ISBN 0-8093-0463-5). S Ill U Pr.

Buddhist & Taoist Influences on Chinese Novels: The Authorship of the Feng Shen Yen I, Vol. 1. Liu Ts'un-Yan. LC 70-222767. 334p. 1962. 32.50x (ISBN 3-447-00564-5). Intl Pubns Serv.

Buddhist Bible, the Favorite Scriptures of the Zen Sect: History of Early Buddhism. 2nd rev. & enl. ed. Ed. by Dwight Goddard. LC 78-72434. 1980. Repr. of 1938 ed. 57.50 (ISBN 0-404-17297-0). AMS Pr.

Buddhist Concept of Hell. Daigan L. Matsunaga & Alicia Matsunaga. LC 73-145466. (Illus.). 1971. 4.95 o.p. (ISBN 0-8022-2048-7). Philos Lib.

Buddhist Conquest of China: The Spread & Adaptation of Buddhism in Early Medieval China, 2 vols. E. Zucher. 470p. 1973. Set. text ed. 73.00x (ISBN 0-391-01961-9). Humanities.

Buddhist Ethics: Essence of Buddhism. H. Saddhatissa. LC 72-138436. 1971. 6.50 o.p. (ISBN 0-8076-0598-0); pap. 2.95 o.p. (ISBN 0-8076-0597-2). Braziller.

Buddhist Experience: Sources & Interpretations. Stephen Beyer. 1974. pap. text ed. 7.95x (ISBN 0-8221-0127-0). Dickenson.

Buddhist Feminine Ideal: Queen Srimala & the Tathagatagarbha American Academy of Religion. Diana Paul. LC 79-12031. (Dissertation Ser.: No. 30). 12.00x (ISBN 0-89130-284-0); pap. 7.50x (ISBN 0-89130-303-0). Scholars Pr CA.

Buddhist Hybrid Sanscrit Reader. Ed. by Franklin Edgerton. 1953. 37.50x (ISBN 0-685-69814-9). Elliots Bks.

Buddhist Logic, 2 vols. Theodore Stcherbatsky. 1930. pap. text ed. 6.00 ea.; Vol. 1. pap. text ed. (ISBN 0-486-20955-5); Vol. 2. pap. text ed. (ISBN 0-486-20956-3). Dover.

Buddhist Mahayana Texts. E. B. Cowell et al. Ed. by F. Max Mueller. LC 68-9450. (Sacred Books of the East Ser). 1969. pap. 6.50 (ISBN 0-486-22093-1). Dover.

Buddhist Mahayana Texts, Vol. 49. Ed. by F. Max Mueller. Tr. by Muller & Fausboll. (Sacred Books of the East Ser.). 15.00x (ISBN 0-8426-1395-1). Verry.

Buddhist Philosophy: A Historical Analysis. David J. Kalupahana. LC 75-20040. 224p. 1976. text ed. 10.00x o.p. (ISBN 0-8248-0360-4, Eastwest Ctr); pap. 3.95x (ISBN 0-8248-0392-2). U Pr of Hawaii.

Buddhist Philosophy of the Middle Way. Shoson Miyamoto. 1981. 9.95 (ISBN 0-914910-07-8); pap. 6.95 (ISBN 0-914910-08-6). Buddhist Bks.

Buddhist Philosophy of Universal Flux. S. Mookerjee. 1975. Repr. 25.00 (ISBN 0-8426-0852-4). Orient Bk Dist.

Buddhist Revival in India: Aspects of the Sociology of Buddhism. Trevor Ling. LC 79-20167. 1980. 22.50x (ISBN 0-312-10681-5). St Martin.

Buddhist Suttas, Vol. 11. Ed. by F. Max Mueller. Tr. by Beal. (Sacred Books of the East Ser.). 15.00x (ISBN 0-8426-1396-X). Verry.

Buddhist Thought in India. Edward Conze. 1967. pap. 3.95 (ISBN 0-472-06129-1, 129, AA). U of Mich Pr.

Buddhist Way of Life. Christmas Humphreys. (Unwin Paperback Ser.). 224p. (Orig.). 1980. pap. 6.50x (ISBN 0-04-294111-3, 9066). Allen Unwin.

Buddhist Wisdom Books: The "Diamond Sutra" & the "Heart Sutra". Edward Conze. 1975. pap. 7.50 (ISBN 0-04-294090-7). Allen Unwin.

Buddhist Wisdom: The Mystery of the Self. 2nd, rev. ed. George Grimm. Ed. by M. Keller-Grimm. Tr. by Carrol Aikins from Ger. 1978. 6.50 (ISBN 0-89684-041-7, Pub. by Motilal Banarsidass India). Orient Bk Dist.

Buddhist Writings of Lafcadio Hearn. Ed. by Kenneth Rexroth. LC 77-2496. 312p. 1977. lib. bdg. 12.95 (ISBN 0-915520-05-2). Ross-Erikson.

Buddhist Yoga. Kanjitsu Iijima. (Illus.). 184p. 1975. pap. 8.95 (ISBN 0-87040-349-4). Japan Pubns.

Buddy Boy. Brian Thompson. LC 77-6109. 1978. 7.95 o.p. (ISBN 0-312-10684-X). St Martin.

Buddy Holly. John Goldrosen. 1979. pap. 7.95 (ISBN 0-8256-3936-0, Quick Fox). Music Sales.

Buddy Paints a Picture. Dina K. Tourneur. (Buddy Books Ser.). (ps). 1978. 1.95 o.p. (ISBN 0-89191-124-3). Cook.

Buddy Plants a Seed. Dina K. Tourneur. (Buddy Books Ser.). (ps). 1978. 1.95 o.p. (ISBN 0-89191-125-1). Cook.

Budgerigar Diseases. Cessa Feyerabend. pap. 4.95 (ISBN 0-87666-413-3, PS671). TFH Pubns.

Budgerigars. William H. Allen, Jr. (Orig.). pap. 2.00 (ISBN 0-87666-415-X, M502). TFH Pubns.

Budgerigars. George A. Radtke. Orig. Title: Wellensittiche-Mein Hobby. (Illus.). 1979. 2.95 (ISBN 0-87666-984-4, KW-011). TFH Pubns.

Budgerigars. Cyril H. Rogers. Ed. by Christina Foyle. (Foyle's Handbooks). 1973. 3.95 (ISBN 0-685-55808-8). Palmetto Pub.

Budgerigars for Pleasure & Profit. Eric Leyland. 6.50x (SpS). Soccer.

Budgerigars in Color - Their Care & Breeding. rev. ed. A. Rutgers. (Color Ser.). (Illus.). 1976. 9.95 (ISBN 0-7137-0813-1, Pub by Blandford Pr England). Sterling.

Budgerigars, Taming & Training. Risa Teitler. (Illus.). 96p. 1979. 2.95 (ISBN 0-87666-887-2, KW-070). TFH Pubns.

Budget - Finance Campaigns. J. William Jones. 1977. pap. 9.50 (ISBN 0-87545-010-5). Natl Sch Pr.

Budget & National Politics. D. S. Ippolito. LC 78-5102. (Illus.). 1978. text ed. 16.95x (ISBN 0-7167-0298-3); pap. text ed. 7.50x o.p. (ISBN 0-7167-0297-5). W H Freeman.

Budget Backpacker. L. A. Zakreski. 1977. 11.95 (ISBN 0-87691-189-0). Winchester Pr.

Budget Book & Much More: Your Money, Goals, Time, Assets, Vital Records. 2nd ed. Robert F. Bohn. 128p. pap. text ed. 5.95 (ISBN 0-8403-2185-6). Kendall-Hunt.

Budget Concepts for Economic Analysis. Ed. by Wilfred Lewis, Jr. LC 68-26185. (Studies of Government Finance). 198p. 1968. pap. 3.95 (ISBN 0-8157-5237-7). Brookings.

Budget Flying. Dan Ramsey. (McGraw-Hill Series in Aviation). (Illus.). 176p. 1980. 16.95 (ISBN 0-07-051202-7). McGraw.

Budget Guide to New York & New England: Special Bicentennial Edition. Ted Kosoy. LC 75-40795. (Illus.). 288p. 1976. pap. 3.95 o.p. (ISBN 0-685-63268-7). St Martin.

Budget Guide Washington, D. C. & the Central Atlantic States: Special Bicentennial Edition. Ted Kosoy. (Illus.). 288p. 1976. 7.95 o.p. (ISBN 0-685-63269-5); pap. 3.95 o.p. (ISBN 0-685-63270-9). St Martin.

Budget Shoppers' Guide to Metropolitan New York. new ed. Thomas L. Widing. (Orig.). 1977. pap. 3.50 o.p. (ISBN 0-917908-02-3). Hamilton Hse.

Budget Shoppers' Guide to the Delaware Valley. Thomas L. Widing. LC 76-43532. (Orig.). 1976. pap. 2.95 o.p. (ISBN 0-917908-01-5). Hamilton Hse.

Budget Shopper's Guide to the Delaware Valley. rev. ed. Thomas L. Widing. LC 80-84929. 160p. (Orig.). 1981. pap. 3.95 (ISBN 0-917908-03-1). Hamilton Hse.

Budgetary Control Procedures for Institutions. Ray M. Powell. LC 78-51520. (Studies in the Managment of Not-for-Profit Institutions: No. 3). (Illus.). 1980. text ed. 12.95x (ISBN 0-268-00658-X). U of Notre Dame Pr.

Budgetary Politics: The Finances of the European Community. Helen Wallace. (Studies on Contemporary Europe Ser.: No. 1). (Illus.). 128p. (Orig.). 1980. text ed. 15.95x (ISBN 0-04-382023-9); pap. text ed. 6.95x (ISBN 0-04-382024-7). Allen Unwin.

Budgeting Municipal Expenditures: A Study in Comparative Policy Making. Lewis B. Friedman. LC 74-11600. (Special Studies). (Illus.). 266p. 1975. text ed. 19.95 o.p. (ISBN 0-275-09630-0). Praeger.

Budgeting: Principles & Practice. Herman C. Heiser. (Illus.). 1959. 24.95 (ISBN 0-8260-4040-3). Ronald Pr.

Budgeting Procedures for Hospitals. 88p. 1971. 8.25 (ISBN 0-686-68590-3, 1130). Hospital Finan.

Budgeting: Profit Planning & Control. 4th ed. Glenn A. Welsch. (Illus.). 656p. 1976. 21.95x (ISBN 0-13-085712-2). P-H.

Budgeting Public Funds: The Decision Process in the Urban School District. Donald Gerwin. LC 69-17326. 1969. 17.50x (ISBN 0-299-05270-2). U of Wis Pr.

Budgeting Techniques for Libraries & Information Centers. Ed. by Michael Koenig. (Professional Development Ser.: No. 1). 1980. pap. write for info. (ISBN 0-87111-278-7). SLA.

Buen Samaritano. Janice Kramer. Tr. by Eliseo Rodriguez from Eng. (Libros Arco Ser.). (Illus.). 32p. (Orig., Span.). (gr. 1-3). 1979. pap. 0.95 (ISBN 0-89922-147-5). Edit Caribe.

Buenos Dias, Judy. Tr. by Jeanne Steuck. (Spanish Bks.). (Span.). 1979. 1.75 (ISBN 0-8297-0496-5). Life Pubs Intl.

Buenos Dias Senor. Tr. by Vance Havner. (Spanish Bks.). (Span.). 1978. 2.25 (ISBN 0-8297-0899-5). Life Pubs Intl.

Buffalo Bill. Mary R. Davidson. (gr. k-6). 1980. pap. 1.25 (ISBN 0-440-40748-6, YB). Dell.

Buffalo Bill. Shannon Garst. (Biography Ser.). (Illus.). (gr. 7 up). 1948. PLB 4.79 o.p. (ISBN 0-671-03840-0). Messner.

Buffalo Bill. Matthew G. Grant. LC 73-10073. 1974. PLB 5.95 (ISBN 0-87191-255-4). Creative Ed.

Buffalo Bill, Last of the Great Scouts: The Life Story of Colonel William F. Cody. Helen C. Wetmore. LC 65-13258. (Illus.). 1965. pap. 2.95 (ISBN 0-8032-5215-3, BB 315, Bison). U of Nebr Pr.

Buffalo Blinkie & the Crazy Circus Caper. Judith J. Mandell. (Illus.). (gr. 3-5). 1977. 5.00 (ISBN 0-89039-196-3); tchr's ed. 4.00 (ISBN 0-686-68523-7). Ann Arbor Pubs.

Buffalo Book: The Full Saga of the American Animal. David D. Dary. LC 73-13211. (Illus.). 374p. 1973. 17.50 (ISBN 0-8040-0653-9, SB); limited ed. o.p. 100.00 (ISBN 0-8040-0717-9). Swallow.

Buffalo Bud: Adventures of an Alberta Cowboy. E. J. Cotton & Ethel Mitchell. (Illus.). 130p. (Orig.). 1981. pap. 9.95 (ISBN 0-88839-095-5). Hancock Hse.

Buffalo Chips. Tom Stratton. (Illus.). 1979. pap. 1.95 (ISBN 0-930000-13-7). Mathom.

Buffalo Creek Revisted: Prolonged Psychological Effects of a Disaster. Goldine C. Gleser et al. (Personality & Psychopathology Ser.). 1981. price not set (ISBN 0-12-286260-0). Acad Pr.

Buffalo Hunter. Zane Grey. 1979. pap. 1.75 (ISBN 0-505-51334-X). Tower Bks.

Buffalo Hunters: The Story of the Hide Men. Mari Sandoz. LC 77-14079. 1978. pap. 4.50 (ISBN 0-8032-5883-6, BB 659, Bison). U of Nebr Pr.

Buffalo Kill. G D. Christensen. (gr. 4-6). 1968. pap. 1.25 (ISBN 0-671-29821-6). Archway.

Buffalo Medicine. Don Coldsmith. LC 80-1690. (Double D Western Ser.). 192p. 1981. 9.95 (ISBN 0-385-15970-6). Doubleday.

Buffalo People. Lee D. Wilby. (Making of America Ser.). (Orig.). 1981. pap. 2.75 (ISBN 0-440-00776-3). Dell.

Buffalo Reproduction & Artificail Insemination. (FAO Animal Production & Health Paper: No. 13). 370p. 1981. pap. 20.00 (ISBN 92-5-100743-8, F2086, FAO). Unipub.

Buffalo Soldiers: A Narrative of the Negro Cavalry in the West. William H. Leckie. (Illus.). 1967. 12.95 (ISBN 0-8061-0734-0); pap. 5.95 (ISBN 0-8061-1244-1). U of Okla Pr.

Buffalo Wallow: A Prairie Boyhood. Charles T. Jackson. LC 52-14022. 1967. pap. 3.25 (ISBN 0-8032-5099-1, BB 373, Bison). U of Nebr Pr.

Buffalo Woman. Dorothy M. Johnson. LC 76-53436. (gr. 5-10). 1977. 6.95 (ISBN 0-396-07423-5). Dodd.

Buffet Catering. Charles Finance. (Illus.). 1958. 19.95 (ISBN 0-8104-9401-9). Hayden.

Buffets and Receptions. Compiled by Pierre Mengelatte et al. Ed. by John Fuller & Michael Small. (Illus.). 1978. 89.95 (ISBN 0-685-90325-7, Virtue & Co.). CBI Pub.

Buffets & Receptions. Ed. by M. Small. (Illus.). 1978. text ed. 99.95 (ISBN 0-685-47808-4). Radio City.

Buffon. Otis E. Fellows & Stephen F. Milliken. LC 76-39777. (World Authors Ser.: France: No. 243). lib. bdg. 10.95 (ISBN 0-8057-2184-3). Twayne.

Buffooneries of Modern Science. Martin Gardner. LC 80-84405. (Critiques of the Paranormal Ser.). 450p. 1981. 19.95 (ISBN 0-87975-144-4); pap. 9.95 (ISBN 0-87975-145-2). Prometheus Bks.

Bug Book. William Dugan. (Illus.). 24p. (ps-4). 1965. PLB 5.38 (ISBN 0-307-68903-4, Golden Pr). Western Pub.

Bug Book. World Book-Childcraft International Staff. (Illus.). 304p. (gr. k-6). 1981. price not set (ISBN 0-7166-0681-X). World Bk-Childcraft.

Bugaku: Japanese Court Dance. Carl Wolz. LC 76-101136. (D (Monographs), No. 1). (Illus.). viii, 181p. (Orig.). 1971. pap. text ed. 9.00x (ISBN 0-913360-03-1). Asian Music Pub.

Bugaku Masks. Kyotaro Nishikawa. Tr. by Monica Bethe. LC 77-75971. (Japanese Arts Library: Vol. 5). (Illus.). 1978. 16.75 (ISBN 0-87011-312-7). Kodansha.

Buganda in Modern History. D. A. Low. LC 73-10019. (Illus.). 1971. 20.00x (ISBN 0-520-01640-8). U of Cal Pr.

Bugbears. Ed. by James D. Clark & Stephen Orgel. LC 78-66768. (Renaissance Drama Ser.). 1979. lib. bdg. 28.50 (ISBN 0-8240-9749-1). Garland Pub.

Buggy-Go-Round. E. Radlauer & R. S. Radlauer. LC 76-15188. (Sports Action Bks). (Illus.). (gr. 3 up). 1971. PLB 5.90 o.p. (ISBN 0-531-01991-8). Watts.

Bugles in the Afternoon. Ernest Haycox. 1981. lib. bdg. 15.95 (ISBN 0-8161-3152-X, Large Print Bks). G K Hall.

Bugles in the Valley: Garnett's Fort Simcoe. rev. ed. H. Dean Guie. LC 77-88149. (Illus.). 216p. 1977. pap. 5.95 (ISBN 0-87595-057-4); 11.95 (ISBN 0-87595-090-6). Oreg Hist Soc.

Bugs-Big & Little. Alice Hopf. LC 80-20705. (Illus.). 64p. (gr. 3-5). 1980. PLB 7.59 (ISBN 0-671-34014-X). Messner.

Bugs Bunny. (Picture Postcards Ser.). (Illus.). (ps-4). 1977. pap. 0.95 o.p. (ISBN 0-307-11100-8, Golden Pr). Western Pub.

Bugs Bunny Book. Kathleen Cowles. (Illus.). 24p. (ps-4). 1977. PLB 5.38 (ISBN 0-307-68913-1, Golden Pr). Western Pub.

Bugs Bunny Comics-Go-Round. (gr. 3 up). 1979. pap. 1.95 o.p. (ISBN 0-307-11196-2, Golden Pr). Western Pub.

Bugs Bunny Goes to the Dentist. Seymour Reit. (Look-Look Bks). (Illus.). 1978. PLB 5.38 (ISBN 0-307-61843-9, Golden Pr); pap. 0.95 (ISBN 0-307-11843-6). Western Pub.

Bugs Bunny-Kingdom of Dimly. Kennon Graham. (Illus.). 24p. (ps-k). 1978. 1.95 (ISBN 0-307-10827-9, Golden Pr). Western Pub.

Bugs Bunny Party Pest. William Johnston. (Tell-a-Tale Readers). (Illus.). (gr. k-3). 1978. PLB 4.77 (ISBN 0-307-68607-8, Whitman). Western Pub.

Bugs Bunny, Pioneer. Fern Brown. (Young Reader Ser.). (Illus.). (gr. k-3). 1979. PLB 5.00 (ISBN 0-307-60144-7, Golden Pr). Western Pub.

Bugs Bunny: Too Many Carrots. Jean Lewis. (Illus.). 24p. (ps-4). 1977. PLB 5.00 (ISBN 0-307-60145-5, Golden Pr). Western Pub.

Bugs Bunny's Carrot Machine. Clark Carlisle. (Illus.). 24p. (gr. k-3). 1976. PLB 5.00 (ISBN 0-307-60127-7, Golden Pr). Western Pub.

Bugs Bunny's Space Carrot. Seymour Reit. (Look-Look Ser.). (Illus.). 1977. PLB 5.38 (ISBN 0-307-61831-5, Golden Pr); pap. 0.95 (ISBN 0-307-11831-2). Western Pub.

Bugs, Snakes & Creepy Things. Annie Mueser. (Pal Paperbacks, - Pal Skills II Ser.). (Illus.). (gr. 5-12). 1980. pap. 1.25 (ISBN 0-8374-6803-5). Xerox Ed Pubns.

Buick: A Complete History. Terry B. Dunham & Lawrence R. Gustin. (Illus.). 444p. 1980. 59.95 (ISBN 0-915038-19-6); leather ed. 79.95 (ISBN 0-915038-27-7). Princeton Pub.

Buick: The Complete History. Terry B. Dunham et al. Ed. by William Doerflinger. (Automobile Quarterly Library Ser.). 444p. 1981. 59.95 (ISBN 0-525-07230-6). Dutton.

Build a Better You-Starting Now, Vol. 7. Ed. by Don M. Dible. LC 79-63064. 1980. 12.95 (ISBN 0-88205-206-3). Showcase Fairfield.

Build a Better You-Starting Now, Vol. 8. Ed. by Don M. Dible. LC 79-63064. 1980. 12.95 (ISBN 0-88205-207-1). Showcase Fairfield.

Build a Fire. Jack London. (Creative's Classics Ser.). (Illus.). 48p. (gr. 4-9). 1980. PLB 6.95 (ISBN 0-87191-769-6). Creative Ed.

Build a Second Income Writing Articles. L. Perry Wilbur. 224p. 1981. pap. text ed. 7.95 (ISBN 0-471-08426-3). Wiley.

Build a Yurt: The Low Cost Mongolian Round House. Len Charney. (Illus.). 160p. 1974. pap. 3.95 o.s.i. (ISBN 0-02-079320-0, Collier). Macmillan.

Build a Yurt: The Low-Cost Mongolian Round House. Len Charney. LC 73-11837. (Illus.). 160p. 1974. 7.95 o.s.i. (ISBN 0-02-523980-5). Macmillan.

Build-It Book of Cabinets & Built-Ins. S. Blackwell Duncan. (Illus.). 1979. 12.95 o.p. (ISBN 0-8306-9854-X); pap. 7.95 (ISBN 0-8306-1002-2, 1002). TAB Bks.

Build-It Book of Learning Plaything. Ruth Wolverton. (Illus.). 1977. pap. 6.95 (ISBN 0-8306-6915-9, 915). TAB Bks.

Build-It Book of Miniature Test & Measurement Instruments. Robert Haviland. LC 75-41720. (Illus.). 238p. 1976. 7.95 o.p. (ISBN 0-8306-6792-X); pap. 4.95 (ISBN 0-8306-5792-4, 792). TAB Bks.

Build-It Book of Optoelectronic Projects. C. K. Adams. (Illus.). 1977. 8.95 (ISBN 0-8306-7935-9); pap. 5.95 (ISBN 0-8306-6935-3, 935). TAB Bks.

Build It: Out of Sight Sewing Center. Joseph D. D'Addario. 1972. pap. 3.95 (ISBN 0-686-01898-2). Classic Furn Kits.

Build on the Rock. Compiled by Claire Lynn. (Illus.). 52p. (Orig.). (ps-7). 1979. pap. 2.50 (ISBN 0-89323-000-6). BMA Pr.

Build Program Technique: A Practical Approach for the Development of Automatic Software Generation Systems. John G. Rice. LC 80-20742. (Business Data Processing Ser.). 375p. 1981. 29.95 (ISBN 0-471-05278-7, Pub. by Wiley-Interscience). Wiley.

Build with Adobe. 2nd rev. & enl. ed. Marcia Southwick. LC 73-1504. (Illus.). 225p. 1974. pap. 5.95 (ISBN 0-8040-0634-2, SB). Swallow.

Build Your Boat with Me. Alec Greeve. 14.95x (ISBN 0-392-07731-0, SpS). Soccer.

Build Your Harvest Kitchen. Ed. by William H. Hylton. (Illus.). 640p. 1980. 24.95 (ISBN 0-87857-316-X). Rodale Pr Inc.

Build Your Own Boats. Percy W. Blandford. (Illus.). 160p. 1972. 17.50x o.p. (ISBN 0-09-080020-6, SpS). Soccer.

Build Your Own Dreamhouse. Paula M. Craig. (Illus.). 44p. (Orig.). 1974. pap. 1.25 o.p. (ISBN 0-87604-076-8). ARE Pr.

Build Your Own High-Quality, Low-Cost Test Equipment. M. J. Salvati. (Illus.). 1976. pap. 7.25 (ISBN 0-8104-5664-8). Hayden.

Build Your Own Sport Plane. Don Dwiggins. 1979. pap. 6.95 (ISBN 0-8015-0971-8, Hawthorn). Dutton.

Build Your Own Woodburning Furnace. Bill White. LC 78-66818. (Illus.). 1978. pap. 3.50 (ISBN 0-9601794-2-9). FireBuilders.

Build Your Own Working Robot. David L. Heiserman. LC 75-41725. 238p. 1976. 9.95 (ISBN 0-8306-6841-1); pap. 5.95 (ISBN 0-8306-5841-6, 841). TAB Bks.

Build Your Own Z-80 Computer. Steve Ciarcia. 473p. 1980. 21.95 (ISBN 0-07-010961-3, BYTE Bks); pap. 15.95 (ISBN 0-07-010962-1). McGraw.

Builder of Bridges. T. Otto Nall. LC 80-50241. 222p. 1980. text ed. 6.95x (ISBN 0-8358-0400-3). Upper Room.

Builders & Humanists: The Renaissance Popes As Patrons of the Arts. Raymond Marcel et al. (Illus.). 1966. pap. 8.00 (ISBN 0-914412-20-5). Inst for the Arts.

Builder's Detail Sheets. Sam Smith. (Series 1). (Illus.). 1973. wirebound 15.95x (ISBN 0-7198-2540-7). Intl Ideas.

Builder's Detail Sheets. Sam Smith. (Series Two). (Illus.). 1977. wirebound 13.50x (ISBN 0-7198-2670-5). Intl Ideas.

Builders' Estimating Fact Book. Roy L. Diez & Lawrence D. Maloney. 132p. 1974. 13.95 (ISBN 0-8436-0115-9). CBI Pub.

Builder's Guide to Government Loans. James E. Newell. (Orig.). 1981. pap. 13.75 (ISBN 0-910460-74-4). Craftsman.

Builder's Office Manual. Michael C. Thomsett. (Illus.). 1981. pap. 13.25 (ISBN 0-910460-73-6). Craftsman.

Builder's Vestpocket Reference Book. William J. Hornung. 1956. 6.95 (ISBN 0-13-085951-6). P-H.

Building a Broader Market: Report of the Twentieth Century Fund Task Force on the Municipal Bond Market. Twentieth Century Fund, Inc. LC 76-28368. 1976. 7.95 (ISBN 0-07-065629-0, P&RB); pap. 3.95 o.p. (ISBN 0-07-065630-4). McGraw.

Building a Career: The Effect of Initial Job Experiences & Related Work Attitudes on Later Employment. Joseph A. Raelin. LC 80-24848. 178p. 1980. text ed. 7.00 (ISBN 0-911558-74-8); pap. text ed. 4.50 (ISBN 0-911558-73-X). Upjohn Inst.

Building a Chamber Music Collection: A Descriptive Guide to Published Scores. Ella M. Forsyth. LC 79-4587. 1979. 10.00 (ISBN 0-8108-1215-0). Scarecrow.

Building a Character. Constantin Stanislavski. 1977. 9.95 (ISBN 0-87830-012-0). Theatre Arts.

Building a Child's Self-Esteem. Donna Foster. 1977. pap. 1.25 (ISBN 0-8307-0489-2, 90-702-06). Regal.

Building a Christian Home. Henry R. Brandt & Homer E. Dowdy. LC 60-53591. 158p. 1960. pap. 2.25 o.p. (ISBN 0-88207-051-7). Victor Bks.

Building a College Vocabulary. Patricia Licklider. 256p. (Orig.). 1981. pap. text ed. 7.95 (ISBN 0-316-52424-7); tchrs'. manual free (ISBN 0-316-52425-5). Little.

Building a Dynamic Corporation Through Grid Organization Development. Robert R. Blake & Jane S. Mouton. Ed. by Edgar Schein et al. (Organization Development Ser). 1969. pap. text ed. 6.50 (ISBN 0-201-00612-X). A-W.

Building a Group Practice. Fred W. Wasserman & Michael C. Miller. 188p. 1973. text ed. 11.75 (ISBN 0-398-02774-9); pap. text ed. 8.50 (ISBN 0-398-02793-5). C C Thomas.

Building a Healthy Heart. Eric F. Powell. 64p. 1961. pap. 3.00x o.p. (ISBN 0-8464-0997-6). Beekman Pubs.

Building a House. Byron Barton. LC 80-22674. (Illus.). 32p. (ps-1). 1981. 7.95 (ISBN 0-688-80291-5); PLB 7.63 (ISBN 0-688-84291-7). Greenwillow.

Building a Just Society. Patrick Bascio. LC 80-27238. 176p. (Orig.). 1981. pap. text ed. 5.95 (ISBN 0-88344-205-1). Orbis Bks.

Building a School Testing Program: Uses & Misuses of Standardized Tests. R. H. Bauernfeind. 226p. 1978. 8.75 (ISBN 0-936224-00-2). Schol Test.

Building a Small Lathe. L. C. Mason. (Illus.). 82p. 1979. 7.50x (ISBN 0-85242-687-9). Intl Pubns Serv.

Building a Strip Canoe: Easy Step-by-Step Instructions & Patterns for 5 Canoe Models. Gil Gilpatrick. (Illus.). 96p. (Orig.). 1979. pap. 8.95 (ISBN 0-89933-000-2). DeLorme Pub.

Building a Successful Marriage. 7th ed. Landis. 1977. 17.95 (ISBN 0-13-087007-2). P-H.

Building a Teachers' Center. Ed. by Kathleen Devaney. 1979. pap. 9.75x (ISBN 0-8077-2566-8, Pub. by Teach Ctr Exchange). Tchrs Coll.

Building a Vocabulary. Robert E. Mehaffy & Dale F. Goodban. 96p. (Orig.). (gr. 9-12). 1981. pap. text ed. 4.95 (ISBN 0-917962-68-0). Peek Pubns.

Building an American Pedigree: A Guide to Family & Local History Research. 2nd, rev. ed. Norman E. Wright. (Illus.). 1981. pap. text ed. 12.95 (ISBN 0-8425-1863-0). Brigham.

Building an Ark: Tools for the Preservation of Natural Diversity Through Land Protection. Phillip M. Hoose. 224p. (Orig.). 1981. pap. 12.00 (ISBN 0-933280-09-2). Island CA.

Building an Effective Vocabulary. Cedric Gale. LC 79-1496. (Orig.). 1979. pap. 3.95 (ISBN 0-8120-2041-3); answer bklet, 1 for every 25 ordered avail. (ISBN 0-8120-2167-3). Barron.

Building & Displaying Model Aircraft. Robert Schleicher. LC 80-70385. 176p. 1981. 13.95 (ISBN 0-686-69512-7); pap. 8.95 (ISBN 0-686-69513-5). Chilton.

Building & Flying Model Aircraft. Robert Schleicher & James R Barr. LC 79-8312. (Illus.). 192p. 1980. 13.95 (ISBN 0-8019-6903-4); pap. 6.95 (ISBN 0-8019-6904-2). Chilton.

Building & Flying Model Airplanes. Walter Musciano. LC 71-146441. (Funk & W Bk.). (Illus.). 192p. 1974. pap. 2.95 o.p. (ISBN 0-308-10136-7, F102, TYC-T). T Y Crowell.

Building & Planning for Industrial Storage & Distribution. Peter Falconer & Jolyon Drury. LC 75-28387. 1975. 44.95 (ISBN 0-470-25355-X). Halsted Pr.

Building & Racing Radio Control Cars & Motorcycles. George G. Siposs. Ed. by Burr Angle. LC 80-84853. (Illus.). 80p. (Orig.). 1981. pap. price not set (ISBN 0-89024-556-8). Kalmbach.

Building Arithmetic Skills. 2nd ed. W. F. Hunter et al. (gr. 8-12). 1976. 5.60 (ISBN 0-07-031322-9, W); tchr's manual 6.64 (ISBN 0-07-031325-3). McGraw.

Building Assertive Skills: A Practical Guide to Professional Development for Allied Dental Health Providers. Judy C. Morton et al. (Illus.). 283p. 1980. pap. text ed. 11.95 (ISBN 0-8016-3520-9). Mosby.

Building Barbecues. 2nd ed. Sunset Editors. LC 76-140161. (Illus.). 80p. 1971. pap. 3.95 (ISBN 0-376-01034-7, Sunset Bks). Sunset-Lane.

Building Basic Sentences. George E. Sullivan & Warren Cox. Ed. by K. West et al. (Writing Skills for Daily Living Ser.). (Illus.). 40p. (gr. 7-12). 1979. pap. text ed. 3.95x (ISBN 0-87453-097-0, 82097). Denoyer.

Building Bicycle Wheels. Robert Wright. LC 75-35277. (Illus.). 48p. 1980. pap. 1.95 (ISBN 0-89037-106-7). Anderson World.

Building Blocks: For Developing Basic Language. Barbara Petersen. 560p. 1977. 34.95 (ISBN 0-86575-036-X). Dormac.

Building Board Directory 1979. (Benn Directories Ser.). 1979. 40.00 (ISBN 0-510-48509-X, Pub by Benn Pubns). Nichols Pub.

Building British Canada. Jack Zondag & Gordon Oosterman. 1978. 3.05 (ISBN 0-87463-336-2). Chr Sch Intl.

Building Care for Hospitality Operations. Bruce H. Axler. 1974. pap. 3.95 (ISBN 0-672-96124-5). Bobbs.

Building Character. Jan Kuzma & Jay Kuzma. LC 79-83592. (Harvest Ser.). 1979. pap. 4.50 (ISBN 0-8163-0233-2, 02625-2). Pacific Pr Pub Assn.

Building Children's Science Concepts Through Experience. Mary Sheckles. LC 58-8243. 1958. pap. text ed. 4.25x (ISBN 0-8077-2149-2). Tchrs Coll.

Building China: Studies in Integrated Development. Ed. by John F. Jones. 158p. 1981. 14.95 (ISBN 0-295-95821-9, Pub. by Chinese Univ Hong Kong). U of Wash Pr.

Building Christian Character. Paul Anderson. (Trinity Teen Curriculum Ser.). 96p. (Orig.). 1980. wkbk. 2.95 (ISBN 0-87123-019-4, 240019). Bethany Fell.

Building Christian Communities: Strategy for Renewing the Church. Stephen B. Clark. LC 75-189990. 192p. 1972. pap. 2.95 (ISBN 0-87793-043-0). Ave Maria.

Building Code Requirements for Reinforced Concrete: ACI 318-63 ANSI A89.1-1964. ACI Committee 318. 1963. 12.00 (ISBN 0-685-85083-8, 318-63). ACI.

Building Code Requirements for Reinforced Concrete: ACI 318-77 ANSI a89.1-1972. ACI Committee 318. 1977. 20.75 (ISBN 0-685-03451-8, 318-77). ACI.

Building Code Requirements for Reinforced Concrete: ACI 318-71 ANSI A89.1-1972. ACI Committee 318. 1971. 19.00 (ISBN 0-685-85075-7, 318-71). ACI.

Building Code Requirements for Reinforced Concrete SI Metric Edition: ACI 318-71. ACI Committee 318. 1975. 20.00 (ISBN 0-685-85081-1, 318-7 SI). ACI.

Building Codes & Residential Construction: An Annotated Bibliography. Diana M. Brown. (Architecture Ser.: Bibliography A-334). 60p. 1980. pap. 6.50. Vance Biblios.

Building College Spelling Skills. Crosby & Emery. 192p. (Orig.). 1981. pap. text ed. 7.95 (ISBN 0-316-16186-1); tchrs'. manual free (ISBN 0-316-16188-8). Little.

Building Colonial Furnishings, Miniatures, & Folk Art. Joseph W. Daniele. LC 76-17006. (Illus.). 256p. 1976. 15.95 (ISBN 0-8117-0451-3). Stackpole.

Building Construction. Melvin Berger. LC 78-6258. (Industry at Work Ser.). (Illus.). (gr. 4-6). 1978. PLB 5.90 s&l (ISBN 0-531-02206-4). Watts.

Building Construction. 2nd ed. Building Research Establishment. (BRE Digests Volumes). 1978. text ed. 20.00x (ISBN 0-904406-42-3). Longman.

Building Construction: An Illustrated Manual for Technicians, Estate Managers & Surveyors. W. Eric Kelsey. (Illus.). 1974. 35.00 (ISBN 0-7153-6287-9). David & Charles.

Building Construction Cost Data, 1981. 39th ed. Robert S. Godfrey. LC 55-20084. 1981. pap. 24.50 (ISBN 0-911950-29-X). Means.

Building Construction Information Sources. Ed. by Howard B. Bentley. LC 64-16502. (Management Information Guide Ser.: No. 2). 1964. 30.00 (ISBN 0-8103-0802-9). Gale.

Building Construction: Materials & Types of Construction. 5th ed. Whitney C. Huntington & Robert E. Mickadeit. LC 79-24467. 1981. text ed. 19.95 (ISBN 0-471-05354-6). Wiley.

Building Contracts for Design & Construction. 2nd ed. Harold D. Hauf. LC 76-2701. 304p. 1976. 27.50 (ISBN 0-471-36003-1, Pub. by Wiley-Interscience). Wiley.

Building Conversion & Rehabilitation. Thomas Markus. 1979. text ed. 42.95 (ISBN 0-408-00313-8). Butterworths.

Building Cost Composites. Otto Fusch. 208p. (Orig.). 1981. pap. 14.25 (ISBN 0-910460-79-5). Craftsman.

Building Cost Control Techniques & Economics. P. E. Bathurst & D. A. Butler. 1973. pap. 14.95x (ISBN 0-434-90101-6). Intl Ideas.

Building Cost Manual Nineteen Eighty-One. Gary Moselle. 240p. (Orig.). 1980. pap. 10.00 (ISBN 0-910460-77-9). Craftsman.

Building Craft Foremanship: A Manual for the Trainee Building Supervisor. R. Howarth. (Illus.). pap. 5.50 o.p. (ISBN 0-7153-5667-4). David & Charles.

Building Defects & Maintenance. 2nd ed. Building Research Establishment. (BRE Digests Volumes). (Illus.). 1978. text ed. 20.00x (ISBN 0-904406-45-8). Longman.

Building Design for Energy Economics. Ove Arup Partnership. 160p. 1981. 38.00 (ISBN 0-86095-850-7). Longman.

Building Early American Furniture. Joseph W. Daniele. LC 74-10953. (Illus.). 256p. 1974. 19.95 (ISBN 0-685-49912-X). Stackpole.

Building Energy Management--Conventional & Solar Approaches: Proceedings of the International Congress, 12-16 May 1980, Povoa de Varzim, Portugal. Fernandes E. De Oliveira et al. LC 80-40415. 800p. 1981. 160.00 (ISBN 0-08-026144-2). Pergamon.

Building English Skills: Silver Level. (gr. 5). 1980. 9.96 (ISBN 0-88343-571-3); tchrs. ed. 9.96 (ISBN 0-88343-572-1); skills practice bk. 3.56 (ISBN 0-88343-574-8); tchrs. ed. with key 3.18 (ISBN 0-88343-575-6); dupl. masters avail. (ISBN 0-88343-576-4); diagnostic & mastery tests 1.83 (ISBN 0-88343-577-2); tchrs. ans. key to tests 1.50 (ISBN 0-88343-578-0). McDougal-Littell.

Building Estimator's Reference Manual. E. Sarviel. 288p. (Orig.). 1981. pap. 14.75 (ISBN 0-910460-76-0). Craftsman.

Building Ethnic Collections: An Annotated Guide for School Media Centers and Public Libraries. Lois Buttlar & Lubomyr R. Wynar. LC 76-55398. 1977. lib. bdg. 22.50x (ISBN 0-87287-130-4). Libs Unl.

Building Failure, Vol. 5. Building Research Establishment. (Construction Press). 1978. 38.00 (ISBN 0-86095-800-0). Longman.

Building Family Strengths: Blueprints for Action. Ed. by Nick Stinnett et al. LC 79-51329. 1979. 19.50x (ISBN 0-8032-4114-3); pap. 9.95x (ISBN 0-8032-9113-2). U of Nebr Pr.

Building Financial Decision-Making Models: An Introduction to Principles & Procedures. Donald R. Moscato. 144p. 1980. 17.95 (ISBN 0-8144-5609-X). Am Mgmt.

Building for Energy Conservation. P. W. O'Callaghan. 1978. text ed. 31.00 (ISBN 0-08-022120-3). Pergamon.

Building for Eternity. rev. ed. Ed. by William A. Kramer. (Units in Religion: Bk. 5, 2-V). (gr. 5-6). 1958. pap. text ed. 3.50 (ISBN 0-86-57525-3, 22-1125); teachers' manual 4.65 (ISBN 0-570-06755-3, 22-1126). Concordia.

Building for School & Community Use: Five Case Studies. (Educational Studies & Documents: No. 26). (Illus.). 1978. pap. 4.75 (ISBN 92-3-101441-2, U761, UNESCO). Unipub.

Building for School & Community: Vol. V, Sweden. Organization for Economic Cooperation & Development. (Programme on Educational Building Ser.). (Illus.). 172p. 1980. pap. text ed. 10.50x (ISBN 92-64-12025-4, 95 80 02 1). OECD.

Building for Women. Ed. by Suzanne Keller. LC 80-8783. 1981. price not set (ISBN 0-669-04368-0). Lexington Bks.

Building in a Broken World. Brother Andrew. 1981. pap. 3.95 (ISBN 0-8423-0184-4). Tyndale.

Building in Hot Dry Climates. Balwant S. Saini. LC 79-41777. 176p. 1980. 44.00 (ISBN 0-471-27764-9, Pub. by Wiley-Interscience). Wiley.

Building in Use Study: Research Report, 2 pts. Harvey Z. Rabinowitz. Incl. Pt. 1. Technical Factors; Pt. 2. Functional Factors. (Publications in Architecture & Urban Planning Ser.). (Illus.). 258p. 1975. 10.00 set (ISBN 0-686-28214-0, R75-1). U of Wis Ctr Arch-Urban.

Building in Visual Concrete. Erwin Heinle & Max Bacher. Tr. by Joseph Berger et al from Ger. (Illus.). 1971. 25.00x (ISBN 0-291-39299-7). Intl Ideas.

Building Independent Learning Skills. Beth S. Atwood. LC 74-16807. (Learning Handbooks Ser.). 1974. pap. 3.95 (ISBN 0-8224-1973-4). Pitman Learning.

Building Language Power with Cloze: Level C. Marjorie S. Frank & P. J. Hutchins. (Skillbooster Ser.). 64p. (gr. 3). 1981. write for info. wkbk. (ISBN 0-87895-516-X). Modern Curr.

Building Language Power with Cloze: Level D. Marjorie S. Frank & P. J. Hutchins. (Skillbooster Ser.). 64p. (gr. 4). 1981. write for info. (ISBN 0-87895-517-8). Modern Curr.

Building Language Power with Cloze: Level E. Marjorie S. Frank & P. J. Hutchins. (Skillbooster Ser.). 64p. (gr. 5). 1981. write for info. wkbk. (ISBN 0-87895-518-6). Modern Curr.

Building Language Power with Cloze, Level F. Marjorie S. Frank & P. J. Hutchins. (Skillbooster Ser.). 64p. (gr. 6). 1981. write for info. (ISBN 0-87895-519-4). Modern Curr.

Building Language Skills. William F. Hunter et al. (Learning Skills Ser: Language Arts). (Illus.). (gr. 7-12). 1978. pap. text ed. 4.92 (ISBN 0-07-031332-6, W); tchr's manual 6.32 (ISBN 0-07-031335-0). McGraw.

Building Library Collections. 5th ed. Wallace J. Bonk & Rose M. Magrill. LC 79-11151. 1979. 12.50 (ISBN 0-8108-1214-2). Scarecrow.

Building Library Collections: Policies & Practices in Academic Libraries. Hugh F. Cline & Loraine T. Sinnott. LC 80-8602. (Illus.). 192p. 1981. 15.95x (ISBN 0-669-04321-4). Lexington Bks.

Building Life Skills, Level D. Alvin Granowsky & Janice H. Mumford. (Skillbooster Ser.: Bk. 1). 64p. (gr. 4). 1981. write for info. wkbk. (ISBN 0-87895-418-X). Modern Curr.

Building Life Skills, Level E. Alvin Granowsky & Janice H. Mumford. (Skillbooster Ser.: Bk. 2). 64p. (gr. 5). 1981. rite for info. wkbk. (ISBN 0-87895-523-2). Modern Curr.

Building Life Skills, Level F. Alvin Granowsky & Janice H. Mumford. (Skillbooster Ser.: Bk. 3). 64p. (gr. 6). 1981. write for info. wkbk. (ISBN 0-87895-617-4). Modern Curr.

Building Maintenance. Jules Oravetz, Sr. LC 76-45885. 1977. 9.95 (ISBN 0-672-23278-2). Audel.

Building Maintenance & Preservation: A Guide for Design & Management. Ed. by Edward D. Mills. (Illus.). 192p. 1980. pap. text ed. 39.95 (ISBN 0-408-00470-3). Butterworths.

Building Maintenance Management. Reginald Lee. 194p. 1976. pap. text ed. 17.50x (ISBN 0-258-96947-4, Pub. by Granada England). Renouf.

Building Masterpiece Miniatures. Joseph Daniele. (Illus.). 352p. 1981. text ed. 24.95 (ISBN 0-8117-0306-1). Stackpole.

Building Materials. V. M. Bhatnager. 300p. 1981. 40.00x (ISBN 0-86095-866-3). Longman.

Building Materials. 2nd ed. Building Research Establishment. (BRE Digests Volumes). (Illus.). 1978. text ed. 20.00x (ISBN 0-904406-43-1). Longman.

Building Math Skills. Foley et al. Incl. Level 1. text ed. 8.32 (ISBN 0-201-13350-4); tchr's manual with ans. 6.00 (13359); test & practice dupl. masters avail.; Level 2. text ed. 8.32; tchr's manual with ans. 6.00 (13379); test & practice dupl. masters avail.. (Gr. 7-12 Basal, Gr. 9-12 Remedial, Gr. 7-12 Supplemental). 1981. A-W.

Building Miniature Furniture. Joseph W. Daniele. (Illus.). 256p. 1981. 24.95 (ISBN 0-8117-1000-9). Stackpole.

Building Motivation in the Classroom: A Structured Approach to Improving Student Achievement. Robert C. Hawley & Isabel I. Hawley. LC 78-69902. 1979. pap. 8.95 (ISBN 0-913636-10-X). Educ Res MA.

Building Number Skills in Dyslexic Children. Ed. by John I. Arena. LC 72-83250. 1972. pap. 4.00x o.p. (ISBN 0-686-57621-7). Acad Therapy.

Building of Detroit: A History. rev. ed. W. Hawkins Ferry. (Illus.). 1980. 40.00 (ISBN 0-8143-1665-4). Wayne St U Pr.

Building of Jalna. Mazo De La Roche. 288p. 1977. pap. 1.50 o.p. (ISBN 0-449-23071-6, Crest). Fawcett.

Building of Oakland with a Section on Piedmont. Robert Bernhardi. 116p. 1979. 14.95 (ISBN 0-9605472-0-7). Forest Hill.

Building of Renaissance Florence: A Social & Economic History. Richard A. Goldthwaite. LC 80-7995. (Illus.). 448p. 1981. text ed. 25.00x (ISBN 0-8018-2342-0). Johns Hopkins.

Building on Springs. R. A. Waller. 1969. 17.25 (ISBN 0-08-006399-3). Pergamon.

Building on the Back Forty. Shirley Cook. LC 78-53324. (Illus.). 1978. pap. 2.95 o.p. (ISBN 0-89636-003-2). Accent Bks.

Building on Your Street. Seymour Simon. LC 72-92583. (Illus.). 48p. (gr. k-3). 1973. reinforced bdg. 3.95 o.p. (ISBN 0-8234-0216-9). Holiday.

Building Peace: Reports of the Commission to Study the Organization of Peace, 1939-1972, 2 vols. Commission to Study the Organization of Peace. LC 73-4845. 1973. Repr. Set. 32.50 (ISBN 0-8108-0621-5). Scarecrow.

Building Physics: Acoustics. H. J. Purkis. 1966. 23.00 (ISBN 0-08-011443-1); pap. 11.25 (ISBN 0-08-011442-3). Pergamon.

Building Physics: Lighting. W. R. Stevens. 1969. 25.00 (ISBN 0-08-006370-5); pap. 13.25 (ISBN 0-08-006369-1). Pergamon.

Building Planning & Design Standards for Architects, Engineers, Designers, Consultants, Building Committees, Draftsman & Students. Harold R. Sleeper. 1955. 31.95 (ISBN 0-471-79761-8, Pub. by Wiley-Interscience). Wiley.

Building Plant & Equipment Sheets. William Davies. (Illus.). 1978. wirebound 13.95x (ISBN 0-7198-2740-X). Intl Ideas.

Building Plastic Models. Robert Schleicher. LC 76-10915. (Orig.). 1976. 4.75 (ISBN 0-89024-527-4). Kalmbach.

Building Plastic Ship Models. James D. Powell. (Illus.). 350p. 1981. cancelled (ISBN 0-498-02286-2). A S Barnes.

Building Playground Sculpture & Homes. Steven H. Pollock. LC 74-20319. (Illus.). pap. 7.95 (ISBN 0-9600818-1-X). Master Pr.

Building Profits Through Organizational Change. Roger J. Howe. 272p. 1981. 17.95 (ISBN 0-8144-5681-2). Am Mgmt.

Building Public Confidence in Your Schools: Ideas That Work. J. William Jones. 1978. pap. 13.95 (ISBN 0-87545-012-1). Natl Sch Pr.

Building Regulations Explained & Illustrated. W. S. Whyte. (Illus.). 1979. 26.95x (ISBN 0-8464-0050-2). Beekman Pubs.

Building Regulations Explained & Illustrated. 5th ed. W. S. Whyte & Vincent Powell-Smith. 299p. 1978. text ed. 34.00 (ISBN 0-246-11273-5, Pub. by Granada England). Renouf.

Building Safe Driving Skills. rev ed. Patrick Kelley. LC 75-186589. (Illus.). (gr. 9-12,RL 3). 1977. text ed. 10.00 (ISBN 0-8224-1104-0); tchrs' guide 2.80 (ISBN 0-8224-1107-5); duplicatable chapter tests 12.00 (ISBN 0-8224-1106-7); student wkbk. 3.96 (ISBN 0-8224-1105-9). Pitman Learning.

Building Science & Materials Two: Checkbook. Pritchard. 1981. text ed. price not set. Butterworth.

Building Science Laboratory Manual. Henry J. Cowan & John Dixon. (Illus.). 1978. text ed. 28.50x (ISBN 0-85334-747-6, Pub. by Applied Science). Burgess-Intl Ideas.

Building Sermons to Meet People's Needs. Harold T. Bryson & James C. Taylor. LC 78-74962. 1980. 5.95 (ISBN 0-8054-2109-2). Broadman.

Building Service & Equipment Four: Checkbook. Hall. 1981. text ed. price not set (ISBN 0-408-00613-7). Butterworth.

Building Services. P. R. Smith & W. G. Julian. (Illus.). 1976. 52.20x (ISBN 0-685-90194-7, Pub. by Applied Science). Burgess-Intl Ideas.

Building Services Engineering: A Review of Its Development. N. S. Billington & B. M. Roberts. (International Series on Building Environmental Engineering: Vol. 1). 500p. 1981. 80.00 (ISBN 0-08-026741-6); pap. 24.00 (ISBN 0-08-026742-4). Pergamon.

Building Snowshoes: Easy Step-by-Step Instructions & Patterns for 4 Snowshoe Styles. Gil Gilpatrick. (Illus.). 96p. 1979. pap. 8.95 (ISBN 0-89933-001-0). DeLorme Pub.

Building Social Change Communities. The Training-Action Affinity Group. 112p. 1979. pap. 2.80 (ISBN 0-686-28496-8). Movement New Soc.

Building Spelling Skills in Dyslexic Children. Ed. by John I. Arena. LC 72-97517. 1968. pap. 4.00x o.p. (ISBN 0-87879-001-2). Acad Therapy.

Building Systems Cost Guide: 1980. 3rd ed. Robert S. Godfrey. LC 76-17689. (Illus.). 1980. pap. 29.50 (ISBN 0-911950-24-9). Means.

Building Systems Cost Guide: 1981. 6th ed. Robert S. Godfrey. LC 76-17689. 375p. 1981. pap. 32.00 (ISBN 0-911950-30-3). Means.

Building Systems Design with Programmable Calculators. Sital Daryanani. 1980. 27.50 (ISBN 0-07-015415-5, P&RB). McGraw.

Building Tables on Tables: A Book About Multiplication. John V. Trivett. LC 74-11263. (Young Math Ser.). (Illus.). 40p. (gr. k-3). 1975. 7.95 (ISBN 0-690-00593-8, TYC-J); PLB 7.89 (ISBN 0-690-00600-4). T Y Crowell.

Building Technology: Mechanical & Electrical Systems. William J. McGuinness & Benjamin Stein. LC 76-14961. 1977. text ed. 27.95 (ISBN 0-471-58433-9); tchrs'. manual avail. (ISBN 0-471-01601-2). Wiley.

Building Technology Three. Jack Bowyer. (Newnes-Butterworths Technician Ser.). 96p. 1980. pap. 9.95 (ISBN 0-408-00411-8). Butterworths.

Building the Allchin. W. J. Hughes. (Illus., Orig.). 1979. pap. 17.50x (ISBN 0-85242-635-6). Intl Pubns Serv.

Building the Herreshoff Dinghy: The Manufacturer's Method. Barry Thomas. (Illus.). 50p. 1977. pap. 4.00 (ISBN 0-913372-13-7). Mystic Seaport.

Building the Maine Guide Canoe. Jerry Stelmok. LC 80-80780. (Illus.). 272p. 1980. 20.00 (ISBN 0-87742-120-X). Intl Marine.

Building the Medieval Cathedrals. P. Watson. LC 74-19525. (Introduction to the History of Mankind). 48p. 1976. pap. 3.95 limp bdg. (ISBN 0-521-08711-2). Cambridge U Pr.

Building the Organizational Society. Ed. by Jerry Israel. LC 70-170872. 1972. 14.95 (ISBN 0-02-915780-3). Free Pr.

Building the Raritan. William H. Morewood. LC 77-89451. (Illus.). 82p. 1977. 17.00 (ISBN 0-914104-04-7); pap. 14.50 (ISBN 0-914104-03-9). Wildwood Pubns MI.

Building the Skiff Cabin Boy: A Step by Step Pictoral Guide. Clemens Kuhlig & Ruth Kuhlig. LC 76-8775. (Illus.). 1977. 15.00 (ISBN 0-87742-064-5). Intl Marine.

Building the Suez Canal. S. C. Burchell. LC 66-21551. (Horizon Caravel Bks). (Illus.). 153p. 1966. 9.95 (ISBN 0-8281-0354-2, J028-0). Am Heritage.

Building the Timber Frame House. Tedd Benson & James Gruber. (Illus.). 1980. 17.95 (ISBN 0-684-16446-9, ScribT). Scribner.

Building the Voice As an Instrument with a Studio Reference Handbook. Pearl S. Wormhoudt. (Illus., Orig.). 1981. pap. text ed. 8.95 (ISBN 0-916358-08-9). Wormhoudt.

Building to Last. (Illus.). 168p. 1981. 24.95 (ISBN 0-8038-0028-2). Hastings.

Building to Last. Herb Greene & Nanine H. Greene. (Illus.). 168p. 1981. 24.95. Architectural.

Building up One Another. Gene A. Getz. 1976. pap. 3.50 (ISBN 0-88207-744-9). Victor Bks.

Building up: The Young Athlete's Guide to Weight Training. Pete Broccoletti. (Illus.). 160p. 1981. 13.95 (ISBN 0-89651-053-0); pap. 8.95 (ISBN 0-89651-054-9). Icarus.

Building Voluntary Support for the Two-Year College. Ed. by John E. Bennett. 1979. pap. 16.50 (ISBN 0-89964-017-6). CASE.

Building with Stone. Charles McRaven. (Illus.). 1980. 14.95 (ISBN 0-690-01879-7); pap. 8.95 (ISBN 0-690-01912-2). Lippincott.

Building with Wood & Other Aspects of Nineteenth Century Building in Central Canada. rev. ed. John I. Rempel. LC 68-71816. (Illus.). 1980. 35.00 (ISBN 0-8020-2280-4); pap. 19.95 (ISBN 0-8020-6428-0). U of Toronto Pr.

Building Work: A Compendium of Occupational Safety & Health. International Labour Office, Geneva. (Occupational Safety & Health Ser.: No. 42). (Illus.). 256p. (Orig.). 1980. pap. 14.25 (ISBN 92-2-101907-1). Intl Labour Office.

Building Wrecking. rev. & enl. ed. Jean P. Colby. LC 72-5484. (Illus.). 96p. (gr. 5 up). 1972. 6.95g (ISBN 0-8038-0717-1). Hastings.

Building Your Alumni Program. Ed. by Patricia L. Alberger. 100p. (Orig.). 1980. pap. 14.50 (ISBN 0-89964-165-2). CASE.

Building Your Dream Boat. Charles E. Wood. (Illus.). 1981. price not set (ISBN 0-87033-259-7, 2597). Cornell Maritime.

Building Your House on the Lord. Steve Brestin & Dee Brestin. LC 76-43127. (Fisherman Bible Study Guides). 87p. 1976. pap. 1.45 (ISBN 0-87788-098-0). Shaw Pubs.

Buildings & Designs of Andrea Palladio, 2 vols. Ottavio Bertotti-Scamozzi. 1976. boxed 400.00x (ISBN 0-685-73875-2); Plates. boxed 200.00x (ISBN 0-686-67583-5); 30 plates 30.00x (ISBN 0-686-67584-3); 10 plates 20.00x (ISBN 0-686-67585-1); eng. trans. only 50.00x (ISBN 0-686-67586-X). U Pr of Va.

Buildings of an Industrial Community: Coalbrookdale & Ironbridge. W. Grant Muter. (Illus.). 69p. 1979. 22.50x (ISBN 0-8476-3039-0). Rowman.

Buildings of Byzantium. Helen Leacroft. LC 76-54979. (gr. 8-12). 1977. PLB 7.95 (ISBN 0-201-09266-2, A-W Childrens). A-W.

Buildings of Detroit: A History. W. Hawkins Ferry. LC 68-20167. (Illus.). 1968. deluxe ed. 100.00 o.p. (ISBN 0-8143-1332-9). Wayne St U Pr.

Buildings of Detroit: Biographical Sketches of 62 Outstanding Blacks. LC 79-65877. 7.00 o.s.i. (ISBN 0-932212-18-2). Avery Color.

Buildings of Renaissance Rome: An American Student Edition. abr. ed. Paul Letarouilly. Ed. by John B. Bayley. (Classical America Series in Art & Architecture). (Illus.). 96p. text ed. cancelled (ISBN 0-8038-0076-2); pap. text ed. cancelled (ISBN 0-8038-0075-4). Architectural.

Built-Ins. (Home Repair & Improvement Ser.). (Illus.). 1979. lib. bdg. 11.97 (ISBN 0-8094-2431-2); kivar bdg. 7.95 (ISBN 0-8094-2432-0). Silver.

Built-Ins. Ed. by Time-Life Books Editors. (Home Repairs & Improvement Ser.). (Illus.). 1980. 10.95 (ISBN 0-8094-2430-4). Time-Life.

Built Upon the Cornerstone. Joseph M. Tewinkel. LC 80-65148. 178p. (Orig.). 1981. pap. 3.95 (ISBN 0-87509-280-2); pap. 1.50 leaders guide (ISBN 0-686-69527-5). Chr Pubns.

Bukom. Bill Marshall. 118p. (Orig.). 1979. pap. 5.00 (ISBN 0-582-64223-X, Drum Deat). Three Continents.

Bulbous Flowers. Henry Budden. (Illus.). 104p. 1980. 15.95x (ISBN 0-19-558055-9). Oxford U Pr.

Bulbs. James U. Crockett. (Encyclopedia of Gardening Ser). (Illus.). 1971. 11.95 (ISBN 0-8094-1101-6). Time-Life.

Bulbs. James U. Crockett. LC 78-140420. (Time-Life Encyclopedia of Gardening). (Illus.). (gr. 6 up). 1971. lib. bdg. 11.97 (ISBN 0-8094-1102-4, Pub. by Time-Life). Silver.

Bulbs, Corms & Such. Millicent E. Selsam. LC 74-5939. (Illus.). 48p. (gr. 2-5). 1974. 7.75 o.p. (ISBN 0-688-21822-9); PLB 7.92 (ISBN 0-688-31822-3). Morrow.

Bulfinch's Mythology. 2nd rev. ed. Thomas Bulfinch. LC 69-11314. (Illus.). 1970. 11.95 (ISBN 0-690-57260-3, TYC-T). T Y Crowell.

Bulgaria in Antiquity. Ralph Hoddinott. LC 74-77766. 1975. 25.00 (ISBN 0-312-10780-3). St Martin.

Bulgaria: Textbook & Reality. Eleanor W. Smollett. (Occasional Papers: No. 28). 1978. 1.25 (ISBN 0-89977-014-2). Am Inst Marxist.

Bulgarian Mural Paintings of the 14th Century. Dora Panayotova. Tr. by Marguerite Alexieva & Theodora Athanassova. (Illus.). 28.50x (ISBN 0-8057-5003-7). Irvington.

Bulk Carrier Register 1979. 11th ed. Ed. by H. Clarkson, Ltd. LC 71-462684. (Illus.). 1979. 160.00x (ISBN 0-8002-2203-2). Intl Pubns Serv.

Bulk Vitamins & Their Major Markets. Ed. by Business Communications Co. 1980. 975.00 (ISBN 0-89336-235-2, GA-036R). BCC.

Bull Hunter. Max Brand. LC 80-20858. 192p. 1981. 8.95 (ISBN 0-396-07916-4). Dodd.

Bull Moose Years: Theodore Roosevelt & the Progressive Party. John A. Gable. (National University Publications in American Studies). 1978. 17.50 (ISBN 0-8046-9187-8). Kennikat.

Bull Wagon. Glen Dines. (gr. 4-6). 1963. 4.25g o.s.i. (ISBN 0-02-730870-7). Macmillan.

Bulldogs. TFH Publications Staff. (Illus.). 125p. 1980. 2.95 (ISBN 0-87666-714-0, KW-101). TFH Pubns.

Bulldozers, Loaders, & Spreaders. Greenvale School, Ninth Grade English Class. LC 73-10799. (Illus.). 64p. (gr. k-3). 1974. PLB 4.95 (ISBN 0-385-02376-6). Doubleday.

Bullet Barricade. Leslie Ernenwein. 1975. pap. 0.95 o.p. (ISBN 0-685-59190-5, LB312, Leisure Bks). Nordon Pubns.

Bullet for a Star. Stuart Kaminsky. 1978. pap. 1.50 o.s.i. (ISBN 0-515-04625-6). Jove Pubns.

Bullet for a Star. Stuart Kaminsky. LC 76-62776. 144p. 1977. 7.95 o.p. (ISBN 0-312-10797-8). St Martin.

Bullet for Cinderella. John D. MacDonald. 1979. pap. 1.75 o.p. (ISBN 0-449-14106-3, GM). Fawcett.

Bullet or a Rope. W. G. Schreiber. 192p. (YA) 1976. 5.95 (ISBN 0-685-64244-5, Avalon). Bouregy.

Bullet Proof. W. F. Bragg. 1981. pap. 1.95 (ISBN 0-8439-0909-9, Leisure Bks). Nordon Pubns.

Bullet Song. W. F. Bragg. 1981. pap. 1.75 (ISBN 0-8439-0880-7, Leisure Bks). Nordon Pubns.

Bulletin Board Book No. 1. Betty Jenkins. (gr. k-3). 5.95 (ISBN 0-916456-15-3, GA72). Good Apple.

Bulletin Board Book No. 2. Betty Jenkins. (gr. k-3). 5.95 (ISBN 0-916456-14-5). Good Apple.

Bulletin Board Ideas. Pat Harrison. (Ideas Ser). (Illus.). 1977. pap. text ed. 1.75 (ISBN 0-87239-119-1, 7959). Standard Pub.

Bulletin Board Ideas. James H. Robinson & Rowena D. Robinson. LC 72-94108. 80p. 1981. pap. 2.95 (ISBN 0-570-03141-9, 12-2525). Concordia.

Bulletin Boards Made the Easy Way. B. M. Harden & D. L. Williams. (Illus.). 64p. 1981. 5.00 (ISBN 0-682-49731-2). Exposition.

Bulletins from a War. Helen Webster. (Illus.). 46p. (Orig.). 1980. pap. 5.95 (ISBN 0-915380-11-0). Word Works.

Bulletins of American Paleontology, Vol. 55. Incl. No. 246. Some Late Cenozoic Stony Corals from Northern Venezuela. N. E. Weisbord. 1968. pap. 8.00 (ISBN 0-87710-184-1); No. 247. Miocene & Pliocene from Trinidad. Peter Jung. 1968. pap. 10.00 (ISBN 0-685-77159-8). (Illus.). 1968. pap. 25.00 set (ISBN 0-87710-284-8). Paleo Res.

Bulletins of American Paleontology, Vol. 56. Incl. No. 248. Names of & Variation in Central American Larger Foraminifera, Particularly the Eocene Pseudophragminids-No. 4. W. S. Cole. (Illus.). 1969. pap. 3.00 (ISBN 0-87710-186-8); No. 249. Report of the North Carolina Geological Survey. E. Emmons. (Illus.). pap. 5.00 (ISBN 0-87710-187-6); No. 250. Revision of R. P. Whitfield's Types of Rugose & Tabulate Corals in the Museum of Paleontology, University of California, & in the United States National Museum. E. C. Stumm. (Illus.). 1969. pap. 1.50 (ISBN 0-87710-188-4); No. 251. Catalogue of Type Specimens of the Belanski Collection. H. L. Strimple & C. O. Levorson. 1969. pap. 0.75 (ISBN 0-87710-189-2); No. 252. Some Late Cenozoic Echinoidea from Cabo Blanco, Venezuela. N. E. Weisbord. (Illus.). 1969. pap. 3.50 (ISBN 0-87710-190-6); No. 253. Neosciadiocapsidae, a New Family of Upper Cretaceous Radiolaria. E. A. Pessagno, Jr. (Illus.). 1969. pap. 4.00 (ISBN 0-87710-191-4); No. 254. Taxonomy, Distribution, & Phylogeny of the Cymatiid Gastropods Argobuccinum, Fusitriton, Mediargo, & Priene. Judith T. Smith. (Illus.). 1970. pap. 8.00 (ISBN 0-87710-192-2). pap. 25.00 set (ISBN 0-87710-285-6). Paleo Res.

Bulletins of American Paleontology, Vol. 57. Incl. No. 255. Ammonite Fauna of the Kialagvik Formation at Wide Bay, Alaska Peninsula. G. E. G. Westermann. 1969. Pt. 2. pap. 12.00 (ISBN 0-87710-193-0); No. 256. New Middle Jurassic Ammonitina from New Guinea. G. E. G. Westermann & T. A. Getty. 1970. pap. 6.00 (ISBN 0-87710-194-9). (Illus.). pap. 25.00 set (ISBN 0-87710-286-4). Paleo Res.

Bulletins of American Paleontology, Vol. 58. Incl. No. 258. Analysis of Some American Upper Cretaceous Larger Foraminifera. W. S. Cole & Esther A. Applin. 1970. pap. 1.75 (ISBN 0-87710-196-5); No. 259. Silicoflagellates from Central North Pacific Core Sediments. Hsin-I Ling. 1970. pap. 1.50 (ISBN 0-87710-197-3); No. 260. Revision of the North American Pleurocystitidae(Rhombifera-Cystoidea) R. L. Parsley. 1970. pap. 3.25 (ISBN 0-87710-198-1); No. 261. Morphology & Taxonomy of Cyclonema Hall (Gastropoda), Upper Ordovician Cincinnatian Province. Esther Thompson. 1970. pap. 2.50 (ISBN 0-685-77175-X); No. 262. New Vasum Species of the Subgenus Hysterivasum. S. C. Hollister. 1971. pap. 1.15 (ISBN 0-87710-199-X). (Illus.). pap. 25.00 set (ISBN 0-87710-200-7). Paleo Res.

Bulletins of American Paleontology, Vol. 59. Incl. No. 263. Bibliography of Cenozoic Echinoidea: Including Some Mesozoic & Paleozoic Titles. N. E. Weisbord. 1971. 1971. pap. 25.00 (ISBN 0-87710-288-0). Paleo Res.

Bulletins of American Paleontology, Vol. 60. Incl. No. 264. Jurassic & Cretaceous Hagiastridae from the Blake-Bahama Basin(Site 5a, Joides Leg 1) & the Great Vlley Sequence, California Coast Ranges. E. A. Pessagno. 1971. pap. 3.75 (ISBN 0-87710-202-3); No. 265. New Species of Cornula(Cirripedia) from the Lower Pliocene of Venezuela. N. E. Weisbord. 1971. pap. 0.80 (ISBN 0-87710-203-1); No. 266. Palynology & the Independence Shale of Iowa. J. B. Urban. 1971. pap. 5.00 (ISBN 0-685-77180-6); No. 267. Trepostomatous Ectopracta (Bryozoa) from the Lower Chickamauga Group(Middle Ordovician), Wills Valley, Alabama. F. K. McKinney. 1971. pap. 8.00 (ISBN 0-87710-205-8). (Illus.). pap. 25.00 set (ISBN 0-87710-289-9). Paleo Res.

Bulletins of American Paleontology, Vol. 61. Incl. No. 268. Catalogue of Murex(Muricinae and Ocenebrinae) Emily H. Vokes. 1971. pap. 6.00 (ISBN 0-685-77184-9); No. 269. Fossil Mollusks from Carriarov, West Indies. Peter Jung. (Illus.). 1971. pap. 7.50 (ISBN 0-87710-207-4); No. 270. Cretaceous Radiolaria, 2 pts. E. A. Pessagno, Jr. (Illus.). 1972. Set. pap. 4.50 (ISBN 0-685-77186-5); Pt. 1. pap. (ISBN 0-685-77187-3); Pt. 2. pap.. pap. 25.00 set (ISBN 0-87710-290-2). Paleo Res.

Bulletins of American Paleontology, Vol. 62. Incl. No. 271. Trace Fossil Zoophycos As an Indicator of Water Depth. R. G. Osgood, Jr. & E. J. Szmuc. 1972. pap. 1.00 (ISBN 0-87710-209-0); No. 272. Mature Modification & Dimorphism in Selected Late Paleozoic Ammonoids. R. A. Davis. 1972. pap. 7.50 (ISBN 0-87710-210-4); No. 274. Siluro-Devonian Microfaunal Biostratigraphyin Nevada. W. A. McClellan. 1973. pap. 6.00 (ISBN 0-87710-212-0). (Illus.). pap. 25.00 (ISBN 0-87710-291-0). Paleo Res.

Bulletins of American Paleontology, Vol. 63. Incl. No. 275. Reexamination of Chitionozoa from the Cedar Valley Formation of Iowa with Observations on Their Morphology & Distribution. J. B. Urban. (Illus.). 1972. pap. 3.00 (ISBN 0-87710-213-9); No. 276. Upper Cretaceous Spumellariina from the Great Valley Sequence, California Coast Ranges. E. A. Pessagno. 1973. pap. 4.00 (ISBN 0-87710-214-7); Tithonian (Jurassic) Ammonite Fauna & Stratigraphy of Sierra Catorce, San Luis Potosi, Mexico. H. M. Verma & G. E. Westermann. 1973. pap. 10.00 (ISBN 0-87710-215-5). pap. 25.00 set (ISBN 0-87710-292-9). Paleo Res.

Bulletins of American Paleontology, Vol. 64. Incl. No. 278. Palynology of the Almond Formation (Upper Cretaceous). Rock Springs Uplift, Wyoming. J. F. Stone. 1973. pap. 7.50 (ISBN 0-87710-216-3); No. 279. Tabulate Corals & Echinoderms from the Pennsylvanian Winterset Limestone, Hogshooter Formation, Northeastern Oklahoma. H. L. Strimple & J. M. Cocke. 1973. pap. 1.00 (ISBN 0-87710-217-1); No. 280. Stratigraphy & Genera of Calcareous Foraminifera of the Fraileys Facies (Mississippian) of Central Kentucky. R. G. Browne & E. R. Pohl. 1973. pap. 3.50 (ISBN 0-87710-218-X); No. 281. Crinoid Studies, 2 pts. R. K. Pabian & H. L. Strimple. 1974. Set. pap. 4.00 (ISBN 0-685-85210-5); Pt. I. Some Pennsylvanian Crinoids From Nebraska. pap. (ISBN 0-685-85211-3); Pt. II. Some Permian Crinoids From Nebraska, Kansas & Oklahoma. pap. (ISBN 0-685-85212-1). pap. 25.00 set (ISBN 0-87710-293-7). Paleo Res.

Bulletins of American Paleontology, Vol. 66. Incl. Middle-Ordovician Crinoids from Southwestern Virginia & Eastern Tennessee. J. C. Brower & Julia Veinus. (Illus.). 1974. pap. 5.00 (ISBN 0-87710-221-X); No. 284. Gastropoda of the Fox Hill Formation (Maestrichtian) of North Dakota. J. M. Erickson. (Illus.). 1977. pap. 4.25 (ISBN 0-87710-222-8); No. 285. Late Cenozoic Corals of South Florida. N. E. Weisbord. (Illus.). 1974. pap. 10.50 (ISBN 0-87710-223-6); No. 286. Neogene Biostratisgraphy (Ostracoda) of Southern Hispaniola. W. A. Van den Bold. (Illus.). 1974. pap. 4.25 (ISBN 0-87710-224-4). pap. 25.00 set (ISBN 0-87710-295-3). Paleo Res.

Bulletins of American Paleontology, Vol. 68. Incl. No. 288. North American Paracrinoidea: Ordovician Echinodermata. R. L. Parsley & L. W. Mintz. (Illus.). 1975. pap. 4.75 (ISBN 0-87710-226-0); No. 289. Ostracodes from the Late Neogene of Cuba. W. A. Van Den Bold. 1975. pap. 2.50 (ISBN 0-87710-227-9); No. 290. Cirripedia of Florida & Surrounding Waters (Acrothracica & Rhizocephala) (Illus.). pap. 2.90 (ISBN 0-87710-228-7). pap. 25.00 set (ISBN 0-87710-297-X). Paleo Res.

Bulletins of American Paleontology, Vol. 70. Incl. No. 292. Bathyal Gastropods of the Family Turridae in the Early Oligocene Keasey Formation in Oregon. C. S. Hickman. (Illus.). 1976. pap. 5.00 (ISBN 0-685-85223-7); No. 293. Two Foraminiteral Assemblages from the Duplin Marl in Georgia & South Carolina. S. M. Herrick. (Illus.). 1976. pap. 2.90 (ISBN 0-87710-231-7); No. 294. Cenozoic Naticidae (Mollusca: Gastropoda) of the Northeastern Pacific. L. Marincovich. (Illus.). pap. 14.00 (ISBN 0-87710-232-5). pap. 25.00 set (ISBN 0-87710-299-6). Paleo Res.

Bullets, Ballots, & Rhetoric: Confederate Policy for the United States Presidential Contest of Eighteen Sixty-Four. Larry E. Nelson. LC 79-27869. 256p. 1980. 17.50x (ISBN 0-8173-0037-6). U of Ala Pr.

Bullnose & Flatnose Morris. Lytton P. Jarman & Robin I. Barraclough. LC 75-42598. (Illus.). 264p. 1976. 21.00 (ISBN 0-7153-6665-3). David & Charles.

Bulls & Chicago: A Stormy Affair. Robert Logan. (Illus.). 256p. 1975. 7.95 o.p. (ISBN 0-695-80619-X). Follett.

Bulozi Under the Luyana Kings: Political Evolution & State Formation in Pre-Colonial Zambia. Mutumba Mainga. LC 73-174757. (Illus.). 296p. (Orig.). 1973. pap. text ed. 7.95x (ISBN 0-582-64088-1). Longman.

Bultaco Service Repair Handbook: 125-370cc, Through 1977. Clymer Publications. (Illus.). 1977. pap. 9.95 (ISBN 0-89287-174-1, M303). Clymer Pubns.

Bum Rap on America's Cities: The Real Causes of Urban Decay. Richard S. Morris. LC 77-17196. 1978. 8.95 o.p. (ISBN 0-13-089227-0). P-H.

Bum Rap on America's Cities: The Real Cause of Urban Decay. Richard S. Morris. 204p. 1980. pap. text ed. 8.50 (ISBN 0-13-089219-X). P-H.

Bum Stories. Dick Bothwell. (Illus.). 60p. (Orig.). 1980. pap. 3.95x (ISBN 0-9605382-0-8). St Petersburg Times.

Bummer Is... Patricia Palla. 1977. pap. 1.50 o.p. (ISBN 0-8431-0415-5). Price Stern.

Bump in the Night. Rockwell. (ps-3). 1980. pap. 1.50 (ISBN 0-590-30071-7, Schol Pap). Schol Bk Serv.

Bumper Book of Things a Boy Can Make. (Illus.). 1978. pap. 4.95 (ISBN 0-8306-1090-1, 1090). TAB Bks.

Bumper Snickers. Bill Hoest. 128p. pap. 0.95 o.p. (ISBN 0-451-07128-X, Q7128, Sig). NAL.

Bumper Tubbs. David McPhail. (gr. k-3). 1980. 8.95 (ISBN 0-395-28477-5). HM.

Bunch from Bananas. David Pownall. LC 80-27422. (Illus.). 96p. (gr. 3-6). 1981. 7.95 (ISBN 0-02-775090-6). Macmillan.

Bunch of Poems & Verses. Beatrice S. De Regniers. LC 76-28324. (Illus.). (gr. 1-5). 1977. 6.95 (ISBN 0-395-28881-9, Clarion). HM.

Bunch of Tagore Poems. Rabindranath Tagore. Tr. by Monika Varma. (Translated from bengali). 8.00 (ISBN 0-89253-611-X); flexible cloth 4.00 (ISBN 0-89253-612-8). Ind-US Inc.

Bunch on McKellahan Street. Carol Farley. LC 75-152736. (Illus.). (gr. 4-6). 1971. PLB 5.88 o.p. (ISBN 0-531-01992-6). Watts.

Buncha Crocs in Surch of Snac. Terry Galloway. LC 80-65065. 1980. 5.95 (ISBN 0-931604-04-4); pap. 2.95 (ISBN 0-931604-05-2). Curbstone Pub NY TX.

Bunches & Bunches of Bunnies. Louise Mathews. LC 78-7625. (Illus.). (gr. k-3). 1978. 6.95 (ISBN 0-396-07601-7). Dodd.

Bunches & Bunches of Bunnies. Louise Mathews. (Illus.). 32p. 1980. Repr. pap. 1.95 (ISBN 0-590-31536-6, Schol Pap). Schol Bk Serv.

Bundling: Its Origin, Progress & Decline in America. Henry R. Stiles. LC 78-167211. 146p. Repr. of 1934 ed. 18.00 (ISBN 0-8103-3204-3). Gale.

Bundy: The Deliberate Stranger. Richard W. Larsen. LC 80-15795. 1980. 10.95 (ISBN 0-13-089185-1). P-H.

Bunglers & Visionaries: Christian Labour at the Crossroads. J. H. Olthuis & G. Vandezande. 1972. pap. 1.50 o.p. (ISBN 0-686-11984-3). Wedge Pub.

Bunjee Venture. McMurty. (gr. 3-5). 1980. pap. 1.25 (ISBN 0-590-30162-4, Schol Pap). Schol Bk Serv.

Bunjil's Cave: Myths, Legends & Superstitions of the Aborigines of South-East Australia. Aldo Massola. (Illus.). 1968. text ed. 14.25x (ISBN 0-391-01962-7). Humanities.

Bunk Among Dragons: Poems & Translanguistic Adaptations. F. Tamminga. 1973. pap. 2.95 o.p. (ISBN 0-686-11994-0). Wedge Pub.

Bunk: Prelude to Depression. William E. Woodward. LC 76-22715. (Social & Intellectual History of American 1920's Ser.). 1976. Repr. of 1923 ed. lib. bdg. 29.50 (ISBN 0-306-70846-9). Da Capo.

Bunker Hill: A Los Angeles Landmark. Arnold Hylen. (L.A. Miscellany Ser.: No. 7). (Illus.). 1976. 22.50 o.p. (ISBN 0-87093-172-5). Dawsons.

Bunko Book. Walter B. Gibson. (Gambler's Book Shelf). 64p. 1976. pap. 2.95 (ISBN 0-89650-565-0). Gamblers.

Bunnell's Surgery of the Hand. 5th ed. Ed. by Joseph H. Boyes. LC 76-126742. (Illus.). 1970. 51.50 (ISBN 0-397-50250-8). Lippincott.

Bunnicula: A Rabbit-Tale of Mystery. Deborah Howe & James Howe. (gr. 3-7). 1980. pap. 1.95 (ISBN 0-380-51094-4, 51094, Camelot). Avon.

Bunny. Illus. by Carolyn Bracken. (Floppies Ser.). (Illus.). 6p. (ps-k). Date not set. 2.95 (ISBN 0-671-42531-5, Little Simon). S&S.

Bunny Book. Patsy Scarry. (Illus.). (ps-3). 1955. PLB 4.57 o.p. (ISBN 0-307-60215-X, Golden Pr). Western Pub.

Bunny Book. Richard Scarry. (Illus.). 24p. (gr. k-1). 1976. PLB 5.38 (ISBN 0-307-68979-4, Golden Pr). Western Pub.

Bunny in the Honeysuckle Patch. Jane Thayer. (Illus.). (ps-3). 1965. 7.75 (ISBN 0-688-21132-1); PLB 7.44 o.p. (ISBN 0-688-31132-6). Morrow.

Bunting & Lyon's Guide to Private Schools. 8th ed. LC 73-77690. (Illus.). 1980. 15.00 o.p. (ISBN 0-913094-03-X). Bunting.

Bunya the Witch. Robert Kraus. LC 80-13252. (Illus.). 32p. (ps-2). 1980. pap. 3.95 (ISBN 0-671-96038-5, Pub. by Windmill). S&S.

Buoy Engineering. H. O. Berteaux. LC 75-20046. (Ocean Engineering Ser). 336p. 1976. 35.00 (ISBN 0-471-07156-0, Pub. by Wiley-Interscience). Wiley.

Buoyancy Effects in Fluids. J. S. Turner. LC 79-7656. (Monographs on Mechanics & Applied Mathematics). (Illus.). 1980. pap. 19.95x (ISBN 0-521-29726-5). Cambridge U Pr.

Buppet Character Book Set, 10 bks. Bob Reese et al. Ed. by Alton Jordan. (Illus.). (gr. k-3). 1981. Set. PLB 45.00 (ISBN 0-89868-088-3, Read Res); pap. 19.50 set (ISBN 0-89868-099-9). ARO Pub.

Burden Is Light. rev. ed. Eugenia Price. 1975. pap. 1.50 (ISBN 0-89129-005-2). Jove Pubns.

Burden Made Light. abr. ed. Alfred Doerffler. LC 74-34213. 128p. 1981. pap. 4.95 (ISBN 0-570-03026-9, 6-1154). Concordia.

Burden of Freedom: Americans and the God of Israel. Paul M Van Buren. 1976. 6.95 (ISBN 0-8164-0318-X). Crossroad NY.

Burden of Guilt: A Short History of Germany, 1914-1945. Hannah Vogt. Tr. by H. Strauss. (Illus.). (gr. 9-12). 1964. pap. 5.95x (ISBN 0-19-501093-0). Oxford U Pr.

Burdens of Progress, 1900-1929. Richard M. Abrams. 1978. pap. text ed. 7.95x (ISBN 0-673-05778-X). Scott F.

Bureaucracy. Guy Benveniste. LC 77-75390. 1977. lib. bdg. 14.00x (ISBN 0-87835-063-2); pap. text ed. 7.95x (ISBN 0-87835-059-4). Boyd & Fraser.

Bureaucracy & Rural Development in Malaysia. Gayl D. Ness. 1967. 20.00x (ISBN 0-520-00922-3). U of Cal Pr.

Bureaucracy in Modern Society. 2nd ed. Peter M. Blau. (Orig.). 1971. pap. text ed. 3.95x (ISBN 0-394-31452-2, RanC). Random.

Bureaucracy, Innovation & Public Policy. George W. Downs, Jr. (Illus.). 1976. 16.95x o.p. (ISBN 0-669-00872-9). Lexington Bks.

Bureaucracy of Han Times. Hans Bielennstein. LC 78-72080. (Cambridge Studies in Chinese History, Literature & Institutions). (Illus.). 1980. 37.50 (ISBN 0-521-22510-8). Cambridge U Pr.

Bureaucracy of Truth. Paul Lendvai. 350p. 1981. lib. bdg. 20.00x (ISBN 0-86531-142-0). Westview.

Bureaucracy Policy & the Public. new ed. Steven T. Seitz. LC 77-26656. (Illus.). 1978. pap. text ed. 4.95 (ISBN 0-8016-4482-8). Mosby.

Bureaucracy: The Career of a Concept. Ed. by Eugene Kamenka & Martin Krygier. 1979. 19.95x (ISBN 0-312-10803-6). St Martin.

Bureaucratic Behavior in the Executive Branch. Louis C. Gawthrop. LC 69-10568. 1969. pap. text ed. 6.95 (ISBN 0-02-911400-4). Free Pr.

Bureaucratic Corruption in Sub-Saharan Africa: Toward a Search for Causes & Consequences. Ed. by Monday U. Ekpo. LC 79-66150. 1979. pap. text ed. 14.50 (ISBN 0-8191-0796-4). U Pr of Amer.

Bureaucratic Corruption in the Third World. David J. Gould. (Policy Studies). 1980. 22.50 (ISBN 0-08-025084-X). Pergamon.

Bureaucratic Culture: Citizens & Administrators in Israel. David Nachmias & David H. Rosenbloom. LC 78-17638. 1978. 17.95x (ISBN 0-312-10808-7). St Martin.

Bureaucratic Justice: Police, Prosecutors, & Plea Bargaining. W. Boyd Littrell. LC 79-18158. (Sage Library of Social Research: Vol. 93). (Illus.). 1979. 18.00x (ISBN 0-8039-1264-1); pap. 8.95x (ISBN 0-8039-1265-X). Sage.

Bureaucratic Leviathan: A Study in the Sociology of Communism. Ed. by Maria Hirszowicz. 224p. 1980. text ed. 27.50x (ISBN 0-8147-3406-5). NYU Pr.

Bureaucratic Opposition: Challenging Abuses at the Workplace. Deena Weinstein. (Pergamon Policy Studies). 1979. 17.75 (ISBN 0-08-023903-X); pap. 6.95 (ISBN 0-08-023902-1). Pergamon.

Bureaucratic Policy Making in a Technological Society. Gerard S. Gryski. 320p. 1981. pap. text ed. 8.95x (ISBN 0-87073-829-1). Schenkman.

Bureaucratic Politics & Administration in Chile. Peter S. Cleaves. 1974. 25.00x (ISBN 0-520-02448-6). U of Cal Pr.

Bureaucratic Politics & Foreign Policy. Morton H. Halperin et al. LC 73-22384. 340p. 1974. 15.95 (ISBN 0-8157-3408-5); pap. 6.95 (ISBN 0-8157-3407-7). Brookings.

Bureaucratic Propaganda. Altheide & Johnson. 1980. text ed. 13.60 (ISBN 0-205-06716-6, 81617168). Allyn.

Bureaucratization of Socialism. Donald C. Hodges. LC 80-23253. 240p. 1981. lib. bdg. 15.00x (ISBN 0-87023-138-3). U of Mass Pr.

Bureaucratization of the World. Henry Jacoby. LC 74-166224. 1973. 23.75x (ISBN 0-520-02083-9); pap. 4.95 (ISBN 0-520-03044-3). U of Cal Pr.

Bureaucrats, Politicians, & Peasants in Mexico: A Case Study in Public Policy. Merilee S. Grindle. LC 76-7759. 1977. 18.00x (ISBN 0-520-03238-1). U of Cal Pr.

Burg: An Italian-American Community at Bay in Trenton. Peter A. Peroni. LC 79-63258. 1979. pap. text ed. 8.00 (ISBN 0-8191-0724-7). U Pr of Amer.

Burge & Minnechaduza Clarendonian Mammalian Faunas of Northcentral Nebraska. David S. Webb. (U. C. Publ. in Geological Sciences: Vol. 78). 1969. pap. 10.95x (ISBN 0-520-09181-7). U of Cal Pr.

Burger Cookery. Pat Jester. LC 77-95176. (Illus.). 1978. 7.95 o.p. (ISBN 0-89586-002-3); pap. 4.95 o.p. (ISBN 0-89586-001-5). H P Bks.

Burger's Daughter. Nadine Gordimer. 362p. 1980. pap. 3.95 (ISBN 0-14-005593-2). Penguin.

Burger's Medicinal Chemistry: The Basis of Medicinal Chemistry, 3 pts. 4th ed. Manfred E. Wolff. LC 78-10791. 1980. Pt. 1. 33.95 (ISBN 0-471-01570-9, Pub. by Wiley-Interscience); Pt. 2. 100.00 (ISBN 0-471-01571-7); Pt. 3. write for info. (ISBN 0-471-01572-5). Wiley.

Burglar at Your Window. 1980. pap. 2.95 (ISBN 0-918734-11-8). Reymont.

Burglar Bill. Allan Ahlberg. LC 76-40339. (Illus.). (gr. k-3). 1977. 8.25 (ISBN 0-688-80078-5); PLB 7.92 (ISBN 0-688-84078-7). Greenwillow.

Burglar in the Closet. Lawrence Block. 1981. pap. write for info. (ISBN 0-671-83581-5). PB.

Burglar Next Door. Jay Williams. LC 76-12422. (Illus.). 128p. (gr. 3-7). 1976. 6.95 (ISBN 0-590-07436-9, Four Winds). Schol Bk Serv.

Burglars Can't Be Choosers. Lawrence Block. 1978. pap. 1.75 o.s.i. (ISBN 0-515-04584-5). Jove Pubns.

Burglary & Theft. J. M. Macdonald. 292p. 1980. 19.75 (ISBN 0-398-03962-3). C C Thomas.

Burgundian Code: Book of Constitutions or Law of Gundobad & Additional Enactments. Tr. by Katherine F. Drew. LC 70-182499. (Middle Ages Ser). (Orig.). 1972. 10.00x (ISBN 0-8122-7654-X); pap. 4.95x (ISBN 0-8122-1035-2, Pa Paperbks). U of Pa Pr.

Burgundy. Anthony Turner & Christopher Brown. 1977. 24.00 (ISBN 0-7134-0889-8). David & Charles.

Burial by Baptism. Derek Prince. 1970. pap. 0.75 o.p. (ISBN 0-934920-15-X, B-22). Derek Prince.

Burial of the Dead: Rite One. 1977. pap. 0.95 (ISBN 0-8164-2153-6). Crossroad NY.

Burial of the Dead: Rite Two. 1977. pap. 0.95 (ISBN 0-8164-2154-4). Crossroad NY.

Burial of the Sardine. Fernando Arrabel. 1980. pap. 4.95 (ISBN 0-7145-0146-8). Riverrun NY.

Burian-Von Noordens Binocular Vision & Ocular Mortility Theory: Management of Strabismas. 2nd ed. Von Noorden. LC 79-19275. 1979. 62.50 (ISBN 0-8016-0898-8). Mosby.

Buried Alive. Ed. by Mary Verdick. (Pal Paperbacks, Pal Skills Ser.). (Illus., Orig.). (gr. 7-12). 1978. pap. text ed. 1.25 (ISBN 0-8374-6705-5). Xerox Ed Pubns.

Buried Cities. rev. ed. Jennie Hall. 1964. 4.95 o.s.i. (ISBN 0-02-741940-1). Macmillan.

Buried for Pleasure. Edmund Crispin. 191p. Repr. of 1948 ed. lib. bdg. 9.70x (ISBN 0-89190-691-6). Am Repr-Rivercity Pr.

Buried Past: An Annotated Bibliography of the Japanese American Research Project Collection. Compiled by Yuji Ichioka et al. 1974. 18.50x (ISBN 0-520-02541-5). U of Cal Pr.

Burke County: A Brief History. Alan D. Watson. (Illus., Orig.). 1979. pap. 2.00 (ISBN 0-86526-130-X). NC Archives.

Burkett: Latest Word from Washington. Melvin L. Barslow. 169p. 1977. pap. 3.00 (ISBN 0-89514-001-2, 10177). Am Voc Assn.

Burlington Route: A History of the Burlington Lines. Richard C. Overton. LC 76-17079. (Illus.). 1976. pap. 8.95 (ISBN 0-8032-5853-4, BB 632, Bison). U of Nebr Pr.

Burma Delta: Economic Development & Social Change on the Rice Frontier, 1852-1941. Michael Adas. LC 73-15256. 288p. 1974. 21.50 (ISBN 0-299-06490-5). U of Wis Pr.

Burma Diary Nineteen Thirty-Eight to Nineteen Forty-Two. Mary O. Johnson. 1981. 5.75 (ISBN 0-8062-1697-2). Carlton.

Burma Rifles: A Story of Merrill's Marauders. Frank Bonham. LC 60-11535. (gr. 5 up). 1960. 7.95 o.p. (ISBN 0-690-16147-6, TYC-J). T Y Crowell.

Burmese Cat. Robine Pocock et al. (Illus.). 182p. 1980. 22.50 (ISBN 0-7134-2937-2, Pub. by Batsford England). David & Charles.

Burmese Days. George Orwell. LC 73-12947. 287p. 1974. pap. 3.95 (ISBN 0-15-614850-1, HPL62, HPL). HarBraceJ.

Burmese Monk's Tales. Ed. by M. Htin Aung. LC 66-10871. 1966. 15.00x (ISBN 0-231-02878-4). Columbia U Pr.

Burn Care for the House Officer. Andrew Munster. (House Officer Ser.). (Illus.). 185p. 1980. softcover 9.95 (ISBN 0-683-06157-7). Williams & Wilkins.

Burn Management. Carole L. Johnson et al. 130p. 1981. 12.50 (ISBN 0-89004-320-5, 466). Raven.

Burn Out: The High Cost of High Achievement. Herbert Freudenberger & Geraldine Richelson. LC 79-6596. 240p. 1980. 9.95 (ISBN 0-385-15664-2, Anchor Pr). Doubleday.

Burn This. Helen McCloy. LC 80-26053. 287p. 1980. Repr. of 1980 ed. large print ed. 10.95 (ISBN 0-89621-261-0). Thorndike Pr.

Burn This. Helen McCloy. LC 80-150. (Dr. Basil Willing Mystery Novel Ser.). 212p. 1980. 7.95 (ISBN 0-396-07806-0). Dodd.

Burned to Life. Mel Kenyon & Mike Christophus. LC 76-1060. (Illus.). 1976. pap. 1.95 (ISBN 0-87123-044-5, 200044). Bethany Fell.

Burnetti Gaetano Seventeen Forty-Four to Seventeen Ninety-Eight: Nine Symphonies. Ed. by Newell Jenkins & Barry S. Brook. LC 79-9531. (Symphony 1720-1840 Ser.: Ser. A, Vol. V). 635p. 1980. lib. bdg. 60.00 (ISBN 0-8240-3801-0). Garland Pub.

Burnham's Celestial Handbook: An Observer's Guide to the Universe Beyond the Solar System. Robert Burnham, Jr. (Illus.). 1980. Repr. of 1978 ed. 16.50x ea. Vintage Bk Co.

Burnham's Celestial Handbook: An Observer's Guide to the Universe Beyond the Solar System, 3 vols. rev. ed. Robert Burnham, Jr. (Illus.). 2000p. 1980. 20.00 ea. Vol. 1 (ISBN 0-486-24063-0). Vol. 2 (ISBN 0-486-24064-9). Vol. 3 (ISBN 0-486-24065-7). Dover.

Burnham's Celestial Handbook: An Observer's Guide to the Universe Beyond the Solar System, Vols. 1 & 2. Robert Burnham, Jr. LC 77-82888. (Illus.). 1978. pap. 8.95 ea. Vol. 1 (ISBN 0-486-23567-X). Vol. 2 (ISBN 0-486-23568-8). Dover.

Burning. Jane Chambers. 1978. pap. 1.50 o.s.i. (ISBN 0-515-04450-4). Jove Pubns.

Burning. Jeff Fain. 1981. pap. 2.25 (ISBN 0-8439-0839-4, Leisure Bks). Nordon Pubns.

Burning Blue Death. Joseph Rosenberger. (Death Merchant Ser.: No. 38). 192p. (Orig.). 1980. pap. 1.95 (ISBN 0-523-41382-3). Pinnacle Bks.

Burning Bud. Ghazala S. Mujtaba. 1981. 5.95 (ISBN 0-533-04532-0). Vantage.

Burning Bush. Geoffrey Spencer. LC 74-84762. 1974. 6.50 (ISBN 0-8309-0129-9). Herald Hse.

Burning Dawn. Elspeth Sandys. (Orig.). Date not set. pap. 3.25 (ISBN 0-440-10882-9). Dell.

Burning Desire. Margaret Mayo. (Harlequin Romances Ser.). 192p. (Orig.). 1981. pap. 1.25 (ISBN 0-373-02385-5, Pub. by Harlequin). PB.

Burning Heart: John Wesley, Evangelist. A. Skevington Wood. LC 78-52837. 1978. pap. 4.95 (ISBN 0-87123-043-7, 210043). Bethany Fell.

Burning Hill. Iona MacGregor. (gr. 5 up). 1970. 6.95 (ISBN 0-571-09318-3, Pub. by Faber & Faber). Merrimack Bk Serv.

Burning in Water, Drowning in Flame. Charles Bukowski. 180p. (Orig.). 1980. 14.00 (ISBN 0-87685-192-8); pap. 6.00 (ISBN 0-87685-191-X). Black Sparrow.

Burning Jungle: An Analysis of Arthur Miller's "Death of a Salesman". Karl Harshbarger. 1978. pap. text ed. 7.50x (ISBN 0-8191-0368-3). U Pr of Amer.

Burning Mad. Mad Magazine Editors. (Mad Ser.). (Illus.). 1975. pap. 1.75 (ISBN 0-446-94360-6). Warner Bks.

Burning Man. Charles R. Pike. LC 80-69220. (Jubal Cade Westerns Ser.). 128p. 1980. pap. 2.95 (ISBN 0-87754-235-X). Chelsea Hse.

Burning Mystery of Ana in Nineteen Fifty-One. Kenneth Koch. LC 78-21608. 1979. 8.95 (ISBN 0-394-50473-9). Random.

Burning of the General Slocum. Claude Rust. (Illus.). 160p. (YA) 1981. 8.95 (ISBN 0-525-66715-6). Elsevier-Nelson.

Burning of Washington: August 1814. Mary K. Phelan. LC 74-30025. (Illus.). (gr. 5-10). 1975. 8.95 (ISBN 0-690-00486-9, TYC-J). T Y Crowell.

Burning Plain & Other Stories. Juan Rulfo. Tr. by George D. Schade. LC 67-25698. (Pan American Paperback Ser.: No. 6). (Illus.). 1957. 8.95x (ISBN 0-292-73685-1); pap. 3.95 (ISBN 0-292-70132-2). U of Tex Pr.

Burning the Years: Special Issue 13. William Childress. pap. 1.00 o.p. (ISBN 0-685-78395-2). The Smith.

Burning Thorn. Ed. by Griselda Greaves. (gr. 7 up). 1971. 5.95 o.s.i. (ISBN 0-02-736740-1). Macmillan.

Burning Valley. J. L. Bouma. 1976. pap. 0.95 o.p. (ISBN 0-685-69511-5, LB378NK, Leisure Bks). Nordon Pubns.

Burning Water: A Novel About George Vancouver, Pacific Explorer. George Bowering. LC 80-21755. 272p. 12.95 (ISBN 0-8253-0005-3). Beaufort Bks NY.

Burning Woman. Margaret Ritter. 1980. pap. 2.75 (ISBN 0-425-04463-7). Berkley Pub.

Burning Wood. Gary Werner. (Illus.). 1980. softcover 6.00 (ISBN 0-686-64446-8); lib. bdg. 10.00 (ISBN 0-915262-53-3). S J Durst.

Burning Wood. David Williams. (Anansi Fiction Ser.: No. 34). 204p. 1975. 12.95 (ISBN 0-88784-435-9, Pub. by Hse Anansi Pr Canada); pap. 6.95 (ISBN 0-88784-054-X). U of Toronto Pr.

Burnish Me Bright. Julia Cunningham. (gr. k-6). 1980. pap. 1.25 (ISBN 0-440-40870-9, YB). Dell.

Burnout: From Tedium to Personal Growth. Ayala Pines et al. LC 80-755. (Illus.). 224p. 1981. 17.95 (ISBN 0-02-925350-0). Free Pr.

Burnout: Funny Car Races. Jay Denan. LC 79-64700. (gr. 5-9). 1979. PLB 5.89 (ISBN 0-89375-256-8); pap. 2.50 (ISBN 0-89375-257-6). Troll Assocs.

Burns Indiana Statutes Annotated, 39 vols. write for info. (ISBN 0-672-83879-6, Bobbs-Merrill Law); write for info 1980 supplement (ISBN 0-672-84244-0). Michie.

Burns of the Upper Extremity. Roger E. Salisbury & Basil A. Pruitt. LC 75-14786. (Major Problems in Clinical Surgery Ser.: Vol. 19). (Illus.). 175p. 1976. text ed. 17.00 (ISBN 0-7216-7902-1). Saunders.

Burns Singer: Selected Poems. Burns Singer. Ed. by Anne Cluysenaar. (Poetry Ser.). 1979. 7.95 o.s.i. (ISBN 0-85635-177-6, Pub. by Carcanet New Pr England). Persea Bks.

Burnside Groups. Ed. by J. L. Mennicke. (Lecture Notes in Mathematics: Vol. 806). 274p. 1980. pap. 16.80 (ISBN 0-387-10006-7). Springer-Verlag.

Burnt Offerings: Parables for Twentieth Century Christians. E. T. Eberhart. LC 77-23158. 1977. pap. 3.95 o.p. (ISBN 0-687-04375-1). Abingdon.

Burnt-Out Case. Graham Greene. 1977. pap. 2.50 (ISBN 0-14-001894-8). Penguin.

Burnt Water. Carlos Fuentes. Tr. by Margaret S. Peden from Span. 295p. 1980. 11.95 (ISBN 0-374-11741-1). FS&G.

Burrowing Birds. Anita Gustafson. LC 80-29058. (Illus.). 64p. (gr. 4-6). 1981. 7.95 (ISBN 0-688-41977-1); PLB 7.63 (ISBN 0-688-51977-6). Morrow.

Burtons of Dunroe, 3 vols. Margaret W. Brew. Ed. by Robert L. Wolff. (Ireland-Nineteenth Century Fiction, Ser. Two: Vol. 69). 1979. Set. lib. bdg. 138.00 (ISBN 0-8240-3518-6). Garland Pub.

Burundi: The Tragic Years. Thomas P. Melady. LC 73-89357. (Illus.). 126p. 1974. 4.95x o.p. (ISBN 0-88344-045-8). Orbis Bks.

Bury the Past. Richard Reinsmith. (Orig.). 1980. pap. 1.75 (ISBN 0-505-51558-X). Tower Bks.

Bus Ride. Marilyn Sachs. LC 79-23596. (Illus.). (gr. 7 up). 1980. PLB 7.95 (ISBN 0-525-27325-5, Skinny Book); pap. 2.50 (ISBN 0-525-45048-3, Skinny Book). Dutton.

Bus Station Mystery. Gertrude C. Warner. LC 74-8293. (Boxcar Children Mysteries-Pilot Bk.). (Illus.). 128p. (gr. 3-7). 1974. 6.95g (ISBN 0-8075-0975-2). A Whitman.

Bus That Went to Church. Jill Tomlinson. (Illus.). (ps-5). 1970. 4.95 o.p. (ISBN 0-571-06337-3, Pub. by Faber & Faber); pap. 2.50 (ISBN 0-571-09407-4). Merrimack Bk Serv.

Bus Them in. Gardiner Gentry. 1976. pap. 2.95 o.p. (ISBN 0-8010-3705-0). Baker Bk.

Bus Trip. Eleanor F. Lattimore. (Illus.). (gr. 2-5). 1965. 7.25 (ISBN 0-688-21133-X). Morrow.

Busch-Reisinger Museum: Harvard University. Charles Haxthausen. LC 80-65261. (Illus.). 152p. (Orig.). 1980. pap. 22.50 (ISBN 0-89659-138-7). Abbeville Pr.

Bush Is Burning. A. Waskow. 1971. pap. 1.95 o.s.i. (ISBN 0-02-089710-3, Collier). Macmillan.

Bush League: A History of Minor League Baseball. Robert Obojski. LC 74-16345. (Illus.). 320p. 1975. 12.95 o.s.i. (ISBN 0-02-591300-X). Macmillan.

Bushcraft: A Serious Guide to Survival & Camping. Richard Graves. (Illus.). 1978. pap. 3.50 (ISBN 0-446-96807-2). Warner Bks.

Bushu: A Key to the 'Radicals' of the Japanese Language. Olov B. Anderson. (Scandinavian Institute of Asian Studies). 1980. pap. text ed. 6.50x (ISBN 0-7007-0127-3). Humanities.

Bushwack. Richard S. Wheeler. LC 78-7772. 1978. 7.95 o.p. (ISBN 0-385-14281-1). Doubleday.

Bushwackers. Lee Floren. (Orig.). 1980. pap. 1.75 (ISBN 0-505-51531-8). Tower Bks.

Bushwhacked Piano. Thomas McGuane. 1973. pap. 1.95 o.p. (ISBN 0-446-89477-X). Warner Bks.

Business. 2nd ed. Charles A. Kirkpatrick & Frederick A. Russ. LC 77-13460. 544p. 1978. pap. text ed. 13.95 (ISBN 0-574-19365-0, 13-2365); instr's guide avail. (ISBN 0-574-19366-9, 13-2366); study guide 5.95 (ISBN 0-574-19367-7, 13-2367); trans. mstrs. 30.00 (ISBN 0-686-60861-5, 13-2367); test booklet 6.50 (ISBN 0-574-19368-5, 13-2368); instructor's presentation notebook 49.95 (ISBN 0-686-52458-6, 13-2309). SRA.

Business. Jack Rudman. (Undergraduate Program Field Test Ser.: UPFT-3). (Cloth bdg. avail. on request). pap. 9.95 (ISBN 0-8373-6003-X). Natl Learning.

Business: An Introduction to American Enterprise. Paul Preston & Thomas W. Zimmerer. 1976. 18.95 (ISBN 0-13-091272-7); student guide 7.95 (ISBN 0-13-091280-8). P-H.

Business Analysis for Marketing Managers. L. A. Rogers. 1978. pap. 14.95x (ISBN 0-434-91738-9). Intl Ideas.

Business & Consumer Mathematics. Michael L. Kovacic. 1978. text ed. 17.80 (ISBN 0-205-05963-5); instr's man. avail. (ISBN 0-205-05964-3). Allyn.

Business & Consumer Mathematics. Thomas F. Saake. (gr. 9-12). 1977. text ed. 14.68 (ISBN 0-201-06775-7, Sch Div); tchr's ed. 18.64 (ISBN 0-201-06776-5). A-W.

Business & Government. Ronald H. Wolf & Vernon A. Mund. 1980. text ed. 19.95 (ISBN 0-89894-006-0). Advocate Pub Group.

Business & Government During the Eisenhower Administration: A Study of the Anti-Trust Policy of the Anti-Trust Division of the Justice Department. Theodore P. Kovaleff. LC 79-25590. x, 313p. 1980. 17.95x (ISBN 0-8214-0416-4). Ohio U Pr.

Business & Personal Taxes. 4th rev. ed. Catherine E. Miles & Joseph E. Lane, Jr. 1977. text ed. 14.95x o.p. (ISBN 0-205-05808-6); instructor's manual avail. o.p. (ISBN 0-205-05809-4). Allyn.

Business & Personal Taxes Nineteen Eighty-One. Miles & Lane. 400p. 1980. text ed. 19.95 (ISBN 0-205-07163-5, 1071637). Allyn.

Business & Politics in India. Stanley A. Kochanek. 1974. 23.75x o.p. (ISBN 0-520-02377-3). U of Cal Pr.

Business & Politics in the Far East. Edith E. Ware. 1932. 27.50x o.p. (ISBN 0-685-89736-2). Elliots Bks.

Business and Professional Communication: Basic Skills and Principles. Vincent Disalvo. (Speech and Drama Ser.). 1977. text ed. 14.95 (ISBN 0-675-08486-5); instrs' manual 3.95 (ISBN 0-675-08486-5). Merrill.

Business & Society: A Managerial Approach. Frederick A. Sturdivant. 1977. 18.95 (ISBN 0-256-01897-9). Irwin.

Business & Society: Environment & Responsibility. Keith Davis & Robert Blomstrom. (Management Ser.). (Illus.). 608p. 1975. text ed. 15.95 o.p. (ISBN 0-07-015524-0, C); instructor's manual 4.95 o.p. (ISBN 0-07-015525-9). McGraw.

Business & Society: Managing Corporate Social Impact. George Sawyer. LC 78-69570. (Illus.). 1978. text ed. 18.50 (ISBN 0-395-26541-X); instr's. manual o.p. (ISBN 0-395-26534-7). HM.

Business & Society: Managing Corporate Social Performance. Archie B. Carroll. text ed. 16.95 (ISBN 0-316-13010-9); training manual free (ISBN 0-316-13011-7). Little.

Business & Technical Writing: An Annotated Bibliography of Books, 1880-1980. Gerald J. Alred et al. LC 80-29211. 249p. 1981. 12.50 (ISBN 0-8108-1397-1). Scarecrow.

Business & the Law. R. Robert Rosenberg & William G. Ott. (Illus.). 280p. 1975. pap. text ed. 12.25 o.p. (ISBN 0-07-053675-9, G); instructor's manual & key 6.00 o.p. (ISBN 0-07-053676-7). McGraw.

Business Applications in Typewriting. Farmer et al. 368p. 1976. text ed. 15.27 (ISBN 0-7715-0878-6); tchr's. manual 7.93 (ISBN 0-7715-0879-4); stationery & business forms 6.60 (ISBN 0-7715-0880-8); Set Of 26 Cassettes. 269.50 (ISBN 0-7715-0882-4). Forkner.

Business Basic. Robert J. Bent & George C. Sethares. LC 79-18502. 1980. pap. text ed. 11.95 (ISBN 0-8185-0359-9). Brooks-Cole.

Business Beat: Its Impact & Its Problems. William McPhatter. LC 80-16599. (ITT Key Issue Lecture Ser.). 168p. pap. text ed. 4.95. Bobbs.

Business Borrowers Complete Success Kit. 2nd ed. Tyler G. Hicks. 596p. 1981. pap. 99.50 (ISBN 0-914306-44-8). Intl Wealth.

Business Brokers' Manual. Howard Benson. 136p. (Orig.). 1977. 15.00 (ISBN 0-686-27499-7). Business Brokers.

Business Budgets & Accounts. 3rd ed. Harold C. Edey. 1966. pap. text ed. 2.75x (ISBN 0-09-022422-1, Hutchinson U Lib). Humanities.

Business Calculator Operations. Joan Elizabeth Warner. (Illus.). 1978. pap. text ed. 13.50 (ISBN 0-87909-097-9); student manual avail. Reston.

Business Capital Sources. 2nd ed. Tyler G. Hicks. 150p. 1981. pap. 15.00 (ISBN 0-914306-47-2). Intl Wealth.

Business Communication. Ed. by W. D. Brooks & R. A. Vogel. LC 76-44138. (Series in Speech Communication). 1977. pap. text ed. 5.95 (ISBN 0-8465-7600-7); instr's guide 3.95 (ISBN 0-8465-7607-4). Benjamin-Cummings.

Business Communication. Richard B. Huseman et al. LC 80-65802. 448p. 1981. text ed. 16.95 (ISBN 0-03-050946-7). Dryden Pr.

Business Communication Dynamics. Bobbye S. Persing. (General Business Ser.). 475p. 1981. text ed. price not set (ISBN 0-675-08153-X). Merrill.

Business Communication: Effective Correspondence Through the Tri-Ask Technique. Virginia L. Hallock. LC 73-80235. (Illus.). 279p. 1980. pap. text ed. 10.15 (ISBN 0-913310-31-X). PAR Inc.

Business Communication: Theory & Application. 3rd ed. Raymond V. Lesikar. 1976. text ed. 16.50x o.p. (ISBN 0-256-01818-9). Irwin.

Business Communication: Theory & Application. 4th ed. Raymond V. Lesikar. 1980. 18.50x (ISBN 0-256-02332-8). Irwin.

Business Communication: Theory & Practice. Dale A. Level, Jr. & William P. Galle, Jr. 1980. 17.95x (ISBN 0-256-02203-8). Business Pubns.

Business Communications. 4th ed. R. T. Chappell & W. L. Read. 232p. (Orig.). 1979. pap. text ed. 13.95x (ISBN 0-7121-0272-8, Pub. by Macdonald & Evans England). Intl Ideas.

Business Communications: Principles & Methods. 5th ed. William C. Himstreet & Wayne M. Baty. 1977. 18.95x (ISBN 0-534-00476-8). Wadsworth Pub.

Business Communications with Writing Improvement Exercises. Charles Hemphill. 256p. 1981. pap. text ed. 11.95 (ISBN 0-13-093880-7). P-H.

Business Computer Systems: An Introduction. David M. Kroenke. (Illus.). 576p. 1980. 15.95x (ISBN 0-938188-00-3). Mitchell Pub.

Business Computer Systems & Applications. 2nd ed. Alan Eliason & Kent D. Kitts. LC 78-18447. 384p. 1979. instr's guide avail. (ISBN 0-574-21215-9, 13-4215); instructor's guide 2.25 (ISBN 0-574-21216-7, 13-4216). SRA.

Business Computers: How to Select Hardware, Software, Services. Dick H. Brandon & Sidney Segelstein. LC 80-26751. 302p. 1981. write for info. (ISBN 0-932648-18-5). Boardroom.

Business Condominium: A New Form of Business Property Ownership. David Clurman. LC 73-10089. (Real Estate for Professional Practitioners Ser.). 185p. 1973. 28.95 (ISBN 0-471-16129-2). Wiley.

Business Control Atlas of the United States & Canada: 1979 Edition. American Map Co. Inc. (Series 6500). 1979. plastic spiral bdg. 9.85 (ISBN 0-8416-9556-3). Am Map.

Business Corporations Laws of the U.S. 1981 ed. 200p. 1981. 7.50 (ISBN 0-87526-196-5). Gould.

Business Correspondence. Waldo C. Wright. **Incl. 1967. 3rd ed. text ed. 10.50 (ISBN 0-672-96007-9); 1963. tchr's manual 6.67 (ISBN 0-685-58241-8). Bobbs.**

Business Cycle Analysis: Papers Presented at the Fourteenth CIRET Conference Proceedings - Lisbon 1979. W. Strigel. 456p. 1980. text ed. 50.00x (ISBN 0-566-00368-6, Pub. by Gower Pub. Co England). Renouf.

Business Cycles & National Income. expanded ed. Alvin H. Hansen. 1964. 14.95x (ISBN 0-393-09726-9, NortonC). Norton.

Business Cycles & Their Causes. Wesley C. Mitchell. (California Library Reprint Series: No. 29). 1971. 15.00x (ISBN 0-520-02071-5). U of Cal Pr.

Business Cycles, Inflation & Forecasting. Geoffrey Moore. 1980. 40.00 (ISBN 0-88410-685-3). Ballinger Pub.

Business Data Processing. 5th ed. Elias M. Awad. (Illus.). 1980. text ed. 19.95 (ISBN 0-13-093807-6); student wkbk. 7.95 (ISBN 0-13-093757-6). P-H.

Business Data Processing. William S. Davis. LC 77-81199. 1978. text ed. 14.95 (ISBN 0-201-01116-6); instr's man. o.p. 2.95 (ISBN 0-201-01001-1); wkbk. o.p. 5.95 (ISBN 0-686-68524-5). A-W.

Business Data Processing. 3rd ed. Mike Murach. 432p. 1980. 15.95 (ISBN 0-574-21275-2, 13-4275); instr's. guide avail. (ISBN 0-574-21276-0, 13-4276); study guide 4.95 (ISBN 0-574-21277-9, 13-4277); transparency masters 3.95 (ISBN 0-574-21278-7, 13-4278); FORTRAN suppl 5.95 (ISBN 0-574-21285-X, 13-4279); BASIC suppl. 5.95 (ISBN 0-574-21290-6, 13-4280); COBOL suppl. 6.95 (ISBN 0-574-21280-9, 13-4281). SRA.

Business Data Processing & Systems Analysis. Pete Kilgannon. (Illus.). 326p. 1980. pap. 21.00 (ISBN 0-7131-2755-4). Intl Ideas.

Business Data Processing Systems, 2 pts. 2nd ed. Lawrence Orilia et al. 1971. Set. text ed. 24.95 (ISBN 0-471-65700-X); tchrs. manual avail. (ISBN 0-471-02612-3). Wiley.

Business Data Systems. D. Clifton. 1979. pap. 16.95 (ISBN 0-13-093963-3). P-H.

Business Decision Theory. Paul Jedamus & R. Frame. LC 69-13609. (Illus.). 1969. text ed. 19.95 (ISBN 0-07-032307-0, C); instructor's manual 4.95 (ISBN 0-07-032311-9). McGraw.

Business Economic Planning: Theory, Practice & Comparison. Gunnar Eliasson. LC 76-5895. 1977. 25.50 (ISBN 0-471-01813-9, Pub. by Wiley-Interscience). Wiley.

Business Economics: A Comprehensive Course, 2 vols. P. H. Turner. 1974. Set. pap. text ed. 19.95x (ISBN 0-685-83708-4) (ISBN 0-245-52375-8). Vol. 1 (ISBN 0-245-52376-6). Vol. 2. Intl Ideas.

Business Economics: Principles & Cases. 5th ed. Marshall R. Colberg et al. 1975. text ed. 19.50x (ISBN 0-256-01547-3). Irwin.

Business English. Roger W. Dow. LC 78-18253. 1979. 14.95 (ISBN 0-471-36661-7); wkbk. 7.95 (ISBN 0-471-04959-X); tchrs' manual avail. (ISBN 0-471-05251-5). Wiley.

Business English. Ed. by Elaine Kornbluh. 1981. pap. text ed. 2.25 (ISBN 0-8120-0669-0). Barron. Postponed.

Business English: A Communications Approach. Mary J. Burnett & Alta Dollar. (gr. 7-12). 1979. pap. text ed. 14.80 (ISBN 0-205-06414-0, 1764144); tchrs'. ed. 4.80 (ISBN 0-205-06415-9). Allyn.

Business English: A Worktext with Programmed Reinforcement. 2nd ed. Keith Slocum. 1981. 7.95 (ISBN 0-672-97310-3); tchrs. manual 6.67 (ISBN 0-672-97311-1). Bobbs.

Business English Basics. Ruth Moyer. LC 80-64. 1980. text ed. 13.95x (ISBN 0-471-04337-0); tchr's manual avail. (ISBN 0-471-08249-X). Wiley.

Business English for the Eighties. Robert E. Barry. (Illus.). 1980. pap. text ed. 12.95 (ISBN 0-13-095372-5). P-H.

Business English Handbook. Joan Warner. 1981. text ed. 14.95 (ISBN 0-8359-0574-8). Reston.

Business Enterprise. Hodgetts. 1977. 11.95 (ISBN 0-7216-4709-X). Dryden Pr.

Business Ethics. Edward Stevens. LC 79-91409. (Orig.). 1980. pap. 7.95 (ISBN 0-8091-2244-8). Paulist Pr.

Business Failures: Causes Remedies & Cures. Ray E. Harrickman. LC 79-84672. 1979. pap. text ed. 17.00 (ISBN 0-8191-0742-5). U Pr of Amer.

Business Finance: The Management Approach. Richards C. Osborn. LC 65-15300. (Illus.). 1965. text ed. 10.95x (ISBN 0-89197-053-3); instructor's manual free (ISBN 0-89197-054-1). Irvington.

Business Forecasting. Charles W. Gross & Robin T. Peterson. LC 75-31029. (Illus.). 320p. 1976. text ed. 20.95 (ISBN 0-395-19505-5). HM.

Business Forecasting. new ed. John E. Hanke & Arthur Reitsch. 416p. 1981. text ed. 23.95 (ISBN 0-205-07139-2, 107139-4); solution's manual free (ISBN 0-205-07140-6). Allyn.

Business Forms: Design & Control. Joseph L. Kish, Jr. 226p. 1971. 25.95 (ISBN 0-8260-5045-X, 57521). Ronald Pr.

Business FORTRAN: A Structured Approach. Robert J. Lewis & David G. Hart. 480p. 1980. pap. text ed. 14.95x (ISBN 0-534-00778-3). Wadsworth Pub.

Business Games. Martin G. Groder & John Von Hartz. LC 80-19095. 250p. 1980. 50.00 (ISBN 0-932648-14-2). Boardroom.

Business Games Directory. Simtek Inc. (Orig.). 1980. pap. 2.95 (ISBN 0-933836-15-5). Simtek.

Business, Government, & the Public. Murray Weidenbaum. LC 76-23088. (Illus.). 1977. 16.95 (ISBN 0-13-099317-4). P-H.

Business History: Selected Readings. Ed. by Kenneth A. Tucker. 442p. 1977. 32.50x (ISBN 0-7146-3030-6, F Cass Co). Biblio Dist.

Business in a Dynamic Environment. John M. Ivancevich et al. (Illus.). 1979. text ed. 17.50 (ISBN 0-8299-0180-9); pap. study guide b Curtis G. Mason 6.95 (ISBN 0-8299-0257-0); instrs.' manual avail. (ISBN 0-8299-0494-8); transparency masters avail. (ISBN 0-8299-0495-6); study guide avail. (ISBN 0-8299-0257-0). West Pub.

Business in Japan: A Guide to Japanese Business Practice & Procedure. Paul Norbury & G. Bownas. LC 74-18421. 351p. 1974. 19.95 (ISBN 0-470-64225-4). Halsted Pr.

Business in Japan: A Guide to Japanese Business Practice & Procedure. Ed. by Paul Norbury & Geoffrey Bownas. (Illus.). 210p. 1980. lib. bdg. 25.00 (ISBN 0-86531-059-9). Westview.

Business in Literature. Ed. by Charles Burden et al. LC 77-573. (English & Humanities Ser.). 1977. pap. text ed. 9.95x (ISBN 0-582-28160-1, Pub. by MacKay). Longman.

Business in the Humane Society. J. J. Corson. 1971. 24.95 o.p. (ISBN 0-07-013185-6, P&RB). McGraw.

Business Information Processing. Alan Eliason. 496p. 1979. text ed. 16.95 (ISBN 0-574-21235-3, 13-4235); instr's guide avail. (ISBN 0-574-21236-1, 13-4236). SRA.

Business Information Processing System. 4th ed. C. Orville Elliot & Robert S. Wasley. 1975. text ed. 18.95 (ISBN 0-256-01579-1). Irwin.

Business Information Processing with BASIC. George Struble. LC 79-1423. 1980. text ed. 13.95 (ISBN 0-201-07640-3); wkbk. 4.50 (ISBN 0-201-07642-X). A-W.

Business Insurance Handbook. Robert F. Cushman et al. 600p. 1981. 37.50 (ISBN 0-87094-237-9). Dow Jones-Irwin.

Business Interruption Insurance: What Is Covered. Frank S. Glendening. LC 79-92558. 245p. 1980. pap. text ed. 20.00 (ISBN 0-87218-304-1). Natl Underwriter.

Business Law. 3rd ed. Hugh W. Babb & Charles Martin. 400p. (Orig.). 1981. pap. 4.95 (ISBN 0-06-460198-6, COS 198, COS). Har-Row.

Business Law. Thomas Harron. 992p. 1981. text ed. 21.95 (ISBN 0-686-69609-3). Allyn.

Business Law. Howell et al. 1978. 20.95 (ISBN 0-03-016711-6). Dryden Pr.

Business Law. 2nd ed. Michael P. Litka. LC 76-2999. (Law Ser.). 1977. text ed. 20.50 (ISBN 0-88244-108-6). Grid Pub.

Business Law. Neinstein & Kornbluh. (High School Exams & Answer Ser.). 1980. pap. 3.95 (ISBN 0-8120-0192-3). Barron.

Business Law: A Practical Approach. Frances E. Zollers & Gail H. Foreman. LC 76-44036. 1978. pap. text ed. 10.80 (ISBN 0-8273-1431-0); instructor's guide 1.60 (ISBN 0-8273-1432-9). Delmar.

Business Law: Alternate Editions. 1978. 21.95 (ISBN 0-03-045481-6). Dryden Pr.

Business Law: An Introduction. rev. ed. Lowell B. Howard. 608p. 1981. pap. text ed. 6.50 (ISBN 0-8120-2260-2). Barron.

Business Law in India. Surajit Sengupta. 894p. (Orig.). 1979. pap. text ed. 9.95x (ISBN 0-19-560658-2). Oxford U Pr.

Business Law: Key Issues & Concepts. Thomas W. Dunfee & J. David Reitzel. LC 78-17091. (Law Ser.). 1978. pap. text ed. 6.95 o.p. (ISBN 0-88244-177-9). Grid Pub.

Business Law: Part One Syllabus. Singleton et al. 1973. pap. text ed. 7.35 (ISBN 0-89420-042-9, 146755); cassette recordings 470.00 (ISBN 0-89420-128-X, 146700). Natl Book.

Business Law: Part Two Syllabus. Singleton et al. 1973. pap. text ed. 7.35 (ISBN 0-89420-054-2, 146757); cassette recordings 470.00 (ISBN 0-89420-128-X, 146700). Natl Book.

Business Law: Principles & Cases, Fourth Uniform Commercial Code Edition. Harold F. Lusk et al. 1978. text ed. 20.95 (ISBN 0-256-02021-3). Irwin.

Business Law: Principles, Documents & Cases. 3rd ed. John R. Goodwin. 1980. 18.50x (ISBN 0-256-02266-6). Irwin.

Business Law: Text & Cases. 4th ed. Townes L. Dawson & Earl W. Mounce. 1979. text ed. 21.95x (ISBN 0-669-01690-X); instructor's manual free (ISBN 0-669-01691-8). Heath.

Business Law: Text & Cases. Joseph L. Frascona. 900p. 1980. text ed. write for info. (ISBN 0-697-08209-1); instructor's manual avail. (ISBN 0-697-08213-X); student study guide avail. (ISBN 0-697-08214-8); transparencies avail. (ISBN 0-697-08212-1). Wm C Brown.

Business Law: Text & Cases. 2nd ed. Rate A. Howell et al. LC 80-65801. 1104p. 1981. text ed. 21.95 (ISBN 0-03-058111-7). Dryden Pr.

Business Law: U.C.C. & C.C.P.A. Principles, Documents & Cases. rev. ed. John R. Goodwin. 1976. text ed. 15.95x o.p. (ISBN 0-256-01781-6); pap. text ed. 5.50x workbk. o.p. (ISBN 0-256-01782-4). Irwin.

Business Law: Uniform Commercial Code Edition. 2nd ed. Hugh W. Babb & Charles Martin. LC 74-77984. 1969. pap. 3.95 (ISBN 0-06-460040-8, CO 40, COS). Har-Row.

Business Laws of Saudi Arabia. Tr. by N. H. Kanam. 500p. 1980. Set. 198.00x (ISBN 0-686-64698-3, Pub. by Graham & Trotman England); Vol. 1. (ISBN 0-86010-222-X); Vol. 2. (ISBN 0-86010-223-8). State Mutual Bk.

Business Leadership in the Large Corporation. Robert A. Gordon. 1945. pap. 2.25 o.p. (ISBN 0-520-00502-3, CAL43). U of Cal Pr.

Business, Legal & Ethical Phases of Engineering. 2nd ed. D. T. Canfield & Bowman. 1954. text ed. 19.50 o.p. (ISBN 0-07-009729-1, C). McGraw.

Business Letter Writing Made Simple. Rosenthal & Rudman. (Span.). pap. 7.95 o.p. (ISBN 0-88332-136-X). Larousse.

Business Letter Writing Made Simple. rev. ed. Irving Rosenthal & Harry W. Rudman. pap. 3.50 (ISBN 0-385-01206-3, Made). Doubleday.

Business Letters for Publishers: Creative Correspondence Outlines. Dan Poynter. 82p. 1981. 14.95 (ISBN 0-915516-28-4); magnetic recorded disc 29.95 (ISBN 0-915516-29-2). Para Pub.

Business Loans: A Guide to Money Sources & How to Approach Them Successfully. 2nd ed. Rick S. Hayes. LC 80-10941. 1980. 22.50 (ISBN 0-8436-0786-6). CBI Pub.

Business Logistics: Physical Distribution & Materials Management. 2nd ed. J. L. Heskett et al. (Illus.). 789p. 1973. 26.95 (ISBN 0-8260-4071-3); instr's manual avail. (ISBN 0-471-07468-3). Wiley.

Business Machine Calculation: Vol. I, Adding Machines & Printing Calculators. Albert Giordano. (Orig.). 1964. Vol. 1. pap. text ed. 9.95 (ISBN 0-13-104943-7). P-H.

Business Machine Practice Set. Dorothy L. Albertson. (Illus.). 192p. (gr. 10-12). 1974. text ed. 7.36 o.p. (ISBN 0-07-000950-3, G); tchr's manual & key 3.95 o.p. (ISBN 0-07-000951-1). McGraw.

Business Management. rev. ed. John A. Shubin. (Orig.). 1957. pap. 3.95 (ISBN 0-06-460092-0, CO 92, COS). Har-Row.

Business Management for Farmers. J. W. Looney. LC 80-67888. (Illus.). 500p. 1981. 24.95 (ISBN 0-932250-11-4). Doane Agricultural.

Business Management Laboratory: Participants' Manual. rev. ed. Ronald Jensen & David J. Cherrington. 1977. pap. 9.95x (ISBN 0-256-01953-3). Business Pubns.

Business Manager in the Independent School. Paul M. Ritter. 1980. pap. 6.50 (ISBN 0-934338-41-8). NAIS.

Business Math. Paul S. Miller. (Illus.). 1980. pap. text ed. 13.95x (ISBN 0-07-042157-9); instructor's manual 8.50 (ISBN 0-07-042158-7). McGraw.

Business Math Basics. Robert E. Swindle. 1979. pap. text ed. 13.95x (ISBN 0-534-00578-0). Wadsworth Pub.

Business Mathematics. 2nd ed. (Illus.). 400p. 1979. pap. 11.95x (ISBN 0-7121-0282-5, Pub. by Macdonald & Evans England). Intl Ideas.

Business Mathematics. Lawrence M Clar et al. Ed. by Calvin Latham. 1980. text ed. 15.95x (ISBN 0-686-65089-1). Macmillan.

Business Mathematics. Funk. 416p. 1980. pap. text ed. 15.95 (ISBN 0-205-06849-9, 1068490). Allyn.

Business Mathematics. 2nd ed. Esther H. Highland. (Illus.). 512p. 1981. text ed. 15.95 (ISBN 0-8359-0585-3); instr's manual free (ISBN 0-8359-0586-1). Reston.

Business Mathematics. George Kevorkian. (Business and Economics Ser.). 288p. 1976. text ed. 14.95 (ISBN 0-675-08587-X); wkbk. 6.95 (ISBN 0-675-08586-1); instructor's manual 3.95 (ISBN 0-686-67425-1). Merrill.

Business Mathematics. 3rd ed. Richard R. McCready. 1978. pap. text ed. 13.95x (ISBN 0-534-00570-5). Wadsworth Pub.

Business Mathematics. Neinstein & Kornbluh. (High School Exams & Answers Ser.). 1980. pap. 3.95 (ISBN 0-8120-0108-7). Barron.

Business Mathematics. Milton C. Olson & F. Barry Haber. 1981. pap. 12.95 (ISBN 0-672-97327-8); answer key 6.67 (ISBN 0-672-97328-6). Bobbs.

Business Mathematics. Qazi Zameeruddin et al. 600p. 1980. text ed. 18.95x (ISBN 0-7069-0752-3, Pub. by Vikas India). Advent Bk.

Business Mathematics - Electronic Calculation. Al Giordano. (Illus.). 304p. 1981. text ed. 17.95 (ISBN 0-13-105163-6); pap. text ed. 13.95 (ISBN 0-13-105155-5). P-H.

Business Mathematics: A Better Course. James Felton. 640p. 1981. pap. 15.95 (ISBN 0-205-07323-9, 1073230); tchr's ed. free (ISBN 0-205-07324-7, 1073249). Allyn.

Business Mathematics: A Consumer Approach. Charles A. Nickerson & Ingeborg A. Nickerson. (Illus.). 256p. 1981. pap. text ed. 13.95 (ISBN 0-675-08071-1); tchr's. manual avail. Merrill.

Business Mathematics: A Programmed Approach, Book 1. Charles D. Miller & Stanley A. Salzman. 1980. pap. text ed. 9.95x (ISBN 0-673-15347-9). Scott F.

Business Mathematics for Colleges. rev ed. Andrew Vazsonyi & Richard Brunell. 1979. pap. text ed. 12.50 (ISBN 0-256-02116-3). Irwin.

Business Maths & Statistics. M. R. Tilley. (Illus.). 1978. pap. text ed. 11.95x (ISBN 0-7131-0152-0). Intl Ideas.

Business, Media & the Law: The Troubled Confluence. Ed. by Robert Lamb et al. LC 78-55569. 1980. 15.00x (ISBN 0-8147-0565-0). NYU Pr.

Business of Business: Private Enterprise & Public Affairs. Myron A. Wright. 1967. 9.50 o.p. (ISBN 0-07-072057-6, P&RB). McGraw.

Business of Crime: Italians & Syndicate Crime in the United States. Humbert S. Nelli. LC 75-32350. (Illus.). 304p. 1976. 17.95 (ISBN 0-19-502010-3). Oxford U Pr.

Business of Crime: Italians & Syndicate Crime in the United States. Humbert S. Nelli. LC 80-27196. xiv, 314p. 1981. pap. 6.95 (ISBN 0-226-57132-7). U of Chicago Pr.

Business of Organized Crime: A Cosa Nostra Family. Annelise G. Anderson. (Publications 201 Ser.). (Illus.). 200p. 1979. 10.95 (ISBN 0-8179-7011-8). Hoover Inst Pr.

Business of Reason. Ed. by J. J. Macintosh & S. C. Coval. LC 68-27430. (International Library of Philosophy & Scientific Method). 1969. text ed. 15.00x (ISBN 0-7100-6528-0). Humanities.

Business of Science. David Fishlock. LC 74-4882. 1975. text ed. 20.95 (ISBN 0-470-26154-4). Halsted Pr.
Business of Shipping. 3rd ed. Lane C. Kendall. LC 79-52466. (Illus.). 1979. text ed. 12.50x (ISBN 0-87033-253-8). Cornell Maritime.
Business of Sports. Ed. by William P. Lineberry. (Reference Shelf Ser.). 1973. 6.25 (ISBN 0-8242-0506-5). Wilson.
Business of Trading in Stocks. John Durand & A. T. Miller. Repr. of 1967 ed. flexible cover 5.00 (ISBN 0-87034-019-0). Fraser Pub Co.
Business One Twenty One. J. R. McCutcheon. 224p. 1981. pap. 9.95 lab manual (ISBN 0-8403-2368-9). Kendall-Hunt.
Business Opportunity Appraiser. Wilfred F. Tetreault et al. (Illus.). 50p. 1980. text ed. 10.00 (ISBN 0-937152-03-X). Am Busn Consult.
Business Organisation & Management. Geoff Handern. 1978. 22.50x (ISBN 0-86003-023-7, Pub. by Allan Pubs England); pap. 11.25x (ISBN 0-86003-124-1). State Mutual Bk.
Business Organization. J. O'Shaughnessy. (Studies in Management). 1966. pap. text ed. 10.95x (ISBN 0-04-658043-3). Allen Unwin.
Business Organizations & Agencies Directory. Ed. by Anthony T. Kruzas & Robert C. Thomas. LC 80-32. 1980. 85.00 (ISBN 0-8103-1135-6). Gale.
Business Policy. R. E. Thomas. 256p. 1977. 36.00x (ISBN 0-86003-502-6, Pub. by Allan Pubs England); pap. 18.00x (ISBN 0-86003-602-2). State Mutual Bk.
Business Policy: A Framework for Analysis. 3rd ed. Robert G. Murdick et al. LC 79-20129. (Management Ser.). 1980. pap. text ed. 10.50 (ISBN 0-88244-204-X). Grid Pub.
Business Policy & Planning: Text & Cases. David C. Rogers. (Illus.). 1977. 21.95 (ISBN 0-13-107409-1). P-H.
Business Policy & Strategic Action: Text, Cases, Management Game. H. Broom. 1969. text ed. 21.95 (ISBN 0-13-107540-3). P-H.
Business Policy & Strategic Management. 3rd ed. William F. Glueck. (Management Ser.). (Illus.). 1980. text ed. 19.95x (ISBN 0-07-023519-8, C). McGraw.
Business Policy & Strategy: Concepts & Readings. rev ed. Daniel J. McCarthy et al. 1979. pap. text ed. 12.95 (ISBN 0-256-02168-6). Irwin.
Business Policy: Case Problems of the General Manager. 3rd ed. Earl Bennett et al. (Marketing & Management Ser.). 1978. text ed. 19.95x (ISBN 0-675-08401-6); manual 3.95 (ISBN 0-686-67971-7). Merrill.
Business Policy: Strategy, Formation & Executive Action. William F. Glueck. 1976. text ed. 18.95 o.p. (ISBN 0-07-023514-7, C). McGraw.
Business Policy: Text & Cases. 4th ed. C. Roland Christensen et al. 1978. text ed. 19.95x (ISBN 0-256-01989-4). Irwin.
Business Practice Set: SAAL Manufacturing Limited Financial Operating Budget. Robert Gilbert. 64p. 1981. pap. text ed. 6.95 (ISBN 0-8403-2346-8). Kendall-Hunt.
Business Problems & Solutions for Proprietors & Partnerships. Luanna C. Blagrove. 160p. 1981. 24.95; pap. 19.95 (ISBN 0-9604466-9-9). Blagrove Pubns.
Business Problems of the Eighties. Jules Backman. (ITT Key Issues Lecture Ser.). 1980. pap. 6.95 (ISBN 0-672-97499-1). Bobbs.
Business Programming in FORTRAN VI & ANSI FORTRAN: A Structured Approach. A. Khailany. 1981. pap. 12.95 (ISBN 0-13-107607-8). P-H.
Business Programming Logic: A Structured Approach. Jay Singelmann & Jean Longhurst. (Illus.). 1978. pap. 12.95 ref. ed. (ISBN 0-13-107631-0). P-H.
Business Programming with BASIC. George Diehr. LC 76-39639. 366p. 1972. 16.95 (ISBN 0-471-21370-5). Wiley.
Business Recordkeeping Practice Set. 2nd ed. N. Fritz. 1974. text ed. 5.48 o.p. (ISBN 0-07-022482-X, G); tchr's. manual & key 1.50 o.p. (ISBN 0-07-022487-0). McGraw.
Business Report Writing. college ed. Burton L. Fischman. LC 75-20317. 200p. (Orig.). 1975. pap. text ed. 10.15 (ISBN 0-913310-40-9). Par Inc.
Business Report Writing. Phillip V. Lewis & William H. Baker. LC 78-50045. (Business English Ser.). 1978. text ed. 17.95 (ISBN 0-88244-084-5). Grid Pub.
Business Reports: Samples from the "Real World". William E. Rivers. (Illus.). 272p. 1981. pap. 9.95 (ISBN 0-13-107656-6). P-H.
Business Research: Concept & Practice. Robert G. Murdick. 226p. 1969. pap. text ed. 8.50 scp o.p. (ISBN 0-7002-2232-4, HarpC). Har-Row.
Business Research Methods. Vernon T. Clover & Howard L. Balsley. LC 78-50046. (Management Ser.). 1979. text ed. 20.95 (ISBN 0-88244-164-7). Grid Pub.
Business Research Methods. C. William Emory. 1976. text ed. 17.50x o.p. (ISBN 0-256-01851-0). Irwin.
Business Research Methods. rev. ed. C. William Emory. 1980. 18.95x (ISBN 0-256-02260-7). Irwin.
Business Responsibility & Social Issues. new ed. Edward A. Nicholson et al. 416p. 1974. text ed. 15.95 (ISBN 0-675-08826-7). Merrill.
Business-School Partnerships: A Plus for Kids. John Chaffee, Jr. 1980. pap. 11.95 (ISBN 0-87545-018-0). Natl Sch PR.
Business Simulation for Decision Making. Ed. by William C. House. LC 77-24080. (Illus.). 1977. text ed. 22.95 (ISBN 0-89433-005-5); pap. text ed. 17.50 (ISBN 0-89433-017-9). Petrocelli.
Business, Society, & the Individual. rev. ed. George A. Smith, Jr. & John B. Matthews, Jr. 1967. text ed. 19.50 (ISBN 0-256-00487-0). Irwin.
Business Spelling & Word Power. 7th ed. A. H. Lass. 1961. text ed. 8.95 (ISBN 0-672-96012-5); tchr's key (2nd ed.) 6.67 (ISBN 0-672-96014-1); tchr's manual (2nd ed.) 5.00 (ISBN 0-672-96013-3); 3.30 (ISBN 0-672-96015-X). Bobbs.
Business Statistics. Herbert F. Spirer. 1975. 18.95 (ISBN 0-256-01672-0). Irwin.
Business Statistics: A Decision-Making Approach. David Groebner & Patrick Shannon. (Illus.). 800p. 1981. text ed. 20.95 (ISBN 0-675-08083-5); tchr's. manual avail.; lab manual avail. (ISBN 0-675-08084-3); test bank avail. Merrill.
Business Statistics: An Introduction. Brent E. Zepke. Ed. by Nancy Cone. LC 78-21440. (College Outline Ser.). 192p. (Orig.). pap. text ed. 4.95 (ISBN 0-06-460180-3, CO 180, COS). Har-Row.
Business Statistics: Basic Concepts & Methodology. 2nd ed. Wayne W. Daniel & James C. Terrell. LC 78-69607. (Illus.). 1979. text ed. 19.50 (ISBN 0-395-26762-5); inst. manual 1.95 (ISBN 0-395-26763-3); study guide 7.95 (ISBN 0-395-26764-1). HM.
Business Statistics: Why & When. Larry E. Richards et al. (Illus.). 1978. text ed. 17.95 (ISBN 0-07-052273-1, C); wkbk. 6.95 (ISBN 0-07-052275-8); instructor's manual 4.95 (ISBN 0-07-052274-X). McGraw.
Business Strategy. Ed. by H. Igor Ansoff. (Education Ser). (Orig.). 1977. pap. 2.95 o.p. (ISBN 0-14-080072-7). Penguin.
Business Survival & Social Change: A Practical Guide to Responsibility & Partnership. John Hargreaves & Jan Dauman. LC 75-5807. 1975. 24.95 (ISBN 0-470-35155-1). Halsted Pr.
Business System Buyer's Guide. Adam Osborne. 600p. (Orig.). 1981. pap. 7.95 (ISBN 0-931988-47-0). Osborne-McGraw.
Business Systems. R. G. Anderson. (Illus.). 240p. (Orig.). 1977. pap. 9.95x (ISBN 0-7121-0254-X, Pub. by Macdonald & Evans England). Intl Ideas.
Business Systems Analysis & Design. Gary B. Shelly & Thomas J. Cashman. LC 74-77398. 1975. 14.95x (ISBN 0-88236-043-4). Anaheim Pub Co.
Business Systems Handbook: Analysis, Designs & Documentation Standards. R. Gilmour. 1979. 24.95 (ISBN 0-13-107755-4). P-H.
Business Tax Traps & How to Avoid Them. Robert S. Holzman. LC 80-23343. 1980. 50.00 (ISBN 0-686-51196-4). Boardroom.
Business: The Process of Enterprise. Gerald H. Graham. LC 76-45808. 580p. 1977. text ed. 16.95 (ISBN 0-574-19300-6, 13-2300); instr's guide avail. (ISBN 0-574-19301-4, 13-2301); study guide 6.50 (ISBN 0-574-19302-2, 13-2302); lecture resource & trans. masters 7.95 (ISBN 0-685-93533-7, 13-2304); filmstrip-tape 35.00 (ISBN 0-685-93534-5, 13-2306); test bank 5.75 (ISBN 0-574-19311-1, 13-2305). SRA.
Business Today. Michael M. Mescon & David J. Rachman. 1976. text ed. 13.95 o.p. (ISBN 0-394-31948-6). Random.
Business Transcription. Farmer & Anderson. 192p. 1973. text ed. 10.60 (ISBN 0-7715-0740-2). Section A, Units 1-10 (6 Cassettes (ISBN 0-7715-0742-9). Section B, Units 11-20 (6 Cassettes (ISBN 0-7715-0743-7). Section C, Units 21-30 (6 Cassettes (ISBN 0-7715-0744-5). Forkner.
Business Traveler's Survival Guides. Business Traveler's Inc. Incl. Business Traveler's Survival Guide to New York. 9.95 (ISBN 0-531-09940-7); Business Traveler's Survival Guide to Atlanta. 8.95 (ISBN 0-531-09941-5). (Illus.). 1981. Watts.
Business Trends & Forecasting Information Sources. Ed. by James B. Woy. LC 65-28351. (Management Information Guide Ser.: No. 9). 1965. 30.00 (ISBN 0-8103-0809-6). Gale.
Business User's Guide to Minicomputers. Dick H. Brandon & Sidney Siegelstein. 300p. 1980. 50.00 (ISBN 0-932648-18-5). Boardroom.
Business Valuation Handbook. Glenn M. Desmond & Richard E. Kelley. LC 77-365976. 1977. 42.50 o.s.i. (ISBN 0-685-83502-2). Valuation.
Business Valuation Handbook. rev ed. Glenn M. Desmond & Richard E. Kelley. LC 80-51554. 1980. 42.50 (ISBN 0-930458-02-8). Valuation.
Business Who's Who of Australia, 1980. 14th ed. Ed. by L. E. Sumner. LC 64-56752. 805p. 1980. write for info (ISBN 0-8002-2741-7). Intl Pubns Serv.
Business Who's Who, 1974-5. Ed. by H. V. Hodson & M. Engel. LC 73-91903. 30.00x (ISBN 0-900537-21-3, H-316, Dist. by Hippocrene Books Inc.). Leviathan Hse.
Business with China. Editors of the Overseas Assignment Directory. LC 79-11413. 1979. pap. 19.95 (ISBN 0-914236-39-3). Knowledge Indus.
Business-Woman's Guide to Thirty American Cities. Patricia Murphy & Elaine Taylor-Gordon. 400p. 1981. 19.95 (ISBN 0-312-92072-5); pap. 9.95 (ISBN 0-312-92073-3). St Martin.
Business Writing. rev. ed. J. Harold Janis & Howard R. Dressner. (Orig.). 1972. pap. 3.95 (ISBN 0-06-460151-X, CO 151, COS). Har-Row.
Business Writing Handbook. William Paxson. 288p. (Orig.). 1981. pap. 3.95 (ISBN 0-553-14344-1). Bantam.
Business Yearbook of Brazil, Mexico & Venezuela 1980. Date not set. 39.50 (ISBN 0-531-03946-3). Watts.
Businessman Answers Questions Asked by College Students. Ira G. Corn, Jr. 1981. 7.95. Green Hill.
Businessman in Public. Kenneth Hudson. LC 75-40414. 153p. 1976. 24.95 (ISBN 0-470-01377-X). Halsted Pr.
Businessman's Complete Checklist. W. C. Shaw & C. J. Day. 1978. text ed. 24.50x (ISBN 0-220-66359-9, Pub. by Busn Bks England). Renouf.
Businessman's Everyday English to Spanish Dictionary: El Mundo De Negocios. Ivan De Renty. 1978. pap. 9.95 (ISBN 0-88332-100-9, 8138). Larousse.
Businessman's Guide to Europe: Country-by-Country Including Eastern Europe & USSR. LC 74-2825. 740p. 1973. 29.95 (ISBN 0-8436-0731-9). CBI Pub.
Businessman's Guide to Letter-Writing & to the Law on Letters. 2nd ed. Ewan Michell. 222p. 1979. text ed. 23.50x (ISBN 0-220-66326-2, Pub. by Busn Bks England). Renouf.
Businessman's Guide to Washington. William Ruder & Raymond Nathan. 320p. 1975. 8.95 o.s.i. (ISBN 0-02-605910-X). Macmillan.
Businessman's Guide to Washington. William Ruder & Raymond Nathan. 320p. 1975. pap. 4.50 o.s.i. (ISBN 0-02-008660-1, Collier). Macmillan.
Businesswoman's Guide to Thirty American Cities. Patricia Murphy & Elaine Taylor-Gordon. 400p. 1980. 17.95 (ISBN 0-312-92072-5); pap. 9.95 (ISBN 0-312-92073-3). St Martin.
Businesswoman's Guide to Thirty American Cities: Vital Information for Women Who Travel in Their Work. Patricia Murphy & Elaine Taylor-Gordon. 400p. 1981. 19.95 (ISBN 0-312-92072-5); pap. 9.95 (ISBN 0-312-92073-3). Congdon & Lattes.
Busing & Backlash: White Against White in an Urban School District. Lillian Rubin. 1972. 16.95x (ISBN 0-520-02198-3); pap. 3.85 (ISBN 0-520-02257-2, CAL252). U of Cal Pr.
Busing Attendant. Ser-Vol-Tel Institute. (Foodservice Career Education Ser.). 1974. pap. 4.95 (ISBN 0-8436-2018-8). CBI Pub.
Busing Coverup. Edward P. Langerton. LC 75-34839. 182p. 1975. pap. 2.95. Quam Pr.
Busing U.S.A. Ed. by Nicolaus Mills. LC 78-31327. 1979. text ed. 15.95x (ISBN 0-8077-2554-4). Tchrs Coll.
Busman's Honeymoon. Dorothy L. Sayers. LC 60-9116. 1960. 12.95 o.s.i. (ISBN 0-06-013765-7, HarpT). Har-Row.
Busqueda De Dios. A. W. Tozer. Tr. by Dardo Bruchez. 130p. (Orig.). 1979. pap. 2.00 (ISBN 0-87509-162-8); pap. 1.50 mass mkt. (ISBN 0-87509-159-8). Chr Pubns.
Busselton Norms. N. S. Stenhouse. 1980. pap. 8.50x (ISBN 0-85564-164-9, Pub. by U of West Australia Pr Australia). Intl Schol Bk Serv.
Bussy D'ambois. George Chapman. Ed. by Robert J. Lordi. LC 64-11358. (Regents Renaissance Drama Ser). 1964. 8.95x (ISBN 0-8032-0256-3); pap. 1.85x (ISBN 0-8032-5257-9, BB 205, Bison). U of Nebr Pr.
Busted. Glen Chase. (Cherry Delight Ser: No. 16). 1974. pap. 1.25 o.p. (ISBN 0-685-51409-9, LB214ZK, Leisure Bks). Nordon Pubns.
Busted Wheeler. Carter Brown. 1979. pap. 1.50 (ISBN 0-505-51414-1). Tower Bks.
Busy Bear. (Photo Board Bks). (Illus.). 22p. (ps). 3.50 (Golden Pr). Western Pub.
Busy Boats. Peter Lippman. LC 79-29636. (Picturebacks Ser.). (Illus.). 32p. (gr. 2-3). 1980. PLB 3.99 (ISBN 0-394-93731-7); pap. 1.25 (ISBN 0-394-83731-2). Random.
Busy Book. Ali Mitgutsch. (Illus.). 1976. 2.95 o.p. (ISBN 0-307-13768-6, Golden Pr); PLB 7.62 o.p. (ISBN 0-307-63768-9). Western Pub.
Busy Bookworm: Good Conduct Book. Herbert Dupree & Sherry Dupree. (Illus.). 1980. pap. 1.10. Displays Sch.
Busy Mother's Cook Book. Patsy Kumm. 1972. 4.95 o.p. (ISBN 0-571-09899-1, Pub. by Faber & Faber). Merrimack Bk Serv.
Busy Wheels. Peter Lippman. (ps-1). 1973. pap. 1.25 (ISBN 0-394-82706-6, BYR). Random.
Busy Woman's Cookbook: Containing Short-Cut Cooking & Make-Ahead Cooking. Editors Of Farm Journal. LC 71-143616. 1971. 8.95 o.p. (ISBN 0-385-02407-X). Doubleday.
Busybody Nora. Johanna Hurwitz. LC 75-25921. (Illus.). 64p. (gr. 1-5). 1976. PLB 6.00 (ISBN 0-688-32057-0). Morrow.
But God! V. Raymond Edman. 1980. 5.95 (ISBN 0-310-24047-6). Zondervan.
But I Didn't Want a Divorce. Andre Bustanoby. 1978. o. p. 6.95 (ISBN 0-310-22170-6); pap. 3.95 (ISBN 0-310-22171-4). Zondervan.
But I'm So Afraid. Dan Day. (Uplook Ser.). 1975. pap. 0.75 (ISBN 0-8163-0171-9, 02655-9). Pacific Pr Pub Assn.
But This Man. G. W. Lane. 105p. 1960. pap. 1.50 (ISBN 0-87148-107-3). Pathway Pr.
But This Night Is Different. Raymond A. Zwerin. (Illus.). 48p. (ps-1). 1981. text ed. 7.95x (ISBN 0-8074-0032-7, 102561). UAHC.
But We Are Not of Earth. Jean Karl. LC 80-21849. (gr. 4-7). 1981. PLB 9.95 (ISBN 0-525-27342-5). Dutton.
But You Look So Well! John R. Ginther. LC 77-26009. 1978. 11.95 (ISBN 0-88229-399-0). Nelson-Hall.
Butch Elects a Mayor. Helene Hanff. LC 78-77784. (Illus.). (gr. 1-4). 1969. 5.95 o.s.i. (ISBN 0-8193-0277-5, Four Winds); PLB 5.41 o.s.i. (ISBN 0-8193-0278-3). Schol Bk Serv.
Butcher, Baker, Cabinetmaker: Photographs of Women at Work. Wendy Saul. LC 77-27668. (Illus.). (gr. k-2). 1978. 7.95 (ISBN 0-690-03899-2, TYC-J); PLB 8.79 (ISBN 0-690-03900-X). T Y Crowell.
Butcher, Number Thirty: Coffin Corner. Stuart Jason. 192p. (Orig.). 1981. pap. 1.95 (ISBN 0-523-41260-6). Pinnacle Bks.
Butter at the Old Price. Marguerite De Angeli. LC 77-116199. 1971. 9.95 (ISBN 0-385-06813-1). Doubleday.
Butter Molds, Identification & Value Guide. Jim Trice. (Illus.). 1980. pap. 7.95 (ISBN 0-89145-131-5). Collector Bks.
Butter Side up! The Delights of Science. Magnus Pyke. (Illus.). 1977. 8.95 o.p. (ISBN 0-8069-0106-3); lib. bdg. 8.29 o.p. (ISBN 0-8069-0107-1). Sterling.
Buttercups & Daisy. Elizabeth Cragoe. LC 76-62760. 1977. 7.95 o.p. (ISBN 0-312-11007-3). St Martin.
Butterflies. Elementary Science Study. 1970. tchr's. guide 8.28 o.p. (ISBN 0-07-017682-5, W). McGraw.
Butterflies. Ruth Heller. (Creative Coloring Activity Pandabacks). (Illus.). 32p. 1981. pap. 1.25 (ISBN 0-448-49624-0). G&D.
Butterflies. Linda Sonntag. (Leprechaun Library). (Illus.). 64p. 1980. 3.95 (ISBN 0-399-12546-9). Putnam.
Butterflies. Paul Whalley. (Illus.). 128p. 1980. 8.95 (ISBN 0-600-31456-1). Transatlantic.
Butterflies & Moths. Susan DeTreville & Stan DeTreville. (Illus.). 32p. (Orig.). 1981. pap. 3.50 (ISBN 0-89844-026-2). Troubador Pr.
Butterflies & Moths. Dean Morris. LC 77-7912. (Read About Animals Ser.). (Illus.). (gr. k-3). 1977. PLB 9.95 (ISBN 0-8393-0010-7). Raintree Child.
Butterflies & Moths Around the World. Eveline Jourdan. LC 80-20086. (Nature & Man Books). (Illus.). (gr. 5 up). 1981. PLB 7.95g (ISBN 0-686-59986-1). Lerner Pubns.
Butterflies Carried Him Home & Other Indian Tales. Ed. by Colette G. Myles. (Illus.). 65p. 1981. 5.00 (ISBN 0-686-28917-X). Artmans Pr.
Butterflies Carried Him Home: And Other Indian Tales. Ed. by Colette G. Myles. LC 80-70506. (Illus.). 65p. (Orig.). 1981. pap. 4.95 (ISBN 0-9605468-1-2). Artmans Pr.
Butterflies in Color. Leif Lyneborg. (European Ecology Ser.). (Illus.). 1974. 9.95 (ISBN 0-7137-0718-6, Pub by Blandford Pr England). Sterling.
Butterflies of Georgia. Lucien Harris, Jr. (Illus.). 326p. 1975. pap. 5.95 (ISBN 0-8061-1295-6). U of Okla Pr.
Butterflies of Oregon. Ernst Dornfeld. 275p. 1980. pap. 24.95x (ISBN 0-917304-58-6, Pub. by Timber Pr). Intl Schol Bk Serv.
Butterflies of Oregon. Ernst Dornfield. 275p. 1980. 25.00 (ISBN 0-917304-58-6, Pub. by Timber Pr). Intl Schol Bk Serv.

Butterflies of Scotland: A Natural History. George Thomson. (Illus.). 267p. 1980. 50.00x (ISBN 0-7099-0383-9, Pub. by Croom Helm Ltd England). Biblio Dist.
Butterflies of the Rocky Mountain States. Ed. by Clifford D. Ferris & F. Martin Brown. LC 80-22274. (Illus.). 500p. 1981. 35.00 (ISBN 0-8061-1552-1); pap. 15.95 (ISBN 0-8061-1733-8). U of Okla Pr.
Butterfly. A. Delaney. LC 77-72651. 32p. (gr. k-1). 1977. 4.95 o.s.i. (ISBN 0-440-00890-5); PLB 4.58 o.s.i. (ISBN 0-440-00891-3). Delacorte.
Butterfly. Paula Z. Hogan. LC 78-26827. (Life Cycles Ser.). (Illus.). (gr. k-3). 1979. PLB 9.95 (ISBN 0-8172-1252-3). Raintree Pubs.
Butterfly. Angela Sheehan. LC 76-49994. (Illus.). (gr. 2-4). 1977. 2.50 (ISBN 0-531-09081-7); PLB 6.45 (ISBN 0-531-09056-6). Watts.
Butterfly & Angelfishes of the World, Vol. 2. Gerald R. Allen. LC 79-17351. 1980. 30.00 (ISBN 0-471-05618-9, Pub. by Wiley-Interscience). Wiley.
Butterfly & the Stone. Lucretia Fisher. (Illus.). 48p. (Orig.). (ps up). 1981. pap. 2.95 (ISBN 0-916144-69-0). Stemmer Hse.
Butterfly Book of Birds. Tr. by Editions des Belles Images Staff. (Butterfly Bks). (Illus.). 16p. (Orig.). (ps-2). 1976. pap. 1.50 (ISBN 0-8467-0226-6, Pub. by Two Continents). Hippocrene Bks.
Butterfly Book of Mammals. Tr. by Editions les Belles Images Staff. (Butterfly Bks). (Orig.). (ps-2). 1976. pap. 1.50 (ISBN 0-8467-0225-8, Pub. by Two Continents). Hippocrene Bks.
Butterfly Books - Little Red Riding Hood. Tr. by Editions les Belles Images Staff. 16p. (Orig.). (ps-2). 1976. pap. 1.50 (ISBN 0-8467-0222-3, Pub. by Two Continents). Hippocrene Bks.
Butterfly Books: The Catnip Family. Tr. by Editions les Belles Images Staff. (Illus., Orig.). (gr. 1-2). 1977. pap. 1.50 (ISBN 0-8467-0330-0, Pub. by Two Continents). Hippocrene Bks.
Butterfly Collector. Naomi Lewis. (ps-2). 1979. 7.95 (ISBN 0-13-108852-1). P-H.
Butterfly Girl. Blossom Elfman. 160p. 1981. pap. 1.95 (ISBN 0-553-14262-3). Bantam.
Butterfly Lions: The Story of the Pekingese in History, Legend & Art. Rumer Godden. (Illus.). 1978. 13.95 o.p. (ISBN 0-670-19788-2, Studio). Viking Pr.
Butterfly of Dinard. Eugenio Montale. Tr. by G. Singh. LC 78-550605. 1971. 9.00x (ISBN 0-8131-1252-4). U Pr of Ky.
Butterfly on Rock: A Study of Themes & Images in Canadian Literature. D. G. Jones. LC 75-133438. 1970. pap. 5.75 (ISBN 0-8020-6186-9). U of Toronto Pr.
Butterfly Ward. Margaret Gibson. LC 79-67815. 135p. 1980. 8.95 (ISBN 0-8149-0834-9). Vanguard.
Butterflyfishes of the World. Warren E. Burgess. (Illus.). 1979. 20.00 (ISBN 0-87666-470-2, H-988). TFH Pubns.
Butterworths: History of a Publishing House. H. Kay Jones. 296p. 1980. text ed. 27.00 (ISBN 0-406-17606-X). Butterworths.
Butterworths Medical Dictionary. 2nd ed. Ed. by Macdonald Critchley. LC 77-30154. 1978. 159.95 (ISBN 0-407-00061-5). Butterworths.
Button-Box Book. Margaret Hutchings. (Make & Play Ser.). (Illus.). 48p. 1976. pap. 1.50 (ISBN 0-685-69138-1). Transatlantic.
Button Eye's Orange. Jan Wahl. LC 80-14429. (Illus.). 48p. (gr. k-3). 1980. 8.95g (ISBN 0-7232-6188-1). Warne.
Button in Her Ear. Ada B. Litchfield. Ed. by Caroline Rubin. LC 75-28390. (Concept Bks.). (Illus.). 32p. (gr. 2-4). 1976. 6.95g (ISBN 0-8075-0987-6). A Whitman.
Button Parade. rev. ed. Dorothy F. Brown. 1969. 14.95 o.p. (ISBN 0-87069-011-6). Wallace-Homestead.
Buttons: A Collector's Guide. Victor Houart. LC 77-79904. (Encore Edition). (Illus.). 1977. 3.95 o.p. (ISBN 0-684-16196-6, ScribT). Scribner.
Buttons: Art in Miniature. Stefan O. Schiff. (Lancaster-Miller Art Ser.). (Illus.). 1980. 9.95 (ISBN 0-89581-013-1). Lancaster-Miller.
Buttons to Chess Sets. Time-Life Books Editors. LC 78-54098. (Encyclopedia of Collectibles Ser.). (Illus.). 1978. lib. bdg. 10.98 (ISBN 0-686-50974-9). Silver.
Buy & Bust. Moore. LC 73-11665. (Illus.). 1977. 15.95 (ISBN 0-669-88179-1). Lexington Bks.
Buy It for Less (Cincinnati) Lois Rosenthal. 144p. 1980. pap. 3.95 (ISBN 0-89879-033-6). Writers Digest.
Buy It for Less (Detroit) Lois Rosenthal. 144p. 1980. pap. 3.95 (ISBN 0-89879-037-9). Writers Digest.
Buy It for Less (Pittsburgh) Lois Rosenthal. 120p. 1980. pap. 3.95 (ISBN 0-89879-038-7). Writers Digest.
Buy It Right. Jan Brown. 1974. pap. 2.95 o.p. (ISBN 0-531-02753-8). Watts.
Buy Jupiter & Other Stories. Isaac Asimov. 1978. pap. 1.95 (ISBN 0-449-23828-8, Crest). Fawcett.
Buy or Sell Your Own Home, Lot, or Farm. Wayne G. Murrison. Orig. Title: Homeowner Sell Your House Yourself. (Illus.). 92p. 1980. pap. text ed. 20.00. Murrison Co.
Buy This Book. Pete Wagner. LC 80-82890. (Illus.). 216p. (Orig.). 1980. pap. 6.95 (ISBN 0-937706-00-0). ME Pubns.
Buy Wisely, Eat Well. Beryl M. Gould. 1969. 10.95 (ISBN 0-571-10328-6, Pub. by Faber & Faber); pap. 4.95 (ISBN 0-571-10665-X). Merrimack Bk Serv.
Buyer Attitudes and Brand Choice Behavior. G. S. Day. LC 74-81374. 1970. 12.95 (ISBN 0-02-907210-7). Free Pr.
Buyer's Guide to the French Ready-to-Wear Industry (Guide D' Achats Du Pret-a Porter) 1978-79, 2 vols. 1978. Set. 30.00x (ISBN 0-8002-2360-8). Intl Pubns Serv.
Buyers Handbook: A Guide to Defensive Shopping. R. Chambers. 1976. 7.95 o.p. (ISBN 0-13-109579-X, Spec); pap. 2.45 o.p. (ISBN 0-13-109561-7). P-H.
Buyer's Manual. 1979. 21.75 (ISBN 0-686-58637-9, M41079). Natl Ret Merch.
Buying a Boat. Colin Jarman. LC 80-68904. (Illus.). 160p. 1981. 19.95 (ISBN 0-7153-7960-7). David & Charles.
Buying a Condominium. Justin W. Heatter. 1981. 10.95 (ISBN 0-938602-01-2); pap. 6.95 (ISBN 0-938602-00-4). Green Hill.
Buying a Secondhand Boat. Dave Gannaway. 104p. 1980. 15.00x (ISBN 0-245-53446-6, Pub. by Nautical England). State Mutual Bk.
Buying a Swimming Pool - Without Getting Drained. Ed. by Lowell E. Edwards. LC 79-57083. 95p. (Orig.). 1980. pap. 4.95 (ISBN 0-936024-00-3). L E Edwards.
Buying & Running Your Own Business. 2nd ed. Ian Ford. 210p. 1977. text ed. 21.00x (ISBN 0-220-66336-X, Pub. by Busn Bks England). Renouf.
Buying & Selling Business Opportunities: A Sales Transaction Handbook. Wilfred F. Tetreault. LC 80-18771. 208p. 1981. text ed. 19.95 (ISBN 0-201-07711-6). A-W.
Buying & Selling Country Land. Daniel Reisman & Sanford J. Durst. (Illus.). 1980. lib. bdg. 30.00 (ISBN 0-915262-40-1). S J Durst.
Buying & Selling Farmland: A Guide to Profitable Investment. Dwight W. Jundt. LC 80-67887. (Illus.). 309p. 1980. 14.95; pap. text ed. 9.95 (ISBN 0-932250-10-6). Doane Agricultural.
Buying & Selling: You & Your Legal Rights. Ann A. Andres & Ann P. Coil. (Orig.). 1981. pap. 2.95 (ISBN 0-671-42131-X). Monarch Pr.
Buying & Using Convenience Foods. Bruce H. Axler. 1974. pap. 3.55 (ISBN 0-672-96122-9). Bobbs.
Buying Country Land. E. Boudreau. 1973. 4.95 o.s.i. (ISBN 0-02-513930-4). Macmillan.
Buying Food. Elsie Fetterman. (Consumer Casebook Ser.). (Illus.). 80p. (gr. 10-12). 1981. pap. text ed. 5.00 (ISBN 0-87005-268-3). Fairchild.
Buying Game: Fashion Buying & Merchandising. Sidney Packard & Miriam Guerreiro. (Illus.). 1979. pap. text ed. 10.00 (ISBN 0-87005-315-9). Fairchild.
Buying Guide to California Wines. 3rd ed. Ed. by John M. Brennan. (Illus.). 1981. 25.00 (ISBN 0-916040-53-4). Wine Consul Calif.
Buying Options: Wall Street on a Shoestring. A. Rodolakis & N. Tetrick. 1976. 12.95 o.p. (ISBN 0-87909-109-6). Reston.
Buying, Owning & Selling a Home in the Nineteen Eighties. R. Kravitol. 1981. pap. 9.95 (ISBN 0-13-109504-8). P-H.
Buying Quality: A Handbook for the Discriminating Shopper & Those Who Sell Fine Merchandise. new ed. Virginia Vose. LC 80-65319. (Illus.). 175p. Date not set. pap. price not set (ISBN 0-9602050-2-0). Freelance Pubns. Postponed.
Buying, Renting & Borrowing in Texas: The Rules of the Game. H. Clyde Farrell & Paul Kens. LC 80-52895. (Illus.). 278p. 1980. 10.95 (ISBN 0-937606-00-6); pap. 6.95 (ISBN 0-937606-01-4). Tex Consumer.
Buzz, Buzz, Buzz. Byron Barton. LC 73-1965. (Illus.). 32p. (gr. k-2). 1973. 7.95 (ISBN 0-02-708450-7). Macmillan.
Buzz: New York in the Fifties. Sandy Darlington. LC 80-69533. 160p. (Orig.). 1981. pap. 4.00 (ISBN 0-9604152-1-1). Arrowhead Bks.
Buzzard Bait. Jack Kane. 192p. (YA) 1975. 5.95 (ISBN 0-685-54482-6, Avalon). Bouregy.
By Accident, Not Design: The Case for Comprehensive Injury Reparations. Eli P. Bernzweig. 238p. 1980. 23.95 (ISBN 0-03-056961-3). Praeger.
By Any Means Necessary: The Revolutionary Struggle at San Francisco State. Robert Smith et al. LC 75-128701. (Higher Education Ser.). 1970. 15.95x o.p. (ISBN 0-87589-075-X). Jossey-Bass.
By Any Other Name: A Comprehensive Checklist of Science Fiction & Fantasy Pseudonyms. R. Reginald. LC 80-10924. (Borgo Reference Library: Vol. 9). 64p. 1981. lib. bdg. 8.95 (ISBN 0-89370-805-4); pap. 2.95x (ISBN 0-89370-905-0). Borgo Pr.
By Blood Alone. Bernhardt Hurwood. 1979. pap. 1.95 (ISBN 0-441-08990-9). Charter Bks.
By Blood & Fire. Thurston Clarke. 288p. 1981. 13.95 (ISBN 0-399-12605-8). Putnam.
By Bullet, Bomb & Dagger: The Story of Anarchism. Richard Suskind. (Illus.). (gr. 7 up). 1971. 5.50 o.s.i. (ISBN 0-02-788730-8). Macmillan.
By Cheyenne Campfires. George B. Grinnell. LC 79-158083. (Illus.). 1971. pap. 3.95 (ISBN 0-8032-5746-5, BB 541, Bison). U of Nebr Pr.
By Command of the Viceroy. Duncan MacNeil. LC 75-9492. 224p. 1975. 8.95 o.p. (ISBN 0-312-11060-X). St Martin.
By Crumbs, It's Mine. Patricia Beatty. LC 75-31574. 256p. (gr. 5-9). 1976. PLB 7.92 (ISBN 0-688-32062-7). Morrow.
By Death or Divorce...It Hurts to Lose. Amy R. Young. LC 78-51382. 1976. pap. 1.95 (ISBN 0-89636-004-0). Accent Bks.
By Freedom's Holy Light. Gordon Palmer. 1980. 3.75 (ISBN 0-8159-5110-8). Devin.
By Furies Possessed. Ted White. 1980. pap. write for info. (ISBN 0-671-83308-1). PB.
By Gaslight in Winter: A Victorian Family History Through the Magic Lantern. Colin Gordon. (Illus.). 128p. 1981. 30.00 (ISBN 0-241-10474-2, Pub. by Hamish Hamilton England). David & Charles.
By Great Waters: A Newfoundland & Labrador Anthology. Ed. by Peter Neary & Patrick O'Flaherty. LC 73-91561. (Social History of Canada Ser.). 1974. pap. 5.95 (ISBN 0-8020-6233-4). U of Toronto Pr.
By Hook & Ladder. John Loeper. LC 80-36738. (Illus.). 96p. (gr. 4-6). 1981. PLB 7.95 (ISBN 0-689-30816-7). Atheneum.
By-Line: Ernest Hemingway. Ernest Hemingway. Ed. by William White. LC 67-15483. 1967. pap. 6.95 (ISBN 0-684-13685-6, SL501, ScribT). Scribner.
By Love Possessed. James G. Cozzens. 1977. pap. 2.25 o.p. (ISBN 0-449-22954-8, Crest). Fawcett.
By My Spirit. Jonathan Goforth. 1967. pap. 2.95 (ISBN 0-87123-034-8, 210034). Bethany Fell.
By Myself. Compiled By Lee B. Hopkins. LC 79-7830. (Illus.). 40p. (ps-3). 1980. 7.95 (ISBN 0-690-04070-9); lib. bdg. 7.89 (ISBN 0-690-04071-7). T y Crowell.
By Passion Possessed. Ralph Hayes. 1978. pap. 1.95 (ISBN 0-505-51240-8). Tower Bks.
By Persons Unknown. George Jonas & Barbara Amiel. 1978. pap. 2.25 o.p. (ISBN 0-440-00893-X, D0893, Dist. by Dell). Grove.
By-Products from Milk. 2nd ed. Byron H. Webb & Earle O. Whittier. (Illus.). 1971. 32.00 o.p. (ISBN 0-87055-085-3). AVI.
By Reason or Force: Chile & the Balancing of Power in South America, 1830-1905. Robert N. Burr. (California Library Reprint Ser.). 1974. 25.75x (ISBN 0-520-02644-6); pap. 6.95x (ISBN 0-520-02629-2). U of Cal Pr.
By Right of Sword. Arthur W. Marchmont. 1976. lib. bdg. 15.30x (ISBN 0-89968-064-X). Lightyear.
By Rope & Lead. Ernest Haycox. 174p. 1975. Repr. of 1951 ed. lib. bdg. 9.95 o.p. (ISBN 0-89190-972-9). Am Repr-Rivercity Pr.
By Sanction of the Victim. Patte Wheat. LC 78-63000. 1978. pap. 6.50 (ISBN 0-931328-02-0). Timely Bks.
By Strange Paths. Sallie L. Bell. 192p. 1974. pap. 2.25 (ISBN 0-310-20992-7). Zondervan.
By the Candelabra's Glare. Lyman F. Baum. Repr. of 1898 ed. write for info. (ISBN 0-8201-1361-1). Schol Facsimil.
By the Late John Brockman. John Brockman. 1969. 6.95 o.s.i. (ISBN 0-02-516390-6). Macmillan.
By the North Gate. Joyce C. Oates. LC 63-13790. 1963. 10.95 (ISBN 0-8149-0174-3). Vanguard.
By the North Gate. Joyce C. Oates. 1978. pap. 1.50 o.p. (ISBN 0-449-22979-3, P2302, Crest). Fawcett.
By the Seat of Their Pants. Phil Ault. LC 78-7738. (Illus.). (gr. 5 up). 1978. 6.95 (ISBN 0-396-07613-0). Dodd.
By the Sweat of Their Brow: Women Workers at Victorian Coal Mines. Angela John. (Illus.). 245p. 1980. 29.00x (ISBN 0-85664-748-9, Pub. by Croom Helm Ltd England). Biblio Dist.
By the Time You Count to Ten. Florence P. Heide. 1981. pap. 3.50 (ISBN 0-570-07797-4, 56-1335). Concordia.
By the Way of the Silverthorns. Grace L. Hill. 1980. pap. cancelled. Bantam.
By Their Own Design. Ed. by Abby Suckle. (Illus.). 1980. 19.95 (ISBN 0-8230-7097-2, Whitney Lib). Watson-Guptill.
By Way of Response. Martin E. Marty. LC 80-20042. (Journeys in Faith Ser.). 1981. 7.95 (ISBN 0-687-04477-4). Abingdon.
By Women. M. M. Folsom & L. H. Kirschner. 1975. pap. text ed. 11.32 (ISBN 0-395-20500-X); instr's. resource bk. 4.64 (ISBN 0-395-20494-1). HM.
By Word & Prayer. George Kraus. 1981. 8.95 (ISBN 0-570-03045-5, 6-1169). Concordia.
Bye-Bye Blackbird. Anita Desai. 266p. 1971. pap. 3.50 (ISBN 0-88253-033-X). Ind-US Inc.
Bye Cadmos: A Journal of Aesthetic Analogies. Serban Andronescu. 5.00 (ISBN 0-686-65394-7). Am Inst Writing Res.
Bygone England: Social Studies in Its Historic Byways & Highways. William Andrews. LC 67-23910. (Social History Reference Ser). (Illus.). 1968. Repr. of 1892 ed. 15.00 (ISBN 0-8103-3246-9). Gale.
Bygones. Frank Wilkinson. 540p. 1981. 14.95 (ISBN 0-399-12572-8). Putnam.
Bylina & Fairytale: The Origins of Russian Heroic Poetry. Alex E. Alexander. LC 72-94439. (Slavistic Printings & Reprintings: No. 281). 1973. 34.10x (ISBN 90-2792-512-7). Mouton.
Byram Succession. Mira Stables. 1978. pap. 1.50 o.p. (ISBN 0-449-23558-0, Crest). Fawcett.
Byrd. Imogen Holst. (Great Composers Ser.). (Illus.). 1972. 7.95 o.p. (ISBN 0-571-09813-4, Pub. by Faber & Faber). Merrimack Bk Serv.
Byrd Thou Never Wert: The Collected Poems & Post Cards of Emmett Byrd. Michael Himden. LC 80-65365. 1980. pap. 4.95 (ISBN 0-89815-023-X). Ten Speed Pr.
Byrne's Standard Book of Pool & Billiards. Robert Byrne. LC 78-53913. (Illus.). 1978. 17.95 (ISBN 0-15-115223-3). HarBraceJ.
Byron. John D. Jump. (Routledge Author Guides). 1972. 16.50x (ISBN 0-7100-7334-8); pap. 6.95 (ISBN 0-7100-7393-3). Routledge & Kegan.
Byron: A Self-Portrait, 2 Vols. George G. Byron. Ed. by Peter Quennell. 1967. Set. 30.00x (ISBN 0-391-00480-8). Humanities.
Byron: A Survey. Bernard Blackstone. 320p. 1975. text ed. 22.00x (ISBN 0-582-48354-9); pap. text ed. 13.95 (ISBN 0-582-48355-7). Longman.
Byron & Europe: The Interplay of Poetry & Politics. Paul G. Trueblood. 1980. write for info. (ISBN 0-391-02164-8). Humanities.
Byron & Joyce Through Homer: Don Juan & Ulysses. Hermione De Almeida. 256p. 1981. 20.00x (ISBN 0-231-05092-5). Columbia U Pr.
Byron & the Bible: A Compendium of Biblical Usage in the Poetry of Lord Byron. Travis Looper. LC 78-1518. 1978. 15.50 (ISBN 0-8108-1123-5). Scarecrow.
Byron & the Theatre. Boleslaw Taborski. (Salzburg Studies in English Literature, Poetic Drama & Poetic Theory: No. 1). (Illus.). 395p. 1972. pap. text ed. 25.00x (ISBN 0-391-01543-5). Humanities.
Byron Criticism Since Nineteen Fifty-Two. R. B. Hearn. (Romantic Reassessment: No. 83: 2). 1980. pap. text ed. 25.00x (ISBN 0-391-02188-5). Humanities.
Byron's Don Juan: A Critical Study. Elizabeth F. Boyd. 1975. Repr. of 1945 ed. 12.50x (ISBN 0-391-00439-5). Humanities.
Byron's Narratice Poems of Eighteen Thirteen. Daniel P. Deneau. (Salzburgstudies in English Literature, Romantic Reassessment Ser.: No. 55). 106p. 1975. pap. text ed. 25.00x (ISBN 0-391-01360-2). Humanities.
Bystander: Behavior, Law & Ethics. Leon S. Sheleff. LC 77-18577. 1978. 18.95 (ISBN 0-669-02110-5). Lexington Bks.
Byte Book of Pascal. Ed. by Blaise W. Liffick. 1980. 25.00 (ISBN 0-07-037823-1, BYTE Bks). McGraw.
Byways in Handweaving. Mary M. Atwater. 1968. 12.95 (ISBN 0-02-504320-X). Macmillan.
Byzantine Altar Epistles. 1980. 77.50 (ISBN 0-911726-37-3); unbound in folded sheets 57.50 (ISBN 0-911726-38-1). Alleluia Pr.
Byzantine Architecture. Cyril Mango. LC 75-4805. (History of World Architecture). (Illus.). 1976. 45.00 (ISBN 0-8109-1004-7). Abrams.
Byzantine Art & the West. Otto Demus. LC 78-88132. (Wrightsman Lectures Ser.: Vol. 3). (Illus.). 1970. 22.50, (ISBN 0-8147-0116-7). NYU Pr.
Byzantine Civilization. Steven Runciman. 1933. 18.75 (ISBN 0-312-11165-7). St Martin.
Byzantine Daily Worship. Joseph Raya & Jose De Vinck. (Illus.). 1969. plastic bdg. 15.75x o.p. (ISBN 0-911726-07-1); deluxe ed. morocco 35.00x o.p. (ISBN 0-911726-09-8); pap. 15.75x o.p. (ISBN 0-911726-00-4). Alleluia Pr.
Byzantine Empire. Robert Browning. 224p. 1980. 25.00 o.p. (ISBN 0-684-16652-6, ScribT). Scribner.
Byzantine Encounter. Andrea Harris. LC 78-71422. 1979. pap. 1.50 o.p. (ISBN 0-87216-504-3). Playboy Pbks.

Byzantine Government in Exile: Government & Society Under the Laskairds of Nicaea 1204-1261. M. J. Angold. 260p. 1975. 29.50x (ISBN 0-19-821854-0). Oxford U Pr.

Byzantine Liturgical Psalters & Gospels. Kurt Weitzmann. 322p. 1980. 200.00x (ISBN 0-86078-064-3, Pub. by Variorum England). State Mutual Bk.

Byzantine Missions Among the Slavs. Francis Dvornik. (Byzantine Ser). (Illus.). 1970. 32.50 (ISBN 0-8135-0613-1). Rutgers U Pr.

Byzantine Silver Stamps. Erica Cruikshank Dodd. LC 61-16953. (Dumbarton Oaks Studies: Vol. 7). (Illus.). 238p. 1961. 15.00 o.p. (ISBN 0-88402-007-X, Ctr Byzantine). Dumbarton Oaks.

Byzantine Studies & Other Essays. Norman H. Baynes. LC 74-11586. (Illus.). 392p. 1974. Repr. of 1955 ed. lib. bdg. 29.75x (ISBN 0-8371-7673-5, BABYS). Greenwood.

Byzantine Theocracy. S. Runciman. LC 76-47405. (Weil Lectures Ser.). 1977. 23.95 (ISBN 0-521-21401-7). Cambridge U Pr.

Byzantium. Philip Sherrard. LC 66-28334. (Great Ages of Man Ser). (Illus.). (gr. 6 up). 1966. PLB 11.97 (ISBN 0-8094-0372-2, Pub. by Time-Life). Silver.

Byzantium & Bulgaria: A Comparative Study Across the Early Medieval Frontier. Robert Browning. LC 73-91665. (Illus.). 1975. 20.00x (ISBN 0-520-02670-5). U of Cal Pr.

Byzantium & the Papacy, Eleven Ninety Eight - Fourteen Hundred. Joseph Gill. 1979. 25.00 (ISBN 0-8135-0864-9). Rutgers U Pr.

Byzantium & the Rise of Russia. John Meyendorff. LC 80-40110. 340p. Date not set. 69.50 (ISBN 0-521-23183-3). Cambridge U Pr.

Byzantium & the World Around It: Economic & Institutional Relations. Robert S. Lopez. 318p. 1980. 50.00x (ISBN 0-86078-030-9, Pub. by Variorum England). State Mutual Bk.

Byzantium for Rome: The Politics of Nostalgia in Umbertian Italy, 1878-1900. Richard Drake. LC 79-16578. 335p. 1980. 20.00x (ISBN 0-8078-1405-9). U of NC Pr.

Byzantium: Its Ecclesiastical History & Relations with the Western World. Donald M. Nicol. 336p. 1980. 60.00x (ISBN 0-902089-35-8, Pub. by Variorum England). State Mutual Bk.

C

C. A. T. Tells Tales. Clarence A. Tryon. 1979. pap. 4.95 (ISBN 0-910286-54-X). Boxwood.

C-Algebra Extensions & K-Homology. R. G. Douglas. 1980. 12.50 (ISBN 0-691-08265-0); pap. 4.50 (ISBN 0-691-08266-9). Princeton U Pr.

C-Algebra Extensions & K-Homology. Ronald G. Douglas. LC 80-424. (Annals of Mathematics Studies: No. 95). (Illus.). 87p. 1980. 12.50x (ISBN 0-691-08265-0); pap. 4.50x (ISBN 0-691-08266-9). Princeton U Pr.

C-Algebras & Applications to Physics: Proceedings Second Japan-USA Seminar, Los Angeles, April 18 - 22, 1977. Ed. by R. V. Kadison. (Lecture Notes in Mathematics: Vol. 650). 1978. pap. 9.40 (ISBN 0-387-08762-1). Springer-Verlag.

C & O Canal Boatmen 1892 to 1929. T. F. Hahn. 1980. 4.75 (ISBN 0-933788-58-4). Am Canal & Transport.

C. C. Slaughter: Rancher, Banker, Baptist. David J. Murrah. (Illus.). 184p. 1981. 14.95 (ISBN 0-292-71067-4). U of Tex Pr.

C. Day Lewis. Joseph N. Riddel. (English Authors Ser.: No. 124). 1971. lib. bdg. 10.95 (ISBN 0-8057-1336-0). Twayne.

C. E. L. Green, Shore & Landscape Painter of Lynn & Newlyn. Frederic A. Sharf & John H. Wright. (Illus.). 49p. 1980. pap. 3.50 (ISBN 0-88389-103-4). Essex Inst.

C. F. A. Voysey: An Architect of Individuality. Duncan Simpson. 160p. 1981. 19.95 (ISBN 0-8230-7483-8, Whitney Lib). Watson-Guptill.

C. G. Montefiore on the Ancient Rabbis: The Second Generation on Reform Judaism in Britain. Joshua B. Stein. LC 77-13194. (Brown University. Brown Judaic Studies: No. 4). 1977. pap. 6.00 (ISBN 0-89130-190-9, 140004). Scholars Pr Ca.

C. I. A. & the American Ethic: An Unfininished Debate. Ernest W. Lefever & Roy Godson. 176p. 1980. 9.50 (ISBN 0-89633-032-X); pap. 5.00 (ISBN 0-89633-031-1). Ethics & Public Policy.

C I B A Collection of Medical Illustrations, 7 vols. Illus. by Frank H. Netter. Incl. Vol. 1. Nervous System. 24.50x (ISBN 0-914168-01-0); Vol. 2. Reproductive System. 34.00x (ISBN 0-914168-02-9); Vol. 3, Pt. 1. Digestive System: Upper Digestive Tract. 27.00x (ISBN 0-914168-03-7); Vol. 3, Pt. 2. Digestive System: Lower Digestive Tract. 29.50x (ISBN 0-914168-04-5); Vol. 3, Pt. 3. Digestive System: Liver, Biliary Tract & Pancreas. 25.00x (ISBN 0-914168-05-3); Vol. 4. Endocrine System & Selected Metabolic Diseases. 34.00x (ISBN 0-914168-06-1); Vol. 5. Heart. 42.00x (ISBN 0-914168-07-X); Vol. 6. Kidneys, Ureters & Urinary Bladder. 44.00x (ISBN 0-914168-08-8). LC 53-2151. (Illus.). 1974. Set. 288.00x (ISBN 0-914168-00-2). C I B A Pharm.

C Is for Cupcake. Carolyn Haywood. LC 73-9282. (Illus.). 192p. (gr. 1-5). 1974. PLB 7.44 (ISBN 0-688-30098-7). Morrow.

C. Jane. Susan Knorr. Ed. by Joseph Lawrence. (Orig.). 1979. pap. 3.25 (ISBN 0-89144-103-4). Crescent Pubns.

C. K. Ogden: A Collective Memoir. Ed. by P. Sargant Florence. 1978. 12.95 o.p. (ISBN 0-301-76061-6, Pub. by Paul Elek); pap. 5.95 o.p. (ISBN 0-301-76062-4). Merrimack Bk Serv.

C. M. B. Questions & How to Answer Them. 5th ed. Vera Da Cruz. (Illus.). 1977. pap. 3.95 (ISBN 0-571-04919-2, Pub. by Faber & Faber). Merrimack Bk Serv.

C M L, Nineteen Eighty. 1980. cancelled (ISBN 0-8218-0071-X). Am Math.

C Notes: A Guide to the C Programming Language. C. T. Zahn. LC 78-63290. (Orig.). 1979. pap. 16.50 (ISBN 0-917072-13-8). Yourdon.

C. P. S. for Kids: A Resource Book for Teaching Creative Problem-Solving to Children. Bob Eberle & Bob Standish. (Illus.). 128p. (Orig.). 1980. tchr's ed 7.95 (ISBN 0-914634-79-8, 8005). DOK Pubs.

C. P. Snow. David Shusterman. LC 74-23949. (World Authors Ser.: No. 179). 1975. lib. bdg. 12.50 (ISBN 0-8057-1510-X). Twayne.

C. P. Snow: The Politics of Conscience. Frederick Karl. LC 63-8905. (Arcturus Books Paperbacks). 175p. 1965. pap. 1.65 (ISBN 0-8093-0161-X). S Ill U Pr.

C. P. Trevelyan, Eighteen Seventy - Nineteen Fifty Eight: Portrait of a Radical. A. J. Morris. 1979. 19.95 (ISBN 0-312-11242-4). St Martin.

C. S. Lewis. Margaret P. Hannay. LC 80-53700. (Modern Literature Ser.). 350p. 1981. 13.50 (ISBN 0-8044-2341-5). Ungar.

C. S. Lewis: A Biography. Roger L. Green & Walter Hooper. 320p. 1974. 6.95 o.p. (ISBN 0-15-123190-7). HarBraceJ.

C. S. Lewis: Mere Christian. rev. ed. Kay Lindskoog. 192p. 1981. pap. 5.95 (ISBN 0-87784-466-6). Inter-Varsity.

C. S. Lewis: Spinner of Tales. Evan K. Gibson. (Orig.). 1980. pap. 8.95 (ISBN 0-8028-1826-9). Eerdmans.

C. S. Lewis: The Art of Enchantment. Donald E. Glover. LC 80-21421. xii, 235p. 1981. 15.00x (ISBN 0-8214-0566-7); pap. 6.95 (ISBN 0-8214-0609-4). Ohio U Pr.

C. S. Lovett: Maranatha Man. C. S. Lovett. (Illus.). 1978. pap. 4.95 (ISBN 0-938148-02-8). Personal Christianity.

C. S. Parnell. Paul Bew. (Gill's Irish Lives Ser.). 152p. 1980. 20.00 (ISBN 0-7171-1079-6, Pub. by Gill & Macmillan); pap. 6.50 (ISBN 0-7171-0963-1). Irish Bk Ctr.

C. W. von Gluck: Orfeo. Patricia Howard. (Cambridge Opera Handbooks Ser.). (Illus.). 200p. Date not set. price not set (ISBN 0-521-22827-1); pap. price not set (ISBN 0-521-29664-1). Cambridge U Pr.

C. Wright Mills. Howard Press. (World Leaders Ser.). 1978. lib. bdg. 12.50 (ISBN 0-8057-7708-3). Twayne.

C-13 NMR Spectroscopy: A Working Manual with Exercises. E. Breitmaier & G. Bauer. Tr. by B. K. Cassels from Ger. (Mmi Press Polymer Monographs). 400p. 1981. 80.00 (ISBN 3-7186-0022-6). Harwood Academic.

Cabal. Philip Dun. (Orig.). 1981. pap. 2.25 (ISBN 0-425-04845-4). Berkley Pub.

Cabal. Norman Garbo. 1980. pap. 2.95 (ISBN 0-440-10883-7). Dell.

Cabala. Bernard Pick. LC 13-26188. 160p. 1974. pap. 2.95 o.p. (ISBN 0-87548-199-X). Open Court.

Caballero de Olmedo. Carpio Lope De Vega. Ed. by I. T. Macdonald. text ed. 6.50x (ISBN 0-521-06676-X). Cambridge U Pr.

Caballos. Virginia Parsons. Tr. by Rene Sanchez from Eng. Orig. Title: Horse Book. (Illus.). 24p. (Span.). (ps-3). 1977. PLB 5.92 o.p. (ISBN 0-307-68837-2, Golden Pr). Western Pub.

Cabanis: Enlightenment & Medical Philosophy in the French Revolution. Martin S. Staum. LC 79-3231. 1980. 27.50x (ISBN 0-691-05301-4). Princeton U Pr.

Cabbage Princess. Errol LeCain. (Illus.). (ps-5). 1969. 6.95 (ISBN 0-571-09155-5, Pub. by Faber & Faber). Merrimack Bk Serv.

Cabby. Leonard Jordan. 1980. pap. 1.95 (ISBN 0-505-51466-4). Tower Bks.

Cabin Comments: A Journal of Life in Jackson Hole. Elisabeth Anderson et al. LC 80-53090. (Illus.). 286p. (gr. 7-12). 1980. 14.95 (ISBN 0-933160-08-9); pap. 7.75 (ISBN 0-933160-07-0). Teton Bkshop.

Cabinda Affair. Matthew Head. LC 80-8715. 256p. 1981. pap. 2.25 (ISBN 0-06-080541-2, P541, PL). Har-Row.

Cabinet. Gerald W. Johnson. (Illus.). (gr. 7 up). 1966. PLB 7.44 (ISBN 0-688-31136-9). Morrow.

Cabinet. Patrick G. Walker. 1972. text ed. 4.95 o.p. (ISBN 0-435-83915-2). Heinemann Ed.

Cabinet-Maker & Upholsterer's Drawing Book. Thomas Sheraton. (Illus.). 13.50 (ISBN 0-8446-4637-7). Peter Smith.

Cabinet Making for Beginners. rev. ed. Charles H. Hayward. LC 78-24432. (Illus.). 1980. pap. 5.95 (ISBN 0-8069-8186-5); lib. bdg. 6.39 o.p. (ISBN 0-8069-8187-3). Sterling.

Cabinet Reform in Britain, 1914-1963. Hans Daalder. 1963. 17.50x (ISBN 0-8047-0139-3). Stanford U Pr.

Cabinetmakers. Leonard E. Fisher. LC 66-10580. (Colonial Americans Ser.). (Illus.). (gr. 4-6). 1966. PLB 4.90 o.p. (ISBN 0-531-01026-0). Watts.

Cabinetmaking. Paul J. Haynie. (Illus.). 272p. 1976. 15.95 (ISBN 0-13-110239-7). P-H.

Cabinetmaking & Millwork. John Feirer. 1977. text ed. 21.28 (ISBN 0-87002-238-5); student guide 4.20 (ISBN 0-87002-176-1). Bennett IL.

Cabinetmaking & Millwork. rev ed. John Feirer. (Illus.). 1977. 37.50 (ISBN 0-684-14914-1, ScribT). Scribner.

Cabinetmaking, Pattermaking, & Millwork. Gaspar J. Lewis. 448p. 1981. 18.95 (ISBN 0-442-24785-0). Van Nos Reinhold.

Cabinetmaking, Patternmaking & Millwork. Gaspar Lewis. LC 79-50917. (Carpentry-Cabinetmaking Ser.). 448p. 1981. text ed. 14.60 (ISBN 0-8273-1814-6); instructor's guide 2.55 (ISBN 0-8273-1815-4). Delmar.

Cabinets & Bookcases. Tom Philbin. Ed. by Shirley M. Horowitz. LC 80-67152. (Illus.). 144p. (Orig.). 1980. 12.95 (ISBN 0-932944-21-3); pap. 5.95 (ISBN 0-932944-22-1). Creative Homeowner.

Cabinets & Built-Ins. H. H. Siegele. LC 80-52589. (Illus.). 104p. 1980. pap. 5.95 o.p. (ISBN 0-8069-8188-1). Sterling.

Cabins & Cottages. (Home Repair & Improvement Ser.). (Illus.). 1978. lib. bdg. 11.97 (ISBN 0-686-51035-6). Silver.

Cabins & Cottages. Time-Life Books Editors. (Home Repair & Improvement). (Illus.). 1979. 12.95 (ISBN 0-8094-2410-X). Time-Life.

Cabins & Vacation Houses. 3rd ed. Sunset Editors. LC 74-20017. (Illus.). 96p. 1975. pap. 2.95 (ISBN 0-376-01064-9, Sunset Bks). Sunset-Lane.

Cable Broadband Communications Book, 1977-1978, Vol. 1. Ed. by Mary L. Hollowell. LC 77-81692. 1977. pap. 15.50x (ISBN 0-89461-027-9). Comm Pr Inc.

Cable-Broadband Communications Book, 1980-1981, Vol. 2. Mary L. Hollowell. (Video Bookshelf Ser.). 300p. 1980. text ed. 29.95x (ISBN 0-914236-79-2). Knowledge Indus.

Cable Broadband Communications Book, 1980-1981, Vol. 2. Ed. by Mary L. Hollowell. LC 77-81692. 1980. 19.50x (ISBN 0-89461-031-7). Comm Pr Inc.

Cable Car Book. Charles Smallwood et al. LC 80-65238. (Illus.). 160p. 1980. 25.00 (ISBN 0-89087-280-5). Celestial Arts.

Cable Harbor. Donald Bowie. 300p. 1981. 11.95 (ISBN 0-87131-347-2). M Evans.

Cable Harbor: A Novel. Donald Bowie. Ed. by Fred Graver. 300p. 1981. 10.95 (ISBN 0-87131-347-2). M Evans.

Cable Structures. H. M. Irvine. (Illus.). 304p. 1981. text ed. 50.00x (ISBN 0-686-69224-1). MIT Pr.

Cable Television: A Comprehensive Bibliography. Felix Chin. 279p. 1978. 45.00 (ISBN 0-306-65172-6). IFI Plenum.

Cable Television: A Guide to Federal Regulations. Steven R. Rivkin. LC 73-90819. (Rand Cable Television Ser.). 1974. 19.50x (ISBN 0-8448-0259-X). Crane-Russak Co.

Cable Television in the Cities: Community Control, Public Access & Minority Ownership. 3rd ed. Ed. by Charles Tate. 192p. 1971. pap. 3.95 o.p. (ISBN 0-87766-020-4). Urban Inst.

Cable Television: Strategy for Penetrating Key Urban Markets. James D. Scott. (Michigan Business Reports: No. 58). 1976. pap. 5.50 o.p. (ISBN 0-87712-172-9). U Mich Busn Div Res.

Cable Television U. S. A. An Analysis of Government Policy: An Analysis of Government Policy. Martin H. Seiden. LC 72-76453. (Special Studies in U. S. Economic, Social, & Political Issues). 1972. 28.00x (ISBN 0-275-28634-7). Irvington.

Cablecasting Production Handbook. Joel Efrein. LC 74-33617. (Illus.). 210p. 1975. 12.95 o.p. (ISBN 0-8306-5768-1, 768). TAB Bks.

Caboose Mystery. Gertrude C. Warner. LC 66-10791. (Boxcar Children Mysteries-Pilot Bk.). (Illus.). 128p. (gr. 3-7). 1966. 6.95g (ISBN 0-8075-1008-4). A Whitman.

Cacti & Succulents. James U. Crockett & Philip Perl. (Time-Life Encyclopedia of Gardening Ser.). (Illus.). 1978. lib. bdg. 11.97 (ISBN 0-686-51057-7). Silver.

Cacti & Succulents. Philip Perl. Ed. by Time-Life Books. (Time-Life Encyclopedia of Gardening Ser.). 1978. 11.95 (ISBN 0-8094-2587-4). Time-Life.

Cacti & Succulents for Modern Living. Laura W. Rice. (Modern Living Ser.). (Illus.). 80p. (Orig.). 1976. pap. 2.95 (ISBN 0-89484-003-7, 10104). Merchants Pub Co.

Cacti & Their Cultivation. Margaret J. Martin et al. 1975. pap. 5.95 o.p. (ISBN 0-684-14365-8, SL601, ScribT). Scribner.

Cacti As Decorative Plants. Jack Kramer. LC 73-172694. (Illus.). 128p. 1974. encore ed. 2.95 o.p. (ISBN 0-684-15711-X, ScribT); pap. 3.95 o.p. (ISBN 0-684-13718-6, SL510, ScribT). Scribner.

Cacti of the Southwest: Texas, New Mexico, Oklahoma, Arkansas, & Louisiana. Del Weniger. (Spencer Foundation Ser.: No. 4). (Illus.). 1970. 29.50 o.p. (ISBN 0-292-70000-8). U of Tex Pr.

Cactus Air Force. Thomas G. Miller, Jr. 256p. 1981. pap. 2.50 (ISBN 0-553-14766-8). Bantam.

Cactus & Succulents. Sunset Editors. LC 77-82873. (Illus.). 80p. 1978. pap. 3.95 (ISBN 0-376-03753-9, Sunset Bks.). Sunset-Lane.

Cactus Country. Edward Abbey. (American Wilderness Ser.). (Illus.). 1973. 12.95 (ISBN 0-8094-1168-7). Time-Life.

Cactus Country. Edward Abbey. LC 72-91599. (American Wilderness Ser). (Illus.). (gr. 6 up). 1973. PLB 11.97 (ISBN 0-8094-1169-5, Pub. by Time-Life). Silver.

Cactus Growing for Beginners. Vera Higgins. (Illus.). 1964. 4.95 (ISBN 0-7137-0128-5, Pub by Blandford Pr England). Sterling.

Cactus Identifier. Helmut Bechtel. (Identifier Ser.). (Illus.). (gr. 6 up). 1977. 6.95 o.p. (ISBN 0-8069-3080-2); PLB 6.69 o.p. (ISBN 0-8069-3081-0). Sterling.

Cactus Identifier. Helmut Bechtel. LC 76-51168. (Illus.). 256p. 1981. pap. 6.95 (ISBN 0-8069-8960-2). Sterling.

Cactus in the Desert. Phyllis Busch. LC 78-4771. (Let's-Read-&-Find-Out Science Bk.). (Illus.). (gr. k-3). 1979. 7.95 (ISBN 0-690-00292-0, TYC-J); PLB 7.89 (ISBN 0-690-01336-1). T Y Crowell.

Cactus Love. Samuel B. Lall. flexible cloth 4.80 (ISBN 0-89253-578-4). Ind-US Inc.

CAD-CAM International Delphi Forecast. Donald Smith et al. LC 80-53001. (Illus.). 181p. 1980. pap. 24.00 (ISBN 0-87263-062-5). SME.

CAD-CAM, Meeting Today's Productivity Challenge. Ed. by Khalil S. Taraman. LC 80-69006. (Manufacturing Update Ser.). (Illus.). 281p. 1980. 29.00 (ISBN 0-87263-063-3). SME.

Cada Muchacho Necesita un Modelo Vivo. Jorge A. Leon. 96p. (Span.). 1981. pap. write for info. (ISBN 0-311-46087-9). Casa Bautista.

Cada Nuevo Dia. Corrie Ten Boom. Tr. by Alejandro Clifford from Eng. 1980. pap. 3.60 (ISBN 0-311-40043-4, Edit Mundo). Casa Bautista.

Cadaveric Renal Transplantation. Ed. by Yoji Iwasaki. (Illus.). 1974. 40.00 (ISBN 0-89640-019-0). Igaku-Shoin.

Caddie Woodlawn. rev. ed. Carol R. Brink. (gr. 4-6). 1970. pap. 2.25 (ISBN 0-02-041880-9). Macmillan.

Caddie Woodlawn. new ed. Carol R. Brink. LC 73-588. (Illus.). 240p. (gr. 4-7). 1973. 8.95 (ISBN 0-02-713670-1). Macmillan.

Caddoan Indians Four. Helen H. Tanner. Ed. by David A. Horr. (American Indian Ethnohistory Ser.). 1978. lib. bdg. 42.00 (ISBN 0-8240-0765-4). Garland Pub.

Caddoan Indians One. Stephen Williams. Ed. by David A. Horr. (American Indian Ethnohistory Ser.). 1978. lib. bdg. 42.00 (ISBN 0-8240-0763-8). Garland Pub.

Caddoan Indians Three: Prehistory of the Caddoan - Speaking Tribes. Jack T. Hughes. (American Indian Ethnohistory Ser.: Plains Indians). (Illus.). lib. bdg. 42.00 (ISBN 0-8240-0815-4). Garland Pub.

Caddoan Indians Two. Robert W. Neuman. Ed. by David A. Horr. (American Indian Ethnohistory Ser.). 1978. lib. bdg. 42.00 (ISBN 0-8240-0764-6). Garland Pub.

Cadillac Modern Encyclopedia. new ed. Ed. by Max S. Shapiro & William Jaber. LC 73-81377. (Illus.). xiv, 1954p. 1973. 39.95 (ISBN 0-87445-000-4). Cadillac.

Cadillac, Standard of the World: The Complete History. 3rd ed. Maurice D. Hendry. LC 72-85846. 1979. 29.95 (ISBN 0-915038-10-2). Princeton Pub.

Cadiz Experiment in Central America, 1808-1826. Mario Rodriguez. 1978. 23.75x (ISBN 0-520-03394-9). U of Cal Pr.

Cadmium in the Environment: Ecological Cycling, Pt. I. Jerome O. Nriagu. LC 79-25087. (Environmental Science & Technology: a Wiley-Interscience Series of Texts & Monographs). 1980. 70.00 (ISBN 0-471-06455-6, Pub. by Wiley-Interscience). Wiley.

Cadres, Bureaucracy, & Political Power in Communist China. Doak A. Barnett. LC 67-15895. 1967. 22.50x (ISBN 0-231-03035-5). Columbia U Pr.

Caduceus Wild. Ward Moore. (Futorian Science Fiction Ser.). 1978. pap. 1.75 o.p. (ISBN 0-523-40246-5). Pinnacle Bks.

Caelius Aurelianus, Gynaecia: Fragments of a Latin version of Soranus' Gynaecia from a thirteenth century manuscript. Ed. by Miriam F. Drabkin & Israel E. Drabkin. (Supplements Bulletin of the History of Medicine Ser: No.13). 136p. 1951. pap. 6.00x o.p. (ISBN 0-8018-0175-3). Johns Hopkins.

Caesar & Cleopatra: A History. George B. Shaw. Ed. by Elizabeth T. Forter. LC 65-14791. (Crofts Classics Ser.). 1965. pap. text ed. 2.95x (ISBN 0-88295-086-X). AHM Pub.

Caesar at the Rubicon: A Play About Politics. Theodore H. White. LC 77-11796. 1978. 8.95 o.s.i. (ISBN 0-06-014602-8, HarpT). Har-Row.

Caesar or Nothing. Pio Baroja. Tr. by Louis How from Span. 337p. 1976. Repr. of 1919 ed. 17.50 (ISBN 0-86527-224-7). Fertig.

Caesars. Thomas DeQuincey. (Illus.). 300p. 1981. 12.95 (ISBN 0-8180-0824-5). Horizon.

Caesar's Army: A Study of the Military Art of the Romans in the Last Days of the Republic. Harry P. Judson. LC 61-12877. (Illus.). 127p. (gr. 7 up). 1888. 8.50x (ISBN 0-8196-0113-6). Biblo.

Caesar's Gallic War. Julius Caesar. Tr. by Joseph Pearl from Latin. (Orig.). (gr. 10 up). 1962. 5.50 (ISBN 0-8120-5014-2); pap. text ed. 3.95 (ISBN 0-8120-0037-4). Barron.

Caesar's Prophet. Charles R. Haynie. Date not set. 8.95 (ISBN 0-533-04844-3). Vantage.

Cafe Society: Photographs & Poetry from San Francisco's North Beach. Photos by Ira Nowinski. LC 78-63332. 1978. pap. 8.95 (ISBN 0-916860-05-1). Bean Pub.

Cage. Roy Brown. LC 77-1586. (gr. 6 up). 1977. 6.95 (ISBN 0-395-28892-4, Clarion). HM.

Cage & Aviary Birds. Cyril H. Rogers. Ed. by Val Clear. LC 75-845. (Illus.). 224p. 1975. 6.98 o.s.i. (ISBN 0-02-604360-2). Macmillan.

Cage of Creatures. Lewis Tureo. (Illus.). 1979. pap. 2.50 (ISBN 0-686-52326-1); pap. 4.50 signed (ISBN 0-918092-08-6). Tamarack Edns.

Cage of Mirrors. Robert J. Ray. LC 80-7867. 320p. 1980. 11.95 (ISBN 0-690-01938-6). Lippincott & Crowell.

Caged Bird Medicine. Charles V. Steiner, Jr. & Richard B. Davis. (Illus.). 176p. 1981. pap. text ed. 17.50 (ISBN 0-8138-1715-3). Iowa St U Pr.

Caged: Eight Prisoners & Their Keepers. Ben H. Bagdikian. LC 74-20398. 438p. (YA) 1976. 12.95 o.s.i. (ISBN 0-06-010174-1, HarpT). Har-Row.

Cages of Glass, Flowers of Time. Charlotte Culin. LC 79-14460. (gr. 7 up). 1979. 9.95 (ISBN 0-87888-157-3). Bradbury Pr.

Caging the Bear: Containment & the Cold War. Charles Gati. LC 73-19522. 1974. pap. text ed. 5.95 (ISBN 0-672-61351-4). Bobbs.

Caging the Raven. William Heffernan. 1981. 12.95 (ISBN 0-671-61056-2, Wyndham Bks). S&S.

Cagney by Cagney. James Cagney. 1981. pap. 2.75 (ISBN 0-671-41757-6). PB.

Cagney: The Actor As Auteur. Patrick McGilligan. LC 73-14028. (Illus.). 192p. 1975. 12.00 o.p. (ISBN 0-498-01462-2). A S Barnes.

Cahiers Du Cinema. Ed. by T. L. French. (Thousand Eyes Ser.). (Illus.). 1978. pap. 3.50 o.p. (ISBN 0-918432-18-9). NY Zoetrope.

Cahiers du Quatrieme Ordre. Pierre Dufournyde Villiers. (Fr.). 1977. lib. bdg. 13.75x o.p. (ISBN 0-8287-0290-X); pap. text ed. 3.75x o.p. (ISBN 0-685-75738-2). Clearwater Pub.

Cahuilla Dictionary. Hansjakob Seiler & Kojiro Hioki. 1979. pap. 15.00 (ISBN 0-686-25243-8). Malki Mus Pr.

Cain's Book. Alexander Trocchi. LC 79-56749. 256p. (Orig.). 1981. pap. 3.50 (ISBN 0-394-17403-8, B-432, BC). Grove.

Cain's Daughters. Doris Shannon. LC 77-15323. 1978. 10.00 o.p. (ISBN 0-312-11390-0). St Martin.

Cairo, Jerusalem, & Damascus, Three Chief Cities of the Egyptian Sultans. David S. Margoliouth. LC 80-1918. (Illus.). 1981. Repr. of 1907 ed. 54.50 (ISBN 0-404-18980-6). AMS Pr.

Caisse De Joseph. J. R. Burne. 1966. text ed. 2.25x (ISBN 0-521-04388-3). Cambridge U Pr.

Caithness. James Miller. 112p. 1980. 14.75x (ISBN 0-7050-0068-0, Pub. by Skilton & Shaw England). State Mutual Bk.

Caiva Siddhanta: Leipzig, 1912. H. W. Schomerus. LC 78-74268. (Oriental Religions Ser.: Vol. 9). 455p. 1981. lib. bdg. 50.00 (ISBN 0-8240-3906-8). Garland Pub.

Cajun Alphabet. James Rice. LC 76-28490. (Illus.). 1976. 9.95 (ISBN 0-88289-136-7). Pelican.

Cajun Columbus. Alice Durio. LC 75-20484. (Illus.). 40p. (gr. 2 up). 1975. 7.95 (ISBN 0-88289-074-3). Pelican.

Cajun Night Before Christmas. Trosclair. Ed. by Howard Jacobs. (Illus.). 48p. (gr. 6-12). 1973. 7.95 (ISBN 0-88289-002-6). Pelican.

Cajun Night Before Christmas Coloring Book. James Rice. 1976. 1.25 (ISBN 0-88289-138-3). Pelican.

Cajuns: From Acadia to Louisiana. William F. Rushton. 1980. pap. 8.95 (ISBN 0-374-51555-7, N 632). FS&G.

Cake Decorating & Sugarcraft. Evelyn Wallace. LC 74-27499. (Illus.). 1975. 12.95 (ISBN 0-668-03766-0). Arco.

Cake Decorating Book. Phylis Magida & Staff of the Culinary Arts Institute. Ed. by Edward G. Finnegan. LC 78-54619. (Adventures in Cooking Ser). (Illus.). 1981. cancelled (ISBN 0-8326-0604-9, 1516); pap. 3.95 (ISBN 0-8326-0603-0, 2516). Delair.

Cake Decorating Ideas & Designs. Louise Spencer. LC 80-54334. (Illus.). 1981. 14.95 (ISBN 0-8069-0214-0); lib. bdg. 13.29 (ISBN 0-8069-0215-9); pap. 9.95 (ISBN 0-8069-7502-4). Sterling.

Cake Design & Decoration. 4th ed. L. J. Hanneman & G. I. Marshall. (Illus.). 1978. text ed. 31.30x (ISBN 0-85334-793-X, Pub. by Applied Science). Burgess-Intl Ideas.

Cal Alley. Ed. by Charles Crawford. LC 72-82797. (Illus.). 382p. 1973. 15.00 (ISBN 0-87870-013-7). Memphis St Univ.

Calabash of Life. Khadambi Asalache. (Orig.). 1967. pap. text ed. 2.25x (ISBN 0-582-64001-6). Humanities.

Calafia: The California Poetry. Ed. by Ishmael Reed. LC 78-51132. 1979. 15.00 (ISBN 0-931676-04-5); pap. 8.95 (ISBN 0-931676-03-7). Y'bird.

Calamities, Catastrophies, & Chaos. Peter Popoff. Ed. by Don Tanner. LC 80-69974. (Illus.). 108p. 1980. pap. 2.50 (ISBN 0-938544-01-2). Faith Messenger.

Calamities of the World. Hubert S. Banner. LC 74-159880. (Tower Bks). (Illus.). 1971. Repr. of 1932 ed. 18.000 (ISBN 0-8103-3918-8). Gale.

Calamity at Devil's Crossing. Denver Bardwell. (YA) 1973. 5.95 (ISBN 0-685-28397-6, Avalon). Bouregy.

Calamity Jane & the Lady Wildcats. Duncan Aikman. 1973. pap. 1.25 o.p. (ISBN 0-345-23507-X). Ballantine.

Calamity Range: Valley of Hunted Men. Paul E. Lehman. 1979. pap. 2.25 (ISBN 0-8439-0679-0). Nordon Pubns.

Calcium & Cell Function: Vol. 1, Calmodulin. Ed. by Wai Yiu Cheung. LC 80-985. (Molecular Biology Ser.). 1980. 46.50 (ISBN 0-12-171401-2). Acad Pr.

Calcium & Phosphoros Metabolism. James T. Irving. 1973. 37.50 (ISBN 0-12-374350-8). Acad Pr.

Calcium Chloride in Concrete: Science & Technology. V. S. Ramachandran. (Illus.). 1976. text ed. 63.30x (ISBN 0-85334-682-8, Pub. by Applied Science). Burgess-Intl Ideas.

Calcium Metabolism. Ed. by John A. Parsons. (Comprehensive Endocrinology Ser.). 1981. 36.00 (ISBN 0-89004-344-2, 393). Raven.

Calcium Metabolism in Renal Failure & Nephrolithiasis. David S. David. LC 76-30308. (Perspectives in Nephrology & Hypertension). 1977. 54.50 (ISBN 0-471-19673-8, Pub. by Wiley Medical). Wiley.

Calcium Movement in Excitable Cells. P. F. Baker & H. Reute. 1976. pap. text ed. 18.25 (ISBN 0-08-018298-4). Pergamon.

Calcium Transfer Mechanisms. Association of Bone & Joint Surgeons. Ed. by Marshall R. Urist & Anthony F. Depalma. (Clinical Orthopaedics & Related Research Ser. No. 78). (Illus.). 1971. 15.00 (ISBN 0-685-24733-3). Lippincott.

Calcul Des Probabilites. 2nd ed. Joseph Bertrand. LC 78-113114. 389p. (Fr.). 1972. text ed. 11.95 (ISBN 0-8284-0262-0). Chelsea Pub.

Calculated Electronic Properties of Metals: Designing Our Career Machines. V. L. Moruzzi et al. LC 79-14183. 1978. 37.00 (ISBN 0-08-022705-8). Pergamon.

Calculating Cat Returns. Eric Gurney. LC 78-61782. (Illus.). 1978. 5.95 (ISBN 0-13-110213-3); pap. 2.95 (ISBN 0-13-110205-2). P-H.

Calculating with Basic. Raymond Guido. (Da Capo Quality Paperbacks Ser.). (Illus.). 80p. 1981. pap. text ed. 8.95 (ISBN 0-306-80144-2). Da Capo.

Calculation of Drug Dosages: A Workbook. 2nd ed. Ruth K. Radcliff & Sheila J. Ogden. 290p. 1980. pap. text ed. 9.95 (ISBN 0-8016-4067-9). Mosby.

Calculation of Molecular Orbitals. John C. Slater. LC 78-323. 1979. 23.95 (ISBN 0-471-03181-X, Pub. by Wiley-Interscience). Wiley.

Calculational Methods of Interacting Arrays of Fissile Material. A. F. Thomas & F. Abbey. LC 73-8604. 144p. 1973. text ed. 28.00 (ISBN 0-08-017660-7). Pergamon.

Calculator Afloat: A Mariner's Guide to the Electronic Calculator. H. H. Shufeldt & Kenneth Newcomer. LC 80-81091. 256p. 1980. 16.95 (ISBN 0-87021-116-1). Naval Inst Pr.

Calculator Calculus. George McCarty. LC 75-27363. 1976. pap. 10.95 o.p. (ISBN 0-8087-3929-8). Burgess.

Calculator Calculus. rev. ed. George McCarty. LC 75-27363. (Illus.). xiv, 258p. 1980. pap. 14.95 (ISBN 0-936356-00-6); pap. text ed. 14.95 (ISBN 0-471-27596-4). Educalc Pubns.

Calculator Clout: Programming Methods for Your Programmable. Maurice D. Weir. (Illus.). 256p. 1981. text ed. 17.95 (ISBN 0-13-110411-X, Spec); pap. text ed. 8.95 (ISBN 0-13-110403-9, Spec). P-H.

Calculator Programs for the Hydrocarbon Processing Industries, Vol. 2. S. Jagannath. 1981. 19.95 (ISBN 0-87201-092-9). Gulf Pub.

Calculator Puzzles, Tricks & Games. Norvin Pallas. LC 76-1166. (Illus.). 96p. (YA) 1976. 5.95 (ISBN 0-8069-4534-6); PLB 6.69 (ISBN 0-8069-4535-4). Sterling.

Calculators in the Classroom. David Moursund. 192p. 1980. pap. text ed. 8.95 (ISBN 0-471-08113-2). Wiley.

Calculators: Readings from the Arithmetic Teacher & the Mathematics Teacher. Compiled by Bruce C. Burt. 1979. pap. 6.25 (ISBN 0-87353-144-2). NCTM.

Calculo. Louis Leithold. (Span.). 1973. pap. 12.00 (ISBN 0-06-315010-7, IntlDept). Har-Row.

Calculo, Vols. I & II. Louis Leithold. (Sp.). 1979. Vol. I. pap. text ed. 7.00 (ISBN 0-06-315008-5, Pub. by HarLA Mexico); Vol. II. pap. text ed. 6.00 (ISBN 0-06-359009-3). Har-Row.

Calculo, Bk. I. 2nd ed. Alvaro Pinzon. (Span.). 1978. pap. text ed. 6.00 (ISBN 0-06-316986-X, Pub. by HarLA Mexico). Har-Row.

Calculo, Bk. II. 2nd ed. Alvaro Pinzon. (Span.). 1978. pap. text ed. 6.00 (ISBN 0-06-316987-8, Pub. by HarLA Mexico). Har-Row.

Calculus. P. Abbott. (Teach Yourself Ser.). 1975. pap. 3.95 o.p. (ISBN 0-679-10391-0). McKay.

Calculus. Jack G. Ceder & David L. Outcalt. 1977. text ed. 27.25 (ISBN 0-205-05560-5); instr's manual avail. (ISBN 0-205-05561-3); study guide 5.95 (ISBN 0-685-74024-2). Allyn.

Calculus. H. Flanders. 1970. text ed. 26.95 (ISBN 0-12-259640-4); ans. manual avail. Acad Pr.

Calculus. Stanley Grossman. 1977. 26.95 (ISBN 0-12-304350-6). Acad Pr.

Calculus. 2nd ed. Lynn H. Loomis. LC 76-12799. (Mathematics Ser). 1977. text ed. 25.95 (ISBN 0-201-04326-2); student supplement 6.95 (ISBN 0-201-04328-9). A-W.

Calculus. Jerrold Marsden & Alan Weinstein. 1979. 26.95 (ISBN 0-8053-6930-9); study guide 6.95. Benjamin-Cummings.

Calculus. 2nd ed. Edwin E. Moise. LC 76-150576. (Mathematics Ser). 1972. text ed. 19.95 (ISBN 0-201-04810-8). A-W.

Calculus. Mustafa Munem & David Foulis. LC 79-770818. (Illus.). 1978. text ed. 27.95 (ISBN 0-87901-087-8); Pt. 1, LC79-64155. 18.95x (ISBN 0-87901-105-X); Pt. 2, LC79-64155. 18.95x (ISBN 0-87901-106-8); study guide 4.95 (ISBN 0-686-68021-9). Worth.

Calculus. rev. ed. Cletus O. Oakley. (Orig.). 1957. pap. 3.95 (ISBN 0-06-460048-3, CO 48, COS). Har-Row.

Calculus, 2 pts. 2nd ed. Saturnino L. Salas & Einar Hille. LC 73-79299. 1974. Pt. 1. text ed. 16.75x o.p. (ISBN 0-471-00888-5); Pt. 2. text ed. 18.95x (ISBN 0-471-01060-X). Wiley.

Calculus. 2nd ed. Michael Spivak. 1980. text ed. 18.50 (ISBN 0-914098-77-2); pap. text ed. 5.75 (ISBN 0-914098-78-0). Publish or Perish.

Calculus. 3rd ed. George B. Thomas, Jr. 1969. text ed. 22.95 (ISBN 0-201-07503-2). A-W.

Calculus: A Genetic Approach. Otto Toeplitz. Ed. by Gottfried Kothe. Tr. by Luise Lange. LC 63-9731. (Illus.). 1963. 8.75x o.s.i. (ISBN 0-226-80665-0). U of Chicago Pr.

Calculus: A Modeling Approach. 2nd ed. Marvin L. Bittinger. LC 79-18272. (Illus.). 1980. text ed. 19.95 (ISBN 0-201-01247-2). A-W.

Calculus: A Modern Approach. Cletus O. Oakley. (Illus., Orig.). 1971. pap. 4.50 (ISBN 0-06-460134-X, CO 134, COS). Har-Row.

Calculus: A Practical Approach. 2nd ed. Kenneth Kalmanson & Patricia C. Kenschaft. LC 77-81756. (Illus.). xiv, 335p. 1978. text ed. 16.95x (ISBN 0-87901-083-5). Worth.

Calculus: A Short Course with Applications to Business, Economics, & the Social Sciences. Gerald Freilich & Frederick P. Greenleaf. LC 75-37569. (Illus.). 1976. 18.95x (ISBN 0-7167-0466-8). W H Freeman.

Calculus: An Intuitive & Physical Approach. 2nd ed. Morris Kline. LC 76-22760. 1977. text ed. 27.95x (ISBN 0-471-49116-0); solutions manual avail. (ISBN 0-471-02396-5). Wiley.

Calculus & Analytic Geometry. Philip S. Clarke. 1974. text ed. 21.95x o.p. (ISBN 0-669-75879-5); instructor's manual free o.p. (ISBN 0-669-85753-X); Vol. 1. study guide by James F. Hurley 7.95x o.p. (ISBN 0-669-94748-2); Vol. 2. study guide 7.95 o.p. (ISBN 0-669-94672-9); transparencies 175.00 o.p. (ISBN 0-669-94748-2). Heath.

Calculus & Analytic Geometry. 3rd ed. Robert C. Fisher & Allen D. Ziebur. (Illus.). 784p. 1975. text ed. 25.95 (ISBN 0-13-112227-4). P-H.

Calculus & Analytic Geometry. Philip Gillet. 928p. 1981. text ed. 28.95 (ISBN 0-669-00641-6); instr's. guide avail. (ISBN 0-669-02702-2); solutions guide vol. 1 6.95 (ISBN 0-669-00642-4); solutions guide vol. 2 6.95 (ISBN 0-669-03212-3); solutions guides vol. 3 6.95 (ISBN 0-669-03213-1). Heath.

Calculus & Analytic Geometry. 3rd ed. Douglas F. Riddle. 1979. text ed. 29.95x (ISBN 0-534-00626-4). Wadsworth Pub.

Calculus & Analytic Geometry. 5th ed. George B. Thomas, Jr. & Ross L. Finney. LC 78-55832. (Illus.). 1979. Combined Ed. text ed. 27.95 (ISBN 0-201-07540-7); Pt. 1. student suppl. & self-study manual avail. 20.95 (ISBN 0-201-07541-5); Pt. 2. 20.95 (ISBN 0-201-07542-3). A-W.

Calculus & Analytic Geometry. 3rd ed. John A. Tierney. 725p. (gr. 12 up). 1975. text ed. 21.95x o.p. (ISBN 0-205-04645-2, 5646456); instr's manual free o.p. (ISBN 0-205-04646-0); student sol. manual 7.95 o.p. (ISBN 0-205-04712-2). Allyn.

Calculus & Analytic Geometry. 4th ed. John A. Tierney. 1979. text ed. 27.25x (ISBN 0-205-06454-X); instr's man. avail. (ISBN 0-205-06455-8); solutions man. avail. (ISBN 0-205-06456-6); self-test supplement avail. (ISBN 0-205-06457-4). Allyn.

Calculus & It's Applications. L. Goldstein. 1980. 21.95 (ISBN 0-13-111963-X). P-H.

Calculus by Discovery. Douglas Downing. 224p. (gr. 10-12). 1981. pap. text ed. 4.50 (ISBN 0-8120-2380-3). Barron.

Calculus: Combined Differential & Integral: Syllabus. Lloyd B. Williams & Allan W. Gray. 1973. text ed. 16.00 (ISBN 0-89420-059-3, 122210); cassette recordings 140.95 (ISBN 0-89420-130-1, 350500). Natl Book.

Calculus: Differential Syllabus, Pt. 1. Lloyd B. Williams & Allan W. Gray. 1973. text ed. 9.25 (ISBN 0-89420-057-7, 122202); cassette recordings 89.20 (ISBN 0-89420-131-X, 350510). Natl Book.

Calculus for Business & Economics. Byrkit & Shamma. 1981. text ed. write for info. (ISBN 0-442-21305-0). D Van Nostrand.

Calculus for Business & Economics. 2nd ed. Robert L. Childress. LC 77-2855. (Illus.). 1978. text ed. 17.95 (ISBN 0-13-111534-0). P-H.

Calculus for Business & Social Science. W. J. Adams. LC 74-5524. 1975. text ed. 18.50 (ISBN 0-471-00988-1). Wiley.

Calculus for Business & the Social Biological Sciences. 2nd ed. David G. Crowdis et al. 1976. text ed. 14.95x (ISBN 0-02-473030-0). Macmillan.

Calculus for Engineering Technology. Walter R. Blakeley. LC 67-29017. 1968. text ed. 20.95 (ISBN 0-471-07931-6). Wiley.

Calculus for the Life Sciences. Rodolfo De Sapio. LC 77-21312. (Illus.). 1978. text ed. 21.95x (ISBN 0-7167-0371-8). W H Freeman.

Calculus: Instructor's Manual. Stanley Grossman. 120p. 1977. 3.00 (ISBN 0-12-304352-2). Acad Pr.

Calculus Made Easy. 3rd ed. Silvanus P. Thompson. 1946. 4.95 (ISBN 0-312-11410-9, Papermac); pap. 5.95 (ISBN 0-686-66541-4). St Martin.

Calculus of Communicating Systems. R. Milner. (Lecture Notes in Computer Science Ser.: Vol. 92). 260p. 1981. pap. 11.80 (ISBN 0-387-10235-3). Springer-Verlag.

Calculus of Consent: Logical Foundations of Constitutional Democracy. James M. Buchanan & Gordon Tullock. 1962. pap. 4.95 (ISBN 0-472-06100-3, 100, AA). U of Mich Pr.

Calculus of Extension. Henry G. Forder. LC 59-1178. 19.50 (ISBN 0-8284-0135-7). Chelsea Pub.

Calculus of Finite Difference. 2nd ed. L. M. Milne-Thomson. LC 80-65906. xxiii, 558p. 1980. text ed. 22.50 (ISBN 0-8284-0308-2). Chelsea Pub.
Calculus of Finite Differences. 3rd ed. Charles Jordan. LC 65-29977. 22.50 (ISBN 0-8284-0033-4). Chelsea Pub.
Calculus of One & Several Variables. Robert T. Seeley. 1973. 16.95x o.p. (ISBN 0-673-07779-9). Scott F.
Calculus of Several Variables. 2nd ed. Serge Lang. LC 78-55822. (Mathematics Ser.). (Illus.). 1979. text ed. 20.95 (ISBN 0-201-04299-1). A-W.
Calculus of Several Variables: An Introduction. Robert T. Seeley. 1970. 15.95x (ISBN 0-673-07543-5). Scott F.
Calculus of Variations. L. E. Elsgolc. 1962. text ed. 6.90 o.p. (ISBN 0-08-009554-2). Pergamon.
Calculus of Variations. Izrail M. Gelfand & S. V. Fomin. Tr. by R. Silverman. (Illus.). 1963. ref. ed. 23.95 (ISBN 0-13-112292-4). P-H.
Calculus of Variations. Robert Weinstock. pap. text ed. 5.00 (ISBN 0-486-63069-2). Dover.
Calculus of Variations & Optimal Control Theory. Magnus R. Hestenes. LC 79-25451. 418p. 1980. Repr. of 1966 ed. lib. bdg. 25.50 (ISBN 0-89874-092-4). Krieger.
Calculus of Vector Functions. 3rd ed. Richard Williamson et al. LC 75-167788. (Illus.). 576p. 1972. ref. ed. 23.95 (ISBN 0-13-112367-X). P-H.
Calculus: One & Several Variables, 2 pts. 3rd ed. S. L. Salas. LC 77-11630. 1978. text ed. 28.95 (ISBN 0-471-74983-4); Pt. 1. text ed. 20.95 (ISBN 0-471-03285-9); Pt. 2. text ed. 20.95 (ISBN 0-471-03286-7); solutions manual 5.95 (ISBN 0-471-04282-X); student supplement 9.95 (ISBN 0-471-02882-7). Wiley.
Calculus: One & Several Variables. 2nd ed. Saturnino L. Salas & Einar Hille. LC 73-79299. 1974. text ed. 22.95x (ISBN 0-471-00956-3). Wiley.
Calculus: One-Variable Calculus with an Introduction to Linear Algebra, Vol. 1. 2nd ed. T. M. Apostol. LC 73-20899. 1967. text ed. 25.50 (ISBN 0-471-00005-1). Wiley.
Calculus Refresher for Technical Men. A. Albert Klaf. 1957. pap. text ed. 5.00 (ISBN 0-486-20370-0). Dover.
Calculus Unlimited. J. Marsden & A. Weinstein. 1980. pap. 6.95 (ISBN 0-8053-6932-5). A-W.
Calculus Unlimited. Jerrold Marsden & Alan Weinstein. 1980. pap. text ed. 6.95 (ISBN 0-8053-6932-5). Benjamin-Cummings.
Calculus with Analytic Geometry. Howard Anton. LC 79-11469. 1980. 27.95 (ISBN 0-471-03248-4); tchrs' manual avail. (ISBN 0-471-06360-6); solution manual avail. Wiley.
Calculus with Analytic Geometry. H. Flanders & J. Price. 1041p. 1978. text ed. 26.95 (ISBN 0-12-259672-2); instr's. manual 3.00 (ISBN 0-12-259673-0). Acad Pr.
Calculus with Analytic Geometry. Daniel J. Fleming & James J. Kaput. 1979. text ed. 26.50 scp (ISBN 0-06-382672-0, HarpC); scp study guide 6.50 (ISBN 0-06-382581-3); solutions manual avail. (ISBN 0-06-382580-5); free instructor's manual (ISBN 0-06-372860-5). Har-Row.
Calculus with Analytic Geometry. John B. Fraleigh. LC 79-18693. (Illus.). 1980. text ed. 26.95 (ISBN 0-201-03041-1). A-W.
Calculus with Analytic Geometry. Roland E. Larson & Robert P. Hostetler. 1979. text ed. 27.95 (ISBN 0-669-01301-3); solution manuals 5.95 ea. Vol. 1 (ISBN 0-669-03187-9). Vol. 2 (ISBN 0-669-03188-7). Vol. 3 (ISBN 0-669-03189-5). Differential Equations suppl. free (ISBN 0-669-03204-2); student manual 6.95 (ISBN 0-669-01705-1); Appendix D free (ISBN 0-669-03190-9); instructor's manual free (ISBN 0-669-01302-1). Heath.
Calculus with Analytic Geometry. Edward M. Pease & George P. Wadsworth. LC 68-56150. 1071p. 1969. 19.95x o.p. (ISBN 0-8260-7055-8). Wiley.
Calculus with Analytic Geometry. 3rd ed. Edwin J. Purcell. LC 77-7977. (Illus.). 1978. 25.95 (ISBN 0-13-112052-2); Solutions Manual by Patterson 4.95 (ISBN 0-13-112037-9); pap. text ed. 1.00 linear algebra suppl. (ISBN 0-13-112029-8). P-H.
Calculus with Analytic Geometry. Burt Rodin. 1969. ref. ed. 25.95 (ISBN 0-13-112060-3). P-H.
Calculus with Analytic Geometry. Abraham Spitzbart. 768p. 1975. 17.95x (ISBN 0-673-07907-4). Scott F.
Calculus with Analytic Geometry, Vol. 1. John M. Olmsted. LC 66-11169. (Century Mathematics Ser.). (Illus.). 1966. 26.50x (ISBN 0-89197-061-4). Irvington.
Calculus with Analytic Geometry: A First Course. 3rd ed. Murray H. Protter & Charles B. Morrey, Jr. LC 76-12801. (Mathematics Ser.). 1977. text ed. 20.95 (ISBN 0-201-06037-X). A-W.
Calculus with Analytic Geometry: A Second Course. Murray H. Protter & Charles B. Morrey, Jr. LC 70-153066. (Mathematics Ser). 1971. text ed. 21.95 (ISBN 0-201-06021-3). A-W.
Calculus with Applications in the Management & Social Sciences. William Thompson. (Illus.). 1977. text ed. 18.95 (ISBN 0-13-112151-0). P-H.
Calculus with Applications to Business & the Life Sciences. Abe Mizrahi & Michael Sullivan. LC 75-17964. 384p. 1976. text ed. 19.95x (ISBN 0-471-61192-1); solutions manual avail. (ISBN 0-471-01607-1). Wiley.
Calculus with Finite Math for Social Sciences. Mary W. Gray. LC 74-174335. 1972. text ed. 17.95 (ISBN 0-201-02573-6); instructor's manual 2.00 (ISBN 0-201-02574-4). A-W.
Calculus with Finite Mathematics for Social Science. Gray. 1972. 17.95 (ISBN 0-201-02573-6); instr's man. 2.00 (ISBN 0-201-02574-4). A-W.
Calculus with Probability. Willard E. Baxter & Clifford W. Sloyer. LC 72-1937. 1973. text ed. 19.95 (ISBN 0-201-00401-1); instructor's manual 2.00 (ISBN 0-201-00404-6). A-W.
Calcutta: People & Empire. Ed. by Nemai S. Bose. LC 75-907962. 1976. 12.50x o.p. (ISBN 0-88386-721-4). South Asia Bks.
Caldecott Aesop-Twenty Fables. Aesop. LC 77-88424. (gr. 3-9). 1978. 12.95 (ISBN 0-385-12653-0); PLB (ISBN 0-385-12654-9). Doubleday.
Caldecott Medal Books, 1938-1957. Ed. by Bertha M. Miller & Elinor W. Field. LC 57-11582. (Illus.). 1957. 17.00 (ISBN 0-87675-001-3). Horn Bk.
Calder, No. 201. (Maeght Gallery: Derriere le Miroir Ser.). 1977. pap. 19.95 (ISBN 0-8120-0923-1). Barron.
Calder, No. 212. (Maeght Gallery: Derriere le Miroire Ser.). 1977. pap. 19.95 (ISBN 0-8120-0924-X). Barron.
Calder, No. 221. (Maeght Gallery: Derriere le Miroir Ser.). 1977. pap. 19.95 (ISBN 0-8120-0895-2). Barron.
Calder, No. 173. (Maeght Gallery: Derriere le Miroir Ser.). 1977. pap. 19.95 (ISBN 0-8120-0920-7). Barron.
Calder, No. 190. (Maeght Gallery: Derriere le Miroir Ser.). 1977. pap. 19.95 (ISBN 0-8120-0921-5). Barron.
Calderon & the Seizures of Honor. Edwin Honig. LC 78-186674. 295p. 1972. 15.00x (ISBN 0-674-09075-6). Harvard U Pr.
Calderon de la Barca. Everett W. Hesse. (World Authors Ser.: Spain: No. 30). 1968. lib. bdg. 10.95 (ISBN 0-8057-2100-2). Twayne.
Calderon de la Barca: El Lcade de Zalemea. Ed. by P. N. Dunn. 1965. 6.00 (ISBN 0-08-011549-7); pap. 5.40 (ISBN 0-08-011548-9). Pergamon.
Calderon: Four Plays. Pedro Calderon De La Barca. Tr. by Edwin Honig. Incl. Secret Vengeance for Secret Insult; Phantom Lady; Mayor of Zalamea; Devotion to the Cross. (Orig.). 1961. pap. 2.95 o.p. (ISBN 0-8090-0721-5, Mermaid). Hill & Wang.
Caldwell Shadow. Dorothy Dahiels. (Orig.). 1975. pap. 1.50 o.s.i. (ISBN 0-446-88560-6). Warner Bks.
Caleb Catlum's America. Vincent McHugh. LC 71-156927. 1971. Repr. of 1936 ed. 18.00 (ISBN 0-8103-3717-7). Gale.
Calendar. Irving Adler & Ruth Adler. LC 67-23865. (Reason Why Ser). (Illus.). (gr. 3-6). 1967. PLB 7.89 (ISBN 0-381-99975-0, A11200, JD-J). John Day.
Calendar Girl. Michael Colmer. LC 76-6265. (Illus.). 1977. Repr. of 1976 ed. 19.95 o.p. (ISBN 0-89104-106-0). A & W Pubs.
Calendar of Country Customs. Richard Whitlock. 1978. 19.95 (ISBN 0-7134-0571-6). David & Charles.
Calendar of Creative Man. John Paxton & Sheila Fairfield. (Illus.). 544p. 1980. 27.50 (ISBN 0-87196-470-8). Facts on File.
Calendar of Soviet Documents on Foreign Policy, 1917-1941. Jane Degras. LC 79-4912. 1981. Repr. of 1948 ed. 19.75 (ISBN 0-88355-962-5). Hyperion Conn.
Calendar of Soviet Treaties, 1917-1957. Robert M. Slusser & Jan F. Triska. 1959. 25.00x (ISBN 0-8047-0587-9). Stanford U Pr.
Calendar of Soviet Treaties: 1958-1973. Robert M. Slusser & George Ginsburgs. LC 80-50453. 990p. 1980. 125.00x (ISBN 90-286-0609-2). Sijthoff & Noordhoff.
Calf. 4th ed. J. H. Roy. LC 79-42840. (Studies in the Agricultural & Food Sciences). 1980. text ed. 79.95 (ISBN 0-408-70941-3). Butterworths.
Calf Is Born. Joanna Cole. LC 75-12408. (Illus.). 48p. (gr. k-3). 1975. PLB 6.48 (ISBN 0-688-32036-8). Morrow.
Caliban Reborn: Renewal in Twentieth-Century Music. Wilfrid Mellers. (Music Reprint Ser.). 1979. Repr. of 1967 ed. lib. bdg. 22.50 (ISBN 0-306-79569-8). Da Capo.
Calibration of Dose Meters Used in Radiotherapy. (Technical Reports Ser.: No. 185). 1979. pap. 7.50 (ISBN 92-0-115079-2, IDC185, IAEA). Unipub.
Caliche-Origin Classification, Morphology & Uses. C. C. Reeves, Jr. LC 76-2234. 1976. text ed. 39.95x (ISBN 0-686-16733-3). Estacado Bks.
Calico Bush. Rachel Field. (gr. 7-9). 1966. 9.95 (ISBN 0-02-734620-X). Macmillan.
Calico Cat at the Zoo. Donald Charles. LC 80-26380. (Calico Cat Storybooks). (Illus.). 32p. (ps-3). 1981. PLB 7.95 (ISBN 0-516-03443-X). Childrens.
Calico Palace. Gwen Bristow. LC 72-106584. 1970. 10.95 (ISBN 0-690-16608-7, TYC-T). T Y Crowell.
Calico Pantry Cookbook. Lois Solomon & Anita Reitman. 320p. 1980. pap. 6.95 (ISBN 0-346-12475-1). Cornerstone.
California. 33.00 (ISBN 0-89770-080-5). Curriculum Info Ctr.
California, 4 vols. Ed. by David G. Delong. (Historic American Buildings). (Illus.). 1980. Set. lib. bdg. 360.00. Vol. 1 (ISBN 0-8240-3197-0). Vol. 2 (ISBN 0-8240-3194-6). Vol. 3 (ISBN 0-8240-3195-4). Vol. 4 (ISBN 0-8240-3196-2). Garland Pub.
California. rev. ed. Ed. by Harry Hansen. Federal Writer's Project. (American Guide Ser). 1967. 12.95 (ISBN 0-8038-1073-3). Hastings.
California! Dana F. Ross. (Wagons West Ser.). 384p. (Orig.). 1981. pap. 2.95 (ISBN 0-553-14260-7). Bantam.
California! Kevin Starr. LC 80-51092. (Illus.). 296p. (gr. 4-9). 1980. text ed. 15.00x (ISBN 0-87905-100-0). Peregrine Smith.
California: A Guide to the Golden State. LC 72-84461. 1939. 54.00 (ISBN 0-403-02157-X). Somerset Pub.
California: A History. 3rd ed. Andrew F. Rolle. LC 77-90674. (Illus.). 1978. text ed. 16.50x (ISBN 0-88295-776-7), AHM Pub.
California: A Programmed History. Susan Berk. (gr. 10-12). 1976. pap. text ed. 5.67 (ISBN 0-87720-617-1). AMSCO Sch.
California-Alaska Oil & Gas Review for 1969. 1970. 30.00 (ISBN 0-686-28269-8). Munger Oil.
California-Alaska Oil & Gas Review for 1971. 30.00 (ISBN 0-686-28270-1). Munger Oil.
California-Alaska Oil & Gas Review for 1972. 30.00 (ISBN 0-686-28271-X). Munger Oil.
California-Alaska Oil & Gas Review for 1973. 1974. 30.00 (ISBN 0-686-28272-8). Munger Oil.
California-Alaska Oil & Gas Review 1975. 1976. 30.00 (ISBN 0-686-28273-6). Munger Oil.
California-Alaska Oil & Gas Review 1976. 1977. 30.00 (ISBN 0-686-28274-4). Munger Oil.
California & the Nation, Eighteen Fifty to Eighteen Sixty-Nine. Joseph Ellison. LC 78-87529. (American Scene Ser.). 1969. Repr. of 1927 ed. lib. bdg. 25.00 (ISBN 0-306-71443-4). Da Capo.
California & the West. Charis Wilson. LC 78-66677. (Illus.). 1978. 25.00 (ISBN 0-89381-034-7); ltd. ed. with print 300.00 (ISBN 0-89381-037-1). Aperture.
California Art Review Books, 3 bks. Ed. by Hank Baum. Incl. Bk. 1. California. LC 80-70751. 272p. pap. 12.95 (ISBN 0-89087-310-0); Bk. 2. Los Angeles. LC 80-70752. 160p. pap. 9.95 (ISBN 0-89087-319-4); Bk. 3. San Francisco. LC 80-70753. 160p. pap. 9.95 (ISBN 0-89087-308-9). (Illus.). Date not set. Celestial Arts.
California Art Review Books. Ed. by Hank Baum. Incl. California Art Review. 272p. pap. 12.95 (ISBN 0-89087-310-0); San Francisco Art Review. 160p. pap. 9.95 (ISBN 0-89087-308-9); Los Angeles Art Review. 160p. pap. 9.95 (ISBN 0-89087-319-4). (Illus., Orig.). 1980. Celestial Arts.
California Beauty Book: A Total Guide to Bringing Out Your Natural Beauty. Trisha Yeager. (Illus.). 240p. 1981. pap. 9.95 (ISBN 0-936602-11-2). Harbor Pub CA.
California Bembecine Sand Wasps in the Genera Bembix, Bicyrtes & Microbembex (Hymenoptera Sphecidae) R. M. Bohart & D. S. Horning. (Bulletin of the California Insect Survey: Vol. 13). 1971. pap. 9.00x (ISBN 0-520-09387-9). U of Cal Pr.
California Brandy: The Wine Drinker's Spirit. Adam Ramos & Joseph Ramos. (Illus.). 1981. 12.95 (ISBN 0-914598-66-X). Padre Prods.
California Bungalow. Robert Winter. LC 80-14078. (Illus.). 96p. 1980. 14.95 (ISBN 0-912158-85-9). Hennessey.
California Catalogue: Everything You Need to Know About Living, Working, Playing, Shopping & Traveling in the Golden State. Roger Rapoport & Margot Lind. LC 76-12524. (Illus.). 1977. pap. 7.95 o.p. (ISBN 0-525-03153-7). Dutton.
California Central Coast Railways. Rick Hamman. (Illus.). 300p. 1980. 39.95 (ISBN 0-87108-553-4). Pruett.
California Civil Code. 1981. 14.00 (ISBN 0-911110-12-7). Parker & Son.
California Code of Civil Procedure. 1981. 14.00 (ISBN 0-911110-13-5). Parker & Son.
California Corporation Laws: Including Current Changes to 1980, 6 vols. R. Bradbury Clark. LC 63-47230. 1980. 350.00 (ISBN 0-911110-00-3). Parker & Son.
California Corporations Code & Corporate Securities Rules. Editorial Staff. 1981. pap. 14.50 (ISBN 0-911110-14-3). Parker & Son.
California County Boundaries. rev. ed. Owen C. Coy. (Illus.). 1973. Repr. 9.95 (ISBN 0-913548-14-6, Valley Calif). Western Tanager.
California Courtroom Evidence. Fulton Haight & Joseph W. Cotchett. LC 72-79475. 375p. 1981. 27.50 (ISBN 0-911110-07-0); 1979 suppl. incl. (ISBN 0-685-26721-0). Parker & Son.
California Coven Project. Bob Stickgold. 192p. 1981. pap. 2.25 (ISBN 0-345-28677-4, Del Rey). Ballantine.
California Crazy. Alan Cartnal. LC 80-27315. 256p. 1981. 9.95 (ISBN 0-395-28213-6). HM.
California Crazy: Roadside Vernacular Architecture. Rip Georges & Jim Heimann. LC 79-24181. (Illus.). 144p. (Orig.). 1980. pap. 7.95 (ISBN 0-87701-171-0). Chronicle Bks.
California Criminal Law: A Guide for Policemen. C. A. Pantaleoni & James C. Bigler. 1969. text ed. 16.95 (ISBN 0-13-112565-6). P-H.
California Criminal Law Manual. 5th ed. Derald D. Hunt. 240p. 1980. pap. 12.95 (ISBN 0-8087-3178-5). Burgess.
California Criminal Procedure. 8th ed. Charles W. Fricke & Arthur L. Alarcon. LC 73-80491. 1981. 16.00x (ISBN 0-910874-26-3). Legal Bk Corp.
California Damages, Law & Proof. 2nd ed. Leland Johns. LC 77-89697. 1977. 49.50 (ISBN 0-911110-24-0); 1980 suppl. incl. Parker & Son.
California Debtor's Handbook. 4th ed. Ralph Warner & Peter Honigsberg. 1981. pap. 6.95 (ISBN 0-917316-34-7). Nolo Pr.
California Debtor's Handbook. 3rd ed. Ralph Warner & Peter Honigsberg. 1979. pap. 5.95 (ISBN 0-917316-14-2). Nolo Pr.
California Desert Wildflowers. Philip A. Munz. (Illus., Orig.). 1962. 14.50 (ISBN 0-520-00898-7); pap. 3.95 (ISBN 0-520-00899-5). U of Cal Pr.
California Dreamers. Norman Bogner. 1981. 13.95 (ISBN 0-671-42877-2, Wyndham Bks). S&S.
California Energy Futures: Two Alternative Societal Scenarios & Their Energy Implications - Consultant Report. SRI International. 206p. 1981. pap. 24.50 (ISBN 0-89934-094-6). Solar Energy Info.
California Environment & Energy. Ed. by Ed Salzman. LC 80-66476. (Illus.). 96p. (Orig.). 1980. pap. text ed. 4.95 (ISBN 0-930302-23-0). Cal Journal.
California Evidence Code. 1981. 9.00 (ISBN 0-911110-15-1). Parker & Son.
California Evidence Code. LC 78-78300. 1981. pap. text ed. 4.00x (ISBN 0-910874-48-4). Legal Bk Corp.
California Factor. Patricia Vernier. (Orig.). 1980. pap. 2.75 (ISBN 0-440-10989-2). Dell.
California Family Law Handbook. L. Ryder Mason. LC 79-90704. 1980. 36.00 (ISBN 0-911110-31-3); 1980 suppl. incl. Parker & Son.
California Fractional Gold. David Doering & Susan Doering. (Illus.). 1980. lib. bdg. 60.00 (ISBN 0-686-64452-2). S J Durst.
California Gas & Oil Exploration: 1963 Annual. 1964. 30.00 (ISBN 0-686-28263-9). Munger Oil.
California Generation. Jacqueline Briskin. 1980. pap. 2.75 (ISBN 0-446-95146-3). Warner Bks.
California Gold Rush. Ralph K. Andrist & Archibald Hanna. LC 61-10677. (American Heritage Junior Library). (Illus.). 153p. (gr. 5 up). 1961. 9.95 (ISBN 0-8281-0388-7, JO06-0). Am Heritage.
California Gold: The Beginning of Mining in the Far West. Rodman W. Paul. LC 47-54111. (Illus.). 1965. pap. 3.95 (ISBN 0-8032-5149-1, BB 313, Bison). U of Nebr Pr.
California Government & Politics. 6th ed. W. W. Crouch et al. 1977. pap. text ed. 8.95 (ISBN 0-13-112458-7). P-H.
California Government & Politics. 7th ed. Winston W. Crouch et al. (Illus.). 288p. 1981. pap. 8.95 (ISBN 0-13-112433-1). P-H.
California Government & Politics Annual, 1980-81. Ed. by Thomas R. Hoeber et al. (Illus.). 128p. (Orig.). 1980. pap. text ed. 3.95x (ISBN 0-930302-24-9). Cal Journal.
California Government & Politics Today. 3rd ed. Charles P. Sohner. 1979. pap. text ed. 4.95x (ISBN 0-673-15242-1). Scott F.
California Government: The Challenge of Change. Noel J. Stowe. 1975. pap. text ed. 5.95x (ISBN 0-02-478720-5, 47872); test bk. free (ISBN 0-685-52459-0, 47871). Macmillan.

California Government Today: Politics of Reform. Charles G. Bell & Charles M. Price. 1980. pap. 9.95x (ISBN 0-256-02185-6). Dorsey.
California Handbook: A Comprehensive Guide to Sources of Current Information & Action. 4th ed. Ed. by Thaddeus C. Trzyna. LC 75-171691. (California Information Guides). (Illus., Orig.). 1981. pap. 20.00x (ISBN 0-912102-44-6). Cal Inst Public.
California Heritage Cookbook. Pasadena Junior League. LC 75-42495. 256p. 1976. 11.95 (ISBN 0-385-03995-6). Doubleday.
California High School Proficiency Examination. Arco Editorial Board. LC 78-4628. 1978. pap. text ed. 6.00 (ISBN 0-668-04412-8, 4412). Arco.
California Iceberg. Harry Harrison. LC 74-78109. (Illus.). 128p. (gr. 3-7). 1975. 5.95 o.s.i. (ISBN 0-8027-6194-1). Walker & Co.
California Indians Five: Sagebrush Corner - Opening of California's Northeast. W. N. Davis. (American Indian Ethnohistory Ser: California & Basin - Plateau Indians). (Illus.). lib. bdg. 42.00 (ISBN 0-8240-0775-1). Garland Pub.
California Indians Four. Harold E. Driver et al. Ed. by David A. Horr. (American Indian Ethnohistory Ser.). 1978. lib. bdg. 42.00 (ISBN 0-8240-0774-3). Garland Pub.
California Indians One: Indians Land Use & Occupancy in California, 3 vols. Harold Driver et al. Ed. by Ralph L. Beals. (American Indian Ethnohistory Ser: California & Basin-Plateau Indians). (Illus.). lib. bdg. 42.00 (ISBN 0-8240-0771-9). Garland Pub.
California Indians Six. Ralph L. Beals. Ed. by David A. Horr. (American Indian Ethnohistory Ser.). 1978. lib. bdg. 42.00 (ISBN 0-8240-0776-X). Garland Pub.
California Indians Three. Erminie Wheeler-Voegelin et al. Ed. by David A. Horr. (American Indian Ethnohistory Ser.). 1978. lib. bdg. 42.00 (ISBN 0-8240-0773-5). Garland Pub.
California Indians Two. Robert F. Heizer. Ed. by David A. Horr. (American Indian Ethnohistory Ser.). 1978. lib. bdg. 42.00 (ISBN 0-8240-0772-7). Garland Pub.
California Indians Vs the U. S. A. Robert F Heizer. (Ballena Press Publications in Archaeology, Ethnology & History Ser.: No. 12). 1979. pap. 5.95 o.p. (ISBN 0-87919-080-9). Ballena Pr.
California Insects. Jerry A. Powell & Charles L. Hogue. (Illus.). 1980. 15.95 (ISBN 0-520-03806-1); pap. 7.95 (ISBN 0-520-03782-0). U of Cal Pr.
California Inter Pocula. Hubert H. Bancroft. LC 67-29422. (Works of Hubert Howe Bancroft Ser.). 1967. Repr. of 1888 ed. 25.00x (ISBN 0-914888-28-5). Bancroft Pr.
California International Trade Register. Ed. by John G. Davis & Phyllis Newman. 750p. 1980. pap. 59.95 (ISBN 0-911510-82-6). Times-M Pr.
California Islands: Proceedings of a Multidisciplinary Symposium. Ed. by Dennis M. Power. LC 80-463. 787p. (Orig.). 1980. pap. text ed. 20.00 (ISBN 0-936494-01-8). Santa Barbara Mus Nat Hist.
California Jewish History: Descriptive Bibliography. Norton B. Stern. 1967. 17.50 o.p. (ISBN 0-87062-056-8). A H Clark.
California Labor Code. 1981. 12.00 (ISBN 0-911110-29-1). Parker & Son.
California: Land of New Beginnings. David Lavender. LC 70-181630. (Regions of America Ser.). (Illus.). 512p. (YA) 1972. 14.95 o.p. (ISBN 0-06-012524-1, HarpT). Har-Row.
California Law Guide. Dan Henke. LC 76-19950. 1976. 50.00 (ISBN 0-911110-21-6); 1980 suppl. incl. Parker & Son.
California Manufacturers Register 1980. 33rd ed. Group-Effort. Ed. by Phyllis Newman. LC 48-3418. 1980. 77.50 o.s.i. (ISBN 0-911510-80-X). Times-M Pr.
California Manufacturers Register, 1981. 34th rev. ed. Ed. by John G. Davis & Phyllis Newman. LC 48-3418. 880p. 1981. 85.00 (ISBN 0-911510-83-4). Times-M Pr.
California Marriage & Divorce Law. 4th ed. Ralph Warner & Toni Ihara. 1981. pap. 7.95 (ISBN 0-917316-16-9). Nolo Pr.
California Mechanics' Lien Law Handbook. 3rd ed. Matthew E. Marsh. LC 72-83952. 1979. 46.00 (ISBN 0-911110-30-5); 1980 suppl. incl. (ISBN 0-685-44105-9). Parker & Son.
California Missions. 2nd ed. Sunset Editors. LC 79-88016. (Illus.). 320p. 1979. pap. 8.95 (ISBN 0-376-05171-X, Sunset Bks). Sunset-Lane.
California Notary Law Primer. 3rd ed. Editors of The National Notary Magazine of the National Notary Assn. 1980. pap. 5.95 (ISBN 0-933134-00-2). Natl Notary.
California Oath Controversy. David P. Gardner. 1967. 17.50x (ISBN 0-520-00455-8). U of Cal Pr.
California Oil & Gas Exploration: 1960 Edition. 1961. 30.00 (ISBN 0-686-28261-2). Munger Oil.
California Oil & Gas Exploration: 1962 Annual. 1963. 30.00 (ISBN 0-686-28262-0). Munger Oil.
California Oil & Gas Exploration: 1964 Annual. 1965. 30.00 (ISBN 0-686-28264-7). Munger Oil.
California Oil & Gas Exploration: 1965 Annual. 1966. 30.00 (ISBN 0-686-28265-5). Munger Oil.
California Oil & Gas Exploration: 1966 Annual. 1967. 30.00 (ISBN 0-686-28266-3). Munger Oil.
California Oil & Gas Exploration: 1967 Annual. 1968. 30.00 (ISBN 0-686-28267-1). Munger Oil.
California Oil & Gas Exploration: 1968 Annual. 1969. 30.00 (ISBN 0-686-28268-X). Munger Oil.
California Paralegal's Handbook. Zella Mack. LC 77-71561. 1977. incl. 1980 suppl. 38.00 (ISBN 0-911110-23-2). Parker & Son.
California: People, Politics, & Government. Katherine Wallace. (Orig.). (gr. 11-12). 1976. pap. text ed. 6.25 (ISBN 0-87720-612-0). AMSCO Sch.
California Pioneers: Tales of Explorers, Indians, & Settlers. Margaret Roberts. (Illus.). 1981. 7.95 (ISBN 0-914598-42-2). Padre Prods.
California Probate Code. 1981. 9.00x (ISBN 0-911110-16-X). Parker & Son.
California Probate Procedure, 3 vols. 4th ed. Arthur K. Marshall. 1979. looseleaf 135.00 (ISBN 0-911110-28-3). Parker & Son.
California Prsonnel Managers Guide to EEO Laws. Simmons. 1980. pap. 25.00 (ISBN 0-917386-40-X). Exec Ent.
California Real Estate Appraisal: Residential Properties. 2nd ed. George H. Miller et al. LC 77-5121. (Illus.). 1977. ref. ed. 18.95 (ISBN 0-13-112599-0). P-H.
California Real Estate Law. Philip B. Bergfield. 1974. text ed. 16.50x o.p. (ISBN 0-256-01571-6). Irwin.
California Real Estate Law: Text & Cases. J. Gordon. (Illus.). 1980. pap. text ed. 14.50 (ISBN 0-13-112524-9). P-H.
California Real Estate Practice. 3rd. ed. Hyman M. Berston. 1977. text ed. 17.95x (ISBN 0-256-01929-0). Irwin.
California Real Estate Principles. 3rd. ed. Hyman M. Berston. 1979. text ed. 17.95x (ISBN 0-256-02149-X). Irwin.
California Real Estate Principles. Dennis J. McKenzie. 416p. 1980. text ed. 13.95 (ISBN 0-471-06316-9). Wiley.
California Real Estate Principles. Dennis J. McKenzie et al. LC 80-23243. (California Real Estate Ser.). 352p. 1981. text ed. 17.95 (ISBN 0-471-01729-9). Wiley.
California Renewable Energy Information Series, 6 vols. California Energy Commission. Incl. Vol. 1. Exploring New Energy Sources for California: The 1980-81 Report of the Legislature. 106p. pap. 17.95 (ISBN 0-89934-085-7); Vol. 2. Comparative Evaluation of Nontraditional Energy Sources. 122p. pap. 17.95 (ISBN 0-89934-086-5); Vol. 3. Wind Energy Overview: Wind-Elastic Power, Wind Energy Program Progress Report & Wind Resource Assessment. 104p. pap. 17.95 (ISBN 0-89934-087-3); Vol. 4. Impact of Large Wind Energy Systems in California. 200p. pap. 19.95 (ISBN 0-89934-088-1); Vol. 5. Solar & Wind Programs, Final Environmental Impact Reports. 195p. pap. 24.50 (ISBN 0-89934-110-1); Vol. 6. Program Plan for the Maximum Implementation of Solar Energy Through 1990. pap. 24.50 (ISBN 0-89934-109-8). 1981. pap. Solar Energy Info.
California Rich. Stephen Birmingham. 1980. 13.95 (ISBN 0-671-24127-3). S&S.
California Services Register, 1981. 2nd ed. Ed. by John G. Davis & Phyllis Newman. 680p. 1981. 60.00 (ISBN 0-911510-84-2). Times-M Pr.
California Slavic Studies, 7 vols. Ed. by Nicholas V. Riasanovsky & Gleb Struve. Incl. Vol. I. 1960 (ISBN 0-520-09037-3); Vol. II. 1963 (ISBN 0-520-09038-1); Vol. V. 1970 (ISBN 0-520-09043-8); Vol. VII. 1974 (ISBN 0-520-09485-9); Vol. VIII. 1975 (ISBN 0-520-09519-7); Vol. IX. 1976 (ISBN 0-520-09541-3); Vol. X. 1977 (ISBN 0-520-09564-2). (Vols. I, II pap. only). Set. 15.75 (ISBN 0-686-63969-3). U of Cal Pr.
California Solar Business Directory. Ed. by J. Yudelson & M. Kitchin. 194p. 1980. pap. 12.00 (ISBN 0-89934-045-8, V055-PD). Solar Energy Info.
California Spring Wildflowers: From the Base of the Sierra Nevada & Southern Mountains to the Sea. Philip A. Munz. (Orig.). 1961. 6.50x o.p. (ISBN 0-520-00895-2); pap. 4.95 (ISBN 0-520-00896-0). U of Cal Pr.
California Story & Coloring Book. Ludwig & Bernal. (Illus.). 32p. (Orig.). pap. 2.50 (ISBN 0-930504-01-1). Polaris Pr.
California Studies in Classical Antiquity, Vol. 12. Ed. by William S. Anderson & Jaan Puhvel. LC 68-26906. (Illus.). 400p. 1981. 15.00x (ISBN 0-520-04055-4). U of Cal Pr.
California Thriller. Max Byrd. 224p. (Orig.). 1981. pap. 2.25 (ISBN 0-553-14508-8). Bantam.
California Through Five Centuries. Katherine Wallace. (gr. 7-12). 1974. pap. text ed. 7.17 (ISBN 0-87720-607-4). AMSCO Sch.
California Tomorrow Plan. Ed. by Alfred Heller. LC 72-85217. (Illus.). 120p. 1972. 5.95 (ISBN 0-913232-01-7). W Kaufmann.
California Uniform Commercial Code. 1980. 8.00 (ISBN 0-911110-17-8). Parker & Son.
California Uninsured Motorist Law Handbook. 3rd ed. Paul Eisler. 1979. 1980 suppl. incl. 60.00 (ISBN 0-911110-27-5). Parker & Son.
California Votes, Nineteen Sixty to Nineteen Seventy-Two: A Review & Analysis of Registration & Voting. new ed. Eugene C. Lee & Bruce E. Keith. LC 74-12271. (Illus.). 172p. 1974. 7.50x (ISBN 0-87772-201-3); 1974 supplement 1.50x (ISBN 0-685-51351-3). Inst Gov Stud Berk.
California Wasps of the Subfamily Philanthinae (Hymenoptera-Specidae) R. M. Bohart & E. E. Grissell. (Bulletin of the California Insect Survey: Vol. 19). 1975. pap. 9.00x (ISBN 0-520-09523-5). U of Cal Pr.
California Water: A New Political Economy. Merrill Goodall et al. LC 77-88255. 128p. 1978. text ed. 18.00 (ISBN 0-916672-86-7). Allanheld.
California Water: A Study in Resource Management. Ed. by David Seckler. LC 76-139773. 1971. 35.00x (ISBN 0-520-01884-2); pap. 7.95 o.p. (ISBN 0-520-02778-7). U of Cal Pr.
California: Where the Twain Did Meet. Anne Loftis. LC 72-11278. 324p. 1973. 7.95 o.s.i. (ISBN 0-02-574100-4). Macmillan.
California Wine Industry: A Study of the Formative Years, 1830-1895. Vincent P. Carosso. (California Library Reprint Ser). 1976. 18.50x (ISBN 0-520-03178-4). U of Cal Pr.
California Woman. Daniel Knapp. (Orig.). 1980. pap. 2.50 o.s.i. (ISBN 0-440-11035-1). Dell.
California Workers' Compensation Law Handbook, 2 vols. Stanford D. Herlick. 1981. Set. incl. 1979 suppl. 92.00 (ISBN 0-911110-25-9). Parker & Son.
California Worker's Compensation Rehabilitation System. Irene Sanchez et al. LC 80-70211. (Illus.). 360p. 1981. 35.00 (ISBN 0-02-927670-5). Macmillan.
California's Architectural Frontier. Harold Kirker. LC 73-77786. (In Search of California Ser). (Illus.). 1973. pap. 4.95 o.s.i. (ISBN 0-87905-011-X). Peregrine Smith.
California's Prodigal Sons: Hiram Johnson & the Progressives. Spencer C. Olin, Jr. 1968. 14.75 (ISBN 0-520-00973-8). U of Cal Pr.
California's Railroad Era Eighteen-Fifty to-Nineteen Eleven. Ward McAfee. LC 73-18280. (Illus.). 296p. 10.95 (ISBN 0-87095-048-7). Golden West.
California's Spanish Place-Names: What They Mean & How They Got There. Barbara Marinacci & Rudy Marinacci. LC 80-11381. (Illus.). 1980. pap. 6.95 (ISBN 0-89141-102-X). Presidio Pr.
Californio. Robert MacLeod. 1979. pap. 1.75 o.p. (ISBN 0-449-14301-5, GM). Fawcett.
Caligula. William Howard. (Illus., Orig.). 1979. pap. 2.50 (ISBN 0-446-91799-0). Warner Bks.
Calila y Digna. (Span.). 7.95 (ISBN 84-241-5618-8). E Torres & Sons.
Calix Stay. Niel Hancock. (Circle of Light Ser.: No. 3). 1977. pap. 2.25 (ISBN 0-445-04047-5). Popular Lib.
Call Adonoi: Manual of Practical Cabalah & Gestalt Mysticism. Albert Schutz. 114p. 1980. pap. 8.95. Ross-Erikson.
Call Adonoi: Manual of Practical Cabalah & Gestalt Mysticism. Albert L. Schutz. Ed. by Anne N. Lowenkopf. LC 80-50264. 200p. (Orig.). 1980. 11.95 (ISBN 0-936596-01-5); pap. 8.95 (ISBN 0-936596-00-7). Quantal.
Call Collect, Ask for Birdman. James Vardaman. (Illus.). 256p. 1980. 10.95 (ISBN 0-312-11425-7). St Martin.
Call for Mr. Sniff. Thomas P. Lewis. LC 79-2679. (I Can Read Bks.). (Illus.). 64p. (gr. k-3). 1981. 6.95 (ISBN 0-06-023814-3, HarpJ); PLB 7.89g (ISBN 0-06-023815-1). Har-Row.
Call for the Destruction of Nixon & Praise for the Chilean Revolution. Pablo Neruda. Tr. by Teresa Anderson. LC 80-53809. (Illus.). 80p. (Orig.). 1980. pap. 3.25 (ISBN 0-931122-22-8). West End.
Call for the Saint. Leslie Charteris. (Saint Ser.). 224p. 1981. pap. 2.25 (ISBN 0-441-09151-2). Charter Bks.
Call from Hibakusha of Hiroshima & Nagasaki: Proceedings of the International Symposium on the Damage & After-Effects of the Atomic Bombing of Hiroshima & Nagasaki, 21 July - 9 August 1977, Tokyo, Hiroshima & Nagasaki. Japan National Preparatory Committee. (Illus.). 1979. pap. 37.00 (ISBN 0-08-024306-1). Pergamon.
Call Home the Heart. Jessica Stirling. LC 76-28059. 416p. 1977. 8.95 o.p. (ISBN 0-312-11427-3). St Martin.
Call It Courage. Armstrong Sperry. (gr. 4-6). 1940. 8.95 (ISBN 0-02-786030-2). Macmillan.
Call It Right! Umpiring in the Little League. Morris A. Shirts & Kent E. Myers. LC 76-51169. (Illus.). 1977. 7.95 (ISBN 0-8069-4108-1); lib. bdg. 7.49 (ISBN 0-8069-4109-X). Sterling.
Call It Treason. George Howe. LC 80-15043. (Great Classic Stories of World War II Ser.). 1980. 8.95 (ISBN 0-396-07870-2); pap. 5.95 (ISBN 0-396-07871-0). Dodd.
Call Me Al Raft. Richard Shaw. LC 75-16313. 160p. (YA) (gr. 6 up). 1975. 7.95 (ISBN 0-525-66464-5). Elsevier-Nelson.
Call Me Counselor. Sara Halbert & Florence Stevenson. 1978. 8.95 o.p. (ISBN 0-397-01239-X). Lippincott.
Call Me Heller, That's My Name. Stella Pevsner. LC 72-90084. (Illus.). 192p. (gr. 3-6). 1973. 7.95 (ISBN 0-395-28874-6, Clarion). HM.
Call Me Margo. Judith St. George. 156p. (gr. 10 up). 1981. 7.95 (ISBN 0-399-20790-2). Putnam.
Call of Destiny: The Epic of the American Republic. Hamilton P. Traub. LC 79-52732. (Illus.). 614p. 1980. 14.95x (ISBN 0-9605364-0-X); pap. 9.95x. Golden Hill.
Call of Gold. Newell D. Chamberlain. (Illus.). 185p. 1981. pap. 5.95 (ISBN 0-934136-12-2). Western Tanager.
Call of San Saba: A History of San Saba Country. Alma W. Namrick. 12.50 (ISBN 0-685-64413-8). Jenkins.
Call of the Heart. Barbara Corcoran. (Orig.). 1981. pap. 1.95 (ISBN 0-345-28668-5). Ballantine.
Call of the Jagadguru. Srngeri Sankaracharya. Ed. by R. Krishnaswami Aiyar. 1961. pap. 1.75 o.p. (ISBN 0-89744-128-1, Pub. by Ganesh & Co India). Auromere.
Call of the Range. Nellie S. Yost. LC 66-30428. 437p. 1966. 16.95 (ISBN 0-8040-0028-X, SB). Swallow.
Call of the Wild. Jack London. (gr. 6 up). 1963. 7.95 (ISBN 0-02-759510-2). Macmillan.
Call of the Wild. Jack London. (Literature Ser). (gr. 7-12). 1969. pap. text ed. 3.33 (ISBN 0-87720-704-6). AMSCO Sch.
Call of the Wild & Selected Stories. Jack London. (RL 6). 1971. pap. 1.75 (ISBN 0-451-51383-5, CE1383, Sig Classics). NAL.
Call of the Wild, White Fang & Other Stories. Jack London. Ed. by Andrew Sinclair. (Penguin American Classics). (Orig.). 1980. pap. 2.95 (ISBN 0-14-039001-4). Penguin.
Call of the Wild with Reader's Guide. Jack London. (Literature Program). (gr. 10-12). 1970. pap. text ed. 3.92 (ISBN 0-87720-804-2); tchrs' ed. 2.60 (ISBN 0-87720-904-9). AMSCO Sch.
Call the Darkness Light. Nancy Zaroulis, 1980. pap. 2.95 (ISBN 0-451-09291-0, E9291, Sig). NAL.
Call to Seriousness: The Evangelical Impact on the Victorians. Ian C. Bradley. LC 75-44282. (Illus.). 288p. 1976. 12.95 o.s.i. (ISBN 0-02-514420-0, 51442). Macmillan.
Call to the Nations: Extracts from the Writings of Shoghi Effendi. Shoghi Effendi. LC 79-670140. 1978. 5.00 (ISBN 0-85398-068-3, 7-08-50); pap. 2.50 (ISBN 0-85398-069-1, 7-08-51). Baha'i.
Callahan. Ed. by John Szarkowski. (Illus.). 1979. pap. 19.50 o.p. (ISBN 0-912334-76-2). Aperture.
Callahan. Intro. by John Szarkowski. LC 76-42104. (Illus.). 1976. 35.00 o.p. (ISBN 0-912334-75-4); ltd. ed. o.p 400.00 o.p. (ISBN 0-89381-010-X). Aperture.
Callahan Rides Alone. Lee Floren. 1977. pap. 1.50 (ISBN 0-505-51206-8). Tower Bks.
Callahan, the Last War Bird. Marvin L. Skelton. 1980. pap. 19.00 (ISBN 0-89126-081-1). Military Aff Aero.
Callaloo & Pastelles Too. Ruth B. Adams. LC 73-93096. 1973. 4.95 o.p. (ISBN 0-8163-0129-8, 03022-1). Pacific Pr Pub Assn.
Callander Square. Anne Perry. 256p. 1981. pap. 2.25 (ISBN 0-449-24365-6, Crest). Fawcett.
Called & Chosen: The Story of Mother Rebecca Jackson & the Philadelphia Shakers. Richard E. Williams. LC 80-25498. (ATLA Monograph Ser.: No. 17). 193p. 1981. 11.00 (ISBN 0-8108-1382-3). Scarecrow.
Called Away. Perdita Buchan. 1980. 10.95 (ISBN 0-316-11407-3, Pub. by Atlantic-Little Brown). Little.

Called for Traveling. Jim McGregor & Ron Rapoport. (Illus.). 1978. 12.95 (ISBN 0-02-583350-2). Macmillan.

Called to Account: The Public Accounts Committee of the House of Commons. Vilma Flegmann. 328p. 1980. text ed. 31.50x (ISBN 0-566-00371-6, Pub. by Gower Pub Co England). Renouf.

Called to Be Friends. Paula Ripple. LC 80-67402. 160p. (Orig.). 1980. pap. 3.95 (ISBN 0-87793-212-3). Ave Maria.

Called to Holy Worldliness. Richard J. Mouw. Ed. by Mark Gibbs. LC 80-8047. (Laity Exchange). 160p. (Orig.). 1980. pap. 5.50 (ISBN 0-8006-1397-X, 1-1397). Fortress.

Called to World: Called to Holy Worldliness. Richard J. Mouw. 1980. pap. 5.95 (ISBN 0-529-05741-7, Pub. by Collins Pubs). Fortress.

Calligrammes. Guillaume Apollinaire. Tr. by Anne H. Greet. 600p. (Fr. & Eng.). 1980. 19.95 (ISBN 0-520-01968-7). U of Cal Pr.

Calligrapher's Reference Book. Anne Leptich & Jacque Evans. pap. 6.00 (ISBN 0-87980-386-X). Wilshire.

Calligraphic Alphabets. Arthur Baker. LC 79-8223. (Pictorial Archive Ser.). (Illus.). 160p. (Orig.). 1974. pap. 4.50 (ISBN 0-486-21045-6). Dover.

Calligraphy. Arthur Baker. (Illus.). 10.00 (ISBN 0-8446-4619-9). Peter Smith.

Calligraphy & Palaeography. Ed. by A. S. Osley. 1965. 19.95 o.p. (ISBN 0-571-06499-X, Pub. by Faber & Faber). Merrimack Bk Serv.

Calligraphy for Fun & Profit. Anne Leptich & Jacque Evans. pap. 6.00 (ISBN 0-87980-385-1). Wilshire.

Calligraphy in the Copperplate Style. Geri Homelsky & Herb Kaufman. (Illus.). 50p. (Orig.). 1981. pap. 1.75 (ISBN 0-486-24037-1). Dover.

Calling All Beginners - a Basic Course in English for Arabic Speaking People. David Hicks. 1976. 14.00x (ISBN 0-917062-01-9). Intl Bk Ctr.

Calling All Girls Party Book. Rubie Saunders. LC 66-10017. (Illus.). (gr. 3-8). 1966. 5.95 o.s.i. (ISBN 0-8193-0131-0, Four Winds); PLB 5.41 o.s.i. (ISBN 0-8193-0132-9). Schol Bk Serv.

Calling Dr. Horowitz. Steve Horowitz & Neil Offen. 1978. pap. 1.95 o.s.i. (ISBN 0-515-04509-8). Jove Pubns.

Calling of Bara. Sheila Sullivan. 304p. 1981. pap. 2.50 (ISBN 0-380-53785-0, 53785). Avon.

Calling: Stories. Mary G. Hughes. LC 80-20981. (Illinois Short Fiction Ser.). 130p. 1980. 10.00 (ISBN 0-252-00842-1); pap. 3.95 (ISBN 0-252-00843-X). U of Ill Pr.

Calling to Mind: An Account of the First Hundred Years of Steel Brothers & Company Ltd. Ed. by H. E. Braund. (Illus.). 1976. 25.00 (ISBN 0-08-017415-9). Pergamon.

Callot's Etchings. Jacques Callot. Ed. by Howard Daniel. (Illus., Orig.). 1974. 10.00 (ISBN 0-486-23081-3); pap. 6.00 (ISBN 0-486-23073-2). Dover.

Calm & Clear. Lama Mi-pham. LC 73-79058. (Tibetan Translation Ser., Vol. 1). (Illus.). 128p. 1973. pap. 4.95 (ISBN 0-913546-02-X). Dharma Pub.

Calming the Mind & Discerning the Real. Alex Wayman. Tr. by Alex Wayman from Sanskrit. (Translations from the Oriental Classics Ser.). 1978. 30.00x (ISBN 0-231-04404-6). Columbia U Pr.

Calor. Harlan Wade. Tr. by Mamie M. Contreras from Eng. LC 78-26916. (Book About Ser.). Orig. Title: Heat. (Illus., Sp.). (gr. k-3). 1979. PLB 7.30 (ISBN 0-8172-1487-9). Raintree Pubs.

Calorie Counter for Six Quick-Loss Diets. William I. Kaufman. 1973. pap. 1.25 o.p. (ISBN 0-515-04903-4, 9137). Jove Pubns.

Calorie Guide to Brand Names. William I. Kaufman. 1973. pap. 1.25 o.p. (ISBN 0-515-04905-0, 9177). Jove Pubns.

Calories & Carbohydrates. 4th, rev. ed. Barbara Kraus. 1981. pap. 5.95 (Z5267, Plume). NAL.

Calories & Carbohydrates. 4th, rev. ed. Barbara Kraus. (Orig.). 1981. pap. 3.50 (ISBN 0-451-09774-2, E9774, Sig). NAL.

Calories & Carbohydrates. rev. ed. Barbara Kraus. 1980. pap. 4.95 (ISBN 0-452-25207-5, 25207, Plume). NAL.

Calories Don't Count When... Sara Parriott. 1979. pap. 2.95 o.p. (ISBN 0-312-90453-3); prepack 29.50 o.p. (ISBN 0-312-90454-1). St Martin.

Calories Don't Count When... Sara Parriott. LC 79-84900. (Illus.). 96p. 1979. pap. 2.95 (ISBN 0-87477-105-6). J P Tarcher.

Calories in - Calories Out Calorie Counter: The Calorie Counter That Counts Both Ways. James Leisy. 96p. (Orig.). 1980. pap. 3.95 (ISBN 0-8289-0401-4). Greene.

Calories in - Calories Out Diary: A Daily Program for Fitness & Weight Control. James Leisy. 256p. (Orig.). 1980. pap. 9.95 (ISBN 0-8289-0412-X). Greene.

Calories in - Calories Out: The Energy Budget Way to Fitness & Weight Control. James Leisy. 128p. 1980. 10.95 (ISBN 0-8289-0413-8); pap. 6.95 (ISBN 0-8289-0414-6). Greene.

Calumny of Apelles: A Study in the Humanist Tradition. David Cast. LC 80-26378. (Publication in the History of Art Ser.: No. 28). (Illus.). 320p. 1981. text ed. 32.50x (ISBN 0-300-02575-0). Yale U Pr.

Calus: Symbolic Transformation in Romanian Ritual. Gail Kligman. LC 80-21372. (Chicago Originals Ser.). (Illus.). 240p. 1981. lib. bdg. 12.00x (ISBN 0-226-44221-7). U of Chicago Pr.

Calvario De Mi Madre. 1981. 8.95 (ISBN 0-686-65726-8); pap. 5.95 span. ed. o.p. (ISBN 0-686-65727-6). Racz Pub.

Calvin, 2 vols. Ed. by John T. McNeil & Institutes of the Christian Religion. (Library of Christian Classics Ser.). 1960. Set. 25.00 (ISBN 0-686-67721-8). Vol. 20 (ISBN 0-664-22020-7). Vol.21 (ISBN 0-664-22021-5). Westminster.

Calvin & Augustine. Benjamin B. Warfield. 1954. 7.95 (ISBN 0-87552-526-1). Presby & Reformed.

Calvin Coolidge. Donald R. McCoy. 1967. 8.95 o.s.i. (ISBN 0-02-583020-1). Macmillan.

Calvinisim & the Religious Wars. Franklin C. Palm. LC 78-80579. 1971. Repr. 12.50 (ISBN 0-86527-020-1). Fertig.

Calvinism & the Amyraut Heresy: Protestant Scholasticism & Humanism in Seventeenth-Century France. Brian G. Armstrong. LC 72-84949. (Illus.). 1969. 27.50 (ISBN 0-299-05490-X). U of Wis Pr.

Calvinist Preaching & Iconoclasm in the Netherlands, 1544-1569. P. Mack Crew. LC 77-77013. (Studies in Early Modern History). 1978. 32.95 (ISBN 0-521-21739-3). Cambridge U Pr.

Calvinistic Temper in English Poetry. James D. Boulger. (De Proprietatibus Litterarum, Ser. Major: No. 21). 1980. text ed. 70.50x (ISBN 90-279-7575-2). Mouton.

Calvin's & the Puritan's View of the Protestant Ethic. Robert M. Mitchell. LC 79-66537. 1979. pap. text ed. 7.00 (ISBN 0-8191-0842-1). U Pr of Amer.

Calvin's Letters. John Calvin. pap. 4.95 (ISBN 0-686-28946-3). Banner of Truth.

Cam Jansen & the Mystery of the Dinosaur Bones. David A Adlr. (Cam Jansen Adventure Ser.). (Illus.). 64p. (gr. 2-5). 1981. 5.95 (ISBN 0-670-20040-9). Viking Pr.

Cam Jansen & the Mystery of the U.F.O. David A. Adler. (Cam Jansen Ser.). (Illus.). 64p. (gr. 7-10). 1980. 4.95 (ISBN 0-670-20041-7). Viking Pr.

Camaro! Chevy's Classy Chassis. Ray Miller. (Illus.). 320p. 1981. write for info. (ISBN 0-913056-10-3). Evergreen Pr.

Camaro Service-Repair Handbook: All Models, 1967-1979. Jim Combs. Ed. by Eric Jorgensen. (Illus.). 1978. pap. 10.95 (ISBN 0-89287-226-8, A136). Clymer Pubns.

Camber of Culdi. Katherine Kurtz. 336p. 1976. pap. 1.95 o.p. (ISBN 0-345-24590-3). Ballantine.

Cambio y Desarrollo En Puerto Rico: La Transformacion Ideologica Del Partido Popular Democratico. Ed. by Gerardo Navas. LC 77-4483. (Planning Ser: G-2). 1978. pap. 10.00 (ISBN 0-8477-2435-2). U of PR Pr.

Cambises: A Critical Edition. Thomas Preston. Ed. by Robert C. Johnson. (Salzburg Studies in English Literature, Elizabethan & Renaissance Studies Ser.: No. 23). 193p. (Orig.). 1975. pap. text ed. 25.00x (ISBN 0-391-01502-8). Humanities.

Cambodia File. Jack Anderson & Bill Pronzini. LC 80-5447. 456p. 1981. 13.95 (ISBN 0-385-14984-0). Doubleday.

Cambodia: Holocaust in Asia. Sobel. 200p. 1981. lib. bdg. 17.50 (ISBN 0-87196-209-8). Facts on File. Postponed.

Cambodia in the Southeast Asian War. Malcolm Caldwell & Lek Tan. LC 79-147877. (Illus.). 1972. 15.00 o.p. (ISBN 0-85345-171-0, CL1710); pap. 4.95 o.p. (ISBN 0-85345-310-1, PB3101). Monthly Rev.

Cambodia in the Southeast War. M. Caldwell. 1979. 24.50 o.p. (ISBN 0-685-67802-4). Porter.

Cambodia: Starvation & Revolution. M. Porter. 1979. 24.50 o.p. (ISBN 0-685-67801-6). Porter.

Cambodia: The Struggle for Survival. Robert J. Myers. 1980. 10.00 o.p. (ISBN 0-531-09914-8). Watts.

Cambodia's Economy & Industrial Development, Data Paper No. 113. Khieu Samphan. Tr. by Laura Summers. 129p. 1979. 6.00 (ISBN 0-87727-111-9). Cornell SE Asia.

Cambrian Bibliography: Containing an Account of Books Printed in the Welsh Language, or Relating to Wales, W. Rowlands. Ed. by Silvan D. Evans. 1970. Repr. of 1869 ed. text ed. 51.50x (ISBN 90-6041-080-7). Humanities.

Cambrian Biography; or Historical Notices of Celebrated Men Among the Ancient Britons. William Owen. Ed. by Burton Feldman & Robert Richardson. LC 78-60896. (Myth & Romanticism Ser.: Vol. 20). (Illus.). 1980. lib. bdg. 66.00 (ISBN 0-8240-3569-0). Garland Pub.

Cambridge Ancient History. Ed. by I. E. Edwards et al. Incl. Vol. 1, Pt. 1. Prolegomena & Prehistory. pap. 29.50 (ISBN 0-521-29821-0); Vol. 1, Pts. 2A & 2B. Early History of the Middle East. pap. 34.50 (ISBN 0-521-29822-9); Vol. 2, Pt. 1. The Middle East & the Aegean Region, c 1800-1380 B.C. pap. 29.50 (ISBN 0-521-29823-7); Vol. 2, Pts. 2A & 2B. The Middle East & the Aegean Region, c 1380-1000 B.C. pap. 34.50 (ISBN 0-521-29824-5). LC 75-85719. (Illus.). Date not set. Cambridge U Pr.

Cambridge Ancient History Series, 12 vols. Incl. Vol. 1, Pt. 1. Prolegomena & Prehistory. 65.00 (ISBN 0-521-07051-1); Vol. 1, Pt. 2. Early History of the Middle East. 86.00 (ISBN 0-521-07791-5); Vol. 2, Pt. 1. History of the Middle East & the Aegean Region, C.1800-1380 B.C. 75.00 (ISBN 0-521-08230-7); Vol.2, Pt. 2. 90.00 (ISBN 0-521-08691-4); Vol. 3. Assyrian Empire. 63.00 (ISBN 0-521-04485-5); Vol. 4. Persian Empire & the West. 55.00 (ISBN 0-521-04486-3); Vol. 5. Athens, Four Seventy-Eight to Four Hundred One B. C. 49.50 (ISBN 0-521-04487-1); Vol. 6. Macedon, Four Hundred One to Three Hundred One B. C. 55.00 (ISBN 0-521-04488-X); Vol. 7. Hellenistic Monarchies & Rise of Rome. 75.00 (ISBN 0-521-04489-8); Vol. 8. Rome & the Mediterranean, Two Hundred Eighteen to One Hundred Thirty-Three B.C. 67.00 (ISBN 0-521-04490-1); Vol. 9. Roman Republic, One Hundred Thirty-Three to Forty-Four B.C. 80.00 (ISBN 0-521-04491-X); Vol. 10. Augustan Empire, Forty-Four B.C.-A.D. Seventy. 80.00 (ISBN 0-521-04492-8); Vol. 11. Imperial Peace, A.D. Seventy to One Ninety-Two. 80.00 (ISBN 0-521-04493-6); Vol. 12. Imperial Crisis & Recovery, A. D. One Ninety-Three to Three Twenty-Four. 66.00 (ISBN 0-521-04494-4); Volume of Plates 1 Illustrating Vol. 1-2. 2nd ed. 36.00 (ISBN 0-521-20571-9); Volume of Plates 2 Illustrating Vols. 5-6. 2nd ed. 42.00 (ISBN 0-521-04495-2); Volume of Plates 3 Illustrating Vols. 7-8. 2nd ed. 47.00 (ISBN 0-521-04496-0); Volume of Plates 4 Illustrating Vols. 9-10. 2nd ed. 47.00 (ISBN 0-521-04497-9); Volume of Plates 5 Illustrating Vols. 11-12. 2nd ed. 33.00 (ISBN 0-521-04498-7). Cambridge U Pr.

Cambridge & Other Memories Nineteen Twenty to Nineteen Fifty-Three. Basil Willey. 1968. text ed. 5.25x (ISBN 0-7011-1430-4). Humanities.

Cambridge Apostles. P. Allen. LC 77-82482. (Illus.). 1979. 38.50 (ISBN 0-521-21803-9). Cambridge U Pr.

Cambridge Before Darwin. Martha M. Garland. LC 80-40327. 224p. 1980. 34.50 (ISBN 0-521-23319-4). Cambridge U Pr.

Cambridge Bibliography of English Literature, 5 vols. Vol. 1. 77.00 (ISBN 0-521-04499-5); Vol. 2. 84.00 (ISBN 0-521-04500-2); Vol. 3. 84.00 (ISBN 0-521-04501-0); Vol. 4. 120.00 (ISBN 0-521-08535-7); Vol. 5. 68.00 (ISBN 0-521-04503-7); Set. 300.00 (ISBN 0-521-08756-2). Cambridge U Pr.

Cambridge CAP Computer & Its Operating System. M. V. Wilkes & R. M. Needham. (Operating & Programming System Ser.: Vol. 6). 1979. 16.95 (ISBN 0-444-00357-6, North Holland); pap. 9.95 (ISBN 0-444-00358-4). Elsevier.

Cambridge Companion to Russian Studies, Vol. 1. Ed. by R. Auty & D. Obolensky. LC 75-10691. 1976. 44.50 (ISBN 0-521-20893-9); pap. 16.95 (ISBN 0-521-28038-9). Cambridge U Pr.

Cambridge Connection & the Elizabethan Settlement of Fifteen Fifty-Nine. Winthrop S. Hudson. LC 79-56513. x, 158p. 1980. 14.75 (ISBN 0-8223-0440-6). Duke.

Cambridge, Corpus Christi College Forty One: The Loricas & the Missal. Raymond J. S. Grant. (Costerus New Ser.: No. XVII). 1979. pap. 17.25x (ISBN 90-6203-762-3). Humanities.

Cambridge Economic History of Europe. Incl. Vol. 1. Agrarian Life of the Middle Ages. 71.50 (ISBN 0-521-04505-3); Vol. 2. Trade & Industry in the Middle Ages. price not set (ISBN 0-685-65802-3); Vol. 3. Economic Organization & Policies in the Middle Ages. 57.50 (ISBN 0-521-04506-1); Vol. 4. Economy of Expanding Europe in the 16th & 17th Centuries. 57.50 (ISBN 0-521-04507-X); Vol. 5. The Economic Organization of Early Europe. 71.50 (ISBN 0-521-08710-4); Vol. 6. Industrial Revolutions & After. 84.50 (ISBN 0-521-04508-8); Vol. 7, Pt. 1. Britain, France, Germany & Scandinavia. 65.50 (ISBN 0-521-21590-0); Vol. 7, Pt. 2. United States, Japan & Russia. 65.50 (ISBN 0-521-21591-9). 1965. Cambridge U Pr.

Cambridge Economic Policy Review. Wynne Godley. 76p. (Orig.). 1979. pap. 12.95 (ISBN 0-686-62424-6, Pub. by Gower Pub Co England). Lexington Bks.

Cambridge Elementary Statistical Tables. Dennis V. Lindley & Jeffrey C. Miller. 1953. text ed. 4.50x (ISBN 0-521-05564-4). Cambridge U Pr.

Cambridge Glass Book. Harold Bennett & Judy Bennett. 1970. pap. 7.95 o.p. (ISBN 0-87069-012-4). Wallace-Homestead.

Cambridge History of Africa, Vols. 2-5. Incl. Vol. 2. From ca. 500 B.C. to A.D. 1050. Ed. by J. D. Fage. 1979. 89.50 (ISBN 0-521-21592-7); Vol. 3. Ca. 1050-1600. Ed. by R. Oliver. 1977. 79.50 (ISBN 0-521-20981-1); Vol. 4. Ed. by R. Gray. 700p. 1975. 79.50 (ISBN 0-521-20413-5); Vol. 5. Ed. by J. E. Flint. 700p. 1977. 79.50 (ISBN 0-521-20701-0). LC 76-2261. (Illus.). Cambridge U Pr.

Cambridge History of China, Vol. II, Pt. 2. John K. Fairbank & Kwang-Ching Liu. LC 76-29852. (Cambridge History of China). (Illus.). 1980. 69.00 (ISBN 0-521-22029-7). Cambridge U Pr.

Cambridge History of English Literature, 15 vols. Incl. Vol. 1. From the Beginnings to the Cycles of Romance (ISBN 0-521-04515-0); Vol. 2. End of the Middle Ages (ISBN 0-521-04516-9); Vol. 3. Renaissance & Reformation (ISBN 0-521-04517-7); Vol. 4. Prose & Poetry-Sir Thomas North to Michael Drayton (ISBN 0-521-04518-5); Vol. 5. Drama to Sixteen Forty-Two: Pt. 1 (ISBN 0-521-04519-3); Vol. 6. Drama: Pt. 2 (ISBN 0-521-04520-7); Vol. 7. Cavalier & Puritan (ISBN 0-521-04521-5); Vol. 8. Age of Dryden (ISBN 0-521-04522-3); Vol. 9. From Steele & Addison to Pope & Swift (ISBN 0-521-04523-1); Vol. 10. Age of Johnson (ISBN 0-521-04524-X); Vol. 11. Period of the French Revolution; Vol. 12. Nineteenth Century, No. 1; Vol. 13. Nineteenth Century, No. 2 (ISBN 0-521-04527-4); Vol. 14. Nineteenth Century, No. 3 (ISBN 0-521-04528-2); Vol. 15. General Index (ISBN 0-521-04529-0). 58.00 ea.; Set. 750.00 (ISBN 0-521-08154-8). Cambridge U Pr.

Cambridge History of Iran. Incl. Vol. 1. The Land of Iran. Ed. by W. B. Fisher. 1968. 62.00 (ISBN 0-521-06935-1); Vol. 4. Ed. by R. N. Frye. 1975. 62.00 (ISBN 0-521-20093-8); Vol. 5. The Saljug & Mongol Periods. Ed. by J. A. Boyle. LC 67-12845. 1968. 62.00 (ISBN 0-521-06936-X). LC 67-12845. (Illus.). Cambridge U Pr.

Cambridge History of Islam. Ed. by P. M. Holt et al. Incl. Vol. 1A. Central Islamic Lands from Pre-Islamic Times to the First World War. 59.00 (ISBN 0-521-21946-9); pap. 19.95 (ISBN 0-521-29135-6); Vol. 1B. Central Islamic Lands Since 1918. 42.00 (ISBN 0-521-21947-7); pap. 14.95 (ISBN 0-521-29136-4); Vol. 2A. The Indian Subcontinent, Southeast Asia, Africa & the Muslim West. 48.00 (ISBN 0-521-21948-5); pap. 18.50 (ISBN 0-521-29137-2); Vol. 2B. Islamic Society & Civilization. 59.00 (ISBN 0-521-21949-3); pap. 21.95 (ISBN 0-521-29138-0). 1977-78. Set. 178.00 (ISBN 0-521-22310-5); Set. pap. 62.00 (ISBN 0-521-08755-4). Cambridge U Pr.

Cambridge History of Islam: Central Islamic Lands from Pre Islamic Times to the First World War, Vol. 1A. Ed. by P. M. Holt & Ann Lambton. (Illus.). 1977. 59.00 (ISBN 0-521-21946-9); pap. 19.95 (ISBN 0-521-29135-6). Cambridge U Pr.

Cambridge History of Islam: Central Islamic Lands Since 1918, Vol. 1B. Ed. by P. M. Holt & Ann Lambton. 1977. 42.00 (ISBN 0-521-21947-7); pap. 14.95 (ISBN 0-521-29136-4). Cambridge U Pr.

Cambridge History of Islam: Islamic Society & Civilisation, Vol. 2B. Ed. by P. M. Holt et al. LC 73-77291. (Illus.). 1978. 59.00 (ISBN 0-521-21949-3); pap. 21.95 (ISBN 0-521-29138-0). Cambridge U Pr.

Cambridge History of Islam: The Indian Sub-Continent, South-East Asia, Africa & the Muslim West, Vol. 2A. Ed. by P. M. Holt et al. (Illus.). 1978. 48.00 (ISBN 0-521-21948-5); pap. 18.50 (ISBN 0-521-29137-2). Cambridge U Pr.

Cambridge History of Later Greek & Early Medieval Philosophy. A. H. Armstrong. 1967. 59.50 (ISBN 0-521-04054-X). Cambridge U Pr.

Cambridge History of the Bible, 3 vols. Incl. Vol. 1. From the Beginnings to Jerome. Ed. by P. R. Ackroyd & C. F. Evans. (ISBN 0-521-07418-5); pap. (ISBN 0-521-09973-0); Vol. 2. The West from the Fathers to the Reformation. Ed. by G. W. Lampe. (ISBN 0-521-04255-0); pap. (ISBN 0-521-29017-1); Vol. 3. The West from the Reformation to the Present Day. Ed. by S. L. Greenslade. (ISBN 0-521-04254-2); pap. (ISBN 0-521-29016-3). LC 63-24435. 45.00 ea.; Set. 144.00 (ISBN 0-521-08778-3); pap. 14.95x ea.; Set. pap. 39.95x (ISBN 0-521-29018-X). Cambridge U Pr.

Cambridge Italian Dictionary. Barbara Reynolds. LC 74-77384. 1962. Vol. 1. Italian-English 1962. 115.00 (ISBN 0-521-06059-1). Cambridge U Pr.

Cambridge Latin Course, 3 bklts, Unit 5, Pupils Books. Cambridge School Classics Project. Incl. Dido et Aeneas; Nero et Agrippina; Words & Phrases. (Illus.). 1974. pap. text ed. 4.50x (ISBN 0-521-08545-4). Cambridge U Pr.

Cambridge Medieval History, 9 vols. Incl. Vol. 1. Christian Roman Empire & the Foundation of the Teutonic Kingdoms. 59.95 (ISBN 0-521-04532-0); Vol. 2. Rise of the Saracens & the Foundation of the Western Empire. 69.95 (ISBN 0-521-04533-9); Vol. 3. Germany & the Western Empire. 64.95 (ISBN 0-521-04534-7); Vol. 4, Pt. 1. Byzantine Empire. 2nd ed. Ed. by J. M. Hussey & D. M. Nicol. 1966. 87.95 (ISBN 0-521-04535-5); Vol. 4, Pt. 2. Government Church & Civilization. 59.95 (ISBN 0-521-04536-3); Vol. 5. Contest of Empire & Papacy. 77.95 (ISBN 0-521-04537-1); Vol. 6. Victory of the Papacy. 77.95 (ISBN 0-521-04538-X); Vol. 7. Decline of the Empire & Papacy. 77.95 (ISBN 0-521-04539-8); Vol. 8. Close of the Middle Ages. 77.95 (ISBN 0-521-04540-1). Cambridge U Pr.

Cambridge Movement. J. F. White. LC 79-50916. (Illus.). 1979. 29.95 (ISBN 0-521-06781-2). Cambridge U Pr.

Cambridge Music: From the Middle Ages to Modern Times. Frida Knight. (Cambridge Town, Gown & Country Ser.: Vol. 29). (Illus.). 1980. 16.50 (ISBN 0-900891-51-3). Oleander Pr.

Cambridge Platonists. Ed. by C. A. Patrides. LC 79-28412. 376p. 1980. 49.50 (ISBN 0-521-23417-4); pap. 12.95 (ISBN 0-521-29942-X). Cambridge U Pr.

Cambridge University Press, Sixteen Ninety-Six to Seventeen Twelve, 2 vols. D. F. McKenzie. Set. 150.00 (ISBN 0-521-05632-2). Cambridge U Pr.

Cambridger Loewenfabel von 1382: Untersuchung und Edition eines defektiven Textes. Hans P. Althaus. (Quellen und Forschungen Zur Sprach-und Kulturgeschichte der Germanischen Voelker Ser.). (Illus.). 238p. 1971. 48.25x (ISBN 3-11-003939-7). De Gruyter.

Cambridgeshire Coprolite Mining Rush. Richard Grove. (Cambridge Town, Gown & County Ser.: Vol. 1). (Illus.). 1976. pap. 4.25 (ISBN 0-902675-61-3). Oleander Pr.

Camel Caravan. Arthur Catherall. LC 68-24733. (Illus.). (gr. 3-7). 1968. 5.95 o.p. (ISBN 0-8164-3009-8, Clarion). HM.

Camel: Its Evolution, Ecology, Behavior, & Relationship to Man. Hilde Gauthier-Pilters & Anne I. Dagg. LC 80-23822. 1981. lib. bdg. 26.00x (ISBN 0-226-28453-0). U of Chicago Pr.

Camelot. Alan J. Lerner & Frederick Loewe. 1961. 6.95 (ISBN 0-394-40521-8). Random.

Camels & Llamas. Olive L. Earle. (Illus.). (gr. 3-7). 1961. PLB 6.48 (ISBN 0-688-31138-5). Morrow.

Camels: Ships of the Desert. John F. Waters. LC 73-14514. (Let's Read-&-Find-Out Science Bk). (Illus.). (ps-3). 1974. 7.95 (ISBN 0-690-00394-3, TYC-J); PLB 7.89 (ISBN 0-690-00395-1). T Y Crowell.

Camera. (Life Library of Photography). (Illus.). 1970. 14.95 (ISBN 0-8094-1007-9). Time-Life.

Camera Age: Essays on Television. Michael J. Arlen. 1981. 12.95 (ISBN 0-374-11822-1). FS&G.

Camera Book. Ed. by Michael J. Langford. (Illus.). 256p. 1980. 25.00 (ISBN 0-87165-073-8). Ziff-Davis Pub.

Camera Lucida: Reflections on Photography. Roland Bathes. Tr. by Richard Howard. (Illus.). 1981. 11.95 (ISBN 0-8090-3340-2). Hill & Wang.

Camera Never Blinks: Adventures of a TV Journalist. Dan Rather & Mickey Herskowitz. 1978. pap. 2.50 (ISBN 0-345-29025-9). Ballantine.

Camera Notes: The Official Organ of the Camera Club of New York, 3 vols. (Photography Ser.). (Repr. of 1897-1903 eds.). 1979. Set. 295.00 (ISBN 0-306-77553-0); 125.00 ea. Vol. 1, 1897-1899 (ISBN 0-306-77554-9). Vol. 2, 1899-1901 (ISBN 0-306-77555-7). Vol. 3, 1901-1903 (ISBN 0-306-77556-5). Da Capo.

Camera Repair Simplified. Jeffrey R. Weber. LC 80-65475. 112p. (Orig.). 1980. pap. text ed. 9.95 (ISBN 0-9604892-0-7). Five Arms Corp.

Camera Sensitive Electrophotography. Helmut Kiess. (Illus.). 100p. 1980. 25.00 (ISBN 0-240-51067-4). Focal Pr.

Camera, Spade & Pen: An Inside View of Southwestern Archaeology. Marnie Gaede & Marc Gaede. LC 80-23751. 1980. 25.00 (ISBN 0-8165-0663-9). U of Ariz Pr.

Camera Techniques in Archaeology. V. M. Conlon. LC 73-82631. (Illus.). 112p. 1973. 19.95 (ISBN 0-312-11445-1). St Martin.

Camera: Victorian Eyewitness; A History of Photography, 1826-1913. Gus MacDonald. LC 79-5296. (Illus.). 1980. 17.95 (ISBN 0-670-20056-5, Studio). Viking Pr.

Camera Work: A Critical Anthology. Ed. by Alfred Stieglitz. LC 73-85257. (Illus.). 1975. 35.00 o.p. (ISBN 0-912334-47-9); pap. 20.00 o.p. (ISBN 0-912334-73-8). Aperture.

Cameraman at War. Ian Grant. (Illus.). 200p. 1981. 31.95 (ISBN 0-85059-489-8). Aztex.

Cameraready. Kenneth A. Caird. 1973. 30.00 (ISBN 0-87703-066-9). Soc Tech Comm.

Camerart Photo Trade Directory 1979. 17th ed. LC 66-98554. (Illus.). 520p. 1979. pap. 25.00x (ISBN 0-8002-2210-5). Intl Pubns Serv.

Cameras. Roald Bostrom. LC 80-17413. (Look Inside Ser.). (Illus.). 48p. (gr. 4-12). 1981. PLB 10.25 (ISBN 0-8172-1404-6). Raintree Pubs.

Cameras: The Facts, a Collector's Guide, 1957-1964. Ed. by Focal Editorial Staff. LC 80-41969. (Illus.). 528p. 1981. 45.00 (ISBN 0-240-51062-3). Focal Pr.

Camilla. Caroline E. Miner & Edward L. Kimball. LC 80-69723. (Illus.). 1980. 5.95 (ISBN 0-87747-845-7). Deseret Bk.

Camille, a Boy in Love with Nature. Camille Kirmser. 4.95 o.p. (ISBN 0-685-58638-3). Vantage.

Camille & Other Plays. Ed. & intro. by Stephen S. Stanton. Incl. Camille. Alexandre Dumas, fils; A Peculiar Position. Scribe; The Glass of Water. Scribe; A Scrap of Paper. Sardou; Olympe's Marriage. Augier. 306p. (Orig.). 1957. pap. 5.95 (ISBN 0-8090-0706-1, Mermaid). Hill & Wang.

Camille Pissarro: The Impressionist Printmaker. Barbara S. Shapiro. (Illus.). 1973. pap. 3.25 (ISBN 0-87846-075-6). Mus Fine Arts Boston.

Camillus: A Study of Indo-European Religion As Roman History. Georges Dumezil. Ed. by Udo Strutynski. Tr. by Annette Aronowicz et al from Fr. 250p. 1980. 16.95x (ISBN 0-520-02841-4). U of Cal Pr.

Caminos Del Comunismo Internacional En las Americas. Comision Especial De Consulta Sobre Seguridad-15th-1971. 50p. (Span.). 1971. pap. 1.00 o.p. (ISBN 0-8270-2920-9). OAS.

Caminos Peligrosos. Emile De Harven. LC 75-38833. (Illus.). 140p. 1976. pap. 4.25 (ISBN 0-88436-259-0). EMC.

Camiones. Ed. by Philip Mann. Tr. by Georgian Kreps from Eng. (Shape Board Play Book). Orig. Title: Trucks. (Illus.). 14p. (Span.). (ps-3). 1981. bds. 3.50 plastic comb bdg (ISBN 0-89828-200-4, 5004SP). Tuffy Bks.

Camp. Jonathan Trask. 1977. pap. 1.50 (ISBN 0-505-51214-9). Tower Bks.

Camp & Community: Manzanar & the Owens Valley. Ed. by Jessie A. Garrett. Ronald C. Larson. 1977. pap. 7.95 (ISBN 0-930046-00-5). CSUF Oral Hist.

Camp at Wallaby Cross: Aboriginal Fringe Dwellers in Darwin. Basil Sansom. 280p. 1980. text ed. 17.00x (ISBN 0-391-01696-2, Pub. by Australian Inst Australia); pap. text ed. 9.75x (ISBN 0-391-01697-0). Humanities.

Camp David Peace Process: A Study of Carter Administration Policies (1977-1980) C. Paul Bradley. LC 81-50100. (Illus.). viii, 79p. 1981. pap. text ed. 4.50 (ISBN 0-936988-03-7). Tompson & Rutter.

Camp-Fire & Cotton-Field. Thomas W. Knox. LC 75-84186. (American Scene Ser.). 1969. Repr. of 1865 ed. lib. bdg. 49.50 (ISBN 0-306-71782-4). Da Capo.

Camp of Death: The Donner Party Mountain Camp, 1846-47. J. Quinn Thornton. Ed. by William R. Jones. 1978. pap. 4.95 (ISBN 0-89646-037-1). Outbooks.

Campaign Against the Underground Press in the United States: 1960-1979. Geoffrey Rips. 80p. 1981. pap. 2.50 (ISBN 0-87286-127-9). City Lights.

Campaign Craftsmanship: A Professional's Guide to Campaigning for Elective Office. Edward Schwartzman. LC 72-91198. (Illus.). 272p. 1973. 10.00x (ISBN 0-87663-173-1); pap. 3.95x o.s.i. (ISBN 0-87663-906-6). Universe.

Campaign for North Africa. Jack Coggins. LC 79-7585. (Illus.). 1980. 15.00 (ISBN 0-385-04351-1). Doubleday.

Campaign for Prohibition in Victorian England: The United Kingdom Alliance Eighteen Seventy-Two to Eighteen Ninety-Five. A. E. Dingle. 240p. 1980. 21.00 (ISBN 0-8135-0909-2). Rutgers U Pr.

Campaign Money: Reform & Reality in the States. Herbert E. Alexander. LC 76-21180. 1976. 12.95 (ISBN 0-02-900410-1); pap. text ed. 3.95 (ISBN 0-02-900420-9). Free Pr.

Campaign of Eighteen Hundred & Twelve in Russia. Karl Von Clausewitz. LC 79-84266. (Illus.). 1977. Repr. of 1843 ed. lib. bdg. 25.00x (ISBN 0-8371-5004-3, CLCA). Greenwood.

Campaign of Lieut. Gen. John Burgoyne & the Expedition of Lieut. Col. Barry St. Leger. W. L. Stone. LC 75-114716. (Era of the American Revolution Ser). 1970. Repr. of 1877 ed. lib. bdg. 42.50 (ISBN 0-306-71925-8). Da Capo.

Campaign of Plataea: Campaign of Plataea: September, Four Hundred & Seventy-Nine B.C. Henry B. Wright. 1904. pap. 27.50x (ISBN 0-685-89737-0). Elliots Bks.

Campaign Organization. Xandra Kayden. 1978. pap. text ed. 5.95x (ISBN 0-669-01782-5). Heath.

Campaign Seventy-Two: The Managers Speak. Ernest R. May & Janet Fraser. LC 73-85182. 318p. 1974. 10.00 (ISBN 0-674-09141-8); pap. 4.95 (ISBN 0-674-09143-4). Harvard U Pr.

Campaign That Won America: The Story of Yorktown. Burke Davis. (Illus.). 319p. (Orig.). 1979. pap. 3.50 (ISBN 0-686-27872-0, Pub. by Eastern Natl Park). Eastern Acorn.

Campaigning in Cuba. George Kennan. LC 75-137918. (American History & Culture in the Nineteenth Century Ser). 1971. Repr. of 1899 ed. 15.00 o.p. (ISBN 0-8046-1484-9). Kennikat.

Campaigns of Napoleon: The Mind & Method of History's Greatest Soldier. David Chandler. 1216p. 1973. 35.00 (ISBN 0-02-523660-1). Macmillan.

Campamentos Cristianos: Manual Para Confidentes. (Illus.). 1978. pap. 2.95 (ISBN 0-311-11030-4, Edit Mundo). Casa Bautista.

Campanus of Novara & Medieval Planetary Theory: Theorica Planetarum. Ed. by Francis S. Benjamin, Jr. & G. J. Toomer. (Medieval Science Ser: No. 16). (Illus.). 1971. 37.50x (ISBN 0-299-05960-X). U of Wis Pr.

Campbell's Kingdom. Hammond Innes. 1979. pap. 1.95 o.p. (ISBN 0-345-27413-X). Ballantine.

Campbell's Operative Orthopaedics, 2 Vols. 6 ed. A. S. Edmonson. LC 80-14731. 1980. Set. 189.50 (ISBN 0-8016-1071-0). Mosby.

Camper's Guide to Texas Parks, Lakes & Forests. Mildred J Little. LC 77-73561. (Illus.). 1978. pap. 5.95 (ISBN 0-88415-097-6). Pacesetter Pr.

Campfire Chillers. Ed. by E. M. Freeman. LC 79-28318. (Illus.). 192p. (Orig.). 1980. lib. bdg. 10.25 o.p. (ISBN 0-686-26886-5). East Woods.

Campfire Cooking. Yvonne Messner. LC 73-90003. (Illus.). 128p. (Orig.). 1973. pap. 1.95 o.p. (ISBN 0-912692-29-4). Cook.

Campground & Trailer Park Guide. Incl. Eastern. pap. 5.95 o.s.i. (ISBN 0-528-84304-4); Western. pap. 4.95 o.s.i. (ISBN 0-528-84302-8); National Edition. pap. 7.95 o.p. (ISBN 0-528-84300-1). 1978. Rand.

Campground & Trailer Park Guide: North American Ed. Incl. Midwestern Campgrounds & Trailer Parks. pap. 3.95 o.p. (ISBN 0-528-84427-X); Northeastern Campgrounds & Trailer Parks. pap. 3.95 o.p. (ISBN 0-686-64857-9); Southeastern Campgrounds & Trailer Parks. pap. 3.95 o.p. (ISBN 0-528-84425-3); Western Campgrounds & Trailer Parks. pap. 4.95 o.p. (ISBN 0-528-84429-6). 1980. pap. 8.95 o.p. (ISBN 0-528-84421-0). Rand.

Campground & Trailer Park Guide: North American Edition. Incl. Midwestern Campgrounds & Trailer Parks. pap. 4.95 (ISBN 0-528-84509-8); Northeastern Campgrounds & Trailer Parks. pap. 4.95 (ISBN 0-528-84505-5); Southeastern Campgrounds & Trailer Parks. pap. 4.95 (ISBN 0-528-84507-1); Western Campgrounds & Trailer Parks. pap. 5.95 (ISBN 0-528-84503-9). 1981. pap. 9.95 set (ISBN 0-528-84501-2). Rand.

Camping. Boy Scouts Of America. LC 19-600. (Illus.). 64p. (gr. 6-12). 1966. pap. 0.70x (ISBN 0-8395-3256-3, 3256). BSA.

Camping. Shirley Zeleznak. Ed. by Howard Schroeder. LC 80-425. (Back to Nature Sports Ser.). (Illus.). 1980. lib. bdg. 5.95 (ISBN 0-89686-071-X). Crestwood Hse.

Camping & Backpacking: A Guide to Information Sources. Ed. by Cecil F. Clotfelter & Mary L. Clotfelter. LC 79-84659. (Sports, Games, & Pastimes Information Guide Ser.: Vol. 2). 1978. 30.00 (ISBN 0-8103-1437-1). Gale.

Camping & Ecology. Paul Neimark. (Wilderness World Ser.). (Illus.). 64p. (gr. 3 up). 1981. PLB 9.25 (ISBN 0-516-02451-5). Childrens.

Camping & Woodcraft. Horace Kephart. (Illus.). 1948. 10.95 (ISBN 0-02-562680-9). Macmillan.

Camping by Backpack & Canoe. Theodore Cheney. LC 69-19649. (Funk & W Bk.). 1970. 7.95 o.s.i. (ISBN 0-308-70404-5, 781340, TYC-T). T Y Crowell.

Camping Caravanning in France. Michelin Guides & Maps Division. (Annual Ser.). 1980. pap. 7.95 (ISBN 2-06-006101-6). Michelin.

Camping Therapy, Its Use in Psychiatry & Rehabilitation. Ed. by Thomas P. Lowry. 160p. 1974. 11.75 (ISBN 0-398-02898-2). C C Thomas.

Camping Together As Christians. John Ensign & Ruth S. Ensign. LC 58-6252. 1958. pap. 1.50 (ISBN 0-8042-1176-0). John Knox.

Camping Trip. Judith Wolman. LC 78-73534. (Illus.). (gr. 1-4). Date not set. price not set (ISBN 0-89799-152-4); pap. price not set (ISBN 0-89799-070-6). Dandelion Pr. Postponed.

Campion Towers. John Beatty & Patricia Beatty. (gr. 7 up). 1965. 4.95g o.s.i. (ISBN 0-02-708670-4). Macmillan.

Camps: Their Planning & Management. Robert E. Wilkinson. (Illus.). 299p. 1981. text ed. 15.95 (ISBN 0-8016-5550-1). Mosby.

Campstoves, Fireplaces & Chimneys. A. D. Taylor. (Illus.). 112p. pap. 6.00 (ISBN 0-8466-6055-5, JJU-55). Shorey.

Campus Art Museums & Galleries: A Profile. Blanche C. Sloan & Bruce R. Swinburne. LC 80-23418. 64p. (Orig.). 1981. pap. price not set (ISBN 0-8093-1005-8). S Ill U Pr.

Campus Nineteen Eighty: The Shape of the Future in American Higher Education. Ed. by Alvin C. Eurich. 1968. 6.95 o.s.i. (ISBN 0-440-01026-8). Delacorte.

Campus Security & Law Enforcement. John W. Powell. 250p. 1981. text ed. 19.95 (ISBN 0-409-95028-9). Butterworth.

Campus Survival Cookbook. Joelyn Gilchrist & Jacqueline Wood. (Illus.). 160p. 1973. 5.95 (ISBN 0-688-00030-4); pap. 4.95 (ISBN 0-688-05030-1). Morrow.

Campustown in the Throes of the Counterculture. Mark Graubard. 420p. 1974. pap. 4.95. Campus Scope.

Campustown U.S.A. at Midcentury. Mark Graubard. 308p. 1971. pap. 3.95. Campus Scope.

CAMS Social-Emotional Program. Helen Casto & Victoria Hoagland. Ed. by Glendon Casto. LC 79-88182. (Curriculum & Monitoring System Ser.). 120p. (For use with early childhood handicapped). 1980. pap. text ed. 12.20 (ISBN 0-8027-9066-6). Walker Educ.

Camus & Sartre: Crisis & Commitment. Germaine Bree. 256p. 1972. 7.95 o.s.i. (ISBN 0-440-01138-8). Delacorte.

Camus' Imperial Vision. Anthony Rizzuto. 1981. price not set (ISBN 0-8093-1002-3). S Ill U Pr.

Camwood on the Leaves & Before the Blackout: Plays. Wole Soyinka. LC 73-92792. 1973. 5.95 (ISBN 0-89388-150-3); pap. 2.95. Okpaku Communications.

Can-Am. Sylvia Wilkinson. (World of Racing Ser.). (Illus.). 48p. (gr. 4 up). 1981. PLB 9.25 (ISBN 0-516-04710-8). Childrens.

Can Cities Survive: A Study of Some Urban Fiscal Problems. Robert B. Pettengill & J. S. Uppal. 128p. 1974. text ed. 14.95 (ISBN 0-312-11515-6); pap. text ed. 6.95 (ISBN 0-312-11480-X). St Martin.

Can-Do Tune-up: Pinto & Vega Cars, 1971-74. Advanced Learning, Inc. 1975. pap. 4.95 (ISBN 0-672-23849-7); pap. 7.95, with cassette tape (ISBN 0-672-23831-4, 23831). Audel.

Can-Do Tune-up: Toyota & Datsun Cars, 1964-74. Advanced Learning, Inc. 1975. pap. 4.95 (ISBN 0-672-23850-0); pap. 7.95, with cassette tape (ISBN 0-672-23835-7, 23835). Audel.

Can Educational Policy Equalise Income Distribution in Latin America. Martin Carnoy et al. 1979. text ed. 16.25x (ISBN 0-566-00255-8, Pub. by Gower Pub Co England). Renouf.

Can Ethics Be Christian? James M. Gustafson. LC 74-11622. 1977. pap. 4.95 (ISBN 0-226-31102-3, P734, Phoen). U of Chicago Pr.

Can God Be Trusted? A. Graham Maxwell. LC 77-10550. 1977. pap. 1.95 (ISBN 0-8127-0155-0). Southern Pub.

Can I Help How I Feel? Carl Morrison & Dorothy V. Morrison. LC 76-4931. (Illus.). (gr. 5-9). 1976. 7.95 (ISBN 0-689-30542-7). Atheneum.

Can Ice Cream & Oranges Prevent the Common Cold & Influenza? Stanley J. Goodwin. (Illus.). 1979. pap. 2.40 (ISBN 0-686-24961-5). Northland Pubns WA.

Can Mormonism Be Proved Experimentally? 2nd rev. ed. Arthur Wallace. 170p. 1973. 4.00 (ISBN 0-937892-00-9); pap. 3.00 (ISBN 0-937892-01-7). LL Co.

Can Organizations Change? Environmental Protection, Citizen Participation, & the Army Corps of Engineers. Daniel A. Mazmanian & Jeanne Nienaber. 1979. 14.95 (ISBN 0-8157-5524-4); pap. 5.95 (ISBN 0-8157-5523-6). Brookings.

Can Public Welfare Keep Pace. Ed. by Malvin Morton. LC 76-89859. 1969. 20.00x (ISBN 0-231-03324-9). Columbia U Pr.

Can Such Things Be? Ambrose Bierce. 314p. 1976. Repr. of 1910 ed. lib. bdg. 13.25 (ISBN 0-89190-195-7). Am Repr-Rivercity Pr.

Can the Red Man Help the White Man. Ed. by Sylvester M. Morey. LC 80-83370. (Illus.). 130p. 1970. pap. 3.50 (ISBN 0-913098-35-3). Myrin Institute.

Can We Explain the Poltergeist. A. R. Owen. LC 64-23925. 1964. 8.50 o.p. (ISBN 0-912326-10-7). Garrett-Helix.

Can We Know? Dale Rhoton & Elaine Rhoton. 1972. pap. 0.95 o.p. (ISBN 0-87508-465-6). Chr Lit.

Can We Know God? R. E. Harlow. pap. 1.95 (ISBN 0-89107-064-8). Good News.

Can We Know God? Ellen G. White. (Uplook Ser.). 1970. pap. 0.75 (ISBN 0-8163-0067-4, 03035-3). Pacific Pr Pub Assn.

Can We Trust the Old Testament? William Neil. 1979. 6.95 (ISBN 0-8164-0435-6). Crossroad NY.

Can Workers Manage? Brian Chiplin et al. (Hobart Papers Ser.: No. 77). 1978. pap. 5.75 (ISBN 0-255-36103-3). Transatlantic.

Can You Do It Until You Need Glasses. Henry G. Felsen. LC 77-6498. (gr. 7 up). 1977. 5.95g (ISBN 0-396-07483-9). Dodd.

Can You Hear Me, God? Vic Merrill. 96p. 1981. 6.00 (ISBN 0-682-49740-1). Exposition.

Can You Retire? D. Dixon. 1968. 8.50 (ISBN 0-08-012725-8). Pergamon.

Can You Run Away from God? James M. Boice. 1977. pap. 1.95 (ISBN 0-88207-501-2). Victor Bks.

Can You Sue Your Parents for Malpractice? Paula Danziger. LC 78-72856. 1979. 7.95 (ISBN 0-440-01050-0). Delacorte.

Can You Talk with Someone Else? Shirley Schwarzrock & C. Gilbert Wrenn. (Coping with Ser.). (Illus.). 36p. (gr. 7-12). 1970. pap. text ed. 1.30 (ISBN 0-913476-22-6). Am Guidance.

Can You Tell Me How What You Are Doing Now Is to Do Something Philosophical? Peter H. Barnett. pap. 5.00 (ISBN 0-686-62107-7). Assembling Pr.

Can You Wait till Friday? The Psychology of Hope. Ken Olson. 288p. 1976. pap. 1.75 o.p. (ISBN 0-449-23022-8, Crest). Fawcett.

Can Your Child Read? Is He Hyperactive? rev. ed. William G. Crook. 1977. pap. 6.95 (ISBN 0-933478-01-1). Prof Bks.

Canaanite Myths and Legends. 2nd ed. John C. Gibson. 208p. 1978. text ed. 32.00x (ISBN 0-567-02351-6). Attic Pr.

Canada. Linda Ferguson. LC 79-15871. (Illus.). (gr. 7 up). 1979. 9.95 (ISBN 0-684-16080-3). Scribner.

Canada. rev. ed. Theo L. Hills & Sarah Jane Hills. LC 77-80448. (American Neighbors Ser.). (Illus.). 224p. (gr. 5 up). 1979. text ed. 9.95 1-4 copies, 5 or more copies 7.96 (ISBN 0-88296-090-3); tchrs'. guide 6.96 (ISBN 0-88296-353-8). Fideler.

Canada. Nina Nelson. (Illus.). 160p. 1980. 24.00 (ISBN 0-7134-1841-9, Pub. by Batsford England). David & Charles.

Canada: A Story of Challenge. rev. ed. James M. Careless. (Illus.). 1963. pap. 7.95 (ISBN 0-312-11620-9). St Martin.

Canada & the Age of Conflict: A History of Canadian External Policies, Vol. II; 1921-48--the Mackenzie King Era. C. P. Stacey. 480p. 1981. 30.00x (ISBN 0-8020-2397-5); pap. 12.50 (ISBN 0-8020-6420-5). U of Toronto Pr.

Canada & the American Presence: The United States Interest in an Independent Canada. John Sloan Dickey. LC 75-10905. (A Council on Foreign Relations Book). 202p. 1975. 14.00x (ISBN 0-8147-1758-6). NYU Pr.

Canada & the Canadian Question. Goldwin Smith. LC 70-163837. 236p. 1971. pap. 5.00 (ISBN 0-8020-6124-9). U of Toronto Pr.

Canada & the French. Ed. by Donald Riseborough. LC 74-75155. 220p. 1975. lib. bdg. 17.50x (ISBN 0-87196-224-1). Facts on File.

Canada & the United States: Transnational & Transgovernmental Relations. Hero N. Fox et al. 1976. 26.00x (ISBN 0-231-04025-3); pap. 10.00x (ISBN 0-231-04026-1). Columbia U Pr.

Canada Before Confederation: A Study in Historical Geography. R. Cole Harris & John Warkentin. (Historical Geography of North America Ser). (Illus.). 368p. 1974. pap. text ed. 7.95x (ISBN 0-19-501791-9). Oxford U Pr.

Canada Handbook. 343p. 1980. pap. 11.75 (ISBN 0-660-10203-X, SSC145, SSC). Unipub.

Canada Handbook: The 48th Annual Handbook of Present Conditions & Recent Progress. Statistics Canada. LC 77-642536. (Illus.). 354p. 1980. pap. 8.95 (ISBN 0-295-95705-0). U of Wash Pr.

Canada in Colour. Ed. by Hounslow Press. (Illus.). 1973. pap. 7.95 o.p. (ISBN 0-684-16372-1, SL694, ScribT). Scribner.

Canada in Pictures. Sterling Publishing Company Editors. LC 66-16200. (Visual Geography Ser.). (Illus.). (gr. 6 up). 1966. PLB 4.99 (ISBN 0-8069-1067-4); pap. 2.95 (ISBN 0-8069-1066-6). Sterling.

Canada in the New Monetary Order: Borrow? Devalue? Restructure! Michael Hudson. 117p. 1978. pap. text ed. 6.95x (ISBN 0-920380-06-9, Pub. by Inst Res Pub Canada). Renouf.

Canada in Transition. Ed. by Grant McClellan. (Reference Shelf Ser.). (Sold on service basis). 1977. 6.25 (ISBN 0-8242-0603-7). Wilson.

Canada Investigates Industrialism: The Royal Commission on the Relations of Labour & Capital. Ed. by Greg Kealey. LC 70-189604. (Social History of Canada Ser.). 1973. pap. 7.50 (ISBN 0-8020-6181-8). U of Toronto Pr.

Canada: Ron Martin & Henry Saxe. (Illus.). 114p. (Orig.). 1978. pap. text ed. 5.00 (ISBN 0-89192-236-9). Interbk Inc.

Canada Since Nineteen Forty-Five: Power, Politics, & Provincialism. Robert Bothwell et al. 496p. 1981. 19.95 (ISBN 0-8020-2417-3). U of Toronto Pr.

Canada-U. S. Relations. Ed. by H. Edward English. LC 76-38067. (Special Studies). 1976. text ed. 22.95 (ISBN 0-275-23300-6). Praeger.

Canada Video. Bruce Ferguson. (Illus.). 112p. 1980. 9.95 (ISBN 0-88884-442-5, 56311-1, Pub. by Natl Mus Canada). U of Chicago Pr.

Canada's Competitive Positon in Copper & Zinc Markets. Brian W. Mackenzie. 60p. (Orig.). 1979. pap. text ed. 4.00x (ISBN 0-686-63143-9, Pub. by Ctr Resource Stud Canada). Renouf.

Canada's Flying Heritage. Frank H. Ellis. 1980. pap. 15.00 (ISBN 0-8020-6417-5). U of Toronto Pr.

Canada's Guns: An Illustrated History of Artillery. Leslie W. Barnes. (Illus.). 1979. pap. 9.95 (ISBN 0-660-00137-3, 56297-2, Pub. by Natl Mus Canada). U of Chicago Pr.

Canada's Indians. James Wilson. (Minority Rights Group: No. 21). 1974. pap. 2.50 (ISBN 0-89192-107-9). Interbk Inc.

Canada's Mineral Trade: The Balance of Payments & Economic Development. 113p. (Orig.). 1978. pap. text ed. 5.00x (ISBN 0-88757-011-9, Pub. by Ctr Resource Stud Canada). Renouf.

Canadian Airmen & the First World War: The Official History of the Royal Canadian Air Force, Vol. 1. S. F. Wise. 980p. 1980. 35.00 (ISBN 0-8020-2379-7). U of Toronto Pr.

Canadian Almanac & Directory 1980. Ed. by Susan Walters. (Illus.). 1980. text ed. 59.95x (ISBN 0-8464-0232-7). Beekman Pubs.

Canadian & Australian Politics in Comparative Perspective. Henry S. Albinski. 448p. 1973. text ed. 15.95x (ISBN 0-19-501682-3). Oxford U Pr.

Canadian Books for Young People. 3rd ed. Irma McDonough. 1980. pap. 15.00x (ISBN 0-8020-4594-4). U of Toronto Pr.

Canadian Brothers: Or the Prophecy Fulfilled: a Tale of the Late American War. John Richardson. Ed. by Carl F. Klinck. 1976. pap. 6.95 (ISBN 0-8020-6264-4). U of Toronto Pr.

Canadian Business Finance. Glen A. Mumey. 1977. 17.50 (ISBN 0-256-01787-5). Irwin.

Canadian Children's Annual, 1980. 1980. 9.95 o.p. (ISBN 0-919676-21-9). Caroline Hse.

Canadian Condition: A Guide to Research in Public Policy. Raymond Breton. 65p. 1977. pap. text ed. 2.95x (ISBN 0-920380-00-X, Pub. by Inst Res Pub Canada). Renouf.

Canadian Conference of the International Foundation of Employee Benifit Plans, Oct. 31-Nov. 3, 1976: Proceedings. Ed. by James J. Neitzel. 1977. spiral bdg 8.75 (ISBN 0-89154-057-1). Intl Found Employ.

Canadian Conference on Employee Benefit Plans, Sept.-Oct. 1975: Proceedings. Ed. by Janice Hatch. (Pensions Canada). 144p. 1976. spiral bdg. 8.75 (ISBN 0-89154-041-5). Intl Found Employ.

Canadian Conference, 10th Annual, Sept. 10-14, 1977: Proceedings. Ed. by James J. Neitzel. 1978. spiral bdg. 8.75 (ISBN 0-89154-071-7). Intl Found Employ.

Canadian Conference, 12th Annual, October 27-31, 1979: Proceedings. Ed. by Mary E. Brennan. 177p. 1980. pap. 10.00 (ISBN 0-89154-129-2). Intl Found Employ.

Canadian Criminal Justice System. Alice Parizeau & Denis Szabo. LC 77-211. (Illus.). 1977. 19.95 (ISBN 0-669-01448-6). Lexington Bks.

Canadian Cultural Nationalism: The Fourth Lester B. Pearson Conference on the Canada-United States Relationship. Ed. by Janice L. Murray. LC 77-15362. 1977. pap. 5.00x (ISBN 0-8147-5421-X). NYU Pr.

Canadian Economics Today, Vol. 1: The Macro View. Edwin G. West & Roger L. Miller. 1978. pap. text ed. 11.50 scp (ISBN 0-685-86365-4, HarpC); tchr's ed. avail. (ISBN 0-06-385472-4); scp study guide 6.50 (ISBN 0-06-385474-0). Har-Row.

Canadian Economy. rev ed. Ian M. Drummond. 1972. pap. text ed. 8.25 (ISBN 0-256-00243-6). Irwin.

Canadian Education: A Sociological Analysis. W. Martin & A. Macdonell. 1978. pap. 11.25 (ISBN 0-13-113092-7). P-H.

Canadian Endangered Species. Darryl Stewart. 12.95 o.s.i. (ISBN 0-685-57292-7). Vanguard. Postponed.

Canadian Frontier, 1534-1760. W. J. Eccles. LC 70-81783. (Histories of the American Frontier Ser.). (Illus.). 234p. 1974. pap. 6.50x (ISBN 0-8263-0311-0). U of NM Pr.

Canadian Government & Politics in Comparative Perspective. Earl H. Fry. LC 78-61913. (Illus.). 1978. pap. text ed. 9.25 (ISBN 0-8191-0627-5). U Pr of Amer.

Canadian History Since Confederation. 2nd ed. Bruce W. Hodgins & Robert J. D. Page. 1979. pap. text ed. 12.50x (ISBN 0-256-02137-6). Dorsey.

Canadian Identity. 2nd ed. William L. Morton. (Orig.). 1972. 17.50x (ISBN 0-299-06130-2); pap. 6.95 (ISBN 0-299-06134-5). U of Wis Pr.

Canadian Industrial Space-Economy. David F. Walker. 261p. 1980. 27.95 (ISBN 0-470-27061-6). Halsted Pr.

Canadian Journal of Psychology, 1947-1968, 22 vols. Repr. 425.00x set o.p. (ISBN 0-685-26286-3); vols. 1-15 20.00x ea. o.p.; vols. 16-22 25.00x ea. o.p. U of Toronto Pr.

Canadian Left: A Critical Analysis. N. Penner. 1977. pap. 9.50 (ISBN 0-13-113126-5). P-H.

Canadian Legislative System: Politicians & Policy-Making. Robert J. Jackson & Michael M. Atkinson. 1980. pap. 8.95x (ISBN 0-7705-0960-6, Pub. by Macmillan of Canada). NYU Pr.

Canadian Library Association Directory. rev. ed. 115p. (Orig.). 1979. pap. text ed. 24.00 (ISBN 0-89664-082-5, Pub. by K G Saur). Gale.

Canadian Marketing Trends. Gerald McCready. 1972. pap. text ed. 3.80x o.p. (ISBN 0-256-01392-6). Irwin.

Canadian Minerals Yearbook, 1977. (Mineral Report Ser.: No. 27). (Illus.). 634p. 1980. 31.00 (ISBN 0-660-10295-1, SSC-1355, SSC). Unipub.

Canadian Music of the Twentieth Century. George A. Proctor. 1980. 27.50 (ISBN 0-8020-5419-6). U of Toronto Pr.

Canadian Nonferrous Metals Industry: An Industrial Organization Study. Elizabeth Urquhart. 159p. (Orig.). 1978. pap. text ed. 8.00x (ISBN 0-88757-005-4, Pub. by Ctr Resource Stud Canada). Renouf.

Canadian Nuclear Policies. G. Bruce Doern. 1980. pap. text ed. 14.95x (ISBN 0-920380-25-5, Pub. by Inst Res Pub Canada). Renouf.

Canadian Official Publications. Olga B. Bishop. (Guides to Official Publications Ser.: Vol. 9). 308p. 1981. 40.00 (ISBN 0-08-024697-4). Pergamon.

Canadian Pacific: The Story of the Famous Shipping Line. George Musk. (Illus.). 272p. 1981. 45.00 (ISBN 0-7153-7968-2). David & Charles.

Canadian Patient's Book of Rights. Lorne E. Rozovsky. LC 79-8942. 176p. 1980. 14.95 (ISBN 0-385-15377-5); pap. 8.95 (ISBN 0-385-15383-X). Doubleday.

Canadian Population Trends & Public Policy Through the 1980's. Leroy O. Stone. 1977. pap. text ed. 4.00x (ISBN 0-7735-0288-2, Pub. by Inst Res Pub Canada). Renouf.

Canadian Private Pilot Manual. (Pilot Training Ser.). (Illus.). 428p. 1981. pap. text ed. price not set (ISBN 0-88487-074-X, JS314131P). Jeppesen Sanderson.

Canadian Provincial Politics. 2nd ed. M. Robin. 1978. pap. 11.25 (ISBN 0-13-113233-4). P-H.

Canadian Public Service: A Physiology of Government, 1867-1970. J. E. Hodgetts. LC 72-90738. 400p. 1973. pap. 8.50 (ISBN 0-8020-6260-1). U of Toronto Pr.

Canadian River Valley. Arrell Gibson. LC 73-96758. 1971. pap. 2.95 (ISBN 0-8077-1422-4). Tchrs Coll.

Canadian Selection: Filmstrips. Helene F. de Rothwell. 516p. 1980. 25.00 (ISBN 0-8020-4586-3). U of Toronto Pr.

Canadian Self-Esteem Inventories for Children & Adults. James Battle. 1981. pap. 45.50 for complete battery (ISBN 0-686-69429-5). Spec Child.

Canadian Short Stories. Ed. by Robert Weaver. (Ser. 3). 1978. pap. 6.95x (ISBN 0-19-540291-X). Oxford U Pr.

Canadian Society: Pluralism, Change & Conflict. R. Ossenberg. 1971. pap. 6.95 o.p. (ISBN 0-13-113282-2). P-H.

Canadian Trade Index 1980. 70th ed. Canadian Manufacturers Association. LC 14-21699. 1400p. 1980. pap. 70.00x (ISBN 0-919102-00-X). Intl Pubns Serv.

Canadian-West Indian Union: A Forty Year Minuet. Robin W. Winks. 1968. pap. text ed. 4.00x (ISBN 0-485-17611-4, Athlone Pr). Humanities.

Canadian Who's Who 1979, Vol. 14. Ed. by Kiernan Simpson. cancelled o.s.i. (ISBN 0-8020-4555-3). Bowker.

Canadian Who's Who, 1980. 15th ed. Ed. by Kieran Simpson. 1980. 75.00 (ISBN 0-8020-4579-0). U of Toronto Pr.

Canadians. Ogden Tanner. (Old West Ser.). (Illus.). (gr. 5 up). 1977. 12.96 (ISBN 0-8094-1543-7, Pub. by Time-Life). Silver.

Canadians. Ed. by Ogden Tanner. (Old West Ser.). 1977. 12.95 (ISBN 0-8094-1541-0). Time-Life.

Canadians: Eighteen Sixty-Seven to Nineteen Sixty-Seven, Pt. 1. James M. Careless & R. Craig Brown. (Illus.). 1969. pap. 9.95 (ISBN 0-312-11795-7). St Martin.

Canadians in the British Flying Service, Nineteen Fourteen to Nineteen Eighteen. S. F. Wise. 1980. 35.00 o.p. (ISBN 0-8020-2379-7). U of Toronto Pr.

Canal. Derek Pratt & Anthony Burton. (Illus.). 96p. 1976. 11.95 (ISBN 0-7153-6932-6). David & Charles.

Canal Age. Charles Hadfield. LC 80-69343. (Illus.). 240p. 1981. 22.50 (ISBN 0-7153-8079-6). David & Charles.

Canal Boat Children on the C & O, Pa., & New York Canals. Hahn & Springer. 1977. 2.50 (ISBN 0-933788-57-6). Am Canal & Transport.

Canal Boats, Interurbans & Trolleys: A History of the Rochester Subway. Ronald Amberger et al. LC 80-82783. (Orig.). 1981. 12.95 (ISBN 0-9605296-1-6). Natl Rail Rochester.

Canal People. Harry Hanson. LC 77-91714. (Illus.). 1978. 19.95 (ISBN 0-7153-7559-8). David & Charles.

Canal People. Anthony Pierce. (Junior Reference Ser.). (Illus.). 64p. (gr. 7 up). 7.95 (ISBN 0-7136-1811-6). Dufour.

Canaletto & His Patrons. J. G. Links. LC 76-39696. (Illus.). 1977. 25.00x, cusa (ISBN 0-8147-4975-5). NYU Pr.

Canaletto: Giovanni Antonio Canal(1697-1768, 2 vols. 2nd ed. W. G. Constable. Ed. by J. G. Links. 1977. Set. 145.00x (ISBN 0-19-817324-5). Oxford U Pr.

Canals of Eastern England. John Boyes & Ronald Russell. 1977. 22.50 (ISBN 0-7153-7415-X). David & Charles.

Canals of North West England, Vols. 1 & 2. Charles Hadfield & Gordon Biddle. (Canals of the British Isles Ser). (Illus.). 496p. 1970. 19.95 ea. Vol. 1 (ISBN 0-7153-4956-2). Vol. 2 (ISBN 0-7153-4992-9). David & Charles.

Canals of South Wales & the Border. 2nd ed. Charles Hadfield. (Canals of the British Isles Ser.). (Illus.). 1967. 22.50 (ISBN 0-7153-4027-1). David & Charles.

Canals of the West Midlands. 2nd ed. Charles Hadfield. (Canals of the British Isles Ser.). (Illus.). 1966. 22.50 (ISBN 0-7153-4030-1). David & Charles.

Canals of Yorkshire & North East England, 2 vols. Charles Hadfield. (Canals of the British Isles Ser.). (Illus.). 19.95 ea. Vol. 1 (ISBN 0-7153-5719-0). Vol. 2 (ISBN 0-7153-5975-4). David & Charles.

Canalside Camera: Eighteen Forty-Five to Nineteen Thirty. Michael E. Ware. LC 75-2916. (Camera Ser.). (Illus.). 95p. 1975. 8.95 (ISBN 0-7153-7001-4). David & Charles.

Canaries. Cyril H. Rogers. Ed. by Christina Foyle. (Foyle's Handbks). (Illus.). 1973. 3.95 (ISBN 0-685-55797-9). Palmetto Pub.

Canaries for Pleasure & Profit. Cliff Newby. (Orig.). 1965. pap. 2.00 (ISBN 0-87666-418-4, AP270). TFH Pubns.

Canaries in Color. George Lynch. (Color Ser.). (Illus.). 1976. 9.95 (ISBN 0-7137-0540-X, Pub by Blandford Pr England). Sterling.

Canary. Tony Cohan. LC 80-2045. 336p. 1981. 13.95 (ISBN 0-385-17086-6). Doubleday.

Canary for King. Joanna Stubbs. (Illus.). (ps-5). 1970. 6.95 (ISBN 0-571-09374-4, Pub. by Faber & Faber). Merrimack Bk Serv.

Canary Islanders: Their Prehistory Conquest & Survival. John Mercer. (Illus.). 285p. 1980. 32.50x (ISBN 0-389-20213-4). B&N.

Canary Red. Robert McKay. (gr. 7-9). 1972. pap. 1.25 o.p. (ISBN 0-590-04435-4, Schol Pap). Schol Bk Serv.

Canary Varieties. Klaus Speicher. Tr. by Christa Ahrens from Ger. Orig. Title: Kanarienrassen. (Illus.). 1979. 2.95 (ISBN 0-87666-993-3, KW-024). TFH Pubns.

Canberra & Walter Burley Griffin: A Bibliography of Eighteen Seventy-Six to Nineteen Seventy-Six & a Guide to Published Sources. Donald Johnson. (Illus.). 128p. (Orig.). 1980. pap. 6.50x (ISBN 0-19-554203-7). Oxford U Pr.

Canberra Model: Essays on Australian Central Government. David E. Butler. LC 73-93820. 200p. 1974. 22.50 (ISBN 0-312-11830-9). St Martin.

Cancan & Barcarolle: The Life & Times of Jacques Offenbach. Arthur Moss & Evalyn Marvel. LC 75-2629. (Illus.). 280p. 1975. Repr. of 1954 ed. lib. bdg. 19.75x (ISBN 0-8371-8045-7, MOCB). Greenwood.

Cancel All Our Vows. John D. MacDonald. 1977. pap. 1.75 o.p. (ISBN 0-449-13764-3, GM). Fawcett.

Cancer. Gail K. Haines. (gr. 4 up). 1980. PLB 6.45 (ISBN 0-531-04159-X). Watts.

Cancer. Eugene McCabe. (Adaptations Ser.). pap. 2.95 (ISBN 0-912262-68-0). Proscenium.

Cancer. Julia Parker. (Pocket Guide to Astrology Ser.). (Orig.). 1980. pap. write for info. (ISBN 0-671-25557-6, Fireside). S&S.

Cancer. rev. ed. Alvin Silverstein & Virginia Silverstein. LC 76-4946. (Illus.). (gr. 3 up). 1976. PLB 7.89 (ISBN 0-381-99604-2, JD-J). John Day.

Cancer. Paula Taylor. (Sun Signs). (Illus.). (gr. 4-12). 1978. PLB 5.95 (ISBN 0-87191-644-4); pap. 2.95 (ISBN 0-89812-074-8). Creative Ed.

Cancer. Michael Weller. 1971. pap. 3.95 o.p. (ISBN 0-571-09765-0, Pub. by Faber & Faber). Merrimack Bk Serv.

Cancer: A Comprehensive Treatise. Ed. by Frederick F. Becker. Incl. Vol. 1. Etiology: Chemical & Physical Carcinogenesis. LC 74-31195. 524p. 1975. 42.50 (ISBN 0-306-35201-X); Vol. 2. Etiology: Viral Carcinogenesis. LC 75-11770. 439p. 1975. 42.50 (ISBN 0-306-35202-8); Vol. 3. Biology of Tumors: Cellular Biology & Growth. LC 74-31196. 473p. 1975. 42.50 (ISBN 0-306-35203-6); Vol. 4, Biology of Tumors: Surfaces,Immunology & Comparative Pathology. 440p. 1975. 42.50 (ISBN 0-306-35204-4); Vol. 5, Chemotherapy. LC 77-1142. 666p. 1977. 42.50 (ISBN 0-306-35205-2); Vol. 6. Radiotherapy, Surgery, & Immunotherapy. LC 74-31196. 544p. 42.50 (ISBN 0-306-35206-0). (Illus., Plenum Pr). Plenum Pub.

Cancer: A Problem of Developmental Biology. G. Barry Pierce et al. (Foundations of Developmental Biology Ser.). 1978. 18.95 (ISBN 0-13-113373-X). P-H.

Cancer: Achievements, Challenges, & Prospects for the 1980's, Vol. 1. Joseph Burchenal & Herbert Oettgen. 1981. write for info. (ISBN 0-8089-1351-4). Grune.

Cancer: Achievements, Challenges, & Prospects for the 1980's, Vol. 2. Ed. by Joseph Burchenal. Herbert Oettgen. 1981. write for info. Grune.

Cancer Among Black Populations: Proceedings. Symposium at Roswell Park Memorial Institute, Buffalo, May 1980. Ed. by Curtis Mettlin & Gerald P. Murphy. (Progress in Clinical & Biological Research Ser.: No. 53). 275p. 1981. 24.00x (ISBN 0-8451-0053-X). A R Liss.

Cancer & Chemicals. Thomas H. Corbett. LC 76-54270. 1977. 12.95 (ISBN 0-88229-305-2); pap. 6.95 (ISBN 0-88229-465-2). Nelson-Hall.

Cancer & Chemotherapy: Antineoplastic Agents, Vol. 3. Ed. by S. T. Crooke & A. W. Prestayko. 1981. write for info. (ISBN 0-12-197803-6). Acad Pr.

Cancer & Chemotherapy: Introduction to Clinical Oncology, Vol. 2. Stanley T. Crooke & Archie W. Prestayko. LC 79-8536. 1981. write for info. (ISBN 0-12-197802-8). Acad Pr.

Cancer & Genetics: Proceedings. Birth Defects Conference-1975, Kansas City, Missouri. Ed. by Daniel Bergsma. LC 75-43622. (Birth Defects-Original Article Ser.: Vol. 12, No. 1). 1976. 23.00x (ISBN 0-8451-1002-0). A R Liss.

Cancer & Nutrition: Etiology & Treatment. Ed. by Guy R. Newell & Neil M. Ellison. 475p. 1981. 45.00 (ISBN 0-89004-631-X). Raven.

Cancer & Related Lesions of the Vulva. Malcolm Stening. (Illus.). 184p. 1980. text ed. 45.00 (ISBN 0-909337-22-5). ADIS Pr.

Cancer & the Environment. Ed. by H. B. Demopoulos & M. A. Mehlman. LC 79-91048. 1980. 33.00 (ISBN 0-930376-13-7). Pathotox Pubs.

Cancer & Vitamin C. Ewan Cameron & Linus Pauling. 1981. pap. 5.95 (ISBN 0-446-97735-7). Warner Bks.

Cancer & You. Ed. by Henry T. Lynch. (Illus.). 338p. 1971. 22.75 (ISBN 0-398-01173-7). C C Thomas.

Cancer Assessment & Monitoring. Tenth Pfizer Intl. Symposium. Ed. by T. Symington et al. (Illus.). 480p. 1980. text ed. 55.00 (ISBN 0-443-01955-X). Churchill.

Cancer Biology Reviews, Vol. 1. Marcholonis. 368p. 1980. 44.50 (ISBN 0-8247-6856-6). Dekker.

Cancer Care: A Guide for Patient Education. Marilee Donavan. 288p. 1981. pap. 11.50 (ISBN 0-8385-1028-0). ACC.

Cancer Care Protocols for Hospital & Home Care Use. Doris N. Ahana & Marilyn M. Kunishi. LC 80-20348. 1980. text ed. 21.50 (ISBN 0-8261-3290-1); pap. text ed. 21.50 (ISBN 0-8261-3291-X). Springer Pub.

Cancer Chemo- & Immunopharmacology, Part I: Chemopharmacology. Ed. by G. Mathe & F. M. Muggia. (Recent Results in Cancer Research Ser.: Vol. 74). (Illus.). 315p. 1981. 66.00 (ISBN 0-387-10162-4). Springer-Verlag.

Cancer Chemo- & Immunopharmacology, Part II: Immunopharmacology, Relations, & General Problems. Ed. by G. Mathe & F. M. Muggia. (Recent Results in Cancer Research Ser.: Vol. 75). (Illus.). 260p. 1981. 52.00 (ISBN 0-387-10163-2). Springer-Verlag.

Cancer Chemotherapy. 3rd ed. Martin J. Cline & Charles M. Haskell. (Illus.). 397p. 1980. text ed. 27.50 (ISBN 0-7216-2609-2). Saunders.

Cancer Chemotherapy. 2nd ed. Edward S. Greenwald. (Medical Outline Ser.). 1973. spiral bdg. 13.50 (ISBN 0-87488-631-7). Med Exam.

Cancer Chemotherapy: A Manual for Nurses. Teresa M. Becker. (Little, Brown Spiral Training Manual Ser.). 1981. pap. text ed. price not set. Little.

Cancer Chemotherapy: Supplement. 2nd. ed. Edward S. Greenwald et al. 1974. pap. 4.00 (ISBN 0-87488-630-9). Med Exam.

Cancer Chemotherapy, Vol. 10: Some Thoughts Regarding the Modes of Action of Drugs on Cells & on Application of Available Pharmacokinetic Data (Anticancer Drugs) Howard E. Skipper. LC 78-24299. (Illus.). 132p. (Orig.). 1980. pap. 14.25 (ISBN 0-8357-0557-9, SS-00140, Pub. by Southern Res Inst). Univ Microfilms.

Cancer Chemotherapy: Vol. 5, Ridgway Osteogenic Sarcoma; Response at Different Stages to Surgery, Single Drugs, Combinatons of Drugs & Surgery - Chemotherapy. Howard E. Skipper. LC 78-24299. (Illus.). 272p. (Orig.). 1979. pap. 22.75 (ISBN 0-8357-0421-1, SS-00097, Pub. by Southern Res Inst). Univ Microfilms.

Cancer Control: International Cancer Congress, 12th, Buenos Aires, 1978, Vol. 2. Ed. by Canonico et al. LC 79-40704. (Advances in Medical Oncology, Research & Education: Vol. II). (Illus.). 68.00 (ISBN 0-08-024385-1). Pergamon.

Cancer Control: Screening, Diagnosis, Therapy. I. Kessler. 1980. 24.50 (ISBN 0-8391-1539-3). Univ Park.

Cancer: Diagnosis & Therapy. James R. Critser, Jr. (Ser. 10CDT - 80). 1981. 60.00 (ISBN 0-914428-77-2). Lexington Data.

Cancer Epidemiology & Prevention: Current Concepts. Ed. by David Schottenfeld. (Illus.). 592p. 1975. 59.75 (ISBN 0-398-03173-8). C C Thomas.

Cancer Genetics. Ed. by H. T. Lynch. (Illus.). 656p. 1976. 64.75 (ISBN 0-398-03222-X). C C Thomas.

Cancer: How to Prevent It, & How to Help Your Doctor Fight It. George Berkley. LC 77-26954. 1978. 10.95 (ISBN 0-13-113399-3, Spec); pap. 5.95 (ISBN 0-13-113381-0, Spec). P-H.

Cancer Immunology: Vol. 7, Immune Function & Dysfunction in Relation to Cancer, Vol. 7. Harold Waters. LC 80-774. 384p. 1980. lib. bdg. 57.50 (ISBN 0-8240-7111-5). Garland Pub.

Cancer in China. Ed. by Henry S. Kaplan & Patricia J. Tsuchitani. LC 78-14486. (Illus.). 240p. 1978. 32.00x (ISBN 0-8451-0202-8). A R Liss.

Cancer in the Young. Levine. 1981. write for info. Masson Pub.

Cancer Incidence in Five Continents Vol. 1. Ed. by R. Doll et al. 1966. 42.50 (ISBN 0-387-03475-7). Springer-Verlag.

Cancer Invasion & Metastasis: Biologic Mechanisms & Therapy. Ed. by Stacey B. Day et al. LC 77-83695. (Progress in Cancer Research & Therapy Ser: Vol. 5). 1977. 43.50 (ISBN 0-89004-184-9). Raven.

Cancer Journals. Audre Lorde. LC 80-53110. 80p. (Orig.). 1980. pap. 4.00 (ISBN 0-933216-03-3). Spinsters Ink.

Cancer Lab. Melvin Berger. LC 74-9369. (gr. 8-11). 1975. PLB 8.79 o.p. (ISBN 0-381-99626-3, JD-J). John Day.

Cancer Markers: Diagnostic & Developmental Significance. Ed. by Stewart Sell. LC 79-91071. (Contemporary Biomedicine Ser.). 1980. 49.50 (ISBN 0-89603-009-1). Humana.

Cancer Mission: Social Contexts of Biomedical Research. Kenneth E. Studer & Daryl E. Chubin. LC 80-10312. (Sage Library of Social Research: Vol. 103). (Illus.). 319p. 1980. 18.00x (ISBN 0-8039-1423-7); pap. 8.95x (ISBN 0-8039-1424-5). Sage.

Cancer: Myths & Realities of Cause & Cure. M. L. Kothari & L. A. Mehta. (Ideas in Progress Ser.). 1979. 12.00 (ISBN 0-7145-2665-7, Pub. by M Boyars); pap. 5.95 (ISBN 0-7145-2666-5). Merrimack Bk Serv.

Cancer Nursing. Ardelina A. Baldonado & Dulcelina A. Stahl. (Nursing Outline Ser.). 1977. spiral bdg. 8.00 o.p. (ISBN 0-87488-374-1). Med Exam.

Cancer Nursing: Surgical. Ed. by Robert Tiffany. (Cancer Nursing Ser.: Vol. 3). (Illus.). 272p. 1980. 39.00 (ISBN 0-571-11364-8, Pub. by Faber & Faber); pap. 12.95 (ISBN 0-571-11365-6, Pub. by Faber & Faber). Merrimack Bk Serv.

Cancer of the Breast. D. W. Smithers et al. 1980. 10.00x (Pub. by Brit Inst Radiology England). State Mutual Bk.

Cancer of the Genitourinary Tract. Ed. by Douglas E. Johnson & Melvin L. Samuels. LC 79-2070. 1979. text ed. 34.50 (ISBN 0-89004-383-3). Raven.

Cancer of the Head & Neck. Ed. by James Y. Suen & Eugene N. Myers. 900p. 1980. text ed. 89.00x (ISBN 0-443-08045-3). Churchill.

Cancer of the Urinary Bladder: With Emphasis on Treatment by Irradiation. William L. Caldwell. LC 72-96980. (Illus.). 128p. 1970. 10.00 o.s.i. (ISBN 0-87527-003-4). Green.

Cancer of the Uterus. Simon & Silverstone. 1981. price not set (ISBN 0-89352-016-0). Masson Pub.

Cancer: Pathophysiology Etiology, Management: Selected Readings. Kruse et al. LC 78-27228. (Illus.). 1979. pap. text ed. 16.95 (ISBN 0-8016-2794-X). Mosby.

Cancer Problem. Armin C. Braun. LC 77-90432. (Molecular Biology Ser). (Illus.). 1969. 20.00x (ISBN 0-231-02938-1). Columbia U Pr.

Cancer Reference Book. Paul Levitt et al. (Orig.). 1980. pap. 4.95 (ISBN 0-440-51353-7, Delta). Dell.

Cancer Reference Book: Direct & Clear Answers to Everyone's Questions. Paul M. Levitt et al. 271p. 1978. 12.95 (ISBN 0-87196-317-5). Facts on File.

Cancer Research: Impact of the Cooperative Groups. Ed. by Barth Hoogstraten. LC 80-82668. 480p. 1980. 44.50 (ISBN 0-89352-092-6). Masson Pub.

Cancer Research Today. I. Berenblum. 1967. 16.50 (ISBN 0-08-012451-8); pap. 8.50 (ISBN 0-08-012452-6). Pergamon.

Cancer: Science & Society. John Cairns. LC 78-16960. (Biology Ser.). (Illus.). 1978. pap. text ed. 8.50x (ISBN 0-7167-0097-2). W H Freeman.

Cancer: Signals & Safeguards. Ed. by Gerald D. Murphy. (Illus.). 364p. 1981. text ed. 27.50 (ISBN 0-88416-229-X). PSG Pub.

Cancer Story. Stewart M. Brooks. LC 71-39355. (Illus.). 176p. 1973. 7.95 o.p. (ISBN 0-498-01180-1). A S Barnes.

Cancer Surgery. Tadeusz Koszarowski. LC 78-27389. (Illus.). 1981. text ed. 25.00 (ISBN 0-8067-1021-7). Urban & S.

Cancer Syndrome. Ralph W. Moss. LC 79-2300. 320p. 1981. pap. 7.95 (ISBN 0-394-17896-3, BC). Grove.

Cancer: The Behavioral Dimensions. Ed. by Joseph W. Cullen et al. LC 75-43192. 1976. 24.50 (ISBN 0-89004-104-0). Raven.

Cancer: The Facts. Ronald B. Scott. 1980. text ed. 11.95x (ISBN 0-19-261149-6). Oxford U Pr.

Cancer Therapy: Prognostic Factors & Criteria of Response. Ed. by Maurice J. Staquet. LC 74-14481. (European Organization for Research on Treatment of Cancer Ser.). 1975. 31.50 (ISBN 0-89004-008-7). Raven.

Cancer Treatment Research. Ed. by Joseph Aisner. Paul Chang. (Developments in Oncology Ser.: Vol. 2). (Illus.). xvi, 272p. 1980. lib. bdg. 44.75 (ISBN 90-247-2358-2, Martinus Nishoff Pubs). Kluwer Boston.

Cancer Treatment: Why So Many Failures? What You Can Do About It. 1980. write for info (ISBN 0-9601644-1-3). GE-PS Cancer.

Cancion Verde. Plenn. 1956. 6.95 (ISBN 0-87751-014-8, Pub by Troutman Press). E Torres & Sons.

Cancionero De la Hisapno-Peruana De 1866. Carlos Garcia-Barron. LC 79-51156. (Coleccion De Estudios Hispanicos: Hispanic Studies Collection). (Illus.). 226p. (Span.). 1980. pap. 12.95 (ISBN 0-89729-225-1). Ediciones.

Cancionero Latinoamericano Para Escolares. (Musica Ser). 64p. (Span.). 1972. pap. 1.00 o.p. (ISBN 0-686-66703-4). OAS.

Canciones. Antonio Machado. Tr. by Robert Bly from Span. LC 80-27641. 20p. 1980. 30.00 (ISBN 0-915124-45-9, Bookslinger); pap. 4.00 (ISBN 0-915124-46-7). Toothpaste.

Canciones de Nuestra Cabana: Songs of Our Cabana. rev. ed. Cabana Committee of World Assoc. of Girl Guides & Girl Scouts. 112p. (Orig.). 1980. pap. 3.75x (ISBN 0-88441-366-7, 23-113). GS.

Canciones Dramatizadas. Pablo Ozaeta. Ed. by Marjorie Frank & Luz P. Lono. LC 75-16545. 20p. (gr. 4-8). 1975. pap. text ed. 2.95 songbook (ISBN 0-88499-240-3); cassette 7.95 (ISBN 0-88499-200-4); program package 79.95 (ISBN 0-88499-239-X). Inst Mod Lang.

Canciones y Juegos de Nuevo Mexico: Songs & Games of New Mexico. Ed. by Dolores Gonzales. LC 73-155. 128p. 1973. 4.95 o.p. (ISBN 0-498-01350-2). A S Barnes.

C&H Complete Dessert Cookbook. Date not set. price not set (ISBN 0-87502-087-9). Benjamin Co.

Candida & How He Lied to Her Husband: Play Manuscripts in Facsimile. George B. Shaw. LC 79-56703. (Bernard Shaw Early Texts Ser.). 1981. lib. bdg. 45.00 (ISBN 0-8240-4579-3). Garland Pub.

Candidate. Gustave Flaubert. Bd. with Castle of Hearts. LC 76-6879. 1978. Repr. of 1904 ed. 17.00 (ISBN 0-86527-225-5). Fertig.

Candidates for Office: Beliefs & Strategies. John W. Kingdon. 6.00 (ISBN 0-8446-2377-6). Peter Smith.

Candidates Nineteen Eighty. Congressional Quarterly Inc. 1980. pap. text ed. 6.95 (ISBN 0-87187-190-4). Congr Quarterly.

Candide. Framcois M. De Voltaire. Ed. by O. R. Taylor. (French Texts Ser.). 1978. pap. text ed. 9.95x (ISBN 0-631-00400-9, Pub. by Basil Blackwell). Biblio Dist.

Candide. Francois M. De Voltaire. LC 62-19952. 1963. pap. text ed. 2.95 (ISBN 0-8120-0038-2). Barron.

Candide. Francois M. De Voltaire. Bd. with Zadig. (Classics Ser). pap. 1.25 (ISBN 0-8049-0117-1, CL-117). Airmont.

Candide. Francois M. De Voltaire. Ed. by J. H. Brumfitt. 1968. pap. 6.95x (ISBN 0-19-832372-7). Oxford U Pr.

Candide. Francois M. De Voltaire. Ed. by Robert M. Adams. (Critical Edition Ser). 1966. pap. 3.95x (ISBN 0-393-09649-1). Norton.

Candide: Bilingual Edition. F. M. Voltaire. Ed. by P. Gay. 300p. (Fr.). 1963. pap. 5.95 o.p. (ISBN 0-312-85190-1). St Martin.

Candido. Alberta Eiseman. (Illus.). (gr. k-2). 1967. 8.95 (ISBN 0-02-733300-0). Macmillan.

Candido or, Dream Dreamed in Sicily. Leonardo Sciascia. Ed. by Helen Wolff. Tr. by Adrienne Foulke. LC 79-1842. (Helen & Kurt Wolff Bk.). 1979. 7.95 (ISBN 0-15-115380-9). HarBraceJ.

Candies, Cookies, Cakes. Aileen Paul & Arthur Hawkins. LC 79-79701. 144p. (gr. 3-7). 1974. 4.95 o.p. (ISBN 0-385-03019-3). Doubleday.

Candle Crafts. Barbara Yonck. (Illus.). (gr. 4-8). 1981. PLB 7.95 (ISBN 0-87460-376-5). Lion.

Candle Light. Edith H. Heflin. (Contemporary Poets of Dorrance). 68p. 1981. 4.50 (ISBN 0-8059-2779-4). Dorrance.

Candle-Making. Susanne Strose. Tr. by Paul Kuttner. LC 68-8759. (Little Craft Book Ser). (Illus.). (gr. 5-10). 1968. 5.95 (ISBN 0-8069-5100-1); PLB 6.69 (ISBN 0-8069-5101-X). Sterling.

Candle of the Wicked. Elizabeth Brown. 1976. pap. 2.25 (ISBN 0-310-21952-3). Zondervan.

Candlelight. T. Lobsang Rampa. 174p. (Orig.). 1974. pap. 2.50 (ISBN 0-685-50987-7). Weiser.

Candles. John Bird & Dorothy Diamond. LC 77-82987. (Teaching Primary Science Ser.). 1977. pap. text ed. 6.95 (ISBN 0-356-05070-X). Raintree Child.

Candles & Candlecrafting. Stanley Leinwoll. LC 72-6556. (Illus.). 128p. 1973. 8.95 o.p. (ISBN 0-684-13187-0, ScribT). Scribner.

Candles & Carnival Lights: The Catholic Sensibility of F. Scott Fitzgerald. Joan M. Allen. LC 77-82752. 1978. 15.00x (ISBN 0-8147-0563-4); pap. 5.00x (ISBN 0-8147-0564-2). NYU Pr.

Candles for Beginners to Make. Alice Gilbreath. LC 74-14968. (Illus.). 64p. (gr. 3-7). 1975. 7.25 (ISBN 0-688-22010-X); PLB 6.96 (ISBN 0-688-32010-4). Morrow.

Candlestick & the Cross. Ruth F. Solomon. 416p. 1980. pap. 2.75 (ISBN 0-515-05249-3). Jove Pubns.

Candy Buyers Directory 1979: Including the Directory of Candy Brokers. 1979. 20.00 o.p. (ISBN 0-686-15692-7). Manufacturing Confectioner.

Candy Buyers Directory, 1981: Includes the Directory of Candy Brokers. 1981. 25.00 (ISBN 0-686-28130-6). Manufacturing Confectioner.

Candy Cookbook. J. H. De Gros. LC 59-13673. (Illus.). 1976. pap. 2.95 o.p. (ISBN 0-668-04003-3). Arco.

Candy Egg Bunny. Weil. (gr. 2-3). 1980. pap. 3.50 incl. record (ISBN 0-590-24001-3, Schol Pap). Schol Bk Serv.

Candy Jones' Complete Book of Beauty & Fashion. Candy Jones. LC 73-4095. (Illus.). 256p. (YA) 1976. 11.95 o.s.i. (ISBN 0-06-012223-4, HarpT). Har-Row.

Candy Man. Steve Bradley. (Pacesetters Ser.). (Illus.). 64p. (gr. 4 up). 1978. PLB 7.95 (ISBN 0-516-02152-4). Childrens.

Candy Stripers. Lee Wyndham. LC 58-11487. (gr. 7up). 1958. PLB 5.79 o.p. (ISBN 0-671-32052-1). Messner.

Candy Technology. Justin J. Alikonis. (Illus.). 1979. lib. bdg. 30.00 (ISBN 0-87055-280-5). AVI.

Candy Witch. Steven Kroll. LC 79-10141. (Illus.). 32p. (gr. k-3). 1979. PLB 8.95 (ISBN 0-8234-0359-9). Holiday.

Cane in Her Hand. Ada B. Litchfield. Ed. by Caroline Rubin. LC 77-14255. (Concept Books Ser.). (Illus.). (gr. 1-3). 1977. 6.95g (ISBN 0-8075-1056-4). A Whitman.

Cane Sugar Handbook: A Manual for Cane Sugar Maufacturers & Their Chemists. 10th ed. George P. Meade & James C. Chen. LC 76-51046. 1977. 70.00 (ISBN 0-471-58995-0, Pub. by Wiley-Interscience). Wiley.

Canek: History & Legends of a Maya Hero. Emilo Abrey. Tr. by Mario L. Davila & Carter Wilson. 1980. 11.50 (ISBN 0-520-03148-2, CAL. NO. 441); pap. 2.95 (ISBN 0-520-03982-3). U of Cal Pr.

Caneville: The Social Structure of a South African Town. Pierre L. Van Den Berghe. LC 63-17796. (Illus.). 1964. 17.50x (ISBN 0-8195-3042-5, Pub. by Wesleyan U Pr). Columbia U Pr.

Canfield Decision. Spiro Agnew. 1977. pap. 1.95 o.p. (ISBN 0-425-03338-4, Medallion). Berkley Pub.

Canine Behavior. M. W. Fox. (Illus.). 152p. 1978. 11.50 (ISBN 0-398-00599-0). C C Thomas.

Canine Genetics: A Definitive Study. Malcolm B. Willis. LC 80-10188. (Illus.). 464p. 1980. 49.95 (ISBN 0-686-61139-X, 4936-9). Arco.

Canine Hip Dysplasia & Orthopedic Problems. Fred L. Lanting. LC 79-54235. (Illus.). 100p. 1981. 12.95 (ISBN 0-931866-06-5). Alpine Pubns.

Canine Neurology: Diagnosis & Treatment. 3rd ed. B. F. Hoerlein. LC 77-72825. (Illus.). 1978. text ed. 39.00 (ISBN 0-7216-4712-X). Saunders.

Canine Pediatrics: Development, Neonatal & Congenital Diseases. M. W. Fox. 160p. 1966. pap. 14.75 photocopy ed. spiral (ISBN 0-398-00600-8). C C Thomas.

Canisy. Jean Follain. Tr. by Louise Guiney & Madeleine Follain. 80p. 1981. text ed. 9.00 (ISBN 0-937406-06-6); pap. 4.00 (ISBN 0-937406-05-8); lib. bdg. 50.00 (ISBN 0-937406-07-4). Logbridge-Rhodes.

Cannabis Experience: An Interpretative Study of the Effects of Marijuana & Hashish. Joseph Berke & Calvin C. Hernton. 288p. 1974. text ed. 17.00x (ISBN 0-7206-0073-1). Humanities.

Cannabis in Costa Rica: A Study of Chronic Marihuana Use. Ed. by William E. Carter. LC 80-14726. (Illus.). 1980. text ed. 17.50x (ISBN 0-89727-008-8). Inst Study Human.

Cannaways. Graham Shelby. LC 76-56335. 1978. 8.95 o.p. (ISBN 0-385-09424-8). Doubleday.

Canned Foods. A. C. Hersom & E. D. Hulland. 1981. text ed. 35.00 (ISBN 0-8206-0288-4). Chem Pub.

Canned Foods: Principles of Thermal Process Control, Acidification & Container Closure Evaluation. rev. 3rd ed. The Food Processors Institute. 224p. 1979. pap. 35.00 (ISBN 0-937774-02-2). Food Processors.

Cannery Row. John Hicks & Regina Hicks. (Pictorial History: No. 1). (Illus.). 48p. 1972. pap. 2.95 (ISBN 0-914606-01-8). Creative Bks.

Cannery Row, a Pictorial History. Date not set. price not set. Creative Bks.

Cannibals of the Heart: A Personal Biography of Louisa Catherine & John Quincy Adams. Jack Shepherd. (Illus.). 300p. 1981. 15.00 (ISBN 0-07-056730-1). McGraw.

Canning, Freezing & Drying. 2nd ed. Sunset Editors. LC 80-53480. (Illus.). 128p. 1981. pap. 4.95 (ISBN 0-376-02213-2, Sunset Books). Sunset-Lane.

Cannon Smoke: The Letters of Captain John J.Good, Good-Douglas Texas Battery, CSA. new ed. Ed. by Lester N. Fitzhugh. LC 73-177902. (Illus.). 1973. 7.50 o.p. (ISBN 0-912172-16-9). Hill Jr Coll.

Cannons' Bibliography of Library Economy, 1876-1920: An Author Index with Citations. Ed. by Anne H. Jordan & Melbourne Jordan. LC 76-3711. 481p. 1976. 22.50 (ISBN 0-8108-0918-4). Scarecrow.

Cannons of Lucknow. V. A. Stuart. (Alex Sheridan Ser., No. 4). 256p. (Orig.). 1974. pap. 1.25 o.p. (ISBN 0-523-00340-4). Pinnacle Bks.

Canoe & Saddle. 2nd ed. Theodore Winthrop. (Illus.). 1981. pap. 5.95 (ISBN 0-8323-0380-1). Binford.

Canoe & White Water: From Essential to Sport. C. E. Franks. LC 77-2611. 1977. 15.00x (ISBN 0-8020-2236-7); pap. 8.95 (ISBN 0-8020-6294-6). U of Toronto Pr.

Canoe Building in Glass-Reinforced Plastic. Alan Byde. (Illus.). 192p. 1974. 15.00 (ISBN 0-7136-1457-9). Transatlantic.

Canoe Camper's Handbook. Ray Bearse. 1974. 9.95 (ISBN 0-87691-094-0). Winchester Pr.

Canoe Camper's Handbook. Ray Bearse. (Illus.). 1979. pap. 7.95 (ISBN 0-87691-281-1). Winchester Pr.

Canoe Country Poems. Marianne R. Giangreco. 1974p. 1981. 4.95 (ISBN 0-935054-05-7). Webb-Newcomb.

Canoe Design & Construction. Alan Byde. (Illus.). 176p. 1976. 16.50 (ISBN 0-7207-0862-1). Transatlantic.

Canoe Guide's Handbook: Planning a Trip for 2 to 20 People. Gil Gilpatrick. (Illus., Orig.). 1981. pap. price not set (ISBN 0-89933-011-8). DeLorme Pub.

Canoe Guide's Handbook: Planning a Trip for 2 to 20 People. Gil Gilpatrick. (Illus., Orig.). 1981. pap. 7.95 (ISBN 0-89933-011-8). DeLorme Pub.

Canoe Racing. Fred Heese. 1979. 12.95 o.p. (ISBN 0-8092-7630-5); pap. 6.95 (ISBN 0-8092-7629-1). Contemp Bks.

Canoe Routes: British Columbia. Richard Wright & Rochelle Wright. (Illus.). 160p. (Orig.). 1977. pap. 6.95 (ISBN 0-916890-61-9). Mountaineers.

Canoe Routes: Yukon Territory. Richard Wright & Rochelle Wright. (Illus.). 122p. (Orig.). 1977. pap. 6.95 (ISBN 0-916890-60-0). Mountaineers.

Canoe Trails Directory. James C. Makens. 1979. pap. 5.95 (ISBN 0-385-12428-7, Dolp). Doubleday.

Canoe Trails of Northern Wisconsin. (Illus.). 64p. (Orig.). 1981. pap. 6.95 (ISBN 0-915024-25-X). Tamarack Edns.

Canoe Tripping with Kids. David Harrison & Judy Harrison. (Illus.). 144p. (Orig.). 1981. pap. 9.95 (ISBN 0-8289-0426-X). Greene.

Canoeing. Boy Scouts Of America. LC 19-600. (Illus.). 72p. (gr. 6-12). 1977. pap. 0.70x (ISBN 0-8395-3308-X, 3308). BSA.

Canoeing for Beginners. Peter Mytton-Davies. 1971. 5.95 (ISBN 0-236-17613-7, Pub. by Paul Elek). Merrimack Bk Serv.

Canoeing (Kayaking) Alan Byde. (Illus.). 1978. 8.95 (ISBN 0-7136-1826-4). Transatlantic.

Canoeing Maine, No. 1. rev. ed. Eben Thomas. LC 79-14500. (Illus.). 1979. lib. bdg. 9.50 o.p. (ISBN 0-89621-035-9); pap. 4.95 (ISBN 0-89621-034-0). Thorndike Pr.

Canoeing Maine, No. 2. rev. ed. Eben Thomas. LC 79-14488. (Illus.). 1979. lib. bdg. 9.50 o.p. (ISBN 0-89621-037-5); pap. 4.95 (ISBN 0-89621-036-7). Thorndike Pr.

Canoeing the Brandywine: A Naturalist's Guide. Charles Aquadro et al. 1980. 2.25x. Brandywine Conserv.

Canoeing the Jersey Pine Barrens. Robert Parnes. LC 77-70413. (Illus.). 288p. (Orig.). 1978. lib. bdg. 10.25 o.p. (ISBN 0-914788-03-5). East Woods.

Canoeing Western Waterways, 2 vols. Ann Schafer. Incl. The Mountain States. LC 74-1851. (Arizona, Colorado, Idaho, Montana, Nevada, New Mexico, Utah & Wyoming). 10.95 o.p. (ISBN 0-06-013797-5); pap. 5.95 (ISBN 0-06-013799-1, TD-281); The Coastal States. LC 76-54410. (California, Oregon, Washington & Hawaii). 10.95 o.p. (ISBN 0-06-013798-3); pap. 5.95 (ISBN 0-06-013806-8, TD-280). (Illus.). 1978 (HarpT). Har-Row.

Canoeing with the Cree. Eric Sevareid. LC 68-63520. (Illus.). 1980. Repr. of 1935 ed. 7.75 (ISBN 0-87351-038-0); pap. 4.50 (ISBN 0-87351-152-2). Minn Hist.

Canoer's Bible. Robert Douglas Mead. LC 74-33610. 176p. 1976. pap. 3.50 (ISBN 0-385-07276-7). Doubleday.

Canoes & Kayaks: A Complete Buyer's Guide. Jack Brosius & Dave LeRoy. 1979. 12.95 o.p. (ISBN 0-8092-7691-7); pap. 5.95 o.p. (ISBN 0-8092-7690-9). Contemp Bks.

Canon Law: A Handbook. rev. ed. Daniel Stevick. 1979. 8.95 (ISBN 0-8164-0347-3). Crossroad NY.

Canon of Sir Thomas Wyatt's Poetry. Richard Harrier. LC 74-82812. 352p. 1975. text ed. 16.50x (ISBN 0-674-09460-3). Harvard U Pr.

Canon of Thomas Middleton's Plays. D. J. Lake. LC 74-25651. (Illus.). 354p. 1975. 49.50 (ISBN 0-521-20741-X). Cambridge U Pr.

Canon SLR Cameras. Carl Shipman. LC 76-50430. (Illus.). 1977. pap. 9.95 (ISBN 0-912656-56-5). H P Bks.

Canones: Values, Crisis, & Survival in a Northern New Mexico Village. Paul Kutsche & John R. Van Ness. (Illus.). 280p. 1981. 17.50x (ISBN 0-8263-0570-9). U of NM Pr.

Canonic Studies. Bernhard Ziehn. Ed. by Ronald Stevenson. 1977. 12.50x (ISBN 0-8008-1232-8, Crescendo). Taplinger.

Canon's Yeoman's Tale. Geoffrey Chaucer. Ed. by M. Hussey et al. (Selected Tales from Chaucer). 1965. text ed. 4.95x (ISBN 0-521-04623-8). Cambridge U Pr.

Can't Catch Me, I'm the Gingerbread Man. Jamie Gilson. LC 80-39748. 160p. (gr. 5-9). 1981. 7.95 (ISBN 0-688-00435-0); PLB 7.63 (ISBN 0-688-00436-9). Morrow.

Cantar de Mio Cid. (Span.). 7.95 (ISBN 84-241-5616-1). E Torres & Sons.

Cantarow & Trumper Clinical Biochemistry. 7th ed. Albert L. Latner. LC 73-89933. 770p. 1975. text ed. 34.00 (ISBN 0-7216-5637-4). Saunders.

Cantatas of Johann Sebastian Bach, Sacred & Secular, 2 vols. W. Gillies Whittaker. 1978. pap. 21.00x (ISBN 0-19-315238-X). Oxford U Pr.

Canterbury Puzzles. Henry E. Dudeney. 1919. pap. 3.50 (ISBN 0-486-20474-X). Dover.

Canterbury Tale: Experiences & Reflections: 1916-1976. John Cogley. 1976. 8.95 (ISBN 0-8164-0322-8). Crossroad NY.

Canterbury Tales. Geoffrey Chaucer. Ed. by John Halverson. LC 79-153880. (Library of Literature Ser: No. 27). 1971. pap. text ed. 8.95 (ISBN 0-672-61006-X). Bobbs.

Canterbury Tales. Geoffrey Chaucer. (Illus.). (gr. 7 up). 10.95 (ISBN 0-385-00028-6). Doubleday.

Canterbury Tales. Geoffrey Chaucer. Ed. by Walter W. Skeat. (World's Classics Ser.). 14.95 (ISBN 0-19-250076-7). Oxford U Pr.

Canterbury Tales. Geoffrey Chaucer. pap. 2.50. Bantam.

Canterbury Tales. Geoffrey Chaucer. LC 80-22141. (Raintree Short Classics). (Illus.). 48p. (gr. 4-8). 1981. PLB 9.95 (ISBN 0-8172-1666-9). Raintree Pubs.

Canterbury Tales: A Facsimile & Transcription of the Hengwrt Manuscript with Variants from the Ellesmere Manuscript. Geoffrey Chaucer. Ed. by Paul G. Ruggiers. LC 77-18611. (Illus.). 1979. 100.00x (ISBN 0-8061-1416-9). U of Okla Pr

Canterbury Tales (Selected) An Interlinear Translation. Geoffrey Chaucer. Ed. by Vincent F. Hopper. LC 70-99791. 1970. 6.00 (ISBN 0-8120-5015-0); pap. text ed. 4.95 (ISBN 0-8120-0039-0). Barron.

Canterbury Under the Angevin Kings. W. Urry. (Univ. of London Historical Studies: No. 19). 1967. text ed. 67.75x (ISBN 0-485-13119-6, Athlone Pr). Humanities.

Canticle for Leibowitz. Walter M. Miller, Jr. (Science Fiction Ser). 336p. 1975. Repr. of 1959 ed. lib. bdg. 14.50 (ISBN 0-8398-2309-6). Gregg.

Canto E Bel Canto P.F. Tosi: Opinioni De Cantori Antchi E Moderni Seventeen Twenty Three. Ed. by Andrea D. Corte. LC 80-2268. 1981. Repr. of 1933 ed. 31.50 (ISBN 0-404-18823-0). AMS Pr.

Canton in Revolution: The Collected Papers of Earl Swisher, 1925-1928. Kenneth Rea. 1977. lib. bdg. 23.50x (ISBN 0-89158-304-1). Westview.

Canton Island. Robert C. Murphy et al. (Museum Pictorial Ser.: No. 10). 1954. pap. 1.10 o.p. (ISBN 0-916278-39-5). Denver Mus Natl Hist.

Cantonese for Beginners, 2 vols. Chiang Ker Chiu. 5.00x (ISBN 0-686-00846-4). Colton Bk.

Cantors. Ed. by Mary Berry. LC 78-56178. (Resources of Music Ser.). 1979. pap. 4.95 (ISBN 0-521-22149-8). Cambridge U Pr.

Cantus Firmus in Mass & Motet Fourteen Twenty to Fifteen Twenty. Edgar H. Sparke. LC 74-31190. (Music Reprint Ser). (Illus.). xi, 504p. 1975. Repr. of 1963 ed. lib. bdg. 42.50 (ISBN 0-306-70720-9). Da Capo.

Canvasback on a Prairie Marsh. H. Albert Hochbaum. LC 80-22699. (Illus.). xx, 208p. 1981. 15.95x (ISBN 0-8032-2300-5); pap. 5.95 (ISBN 0-8032-7200-6, BB 681, Bison). U of Nebr Pr.

Canvases & Cathedrals. Donald F. Gill. 1977. 4.50 o.p. (ISBN 0-685-86616-5). Vantage.

Canyon Christian Academy: An Alternate Education K-12. Dorie A. Erickson. LC 80-51386. (Illus.). 55p. (Orig.). 1980. pap. 9.95 (ISBN 0-937242-01-2). Scandia Pubs.

Canyon De Chelly: The Story Behind the Scenery. Anderson et al. LC 79-157461. (Illus.). 1971. 7.95 (ISBN 0-916122-34-4); pap. 2.50 (ISBN 0-916122-09-3). K C Pubns.

Canyon of the Gun. T. V. Olsen. 1978. pap. 1.75 (ISBN 0-449-13943-3, GM). Fawcett.

Canyon Winter. Walt Morey. (gr. 4 up). 1972. PLB 10.95 (ISBN 0-525-27410-3). Dutton.

Canyons & Mesas. Jerome Doolittle. LC 74-77772. (American Wilderness). (Illus.). (gr. 6 up). 1974. PLB 11.97 (ISBN 0-8094-1238-1, Pub. by Time-Life). Silver.

Canyons & Mesas. Jerry Doolittle. (American Wilderness Ser). (Illus.). 184p. 1974. 12.95 (ISBN 0-8094-1237-3). Time-Life.

Canzoni: Testi E Commento a Cura Di Mauro Braccini. Rigaut De Barbezieux. LC 80-2188. 1981. Repr. of 1960 ed. 26.00 (ISBN 0-404-19017-0). AMS Pr.

Cap of Darkness. Diane Wakoski. 117p. 1980. 14.00 (ISBN 0-87685-454-4); pap. 5.00 (ISBN 0-87685-453-6); signed ed. 20.00 (ISBN 0-87685-455-2). Black Sparrow.

Cap That Mother Made. Christine Westerberg. LC 76-48301. (Illus.). (ps-2). 1977. 6.95 (ISBN 0-13-113365-9); pap. 2.50 (ISBN 0-13-113274-1). P-H.

Capability Brown. Dorothy Stroud. 1975. 43.00 (ISBN 0-571-10267-0, Pub. by Faber & Faber). Merrimack Bk Serv.

Capability Brown & Humphry Repton. Edward Hyams. LC 71-123850. (Illus.). 1971. 12.95x o.p. (ISBN 0-912158-83-2). Hennessey.

Capablanca's Best Chess Endings. Irving Chernev. (Illus.). 1978. 23.95 o.p. (ISBN 0-19-217553-X); pap. 8.95 o.p. (ISBN 0-19-217554-8). Oxford U Pr.

Capablanca's One Hundred Best Games of Chess. H. Golombek. (Illus.). 1978. pap. 5.95 (ISBN 0-679-14044-1, Tartan). McKay.

Capacity & Extent of Human Understanding, Exemplified in the Extraordinary Case of Automathes. John Kirkby. (Flowering of the Novel, 1740-1775 Ser: Vol. 15). 1974. Repr. of 1745 ed. lib. bdg. 50.00 (ISBN 0-8240-1114-7). Garland Pub.

Capacity Utilization: A Theoretical & Empirical Analysis. Roger Betancourt & Christopher Clague. LC 80-22410. (Illus.). 320p. Date not set. price not set (ISBN 0-521-23583-9). Cambridge U Pr.

CAPD Update: Continuous Ambulatory Peritoneal Dialysis, Vol. 1. Greifer et al. (Modern Problems in Kidney Disease Ser.). 1981. price not set (ISBN 0-89352-134-5). Masson Pub.

Cape Ann: Cape America. Herbert A. Kenny. LC 70-14190. 1971. 6.95 o.p. (ISBN 0-397-00694-2). Lippincott.

Cape Cod. Henry D. Thoreau. (Apollo Eds.). (YA) (gr. 9-12). pap. 4.95 (ISBN 0-8152-0116-8, A116, TYC-T). T Y Crowell.

Cape Cod Fisherman. Phil Schwind. LC 74-19999. (Illus.). 1974. 12.50 (ISBN 0-87742-045-9). Intl Marine.

Cape Cod: The Story Behind the Scenery. Glen Kaye. Ed. by Gweneth R. DenDooven. LC 80-81370. (Illus.). 1981. 7.95 (ISBN 0-916122-74-3); pap. 3.00 (ISBN 0-916122-73-5). K C Pubns.

Cape Colour Question. W. M. Macmillan. 1968. Repr. of 1927 ed. text ed. 17.00x (ISBN 0-391-01964-3). Humanities.

Cape Hatteras Seashore. Bruce Robert & David Stick. LC 64-23727. (Illus.). 3.95 (ISBN 0-87461-950-5). McNally.

Cape Horn to Port. Errol Bruce. (Nautical). (Illus.). Date not set. cancelled (ISBN 0-679-50951-8). McKay.

Capetian France Nine Hundred Thirty-Seven to Thirteen Hundred Twenty-Eight. Elizabeth M. Hallam. (Illus.). 368p. 1980. text ed. 45.00 cased (ISBN 0-582-48909-1). Longman.

Capetian Kings of France: Monarchy & Nation, 987-1328. Robert Fawtier. (Illus.). 1960. pap. 7.95 (ISBN 0-312-11900-3). St Martin.

Capital. Karl Marx. Tr. by Eden & Cedar Paul. 1979. 16.00x (ISBN 0-460-00848-X, Evman). Dutton.

Capital, 3 vols. Karl Marx. Ed. by Frederick Engels. Incl. Vol. 1. Process of Capitalist Production. 820p; Vol. 2. Process of Circulation of Capital. 558p; Vol. 3. Process of Capitalist Production As a Whole. 960p. LC 67-19754. 1967. 35.00 set (ISBN 0-7178-0019-9); pap. 15.00 set (ISBN 0-7178-0018-0). Intl Pub Co.

Capital: A Critical Analysis of Capitalistic Production. Karl Marx. 1946. text ed. 12.50x o.p. (ISBN 0-04-331018-4). Allen Unwin.

Capital Adequacy Requirements & Bank Holding Companies. Itzhak Swary. Ed. by Gunter Dufey. (Research for Business Decisions). 161p. 1980. 24.95 (ISBN 0-8357-1129-3, Pub. by UMI Res Pr). Univ Microfilms.

Capital & Credit in British Overseas Trade: The View from the Chesapeake 1770-1776. Jacob M. Price. LC 80-13815. 1980. text ed. 18.50x (ISBN 0-674-09480-8). Harvard U Pr.

Capital & Growth. John Hicks. 352p. 1972. pap. 5.95 (ISBN 0-19-877001-4, GB375, GB). Oxford U Pr.

Capital & Growth. John R. Hicks. (Illus.). 1965. 22.50x (ISBN 0-19-828150-1). Oxford U Pr.

Capital & Its Structure. Ludwig M. Lachmann. LC 77-82807. (Studies in Economic Theory). 130p. 1977. 15.00; pap. 4.95. NYU Pr.

Capital & Labour in South Africa. Darcy Du Toit. (Monographs from the African Studies Centre, Leiden). 480p. 1981. price not set (ISBN 0-7103-0001-8). Routledge & Kegan.

Capital & Labour in the Nigerian Tin Mines. Bill Freund. (Ibadan History Ser.). 1980. text ed. write for info. (ISBN 0-391-02155-9). Humanities.

Capital & Time: A Neo-Austrian Theory. John R. Hicks. (Illus.). 226p. 1973. text ed. 22.50x (ISBN 0-19-828179-X). Oxford U Pr.

Capital Budgeting. Joel Dean. LC 51-11344. (Illus.). 1951. 20.00x (ISBN 0-231-01847-9). Columbia U Pr.

Capital Budgeting: A Quantitative Evaluation of Investment Alternatives. Robert V. Oakford. 1970. 19.95 o.p. (ISBN 0-8260-6815-4). Wiley.

Capital Budgeting & Company Finance. 2nd ed. A. J. Merrett et al. LC 73-86116. 1974. pap. text ed. 6.00x o.p. (ISBN 0-582-45058-6). Longman.

Capital Budgeting: Long-Term Asset Selection. 2nd ed. Jerome S. Osteryoung. LC 77-85044. (Finance Ser.). 1979. text ed. 20.95 (ISBN 0-88244-139-6). Grid Pub.

Capital Budgeting Under Conditions of Uncertainty. Ed. by Roy L. Crum & Frans G. Derkinderen. (Nijenrode Studies in Business: Vol. 5). 240p. 1980. lib. bdg. 20.00 (ISBN 0-89838-045-6, Pub. by Martinus Nijhoff). Kluwer Boston.

Capital, Expectations, & the Market Process: Essays on the Theory of the Market Economy. Ludwig M. Lachmann. LC 77-1357. (Studies in Economic Theory). 352p. 1977. 15.00; pap. 4.95. NYU Pr.

Capital, Expectations, & the Market Process: Essays on the Theory of the Market Economy. Ludwig M. Lachmann. Ed. & intro. by Walter E. Grinder. 1977. write for info. NYU Pr.

Capital Expenditure Analysis. Suk H. Kim & Henry J. Guithues. LC 80-6070. 338p. 1981. 20.00 (ISBN 0-8191-1462-6); pap. 11.25. U Pr of Amer.

Capital Expenditure Analysis: For Managers & Engineers. Mayer. LC 77-84052. 1978. text ed. 17.95x (ISBN 0-917974-12-3). Waveland Pr.

Capital Exports & Growth Among U.S. Regions. J. Thomas Romans. LC 65-21131. (New England Research Ser: No. 1). 1965. 17.50x (ISBN 0-8195-8009-0, Pub. by Wesleyan U Pr). Columbia U Pr.

Capital Financing for Hospitals. American Hospital Association. LC 73-87100. (Financial Management Ser.). 60p. (Orig.). 1974. pap. 8.75 (ISBN 0-87258-139-X, 1175). Am Hospital.

Capital Formation & Economic Development. Ed. by P. N. Rosenstein-Rodan. (Studies in the Economic Development of India). 1964. text ed. 10.95x o.p. (ISBN 0-04-330082-0). Allen Unwin.

Capital Formation in Mainland China, 1952-1965. Kang Chao. 1974. 23.75x (ISBN 0-520-02304-8). U of Cal Pr.

Capital Formation Through Life Insurance. George Bishop. 1976. text ed. 9.25x o.p. (ISBN 0-256-01850-2). Irwin.

Capital, Inflation & the Multinationals. Charles Levinson. 1971. text ed. 12.50x o.p. (ISBN 0-04-330196-7). Allen Unwin.

Capital, Interest & Rent: Essays in the Theory of Distribution. Frank A. Fetter. Ed. by Murray N. Rothbard. LC 76-25587. (Studies in Economic Theory). 400p. 1976. 12.00; pap. 4.95. NYU Pr.

Capital, Interest, & Rent: Essays in the Theory of Distribution. Frank A. Fetter. Ed. & intro. by Murray N. Rothbard. 1977. write for info. NYU Pr.

Capital Investment & Financial Decisions. H. Levy & M. Sarnat. 1978. 21.95 (ISBN 0-13-113423-X). P-H.

Capital Investment in Africa: Its Course & Effects. S. Herbert Frankel. LC 68-9593. (Illus.). 1970. Repr. 22.50 (ISBN 0-86527-021-X). Fertig.

Capital Investment in the Middle East: The Use of Surplus Funds for Regional Development. Ragaei El-Mallakh et al. LC 77-7806. (Praeger Special Studies). 1977. text ed. 25.95 (ISBN 0-03-021986-8). Praeger.

Capital Market Equilibrium & Efficiency: Implications for Accounting, Finance, & Portfolio Decision Making. Ed. by James L. Bicksler. 1977. 38.50 (ISBN 0-669-86660-1). Lexington Bks.

Capital Markets & Industrial Investment in Germany & France: Lessons for the U. K. B. T. Bayliss & A. Butt Philip. 1979. text ed. 29.50x (ISBN 0-566-00335-X, Pub. by Gower Pub Co England). Renouf.

Capital Markets & Institutions. 4th ed. Herbert E. Dougall & Jack E. Gaumnitz. (Foundations of Finance Ser.). (Illus.). 1980. pap. text ed. 10.95 (ISBN 0-13-113670-4). P-H.

Capital Markets & Institutions. 3rd ed. Herbert E. Dougall & Jack E. Graumnitz. (Foundations of Finance Ser.). 240p. 1975. pap. text ed. 9.95 o.p. (ISBN 0-13-113654-2). P-H.

Capital Markets in the E.E.C. E. Victor Morgan & Richard Harrington. LC 76-27854. 1977. lib. bdg. 47.50x (ISBN 0-89158-700-4). Westview.

Capital Needs in the Seventies. Barry Bosworth et al. 70p. 1975. pap. 3.95 (ISBN 0-8157-1031-3). Brookings.

Capital Projects for Health Care Facilities. W. Thomas Berriman et al. LC 76-15771. 1976. 27.50 (ISBN 0-912862-24-6). Aspen Systems.

Capital Punishment. Antony James. 1977. pap. 1.75 (ISBN 0-505-51189-4). Tower Bks.

Capital Structure & the Cost of Capital. I. M. Pandey. 600p. 1980. text ed. 20.00x (ISBN 0-7069-0999-2, Pub. by Vikas India). Advent Bk.

Capital Theory & Dynamics. E. Burmeister. LC 79-28412. (Cambridge Surveys of Economic Literature Ser.). 224p. 1980. 37.00 (ISBN 0-521-22889-1); pap. 12.95 (ISBN 0-521-29703-6). Cambridge U Pr.

Capital Versus the Regions. Stuart Holland. LC 77-70277. 1977. 17.95x (ISBN 0-312-11945-3). St Martin.

Capitalism: A Cooperative Venture. Thomas Katsaros & John Teluk. LC 80-8163. 161p. 1981. lib. bdg. 17.50 (ISBN 0-8191-1484-7); pap. text ed. 8.50 (ISBN 0-8191-1485-5). U Pr of Amer.

Capitalism & Catastrophe. S. Rousseas. LC 78-11996. (Illus.). 1979. 18.95 (ISBN 0-521-22333-4). Cambridge U Pr.

Capitalism & Colonialism in Mozambique: A Study of the Quelimane District. Leroy Vail & Landeg White. LC 80-22702. (Illus.). 424p. 1981. 45.00x (ISBN 0-8166-1039-8). U of Minn Pr.

Capitalism & Human Obsolescence: Corporate Control vs. Individual Survival in Rural America. John Young & Jan Newton. LC 78-71099. (LandMark Study). 272p. 1981. text ed. 21.50 (ISBN 0-916672-22-0). Allanheld.

Capitalism & Modern Social Theory: An Analysis of the Writings of Marx, Durkheim & Max Weber. Anthony Giddens. LC 70-161291. 1971. 29.95 (ISBN 0-521-08293-5); pap. 8.95x (ISBN 0-521-09785-1). Cambridge U Pr.

Capitalism & Politics in Russia: A Social History of the Moscow Merchants, 1855 to 1905. Thomas C. Owen. LC 80-11279. (Illus.). 352p. Date not set. 35.00 (ISBN 0-521-23173-6). Cambridge U Pr.

Capitalism & Progress: A Diagnosis of Western Society. Bob Goudzwaard. 1979. pap. 9.95 (ISBN 0-88906-106-8). Radix Bks.

Capitalism & Revolution in Iran: Selected Writings. Bizhan Jazani. 1981. 17.00 (ISBN 0-905762-82-7, Pub. by Zed Pr); pap. 7.95 (ISBN 0-905762-57-6). Lawrence Hill.

Capitalism & the Chinese Peasant: Social & Economic Change in a Hong Kong Village. J. M. Potter. (Center for Chinese Studies, UC Berkeley). 1968. 18.50x (ISBN 0-520-01024-8). U of Cal Pr.

Capitalism & the National Question in Canada. Ed. by Gary Teeple. LC 72-91690. 1972. pap. 6.50 (ISBN 0-8020-6171-0). U of Toronto Pr.

Capitalism & the State in Modern France: Renovation & Economic Management in the Twentieth Century. Richard F. Kuisel. 352p. Date not set. price not set (ISBN 0-521-23474-3). Cambridge U Pr.

Capitalism & Underdevelopment in Latin America. F. Frank. 1979. 24.50 o.p. (ISBN 0-685-67803-2). Porter.

Capitalism &Socialism: A Theological Inquiry. Ed. by Michael Novak. 1979. 12.25 (ISBN 0-8447-2153-0); pap. 6.25 (ISBN 0-8447-2154-9). Am Enterprise.

Capitalism: Economic Individualism to Today's Welfare State. James D. Forman. LC 72-6739. (Studies in Contemporary Politics). 128p. (gr. 7-12). 1972. 5.90 o.p. (ISBN 0-531-02570-5). Watts.

Capitalism for Beginners. Robert Lekachman. Tr. by Bron Van Loon. (Pantheon Documentary Comic Books). 1981. 8.95 (ISBN 0-394-51027-5); pap. 2.95 (ISBN 0-394-73863-2). Pantheon.

Capitalism in Argentine Culture: A Study of Torcuato Di Tella & S.I.A.M. Thomas C. Cochran & Reuben E. Reina. LC 62-18996. Orig. Title: Entrepreneurship in Argentine Culture. (Illus.). 1971. pap. 4.95x o.p. (ISBN 0-8122-1005-0, Pa Paperbks). U of Pa Pr.

Capitalism in Crisis & Everyday Life. Michel Bosquet. (Marxist Theory & Contemporary Capitalism: No. 6). 1977. text ed. 22.75x (ISBN 0-391-00670-3); pap. text ed. 9.25x (ISBN 0-391-01061-1). Humanities.

Capitalism in the UK: A Marxist Perspective. Mike Campbell. 216p. 1981. 28.00x (ISBN 0-7099-0089-9, Pub. by Croom Helm LTD England). Biblio Dist.

Capitalism: Opposing Viewpoints. Ed. by Bruno Leone. (ISMS Ser.). (Illus.). (gr. 9-12). 1978. 8.95 (ISBN 0-912616-51-2); pap. 3.95 (ISBN 0-912616-50-4). Greenhaven.

Capitalism or Worker Control: An Ethical & Economic Appraisal. David Schweickart. 266p. 1980. 22.95 (ISBN 0-03-056724-6). Praeger.

Capitalism, Socialism & Democracy. Joseph A. Schumpeter. pap. 4.95x (ISBN 0-06-133008-6, TB 3008, Torch). Har-Row.

Capitalism, Socialism & the Environment. H. Stretton. (Illus.). 368p. 1976. 34.50 (ISBN 0-521-21057-7); pap. 10.95x (ISBN 0-521-29025-2). Cambridge U Pr.

Capitalism, State Formation & Marx Theory. Philip Corrigan. 258p. 1980. 9.95 (ISBN 0-7043-3311-2, Pub. by Quartet England). Horizon.

Capitalism, the Family & Personal Life. Eli Zaretsky. 1976. pap. 3.95 (ISBN 0-06-090538-7, CN538, CN). Har-Row.

Capitalism's Inflation & Unemployment Crisis. Sidney Weintraub. LC 77-73955. (Economics Ser.): (Illus.). 7.95 (ISBN 0-201-08502-X). A-W.

Capitalist Enterprise & Social Progress. Maurice H. Dobb. LC 79-1577. 1981. Repr. of 1925 ed. 27.50 (ISBN 0-88355-883-1). Hyperion Conn.

Capitalist Patriarchy & Socialist Feminism. Ed. by L. Eisenstein. 1979. 24.50 o.p. (ISBN 0-685-67804-0). Porter.

Capitalist Patriarchy & the Case for Socialist Feminism. Ed. by Zillah R. Eisenstein. LC 77-76162. 1978. 16.50 o.p. (ISBN 0-85345-419-1, CL4191). Monthly Rev.

Capitalist Society: Readings for a Critical Sociology. Richard Quinney. 1979. pap. text ed. 11.50x (ISBN 0-256-02233-X). Dorsey.

Capitalist World Economy. I. Wallerstein. LC 78-1161. (Studies in Modern Capitalism). 1979. 49.00 (ISBN 0-521-22085-8); pap. 11.95x (ISBN 0-521-29358-8). Cambridge U Pr.

Capitalization Theory & Techniques Study Guide. Charles B. Akerson. 1980. pap. 10.00 (ISBN 0-911780-48-3). Am Inst Real Estate Appraisers.

Capitol & the Campus: State Responsibility for Postsecondary Education. Carnegie Commission On Higher Education. 1971. 4.50 o.p. (ISBN 0-07-010025-X, P&RB). McGraw.

Capitol, Courthouse & City Hall. 5th ed. Robert L. Morlan. LC 76-13093. (Illus.). 384p. 1977. pap. text ed. 10.95 (ISBN 0-395-24331-9). HM.

Capitol, Courthouse, & City Hall. 6th ed. Robert L. Morlan & David L. Martin. LC 80-82016. (Illus.). 480p. 1981. pap. text ed. 11.50 (ISBN 0-395-29186-0). HM.

Capitol Names: Individuals Woven into Oregon's History. Philip Cogswell, Jr. LC 76-56657. (Illus.). 144p. 1977. 4.95 (ISBN 0-87595-076-0); pap. 2.95 (ISBN 0-87595-054-X). Oreg Hist Soc.

Capitol Press Corps: Newsmen & the Governing of New York State. David Morgan. LC 77-84771. (Contributions in Political Science: No. 2). 1978. lib. bdg. 16.95 (ISBN 0-8371-9883-6, MCP/). Greenwood.

Capitol Reef: The Story Behind the Scenery. Virgil J. Olson. Ed. by Gweneth R. DenDooven. LC 75-184671. (Illus.). 1972. 7.95 (ISBN 0-916122-36-0); pap. 2.50 (ISBN 0-916122-11-5). K C Pubns.

Cap'n Smudge. (gr. 1-6). 1977. pap. 1.50 (ISBN 0-8431-0551-8). Serendipity Pr.

Cap'n Smudge. Steve Cosgrove. (Serendipity Bks). (Illus.). (gr. k-4). 1978. PLB 6.95 (ISBN 0-87191-659-2). Creative Ed.

Capone. John Kobler. 416p. 1977. pap. 1.95 o.p. (ISBN 0-449-22824-X, C2824, Crest). Fawcett.

Cappy Dee Stories. Pierre Geaugue. 1979. cancelled —(ISBN 0-685-96676-3). Wake-Brook.

Capri Affair. David Hanna. (Orig.). 1980. pap. 1.95 (ISBN 0-505-51547-4). Tower Bks.

Capri Service Repair Handbook All Models, 1970-1976. 2nd ed. Alan Ahlstrand. Ed. by Jeff Robinson. (Illus.). 1976. pap. text ed. 10.95 (ISBN 0-89287-110-5, A143). Clymer Pubns.

Capricorn. Julia Parker. (Pocket Guide to Astrology Ser.). (Orig.). 1980. pap. (ISBN 0-671-25548-7, Fireside). S&S.

Capricorn. Paula Taylor. (Sun Signs Ser.). (Illus.). (gr. 4-12). 1978. PLB 5.95 (ISBN 0-87191-650-9); pap. 2.95 (ISBN 0-89812-080-2). Creative Ed.

Capricorn One. Ron Goulart. 1978. pap. 1.75 o.p. (ISBN 0-449-14024-5, GM). Fawcett.

Capricorn Run. Denis J. Cleary & Frank J. Maher. LC 78-70355. 1979. pap. 1.50 o.p. (ISBN 0-87216-513-2). Playboy Pbks.

Caps for Sale. Esphyr Slobodkina. (gr. k-3). 1976. pap. 1.50 (ISBN 0-590-31401-7, Schol Pap); pap. 3.50 bk. & record (ISBN 0-590-04418-4). Schol Bk Serv.

Capsize in a Trimaran: A Story of Survival in the North Atlantic. Nicholas Angel. (Illus.). 1981. 15.95 (ISBN 0-393-03264-7). Norton.

Capsule Reviews. Lynne Holdom. LC 80-20445. 51p. 1980. Repr. of 1977 ed. lib. bdg. 9.95 (ISBN 0-89370-056-8). Borgo Pr.

Capt. Joshua Slocum: The Life & Voyages of America's Best Known Sailor. Victor Slocum. LC 80-28585. (Illus.). 384p. 1981. Repr. of 1950 ed. 16.50 (ISBN 0-911378-04-9). Sheridan.

Capt. Nat Herreshoff: The Wizard of Bristol. L. F. Herreshoff. LC 80-28519. (Illus.). 350p. 1981. Repr. of 1953 ed. 17.50 (ISBN 0-911378-32-4). Sheridan.

Captain & Tennille. James Spada. (Rock 'n Pop Stars Ser). (Illus.). (gr. 4-12). PLB 5.95 (ISBN 0-87191-615-0); pap. 2.95 (ISBN 0-89812-119-1). Creative Ed.

Captain at Fifteen. Jules Verne. 1977. 5.50 (ISBN 0-200-72360-X); pap. 1.95 o.p. (ISBN 0-200-72361-8). Transatlantic.

Captain Brassbound's Conversion. George B. Shaw. Ed. by Rodelle Weintraub. LC 79-56711. (Bernard Shaw Early Texts: Play Manuscripts in Facsimile). 1981. lib. bdg. 45.00 (ISBN 0-8240-4586-6). Garland Pub.

Captain Caution. Kenneth Roberts. 1977. pap. 1.50 o.p. (ISBN 0-449-30739-5, Q739, Prem). Fawcett.

Captain Caution. Kenneth Roberts. 11.95 (ISBN 0-385-04794-0). Doubleday.

Captain Clint: Peoples Texas Ranger. James M. Day. 1980. 17.50 (ISBN 0-87244-055-9). Texian.

Captain Cook. (gr. 1). 1974. pap. text ed. 2.80 (ISBN 0-205-03871-9, 8038716); tchrs' guide 12.00 (ISBN 0-205-03866-2, 803866X). Allyn.

Captain Cook. (MacDonald Educational Ser.). (Illus., Arabic.). 3.50 (ISBN 0-686-53095-0). Intl Bk Ctr.

Captain Cutlass. Gordon Shirreffs. 1978. pap. 1.95 o.p. (ISBN 0-449-14001-6, GM). Fawcett.

Captain Departs: Ulysses S. Grant's Last Campaign. Thomas M. Pitkin. LC 73-4321. 185p. 1973. 10.95x (ISBN 0-8093-0637-9). S Ill U Pr.

Captain Elias Pelletreau, Long Island Silversmith. M. C. Weaks. 1966. pap. 3.95 (ISBN 0-911660-04-6). Yankee Peddler.

Captain Gaius Sees a Miracle. Ardith Zook. 1980. pap. 0.79 (ISBN 0-570-06133-4, 59-1251, Arch Bk). Concordia.

Captain Grownup. Kit Reed. 1978. pap. 1.95 o.p. (ISBN 0-449-23692-7, Crest). Fawcett.

Captain Incognito. George Gibson. 224p. 1980. 12.00x (ISBN 0-245-53040-1, Pub. by Nautical England). State Mutual Bk.

Captain James Cook. lib. rep. ed. Alan Villiers. 1970. Repr. 20.00x (ISBN 0-684-15553-2, ScribT). Scribner.

Captain John Ericsson: Father of the Monitor. Constance B. Burnett. LC 60-15070. (gr. 7 up). 6.95 (ISBN 0-8149-0284-7). Vanguard.

Captain John Sinclair of Virginia. Claude O. Lanciano, Jr. LC 72-93109. (Illus.). 1973. 7.50 (ISBN 0-9603558-2-0). Lands End Bks.

Captain John Smith. Everett H. Emerson. (U. S. Authors Ser.: No. 177). lib. bdg. 10.95 (ISBN 0-8057-0676-3). Twayne.

Captain John Smith. Henry I. Kurtz. LC 75-20148. (Visual Biographies Ser). (Illus.). 64p. (gr. 4-6). 1976. PLB 4.90 o.p. (ISBN 0-531-01105-4). Watts.

Captain John Smith's History of Virginia. John Smith. Ed. by David F. Hawke. LC 74-12083. (American History Landmarks Ser.). 1970. 5.50 (ISBN 0-672-60881-2). Bobbs.

Captain Jones's Wormslow: A Historical, Archaeological, & Architectural Study of an Eighteenth-Century Plantation Site Near Savannah, Georgia. William M. Kelso. LC 78-2288. (Wormsloe Foundations Publications Ser.: No. 13). (Illus.). 208p. 1979. 20.00x (ISBN 0-8203-0447-6). U of Ga Pr.

Captain LeVrier Believes in Miracles. Kathryn Kuhlman. 90p. 1973. pap. 0.95 (ISBN 0-87123-077-1, 200077). Bethany Fell.

Captain Mayne Reid. Joan Steele. (English Authors Ser: No. 229). 1978. lib. bdg. 12.50 (ISBN 0-8057-6700-2). Twayne.

Captain Medwin: Friend of Byron & Shelley. Ernest J. Lovell, Jr. 1962. pap. 6.95 (ISBN 0-292-73180-9). U of Tex Pr.

Captain Mike's Complete Guide to Grunion Hunting. Mike Ambrose & Nora S. Walker. (Illus.). 93p. (Orig.). 1981. pap. 3.95 (ISBN 0-916392-70-8). Oak Tree Pubns.

Captain Nash & the Wroth Inheritance. Raymond R. Butler. LC 76-29856. 1977. 7.95 o.p. (ISBN 0-312-11970-4). St Martin.

Captain Nemo's Fantastic Voyage. abr. ed. Verne. (gr. 3-5). pap. 1.25 (ISBN 0-590-05811-8, Schol Pap). Schol Bk Serv.

Captain of the Planter. Dorothy Sterling. LC 58-5582. (gr. 8-12). 1958. 4.95 o.p. (ISBN 0-385-11394-3). Doubleday.

Captain Pugwash: A Pirate Story. John Ryan. (Illus.). (gr. k-3). 1979. 7.50 (ISBN 0-370-00706-9, Pub. by Chatto Bodley Jonathan). Merrimack Bk Serv.

Captain Pugwash: Cartoon Bk. John Ryan. (Illus.). (gr. 1 up). 1979. 7.50 (ISBN 0-370-30030-0, Pub. by Chatto Bodley Jonathan). Merrimack Bk Serv.

Captain Swing: A Social History of the Great English Agricultural Uprising of 1830. Eric Hobsbawm & George Rude. (Illus.). 384p. 1975. pap. 5.95 (ISBN 0-393-00793-6, Norton Lib). Norton.

Captain Wunder. Donald Thomas. 300p. 1981. 12.95 (ISBN 0-670-20355-6). Viking Pr.

Captain Zomo. Alta M. Rymer. LC 79-67651. (Tales of Planet Artembo Ser.: Bk. 2). (Illus.). (gr. 4-7). Date not set. pap. 6.95 (ISBN 0-9600792-2-X). Rymer Bks. Postponed.

Captains & the Kings. Taylor Caldwell. 1977. pap. 2.95 (ISBN 0-449-24089-4, Crest). Fawcett.

Captain's Best Mate: The Journal of Mary Chipman Lawrence on the Whaler Addison, 1856-1860. Mary C. Lawrence. Ed. by Stanton Garner. LC 66-19585. (Illus.). 311p. 1966. 15.00 (ISBN 0-87057-099-4, Pub. by Brown U Pr). Univ Pr of New England.

Captains Courageous. Rudyard Kipling. (Classics Ser). (gr. 6 up). 1964. pap. 1.25 (ISBN 0-8049-0027-2, CL-27). Airmont.

Captains Courageous. Rudyard Kipling. (Literature Ser.). (gr. 10-12). 1970. pap. text ed. 3.33 (ISBN 0-87720-722-4). AMSCO Sch.

Captains Courageous: Student Activity Book. Marcia Sohl & Gerald Dackerman. (Now Age Illustrated Ser.). (Illus.). 1976. wkbk. 0.95 (ISBN 0-88301-286-3). Pendulum Pr.

Captains of Industry. Bernard A. Weisberger & Allan Nevins. (American Heritage Junior Library). (Illus.). (gr. 5 up). 1966. 9.95 (ISBN 0-8281-0398-4, Dist. by Har-Row); PLB 12.89 (ISBN 0-06-026379-2). Am Heritage.

Captain's Pleasure. Mary R. Myers. (Orig.). 1981. pap. 2.75 (ISBN 0-449-14399-6, GM). Fawcett.

Captain's Rangers. Elmer Kelton. 1981. pap. 1.95 (ISBN 0-553-14990-3). Bantam.

Captain's Vixen. Wanda Owen. 400p. (Orig.). 1981. pap. 2.50 (ISBN 0-89083-709-0). Zebra.

Captive. Robert Stallman. (Orig.). 1981. pap. 2.25 (ISBN 0-671-41382-1). PB.

Captive Americans: Prisoners During the American Revolution. Larry G. Bowman. LC 75-36984. viii, 146p. 1976. 9.00x (ISBN 0-8214-0215-3); pap. 4.50x (ISBN 0-8214-0229-3). Ohio U Pr.

Captive & the Free. Joyce Cary. 369p. 1976. Repr. of 1959 ed. lib. bdg. 15.75x (ISBN 0-89244-071-6). Queens Hse.

Captive City. Daniel Da Cruz. 224p. (Orig.). 1976. pap. 1.50 o.p. (ISBN 0-345-24769-8). Ballantine.

Captive Flame. Patricia Phillips. 384p. (Orig.). 1980. pap. 2.50 (ISBN 0-515-05190-X). Jove Pubns.

Captive Heart. Patti Beckman. 192p. (Orig.). 1980. pap. 1.50 (ISBN 0-671-57008-0). S&S.

Captive Heart. Barbara Cartland. pap. 1.75 (ISBN 0-515-05566-2). Jove Pubns.

Captive Insurance Companies. Paul Bawcutt. 160p. 1980. 54.00x (ISBN 0-85941-077-3, Pub. by Woodhead-Faulkner England). State Mutual Bk.

Captive Lion & Other Poems. William H. Davies. 1921. 17.50x (ISBN 0-685-89738-9). Elliots Bks.

Captive Moments. Amaresh Datta. (Redbird Bk.). 1976. 8.00 (ISBN 0-89253-528-8); flexible bdg. 4.00 (ISBN 0-89253-082-0). Ind-US Inc.

Captive on the Ho Chi Minh Trail. Marjorie A. Clark. 160p. 1974. pap. 2.25 (ISBN 0-8024-1170-3). Moody.

Captive Passions. Fern Michaels. LC 76-56142. 1977. pap. 2.50 (ISBN 0-345-29081-X). Ballantine.

Captive Queen of Scots. Jean Plaidy. 448p. 1977. pap. 1.75 o.p. (ISBN 0-449-23287-5, Crest). Fawcett.

Captive Splendors. Fern Michaels. 1980. pap. 2.50 (ISBN 0-345-28847-5). Ballantine.

Captive Thunder. Beverly Butler. LC 69-16204. (gr. 8 up). 1969. 3.95 (ISBN 0-396-05880-9). Dodd.

Captive Universe. Harry Harrison. pap. 1.25 o.p. (ISBN 0-425-03072-5). Berkley Pub.

Captive Wife. Hannah Gavron. (International Library of Sociology & Social Reconstruction Ser.). 1966. text ed. 17.00x (ISBN 0-7100-3457-1). Humanities.

Captive Wild. Lois Crisler. LC 68-28191. (Illus.). (YA) 1968. 10.00 o.s.i. (ISBN 0-06-010916-5, HarpT). Har-Row.

Captives' Mansion. S. R. Slaymaker, 2nd. LC 72-9155. (Illus.). 256p. 1973. 10.95 o.p. (ISBN 0-06-013923-4, HarpT). Har-Row.

Captivity & Sufferings of Gen. Freegift Patchin... Among the Indians... During the Border Warfare in the Time of the American Revolution, Repr. Of 1833 Ed. Bd. with U.S. Congress. House. Committee on Claims. Samuel Cozad... Report Made by Mr. E. Whittlesey from the Committee of Claims. Repr. of 1835 ed; Narrative of the Massacre by the Savages of the Wife & Children of Thomas Baldwin. (Incl. 2nd ed. of 1836). Repr. of 1835 ed; Authentic Narrative of the Seminole War. Repr. of 1836 ed; Captivity & Sufferings of Mrs. Mason, with an Account of the Massacre of Her Youngest Child. Repr. of 1836 ed; Stories of the Revolution: With an Account of the Lost Child of the Delaware. Josiah Priest. Repr. of 1836 ed; Indian Captive (Charles Eaton) The Perilous Adventure (Captivity of David Morgan) in: Columbian Almanac for 1838. LC 75-7074. (Indian Captivities Ser.: Vol. 52). 1977. lib. bdg. 44.00 (ISBN 0-8240-1676-9). Garland Pub.

Captivity of Father Peter Milet: Among the Oneida Indians. His Own Narrative with Supplementary Documents, Repr. Of 1888 Ed. Pierre Miller. Bd. with Captivity Among the Oneidas in 1690-91 of Father Pierre Milet of the Society of Jesus. Repr. of 1897 ed; Lost & Found: Or 3 Months with the Wild Indians; a Brief Sketch of the Life of Ole T. Nystel, Embracing His Experience While in Captivity to the Comanches & Subsequent Liberation from Them. Repr. of 1888 ed; Wehman's Book on the Scalping Knife: Or the Log Cabin in Flames. Henry J. Wehman. Repr. of 1890 ed; Left by the Indians. Story of My Life. Emeline L. Fuller. Repr. of 1892 ed. LC 75-7123. (Indian Captivities Ser.: Vol. 96). 1976. lib. bdg. 44.00 (ISBN 0-8240-1720-X). Garland Pub.

Capture & Care of Wild Animals. Ed. by E. Young. LC 75-21985. (Illus.). 224p. 1976. 20.00 o.p. (ISBN 0-88359-010-7). R Curtis Bks.

Capture & Escape: Or, Life Among the Sioux. Sarah L. Larimer. LC 75-7110. (Indian Captivities Ser.: Vol. 84). 1976. Repr. of 1870 ed. lib. bdg. 44.00 (ISBN 0-8240-1708-0). Garland Pub.

Capture, Management & Display of Geological Data: With Special Emphasis on Energy & Mineral Resources. Ed. by D. F. Merriam. LC 76-56893. 1977. pap. text ed. 41.25 (ISBN 0-08-021422-3). Pergamon.

Captured by Love. Jean Hager. (Orig.). 1981. pap. 1.50 (ISBN 0-440-11122-6). Dell.

Captured by the Indians: Reminiscences of Pioneer Life in Minnesota, Repr. Of 1907 Ed. Minnie B. Carrigan. Bd. with Eastern Kentucky Papers: The Founding of Harman's Station with an Account of the Indian Captivity of Mrs. Jennie Wiley. William E. Connelley. Repr. of 1910 ed. LC 75-7134. (Indian Captivities Ser.: Vol. 106). (Incl. rev. ed. of 1912). 1977. lib. bdg. 44.00 (ISBN 0-8240-1730-7). Garland Pub.

Capuchin. O. J. Seiden. Ed. by Bob Emmet. 240p. 1980. 12.95 (ISBN 0-917224-08-6). Gregory Pubns.

Capyboppy. Bill Peet. (Illus.). (gr. 2-4). 1966. reinforced bdg. 6.95 (ISBN 0-395-24378-5); pap. 3.00 o.p. (ISBN 0-395-07019-8). HM.

Caqueza: Living Rural Development. 1979. 15.00 (ISBN 0-88936-167-3, IDRC107, IDRC). Unipub.

Car Buyer's Illustrated Fact & Figure Guidebook 1981. Ed. by Warren E. Benson, Jr. LC 80-319. (Illus.). 160p. (Orig.). 1981. pap. 5.00 (ISBN 0-394-17881-5, E 761, Ever). Grove.

Car Buyer's Illustrated Fact & Figure Book 1980. Ed. by Warren E. Benson, Jr. (Illus.). 1981. pap. 5.00 (ISBN 0-394-17881-5, E761, Ever). Grove.

Car Clouting: The Crime, the Criminal & the Police. A. T. Nelson & Howard Smith. 180p. 1958. pap. 6.00 spiral (ISBN 0-398-01390-X). C C Thomas.

Car Facts & Feats. Ed. by Anthony Harding. LC 76-51170. (Guinness Family Ser.). (Illus.). 1977. 17.95 (ISBN 0-8069-0108-X); lib. bdg. 15.99 (ISBN 0-8069-0109-8). Sterling.

Car Facts, 1981. rev. ed. Ed. by Michael L. Green. (Buyer's Guide Ser.). 96p. (Orig.). Date not set. pap. 2.50 (ISBN 0-89552-069-9). DMR Pubns.

Car Maintenance & Repair. 6th ed. Arthur W. Judge. LC 67-31004. (Motor Manuals Ser.: Vol. 4). text ed. 10.95x o.p. (ISBN 0-8376-0067-7). Bentley.

Car Owner's Handbook. Ray Stapley. LC 73-75166. 312p. 1973. pap. 3.95 (ISBN 0-385-05097-6, Dolp). Doubleday.

Car Values: 1981 Edition. 4th ed. Brian N. Jones. (Illus.). 272p. (Orig.). 1981. pap. 12.95 (ISBN 0-528-88138-8). Rand.

CAR Yearbook: 1979, Vol. 89. Ed. by Elliot L. Stevens. 1980. 15.00. Central Conf.

Cara. Dennis Fradin. (Illus.). (gr. 2-4). 1977. PLB 7.95 o.p. (ISBN 0-516-03438-3). Childrens.

Caracolitos, 54 bks. Rosa Flores. (Crossties Ser.). (gr. k-3). 1979. Set. pap. text ed. 129.90 (ISBN 0-8332-1135-8). Economy Co.

Caravaggio. John Gash. (Oresko-Jupiter Art Bks). (Illus.). 96p. 1981. 17.95 (ISBN 0-933516-83-5, Pub. by Oresko-Jupiter England). Hippocrene Bks.

Caravan Journeys & Wanderings in Persia, Afghanistan, Turkistan & Beloochistan. J. P. Ferrier. (Oxford in Asia Historical Reprints Ser.). (Illus.). 1977. 26.00x (ISBN 0-19-577214-8). Oxford U Pr.

Caravan to Vaccares. Alistair MacLean. 224p. 1977. pap. 2.25 (ISBN 0-449-24082-7, Crest). Fawcett.

Caravan to Xanadu. Edison Marshall. 1972. pap. 1.75 (ISBN 0-380-00873-4, 31401). Avon.

Caravans. James Michener. 1979. pap. 2.75 (ISBN 0-449-23959-4, Crest). Fawcett.

Caravans to Tartary. Roland Michaud & Sabrina Michaud. (Illus.). 1978. 37.50 o.p. (ISBN 0-670-20384-X, Studio). Viking Pr.

Carbanions in Organic Synthesis. John C. Stowell. LC 79-373. 1979. 24.50 (ISBN 0-471-02953-X, Pub. by Wiley-Interscience). Wiley.

Carbene Chemistry. 2nd ed. Wolfgang Kirmse. (Organic Chemistry Ser.: Vol. 1). 1971. 55.50 o.p. (ISBN 0-12-409956-4). Acad Pr.

Carbenes, Vol. 1. Ed. by Maitland Jones, Jr. & Robert A. Moss. LC 80-11836. 364p. 1981. Repr. of 1973 ed. lib. bdg. write for info. (ISBN 0-89874-216-1). Krieger.

Carbenes, Vol. 2. Robert A. Moss & Maitland Jones, Jr. LC 80-11836. (Reactive Intermediates in Organic Chemistry Ser.). 390p. 1981. Repr. of 1975 ed. lib. bdg. write for info. (ISBN 0-89874-160-2). Krieger.

Carbine & Lance: The Story of Old Fort Sill. rev. centennial ed. Wilbur S. Nye. 1937. 14.95 (ISBN 0-8061-0856-8). U of Okla Pr.

Carbine: The Story of David Marshall Williams. Ross E. Beard, Jr. LC 76-20847. 1977. 12.50 (ISBN 0-87844-036-4); ltd ed, signed 25.00 (ISBN 0-87844-047-X). Sandlapper Store.

Carbo-Calorie Diet. Donald S. Mart. LC 72-92396. 120p. 1973. pap. 1.95 (ISBN 0-385-00615-2, Dolp). Doubleday.

Carbo-Calorie Diet Cookbook. Donald S. Mart. LC 75-36617. 160p. 1976. pap. 2.95 (ISBN 0-385-09908-8, Dolp). Doubleday.

Carbocationic Polymerization. Joseph P. Kennedy & Ernest Marechal. 675p. 1981. 65.00 (ISBN 0-471-01787-6, Pub. by Wiley-Interscience). Wiley.

Carbohydrate Metabolism & Its Disorders, 2 Vols. Ed. by Frank Dickens et al. 1968. Vol. 1. o. s. i. 74.00 (ISBN 0-12-214901-7); Vol. 2. 54.50 (ISBN 0-12-214902-5). Acad Pr.

Carbohydrate Metabolism: Quantitative Physiology & Mathematical Modelling. E. Cobelli & R. N. Bergman. 432p. 1981. 77.00 (ISBN 0-471-27912-9, Pub. by Wiley Interscience). Wiley.

Carbohydrate Metabolism: Regulation & Physiological Role, Vol. 1. Ed. by Carolyn D. Berdanier. LC 76-27944. (Advances in Modern Nutrition Ser.). 1976. 24.50 o.p. (ISBN 0-470-15047-5). Halsted Pr.

Carbohydrates. 2nd ed. W. Pigman & D. Horton. Incl. Vol. 1A. 1972. 68.50 (ISBN 0-12-556301-9); subscription 58.75 (ISBN 0-686-66782-4); Vol. 2A. 1970. 56.00, subscription 48.00 (ISBN 0-12-556302-7); Vol. 2B. 1970. 72.50, subscription 62.00 (ISBN 0-12-556352-3). Acad Pr.

Carbohydrates & Health. Lamartine F. Hood & E. K. Wardrip. (Illus.). 1977. text ed. 23.50 (ISBN 0-87055-223-6). AVI.

Carbohydrates: Chemistry & Biochemistry, Vol. 1b. 2nd ed. W. Pigman. LC 68-26647. 1981. 69.50 (ISBN 0-12-556351-5). Acad Pr.

Carbohydrates in Human Nutrition. (Food & Nutrition Paper Ser.: No. 15). 82p. 1980. pap. 6.00 (ISBN 92-5-100903-1, F2040, FAO). Unipub.

Carbon Dioxide, Climate & Society: Proceedings of an IIASA Workshop, Feb. 1978. Ed. by J. Williams. 1978. text ed. 45.00 (ISBN 0-08-023252-3). Pergamon.

Carbon Fourteen. V. F. Raaen et al. (Advanced Chemistry Ser.). 1968. text ed. 27.00 o.p. (ISBN 0-07-051085-7, C). McGraw.

Carbon Monoxide in Organic Synthesis. J. Falbe. Tr. by C. R. Adams. LC 77-108917. (Illus.). 1970. 37.10 (ISBN 0-387-04814-6). Springer-Verlag.

Carbon Monoxide, Industry & Performance. Ed. by W. H. Walton. 1976. pap. text ed. 27.50 (ISBN 0-08-019966-6). Pergamon.

Carbon Monoxide: Medical & Biological Effects of Environmental Pollutants. 1977. pap. 9.75 (ISBN 0-309-02631-8). Natl Acad Pr.

Carbon Stars. rev. ed. Z. K. Alksne & Ya Y. Ikaunieks. Ed. by J. H. Baumert. (Astronomy & Astrophysics Ser.: Vol. 11). Orig. Title: Uglerodnye Zvevdy. (Illus.). 192p. pap. 24.00 (ISBN 0-912918-16-0). Pachart Pub Hse.

Carbon-Thirteen NMR Based Organic Spectral Problems. P. L. Fuchs & C. A. Bunnell. LC 78-20668. 1979. pap. text ed. 13.95 (ISBN 0-471-04907-7); answer booklet avail. (ISBN 0-471-05138-1). Wiley.

Carbon-Thirteen NMR Spectral Problems. Robert B. Bates & William A. Beavers. LC 79-92216. (Organic Chemistry Ser.). 288p. 1981. text ed. 24.50x (ISBN 0-89603-010-5); pap. text ed. 12.50x (ISBN 0-89603-016-4). Humana.

Carbon-Thirteen Nuclear Magnetic Resonance. 2nd ed. George C. Levy et al. LC 80-17289. 300p. 1980. 22.50 (ISBN 0-471-53157-X, Pub. by Wiley-Interscience). Wiley.

Carbonate Chemistry of Aquatic Systems, Vol. 2. R. E. Loewenthal & G. V. Marais. LC 76-24963. 1981. price not set (ISBN 0-250-40150-9). Ann Arbor Science. Postponed.

Carbonate Facies in Geologic History. J. L. Wilson. (Illus.). 485p. 1975. 44.60 o.p. (ISBN 0-387-07236-5). Springer-Verlag.

Carboniferous of the Southeastern United States. Ed. by Garrett Briggs. LC 73-87234. (Special Paper: No. 148). (Illus., Orig.). 1974. pap. 10.00x (ISBN 0-8137-2148-2). Geol Soc.

Carboniferous Rocks of the Llano Region of Central Texas. F. B. Plummer. (Illus.). 170p. 1943. 2.00 (PUB 4329). Bur Econ Geology.

Carburetors & Carburetion. Walter B. Larew. LC 66-27600. (Illus.). 1967. 9.50 o.p. (ISBN 0-8019-5224-7). Chilton.

Carburizing & Carbonitriding. (Illus., 76-55702). 1977. 34.00 (ISBN 0-87170-044-1). ASM.

Carcinogenesis. Ed. by Canonico & G. P. Margison. (Illus.). 1979. 68.00 (ISBN 0-08-024379-7). Pergamon.

Carcinogenesis & Mutagenesis. Myron A. Mehlman et al. (Journal of Environmental Pathology & Toxicology: Vol. 1, No. 2, Nov.-Dec. 1977). (Illus.). 388p. (Orig.). 1978. text ed. 23.00x (ISBN 0-930376-02-1); pap. 18.50x (ISBN 0-686-64026-8). Pathotox Pubs.

Carcinogenesis & Radiation Risk: A Biomathematical Reconnaissance. W. V. Mayneord & R. H. Clark. 1980. 35.00x (Pub. by Brit Inst Radiology England). State Mutual Bk.

Carcinogenesis: Fundamental Mechanisms & Environmental Effects. Ed. by Bernard Pullman et al. (Jerusalem Symposium: No. 13). 560p. PLB 63.00 (ISBN 90-277-1171-2, Pub. by D. Reidel). Kluwer Boston.

Carcinogens: Identification & Mechanisms of Action. Annual Symposium on Fundamental Cancer Research, No. 31. Ed. by A. Clark Griffin & Charles R. Shaw. LC 78-23366. 1979. text ed. 45.00 (ISBN 0-89004-286-1). Raven.

Carcinoma of the Bladder. Ed. by John G. Connolly. (Progress in Cancer Research & Therapy Ser.). 275p. 1981. 27.00 (ISBN 0-89004-536-4). Raven.

Card, 2 vols. in 1. John Kidgell. (Flowering of the Novel, 1740-1775 Ser: Vol. 43). 1974. Repr. of 1755 ed. lib. bdg. 50.00 (ISBN 0-8240-1142-2). Garland Pub.

Card & Cardboard. LC 71-158980. (Color Crafts Ser.). (Illus.). (gr. 1-4). 1971. 6.95 o.p. (ISBN 0-531-02002-9). Watts.

Card Catalog of the Manuscript Collections of the Archives of American Art, 10 vols. LC 80-53039. 5000p. 1981. lib. bdg. 595.00 (ISBN 0-8420-2174-4). Scholarly Res Inc.

Card Game. Aaron Fletcher. 1980. pap. 1.75 (ISBN 0-505-51456-7). Tower Bks.

Card Games. John Belton & Joella Cramblit. LC 75-42319. (Games & Activities Ser.). (Illus.). 48p. (gr. 3 up). 1976. PLB 9.30 (ISBN 0-8172-0021-5). Raintree Pubs.

Card Games. Ken Reisberg. LC 78-11646. (First Bks.). (Illus.). (gr. 4 up). 1979. PLB 6.45 s&l (ISBN 0-531-02253-6). Watts.

Card Play Technique. rev. ed. Victor Mollo & Nico Gardener. 1971. 10.95 (ISBN 0-571-09744-8, Pub. by Faber & Faber). Merrimack Bk Serv.

Card Tricks. Geoffrey Lamb. LC 72-13357. (Illus.). 80p. (gr. 6 up). 1973. 6.95 o.p. (ISBN 0-525-66300-2). Elsevier-Nelson.

Card Tricks. Ken Reisberg. (gr. 1-3). 1980. PLB 7.90 (ISBN 0-531-04137-9). Watts.

Cardboard Carpentry. Janet D'Amato & Alex D'Amato. (Activity Bks). (Illus.). (gr. 2-5). PLB 7.21 (ISBN 0-87460-085-5). Lion.

Cardenio und Celine. 2nd ed. Andreas Gryphius. Ed. by Hugh Powell. (Ger.). 1967. pap. text ed. 4.75x (ISBN 0-7185-1028-3, Leicester). Humanities.

Cardiac Arrest & CPR: Assessment, Planning & Intervention. Joseph J. Bander et al. 232p. 1980. text ed. cancelled (ISBN 0-89443-328-8). Aspen Systems.

Cardiac Arrhythmias. Ed. by Dennis M. Krikler & John F. Goodwin. LC 75-11582. (Illus.). 255p. 1975. text ed. 26.00 (ISBN 0-7216-5516-5). Saunders.

Cardiac Arrhythmias. 3rd ed. Brendan Phibbs. LC 78-7265. 1978. pap. text ed. 17.50 (ISBN 0-8016-3911-5). Mosby.

Cardiac Arrhythmias: A Symposium. Ed. by Jaok Han. (Illus.). 320p. 1972. 31.50 (ISBN 0-398-02305-0). C C Thomas.

Cardiac Arrhythmias: Exercises in Pattern Interpretation. 2nd ed. Mary H. Conover. LC 77-24509. (Illus.). 1978. pap. text ed. 11.50 (ISBN 0-8016-1024-9). Mosby.

Cardiac Arrhythmias: Their Mechanisms, Diagnosis, & Management. Ed. by William J. Mandel. (Illus.). 592p. 1980. text ed. 55.00 (ISBN 0-397-50473-X). Lippincott.

Cardiac Care: A Guide for Patient Education. Amy M. Karch. (Patient Education Series). 1981. pap. 11.50 (ISBN 0-8385-1041-8). ACC.

Cardiac Catheterization & Angiography. 2nd ed. Ed. by William Grossman. LC 80-10331. (Illus.). 427p. 1980. text ed. 34.50 (ISBN 0-8121-0714-4). Lea & Febiger.

Cardiac Conducting System & the HIS Bundle Electrogram. Roberts. 1975. 18.50 o.p. (ISBN 0-8385-1040-X). ACC.

Cardiac Emergency Care. 2nd ed. Ed. by Edward K. Chung. LC 79-28235. (Illus.). 475p. 1980. text ed. 25.00 (ISBN 0-8121-0690-3). Lea & Febiger.

Cardiac Pacemakers. H. Siddons & E. Sowton. (Amer. Lec. in Living Chemistry Ser.). (Illus.). 352p. 1974. 18.50 (ISBN 0-398-03091-X). C C Thomas.

Cardiac Receptors. Ed. by R. Hainsworth et al. LC 77-12404. (Illus.). 1980. 83.50 (ISBN 0-521-21853-5). Cambridge U Pr.

Cardiac Rehabilitation. Lou Amundsen. (Clinics in Physical Therapy Ser.). (Illus.). 224p. 1981. lib. bdg. 18.00 (ISBN 0-443-08147-6). Churchill.

Cardiac Rehabilitation, Adult Fitness & Exercise Testing. Philip K. Wilson et al. LC 80-16556. (Illus.). 462p. 1981. text ed. 29.50 (ISBN 0-8121-0687-3). Lea & Febiger.

Cardiac Rehabilitation for the Patient & Family. Judy Davis & Shirley Spellman. (Illus.). 176p. 1980. text ed. 10.95 (ISBN 0-8359-0679-5). Reston.

Cardiac Rehabilitation: Implications for the Nurse & Other Allied Health Professionals. Paul S. Fardy et al. LC 80-16296. (Illus.). 283p. 1980. pap. text ed. 14.95 (ISBN 0-8016-1610-7). Mosby.

Cardiac Rhythms: A Systematic Approach to Interpretation. Raymond E. Phillips & Mary K. Feeney. LC 72-86451. (Illus.). 320p. 1973. text ed. 15.50 o.p. (ISBN 0-7216-7220-5). Saunders.

Cardiac Roentgenology: Plain Films & Angiographic Findings. William Meszaros. (Amer. Lec. Roentgen Diagnosis Ser.). 600p. 1969. pap. 65.00 spiral (ISBN 0-398-01297-0). C C Thomas.

Cardiac Surgery One. Dwight. Harken. (Illus.). 1971. 15.00 (ISBN 0-8036-4567-8). Davis Co.

Cardiac Ultrasound. Raymond Gramiak & Robert C. Waag. LC 75-29250. (Illus.). 308p. 1975. 41.50 o.p. (ISBN 0-8016-1956-4). Mosby.

Cardiac Valve Prostheses. Edward Lefrak & Albert Starr. LC 79-46. (Illus.). 1979. 25.50 (ISBN 0-8385-1049-3). ACC.

Cardigan Bay: The Horse That Won a Million Dollars. Ron Bisman. (Illus.). 154p. 1972. 6.95 o.p. (ISBN 0-668-02840-8). Arco.

Cardinal & the Queen. Evelyn Anthony. 1977. pap. 1.50 o.p. (ISBN 0-425-03591-3, Medallion). Berkley Pub.

Cardinal & the Secretary: Thomas Wolsey & Thomas Cromwell. Neville Williams. (Illus.). 288p. 1976. 9.95 o.s.i. (ISBN 0-02-629070-7). Macmillan.

Cardinal De Retz: The Ambiguities of a Seventeenth-Century Mind. Derek A. Watts. 308p. 1980. text ed. 39.95x (ISBN 0-19-815762-2). Oxford U Pr.

Cardinal in Armor: The Story of Richelieu & His Times. Burke Wilkinson. (gr. 7 up). 1966. 4.50g o.s.i. (ISBN 0-02-792930-2). Macmillan.

Cardinal Newman & His Influence on Religious Life & Thought. Charles Sarolea. 182p. Repr. of 1908 ed. 3.50 (ISBN 0-567-04523-4). Attic Pr.

Cardinal Points of Borges. Lowell Dunham & Ivar Ivask. LC 76-163635. (Illus.). 1971. 9.95 (ISBN 0-8061-0983-1); pap. 4.95 (ISBN 0-8061-0984-X). U of Okla Pr.

Cardinal Protectors of England, Rome & the Tudors Before the Reformation. W. E. Wilkie. LC 73-82462. 224p. 1974. 35.50 (ISBN 0-521-20332-5). Cambridge U Pr.

Cardinal Sins. Andrew Greeley. (Orig.). 1981. 12.95 (ISBN 0-446-51236-2). Warner Bks.

Cardinals & Saints. Arlene Zekowski & Stanley Berne. LC 58-11713. 1958. 75.00 (ISBN 0-913844-10-1). Am Canadian.

Cardio Active Drugs: Pharmachlogical Basis for Practice. Dennis A. Bloomfield & Hansjorg Simon. 1981. price not set. Urban & S.

Cardiogenic Shock. Anna L. Seal. (Myocardial Infarction Ser.). 100p. 1980. pap. 6.95x (ISBN 0-8385-1056-6). ACC.

Cardiology Case Studies. 2nd ed. Nicholas P. DePasquale & Michael S. Bruno. LC 79-91847. 1980. pap. 15.00 (ISBN 0-87488-001-7). Med Exam.

Cardiology Case Studies. Ed. by Nicholas P. DePasquale & Michael S. Bruno. 1973. spiral bdg. 12.00 o.p. (ISBN 0-87488-001-7). Med Exam.

Cardiology for the House Officer. Joel Heger. (House Officer Ser.). (Illus.). 200p. 1981. price not set softcover (ISBN 0-683-03946-6). Williams & Wilkins.

Cardiology Review. 2nd. ed. Ed. by Jami G. Shakibi & Philip R. Liebson. 1976. spiral bdg. 14.00 (ISBN 0-87488-337-7). Med Exam.

Cardiology Specialty Board Review. James W. Holsinger, Jr. & Vincent F. Miscia. 1975. spiral bdg. 16.50 (ISBN 0-87488-314-8). Med Exam.

Cardiology: 81. William C. Roberts et al. (Illus.). 400p. 1981. text ed. 35.00 (ISBN 0-914316-22-2). Yorke Med.

Cardiopulmonary Pathology & Pathophysiology Case Studies. Rickert E. Goyette. 1976. spiral bdg. 12.00 o.p. (ISBN 0-87488-075-0). Med Exam.

Cardiopulmonary Resusitation: Procedures for Basic & Advanced Life Support. Diane Ellis & Diane Billings. LC 79-19356. 1979. pap. text ed. 10.50 (ISBN 0-8016-1557-7). Mosby.

Cardiopulmonary Technology Examination Review Book, Vol. 1. Frank G. Simmons & Susan E. Coombes. 1980. pap. 12.50 (ISBN 0-87488-473-X). Med Exam.

Cardiopulmonary Technology Examination Review Book, Vol. 1. Frank G. Simmons & Susan E. Coombs. 1971. spiral bdg. 8.50 o.p. (ISBN 0-87488-473-X). Med Exam.

Cardiothoracic Surgery. 3rd ed. J. W. Jackson. (Operative Surgery Ser.). 1978. 135.00 (ISBN 0-407-00604-4). Butterworths.

Cardiovascular Assessment: Guide for Nurses & Health Professionals. Donald A. Thompson. (Illus.). 185p. 1981. pap. text ed. 10.95 (ISBN 0-8016-4954-4). Mosby.

Cardiovascular Care Unit: A Guide for Planning & Operation. Glen O. Turner. LC 77-14215. 1978. 27.50 o.p. (ISBN 0-471-03022-8, Pub. by Wiley Medical). Wiley.

Cardiovascular Disease - Epidemiology, Prevention & Rehabilitation: A Guide to the Literature, Vol. 1, 1960-1973. Ed. by Senta S. Rogers & Irvin C. Mohler. 606p. 1974. 65.00 (ISBN 0-306-67191-3). IFI Plenum.

Cardiovascular Diseases. Ed. by Kalman Greenspan & John Fischer. (Medical Examination Review Ser.: No. 28). 1973. spiral bdg. 15.00 o.s.i. (ISBN 0-87488-138-2). Med Exam.

Cardiovascular Diseases & Therapy, 6 vols. 2nd ed. J. Alan Herd. Incl. Bk. 1. The Circulatory System & Blood Pressure Control. pap. text ed. 13.50 (ISBN 0-89147-041-7); Bk. 2. Hypertension & Anti-Hypertensive Agents. pap. text ed. 16.50 (ISBN 0-89147-042-5); Bk. 3. Beta-Adrenergic Blocking Agents. pap. text ed. 16.50 (ISBN 0-89147-043-3); Bk. 4. Electrolyte Balance & Diffusion of Body Fluids. pap. text ed. 13.50 (ISBN 0-89147-044-1); Bk. 5. Kidney Structure & Function. pap. text ed. 13.50 (ISBN 0-89147-045-X); Bk. 6. Diuretics. (Illus.). pap. text ed. 13.50 (ISBN 0-89147-046-8). 1976. Set. pap. text ed. 75.00 (ISBN 0-89147-040-9). CAS.

Cardiovascular Effects of Mood-Altering Drugs. Barry Stimmel. LC 77-91582. 1979. text ed. 27.00 (ISBN 0-89004-287-X). Raven.

Cardiovascular Hemorheology. S. Oka. (Illus.). 200p. Date not set. price not set (ISBN 0-521-23650-9). Cambridge U Pr.

Cardiovascular Nuclear Medicine. Ed. by A. Donath & A. Righetti. (Progress in Nuclear Medicine: Vol. 6). (Illus.). viii, 228p. 1980. 88.75 (ISBN 3-8055-0618-X). S Karger.

Cardiovascular Nuclear Medicine. 2nd ed. H. William Strauss & Bertram Pitt. LC 79-18410. (Illus.). 1979. text ed. 54.50 (ISBN 0-8016-2409-6). Mosby.

Cardiovascular Pathology. Ed. by J. M. Budinger. (AP Slide Seminar Ser.). (Illus.). 1978. pap. text ed. 15.00 o.p. (ISBN 0-89189-051-3, 50-1-042-00); slides 75.00 o.p. (ISBN 0-686-67355-7, 01-1-076-01). Am Soc Clinical.

Cardiovascular Pathophysiology. Tjeerd Van der Werf. (Illus.). 320p. 1980. 19.95 (ISBN 0-19-261153-4); pap. text ed. 10.95x (ISBN 0-19-261229-8). Oxford U Pr.

Cardiovascular Pharmacology. Ed. by Michael J. Antonaccio. LC 74-14469. 1977. 31.00 (ISBN 0-89004-063-X). Raven.

Cardiovascular Physiolgy. 4th ed. Robert M. Berne & Matthew N. Levy. (Illus.). 304p. 1981. pap. text ed. 16.50 (ISBN 0-8016-0655-1). Mosby.

Cardiovascular Physiology. Lois J. Heller & David E. Mohrman. Ed. by Richard W. Mixter. (Illus.). 176p. 1980. pap. text ed. 9.95 (ISBN 0-07-027973-X). McGraw.

Cardiovascular Physiology, Heart, Peripheral Circulation & Methodology: Proceedings of the 28th International Congress of Physiological Sciences, Budapest, Hungary, 1980. Ed. by A. G. B. Kovach et al. LC 80-41875. (Advances in Physiological Sciences). (Illus.). 400p. 1981. 50.00 (ISBN 0-08-026820-X). Pergamon.

Cardiovascular Physiology, Microcirculation & Capillary Exchange: Proceedings of the 28th International Congress of Physiological Sciences, Budapest, 1980. Ed. by A. G. B. Kovach et al. LC 80-41873. (Advances in Physiological Sciences: Vol. 7). (Illus.). 400p. 1981. 50.00 (ISBN 0-08-026819-6). Pergamon.

Cardiovascular Physiology-Neural Control Mechanisms: Proceesings of the 28th International Congress of Physiological Sciences, Budapest, 1980. Ed. by A. G. B. Kovach et al. LC 80-41927. (Advances in Physiological Sciences: Vol. 9). (Illus.). 400p. 1981. 50.00 (ISBN 0-08-026821-8). Pergamon.

Cardiovascular Problems: A Critical Care Nursing Focus. Mary Jackle & Marney Halligan. (Illus.). 1980. pap. text ed. 19.95 (ISBN 0-87619-667-9). R J Brady.

Cardiovascular Psychophysiology: Current Issues in Response Mechanisms, Biofeedback & Methodology. Ed. by Paul A. Obrist et al. LC 73-89517. 624p. (Orig.). 1974. 29.95x (ISBN 0-202-25116-0). Aldine Pub.

Cardiovascular System: Disease, Diagnosis, Treatment. K. G. Swan. (Clinical Monographs Ser.). (Illus.). 1973. pap. 7.95 (ISBN 0-87618-058-6). R J Brady.

Cardiovascular System, Vol. 2: Vascular Smooth Muscle. American Physiological Society et al. (APS Handbk. of Physiology: Section 2). (Illus.). 700p. 1980. lib. bdg. 95.00 (ISBN 0-683-00606-1). Williams & Wilkins.

Cards of Identity. Nigel Dennis. LC 55-10479. 1955. 9.95 (ISBN 0-8149-0083-6). Vanguard.

Cards of Love. Clarence W. Duff. 1980. pap. 6.95 (ISBN 0-87552-248-3). Presby & Reformed.

Cards on the Table. Agatha Christie. 1980. pap. 2.25 (ISBN 0-440-11052-1). Dell.

Care & Conservation of Collections: A Bibliography on Historical Organization Practices, Vol. 2. Ed. by Frederick L. Rath, Jr. & Merrilyn O'Connell. LC 75-26770. 1977. 10.00x (ISBN 0-910050-28-7). AASLH.

Care & Counseling of the Aging. William M. Clements. Ed. by Howard J. Clinebell & Howard W. Stone. LC 78-54547. (Creative Pastoral Care & Counseling Ser). 96p. 1979. pap. 2.95 (ISBN 0-8006-0561-6, 1-1561). Fortress.

Care & Counseling of Youth in the Church. Paul B. Irwin. Ed. by Howard J. Clinebell & Howard W. Stone. LC 74-26334. (Creative Pastoral Care & Counseling Ser.). 96p. 1975. pap. 3.25 (ISBN 0-8006-0552-7, 1-552). Fortress.

Care & Education in Young Children in America: Policy, Politics & Social Science. Ed. by Ron Haskins & James J. Gallagher. LC 80-11788. (Illus.). 224p. 1980. text ed. 19.95 (ISBN 0-89391-040-6). Ablex Pub.

Care & Feeding of Power Grid Tubes. Robert I. Sutherland & EIMAC Division of Varian Laboratory Staff. (Illus.). 158p. 1967. 5.95 (ISBN 0-933616-06-6). Radio Pubns.

Care & Feeding of the Offshore Crew. Lin Pardey & Larry Pardey. (Illus.). 1980. 17.95 (ISBN 0-393-03249-3). Norton.

Care & Handling of the 1000 LB. Dog. Douglas H. Eads. (Illus.). 96p. (Orig.). 1980. pap. 4.95 (ISBN 0-89769-019-2). Pine Mntn.

Care & Management of Spinal Cord Injuries. Ed. by G. Bedbrook. (Illus.). 351p. 1981. 39.80 (ISBN 0-387-90494-8). Springer-Verlag.

Care & Management of the Sick & Incompetent Physician. Robert C. Green, Jr. et al. (Illus.). 116p. 1978. 12.75 (ISBN 0-398-03727-2). C C Thomas.

Care & Operation of Small Engines, 2 vols. 4th ed. J. Howard Turner. Vol. 1. 7.95 (ISBN 0-914452-23-1); Vol. 2. 9.95 (ISBN 0-914452-24-X). Green Hill.

Care & Rehabilitation of the Stroke Patient. Benjamin G. Cox, Jr. (Illus.). 100p. 1973. pap. 14.75 spiral (ISBN 0-398-02890-7). C C Thomas.

Care & Repair of Boat Auxiliary Systems: Boatowner's How-to Guides, Vol. 6. 144p. 1980. 5.95 (ISBN 0-8306-9751-9, 947). Tab Bks.

Care & Repair of Fishing Tackle. Mel Marshall. 1976. 12.95 (ISBN 0-87691-183-1). Winchester Pr.

Care & Repair of Furniture. Desmond Gaston. LC 78-55622. 1978. 9.95 o.p. (ISBN 0-385-14466-0). Doubleday.

Care & Use of Japanese Woodworking Tools. Kip Mesirow. LC 78-60055. (Illus.). 1980. pap. 8.95 (ISBN 0-918036-08-9). Woodcraft Supply.

Care for the Dying. Richard N. Soulen. LC 74-19968. 120p. 1975. pap. 4.95 (ISBN 0-8042-1098-5). John Knox.

Care of Books: An Essay on the Development of Libraries & Their Fittings, from the Earliest Times to the End of the 18th Century. John W. Clark. 442p. 1980. 50.00x (ISBN 0-902089-78-1, Pub. by Variorum England). State Mutual Bk.

Care of Cogenital Hand Anomalies. Adrian E. Flatt. LC 77-5932. (Illus.). 1977. text ed. 39.50 (ISBN 0-8016-1586-0). Mosby.

Care of Converts. Keith M. Baily. 95p. (Orig.). 1979. pap. 1.75 (ISBN 0-87509-157-1); leader's guide 0.75 (ISBN 0-686-65443-9). Chr Pubns.

Care of Minor Hand Injuries. 4th ed. Adrian E. Flatt. LC 79-12082. (Illus.). 1979. text ed. 38.50 (ISBN 0-8016-1581-X). Mosby.

Care of Patients with Emotional Problems. 3rd ed. Dolores F. Saxton & Phyllis W. Haring. LC 78-31641. (Illus.). 1979. pap. text ed. 8.50 (ISBN 0-8016-4341-4). Mosby.

Care of the Adult Patient. Dorothy Smith & Carol P. Germain. (Illus.). 1975. 21.75 o.p. (ISBN 0-397-54165-1); pap. 21.00 o.p. (ISBN 0-397-54171-6). Lippincott.

Care of the Burn-Injured Patient: A Multidisciplinary Involvement. Ed. by Mary M. Wagner. 320p. 1981. 24.00 (ISBN 0-88416-249-4). PSG Pub.

Care of the Cancer Patient. L. G. Capra. (Illus.). 1972. pap. text ed. 21.00x (ISBN 0-433-05145-0). Intl Ideas.

Care of the Child Facing Death. Ed. by Lindy Burton. 1974. 18.50 (ISBN 0-7100-7863-3). Routledge & Kegan.

Care of the Critically Ill. 2nd ed. Ayres. 1974. 17.50 o.p. (ISBN 0-8385-1053-1). ACC.

Care of the Elderly Person: A Guide for the Licensed Practical Nurse. 3rd. ed. Maureen O. Flaherty. LC 80-11236. (Illus.). 1980. pap. text ed. 9.95 (ISBN 0-8016-3706-6). Mosby.

Care of the Fetus. Robert C. Goodlin. LC 78-62542. (Illus.). 580p. 1979. 43.50 (ISBN 0-89352-021-7). Masson Pub.

Care of the Mentally Retarded. Marian Blackwell. 1979. 15.95 (ISBN 0-316-09890-6). Little.

Care of the Neurologically Handicapped Child. Arthur L. Prensky & Helen Palkes. (Illus.). 350p. 1981. text ed. 18.95x (ISBN 0-19-502917-8). Oxford U Pr.

Care of the Newborn. Ed. by Richard L. Schreiner. 318p. 1980. text ed. 24.00 (ISBN 0-89004-518-6). Raven.

Care of the Older Adult. Joan Breitung. LC 80-51870. (Illus.). 344p. (gr. 12). 1981. pap. text ed. 9.90 (ISBN 0-913292-05-2). Tiresias Pr.

Care of the Ostomy Patient. 2nd ed. Virginia C. Vukovich & Reba G. Grubb. LC 76-58498. (Illus.). 1977. pap. text ed. 9.50 (ISBN 0-8016-5276-6). Mosby.

Care of the Patient with Neurogenic Bladder. Saul Boyarsky et al. 1978. text ed. 13.95 (ISBN 0-316-10431-0). Little.

Care of the Wild Feathered & Furred: A Guide to Wildlife Handling & Care. Mae Hickman & Maxine Guy. LC 73-76970. (Illus.). 175p. (Orig.). 1973. 8.95 o.p. (ISBN 0-913300-29-2); pap. 5.95 (ISBN 0-913300-26-8). Unity Pr.

Care of Water Pets. Gertrude Pels. LC 54-9768. (Illus.). (gr. 2-5). 1955. 8.95 (ISBN 0-690-17070-X, TYC-J); PLB 8.79 (ISBN 0-690-17071-8). T Y Crowell.

Care to Communicate. Pat M. Ashworth. (RCN Research Monographs). 184p. (Orig.). 1980. pap. 10.00 (ISBN 0-443-02412-X). Churchill.

Career: A Handbook of Ideas to Motivate the Teaching of Career Education. (Spice Ser.). 1977. 6.50 (ISBN 0-89273-123-0). Educ Serv.

Career Adaptive Behavior Inventory Activity Book. Thomas P. Lombardi. Ed. by J. B. Preston. 88p. (Orig.). 1980. pap. text ed. 10.00x (ISBN 0-87562-066-3). Spec Child.

Career & Motherhood: Struggles for a New Identity. Alan Roland & Barbara Harris. LC 78-8026. 1978. 16.95 (ISBN 0-87705-372-3). Human Sci Pr.

Career Astrology: Vocational Counseling for the Nineteen Eighties. C. J. Puotinen. 240p. 1980. pap. 8.95 (ISBN 0-930840-10-0). Ninth Sign.

Career Choices for the Seventies. Arnold Arnold. LC 79-132860. (gr. 7 up). 1971. 7.95 (ISBN 0-02-705670-8, CCPr). Macmillan.

Career Conflict: Management's Inelegant Dysfunction. Robert K. Mueller. LC 78-19240. (Arthur D. Little Books). 1978. 15.95 (ISBN 0-669-02471-6). Lexington Bks.

Career Counseling. Vernon G. Zunker. LC 80-23030. 357p. 1980. text ed. 16.95 (ISBN 0-8185-0428-5). Brooks-Cole.

Career Counseling in the Community College. C. Healy. (Illus.). 160p. 1974. 14.75 (ISBN 0-398-03096-0); pap. 8.50 (ISBN 0-398-03097-9). C C Thomas.

Career Counseling: Models, Methods & Materials. John O. Crites. (Illus.). 240p. 1981. text ed. 14.95x (ISBN 0-07-013781-1, C). McGraw.

Career Development Activities. Larry Kenneke. 1973. pap. 6.00 o.p. (ISBN 0-672-97621-8). Bobbs.

Career Development & Job Training: A Manager's Handbook. new ed. James G. Stockard. 1978. 24.95 (ISBN 0-8144-5449-6). Am Mgmt.

Career Development for the College Student. Ed. by Philip W. Dunphy. LC 76-8405. (gr. 9-12). 1976. pap. 4.75 o.p. (ISBN 0-910328-02-1). Carroll Pr.

Career Development for the College Student. 5th ed. Ed. by Philip W. Dunphy. 128p. 1981. pap. 6.50 (ISBN 0-910328-02-1). Carroll Pr.

Career Development: Growth & Crisis. Arthur M. Kroll et al. LC 79-96048. 1970. 20.00 (ISBN 0-471-50850-0, Pub. by Wiley-Interscience). Wiley.

Career Development: Self-Concept Theory. Donald E. Super et al. (Research Monograph: No. 4). 1963. pap. 6.00 (ISBN 0-87447-010-2, 213815). College Bd.

Career Directory. 1981. pap. 9.95 (ISBN 0-686-69085-0). Dial.

Career Dynamics: Matching Individual & Organizational Needs. Edgar H. Schein. 1978. pap. text ed. 7.50 (ISBN 0-201-06834-6). A-W.

Career Edition for Exceptional Children & Youth: Career Edition for Excepional Children & Youth. Pamela Gillet. LC 80-84931. 340p. 1981. text ed. 18.95 (ISBN 0-913420-90-5). Olympus Pub Co.

Career Education: A Lifelong Process. Ed. by Jack W. Fuller & Terry O. Whealon. LC 78-1994. 1978. text ed. 19.95 (ISBN 0-88229-200-5). Nelson-Hall.

Career Education & Rehabilitation for the Mentally Handicapped. T. F. Riggar & S. W. Riggar. (Illus.). 272p. 1980. text ed. 24.75 (ISBN 0-398-04137-7). C C Thomas.

Career Education & the Art Teaching Profession. Ed. by Kent Anderson. 48p. 1980. 4.50 (ISBN 0-686-27491-1). Natl Art Ed.

Career Education & the Elementary School Teacher. Kenneth B. Hoyt et al. LC 73-78952. 200p. 1973. pap. 5.95 o.p. (ISBN 0-913420-06-9). Olympus Pub Co.

Career Education for Handicapped Children & Youth. Donn E. Brolin & Charles J. Kokaska. (Special Education Ser.). 1979. text ed. 19.50 (ISBN 0-675-08278-1). Merrill.

Career Education in the Visual Arts: Representative Programs & Projects. Ed. by George Geahigan. 127p. 1980. 6.75 (ISBN 0-686-27492-X). Natl Art Ed.

Career Education: New Approaches to Human Development. Larry J. Bailey & Ronald W. Stadt. 403p. 1974. pap. 16.09 (ISBN 0-87345-601-7). McKnight.

Career Education: Where It Is & Where It's Going. Kenneth Hoyt. 280p. 1981. text ed. price not set (ISBN 0-913420-92-1). Olympus Pub Co.

Career Exploration: You & Your Future. Ted Elsberg. LC 75-10352. (Illus.). 1975. 6.95 (ISBN 0-87005-145-8); wkbk. 3.50 (ISBN 0-87005-152-0). Fairchild.

Career Guidance for a New Age. Henry Borow et al. (Illus.). 336p. 1973. text ed. 17.75 (ISBN 0-395-14362-4, 3-05191). HM.

Career in Catering--Choosing a Course. Roy Hayter. LC 79-41628. (Illus.). 232p. 1980. 33.00 (ISBN 0-08-024708-3); pap. 14.50 (ISBN 0-08-024707-5). Pergamon.

Career in Speech Pathology. Charles Van Riper. LC 78-9678. 1979. pap. 7.95 ref. (ISBN 0-13-114769-2). P-H.

Career Information in Counseling & Teaching. 3rd ed. Lee E. Isaacson. 1977. text ed. 18.95 (ISBN 0-205-05785-3). Allyn.

Career Management for the Organization: The Individual. Ed. by Mariann Jelinek. 1979. pap. text ed. 12.50 (ISBN 0-914292-18-8); teacher's manual avail. (ISBN 0-471-06292-8). Wiley.

Career Mathematics: Practical Applications for Nonmechanical & Business Occupations. Sidney Rock & Samuel I. Miller. (gr. 10 up). 1978. text ed. 13.95x (ISBN 0-8104-5536-6); pap. text ed. 10.95x (ISBN 0-8104-5535-8); tchrs'. guide 1.95 (ISBN 0-8104-5625-7). Hayden.

Career of a Radical Rightist: A Study in Failure. Scott G. McNall. 1975. 15.00 (ISBN 0-8046-9099-5, Natl U). Kennikat.

Career of a Tsarist Officer: Memoirs, 1872-1916. Anton I. Denikin. Tr. by Margaret Patoski from Rus. LC 75-14625. (Illus.). 355p. 1975. 22.50x (ISBN 0-8166-0698-6). U of Minn Pr.

Career of Philosophy Vol. 1: From the Middle Ages to the Enlightenment. John H. Randall. LC 62-10454. 1970. 27.50x (ISBN 0-231-08677-6); pap. 12.50x (ISBN 0-231-08637-7). Columbia U Pr.

Career of Philosophy Vol. 2. From the German Enlightenment to the Age of Darwin. John H. Randall. LC 62-10454. 1970. 20.00x (ISBN 0-231-08678-4); pap. 12.50x (ISBN 0-231-08639-3). Columbia U Pr.

Career of William Beaumont & the Reception of His Discovery: An Original Anthology. William Beaumont. Ed. by I. Bernard Cohen. LC 79-7949. (Three Centuries of Science in America Ser.). (Illus.). 1980. lib. bdg. 20.00x (ISBN 0-405-12530-5). Arno.

Career Patterns of Liberal Arts Graduates. Robert Calvert, Jr. LC 73-84568. (gr. 12). 1973. 10.00x o.p. (ISBN 0-910328-00-5). Carroll Pr.

Career Patterns of Women Librarians with Doctorates. Doris Dale. (Occasional Papers: No. 147). 1980. pap. 3.00. U of Ill Lib Sci.

Career Planning & Decision-Making for College Students. 5.95; instrs'. 7.50. McKnight.

Career Planning for Salesmen. 2nd ed. Ed Roseman. 56p. 1981. spiral bdg 7.95 (ISBN 0-89047-041-3). Herman Pub.

Career Planning for the Blind. Fred L. Crawford. (Keith Jennison Large Type Bks). 8.95 o.p. (ISBN 0-531-00171-7). Watts.

Career Planning for the Blind: A Manual for Students & Teachers. Fred L. Crawford. 189p. 1966. 3.95 (ISBN 0-374-11905-8). FS&G.

Career Planning: Freedom to Choose. 2nd ed. Bruce Shertzer. LC 80-81846. (Illus.). 416p. 1981. pap. text ed. 9.25 (ISBN 0-395-29738-9); 0.80 (ISBN 0-395-29739-7). HM.

Career Planning: Skills to Build Your Future. Carney et al. (Orig.). 1980. 8.95 (ISBN 0-442-23350-7); instr's. manual 2.50 (ISBN 0-442-25860-7). D Van Nostrand.

Career Potentials in Physical Activity. Bryant J. Cratty. LC 79-136631. (Physical Education Ser). 1971. ref. ed. 15.95 (ISBN 0-13-114710-2). P-H.

Career Power. Richard J. Rinella & Claire C. Robbins. 281p. 1981. 14.95 (ISBN 0-8144-5630-8); comb-bound 16.95 (ISBN 0-8144-7009-2). Am Mgmt.

Career Satisfaction & Success: A Guide to Job Freedom. Bernard Haldane. (AMACOM Executive Books). 1978. pap. 4.95 (ISBN 0-8144-7501-9). Am Mgmt.

Career Search. Elwood N. Chapman. LC 75-35758. (Illus.). 200p. 1976. pap. text ed. 6.50 (ISBN 0-574-20005-3, 13-3005); instr's guide avail. (ISBN 0-574-20006-1, 13-3006). SRA.

Career Sevices Today: A Dynamic College Profession. C Randall Powell & Donald K. Kirts. LC 79-54801. 1980. pap. 11.95 (ISBN 0-913936-13-8). Coll Placement.

Career Strategies: Planning for Personal Achievement. new ed. Andrew H. Souerwine. LC 77-28087. 1978. 15.95 (ISBN 0-8144-5454-2); pap. 6.95 (ISBN 0-8144-6963-9). Am Mgmt.

Career Success - Personal Failure. Abraham Korman & Rhoda Korman. 150p. 1980. text ed. 12.95 (ISBN 0-13-114777-3). P-H.

Career Training in Child Psychiatry. Conference on Training in Child Psychiatry, 1963. 1964. 3.00 o.p. (ISBN 0-685-24854-2, 161). Am Psychiatric.

Careers & Career Education in the Performing Arts: An Annotated Bibliography. Ed. by William L. Waack. 57p. 3.50. Am Theatre Assoc.

Careers & Disabilities: A Career Education Approach. David C. Gardner & Sue A. Warren. LC 78-62312. (Orig.). 1978. text ed. 9.95x (ISBN 0-89223-020-7). Greylock Pubs.

Careers & Professions. pap. 3.95 o.p. (ISBN 0-8092-9354-4). Contemp Bks.

Careers at a Zoo. Mark Lerner. LC 80-19614. (Early Career Bks.). (Illus.). (gr. 2-5). 1980. PLB 4.95g (ISBN 0-8225-0342-5). Lerner Pubns.

Careers, Eighty - Eighty-One: A Human Resource Consultants' Views of Career Management & a Guide to 600 Current Books & Articles. Donald B. Miller. (Orig.). 1980. pap. 11.95 (ISBN 0-930918-02-9). Vitality Assocs.

Careers Encyclopedia. Ed. by Craig T. Norback. 360p. 1980. 27.50 (ISBN 0-87094-203-4). Dow Jones-Irwin.

Careers for a Small World: Working & Living with Appropriate Technology. Robert V. Doyle. (Illus.). 190p. (gr. 9-12). 1981. PLB price not set. Messner.

Careers for Humanities - Liberal Arts Majors: A Guide to Programs & Resources. Ed. by Thomas N. Trzyna et al. LC 80-50352. 188p. (Orig.). 1980. pap. 22.50x (ISBN 0-9604078-0-4). Weatherford.

Careers for the Seventies: Dance. Walter Terry. (gr. 9 up). 1971. 4.95g o.s.i. (ISBN 0-02-789150-X, CCPr). Macmillan.

Careers in a Department Store. Lavinia Stanhope. LC 76-4836. (Whole Works Ser.). (Illus.). 48p. (gr. 3-7). 1976. PLB 9.65 (ISBN 0-8172-0703-1). Raintree Pubs.

Careers in a Fire Department. Margaret Reuter. LC 77-8151. (Whole Works Ser.). (Illus.). (gr. 3-7). 1977. PLB 9.65 (ISBN 0-8172-0954-9). Raintree Pubs.

Careers in a Hospital. Joy Schaleben-Lewis. LC 76-12487. (Whole Works Ser.). (Illus.). 48p. (gr. 3-7). 1976. PLB 9.65 (ISBN 0-8172-0709-0). Raintree Pubs.

Careers in a Police Department. Margaret Reuter. LC 77-8113. (Whole Works Ser.). (Illus.). (gr. 3-7). 1977. PLB 9.65 (ISBN 0-8172-0956-5). Raintree Pubs.

Careers in a Supermarket. Joy Schaleben-Lewis. LC 76-44915. (Whole Works Ser). (Illus.). 48p. (gr. 3-7). 1977. PLB 9.65 (ISBN 0-8172-0713-9). Raintree Pubs.

Careers in Agribusiness & Industry. 2nd ed. Archie A. Stone. LC 76-106341. (Illus.). (gr. 9-12). 1980. 12.65 o.p. (ISBN 0-8134-2073-3); text ed. 9.50x o.p. (ISBN 0-685-03875-0, 2073). Interstate.

Careers in Agribusiness & Industry. 3rd ed. Archie A. Stone. LC 76-106341. (Illus.). (gr. 9-12). 12.65 (ISBN 0-8134-2073-3); text ed. 9.50x. Interstate.

Careers in an Airport. Gary Paulsen. LC 76-44241. (Whole Works Ser.). (Illus.). (gr. 3-7). 1977. PLB 9.65 (ISBN 0-8172-0707-4). Raintree Pubs.

Careers in Art. rev. ed. National Art Education Association. 1971. pap. 1.00 (ISBN 0-686-00141-9, 061-25834). Natl Art Ed.

Careers in Auto Racing. Mark Lerner. LC 80-12047. (Illus.). (gr. 2-5). 1980. PLB 4.95 (ISBN 0-8225-0343-3). Lerner Pubns.

Careers in Business: Selecting & Planning Your Career Path. Lila B. Stair. 1980. 6.95x (ISBN 0-256-02368-9). Irwin.

Careers in Computers & Data Processing. Herman McDaniel. LC 77-25076. 1978. 11.50 (ISBN 0-89433-029-2); pap. 8.95 (ISBN 0-89433-030-6). Petrocelli.

Careers in Conservation: Opportunities in Natural Resource Management. 2nd ed. Henry Clepper. LC 78-21917. 1979. 15.50 (ISBN 0-471-05163-2). Ronald Pr.

Careers in Conservation: Profiles of People Working for the Environment. Ada Graham & Frank Graham. LC 79-20793. (Illus.). (gr. 5 up). 1980. 9.95 (ISBN 0-684-16472-8). Scribner.

Careers in Counseling & Guidance. Shelley C. Stone & Bruce Shertzer. LC 72-185792. 160p. (Orig.). 1972. pap. text ed. 9.75 (ISBN 0-395-13494-3). HM.

Careers in Engineering & Engineering Technology. Mary McHugh. (Career Concise Guides Ser.). (Illus.). (gr. 7 up). 1978. PLB 6.45 s&l (ISBN 0-531-01424-X). Watts.

Careers in Food Services. Ann Cavallaro. 160p. (YA) 1981. 9.95 (ISBN 0-525-66698-2). Elsevier-Nelson.

Careers in Health Sciences. Diane Seide. 160p. Date not set. 7.95 (ISBN 0-525-66679-6). Elsevier-Nelson. Postponed.

Careers in Management for the New Woman. Gloria Shashower. (Choosing Careers & Life-Styles Ser.). (Illus.). (gr. 7 up). 1978. PLB 7.90 s&l (ISBN 0-531-01350-2). Watts.

Careers in Medicine for the New Woman. Carol Jochnowitz. (Choosing Careers & Life-Styles Ser.). (Illus.). (gr. 7 up). 1978. PLB 7.90 s&l (ISBN 0-531-01444-4). Watts.

Careers in Music. rev. ed. Ed. by Betty Stearns & Clara Degen. LC 76-150516. (Illus.). 1980. pap. text ed. 2.00 (ISBN 0-918196-00-0). American Music.

Careers in Office Work. Louise Horton. (Career Concise Guides Ser.). (Illus.). (gr. 7 up). 1977. PLB 6.45 s&l (ISBN 0-531-01308-1). Watts.

Careers in Photography. Ted Schwarz. 1981. 12.95 (ISBN 0-8092-7019-6); pap. 5.95 (ISBN 0-8092-7018-8). Contemp Bks.

Careers in Physical Rehabilitation Therapy. Toure Halima. (Career Concise Guides Ser.). (Illus.). (gr. 7 up). 1977. PLB 6.45 s&l (ISBN 0-531-01306-5). Watts.

Careers in Politics for the New Woman. Alice L. Booth. (Choosing Careers & Life-Styles Ser.). (Illus.). (gr. 7 up). 1978. PLB 7.90 s&l (ISBN 0-531-01313-8). Watts.

Careers in Publishing & Printing. Eleanor Felder. LC 76-5903. (Whole Works Ser). (Illus.). 48p. (gr. 3-7). 1976. PLB 9.65 (ISBN 0-8172-0701-5). Raintree Pubs.

Careers in Shanghai: The Social Guidance of Personal Energies in a Developing Chinese City, 1949-1966. Lynn T. White, 3rd. 1978. 20.00x (ISBN 0-520-03361-2). U of Cal Pr.

Careers in State & Local Government. John W. Zehring. LC 80-67448. (Illus.). 236p. 1980. pap. 10.95 (ISBN 0-912048-15-8). Garrett Pk.

Careers in the Beauty Industry. Doris Cassiday & Bruce Cassiday. (Career Concise Guides Ser.). (Illus.). (gr. 7 up). 1978. PLB 6.45 s&l (ISBN 0-531-01419-3). Watts.

Careers in the Energy Industry. Betsy H. Kraft. (Career Concise Guides Ser.). (Illus.). (gr. 7 up). 1977. PLB 6.45 s&l (ISBN 0-531-01305-7). Watts.

Careers in the Insurance Industry. Patricia Van Gelder. (Career Concise Guides Ser.). (Illus.). (gr. 7 up). 1978. PLB 6.45 s&l (ISBN 0-531-01421-5). Watts.

Careers in the Legal Profession. Elinor Porter Swiger. LC 77-811. (Career Concise Guides Ser.). (gr. 7 up). 1977. PLB 6.45 (ISBN 0-531-01294-8). Watts.

Careers in the Services. W. E. Butterworth. LC 76-9816. (Career Concise Guides Ser.). (Illus.). 72p. (gr. 7 up). 1976. PLB 6.45 (ISBN 0-531-00324-8). Watts.

Careers in the Sports Industry. Barbara Fenten & D. X. Fenten. LC 76-44506. (Career Concise Guides Ser.). (Illus.). (gr. 7 up). 1977. PLB 6.45 (ISBN 0-531-00372-8). Watts.

Careers in the Visual Arts: Options, Training & Employment. Ed. by Theodore Zernich. 64p. 1980. 4.75 (ISBN 0-686-27493-8). Natl Art Ed.

Careers in the Visual Arts: Talking with Professionals. Dian G. Smith. LC 80-17848. (Career Bks.). (Illus.). 224p. (gr. 7 up). 1980. PLB 9.29 (ISBN 0-671-33080-2). Messner.

Careers in Theatre, Music & Dance. Louise Horton. (Career Concise Guides Ser.). (Illus.). 72p. (gr. 7 up). 1976. PLB 6.45 (ISBN 0-531-01205-0). Watts.

Careers in Toy Making. Mark Lerner. LC 80-11293. (Early Career Bks.). (Illus.). (gr. 2-5). 1980. PLB 4.95g (ISBN 0-8225-0340-9). Lerner Pubns.

Careers Nineteen Seventy-Nine: A Guide to Books & Information About Career Management & Planning. Donald B. Miller. 1978. pap. 5.00 o.p. (ISBN 0-930918-01-0). Vitality Assocs.

Careers of PhD's. National Academy Of Sciences Office Of Scientific Personnel. 1968. 7.25 o.p. (ISBN 0-309-01577-4). Natl Acad Pr.

Careers of Professional Women. Ed. by Rosalie Silverstone & Audrey Ward. 227p. 1980. 30.00x (ISBN 0-85664-923-6, Pub. by Croom Helm Ltd England). Biblio Dist.

Careers of Social Studies Students. Barbara N. Rodgers. 75p. 1964. pap. text ed. 3.75x (Pub. by Bedford England). Renouf.

Careers Through Cooperative Work Experience. Robert L. Bennett. 1977. 11.95 (ISBN 0-471-06634-6); tchrs'. manual (ISBN 0-471-02416-3). Wiley.

Careers to Explore for Brownie & Junior Girl Scouts. Girl Scouts of the U.S.A. Program Dept. (GS Catalogue: No. 20-813). 80p. (Orig.). (gr. 6-12). 2.75 (ISBN 0-88441-324-1). GS.

Careers to Preserve Our Shrinking World: Working & Living with Appropriate Technology. 192p. (gr. 7 up). 1981. write for info. Messner.

Carefree Cookbook. Christine Cooper & Angela Hildesley. 1976. 8.95 (ISBN 0-600-31879-6). Transatlantic.

Careful Consumer. 2nd ed. Jean Stewart. 1978. pap. text ed. 3.00 o.p. (ISBN 0-435-42281-2). Heinemann Ed.

Careful Melinda, That Footstep Belongs to... !! Dina Anastasio. (Write-It-Yourself Bks.). (Illus.). 48p. 1981. pap. 1.75 (ISBN 0-8431-0282-9). Price Stern.

Caregiver Training for Child Care: A Multimedia Program. LaVisa C. Wilson. (Elementary Education Ser.). 1977. pap. text ed. 7.95 (ISBN 0-675-08482-2); instr's manual 3.95 (ISBN 0-686-67613-0). Merrill.

Careless Animal. Ada Graham & Frank Graham, Jr. LC 73-14222. 112p. (gr. 3-5). 1975. PLB 4.95 (ISBN 0-385-01828-2). Doubleday.

Careless Husband. Colley Cibber. Ed. by William W. Appleton. LC 66-15482. (Regents Restoration Drama Ser). 1966. 8.50x (ISBN 0-8032-0352-7); pap. 1.65x (ISBN 0-8032-5352-4, BB 257, Bison). U of Nebr Pr.

Caresse. Pamela Wallace. 1979. pap. 2.50 o.p. (ISBN 0-523-40516-2). Pinnacle Bks.

Caretaker. Arthur Roth. LC 80-66249. 224p. (gr. 7 up). 1980. 9.95 (ISBN 0-590-07631-0, Four Winds). Schol Bk Serv.

Caretaker Wife. Barbara Whitehead. 1979. pap. 1.95 o.p. (ISBN 0-425-04038-0). Berkley Pub.

Caretakers of Wonder. Cooper Edens. (Illus.). 40p. (Orig.). 1980. pap. 6.95 (ISBN 0-914676-76-8). Green Tiger.

Caretakers of Wonder. Cooper Edens. (Illus.). 40p. 1981. 10.95 (ISBN 0-914676-78-4). Green Tiger.

Caretakers: Treating Emotionally Disturbed Children. David R. Buckholdt & Jaber F. Gubrium. LC 79-10000. (Sociological Observations: No. 7). 1979. 18.95x (ISBN 0-8039-1202-1); pap. 8.95x (ISBN 0-8039-1203-X). Sage.

Cargo Handling in a Modern Port. R. B. Oram. 1965. 27.00 (ISBN 0-08-011306-0); pap. 14.00 (ISBN 0-08-011305-2). Pergamon.

Cargo Loss Prevention Recommendation. 3rd ed. International Union of Marine Insurance. 1980. pap. 2.00 (ISBN 0-685-64826-5). Helios.

Cargo Risk. Michael Kirk. LC 80-1123. (Crime Club Ser.). 1980. 8.95 (ISBN 0-385-17272-9). Doubleday.

Cargo Ships. Herbert S. Zim & James R. Skelly. (How Things Work). (Illus.). (gr. 3-7). 1970. PLB 5.71 (ISBN 0-688-31143-1). Morrow.

Cargoes: Matson's First Century in the Pacific. William L. Worden. 208p. 1981. 12.95 (ISBN 0-8248-0708-1). U Pr of Hawaii.

Carian Inscriptions from North Sacqara & Buhen. O. Masson. 120p. 1979. 75.00x (ISBN 0-686-61264-7, Pub. by Aris & Phillips). Intl Schol Bk Serv.

Caribbean Bargain Book, 1980-81. 656p. pap. 6.95 (ISBN 0-671-25494-4). Frommer-Pasmantier.

Caribbean: British, Dutch, French, United States. Ed. by A. Curtis Wilgus. LC 51-12532. (Caribbean Conference Ser: Vol. 8). 1958. 9.00 o.p. (ISBN 0-8130-0248-6). U Presses Fla.

Caribbean Co-Operation for Curriculum Develoment & Reform in Teacher Training. (Experiments & Innovations in Education Ser.: No. 39). 46p. 1980. pap. 3.50 (U 1041, UNESCO). Unipub.

Caribbean Dependence on the United States Economy. Ransford W. Palmer. LC 78-19770. (Praeger Special Studies). 1979. 22.95 (ISBN 0-03-041426-1). Praeger.

Caribbean, English Speaking Islands, in Pictures. Sterling Publishing Company Editors. LC 68-18795. (Visual Geography Series). (Illus., Orig.). (gr. 4-12). 1968. PLB 4.99 (ISBN 0-8069-1097-6); pap. 2.95 o.p. (ISBN 0-8069-1096-8). Sterling.

Caribbean Family: Legitimacy in Martinique. Mariam K. Slater. LC 76-28118. 1976. text ed. 15.95x (ISBN 0-312-12075-3); pap. text ed. 7.95x (ISBN 0-312-12110-5). St Martin.

Caribbean Georgian: The Great Houses & Small of the Caribbean. Pamela Gosner. LC 78-72966. (Illus.). 324p. (Orig.). 1981. 30.00x (ISBN 0-89410-011-4); pap. 12.00x (ISBN 0-89410-012-2). Three Continents.

Caribbean History in Maps. Peter Ashdown. (Illus.). 84p. 1979. pap. text ed. 9.95 (ISBN 0-582-76541-2). Longman.

Caribbean Islands. Helmut Blume. Tr. by J. Maczewski & A. V. Norton. Orig. Title: Die Westindischen Inseln. (Illus.). 448p. 1977. pap. text ed. 14.95x (ISBN 0-582-48574-6). Longman.

Caribbean Isles. Peter Wood. (American Wilderness Ser). (Illus.). 184p. 1975. 12.95 (ISBN 0-8094-1213-6). Time-Life.

Caribbean Isles. Peter Wood. LC 74-24663. (American Wilderness Ser.). (Illus.). 184p. (gr. 6 up). 1975. lib. bdg. 11.97 (ISBN 0-8094-1214-4). Silver.

Caribbean Issues of Emergence: Socio-Economic & Political Perspectives. Vincent R. McDonald. LC 79-6604. 1980. text ed. 22.00 (ISBN 0-8191-0925-8); pap. text ed. 12.25 (ISBN 0-8191-0926-6). U Pr of Amer.

Caribbean Lands. rev. ed. John P. Augelli. LC 77-84154. (American Neighbors Ser.). (Illus.). (gr. 5 up). 1978. text ed. 9.95 ea. 1-4 copies (ISBN 0-88296-112-8); text ed. 7.96 ea. 5 or more; tchrs'. guide 6.96 (ISBN 0-88296-353-8). Fideler.

Caribbean Lands. rev. 3rd ed. John Macpherson. (Illus.). 192p. 1973. pap. text ed. 6.95x o.p. (ISBN 0-582-76615-X). Longman.

Caribbean Lands. 4th ed. John Macpherson. (Illus.). 192p. 1980. pap. text ed. 6.95x (ISBN 0-582-76565-X). Longman.

Caribbean Mass Communications: A Comprehensive Bibliography. John A. Lent. (Archival & Bibliographic Ser.). 152p. 1981. pap. 20.00 (ISBN 0-918456-39-8). African Studies Assn.

Caribbean Mystery. Agatha Christie. 1980. pap. write for info. (ISBN 0-671-83052-X). PB.

Caribbean Reef Invertebrates & Plants. Patrick I. Colin. (Illus.). 1978. 20.00 (ISBN 0-87666-460-5, H-971). TFH Pubns.

Caribbean Story: Foundations, Bk. 1. William Claypole & John Robottom. (Longman Caribbean Ser.). (Illus.). 198p. (Orig.). 1981. pap. text ed. 9.95 (ISBN 0-582-76534-X). Longman.

Caribbean: The Genesis of a Fragmented Nationalism. Franklin W. Knight. (Latin American History Ser.). 1978. 14.95 (ISBN 0-19-502242-4); pap. 4.95x (ISBN 0-19-502243-2). Oxford U Pr.

Caribbean Transformations. Sidney W. Mintz. LC 74-82602. 360p. 1974. lib. bdg. 23.95x (ISBN 0-202-01125-9). Aldine Pub.

Caribbean Year Book 1979-1980. 50th ed. Ed. by Colin Rickards. (Illus.). 1980. pap. 45.00x (ISBN 0-8002-2717-4). Intl Pubns Serv.

Caribbean...the Inn Way. rev. ed. Margaret Zellers. 240p. 1980. 4.95 (ISBN 0-937334-00-6). Berkshire Traveller.

Caribe. Lindsay Maracotta. (Orig.). 1980. pap. 2.25 (ISBN 0-515-04692-2). Jove Pubns.

Caricature of Today. Geoffrey Holme. LC 73-20081. (Illus.). 136p. 1974. Repr. of 1928 ed. 18.00 (ISBN 0-8103-3969-2). Gale.

Caricature: The Wit & Humor of a Nation in Picture, Song, & Story. LC 74-14535. (Illus.). 260p. 1976. Repr. of 1903 ed. 24.00 (ISBN 0-8103-4057-7). Gale.

Caril. Ninette Beaver et al. LC 74-9843. 1974. 10.00 o.p. (ISBN 0-397-00997-6). Lippincott.

Caring. Jane B. Mancure. Ed. by Jane Buerger. 1980. 4.95 (4928). Standard Pub.

Caring. Jane B. Moncure. LC 80-14200. (What Does the Bible Say? Ser.). (Illus.). 32p. (ps-2). 1980. PLB 4.95. Childs World.

Caring. rev. ed. Jane B. Moncure. LC 80-27506. (What Is It? Ser.). (Illus.). (gr. k-3). 1981. PLB 5.50 (ISBN 0-89565-201-3). Childs World.

Caring & Cooking for the Allergic Child. rev. ed. Linda Thomas. LC 79-91379. (Illus.). 144p. 1980. 12.95 (ISBN 0-8069-5552-X); lib. bdg. 11.69 (ISBN 0-8069-5553-8); pap. 5.95 (ISBN 0-8069-8906-8). Sterling.

Caring & Cooking for the Hyperactive Child. Mary J. Finsand. LC 80-54335. 192p. 1981. 12.95 (ISBN 0-8069-5560-0); lib. bdg. 11.69 (ISBN 0-8069-5561-9); pap. 6.95 (ISBN 0-8069-8980-7). Sterling.

Caring & Curing: A Philosophy of Medicine & Social Work. R. S. Downie & Elizabeth Telfer. LC 80-40246. 180p. 1980. 19.95 (ISBN 0-416-71800-0, 2063). Methuen Inc.

Caring Enough to Forgive. David Augsburger. LC 80-50545. 1981. pap. 4.95 (ISBN 0-8307-0749-2). Regal.

Caring for Babies. Joan Leach & Patricia St. Louis. LC 78-52432. (Illus.). 1978. pap. 3.50 (ISBN 0-87239-220-1, 7963). Standard Pub.

Caring for Children. Draper. 1979. text ed. 13.60 (ISBN 0-87002-281-4); tchr's guide 8.56 (ISBN 0-87002-286-5); student's guide 3.16 (ISBN 0-87002-291-1). Bennett IL.

Caring for Children: A Symposium on Co-Operation in Child Care. Ed. by M. L. Pringle. (Studies in Child Development). (Orig.). 1969. pap. text ed. 4.50x (ISBN 0-582-32439-4). Humanities.

Caring for Children in Trouble. Julius Carlebach. (International Library of Sociology & Social Reconstruction). 1970. text ed. 8.50x (ISBN 0-7100-6564-7). Humanities.

Caring for Deprived Children: International Case Studies of Residential Setting. Ed. by C. J. Payne & K. J. White. 1979. 19.95 (ISBN 0-312-12166-0). St Martin.

Caring for Elderly People: Understanding & Practical Help. Susan Hooker. (Illus.). 1976. 14.00 (ISBN 0-7100-8376-9); pap. 6.95 (ISBN 0-7100-8826-4). Routledge & Kegan.

Caring for Patients with Chronic Renal Disease. Ginny L. Hansen et al. 132p. 1974. pap. text ed. 5.75x o.p. (ISBN 0-397-54157-0). Lippincott.

Caring for Photographs: Display, Storage, & Restoration. LC 72-84344. (Life Library of Photography). (Illus.). 1972. 14.95 (ISBN 0-8094-1066-4). Time-Life.

Caring for the Mentally Handicapped Child. David Wilkin. 192p. 1980. 30.00x (ISBN 0-85664-648-2, Pub. by Croom Helm England). State Mutual Bk.

Caring for the Mentally Ill in the Community. C. A. Butterworth & D. Skidmore. 160p. 1980. 27.00x (Pub by Croom Helm England). State Mutual Bk.

Caring for Your Child: A Complete Medical Guide. Consumer's Guide Editors. (Illus.). 1979. 10.95 (ISBN 0-517-53957-8, Harmony); pap. 5.95 (ISBN 0-517-53910-1). Crown.

Caring: Home Treatment for the Emotionally Disturbed. Fredric Neuman. 245p. 1980. 10.95 (ISBN 0-8037-0969-2). Dial.

Caring: How Can We Love Each Other? Morton T. Kelsey. 192p. (Orig.). 1981. pap. 6.95 (ISBN 0-8091-2366-5). Paulist Pr.

Carini & Owens' Neurological & Neurosurgical Nursing. 7th ed. Barbara L. Conway. 1978. text ed. 18.95 (ISBN 0-8016-0946-1). Mosby.

Carinthian Love Songs. Margarethe Herzele. Tr. by Herbert Kuhner. LC 78-56886. (Bilingual Poetry Ser.: No. 2). (Illus., Ger.). 1978. 10.00x (ISBN 0-89304-025-8, CCC113); signed ed. o.p. 10.50x (ISBN 0-89304-040-1); special signed ed. o.p. 25.00 (ISBN 0-89304-027-4); pap. 4.50x (ISBN 0-89304-026-6); pap. 6.50x signed ed. o.p. (ISBN 0-89304-041-X). Cross Cult.

Carl Akers' Colorado. Carl Akers. Date not set. pap. 9.50 (ISBN 0-933472-53-6). Johnson Colo.

Carl Friedrich Gauss: Prince of Mathematicians. William L. Schaaf. LC 64-11913. (Biography Ser). (Illus.). (gr. 7 up). 1964. PLB 5.90 o.p. (ISBN 0-531-00877-0). Watts.

Carl Gustav Jung: Nine Memorial Messages by Edinger, Harding, McCormick, Murray, Northrup & Tillich. 53p. 1962. pap. 3.00 o.p. (ISBN 0-685-40690-3). Spring Pubns.

Carl H. Milam & the United Nations Library. Ed. by Doris C. Dale. LC 76-14866. 149p. 1976. 10.00 (ISBN 0-8108-0941-9). Scarecrow.

Carl Jonas Love Almqvist. Bertil Romberg. LC 76-16859. (World Authors Ser: No. 401). 1977. lib. bdg. 12.50 (ISBN 0-8057-6241-8). Twayne.

Carl Maria Von Weber. 2nd ed. William Saunders. LC 69-11670. (Music Reprint Ser). 1969. Repr. of 1940 ed. lib. bdg. 29.50 (ISBN 0-306-71200-8). Da Capo.

Carl Maria Von Weber. 2nd ed. J. Warrack. LC 76-12915. (Illus.). 1976. 39.50 (ISBN 0-521-21354-1); pap. 13.95 (ISBN 0-521-29121-6). Cambridge U Pr.

Carl Purcell's Complete Guide to Travel Photography. Carl Purcell. (Illus.). 1980. 14.95 (ISBN 0-87165-053-3); pap. 7.95 (ISBN 0-87165-054-1). Ziff-Davis Pub.

Carl Sandburg. Richard Crowder. (U. S. Author's Ser.: No. 47). 1963. lib. bdg. 9.95 (ISBN 0-8057-0648-8). Twayne.

Carl Sandburg: Lincoln of Our Literature: A Biography. North Callahan. LC 76-92521. (Illus.). 1970. 15.00x (ISBN 0-8147-0069-1); pap. 5.95x (ISBN 0-8147-0070-5). NYU Pr.

Carl Sandburg Remembered. William A. Sutton. LC 78-31298. 1979. 13.50 (ISBN 0-8108-1202-9). Scarecrow.

Carl Sternheim Plays: The Bloomers, The Snob, Paul Schiffel, 1913 & The Fossil. Carl Sternheim. 1980. pap. 6.95 (ISBN 0-7145-0027-5). Riverrun NY.

Carl Van Vechten & the Irreverant Decades. Bruce Kellner. (Illus.). 1968. 17.95 (ISBN 0-8061-0808-8). U of Okla Pr.

Carl von Linnaeus's Plants. Carl von Linnaeus. Ed. by David Black. (Encore Edition). (Illus.). 1979. pap. 4.95 (ISBN 0-684-16821-9, ScribT). Scribner.

Carl Zuckmayer. Arnold Bauer. LC 75-29600. (Modern Literature Ser.). 1976. 10.95 (ISBN 0-8044-2026-2). Ungar.

Carleton's Histological Technique. 4th ed. H. M. Carleton. Ed. by R. A. Drury & E. A. Wallington. 1967. 46.50x o.p. (ISBN 0-19-261205-0). Oxford U Pr.

Carleton's Histological Technique. 5th ed. Ed. by H. M. Carleton & R. A. Drury. (Illus.). 592p. 1980. text ed. 59.50 (ISBN 0-19-261310-3). Oxford U Pr.

Carlism & Crisis in Spain: 1931-1939. M. Blinkhorn. LC 75-2727. (Illus.). 408p. 1975. 51.50 (ISBN 0-521-20729-0). Cambridge U Pr.

Carlos Arniches. Douglas R. McKay. (World Authors Ser.: Spain: No. 188). lib. bdg. 10.95 (ISBN 0-8057-2068-5). Twayne.

Carlos at the Fiesta (Carlos En la Fiesta) Rebecca Lovato. Tr. by Consuelo M. Cardona. LC 76-42856. (gr. 6-12). 1976. pap. 1.95 (ISBN 0-89430-000-8). Morgan-Pacific.

Carlos Goes to School. Eloise Anderson. LC 72-89478. (Illus.). 32p. (gr. 1-3). 1973. PLB 4.95 (ISBN 0-7232-6095-8). Warne.

Carlos Pellicer. Edward J. Mullen. (World Authors Ser.: Noo. 451). 1977. 12.50 (ISBN 0-8057-6288-4). Twayne.

Carlota. Scott O'Dell. LC 77-9468. (gr. 5-9). 1977. 10.95 (ISBN 0-395-25487-6). HM.

Carlotta & the Scientist. 2nd ed. Patricia R. Lenthall. LC 76-20841. 47p. (gr. k-4). 1976. 6.50 (ISBN 0-914996-14-2); pap. 2.75 (ISBN 0-914996-12-6). Lollipop Power.

Carlotta Corpron: Designer with Light. Carlotta Corpron & Martha A. Sandweiss. 64p. 1980. 14.95 (ISBN 0-292-71064-X); pap. 9.95 (ISBN 0-292-71065-8). U of Tex Pr.

Carlson Wade's Lecithin Book. Carlson Wade. LC 80-82319. 128p. (Orig.). 1980. pap. 2.25 (ISBN 0-87983-226-6). Keats.

Carlstadts Ordinaciones & Luther's Liberty. James S. Preus. (Harvard Theological Review & Studies). 1974. pap. 6.00 (ISBN 0-89130-223-9, 020027). Scholars Pr Ca.

Carlton's Complete Reference Book of Music. Joseph R. Carlton. LC 44-181. (Illus.). 729p. 1980. PLB 40.00 (ISBN 0-937348-00-7). Carlton Pubns CA.

Carly Simon. Charles Morse & Ann Morse. LC 74-14550. (Rock'n Pop Stars Ser.). 32p. (gr. 4-12). 1974. PLB 5.95 (ISBN 0-87191-393-3); pap. 2.95 (ISBN 0-89812-101-9). Creative Ed.

Carlyle Marney: A Pilgrim's Progress. John J. Carey. LC 80-82573. xii, 156p. 1980. 11.95 (ISBN 0-86554-001-2). Mercer Univ Pr.

Carlyle's Dubliners. Ed. by Grace J. Calder. 1980. 22.50x (ISBN 0-85105-268-1, Dolmen Pr). Humanities.

Carm-Chilton's Automotive Repair Manual: 1972-79. 1154p. 1980. 18.00 (ISBN 0-8019-6914-X). Chilton.

Carmel Mission, from Founding to Rebuilding. Sydney Temple. LC 79-57168. (Illus.). 176p. 1980. pap. 5.95 (ISBN 0-913548-71-5, Valley Calif). Western Tanager.

Carmen. Georges Bizet. Ed. & tr. by Ellen Bleiler. LC 68-10868. (Opera Guide & Libretto Ser). (Illus., Orig.). 1970. pap. 4.00 (ISBN 0-486-22111-3). Dover.

Carmen Conde y el Mar - Carmen Conde & the Sea. Josefina Inclan. Tr. by Manuel J. Santayana. LC 80-69623. (Coleccion Polymita). 81p. (Orig., Span. & Eng.). 1980. pap. 8.95 (ISBN 0-89729-277-4). Ediciones.

Carmen Gratulans Adventu Serenissimi Principis Federici Comitis Palatini Ad Academian Cantalrig En Sem: An Edition with Introduction, Translation & Commentary, 2 vols. Ed. by Phillip Dust. (Salzburg Studies in English Literature, Elizabethan & Renaissance Studies Ser.: No. 8). 1975. pap. text ed. 50.25x (ISBN 0-391-01367-X). Humanities.

Carmen Laforet. Roberta Johnson. (World Authors Ser: No. 601). 1981. lib. bdg. 14.50 (ISBN 0-8057-6443-7). Twayne.

Carmen Miranda Memorial Flagpole. Gerald Rosen. LC 77-73554. 1977. 8.95 o.s.i. (ISBN 0-89141-032-5); pap. 3.95 o.s.i. (ISBN 0-89141-033-3). Presidio Pr.

Carmichael's Manual of Child Psychology, 2 vols. 3rd ed. P. H. Mussen. LC 69-16127. 1970. Set. 99.95 (ISBN 0-471-62697-X); Vol. 1. 69.95 (ISBN 0-471-62695-3); Vol. 2. 45.95 (ISBN 0-471-62696-1). Wiley.

Carmina Cum Fragmentis. Pindar. Ed. by C. M. Bowra. (Oxford Classical Texts Ser). 1935. 18.95x (ISBN 0-19-814539-X). Oxford U Pr.

Carnahan Conference on Crime Countermeasures: Proceedings Nineteen Seventy-Nine. Ed. by R. William De Vore. J. S. Jackson. LC 79-64890. (Illus., Orig.). 1979. pap. 22.50 (ISBN 0-89779-018-9, UKY BU117); microfiche 3.50 (ISBN 0-89779-019-7). OES Pubns.

Carnahan Conference on Crime Countermeasures: Proceedings, 1980. Ed. by R. William De Vore & J. S. Jackson. LC 79-644630. (Illus.). 160p. (Orig.). 1980. pap. 22.50 (ISBN 0-89779-030-8, UKY BU120); microfiche 2.50 (ISBN 0-89779-031-6). OES Pubns.

Carnahan Conference on Crime Countermeasures, 1978: Proceedings. Ed. by R. William De Vore & John S. Jackson. 1978. pap. text ed. 22.50 (ISBN 0-89779-000-6); microfiche 3.50 (ISBN 0-89779-001-4). OES Pubns.

Carnal Christian: What Should We Think of the Carnal Christian? Ernest C. Reisinger. 75p. Date not set. 0.75. Banner of Truth.

Carnal Musings of Sylvia Savage. Ruth M. Kempher. 1980. 2.00. Windless Orchard.

Carnegie Council on Policy Studies in Higher Education: A Summary of Reports & Recommendations. Carnegie Council on Policy Studies in Higher Education. LC 80-7999. (Carnegie Council Ser.). 1981. text ed. 25.00x (ISBN 0-87589-474-7). Jossey-Bass.

Carnelian Throne. Janet E. Morris. 256p. (Orig.). 1981. pap. 2.50 (ISBN 0-553-14924-5). Bantam.

Carnets Du Major W. Marmaduke Thompson. Pierre Daninos. (Illus.). 1963. pap. text ed. 5.95x (ISBN 0-521-04767-6). Cambridge U Pr.

Carnival. Julian Rathbone. LC 76-27622. 1976. 7.95 o.p. (ISBN 0-312-12250-0). St Martin.

Carnival & Coca-Leaf: Some Traditions of the Quechua Ayllu. Douglas Gifford & Pauline Hoggarth. LC 76-1302. 200p. 1976. 18.95 (ISBN 0-312-12215-2). St Martin.

Carnival Gaffs. Walter B. Gibson. (Gambler's Book Shelf). 64p. 1976. pap. 2.95 (ISBN 0-89650-566-9). Gamblers.

Carnival Glass. Regina Stewart & Geraldine Cosentino. (Handbook of Collectibles Ser.). (Illus.). 1977. pap. 3.95 o.p. (ISBN 0-307-43175-4, Golden Pr). Western Pub.

Carnival Glass Collector's Price Guide. Marian Klamkin. LC 77-92365. (Illus., Orig.). 1978. pap. 5.95 (ISBN 0-8015-1094-5, Hawthorn). Dutton.

Carnival Glass Price Guide. 7th ed. Sherman Hand. (Illus.). 1979. pap. 3.95 o.p. (ISBN 0-89145-023-8). Collector Bks.

Carnival in Rio. Albert Goldman. LC 78-52280. (Illus.). 1978. 19.95 o.p. (ISBN 0-8015-1000-7). Dutton.

Carnival Kidnap Caper. Fitzhugh Dodson & Paula Reuben. LC 79-20260. (gr. 5-9). 1979. 7.95 (ISBN 0-916392-40-6). Oak Tree Pubns.

Carnival of Souls: Religious Cults & Young People. Joel A. MacCollam. 1979. 10.95 (ISBN 0-8164-0436-4); pap. 4.95 (ISBN 0-8164-2211-7). Crossroad NY.

Carnivores of Europe. Robert Burton. 1979. 38.00 (ISBN 0-7134-0690-9, Pub. by Batsford England). David & Charles.

Carnivorous Plants. Adrian Slack. (Illus.). 240p. 1980. 19.95 (ISBN 0-262-19186-5). MIT Pr.

Carnivorous Plants. John F. Waters. LC 73-21976. (First Bks). (Illus.). 72p. (gr. 4-6). 1974. PLB 4.90 o.p. (ISBN 0-531-02700-7). Watts.

Carny. Thomas Baum. 224p. (Orig.). 1980. pap. 2.50 (ISBN 0-515-05431-3). Jove Pubns.

Carol Burnett. David Paige. (Stars of Stage & Screen Ser.). (Illus.). (gr. 3-8). 1977. PLB 5.95 (ISBN 0-87191-555-3). Creative Ed.

Carol Burnett: Star of Comedy. Carol B. Church. Ed. by David L. Bender & Gary E. Mc Cuen. (Focus on Famous Women Ser). (Illus.). (gr. 3-9). 1976. 6.95 (ISBN 0-912616-42-3); read-along cassette 9.95 (ISBN 0-89908-241-6). Greenhaven.

Carole King. Paula Taylor. (Rock 'n Pop Stars Ser.). (Illus.). (gr. 4-12). 1976. PLB 5.95 (ISBN 0-87191-465-4); pap. 2.95 (ISBN 0-89812-111-6). Creative Ed.

Carolina. Thomas Shipman. LC 80-17666. 1980. Repr. of 1683 ed. 30.00x (ISBN 0-8201-1355-7). Schol Facsimiles.

Carolina Adventures: Brief Sketches of Growing up in Eastern North Carolina at the Turn of the Century (1889-1915) Melvin B. Andrews. Ed. by J. David Andrews. (Illus.). 92p. (Orig.). 1979. pap. 5.00. Planetary Pr.

Carolina Goldrush: America's First. Bruce Roberts. LC 70-165464. 4.50 (ISBN 0-87461-958-0). McNally.

Carolina Hurricane. Marian Rumsey. LC 77-5622. (Illus.). (gr. 3-7). 1977. 7.75 (ISBN 0-688-22128-9); PLB 7.44 (ISBN 0-688-32128-3). Morrow.

Carolina's Courage. Elizabeth Yates. (Illus.). (gr. 3-5). 1964. PLB 7.50 o.p. (ISBN 0-525-27480-4). Dutton.

Caroline & Her Kettle Named Maud. Miriam E. Mason. (Illus.). (gr. 4-6). 1951. 3.95g o.s.i. (ISBN 0-02-763280-6). Macmillan.

Caroline & the King's Hunt. Jean Le Paillot. Tr. by Rubie Saunders. LC 72-673. (Illus.). 36p. (ps-3). 1972. Repr. 5.95 o.s.i. (ISBN 0-8193-0604-5, Four Winds); PLB 5.41 o.s.i. (ISBN 0-8193-0605-3). Schol Bk Serv.

Caroline & the Seven Little Words. Miriam E. Mason. (gr. 2-4). 1967. 4.95 o.s.i. (ISBN 0-02-763330-6). Macmillan.

Caroline at the King's Ball. Jean Le Paillot. Tr. by Rubie Saunders from Fr. LC 75-183378. Orig. Title: Caroline Au Bal Du Roi. (Illus.). (gr. k-3). 1972. Repr. of 1968 ed. 5.95 o.s.i. (ISBN 0-8193-0551-0, Four Winds); PLB 5.41 o.s.i. (ISBN 0-8193-0552-9). Schol Bk Serv.

Caroline Gordon. W. J. Stuckey. (U. S. Authors Ser.: No. 200). lib. bdg. 10.95 (ISBN 0-8057-0332-2). Twayne.

Caroline M. Kirkland. William S. Osborne. (U. S. Authors Ser.: No. 207). lib. bdg. 10.95 (ISBN 0-8057-0424-8). Twayne.

Caroline R. David Lancaster. 1980. 11.95 (ISBN 0-87795-285-X). Arbor Hse.

Caroline Silver. Charles Oman. 1970. 31.95 (ISBN 0-571-09442-2, Pub. by Faber & Faber). Merrimack Bk Serv.

Caroline's Waterloo. Betty Neels. (Harlequin Romances). 192p. 1981. pap. 1.25 (ISBN 0-373-02393-6, Pub. by Harlequin). PB.

Caroling Dusk: An Anthology of Verse by Negro Poets. Ed. by Countee Cullen. LC 73-18651. 256p. (YA) 1974. 10.95 o.s.i. (ISBN 0-06-010926-2, HarpT). Har-Row.

Carolingian Lord. Dennis H. Green. 1965. 90.00 (ISBN 0-521-05138-X). Cambridge U Pr.

Carolingians & the Frankish Monarchy: Studies in Carolingian History. F. L. Ganshof. Tr. by Janet Sondheimer. LC 72-147074. (Illus.). 1971. 22.50x o.p. (ISBN 0-8014-0635-8). Cornell U Pr.

Carolus Stuardus. Andreas Gryphius. 1963. Repr. of 1955 ed. text ed. 6.50x (ISBN 0-7185-1004-6, Leicester). Humanities.

Carolyn Wells' Book of American Limericks. Carolyn Wells. LC 77-174140. (Tower Bks). (Illus.). viii, 91p. 1972. Repr. of 1925 ed. 18.00 (ISBN 0-8103-3929-3). Gale.

Carotenoid As Colorants & Vitamin A Precursors: Technological & Nutritional Applications. Ed. by Jack C. Bauerfeind. LC 79-8850. (Food Science & Technology Ser.). 1981. write for info. (ISBN 0-12-082850-2). Acad Pr.

Carotenoids Five. International Symposium on Carotenoids, Madison, 5th, U. S. A., July 23-28 1978. Ed. by T. W. Goodwin. (IUPAC Symposium Ser.). (Illus.). 1979. 50.00 (ISBN 0-08-022359-1). Pergamon.

Carotenoproteins in Animal Colorations. Ed. by Welton L. Lee. (Benchmark Papers in Biological Concepts Ser.: Vol. 3). 1977. 42.50 (ISBN 0-12-786935-2). Acad Pr.

Carpaccio. Sgarbi. 1980. pap. cancelled (ISBN 0-8120-2304-8). Barron.

Carpenter of the Sun. Nancy Willard. 55p. 1974. 6.95 o.p. (ISBN 0-87140-602-0); pap. 2.50 o.p. (ISBN 0-87140-098-7). Liveright.

Carpenters & Builders Library. John E. Ball. LC 76-24079. 1977. 35.95 set (ISBN 0-672-23244-8); 9.95 ea. Vol. 1 (ISBN 0-672-23240-5). Vol. 2 (ISBN 0-672-23241-3). Vol. 3 (ISBN 0-672-23242-1). Vol. 4 (ISBN 0-672-23243-X). Audel.

Carpenter's Manifesto. Jeffrey Ehrlich & Marc Mannheimer. LC 77-73865. 1977. 12.95 o.p. (ISBN 0-03-016756-6); pap. 7.95 (ISBN 0-03-016761-2). HR&W.

Carpenter's Son. Rosemary Haughton. (gr. 5-8). 1967. 4.95g o.s.i. (ISBN 0-02-743430-3). Macmillan.

Carpenter's Wife. B. A. Tompkins. 1977. pap. 1.00 o.p. (ISBN 0-931832-05-5). No Dead Lines.

Carpentry. Byron J. Alpers & Mitchell L. Afrow. (Shoptalk - Vocational Reading Skills). (gr. 9-12). 1978. pap. text ed. 5.12 (ISBN 0-205-05820-5, 4958209); 5.40 (ISBN 0-205-05824-8). Allyn.

Carpentry & Building. Harry F. Ulrey. LC 66-29074. 10.95 (ISBN 0-672-23142-5, 23142). Audel.

Carpentry & Building Constructions. rev. ed. John Feirer & Gilbert R. Hutchings. (Illus.). 1981. 37.50 (ISBN 0-684-16981-9, ScribT). Scribner.

Carpentry Building & Construction. John Feirer & Gilbert Hutchings. (gr. 10-12). 1976. text ed. 22.60 (ISBN 0-87002-004-8); student guide 3.92 (ISBN 0-87002-277-6). Bennett IL.

Carpentry Construction & Building. rev. ed. Feirer & Hutchings. 1981. text ed. 24.60 (ISBN 0-87002-327-6). Bennett IL.

Carpentry for Beginners. Charles Hayward. LC 77-18406. (Drake Home Craftsman Ser.). (Illus.). 1978. pap. 5.95 (ISBN 0-8069-8196-2, 031250). Sterling.

Carpentry for Builders. A. B. Amary. (Drake Home Craftsman Ser.). (Illus.). 204p. (Orig.). 1976. pap. 5.95 (ISBN 0-8069-8198-9). Sterling.

Carpentry for Kids. D. J. Herda & Judy B. Herda. LC 79-26793. (Illus.). 96p. (gr. 4 up). 1980. PLB 7.29 (ISBN 0-671-33042-X). Messner.

Carpentry for the Home. Alex Leggatt. (Illus.). 144p. 1981. 22.50 (ISBN 0-7134-1886-9, Pub. by Batsford England). David & Charles.

Carpentry: Framing & Finishing. Byron Maguire. (Illus.). 1979. 18.95 (ISBN 0-8359-0701-5); instrs'. manual avail. (ISBN 0-8359-0702-3). Reston.

Carpentry Fundamentals. Glenn E. Baker & Rex Miller. (Contemporary Construction Ser.). (Illus.). 512p. (gr. 10-12). 1981. 16.95 (ISBN 0-07-003361-7, G); tchrs. manual & key 1.50 (ISBN 0-07-003363-3); write for info wkbk. (ISBN 0-07-003362-5). McGraw.

Carpentry in Commercial Construction. 2nd ed. S. Badzinski. 1980. 14.95 (ISBN 0-13-115220-3). P-H.

Carpentry in Commercial Construction. B. Maguire. 1976. 17.00 (ISBN 0-87909-124-X); text ed. 13.50 (ISBN 0-87909-124-X). Reston.

Carpentry in Residential Construction. S. Badzinski, Jr. 1981. 16.95 (ISBN 0-13-115238-6). P-H.

Carpentry in Residential Construction. Byron W. Maguire. (Illus.). 416p. 1975. 18.95 (ISBN 0-87909-118-5). Reston.

Carpet Annual 1980. (Illus.). 1979. 42.50x (ISBN 0-8002-2745-X). Intl Pubns Serv.

Carpet Annual 1980: Year Book & Directory of the World's Carpet Industries & Trade. 45th ed. 372p. 1979. 42.50x (ISBN 0-8002-2745-X). Intl Pubns Serv.

Carpet Garden. Renee Rockmore & Steve Rockmore. LC 77-27434. (Illus.). 1978. 7.95 o.p. (ISBN 0-690-01679-4, TYC-T); pap. 4.95 o.p. (ISBN 0-690-01747-2, TYC-T). T Y Crowell.

Carpeting Simplified. Donald R. Brann. LC 72-91055. (Illus.). 1980. pap. 5.95 (ISBN 0-87733-683-0). Easi-Bild.

Carreta Made a U-Turn. Tato Laviera. LC 79-90764. (Orig.). 1980. pap. 5.00x (ISBN 0-934770-01-8). Arte Publico.

Carribean Cultural Identity: The Case of Jamaica. Rex Nettleford. Ed. by Robert A. Hill & Johannes Wilbert. LC 79-54305. (Afro-American Culture & Society Monograph: No. 1). Orig. Title: Cultural Action & Social Change: the Case of Jamaica. (Illus.). 239p. 1980. 13.95x (ISBN 0-934934-00-2, Co-Pub by UCLA Lat Am Ctr); pap. 8.00x (ISBN 0-934934-02-9, Co-Pub by UCLA Lat Am Ctr). Ctr Afro-Am Stud.

Carribean Heritage. Virginia Radcliffe. LC 75-12189. (Illus.). 288p. 1976. 17.50 (ISBN 0-8027-0518-9). Walker & Co.

Carrie. Stephen King. LC 73-9037. 216p. 1974. 7.95 (ISBN 0-385-08695-4). Doubleday.

Carrier Fighters. David Brown. 1981. 8.95 (ISBN 0-356-08095-1, Pub. by MacDonald & Jane's England). Hippocrene Bks.

Carrier of Ladders. W. S. Merwin. LC 72-124964. 1970. pap. 5.95 (ISBN 0-689-10343-3). Atheneum.

Carrier Operations in World War II: The Royal Navy, Vol. 1. David Brown. LC 74-33800. 1975. Vol. 1. 12.95 o.s.i. (ISBN 0-87021-814-X). Naval Inst Pr.

Carrie's War: T.V. Ed. Nina Bawden. (Illus.). 1980. pap. 2.95 (ISBN 0-14-005581-9). Penguin.

Carroll College, the First Century, 1846-1946. Ellen Langill. LC 79-54879. (Illus.). 1980. text ed. 20.95 (ISBN 0-916120-06-6). Carroll Coll.

Carroll's First Book of Proverbs or Life Is a Fortune Cookie. Carroll Carroll. (Illus.). 96p. 1981. pap. 4.95 (ISBN 0-87786-004-1). Gold Penny.

Carrot Cake. Nonny Hogrogian. LC 76-17628. (Illus.). (ps-3). 1977. 7.50 (ISBN 0-688-80061-0); PLB 7.63 (ISBN 0-688-84061-2). Greenwillow.

Carry Me Back: Slavery & Servitude in Seventeenth Century Virginia. Robert S. Cope. (Illus.). xv, 179p. 1973. 2.00. Pikeville Coll.

Carry-Me Shape Books, 6 bks. (Boxed Golden Bks. Ser.). (ps-2). 1977. 3.50 set (ISBN 0-307-13634-5, Golden Pr). Western Pub.

Carry Nation. Arnold Madison. LC 76-58839. (gr. 8 up). 1977. Repr. 7.95 o.p. (ISBN 0-525-66540-4). Elsevier-Nelson.

Carry-on Book. Kenneth Eastaugh. 1978. 10.95 (ISBN 0-7153-7403-6). David & Charles.

Carry on Jeeves. P. G. Wodehouse. 240p. 1975. pap. 2.95 (ISBN 0-14-001174-9). Penguin.

Carrying Capacity of a Nation: Growth & the Quality of Life. Peter W. House & Edward R. Williams. LC 75-16623. 1976. 22.95 (ISBN 0-669-00056-6). Lexington Bks.

Cars. (MacDonald Educational Ser.). (Illus., Arabic.). 3.50 (ISBN 0-686-53083-7). Intl Bk Ctr.

Cars. James Clark. LC 80-17876. (Look Inside Ser.). (Illus.). 48p. (gr. 4-12). 1981. PLB 10.25 (ISBN 0-8172-1405-4). Raintree Child.

Cars. Laura Hobbs. (Easy-Read Fact Books). (Illus.). (gr. 2-4). 1977. PLB 6.45 s&l (ISBN 0-531-00375-2). Watts.

Cars. Bob Ottum. (Illus.). (ps-1). 1973. PLB 5.00 (ISBN 0-307-60566-3, Golden Pr). Western Pub.

Cars. John Ray. (Junior Reference Ser.). (Illus.). 96p. (gr. 7 up). 7.96 (ISBN 0-7136-1322-X). Dufour.

Cars, Boats, Trains & Planes of Today & Tomorrow. Thomas G. Aylesworth. LC 74-31906. (Illus.). 128p. (gr. 3-7). 1975. 6.95 o.s.i. (ISBN 0-8027-6236-0). Walker & Co.

Cars! Cars! Cars! Featuring "The Love Bug" & Other Fun on Wheels. Walt Disney Productions. LC 77-74465. (Disney's World of Adventure). (Illus.). (gr. 2-6). 1977. 3.95 (ISBN 0-394-83598-0, BYR); PLB 4.99 (ISBN 0-394-93598-5). Random.

Cars of Pacific Electric, Vol. 2. Ira Swett. Ed. by Jim Walker. (Special Ser.: No. 36). (Illus.). 212p. 1976. pap. 10.00 o.p. (ISBN 0-916374-24-6). Interurban.

Cars of Pacific Electric: City & Suburban Cars, Vol. 1. 2nd rev. ed. Ira L. Swett. Ed. by Mac Sebree. (Special Ser.: No. 28). (Illus.). 1975. pap. 10.00 (ISBN 0-916374-03-3). Interurban.

Cars of Pacific Electric: Locomotives, Combination Cars, Etc, Vol. 3. Ira L. Swett. Ed. by Jim Walker. (Special Ser.: No. 37). (Illus.). 1978. pap. 12.00 (ISBN 0-916374-30-0). Interurban.

Cars That Henry Ford Built. Beverly R. Kimes. LC 78-51029. 1978. 19.95 (ISBN 0-915038-08-0). Princeton Pub.

Cars That Hudson Built. John A. Conde. (Illus.). 224p. 1980. 19.95 (ISBN 0-9605048-0-X). Arnold-Porter Pub.

Carso de Filosofia. rev., 2nd ed. Angel J. Casares. 238p. 1980. text ed. write for info. (ISBN 0-8477-2821-8); pap. text ed. write for info. (ISBN 0-8477-2822-6). U of PR Pr.

Carson Inheritance. Dorothy Daniels. 160p. (Orig.). 1975. pap. 0.95 o.s.i. (ISBN 0-446-75562-1). Warner Bks.

Carson McCullers. Richard M. Cook. LC 75-2789. (Modern Literature Ser.). 160p. 1975. 10.95 (ISBN 0-8044-2128-5). Ungar.

Carson McCullers: A/Descriptive Listing & Annotated Bibliography of Criticism. Adrian M. Shapiro et al. LC 79-7909. (Garland Reference Library of Humanities). 250p. 1980. lib. bdg. 35.00 (ISBN 0-8240-9534-0). Garland Pub.

Cartanian Geometry, Nonlinear Waves, & Control Theory, Pt. B. Robert Hermann. Tr. by Michael Ackerman. (Interdisciplinary Mathematics Ser.: Vol. 21). 585p. 1980. text ed. 60.00x (ISBN 0-915692-29-5, QA649.H46). Math Sci Pr.

Cartas Da Prisao. Tr. by Corrie Ten Boom. (Portugese Bks.). (Port.). 1979. 1.20 (ISBN 0-8297-0734-4). Life Pubs Intl.

Cartas De Gabriela Mistral a Juan Ramon Jimnez. Gabriela Mistral. pap. 0.50 o.p. (ISBN 0-8477-3139-1). U of PR Pr.

Cartas De Zaragoza. Lawrence Shaw & Carmen Ibanez. (Illus.). (gr. 7-10). 1970. pap. text ed. 4.95 (ISBN 0-312-12285-3). St Martin.

Carteggio (Political Correspondence), 1916-1922. Sidney Sonnino. Ed. by Pietro Pastorelli. (Complete Works of Sidney Sonnino Ser). (It.). 1976. 15.00x o.p. (ISBN 0-7006-0150-3). Regents Pr KS.

Carter Glass: A Biography. R. Smith & N. Beasley. LC 72-172012. (FDR & the Era of the New Deal Ser). (Illus.). 520p. 1972. Repr. of 1939 ed. lib. bdg. 49.50 (ISBN 0-306-70392-0). Da Capo.

Carter on the Arts. Intro. by Joan Mondale. 1977. pap. 2.50 o.p. (ISBN 0-686-67828-1). Interbk Inc.

Carter Presidency. National Journal. 1979. 2.35 o.s.i. (ISBN 0-89234-004-5). Natl Journal.

Cartesian Tensors. Harold Jeffreys. (Orig.). 1931-1962. 17.95 (ISBN 0-521-05423-0); pap. 6.95x (ISBN 0-521-09191-8, 191). Cambridge U Pr.

Cartesian Tensors in Engineering Science. L. G. Jaeger. 1966. 23.00 (ISBN 0-08-011222-6); pap. 11.25 (ISBN 0-08-011221-8). Pergamon.

Cartier: Finder of the St. Lawrence. Ronald Syme. (Illus.). (gr. 3-7). 1958. PLB 6.24 (ISBN 0-688-31146-6). Morrow.

Cartographic Design & Production. J. S. Keates. LC 72-9251. 240p. 1976. pap. 27.95 (ISBN 0-470-15106-4). Halsted Pr.

Cartography. Debora Greger. 1980. signed 35.00 (ISBN 0-686-28114-4). Penumbra Press.

Carton Crafts. Helen Fletcher. (Illus.). 64p. (gr. 3-7). 1981. PLB 7.95 (ISBN 0-87460-268-8). Lion.

Cartoon Animation for Everyone. Alan Cleave. 1977. pap. 8.95 o.p. (ISBN 0-85242-566-X, Pub. by Fountain). Morgan.

Cartoon Classics, 2 bks. Medical Economics Company. (Illus.). 1963. 29.50 set (ISBN 0-87489-028-4). Med Economics.

Cartooning Fundamentals. Al Ross. LC 77-1201. (Illus.). 1977. 11.95 (ISBN 0-87396-080-7). Stravon.

Cartoonist. Betsy Byars. (gr. k-6). 1981. pap. 1.25 (ISBN 0-440-41046-0, YB). Dell.

Cartoons by Guindon. Richard Guindon. (Illus.). 1980. pap. 6.95 (ISBN 0-8256-3180-7, Quick Fox). Music Sales.

Cartoons for Kids. Mamoru Funai. LC 76-44273. (Illus.). (gr. 1-4). 1977. 7.95 (ISBN 0-13-115154-1); pap. 1.95 (ISBN 0-13-115147-9). P-H.

Cartulary of Cirencester Abbey, Gloucestershire, Vol. 3. Ed. by Mary Devine. 1977. 45.00x (ISBN 0-19-711637-X). Oxford U Pr.

Cartulary of the Order of St. John of Jerusalem (Hospitalers) in England. Ed. by Michael Gervers. (Records of Social & Economic History Ser.). 618p. 1980. 169.00 (ISBN 0-19-725996-0). Oxford U Pr.

Cartwrightiana. Ed. by Leland H. Carlson. Albert Peel. (Elizabethan Nonconformist Texts). 1951. text ed. 8.95x o.p. (ISBN 0-04-274001-0). Allen Unwin.

Carved & Decorated European Art Glass. Ray Grover & Lee Grover. LC 71-94025. (Illus.). 1970. 55.00 (ISBN 0-8048-0707-8). C E Tuttle.

Carved Masonry Domes of Mediaeval Cairo. Christel Kessler. 1976. pap. 15.00x (ISBN 0-686-19945-6). Intl Learn Syst.

Carver Effect: A Paranormal Experience. Wolffgang On Bober. (Illus.). 224p. 1979. 11.95 (ISBN 0-8117-0329-0). Stackpole.

Carver's Kingdom. Fredrick Nolan. 1980. pap. 2.50 (ISBN 0-446-81201-3). Warner Bks.

Carving Duck Decoys, with Full-Size Patterns for Hollow Contruction. Harry V. Shourds & Anthony Hillman. (Illus.). 64p. (Orig.). 1981. pap. price not set (ISBN 0-486-24083-5). Dover.

Carving Flora & Fables in Wood. E. J. Tangerman. LC 80-54336. (Illus.). 128p. 1981. pap. 5.95 (ISBN 0-8069-8982-3). Sterling.

Caryapadas: Tantric Poems of the Eighty-Four Mahasiddhas (Siddhacaryas) 2nd rev. ed. Tr. by Atindra Mojumder from Bengali. 225p. 1980. text ed. 13.95x (ISBN 0-935548-03-3). Santarasa Pubns.

Caryl Chessman: The Red Light Bandit. Frank J. Parker. LC 75-8760. (Illus.). 245p. 1975. 13.95 (ISBN 0-88229-188-2). Nelson-Hall.

Casa Apinada. David Lewis. (Calle Lucas). 1978. pap. 0.40 o.p. (ISBN 0-311-38520-6, Edit Mundo). Casa Bautista.

Casa Del Cobrador. David Lewis. (Calle Lucas). 1978. pap. 0.40 o.p. (ISBN 0-311-38524-9, Edit Mundo). Casa Bautista.

Casa Del Lider. David Lewis. (Calle Lucas). 1978. pap. 0.40 o.p. (ISBN 0-311-38522-2, Edit Mundo). Casa Bautista.

Casa Del Rico. David Lewis. (Calle Lucas). 1978. pap. 0.40 o.p. (ISBN 0-311-38521-4, Edit Mundo). Casa Bautista.

Casa En las Afueras. David Lewis. 1978. pap. 0.40 o.p. (ISBN 0-311-38526-5, Edit Mundo). Casa Bautista.

Casa Guidi Windows. Elizabeth B. Browning. Ed. by Julia Markus. LC 77-24944. (Illus.). 1977. 11.50x (ISBN 0-930252-00-4, Pub by Browning Inst). Pub Ctr Cult Res.

Casa Hospedadora. David Lewis. (Calle Lucas). pap. 0.40 o.p. (ISBN 0-311-38523-0, Edit Mundo). Casa Bautista.

Casa Madrone. Mignon G. Eberhart. 256p. 1981. pap. 2.25 (ISBN 0-445-04645-7). Popular Lib.

Casa Secreta. David Lewis. (Calle Lucas). 1978. pap. 0.40 o.p. (ISBN 0-311-38525-7, Edit Mundo). Casa Bautista.

Casa Triste. David Lewis. (Calle Lucas). 1978. pap. 0.40 o.p. (ISBN 0-311-38519-2, Edit Mundo). Casa Bautista.

Casals & the Art of Interpretation. David Blum. LC 77-1444. text ed. 24.50x o.p. (ISBN 0-8419-0307-7). Holmes & Meier.

Cascade Alpine Guide: Climbing & High Routes-Rainy Pass to Fraser River, Vol. III. Fred Beckey. Ed. by Peggy Ferber. (Illus.). 356p. (Orig.). 1981. pap. 12.95 (ISBN 0-89886-002-4). Mountaineers.

Cascades. Jared Angira. 143p. (Orig.). (gr. 10 up). 1979. pap. 5.00 (ISBN 0-582-64225-6, Drum Beat). Three Continents.

Cascades. Richard L. Williams. (American Wilderness Ser.). (Illus.). 1974. 12.95 (ISBN 0-8094-1245-4). Time-Life.

Cascades. Richard L. Williams. LC 74-13323. (American Wilderness). (Illus.). (gr. 6 up). 1974. PLB 11.97 (ISBN 0-8094-1246-2, Pub. by Time-Life). Silver.

Case Against a Libertarian Political Party. Erwin S. Strauss. 1980. pap. 4.50. Loompanics.

Case Against Assertion Training. Albert Eglash. (Beyond Assertion Training Ser.: No. 5). 180p. (Orig.). 1981. pap. 20.00 (ISBN 0-935320-12-1). Quest Pr.

Case Against Joining the Common Market. Paul Einzig. 144p. 1971. 21.95 (ISBN 0-312-12320-5). St Martin.

Case Against Pornography. Ed. by David Holbrook. LC 72-5279. 294p. 1973. 17.50 (ISBN 0-912050-28-4, Library Pr); pap. 5.95. Open Court.

Case Against Religion: A Psychotherapist's View. Albert Ellis. 1976. pap. 3.00. Am Atheist.

Case-Book of Astral Projection, 545-746. Robert Crookall. 160p. 1980. pap. 3.95 (ISBN 0-8065-0730-6). Citadel Pr.

Case Book of Sherlock Holmes. Arthur Conan Doyle. (gr. 10 up). pap. 1.95 (ISBN 0-425-04822-5, Medallion). Berkley Pub.

Case Exercises in Operations Research. Ed. by M. J. Martin & R. A. Denison. LC 75-146548. 1971. 21.00 (ISBN 0-471-57355-8, Pub. by Wiley-Interscience). Wiley.

Case for Astral Projection. Sylvan Muldoon. 1936. 3.00 (ISBN 0-933646-05-4). Aries Pr.

Case for Christian Theism: An Introduction to Apologetics. A. J. Hoover. 272p. 1981. pap. 6.95 (ISBN 0-8010-4251-8). Baker Bk.

Case for Christianity. C. S. Lewis. 1943. 7.95 (ISBN 0-02-570490-7). Macmillan.

Case for Colour. S. P. Adinarayan. 1964. 10.00x (ISBN 0-210-26896-4). Asia.

Case for English Student's Book. Diana Hicks et al. (Cambridge English Language Learning Ser.). 112p. 1980. pap. 5.95x (ISBN 0-521-22291-5); cassette 13.95x (ISBN 0-521-22527-2); tchr's bk. 8.95x (ISBN 0-521-22526-4, 84 PAGES). Cambridge U Pr.

Case for Foreign Language Study: A Collection of Readings. Ed. by James W. Dodge. 52p. 1971. pap. 2.00x o.p. (ISBN 0-915432-01-3). NE Conf Teach Foreign.

Case for Liberal Christianity. Donald E. Miller. LC 80-8355. 160p. 1980. 9.95 (ISBN 0-06-065753-7). Har-Row.

Case for Modern Man. Charles Frankel. 1959. pap. 2.95 o.p. (ISBN 0-8070-5089-X, BP74). Beacon Pr.

Case for Polygamy. Michael H. Brown. 1976. pap. 4.95 (ISBN 0-685-63906-1). Madison Pub.

Case for Surface Case. Anna Wierzbicka. (Linguistica Extranea: Studia: No. 9). 201p. 1980. 13.50 (ISBN 0-89720-027-6); pap. 7.50 (ISBN 0-89720-028-4). Karoma.

Case for the Burial of Ancestors, Bk. 1. Paul Zelevansky. 1981. 25.00 (ISBN 0-9605610-3-X); pap. 15.00 (ISBN 0-9605610-2-1). Zartscorp.

Case for the Multinational Corporation. Ed. by Carl H. Madden. LC 76-12863. (Special Studies). 1976. text ed. 25.95 (ISBN 0-275-23980-2). Praeger.

Case for the Sea Serpent. Rupert T. Gould. LC 72-75791. 1969. Repr. of 1930 ed. 15.00 (ISBN 0-8103-3833-5). Gale.

Case for the UFO. M. K. Jessup. 1973. pap. 32.50 (ISBN 0-685-37599-4). Saucerian.

Case for the Welfare State: From Social Security to Social Equality. Norman Furniss & Timothy Tilton. LC 76-26414. 256p. 1977. 14.00x (ISBN 0-253-31322-8); pap. 5.95x (ISBN 0-253-20230-2). Ind U Pr.

Case Histories in Construction Law: A Guide for Architects, Engineers, Contractors, Builders. William Jabine. LC 72-81985. 1973. 15.95 o.p. (ISBN 0-8436-0113-2). CBI Pub.

Case-Histories in Engineering Geology. H. G. Anderson & C. F. Trigg. (Illus.). 1977. 35.00 (ISBN 0-236-40049-5, Pub. by Paul Elek). Merrimack Bk Serv.

Case Histories in Failure Analysis. 1979. 62.00 (ISBN 0-87170-078-6). ASM.

Case History Method in the Study of Family Process, Vol. 7. GAP Committee on Family. LC 62-2872. (Report No. 76). 1970. pap. 5.00 (ISBN 0-87318-105-0). Adv Psychiatry.

Case in Camera. Oliver Onions. 320p. 1980. Repr. of 1918 ed. lib. bdg. 15.50x (ISBN 0-89968-205-7). Lightyear.

Case Is Altered. Ben Jonson. Ed. by W. E. Selin. 1917. pap. 34.50x (ISBN 0-685-89739-7). Elliots Bks.

Case of Authors by Profession or Trade, 1758, Champion 1739. James Ralph. LC 66-10008. 1966. 26.00x (ISBN 0-8201-1037-X). Schol Facsimiles.

Case of Jenny Brice. Mary R. Rinehart. 1976. lib. bdg. 12.95x (ISBN 0-89968-182-4). Lightyear.

Case of Leonid Plyushch. Ed. by T. Khodorovich. LC 76-6094. 1976. 18.50x (ISBN 0-89158-600-8). Westview.

Case of Nora: Body Awareness As Healing Therapy. Moshe Feldenkrais. LC 76-62935. 1977. 6.95 o.p. (ISBN 0-06-062346-2, HarpR). Har-Row.

Case of Princess Tomorrow. Sid Fleischman. LC 80-19518. (Bloodhound Gang Ser.). (Illus.). 64p. (gr. 2-5). 1981. PLB 4.99 (ISBN 0-394-84674-5); pap. 1.75 (ISBN 0-394-84674-5). Random.

Case of Rape. Doug Warren. (Orig.). 1975. pap. 1.75 o.s.i. (ISBN 0-515-03617-X, A3617). Jove Pubns.

Case of the Ancient Astronauts. I. J. Gallagher. LC 77-10822. (Great Unsolved Mysteries Ser.). (Illus.). (gr. 4-5). 1977. PLB 9.65 (ISBN 0-8172-1059-8). Raintree Pubs.

Case of the Baker Street Irregular. Robert Newman. 176p. 1981. pap. 1.75 (ISBN 0-553-14272-0). Bantam.

Case of the Bashful Bank Robber. E. W. Hildick. LC 80-27422. (McGurk Mystery Ser.). (Illus.). 128p. (gr. 3-6). 1981. PLB 8.95 (ISBN 0-02-743870-8). Macmillan.

Case of the Black Family: A Sociological Inquiry. new ed. Jerold Heiss. LC 74-34418. 288p. 1975. 17.50x (ISBN 0-231-03782-1). Columbia U Pr.

Case of the Blackmail Boys. Terrance Dicks. (gr. 4 up). 1981. 7.95 (ISBN 0-525-66710-5). Elsevier-Nelson.

Case of the Cackling Ghost. Sid Fleischman. LC 80-20059. (Bloodhound Gang Ser.). (Illus.). 64p. (gr. 2-4). 1981. PLB 4.99 (ISBN 0-394-94673-1); pap. 1.75 (ISBN 0-394-84673-7). Random.

Case of the Condemned Cat: A McGurk Mystery. E. W. Hildick. LC 75-14196. (Illus.). 112p. (gr. 3-6). 1975. 6.95 o.s.i. (ISBN 0-02-743810-4, 74381). Macmillan.

Case of the Condemned Cat: A McGurk Mystery, No. 2. E. W. Hildick. (gr. 3-5). 1978. pap. 1.75 (ISBN 0-671-41404-6). Archway.

Case of the Counterfeit Racehorse. Elizabeth Levy. (Jody & Jake Mystery Bk.: No. 2). (Orig.). (gr. 5-7). 1980. pap. 1.95 (ISBN 0-671-29965-4). Archway.

Case of the Crimson Kiss. Erle S. Gardner. 1971. 6.95 (ISBN 0-688-01275-2). Morrow.

Case of the Crooked Kids. Terrance Dicks. (gr. 4 up). 1980. 7.95 (ISBN 0-525-66702-4). Elsevier-Nelson.

Case of the Crying Swallow. Erle S. Gardner. 1971. 6.95 (ISBN 0-688-01274-4). Morrow.

Case of the Daring Divorcee. Erle S. Gardner. 192p. 1981. pap. 1.95 (ISBN 0-345-29499-8). Ballantine.

Case of the Dark Horse: A Judy & Jake Mystery, No. 2. Elizabeth Levy. (Orig.). (gr. 4-7). 1980. pap. write for info. PB.

Case of the Deadly Diamonds. Christopher Bush. 1969. 8.95 (ISBN 0-02-519280-9). Macmillan.

Case of the Deadly Toy. Erle S. Gardner. LC 80-27287. 288p. Repr. of 1959 ed. lib. bdg. 10.00x (ISBN 0-8376-0397-8). Bentley.

Case of the Double Cross. Crosby Bonsall. LC 80-7768. (I Can Read Bks.). (Illus.). 64p. (gr. k-3). 1980. 6.95 (ISBN 0-06-020602-0, HarpJ); PLB 7.89 (ISBN 0-06-020603-9). Har-Row.

Case of the Fabulous Fake. Erle S. Gardner. LC 70-90761. 1969. 6.95 (ISBN 0-688-01276-0). Morrow.

Case of the Fenced-in Woman. Erle S. Gardner. 1972. 6.95 (ISBN 0-688-00059-2). Morrow.

Case of the Fiery Fingers. Erle S. Gardner. 1981. pap. 1.95 (ISBN 0-345-29494-7). Ballantine.

Case of the Fired-up Gang. Elizabeth Levy. (Jody & Jake Mystery: No. 3). (gr. 3-6). 1981. pap. 1.95 (ISBN 0-671-41140-3). Archway.

Case of the Five Orange Pips. Arthur Conan Doyle. Ed. by Walter Pauk & Raymond Harris. (Classics Ser). (Illus.). (gr. 6-12). 1976. pap. text ed. 1.60x (ISBN 0-89061-062-2, 545); tchrs. ed. 3.00 (ISBN 0-89061-063-0, 547). Jamestown Pubs.

Case of the Frightened Rock Star: A Jody & Jake Mystery Bk. Elizabeth Levy. (No. 1). (Orig.). 1980. pap. 1.95 (ISBN 0-671-29964-6). Archway.

Case of the Frozen Scream. Tom B. Haughey. LC 79-50829. (Baker Street Mystery Ser.). 1979. pap. 2.50 (ISBN 0-87123-045-3, 200045). Bethany Fell.

Case of the Gilded Fly. Edmund Crispin. 1980. lib. bdg. 13.95 (ISBN 0-8161-3018-3). G K Hall.

Case of the Gilded Fly. Edmund Crispin. LC 79-52173. (Walker Mystery Ser.). 223p. 1979. Repr. 8.95 o.s.i. (ISBN 0-8027-5410-4). Walker & Co.

Case of the Gilded Lily. Erle S. Gardner. LC 80-27291. 256p. Repr. of 1956 ed. lib. bdg. 10.00x (ISBN 0-8376-0396-X). Bentley.

Case of the Hijacked Moon. Thomas B. Haughey. (Baker Street Mystery Ser.). 144p. 1981. pap. 2.50 (ISBN 0-87123-143-3, 200143). Bethany Fell.

Case of the Horrified Heirs. Erle S. Gardner. 1964. 4.50 o.p. (ISBN 0-688-01264-7). Morrow.

Case of the Ice Cold Hands. Erle S. Gardner. 1980. lib. bdg. 11.95 (ISBN 0-8161-3174-0, Large Print Bks). G K Hall.

Case of the Iceland Dogs. Cora Cheney. LC 76-53635. (gr. 4 up). 1977. 5.95 (ISBN 0-396-07398-0). Dodd.

Case of the Invisible Dog: A McGurk Mystery. E. W. Hildick. LC 77-4466. ("McGurk Mystery" Ser.). (Illus.). (gr. 3-6). 1977. 8.95 (ISBN 0-02-743830-9, 74383). Macmillan.

Case of the Invisible Dog: A McGurk Mystery, No. 5. E. W. Hildick. (gr. 3-5). 1978. pap. 1.75 (ISBN 0-671-41406-2). PB.

Case of the Invisible Thief. Thomas Brace Haughey. LC 78-68424. (Baker Street Mystery Ser.). 1978. pap. 2.50 (ISBN 0-87123-086-0, 200086). Bethany Fell.

Case of the Irate Witness. Erle S. Gardner. 1972. 6.95 (ISBN 0-688-00102-5). Morrow.

Case of the Kidnapped Shadow. Thomas B. Haughey. (Baker Street Mysteries Ser.). (Orig.). 1980. pap. 2.50 (ISBN 0-87123-112-3, 200112). Bethany Fell.

Case of the Maltese Treasure. Thomas B. Haughey. LC 79-54939. (Baker Street Mysteries). 1979. pap. 2.50 (ISBN 0-87123-048-8, 200048). Bethany Fell.

Case of the Midwife Toad. Arthur Koestler. 1972. 8.95 o.p. (ISBN 0-394-48037-6). Random.

Case of the Mischievous Doll. Erle S. Gardner. 1981. lib. bdg. 11.95 (ISBN 0-8161-3215-1, Large Print Bks). G K Hall.

Case of the Missing Dinosaur. Bernard Palmer. LC 80-65059. (Powell Family Ser.). 160p. (Orig.). (gr. 7-10). 1981. pap. 2.25 (ISBN 0-89636-050-4). Accent Bks.

Case of the Murderer's Bride. Erle S. Gardner. Intro. by Ellery Queen. LC 77-81936. 1977. pap. 1.50 o.p. (ISBN 0-89559-003-4). Davis Pubns.

Case of the Mythical Monkeys. Erle S. Gardner. LC 80-27190. 288p. Repr. of 1959 ed. lib. bdg. 10.00x (ISBN 0-8376-0398-6). Bentley.

Case of the Nervous Newsboy: A McGurk Mystery. E. W. Hildick. LC 75-35873. (Illus.). 112p. (gr. 4-6). 1976. 7.95 (ISBN 0-02-743790-6, 74379). Macmillan.

Case of the Nervous Newsboy: A McGurk Mystery, No. 3. E. W. Hildick. (gr. 3-5). 1978. pap. 1.75 (ISBN 0-671-41405-4). Archway.

Case of the Nervous Newsboy: A McGurk Mystery, No. 3. E. W. Hildick. (Illus.). (gr. 3-5). 1978. pap. 1.75 (ISBN 0-671-41405-4). PB.

Case of the Phantom Frog. E. W. Hildick. LC 78-10836. (McGurk Mystery Ser.). (Illus.). (gr. 3-6). 1979. 7.95 (ISBN 0-02-743840-6). Macmillan.

Case of the Postponed Murder. Erle S. Gardner. LC 72-1344. 1973. 6.95 (ISBN 0-688-00033-9). Morrow.

Case of the Queenly Contestant. Erle S. Gardner. 1967. 6.95 (ISBN 0-688-01280-9). Morrow.

Case of the Russian Diplomat. E. V. Cunningham. 1979. pap. 1.75 o.s.i. (ISBN 0-515-04881-X, 04881-X). Jove Pubns.

Case of the Secret Scribbler. E. W. Hildick. LC 78-2340. (McGurk Mystery Ser.). (Illus.). (gr. 3-6). 1978. 7.95 (ISBN 0-02-743780-9). Macmillan.

Case of the Secret Scribbler: A McGurk Mystery, No. 6. E. W. Hildick. (Illus.). (gr. 3-5). 1979. pap. 1.75 (ISBN 0-671-43293-1). PB.

Case of the Shapely Shadow. Erle S. Gardner. 1981. pap. 1.95 (ISBN 0-345-29498-X). Ballantine.

Case of the Silver Skull. Scott Corbett. (Illus.). 128p. (gr. 4-6). 1974. 5.95 (ISBN 0-316-15711-2, Pub. by Atlantic Monthly Pr). Little.

Case of the Singing Skirt. Erle S. Gardner. LC 80-27263. 256p. Repr. of 1959 ed. lib. bdg. 10.00x (ISBN 0-8376-0399-4). Bentley.

Case of the Six Napoleons. Arthur Conan Doyle. Ed. by Walter Pauk & Raymond Harris. (Classics Ser). (Illus.). (gr. 6-12). 1976. pap. text ed. 1.60x (ISBN 0-89061-058-4, 537); tchrs. ed. 3.00 (ISBN 0-89061-059-2, 539). Jamestown Pubs.

Case of the Smiley Faces. Larry Sutton. (Carolrhoda Mini-Mysteries Ser.). (Illus.). 32p. (gr. 1-4). 1981. PLB 4.95 (ISBN 0-87614-133-5). Carolrhoda Bks.

Case of the Somerville Secret. Robert Newman. LC 80-18584. 192p. (gr. 4-6). 1981. PLB 9.95 (ISBN 0-689-30825-6). Atheneum.

Case of the Treetop Treasure: A McGurk Mystery No. 8. E. W. Hildick. (McGurk Mystery Bk.: No. 8). 1981. pap. write for info. (ISBN 0-671-41868-8). Archway.

Case of the Trick Note. Larry Sutton. (Carolrhoda Mini-Mysteries Ser.). (Illus.). 32p. (gr. 1-4). 1980. PLB 4.95 (ISBN 0-87614-134-3). Carolrhoda Bks.

Case of the Vanishing Boy. Alexander Key. (gr. 5-7). 1979. pap. 1.75 (ISBN 0-671-56006-9). PB.

Case of Thomas J. Mooney & Warren K. Billings. Henry T. Hunt. LC 72-122166. (Civil Liberties in American History Ser). (Illus.). 1970. Repr. of 1929 ed. lib. bdg. 42.50 (ISBN 0-306-71976-2). Da Capo.

Case of Victor L. Berger of Wisconsin, 2 vols. United States, 66th Congress, House of Representatives, 1st. Session. LC 78-39129. (Civil Liberties in American History Ser). 1972. Repr. of 1920 ed. lib. bdg. 105.00. Vol. 1 (ISBN 0-306-70465-X). Vol. 2 (ISBN 0-306-70466-8). Set. lib. bdg. 85.00 (ISBN 0-686-57599-7). Da Capo.

Case of Walter Bagehot. C. H. Sisson. 140p. 1972. text ed. 10.50x (ISBN 0-571-09501-1). Humanities.

Case of Walter Lippmann: A Presidential Strategy, Vol. 3. Lyndon H. LaRouche, Jr. Ed. by Kathy Stevens. (American History Ser.). 1978. pap. 5.95 (ISBN 0-918388-06-6, Univ Edns). New Benjamin.

Case Organizational Strategy Policy. Naumes. 1978. pap. 12.95 (ISBN 0-7216-6662-0). Dryden Pr.

Case Problems in Business Logistics. J. L. Heskett et al. 1973. 16.95x (ISBN 0-8260-4072-1). Wiley.

Case Problems in Finance. 7th ed. J. Keith Butters et al. 1975. text ed. 18.95x (ISBN 0-256-01756-5). Irwin.

Case Problems in Management. Randall S. Schuler & Edgar F. Huse. (Management Ser.). (Illus.). 1979. pap. text ed. 9.50 (ISBN 0-8299-0242-2); instrs.' manual avail. (ISBN 0-8299-0604-5). West Pub.

Case Problems in Marketing. David Leighton & Kenneth Simmonds. 1973. pap. text ed. 12.95 (ISBN 0-17-771026-8). Intl Ideas.

Case Studies from the Distribution Trades. E. P. Gostling & K. Ambrose. 1972. text ed. 14.95x (ISBN 0-07-002016-7). Intl Ideas.

Case Studies in American Industry. 3rd ed. Leonard W. Weiss. LC 78-31149. (Introduction to Economics Ser.). 1980. pap. text ed. 10.50 (ISBN 0-471-03159-3). Wiley.

Case Studies in Anatomy. 3rd ed. Ernest Lachman & Kenneth K. Faulkner. (Illus.). 432p. 1981. pap. text ed. 9.95x (ISBN 0-19-502813-9). Oxford U Pr.

Case Studies in Behaviour Therapy. Ed. by H. J. Eysenck. 400p. 1976. 30.00x (ISBN 0-7100-8164-2). Routledge & Kegan.

Case Studies in Classroom Management. David M. Galloway. 1976. pap. text ed. 7.95 (ISBN 0-582-48562-2). Longman.

Case Studies in Clinical Social Work. Ed. by Mary Gottesfeld. LC 78-71807. 1979. pap. 6.95x (ISBN 0-87705-397-9). Human Sci Pr.

Case Studies in Curriculum Change. Ed. by William A. Reid & Decker F. Walker. 1975. 24.00x (ISBN 0-7100-8037-9); pap. 10.00 (ISBN 0-7100-8038-7). Routledge & Kegan.

Case Studies in Deviant Behavior: An Interactional Perspective. 2nd ed. Gloria R. Leon. 1977. pap. 11.95 (ISBN 0-205-05847-7, 795847-1). Allyn.

Case Studies in Elementary School Administration. Morris Hamburg. LC 57-12480. 1957. pap. text ed. 4.75x (ISBN 0-8077-1485-2). Tchrs Coll.

Case Studies in Genetics. Michael A. Tribe et al. LC 77-75778. (Basic Biology Course Ser.: Bk. 12). (Illus.). 1977. 29.95 (ISBN 0-521-21373-8); pap. 11.95x (ISBN 0-521-21372-X). Cambridge U Pr.

Case-Studies in Groundwater Resources Evaluation. J. W. Lloyd. (Illus.). 250p. 1981. 82.50 (ISBN 0-19-854530-4). Oxford U Pr.

Case Studies in Health Administration, 2 vols. J. O. Hepner. Incl. Vol. 1. Health Planning for Emergency Multi-Hospital Systems. LC 77-17008. (Illus.). 1978. pap. text ed. 15.95 (ISBN 0-8016-2156-9); Vol. 2. Hospital Administrator-Physician Relationships. LC 80-16073. 1980. pap. text ed. 21.95 (ISBN 0-8016-2158-5). Mosby.

Case Studies in Institutional Licensee Management. Robert F. Schenkkan et al. 75p. 1980. pap. 4.00 (Pub Telecom). NAEB.

Case Studies in Marketing & Distribution. Patricia M. Rath et al. (Illus.). (gr. 9-12). 1965. pap. text ed. 2.95x (ISBN 0-8134-0835-0, 835). Interstate.

Case Studies in Personnel Management. Michael Armstrong. 1979. 30.00x (ISBN 0-85038-243-2). Nichols Pub.

Case Studies in Pollution Control in the Textile Dyeing & Finishing Industries: A Study in Non-Technical Language of Essential Information on the Economics of Control, the Problems & Their Solutions. M. H. Atkins & J. F. Lowe. 1979. 45.00 (ISBN 0-08-022457-1). Pergamon.

Case Studies in Quantitative Management. C. Wilson. 1972. text ed. 14.95x (ISBN 0-7002-0166-1). Intl Ideas.

Case Studies in Radiology. Daffner. 1975. pap. 15.50 o.p. (ISBN 0-8385-1072-8). ACC.

Case Studies in Reading Disability. new ed. George D. Spache et al. 250p. 1980. text ed. 13.50 (237258-4). Allyn.

Case Studies in Regulation: Revolution & Reform. Weiss & Klass. 1981. pap. text ed. 9.95 (ISBN 0-316-92893-3). Little.

Case Studies in Spirit Possession. V. Crapanzano & V. Garrison. LC 76-26653. 1977. 29.50 (ISBN 0-471-18460-8). Wiley.

Case Studies in Systems Design. R. G. Anderson. (Illus.). 208p. (Orig.). 1980. pap. text ed. 10.00x (ISBN 0-7121-0387-2). Intl Ideas.

Case Studies of the Clinical Interpretation of the Bender Gestalt Test: Illustrations of the Interpretive Process for Graduate Training & Continuing Professional Education. Clifford M. DeCato & Robert J. Wicks. (Illus.). 152p. 1976. 14.50 (ISBN 0-398-03554-7). C C Thomas.

Case Study II: MEDCO, Inc. Peter P. Dawson & Frederick Gallegos. (Illus.). 89p. 1973. pap. text ed. 5.95 (ISBN 0-574-17920-8, 13-0920); instr's guide avail. (ISBN 0-574-17921-6, 13-0921). SRA.

Case Study in Auditing. Donald H. Taylor & G. William Glezen. LC 78-27496. 1979. pap. text ed. 13.50x (ISBN 0-471-04626-4); tchrs. manual avail. (ISBN 0-471-05297-3). Wiley.

Case Study in Business System Design. SRA Data Processing & Curriculum Group. (Illus.). 1970. pap. text ed. 5.95 (ISBN 0-574-16094-9, 13-0782); instr's guide avail. (ISBN 0-574-16095-7, 13-0783). SRA.

Case Study in Risk Management. Jerry Rosenbloom. 160p. 1972. pap. 11.95 (ISBN 0-13-116061-3). P-H.

Case Study in Syntactic Markedness: The Binding Nature of Prepositional Phrases. H. C. Riemsdijk. 1978. pap. text ed. 23.00x o.p. (ISBN 90-316-0160-8). Humanities.

Case Study: Mr. Paranoid. George A. Jackson. 64p. 1981. 4.00 (ISBN 0-682-49692-8). Exposition.

Case Study of a Soviet Republic: The Estonian SSR. Ed. by Tonu Parming & Elmar Jarvesoo. LC 77-671. (Westview Special Studies on the Soviet Union & Eastern Europe). 1978. lib. bdg. 30.00x (ISBN 0-89158-247-9). Westview.

Case Worker. 5th ed. Arco Editorial Board. LC 75-21849. 1975. pap. 8.00 o.p. (ISBN 0-668-01528-4). Arco.

Case Worker. 7th ed. LC 80-18006. 256p. 1980. pap. 8.00 (ISBN 0-668-04979-0, 4979-0). Arco.

Casebook for Management Information Systems. 2nd ed. Henry Lucas & Cyrusf. Gibson. (Management Information Systems Ser.). (Illus.). 480p. 1980. pap. text ed. 10.95 (ISBN 0-07-038939-X, C) (ISBN 0-686-68691-8). McGraw.

Casebook for Special Education & Elementary Education. Thomas Hughes & Kendall S. Hughes. LC 76-57115. 1977. pap. 7.50x (ISBN 0-8134-1905-0, 1905). Interstate.

Casebook in Business Policy & Planning. Charles W. Hofer et al. 150p. Date not set. price not set instr's. manual (ISBN 0-8299-0614-2). West Pub.

Casebook in Commercial Banking. Edward W. Reed et al. (Illus.). 1977. ref. ed. 9.95 (ISBN 0-13-117473-8). P-H.

Casebook in Group Therapy: A Behavioral-Cognitive Approach. Sheldon D. Rose. (Social Work Practice Ser.). (Illus.). 1979. text ed. 14.95 (ISBN 0-13-117408-8). P-H.

Casebook of a UFO Investigator. Raymond E. Fowler. 1980. 11.95 (ISBN 0-13-117432-0). P-H.

Casebook of Diagnosis & Evaluation in Speech Pathology. Lon L. Emerick. (Illus.). 224p. 1981. pap. text ed. 11.95 (ISBN 0-13-117358-8). P-H.

Casebook of Economic, Microeconomic Problems & Policies: Practice in Thinking. 4th ed. Fels et al. 112p. 1978. 5.95 (ISBN 0-8299-0479-4); staff notes avail. West Pub.

Casebook of Grant Proposals in the Humanities. Ed. by William Coleman et al. 350p. 1981. 24.95 (ISBN 0-918212-45-6). Neal-Schuman.

Casebook of Methods of Computation of Quantitative Changes in the Hydrological Regime of River Basins Due to Human Activities. (Studies & Reports in Hydrology: No. 28). 330p. 1980. pap. 24.25 (ISBN 92-3-101798-5, U1037, UNESCO). Unipub.

Casebook of Professional Practices in Special Education. Jean R. Hebeler & Maynard C. Reynolds. 1976. pap. text ed. 4.00x o.p. (ISBN 0-86586-009-2). Coun Exc Child.

Casebook of Self-Timed Exercises. Conal P. Keogh. (gr. 11-12). 1970. pap. text ed. 5.75x (ISBN 0-88334-025-9). Ind Sch Pr.

Casebook of Test Interpretation in Counseling. Harley D. Christiansen. (Illus.). 96p. (Orig.). 1981. pap. text ed. 8.95 (ISBN 0-915456-05-2). P Juul Pr.

Casebook of the Black Widowers. Isaac Asimov. 256p. 1981. pap. 2.25 (ISBN 0-449-24384-2, Crest). Fawcett.

Casebook on Church & Society. Ed. by Keith R. Bridston et al. LC 74-13419. 224p. (Orig.). 1974. pap. 5.95 o.p. (ISBN 0-687-04709-9). Abingdon.

Casenotes of a Medical Astrologer. Margaret Millard. 1980. pap. 7.95 (ISBN 0-87728-484-9). Weiser.

Cases & Comments on Criminal Procedure. 2nd ed. Fred E. Inbau et al. LC 80-17843. (University Casebooks Ser.). 1598p. text ed. write for info. (ISBN 0-88277-011-X). Foundation Pr.

Cases & Comments on Criminal Procedure. Andre A. Moenssens et al. (Contemporary Legal Education Ser.). 900p. 1979. text ed. 21.00 (ISBN 0-672-83683-1). Bobbs.

Cases & Comments on Juvenile Law. Senna & Siegel. (Criminal Justice Ser.). 600p. 1976. pap. text ed. 17.95 (ISBN 0-8299-0629-0). West Pub.

Cases & Concepts in Corporate Strategy. Robert L. Katz. 1970. ref. ed 21.95 (ISBN 0-13-118422-9). P-H.

Cases & Excercises in Personnel. rev. ed. William F. Glueck. 1978. pap. 9.95x (ISBN 0-256-01952-5). Business Pubns.

Cases & Materials on Civil Rights. Charles F. Abernathy. LC 79-24759. (American Casebook Ser.). 700p. 1980. text ed. 17.95 (ISBN 0-8299-2076-5). West Pub.

Cases & Materials on Constitutional Law. 10th ed. Gerald Gunther. LC 80-20484. (University Casebook Ser.). 1839p. 1980. text ed. write for info. (ISBN 0-88277-010-1). Foundation Pr.

Cases & Materials on Constitutional Rights & Liberties. 5th ed. William B. Lockhart et al. LC 80-54541. (American Casebook Ser.). 1298p. 1980. text ed. 21.95 (ISBN 0-8299-2135-4). West Pub.

Cases & Materials on Contracts. 3rd ed. E. Allan Farnsworth & William F. Young. LC 80-15040. (University Casebook Ser.). 1203p. write for info. (ISBN 0-88277-009-8). Foundation Pr.

Cases & Materials on Copyright & Other Aspects of Law Pertaining to Literary, Musical & Artistic Works. 2nd ed. Melville B. Nimmer. LC 79-13515. (American Casebook Ser.). (Illus.). 1023p. 1979. text ed. 21.95 (ISBN 0-8299-2038-2). West Pub.

Cases & Materials on Corporations. 5th ed. William Cary & Melvin A. Eisenberg. LC 80-18042. (University Casebook Ser.). 1829p. pap. 2.50 (ISBN 0-88277-012-8). Foundation Pr.

Cases & Materials on Corporations. abr. 5th ed. William L. Cary & Melvin A. Eisenberg. LC 80-68866. (University Casebook Ser.). 1085p. 1980. text ed. 21.50 (ISBN 0-88277-017-9). Foundation Pr.

Cases & Materials on Corporations. 5th ed. Richard W. Jennings & Richard M. Buxbaum. LC 79-9237. (American Casebook Ser.). 1397p. 1979. text ed. 23.95 (ISBN 0-8299-2054-4). West Pub.

Cases & Materials on Creditors' Remedies & Debtors' Protection. 3rd ed. Stefan A. Riesenfeld. LC 79-9357. (American Casebook Ser.). 810p. 1979. text ed. 20.95 (ISBN 0-8299-2060-9). West Pub.

Cases & Materials on Criminal Law. 2nd ed. George E. Dix & M. Michael Sharlot. LC 79-16929. (American Casebook Ser.). 764p. 1979. text ed. 19.95 (ISBN 0-8299-2056-0). West Pub.

Cases & Materials on Debtor-Creditor Relations. Pierre R. Loiseaux & William Hawkland. (Contemporary Legal Education Ser.). 1979. 22.50 (ISBN 0-672-82028-5, Bobbs-Merrill Law); statutory appendix 4.50 (ISBN 0-672-83731-5). Michie.

Cases & Materials on Employment Discrimination Law. Mack A. Player. LC 79-28069. (American Casebook Ser.). 915p. 1980. text ed. 18.95 (ISBN 0-8299-2075-7). West Pub.

Cases & Materials on Energy & Natural Resources Law. William H. Rodgers, Jr. LC 78-31515. (American Casebook Ser.). 995p. 1979. text ed. 23.95 (ISBN 0-8299-2029-3). West Pub.

Cases & Materials on Equitable Remedies & Restitution. 3rd ed. Robert N. Leavell et al. LC 79-27903. (American Casebook Ser.). 736p. 1980. text ed. 19.95 (ISBN 0-8299-2084-6). West Pub.

Cases & Materials on Evidence. 4th ed. David W. Louisell & John Kaplan. (University Casebook Ser.). 899p. 1981. write for info. (ISBN 0-88277-018-7). Foundation Pr.

Cases & Materials on Evidence. 5th ed. Charles T. McCormick et al. LC 80-22463. 1083p. 1980. text ed. write for info. (ISBN 0-8299-2112-5). West Pub.

Cases & Materials on Family Law. 2nd ed. Caleb Foote et al. 1976. 24.50 (ISBN 0-316-28850-0); pap. 5.95 1980 suppl. (ISBN 0-316-28852-7). Little.

Cases & Materials on Federal Income Taxation: Taxation of Corporations, Shareholders, Partnerships & Partners, Vol. II. Adrian A. Kragen & John K. McNulty. (American Casebook Ser.). 976p. 1981. text ed. 24.95 (ISBN 0-8299-2133-8). West Pub.

Cases & Materials on Federal Income Taxation: Taxation of Individuals, Vol. 1. 3rd ed. Adrian A. Kragen & John K. McNulty. LC 79-16910. (American Casebook Ser.). 1236p. 1979. text ed. 24.95 (ISBN 0-8299-2058-7). West Pub.

Cases & Materials on Federal Indian Law. David H. Getches et al. LC 79-3906. (American Casebook Ser.). 600p. 1979. text ed. 19.95 (ISBN 0-8299-2027-7). West Pub.

Cases & Materials on Individual Rights in Constitutional Law. 3rd, abr. ed. Gerald Gunther. LC 80-70238. (University Casebook Ser.). 1337p. 1980. text ed. write for info. (ISBN 0-88277-021-7). Foundation Pr.

Cases & Materials on International Law. 2nd ed. Louis Henkin et al. LC 80-17731. (American Casebook Ser.). 1210p. 1980. text ed. 22.95 (ISBN 0-8299-2099-4). West Pub.

Cases & Materials on International Law. 2nd ed. Lester B. Orfield & E. D. Re. 1965. 20.00 (ISBN 0-672-80979-6, Bobbs-Merrill Law). Michie.

Cases & Materials on Labor Law. Douglas Leslie. 1979. 21.00 (ISBN 0-316-52157-4); pap. 3.95 statutory supplement (ISBN 0-316-52158-2). Little.

Cases & Materials on Labor Law: Collective Bargaining in a Free Society. 2nd ed. Walter E. Oberer et al. LC 78-20988. (American Casebook Ser.). 1168p. 1979. text ed. 23.95 (ISBN 0-8299-2024-2). West Pub.

Cases & Materials on Law & Medicine. David J. Sharpe et al. LC 78-12529. (American Casebook Ser.). 882p. 1978. text ed. 19.95 (ISBN 0-8299-2015-3). West Pub.

Cases & Materials on Law & Medicine. Walter J. Wadlington et al. LC 80-23725. (University Casebook Ser.). 1077p. 1980. text ed. write for info. (ISBN 0-88277-015-2). Foundation Pr.

Cases & Materials on Patent Law, Also Including Trade Secrets - Copyrights - Trademarks. 2nd ed. Robert A. Choate & William H. Francis. (American Casebook Ser.). 1100p. 1981. text ed. 23.95 (ISBN 0-8299-2124-9). West Pub.

Cases & Materials on Pharmacy Law. Helen Wetherbee & Bruce D. White. LC 80-14608. 612p. 1980. text ed. 17.95 (ISBN 0-8299-2091-9). West Pub.

Cases & Materials on Products Liability. Marshall S. Shapo. LC 80-11639. (University Casebook Ser.). 906p. 1980. text ed. write for info. (ISBN 0-88277-001-2). Foundation Pr.

Cases & Materials on Public Planning & Control of Urban & Land Development. 2nd ed. Donald G. Hagman. LC 80-36684. (American Casebook Ser.). 1301p. 1980. text ed. 23.95 (ISBN 0-8299-2100-1). West Pub.

Cases & Materials on Remedies. 3rd ed. Kenneth H. York & John A. Bauman. LC 78-23510. (American Casebook Ser.). 1250p. 1979. text ed. 23.95 (ISBN 0-8299-2021-8). West Pub.

Cases & Materials on State & Local Taxation. 4th ed. Jerome R. Hellerstein & Walter Hellerstein. LC 78-2418. (American Casebook Ser.). 1041p. 1978. text ed. 21.95 (ISBN 0-8299-2000-5). West Pub.

Cases & Materials on the English Legal System. Michael Zander. (Law in Context Ser.). 484p. 1973. 19.50x o.p. (ISBN 0-297-99547-2). Rothman.

Cases & Materials on the English Legal System. 3rd ed. Michael Zander. (Law in Context Ser.). xxvii, 476p. 1980. 47.95x (ISBN 0-297-77822-6, Pub. by Weidenfeld & Nicholson England). Rothman.

Cases & Materials on the Law of Corrections & Prisoners' Rights. 2nd ed. Sheldon Krantz. (American Casebook Ser.). 786p. 1981. text ed. 22.95 (ISBN 0-8299-2127-3). West Pub.

Cases & Materials on the Law of Deprivation of Liberty: A Study in Social Control. Fred Cohen. LC 79-26667. (American Casebook Ser.). 793p. 1980. text ed. 18.95 (ISBN 0-8299-2079-X). West Pub.

Cases & Materials on Trial Practice. Joseph R. Nolan. (American Casebook Ser.). 514p. 1981. text ed. 17.95 (ISBN 0-686-69319-1). West Pub.

Cases & Materials on Water Law. 3rd ed. Frank J. Trelease. LC 79-22224. (American Casebook Ser.). 833p. 1979. text ed. 20.95 (ISBN 0-8299-2063-3). West Pub.

Cases & Materials on Workers' Compensation & Employment Rights. 2nd ed. Wex S. Malone et al. LC 80-11963. (American Casebook Ser.). Orig. Title: Cases & Materials on the Employment Relation. 1043p. 1980. text ed. 21.95 (ISBN 0-8299-2088-9). West Pub.

Cases & Other Materials on Civil Procedure. Austin W. Scott & Robert B. Kent. 1117p. 1967. 18.50 o.p. (ISBN 0-316-77642-4). Little.

Cases & Policies in Human Resources Management. 3rd ed. Raymond L. Hilgert et al. LC 77-72903. (Illus.). 1977. pap. text ed. 10.95 (ISBN 0-395-25070-6); inst. manual 0.75 (ISBN 0-395-25071-4). HM.

Cases & Problems on Contracts. John D. Calamari & Joseph M. Perillo. LC 78-18757. (American Casebook Ser.). 1061p. 1978. text ed. 21.95 (ISBN 0-8299-2010-2). West Pub.

Cases & Problems on Domestic Relations. 3rd ed. Homer H. Clark, Jr. LC 80-19763. (American Casebook Ser.). 1193p. 1980. text ed. 22.95 (ISBN 0-8299-2104-4). West Pub.

Cases & Readings in Marketing. Richard Buskirk. LC 71-118233. 1976. text ed. 6.20 o.p. (ISBN 0-913310-47-6). Par Inc.

Cases & Text Materials on Legal Method: Successor Edition. Harry W. Jones et al. LC 80-13230. (University Casebook Ser.). Orig. Title: Materials for Legal Method. 817p. 1980. text ed. write for info. (ISBN 0-88277-004-7). Foundation Pr.

Cases for Analysis in Marketing. 2nd ed. Wayne Talarzyk. LC 80-65809. 384p. 1981. pap. text ed. 8.95 (ISBN 0-03-058179-6). Dryden Pr.

Cases for Discussion. J. R. Lewis. 1966. 13.75 (ISBN 0-08-011352-4); pap. 6.25 (ISBN 0-08-011351-6). Pergamon.

Cases in Accountability: The Work of the Gao. Ed. by Erasmus H. Kloman. 1979. lib. bdg. 24.50x (ISBN 0-89158-395-5); pap. text ed. 9.50x (ISBN 0-89158-494-3). Westview.

Cases in Administrative Policies & Contemporary Issues. 4th ed. Merwin M. Hargrove et al. 1973. text ed. 18.50 (ISBN 0-256-01433-7). Irwin.

Cases in Advertising & Communications Management. Stephen A. Greyser. LC 74-158911. (Illus.). 1972. ref. ed. 19.95 (ISBN 0-13-118497-0). P-H.

Cases in Advertising & Communications Management. 2nd ed. Stephen A. Greyser. 300p. 1981. text ed. 19.95 (ISBN 0-13-118513-6). P-H.

Cases in Basic Financial Management. John D. Martin et al. 1979. pap. text ed. 10.95 (ISBN 0-13-117556-4). P-H.

Cases in Business Ethics. Thomas M. Garrett. 1968. pap. text ed. 10.95 (ISBN 0-13-118703-1). P-H.

Cases in Collective Bargaining & Industrial Relations: A Decisional Approach. 3rd ed. Sterling H. Schoen & Raymond L. Hilgert. 1978. pap. text ed. 10.95 (ISBN 0-256-02002-7). Irwin.

Cases in Constitutional Law. 6th ed. Dayid L. Keir & Frederick H. Lawson. Ed. by D. J. Bentley. 592p. 1979. text ed. 43.50x (ISBN 0-19-876065-5). Oxford U Pr.

Cases in Consumer Behavior. S. Ward & S. De Bruicker. 1980. pap. 13.95 (ISBN 0-13-118356-7). P-H.

Cases in Diagnostic Ultrasound. I. H. Leopold. 224p. 1980. 22.00 (ISBN 0-471-08731-9, Pub. by Wiley Med). Wiley.

Cases in Economic Development Projects: Policies & Statistics. Stern Roemer. 1981. text ed. price not set (ISBN 0-408-10730-8); pap. text ed. price not set (ISBN 0-408-10729-4). Butterworth.

Cases in Finance. D. F. Scott, Jr. et al. (Illus.). 1977. pap. 10.95x ref. ed. (ISBN 0-13-115337-4). P-H.

Cases in Financial Management. Vincent P. Apilado et al. 1977. pap. text ed. 9.50 (ISBN 0-8299-0120-5); instrs.' manual avail. (ISBN 0-8299-0456-5). West Pub.

Cases in Financial Management. Avery B. Cohan & Harold E. Wyman. LC 72-39508. (Illus.). 256p. 1972. pap. text ed. 10.95x (ISBN 0-13-118745-7). P-H.

Cases in Financial Management. Jerry Viscione & George Aragon. LC 79-87854. 1979. text ed. 18.50 (ISBN 0-395-26715-3); instructor's manual 3.00 (ISBN 0-395-26716-1). HM.

Cases in Financial Management. Bernard J. Winger. LC 80-11532. (Finance Ser.). 115p. 1981. pap. 8.50 (ISBN 0-88244-224-4). Grid Pub.

Cases in Labor Law. D. Nordlinger Stern & Joseph P. Yaney. LC 76-5617. (Law Ser.). 1977. pap. text ed. 11.95 o.p. (ISBN 0-88244-110-8). Grid Pub.

Cases in Labor Relations: An Arbitration Experience. John Abersold & Wayne Howard. (Orig.). 1967. pap. text ed. 10.95 (ISBN 0-13-118794-5). P-H.

Cases in Learning & Behavior Problems: A Guide to Individualized Education Programs. Janet Lerner et al. LC 79-88101. 1979. pap. text ed. 9.50 (ISBN 0-395-28493-7); instructor's manual 0.25 (ISBN 0-395-28494-5). HM.

Cases in Managerial Economics. Bernard J. Winger. LC 78-27382. (Grid Series in Economics). 1979. pap. text ed. 7.95 (ISBN 0-88244-183-3). Grid Pub.

Cases in Managerial Finance. 4th ed. Brigham et al. 1980. pap. 9.95 (ISBN 0-03-054786-5). Dryden Pr.

Cases in Manufacturing Management. Albert N. Schreiber. (Management Ser.). (Illus.). 1965. text ed. 16.95 o.p. (ISBN 0-07-055608-3, C). McGraw.

Cases in Marketing: Decision, Policies, Strategies. Richard Still & Clyde E. Harris, Jr. (Illus.). 304p. 1972. pap. text ed. 9.95 (ISBN 0-13-118877-1). P-H.

Cases in Marketing Management. Kenneth L. Bernhardt & Thomas C. Kinnear. 1978. 19.95x (ISBN 0-256-02081-7). Business Pubns.

Cases in Marketing Management. Subhash C. Jain & Iqbal Mathur. LC 77-81539. (Marketing Ser.). 1978. text ed. 19.95 o.p. (ISBN 0-88244-129-9). Grid Pub.

Cases in Marketing Management. Dale Varble. (Business Ser.). 272p. 1976. pap. text ed. 12.50 (ISBN 0-675-08638-8); instructor's manual 3.95 (ISBN 0-686-67246-1). Merrill.

Cases in Marketing Research. Walter B. Wentz. 290p. 1975. pap. text ed. 10.95 scp (ISBN 0-06-047008-9, HarpC). Har-Row.

Cases in Medical Staff Administration. Nathan Hershey et al. 350p. 1981. text ed. price not set (ISBN 0-89443-282-6). Aspen Systems.

Cases in Modern Financial Management: Public & Private Sector Perspectives. Ronald F. Wippern. 1980. 17.95x (ISBN 0-256-02363-8). Irwin.

Cases in Nursing Management. Warren Ganong & Joan Ganong. LC 79-2572. 1979. text ed. 23.95 (ISBN 0-89443-152-8). Aspen Systems.

Cases in Operations Management. James L. McKenney & Richard S. Rosenbloom. LC 69-13680. (Management & Administration Ser). 1969. pap. text ed. 14.50x o.p. (ISBN 0-471-58451-7). Wiley.

Cases in Operations Research. Christoph Haehling von Lanzenauer. 1975. 12.95x (ISBN 0-8162-3546-5); manual 4.50instr's (ISBN 0-8162-3556-2). Holden-Day.

Cases in Organizational & Administrative Behavior. Robert Wegner & Leonard Sayles. LC 71-158913. 1972. pap. text ed. 10.95 (ISBN 0-13-118562-4). P-H.

Cases in Personnel Management. Arno F. Knapper. LC 76-11577. (Management Ser.). 1977. pap. text ed. 6.95 o.p. (ISBN 0-88244-121-3). Grid Pub.

Cases in Personnel Management & Supervision. 2nd ed. R. Calhoun. 1971. pap. text ed. 10.95 (ISBN 0-13-120352-5). P-H.

Cases in Production & Operations Management. Joe C. Iverstine & Jerry Kinard. 1977. pap. text ed. 12.95 (ISBN 0-675-08521-7). Merrill.

Cases in Profit Planning & Control. Glenn A. Welsch. 1970. pap. text ed. 9.95 (ISBN 0-13-118471-7). P-H.

Cases in Promotional Strategy. James F. Engel et al. 1971. pap. text ed. 10.50 (ISBN 0-256-00611-3). Irwin.

Cases in Retail Management Attitude Development. Larry K. Christiansen & James W. Strate. (Gregg-McGraw-Hill Marketing Ser.). (Illus.). 256p. Date not set. wkbk. 5.75 (ISBN 0-07-010820-X, G). McGraw.

Cases in Sales Management. Charles M. Futrell. LC 80-65797. 320p. 1981. pap. text ed. 10.95 (ISBN 0-03-054736-9). Dryden Pr.

Cases in Written Communication II. Mary C. Bromage & Bruce A. Nelson. (Michigan Business Cases Ser.: No. 2). 1967. pap. 5.50 o.p. (ISBN 0-87712-131-1). U Mich Busn Div Res.

Cases of Conscience. E. Rose. LC 74-76947. 272p. 1975. 35.50 (ISBN 0-521-20462-3). Cambridge U Pr.

Cases of the Reincarnation Type: Twelve Cases in Lebanon & Turkey, Vol. 3. Ian Stevenson. LC 74-28263. 1980. 25.00x (ISBN 0-8139-0816-7). U Pr of Va.

Cases on Constitutional Law: Political Roles of the Supreme Court. Ed. by Victor G. Rosenblum & A. Didrick Castberg. 1973. pap. text ed. 19.95x (ISBN 0-256-01165-6). Dorsey.

Cases on Financial Institutions. Dixon C. Cunningham et al. LC 77-90644. (Finance Ser.). 1979. text ed. 18.50 (ISBN 0-88244-120-5). Grid Pub.

Cases on Restitution. 2nd ed. John Dawson & George Palmer. 1969. 22.00 (ISBN 0-672-81193-6, Bobbs-Merrill Law). Michie.

Casework: A Psychological Therapy. 3rd ed. F. Hollis & M. E. Woods. 552p. 1981. text ed. 16.95 (ISBN 0-394-32368-8). Random.

Casework in Context: A Basis for Practice. Fred Tilbury & Derek Edward. 250p. 1977. text ed. 25.00 (ISBN 0-08-019744-2); pap. text ed. 14.00 (ISBN 0-08-019743-4). Pergamon.

Casey & the Great Idea. Joan L. Nixon. (Illus.). (gr. 4-6). 1980. PLB 9.95 (ISBN 0-525-27525-8). Dutton.

Casey at the Bat. Ernest L. Thayer. (Illus.). (gr. 4 up). 1964. pap. 2.50 (ISBN 0-13-120402-5). P-H.

Casey! Charles Stengel. James Hahn & Lynn Hahn. Ed. by Howard Schroeder. (Sports Legends Ser.). (Illus.). 48p. (Orig.). (gr. 3-5). 1981. PLB 5.95 (ISBN 0-89686-126-0); pap. text ed. 2.95 (ISBN 0-89686-141-4). Crestwood Hse.

Cash from Trash. Edwin G. Warman. (Illus.). 3.95 o.p. (ISBN 0-685-21844-9). Warman.

Cash Management. Richard B. Homonoff & David W. Mullins, Jr. LC 74-23318. (Illus.). 1975. 13.00 o.p. (ISBN 0-669-97485-4). Lexington Bks.

Cash Operations Management: Profit from Within. Gerald R. Sinn. 1980. 19.00 (ISBN 0-89433-116-7). Petrocelli.

Cash: Planning, Forecasting & Control. W. C. Hartley. 210p. 1976. text ed. 24.50x (ISBN 0-220-66288-6, Pub. by Busn Bks England). Renouf.

Cashews & Lentils, Apples & Oats. Diana Dalsass. (Illus.). 1981. 14.95 (ISBN 0-8092-5935-4); pap. 7.95 (ISBN 0-8092-5934-6). Contemp Bks.

Cashiering. Ser-Vol-Tel Institute. (Foodservice Career Education Ser.). 1974. pap. 4.95 (ISBN 0-8436-2011-0). CBI Pub.

Cashing in at the Checkout. Susan J. Samtur & Tad Tuleja. 1980. pap. 1.95 (ISBN 0-446-90585-2). Warner Bks.

Cashing in on the Auction Boom: How to Buy Today's Goods at Yesterday's Prices. James Wagenvoord. 1980. 13.95 (ISBN 0-89256-149-1); pap. 6.95 (ISBN 0-89256-151-3). Rawson Wade.

Cashless Society: EFTS at the Crossroads. August Bequai. LC 80-21517. 350p. 1981. 19.95 (ISBN 0-471-05654-5, Pub. by Wiley-Interscience). Wiley.

Casilda of the Rising Moon. Elizabeth B. De Trevino. LC 67-10389. 224p. (gr. 7 up). 1967. 3.95 (ISBN 0-374-31188-9). FS&G.

Casino. Robert Kirsch. Date not set. pap. 2.75 (ISBN 0-671-82931-9). PB.

Casino. Marilyn Lynch. 1979. pap. 2.50 (ISBN 0-441-09229-2). Ace Bks.

Casino Gambling. Jeffrey Feinman. 128p. (Orig.). 1981. pap. 2.95 (ISBN 0-668-05172-8, 5172). Arco.

Casino Greystone, No. 4. Louisa Bronte. 256p. (Orig.). 1976. pap. 1.50 o.p. (ISBN 0-345-24962-3). Ballantine.

Casino Management. 384p. 1981. 75.00 (ISBN 0-8184-0311-X). Lyle Stuart.

Casino Royale. Ian Fleming. (James Bond Agent 007 Ser.). pap. 2.25 (ISBN 0-515-05895-5). Jove Pubns.

Cask. Freeman W. Crofts. lib. bdg. 12.95x (ISBN 0-89966-245-5). Buccaneer Bks.

Cask of Amontillado. Edgar A. Poe. (Creative's Classics Ser.). (Illus.). 32p. (gr. 5-9). 1980. lib. bdg. 6.95 (ISBN 0-87191-773-4). Creative Ed.

Caslon Old Face: Roman & Italic. (Illus.). 64p. 1979. 80.00x (ISBN 0-85667-075-8, Pub. by Sotheby Parke Bernet England). Biblio Dist.

Caspar David Friedrich Seventeen Seventy-Four to Eighteen Forty. William Vaughan. (Tate Gallery Art Ser.). (Illus.). 1977. 11.95 o.p. (ISBN 0-8120-5145-9). Barron.

Casper Far Out Fables. Harvey Comics. 1981. pap. 1.25 (ISBN 0-448-17251-8, Tempo). G&D.

Casper Site: A Hell Gap Bison Kill on the High Plains. Ed. by George Frison. 1974. 25.00 (ISBN 0-12-268550-4). Acad Pr.

Casper: TV Tales. Harvey Comics. (Casper the Friendly Ghost Cartoon Bks.). 128p. (gr. 4-9). 1981. pap. text ed. 1.25 (ISBN 0-448-17119-8, Tempo). G&D.

Cassandra. Claudette Williams. 1979. pap. 2.25 o.p. (ISBN 0-449-23895-4, Crest). Fawcett.

Cassandra Crossing. Robert Katz. (Orig.). 1977. pap. 1.50 o.p. (ISBN 0-345-24283-1). Ballantine.

Cassava Cultural Practices. 152p. 1980. pap. 10.00 (ISBN 0-88936-245-9, IDRC151, IDRC). Unipub.

Cassell Book of Austin Farina. S. F. Page. 8.50x (ISBN 0-392-05820-0, SpS). Soccer.

Cassell Book of English Poetry. Ed. by James Reeves. LC 65-20998. (YA) 1965. 15.00x o.s.i. (ISBN 0-06-005910-9, HarpT). Har-Row.

Cassell's Colloquials, 4 bks. Cassell. Incl. French. 160p. pap. 3.95 (ISBN 0-02-079420-7); German. 176p. pap. 3.95 (ISBN 0-02-079410-X); Spanish. 256p. pap. 4.95 (ISBN 0-02-079430-4); Italian. 192p. pap. 3.95 (ISBN 0-02-079440-1). 1981. Macmillan.

Casserole Cook Book. 3rd ed. Sunset Editors. LC 80-80854. (Illus.). 96p. 1980. pap. 3.95 (ISBN 0-376-02254-X, Sunset Bks). Sunset-Lane.

Casseroles & Vegetables for Foodservice Menu Planning. Eulalia C. Blair. LC 76-29357. (Cahners Foodservice Menu Planning Ser). 1976. 16.50 (ISBN 0-8436-2121-4). CBI Pub.

Cassilee. Susan Coon. 1980. pap. 2.25 (ISBN 0-686-69246-2, 75887). Avon.

Cassiodorus. James J. O'Donnell. LC 77-93470. 1979. 20.00x (ISBN 0-520-03646-8). U of Cal Pr.

Cassis. Mark Walker. 1979. 8.95 o.s.i. (ISBN 0-8027-5405-8). Walker & Co.

Cassius Marcellus Clay: Firebrand of Freedom. H. Edward Richardson. LC 74-7882. (Kentucky Bicentennial Bookshelf Ser.). (Illus.). 168p. 1980. Repr. of 1976 ed. 5.95 (ISBN 0-8131-0205-7). U Pr of Ky.

Cast a Long Shadow. Laura Conway. 1978. 6.95 o.p. (ISBN 0-525-07790-1). Dutton.

Cast a Long Shadow. Wayne D. Overholser. Date not set. pap. 1.95 (ISBN 0-440-11423-3). Dell.

Cast in Order of Disappearance. Simon Brett. 1979. pap. 2.25 (ISBN 0-425-04934-5). Berkley Pub.

Cast Iron: Physical & Engineering Properties. H. T. Angus. 542p. 1976. 89.00 (ISBN 0-408-70933-2). Butterworths.

Cast Metals Technology. J. Gerin Sylvia. LC 74-153067. 1972. text ed. 18.95 (ISBN 0-201-07395-1). A-W.

Cast the Spear. Netta Muskett. 1978. pap. 1.50 o.s.i. (ISBN 0-515-04537-3). Jove Pubns.

Castastrophe Theory. Alexander Woodcock & Monte Davis. 1979. pap. 2.75 (ISBN 0-380-48397-1, 48397). Avon.

Castaway. Frances Murray. LC 78-12633. 1979. 8.95 o.p. (ISBN 0-684-16064-1, ScribT). Scribner.

Castaway. Frances Murray. 208p. 1981. pap. 1.95 (ISBN 0-345-28684-7). Ballantine.

Castaway & Wrecked. Rex Cowan. (Illus.). 1978. pap. 6.75 o.p. (ISBN 0-7156-1146-1, Pub. by Duckworth England). Biblio Dist.

Castaways in Time. Robert Adams. Ed. by Polly Freas & Kelly Freas. LC 79-11600. (Illus.). 1980. pap. 4.95 (ISBN 0-915442-96-5, Starblaze). Donning Co.

Castaways of Tangar. Brian M. Stableford. (Science Fiction Ser.). 1981. pap. 2.50 (ISBN 0-87997-609-8, UE1609). DAW Bks.

Castaways, One Hundred Thousand Dollar Nineteen Seventy-Nine Pro Football Handicapping Championship. Martin Mendelsohn. 64p. (Orig.). 1980. pap. 2.95 (ISBN 0-89650-644-4). Gamblers.

Caste & Family in the Politics of the Sinhalese. Janice Jiggins. LC 78-54715. (Illus.). 1979. 24.95 (ISBN 0-521-22069-6). Cambridge U Pr.

Caste & the Economic Frontier. Frederick G. Bailey. 1957. text ed. 10.50x (ISBN 0-7190-0249-4). Humanities.

Caste, Class & Power: Changing Patterns of Stratification in a Tanjore Village. Andre Beteille. 1965. pap. 7.50x (ISBN 0-520-02053-7). U of Cal Pr.

Caste Dynamics Among the Bengali Hindus. Jyotimoyee Sarma. 1980. 11.50x (ISBN 0-8364-0633-8, Pub. by Mukhopadhyay India). South Asia Bks.

Caste: Identity & Continuity. V. C. Channa. 1979. text ed. 10.00x (ISBN 0-391-01871-X). Humanities.

Caste in a Changing World: The Chitrapur Saraswat Brahmans, 1700-1935. Frank F. Conlon. LC 75-7192. 1977. 20.00x (ISBN 0-520-02998-4). U of Cal Pr.

Caste in Contemporary India. Pauline Kolenda. LC 77-74109. 1978. pap. text ed. 6.95 (ISBN 0-8053-5602-9). Benjamin-Cummings.

Castigations of Mr. Hobbes. John Bramhall. Ed. by Rene Wellek. LC 75-11199. (British Philosophers & Theologians of the 17th & 18th Centuries: Vol. 6). 1976. Repr. of 1658 ed. lib. bdg. 42.00 (ISBN 0-8240-1755-2). Garland Pub.

Castiglione: A Reassessment of the Courtier. J. Woodhouse. (Writers of Italy: No. 7). 229p. 1979. 12.50x (ISBN 0-85224-346-4, Pub. by Edinburgh U Pr Scotland). Columbia U Pr.

Casting a Spell. Vaune Ainsworth-Land & Norma Fletcher. (Illus., Orig.). 1980. pap. text ed. 7.95 (ISBN 0-914634-65-8, 7909). DOK Pubs.

Casting for the Cutthroat & Other Poems. Charles Entrekin. 46p. (Orig.). 1980. pap. 3.95 (ISBN 0-917658-13-2). Berkeley Poets.

Casting Out Anger. Grace G. Harris. LC 77-80837. (Studies in Anthropology: No. 21). (Illus.). 1978. 24.95 (ISBN 0-521-21729-6). Cambridge U Pr.

Casting Spells. Serge Hutin. 1978. 9.50 o.p. (ISBN 0-214-20522-3, 8064, Dist. by Arco). Barrie & Jenkins.

Casting Techniques for Sculpture. Glynis Beecroft. 1979. 24.00 (ISBN 0-7134-3314-0, Pub. by Batsford England). David & Charles.

Casting the Horoscope. Alan Leo. (Astrologer's Library). 1979. pap. 6.95 (ISBN 0-89281-176-5). Inner Tradit.

Castle Craneycrow. George B. McCutcheon. 1976. lib. bdg. 17.25x (ISBN 0-89968-059-3). Lightyear.

Castle Daly: The Story of an Irish Home Thirty Years Ago. Annie Keary. (Nineteenth Century Fiction Ser.: Ireland: Vol. 65). 1004p. 1979. lib. bdg. 46.00 (ISBN 0-8240-3514-3). Garland Pub.

Castle Diaries Nineteen Seventy-Four to Seventy-Six. Barbara Castle. 788p. 1981. text ed. 40.00 (ISBN 0-8419-0689-0). Holmes & Meier.

Castle D'or. Arthur Quiller-Couch & Daphne Dumaurier. 274p. 1976. Repr. of 1962 ed. lib. bdg. 9.50x (ISBN 0-89244-091-0). Queens Hse.

Castle Heritage. Elisabeth Barr. 1979. pap. 1.75 (ISBN 0-87216-669-4). Playboy Pbks.

Castle in the Air. Donald Westlake. 288p. 1981. pap. 2.50 (ISBN 0-449-24382-6, Crest). Fawcett.

Castle Light. Evelyn McKenna. (YA) 1976. 4.95 o.p. (ISBN 0-685-69051-2, Avalon). Bouregy.

Castle Malindine. Hilary Ford. 1977. pap. 1.75 o.p. (ISBN 0-345-25315-9). Ballantine.

Castle Mirage. Alice Brennan. 1976. pap. 1.25 o.p. (ISBN 0-685-72570-7, LB392, Leisure Bks). Nordon Pubns.

Castle Morvant. Dorothy Daniels. 1972. pap. 1.75 o.s.i. (ISBN 0-446-84828-X). Warner Bks.

Castle Mystery. Marjorie Zimmerman. LC 77-78494. (Illus.). (gr. 3-6). 1977. pap. 1.95 o.p. (ISBN 0-89191-080-8, 15289). Cook.

Castle of Foxes. Alanna Knight. LC 80-952. 312p. 1981. 11.95 (ISBN 0-385-15327-9). Doubleday.

Castle of Knowledge. Robert Record. LC 74-28882. (English Experience Ser.: No. 760). 1975. Repr. of 1556 ed. 44.00 (ISBN 90-221-0760-4). Walter J Johnson.

Castle of Llyr. Lloyd Alexander. (gr. 4-8). 1969. pap. 1.50 (ISBN 0-440-41125-4, YB). Dell.

Castle of Love. Diego de San Pedro. LC 51-634. Repr. of 1549 ed. 23.00x (ISBN 0-8201-1217-8). Schol Facsimiles.

Castle of Otranto. Horace Walpole. 1963. pap. 1.95 (ISBN 0-02-055200-9, Collier). Macmillan.

Castle or Picture of Policy. William Blandy. LC 71-38157. (English Experience Ser.: No. 436). 68p. 1972. Repr. of 1581 ed. 9.50 (ISBN 90-221-0436-2). Walter J Johnson.

Castle Rackrent. Maria Edgeworth. Ed. by Robert L. Wolff. (Ireland Nineteenth Century Fiction - Ser. 2). 1979. Repr. of 1800 ed. lib. bdg. 46.00 (ISBN 0-8240-3450-3). Garland Pub.

Castle Richmond. Anthony Trollope. Ed. by Robert L. Wolff. (Ireland Nineteenth Century Fiction Ser. 2: Vol. 55). 912p. 1979. lib. bdg. 32.00 (ISBN 0-8240-3504-6). Garland Pub.

Castle Roogna. Piers Anthony. 1979. pap. 2.50 (ISBN 0-345-29421-1, Del Rey Bks). Ballantine.

Castlereagh. John W. Derry. LC 75-29820. (British Political Biography Ser.). 250p. 1976. 18.95 (ISBN 0-312-12355-8). St Martin.

Castlereagh & Adams: England & the United States, 1812-1823. Bradford Perkins. 1964. 20.00x (ISBN 0-520-00997-5). U of Cal Pr.

Castles: A History & a Guide. Ed. by R. Allen Brown. (Illus.). 196p. 1980. 24.95 o.p. (ISBN 0-7137-0953-7, Pub. by Blandford Pr England). Sterling.

Castles & Historic Places in Wales. Automobile Association - British Tourist Authority. (Illus.). 1979. pap. 3.95 o.p. (ISBN 0-900784-63-6, Pub. by B T A). Merrimack Bk Serv.

Castles & Historic Places in Wales. rev. ed. Wales Tourist Board. (Illus.). 104p. 1981. pap. write for info. (ISBN 0-900784-77-6, Pub. by Auto Assn-British Tourist Authority England). Merrimack Bk Serv.

Castles of Britain. Christina Gasciogne. (Illus.). 224p. 1980. 19.95 (ISBN 0-500-24098-1). Thames Hudson.

Castrati. Sven Delblac. 7.95 (ISBN 0-89720-020-9). Green Hill.

Castrati in Opera. Angus Heriot. LC 74-1332. (Music Ser.). 243p. 1974. Repr. of 1956 ed. lib. bdg. 22.50 (ISBN 0-306-70650-4). Da Capo.

Castro's Cuba in the 1970's. Ed. by Lester Sobel. 1977. lib. bdg. 17.50x (ISBN 0-87196-151-2). Facts on File.

Casual Entertaining Cook Book. Ed. by Better Homes & Gardens Editors. (Illus.). 96p. 1981. 4.95 (ISBN 0-696-00490-9). Meredith Corp.

Casual Models in Marketing. Richard P. Bagozzi. LC 79-11622. (Theories in Marketing Ser.). 1980. text ed. 21.95 (ISBN 0-471-01516-4). Wiley.

Casualty: A Memoir of Love & War. Corinne Browne. 1981. 12.95 (ISBN 0-393-01422-3). Norton.

Casualty Claim Practice. 3rd ed. James H. Donaldson. 1976. text ed. 23.50x (ISBN 0-256-00116-2). Irwin.

Casualty Insurance. 4th ed. C. A. Kulp & J. W. Hall. 1072p. 1968. 28.95 (ISBN 0-471-06568-4). Wiley.

Casualty Insurance. 4th ed. C. A. Kulp & John W. Hall. LC 68-30893. 1968. 28.95 (ISBN 0-8260-5165-0, 58871). Ronald Pr.

Casualty Officer's Handbook. 3rd ed. M. Ellis. 1970. 13.95 o.p. (ISBN 0-407-13052-7). Butterworths.

Casualty Officer's Handbook. 4th ed. David H. Wilson & Malcolm H. Hall. (Illus.). 1979. text ed. 29.95 (ISBN 0-407-00140-9). Butterworths.

Casuistical Tradition in Shakespeare, Donne, Herbert, & Milton. Camille W. Slights. LC 80-8576. 352p. 1981. 26.50x (ISBN 0-691-06463-6). Princeton U Pr.

Cat. Helen Chetin. 1977. pap. 1.00 o.p. (ISBN 0-931832-06-3). No Dead Lines.

Cat. Owen Ely. 320p. 1980. cancelled 9.95 (ISBN 0-906071-50-X). Proteus Pub NY.

Cat. B. Kliban. LC 75-7285. (Illus.). 160p. (Orig.). 1975. pap. 3.50 (ISBN 0-911104-54-2). Workman Pub.

Cat-Alog. Carolyn London. (Children's Bks). (Illus.). 128p. (gr. 5 up). 1971. pap. 1.50 (ISBN 0-8024-1120-7). Moody.

Cat: An Owner's Maintenance Manual. (Illus.). 96p. (Orig.). 1980. pap. 3.50 (ISBN 0-04-636011-5). Allen Unwin.

Cat & Dog & the Mixed-up Week. Elizabeth Miller & Jane Cohen. (ps). 1980. 2.95 (ISBN 0-531-03529-8); PLB 5.95 (ISBN 0-531-04123-9). Watts.

Cat & Dog Give a Party. Elizabeth Miller & Jane Cohen. (ps). 1980. 2.95 (ISBN 0-531-03527-1); PLB 5.95 (ISBN 0-531-04126-3). Watts.

Cat & Dog Have a Contest. Elizabeth Miller & Jane Cohen. (ps). 1980. 2.95 (ISBN 0-531-03528-X); PLB 5.95 (ISBN 0-531-04125-5). Watts.

Cat & Dog Raise the Roof. Elizabeth Miller & Jane Cohen. (ps). 1980. 2.95 (ISBN 0-531-03530-1); PLB 5.95 (ISBN 0-531-04124-7). Watts.

Cat & Dog Take a Trip. Elizabeth Miller & Jane Cohen. (ps). 2.95 (ISBN 0-531-03531-X); PLB 5.95 (ISBN 0-531-04127-1). Watts.

Cat & Shakespeare: A Tale of Modern India. Raja Rao. (Orient Paperback Ser.). 119p. 1975. pap. 2.00 o.p. (ISBN 0-88253-775-X). Ind-US Inc.

Cat & the Captain. Elizabeth Coatsworth. LC 73-6041. (Illus.). 64p. (gr. 1-3). 1974. 6.95 (ISBN 0-02-719070-6). Macmillan.

Cat & the Fiddler. Jacky Jeter. LC 68-11654. (Illus.). (ps-3). 1968. 5.95 o.s.i. (ISBN 0-8193-0203-1, Four Winds); PLB 5.41 o.s.i. (ISBN 0-8193-0204-X). Schol Bk Serv.

Cat & the King. Louis Auchincloss. 192p. 1981. 9.95 (ISBN 0-395-30225-0). HM.

Cat Astrology. Mary Daniels. 96p. 1976. 5.95 o.p. (ISBN 0-688-03024-6). Morrow.

Cat Ate My Gymsuit. Paula Danziger. LC 74-5501. 160p. (gr. 5-9). 1974. 7.95 (ISBN 0-440-01612-6); PLB 6.46 (ISBN 0-440-01696-7). Delacorte.

Cat Ate My Gymsuit. Paula Danziger. (gr. k-6). 1980. pap. 1.50 (ISBN 0-440-41612-4, YB). Dell.

Cat Book. Kathleen Daly. (Illus.). (ps-2). 1974. PLB 7.62 (ISBN 0-307-60837-9, Golden Pr). Western Pub.

Cat Book. Jan Pfloog. (Illus.). (ps-1). 1964. PLB 5.38 (ISBN 0-307-68901-8, Golden Pr). Western Pub.

Cat Breeding. Dagmar Thies. Tr. by Christa Ahrens from Ger. (Illus.). 128p. 1980. text ed. 2.95 (ISBN 0-87666-863-5, KW065). TFH Pubns.

Cat Calender Book. B. Kliban. LC 80-54618. 144p. 1981. 17.50 (ISBN 0-89480-155-4). Workman Pub.

Cat Called Amnesia. E. W. Hildick. (gr. 5-7). 1977. pap. 1.75 (ISBN 0-671-42132-8). Archway.

Cat Called Amnesia. E. W. Hildick. (Illus.). (gr. 5-7). 1977. pap. 1.50 (ISBN 0-671-56003-4). PB.

Cat Called Camouflage. Cordelia Jones. LC 79-166339. (Illus.). (gr. 7 up). 1971. 9.95 (ISBN 0-87599-189-0). S G Phillips.

Cat Care. Dagmar Thies. Tr. by Thomas P. Madero from Ger. Orig. Title: Katzenhaltung, Katzenpflege. (Illus.). 96p. 1980. 2.95 (ISBN 0-87666-862-7, KW 064). TFH Pubns.

Cat Catalog. Ed. by Judy Fireman. LC 76-25473. (Illus.). 1976. 12.50 (ISBN 0-911104-81-X); pap. 7.95 (ISBN 0-911104-82-8). Workman Pub.

Cat Claws & Tree Bark. Virginia C. Turner. 111p. 1972. 2.00. Pikeville Coll.

Cat Count. Betsy Lewin. LC 80-25849. (Illus.). 32p. (ps-2). 1981. PLB 5.95 (ISBN 0-396-07928-8). Dodd.

Cat Diseases. Percy M. Soderberg. (Orig.). pap. 2.50 (ISBN 0-87666-171-1, AP4800). TFH Pubns.

Cat Family. Robert Burton. LC 78-64654. (Fact Finders Ser.). (Illus.). 1979. lib. bdg. 3.96 (ISBN 0-686-51125-5). Silver.

Cat from Outer Space. Ted Key. (gr. 5-7). pap. 1.75 (ISBN 0-671-56106-5). Archway.

Cat in a Monastery. Karle F. Berger. 63p. 1981. 5.95 (ISBN 0-533-04717-X). Vantage.

Cat in the Hat Beginner Book Dictionary in French. Philip D. Eastman. (ps-2). 1965. 7.95 (ISBN 0-394-81063-5, BYR); PLB 8.99 (ISBN 0-394-91063-X). Random.

Cat Manners & Mysteries. Nina Epton. 1973. 8.95 o.p. (ISBN 0-7181-1148-6, Pub. by Michael Joseph). Merrimack Bk Serv.

Cat Notebook: Being an Illlustrated Book with Quotes. Ed. by Lawrence Teacher. (Illus.). 96p. (Orig.). 1981. lib. bdg. 12.90 (ISBN 0-89471-131-8); pap. 4.95 (ISBN 0-89471-133-4). Running Pr.

Cat People. Bill Hayward. LC 77-16921. 1978. 12.95 o.p. (ISBN 0-385-14313-3). Doubleday.

Cat Sun Signs. Vivian Buchan. LC 79-65117. (Illus.). 156p. 1981. pap. 5.95 (ISBN 0-8128-6097-7). Stein & Day.

Cat Testrophy. Al Kaeppel. LC 79-91599. (Illus., Orig.). 1981. 3.95 (ISBN 0-89896-000-2). Larksdale.

Cat That Came in from the Cold. Philip Brown. 1978. 7.95 o.p. (ISBN 0-684-15909-0, ScribJ). Scribner.

Cat That Never Died. William MacKellar. LC 75-38358. (Illus.). (gr. 5 up). 1976. 5.95 (ISBN 0-396-07303-4). Dodd.

Cat Who Stamped His Feet. Betty R. Wright. (Eager Readers Ser.). (Illus.). (gr. k-3). 1975. PLB 5.00 (ISBN 0-307-60806-9, Golden Pr). Western Pub.

Cat Who Went to Heaven. Elizabeth Coatsworth. LC 58-10917. (gr. 3-6). 1972. pap. 2.95 (ISBN 0-02-042580-5, Collier). Macmillan.

Cat You Care for. Felicia Ames. Date not set. pap. 1.75 o.p. (ISBN 0-451-07862-4, E7862, Sig). NAL.

Catabasis: Vergil & the Wisdom Tradition. Raymond J. Clark. 1979. pap. text ed. 34.25x (ISBN 9-0603-2104-9). Humanities.

Cataclimo. Tr. by Phil Saint. (Spanish Bks.). (Span.). 1978. 1.00 (ISBN 0-8297-0435-3). Life Pubs Intl.

Cataclysms of the Earth. Hugh A. Brown. (Illus.). 288p. pap. 5.50 (ISBN 0-8334-1778-9). Steinerbks.

Catalans. Jan Read. 1979. 21.95 (ISBN 0-571-10969-1, Pub. by Faber & Faber). Merrimack Bk Serv.

Cataline. Sallust. Ed. by C. Merivale. (Classical Ser). (Lat). 1870. pap. text ed. 7.95 (ISBN 0-312-12460-0). St Martin.

Catalog. Jasper Thomkins. (Illus.). 60p. (Orig.). 1981. pap. 5.95 (ISBN 0-914676-54-7). Green Tiger.

Catalog of American Antiques. William C. Ketchum, Jr. LC 77-1118. (Illus.). 1979. pap. 8.95 o.p. (ISBN 0-88332-109-2, 8147). Larousse.

Catalog of Books Relating to the Discovery & Early History of North & South America, 5 vols. E. D. Church. Compiled by G. W. Cole. Set. 100.00 (ISBN 0-8446-1113-1). Peter Smith.

Catalog of Chamber Music for Wind Instruments. rev. ed. Sanford M. Helm. LC 70-86597. (Music Reprint Ser). 1969. Repr. of 1952 ed. lib. bdg. 14.50 (ISBN 0-306-71490-6). Da Capo.

Catalog of Chess Mistakes. 1981. 10.95 (ISBN 0-679-13250-3); pap. 5.95 (ISBN 0-679-14151-0). McKay.

Catalog of Crime. Jacques Barzun & Wendell H. Taylor. LC 73-20705. (Illus.). 864p. 1974. 25.00 o.p. (ISBN 0-06-010266-7, HarpT). Harrow.

Catalog of Modern World Coins. R. S. Yeoman. 1979. pap. 5.95 o.p. (ISBN 0-307-09053-1, Golden Pr). Western Pub.

Catalog of Museum Publications & Media. 2nd ed. Ed. by Paul Wasserman. LC 79-22633. 1980. 120.00 (ISBN 0-8103-0388-4). Gale.

Catalog of Published Concert Music by American Composers. Angelo Eagon. LC 68-9327. (Suppl. to 2nd ed.). 1971. 10.00 (ISBN 0-8108-0387-9). Scarecrow.

Catalog of Published Concert Music by American Composers. Angelo Eagon. LC 68-9327. (2nd suppl. to 2nd ed.). 1974. 10.00 (ISBN 0-8108-0728-9). Scarecrow.

Catalog of Special Plane Curves. J. Dennis Lawrence. LC 72-80280. (Illus.). 218p. 1972. pap. text ed. 4.50 (ISBN 0-486-60288-5). Dover.

Catalog of the Avery Memorial Architectural Library, Second Edition, Fourth Supplement. Columbia University. 1979. lib. bdg. 325.00 (ISBN 0-8161-0283-X). G K Hall.

Catalog of the E. Azalia Hackley Memorial Collection of Negro Music, Dance & Drama. Detroit Public Library. 1979. lib. bdg. 100.00 (ISBN 0-8161-0299-6). G K Hall.

Catalog of the Farlow Reference Library of Cryptogamic Botany. Harvard University. 1979. lib. bdg. 660.00 (ISBN 0-8161-0279-1). G K Hall.

Catalog of the Latin American Collection, University of Florida Libraries, First Supplement. University of Florida. 1979. lib. bdg. 950.00 (ISBN 0-8161-1090-5). G K Hall.

Catalog of the Latin American Library of the Tulane University Library: Third Supplement, 2 vols. Tulane University, New Orleans. 1978. Set. lib. bdg. 260.00 (ISBN 0-8161-0005-5). G K Hall.

Catalog of the Manuscript & Archival Collections & Index to the Correspondence of John Torrey. The New York Botanical Garden Library. 1973. 50.00 (ISBN 0-8161-1018-2). G K Hall.

Catalog of the Mosquitos of the World, Vol. 6. 2nd ed. Kenneth L. Knight & Alan Stone. LC 77-82735. 1977. 20.50 (ISBN 0-686-04889-X); supplement 1978 3.35 (ISBN 0-686-28524-7). Entomol Soc.

Catalog of the Photographs in the Collection of the Sheldon Memorial Gallery at the University of Nebraska-Lincoln. Sheldon Memorial Gallery. LC 77-89862. (Illus.). 1977. 27.50 o.p. (ISBN 0-8032-7644-3); pap. 17.50 o.p. (ISBN 0-8032-5877-1). U of Nebr Pr.

Catalog of the Police Library of the Los Angeles Public Library, First Supplement. Los Angeles Public Library. (Library Catalogs). 1980. lib. bdg. 220.00 (ISBN 0-8161-0328-3). G K Hall.

Catalog of the Texas Collection in the Barker Texas History Center. University of Texas. (Library Catalogs-Bib. Guides). 1979. lib. bdg. 1200.00 (ISBN 0-8161-0273-2). G K Hall.

Catalog of the Works of Arthur William Foote, Eighteen Fifty-Three to Nineteen Thirty-Seven. Wilma Cipolla. LC 79-92139. (Bibliographies in American Music: No. 6). 1980. 17.50 (ISBN 0-911772-99-5). Info Coord.

Catalog Sources for Creative People: Where to Buy Craft, Needlework & Hobby Supplies by Mail. Margaret A. Boyd. (Orig.). 1981. pap. 10.95 (ISBN 0-938814-01-X). Barrington.

Catalog Translators Library, Vols. 1-4. Her Majesty's Stationary Office. 1976. Set. 9.00 (ISBN 0-379-00651-0). Oceana.

Cataloging & Classification: An Introduction. Lois M. Chan. (Library Education Ser.). (Illus.). 416p. 1980. text ed. 18.95 (ISBN 0-07-010498-0, C). McGraw.

Cataloging & Classification of Non-Western Materials: Concerns, Issues, & Practices. Ed. by Mohammed M. Aman. 1980. lib. bdg. 18.50x (ISBN 0-912700-06-8). Oryx Pr.

Cataloging Made Easy: How to Organize Your Congregation's Library. Ruth S. Smith. (Orig.). 1978. pap. 4.95 (ISBN 0-8164-2191-9). Crossroad NY.

Cataloging of Audiovisual Materials: A Manual Using AACR2, with an Appendix Containing OCLC Worksheets for All Examples Given in the Text. Nancy B. Olson. LC 79-73907. 1980. 17.50 (ISBN 0-933474-07-5). Minn Scholarly.

Cataloging with Copy: A Decision-Makers Handbook. Arlene Taylor Dowell. LC 76-1844. (Illus.). 295p. 1976. lib. bdg. 22.50x (ISBN 0-87287-153-3). Libs Unl.

Catalogo De Extranjeros Residentes En Puerto Rico En el Siglo XIX. Estela Cifre De Loubriel. 3.10 o.p. (ISBN 0-8477-0822-5); pap. 1.85 (ISBN 0-8477-0823-3). U of PR Pr.

Catalogue & Reclassification of the Eastern Palearctic Ichneumonidae. Henry Townes et al. (Memoirs Ser.: No. 5). 661p. 1965. 40.00 (ISBN 0-686-00414-0). Am Entom Inst.

Catalogue & Reclassification of the Indo-Australian Ichneumonidae. Henry Townes et al. (Memoirs Ser: No. 1). 522p. 1961. 33.00 (ISBN 0-686-00415-9). Am Entom Inst.

Catalogue & Reclassification of the Neotropic Ichneumonidae. Henry Townes & Marjorie Townes. (Memoirs Ser: No. 8). 1966. 25.00 (ISBN 0-686-00416-7). Am Entom Inst.

Catalogue De L'qeuve Comblet De Fantin Latour. Victoria Fantin-Latour. (Graphic Art Ser.). 320p. (Fr.). 1970. Repr. of 1911 ed. 47.50 (ISBN 0-306-71924-X). Da Capo.

Catalogue Des Ouvrages Imprimes Au XVIe Siecle: Science, Techniques, Medicine. Ed. by Jacqueline Rinet & Denise Hillard. 450p. 1980. text ed. 45.00 (ISBN 3-598-10119-8). K G Saur.

Catalogue Du Fonds De Musique Ancienne De la Bibliotheque Nationale, 4 vols. Jules A. Ecorcheville. LC 79-166103. (Music Ser). (Illus.). 1973. Repr. of 1914 ed. Set. lib. bdg. 165.00 (ISBN 0-306-70280-0). Da Capo.

Catalogue for the Qualitative Interpretation of the House-Tree-Person (H-T-P) rev. ed. Isaac Jolles. LC 79-57217. 1971. pap. 7.50x (ISBN 0-87424-001-8). Western Psych.

Catalogue of African Herbs. J. O. Lambo. (Traditional Healing Ser.: Vol. 5). 1981. 39.50 (ISBN 0-932426-04-2). Trado-Medic.

Catalogue of Books Printed for Private Circulation. Bertram Dobell. LC 66-25693. 1966. Repr. of 1906 ed. 15.00 (ISBN 0-8103-3303-1). Gale.

Catalogue of Books Printed on the Continent of Europe, 2 Vols. H. M. Adams. 1967. Set. 350.00 (ISBN 0-521-06951-3). Cambridge U Pr.

Catalogue of British Parliamentary Papers 1801 - 1900. 310p. 1977. 45.00x (ISBN 0-686-19005-X, Pub. by Irish Academic Pr Ireland). Biblio Dist.

Catalogue of Chamber Music for Woodwind Instruments. Roy Houser. LC 76-166093. (Music Ser). 1973. Repr. of 1960 ed. lib. bdg. 17.00 (ISBN 0-306-70257-6). Da Capo.

Catalogue of Chinese Greenware in the Ashmolean Museum-Oxford. Mary Tregear. (Illus.). 1977. 79.00x (ISBN 0-19-813167-4). Oxford U Pr.

Catalogue of Chinese Manuscripts in the Danish Archives: Chinese Diplomatic Correspondence from the Ch'ing Dynasty (1644-1911) Erik Baark. (Studies on Asian Topics: No. 2). (Orig.). 1979. pap. text ed. 11.00x (ISBN 0-7007-0120-6). Humanities.

Catalogue of Coins of the Roman Empire in the Ashmolean Museum: Augustus (c. 31 B.C. - A.D. 14, Pt. 1. C. H. Sutherland & C. M. Kraay. (Illus.). 60p. 1975. 65.00x (ISBN 0-19-813189-5). Oxford U Pr.

Catalogue of Colubrine Snakes in the Collection of the British Museum. Albert Gunther. xvi, 281p. 1971. Repr. of 1858 ed. 4.50x (ISBN 0-565-00709-2, Pub. by British Mus Nat Hist England). Sabbot-Natural Hist Bks.

Catalogue of Drawings & Watercolour in the Fitzwilliam Museum, Cambridge. M. W. Turner, R. A., 1775-1851. M. Cormack. LC 75-12158. (Illus.). 132p. 1975. 32.50 (ISBN 0-521-20955-2). Cambridge U Pr.

Catalogue of Drawings by Camille Pissarro in the Ashmolean Museum, Oxford. Ed. by Richard Brettell & Christopher Lloyd. (Illus.). 440p. 1980. 115.00x (ISBN 0-19-817357-1). Oxford U Pr.

Catalogue of Drawings of Willem Van de Velde Senior & Junior, 2 vols. M. S. Robinson. (Illus.). 240p. 1958. Vol. 1. 110.00 (ISBN 0-521-06114-8); Vol. 2, 1974. 110.00 (ISBN 0-521-06115-6). Cambridge U Pr.

Catalogue of Early Books on Music (Before 1800) Hazel Bartlett & Julia Gregory. LC 69-12684. (Music Ser). 1969. Repr. of 1913 ed. lib. bdg. 32.50 (ISBN 0-306-71223-7). Da Capo.

Catalogue of Egyptian Revenue Stamps. Peter R. Feltus. (Illus.). 240p. 1981. 30.00 (ISBN 0-9605286-0-1). P R Feltus.

Catalogue of English & American Chap-Books & Broadside Ballads in Harvard College Library. Harvard University Library. LC 67-23932. 1968. Repr. of 1905 ed. 15.00 (ISBN 0-8103-3420-8). Gale.

Catalogue of First Editions of Edward MacDowell. Oscar G. Sonneck. LC 72-155232. (Music Ser). 1971. Repr. of 1917 ed. lib. bdg. 15.00 (ISBN 0-306-70161-8). Da Capo.

Catalogue of First Editions of Stephen C. Foster. W. R. Whittlesey & O. G. Sonneck. LC 76-155233. (Music Ser). 1971. Repr. of 1915 ed. lib. bdg. 15.00 (ISBN 0-306-70162-6). Da Capo.

Catalogue of Fossil Hominids: Nineteen Eighty, 3 vols. Ed. by Kenneth Oakley & Bernard Campbell. Incl. Pt. 1. Africa. 223p. pap. 27.50 (ISBN 0-87474-700-7); Pt. 2. Europe. 379p. pap. 42.50 (ISBN 0-87474-701-5); Pt. 3. Americas, Asia, Australia. 226p. pap. 30.00 (ISBN 0-87474-702-3). (Illus.). 1980. Set. pap. 87.50 (ISBN 0-87474-699-X, Pub. by Trustees Brit. Mus. Nat. Hist.). Smithsonian.

Catalogue of Meteorological Data for Research, Pt. IV. 117p. 1980. pap. 17.00 (ISBN 0-686-65617-2, W448, WMO). Unipub.

Catalogue of Nineteenth Century Printing Presses. Harold E. Sterne. LC 78-63314. (Illus.). 384p. 1978. 19.95 (ISBN 0-932606-00-8). Ye Olde Print.

Catalogue of Persons Named in Germanic Heroic Literature 700-1600, Including Named Animals & Objects & Ethnic Names. George T. Gillespie. 1973. 33.75x o.p. (ISBN 0-19-815718-5). Oxford U Pr.

Catalogue of Primates in the British Museum (Natural History) & Elsewhere in the British Isles, Part 2: Family Cercopithecidae, Subfamily Cercopthecinae. P. H. Napier. 120p. 1980. pap. 25.00x (ISBN 0-565-00815-3). Sabbot-Natural Hist Bks.

Catalogue of Printed Music in the British Library to 1980, 62 vols. 1980. Set. 1200.00 (ISBN 0-85157-900-0, Dist. by Gale Research Co.). K G Saur.

Catalogue of Printing Presses & Printers' Materials, Lithographic Presses, Stereotyping & Electrotyping Machinery, Binders' Presses & Materials. R. Hoe & Co. Ed. by John Bidwell. LC 78-74397. (Nineteenth-Century Book Arts & Printing History Ser.: Vol. 11). (Illus.). 1980. lib. bdg. 22.00 (ISBN 0-8240-3885-1). Garland Pub.

Catalogue of Rembrandt's Etchings 2 Vols. 2nd ed. Arthur M. Hind. LC 67-27456. (Graphic Art Ser). 1967. Repr. of 1923 ed. lib. bdg. 35.00 (ISBN 0-306-70977-5). Da Capo.

Catalogue of Specimens of Printing Types by English & Scottish Printers & Founders 1665-1830. Turner W. Berry & A. F. Johnson. LC 78-74404. (Nineteenth-Century Book Arts & Printing History Ser.: Vol. 12). 1980. lib. bdg. 38.00 (ISBN 0-8240-3886-X). Garland Pub.

Catalogue of Such English Books As Lately Have Been, or Now Are, in Printing for Publication. William Jaggard. LC 78-26323. (English Experience Ser.: No. 196). 1969. Repr. of 1618 ed. 7.00 (ISBN 90-221-0196-7). Walter J Johnson.

Catalogue of Technical Reports & Documents of the Oas, 1974-1976. (Eng. & Span.). 1977. 4.00 (ISBN 0-8270-0200-9). OAS.

Catalogue of the Anglo-Saxon Ornamental Metalwork 700-1100 in the Department of Antiquities, Ashmolean Museum. David A. Hinton. (Illus.). 140p. 1974. 30.50x o.p. (ISBN 0-19-813187-9). Oxford U Pr.

Catalogue of the Byzantine & Early Mediaeval Antiquities in the Dumbarton Oaks Collection, 2 vols. Incl. Vol. I. Metalwork, Ceramics, Glass, Glyptics, Paintings. Marvin C. Ross. 115p. 1962. 20.00 (ISBN 0-88402-009-6); Vol. III. Ivories & Steatites. Kurt Weitzmann. 126p. 1972. 25.00 (ISBN 0-88402-038-X). LC 68-25. (Illus., Ctr Byzantine). Dumbarton Oaks.

Catalogue of the Chaetopoda in the British Museum (Natural History) A. Polychaeta. J. H. Ashworth. (Illus.). xii, 175p. 1912. 15.00x (ISBN 0-565-00102-7, Pub. by British Mus Nat Hist England). Sabbot-Natural Hist Bks.

Catalogue of the Coins of Dalmatia et Albania (1410-1797) (Illus.). 1980. pap. 5.00 (ISBN 0-916710-67-X). Obol Intl.

Catalogue of the Colonial Office Library: Third Supplement, 4 vols. Foreign & Commonwealth Office, London. 1979. Set. lib. bdg. 520.00 (ISBN 0-8161-0010-1). G K Hall.

Catalogue of the Comparative Education Library: Second Supplement. University of London, Institute of Education. (Library Catalogs-Bib. Guides). 1979. lib. bdg. 350.00 (ISBN 0-8161-0285-6). G K Hall.

Catalogue of the Diptera of the Afrotropical Region. Ed. by R. W. Crosskey. 1437p. 1980. 140.50x (ISBN 0-565-00821-8, Pub. by Brit Mus Nat Hist England). Sabbot-Natural Hist Bks.

Catalogue of the Earlier Italian Paintings in the Ashmolean Museum. Christopher Lloyd. (Illus.). 1977. 49.50x (ISBN 0-19-817342-3). Oxford U Pr.

Catalogue of the Emma B. King Library of the Shaker Museum. Compiled by Robert F. Meader. (Illus.). 63p. 1970. pap. 1.75 (ISBN 0-937942-00-6). Shaker Mus.

Catalogue of the Engraved Gems & Finger Rings in the Ashmoleaw Museum, Vol. I: Green & Etruscan. John Boardman & Marie-Louise Vollenweider. (Illus.). 1978. 79.00 (ISBN 0-19-813195-X). Oxford U Pr.

Catalogue of the Evelyn Waugh Collection at the Humanities Research Center: The Universtiy of Texas at Austin. Robert M. Davis. LC 80-50840. 375p. 1981. 25.00x (ISBN 0-87875-194-7). Whitston Pub.

Catalogue of the Flora of Arizona. J. Harry Lehr. 1978. 4.75 (ISBN 0-9605656-0-4). Desert Botanical.

Catalogue of the Fossil & Recent Genera & Species of Diatoms & Their Synonyms. S. L. Van Landingham. Incl. Pt. 1. Acanthoceras - Bacillaria. 1967 (ISBN 3-7682-0471-5); Pt. 2. Bacteriastrum - Coscinodiscus. 1968 (ISBN 3-7682-0472-3); Pt. 3. Coscinophaena - Fibula. 1969 (ISBN 3-7682-0473-1); Pt. 4. Fragilaria - Maunema. 1971 (ISBN 3-7682-0474-X). pap. 50.00 ea. (ISBN 0-686-22227-X). Lubrecht & Cramer.

Catalogue of the Genealogical & Historical Library of the Colonial Dames of the State of New York. National Society Of The Colonial Dames Of America. LC 76-149778. 1971. Repr. of 1912 ed. 34.00 (ISBN 0-8103-3713-4). Gale.

Catalogue of the Gennadius Library: American School of Classical Studies at Athens. American School of Classical Studies at Athens. (Library Catalogs: Supplement 2). 1981. lib. bdg. 160.00 (ISBN 0-8161-0011-X). G K Hall.

Catalogue of the Icelandic Collection: Additions 1913-1926. Ed. by Halldor Hermannsson. (University Library Publications). 1960. soft cover 25.00x (ISBN 0-8014-9817-1). Cornell U Pr.

Catalogue of the Icelandic Collection: Additions 1927-1942. Ed. by Halldor Hermannsson. (University Library Publications). 1960. soft cover 25.00x (ISBN 0-8014-9818-X). Cornell U Pr.

Catalogue of the Icelandic Collection Bequeathed by Willard Fiske. Ed. by Halldor Hermannsson. (University Library Publications). 1960. soft cover 35.00x (ISBN 0-8014-9816-3). Cornell U Pr.

Catalogue of the Irwin Untermyer Collection, Vols. 2, 5, 6. Yvonne Hackenbroch. Incl. Vol. 1. Meissen & Other Continental Porcelain, Faience & Enamel. (Illus.). 1956. write for info. (ISBN 0-87099-103-5); Vol. 2. Chelsea & Other English Porcelain, Pottery, & Enamel. (Illus.). 1957. 12.50 (ISBN 0-87099-102-7); Vol. 5. Bronzes, Other Metalwork & Sculpture. 2nd ed. (Illus.). 1962. 27.50 (ISBN 0-87099-101-9); English & Other Silver. 2nd ed. (Illus.). 1969. Vol. 6. write for info (ISBN 0-87099-104-3). Metro Mus Art.

Catalogue of the Library of the Arctic Institute of North America, Third Supplement. Arctic Institute of North America (Montreal, Canada) 1980. lib. bdg. 395.00 (ISBN 0-8161-1162-6). G K Hall.

Catalogue of the Library of the Freshwater Biological Association. Freshwater Biological Association, Cumbria England. 1979. lib. bdg. 630.00 (ISBN 0-8161-0289-9). G K Hall.

Catalogue of the Library of the Graduate School of Design, Harvard University: Third Supplement. Harvard University. (Library Catalogs-Bib. Guides). 1979. lib. bdg. 425.00 (ISBN 0-8161-0284-8). G K Hall.

Catalogue of the Library of the Institute of Advanced Legal Studies, 6 vols. Institute of Advanced Legal Studies, University of London. 1978. lib. bdg. 480.00 (ISBN 0-8161-0099-3). G K Hall.

Catalogue of the Manuscript Collections of the American Antiquarian Society. American Antiquarian Society. 1979. lib. bdg. 375.00 (ISBN 0-8161-0258-9). G K Hall.

Catalogue of the Pepys Library, Vol. 1. Ed. by Robert Latham. (Printed Bks.). 201p. 1978. 89.50x (ISBN 0-87471-819-8). Rowman.

Catalogue of the Pepys Library at Magdalene College, Cambridge, Vol. 3: Pt. 1 - Prints & Drawings (General) Robert Latham. Ed. by A. Aspitall. 160p. 1981. 135.00x (ISBN 0-8476-3637-2). Rowman.

Catalogue of the Population Council Library. Population Council. 1979. lib. bdg. 280.00 (ISBN 0-8161-0278-3). G K Hall.

Catalogue of the Prehistoric Metalwork in Merseyside County Museum, No. 2. Susan M. Nicholson. (Worknotes Ser.). (Illus.). 148p. (Orig.). 1981. pap. 12.50x (ISBN 0-87474-675-2). Smithsonian.

Catalogue of the Public Archives of Canada: Collection of Published Material with a Chronological List of Pamphlets. Public Archives of Canada. 1979. lib. bdg. 1200.00 (ISBN 0-8161-0316-X). G K Hall.

Catalogue of the Recent Sea-Urchins (Echinoidea) in the Collection of the British Museum (Natural History) Hubert L. Clark. (Illus.). xxviii, 250p. 1925. 21.00x (ISBN 0-565-00165-5, Pub. by British Mus Nat Hist England). Sabbot-Natural Hist Bks.

Catalogue of the Strandell Collection at the Hunt Institute for Botanical Documentation. G. H. Lawrence et al. 1000p. 1980. 180.00 (ISBN 0-913196-21-5). Hunt Inst Botanical.

Catalogue of the Tate Gallery's Collection of Modern Art Other Than Works by British Artists. Ed. by Ronald Alley. (Illus.). 800p. 1981. 120.00x (ISBN 0-85667-102-9, Pub. by Sotheby Parke Bernet England). Biblio Dist.

Catalogue of the World's Most Popular Coins. 10th ed. Fred Reinfeld & Burton Hobson. LC 78-66299. (Illus.). 1979. 19.95 (ISBN 0-8069-6070-1); lib. bdg. 17.59 (ISBN 0-8069-6071-X). Sterling.

Catalogue of Type & Figured Fossil Crustacea (Exc. Ostracoda), Chelicerata & Myriapoda in the British Museum (Natural History) S. F. Morris. (Illus.). 56p. 1980. pap. 13.00x (ISBN 0-565-00828-5). Sabbot-Natural Hist Bks.

Cataloguing Audiovisual Materials: A Manual Based on the AACR II. Eugene Fleischer & Helen Goodman. LC 80-18782. (Illus.). 1980. pap. 19.95 (ISBN 0-918212-39-1). Neal-Schuman.

Catalogus Dissertationum Philologicarum Classicarum. 3rd ed. 1937. 12.50 (ISBN 0-685-13367-2); 46.00, bound with 1910 ed. (ISBN 0-685-13368-0). Johnson Repr.

Catalysis by Electron Donor-Acceptor Complexes: Their General Behavior & Biological Roles. K. Tamaru & M. Ichikawa. LC 75-28051. 1976. 30.95 (ISBN 0-470-84435-3). Halsted Pr.

Catalysis, C-023: New Directions. Business Communication Co. 1981. 800.00 (ISBN 0-89336-271-9). BCC.

Catalyst. Fay Angus. 1979. pap. 3.95 (ISBN 0-8423-0210-7). Tyndale.

Catalytic Activation of Carbon Monoxide. Ed. by Peter Ford. (ACS Symposium Ser.: No. 152). 1981. price not set (ISBN 0-8412-0620-1). Am Chemical.

Catamaran Sailing to Win. Chris Wilson & Max Press. LC 73-3767. (Illus.). 160p. 1976. 7.95 o.p. (ISBN 0-498-01392-8). A S Barnes.

Catamarans for Cruising. Jim Andrews. (Illus.). 224p. 1976. 14.00 (ISBN 0-370-10339-4); pap. 8.95 (ISBN 0-370-10294-0). Transatlantic.

Catamog: Concepts & Techniques in Modern Geography, 24 vols. Incl. Vol. 1. Introduction to Markov Chain Analysis. L. Callins; Vol. 2. Distance Decay in Spatial Interactions. P. J. Taylor; Vol. 3. Understanding Canonical Correlation Analysis. D. Clark; Vol. 4. Some Theoretical & Applied Aspects of Spatial Interaction Shopping Models. S. Openshaw; Vol. 5. Introduction to Trend Surface: Analysis. D. Unwin; Vol. 6. Classification in Geography. R. J. Johnson; Vol. 7. Introduction to Factor Analysis. J. B. Goddard & A. Kirby; Vol. 8. Principal Components Analysis. S. Daultrey; Vol. 9. Causal Interferences from Dichotomous Variables. N. Davidson; Vol. 10. Introduction to the Use of Logit Models in Geography. N. Wrigley; Vol. 11. Linear Programming: Elementary Geographical Applications of the Transportation Problem. A. Hay; Vol. 12. Introduction to Quadrat Analysis. 2nd ed. R. W. Thomas; Vol. 13. Introduction to Time-Geography. N. J. Thrift; Vol. 14. Introduction to Graph Theoretical Methods in Geography. K. J. Tinkler; Linear Regression in Geography. R. Ferguson; Vol. 16. Probability Surface Mapping: An Introduction with Examples & FORTRAN Programs. N. Wrigley; Vol. 17. Sampling Methods for Geographical Research. C. Dixon & B. Leach; Vol. 18. Questionaires & Interviews in Geographical Research. C. Dixon & B. Leach; Vol. 19. Analysis of Frequency Distributions. Y. Gardiner & G. Gardiner; Vol. 20. Anlaysis of Covariance & Comparison of Regression Lines. J. Silk; Vol. 21. Introduction to the Use of Simultataneous Equation Regression Analysis in Geography. D. Todd; Vol. 22. Transfer Function Modelling: Relationship Between Time Series Variables. Pong-Wai Lai; Vol. 23. Stochastic Processes in One Dimensional Series: An Introduction. K. S. Richards; Vol. 24. Linear Programming: The Simplex Method with Geographical Applications. James E. Killen. 1980. Set. pap. text ed. 168.00x (ISBN 0-686-64924-9, Pub. by GEO Abstracts England); pap. text ed. 8.00x ea. State Mutual Bk.

Cataract. Mykhaylo Osadchy. Tr. by Marco Carynnyk from Ukrainian. LC 75-34371. (Helen & Kurt Wolff Bk.). 264p. 1976. 8.95 o.p. (ISBN 0-15-615550-8). HarBraceJ.

Cataracts & Their Treatment. Joe W. Morgan. 144p. 1981. 6.95 (ISBN 0-8059-2775-1). Dorrance.

Catastrophe Cat. Dennis Panek. LC 77-90951. (Illus.). (ps-1). 1978. 8.95 (ISBN 0-87888-130-1). Bradbury Pr.

Catastrophe Cat at the Zoo. Dennis Panek. LC 78-26369. (Illus.). (ps-1). 1979. 8.95 (ISBN 0-87888-147-6). Bradbury Pr.

Catastrophe in the Opening. Ed. by Yakov Nieshtadt. (Pergamon Chess Ser.). (Illus.). 1980. 17.25 (ISBN 0-08-023121-7); pap. 9.60 (ISBN 0-08-024097-6). Pergamon.

Catastrophe Survived: Euripides' Plays of Mixed Reversal. Anne P. Burnett. 244p. 1971. 23.50x o.p. (ISBN 0-19-814186-6). Oxford U Pr.

Catastrophe Theory. Alexander Woodcock. 1980. pap. 2.75 (ISBN 0-380-48397-1, 48397). Avon.

Catastrophe Theory for Scientists & Engineers. Robert Gilmore. LC 80-22154. 700p. 1981. 45.00 (ISBN 0-471-05064-4, Pub. by Wiley-Interscience). Wiley.

Catastrophe Theory: Selected Papers (1972-1977) E. C. Zeeman. LC 77-21459. 1977. text ed. 33.50 (ISBN 0-201-09014-7, Adv Bk Prog); pap. text ed. 21.50 (ISBN 0-201-09015-5). A-W.

Catastrophic Diseases: Who Decides What? Jay Katz & Alexander M. Capron. 273p. 1982. pap. 7.95 (ISBN 0-87855-686-9). Transaction Bks. Postponed.

Catastrophies. Walter R. Brown et al. LC 79-19141. (Illus.). (gr. 5 up). 1979. pap. 6.95 (ISBN 0-201-00791-6, 0791, A-W Childrens). A-W.

Catboat Book. Ed. by John Leavens. LC 73-88648. 168p. 1973. 15.00 (ISBN 0-87742-034-3). Intl Marine.

Catch a Little Fox. Beatrice S. De Regnier. LC 75-97036. (Illus.). (ps-2). 1970. 6.50 (ISBN 0-395-28821-5, Clarion). HM.

Catch a Red Leaf. Gladis DePree & Gordon DePree. (Illus.). 128p. (Orig.). 1980. pap. 3.95 (ISBN 0-310-23671-1, 9485P). Zondervan.

Catch an Angel's Wing. Gene Van Note. 76p. 1979. pap. 1.95 (ISBN 0-8341-0559-4, Beacon). Nazarene.

Catch Me a Colobus. Gerald Durrell. 1977. pap. 1.95 o.s.i. (ISBN 0-14-004337-3). Penguin.

Catch Rides. Sara McAuley. 1975. 7.95 o.p. (ISBN 0-394-49553-5). Knopf.

Catch That Catch Can. John Hilton. LC 75-87492. (Music Ser). 1970. Repr. of 1652 ed. lib. bdg. 17.50 (ISBN 0-306-71498-1). Da Capo.

Catch That Pass. Matt Christopher. (Illus.). (gr. 3-5). 1974. pap. 0.75 (ISBN 0-671-29612-4). PB.

Catch the Sun. Eve Cowen. (Storytellers Ser,). (Illus.). 64p. (gr. 5 up). 1981. PLB 7.95 (ISBN 0-516-02261-X). Childrens.

Catch the Wind: A Book of Windmills & Windpower. Landt Dennis. LC 75-45002. (Illus.). 128p. (gr. 5 up). 1976. 8.95 (ISBN 0-590-07414-8, Four Winds). Schol Bk Serv.

Catch Trap. Marion Z. Bradley. 1979. 10.95 (ISBN 0-345-28090-3). Ballantine.

Catch Twenty-Two. Joseph Heller. 1976. pap. 2.95 (ISBN 0-440-11120-X). Dell.

Catcher in the Rye by J. D. Salinger. Richard Lettis. LC 63-17168. (Orig.). 1964. pap. text ed. 1.95 (ISBN 0-8120-0001-3). Barron.

Catcher in the Wry. Bob Uecker & Mickey Herskowitz. 320p. 1981. 10.95 (ISBN 0-399-12586-8). Putnam.

Catchers. Anthony Tuttle. LC 76-8456. (Stars of the Nl & Al Ser). (Illus.). (gr. 4-12). 1976. PLB 7.50 o.p. (ISBN 0-87191-519-7). Creative Ed.

Catching Salmon. Richard Waddington. LC 77-85034. (Illus.). 1978. 17.95 (ISBN 0-7153-7533-4). David & Charles.

Catching Up: Remedial Education. John E. Roueche & R. Wade Kirk. LC 73-1851. (Higher Education Ser.). 1973. 9.95x o.p. (ISBN 0-87589-170-5). Jossey-Bass.

Catchworld. Chris Boyce. 1978. pap. 1.75 o.p. (ISBN 0-449-23635-8, Crest). Fawcett.

Catechesis of Revelation. Gabriel Moran. 1968. pap. 3.95 (ISBN 0-8164-2502-7). Crossroad NY.

Catechesis of the Orthodox Church. rev. ed. Apostolos Makrakis. Ed. by Orthodox Christian Educational Society. 239p. 1969. pap. text ed. 4.00x (ISBN 0-938366-14-9). Orthodox Chr.

Catechetical Helps. Edwin W. Kurth. (gr. 4-12). 1981. pap. text ed. 4.50 (ISBN 0-570-03507-4, 14-1261). Concordia.

Catechetics for the Future. Alois Muller. (Concilium Ser.: Religion in the Seventies: Vol. 53). 1970. pap. 4.95 (ISBN 0-8164-2509-4). Crossroad NY.

Catechism for Adults. James Alberione. LC 75-160578. (Illus.). 1971. pap. 2.25 o.s.i. (ISBN 0-8198-0352-9). Dghtrs St Paul.

Catechists Never Stop Learning. 97p. 1972. 2.00. Natl Cath Educ.

Catecholamines & Their Enzymes in the Neuropathology of Schizophrenia. Steven Matthysse & Seymour S. Kety. LC 75-4093. (Illus.). 382p. 1975. text ed. 57.00 (ISBN 0-08-018242-9). Pergamon.

Catecholamines: Basic & Clinical Frontiers: Proceedings of the Fourth International Catecholamine Symposium; Asilomar Conference Center, Pacific Grove, California; September 17-22, 1978, 2 vols. Ed. by Earl Usdin et al. 1979. 220.00 (ISBN 0-08-022650-7). Pergamon.

Catecholamines of Developing Brain: Preconditioning of Behavior. Clara Torda. 1977. 14.95 (ISBN 0-686-27726-0). W Torda.

Categorical Imperative: A Study in Kant's Moral Philosophy. H. J. Paton. 1971. pap. 4.95x (ISBN 0-8122-1023-9, Pa Paperbks). U of Pa Pr.

Categorically Speaking. Photos by Lynn Lennon. (Illus.). 128p. (Orig.). 1981. pap. 6.95 (ISBN 0-670-20685-7, Studio). Viking Pr.

Categories & De Interpretatione. Aristotle. Tr. by J. L. Ackrill. (Clarendon Aristotle Ser.). 1963. pap. 12.50x (ISBN 0-19-872086-6). Oxford U Pr.

Categories Et Liber De Interpretatione. Aristotle. Ed. by L. Minio-Paluello. (Oxford Classical Texts Ser). 1949. 14.95 (ISBN 0-19-814507-1). Oxford U Pr.

Categories for the Working Mathematician. S. MacLane. LC 78-166080. (Graduate Texts in Mathematics: Vol. 5). 272p. 1972. 19.80 o.p. (ISBN 0-387-90035-7); pap. 9.50 o.p. (ISBN 0-387-90036-5). Springer-Verlag.

Categorization & Social Judgment. Ed. by J. R. Eiser & Wolfgang Strobe. (European Monographs in Social Psychology Ser.: No. 3). 1973. 24.50 (ISBN 0-12-235350-1). Acad Pr.

Category Formation & the History of Religions. Robert D. Baird. (Religion & Reason Ser: No. 1). 178p. 1971. text ed. 22.95x (ISBN 90-2796-889-6). Mouton.

Cateract Surgery & Its Complications. 3rd ed. Norman S. Jaffe. LC 80-19355. (Illus.). 611p. 1980. text ed. 69.50 (ISBN 0-8016-2404-5). Mosby.

Catering Eleven Houston. V. T. Abercrombie & Louise Gaylord. Date not set. price not set. Brown Rabbit.

Catering Equipment & Systems Design. G. Glew. (Illus.). 1977. 102.60x (ISBN 0-85334-730-1, Pub. by Applied Science). Burgess-Intl Ideas.

Catering Handbook. Hal Weiss & Edith Weiss. (Illus.). 1971. 16.95 (ISBN 0-8104-9452-3). Hayden.

Caterpillar & the Cross. new ed. Flint Russ. LC 74-81137. (Illus.). (gr. 1-6). 1979. cancelled (ISBN 0-914850-47-4, MO520). Impact Tenn.

Caterpillar Caper. Nell Nale et al. (Kindergarten Keys Ser.). (Illus.). 1975. pap. text ed. 2.49 (ISBN 0-87892-656-9); 2.49 (ISBN 0-87892-657-7); prereading skills test 7.29 (ISBN 0-87892-664-X). Economy Co.

Caterpillars or Butterflies. Jane McWhorter. 1977. pap. 3.75 (ISBN 0-89137-410-8). Quality Pubns.

Catfish Hunter. Paul Deegan. (Sports Superstars Ser.). (Illus.). (gr. 3-9). 1979. PLB 5.95 (ISBN 0-87191-720-3); pap. 2.95 (ISBN 0-89812-159-0). Creative Ed.

Catfishes for the Advanced Hobbyist. C. W. Emmens & Herbert Axelrod. pap. 4.95 (ISBN 0-87666-758-2, PS650). TFH Pubns.

Catharine Maria Sedgwick. Edward H. Foster. (U. S. Authors Ser.: No. 233). 1974. lib. bdg. 10.95 (ISBN 0-8057-0658-5). Twayne.

Catharsis in Healing, Ritual & Drama. Thomas J. Scheff. 1980. 14.95x (ISBN 0-520-03710-3); pap. 4.95x (ISBN 0-520-04125-9, CAMPUS NO. 249). U of Cal Pr.

Cathechisme Du Genre Humain. 2nd ed. Francois Boissel. (Fr.). 1977. lib. bdg. 30.50x o.p. (ISBN 0-8287-0102-4); pap. text ed. 20.50x o.p. (ISBN 0-685-74920-7). Clearwater Pub.

Cathedral: A Gothic Pilgrimage. Helen H. Parkhurst. 304p. 1980. Repr. of 1936 ed. lib. bdg. 40.00 (ISBN 0-8492-2174-9). R West.

Cathedral & City: St. Albans Ancient & Modern. Ed. by Robert Runcie. 1977. text ed. 13.00x (ISBN 0-85422-149-2). Humanities.

Cathedral Architecture. H. Braun. LC 72-86608. (Illus.). 272p. 1972. 19.50x (ISBN 0-8448-0100-3). Crane-Russak Co.

Cathedrals. Mervyn Blatch. (Illus.). 176p. 1980. 12.95 (ISBN 0-7137-0943-X, Pub. by Blandford Pr England); pap. 6.95 (ISBN 0-7137-1081-0, Pub. by Blandford Pr England). Sterling.

Cathedrals. Neil Grant. LC 79-183939. (First Bks). (Illus.). 96p. (gr. 4-6). 1972. PLB 4.90 o.p. (ISBN 0-531-00755-3). Watts.

Cathedrals of France. rev. ed. Auguste Rodin. Tr. by Elisabeth C. Geissbuhler from Fr. (Illus.). 278p. 20.00x (ISBN 0-933806-07-8). Black Swan CT.

Catherine & Igor Stravinsky. Theodore Stravinsky. LC 72-95737. 1973. 15.00 (ISBN 0-85162-008-6). Boosey & Hawkes.

Catherine Furze, 1893. William H. White. Ed. by Robert L. Wolff. Bd. with Clara Hopgood, 1896. LC 75-1516. (Victorian Fiction Ser.). 1975. lib. bdg. 66.00 (ISBN 0-8240-1589-4). Garland Pub.

Catherine of Genoa: Purgation & Purgatory, the Spiritual Dialogue. Catherine Of Genoa. Tr. by Serge Hughes. (Classics of Western Spirituality Ser). 1979. 11.95 (ISBN 0-8091-0285-4); pap. 7.95 (ISBN 0-8091-2207-3). Paulist Pr.

Catherine of Sienna: The Dialogue. Ed. by Suzanne Noffke. (Classics of Western Spirituality Ser.). 398p. 1980. 11.95 (ISBN 0-8091-0295-1); pap. 7.95 (ISBN 0-8091-2233-2). Paulist Pr.

Catherine the Great. L. S. Oliva. 1971. 8.95 o.p. (ISBN 0-13-121160-9, Spec). P-H.

Catherine the Great: A Profile. Ed. by Marc Raeff. LC 77-163575. (World Profiles Ser.). 1972. 7.95 o.p. (ISBN 0-8090-3367-4); pap. 5.95 o.p. (ISBN 0-8090-1400-9). Hill & Wang.

Catherine the Great & the Russian Nobility. P. Dukes. 1968. 38.50 (ISBN 0-521-04858-3). Cambridge U Pr.

Catherine's Time for Love. Juliette Benzoni. 1973. pap. 1.95 (ISBN 0-380-40949-6, 40949). Avon.

Catherine's Twins. Larry Raygor. (Orig.). 1979. pap. 1.95 (ISBN 0-532-23107-4). Manor Bks.

Cathexis Reader: Transactional Analysis Treatment of Psychosis. Jacqui L. Schiff & Cathexis Institute. 1975. text ed. 13.95 scp (ISBN 0-06-045773-2, HarpC). Har-Row.

Cathlamet on the Columbia. new ed. Thomas N. Strong. (Illus.). 1981. pap. 4.95 (ISBN 0-8323-0378-X). Binford.

Cathletics: Ways to Amuse & Exercise Your Cat. Jo Loeb & Paul Loeb. LC 80-39813. (Illus.). 96p. 81. pap. 4.50 (ISBN 0-13-121004-1). P-H.

Catholic America. John Cogley. 240p. 1974. pap. 2.95 (ISBN 0-385-08916-3, Im). Doubleday.

Catholic & Reformed: Selected Writings of John Williamson Nevin. Ed. by Charles Yrigoyen, Jr. & George H. Bricker. LC 78-2567. (Pittsburgh Original Texts & Translations: No. 3). 1978. pap. text ed. 9.50 (ISBN 0-915138-37-9). Pickwick.

Catholic Bible Study Course, 6 vols. 1980. Set. pap. text ed. 125.00 (ISBN 0-8434-0766-2, Consortium); 6 wkbks. incl. McGrath.

Catholic Bible Study Course, 12 vols. Incl. Vol. 1. Pentateuch. Glendon E. Bryce. 250p (ISBN 0-8434-0745-X); Vol. 2. Guide Through Pentateuch (ISBN 0-8434-0746-8); Vol. 3. Historical Literature. Ed. by Charles Miller. 250p (ISBN 0-8434-0747-6); Vol. 4. Guide Through Historical Literature (ISBN 0-8434-0748-4); Vol. 5. Wisdom Literature. Betty J. Lillie. 250p (ISBN 0-8434-0749-2); Vol. 6. Guide Through Wisdom Literature (ISBN 0-8434-0750-6); Vol. 7. Prophetic Literature. Vincent Branick. 250p (ISBN 0-8434-0751-4); Vol. 8. Guide Through Prophetic Literature (ISBN 0-8434-0752-2); Vol. 9. Mark-Matthew-Luke. Ed. by Robert Sargent. 250p (ISBN 0-8434-0754-9); Vol. 10. Guide Through Mark-Matthew-Luke (ISBN 0-8434-0754-9); Vol. 11. John & Epistles. Ed. by Joseph Grassi. 250p (ISBN 0-8434-0755-7); Vol. 12. Guide Through John & Epistles (ISBN 0-8434-0756-5). Date not set. Set. 125.00 (ISBN 0-686-68786-8); Vols. 1 & 2. 25.00; Vols. 3 & 4. 25.00; Vols. 5 & 6. 25.00; Vols. 7 & 8. 25.00; Vols. 9 & 10. 25.00; Vols. 11 & 12. 25.00. McGrath.

Catholic Church & the Race Question. Yves M. J. Congar. 1966. pap. 2.50 (ISBN 92-3-100415-8, U68, UNESCO). Unipub.

Catholic Church Story. rev ed. Edward Day. LC 75-27612. (Illus.). 192p. (Orig.). 1975. pap. 3.50 (ISBN 0-89243-105-9, 65300). Liguori Pubns.

Catholic Church Through the Ages. Martin P. Harney. LC 73-76312. 1974. 12.00 (ISBN 0-8198-0500-9); pap. 11.00 (ISBN 0-8198-0501-7). Dghtrs St Paul.

Catholic Education in America: A Documentary History. Ed. by Neil G. McCluskey. LC 64-23904. (Orig.). 1964. text ed. 8.75 (ISBN 0-8077-1731-2); pap. text ed. 4.00x (ISBN 0-8077-1728-2). Tchrs Coll.

Catholic Left in Latin America: A Comprehensive Bibliography. Therrin C. Dahlin et al. (Reference Bks.). 1981. lib. bdg. 35.00 (ISBN 0-8161-8396-1). G K Hall.

Catholic Power in the Netherlands. Herman Bakvis. (Illus.). 550p. 1981. 35.95x (ISBN 0-7735-0367-6); pap. 18.95x (ISBN 0-7735-0368-4). McGill-Queens U Pr.

Catholic Question in America. William Sampson. LC 73-22105. (Civil Liberties in American History Ser.). 122p. 1974. Repr. of 1813 ed. lib. bdg. 17.50 (ISBN 0-306-70600-8). Da Capo.

Catholic Reformation. J. C. Olin. 1969. 8.50 o.p. (ISBN 0-87061-001-5). Chr Classics.

Catholic Schools in a Declining Church. Andrew M. Greeley et al. (Illus.). 488p. 1975. 15.00 o.p. (ISBN 0-8362-0648-7). Andrews & McMeel.

Catholic Sex Manual for Teenagers. Charles B. Muse. (Illus.). 1980. 21.50 (ISBN 0-89266-217-4). Am Classical Coll Pr.

Catholic Theology in the Nineteenth Century: The Quest for a Unitary Method. Gerald A. McCool. 1977. 14.95 (ISBN 0-8164-4710-1). Crossroad NY.

Catholic Theories of Biblical Inspiration, 1810 to the Present: A Review Critique. J. T. Burtchaell. 1969. 44.50 (ISBN 0-521-07485-1). Cambridge U Pr.

Catholicism. John P. Dolan. LC 67-28536. (Orig.). 1968. text ed. 10.00 (ISBN 0-8120-6013-X); pap. text ed. 3.75 (ISBN 0-8120-0273-3). Barron.

Catholicism, 2 vols. Richard P. McBrien. 1368p. 1980. Set. 37.50 (ISBN 0-03-056907-9). Winston Pr.

Catholicism Against Itself, Vol. 1. O. C. Lambert. 7.50 (ISBN 0-89315-005-3). Lambert Bk.

Catholicism Against Itself, Vol. 2. O. C. Lambert. 7.50 (ISBN 0-89315-006-1). Lambert Bk.

Catholicism & History. O. Chadwick. LC 77-77740. 1978. 18.95 (ISBN 0-521-21708-3). Cambridge U Pr.

Catholicism & Modernity: Confrontation or Capitulation? James Hitchcock. 1979. 13.95 (ISBN 0-8164-0427-5). Crossroad NY.

Catholicism in Gothic Fiction. Sr. Mary Tarr. Ed. by E. F. Bleiler. LC 78-60815. (Fiction of Popular Culture Ser.: Vol. 16). 148p. 1979. lib. bdg. 15.00 (ISBN 0-8240-9652-5). Garland Pub.

Catholicism, Judaism & the Effort at World Domination, 2 vols. in one. Victor Marx. (Institute for Economic & Political World Strategic Studies). (Illus.). 191p. 1975. Set. 65.00 (ISBN 0-913314-61-7). Am Classical Coll Pr.

Catholicism, Judaism & the Effort at World Domination. Victor Marx. (Illus.). 1980. 65.00 (ISBN 0-89266-216-6). Am Classical Coll Pr.

Catholicism Today. Matthew F. Kohmescher. LC 80-82085. 160p. (Orig.). 1980. pap. 3.50 (ISBN 0-8091-2335-5). Paulist Pr.

Catholicity of Protestantism: Being a Report Presented to His Grace the Archbishop of Canterbury by a Group of Free Churchmen. Ed. by Robert N. Flew & Rupert E. Davies. LC 80-29108. 159p. 1981. Repr. of 1950 ed. lib. bdg. 17.50x (ISBN 0-313-22825-6, FLCAT). Greenwood.

Catholics & Radicals: The Association of Catholic Trade Unionists & the American Labor Movement, from Depression to Cold War. Douglas P. Seaton. 300p. 1981. 18.50 (ISBN 0-8387-2193-1). Bucknell U Pr.

Catholics & the Left: The Slant Manifesto. Ed. by Neil Middleton. Date not set. pap. cancelled (ISBN 0-87243-018-9). Templegate.

Catholics in Colonial Days. Thomas P. Phelan. LC 74-145706. Repr. of 1935 ed. 18.00 (ISBN 0-8103-3685-5). Gale.

Catholics, Peasants & Chewa Resistance in Nyasaland, 1889-1939. Ian Linden & Jane Linden. 1974. 23.75x (ISBN 0-520-02500-8). U of Cal Pr.

Catholocism Confronts Modernity: A Protestant View. Langdon Gilkey. 1975. 8.95 (ISBN 0-8164-1163-8). Crossroad NY.

Cathredrals of England & Wales. John Harvey. 1974. 38.00 (ISBN 0-7134-0616-X). David & Charles.

Cathy & Company & Hank, the Horse. Alice Schertle. LC 79-19179. (Cathy & Company Ser.). (Illus.). 48p. (gr. 2 up). 1980. PLB 7.95 (ISBN 0-516-07725-2, Elk Grove Bks.). Childrens.

Cathy Leonard Calling. Catherine Woolley. (Illus.). (gr. 3-7). 1961. 7.75 o.p. (ISBN 0-688-21154-2). Morrow.

Cathy's Little Sister. Catherine Woolley. (Illus.). (gr. 3-7). 1964. 8.25 (ISBN 0-688-21155-0). Morrow.

Cationic Graft Copolymerization, No. 30. Ed. by J. P. Kennedy. (Journal of Applied Polymer Science). 1977. pap. 22.95 (ISBN 0-471-04426-1, Pub. by Wiley-Interscience). Wiley.

Cationic Polymerisation. A. Gandini & H. Cheradame. (Advances in Polymer Science Ser.: Vol. 34, 35). (Illus.). 360p. 1980. 79.80 (ISBN 0-387-10049-0). Springer-Verlag.

Cationic Ring-Opening Polymerization of Heterocyclic Monomers. S. Penczek et al. (Advances in Polymer Science Ser.: Vol. 37). (Illus.). 156p. 1981. 46.00 (ISBN 0-387-10209-4). Springer-Verlag.

Catlin. Don Higgins. 1980. 9.95 (ISBN 0-312-12471-6). St Martin.

Catlin's North American Indian Portfolio: A Reproduction. facs ed. George Catlin. LC 78-132585. (Reproduction). 1970. Repr. of 1845 ed. 250.00 (ISBN 0-8040-0029-8, SB). Swallow.

Catnapped! the Further Adventures of Undercover Cat. The Gordons. LC 74-5915. 192p. 1974. 5.95 o.p. (ISBN 0-385-08901-5). Doubleday.

Catnip Re. Jerome Salzman. LC 79-20289. (Illus.). 1980. 6.00 (ISBN 0-916906-24-8). Konglomerati.

Cato the Censor. Nels W. Forde. LC 74-28128. (World Leaders Ser: No. 49). 1975. lib. bdg. 10.95 (ISBN 0-8057-3017-6). Twayne.

Catrin in Wales. Mabel E. Allan. LC 61-9009. (gr. 7-11). 1960. 5.95 (ISBN 0-8149-0258-8). Vanguard.

Cats. (Wild, Wild World of Animals Ser.). (Illus.). 1976. 10.95 (ISBN 0-913948-02-0). Time-Life.

Cats. LC 75-29831. (Wild, Wild World of Animals). (Illus.). (gr. 5 up). 1976. lib. bdg. 11.97 (ISBN 0-685-73289-4, Pub. by Time-Life Television). Silver.

Cats. Laura French. (Illus.). 24p. (gr. k-2). 1976. PLB 5.00 (ISBN 0-307-60150-1, Golden Pr). Western Pub.

Cats. Ruth Heller. (Creative Coloring Activity Pandabacks). (Illus.). 32p. 1981. pap. 1.25 (ISBN 0-448-49626-7). G&D.

Cats. Henrie. (gr. 2-5). 1980. PLB 5.90 (ISBN 0-531-04119-0, E18). Watts.

Cats. Michael Holman. (Easy-Read Fact Book Ser.). (Illus.). 48p. (gr. 2-4). 1976. PLB 6.45 (ISBN 0-531-01220-4). Watts.

Cats. Dean Morris. LC 77-8118. (Read Animals Ser.). (Illus.). (gr. k-3). 1977. PLB 9.95 (ISBN 0-8393-0002-6). Raintree Child.

Cats. Louise B. Van Der Meid. (Orig.). pap. 2.00 (ISBN 0-87666-173-8, M503). TFH Pubns.

Cats - in Fact & Legend. Adele Millard. LC 76-1173. (Illus.). 128p. 1976. 5.95 o.p. (ISBN 0-8069-3728-9); PLB 5.89 o.p. (ISBN 0-8069-3729-7). Sterling.

Cats & Bats & Things Like That. Gil Beers. 32p. (gr. 1-3). 1972. 4.95 (ISBN 0-8024-1211-4). Moody.

Cats & Kittens. Grace Pond. 1976. pap. 5.95 (ISBN 0-7134-3247-0, Pub. by Batsford England). David & Charles.

Cats & Kittens. Jane Rockwell. LC 73-14560. (First Bks). (Illus.). 72p. (gr. 4-7). 1974. PLB 6.45 (ISBN 0-531-00812-6). Watts.

Cat's Cradle. Kurt Vonnegut, Jr. pap. 2.50 (ISBN 0-440-11149-8). Dell.

Cat's Elbow & Other Secret Languages. Alvin Schwartz. (Illus.). 96p. (gr. 3 up). Date not set. 8.95 (ISBN 0-374-31224-9). FS&G.

Cat's-Eye. Michael Rothberg. 12p. (Orig.). 1980. pap. 2.00 (ISBN 0-938370-00-6). Wildflower.

Cats' Eyes. Anthony Taber. (Illus.). 1978. 9.95 o.p. (ISBN 0-525-07814-2). Dutton.

Cat's Eyes. Anthony Taber. (Illus.). 1980. pap. 6.95 (ISBN 0-525-03162-6, Thomas Congdon Book). Dutton.

Cats from Summer Island. Edith Unnerstad. (gr. 2-4). 1963. 3.95g o.s.i. (ISBN 0-02-789680-3). Macmillan.

Cat's Got Our Tongue. Claire Necker. 1973. 10.00 (ISBN 0-8108-0545-6). Scarecrow.

Cats in May. Doreen Tovey. 1976. 9.95 (ISBN 0-236-40079-7, Pub. by Paul Elek). Merrimack Bk Serv.

Cats in the Belfry. Doreen Tovey. 1978. 9.95 (ISBN 0-236-30847-5, Pub. by Paul Elek). Merrimack Bk Serv.

Cat's Magic. Margaret Greaves. LC 80-8451. 192p. (gr. 5 up). 1981. 8.95 (ISBN 0-06-022122-4, HarpJ); PLB 8.79g (ISBN 0-06-022123-2). Har-Row.

Cats to Come. Geoffrey Household. (Greenwich Ed.). 1975. 5.95 o.p. (ISBN 0-7181-1347-0, Pub. by Michael Joseph). Merrimack Bk Serv.

Cat's Whisker: Fifty Years of Wireless Design. Jonathan Hill. LC 78-52365. (Art Bks). (Illus.). 1978. 15.95 (ISBN 0-8467-0477-3, Pub. by Two Continents); pap. 9.95 (ISBN 0-8467-0478-1). Hippocrene Bks.

Cat's Whiskers. Bill Charmatz. LC 75-78085. (Illus.). (gr. k-2). 1969. 5.95g o.s.i. (ISBN 0-02-718170-7). Macmillan.

Catskill Country Cooking. Beverly Borwick. LC 75-40761. (Illus.). 192p. 1976. pap. 4.95 o.s.i. (ISBN 0-8027-0528-6). Walker & Co.

Catskill Flytier: My Life, Times, & Techniques. Harry Darbee & Mac Francis. LC 77-22503. (Illus.). 1977. 8.95 o.p. (ISBN 0-397-01214-4). Lippincott.

Catskills. T. Morris Longstreth. LC 75-118782. (Empire State Historical Publications Ser: No. 85). 1970. Repr. of 1918 ed. 10.00 o.p. (ISBN 0-87198-085-1). Friedman.

Cattafi Selected Poems. Bartolo Cattafi. Tr. by Brian Swann & Ruth Feldman. 228p. 1981. 14.00 (ISBN 0-931556-04-X); pap. 6.00 (ISBN 0-931556-05-8). Translation Pr.

Cattle Baron. Jack Slade. (Lassiter Ser). 1977. pap. 1.25 (ISBN 0-505-51163-0). Tower Bks.

Cattle Car Express: A Prisoner of War in Siberia. Emil Lengyel. LC 79-53452. (Short Story Index in Reprint Ser.). Date not set. Repr. of 1931 ed. 21.50x (ISBN 0-8486-5008-5). Core Collection. Postponed.

Cattle, Economics & Development. 253p. 1981. 62.50 (ISBN 0-85198-452-5, CAB 14, CAB). Unipub.

Cattle King. Edward F. Treadwell. (Illus.). xii, 375p. 1981. pap. 6.95 (ISBN 0-934136-10-6). Western Tanager.

Cattle Management. Cheryl May. 350p. 1981. text ed. 16.95 (ISBN 0-8359-0721-X); instr's. manual free. Reston.

Cattle Mutilations. Ian Summers & Dan Kagan. 288p. (Orig.). 1981. pap. 2.95. Bantam.

Cattle Mutilators. John J. Dalton. (Orig.). 1980. pap. 1.95 (ISBN 0-532-23117-1). Manor Bks.

Cattle Pricing Guide. 3rd rev. ed. Hugh Cleveland. (Illus.). 1980. pap. 7.95 (ISBN 0-89145-137-4). Collector Bks.

Cattle, Sheep, & Hogs. (Country Home Ser.). 96p. 2.95 (ISBN 0-88453-005-1). Berkshire Traveller.

Cattle, Sheep & Hogs. Hollis Lee. (Country Home & Small Farm Guides Ser.). (Illus.). 1978. pap. 2.95 (ISBN 0-88453-005-1). Barrington.

Cattle Trails to Trenches. Howard G. Smith. (Illus.). 8.95 (ISBN 0-8363-0020-3). Jenkins.

Cattlemen. Mari Sandoz. 1975. Repr. 11.95 (ISBN 0-8038-1087-3). Hastings.

Cattlemen: From the Rio Grande across the Far Marias. Mari Sandoz. LC 77-14078. 1978. pap. 7.95 (ISBN 0-8032-5882-8, BB 660, Bison). U of Nebr Pr.

Catullan Revolution. Kenneth Quinn. 1971. pap. 1.95 o.p. (ISBN 0-472-06175-5, 175, AA). U of Mich Pr.

Catullus: A Commentary. Ed. by C. J. Fordyce. 1961. 22.50x (ISBN 0-19-814430-X). Oxford U Pr.

Catullus & the Traditions of Ancient Poetry. Arthur L. Wheeler. (Sather Classical Lectures: Vol. 9). 1974. 20.00x (ISBN 0-520-02640-3). U of Cal Pr.

Catullus of William Hull. Catullus. Tr. by William Hull. 7.00 (ISBN 0-89253-791-4); flexible cloth 4.00 (ISBN 0-89253-792-2). Ind-US Inc.

Catullus: Selections from the Poems. Ed. by F. Kinchin & J. W. Melluish. (Roman World Ser.). 1956. pap. text ed. 3.95x (ISBN 0-04-874001-2). Allen Unwin.

Catundra. Stephen Cosgrove. (Creative Fantasies Ser.). (Illus.). (gr. k-4). 1979. PLB 6.95 (ISBN 0-87191-692-4). Creative Ed.

Caucasians Only: The Supreme Court, the NAACP, & the Restrictive Covenant Cases. Clement E. Vose. LC 59-8758. 1959. 19.50x (ISBN 0-520-01308-5); pap. 4.95x (ISBN 0-520-01309-3, CAMPUS1). U of Cal Pr.

Caudillism & Militarism in Venezuela, 1810-1910. Robert L. Gilmore. LC 64-22887. 1964. 12.00 o.p. (ISBN 0-8214-0003-7). Ohio U Pr.

Caught in the Rain. Beatriz Ferro. LC 79-2513. (gr. 2). 1980. 6.95a (ISBN 0-385-15624-3); PLB (ISBN 0-385-15625-1). Doubleday.

Caught in the Web of Words: James A. H. Murray & the "Oxford English Dictionary". K. M. Murray. LC 77-76309. (Illus.). 1977. 20.00x (ISBN 0-300-02131-3). Yale U Pr.

Causa. G. Horwitz & P. Fusco. 1970. 7.95 o.s.i. (ISBN 0-02-554120-X). Macmillan.

Causa. G. Horwitz & P. Fusco. 1970. pap. 3.95 o.s.i. (ISBN 0-02-073560-X, Collier). Macmillan.

Causal Analysis. David R. Heise. LC 75-20465. 301p. 1975. 24.95 (ISBN 0-471-36898-9, Pub. by Wiley-Interscience). Wiley.

Causal Models in the Social Sciences. Ed. by H. M. Blalock, Jr. LC 70-133304. 1971. text ed. 26.95x (ISBN 0-202-30076-5); pap. text ed. 13.95x (ISBN 0-202-30228-8). Aldine Pub.

Causal Theories of Mind. Ed. by Steven Davis. (Foundations of Communications Ser.). 400p. 1980. 81.50x (ISBN 3-11-007730-2). De Gruyter.

Causality & Chance in Modern Physics. David Bohm. LC 57-28894. 1971. pap. 4.95x (ISBN 0-8122-1002-6, Pa Paperbks). U of Pa Pr.

Causality & Determinism. Georg H. Von Wright. 128p. 1974. 15.00x (ISBN 0-231-03758-9). Columbia U Pr.

Causality & Scientific Explanation: Classical & Contemporary Science, Vol. 2. William A. Wallace. 432p. 1981. lib. bdg. 22.75 (ISBN 0-8191-1480-4); pap. text ed. 13.75 (ISBN 0-8191-1481-2). U Pr of Amer.

Causality & Scientific Explanation: Medieval & Early Classical Science, Vol. 1. William A. Wallace. 298p. 1981. lib. bdg. 19.25 (ISBN 0-8191-1478-2); pap. text ed. 10.50 (ISBN 0-8191-1479-0). U Pr of Amer.

Causality: Lectures. University Of California Philosophical Union - 1932. (Publications in Philosophy Ser: Vol. 15). pap. 17.00 (ISBN 0-384-07040-X). Johnson Repr.

Causation in the Law. Herbert L. Hart & Antony M. Honore. 1959. 37.50x (ISBN 0-19-825147-5). Oxford U Pr.

Cause & Meaning in the Social Sciences. Ernest Gellner. Ed. by I. C. Jarvie & Joseph Agassi. 240p. 1973. 20.00x (ISBN 0-7100-7599-5). Routledge & Kegan.

Cause for Wonder. Wright Morris. LC 77-14594. 1978. 12.50x (ISBN 0-8032-0966-5); pap. 3.95 (ISBN 0-8032-5885-2, BB 656, Bison). U of Nebr Pr.

Cause of God & Truth. John Gill. (Giant Summit Ser.). 336p. 1981. pap. 7.95 (ISBN 0-8010-3761-1). Baker Bk.

Cause of World Unrest. Intro. by H. A. Gwynne. 1978. pap. 5.00x (ISBN 0-911038-40-X). Noontide.

Causes & Cures of Unemployment. William H. Beveridge. LC 75-41030. 1976. Repr. of 1931 ed. 9.00 (ISBN 0-685-70886-1). Ams Pr.

Causes & Effects of Smoking. H. J. Eysenck & L. J. Eaves. LC 79-48085. (Illus.). 400p. 1980. 39.95 (ISBN 0-8039-1454-7). Sage.

Causes & Prevention of Blindness. Ed. by I. C. Michaelson & Elaine R. Berman. 1973. 25.00 (ISBN 0-12-493650-4). Acad Pr.

Causes, Ecology & Prevention of Traffic Accidents: With Emphasis Upon Traffic Medicine, Epidemiology Sociology & Logistics. H. J. Roberts. (Illus.). 1200p. 1971. 54.75 (ISBN 0-398-02169-4). C C Thomas.

Causes Financieres De la Revolution Francaise, 2 vols. Charles Gomel. 1892-93. Set. 55.00 (ISBN 0-8337-1374-4); 30.00 ea. (ISBN 0-8337-1374-4). B Franklin.

Causes, Mechanism, & Control of Cracking in Concrete. ACI Committee 224. (Bibliography: No. 9). 1971. pap. 26.25 (ISBN 0-685-85148-6, B-9). ACI.

Causes of & Solutions to Coastal Erosion in Benin & Togo. Un. Date not set. price not set. Gordon.

Causes of Climate. John G. Lockwood. 1979. 32.95 o.p. (ISBN 0-470-26657-0); pap. 16.95 (ISBN 0-470-26658-9). Halsted Pr.

Causes of Delinquency. Travis Hirschi. 1969. 18.50x (ISBN 0-520-01487-1); pap. 4.95x (ISBN 0-520-01901-6, CAMPUS47). U of Cal Pr.

Causes of Suicide. Maurice Halbwachs. Tr. by Harold Goldblatt. LC 78-54110. (Illus.). 1978. 19.95 (ISBN 0-02-913540-0). Free Pr.

Causes of the Present Inflation: An Interdisciplinary Explanation Centered on Britain, Germany & the United States. Andrew Tylecote. 180p. 1980. text ed. 24.95x (ISBN 0-470-26953-7). Halsted Pr.

Causes of the War of Independence. Claude H. Van Tyne. 8.50 (ISBN 0-8446-1459-9). Peter Smith.

Causes of War. Geoffrey Blainey. LC 73-2016. 1975. pap. 6.95 (ISBN 0-02-903590-2). Free Pr.

Cautantowwit's House: An Indian Burial Ground on the Island of Conanicut in Narragansett Bay. William S. Simmons. LC 77-111456. (Illus.). 1970. 10.00 (ISBN 0-87057-122-2, Pub. by Brown U Pr). Univ Pr of New England.

Caution: Christians Under Construction. Bill Hybels & Jay Caress. 1978. pap. 2.50 (ISBN 0-88207-759-7). Victor Bks.

Caution: Kindness Can Be Dangerous to the Alcholic. Abraham J. Twerski. 1981. 10.95 (ISBN 0-13-121244-3); pap. 4.95 (ISBN 0-13-121236-2). P-H.

Cautionary Tales. Hilaire Belloc. (Children's Literature Ser.). 1980. PLB 5.95 (ISBN 0-8398-2602-8). Gregg.

Cautionary Verses. Hilaire Belloc. (Illus.). 1959. 10.00 (ISBN 0-394-40314-2). Knopf.

Cavaille-Coll & the Musicians. Fenner Douglass. (Illus.). 48p. 78.00 (ISBN 0-915548-09-7). Sunbury Pr.

Cavalcade: Negro American Writing from 1760 to the Present. Ed. by Arthur P. Davis & Saunders Redding. LC 70-20257. 1971. text ed. 19.50 (ISBN 0-395-04345-X); tchrs. manual pap. 2.00 (ISBN 0-395-04346-8). HM.

Cavalier & Yankee. William R. Taylor. LC 61-15493. 1961. 6.00 o.s.i. (ISBN 0-8076-0152-7). Braziller.

Cavalier King Charles Spaniels. Eiliah M. Stenning. Ed. by Christina Foyle. (Foyle's Handbks). (Illus.). 1973. 3.95 (ISBN 0-685-55793-6). Palmetto Pub.

Cavalletti. Reiner Klimke. Tr. by Daphne M. Goodall. (Illus.). pap. 7.85 (ISBN 0-85131-192-X, Dist. by Sporting Book Center). J A Allen.

Cavalli. Jane Glover. LC 77-23638. (Illus.). 1978. 18.95 (ISBN 0-312-12546-1). St Martin.

Cavalry: Confederate & Union Troops & Their Leaders in the Civil War. Samuel Carter. LC 76-62758. 1979. 15.00 o.p. (ISBN 0-685-96173-7). St Martin.

Cavalry of World War II. Janusz Piekalkiewicz. LC 80-5800. (Illus.). 256p. 1980. 25.00 (ISBN 0-8128-2749-X). Stein & Day.

Cavalry Uniforms of Britain & the Commonwealth. Robert Wilkinson-Latham & Christopher Wilkinson-Latham. (Color Ser.). (Illus.). 1969. 9.95 (ISBN 0-7137-0134-X, Pub by Blandford Pr England). Sterling.

Cavanaugh Quest. Thomas Gifford. 1977. pap. 2.50 (ISBN 0-345-29065-8). Ballantine.

Cave Bear Story. Life & Death of a Vanished Animal. Bjory Kurten. LC 76-3723. (Illus.). 144p. 1976. 15.00x (ISBN 0-231-04017-2). Columbia U Pr.

Cave Children. A. T. Sonnleitner. Tr. by Anthea Bell from Ger. LC 70-120785. (Illus.). (gr. 8 up). 1971. 9.95 (ISBN 0-87599-169-6). S G Phillips.

Cave Divers. Robert F. Burgess. LC 75-22130. (Illus.). 1976. 9.95 (ISBN 0-396-07204-6). Dodd.

Cave Exploring. Jennifer Anderson. (Illus.). 128p. 1974. pap. 4.95 o.p. (ISBN 0-8096-1889-3, Assn Pr). Follett.

Cave Girl. Edgar R. Burroughs. Ed. by Wendy Wallace. 224p. 1981. pap. 1.95 (ISBN 0-448-17176-7, Tempo). G&D.

Cave In! Lael Littke. (Prime Time Adventures Ser.). (Illus.). 64p. (gr. 4 up). 1981. PLB 7.95 (ISBN 0-516-02102-8). Childrens.

Cave-in at Mason's Mine. Bessie H. Heck. LC 80-18637. (Illus.). 64p. (gr. 2-6). 1980. 7.95 (ISBN 0-684-16718-2). Scribner.

Cave of Night. Vincente Aleixandre. 1980. 3.95. Solo Pr.

Cave of the Ancients. T. Rampa. pap. 2.50 (ISBN 0-685-88123-7). Weiser.

Cave of the Moaning Winds. Jean DeWeese. 1976. pap. 1.25 o.p. (ISBN 0-345-25160-1). Ballantine.

Cave Temples of Maichishan. Michael Sullivan. LC 69-15829. (Illus.). 1969. 46.50x (ISBN 0-520-01448-0). U of Cal Pr.

Cavender's Balkan Quest. Elliot Tokson. 1977. pap. 1.75 o.p. (ISBN 0-449-13917-4, GM). Fawcett.

Cavendish Laboratory: 1874-1974. J. G. Crowther. 349p. 1974. text ed. 50.00x o.p. (ISBN 0-88202-029-3, Sci Hist). N Watson.

Cavendish Square. Kathryn Douglas. 224p. (Orig.). 1976. pap. 1.50 o.p. (ISBN 0-345-24910-0). Ballantine.

Caverns: The Journeys of McGill Feighan, Bk. I. Kevin O'Donnell, Jr. (Orig.). 1981. pap. 2.25 (ISBN 0-425-04730-X). Berkley Pub.

Caves. Roma Gans. LC 76-4881. (Let's Read & Find Out Science Book Ser.). (Illus.). (gr. k-3). 1977. PLB 7.89 (ISBN 0-690-01070-2, TYC-J). T Y Crowell.

Caves. George Laycock. LC 76-15194. (Illus.). 112p. (gr. 5-9). 1976. 6.95 (ISBN 0-590-07392-3, Four Winds). Schol Bk Serv.

Caves & Canyons. M. A. Toigo. LC 79-54772. (Illus.). 52p. 1979. 5.00 (ISBN 0-913180-02-5). Benedict Con Adoration.

Caves of Darkness. Joyce Schenk. (YA) 1977. 5.95 (ISBN 0-685-73814-0, Avalon). Bouregy.

Caves of Drach. Hugh Walters. LC 79-670249. (gr. 8-11). 1979. 9.95 (ISBN 0-571-11037-1, Pub. by Faber & Faber). Merrimack Bk Serv.

Caves of Fire & Ice. Shirley R. Murphy. LC 80-12887. 180p. (gr. 6 up). 1980. 9.95 (ISBN 0-689-30784-5, Argo). Atheneum.

Caves of the Great Hunters. rev. ed. Hans Baumann. (Illus.). (gr. 5 up). 1962. PLB 6.99 o.s.i. (ISBN 0-394-91006-0). Pantheon.

Cavitation & Multiphase Flow Phenomena. Frederick G. Hammitt. 448p. 1980. text ed. 48.00 (ISBN 0-07-025907-0). McGraw.

Cavitation & Polyphase Flow Forum - 1979: Book No. 600143. Robert L. Waid. 1979. pap. text ed. 4.00 (ISBN 0-685-81925-6). ASME.

Cawdor & Medea. Robinson Jeffers. LC 76-103374. 1970. pap. 5.95 (ISBN 0-8112-0073-6, NDP293). New Directions.

Cay. Theodore Taylor. (gr. 3 up). 1977. pap. 1.75 (ISBN 0-380-00142-X, 51037, Camelot). Avon.

Cayuse Indians: Imperial Tribesmen of Old Oregon. Robert H. Ruby & John A. Brown. LC 74-177345. (Civilization of the American Indian Ser.: Vol. 120). (Illus.). 320p. 1972. 16.95 (ISBN 0-8061-0995-5); pap. 7.95 (ISBN 0-8061-1316-2). U of Okla Pr.

Caza Del Lobo. 1969. 2.50 o.p. (ISBN 0-312-46200-X). St Martin.

CB. James L. Collier. (Career Concise Guides Ser.). (Illus.). (gr. 7 up). 1977. PLB 6.45 s&l (ISBN 0-531-00095-8). Watts.

CB Bible. Porter Bibb et al. 1976. pap. 4.95 (ISBN 0-385-12323-X). Doubleday.

CB Convoy Caper. M. Blount Christian. (The Goosehill Gang Series: No. 2). (gr. 2-5). 1981. pap. 1.10 (ISBN 0-570-07352-9, 39-1042). Concordia.

CB Picture Dictionary. Joan Murray. LC 80-1725. (Illus.). 64p. (gr. 5 up). 8.95a (ISBN 0-385-14782-1); PLB (ISBN 0-385-14783-X). Doubleday.

CB Radio Caper. Gary Paulsen. LC 76-47631. (Mallard Mystery Ser.). (Illus.). (gr. 3-6). 1977. PLB 7.75 (ISBN 0-8172-0926-3). Raintree Pubs.

CB Radio Schematic-Servicing Manual, Vol. 3. Tab Editorial Staff. LC 75-41727. 200p. 1976. vinyl o.p. 8.95 (ISBN 0-8306-6858-6); pap. 5.95 (ISBN 0-8306-5858-0, 858). TAB Bks.

CBers' How-to Book. rev., 2nd ed. Leo G. Sands. (Illus.). Date not set. pap. cancelled (ISBN 0-8104-0828-7). Hayden.

CBers' SSB Handbook. Tom Kneitel. (gr. 10 up). 1977. pap. 7.15 (ISBN 0-8104-0857-0). Hayden.

CCAR Yearbook: 1978, Vol. 88. Ed. by Elliot L. Stevens & Donald A. Weber. 1979. 15.00x o.p. (ISBN 0-916694-58-5). Central Conf.

Ce Que la Bible Enseigne. Tr. by R. A. Torrey. (French Bks.). (Fr.). 1979. 6.00 (ISBN 0-686-28818-1). Life Pubs Intl.

Cebuano Sorcery: Malign Magic in the Philippines. Richard W. Lieban. 1967. 14.75x (ISBN 0-520-00749-2); pap. 3.95x (ISBN 0-520-03420-1). U of Cal Pr.

Cecco Angiolieri: A Study. Gifford P. Orwen. (Studies in the Romance Languages & Literatures: No. 215). 104p. 1980. pap. 7.50 (ISBN 0-8078-9215-7). U of NC Pr.

Cecil Textbook of Medicine, 2 vols. 15th ed. Paul B. Beeson et al. (Illus.). 2478p. 1979. Single Vol. Ed. 49.00 (ISBN 0-7216-1663-1); Two Vol. Set. 60.00 (ISBN 0-7216-1667-4); Vol. 1. 30.00 (ISBN 0-7216-1664-X); Vol. 2. 30.00 (ISBN 0-7216-1666-6). Saunders.

Cedar Light. Allen Hoey. 10.00 (ISBN 0-686-65776-4); pap. 2.00 (ISBN 0-935252-16-9). Street Pr.

Cedric Willson Symposium on Expansive Cement. 1980. 30.60 (SP-64). ACI.

Celebrate! No. V. Ed. by Eugene T. Sullivan & Marilynn C. Sullivan. LC 75-24148. 1978. 12.95 (ISBN 0-912696-14-1). Wilton.

Celebrate! No. VI. Ed. by Marilynn C. Sullivan & Eugene T. Sullivan. LC 76-48542. 160p. 1980. 12.95 (ISBN 0-912696-17-6). Wilton.

Celebrate the Sun. James Kavanaugh. 1973. 6.95 (ISBN 0-87690-163-1). Dutton.

Celebrate with Sesame Street. Date not set. pap. 6.50 boxed set (ISBN 0-307-13628-0, Golden Pr). Western Pub.

Celebrate Yourself: The Secret to a Life of Hope & Joy. Bryan J. Cannon. LC 76-48542. 1977. pap. 3.95 o.p. (ISBN 0-87680-802-X, 98107). Word Bks.

Celebrated Cases of Dick Tracy Nineteen Thirty-One to Nineteen Fifty-One. abr. ed. Chester Gould. Ed. by Herb Galewitz. LC 70-127010. (Illus.). 290p. 1981. pap. 12.50 (ISBN 0-87754-220-1). Chelsea Hse.

Celebrated Thoughts. Marylou Johnson. 60p. 1980. 3.95 (ISBN 0-8059-2737-9). Dorrance.

Celebrating Mass with Children: A Commentary on the Directory of Masses with Children. Edward Matthews. LC 78-58564. 1978. pap. 6.95 (ISBN 0-8091-2160-3). Paulist Pr.

Celebrating the Church Year: A Children's Worship Service. Carl B. Rife. 1980. pap. text ed. 0.95 (ISBN 0-89536-443-3). CSS Pub.

Celebrating with Books. Nancy Polette & Marjorie Hamlin. LC 77-3862. (Illus.). 1977. 10.00 (ISBN 0-8108-1032-8). Scarecrow.

Celebration & Blessing of a Marriage. 1977. pap. 0.95 (ISBN 0-8164-2152-8). Crossroad NY.

Celebration in the Bedroom. Charlie Shedd & Martha Shedd. 128p. 1981. pap. 2.50 (ISBN 0-553-14436-7). Bantam.

Celebration of Adulthood. Donald Deffner. LC 80-81839. pap. 4.50 (ISBN 0-933350-41-4). Morse Pr.

Celebration of Awareness. Ivan D. Illich. LC 71-113986. 1971. pap. 1.95 (ISBN 0-385-07386-0, Anch). Doubleday.

Celebration of Christmas. Gillian Cooke. 1980. 16.95 (ISBN 0-686-68353-6). Putnam.

Celebration of Heroes: Prestige As a Social Control System. William J. Goode. LC 77-20322. 1979. 20.00x (ISBN 0-520-03602-6); pap. 7.95x (ISBN 0-520-03811-8). U of Cal Pr.

Celebration of Sexuality. (Illus.). pap. 5.00 (ISBN 0-910550-31-X). Centurion Pr.

Celebration of the Gospel. Hardin Q. White, Jr. et al. 1978. 3.95 (ISBN 0-687-04800-1). Abingdon.

Celebrations. Alan Burns. 1980. pap. cancelled (ISBN 0-7145-0072-0). Riverrun NY.

Celebrations & Attacks. Irving Howe. LC 80-14048. 1980. pap. 4.95 (ISBN 0-15-616248-2, Harv). HarBraceJ.

Celebrations of Death. R. Huntington & P. Metcalf. LC 79-478. (Illus.). 1979. 27.50 (ISBN 0-521-22531-0); pap. 7.95x (ISBN 0-521-29540-8). Cambridge U Pr.

Celebrations of Life. Ed. by Loren B. Mead. 1974. pap. 5.95 (ISBN 0-8164-2092-0). Crossroad NY.

Celebrities of the Century: Being a Dictionary of Men & Women of the Nineteenth Century. Lloyd C. Sanders. LC 68-27185. 1971. Repr. of 1887 ed. 54.00 (ISBN 0-8103-3774-6). Gale.

Celebrity Exercise. Ann Smith. LC 75-12188. (Illus.). 160p. 1976. 10.00 o.s.i. (ISBN 0-8027-0501-4). Walker & Co.

Celebrity Homes. Ed. by Architectural Digest Editors. (Studio Bk). (Illus.). 1977. 35.00 o.p. (ISBN 0-670-20964-3). Viking Pr.

Celebrity Vegetarian Cookbook. J. L. Barkas. LC 78-3837. (Illus.). 1978. pap. 2.50 o.p. (ISBN 0-668-04616-3, 4616). Arc Bks.

Celery. 93p. 1980. pap. 9.95x (ISBN 0-901361-29-1, Pub. by Grower Bks England). Intl Schol Bk Serv.

Celestial Democracy. Vossa E. Wysinger. LC 66-24014. 1966. text ed. 12.00 (ISBN 0-686-24366-8); pap. text ed. 9.00 (ISBN 0-686-24367-6). V E Wysinger.

Celestial Harmony: A Guide to Horoscope Interpretation. Martin Schulman. 1980. pap. 7.95 (ISBN 0-87728-495-4). Weiser.

Celestial Horizons: A Concise View of the Universe. John C. Rosemergy. 1977. pap. text ed. 12.95x (ISBN 0-205-05571-0); instr's manual avail. (ISBN 0-205-05572-9). Allyn.

Celestial Influences, 1981: Eastern Time. Jim Maynard. pap. 4.95 (ISBN 0-930356-24-1). Quicksilver Prod.

Celestial Influences: 1981, Pacific Time. Jim Maynard. 1981. 4.95 (ISBN 0-930356-21-7). Quicksilver Prod.

Celestial Journey & the Harmony of the Spheres. Carrie E. Hammill. LC 79-28416. 183p. 1980. pap. 13.50 (ISBN 0-912646-53-5). Carrollton Pr.

Celestial Lancets: History & Rationale of Acupuncture & Moxa. Gwei-Djen Lu & J. Needham. LC 79-41734. (Illus.). 400p. 1980. 97.50 (ISBN 0-521-21513-7). Cambridge U Pr.

Celestial Masers. A. H. Cook. LC 76-14028. (Cambridge Monographs on Physics). (Illus.). 1977. 28.95 (ISBN 0-521-21344-4). Cambridge U Pr.

Celestial Mechanics, Vols. 1-4. Pierre S. Laplace. LC 69-11316. Set. text ed. 175.00 (ISBN 0-8284-0194-2). Chelsea Pub.

Celestial Mechanics, Vol. 5. Pierre S. Laplace. LC 63-11316. (Mecanique Celeste, Tome V, Fr). 1969. Repr. of 1832 ed. text ed. 20.00 (ISBN 0-8284-0214-0). Chelsea Pub.

Celestial Navigation. 1981. pap. 7.95 (ISBN 0-679-50965-8). McKay.

Celestial Navigation for Beginners. Jeff Toghill. (Illus.). 112p. (Orig.). 1978. pap. 6.75 (ISBN 0-589-50042-2, Pub. by Reed Books Australia). C E Tuttle.

Celestial Navigation for Beginners. Jeff Toghill. (Orig.). 1980. pap. 8.95 (ISBN 0-8464-0998-4). Beekman Pubs.

Celestial Navigation for Yachtsmen. Mary Blewitt. LC 67-25097. 1967. 6.95 (ISBN 0-8286-0028-7). De Graff.

Celestial Navigation with a Pocket Calculator. G. A. Patterson. 1980. softbound 14.95 (ISBN 0-917410-03-3). Basic Sci Pr.

Celestial Passengers: UFOs & Space Travel. Margaret Sachs & Ernest Jahn. (Orig.). 1977. pap. 2.95 o.p. (ISBN 0-14-004483-3). Penguin.

Celestial Shaggy Dog Joke, No.2. Lombard Sayre. (Illus.). 51p. (Orig.). 1980. pap. 3.95 (ISBN 0-89260-194-9). Hwong Pub.

Celestina: A Play in Twenty-One Acts Attributed to Fernando De Rojas. Tr. by Mack H. Singleton. 1958. pap. 7.95 (ISBN 0-299-01774-5). U of Wis Pr.

Celia. Marilyn Granbeck. 1977. pap. 1.95 (ISBN 0-515-03951-9). Jove Pubns.

Celia Garth. Gwen Bristow. LC 59-10435. 1959. 10.95 (ISBN 0-690-18348-8, TYC-T). T Y Crowell.

Celia's House. D. E. Stevenson. LC 76-29915. 1977. 7.95 o.p. (ISBN 0-03-020441-0). HR&W.

Celibacy in the Church. Ed. by William W. Bassett & Peter J. Huizing. LC 72-3943. (Concilium Ser.: Religion in the Seventies: Vol. 78). 156p. 1972. pap. 4.95 (ISBN 0-8164-2534-5). Crossroad NY.

Celine et les mots: Etude stylistique des effets de mots dans le Voyage au bout de la nuit. Yves de La Queriere. LC 70-160050. (Studies in Romance Languages: No. 7.). 172p. 1973. 10.00x (ISBN 0-8131-1268-0). U Pr of Ky.

Celine: The Novel As Delirium. Allen Thiher. LC 77-185394. 1972. 18.50 (ISBN 0-8135-0717-0). Rutgers U Pr.

Cell. Horst Bienek. Tr. by Mahlendorf from Ger. LC 74-134739. 1973. 7.50 (ISBN 0-87775-024-6); pap. 2.95 (ISBN 0-87775-070-X). Unicorn Pr.

Cell. 2nd ed. Don Fawcett. (Illus.). 928p. 1981. text ed. write for info. (ISBN 0-7216-3584-9). Saunders.

Cell. John Kirn. (Orig.). 1960. pap. 0.90 (ISBN 0-8054-9706-4). Broadman.

Cell. rev. ed. John Pfeiffer. LC 64-15570. (Life Science Library). (Illus.). (gr. 5 up). 1969. PLB 8.97 o.p. (ISBN 0-8094-0462-1, Pub. by Time-Life). Silver.

Cell. 4th ed. Carl P. Swanson & Peter Webster. (Foundation of Modern Biology Ser). (Illus.). 1977. 15.95 (ISBN 0-13-121707-0); pap. text ed. 13.95 (ISBN 0-13-121699-6). P-H.

Cell & Tissue Interactions. Ed. by James Lash & Max M. Burger. LC 77-83689. (Society of General Physiologists Ser: Vol. 32). 1977. 29.50 (ISBN 0-89004-180-6). Raven.

Cell: Biochemistry, Physiology, Morphology, 6 vols. Ed. by Jean Brachet & A. E. Mirsky. Incl. Vol. 1. Methods: Problems of Cell Biology. 1959. 62.00 (ISBN 0-12-123301-4); Vol. 2. Cells & Their Component Parts. 1961. 62.00 (ISBN 0-12-123302-2); Vol. 3. Meiosis & Mitosis. 1961. 47.00 (ISBN 0-12-123303-0); Vol. 4. Specialized Cells, Part 1. 1960. 51.00 (ISBN 0-12-123304-9); Vol. 5. Specialized Cells, Part 2. 1961. 55.50 (ISBN 0-12-123305-7); Vol. 6. Supplementary Volume. 1964. 55.50 (ISBN 0-12-123306-5). Set. 281.00 (ISBN 0-685-23120-8). Acad Pr.

Cell Biological Aspects of Disease: The Plasma Membrane & Lysosomes. Ed. by W. T. Daems et al. (Boerhaave Series for Postgraduate Medical Education: No. 19). 330p. 1981. PLB 68.50 (ISBN 90-6021-466-8, Pub. by Leiden U Pr). Kluwer Boston.

Cell Biology. E. J. Ambrose & Dorothy M. Easty. LC 79-140833. (Biology Ser). 1970. text ed. 18.95 (ISBN 0-201-00233-7). A-W.

Cell Biology. 2nd ed. Charlotte J. Avers. 1981. text ed. price not set (ISBN 0-442-25770-8). D Van Nostrand.

Cell Biology. 2nd ed. John W. Kimball. LC 77-77742. (Life Sciences Ser.). (Illus.). 1978. pap. text ed. 16.95 (ISBN 0-201-03628-2). A-W.

Cell Biology: A Comprehensive Treatise, 2 vols. Ed. by L. Goldstein & David Prescott. Incl. Vol. 1. 1978. 47.00 (ISBN 0-12-289501-0); by subscription 40.50 (ISBN 0-686-61588-3); Vol. 2. The Structure & Replication of Genetic Material. 1979. 47.00, by subscription 40.50 (ISBN 0-12-289502-9). LC 78-10457. Acad Pr.

Cell Biology: A Molecular Approach. 2nd ed. Robert D. Dyson. 1978. text ed. 20.95 (ISBN 0-205-05942-2). Allyn.

Cell Biology of Brain. W. E. Watson. LC 76-1921. 1976. 48.95 o.p. (ISBN 0-470-15042-4). Halsted Pr.

Cell Biology of Breast Cancer. Ed. by Charles M. McGrath et al. LC 80-13804. 1981. 33.00 (ISBN 0-12-483940-1). Acad Pr.

Cell Cycle in Development & Differentiation. Ed. by M. Balls & F. S. Billett. (British Society for Developmental Biological Symposia Ser.). (Illus.). 450p. 1973. 71.50 (ISBN 0-521-20136-5). Cambridge U Pr.

Cell Differentiation & Neoplasia. Ed. by Grady F. Saunders. LC 77-17694. (M.D. Anderson Symposia on Fundamental Cancer Research). 1978. 49.00 (ISBN 0-89004-200-4). Raven.

Cell Division & Heredity. Roger Kemp. 1971. text ed. 14.95 (ISBN 0-312-12635-2). St Martin.

Cell Electrophoresis: Clinical Application & Methodology. Ed. by A. W. Preece & D. Sabolovic. 496p. 1979. 56.00 (ISBN 0-7204-0674-9). Elsevier.

Cell Lineage, Stem Cells & Cell Determination. Ed. by N. Le Douarin. (INSERM: No. 10). 378p. 1979. 56.00 (ISBN 0-7204-0673-0, North Holland). Elsevier.

Cell Markers. Ed. by G. Jasmin. (Methods & Achievements in Experimental Pathology: Vol. 10). (Illus.). vi, 294p. 1981. 90.00 (ISBN 3-8055-1736-X). S Karger.

Cell Mediated Reactions: Vol. 3, PAR. Pseudo-Allergic Reactions. Involvement of Drugs & Chemicals. Ed. by P. Dukor et al. (Illus.). 250p. 1981. 72.00 (ISBN 3-8055-0960-X). S Karger.

Cell Membrane Receptors for Drugs & Hormones. Ed. by Ralph W. Straub & Liana Bolis. LC 77-87454. 1978. 36.50 (ISBN 0-89004-227-6). Raven.

Cell Membrane Receptors for Viruses, Anticens & Antibodies, Polypeptide Hormones, & Small Molecules. Ed. by Roland F. Beers, Jr. & Edward G. Bassett. LC 75-25108. (Miles International Symposium Ser.: No.9). 1976. 49.50 (ISBN 0-89004-091-5). Raven.

Cell Membranes & Ion Transport. J. L. Hall & D. A. Baker. (Integrated Themes in Biology Ser.). (Illus.). 1978. pap. text ed. 10.50x (ISBN 0-582-44192-7). Longman.

Cell Movement & Neoplasia: Proceedings of the Annual Meeting of the Cell Tissue & Organ Culture Study Group, Held at the Janssen Research Foundation, Beerse, Belgium, May 1979. Ed. by M. De Brabander et al. (Illus.). 174p. 1980. 35.00 (ISBN 0-08-025534-5). Pergamon.

Cell Nucleus: Metabolism & Radiosensitivity. Ed. by H. M. Klouwen et al. 1966. pap. text ed. 17.95x (ISBN 0-685-83716-5). Intl Ideas.

Cell Nucleus: Nuclear Particles, Vol. 8. Ed. by Harris Busch. 1981. write for info. (ISBN 0-12-147608-1). Acad Pr.

Cell Physiology: Molecular Dynamics. Henry Tedeschi. 1974. 23.50 (ISBN 0-12-685150-6). Acad Pr.

Cell Populations. E. Reid. LC 79-40729. (Methodological Surveys in Biochemistry Ser.: Vol. 8). 1979. 59.95x (ISBN 0-470-26809-3). Halsted Pr.

Cell Potassium. Roderick P. Kernan. LC 80-133320. (Transport in the Life Sciences Ser.). 1980. 32.50 (ISBN 0-471-04806-2, Pub. by Wiley-Interscience). Wiley.

Cell Structure & Function. A. T. Varute & K. S. Bhatia. 1976. 15.00 (ISBN 0-7069-0461-3, Pub. by Vikas India). Advent Bk.

Cell Surface, Vol. IV. Ed. by Peter Knox. (Biochemistry of Cellular Regulation). 304p. 1981. 69.95 (ISBN 0-8493-5457-9). CRC Pr.

Cell Surface Carbohydrates & Biological Recognition: Proceedings of the ICN-UCLA Symposium Held at Keystone, Col., Feb. 1977. Ed. by Vincent T. Marchesi et al. LC 78-417. 690p. 1978. 76.00 (ISBN 0-8451-0023-8). A R Liss.

Cell Surface in Development. Ed. by Aron Moscona. LC 74-7308. 1974. 48.95 (ISBN 0-471-61855-1, Pub. by Wiley Medical). Wiley.

Cell Surface Labeling. Robert P. Becker & Om Johari. (Illus.). 100p. 1979. pap. text ed. 10.00 (ISBN 0-931288-07-X). Scanning Electron.

Cell Surface Receptors: Proceedings. ICN-UCLA Conference, Squaw Valley, Calif., March 2-7, 1975. Ed. by Garth L. Nicolson et al. LC 76-8160. (Progress in Clinical & Biological Research: Vol. 8). 1976. 49.00x (ISBN 0-8451-0008-4). A R Liss.

Cell Survival After Low Doses of Radiation: Theoretical & Clinical Implications. T. Alper. LC 75-25578. (Sixth L. H. Gray Memorial Conference). 1975. 63.00 o.p. (ISBN 0-471-02513-5, Pub. by Wiley-Interscience). Wiley.

Cell System of Production. David Jackson. 170p. 1978. text ed. 23.50x (ISBN 0-220-66345-9, Pub. by Busn Bks England). Renouf.

Cell Three Fifty. Francisco V. Gorga. LC 73-93096. (Stories That Win Ser.). 1974. pap. 0.95 o.p. (ISBN 0-8163-0130-1, 03075-9). Pacific Pr Pub Assn.

Cell: Three Tales of Horror. David Case. 1969. 5.00 o.p. (ISBN 0-8090-3383-6). Hill & Wang.

Cell, Tissue & Organ Cultures in Neurobiology. Ed. by S. Fedoroff & Leif Hertz. 1978. 40.50 (ISBN 0-12-250450-X). Acad Pr.

Cell Wall Biochemistry Related to Specificity in Host-Plant Pathogen Interactions. B. Solheim. 1977. pap. 43.00x (ISBN 82-00-05141-2, Dist. by Columbia U Pr). Universitet.

Cellar. Richard Laymon. (Orig.). 1980. pap. 2.25 (ISBN 0-446-92246-3). Warner Bks.

Cellars & Attics. Michele Brailow. 48p. 1981. 6.95 (ISBN 0-87881-099-4). Mojave Bks.

Cellars of the Dead. Marilyn Ross. (Stewarts of Stormhaven Ser.: No. 2). 1976. pap. 1.25 o.p. (ISBN 0-445-00410-X). Popular Lib.

Cellist Music. Gregor Piatagorsky. 1979. Repr. of 1965 ed. 27.50 (ISBN 0-306-70822-1). Da Capo.

Cello. Elizabeth Cowling. 1977. pap. 4.95 o.p. (ISBN 0-684-14784-X, ScribT). Scribner.

Cells. Michael W. Berns. LC 77-2815. 163p. 1977. pap. text ed. 5.50 (ISBN 0-03-013456-0, HoltC). HR&W.

Cells & Tissues in Culture: Methods, Biology, & Physiology, 3 Vols. E. N. Willmer. 1965-1967. Vol. 1. 98.00, by subscription 69.00 (ISBN 0-12-757601-0); Vol. 2. 98.00, by subscription 69.00 (ISBN 0-12-757602-9); Vol. 3. 98.00, by subscription 69.00 (ISBN 0-12-757603-7). Acad Pr.

Cells & Tissues of the Immune System: Structure, Functions, Interactions. Leon Weiss. (Foundations of Immunology Ser). (Illus.). 1972. ref. ed. 22.95x (ISBN 0-13-121772-0). P-H.

Cells into Organs: The Forces That Shape the Embryo. J. P. Trinkaus. 1969. pap. 11.95x ref. ed. (ISBN 0-13-121640-6). P-H.

Cellular Analogues of Conditioning & Neural Plasticity: Proceedings of a Satellite Symposium of the 28th International Congress of Physiological Sciences, Szeged, Hungary, 1980. Ed. by O. Feher & F. Joo. LC 80-41992. (Advances in Physiological Sciences: Vol. 36). (Illus.). 300p. 1981. 40.00 (ISBN 0-08-027372-6). Pergamon.

Cellular & Molecular Bases of Neuroendocrine Processes. Endroczi. 1976. 41.50 (ISBN 0-9960007-1-2, Pub. by Kaido Hungary). Heyden.

Cellular & Molecular Bases of Neuroendoctrine Processes: Proceedings. Symposium of the International Society of Psychoneuroendocrinology Visgrad, Hungary, Dec. 1975 & E Endroczi. 1977. 40.00x (ISBN 0-8002-0436-0). Intl Pubns Serv.

Cellular & Molecular Laboratory Manual. Charlene A. Jope. 64p. 1981. pap. text ed. 5.95 (ISBN 0-8403-2353-0). Kendall-Hunt.

Cellular & Molecular Regulation of Hemoglobin Switching. Ed. by G. Stamatoyannopoulos & A. Nienhuis. 1979. 68.50 (ISBN 0-686-63983-9). Grune.

Cellular & Organismal Biology: Readings from Scientific American. Intro. by Donald Kennedy. LC 74-775. (Illus.). 1974. text ed. 19.95x (ISBN 0-7167-0894-9); pap. text ed. 9.95x (ISBN 0-7167-0893-0). W H Freeman.

Cellular Aspects of Neural Growth & Differentiation. Ed. by Daniel C. Pease. LC 73-126760. (UCLA Forum in Medical Sciences: No. 14). (Illus.). 1971. 50.00x (ISBN 0-520-01793-5). U of Cal Pr.

Cellular Basis & Aetiology of Late Somatic Effects of Ionizing Radiations: Proceedings. Ed. by Robert J. Harris. 1962. 50.00 (ISBN 0-12-327174-6). Acad Pr.

Cellular Basis of Behavior: An Introduction to Behavioral Neurobiology. Eric R. Kandel. LC 76-8277. (Psychology Ser.). (Illus.). 1976. text ed. 56.00x (ISBN 0-7167-0523-0); pap. text ed. 27.95x (ISBN 0-7167-0522-2). W H Freeman.

Cellular Basis of the Immune Response: An Approach to Immunobiology. Edward S Golub. LC 77-3728. (Illus.). 1977. pap. text ed. 12.00x (ISBN 0-87893-210-0). Sinauer Assoc.

Cellular Basis of the Immune Response. rev. & 2nd ed. Edward S. Golub. LC 80-28080. (Illus.). 325p. 1981. pap. text ed. price not set (ISBN 0-87893-212-7). Sinauer Assoc.

Cellular Biochemistry & Physiology. N. A. Edwards & K. A. Hassall. 1972. text ed. 19.95 o.p. (ISBN 0-07-094136-X, C). McGraw.

Cellular Defence Reactions of Insects. George Salt. LC 71-118067. (Monographs in Experimental Biology: No. 16). (Illus.). 1970. 24.95 (ISBN 0-521-07936-5). Cambridge U Pr.

Cellular Immunology, 2 bks. in 1. F. Macfarlane Burnet. LC 69-12162. (Illus.). 1969. 74.50 (ISBN 0-521-07217-4). Cambridge U Pr.

Cellular Pathology. Brewer. (Postgraduate Pathology Ser.). 1981. price not set (ISBN 0-407-00050-X). Butterworths. Postponed.

Cellular Pharmacology of Excitable Tissues. Toshio Narahashi. (Illus.). 552p. 1975. 47.50 (ISBN 0-398-03358-7). C C Thomas.

Cellular Plastics. Advisory Board on Military Personnel Supplies. 1967. 13.00 o.p. (ISBN 0-309-01462-X). Natl Acad Pr.

Cellular Radiobiology. T. Alper. LC 78-68331. (Illus.). 1979. 47.50 (ISBN 0-521-22411-X); pap. 14.95x (ISBN 0-521-29479-7). Cambridge U Pr.

Cellular Selection & Regulation in the Immune Response. Ed. by Gerald M. Edelman. LC 73-93857. (Society of General Physiologists Ser.: Vol. 29). 1974. 34.50 (ISBN 0-911216-71-5). Raven.

Cellulite: Defeat It Through Diet & Exercise. Beverly Cox & George Benois. (Illus.). 192p. 1981. 12.50 (ISBN 0-8149-0845-4); pap. 9.95 (ISBN 0-8149-0846-2). Vanguard.

Celluloid Closet: Homosexuality in the Movies. Vito Russo. LC 79-1682. (Illus.). 256p. 1981. 15.00 (ISBN 0-06-013704-5, HarpT). Har-Row.

Celluloid Closet: Homosexuality in the Movies. Vito Russo. LC 79-1682. (Illus.). 256p. 1981. pap. 7.95 (ISBN 0-06-090871-8, CN). Har-Row.

Celluloid Literature: Film in the Humanities. 2nd ed. William Jinks. LC 73-7361. (Illus.). 208p. 1974. pap. text ed. 6.95x (ISBN 0-02-474910-9, 47490). Macmillan.

Cellulose & Cellulose Derivatives, Vol. 5, Pts. 4 & 5. N. M. Bikales & L. Segal. 1411p. 1971. Set. 130.00 (ISBN 0-471-39038-0). Wiley.

Celsius Thermometer. Jerolyn Nentle. LC 76-24205. (Metrics America Ser.). (gr. 4). 1976. 5.95 (ISBN 0-913940-48-8). Crestwood Hse.

Celtic: A Comparative Study. Douglas B. Gregor. (Language & Literature Ser.). 1980. 36.00 (ISBN 0-900891-41-6). Oleander Pr.

Celtic & Anglo-Saxon Painting: Book Illumination in the British Isles 600-800. Carl Nordenfalk. 1977. 19.95 (ISBN 0-8076-0825-4); pap. 9.95 (ISBN 0-8076-0826-2). Braziller.

Celtic Art: The Methods of Construction. George Bain. (Illus.). 160p. 1973. pap. 5.00 (ISBN 0-486-22923-8). Dover.

Celtic Britain in the Early Middle Ages: Studies in Scottish & Welsh Sources. Kathleen Hughes. Ed. by David Dumville. (Studies in Celtic History). 123p. 1980. 35.00x (ISBN 0-8476-6771-5). Rowman.

Celtic Craftsmanship in Bronze. H. E. Kilbride-Jones. LC 80-10520. (Illus.). 320p. 1980. 35.00 (ISBN 0-312-12698-0). St Martin.

Celtic Dragon Myth. J. F. Campbell & George Henderson. (Newcastle Mythology Library: Vol. 4). 1981. pap. 5.95 (ISBN 0-87877-048-8). Newcastle Pub.

Celtic Dragon Myth. George Henderson. (Newcastle Mythology Library: Vol. 4). 160p. 1981. Repr. lib. bdg. 12.95 (ISBN 0-89370-648-5). Borgo Pr.

Celtic Heart. Eileen Sherman. LC 80-50889. 328p. (YA) 1980. 12.95 (ISBN 0-9604382-0-3); pap. 4.00. Resolute Pr.

Celtic Heritage: Ancient Tradition in Ireland & Wales. Alwyn Rees & Brinley Rees. (Illus.). 1977. pap. 8.95 (ISBN 0-500-27039-2). Thames Hudson.

Celtic Myth & Legend, Poetry & Romance. Charles Squire. LC 80-53343. (Newcastle Mythology Library: Vol. 1). 450p. 1980. Repr. of 1975 ed. lib. bdg. 12.95x (ISBN 0-89370-630-2). Borgo Pr.

Celtic Quest: Soul & Sexuality in Individuation. John Layard. (Seminar Ser.). 220p. 1975. 12.00 o.p. (ISBN 0-88214-110-4). Spring Pubns.

Celtic Researches, on the Origin, Traditions & Language, of the Ancient Britons. Edward Davies. Ed. by Burton Feldman & Robert D. Richardson. LC 78-60902. (Myth & Romanticism Ser.: Vol. 8). (Illus.). 1979. lib. bdg. 66.00 (ISBN 0-8240-3557-7). Garland Pub.

Celtic Way of Life. Ed. by Agnes McMahon & Curriculm Development Unit Dublin Vocation Ed. Comm. (Illus.). 1977. pap. text ed. 4.95 (ISBN 0-905140-16-8). Irish Bk Ctr.

Celts. Robin Place & Anne Ross. LC 77-86183. (Peoples of the Past Ser.). (Illus.). 1977. lib. bdg. 7.95 (ISBN 0-686-51155-7). Silver.

Celts. Duncan N. Taylor. LC 74-17779. (Emergence of Man Ser.). (gr. 6 up). 1974. PLB 9.63 o.p. (ISBN 0-8094-1286-1, Pub. by Time-Life). Silver.

Cement & Concrete Terminology. ACI Committee 116. 1967. pap. 11.25 (ISBN 0-685-85102-8, SP-19) (ISBN 0-685-85103-6). ACI.

Cement & Concrete Thesaurus. 1969. pap. 12.95 (ISBN 0-685-85158-3, CCT). ACI.

Cement & Mortar Technology & Additives: Developments Since 1977. Ed. by M. H. Gutcho. LC 80-19343. (Chemical Tech. Rev. 173). 540p. (Orig.). 1981. 54.00 (ISBN 0-8155-0822-0). Noyes.

Cement Industry: 1796-1914. Francis. 1978. 25.00 (ISBN 0-7153-7386-2). David & Charles.

Cemetery Box. Don Mitchell & Gary Grimm. (gr. 3-8). 1976. 10.95 (ISBN 0-916456-01-3, GA62). Good Apple.

Cenci. Percy B. Shelley. Ed. by Roland A. Duerksen. (Library of Liberal Arts Ser). 1970. 6.95 o.p. (ISBN 0-672-51322-6, LLA170); pap. 3.80 o.p. (ISBN 0-672-60398-5). Bobbs.

Cendrillon (Cinderella) Levater. Date not set. 12.95 (ISBN 0-8120-5311-7). Barron. Postponed.

Cenerentola: Rossini. Gossett et al. Tr. by Arthur Jacobs. 1980. pap. 4.95 (ISBN 0-7145-3819-1). Riverrun NY.

Cenodoxus. Jacob Bidermann. Tr. by D. G. Dyer & Cecily Longrigg. LC 74-15527. (Edinburgh Bilingual Library: No. 9). 203p. 1976. 9.50x (ISBN 0-292-71027-5); pap. 4.95x (ISBN 0-292-71028-3). U of Tex Pr.

Cenozoic Era. C. Pomerol. 280p. 1981. 74.95 (ISBN 0-470-27140-X). Halsted Pr.

Censor Marches on. M. L. Ernst & A. Lindey. LC 73-164512. (Civil Liberties in American History Ser.). 346p. 1971. Repr. of 1940 ed. lib. bdg. 32.50 (ISBN 0-306-70295-9). Da Capo.

Censors in the Classroom: The Mind Benders. Edward B. Jenkinson. LC 79-17417. 206p. 1979. 13.95 (ISBN 0-8093-0929-7). S Ill U Pr.

Censorship & the Media: Mixed Blessing or Dangerous Threat. Fred R. Czarra & Joseph F. Heaps. Ed. by Jack R. Fraenkel. (Crucial Issues in American Government Ser.). (gr. 9-12). 1977. pap. text ed. 4.96 (ISBN 0-205-04910-9, 764910X). Allyn.

Censorship in America. Olga G. Hoyt & Edwin P. Hoyt. LC 73-125833. (gr. 6 up). 1970. 6.95 o.p. (ISBN 0-8164-3013-6, Clarion). HM.

Censorship in Russia, Eighteen Sixty-Five to Nineteen Five. Daniel Balmuth. LC 79-52510. 1979. pap. text ed. 10.50 (ISBN 0-8191-0773-5). U Pr of Amer.

Censorship in the United States. Ed. by Grant S. McClellan. (Reference Shelf Ser: Vol. 39, No. 3). 1967. 6.25 (ISBN 0-8242-0096-9). Wilson.

Censorship Nineteen Seventeen. James R. Mock. LC 74-37864. (Civil Liberties in American History Ser). 250p. 1972. Repr. of 1941 ed. lib. bdg. 25.00 (ISBN 0-306-70436-6). Da Capo.

Censorship of English Drama, 1824-1901. J. R. Stephens. LC 79-41601. (Illus.). 230p. Date not set. 39.50 (ISBN 0-521-23021-7). Cambridge U Pr.

Censorship of the Movies: The Social & Political Control of a Mass Medium. Richard S. Randall. LC 68-14035. 1968. 22.50 (ISBN 0-299-04731-8); pap. 6.95x (ISBN 0-299-04734-2). U. of Wis Pr.

Censorship: The Irish Experience. Michael Adams. 265p. 1968. 15.00x (ISBN 0-686-28344-9, Pub. by Irish Academic Pr). Biblio Dist.

Censos de Poblacion: Temas, Definiciones, Classificaciones & Cuestionarios Utilizados Por los Paises de la Region Americana. (Illus.). 1977. pap. text ed. 8.00 o.p. (ISBN 0-685-82130-7). OAS.

Census. Madelyn K. Anderson. LC 79-67813. (Illus.). (gr. 4-7). 1980. 7.95 (ISBN 0-8149-0824-1). Vanguard.

Census Catalogue of World Members of the Bolbitiaceae. Roy Watling & Norma Gregory. (Bibliotheca Mycologica). 300p. 1981. lib. bdg. 40.00x (ISBN 3-7682-1279-3, Pub. by Cramer Germany). Lubrecht & Cramer.

Census, U. S. A. Fact Finding for the American People, 1790-1970. Ann H. Scott. LC 68-24734. (Illus.). (YA) (gr. 9 up). 1968. 8.95 (ISBN 0-395-28924-6, Clarion). HM.

Centaurs of Many Lands. Edward L. Tinker. (Illus.). 5.25 (ISBN 0-85131-072-9, Dist. by Sporting Book Center). J A Allen.

Centenary Tribute Sir Alfred Munnings 1878-1959: An Appreciation of the Artist & a Selection of His Paintings. Stanley Booth. (Illus.). 218p. 1978. 120.00 (ISBN 0-85667-043-X, Pub. by Sotheby Parke Bernet England). Biblio Dist.

Centenary Tribute to John Millington Synge 1871-1909: Sunshine & the Moon's Delight. Ed. by S. B. Bushrui. 1972-1978. pap. text ed. 6.00x (ISBN 0-391-00854-4). Humanities.

Centennial Ball. Lee S. Teller. (Historical Romance). 368p. (Orig.). 1981. pap. 2.75 (ISBN 0-515-05864-5). Jove Pubns.

Centennial History of Graham. Young County Historical Survey Committee. 7.95 o.p. (ISBN 0-685-48797-0). Nortex Pr.

Centennial History of the American Society of Mechanical Engineers: 1880-1980. Bruce Sinclair. 256p. 1980. text ed. 15.00 (H0175H); pap. text ed. 10.00 (H0175P). ASME.

Centennial of Life & Faith in Del Norte Country (Cal.) 1854-1954. (Illus.). 1954. pap. 3.00 (ISBN 0-918634-25-3). D M Chase.

Centennial of the Sheffield Scientific School (Yale University) Ed. by George A. Baitsell. 1950. 32.50x (ISBN 0-686-51350-9). Elliots Bks.

Center for International Affairs, Harvard University: The Politics of Participation & Control. Henry Bienen. LC 73-2461. 192p. 1974. 14.00x (ISBN 0-691-03096-0); pap. 4.95 o.p. (ISBN 0-691-00022-0). Princeton U Pr.

Center of Attention. Daniel Hoffman. 96p. Date not set. pap. 1.95 (ISBN 0-394-71988-3, Vin). Random.

Center Stage: An Anthology of 21 Contemporary Black American Plays. Ed. by Eileen J. Ostrow. LC 80-53143. (Illus.). 352p. (Orig.). 1981. pap. price not set. Sea Urchin.

Centerbeam. Otto Piene et al. (Illus.). 1980. pap. 15.00 (ISBN 0-262-66047-4). MIT Pr.

Centered Teacher: Awareness Activities for Teachers & Their Students. Gay Hendricks. (Transformation Ser.). 192p. 1981. 9.95 (ISBN 0-13-122234-1, Spec); pap. 4.95 (ISBN 0-13-122226-0). P-H.

Centering Book: Awareness Activities for Children, Parents & Teachers. C. G. Hendricks & Russell Wills. (Transpersonal Bks.). (Illus.). 192p. 1975. 11.95 (ISBN 0-13-122192-2, Spec); pap. 4.95 (ISBN 0-13-122184-1, Spec). P-H.

Centering in Pottery, Poetry, & the Person. Mary C. Richards. LC 64-22372. 1969. pap. 6.95 (ISBN 0-8195-6011-1, Pub. by Wesleyan U Pr). Columbia U Pr.

Centering Moment. Howard Thurman. LC 80-67469. 1980. pap. 3.95 (ISBN 0-913408-64-6). Friends United.

Centering: Your Guide to Inner Growth. Sanders Laurie et al. 1978. 2.25 (ISBN 0-446-82750-9). Inner Tradit.

Centerman from Quebec. Sheldon Ilowite. (Illus.). 128p. (gr. 4-7). 1972. 5.95g (ISBN 0-8038-1174-8). Hastings.

Centers. Robert Armstrong. (Stars of the NBA Ser.). (Illus.). (gr. 4-12). 1977. PLB 7.50 o.p. (ISBN 0-87191-565-0). Creative Ed.

Centers of Learning: Britain, France, Germany, United States. Carnegie Commission on Higher Education & Joseph Ben-David. LC 76-45798. (Illus.). 1977. 15.95 o.p. (ISBN 0-07-010133-7). McGraw.

Centinel: Warnings of a Revolution. Ed. by Elizabeth I. Nybakken. LC 77-92570. 240p. 1980. 19.50 (ISBN 0-87413-141-3). U Delaware Pr.

Centrafugal Pump Clinic. Karasik. 488p. 1981. 39.50 (ISBN 0-8247-1016-9). Dekker.

Central Action of Drugs in the Regulation of Blood Pressure. Ed. by D. Davies. (Illus.). 1976. 39.50 (ISBN 0-8391-0800-1). Univ Park.

Central Administration in Nigeria, Nineteen Fourteen to Nineteen Fifty-One: The Problem of Polarity. Jeremy J. White. 250p. 1981. 39.00x (ISBN 0-686-28430-5, Pub. by Irish Academic Pr Ireland). Biblio Dist.

Central Adrenaline Neurons: Basic Aspects & Their Role in Cardiovascular Disease: Proceedings of an International Symposium 27-28 August 1979, Wenner-Gren Center, Stockholm. Ed. by Kjell Fuxe et al. (Wenner-Gren Ser.: Vol. 33). (Illus.). 356p. 1980. 53.00 (ISBN 0-08-025927-8). Pergamon.

Central Air Conditioning Service. Ed. by A. Ross Sabin. (Illus.). 218p. (gr. 11). 1974. 20.00 (ISBN 0-938336-03-7). Whirlpool.

Central America Guide. Cliff Cross. LC 72-15593. 1974. pap. 4.95 o.p. (ISBN 0-912656-37-9). H P Bks.

Central American Jungles. Don Moser. (American Wilderness Ser.). (Illus.). 1975. 12.95 (ISBN 0-8094-1342-6). Time-Life.

Central American Jungles. Don Moser. LC 75-14284. (American Wilderness). (Illus.). (gr. 6 up). 1975. PLB 11.97 (ISBN 0-8094-1343-4, Pub. by Time-Life). Silver.

Central & Peripheral Regulation of Prolactin Function. Ed. by Robert MacLeod & Umberto Scapagnini. 424p. 1980. text ed. 39.00 (ISBN 0-89004-489-9). Raven.

Central Asia. Ed. by Edward Allworth. LC 66-16288. (Illus.). 1967. 27.00x (ISBN 0-231-02695-1). Columbia U Pr.

Central Asia. Alexandr Belenitsky. Tr. by James Hogarth from Rus. (Archaeologia Mundi Ser.). 256p. 1968. 29.50 (ISBN 0-88254-147-1). Hippocrene Bks.

Central Asia. Ed. by Gavin Hambly. (World History Ser). 1970. 9.95 o.p. (ISBN 0-440-01219-8). Delacorte.

Central Asians Under Russian Rule: A Study in Cultural Change. Elizabeth Bacon. LC 66-16739. (Cornell Paperback Ser.). (Illus.). 291p. 1980. pap. 5.95 (ISBN 0-8014-9211-4). Cornell U Pr.

Central Auditory & Language Disorders in Children. Ed. by Robert W. Keith. (Illus.). 264p. 1981. text ed. 29.00 (ISBN 0-933014-61-9). College-Hill.

Central Axis Depth Dose Data for Use in Radiotherapy. Ed. by M. Cohen et al. 1980. 25.00x (Pub. by Brit Inst Radiology England). State Mutual Bk.

Central Banking. 4th ed. M. H. DeKock. LC 74-78896. 318p. 1974. 25.00 (ISBN 0-312-12740-5). St Martin.

Central Cholinergic Systems & Behavior. F. V. De Feudis. 1975. 32.50 (ISBN 0-12-208750-X). Acad Pr.

Central City - Spread City: The Metropolitan Regions Where More & More of Us Spend Our Lives. Alvin Schwartz. LC 72-81068. (Illus.). 160p. (gr. 5-9). 1973. PLB 4.95 o.s.i. (ISBN 0-02-781320-7). Macmillan.

Central City Malls. Harvey M. Rubenstein. LC 78-7536. 1978. 27.50 (ISBN 0-471-03098-8, Pub. by Wiley-Interscience). Wiley.

Central Edinburgh & Royal Mile Visitors Map. Alan Hamilton. 1977. pap. 4.50 (ISBN 0-8277-5357-8). British Bk Ctr.

Central Eskimo. Franz Boas. LC 64-63593. (Illus.). 1964. pap. 3.75 (ISBN 0-8032-5016-9, BB 196, Bison). U of Nebr Pr.

Central Heating. John Bowyer. LC 76-40808. (Illus.). 1977. 13.50 (ISBN 0-7153-7037-5). David & Charles.

Central Heating with Wood & Coal. Larry Gay. (Illus.). 128p. 1980. write for info. (ISBN 0-8289-0419-7); pap. write for info. (ISBN 0-8289-0420-0). Greene.

Central Ideas in Sociology: An Introduction. David Berry. 185p. 1975. pap. text ed. 5.95 o.p. (ISBN 0-87581-181-7). Peacock Pubs.

Central Limit Theorem for Real & Banach Valued-Random Variables. Aloisio Araujo & Evarist Gine. (Ser. in Probability & Mathematical Statistics). 1980. 26.95 (ISBN 0-471-05304-X, Pub. by Wiley-Interscience). Wiley.

Central Mechanisms of Anorectic Drugs. Ed. by S. Garattini & R. Samanin. LC 77-17749. (Monographs of the Mario Negri Institute for Pharmacological Research). 1978. 40.00 (ISBN 0-89004-219-5). Raven.

Central Nervous Control Mechanisms in Breathing--Physiological & Clinical Aspects of Regular, Periodic & Irregular Breathing in Adults & in the Perinatal Period: Proceedings of the International Symposium Held at the Wenner-Gren Center, Stockholm, Sweden, Sept. 4-6, 1978. Ed. by C. Von Euler & H. Lagercrantz. (Wenne-Gren International Symposium Ser.: Vol. 32). (Illus.). 1979. 82.00 (ISBN 0-08-024942-6). Pergamon.

Central Nervous System. Kenneth M. Earle & Lucien J. Rubinstein. (Anatomic Pathology Seminars). (Illus.). 1976. atlas slides 55.00 (ISBN 0-89189-052-1, 15-1-015-00); proceedings 5.00 (ISBN 0-89189-003-3, 50-1-040-00). Am Soc Clinical.

Central Nervous System Effects of Hypothalamic Hormones. Ed. by Robert Collu et al. LC 77-94310. 1978. text ed. 41.00 (ISBN 0-89004-347-7). Raven.

Central Nervous System Mechanisms in Hypertension. Ed. by Joseph P. Buckley & Carlos Ferrario. 425p. 1981. 39.95 (ISBN 0-89004-545-3). Raven.

Central Neurotransmitter Turnover. Ed. by C. J. Pycock & P. V. Taberner. 200p. 1980. 30.00x (Pub. by Croom Helm England). State Mutual Bk.

Central North Atlantic Ocean Basin & Continental Margins: Geology, Geophysics, Geochemistry, & Resources, Including the Trans-Atlantic Geotraverse (TAG) Peter A. Rona. (Illus.). 99p. 1980. pap. 45.00 (ISBN 0-08-026259-7). Pergamon.

Central Place Theory: A Reinterpretation. K. S. Beavon. LC 76-42282. (Illus.). 1977. text ed. 16.95x (ISBN 0-582-48678-5); pap. text ed. 12.95x (ISBN 0-582-48683-1). Longman.

Central Problems in Social Theory: Action, Structure & Contradiction in Social Analysis. Anthony Giddens. 1979. 23.75x (ISBN 0-520-03972-6); Campus No. 241. pap. 8.95x (ISBN 0-520-03975-0). U of Cal Pr.

Central Self: A Study in Romantic & Victorian Imagination. Patricia M. Ball. 1968. text ed. 23.50x (ISBN 0-485-11102-0, Athlone Pr). Humanities.

Central Society of Education: 1837-1839, 3 vols. (First Ser. in the Social History of Education Ser.: No. 3). 1968. Repr. of 1837 ed. Set. 82.50x (ISBN 0-7130-0002-3, Pub. by Woburn Pr England); 27.50x ea.; Vol. 1. (ISBN 0-7130-0002-3); Vol. 2. (ISBN 0-7130-0003-1); Vol. 3. (ISBN 0-7130-0004-X). Biblio Dist.

Centralia Case: Three Views of the Armistice Day Tragedy at Centralia, Washington, November 11, 1919. R. Chaplin et al. LC 77-160845. (Civil Liberties in American History Ser). 1971. Repr. of 1924 ed. lib. bdg. 29.50 (ISBN 0-306-70211-8). Da Capo.

Centralised Legislation-Legislative System of British India 1834-1861. S. V. Desika Char. 9.00x o.p. (ISBN 0-210-34010-X). Asia.

Centralization vs. Decentralization in Organizing the Controller's Department. Herbert A. Simon et al. LC 77-90343. 1978. Repr. of 1954 ed. text ed. 10.00 (ISBN 0-914348-24-8). Scholars Bk.

Centralized Book Processing: A Feasibility Study Based on Colorado Academic Libraries. Lawrence E. Leonard et al. LC 77-4903. 1969. 13.50 (ISBN 0-8108-0263-5). Scarecrow.

Centralized Processing for Academic Libraries. Richard M. Dougherty & Joan M. Maier. LC 73-155716. 1971. 16.50 (ISBN 0-8108-0381-X). Scarecrow.

Centre & Periphery: Spatial Variation in Politics. Ed. by Jean Gottmann. LC 79-21564. (Sage Focus Editions: Vol. 19). 1980. 18.95x (ISBN 0-8039-1344-3); pap. 9.95x (ISBN 0-8039-1345-1). Sage.

Centre-State Relations in Agricultural Development. S. P. Singh. 1973. 15.00 (ISBN 0-7069-0182-7, Pub. by Vikas India). Advent Bk.

Centrifugal Analysers in Clinical Chemistry. Ed. by Christopher P. Price & Kevin Spencer. 520p. 1980. 59.95 (ISBN 0-03-058854-5). Praeger.

Centrifugal & Axial Flow Pumps: Theory, Design & Application. 2nd ed. A. J. Stepanoff. LC 57-10815. 462p. 1957. 36.50 (ISBN 0-471-82137-3, Pub. by Wiley-Interscience). Wiley.

Centrifugal Model Testing of Waste-Heap Embankment. Yu N. Malushitsky. Ed. by A. N. Schofield. LC 78-67431. (Illus.). Date not set. price not set (ISBN 0-521-22423-3). Cambridge U Pr.

Centrifugal Pump Problems. S. Yedidiah. 232p. 1980. 35.00 (ISBN 0-87814-131-6). Pennwell Pub.

Centrifugal Seperations in Molecular & Cell Biology. G. D. Birnie & D. Rickwood. (Illus.). 1978. 29.95 (ISBN 0-408-70803-4). Butterworths.

Centrifugation: A Practical Approach. 224p. 16.00 (ISBN 0-904147-10-X); pap. 9.00 (ISBN 0-904147-11-8). Info Retrieval.

Centrist. Bea Clark. 1981. 6.50 (ISBN 0-8062-1577-1). Carlton.

Century. Fred M. Stewart. LC 80-22417. 576p. 1981. 13.95 (ISBN 0-688-00398-2). Morrow.

Century of American Diplomacy. John W. Foster. LC 79-87542. (American History, Politics & Law Ser). 1970. Repr. of 1900 ed. lib. bdg. 45.00 (ISBN 0-306-71458-2). Da Capo.

Century of American Sculpture: Treasures from Brookgreen Gardens. Intro. by A. Hyatt Mayor. (Illus.). 128p. 1981. 29.95 (ISBN 0-89659-185-9); pap. 16.95 (ISBN 0-89659-150-6). Abbeville Pr.

Century of Australian Short Stories. Ed. by C. Hadgraft & R. Wilson. 1964. pap. text ed. 4.50x o.p. (ISBN 0-686-65313-0). Heinemann Ed.

Century of Ballads. John Ashton. LC 67-23925. 1968. Repr. of 1887 ed. 18.00 (ISBN 0-8103-3406-2). Gale.

Century of Bank Rate. Ralph G. Hawtrey. Repr. of 1939 ed. 22.50x (ISBN 0-678-05175-5). Kelley.

Century of Cameras. rev. ed. Eaton S. Lothrop, Jr. 1981. pap. 12.95 (ISBN 0-87100-163-2). Morgan.

Century of Children's Books. Florence V. Barry. LC 68-23467. 18.00 (ISBN 0-8103-3472-0). Gale.

Century of Civil Rights. Milton R. Konvitz. LC 61-8988. 1967. pap. 6.00x (ISBN 0-231-08577-X). Columbia U Pr.

Century of Dishonor: The Early Crusade for Indian Reform. Helen H. Jackson. Ed. by Rolle. 8.00 (ISBN 0-8446-2298-2). Peter Smith.

Century of DNA. Franklin H. Portugal & Jack S. Cohen. (Illus.). 400p. 1980. 20.00 (ISBN 0-262-16067-6); pap. 6.95 (ISBN 0-262-16067-6). MIT Pr.

Century of Doctorates. Commission on Human Resources. LC 78-5644. 1978. pap. text ed. 10.50 (ISBN 0-309-02738-1). Natl Acad Pr.

Century of Dutch Manuscript Illumination. L. M. Delaisse. (California Studies in the History of Art: No. VI). (Illus.). 1968. 52.50x (ISBN 0-520-00315-2). U of Cal Pr.

Century of Entomology in the Pacific Northwest. Melville H. Hatch. (Illus.). 51p. 1949. pap. 5.00 (ISBN 0-295-73733-6). U of Wash Pr.

Century of Friedel-NCrafts Alkylations & Re-Arrangements. Roberts. Date not set. price not set (ISBN 0-8247-6433-1). Dekker.

Century of Growth: The Kachin Baptist Church of Burma. Herman Tegenfeldt. LC 74-4415. 540p. 1974. 10.95 (ISBN 0-87808-416-9). William Carey Lib.

Century of Healing Arts-Eighteen Fifty to Nineteen Fifty. Ed. by John W. Ripley & Robert W. Richmind. (Illus.). 176p. 1980. pap. 5.95. Shawnee County Hist.

Century of Indian Orchids. J. D. Hooker. (Calutta Royal Bot. Gard. Ser.). (Illus.). 1967. 100.00 (ISBN 3-7682-0464-2). Lubrecht & Cramer.

Century of Innovation: A History of European & American Theatre & Drama, 1870-1970. O. Brockett & R. Findlay. (Theater & Drama Ser.). 1973. 24.95 (ISBN 0-13-122747-5). P-H.

Century of Japanese Photography. Japan Photographers Association. (Illus.). 1981. 45.00 (ISBN 0-394-51232-4). Pantheon. Postponed.

Century of Law Reform: 1971-1978. LC 71-181888. ix, 431p. 1979. Repr. of 1901 ed. text ed. 22.50x (ISBN 0-8377-2005-2). Rothman.

Century of Light. James A. Cox. LC 78-19104. (Illus.). 1979. 17.50 (ISBN 0-87502-062-3). Larousse.

Century of Moral Philosophy. Donald Hudson. 1980. 18.95 (ISBN 0-312-12777-4). St Martin.

Century of Music-Making: The Lives of Josef & Rosina Lhevinne. Robert K. Wallace. LC 75-28908. (Illus.). 384p. 1976. 17.50x o.p. (ISBN 0-253-31330-9). Ind-U Pr.

Century of Parody & Imitation. Walter C. Jerrold & R. M. Leonard. LC 68-30585. 1968. Repr. of 1913 ed. 20.00 (ISBN 0-8103-3215-9). Gale.

Century of Portland Architecture. Thomas Vaughan & George A. McMath. (Illus.). 250p. 1981. pap. write for info. (ISBN 0-87595-005-1). Oreg Hist Soc.

Century of Protestant Theology. Alasdair I. Heron. LC 80-17409. (Orig.). 1980. pap. write for info. (ISBN 0-664-24346-0). Westminster.

Century of Psychical Research: The Continuing Doubts & Affirmations; Proceedings. International Conference, France, 1970. LC 73-153407. 1971. 7.00 (ISBN 0-912328-19-3). Parapsych Foun.

Century of Servitude: Pribilof Aleuts Under U. S. Rule. Dorothy K. Jones. LC 80-1407. 198p. 1980. lib. bdg. 17.75 (ISBN 0-8191-1348-4); pap. text ed. 9.00 (ISBN 0-8191-1349-2). U Pr of Amer.

Century of Soil Mechanics. Thomas Telford Editorial Staff, Ltd. 490p. 1980. 35.00x (ISBN 0-901948-15-2, Pub. by Telfor England). State Mutual Bk.

Century of Surgery: History of the American Surgical Association, 2 vols. Mark M. Ravitch. (Illus.). 1600p. 1981. Set. 195.00. Lippincott.

Century of the Detective. Jurgen Thorwald. LC 64-18296. (Helen & Kurt Wolff Bk). (Illus.). 1965. 12.50 o.p. (ISBN 0-15-116350-2). HarBraceJ.

Century of the English Novel. Cornelius Weygandt. 1980. Repr. of 1925 ed. write for info. (ISBN 0-89760-916-6). Telegraph Bks.

Century Readings in English Literature. 5th ed. Ed. by John W. Cunliffe et al. 1955. 35.00x (ISBN 0-89197-068-1); pap. text ed. 14.95x (ISBN 0-89197-694-9). Irvington.

Century Readings in the American Short Story. Ed. by Fred L. Pattee. 562p. 1980. Repr. of 1927 ed. lib. bdg. 40.00 (ISBN 0-89760-708-2). Telegraph Bks.

Cenzoic Geology of the Trans-Pecos Volcanic Field of Texas. Ed. by A. W. Walton & C. D. Henry. 202p. 1979. write for info. (GB 19). Bur Econ Geology.

Cephid Stem Borers of California (Hymenoptera: Cephidae) Woodrow W. Middlekauff. (Bulletin of the California Insect Survey: Vol. 11). 1969. pap. 5.00x (ISBN 0-520-09036-5). U of Cal Pr.

Ceramic & Graphic Fibers & Whiskers: A Survey of Technology. L. R. McCreight et al. (Refractory Materials Ser., Vol. 1). 1965. 41.00 (ISBN 0-12-482950-3). Acad Pr.

Ceramic Formulas: A Guide to Clay, Glaze, Enamel, Glass & Their Colours. John W. Conrad. 160p. 1973. 14.95 (ISBN 0-02-527610-7). Macmillan.

Ceramic Furniture & Silver Collectors' Glossary. Edwin A. Barber. LC 76-8172. (Architecture & Decorative Art Ser). 1967. Repr. of 1914 ed. 14.50 (ISBN 0-306-70967-8). Da Capo.

Ceramic Glazemaking. Richard Behrens. 3.95 (ISBN 0-934706-07-7). Prof Pubns Ohio.

Ceramic Glazes. 3rd ed. C. W. Parmelee. Ed. by Cameron G. Harman. LC 70-183371. 1973. 21.50 (ISBN 0-8436-0609-6). CBI Pub.

Ceramic Microstructures 1976: With Emphasis on Energy Related Applications. Ed. by Richard M. Fulrath. Joseph A. Pask. LC 77-5232. 1977. lib. bdg. 75.00x (ISBN 0-89158-307-6). Westview.

Ceramic Processing. Materials Advisory Board. (Illus.). 1968. 16.00 (ISBN 0-309-01576-6). Natl Acad Pr.

Ceramic Projects. Ed. by Thomas Sellers. 2.95 (ISBN 0-934706-08-5). Prof Pubns Ohio.

Ceramic Sequence in Colima: Capacha, an Early Phase. Isabel Kelly. (Anthropological Papers: No. 37). 1980. pap. text ed. 9.95x (ISBN 0-8165-0565-9). U of Ariz Pr.

Ceramics for the Archaeologist. Anna O. Shepard. (Illus.). 1980. pap. 11.00 (ISBN 0-87279-620-5, 609). Carnegie Inst.

Ceramics for the Artist Potter. Frederick H. Norton. 1956. 18.95 (ISBN 0-201-05300-4). A-W.

Ceramics, from Clay to Kiln. Harvey Weiss. LC 64-13583. (Beginning Artist's Library Ser.). (gr. 5-9). 1964. PLB 7.95 o.p. (ISBN 0-201-09153-4, A-W Childrens). A-W.

Ceramics from the World of Islam. Esin Atil. LC 73-92017. (Illus.). 225p. 1973. pap. 12.50x (ISBN 0-87474-217-X). Smithsonian.

Ceramics Handbook. Richard Hyman. (Illus.). 1977. 4.95 o.p. (ISBN 0-668-00347-2); pap. 2.50 o.p. (ISBN 0-668-04066-1). Arco.

Ceramics in America: Winterthur Conference Report 1972. Ed. by Ian M. Quimby. LC 72-96715. (Winterthur Conference Report). 350p. 1980. 12.50x (ISBN 0-8139-0870-1); pap. 6.95x (ISBN 0-8139-0476-5). U Pr of Va.

Ceramics in the Pacific Northwest: A History. LaMar Harrington. LC 78-4369. (Index of Art in the Pacific Northwest: No. 10). (Illus.). 128p. 1979. 15.95 (ISBN 0-295-95623-2). U of Wash Pr.

Ceramics, Mosaics, Stained Glass. Ed. by Saul Lapidus. 1977. 9.95 o.p. (ISBN 0-679-50761-2); pap. 6.95 o.p. (ISBN 0-679-50762-0). McKay.

Ceramics of Altar De Sacrificios. Richard E. Adams. LC 72-126638. (Peabody Museum Papers: Vol. 63, No. 1). 1971. pap. text ed. 25.00 (ISBN 0-87365-180-4). Peabody Harvard.

Ceramics of the Mosque of Rustem Pasha & the Environment of Change. Walter B. Denny. LC 76-23612. (Outstanding Dissertations in the Fine Arts Ser.). 1977. lib. bdg. 67.00x (ISBN 0-8240-2684-5). Garland Pub.

Ceramics, Step by Step. Jolyon Hofstead. (Step by Step Craft Ser). 1974. PLB 9.15 o.p. (ISBN 0-307-62001-8, Golden Pr); pap. 2.95 o.p. (ISBN 0-307-42001-9). Western Pub.

Ceratomorpha & Ancylopoda (Perissodactyla) from the Lower Eocene Paris Basin, France. D. E. Savage et al. (U. C. Publ. in Geological Sciences: Vol. 66). 1966. pap. 5.00x (ISBN 0-520-09167-1). U of Cal Pr.

Cerbral Arterial Spasm: Proceedings of Second International Workshop. Robert H. Wilkins. (Illus.). 706p. 1981. write for info. (ISBN 0-683-09086-0). Williams & Wilkins.

Cereal Technology. Samuel A. Matz. (Illus.). 1970. 26.50 o.p. (ISBN 0-87055-071-3). AVI.

Cereals in the United Kingdom. D. K. Britton. 1969. 104.00 o.p. (ISBN 0-08-013896-9). Pergamon.

Cerebellar Stimulation in Man. Ed. by I. S. Cooper. LC 77-76925. 1978. 28.00 (ISBN 0-89004-206-3). Raven.

Cerebellum, Posture & Cerebral Palsy. (Clinics in Developmental Medicine Ser. No. 8). 1962p. 1962. 5.00 o.p. (ISBN 0-685-24714-7). Lippincott.

Cereberal Cortex: Proceedings of a Neurosciences Research Program Colloquium. Ed. by F. O. Schmitt et al. (Illus.). 576p. 1981. text ed. 50.00x (ISBN 0-262-19189-X). MIT Pr.

Cerebral Death. 2nd ed. A. Earl Walker. LC 80-26410. (Illus.). 1981. text ed. 32.50 (ISBN 0-8067-2142-1). Urban & S.

Cerebral Degenerations in Childhood. Robert P. Sedgwick et al. 1975. spiral bdg. 12.00 (ISBN 0-87488-759-3). Med Exam.

Cerebral Hemodynamics in Man & Monkey: Some Considerations in Cerebrovascular Disease, Subarachnoid Hemorrhage, & Intracranial Pressure. Byron M. Bloor. (Illus.). 132p. 1981. 19.75 (ISBN 0-398-04066-4). C C Thomas.

Cerebral Hypoxia & Its Consequences. Ed. by Stanley Fahn et al. LC 78-57236. (Advances in Neurology Ser.: Vol. 26). 1979. text ed. 36.50 (ISBN 0-89004-296-9). Raven.

Cerebral Logic: Solving the Problem of Mind & Brain. Charles W. Needham. (Illus.). 232p. 1978. 23.50 (ISBN 0-398-03754-X). C C Thomas.

Cerebral Metabolism & Neural Function. Janet V. Passonneau & Richard A. Hawkins. (Illus.). 370p. 1980. lib. bdg. 57.00 (ISBN 0-683-06788-5). Williams & Wilkins.

Cerebral Microcirculation & Metabolism. Ed. by J. Cervos-Navarro & E. Fritschka. 1981. text ed. price not set (ISBN 0-89004-590-9). Raven.

Cerebral Palsied & Learning Disabled Children: A Handbook Guide to Treatment, Rehabilitation & Education. Nancy C. Marks. (Illus.). 424p. 1974. 23.75 (ISBN 0-398-02911-3). C C Thomas.

Cerebral Palsy. Daniel Boone. LC 76-190708. (Studies in Communicative Disorders Ser). 1972. text ed. 2.50 (ISBN 0-672-61290-9). Bobbs.

Cerebral Palsy. Sidney Keats. (Illus.). 384p. 1977. 18.75 (ISBN 0-398-00992-9). C C Thomas.

Cerebral Palsy: A Clinical & Neuropathological Study. (Clinics in Developmental Medicine Ser. No. 25). 134p. 1967. 5.00 o.p. (ISBN 0-685-24724-4). Lippincott.

Cerebral Palsy: A Developmental Disability. rev. 3rd ed. Ed. by William M. Cruickshank. LC 75-34275. 1976. text ed. 26.00x (ISBN 0-8156-2168-X). Syracuse U Pr.

Cerebral Palsy, Spina Bifida: No Cause for Life Long Handicap. Hildegard Winky-Lotz. (Illus.). 85p. Date not set. pap. 4.40 (ISBN 0-936112-04-2). Willyshe Pub. Postponed.

Cerebral Palsy-the Preschool Years: Diagnosis, Treatment & Planning. Eric Denhoff. 144p. 1968. pap. 14.75 photocopy ed. spiral (ISBN 0-398-00432-3). C C Thomas.

Cerebral Vasospasm. David J. Boullin. LC 79-40735. 1980. 51.75 (ISBN 0-471-27639-1, Pub. by Wiley-Interscience). Wiley.

Cerebral Vessel Wall. Ed. by H. Cervos-Navarro et al. LC 75-25110. 1976. 31.50 (ISBN 0-89004-071-0). Raven.

Cerebrovascular Diseases. Princeton Conferences on Cerebrovascular Diseases, 10th. Ed. by Peritz Scheinberg. LC 75-25125. 1976. 27.00 (ISBN 0-89004-095-8). Raven.

Cerebrovascular Disorders & Stroke. Ed. by Murray Goldstein et al. LC 78-62496. (Advances in Neurology Ser.: Vol. 25). 1979. text ed. 41.50 (ISBN 0-89004-294-2). Raven.

Ceremonial Chemistry: The Ritual Persecution of Drugs, Addicts, & Pushers. Szasz, Thomas S., M.D. LC 74-2834. 240p. 1975. pap. 2.95 o.p. (ISBN 0-385-06636-8, 1004, Anch). Doubleday.

Ceremonial Costume: Court, Civil & Civic Costume from Sixteen Sixty to the Present Day. Alan Mansfield. (Illus.). 304p. 1980. 36.00x (ISBN 0-389-20124-3). B&N.

Ceremonial Magic. Daniel Cohen. LC 78-20429. (Illus.). 160p. (gr. 7 up). 1979. 7.95 (ISBN 0-590-07466-0, Four Winds). Schol Bk Serv.

Ceremonial Ox of India: The Mithan in Nature, Culture, & History. Frederick J. Simoons & Elizabeth S. Simoons. LC 68-9023. (Illus.). 1968. 27.50x (ISBN 0-299-04980-9). U of Wis Pr.

Ceremonial Spirit Possession in Africa & Afro-America: Forms, Meanings & Functional Significance for Individuals & Social Groups. Sheila S. Walker. 179p. 1972. text ed. 31.00x (ISBN 90-040-3584-2). Humanities.

Ceremonial, Stories 1936-1940: The Collected Stories of Paul Goodman, Vol. 2. Paul Goodman. Ed. by Taylor Stoehr. 273p. 1978. 14.00 (ISBN 0-87685-354-8); deluxe ed. 25.00 (ISBN 0-87685-355-6); pap. 7.50 (ISBN 0-87685-353-X). Black Sparrow.

Ceremonies in Dark Old Men. Lonne Elder, 3rd. LC 70-87212. (Orig.). 1969. pap. 4.95 (ISBN 0-374-50792-9, N372). FS&G.

Ceremony in Lone Tree. Wright Morris. LC 60-7775. viii, 308p. 1973. pap. 3.25 (ISBN 0-8032-5782-1, BB 560, Bison). U of Nebr Pr.

Ceremony of the Innocent. Taylor Caldwell. LC 75-36582. 1976. 10.95 o.p. (ISBN 0-385-07042-X). Doubleday.

Ceremony of the Innocent. Taylor Caldwell. 1978. pap. 2.75 (ISBN 0-449-23977-2, Crest). Fawcett.

Ceres in an Open Field. Jane Creighton. LC 79-26248. (Illus.). 80p. 1980. pap. 3.50 (ISBN 0-918314-12-7). Out & Out.

Cerissa. Jessica St. Claire. Date not set. pap. 2.25 (ISBN 0-686-66186-9, Leisure Bks). Nordon Pubns.

Cerre Colorade: A Case Study of the Role of Canadian Crown Corporations in Foreign Mineral Development. C. George Miller et al. 60p. (Orig.). 1978. pap. text ed. 3.00x (ISBN 0-686-63142-0, Pub. by Ctr Resource Stud Canada). Renouf.

Cerro Prieto Geothermal Field: Prodeedings of the First Symposium Held at San Diego, California, Sept. 1978. Ed. by E. Barbier. (Illus.). 300p. 1981. 77.00 (ISBN 0-08-026241-4). Pergamon.

Certain Aspects of the Action of Radiation on Living Cells. Ed. by F. G. Spear. 1980. 10.00x (Pub. by Brit Inst Radiology England). State Mutual Bk.

Certain Blindness. Roy Lewis. 180p. 1981. 9.95 (ISBN 0-312-12782-0). St Martin.

Certain Considerations in Order to a More Speedy, Cheap, and Equal Distribution of Justice Throughout the Nation. Henry Robinson et al. Ed. by David S. Berkowitz & Samuel E. Thorne. LC 77-86668. (Classics of English Legal History in the Modern Era Ser.: Vol. 49). 317p. 1979. lib. bdg. 40.00 (ISBN 0-8240-3098-2). Garland Pub.

Certain Crossroad. Emilie Loring. 224p. 1981. pap. 1.95 (ISBN 0-553-14511-8). Bantam.

Certain Journey. Charles W. Conn. 152p. 1965. 2.95 (ISBN 0-87148-000-X); pap. 2.25 (ISBN 0-87148-001-8). Pathway Pr.

Certain Language Skills in Children: Their Development & Interrelationships. Mildred C. Templin. LC 57-8922. (Child Welfare Monograph Ser: No. 26). (Illus.). 1957. 10.95x (ISBN 0-8166-0152-6). U of Minn Pr.

Certain Life: Contemporary Meditations on the Way of Christ. Herbert O'Driscoll. 96p. (Orig.). 1980. pap. 3.95 (ISBN 0-8164-2040-8). Crossroad NY.

Certain Necessary Directions Aswell for the Cure of the Plague As for Preventing the Infection: Also Certaine Select Statutes, London College of Physicians. LC 79-84120. (English Experience Ser.: No. 939). 148p. 1979. Repr. of 1636 ed. lib. bdg. 14.00 (ISBN 90-221-0939-9). Walter J Johnson.

Certain People of the Book. Maurice Samuel. 1977. pap. 7.50 (ISBN 0-8074-0082-3, 388350). UAHC.

Certain Rich Girls. Ann Pinchot. 288p. 1980. pap. 2.50 (ISBN 0-553-13195-8). Bantam.

Certain Rich Man. William A. White. LC 79-104763. (Novel As American Social History Ser.). 446p. 1970. 10.00x (ISBN 0-8131-1206-0); pap. 4.50 (ISBN 0-8131-0127-1). U Pr of Ky.

Certain Small Works. Robert H. Taylor. LC 79-3891. (Illus.). 164p. 1980. 12.00 (ISBN 0-87811-023-2). Princeton Lib.

Certain Smile. Marjorie Lewty. (Harlequin Romances Ser.). (Orig.). 1980. pap. 1.25 o.p. (ISBN 0-373-02331-6, Pub. by Harlequin). PB.

Certaine Aduertisements Out of Ireland, Concerning the Losses to the Spanish Nauie. LC 72-6009. (English Experience Ser.: No. 535). 1973. Repr. of 1588 ed. 6.00 (ISBN 90-221-0535-0). Walter J Johnson.

Certaine Excellent Knots & Mazes, for Plots of Gardens. LC 73-6148. (English Experience Ser.: No. 611). 1973. Repr. of 1623 ed. 5.00 (ISBN 90-221-0611-X). Walter J Johnson.

Certaine Miscellany Works. Francis Bacon. LC 79-25440. (English Experience Ser.: No. 222). 166p. Repr. of 1629 ed. 21.00 (ISBN 90-221-0222-X). Walter J Johnson.

Certainty & Uncertainty in Biochemical Techniques. Harold H. Hillman. 1972. 22.50x (ISBN 0-903384-00-0). Intl Ideas.

Certayne News of Christian Princes. LC 74-38155. (English Experience Ser.: No. 442). 16p. 1972. Repr. of 1547 ed. 7.00 (ISBN 90-221-0442-7). Walter J Johnson.

Certificate Chemistry: Multiple Choice Questions. M. M. Oblitas. 1976. pap. text ed. 3.95x o.p. (ISBN 0-435-64650-8). Heinemann Ed.

Certificate in Data Processing Examination. rev. ed. James W. Morrison. LC 80-16390. 368p. 1980. pap. 12.00 (ISBN 0-668-04922-7, 4922-7). Arco.

Certificate in Management Accounting Review, 6 vols. Grant W. Newton. 1979. scp package set 89.50 (ISBN 0-06-453735-8, HarpC). Har-Row.

Certified Internal Auditor Examination--May 1979: Questions & Suggested Solutions. Board of Regents of IIA. 1979. pap. text ed. 3.00 (ISBN 0-89413-081-1). Inst Inter Aud.

Certified Internal Auditor Examination, May 1980: Questions & Suggested Solutions, No. 7. Board of Regents of IIA. (Illus.). 57p. 1980. pap. text ed. 3.00 (ISBN 0-89413-089-7). Inst Inter Aud.

Certified Professional Social Worker (CPSW) Jack Rudman. (Admission Test Ser.: AT-88). (Cloth bdg. avail. on request). pap. 17.95 (ISBN 0-8373-5088-3). Natl Learning.

Certified Public Accounting: A Sociological View of a Profession in Change. Paul D. Montagna. LC 73-90140. 1975. text ed. 13.00 (ISBN 0-914348-14-0). Scholars Bk.

Cervantes. Manuel Duran. LC 74-7006. (World Author's Ser.: Spain: No. 329). 1974. lib. bdg. 9.95 (ISBN 0-8057-2206-8). Twayne.

Cervantes. Melveena McKendrick. Ed. by J. H. Plumb. (Library of World Biography). 288p. 1980. 11.95 (ISBN 0-316-56054-5). Little.

Cervantes' Novelas Ejemplares: A Selective, Annotated Bibliography. 2nd,rev. ed. Dana B. Drake. LC 80-8492. 250p. 1981. lib. bdg. 35.00 (ISBN 0-8240-9473-5). Garland Pub.

Cervantes' Place-Names: A Lexicon. Eugene C. Torbert. LC 78-6111. 1978. lib. bdg. 11.50 (ISBN 0-8108-1139-1). Scarecrow.

Cervantes: Relatos Ilustrados. (Span.). 7.95 (ISBN 84-241-5411-8). E Torres & Sons.

Cervical Pain. C. Hirsch. Ed. by Y. Zotterman. 232p. 1972. text ed. 50.00 (ISBN 0-08-016875-2). Pergamon.

Cervical Spondylosis. Ed. by Stewart Dunsker. (Seminars in Neurological Surgery). 229p. 1980. text ed. 25.00 (ISBN 0-89004-421-X). Raven.

Cervical Syndrome. 4th ed. Ruth Jackson (Amer. Lec. in Orthopaedic Surgery Ser.). (Illus.). 416p. 1978. 26.50 (ISBN 0-398-03696-9). C C Thomas.

Cervix. Ed. by Joseph A. Jordan & Albert Singer. LC 76-8579. (Illus.). 529p. 1976. text ed. 32.00 (ISBN 0-7216-5227-1). Saunders.

Cesar Franck & His Circle. Laurence Davies. LC 77-4231. (Music Reprint Ser.). (Illus.). 1977. Repr. of 1970 ed. lib. bdg. 27.50 (ISBN 0-306-77410-0). Da Capo.

Cesar Vallejo: An Anthology of Poetry. Ed. by J. Higgins. 1970. 22.00 (ISBN 0-08-015762-9); pap. 10.75 (ISBN 0-08-015761-0). Pergamon.

Cesar Vallejo En Trilce. Jose L. Vega. LC 79-26380. (Coleccion UPREX, 60 Ser.: Estudios Literarios). ix, 132p. Date not set. pap. write for info. (ISBN 0-8477-0060-7). U of PR Pr.

Cesar Vallejo: The Complete Posthumous Poetry. Cesar Vallejo. Tr. by Clayton Eshleman & Jose R. Barcia. LC 77-93472. 1978. 20.00 (ISBN 0-520-03648-4); pap. 6.95. U of Cal Pr.

Cesare Borgia. Sarah Bradford. (Illus.). 352p. 1976. 10.95 o.s.i. (ISBN 0-02-514400-6). Macmillan.

Cesarean Birth: A Couple's Guide for Decision & Preparation. Kathleen Mitchell & Marty Nason. 208p. 1981. pap. 7.95 (ISBN 0-936602-17-1). Harbor Pub CA.

Cesarean Childbirth: A Handbook for Parents. rev., expanded ed. Christine C. Wilson & Wendy R. Hovey. LC 78-22792. (Illus.). 312p. (Orig.). 1980. pap. 6.95 (ISBN 0-385-15154-3, Dolp). Doubleday.

Cesarean (R) Evolution: A Handbook for Parents & Professionals. rev., 2nd ed. Linda D. Meyer. (Illus.). 150p. 1981. pap. 5.95 (ISBN 0-9603516-1-2). C Franklin Pr.
Cesarean Revolution: A Handbook for Parents & Professionals. rev. & expanded ed. Linda D. Meyer. (Illus.). 1979. pap. 5.95 (ISBN 0-9603516-0-4). C Franklin Pr.
Ceskoslovenska Vlastiveda, 14 vols. (Czech.). 1930-1937. 620.00 (ISBN 0-8277-3065-9). Maxwell Sci Intl.
C'Est-a-Dire. Edward C. Knox & Carol D. Rifelj. 352p. 1980. pap. text ed. write for info. (HC). HarBraceJ.
Cest Daucasi&De Nicolete. Ed. by F. W. Bourdillon. LC 80-2241. (Illus.). 1981. Repr. of 1896 ed. 17.50 (ISBN 0-404-19036-7). AMS Pr.
Cestello: A Cistercian Church of the Florentine Renaissance. Allison Luchs. LC 76-23642. (Outstanding Dissertations in the Fine Arts - 2nd Series - 15th Century). (Illus.). 1977. Repr. lib. bdg. 63.00 (ISBN 0-8240-2706-X). Garland Pub.
Ceta: Assessment of Public Service Employment Programs. William Mirengoff et al. xxl, 197p. 1980. pap. text ed. 10.50 (ISBN 0-309-02925-2). Natl Acad Pr.
CETA: Manpower Programs Under Local Control. William Mirengoff & Lester Rindler. 1978. pap. text ed. 10.50x (ISBN 0-309-02792-6). Natl Acad Pr.
Ceylon. Zeylancius. 1970. 19.95 (ISBN 0-236-17657-9, Pub. by Paul Elek). Merrimack Bk Serv.
Ceylon & Malaysia. Serarat Paranavitana. (Illus.). 234p. 1975. text ed. 10.00x o.p. (ISBN 0-8426-0791-9). Verry.
Cezanne. (Artists Ser.). (Illus.). 1977. pap. 5.95 (ISBN 0-8120-0762-X). Barron.
Cezanne. Meyer Schapiro. (Library Great Painters Ser). (Illus.). 1952. 35.00 (ISBN 0-8109-0052-1). Abrams.
Cezanne & the Post-Impressionists. (Illus.). 1975. Repr. 5.95 o.p. (ISBN 0-88308-004-4). Lamplight Pub.
Cezanne in Perspective. Judith Weschler. (Artists in Perspective Ser). (Illus.). 192p. 1975. 8.95 o.p. (ISBN 0-13-123356-4, Spec); pap. 1.95 o.p. (ISBN 0-13-123349-1). P-H.
Cezanne: The Late Work. Ed. by William Rubin. LC 77-77287. (Illus.). 1977. 45.00 (ISBN 0-87070-278-5, 134619, Pub. by Museum of Modern Art). NYGS.
C.F.A. Personal Trust Investment Management. Ed. by Chartered Financial Analysts. (Illus.). 1968. text ed. 5.55x o.p. (ISBN 0-256-00245-2). Irwin.
CH-Acids. O. A. Reutov et al. LC 77-30618. (Illus.). 1979. 41.00 (ISBN 0-08-021610-2). Pergamon.
Chaco Canyon: Archaeology & Archaeologists. Robert H. Lister & Florence C. Lister. (Illus.). 312p. 1981. 29.95 (ISBN 0-8263-0574-1). U of NM Pr.
Chadbourne Luck. Lucia Curzon. (Second Chance at Love, Regency Ser.: No. 3). 192p. (Orig.). 1981. pap. 1.75 (ISBN 0-515-05624-3). Jove Pubns.
Chaff & Grain. Badr-Ud-Din Tyabji. 10.00x (ISBN 0-210-26979-0). Asia.
Chaff & the Wheat: Nineteen Twenty-Nine Seventy-Nine. Gregory J. Palma. LC 79-56716. (Orig.). 1979. 12.00 (ISBN 0-933402-08-2); pap. 6.95 (ISBN 0-933402-01-5). Charisma Pr.
Chafing Dish Specialties. Nedda C. Anders. LC 54-11633. 2.50 o.p. (ISBN 0-685-56521-1, 8208-0205). Hearthside.
Chaga. Will & Nicholas. LC 55-7615. (Illus.). (gr. k-3). 1945. 4.95 o.p. (ISBN 0-15-215894-4, HJ). HarBraceJ.
Chagall. Werner Haftmann. LC 73-7657. (Library of Great Painters). (Illus.). 160p. 1974. 35.00 (ISBN 0-8109-0074-2). Abrams.
Chagaynu, Vols. 1 & 2. Eliezer Wenger. (Illus.). 104p. (gr. 4 up). 1975. Set. pap. text ed. 3.00 (ISBN 0-89655-100-8); wkbk. 0.50 (ISBN 0-89655-101-6); answer key 0.25 (ISBN 0-89655-102-4). BRuach HaTorah.
Chain Gang Kill. Paul Ledd. (Shelter Ser.: No. 3). 256p. (Orig.). 1980. pap. 1.95 (ISBN 0-89083-658-2). Zebra.
Chain of Chance. Stanislaw Lem. 1979. pap. 1.75 (ISBN 0-515-05138-1). Jove Pubns.
Chain of Tradition Series, 5 vols. Louis Jacobs. Incl. Vol. 1. Jewish Law. LC 68-27329. pap. text ed. 3.95x (ISBN 0-87441-211-0); Vol. 2. Jewish Ethics, Philosophy & Mysticism. LC 71-80005. pap. text ed. 3.95x (ISBN 0-87441-212-9); Vol. 3. Jewish Thought Today. LC 73-116679. (Illus.). 1974. pap. text ed. 3.95x (ISBN 0-87441-213-7); Vol. 4. Hasidic Thought. pap. text ed. o.p. (ISBN 0-87441-242-0); Vol. 5. Jewish Biblical Exegesis. pap. text ed. 4.50x o.p. (ISBN 0-685-63822-7). LC 78-1487. (Illus.). (gr. 8 up). 1974. Behrman.
Chain Reaction. Gordon Pape & Tony Aspler. 1978. 9.95 o.p. (ISBN 0-670-21102-8). Viking Pr.
Chain-Restaurant Industry. D. Daryl Wyckoff & W. Earl Sasser. LC 77-2048. (Lexington Casebook Series in Industry Analysis). 1978. 19.95x (ISBN 0-669-01440-0); instructors manual free (ISBN 0-669-03248-4). Lexington Bks.
Chain Saw Craft Book. Harold C. MacIntosh. (Illus.). 1980. pap. 6.95 (ISBN 0-87108-516-X). Pruett.
Chain Saw Manual. America Pulpwood Association. 118p. 1980. pap. text ed. 4.95 (ISBN 0-8134-2133-0). Interstate.
Chained Reaction. Warren Murphy. (Destroyer Ser.: No. 34). 1978. pap. 1.50 (ISBN 0-523-40156-6, Dist. by Independent News Co.). Pinnacle Bks.
Chains. Gerald Green. 528p. 1981. pap. 3.50 (ISBN 0-553-13419-1). Bantam.
Chains of Protection: The Judicial Response to Women's Labor Legislation. Judith A. Baer. LC 77-82695. (Contributions in Women's Studies: No. 1). 1978. lib. bdg. 18.95x (ISBN 0-8371-9785-6, BCP/). Greenwood.
Chair: The Complete State of the Art. Ed. by Peter Bradford & Barbara Prete. LC 78-60172. (Illus.). 1978. 19.95 o.p. (ISBN 0-690-01783-9, TYC-T). T Y Crowell.
Chairman. William Flanagan. (Orig.). 1981. pap. 2.50 (ISBN 0-440-11546-9). Dell.
Chairman Mao & the Chinese Communist Party. Andres D. Onate. LC 78-11049. (Illus.). 1979. 18.95 (ISBN 0-88229-250-1); pap. 9.95 (ISBN 0-88229-646-9). Nelson-Hall.
Chairman's New Clothes: Mao & the Cultural Revolution. Simon Leys. LC 77-12772. 1978. 18.95 (ISBN 0-312-12791-X). St Martin.
Chairs in Color. Lanto Synge. (Illus.). 1979. 12.95 (ISBN 0-7137-0828-X, Pub. by Blandford Pr England). Sterling.
Chairwoman's New Clothes: Mao & the Cultural Revolution. Simon Leys. (Allison & Busby Motive Ser.). 270p. 1981. pap. 8.95 (ISBN 0-8052-8080-4, Pub. by Allison & Busby England). Schocken.
Chaitanya Movement: 011calcutta & London, 1925. Melville R. Kennedy. LC 78-74267. (Oriental Religions Ser.: Vol. 6). 283p. 1981. lib. bdg. 33.00 (ISBN 0-8240-3904-1). Garland Pub.
Chakras. 10th ed. Charles W. Leadbeater. 1973. 7.25 (ISBN 0-8356-7016-3). Theos Pub Hse.
Chaldean-Americans Changing Conceptions of Ethnic Identity. Mary C. Sengstock. (Illus.). 220p. Date not set. 7.95x (ISBN 0-913256-42-0). Ctr Migration.
Chaldean Arabic, English Picture Dictionary. pap. 4.95 (ISBN 0-685-88941-6). Intl Bk Ctr.
Chaleur. Harlan Wade. Tr. by Claude Potvin & Rose-Ella Potvin. (Book About Ser.). Orig. Title: Heat. (Illus., Fr.). (gr. k-3). 1979. PLB 7.30 (ISBN 0-8172-1462-3). Raintree Pubs.
Chaleur Network. Richard Stern. 244p. 1981. Repr. of 1962 ed. 15.95 (ISBN 0-933256-18-3). Second Chance.
Chalk Cross. Berthe Amoss. LC 75-4778. 192p. (gr. 5-12). 1976. 6.95 (ISBN 0-395-28887-8, Clarion). HM.
Chalk Garden. F. C. Stern. (Illus.). 1974. 13.95 (ISBN 0-571-10189-5, Pub. by Faber & Faber). Merrimack Bk Serv.
Chalk Giants. Keith Roberts. LC 75-10687. (YA) 1975. 6.95 o.p. (ISBN 0-399-11559-5, Dist. by Putnam). Berkley Pub.
Challange of Cancer. George Javor. LC 79-29674. (Orion Ser.). 96p. 1980. pap. 2.50 (ISBN 0-8127-0275-1). Southern Pub.
Challenge. Kerry Allyne. (Harlequin Romances). 192p. 1981. pap. 1.25 (ISBN 0-373-02389-8, Pub. by Harlequin). PB.
Challenge! rev. ed. Ronald J. Wilkins. (To Live Is Christ Ser). 1978. pap. 4.10 (ISBN 0-697-01683-8). Wm C Brown.
Challenge: A Handbook of Classroom Ideas to Motivate the Teaching of Intermediate Math. (Spice Ser.). 1975. 6.50 (ISBN 0-89273-116-8). Educ Serv.
Challenge & Change in American Education. Seymour E. Harris. 1965. text ed. 12.50x o.p. (ISBN 0-8211-0713-5); text ed. 10.00x ten or more copies o.p. (ISBN 0-686-66475-2). McCutchan.
Challenge & Choice in Contemporary Education. Christopher J. Lucas. (Illus.). 1976. text ed. 9.25 (ISBN 0-02-372180-4). Macmillan.
Challenge & Response: Education in American Culture. John M. Rich. LC 73-22100. 300p. 1974. text ed. 17.95 o.p. (ISBN 0-471-71900-5). Wiley.
Challenge & Response: Study of Famines in India. Kesharichand D. Gangrade. LC 73-903461. xiii, 124p. 1973. 8.00x o.p. (ISBN 0-88386-406-1). South Asia Bks.
Challenge & Stagnation: The Indian Mass Media. Chanchal Sarkar. 1969. 5.00x o.p. (ISBN 0-8426-1501-6). Verry.
Challenge Duplicating Masters, 2 vols. (Spice Duplicating Masters Ser). 1975. Vol. 1, Grades 4-6. 5.95 (ISBN 0-89273-523-6); Vol. 2, Grades 6-8. (ISBN 0-89273-524-4). Educ Serv.
Challenge of Achievement: Helping Your Child Succeed. Shirley Gould. LC 78-53400. 1979. 7.95 o.p. (Hawthorn); pap. 4.95 (ISBN 0-8015-3386-4). Dutton.
Challenge of Administering Health Services. Lowell E. Bellin. Ed. by Lewis E. Weeks. (Illus.). 400p. 1981. write for info. (ISBN 0-914904-64-7). Health Admin Pr.
Challenge of American Democracy 1974. new rev. ed. Dell Felder. (gr. 9-12). 1974. text ed. 13.20 (ISBN 0-205-04371-2, 7643713); tchrs'. guide 3.40 (ISBN 0-205-04372-0, 7643721). Allyn.
Challenge of Basic Christian Communities. Ed. by Sergio Torres & John Eagleson. Tr. by John Drury. 192p. (Orig.). 1981. pap. 7.95 (ISBN 0-88344-503-4). Orbis Bks.
Challenge of Change. T. Evans. LC 71-104788. 1970. 16.00 (ISBN 0-08-015825-0); pap. 7.75 (ISBN 0-08-015824-2). Pergamon.
Challenge of Change. The Educational Research Council. (Human Adventure Concepts and Inquiry Ser). (gr. 6). 1975. pap. text ed. 7.20 (ISBN 0-205-04456-5, 8044562); tchrs'. guide 5.20 (ISBN 0-205-04457-3, 8044570). Allyn.
Challenge of Change: A Multi-Disciplinary Symposium. Ed. by M. Kogan & M. Pope. Lord Cohen of Birkenhead. (General Ser.). 110p. 1972. pap. text ed. 9.50x (ISBN 0-85633-013-2, NFER). Humanities.
Challenge of Child Training. Rudolf Dreikurs. 1972. pap. 4.50 (ISBN 0-8015-1146-1, Hawthorn). Dutton.
Challenge of Crime in a Free Society. H. Ruth et al. LC 79-152126. (Symposia on Law & Society Ser). 1971. Repr. of 1968 ed. lib. bdg. 19.50 (ISBN 0-306-70124-3). Da Capo.
Challenge of Daycare. Sally Provence et al. LC 75-43331. 1977. 20.00x (ISBN 0-300-01964-5); pap. 7.95x (ISBN 0-300-02354-5). Yale U Pr.
Challenge of Effective Speaking. 4th ed. Rudolph F. Verderber. 1979. pap. text ed. 10.95x (ISBN 0-534-00611-6). Wadsworth Pub.
Challenge of Friendship: Helping Your Child Become a Friend. Shirley Gould. 124p. 1981. 16.95 (ISBN 0-8015-1172-0, Hawthorn). Dutton.
Challenge of Ideas: An Essay Reader. rev. ed. Ed. by John Gehlmann. LC 61-1143. 1961. 5.50 (ISBN 0-672-73247-5). Odyssey Pr.
Challenge of Interior Design. Walter Kleeman. 304p. 1981. 19.95 (ISBN 0-8436-0133-7). CBI Pub.
Challenge of Islam. Ed. by Altaf Gauhar. 393p. 1980. 35.00x (ISBN 0-906041-02-3, Pub. by Islamic Council of Europe England); pap. 14.95x (ISBN 0-906041-03-1). Intl Schol Bk Serv.
Challenge of Jesus. John Shea. 1977. pap. 2.45 (ISBN 0-385-12439-2, Im). Doubleday.
Challenge of Law Reform. Arthur T. Vanderbilt. LC 76-3784. 194p. 1976. Repr. of 1955 ed. lib. bdg. 18.75x (ISBN 0-8371-8809-1, VALR). Greenwood.
Challenge of Management: A Behavioral Orientation. Alan M. Glassman. LC 77-16095. 1978. text ed. 9.95 (ISBN 0-471-02767-7); tchrs. manual avail. (ISBN 0-471-02766-9). Wiley.
Challenge of Marriage. Rudolf Dreikurs. 1978. 9.95 o.p. (ISBN 0-8015-1176-3, Hawthorn); pap. 4.95 (ISBN 0-8015-1177-1, Hawthorn). Dutton.
Challenge of Marxism. Klaus Bockmuehl. LC 79-9701. 1980. pap. 4.95 (ISBN 0-87784-816-5). Inter-Varsity.
Challenge of Nursing: A Book of Readings. Margaret E. Auld & Linda H. Birum. LC 72-87648. 224p. 1973. pap. text ed. 8.95 o.p. (ISBN 0-8016-0410-9). Mosby.
Challenge of Our Age. H. Hart. LC 68-9843. 1974. pap. 3.25 (ISBN 0-686-11982-7). Wedge Pub.
Challenge of Partnership: Working with Parents of Children in Foster Care. Ed. by Anthony N. Maluccio & Paula A. Sinanoglu. (Orig.). 1981. pap. text ed. price not set (ISBN 0-87868-181-7). Child Welfare.
Challenge of Reading Failure. Margaret Cox. (Exploring Education Ser.). 1968. pap. text ed. 3.25x (ISBN 0-901225-16-9, NFER). Humanities.
Challenge of Red China. Guenther Stein. LC 74-34407. (China in the 20th Century Ser). (Illus.). x, 490p. 1975. Repr. of 1945 ed. lib. bdg. 35.00 (ISBN 0-306-70736-5). Da Capo.
Challenge of Skiing. Jane Sholinsky. LC 74-3073. (gr. 5-8). 1974. PLB 4.47 o.p. (ISBN 0-531-02736-8). Watts.
Challenge of the Land. C. Little. 1969. 12.25 (ISBN 0-08-006913-4). Pergamon.
Challenge of the New International Economic Order. Ed. by Edwin P. Reubens. (Westview Special Studies in International Economics & Business). 220p. 1981. lib. bdg. 25.00x (ISBN 0-89158-762-4); pap. text ed. 11.50x (ISBN 0-86531-078-5). Westview.
Challenge of the Spaceship. Arthur C. Clarke. 1980. pap. 2.50 (ISBN 0-671-82139-3). PB.
Challenge of the Third World. Joseph Hutchinson. (Eddington Memorial Lecture Ser.: No. 2). 80p. 1975. 12.50 (ISBN 0-521-20853-X); pap. 4.50 (ISBN 0-521-09996-X). Cambridge U Pr.
Challenge of Urinary Tract Infections. A. W. Asscher. 1980. 34.50 (ISBN 0-8089-1268-2). Grune.
Challenge of Venezuelan Democracy. Jose A. Yepes. 175p. 1981. 19.95 (ISBN 0-87855-401-7); text ed. 19.95 (ISBN 0-686-68055-3). Transaction Bks.
Challenge of Violence. Derek Richter. 1973. text ed. 12.25 (ISBN 0-08-017809-X). Pergamon.
Challenge to a Liberal International Economic Order. Ed. by Amacher et al. 1979. 16.25 (ISBN 0-8447-2151-4); pap. 9.25 (ISBN 0-8447-2152-2). Am Enterprise.
Challenge to Governance: Studies in Overloaded Polities. Ed. by Richard Rose. LC 80-40148. 238p. 1980. 20.00 (ISBN 0-8039-9816-3); pap. 9.95 (ISBN 0-8039-1508-X). Sage.
Challenge to Leadership: Managing in a Changing World. The Conference Board. LC 73-1861. (Orig.). 1973. pap. 5.95 (ISBN 0-02-906570-4). Free Pr.
Challenge to Liberty. Herbert Hoover. LC 72-2373. (FDR & the Era of the New Deal Ser.). 212p. 1973. Repr. of 1934 ed. lib. bdg. 25.00 (ISBN 0-306-70499-4). Da Capo.
Challenge to Management Control. John Storey. 160p. 1980. 30.00x (ISBN 0-85038-187-8). Nichols Pub.
Challenge to Musical Tradition. Adele T. Katz. LC 79-180046. 408p. 1972. Repr. of 1945 ed. lib. bdg. 32.50 (ISBN 0-306-70428-5). Da Capo.
Challenge to Parents: Improve Your Child's Reading. Vilma R. Oxenford. LC 77-84744. (Illus.). 1977. pap. 8.95 (ISBN 0-9601474-1-1). Point Pr.
Challenge to Science: The UFO Enigma. Jacques Vallee & Janine Vallee. (Illus.). 352p. (Orig.). 1974. pap. 2.25 (ISBN 0-345-27086-X). Ballantine.
Challenge to Survival. Leonard Williams. LC 76-51920. 170p. 1977. 12.00x (ISBN 0-8147-9172-7). NYU Pr.
Challenge to Urban Liberalism: Federal-City Relations During World War II. Philip J. Funigiello. LC 78-2670. (Twentieth-Century America Ser). 1978. 14.50x (ISBN 0-87049-228-4). U of Tenn Pr.
Challenger Sketchbook: B. Shephard's Sketchbook of the H.M.S. Challenger Expedition 1872-1874. Ed. by Harris B. Stewart, Jr. & J. Welles Henderson. (Illus.). 34p. 1972. 25.00 (ISBN 0-913346-01-2). Phila Maritime Mus.
Challenges & Strategies in Health: The Coming of Post-Clinical Medicine. Alfred E. Miller. (Health, Medicine, & Society Ser.). 504p. 1981. 27.50 (ISBN 0-471-60409-7, Pub. by Wiley-Interscience). Wiley.
Challenges in Mental Retardation. Gunnar Dybwad. 1964. 15.00 o.p. (ISBN 0-231-02702-8). Columbia U Pr.
Challenges in Mental Retardation: Progressive Ideology & Services. Frank J. Menolascino. LC 76-6947. 1977. text ed. 24.95 (ISBN 0-87705-295-6). Human Sci Pr.
Challenges of Aging. Otto Pollak & Nancy L. Kelley. 224p. 1981. 9.95 (ISBN 0-88427-045-9, Dist. by Caroline Hse). North River.
Challenges of Israel. Ora Shem-Ur. LC 80-52915. 80p. 1980. 4.95 (ISBN 0-88400-071-0). Shengold.
Challenges to Empiricism. Harold Morick. 320p. 1972. pap. 10.95x o.p. (ISBN 0-534-00187-4). Wadsworth Pub.
Challenges to Empiricism. Harold Morick. LC 72-806552. 329p. 18.50 (ISBN 0-915144-89-1); pap. text ed. 7.95 (ISBN 0-915144-90-5). Hackett Pub.
Challenges to Graduate Schools. Ann M. Heiss. LC 73-129770. (Higher Education Ser). 1970. 14.95x o.p. (ISBN 0-87589-072-5). Jossey-Bass.
Challenges to the Criminal Justice System: The Perspectives of Community Psychology. Ed. by Theodore R. Sarbin & Daniel Adelson. LC 78-32181. (Community Psychology Ser.: Vol. V). 166p. 1979. 14.95 (ISBN 0-87705-380-4). Human Sci Pr.
Challenging & Highly Profitable Business Careers for the New College Graduate Eager for Success & Adventure. Ken Carlyle. (Illus.). 1977. 37.50 (ISBN 0-89266-078-3). Am Classical Coll Pr.
Challenging Careers in Urban Affairs. Sterling McLeod & Science Book Associates Editors. LC 76-26977. (Messner Career Bks.). (Illus.). 192p. (gr. 7-12). 1976. PLB 7.79 (ISBN 0-671-32810-7). Messner.
Challenging Strategic Planning Assumptions: Theory, Cases & Techniques. Richard O. Mason & Ian I. Mitroff. 300p. 1981. 24.95 (ISBN 0-471-08219-8, Pub. by Wiley-Interscience). Wiley.

Challenging the Deep: Thirty Years of Undersea Adventure. Hans Hass. (Illus.). 88p. 1972. 11.95 o.p. (ISBN 0-688-00140-8). Morrow.

Chamars of Uttar Pradesh: A Study in Social Geography. A. B. Mukerji. 155p. 1980. text ed. 11.25x (ISBN 0-391-02124-9). Humanities.

Chamber Music. 2nd ed. Homer Ulrich. LC 66-17909. 1966. 22.50x (ISBN 0-231-02763-X); pap. text ed. 10.00x (ISBN 0-231-08617-2). Columbia U Pr.

Chamber Music, Pomes Penyeach, & Occasional Verse: A Facsimile of Manuscripts by James Joyce, Typescripts & Proofs, Vol. 1. Ed. by Hans W. Gabler. LC 78-10445. (James Joyce Archive Ser.). 1979. lib. bdg. 74.00 (ISBN 0-8240-2800-7). Garland Pub.

Chamber Plays. 2nd, rev. ed. August Strindberg. Tr. by Evert Sprinchorn et al from Swedish. 288p. 1981. 15.00 (ISBN 0-8166-1028-2); pap. 6.95 (ISBN 0-8166-1031-2). U of Minn Pr.

Chambers. Alvin Lucier & Douglas Simon. 173p. 1980. 15.00x (ISBN 0-8195-5042-6, Pub. by Wesleyan U Pr). Columbia U Pr.

Chambers Atlas of World History. 136p. 1980. 25.00x (ISBN 0-550-14001-8, Pub. by W & R Chambers Scotland). State Mutual Bk.

Chambers Biographical Dictionary. Ed. by J. O. Thorne & T. C. Collocott. LC 78-56110. 1974. 25.00 (ISBN 0-8467-0510-9, Pub. by Two Continents). Hippocrene Bks.

Chambers Compact Dictionary. LC 77-83851. 1978. 3.95 (ISBN 0-8467-0394-7, Pub. by Two Continents). Hippocrene Bks.

Chambers Dictionary of Science & Technology. (Illus.). 1978. 25.00 (ISBN 0-8467-0520-6, Pub. by Two Continents); pap. 10.95 (ISBN 0-8467-0530-3). Hippocrene Bks.

Chambers Everyday Dictionary. LC 77-84354. 1978. 6.95 (ISBN 0-8467-0395-5, Pub. by Two Continents); text ed. 3.95 (ISBN 0-8467-0396-3). Hippocrene Bks.

Chambers Scots Dictionary. Alexander Warrack. Repr. of 1911 ed. 14.95 (ISBN 0-550-11801-2, Pub. by Two Continents). Hippocrene Bks.

Chambers Spell Well. E. M. Kirkpatrick & C. M. Schwartz. 256p. 1980. 10.00x (ISBN 0-550-11821-7, Pub. by W & R Chambers Scotland). State Mutual Bk.

Chambers Twentieth Century Dictionary. LC 77-83852. 1978. 10.95 (ISBN 0-8467-0393-9, Pub. by Two Continents). Hippocrene Bks.

Chambers Universal Learners' Dictionary. Ed. by E. M. Kirkpatrick. 928p. 1980. 25.00x (ISBN 0-550-10632-4, Pub. by W & R Chambers Scotland). State Mutual Bk.

Chambers's Encyclopedia, 15vols. 1973. 375.00 (ISBN 0-685-56975-6). Maxwell Sci Intl.

Chameleon Was a Spy. Diane R. Massie. LC 78-19510. (Illus.). (gr. 2-6). 1979. 6.95 (ISBN 0-690-03909-3, TYC-J); PLB 7.89 (ISBN 0-690-03910-7). T Y Crowell.

Champ-Arrow-Sapporo 1978-81. LC 80-70347. (Illus.). 208p. 1980. pap. 8.95. Chilton.

Champagne Blues. Nan Lyons & Ivan Lyons. 1980. pap. 2.25 (ISBN 0-449-24317-6, Crest). Fawcett.

Champagne Spring. Margaret Rome. (Harlequin Romances Ser.). (Orig.). 1980. pap. 1.25 o.p. (ISBN 0-373-02332-4, Pub. by Harlequin). PB.

Champignons du Jura et des Vosges, 22 pts. in 1 vol. Lucien Quelet. (Illus.). 1964. 76.80 o.p. (ISBN 0-686-21595-8). Lubrecht & Cramer.

Champion Cats of the World. Catherine Ing & Grace Pond. LC 70-188397. (Illus.). 1978. 17.50 o.p. (ISBN 0-312-12846-0). St Martin.

Champion Horses & Riders of North America: A Picture Yearbook. Ed. by John H. Fritz. (Illus.). 1975. 10.00 o.p. (ISBN 0-397-01083-4). Lippincott.

Champion of Garathoram. Michael Moorcock. 1981. pap. 2.25 (ISBN 0-440-11173-0). Dell.

Champion Pig: Great Moments in Everyday Life. Barbara Norfleet. (Illus.). 123p. 1980. pap. 8.95 (ISBN 0-14-005551-7). Penguin.

Champions All. Ed. by Ken Lane. (Pal Paperbacks Ser., Kit B). (Illus., Orig.). (gr. 7-12). 1972. pap. text ed. 1.25 (ISBN 0-8374-3510-2). Xerox Ed Pubns.

Champions & the All Americans. Jerry L. Preas. (Illus.). 1979. pap. 4.95 (ISBN 0-686-26660-9). Texan-Am Pub.

Champions at Speed. Richard Corson. LC 78-25853. (Illus.). (gr. 6 up). 1979. 5.95 (ISBN 0-396-07656-4). Dodd.

Champions in Sports Learning Module. Mary Manoni et al. LC 76-731377. 1976. pap. text ed. 175.00 (ISBN 0-89290-112-8, CM-36). Soc for Visual.

Champions in the Making: Quality Training for Track & Field. Payton Jordan & Bud Spencer. LC 68-28877. 1968. text ed. 14.95 (ISBN 0-13-125401-4). P-H.

Champions of the Indianapolis 500. Bill Libby. LC 76-87. (Illus.). 1976. 7.95 (ISBN 0-396-07306-9). Dodd.

Championship Baseball. Hank Bauer. LC 67-15347. 1968. 6.95 o.p. (ISBN 0-385-08573-7). Doubleday.

Championship Bowls. Bill Irish. LC 78-74073. 1979. 8.95 (ISBN 0-7153-7469-9). David & Charles.

Championship Teams of the N. F. L. Phil Berger. LC 68-23667. (NFL Punt, Pass & Kick Library: No. 10). (Illus.). (gr. 5-9). 1968. 2.50 o.p. (ISBN 0-394-80640-9, BYR). Random.

Championship Tennis by the Experts. Ed. by Paul Assaiante. LC 80-83978. (West Point Sports Fitness Ser.: Vol. 13). (Illus.). 208p. (Orig.). 1981. pap. text ed. 6.95 (ISBN 0-918438-23-3). Leisure Pr.

Champlain. Matthew G. Grant. LC 73-13714. 1974. PLB 5.95 (ISBN 0-87191-287-2). Creative Ed.

Champlain Monster. Jeff Danziger. (Illus.). 64p. 1981. pap. 3.95 (ISBN 0-9603900-7-3). Lanser Pr.

Chan Chan: Andean Desert City. Ed. by Micheal E. Moseley & Kent C. Day. (School of American Research Advanced Seminar Ser.). (Illus.). 440p. 1981. 29.95x (ISBN 0-8263-0575-X). U of NM Pr.

Chan-Ese Way. Titus Chan. LC 74-16221. 1974. 12.95 (ISBN 0-87909-117-7). Reston.

Chan-Kuo Ts'e. Tr. by J. I. Crump, Jr. (Oxford Library of East Asian Literature). 1970. 48.00x (ISBN 0-19-815439-9). Oxford U Pr.

Chance Child. Jill Paton Walsh. 144p. (YA) 1980. pap. 1.95 (ISBN 0-380-48561-3, 48561). Avon.

Chance for Love: No. 36. Iris Bromige. 224p. (Orig.). 1975. pap. 0.95 o.p. (ISBN 0-345-26712-5). Ballantine.

Chance, Love & Logic. Charles S. Peirce. 317p. 1980. Repr. of 1923 ed. lib. bdg. 50.00 (ISBN 0-89984-386-7). Century Bookbindery.

Chance McGraw. Mary L. Manning. (Orig.). 1980. pap. 2.75 (ISBN 0-440-11523-X). Dell.

Chance Meeting. Kay Thorpe. (Harlequin Romance Ser.). 192p. 1980. pap. 1.50 (ISBN 0-373-10378-6, Pub. by Harlequin). PB.

Chance to Sit Down. Meredith Daneman. 176p. 1981. pap. 2.25 (ISBN 0-380-54163-7, 54163). Avon.

Chance Tomorrow. Dixie Browning. 192p. 1981. pap. 1.50 (ISBN 0-671-57053-6). S&S.

Chancellor's Spy: The Revelations of the Chief of Bismarck's Secret Service. Wilhelm J. Stieber. Tr. by Jan Van Heurck from German. LC 79-52090. Orig. Title: Spion Des Kanzlers. 272p. 1981. 12.50 (ISBN 0-394-50869-6). Grove.

Chances of Rhyme: Device & Modernity. Donald Wesling. 1980. 14.75x (ISBN 0-520-03861-4). U of Cal Pr.

Chandler. William Denbow. 1977. pap. 1.50 (ISBN 0-505-51169-X). Tower Bks.

Chandranath. Saratchandra Chattopadhyaya. 101p. 1969. pap. 2.50 (ISBN 0-88253-027-5). Ind-US Inc.

Chaneysville Incident. David Bradley. LC 80-8225. 480p. 1981. 12.95 (ISBN 0-06-010491-0, HarpT). Har-Row.

Change. Laura Greene. 32p. 1980. 8.95 (ISBN 0-87705-401-0). Human Sci Pr.

Change & Adaptation in Soviet & East European Politics. Ed. by Jane P. Shapiro & Peter J. Potichnyj. LC 76-8415. (Special Studies). (Illus.). 275p. 1976. text ed. 27.95 (ISBN 0-275-56190-9). Praeger.

Change & Choice: Women & Middle Age. Ed. by Beatrice Musgrave & Zoe Menell. 186p. 1980. text ed. 18.50x (ISBN 0-7206-0539-3). Humanities.

Change & Continuity in India's Villages. Ed. by K. Ishwaran. LC 79-110604. 1970. 17.50x (ISBN 0-231-03323-0). Columbia U Pr.

Change & Continuity in Seventeenth-Century England. Christopher Hill. LC 74-12878. 1975. 16.50x (ISBN 0-674-10765-9). Harvard U Pr.

Change & Decline: Roman Literature in the Early Empire. Gordon Williams. LC 76-24598. (Sather Classical Lectures: No. 45). 1978. 17.75x (ISBN 0-520-03333-7). U of Cal Pr.

Change & Other Plays. Wolfgang Bauer. 249p. 1973. 10.00 (ISBN 0-8090-3403-4, Mermaid); pap. 3.95 o.p. (ISBN 0-8090-0750-9). Hill & Wang.

Change & the Churches: An Anatomy of Religion in Britain. David Perman. 1978. 18.00 (ISBN 0-370-10329-7). Transatlantic.

Change & the Future International System. Ed. by David S. Sullivan & Martin J. Sattler. 1972. 20.00 (ISBN 0-231-03565-9); pap. 5.00 (ISBN 0-231-08304-1). Columbia U Pr.

Change & Tradition in Rural England: An Anthology of Writings on Country Life. Denys Thompson. LC 79-41613. 288p. 1981. 27.50 (ISBN 0-521-22546-9). Cambridge U Pr.

Change at Jamaica: A Commuter's Guide to Survival. Warren Goodrich. LC 57-12254. (Illus.). 5.95 (ISBN 0-8149-0109-3). Vanguard.

Change for Heart: Your Family & the Food You Eat. James M. Ferguson & C. Barr Taylor. 1978. pap. 5.95 (ISBN 0-915950-22-7). Bull Pub.

Change for the Worse. Elizabeth Lemarchand. 192p. 1981. 9.95 (ISBN 0-8027-5429-5). Walker & Co.

Change in Art Education. Dick Field. (Students Library of Education). 1970. text ed. 4.75x (ISBN 0-7100-6675-9). Humanities.

Change in Bengal Agrarian Society, Seventeen Sixty to Eighteen Fifty. Ratnalakha Ray. 1980. 20.00x (ISBN 0-8364-0646-X, Pub. by Manohar India). South Asia Bks.

Change in Public Bureaucracies. M. W. Meyer. LC 76-47193. (Illus.). 1979. 22.50 (ISBN 0-521-22670-8). Cambridge U Pr.

Change in Rural America: Causes, Consequences & Alternatives. Richard D. Rodefeld et al. LC 78-4644. (Illus.). 1978. pap. text ed. 17.95 (ISBN 0-8016-4145-4). Mosby.

Change in Rural Appalachia: Implications for Action Programs. Ed. by John D. Photiadis & Harry K. Schwarzweller. LC 75-122381. (Illus.). 1971. 17.00x (ISBN 0-8122-7618-3). U of Pa Pr.

Change in the International System. Ed. by Ole R. Holsti et al. 460p. 1980. lib. bdg. 27.50x (ISBN 0-89158-846-9); pap. text ed. 12.50x (ISBN 0-89158-895-7). Westview.

Change in University Organization: 1964-1971. Carnegie Commission on Higher Education. Ed. by Edward Gross. Paul V. Grambsch. LC 73-13634. (Illus.). 288p. 1974. 12.50 o.p. (ISBN 0-07-010066-7, P&RB). McGraw.

Change Lobsters & Dance: The Autobiography of Lilli Palmer. Lilli Palmer. LC 75-15924. (Illus.). 336p. 1975. 8.95 o.s.i. (ISBN 0-02-594610-2, 59461). Macmillan.

Change of Gods. Neal Oxenhandler. LC 62-16727. 1962. 4.50 o.p. (ISBN 0-15-116640-4). HarBraceJ.

Change of Heart. Faith Baldwin. 1980. pap. write for info. (ISBN 0-671-83091-0). PB.

Change of Heart. Sally Mandell. 1981. pap. 2.95 (ISBN 0-440-11355-5). Dell.

Change of Life. Barbara Evans. LC 79-89935. (Illus.). 1980. pap. cancelled (ISBN 0-89793-012-6). Hunter Hse.

Change of Light & Other Stories. Julio Cortazar. Tr. by Gregory Rabassa from Span. LC 80-7656. 288p. 1980. 11.95 (ISBN 0-394-50721-5). Knopf.

Change Resisters: How They Prevent Progress & What Managers Can Do About Them. Geogre S. Odiorne. (Illus.). 304p. 1981. 16.95 (ISBN 0-13-127902-5, Spec); pap. 7.95 (ISBN 0-13-127894-0). P-H.

Change Without War: The Shifting Structure of World Power. Alastair Buchan. LC 74-19962. 112p. 1975. 17.95 (ISBN 0-312-12880-0). St Martin.

Change Your Job, Change Your Life. Arbie M. Dale. 1978. pap. 1.95 (ISBN 0-87216-721-6). Playboy Pbks.

Change Your Life. Willis A. Jewell. 1977. 17.95 o.p. (ISBN 0-686-22159-1). W A Jewell.

Changed into His Likeness. Watchman Nee. 1969. 3.00 (ISBN 0-87508-411-7); pap. 2.50 (ISBN 0-87508-410-9). Chr Lit.

Changeling. Thomas Middleton & William Rowley. Ed. by George W. Williams. LC 65-15340. (Regents Renaissance Drama Ser). 1966. 7.50x (ISBN 0-8032-0281-4); pap. 2.25x (ISBN 0-8032-5281-1, BB 214, Bison). U of Nebr Pr.

Changeling. Roger Zelazny. 1980. pap. 6.95 (ISBN 0-441-10256-5). Ace Bks.

Changement: Understanding & Managing Business. Peter H. Burgher. 1979. 16.95 (ISBN 0-669-02569-0). Lexington Bks.

Changes. Samuel F. Morse. LC 64-25346. 91p. 1964. 5.95 (ISBN 0-8040-0034-4). Swallow.

Changes in British Aid Policy: 1951-1970, Vol. 4. D. J. Morgan. 1980. text ed. cancelled (ISBN 0-391-01687-3). Humanities.

Changes in Community Institutions & Income Distribution in a West Java Village. (IRRI Research Paper Ser.: No. 50). 16p. 1981. pap. 5.00 (R131, IRRI). Unipub.

Changes in Food Habits in Relation to Increase of Productivity. 370p. 1973. 13.75 (APO14, APO). Unipub.

Changes in Location of Manufacturing in the United States Since 1929. Victor R. Fuchs. 1962. 65.00x o.p. (ISBN 0-685-69819-X). Elliots Bks.

Changes in Occupational Characteristics: Planning Ahead for the 1980's. Leonard A. Lecht et al. LC 76-20179. (Report Ser.: No. 691). (Illus.). 1976. pap. 30.00 o.p. (ISBN 0-8237-0125-5). Conference Bd.

Changes in Rice Farming in Selected Areas of Asia. 377p. 1975. pap. 16.00 (R011, IRRI). Unipub.

Changes in Rice Harvesting Systems in Central Luzon & Laguna. (IRRI Research Paper Ser.: No. 31). 24p. 1979. pap. 5.00 (R071, IRRI). Unipub.

Changes in Scottish Education. G. S. Osborne. 1968. text ed. 3.25x (ISBN 0-582-32415-7). Humanities.

Changes in Secondary Education & Their Implications for Continuing Education in Canada. (Experiments & Innovations in Education, No. 5). 27p. (Orig.). 1973. pap. 2.50 (ISBN 9-231-01122-7, U70, UNESCO). Unipub.

Changes in Secondary School Mathematics in Australia, 1964-1978. M. J. Rosier. (ACER Research Monographs: No. 8). 1980. pap. 20.00 (ISBN 0-85563-208-9). Verry.

Changes in the Japanese University: A Comparative Perspective. William K. Cummings et al. LC 78-19787. 1979. 25.95 (ISBN 0-03-045546-4). Praeger.

Changes in the 1981 National Electrical Code. George W. Flach. 144p. 1981. pap. 6.95 (ISBN 0-13-127852-5). P-H.

Changes in Working Life. Ed. by K. D. Duncan et al. LC 80-40129. 1981. 68.75 (ISBN 0-471-27777-0, Fpub. by Wiley-Interscience). Wiley.

Changes, Issues & Prospects in Australian Education. 2nd ed. Ed. by S. D'Urso & R. A. Smith. (Illus.). 333p. 1981. pap. text ed. 19.95x (ISBN 0-7022-1582-1). U of Queensland Pr.

Changes: Stage 3. Don Radford. LC 77-83001. (Science 5-13 Ser.). (Illus.). 1977. pap. text ed. 9.30 (ISBN 0-356-04346-0). Raintree Child.

Changes: Stages 1 & 2 & Background. Don Radford. LC 77-83001. (Science 5-13 Ser.). (Illus.). 1977. pap. text ed. 9.30 (ISBN 0-356-04105-0). Raintree Child.

Changing Administrations: The 1961 & 1964 Transitions in Six Departments. David T. Stanley. 1965. 8.95 (ISBN 0-8157-8100-8). Brookings.

Changing Aims in Religious Education. Edwin Cox. (Students Library of Education Ser.). 1966. pap. text ed. 3.00x (ISBN 0-7100-4207-8). Humanities.

Changing American Legal System: Some Selected Phases. Francis R. Aumann. LC 79-92625. (Law, Politics, & History Ser). 1969. Repr. of 1940 ed. 29.50 (ISBN 0-306-71762-X). Da Capo.

Changing & Unchanging Harvest. W. E. La Farge. (Orig.). 1980. pap. 4.95 (ISBN 0-935598-00-6). Heartwork Pr.

Changing Aspects of Rural Relief. A. R. Mangus. LC 74-165685. (FDR & the Era of the New Deal Ser.). 1971. Repr. of 1938 ed. lib. bdg. 25.00 (ISBN 0-306-70346-7). Da Capo.

Changing Attitudes: Student Booklet. American Psychological Association. (Human Behavior Curriculum Project Ser.). 64p. (Orig.). (gr. 9-12). 1981. pap. text ed. 3.95 (ISBN 0-8077-2621-4). Tchrs Coll.

Changing Attitudes: Teachers Handbook & Duplication Masters. American Psychological Association. (Human Behavior Curriculum Project Ser.). 48p. (Orig.). (gr. 9-12). 1981. 9.95 (ISBN 0-8077-2622-2). Tchrs Coll.

Changing Bodies, Changing Lives: A Book for Teens on Sex & Relationships. Ruth Bell et al. (Illus.). 1981. 14.95 (ISBN 0-394-50304-X); pap. 7.95 (ISBN 0-394-73632-X). Random.

Changing British Party System 1945-1979. S. E. Finer. 1980. pap. 7.25 (ISBN 0-8447-3368-7). Am Enterprise.

Changing Campaign Techniques: Elections & Values in Contemporary Democracies. Ed. by Louis Maisel. LC 76-6311. (Sage Electoral Studies Yearbook: Vol. 2). 1976. 20.00x (ISBN 0-8039-0683-8); pap. 9.95x (ISBN 0-8039-0684-6). Sage.

Changing Careers After Thirty-Five: New Horizons Through Professional & Graduate Study. Dale L. Hiestand. LC 73-142890. 1971. 17.50x (ISBN 0-231-03482-2). Columbia U Pr.

Changing Channels: On Channeling the Direction of Your Life. Robert Gordon. LC 79-66609. 111p. 1980. 12.00 (ISBN 0-936654-00-7). Wilmington Pr.

Changing Children's Behavior. John D. Krumboltz & Helen Krumboltz. (Counseling & Guidance Ser). 1972. 14.95 (ISBN 0-13-127951-3); pap. text ed. 10.50 (ISBN 0-13-127944-0). P-H.

Changing Cities: A Challenge to Planning. Ed. by M. Pierre Laconte & Richard D. Lambert. (Annals of the American Academy of Political & Social Science Ser.: No. 451). 250p. 1980. 7.50 (ISBN 0-87761-254-4); pap. text ed. 6.00 (ISBN 0-87761-255-2). Am Acad Pol Soc Sci.

Changing Climate. Arthur Bloomfield. LC 77-80427. 1977. pap. 1.95 (ISBN 0-87123-060-7, 200060). Bethany Fell.

Changing College Classroom. Ed. by Philip Runkel et al. LC 70-92896. (Higher Education Ser.). 1969. 14.95x o.p. (ISBN 0-87589-047-4). Jossey-Bass.

Changing Concepts of Business Income. Percival F. Brundage. LC 75-21163. 1975. Repr. of 1952 ed. text ed. 10.00 (ISBN 0-914348-18-3). Scholars Bk.

Changing Demography of Spanish Americans. Abraham J. Jaffe et al. (Studies in Population Ser.). 1980. 31.00 (ISBN 0-12-379580-X). Acad Pr.

Changing Dietary Patterns & Habits. L. P. Vidyarthi et al. 1979. text ed. 15.00x (ISBN 0-391-01928-7). Humanities.

Changing Dimensions of U. S. Agricultural Policy. A. Desmond O'Rourke. (Illus.). 1978. ref. ed. 14.95 (ISBN 0-13-127936-X). P-H.

Changing Economic Role of Central Cities. J. Thomas Black. LC 78-66446. (Issue Paper Ser.). 30p. 1978. pap. text ed. 4.75 (ISBN 0-87420-577-8). Urban Land.

Changing Energy Use Futures: Second International Conference on Energy Use Management, October 1979, L. A., Ca. Rocco A. Fazzolare & Craig B. Smith. (Illus.). 1979. 440.00 (ISBN 0-08-025099-8); pap. 350.00 (ISBN 0-08-025100-5). Pergamon.

Changing English. S. Potter. (Andre Deutsch Language Library). 1977. lib. bdg. 12.50x (ISBN 0-233-96648-X). Westview.

Changing Environment of Business. Starling. (Illus.). 1980. text ed. 16.95 (ISBN 0-87872-251-3). Duxbury Pr.

Changing Eskimos. Gerald Newman. LC 78-15956. (Easy-Read Fact Book). (Illus.). (gr. 2-4). 1979. PLB 6.45 s&l (ISBN 0-531-02271-4). Watts.

Changing Face of Brazil. Kempton Webb. 1974. 22.50x (ISBN 0-231-03767-8). Columbia U Pr.

Changing Face of Southeast Asia. Amry Vandenbosch & Richard Butwell. LC 66-16234. (Illus.). 448p. 1966. 15.00x (ISBN 0-8131-1124-2); pap. 6.50 (ISBN 0-8131-0112-3). U Pr of Ky.

Changing Face of the Constitution. Don Lawson. LC 78-11570. (gr. 7 up). 1979. PLB 7.45 s&l (ISBN 0-531-02923-9). Watts.

Changing Face of Tibet: The Impact of Chinese Communist Ideology on the Landscape. Pradyumna P. Karan. LC 74-18935. (Illus.). 128p. 1976. 22.50x (ISBN 0-8131-1318-0). U Pr of Ky.

Changing Face of Western Communism. Ed. by David Childs. 1980. 27.50 (ISBN 0-312-12951-3). St Martin.

Changing Faces. Betsy Sholl. LC 74-81379. 72p. 1974. pap. 4.95 (ISBN 0-914086-05-7). Alicejamesbooks.

Changing Faces of Juvenile Justice. Ed. by V. Lorne Stewart. LC 77-87578. 1978. 12.00x (ISBN 0-8147-7788-0). NYU Pr.

Changing Faces of Rural Spain. Ed. by J. B. Aceves & W. A. Douglass. LC 75-33744. 1976. text ed. 15.95 (ISBN 0-470-00236-0); pap. text ed. 8.95 (ISBN 0-470-00237-9). Halsted Pr.

Changing Family: A Sociological Perspective. Betty G. Yorburg. LC 72-7284. 1973. 17.50x (ISBN 0-231-03461-X); pap. 6.00x (ISBN 0-231-08317-3). Columbia U Pr.

Changing Family: Adaptation & Diversity. Ed. by Gordon F. Streib. LC 72-11076. 1973. pap. text ed. 5.50 (ISBN 0-201-07320-X). A-W.

Changing Family: Its Function & Future. 2nd ed. David A. Schulz. (Illus.). 432p. 1976. 17.95 (ISBN 0-13-127977-7). P-H.

Changing Forms in Modern Music. 2nd ed. Karl Eschman. LC 67-26898. (Illus.). 213p. 1967. 5.00 (ISBN 0-911318-01-1). E C Schirmer.

Changing Gas Industry: Good & Bad-E-019. Business Communications Co., Inc. 1976. 450.00 o.p. (ISBN 0-89336-018-X). BCC.

Changing Health Care: Perspectives from a New Medical Care Setting. Gerald T. Perkoff. 1980. 18.50 (ISBN 0-914904-38-8). Health Admin Pr.

Changing Human Service Organizations: Politics & Practice. George Brager & Stephen Holloway. LC 77-87572. 1978. text ed. 15.95 (ISBN 0-02-904620-3). Free Pr.

Changing Image of India: The Twenty-Point Programme. S. K. Das. 1977. 7.50 o.p. (ISBN 0-88386-965-9). South Asia Bks.

Changing Image of the Magistracy: 1974-1977. Thomas Skyrme. 1979. text ed. 23.25x (ISBN 0-391-01123-5). Humanities.

Changing Images of the Family. Ed. by Virginia Tufte & Barbara Myerhoff. LC 79-537. 1979. 25.00 (ISBN 0-300-02361-8). Yale U Pr.

Changing Images of the Family: Multidisciplinary Perspectives. Virginia Tufte & Barbara Myerhoff. LC 79-537. (Illus.). 413p. 1981. pap. 6.95 (ISBN 0-300-02671-4). Yale U Pr.

Changing Information Environment. John McHale. (Westview Environmental Studies: Vol. 4). 1976. 18.00x (ISBN 0-89158-623-7). Westview.

Changing International Community: Some Problems of Its Laws, Structures, & Peace Research & the Middle East Conflict. Ed. by Charles Boasson & Max Nurock. (New Babylon Studies in Social Sciences: No. 18). 1973. text ed. 37.75x (ISBN 90-2797-292-3). Mouton.

Changing Interpretations & New Sources in Naval History. Ed. by Robert W. Love. LC 80-5. (Papers from the Third United States Naval Academy History Symposium). 500p. 1980. lib. bdg. 44.00 (ISBN 0-8240-9517-0). Garland Pub.

Changing Jamaica. Adam Kuper. 160p. 1975. 18.50x (ISBN 0-7100-8241-X). Routledge & Kegan.

Changing Land. Roger Zelany. 224p. 1981. pap. 2.50 (ISBN 0-345-25389-2, Del Rey). Ballantine.

Changing Land Use in Britain. J. T. Coppock & Robin H. Best. (Illus.). 1962. 9.95 (ISBN 0-571-05239-8, Pub. by Faber & Faber). Merrimack Bk Serv.

Changing Landscape of South Etruria. T. W. Potter. (Illus.). 1979. 27.50 (ISBN 0-312-12953-X). St Martin.

Changing Life in Scotland 1760 - 1820. Ed. by Michael Moss & Andrew Forrester. (History Broadsheets Ser.). (Illus.). 1977. pap. text ed. 6.95x o.p. (ISBN 0-435-31641-9). Heinemann Ed.

Changing Marketing Strategies in a New Economy. John Czepiel & Jules Backman. LC 77-11109. (Key Issues Lecture Ser). 1977. pap. 5.50 (ISBN 0-672-97199-2). Bobbs.

Changing Middle Eastern City. Ed. by G. H. Blake & R. I. Lawless. (Illus.). 273p. 1980. 28.50x. B&N.

Changing Migration Patterns Within the United States. Curtis C. Roseman. Ed. by Salvatore J. Natoli. LC 76-57033. (Resource Papers for College Geography Ser.). (Illus.). 1977. pap. text ed. 4.00 (ISBN 0-89291-123-9). Assn Am Geographers.

Changing Mile. James R. Hastings & Raymond Turner. LC 65-25019. (Illus.). 1965. 18.00x (ISBN 0-8165-0014-2). U of Ariz Pr.

Changing Mind. Vincent G. Stuart. LC 80-53447. 80p. 1981. 5.95 (ISBN 0-394-51791-1). Shambhala Pubns.

Changing More Than the Channel: How to Form a Media Access Group. Evonne Ianacone. pap. 6.00 (ISBN 0-9603466-2-7). NCCB.

Changing Munda. Sachchidananda. 1979. text ed. 25.00x (ISBN 0-391-01932-5). Humanities.

Changing Nature of Geography. Roger Minshull. 1970. pap. text ed. 7.25x (ISBN 0-09-102711-X, Hutchinson U Lib). Humanities.

Changing of the Gods: Feminism & the End. Naomi R. Goldenberg. LC 78-19602. 1979. 9.95 (ISBN 0-8070-1110-X); pap. 5.95 (ISBN 0-8070-1111-8, BP600). Beacon Pr.

Changing of the Guard. David S. Broder. 1980. 14.95 (ISBN 0-671-24566-X). S&S.

Changing Opera. Paul Bekker. Tr. by Arthur Mendel. LC 80-2256. 1981. Repr. of 1935 ed. 35.50 (ISBN 0-404-18803-6). AMS Pr.

Changing Pattern of Distribution. Nicholas A. Stacey & Wilson Aubrey. 1965. 16.50 (ISBN 0-08-010654-4); pap. 7.75 (ISBN 0-08-010653-6). Pergamon.

Changing Patterns of Military Politics. Ed. by Samuel P. Huntington. LC 61-18255. 1962. 9.95 o.s.i. (ISBN 0-02-915530-4). Free Pr.

Changing Perspectives in Special Education. Rebecca D. Kneedler & Sara G. Tarver. 1977. pap. text ed. 12.50 (ISBN 0-675-08529-2). Merrill.

Changing Politics of Education Prospects for the 1980's. Ed. by Edith K. Mosher & Jennings L. Wagoner, Jr. LC 77-75609. (Education Ser.). 1978. 19.00 (ISBN 0-8211-1252-X); text ed. 17.00 ten copies (ISBN 0-685-04968-X). McCutchan.

Changing Priorities on the International Agenda: The New International Economic Order. Ed. by Karl P. Sauvant. (Systems Science & World Order Library: Explorations of World Order). (Illus.). 272p. 1981. 52.00 (ISBN 0-08-023117-9). Pergamon.

Changing Problems into Challenges. Carol Amen. (Uplook Ser.). 1972. pap. 0.75 (ISBN 0-8163-0068-2, 03109-6). Pacific Pr Pub Assn.

Changing Role & Concepts of the International Civil Service. Ed. by Norman A. Graham & Robert S. Jordan. (Pergamon Policy Studies). 1980. 27.00 (ISBN 0-08-024643-5). Pergamon.

Changing Role of the Hospital: Options for the Future. Compiled by Minnesota Hospital Association. 336p. (Orig.). 1980. pap. 35.00 (ISBN 0-87258-310-4, 1186). Am Hospital.

Changing Role of the Individual Investor: A Twentieth Century Fund Report. Marshall E. Blume & Irwin Friend. LC 78-18303. 1978. 24.95 (ISBN 0-471-04547-0, Pub. by Wiley-Interscience). Wiley.

Changing Roles of Men & Women. Shirley Schwarzrock & C. Gilbert Wrenn. (Coping with Ser.). (Illus.). 31p. (gr. 7-12). 1970. pap. text ed. 1.30 (ISBN 0-913476-29-3). Am Guidance.

Changing Rural Village of America. Johansen Harley & Glen V. Fugitt. 1981. price not set (ISBN 0-88410-692-6). Ballinger Pub.

Changing Sexual Values & the Family. G. Pirooz Sholevar (Illus.). 192p. 1977. 16.50 (ISBN 0-398-03519-9). C C Thomas.

Changing Sixth-Form in the Twentieth Century. A. D. Edwards. (Students Library of Education Ser.). 1970. text ed. 5.50x (ISBN 0-7100-6742-9); pap. text ed. 2.75x (ISBN 0-7100-6743-7). Humanities.

Changing Small-Town in South India. P. K Geevarghese. LC 78-71371. (Illus.). 1979. pap. text ed. 11.50 (ISBN 0-8191-0666-6). U Pr of Amer.

Changing Societal Roles & Teaching. R. Dow. LC 76-39645. 1977. pap. 2.50 (ISBN 0-686-21734-9, 261-08428). Home Econ Educ.

Changing Society of China. Ch'U Chai & Winberg Chai. (Orig.). 1962. pap. 1.50 (ISBN 0-451-61205-1, MW1205, Ment). NAL.

Changing Soviet Navy. Barry M. A. Blechman. (Studies in Defense Policy). 1973. pap. 3.95 (ISBN 0-8157-0995-1). Brookings.

Changing States. Barbara Rogan. 192p. 1981. 10.95 (ISBN 0-385-17373-3). Doubleday.

Changing Status of the Blind: From Separation to Integration. Berthold Lowenfeld. 352p. 1975. 31.75 (ISBN 0-398-03189-4). C C Thomas.

Changing Supervisor Behavior. Arnold P. Goldstein & Melvin Sorcher. LC 73-10059. 1974. text ed. 12.75 (ISBN 0-08-017742-5); pap. text ed. 6.75 (ISBN 0-08-017769-7). Pergamon.

Changing System of Industrial Relations in Great Britain: A Completely Rewritten Version of "the System of Industrial Relations in Great Britain". Hugh A. Clegg. 1979. 45.50x (ISBN 0-631-11091-7, Pub. by Basil Blackwell England); pap. 21.00x (ISBN 0-631-11101-8). Biblio Dist.

Changing Technology & Employment in Agriculture. John A. Hopkins. LC 73-174470. (FDR & the Era of the New Deal Ser.). 242p. 1973. Repr. of 1941 ed. lib. bdg. 20.00 (ISBN 0-306-70380-7). Da Capo.

Changing the American Schoolbook. Paul Goldstein. LC 77-13572. (Politics of Education Ser.). 160p. 1978. 15.95 (ISBN 0-669-01984-4). Lexington Bks.

Changing the Body: Psychological Effects of Plastic Surgery. John M. Goin & Maria K. Goin. 240p. 1981. write for info. soft cover (3630-0). Williams & Wilkins.

Changing the Lawbreaker. Don C. Gibbons. 1981. pap. text ed. 8.95 (ISBN 0-86598-017-9). Allanheld.

Changing the Windows: Poems. Jerome Mazzaro. LC 66-21764. 1966. 4.75 o.p. (ISBN 0-8214-0020-7). Ohio U Pr.

Changing Times: Ireland Since Eighteen Ninety-Eight. Edward MacLysaght. 1978. text ed. 16.50x (ISBN 0-901072-88-5). Humanities.

Changing United Nations: Options for the United States. Ed. by David A. Kay. LC 77-89037. (Praeger Special Studies). 1978. 24.95 (ISBN 0-03-043706-7). Praeger.

Changing University: A Report on the Staff Development in Universities Programme 72-74. David W. Piper & Ron Glatter. (General Ser.). (Illus., Orig.). 1977. pap. text ed. 38.50x (ISBN 0-85633-121-X, NFER). Humanities.

Changing Views About the Principles of Scientific Theory Evaluation. Ed. by G. Buchdahl. 90p. 1980. pap. 16.50 (ISBN 0-08-027408-0). Pergamon.

Changing Workplace: Modern Technology & the Working Environment. Edward D. Mills. 1972. text ed. 15.95x (ISBN 0-7114-3304-6). Intl Ideas.

Changing World in Plays & Theatre. A. Block. LC 73-77721. 448p. 1971. Repr. of 1939 ed. lib. bdg. 37.50 (ISBN 0-306-71359-4). Da Capo.

Changing World of Anthony Trollope. Robert M. Polhemus. 1968. 16.75x (ISBN 0-520-01021-3). U of Cal Pr.

Changing World of Fashion: 1900 to the Present. Carter. Date not set. price not set (ISBN 0-517-31110-0). Bonanza.

Changing World of the American Military. Ed. by Franklin D. Margiotta. (Westview Special Studies in Military Affairs). 1978. lib. bdg. 27.50x (ISBN 0-89158-331-9); pap. 12.00x (ISBN 0-89158-309-2). Westview.

Changing Years: The Menopause Without Fear. rev. ed. Madeline Gray. LC 77-16917. 280p. 1981. 12.95 (ISBN 0-385-12635-2). Doubleday.

Channel Harbours & Anchorages. 5th ed. K. A. Coles. 198p. 1980. 24.00 (ISBN 0-245-53086-X, Pub. by Nautical England). State Mutual Bk.

Channel Island Pilot. Malcolm Robson. 176p. 1980. 27.00 (ISBN 0-245-53413-X, Pub. by Nautical England). State Mutual Bk.

Channel Islands: A New Study. Victor Coysh. 1977. 25.00 (ISBN 0-7153-7333-1). David & Charles.

Channels Worth Watching. Madeline Johnston. Ed. by Bobbie J. Van Dolson. 64p. 1981. pap. write for info. (ISBN 0-8280-0030-1). Review & Herald.

Channing of Concord: A Life of William Ellery Channing 2nd. Frederick T. McGill, Jr. 1967. 15.00 (ISBN 0-8135-0558-5). Rutgers U Pr.

Channings of Everleigh. Margaret Maitland. 1977. pap. 1.95 (ISBN 0-505-51199-1). Tower Bks.

Chanson Albums of Marguerite of Austria. Martin Picker. 1965. 55.00x (ISBN 0-520-01009-4). U of Cal Pr.

Chanson D'Antioche, Chanson De Geste: Le Cycle de la Croisade Estil Epique? Robert F. Cook. (Purdue University Monographs in Romance Languages: No. 2). 115p. 1980. text ed. 17.25x (ISBN 90-272-1712-2, Athlone Pr). Humanities.

Chanson de Roland. Ed. by William C. Calin. LC 67-29335. (Medieval French Literature Ser.). (Fr.). 1968. pap. text ed. 8.95x (ISBN 0-89197-071-1). Irvington.

Chanson De Roland. Ed. by F. Whitehead. (French Texts Ser.). 1975. pap. text ed. 9.95x (ISBN 0-631-00390-8, Pub. by Basil Blackwell). Biblio Dist.

Chanson de Roland: Edition bilingue. Ed. by Gerard Maignet. (Du texte a l'idee). (Old fr. & mod. fr.). 1969. pap. 5.50x o.p. (ISBN 0-685-13820-8, 3023). Larousse.

Chansons Attribuees Aux Seigneurs De Craon. Maurice Amauri & Pierre Decraon. Ed. by Arthur Langfors. LC 80-2160. (Societe Neo-Philologique De Helsingfors, Memoires Ser.: Vol. 6). 1981. Repr. of 1917 ed. 17.50 (ISBN 0-404-19020-0). AMS Pr.

Chansons Francaises Du XIIIe Siecle. Holger N. Petersen-Dyggve. LC 80-2167. 1981. 29.50 (ISBN 0-404-19030-8). AMS Pr.

Chantal. Claire Lorimer. 480p. (Orig.). 1981. pap. 2.95 (ISBN 0-553-13992-4). Bantam.

Chanters Chase. Jill Tattersall. LC 77-10910. 1978. 7.95 o.p. (ISBN 0-688-03262-1). Morrow.

Chanticleer & the Fox. Geoffrey Chaucer. LC 58-10449. (Illus.). (gr. k-3). 1958. 6.95 (ISBN 0-690-18561-8, TYC-J); PLB 7.89 (ISBN 0-690-18562-6). T Y Crowell.

Chanukah: The Festival of Lights. Sophia Cedarbaum. (Illus.). (gr. k-2). 1960. 2.00 o.p. (ISBN 0-685-20730-7, 301572). UAHC.

Chao Lun: The Treatises of Chao. 2nd ed. 15.00x o.p. (ISBN 0-685-56358-8, Hong Kong U Pr). Paragon.

Chaos & Context: A Study in William James. Charlene H. Seigfried. LC 77-86346. xiii, 137p. 1978. 12.00x (ISBN 0-8214-0378-8). Ohio U Pr.

Chaos Weapon. Colin Kapp. (Del Rey Bks.). (Orig.). 1977. pap. 1.50 o.p. (ISBN 0-345-27115-7). Ballantine.

Chaotic Kitchen. LaVada Weir. LC 74-858. (Laurie Newman Adventures Ser). 32p. (gr. 3-9). 1974. 5.95 (ISBN 0-87191-334-8). Creative Ed.

Chap-Book Chaplets 1883. Joseph Crawhall. (Illus.). 1976. Repr. of 1883 ed. 40.00x (ISBN 0-85967-260-3, Pub. by Scolar Pr England). Biblio Dist.

Chapel of Our Lady of Talpa. William Wroth. 1979. pap. 7.50. Taylor Museum.

Chapel of the Cardinal of Portugal. Frederick Hartt et al. LC 62-17064. (Illus.). 1964. 25.00x o.p. (ISBN 0-8122-7332-X). U of Pa Pr.

Chapel Talks. C. B. Eavey. (Pocket Pulpit Library). 120p. 1981. pap. 2.95 (ISBN 0-8010-3365-9). Baker Bk.

Chaperone. Ethel Gordon. (Orig.). 1981. pap. 1.50 o.s.i. (ISBN 0-440-12076-4). Dell.

Chaplaincy: Love on the Line. Walker Knight & Steve Wall. Ed. by Elaine S. Furlow. (Human Touch Photo-Text Ser.). (Illus.). 1978. 6.95 (ISBN 0-937170-12-7). Home Mission.

Chapman's Log & Owner's Manual. John Whiting. 128p. 1980. 12.95 (ISBN 0-87851-801-0); deluxe ed. 75.00 (ISBN 0-87851-801-0). Hearst Bks.

Chappaquiddick Decision. Larryanne Willis. (Illus., Orig.). 1980. pap. 2.95 (ISBN 0-937980-00-5). Better Bks.

Chappie & Me. John Craig. LC 79-664. 1979. 8.95 (ISBN 0-396-07660-2). Dodd.

Chapters from an Autobiography. Samuel M. Steward. LC 80-26602. 160p. 1981. 12.00 (ISBN 0-912516-59-3); pap. 5.95 (ISBN 0-912516-60-7). Grey Fox.

Chapters in Church History. rev. ed. Powel M. Dawley. (Orig.). 1963. pap. 3.95 (ISBN 0-8164-2004-1, SP2). Crossroad NY.

Chapters of Life. T. Lobsang Rampa. pap. 2.50 (ISBN 0-685-22170-9). Weiser.

Chapters of Opera. Henry Krehbiel. (Music Reprint Ser.). (Illus.). xvii, 435p. 1980. Repr. of 1909 ed. lib. bdg. 45.00 (ISBN 0-306-76036-3). Da Capo.

Chapters on Mental Physiology. Henry Holland. Bd. with On Man's Power Over Himself to Prevent or Control Insanity. John Barlow. (Contributions to the History of Psychology Ser., Vol. VI, Pt. C: Medical Psychology). 1980. Repr. of 1858 ed. 30.00 (ISBN 0-89093-321-9). U Pubns Amer.

Characoids of the World. Jacques Gery. (Illus.). 1978. 20.00 (ISBN 0-87666-458-3, H-961). TFH Pubns.

Character: A Novel of Father & Son. Ferdinand Bordewijk. Tr. by E. M. Price. 1966. 12.95 (ISBN 0-7206-1611-5). Dufour.

Character Analysis. Wilhelm Reich. Tr. by Vincent R. Carfagno. 1980. pap. 7.95 (ISBN 0-374-50980-8). FS&G.

Character in English Literature. Christopher Gillie. 1965. text ed. 6.25x (ISBN 0-7011-0715-4). Humanities.

Character in Relation to Action in the Tragedies of George Chapman. Derek Crawley. (Salzburg Studies in English Literature, Jacobean Drama Studies: No. 16). 202p. 1974. pap. text ed. 25.00x (ISBN 0-391-01353-X). Humanities.

Character Names in Dostoevsky's Fiction. Charles Passage. 1981. 16.00 (ISBN 0-88233-616-9). Ardis Pubs.

Character of American History. 2nd ed. W. R. Brock. (Illus.). 1965. 18.95 (ISBN 0-312-12985-8). St Martin.

Character of Americans: A Book of Readings. rev. ed. Ed. by Michael McGiffert. (Orig.). 1970. pap. text ed. 9.50x (ISBN 0-256-01138-9). Dorsey.

Character of the Year Project: A Catalog. (Bologna Children's Book Fair). pap. 10.00. Boston Public Lib.

Character People. Ken D. Jones et al. LC 74-30972. (Illus.). 256p. 1976. 17.50 o.p. (ISBN 0-498-01697-8). A S Barnes.

Character Text for Intermediate Chinese. John DeFrancis. (Illus.). 1965. pap. text ed. 8.95x (ISBN 0-300-00062-6). Yale U Pr.

Character Variation & Evolution of Sibling Species in the Empidonax Difficilis-Flavescens Complex (Aves: Tyrannidae) Ned K. Johnson. (University of California Publications in Zoology: Vol. 112). 1980. monograph 10.50x (ISBN 0-520-09599-5). U of Cal Pr.

Character Workbook for Beginning Chinese for Intermediate Schools, 2 vols. Juliet Choi & John Defrancis. viii, 115p. (Orig.). (gr. 7-12). 1980. Set. pap. text ed. 15.45x (ISBN 0-89644-640-9). Chinese Materials.

Characteristics & Needs of Adults in Postsecondary Education. Lewis C. Solmen & Joanne J. Gordon. 1981. 20.95 (ISBN 0-669-04361-3). Lexington Bks.

Characteristics & Peculiarities of the Arabic Language. Emir Nasiruddin. (Arabic.). 1968. 13.00x (ISBN 0-685-72031-4). Intl Bk Ctr.

Characteristics of Children's Behavior Disorders. 2nd ed. James M. Kauffman. (Special Education Ser.). (Illus.). 352p. 1981. pap. text ed. 17.95 (ISBN 0-675-08055-X); write for info. instrs'. manual. Merrill.

Characteristics of Local Media Audiences. Ray Brown. 1978. text ed. 23.00x (ISBN 0-566-00218-3, Pub. by Gower Pr England). Renouf.

Characteristics of Nursing Home Residents Health Status, & Care Received: National Nursing Home Survey, May-December 1977. Ester Hing. Ed. by Klaudia Cox. 60p. 1981. pap. 1.95 (ISBN 0-8406-0212-X). Natl Ctr Health Stats.

Characteristics of Preschoolers. Marie Frost. (Peter Panda Ser.). 1977. pap. 1.25 (ISBN 0-87239-143-4, 42035). Standard Pub.

Characteristics of Solidified High-Level Waste Products. 1979. pap. 14.00 (ISBN 92-0-125079-7, IDC187, IAEA). Unipub.

Characteristics of the Population in New York City Health Areas: Family Composition, No. 3. 1973. 4.00 (ISBN 0-86671-014-0). Comm Coun Great NY.

Characteristics of the Present Age. Johann G. Fichte. Tr. by W. Smith. Bd. with Way Towards the Blessed Life. (Contributions to the History of Psychology Ser., Pt. A: Orientations). 1978. Repr. of 1889 ed. 30.00 (ISBN 0-89093-151-8). U Pubns Amer.

Characterization & Individuality in Wolfram's Parzival. David Blamires. 1966. 78.00 (ISBN 0-521-04271-2). Cambridge U Pr.

Characterization of Catalysts. J. M. Thomas & R. M. Lambert. 1980. write for info. (ISBN 0-471-27874-2, Pub. by Wiley-Interscience). Wiley.

Characterization of Immobilized Biocatalysts. Ed. by DECHEMA, Deutsche Gesellschaft Fuer Chemisches Apparatewesen E. V. (DECHEMA Monographs: Vol. 84). 400p. (Orig.). 1979. pap. text ed. 46.00 (ISBN 3-527-10767-3). Verlag Chemie.

Characterization of Macromolecular Structure. Division of Chemistry and Chemical Technology. (Illus.). 1968. 16.00 (ISBN 0-309-01573-1). Natl Acad Pr.

Characterization of Metal & Polymer Surfaces, 2 vols. Ed. by L. H. Lee. 1977. Vol. 1. 37.00 (ISBN 0-12-442101-6); Vol. 2. 36.00 (ISBN 0-12-442102-4). Acad Pr.

Characterization of Soils in Relation to Their Classification & Management. D. J. Greenland. 450p. 1981. 98.00x (ISBN 0-19-854538-X). Oxford U Pr.

Characterization Problems in Mathematical Statistics. A. M. Kagan et al. Tr. by B. Ramachandran. LC 73-9643. (Ser. in Probability & Mathematical Statistics Ser.). 499p. 1973. 37.95 (ISBN 0-471-45421-4). Wiley.

Characterizations of the Normal Probability Law. A. M. Mathai & G. Pederzoli. LC 77-13038. 1978. 11.95 (ISBN 0-470-99322-7). Halsted Pr.

Characters Make Your Story. Maren Elwood. 1973. text ed. 11.95 (ISBN 0-87116-080-3). Writer.

Charades. Kelrich. 1979. pap. 2.50 (ISBN 0-441-10261-1). Ace Bks.

Charcoal Burner & Other Poems: Classical Chinese Poetry. Tr. by Henry H. Hart from Chinese. 1974. pap. 5.95 (ISBN 0-8061-1475-4). U of Okla Pr.

Charcoal Drawing. Henry C. Pitz. LC 73-133980. (Illus.). 1971. 13.95 o.p. (ISBN 0-8230-0615-8); pap. 9.95 o.p. (ISBN 0-8230-0616-6). Watson-Guptill.

Charcoal Horse. Edward Loomis. LC 59-8210. 124p. 1959. 4.50 (ISBN 0-8040-0035-2). Swallow.

Charcoal's World. Hugh A. Dempsey. LC 79-14920. (Illus.). 1979. 11.95 (ISBN 0-8032-1651-3); pap. 3.95 (ISBN 0-8032-6552-2, BB 717, Bison). U of Nebr Pr.

Chardin. Pierre Rosenberg. LC 78-74107. (Illus.). 428p. 1979. 47.50x (ISBN 0-910386-48-X, Pub. by Cleveland Mus Art); pap. 32.50x (ISBN 0-910386-49-8, Pub. by Cleveland Mus Art). Ind U Pr.

Chardin & the Still-Life Tradition in France. Gabriel P. Weisberg & William S. Talbot. LC 79-63386. (Themes in Art Ser.). (Illus.). 128p. (Orig.). 1979. pap. 7.95x (ISBN 0-910386-51-X, Pub. by Cleveland Mus Art). Ind U Pr.

Charg, Monster, No. 20. Maxwell Grant. 1977. pap. 1.25 o.s.i. (ISBN 0-515-04284-6). Jove Pubns.

Charge It: Inside the Credit Card Conspiracy. Terry Galanoy. 264p. 1981. 11.95 (ISBN 0-399-12555-8). Putnam.

Charge Nurse. Patricia Rae. 368p. (Orig.). 1980. pap. 2.50 (ISBN 0-89083-663-9). Zebra.

Charge of Sir F. Bacon Touching Duells. Francis Bacon. LC 68-27475. (English Experience Ser.: No. 7). 62p. Repr. of 1614 ed. 8.00 (ISBN 90-221-0007-3). Walter J Johnson.

Charge Transfer Devices. G. S. Hobson. LC 78-40587. (Contemporary Electrical Engineering Ser.). 1978. 42.95 (ISBN 0-470-26458-6). Halsted Pr.

Charged-Particle-Induced Radiative Capture. (Illus.). 384p. (Orig.). 1974. pap. 24.75 (ISBN 92-0-131074-9, IAEA). Unipub.

Charges. Albert Cook. LC 70-112872. 154p. 1970. 8.95 (ISBN 0-8040-0036-0); pap. 4.95 (ISBN 0-8040-0037-9). Swallow.

Charges & Addresses. John C. Ryle. 1978. 14.95 (ISBN 0-85151-267-4). Banner of Truth.

Charging for Computer Services: Principles & Guidelines. Ed. by Dan Bernard et al. James C. Emery & Richard Nolan. LC 77-23811. (Computer & Data Processing Professionals Ser). 1977. text ed. 14.00 (ISBN 0-89433-055-1); pap. text ed. 12.00 (ISBN 0-89433-051-9). Petrocelli.

Charging for Social Care. Ken Judge & James Matthews. (National Institute Social Services Library: No. 39). (Illus.). 168p. (Orig.). 1980. text ed. 27.50x (ISBN 0-04-361040-4, 2528); pap. text ed. 12.95x (ISBN 0-04-361041-2, 2529). Allen Unwin.

Charging the Jury: A Monograph. Seymour D. Thompson. 196p. 1980. Repr. lib. bdg. 20.00x (ISBN 0-8377-2628-X). Rothman.

Charisma: A Psychoanalytic Look at Mass Society. Irvine Schiffer. LC 72-95816. 1973. pap. 4.00 (ISBN 0-8020-6221-0). U of Toronto Pr.

Charisma Campaigns. Jack Matthews. LC 71-174511. 1972. 5.95 o.p. (ISBN 0-15-116800-8). HarBraceJ.

Charismatic Church. W. G. Olson. LC 74-10600. 1974. pap. 3.50 (ISBN 0-87123-080-1, 210080). Bethany Fell.

Charismatic Figure As Miracle Worker. David L. Tiede. LC 72-87359. (Society of Biblical Literature. Dissertations Ser.: No. 1). (Illus.). pap. 10.50 (ISBN 0-89130-158-5, 060101). Scholars Pr Ca.

Charismatic Gifts. Kurt E. Koch. 1975. pap. 2.95 (ISBN 0-8254-3023-2). Kregel.

Charismatic Renewal Among Lutherans. Larry Christenson. 1976. pap. 3.95 (ISBN 0-87123-081-X, 210081). Bethany Fell.

Charismatic Renewal & the Churches. Kilian McDonnell. 1976. 8.95 (ISBN 0-8164-0293-0). Crossroad NY.

Charismatica. (Illus.). 1979. 6.50 (ISBN 0-911346-03-1). Christianica.

Charismatics. James Hitchcock & Gloriana Bednarski. (Catholic Perspectives Ser.). 104p. (Orig.). 1980. pap. 3.95 (ISBN 0-88347-114-0). Thomas More.

Charismatics: A Doctrinal Perspective. John F. MacArthur, Jr. 224p. (Orig.). (YA) 1980. pap. 4.95 (ISBN 0-310-28491-0). Zondervan.

Charisms in the Church Concilium, Vol. 109. Ed. by Casiano Floristan & Christian Duquoc. 1978. pap. 4.95 (ISBN 0-8164-2168-4). Crossroad NY.

Chariton. Gareth L. Schmeling. (World Authors Ser.: Greece: No. 295). 1974. lib. bdg. 10.95 (ISBN 0-8057-2207-6). Twayne.

Charity & Correction in New Jersey: A History of State Welfare Institutions. James Leiby. 1967. 27.50 (ISBN 0-8135-0560-7). Rutgers U Pr.

Charity & Its Fruits. Jonathan Edwards. 1978. 9.95 (ISBN 0-85151-009-4). Banner of Truth.

Charity Cook. Algie Newlin. 1981. write for info. (ISBN 0-913408-66-2). Friends United.

Charity Costume: Of Children, Scholars, Almsfolk, Pensioners. Phillis Cunnington & Catherine Lucas. (Illus.). 331p. 1978. 26.50x (ISBN 0-06-491346-5). B&N.

Charity Law & Voluntary Organisations. Report of the Goodman Committee. 150p. 1976. pap. text ed. 5.00x (ISBN 0-7199-0910-4, Pub. by Bedford England). Renouf.

Charity Under Siege: Government Regulation of Fund Raising. Bruce Hopkins. LC 80-23987. 350p. 1980. 42.00 (ISBN 0-471-08170-1, Pub. by Ronald). Wiley.

Charlemagne. Monroe Stearns. LC 77-132069. (Biography Ser). (Illus.). (gr. 7 up). 1971. PLB 5.90 o.p. (ISBN 0-531-00960-2). Watts.

Charlemagne. Richard Winston & Harry Bober. LC 68-13721. (Horizon Caravel Bks). (Illus.). 153p. (gr. 6 up). 1968. 9.95 (ISBN 0-8281-0475-1, Dist. by Har-Row); PLB 12.89 (ISBN 0-06-026543-4). Am Heritage.

Charles A. Lindbergh: An American Life. Tom D. Crouch. LC 77-14537. (Illus.). 128p. 1977. 8.95 (ISBN 0-87474-342-7); pap. 4.95 (ISBN 0-87474-343-5). Smithsonian.

Charles Ammi Cutter: Library Systematizer. Ed. by Francis Miksa. LC 76-58870. (Heritage of Librarianship: No. 3). 1977. lib. bdg. 20.00x (ISBN 0-87287-112-6). Libs Unl.

Charles & Mary Stories. Marie W. O'Dell. 1981. 4.95 (ISBN 0-8062-1582-8). Carlton.

Charles-Augustin Sainte Beuve. Richard M. Chadbourne. (World Authors Ser.: No. 453). 1978. lib. bdg. 12.50 (ISBN 0-8057-6290-6). Twayne.

Charles Babbage: Father of the Computer. Dan Halacy. LC 79-119618. (Surveyor Bks). (Illus.). (gr. 7-12). 1970. 4.95 o.s.i. (ISBN 0-02-741370-5). Macmillan.

Charles Baudelaire. A. E. Carter. (World Authors Ser.: No. 429). 1977. lib. bdg. 9.95 (ISBN 0-8057-6269-8). Twayne.

Charles Baudelaire. Theophile Gautier. Tr. by Guy Thorne. LC 77-10264. (Illus.). 1977. Repr. of 1915 ed. 27.50 (ISBN 0-685-87692-6). Ams Pr.

Charles Boettcher: A Study in Pioneer Western Enterprise. Geraldine Bean. LC 76-6472. 1976. 19.00x (ISBN 0-89158-049-2). Westview.

Charles Bridgeman & the English Landscape Garden. Peter Willis. (Studies in Architecture: Vol. 17). (Illus.). 1978. 100.00 o.p. (ISBN 0-8390-0223-8). Allanheld & Schram.

Charles Bulfinch: Architect & Citizen. Charles A. Place. LC 68-27717. (Architecture & Decorative Art Ser). (Illus.). 1968. Repr. of 1925 ed. lib. bdg. 29.50 (ISBN 0-306-71150-8). Da Capo.

Charles Chapin Story. Charles Chapin. (American Newspapermen 1790-1933 Ser.). xxv, 334p. 1974. Repr. of 1920 ed. 17.50x o.s.i. (ISBN 0-8464-0028-6). Beekman Pubs.

Charles Churchill. Raymond J. Smith. (English Authors Ser.: No. 197). 1977. lib. bdg. 10.95 (ISBN 0-8057-6669-3). Twayne.

Charles Darwin. L. Robert Stevens. (English Authors Ser.: No. 240). 1978. 12.50 (ISBN 0-8057-6718-5). Twayne.

Charles Darwin & Natural Selection. Alice Dickinson. LC 64-11921. (Biography Ser). (gr. 7 up). 1964. PLB 5.90 o.p. (ISBN 0-531-00865-7). Watts.

Charles Darwin & the Origin of Species. Walter Karp & J. W. Burrow. LC 68-12439. (Horizon Caravel Bks). (Illus.). 153p. (gr. 7 up). 1968. 9.95 (ISBN 0-06-023094-0, Dist. by Har-Row); PLB 12.89 o.p. (ISBN 0-06-023095-9). Am Heritage.

Charles Demuth: Behind a Laughing Mask. Emily Farnham. LC 70-108804. (Illus.). 1971. 13.95 (ISBN 0-8061-0913-0). U of Okla Pr.

Charles Dickens. Ed. by William R. Clark. (Discussions of Literature). 1961. pap. text ed. 2.95x o.p. (ISBN 0-669-21832-4). Heath.

Charles Dickens & His Original Illustrators. Jane R. Cohen. LC 79-21570. (Illus.). 320p. 1980. 32.50 (ISBN 0-686-65921-X). Ohio St U Pr.

Charles Dickens As a Familiar Essayist. Gordon Spence. (Salzburg Studies in English Literature: Romantic Reassessment Ser.: No. 71). 1977. pap. text ed. 25.00x (ISBN 0-391-01530-3). Humanities.

Charles Dickens: Interviews & Recollections, 2 vols. Ed. by Philip Collins. (Illus.). 1981. 26.50x ea. Vol. 1, 160pgs (ISBN 0-389-20042-5). Vol. 2, 160 Pgs (ISBN 0-389-20043-3). B&N.

Charles Drew. Roland Bertol. LC 77-94789. (Biography Ser.). (Illus.). (gr. 2-5). 1970. PLB 7.89 o.p. (ISBN 0-690-18598-7, TYC-J). T Y Crowell.

Charles Eldred: Sculpture & Drawing. Ed. by Roslyn Tunis. LC 80-80820. (Illus.). 1980. 10.00 (ISBN 0-89062-078-4, Pub. by Roberson Ctr). Pub Ctr Cult Res.

Charles Fenderich: Lithographer of American Statesmen. Library of Congress. Ed. by Lillian B. Miller. (Illus.). 1978. text ed. 25.00 incl. microfiche (ISBN 0-226-69243-4). U of Chicago Pr.

Charles-Ferdinand Ramuz. David Bevan. (World Authors Ser.: No. 512). 1979. lib. bdg. 14.95 (ISBN 0-8057-6353-8). Twayne.

Charles Fifth. Neil Grant. LC 79-104187. (Biography Ser). (gr. 7 up). 1970. PLB 5.90 o.p. (ISBN 0-531-00937-8). Watts.

Charles Francis Adams. Charles F. Adams, Jr. LC 80-24115. (American Statesmen Ser.). 425p. 1980. pap. 6.95 (ISBN 0-87754-181-7). Chelsea Hse.

Charles G. Finney. Basil Miller. 1969. pap. 1.95 (ISBN 0-87123-061-5, 200061). Bethany Fell.

Charles Gwathmey & Robert Siegel: Residential Works Nineteen Sixty-Six to Nineteen Seventy-Seven. Kay Breslow & Paul Breslow. (Illus.). 172p. 1980. 49.95 (ISBN 0-8038-0045-2). Architectural.

Charles Gwathmey & Robert Siegel: Residential Works Nineteen Sixty-Six to Nineteen Seventy-Seven. Kay Breslow & Paul Breslow. 1980. 49.95 (ISBN 0-8038-0045-2). Hastings.

Charles Haddon Spurgeon: Autobiography, Vol. 1 The Early Years, 1834-1860. Charles H. Spurgeon. 1976. 14.95 (ISBN 0-85151-076-0). Banner of Truth.

Charles Haddon Spurgeon: Autobiography, Vol. 2 The Full Harvest, 1861-1892. Charles H. Spurgeon. 1975. 14.95 (ISBN 0-85151-182-1). Banner of Truth.

Charles Heaney: Master of the Oregon Scene. Ed. by Barbara L. Mc Larty. Tr. by Jack McLarty. (Illus.). 65p. (Orig.). 1980. pap. 9.50. Image Gallery.

Charles III & the Revival of Spain. Anthony H. Hull. LC 80-491. (Illus.). 416p. 1980. text ed. 22.00 (ISBN 0-8191-1021-3); pap. text ed. 14.00 (ISBN 0-8191-1022-1). U Pr of Amer.

Charles II's Escape from Worcester: A Collection of Essays Assembled by Samuel Pepys. William Matthews. 1966. 16.50x (ISBN 0-520-00831-6). U of Cal Pr.

Charles Ives & His Music. Henry Cowell & Sidney Cowell. LC 54-10000. (Illus.). 1969. pap. 4.95 o.p. (ISBN 0-19-500780-8, GB). Oxford U Pr.

Charles James Fox. John W. Derry. 1972. 42.00 (ISBN 0-7134-1118-X, Pub. by Batsford England). David & Charles.

Charles James Fox & the Disintegration of the Whig Party, 1782-1794. L. G. Mitchell. (Oxford Historical Monographs). 1971. 29.95x (ISBN 0-19-821838-9). Oxford U Pr.

Charles Kingsley. Larry K. Uffelman. (English Authors Ser.: No. 273). 1979. 13.50 (ISBN 0-8057-6752-5). Twayne.

Charles Kingsley: A Reference Book. Styron Harris. (Reference Books Ser.). 1981. 26.00 (ISBN 0-8161-8166-7). G K Hall.

Charles Lamb. George L. Barnett. (English Author Ser.). 1976. lib. bdg. 12.50 (ISBN 0-8057-6668-5). Twayne.

Charles Lamb in Essays & Letters. Maurice G. Fulton. 349p. 1980. Repr. of 1930 ed. lib. bdg. 30.00 (ISBN 0-89984-203-8). Century Bookbindery.

Charles Lamb's Children's Literature. Jospeh E. Riehl. (Romantic Reassessment Ser.: No. 94). 1980. pap. text ed. 25.00x (ISBN 0-391-02189-3). Humanities.

Charles M. Russell. concise ed. Frederic G. Renner. (Illus.). 1977. 17.50 o.p. (ISBN 0-8109-1590-1). Abrams.

Charles Metcalfe in India-Ideas & Administration, 1806-35. D. Panigrahi. 1968. 8.75x o.p. (ISBN 0-8426-1463-X). Verry.

Charles Moore. Gerald Allen. (Illus.). 128p. 1980. 18.95 (ISBN 0-8230-7375-0). Watson-Guptill.

Charles Nodier. Hilda Nelson. (World Authors Ser.: France: No. 242). lib. bdg. 10.95 (ISBN 0-8057-2654-3). Twayne.

Charles of Orleans: Selected Poems. Ed. by Sally Purcell. (Fyfield). 112p. 1979. 6.95 (ISBN 0-902145-68-1, Pub. by Carcanet New Pr England); pap. 3.95 o.s.i. (ISBN 0-902145-69-X). Persea Bks.

Charles Olson & Robert Creeley: The Complete Correspondence, Vol. 3. Charles Olson & Robert Creeley. Ed. by George F. Butterick. (Illus.). 200p. (Orig.). 1981. 20.00 (ISBN 0-87685-483-8); deluxe ed. 30.00 (ISBN 0-87685-484-6); pap. 7.50 (ISBN 0-87685-482-X). Black Sparrow.

Charles Olson & Robert Creeley: The Complete Correspondence, Vol. 3. Charles Olson & Robert Creeley. Ed. by George F. Butterick. (Illus.). 200p. (Orig.). 1981. 20.00 o.p. (ISBN 0-87685-483-8); deluxe ed. 30.00 o.p. (ISBN 0-87685-484-6); pap. 7.50 o.p. (ISBN 0-87685-501-X). Black Sparrow.

Charles Olson in Connecticut. Charles Boer. LC 73-13214. (Illus.). 146p. 1975. 8.95 (ISBN 0-8040-0649-0). Swallow.

Charles Peguy. F. C. St Aubyn. (World Authors Ser.: France: No. 467). 1977. lib. bdg. 12.50 (ISBN 0-8057-6304-X). Twayne.

Charles Press Handbook of Current Medical Abbreviatons. 1977. 6.95 (ISBN 0-913486-80-9). Charles.

Charles Rennie Mackintosh & the Modern Movement. T. Howarth. 1977. 60.00 (ISBN 0-7100-8538-9). Routledge & Kegan.

Charles Rennie Mackintosh & the Modern Movement. Thomas Howarth. LC 76-17782. (Aesthetic Movement & the Arts & Crafts Movement Ser.: Vol. 38). (Illus.). 1977. Repr. of 1932 ed. lib. bdg. 44.00 (ISBN 0-8240-2487-7). Garland Pub.

Charles Rex. Ethel M. Dell. (Barbara Cartland's Library of Love: Vol. 18). 216p. 1980. 12.95x (ISBN 0-7156-1478-9, Pub. by Duckworth England). Biblio Dist.

Charles Richard Drew: Pioneer in Blood Research. Richard Hardwick. LC 67-24049. 1967. 5.95 o.p. (ISBN 0-684-92299-1, ScribJ). Scribner.

Charles Robert Maturin. Dale Kramer. (English Authors Ser.: No. 156). 1973. lib. bdg. 10.95 (ISBN 0-8057-1382-4). Twayne.

Charles Robert Maturin: The Forgotten Imitator. John B. Harris. Ed. by Devendra P. Varma. LC 79-8456. (Gothic Studies & Dissertations Ser.). 1980. lib. bdg. 33.00x (ISBN 0-405-12646-8). Arno.

Charles: Royal Adventurer. Don Coolican & Serge Lemoine. (Illus.). 1978. 10.00 (ISBN 0-7207-1056-1, Pub. by Two Continents). Hippocrene Bks.

Charles S. Peirce: Selected Writings. Charles S. Peirce. Ed. by Philip P. Wiener. Orig. Title: Values in a Universe of Chance: Selected Writings of Charles S. (Peirce). pap. text ed. 6.00 (ISBN 0-486-21634-9). Dover.

Charles Sanders Peirce: Contributions to the Nation Part One: 1869-1893. Compiled by Kenneth L. Ketner & James E. Cook. (Graduate Studies: No. 10). 1975. 15.00 (ISBN 0-89672-020-9); pap. 10.00 (ISBN 0-89672-019-5). Tex Tech Pr.

Charles Sanders Peirce: From Pragmatism to Pragmaticism. Karl-Otto Apel. Tr. by John M. Krois from Ger. Orig. Title: Denkweg Von Charles Sanders Peirce. 336p. 1981. lib. bdg. 20.00x (ISBN 0-87023-177-4). U of Mass Pr.

Charles Sheeler: Artist in the American Tradition. Constance Rourke. LC 70-87603. (Library of American Art Ser). 1969. Repr. of 1938 ed. lib. bdg. 22.50 (ISBN 0-306-71634-8). Da Capo.

Charles Simeon of Cambridge. Hugh E. Hopkins. 1977. 7.95 o.p. (ISBN 0-8028-3498-1). Eerdmans.

Charles Stewart Parnell. F. S. Lyons. 1977. 25.00 (ISBN 0-19-519949-9). Oxford U Pr.

Charles Stewart Parnell: The Man & His Family. R. R. Foster. 320p. 1976. text ed. 31.25x (ISBN 0-391-00909-5). Humanities.

Charles Sumner. Moorfield Storey. LC 80-25284. (American Statesmen Ser.). 470p. 1981. pap. 6.95 (ISBN 0-87754-197-3). Chelsea Hse.

Charles the King. Evelyn Anthony. 427p. 1976. Repr. of 1961 ed. lib. bdg. 15.95x (ISBN 0-89244-067-8). Queens Hse.

Charles Virion's French Country Cookbook. Charles Virion. Ed. by Beth Backman. (Illus.). 416p. 1980. pap. 7.95 (ISBN 0-8015-1198-4, Hawthorn). Dutton.

Charles W. Eliot & Popular Education. Ed. by Edward A. Krug. LC 61-17886. (Orig.). 1961. text ed. 8.75 (ISBN 0-8077-1656-1); pap. text ed. 4.00x (ISBN 0-8077-1653-7). Tchrs Coll.

Charles W. Morgan. John F. Leavitt. LC 73-83835. (Illus.). 131p. 1973. 14.00 (ISBN 0-913372-09-9); pap. 8.00 (ISBN 0-913372-10-2). Mystic Seaport.

Charles Wesley & His Colleagues. Charles Flint. 7.00 (ISBN 0-8183-0230-5). Pub Aff Pr.

Charles X. Vincent Beach. LC 69-14471. (Illus.). 1970. 25.00x (ISBN 0-87108-103-2). Pruett.

Charleston. Ed. by Alexandra Ripley. LC 79-8568. 504p. 1981. 14.95 (ISBN 0-385-14572-1). Doubleday.

Charley Dickey's Bobwhite Quail Hunting. Charley Dickey. LC 74-79232. (Illus.). 200p. 1975. 9.95 o.p. (ISBN 0-8487-0397-9). Oxmoor Hse.

Charley O'Toole the Leprechaun. Helen Piper. 1980. pap. 2.00 (ISBN 0-89502-041-6). FEB.

Charley Patton. John Fahey. (Paul Oliver Blues Ser.). pap. 2.95 (ISBN 0-913714-29-1). Legacy Bks.

Charley Pride. Pamela Barclay. LC 74-14659. (Rock'n Pop Stars Ser.). (Illus.). 32p. (gr. 4-12). 1974. PLB 5.95 (ISBN 0-87191-397-6); pap. 2.95 (ISBN 0-89812-108-6). Creative Ed.

Charlie: A Novel. George Mikes. 1977. 10.00 (ISBN 0-233-96842-3). Transatlantic.

Charlie & the Chocolate Factory. Roald Dahl. 176p. (gr. 4-6). 1981. pap. 2.25 (ISBN 0-553-15097-9, Skylark). Bantam.

Charlie Brown & Snoopy: Selected Cartoons from "As You Like It", Charlie Brown, Vol. 1. Charles M. Schulz. (Illus.). 1978. pap. 1.50 (ISBN 0-449-24049-5, Crest). Fawcett.

Charlie Brown Dictionary. Charles M. Schulz. (Illus.). (ps-3). 1973. text ed. 11.52 (ISBN 0-13-084269-9). P-H.

Charlie Brown Paint with Water Book. (Illus.). 48p. (ps-5). 1979. pap. 1.25 (ISBN 0-448-16770-0). G&D.

Charlie Brown, Snoopy & Me & All the Other Peanuts Characters. Charles M. Schulz & R. Smith Kiliper. LC 80-923. (Illus.). 128p. 1980. 7.95a (ISBN 0-385-15805-X); PLB (ISBN 0-385-15806-8). Doubleday.

Charlie Brown's Second Super Book of Questions & Answers: About the Earth & Space from Plants to Planets. Charles M. Schulz. LC 77-74455. (Illus.). (gr. 3-6). 1977. 6.95 (ISBN 0-394-83491-7, BYR); PLB 7.39 (ISBN 0-394-93491-1). Random.

Charlie Brown's Third Super Book of Questions & Answers: About All Kinds of Boats & Trains, Cars & Planes & Other Things That Move! Charles M. Schulz. LC 78-7404. (Illus.). (gr. 4-7). 1978. 6.95 (ISBN 0-394-83729-0, BYR); PLB 7.39 (ISBN 0-394-93729-5). Random.

Charlie Chan: Great Stories from the Saturday Evening Post. LC 77-90936. 1977. 5.95 (ISBN 0-89387-015-3). Sat Eve Post.

Charlie Chaplin. Raj Sacranie. (Profiles Ser.). (Illus.). 64p. (gr. 3-6). 1981. 7.95 (ISBN 0-241-10481-5, Pub. by Hamish Hamilton England). David & Charles.

Charlie Churchmouse. Violet Hodson. (Illus.). 40p. (gr. k-4). 1976. pap. 1.95 o.p. (ISBN 0-87239-104-3, 2761). Standard Pub.

Charlie Hammond's Sketch-Book. Charlie Hammond. (Illus.). 84p. 1980. 19.95 (ISBN 0-19-212974-0). Oxford U Pr.

Charlie M. Brian Freemantle. LC 77-75383. 1977. 7.95 o.p. (ISBN 0-385-13021-X). Doubleday.

Charlie Needs a Cloak. T. De Paola. 1974. 6.95 (ISBN 0-13-128355-3). P-H.

Charlie Rich. Judy Eron & Geoffrey Morgan. (Rock 'n Pop Stars Ser.). (Illus.). (gr. 4-12). 1975. PLB 5.95 (ISBN 0-87191-463-8); pap. 2.95 (ISBN 0-89812-116-7). Creative Ed.

Charlie the Mole & Other Droll Souls. Howard Jacobs. LC 73-12219. (Illus.). 288p. 1973. 5.95 (ISBN 0-88289-001-8). Pelican.

Charlie the Tramp. Russell Hoban & Lillian Hoban. (gr. 2-3). 1970. pap. 1.50 (ISBN 0-590-02254-7, Schol Pap); pap. 3.50 bk. & record (ISBN 0-590-04392-7). Schol Bk Serv.

Charlie's Angels, No. 4. Max Franklin. 1977. pap. 1.50 o.p. (ISBN 0-345-27182-3). Ballantine.

Charlie's Angels, No. 3: Angels on a String. Max Franklin. 1977. pap. 1.50 o.p. (ISBN 0-345-25691-3). Ballantine.

Charlie's Dream. Rachi Farrow. LC 77-4320. (gr. 1-5). 1978. PLB 5.99 (ISBN 0-394-83595-6); 5.99g (ISBN 0-394-93595-0). Pantheon.

Charlotte. Amanda H. Douglass. 1978. pap. 1.95 (ISBN 0-505-51271-8). Tower Bks.

Charlotte & Emily Bronte. Norman Sherry. LC 73-101773. (Literary Critiques Ser.). (Illus., Orig.). 1970. lib. bdg. 4.95 o.p. (ISBN 0-668-02184-5). Arco.

Charlotte & Mecklenburg County: A Pictorial History. W. T. Simmons & L. Brooks Lindsay. LC 77-12680. (Illus.). 1977. 15.95 (ISBN 0-915442-33-7). Donning Co.

Charlotte Bronte. Margaret Blom. (English Authors Ser.: No. 203). 1977. lib. bdg. 10.95 (ISBN 0-8057-6673-1). Twayne.

Charlotte Bronte & Her Circle. Clement K. Shorter. LC 78-78241. 1969. Repr. of 1896 ed. 26.00 (ISBN 0-8103-3138-1). Gale.

Charlotte Hughes Herbert's Cookery for Special Occasions. Charlotte H. Herbert. (Illus.). 1980. pap. 7.85 (ISBN 0-9604928-0-1). Sullivan Prod.

Charlotte Mary Yonge, Her Life & Letters. Christabel Coleridge. LC 77-75961. (Library of Lives & Letters). 1969. Repr. of 1903 ed. 20.00 (ISBN 0-8103-3891-2). Gale.

Charlotte Perkis Gilman Reader: "The Yellow Wallpaper" & Other Fiction. Ed. by Ann Lane. 1980. 10.95 (ISBN 0-394-51085-2); pap. 5.95 (ISBN 0-394-73933-7). Pantheon.

Charlotte Smith, Popular Novelist. Carroll L. Fry. Ed. by Devendra P. Varma. LC 79-8453. (Gothic Studies & Dissertations Ser.). 1980. lib. bdg. 24.00x (ISBN 0-405-12667-0). Arno.

Charlotte: Spirit of the New South. Mary Kratt. Ed. by Ellen S. Blakey & Larry P. Silvey. LC 80-66341. (American Portrait Ser.). (Illus.). 224p. 1980. 24.95 (ISBN 0-932986-14-5). Continent Herit.

Charlotte's Web. White. (Illus.). (gr. 5). Date not set. pap. cancelled (ISBN 0-590-30271-X, Schol Pap). Schol Bk Serv.

Charm & Charisma: A Personal Guide. Virginia L. Hallock & Susan L. Ferguson. LC 74-18094. (Illus.). 272p. 1974. pap. text ed. 9.55 (ISBN 0-913310-36-0). PAR Inc.

Charm Course for College Coeds. Katrina Davis. (Illus.). 80p. (Orig.). 1981. pap. 9.95 (ISBN 0-937242-05-5). Scandia Pubs.

Charm of the English Village. P. H. Ditchfield & Sydney Jones. 1977. 24.00 (ISBN 0-7134-1068-X, Pub. by Batsford England). David & Charles.

Charm of Your Children. Mildred Scott-Washburn. (Illus.). 176p. 1980. 8.00 (ISBN 0-682-49615-4). Exposition.

Charmaine. Lynn Lowry. 432p. (Orig.). 1981. pap. 2.75 (ISBN 0-553-14150-3). Bantam.

Charmed Life. Diana W. Jones. LC 77-18414. (gr. 5-9). 1978. 7.95 (ISBN 0-688-80138-2); PLB 7.73 (ISBN 0-688-84138-4). Greenwillow.

Charmed Life. Mary McCarthy. 256p. 1981. pap. 2.95 (ISBN 0-380-53884-9, Bard). Avon.

Charmed Life. Jack B. Yeats. 1974. 16.00 (ISBN 0-7100-7667-3). Routledge & Kegan.

Charmed Lives. Michael Korda. 560p. 1981. pap. 3.50 (ISBN 0-380-53017-1, 53017). Avon.

Charmes ou Poemes. Paul Valery. Ed. by Charles G. Whiting. (French Poets Ser.). 146p. 1973. text ed. 16.25x (ISBN 0-485-14701-7, Athlone Pr); pap. text ed. 8.75x (ISBN 0-485-12701-6, Athlone Pr). Humanities.

Charms. Jonathan Cott. 24p. 1980. pap. 4.00 (ISBN 0-915124-48-3). Toothpaste.

Charro! Harry Whittington. 1981. pap. 1.75 (ISBN 0-449-14189-6, GM). Fawcett.

Chart of Accounts for Hospitals. LC 76-6469. (Financial Management Ser.). (Illus.). 168p. (Orig.). 1976. 20.00 (ISBN 0-87258-176-4, 2830). Am Hospital.

Chart of Accounts for Hospitals. 157p. 1976. 10.75 (ISBN 0-686-68594-6, 2830). Hospital Finan.

Charter Controversy in the City of London, 1660-1688, & Its Consequence. Jennifer Levin. 1969. text ed. 17.50x (ISBN 0-485-13409-8, Athlone Pr). Humanities.

Charter for a New Age: An Inside View of the Sixth Illinois Constitutional Convention. Elmer Gertz & Joe Pisciotte. LC 80-10837. (Studies in Illinois Constitution Making Ser.). 368p. 1980. 15.00 (ISBN 0-252-00820-0). U of Ill Pr.

Charter for Choice: A Study of Options Schemes. Ann Hurman. (General Ser.). 1979. pap. text ed. 25.00x (ISBN 0-85633-161-9, NFER). Humanities.

Charter for the Disabled: The Chronically Sick & Disabled Persons Act 1970. Eda Topliss & Bryan Gould. (Aspects of Social Policy Ser.). 160p. 1981. 19.95x (ISBN 0-631-12833-6, Pub. by Basil Blackwell England). Biblio Dist.

Charter Game: How to Make Money Sailing Your Own Boat. Ross Norgrove. LC 78-55784. (Illus.). 1979. 17.50 (ISBN 0-87742-092-0). Intl Marine.

Charter of the Organization of American States, Bogota, 1948. Organization of American States. (Treaty Ser.: No. 1). (Eng., Span., Port. & Fr.). 1948. pap. 1.00 (ISBN 0-8270-0245-9). OAS.

Charter of the United Nations: Commentary & Documents. 3rd ed. Leland M. Goodrich et al. LC 79-87146. 1969. 27.50x (ISBN 0-231-03218-8). Columbia U Pr.

Chartering & Charter Parties. 2nd ed. H. B. Cooley. LC 47-27564. 1974. pap. 6.00x (ISBN 0-87033-012-8). Cornell Maritime.

ChartGuide for Southern California 1980-81. rev. ed. Edmond Winlund. LC 74-29812. (Illus.). 138p. (Orig.). 1979. pap. 17.25 (ISBN 0-938206-00-1). ChartGuide.

Charting a New Course: Mike Mansfield & U. S. Asian Policy, Four Reports. Mike Mansfield. LC 77-83044. (Illus.). 1977. pap. 3.95 (ISBN 0-8048-1256-X). C E Tuttle.

Charting Compass Points. Walter B. Barbe et al. (Design for Reading Ser). (Illus.). (gr. 8). 1972. text ed. 13.28 (ISBN 0-06-516011-8, SchDept); tchr's. manual 13.80 (ISBN 0-06-516209-9). Har-Row.

Charting Intellectual Development: A Practical Guide to Piagetian Tasks. protocopy ed. Ruth Formanek & Anita Gurian. (Illus.). 120p. 1976. 13.50 (ISBN 0-398-03449-4); pap. 8.00 o.p. (ISBN 0-398-03450-8). C C Thomas.

Charting Intellectual Development: A Practical Guide to Piagetian Tasks. 2nd ed. Ruth Formanek & Anita Gurian. write for info. (ISBN 0-398-04476-7). C C Thomas.

Charting the Oceans. Ruth Brindze. LC 77-134674. (Illus.). 128p. (gr. 6-12). 1972. 6.95 (ISBN 0-8149-0002-X). Vanguard.

Chartism: A New Organization of the People. William Lovett & John Collins. (Victorian Library). 1969. Repr. of 1840 ed. text ed. 5.50x (ISBN 0-7185-5006-4, Leicester). Humanities.

Chartism & Society. Ed. by F. C. Mather. LC 80-15587. 488p. 1980. text ed. 45.00x (ISBN 0-8419-0625-4). Holmes & Meier.

Chartist Land Company. 2nd ed. Alice M. Hadfield. (Illus.). 248p. 1970. 8.95 (ISBN 0-7153-4872-8); pap. 3.95 (ISBN 0-7153-5809-X). David & Charles.

Chartist Studies. Asa Briggs. 1959. pap. 9.95 (ISBN 0-312-13125-9, Papermac). St Martin.

Chartres Cathedral. Ed. by Robert Branner. (Norton Critical Studies in Art History). (Illus.). 1969. pap. 7.95x (ISBN 0-393-09851-6, NortonC). Norton.

Charts You Can Use in Preaching, Teaching & Studying on Divorce & Remarriage. Thomas B. Warren. 1978. pap. 9.95 (ISBN 0-934916-29-2). Natl Christian Pr.

Chase! Sylvia R. Tester. LC 80-14509. (Picture Word Bks.). (Illus.). 32p. (ps-1). 1980. PLB 5.50 (ISBN 0-89565-157-2). Childs World.

Chase, Chance, & Creativity. James H. Austin. LC 77-23011. 1978. 15.00x (ISBN 0-231-04294-9). Columbia U Pr.

Chase Me, Catch Nobody! Erik C. Haugaard. (gr. 7 up). 1980. 7.95 (ISBN 0-395-29208-5). HM.

Chase the Game. Pat Jordan. LC 78-31848. (Illus.). 1979. 8.95 (ISBN 0-396-07632-7). Dodd.

Chase's Calendar of Annual Events: Special Days, Weeks & Months in 1981. rev. ed. William D. Chase & Helen M. Chase. (Illus., Orig.). 1980. pap. 12.95 (ISBN 0-913082-28-7). Apple Tree.

Chasidic Dance. Fred Berk. (gr. 9 up). 1975. pap. 5.00 (ISBN 0-8074-0083-1, 582050). UAHC.

Chasin the Trane. J. C. Thomas. LC 76-6560. 1976. pap. 6.95 (ISBN 0-306-80043-8). Da Capo.

Chasing After Annie. Marjorie W. Sharmat. LC 80-7906. (Illus.). 64p. (gr. 2-7). 1981. 7.95 (ISBN 0-06-025562-5, HarpJ); PLB 7.89g (ISBN 0-06-025567-6). Har-Row.

Chasing Dad. Candace Flynt. 274p. 1980. 9.95 (ISBN 0-8037-1392-4). Dial.

Chasing Gold: For Fun & Profit. Gertrude Wire. LC 78-62651. (Illus.). 210p. 1980. 9.95 (ISBN 0-86533-003-4). Amber Crest.

Chasing the Wind. William MacDonald. 1981. pap. 1.95 (ISBN 0-937396-07-9). Walterick Pubs.

Chasing Trouble. Harriet Luger. (YA) (gr. 7-12). 1981. pap. price not set (ISBN 0-440-91568-6, LE). Dell.

Chasm Ahead. A. Peccei. 1969. 7.50 o.s.i. (ISBN 0-02-595360-5). Macmillan.

Chaste, Silent & Obedient: English Books for Women, 1475-1640. Suzanne W. Hull. (Illus.). 1980. write for info. (ISBN 0-87328-115-2). Huntington Lib.

Chateau de ma Mere. Pagnol. (Easy Reader, C). pap. 3.75 (ISBN 0-88436-045-8, FRA201055). EMC.

Chateau Laurens. Esther L. Neely. (Orig.). 1980. pap. 1.95 (ISBN 0-505-51515-6). Tower Bks.

Chateaubriand's Travels in America. Francois R. Chateaubriand. Ed. & tr. by Richard Switzer. LC 68-55043. (Illus.). 248p. 1969. 12.00x (ISBN 0-8131-1178-1). U Pr of Ky.

Chateaux de l'Industrie: Lille, 1830-1930, Vol. 2. Lise Grenier & Hans Wieser-Benedetti. (Archives d'Architecture Moderne Ser.). (Illus.). 250p. (Fr.). 1979. pap. 27.50x (ISBN 0-8150-0920-8). Wittenborn.

Chatham House Annual Review: International Economic & Monetary Issues, Vol. 1. Ed. by The Royal Institute of International Affairs. (PPS on International Politics). (Illus.). 200p. 1981. 20.00 (ISBN 0-08-027532-X). Pergamon.

Chatiments. Victor Hugo. Ed. by P. J. Yarrow. (French Poets Ser). 312p. 1975. text ed. 22.50x (ISBN 0-485-14707-6, Athlone Pr); pap. text ed. 9.00x (ISBN 0-485-12707-5). Humanities.

Chatter with the Angels. Shirley McRae. 1980. pap. 5.50 (ISBN 0-918812-09-7). Magnamusic.

Chatterbox. Ann Thwaite. (Illus.). (ps-3). 1979. PLB 7.95 (ISBN 0-233-96967-5). Andre Deutsch.

Chaturanga. Rabindranath Tagore. Tr. by Ashok Mitra from Bengali. 101p. 1974. Repr. bds. 4.95 (ISBN 0-88253-279-0). Ind-US Inc.

Chaucer: A Norfolk Man. Walter Rye. 104p. 1980. Repr. of 1915 ed. lib. bdg. 20.00 (ISBN 0-8495-4636-2). Arden Lib.

Chaucer: A Selected Bibliography. Ed. by John Leyerle & Anne Quick. (Toronto Medieval Bibliographies). 224p. 1981. 20.00x (ISBN 0-8020-2375-4); pap. 8.95x (ISBN 0-8020-6408-6). U of Toronto Pr.

Chaucer & His Poetry. Edward W. Edmunds. 218p. 1980. Repr. of 1920 ed. lib. bdg. 8.00 (ISBN 0-8495-1349-9). Arden Lib.

Chaucer & His Poetry. George L. Kittredge. LC 78-135544. 1970. 10.00x (ISBN 0-674-11201-6); pap. 2.95 (ISBN 0-674-11210-5). Harvard U Pr.

Chaucer & His World. Derek Brewer. LC 77-10790. (Illus.). 1978. 20.00 (ISBN 0-396-07519-3). Dodd.

Chaucer & Medieval Estates Satire. Jill Mann. LC 72-90490. 384p. 1972. 49.50 (ISBN 0-521-20058-X); pap. 13.95x (ISBN 0-521-09795-9). Cambridge U Pr.

Chaucer & Menippean Satire. F. Anne Payne. LC 79-5412. 320p. 1981. 22.50 (ISBN 0-299-08170-2). U of Wis Pr.

Chaucer & the English Tradition. Ian Robinson. LC 79-163179. 1972. 44.00 (ISBN 0-521-08231-5); pap. 9.95x (ISBN 0-521-09899-8). Cambridge U Pr.

Chaucer & the Fifteenth Century. Henry S. Bennett. (Oxford History of English Literature Ser.). 1947. 37.50x (ISBN 0-19-812201-2). Oxford U Pr.

Chaucer & the French Tradition: A Study in Style & Meaning. Charles Muscatine. 1957. 15.75x (ISBN 0-520-01434-0); pap. 4.95 (ISBN 0-520-00908-8, CAL104). U of Cal Pr.

Chaucer & the Making of English Poetry, 2 vols. P. M. Kean. Incl. Vol. 1. Love Vision & Debate. 18.00 (ISBN 0-7100-7046-2); Vol. 2. The Art of Narrative. 18.00 (ISBN 0-7100-7250-3). (Illus.). 1972. Set. 35.00 (ISBN 0-685-25613-8). Routledge & Kegan.

Chaucer Glossary. Norman Davis et al. 1979. 19.95x (ISBN 0-19-811168-1); pap. 9.95x (ISBN 0-19-811171-1). Oxford U Pr.

Chaucer in His Time. D. S. Brewer. LC 74-159930. 244p. (Orig.). 1973. pap. text ed. 11.50x (ISBN 0-582-48511-8). Longman.

Chaucer: Modern Essays in Criticism. Ed. by Edward Wagenknecht. (Orig.). 1959. pap. 6.95 (ISBN 0-19-500683-6, GB). Oxford U Pr.

Chaucer-the Critical Heritage, 2 vols. Ed. by Derek Brewer. Incl. Vol. 1. 1385-1837. 27.00 (ISBN 0-7100-8497-8); Vol. 2. 1837-1933. 35.00 (ISBN 0-7100-8498-6). (Critical Heritage Ser). 1978. Set. 50.00 (ISBN 0-685-86576-2). Routledge & Kegan.

Chaucer the Maker. 2nd ed. John Speirs. 1964. pap. text ed. 3.25x (ISBN 0-571-05814-0). Humanities.

Chaucerian Problems & Perspectives. Ed. by Edward Vasta & Zacharias Thundy. LC 78-62971. 1979. text ed. 19.95 (ISBN 0-268-00728-4). U of Notre Dame Pr.

Chaucer's English. Ralph Elliot. (Andre Deutsch Language Library). 1977. lib. bdg. 20.50x (ISBN 0-233-96539-4). Westview.

Chaucer's Legend of Good Women. Harold C. Goddard. 107p. 1980. Repr. of 1908 ed. lib. bdg. 20.00 (ISBN 0-8495-1959-4). Arden Lib.

Chaucer's London. Durant W. Robertson, Jr. LC 68-30920. (New-Dimensions Historical Cities Ser). (Illus.). 1968. pap. text ed. 9.50x o.p. (ISBN 0-471-72731-8). Wiley.

Chaucers Major Poetry. Ed. by A. Baugh. 1963. 18.95 (ISBN 0-13-128223-9). P-H.

Chaucer's Poetry: An Anthology for the Modern Reader. 2nd ed. Ed. by E. T. Donaldson. LC 74-22536. 1975. 21.95 (ISBN 0-8260-2781-4). Wiley.

Chaucer's Prosody. Ian Robinson. LC 79-116841. 1971. 42.50 (ISBN 0-521-07920-9). Cambridge U Pr.

Chaucer's "Troilus & Criseyde" & the Critics. Alice R. Kaminsky. LC 79-27535. xiv, 245p. 1980. 15.00x (ISBN 0-8214-0428-8, 0428E). Ohio U Pr.

Chaucer's "Troilus": Essays in Criticism. Ed. by Stephen Barney. 323p. 1980. 22.50 (ISBN 0-208-01822-0, Archon). Shoe String.

Chaucer's World. Ed. by Edith Rickert et al. LC 48-6059. 1948. 25.00x (ISBN 0-231-01568-2); pap. 12.50x (ISBN 0-231-08530-3, 30). Columbia U Pr.

Chaucer's World: A Pictorial Companion. Geoffrey Chaucer. Ed. by M. Hussey. (Selected Tales from Chaucer). (Orig.). 1967. 23.95 (ISBN 0-521-05354-4); pap. 7.95x (ISBN 0-521-09430-5, 430). Cambridge U Pr.

Chauncy Lively's Flybox: A Portfolio of Modern Trout Flies. Chauncy K. Lively. (Illus.). 96p. 1980. pap. 9.95 (ISBN 0-8117-2078-0). Stackpole.

Chavurah: A Contemporary Jewish Experience. Bernard Reisman. 1977. pap. 5.50 (ISBN 0-8074-0048-3, 140050). UAHC.

Che Figurato Muore. Luigi Ballerini. Tr. by Richard Milazzo from It. LC 78-58982. 1981. 7.95 (ISBN 0-915570-11-4). Oolp Pr.

Cheap & Cheaper Restaurant Guide to Manhattan. Peebles Press International & Ann Zabronski. 192p. 1980. 8.95 (ISBN 0-13-128421-5, Spec); pap. 3.95 (ISBN 0-13-128413-4). P-H.

Cheap & Cheaper Restaurant Guide to Manhattan. Peebles Press International & Ann Zabronski. 192p. 1980. 8.95 (ISBN 0-686-69278-0, Spec); pap. 3.95 (ISBN 0-686-69279-9). P-H.

Cheap & Cheaper Restaurant Guide to Paris. Peebles Press International. 192p. 1980. 8.95 (ISBN 0-13-128488-6, Spec); pap. 3.95 (ISBN 0-13-128470-3). P-H.

Cheap Thrills. Ronald Koertge. 28p. 1976. pap. 2.00 (ISBN 0-935390-01-4). Wormwood Rev.

Cheaper by the Dozen. rev. ed. Frank B. Gilbreth & Ernestine G. Carey. LC 63-20411. (Illus.). 1963. 10.95 (ISBN 0-690-18632-0, TYC-T). T Y Crowell.

Chebyshev Polynomials. Theodore J. Rivlin. LC 74-10876. (Pure & Applied Mathematics Ser). 192p. 1974. 27.95 (ISBN 0-471-72470-X, Pub. by Wiley-Interscience). Wiley.

Check-Forgers. John F. Klein & Arthur Montague. LC 77-14869. 1978. 16.95 (ISBN 0-669-01993-3). Lexington Bks.

Check in-Check Out: Principles of Effective Front Office Management. 2nd ed. Jerome J. Vallen. 370p. 1980. pap. text ed. write for info. (ISBN 0-697-08412-4); instrs' manual avail. Wm C Brown.

Check List for Better Tennis. William Bockus. LC 72-97268. 160p. 1973. pap. 1.95 (ISBN 0-385-04612-X, Dolp). Doubleday.

Check List of Plant & Soil Nematodes: A Nomenclatorial Compilation. Armen C. Tarjan. LC 60-10226. xiii, 115p. 1960. 8.25 (ISBN 0-8130-0223-0); suppl. 1967 6.75 (ISBN 0-8130-0224-9). U Presses Fla.

Check-List of the Fishes of the North-Eastern Atlantic & the Mediterranean: With Supplement. (CLOFAM I & II Ser.). 1077p. 1980. pap. 89.25 (ISBN 92-3-001100-2, U 980, UNESCO). Unipub.

Check Your Chances of Success in a Mixed Marriage. Bilnitzer. pap. 1.00 o.p. (ISBN 0-686-12318-2). Christs Mission.

Check Your Character (Instructor) Julia Staton & Knofel Staton. LC 80-199950. 132p. (Orig.). 1980. pap. 2.50 (ISBN 0-87239-421-2, 39992). Standard Pub.

Check Your Character (Student) Knofel Staton. 116p. (Orig.). 1980. pap. 2.25 (ISBN 0-87239-422-0, 39993). Standard Pub.

Check Your Lifestyle. Knofel Staton. LC 78-66436. (Illus.). 1978. instr's manual o.s.i. 2.50 (ISBN 0-87239-232-5, 39996); pap. 2.25 student (ISBN 0-87239-233-3, 39997). Standard Pub.

Check Yourself Out. Craig Norback. 256p. 1981. 8.95 (ISBN 0-8129-0935-6). Times Bks.

Checker Players. Alan Venable. LC 73-2883. (Illus.). 48p. (gr. k-3). 1973. 6.50 o.p. (ISBN 0-397-31479-5). Lippincott.

Checkered Flag Ser. H. Bamman & R. Whitehead. (gr. 6-12). 1968. pap. text ed. 7.52 ea. (Sch Div); tchr's. manual o.p. 2.72 (ISBN 0-685-83973-7); o.p. Vol. 2 (ISBN 0-201-40102-9). Vol. 3 (ISBN 0-201-40103-7). Vol. 4 (ISBN 0-201-40104-5). Vol. 5 (ISBN 0-201-40105-3). Vol. 6 (ISBN 0-201-40106-1). Vol. 7. o.p. (ISBN 0-201-40107-X). A-W.

Checkering & Carving of Gunstocks. rev. ed. Monty Kennedy. (Illus.). 352p. 1952. 21.95 (ISBN 0-8117-0630-3). Stackpole.

Checking & Defensive Play. Paul J. Deegan. LC 76-13849. (Sports Instruction Ser.). (Illus.). (gr. 3-9). 1976. PLB 5.95 (ISBN 0-87191-525-1); pap. 2.95 (ISBN 0-686-67439-1). Creative Ed.

Checklist for a Perfect Wedding. rev. ed. Barbara Lee Follett. LC 72-97272. 120p. 1973. pap. 1.95 (ISBN 0-385-04251-5, Dolp). Doubleday.

Checklist for a Working Wife. Marilyn Cooley. LC 78-8205. 1979. pap. 2.50 (ISBN 0-385-14205-6, Dolp). Doubleday.

Checklist-Guide to Selecting a Small Computer. Wilma E. Bennett. LC 80-13996. 1980. pap. 5.00 (ISBN 0-87576-091-0). Pilot Bks.

Checklist Guide to Successful Acquisitions. Victor Harold. LC 77-180209. 54p. (Orig.). 1980. pap. 3.50 (ISBN 0-87576-039-2). Pilot Bks.

Checklist of American Coverlet Weavers. Ed. by John Heisey et al. LC 77-15968. 1980. Repr. of 1978 ed. 15.00x (ISBN 0-87935-048-2). U Pr of Va.

Checklist of American Imprints, Vol. 1828. Richard H. Shoemaker. Ed. by Gayle Cooper. 1971. 20.00 (ISBN 0-8108-0377-1). Scarecrow.

Checklist of American Imprints, Vol. 1820. Richard H. Shoemaker. LC 64-11784. 1964. 12.50 (ISBN 0-8108-0153-1). Scarecrow.

Checklist of American Imprints, Vol. 1825. Richard H. Shoemaker. LC 64-11784. 1969. 12.00 (ISBN 0-8108-0259-7). Scarecrow.

Checklist of American Imprints, Vol. 1826. Richard H. Shoemaker. LC 64-11784. 1970. 16.00 (ISBN 0-8108-0323-2). Scarecrow.

Checklist of American Imprints, Vol. 1829. Richard H. Shoemaker. LC 64-11784. 1971. 16.00 (ISBN 0-8108-0395-X). Scarecrow.

Checklist of American Imprints, Vol. 1821. Richard H. Shoemaker. LC 64-11784. 1967. 12.00 (ISBN 0-8108-0154-X). Scarecrow.

Checklist of American Imprints, Vol. 1822. Richard H. Shoemaker. LC 64-11784. 1967. 12.00 (ISBN 0-8108-0155-8). Scarecrow.

Checklist of American Imprints, Vol. 1823. Richard H. Shoemaker. LC 64-11784. 1968. 12.00 (ISBN 0-8108-0156-6). Scarecrow.

Checklist of American Imprints, Vol. 1827. Ed. by Richard H. Shoemaker. LC 64-11784. 1970. 14.00 (ISBN 0-8108-0336-4). Scarecrow.

Checklist of American Imprints, Vol. 1824. Ed. by Richard H. Shoemaker. LC 64-11784. 1969. 15.50 (ISBN 0-8108-0246-5). Scarecrow.

Checklist of American Imprints Eighteen Twenty to Eighteen Twenty-Nine: Title Index. M. Frances Cooper. (Checklist of American Imprints Ser.). 1972. 22.00 (ISBN 0-8108-0513-8). Scarecrow.

Checklist of American Imprints Eighteen Twenty to Eighteen Twenty-Nine: Author Index, Corrections & Sources. M. Frances Cooper. 1973. 11.00 (ISBN 0-8108-0567-7). Scarecrow.

Checklist of American Imprints for 1833: Items 17208-22795. Scott Bruntjen & Carol R. Bruntjen. LC 64-11784. (Checklist of American Imprints Ser.: Vol. 1833). 1979. lib. bdg. 27.50 (ISBN 0-8108-1191-X). Scarecrow.

Checklist of American Imprints for 1830: Items 1-5609. Gayle Cooper. (Checklist of American Imprints Ser.: Vol. 1830). 1972. 20.00 (ISBN 0-8108-0520-0). Scarecrow.

Checklist of American Imprints for 1831. Scott Bruntjen & Carol R. Bruntjen. LC 64-11784. (Checklist of American Imprints Ser.: Vol. 1831). 433p. 1975. 20.00 (ISBN 0-8108-0828-5). Scarecrow.

Checklist of American Imprints for 1832. Compiled by Scott Bruntjen & Carol R. Bruntjen. LC 64-11784. (Checklist of American Imprints Ser.: Vol. 1832). 1977. 22.50 (ISBN 0-8108-1019-0). Scarecrow.

Checklist of British Parliamentary Papers in the Irish University Press: One Thousand Volume Series 1801-1899. 230p. 1972. 45.00x (ISBN 0-7165-0059-0, Pub. by Irish Academic Pr Ireland). Biblio Dist.

Checklist of Economic Plants in Australia. 214p. 1980. pap. 9.00 (ISBN 0-643-02551-0, CO04, CSIRO). Unipub.

Checklist of Economic Plants in Australia. W. Hartley. 214p. 1980. pap. 7.50x (ISBN 0-643-02551-0, Pub. by CSIRO Australia). Intl Schol Bk Serv.

Checklist of Editions of Greek Papyri & Ostraca. John F. Oates et al. LC 78-26003. (Bulletin of the American Society of Papyrologists Supplements: No. 1). 1978. pap. 6.00 (ISBN 0-89130-272-7, 311101). Scholars Pr Ca.

Checklist of Monographs & Periodicals on the Japanese Colonial Empire. Michiko Kiyohara. LC 80-84459. (Special Project Ser.: No. 28). 352p. 1981. pap. 11.95 (ISBN 0-8179-4284-X). Hoover Inst Pr.

Checklist of Monographs & Periodicals on the Japanese Colonial Empire. Compiled by Michiko Kiyohara. (Special Project: No.28). 352p. 1981. pap. 11.95 (ISBN 0-8179-4284-X). Hoover Inst Pr.

Checklist of North American Plants for Wildlife Biologists. Thomas G. Scott & Clinton H. Wasser. LC 79-89208. 58p. (Orig.). 1979. pap. 4.50 (ISBN 0-933564-07-4). Wildlife Soc.

Checklist of the American Engravings of John Hill, 1770-1850. Richard J. Koke. LC 61-66305. (Illus.). 1961. pap. 4.50x o.p. (ISBN 0-685-73878-7, New York Historical Society). U Pr of Va.

Checklist of the Paintings, Prints, & Drawings in the Collection of the Robert Hull Fleming Museum. Compiled by Nina G. Parris. (Illus.). 166p. (Orig.). 1977. pap. 7.50 (ISBN 0-87451-989-6). U Pr of New Eng.

Checklist of the Robert A Feer Collection of World Fairs of North America. Compiled by Earl R. Taylor. pap. 3.00. Boston Public Lib.

Checklist of the Science Fiction Magazines: Through 1980. 112p. (Orig.). 1981. pap. 5.50 (ISBN 0-935064-10-9). H W Hall.

Checklist of Toronto Cabinet & Chair Makers, 1800 to 1865. Joan Mackinnon. (Illus.). 202p. 1975. pap. text ed. 3.95x (ISBN 0-660-00111-X, 56305-7, Pub. by Natl Mus Canada). U of Chicago Pr.

Checklist of Vascular Plants of the Ottawa-Hull Region, Canada. John M. Gillett & David J. White. (Illus.). 1978. pap. text ed. 4.50x (ISBN 0-660-00091-1, 56300-6, Pub. by Natl Mus Canada). U of Chicago Pr.

Checklist of Works on John Stuart Mill. Michael Laine. 176p. 1981. 25.00x (ISBN 0-686-69479-1). U of Toronto Pr.

Checklist of Writings About John Dewey, 1887-1977. 2nd, enl. ed. Ed. by Jo Ann Boydston & Kathleen Poulos. LC 77-17136. 488p. 1978. 19.95x (ISBN 0-8093-0842-8). S Ill U Pr.

Checklists: A Personal Organizer. Beth Walker. 192p. (Orig.). Date not set. leatherette spiral binding 9.95 (ISBN 0-8027-7164-5). Walker & Co.

Checklists of Basic American Legal Publications, 5 pts. Ed. by M. G. Pimsleur. Incl. Pt. 1. Statutes; Pt. 2. Session Laws; Pt. 3. Attorneys General Opinions & Reports; Pt. 4. Judicial Councils; Pt. 5. Restatements. (AALL Publications Ser: No. 4). (5 sections with 1978 supplement). looseleaf bdg., 1978 supplement incl. 140.00x (ISBN 0-8377-0104-X). Rothman.

Checkmate. Dorothy Dunnett. 1976. pap. 2.50 o.p. (ISBN 0-445-08483-9). Popular Lib.

Checkmate. Dorothy Dunnett. 736p. 1981. pap. 2.95 (ISBN 0-445-08483-9). Popular Lib.

Checkmate in Prague: The Memoirs of a Grand Master. Ludek Pachman. Tr. by Marian Sling. (Illus.). 216p. 1975. 8.95 o.s.i. (ISBN 0-02-594300-6). Macmillan.

Checkmate in Rio. (Nick Carter Ser.). 1979. pap. 1.95 (ISBN 0-441-10325-1). Charter Bks.

Checks from God. Leila Ashton. (My Church Teaches Ser.). 32p. (ps-1). 1981. pap. 1.50 (ISBN 0-8127-0314-6). Southern Pub.

Cheech & Chong's Next Movie. Chong & Marin. 1980. pap. 2.50 (ISBN 0-515-05709-6). Jove Pubns.

Cheeks on Fire. Raymond Radiquet. Tr. by Alan Stone. 1980. pap. 4.95 (ISBN 0-686-68795-7). Riverrun NY.

Cheerleading. Nancy Robison. LC 80-80607. (Free Time Fun Ser.). (Illus.). 48p. (gr. 5 up). 1981. 6.79 (ISBN 0-8178-0005-0). Harvey.

Cheerleading & Songleading. Barbara Egbert. LC 80-52322. (Illus.). 128p. (gr. 8 up). 1980. 12.95 (ISBN 0-8069-4626-1); PLB 11.69 (ISBN 0-8069-4627-X); pap. 7.95 (ISBN 0-8069-8950-5). Sterling.

Cheerleading Is for Me. Jim W. Hawkins. (Sports for Me Bks.). (Illus.). (gr. 2-5). 1981. PLB 5.95 (ISBN 0-8225-1127-4). Lerner Pubns.

Cheese. L. L. Van Slyke & W. V. Price. (Illus.). 522p. 1980. 35.00 (ISBN 0-917930-21-5); lib. bdg. 28.00 (ISBN 0-917930-31-2); pap. 18.00 (ISBN 0-917930-51-7); pap. text ed. 14.00x (ISBN 0-917930-11-8). Ridgeview.

Cheese Making at Home: The Complete Illustrated Guide. Don Radke. LC 74-1505. 168p. 1974. 5.95 o.p. (ISBN 0-385-01887-8). Doubleday.

Cheese Stands Alone. Marjorie M. Prince. LC 73-6737. (Illus.). 176p. (gr. 5 up). 1973. 7.95 (ISBN 0-395-17511-9). HM.

Cheese Stands Alone. Marjorie M. Prince. (gr. 7-9). 1975. pap. 1.95 (ISBN 0-671-42449-1). Archway.

Cheese Stands Alone. Marjorie M. Prince. (Illus.). (YA) (gr. 7-9). 1979. pap. 1.75 (ISBN 0-671-56042-5). PB.

Cheeses & Wines of England & France with Notes on Irish Whiskey. John Ehle. LC 72-79659. (Illus.). 320p. 1972. 10.95 o.s.i. (ISBN 0-06-011167-4, HarpT). Har-Row.

Cheetah: The Biology, Ecology, & Behavior of an Endangered Species. Randall L. Eaton. 178p. 1974. 13.95 (ISBN 0-442-22229-7). Krieger.

Chef's Dessert Cookbook. Dominique D'Ermo. LC 75-13679. 1976. pap. 5.95 (ISBN 0-689-70571-9, 239). Atheneum.

Chef's Manual of Kitchen Management. John Fuller. 1977. pap. 22.50 (ISBN 0-7134-0551-1, Pub. by Batsford England). David & Charles.

Cheirolumbar Dysostosis. A. Wackenheim et al. (Illus.). 102p. 1981. pap. 34.30 (ISBN 0-387-10371-6). Springer-Verlag.

Cheiro's Language of the Hand. Cheiro. LC 62-16458. (Illus.). 1968. pap. 1.95 (ISBN 0-668-01780-5). Arc Bks.

Chekhov. B. Hahn. 300p. 1977. 44.00 (ISBN 0-521-20951-X). Cambridge U Pr.

Chekhov. Beverly Hahn. LC 75-22557. (Major European Authors Ser.). 1979. pap. 10.95x (ISBN 0-521-29670-6). Cambridge U Pr.

Chekhov in Performance: A Commentary of the Major Plays. J. L. Styan. LC 73-134614. (Illus.). 1971. 42.00 (ISBN 0-521-07975-6); pap. 11.95 (ISBN 0-521-29345-6). Cambridge U Pr.

Chekhov: The Critical Heritage. Ed. by Victor Emeljanow. (Critical Heritage Ser.). 496p. 1981. 50.00 (ISBN 0-7100-0374-9). Routledge & Kegan.

Chekhov the Man. Beatrice Saunders. 1961. 13.95 (ISBN 0-900000-66-X). Dufour.

Chekhov's Art: A Stylistic Analysis. Peter Bitsilli. Tr. by Toby Clyman & Edwina Cruise. 1981. 15.00 (ISBN 0-88233-100-0). Ardis Pubs.

Chelation of Heavy Metals. Ed. by W. G. Levine. 1979. text ed. 9.00 (ISBN 0-08-017719-0). Pergamon.

Chem Sources-Europe. 6th ed. 1980. 100.00 (ISBN 0-937020-01-X). Directories Pub.

Chem Sources USA. 22nd ed. 1981. 120.00 (ISBN 0-937020-00-1). Directories Pub.

Chem Sources-USA. 21st ed. 1980. 120.00 o.p. (ISBN 0-686-26931-4). Directories Pub.

Chemehuevi: A Grammar & Lexicon. Margaret L. Press. (U. C. Publications in Linguistics Ser.: Vol. 92). 1980. pap. 12.00 (ISBN 0-520-09600-2). U of Cal Pr.

Chemehuevi Indians of Southern California. Ron Miller & Peggy Jean Miller. 1973. 1.00 (ISBN 0-686-25507-0). Malki Mus Pr.

Chemical After Treatment of Textiles. Ed. by H. Mark et al. LC 70-147234. 1971. 63.50 o.p. (ISBN 0-471-56989-5, Pub. by Wiley-Interscience). Wiley.

Chemical Analyses for Medical Technologists. C. I Wynter. (Illus.). 232p. 1975. 19.75 (ISBN 0-398-03236-X); pap. 13.50 (ISBN 0-398-03238-6). C C Thomas.

Chemical Analysis by Microwave Rotational Spectroscopy. Ravi Varma & Lawrence W. Hrubesh. LC 78-17415. (Chemical Analysis Series of Monographs on Analytical Chemistry & Its Application). 1979. 27.50 (ISBN 0-471-03916-0, Pub. by Wiley-Interscience). Wiley.

Chemical Analysis, Chromatography, & Ion Exchange. R. T. Allsop & J. A. Healey. 1974. pap. text ed. 4.95x (ISBN 0-435-65954-5); tchr's guide 3.25x (ISBN 0-435-65955-3). Heinemann Ed.

Chemical Analysis of Ecological Materials. Stewart Allen et al. LC 74-9819. 1975. 52.95 (ISBN 0-470-02318-X). Halsted Pr.

Chemical Analysis of Ores & Minerals for Copper, Silver, Gold, & the Platinum Metals. George F. Muns. (Illus.). 53p. (Orig.). 1980. pap. 6.50 (ISBN 0-9604924-0-2). Muns.

Chemical & Biochemical Applications of Lasers, Vol. 5. Ed. by C. Bradley Moore. 1980. 23.00 (ISBN 0-12-505405-X). Acad Pr.

Chemical & Biochemical Aspects of Electron Spin Resonance Spectroscopy. M. C. Symons. LC 78-2837. 1978. 24.95 (ISBN 0-470-26359-8). Halsted Pr.

Chemical & Biological Action of Radiations. Ed. by M. Haissinsky. 1961. Vol. 5. 38.50 (ISBN 0-12-316505-9). Acad Pr.

Chemical & Biological Aspects of Pyridoxal Catalysis. Ed. by E. E. Snell et al. 1963. 45.00 (ISBN 0-08-010423-1). Pergamon.

Chemical & Botanical Guide to Lichen Products. Chicita F. Culberson. 1979. pap. text ed. 78.00 (ISBN 3-87429-165-0). Lubrecht & Cramer.

Chemical & Engineering Thermodynamics. Stanley I. Sandler. LC 77-1312. 1977. text ed. 29.95x (ISBN 0-471-01774-4); solutions manual avail. (ISBN 0-471-02736-7). Wiley.

Chemical & Molecular Basis of Nerve Activity. 2nd & rev. ed. David Nachmanpohn. 1975. 31.50 (ISBN 0-12-512757-X). Acad Pr.

Chemical & Nonchemical Methods of Wastewater Disinfection. Nicholas P. Cheremisinoff et al. (Illus.). 170p. 1981. 29.50 (ISBN 0-250-40390-0). Ann Arbor Science.

Chemical & Petro-Chemical Industries of Russia & Eastern Europe, 1960-1980. Cecil Rajana. 1975. 62.50 (ISBN 0-85621-040-4, Pub. by Scottish Academic Pr Scotland). Columbia U Pr.

Chemical & Process Plant: A Guide to the Selection of Engineering Materials. 2nd ed. L. S. Evans. LC 80-20355. 190p. 1981. 34.95 (ISBN 0-470-27064-0). Halsted Pr.

Chemical Applications of Thermal Neutron Scattering. B. T. Willis. (Harwell Ser.). (Illus.). 328p. 1973. 45.00x (ISBN 0-19-851709-2). Oxford U Pr.

Chemical Basis of Life: An Introduction to Molecular & Cell Biology: Readings from Scientific American. Intro. by Philip C. Hanawalt & Robert H. Haynes. LC 73-8899. (Illus.). 405p. 1973. text ed. 19.95x (ISBN 0-7167-0882-5); pap. text ed. 9.95x (ISBN 0-7167-0881-7). W H Freeman.

Chemical Binding & Structure. J. E. Spice. 1964. 9.35 (ISBN 0-08-010568-8); pap. 10.75 (ISBN 0-08-010567-X). Pergamon.

Chemical Bond: A Brief Introduction to Modern Structural Chemistry. abr. ed. Linus C. Pauling. (Illus.). 278p. (gr. 11-12). 1967. text ed. 20.00x (ISBN 0-8014-9829-5); pap. text ed. 7.95x (ISBN 0-8014-9829-5). Cornell U Pr.

Chemical Carcinogens & DNA, 2 vols. Philip L. Grover. 1979. Vol. 1, 256p. 59.95 (ISBN 0-8493-5303-3); Vol. 2, 224p. 59.95 (ISBN 0-8493-5304-1). CRC Pr.

Chemical Concepts in Pollutant Behavior. Ian J. Tinsley. LC 78-24301. (Environmental Science & Technology Ser.). 1979. 26.95 (ISBN 0-471-03825-3, Pub. by Wiley-Interscience). Wiley.

Chemical Contraception. John P. Bennett. LC 73-7910. 272p. 1973. 25.00x (ISBN 0-231-03434-2). Columbia U Pr.

Chemical Dynamics. Committee for the Survey of Chemistry. 1966. pap. 4.00 (ISBN 0-309-01292-9). Natl Acad Pr.

Chemical Economy. B. G. Reuben & M. L. Burstall. LC 73-85210. (Illus.). 400p. 1974. text ed. 30.00x (ISBN 0-582-46307-6). Longman.

Chemical Effects of Nuclear Transformations - 1964, 2 vols. (Illus.). 1965. Vol. 1. 21.00 (ISBN 92-0-040065-5, ISP91-1, IAEA); Vol. 2. 26.25 (ISBN 92-0-040165-1, ISP91-2). Unipub.

Chemical (Electroless) Nickel Plating. G. G. Gawrilov. (Illus.). 189p. 1979. 42.50x (ISBN 0-86108-023-8). Intl Pubns Serv.

Chemical Elements & Man: Measurements, Perspectives, Applications. E. I. Hamilton. (Am. Lec. Living Chemistry Ser.). (Illus.). 512p. 1979. 44.75 (ISBN 0-398-03732-9). C C Thomas.

Chemical Engineering. Ed. by J. R. Richardson & D. G. Peacock. (Chemical Engineering Ser.: Vol. 3). (Illus.). 1979. text ed. 75.00 (ISBN 0-08-023818-1); pap. text ed. 24.00 (ISBN 0-08-023819-X). Pergamon.

Chemical Engineering & the Environment. A. S. Teja. (Critical Reports on Applied Chemistry). 115p. 1981. 27.95 (ISBN 0-470-27106-X). Halsted Pr.

Chemical Engineering & the Environments. A. S. Teja. LC 80-26427. 115p. 1981. 27.95 (ISBN 0-470-27106-X). Halsted Pr.

Chemical Engineering Costs. O. T. Zimmerman & Irvin Lavine. 1950. 19.50 (ISBN 0-686-20565-0). Indus Res Serv.

Chemical Engineering Drawing Symbols. D. G. Austin. 1979. 22.95 (ISBN 0-470-26601-5). Halsted Pr.

Chemical Engineering in Practice. G. Nonhebel & M. Berry. LC 73-77793. (Wykeham Science Ser.: No. 28). 1973. pap. 6.25x (ISBN 0-8448-1155-6). Crane-Russak Co.

Chemical Engineering Kinetics. 2nd ed. Joe M. Smith. (Chemical Engineering Ser.). 1970. text ed. 24.95 o.p. (ISBN 0-07-058693-4, C). McGraw.

Chemical Engineering Kinetics. 3rd ed. Joseph M. Smith. (Chemical Engineering Ser.). (Illus.). 704p. 1980. text ed. 27.95 (ISBN 0-07-058710-8, C); solution manual 8.95 (ISBN 0-07-058711-6). McGraw.

Chemical Engineering Laboratory Equipment. 2nd ed. O. T. Zimmerman & Irvin Lavine. 1955. 17.50 (ISBN 0-686-20566-9). Indus Res Serv.

Chemical Engineering S.I. Ed, Vol. 1. 3rd ed. J. M. Coulson et al. LC 75-42295. (Illus.). 412p. 45.00 (ISBN 0-08-020614-X); pap. 17.50 (ISBN 0-08-021015-5). Pergamon.

Chemical Engineering Thermodynamics. R. E. Balzhiser et al. (International Physical & Chemical Engineering Sciences Ser). (Illus.). 1972. ref. ed. 27.95 (ISBN 0-13-128603-X). P-H.

Chemical Engineering, Vol. 5: Solutions to the Problems in Volume Two. 3rd ed. J. M. Coulson et al. LC 78-40923. (Chemical Engineering Technical Ser.). (Illus.). 1979. 37.00 (ISBN 0-08-022951-4); pap. 16.50 (ISBN 0-08-022952-2). Pergamon.

Chemical Equilibria in Soils. Willard L. Lindsay. LC 79-12151. 1979. 28.95 (ISBN 0-471-02704-9, Pub. by Wiley-Interscience). Wiley.

Chemical Equilibrium. 3rd ed. Kenneth Denbigh. LC 74-152638. (Illus.). 1971. text ed. 47.50 (ISBN 0-521-08151-3); pap. text ed. 15.95x (ISBN 0-521-09655-3). Cambridge U Pr.

Chemical Equilibrium & Analysis. Richard W. Ramette. (Chemistry Ser). (Illus.). 672p. 1981. text ed. 23.95 (ISBN 0-201-06107-4). A-W.

Chemical Experimentation: An Integrated Course in Inorganic, Analytical & Physical Chemistry. Ursula A. Hofacker. (Illus.). 1972. lab. manual 10.95x (ISBN 0-7167-0166-9). W H Freeman.

Chemical Experiments. R. H. Warring. (Pegasus Books: No. 33). (Illus.). 152p. 1974. 10.50x (ISBN 0-234-77684-6). Intl Pubns Serv.

Chemical Feedstocks from Coal. Jurgen Falbe. 730p. 1981. 50.00 (ISBN 0-471-05291-4, Pub by Wiley-Interscience). Wiley.

Chemical Formulary, 22 vols. Ed. by H. Bennett. Incl. Vol. 1, 1933 (ISBN 0-8206-0259-0). Vol. 2, 1935 (ISBN 0-8206-0260-4). Vol. 3, 1936 (ISBN 0-8206-0261-2). Vol. 4, 1939 (ISBN 0-8206-0262-0). Vol. 5, 1941 (ISBN 0-8206-0263-9). Vol. 6, 1943 (ISBN 0-8206-0264-7). Vol. 7, 1945 (ISBN 0-8206-0265-5); Vol. 8, 1948 (ISBN 0-8206-0266-3). Vol. 9, 1950 (ISBN 0-8206-0267-1). Vol. 10, 1957 (ISBN 0-8206-0268-X). Vol. 11, 1961 (ISBN 0-8206-0269-8). Vol. 12, 1965 (ISBN 0-8206-0270-1). Vol. 13, 1967 (ISBN 0-8206-0271-X). Vol. 14, 1968 (ISBN 0-8206-0272-8); Vol. 15, 1970 (ISBN 0-8206-0273-6). Vol. 16, 1971 (ISBN 0-8206-0274-4). Vol. 17, 1973 (ISBN 0-8206-0275-2). Vol. 18, 1975 (ISBN 0-8206-0276-0). Vol. 19, 1976 (ISBN 0-8206-0277-9). Vol. 20, 1977 (ISBN 0-8206-0278-7). Vol. 21, 1979 (ISBN 0-8206-0279-5). Vol. 22, 1979 (ISBN 0-8206-0280-9). 22.50 ea. Chem Pub.

Chemical Formulary, Vol. 23. Ed. by H. Bennett. 1981. 22.50 (ISBN 0-8206-0282-5). Chem Pub.

Chemical Foundations: The Alkali Industry in Britain to Nineteen Twenty-Six. Kenneth Warren. (Oxford Research Studies in Geography). (Illus.). 220p. 1980. text ed. 46.00x (ISBN 0-19-823231-4). Oxford U Pr.

Chemical Hazards in the Workplace: Measurement & Control. Ed. by G. Choudhary. (ACS Symposium Ser.: No. 149). 1981. price not set (ISBN 0-8412-0608-2). Am Chemical.

Chemical Industries Information Sources. Ed. by Theodore P. Peck. LC 76-6891. (Management Information Guide Ser.: No. 29). 1979. 30.00 (ISBN 0-8103-0829-0). Gale.

Chemical Industry During the Nineteenth Century: A Study of the Economic Aspect of Applied Chemistry in Europe & North America. L. F. Haber. 1958. 19.95x (ISBN 0-19-858102-5). Oxford U Pr.

Chemical Industry Nineteen Seventy-Eight. 56p. (Fr. & Eng.). 1980. 6.50 (ISBN 92-64-02091-8). OECD.

Chemical Information Systems. Ed. by J. Ash & E. Hyde. LC 74-14904. 309p. 1975. 49.95 (ISBN 0-470-03444-0). Halsted Pr.

Chemical Instrumentation. 2nd ed. H. A. Strobel. 1973. 26.95 (ISBN 0-201-07301-3). A-W.

Chemical Investigations for the Nonscientist. John Tonnis & Gerald Rausch. 1980. coil binding 6.95 (ISBN 0-88252-109-8). Paladin Hse.

Chemical Kinetics. Ralph Weston & Harold Schwarz. (Fundamental Topics in Physical Chemistry Ser). (Illus.). 1972. ref. ed. 17.95 (ISBN 0-13-128660-9). P-H.

Chemical Kinetics: A Modern Survey of Gas Reactions. J. E. Nicholas. LC 75-17433. 1976. 24.95 (ISBN 0-470-63686-6). Halsted Pr.

Chemical Kinetics & Surface & Colloid Chemistry. A. F. Trotman-Dickenson & G. D. Parfitt. (Illus.). 1966. 15.00 (ISBN 0-08-011257-9); pap. 7.00 (ISBN 0-08-011256-0). Pergamon.

Chemical Kinetics for Chemical Engineers. 2nd ed. Bohdan W. Wojciechowski. (Illus.). 333p. 1981. pap. text ed. 11.95 (ISBN 0-88408-130-3). Sterling Swift.

Chemical Kinetics (Homogenous Reactions) N. M. Emanuel' & D. G. Knorre. Ed. by D. Slutzkin. Tr. by R. Kondor from Rus. LC 73-12689. 413p. 1973. text ed. 34.95 (ISBN 0-470-23890-9). Halsted Pr.

Chemical Kinetics of Gas Reactions. V. N. Kondratiev. 1964. text ed. 37.00 o.p. (ISBN 0-08-010108-9). Pergamon.

Chemical Mechanisms of Drug Action. Curt C. Porter. (American Lectures in Living Chemistry Ser). (Illus.). 184p. 1970. 15.50 (ISBN 0-398-01509-0). C C Thomas.

Chemical Mediators in the Acute Inflammatory Reaction. M. Rocha E Silva & J. Garcia Leme. 374p. 1973. text ed. 42.00 (ISBN 0-08-017040-4). Pergamon.

Chemical, Medical, & Pharmaceutical Books Printed Before 1800: In the Collections of the University of Wisconsin Libraries. Ed. by John Neu et al. 1965. 27.50x (ISBN 0-299-03680-4). U of Wis Pr.

Chemical Methods of Rock Analysis. 2nd ed. P. G. Jeffery. Ed. by R. Belcher & H. Freiser. LC 74-16500. 526p. 1975. text ed. 75.00 (ISBN 0-08-018076-0). Pergamon.

Chemical Microstructure of Polymer Chains. Jack L. Koenig. LC 80-15165. 450p. 1980. 42.50 (ISBN 0-471-07725-9, Pub. by Wiley Interscience). Wiley.

Chemical Milling: The Technology of Cutting Materials by Etching. William T. Harris. (Oxford Series on Advanced Manufacturing). (Illus.). 1977. 59.00x (ISBN 0-19-859115-2). Oxford U Pr.

Chemical Modulation of Brain Function. Ed. by H. Sabelli. LC 72-96825. (Illus.). 331p. 1973. 24.50 (ISBN 0-685-92920-5). Raven.

Chemical Pathology: A Progressive, Three Level Approach. M. Desmond Burke & Robert C. Rock. 1980. pap. 8.50 study guide (ISBN 0-89189-075-0, 45-2-038-00). Am Soc Clinical.

Chemical Physics of Ice. Neville H. Fletcher. LC 74-75825. (Monographs on Physics). (Illus.). 1970. 41.95 (ISBN 0-521-07597-1). Cambridge U Pr.

Chemical Physics of Surfaces, Catalysis & Membranes. Per-Olov Lowdin et al. (International Journal of Quantum Chemistry Ser.: Supplement 2). 1978. pap. 21.95 (ISBN 0-471-05247-7, Pub. by Wiley-Interscience). Wiley.

Chemical Plant & Its Operation (Including Safety & Health Aspects) 2nd ed. T. M. Cook & D. J. Cullen. (Illus.). 1980. text ed. 19.00 (ISBN 0-08-023812-2); pap. text ed. 8.50 (ISBN 0-08-023813-0). Pergamon.

Chemical Principles. Robert S. Boikess & Edward Edelson. (Illus.). 1978. pap. text ed. 22.95 scp (ISBN 0-06-040807-3, HarpC); scp lab manual 8.95 (ISBN 0-06-044626-9); scp solution manual 5.50 (ISBN 0-06-040806-5); scp student guide & glossary 7.50 (ISBN 0-06-044572-6); inst. manual avail. (ISBN 0-06-360790-5); ans. bk. free (ISBN 0-06-360791-3). Har-Row.

Chemical Principles. 3rd ed. Richard E. Dickerson et al. LC 77-87336. 1979. pap. text ed. 22.95 (ISBN 0-8053-2398-8); instr's guide 3.95 (ISBN 0-8053-2410-0); programmed reviews 99.95 (ISBN 0-8053-6027-1); problems 10.95 (ISBN 0-8053-1587-X); study guide 7.95 (ISBN 0-8053-2399-6); transparency masters 50.00 (ISBN 0-8053-2396-1). Benjamin-Cummings.

Chemical Principles for the Life Sciences. 2nd ed. Ralph J. Fessenden & Joan S. Fessenden. 1979. text ed. 20.95x (ISBN 0-205-06506-6); instr's manual (ISBN 0-205-06533-3). Allyn.

Chemical Problem Solving by Dimensional Analysis. 2nd ed. Arnold B. Loebel. LC 77-78565. (Illus.). 1978. pap. text ed. 9.50 (ISBN 0-395-25516-3). HM.

Chemical Problem Solving Using Dimensional Analysis. Robert Nakon. (Illus.). 1978. pap. 9.95 (ISBN 0-13-128645-5). P-H.

Chemical Problems for Changing Times. Leon M. Zaborowski & John W. Hill. 1973. pap. text ed. 3.95 o.p. (ISBN 0-8087-2600-5). Burgess.

Chemical Process Control: Theory & Applications. Leonard A. Gould. (Chemical Engineering Ser). 1969. text ed. 21.95 (ISBN 0-201-02562-0). A-W.

Chemical Process Development, 2 pts. 2nd ed. Donald G. Jordan. LC 78-23432. 1979. Repr. of 1968 ed. Pt. 1 428p. lib. bdg. 39.50 (ISBN 0-89874-064-9); Pt. 2 628p. lib. bdg. 45.50 (ISBN 0-88275-806-3); Set 1056p. lib. bdg. 76.50 (ISBN 0-89874-064-9). Krieger.

Chemical Process Industries. 4th ed. R. Norris Shreve & Joseph Brink. (Illus.). 1977. 28.50 (ISBN 0-07-057145-7, P&RB). McGraw.

Chemical Process Principles, 3 pts. O. A. Hougen et al. Incl. Pt. 1. Material & Energy Balances. 2nd ed. 525p. 1954. 33.50x (ISBN 0-471-41283-X); Pt. 2. Thermodynamics. 2nd ed. 624p. 1959. 33.50x (ISBN 0-471-41382-8); Pt. 3. Kinetics & Catalysis. 303p. 1947. o.p. (ISBN 0-471-41415-8). LC 54-13512. Wiley.

Chemical Psychoses: LSD & Related Drugs. Leo E. Hollister. (Amer. Lec. Living Chemistry Ser). (Illus.). 200p. 1972. 11.75 (ISBN 0-398-00860-4). C C Thomas.

Chemical Reaction Engineering: International Symposium on Chemical Reaction Engineering, Nice, France, March 25-27, 1980, Vol. 1, Contributed Papers. Ed. by J. Villermaux & P. Trambouze. LC 79-41749. 540p. 1980. 77.00 (ISBN 0-08-024018-6). Pergamon.

Chemical Reaction Engineering: Proceedings of the Fourth International Symposium. Ed. by R. Jottrand. 1971. 105.00 (ISBN 0-08-013182-4). Pergamon.

Chemical Reaction Engineering: Sixth International Symposium on Chemical Reaction Engineering--Plenary Lectures, Vol. 2. Ed. by J. Villermaux & P. Trambouze. LC 79-41749. (Illus.). 259p. 1980. pap. 40.00 (ISBN 0-08-026234-1). Pergamon.

Chemical Reactions in Solvents & Melts. G. Charlot & B. Tremillon. 1969. 79.00 (ISBN 0-08-012678-2). Pergamon.

Chemical Reactions of Polymers, Vol. 19. E. M. Fettes. 1304p. 1964. 90.00 (ISBN 0-470-39305-X). Wiley.

Chemical Reactivity & Reaction Paths. Ed. by Gilles Klopman. LC 73-17325. 369p. 1974. 32.50 (ISBN 0-471-49355-4, Pub. by Wiley-Interscience). Wiley.

Chemical Reactor Analysis & Design. Gilbert F. Froment & Kenneth B. Bischoff. LC 78-12465. 1979. text ed. 35.95 (ISBN 0-471-02447-3). Wiley.

Chemical Reactor Design for Process Plants, 2 vols. Howard F. Rase. Incl. Vol. 1. Principles & Techniques. 50.00 (ISBN 0-471-01891-0); Vol. 2. Case Studies & Design Data. 27.95 (ISBN 0-471-01890-2). LC 77-1285. 1977 (Pub. by Wiley-Interscience). Wiley.

Chemical Recognition in Biology. Ed. by F. Chapeville & A. O. Haenni. (Molecular Biology, Biochemistry & Biophysics: Vol. 32). (Illus.). 430p. 1980. 57.80 (ISBN 0-387-10205-1). Springer-Verlag.

Chemical Signals: Vertebrates & Aquatic Invertebrates. Ed. by D. Muller-Schwarze & R. M. Silverstein. 450p. 1980. 39.50 (ISBN 0-306-40339-0, Plenum Pr). Plenum Pub.

Chemical Structure - Biological Activity Relationships, Quantitative Approaches: Proceedings of the Third Congress of the Hungarian Pharmacological Society, Budapest, 1979. Ed. by F. Darvas & J. Knoll. LC 80-41281. (Advances in Pharmacological Research & Practice Ser.: Vol. III). 355p. 1981. 67.00 (ISBN 0-08-026388-7). Pergamon.

Chemical Structure Information Handling: A Review of the Literature, 1962-1968. Division Of Chemistry And Chemical Technology. LC 70-602073. (Orig.). 1969. pap. 6.95 (ISBN 0-309-01733-5). Natl Acad Pr.

Chemical Tables. Bela A. Nemeth. LC 75-19223. 1975. 37.95 (ISBN 0-470-63161-9). Halsted Pr.

Chemical Tables for Laboratory & Industry. Wolfgang Helbing & Adolf Burkart. LC 79-26137. 1980. 19.95x (ISBN 0-470-26910-3). Halsted Pr.

Chemical Technicians' Ready Reference Handbook. 2nd ed. Gershon Shugar et al. 864p. 1981. 39.50 (ISBN 0-07-057176-7, P&RB). McGraw.

Chemical Technology. F. A. Henglein. 1969. 105.00 (ISBN 0-08-011848-8). Pergamon.

Chemical Technology: An Encyclopedic Treatment, 7 vols. Intro. by John J. McKetta. Jr. Incl. Vol. 1. Air, Water, Inorganic Chemicals & Nucleonics. 1968. o.p. (ISBN 0-06-491102-0); Vol. 2. Non-Metallic Ores, Silicate Industries & Solid Minerals Fuels. 1971 (ISBN 0-06-491103-9); Vol. 3. Metals & Ores. 1970 (ISBN 0-06-491104-7); Vol. 4. Petroleum & Organic Chemicals. 1972 (ISBN 0-06-491105-5); Vol. 5. Natural Organic Materials & Related Synthetic Products. 1972 (ISBN 0-06-491106-3); Vol. 6. Wood, Paper, Textiles, Plastics & Photographic Materials. 1973 (ISBN 0-06-491107-1); Vol. 7. Vegetable Food Products & Luxuries. 1975 (ISBN 0-06-491108-X); Vol. 8. Edible Oils & Fats & Animal Food Products. 1975 (ISBN 0-06-491109-8). (Illus.). 40.00x ea. B&N.

Chemical Thermodynamics. 3rd ed. Irving M. Klotz & R. M. Rosenberg. 1972. 21.95 (ISBN 0-8053-5506-5). Benjamin-Cummings.

Chemical Thermodynamics - 4: Proceedings. Ed. by J. Rouquerol & R. Sabbah. LC 76-44615. 1977. text ed. 27.00 (ISBN 0-08-021366-9). Pergamon.

Chemical Thermodynamics: A Course of Study. 3rd ed. Frederick T. Wall. LC 73-13808. (Chemistry Ser.). (Illus.). 1974. text ed. 27.95x (ISBN 0-7167-0173-1); answers to problems avail. (ISBN 0-685-39026-8). W H Freeman.

Chemical Thermodynamics of Actinide Elements & Compounds, 2 vols. Incl. Vol. 1. Actinide Elements. F. L. Oetting et al. pap. 10.75 (ISBN 92-0-149076-3); Vol. 2. Actinide Aqueous Ions. J. Fuger & F. L. Oetting. pap. 8.25 (ISBN 92-0-149176-X). (Illus.). 1977 (IAEA). Unipub.

Chemical Thermodynamics of Actinide Elements & Compounds: Part 3, Miscellaneous Actinide Compounds. 1978. pap. 8.75 (ISBN 92-0-149078-X, ISP424-3, IAEA). Unipub.

Chemical Thermodynamics of Organic Compounds. Daniel R. Stull et al. LC 68-9250. 1969. 60.00 (ISBN 0-471-83490-4, Pub. by Wiley-Interscience). Wiley.

Chemical Treatment of Boiler Water. James W. McCoy. (Illus.). 1981. 40.00 (ISBN 0-8206-0284-1). Chem Pub.

Chemical Treatment of Radioactive Wastes. (Technical Reports Ser.: No. 89). (Illus., Orig.). 1968. pap. 6.00 (ISBN 92-0-125468-7, IAEA). Unipub.

Chemical Trends in Wildlife: An International Cooperative Study. (Illus.). 1980. pap. 7.00 (ISBN 9-2641-2105-6). OECD.

Chemical Warfare: A Study in Restraints. Frederic J. Brown. LC 80-27993. xix, 355p. 1981. Repr. of 1968 ed. lib. bdg. 31.75x (ISBN 0-313-22823-X, BRCHW). Greenwood.

Chemical Warfare, Pyrotechnics & the Fireworks Industry. T. F. Watkins et al. 1968. 16.50 (ISBN 0-08-012811-4); pap. 7.75 (ISBN 0-08-012810-6). Pergamon.

Chemical Weapons: Destruction & Conversion. SIPRI. LC 80-13956. 1980. pap. 19.50x (ISBN 0-8448-1349-4). Crane-Russak Co.

Chemical Zoology, 11 vols. Ed. by Marcel Florkin & Bradley T. Sheer. Incl. Vol. 1. 1967. 72.50 (ISBN 0-12-261031-8); Vol. 2. 1968. 62.50 (ISBN 0-12-261032-6); Vol. 3. 1968. 68.50 (ISBN 0-12-261033-4); Vol. 4. 1969. 58.50 (ISBN 0-12-261034-2); Vol. 5. 1970. 52.50 (ISBN 0-12-261035-0); Vol. 6. 1971. 58.50 (ISBN 0-12-261036-9); Vol. 7. 1972. 57.00 (ISBN 0-12-261037-7); Vol. 8. 1974. 75.00 (ISBN 0-12-261038-5); Vol. 9. 1974. 72.50 (ISBN 0-12-261039-3); Vol. 10. 1978. 56.50 (ISBN 0-12-261040-7); Vol. 11. Mammalia. 1979. 49.50 (ISBN 0-12-261041-5). LC 67-23158. Set. 588.75. Acad Pr.

Chemicals for the Semiconductor Industry C-028. 1981. 850.00 (ISBN 0-89336-250-6). BCC.

Chemicals from Petroleum. 3rd ed. A. L. Waddams. LC 73-3397. 1973. pap. 14.95 (ISBN 0-470-91303-7). Halsted Pr.

Chemicals from Petroleum. 4th ed. A. L. Waddams. (Illus.). 375p. 1980. 12.95 (ISBN 0-87201-104-6). Gulf Pub.

Chemicals in the Forest. Michael Newton. 160p. 1980. pap. 10.95 (ISBN 0-917304-25-X, Pub. by Timber Pr). Intl Schol Bk Serv.

Chemins Dangereux. Emile De Harven. LC 75-38836. (Illus.). 140p. 1976. pap. 4.25 (ISBN 0-88436-260-4). EMC.

Chemische Farbreaktion von Pilzen. A. Meixner. 1975. 14.75 o.p. (ISBN 3-7682-0956-3). Lubrecht & Cramer.

Chemisorption: An Experimental Approach. G. Welder. Tr. by D. Klemperer. 1977. text ed. 24.95 (ISBN 0-408-10611-5). Butterworths.

Chemist in Industry, One: Fine Chemicals for Polymers. Ed. by E. S. Stern. (Oxford Chemistry Ser.). (Illus.). 96p. 1973. pap. text ed. 4.95x o.p. (ISBN 0-19-855415-X). Oxford U Pr.

Chemist in Industry Two: Human Health & Plant Protection. J. F. Cavalla & Jones D. Price. (Oxford Chemistry Ser). (Illus.). 96p. 1974. pap. 4.95x o.p. (ISBN 0-19-855416-8). Oxford U Pr.

Chemist in Industry (3) Management & Economics. M. H. Freemantle. (Oxford Chemistry Ser). (Illus.). 96p. 1975. 14.95x (ISBN 0-19-855497-4). Oxford U Pr.

Chemistry. John C. Bailar et al. 940p. 1978. 21.95 (ISBN 0-12-072850-8); instr's. manual 3.00 (ISBN 0-12-072852-4); study guide 6.95 (ISBN 0-12-072854-0). Acad Pr.

Chemistry. Boy Socuts of America. LC 19-600. (Illus.). 48p. (gr. 6-12). 1973. pap. 0.70x (ISBN 0-8395-3367-5, 3367). BSA.

Chemistry. 2nd ed. Daryle H. Busch et al. 1978. text ed. 21.95 (ISBN 0-205-05704-7); instr's manual (ISBN 0-205-05705-5). Allyn.

Chemistry. Raymond Chang. Incl. Eugene Losey. wkbk. 6.95 (ISBN 0-394-32447-1); Harold Goldwhite & John Spielman. solutions to problem sets 4.95 (ISBN 0-394-32519-2). 815p. 1981. text ed. 23.95 (ISBN 0-394-31224-4). Random.

Chemistry. (Undergraduate Program Field Test Ser.: UPFT-4). (Cloth bdg. avail. on request). pap. 9.95 (ISBN 0-8373-6004-8). Natl Learning.

Chemistry. Eugene Cordes & Riley S. Schaeffer. (Rice Chemistry Ser.). (Illus.). 702p. 1973. text ed. 23.50 scp (ISBN 0-06-041359-X, HarpC); instructor's manual avail. (ISBN 0-06-361393-X). Har-Row.

Chemistry. 2nd ed. T. L. Cottrell. (Oxford Paperbacks University Ser). 1970. pap. 1.95x o.p. (ISBN 0-19-888047-2). Oxford U Pr.

Chemistry. King. 1979. 19.95 (ISBN 0-525-07926-2). Dutton.

Chemistry. Edward L. King. 1100p. 1981. text ed. 23.95 (ISBN 0-394-32761-6). Random.

Chemistry. Gary E. Maciel et al. 1978. text ed. 21.95x (ISBN 0-669-84830-1); inst. manual free (ISBN 0-669-99945-8); lab manual 7.95x (ISBN 0-669-00999-7); study guide 6.95x (ISBN 0-669-01000-6); solutions manual 3.99 (ISBN 0-669-01027-8). Heath.

Chemistry. Linus Pauling & Peter Pauling. LC 74-34071. (Chemistry Ser.). (Illus.). 770p. 1975. 23.95x (ISBN 0-7167-0176-6); ans. bk. avail. (ISBN 0-685-55250-0). W H Freeman.

Chemistry. 3rd ed. James Quagliano & L. Vallarino. 1969. ref. ed. 21.95x (ISBN 0-13-128926-8); answers to selected problems 0.25 (ISBN 0-13-128934-9). P-H.

Chemistry. A. Truman Schwartz. 1973. text ed. 18.50 (ISBN 0-12-632950-8). Acad Pr.

Chemistry. Michael J. Walsh. Ed. by Stanley H. Kaplan. LC 57-58729. (High School Regents Exams & Answer Ser.). (gr. 9-12). 1977. pap. 3.95 (ISBN 0-8120-0109-5). Barron.

Chemistry. George W. Watt et al. (Illus.). 1964. 15.95x (ISBN 0-393-09511-8, NortonC); pap. labaratory manual. 9.95x (ISBN 0-393-09626-2). Norton.

Chemistry: A Basic Introduction. G. Tyler Miller. 1978. text ed. 18.95x o.p. (ISBN 0-534-00527-6); study guide 6.95x o.p. (ISBN 0-534-00623-X); lab manual 8.95x o.p. (ISBN 0-534-00529-2). Wadsworth Pub.

Chemistry: A Basic Introduction. 2nd ed. G. Tyler Miller, Jr. 560p. 1980. text ed. 18.95x (ISBN 0-534-00878-X). Wadsworth Pub.

Chemistry: A Contemporary Approach. G. Tyler Miller, Jr. 1976. text ed. 19.95x (ISBN 0-534-00456-3). Wadsworth Pub.

Chemistry: A Quantitative Approach. R. Nelson Smith. LC 71-75642. 639p. 1969. 24.50x o.p. (ISBN 0-8260-8300-5); lab. manual 9.95x o.p. (ISBN 0-8260-8301-3). Wiley.

Chemistry: A Structural View. D. R. Stranks et al. LC 74-31783. 500p. 1975. 41.50 (ISBN 0-521-20707-X); pap. 19.95x (ISBN 0-521-09928-5). Cambridge U Pr.

Chemistry, a Study of Matter. 3rd ed. W. T. Lippincott. 1977. 21.95x (ISBN 0-471-29246-X); study guide 7.95 (ISBN 0-471-02221-7); tchrs'. manual avail. (ISBN 0-471-02689-1). Wiley.

Chemistry: A Unified Approach. J. W. Buttle et al. 1981. text ed. price not set (ISBN 0-408-70938-3). Butterworth.

Chemistry Achievement Test. Leo Spector & Richard Weiss. LC 65-23057. (College Board Ach. Test Ser.). 318p. 1966. lib. bdg. 4.50 o.p. (ISBN 0-668-01261-7). Arco.

Chemistry: An Experimental Science. Ed. by George C. Pimentel. LC 63-18323. (Chemical Education Material Study). (Illus.). 1963. text ed. 11.95x (ISBN 0-7167-0001-8); tchrs guide o.p. 14.95x (ISBN 0-7167-0003-4); lab manual ed. by Lloyd E Malm 2.00x (ISBN 0-7167-0002-6). W H Freeman.

Chemistry: An Introduction to General, Organic, & Biological Chemistry. Joanne M. Widom & Stuart J. Edelstein. LC 80-23816. (Illus.). 1981. text ed. 22.95x (ISBN 0-7167-1224-5); instr's. manual avail.; study guide 4.95x. W H Freeman.

Chemistry & Biochemistry of Estuaries. Eric Olausson & Ingemar Cato. LC 79-41211. 432p. 1980. 80.00 (ISBN 0-471-27679-0, Pub. by Wiley-Interscience). Wiley.

Chemistry & Biochemistry of the Sulfhydryl Group in Amino Acids, Peptides & Proteins. Mendel Friedman. 1973. text ed. 72.00 (ISBN 0-08-016845-0). Pergamon.

Chemistry & Biology of the Starch Granule. N. P. Badenhuizen. (Protoplasmatologia Ser.: Vol. 2B, Pt. 2bs). (Illus.). 1959. pap. 26.00 o.p. (ISBN 0-387-80522-2). Springer-Verlag.

Chemistry & Chemical Engineering of Catalytic Processes. Ed. by G. G. Schuit & R. Prins. (NATO-Advanced Study Institute Ser.). 660p. 1980. 75.00x (ISBN 9-0286-0730-7). Sijthoff & Noordhoff.

Chemistry & Cytochemistry of Nucleic Acids & Nuclear Proteins. C. Scholtissek et al. (Protoplasmatologia: Vol. 5, Pt. 3A-D). (Illus.). 1966. pap. 57.90 o.p. (ISBN 0-387-80782-9). Springer-Verlag.

Chemistry & Fertility of Sea Waters. 2nd ed. Hildebrande W. Harvey. 1957. 43.00 (ISBN 0-521-05225-4). Cambridge U Pr.

Chemistry & Function of Proteins. 2nd ed. Felix Haurowitz. 455p. 1963. text ed. 19.50 (ISBN 0-12-332956-6). Acad Pr.

Chemistry & Metabolism of the Vitamin B6 Antagonist, 4' Deoxypyridoxine. Stephen P. Coburn. 224p. 1981. 69.95 (ISBN 0-8493-5783-7). CRC Pr.

Chemistry & Physics of Anesthesia. 2nd ed. John Adriani. (Illus.). 862p. 1979. 39.75 (ISBN 0-398-00011-5). C C Thomas.

Chemistry & Physics of Carbon, Vol. 16. Walker & Thrower. 376p. 1981. 42.50 (ISBN 0-8247-6991-0). Dekker.

Chemistry & Physics of Clays. 4th ed. R. W. Grimshaw. LC 76-178139. 1032p. 1971. 49.95 (ISBN 0-471-32780-8). Halsted Pr.

Chemistry & Physiology of Mitochondria & Microsomes. O. Lindberg & L. Ernster. (Protoplasmatologia: Vol. 3, Pt. 4). (Illus.). 1954. 30.70 o.p. (ISBN 0-387-80346-7). Springer-Verlag.

Chemistry & Physiology of the Human Plasma Proteins: Proceedings of a Conference Held November 19-21 1978 in Boston, Massachusetts, USA. rev. ed. Sponsored by the Center for Blood Research. Ed. by David H. Bing. LC 79-10742. (Illus.). 416p. 1979. 44.00 (ISBN 0-08-023860-2). Pergamon.

Chemistry & Technology of Cellulose Copolymers. A. Hebeisch & J. T. Guthrie. (Polymers - Properties & Applications Ser.: Vol. 4). (Illus.). 340p. 1981. 87.30 (ISBN 0-387-10164-0). Springer-Verlag.

Chemistry & Technology of Lime & Limestone. 2nd ed. Robert S. Boynton. LC 79-16140. 1980. 54.00 (ISBN 0-471-02771-5, Pub. by Wiley-Interscience). Wiley.

Chemistry & Testing of Dairy Products. 4th ed. Henry V. Atherton & John A. Newlander. (Illus.). 1977. text ed. 17.00 (ISBN 0-87055-253-8). AVI.

Chemistry & the Food System. ACS Committee on Chemistry & Public Affairs. LC 80-11194. 1980. 15.00 (ISBN 0-8412-0557-4); pap. 9.00 (ISBN 0-8412-0563-9). Am Chemical.

Chemistry & Unit Operations in Sewage Treatment. D. Barnes & F. Wilson. (Illus.). 1978. text ed. 51.30x (ISBN 0-85334-783-2, Pub. by Applied Science). Burgess-Intl Ideas.

Chemistry, Biochemistry & Pharmacology of Prostanoids. Ed. by S. M. Roberts & F. Scheinmann. 1978. text ed. 90.00 (ISBN 0-08-023799-1). Pergamon.

Chemistry by Concept. Antony Spiers & Derek Stebbens. 1973. pap. text ed. 8.95x o.p. (ISBN 0-435-64830-6). Heinemann Ed.

Chemistry by Discovery. G. Van Praagh. (gr. 8-12). 5.95 (ISBN 0-7195-1439-8). Transatlantic.

Chemistry by Inquiry. Derek Stebbens. pap. text ed. 4.95x o.p. (ISBN 0-435-64841-1); tchr's guide 4.95x o.p. (ISBN 0-435-64842-X). Heinemann Ed.

Chemistry Careers. L. B. Taylor, Jr. (Career Concise Guides Ser.). (Illus.). (gr. 7 up). 1978. PLB 6.45 s&l (ISBN 0-531-01420-7). Watts.

Chemistry Check-up. A. H. Johnstone & I. M. Duncan. 1974. pap. text ed. 3.95x o.p. (ISBN 0-435-64183-2). Heinemann Ed.

Chemistry: Elementary Principles. P. F. Weller & J. H. Supple. 1971. 17.95 (ISBN 0-201-08596-8). A-W.

Chemistry, Energy, & Human Ecology. Frederick Kabbe & Lois Kabbe. LC 75-27126. (Illus.). 464p. 1976. pap. text ed. 16.95 (ISBN 0-395-19833-X); instr. manual 1.00 (ISBN 0-395-19831-3); slides o.p. 11.25 (ISBN 0-395-19832-1). HM.

Chemistry Experiments. A. Kemper. (Science Experiments Ser). (Illus.). 1965. 17.50x (ISBN 0-222-69371-1). Intl Pubns Serv.

Chemistry Explained. Robert L. Wolke. (Illus.). 1980. text ed. 18.95 (ISBN 0-13-129163-7). P-H.

Chemistry for Biologists. J. G. Stamper & M. A. Stamper. 1971. pap. text ed. 5.95x (ISBN 0-04-540006-7). Allen Unwin.

Chemistry for Health-Related Sciences: Concepts & Correlations. Conrad L. Stanitski & Curtis T. Sears. 1976. 19.95 (ISBN 0-13-129429-6); lab. manual 8.95 (ISBN 0-13-129437-7); student guide 6.95 (ISBN 0-13-129403-2). P-H.

Chemistry for Technologists. G. R. Palin. LC 70-142175. 355p. 1972. text ed. 25.00 (ISBN 0-08-016385-8); pap. text ed. 12.75 (ISBN 0-08-016386-6). Pergamon.

Chemistry for the Allied Health Sciences. R. Bauer & R. Loeschen. 1980. 19.95 (ISBN 0-13-129205-6); lab manual 7.95 (ISBN 0-13-129213-7); student guide 6.95 (ISBN 0-13-129197-1). P-H.

Chemistry for the Engineering & Applied Sciences: Second Edition of Chemistry for the Applied Sciences. 2nd ed. W. Steedman et al. 1980. 69.00 (ISBN 0-08-022851-8); pap. 19.25 (ISBN 0-08-022852-6). Pergamon.

Chemistry for the Health Professions. Charles Henrickson & Larry Byrd. (Illus.). 798p. 1980. text ed. 21.95 (ISBN 0-442-23258-6); instr's. manual 3.50 (ISBN 0-442-26252-3); Student Self Study Guide by John R. Wilson 7.95. D Van Nostrand.

Chemistry for the Life Sciences. Lee R. Summerlin. Incl. P. S. Associates. wkbk. 6.95 (ISBN 0-394-32457-9); William Hendrickson & Juanita Healy. lab manual 6.95 (ISBN 0-394-32520-6). 631p. 1981. text ed. 19.95 (ISBN 0-394-32215-0). Random.

Chemistry for the Million. Richard F. Smith. LC 77-37219. 1974. pap. 2.95 o.p. (ISBN 0-684-13692-9, SL507, ScribT). Scribner.

Chemistry for the Modern Mind. Joachim Rudolph. Tr. by H. C. Grinter. LC 73-6202. (Science for the Modern Mind Ser.). (Illus.). 358p. 1974. 12.95 (ISBN 0-02-605850-2). Macmillan.

Chemistry: Ideas to Interpret Your Changing Environment. Tom Hughes. 1975. text ed. 19.95x (ISBN 0-8221-0138-6). Dickenson.

Chemistry in Modern Perspective. G. E. Gordon & W. H. Zoller. 1975. 18.95 (ISBN 0-201-02561-2); lab manual 6.95 (ISBN 0-201-03154-X). A-W.

Chemistry in Two Dimensions: Surfaces. Gabor A. Somorjai. LC 80-21443. (George Fisher Baker Non-Resident Lectureship in Chemistry at Cornell University Ser.). (Illus.). 552p. 1981. 48.50 (ISBN 0-8014-1179-3). Cornell U Pr.

Chemistry in Water Reuse, Vol. 1. Ed. by William J. Cooper. 350p. 1981. text ed. 39.95 (ISBN 0-686-69578-X). Ann Arbor Science.

Chemistry in Water Reuse, Vol. 2. William J. Cooper. 1981. text ed. 39.95 (ISBN 0-250-40391-9). Ann Arbor Science.

Chemistry: Inorganic, Organic & Biological. Philip S. Chen. (Orig.). 1968. pap. 3.95 o.p. (ISBN 0-06-460082-3, 82, COS). Har-Row.

Chemistry: Inorganic, Organic & Biological. 2nd ed. Philip S. Chen. (College Outline Ser.). 288p. 1980. pap. text ed. 4.95 (ISBN 0-06-460182-X, CO 182, COS). Har-Row.

Chemistry: Its Role in Society. James S. Chickos et al. 1973. pap. text ed. 7.95x o.p. (ISBN 0-669-83030-5); instructor's guide free o.p. (ISBN 0-669-83048-8). Heath.

Chemistry Made Simple. Fred C. Hess. 1955. pap. 3.50 (ISBN 0-385-01207-1, Made). Doubleday.

Chemistry, Matter, & the Universe. Richard E. Dickerson & Irving Geis. 1976. 21.95 (ISBN 0-8053-2369-4); study guide 5.25 (ISBN 0-8053-5260-0); instr's guide 3.95 (ISBN 0-8053-2380-5). Benjamin-Cummings.

Chemistry of Arsenic, Antimony & Bismuth. J. D. Smith. (Pergamon Texts in Inorganic Chemistry: Vol. 2). 138p. 1975. text ed. 27.00 (ISBN 0-08-018778-1); pap. text ed. 14.00 (ISBN 0-08-018777-3). Pergamon.

Chemistry of Art. 1980. 3.00 (ISBN 0-910362-13-0). Chem Educ.

Chemistry of Boron. N. N. Greenwood. (Pergamon Texts in Inorganic Chemistry: Vol. 8). 328p. 1975. text ed. 46.00 (ISBN 0-08-018790-0); pap. text ed. 26.00 (ISBN 0-08-018789-7). Pergamon.

Chemistry of Building Materials. R. M. Diamant. (Illus.). 258p. 1970. 19.50x (ISBN 0-8464-0240-8). Beekman Pubs.

Chemistry of Catalytic Hydrocarbon Conversions. Herman Pines. 1981. price not set (ISBN 0-12-557160-7). Acad Pr.

Chemistry of Chalcones & Related Compounds. D. N. Dhar. 300p. 1981. 29.50 (ISBN 0-471-08007-1, Pub. by Wiley-Interscience). Wiley.

Chemistry of Chelation in Cancer. Arthur Furst. 160p. 1963. pap. 14.75 photocopy ed. spiral (ISBN 0-398-00633-4). C C Thomas.

Chemistry of Chlorine, Bromine, Iodine & Astatine. A. J. Downs & C. J. Adams. (Pergamon Texts in Inorganic Chemistry: Vol. 7). 488p. 1975. text ed. 64.00 (ISBN 0-08-018788-9); pap. text ed. 35.00 (ISBN 0-08-018787-0). Pergamon.

Chemistry of Chromium, Molybdenum & Tungsten. C. L. Rollinson. (Pergamon Texts in Inorganic Chemistry: Vol. 21). 148p. 1975. text ed. 28.00 (ISBN 0-08-018868-0); pap. text ed. 14.50 (ISBN 0-08-018867-2). Pergamon.

Chemistry of Clay-Organic Reactions. Benny K. Theng. LC 74-12524. 343p. 1974. 67.95 o.p. (ISBN 0-470-85852-4). Halsted Pr.

Chemistry of Coal Utilization, Vols. 1 & 2. H. H. Lowry. LC 45-5498. 1945. Set. 69.50 (ISBN 0-471-02494-5, Pub. by Wiley-Interscience); suppl. vol. (1963) 80.00 (ISBN 0-471-55158-9). Wiley.

Chemistry of Coal Utilization: Supplementary Volume 2. Ed. by Martin A. Elliott. LC 80-13296. 1981. 150.00 (ISBN 0-471-07726-7, Pub. by Wiley-Interscience). Wiley.

Chemistry of Cyclo-Octatetraene & Its Derivatives. G. I. Fray & R. G. Saxton. LC 76-57096. 1978. 95.00 (ISBN 0-521-21580-3). Cambridge U Pr.

Chemistry of Death. W. E. Evans. 120p. 1963. pap. 14.75 photocopy ed. spiral (ISBN 0-398-00530-3). C C Thomas.

Chemistry of Diacetylenes. M. F. Shostakovskii. Ed. by N. Lederman. Tr. by N. Mandel from Rus. Ed. by A. V. Bogdanova. LC 74-8274. 493p. 1974. 64.95 (ISBN 0-470-78854-2). Halsted Pr.

Chemistry of Effluent Treatment. Ed. by George Kakabadse. (Illus.). 1979. 36.30x (ISBN 0-85334-840-5, Pub. by Applied Science). Burgess-Intl Ideas.

Chemistry of Electrode Processes. Ilana Fried. 1974. 30.50 (ISBN 0-12-267650-5). Acad Pr.

Chemistry of Fire & Hazardous Materials. Turner & McCreery. 1980. text ed. 16.95 (ISBN 0-205-06912-6, 826912-2). Allyn.

Chemistry of Fluorine. T. A. O'Donnell. (Pergamon Texts in Inorganic Chemistry: Vol. 5). 98p. 1975. text ed. 18.75 (ISBN 0-08-018784-6); pap. text ed. 10.75 (ISBN 0-08-018783-8). Pergamon.

Chemistry of Free Atoms & Particles. Kenneth J. Klabunde. 1980. 29.50 (ISBN 0-12-410750-8). Acad Pr.

Chemistry of Germanium, Tin & Lead. E. G. Rochow & E. W. Abel. (Pergamon Texts in Inorganic Chemistry: Vol. 14). 146p. 1975. text ed. 27.00 (ISBN 0-08-018854-0); pap. text ed. 14.00 (ISBN 0-08-018853-2). Pergamon.

Chemistry of Heterocyclic Compounds, Vols. 5, 13, 14 & 30. Incl. Vol. 5. Pyridazine & Pyrazine Rings. J. C. Simpson. LC 52-6641. 1953. 42.50 o.p. (ISBN 0-470-37620-1); Vol. 13. S-Triazines. L. Rapoport & E. M. Smolin. 1959. 56.95 o.p. (ISBN 0-470-37884-0); Vol. 14. Thiophene, 2 pts. R. E. Abramovitch. 552p. 1954. Pt. 1. 70.00 o.p. (ISBN 0-471-37913-1); Pt. 2. 79.50 o.p. (ISBN 0-471-37914-X); Vol. 30. Special Topics in Heterocyclic Chemistry0. A. Weissberger & E. C. Taylor. LC 76-10672. 1957. 75.00 (ISBN 0-471-67253-X). Pub. by Wiley-Interscience). Wiley.

Chemistry of Heterocyclic Compounds: Indoles. William J. Houlihan. LC 76-154323. (Chemistry of Heterocyclic Compounds: Monographs: Vol. 25, Pt. 3). 1979. 93.50 (ISBN 0-471-05132-2, Pub. by Wiley-Interscience). Wiley.

Chemistry of Human Behavior. Herbert L. Meltzer. LC 77-19195. (Illus.). 1978. 18.95 (ISBN 0-88229-177-7). Nelson-Hall.

Chemistry of Interfaces. M. J. Jaycock & G. D. Parfitt. LC 80-40387. (Physical Chemistry Ser.). 370p. Date not set. 90.00 (ISBN 0-470-27013-6, Pub. by Halsted Pr). Wiley.

Chemistry of Iron, Cobalt & Nickel. D. Nicholls. (Pergamon Texts in Inorganic Chemistry: Vol. 24). 184p. 1975. text ed. 32.00 (ISBN 0-08-018874-5); pap. text ed. 17.50 (ISBN 0-08-018873-7). Pergamon.

Chemistry of Life: Eight Lectures on the History of Biochemistry. Joseph Needham. LC 78-85733. (Illus.). 1970. 32.95 (ISBN 0-521-07379-0). Cambridge U Pr.

Chemistry of Lithium, Sodium, Potassium, Rubidium, Cesium & Francium. W. A. Hart et al. (Pergamon Texts in Inorganic Chemistry: Vol. 13). 200p. 1975. text ed. 28.00 (ISBN 0-08-018852-4); pap. text ed. 17.50 (ISBN 0-08-018799-4). Pergamon.

Chemistry of Living Systems. Robert Steiner et al. 1981. text ed. write for info. (ISBN 0-442-20052-8). D Van Nostrand.

Chemistry of Manganese, Technetium & Rhenium. Ed. by R. Kemmit. R. Peacock. (Pergamon Texts in Inorganic Chemistry: Vol. 22). 208p. 1975. text ed. 28.00 (ISBN 0-08-018870-2); pap. text ed. 17.50 (ISBN 0-08-018869-9). Pergamon.

Chemistry of Monatomic Gases. A. H. Cockett et al. (Pergamon Texts in Inorganic Chemistry: Vol. 4). 192p. 1975. text ed. 28.00 (ISBN 0-08-018782-X); pap. text ed. 17.50 (ISBN 0-08-018781-1). Pergamon.

Chemistry of Natural Products, Eleven: International Symposium on Chemistry of Natural Products, 11th, Golden Sands, Bulgaria, 17-23 September, 1978. Ed. by R. Vlahov. 1979. 41.00 (ISBN 0-08-022366-4). Pergamon.

Chemistry of Natural Waters. Aly Faust. 450p. 1981. text ed. 40.00 (ISBN 0-250-40387-0). Ann Arbor Science.

Chemistry of Nitrogen. K. Jones. (Pergamon Texts in Inorganic Chemistry: Vol. 11). 242p. 1975. text ed. 37.00 (ISBN 0-08-018796-X); pap. text ed. 22.00 (ISBN 0-08-018795-1). Pergamon.

Chemistry of One, Two, Three-Triazines & One, Two, Four-Triazines, Tetrazines & Pentazines. Hans Neunhoeffer & Paul F. Wiley. LC 77-18932. (Chemistry of Heterocyclic Compounds Ser.: Vol. 33). 1978. Vol. 33. 132.95 (ISBN 0-471-03129-1, Pub. by Wiley-Interscience). Wiley.

Chemistry of Organic Fluorine Compounds. Milos Hudlicky. LC 73-14377. 903p. 1976. text ed. 145.95 (ISBN 0-470-41835-4). Halsted Pr.

Chemistry of Organolithium Compounds. B. J. Wakefield. LC 73-10091. 336p. 1974. text ed. 49.00 (ISBN 0-08-017640-2). Pergamon.

Chemistry of Our Environment. R. A. Horne. LC 77-1156. 1978. 37.50 (ISBN 0-471-40944-8, Pub. by Wiley-Interscience). Wiley.

Chemistry of Oxygen. E. A. Ebsworth et al. (Pergamon Texts in Inorganic Chemistry: Vol. 16). 110p. 1975. text ed. 23.00 (ISBN 0-08-018858-3); pap. text ed. 13.25 (ISBN 0-08-018857-5). Pergamon.

Chemistry of Penicillins & Other Beta-Lactams. Maghar S. Manhas. Ed. by Bose K. Ajay. LC 78-27100. 248p. 1981. Repr. of 1971 ed. write for info. (ISBN 0-88275-830-6). Krieger.

Chemistry of Phosphorous. A. D. Toy. (Pergamon Texts in Inorganic Chemistry: Vol. 3). 158p. 1975. text ed. 27.00 (ISBN 0-08-018780-3); pap. text ed. 14.00 (ISBN 0-08-018779-X). Pergamon.

Chemistry of Phosphorus. John Emsley & Dennis Hall. LC 75-17432. 1976. 54.95 (ISBN 0-470-23869-0). Halsted Pr.

Chemistry of Platinum & Palladium: With Particular Reference to Complexes of the Elements. F. R. Hartley. LC 72-11319. 1973. 59.95 (ISBN 0-470-35658-8). Halsted Pr.

Chemistry of Radiopharmaceuticals. 3rd ed. Ed. by Ned D. Heindel et al. LC 77-94827. (Cancer Management Ser.). (Illus.). 1978. 37.75 (ISBN 0-89352-019-5). Masson Pub.

Chemistry of Ruthenium, Rhodium, Palladium, Osmium, Iridium & Platinum. S. E. Livingstone. (Pergamon Texts in Inorganic Chemistry: Vol. 25). 208p. 1975. text ed. 32.00 (ISBN 0-08-018876-1); pap. text ed. 17.50 (ISBN 0-08-018875-3). Pergamon.

Chemistry of Silicon. E. G. Rochow. (Pergamon Texts in Inorganic Chemistry: Vol. 9). 146p. 1975. text ed. 27.00 (ISBN 0-08-018792-7); pap. text ed. 14.00 (ISBN 0-08-018791-9). Pergamon.

Chemistry of Soil Processes. D. J. Greenland & M. H. Hayes. LC 79-42908. 618p. 1981. 92.95 (ISBN 0-471-27693-6, Pub. by Wiley-Interscience). Wiley.

Chemistry of Sphingolipids. David Shapiro. LC 70-451052. (Chemistry of Natural Products Ser.). 111p. 1969. 18.50x (ISBN 0-8002-0293-7). Intl Pubns Serv.

Chemistry of Sulphoniom Group, Part 2. C. J. Stirling. (Chemistry of Functional Group Ser.). 1400p. 1981. 130.00 (ISBN 0-471-27770-3, Pub.by Wiley-Interscience); Set. 240.00 (ISBN 0-471-27655-3). Wiley.

Chemistry of Sulphur, Selenium, Tellurium & Polonium. M. Schmidt et al. (Pergamon Texts in Inorganic Chemistry: Vol. 15). 214p. 1975. text ed. 32.00 (ISBN 0-08-018856-7); pap. text ed. 17.50 (ISBN 0-08-018855-9). Pergamon.

Chemistry of Synthethic Dyes, 8 vols. Ed. by Krishnasami Venkataraman. Incl. Vol. 1. 1952. 62.50 (ISBN 0-12-717001-4); Vol. 2. 1952. 62.50 (ISBN 0-12-717001-4); Vol. 3. 1970. 62.50 (ISBN 0-12-717003-0); Vol. 4. 1971. 62.50 (ISBN 0-12-717004-9); Vol. 5. 1972. 68.00 (ISBN 0-12-717005-7); Vol. 6. 1973. 62.50 (ISBN 0-12-717006-5); Vol. 7. 1974. 62.50 (ISBN 0-12-717007-3); Vol. 8. 1978. 62.50 (ISBN 0-12-717008-1). (Organic & Biological Chemistry Ser.). Set. 412.00 (ISBN 0-12-717002-2). Acad Pr.

Chemistry of Thallium. A. G. Lee. (Illus.). 1971. text ed. 59.60x (ISBN 0-444-20112-2, Pub. by Applied Science). Burgess-Intl Ideas.

Chemistry of the Actinides. S. Ahrland et al. (Pergamon Texts in Inorganic Chemistry: Vol. 10). 636p. 1975. text ed. 75.00 (ISBN 0-08-018794-3); pap. text ed. 35.00 (ISBN 0-08-018793-5). Pergamon.

Chemistry of the Atmosphere. M. J. McEwan & L. F. Phillips. LC 75-14487. 1975. 39.95x (ISBN 0-470-58393-2). Halsted Pr.

Chemistry of the Lanthanides. T. Moeller. (Pergamon Texts in Inorganic Chemistry: Vol. 26). 104p. 1975. text ed. 23.00 (ISBN 0-08-018878-8); pap. text ed. 13.25 (ISBN 0-08-018877-X). Pergamon.

Chemistry of the Nitro & Nitroso Groups. Ed. by H. Feuer. LC 68-29395. (Chemistry of Functional Groups Ser: Pt. 2). 1970. 37.95 o.p. (ISBN 0-471-25791-5, Pub. by Wiley-Interscience). Wiley.

Chemistry of the Nitro & Nitroso Groups: Part 1. Ed. by Henry Feuer. LC 80-21491. 996p. 1981. Repr. of 1969 ed. text ed. write for info. (ISBN 0-89874-271-4). Krieger.

Chemistry of the Nitro & Nitroso Groups: Part 2. Ed. by Henry Feuer. LC 80-21491. 450p. 1981. Repr. text ed. write for info. (ISBN 0-89874-272-2). Krieger.

Chemistry of the Non-Metallic Elements. E. Sherwin & G. J. Weston. 1966. 15.00 (ISBN 0-08-011296-X); pap. 7.00 (ISBN 0-08-011295-1). Pergamon.

Chemistry of the O-Glycosidic Bond: Formation & Cleavage. A. E. Bochkov & G. E. Zaikov. 1979. 45.00 (ISBN 0-08-022949-2). Pergamon.

Chemistry of the Sulphonium Group, 2 pts. C. J. Stirling. (Chemistry of Functional Groups). 1981. Pt. 1. 110.00 (ISBN 0-471-27769-X, Pub. by Wiley-Interscience); Pt. 2. write for info. (ISBN 0-471-27770-3). Wiley.

Chemistry of the Transition Elements. A. Earnshaw & T. J. Harrington. (Oxford Chemistry Ser.). (Illus.). 112p. 1973. pap. 8.95x (ISBN 0-19-855425-7). Oxford U Pr.

Chemistry of Titanium, Zirconium & Hafnium. R. Clark et al. (Pergamon Texts in Inorganic Chemistry: Vol. 19). 136p. 1975. text ed. 27.00 (ISBN 0-08-018864-8); pap. text ed. 14.00 (ISBN 0-08-018863-X). Pergamon.

Chemistry of Vanadium, Niobium & Tantalum. R. Clark & D. Brown. (Pergamon Texts in Inorganic Chemistry: Vol. 20). 132p. 1975. text ed. 27.00 (ISBN 0-08-018866-4); pap. text ed. 14.00 (ISBN 0-08-018865-6). Pergamon.

Chemistry of Viruses. C. A. Knight. (Protoplasmatologia: Vol. 4, Pt. 2). (Illus.). 1963. pap. 29.50 o.p. (ISBN 0-387-80652-0). Springer-Verlag.

Chemistry: Opportunities & Needs. Committee For The Survey Of Chemistry. 1965. pap. 6.00 (ISBN 0-309-01292-9). Natl Acad Pr.

Chemistry: Principles & Properties. 2nd ed. Michell J. Sienko & Robert A. Plane. (Illus.). 736p. 1974. text ed. 19.00 o.p. (ISBN 0-07-057364-6, C); instructor's manual 6.50 o.p. (ISBN 0-07-057365-2); study guide 7.00 o.p. (ISBN 0-686-57683-7). McGraw.

Chemistry Problems. 2nd ed. Michael J. Sienko. LC 70-151306. (Chemistry Ser.). 1972. pap. text ed. 8.95 (ISBN 0-8053-8808-7). Benjamin-Cummings.

Chemistry Problems & How to Solve Them. 7th ed. Paul R. Frey. (Illus., Orig.). 1969. pap. 4.95 (ISBN 0-06-460046-7, CO 46, COS). Har-Row.

Chemistry: Process & Prospect. Mary A. Merrill. LC 72-90998. (gr. 9-12). 1973. text ed. 17.95x (ISBN 0-675-09023-7); wkbk. 9.95 (ISBN 0-675-09026-1). Merrill.

Chemistry Research & Chemical Techniques Based on Research Reactors. (Technical Reports Ser.: No. 17). (Illus., Orig.). 1963. pap. 10.75 (ISBN 92-0-045063-6, IAEA). Unipub.

Chemistry Takes Shape. A. H. Johnstone & T. I. Morrison. Incl. Book 1. 1964. pap. text ed. 4.50x o.p. (ISBN 0-435-64482-3); tchrs guide 2.50x o.p. (ISBN 0-435-64484-X); Book 2. 1965. pap. text ed. 4.50x o.p. (ISBN 0-435-64486-6); Book 3. 1966. pap. text ed. 5.50x o.p. (ISBN 0-435-64490-4); Book 4. pap. text ed. 5.50x o.p. (ISBN 0-435-64494-7); tchrs guide 2.50x o.p. (ISBN 0-435-64495-5); Book 5. 1970. pap. text ed. 6.50x o.p. (ISBN 0-435-64497-1); tchrs. ed. 2.50x o.p. (ISBN 0-435-64498-X). Heinemann Ed.

Chemistry: The Central Science. T. L. Brown & H. Eugene LeMay, Jr. LC 76-22159. (Illus.). 1977. text ed. 21.95 (ISBN 0-13-128769-9); students guide 7.95 (ISBN 0-13-128512-2); lab. exp. 9.95 (ISBN 0-13-128751-6); solutions 4.95 (ISBN 0-13-128793-1); pap. 9.95 lab manual (ISBN 0-13-128520-3). P-H.

Chemistry: The Central Science. 2nd ed. Theodore L. Brown & H. Eugene LeMay. 832p. 1981. text ed. 22.95 (ISBN 0-13-128504-1). P-H.

Chemistry, The Central Science: Solutions to Exercises. Theodore L. Brown & H. E. LeMay. 272p. 1980. 6.96 (ISBN 0-13-128538-6). P-H.

Chemistry: The Science & the Scene. Ronald D. Clark & Robert L. Amai. LC 74-13782. 355p. 1975. text ed. 16.50x o.p. (ISBN 0-471-15857-7). Wiley.

Chemistry Through Models. C. J. Suckling et al. LC 77-71429. (Illus.). 1978. 47.50 (ISBN 0-521-21661-3). Cambridge U Pr.

Chemistry Through Models. Colin J. Suckling et al. LC 77-71429. (Illus.). 321p. 1980. pap. 13.95x (ISBN 0-521-29932-2). Cambridge U Pr.

Chemmeen. Thakazhi S. Pillai. Tr. by Narayana Menon. 221p. 1964. pap. 3.00 (ISBN 0-88253-066-6). Ind-US Inc.

Chemodynamics: Environmental Movement of Chemicals in Air, Water, & Soil. Louis J. Thibodeaux. LC 78-31637. 1979. 36.00 (ISBN 0-471-04720-1, Pub. by Wiley-Interscience). Wiley.

Chemonucleolysis. Association of Bone & Joint Surgeons. Ed. by M. R. Urist. (Clinical Orthopaedics Ser, Vol. 67). 1969. 12.00 o.p. (ISBN 0-685-14224-8). Lippincott.

Chemosurgery: Microscopically Controlled Surgery for Skin Cancer. Frederic E. Mohs. (Illus.). 400p. 1978. 49.75 (ISBN 0-398-03725-6). C C Thomas.

Chemotherapy: A Manual for Patients & Their Families. M. V. Scoy-Mosher. Date not set. Set Of 100. pap. 40.00. Masson Pub.

Chemotherapy of Cancer. 2nd ed. Carter. 400p. 1981. 15.75 (ISBN 0-471-08045-4, Pub. by Wiley Medical). Wiley.

Chemotherapy of Cancer. Stephen K. Carter et al. LC 77-8142. 1977. 17.95 (ISBN 0-471-02935-1, Pub by Wiley-Medical). Wiley.

Chemotherapy of Cancer Dissemination & Metastasis. Ed. by S. Garattini & G. Franchi. LC 72-96335. (Monographs of the Mario Negri Institute for Pharmacological Research). (Illus.). 400p. 1973. 34.50 (ISBN 0-911216-46-4). Raven.

Chemotherapy of Helminthiasis. Ed. by R. Cavier. LC 72-86179. 532p. 1973. text ed. 90.00 (ISBN 0-08-015755-6). Pergamon.

Chemotherapy of Urogenital Tumors. Gerald P. Murphy & Arnold Mittelman. (Illus.). 288p. 1975. 32.75 (ISBN 0-398-03319-6). C C Thomas.

ChemThermo: A Statistical Approach to Thermodynamics. Leonard K. Nash. 1972. pap. text ed. 6.95 (ISBN 0-201-05237-7). A-W.

Chen Chi Watercolors, Drawings, Sketches: Deluxe Edition. Chi Chen. (Illus.). 108p. 1980. leather bound 100.00 (ISBN 0-9604652-1-9). Chen Chi Studio.

Chequered Career of Ferdinand Rudolph Hassler: First Superintendent of the U. S. Coast Survey. Florian Cajori. Ed. by I. Bernard Cohen. LC 79-7954. 1980. Repr. of 1929 ed. lib. bdg. 18.00x (ISBN 0-405-12535-6). Arno.

Cheremis Literary Reader: With Glossary. Thomas A. Sebeok. (Indiana University Uralic & Altaic Ser.: Vol. 132). 120p. 1978. 17.00 (ISBN 2-8017-0096-7). Ind U Res Inst.

Cherishable: Love & Marriage. David Augsburger. 1975. pap. 1.25 (ISBN 0-89129-065-6, PV065). Jove Pubns.

Chern Symposium Nineteen Seventy Nine. Ed. by W. Hsiang et al. (Illus.). 259p. 1981. 29.50 (ISBN 0-387-90537-5). Springer-Verlag.

Cherokee & Creek Indians. Incl. Ethnographic Report on Royce Area 79, Docket 275, Chicasaw, Cherokee, & Creek. Charles H. Fairbanks; Cherokee Treaties. John H. Goff; Findings of Fact, & Opinion. Indian Claims Commission. (American Indian Ethnohistory Ser: Southern & Southeast Indians). (Illus.). lib. bdg. 42.00 (ISBN 0-8240-0757-3). Garland Pub.

Cherokee Archaeology: A Study of the Appalachian Summit. Bennie C. Keel. LC 75-41444. (Illus.). 1976. 14.50x (ISBN 0-87049-189-X). U of Tenn Pr.

Cherokee Cavaliers: Forty Years of Cherokee History As Told in the Correspondence of the Ridge-Watie-Boudinot Family. E. E. Dale & Gaston Litton. (Civilization of the American Indian Ser.: No. 19). (Illus.). 1969. Repr. of 1939 ed. 16.95 o.p. (ISBN 0-8061-0085-0). U of Okla Pr.

Cherokee Excavations: Holocene Ecology & Human Adaptations in Northwestern Iowa. Ed. by Duane C. Anderson & Holmes Semken. (Studies in Archaeology). 1980. 23.00 (ISBN 0-12-058260-0). Acad Pr.

Cherokee: Indians of the Mountains. Sonia Bleeker. (Illus.). (gr. 3-6). 1952. PLB 6.67 (ISBN 0-688-31160-1). Morrow.

Cherokee Nation of Indians. Charles Royce. LC 75-20708. (Illus.). 272p. 1975. 12.50x (ISBN 0-87474-814-3); pap. 5.95x (ISBN 0-87474-815-1). Smithsonian.

Cherokee Prehistory: The Pisgah Phase in the Appalachian Summit Region. Roy S. Dickens, Jr. LC 76-1972. 1976. 16.50x (ISBN 0-87049-193-8). U of Tenn Pr.

Cherokee Removal 1838: An Entire Indian Nation Is Forced Out of Its Homeland. Glen H. Fleischmann. LC 75-135396. (Focus Bks). (Illus.). (gr. 7 up). 1971. PLB 4.90 o.p. (ISBN 0-531-01024-4); pap. 1.25 o.p. (ISBN 0-531-02328-1). Watts.

Cherokee Sunset- Nation Betrayed. Samuel Carter, III. LC 74-33634. 336p. 1976. 9.95 o.p. (ISBN 0-385-06735-6). Doubleday.

Cherokee Tragedy. Thurman Wilkins. LC 73-92077. 1970. 10.00 o.s.i. (ISBN 0-02-628670-X). Macmillan.

Cherokees. Grace S. Woodward. (Civilization of the American Indian Ser.: No. 65). (Illus.). 1979. Repr. of 1963 ed. 14.95 (ISBN 0-8061-0554-2). U of Okla Pr.

Cherokees: A Critical Bibliography. Raymond D. Fogelson. LC 78-3254. (Newberry Library Center for the History of the American Indian Bibliographical Ser.). 112p. 1978. pap. 4.95x (ISBN 0-253-31346-5). Ind U Pr.

Cherries & Lemons. Joe Troise. 1980. pap. 1.95 (ISBN 0-446-90547-X). Warner Bks.

Cherron. Sharon Combes. 336p. (Orig.). 1980. pap. 2.75 (ISBN 0-89083-700-7). Zebra.

Cherry Delight up Your Ante. Glen Chase. 1976. pap. 1.25 o.p. (ISBN 0-685-72568-5, LB407, Leisure Bks). Nordon Pubns.

Cherry Grove. William Delligan. 1976. pap. 1.75 o.p. (ISBN 0-445-08485-5). Popular Lib.

Cherry Hill: The History & Collections of a Van Rensselaer Family. Roderic H. Blackburn. LC 75-44844. (Illus.). 186p. 1976. 16.00x (ISBN 0-89062-098-9, Pub. by Historic Cherry); pap. 11.95x (ISBN 0-89062-099-7). Pub Ctr Cult Res.

Cherry Orchard. Anton Chekhov. Ed. by John Gielgud. (Orig.). 1963. pap. 3.25x (ISBN 0-87830-510-6, 10). Theatre Arts.

Cherry Valley Massacre, November 11, 1778: The Frontier Atrocity That Shocked a Young Nation. David Goodnough. LC 68-24489. (Focus Bks). (Illus.). (gr. 7 up). 1968. PLB 4.90 o.p. (ISBN 0-531-00998-X). Watts.

Cherubini: Memorials Illustrative of His Life & Work. Edward Bellasis. LC 70-138497. (Music Ser). 1971. Repr. of 1912 ed. lib. bdg. 29.50 (ISBN 0-306-70071-9). Da Capo.

Cheryl Prewitt Story. Cheryl Prewitt & Kathryn S. Slattery. LC 80-2896. (Illus.). 216p. 1981. 11.95 (ISBN 0-385-17021-1, Galilee). Doubleday.

Chesapeake Bay Fish & Fowl Cookbook: A Treasury of Old & New Recipes from Maryland's Eastern Shore. Joseph Foley & Joan Foley. (Illus.). 192p. 1981. 13.95 (ISBN 0-02-539560-2). Macmillan.

Chesapeake Bay: Notes & Sketches. Carvel H. Blair & Willits D. Ansel. LC 76-124311. (Illus.). 1970. 6.00 (ISBN 0-87033-148-5, Pub. by Tidewater). Cornell Maritime.

Chesapeake Bay Retriever. Arthur Beaman. 1980. 19.95 (ISBN 0-87714-075-8). Caroline Hse.

Chesapeake Charlie & Blackbeard's Treasure. William Coleman. (Chesapeake Charlie Ser.). 112p. (Orig.). (gr. 5-9). 1981. pap. 2.50 (ISBN 0-87123-116-6, 200116). Bethany Fell.

Chesapeake Charlie & the Bay Bank Robbers. William Coleman. (Chesapeake Charlie Ser.). 112p. (Orig.). 1980. pap. 2.50 (ISBN 0-87123-113-1, 200113). Bethany Fell.

Chesapeake Kaleidoscope. Anne M. Hays & Harriet R. Hazleton. LC 75-23447. (Illus.). 1975. pap. 5.00 (ISBN 0-87033-214-7, Pub. by Tidewater). Cornell Maritime.

Chesapeake Politics, Seventeen Eighty One-Eighteen Hundred. Norman K. Risjord. LC 78-7996. 1978. 30.00x (ISBN 0-231-04328-7). Columbia U Pr.

Cheshire Grand Jury, 1625-1959: A Social & Administrative Study. J. S. Morrill. (Occasional Papers in English Local History, Third Series: No. 1). (Illus., Orig.). 1976. pap. text ed. 6.75x (ISBN 0-7185-2031-9, Leicester). Humanities.

Cheshire Sixteen Thirty to Sixteen Sixty: County Government & Society During the English Revolution. J. S. Morrill. (Oxford Historical Monographs Ser). 367p. 1974. 37.50x (ISBN 0-19-821855-9). Oxford U Pr.

Chess. rev. ed. R. F. Green. (Illus.). 113p. 1974. 7.50 (ISBN 0-7135-0506-0). Transatlantic.

Chess. Richard Roberts. (Quick & Easy Ser). (Orig.). 1965. pap. 1.95 o.s.i. (ISBN 0-02-081260-4, Collier). Macmillan.

Chess Battle Strategies. John Love & John Hodgkins. LC 79-65066. (Illus.). 1979. 9.95 (ISBN 0-8069-4952-X); lib. bdg. 9.29 (ISBN 0-8069-4953-8). Sterling.

Chess Combination from Philidor to Karpov. R. D. Keene. LC 77-4379. 1977. text ed. 12.25 (ISBN 0-08-019758-2); pap. text ed. 5.50 o.p. (ISBN 0-08-019757-4). Pergamon.

Chess Competitors Handbook. Bozidar Kazic. 1980. 22.50 (ISBN 0-7134-2035-9); pap. 14.50. David & Charles.

Chess Endings - Essential Knowledge. Y. Averbakh. text ed. 11.50 (ISBN 0-08-011823-2); pap. text ed. 5.75 (ISBN 0-08-011822-4). Pergamon.

Chess Endings: Essential Knowledge. Y. Averbakh. (Pergamon Chess Ser.). (Illus.). 1966. 11.50 (ISBN 0-08-011823-2); pap. 5.75 (ISBN 0-08-011822-4). Pergamon.

Chess for Beginners: A Picture Guide. Al Horowitz. (Illus.). 1959. pap. 3.50 (ISBN 0-06-463223-7, EH 223, EH). Har-Row.

Chess for Children. rev. ed. Fred Reinfeld. LC 58-7612. (Illus.). 72p. (gr. 3-12). 1980. 6.95 (ISBN 0-8069-4904-X); PLB 6.69 (ISBN 0-8069-4905-8). Sterling.

Chess for Fun & Chess for Blood. 2nd ed. Edward Lasker. (Illus.). 1942. pap. 3.50 (ISBN 0-486-20146-5). Dover.

Chess for Pleasure. Elaine Pritchard. (Illus.). 1971. 7.95 (ISBN 0-571-09201-2, Pub. by Faber & Faber). Merrimack Bk Serv.

Chess for Young Beginners. (Illus.). 1977. PLB 10.69 o.p. (ISBN 0-307-63772-7, Golden Pr); pap. 2.95 (ISBN 0-307-13772-4). Western Pub.

Chess from Morphy to Botwinnik. 2nd ed. Imre Konig. LC 77-72873. 1977. pap. 3.75 (ISBN 0-486-23503-3). Dover.

Chess Fundamentals. Jose R. Capablanca. (Illus.). 1967. pap. 4.95 (ISBN 0-679-14004-2, 27, Tartan). McKay.

Chess: How to Improve Your Technique. Frank Brady. LC 74-4103. (Career Concise Guides Ser.). (Illus.). 72p. (gr. 5 up). 1974. PLB 4.90 o.p. (ISBN 0-531-02730-9). Watts.

Chess in a Nutshell. Fred Reinfeld. LC 58-11323. 1958. 5.95 o.p. (ISBN 0-385-01754-5). Doubleday.

Chess in the Mirror: A Study of Theatrical Cubism in Francis Warner's Requiem & Its Maquettes. Rosalind Jeffrey. 1981. text ed. 13.00 (ISBN 0-85455-020-8). Humanities.

Chess Is an Easy Game. Fred Reinfeld. LC 61-18952. (gr. 5 up). 1962. 6.95 (ISBN 0-8069-4906-6); PLB 6.69 (ISBN 0-8069-4907-4). Sterling.

Chess Made Simple. Milton L. Hanauer. 1967. pap. 3.50 (ISBN 0-385-01215-2, Made). Doubleday.

Chess Move by Move. L. Abramov & B. Cafferty. (Chess Player Ser.). 1977. pap. 4.95 o.p. (ISBN 0-900928-67-0, H-1188). Hippocrene Bks.

Chess Olympiad Skopje Nineteen Seventy-Two. Robert Bellin. 1977. 17.25 o.p. (ISBN 0-7134-3211-X). David & Charles.

Chess Olympiad Skopje Nineteen Seventy-Two. Bernard Cafferty. 1979. 14.95 o.p. (ISBN 0-7134-1976-8); pap. 9.25 o.p. (ISBN 0-7134-1977-6). David & Charles.

Chess Olympiad Skopje Nineteen Seventy-Two. R. D. Keene & David Levy. 1973. 19.95 (ISBN 0-7134-0373-X). David & Charles.

Chess Olympiad Skopje Nineteen Seventy-Two. R. D. Keene & David Levy. 1975. 9.25 o.p. (ISBN 0-7134-3055-9). David & Charles.

Chess Openings for You. Cafferty. 16.95 (ISBN 0-7134-1976-8, Pub. by Batsford England); pap. 10.95 (ISBN 0-7134-1977-6). David & Charles.

Chess Players Bedside Book. Keene & Edwards. 14.95 (Pub. by Batsford England); pap. 10.95. David & Charles.

Chess Questions Answered. Larry Evans. (Illus.). 1971. 7.95 o.p. (ISBN 0-571-09707-3, Pub. by Faber & Faber). Merrimack Bk Serv.

Chess Scandals: The Nineteen Seventy-Eight World Championship Match. E. B. Edmondson. (Pergamon Chess Ser.). (Illus.). 260p. 1981. 24.00 (ISBN 0-08-024145-X); pap. 14.40 (ISBN 0-08-024144-1). Pergamon.

Chess Self-Teacher. Al Horowitz. (Orig.). 1961. pap. 2.95 (ISBN 0-06-463257-1, EH 257, EH). Har-Row.

Chess Struggle in Practice. 1980. 17.95 (ISBN 0-679-13064-0); pap. 7.95 (ISBN 0-679-14152-9). McKay.

Chess Tactics & Attacking Techniques. Raymond Edwards. (Chess Handbooks: Vol. 5). 1978. pap. 4.95 (ISBN 0-7100-8821-3). Routledge & Kegan.

Chess Techniques. A. R. B. Thomas. 1975. 15.00 (ISBN 0-7100-8098-0); pap. 6.50 (ISBN 0-7100-8099-9). Routledge & Kegan.

Chess Training. Nigel Povah. 176p. 1981. 19.95 (ISBN 0-571-11604-3, Pub. by Faber & Faber); pap. 8.95 (ISBN 0-571-11608-6). Merrimack Bk Serv.

Chessman of Mars. Edgar R. Burroughs. 1973. pap. 1.95 (ISBN 0-345-27838-0). Ballantine.

Chest Disease Case Studies. Ed. by Oscar J. Balchum & Ralph C. Jung. 1973. spiral bdg. 12.00 o.s.i. (ISBN 0-87488-012-2). Med Exam.

Chest Nuclear Medicine Case Studies. Marvin Guter & Aldo Serafini. 1979. spiral bdg. 14.50 (ISBN 0-87488-083-1). Med Exam.

Chest Trauma: Diagnosis & Management. W. Glinz. (Illus.). 310p. 1981. 58.00 (ISBN 0-387-10409-7). Springer-Verlag.

Chester & Holyhead Railway: The Main Line up 1880, Vol. 1. Peter E. Baughan. (Railway History Ser.). (Illus.). 17.95 (ISBN 0-7153-5617-8). David & Charles.

Chester Chipmunk's Thanksgiving. Barbara Williams. LC 77-20812. (Illus.). (gr. k-3). 1978. PLB 7.95 (ISBN 0-525-27655-6). Dutton.

Chester County Historical Society. Peter B. Schiffer. (Illus.). 70p. 1970. pap. 3.50. Schiffer.

Chester Cricket's Pigeon Ride. George Selden. LC 80-20326. (gr. 1 up). 1981. 9.95 (ISBN 0-374-31239-7). FS&G.

Chester Himes. James Lundquist. LC 75-42864. (Modern Literature Ser.). 170p. 1976. 10.95 (ISBN 0-8044-2561-2). Ungar.

Chester Mystery Plays. Ed. by Maurice Hussey. pap. 3.25x (ISBN 0-87830-572-6). Theatre Arts.

Chester the Worldly Pig. Bill Peet. (Illus.). (gr. k-3). 1965. reinforced bdg. 10.95 (ISBN 0-395-18470-3). HM.

Chester Through Derry Conodonts & Stratigraphy of Northern Clark & Southern Lincoln Counties, Nevada. G. D. Webster. (U. C. Publ. in Geological Sciences: Vol. 79). 1969. pap. 8.00x (ISBN 0-520-09182-5). U of Cal Pr.

Chestnut Farm Eighteen Sixty. Geoffrey Patterson. (Illus.). (gr. k-3). 1980. 8.95 (ISBN 0-233-97208-0). Andre Deutsch.

Chet Atkins Note-for-Note. Chet Atkins & John Knowles. LC 75-14957. 72p. (Orig.). 1978. pap. 5.95 (ISBN 0-8256-9510-4). Guitar Player.

Chetifs. Geoffrey M. Myers. Ed. by Jan A. Nelson & Emanuel J. Mickel, Jr. (Old French Crusade Cycle Ser.: Vol. V). 352p. Date not set. 25.00 (ISBN 0-8173-0023-6). U of Ala Pr.

Chetki. Anna Akhmatova. 1972. pap. 3.00 (ISBN 0-88233-029-2). Ardis Pubs.

Chevalier Bayard. Samuel Shellabarger. LC 76-156738. (Illus.). 1971. Repr. of 1928 ed. 15.00x (ISBN 0-8196-0272-8). Biblo.

Chevette, Nineteen Seventy-Six to Nineteen Eighty. Chilton's Automotive Editorial Dept. LC 78-20248. (Chilton's Repair & Tune-Up Guides). (Illus.). 1128p. 1979. pap. 8.95 (ISBN 0-8019-6836-4, 6836). Chilton.

Chevette Service Repair Handbook: All Models 1976-1978. Eric Jorgensen. Ed. by Jeff Robinson. (Illus.). 1978. pap. 11.95 (ISBN 0-89287-145-8, A290). Clymer Pubns.

Chevrolet & GMC--4-Wheel Drive Maintenance: Blazer, Jimmy, Pickups & Suburbans, 1967-1979. Mike Bishop. Ed. by Jeff Robinson. (Illus.). 1978. pap. 7.95 (ISBN 0-89287-159-8, A230). Clymer Pubns.

Chevrolet & GMC Tune-up-Maintenance: Vans, Pickups, & Suburban, 1967-1980. 2nd ed. Mike Bishop. Ed. by Jeff Robinson. (Illus.). 1977. pap. text ed. 10.95 o.p. (ISBN 0-89287-207-1, A238). Clymer Pubns.

Chevrolet-GMC Pick-Ups: Nineteen Seventy to Eighty Repair & Tune-up Guide. LC 79-8304. (New Automotive Bks.). 272p. 1980. 8.95 (ISBN 0-8019-6936-0). Chilton.

Chevrolet-GMC Vans: Nineteen Sixty Seven to Eighty. LC 78-20260. (New Automotive Bks.). 224p. 1980. 8.95 (ISBN 0-8019-6930-1). Chilton.

Chevrolet High Performance. Editors of Hot Rod Magazine. LC 80-80176. (Illus.). 256p. (gr. 9-12). 1980. pap. 7.95 (ISBN 0-8227-6005-3). Petersen Pub.

Chevrolet Mid-Size Nineteen Sixty-Four to Nineteen Seventy-Nine. Chilton's Automotive Editorial Dept. LC 78-20252. (Chilton's Repair & Tune-Up Guides). (Illus.). 1979. pap. 8.95 (ISBN 0-8019-6840-2, 6840). Chilton.

Chevrolet, Nineteen Sixty-Eight to Nineteen Seventy-Nine. Chilton's Automotive Editorial Dept. LC 78-20251. (Chilton's Repair & Tune-Up Guides). (Illus.). 1979. pap. text ed. 8.95 (ISBN 0-8019-6839-9, 6839). Chilton.

Chevrolet Nineteen Sixty-Eight to Seventy-Nine. (Illus.). 268p. (Spanish.). 1979. pap. 8.95. Chilton.

Chevrolet Tune-up Maintenance: All Models, 1966-1980. Jim Combs. Ed. by Jeff Robinson. (Illus.). 152p. 1977. pap. text ed. 7.95 (ISBN 0-89287-191-1, A137). Clymer Pubns.

Chevy. LC 80-80770. (Saturday Mechanic Car Care Guides). (Illus.). 176p. 12.95 (ISBN 0-87851-933-5); pap. 6.95 (ISBN 0-87851-925-4). Hearst Bks.

Chevy & GMC Vans Nineteen Sixty-Seven to Nineteen Eighty Shop Manual. Mike Bishop. Ed. by Eric Jorgensen. (Illus.). 1979. pap. text ed. 10.95 (ISBN 0-89287-300-0, A239). Clymer Pubns.

Chevy GMC Pickups Nineteen Sixty-Seven to Nineteen Eighty: Includes Suburbans Shop Manual. Mike Bishop. Ed. by Eric Jorgensen. (Illus.). 1979. pap. text ed. 9.95 (ISBN 0-89287-207-1, A238). Clymer Pubns.

Chevy Luv: 1972-1980--Service, Repair Handbook. Ed Scott. Ed. by Eric Jorgensen. (Illus.). 1978. pap. 10.95 (ISBN 0-89287-274-8, A145). Clymer Pubns.

Chevy Malibu Chevelle MonteCarlo: 1970-1980 Shop Manual. Jim Combs. Ed. by Eric Jorgensen. (Illus.). 360p. (Orig.). 1980. pap. text ed. 10.95 (ISBN 0-89287-319-1, A246). Clymer Pubns.

Chevy Nova Nineteen Seventy-One to Nineteen Seventy-Nine: Shop Manual. Alan Ahlstrand. Ed. by Eric Jorgensen. (Illus.). 362p. (Orig.). 1980. pap. text ed. 10.95 (ISBN 0-89287-317-5, A133). Clymer Pubns.

Chevy Super Sports. Terry V. Boyce. (Illus.). 1981. pap. 13.95 (ISBN 0-87938-096-9). Motorbooks Intl.

Chevy Two & Nova, Nineteen Sixty-Two to Nineteen Seventy-Nine. Chilton's Automotive Editorial Department. LC 78-20253. (Chilton's Repair & Tune-up Guides). (Illus.). 1979. pap. 8.95 (ISBN 0-8019-6841-0, 6841). Chilton.

Cheyenne Artist: The Story of Richard West. Charles A. Waugaman. LC 70-130779. (Bold Believers Ser). (Orig.). 1970. pap. 0.95 o.p. (ISBN 0-377-84211-7). Friend Pr.

Cheyenne Autumn. Mari Sandoz. 1969. pap. 2.95 (ISBN 0-380-01094-1, 52621, Discus). Avon.

Cheyenne Autumn. Mari Sandoz. 1975. Repr. 9.95 (ISBN 0-8038-1094-6). Hastings.

Cheyenne Manhunt. Lester Merha. (Orig.). 1980. pap. 1.75 (ISBN 0-8439-0742-8, Leisure Bks). Nordon Pubns.

Cheyenne Memories. John Stands In Timber & Margot Liberty. LC 67-24515. (Illus.). 1972. pap. 3.95 (ISBN 0-8032-5751-1, BB 544, Bison). U of Nebr Pr.

Cheyenne Memories. John Stands In Timber et al. (Western Americana Ser.: No. 17). (Illus.). 1967. 22.00x o.p. (ISBN 0-300-00971-2). Yale U Pr.

Cheyenne Payoff. Brad Spear. 1981. pap. 2.25 (ISBN 0-440-01269-4). Dell.

Cheyennes, Ma Heo O's People: A Critical Bibliography. Peter J. Powell. LC 80-8033. (Newberry Library Center for the History of the American Indian Bibliographical Ser.). 128p. 1980. pap. 4.95x (ISBN 0-253-30416-4). Ind U Pr.

Cheyne Mystery. Freeman W. Crofts. (Crime Ser). 1978. pap. 2.50 (ISBN 0-14-000917-5). Penguin.

Chez Nous: A Domestic Comedy in Two Acts. Peter Nichols. 1974. 8.50 (ISBN 0-571-10583-1, Pub. by Faber & Faber); pap. 4.95 (ISBN 0-571-10602-1). Merrimack Bk Serv.

Ch'i Heavy Sword Coins of the Chou Dynasty, Vol. 5. Arthur B. Coole. LC 72-86801. (Encyclopedia of Chinese Coins Ser.: Vol. 5). (Illus.). 1976. 35.00x (ISBN 0-88000-014-7). Quarterman.

Chia-Ting Loyalists: Confucian Leadership & Social Change in Seventeenth-Century China. Jerry Dennerline. LC 80-21417. (Historical Publications Miscellany Ser.: No. 126). (Illus.). 416p. 1981. text ed. 35.00 (ISBN 0-300-02548-3). Yale U Pr.

Chiang Kai-Shek: Marshal of China. Sven Hedin. Tr. by Bernard Norbelle from Swedish. LC 74-31277. (China in the 20th Century Ser). (Illus.). xiv, 290p. 1975. Repr. of 1940 ed. lib. bdg. 22.50 (ISBN 0-306-70690-3). Da Capo.

Chiang Kuei. Timothy A. Ross. LC 74-2172. (World Authors Ser.: China: No. 320). 1974. lib. bdg. 12.50 (ISBN 0-8057-2214-9). Twayne.

Chicago. Finis Farr. LC 72-78486. (Illus.). 1973. 12.95 o.s.i. (ISBN 0-87000-179-5). Arlington Hse.

Chicago. Mary J. O'Shea. (Rock 'n Pop Stars Ser.). (Illus.). (gr. 4-12). 1975. PLB 5.95 (ISBN 0-87191-458-1); pap. 2.95 (ISBN 0-89812-114-0). Creative Ed.

Chicago: A Historical Guide to Neighborhoods. Glen Holt & Dominic A. Pacyga. 1980. pap. 8.95 (ISBN 0-686-65047-6, 10413-3). U of Chicago Pr.

Chicago: a Historical Guide to the Neighborhoods: Vol. I: the Loop & South Side, Vol. 1. Glen E. Holt & Dominic A. Pacyga. LC 78-60184. (Illus.). 174p. 1979. pap. 8.95 (ISBN 0-913820-07-5). Chicago Hist.

Chicago & Beyond: Twenty-Six Bike Tours. Linda Nash & Steve Nash. 224p. 1981. pap. 6.95 (ISBN 0-695-81561-X). Follett.

Chicago & Other Plays. Sam Shepard. LC 80-27628. 1981. 15.00 (ISBN 0-89396-042-X); pap. 6.95 (ISBN 0-89396-043-8). Urizen.

Chicago Architects: A Revisionist View of Chicago Architecture. Stuart E. Cohen. LC 76-2194. (Illus.). 1976. 25.00 o.s.i. (ISBN 0-8040-0732-2); pap. 10.00 o.s.i. (ISBN 0-8040-0731-4). Swallow.

Chicago Book. Don Klimovitch et al. (Illus., Orig.). 1981. pap. 5.95 (ISBN 0-8092-5893-5). Contemp Bks.

Chicago Breakdown. Mike Rowe. (Roots of Jazz Ser.). (Illus.). 1979. Repr. of 1974 ed. lib. bdg. 21.50 (ISBN 0-306-79532-9). Da Capo.

Chicago Ceramics & Glass. Sharon S. Darling. LC 79-91566. (Illus.). 240p. 1980. 25.00 (ISBN 0-913820-10-5). Chicago Hist.

Chicago Ceramics & Glass: An Illustrated History from 1871 to 1933. Sharon S. Darling. LC 79-91566. (Illus.). xiv, 222p. 1980. 25.00 o.p. (ISBN 0-913820-10-5). Chicago Hist.

Chicago, Cook County & Illinois Industrial Directory. 1980. 85.00 (ISBN 0-686-21882-5). Natl Pub IL.

Chicago: Creating New Traditions. Perry Davis. LC 76-45167. (Illus.). 1976. 12.50 (ISBN 0-913820-03-2); pap. 7.95 (ISBN 0-913820-05-9). Chicago Hist.

Chicago Giant: A Biography of Long John Wentworth. Don E. Fehrenbacher. (Illus.). 278p. 1957. 10.00 (ISBN 0-87057-042-0, Pub. by Brown U Pr). Univ Pr of New England.

Chicago Great Western. Phil Hastings. (Carstens Hobby Bks.: No. C39). 1980. pap. 9.95 (ISBN 0-911868-39-9). Carstens Pubns.

Chicago: Growth of a Metropolis. Harold M. Mayer & Richard C. Wade. LC 68-54054. (Illus.). 1969. 35.00 (ISBN 0-226-51273-8). U of Chicago Pr.

Chicago: Growth of a Metropolis. Harold M. Mayer & Richard C. Wade. LC 68-54054. (Illus.). 1973. pap. 12.50 (ISBN 0-226-51274-6, P546, Phoen). U of Chicago Pr.

Chicago Jewish Source Book. Rachel B. Heimovics. 336p. 1981. pap. 6.95 (ISBN 0-695-81568-7). Follett.

Chicago Job Bank: A Comprehensive Guide to Major Employers Throughout Greater Chicago. Ed. by Robert Lang Adams & Associates. (Job Bank Ser.). 300p. (Orig.). 1981. pap. 9.95 (ISBN 0-937860-05-0). Adams Inc MA.

Chicago Performs: A Guide to Theatre & Dance. Ed. by Brenda Schnede. LC 77-87358. (Illus.). 93p. (Orig.). 1977. pap. 5.95 (ISBN 0-8040-0795-0). Swallow.

Chicago Psychoanalytic Literature Index 1979. Chicago Institute for Psychoanalysis. Ed. by Glenn E. Miller. LC 76-182629. 1980. lib. bdg. 50.00 (ISBN 0-918568-06-4). Chicago Psych.

Chicago Psychoanalytic Literature Index Nineteen Seventy-Five. Ed. by Glenn E. Miller. 1975. write for info. Chicago Psych.

Chicago Psychoanalytic Literature Index 1980: Chicago Institute for Psychoanalysis. Ed. by Glenn E. Miller. 1981. lib. bdg. 50.00 (ISBN 0-918568-07-2). Chicago Psych.

Chicago School of Architecture. Carl W. Condit. LC 64-13287. (Illus.). xvii, 238p. 1973. pap. 9.95 (ISBN 0-226-11455-4, P540, Phoen). U of Chicago Pr.

Chicago Tribune Tower Competition & Late Entries, 2 vols. Stanley Tigerman. LC 80-51371. (Orig.). 1980. Set. pap. 30.00 (ISBN 0-8478-0333-3). Vol. 1, 193p. Vol. 2, 113p. Rizzoli Intl.

Chicago World's Fair of Eighteen Ninety-Three: A Photographic Record. Stanley Appelbaum. (Illus.). 144p. (Orig.). 1980. pap. 6.00 (ISBN 0-486-23990-X). Dover.

Chicago's Catholics: An Evolution of an American Identity. Charles Shanabruch. LC 80-53071. (Studies in American Catholicism: Vol. 4). 288p. 1981. text ed. 18.95 (ISBN 0-268-01840-5). U of Notre Dame Pr.

Chicago's Famous Buildings: A Photographic Guide to the City's Architectural Landmarks & Other Notable Buildings. 2nd ed. Arthur Siegel et al. LC 69-15367. (Illus.). 1970. pap. 3.25 o.s.i. (ISBN 0-226-75685-8). U of Chicago Pr.

Chicana: The Mexican-American Woman. Alfredo Mirande & Evangelina Enriquez. LC 79-13536. (Illus.). x, 284p. 1981. pap. 6.95 (ISBN 0-226-53160-0). U of Chicago Pr.

Chicano English. Alan A. Metcalf. (Language in Education Ser.: No. 21). 1979. 2.95 (ISBN 0-87281-107-7). Ctr Appl Ling.

Chicano: Essays from the Pacific Historical Review. Ed. by Norris Hundley, Jr. LC 75-2354. 168p. 1975. 11.80 (ISBN 0-87436-212-1); pap. 5.20 (ISBN 0-87436-213-X). ABC-Clio.

Chicano Experience. Stanley A. West & June Macklin. (Special Studies in Contemporary Social Issues). 1979. lib. bdg. 26.50x (ISBN 0-89158-489-7). Westview.

Chicano Girl. Hila Colman. 192p. (gr. 7 up). 1973. 6.75 o.p. (ISBN 0-688-20082-6). Morrow.

Chicano Manifesto. A. Rendon. 1972. pap. 2.95 o.s.i. (ISBN 0-02-096330-0, Collier). Macmillan.

Chicano Poetry Anthology. Ed. by Toni Empringham. 128p. (Orig.). 1981. pap. 6.50 (ISBN 0-88496-164-8). Capra Pr.

Chicano Politics. Maurilio Vigil. 1977. pap. text ed. 10.75x (ISBN 0-8191-0110-9). U Pr of Amer.

Chicano Psychology. Ed. by J. L. Martinez, Jr. 1978. 12.50 (ISBN 0-12-475650-6). Acad Pr.

Chicano Scholars & Writers: A Bio-Bibliographical Directory. Compiled by Julio A. Martinez. LC 78-32076. 589p. 1979. 29.00 (ISBN 0-8108-1205-3). Scarecrow.

Chicano Sports Heroes: Athletes & Athletics in the Spanish Speaking Community. D. Villanveva. 1975. 8.95 o.p. (ISBN 0-13-129809-7). P-H.

Chicanos in a Changing Society: From Mexican Pueblos to American Barrios in Santa Barbara & Southern California, 1848-1930. Albert Camarillo. LC 79-10687. 1979. 17.50x o.p. (ISBN 0-674-11395-0); pap. 7.95x (ISBN 0-674-11396-9). Harvard U Pr.

Chicanos: Life & Struggles of the Mexican Minority in the United States, with Readings. Gilberto L. Rivas. Ed. by Elizabeth Martinez. LC 73-8056. 224p. (Bilingual). 1974. 7.95 o.p. (ISBN 0-85345-298-9, CL2989); pap. 4.95 (ISBN 0-85345-329-2, PB3292). Monthly Rev.

Chicanos: Social & Psychological Perspectives. 2nd ed. Carrol A. Hernandez et al. LC 75-37769. (Illus.). 376p. 1976. pap. 12.00 (ISBN 0-8016-5316-9). Mosby.

Chichee's Trunk: A Story of Roots & Branches. J. W. Van De Water. (Illus.). 130p. (Orig.). pap. 5.00x (ISBN 0-686-27489-X). Jonsalvania.

Chichen Itza & Its Cenote of Sacrifice: A Comparative Study of Contemporaneous Maya & Toltec. Alfred M. Tozzer. LC 58-1778. (Peabody Museum Memoirs: Vols. 11-12). 1957. pap. 50.00 (ISBN 0-87365-684-9). Peabody Harvard.

Chick & the Duckling. Mirra Ginsburg. LC 74-188773. (ps-1). 1972. 9.95 (ISBN 0-02-735940-9). Macmillan.

Chick Hatches. Joanna Cole. (Illus.). 48p. (gr. k-3). 1976. PLB 7.92 (ISBN 0-688-32087-2). Morrow.

Chickasaw Freedmen: A People Without a Country. Daniel F. Littlefield, Jr. LC 79-6192. (Contributions in Afro-American and African Studies: No. 54). xii, 248p. 1980. lib. bdg. 25.00 (ISBN 0-313-22313-0, LCF/). Greenwood.

Chickasaws. Arrell M. Gibson. (Civilization of the American Indian Ser.: Vol. 109). (Illus.). 320p. 1971. 16.95 o.p. (ISBN 0-8061-0945-9); pap. 7.95 (ISBN 0-8061-1042-2). U of Okla Pr.

Chicken & Fish. Mary Bayramian. (Illus.). 1978. 3.95 (ISBN 0-912300-85-X, 85-X). Troubador Pr.

Chicken at the Window. Ann K. Weinhaus. LC 78-19482. (Illus.). 32p. (gr. k-3). 1981. 8.95 (ISBN 0-06-026390-3, HarpJ); PLB 8.79g (ISBN 0-06-026391-1). Har-Row.

Chicken Cookbook. Sophie Kay & Consumer Guide Editors. 160p. (Orig.). 1981. pap. 6.95 (ISBN 0-449-90049-5, Columbine). Fawcett.

Chicken Cookbook. National Chicken Cooking Contest & National Broiler Council. 128p. 1975. pap. 1.25 o.p. (ISBN 0-445-08367-0). Popular Lib.

Chicken Favorites. Mary K. Hollander. Ed. by Susan H. Herbert. (Illus.). 64p. (Orig.). 1981. pap. 2.50 (ISBN 0-915942-18-6). Owlswood Prods.

Chicken for Every Pot: San Francisco's Famous Chicken Diet. Rudolf E. Noble. 124p. 1980. pap. 4.95 (ISBN 0-930306-35-X). Delphi Info.

Chicken in Every Pot. Edith Vanocur. LC 75-46581. (Illus.). 176p. 1976. 6.95 o.s.i. (ISBN 0-690-00391-9, TYC-T). T Y Crowell.

Chicken Licken. (Ladybird Stories Ser.). (Illus., Arabic.). 2.50x (ISBN 0-686-53064-0). Intl Bk Ctr.

Chicken Little. Ruth Ruhman. (Illus.). (ps-2). 1974. PLB 5.38 (ISBN 0-307-68924-7, Golden Pr). Western Pub.

Chicken Pox Papers. Susan Terris. 1978. pap. 1.50 (ISBN 0-440-41402-4, YB). Dell.

Chicken Pox Papers. Susan Terris. (Illus.). 128p. (gr. 4-6). 1976. PLB 5.90 o.p. (ISBN 0-531-00332-9). Watts.

Chicken Riddle. Ann Bishop. LC 72-83681. (Riddle Bk.). (Illus.). 40p. (gr. 1-3). 1972. 5.75g (ISBN 0-8075-1140-4). A Whitman.

Chicken Soup & Other Medical Matters. Sidney Harris. (Illus.). 108p. 1979. 7.95 o.p. (ISBN 0-913232-75-0); pap. 3.95 (ISBN 0-913232-74-2). W Kaufmann.

Chickencoop Chinaman & the Year of the Dragon: Two Plays. 1981. price not set o.p. U of Wash Pr.

Chickens, Chickens, Chickens. Peter R. Limburg. LC 75-16378. (Illus.). 160p. (gr. 5 up). 1975. 7.95 (ISBN 0-525-66463-7). Elsevier-Nelson.

Chicken's Child. Margaret A. Hartelius. LC 74-18884. 40p. (ps-k). 1975. PLB 5.95 (ISBN 0-385-07370-4). Doubleday.

Chicoral Index to Reading & Learning Disabilities: Books, 1978 Annual, Vol. 14A. 400p. 1980. 85.00 (ISBN 0-934598-09-6). Am Lib Pub Co.

Chicorel Abstracts to Reading & Learning Disabilities: Periodicals, 1978 Annual, Vol. 19. 400p. 1979. 85.00 (ISBN 0-934598-16-9). Am Lib Pub Co.

Chicorel Abstracts to Reading & Learning Disabilities: Periodicals, 1979 Annual, Vol. 19. 400p. 1980. 85.00 (ISBN 0-934598-10-X). Am Lib Pub Co.

Chicorel Abstracts to Reading & Learning Disabilities, 1976 Annual. annual ed. Marietta Chicorel. (Chicorel Index Ser.). 1000p. 1976. text ed. 85.00 ca. (ISBN 0-934598-15-0); Vol. 19. text ed. (ISBN 0-934598-15-0); Vol. 19A. text ed. o.p. Am Lib Pub Co.

Chicorel Index to Abstracting & Indexing, Vols. 11 & 11a. 2nd ed. Marietta Chicorel. (Chicorel Index Ser.). 1978. text ed. 190.00x set (ISBN 0-934598-20-7). Am Lib Pub Co.

Chicorel Index to Mental Health Book Reviews, 1976, Vol. 26. annual ed. Ed. by Marietta Chicorel. (Chicorel Index Ser). 1977. text ed. 85.00 ca. (ISBN 0-934598-08-8). Am Lib Pub Co.

Chicorel Index to Mental Health Book Reviews: 1977 Annual, Vol. 26. 400p. 1978. 85.00 (ISBN 0-934598-77-0). Am Lib Pub Co.

Chicorel Index to Mental Health Book Reviews: 1978 Annual, Vol. 26. 400p. 1980. 85.00 (ISBN 0-934598-08-8). Am Lib Pub Co.

Chicorel Index to Poetry Nineteen Seventy Five - Nineteen Seventy Seven, 2 vols, Vols. 5 & 5a. Ed. by Marietta Chicorel. (Chicorel Index Ser.). 1979. Set. text ed. 170.00 (ISBN 0-934598-13-4). Am Lib Pub Co.

Chicorel Index to the Spoken Arts on Discs, Tapes, & Cassettes, Vol. TA. 500p. 1974. 85.00. Am Lib Pub Co.

Chicorel Index to Urban Planning & Environmental Design, Vols. 17 & 17a. Ed. by Marietta Chicorel. LC 75-30637. (Index Ser.). 1000p. 1975. Set. 170.00 (ISBN 0-934598-65-7). Am Lib Pub Co.

Chicorel Theater Index to Plays for Young People, Vol. 9. Ed. by Marietta Chicorel. 500p. 1974. 85.00 (ISBN 0-934598-34-7). Am Lib Pub Co.

Chief. Frank Bonham. (gr. 6 up). 1971. PLB 7.95 o.p. (ISBN 0-525-27673-4). Dutton.

Chief Executive Officer. Robert H. Rock. LC 77-6505. (Illus.). 1977. 15.95 (ISBN 0-669-01599-7). Lexington Bks.

Chief Executive: Realities of Corporate Leadership. Chester Burger. LC 77-2844. 1978. 19.95 (ISBN 0-8436-0747-5). CBI Pub.

Chief Executives. Isadore Barmash. 10.95 o.s.i. (ISBN 0-397-01285-3). Lippincott.

Chief Factors for the Gods: From Trial to Triumph, Vol. 2. S. J. Freebairn-Smith & G. N. Littlejohn. 1977. pap. text ed. 5.25x (ISBN 0-435-36321-2). Heinemann Ed.

Chief: Field Marshal Lord Wavell, Commander-in-Chief & Viceroy 1939-47. Ronald Lewin. 1980. 10.95 (ISBN 0-374-12112-5). FS&G.

Chief Glory of Every People: Essays on Classic American Writers. Ed. by Matthew J. Bruccoli. LC 73-1783. 310p. 1973. 14.95x (ISBN 0-8093-0615-8). S Ill U Pr.

Chief Inspector's Daughter. Sheila Radley. 256p. 1981. 9.95 (ISBN 0-684-16730-1, ScribT). Scribner.

Chief Joseph. Matthew G. Grant. LC 73-9816. 1974. PLB 5.95 (ISBN 0-87191-251-1). Creative Ed.

Chief Joseph. Harrison et al. 35p. (gr. 1-9). 1981. 2.95. Dormac.

Chief Joseph: War Chief of the Nez Perce. Russell G. Davis & B. Ashabranner. (gr. 5-7). 1962. PLB 7.95 o.p. (ISBN 0-07-015926-2, GB). McGraw.

Chief Justice John Marshall: A Reappraisal. Ed. by W. M. Jones. LC 70-152688. (American Constitutional & Legal History Ser). 1971. Repr. of 1956 ed. lib. bdg. 22.50 (ISBN 0-306-70132-4). Da Capo.

Chief Justice: John Marshall & the Growth of the Republic. David G. Loth. Repr. of 1949 ed. lib. bdg. 18.75x (ISBN 0-8371-2450-6, LOJM). Greenwood.

Chief Left Hand: Southern Arapaho. Margaret Coel. LC 80-5940. (Civilization of the American Indian Ser.: Vol. 159). (Illus.). 482p. 1981. 15.95 (ISBN 0-8061-1602-1). U of Okla Pr.

Chief Multiple Residence Inspector. Jack Rudman. (Career Examination Ser.: C-2844). (Cloth bdg. avail. on request). 1980. pap. 14.00 (ISBN 0-8373-2844-6). Natl Learning.

Chief Red Horse Tells About Custer. Jessie B. McGaw. (Illus.). 64p. (gr. 4 up). 1981. 8.95 (ISBN 0-525-66713-X). Elsevier-Nelson.

Chief Sarah. Dorothy N. Morrison. LC 79-22545. (Illus.). (gr. 6-7). 1980. 9.95 (ISBN 0-689-30752-7). Atheneum.

Chiefdom Politics & Alien Law. Sandra Burman. LC 79-25600. 1981. text ed. 38.00x (ISBN 0-8419-0591-6, Africana). Holmes & Meier.

Chiefs: A Novel. Stuart Woods. 1981. 15.95 (ISBN 0-393-01461-4). Norton.

Chiefs & Challengers. George H. Phillips. 1975. 15.95 (ISBN 0-520-02719-1). U of Cal Pr.

Chiefs & Clerics: Abdul Bokar Kan & the History of Futa Toro 1853-1891. David Robinson. (Studies in African Affairs). (Illus.). 306p. 1975. 19.50x o.p. (ISBN 0-19-822701-9). Oxford U Pr.

Chiefs & Politicians: Regional & Political Development in North Ghana. Paul A. Ladouceur. (LEGON History Ser.). (Illus.). 1979. text ed. 40.00 (ISBN 0-582-64646-4). Longman.

Chiefs of Naval Operations. Robert W. Love, Jr. LC 80-12253. 1980. 28.95x (ISBN 0-87021-115-3). Naval Inst Pr.

Chieftan. George Forty. (Illus.). 1980. 14.95 (ISBN 0-684-16433-7, ScribT). Scribner.

Chiffon Scarf. Mignon G. Eberhart. 1975. pap. 0.95 o.p. (ISBN 0-445-00679-X). Popular Lib.

Chihabi's Dictionary of Agricultural & Forestry Terms: English-Arabic. Ahmad Khatib. 1978. 40.00x. Intl Bk Ctr.

Chihuahua Guide. Hilary Harmar. 6.98 o.p. (ISBN 0-385-01569-0). Doubleday.

Chihuahua, Nineteen Sixteen. Otis Carney. 1980. 9.95 (ISBN 0-13-130286-8). P-H.

Chihuahuas. Beverly Pisano & Tressa E. Thurmer. (Illus.). 128p. 1980. 2.95 (ISBN 0-87666-701-9, KW-087). TFH Pubns.

Chike & the River. Chinua Achebe. 1966. text ed. 2.95x (ISBN 0-521-04003-5). Cambridge U Pr.

Child. W. Kessen. LC 65-14253. (Perspectives in Psychology Ser.). 1965. pap. 11.50 (ISBN 0-471-47306-5, Pub. by Wiley-Interscience). Wiley.

Child Abuse: A Crying Shame. Shirley O'Brien. LC 80-23708. 184p. 1980. 15.95x (ISBN 0-8425-1829-0). Brigham.

Child Abuse: An Annotated Bibliography. Ed. by Dorothy P. Wells. LC 79-21641. 458p. 1980. 20.00 (ISBN 0-8108-1264-9). Scarecrow.

Child Abuse: An Interactional Event. Alfred Kadushin & Judith A. Martin. (Illus.). 360p. 1981. 25.00x (ISBN 0-231-04774-6). Columbia U Pr.

Child Abuse & Neglect: An Annotated Bibliography. Beatrice J. Kalisch. LC 78-3123. (Contemporary Problems of Childhood: No. 2). 1978. lib. bdg. 29.95 (ISBN 0-313-20376-8, KBA/). Greenwood.

Child Abuse & Neglect Case Studies. Abe R. Fosson & H. Otto Kaak. 1977. 13.00 (ISBN 0-87488-062-9). Med Exam.

Child Abuse & Neglect: Legislation, Reporting & Prevention. Joseph H. Costa & Gordon K. Nelson. LC 77-3836. 1978. 26.95 (ISBN 0-669-01670-5). Lexington Bks.

Child Abuse & Neglect: The Family & the Community. Ed. by Ray E. Helfer & C. Henry Kempe. LC 76-8891. 1976. 25.00 (ISBN 0-88410-217-3); pap. text ed. 9.95 (ISBN 0-88410-240-8). Ballinger Pub.

Child Abuse Predictions: Policy Implications. Ed. by R. H. Starr. 1981. pns professional reference (ISBN 0-88410-378-1). Ballinger Pub.

Child Advocacy Handbook. Happy Fernandez. LC 80-24053. 1981. pap. 6.95 (ISBN 0-8298-0403-X). Pilgrim NY.

Child Analysis & Therapy. Jules Glenn. LC 78-65122. 1978. 35.00 (ISBN 0-87668-356-1). Aronson.

Child & Adolescent Development. Jason W. Brunk. LC 74-16258. 464p. 1975. pap. text ed. 13.95x o.p. (ISBN 0-471-11430-8). Wiley.

Child & Adolescent Development. Gander & Gardiner. 1981. text ed. 16.95 (ISBN 0-316-30322-4); tchrs'. manual free (ISBN 0-316-30319-4); study guide 5.95 (ISBN 0-316-30318-6). Little.

Child & Adolescent Psychiatry Continuing Education Review. Ed. by Pirooz G. Sholevar. 1977. spiral bdg. 14.00 (ISBN 0-87488-343-1). Med Exam.

Child & Death. Olle J. Sahler. LC 78-18239. (Illus.). 1978. pap. text ed. 14.95 (ISBN 0-8016-4288-4). Mosby.

Child & Family Genealogy Reporting System. 2nd ed. Edward J. Bradley. 1979. 9.95 (ISBN 0-935202-01-3). Child & Family Ent.

Child & His Image: Self Concept in the Early Years. Ed. by Kaoru Yamamoto. LC 72-163283. (Illus., Orig.). 1972. pap. text ed. 10.95 (ISBN 0-395-12571-5, 3-60986). HM.

Child & His Welfare. 3rd ed. Hazel Fredericksen & Raymond A. Mulligan. LC 70-172242. (Illus.). 1972. text ed. 21.95x (ISBN 0-7167-0905-8). W H Freeman.

Child & Play. (Educational Studies & Documents: No. 34). 68p. 1980. pap. 4.00 (ISBN 92-3-101658-X, U1030, UNESCO). Unipub.

Child & Story: The Literary Connection. Kay E. Vandergrift. Ed. by Jane Anne Hannigan. (Diversity & Directions in Children's Literature Ser.). 349p. 1980. 14.95x (ISBN 0-918212-42-1). Neal-Schuman.

Child & the Book. N. Tucker. 275p. Date not set. 29.95 (ISBN 0-521-23251-1). Cambridge U Pr.

Child & the Republic: The Dawn of Modern American Child Nurture. Bernard Wishy. LC 67-26223. 1972. 10.00x (ISBN 0-8122-7556-X); pap. 5.95x (ISBN 0-8122-1026-3, Pa Paperbks). U of Pa Pr.

Child & the Serpent: Refelctions on Popular Indian Symbols. Jyoti Sahi. (Illus.). 192p. (Orig.). 1980. pap. 18.50 (ISBN 0-7100-0704-3). Routledge & Kegan.

Child As Critic: Teaching Literature in the Elementary School. Glenna Sloan. LC 75-23360. 1975. pap. text ed. 6.50x (ISBN 0-8077-2482-3). Tchrs Coll.

Child Behavior. rev. ed. Frances L. Ilg et al. LC 80-8371. (Illus.). 1981. 14.95 (ISBN 0-06-014829-2, HarpT). Har-Row.

Child Behavior. Grover J. Whitehurst & Ross F. Vasta. LC 76-14009. (Illus.). 1977. text ed. 19.50 (ISBN 0-395-24446-3); test item manual 1.00 (ISBN 0-395-24447-1); wkbk. 6.75 (ISBN 0-395-25794-8). HM.

Child Behavior Analysis & Therapy. Donna L. Gelfand & Donald P. Hartmann. LC 74-14707. 1975. text ed. 23.00 (ISBN 0-08-018229-1); pap. text ed. 12.50 (ISBN 0-08-018228-3). Pergamon.

Child Behavior Modification: A Manual for Teachers, Nurses & Parents. L. S. Watson, Jr. 1973. pap. text ed. 9.25 (ISBN 0-08-017061-7). Pergamon.

Child Captives: A True Tale of Life Among the Indians of the West. Margaret K. Hosmer. LC 75-7109. (Indian Captivities Ser.: Vol. 83). 1976. Repr. of 1870 ed. lib. bdg. 44.00 (ISBN 0-8240-1707-2). Garland Pub.

Child Care: A Comprehensive Guide, 2 vols. Ed. by Stevanne Auerbach. Incl. Vol. 1. Rationale for Child Care: Programs Vs. Politics. LC 74-11877. 215p. 1975. text ed. 16.95 (ISBN 0-87705-218-2); Vol. 2. Model Programs & Their Components. LC 76-10121. 297p. 1976. 19.95 (ISBN 0-87705-256-5). Human Sci Pr.

Child Care Alternatives & Emotional Well-Being. Judith D. Schiller. 204p. 1980. 21.95 (ISBN 0-03-056139-6). Praeger.

Child Care & Mediating Structures. Ed. by Brigitte Berger & Sidney Callahan. 1979. 9.25 (ISBN 0-8447-2162-X); pap. 4.25. Am Enterprise.

Child Care & Public Policy. Ed. by Philip K. Robins & Samuel Weiner. LC 77-17724. (Illus.). 1978. 21.00 (ISBN 0-669-02088-5). Lexington Bks.

Child Care & the Family. H. R. Schaffer. 88p. 1968. pap. text ed. 5.00x (ISBN 0-7135-1511-2, Pub. by Bedford England). Renouf.

Child Care, Family Benefits & Working Parents. Sheila B. Kamerman & Alfred J. Kahn. (Illus.). 352p. 1981. text ed. 25.00x (ISBN 0-231-05170-0). Columbia U Pr.

Child Care: Needs & Numbers. Jean Packman. (National Institute Social Services Library). 1969. text ed. 27.50x (ISBN 0-04-360016-6). Allen Unwin.

Child Christopher & Goldilind the Fair. William Morris. Ed. by R. Reginald & Douglas Menville. LC 80-19163. (Newcastle Forgotten Fantasy Library: Vol. 12). 219p. 1980. Repr. of 1977 ed. lib. bdg. 10.95x (ISBN 0-89370-511-X). Borgo Pr.

Child Development. G. Craig. 1979. 18.95 (ISBN 0-13-131250-2); study guide & wkbk. 6.95 (ISBN 0-13-131268-5). P-H.

Child Development. Greta Fein. (Illus.). 1978. text ed. 18.95 (ISBN 0-13-132571-X); study guide & wkbk. 6.95 (ISBN 0-13-132555-8). P-H.

Child Development. Mary J. Tudor. 544p. 1981. text ed. 22.95 (ISBN 0-07-065412-3, HP). McGraw.

Child Development - an Introduction. Robert F. Biehler. LC 75-31014. 1976. text ed. 17.95 (ISBN 0-395-20650-2); inst. manual 3.50 (ISBN 0-395-20651-0); inst. suppl. 1.25 (ISBN 0-395-25079-X); study guide 6.60 (ISBN 0-395-20652-9). HM.

Child Development: An Introduction. 2nd ed. Robert F. Biehler. LC 80-82347. (Illus.). 704p. 1981. text ed. write for info. (ISBN 0-395-29833-4); price not set study guide (ISBN 0-395-29835-0); price not set instr's. manual (ISBN 0-395-29834-2). HM.

Child Development & Curriculum Materials. University of Missouri - Home Economics Resource Unit. text ed. 1.75x spiral bdg. (ISBN 0-87543-022-8). Lucas.

Child Development & Developmental Disabilities. Stewart Gabel & Marilyn T. Erickson. (Little, Brown Ser. in Clinical Pediatrics). 1980. text ed. 24.50 (ISBN 0-316-30100-0). Little.

Child Development & Individually Guided Education. Glenn E. Tagatz. LC 75-12103. (Individually Guided Education-Leadership Ser.). (Illus.). 224p. 1976. pap. text ed. 7.95 (ISBN 0-201-19111-3); tchrs guide 2.95 (ISBN 0-201-19121-0). A-W.

Child Development for Day Care Workers. Ruth Highberger & Carol Schramm. LC 75-31008. (Illus.). 288p. 1976. text ed. 14.50 (ISBN 0-395-20631-6); resource manual 1.50 (ISBN 0-395-20632-4). HM.

Child Development: The Human, Cultural, & Educational Context. W. H. Schmidt. (Holtzman Series). 191p. 1973. pap. text ed. 9.50 scp (ISBN 0-06-045781-3, HarpC). Har-Row.

Child: Development Through Adolescence. B. Fong & M. Resnick. 1980. 16.95 (ISBN 0-8053-9010-3); instrs guide-test item file 3.95 (ISBN 0-8053-9011-1); study guide 6.95 (ISBN 0-8053-9012-X); project & film guide 1.95 (ISBN 0-686-65168-5). A-W.

Child: Development Through Adolescence. Bernadine Fong & Miriam Resnick. 1980. 16.95 (ISBN 0-8053-9010-3); study guide 6.95 (ISBN 0-8053-9012-X). Benjamin-Cummings.

Child Development Through Physical Education. J. H. Humphrey. (Illus.). 200p. 1980. 15.75 (ISBN 0-398-03981-X). C C Thomas.

Child Drama. P. Slade. 1979. pap. 25.00 (ISBN 0-340-20968-2). Verry.

Child, Family & State, Cases & Materials on Children & the Law. Robert Mnookin. 857p. (Orig.). 1978. text ed. 23.25 (ISBN 0-316-57650-6). Little.

Child Figure in English Literature. Robert Pattison. LC 76-2893. 190p. 1978. 13.50x (ISBN 0-8203-0409-3). U of Ga Pr.

Child from Three to Eighteen. Olle J. Sahler. (Illus.). 260p. 1981. softcover 12.50 (ISBN 0-8016-4290-6). Mosby.

Child Grows Up: A New Approach to Child Development. Candida C. Peterson. LC 73-89779. 1974. pap. text ed. 7.95x (ISBN 0-88284-012-6). Alfred Pub.

Child Growth. W. M. Krogman. (Ann Arbor Science Library). 1972. pap. 5.50 (ISBN 0-472-05019-2, AA). U of Mich Pr.

Child Health: America's Future. George A. Silver. LC 78-14217. 1978. text ed. 22.50 (ISBN 0-89443-043-2). Aspen Systems.

Child Health & the Community. Robert J. Haggerty et al. LC 75-1139. (Wiley Series in Health, Medicine & Society). 388p. 1975. 25.95 (ISBN 0-471-33871-0, Pub. by Wiley-Interscience). Wiley.

Child Health: Basics for Primary Care. Margaret C. Heagarty et al. 454p. 1980. pap. text ed. 16.95 (ISBN 0-8385-1111-2). ACC.

Child Health in the Community. 2nd ed. Ed. by Rose G. Mitchell & James Mackenzie. (Illus.). 352p. 1980. text ed. 37.50 (ISBN 0-443-02195-3). Churchill.

Child Health Maintenance: A Guide to Clinical Assessment. 2nd ed. Peggy L. Chinn & Cynthia J. Leitch. LC 78-11964. 1979. pap. text ed. 10.50 (ISBN 0-8016-0949-6). Mosby.

Child Health Nursing: Care of the Growing Family. 2nd ed. Adele Pillitteri. 1981. text ed. write for info (ISBN 0-316-70793-7). Little.

Child Health Nursing: Concepts & Management. Steele. 1981. price not set (ISBN 0-89352-035-7). Masson Pub.

Child: His Origin, Development & Care. Florence B. Sherbon. 707p. 1980. Repr. of 1934 ed. lib. bdg. 50.00 (ISBN 0-89984-422-7). Century Bookbindery.

Child in His Family. E. James Anthony et al. Incl. Vol. 2. The Impact of Disease & Death. 1973. 30.50 o.p. (ISBN 0-471-03226-3); Vol. 3. Children at Psychiatric Risk. LC 74-6169. 1974. 28.50 (ISBN 0-471-03228-X); Vol. 4. Vulnerable Children. LC 78-120701. 1978. 31.50 (ISBN 0-471-04433-4); Vol. 5. Children & Their Parents in a Changing World. LC 78-120701. 1978. 29.95 (ISBN 0-471-04432-6); Vol. 6. Preventative Child Psychiatry in an Age of Transition. 1980. 32.50 (ISBN 0-471-08403-4). LC 72-11702. (International Association for Child Psychiatry & Allied Professions Yearbook, Pub. by Wiley-Interscience). Wiley.

Child in Primitive Society. Nathan Miller. LC 76-167074. 1975. Repr. of 1928 ed. 21.00 (ISBN 0-8103-3995-1). Gale.

Child in Prison Camp. Shizuye Takashima. (Illus.). 64p. (gr. 5 up). 1974. 9.25 (ISBN 0-688-20113-X); PLB 8.88 (ISBN 0-688-30113-4). Morrow.

Child in the Bamboo Grove. Rosemary Harris. LC 72-4064. (Illus.). (gr. 1-3). 1972. 8.95 (ISBN 0-87599-194-7). S G Phillips.

Child in the World of Tomorrow: a Window into the Future: Proceedings. Institute of Child Health Athens International Symposium 2-8, July 1978 Athens, Greece. Ed. by Spyros Doxiadis & Jaqueline Tyrwhitt. (Illus.). 1979. 45.00 (ISBN 0-686-67666-1). Pergamon.

Child Is Born: The Drama of Life Before Birth. Claes Wirsen et al. 1969. pap. 6.95 (ISBN 0-440-51214-X, Dell Trade Pbks). Dell.

Child Is Missing. Charlotte Paul. 1978. pap. 2.75 (ISBN 0-425-04354-1, Medallion). Berkley Pub.

Child Killer. Edson T. Hamill. (Ryker Ser: No. 5). (Orig.). 1975. pap. 1.25 o.p. (ISBN 0-685-52936-3, LB266ZK, Leisure Bks). Nordon Pubns.

Child Language. Alison J. Elliot. (Cambridge Textbooks in Linguistics). 180p. Date not set. text ed. price not set (ISBN 0-521-22518-3); pap. text ed. price not set (ISBN 0-521-29556-4). Cambridge U Pr.

Child Language, Learning, & Linguistics: An Overview for the Teaching & Therapeutic Professions. David Crystal. 1976. pap. 9.95x (ISBN 0-7131-5890-5). Intl Ideas.

Child Learns to Speak: A Guide for Parents & Teachers of Preschool Children. Susan M. Leitch. (Illus.). 104p. 1977. 11.75 (ISBN 0-398-03599-7); pap. 8.25 (ISBN 0-398-03602-0). C C Thomas.

Child Life in Hospitals. Richard A. Thompson & Gene Stanford. 1981. write for info (ISBN 0-398-04445-7). C C Thomas.

Child Maltreatment: Developing a Community Team Approach. Ed. by Brent Q. Hafen. 1981. cancelled (ISBN 0-88416-320-2). PSG Pub.

Child Maltreatment in the United States. Saad Z. Nagi. LC 77-22121. 1977. 15.00x (ISBN 0-231-04394-5). Columbia U Pr.

Child Management: A Program for Parents & Teachers. Judith M. Smith & Donald E. Smith. LC 76-22829. 1976. pap. text ed. 5.95 (ISBN 0-87822-125-5); discussion guide 2.95 (ISBN 0-87822-126-3). Res Press.

Child Management Program for Abusive Parents. David Wolfe et al. (Illus.). 192p. (Orig.). 1981. pap. write for info. (ISBN 0-89305-035-0). Anna Pub.

Child of an Oak. Alan Katz. (Poetry Ser.). (Illus.). (gr. 9-12). 1971. pap. 3.00x o.p. (ISBN 0-89304-000-2, CCC099). Cross Cult.

Child of Gentle Courage. Sarah Shears. 1974. 8.95 (ISBN 0-236-31065-8, Pub. by Paul Elek). Merrimack Bk Serv.

Child of Nature, 1774, 2 vols. in 1. Claude Helvetius. Ed. by Michael F. Shugrue. (Flowering of the Novel, 1740-1775 Ser: Vol. 105). 1974. lib. bdg. 50.00 (ISBN 0-8240-1204-6). Garland Pub.

Child of Night. Anne Edwards. 1978. pap. 1.75 o.p. (ISBN 0-445-04156-0). Popular Lib.

Child of Scorn: A Mind Play in Three Parts & Numerous Voices. Carol A. Morizot. LC 78-52256. (Orig.). 1978. pap. 3.95 o.p. (ISBN 0-930138-02-3). Harold Hse.

Child of Six Could Do It! Cartoons About Modern Art. George Melly & J. R. Glaves-Smith. (Tate Gallery Art Ser.). (Illus.). 1977. pap. 1.95 (ISBN 0-8120-0854-5). Barron.

Child of the Age. Francis Adams. Ed. by Ian Fletcher & John Stokes. LC 76-20045. (Decadent Consciousness Ser.: Vol. 1). 1977. Repr. of 1894 ed. lib. bdg. 38.00 (ISBN 0-8240-2750-7). Garland Pub.

Child of the Revolution. 2nd ed. Leonhard Wolfgang. Tr. by C. M. Woodhouse from Ger. 448p. 1980. pap. text ed. 13.00x (ISBN 0-906133-26-2). Humanities.

Child of the Temple. Lucy Diamond. (Ladybird Ser). (Illus.). 1955. bds. 1.49 (ISBN 0-87508-836-8). Chr Lit.

Child Personality & Psychopathology: Current Topics, 3 vols. Ed. by Anthony Davids. LC 74-7030. 256p. Vol. 1, 1974. 23.95 o.p. (ISBN 0-471-19696-7); Vol. 2, 1975. 25.95 o.p. (ISBN 0-471-19700-9); Vol. 3, 1976. 28.95 o.p. (ISBN 0-471-19702-5, Pub. by Wiley-Interscience). Wiley.

Child Phonology: Vol. I Production. Ed. by Grace H. Yeni-Komshian et al. LC 79-8867. (Perspectives in Neurolinguistics Psycho-Linguistics Ser.). 1980. write for info. (ISBN 0-12-770601-1). Acad Pr.

Child Phonology: Vol. 2, Perception. Ed. by Grace H. Yeni-Komshian et al. (Perspectives in Neurolinguistics & Psycholinguistics Ser.). 1980. 24.00 (ISBN 0-12-770602-X). Acad Pr.

Child Placement Through Clinically Oriented Casework. Esther Glickman. LC 56-10783. 1957. 20.00x (ISBN 0-231-02127-5). Columbia U Pr.

Child Player. William Dobson. (Orig.). 1981. pap. 1.95 (ISBN 0-451-09604-5, J9604, Sig). NAL.

Child Psychiatry. 3rd ed. John C. Duffy. (Medical Examination Review Bks.: Vol. 23). 1977. spiral bdg. 16.50 (ISBN 0-87488-126-9). Med Exam.

Child Psychiatry. 2nd ed. Ed. by John C. Duffy. (Medical Outline Ser.). 1977. spiral bdg 13.50 (ISBN 0-87488-613-9). Med Exam.

Child Psychiatry. 4th ed. Leo Kanner. (Illus.). 768p. 1979. 22.75 (ISBN 0-398-02199-6). C C Thomas.

Child Psychiatry Case Studies. R. Dean Coddington et al. 1973. spiral bdg. 14.00 (ISBN 0-87488-029-7). Med Exam.

Child Psychiatry Observed. Elizabeth Gore. Ed. by Jean Nursten. LC 75-6926. 264p. 1975. text ed. 26.00 (ISBN 0-08-017277-6); pap. text ed. 14.00 (ISBN 0-08-017278-4). Pergamon.

Child Psychology. Lester D. Crow & Alice Crow. 1953. pap. 3.75 o.p. (ISBN 0-06-460079-3, CO 79, COS). Har-Row.

Child Psychology. 7th ed. Arthur T. Jersild et al. LC 74-20723. (Illus.). 640p. 1975. text ed. 18.95 (ISBN 0-13-130971-4). P-H.

Child Psychology: A Developmental Perspective. William J. Meyer & Jerome B. Dusek. 1979. text ed. 16.95x (ISBN 0-669-88971-7). Heath.

Child Psychology: Behavior & Development. 3rd ed. Ronald C. Johnson & Gene R. Medinnus. LC 73-22298. 576p. 1974. text ed. 21.95x (ISBN 0-471-44624-6). Wiley.

Child Psychology in Contemporary Society. John R. Dill. 1978. text ed. 18.95 (ISBN 0-205-05775-6, 795775-0). Allyn.

Child Psychopathology: Assessment, Etiology & Treatment. Marilyn T. Erickson. 1978. ref. ed. 19.95 (ISBN 0-13-131102-6). P-H.

Child Rearing Values: A Cross National Study. Wallace E. Lambert et al. LC 78-19747. 1979. 29.95 (ISBN 0-03-049086-3). Praeger.

Child Savers. Peter S. Prescott. LC 80-2705. 320p. 1981. 12.95 (ISBN 0-394-50235-3). Knopf.

Child Sellers. Wendy Leeds. 1981. pap. 2.25 (ISBN 0-8439-0889-0, Leisure Bks). Nordon Pubns.

Child Sexual Abuse: Analysis of a Family Therapy Approach. Jerome A. Kroth. (Illus.). 216p. 1979. text ed. 19.25 (ISBN 0-398-03906-2). C C Thomas.

Child-Snatched. Margaret Strickland. LC 79-91709. 112p. 1979. pap. 4.95 (ISBN 0-935834-00-1). Rainbow-Betty.

Child Support & Public Policy. Judith Cassetty. LC 77-4541. (Illus.). 1978. 17.95 (ISBN 0-669-01486-9). Lexington Bks.

Child, the Family & the Outside World. D. W. Winnicott. lib. bdg. 8.50x o.p. (ISBN 0-88307-484-2). Gannon.

Child, the Family, & the Outside World. D. W. Winnicott. 240p. 1964. pap. 1.95 o.p. (ISBN 0-14-020668-X, Pelican). Penguin.

Child Under Six. Jesild Hymes, Jr. 1963. 9.95 (ISBN 0-13-132209-5). P-H.

Child Welfare Forecasting: Context & Technique. John L. Craft et al. (Illus.). 216p. 1980. 21.75 (ISBN 0-398-04045-1). C C Thomas.

Child Who Does Not Talk. (Clinics in Developmental Medicine Ser. No. 13). 220p. 1964. 6.75 o.p. (ISBN 0-685-24735-X). Lippincott.

Child Who Never Grew. Pearl S. Buck. (Special Education Bks). 1950. 3.95 (ISBN 0-381-98020-0, A12200, JD-J). John Day.

Child Who Walks Alone: Case Studies of Rejection in the Schools. Anne Stilwell & Hart Stilwell. LC 79-38569. 218p. 1972. 10.00 (ISBN 0-292-71002-X). U of Tex Pr.

Child with a Chronic Medical Problem: Cardiac Disorders, Diabetes, Haemophilia, Social, Emotional, & Educational Adjustment. Doria Pilling. (General Ser.). 60p. 1973. pap. text ed. 6.25x (ISBN 0-85633-027-2, NFER). Humanities.

Child with an Acquired Amputation. Committee on Prosthetics Research & Development. (Illus.). 176p. 1972. pap. 7.75 (ISBN 0-309-02047-6). Natl Acad Pr.

Child with Asthma: Social, Emotional & Educational Adjustment - an Annotated Bibliography. Doria Pilling. (General Ser.). 84p. 1975. pap. text ed. 7.00x (ISBN 0-85633-071-X, NFER). Humanities.

Child with Cancer: Clinical Approaches to Psychosocial Care - Research in Psychosocial Aspects. Jerome L. Schulman & Mary J. Kupst. (Illus.). 232p. 1980. text ed. 19.50 (ISBN 0-398-03944-5). C C Thomas.

Child with Cerebral Palsy: Social, Emotional & Educational Adjustment: an Annotated Bibliography. Doria Pilling. (General Ser.). 61p. (Orig.). 1973. pap. text ed. 7.00x (ISBN 0-85633-016-7, NFER). Humanities.

Child with Delayed Speech. Michael Rutter & J. A. Martin. (Clinics in Developmental Medicine Ser.: Vol. 43). 1972. 29.00 (ISBN 0-685-34615-3). Lippincott.

Child with Down's Syndrome (Mongolism) David W. Smith & Ann C. Wilson. LC 72-88852. (Illus.). 120p. 1973. pap. 7.95 (ISBN 0-7216-8420-3). Saunders.

Child with Spinal Bifida: Social, Emotional, & Educational Adjustment, an Annotated Bibliography. Doria Pilling. (General Ser.). 1973. pap. text ed. 6.25x (ISBN 0-85633-021-3, NFER). Humanities.

Child Without Tomorrow. Anthony M. Graziano. LC 73-3394. 1974. 23.00 (ISBN 0-08-017085-4). Pergamon.

Childbearing: A Guide for Pregnant Parents. Sherry L. Jimenez. (Illus.). 176p. 1980. 12.95 (Spec); pap. 5.95. P-H.

Childbearing Family: A Nursing Perspective. Mary Anne Miller & Dorothy Brooten. 1977. text ed. 16.95 (ISBN 0-316-57146-6, Little Med Div). Little.

Childbirth: A Source Book for Conception, Pregnancy, Birth & the First Weeks of Life. Sharron Hannon. (Illus.). 256p. 1980. pap. 9.95 (ISBN 0-87131-291-3). M Evans.

Childbirth Education. Mary J. Hungerford. (Illus.). 344p. 1972. pap. text ed. 17.50 (ISBN 0-398-02321-2). C C Thomas.

Childbirth Education: A Nursing Perspective. Jeanette L. Sasmor. LC 78-32177. 1979. 14.95 (ISBN 0-471-75490-0, Pub. by Wiley Medical). Wiley.

Childbirth Without Fear: The Original Approach to Natural Childbirth. new, 4th ed. Grantly Dick-Read. Ed. by Helen Wessel & Harlan F. Ellis. LC 77-181616. (Illus.). 352p. 1972. 13.95 o.s.i. (ISBN 0-06-011034-1, HarpT). Har-Row.

Childcraft-the How & Why Library, 15 vols. Ed. by World Book-Childcraft International Inc. Incl. Vol. 1. Poems & Rhymes; Vol. 2. Stories & Fables; Vol. 3. Children Everywhere; Vol. 4. World & Space; Vol. 5. About Animals; Vol. 6. The Green Kingdom; Vol. 7. How Things Work; Vol. 8. About Us; Vol. 9. Holidays & Birthdays; Vol. 10. Places to Know; Vol. 11. Make & Do; Vol. 12. Look & Learn; Vol. 13. Mathemagic; Vol. 14. About Me; Vol. 15. Guide for Parents. (Illus.). (gr. k-6). 1981. PLB write for info. (ISBN 0-7166-0181-8). World Bk Child.

Childers' Diet to Stop Arthritis: The Nightshades & Ill Health. 2nd rev. ed. 200p. 1981. pap. 9.95 (ISBN 0-938378-00-7). Horticult Pubns.

Childhood: A Sociological Perspective. Marten Shipman. (Exploring Education Ser.). 115p. (Orig.). 1972. pap. text ed. 5.00x (ISBN 0-85633-006-X, NFER). Humanities.

Childhood & Adolescence: A Psychology of the Growing Person. 4th ed. L. Joseph Stone & Joseph Church. LC 78-10730. 1979. text ed. 15.95x (ISBN 0-394-32086-7); study guide 5.95x (ISBN 0-394-32170-7). Random.

Childhood & Movement. Diana Jordon. (gr. 9 up). 1972. 8.50x o.p. (ISBN 0-392-02545-0, SpS). Soccer.

Childhood Deprivation. Ed. by Albert R. Roberts. 232p. 1974. 14.75 (ISBN 0-398-03149-5). C C Thomas.

Childhood Diabetes. 2nd ed. Oman Craig & John Apley. (Postgraduate Pediatric Ser.). 1981. text ed. price not set (ISBN 0-407-00209-X). Butterworth.

Childhood Disorder: A Psychosomatic Approach. Philip Pinkerton. (Illus.). 200p. 1975. 15.00x (ISBN 0-231-03955-7). Columbia U Pr.

Childhood in China. Ed. by William Kessen. LC 75-8151. 320p. 1975. 15.00x (ISBN 0-300-01910-6); pap. 4.95x (ISBN 0-300-01917-3). Yale U Pr.

Childhood in Poetry: First Supplement, 3 Vols. Ed. by John M. Shaw. LC 67-28092. (Illus.). 1972. Set. 130.00 (ISBN 0-8103-0476-7). Gale.

Childhood in Poetry: Second Supplement-a Catalogue, with Biographical & Critical Annotations, of the Books of English & American Poets Comprising the Shaw Childhood in Poetry Collection in the Library of the Fla. St. U, 2 vols. Ed. by John M. Shaw. LC 67-28092. 1500p. 1976. Set. 130.00 (ISBN 0-8103-0477-5); Vol. 1. 42.50 (ISBN 0-8103-0479-1); Vol. 2. index 58.00 (ISBN 0-686-67256-9). Gale.

Childhood in Poetry: Third Supplement. Ed. by John M. Shaw. LC 67-28092. (Childhood in Poetry Ser.). (Illus.). 75.00 (ISBN 0-8103-0480-5). Gale.

Childhood of Fiction. John A. MacCulloch. LC 74-78208. 1971. Repr. of 1905 ed. 28.00 (ISBN 0-8103-3628-6). Gale.

Childhood: Pathways of Discovery. Sheldon White & Barbara N. White. (Life Cycle Ser.). 1979. pap. text ed. 4.95 scp (ISBN 0-06-384743-4, HarpC). Har-Row.

Childhood Prevention of Atherosclerosis. Ed. by R. M. Lauer & R. B. Shekelle. 1979. 48.50 (ISBN 0-89004-381-7). Raven.

Childhood Psychopathology: A Developmental Approach. Irwin J. Knopf. (Illus.). 1979. text ed. 19.95 (ISBN 0-13-130336-8). P-H.

Childhood Sexual Learning: The Unwritten Curriculum. Elizabeth Roberts. 1980. 22.50 (ISBN 0-88410-374-9). Ballinger Pub.

Childhood Songs. Lucy Larcom. LC 77-20397. (Granger Poetry Library Ser.). (Illus.). 1978. Repr. of 1874 ed. 19.00x (ISBN 0-89609-069-8). Granger Bk.

Childhood, the Biography of a Place. Harry Crews. 1979. lib. bdg. 12.95 (ISBN 0-8161-6752-4). G K Hall.

Childhood, Welfare & Justice. Michael King. 160p. 1981. pap. 16.95 (ISBN 0-7134-3713-8, Pub. by Batsford England). David & Charles.

Childmare. A. G. Scott. (Orig.). 1981. pap. 2.25 (ISBN 0-451-09807-2, E9807, Signet Bks). NAL.

Children & Adolescents. 3rd ed. David Elkind. 272p. 1981. text ed. 15.95x (ISBN 0-19-502820-1); pap. text ed. 5.95x (ISBN 0-19-502821-X). Oxford U Pr.

Children & Adolescents with Learning Disabilities. Cecil D. Mercer. (Special Education Ser.). 1979. text ed. 18.50 (ISBN 0-675-08272-2). Merrill.

Children & Adults: Activities for Growing Together. Joseph Braga & Laurie Braga. (Human Development Bks.). (Illus.). 1978. 15.95 (ISBN 0-13-130351-1, Spec); pap. 7.95 (ISBN 0-13-130344-9). P-H.

Children & Ancestors. Stanley L. Weinberg & Herbert J. Stoltze. (Action Biology Ser.). (gr. 9-12). 1974. pap. text ed. 3.20 (ISBN 0-205-04143-4, 6741436). Allyn.

Children & Books. 5th ed. Zena Sutherland & May H. Arbuthnot. 1977. 18.95x (ISBN 0-673-15037-2). Scott F.

Children & Books. 6th ed. Zena Sutherland et al. 1981. text ed. 18.95x (ISBN 0-673-15377-0). Scott F.

Children & Communication: Verbal & Nonverbal Language Development. 2nd ed. Barbara S. Wood. (Illus.). 320p. 1981. text ed. 15.95 (ISBN 0-13-131920-5). P-H.

Children & Communication: Verbal & Non-Verbal Language Development. Barbara Wood. LC 75-22452. (Speech Communication Ser.). (Illus.). 336p. 1976. text ed. 15.95x (ISBN 0-13-131896-9). P-H.

Children & Divorce. Martin Wilkinson. (Practice of Social Work Ser.: No. 6). 288p. 1981. 25.00x (ISBN 0-631-12514-0, Pub. by Basil Blackwell England); pap. 12.50x (ISBN 0-631-12524-8). Biblio Dist.

Children & Drama. 2nd ed. Nellie McCaslin. 320p. 1981. text ed. 9.95 (ISBN 0-686-28848-3). Longman.

Children & Drama. Ed. by Nellie McCaslin. LC 74-84081. 1975. pap. 8.95x (ISBN 0-679-30269-7, Pub. by MacKay). Longman.

Children & Mental Health Centers: Programs, Problems, Prospects, 1972. Raymond M. Glasscote et al. 257p. 1972. pap. 7.50 (P172-0). Am Psychiatric.

Children & Parents in Hospitals. Ed. by J. Lind et al. (Journal: Pediatrician: Vol. 9, No. 3-4). (Illus.). 120p. 1980. pap. 12.00 (ISBN 3-8055-1476-X). S Karger.

Children & Plastics: Stages 1 & 2 & Background. Mary Horn. LC 77-83010. (Science 5-13 Ser.). 1977. pap. text ed. 9.30 (ISBN 0-356-04352-5). Raintree Child.

Children & Science. Lazer Goldberg. LC 70-106554. 1970. 6.95 o.p. (ISBN 0-684-10207-2, ScribT). Scribner.

Children & Science: The Process of Teaching & Learning. David P. Butts & Gene E. Hall. (Illus.). 368p. 1975. ref. ed. 15.95 (ISBN 0-13-132258-3); pap. text ed. 11.95 (ISBN 0-13-132241-9). P-H.

Children & Television. Ed. by Ray Brown. LC 76-50500. (Illus.). 1976. 20.00x (ISBN 0-8039-0821-0); pap. 9.95x (ISBN 0-8039-0822-9). Sage.

Children & Television. Ed. by Sara Lake. (Special Interest Resource Guides in Education Ser.). (Orig.). 1981. pap. 8.50x (ISBN 0-912700-87-4). Oryx Pr.

Children & the Faces of Television: Teaching, Violence, Selling. Edward L. Palmer. 1980. 24.50 (ISBN 0-12-544480-X). Acad Pr.

Children & the Urban Environment: Evaluation of the WGBH-TV Educational Project. Gans Marshall Kaplan & Kahn. LC 70-187397. (Special Studies in U. S. Economic, Social & Political Issues). 1973. 28.00x (ISBN 0-275-28687-8). Irvington.

Children & Their Books. 2nd rev. ed. Gladys Williams. 1981. pap. 3.95x (ISBN 0-7156-0535-6, Pub. by Duckworth England). Biblio Dist.

Children & Their Literature. Constantine Georgiou. LC 69-10223. (Education Ser). 1969. text ed. 18.95x (ISBN 0-13-132167-6). P-H.

Children & TV: Television's Impact on the Child. Ed. by Sylvia Sunderlin. (Illus.). 1967. pap. 1.25x o.p. (ISBN 0-87173-016-2). ACEI.

Children & War: Political Socialization to International Conflict. Howard B. Tolley, Jr. LC 72-90521. (Illus.). 274p. 1973. pap. text ed. 6.50x (ISBN 0-8077-2280-4). Tchrs Coll.

Children Are People: The Librarian in the Community. Janet Hill. LC 73-16277. (Illus.). 1974. 8.95 o.s.i. (ISBN 0-690-00475-3, TYC-T). T Y Crowell.

Children As Poets. Ed. by Denys Thompson. 1972. pap. text ed. 11.95x (ISBN 0-435-14893-1). Heinemann Ed.

Children As Writers. Incl. 15th Competition. Frwd. by Jack Longland. 1974. pap. text ed. 3.95x o.p. (ISBN 0-435-13401-9); 16th Competition. Frwd. by Ted Hughes. 1975. pap. text ed. 3.95x o.p. (ISBN 0-435-13403-5); 17th Competition. Frwd. by Marjorie Hourd. 1976. pap. text ed. 4.95x o.p. (ISBN 0-435-13405-1). Heinemann Ed.

Children As Writers, No. 5. British Daily Mirror Children's Lit. Competitions. Ed. by Ed J. Longland. 1979. pap. text ed. 4.95 o.p. (ISBN 0-686-60336-2). Heinemann Ed.

Children at Play. Heidi Britz-Crecelius. (Illus.). 1979. 12.50 (ISBN 0-903540-24-X, Pub. by Floris Books); pap. 6.95 (ISBN 0-903540-27-4, Pub. by Floris Books). St George Bk Serv.

Children at School: Primary Education in Britain Today. Ed. by Geoffrey Howson. LC 75-106645. (Illus.). 1970. pap. text ed. 6.50x (ISBN 0-8077-1523-9). Tchrs Coll.

Children at Work. International Labour Office, Geneva. Ed. by Elias Mendelievich. (Illus.). 176p. 1979. 16.25 (ISBN 9-22-102165-3); pap. 11.25 (ISBN 9-22-102072-X). Intl Labour Office.

Children at Work. Jennifer Tann. (History in Focus Ser.). (Illus.). 72p. (gr. 6 up). 1981. 14.95 (ISBN 0-7134-3553-4, Pub. by Batsford England). David & Charles.

Children Australia. Ed. by Ray Brown. 320p. 1981. text ed. 22.50x (ISBN 0-86861-186-7, 2567); pap. text ed. 12.50x (ISBN 0-86861-194-8, 2568). Allen Unwin.

Children Away from Home: A Sourcebook in Residential Treatment. Ed. by James K. Whittaker & Albert E. Trieschman. LC 72-140014. 1972. 24.95x (ISBN 0-202-36010-5). Aldine Pub.

Children, Celebrate! Maria Rabalais & Howard Hall. LC 73-94242. (Orig.). 1974. pap. 5.95 (ISBN 0-8091-1820-3). Paulist Pr.

Children Discover Music & Dance. Emma D. Sheehy. LC 68-24571. 1968. pap. text ed. 7.25x (ISBN 0-8077-2150-6). Tchrs Coll.

Children, Dying, & Grief. Ed. by Margot Tallmer et al. (Thanatology Service Ser.). 200p. 1981. pap. 9.95 (ISBN 0-930194-26-8). Highly Specialized.

Children, Family & Foster Care: New Insights from Research in New York City. 1976. 3.00 (ISBN 0-86671-029-9). Comm Coun Great NY.

Children, Go Where I Send Thee: An American Spiritual. Illus. by Kathryn E. Shoemaker. (Illus.). 32p. (Orig.). 1980. pap. 6.95 (ISBN 0-03-056673-8). Winston Pr.

Children, Grief & Social Work. Gill Lonsdale et al. (Practice of Social Work Ser.: Vol. 4). 130p. 1979. 21.95x (ISBN 0-631-12191-9, Pub. by Basil Blackwell); pap. 9.95x (ISBN 0-631-12181-1). Biblio Dist.

Children in Classrooms: An Investigation of Person-Environment Interaction. Daniel Solomon & Arthur J. Kendall. (Praeger Special Studies). 1979. 25.95 (ISBN 0-03-047071-4). Praeger.

Children in Crisis: A Time for Caring, a Time for Change. Carmie T. Cochrane & David V. Myers. LC 79-20132. (Sage Human Service Guides: Vol. 12). 95p. 1980. pap. 6.00 (ISBN 0-8039-1386-9). Sage.

Children in Danger. Jean Renvoize. 1975. 13.00x (ISBN 0-7100-7892-7). Routledge & Kegan.

Children in Fear. Stephen Joseph. LC 72-91587. 224p. 1974. 6.95 o.p. (ISBN 0-03-007711-7). HR&W.

Children in Foster Care: A Longitudinal Investigation. David Fanshel & Eugene Shinn. LC 77-3176. 1978. 27.50x (ISBN 0-231-03576-4). Columbia U Pr.

Children in Foster Care: Destitute, Neglected...Betrayed. Alan R. Gruber. LC 77-521. 1977. 19.95 (ISBN 0-87705-265-4). Human Sci Pr.

Children in Foster Homes: Achieving Continuity of Care. Theodore J. Stein et al. LC 78-16927. 1978. 28.95 (ISBN 0-03-046421-8). Praeger.

Children in Libraries: Patterns of Access to Materials & Services in Schools & Public Libraries. Ed. by Zena Sutherland. LC 80-53135. (Studies in Library Science). 128p. 1981. lib. bdg. 10.00x (ISBN 0-226-78063-5). U of Chicago Pr.

Children in Search of Meaning. Violet Madge. (Orig.). 1966. pap. 3.25 o.p. (ISBN 0-8192-1051-X). Morehouse.

Children in the Worshipping Community. David Ng & Virginia Thomas. LC 80-84653. (Illus.). 128p. (Orig.). 1981. pap. 6.50 (ISBN 0-8042-1688-6). John Knox.

Children in Time & Space. Ed. by Kaoru Yamamoto. LC 79-91. 1979. pap. text ed. 9.95 (ISBN 0-8077-2553-6). Tchrs Coll.

Children in Your Life: A Guide to Child Care & Parenting. Deanna J. Radeloff & Roberta Zechman. LC 80-67826. (Home Economics Ser.). 384p. 1981. pap. 12.40 (ISBN 0-8273-1748-4); instr's. guide 1.10 (ISBN 0-8273-1749-2). Delmar.

Children Learn to Communicate: Language Arts Through Creative Problem Solving. S. Lundsteen. (Illus.). 1976. ref. ed. 18.95 (ISBN 0-13-131888-8); ideas into practice companion guide 5.95 (ISBN 0-13-449231-5). P-H.

Children Learn to Measure. 1980. text ed. 15.70 (ISBN 0-06-318155-X, IntlDept); pap. text ed. 7.80 (ISBN 0-06-318156-8). Har-Row.

Children Learning by Doing. Charles Nagel. (Illus.). (gr. k-3). 1973. 3.25x (ISBN 0-933892-01-2). Child Focus Co.

Children Moving: A Reflective Approach to Teaching Physical Education. George Graham et al. LC 79-91832. (Illus.). 497p. 1980. text ed. 15.95 (ISBN 0-87484-467-3). Mayfield Pub.

Children, My Children. Celestine Sibley. LC 80-8231. 210p. 1981. 9.95 (ISBN 0-06-014872-1, HarpT). Har-Row.

Children of a Lesser God. Mark Medoff. LC 80-24379. xxii, 91p. 1980. 8.98 (ISBN 0-88371-032-3); pap. 4.95 (ISBN 0-88371-034-X). J T White.

Children of Ancient Gaul. Louise Lamprey. LC 60-16708. (Illus.). (gr. 7-11). 8.50x (ISBN 0-8196-0109-8). Biblo.

Children of Ancient Rome. Louise Lamprey. LC 61-12876. (Illus.). (gr. 7-11). 8.50x (ISBN 0-8196-0114-4). Biblo.

Children of Appalachia. Peg Shull. LC 79-81386. (Illus.). (gr. 3-6). 1969. PLB 3.64 o.p. (ISBN 0-671-32134-X). Messner.

Children of Change. Don Fabun. (Illus.). 1970. pap. text ed. 2.50 (ISBN 0-02-475230-4, 47523). Macmillan.

Children of Conflict: A Study of Interracial Sex & Marriage. Fernando Henriques. 224p. 1975. 8.95 (ISBN 0-525-07996-3); pap. 3.95 o.p. Dutton.

Children of Darkness: Some Heretical Reflections on the Kid Cult. Richard S. Wheeler. 1973. 7.95 o.p. (ISBN 0-87000-208-2). Arlington Hse.

Children of Dune. Frank Herbert. (YA) 1976. 2.50 (ISBN 0-425-04383-5, Dist. by Putnam). Berkley Pub.

Children of Fantasy: The First Rebels of Greenwich Village. Robert E. Humphrey. LC 77-28242. 1978. 19.95 (ISBN 0-471-42100-6, Pub. by Wiley-Interscience). Wiley.

Children of Gebelawi. Naguib Mahfouz. Tr. by Philip Stewart from Arabic. (Arab Writers Series). 400p. (Orig.). 1980. 14.00x (ISBN 0-89410-212-5); pap. 7.00x (ISBN 0-686-64483-2). Three Continents.

Children of Heroin Addicts. Barbara J. Sowder & Marvin R. Burt. 200p. 1980. 18.95 (ISBN 0-03-057033-6). Praeger.

Children of India. Sumana Chandavarkar. LC 74-120167. (Illus.). (gr. 4-6). 1971. 7.75 (ISBN 0-688-41291-2); PLB 6.96 o.p. (ISBN 0-688-51291-7). Lothrop.

Children of Infinity: Original Science Fiction Stories for Young Readers. Ed. by Roger Elwood. LC 72-8930. (Illus.). 192p. (gr. 6 up). 1973. PLB 5.88 o.p. (ISBN 0-531-02599-3). Watts.

Children of Ishmael: Critical Perspectives on Juvenile Delinquency. Ed. by Barry Krisberg & James Austin. LC 77-89919. 1978. pap. text ed. 11.95 (ISBN 0-87484-387-1). Mayfield Pub.

Children of Israel. Tamar Grand & Samuel Grand. (gr. 3-4). 1972. text ed. 5.50 (ISBN 0-8074-0131-5, 121320); tchr's guide 2.25 (ISBN 0-8074-0132-3, 201320); fun & act bk. 3.00 (ISBN 0-8074-0133-1, 121322). UAHC.

Children of Jonestown. Ed. by Kenneth Wooden. (Paperbacks Ser.). 1980. pap. 4.95 (ISBN 0-07-071641-2, GB). McGraw.

Children of Master O'Rourke. John C. Smith. LC 77-23278. 1977. 10.95 o.p. (ISBN 0-03-016916-X). HR&W.

Children of Mount Vernon: A Guide to George Washington's Home. Miriam A. Bourne. LC 80-974. (Illus.). 64p. (gr. 4-6). 1981. PLB 8.95 (ISBN 0-385-15535-2); pap. 4.95 (ISBN 0-385-15534-4). Doubleday.

Children of Naples. Geoffrey Hanks. 1976. 1.55 (ISBN 0-08-017619-4). Pergamon.

Children of Nazareth. E. Le Camus. 131p. 1901. text ed. 2.95 (ISBN 0-567-02162-9). Attic Pr.

Children of Odin. Padraic Colum. (Illus.). (gr. 4-6). 1962. 6.95g o.s.i. (ISBN 0-02-723370-7). Macmillan.

Children of Oedipus & Other Essays on the Imitation of Greek Tragedy Fifteen Fifty to Eighteen Hundred. Martin Mueller. 1980. 25.00x (ISBN 0-8020-5478-1); pap. 12.50 (ISBN 0-8020-6381-0). U of Toronto Pr.

Children of Our Time. Ed. by New Inc.-Fourth World Movement. (Symposium Ser.: Vol. 7). (Illus., Orig.). 1981. soft cover 9.95x (ISBN 0-88946-911-3). E Mellen.

Children of Parting Parents. Lora Heims Tessman. LC 77-94094. 1978. 35.00x (ISBN 0-87668-307-3). Aronson.

Children of Poverty with Handicapping Conditions: How Teachers Can Cope Humanistically. Nancy P. Dixon. write for info. (ISBN 0-398-04478-3). C C Thomas.

Children of Power. Susan R. Shreve. 1979. 8.95 o.s.i. (ISBN 0-02-610510-1). Macmillan.

Children of Skylard Ward. Ann Hales. LC 77-80836. 1978. 12.95 (ISBN 0-521-21752-0). Cambridge U Pr.

Children of Strangers: The Stories of a Black Family. Kathryn L. Morgan. (Illus.). 160p. 1980. 9.95 (ISBN 0-87722-203-7). Temple U Pr.

Children: Of Such Is the Kingdom of God. Ed. by Barbara Howard. LC 79-7102. 1979. pap. 8.00 (ISBN 0-8309-0243-0). Herald Hse.

Children of the Dragon. Frank S. Robinson. 1977. pap. 1.95 (ISBN 0-380-01819-5, 35774). Avon.

Children of the Dream. Bruno Bettelheim. 1970. pap. 2.50 (ISBN 0-380-01097-6, 49130, Discus). Avon.

Children of the Ghetto. x1893 ed. Israel Zangwill. (Victorian Library Ser). (Illus.). 448p. 1977. Repr. of 1893 ed. text ed. 15.75x (ISBN 0-7185-5028-5, Leicester). Humanities.
Children of the Ladybug: A Drama in 2 Acts. Robert Thom. 1956. 17.50x (ISBN 0-685-69875-0). Elliots Bks.
Children of the Lens. Edward E. Smith. 1970. pap. 1.75 (ISBN 0-515-05326-0, V3251). Jove Pubns.
Children of the Lion. Peter Danielson. 480p. (Orig.). 1980. pap. 2.95 (ISBN 0-553-14249-6). Bantam.
Children of the Moon. Deena Metzger et al. (Valhalla Ser., No. 2). (300 copies on pearl paper). 1973. 2.00 o.p. (ISBN 0-686-09147-7). Merging Media.
Children of the Resistance. Lore Cowan. (YA) (gr. 7-9). 1971. pap. 1.25 (ISBN 0-671-29834-8). PB.
Children of the Revels: The Boy Companies of Shakespeare's Time and Their Plays. Michael Shapiro. LC 76-47585. 1977. 20.00x (ISBN 0-231-04112-8). Columbia U Pr.
Children of the River. William Lavendar. 448p. (Orig.). 1980. pap. 2.50 (ISBN 0-515-05388-0). Jove Pubns.
Children of the Seventh Prophecy. Amy K. Rubin. LC 80-23522. 192p. (gr. 4-7). 1981. 8.95 (ISBN 0-7232-6200-4). Warne.
Children of the Sun. Jan Carew. (Illus.). 40p. (gr. k up). 1980. 9.95 (ISBN 0-316-12848-1). Little.
Children of the Twenty Third Century Beautiful As You Will Be I Know Your Hair. Jack Libert. (Illus.). 69p. 1980. pap. 4.00 (ISBN 0-911732-08-X). Irego.
Children of the Uprooted. Ed. by Oscar Handlin. LC 66-12905. 8.50 o.s.i. (ISBN 0-8076-0361-9). Braziller.
Children of the Volga. George G. Bruntz. 144p. 1981. 6.95 (ISBN 0-8059-2763-8). Dorrance.
Children of Theatre Street. Earle Mack & Patricia Barnes. (Large Format Ser.). (Illus.). 1978. pap. 7.95 o.p. (ISBN 0-14-005019-1). Penguin.
Children of Very Low Birthweight, Vol. 1. Alison MacDonald. (Clinics in Developmental Medicine Research Monographs). 1967. 4.50 o.p. (ISBN 0-685-34618-8). Lippincott.
Children of Woot: A History of the Kuba Peoples. Jan Vansina. LC 77-91061. (Illus.). 1978. 30.00 (ISBN 0-299-07490-0). U of Wis Pr.
Children on Troublemaker Street. Astrid Lindgren. Tr. by Gerry Bothner. (Illus.). (gr. 2-5). 1964. 7.95g (ISBN 0-02-759100-X). Macmillan.
Children, School & Society in Nineteenth Century England. Anne Digby & Peter Searby. (Illus.). 282p. 1980. text ed. 24.00x (ISBN 0-333-24678-0). Humanities.
Children Sing. Mackinlay Kantor. 1977. pap. 1.75 (ISBN 0-505-51108-8). Tower Bks.
Children: The Challenge. Rudolf Dreikurs & Vicki Soltz. 1964. 9.95 (ISBN 0-8015-1248-4, Hawthorn); pap. 5.95 (ISBN 0-8015-1249-2). Dutton.
Children Who Read Early. Dolores Durkin. LC 66-25980. 1966. text ed. 8.75x (ISBN 0-8077-1260-4). Tchrs Coll.
Children with Chronic Arthritis: A Primer for Patients & Parents. Gordon F. Williams. LC 80-14190. 350p. 1981. 22.50 (ISBN 0-88416-273-7, 273). PSG Pub.
Children with Handicaps: A Medical Primer. Mark L. Batshaw & Yvonne M. Perret. (Illus.). 300p. 1981. price not set (ISBN 0-933716-16-8). P H Brookes.
Children with Learning & Behavior Problems: A Behavior Management Approach. 2nd ed. William I. Gardner. 1978. text ed. 19.95 (ISBN 0-205-06067-6); pap. text ed. 12.50 (ISBN 0-205-06066-8). Allyn.
Children with Learning Disabilities. 2nd ed. Janet W. Lerner. LC 75-26085. (Illus.). 448p. 1976. text ed. 17.95 (ISBN 0-395-20474-7); inst. manual 1.25 (ISBN 0-395-20473-9). HM.
Children with Learning Problems: A Handbook for Teachers. Larry A. Faas. LC 79-89741. (Illus.). 1980. text ed. 14.95 (ISBN 0-395-28352-3); inst. manual 0.65 (ISBN 0-395-28353-1). HM.
Children with Specific Learning Difficulties. 2nd ed. Jesse Francis-Williams. LC 74-4021. 240p. 1974. text ed. 23.00 (ISBN 0-08-017967-3); pap. text ed. 10.75 (ISBN 0-08-017968-1). Pergamon.
Children with Specific Reading Disability. Che Kan Leong (Modern Approaches to the Diagnosis & Instruction of Mnulti-Handicapped Children Ser.). 160p. Date not set. text ed price not set (Pub. by Swets Pub Serv Holland). Swets North Am.
Children You Gave Us. Jacqueline Bernard. LC 72-87122. (Illus.). 1972. 6.95 (ISBN 0-8197-0356-7). Bloch.
Children's Acquisition of Mathemathics. Ernest Choat. (General Ser.). (Illus.). 1978. pap. text ed. 14.50x (ISBN 0-685-90799-6, NFER). Humanities.
Children's Art: A Study of Normal Development in Children's Modes of Visualization. Miriam Lindstrom. LC 57-10499. (Illus.). 1957. 10.00 o.p. (ISBN 0-520-01441-3); pap. 3.95 (ISBN 0-520-00752-2, CAL8). U of Cal Pr.
Children's Art Education. Estelle H. Knudsen & Christensen. (YA) (gr. 9 up). 1971. 11.52 (ISBN 0-87002-060-9). Bennett IL.
Children's Astrologer. Dodie Edmands & Allen Edmands. LC 78-53406. (Illus.). 1978. 7.95 o.p. (ISBN 0-8015-1227-1). Dutton.
Children's Authors & Illustrators: An Index to Biographical Dictionaries. 3rd, rev. ed. Ed. by Adele Sarkissian. (Gale Biographical Index Ser.: No. 2). 1981. 85.00 (ISBN 0-8103-1084-8). Gale.
Children's Bible: Selections from the Good News Bible. Adapted by David L. Edwards. (Illus.). 1978. 8.95 (ISBN 0-529-05623-2, Pub. by Collins Pubs). World Bible.
Children's Bible Stories. Edward G. Finnegan. LC 75-18758. (Treasure House Bks). (Illus.). (ps-12). 1978. 8.95 (ISBN 0-8326-1803-9, 3602); deluxe ed. 7.95 (ISBN 0-686-66397-7). Delair.
Children's Book & Recordings, Nineteen Seventy-Eight. annual Office of Children's Services. 1978. pap. 2.00 o.p. (ISBN 0-87104-632-6, Branch Lib). NY Pub Lib.
Children's Book of Comic Verse. Ed. by Christopher Logue. (Illus.). 1979. 10.25 o.s.i. (ISBN 0-7134-1528-2, Pub. by Batsford). Hippocrene Bks.
Children's Book of Comic Verse. Compiled by Christopher Logue. (Illus.). 160p. 1980. 17.95 (ISBN 0-7134-1528-2, Pub. by Batsford England). David & Charles.
Children's Book of the Earth. Lisa Watts & Jenny Tyler. LC 77-13212. (Children's Guides). (Illus.). (gr. 3 up). 1978. PLB 6.95 (ISBN 0-88436-466-6). EMC.
Children's Book of the Seas. Jenny Tyler & Lisa Watts. LC 77-15549. (Children's Guides Ser.). (Illus.). (gr. 3 up). 1978. PLB 6.95 (ISBN 0-88436-464-X). EMC.
Children's Book Review Index: Annual Clothbound Volumes. Ed. by Gary C. Tarbert. LC 75-27408. 42.00 ea.; Annual 1975. (ISBN 0-8103-0626-3); Annual 1976. (ISBN 0-8103-0627-1); Annual 1977. (ISBN 0-8103-0628-X); Annual 1978. (ISBN 0-8103-0629-8); Annual 1979. (ISBN 0-8103-0630-1). Gale.
Children's Book Review Index: Nineteen-Eighty Annual. Ed. by Gary C. Tarbert. LC 75-27408. (Children's Book Review Index Ser.). 350p. 1981. 46.00 (ISBN 0-8103-0631-X). Gale.
Children's Books & Reading. Montrose J. Moses. LC 74-23680. 1975. Repr. of 1907 ed. 20.00 (ISBN 0-8103-3767-3). Gale.
Children's Books in Print 1980-1981. 935p. 1980. 35.00 (ISBN 0-8352-1311-0). Bowker.
Children's Books in Print 1980-1981. 12th ed. 889p. 1980. 35.00 (ISBN 0-8352-1311-0). Bowker.
Children's Books International III: Proceedings. 1978. 7.50. Boston Public Lib.
Children's Books International IV: Proceedings. 1979. 7.50. Boston Public Lib.
Children's Books of the Year: 1979. Elaine Moss & Barbara Sherrard-Smith. 1980. 10.95 (ISBN 0-531-04178-6). Watts.
Children's Books of Yesterday. Philip James. Ed. by C. Geoffrey Holme. LC 79-174059. (Illus.). 128p. 1976. Repr. of 1933 ed. 22.00 (ISBN 0-8103-4135-2). Gale.
Children's Books of Yesterday. National Book League. Ed. by Percy H. Muir. LC 76-89280. 1970. Repr. of 1946 ed. 15.00 (ISBN 0-8103-3550-6). Gale.
Children's Books to Comics. Time-Life Books Editors. LC 77-99201. (Encyclopedia of Collectibles Ser.). (Illus.). 1978. lib. bdg. 10.98 (ISBN 0-686-50975-7). Silver.
Childrens Books Too Good to Miss: Revised Edition 1979. 7th ed. May H. Arbuthnot et al. LC 79-53812. (Illus.). 125p. 1980. 7.95 (ISBN 0-8295-0287-4). UPBS.
Children's Cartoons. 48p. 1.00 (ISBN 0-913452-04-1). Jesuit Bks.
Children's Cause. Gilbert Y. Steiner. 1976. 14.95 (ISBN 0-8157-8120-2); pap. 5.95 (ISBN 0-8157-8119-9). Brookings.
Children's Clothes Nineteen Thirty Nine to Nineteen Seventy: The Advent of Fashion. Alice Guppy. (Illus.). 1978. 23.95 (ISBN 0-7137-0896-4, Pub. by Blandford Pr England). Sterling.
Children's Cognitive Development: Piaget's Theory & the Process Approach. Ruth L. Ault. (Illus.). 1977. text ed. 11.95x (ISBN 0-19-502092-8); pap. text ed. 4.95x (ISBN 0-19-502093-6). Oxford U Pr.
Children's Costume in America Sixteen Hundred & Seven to Nineteen Ten. Estelle A. Worrell. (Illus.). 224p. 1981. 25.00 (ISBN 0-684-16645-3, ScribT). Scribner.
Children's Costume in England. P. Cunnington. 1972. text ed. 17.00x (ISBN 0-7136-0371-2). Humanities.
Children's Crusade. Paul Thompson. 1975. pap. text ed. 2.95 (ISBN 0-435-23880-9). Heinemann Ed.
Children's Developmental Progress from Birth to Five Years: The Stycar Sequences. M. D. Sheridan. (General Ser). (Illus.). 72p. 1975. pap. text ed. 6.25x (ISBN 0-85633-018-3, NFER). Humanities.
Children's Experience of Place: A Developmental Study. Roger Hart. LC 77-21507. 1979. 27.50 (ISBN 0-470-99190-9). Halsted Pr.
Children's Experience with Death. Rose Zeligs. 264p. 1974. 14.75 (ISBN 0-398-02984-9). C C Thomas.
Children's Fiction About Africa in English. Nancy J. Schmidt. LC 80-18491. 300p. 1981. 35.00 (ISBN 0-914970-63-1). Conch Mag.
Children's History of India. 7th rev. ed. Sheila Dhar. (Illus.). 178p. (gr. 5-7). pap. text ed. 1.50x (ISBN 0-88253-919-1). Ind-US Inc.
Children's History of Texas: Text & Coloring Book. Sarah Jackson & Mary Ann Patterson. (Illus.). (gr. 1-6). 2.50 (ISBN 0-685-48834-9). Nortex Pr.
Children's Humour. Paul E. McGhee & Antony J. Chapman. LC 79-40648. 1980. 40.25 (ISBN 0-471-27638-3, Pub. by Wiley-Interscience). Wiley.
Children's Illustrated Bible Dictionary. Gilbert Beers. Tr. by Alvaro Mairani. LC 77-12650. (Illus.). 1977. 8.95 o.p. (ISBN 0-8407-4987-2). Nelson.
Children's Illustrated Bible Dictionary. V. Gilbert Beers. 1981. pap. 6.95 (ISBN 0-8407-5755-7). Nelson.
Children's Language. Ed. by Keith E. Nelson. LC 77-26226. (Children's Language Ser.: Vols. 1 & 2). Vol. 1, 1978. 24.95 (ISBN 0-470-99385-5); Vol. 2, 1979. 29.95 (ISBN 0-470-26716-X). Halsted Pr.
Children's Language & Learning. Judith W. Lindfors. (Illus.). 1980. text ed. 17.95 (ISBN 0-13-131953-1). P-H.
Children's Language Disorders: An Integrated Approach. Robert D. Hubbell. (Illus.). 432p. 1981. text ed. 18.95 (ISBN 0-13-132001-7). P-H.
Children's Learning. Harold W. Stevenson. (Illus.). 425p. 1972. 16.95 (ISBN 0-13-132472-1). P-H.
Children's Libraries. A. Fleet. (Grafton Books on Library Science). 1977. lib. bdg. 12.00x (ISBN 0-233-96229-8). Westview.
Children's Literature: An Issues Approach. Masha Rudman. 1976. text ed. 11.95x o.p. (ISBN 0-669-00322-0); pap. text ed. 9.95x (ISBN 0-669-93203-5). Heath.
Children's Literature: Annual of the Modern Language Association Division on Children's Literature Association, Vol. 9. Ed. by Francelia Butler et al. LC 79-711. (Illus.). 272p. 1981. text ed. 27.50x (ISBN 0-300-02623-4); pap. 8.95 (ISBN 0-300-02642-0). Yale U Pr.
Children's Literature Review: Excerpts from Critical Commentaries on Juvenile & Young People's Authors & Their Books, 3 vols. Ed. by Gerard J. Senick. Incl. Vol. 1. 1976 (ISBN 0-8103-0077-X); Vol. 2. 1976 (ISBN 0-8103-0078-8); Vol. 3 (ISBN 0-8103-0079-6). LC 75-34953. (Children's Literature Review Ser.). 44.00 ea. Gale.
Children's Literature: Strategies of Teaching. Robert Whitehead. (Orig.). 1968. pap. text ed. 10.95 (ISBN 0-13-132589-2). P-H.
Children's Magic Kit: Sixteen Easy-to-Do Tricks Complete with Cardboard Cutouts. Karl Fulves. (Illus.). 32p. (Orig.). (gr. 3-6). Date not set. pap. price not set (ISBN 0-486-24019-3). Dover. Postponed.
Children's Manners Book. Alida Allison. (Illus.). 32p. (Orig.). 1981. pap. 3.95 (ISBN 0-8431-0437-6). Price Stern.
Children's Mathematical Concepts: Six Piagetian Studies in Mathematical Education. Ed. by Myron F. Rosskopf. LC 75-12872. 1975. text ed. 14.95x (ISBN 0-8077-2447-5). Tchrs Coll.
Children's Media Market Place. 2nd ed. 450p. 1981. pap. text ed. 24.95 (ISBN 0-918212-33-2). Neal-Schuman.
Children's Minds. Margaret Donaldson. (Illus.). 1979. 10.95 (ISBN 0-393-01185-2); pap. 3.95x (ISBN 0-393-95101-4). Norton.
Children's Moment. Julius Fishbach. (gr. 3-7). 1966. bds. 3.95 o.p. (ISBN 0-8170-0355-X). Judson.
Children's Museum Activity Book: Ball-Point Pens. Bernie Zubrowski. LC 78-31622. (Children's Museum Bks.). (Illus.). (gr. 5-7). 1979. 6.95g (ISBN 0-316-98882-0); pap. 3.95 (ISBN 0-316-98883-9). Little.
Children's Oral Communication Skills. Ed. by W. Patrick Dickson. (Developmental Psychology Ser.). 1981. write for info. (ISBN 0-12-215450-9). Acad Pr.
Children's Perceptions of Elderly Persons. Lillian A. Phenice. LC 80-65604. 145p. 1981. perfect bdg. 10.50 (ISBN 0-86548-054-0). Century Twenty One.
Children's Perceptions of Gender & Work Roles. Gloria M. Nemerowicz. LC 79-11783. 1979. 24.95 (ISBN 0-03-049811-2). Praeger.
Children's Picture Atlas. Tessa Campbell. LC 77-17968. (Children's Guides Ser.). (Illus.). (gr. 3 up). 1978. PLB 6.95 (ISBN 0-88436-465-8). EMC.
Children's Pictures of God. Ed. by V. Peter Pitts. (Illus.). (gr. 1-4). 1979. pap. 3.95 (ISBN 0-915744-20-1). Character Res.
Children's Play & Playgrounds. Joe L. Frost & Barry L. Klein. 1979. pap. text ed. 10.50 (ISBN 0-205-06586-4). Allyn.
Children's Play Spaces. Jacques Simon & Marguerite Rouard. LC 76-57882. (Illus.). 1977. 30.00 (ISBN 0-87951-056-0). Overlook Pr.
Children's Rhymes, Children's Games, Children's Songs, Children's Stories. Robert Ford. LC 69-16067. 1968. Repr. of 1904 ed. 18.00 (ISBN 0-8103-3526-3). Gale.
Children's Rights & the Mental Health Professions. Ed. by Gerald P. Koocher. LC 76-16062. (Personality Processes Ser.). 1976. 26.95 (ISBN 0-471-01736-1, Pub. by Wiley-Interscience). Wiley.
Children's Rights: Contemporary Perspectives. Ed. by Patricia Vardin & Ilene Brody. LC 78-12584. (Orig.). 1978. pap. 8.95x (ISBN 0-8077-2550-1). Tchrs Coll.
Children's Rights Movement: Overcoming the Oppression of Young People. Ed. by Beatrice Gross & Ronald Gross. LC 75-40753. 1977. 9.95 (ISBN 0-385-11027-8, Anchor Pr); pap. 3.95 (ISBN 0-385-11028-6). Doubleday.
Children's Rooms & Play Yards. Sunset Editors. LC 79-90336. (Illus.). 96p. 1980. pap. 3.95 (ISBN 0-376-01054-1, Sunset Bks). Sunset-Lane.
Childrens Songs & Rhymes. 256p. 1981. pap. 2.49 (ISBN 0-8256-3209-9, Quick Fox). Music Sales.
Children's Spatial Development. J. Eliot & N. Salkind. (Illus.). 312p. 1975. 32.50 (ISBN 0-398-03210-6). C C Thomas.
Children's Stories & How to Tell Them. Woutrina A. Bone. LC 75-28363. (Illus.). xviii, 200p. 1975. Repr. of 1924 ed. 18.00 (ISBN 0-8103-3747-9). Gale.
Childrens Stories for Teenage Adults. rev. ed. Robert F. Brooks. (Illus.). 32p. (Orig.). (gr. 5-9). pap. 3.00 (ISBN 0-936868-05-8). Freeland Pubns.
Children's Television: An Analysis of Programming & Advertising. F. Earle Barcus & Rachel Wolkin. LC 76-12843. (Special Studies). 1977. text ed. 25.95 (ISBN 0-275-23210-7). Praeger.
Children's Treasure Hunt Travel to Belgium & France. Frances Goldstein. LC 80-85012. (Children's Treasure Hunt Travel Guide Ser.). (Illus.). 230p. (Orig.). (gr. k-12). 1981. pap. 4.95 (ISBN 0-933334-02-8). Paper Tiger Pap.
Children's Understanding of Social Interaction. Dorothy Flapan. LC 67-25065. 1968. pap. text ed. 4.75x (ISBN 0-8077-1357-0). Tchrs Coll.
Children's Ways of Knowing: Nathan Isaacs on Education, Psychology & Piaget. Ed. by Mildred Hardeman. LC 74-3103. 1974. pap. text ed. 7.25x (ISBN 0-8077-2467-X). Tchrs Coll.
Children's Well-Being. John Brierley. 171p. 1981. pap. text ed. 18.75x (ISBN 0-85633-218-6, NFER). Humanities.
Children's Writing. David Holbrook. 1967. 22.50 (ISBN 0-521-05284-X); pap. 7.95x (ISBN 0-521-09434-8, 434). Cambridge U Pr.
Child's Acquisition of Language. June Derrick. (Orig.). 1977. pap. text ed. 5.75x (ISBN 0-85633-110-4, NFER). Humanities.
Child's Book of Glass. Barry Nord & Elaine Nord. (Illus.). 64p. (Orig.). (gr. 7-9). Date not set. pap. price not set (101E). Chrome Yellow.
Child's Book of Seasons. Satomi Ichikawa. LC 74-31047. (Illus.). (gr. k-3). 1976. 5.95 o.s.i. (ISBN 0-8193-0795-5, Four Winds); PLB 5.41 o.s.i. (ISBN 0-8193-0796-3). Schol Bk Serv.
Child's Christmas Cookbook. Betty Chancellor. (Illus.). 32p. (gr. 4-7). 1974. PLB 5.79 (ISBN 0-8178-5362-6). Harvey.
Child's Christmas in Wales. Dylan Thomas. LC 59-13174. (Illus.). 1969. gift ed. 12.00 (ISBN 0-8112-0391-3). New Directions.
Child's Conception of Geometry. Jean Piaget et al. Tr. by E. A. Lunzer. 432p. 1981. pap. 8.95 (ISBN 0-393-00057-5). Norton.
Child's Conception of Language. A. Sinclair et al. (Springer Ser. in Language & Communication: Vol. 2). (Illus.). 1979. 22.50 (ISBN 0-387-09153-X). Springer-Verlag.

Child's Conception of Physical Causality. Jean Piaget. 1966. Repr. of 1930 ed. text ed. 17.75x (ISBN 0-7100-3068-1). Humanities.

Child's Cookbook. B. Veitch & T. Harms. (ps-4). 1981. 8.95 (ISBN 0-201-09430-4, 09426, Sch Div); tchr's guide free; recipe step book 15.00 (ISBN 0-686-69466-X). A-W.

Child's Discovery of Himself. Clark Moustakas. 1975. pap. 1.75 o.p. (ISBN 0-345-24892-9). Ballantine.

Child's Eye View of the World. Marc Simont & Boston Children's Medical Center Staff. (Illus.). 128p. 1972. 4.95 o.p. (ISBN 0-440-01221-X, Sey Lawr). Delacorte.

Child's Garden of Bible Stories. Arthur W. Gross. (Concordia Primary Religion Ser.). (gr. 1-3). 1981. 6.50 (ISBN 0-570-03414-0, 56-1001); pap. 4.95 (ISBN 0-570-03402-7, 56-1012). Concordia.

Child's Garden of Prayer. Ed. by Herman W. Gockel & Edward J. Saleska. (Illus.). (gr. k-2). 1981. pap. 0.99 (ISBN 0-570-03412-4, 56-1016). Concordia.

Child's Garden of Verses. Robert L. Stevenson. (Illus.). (gr. k-3). 1951. PLB 7.62 o.p. (ISBN 0-307-65557-1, Golden Pr). Western Pub.

Child's Garden of Verses. Robert L. Stevenson. (Children's Library of Picture Bks.). (Illus.). 10p. (ps). 1979. 1.95 (ISBN 0-89346-178-4, TA60, Pub. by Froebel-Kan Japan). Heian Intl.

Child's Garden of Yoga. Baba Hari Dass. LC 80-80299. (Illus.). 108p. (Orig.). (gr. 3-12). 1980. pap. 5.95 (ISBN 0-918100-02-X). Starmont Hse.

Child's Garland. Jane Carton. 1942. 6.95 o.p. (ISBN 0-571-05352-1, Pub. by Faber & Faber). Merrimack Bk Serv.

Child's Generation: Child Care Policy from Curtis to Houghton. Jean Packman. (Aspects of Social Policy Ser.). 1975. 15.00x (ISBN 0-631-16590-8, Pub. by Basil Blackwell); pap. 11.95x (ISBN 0-631-16600-9). Biblio Dist.

Child's Generation: Child Care Policy in Britain. 2nd ed. Jean Packman. (Aspects of Social Policy Ser.). 200p. 1981. pap. 12.50x (ISBN 0-631-12664-3, Pub. by Basil Blackwell England). Biblio Dist.

Child's History of America: Some Ribs & Riffs for the Sixties. Charles Newman. LC 73-5951. 307p. 1973. 13.95 (ISBN 0-8040-0644-X). Swallow.

Child's History of England. Charles Dickens. (gr. 4-6). 1970. 12.95x (ISBN 0-460-00291-0, Evman). Dutton.

Child's Look at the Twenty-Third Psalm. W. Phillip Keller. LC 80-976. (Illus.). 96p. 1981. 7.95 (ISBN 0-385-15456-9, Galilee). Doubleday.

Child's Mind. Muriel Beadle. LC 75-89079. 1971. pap. 3.50 (ISBN 0-385-08228-2, Anch). Doubleday.

Child's Parent Dies: Studies in Childhood Bereavement. Erna Furman. LC 73-86894. 1974. 25.00x (ISBN 0-300-01719-7). Yale U Pr.

Child's Parent Dies: Studies in Childhood Bereavement. Erna Furman. LC 73-86894. 352p. 1981. pap. 7.95x (ISBN 0-300-02645-5). Yale U Pr.

Child's Play. Warren Murphy. (Destroyer No. 23). 192p. 1976. pap. 1.95 (ISBN 0-523-41238-X). Pinnacle Bks.

Childs Play: Collected Readings on the Biology, Ecology, Psychology & Sociology of Play. Ed. by Robin Herron & Brian Sutton-Smith. LC 73-136714. 1971. 25.50 (ISBN 0-471-37330-3). Wiley.

Child's Psychosocial Development: From Birth to Early Adolescence. Margot B. Nadien. 160p. (Orig.). 1980. pap. 6.95 (ISBN 0-89529-115-0). Avery Pub.

Child's Very Own First Book. Jody Taylor. (Gingerbread Bks.). (Illus.). (ps-2). 1980. 2.50 (ISBN 0-525-69035-2, Gingerbread); PLB 5.95 (ISBN 0-525-69036-0, Gingerbread). Dutton.

Child's World: Infancy Through Adolescence. Diane E. Papalia & Sally W. Olds. LC 74-31496. (Illus.). 672p. 1975. text ed. 15.95 (ISBN 0-07-048458-9, C); instructors' manual 2.95 (ISBN 0-685-50939-7); test file 5.95 (ISBN 0-07-048459-7). McGraw.

Child's World of Stamps: Stories, Poems, Fun & Facts from Many Lands. Mildred DePree. LC 72-10178. (Illus.). 128p. (gr. 3 up). 1973. 5.95 o.s.i. (ISBN 0-8193-0661-4, Four Winds); PLB 5.41 o.s.i. (ISBN 0-8193-0662-2). Schol Bk Serv.

Childsong. Barbara Wood. LC 80-1821. 288p. 1981. 12.95 (ISBN 0-385-15560-3). Doubleday.

Childwold. Joyce C. Oates. LC 76-42086. 380p. 1976. 10.95 (ISBN 0-8149-0777-6). Vanguard.

Chile, A Geographic Extravaganza. Benjamin Subercaseaux. Tr. by Angel Flores from Span. 1971. Repr. of 1943 ed. 14.75 o.s.i. (ISBN 0-02-853090-X). Hafner.

Chile: The Legacy of Hispanic Capitalism. Brian Loveman. LC 78-13965. (Latin American Histories Ser.). (Illus.). 1979. 14.95x (ISBN 0-19-502518-0); pap. text ed. 6.95x (ISBN 0-19-502520-2). Oxford U Pr.

Chilean Rural Society from the Spanish Conquest to 1930. A. J. Bauer. LC 75-2724. (Cambridge Latin American Studies: No. 21). (Illus.). 311p. 1975. 32.95 (ISBN 0-521-20727-4). Cambridge U Pr.

Chilean Senate: Internal Distribution of Influence. Weston H. Agor. (Latin American Monograph Ser.: No. 23). 1971. 11.95 (ISBN 0-292-70146-2). U of Tex Pr.

Chilean Voices: Activists Describe Their Experiences of the Popular Unity Period. Ed. by Colin Henfrey & Sorj Bernardo. (Marxist Theory & Contemporary Capitalism). (Illus.). 1977. text ed. 13.00x (ISBN 0-391-00697-5); pap. text ed. 9.25x (ISBN 0-391-00698-3). Humanities.

Chile's Marxist Experiment. Robert Moss. LC 74-558. 225p. 1973. 13.95 (ISBN 0-470-61910-4). Halsted Pr.

Chili-Lovers' Cook Book. Mildred Fischer & Al Fischer. 1978. pap. 3.00 plastic (ISBN 0-914846-06-X). Golden West Pub.

Chill Factor. Aaron Marc Stein. LC 77-11754. 1978. 7.95 o.p. (ISBN 0-385-13556-4). Doubleday.

Chilly Scenes of Winter. Ann Beattie. 1978. pap. 2.75 (ISBN 0-445-04261-3). Popular Lib.

Chilton's Auto Repair Manual, 1964-1971. Chilton's Automotive Editorial Department. LC 54-17274. (Illus.). 1536p. 1974. 19.95 (ISBN 0-8019-5974-8). Chilton.

Chilton's Chevrolet Luv: 1972-1979, Repair & Tune-up Guide. Chilton's Automotive Editorial Dept. LC 78-20241. (Repair & Tune-up Guides Ser.). 1979. pap. 8.95 (ISBN 0-8019-6815-1). Chilton.

Chilton's Complete Guide to Motorcycles & Motorcycling. Donald Koch. LC 74-17365. (Illus.). 240p. 1974. pap. 5.95 o.p. (ISBN 0-8019-6089-4). Chilton.

Chilton's Complete Home Wiring & Lighting Guide. L. D. Meyers. LC 80-971. Date not set. 14.95 (ISBN 0-8019-6790-2); pap. 10.95 (ISBN 0-8019-6791-0). Chilton.

Chilton's Datsun Pick-Ups: 1970-1979 Repair & Tune-up Guide. Chilton's Automotive Editorial Dept. LC 78-20245. (Repair & Tune-up Guides Ser.). 1979. pap. 8.95 (ISBN 0-8019-6816-X). Chilton.

Chilton's Diesel Guide. LC 78-22145. (New Automotive Bks.). 224p. Date not set. 11.95 (ISBN 0-8019-6753-8); pap. 8.95 (ISBN 0-8019-6754-6). Chilton.

Chilton's Easy Car Care. Chilton Automotive Staff. LC 78-7152. (Illus.). 1978. 9.95 (ISBN 0-8019-6784-8); pap. 8.95 o.p. (ISBN 0-8019-6729-5). Chilton.

Chilton's Easy Car Care. 2nd ed. Orig. Title: La Cautela Facil Del Automovil Chilton. (Illus.). 384p. (Spanish.). pap. 9.95. Chilton.

Chilton's Guide to Consumers' Auto Repairs & Prices. (New Automotive Bks.). 176p. 1980. 10.95 (ISBN 0-8019-6941-7); pap. 7.95 (ISBN 0-8019-6942-5). Chilton.

Chilton's Guide to Emission Controls & How They Work. Chilton's Automotive Editorial Department. LC 74-6332. (Illus.). 160p. 1974. pap. 8.95 (ISBN 0-8019-6084-3). Chilton.

Chilton's Import Car Repair Manual. Ed. by Chilton's Editorial Dept. LC 78-20243. (Illus.). 1536p. 1981. 19.95 (ISBN 0-8019-7029-6). Chilton.

Chilton's Jeep CJ: 1953-1979, Repair & Tune-up Guide. Chilton's Automotive Editorial Dept. LC 78-19732. (Repair & Tune-up Guides Ser.). (Illus.). 1979. pap. 8.95 (ISBN 0-8019-6817-8). Chilton.

Chilton's Mechanics' Handbook: Automobile Sheet Metal Repair, Vol. III. Ed. by Chilton's Editorial Dept. (Illus.). 300p. 1981. pap. 14.95 (ISBN 0-686-69516-X). Chilton.

Chilton's Mechanics' Handbook: Engine Rebuilding, Engine Repair, Engine Theory, Vol. II. Ed. by Chilton's Editorial Dept. (Illus.). 300p. (Orig.). 1981. pap. text ed. 14.95 (ISBN 0-686-69515-1). Chilton.

Chilton's More Miles per Gallon. (New Automotive Bks.). 176p. 1980. 10.95 (ISBN 0-8019-6907-7); pap. 7.95 (ISBN 0-8019-6908-5). Chilton.

Chilton's Motor Age Professional Truck & Van Repair Manual: Gasoline & Diesel Engines. Chilton's Automotive Editorial Dept. (Illus.). 1980. 27.00x (ISBN 0-8019-6925-5). Chilton.

Chilton's Motorcycle Owner's Handbook. Chilton's Automotive Editorial Dept. (Illus.). 1979. 10.95 (ISBN 0-8019-6894-1); pap. 8.95 (ISBN 0-8019-6867-4, 795). Chilton.

Chilton's Motorcycle Troubleshooting Guide. 2nd ed. Chilton Book Company Auto. Ed. Dept. LC 77-121. 1977. pap. 7.95 (ISBN 0-8019-6587-X, 6587). Chilton.

Chilton's Mustang II: 1974-1978, Repair & Tune-up Guide. Chilton's Automotive Editorial Dept. LC 78-22143. (Repair & Tune-up Guides Ser.). (Illus.). 1979. pap. 8.95 (ISBN 0-8019-6812-7). Chilton.

Chilton's Pinto-Bobcat: 1971-1979, Repair & Tune-up Guide. Chilton's Automotive Editorial Dept. LC 78-22144. (Repair & Tune-up Guides Ser.). (Illus.). 1979. pap. 8.95 (ISBN 0-8019-6813-5). Chilton.

Chilton's Repair & Tune-up Guide, Bronco 1966-1973. Chilton's Automotive Editorial Department. LC 74-2472. (Illus.). 1974. 8.95 (ISBN 0-8019-5920-9); pap. 8.95 (ISBN 0-8019-5921-7). Chilton.

Chilton's Repair & Tune-up Guide for Aspen-Volare, 1976-1978. Chilton's Automotive Ed. Dept. (Chilton's Repair & Tune-up Guides). (Illus., Orig.). 1977. pap. 8.95 (ISBN 0-8019-6637-X, 6637). Chilton.

Chilton's Repair & Tune-up Guide for Audi, 1970-1973. Chilton's Automotive Editorial Department. (Illus.). 190p. 1973. 8.95 (ISBN 0-8019-5864-4); pap. 8.95 (ISBN 0-8019-5902-0). Chilton.

Chilton's Repair & Tune-up Guide for Barracuda & Challenger: 1965-1972. Chilton's Automotive Editorial Department. LC 72-7036. (Illus.). 128p. 1972. 8.95 (ISBN 0-8019-5721-4); pap. 8.95 (ISBN 0-8019-5807-5). Chilton.

Chilton's Repair & Tune-up Guide: For Blazer-Jimmy, 1969-1977. Chilton Book Company. Automotive Editorial Dept. LC 76-53144. (Chilton's Repair & Tune up Guides). 1977. pap. 8.95 (ISBN 0-8019-6558-6). Chilton.

Chilton's Repair & Tune-up Guide for Bultaco, Montesa, & Ossa 1963-1972. Chilton's Automotive Editorial Department. LC 74-4029. (Illus.). 1974. 8.95 (ISBN 0-8019-5817-2); pap. 8.95 (ISBN 0-8019-5888-1). Chilton.

Chilton's Repair & Tune-up Guide for Bmw Motorcycle Through 1972. Chilton's Automotive Editorial Department. LC 72-8340. (Illus.). 150p. 1973. 8.95 (ISBN 0-8019-5738-9); pap. 8.95 (ISBN 0-8019-6049-5). Chilton.

Chilton's Repair & Tune-up Guide for BSA Thru 1972. Chilton's Automotive Editorial Department. LC 72-6147. (Illus.). 176p. 1972. 8.95 (ISBN 0-8019-5713-3); pap. 8.95 (ISBN 0-8019-6048-7). Chilton.

Chilton's Repair & Tune-Up Guide for BMW: 1959-1970. Chilton's Automotive Editorial Department. LC 78-143690. (Illus.). 1971. 8.95 (ISBN 0-8019-5576-9). Chilton.

Chilton's Repair & Tune-up Guide for Bronco, 1966-77. (Illus.). 1978. pap. 8.95 (ISBN 0-8019-6701-5). Chilton.

Chilton's Repair & Tune-up Guide for BMW 2, 1969-1974. Chilton's Automotive Editorial Department. LC 74-17352. (Illus.). 224p. 1974. 8.95 (ISBN 0-8019-5979-9); pap. 8.95 (ISBN 0-8019-5980-2). Chilton.

Chilton's Repair & Tune-up Guide for Charger, Coronet 1971-1975. Chilton's Automotive Editorial Department. (Illus.). 190p. 1975. 8.95 (ISBN 0-8019-6315-X); pap. 8.95 (ISBN 0-8019-6316-8). Chilton.

Chilton's Repair & Tune-up Guide for Chevelle, el Camino, Monte Carlo 1964-1977. Chilton's Automotive Ed. Dept. LC 76-57314. (Chilton's Repair & Tune-up Guides Ser.). (Illus., Orig.). 1977. pap. 8.95 (ISBN 0-8019-6611-6, 6611). Chilton.

Chilton's Repair & Tune-up Guide for Chevrolet-Gmc Pick-Ups, 1970-78. (Illus.). 1978. pap. 8.95 (ISBN 0-8019-6700-7). Chilton.

Chilton's Repair & Tune-up Guide for Chevrolet-GMC Vans, 1967-1974. Chilton's Automotive Editorial Department. LC 74-12293. (Illus.). 256p. 1974. 8.95 (ISBN 0-8019-6011-8); pap. 8.95 (ISBN 0-8019-6012-6). Chilton.

Chilton's Repair & Tune-Up Guide for Camaro 1967-1979. Chilton's Automotive Ed. Dept. (Repair & Tune-up Guides Ser.). (Illus.). 1978. pap. 8.95 (ISBN 0-8019-6735-X). Chilton.

Chilton's Repair & Tune-up Guide for Capri, 1970-1976. Chilton's Automotive Editorial Department. (Illus.). 192p. 1975. 8.95 (ISBN 0-8019-6403-2); pap. 8.95 (ISBN 0-8019-6404-0). Chilton.

Chilton's Repair & Tune-up Guide for Colt, 1971-1976. Ed. by Chilton's Automotive Editorial Department. (Illus.). 1976. 8.95 (ISBN 0-8019-6474-1); pap. 8.95 (ISBN 0-8019-6475-X). Chilton.

Chilton's Repair & Tune-up Guide for Capri 1970-1978. LC 77-90926. (Illus.). 1978. pap. 8.95 (ISBN 0-8019-6695-7). Chilton.

Chilton's Repair & Tune-up Guide for Corvair, 1960-1969. LC 70-161623. (Illus.). 1978. pap. 8.95 (ISBN 0-8019-6691-4). Chilton.

Chilton's Repair & Tune-up Guide for Cutlass-442, 1970-1977. Chilton's Automotive Ed. Dept. LC 77-89117. (Chilton's Repair & Tune-up Guides). (Illus., Orig.). 1978. pap. 8.95 (ISBN 0-8019-6597-7, 6597). Chilton.

Chilton's Repair & Tune-up Guide for Dodge Dart & Demon, 1968-1976. Chilton's Automotive Editorial Dept. (Illus.). 190p. 1976. 8.95 (ISBN 0-8019-6323-0); pap. 8.95 (ISBN 0-8019-6324-9). Chilton.

Chilton's Repair & Tune-up Guide for Dodge-Plymouth Vans 1967-1977. Chilton's Automotive Ed. Dept. LC 77-71692. (Chilton's Repair & Tune-up Guides). (Illus., Orig.). 1977. pap. 8.95 (ISBN 0-8019-6599-3, 6599). Chilton.

Chilton's Repair & Tune-up Guide for Dodge 1968-1977. Chilton's Automotive Ed. Dept. LC 77-71635. (Chilton's Repair & Tune-up Guides Ser.). (Illus.). 1977. pap. 8.95 (ISBN 0-8019-6554-3). Chilton.

Chilton's Repair & Tune-up Guide for Dasher, 1974-1975. Chilton's Automotive Editorial Department. (Illus.). 190p. 1975. 8.95 (ISBN 0-8019-6212-9); pap. 8.95 (ISBN 0-8019-6213-7). Chilton.

Chilton's Repair & Tune-up Guide for Datsun, 1973-1978. LC 77-90862. (Illus.). 1978. pap. 8.95 (ISBN 0-8019-6694-9). Chilton.

Chilton's Repair & Tune-up Guide for Datsun 2, 1973-1975, Vol. 2. Chilton's Automotive Editorial Department. (Illus.). 224p. 1975. pap. 8.95 (ISBN 0-8019-6311-7). Chilton.

Chilton's Repair & Tune-up Guide for Datsun, 240-260z, 1970-1974. Chilton's Automotive Editorial Department. (Illus.). 224p. 1975. 8.95 (ISBN 0-8019-6214-5); pap. 8.95 (ISBN 0-8019-6215-3). Chilton.

Chilton's Repair & Tune-up Guide for Datsun 240-260-280z, 1970-1977. Chilton's Automotive Ed. Dept. LC 77-85345. (Chilton's Repair & Tune-up Guides). (Illus., Orig.). 1977. pap. 8.95 (ISBN 0-8019-6638-8, 6638). Chilton.

Chilton's Repair & Tune-up Guide for Fairlane & Torino, 1962-1975. Chilton's Automotive Editorial Dept. (Illus.). 250p. 1975. 8.95 (ISBN 0-8019-6319-2); pap. 8.95 (ISBN 0-8019-6320-6). Chilton.

Chilton's Repair & Tune-up Guide for Ford Courier, 1972-1975. Chilton's Automotive Editorial Department. (Illus.). 224p. 1975. 8.95 (ISBN 0-8019-6202-1); pap. 8.95 (ISBN 0-8019-6203-X). Chilton.

Chilton's Repair & Tune-up Guide for Ford Courier 1972-78. Chilton's Automotive Ed. Dept. (Repair & Tune-up Guides Ser.). (Illus.). pap. 8.95 (ISBN 0-8019-6723-6). Chilton.

Chilton's Repair & Tune-up Guide for Ford Mid-Size 1971-1978. LC 77-92361. (Illus.). 1978. pap. 8.95 (ISBN 0-8019-6696-5). Chilton.

Chilton's Repair & Tune-up Guide for Ford Vans 1966-1977. Chilton's Automotive Ed. Dept. LC 76-57320. (Chilton's Repair & Tune-up Guides). (Illus., Orig.). 1977. pap. 8.95 (ISBN 0-8019-6585-3, 6585). Chilton.

Chilton's Repair & Tune-up Guide for Fiat 1969-1978. Chilton's Automotive Ed. Dept. (Repair & Tune-up Guides Ser.). (Illus.). 1978. pap. 8.95 (ISBN 0-8019-6734-1). Chilton.

Chilton's Repair & Tune-up Guide for Firebird, 1967-1974. Chilton's Automotive Editorial Department. LC 74-16191. (Illus.). 190p. 1974. 8.95 (ISBN 0-8019-5995-0, 16191); pap. 8.95 (ISBN 0-8019-5996-9). Chilton.

Chilton's Repair & Tune-up Guide for Gremlin & Hornet, 1970-1974. 2nd ed. Chilton's Automotive Editorial Department. LC 74-10693. (Illus.). 224p. 1974. 8.95 (ISBN 0-8019-5993-4); pap. 8.95 (ISBN 0-8019-5994-2). Chilton.

Chilton's Repair & Tune-up Guide for Granada-Monarch, 1975-1977. Chilton's Automotive Ed. Dept. LC 77-89116. (Chilton's Repair & Tune-up Guides). (Illus., Orig.). 1977. pap. 8.95 (ISBN 0-8019-6636-1, 6636). Chilton.

Chilton's Repair & Tune-up Guide for Honda Elsinores, 1973-1975. Chilton's Automotive Editorial Department. (Illus.). 152p. 1975. 8.95 (ISBN 0-8019-6283-8); pap. 8.95 (ISBN 0-8019-6284-6). Chilton.

Chilton's Repair & Tune-up Guide for Honda Fours, 1969-1974. 2nd ed. Chilton's Automotive Editorial Department. (Illus.). 200p. 1974. 8.95 (ISBN 0-8019-6029-0); pap. 8.95 (ISBN 0-8019-6030-4). Chilton.

Chilton's Repair & Tune-up Guide for Honda Singles, 1968-1975. Chilton's Automotive Editorial Department. (Illus.). 1975. 8.95 (ISBN 0-8019-6033-9); pap. 8.95 (ISBN 0-8019-6034-7). Chilton.

Chilton's Repair & Tune-up Guide for Honda Twins, 1966-1972. Chilton's Automotive Editorial Department. LC 72-7035. (Illus.). 148p. 1972. 8.95 (ISBN 0-8019-5736-2); pap. 8.95 (ISBN 0-8019-5799-0). Chilton.

Chilton's Repair & Tune-up Guide for Hodaka, 1964-1973. Chilton's Automotive Editorial Department. LC 74-8643. (Illus.). 220p. 1974. 8.95 (ISBN 0-8019-6026-6); pap. 8.95 (ISBN 0-8019-6027-4). Chilton.

Chilton's Repair & Tune-up Guide for Honda 125-200 Twins, 1969-1976. Chilton's Automotive Editorial Department. LC 75-38656. (Illus.). 175p. 1975. 8.95 (ISBN 0-8019-6468-7); pap. 8.95 (ISBN 0-8019-6469-5). Chilton.

Chilton's Repair & Tune-up Guide for Honda 350-360 Twins, 1968-1975. Chilton's Automotive Editorial Department. (Illus.). 1975. 8.95 (ISBN 0-8019-6037-1); pap. 8.95 (ISBN 0-8019-6038-X). Chilton.

Chilton's Repair & Tune-up Guide for Honda 350-360, 1968-77: Motorcycle. (Repair & Tune-up Guides Ser.). (Illus.). 1978. pap. 8.95 (ISBN 0-8019-6705-8). Chilton.

Chilton's Repair & Tune-Up Guide for Honda 350-550, 1972-1977. Chilton's Automotive Ed. Dept. LC 77-89115. (Chilton's Repair & Tune-up Guides). (Illus., Orig.). 1977. pap. 8.95 (ISBN 0-8019-6603-5, 6603). Chilton.

Chilton's Repair & Tune-up Guide for Honda 750 1969-1977. Chilton's Automotive Ed. Dept. LC 76-57321. (Chilton's Repair & Tune-up Guides). (Illus., Orig.). 1977. pap. 8.95 (ISBN 0-8019-6589-6, 6598). Chilton.

Chilton's Repair & Tune-up Guide for Inboard-Outdrives: 1968-1972. Chilton's Automotive Editorial Department. LC 73-1268. (Illus.). 251p. 1973. 8.95 (ISBN 0-8019-5781-8). Chilton.

Chilton's Repair & Tune-up Guide for International Scout, 1967-1973: International Scout. Chilton's Automotive Editorial Department. LC 74-5077. (Illus.). 200p. 1974. 8.95 (ISBN 0-8019-5878-4); pap. 8.95 (ISBN 0-8019-5912-8). Chilton.

Chilton's Repair & Tune-up Guide for Jeep Universal, 1953-1976. Ed. by Chilton's Automotive Editorial Department. 1976. 8.95 (ISBN 0-8019-6555-1); pap. 8.95 (ISBN 0-8019-6556-X). Chilton.

Chilton's Repair & Tune-up Guide for Jeep Wagoneer, Commando & Cherokee 1966-79. Chilton's Automotive Ed. Dept. (Repair & Tune-up Guides Ser.). (Illus.). 1978. pap. 8.95 (ISBN 0-8019-6739-2). Chilton.

Chilton's Repair & Tune-up Guide for Jaguar, 1969-1974. Chilton's Automotive Editorial Department. LC 74-10545. (Illus.). 220p. 1974. 8.95 (ISBN 0-8019-5997-7); pap. 8.95 (ISBN 0-8019-5998-5). Chilton.

Chilton's Repair & Tune-up Guide for Kawasaki Triples, 1969-1975. Chilton's Automotive Editorial Department. Ed. by Charles Martinell. (Illus.). 175p. 1975. 8.95 (ISBN 0-8019-6264-1); pap. 8.95 (ISBN 0-8019-6265-X). Chilton.

Chilton's Repair & Tune-up Guide for Kawasaki, 1966-1972. Chilton's Automotive Editorial Department. LC 72-6444. (Illus.). 171p. 1972. 8.95 (ISBN 0-8019-5696-X); pap. 8.95 (ISBN 0-8019-6044-4). Chilton.

Chilton's Repair & Tune-up Guide for Kawasaki 900 Z1, 1973-1974. Chilton's Automotive Editorial Department. LC 74-8628. (Illus.). 200p. 1974. 8.95 (ISBN 0-8019-6024-X); pap. 8.95 (ISBN 0-8019-6025-8). Chilton.

Chilton's Repair & Tune-up Guide for Kawasaki 900-1000, 1973-1977. (Repair & Tune-up Guides Ser.). (Illus.). 1978. pap. 8.95 (ISBN 0-8019-6605-1). Chilton.

Chilton's Repair & Tune-up Guide for Maverick & Comet 1970-1977. Chilton's Automotive Ed. Dept. LC 77-75991. (Chilton's Repair & Tune-up Guides). (Illus., Orig.). 1977. pap. 8.95 (ISBN 0-8019-6634-5, 6634). Chilton.

Chilton's Repair & Tune-up Guide for Moto Guzzi, 1966-1972. Chilton's Automotive Editorial Department. LC 73-17292. (Illus.). 224p. 1973. 8.95 (ISBN 0-8019-5866-0); pap. 8.95 (ISBN 0-8019-5908-X). Chilton.

Chilton's Repair & Tune-up Guide for Mazda Pick-up, 1972-1975. Chilton's Automotive Editorial Department. (Illus.). 1975. 8.95 (ISBN 0-8019-6273-0); pap. 8.95 o.p. (ISBN 0-8019-6274-9). Chilton.

Chilton's Repair & Tune-up Guide for Mustang: 1965-1973. Chilton's Automotive Editorial Department. (Illus.). 271p. 1972. 8.95 o.p. (ISBN 0-8019-6541-1); pap. 8.95 (ISBN 0-8019-6542-X). Chilton.

Chilton's Repair & Tune-up Guide for Mazda, 1971-1973. Chilton's Automotive Editorial Department. (Illus.). 190p. 1974. 8.95 (ISBN 0-8019-5862-8); pap. 8.95 (ISBN 0-8019-5906-3). Chilton.

Chilton's Repair & Tune-up Guide for Mazda 1971-78. Chilton's Automotive Ed. Dept. (Repair & Tune-up Guides Ser.). (Illus.). 1978. pap. 8.95 (ISBN 0-8019-6746-5). Chilton.

Chilton's Repair & Tune-up Guide for Norton 750 & 850, 1966-1973. Chilton's Automotive Editorial Department. LC 73-16164. (Illus.). 224p. 1973. 8.95 (ISBN 0-8019-5816-4); pap. 8.95 (ISBN 0-8019-5913-6). Chilton.

Chilton's Repair & Tune-up Guide for Outboard Motors 30 Horsepower & Over: 1966-1972. Chilton's Automotive Editorial Department. LC 72-11533. (Illus.). 284p. 1973. 8.95 (ISBN 0-8019-5722-2); pap. 8.95 (ISBN 0-8019-5803-2). Chilton.

Chilton's Repair & Tune-up Guide for Opel: 1964-1970. Chilton's Automotive Editorial Department. LC 72-153140. (Illus.). 170p. 1971. pap. 8.95 (ISBN 0-8019-5792-3). Chilton.

Chilton's Repair & Tune-up Guide for Ramcharger - Trailduster, 1974-1975. Chilton's Automotive Editorial Department. (Illus.). 1975. 8.95 (ISBN 0-8019-6330-3); pap. 8.95 (ISBN 0-8019-6331-1). Chilton.

Chilton's Repair & Tune-up Guide for Rebel-Matador, 1967-1974. Chilton's Automotive Editorial Department. LC 74-13402. (Illus.). 190p. 1974. 8.95 (ISBN 0-8019-5985-3); pap. 8.95 (ISBN 0-8019-5986-1). Chilton.

Chilton's Repair & Tune-up Guide for Road Runner, Satellite, Belvedere, GTX, 1968-1973. Chilton's Automotive Editorial Department. LC 73-4347. (Illus.). 224p. 1973. 8.95 (ISBN 0-8019-5810-5); pap. 8.95 (ISBN 0-8019-5821-0). Chilton.

Chilton's Repair & Tune-up Guide for Rabbit-Scirocco 1975-1978. Chilton's Automotive Ed. Dept. (Repair & Tune-up Guides Ser.). (Illus.). 1978. pap. 8.95 (ISBN 0-8019-6736-8). Chilton.

Chilton's Repair & Tune-up Guide for Suzuki Triples, 1972-1974. Chilton's Automotive Editorial Department. LC 74-14579. (Illus.). 175p. 1974. 8.95 (ISBN 0-8019-6031-2); pap. 8.95 (ISBN 0-8019-6032-0). Chilton.

Chilton's Repair & Tune-up Guide for Suzuki, 1963-1972. Chilton's Automotive Editorial Department. LC 72-8075. (Illus.). 247p. 1972. 8.95 (ISBN 0-8019-5695-1); pap. 8.95 (ISBN 0-8019-5800-8). Chilton.

Chilton's Repair & Tune-up Guide for Snowmobiles, 1969-1976. Chilton's Automotive Editorial Department. (Illus.). 240p. 1975. 8.95 (ISBN 0-8019-6007-X); pap. 8.95 (ISBN 0-8019-6008-8). Chilton.

Chilton's Repair & Tune-up Guide for Subaru, 1970-78. (Illus.). 1978. pap. 8.95 (ISBN 0-8019-6693-0). Chilton.

Chilton's Repair & Tune-up Guide for Tempest, GTO & Le Mans, 1968-1973. Chilton's Automotive Editorial Department. LC 73-10219. (Illus.). 190p. 1973. 8.95 (ISBN 0-8019-5809-1); pap. 8.95 (ISBN 0-8019-5905-5). Chilton.

Chilton's Repair & Tune-up Guide for Toyota Hi Lux, 1970-1974. Chilton's Automotive Editorial Department. (Illus.). 224p. 1974. 8.95 (ISBN 0-8019-6204-8); pap. 8.95 (ISBN 0-8019-6205-6). Chilton.

Chilton's Repair & Tune-up Guide for Toyota Land Cruiser, 1966-1974. Chilton's Automotive Editorial Department. (Illus.). 224p. 1974. 8.95 (ISBN 0-8019-6275-7); pap. 8.95 (ISBN 0-8019-6276-5). Chilton.

Chilton's Repair & Tune-up Guide for Triumph Motorcycle Through 1972. Chilton's Automotive Editorial Department. LC 72-5158. (Illus.). 201p. 1972. 8.95 (ISBN 0-8019-5712-5); pap. 8.95 (ISBN 0-8019-6046-0). Chilton.

Chilton's Repair & Tune-up Guide for Toyota Pick-Ups, 1970-1978. LC 77-18305. (Illus.). 1978. pap. 8.95 (ISBN 0-8019-6692-2). Chilton.

Chilton's Repair & Tune-up Guide for Toyota 1970-1977. Chilton's Automotive Ed. Dept. LC 76-57318. (Chilton's Repair & Tune-up Guides). (Illus., Orig.). 1977. pap. 8.95 (ISBN 0-8019-6617-5, 6617). Chilton.

Chilton's Repair & Tune-up Guide for Triumph 2, 1969-1973. Chilton's Automotive Editorial Department. LC 73-18387. (Illus.). 224p. 1974. 8.95 (ISBN 0-8019-5863-6); pap. 8.95 (ISBN 0-8019-5910-1). Chilton.

Chilton's Repair & Tune-up Guide for Valiant & Duster, 1968-1976. Chilton's Automotive Editorial Dept. (Illus.). 190p. 1975. 8.95 (ISBN 0-8019-6325-7); pap. 8.95 (ISBN 0-8019-6326-5). Chilton.

Chilton's Repair & Tune-up Guide for Volkswagen 1970-1977. Chilton's Automotive Ed. Dept. LC 76-57319. (Chilton's Repair & Tune-up Guides). (Illus., Orig.). 1977. pap. 8.95 (ISBN 0-8019-6619-1, 6619). Chilton.

Chilton's Repair & Tune-up Guide for Vega 1971-1977. Chilton's Automotive Ed. Dept. LC 76-53150. (Chilton's Repair & Tune-up Guides). (Illus., Orig.). 1977. pap. 8.95 (ISBN 0-8019-6609-4, 6609). Chilton.

Chilton's Repair & Tune-up Guide for Volkswagen: 1949-1971. Chilton's Automotive Editorial Department. LC 74-154691. (Illus.). 212p. 1971. 8.95 (ISBN 0-8019-5624-2); pap. 8.95 (ISBN 0-8019-5796-6). Chilton.

Chilton's Repair & Tune-up Guide for Volvo, 1970-1973. Chilton's Automotive Editorial Department. LC 73-3398. (Illus.). 224p. 1973. 8.95 o.p. (ISBN 0-8019-5813-X); pap. 8.95 (ISBN 0-8019-5850-4). Chilton.

Chilton's Repair & Tune-up Guide for Winnebago Motor Homes, 1968-1974. Chilton's Automotive Editorial Department. LC 74-17354. (Illus.). 224p. 1974. 8.95 (ISBN 0-8019-6013-4); pap. 8.95 (ISBN 0-8019-6014-2). Chilton.

Chilton's Repair & Tune-up Guide for Yamaha Enduros, 1968-1974. Chilton's Automotive Editorial Department. (Illus.). 1975. 8.95 (ISBN 0-8019-6085-1); pap. 8.95 (ISBN 0-8019-6086-X). Chilton.

Chilton's Repair & Tune-up Guide for Yamaha Four-Strokes, 1970-1974. Chilton's Automotive Editorial Department. LC 74-16276. (Illus.). 200p. 1974. 8.95 (ISBN 0-8019-6087-8); pap. 8.95 (ISBN 0-8019-6088-6). Chilton.

Chilton's Repair & Tune-up Guide for Yamaha 360-400 1976-78. Chilton's Automotive Ed. Dept. (Repair & Tune-up Guides Ser.). (Illus.). 1978. pap. 8.95 (ISBN 0-8019-6738-4). Chilton.

Chimaera of His Age: Studies in Medieval Cistercian History V. Ed. by E. Rozanne Elder & John R. Sommerfeldt. (Cistercian Studies Ser.: No. 63). 146p. 1980. pap. 8.95 (ISBN 0-87907-863-4). Cistercian Pubns.

Chime Child: Or, Somerset Singers - Being an Account of Some of Their Songs Collected Over Sixty Years. Ruth L. Tongue. LC 68-77292. x, 102p. Repr. of 1968 ed. 15.00 (ISBN 0-8103-5022-X). Gale.

Chimeres. Gerard De Nerval. Ed. by Norma Rinsler. 1973. text ed. 19.50x (ISBN 0-485-14702-5, Athlone Pr); pap. text ed. 10.50x (ISBN 0-485-12702-4, Athlone Pr). Humanities.

Chimney Farm Bedtime Stories. Beston & Coatsworth. 1977. pap. 3.50 (ISBN 0-89272-040-9). Down East.

Chimney Swifts & Their Relatives. Margaret Whittemore. 176p. 1981. pap. 5.95 (ISBN 0-912542-02-0). Nature Bks Pub.

Chimpanzees. Ralph Whitlock. LC 77-13965. (Animals of the World Ser.). (Illus.). (gr. 4-5). 1977. PLB 10.65 (ISBN 0-8172-1077-6). Raintree Pubs.

China. Ed. by Congressional Quarterly Inc. (Orig.). 1980. pap. text ed. 10.95 (ISBN 0-87187-188-2). Congr Quarterly.

China. Jonathan Hammond. LC 75-44869. (Macdonald Countries). (Illus.). (gr. 6 up). 1976. PLB 7.95 (ISBN 0-382-06101-2, Pub. by Macdonald Ed). Silver.

China. Huang Jiemin. 83p. Date not set. 50.00 (ISBN 0-07-056830-8). McGraw.

China. Charles McNulty. (Orig.). (gr. 9-12). 1975. pap. text ed. 4.92 (ISBN 0-87720-615-5). AMSCO Sch.

China. Mortimer Menpes. 139p. 1980. Repr. of 1909 ed. lib. bdg. 35.00 (ISBN 0-89987-562-9). Darby Bks.

China. Zheng Shifeng et al. LC 80-23641. (Illus.). 230p. 1980. 50.00 (ISBN 0-07-056830-8); until Dec. 1980 50.00 (ISBN 0-686-64507-3). McGraw.

China: A Brief History. Nancy F. Sizer & Rebecca S. Rudd. (Illus.). 210p. (Orig.). (gr. 9-12). 1979. pap. text ed. 4.50x (ISBN 0-88334-119-0). Ind Sch Pr.

China: A Business Guide. Japan External Trade Organization & Press International, Ltd. (Tokyo) (Illus.). 216p. (Orig.). 1979. pap. 30.00x (ISBN 0-8002-2235-0). Intl Pubns Serv.

China: A Geographical Survey. Thomas R. Tregear. 372p. 1980. 42.50x (ISBN 0-470-26925-1); pap. text ed. 19.95x (ISBN 0-470-26926-X). Halsted Pr.

China: A History of the Laws, Manners & Customs of the People, 2 vols. J. H. Gray. Ed. by W. G. Gregor. (Illus.). 800p. 1972. Repr. of 1878 ed. 70.00x (ISBN 0-7165-2030-3, Pub. by Irish Academic Pr Ireland). Biblio Dist.

China: A Political History. Richard C. Thornton. 500p. (Orig.). 1981. lib. bdg. 27.50x (ISBN 0-86531-197-8); pap. text ed. 12.00x (ISBN 0-86531-198-6). Westview.

China: A Short Cultural History. C. P. Fitzgerald. 1978. 19.95 o.p. (ISBN 0-248-98299-0, 8018, Dist. by Arco). Barrie & Jenkins.

China: A Workbook in World Cultures. John M. Cassebaum et al. LC 72-95839. (gr. 8-10). 1973. pap. 2.25 o.p. (ISBN 0-931992-29-X). Penns Valley.

China After the Cultural Revolution. Jurgen Domes. Tr. by David Goodman from Ger. 1977. 21.50x (ISBN 0-520-03064-8). U of Cal Pr.

China-An Interpretive History: From the Beginnings to the Fall of Han. Joseph R. Levenson & Franz Schurmann. 1969. 14.50x (ISBN 0-520-01440-5); pap. 4.75x (ISBN 0-520-01892-3, CAMPUS46). U of Cal Pr.

China: An Uncensored Look. rev. ed. Julian Schuman. LC 79-63789. 1979. 15.95 (ISBN 0-933256-01-9); pap. 7.95 (ISBN 0-933256-04-3). Second Chance.

China & Africa in the Middle Ages. Tr. by Teobaldo Filesi & D. L. Morrison. (Illus.). 104p. 1972. 24.00x (ISBN 0-7146-2604-X, F Cass Co). Biblio Dist.

China & America: Past & Future. Michel Oksenberg & Robert B. Oxnam. (Headline Ser.: 235). 1977. pap. 2.00 (ISBN 0-87124-041-6, 77-77822). Foreign Policy.

China & Her Unfinished Revolution. Helen G. Pratt. (Studies in Chinese History & Civilization). 173p. 1977. Repr. of 1937 ed. 16.00 (ISBN 0-89093-091-0). U Pubns Amer.

China & Japan: A New Balance of Power. Commission on Critical Choices & Donald C. Hellman. LC 75-44730. (Critical Choices for Americans Ser.: Vol. XII). 1976. 19.95 (ISBN 0-669-00426-X). Lexington Bks.

China & Japan at War, 1937-1945: The Politics of Collaboration. John H. Boyle. LC 76-183886. (Illus.). 416p. 1972. 18.50x (ISBN 0-8047-0800-2). Stanford U Pr.

China & Japan: Emerging Global Powers. Peter G. Mueller & Douglas A. Ross. LC 74-33039. (Special Studies). (Illus.). 240p. 1975. text ed. 24.95 (ISBN 0-275-05400-4); pap. text ed. 9.95 (ISBN 0-275-89390-1). Praeger.

China & Japan Nineteen Forty-Nine to Nineteen Seventy-Six. R. K. Jain. LC 77-70008. 1977. text ed. 17.50x (ISBN 0-391-00749-1). Humanities.

China & Parian Dolls. Patricia Smith. (Illus.). 1980. pap. 9.95 (ISBN 0-89145-144-7). Collector Bks.

China & Russia: The Great Game. O. Edmund Clubb. LC 72-155362. (Illus.). 1970. 22.50x (ISBN 0-231-02740-0); pap. 9.00x (ISBN 0-231-08305-X, 138). Columbia U Pr.

China & Southeast Asia: Peking's Relations with Revolutionary Movements. expanded & updated ed. Jay Taylor. LC 76-3679. (Praeger Special Studies Ser.). 416p. 1976. text ed. 27.95 (ISBN 0-275-56830-X); pap. text ed. 11.95 (ISBN 0-275-64490-1). Praeger.

China & the Cold War: A Study in International Politics. Michael Lindsay. LC 79-2834. 286p. 1981. Repr. of 1955 ed. 22.50 (ISBN 0-8305-0011-1). Hyperion Conn.

China & the Great Powers: Relations with the U. S., the Soviet Union & Japan. Ed. by Francis O. Wilcox. LC 74-1736. (Special Studies). 96p. 1974. text ed. 15.95 o.p. (ISBN 0-275-08770-0). Praeger.

China & the Major Powers in East Asia. A. Doak Barnett. 1977. 15.95 (ISBN 0-8157-0824-6); pap. 6.95 (ISBN 0-8157-0823-8). Brookings.

China & the Overseas Chinese: A Study of Peking's Changing Policy, 1949-1970. S. Fitzgerald. LC 77-177938. (Cambridge Studies in Chinese History, Literature & Institutions). (Illus.). 250p. 1972. 41.00 (ISBN 0-521-08410-5); pap. 13.95 (ISBN 0-521-29810-5). Cambridge U Pr.

China & the Politics of Disarmament, 1949 to 1980: A Documentary Study. R. K. Jain. 400p. 1980. text ed. 20.50x (ISBN 0-391-02118-4). Humanities.

China & the Powers: A Narrative of the Outbreak of 1900. Harry C. Thomson. LC 79-2840. (Illus.). 285p. 1981. Repr. of 1902 ed. 26.50 (ISBN 0-8305-0017-0). Hyperion Conn.

China & the Taiwan Issue. Hungdah Chiu. LC 79-14270. (Praeger Special Studies Ser.). 1980. 27.95 (ISBN 0-03-048911-3). Praeger.

China & the United States: What Next? Allen S. Whiting. (Headline Ser.: 230). (Illus.). 1976. pap. 2.00 (ISBN 0-87124-035-1, 76-4299). Foreign Policy.

China & the West: Comparative Literature Studies. Ed. by William Tay. (New Asia Economic Bulletin Ser.). 306p. 1980. 18.50 (ISBN 0-295-95694-1, Pub. by Chinese Univ Hong Kong). U of Wash Pr.

China & the West: Mankind Evolving. Robert Jungk et al. (Teilhard Study Library). 1970. text ed. 6.25x (ISBN 0-391-00023-3). Humanities.

China & the West: Society & Culture 1815-1937. Jerome Ch'en. LC 79-2704. (Illus.). 488p. 1980. 22.50x (ISBN 0-253-12032-2). Ind U Pr.

China & the World Food System. A. Doak Barnett. LC 79-87912. (Monographs: No. 12). 128p. 1979. 5.00 (ISBN 0-686-28683-9). Overseas Dev Council.

China & the World War. Thomas E. LaFargue. 16.50 (ISBN 0-86527-023-6). Fertig.

China & Yugoslavia, Nineteen Forty-Nine to Nineteen-Eighty. R. K. Jain. 400p. 1980. text ed. 20.50x (ISBN 0-391-02117-6). Humanities.

China Beginner's Traveler's Dictionary. Richard L. Kimball. 1980. pap. 6.95 (ISBN 0-8351-0732-9). China Bks.

China Briefing Nineteen Eighty. Ed. by Robert B. Oxnam & Richardc. Bush. 120p. (Published in cooperation with the China Council of the Asia Society, Inc.). 1980. lib. bdg. 14.50x (ISBN 0-86531-028-9); pap. text ed. 6.50x (ISBN 0-86531-070-X). Westview.
China-Burma-India. Don Moser. Ed. by Time Life Books. (World War II Ser.). 1978. 12.95 (ISBN 0-8094-2482-7). Time-Life.
China Business Directory. Phillip M. Perry. LC 80-52703. (Illus.). 352p. 1980. 55.00 (ISBN 0-87762-286-8). Technomic.
China Card. Donald Freed. 1980. 12.95 (ISBN 0-87795-281-7). Arbor Hse.
China Challenge. Albert Axelbank. (Illus.). (gr. 7 up). 1978. PLB 5.90 s&l o.p. (ISBN 0-531-01478-9). Watts.
China Collecting in America. Alice M. Earle. LC 77-99044. 1970. Repr. of 1892 ed. 18.00 (ISBN 0-8103-3579-4). Gale.
China Connection. Warren I. Cohen. (Studies of the East Asian Institute). 1978. 20.00x (ISBN 0-231-04444-5). Columbia U Pr.
China Court. Rumer Godden. 1974. pap. 1.25 o.s.i. (ISBN 0-380-00114-4, 20412). Avon.
China: Development of Olive Production. 163p. 1981. pap. 8.75 (ISBN 92-5-100995-3, F2097, FAO). Unipub.
China Diary: Crisis Diplomacy in Dairen. Paul Paddock. 1977. 3.75 (ISBN 0-8138-0240-7). Iowa St U Pr.
China Directory-1971. 9th ed. Ed. by Radiopress-Tokyo. 657p. 1980. 85.00x (ISBN 0-8002-2752-2). Intl Pubns Serv.
China Doll. Paul Ledd. (Shelter Ser.: No. 5). 1980. pap. 1.95 (ISBN 0-89083-682-5, Kable News Co). Zebra.
China Enters the United Nations: A New Era for the World Organization. Peter A. Poole. LC 74-584. (World Focus Bks.). (Illus.). 96p. (gr. 7 up). 1974. PLB 6.45 (ISBN 0-531-02713-9). Watts.
China Facts & Figures Annual (CHIFFA, Vol. 3, 1981. Ed. by John L. Scherer. 37.00 (ISBN 0-87569-036-X). Academic Intl.
China for America: Export Porcelain of the 18th & 19th Centuries. Herbert Schiffer & Peter Schiffer. LC 79-88254. 1979. 27.50 (ISBN 0-916838-23-4). Schiffer.
China from Manchu to Mao. John R. Roberson. LC 79-22269. (Illus.). 208p. (gr. 5 up). 1980. 10.95 (ISBN 0-689-30758-6). Atheneum.
China Geographer. Ed. by Clifton W. Pannell & Christopher L. Salter. (Illus.). 200p. 1981. lib. bdg. 24.50x (ISBN 0-89158-860-4). Westview.
China Guide Book: A Travel Guide to the People's Republic of China, 1979-80 Ed. Arne J. de Keijzer & Fredric Kaplan. 1979. 12.95 o.p. (ISBN 0-397-01358-2); pap. 8.95 (ISBN 0-397-01359-0). Lippincott.
China Guidebook: 1980-81 Edition. rev. ed. Arne J. Dekeijzer & Frederic M. Kaplan. LC 80-7860. (Illus.). 448p. 1980. 14.95 (ISBN 0-690-01953-X); pap. 10.95 (ISBN 0-690-01955-6). Lippincott & Crowell.
China Half-Figures Called Pincushion Dolls. Frieda Marion. LC 74-178257. (Illus.). 1977. Repr. 7.95 (ISBN 0-89145-058-0). J Palmer.
China Hand. Bruno Skoggard. LC 79-522. 1979. 8.95 (ISBN 0-396-07662-9). Dodd.
China Hand. Bruno Skoggard. LC 80-85112. 288p. 1981. pap. 2.95 (ISBN 0-87216-838-7). Playboy Pbks.
China Handbook, Nineteen Thirty-Seven to Nineteen Forty-Five: A Comprehensive Survey of Major Developments in China. rev. enl. ed. Compiled by The Chinese Ministry of Information & Hollington K. Tong. (China in the 20th Century Ser). (Illus.). xvi, 862p. 1975. Repr. of 1947 ed. lib. bdg. 75.00 (ISBN 0-306-70701-2). Da Capo.
China in Convulsion, 2 vols. Arthur H. Smith. (Illus.). 770p. 1972. Repr. of 1901 ed. 70.00x (ISBN 0-686-28324-4, Pub. by Irish Academic Pr). Biblio Dist.
China in Disintegration: The Republican Era in Chinese History, 1912-1949. James E. Sheridan. LC 74-28940. (Transformation of Modern China Ser.). 1977. 15.95 (ISBN 0-02-928610-7); pap. text ed. 7.95 (ISBN 0-02-928650-6). Free Pr.
China in Old Photographs, Eighteen Sixty-Five to Nineteen Ten. Burton F. Beers. (Illus.). 1978. 5.95 (ISBN 0-684-16532-5, ScribT). Scribner.
China in Pictures. Sterling Publishing Company Editors. LC 73-83436. (Visual Geography Ser.). (Illus.). 64p. (gr. 6 up). 1973. PLB 4.99 (ISBN 0-8069-1171-9); pap. 2.95 (ISBN 0-8069-1170-0). Sterling.
China in Revolt: How a Civilization Became a Nation. Leang-Ti T'Ang. (Studies in Chinese History & Civilization). 176p. 1977. Repr. of 1927 ed. 18.00 (ISBN 0-89093-070-8). U Pubns Amer.
China in the Global Community. Ed. by James C. Hsiung & Samuel S. Kim. 288p. 1980. 27.95 (ISBN 0-03-057009-3). Praeger.
China in the Twentieth Century. Jules Archer. LC 73-6050. (Illus.). 240p. (gr. 7 up). 1974. 9.95 (ISBN 0-02-705620-1, 70562). Macmillan.
China in the Twentieth Century. Peter Lane. 16.95 (ISBN 0-7134-0973-8, Pub. by Batsford England). David & Charles.
China in the Twentieth Century. Peter Lane. 1978. 14.00 (ISBN 0-7134-0973-8, Pub. by Batsford England). David & Charles.
China in World Politics. 2nd ed. Jagdish P. Jain. 1980. text ed. 15.00x (ISBN 0-391-01691-1). Humanities.
China Is Farther Than the Sun? A Beginning Chinese-English Reader. Florence C. Chang. LC 80-68256. (Chinese Can Be Fun Ser.: Bk. 1). (Illus.). 51p. (gr. 3-5). 1980. pap. 3.00 (ISBN 0-936620-00-5). Ginkgo Hut.
China: Its History & Culture. Morton. 1981. 10.95 (ISBN 0-690-01863-0). Lippincott & Crowell.
China: It's History & Culture. W. Scott Morton. (Illus.). 1980. 16.95 (ISBN 0-690-01863-0). Lippincott.
China, Japan, & Nineteenth Century Britain. I Nish & D. Steeds. (Government & Society in Nineteenth Century Britain Ser.). 1977. 20.00x (ISBN 0-7165-2225-X, Pub. by Irish Academic Pr Ireland). Biblio Dist.
China Journal: Glimpses of a Nation in Transition. Robert Lee. (Illus., Orig.). 1980. 9.25 (ISBN 0-934788-00-6); pap. 5.25 (ISBN 0-686-28891-2). E-W Pub Co.
China: Liberation & Transformation 1942-1962. Bill Brugger. (Illus.). 288p. 1981. 27.50x (ISBN 0-389-20086-7). B&N.
China Lobby in American Politics. Ross Y. Koen. 1974. pap. 4.95x o.p. (ISBN 0-06-138885-8, HR1833, Torch). Har-Row.
China Men. Maxine H. Kingston. 288p. 1981. pap. 3.50 (ISBN 0-345-29482-3). Ballantine.
China Mending: A Guide to Repairing & Restoration. Echo Evetts. (Illus.). 1978. 15.95 (ISBN 0-571-10822-9, Pub. by Faber & Faber). Merrimack Bk Serv.
China: Multiple Cropping & Related Crop Production Technology. (FAO Plant Protection Paper Ser.: No. 22). 66p. 1981. pap. 6.00 (ISBN 92-5-100977-5, F2108, FAO). Unipub.
China: New Age & New Outlook. Ping-Chia Kuo. LC 74-30084. (China in the 20th Century Ser). xix, 231p. 1975. Repr. of 1956 ed. lib. bdg. 22.50 (ISBN 0-306-70679-2). Da Capo.
China: New Force in World Affairs, Vol. 44, No. 5. Ed. by Irwin Isenberg. (Reference Shelf Ser.: Vol. 44, No. 5). 200p. 1972. 6.25 (ISBN 0-8242-0468-9). Wilson.
China Notebook, Nineteen Seventy-Five to Nineteen Seventy-Eight. Jan Myrdal. Tr. by Rolf Von Dorp from Swedish. LC 79-88412. (Illus.). lib. bdg. 8.95 (ISBN 0-930720-59-8); pap. 3.95 (ISBN 0-930720-58-X). Liberator Pr.
China Nurse. Mary S. Ogle. LC 74-79164. (Destiny Ser.). 1975. pap. 4.95 (ISBN 0-8163-0168-9, 03195-5). Pacific Pr Pub Assn.
China, Oil, & Asia: Conflict Ahead? Selig S. Harrison. LC 77-8185. 1977. 15.00x (ISBN 0-231-04378-3). Columbia U Pr.
China: Past, Present & Personal. C. M. Fraser. LC 80-67728. 141p. 1980. 8.95 (ISBN 0-8059-2736-0). Dorrance.
China Policy: Old Problems & New Challenges. A. Doak Barnett. LC 76-51538. 1977. 9.95 (ISBN 0-8157-0822-X); pap. 3.95 (ISBN 0-8157-0821-1). Brookings.
China Profiles. Michael Dillon. 1981. 25.00x (ISBN 0-7146-3152-3, F Cass Co). Biblio Dist.
China: Pushing Toward the Year 2000. Gil Loescher & Ann D. Loescher. LC 80-8802. (Illus.). 160p. (gr. 7 up). 1981. 10.95 (ISBN 0-15-217506-7, HJ). HarBraceJ.
China: Radicalism to Revisionism 1962-1979. Bill Brugger. (Illus.). 275p. 1981. 27.50x (ISBN 0-389-20087-5). B&N.
China: Railway Patterns & National Goals. Chi-Keung Leung. LC 80-17030. (Research Papers). (Illus.). 233p. 1980. pap. 8.00 (ISBN 0-89065-102-7). U Chicago Dept Geog.
China: Regional Study. 2nd ed. Hyman Kublin. Ed. by Howard R. Anderson. (World Regional Studies). (gr. 7-12). 1976. pap. text ed. 6.60 (ISBN 0-395-21686-9, 2-31023). HM.
China Scapegoat: The Diplomatic Ordeal of John Carter Vincent. Gary May. LC 79-4129. (Illus.). 1979. 15.95 o.p. (ISBN 0-915220-49-0). New Republic.
China: Selected Readings. 2nd ed. Hyman Kublin. Ed. by Howard R. Anderson. (World Regional Studies). (gr. 7-12). 1976. pap. text ed. 6.60 (ISBN 0-395-21686-9, 2-31029). HM.
China: Selected Readings on the Middle Kingdom. Ed. by Leon Hellerman et al. (Illus.). 1971. pap. 1.25 o.s.i. (ISBN 0-671-48111-8). WSP.
China Since Mao. Ed. by Lester Sobel. 200p. 1980. lib. bdg. 17.50 (ISBN 0-87196-210-1). Facts on File.
China-South Asian Relations: 1949-1980, 2 vols. Ed. by Rajendra K. Jain. 1400p. 1980. Set. text ed. write for info. (ISBN 0-391-01896-5). Humanities.
China Station: War & Diplomacy 1830-1860. Gerald S. Graham. (Illus.). 1978. 54.00x (ISBN 0-19-822472-9). Oxford U Pr.
China Tangle: The American Effort in China from Pearl Harbor to the Marshall Mission. Herbert Feis. 456p. 1953. 20.00x (ISBN 0-691-05606-4); pap. 6.95 o.p. (ISBN 0-691-01064-1). Princeton U Pr.
China: The Agricultural Training System. (FAO Economic & Social Development Paper Ser.: No. 11). 141p. 1980. pap. 7.50 (ISBN 92-5-100898-1, F1941, FAO). Unipub.
China: The History, Diplomacy & Commerce from the Earliest Times to the Present Day. E. H. Parker. LC 78-74314. (Modern Chinese Economy Ser.: Vol. 6). 394p. 1980. lib. bdg. 44.00 (ISBN 0-8240-4255-7). Garland Pub.
China: The Land & Its People. R. C. Decrespigny. 1973. pap. 7.95 (ISBN 0-312-13265-4). St. Martin.
China, the Land & the People: A Human Geography. Leonard H. Buxton. LC 79-2818. (Illus.). 333p. 1981. Repr. of 1929 ed. 27.50 (ISBN 0-8305-0000-6). Hyperion Conn.
China-the Sick Dragon. LC 78-65281. 1979. write for info. Sundowner Serv.
China, the Soviet Union & the West: Strategic & Political Dimensions for the Nineteen Eighties. Ed. by Douglas T. Stuart & William T. Tow. (Special Studies in International Relations). 320p. (Orig.). 1981. lib. bdg. 27.50x (ISBN 0-86531-091-2); pap. text ed. 12.50x (ISBN 0-86531-168-4). Westview.
China, the Struggle for Power, 1917-1972. Richard C. Thornton. LC 73-77856. 416p. 1974. 15.00x (ISBN 0-253-31353-8). Ind U Pr.
China: The Turning Point. Ed. by Edwin J. Feulner, Jr. 1976. pap. 10.00 (ISBN 0-685-79961-1). Coun Am Affairs.
China This Century. R. R. De Crespigny. LC 75-10977. 300p. 1975. text ed. 19.95 (ISBN 0-312-13335-9). St Martin.
China to Eighteen Fifty: A Short History. Charles O. Hucker. LC 77-79998. 1978. 8.50x (ISBN 0-8047-0957-2); pap. 2.95x (ISBN 0-8047-0958-0). Stanford U Pr.
China to Me: A Partial Autobiography. Emily Hahn. LC 74-23432. (China in the 20th Century Ser). 429p. 1975. Repr. of 1944 ed. lib. bdg. 35.00 (ISBN 0-306-70695-4). Da Capo.
China Today. Nigel Cameron. LC 73-21234. (International Library). (Illus.). 128p. (gr. 7 up). 1974. PLB 6.90 o.p. (ISBN 0-531-02712-0). Watts.
China Today. Marie-Ange Donze & Claude Sauvageot. (Illus.). 255p. 1980. 14.95 (ISBN 0-686-64605-3, Pub. by Two Continents). Hippocrene Bks.
China Trace. Charles Wright. LC 77-74604. (Wesleyan Poetry Program: Vol. 88). 1977. pap. 10.00x (ISBN 0-8195-2088-8, Pub. by Wesleyan U Pr); pap. 4.95 (ISBN 0-8195-1088-2). Columbia U Pr.
China Trade: A Guide to Doing Business with the People's Republic of China. Herbert B. Azif. LC 80-84105. (Illus.). 200p. (Orig.). Date not set. pap. price not set (ISBN 0-9605190-0-9). Intraworld Trade.
China Trade Porcelain: Patterns of Exchange. Clara Le Corbeiller. LC 74-2097. (Illus.). 1974. 15.00 o.p. (ISBN 0-87099-089-6, 139092). Metro Mus Art.
China: Tradition & Transformation. John K. Fairbank & Edwin O. Reischauer. LC 77-77980. (Illus.). 1977. text ed. 14.25 (ISBN 0-395-25813-8). HM.
China Traveler's Phrasebook. Bennett Lee & Geremie Barme. 1980. pap. 5.95 (ISBN 0-8351-0729-9). China Bks.
China Under Mongol Rule. Ed. by John D. Langlois, Jr. LC 80-8559. (Illus.). 532p. 1981. 30.00x (ISBN 0-691-03127-4); pap. 12.50x (ISBN 0-691-10110-8). Princeton U Pr.
Chinaberry. William Lavender. (Orig.). 1976. pap. 2.95 (ISBN 0-515-05838-6). Jove Pubns.
Chinaglia. Giorgio Chinaglia & Basil Kane. 1980. 11.95 (ISBN 0-671-25049-3). S&S.
China's African Revolution. Alan Hutchison. LC 75-45233. 1976. 21.50x (ISBN 0-89158-025-5). Westview.
China's Crafts: The Story of How They're Made & What They Mean. Roberta Stalberg & Ruth Nesi. 1980. pap. 10.95 (ISBN 0-8351-0740-X). China Bks.
China's Cultural Revolution. Gargi Dutt & V. P. Dutt. 1970. 10.00x (ISBN 0-210-98192-X). Asia.
China's Development Experience in Comparative Perspective: A Social Science Research Council Study. Ed. by Robert Dernberger. LC 80-418. (East Asian Ser.: No. 93). 1980. text ed. 30.00x (ISBN 0-674-11890-1). Harvard U Pr.
China's Economic Development: The Interplay of Scarcity & Ideology. Alexander Eckstein. LC 74-25951. (Michigan Studies on China Ser.). (Illus.). 1975. 16.50 o.p. (ISBN 0-472-29872-0); pap. 7.95x (ISBN 0-472-08310-4). U of Mich Pr.
China's Economic Revolution. A. Eckstein. LC 76-9176. (Illus.). 1977. 41.95 (ISBN 0-521-21283-9); pap. 9.95x (ISBN 0-521-29189-5). Cambridge U Pr.
China's Energy: Achievements, Problems, Prospects. Vaclav Smil. LC 75-44939. (Illus.). 1976. text ed. 26.95 (ISBN 0-275-23050-3). Praeger.
China's Examination Hell: The Civil Service Examinations of Imperial China. Ichisada Miyazaki. Tr. by Conrad Schirokauer from Chinese. LC 80-54223. 142p. 1981. pap. 4.95 (ISBN 0-300-02639-0). Yale U Pr.
China's Foreign Aid: An Instrument of Peking's Foreign Policy. John F. Copper. LC 75-39318. (Illus.). 1976. 21.95 (ISBN 0-669-00441-3). Lexington Bks.
China's Four Modernizations: The New Technological Revolution. Ed. by Richard Baum. (Westview Special Studies on China & East Asia). 276p. 1980. lib. bdg. 22.00x (ISBN 0-89158-673-3); pap. 9.50x (ISBN 0-89158-755-1). Westview.
China's Gentry: Essays in Rural-Urban Relations with Six Life-Histories of Chinese Gentry Families. Ed. by Hsiao-Tung Fei & Margaret Redfield. LC 53-11440. (Midway Reprint Ser.). 296p. 1980. pap. 9.00x (ISBN 0-226-23957-8). U of Chicago Pr.
China's Global Role: An Analysis of Peking's National Power Capabilities in the Context of an Evolving International System. John F. Copper. LC 79-88585. (Publication: No. 226). 1980. pap. 7.95 (ISBN 0-8179-7262-5). Hoover Inst Pr.
China's Higher Leadership in the Socialist Transition. Paul Wong. LC 76-7179. 1976. 25.00 (ISBN 0-02-935600-8). Free Pr.
China's Island Frontier: Studies in the Historical Geography of Taiwan. Ed. by Ronald G. Knapp. LC 80-18578. 368p. 1980. text ed. 20.00x (ISBN 0-8248-0705-7). U Pr of Hawaii.
China's New Constitution & International Problems. Min-Chi'En T. Tyau. (Studies in Chinese Government & Law). 286p. 1977. Repr. of 1918 ed. 19.50 (ISBN 0-89093-064-3). U Pubns Amer.
China's Oil Future: A Case of Modest Expectations. Randall W. Hardy. LC 77-27555. (Westview Special Studies on China & East Asia Ser.). 1978. lib. bdg. 23.50x (ISBN 0-89158-156-1). Westview.
China's Oil: Problems & Prospects. Sevinc Carlson. LC 79-92159. (CSIS Monograph). 128p. 1979. 77.00 (ISBN 0-89206-010-7). CSI Studies.
China's Own Critics. Shih Hu & Yu-T'Ang Lin. LC 79-2829. 166p. 1981. Repr. of 1931 ed. 16.00 (ISBN 0-8305-0006-5). Hyperion Conn.
China's Quest for Independence: Policy Evolution in the Nineteen Seventy's. Ed. by Thomas Fingar. (Westview Special Studies on China & East Asia). 245p. 1980. 22.00x (ISBN 0-89158-570-2). Westview.
China's Road to Development. Neville Maxwell. 1976. pap. text ed. 20.00 o.p. (ISBN 0-08-019979-8). Pergamon.
China's Road to Development. 2nd ed. Neville Maxwell. 1979. text ed. 55.00 (ISBN 0-08-023140-3); pap. text ed. 12.75 (ISBN 0-08-023139-X). Pergamon.
China's Role in World Affairs. Michael B. Yahuda. LC 78-19218. 1978. 20.00 (ISBN 0-312-13358-8). St Martin.
China's Silk Trade: A Traditional Industry & the International Market, 1842-1937. Lillian Ming-tse Li. (Harvard East Asian Monograph: No. 97). 1981. text ed. 15.00x (ISBN 0-674-11962-2). Harvard U Pr.
China's Socialist Revolution. John Collier & Elsie Collier. LC 74-7782. 272p. 1975. 8.95 o.p. (ISBN 0-85345-336-5, CL3365). Monthly Rev.
China's Struggle for Railroad Development. Chang Kia-ngau, pseud. LC 74-34331. (China in the 20th Century Ser). (Illus.). vii, 340p. 1975. Repr. of 1943 ed. lib. bdg. 29.50 (ISBN 0-306-70689-X). Da Capo.
China's Three Thousand Years: The Story of a Great Civilisation. Louis Heren & C. P. Fitzgerald. LC 73-12638. (Illus.). 240p. 1974. pap. 3.95 o.s.i. (ISBN 0-02-032200-3, Collier). Macmillan.
China's Three Thousand Years: The Story of a Great Civilization. Louis Heren et al. (Illus.). 240p. 1974. 8.95 o.s.i. (ISBN 0-02-550080-5). Macmillan.
China's Transition to Industrialism: Producer Goods & Economic Development in the Twentieth Century. Thomas G. Rawski. (Michigan Studies on China). (Illus.). 226p. 1980. 16.50x (ISBN 0-472-08755-X). U of Mich Pr.

China's Watergate: Political & Economic Conflicts in China 1969-1977. Leo Goodstadt. 1979. text ed. 15.00x (ISBN 0-7069-0725-6). Humanities.

China's Watergate: Political & Economic Conflicts, 1969-1977. Leo Goodstadt. LC 79-902871. 219p. 1979. 13.50x (ISBN 0-7069-0725-6). Intl Pubns Serv.

China's World: The Foreign Policy of a Developing State. J. D. Simmonds. LC 75-126932. 1971. 18.50x (ISBN 0-231-03511-X). Columbia U Pr.

Chinchilla. Robert D. MacDonald. (Phoenix Theatre Ser.). pap. 2.95 (ISBN 0-912262-73-7). Proscenium.

Chindi. Brad Steiger. (Orig.). 1980. pap. 2.75 (ISBN 0-440-11119-6). Dell.

Chinese Acupuncture. W. Wei-Ping. 7.50 o.p. (ISBN 0-685-47283-3). Weiser.

Chinese Acupuncture. Wu Wei-P'Ing. Tr. by Philip Chancellor from Fr. 184p. 1962. text ed. 10.35x (ISBN 0-8464-0999-2). Beekman Pubs.

Chinese Acupuncture: Do-It Yourself, a Text Book for Practitioners. 4th ed. Charles A. Meeker. LC 60-972. (Illus.). 210p. Date not set. 15.50 (ISBN 0-935068-07-4). Meeker Pub.

Chinese Agent. Michael Moorcock. Ed. by Howard Sandum. LC 79-96746. (Cock Robin Mystery). 1970. 4.50 o.s.i. (ISBN 0-02-585790-8). Macmillan.

Chinese American Story. Edward W. Ludwig. (Illus.). 32p. (Orig.). (gr. 4-12). 1981. pap. 2.95 (ISBN 0-930504-02-X). Polaris Pr. Postponed.

Chinese Americans. Ed. by Integrated Education Associates Editorial Staff. LC 72-83395. pap. 2.70 (ISBN 0-912008-04-0). Integrated Ed Assoc.

Chinese Americans. Stanford Lyman. (Rose Ser: Ethnic Groups in Comparative Perspective). 1974. pap. text ed. 4.95 (ISBN 0-394-31157-4). Random.

Chinese Amusement: The Lively Plays of Li Yu. Eric Henry. 1980. 23.50 (ISBN 0-208-01837-9, Archon). Shoe String.

Chinese Anarchist Movement. Robert A. Scalapino & George T. Yu. LC 80-23499. (University of California Institute of International Studies, Center for Chinese Studies, Research Ser.). vi, 81p. 1980. Repr. of 1961 ed. lib. bdg. 19.75x (ISBN 0-313-22586-9, SCCM). Greenwood.

Chinese & Indian Architecture. Nelson I. Wu. LC 63-7513. (Great Ages of World Architecture Ser). 1963. 7.95 o.p. (ISBN 0-8076-0210-8); pap. 3.95 o.p. (ISBN 0-8076-0339-2). Braziller.

Chinese & Japanese Cloisonne Enamels. Harry M. Garner. (Illus.). 1962. 41.50 (ISBN 0-8048-0093-6). C E Tuttle.

Chinese & Soviet Aid to Africa. Ed. by Warren Weinstein. LC 74-3512. (Special Studies). (Illus.). 316p. 1975. text ed. 32.50 (ISBN 0-275-09050-7). Praeger.

Chinese & Their Rebellions. T. T. Meadows. (Illus.). 716p. 1972. Repr. of 1856 ed. 55.00x (ISBN 0-7165-2038-9, Pub. by Irish Academic Pr Ireland). Biblio Dist.

Chinese Armorial Porcelain. David S. Howard. 1974. 185.00 (ISBN 0-571-09811-8, Pub. by Faber & Faber). Merrimack Bk Serv.

Chinese Art. LC 76-14077. (Garland Library of the History of Art: Vol.XIV). 1977. lib. bdg. 50.00 (ISBN 0-8240-2424-9). Garland Pub.

Chinese Arts & Crafts. (Illus.). 1973. 35.00 (ISBN 0-8351-0031-6). China Bks.

Chinese Astrology. Paula Delsol. 1976. pap. 2.50 (ISBN 0-446-91800-8). Warner Bks.

Chinese Bandit. Stephen Becker. 1977. pap. 1.95 o.p. (ISBN 0-425-03403-8, Medallion). Berkley Pub.

Chinese Bell Murders. Robert Van Gulik. LC 77-80378. 1977. pap. 3.25 (ISBN 0-226-84862-0). U of Chicago Pr.

Chinese Book of Table Tennis. Ding Shu De et al. LC 80-65996. 1981. 10.95 (ISBN 0-689-11082-0). Atheneum.

Chinese Bronze Mirrors. Milan Rupert & O. J. Todd. (Illus.). 1966. 15.00 o.p. (ISBN 0-8188-0077-1). Paragon.

Chinese Brush Painting for Children. Vickey Aubrey. (Illus.). 32p. (gr. 2 up). 1981. 9.95 (ISBN 0-8149-0851-9). Vanguard.

Chinese Brushwork. Ed. by David Kwo. 200p. 1981. text ed. 46.50 (ISBN 0-8390-0267-X). Allanheld.

Chinese Brushwork: Its History, Aesthetics, & Techniques. Kwo Da-Wei. (Illus.). 220p. 1981. 37.50 (ISBN 0-8390-0267-X). Alanheld & Schram.

Chinese Buddhism: Aspects of Interaction & Reinterpretation. W. Pachow. LC 80-5432. 275p. 1980. lib. bdg. 19.00 (ISBN 0-8191-1090-6); pap. text ed. 10.50 (ISBN 0-8191-1091-4). U Pr of Amer.

Chinese Buddhist Monasteries. Johannes Prip-Moller. (Illus.). 410p. 1981. 65.00 (ISBN 0-85656-034-0). Great Eastern.

Chinese Carpets & Rugs. Adolf Hackmack. LC 77-83943. (Illus.). 1981. 17.50 (ISBN 0-8048-1258-6). C E Tuttle.

Chinese Celadon Wares. 2nd ed. G. M. Gompertz. (Illus.). 1980. 48.00 (ISBN 0-571-18003-5, Pub. by Faber & Faber). Merrimack Bk Serv.

Chinese Ceramics. Harry Garner. LC 75-18991. 1976. 20.00 o.p. (ISBN 0-312-13370-7). St Martin.

Chinese Ceramics from Japanese Collections. Seizo Hayashiya & Henry Trubner. LC 77-1654. (Illus.). 136p. 1977. 19.95 (ISBN 0-87848-049-8). Asia Soc.

Chinese Character Indexes: Vol. 1: Telegraphic Code Index. Vol. 2: Romanization Index. Vol. 3: Radical Index. Vol. 4: Total Stroke Count Index. Vol. 5: Four Corner System Index. Ching-yi Dougherty et al. 1963. 82.50x (ISBN 0-520-00346-2). U of Cal Pr.

Chinese Characteristics. A. H. Smith. (Illus.). 344p. 1972. Repr. of 1900 ed. 29.00x (ISBN 0-7165-2043-5, Pub. by Irish Academic Pr Ireland). Biblio Dist.

Chinese Characteristics. Arthur H. Smith. 342p. 1980. Repr. of 1894 ed. lib. bdg. 40.00 (ISBN 0-89760-849-6). Telegraph Bks.

Chinese Characters, Their Origin, Etymology, History, Classification & Signification. 2nd ed. L. Wieger. Tr. by L. Davrout. 1927. pap. 10.00 (ISBN 0-486-21321-8). Dover.

Chinese Civil Law. V. A. Riasanovsky. (Studies in Chinese Government & Law). 1977. Repr. of 1938 ed. 22.50 (ISBN 0-89093-061-9). U Pubns Amer.

Chinese Civilization & Society: A Sourcebook. Ed. by Patricia B. Ebrey. LC 80-639. 1981. 19.95 (ISBN 0-02-908750-3); pap. text ed. 10.95 (ISBN 0-02-908760-0). Free Pr.

Chinese Classical Prose: The Eight Masters of the T'ang-Sung Period. Tr. by Shih S. Liu from Chinese. LC 79-129782. (Renditions Bk.). (Illus.). 3384p. 1980. 20.00 (ISBN 0-295-95662-3). U of Wash Pr.

Chinese Classical Work Commonly Called the Four Books, 1828. Ssu Shu. Ed. by David Collie. LC 75-122487. 1970. Repr. of 1828 ed. 36.00x (ISBN 0-8201-1079-5). Schol Facsimiles.

Chinese Communism. Robert C. North. (Illus., Orig.). (gr. 9-12). 1966. pap. 2.95 o.p. (ISBN 0-07-047450-8, SP). McGraw.

Chinese Communist Army in Action: The Korean War & Its Aftermath. Alexander L. George. LC 67-12659. 1969. 20.00x (ISBN 0-231-03020-7); pap. 7.50x (ISBN 0-231-08595-8). Columbia U Pr.

Chinese Communist Party in Power, Nineteen Forty-Nine to Nineteen Seventy-Eight. Jacques Guillermaz. LC 76-7593. 1976. 32.50x (ISBN 0-89158-041-7); pap. 14.50x (ISBN 0-89158-348-3). Westview.

Chinese Communist Power & Policy in Xinjiang, 1949-1977. Donald H. McMillen. 1979. lib. bdg. 27.50 o.p. (ISBN 0-89158-452-8). Westview.

Chinese Connection. Pai Ye Loh. 1978. 6.95 o.p. (ISBN 0-8007-0954-3). Revell.

Chinese Connoisseurship. Ed. by Percival David. 1971. 68.00 (ISBN 0-571-09979-3, Pub. by Faber & Faber). Merrimack Bk Serv.

Chinese Constitution: A Study of Forty Years of Constitution-Making in China. P'an Wei-Tung. LC 79-1639. 1981. Repr. of 1945 ed. 25.00 (ISBN 0-88355-942-0). Hyperion Conn.

Chinese Cookbook. Craig Claiborne & Virginia Lee. 1976. pap. 9.95 (ISBN 0-397-01173-3). Lippincott.

Chinese Cookbook. Fu Pei Mei. (Eng. & Chinese.). 1969. deluxe ed. 17.50 (ISBN 0-911268-14-6). Rogers Bk.

Chinese Cookbook. Yamei Tsai. 1978. 9.95 o.p. (ISBN 0-214-20506-1, 8067, Dist. by Arco). Barrie & Jenkins.

Chinese Cookbook, Vol. 2. Fu Pei Mei. 1974. 17.50 (ISBN 0-911268-18-9). Rogers Bk.

Chinese Cooking. Emily Hahn. LC 68-56965. (Foods of the World Ser.). (Illus.). 200p. (gr. 6 up). 1968. lib. bdg. 11.97 (ISBN 0-8094-0062-6, Time-Life). Silver.

Chinese Cooking at Home. Constance D. Chang. (Illus., Orig.). 1977. pap. 4.95 (ISBN 0-87040-408-3). Japan Pubns.

Chinese Cooking for Beginners. Alice Schryver. LC 73-11986. (gr. 7 up). 1974. 6.95 (ISBN 0-396-06875-8). Dodd.

Chinese Cooking for Everyone. Mariko Tsujita & Kyoko Ikeda. (Illus.). 96p. 1980. 4.50 (ISBN 0-86628-003-0). Ridgefield Pub.

Chinese Cooking Jenny Kim's Way. Jenny Kim. LC 78-71036. (Illus.). 1979. pap. 5.95 o.p. (ISBN 0-916076-29-6). Writing.

Chinese Cooking Lessons. Constance D. Chang. LC 76-21508. 1977. 6.95 o.p. (ISBN 0-385-12455-4). Doubleday.

Chinese Cooking Made Easy. Rosy Tseng. LC 63-21064. (Illus.). 1964. bds. 4.95 (ISBN 0-8048-0097-9). C E Tuttle.

Chinese Costume in Transition. A. C. Scott. (Illus., Orig.). 1960. pap. 3.25 (ISBN 0-87830-017-1). Theatre Arts.

Chinese Cultural Revolution. Adrian Hsia. LC 72-3940. 1972. 8.95 o.p. (ISBN 0-8164-9107-0); pap. 3.95 o.p. (ISBN 0-8164-9213-1). Continuum.

Chinese Cut-Out Design Coloring Book: Designs from the World of Nature. Ramona Jablonski. (International Design Library). (Illus.). 48p. 1980. pap. 2.95 (ISBN 0-916144-55-0). Stemmer Hse.

Chinese Domestic Furniture. Gustav Ecke. LC 62-21540. (Illus.). 1962. boxed 59.50 (ISBN 0-8048-0098-7). C E Tuttle.

Chinese Domestic Politics & Foreign Policy in the 1970s. Allen S. Whiting. LC 78-31865. (Michigan Papers in Chinese Studies: No. 36). (Orig.). 1979. pap. text ed. 4.00 (ISBN 0-89264-036-7). U of Mich Ctr Chinese.

Chinese Economy, Ca. Eighteen Seventy to Nineteen Eleven. Albert Feuerwerker. (Michigan Papers in Chinese Studies Ser.: No. 5). (Illus.). 77p. 1969. pap. 4.00 (ISBN 0-89264-005-7). U of Mich Ctr Chinese.

Chinese Education Since the Revolution: Development, Modernization or Revolutionary Communism. Theodore Hsi-en Chen. (Pergamon Policy Studies). Date not set. 25.01 (ISBN 0-08-023861-0). Pergamon.

Chinese Education Under Communism. 2nd ed. Ed. by C. T. Hu. LC 62-20698. 1974. text ed. 9.75 (ISBN 0-8077-2462-9); pap. text ed. 4.25x (ISBN 0-8077-2461-0). Tchrs Coll.

Chinese Encounters. Arthur Miller & Inge Morath. (Illus.). 256p. 1981. pap. 9.95 (ISBN 0-14-005781-1). Penguin.

Chinese-English Dictionary. 8.50 (ISBN 0-685-00818-5). Saphrograph.

Chinese-English, English-Chinese Dictionary, 2 vols. Set. 40.00 (ISBN 0-685-79110-6). Heinman.

Chinese-English Phrase Book for Travellers. John S. Montanare. 200p. 1981. pap. text ed. 4.95 (ISBN 0-471-08298-8). Wiley.

Chinese-English Phrase Book for Travellers. John S. Montanaro. 200p. 1981. pap. text ed. 4.95 (ISBN 0-471-08298-8). Wiley.

Chinese Experience. Raymond Dawson. (Illus.). 1978. 20.00 o.p. (ISBN 0-684-15912-0, ScribT). Scribner.

Chinese Export Porcelain: Standard Patterns & Forms, 1780-1880. H. Schiffer et al. 256p. 1980. 59.85x (ISBN 0-903485-96-6, Pub. by Allan Pubs England). State Mutual Bk.

Chinese Fairy Tales. Tr. by Marie Ponsot from Chinese. (Illus.). (gr. 4-6). 1974. PLB 10.69 o.p. (ISBN 0-307-66820-7, Golden Pr). Western Pub.

Chinese Family & Kinship. Hugh Baker. LC 78-26724. 1979. 20.00x (ISBN 0-231-04768-1). Columbia U Pr.

Chinese Family & Kinship. Hugh R. Baker. 1980. pap. 7.50x (ISBN 0-231-04769-X). Columbia U Pr.

Chinese Folk Toys & Ornaments. 1980. pap. 4.95 (ISBN 0-8351-0735-3). China Bks.

Chinese for Advanced Beginners. Ellie M. Mok & Jean Jofen. LC 80-5492. 110p. (Orig.). 1980. pap. 6.95 (ISBN 0-8044-6506-1). Ungar.

Chinese for Beginners. Ellie M. Mok & Jean Jofen. LC 80-5492. 110p. (Orig.). 1980. pap. 6.95 (ISBN 0-8044-6505-3). Ungar.

Chinese Foreign Policy After Mao, Vol. 1. R. K. Jain. 450p. 1980. text ed. 25.75x (ISBN 0-391-02113-3). Humanities.

Chinese Foreign Policy After Mao: Volume 3, 1979. R. K. Jain. 500p. 1980. text ed. 30.75x (ISBN 0-391-02115-X). Humanities.

Chinese Foreign Policy After Mao: Volume 2, 1978. R. K. Jain. 500p. 1980. text ed. 30.75x (ISBN 0-391-02114-1). Humanities.

Chinese Foreign Policy After the Cultural Revolution: 1966-1977. Robert G. Sutter. LC 77-7018. (Special Studies on China & East Asia Ser.). 1978. lib. bdg. 22.50x (ISBN 0-89158-342-4). Westview.

Chinese Government in Ming Times: Seven Studies. Ed. by Charles O. Hucker. LC 69-14265. (Oriental Culture Ser.: No. 2). 1969. 20.00x (ISBN 0-231-03172-6). Columbia U Pr.

Chinese Household Furniture. George Kates. (Illus.). 1948. pap. 3.50 (ISBN 0-486-20958-X). Dover.

Chinese in America. Betty L. Sung. LC 78-188774. (Illus.). (gr. 4-7). 1972. 6.95 o.s.i. (ISBN 0-02-788670-0). Macmillan.

Chinese in Chicago: The First Hundred Years. Susan L. Moy. 1980. pap. write for info. (ISBN 0-934584-12-5). Pacific-Asian.

Chinese in Indonesia. Ed. by J. A. Mackie. LC 76-139. 296p. 1976. text ed. 12.00x (ISBN 0-8248-0449-X). U Pr of Hawaii.

Chinese in Indonesia, the Philipines & Malaysia. (Minority Rights Group: No. 10). 1972. pap. 2.50 (ISBN 0-89192-099-4). Interbk Inc.

Chinese in Southeast Asia. 2nd ed. Victor Purcell. (Royal Institute of International Affairs Ser.). (Illus.). 640p. 1980. pap. 22.00x (ISBN 0-19-580463-5). Oxford U Pr.

Chinese Inflation, Nineteen Thirty-Seven to Nineteen Forty-Nine. Chou Shun-Hsin. LC 62-18260. 1963. 18.50x (ISBN 0-231-02565-3). Columbia U Pr.

Chinese Jade from Southern California Collections. George Kuwayama. LC 76-43233. (Illus.). 1976. pap. 4.95 o.p. (ISBN 0-87587-074-0). LA Co Art Mus.

Chinese Jade Throughout the Ages: A Review of Its Characteristics, Decoration, Folklore & Symbolism. Stanley C. Nott. LC 62-8839. (Illus.). 1962. 47.50 (ISBN 0-8048-0100-2). C E Tuttle.

Chinese Jades & Other Hardstones. Pierre-F. Schneeberger. Tr. by Katherine Watson from Fr. (Illus.). 1976. 225.00 (ISBN 0-7100-0455-9). Routledge & Kegan.

Chinese Jades: Archaic & Modern. Na Chih-Liang. (Illus.). 1977. 25.00 o.p. (ISBN 0-685-67980-2). Minneapolis Inst Arts.

Chinese Jades from Han to Ch'ing. James C. Watt. LC 80-20115. (Illus.). 236p. 1980. 22.50 (ISBN 0-87848-057-9). Asia Soc.

Chinese Jews: A Compilation of Matters Relating to the Jews of K'ai-feng Fu. abr., 2nd ed. William C. White. 9.95 (ISBN 0-8037-1252-9). Dial.

Chinese Labor Movement, 1919-1927. Jean Chesneaux. Tr. by H. M. Wright. 1968. 25.00x (ISBN 0-8047-0644-1). Stanford U Pr.

Chinese Labour: An Economic & Statistical Survey of the Labour Conditions & Labour Movements in China. Fu-An Fang. LC 78-22780. (Modern Chinese Economy Ser.: Vol. 34). 185p. 1980. lib. bdg. 20.00 (ISBN 0-8240-4282-4). Garland Pub.

Chinese Landscape Painting. Sherman E. Lee. LC 62-11141. (Illus.). 168p. 1962. 15.00x (ISBN 0-910386-02-1, Pub. by Cleveland Mus Art). Ind U Pr.

Chinese Landscape Painting in the Sui & T'ang Dynasties. Michael Sullivan. (Illus.). 1980. 38.50 (ISBN 0-520-03558-5). U of Cal Pr.

Chinese Language. 3rd ed. R. A. Forrest. (Great Language Ser.). 1973. text ed. 19.50x (ISBN 0-571-04815-3). Humanities.

Chinese Language Study in American Higher Education: State of the Art. Peter Eddy et al. (Language in Education Ser.: No. 30). 1980. pap. text ed. 7.95 (ISBN 0-87281-129-8). Ctr Appl Ling.

Chinese Language Today: Features of an Emerging Standard. Paul Kratochvil. (Illus.). 1968. pap. text ed. 6.00x (ISBN 0-09-084651-6, Hutchinson U Lib). Humanities.

Chinese Letters, Seventeen Forty-One. Jean Baptiste De Boyer Argens. (Flowering of the Novel, 1740-1775 Ser: Vol. 4). 1974. lib. bdg. 50.00 (ISBN 0-8240-1103-1). Garland Pub.

Chinese Lineage & Society: Fukien & Kwangtung. M. Freedman. (Monographs on Social Anthropology: No. 33). (Illus.). 206p. 1971. pap. text ed. 10.00x (ISBN 0-391-00199-X, Athlone Pr). Humanities.

Chinese Literature: An Anthology from the Earliest Times to the Present Day. Ed. by William McNaughton. LC 73-75284. 1974. pap. 11.75 (ISBN 0-8048-0882-1). C E Tuttle.

Chinese Literature: Nature Poetry, Vol. 2. Tr. by H. C. Chang from Chinese. LC 73-79265. (Chinese Literature Ser.). 1977. 12.50x (ISBN 0-231-04288-4). Columbia U Pr.

Chinese Literature: Popular Fiction & Drama, Vol. 1. Ed. by H. C. Chang. LC 73-79265. 1973. text ed. 27.50x (ISBN 0-85224-240-9). Columbia U Pr.

Chinese Look at Literature: The Literary Values of Chou Tso-Jen in Relation to the Tradition. David E. Pollard. 1974. 20.00x (ISBN 0-520-02409-5). U of Cal Pr.

Chinese Looking Glass. rev. ed. Dennis Bloodworth. 1980. 15.00 (ISBN 0-374-12241-5); pap. 8.95 (ISBN 0-374-51493-3). FS&G.

Chinese Lyricism: Shih Poetry from the Second to Twelfth Century. Tr. by Burton Watson from Chinese. LC 71-109252. (Companions to Asian Studies). 1971. 16.00x (ISBN 0-231-03464-4); pap. 5.00 (ISBN 0-231-03465-2). Columbia U Pr.

Chinese Mafia. Fenton Bresler. LC 80-5797. (Illus.). 256p. 1981. 12.95 (ISBN 0-8128-2752-X). Stein & Day.

Chinese Man...& the Chinese Woman. John Lewis. (Chinese Word for...Ser). (Illus.). 1977. pap. 3.95 (ISBN 0-8467-0384-X, Pub. by Two Continents). Hippocrene Bks.

Chinese Medicine: New Medicine. Ed. by Frederick F. Kao & John J. Kao. (Illus.). 1977. 9.95 (ISBN 0-88202-174-5). N Watson.

Chinese Micro-Massage. J. Lavier. 1978. pap. 3.95 o.s.i. (ISBN 0-7225-0362-8). Newcastle Pub.

Chinese Military System: An Organizational Study of the Chinese People's Liberation Army. Harvey W. Nelsen. (Special Studies on China & East Asia). (Illus.). 266p. (Orig.). 1981. lib. bdg. 25.00x (ISBN 0-86531-069-6); pap. text ed. 15.00x (ISBN 0-86531-192-7). Westview.

Chinese Mushroom (Volvariella volvacea) Morphology, Cytology, Genetics, Nutrition, & Cultivation. Chang Shu-Ting. (Illus.). 118p. 1972. 8.95 (ISBN 0-295-95743-3, Pub by Chinese Univ Hong Kong). U of Wash Pr.
Chinese Music: An Annotated Bibliography. Fredric Lieberman. LC 72-101135. (A (Bibliographies), No. 1). xii, 158p. (Orig.). 1970. pap. text ed. 7.50x (ISBN 0-913360-02-3). Asian Music Pub.
Chinese Nail Murders. Robert Van Gulik. LC 77-80379. 1977. pap. 3.25 (ISBN 0-226-84863-9). U of Chicago Pr.
Chinese Novel at the Turn of the Century. Ed. by Milena Dolezelova-Velingerova. (Modern East Asian Studies). 1980. 30.00x (ISBN 0-8020-5473-0). U of Toronto Pr.
Chinese of America. Jack Chen. LC 80-7749. (Illus.). 288p. 1981. 15.95 (ISBN 0-06-250140-2, HarpR). Har-Row.
Chinese Opium Wars. Jack Beeching. LC 75-16414. (Illus.). 368p. 1976. 14.95 o.p. (ISBN 0-15-117650-7). HarBraceJ.
Chinese Orange Mystery. Ellery Queen. 1979. 1.75 o.p. (ISBN 0-686-63173-0, Sig). NAL.
Chinese Painting: A Comprehensive Guide. Chow Chien-chiu & Chow L. Chen-ying. (Illus.). 240p. 1980. 45.00 (ISBN 0-89955-139-4, Pub. by Art Bk Co Taiwan). Intl Schol Bk Serv.
Chinese Pavilion Architecture. Werner Blaser. Date not set. 45.00 o.p. (ISBN 0-8038-0043-6). Hastings.
Chinese Perspectives on the Nien Rebellion. Elizabeth J. Perry. 150p. 1981. 18.50 (ISBN 0-87332-191-X). M E Sharpe.
Chinese Poetry: Major Modes & Genres. Wai-Lim Yip. LC 74-76394. 1976. 23.75x (ISBN 0-520-02727-2). U of Cal Pr.
Chinese Political Philosophy. William S. Pott. LC 79-2290. 1981. Repr. of 1925 ed. 13.50 (ISBN 0-88355-966-8). Hyperion Conn.
Chinese Popular Literature & the Child. Dorothea H. Scott. LC 80-10412. 192p. 1980. 15.00 (ISBN 0-8389-0289-8). ALA.
Chinese Porcelain Industry. Michael Dillon. 1981. 27.50x (ISBN 0-7146-3148-5, F Cass Co). Biblio Dist.
Chinese Porcelains from the Ardebil Shrine. 2nd ed. John A. Pope. (Illus.). 496p. 1981. 100.00x (ISBN 0-85667-097-9, Pub. by Sotheby Parke Bernet England). Biblio Dist.
Chinese: Portrait of a People. John Fraser. LC 80-26314. (Illus.). 463p. 1980. 14.95 (ISBN 0-671-44873-0). Summit Bks.
Chinese Reader's Manual. William F. Mayers. LC 68-30660. 1968. Repr. of 1910 ed. 20.00 (ISBN 0-8103-3335-X). Gale.
Chinese Regional Cooking. Kenneth Lo. 1981. pap. 4.95 (ISBN 0-394-73870-5). Pantheon.
Chinese Regional Cooking: Authentic Recipies of the Liang School. Lucille Liang. LC 79-65067. (Illus.). 1979. 12.95 (ISBN 0-8069-0148-9); lib. bdg. 11.69 (ISBN 0-8069-0149-7). Sterling.
Chinese Restaurant Cookbook. Barbara Myers. LC 80-6229. 348p. 1981. 14.95 (ISBN 0-8128-2803-8). Stein & Day.
Chinese Restaurant Experience. Jennie Low & Diane Yee. Ed. by Sharon Silva. LC 80-66946. 192p. 1981. pap. 5.95 (ISBN 0-89395-058-0). Cal Living Bks.
Chinese Revolution. Anthony Weston. Ed. by Malcolm Yapp et al. (World History Ser.). (Illus.). 32p. (gr. 10). 1980. Repr. of 1977 ed. lib. bdg. 5.95 (ISBN 0-89908-139-8); pap. text ed. 1.95 (ISBN 0-89908-114-2). Greenhaven.
Chinese Revolution: A Phase in the Regeneration of a World Power. Arthur N. Holcombe. LC 76-80557. xii, 401p. 1974. Repr. of 1930 ed. 19.00 (ISBN 0-86527-024-4). Fertig.
Chinese Revolution: The Early Stages. 1977. pap. 8.95 set (ISBN 0-8351-0039-1). China Bks.
Chinese Revolutionary, Memoirs 1919-49. Wang Fan-Hsi. Tr. by Gregor Benton. 256p. 1980. 45.00 (ISBN 0-19-211746-7). Oxford U Pr.
Chinese Rhyme-Prose: Poems in the Fu Form from the Han & Six Dynasties Period. Tr. by Burton Watson from Chinese. LC 75-159674. 1971. 12.50x (ISBN 0-231-03553-5); pap. 2.95 o.p. (ISBN 0-231-03554-3). Columbia U Pr.
Chinese-Russian Relations. Michel N. Pavlovsky. Tr. by Ruth Krader from Fr. LC 79-5209. (Illus.). 194p. 1981. Repr. of 1949 ed. 19.00 (ISBN 0-8305-0088-X). Hyperion Conn.
Chinese Sayings. William M. Bueler. LC 79-182059. (YA) 1972. pap. 4.50 (ISBN 0-8048-1018-4). C E Tuttle.
Chinese Seafood Cooking. Stella L. Fessler. 1981. pap. price not set (ISBN 0-452-25265-2, Z5265, Plume). NAL.
Chinese Seals. T. C. Lai. LC 76-7789. (Illus.). 224p. 1976. 10.00 (ISBN 0-295-95517-1). U of Wash Pr.
Chinese Secret Service. Richard Deacon. (Illus.). 544p. 1976. pap. 2.25 o.p. (ISBN 0-345-24901-1). Ballantine.
Chinese Secrets of Longevity. Chuang Shu Chi & Joe Deisher. (Illus.). 126p. (Orig.). 1979. pap. 3.50 o.p. (ISBN 0-686-65533-8). C E Tuttle.
Chinese Secrets of Longevity. Chuang Shu Chih & Joe Deisher. (Illus., Orig.). 1973. pap. 3.50 o.p. (ISBN 0-8048-1338-8, Pub. by Shufunotomo Co Ltd Japan). C E Tuttle.
Chinese Shar-Pei. Paul Strang. 1980. 19.95 (ISBN 0-87714-072-3). Caroline Hse.
Chinese Shari-Pei. Paul D. Strang & Eve C. Olsen. 19.95 (ISBN 0-87714-072-3). Green Hill.
Chinese Snuff Bottles. Lilla S. Perry. LC 60-12196. (Illus.). 1960. 35.00 (ISBN 0-8048-0106-1). C E Tuttle.
Chinese Society in Nineteenth Century Singapore. Lee Poh Ping. (East Asian Historical Monographs). (Illus.). 1978. 19.95x (ISBN 0-19-580384-1). Oxford U Pr.
Chinese Stories from Taiwan, Nineteen Sixty to Nineteen Seventy. Ed. by Joseph S. Lau & Timothy A. Ross. 336p. 1976. 22.50x (ISBN 0-231-04007-5); pap. 10.00x (ISBN 0-231-04008-3). Columbia U Pr.
Chinese Supreme Court Decisions: Relating to General Principles of Civil Law, Obligations & Commercial Law. Tr. by F. T. Cheng from Chinese. 229p. 1979. Repr. of 1923 ed. 22.50 (ISBN 0-89093-065-1). U Pubns Amer.
Chinese Symbols & Superstitions. Harry T. Morgan. LC 74-167079. (Illus.). 192p. 1972. Repr. of 1942 ed. 22.00 (ISBN 0-8103-3069-5). Gale.
Chinese: Their History & Culture, 2 Vols in 1. 4th, rev. ed. Kenneth S. Latourette. 1964. 15.95 o.s.i. (ISBN 0-02-568920-7). Macmillan.
Chinese Thought from Confucius to Mao Tse-Tung. Herrlee G. Creel. LC 53-10054. 1971. pap. 5.95 (ISBN 0-226-12030-9, P394, Phoen). U of Chicago Pr.
Chinese Village: Taitou, Shantung Province. Martin C. Yang. LC 45-4581. 1945. pap. 6.00x (ISBN 0-231-08561-3). Columbia U Pr.
Chinese Walled Cities: A Collection of Maps from Shina Jokaku No Gaiyo. Ed. by Benjamin F. Wallacker et al. (Illus.). 266p. 1979. Repr. of 1940 ed. 50.00 (ISBN 0-295-95698-4, Pub. by Chinese Univ Press Hong Kong). U of Wash Pr.
Chinese Way in Religion. Laurence G. Thompson. (Religious Life of Man Ser.). 1973. pap. 7.95x (ISBN 0-8221-0109-2). Dickenson.
Chinese Weapons. E. T. Werner. Ed. by Pat Alston. (Series 308). (Illus.). 1972. pap. 4.95 (ISBN 0-89750-036-9). Ohara Pubns.
Chinese-Western Comparative Literature & Strategy. Ed. by John J. Deeney. 220p. 1981. 17.50 (ISBN 0-295-95810-3, Pub. by Chinese Univ Hong Kong). U of Wash Pr.
Chinese Women: Yesterday & Today. Florence Ayscough. LC 74-32095. (China in the 20th Century Ser). (Illus.). xiv, 324p. 1975. Repr. of 1937 ed. lib. bdg. 29.50 (ISBN 0-306-70700-4). Da Capo.
Chinese Word for Horse. John Lewis. (Chinese Word for...Ser.). (Illus.). 1977. pap. 3.95 (ISBN 0-8467-0383-1, Pub. by Two Continents). Hippocrene Bks.
Chinese Word for Thief. John Lewis. (Chinese Word for...Ser.). (Illus., Orig.). 1978. pap. 3.95 (ISBN 0-8467-0431-5, Pub. by Two Continents). Hippocrene Bks.
Chinese World. Richard Yang & Edward J. Lazzerini. LC 77-81184. (World of Asia Ser.). (Illus., Orig.). 1978. pap. 3.95 (ISBN 0-88273-504-7). Forum Pr MO.
Chinese Zither Tutor: The Mei-an Ch'in-p'u. Fred Lieberman. 1981. write for info. U of Wash Pr.
Chinesische Landwirtschaft. Wilhelm Wagner. LC 78-74338. (Modern Chinese Economy Ser.: Vol. 15). 659p. 1980. lib. bdg. 72.00 (ISBN 0-8240-4263-8). Garland Pub.
Chingada. Jane L. Brandt. 1980. pap. write for info. PB.
Chingis Khan & the Mongol Empire. Malcolm Yapp. Ed. by Margaret Killingray & Edmund O'Connor. (World History Ser.). (Illus.). 32p. (gr. 10). 1980. Repr. of 1977 ed. lib. bdg. 5.95 (ISBN 0-89908-030-8); pap. text ed. 1.95 (ISBN 0-89908-005-7). Greenhaven.
Chino en el Habla Cubana. Beatriz Varela. LC 79-54025. (Coleccion Polymita). (Illus.). 64p. (Orig., Span.). 1980. pap. 6.95 (ISBN 0-89729-233-2). Ediciones.
Chinoiserie: The Vision of Cathay. Hugh Honour. LC 73-4090. (Icon Editions). (Illus.). 306p. 1973. pap. 6.95x o.s.i. (ISBN 0-06-430039-0, IN-39, HarpT). Har-Row.
Chinto, the Chaparral Cock. Emilie Toepperwein & Fritz Toepperwein. (gr. 4-7). 2.00 (ISBN 0-910722-04-8). Highland Pr.
Chinua Achebe. David Carroll. (World Authors Ser.: Nigeria: No. 101). lib. bdg. 9.95 (ISBN 0-8057-2004-9). Twayne.
Chip Carving. Harris W. Moore. LC 75-19755. (Illus.). 48p. 1976. pap. 1.75 (ISBN 0-486-23256-5). Dover.
Chip, Oh Brother! Vivian Greene. (Illus.). (gr. 3-5). 1979. 2.95 (ISBN 0-531-02510-1); PLB 5.90 s&l (ISBN 0-531-04089-5). Watts.
Chipewa Indians I: Red Lake & Pembina Chippewa. Erminie Wheeler-Voegelin. (American Indian Ethnohistory Ser: North Central & Northeastern Indians). (Illus.). lib. bdg. 42.00 (ISBN 0-8240-0808-1). Garland Pub.
Chipmunk Portrait. B. A. Henisch & H. K. Henisch. LC 78-88029. (Illus.). 98p. 1970. 11.95 (ISBN 0-87601-003-6). Carnation.
Chipmunks. B. Kohn. 1979. pap. 1.50 (ISBN 0-13-133090-X). P-H.
Chipmunk's ABC. Roberta Miller. (Illus.). 24p. (gr. k-1). 1976. PLB 4.57 o.p. (ISBN 0-307-60512-4, Golden Pr). Western Pub.
Chipmunks on the Doorstep. Edwin Tunis. LC 73-13205. (Illus.). (gr. 5-8). 1971. 7.95 o.p. (ISBN 0-690-19044-1, TYC-J); PLB 7.89 (ISBN 0-690-19045-X). T Y Crowell.
Chipper's Choices. Betty Boegehold. (Illus.). 64p. (gr. 6-9). 1981. PLB 6.99 (ISBN 0-698-30725-9). Coward.
Chippewa & Dakota Indians: A Subject Catalog of Books, Pamphlets, Periodical Articles & Manuscripts in the Minnesota Historical Society. Minnesota Historical Society. LC 70-102272. 131p. 1969. pap. 7.50 (ISBN 0-87351-056-9). Minn Hist.
Chippewa Customs. Frances Densmore. LC 79-15400. (Illus.). 204p. 1979. pap. 7.50 (ISBN 0-87351-142-5). Minn Hist.
Chippewa Indians II: Ethnohistory of Mississippi Bands, & Pillager & Winnibigoshish Bands of Chippewa. Harold Hickerson. (American Indian Ethnohistory Ser: North Central & Northeastern Indians). (Illus.). lib. bdg. 42.00 (ISBN 0-8240-0809-X). Garland Pub.
Chippewa Indians III. Harold Hickerson. Ed. by David A. Horr. (American Indian Ethnohistory Ser.). 1978. lib. bdg. 42.00 (ISBN 0-8240-0810-3). Garland Pub.
Chippewa Indians IV: Ethnohistory of Chippewa in Central Minnesota. Harold Hickerson. (American Indian Ethnohistory Ser: North Central & Northeastern Indians). (Illus.). lib. bdg. 42.00 (ISBN 0-8240-0811-1). Garland Pub.
Chippewa Indians: Rice Gatherers of the Great Lakes. Sonia Bleeker. (Illus.). (gr. 3-6). 1955. PLB 6.67 (ISBN 0-688-31167-9). Morrow.
Chippewa Indians V. Erminie Wheeler-Voegelin et al. Ed. by David A. Horr. (American Indian Ethnohistory Ser.). 1978. lib. bdg. 42.00 (ISBN 0-8240-0812-X). Garland Pub.
Chippewa Indians VI. John C. Ewers. Ed. by David A. Horr. (American Indian Ethnohistory Ser.). 1978. lib. bdg. 42.00 (ISBN 0-8240-0813-8). Garland Pub.
Chippewa Indians VII: Findings of Fact, & Opinion. Indian Claims Commission. (American Indian Ethnohistory Ser: North Central & Northeastern Indians). (Illus.). lib. bdg. 42.00 (ISBN 0-8240-0814-6). Garland Pub.
Chippewa Music, 2 vols. Frances Densmore. LC 77-164513. (Illus.). 1972. Repr. of 1913 ed. Set. lib. bdg. 45.00 (ISBN 0-306-70459-5). Da Capo.
Chips from a Wilderness Log. Calvin Rutstrum. LC 77-20847. 256p. 1981. pap. 6.95 (ISBN 0-8128-6124-8). Stein & Day.
Chiricahua. Will Henry. LC 78-38941. (YA) 1972. 6.95 (ISBN 0-397-00887-2). Lippincott.
Chirologia; or the Natural Language of the Hand. Chironomia; or the Art of Manual Rhetoric. John Bulwer. Ed. by James W. Cleary. LC 76-132492. (Landmarks in Rhetoric & Public Address Ser.). 380p. 1974. 19.50x (ISBN 0-8093-0497-X). S Ill U Pr.
Chironomidae-Ecology Systematics Cytology & Physiology: Proceedings. International Symposium on Chironomidae, 7th, Dublin, August 1979. Ed. by D. A. Murray. (Illus.). 380p. 1980. 69.00 (ISBN 0-08-025889-1). Pergamon.
Chiropractic Alternative. Nathaniel Altman. LC 79-93020. 208p. 1981. 10.00 (ISBN 0-87477-132-3). J P Tarcher.
Chiropractic Analysis Through Palpation. F. P. DeGiacomo. Ed. by James McDonnell. (Illus.). 192p. 1980. 12.00 (ISBN 0-938470-00-0). NY Chiro Coll.
Chiropractic Physical & Spinal Diagnosis. Ed. by R. C. Schafer. (Illus.). 578p. 1980. text ed. 30.00 (ISBN 0-936948-00-0). Am Chiro Acad.
Chiropractic Theories: A Synopsis of Scientific Research. Robert A. Leach. LC 79-92761. (Illus.). 300p. 1980. pap. text ed. 16.95 (ISBN 0-935974-00-8). Mid South Sci Pubs.
Chiroptera & Dermoptera of the French Early Eocene. Donald E. Russell et al. (U. C. Publ. in Geological Sciences: Vol. 95). 1973. pap. 7.50x (ISBN 0-520-09423-9). U of Cal Pr.
Chisel-Tooth the Beaver. Joseph W. Lippincott. (Illus.). (gr. 4-6). 1936. 3.95 o.p. (ISBN 0-397-30028-X). Lippincott.
Chisholm Trail. Wayne Gard. (Illus., Orig.). 1954. 13.50 (ISBN 0-8061-0291-8); pap. 6.95 (ISBN 0-8061-1536-X). U of Okla Pr.
Chisholm Trail. Donald E. Worcester. LC 80-12412. xx, 201p. 1981. 14.50 (ISBN 0-8032-4710-9). U of Nebr Pr.
Chisholms: A Novel of the Journey West. Evan Hunter. LC 75-25086. 288p. (YA) 1976. 8.95 o.s.i. (ISBN 0-06-012013-4, HarpT). Har-Row.
Chitin. Riccardo A. Muzzarelli. LC 76-52421. 365p. 1977. text ed. 57.00 (ISBN 0-08-020367-1). Pergamon.
Chitralekha. Bhawati C. Verma. Tr. by Chandra B. Karki. 1966. pap. 2.50 (ISBN 0-88253-198-0). Ind-US Inc.
Chitty Chitty Bang Bang. Fleming. (gr. 3-5). 1980. pap. 1.50 (ISBN 0-590-03428-6, Schol Pap). Schol Bk Serv.
Chitty-Chitty-Bang-Bang. Ian Fleming. (gr. 2-4). 1964. 4.95 (ISBN 0-394-81021-X). Random.
Chitty Chitty Bang Bang. Ian Fleming. 159p. Repr. of 1964 ed. lib. bdg. 8.75x (ISBN 0-88411-983-1). Amereon Ltd.
Chivalric Literature: Essays on Relations Between Literature and Life in the Later Middle Ages. Ed. by Larry D Benson & John Leyerle. LC 80-17514. (Studies in Medieval Culture: XIV). (Illus.). 176p. (Orig.). 1980. pap. 10.80 (ISBN 0-918720-09-5). Medieval Inst.
Chivalrous Society. Georges Duby. Tr. by Cynthia Postan from Fr. LC 74-81431. 1978. 29.50x (ISBN 0-520-02813-9); pap. 4.95 (ISBN 0-520-04271-9). U of Cal Pr.
Chlamydia & Chlamydia-Induced Diseases. Johannes Storz. (Illus.). 376p. 1971. 26.75 (ISBN 0-398-01870-7). C C Thomas.
Chlorinated Insectides, 2 vols. G. T. Brooks. Incl. Vol. 1. Technology & Applications. 249p (ISBN 0-8493-5062-X); Vol. 2. Biological & Environmental Aspects (ISBN 0-8493-5063-8). LC 73-90535. (Uniscience Ser.). 1974. 49.95 ea. CRC Pr.
Chlorine & Hydrogen Chloride. Division of Medical Sciences, Assembly of Life Sciences, National Research Council. LC 76-39940. (Medical & Biological Effects of Environmental Pollutants Ser.). 1976. pap. 10.00 (ISBN 0-309-02519-2). Natl Acad Pr.
Chloroform, Carbon Tetrachloride & Other Halomethanes. Environmental Studies Board. 1978. pap. 8.75 (ISBN 0-309-02763-2). Natl Acad Pr.
Chlorophyll Organization & Energy Transfer in Photosynthesis. Ciba Foundation. (Ciba Foundation Symposium: No. 61). 1979. 42.00 (ISBN 0-444-90044-6, Excerpta Medica). Elsevier.
Chocolate & Chortles. Edwina G. Lashings. 64p. (Orig.). 1975. pap. 1.95 (ISBN 0-686-10979-1). MTM Pub Co.
Chocolate Cocoa and Confectionery: Science & Technology. Bernard W. Minifie. 1970. 29.00 o.p. (ISBN 0-87055-097-7). AVI.
Chocolate, Cocoa & Confectionery: Science & Technology. 2nd ed. Bernard W. Minifie. (Illus.). 1980. lib. bdg. 45.00 (ISBN 0-87055-330-5). AVI.
Chocolate Cookery. Mable Hoffman. LC 78-61007. (Illus.). 1978. pap. 5.95 (ISBN 0-89586-017-1). H P Bks.
Chocolate Fever. Robert K. Smith. 1978. pap. 1.25 (ISBN 0-440-41369-9, YB). Dell.
Chocolate Marshmelephant Sundae. Mike Thaler. 1980. pap. 1.50 (ISBN 0-380-49320-9, 49320, Camelot). Avon.
Chocolate Touch. Patrick S. Catling. LC 78-31100. (Illus.). (gr. 4-6). 1979. Repr. of 1952 ed. 6.50 (ISBN 0-688-22187-4); PLB 6.24 (ISBN 0-688-32187-9). Morrow.
Chocolate Touch. Patrick S. Catling. (Skylark Ser.). 96p. 1981. pap. 1.75 (ISBN 0-553-15075-8). Bantam.
Choctaw Music. Frances Densmore. LC 72-1883. (Music Ser.). (Illus.). 110p. 1972. Repr. of 1943 ed. lib. bdg. 14.00 (ISBN 0-306-70511-7). Da Capo.
Choctaws: A Critical Bibliography. Clara S. Kidwell & Charles Roberts. LC 80-8037. (Newberry Library Center for the History of the American Indian Bibliographical Ser.). 96p. 1980. pap. 3.95 (ISBN 0-253-34412-3). Ind U Pr.
Choderlos De Laclos. Ronald C. Rosbottom. (World Authors Ser.: No. 502 (France)). 1978. 13.95 (ISBN 0-8057-6343-0). Twayne.
Choephoroe. Aeschylus. Tr. by Gilbert Murray. 1923. pap. text ed. 3.95x (ISBN 0-04-882004-0). Allen Unwin.
Choice. Harold Myra. 1980. 9.95 (ISBN 0-8423-0249-2). Tyndale.
Choice Against Chance: An Introduction to Statistical Decision Theory. John Aitchison. LC 70-109505. (Business & Economics Ser). 1970. text ed. 17.95 (ISBN 0-201-00141-1). A-W.
Choice: An Introduction to Economics. 2nd ed. Augustus J. Rogers, 3rd. (Illus.). 258p. 1974. pap. text ed. 11.95 (ISBN 0-13-133223-6). P-H.

Choice & Change: An Introduction to Economics. William C. Dickneider, Jr. & David Kaplan. (Illus.). 1978. pap. text ed. 12.50 (ISBN 0-8299-0165-5); test bank avail. (ISBN 0-8299-0475-1). West Pub.

Choice & Change: An Introduction to the Psychology of Growth. V. O'Connell & A. O'Connell. 1974. pap. 12.95 o.p. (ISBN 0-13-133165-5); wkbk. 5.95 o.p. (ISBN 0-13-133140-X). P-H.

Choice & Change: Essays in Honour of Lucy Mair. Ed. by J. Davis. (London School of Economics Monographs on Social Anthropology Ser: No. 50). 264p. 1974. text ed. 13.50x (ISBN 0-391-00328-3, Athlone Pr). Humanities.

Choice & Change: Psychology of Adjustment, Growth & Creativity. rev. ed. April O'Connell & Vincent O'Connell. (Illus.). 1980. pap. text ed. 14.95 (ISBN 0-13-133066-7); study guide & wrk bk 5.95 (ISBN 0-13-133082-9). P-H.

Choice & Demand. Peter J. Simmons. LC 73-23035. 1974. text ed. 16.95 (ISBN 0-470-79179-9). Halsted Pr.

Choice, Class & Conflict: A Study of Southern Nigerian Factory Workers. Adrian J. Peace. LC 79-12658. (Harvester Studies in African Political Economy.). 1979. text ed. 38.75x (ISBN 0-391-01027-1). Humanities.

Choice, Complexity & Ignorance. B. J. Loasby. LC 75-22558. 1976. 38.50 (ISBN 0-521-21065-8). Cambridge U Pr.

Choice: Handbook of Activities to Motivate Teaching of Elementary Economics. 1975. 6.50 (ISBN 0-89273-120-6). Educ Serv.

Choice of Anglo-Saxon Verse. Compiled by & intro. by Richard Hamer. 207p. (Orig.). 1970. pap. text ed. 5.50x (ISBN 0-571-08765-5). Humanities.

Choice of Attitudes. Gray Burr. LC 69-17790. (Wesleyan Poetry Program: Vol. 44). 1969. 10.00x (ISBN 0-8195-2044-6, Pub. by Wesleyan U Pr); pap. 4.95x (ISBN 0-8195-1044-0). Columbia U Pr.

Choice of Blake's Verse. Robert Blake. Ed. by Kathleen Raines. 1970. pap. 5.95 (ISBN 0-571-09268-3, Pub. by Faber & Faber). Merrimack Bk Serv.

Choice of Burns' Poems & Songs. Robert Burns. Ed. by Sydney G. Smith. 1966. pap. 5.50 (ISBN 0-571-06835-9, Pub. by Faber & Faber). Merrimack Bk Serv.

Choice of Byron's Verse. Lord Byron. Ed. by Douglas Dunn. 1974. pap. 5.95 (ISBN 0-571-10589-0, Pub. by Faber & Faber). Merrimack Bk Serv.

Choice of Catastrophes. Isaac Asimov. 384p. 1981. pap. 6.95 (ISBN 0-449-90048-7, Columbine). Fawcett.

Choice of Chaucer's Verse. Geoffrey Chaucer. Ed. by Nevill Coghill. 1972. pap. 4.95 (ISBN 0-571-09691-3, Pub. by Faber & Faber). Merrimack Bk Serv.

Choice of Clough's Verse. Arthur H. Clough. Ed. by Michael Thorpe. 1969. pap. 5.95 (ISBN 0-571-08685-3, Pub. by Faber & Faber). Merrimack Bk Serv.

Choice of Crimes. Lesley Egan. LC 80-1121. (Crime Club Ser.). 1980. 8.95 (ISBN 0-385-17269-9). Doubleday.

Choice of Dryden's Verse. John Dryden. Ed. by W. H. Auden. 1973. 8.95 (ISBN 0-571-10238-7, Pub. by Faber & Faber); pap. 3.95 (ISBN 0-571-10255-7). Merrimack Bk Serv.

Choice of George Herbert's Verse. Ed. by R. S. Thomas. George Herbert. 1967. pap. 4.95 (ISBN 0-571-08189-4, Pub. by Faber & Faber). Merrimack Bk Serv.

Choice of God. Hubert Van Zeller. 1973. pap. 3.95 (ISBN 0-87243-047-2). Templegate.

Choice of Pope's Verse. Alexander Pope. Ed. by Peter Porter. 1971. 7.50 (ISBN 0-571-09291-8, Pub. by Faber & Faber); pap. 3.95 (ISBN 0-571-09292-6). Merrimack Bk Serv.

Choice of Scottish Verse. Ed. by John MacQueen & Winifred MacQueen. 1972. 8.95 (ISBN 0-571-09532-1, Pub. by Faber & Faber); pap. 4.95 (ISBN 0-571-09686-7). Merrimack Bk Serv.

Choice of Shakespeare's Verse. William Shakespeare. Ed. by Ted Hughes. 1971. 7.95 (ISBN 0-571-09426-0, Pub. by Faber & Faber); pap. 3.95 o.p. (ISBN 0-571-09427-9). Merrimack Bk Serv.

Choice of Sir Walter Raleigh's Verse. Walter Raleigh. Ed. by Robert Nye. 1972. 7.95 (ISBN 0-571-08253-X, Pub. by Faber & Faber); pap. 3.95 (ISBN 0-571-08753-1). Merrimack Bk Serv.

Choice of Southey's Verse. Robert Southey. Ed. by Geoffrey Grigson. 1971. 4.95 o.p. (ISBN 0-571-09055-9, Pub. by Faber & Faber); pap. 3.95 (ISBN 0-571-09056-7). Merrimack Bk Serv.

Choice of Swinburne's Verse. Ed. by Robert Nye. Algernon C. Swinburne. 1973. 7.50 (ISBN 0-571-09260-8, Pub. by Faber & Faber); pap. 2.95 o.p. (ISBN 0-571-09261-6). Merrimack Bk Serv.

Choice of Tennyson's Verse. Alfred L. Tennyson. Ed. by David Cecil. 1971. pap. 3.95 (ISBN 0-571-09184-9, Pub. by Faber & Faber). Merrimack Bk Serv.

Choice of Weapons. Gordon Parks. LC 64-25119. 1966. 9.95 o.s.i. (ISBN 0-06-013281-7, HarpT). Har-Row.

Choice of Whitman's Verse. Walt Whitman. Ed. by Donald Hall. 1968. 4.95 o.p. (ISBN 0-571-08403-6, Pub. by Faber & Faber); pap. 4.95 (ISBN 0-571-08613-6). Merrimack Bk Serv.

Choice of William Morris' Verse. William Morris. Ed. by Geoffrey Grigson. 1969. 7.50 (ISBN 0-686-16375-3, Pub. by Faber & Faber); pap. 3.95 (ISBN 0-571-08980-1). Merrimack Bk Serv.

Choice of Wordsworth's Verse. William Wordsworth. Ed. by R. S. Thomas. 1971. 5.95 o.p. (ISBN 0-571-09258-6, Pub. by Faber & Faber); pap. 3.95 (ISBN 0-571-09259-4). Merrimack Bk Serv.

Choice Readings. Ruth Vaughn. LC 63-7338. (Orig.). 1962. pap. 0.80 (ISBN 0-8054-9912-1). Broadman.

Choice Sequences: A Chapter of Intuitionistic Mathematics. A. S. Troelstra. (Oxford Logic Guides Ser.). 1977. 21.00x (ISBN 0-19-853163-X). Oxford U Pr.

Choices. Corinne Gerson. (Orig.). 1980. pap. 1.75 (ISBN 0-505-51476-1). Tower Bks.

Choices. Nancy Toder. LC 80-20836. 320p. (Orig.). 1980. pap. 6.00 (ISBN 0-930436-05-9). Persephone.

Choices & Decisions: A Guidebook for Constructing Values. Michael Bargo, Jr. LC 79-67019. 164p. 1980. pap. 12.00 (ISBN 0-88390-153-6); facilitator's manual with guidebook 25.00 (ISBN 0-88390-152-8). Univ Assocs.

Choices & Decisions: Economics & Society. new ed. Educational Research Council of America. (Challenges of Our Time Ser.). (Orig.). (gr. 7). 1972. pap. text ed. 9.32 (ISBN 0-205-05035-2, 805035X); tchrs'. guide 6.60 (ISBN 0-205-05036-0, 8050368). Allyn.

Choices: Coping Creatively with Personal Change. Frederic Flach. LC 77-22923. 1977. 8.95 o.p. (ISBN 0-397-01234-9). Lippincott.

Choices for Tomorrow. Gerald P. Cosgrave. 1978. pap. text ed. 4.25x (ISBN 0-8077-8065-0, Guidance Center). Tchrs Coll.

Choir Ideas. Flora E. Breck. (Interlude Bks). 1971. pap. 1.95 o.p. (ISBN 0-8010-0545-0). Baker Bk.

Choirboys. Joseph Wambaugh. pap. 2.95 (ISBN 0-440-11188-9). Dell.

Choiseul Marble. W. Kendrick Pritchett. (U. C. Publ. in Classical Studies: Vol. 5). 1970. pap. 7.50x (ISBN 0-520-09051-9). U of Cal Pr.

Cholera, Fever & English Medicine, 1825 - 1865. Margaret Pelling. (Historical Monographs). 1978. text ed. 29.95x (ISBN 0-19-821872-9). Oxford U Pr.

Cholesterol: Chemistry, Biochemistry, & Pathology. Ed. by Robert P. Cook. 1958. 55.00 o.s.i. (ISBN 0-12-187350-1). Acad Pr.

Cholesterol, Children, & Heart Disease: An Analysis of Alternatives. Donald M. Berwick et al. (Illus.). 416p. 1980. 32.95x (ISBN 0-19-502669-1). Oxford U Pr.

Cholesterol Control Gram Counter. W. I. Kaufman. (Orig.). 1975. pap. 1.25 o.p. (ISBN 0-515-04936-0). Jove Pubns.

Cholesterol Counter. Elizabeth Weiss & Rita Wolfson. (Health Ser.). (Orig.). 1973. pap. 1.50 (ISBN 0-515-05689-8, P3208). Jove Pubns.

Choline & Acetylcholine: Handbook of Chemical Assay Methods. Ed. by Israel Hanin. LC 73-79289. 246p. 1974. 24.50 (ISBN 0-911216-51-0). Raven.

Choline & Lecithin in Brain Disorders. Ed. by Andre Barbeau et al. LC 78-68608. (Nutrition & the Brain Ser.: Vol. 5). 1979. text ed. 47.50 (ISBN 0-89004-366-3). Raven.

Cholinergic Mechanisms. Ed. by P. Waser. LC 74-14485. 1975. 45.00 (ISBN 0-89004-009-5). Raven.

Cholinergic Synapse: Proceedings. International Conference on the Synapse, Czechoslovakia, May, 1978. Ed. by S. Tucek et al. LC 79-577. (Progress in Brain Research Ser.: Vol. 49). 1979. 92.75 (ISBN 0-444-80105-7, North Holland). Elsevier.

C.H.O.M.P.S. Crumne. (gr. 3-5). 1980. pap. 1.50 (ISBN 0-590-30528-X, Schol Pap). Schol Bk Serv.

Chomsky: Selected Readings. Ed. by J. P. Allen & Paul Van Buren. 166p. 1981. pap. 6.95 (ISBN 0-19-437046-1). Oxford U Pr.

Chon-Ji of Tae Kwon Do Hyung. Jhoon Rhee. Tr. by Roberto Alvarez. LC 74-120124. (Series 102). (Illus., Sp. & Eng.). 1970. pap. text ed. 5.95 (ISBN 0-89750-000-8). Ohara Pubns.

Chonroid Bone, Secondary Cartilage & Metaplasia. W. A. Beresford. LC 80-13411. (Illus.). 360p. (Orig.). 1980. text ed. 42.50 (ISBN 0-8067-0261-3). Urban & S.

Choogoowarra: Australian Sheep Station. John Kiddell. LC 79-165575. (gr. 3-6). 1972. 4.95g o.s.i. (ISBN 0-02-750300-3). Macmillan.

Choose Once Again. Ed. by Julius J. Finegold & William N. Thetford. LC 76-20363. (Illus.). 112p. 1981. 8.95 (ISBN 0-89087-285-6). Celestial Arts.

Choosing a Nursing Home: The Problems & Their Solutions. Thomas A. Routh. 172p. 1970. text ed. 11.75 (ISBN 0-398-01617-8). C C Thomas.

Choosing a Sports Camp for Your Child. Gregg T. Weinlein. (Illus.). 1980. cancelled (ISBN 0-8092-7376-4); pap. 6.95 (ISBN 0-8092-7375-6). Contemp Bks.

Choosing an Automated Library System: A Planning Guide. Joseph R. Matthews. LC 80-17882. 128p. 1980. 11.00 (ISBN 0-8389-0310-X). ALA.

Choosing & Caring for Garden Shrubs. Ray Edwards. pap. 4.50 (ISBN 0-7153-7902-X). David & Charles.

Choosing & Changing: A Guide to Self Reliance. Richard Grossman. 1978. 7.95 o.p. (ISBN 0-525-07940-8). Dutton.

Choosing & Managing Information Systems for Public Administration. G. Norris & W. Ewart. 1979. text ed. 19.25x (ISBN 0-566-00244-2, Pub. by Gower Pub Co England). Renouf.

Choosing Books for Children. Peter Hollindale. 1974. 9.95 o.p. (ISBN 0-236-15482-6, Pub. by Paul Elek). Merrimack Bk Serv.

Choosing Books for Children: A Commonsense Guide. Betsy Hearne. LC 80-66203. 228p. 1981. 8.95 (ISBN 0-440-01930-3). Delacorte.

Choosing College Major in Education. 10.95 (ISBN 0-679-50957-7); pap. 5.95 (ISBN 0-679-50958-5). McKay.

Choosing Evaluation Techniques. H. Spitze & M. Griggs. LC 75-32848. 1976. pap. 3.50 (ISBN 0-686-15326-X, 261-08424). Home Econ Educ.

Choosing Techniques for Teaching & Learning. 2nd ed. H. Spitze. LC 78-68514. 1979. pap. 2.50 (ISBN 0-686-14992-0, 261-08402). Home Econ Educ.

Choosing the Best Form for Your Poem: An Illustrated Guide to Fifteen Noteworthy Verse Forms. J. David Andrews. 92p. (gr. 6-12). 1979. pap. 6.50; pap. text ed. 5.50. Planetary Pr.

Choosing the College for You. Robert B. Ewen. LC 75-25794. (Career Concise Guides Ser.). (Illus.). 72p. (gr. 8 up). 1976. PLB 6.45 (ISBN 0-531-00290-X). Watts.

Choosing the President. League of Women Voters Education Fund. 108p. 1980. pap. 1.95 (ISBN 0-8407-5726-3). Nelson.

Choosing the President: 1980 Edition. League of Women Voters Education Fund. (Illus.). 1980. pap. 1.95 (ISBN 0-89959-100-0, 420). LWV US.

Choosing the Right College. Lester J. Schwartz. 128p. Date not set. pap. 4.95 (ISBN 0-553-01276-2). Bantam.

Choosing to Work. Leonard Cohen. 1979. case bdg. 11.95 (ISBN 0-8359-0764-3); pap. 6.95 (ISBN 0-8359-0762-7); instrs'. manual avail. Reston.

Chopin. Bernard Gavoty. Tr. by Martin Sokolinsky. LC 77-3966. (Illus.). 1977. encore edition 5.95 o.p. (ISBN 0-684-16354-3, ScribT). Scribner.

Chopin: An Index of His Works in Chronological Order. 2nd ed. Maurice J. Brown. LC 70-39498. (Music Ser.). 1972. Repr. of 1960 ed. 22.50 (ISBN 0-306-70500-1). Da Capo.

Chopin: His Life & Times. Ates Orga. (Illus.). 1978. 16.95 (ISBN 0-8467-0415-3, Pub. by Two Continents); pap. 5.95 (ISBN 0-8467-0416-1). Hippocrene Bks.

Chopin: Man & His Music. James G. Huneker. Ed. by Herbert Weinstock. (Illus.). 1966. pap. 3.50 (ISBN 0-486-21687-X). Dover.

Chopin Preludes Opus. Frederick F. Chopin. Ed. by Thomas Higgins. (Critical Scores Ser). 1974. 7.95x (ISBN 0-393-02161-0); pap. 4.95x (ISBN 0-393-09699-8). Norton.

Chopin, Preludes, Opus 28. Ed. by Thomas Higgins. (Illus.). 101p. 1974. 7.95x (ISBN 0-393-02161-0); pap. 4.95x (ISBN 0-393-09699-8). Norton.

Chopin: The Man & His Music. Herbert Weinstock. (Music Ser.). (Illus.). xiv, 336p. 1981. Repr. of 1949 ed. lib. bdg. 27.50 (ISBN 0-306-76081-9). Da Capo.

Chopper Bunch. Jay Schleifer. Ed. by Thomas J. Mooney. (Pal Paperbacks Ser., Kit A). (Illus., Orig.). (gr. 7-12). 1976. pap. text ed. 1.25 (ISBN 0-8374-3492-0). Xerox Ed Pubns.

Chopper Cycle. E. Radlauer & R. S. Radlauer. LC 79-180239. (Sports Action Bks). (Illus.). 48p. (gr. 3 up). 1972. PLB 5.90 o.p. (ISBN 0-531-02033-9). Watts.

Choral Conducting: A Symposium. Ed. by Harold A. Decker & Julius Herford. LC 72-94347. (Illus.). 320p. 1973. 18.50 (ISBN 0-13-133355-0). P-H.

Choral Experience: Literature, Materials, & Methods. Ray Robinson & Allen Winold. 1976. text ed. 14.95x scp (ISBN 0-06-161419-X, HarpC). Har-Row.

Choral Music Education. Paul F. Roe. LC 77-100403. (Music Ser). 1970. ref. ed. 18.50 (ISBN 0-13-133348-8). P-H.

Choral Music of the Church. Elwyn A. Wienandt. (Music Reprint Ser.). xi, 494p. 1980. Repr. of 1965 ed. lib. bdg. 32.50 (ISBN 0-306-76002-9). Da Capo.

Choral Tradition. rev. ed. Percy M. Young. 400p. 1981. pap. 8.95 (ISBN 0-393-00058-3). Norton.

Chord Dictionary. Albert DeVito. LC 75-40685. 1980. 3.95 (ISBN 0-934286-01-9). Kenyon.

Chord Encyclopedia. Albert DeVito. LC 75-43441. 1980. 4.95 (ISBN 0-934286-02-7). Kenyon.

Chordates. R. McNeill Alexander. LC 74-76580. (Illus.). 496p. 1975. 65.50 (ISBN 0-521-20472-0); pap. 18.95x (ISBN 0-521-09857-2). Cambridge U Pr.

Chordates. Alexander R. McNeill. (Illus.). 500p. Date not set. text ed. price not set (ISBN 0-521-23658-4); pap. text ed. price not set (ISBN 0-521-28141-5). Cambridge U Pr.

Choriocarcinoma & Related Gestational Trophoblastic Tumors in Women. Roy Hertz. LC 75-31481. 1978. 19.50 (ISBN 0-89004-086-9). Raven.

Chorionic Gonadotropin. Ed. by Sheldon J. Segal. 485p. 1981. 42.50 (ISBN 0-306-40563-6, Plenum Pr). Plenum Pub.

Chorti (Mayan) Texts: I. John G. Fought. LC 72-80380. (Folklore & Folklife Ser). 592p. 1973. 18.00x (ISBN 0-8122-7667-1). U of Pa Pr.

Chorus in Sopocles Tragedies. R. W. B. Burton. 312p. 1980. 48.00x (ISBN 0-19-814374-5). Oxford U Pr.

Chosen. Lee Amber. 1978. pap. 2.98 o.s.i. (ISBN 0-88449-072-6). Vision Hse.

Chosen. Chaim Potok. 1978. pap. 2.50 (ISBN 0-449-24200-5, Crest). Fawcett.

Chosen Days: Celebrating Jewish Festivals in Poetry & Art. David Rosenberg. LC 79-7906. (Illus.). 224p. 1980. 14.95 (ISBN 0-385-14365-6). Doubleday.

Chosen for Children. 3rd ed. Ed. by M. Crouch & A. Ellis. 1977. 15.50x (ISBN 0-85365-349-6, Pub. by Lib Assn England). Oryx Pr.

Chosen for Riches. Bob Hendren. LC 77-25775. (Journey Bks.). 1978. 2.35 (ISBN 0-8344-0096-0). Sweet.

Chosen Highway. Lady Blomfield. Ed. by David Hofman. LC 67-16026. (Illus.). 7.95 o.p. (ISBN 0-87743-015-2, 7-31-07); pap. 4.95 o.p. (ISBN 0-87743-037-3, 7-31-08). Baha'i.

Chosen Light. John Montague. LC 71-81498. 69p. 1970. 6.50 (ISBN 0-8040-0040-9). Swallow.

Chosen to Serve: The Deacon. Andrew A. Jumper. LC 61-18257. (Orig.). 1961. pap. 3.00 (ISBN 0-8042-3912-6). John Knox.

Chosen Twelve Plus One. Clarence E. Macartney. LC 80-17881. (Illus.). 124p. 1980. 39.95 (ISBN 0-930014-43-X); ltd. ed. 200.00 (ISBN 0-930014-52-9). Multnomah.

Chou. John McCook Roots. LC 74-27588. 1978. 8.95 o.p. (ISBN 0-385-03804-6). Doubleday.

Chow Chows. Beverly Pisano. (Illus.). 125p. 2.95 (ISBN 0-87666-702-7, KW-089). TFH Pubns.

Choy Lay Fut Kung-Fu. Leo T. Fong. Ed. by Pat Alston. LC 70-181999. (Series 307). (Illus.). 1972. pap. text ed. 6.95 (ISBN 0-89750-035-0). Ohara Pubns.

Chrestomathie de la Langue Francaise au Quinzieme Siecle. Ed. by P. Rickard. LC 74-12976. 464p. 1976. 115.00 (ISBN 0-521-20685-5). Cambridge U Pr.

Chrestomathie de l'Ancien Francais (VIII-XV Siecles) 12th rev. ed. K. Bartsch. 1969. 14.25 (ISBN 0-02-841100-5). Hafner.

Chretien de Troyes. L. T. Topsfield. 300p. Date not set. 49.50 (ISBN 0-521-23361-5). Cambridge U Pr.

Chris Evert. Jay H. Smith. LC 75-8739. (New Creative Education Superstar Bks.). (Illus.). 32p. (gr. 3-9). 1975. PLB 5.95 (ISBN 0-87191-439-5); pap. 2.95 (ISBN 0-89812-176-0). Creative Ed.

Chris Evert: Princess of Tennis. Julian May. LC 75-28936. (Sports Close-up Ser.). (gr. 3-9). 1975. PLB 5.95 o.p. (ISBN 0-913940-35-6); pap. 2.50 o.p. (ISBN 0-89686-001-9). Crestwood Hse.

Chris Evert: Women's Tennis Champion. Dorothy C. Schmitz. LC 77-70891. (Pros Ser.). (Illus.). (gr. 2). 1977. PLB 6.45 (ISBN 0-913940-64-X). Crestwood Hse.

Chrisitan Family Almanac. Margot K. Hover & Monica E. Breidenbach. 128p. (Orig.). 1980. pap. 9.95 (ISBN 0-697-01740-0). Wm C Brown.

Christ. Piet Schoonenberg. LC 74-127873. 1971. 8.95 (ISBN 0-8164-1006-2). Crossroad NY.

Christ & Baha'u'llah. George Townshend. LC 68-168. 1966. 5.50 (ISBN 0-85398-016-0, 7-31-09, Pub. by G Ronald England); pap. 2.00 o.s.i. (ISBN 0-85398-005-5, 7-31-10). Baha'i.
Christ & Christmas, Poem. Mary B. Eddy. (Illus.). 12.50 (ISBN 0-686-00511-2). First Church.
Christ & His Church. Larry Christenson. (Trinity Bible Ser.). 1973. pap. 4.95 spiral wkbk. (ISBN 0-87123-550-1, 240550). Bethany Fell.
Christ & Power. Martin Hengel. Tr. by Everett R. Kalin from Ger. LC 76-62608. 96p. (Orig.). 1977. pap. 3.25 (ISBN 0-8006-1256-6, 1-1256). Fortress.
Christ & Spirit in the New Testament. B. Lindars & S. S. Smalley. LC 72-91367. 300p. 1974. 63.00 (ISBN 0-521-20148-9). Cambridge U Pr.
Christ & the Crowds. James E. Carter. 1981. 3.25 (ISBN 0-8054-5181-1). Broadman.
Christ & the Kingdom: What Scripture Says About Living in the Kingdom of God. A. M. Hunter. 120p. 1980. pap. 3.95 (ISBN 0-89283-092-1). Servant.
Christ & the Patriarchs. Marcus Von Wellnitz. LC 80-83035. 400p. 1981. 6.95 (ISBN 0-88290-164-8, 2045). Horizon Utah.
Christ & the World of Thought. 2nd ed. Daniel Lamont. 309p. 1935. text ed. 6.50 (ISBN 0-567-02160-2). Attic Pr.
Christ at Corinth. rev. ed. Gussie Lambert. pap. 3.95 (ISBN 0-89315-008-8). Lambert Bk.
Christ Book: What Did He Really Say? Christopher Hills. Ed. by Norah Hills. LC 80-5865. (Illus.). 204p. 1980. text ed. 10.95 (ISBN 0-916438-37-6). Univ of Trees.
Christ-Centered Family. Raymond T. Brock. (Radiant Life Ser.). 1977. pap. 1.95 (ISBN 0-88243-903-0, 02-0903); teacher's ed 2.50 (ISBN 0-88243-173-0, 32-0173). Gospel Pub.
Christ Commission. Og Mandino. 272p. 1981. pap. 2.75 (ISBN 0-553-14515-0). Bantam.
Christ, Faith & History. S. W. Sykes & J. P. Clayton. LC 70-176257. (Cambridge Studies in Christology). (Illus.). 280p. 1972. 44.00 (ISBN 0-521-08451-2); pap. text ed. 10.95x (ISBN 0-521-29325-1). Cambridge U Pr.
Christ in Christian Tradition: From the Apostolic Age to Chalcedon, Vol. 1. rev. ed. Aloys Grillmeier. Tr. by John S. Bowden from Ger. LC 75-13456. 451p. 1975. 28.00 (ISBN 0-8042-0492-6). John Knox.
Christ in Concrete. Pietro di Donato. LC 39-10762. 320p. 1975. 8.95 (ISBN 0-672-52161-X); pap. 5.95 (ISBN 0-672-52187-3). Bobbs.
Christ in Eastern Christian Thought. John Meyendorff. LC 75-31977. Orig. Title: Christ Dans la Theologie Byzantine. 248p. 1975. pap. 6.95 (ISBN 0-913836-27-3). St Vladimirs.
Christ in His Sanctuary. Ellen G. White. LC 70-94869. (Dimension Ser.). 1969. pap. 5.95 (ISBN 0-8163-0128-X, 03254-0). Pacific Pr Pub Assn.
Christ in Jesus. Stanley B. Marrow. LC 68-16666. (Orig.). 1968. pap. 1.95 (ISBN 0-8091-1521-2, Deus). Paulist Pr.
Christ in the Psalms. Brian McNeil. 90p. 1980. pap. 2.95 (ISBN 0-8091-2341-X). Paulist Pr.
Christ in Your Shoes. Buckner Fanning. LC 74-117305. 1970. 3.50 o.p. (ISBN 0-8054-1913-6). Broadman.
Christ Is Alive. Michel Quoist. LC 71-131101. 1972. pap. 1.95 (ISBN 0-385-09484-1, Im). Doubleday.
Christ Is in Our Midst: Letters from a Russian Monk. John Skhi-Igumen. Tr. by Esther Williams from Rus. LC 80-10530. 168p. (Orig.). 1980. pap. 4.95 (ISBN 0-913836-64-8). St Vladimirs.
Christ Legends. Selma Lagerlof. 1977. 8.95 (ISBN 0-903540-06-1, Pub. by Floris Books). St George Bk Serv.
Christ Life. Albert B. Simpson. LC 80-69301. 96p. pap. 1.75 (ISBN 0-87509-291-8). Chr Pubns.
Christ Lore: Being the Legends, Traditions, Myths, Symbols, Customs, & Superstitions of the Christian Church. Frederick W. Hackwood. LC 69-16064. (Illus.). 1971. Repr. of 1902 ed. 18.00 (ISBN 0-8103-3528-X). Gale.
Christ of Faith & the Jesus of History: A Critique of Schleiermacher's The Life of Jesus. David F. Strauss. Tr. & intro. by Leander E. Keck. LC 75-37152. (Lives of Jesus Ser.). 288p. 1976. pap. 9.95 (ISBN 0-8006-1273-6, 1-1273). Fortress.
Christ of the Covenants. O. Palmer Robertson. 385p. (Orig.). 1981. pap. 7.50 (ISBN 0-8010-7699-4). Baker Bk.
Christ of the Mount. E. Stanley Jones. (Festival Ser.). 336p. 1981. pap. 2.45 (ISBN 0-687-06925-4). Abingdon.
Christ Story. William Corlett & John Moore. LC 79-15687. (Questions Ser.). 1980. 8.95 (ISBN 0-87888-150-6). Bradbury Pr.
Christ the Center: A New Translation. new ed. Dietrich Bonhoeffer. LC 78-4747. (Harper's Ministers Paperback Library Ser.). 1978. pap. 3.95 (ISBN 0-06-060815-3, RD 285, HarpR). Har-Row.
Christ: The Christian Experience in the Modern World. Edward Schillebeeck. 900p. 1980. 29.50 (ISBN 0-8245-0136-5). Crossroad NY.
Christ: The Fulfillment of the Law & Prophets. Bales. pap. 3.95 (ISBN 0-89315-009-6). Lambert Bk.
Christ the Lord. Gerard S. Sloyan. pap. 0.95 (ISBN 0-385-00620-9, E6, Echo). Doubleday.
Christ the Savior. Swami Prajnanananda. 1.25 o.p. (ISBN 0-87481-627-0). Vedanta Pr.
Christ the Way: The Christology of Guerric of Igny. John Morson. (Cistercian Studies: N0.25). 1978. 11.95 (ISBN 0-87907-825-1). Cistercian Pubns.
Christabel. Amanda H. Douglass. 1978. pap. 2.25 (ISBN 0-505-51310-2). Tower Bks.
Christabel: A Brief Critical History & Reconsideration. Michael D Patrick et al. (Salzburg Studies in English Literature, Romantic Reassessment: No. 11). 118p. (Orig.). 1973. pap. text ed. 25.00x (ISBN 0-391-01494-3). Humanities.
Christabel's Room. Abigail Clement. 176p. 1977. pap. 1.25 o.p. (ISBN 0-449-13820-8, GM). Fawcett.
Christable As Dream Reverie. Susan M. Luther. (Salzburg Studies: Romantic Reassessment, Ser.: No. 61). 1976. pap. text ed. 25.00x (ISBN 0-391-01464-1). Humanities.
Christendom: A Short History of Christianity & Its Impact on Western Civilization, Vol. 1. rev. ed. Roland H. Bainton. (Illus.). pap. 5.50x (ISBN 0-06-130131-0, TB131, Torch). Har-Row.
Christening Pagan Mysteries: Erasmus in Pursuit of Wisdom. Marjorie O. Boyle. (Erasmus Studies). 168p. 1981. 15.00x (ISBN 0-8020-5525-7). U of Toronto Pr.
Christening: The Making of Christians. Mark Searle. 185p. (Orig.). 1980. pap. text ed. 6.50 (ISBN 0-8146-1183-4). Liturgical Pr.
Christentum am Roten Meer, Vol. 2. Franz Altheim & Ruth Stiehl. 1973. 170.55x (ISBN 3-11-003791-2). De Gruyter.
Christian Agnostic. Leslie D. Weatherhead. 1972. Repr. of 1965 ed. 3.50 o.p. (ISBN 0-687-06977-7, Apex). Abingdon.
Christian Anthropology & Ethics. James M. Childs, Jr. LC 77-78626. 192p. 1978. pap. 5.95 (ISBN 0-8006-1316-3, 1-1316). Fortress.
Christian Art in Asia. W. A. Dyrness. 1979. pap. text ed. 11.50x (ISBN 0-391-01157-X). Humanities.
Christian at the Crossroads. Karl Rahner. Tr. by Jeremy Moiser from Ger. 250p. 1976. 5.95 (ISBN 0-8164-4712-8). Crossroad NY.
Christian Baptism. John Murray. pap. 2.50 (ISBN 0-87552-343-9). Presby & Reformed.
Christian Baptism, Feet Washing & the Lord's Supper. H. M. Riggle. 264p. 3.50. Faith Pub Hse.
Christian Blessedness (with) Reflections Upon a Late Essay Concerning Human Understanding. John Norris. Ed. by Rene Wellek. LC 75-11241. (British Philosophers & Theologians of the 17th & 18th Centuries Ser.). 1978. Repr. of 1690 ed. lib. bdg. 42.00 (ISBN 0-8240-1793-5). Garland Pub.
Christian Calendar & the Gregorian Reform. Peter Archer. 1941. 20.00 o.p. (ISBN 0-8232-0001-9). Fordham.
Christian Capitalism. Arthur F. Hallam. 182p. (Orig.). 1981. pap. 14.95 (ISBN 0-938770-00-4). Capitalist Pr OH.
Christian Catalogue. McCollister. LC 77-29136. 1981. 12.50 (ISBN 0-8246-0226-9). Jonathan David.
Christian: Celebrate Your Sexuality. Dwight Hervey Small. 224p. 1974. 7.95 o.p. (ISBN 0-8007-0661-7). Revell.
Christian Church (Disciples of Christ) in Florida: Its History & Development. John C. Updegraff. 384p. 1981. write for info. (ISBN 0-89305-034-2). Anna Pub.
Christian Church: Its Rise & Progress. H. M. Riggle. 488p. 5.00. Faith Pub Hse.
Christian Churches at the Crossroads. Ben Coe. 1980. pap. write for info. (ISBN 0-87808-178-X). William Carey Lib.
Christian Churches at the Crossroads. Frwd. by Donald McGavran. 160p. (Orig.). 1980. pap. write for info. (ISBN 0-87808-178-X). William Carey Lib.
Christian Converts & Social Protest in Meiji Japan. Irwin Scheiner. LC 74-94981. (Center for Japanese & Korean Studies, UC Berkeley). 1970. 18.50x (ISBN 0-520-01585-1). U of Cal Pr.
Christian Counseling & Occultism. Kurt E. Koch. LC 65-23118. 1972. pap. 5.95 (ISBN 0-8254-3010-0). Kregel.
Christian Counsellor. Charles E. Cobb. 3.00 o.p. (ISBN 0-89225-062-3). Gospel Advocate.
Christian Counselor's Starter Packet. J. Adams. 12.50 o.p. (ISBN 0-87552-015-4). Presby & Reformed.
Christian Couple. Larry Christenson & Nordis Christenson. LC 77-24085. 1977. pap. 3.95 (ISBN 0-87123-051-8); 0.95 (ISBN 0-87123-046-1, 210046). Bethany Fell.
Christian Criticism in the Twentieth Century. Norman R. Cary. (National University Publications Literary Criticism Ser.). 1976. 11.50 (ISBN 0-8046-9104-5, Natl U). Kennikat.
Christian Critique of Art & Literature. C. Seerveld. 1976. pap. 3.95 (ISBN 0-88958-004-9). Wedge Pub.
Christian Democracy in France. R. E. Irving. 1973. text ed. 27.50x o.p. (ISBN 0-04-320085-0). Allen Unwin.
Christian Dietrich Grabbe. Roy C. Cowen. (World Authors Ser.: Germany: No. 206). lib. bdg. 10.95 (ISBN 0-8057-2396-X). Twayne.
Christian Discourses. Soren Kierkegaard. Tr. by W. Lowrie. 1971. pap. 5.95 (ISBN 0-691-01973-8). Princeton U Pr.
Christian Doctrine. John S. Whale. 1941. 19.95 (ISBN 0-521-06774-X); pap. 5.95x (ISBN 0-521-09642-1). Cambridge U Pr.
Christian Doctrine of Man. H. Wheeler Robinson. 392p. Repr. of 1926 ed. 10.00x (ISBN 0-567-22219-5). Attic Pr.
Christian Doctrine: Teachings of the Christian Church. Shirley C. Guthrie, Jr. (Orig.). 1969. pap. 5.95 (ISBN 0-8042-9051-2). John Knox.
Christian Education for the Local Church. Herbert W. Byrne. 14.95 (ISBN 0-310-22230-3). Zondervan.
Christian Education Handbook. Ed. by Bruce P. Powers. 1981. pap. 7.95 (ISBN 0-8054-3229-9). Broadman.
Christian Education Public Schools: A Teacher's Interpretation. Elizabeth M. Machen. 1978. 5.00 o.p. (ISBN 0-682-48990-5). Exposition.
Christian England: Its Story to the Reformation. David L. Edwards. (Illus.). 356p. 1981. 19.95 (ISBN 0-19-520229-5). Oxford U Pr.
Christian Ethics & Economics: The North South Conflict, Concilium 140. Ed. by Dietmar Mieth & Jacques Pohier. (New Concilium 1980). 128p. 1980. pap. 5.95 (ISBN 0-8245-4773-X). Crossroad NY.
Christian Ethics-Sources of the Living Tradition. 2nd ed. Ed. by Waldo Beach & H. Richard Niebuhr. 550p. 1973. text ed. 16.95 (ISBN 0-8260-0786-4). Wiley.
Christian Experience, Concilium 139. Ed. by Casiano Floristan & Christian Duquoc. (New Concilium 1980). 128p. 1980. pap. 5.95 (ISBN 0-8245-4772-1). Crossroad NY.
Christian Faith & Other Faiths: The Christian Dialogue with Other Religions. 2nd ed. Stephen Neill. 1970. 10.95 (ISBN 0-19-213305-5); pap. 6.95x (ISBN 0-19-283011-2, OPB196). Oxford U Pr.
Christian Faith in a Neo-Pagan Society: Proceedings of the Fellowship of Catholic Scholars. Ed. by Paul L. Williams. LC 81-80229. 128p. (Orig.). 1981. pap. 5.95 (ISBN 0-937374-02-4); pap. text ed. 4.50 (ISBN 0-937374-03-2). NE Bks.
Christian Faith: The Challenge of the Call. Ronald J. Wilkins. 72p. 1978. pap. 3.00 (ISBN 0-697-01684-6); tchr's. manual 3.50 (ISBN 0-697-01688-9). Wm C Brown.
Christian Family Almanac. Margot K. Hover & Monica E. Breidenbarn. 128p. 1980. pap. 9.95 (ISBN 0-697-01740-0). Wm C Brown.
Christian Family Classics. LC 74-13327. 128p. (gr. 5-8). 1974. pap. 1.25 o.p. (ISBN 0-912692-47-2). Cook.
Christian Family in Action. Mike Phillips. LC 77-1887. 1977. pap. 2.95 (ISBN 0-87123-085-2, 210085). Bethany Fell.
Christian Future. Eugen Rosenstock-Huessy. pap. 3.50 (ISBN 0-912148-10-1). Argo Bks.
Christian Handbook. L. Davis. 5.00 o.p. (ISBN 0-8062-1218-7). Carlton.
Christian Healing Rediscovered. Roy Lawrence. LC 80-7470. 128p. (Orig.). 1980. pap. 3.95 (ISBN 0-87784-621-9). Inter-Varsity.
Christian Higher Education in Changing China. William Fenn. 256p. 1976. 5.95 o.p. (ISBN 0-8028-1662-2). Eerdmans.
Christian History & Interpretation. William R. Farmer et al. 1967. 42.50 (ISBN 0-521-04981-4). Cambridge U Pr.
Christian Home Birth: A Preparation for Spirit, Soul & Body. Joy Young. (Illus.). 208p. (Orig.). 1980. pap. 6.00x (ISBN 0-686-28082-2). J Young.
Christian Hope. John Macquarrie. 1978. 7.95 (ISBN 0-8164-0388-0). Crossroad NY.
Christian Hope & the Future. Stephen H. Travis. Ed. by I. Howard Marshall. LC 80-7471. (Issues in Contemporary Theology Ser.). 160p. (Orig.). 1980. pap. 4.95 (ISBN 0-87784-463-1). Inter-Varsity.
Christian Humanism of Flannery O'Connor. David Eggenschwiler. LC 79-179560. 156p. 1972. 9.95x (ISBN 0-8143-1463-5). Wayne St U Pr.
Christian Iconography: A Study of Its Origins. Andre Grabar. LC 67-31114. (A. W. Mellon Lectures in the Fine Arts Bollingen Ser: No. XXXV: 10). (Illus.). 432p. (Orig.). 1980. 30.00x (ISBN 0-691-09716-X); pap. 8.95 (ISBN 0-691-01830-8). Princeton U Pr.
Christian Imagination: Essays on Literature & the Arts. Ed. by Leland Ryken. 344p. (Orig.). 1981. pap. 9.95 (ISBN 0-8010-7702-8). Baker Bk.
Christian in Complete Armour. William Gurnall. 1979. 22.95 (ISBN 0-85151-196-1). Banner of Truth.
Christian in Mid-Life. Jerry White & Mary White. LC 80-83388. (Orig.). 1980. pap. 4.95 (ISBN 0-89109-448-2). NavPress.
Christian in the Making. Rodney Sargent. (Orig.). 1981. pap. price not set. NavPress.
Christian in Today's World: Inner City to World Community. Lewis Smythe. 1974. 6.50 o.p. (ISBN 0-682-48055-X). Exposition.
Christian Knowledge of God. H. P. Owen. 1969. text ed. 34.00x (ISBN 0-485-11107-1, Athlone Pr). Humanities.
Christian Leaders of the Eighteenth Century: Includes Whitefield, Wesley, Grimshaw, Romaine, Rowlands, Berridge, Venn, Walker, Harvey, Toplady, & Fletcher. J. C. Ryle. 1978. pap. 5.45 (ISBN 0-85151-268-2). Banner of Truth.
Christian Life. Karl Barth. Ed. by Geoffrey W. Bromiley. LC 80-39942. 328p. 1981. 14.95 (ISBN 0-8028-3523-6). Eerdmans.
Christian Life Patterns: The Psychological Challenges & Religious Invitations of Adult Life. Evelyn E. Whitehead & James D. Whitehead. LC 78-22543. 1979. 9.95 (ISBN 0-385-15130-6). Doubleday.
Christian Living. Stephen F. Bayne, Jr. (Orig.). 1956. pap. 4.95 (ISBN 0-8164-2007-6, SP5). Crossroad NY.
Christian Living: The Challenge of Response. 80p. 1978. pap. 3.00 o.p. (ISBN 0-697-01686-2); tchrs' manual 3.50 o.p. (ISBN 0-697-01689-7). Wm C Brown.
Christian Living Today: A Personal Credo. Terry J. Tekippe. LC 77-14805. 1977. pap. 2.45 (ISBN 0-8091-2060-7). Paulist Pr.
Christian Married Love: Five Contributions. Malcolm Muggeridge et al. Tr. by Sergia Englund & Erasmo Leiva. 150p. (Orig.). 1981. pap. price not set (ISBN 0-89870-008-6). Ignatius Pr.
Christian Maturity Manual. rev. ed. David Wilkerson. LC 79-169590. 1977. 2.95 (ISBN 0-8307-0496-5, 5200121). Regal.
Christian Message in a Non-Christian World. Hendrik Kraemer. LC 56-10732. 1961. 12.95 (ISBN 0-8254-3002-X). Kregel.
Christian Ministry. Charles Bridges. 1980. 11.95 (ISBN 0-85151-087-6). Banner of Truth.
Christian Ministry & the Social Order: Lectures Delivered in the Course in Pastoral Functions at the Yale Divinity School, 1908-1909. Charles S. MacFarland. 1913. 27.50x o.p. (ISBN 0-686-51352-5). Elliots Bks.
Christian Morgenstern. Erich P. Hofacker. (World Authors Ser.: No. 508 (Germany)). 1978. 12.50 (ISBN 0-8057-6349-X). Twayne.
Christian Morgenstern's Galgenlieder (Gallows Songs) bilingual ed. Christian Morgenstern. Tr. & intro. by Max Knight. (Illus.). (gr. 9 up). 1963. 12.95x (ISBN 0-520-00883-9, CAL 101); pap. 4.95 (ISBN 0-520-00884-7). U of Cal Pr.
Christian Mother Goose Treasury: Part II of the Original Christian Mother Goose Book. Marjorie A. Decker. LC 80-69167. (Three Part Series: Vol. II). (Illus.). 112p. (gr. k-4). 1980. PLB 10.95 (ISBN 0-933724-01-2). CMG Prods.
Christian, Non-Christian Dialogue: The Vision of Robert C. Zaehner. Richard L. Schebera. LC 78-64369. 1978. pap. text ed. 9.00 (ISBN 0-8191-0629-1). U Pr of Amer.
Christian Non-Resistance. Adin Ballou. LC 70-121104. (Civil Liberties in American History Ser). 1970. Repr. of 1910 ed. lib. bdg. 29.50 (ISBN 0-306-71980-0). Da Capo.
Christian Occasions: A Photographic Study of Unusual Styles of Religion in American Life. Alan Whitman. LC 77-76286. 1979. pap. 6.95 (ISBN 0-385-12597-6, Dolp). Doubleday.
Christian Pacifism. Mike Snow. 1981. write for info. (ISBN 0-913408-67-0). Friends United.
Christian Pacifism & History. G. Nuttall. pap. 1.25 (ISBN 0-8164-9235-2). Crossroad NY.
Christian Pacifism in History. G. Nuttall. pap. 1.25 (ISBN 0-8164-9235-2). Continuum.
Christian Path of Intuitive Wisdom. Irvin Holmes. 80p. (Orig.). 1981. pap. 3.50 (ISBN 0-87516-408-0). De Vorss.
Christian Paths of Self Acceptance. R. H. Bonthius. 20.00x o.p. (ISBN 0-231-09863-4). Columbia U Pr.
Christian Perfection. Francois Fenelon. Ed. by Charles F. Whiston. Tr. by Mildred W. Stillman from Fr. LC 75-22545. 224p. 1976. pap. 2.95 (ISBN 0-87123-083-6, 200083). Bethany Fell.
Christian Perfection. Mahan. pap. 3.95 o.p. (ISBN 0-686-12855-9). Schmul Pub Co.
Christian Perspectives on Dating & Marriage. David Chadwell. 1980. pap. 3.95 (ISBN 0-89137-523-6). Quality Pubns.

Christian Persuader. Ford Leighton. LC 66-22043. 1977. pap. 4.95 (ISBN 0-06-062679-8, RD 157, HarpR). Har-Row.

Christian Philosopher: A Collection of the Best Discoveries in Nature, with Religious Improvements. Cotton Mather. LC 68-29082. 1968. Repr. of 1721 ed. 33.00x (ISBN 0-8201-1033-7). Schol Facsimiles.

Christian Poet in Paradise Lost. William G. Riggs. 1972. 16.50x (ISBN 0-520-02081-2). U of Cal Pr.

Christian Political Option. B. Goudzwaard. 1973. pap. 2.75 o.p. (ISBN 0-686-11981-9). Wedge Pub.

Christian Political Options. C. Den Hollander. 1980. pap. 9.00x o.p. (ISBN 0-686-27478-4). Radix Bks.

Christian Political Theory & Church Politics in the Mid-Twelfth Century: The Ecclesiology of Gratian's Decretum. Stanley Chodorow. (UCLA Center for Medieval & Renaissance Studies). 1972. 26.50x (ISBN 0-520-01850-8). U of Cal Pr.

Christian Prayer. Ladislaus Boros. 1976. 5.95 (ISBN 0-8164-1199-9). Crossroad NY.

Christian Prayer Through the Centuries. Josef Jungmann. LC 78-61729. Orig. Title: Christliches Beten. 1978. pap. 2.95 (ISBN 0-8091-2167-0). Paulist Pr.

Christian Realism & Liberation Theology: Practical Theologies in Conflict. Dennis P. McCann. LC 80-23163. 256p. (Orig.). 1981. pap. 9.95 (ISBN 0-88344-086-5). Orbis Bks.

Christian Religion. Georg W. Hegel. Ed. by Georg Lasson. Tr. by Peter C. Hodgson from Ger. LC 79-424. (American Academy of Religion, Texts & Translation Ser.: No. 2). Orig. Title: Vorlesungen Uber Die Philosophie der Religion. 1979. 13.50 (ISBN 0-89130-276-X, 010202); pap. 9.00 (ISBN 0-89130-351-0). Scholars Pr Ca.

Christian Religion in Its Doctrinal Expression. Edgar Y. Mullins. 7.95 o.p. (ISBN 0-8170-0042-9). Judson.

Christian Religious Education: Sharing Our Story & Vision. Thomas H. Groome. LC 80-7755. 288p. 1980. 12.95 (ISBN 0-06-063491-X, HarpR). Har-Row.

Christian Revolutionary: John Milton. Hugh M. Richmond. 1975. 16.50x (ISBN 0-520-02443-5). U of Cal Pr.

Christian Rohlfs: Watercolors, Drawings & Prints. Tr. by David Wilson from German. 80p. 1968. 5.00 (ISBN 0-88397-018-X). Intl Exhibit Foun.

Christian Science. Walter Martin. 1957. pap. 1.25 (ISBN 0-87123-064-X, 210064). Bethany Fell.

Christian Society & the Crusades, 1198-1229: Sources in Translation, Including the Capture of Damietta. Ed. by Edward Peters. LC 78-163385. (Middle Ages Ser). 1971. 7.50x (ISBN 0-8122-7644-2); pap. 4.95x (ISBN 0-8122-1024-7, Pa Paperbks). U of Pa Pr.

Christian Spirituality: A Theological History from the New Testament to Luther & St. John of the Cross. Rowan Williams. LC 80-82190. 193p. 1980. 15.00 (ISBN 0-8042-0660-0); pap. 7.50 (ISBN 0-8042-0508-6). John Knox.

Christian Sunday: A Biblical & Historical Study. Roger T. Beckwith & Wilfrid Stott. (Canterbury Ser.). 192p. 1980. pap. 4.95 (ISBN 0-8010-0784-4). Baker Bk.

Christian Symbols & How to Use Them. Sr. Justina Knapp. LC 74-8172. (Illus.). 164p. 1975. Repr. of 1935 ed. 20.00 (ISBN 0-8103-4050-X). Gale.

Christian Theistic Ethics. Cornelius Van Til. syllabus 4.50 (ISBN 0-87552-478-8). Presby & Reformed.

Christian Theology. Emery Bancroft. Pref. by Ronald B. Mayers. 1976. 12.95 (ISBN 0-310-20440-2). Zondervan.

Christian Theology: A Case Method Approach. Ed. by Robert A. Evans & Thomas D. Parker. LC 76-9963. 1976. 10.00 o.p. (ISBN 0-06-062251-2, HarpR); pap. 5.95x (ISBN 0-06-062252-0, RD 176, HarpR). Har-Row.

Christian Theology of Judaism. Clemens Thoma. Tr. by Helga Croner & Lawrence Frizzell. LC 80-82252. (Studies in Judaism & Christianity). 212p. 1980. pap. 7.95 (ISBN 0-8091-2310-X). Paulist Pr.

Christian Tradition, a History of the Development of Doctrine: The Spirit of Eastern Christendom (600-1700, Vol. 2. Jaroslav Pelikan. LC 79-142042. 1977. pap. 7.50 (ISBN 0-226-65373-0, P738, Phoen). U of Chicago Pr.

Christian Tradition: A History of the Development of Doctrine, Vol. 1: Emergence of the Catholic Tradition, 100-600. Jaroslav Pelikan. LC 79-142042. 1971. 20.00 (ISBN 0-226-65370-6). U of Chicago Pr.

Christian Tradition in Modern British Verse Drama: The Poetics of Sacramental Time. William V. Spanos. 1967. 22.00 o.p. (ISBN 0-8135-0554-2). Rutgers U Pr.

Christian Unity: An Exposition of Ephesians 4: 1-16. D. Martyn Lloyd-Jones. 280p. 1981. 9.95 (ISBN 0-8010-5607-1). Baker Bk.

Christian View of Man. J. Gresham Machen. pap. 1.95 o.p. (ISBN 0-686-12511-8). Banner of Truth.

Christian View of Men & Things. Gordon H. Clark. (Twin Brooks Ser.). 325p. 1981. pap. 8.95 (ISBN 0-8010-2466-8). Baker Bk.

Christian View of the World. George J. Blewett. 1912. 32.50x (ISBN 0-685-89741-9). Elliots Bks.

Christian Vogt: Photographs. Christian Vogt. (Living Photographers Ser.). (Illus.). 1981. 35.00 (ISBN 0-686-69478-3, Pub. by Roto-Vision). Norton.

Christian Way: A Book of Instructions & Devotions for Members of the Episcopal Church. Frank D. Gifford. (Orig.). pap. 3.25 (ISBN 0-8192-1033-1). Morehouse.

Christian Wholeness. Thomas A. Langford. LC 78-58011. 1979. pap. 3.50x (ISBN 0-8358-0383-X). Upper Room.

Christian World Mission: Today & Tomorrow. J. Herbert Kane. 240p. 1981. 9.95 (ISBN 0-8010-5426-5). Baker Bk.

Christian Year; Its Purpose & Its History. Walker Gwynne. LC 74-89269. xiv, 143p. 1972. Repr. of 1917 ed. 20.00 (ISBN 0-8103-3814-9). Gale.

Christian Year: Thoughts in Verse for the Sundays & Holidays Throughout the Year. John Keble. LC 70-167019. (Illus.). 291p. 1975. Repr. of 1896 ed. 20.00 (ISBN 0-8103-4095-X). Gale.

Christian Zen. William Johnston. 1974. pap. 3.95 o.p. (ISBN 0-06-090368-6, CN368, CN). Har Row.

Christian Zen: A Way of Meditation. 2nd ed. William Johnston. LC 80-8430. (Illus.). 144p. 1981. pap. 4.95 (ISBN 0-06-064198-3, RD 343, HarpR). Har-Row.

Christianica. Christianica Center. LC 74-13005. (Illus.). 1975. 6.50 (ISBN 0-911346-02-3). Christianica.

Christianismo...y Nada Mas. C. S. Lewis. Tr. by Julio Orozco from Eng. LC 77-85609. 216p. (Orig., Span.). 1977. pap. 3.50 (ISBN 0-89922-096-7). Edit Caribe.

Christianity Among the Arabs in Pre-Islamic Times. J. Spencer Trimingham. (Arab Background Ser). (Illus.). 1979. text ed. 30.00x (ISBN 0-582-78081-0). Longman.

Christianity & Classical Culture: A Study of Thought & Action from Augustus to Augustine. Charles N. Cochrane. 1957. pap. 7.95 (ISBN 0-19-500207-5, GB). Oxford U Pr.

Christianity & History. Herbert Butterfield. 1950. 5.95 o.p. (ISBN 0-684-12423-8, ScribT). Scribner.

Christianity & Islam: A Battle for the True Image of Man. Rudolf Frieling. 1978. 8.95 (ISBN 0-903540-11-8, Pub. by Floris Bks). St George Bk Serv.

Christianity & Life. James V. Schall. LC 79-89759. 130p. (Orig.). 1981. pap. write for info. (ISBN 0-89870-004-3). Ignatius Pr.

Christianity & Naturalism: Essays in Criticism, Second Series. Robert Shafer. 1926. 11.50x (ISBN 0-686-51353-3). Elliots Bks.

Christianity & Occult Mysteries of Antiquity. Rudolf Steiner. LC 72-175057. (Illus.). 256p. 1972. pap. 6.95 (ISBN 0-8334-1719-3). Steinerbks.

Christianity & Other Religions: Selected Readings. Ed. by John Hick & Brian Hebblethwaite. LC 80-2383. 256p. 1981. pap. 6.95 (ISBN 0-8006-1444-5, 1-1444). Fortress.

Christianity & Paradox: Critical Studies in Twentieth-Century Theology. Ronald W. Hepburn. LC 68-17550. 1968. pap. 3.50 (ISBN 0-672-63723-5). Bobbs.

Christianity & Political Philosophy. Frederick D. Wilhelmsen. LC 77-22754. 243p. 1978. 14.50 (ISBN 0-8203-0431-X). U of Ga Pr.

Christianity & Real Life. William E. Diehl. LC 76-7860. 128p. 1976. pap. 3.95 (ISBN 0-8006-1231-0, 1-1231). Fortress.

Christianity & Reincarnation. Rudolf Frieling. 1977. pap. 7.95 (ISBN 0-903540-05-3, Pub. by Floris Books). St George Bk Serv.

Christianity & Social Order. William Temple. 1977. 5.95 (ISBN 0-8164-0348-1). Crossroad NY.

Christianity & Socialism. J. B. Metz & J. P. Jossua. (Conciliums Ser.: Vol. 105). 1978. pap. 4.95 (ISBN 0-8164-2148-X). Crossroad NY.

Christianity & the Encounter of the World Religions. Paul J. Tillich. LC 63-7508. 1963. 12.50x (ISBN 0-231-02602-1); pap. 3.00 (ISBN 0-231-08555-9). Columbia U Pr.

Christianity & the French Revolution. Alphonse Aulard. 1966. 15.00 (ISBN 0-86527-025-2). Fertig.

Christianity & the Shona. M. W. Murphree. LC 68-18053. (Monographs on Social Anthropology Ser: No. 36). 1969. text ed. 12.50x (ISBN 0-485-19536-4, Athlone Pr). Humanities.

Christianity & the World Order. E. R. Norman. 1979. 9.95 (ISBN 0-19-215510-5); pap. 4.95 (ISBN 0-19-283019-8). Oxford U Pr.

Christianity & World Issues. T. B. Maston. 1957. 5.95 o.s.i. (ISBN 0-02-581790-6). Macmillan.

Christianity As Mystical Fact & the Mysteries of Antiquity. Rudolf Steiner. 1972. 9.75 (ISBN 0-85440-252-7); pap. 6.95 (ISBN 0-910142-04-1). Anthroposophic.

Christianity As Old Creation or the Gospel. Matthew Tindal. Ed. by Rene Wellek. LC 75-11256. (British Philosophers & Theologians of the 17th & 18th Centuries Ser.). 1978. lib. bdg. 42.00 (ISBN 0-8240-1806-0). Garland Pub.

Christianity Challenges the University. Ed. by Peter Wilkes. 108p. 1981. pap. 3.95 (ISBN 0-87784-474-7). Inter Varsity.

Christianity Confronts Culture. Marvin Mayers. (Contemporary Evangelical Perspectives Ser.). 8.95 (ISBN 0-310-28891-6). Zondervan.

Christianity for the Tough-Minded. Ed. & intro. by John W. Montgomery. LC 73-4842. 300p. 1973. kivar 5.95 (ISBN 0-87123-076-3, 210079). Bethany Fell.

Christianity in European History. William Clebsch. 1979. 15.95 (ISBN 0-19-502471-0); pap. text ed. 4.95x (ISBN 0-19-502472-9). Oxford U Pr.

Christianity in the World: Its Status & Future. pap. 1.90 (ISBN 0-912552-28-X). MARC.

Christianity Is Christ. W. Griffith Thomas. (Shepherd Illustrated Classics). (Illus.). 200p. Date not set. pap. 5.95 (ISBN 0-87983-238-X). Keats.

Christianity Is Christ. W. Griffith Thomas. (Shepherd Illustrated Classics Ser.). (Illus.). 200p. 1979. pap. 5.95 (ISBN 0-87983-238-X). Keats.

Christianity Is Jewish. Edith Schaeffer. 1975. pap. 2.95 (ISBN 0-8423-0242-5). Tyndale.

Christianity, Islam, & the Negro. Edward Blyden. Ed. by C. Fyfe. 1967. 24.50x (ISBN 0-85224-085-6, Pub. by Edinburgh U Pr Scotland). Columbia U Pr.

Christianity Not Mysterious. John Toland. Ed. by Rene Wellek. LC 75-11257. (British Philosophers & Theologians of the 17th & 18th Centuries Ser.). 1978. lib. bdg. 42.00 (ISBN 0-8240-1807-9). Garland Pub.

Christianity, Social Tolerance, & Homosexuality. John Boswell. LC 79-11171. 1980. 27.50 (ISBN 0-226-06710-6). U of Chicago Pr.

Christianity Through the Thirteenth Century. Ed. by Marshall W. Baldwin. 15.00x o.s.i. (ISBN 0-8027-2003-X). Walker & Co.

Christians & Jews: Concilium Ser.: Religion in the Seventies. Ed. by Hans Kung & Walker Kasper. (Vol. 98). 1976. pap. 4.95 (ISBN 0-8164-2095-5). Crossroad NY.

Christians & Jews in the Ottoman Empire, Vol. 1: The Central Lands. Ed. by Benjamin Braude & Bernard Lewis. LC 80-11337. 1981. text ed. 40.00x (ISBN 0-8419-0519-3). Holmes & Meier.

Christians & Jews in the Ottoman Empire, Vol. 2: The Arabic-Speaking Lands. Ed. by Benjamin Braude & Bernard Lewis. LC 80-11337. 1981. text ed. 30.00x (ISBN 0-8419-0520-7). Holmes & Meier.

Christians for Christians Inscriptions of Phrygia. Elsa Gibson. LC 78-12688. (Harvard Theological Studies: No. 32). 1978. pap. 7.50 (ISBN 0-89130-262-X, 020032). Scholars Pr Ca.

Christians' God. Stephen Neill. 1980. 1.25 (ISBN 0-686-28774-6). Forward Movement.

Christians Grieve Too. Donald Howard. 1980. pap. 1.45 (ISBN 0-85151-315-8). Banner of Truth.

Christian's Guide Great Interest. William Guthrie. pap. 1.95 o.p. (ISBN 0-686-12510-X). Banner of Truth.

Christians in the Shadow of the Kremlin. Anita Deyneka & Peter Deyneka, Jr. LC 74-17730. (Illus.). 112p. 1975. pap. 1.95 (ISBN 0-912692-48-0). Cook.

Christian's Knowledge of God. W. W. Bryden. 5.50 (ISBN 0-227-67434-0). Attic Pr.

Christians Only: A Study in Prejudice. Heywood Broun & George Britt. LC 73-19688. (Civil Liberties in American History Ser). 333p. 1974. Repr. of 1931 ed. lib. bdg. 29.50 (ISBN 0-306-70599-0). Da Capo.

Christians Will Go Through the Tribulation. Jim McKeever. LC 78-55091. (Illus.). 1978. 10.95 (ISBN 0-931608-01-5); pap. 5.95 (ISBN 0-931608-02-3). Omega Pubns OR.

Christians with Secular Power. LC 80-8048. (Laity Exchange). 144p. (Orig.). Date not set. pap. 4.95 (ISBN 0-8006-1389-9, 1-1389). Fortress. Postponed.

Christians: World Citizens. Ed. by Margaret A. Nash. 1965. pap. 0.75 o.p. (ISBN 0-377-82551-4). Friend Pr.

Christiarisme en Orient. Hajjar French. 9.00x (ISBN 0-685-85421-3). Intl Bk Ctr.

Christie's Review of the Season 1977. 1978. 45.00 (ISBN 0-02-525260-7). Macmillan.

Christie's Review of the Season 1978. Christie's. Ed. by John Herbert. (Illus.). 1979. 45.00 (ISBN 0-02-525270-4). Macmillan.

Christina. Caroline Arnett. (Coventry Romance Ser.: No. 65). 224p. 1980. pap. 1.75 (ISBN 0-449-50096-9, Coventry). Fawcett.

Christina Rossetti. Ralph A. Bellas. (English Authors Ser.: No. 201). 1977. lib. bdg. 9.95 (ISBN 0-8057-6671-5). Twayne.

Christina Rossetti. Lona M. Packer. (Illus.). 1963. 25.00x o.p. (ISBN 0-520-00980-0). U of Cal Pr.

Christina Stead. R. G. Geering. (World Authors Ser.: Australia: No. 95). lib. bdg. 12.50 (ISBN 0-8057-2858-9). Twayne.

Christina's Desire. Blakely St. James. LC 77-88263. (Christina Van Bell Ser.: No. 7). 1978. pap. 2.25 (ISBN 0-87216-734-8). Playboy Pbks.

Christina's Ecstasy. Blakely St. James. LC 80-82855. (Christina Ser.). 256p. (Orig.). 1981. pap. 2.50 (ISBN 0-87216-782-8). Playboy Pbks.

Christinas Escape. Blakely St. James. LC 80-85112. (Christina Van Bell Ser.). 256p. (Orig.). 1981. pap. 2.50 (ISBN 0-87216-820-4). Playboy Pbks.

Christina's Nights. Blakely St. James. LC 77-72969. (Christina Van Bell Ser.: No. 6). (Orig.). 1977. pap. 2.25 (ISBN 0-87216-739-9). Playboy Pbks.

Christina's Obsession. Blakely St. James. LC 81-80095. 256p. (Orig.). 1981. pap. 2.75 (ISBN 0-87216-853-0). Playboy Pbks.

Christina's Sins. Blakely St. James. LC 80-81522. (Christina Ser.). 256p. 1980. pap. 2.25 (ISBN 0-87216-729-1). Playboy Pbks.

Christine: A Search for Christine Granville. Madeleine Masson. 1978. 19.95 (ISBN 0-241-89274-0, Pub. by Hamish Hamilton England). David & Charles.

Christman Programs for the Church, No. 14. Ed. by Judith Sparks. 64p. (Orig.). 1981. pap. 2.75 (ISBN 0-87239-437-9, 8614). Standard Pub.

Christmas. Barbara Cooney. LC 67-18510. (Holiday Ser.). (Illus.). (gr. k-3). 1967. PLB 7.89 (ISBN 0-690-19201-0, TYC-J). T Y Crowell.

Christmas. Cass R. Sandak. (gr. 2-4). 1980. PLB 7.90 (ISBN 0-531-04147-6). Watts.

Christmas. Alana Willoughby. Ed. by Alton Jordan. (Holidays Ser.). (Illus.). (gr. k-3). 1977. PLB 3.50 (ISBN 0-89868-025-5, Read Res); pap. text ed. 1.75 boxed (ISBN 0-89868-058-1, Read Res). ARO Pub.

Christmas, Vol. 47. Ed. by Randolph Haugan. LC 32-30914. 1977. 8.95 (ISBN 0-8066-8951-X, 17-0115); pap. 4.75 (ISBN 0-8066-8950-1, 17-0114). Augsburg.

Christmas: An American Annual of Christmas Literature & Art, Vol. 45. Ed. by Randolf E. Haugan. LC 32-30914. (Illus.). 68p. (Orig.). 1975. 8.95 (ISBN 0-8066-8946-3, 17-0110); pap. 4.75 (ISBN 0-8066-8945-5, 17-0109). Augsburg.

Christmas: An American Annual of Christmas Literature & Art, Vol. 46. Ed. by Randolph E. Haugan. LC 32-30914. 1976. 8.95 (ISBN 0-8066-8948-X, 17-0113); pap. 4.75 (ISBN 0-8066-8947-1, 17-0112). Augsburg.

Christmas: An American Annual of Christmas Literature & Art, Vol. 49. Ed. by Randolph E. Haugan. LC 32-30914. (Illus.). 64p. 1979. 8.95 (ISBN 0-8066-8955-2, 17-0119); pap. 4.75 (ISBN 0-8066-8954-4, 17-0118). Augsburg.

Christmas: An American Annual of Christmas & Art, Vol. 48. Ed. by Randolph E. Haugan. LC 32-30914. (Illus.). 1978. 8.95 (ISBN 0-8066-8953-6, 17-0117); pap. 4.75 (ISBN 0-8066-8952-8, 17-0116). Augsburg.

Christmas & Christmas Lore. Thomas G. Crippen. LC 69-16067. (Illus.). x, 223p. 1972. Repr. of 1923 ed. 24.00 (ISBN 0-8103-3029-6). Gale.

Christmas Bells Are Ringing. Sara Brewton & John E. Brewton. (Illus.). (gr. 4-6). 1964. 4.95g o.s.i. (ISBN 0-02-712790-7). Macmillan.

Christmas Book. Moira Eastman & Wendy Poussard. LC 80-68368. (Illus.). 40p. 1980. 5.95 (ISBN 0-87793-214-X). Ave Maria.

Christmas Book. Ed. by David Larkin. (Encore Ed.). (Illus.). 1975. 3.95 o.p. (ISBN 0-685-99258-6, ScribT). Scribner.

Christmas Carol. Sheila L. Burns. LC 78-72141. (Illus.). (gr. 2-5). Date not set. price not set (ISBN 0-89799-093-5); pap. price not set (ISBN 0-89799-064-1). Dandelion Pr. Postponed.

Christmas Carol. Charles Dickens. (Illus.). 1979. 9.95 (ISBN 0-312-13403-7). St Martin.

Christmas Carol. Charles Dickens. (Illus.). (gr. 7-9). 1952. 8.95 o.s.i. (ISBN 0-397-00033-2). Lippincott.

Christmas Carol. Charles Dickens. (gr. 4 up). 1963. 3.95g o.s.i. (ISBN 0-02-730300-4). Macmillan.

Christmas Carol. Charles Dickens. 1976. deluxe ed. 9.95 o.p. (ISBN 0-385-12816-9). Doubleday.

Christmas Carol. Charles Dickens. 150p. 1980. Repr. PLB 11.95x (ISBN 0-89967-017-2). Harmony & Co.

Christmas Carol. Darwin R. Payne. LC 80-18827. 128p. 1981. pap. price not set (ISBN 0-8093-0999-8). S Ill U Pr.

Christmas Carol: And Other Christmas Books. Charles Dickens. 1979. 10.00x (ISBN 0-460-00239-2, Evman). Dutton.

Christmas Carol: Retold by A. Sweaney. Charles Dickens. (Oxford Progressive English Readers Ser.). (gr. k-6). 1975. pap. text ed. 2.95x (ISBN 0-19-580724-3). Oxford U Pr.

Christmas Carol: The Original Manuscript. Charles Dickens. 8.50 (ISBN 0-8446-0078-4). Peter Smith.

Christmas Carols for Young Children. Illus. by Henriette W. Le Mair. (Illus.). 32p. pap. 4.95 o.s.i. (ISBN 0-914676-42-3). Green Tiger.

Christmas Cookbook. Shona C. Poole. LC 79-63631. 259p. 1981. pap. 5.95 (ISBN 0-689-70606-5, 267). Atheneum.

Christmas Cookie Sprinkle Snitcher. Robert Kraus. LC 80-13641. (Illus.). 32p. (gr. k-3). 1980. pap. 3.95 (ISBN 0-671-41199-3, Pub. by Windmill). S&S.

Christmas Crackers. Willis Hall. 1978. pap. text ed. 2.95 (ISBN 0-435-23369-6). Heinemann Ed.

Christmas Crafts Book. Sterling Editors. LC 79-65064. (Illus.). 1979. 16.95 (ISBN 0-8069-5396-9); lib. bdg. 13.99 (ISBN 0-8069-5397-7). Sterling.

Christmas Customs & Traditions: Their History and Significance. Clement A. Miles. LC 76-9183. Orig. Title: Christmas in Ritual and Tradition. (Illus.). 1976. pap. 5.00 (ISBN 0-486-23354-5). Dover.

Christmas Decorations for You to Make. Susan Purdy. LC 65-21673. (Illus.). (gr. 1-9). 1965. 9.79 (ISBN 0-397-31486-8). Lippincott.

Christmas Entertaining. Barbara Myers. LC 80-51252. 256p. 1980. 13.95 (ISBN 0-686-62320-7). Rawson Wade.

Christmas Eve Mystery. Joan L. Nixon. Ed. by Ann Fay. (First Read-Alone Mysteries Ser.). (Illus.). 32p. (gr. 1-3). 1981. 5.50 (ISBN 0-8075-1150-1). A Whitman.

Christmas Fantasy. Carolyn Haywood. LC 71-184244. (Illus.). 32p. (gr. k-3). 1972. lib. bdg. 8.25 (ISBN 0-688-20094-X); PLB 7.92 (ISBN 0-688-30094-4). Morrow.

Christmas Feast: A Delightful Treasury of Yuletide Stories and Poems for the Whole Family. Ed. by James Charlton & Barbara Gilson. LC 76-20833. 1976. 7.95 o.p. (ISBN 0-385-12512-7). Doubleday.

Christmas Games & Crafts for Children. Shirley Beegle. (Standard Ideas Ser.). 1978. pap. 1.75 (ISBN 0-87239-215-5, 2816). Standard Pub.

Christmas Ghosts. Seon Manley. LC 77-26517. (gr. k up). 1978. 8.95a (ISBN 0-385-14032-0); PLB (ISBN 0-385-14033-9). Doubleday.

Christmas Gifts for You to Make. Susan Purdy. LC 76-10160. (Illus.). (gr. 5-12). 1976. 8.79 (ISBN 0-397-31695-X); pap. 4.95 (ISBN 0-397-31696-8). Lippincott.

Christmas Grump. Joseph Low. LC 77-3903. (Illus.). (ps-3). 1977. 7.95 (ISBN 0-689-50092-0, McElderry Bk). Atheneum.

Christmas Here, There & Everywhere. Frank Jupo. LC 77-3893. (gr. 1 up). 1977. 5.95 (ISBN 0-396-07462-6). Dodd.

Christmas in All the World. LC 79-50087. (Illus.). 1979. pap. 3.50 (ISBN 0-8066-1704-7, 10-11238). Augsburg.

Christmas in Context. Virgil C. Feerer. 1980. 4.95 (ISBN 0-533-04785-4). Vantage.

Christmas in France. World Book-Childcraft International, Inc. LC 80-50994. (Around the World Christmas Program Ser.). (Illus.). 80p. (ps-9). 1980. write for info. (ISBN 0-7166-3106-7). World Bk-Childcraft.

Christmas in Latin America. (Eng.). 1976. pap. 1.00 (ISBN 0-8270-3960-3). OAS.

Christmas in Norway. V. Hendriksen. (Tanum of Norway Tokens Ser). pap. 7.50x (ISBN 82-518-1375-1, N501). Vanous.

Christmas in Old New England. Irving Bell. 54p. (gr. 3-8). 1981. 8.95 (ISBN 0-917780-02-7). April Hill.

Christmas in Ritual & Tradition, Christian & Pagan. Clement A. Miles. LC 68-54858. 1968. Repr. of 1912 ed. 20.00 (ISBN 0-8103-3354-6). Gale.

Christmas in Texas. Ed. by V. T. Abercrombie & Helen Williams. LC 79-66212. (Illus., Orig.). 1979. pap. 4.50 (ISBN 0-933988-00-1). Brown Rabbit.

Christmas in the Barn. Margaret W. Brown. LC 52-7858. (Illus.). (gr. k-3). 1949. 7.95 (ISBN 0-690-19272-X, TYC-J); pap. 7.89 (ISBN 0-686-68499-0). T Y Crowell.

Christmas in the Forest. Jan Wahl. (Illus.). (gr. k-2). 1967. 4.95g o.s.i. (ISBN 0-02-792370-3). Macmillan.

Christmas in the Mountains: Southwest Virginia Christmas Customs & Their Origins. Hubert J. Davis. (Illus.). 144p. 1972. 7.50 (ISBN 0-930230-06-X). Johnson NC.

Christmas in Williamsburg. rev. ed. Taylor B. Lewis, Jr. & Joanne B. Young. LC 76-11598. 1976. 5.95 o.p. (ISBN 0-03-089945-1). HR&W.

Christmas Is a Happy Time. Jane B. Moncure. Ed. by Jane Buerger. 1980. 4.95 (ISBN 0-89565-171-8, 4922). Standard Pub.

Christmas, Its Origin & Associations, Together with Its Historical Events & Festive Celebrations During Nineteen Centuries. William F. Dawson. LC 68-54857. 1968. Repr. of 1902 ed. 26.00 (ISBN 0-8103-3351-1). Gale.

Christmas Lamb. Barbara Witter. (Illus.). (gr. k-6). 1977. pap. 1.50 o.p. (ISBN 0-917726-18-9). Hunter Bks.

Christmas Mice. Elizabeth Smith. 1979. 4.00 (ISBN 0-8062-1287-X). Carlton.

Christmas: More Than a Season. Wilson O. Weldon. LC 80-51313. 75p. (Orig.). 1980. pap. 1.95x (ISBN 0-8358-0402-X). Upper Room.

Christmas Music from Baroque Mexico. Robert Stevenson. (Illus.). 1974. 35.00x o.p. (ISBN 0-520-02036-7). U of Cal Pr.

Christmas: New Ideas for an Old-Fashioned Celebration. Barbara Rosenthal & Nadia Rosenthal. 1980. 12.95 (ISBN 0-517-53695-1). Potter.

Christmas Pageant. Ed. by Winston Press Editorial Staff. (Illus.). 1979. 7.95 (ISBN 0-03-046356-4). Winston Pr.

Christmas Party Games. Richard Mullin. (Standard Ideas Ser.). 1978. pap. 1.75 (ISBN 0-87239-216-3, 2817). Standard Pub.

Christmas Pinata. Jack Kent. LC 74-30450. (Illus.). 40p. (gr. k-3). 1975. 5.95 o.s.i. (ISBN 0-8193-0815-3, Four Winds); PLB 5.41 o.s.i. (ISBN 0-8193-0816-1). Schol Bk Serv.

Christmas Plays for Older Children. Linda Berry. (gr. 5-7). 1981. saddle wire 1.65 (ISBN 0-8054-9733-1). Broadman.

Christmas Programs for the Church, No. 12. Ed. by Jacqueline Westers. (Special-Day Program Bks). 64p. (Orig.). 1979. pap. 2.75 (ISBN 0-87239-252-X, 8612). Standard Pub.

Christmas Programs for the Church, No. 13. Ed. by Judith Sparks. 64p. (Orig.). 1980. pap. 2.75 (ISBN 0-87239-392-5, 8613). Standard Pub.

Christmas Reflections. Mary B. Christian. 1980. pap. 3.50 (ISBN 0-570-03494-9, 56-1711). Concordia.

Christmas Spider: A Puppet Play from Poland & Other Traditional Games, Crafts & Activities. Loretta Holz. (gr. 3-7). 5.95 (ISBN 0-399-20754-6); lib. bdg. 5.99g (ISBN 0-399-61164-9). Philomel.

Christmas Stories. Charles Dickens. 1979. 6.00x (ISBN 0-460-00414-X, Evman); pap. 2.75 (ISBN 0-460-01414-5). Dutton.

Christmas Stories Round the World. Lois Johnson. (Illus.). (gr. 3-7). 1970. pap. 2.95 o.s.i. (ISBN 0-528-87032-7). Rand.

Christmas Story. LC 76-47915. (Sunshine Books Ser.). (Illus.). 1977. pap. 1.00 o.p. (ISBN 0-8006-1579-4, 1-1579). Fortress.

Christmas Story. G. A. Pottebaum. (Little People's Paperbacks Ser.). 1979. pap. 0.99 (ISBN 0-8164-2241-9). Crossroad NY.

Christmas Surprise. Sharon Gordon. (Illus.). 32p. (gr. k-2). 1980. PLB 2.96 (ISBN 0-89375-373-4); pap. 0.95 (ISBN 0-89375-273-8). Troll Assocs.

Christmas Tree. A. C. Greene. (Illus.). 40p. 1973. 9.50 o.p. (ISBN 0-88426-035-6). Encino Pr.

Christmas Tree Farm. David Budbill. LC 73-6051. (Illus.). 32p. (gr. k-2). 1974. 5.95g o.s.i. (ISBN 0-02-715330-4, 71533). Macmillan.

Christmas with Tamworth Pig. Gene Kemp. LC 78-300034. (Illus.). (gr. 8-12). 1979. 8.95 (ISBN 0-571-11117-3, Pub. by Faber & Faber). Merrimack Bk Serv.

Christobel. large type ed. Mary L. Roby. pap. 1.50 o.p. (ISBN 0-425-03141-1). Berkley Pub.

Christological Controversy. Ed. by Richard A. Norris, Jr. & William G. Rusch. Tr. by Richard A. Norris. LC 79-8890. (Sources of Early Christian Thought). 176p. 1980. pap. 6.95 (ISBN 0-8006-1411-9, 1-1411). Fortress.

Christology After Auschwitz. Michael B. McGarry. LC 77-73977. 1977. pap. 3.95 (ISBN 0-8091-2024-0). Paulist Pr.

Christology & a Modern Pilgrimage: A Discussion with Norman Perrin. Hans D. Betz. LC 75-31605. (Scholars Press Homage Ser.: No. 1). 1974. pap. 7.50 (ISBN 0-89130-185-2, 001601). Scholars Pr Ca.

Christology in the Making: A New Testament Inquiry into the Origins of the Doctrine of the Incarnation. James D. Dunn. LC 80-16968. 1980. pap. 24.50 (ISBN 0-664-24356-8). Westminster.

Christology of Early Jewish Christianity. Richard N. Longenecker. (Twin Brooks Ser.). 178p. 1981. pap. 5.95 (ISBN 0-8010-5610-1). Baker Bk.

Christology of the New Testament. rev. ed. Oscar Cullmann. Tr. by Shirley C. Guthrie & Charles A. Hall. LC 59-10178. pap. 11.95. Westminster.

Christoph Martin Wieland. John A. McCarthy. (World Authors Ser.: No. 528). 1979. lib. bdg. 13.95 (ISBN 0-8057-6369-4). Twayne.

Christopher Columbus. Sue Heimann. LC 72-10402. (Visual Biography Ser). (Illus.). 64p. (gr. 4-5). 1973. PLB 4.90 o.p. (ISBN 0-531-00971-8); pap. 1.95 o.p. (ISBN 0-531-02707-4). Watts.

Christopher Columbus: Man of Destiny & Vision. C. F. Nagro. 1981. 9.50 (ISBN 0-533-04809-5). Vantage.

Christopher for President. Addie. (Illus.). (gr. 2-5). 1973. PLB 10.69 o.p. (ISBN 0-307-65776-0, Golden Pr). Western Pub.

Christopher Isherwood. Carolyn Heilbrun. LC 73-126543. (Columbia). (Orig.). 1970. pap. 2.00 (ISBN 0-231-03257-9, MW53). Columbia U Pr.

Christopher Isherwood. Claude J. Summers. LC 80-5335. (Modern Literature Ser.). 192p. 1980. 10.95 (ISBN 0-8044-2846-8). Ungar.

Christopher Isherwood: Myth & Anti-Myth. Paul Piazza. LC 77-14271. 1978. 15.00x (ISBN 0-231-04118-7). Columbia U Pr.

Christopher Marlowe. Philip Henderson. Ed. by Bonamy Dobree et al. Bd. with Ben Jonson. J. B. Bamborough; John Webster. Ian Scott-Kilvert; John Ford. Clifford Leech. LC 63-63096. (British Writers & Their Work Ser: Vol. 11). 1966. pap. 3.25x (ISBN 0-8032-5661-2, BB 460, Bison). U of Nebr Pr.

Christopher Marlowe. Robert E. Knoll. LC 68-17237. (English Authors Ser.: No. 74). 1969. lib. bdg. 10.95 (ISBN 0-8057-1376-X). Twayne.

Christopher Marlowe. Judith Weil. LC 76-26586. 1977. 34.00 (ISBN 0-521-21554-4). Cambridge U Pr.

Christopher Marlowe: An Annotated Bibliography of Criticism Since 1950. Kenneth Friedenreich. LC 79-17646. (Scarecrow Author Bibliographies Ser.: No. 43). 1979. 10.00 (ISBN 0-8108-1239-8). Scarecrow.

Christopher Marlowe & the Politics of Power. Claude J. Summers. (Salzburg Studies in English Literature, Elizabethan & Renaissance Studies: No. 22). 208p. 1974. pap. text ed. 25.00x (ISBN 0-391-01542-7). Humanities.

Christopher Marlowe: Five Plays. Ed. by Brian Morris. LC 77-7525. 1969. pap. 4.50 o.p. (ISBN 0-8090-0701-0). Hill & Wang.

Christopher Marlowe: The Over-Reacher. Harry Levin. (Orig.). 1965. pap. 2.95 o.p. (ISBN 0-571-07028-0, Pub. by Faber & Faber). Merrimack Bk Serv.

Christopher Marlowe's Tragic Vision: A Study in Damnation. Charles G. Masinton. LC 77-181683. x, 168p. 1972. 10.95x (ISBN 0-8214-0101-7). Ohio U Pr.

Christopher Morley. Mark I. Wallach & Jon Bracker. LC 76-17922. (U.S. Authors Ser.: No. 278). 1976. lib. bdg. 10.95 (ISBN 0-8057-7178-6). Twayne.

Christopher Smart. Frances E. Anderson. (English Authors Ser.: No. 161). 1974. lib. bdg. 10.95 (ISBN 0-8057-1502-9). Twayne.

Christopher Uptake. Susan Price. 208p. (gr. 5-12). 1981. 14.95 (ISBN 0-571-11660-4, Pub. by Faber & Faber). Merrimack Bk Serv.

Christopher Wren & St. Paul's Cathedral. R. Gray. LC 77-94370. (Cambridge Introduction to the History of Mankind Ser.). (Illus.). (YA) 1980. pap. 3.95 (ISBN 0-521-21666-4). Cambridge U Pr.

Christopher's Parade. Richard Hefter & Martin S. Moskof. LC 72-394. (Illus.). 40p. (ps-3). 1972. 5.95 o.s.i. (ISBN 0-8193-0586-3, Four Winds); PLB 5.41 o.s.i. (ISBN 0-8193-0587-1). Schol Bk Serv.

Christotherapy: Healing Through Enlightenment. Bernard Tyrrell. 250p. 1975. 8.95 (ISBN 0-8164-0278-7). Crossroad NY.

Christ's Comfort for Those Who Sorrow. A. M. Coniaris. 1978. pap. 2.95 (ISBN 0-937032-00-X). Light & Life Pub Co MN.

Christ's Coming--Satan's Kingdom. David A. Duke. 220p. (Orig.). 1981. pap. 2.95 (ISBN 0-9605056-0-1). D A Duke.

Christs' Company. R. W. Dixon. Ed. by Ian Fletcher & John Stokes. LC 76-20033. (Decadent Consciousness Ser.). 1978. lib. bdg. 38.00 (ISBN 0-8240-2776-0). Garland Pub.

Christ's Life: Our Life. John B. Coburn. 1979. pap. 3.95 (ISBN 0-8164-2616-3). Crossroad NY.

Christ's Life, Our Life. John B. Coburn. LC 77-17172. 1978. 6.95 (ISBN 0-8164-0384-8). Crossroad NY.

Christ's Lordship & Religious Pluralism. Gerald H. Anderson & Thomas F. Stransky. LC 80-25406. 256p. (Orig.). 1981. pap. 8.95 (ISBN 0-88344-088-1). Orbis Bks.

Christ's Object Lessons. large print ed. 1980. pap. 5.95 (ISBN 0-8280-0044-1, 03364-7). Review & Herald.

Christ's Promise Fulfilled. Abdu'l-Baha. 1954. pap. 2.50 (ISBN 0-87743-049-7, 7-06-01). Baha'i.

Christy. Johnson. (gr. 7-12). 1980. pap. 1.50 (ISBN 0-590-31261-8, Schol Pap). Schol Bk Serv.

Christy. Catherine Marshall. 1968. pap. 2.50 (ISBN 0-380-00141-1, 44032). Avon.

Chromatic Harmony. J. Shir-Cliff et al. LC 64-23079. 1965. text ed. 10.95 (ISBN 0-02-928630-1); wkbk. 9.95 (ISBN 0-02-928640-9). Free Pr.

Chromatin Structure & Function, Pt. B: Levels of Organization & Cell Function. Ed. by Claudio Nicolini. (NATO Advanced Study Institutes Ser.; Series A, Life Sciences: Vol. 21B). 502p. 1979. 42.50 (ISBN 0-306-40076-6, Plenum Pr). Plenum Pub.

Chromatography: An Adventure in Graduate School. Guy B. Alexander. LC 77-8637. (Chemistry in Action Ser.). 1977. 7.50 o.p. (ISBN 0-8412-0277-X); pap. 4.50 (ISBN 0-8412-0616-3). Am Chemical.

Chromatography of Hemoglobin. Schreeder & Huisman. 320p. 1980. 29.75 (ISBN 0-8247-6941-4). Dekker.

Chromatography of Steroids. I. E. Bush et al. 1961. 38.00 (ISBN 0-08-009544-5). Pergamon.

Chromatography of Synthetic & Biological Polymers: Hydrophobic, Ion-Exchange & Affinity Methods, Vol. II. Ed. by Roger Epton. LC 77-40142. 1978. 59.95 (ISBN 0-470-26366-0). Halsted Pr.

Chrome. George Nader. 1979. pap. 1.75 (ISBN 0-515-04846-1). Jove Pubns.

Chrome Colossus: General Motors & Its Times. Ed Cray. (Illus.). 548p. 1980. 14.95 (ISBN 0-07-013493-6). McGraw.

Chromenes, Chromanones, & Chromones: Chemistry of Heterocyclic Compounds-A Series of Monographs. G. P. Ellis. (Vol. 31). 1977. 155.00 (ISBN 0-471-38212-4). Wiley.

Chromium. Medical Sciences Division. LC 74-3493. (Medical & Biologic Effects of Environmental Pollutants Ser.). 168p. 1974. pap. 9.00 (ISBN 0-309-02217-7). Natl Acad Pr.

Chromium in Nutrition & Disease. Ed. by Gunay Saner. LC 80-81854. (Current Topics in Nutrition & Disease: Vol. 2). 146p. 1980. 16.00 (ISBN 0-8451-1601-0). A R Liss.

Chromium: Its Physicochemical Behaviour & Petrologic Significance: Proceedings of the Carnegie Institute of Washington Conference, Geophysical Laboratory. Ed. by T. N. Irvine. LC 75-33383. 1977. text ed. 47.00 (ISBN 0-08-019954-2). Pergamon.

Chromogenic Peptide Substrates. Michael F. Scully & Vijay V. Kakkar. (Illus.). 1979. text ed. 37.50 o.s.i. (ISBN 0-443-01840-5). Churchill.

Chromosomal Variations in Man: A Catalog of Chromosomal Variants & Anomalies. 3rd ed. Digamber S. Borgaonkar. LC 80-81466. 846p. 1980. 58.00x (ISBN 0-8451-0206-0). A R Liss.

Chromosome Botany & the Origins of Cultivated Plants. 3rd ed. C. D. Darlington. (Illus.). 1973. text ed. 25.00x (ISBN 0-04-581011-7). Allen Unwin.

Chromosome Complement. B. John & K. R. Lewis. (Protoplasmatologia: Vol. 6, Pt. A). (Illus.). 1968. pap. 57.90 o.p. (ISBN 0-387-80881-7). Springer-Verlag.

Chromosome Cycle. B. John & K. R. Lewis. (Protoplasmatologia: Vol. 6, Pt. B). (Illus.). 1969. 42.50 o.p. (ISBN 0-387-80918-X). Springer-Verlag.

Chromosome Numbers of Flowering Plants. Ed. by A. Fedorov. 926p. 1969. Repr. of 1974 ed. lib. bdg. 121.00x (ISBN 3-87429-067-0). Lubrecht & Cramer.

Chromosome Studies. G. W. Shaw. (Investigations in Biology Ser.). 1973. pap. text ed. 3.95x o.p. (ISBN 0-435-60286-1). Heinemann Ed.

Chromosome Techniques. 3rd ed. Sharma & Sharma. LC 79-41279. 1980. 135.00 (ISBN 0-408-70942-1). Butterworths.

Chromosome Variation in Human Evolution. A. J. Boyce. LC 75-25643. (Symposia for the Study of Human Biology Ser: Vol. 14). 131p. 1976. 24.95 (ISBN 0-470-09330-7). Halsted Pr.

Chromosome Variation in Human Evolution, Vol. 14. A. J. Boyce. 131p. 1975. 24.95 (ISBN 0-470-09330-7). Wiley.

Chromosomes - from Simple to Complex: Proceedings. Biology Colloquium, 35th,Oregon State University,1974. Ed. by Paul Roberts. LC 76-5880. (Illus.). 96p. 1977. pap. text ed. 6.00 (ISBN 0-87071-174-1). Oreg St U Pr.

Chromosomes, Giant Molecules, & Evolution. Bruce Wallace. (Illus.). 1966. 5.00x (ISBN 0-393-06343-7); pap. 3.95x (ISBN 0-393-09677-7, NortonC). Norton.

Chromosomes in Human Cancer. Jaroslav Cervenka & Lucien Koulischer. (Illus.). 212p. 1973. 19.75 (ISBN 0-398-02629-7). C C Thomas.

Chromosomes in Human Cancer & Leukemia. A. A. Sanberg. LC 79-22474. 776p. 1979. 97.50 (ISBN 0-444-00289-8, North Holland). Elsevier.

Chromosomes in Medicine. (Clinics in Developmental Medicine Ser. No. 5). 203p. 1961. 7.50 o.p. (ISBN 0-685-24712-0). Lippincott.
Chromosomes of the Algae. Maud B. Godward. (Illus.). 1969. 21.95 (ISBN 0-312-13440-1). St Martin.
Chromosomes of the California Liliaceae. Marion S. Cave. (U. C. Publ. in Botany: Vol. 57). 1970. pap. 5.50x (ISBN 0-520-09031-4). U of Cal Pr.
Chromosomes Today, Vol. 4. Ed. by J. Wahrman & K. R. Lewis. LC 74-831. 441p. 1973. 59.95 (ISBN 0-470-91630-3). Halsted Pr.
Chromosomes Today, Vol. 5. Ed. by P. L. Pearson & K. R. Lewis. LC 75-43619. 1976. 74.95 (ISBN 0-470-14997-3). Halsted Pr.
Chronic Care Nursing. Seigina M. Frik et al. 304p. 1981. text ed. price not set (ISBN 0-8261-3010-0); pap. text ed. price not set (ISBN 0-8261-3011-9). Springer Pub.
Chronic Cholecystitis: Its Pathology & the Role of Vascular Factors in Its Pathogenesis. Talya Levine. LC 75-6842. 1975. 33.95 (ISBN 0-470-53122-3). Halsted Pr.
Chronic Ear Disease. D. S. Smyth & D. L. Gordon. (Monographs in Clinical Otolaryngology). (Illus.). 224p. 1980. text ed. 28.00x (ISBN 0-443-08071-2). Churchill.
Chronic Illness & the Quality of Life. Anselm A. Strauss. LC 75-2458. 1975. pap. text ed. 10.50 (ISBN 0-8016-4837-8). Mosby.
Chronic Leukemias: Chemistry, Pathophysiology & Treatment. John R. Durant & Richard V. Smalley. (Amer. Lec. Living Chemistry Ser). (Illus.). 240p. 1972. 19.75 (ISBN 0-398-02275-5). C C Thomas.
Chronic Mental Patient in the Community: Vol. 10. GAP Committee on Psychiatry & the Community. LC 78-55381. (Publication No. 102). 1978. pap. 4.00 (ISBN 0-87318-139-5). Adv Psychiatry.
Chronic Mental Patient: Problems, Solutions, & Recommendations for a Public Policy. Report of a Conference Held in January 1979. Ed. by John A. Talbott. LC 78-73984. 1979. pap. 11.00x (ISBN 0-685-95862-0, P242-0). Am Psychiatric.
Chronic Mentally Ill. Talbott. 1980. pap. text ed. 29.95x (ISBN 0-87705-086-4). Human Sci Pr.
Chronic Obstructive Lung Disease: Clinical Treatment & Management. new ed. Richard E. Brashear & Mitchell L. Rhodes. LC 77-18551. (Illus.). 1978. text ed. 37.50 (ISBN 0-8016-0753-1). Mosby.
Chronic Obstructive Pulmonary Disease. Warren C. Miller. LC 79-91977. (Discussions in Pateint Managemenrt Ser.). 1980. pap. 12.00 (ISBN 0-87488-872-7). Med Exam.
Chronic Psychiatric Illness. Judith B. Krauss & Ann T. Slavinsky. (Illus.). 288p. 1981. text ed. 14.95 (ISBN 0-86542-006-8). Blackwell Sci.
Chronic Schizophrenias. Christian Astrup. (Orig.). 1979. pap. 18.00x (ISBN 82-00-01810-5, Dist. by Columbia U. Pr.). Universitet.
Chronically-Distressed Client: A Model for Intervention in the Community. Frances P. Rowan. LC 79-22475. 1980. pap. 10.00 (ISBN 0-8016-4204-3). Mosby.
Chronicle. Joel Zoss. (Orig.). 1980. pap. write for info. (ISBN 0-671-41458-5). PB.
Chronicle & Works, 5 vols. H. C. Landon. Incl. Haydn: The Early Years, 1732-1765. Vol. 1 Haydn: the Early Years, 1732-1765. 640p. 1980. 75.00x (ISBN 0-253-37001-9); Vol. 2. Haydn at Eszterhaza; 1766-1790. 820p. 1978. 60.00x (ISBN 0-253-37002-7); Vol. 3. Haydn in England, 1791-1795. 640p. 1976. 55.00x (ISBN 0-253-37003-5); Vol. 4. Haydnn: the Years of "The Creation" 1796-1800. 640p. 1976. 55.00x (ISBN 0-253-37004-3); Vol. 5. Haydn: the Late Years, 1801-1809. 496p. 1977. 55.00x (ISBN 0-253-37005-1). Set. 300.00x. Ind U Pr.
Chronicle into History: An Essay on the Interpretation of History in Florentine Fourteenth Century Cronicles. Louis Green. LC 71-186249. (Cambridge Studies in Early Modern History). 180p. 1972. 26.95 (ISBN 0-521-08517-9). Cambridge U Pr.
Chronicle of Ernoul & the Continuations of William of Tyre. M. R. Morgan. (Oxford Historical Monographs). 214p. 1974. 22.50x (ISBN 0-19-821851-6). Oxford U Pr.
Chronicle of Gods & Sovereigns: Jinno Shotoki of Kitabatake Chikafusa. Tr. by H. Paul Varley from Japanese. (Translations from Oriental Classics Ser.). 1980. 22.50x (ISBN 0-231-04940-4). Columbia U Pr.
Chronicle of Leopold & Molly Bloom: "Ulysses" As Narrative. John H. Raleigh. 1978. 17.50x (ISBN 0-520-03301-9). U of Cal Pr.
Chronicle of the Guayaki Indians. Pierre Clastres. Tr. by Paul Auster & Lydia Davis. 1981. 20.00 (ISBN 0-89396-031-4). Urizen Bks.
Chronicle Two-Year College Databook Nineteen Eighty. Chronicle Guidance Publications, Inc. 1980. pap. 11.00 (ISBN 0-912578-43-2). Chron Guide.
Chroniclers. Keith Wheeler. (Old West Ser.). (Illus.). 1976. 12.95 (ISBN 0-8094-1529-1). Time-Life.
Chroniclers. Keith Wheeler. LC 75-34961. (Old West). (Illus.). (gr. 5 up). 1976. kivar 12.96 (ISBN 0-8094-1531-3, Pub. by Time-Life). Silver.
Chronicles, I & II. E. L. Curtis & A. A. Madsen. LC 10-14958. (International Critical Commentary Ser.). 560p. Repr. of 1910 ed. text ed. 23.00x (ISBN 0-567-05007-6). Attic Pr.
Chronicles of America, 27 vols, Vols. 30-56. Ed. by Allen Johnson & Allan Nevins. Incl. Vol. 30. Day of the Confederacy. Nathaniel W. Stephenson (ISBN 0-911548-29-7); Vol. 31. Captains of the Civil War. William Wood (ISBN 0-911548-30-0); Vol. 32. Sequel of Appomattox. Walter L. Fleming (ISBN 0-911548-31-9); Vol. 33. American Spirit in Education. Edwin E. Slosson (ISBN 0-911548-32-7); Vol. 34. American Spirit in Literature. Bliss Perry (ISBN 0-911548-33-5); Vol. 35. Our Foreigners. Samuel P. Orth (ISBN 0-911548-34-3); Vol. 36. Old Merchant Marine. Ralph D. Paine (ISBN 0-911548-35-1); Vol. 37. Age of Invention. Holland Thompson (ISBN 0-911548-36-X); Vol. 38. Railroad Builders. John Moody (ISBN 0-911548-37-8); Vol. 39. Age of Big Business. Burton J. Hendrick (ISBN 0-911548-38-6); Vol. 40. Armies of Labour. Samuel P. Orth (ISBN 0-911548-39-4); Vol. 41. Masters of Capital. John Moody (ISBN 0-911548-40-8); Vol. 42. New South. Holland Thompson (ISBN 0-911548-41-6); Vol. 43. Boss & the Machine. Samuel P. Orth (ISBN 0-911548-42-4); Vol. 44. Cleveland Era. Henry J. Ford (ISBN 0-911548-43-2); Vol. 45. Agrarian Crusade. Solon J. Buck (ISBN 0-911548-44-0); Vol. 46. Path of Empire. Carl R. Fish (ISBN 0-911548-45-9); Vol. 47. Theodore Roosevelt & His Times. Harold Howland (ISBN 0-911548-46-7); Vol. 48. Woodrow Wilson & the World War. Charles Seymour (ISBN 0-911548-47-5); Vol. 49. Canadian Dominion. Oscar D. Skelton (ISBN 0-911548-48-3); Vol. 50. Hispanic Nations of the New World. William R. Shepherd (ISBN 0-911548-49-1); Vol. 51. From Versailles to the New Deal. Harold U. Faulkner (ISBN 0-911548-50-5); Vol. 52. Era of Franklin D. Roosevelt. Denis W. Brogan (ISBN 0-911548-51-3); Vol. 53. Struggle for Survival. Eliott Janeway (ISBN 0-911548-52-1); Vol. 54. War for the World. Fletcher Pratt (ISBN 0-911548-53-X); Vol. 55. United States in a Chaotic World. Allan Nevins (ISBN 0-911548-54-8); Vol. 56. New Deal & World Affairs. Allan Nevins (ISBN 0-911548-55-6). 8.95 ea.; 56 vols. 445.00 set (ISBN 0-911548-71-8). US Pubs.
Chronicles of American Indian Protest. 2nd, rev. ed. Council on Interracial Books for Children, Inc. 400p. (gr. 11-12). pap. 5.95 (ISBN 0-930040-30-9). CIBC.
Chronicles of Castles Cloyne: Pictures of Munster Life, 3 vols. Margaret W. Brew. Ed. by Robert L. Wolff. (Ireland-Nineteenth Century Fiction, Ser. Two: Vol. 70). 1979. lib. bdg. 46.00 (ISBN 0-8240-3519-4); lib. bdg. 42.00 (ISBN 0-686-66181-8). Garland Pub.
Chronicles of Kedaram. K. Nagarajan. 8.00x (ISBN 0-210-33818-0). Asia.
Chronicles of Pennsylvania, 3 Vols. Charles P. Keith. LC 69-18291. (Keystone State Historical Publications Ser: No. 3). 1969. Repr. of 1917 ed. Set. 45.00x (ISBN 0-87198-503-9). Friedman.
Chronicles of the Crusades. Geoffrey De Villehardouin & Jean De Joinville. Tr. by Margaret R. Shaw. (Classics Ser.). (Orig.). 1963. pap. 3.95 (ISBN 0-14-044124-7). Penguin.
Chronicles of the First Planters of the Colony of Massachusetts Bay, 1623-1636. Alexander Young. LC 78-87667. (Law, Politics & History Ser.). 1970. Repr. of 1846 ed. lib. bdg. 55.00 (ISBN 0-306-71759-X). Da Capo.
Chronicon Adae de Usk, A.D. 1377 to 1421. Adam, of Usk. Ed. by Edward M. Thompson. (Pilgrimages Ser.). 392p. 1980. Repr. of 1904 ed. 44.50 (ISBN 0-404-16367-X). AMS Pr.
Chronik: Des Salimbene Von Parma Nach der Ausgabe der Monuments Germaniae, 2 Vols. Salimbene Ognibene Di Guido Di Adamo. Ed. by A. Doren. Repr. of 1914 ed. pap. 36.50 set (ISBN 0-384-53125-3). Johnson Repr.
Chronobiology in Allergy & Immunology. John P. McGovern et al. (Illus.). 308p. 1977. 27.75 (ISBN 0-398-03583-0). C C Thomas.
Chronobiology: Principles & Applications to Shifts in Schedules. Lawrence E. Scheving & Franz Halberg. (NATO Advanced Study Institute: Behavioral Social Sciences, No. 3). 597p. 1980. 65.00x (ISBN 90-286-0940-7). Sijthoff & Noordhoff.
Chronogenetics: The Inheritance of Biological Time. Luigi Gedda & Gianni Brenci. (Illus.). 232p. 1978. 27.75 (ISBN 0-398-03641-1). C C Thomas.
Chronolgy of the Larsa Dynasty. Bd. with Pt. 1. Ettalene M. Grice; Patesis of the Ur Dynasty, Pt 2. Clarence E. Kelser; An Old Babylonian Version of the Gilgamesh Epic on the Basis of Recently Discovered Texts, Pt 3. Morris Jastrow & Albert T. Clay. 200p. 1980. Repr. of 1920 ed. 37.50 (ISBN 0-404-60274-6). AMS Pr.
Chronological Account of Nearly Four Hundred Irish Writers. E. O'Reilly. 256p. 1969. Repr. of 1820 ed. 25.00x (ISBN 0-7165-0026-4, Pub. by Irish Academic Pr Ireland). Biblio Dist.
Chronological History of the Negro in America. Ed. by Bergman Publ. Co. (RL 7). pap. 1.50 o.p. (ISBN 0-451-60937-9, MW937, Ment). NAL.
Chronological Outlines of American Literature. Selden L. Whitcomb. LC 68-30590. 1968. Repr. of 1894 ed. 18.00 (ISBN 0-8103-3227-2). Gale.
Chronological Outlines of English Literature. Frederick Ryland. LC 68-30587. 1968. Repr. of 1914 ed. 22.00 (ISBN 0-8103-3223-X). Gale.
Chronological Tables of the Chinese Dynasties. Theodore R. Wong. Ed. by E. R. Lyman. (Studies in Chinese History & Civilization). 103p. 1977. Repr. of 1902 ed. 12.00 (ISBN 0-89093-092-9). U Pubns Amer.
Chronologisches Verzeichnis Franzosischer Grammatiken Vom Ende Des 14 Bis Zum Ausgange Des 18 Jahrhunderts, Nebst Angabe der Bisher Ermittelten Fundortet Derselben. Ed. by Edmund Stengel. (Studies in the History of Linguistics: No. 8). 1976. text ed. 34.25x (ISBN 0-391-01643-1). Humanities.
Chronology & Documentary Handbook of the State of New York. 1978. 8.50. Oceana.
Chronology & Documentary Handbook of the State of Hawaii. W. F. Swindler. 1978. 8.50 (ISBN 0-379-16136-2). Oceana.
Chronology & Documentary Handbook of the State of Virginia. W. F. Swindler. 1978. 8.50 (ISBN 0-379-16157-5). Oceana.
Chronology, Migration & Drought in Interlacustrine Africa. Ed. by J. B. Webster. LC 78-7050. (Dalhousie African Studies). 1979. text ed. 44.50x (ISBN 0-8419-0377-8, Africana); pap. text ed. 22.45x (ISBN 0-8419-0388-3, Africana). Holmes & Meier.
Chronology of Canadian Military Aviation. H. A. Halliday. (Illus.). 1975. pap. text ed. 3.00x (ISBN 0-660-00149-7, 56301-4, Pub. by Natl Mus Canada). U of Chicago Pr.
Chronology of Librarianship. Josephine M. Smith. LC 67-12062. 1968. 10.00 (ISBN 0-8108-0024-1). Scarecrow.
Chronology of Oral Tradition: Quest for a Chimera. David P. Henige. (Oxford Studies in African Affairs). (Illus.). 266p. 1974. 27.00x (ISBN 0-19-821694-7). Oxford U Pr.
Chronology of Photography: A Critical Survey of the History of Photography As a Medium of Art. Arnold Gassan. 380p. (Orig.). 1981. text ed. 19.95 (ISBN 0-87992-022-X); pap. text ed. 12.95 (ISBN 0-87992-021-1). Light Impressions.
Chronology of Substances of Abuse. Martin W. Fulton. LC 78-62253. 1978. pap. text ed. 8.50 (ISBN 0-8191-0566-X). U Pr of Amer.
Chronology of the Federal Emergency Relief Administration: May 12, 1933 to December 31, 1935. Doris Carothers. LC 70-165681. (FDR & the Era of the New Deal Ser.). 1971. Repr. of 1937 ed. lib. bdg. 15.00 (ISBN 0-306-70338-6). Da Capo.
Chronology of the Hebrew Kings. Edwin R. Thiele. 1977. pap. 3.95 (ISBN 0-310-36001-3). Zondervan.
Chronology of the Origin & Progress of Paper & Paper-Making. Joel Munsell. Ed. by John Bidwell. LC 78-74389. (Nineteenth-Century Book Arts & Printing History Ser.: Vol. 4). 1980. lib. bdg. 27.50 (ISBN 0-8240-3878-9). Garland Pub.
Chronology of the People's Republic of China from October 1, 1949. Peter P. Cheng. LC 70-184667. (Quality Paperbacks Ser.: No. 250). 347p. (Orig.). 1972. pap. 4.95 (ISBN 0-8226-0250-4). Littlefield.
Chronopolis. J. G. Ballard. 1979. pap. 2.25 (ISBN 0-425-04191-3). Berkley Pub.
Chrysal, or the Adventures of a Guinea, 4 vols. Charles Johnstone. Ed. by Ronald Paulson. LC 78-60839. (Novel 1720-1805 Ser.: Vol. 5). 1979. Set. lib. bdg. 124.00 (ISBN 0-8240-3654-9). Garland Pub.
Chrysalis. Joyce E. Davis. Ed. by Heather Bennett. LC 80-84927. 170p. 1981. write for info. (ISBN 0-913420-91-3). Olympus Pub Co.
Chrysalis Eight. Roy Torgeson. LC 80-649. (Double D Science Fiction Ser.). 192p. 1980. 9.95 (ISBN 0-385-17040-8). Doubleday.
Chrysanthemum & the Bat. Robert Whiting. LC 76-27708. (Illus.). 352p. 1977. 10.00 (ISBN 0-396-07317-4). Dodd.
Chrysanthemums. James F. Smith. (Illus.). 224p. 1975. 16.50 o.s.i. (ISBN 0-7134-2936-4). Hippocrene Bks.
Chrysanthemums: Year Round Growing. Barrie Machin & Nigel Scopes. (Illus.). 1978. 24.95 (ISBN 0-7137-0885-9, Pub. by Blandford Pr England). Sterling.
Chrysler Outboards, Three and One Half to Twenty Hp: 1966-1977. 184p. 8.00 o.p. (ISBN 0-89287-221-7, B655). Western Marine Ent.
Chrysler Outboards, Twenty-Five to One Hundred -Thirty-Five HP: 1966-1977. 192p. 8.00 o.p. (ISBN 0-686-62676-1, B657). Western Marine Ent.
Chryssa. Pierre Restany. LC 77-1916. (Contemporary Artist Ser.). (Illus.). 1978. 55.00 o.p. (ISBN 0-8109-0366-0). Abrams.
Chrystal Beauty & Other Poems. Jon Kochis. 1981. 5.75 (ISBN 0-8062-1688-3). Carlton.
Chu-Shu-Chi-Nien As a Source to the Social History of Ancient China. LC 79-2822. 101p. 1981. Repr. of 1956 ed. 12.00 (ISBN 0-8305-0002-2). Hyperion Conn.
Chuang Tzu. Tr. by Herbert A. Giles from Chinese. (Unwin Paperbacks Ser.). 336p. (Orig.). 1980. pap. 7.50x (ISBN 0-04-299009-2, 2572). Allen Unwin.
Chuang Tzu: Basic Writings. Chuang Tzu. Tr. by Burton Watson. LC 64-21079. pap. 5.00x (ISBN 0-231-08606-7). Columbia U Pr.
Chuck Berry: Rock'n'roll Music. Howard A. Dewitt. (Illus.). 120p. (Orig.). 1981. 12.95 (ISBN 0-938840-01-0); pap. 5.95 (ISBN 0-938840-00-2). Horizon Bks CA.
Chuck Foreman. John De Rosier. (Sports Superstars Ser.). (Illus.). (gr. 3-9). 1976. o. p. 5.95 (ISBN 0-87191-543-X); pap. 2.95 (ISBN 0-89812-168-X). Creative Ed.
Chuck Wagon Cookbook. Beth McElfresh. LC 60-8068. 72p. 1960. pap. 3.50 (ISBN 0-8040-0042-5, 1, SB). Swallow.
Church. Hans Kung. 600p. 1976. pap. 3.95 (ISBN 0-385-11367-6, Im). Doubleday.
Church. Russell P. Spittler. LC 77-83982. (Radiant Life Ser.). 1977. pap. 1.50 (ISBN 0-88243-910-3, 02-0910); 2.50 (ISBN 0-88243-180-3, 32-0180). Gospel Pub.
Church: A Believing Fellowship. rev. ed. John Leith. LC 80-82192. 1980. 6.95 (ISBN 0-8042-1813-7). John Knox.
Church, a Believing Fellowship. John H. Leith. LC 80-82192. 192p. 1981. pap. 6.95 (ISBN 0-8042-0518-3). John Knox.
Church According to the Bible. J. J. Turner. pap. 1.95 (ISBN 0-89315-016-9). Lambert Bk.
Church & Chapel, 1863, 3 vols. in 1. Frederick W. Robinson. Ed. by Robert L. Wolff. LC 75-1500. (Victorian Fiction Ser.). 1975. lib. bdg. 66.00 (ISBN 0-8240-1575-4). Garland Pub.
Church & China: Toward Reconciliation? Joseph J. Spae. 168p. 1980. pap. 10.00 (ISBN 0-936078-01-4). Chicago Theology & Culture.
Church and Community Resources. Marcus D. Bryant & Charles F. Kemp. 96p. 1977. pap. 1.95 (ISBN 0-8272-0441-8). Bethany Pr.
Church & Cultures: An Applied Anthropology for the Religious Worker. Louis J. Luzbetak. LC 75-108055. (Applied Cultural Anthropology Ser). 448p. 1976. pap. 6.95x (ISBN 0-87808-725-7). William Carey Lib.
Church & Government in the Middle Ages. Ed. by C. Brooke et al. LC 75-41614. (Illus.). 1977. 55.00 (ISBN 0-521-21172-7). Cambridge U Pr.
Church & Human Rights. Ed. by Norbert Greinacher & Alois Muller. (Concilium Ser.: Vol. 124). 1979. pap. 4.95 (ISBN 0-8164-2232-X). Crossroad NY.
Church & Its Order According to Scripture. Samuel Ridout. Date not set. pap. 1.95 (ISBN 0-87213-711-2). Loizeaux.
Church & Its Youth. Lamar Vest. (CTC Ser.). 1980. 4.50 (ISBN 0-87148-170-7); pap. 3.50 (ISBN 0-87148-171-5); instr's guide 7.95 (ISBN 0-87148-172-3). Pathway Pr.
Church & Man's Struggle for Unity. Herbert Waddams. 1973. pap. 5.95 (ISBN 0-7137-0480-2). Transatlantic.
Church & People, 1450-1600. Claire Cross. LC 76-25005. (Fontana Library of English History). 288p. 1976. text ed. 18.25x (ISBN 0-391-00649-5). Humanities.
Church & Politics: From Theology to a Case History of Zimbabwe. Edna McDonagh. LC 80-53070. 200p. 1980. text ed. 12.95 (ISBN 0-268-00734-9); pap. text ed. 5.95 (ISBN 0-268-00736-5). U of Notre Dame Pr.
Church & Society in Catholic Europe of the Eighteenth Century. W. J. Callahan & D. Higgs. LC 78-12165. 1979. 22.50 (ISBN 0-521-22424-1). Cambridge U Pr.
Church & Society in England, 1770-1970: A Historical Survey. E. R. Norman. 1976. 54.00x (ISBN 0-19-826435-6). Oxford U Pr.
Church & Society in the Last Centuries of Byzantium. D. M. Nicol. LC 78-72092. (Birkbeck Lectures, 1977). 1979. 23.95 (ISBN 0-521-22438-1). Cambridge U Pr.

Church & State from Constantine to Theodosius. Stanley L. Greenslade. LC 79-8712. 93p. 1981. Repr. of 1954 ed. lib. bdg. 19.50x (ISBN 0-313-20793-3, GRCS). Greenwood.

Church & State in Early Maryland. George Petrie. 1973. Repr. of 1892 ed. pap. 7.00 (ISBN 0-384-45970-6). Johnson Repr.

Church & State in Europe. Ed. by Ernst Helmrich. LC 78-68021. (Problems in Civilization Ser.). 1979. pap. 3.95 (ISBN 0-88273-405-9). Forum Pr MO.

Church & State in Fascist Italy. D. A. Binchy. (Royal Institute of International Affairs Ser.). 1941. 39.50x (ISBN 0-19-821486-3). Oxford U Pr.

Church & State in North Carolina. Stephen B. Weeks. Repr. of 1893 ed. pap. 7.00 (ISBN 0-384-66391-5). Johnson Repr.

Church & State in Scotland: Sixteen Sixty to Sixteen Eighty-One. Julia Buckroyd. 1980. text ed. 32.50x (ISBN 0-85976-042-1). Humanities.

Church & State in Yugoslavia Since Nineteen Forty-Five. Stella Alexander. LC 77-88668. (Soviet & East European Studies). 1979. 41.50 (ISBN 0-521-21942-6). Cambridge U Pr.

Church & the Law in the Earlier Middle Ages. Walter Ullman. 406p. 1980. 60.00x (ISBN 0-902089-79-X, Pub. by Variorum England). State Mutual Bk.

Church & the Public Conscience. Edgar M. Carlson. LC 79-8710. xii, 104p. 1981. Repr. of 1956 ed. lib. bdg. 17.50x (ISBN 0-313-22195-2, CACH). Greenwood.

Church & the Secular Order in Reformation Thought. John M. Tonkin. LC 73-143390. 236p. 1971. 17.50x (ISBN 0-231-03374-5). Columbia U Pr.

Church & the Tribulation. Robert H. Gundry. 224p. 1973. text ed. 6.95 (ISBN 0-310-25401-9). Zondervan.

Church & the Two Nations in Medieval Ireland. J. A. Watt. LC 72-120196. (Cambridge Studies in Medieval Life & Thought: Vol. 3). (Illus.). 1970. 42.00 (ISBN 0-521-07738-9). Cambridge U Pr.

Church Architecture. Henry H. Holly. 1980. lib. bdg. 75.00 (ISBN 0-8490-3141-9). Gordon Pr.

Church As Institution. Gregory Baum & Andrew Greeley. LC 73-6430. (Concilium Ser.: Religion in the Seventies: Vol. 91). 156p. 1974. pap. 4.95 (ISBN 0-8164-2575-2). Crossroad NY.

Church As Moral Decision-Maker. James M. Gustafson. LC 74-124454. 1970. 5.95 o.p. (ISBN 0-8298-0178-2). Pilgrim NY.

Church Authority & Intellectual Freedom. Christopher Derrick. LC 81-80129. 95p. (Orig.). 1981. pap. price not set (ISBN 0-89870-011-6). Ignatius Pr.

Church Banquets Made Easy. Joanne Fields & Lois Otto. LC 76-19480. (Illus.). 1976. pap. 2.25 (ISBN 0-87239-115-9, 2766). Standard Pub.

Church Before the Watching World. Francis A. Schaeffer. LC 76-166121. (Orig.). 1971. pap. 1.95 o.p. (ISBN 0-87784-542-5). Inter-Varsity.

Church Between Revolution & Restoration. Ed. by Hubert Jedin & John P. Dolan. (History of the Church: Vol. 7). 1980. 37.50 (ISBN 0-8245-0446-1). Crossroad NY.

Church Bulletin Bits. George W. Knight. 160p. 1976. pap. 3.45 (ISBN 0-8010-5368-4). Baker Bk.

Church Cat Abroad. Graham Oakley. 1980. pap. 2.95 (ISBN 0-689-70472-0, Aladdin). Atheneum.

Church, Change & Development. Ivan Illich. 4.95 o.p. (ISBN 0-8164-1010-0); pap. 2.45 (ISBN 0-8164-2505-1). Crossroad NY.

Church Courts & the People During the English Reformation Fifteen-Twenty to Fifteen Seventy. Ralph Houlbrooke. (Oxford Historical Monographs). 1979. 29.95x (ISBN 0-19-821876-1). Oxford U Pr.

Church Cyclopaedia: A Dictionary of Church Doctrine, History, Organization & Ritual, & Containing Original Articles on Special Topics, Written Expressly for This Work by Bishops, Presbyters, & Laymen. Angelo Ames Benton. LC 74-31499. 810p. 1975. Repr. of 1883 ed. 32.00 (ISBN 0-8103-4204-9). Gale.

Church Dogmatics. Karl Barth. Incl. Vol. 4. Doctrine of Reconcilliation, 2 pts. Pt. 3, Repr. Of 1962 Ed., 492p. 23.00x (ISBN 0-567-09044-2); Pt. 4, Repr. Of 1969 Ed., 240p. 12.95x (ISBN 0-567-09045-0); Vol. 5. Index: with Aids to the Preacher. G. W. Bromiley & G. F. Torrance. 584p. Repr. of 1977 ed. 32.00x (ISBN 0-567-09046-9). Attic Pr.

Church Dogmatics: The Doctrine of Creation, Vol. III, Pt. I. Karl Barth. 440p. 1958. text ed. 23.00x (ISBN 0-567-09031-0). Attic Pr.

Church Dogmatics: The Doctrine of Creation, Vol. III, Pt. II. 680p. 1960. text ed. 23.00x (ISBN 0-567-09032-9). Attic Pr.

Church Dogmatics: The Doctrine of God, Vol. II, Pt. I. Karl Barth. Tr. by T. H. Parker et al from Ger. 710p. 1957. text ed. 23.00x (ISBN 0-567-09021-3). Attic Pr.

Church Dogmatics: The Doctrine of God, Vol. II, Pt. II. Karl Barth. Tr. by G. W. Bromiley from Ger. 820p. 1957. text ed. 23.00x (ISBN 0-567-09022-1). Attic Pr.

Church Dogmatics: The Doctrine of the Word of God (Prolegomena to Church Dogmatics, Vol. 1, Pt. 2. Karl Barth. Ed. by G. T. Thomson & Harold Knight. 924p. 1956. text ed. 23.00x (ISBN 0-567-09012-4). Attic Pr.

Church Dogmatics, Vol. III: The Doctrine of Creation, Pt. 3. Karl Barth. 560p. Repr. of 1961 ed. text ed. 23.00x (ISBN 0-567-09033-7). Attic Pr.

Church Dogmatics Vol. III: The Doctrine of Creation Pt. 4. Karl Barth. 720p. Repr. of 1961 ed. text ed. 23.00 (ISBN 0-567-09034-5). Attic Pr.

Church Dogmatics, Vol IV: The Doctrine of Reconciliation-Part 1. Karl Barth. 814p. Repr. of 1956 ed. text ed. 23.00x (ISBN 0-567-09041-8). Attic Pr.

Church Dogmatics, Vol. IV: The Doctrine of Reconciliation-Part 2. Karl Barth. 882p. Repr. of 1958 ed. text ed. 23.00x (ISBN 0-567-09042-6). Attic Pr.

Church Dogmatics, Vol. IV: The Doctrine of Reconciliation-Part 3, (I) Karl Barth. 496p. Repr. of 1961 ed. text ed. 23.00 (ISBN 0-567-09043-4). Attic Pr.

Church Dogmatics, Vol. 1: The Doctrine of the Word of God (Prolegomena to Church Dogmatics), Pt. 1. 2nd ed. Karl Barth. Tr. by G. W. Bromiley from Ger. 592p. Repr. of 1975 ed. text ed. 23.00x (ISBN 0-567-09013-2). Attic Pr.

Church Emerging: A U. S. Lutheran Case Study. Ed. by John Reumann. LC 76-62618. 288p. 1977. pap. 9.95 (ISBN 0-8006-1259-0, 1-1259). Fortress.

Church Feasts & Seasons. Maureen Curley. (Children of the Kingdom Activities Ser.). (gr. 1-4). 1974. 7.95 (ISBN 0-686-13684-5). Pflaum Pr.

Church Fellowship. Becker Erlandson. 1980. 0.80 (ISBN 0-8100-0113-6). Northwest Pub.

Church Festival Decorations. 2nd enl. ed. Ernest Suffling. LC 74-6266. (Illus.). vi, 156p. 1974. Repr. of 1907 ed. 20.00 (ISBN 0-8103-4015-1). Gale.

Church Furnishings: The Nadfas Guide. Patricia Dirsztay. (Illus.). 1978. 16.00 (ISBN 0-7100-8820-5); pap. 7.95 (ISBN 0-7100-8897-3). Routledge & Kegan.

Church: God's People. Bruce Shelley. 1978. pap. 3.95 (ISBN 0-88207-770-8). Victor Bks.

Church Growth - a Mighty River. Delos Miles. 1981. pap. 5.95 (ISBN 0-8054-6227-9). Broadman.

Church Growth & Group Conversion. new ed. Donald A. McGavran. LC 73-80163. 128p. 1973. pap. 3.95 (ISBN 0-87808-712-5). William Carey Lib.

Church Growth Is Not the Point. Robert K. Hudnut. LC 74-25692. 160p. 1975. 7.95 o.p. (ISBN 0-06-064062-6, HarpR). Har-Row.

Church History. Earle Cairns. pap. 1.50 (ISBN 0-8024-1483-4). Moody.

Church History in Future Perspective. Ed. by Roger Aubert. (Concilium Ser.; Religion in the Seventies: Vol. 57). 1970. pap. 4.95 (ISBN 0-8164-2513-2). Crossroad NY.

Church Hymnary: With Music. 3rd ed. 1055p. 1973. 18.50x (ISBN 0-19-146605-0). Oxford U Pr.

Church in History. John E. Booty. (Church's Teaching Ser.: Vol. 3). 1979. 9.50 (ISBN 0-8164-0420-8); pap. 3.95 (ISBN 0-8164-2216-8). Crossroad NY.

Church in Italy in the Fifteenth Century. Denys Hay. LC 76-47409. (Birkbeck Lectures: 1971). 1977. 27.50 (ISBN 0-521-21532-3). Cambridge U Pr.

Church in the Age of Absolutism & Enlightenment. Ed. by Hubert Jedin & John P. Dolan. (History of the Church: Vol. 6). 1981. 37.50 (ISBN 0-8245-0445-3). Crossroad NY.

Church in the Age of Feudalism. Ed. by Hubert Jedin & John P. Dolan. (History of the Church: Vol. 3). 1980. 37.50 (ISBN 0-8164-1039-9). Crossroad NY.

Church in the Age of Liberalism. Ed. by Hubert Jedin & John P. Dolan. (History of the Church: Vol. 8). 1981. 37.50 (ISBN 0-8245-0447-X). Crossroad NY.

Church in the Bible. Don DeWelt. (Bible Study Textbook Ser.). (Illus.). 1958. 13.00 (ISBN 0-89900-049-5). College Pr Pub.

Church in the Industrial Age. Ed. by Hubert Jedin & John P. Dolan. (History of the Church: Vol. 9). 1981. 37.50 (ISBN 0-8245-0448-8). Crossroad NY.

Church in the Modern Age. Ed. by Hubert Jedin & John P. Dolan. (History of the Church: Vol. 10). 1980. 37.50 (ISBN 0-8245-0452-6). Crossroad NY.

Church in the New Testament. Rudolph Schnackenburg. pap. 5.95 (ISBN 0-8164-2585-X). Crossroad NY.

Church in the Roman Empire. Erwin R. Goodenough. LC 77-122754. 1970. Repr. of 1931 ed. lib. bdg. 12.50x (ISBN 0-8154-0337-2). Cooper Sq.

Church in the Theology of the Reformers. Paul D. Avis. Ed. by Peter Toon & Ralph Martin. LC 80-16186. (New Foundations Theological Library). 256p. 1981. 18.50 (ISBN 0-8042-3708-5); pap. 11.95 (ISBN 0-8042-3728-X). John Knox.

Church in Town & Countryside: Papers Read at the Seventeenth Summer Meeting & the Eighteenth Winter Meeting of the Ecclesiastical History Society. Ed. by Derek Baker. (Studies in Church History: Vol. 16). 1980. 36.00x (ISBN 0-631-11421-1, Pub. by Basil Blackwell). Biblio Dist.

Church: Its Changing Image Through Twenty Centuries. Eric G. Jay. LC 79-92070. 1980. 18.00 (ISBN 0-8042-0877-8); pap. 9.95 (ISBN 0-8042-0878-6). John Knox.

Church Library Workbook. Francine E. Walls. 152p. 1980. pap. 4.95 (ISBN 0-89367-048-0). Light & Life.

Church-Maintained in Truth: A Theological Meditation. Hans Kung. 87p. 1980. 6.95 (ISBN 0-8164-0454-2). Crossroad NY.

Church Mice at Christmas. Graham Oakley. LC 80-14518. (Illus.). 40p. (gr. k up). 1980. 10.95 (ISBN 0-689-30797-7). Atheneum.

Church Monuments in Romantic England. Nicholas Penny. LC 76-58912. (Studies in British Art). (Illus.). 1977. 27.50x (ISBN 0-300-02075-9). Yale U Pr.

Church Music: An International Bibliography. Richard C. Von Ende. LC 79-23697. 473p. 1980. lib. bdg. 22.00 (ISBN 0-8108-1271-1). Scarecrow.

Church Music Handbook. Lynn W. Thayer. 9.95 (ISBN 0-310-36880-4). Zondervan.

Church Music of William Billings. Murray Barbour. LC 72-39000. 168p. 1972. Repr. of 1960 ed. lib. bdg. 15.00 (ISBN 0-306-70434-X). Da Capo.

Church Music Transgressed: Reflections on Reform. Francis P. Schmitt. LC 77-9424. 1977. 7.95 (ISBN 0-8164-0355-4). Crossroad NY.

Church Musicians Enchiridon. A. Lehmann. 1979. 3.25 (ISBN 0-8100-0111-X). Northwest Pub.

Church of Christ, 2 vols. James Bannerman. Set. 15.95 o.p. (ISBN 0-686-12499-5). Banner of Truth.

Church of England. Jan Baker. 1978. pap. 2.90 (ISBN 0-08-021408-8). Pergamon.

Church of England. Edward W. Watson. LC 80-22643. (Home University Library of Modern Knowledge: No. 90). 192p. 1981. Repr. of 1961 ed. lib. bdg. 25.00x (ISBN 0-313-22683-0, WAEN). Greenwood.

Church of God Doctrines. C. C. Carver. 180p. 1948. pap. 2.00. Faith Pub Hse.

Church of the Earth: The Ecology of a Creative Community. Robert S. De Ropp. (Illus.). 288p. 1974. 8.95 o.p. (ISBN 0-440-01232-5, Sey Lawr). Delacorte.

Church of the Old Testament. rev. ed. John Tvedtnes. LC 80-18595. 111p. 1980. 5.95 (ISBN 0-87747-827-9). Deseret Bk.

Church Officers at Work. Glenn H. Asquith. pap. 2.50 (ISBN 0-8170-0048-8). Judson.

Church School Student's Bibles: Revised Standard Version. 7.95 ea. (Pub. by Collins Pubs). Black (RS4). Burg (RS4R). White (RS4W). Blue (RS4B). Brown (RS4BR). World Bible.

Church School Teaching Can Be Fun! Proven Ways to Make Your Class More Interesting. Carol Schmelzel. 1979. pap. 6.95 (ISBN 0-8164-2190-0); wkbk. avail. (ISBN 0-685-59465-3). Crossroad NY.

Church Shall Be Free: A Glance at Eight Centuries of Church & State. Arthur E. Sutherland. LC 65-24000. (Orig.). 1965. pap. 1.95x (ISBN 0-8139-0232-0). U Pr of Va.

Church Society & Politics. Ed. by Derek Baker. (Studies in Church History Ser.: Vol. 12). 1975. 36.00x (ISBN 0-631-16970-9, Pub. by Basil Blackwell). Biblio Dist.

Church, State & Opposition in U. S. S. R. Gerhard Simon. 1974. 20.00x (ISBN 0-520-02612-8). U of Cal Pr.

Church State & Public Policy. Ed. by Jay Mechling. 1979. 10.25 (ISBN 0-8447-2159-X); pap. 5.25 (ISBN 0-8447-2160-3). Am Enterprise.

Church Symbolism: An Explanation of the More Important Symbols of the Old & New Testament, the Primitive, the Mediaeval & the Modern Church. rev. 2nd ed. Frederick R. Webber. LC 79-107627. (Illus.). 1971. Repr. of 1938 ed. 28.00 (ISBN 0-8103-3349-X). Gale.

Church That Glowed. Wynelle Gardner. 1978. pap. 2.95 o.p. (ISBN 0-88270-129-0). Logos.

Church, the Beautiful Bride of Christ. Ed. by Thomas B. Warren & Garland Elkins. 1980. pap. 16.95. Natl Christian Pr.

Church Through the Ages, Pt. 1. Morris Womack. (Living Word Paperback Ser.). (Orig.). 1965. Pt. 1. pap. 2.25 (ISBN 0-8344-0052-9). Sweet.

Church Under the Law. R. A. Marchant. LC 79-80819. (Illus.). 1969. 47.50 (ISBN 0-521-07460-6). Cambridge U Pr.

Church, University, Enlightenment: The Moderate Literati of Edinburgh, 1720-1793. Richard B. Sher. 1980. text ed. write for info. (ISBN 0-391-01208-8). Humanities.

Church Usher: Servant of God. David R. Enlow. LC 80-66769. 64p. (Orig.). 1980. pap. 1.95 (ISBN 0-87509-284-5). Chr Pubns.

Church Ushers' Manual. Willis O. Garrett. pap. 1.95 (ISBN 0-8007-0048-1). Revell.

Church Wealth & Business Income. Martin A. Larson. LC 65-20799. 1965. 3.95 o.p. (ISBN 0-8022-0930-0). Philos Lib.

Church Without Walls. Odin K. Stenberg. LC 76-7702. 1976. pap. 2.45 (ISBN 0-87123-056-9, 200056). Bethany Fell.

Churched & Unchurched in America: A Comparative Profile. David A. Roozen. LC 77-94682. 1978. pap. 2.00 (ISBN 0-914422-07-3). Glenmary Res Ctr.

Churches & Churchgoers: Patterns of Church Growth in the British Isles Since 1700. Robert Currie et al. (Illus.). 1978. 45.00x (ISBN 0-19-827218-9). Oxford U Pr.

Churches & Politics in Germany. Frederic Spotts. LC 72-11050. 352p. 1973. 25.00x (ISBN 0-8195-4059-5, Pub. by Wesleyan U Pr). Columbia U Pr.

Churches & Politics in Latin America. Ed. by Daniel H. Levine. LC 79-23827. (Sage Focus Editions: Vol. 14). 288p. 1980. 18.95 (ISBN 0-8039-1298-6); pap. 9.95x (ISBN 0-8039-1299-4). Sage.

Churches & the Indian Schools, 1888-1912. Francis P. Prucha. LC 79-12220. (Illus.). 1979. 16.50x (ISBN 0-8032-3657-3). U of Nebr Pr.

Churches in Cultural Captivity: A History of the Social Attitudes of Southern Baptists. John L. Eighmy. LC 70-111047. 1972. 14.50x (ISBN 0-87049-115-6). U of Tenn Pr.

Churches in the Nineteenth Century. Josef L. Altholz. LC 66-30446. (Orig.). 1967. 7.15 o.p. (ISBN 0-672-51130-4); pap. 5.95 (ISBN 0-672-60682-8). Bobbs.

Churches of Africa. Claude Geffre. (Concilium Ser.: Vol. 106). pap. 4.95 (ISBN 0-8164-2150-1). Crossroad NY.

Churches of Mexico, 1530-1810. Joseph A. Baird, Jr. (Illus.). 1962. 35.00x (ISBN 0-520-00066-8). U of Cal Pr.

Churchill. Madeline Jones. (Leaders Ser.). (Illus.). 96p. (gr. 9-12). 1980. 14.95 (ISBN 0-7134-1922-9, Pub. by Batsford England). David & Charles.

Churchill: A Profile. Ed. by Peter Stansky. (World Profiles Ser.). 1973. 7.95 o.p. (ISBN 0-8090-3447-6). Hill & Wang.

Churchill & His Generals. Barrie Pitt. 224p. 1981. pap. 2.50 (ISBN 0-553-14610-6). Bantam.

Churchill & the Admirals. Stephen Roskill. LC 78-57070. (Illus.). 1978. 12.95 o.p. (ISBN 0-688-03364-4). Morrow.

Churchill & the Montgomery Myth. R. W. Thompson. LC 68-18714. 272p. 1968. 5.95 (ISBN 0-87131-001-5). M Evans.

Churchill As Warlord. Ronald Lewin. LC 72-96544. (Illus.). 308p. 1981. pap. 6.95 (ISBN 0-8128-6099-3). Stein & Day.

Churchill Coalition, Nineteen Forty to Nineteen Forty-Five. J. M. Lee. 192p. 1980. 20.00 (ISBN 0-208-01880-8, Archon). Shoe String.

Churchill, Cripps, & India, Nineteen Thirty-Nine to Nineteen Forty-Five. R. J. Moore. 1979. 29.50x (ISBN 0-19-822485-0). Oxford U Pr.

Churchill, Roosevelt, Stalin: The War They Waged & the Peace They Sought. 2nd ed. Herbert Feis. 1967. 23.50x (ISBN 0-691-05607-2); pap. 5.95 (ISBN 0-691-01050-1). Princeton U Pr.

Churchill Speaks: Winston S. Churchill in Peace & War Collected Speeches, 1897-1963. abr. ed. Ed. by Robert R. James. LC 80-21880. 1000p. 1980. pap. 25.00 (ISBN 0-87754-256-2). Chelsea Hse.

Churchill's Gold. James Follett. 228p. 1981. 9.95 (ISBN 0-395-30526-8). HM.

Church's Amazing Story. Ed. by Daughters Of St. Paul. LC 68-59043. (Divine Master Ser., Vol. 2). (gr. 10). 1969. 5.00 (ISBN 0-8198-0028-7); pap. 4.00 (ISBN 0-8198-0029-5); discussion questions & projects 0.50 (ISBN 0-8198-0030-9). Dghtrs St Paul.

Church's Confession Under Hitler. 2nd ed. Arthur C. Cochrane. LC 76-57655. (Pittsburgh Reprint Ser.: No. 4). 1977. pap. text ed. 7.50 (ISBN 0-915138-28-X). Pickwick.

Church's Ministry with Senior Highs. Rowena Ferguson. 1963. 1.50 o.p. (ISBN 0-687-08533-0). Abingdon.

Chushingura: The Treasury of Loyal Retainers. Tr. by Donald Keene from Japanese. LC 78-142283. 1971. 17.50x (ISBN 0-231-03530-6); pap. 6.00x (ISBN 0-231-03531-4). Columbia U Pr.

Chymia, Vols. 7, 9-12, 1961-1967. Ed. by Henry M. Leicester. LC 48-7051. (Vol. 8 o.p.). 10.00x ea. o.p. U of Pa Pr.

C.I.-Crisis Intervention. Harvey L. Ruben. 1976. pap. 1.75 o.p. (ISBN 0-445-08522-3). Popular Lib.

CIA: A Bibliography. Robert Goehlert & Elizabeth R. Hoffmeister. (Public Administration Ser.: Bibliography P-498). 79p. 1980. pap. 8.50. Vance Biblios.

CIA & the Third World: A Study in Cryptodiplomacy. 22.50 (ISBN 0-7069-1292-6, Pub. by Vikas India). Advent Bk.

CIA Energy Information Reprint Series, 5 vols. Central Intelligence Agency. Ed. by J. A. Bereny. Incl. Vol. I. International Energy Situation: Outlook to 1985; Vol. 2. Prospects for Soviet Oil Production; Vol. 3. Prospects for Soviet Oil Production: A Supplemental Analysis; Vol. 4. China: Oil Production Prospects; Vol. 5. World Petroleum Outlook. 89p. 1979. 49.00 (ISBN 0-930978-57-9); pap. 38.00 (ISBN 0-89934-000-8). Solar Energy Info.

CIA in America. John Kelly. LC 78-24776. 256p. 1981. 14.95 (ISBN 0-88208-102-0); pap. 6.95 (ISBN 0-88208-103-9). Lawrence Hill.

CIA: The Cult of Intelligence. Victor Marchetti & John D. Marks. 1980. pap. 2.95 (ISBN 0-440-11329-6). Dell.

CIAMDA Eighty: An Index to the Literature on Atomic & Molecular Collision Data Relevant to Fusion Research. 498p. 1980. pap. 31.25 (ISBN 92-0-039080-3, ISP550, IAEA). Unipub.

Ciascuno Il Suo. Iole F. Magri. LC 75-29713. 1976. pap. text ed. 7.20 (ISBN 0-395-13398-X). HM.

Cicada. John Haines. LC 77-74602. (Wesleyan Poetry Program: Vol. 86). 1977. pap. 10.00x (ISBN 0-8195-2086-1, Pub. by Wesleyan U Pr); pap. 4.95 (ISBN 0-8195-1086-6). Columbia U Pr.

Cicero: A Biography. Torsten Petersson. LC 63-10768. 1920. 15.00x (ISBN 0-8196-0119-5). Biblo.

Cicero, Epistulae Ad Familiares: 47-43 B.C, Vol. II. Ed. by D. R. Shackleton-Bailey. LC 76-11079. (Classical Texts & Commentaries Ser.: No. 17). 1977. 82.00 (ISBN 0-521-21152-2). Cambridge U Pr.

Cicero, Epistulae Ad Familiares: 62-47 B.C, Vol. 1. Ed. by D. R. Shackleton-Bailey. LC 76-11079. (Classical Texts & Commentaries Ser.: No. 16). 1977. 82.00 (ISBN 0-521-21151-4). Cambridge U Pr.

Cicero: Epistulae Ad Quintum Fratrem et M. Brutum. Ed. by D. R. Bailey. (Cambridge Classical Texts & Commentaries Ser.: No. 22). 300p. Date not set. 49.50 (ISBN 0-521-23053-5). Cambridge U Pr.

Cicero on Moral Obligation: A New Translation of Cicero's De Officiis. Tr. & annotations by John Higginbotham. 1967. 16.50x (ISBN 0-520-00556-2). U of Cal Pr.

Cicero: Pro Archia. Cicero. Ed. by G. H. Nall. (Elementary Classics Ser.). (Latin). 1962. Repr. of 1901 ed. 5.95 (ISBN 0-312-13685-4). St Martin.

Cicero: Pro Milone. Cicero. Ed. by Francis M. Colson. (Classical Ser.). (Latin). 1954. Repr. of 1893 ed. 5.95 (ISBN 0-312-13720-6). St Martin.

Cicero: Pro Murena. Ed. by C. Macdonald. (Modern School Classics Ser). (Illus.). (gr. 10-12). 1969. text ed. 5.95 (ISBN 0-312-13755-9). St Martin.

Cicero: Speeches Against Antony, Philippics 4, 5, 6. J. Terry & D. Upton. (Modern School Classics Ser.). 1.75 1970. 5.95 (ISBN 0-312-13650-1). St Martin.

Cicero: Verrine Orations V. R. G. Levens. 1946. 6.95 (ISBN 0-312-13825-3). St Martin.

Cicerone: An Art Guide to Painting in Italy for the Use of Travellers & Students. Jakob Burckhardt. Ed. by Sydney J. Freedberg. LC 77-18677. (Connoisseurship, Criticism & Art History Ser.: Vol. 3). 305p. 1979. lib. bdg. 30.00. Garland Pub.

Ciceronis Amor: Tullie's Love, a Critical Edition. Robert Greene. Ed. by Charles H. Larson. (Salzburg Studies in English Literature, Elizabethan & Renaissance Studies: No. 36). 216p. 1974. pap. text ed. 25.00x (ISBN 0-391-01392-0). Humanities.

Cicero's Letters to Atticus, 16 bks. in 6 vols. Cicero. Ed. by D. R. Bailey. (Cambridge Classical Texts & Commentaries). (Lat.). Vol. 1, Bks. 1 & 2. 52.00 (ISBN 0-521-04643-2); Vol. 2, Bks. 3 & 4. 32.50 (ISBN 0-521-04644-0); Vol. 3, Bks. 5-7. 44.50 (ISBN 0-521-06927-0); Vol. 4, Bks. 8-10. 59.00 (ISBN 0-521-06928-9); Vol. 5, Bks. 11-13. 54.00 (ISBN 0-521-04645-9); Vol. 6, Bks. 14-16. 44.50 (ISBN 0-521-04646-7); Vol. 7, Indices To Vols. 1-6. 19.95 (ISBN 0-521-07840-7); 265.00 (ISBN 0-521-08773-2). Cambridge U Pr.

Cicero's Tusculan Disputations, Bk. 1. Ed. & intro. by Frank E. Rockwood. Bd. with Scipio's Dream. xiv, 22p. xiv, 109p. 1966. 5.95x (ISBN 0-8061-0718-9). U of Okla Pr.

Cichlid Fishes of the Great Lakes of Africa, Their Biology & Evolution. G. Fryer & T. D. Iles. (Illus.). 641p. 1981. Repr. of 1972 ed. lib. bdg. 104.50x (ISBN 3-87429-169-3). Lubrecht & Cramer.

Cichlids of the World. Robert J. Goldstein. (Illus.). 382p. 1973. 20.00 (ISBN 0-87666-032-4, H-945). TFH Pubns.

CIC's School Directory Nineteen Seventy-Eight to Nineteen Seventy-Nine, 7 vols. Curriculum Information Center Staff. LC 77-88521. 1978. 48.00 ea. o.p. (ISBN 0-89770-023-6); 295.00 set o.p. (ISBN 0-685-58438-0). Curriculum Info Ctr.

Cid. Pierre Corneille. Ed. & tr. by John C. Lapp. LC 55-9014. (Crofts Classics Ser.). 1955. pap. text ed. 2.75x (ISBN 0-88295-026-6). AHM Pub.

Cid, Cinna, the Theatrical Illusion. Pierre Corneille. Tr. by John Cairncross from Fr. (Penguin Classics). 1980. pap. 3.95 (ISBN 0-14-044312-6). Penguin.

Cider. Annie Proulx & Lew Nichols. (Illus.). 272p. 1980. pap. 9.95 (ISBN 0-88266-242-2). Garden Way Pub.

Cider Book. Lila Gault & Betsy Sestrap. LC 80-18267. 200p. 1980. pap. 5.95 (ISBN 0-914842-48-X). Madrona Pubs.

Cider Vinegar. Cyril Scott. 1980. pap. 1.95 (ISBN 0-87904-011-4). Lust.

Cielo Baja Al Infierno. Tr. by Merlin Carothers. (Spanish Bks.). (Span.). 1978. 1.75 (ISBN 0-8297-0766-2). Life Pubs Intl.

Ciencia y Practica de la Iridologia. Bernard Jensen. Orig. Title: Science & Practice of Iridology. (Spanish.). 18.50 o.s.i. (ISBN 0-89557-027-0). Bi World Indus.

Cigarette End. Carola Halhuber. 1978. pap. 3.95 o.s.i. (ISBN 0-7225-0423-3). Newcastle Pub.

Cigarette Papers: Snip the Strings to Your Habit. Diane DuCharme et al. LC 79-54085. (Illus., Orig.). 1981. pap. 5.95 (ISBN 0-89638-039-4). CompCare.

Cihuatan: An Early Postclassic Town of El Salvador: the 1977-78 Excavations. Karen O. Bruhns. Ed. by Lawrence Feldman. (Monographs in Anthropology Ser.: No. 5). (Illus.). vii, 171p. (Orig.). 1980. pap. 8.60 (ISBN 0-913134-82-1). Mus Anthro MO.

Ciid Beetles of California: Coleoptera, Ciid. John F. Lawrence. (California Insect Survey Bulletin, Vol. 17). 1974. pap. 6.25x (ISBN 0-520-09489-1). U of Cal Pr.

Ciliated Protozoa: Characterization, Classification & Guide to the Literature. 2nd ed. John O. Corliss. LC 78-41075. (Illus.). 1979. text ed. 49.50 (ISBN 0-08-018752-8). Pergamon.

Ciliates. A. R. Jones. (Illus.). 1973. pap. text ed. 6.00x (ISBN 0-09-117301-9, Hutchinson U Lib). Humanities.

Ciliates. Alick R. Jones. LC 73-87077. (Illus.). 160p. 1974. 16.95 (ISBN 0-312-13860-1). St Martin.

Cilician Kingdom of Armenia. Ed. by T. S. Boase. LC 74-22291. 1979. text ed. 20.00 (ISBN 0-312-13895-4). St Martin.

Cimarron. Ricardo Alonso. LC 78-25876. (Wesleyan Poetry Program: Vol. 94). 1979. 10.00x (ISBN 0-8195-2094-2, Pub. by Wesleyan U Pr); pap. 4.95 (ISBN 0-8195-1094-7). Columbia U Pr.

Cimarron. Edna Ferber. LC 30-8609. 1951. 11.95 (ISBN 0-385-04069-5). Doubleday.

Cimarron Thunder. E. E. Halleran. 1981. pap. 1.75 (ISBN 0-345-29492-0). Ballantine.

Cincinnati: A Guide to the Queen City & Its Neighbors. LC 72-84462. 1943. 45.00 (ISBN 0-403-02201-0). Somerset Pub.

Cincinnati & Lake Erie. Jack Keenan. LC 74-23814. (Illus.). 224p. 1975. 21.95 o.p. (ISBN 0-87095-055-X). Golden West.

Cincinnati Bengals. Julian May. (NFL Today Ser.). (gr. 4-8). 1980. PLB 6.45 (ISBN 0-87191-734-3); pap. 2.95 (ISBN 0-89812-237-6). Creative Ed.

Cincinnati Companion. Tom Beckman. (Illus.). 1979. pap. text ed. 4.95 o.p. (ISBN 0-930556-00-3). T Beckman & Assoc.

CINDA Eighty: An Index to the Literature on Microscopic Neutron Data. 442p. 1980. pap. 38.75 (ISBN 92-0-039180-X, ICIN77/80, IAEA). Unipub.

CINDA: Nineteen Seventy-Eight, an Index to the Literature on Microscopic Neutron Data, Suppl. 4. 1979. pap. 24.25 (ISBN 92-0-039078-1, ICIN78-4, IAEA). Unipub.

CINDA: Nineteen Thirty-Five to Nineteen Seventy-Six, 2 vols. 1929p. 1980. Set. pap. 86.75 (ISBN 0-686-60074-6, ICIN 35-76, IAEA); Vol. 1 Z-50. pap. (ISBN 92-0-039079-X); Vol. 2 Z-51. pap. (ISBN 92-0-039179-6). Unipub.

CINDA Seventy-Nine: An Index to the Literature on Microscopic Neutron Data. 1977-1979. 376p. 1980. pap. 29.00 (ISBN 92-0-039279-2, ICIN 77-79, IAEA); free supplement (ISBN 92-0-039379-9). Unipub.

CINDA: 1976-1977 Index to the Literature on Microscopic Neutron Data, 2 vols. USA National Neutron Cross-Section Center & USSR Nuclear Data Centre. (Orig.). 1976. pap. 92.25 ea. (IAEA). Vol. 1 (ISBN 92-0-039076-5, Z52). Vol. 2 (Z53). Unipub.

CINDA: 1978 Index to the Literature on Microscopic Neutron Data, Suppl. 5. 1979. pap. 25.75 (ISBN 92-0-039178-8, ICIN78-5, IAEA). Unipub.

Cinder Path. Catherine Cookson. LC 78-54993. 1978. 9.95 o.p. (ISBN 0-688-03339-3). Morrow.

Cinderella. Brothers Grimm. LC 80-15394. (Illus.). 32p. (gr. k-3). 1981. 7.95 (ISBN 0-688-80299-0); PLB 7.63 (ISBN 0-688-84299-2). Greenwillow.

Cinderella. Marcia Brown & Charles Perrault. (Illus.). 32p. (gr. k-3). pap. 2.95 (ISBN 0-689-70484-4, A-111, Aladdin). Atheneum.

Cinderella. (Illus.). Arabic 2.50x (ISBN 0-685-82816-6). Intl Bk Ctr.

Cinderella. new ed. Charles Perrault. LC 78-18067. (Illus.). (gr. 1-4). 1979. PLB 5.21 (ISBN 0-89375-120-0); pap. 1.50 (ISBN 0-89375-098-0). Troll Assocs.

Cinderella. Anne Rogers. LC 78-50997. (Grimm Ser.). (Illus.). 24p. (gr. 2). 1978. lib. bdg. 6.95 o.p. (ISBN 0-88332-093-2, 8130). Larousse.

Cinderella & Snow White & Rose Red. Illus. by Jordon Laite. (Illus.). 24p. (gr. k-3). 1976. PLB 7.15 o.p. (ISBN 0-307-69052-0, Golden Pr). Western Pub.

Cinderella Complex: Women's Hidden Fear of Independence. Colette Dowling. 288p. 1981. 13.95 (ISBN 0-671-40052-5). Summit Bks.

Cinderella Syndrome. Septima Palm & Ingrid Brewer. (Illus.). 1980. pap. 3.50 (ISBN 0-686-28643-X). Septima.

Cindy. John Benton. 1978. pap. 2.50 (ISBN 0-8007-8319-0, Spire). Revell.

Cindy, a Hearing Ear Dog. Patricia Curtis. LC 80-24487. (Illus.). (gr. 3-5). 1981. PLB 9.95 (ISBN 0-525-27950-4). Dutton.

Cindy on Fire. Burt Hirschfeld. 1971. pap. 2.50 (ISBN 0-380-00267-1, 49270). Avon.

Cinema & History: British Newsreels & the Spanish Civil War. Anthony Aldgate. (Illus.). 1979. text ed. 31.25x (ISBN 0-85967-485-1). Humanities.

Cinema & Theatre Organ. Reginald Whitworth. (Illus.). 144p. 1981. pap. 15.00x (ISBN 0-913746-14-2). Organ Lit.

Cinema & Theatre Organ: A Comprehensive Description of This Instrument, Its Constituent Parts, & Its Use. Reginald Whitworth. (Illus.). 144p. 1981. pap. 15.00x (ISBN 0-913746-14-2). Organ Lit.

Cinema Beyond the Danube: The Camera & Politics. Michael J. Stoil. LC 74-5274. 1974. 10.00 (ISBN 0-8108-0722-X). Scarecrow.

Cinema Booklist: Supplement One. George Rehrauer. LC 70-188378. 1974. 11.00 o.p. (ISBN 0-8108-0696-7). Scarecrow.

Cinema Booklist: Supplement Two. George Rehrauer. LC 70-188378. 1977. 16.50 o.p. (ISBN 0-8108-0997-4). Scarecrow.

Cinema of Francois Truffaut. Graham Petrie. LC 72-106791. (Film Guide Ser). (Illus.). 1970. pap. 3.50 o.p. (ISBN 0-498-07649-0). A S Barnes.

Cinema of Joseph Losey. James Leahy. (Film Guide Ser.). 1967. pap. 4.95 o.p. (ISBN 0-498-06749-1). A S Barnes.

Cinema Seventy Nine. Ed. by David Castell. (Illus.). 1978. pap. 7.95 (ISBN 0-8467-0504-4, Pub. by Two Continents). Hippocrene Bks.

Cinema, the Magic Vehicle-A Guide to Its Achievement-Journey One: The Cinema Through 1949. Adam Garbicz & Jacek Klinowski. LC 75-2183. 551p. 1975. 22.50 (ISBN 0-8108-0801-3). Scarecrow.

Cinema, the Magic Vehicle-A Guide to Its Achievement-Journey Two: The Cinema in the Fifties. Adam Garbicz & Jacek Klinowski. LC 75-2183. 551p. 1979. 27.50 (ISBN 0-8108-1241-X). Scarecrow.

Cinematic Apparatus. Ed. by Teresa DeLaurentis & Stephen Heath. 1980. 18.95 (ISBN 0-312-13907-1). St Martin.

Cinematographer's Field Guide. 3rd ed. Ed. by Eastman Kodak Company. (Illus.). 1980. 6.95 (ISBN 0-87985-276-3, H-2). Eastman Kodak.

Cinematographer's Field Guide, (H-2) 3rd rev. ed. Ed. by Eastman Kodak. (Illus.). 100p. Date not set. text ed. 6.95 (ISBN 0-87985-276-3). Eastman Kodak.

Cinematographic Techniques in Biology & Medicine. Ed. by Alexis L. Burton. 1971. 49.00 o.p. (ISBN 0-12-147250-7). Acad Pr.

Cinna, the Poet & Other Roman Essays. T. P. Wiseman. 224p. 1974. text ed. 14.50x (ISBN 0-7185-1120-4, Leicester). Humanities.

Cinnabar. Edward Bryant. LC 75-20160. 1976. 7.95 o.s.i. (ISBN 0-02-518000-2, 51800). Macmillan.

Cinnabar, the One O'Clock Fox. Marguerite Henry. LC 56-11343. (Illus.). 1956. pap. 2.95 (ISBN 0-528-87768-2). Rand.

Cinnamon Clouds. Linda Wilkinson. LC 78-55222. 1979. padded gift ed. 8.95 (ISBN 0-89081-139-3, 1393). Harvest Hse.

Cinq Livres Des Hieroglyphiques. Pierre Dinet. Ed. by Stephen Orgel. LC 78-68199. (Philosophy of Images Ser.: Vol. 11). 1980. lib. bdg. 66.00 (ISBN 0-8240-3685-9). Garland Pub.

Cinq Nouvelles Nouvelles. Ed. by Raymond Federman. LC 70-115011. (Illus., Orig., Fr.). 1970. pap. text ed. 5.95x (ISBN 0-89197-079-7). Irvington.

Circe Factor. Barry Nazarian. LC 80-52407. 320p. 1981. 11.95 (ISBN 0-87223-664-1). Seaview Bks.

Circle, Crescent, Star. Ansen Dibell. (Science Fiction Ser.). 1981. pap. 2.25 (ISBN 0-87997-603-9, UE1603). Daw Bks.

Circle Fine Art: Editions Catalog. Circle Fine Art. LC 80-54149. (Orig.). 1980. pap. write for info. (ISBN 0-932240-01-1). Circle Fine Art.

Circle Game. Margaret Atwood. (House of Anansi Poetry Ser.: No. 3). 80p. 1967. 8.95 (ISBN 0-88784-103-1, Pub. by Hse Anansi Pr Canada). U of Toronto Pr.

Circle of Children. Mary MacCracken. LC 73-10054. 192p. 1973. 7.95 o.s.i. (ISBN 0-397-00994-1). Lippincott.

Circle of Fires: Life Among the Yanomami. Jacques Lizot. Tr. by Ernest Simon from Fr. 224p. 1981. 22.50x (ISBN 0-8476-6968-8). Rowman.

Circle of Iron. Robert Weverka. (Orig.). 1979. pap. 1.95 o.s.i. (ISBN 0-446-89928-3). Warner Bks.

Circle of Life: The Miccosukee Indian Way. Nancy Henderson & Jane Dewey. LC 73-19325. (Illus.). (gr. 3-6). 1974. PLB 5.29 o.p. (ISBN 0-671-32658-9). Messner.

Circle of Quiet. Madeleine L'Engle. 246p. 1972. 10.95 (ISBN 0-374-12374-8). FS&G.

Circle of Seasons. Dennis Stock & Josephine W. Johnson. LC 73-20661. (Illus.). 108p. 1974. 16.95 o.p. (ISBN 0-670-22263-1, Studio). Viking Pr.

Circle of Warmth: Family Program. Gerry Ball. 1980. 34.95 (ISBN 0-86584-040-7). Human Dev Train.

Circle Round the Zero: Play Chants & Singing Games of City Children. Ed. by Maureen Kenney. (Illus.). 1975. pap. 6.95 (ISBN 0-918812-08-9). Magnamusic.

Circle to Circle: The Poetry of Robert Lowell. Stephen Yenser. LC 74-79778. 400p. 1976. 23.75x (ISBN 0-520-02790-6). U of Cal Pr.

Circle Without End: A Sourcebook of American Indian Ethics. Gerald S. Lombardi & Frances G. Lombardi. (Illus.). 212p. 1981. lib. bdg. 9.95 (ISBN 0-87961-114-6); pap. 5.95 (ISBN 0-87961-117-0). Naturegraph.

Circles. Mindel Sitomer & Harry Sitomer. LC 71-113856. (Young Math Ser.). (Illus.). (gr. 1-4). 1971. 6.95 (ISBN 0-690-19430-7, TYC-J); PLB 7.89 (ISBN 0-690-19431-5). T Y Crowell.

Circles, a Mathematical View. Dan Pedoe. LC 78-73522. (Illus.). 1979. pap. text ed. 2.75 (ISBN 0-486-63698-4). Dover.

Circles of Friends: Two Hundred New Ways to Make Friends in Washington D. C. Dorothy O'Callaghan. LC 76-25316. 1981. pap. 4.00 (ISBN 0-914694-02-2). Mail Order.

Circles, Triangles & Squares. Tana Hoban. LC 72-93305. (Illus.). 32p. (ps-2). 1974. 8.95 (ISBN 0-02-744830-4, 74483). Macmillan.

Circuit. Ralph M. Demers. 1977. pap. 1.95 o.p. (ISBN 0-345-25722-7). Ballantine.

Circuit Analysis. John R. O'Malley. 1980. text ed. 20.95 (ISBN 0-13-133827-7). P-H.

Circuit & System Theory. G. Lago & L. M. Benningfield. LC 79-10878. 1979. text ed. 29.95 (ISBN 0-471-04927-1). Wiley.

Circuit Cellar, Vol. II. Steve Ciarcia. 190p. 1981. pap. 11.95 (ISBN 0-07-010963-X). McGraw.

Circuit Concepts: Direct & Alternating Current. T. S. Kubala. LC 75-19521. 1976. pap. 8.80 (ISBN 0-8273-1169-9); instructor's guide 1.60 (ISBN 0-8273-1170-2). Delmar.

Circuit Design Idea Handbook. Ed. by Bill Furlow. LC 73-76440. 1972. 21.50 (ISBN 0-8436-0205-8). CBI Pub.

Circuit Electronics. Brian Jones. 1974. text ed. 18.95 (ISBN 0-201-03374-7). A-W.

Circuit Hikes in Shenandoah National Park. 11th ed. James Denton. LC 80-81762. 86p. 1980. pap. write for info. (ISBN 0-915746-15-8). Potomac Appalach.

Circuit Hikes in the Shenandoah National Park. 10th ed. Ed. by James W. Denton. LC 76-21937. 1976. pap. 2.00 o.p. (ISBN 0-915746-08-5). Potomac Appalach.

Circuit Problems & Solutions, Vol. 2: Network Theorems. Gerard Lippin. 128p. 1971. pap. 6.45 o.p. (ISBN 0-8104-5755-5). Hayden.

Circuit Problems & Solutions, Vol. 3: Transistor & Tube Circuits. Gerard Lippin. 96p. 1971. pap. 5.95 o.p. (ISBN 0-8104-5756-3). Hayden.

Circuit Rider. Edward Eggleston. LC 77-104768. (Novel As American Social History Ser.). 344p. 1970. 10.00x (ISBN 0-8131-1209-5); pap. 4.50 (ISBN 0-8131-0133-6). U Pr of Ky.

Circuit Rider Dismounts, a Social History of Southern Methodism 1865-1900. Hunter D. Farish. LC 77-87534. (American Scene Ser). 1969. Repr. of 1938 ed. 35.00 (ISBN 0-306-71450-7). Da Capo.

Circuit Theory & Design. Ed. by G. S. Moschytz & J. Neirynck. 1978. text ed. 84.00x (ISBN 2-604-00033-4). Renouf.

Circuit Theory Fundamentals & Applications. Aram Budak. LC 77-22344. (Illus.). 1978. 27.95 (ISBN 0-13-133975-3). P-H.

Circuit Theory: The Computational Approach. S. W. Director. LC 75-2016. 679p. 1975. text ed. 31.95 (ISBN 0-471-21580-5); tchrs manual avail. (ISBN 0-471-21582-1). Wiley.

Circuits for Electronics Engineers. Electronics Magazine. Ed. by Samuel Weber. LC 76-57777. (Illus.). 1977. pap. text ed. 15.95 (ISBN 0-07-099706-3, R-711). McGraw.

Circulant Matrices. Philip J. Davis. LC 79-10551. (Pure & Applied Mathematics: Texts, Monographs, & Tracts). 1979. 19.95 (ISBN 0-471-05771-1, Pub. by Wiley-Interscience). Wiley.

Circular Staircase. Mary R. Rinehart. 1976. lib. bdg. 12.95x (ISBN 0-89968-181-6). Lightyear.

Circular Study. Anna K. Green. 1976. lib. bdg. 12.95x (ISBN 0-89968-170-0). Lightyear.

Circulation of Skeletal Muscle. O. Hudlicka. 1968. 27.50 o.p. (ISBN 0-08-012466-6). Pergamon.

Circulation of the Blood. G. James. 1978. 59.50 (ISBN 0-8391-1241-6). Univ Park.

Circulation of the Brain & Spinal Cord, Vol. 18. Association for Research in Nervous Mental Disease. 1966. 27.50 (ISBN 0-02-842900-1). Hafner.

Circulation Procedures. 2nd ed. 75p. 1972. 3.00. Inglewood Ca.

Circulatory & Developmental Aspects of Brain Metabolism. Ed. by M. Spatz et al. 445p. 1980. 49.50 (ISBN 0-306-40542-3, Plenum Pr). Plenum Pub.

Circulatory Control & Management, Vol. I. Herman Turndorf & Jack Chalon. (Current Problems in Anesthesiology Ser.). (Illus.). 300p. 1980. lib. bdg. cancelled (ISBN 0-683-08473-9). Williams & Wilkins.

Circulatory Physiology: The Essentials. James L. Smith & John P. Kampine. 344p. 1980. softcover 14.95 (ISBN 0-683-07885-2). Williams & Wilkins.

Circulatory Physiology Two: Dynamics & Control of the Body Fluids. Arthur C. Guyton et al. LC 74-24844. (Illus.). 397p. 1975. text ed. 27.50 (ISBN 0-7216-4361-2). Saunders.

Circumpolar Problems: Habitat, Economy & Social Relations in the Arctic. C. Berg. 1973. text ed. 46.00 (ISBN 0-08-017038-2). Pergamon.

Circumstantial Evidence. Eugene Fitzmaurice. 1978. pap. 1.95 o.s.i. (ISBN 0-515-04265-X). Jove Pubns.

Circus. Rupert Croft-Cooke & Peter Cotes. (Illus.). 1977. 6.95 o.s.i. (ISBN 0-02-528860-1, 52886). Macmillan.

Circus. Netta Gillespie. Ed. by Robert Bensen. (Chapbook: No. 6). 1980. pap. 3.50. Red Herring.

Circus. Jack Prelutsky. LC 73-6055. (Illus.). 32p. (gr. k-3). 1974. 7.95g (ISBN 0-02-775060-4). Macmillan.

Circus. Youldon. (ps-2). 1980. cancelled (ISBN 0-531-04167-0); PLB cancelled (ISBN 0-531-03525-5). Watts.

Circus: A Book to Begin On. Mary K. Phelan. LC 63-9083. (Book to Begin on Ser.). 48p. (gr. k-4). 1963. pap. 0.95 o.p. (ISBN 0-03-080113-3). HR&W.

Circus Baby. Maud Petersham & Miska Petersham. (Illus.). (gr. k-3). 1950. 9.95g (ISBN 0-02-771670-8). Macmillan.

Circus Book Featuring "Toby Tyler". Walt Disney Productions. LC 77-74462. (Disney's World of Adventure). (Illus.). (gr. 2-6). 1978. 3.95 (ISBN 0-394-83597-2, BYR); PLB 4.99 (ISBN 0-394-93597-7). Random.

Circus Cannonball. Judy Varga. LC 74-26796. (Illus.). 32p. (gr. k-3). 1975. 7.75 (ISBN 0-688-22026-6); PLB 7.44 (ISBN 0-688-32026-0). Morrow.

Circus: From Rome to Ringling. Marian Murray. LC 74-171420. (Illus.). 354p. 1956. Repr. of 1956 ed. lib. bdg. 29.75x (ISBN 0-8371-6259-9, MUCI). Greenwood.

Circus Is Coming. Hilary Knight. (Illus.). (ps-2). 1979. 3.95 (ISBN 0-307-13737-6, Golden Pr); PLB 9.15 (ISBN 0-307-63377-2). Western Pub.

Circus Is in Town. David L. Harrison. (Young Reader Ser.). (Illus.). (gr. k-3). 1979. PLB 5.00 (ISBN 0-307-60168-4, Golden Pr). Western Pub.

Circus, Its Origin & Growth Prior to 1835. Isaac J. Greenwood. (Illus.). 1962. 5.00 o.p. (ISBN 0-87588-021-5). Hobby Hse.

Circus Numbers. Rodney Peppe. LC 75-86381. (Illus.). (ps-3). 1969. 5.95 o.p. (ISBN 0-440-01288-0); PLB 5.47 o.p. (ISBN 0-440-01289-9). Delacorte.

Circus of Love. Mary A. Dasgupta. 8.00 (ISBN 0-89253-463-X); flexible cloth 4.80 (ISBN 0-89253-464-8). Ind-US Inc.

Circus Techniques. Hovey Burgess. (Illus.). 1977. 11.95 o.s.i. (ISBN 0-690-01463-5, TYC-T); pap. 7.95 o.s.i. (ISBN 0-690-01464-3, TYC-T). T Y Crowell.

Circus Villains: Poems. Richard Frost. LC 65-24647. 55p. 1965. 5.95 (ISBN 0-8214-0010-X). Ohio U Pr.

Circus Workin's. Martin Hintz. LC 80-19784. (Illus.). 96p. (gr. 4-6). 1980. PLB 7.79 (ISBN 0-671-34006-9). Messner.

Ciris: A Poem Attributed to Vergil. Ed. by R. O. Lyne. LC 77-80845. (Classical Texts & Commentaries Ser.: No. 20). (Illus.). 1978. 65.00 (ISBN 0-521-21727-X). Cambridge U Pr.

Cirque. Terry Carr. 1978. pap. 1.75 o.p. (ISBN 0-449-23556-4, Crest). Fawcett.

Cirripedia Thoracica & Acrothoracica. Carl A. Nilsson-Cantell. (Illus.). 1978. pap. 16.50 (ISBN 82-00-01670-6, Dist. by Columbia U Pr). Universitet.

CIS U.S. Congressional Committee Prints Index, 5 vols. Congressional Information Service. 3172p. 1980. lib. bdg. 1475.00 (ISBN 0-912380-57-8). Cong Info.

Ciskei: Economics & Politics of Dependence in a South African Homeland. Ed. by Nancy Charton. 253p. 1980. 32.50x (ISBN 0-7099-0332-4, Pub. by Croom Helm Ltd England). Biblio Dist.

Cisplatin Derzeitiger Stand und Neue Entwicklungen in der Chemotherapie Maligner Neoplasien. Ed. by S. Seeber et al. (Beitraege zur Onkologie: Band 3). (Illus.). 184p. 1980. pap. 21.00 (ISBN 3-8055-1364-X). S Karger.

Cistercians & Cluniacs: The Case for Citeaux. Idung Of Prufening. Tr. by Jeremiah F. O'Sullivan & Joseph Leahey. LC 77-9289. 1977. 12.95 (ISBN 0-87907-633-X). Cistercian Pubns.

Cistercians in the Late Middle Ages. Ed. by E. Rozanne Elder. (Cistercian Studies: No. 64). (Illus., Orig.). 1980. pap. 8.95 (ISBN 0-87907-865-0). Cistercian Pubns.

Cistercians in the Late Middle Ages: Studies in Medievel Cistercian History VI. Ed. by E. Rozanne Elder et al. (Cistercian Studies: No. VI). 161p. (Orig.). 1981. pap. 8.97 (ISBN 0-87907-864-2). Cistercian Pubns.

Cisternography & Hydrocephalus: A Symposium. Ed. by John C. Harbert. (Illus.). 670p. 1972. 58.75 (ISBN 0-398-02308-5). C C Thomas.

Cities. Richard Tames. Ed. by Malcolm Yapp et al. (World History Ser.). (Illus.). 32p. (gr. 10). 1980. Repr. of 1977 ed. lib. bdg. 5.95 (ISBN 0-89908-140-1); pap. text ed. 1.95 (ISBN 0-89908-115-0). Greenhaven.

Cities Advocate: Whether Apprentiship Extinguisheth Gentry? Edmund Bolton. LC 74-28834. (English Experience Ser.: No. 715). 1975. Repr. of 1629 ed. 7.00 (ISBN 90-221-0715-9). Walter J Johnson.

Cities & Firms. Ed. by Herrington J. Bryce. LC 80-8367. (Urban Roundtable Ser.). 272p. 1980. 18.95x (ISBN 0-669-04042-8). Lexington Bks.

Cities & Metropolitan Areas. Samuel L. Arbital. Ed. by Etta S. Ress. LC 67-25673. (Illus.). (gr. 4-9). 1968. PLB 7.50 o.p. (ISBN 0-87191-004-7). Creative Ed.

Cities & Planning in the Ancient Near East. Paul Lampl. LC 68-14699. (Planning & Cities Ser). (Illus., Orig.). (YA) (gr. 9-12). 1968. 7.95 (ISBN 0-8076-0465-8); pap. 4.95 (ISBN 0-8076-0469-0). Braziller.

Cities & Schools in the Gilded Age: The Evolution of an Urban Institution. William A. Bullough. LC 74-80592. 1974. 14.50 (ISBN 0-8046-9094-4, Natl U). Kennikat.

Cities & Suburbs. Illus. by Mac Conner et al. (Bowmar-Noble Social Studies Program). Orig. Title: Man & His World. (Illus.). (gr. 3). text ed. 7.86 (ISBN 0-8372-3684-3); tchrs. ed. 11.28 (ISBN 0-8372-3685-1); tests 9.30 (ISBN 0-8372-3727-0). Bowmar-Noble.

Cities & Suburbs: Urban Life in West Africa. Margaret Peil. LC 80-26440. (New Library of African Affairs). 330p. 1981. text ed. 24.00x (ISBN 0-8419-0685-8). Holmes & Meier.

Cities by Contract: The Politics of Municipal Incorporation. Gary J. Miller. 256p. 1981. text ed. 22.50x (ISBN 0-262-13164-1). MIT Pr.

Cities Fit to Live In. Ed. by Walter McQuade. 1971. pap. 3.50 o.s.i. (ISBN 0-02-087700-5, Collier). Macmillan.

Cities in a Larger Context. Ed. by Thomas W. Collins. LC 79-54361. (Southern Anthropological Society Proceedings Ser.: No. 14). (Illus.). 168p. 1980. 12.00x (ISBN 0-8203-0504-9); pap. 5.95x (ISBN 0-8203-0505-7). U of Ga Pr.

Cities in Action. E. Van Cleef. LC 79-84197. 1971. 21.00 (ISBN 0-08-015622-3); pap. 12.75 (ISBN 0-08-016417-X). Pergamon.

Cities in Change: Studies on the Urban Condition. 2nd ed. John Walton & Donald Carns. 1977. pap. text ed. 13.60x (ISBN 0-205-05579-6). Allyn.

Cities in Flight. James Blish. 1970. pap. 2.50 (ISBN 0-380-00998-6, 49908). Avon.

Cities in Revolt: Urban Life in America, 1743-1776. Carl Bridenbaugh. (Illus.). 1970. pap. 6.95 (ISBN 0-19-501362-X, GB). Oxford U Pr.

Cities in the March of Civilization. Barbara Habenstreit. LC 73-2302. (International Library). (Illus.). 128p. (gr. 7 up). 1974. PLB 6.90 o.p. (ISBN 0-531-02114-9). Watts.

Cities in the Wilderness: The First Century of Urban Life in America, 1625-1742. Carl Bridenbaugh. (Illus.). 1971. pap. 6.95 (ISBN 0-19-501361-1, GB). Oxford U Pr.

Cities in Transition: From the Ancient World to Urban America. Ed. by Frank J. Coppa & Philip C. Dolce. LC 73-84778. 1974. 17.95 (ISBN 0-911012-95-8). Nelson-Hall.

Cities of Mughul India. 1968. 21.95 (ISBN 0-236-31092-5, Pub. by Paul Elek). Merrimack Bk Serv.

Cities of Sin. Hendrik DeLeeuw. Ed. by Charles Winick. LC 78-60861. (Prostitution Ser.: Vol. 5). 297p. 1979. lib. bdg. 30.00 (ISBN 0-8240-9723-8). Garland Pub.

Cities of the Blue Distance. Harold L. Johnson. (Illus.). 104p. 1980. 10.50x (ISBN 0-937308-01-3); pap. 7.25 (ISBN 0-937308-02-1). Hearthstone.

Cities of the Interior, 5 vols. in 1. Anais Nin. Incl. Ladders to Fire; Children of the Albatross; Four-Chambered Heart; Spy in the House of Love; Seduction of the Minotaur. LC 74-21884. (Illus.). xx, 589p. 1975. 19.95 (ISBN 0-8040-0665-2); pap. 12.95 (ISBN 0-8040-0666-0). Swallow.

Cities of the Red Night. William S. Burroughs. LC 80-13637. 448p. 1981. 14.95 (ISBN 0-03-053976-5). HR&W.

Cities of Vision. Rolf Jensen. (Illus.). 1974. 40.90x (ISBN 0-85334-569-4, Pub. by Applied Science). Burgess-Intl Ideas.

Cities, Space & Behavior: The Elements of Urban Geography. Leslie J. King & Reginald G. Golledge. (Illus.). 1978. ref. 20.95 (ISBN 0-13-134601-6). P-H.

Cities, Suburbs & States: Governing & Financing Urban America. William G. Colman. LC 75-2810. (Illus.). 1975. 17.95 (ISBN 0-02-906490-2). Free Pr.

Cities with Little Crime. M. B. Clinard. LC 77-88672. (ASA Rose Monograph Ser.). 1978. 19.95 (ISBN 0-521-21960-4); pap. 6.95x (ISBN 0-521-29327-8). Cambridge U Pr.

Citizen & State: Vol. 1 of Political Participation in Latin America. Ed. by John A. Booth & Mitchell A. Seligson. LC 77-16666. 260p. 1978. 27.00x (ISBN 0-8419-0334-4); pap. text ed. 10.50x (ISBN 0-8419-0376-X). Holmes & Meier.

Citizen Band Transceivers: Installation & Troubleshooting. Mannie Horowitz. (Illus.). 1978. ref. 17.95 (ISBN 0-87909-102-9). Reston.

Citizen Genet Affair: A Chapter in the Formation of American Foreign Policy. Harold C. Vaughan. LC 76-114928. (Focus Bks). (Illus.). (gr. 7 up). 1970. PLB 4.90 o.p. (ISBN 0-531-01014-7). Watts.

Citizen Groups in Local Politics: A Bibliographic Review. John D. Hutcheson, Jr. & Jann Shevin. LC 76-23441. 275p. 1976. text ed. 8.75 (ISBN 0-87436-231-8). ABC-Clio.

Citizen Hearst. W. A. Swanberg. (Illus.). 1961. lib. rep. ed. 25.00x (ISBN 0-684-14503-0, ScribT). Scribner.

Citizen Hoover: A Critical Study of the Life & Times of J. Edgar Hoover & His FBI. Jay R. Nash. LC 72-76266. (Illus.). 240p. 1972. 14.95 (ISBN 0-911012-60-5). Nelson-Hall.

Citizen in Court: Litigant, Witness, Juror, Judge. Delmar Karlen. LC 73-19739. (American Constitutional & Legal History Ser.). 211p. 1974. Repr. of 1964 ed. lib. bdg. 22.50 (ISBN 0-306-70614-8). Da Capo.

Citizen Inspectors in the Soviet Union: The Peoples Control Committee. Jan S. Adams. LC 77-83460. (Praeger Special Studies). 1978. 27.95 (ISBN 0-03-023201-5). Praeger.

Citizen Involvement in Crime Prevention. George J. Washnis. LC 75-5238. 160p. 1976. 16.95x (ISBN 0-669-99812-5). Lexington Bks.

Citizen Involvement in Land Use Governance: Issues & Methods. Nelson M. Rosenbaum. 82p. 1976. pap. 3.50 (ISBN 0-87766-140-5, 11500). Urban Inst.

Citizen Monitoring: A Guide for Social Change. 1979. 5.00. Comm Coun Great NY.

Citizen of the Galaxy. Robert A. Heinlein. (Del Rey Bks.). 1978. pap. 1.75 o.p. (ISBN 0-345-26074-0). Ballantine.

Citizen Participation & Public Library Policy. Jane Robbins. LC 74-34248. 191p. 1975. 10.00 (ISBN 0-8108-0796-3). Scarecrow.

Citizen Participation in America. Ed. by Stuart Langton. LC 78-19913. 1978. 14.95 (ISBN 0-669-02651-4); pap. 9.95 (ISBN 0-669-02465-1). Lexington Bks.

Citizen Participation in American Communities: Strategies for Success. Daniel M. Barber. LC 80-83336. 144p. 1980. pap. 8.95 (ISBN 0-8403-2299-2). Kendall-Hunt.

Citizen Participation in Education: Annotated Bibliography. Ed. by Don Davies & Ross Zerchykov. 386p. (Orig.). 1978. pap. text ed. 15.00 (ISBN 0-917754-05-0). Inst Responsive.

Citizen Participation in Planning. Michael Fagence. 1977. text ed. 26.00 (ISBN 0-08-020397-3); pap. text ed. 14.50 (ISBN 0-08-020398-1). Pergamon.

Citizen Participation: The Local Perspective. Melvin B. Mogulof. 1970. pap. 3.00 o.p. (ISBN 0-87766-065-4, 80002). Urban Inst.

Citizen Soldier & United States Military Policy. James B. Whisker. 7.50 (ISBN 0-88427-035-1); pap. 4.95 (ISBN 0-88427-036-X). Green Hill.

Citizen Soldier of the American Revolution: The Diary of Benjamin Gilbert in Massachusettes & New York. 1980. 8.95 (ISBN 0-917334-03-5). Fenimore Bk.

Citizen Soldiers: The Plattsburg Training Camp Movement, 1913-1920. John G. Clifford. LC 71-183350. 336p. 1972. 14.00x (ISBN 0-8131-1262-1). U Pr of Ky.

Citizen Vampire. Les Daniels. 204p. 1981. 9.95 (ISBN 0-684-16827-8, ScribT). Scribner.

Citizen Vampire. Les Daniels. 228p. 1980. cancelled (ISBN 0-684-16827-8, ScribT). Scribner.

Citizens & Waste. 4.00 set (ISBN 0-686-27466-0); Vol. 1. 2.00 (ISBN 0-686-27467-9); Vol. 2. 3.00 (ISBN 0-686-27468-7). Tech Info Proj.

Citizens As Sovereigns. Paul H. Appleby. LC 62-10727. 1962. 10.00x (ISBN 0-8156-0024-0). Syracuse U Pr.

Citizens Band Radio Service Manual. Robert F. Burns & Leo G. Sands. LC 77-170665. 1971. 8.95 o.p. (ISBN 0-8306-1581-4); pap. 5.95 (ISBN 0-8306-0581-9, 581). TAB Bks.

Citizens' Committees in the Public Schools. Herbert M. Hamlin. (Illus.). 1952. text ed. 4.25x (ISBN 0-8134-0084-8, 84). Interstate.

Citizens' Energy Directory. 2nd, rev. ed. Jan Simpson. (Illus.). 185p. 1980. pap. 11.00 (ISBN 0-89988-055-X). Citizens Energy.

Citizens Guide to the Proposed New Texas Constitution. George D. Braden. LC 75-25764. (Orig.). 1975. 3.25 o.p. (ISBN 0-88408-026-9). Sterling Swift.

Citizen's Guide to the Social Sciences. Bernard Mausner. LC 78-16626. 1979. text ed. 16.95 (ISBN 0-88229-401-6); pap. 7.95 (ISBN 0-88229-650-7). Nelson-Hall.

Citizens Media Directory. Ed. by Pamela Draves. 1977. pap. 3.50 (ISBN 0-9603466-3-5); 1980 update avail. NCCB.

Citizens of Rome: Reflections from the Life of a Roman Catholic. Frederick Wilhelmsen. 12.95 (ISBN 0-89385-010-1); pap. 4.95 (ISBN 0-89385-005-5). Green Hill.

Citizenship & Conscience: A Study in the Theory & Practice of Religious Toleration in England During the Eighteenth Century. Richard B. Barlow. LC 62-7197. 1963. 12.00x o.p. (ISBN 0-8122-7395-8). U of Pa Pr.

Citizenship & Consumer Education: Key Assumptions & Basic Competencies. Richard C. Remy. LC 79-93121. (Fastback Ser.: No. 144). (Orig.). 1980. pap. 0.75 (ISBN 0-87367-144-9). Phi Delta Kappa.

Citizenship Between Elections. James N. Rosenau. LC 73-16907. (Illus.). 1974. 19.95 (ISBN 0-02-926970-9). Free Pr.

Citizenship in Africa: The Role of Adult Education in the Political Socialization of Tanganyikans, 1891-1961. Joel C. Millonzi. LC 75-30644. (Foreign and Comparative Studies Eastern African Series XIX). 119p. 1975. pap. text ed. 4.50x (ISBN 0-915984-16-4). Syracuse U Foreign Comp.

Citizenship in an Age of Science: A Public Opinion Survey of Young Adults. Jon D. Miller et al. (Pergamon Policy Studies). 1980. 39.00 (ISBN 0-08-024662-1). Pergamon.

Citizenship in the Community. Boy Scouts of America. LC 19-600. (Illus.). 48p. (gr. 6-12). 1972. pap. 0.70x (ISBN 0-8395-3253-9, 3253). BSA.

Citizenship in the Nation. Boy Scouts of America. LC 19-600. (Illus.). 64p. (gr. 6-12). 1972. pap. 0.70x (ISBN 0-8395-3252-0, 3252). BSA.

Citizenship in the World. Boy Scouts of America. LC 19-600. (Illus.). 64p. (gr. 6-12). 1972. pap. 0.70x (ISBN 0-8395-3254-7, 3254). BSA.

Citizenship of the United States. Frederick Van Dyne. xxvii, 385p. 1980. Repr. of 1904 ed. lib. bdg. 28.50x (ISBN 0-8377-1229-7). Rothman.

Citroen, the Great Marque of France: 1961-1976. Pierre Dumont. Tr. by Tom Ellaway from Fr. LC 80-22034. Orig. Title: Quai De Javel Quai Andre Citroen. (Illus.). 1976. 35.00 (ISBN 0-903192-72-1, EPA France). Motorbooks Int.

Citrus. Richard Ray & Lance Walheim. (Gardening Ser.). (Orig.). 1980. pap. 7.95 (ISBN 0-89586-076-7). H P Bks.

Citrus Fruit. (International Standardisation of Fruit & Vegetables Ser.). 103p. (Orig.). 1980. pap. 17.50 (ISBN 9-2640-2112-4). OECD.

Citrus Nutrition & Quality. Ed. by Steven Nagy & John Attaway. LC 80-22562. (ACS Symposium Ser.: No. 143). 1980. 36.25 (ISBN 0-8412-0595-7). Am Chemical.

Citrus Science & Technology, Vol. 1. Steven Nagy et al. (Illus.). 1977. lib. bdg. 39.50 (ISBN 0-87055-221-X). AVI.

Citrus Science & Technology, Vol. 2. Steven Nagy et al. (Illus.). 1977. lib. bdg. 42.50 (ISBN 0-87055-222-8). AVI.

Citrus Seed Grower's Indoor How-to Book. Hazel Perper. LC 73-179694. (Illus.). 1971. 4.50 (ISBN 0-396-06434-5). Dodd.

City. Jane Gaskell. LC 77-23530. 1978. 8.95 o.p. (ISBN 0-312-13982-9). St Martin.

City. Robert E. Park & Ernest W. Burgess. Ed. by Morris Janowitz. LC 66-23694. (Heritage of Sociology Ser). 1967. 12.50x o.s.i. (ISBN 0-226-64607-6). U of Chicago Pr.

City. Max Weber. LC 58-6492. 1958. 12.95 (ISBN 0-02-934200-7); pap. text ed. 4.95 (ISBN 0-02-934210-4). Free Pr.

City & Social Theory. Michael P. Smith. LC 77-86294. 1979. text ed. 14.95 (ISBN 0-312-14000-2); pap. text ed. 7.95 (ISBN 0-312-14035-5). St Martin.

City & Suburb: Exploring an Ecosystem. Laurence Pringle. LC 75-16161. (Illus.). 69p. (gr. 3-6). 1975. 9.95 (ISBN 0-02-775350-6, 77535). Macmillan.

City & Suburban Architect. Samuel Sloan. LC 75-31711. (Architecture & Decorative Art Ser.). (Illus.). 1975. Repr. of 1859 ed. lib. bdg. 65.00 (ISBN 0-306-70745-4). Da Capo.

City & Suburban Gardens: Frontyards, Backyards, Terraces, Rooftops & Window Boxes. Tom Riker. LC 76-58532. (Illus.). 1977. 12.95 (ISBN 0-13-134544-3); pap. 8.95 o.p. (ISBN 0-13-134536-2). P-H.

City & the Court: Sixteen Hundred & Three to Sixteen Forty-Three. R. Ashton. LC 78-67296. 1979. 29.50 (ISBN 0-521-22419-5). Cambridge U Pr.

City & the Stars. Arthur Clarke. 192p. (RL 7). 1973. pap. 1.75 (ISBN 0-451-09232-5, E9232, Sig). NAL.

City Behind a Fence: Oak Ridge, Tennessee, 1942-1946. Charles O. Johnson & Charles W. Jackson. LC 80-15897. (Illus.). 272p. 1981. 18.50 (ISBN 0-87049-303-5); pap. 9.50 (ISBN 0-87049-309-4). U of Tenn Pr.

City Below the Hill. H. B. Ames. LC 78-163831. (Social History of Canada Ser.). 112p. 1972. pap. 3.50 (ISBN 0-8020-6142-7). U of Toronto Pr.

City Bias & Rural Neglect: The Dilemma of Urban Development. Michael P. Todaro & Jerry Stilkind. LC 80-26071. (Public Issues Papers). (Illus.). xiv, 93p. (Orig.). 1981. pap. text ed. 2.50 (ISBN 0-87834-042-4). Population Coun.

City Book. Lucille Corcos. (Illus.). (gr. 1-6). 1972. PLB 10.69 o.p. (ISBN 0-307-65772-8, Golden Pr). Western Pub.

City Boy. Herman Wouk. 1980. pap. write for info. (ISBN 0-671-41511-5). PB.

City Boy: The Adventures of Herbie Bookbinder. Herman Wouk. LC 69-10961. 1969. 8.95 (ISBN 0-385-04072-5). Doubleday.

City Cat. Najaka. 110p. Date not set. 2.95 (ISBN 0-07-045858-8). McGraw.

City Centre Redevelopment. Ed. by J. Holliday. LC 73-17764. (Illus.). 1973. 27.95 (ISBN 0-470-40644-5). Halsted Pr.

City, Class & Power. Manuel Castells. Tr. by Elizabeth Lebas from Fr. 1979. 20.00 (ISBN 0-312-13989-6). St Martin.

City Classification Handbook: Methods & Applications. B. J. Berry. LC 71-171911. (Urban Research Ser.). 394p. 1972. 38.00 (ISBN 0-471-07115-3, Pub. by Wiley-Interscience). Wiley.

City College & the Jewish Poor: Education in New York, 1880-1924. Sherry Goerlick. (Illus.). 256p. 1981. 14.95 (ISBN 0-8135-0905-X). Rutgers U Pr.

City Cop. Fred J. Cook. (YA) (gr. 7-12). 1981. pap. 1.25 (ISBN 0-440-90974-0, LE). Dell.

City-County Index to Eighteen-Fifty Census Schedules. Ed. by J. Carlyle Parker. LC 79-11644. (Genealogy & Local History Ser.: Vol. 6). 1979. 30.00 (ISBN 0-8103-1385-5). Gale.

City Directory 1980-1981: An Investors Chronicle Guide to Financial & Professional Services Allied to the City of London. Investors Chronicle. 376p. 1980. pap. 20.00 (ISBN 0-85941-083-8). Herman Pub.

City Directory 1980-81: An Investors Chronicle Guide to Financial & Professional Services Allied to the City of London. Ed. by Woodhead-Faulkner. 432p. 1980. 45.00x (ISBN 0-85941-135-4, Pub. by Woodhead-Faulkner England); pap. 36.00x (ISBN 0-85941-136-2). State Mutual Bk.

City Dog. Richard A. Wolters. 1975. 8.95 (ISBN 0-87690-148-8). Dutton.

City for Lincoln. John R. Tunis. LC 45-35202. (gr. 7 up). 4.95 o.p. (ISBN 0-15-218579-8, HJ). HarBraceJ.

City Fun. Margaret Hillert. (Just Beginning-to-Read Ser.). 32p. 1980. PLB 4.39 (ISBN 0-695-41457-7); pap. 1.50 (ISBN 0-695-31457-2). Follett.

City Government in Georgia. Mary A. Hepburn et al. LC 79-24128. 150p. (Orig.). (gr. 8-12). 1980. pap. 7.50 (ISBN 0-89854-052-6). U of GA Inst Govt.

City Governments & Urban Problems: A New Introduction to Urban Politics. Demetrios Caraley. LC 76-28327. (Illus.). 1977. 16.95 (ISBN 0-13-134973-2). P-H.

City Green. Eleanor Schick. LC 73-8574. (Illus.). 40p. (ps-3). 1974. 4.95g o.s.i. (ISBN 0-02-781170-0). Macmillan.

City House. Commission on Chicago Historical & Architectural Landmarks. LC 79-51990. (Illus.). 100p. (Orig.). 1979. pap. 4.95 (ISBN 0-934076-25-1). Comm Chi Hist & Arch.

City in Ancient Israel. Frank S. Frick. LC 77-21984. (Society of Biblical Literature. Dissertation Ser.: No. 36). 1977. pap. 7.50 (ISBN 0-89130-149-6, 060136). Scholars Pr Ca.

City in Print: An Urban Studies Bibliography. R. Charles Bryfogle. Incl. City in Print Supplement One. 1975. (ISBN 0-88874-046-8). 1974. 35.00 set (ISBN 0-88874-003-4). Dawson & Co.

City in Print: An Urban Studies Bibliography, Supplement Two. R. Charles Bryfogle. 1977. pap. 12.00 (ISBN 0-918010-00-4). Dawson & Co.

City in Print: An Urban Studies Bibliography, Supplement Three. R. Charles Bryfogle. 1979. pap. 15.00 (ISBN 0-918010-01-2). Dawson & Co.

City in Russian History. Ed. by Michael F. Hamm. LC 75-3544. 362p. 1976. 19.50x (ISBN 0-8131-1328-8). U Pr of Ky.

City in South Asia. Ed. by K. Ballhatchet & J. Harrison. 1980. text ed. 15.75x (ISBN 0-391-01129-4). Humanities.

City in Southern History: The Growth of Urban Civilization in the South. Ed. by Blaine A. Brownell & David R. Goldfield. (Interdisciplinary Urban Ser.). 1976. pap. 8.50 (ISBN 0-8046-9160-6, Natl U). Kennikat.

City in Summer. Eleanor Schick. LC 69-11306. (Illus.). (gr. k-2). 1969. 5.95g o.s.i. (ISBN 0-02-781270-7). Macmillan.

City in the Stars. Victor Appleton. Ed. by Wendy Barish. (Tom Swift Ser.). 192p. (Orig.). (gr. 2-7). 1981. 7.95 (ISBN 0-671-41120-9); pap. 1.95 (ISBN 0-671-41115-2). Wanderer Bks.

City in the Winter. Eleanor Schick. LC 69-18237. (Illus.). (gr. k-3). 1973. 5.95g o.s.i. (ISBN 0-02-781280-4). Macmillan.

City in West Europe. D. Burtenshaw. 320p. 1981. 47.50 (ISBN 0-471-27929-3, Pub. by Wiley-Interscience). Wiley.

City Kid. MacCracken. 288p. 1981. 12.95 (ISBN 0-316-54186-9). Little.

City-Kid Farmer. Jeanette Gilge. LC 75-4454. (Illus.). 128p. (Orig.). (gr. 6-7). 1975. pap. 1.95 (ISBN 0-912692-67-7). Cook.

City Life in Japan: A Study of a Tokyo Ward. Ronald P. Dore. (Illus.). 1958. pap. 4.85x (ISBN 0-520-00343-8, CAMPUS49). U of Cal Pr.

City Life: Writing from Experience. William O. Makely. 256p. 1974. 7.95 (ISBN 0-312-14105-X). St Martin.

City Lights: An Introduction to Urban Studies. E. Barbara Phillips & Richard T. LeGates. (Illus.). 608p. 1981. pap. text ed. 14.95x (ISBN 0-19-502797-3). Oxford U Pr.

City Limits. Paul E. Peterson. 288p. 1981. lib. bdg. price not set (ISBN 0-226-66292-6); pap. price not set (ISBN 0-226-66293-4). U of Chicago Pr.

City Limits: Emerging Constraints on Urban Growth. Kathleen Newland. LC 80-52951. (Worldwatch Papers). 1980. pap. 2.00 (ISBN 0-916468-37-2). Worldwatch Inst.

City Madam. Phillip Massinger. Ed. by Cyrus Hoy. LC 64-11357. (Regents Renaissance Drama Ser). 1964. 6.95x (ISBN 0-8032-0278-4); pap. 1.65x (ISBN 0-8032-5277-3, BB 204, Bison). U of Nebr Pr.

City Man. Rachel Rivers-Coffey. LC 77-97. 1978. 7.95 o.s.i. (ISBN 0-06-013576-X, HarpT). Harrow.

City Mouse - Country Mouse & Two More Mouse Tales from Aesop. Illus. by Marian Parry. (Illus.). (gr. 2-3). 1971. pap. 1.50 (ISBN 0-590-04438-9, Schol Pap); pap. 3.50 bk. & record (ISBN 0-590-04353-6). Schol Bk Serv.

City-Night Cap. Robert Davenport. Ed. by Willis J. Monie & Stephen Orgel. LC 78-66832. (Renaissance Drama Ser.). 1979. lib. bdg. 22.00 (ISBN 0-8240-9738-6). Garland Pub.

City of Beirut: A Socio-Economic Survey. Ed. by Charles Churchill. 78p. 1954. pap. 10.00x (ISBN 0-8156-6023-5, Am U Beirut). Syracuse U Pr.

City of God, 2 Vols. Saint Augustine. Ed. by R. V. Tasker. Tr. by John Healey. 1957. 10.50x ea. (ISBN 0-686-66408-6, Evman). Vol. 1 (ISBN 0-460-00982-6). Vol. 2 (ISBN 0-460-00983-4). Dutton.

City of God. Cecelia Holland. 320p. 1981. pap. 2.50 (ISBN 0-446-91517-3). Warner Bks.

City of God. St. Augustine. LC 58-5717. 4.50 (ISBN 0-385-02910-1). Doubleday.

City of God, Bks. 1-7. St. Augustine. (Fathers of the Church Ser.: Vol. 8). 24.00 (ISBN 0-8132-0008-3). Cath U Pr.

City of God & the City of Man in Africa. Edgar H. Brookes & Amry Vandenbosch. LC 64-13998. (Illus.). 144p. 1964. 7.00x (ISBN 0-8131-1091-2). U Pr of Ky.

City of Gold & Lead. John Christopher. (gr. 7 up). 1967. 8.95 (ISBN 0-02-718380-7). Macmillan.

City of Gold & Other Stories from the Old Testament. Peter Dickinson. (Illus.). 1980. 13.95 (ISBN 0-394-51385-1). Pantheon.

City of Golden Cages. Jo Germany. LC 78-3967. 1978. 7.95 o.p. (ISBN 0-312-14115-7). St Martin.

City of Illusion. Ursula K. Leguin. 160p. (Orig.). 1976. pap. 2.25 (ISBN 0-441-10705-2). Ace Bks.

City of London: A Financial & Commercial History. Robert Gibson-Jarvie. (Illus.). 128p. 1980. 17.50 (ISBN 0-85941-090-0). Herman Pub.

City of London: Its Architectual Heritage. David Crawford. (Illus.). 144p. 1980. 15.00 (ISBN 0-85941-049-8); pap. 9.95 (ISBN 0-85941-043-9). Herman Pub.

City of Many Days. Shulamith Hareven. 1978. pap. 1.95 o.p. (ISBN 0-445-04251-6). Popular Lib.

City of Peace. (Sharazad Stories Ser.). (Illus., Arabic.). pap. 3.50 (ISBN 0-686-53105-1). Intl Bk Ctr.

City of Peril. Arthur Stringer. 1976. lib. bdg. 14.85x (ISBN 0-89968-118-2). Lightyear.

City of Revelation. John Michell. 1977. pap. 1.75 o.p. (ISBN 0-345-25875-4). Ballantine.

City of the Dagger. H. H. Keely & Christine Price. LC 70-161066. (Illus.). (gr. 3-6). 1971. 4.95 o.p. (ISBN 0-7232-6077-X). Warne.

City of the Sun: A Poetical Dialogue of Tommaso Campanella. Tommaso Campanella. Ed. by Daniel J. Donno. (Biblioteca Italiana Ser.). 1981. 12.50x (ISBN 0-520-04034-1); pap. 3.50x (ISBN 0-520-04036-8). U of Cal Pr.

City of Worcester in the Sixteenth Century. Alan D. Dyer. 320p. 1971. text ed. 15.00x (ISBN 0-7185-1102-6, Leicester). Humanities.

City of Zion--the Human Society in Christ, i.e., the Church Built Upon a Rock. Apostolos Makrakis. Ed. by Orthodox Christian Educational Society. Tr. by Denver Cummings from Hellenic. 109p. 1958. pap. 3.00x (ISBN 0-938366-16-5). Orthodox Chr.

City Outside the World. Lin Carter. 1977. pap. 1.50 o.p. (ISBN 0-425-03549-2, Medallion). Berkley Pub.

City Parables. William Heyen. 43p. 1980. 10.95 (ISBN 0-912348-06-2). Croissant & Cot.

City People. Barbara Lamont. 224p. 1975. 7.95 o.s.i. (ISBN 0-02-567690-3). Macmillan.

City People's Guide to Country Living. Betsy Cobb & Hubbard Cobb. LC 72-85757. 224p. 1973. pap. 1.50 o.s.i. (ISBN 0-02-079360-X, Collier). Macmillan.

City Planning: A Selected List of Books, 1970-1978. Mary Vance. (Architecture Ser.: Bibliography A-224). 99p. 1980. pap. 10.50. Vance Biblios.

City Planning Bibliography. Compiled By American Society of Civil Engineers et al. 536p. 1972. pap. text ed. 16.75 (ISBN 0-87262-036-0). Am Soc Civil Eng.

City Planning Process: A Political Analysis. Alan A. Altshuler. LC 65-25498. 1966. 25.00x (ISBN 0-8014-0007-4); pap. 6.95 (ISBN 0-8014-9081-2, CP81). Cornell U Pr.

City Police. Jonathan Rubinstein. 1973. 12.95 (ISBN 0-374-12411-6); pap. 8.95 (ISBN 0-374-51555-7). FS&G.

City Police. Jonathan Rubinstein. 480p. 1975. pap. 2.25 (ISBN 0-345-28409-7). Ballantine.

City Politics & Planning. Francine F. Rabinovitz. LC 69-19454. 1970. 15.95x (ISBN 0-202-24091-6). Aldine Pub.

City Politics & the Press. H. Cox & D. Morgan. LC 72-96678. (Illus.). 200p. 1973. 23.95 (ISBN 0-521-20162-4). Cambridge U Pr.

City Politiques. John Crowne. Ed. by John H. Wilson. LC 67-12641. (Regents Restoration Drama Ser). 1967. 9.75x (ISBN 0-8032-0355-1); pap. 1.65x (ISBN 0-8032-5355-9, BB 262, Bison). U of Nebr Pr.

City Sandwich. Frank Asch. LC 77-18902. (Illus.). (gr. 1-4). 1978. 6.95 (ISBN 0-688-80156-0); PLB 6.67 (ISBN 0-688-84156-2). Greenwillow.

City Scenes: Problems & Prospects. 2nd ed. Palen. 1981. pap. text ed. 9.95 (ISBN 0-316-68871-1). Little.

City Spreads Its Wings. Ed. by Lee B. Hopkins. LC 73-117179. (gr. k-3). 1970. PLB 4.90 o.p. (ISBN 0-531-01942-X). Watts.

City Sun. Eleanor Schick. (Illus.). 40p. (gr. 1-3). 1974. 4.95g o.s.i. (ISBN 0-02-781200-6). Macmillan.

City That Was. Stephen Smith. Bd. with Report of the General Committee of Health, New York City, 1806. LC 73-1827. (History of Medicine Ser.: No. 36). 1973. Repr. of 1911 ed. 11.00 (ISBN 0-8108-0598-7). Scarecrow.

City: The Hope of Democracy. Frederic C. Howe. LC 68-1361. (American Library Ser: No. 1). 350p. 1967. Repr. of 1905 ed. 11.50 (ISBN 0-295-97858-9). U of Wash Pr.

City, the Immigrant, & American Fiction, 1880-1920. David M. Fine. LC 77-6297. 1977. 10.00 (ISBN 0-8108-1038-7). Scarecrow.

City Trucks. Robert Quackenbush. Ed. by Kathleen Tucker. (Illus.). 40p. (ps-4). 1981. 6.95 (ISBN 0-8075-1163-3). A Whitman.

City Under Ground. Suzanne Martel. (gr. 4-6). 1975. pap. 0.95 o.s.i. (ISBN 0-671-29730-9). Archway.

City Under the Sea. Kenneth Bulmer. 1979. pap. 1.95 (ISBN 0-380-48348-3, 48348, Discus). Avon.

City Underground. Suzanne Martel. (Illus.). (gr. 4-6). 1975. pap. 0.95 (ISBN 0-671-29730-9). PB.

City Zoning. Clifford L. Weaver & Richard F. Babcock. LC 79-90347. 328p. (Orig.). 1980. pap. 16.95 (ISBN 0-918286-17-4). Planners Pr.

Cityward Migration: Swedish Data. Jane Moore. 1938. 32.50x (ISBN 0-686-51354-1). Elliots Bks.

Ciudadania en Puerto Rico. 2nd ed. Reece B. Bothwell. LC 78-24031. (Sp.). 1979. pap. 1.85 (ISBN 0-8477-2451-4). U of PR Pr.

Civic Education in Ten Countries: An Empirical Study. Judith Torney et al. LC 75-42147. (International Studies in Evaluation: Vol. 6). 1976. pap. 28.95 (ISBN 0-470-14989-2). Halsted Pr.

Civic Ritual in Renaissance Venice. Edward Muir. LC 80-8568. (Illus.). 368p. 1981. 17.50x (ISBN 0-691-05325-1). Princeton U Pr.

Civics for New Mexicans. Susan A. Roberts et al. LC 80-52284. 375p. 1980. 25.00 (ISBN 0-8263-0547-4). U of NM Pr.

Civil Aircraft of the World. Swanborough. 1980. 12.95 (ISBN 0-684-16616-X, ScribT). Scribner.

Civil Aircraft of the World. 3rd. ed. John W. Taylor & Gordon Swanborough. LC 77-74718. (Illus.). 1978. 9.95 (ISBN 0-684-15224-X, ScribT). Scribner.

Civil & Environmental Aspects of Energy Complexes: Proceedings. Engineering Foundation Conference, Aug. 1975. Compiled By American Society of Civil Engineers. 456p. 1976. pap. text ed. 14.00 (ISBN 0-87262-153-7). Am Soc Civil Eng.

Civil Aviation Development: A Policy & Operation Analysis. Arthur D. Little, Inc. et al. LC 70-185656. (Special Studies in U.S. Economic, Social & Political Issues). 1980. Repr. of 1972 ed. 39.50x (ISBN 0-89197-697-3). Irvington.

Civil Code of the Republic of China. Tr. by Yu-Kon Chang et al from Chinese. Ching-Lin Hsia. (Studies in Chinese Government & Law). 400p. 1977. Repr. of 1930 ed. 26.50 (ISBN 0-89093-055-4). U Pubns Amer.

Civil Commitment & Social Control. Martin L. Forst. LC 77-14626. (Illus.). 1978. 17.95 (ISBN 0-669-01988-7). Lexington Bks.

Civil Disobedience & Democratic Theory. Elliot M. Zashin. LC 74-122283. 1972. 7.95 o.s.i. (ISBN 0-02-935710-1). Free Pr.

Civil Disobedience & Moral Law in Nineteenth-Century American Philosophy. Edward H. Madden. LC 68-11043. 222p. 1970. pap. 2.95 (ISBN 0-295-95070-6). U of Wash Pr.

Civil Disobedience: Conscience, Tactics & the Law. Carl Cohen. LC 14-7897. 1971. 15.00x (ISBN 0-231-03470-9); pap. 5.00x (ISBN 0-231-08646-6). Columbia U Pr.

Civil Disobedience: Theory & Practice. Ed. by Hugo A. Bedau. LC 69-27984. (Orig.). 1969. pap. 6.95 (ISBN 0-672-63514-3). Pegasus.

Civil Engineering Classics: Outstanding Papers of Thomas R. Camp. Compiled By American Society of Civil Engineers. 418p. pap. text ed. 16.00 (ISBN 0-87262-053-0). Am Soc Civil Eng.

Civil Engineering Contracts. Haswell & Silva. 1981. text ed. price not set (ISBN 0-408-00526-2). Butterworth.

Civil Engineering Education. Compiled By American Society of Civil Engineers. 1024p. 1979. pap. text ed. 48.00 (ISBN 0-87262-195-2). Am Soc Civil Eng.

Civil Engineering Education: Engineering Practice & Nations Needs, Vol. 3. Compiled By American Society of Civil Engineers. 1975. pap. text ed. 48.00 (ISBN 0-87262-110-3). Am Soc Civil Eng.

Civil Engineering in the Oceans III. Compiled By American Society of Civil Engineers. 1560p. 1976. pap. text ed. 59.00 (ISBN 0-87262-162-6). Am Soc Civil Eng.

Civil Engineering Materials. Neil Jackson. LC 76-381536. (Illus.). 1977. pap. 17.50x (ISBN 0-333-19310-5). Scholium Intl.

Civil Engineering Procedure. 3rd ed. 112p. 1980. 25.00x (ISBN 0-7277-0113-4, Pub. by Telford England). State Mutual Bk.

Civil Engineering Review Manual. 2nd ed. Michael R. Lindeburg. LC 80-81798. (Engineering Review Manual Ser.). (Illus.). 688p. (Orig.). 1980. pap. 29.50 (ISBN 0-932276-15-6); wkbk. 4.00 (ISBN 0-932276-17-2). Prof Engine.

Civil Engineering Software Center. Compiled By American Society of Civil Engineers. 116p. 1973. pap. text ed. 16.50 (ISBN 0-87262-052-2). Am Soc Civil Eng.

Civil Engineer's Role in Productivity in the Construction Industry: Proceedings, 2 vols. ASCE Committee on Engineering Management, Aug. 1976. Compiled By American Society of Civil Engineers. 408p. 1976. Set. pap. text ed. 17.75 (ISBN 0-87262-075-1). Am Soc Civil Eng.

Civil Engineer's Technical Reference Book. 3rd ed. B. Fletcher & S. Lavan. (Technician Ser.). (Illus.). 1980. 14.50 (ISBN 0-408-00426-6). Butterworths.

Civil Law in Its Natural Order, 2 vols. Jean Domat. Ed. by Luther S. Cushing. Tr. by William Strahan from Fr. 1763p. 1981. Repr. of 1850 ed. Set. lib. bdg. 97.50x (ISBN 0-8377-0511-8). Rothman.

Civil Liability of Law Enforcement Officers. Joyce Blalock. 248p. 1974. photocopy ed. spiral 15.75 (ISBN 0-398-02864-8). C C Thomas.

Civil Liberties & the Constitution. 3rd ed. L. Barker & T. Barker. 1978. pap. 12.95 (ISBN 0-13-134957-0). P-H.

Civil Liberties: Policy & Policy Making. Ed. by Stephen L. Wasby. LC 76-43318. 256p. 1977. pap. 7.95 (ISBN 0-8093-0817-7). S Ill U Pr.

Civil Litigation. Delmar Karlen. 1978. text ed. 17.00 (ISBN 0-672-82898-7, Bobbs-Merrill Law). Michie.

Civil Litigation & the Police: A Method of Communication. Robert H. Sulnick. 168p. 1976. 14.75 (ISBN 0-398-03494-X). C C Thomas.

Civil-Military Relations, an Annotated Bibliography, 1940-1952. Social Science Research Council. LC 75-3796. 140p. 1975. Repr. of 1954 ed. lib. bdg. 13.75x (ISBN 0-8371-8076-7, CIMR). Greenwood.

Civil-Military Relations: Changing Concepts in the Seventies. Charles L. Cochran. LC 73-17646. 1974. 17.95 (ISBN 0-02-905670-5). Free Pr.

Civil-Military Relations in Communist Systems. Ed. by Dale R. Herspring & Ivan Volgyes. 1978. lib. bdg. 28.50x (ISBN 0-89158-165-0, Dawson). Westview.

Civil Practice & Procedure: (N.Y.) Louis A. Kass. 150p. 1980. 6.50 (ISBN 0-87526-093-4). Gould.

Civil Practice Law & Rules of New York. (Supplemented annually). 1980. looseleaf 12.50 (ISBN 0-87526-155-8). Gould.

Civil Prisoners. Meriol Trevor. 1977. 7.95 o.p. (ISBN 0-525-08175-5). Dutton.

Civil Procedure, Cases & Materials. 3rd ed. John L. Cound et al. LC 80-14621. (American Casebook Ser.). 1223p. 1980. text ed. 22.95 (ISBN 0-8299-2092-7). West Pub.

Civil Rights. Ed. by Grant S. McClellan. (Reference Shelf Ser: Vol. 36, No. 6). 1964. 6.25 (ISBN 0-8242-0083-7). Wilson.

Civil Rights & Liberties in the 1970's. Richard M. Pious. 1973. pap. text ed. 3.95 (ISBN 0-394-31707-6). Random.

Civil Rights & the Crisis of Liberalism: The Democratic Party, 1945-1976. John F. Martin. 1979. lib. bdg. 24.50x (ISBN 0-89158-454-4). Westview.

Civil Rights & the South: A Symposium. A. E. Sutherland, Jr. LC 78-151047. (Symposia on Law & Society Ser.). 1971. Repr. of 1963 ed. lib. bdg. 17.50 (ISBN 0-306-70116-2). Da Capo.

Civil Rights Injunction. Owen M. Fiss. LC 78-2052. 128p. 1978. 10.95x (ISBN 0-253-31356-2). Ind U Pr.

Civil Rights of Students. David Schimmel & Louis Fischer. (Critical Issues in Education Ser.). 347p. 1975. pap. text ed. 9.50 scp (ISBN 0-06-045776-7, HarpC). Har-Row.

Civil Service Arithmetic & Vocabulary. Barbara Erdsneker & Margaret Haller. 320p. 1981. lib. bdg. 9.00 (ISBN 0-668-05116-7, 4872-7); pap. 6.00 (ISBN 0-668-04872-7). Arco.

Civil Service Careers. Virginia N. McCall. (Career Concise Guides Ser.). (Illus.). (gr. 7 up). 1977. PLB 6.45 s&l (ISBN 0-531-01302-2). Watts.

Civil Service Handbook. 7th ed. Editorial Board. 128p. (Orig.). 1981. pap. 4.00 (ISBN 0-668-05166-3, 5166). Arco.

Civil Service in Great Britain. S. R. Maheshawari. 1977. 7.00x o.p. (ISBN 0-88386-948-9). South Asia Bks.

Civil Service Reform in Brazil: Principles Versus Practice. Lawrence S. Graham. (Latin American Monographs: No. 13). 1968. 9.95x (ISBN 0-292-78356-6). U of Tex Pr.

Civil Service Reform in Lebanon. Iskandar Bashir. 1977. 15.00x (ISBN 0-8156-6050-2, Am U Beirut). Syracuse U Pr.

Civil Services of the United Kingdom, 1855-1970. Edgar N. Gladden. LC 67-16352. 1967. 17.50x (ISBN 0-678-05048-1). Kelley.

Civil Tongue. Edwin Newman. LC 76-11607. 1976. 9.95 (ISBN 0-672-52267-5). Bobbs.

Civil Tongue. Edwin Newman. 1977. pap. 2.75 (ISBN 0-446-95954-5). Warner Bks.

Civil War. Julius Caesar. Tr. by Jane F. Mitchell. (Classics Ser.). 1976. pap. 3.50 (ISBN 0-14-044187-5). Penguin.

Civil War: A Concise History of the War Between the States. Ed. by Maurice Matloff. 1978. 6.95 o.p. (ISBN 0-679-50840-6). McKay.

Civil War & Reconstruction, 1850-1877. Ed. by I. A. Newby. (Literature of History Ser). (Orig.). 1971. 18.95x (ISBN 0-89197-080-0); pap. text ed. 7.95x (ISBN 0-89197-081-9). Irvington.

Civil War & the American System: America's Battle with Britain 1860-76, Vol. 2. Allen Salisbury. Ed. by Kathy Stevens. (American History Ser.). 1978. pap. 5.95 (ISBN 0-918388-02-3, E469S24, Univ Edns). New Benjamin.

Civil War Day by Day: An Almanac 1861-1865. E. B. Long & Barbara Long. LC 73-163653. 1971. 11.95 (ISBN 0-385-01264-0). Doubleday.

Civil War Dictionary. Mark M. Boatner, 3rd. (Illus., Maps & diagrams). 22.50 (ISBN 0-679-50013-8). McKay.

Civil War in America. Alan Barker. LC 61-11594. pap. 1.95 (ISBN 0-385-09871-5, A274, Anch). Doubleday.

Civil War in China: The Political Struggle, 1945-1949. Suzanne Pepper. 1978. 20.00x (ISBN 0-520-02440-0); pap. 6.95x (ISBN 0-520-04085-6). U of Cal Pr.

Civil War in France. Marx. 1977. 3.95 (ISBN 0-8351-0562-8); pap. 2.25 (ISBN 0-8351-0044-8). China Bks.

Civil War in Kentucky. Lowell Harrison. LC 75-3545. (Kentucky Bicentennial Bookshelf Ser.). (Illus.). 136p. 1980. Repr. of 1975 ed. 5.95 (ISBN 0-8131-0209-X). U Pr of Ky.

Civil War in Louisiana. John D. Winters. LC 63-9647. 552p. 1979. 25.00 (ISBN 0-8071-0834-0). La State U Pr.

Civil War in Russia, 1917-20. John Bradley. LC 75-18594. 200p. 1975. 19.95 (ISBN 0-312-14140-8). St Martin.

Civil War in South Russia, 1918: The First Year of the Volunteer Army. Peter Kenez. LC 78-114339. 1971. 21.50c (ISBN 0-520-01709-9). U of Cal Pr.

Civil War in Spain. Frank Jellinek. 1969. Repr. of 1938 ed. 23.50 (ISBN 0-86527-028-7). Fertig.

Civil War in the United States. Karl Marx & Frederick Engels. pap. 3.25 o.p. (ISBN 0-7178-0028-8). Intl Pub Co.

Civil War Letters of General Frank "Bull" Paxton: A Lieutenant of Lee & Jackson. Ed. by John G. Paxton. LC 78-68427. 1978. 8.50 (ISBN 0-912172-23-1). Hill Jr Coll.

Civil War Letters of General Robert McAllister. Robert McAllister. Ed. by James I. Robertson, Jr. (Illus.). 1965. 30.00 (ISBN 0-8135-0496-1). Rutgers U Pr.

Civil War Nurse: The Diary & Letters of Hannah Ropes. Ed. by John R. Brumgardt. LC 79-28372. 200p. 1980. 12.50x (ISBN 0-87049-280-2). U of Tenn Pr.

Civil War on the Screen & Other Essays. Jack Spears. LC 75-5176. 1977. 17.50 o.p. (ISBN 0-498-01728-1). A S Barnes.

Civil War Sketchbook of Charles Ellery Stedman, Surgeon, United States Navy. Jim D. Hill. LC 76-4164. (Illus.). 217p. 1976. 24.95 o.p. (ISBN 0-89141-001-5). Presidio Pr.

Civil War Washington: A Guide to Mr. Lincoln's City. Richard M. Lee. 272p. 1981. pap. price not set (ISBN 0-914440-48-9). EPM Pubns.

Civil Wars. June Jordan. LC 80-68164. 192p. 1981. 12.95 (ISBN 0-8070-3232-8). Beacon Pr.

Civil Wars, Bk. 1. Appian. Ed. by J. L. Strachan-Davidson. 1902. 2.50x o.p. (ISBN 0-19-814104-1). Oxford U Pr.

Civil Wars in the Twentieth Century. Ed. by Robin Higham. LC 78-160044. 272p. 1972. 12.00x (ISBN 0-8131-1261-3). U Pr of Ky.

Civil Works Administration. Forrest A. Walker. Ed. by Frank Freidel. LC 78-62516. (Modern American History Ser.: Vol. 18). 1979. lib. bdg. 23.00 (ISBN 0-8240-3641-7). Garland Pub.

Civilisation: A Personal View. Kenneth Clark. LC 75-97174. (Illus.). 1970. 25.00 (ISBN 0-06-090787-8, CN 787, HarpT); pap. 10.95 (ISBN 0-06-010801-0, TD-113, HarpT). Har-Row.

Civilities & Civil Rights: Greensboro, North Carolina, & the Black Struggle for Freedom. William H. Chafe. (Illus.). 1980. 15.95 (ISBN 0-19-502625-X). Oxford U Pr.

Civilities & Civil Rights: Greensboro, North Carolina, & the Black Struggle for Freedom. William H. Chafe. (Illus.). 320p. 1981. pap. 5.95 (ISBN 0-19-502919-4, GB 644, GB). Oxford U Pr.

Civilization & Progress. Radoslav A. Tsanoff. LC 74-160051. 384p. 1971. 17.00x (ISBN 0-8131-1255-9). U Pr of Ky.

Civilization & Society in the West. Carolly Erickson. 1978. pap. 13.95x (ISBN 0-673-15123-9). Scott F.

Civilization in Crisis. J. A. Camilleri. LC 76-4240. (Illus.). 1977. 28.95 (ISBN 0-521-21248-0); pap. 11.50x (ISBN 0-521-29078-3). Cambridge U Pr.

Civilization in the West, Pt. II. 4th ed. John B. Christopher et al. (Illus.). 512p. 1981. pap. text ed. 13.95 (ISBN 0-13-134932-5). P-H.

Civilization: Its Cause & Cure. Edward Carpenter. 44p. pap. 1.50 (ISBN 0-934676-01-1). Greenlf Bks.

Civilization: Lectures. University Of California Philosophical Union - 1941. (Publications in Philosophy Ser: Vol. 23). 1941. pap. 17.00 (ISBN 0-384-07050-7). Johnson Repr.

Civilization of Ancient Crete. R. F. Willetts. 1978. 31.50x (ISBN 0-520-03406-6). U of Cal Pr.

Civilization of the Old South: Writings of Clement Eaton. Clement Eaton. Ed. by Albert D. Kirwan. LC 68-29638. 328p. 1968. 11.00x (ISBN 0-8131-1162-5). U Pr of Ky.

Civilization Past & Present. 7th ed. T. Walter Wallbank et al. 1976. pap. 9.95x ea.; Bk. 1. o.p. (ISBN 0-673-15078-X); Bk. 2. (ISBN 0-673-15079-8); Bk. 3. (ISBN 0-673-15080-1). Scott F.

Civilization Past & Present. 5th ed. T. Walter Wallbank et al. 1978. 19.95x (ISBN 0-673-07951-1). Scott F.

Civilization Past & Present: Prehistory to 1650. 5th ed. T. Walter Wallbank et al. 1979. Vol. 1. pap. text ed. 12.95x (ISBN 0-673-15246-4). Scott F.

Civilization Past & Present: Prehistory to Sixteen Fifty, Vol. 1. T. Walter Wallbank et al. 1981. pap. text ed. 13.95x (ISBN 0-673-15235-9). Scott F.

Civilization Past & Present: 1650 to the Present. 5th ed. T. Walter Wallbank et al. 1979. Vol. 2. pap. text ed. 12.95x (ISBN 0-673-15247-2). Scott F.

Civilization: Readings from Scientific American. Intro. by Brian M. Fagan. LC 78-15780. (Illus.). 1979. text ed. 17.95x (ISBN 0-7167-1024-2); pap. text ed. 8.95x (ISBN 0-7167-1023-4). W H Freeman.

Civilizations of Ancient America. International Congress Of Americanists - 29th. Ed. by Sol Tax. (Illus.). 328p. 1952. Repr. 17.50x (ISBN 0-8154-0231-7). Cooper Sq.

Civilizations of Black Africa. Jacques Maquet. Tr. by Joan Rayfield. 1972. pap. 5.95 (ISBN 0-19-501464-2, GB368, GB). Oxford U Pr.

Civilizations of Europe. Michael Grant. 4.95 o.p. (ISBN 0-452-25039-0, Z5039, Plume). NAL.

Civilized Man's Eight Deadly Sins. Konrad Lorenz. Tr. by Marjorie Kerr-Wilson. LC 73-20189. (Helen & Kurt Wolff Bk). 1974. 4.95 o.p. (ISBN 0-15-118061-X). HarBraceJ.

Civilized Wilderness: Backgrounds to American Literature, 1817-1860. Edward H. Foster. LC 74-33091. (Illus.). 1975. 12.95 (ISBN 0-02-910350-9). Free Pr.

Civilizing American Cities: A Selection of Frederick Law Olmsted's Writings on City Landscapes. Ed. by S. B. Sutton. (Illus.). 1971. pap. 7.95 (ISBN 0-262-65012-6). MIT Pr.

Civilizing Process: The/Development of Manners, Vol. 1. Norbert Elias. Tr. by Edmund Jephcott from Ger. 1977. 20.00 (ISBN 0-916354-32-6). Urizen Bks.

Civilizing Process: The Dynamics of the State, Vol. II. Date not set. 20.00 (ISBN 0-916354-33-4). Urizen Bks.

Civis Romanus: Reader for the First Two Years of Latin. J. M. Cobban & R. Colebourn. (Illus., Lat.). (gr. 8-10). 1969. text ed. 5.95 (ISBN 0-312-14175-0); key s.p. 3.95 (ISBN 0-312-14210-2). St Martin.

CJB International Council for Building Research, Studies & Documentation Sixth Congress, Budapest 1974. 1730p. 1980. 285.00x (ISBN 0-85950-035-7, Pub. by Thornes England). State Mutual Bk.

Claes Oldenburg. Barbara Rse. 224p. 1979. 12.50 (ISBN 0-87070-509-1). NYGS.

Claes Oldenburg: Drawings & Prints. Intro. By Gene Baro. LC 68-8894. (Illus.). 274p. 1981. pap. 19.95 (ISBN 0-87754-202-3). Chelsea Hse.

Claiborne County. Edgar A. Holt. Ed. by Joy B. Dunn & Charles W. Crawford. (Tennessee County History Ser.: No. 13). (Illus.). 144p. 1981. 12.50x (ISBN 0-87870-101-X). Memphis St Univ.

Claimed by Vesuvius. Walter H. Marx. (Illus.). 164p. 1975. pap. text ed. 4.95x (ISBN 0-88334-069-0). Ind Sch Pr.

Claiming a Frontier: Ministry & Older People. Robert W. McClellan. LC 77-85413. 1977. 4.50 (ISBN 0-88474-040-4). USC Andrus Geron.

Claiming an Identity They Taught Me to Despise. Michelle Cliff. LC 80-23137. (Orig.). 1980. pap. 4.00 (ISBN 0-930436-06-7). Persephone.

Claiming Kin. Ellen B. Voigt. LC 76-5944. (Wesleyan Poetry Program: Vol.83). 1976. lib. bdg. 10.00x (ISBN 0-8195-2083-7, Pub. by Wesleyan U Pr); pap. 4.95 (ISBN 0-8195-1083-1). Columbia U Pr.

Claims of Labour. Arthur Helps. 288p. 1971. Repr. of 1845 ed. 21.00x (ISBN 0-686-28329-5, Pub. by Irish Academic Pr). Biblio Dist.

Claims to Territory in International Law & Relations. Norman L. Hill. LC 75-25488. (Illus.). 248p. 1976. Repr. of 1945 ed. lib. bdg. 20.25x (ISBN 0-8371-8430-4, HICT). Greenwood.

Clairvoyance. 10th ed. Charles W. Leadbeater. 1968. 4.50 (ISBN 0-8356-7095-3). Theos Pub Hse.

Clairvoyant Countess. Dorothy Gilman. 224p. 1978. pap. 1.95 (ISBN 0-449-23561-0, Crest). Fawcett.

Clam Lover's Cookbook. 2nd ed. William G. Flagg. LC 80-10619. (Illus., Orig.). 1980. pap. 5.95 (ISBN 0-88427-041-6, Dist. by Caroline Hse). North River.

Clam Plate Orgy & Other Subliminal Techniques for Manipulating Your Behavior. Wilson B. Key. (Illus.). 1981. pap. 2.95 (ISBN 0-686-69108-3, E9723, Sig). NAL.

Clam Theater. Russell Edson. LC 72-11052. (Wesleyan Poetry Program: Vol. 64). 1973. 10.00x (ISBN 0-8195-2064-0, Pub. by Wesleyan U Pr). Columbia U Pr.

Clan Donald. Donald J. MacDonald. (Illus.). 437p. 1980. 59.95 (ISBN 0-904265-21-8). Pelican.

Clan Leaders & Colonial Chiefs in Lango: The Political History of an East African Stateless Society, 1800-1939. John Tosh. (Studies in African Affairs). (Illus.). 1979. 42.00x (ISBN 0-19-822711-6). Oxford U Pr.

Clandestine Armament, 1941-1944. Pierre Lorain. (Illus.). 192p. 1981. 12.50 (ISBN 0-02-575200-6). Macmillan.

Clandestine Betrothal. Alice C. Ley. 192p. (Orig.). 1976. pap. 1.50 (ISBN 0-345-28576-X). Ballantine.

Clandestine Essays. Ievhen Sverstiuk. Tr. by George S. Luckyj from Ukrainian. Orig. Title: Ivan Kotliarevsky Smietsia. 100p. 1976. PLB 10.00x (ISBN 0-87287-151-7); pap. 7.50 (ISBN 0-87287-158-4). Ukrainian Acad.

Clansman: An Historical Romance of the Ku Klux Klan. Thomas Dixon, Jr. LC 71-104761. (Novel As American Social History Ser.). 392p. 1970. pap. 7.00x (ISBN 0-8131-0126-3). U Pr of Ky.

Clara Barton. Matthew G. Grant. LC 73-15869. 1974. PLB 5.95 (ISBN 0-87191-306-2). Creative Ed.

Clara Barton. new ed. Robert Kraske. (Stories About Christian Heroes Ser.). (Illus.). (gr. 1-3). 1980. pap. 1.95 (ISBN 0-03-049436-2). Winston Pr.

Clara Butt: Her Life Story. Winifred Ponder. LC 77-16530. (Music Reprint Ser.: 1978). (Illus.). 1978. Repr. of 1928 ed. lib. bdg. 27.50 (ISBN 0-306-77529-8). Da Capo.

Clara Novello. Averil Mackenzie-Grieve. (Music Reprint Ser.). 1980. Repr. of 1955 ed. lib. bdg. 29.50 (ISBN 0-306-76009-6). Da Capo.

Clara Reeve. Leonie Hargrave. 496p. 1976. pap. 1.95 o.p. (ISBN 0-345-25070-2). Ballantine.

Clara Schumann: An Artist's Life, 2 vols. Berthold Litzmann. (Music Reprint Ser.). 1979. Repr. of 1913 ed. Set. lib. bdg. 69.50 (ISBN 0-306-79582-5). Da Capo.

Clara Weaver Parrish. C. Reynolds Brown. LC 80-82147. (Illus.). 1980. pap. 4.00 (ISBN 0-89280-016-X). Montgomery Mus.

Clarastella Together with Poems Occasional, Elegies, Epigrams, Satyrs, 1650. Robert Heath. LC 74-119866. 1970. Repr. of 1650 ed. 21.00x (ISBN 0-8201-1073-6). Schol Facsimiles.

Clare: The Critical Heritage. Ed. by Mark Storey. (Critical Heritage Ser). 474p. 1973. 38.00x (ISBN 0-7100-7389-5). Routledge & Kegan.
Clarel. Ed. by Walter E. Bezanson. 772p. 1959. 12.50 (ISBN 0-87532-011-2). Hendricks House.
Clarence Darrow. Miriam Gurko. LC 65-13138. (gr. 7 up). 1965. 8.95 o.p. (ISBN 0-690-19484-6, TYC-J). T Y Crowell.
Clarence Darrow: A Bibliography. Willard D. Hunsberger. LC 80-26317. viii, 215p. 1981. 12.50 (ISBN 0-8108-1384-X). Scarecrow.
Clarence Darrow: The Sentimental Rebel. Arthur Weinberg & Lila Weinberg. 1980. 17.95 (ISBN 0-399-11936-1). Putnam.
Clarence White. Intro. by Maynard P. White. (Aperture History of Photography Ser.: No. 11). (Illus.). 1979. over boards 8.95 (ISBN 0-89381-019-3). Aperture.
Clare's Choice. new ed. Melissa C. Flannery. (Stories About Christian Heroes Ser.). (Illus.). (gr. 1-3). 1980. pap. 1.95 (ISBN 0-03-049431-1). Winston Pr.
Claret & Cross-Buttock: Rafferty's Prize-Fighters. Joe Robinson. 1976. 13.50 o.p. (ISBN 0-04-920048-8). Allen Unwin.
Clarification & Enlightenment: Essays in Comparative Philosophy. Joseph S. Wu. LC 78-62175. 1978. pap. text ed. 9.75 o.p. (ISBN 0-8191-0425-6). U Pr of Amer.
Clarification of the Status of the Type Specimens of Diabroticites (Coleoptera, Chrysomelidae, Galerocinae) R. F. Smith & J. F. Lawrence. (U. C. Publ. in Entomology: Vol. 45). 1967. pap. 8.50x (ISBN 0-520-09117-5). U of Cal Pr.
Clarinet. Jack Brymer. LC 77-275. (Yehudi Menuhin Music Guides Ser.). (Illus.). 1977. 12.95 (ISBN 0-02-871430-X); pap. 6.95 (ISBN 0-02-871440-7). Schirmer Bks.
Clarinet & Clarinet Playing. David Pino. (Illus.). 288p. 1980. 15.95 (ISBN 0-684-16624-0, ScribT). Scribner.
Clarinet & Saxophone Experience. Stanley Richmond. LC 70-183051. (Illus.). 1972. 8.95 o.p. (ISBN 0-312-14245-5, C30000). St Martin.
Clarinet & Sax0 Phone Experience. Stanley Richmond. 1980. 25.00x (Pub.by Darton-Longman-Todd England). State Mutual Bk.
Clarinet Technique. 3rd ed. Frederick Thurston. Ed. by Thea King. (Technique Books). 1977. 7.75 (ISBN 0-19-318610-1). Oxford U Pr.
Clarion Cook Book for Boys & Girls. Eva Moore. LC 79-129210. (Illus.). (gr. 1-4). 1971. 5.95 (ISBN 0-395-28818-5, Clarion). HM.
Clarita's Cocina: Great Traditional Recipes from a Spanish Kitchen. Clarita Garcia. LC 74-113069. (Illus.). 1970. 10.95 (ISBN 0-385-04657-X). Doubleday.
Clark Inheritance: A Coal Country Saga. Sophia Yarnall. LC 80-54812. 224p. 1981. 11.95 (ISBN 0-8027-0679-7). Walker & Co.
Clarke Papers, 4 Vols. William Clarke. Ed. by C. H. Firth. Set. 89.50 (ISBN 0-384-09232-2); 22.50 ea. Johnson Repr.
Clark's Positioning in Radiography, Vol. 1. 10th ed. Louis Kreal. (Illus.). 500p. 1980. 45.95 (ISBN 0-8151-5190-X). Year Bk Med.
Clary Genealogy: Four Early American Lines & Related Families. Ralph S. Rowland & Star W. Rowland. LC 80-54651. 1980. write for info. R & S Rowland.
Clary Genealogy: Four Early American Lines & Related Families. Ralph S. Rowland & Star W. Rowland. 1980. 17.50. R & S Rowland.
Clash of Cultures: Christian Missionaries & the Shona of Rhodesia. Geoffrey Z. Kapenzi. LC 78-68799. 1979. pap. text ed. 7.50 (ISBN 0-8191-0704-2). U Pr of Amer.
Clash of the Titans. Ed. by Don Glut. (Big Little Book Special Ser.). (Illus.). 256p. (gr. 3-7). 2.50 (Golden Pr). Western Pub.
Clash of the Titans Storybook. Hans Pemsteen. (Illus.). 32p. (gr. 4-6). 1981. 4.95 (ISBN 0-307-16801-8, Golden Pr). Western Pub.
Clash of Titans: Africa & U. S. Foreign Policy. Edward W. Chester. LC 73-80518. 320p. 1974. 12.95x o.p. (ISBN 0-88344-065-2). Orbis Bks.
Clash: The Conflict of Modern Youth. C. M. Ward. 1955. pap. 0.50 o.p. (ISBN 0-88243-701-1, 02-0701). Gospel Pub.
Clashing Myths in German Literature: From Heine to Rilke. Henry Hatfield. LC 73-83964. 256p. 1974. text ed. 14.00x (ISBN 0-674-13375-7). Harvard U Pr.
Clasificacion Decimal de Dewey Para Pequenas Bibliotecas Publicas y Escolares. Melvil Dewey. (Span). 1967. pap. 2.00x, public & school lib. ed (ISBN 0-910608-08-3). Forest Pr.
Class. Jilly Cooper. LC 80-2718. (Illus.). 288p. 1981. 12.95 (ISBN 0-394-51414-9). Knopf.
Class Act. Terry Fisher. (Orig.). 1976. pap. 1.75 o.s.i. (ISBN 0-446-84242-7). Warner Bks.
Class-Action Suit That Worked. new ed. Thomas C. Bartsh et al. LC 78-58814. 1978. 19.95 (ISBN 0-669-02409-0). Lexington Bks.
Class Against Itself. D. McEachern. 245p. 1980. 29.50 (ISBN 0-521-22985-5); pap. cancelled (ISBN 0-521-28054-0). Cambridge U Pr.
Class & Character in Faulkners South. Myra Jehlen. LC 76-3519. 176p. 1976. 12.50x (ISBN 0-231-04011-3). Columbia U Pr.
Class & Class Consciousness in the Industrial Revolution, 1780-1850. R. J. Morris. (Studies in Economic & Social History). 80p. 1979. pap. text ed. 4.75x (ISBN 0-333-15454-1). Humanities.
Class & Class Structure. Ed. by Alan Hunt. 1977. pap. text ed. 7.75x (ISBN 0-85315-402-3). Humanities.
Class & Community: The Industrial Revolution in Lynn. Alan Dawley. LC 75-29049. (Harvard Studies in Urban History Ser.). (Illus.). 1979. 17.50x (ISBN 0-674-13390-0); pap. 6.95x (ISBN 0-674-13395-1). Harvard U Pr.
Class & Conflict in Nineteenth-Century England, 1815-1850. Ed. by Patricia Hollis. (Birth of Modern Britain Ser). 402p. 1973. 20.00x (ISBN 0-7100-7419-0); pap. 10.00 (ISBN 0-7100-7420-4). Routledge & Kegan.
Class & Economic Change in Kenya: The Making of an African Petite Bourgeoisie, 1905-1970. Gavin Kitching. LC 79-21804. 448p. 1980. text ed. 35.00x (ISBN 0-300-02385-5). Yale U Pr.
Class & Hierarchy: The Social Meaning of Occupations. Anthony P. Coxon & Charles L. Jones. (Illus.). 1979. 21.95 (ISBN 0-312-14256-0). St Martin.
Class & Nation, Historically & in the Current Crisis. LC 79-3022. 292p. 1981. pap. 6.50 (ISBN 0-85345-523-6). Monthly Rev.
Class & Politics in the United States. R. F. Hamilton. LC 72-1951. 1972. pap. 15.95x (ISBN 0-471-34709-4). Wiley.
Class & Society in Early America. Gary B. Nash. (Interdisciplinary Approaches to History). (Illus.). 1970. ref. ed. 11.95 (ISBN 0-13-135111-7); pap. text ed. 9.95 o.p. (ISBN 0-13-135103-6). P-H.
Class & Status in France: Economic Change & Social Immobility, 1945-1975. Jane Marceau. 1977. 24.00x (ISBN 0-19-827217-0). Oxford U Pr.
Class Book of Problems in "A" Level Chemistry. 3rd ed. A. Holderness & J. Lambert. 1971. pap. text ed. 3.95x o.p. (ISBN 0-435-65431-4). Heinemann Ed.
Class, Codes & Control Vol. 1: Theoretical Studies Towards a Sociology of Language. Basil Bernstein. (Primary Socialization, Language & Education Ser.). 1971. 30.00 (ISBN 0-7100-7060-8). Routledge & Kegan.
Class, Codes & Control, Vol. 2: Applied Studies Towards a Sociology of Language. Ed. by Basil Bernstein. (Primary Socialization, Language & Education Ser). 1973. 30.00 (ISBN 0-7100-7396-8). Routledge & Kegan.
Class, Codes & Control, Vol. 3: Towards a Theory of Educational Transmissions. Basil Bernstein. (Primary Socialization, Language & Education Ser.). 1977. pap. 6.95 (ISBN 0-7100-8666-0). Routledge & Kegan.
Class Conflict in Egypt, 1945-1970. Mahmoud Hussein. Tr. by Alfred Ehrenfeld et al from Fr. LC 72-81767. (Illus.). 416p. 1973. 13.95 o.p. (ISBN 0-85345-233-4, CL2334). Monthly Rev.
Class Crystallization. Werner S. Landecker. 272p. 1981. 19.00 (ISBN 0-8135-0918-1). Rutgers U Pr.
Class, Culture & Social Change: A Reconsideration of the 1930's. Frank Gloversmith. 1980. text ed. 42.50x (ISBN 0-391-01739-X). Humanities.
Class, Culture & the Curriculum. Denis Lawton. (Students Library of Education). 1975. 12.75x o.s.i. (ISBN 0-7100-8053-0); pap. 7.00 (ISBN 0-7100-8054-9). Routledge & Kegan.
Class Devotions: For Use with the 1981-82 International Lessons. Harold L. Fair. 1981. pap. 3.95 (ISBN 0-687-08621-3). Abingdon.
Class, Ethnicity & Politics in Liberia: Analysis of Power Struggles in the Tubman & Tolbert Administrations from 1944-1975. Stephen S. Hlope. LC 79-63261. 1979. pap. text ed. 11.25 (ISBN 0-8191-0721-2). U Pr of Amer.
Class: Image & Reality in Britain, France & the U. S. A. Since 1930. Arthur Marwick. 1980. 19.95 (ISBN 0-19-520203-1). Oxford U Pr.
Class in American Society. Leonard Reissman. 1960. text ed. 12.95 (ISBN 0-02-926270-4). Free Pr.
Class in English History: 1680-1850. R. S. Neale. 1981. 28.50x (ISBN 0-389-20177-4). B&N.
Class Inequality & Health Care: The Origins & Impact of the National Health Service. Vivienne Walters. 175p. 1980. 26.00x (ISBN 0-85664-685-7, Pub. by Croom Helm Ltd England). Biblio Dist.
Class J. Mills & Broughton. (Bliss Education Classification Ser.). 1977. text ed. 19.95 (ISBN 0-408-70829-8). Butterworths.
Class P: Religion, the Occult, Morals & Ethics. Mills & Broughton. (Bliss Bibliographic Classification Ser.). 1977. 19.95 (ISBN 0-408-70832-8). Butterworths.
Class Pictures. Marilyn Sachs. LC 80-390. 144p. (gr. 4-7). 1980. PLB 9.95 (ISBN 0-525-27985-7). Dutton.
Class, Politics, & Culture. Stanley Aronowitz. 256p. 1981. 25.95 (ISBN 0-03-059031-0). Praeger.
Class, Race & Black Liberation. Henry Winston. LC 77-923. 1977. 8.00 (ISBN 0-7178-0484-4); pap. 2.75 o.p. (ISBN 0-7178-0491-7). Intl Pub Co.
Class, Race & Worker Insurgency. J. A. Geschwender. LC 76-62581. (ASA Rose Monographs). (Illus.). 1977. 22.95 (ISBN 0-521-21584-6); pap. 6.95x (ISBN 0-521-29191-7). Cambridge U Pr.
Class, Religion, & Local Politics: The Centre Party in Wurttemberg Before 1914. David Blackbourn. LC 80-11878. 288p. 1980. text ed. 25.00x (ISBN 0-300-02464-9). Yale U Pr.
Class Reunion. Rona Jaffe. 1980. pap. 2.75 o.s.i. (ISBN 0-440-11408-X). Dell.
Class, Sex, & the Woman Worker. Ed. by Milton Cantor & Bruce Laurie. LC 76-15304. (Contributions in Labor History Ser.: No. 1). 1977. lib. bdg. 16.95x (ISBN 0-8371-9032-0, CCS/). Greenwood.
Class, State & Industrial Structure: The Historical Process of South American Industrial Growth. Frederick S. Weaver. LC 79-6571. (Contributions in Economics & Economic History: No. 32). (Illus.). xiv, 247p. 1980. lib. bdg. 28.50 (ISBN 0-313-22114-6, WCI/). Greenwood.
Class, State & Power in the Third World: With Case Studies on Class Conflict in Latin America. James Petras. 300p. 1981. text ed. 19.95 (ISBN 0-86598-018-7). Allanheld.
Class, Status & Power: A Reader in Social Stratification. rev. ed. Ed. by Reinhard Bendix & S. M. Lipset. LC 65-23025. 1966. text ed. 17.95 (ISBN 0-02-902630-X). Free Pr.
Class Structure & Economic Growth: India & Pakistan Since the Moghuls. Angus Maddison. 1972. 7.95x (ISBN 0-393-05467-5, 05467); pap. 3.95x (ISBN 0-393-09399-9). Norton.
Class, Structure & Knowledge: Problems in the Sociology of Knowing. Nicholas Abercrombie. LC 79-9650. 1980. 20.00x (ISBN 0-8147-0571-5). NYU Pr.
Class Structure in the Social Consciousness. Stanislaw Ossowski. LC 63-13183. 1963. 14.95 (ISBN 0-02-923500-6). Free Pr.
Class Struggle in the First French Republic: Bourgeois & Bras Nus 1793-1795. Daniel Guerin. Tr. by Ian Patterson from Fr. 1977. text ed. 17.25x (ISBN 0-904383-30-X). Humanities.
Class Struggle in the Pale. Ezra Mendelsohn. LC 71-96097. 1970. 23.50 (ISBN 0-521-07730-3). Cambridge U Pr.
Class Struggles in Ancient Greece. Margaret O. Wason. LC 72-80600. 262p. 1973. Repr. of 1947 ed. 13.50 o.p. (ISBN 0-86527-029-5). Fertig.
Class Struggles in France, 1848-1850. Karl Marx. LC 64-19792. 1964. pap. 2.25 (ISBN 0-7178-0030-X). Intl Pub Co.
Class Theory & the Division of Labour. Gavin Mackenzie. (Studies in Sociology). 1980. pap. write for info. (ISBN 0-391-01128-6). Humanities.
Classes Rurales et le Regime Domanial En France Au Moyen Age. Henri E. See. LC 80-2003. 1981. Repr. of 1901 ed. 61.50 (ISBN 0-404-18594-0). AMS Pr.
Classes, Strata & Power. Wlodsimierz Wesolowki. (International Library of Sociology). 1979. 20.00 (ISBN 0-7100-8845-0). Routledge & Kegan.
Classic Airplanes of the Thirties - Aircraft of the Roaring Twenties. Antique Airplane Association. Ed. by James Gilbert. LC 79-7238. (Flight: Its First Seventy-Five Years Ser.). (Illus.). 1979. Repr. of 1965 ed. lib. bdg. 15.00x (ISBN 0-405-12153-9). Arno.
Classic American Patchwork Quilt Patterns. Maggie Malone. LC 77-80195. (Illus.). pap. 6.95 (ISBN 0-8069-8212-8). Sterling.
Classic American Philosophers. Ed. by Max H. Fisch. (Orig.). 1966. pap. text ed. 13.95 (ISBN 0-13-135186-9). P-H.
Classic American Railroad Stations. Julien Cavalier. LC 78-69669. (Illus.). 1980. 17.50 (ISBN 0-498-02216-1). A S Barnes.
Classic Ballroom Dances. Charles Simic. LC 80-14470. 1980. 8.95 (ISBN 0-8076-0973-0); pap. 4.95 (ISBN 0-8076-0974-9). Braziller.
Classic Boat. Ed. by Time-Life Books. (Time-Life Library of Boating). 1977. 14.95 (ISBN 0-8094-2144-5). Time-Life.
Classic Boat. Ed. by Time Life Books. LC 76-55862. (Illus.). (gr. 6 up). 1977. PLB 13.95 (ISBN 0-8094-2145-3, Pub. by Time-Life). Silver.
Classic Chinese Novel: A Critical Introduction. Hsia Chih-Tsing. LC 68-18997. (Companions to Asian Studies). 1968. 20.00x o.p. (ISBN 0-231-03109-2); pap. 7.50 o.p. (ISBN 0-231-08669-5). Columbia U Pr.
Classic Clitoris. Ed. by Thomas P. Lowry. LC 78-18298. (Illus.). 1978. text ed. 15.95 (ISBN 0-88229-387-7). Nelson-Hall.
Classic Contributions in the Addictions. Ed. by Howard Shaffer & Milton E. Burglass. 600p. 1981. 30.00 (ISBN 0-87630-260-6). Brunner-Mazel.
Classic Country Inns of America, 3 vols. Ed. by Peter Andrews. LC 77-71352. (Illus.). 1978. Set. slip-cased 49.95x o.s.i. (ISBN 0-03-045556-1). Knapp Pr.
Classic Cuisine of Vietnam. Bach Ngo & Gloria Zimmerman. LC 79-20323. (Illus.). 1979. 17.95 (ISBN 0-8120-5309-5). Barron.
Classic Descriptions of Disease: With Biographical Sketches of the Authors. 3rd ed. Ralph H. Major. (Illus.). 712p. 1978. 16.50 (ISBN 0-398-01202-4). C C Thomas.
Classic Desserts. The Editors of Time-Life Books. (Good Cook Ser.). (Illus.). 1980. 12.95 (ISBN 0-8094-2870-9). Time-Life.
Classic Essays on Photography. Alan Trachtenberg. LC 78-61844. 1980. 12.95 (ISBN 0-918172-07-1); pap. 8.95 (ISBN 0-918172-08-X). Leetes Isl.
Classic Essays on the Culture of Cities. Ed. by Richard Sennett. (Orig.). 1969. pap. text ed. 10.95 (ISBN 0-13-135194-X). P-H.
Classic Fairy Tales. Iona Opie & Peter Opie. (Illus.). 1974. 22.50x (ISBN 0-19-211559-6). Oxford U Pr.
Classic Fairy Tales. Iona Opie & Peter Opie. (Illus.). 352p. 1980. pap. 7.95 (ISBN 0-19-520219-8). Oxford U Pr.
Classic French Cooking. Craig Claiborne & Pierre Franey. LC 79-124640. (Foods of the World Ser.). (Illus.). (gr. 6 up). 1970. PLB 14.94 (ISBN 0-8094-0074-X, Pub. by Time-Life). Silver.
Classic Guitar Construction. Irving Sloane. (Illus.). 1966. 10.95 o.p. (ISBN 0-525-08200-X). Dutton.
Classic Indian Cooking. Julie Sahni. LC 80-19475. (Illus.). 320p. 1980. 15.95 (ISBN 0-688-03721-6). Morrow.
Classic Movie Monsters. Donald F. Glut. LC 77-16014. (Illus.). 1978. 18.00 (ISBN 0-8108-1049-2). Scarecrow.
Classic Music: A Handbook for Analysis. Leonard Ratner. LC 76-57808. (Illus.). 1980. 35.00 (ISBN 0-02-872020-2). Schirmer Bks.
Classic Myths in English Literature & in Art. rev. & enlarged ed. Charles M. Gayley. 1939. 18.50 (ISBN 0-471-00191-0). Wiley.
Classic Philosophical Questions. 3rd ed. James A. Gould. (Philosophy Ser.). 1979. pap. text ed. 12.95 (ISBN 0-675-08308-7); instructor's manual free. Merrill.
Classic Piano Rags. Rudi Blesh. (Orig.). 1973. pap. 8.95 (ISBN 0-486-20469-3). Dover.
Classic Rods & Rodmakers. Martin J. Keane. 1976. 17.95 (ISBN 0-87691-178-5). Winchester Pr.
Classic, Romantic & Modern. Jacques Barzun. xvi, 256p. 1975. pap. 5.50 (ISBN 0-226-03852-1, P643, Phoen). U of Chicago Pr.
Classic Secrets of Magic. Bruce Elliot. (Illus., Orig.). 1969. pap. 4.95 (ISBN 0-571-09019-2, Pub. by Faber & Faber). Merrimack Bk Serv.
Classic Short Fiction: An International Collection. Ed. by James K. Bowen. Richard Vanderbeets. LC 70-183111. 1972. pap. 6.95 (ISBN 0-672-61240-2). Bobbs.
Classic Snooker. Ray Reardon. LC 76-20094. 1976. 10.50 (ISBN 0-7153-7244-0). David & Charles.
Classic Tales from Modern Spain. Tr. by William E. Colford from Span. LC 63-23445. 1964. 6.95 (ISBN 0-8120-5022-3); pap. text ed. 3.50 (ISBN 0-8120-0046-3). Barron.
Classic Tales from Spanish America. Tr. by William E. Colford from Span. LC 61-18356. 1963. pap. 3.50 (ISBN 0-8120-0045-5). Barron.
Classic Techniques. Time Life Bks Editors. LC 73-85529. (Art of Sewing Ser.). (Illus.). 208p. (gr. 6 up). 1973. lib. bdg. 11.97 (ISBN 0-8094-1703-0). Silver.
Classic World of Horses. Robert Magee. LC 73-93951. (Orig.). 1974. 15.00 o.p. (ISBN 0-668-03466-1). Arco.
Classical & Biblical Reference Book. Henry A. Treble. (YA) (gr. 9 up). 1959. 6.00 (ISBN 0-7195-1426-6). Transatlantic.
Classical & Christian Ideas in English Renaissance Poetry. Isabel Rivers. 1979. text ed. 24.95x (ISBN 0-04-807002-5); pap. text ed. 8.95x (ISBN 0-04-807003-3). Allen Unwin.
Classical & Contemporary Readings in the Philosophy of Religion. 2nd ed. John Hick. LC 75-98092. (Philosophy Ser). 1969. text ed. 18.95 (ISBN 0-13-135269-5). P-H.
Classical & Foreign Quotations. 3rd ed. Francis H. King. LC 68-30647. 1968. Repr. of 1904 ed. 18.00 (ISBN 0-8103-3185-3). Gale.

Classical & Modern Physics, 3 vols. Kenneth Ford. Incl. Vol. 1. 1972. text ed. 19.95x (ISBN 0-471-00723-4); Vol. 2. text ed. 19.95x (ISBN 0-471-00724-2); answer manual 5.95 (ISBN 0-471-00945-8); Vol. 3. 1974. text ed. 21.95x (ISBN 0-471-00878-8); answer manual 5.95 (ISBN 0-471-00946-6). LC 76-161385. combined ed. for vols. 1 & 2 27.95 (ISBN 0-471-00666-1). Wiley.

Classical & Romantic. D. Stevens & Robertson. 1968. pap. 2.50 o.p. (ISBN 0-14-020494-6). Penguin.

Classical Art Forms & Celtic Mutations: Figural Art in Roman Britain. Claire Lindgren. LC 80-18987. (Illus.). 244p. (Orig.). 1981. 24.00 (ISBN 0-8155-5057-X, NP). Noyes.

Classical Brain Stem Syndromes: Translations of the Original Papers with Notes on the Evolution of Clinical Neuroanatomy. John K. Wolf. (Illus.). 186p. 1971. text ed. 13.75 (ISBN 0-398-02170-8). C C Thomas.

Classical Charged Particles. F. Rohrlich. 1965. text ed. 24.50 (ISBN 0-201-06492-8, Adv Bk Prog). A-W.

Classical Chess Matches, 1907-1913. Ed. by Fred Wilson. LC 74-79463. (Illus.). viii, 227p. (Orig.). 1975. pap. 3.00 o.p. (ISBN 0-486-23145-3). Dover.

Classical Chinese Plays. rev. ed. Josephine Huang Hung. 288p. 1980. 7.95x (ISBN 0-89955-152-1, Pub. by Mei Ya China); pap. 6.95x (ISBN 0-89955-186-6). Intl Schol Bk Serv.

Classical Conditioning. Ed. by William F. Prokasy. LC 65-16466. (Century Psychology Ser.). (Illus.). 1965. 24.50x (ISBN 0-89197-082-7); pap. text ed. 8.95x (ISBN 0-89197-083-5). Irvington.

Classical Conditioning & Instrumental Learning: A Contemporary Approach. John F. Hall. LC 75-32539. 528p. 1976. text ed. 13.00 o.p. (ISBN 0-397-47346-X). Lippincott.

Classical Dictionary of Hindu Mythology. 10th ed. John Dowson. 1968. Repr. of 1961 ed. 27.00 (ISBN 0-7100-1302-7). Routledge & Kegan.

Classical Dutch. Bellin. 19.95 (ISBN 0-7134-3211-X, Pub. by Batsford England). David & Charles.

Classical Dutch. Robert Bellin. (Batsford Chess Ser.). (Illus.). 1977. 12.95 o.s.i. (ISBN 0-7134-3211-X). Hippocrene Bks.

Classical Dynamics. D. Greenwood. 1977. 26.95 (ISBN 0-13-136036-1). P-H.

Classical Dynamics & Its Quantum Analogues. D. A. Park. (Lecture Notes in Physics: Vol. 110). 339p. 1980. pap. 18.00 (ISBN 0-387-09565-9). Springer-Verlag.

Classical Dynamics of Particles & Systems. 2nd ed. Jerry Marion. 1970. text ed. 22.95 (ISBN 0-12-472252-0). Acad Pr.

Classical Electricity & Magnetism. 2nd ed. Wolfgang K. Panofsky & Melba Phillips. 1962. 24.95 (ISBN 0-201-05702-6). A-W.

Classical Electrodynamics. 2nd ed. J. D. Jackson. LC 75-9962. 864p. 1975. text ed. 29.50 (ISBN 0-471-43132-X). Wiley.

Classical Electromagnetic Field. Leonard Eyges. (Illus.). 432p. 1980. pap. text ed. 7.00 (ISBN 0-486-63947-9). Dover.

Classical Electromagnetic Radiation. Jerry B. Marion. 1965. text ed. 21.50 o.p. (ISBN 0-12-472256-3). Acad Pr.

Classical Evangelical Essays in Old Testament Interpretation. Walter C. Kaiser, Jr. 1972. pap. 6.95 (ISBN 0-8010-5314-5). Baker Bk.

Classical Faces & Figures from the 16th to the 19th Century Fully Illustrated & Described. S. Del Borgo. (Science of Man Library Bks.). (Illus.). 115p. 1981. 47.85 (ISBN 0-89901-028-8). Found Class Reprints.

Classical Field Theory. Davison E. Soper. LC 75-37659. 300p. 1976. text ed. 30.95 (ISBN 0-471-81368-0, Pub. by Wiley-Interscience). Wiley.

Classical Greece. C. M. Bowra. LC 65-17305. (Great Ages of Man). (Illus.). (gr. 6 up). 1965. PLB 11.97 (ISBN 0-8094-0363-3, Pub. by Time-Life). Silver.

Classical Greece. C. M. Bowra. (Great Ages of Man Ser). (Illus.). 1965. 12.95 (ISBN 0-8094-0341-2); lib. bdg. avail. (ISBN 0-685-20546-0). Time-Life.

Classical Greek Art. Jean Charbonneaux et al. LC 72-80015. (Arts of Mankind Ser). (Illus.). 422p. 1973. 45.00 o.s.i. (ISBN 0-8076-0627-8). Braziller.

Classical Groups for Physicists. Brian G. Wybourne. LC 73-17363. 416p. 1974. 33.95 (ISBN 0-471-96505-7, Pub. by Wiley-Interscience). Wiley.

Classical Hebrew Composition. Jacob Weingreen. 1957. 13.95x (ISBN 0-19-815423-2). Oxford U Pr.

Classical Heritage & Its Beneficiaries. R. R. Bolgar. LC 54-13284. 1977. 74.00 (ISBN 0-521-04277-1); pap. 17.50x (ISBN 0-521-09812-2). Cambridge U Pr.

Classical Heritage in Islam. Franz Rosenthal. Tr. by Emile Marmorstein. LC 69-12476. 1975. 25.75x (ISBN 0-520-01997-0). U of Cal Pr.

Classical Indian Sculpture. Chintamoni Kar. (Illus.). 112p. 1974. pap. 6.95 (ISBN 0-685-50124-8). Transatlantic.

Classical Influence on European Culture, A.D. 500-1500. Ed. by R. R. Bolgar. LC 77-113599. (Illus.). 1971. 54.00 (ISBN 0-521-07842-3). Cambridge U Pr.

Classical Influences on European Culture: 1500-1700. Ed. by R. R. Bolgar. (Illus.). 300p. 1976. 63.00 (ISBN 0-521-20840-8). Cambridge U Pr.

Classical Influences on Western Thought A.D. 1650-1870. R. R. Bolgar. LC 77-91078. 1979. 65.00 (ISBN 0-521-21964-7). Cambridge U Pr.

Classical Keynesianism: Monetary Theory & the Price Level. Sidney Weintraub. LC 72-2573. (Illus.). 190p. 1961. Repr. lib. bdg. 18.75x (ISBN 0-8371-6421-4, WECK). Greenwood.

Classical Kinetic Theory of Fluids. P. Resibois & M. F. De Leener. LC 76-58852. 1977. 39.95 (ISBN 0-471-71694-4, Pub. by Wiley-Interscience). Wiley.

Classical Law of India. Robert Lingat. Tr. by J. Duncan Derrett from Fr. LC 76-81798. Orig. Title: Sources Du Droit Dans le Systeme Traditionnel De L'inde. 1973. 25.00x (ISBN 0-520-01898-2). U of Cal Pr.

Classical Lexicon for Finnegans Wake: A Glossary of the Greek & Latin in Major Works of Joyce. Brendan O'Hehir & John M. Dillon. 1977. 30.00x (ISBN 0-520-03082-6). U of Cal Pr.

Classical Mathematics. Joseph E. Hoffmann. 4.75 o.p. (ISBN 0-685-28345-3). Philos Lib.

Classical Mechanics. 2nd ed. Herbert Goldstein. LC 79-23456. (Illus.). 1980. text ed. 25.95 (ISBN 0-201-02918-9). A-W.

Classical Mechanics. 2nd ed. T. W. Kibble. LC 73-8910. 254p. 1973. text ed. 19.95 (ISBN 0-470-47395-9). Halsted Pr.

Classical Monologues 2: Shakespeare & Friends. Ed. by Stefan Rudnicki. LC 79-16079. 1980. pap. 3.95x (ISBN 0-89676-022-7). Drama Bk.

Classical Monologues 3: The Age of Style. Ed. by Stefan Rudnicki. 128p. (Orig.). 1981. pap. 3.95x (ISBN 0-89676-036-7). Drama Bk.

Classical Monologues 4: Shakespeare & Friends Encore. Ed. by Stefan Rudnicki. 144p. (Orig.). 1981. pap. text ed. 4.95x (ISBN 0-89676-037-5). Drama Bk.

Classical Monologues 5: Warhorses. Ed. by Stefan Rudnicki. 96p. (Orig.). 1981. pap. text ed. 4.95x (ISBN 0-89676-038-3). Drama Bk.

Classical Music Quiz with Richard Baker. Roy Carter. LC 80-67581. 128p. 1980. 11.95 (ISBN 0-7153-7819-8). David & Charles.

Classical Mythology. 2nd ed. Mark P. Morford & Robert J. Lenardon. 1977. pap. 11.95x (ISBN 0-582-28004-4). Longman.

Classical Mythology in Literature, Art, & Music. Philip Mayerson. 1971. text ed. 20.95 (ISBN 0-471-00365-4). Wiley.

Classical Mythology in Twentieth-Century Thought & Literature. Ed. by Wendell M. Aycock & Theodore M. Klein. (Proceedings of the Comparative Literature Symposium). (Illus.). 221p. (Orig.). 1980. pap. 12.00 (ISBN 0-89672-079-9). Tex Tech Pr.

Classical Political Economy & British Policy in India. S. Ambirajan. LC 76-21020. (South Asian Studies: No. 21). (Illus.). 1978. 44.50 (ISBN 0-521-21415-7). Cambridge U Pr.

Classical Riding School. Reis D'Eisenberg. (Illus.). 1979. 9.95 o.p. (ISBN 0-670-22509-6, The Vendome Pr.). Viking Pr.

Classical Samkhya. Gerald Larsen. LC 79-26238. 332p. 1980. pap. 8.95 (ISBN 0-915520-27-3). Ross-Erikson.

Classical Sanskrit Love Poetry. Ed. by W. S. Merwin & J. Moussaieff Masson. LC 77-13407. 1977. 17.50x (ISBN 0-231-04282-5). Columbia U Pr.

Classical Subjects 1: Satire & Burlesque. Ed. by Walter H. Rubsamen. (Ballad Opera Ser.). 1974. lib. bdg. 50.00 (ISBN 0-8240-0906-1). Garland Pub.

Classical Subjects 2: Pastoral & Comedy. Ed. by Walter H. Rubsamen. (Ballad Opera Ser.). 1974. lib. bdg. 50.00 (ISBN 0-8240-0907-X). Garland Pub.

Classical Theories of Value: From Smith to Sraffa. Jeffrey T. Young. 1978. lib. bdg. 18.00 o.p. (ISBN 0-89158-287-8). Westview.

Classical Theory of Structures. Peter G. Lowe. (Illus.). 1971. 40.75 (ISBN 0-521-08089-4). Cambridge U Pr.

Classical Thermodynamics of Deformable Materials. A. G. McLellan. LC 76-2277. (Cambridge Monographs on Physics). (Illus.). 1980. 74.50 (ISBN 0-521-21237-5). Cambridge U Pr.

Classical Topology & Combinatorial Group Theory. J. Stillwell. (Graduate Texts in Mathematics Ser.: Vol. 72). (Illus.). 301p. 1980. 32.00 (ISBN 0-387-90516-2). Springer-Verlag.

Classical Tradition in Norway. Sigmund Skard. 204p. 1980. pap. 20.00x (ISBN 8-20001-972-1). Universitet.

Classical World. Colin McEvedy & Sarah McEvedy. LC 75-653786. (Atlas of World History Ser.). (Illus.). 64p. (gr. 6-12). 1974. 9.95 (ISBN 0-02-765550-4, 76555, CCPr). Macmillan.

Classical World Bibliography of Greek & Roman History. Intro. by Walter Donlan. LC 76-52511. (Library of Humanities Reference Bks.: No. 94). lib. bdg. 27.00 (ISBN 0-8240-9879-X). Garland Pub.

Classics: An Outline for the Intending Student. Ed. by B. R. Rees. (Outlines Ser). 1970. 8.25 (ISBN 0-7100-6914-6); pap. 7.50 (ISBN 0-7100-6915-4). Routledge & Kegan.

Classics in Arterial Hypertension. Arthur Ruskin. (Amer. Lec. Classics in Science & Medicine Ser.). (Illus.). 400p. 1956. pap. 36.00 spiral (ISBN 0-398-01633-X). C C Thomas.

Classics in Cardiology. Thomas E. Keys. 1981. Vol. 3. write for info. Krieger.

Classics in Clinical Dermatology: With Biographical Sketches. Walter B. Shelley & John T. Crissey. (Illus.). 496p. 1970. 20.75 (ISBN 0-398-01741-7). C C Thomas.

Classics in Consumer Behavior. new ed. Gene Boone. (Orig.). 1977. pap. 11.95 (ISBN 0-87814-092-1). Pennwell Pub.

Classics in Coordination Chemistry: Selected Papers (1798-1899, Pt. II. Ed. by George B. Kauffman. (Illus.). 1976. pap. text ed. 4.50 (ISBN 0-486-63343-8). Dover.

Classics in Coordination Chemistry: Twentieth-Century Papers (1904-1935, Pt. III. Ed. by George B. Kauffman. LC 67-26870. (Classics of Science Ser.). (Illus.). 1978. pap. text ed. 6.00 (ISBN 0-486-63496-5). Dover.

Classics in Coordination Chemistry: The Selected Papers of Alfred Werner, Pt. I. George Kauffman. (Illus.). 1974. pap. text ed. 2.50 (ISBN 0-486-61870-6). Dover.

Classics in Neurology. H. S. Burr. 184p. 1963. pap. 14.50 photocopy ed. spiral (ISBN 0-398-00263-0). C C Thomas.

Classics in Psychoanalytic Technique. Ed. by Robert Langs. LC 80-66919. 750p. 1981. 50.00 (ISBN 0-87668-417-7). Aronson.

Classics in the Education of Girls & Women. Shirley N. Kersey. LC 80-20711. 335p. 1981. 17.50 (ISBN 0-8108-1354-8). Scarecrow.

Classics in the History of Thought, 2 vols. Ed. by Paul W. Kurtz. Incl. Vol. 1. American Thought Before 1900. text ed. 5.95 (ISBN 0-685-22913-0, 56654); Vol. 2. American Philosophy in the Twentieth Century. text ed. 6.95 (ISBN 0-02-566550-2, 56655). 1966. Macmillan.

Classics in Translation, 2 vols. Ed. by Paul L MacKendrick & Herbert M Howe. Incl. Vol. 1. Greek Literature. 440p (ISBN 0-299-80895-5); Vol. 2. Latin Literature. 448p (ISBN 0-299-80896-3). 1952. text ed. 7.95 ea. U of Wis Pr.

Classics: Major & Minor. Eric Blom. LC 74-166098. 212p. 1972. Repr. of 1958 ed. lib. bdg. 19.50 (ISBN 0-306-70293-2). Da Capo.

Classics of Greek Literature. Harry E. Wedeck. LC 63-11490. 1963. 6.00 (ISBN 0-8022-1826-1). Philos Lib.

Classics of Spanish Literature, 2 levels. Incl. Level 1, 4 bks. Adapted by Alberto Romo; Bk. 1. Fuenteovejuna. (Vocab. range: 875 words). 1963. pap. text ed. 2.75 (ISBN 0-88345-057-7, 17449); Bk. 2. Marianela. (Vocab. range: 1100 words). 1964. pap. text ed. 2.75 (ISBN 0-88345-098-4, 17451); Bk. 3. Pepita Jimenez. (Vocab. range: 1350 words). 1967. pap. text ed. 2.75 (ISBN 0-88345-127-1, 17457); Bk. 4. Sombrero De Tres Picos. (Vocab. range: 1600 words). 1970. pap. text ed. 3.50 (ISBN 0-88345-151-4, 17458); Level 2, 2 bks. Ed. by Juan Gamez-Garcia. pap. text ed. 3.50 ea.; Bk. 1. Amantes De Teruel. Juan E. Hartzenbusch. 1974 (ISBN 0-88345-011-9); Bk. 2. Don Juan Tenorio. Jose Zorilla. 1974 (ISBN 0-88345-042-9, 17764). (gr. 9 up). Regents Pub.

Classification & Cataloging of Picture & Slides. Stanford J. Green. 200p. (Orig.). pap. write for info. (ISBN 0-9604656-0-X). S Green.

Classification & Fourier Inversion for Parabolic Subgroups with Square Integrable Nilradical. Joseph Wolf. LC 79-21155. (Memoirs: No. 225). 1979. 7.60 (ISBN 0-8218-2225-X). Am Math.

Classification & Indexing in Science. 3rd ed. B. C. Vickery. 228p. 1975. 27.95 (ISBN 0-408-70662-7). Butterworths.

Classification & Nomenclature of Beads & Pendants. Horace Beck. (Illus.). 80p. 1973. pap. 10.00 (ISBN 0-87387-083-2). Shumway.

Classification & Nomenclature of Viruses: Report of the International Committee on Taxonomy of Viruses, 3rd. Ed. by R. E. Matthews. (Intervirology: Vol. 12, Nos. 3-5, 1979). 1980. pap. 6.00 (ISBN 3-8055-0523-X). S Karger.

Classification & Structure of C-Algebra Bundles. N. J. Dupre. LC 79-17975. (Memoirs Ser.: No. 222). 1979. 6.40 (ISBN 0-8218-2222-5). Am Math.

Classification Decimale de Dewey et Index, 2 vols. Melvil Dewey. Incl. Vol. 1. Tables Generales (ISBN 0-910608-14-8); Vol. 2. Index (ISBN 0-910608-15-6). (Fr.). 1974. Set. 60.00x (ISBN 0-685-47821-1); 30.00x ea. Forest Pr.

Classification for a General Indexing Language. D. Foskett. 1970. pap. 4.50x (ISBN 0-85365-032-2, Pub. by Lib Assn England). Oryx Pr.

Classification of Flowering Plants, 2 bks. Alfred B. Rendle. Incl. Bk. 1. Gymnosperms & Monocotyledons. 72.50 (ISBN 0-521-06056-7); Bk. 2. Dicotyledons. 85.00 (ISBN 0-521-06057-5). Cambridge U Pr.

Classification of Nursing Diagnoses. Ed. by Kristine M. Gebbie & Mary A. Lavin. LC 74-14869. 1975. pap. text ed. 9.50 (ISBN 0-8016-1769-3). Mosby.

Classification of the Greek Manuscripts of the Johannine Epistles. William L. Richards. LC 77-23469. (Society of Biblical Literature. Dissertation Ser.). 1977. pap. 7.50 (ISBN 0-89130-140-2, 060135). Scholars Pr Ca.

Classification of the Large Carpenter Bees (Hylocopini) (Hymenoptera: Apoidea) P. D. Hurd, Jr. & J. S. Moure. (U. C. Publ. in Entomology: Vol. 29). 1963. pap. 12.00x (ISBN 0-520-09096-9). U of Cal Pr.

Classification of the Squash & Gourd Bees Peponapis & Xenoglossa (Hymenoptera: Apoidea) Paul D. Hurd, Jr. & E. Gorton Linsley. (U. C. Publ. in Entomology: Vol. 62). 1970. pap. 6.00x (ISBN 0-520-09356-9). U of Cal Pr.

Classification Scheme & List of Subject Headings for the Squire Library of the Library of Cambridge. University of Cambridge. 1974. 20.00 (ISBN 0-379-20060-0). Oceana.

Classification System to Describe Workpieces, Classification System. H. Opitz. Tr. by R. A. Taylor. LC 71-112891. 1970. Set. 64.00 (ISBN 0-08-015758-0). Pergamon.

Classified Catalog of the Ecumenical Movement: First Supplement. World Council of Churches. (Library Catalogs-Supplements Ser.). 1981. lib. bdg. 95.00 (ISBN 0-686-69558-5). G K Hall.

Classified Directory of Artists' Signatures, Symbols, & Monograms. Ed. by H. H. Caplan. (Illus.). 1976. 110.00 (ISBN 0-8103-0985-8). Gale.

Classified Spanish Vocabulary. G. J. Chayne. LC 78-670001. 1964. text ed. 12.95x (ISBN 0-245-55575-7). Intl Ideas.

Classifying Criminal Offenders: A New System Based on the MMPI. Edwin I. Megargee & Martin J. Bohn, Jr. LC 79-11677. (Sage Library of Social Research: Vol. 82). 288p. 1979. 18.00 (ISBN 0-8039-1168-8); pap. 8.95 (ISBN 0-8039-1167-X). Sage.

Classifying Spaces & Fibrations. J. Peter May. (Memoirs: No. 155). 98p. 1980. pap. 5.60 (ISBN 0-8218-1855-4, MEMO-155). Am Math.

Classless Profession: American Schoolmen of the Nineteenth Century. Paul H. Mattingly. LC 74-29126. (New York University Series in Education & Socialization in American History). 235p. 1975. 15.00x (ISBN 0-8147-5400-7); pap. 6.00x (ISBN 0-8147-5420-1). NYU Pr.

Classroom Activities for Auditory Perceptual Disorders. Donald L. Rampp. 1976. pap. text ed. 2.95x (ISBN 0-8134-1794-5, 1794). Interstate.

Classroom & the Chancellery: State Educational Reform in Russia Under Count Dmitry Tolstoi. Allen Sinel. LC 72-95185. (Russian Research Center Studies: No. 72). 352p. 1973. text ed. 16.50x (ISBN 0-674-13481-8). Harvard U Pr.

Classroom Application Theory & Practice in Secondary School Social Studies. John R. Popenfus. LC 78-60694. 1978. pap. text ed. 9.00 o.p. (ISBN 0-8191-0563-5). U Pr of Amer.

Classroom Approaches to Remedial Reading. 2nd ed. Eddie C. Kennedy. LC 76-53238. 1977. text ed. 14.95 (ISBN 0-87581-210-4, 210). Peacock Pubs.

Classroom Cartoons. 48p. 1.00 (ISBN 0-913452-05-X). Jesuit Bks.

Classroom Creativity: An Idea Book for Religion Teachers. Elizabeth Jeep. LC 77-24719. 1977. pap. 4.95 (ISBN 0-8164-2160-9). Crossroad NY.

Classroom Discipline: A Positive Approach. Susan B. Stainback & William C. Stainback. 180p. 1977. pap. 11.75 (ISBN 0-398-02814-1). C C Thomas.

Classroom Encounters: Language & English Teaching. Mike Torbe & Robert Protherough. 214p. 1979. pap. text ed. 7.45x (ISBN 0-7062-3482-0, 6064-5, Pub. by Ward Lock Educational England). Hayden.

Classroom Evaluation Strategies. Elizabeth C. King. LC 79-13907. (Illus.). 1979. pap. text ed. 11.50 (ISBN 0-8016-2674-9). Mosby.

Classroom Hanukah. Jacqueline Greene. (Illus., Orig.). (gr. k-4). 1980. pap. 3.00x (ISBN 0-938836-01-3). Pascal Pubs.

Classroom Language Assessment. (Teacher Idea Ser.). 96p. (Orig.). 1981. pap. text ed. 7.95 (ISBN 0-88499-625-5). Inst Mod Lang.

Classroom-Made Movement Materials: A Perceptual-Motor Program with Classroom-Made Materials. Tom Hall. Ed. by Frank Alexander & Diane Alexander. (Illus., Orig.). 1981. pap. 5.95 (ISBN 0-915256-09-6). Front Row.

Classroom Management & Behavioral Objectives. Terrence Piper. LC 73-91797. 1974. pap. 4.95 (ISBN 0-8224-1412-0); duplicatable materials 4.95. Pitman Learning.

Classroom Management & Teaching: Persistent Problems & Rational Solutions. Charlotte Epstein. 1979. text ed. 13.95 (ISBN 0-8359-0824-0). Reston.

Classroom Management: Remediation & Prevention. Howard N. Sloane. LC 75-35987. 1976. pap. text ed. 10.95 (ISBN 0-471-79857-6). Wiley.

Classroom Management: The Successful Use of Behavior Modification. 2nd ed. Ed. by K. Daniel O'Leary & Susan G. O'Leary. LC 76-41004. 1977. text ed. 32.00 (ISBN 0-08-021396-0); pap. text ed. 9.95 (ISBN 0-08-021395-2). Pergamon.

Classroom Measurement & Evaluation. Charles D. Hopkins & Richard L. Antes. LC 77-83367. 1978. text ed. 14.95 (ISBN 0-87581-224-4). Peacock Pubs.

Classroom Observation of Primary School Children: All in a Day. Richard W. Mills. (Unwin Education Bks). (Illus.). 248p. (Orig.). 1980. text ed. 22.50x (ISBN 0-04-372028-5); pap. text ed. 9.95x (ISBN 0-04-372029-3). Allen Unwin.

Classroom Observer: Guide to Developing Observation Skills. Ann E. Boehm & Richard A. Weinberg. LC 77-4316. (Illus.). 1977. pap. text ed. 7.50x (ISBN 0-8077-2506-4). Tchrs Coll.

Classroom Practices in Teaching English, 1980-1981: Dealing with Differences. Ed. by Editors of NCTE Committee & Gene Stanford. (Classroom Practices in Teaching English Ser.). 144p. 1980. 5.00 (ISBN 0-8141-0690-0, 06900). NCTE.

Classroom Skills for Preschool Teachers: A Self-Taught Modular Training Program. Janice J. Beaty. (Early Childhood Education Ser.). 1979. pap. 8.95 (ISBN 0-675-08283-8). media 195.00 (ISBN 0-675-08282-X); 2-4 sets 155.00 (ISBN 0-686-67284-4); 6 or more 125.00 (ISBN 0-686-67285-2); manual 3.95 (ISBN 0-686-67286-0). Merrill.

Classroom Skills Through Games for the Middle School, Vol. 1. Jeanne E. Wieckert & Irene W. Bell. (Illus.). 300p. 1981. lib. bdg. 17.50x (ISBN 0-87287-227-0). Libs Unl.

Classroom Skills Through Games for the Middle School, Vol. 2. Jeanne E. Wieckert & Irene W. Bell. (Illus.). 250p. 1981. lib. bdg. 17.50x (ISBN 0-87287-236-X). Libs Unl.

Classroom Teachers' Guide for Elementary Physical Education: Games-Relays-Stunts. George W. Cross. (Brighton Series in Health & Physical Education). 1979. pap. text ed. 7.95 (ISBN 0-89832-010-0). Brighton Pub Co.

Classroom Teaching Skills: A Handbook. James M. Cooper et al. 1977. pap. text ed. 12.95x (ISBN 0-669-94722-9); instructor's manual free (ISBN 0-669-97899-X); wkbk. 8.95x (ISBN 0-669-94730-X). Heath.

Classroom Test Construction. John C. Marshall & Loyde W. Hales. LC 70-133892. (Education Ser). 1971. text ed. 14.95 (ISBN 0-201-04506-0). A-W.

Classrooms & Corridors: The Crisis of Authority in Desegregated Secondary Schools. Mary H. Metz. 1978. 17.95x (ISBN 0-520-03396-5); pap. 4.95 (ISBN 0-520-03941-6). U of Cal Pr.

Classrooms Observed: The Teacher's Perception & the Pupil's Performance. Roy Nash. (Students Library of Education). 1973. cased 8.75x (ISBN 0-7100-7679-7); pap. 6.95 (ISBN 0-7100-7694-0). Routledge & Kegan.

Clauberg Trigger. John Tarrant. (Orig.). 1980. pap. 1.95 (ISBN 0-505-51523-7). Tower Bks.

Claude & Pepper. Dick Gackenbach. LC 75-25507. (Illus.). 32p. (ps-2). 1976. 6.95 (ISBN 0-395-28793-6, Clarion). HM.

Claude Bernard & Animal Chemistry. Frederick L. Holmes. LC 73-88497. (Commonwealth Fund Publications Ser). 640p. 1974. text ed. 25.00x (ISBN 0-674-13485-0). Harvard U Pr.

Claude Bernarde & the Internal Environment. E. D. Robin. 1979. 34.50 (ISBN 0-8247-6894-9). Dekker.

Claude Debussy: A Bibliography. Claude Abravanel. LC 72-90430. (Detroit Studies in Music Bibliography Ser.: No. 29). 1974. 9.50 (ISBN 0-685-26717-2); pap. 8.00 (ISBN 0-685-26717-2). Info Coord.

Claude Debussy & the Poets. Arthur B. Wenk. LC 74-82854. 1976. 31.50x (ISBN 0-520-02827-9). U of Cal Pr.

Claude Levi-Strauss. rev. ed. Edmund Leach. (Modern Masters Ser.). 1976. pap. 3.50 (ISBN 0-14-004300-4). Penguin.

Claude Lorrain: Liber Veritatis. Michael Kitson. (Illus.). 1978. 40.00 o.p. (ISBN 0-684-15784-5, ScribT). Scribner.

Claude Lorrain: The Drawings, 2 vols., boxed. Marcel Roethlisberger. Incl. Vol. 1. Catalogue (ISBN 0-520-01458-8); Vol. 2. Plates (ISBN 0-520-01805-2). LC 66-24050. (Studies in the History of Art: No. 8). (Illus.). 1969. 70.00x ea. U of Cal Pr.

Claude McKay. James R. Giles. LC 76-10154. (U.S. Authors Ser.: No. 271). 1976. lib. bdg. 10.95 (ISBN 0-8057-7171-9). Twayne.

Claude Monet. Compiled By Anna Barskaya. (Illus.). 50p. 1980. pap. 4.95 (ISBN 0-686-62716-4, 2219-3). Abrams.

Claude Monet. (Illus.). 1973. pap. 0.25 o.p. (ISBN 0-88401-015-5). Fine Arts Mus.

Claude Simon. Salvador Jimenez-Fajardo. LC 74-30154. (World Authors Ser.: France: No. 346). 1975. lib. bdg. 12.50 (ISBN 0-8057-2828-7). Twayne.

Claude the Dog. Dick Gackenbach. LC 74-3403. (Illus.). 32p. (ps-2). 1974. 6.95 (ISBN 0-395-28792-8, Clarion). HM.

Claude Tillier. Melvin B. Yoken. LC 75-22346. (World Author Ser.: France: No. 376). 1976. lib. bdg. 10.95 (ISBN 0-8057-6222-1). Twayne.

Claudel's Immortal Heroes: A Choice of Deaths. Harold M. Watson. LC 73-160572. 1971. 14.50 (ISBN 0-8135-0695-6). Rutgers U Pr.

Claude's Confession. Emile Zola. Tr. by George D. Cox from Fr. 1979. Repr. of 1882 ed. 16.50 (ISBN 0-86527-030-9). Fertig.

Claudia. Caroline Arnett. 1978. pap. 1.75 o.p. (ISBN 0-449-23647-1, Crest). Fawcett.

Claudia, Where Are You? Hila Colman. (gr. 7 up). 1969. PLB 6.96 (ISBN 0-688-31174-1). Morrow.

Claudia, Where Are You? Hila Colman. (gr. 7-9). 1976. pap. 1.95 (ISBN 0-671-42450-5). Archway.

Claudia, Where Are You? Hila Colman. (YA) (gr. 7-9). 1976. pap. 1.75 (ISBN 0-671-56071-9). PB.

Claudian: De Raptu Proserpinae. J. B. Hall. LC 69-14395. (Cambridge Classical Texts & Commentaries Ser). 1969. 44.00 (ISBN 0-521-07442-8). Cambridge U Pr.

Claudia's Secret. Louise Bergstrom. (YA) 1969. 5.95 (ISBN 0-685-07426-9, Avalon). Bouregy.

Claudius, the Emperor & His Achievement. rev. ed. Arnaldo Momigliano. Tr. by W. D. Hogarth from Ital. LC 80-26158. xv, 143p. 1981. Repr. of 1961 ed. lib. bdg. 17.50x (ISBN 0-313-20813-1, MOCE). Greenwood.

Clausewitz & the State. Peter Paret. LC 75-16901. (Illus.). 560p. 1976. 25.95x (ISBN 0-19-501988-1). Oxford U Pr.

Clave Para Identificar los Peces Del Peru. F. Norma Chirichigno. (Institut del Mar del Peru Ser.: Informe 44). (Illus.). 388p. (Span.). 1978. pap. text ed. 72.80x (ISBN 3-87429-131-6). Lubrecht & Cramer.

Clavicle. Association of Bone & Joint Surgeons. Ed. by Marshall R. Urist. (Clinical Orthopaedics Series, Vol. 58). 1968. 12.00 o.p. (ISBN 0-685-14225-6). Lippincott.

Clavier-Buchlein Vor Wilhelm Friedmann Bach. Johann S. Bach. (Music Reprint Ser.). 1979. Repr. of 1959 ed. 19.50 (ISBN 0-306-79558-2). Da Capo.

Clavis Universalis: New Inquiry After Truth, Being a Demonstration of the Non-Existence or Impossibility of an External World, 1713. Arthur Collier. Ed. by Rene Wellek. LC 75-11208. (British Philosophers & Theologians of the 17th & 18th Centuries Ser.). lib. bdg. 42.00 (ISBN 0-8240-1763-3). Garland Pub.

Claw of the Bear. Larry Healey. (gr. 6 up). 1978. PLB 8.90 s&l (ISBN 0-531-01469-X). Watts.

Claw of the Conciliator. Gene Wolfe. (Book of the New Sun Ser.: Vol. II). 1981. 12.95 (ISBN 0-671-41370-8). S&S.

Claws of a Young Century. Irene Hunt. LC 80-10571. (gr. 7 up). 1980. 9.95 (ISBN 0-686-59963-2). Scribner.

Clay. Rolf Hartung. 1972. 15.95 (ISBN 0-7134-2383-8, Pub. by Batsford England). David & Charles.

Clay-Dough, Play-Dough. Goldie T. Chernoff. LC 73-92449. (Illus.). 24p. (gr. k-3). 1974. 3.95 o.s.i. (ISBN 0-8027-6178-X). Walker & Co.

Clay Fills. Ed. by Thomas Telford Editorial Staff, Ltd. 330p. 1980. 90.00x (ISBN 0-7277-0069-3, Pub. by Telford England). State Mutual Bk.

Clay Giants II. Lyndon Viel. (Illus.). 12.95 (ISBN 0-87069-314-X); pap. 1.50 Price Guide (ISBN 0-87069-315-8). Wallace-Homestead.

Clay in the Primary School. Warren Farnworth. 1973. 17.95 (ISBN 0-7134-2323-4, Pub. by Batsford England). David & Charles.

Clay Is the Word: Patrick Kavanagh 1904-1967. Alan Warner. 1974. text ed. 11.00x (ISBN 0-85105-210-X, Dolmen Pr); pap. text ed. 4.50x (ISBN 0-85105-206-1). Humanities.

Clay Target Games. Edward C. Migdalski. (Illus.). 1978. pap. 8.95 (ISBN 0-87691-277-3). Winchester Pr.

Clays & Ceramic Raw Materials. W. E. Worrall. LC 75-12684. 203p. 1975. 29.95 (ISBN 0-470-96085-X). Halsted Pr.

Clayton: Not Quite Shangri-la. George A. Pettitt. LC 79-76597. (Illus.). 1969. 5.00 o.p. (ISBN 0-685-72718-1). Brooks-Sterling.

Clea. Lawrence Durrell. 1961. pap. 2.50 o.p. (ISBN 0-525-47083-2). Dutton.

Clean & Decent: The Fascinating History of the Bathroom & the Water Closet. Lawrence Wright. 224p. (Orig.). 1980. pap. 7.95 (ISBN 0-7100-0647-0). Routledge & Kegan.

Clean Brook. Margaret F. Bartlett. LC 60-8257. (Let's-Read-&-Find-Out Science Bk). (Illus.). (gr. k-3). 1960. PLB 7.89 (ISBN 0-690-19556-7, TYC-J). T Y Crowell.

Clean Coal - Dirty Air. Bruce A. Ackerman & William T. Hassler. (Illus.). 175p. 1981. 20.00x (ISBN 0-300-02628-5); pap. 5.95 (ISBN 0-300-02643-9). Yale U Pr.

Clean: The Meaning of Christian Baptism. William G. Johnsson. LC 80-15681. (Horizon Ser.). 96p. 1980. pap. write for info. (ISBN 0-8127-0293-X). Southern Pub.

Clean Water for Our Future Environment. Compiled By American Society of Civil Engineers. 384p. 1971. pap. text ed. 14.50 (ISBN 0-87262-030-1). Am Soc Civil Eng.

Cleaning & Repairing Books: A Practical Home Manual. LC 80-21244. (Illus.). 112p. 1980. pap. 7.95 (ISBN 0-914046-00-4). R L Shep.

Cleaning & Sanitation. Ser-Vol-Tel Institute. (Foodservice Career Education Ser.). 1974. pap. 4.95 (ISBN 0-8436-2009-9). CBI Pub.

Cleaning, Repairing, Lining & Restoring of Oil Paintings: A Practical Guide for Their Better Care & Preservation. Alphonse Ford. (Library of the Arts). (Illus.). 1977. Repr. of 1867 ed. 55.25 (ISBN 0-89266-074-0). Am Classical Coll Pr.

Cleaning Up Europe's Waters: Economics, Management, Policies. Ralph W. Johnson & Gardner M. Brown. LC 76-23193. 1976. 35.00 (ISBN 0-275-56930-6). Praeger.

Cleaning Up: The Cost of Refinery Pollution Control. Council on Economic Priorities & Joan N. Boothe. LC 75-10535. (Praeger Special Studies). 1977. 20.95 (ISBN 0-03-040936-5). Praeger.

Cleanness, Patience & Sir Gawain. Pearl. (Early English Text Society Ser.). 1923. 69.00x (ISBN 0-19-722162-9). Oxford U Pr.

Cleansing of the Sanctuary. D. S. Warner & H. M. Riggle. 541p. Repr. 5.50. Faith Pub Hse.

Clear & Simple Guide to Bookkeeping. B. G. Quint. (Clear & Simple Guides Ser.). (Illus.). 96p. (Orig.). 1981. pap. 4.95 (ISBN 0-671-42108-5). Monarch Pr.

Clear & Simple Guide to Business Spelling. A. De Capno. (Clear & Simple Guides Ser.). 96p. (Orig.). 1981. pap. 4.95 (ISBN 0-686-68915-1). Monarch Pr.

Clear & Simple Guide to Touch Typing. Yacht. (Clear & Simple Guides Ser.). (Illus.). 96p. (Orig.). 1981. pap. 5.95 (ISBN 0-671-42223-5). Monarch Pr.

Clear Creek Bike Book. Hal Aigner et al. Ed. by Peter Lawlor & Clear Creek Editors. 192p. 1973. pap. 1.25 o.p. (ISBN 0-451-05459-8, Y5459, Sig). NAL.

Clear for Action. Stephen W. Meader. LC 40-27736. (Illus.). (gr. 7 up). 1940. 4.95 o.p. (ISBN 0-15-218937-8, HJ). HarBraceJ.

Clear Introduction to Business Mathematics. 2nd ed. Horace M. King. 580p. pap. text ed. 15.95x (ISBN 0-89863-035-5). Star Pub CA.

Clear Light of Day. Anita Desai. LC 80-7603. 224p. 1980. 11.95 (ISBN 0-06-010984-X, HarpT). Har-Row.

Clear Print. 65p. 1972. pap. 5.50x (ISBN 0-85365-475-1, Pub. by Lib Assn England). Oryx Pr.

Clear Skin, Healthy Skin. Alan E. Nourse. LC 76-12640. (Career Concise Guides Ser.). (Illus.). 72p. (gr. 7 up). 1976. PLB 6.45 (ISBN 0-531-00343-4). Watts.

Clear Sky, Pure Light: Encounters with Henry David Thoreau. Henry D. Thoreau. Ed. by Christopher Childs. LC 78-56627. 1978. 12.00 (ISBN 0-915778-27-0); deluxe ed. 50.00x (ISBN 0-915778-26-2). Penmaen Pr.

Clear Synthesis: A Study of William Wordsworth's Stylistic Development As a Descriptive Poet from 1793 to 1808. Bowman G. Wiley. (Salzburg Studies in English Literature, Romantic Reassessment: No. 16). 1974. pap. text ed. 25.00x (ISBN 0-391-01571-0). Humanities.

Clear the Bridge. Richard H. O'Kane. 496p. 1981. pap. 2.95 (ISBN 0-553-14516-9). Bantam.

Clear the Track. Louis Slobodkin. (gr. k-3). 1967. 4.95g o.s.i. (ISBN 0-02-783680-0). Macmillan.

Clear Thinking About Sexual Deviations: A New Look at an Old Problem. James L. Mathis. LC 72-80165. 1972. 11.95 (ISBN 0-911012-40-0). Nelson-Hall.

Clear Thinking for All. A. Russell. 1967. pap. text ed. 2.00 o.p. (ISBN 0-08-012281-7). Pergamon.

Clear View - Guide to Industrial Pollution Control. James Connon. LC 75-15321. 1975. pap. 4.00. Inform.

Clearance. Joan Lingard. LC 74-1289. 160p. (gr. 7 up). 1974. 6.95 o.p. (ISBN 0-525-66400-9). Elsevier-Nelson.

Cleared for Takeoff: Flying for Beginners. Gordon Stokes. LC 78-595. (Illus.). 1978. 9.95 o.p. (ISBN 0-684-15787-X, ScribT). Scribner.

Clearing. Gary Clark. (Norwegian Trilolgy Ser.). 200p. (Orig.). Date not set. price not set (ISBN 0-913124-45-1). Nordland Pub.

Clearing. Therese de Saint-Phalle. 1978. pap. 1.75 o.p. (ISBN 0-445-04234-6). Popular Lib.

Clearing & Beyond. May Miller. LC 73-93070. 1974. 7.50 (ISBN 0-685-41659-3). Charioteer.

Cleft Craft: Alveolar & Palatal Deformities, Vol. III. D. Ralph Millard, Jr. 1980. 125.00 (ISBN 0-316-57139-3). Little.

Cleft Craft: the Evolution of Its Surgery, Vol. 1: The Unilateral Deformity. D. Ralph Millard, Jr. 1976. text ed. 95.00 (ISBN 0-316-57137-7). Little.

Cleft Palate. Gene R. Powers. LC 72-86554. (Studies in Communicative Disorders Ser.). 37p. 1973. pap. text ed. 3.50 (ISBN 0-672-61288-7). Bobbs.

Cleft Palate & Communication. Ed. by C. Spriestersbach & Dorothy Sherman. LC 68-18682. 1968. text ed. 20.50 (ISBN 0-12-658850-3). Acad Pr.

Cleft Palate Deformation: Causation & Prevention. J. J. Longacre. 128p. 1970. pap. 16.25 photocopy ed. spiral (ISBN 0-398-01142-7). C C Thomas.

Cleft Palate Team Addresses the Speech Clinician. Ed. by Mervyn L. Falk. 248p. 1971. 22.50 (ISBN 0-398-00542-7). C C Thomas.

Clem the Clam & His Friends. Marcie Stanton. Date not set. 5.95 (ISBN 0-533-04852-4). Vantage.

Clement Marot & the Inflections of Poetic Voice. Robert Griffin. 1976. 22.50x (ISBN 0-520-02586-5). U of Cal Pr.

Clement of Alexandria. John Ferguson. (World Authors Ser.: Greece: No. 289). 1974. lib. bdg. 10.95 (ISBN 0-8057-2231-9). Twayne.

Clement Vision: Poetic Realism in Turgenev & James. Dale E. Peterson. (National University Publications Literary Criticism Ser.). 1975. 12.00 (ISBN 0-8046-9107-X, Natl U). Kennikat.

Clemente! Kal Wagenheim. 1974. pap. 1.45 o.s.i. (ISBN 0-671-48355-2). WSP.

Clemente Rebora. Margherita Marchione. (World Authors Ser.: No. 521). 1979. lib. bdg. 13.95 (ISBN 0-8057-6362-7). Twayne.

Clementine. Robert Quackenbush. LC 73-13990. (Illus.). 40p. (gr. k-3). 1974. 8.79 (ISBN 0-397-31506-6). Lippincott.

Clemmie. John D. MacDonald. 1978. pap. 1.75 o.p. (ISBN 0-449-14015-6, GM). Fawcett.

Cleo Catra's Riddle Book. Ann Bishop. (Illus.). (gr. 2-5). 1981. 6.95 (ISBN 0-525-66706-7). Elsevier-Nelson.

CLEP General & Subject Examinations: Descriptions & Sample Questions. College Entrance Examination Board. 1980. pap. 1.00 (ISBN 0-87447-013-7, 200631). College Bd.

CLEP Scores: Interpretation & Use. 1980. pap. 2.50 (ISBN 0-87447-014-5, 217434). College Bd.

Clergy & Clients: The Practice of Pastoral Psychotherapy. Ronald R. Lee. 1980. 9.95 (ISBN 0-8164-0115-2). Crossroad NY.

Clergy & The Great Awakening in New England. David Harlan. Ed. by Robert Berkhofer. (Studies in American History & Culture). 180p. 1980. 23.95 (ISBN 0-8357-1097-1, Pub. by UMI Res Pr). Univ Microfilms.

Clergy, Ministers & Priests. Stewart Ransom et al. (International Library of Sociology Ser.). 1977. 20.00 (ISBN 0-7100-8713-6). Routledge & Kegan.

Clergyman & the Psychiatrist: When to Refer. Robert L. Mason et al. LC 77-22597. 1978. 15.95x (ISBN 0-88229-260-9). Nelson-Hall.

Clergyman's Daughter. George Orwell. LC 60-10943. 1969. pap. 3.95 (ISBN 0-15-618065-0, HPL37, HPL). HarBraceJ.

Clergymen of the Church of England. Anthony Trollope. (Victorian Library). 134p. 1974. Repr. of 1866 ed. text ed. 14.50x (ISBN 0-7185-5023-4, Leicester). Humanities.

Clerical & Commercial Training Handbook. Peter Gabe. 1974. 21.00x o.p. (ISBN 0-8464-0249-1). Beekman Pubs.

Clerical & Secretarial Systems for the Office. Richard J. Dallas & James M. Thompson. (Office Occupations Ser.). (Illus.). 448p. 1975. ref. ed. 16.95 (ISBN 0-13-136390-5). P-H.

Clerical Office Practice Set. 2nd ed. Esther Sandry. (gr. 9-12). 1973. pap. 2.96 (ISBN 0-8224-1741-3); supplies 6.20 (ISBN 0-8224-2082-1); tchrs'. manual 1.72 (ISBN 0-8224-2081-3). Pitman Learning.

Clerical Practice Skills. Calman Goozner. (gr. 10 up). 1978. pap. text ed. 7.08 (ISBN 0-87720-403-9). AMSCO Sch.

Clerical Techniques for a Business Career. Jack Kestenbaum. (Orig.). (gr. 9-12). 1975. text ed. 13.20 (ISBN 0-205-04507-3, 1745077); tchrs'. guide 3.80 (ISBN 0-205-04508-1, 1745085); workbook 5.92 (ISBN 0-205-04509-X, 1745093). Allyn.

Clerks & Craftsmen in China & the West: Lectures & Addresses on the History of Science & Technology. Joseph Needham. (Illus.). 1970. 65.00 (ISBN 0-521-07235-2). Cambridge U Pr.

Clerk's Prologue & Tale. Geoffrey Chaucer. Ed. by J. Winny. (Selected Tales from Chaucer). 1966. text ed. 4.95x (ISBN 0-521-04632-7). Cambridge U Pr.

Cleveland Bay Horses. Anthony Dent. (Illus.). 1978. 7.85 (ISBN 0-85131-283-7, Dist. by Sporting Book Center). J A Allen.

Cleveland Benjamin's Dead. Patsy Sims. LC 79-84669. (Illus.). cancelled (ISBN 0-8015-0586-0, Hawthorn). Dutton.

Cleveland Museum of Art's Tuti-Nama. Ziya'U'D-Din Nakhshabi. Tr. by Muhammed A. Simsar from Persian. LC 76-55714. (Illus.). 362p. 1979. 45.00x (ISBN 0-910386-29-3, Pub. by Cleveland Mus Art). Ind U Pr.

Cleveland Rockwell: Scientist & Artist, Eighteen Thirty-Seven to Nineteen Hundred & Seven. Franz Stenzel. LC 72-80732. (Illus.). 168p. 1972. pap. 9.95 (ISBN 0-87595-037-X); 10.95. Oreg Hist Soc.

Cleveland, the Disco King. Vivian Greene. (Illus.). (gr. 3-5). 1979. 2.95 (ISBN 0-531-02513-6); PLB 5.90 s&l (ISBN 0-531-04095-X). Watts.

Cleveland: Where the East Coast Meets the Midwest. Peter Jedick. (Illus.). 105p. (Orig.). 1980. pap. 11.95 (ISBN 0-9605508-1-X). Jedick Ent.

Clever Cooks: A Ready-Mix of Stories, Recipes, & Riddles. Ellin Greene. (gr. 4-6). 1977. pap. 1.25 o.p. (ISBN 0-590-02352-7, Schol Pap). Schol Bk Serv.

Clever Coyote. Stanley P. Young & Hartley H. Jackson. LC 77-14026. (Illus.). 1978. 19.50x (ISBN 0-8032-0976-2); pap. 5.50 (ISBN 0-8032-5893-3, BB 662, Bison). U of Nebr Pr.

Clever Kate. Adapted by Elizabeth Shub. LC 72-81063. (Ready-to-Read Ser.). (Illus.). 64p. (gr. 1-4). 1973. 7.95g (ISBN 0-02-782490-X). Macmillan.

Clever Moron. R. S. Scorer. 1977. 15.00 (ISBN 0-7100-8552-4). Routledge & Kegan.

Clever Princess. Ann Tompert. LC 77-72559. (Illus.). 39p. (gr. k-4). 1977. 6.75 (ISBN 0-914996-15-0); pap. 3.00 (ISBN 0-914996-13-4). Lollipop Power.

Clever Raccoon. Jane Thayer. LC 80-23119. (Junior Bks.). (Illus.). 32p. (gr. k-3). 1981. 7.95 (ISBN 0-688-00238-2); PLB 7.63 (ISBN 0-688-00239-0). Morrow.

Clever Woman of the Family, 1865. Charlotte M. Yonge. Ed. by Robert L. Wolff. LC 75-1523. (Victorian Fiction Ser.). 1975. lib. bdg. 66.00 (ISBN 0-8240-1595-9). Garland Pub.

Clewiston Test. Kate Wilhelm. LC 75-31683. 256p. 1976. 8.95 o.p. (ISBN 0-374-12500-7). FS&G.

Clewiston Test. Kate Wilhelm. 1980. pap. write for info. (ISBN 0-671-83503-3). PB.

CLIBOC: Chinese Linguistics Bibliography on Computer. Ed. by William S-Y Wang & Anatole Lyovin. LC 74-85740. (Princeton-Cambridge Studies in Chinese Linguistic Ser). 1970. 90.00 (ISBN 0-521-07455-X). Cambridge U Pr.

Client Centered Therapy. Carl R. Rogers. LC 51-9139. 1951. pap. text ed. 13.50 (ISBN 0-395-05322-6). HM.

Client-Clinician Relationship: Essays on Interpersonal Sensitivity in the Therapeutic Transaction. Ed. by Lon L. Emerick & Stephen B. Hood. (Illus.). 128p. 1974. 12.75 (ISBN 0-398-03016-2). C C Thomas.

Client Speaks: Working Class Impressions of Casework. John E. Mayer & Noel Timms. 1970. 16.00 (ISBN 0-7100-6906-5); pap. 9.50 (ISBN 0-7100-7673-8). Routledge & Kegan.

Client-Worker Transactions. William Jordan. (Library of Social Work). 1970. 8.95 (ISBN 0-7100-6836-0). Routledge & Kegan.

Cliff, America's First Great Copper Mine. Donald Chaput. LC 75-146505. (Illus.). 116p. 1971. 14.95 (ISBN 0-910726-90-6). Hillsdale Educ.

Cliff Castles & Cave Dwellings of Europe. Sabine Baring-Gould. LC 68-17983. (Illus.). 1968. Repr. of 1911 ed. 15.000 (ISBN 0-8103-3423-2). Gale.

Clifford Odets. Margaret Brenman-Gibson. LC 80-7927. 1981. 25.00 (ISBN 0-689-10827-3). Atheneum.

Clifford Odets: Playwright-Poet. Harold Cantor. LC 77-27284. 1978. 12.00 (ISBN 0-8108-1107-3). Scarecrow.

Clifford the Big Red Dog. Norman Bridwell. (Illus.). (gr. k-3). 1969. pap. 1.25 (ISBN 0-590-08028-8, Schol Pap); pap. 3.95 clifford the big red dog & witch's christmas (2 bks.) & 1 record (ISBN 0-590-04385-4). Schol Bk Serv.

Clifford, the Small Red Puppy. Norman Bridwell. (Illus.). (gr. k-3). 1973. pap. 0.95 (ISBN 0-590-09349-5, Schol Pap); pap. 3.50 bk. & record (ISBN 0-590-20696-6). Schol Bk Serv.

Clifford W. Beers: Advocate for the Insane. Norman Dain. LC 79-24290. (Contemporary Community Health Ser.). 1980. 19.95 (ISBN 0-8229-3419-1). U of Pittsburgh Pr.

Clifford's Good Deeds. Bridwell. (ps-3). pap. 1.25 (ISBN 0-590-01379-3, Schol Pap). Schol Bk Serv.

Clifford's Good Deeds. Norman Bridwell. LC 75-15463. (Illus.). 48p. (gr. k-3). 1976. 5.95 (ISBN 0-590-07439-3, Four Winds). Schol Bk Serv.

Clifford's Good Deeds. Norman Bridwell. pap. 3.50 incl. record (ISBN 0-590-20792-X, Schol Pap). Schol Bk Serv.

Clifford's Halloween. Norman Bridwell. (Illus.). (gr. k-3). 1970. pap. 1.25 (ISBN 0-590-01466-8, Schol Pap); pap. 3.50 bk. & record (ISBN 0-590-20603-6). Schol Bk Serv.

Clifford's Tricks. Norman Bridwell. (Illus.). (gr. k-3). 1971. pap. 1.25 (ISBN 0-590-04439-7, Schol Pap); pap. 3.50 bk. & record (ISBN 0-590-04395-1). Schol Bk Serv.

Cliffs of Cairo. Elsa Marston. LC 80-26785. 160p. (gr. 7 up). 1981. 7.95 (ISBN 0-8253-0032-0). Beaufort Bks NY.

Cliffs of Fall: Paradox & Polyvalence in the Parables of Jesus. John D. Crossan. 128p. 1980. 8.95 (ISBN 0-8164-0113-6). Crossroad NY.

Climate & Food: Climatic Fluctuation & U. S. Agricultural Production. Board on Agriculture & Renewable Resources, National Research Council. LC 76-46195. 1976. pap. 7.75 (ISBN 0-309-02522-2). Natl Acad Pr.

Climate & Human Variability. 2nd ed. D. F. Roberts. LC 76-2227. 1978. pap. text ed. 5.95 o.p. (ISBN 0-8465-6625-7). Benjamin-Cummings.

Climate & Man: Nineteen Forty-One Yearbook of Agriculture, House Document No. 27, 77th Congress, 1st Session. U. S. Department of Agriculture. LC 74-6297. 1248p. 1975. Repr. of 1941 ed. 60.00 (ISBN 0-8103-4016-X). Gale.

Climate & Man's Environment: An Introduction to Applied Climatology. John E. Oliver. LC 73-5707. 517p. 1973. text ed. 24.95x (ISBN 0-471-65338-1). Wiley.

Climate & the Affairs of Men. 2nd ed. Nels Winkless, III & Iben Browning. 1980. flexible cover 10.00 (ISBN 0-87034-059-X). Fraser Pub Co.

Climate Change & Society: Consequences of Increasing Atmospheric Carbon Dioxide. William W. Kellogg & Robert Schware. (Special Study Ser.). 170p. (Orig.). 1981. lib. bdg. 15.00x (ISBN 0-86531-179-X); pap. 8.00x (ISBN 0-86531-180-3). Westview.

Climate Change & World Affairs. Chrispin Tickell. 1978. text ed. 13.25 (ISBN 0-08-022228-5). Pergamon.

Climate, Climatic Change & Water Supply. Geophysics Research Board. 1977. pap. 7.75 (ISBN 0-309-02625-3). Na'' Acad Pr.

Climate for Creativity. Ed. by C. W. Taylor. 312p. 1972. text ed. 23.00 (ISBN 0-08-016329-7). Pergamon.

Climate in Review. Geoffrey McBoyle. LC 72-3536. 1973. pap. text ed. 10.95 (ISBN 0-395-16007-3, 3-35100). HM.

Climate Mandate. Walter O. Roberts & Henry Lansford. LC 78-25677. (Illus.). 1979. text ed. 16.95x (ISBN 0-7167-1054-4); pap. text ed. 8.95x (ISBN 0-7167-1055-2). W H Freeman.

Climate of the British Isles. T. J. Chandler & S. Gregory. (Illus.). 1977. text ed. 24.00x (ISBN 0-582-48558-4). Longman.

Climate, Water and Agriculture in the Tropics. Ian J. Jackson. LC 76-53759. (Illus.). 1977. pap. text ed. 11.95x (ISBN 0-582-48529-0). Longman.

Climate Water Budget in Environmental Analysis. John R. Mather. LC 77-17726. (Illus.). 1978. 23.95 (ISBN 0-669-02087-7). Lexington Bks.

Climate's Impact on Food Supplies. Ed. by Lloyd E. Slater & Susan K. Levin. (Selected Symposium Ser.: No. 62). 250p. 1981. lib. bdg. 20.00x (ISBN 0-86531-166-8). Westview.

Climates of Hunger: Mankind & the World's Changing Weather. Reid A. Bryson & Thomas J. Murray. (Illus.). 1979. pap. 6.95 (ISBN 0-299-07374-2). U of Wis Pr.

Climates of Hunger: Mankind & the World's Changing Weather. Reid A. Bryson & Thomas J. Murray. LC 76-53649. 1977. 15.00 (ISBN 0-299-07370-X). U of Wis Pr.

Climates of the Mind. Carolyn M. Kleefeld. Ed. by Patricia Karahan. LC 78-73648. 240p. 1980. signed ed. 27.00 (ISBN 0-9602214-1-7); pap. 8.95 (ISBN 0-9602214-2-5). Horse & Bird.

Climates of the States, 2 vols. Rev. by James Ruffner. LC 76-11672. 1400p. 1978. 59.00 o.p. (ISBN 0-8103-1042-2). Gale.

Climates of West Africa. Oyedrian Ojo. 1977. text ed. 29.50 (ISBN 0-435-95700-7); pap. text ed. 14.50 (ISBN 0-435-95701-5). Heinemann Ed.

Climates Past & Present. Ed. by Brian J. Skinner. (Earth & Its Inhabitants: Selected Readings from American Scientist Ser.). (Illus.). 200p. (Orig.). 1981. pap. 9.95 (ISBN 0-913232-91-2). W Kaufmann.

Climatic Accidents in Landscape Making. C. A. Cotton. (Illus.). 1969. Repr. of 1947 ed. 21.75 o.p. (ISBN 0-02-843200-2). Hafner.

Climatic Atlas of the Indian Ocean, 2 vols. Stefan Hastenrath & Peter J. Lamb. LC 78-65016. (Illus.). 100.00 (ISBN 0-299-07814-0). U of Wis Pr.

Climatic Atlas of the Tropical Atlantic & Eastern Pacific Oceans. Stefan L. Hastenrath & Peter Lamb. 1977. pap. 50.00 (ISBN 0-299-07234-7). U of Wis Pr.

Climatic Change. Ed. by J. Gribbin. LC 76-52185. 1978. 68.50 (ISBN 0-521-21594-3); pap. 19.50x (ISBN 0-521-29205-0). Cambridge U Pr.

Climatic Change & Variability: A Southern Perspective. Ed. by A. B. Pittock et al. LC 76-53521. (Illus.). 1978. 65.50 (ISBN 0-521-21562-5). Cambridge U Pr.

Climatic Cycle & Tree Growth, 3 vols. in one. A. E. Douglass. (Vols. 1 & 2, A Study of the Annual Rings of Trees in Relation to Climate & Solar Activity; Vol. 3, A Study of Cycles). 1971. 75.00 (ISBN 3-7682-0720-X). Lubrecht & Cramer.

Climatic Races & Descent Groups. Grover S. Krantz. 288p. 1980. 14.95 (ISBN 0-8158-0390-7). Chris Mass.

Climatic Resources & Economic Activity. J. A. Taylor. LC 74-823. (Illus.). 264p. 1974. 21.95 (ISBN 0-470-84826-X). Halsted Pr.

Climax of French Imperial Expansion, 1914-1924. Christopher M. Andrew & A. S. Kanya-Forstner. (Illus.). 304p. 1981. 29.50x (ISBN 0-8047-1101-1). Stanford U Pr.

Climax of Populism: The Election of 1896. Robert F. Durden. LC 65-11824. 208p. 1965. pap. 3.00x (ISBN 0-8131-0103-4). U Pr of Ky.

Climb. Carol Carrick. 32p. (gr. k-4). 1980. 8.95 o.p. (ISBN 0-395-29431-2, Clarion). HM.

Climb Mount Moriah. Pat Brooks. 1974. pap. 1.25 o.p. (ISBN 0-88368-024-6). Whitaker Hse.

Climb the Highest Mountain. Mark Prophet & Elizabeth Prophet. LC 72-175101. (Illus.). 1978. pap. 9.95 (ISBN 0-916766-26-8). Summit Univ.

Climb to the Top. Matthew Kostka. LC 62-14787. (gr. 6-9). 1962. 5.95 o.p. (ISBN 0-385-02581-5). Doubleday.

Climb up Through Your Valleys. Evaline Echols. 1980. 6.95; pap. 5.95. Pathway Pr.

Climber & Fellwaker in Lakeland. Frank Monkhouse & Joe Williams. (Climbing & Walking). (Illus.). 216p. 1971. 13.50 (ISBN 0-7153-5459-0). David & Charles.

Climber's Sourcebook. Anne Schneider & Steven Schneider. LC 75-21251. 321p. 1976. pap. 4.95 (ISBN 0-385-11081-2, Anch). Doubleday.

Climbing. James Lovelock. 1975. 7.50 o.p. (ISBN 0-7134-0326-8). Hippocrene Bks.

Climbing & Hiking in the Wind River Mountains: Wyoming. Joe Kelsey. LC 79-23882. (Illus.). 400p. (Totebook). 1980. pap. 8.95 (ISBN 0-87156-267-7). Sierra.

Climbing Ghetto Walls: Disadvantagement, Delinquency & Rehabilitation. Ed. by Richard E. Hardy & John G. Cull. (American Lectures in Social & Rehabilitation Psychology Ser.). (Illus.). 210p. 1973. 12.75 (ISBN 0-398-02865-6). C C Thomas.

Climbing Higher. Ed. by Al Bryant. LC 77-24978. 1977. 7.95 (ISBN 0-87123-052-6); pap. 4.95 (ISBN 0-87123-054-2, 210054). Bethany Fell.

Climbing into the Roots. Reg Saner. LC 75-7953. 96p. 1976. 7.95 o.p. (ISBN 0-06-013762-2, HarpT); pap. 3.50 (ISBN 0-06-013763-0, TD233, HarpT). Har-Row.

Climbing Sun: The Story of a Hopi Indian Boy. Marjorie Thayer & Elizabeth Emanuel. LC 80-13743. (Illus.). 96p. (gr. 5 up). 1980. 6.95g (ISBN 0-396-07844-3). Dodd.

Climbing the Academic Ladder: Doctoral Women Scientists in Academe. Commission on Human Resources, Nat. Research Council. 1979. pap. text ed. 8.00 (ISBN 0-309-02880-9). Natl Acad Pr.

Climbing the Heights. Al Bryant. 1956. pocket ed. 5.95 o.p. (ISBN 0-310-22060-2). Zondervan.

Climbing the Heights. Ed. by Al Bryant. 384p. 1981. pap. 4.95 (ISBN 0-310-22061-0). Zondervan.

Climbing to the Sun. Jeffrey Carroll. LC 77-8617. (gr. 5 up). 1977. 6.95 (ISBN 0-395-28898-3, Clarion). HM.

Climbing up to Nowhere. Ed. by Sibyl Hancock. (I Can Read a Bible Story Ser.: No. 2). (Illus.). (gr. 7-9). 1977. 3.95 (ISBN 0-570-07322-7, 56-1513); pap. 1.95 (ISBN 0-686-67848-6, 56-1413). Concordia.

Clinical Voice Disorders. Arnold E. Aronson. 1980. 19.50. Thieme Stratton.

Clinging. Ernest T. Jahn. 336p. (Orig.). 1981. pap. 2.50 cancelled (ISBN 0-89083-705-8). Zebra.

Clinic. Eleanor Kay. LC 70-139486. (First Bks). (Illus.). (gr. 4-6). 1971. PLB 4.90 o.p. (ISBN 0-531-00721-9). Watts.

Clinic. Anthony Pietropinto & Elaine Congress. 1981. 11.95 (ISBN 0-8129-0887-2). Times Bks.

Clinical Anatomy for Medical Students. 2nd ed. Richard S. Snell. 1981. text ed. price not set. Little.

Clinical & Diagnostic Veterinary Toxicology. 2nd ed. William B. Buck et al. 1976. pap. 13.95 (ISBN 0-8403-0720-9). Kendall-Hunt.

Clinical & Experimental Applications of Krypton 81m. Ed. by J. P. Lavender. 1980. 75.00x (Pub. by Brit Inst Radiology England). State Mutual Bk.

Clinical Anesthesia: Case Selections from the University of California, San Francisco. Wilkinson et al. LC 79-23938. (Illus.). 1980. 37.50 (ISBN 0-8016-3423-7). Mosby.

Clinical Anesthesia Procedures of the Massachusetts General Hospital. Massachusetts General Hospital. Ed. by Philip W. Lebowitz. 1978. pap. text ed. 10.95 (ISBN 0-316-54957-6). Little.

Clinical Application of Projective Drawings. Emanuel F. Hammer. (Illus.). 688p. 1980. 28.75 (ISBN 0-398-00768-3). C C Thomas.

Clinical Applications of Biofeedback: Appraisal & Status. Ed. by Robert J. Gatchel & Kenneth P. Price. LC 78-26959. (Pergamon General Psychology Ser.: Vol. 75). (Illus.). 1979. text ed. 33.00 (ISBN 0-08-022978-6); pap. text ed. 11.00 (ISBN 0-08-022977-8). Pergamon.

Clinical Applications of Evoked Potentials in Neurology. Ed. by Jean Courjon et al. 1981. text ed. price not set (ISBN 0-89004-619-0). Raven.

Clinical Applications of the Acid Etch Technique. Richard J. Simonsen. (Illus.). 123p. 1978. 42.00 (ISBN 0-931386-01-2). Quint Pub Co.

Clinical Approach to Marital Problems: Diagnosis, Prevention & Treatment. 2nd ed. Bernard L. Greene. (Illus.). 528p. 1981. text ed. 53.75 (ISBN 0-398-04138-5). C C Thomas.

Clinical Approach to Training the Educable Mentally Retarded: A Handbook. Isaac Jolles & Selma I. Southwick. LC 70-95255. (Professional Handbook Ser.). (Illus.). 31p. 1971. pap. 7.00x (ISBN 0-87424-113-8). Western Psych.

Clinical Art Therapy. Helen B. Landgarten. 416p. 1981. 27.50 (ISBN 0-87630-237-1). Brunner-Mazel.

Clinical Aspects & Treatment of Cysts of the Jaws. Herbert Harnisch. (Illus.). 237p. 1974. 38.00. Quint Pub Co.

Clinical Aspects of Alzheimer's Disease & Senile Dementia. Ed. by Nancy Miller & Gene D. Cohen. (Aging Ser.: Vol. 15). 350p. 1981. text ed. 33.00 (ISBN 0-89004-326-4). Raven.

Clinical Aspects of Blood Viscosity & Ceell Deformability. Ed. by G. D. Love et al. (Illus.). 250p. 1981. 41.30 (ISBN 0-387-10299-X). Springer-Verlag.

Clinical Aspects of Dermatological Photobiology. I. A. Magnus. (Blackwell Scientific Pubns.). (Illus.). 1976. 40.00 (ISBN 0-8016-3082-7, Blackwell). Mosby.

Clinical Aspects of Inhaled Particles. Ed. by D. C. Muir. (Illus.). 1972. 17.95x (ISBN 0-433-22700-1). Intl Ideas.

Clinical Aspects of Remedial Reading. Clifford J. Kolson & George Kaluger. (Illus.). 160p. 1972. pap. 14.95 photocopy ed., spiral (ISBN 0-398-01038-2). C C Thomas.

Clinical Aspects of Respiratory Physiology. Clarence A. Guenter et al. LC 78-498. 1978. soft cover 12.95 (ISBN 0-397-50400-4). Lippincott.

Clinical Aspects of the Violent Individual. (Task Force Report: No. 8). 46p. 1974. pap. 5.00 (ISBN 0-685-65580-6, P214-0). Am Psychiatric.

Clinical Assays. James R. Critser, Jr. (Ser. 10CA 80). 1981. 80.00 (ISBN 0-914428-78-0). Lexington Data.

Clinical Assays. James R. Critser, Jr. (Ser. 10CA-79). 122p. 1980. 80.00 (ISBN 0-914428-65-9). Lexington Data.

Clinical Assessment of Learning Problems: Model, Process & Remedial Planning. new ed. Marion Sanders. 1978. text ed. 18.95 (ISBN 0-205-06149-4). Allyn.

Clinical Atlas of Human Chromosomes. Jean De Grouchy & Catherine Turleau. LC 77-2282. 1977. 49.95 (ISBN 0-471-01704-3, Pub. by Wiley Medical). Wiley.

Clinical Atlas of Muscle & Musculocutaneous Flaps. Stephen J. Mathes & Foad Nahai. LC 79-10739. (Illus.). 1979. text ed. 44.50 (ISBN 0-8016-3141-6). Mosby.

Clinical Audiometry & Masking. Frederick Martin. LC 74-183115. (Studies in Communicative Disorders Ser). 1972. pap. 2.95 (ISBN 0-672-61282-8). Bobbs.

Clinical Bacteriology. Ed. by John Scimone. (Functional Medical Laboratory Manual). (Illus.). 1978. pap. 10.00 (ISBN 0-87055-267-8). AVI.

Clinical Behavior: Therapy & Behavior Modification, Vol. 2. Reid J. Daitzman. LC 79-14455. 304p. 1980. lib. bdg. 32.50 (ISBN 0-8240-7217-0). Garland Pub.

Clinical Behavior Therapy & Behavior Modification, Vol. 2. Reid J. Daitzman. 304p. 1981. lib. bdg. 32.50 (ISBN 0-8240-7217-0). Garland Pub.

Clinical Behavioral Science. Frederick Sierles. 1981. text ed. write for info. (ISBN 0-89335-131-8). Spectrum Pub.

Clinical Biochemical & Hematological Reference Values in Normal Experimental Animals. Brij M. Mitruka & Howard M. Rawnsley. LC 77-84608. (Illus.). 286p. 1977. 28.75 (ISBN 0-89352-006-3). Masson Pub.

Clinical Biochemistry of Cancer: Proceedings of the Second Arnold O. Beckman Conference in Cliniical Chemistry. Ed. by Martin Fleisher. LC 79-14027. 405p. 1979. 31.95 (ISBN 0-915274-09-4). Am Assn Clinical Chem.

Clinical Biochemistry of Domestic Animals. 3rd ed. Ed. by Jiro J. Kaneko. LC 79-8873. 1980. 60.00 (ISBN 0-12-396350-8). Acad Pr.

Clinical Biochemistry of Domestic Animals, Vols. 1 & 2. 2nd ed. Ed. by J. J. Kaneko & C. E. Cornelius. 1970. Set. 84.00 (ISBN 0-685-02413-X); Vol. 1. 52.50 (ISBN 0-12-396301-X); Vol. 2. 50.50 (ISBN 0-12-396302-8). Acad Pr.

Clinical Biochemistry Review, Vol. 2. David M. Goldberg. 416p. 1981. 24.00 (ISBN 0-471-08297-X, Pub. by Wiley Med). Wiley.

Clinical Biomechanics: A Case History Approach. Jonathan Black & John Dumbleton. (Illus.). 416p. 1980. text ed. 40.00x (ISBN 0-443-08022-4). Churchill.

Clinical Biomechanics of the Spine. Augustus A. White & Manohar Panjabi. LC 78-15708. (Illus.). 1978. 51.75 (ISBN 0-397-50388-1). Lippincott.

Clinical Burn Therapy: A Complete Guide for Physicians & Surgeons in a Community Hospital Setting. Robert P. Hummel, Jr. 500p. 1981. 49.00 (ISBN 0-88416-284-2). PSG Pub.

Clinical Cancer - Principal Sites One: International Cancer Congress, 12th, Buenos Aires, 1978. Ed. by S. Kumar et al. LC 79-40710. (Advances in Medical Oncology, Research & Education: Vol. X). (Illus.). 1979. 68.00 (ISBN 0-08-024393-2). Pergamon.

Clinical Cancer Chemotherapy. Ed. by E. Greenspan. LC 75-14575. 432p. 1975. 26.00 (ISBN 0-89004-069-9). Raven.

Clinical Cancer Medicine: Treatment Tactics. Jacob J. Lokich. (Medical Bks.). 1980. lib. bdg. 37.50 (ISBN 0-8161-2103-6, Hall Medical). G K Hall.

Clinical Cardiac Radiology. 2nd ed. Rees Jefferson. LC 79-40913. (Illus.). 1980. text ed. 75.95 (ISBN 0-407-13576-6). Butterworths.

Clinical Cardiology & Diabetes: Clinical Pharmacology & Use of Selected Drugs, Vol. 2. Ralph C. Scott. LC 79-91228. (Illus.). 1980. 42.00 (ISBN 0-87993-136-1). Futura Pub.

Clinical Cardiovascular Pharmacology. David D. Shand. (Monographs in Clinical Pharmacology). (Illus.). Date not set. text ed. price not set (ISBN 0-443-08040-2). Churchill. Postponed.

Clinical Cellular Immunology. Ed. by Albert Luderer & Howard Weetall. (Contemporary Immunology Ser.). (Illus.). 1981. 44.50 (ISBN 0-89603-011-3). Humana.

Clinical Chemistry. Muriel Kanter. LC 75-4050. (Allied Health Ser). 1975. pap. 8.35 (ISBN 0-672-61380-8). Bobbs.

Clinical Chemistry & Automation: A Study in Laboratory Proficiency. R. Robinson. 188p. 1971. 21.95x (ISBN 0-85264-204-0, Pub. by Griffin England). State Mutual Bk.

Clinical Chemistry: Functional Medical Laboratory Manual. John Scimone & Robert Rothstein. (Illus.). 1978. lab. manual 10.00 (ISBN 0-87055-271-6). AVI.

Clinical Chemistry in Diagnosis & Treatment. 3rd ed. Joan F. Zilva & P. R. Pannall. (Illus.). 1979. pap. 24.95 (ISBN 0-8151-9869-8). Year Bk Med.

Clinical Chemistry: Theory, Practice & Interpretation. R. Richterich. Ed. by J. P. Colombo. 672p. 1981. price not set (ISBN 0-471-27809-2, Pub. by Wiley-Interscience). Wiley.

Clinical Child Psychology: Current Practices & Future Perspectives. Ed. by Gertrude Williams & Sol Gordon. LC 73-13511. 632p. 1974. text ed. 29.95 (ISBN 0-87705-125-9). Human Sci Pr.

Clinical Cognitive Psychology. Ed. by Louis Breger. LC 70-85956. 1969. 24.50x (ISBN 0-13-137620-9). Irvington.

Clinical Companion to Biochemical Studies. Victor Schwarz. LC 77-17132. (Illus.). 1978. 19.95x (ISBN 0-7167-0078-6); pap. text ed. 9.95x (ISBN 0-7167-0077-8). W H Freeman.

Clinical Core of Respiratory Medicine. Colin R. Woolf. (Illus.). 224p. 1981. pap. text ed. write for info (ISBN 0-397-50501-9). Lippincott.

Clinical Decision Analysis. Milton C. Weinstein & Harvey V. Fineberg. (Illus.). 400p. 1980. text ed. 215.00 (ISBN 0-7216-9166-8). Saunders.

Clinical Dental Hygiene. 4th ed. Ed. by Shailer Peterson. LC 72-77196. (Illus.). 448p. 1972. text ed. 15.95 o.p. (ISBN 0-8016-3810-0). Mosby.

Clinical Dermatology of Small Animals: A Stereoscopic Presentation. George G. Doering & Harlan E. Jensen. LC 73-14545. 1973. 61.50 o.p. (ISBN 0-8016-1404-X). Mosby.

Clinical Diabetes: Modern Management. Ed. by Stephen Podolsky. 608p. 1980. 30.00x (ISBN 0-8385-1123-6). ACC.

Clinical Diagnosis in Pediatric Cardiology. J. R. Zuberbuhler. (Modern Pediatric Cardiology Ser.). (Illus.). 192p. 1981. text ed. 50.00 (ISBN 0-686-28921-8). Churchill.

Clinical Diagnosis in Pediatric Cardiology. J. R. Zuberbuhler. (Modern Pediatric Cardiology Ser.). (Illus.). 192p. 1981. 50.00 (ISBN 0-443-01889-8). Churchill.

Clinical Diagnosis of Mental Disorders: A Handbook. Ed. by Benjamin B. Wolman. LC 78-14969. (Illus.). 933p. 1978. 50.00 (ISBN 0-306-31141-0, Plenum Pr). Plenum Pub.

Clinical Diagnostic Manual for the House Officer. Kenneth L. Baughman & Bruce L. Greene. (House Officer Ser.). (Illus.). 110p. 1981. write for info. (ISBN 0-683-03553-3). Williams & Wilkins.

Clinical Diagnostic Manual for the House Officer. Kenneth L. Baughman & Bruce M. Greene. 110p. 1981. write for info. soft cover (3553-3). Williams & Wilkins.

Clinical Diagnostic Pearls. Jason C. Birnholz. 1971. spiral bdg. 7.50 (ISBN 0-87488-730-5). Med Exam.

Clinical Disorders in Pediatric Gastroenterology & Nutrition. Lifshitz. 488p. 1980. 44.50 (ISBN 0-8247-6954-6). Dekker.

Clinical Disorders of Fluid & Electrolyte Metabolism. 2nd ed. Morton H. Maxwell & Charles R. Kleeman. (Illus.). 1972. text ed. 60.00 o.p. (ISBN 0-07-040993-5, HP). McGraw.

Clinical Dysmorphology of Oral-Facial Structures. Ed. by Michael Melnick, Edward D. Shields & Norbert J. Burzynski. (Post Graduate Dental Handbook Ser.: Vol. 12). 1981. 49.50 (ISBN 0-88416-169-2). PSG Pub.

Clinical Echocardiography. Navin C. Nanda & Raymond Gramiak. LC 78-4116. 1978. text ed. 41.50 (ISBN 0-8016-3622-1). Mosby.

Clinical Education for the Allied Health Professions. Charles W. Ford. LC 78-3620. 1978. text ed. 15.95 (ISBN 0-8016-1623-9). Mosby.

Clinical Electrocardiography: A Simplified Approach. 2nd ed. Ary L. Goldberger & Emanuel Goldberger. LC 80-27024. (Illus.). 278p. 1981. text ed. 14.95 (ISBN 0-8016-1865-7). Mosby.

Clinical Electroencephalography. 4th ed. L. G. Kiloh et al. 1981. text ed. price not set (ISBN 0-407-00160-3). Butterworth.

Clinical Endocrinology: A Survey of Current Practice. Ezrin. 1977. 24.50 o.p. (ISBN 0-8385-1137-6). ACC.

Clinical Endocrinology: Pituitary, Vol. 1. C. Beardwell. (Butterworths International Medical Reviews Ser.). 1981. text ed. price not set (ISBN 0-407-02272-4). Butterworth.

Clinical Endodontology: A Comprehensive Guide to Diagnosis, Treatment & Prevention. Donald R. Morse. (Illus.). 664p. 1974. 39.75 (ISBN 0-398-03121-5). C C Thomas.

Clinical Engineering: Principles & Practices. Ed. by Albert M. Cook & John G. Webster. (Illus.). 1979. text ed. 27.95 (ISBN 0-13-137737-X). P-H.

Clinical Enzymology. John C. Griffiths. LC 79-84461. (Illus.). 222p. 1979. 22.50 (ISBN 0-89352-030-6). Masson Pub.

Clinical Enzymology Symposia, Vol. 2. Ed. by A. Burlina & L. Galzigna. (Illus.). 646p. 1980. text ed. 49.50 (ISBN 88-212-0772-2, Pub. by Piccin Italy). J K Burgess.

Clinical Examination of Cattle. Gustav Rosenberger. (Illus.). 469p. 1980. 95.00 (ISBN 0-7216-7705-3). Saunders.

Clinical Experience Record & Nursing Care Planning: A Guide for Student Nurses. 2nd ed. Sr. Mary T. Fuhr. LC 77-22532. 1978. pap. text ed. 9.50 (ISBN 0-8016-1711-1). Mosby.

Clinical Experiences in Collegiate Nursing Education: Selection of Nursing Agencies. Joellen W. Hawkins. LC 80-23401. (Springer Series on the Teaching of Nursing: Vol. 7). 128p. 1980. text ed. cancelled (ISBN 0-8261-3390-8); pap. text ed. 11.50 (ISBN 0-8261-3391-6). Springer Pub.

Clinical Gastroenterology. 2nd ed. Sir F. Avery Jones et al. (Illus.). 900p. 1968. 21.50 (ISBN 0-397-60057-7, Dist. by Mosby). Lippincott.

Clinical Genetics. 2nd ed. A. Sorsby. 1973. 77.95 (ISBN 0-407-13651-7). Butterworths.

Clinical Genetics: A Sourcebook for Physicians. Laird G. Jackson & R. Neil Schimke. LC 78-24414. 1979. 42.95 (ISBN 0-471-01943-7, Pub. by Wiley Medical). Wiley.

Clinical Genetics & Genetics Counseling. Thaddeus E. Kelly. (Illus.). 400p. 1980. 29.50 (ISBN 0-8151-5011-3). Year Bk Med.

Clinical Gynecologic Oncology. Philip J. DiSaia & William T. Creasman. LC 80-18687. (Illus.). 478p. 1980. text ed. 29.50 (ISBN 0-8016-1314-0). Mosby.

Clinical Handbook of Antipsychotic Drug Therapy. Aaron S. Mason & Robert P. Granacher. LC 80-11235. 1980. 25.00 (ISBN 0-87630-215-0). Brunner Mazel.

Clinical Handbook of Pediatric Nursing. Donna L. Wong & Lucille F. Whaley. (Illus.). 316p. 1981. pap. text ed. 10.95 (ISBN 0-8016-5545-5). Mosby.

Clinical Handbook of Psychopharmacology. Ed. by Alberto DiMascio & Richard Shader. LC 75-118581. 1970. 30.00x (ISBN 0-87668-033-3). Aronson.

Clinical Heart Disease. Samuel Oram. (Illus.). 1971. 65.00x (ISBN 0-685-83723-8). Intl Ideas.

Clinical Hypertension & Hypotension. Brunner & Gravas. Date not set. price not set (ISBN 0-8247-1279-X). Dekker.

Clinical Hypnosis Primer. George J. Pratt et al. LC 79-92665. 1980. 12.95 (ISBN 0-930626-07-9). Psych & Consul Assocs.

Clinical Immunology of the Heart. John Zabriskie. (Perspectives in Clinical Immunology Ser.). 230p. 1981. 32.50 (ISBN 0-471-02676-X, Pub. by Wiley Med). Wiley.

Clinical Implications of Drug Use, 2 vols. T. K. Basu. 1981. Vol. 1, 160p. 49.95 (ISBN 0-8493-5391-2); Vol. 2, 144p. 49.95 (ISBN 0-8493-5392-0). CRC Pr.

Clinical Implications of Laboratory Tests, Nineteen Seventy-Nine. 2nd ed. Sarko M. Tilkian et al. LC 78-16221. (Illus.). 1979. pap. text ed. 12.95 (ISBN 0-8016-4962-5). Mosby.

Clinical Importance of Surfactant Defects. Ed. by P. Von Wichert. (Progress in Respiration Research: Vol. 15). (Illus.). 210p. 1980. 48.00 (ISBN 3-8055-1011-X). S Karger.

Clinical Instrument Report. Nelson Alpert. LC 75-25432. 1976. 24.50 (ISBN 0-912920-45-9). North Am Pub Co.

Clinical Interpretation & Practice of Cancer Chemotherapy. Ezra Greenspan. 1981. text ed. price not set (ISBN 0-89004-566-6). Raven.

Clinical Kidney Disease & Hypertension. McDonald. 1980. 32.00. Thieme Stratton.

Clinical Laboratories & the Practice of Medicine: An Economic Perspective. Richard M. Bailey. LC 78-70545. (Health Care Ser.). 1979. 20.50 (ISBN 0-8211-0132-3); text ed. 18.50 in ten or more copies (ISBN 0-685-63680-1). McCutchan.

Clinical Laboratory in Nursing Education. Mary S. Infante. LC 74-12454. 112p. 1975. text ed. 13.50 (ISBN 0-471-42715-2, Pub. by Wiley Medical). Wiley.

Clinical Laboratory Methods. 8th ed. John D. Bauer et al. LC 73-6928. 1974. pap. 36.50 (ISBN 0-8016-0507-5). Mosby.

Clinical Laboratory Statistics. 2nd ed. Roy N. Barnett. (Series in Laboratory Medicine). 224p. 1978. 17.95 (ISBN 0-316-08196-5). Little.

Clinical Laboratory Tests: A Manual for Nurses. 2nd ed. Marcella M. Strand & Lucille A. Elmer. LC 79-29765. 1980. pap. text ed. 7.50 (ISBN 0-8016-4827-0). Mosby.

Clinical Laparoscopy. Giorgio Dagnini. (Illus.). xii, 307p. 1980. 130.00 (ISBN 88-212-0746-3, Pub. by Piccin Italy). J K Burgess.

Clinical Leprosy. V. N. Sehgal. (Illus.). 1980. text ed. 13.50x (ISBN 0-7069-0785-X, Pub. by Vikas India). Advent Bk.

Clinical Management of Articulation Disorders. Curtis E. Weiss & Gordon Lillywhite. LC 80-17348. (Illus.). 303p. 1980. pap. text ed. 11.95 (ISBN 0-8016-5391-6). Mosby.

Clinical Manifestations--Medical Management, Vol. III, Pt. I. Ed. by Ralph C. Scott. (Clinical Cardiology & Diabetes Monographs). (Illus.). 448p. 1981. 39.50 (ISBN 0-87993-137-X). Futura Pub.

Clinical Manual of Health Assessment. June M. Thompson & Arden C. Bowers. (Illus.). 1980. pap. text ed. 17.95 (ISBN 0-8016-4935-8). Mosby.

Clinical Medical Assistant. Bonnie J. Lindsey. (Illus.). 169p. (Orig.). 1980. pap. text ed. 9.95 (ISBN 0-87619-714-4). R J Brady.

Clinical Methods. 2nd ed. Walker et al. 1980. 39.95 (ISBN 0-409-95190-0). Butterworths.

Clinical Methods in Psychology. Irving B. Weiner. LC 75-28366. (Personality Processes Ser). 678p. 1976. 35.95 (ISBN 0-471-92576-4, Pub. by Wiley-Interscience). Wiley.

Clinical Methods: The History, Physical, & Laboratory Examinations, 2 vols. H. K. Walker et al. LC 76-44215. 1977. 39.95 o.p. (ISBN 0-409-95006-8). Butterworths.

Clinical Microbiology. Leo R. DiLiello. (Illus.). 1979. pap. text ed. 12.00 (ISBN 0-87055-325-9). AVI.

Clinical Microbiology. 2nd ed. Hugh L. Moffet. 1980. text ed. 17.75 (ISBN 0-397-50450-0). Lippincott.

Clinical Neuroanatomy for Medical Students. Richard S. Snell. 1980. text ed. 21.95 (ISBN 0-316-80213-1). Little.

Clinical Neuroendocrinology: A Pathophysiological Approach. Ed. by George Tolis et al. LC 78-64844. 1979. text ed. 50.00 (ISBN 0-89004-355-8). Raven.

Clinical Neurology. 4th ed. Francis M. Forster. LC 78-7343. 1978. pap. text ed. 10.95 (ISBN 0-8016-1637-9). Mosby.

Clinical Neurology for Psychiatrists. David M. Kaufman. 1981. write for info. (ISBN 0-8089-1321-2). Grune.

Clinical Neuropharmacology, Vol. 1. Ed. by Harold L. Klawans. LC 75-14581. 1976. 26.00 (ISBN 0-89004-035-4). Raven.

Clinical Neuropharmacology, Vol. 2. Ed. by Harold L. Klawans. LC 75-14581. 1977. 24.00 (ISBN 0-89004-171-7). Raven.

Clinical Neuropharmacology, Vol. 3. Ed. by Harold L. Klawans. LC 75-14581. 1978. 24.50 (ISBN 0-89004-266-7). Raven.

Clinical Neuropharmacology, Vol. 4. Harold L. Klawans. 1979. 24.50 (ISBN 0-89004-350-7). Raven.

Clinical Neuropharmacology, Vol. 5. Ed. by Harold L. Klawans. 1981. text ed. price not set (ISBN 0-89004-648-4). Raven.

Clinical Neurophysiological Aspects of Psychopathological Conditions. Ed. by C. Perris & L. Von Knorring. (Advances in Biological Psychiatry: Vol. 4). (Illus.). viii, 192p. 1980. pap. 36.75 (ISBN 3-8055-0604-X). S Karger.

Clinical Neurosis. Philip Snaith. 240p. 1981. text ed. 16.95x. Oxford U Pr.

Clinical Neurosurgery, Vol. 27. Peter W. Carmel. (Illus.). 600p. 1981. write for info. (2022-6). Williams & Wilkins.

Clinical Nuclear Cardiology. Danieal S. Berman & Dean T. Mason. (Clinical Cardiology Monographs Ser.). 1981. write for info. (ISBN 0-8089-1356-5). Grune.

Clinical Nuclear Cardiology. Ed. by Robert W. Parkey et al. LC 78-12673. 1978. 34.50 (ISBN 0-8385-1146-5). ACC.

Clinical Nursing Techniques. 3rd ed. Norma Dison. LC 74-28411. 1975. pap. text ed. 10.50 o.p. (ISBN 0-8016-1307-8). Mosby.

Clinical Nursing Techniques. 4th ed. Norma Dison. LC 78-31262. (Illus.). 1979. pap. text ed. 14.95 (ISBN 0-8016-1308-6). Mosby.

Clinical Nutrition. 2nd ed. Victoria Thiele. LC 80-13265. (Illus.). 300p. 1980. pap. text ed. 11.95 (ISBN 0-8016-4901-3). Mosby.

Clinical Nutrition & Dietetics. Ed. by G. A. Goldsmith. 1976. text ed. write for info. o.p. (ISBN 0-08-016469-2). Pergamon.

Clinical Oncology: A Manual for Students & Doctors. International Union Against Cancer - Committee on Professional Education - Geneva. Ed. by U. Veronesi et al. (Illus.). xvii, 321p. 1973. pap. 14.10 o.p. (ISBN 0-387-05851-6). Springer Verlag.

Clinical Oncology: A Quantitative Approach. N. M. Emanuel & D. S. Evseenko. Ed. by J. H. Abramson. Tr. by N. Kaner from Rus. LC 73-16436. 272p. 1974. 45.95 (ISBN 0-470-23891-7). Halsted Pr.

Clinical Oncology: The Foundations of Current Patient Management, Vol. 4. Ed. by Jesus Vicente et al. LC 80-80729. (Cancer Management Series). (Illus.). 224p. 1980. 43.50 (ISBN 0-89352-083-7). Masson Pub.

Clinical Ophthalmology, 5 vols. & index. Loose Leaf Reference Service. Ed. by Thomas Duane. (Illus.). Set. looseleaf bdg. 325.00 (ISBN 0-06-148007-X, Harper Medical); annual revision pages 50.00 (ISBN 0-685-71848-4). Har-Row.

Clinical Oral Periatrics. White. 148p. 1981. 68.00 (ISBN 0-931386-32-2). Quint Pub Co.

Clinical Orthopaedics & Related Research: Vol. 85, AOFS Surgery of the Foot. Association of Bone & Joint Surgeons. Ed. by Marshall R. Urist. 1972. 15.00 (ISBN 0-685-27031-9). Lippincott.

Clinical Orthopaedics & Related Research: Vol. 86, Progress in Hip Joint Surgery. Association of Bone & Joint Surgeons. Ed. by Marshall R. Urist. 1972. 15.00 (ISBN 0-685-27032-7). Lippincott.

Clinical Orthopaedics & Related Research: Vol. 80, Problems of Unusual Interest. Association of Bone & Joint Surgeons. Ed. by Marshall R. Urist. 1971. 15.00 (ISBN 0-685-27028-9). Lippincott.

Clinical Orthopaedics & Related Research: Vol. 81, Spinal Column. Association of Bone & Joint Surgeons. Ed. by Marshall R. Urist. 1971. 12.00 o.p. (ISBN 0-685-27029-7). Lippincott.

Clinical Orthopaedics & Related Research: Vol. 82, Subjects of Current Interest. Association of Bone & Joint Surgeons. Ed. by Marshall R. Urist. 1972. 12.00 o.p. (ISBN 0-685-27030-0). Lippincott.

Clinical Otolaryngology. Vijay S. Dayal. (Illus.). 304p. 1981. pap. text ed. write for info (ISBN 0-397-50499-3). Lippincott.

Clinical Pathology Continuing Education Review. David H. Buss et al. LC 79-91972. 1980. pap. 14.75 (ISBN 0-87488-320-2). Med Exam.

Clinical Pathology for Medical Students. Neelam Batra. 240p. 1981. text ed. 18.95x (ISBN 0-7069-1117-2, Pub. by Vikas India). Advent Bk.

Clinical Pediatric Dermatology. Sidney Hurwitz. (Illus.). 656p. 1980. write for info. (ISBN 0-7216-4872-X). Saunders.

Clinical Performance Examination. Carrie Lenburg. 384p. 1979. 14.75 (ISBN 0-8385-1168-6). ACC.

Clinical Perinatal Biochemical Monitoring. Neils H. Lauersen & Howard Hochberg. 271p. 1981. write for info. (1901-1). Williams & Wilkins.

Clinical Perinatology. Ed. by Silvio Aladjem & Audrey K. Brown. LC 74-8599. (Illus.). 1974. 45.00 o.p. (ISBN 0-8016-0100-2). Mosby.

Clinical Perinatology. 2nd ed. Silvio Aladjem et al. LC 79-24340. (Illus.). 1979. text ed. 52.50 (ISBN 0-8016-0103-7). Mosby.

Clinical Perspectives in Nursing Research: Relevance, Suffering, Recovery. Ed. by M. Janice Nelson. LC 78-18242. 1978. pap. text ed. 5.75x (ISBN 0-8077-2549-8). Tchrs Coll.

Clinical Pharmacokinetics. LC 74-16725. 1974. 5.00 o.p. (ISBN 0-917330-14-5). Am Pharm Assn.

Clinical Pharmacokinetics: Concepts & Applications. Malcolm Rowland & Thomas N. Tozer. LC 79-10735. (Illus.). 330p. 1980. text ed. 29.50 (ISBN 0-8121-0681-4). Lea & Febiger.

Clinical Pharmacology, 2 Vols. Ed. by Louis Lasagna. 1966. Set. 34.00 (ISBN 0-08-012067-9). Pergamon.

Clinical Pharmacology. 3rd ed. John Reinhard. (Illus.). 1977. pap. text ed. 20.50 (ISBN 0-89147-039-5). CAS.

Clinical Pharmacology & the Aged Patient. Ed. by L. F. Jarvik et al. (Aging Ser.: Vol. 16). 256p. 1981. text ed. 25.00 (ISBN 0-89004-340-X). Raven.

Clinical Pharmacology & the Aged Patient. Ed. by L. F. Jarvik et al. (Aging Ser.). 1980. 25.00 (ISBN 0-89004-340-X, 349). Raven.

Clinical Pharmacology for Nurses. 9th ed. J. R. Trounce. (Illus.). 432p. 1981. pap. text ed. 10.00 (ISBN 0-443-02333-6). Churchill.

Clinical Pharmacology for Nurses. 9th ed. Ed. by J. R. Trounce. (Illus.). Date not set. text ed. price not set (ISBN 0-443-02333-6). Churchill.

Clinical Pharmacology in Dental Practice. 2nd ed. Ed. by Sam V. Holroyd. LC 77-22265. (Illus.). 1978. pap. text ed. 19.95 (ISBN 0-8016-2241-7). Mosby.

Clinical Pharmacology of Antieliptic Drugs. (Illus.). 340p. 62.70 (ISBN 0-387-06987-9). Springer-Verlag.

Clinical Pharmacology of Prostacyclin. Ed. by Peter J. Lewis & John M. O'Grady. 1981. price not set (ISBN 0-89004-591-7). Raven.

Clinical Pharmacology of the Beta-Adrenocepter Blocking Drugs. William H. Frishman. 288p. 1980. 16.95x (ISBN 0-8385-1143-0). ACC.

Clinical Pharmacology: Symposium Proceedings. Ed. by William A. Creasey. 248p. 1976. text ed. 30.00 (ISBN 0-08-018949-0). Pergamon.

Clinical Physics & Physiology of Chronic Lung Disease, Inhalation Therapy, & Pulmonary Function Testing. D. S. Tysinger, Jr. (Illus.). 264p. 1973. text ed. 17.50 (ISBN 0-398-02777-3). C C Thomas.

Clinical Physiology of Physical Fitness & Rehabilitation. Ernst Jokl. (American Lecture Sportsmedicine Ser). (Illus.). 208p. 1971. photocopy ed., spiral 19.75 (ISBN 0-398-02198-8). C C Thomas.

Clinical Podiatric Laboratory Diagnosis. Murray J. Politz. Ed. by Morton D. Fielding. LC 77-80657. (Podiatric Medicine & Surgery Ser.: Vol. 9). 1977. 27.50 (ISBN 0-87993-096-9). Futura Pub.

Clinical Podogeriatrics. Arthur E. Helfand. (Illus.). 248p. 1981. write for info. (3951-2). Williams & Wilkins.

Clinical Practice in Pediatric Radiology: The Heart & Great Vessels, Vol. I. Jacques Lefebvre. Ed. by Herbert J. Kaufmann. LC 79-83739. (Great Pediatric Radiology Ser.). Orig. Title: Radiopediatrie. 1979. 54.50 (ISBN 0-89352-015-2). Masson Pub.

Clinical Practice in Pediatric Radiology: The Respiratory System, Vol. II. Jacques Lefebvre. Ed. by Herbert J. Kaufman. LC 79-83739. 448p. 1979. 65.50 (ISBN 0-89352-066-7). Masson Pub.

Clinical Practice of Adolescent Medicine. Jerome T. Shen. 750p. 1979. 36.50x (ISBN 0-8385-1148-1). ACC.

Clinical Practice of Blood Transfusion. Petz & Swisher. Date not set. text ed. price not set (ISBN 0-443-08067-4). Churchill.

Clinical Practice of Blood Transfusion. Ed. by Lawrence D. Petz & Scott N. Swisher. (Illus.). 640p. 1981. lib. bdg. 55.00 (ISBN 0-443-08067-4). Churchill.

Clinical Practice of Psychology: A Practical Guide for Mental Health Professionals. Ed. by C. Eugene Walker. (Pergamon General Psychology Ser.). Date not set. 27.51 (ISBN 0-08-025591-4); pap. 15.91 (ISBN 0-08-025590-6). Pergamon.

Clinical Problems with Drugs. Leighton E. Cluff et al. (Major Problems in Internal Medicine Ser., Vol. 5). (Illus.). 308p. 1975. text ed. 18.00 (ISBN 0-7216-2613-0). Saunders.

Clinical Procedures: A Concise Guide for Students of Medicine. Jack C. Fisher. (Illus.). 1970. pap. 6.95 o.p. (ISBN 0-683-03239-9). Williams & Wilkins.

Clinical Procedures: A Concise Guide for Students of Medicine. 2nd ed. Jack C. Fisher & Thomas Wachtel. (Illus.). 251p. 1980. 13.50 (ISBN 0-683-03240-2). Williams & Wilkins.

Clinical Procedures for Behavior Therapy. C. Eugene Walker et al. (Illus.). 464p. 1981. text ed. 18.95 (ISBN 0-13-137794-9). P-H.

Clinical Procedures for Medical Assistants. Kathy Bonewit. 1979. text ed. 18.50 (ISBN 0-7216-1846-4). Saunders.

Clinical Psychiatry. Emil Kraepelin. LC 80-25289. (History of Psychology Ser.). 1981. write for info. (ISBN 0-8201-1352-2). Schol Facsimilies.

Clinical Psychiatry in Primary Care. Steven L. Dubovsky. 1978. pap. 12.95 (ISBN 0-683-02671-2); package set o.p. 49.50 (ISBN 0-686-67997-0). Williams & Wilkins.

Clinical Psychiatry: Problems of Treatment, Research & Prevention. Group For The Advancement Of Psychiatry. LC 67-8140. 1967. 25.00x (ISBN 0-87668-003-1). Aronson.

Clinical Psychoanalysis. Ed. by Shelly Orgel & Bernard D. Fine. (Downstate Psychoanalytic Institute Twenty-Fifth Anniversary Ser: Vol. III). 1979. 25.00x (ISBN 0-87668-368-5). Aronson.

Clinical Psychology. 2nd ed. Julian B. Rotter. LC 74-110493. (Foundations of Modern Psychology Ser). (Illus.). 1971. pap. 7.95x ref. ed. (ISBN 0-13-137836-8). P-H.

Clinical Psychology & Medicine: An Interdisciplnary Approach. Frank J. Vingoe. (Illus.). 480p. 1981. text ed. 35.00x. Oxford U Pr.

Clinical Psychology: Concepts, Methods, & Profession. E. Jerry Phares. 1979. 18.95x (ISBN 0-256-02190-2). Dorsey.

Clinical Psychology: Expanding Horizons. 2nd ed. Norman D. Sundberg et al. (Century Psychology Ser.). (Illus.). 1973. 20.95x (ISBN 0-13-137877-5). P-H.

Clinical Psychology: The Study of Personality & Behavior. Sol L. Garfield. LC 73-89520. 1974. lib. bdg. 22.95x (ISBN 0-202-26073-9); pap. text ed. 12.95x (ISBN 0-202-26077-1). Aldine Pub.

Clinical Radioimmunoassy: State of the Art. Jeffrey C. Travis. (Illus.). 1980. 39.00 (ISBN 0-930914-06-6). Sci Newsletters.

Clinical Recognition & Treatment of Diabetic Vascular Disease. John A. Colwell. (Amer. Lec. Circulation Ser.). (Illus.). 104p. 1975. 12.75 (ISBN 0-398-03251-3). C C Thomas.

Clinical Repertory. John H. Clarke. 346p. 1979. text ed. 24.95x (ISBN 0-8464-1000-1). Beekman Pubs.

Clinical Research in Alcoholism: PRR 24. Ed. by Jonathan O. Cole. 178p. 1968. pap. 5.00 (ISBN 0-685-24867-4, P024-0). Am Psychiatric.

Clinical Rheumatology. 2nd ed. Ed. by Michael Mason & H. L. Currey. LC 75-32623. (Illus.). 1975. 24.00 o.p. (ISBN 0-397-58186-6). Lippincott.

Clinical Science for Surgeons. William Burnett. 1981. text ed. price not set (ISBN 0-407-00181-6). Butterworth.

Clinical Serology. Clois W. Bennett. (Illus.). 304p. 1980. text ed. 13.50 (ISBN 0-398-00130-8). C C Thomas.

Clinical Sialography. Gordon B. Manashil. (Illus.). 112p. 1978. 19.50 (ISBN 0-398-03770-1). C C Thomas.

Clinical Simulations in Pediatrics. Floy Helnig. (Clinical Simulation Ser.). 218p. 1979. pap. 33.50x (ISBN 0-8385-1173-2). ACC.

Clinical Simulations in Surgery. Bernard Sigel. Ed. by Phillip M. Forman. 352p. 1980. pap. 38.50 (ISBN 0-8385-1174-0). ACC.

Clinical Simulations: Selected Problems in Patient Management. 2nd ed. McGuire. 1976. pap. 25.50 (ISBN 0-8385-1161-9). ACC.

Clinical Skills & Assisting Techniques for the Medical Assistant. Sharron Zakus. (Illus.). 536p. 1981. pap. text ed. 15.95 (ISBN 0-8016-5672-9). Mosby.

Clinical Social Work: Theory & Practice. Herbert S. Strean. LC 77-90147. 1978. text ed. 14.95 (ISBN 0-02-932210-3). Free Pr.

Clinical Studies in Behavior Therapy with Children, Adolescents, & Their Families. James M. Stedman et al. (Illus.). 412p. 1973. 26.75 (ISBN 0-398-02736-6); pap. 20.50 (ISBN 0-398-02763-3). C C Thomas.

Clinical Studies in Infant Mental Health: The First Year of Life. Selma Fraiberg. (Illus.). 279p. 1980. text ed. 17.50x (ISBN 0-465-01170-5). Basic.

Clinical Studies in Neurology. Harry L. Parker. 384p. 1969. 12.75 (ISBN 0-398-01449-3). C C Thomas.

Clinical Study of Human Equilibrium by Electonystagmography & Allied Tests. Claus F. Claussen & Joe V. Desa. (Illus.). xiii, 437p. 1980. text ed. 50.00x (ISBN 0-86590-002-7). Apt Bks.

Clinical Supervision. Morris L. Cogan. LC 72-85906. 250p. 1973. text ed. 19.95 (ISBN 0-395-14027-7). HM.

Clinical Supervision. David J. Powell. LC 79-20586. 1979. manual 19.95x (ISBN 0-87705-406-1); trainee wkbk. 7.95x (ISBN 0-87705-407-X). Human Sci Pr.

Clinical Surgery: Eye. Stewart Duke-Elder. (Illus.). 1964. 18.75 o.p. (ISBN 0-397-58001-0). Lippincott.

Clinical Surgery: Gynaecology & Obstetrics, Vol. 15. David W. Roberts. Ed. by Charles Rob & Rodney Smith. (Illus.). 1968. 12.00 o.p. (ISBN 0-397-58017-7). Lippincott.

Clinical Surgery: Orthopaedics. G. C. Lloyd-Roberts. (Illus.). 1968. 22.50 o.p. (ISBN 0-397-58016-9). Lippincott.

Clinical Surgery: Vascular Surgery & Reticulo-Endothelial System, Vol. 14. Gerard W. Taylor & John F. Wilkinson. (Illus.). 1967. 22.00 o.p. (ISBN 0-397-58012-6). Lippincott.

Clinical Training of Doctors: An Essay of 1793. Philippe Pinel. Ed. & tr. by Dora B. Weiner. LC 80-14500. (Henry E. Sigerist Supplements to the Bulletin of the History of Medicine, New Ser.: No. 3). 108p. 1981. pap. text ed. 7.50x (ISBN 0-8018-2448-6). Johns Hopkins.

Clinical Transcutaneous Electrical Nerve Stimulation. Jeffrey S. Mannheimer & Gerald N. Lampe. 1981. 22.50 (ISBN 0-8036-5832-X). Davis Co.

Clinical Transplantation in Dental Specialties. Guernsey Robinson. 1979. 45.00 (ISBN 0-8016-4142-X). Mosby.

Clinical Treatment of Back & Neck Pain. Hans Kraus. LC 70-79496. (Illus.). 1970. 23.50 o.p. (ISBN 0-07-035415-4, HP). McGraw.

Clinical Ultrasound Review, Vol. 1. Fred Winsberg. LC 80-19595. (Annual Review of Ultrasound). 300p. 1980. 32.00 (ISBN 0-471-05738-X, Pub. by Wiley Med). Wiley.

Clinical Use of Psychotherapeutic Drugs. Leo E. Hollister. 200p. 1977. 12.75 (ISBN 0-398-02749-8). C C Thomas.

Clinical Uses of Dreams: Jungian Interpretation & Enactments. James A. Hall. 1978. 31.25 (ISBN 0-8089-1053-1). Grune.

Clinical Uses of Whole-Body Counting. (Illus., Orig.). 1966. pap. 13.50 (ISBN 92-0-111066-9, IAEA). Unipub.

Clinical Venereology. B. Schwartz. 1965. pap. 9.75 (ISBN 0-08-011601-9). Pergamon.

Clinical Veterinary Anesthesia: A Guide for the Practitioner. Charles Short. LC 74-8001. 1974. 29.50 o.p. (ISBN 0-8016-4601-4). Mosby.

Clinical Workbook in Medical-Surgical Nursing. Rosemary B. Kurtz & Nancy F. Miller. (Illus.). 1978. pap. text ed. 9.95 (ISBN 0-7216-5580-7). Saunders.

Clinical Writing for Health Professionals. Alice M. Robinson & Lucille Notter. (Illus.). 128p. (Orig.). 1981. pap. price not set (ISBN 0-87619-893-0). R J Brady.

Clinically Adapted Instruments for the Multiply Handicapped: A Sourcebook. rev. ed. Compiled by Cynthia Clark & Donna Chadwick. 1980. Repr. of 1979 ed. 12.95 (ISBN 0-918812-13-5). Magnamusic.

Clinically Oriented Anatomy. Keith L. Moore. (Illus.). 950p. 1980. lib. bdg. 26.95 (ISBN 0-683-06146-1). Williams & Wilkins.

Clinician's Guide to Research Design. Gerald Goldstein. LC 79-18818. 288p. 1981. text ed. 24.95 (ISBN 0-88229-340-0). Nelson-Hall.

Clinician's Handbook of Childhood Psychopathology. Martin M. Josephson & Robert T. Porter. 30.00x (ISBN 0-87668-359-6). Aronson.

Clinicopathologic Correlation of Ocular Disease: A Stereoscopic Atlas. 2nd ed. David J. Apple & Maurice F. Rabb. LC 78-15635. 1978. text ed. 115.00 (ISBN 0-8016-0272-6). Mosby.

Clinics, Contraception & Communication: Evaluation Studies of Family Planning Programs in Four Latin American Countries. Ed. by J. Mayone Stycos. LC 79-184865. (Illus.). 1973. 20.00x (ISBN 0-89197-625-6); pap. text ed. 8.95x (ISBN 0-89197-700-7). Irvington.

Clip Book Number Eleven: Communicate the Action. Norman H. Ludlow, Jr. (Illus.). 64p. (Orig.). 1980. pap. 13.95 (ISBN 0-916706-22-2). N H Ludlow.

Clipart Book of Promotional & Program Artwork. Lauren Reinertsen. LC 74-84398. (Illus.). 64p. 1974. pap. 9.95 (ISBN 0-87874-013-9). Galloway.

Clipper Ships. A. B. Whipple. Ed. by Time-Life Bks. (Seafarers Ser.). (Illus.). 176p. 1980. 14.95 (ISBN 0-8094-2677-3). Time-Life.

Clive: Proconsul of India. James P. Lawford. 1976. text ed. 25.00x o.p. (ISBN 0-04-923067-0). Allen Unwin.

Cloak & Dagger Bibliography: An Annotated Guide to Spy Fiction, 1937-1975. Myron J. Smith. 1975. 10.00 (ISBN 0-8108-0897-8). Scarecrow.

Clock Book. Donna Kelly. (Golden Book for Early Childhood Ser.). (Illus.). (gr. k-3). 1979. PLB 5.38 (ISBN 0-307-68962-X, Golden Pr). Western Pub.

Clock Book. Wallace Nutting. LC 70-178648. (Illus.). 1975. Repr. of 1924 ed. 28.00 (ISBN 0-8103-4145-X). Gale.

Clock Guide: Identification with Prices. rev. & enl. ed. Robert W. Miller. (Illus.). 1978. 8.95 o.p. (ISBN 0-87069-251-8). Wallace-Homestead.

Clock of Dreams. Brian Lumley. 1978. pap. 1.75 o.s.i. (ISBN 0-685-86423-5). Jove Pubns.

Clock Price Up-Date & Index to Clock Identification & Price Guide, 1979, Bk. 1. Roy Ehrhardt. 1979. 4.00 (ISBN 0-913902-28-4). Heart Am Pr.

Clock Types. E. J. Tyler. 1980. pap. 10.95 (ISBN 0-85936-159-4, Pub. by Midas Bks England). Intl Schol Bk Serv.

Clockmakers' Library: The Catalogue of the Books & Manuscripts in the Library of the Worshipful Company of Clockmakers. Ed. by John Bromley. (Illus.). 136p. 1977. 52.50x (ISBN 0-85667-033-2, Pub. by Sotheby Parke Bernet England). Biblio Dist.

Clocks & More Clocks. Pat Hutchins. (Illus.). (gr. k-3). 1970. 8.95 (ISBN 0-02-745860-1). Macmillan.

Clocks & Watches: The Collection of the Worshipful Company of Clockmakers. Ed. by George Daniels & Cecil Clutton. (Illus.). 160p. 1975. 52.50x (ISBN 0-85667-019-7, Pub. by Sotheby Park Bernet England). Biblio Dist.

Clocks for the Ages: How Scientists Date the Past. Robert Silverberg. (Illus.). (gr. 7 up). 1971. 6.95 o.s.i. (ISBN 0-02-782680-5). Macmillan.

Clocks in Color. Andrew Nicholls. LC 75-17890. (Illus.). 176p. 1976. 6.95 o.s.i. (ISBN 0-02-589460-9, 58946). Macmillan.

Clocks of Columbus: The Literary Career of James Thurber. Charles S. Holmes. LC 72-78287. (Illus.). 1978. pap. 6.95 (ISBN 0-689-70574-3, 242). Atheneum.

Clockwork Debt: Trade & the External Debt of Developing Countries. Pierre Dhonte. LC 79-1753. 144p. 1979. 16.95 (ISBN 0-669-02925-4). Lexington Bks.

Clockwork Image. Donald MacKay. LC 74-8347. 112p. (Orig.). 1974. pap. 3.95 o.p. (ISBN 0-87784-557-3). Inter-Varsity.

Clockwork Orange. Anthony Burgess. 1963. 9.95 (ISBN 0-393-08519-8, Norton Lib); pap. 3.50 (ISBN 0-393-00224-1). Norton.

Clockwork Orange. Anthony Burgess. 1976. pap. 2.25 (ISBN 0-345-28411-9). Ballantine.

Clockwork Traitor. (Family D'Alembert Ser.: No. 3). 1977. pap. 1.75 (ISBN 0-515-04824-0). Jove Pubns.

Clockwork Universe. Ed. by Otto Mayr. 1980. lib. bdg. 55.00 (ISBN 0-88202-188-5); prepub. 45.00 prepub. N Watson.

Cloisonne Enameling & Jewelry. Felicia Liban & Louise K. Mitchell. 256p. 1980. 18.95 (ISBN 0-8019-6900-X). Chilton.

Cloister & the Hearth. Charles Reade. 1955. 7.50x o.p. (ISBN 0-460-00029-2, Evman). Dutton.

Cloning: A Biologist Reports. Robert C McKinnell. LC 79-10569. (Illus.). 1979. 8.95 (ISBN 0-8166-0883-0). U of Minn Pr.

Cloning of Human Tumor Stem Cells. Ed. by Sydney E. Salman. LC 80-19600. (Progress in Clinical & Biological Research: Vol. 48). 366p. 1980. 44.00 (ISBN 0-8451-0048-3). A R Liss.

Close Associates. Catherine Linden. 1980. pap. 1.95 (ISBN 0-380-75473-8, 75473). Avon.
Close but Not Quite. Paul J. Deegan. LC 74-16334. (Dan Murphy Sports Ser.). 40p. (gr. 3-6). 1975. PLB 5.95 (ISBN 0-87191-405-0); pap. 2.95 (ISBN 0-89812-152-3). Creative Ed.
Close Encounters: A Factual Report on UFOs. Sherman J. Larsen. LC 78-2322. (Illus.). (gr. 4-12). 1978. PLB 16.50 (ISBN 0-8172-1200-0). Raintree Pubs.
Close Encounters of the Highest Kind. Jim McKeever. LC 78-70089. 1978. 7.95 (ISBN 0-931608-04-X); pap. 3.95 (ISBN 0-931608-03-1). Omega Pubns OR.
Close Encounters of the Third Kind. Steven Spielberg. 1977. 8.95 o.s.i. (ISBN 0-440-01373-9). Delacorte.
Close Encounters of the Third Kind. Steven Spielberg. 1977. pap. 2.50 (ISBN 0-440-11332-6). Dell.
Close Look at Close Encounters. Daniel Cohen. LC 80-2784. (Illus.). 192p. (gr. 7 up). 1981. PLB 7.95 (ISBN 0-396-07927-X). Dodd.
Close Radio Catalog. Ed. by Paul McCarthy & John Duncan. LC 81-65198. (Illus.). 100p. (Orig.). 1981. pap. 5.00 (ISBN 0-937122-01-7). Astro Artz.
Close the Forty-Ninth Parallel Etc. The Americanization of Canada. Ed. by Ian Lumsden. LC 79-477171. 1970. pap. 6.50 (ISBN 0-8020-6111-7). U of Toronto Pr.
Close to Critical. Hal Clement. 192p. (Orig.). 1975. pap. 1.95 (ISBN 0-345-29168-9). Ballantine.
Close to Critical. Hal Clement. 192p. 1981. pap. 1.95 (ISBN 0-345-29168-9, Del Rey). Ballantine.
Close to Death: A Buena Costa Country Mystery. John Crowe. LC 79-1213. (Red Badge Novel of Suspense Ser.). 1979. 7.95 (ISBN 0-396-07675-0). Dodd.
Close to Home. Ellen Goodman. 1980. pap. 2.50 (ISBN 0-449-24351-6, Crest). Fawcett.
Close to the Heart. Helen Lowrie Marshall. 1958. 2.50 o.p. (ISBN 0-385-08261-4). Doubleday.
Close-up on Composition. Linda Stanley et al. 464p. 1980. pap. text ed. 9.95x (ISBN 0-534-00745-7). Wadsworth Pub.
Close-up Photography & Photomacrography. Ed. by Staff of Eastman Kodak Co., LC 77-88930. (Kodak Publication). (Illus.). 1977. pap. 8.00 (ISBN 0-87985-206-2, N-12). Eastman Kodak.
Close-Up: The Contemporary Director. Ed. by Jon Tuska et al. LC 80-23551. 437p. 1981. 22.50 (ISBN 0-8108-1366-1). Scarecrow.
Close up: The Contract Director. Ed. by Jon Tuska et al. LC 76-41345. 1976. 21.00 (ISBN 0-8108-0961-3). Scarecrow.
Close-up: The Hollywood Director. Ed. by Jon Tuska et al. LC 77-14114. 1978. 21.00 (ISBN 0-8108-1085-9). Scarecrow.
Closed Book. Richard Blessing. LC 80-50865. 80p. 1980. 8.95 (ISBN 0-295-95757-3). U of Wash Pr.
Closed Functional Treatment of Fractures. A. Sarmiento & L. Latta. (Illus.). 650p. 1981. 148.00 (ISBN 0-387-10384-8). Springer-Verlag.
Closed-List Classes of Colloquial Egyptian Arabic. Zaki N. Abdel-Malek. (Janua Linguarum, Ser. Practica: No. 128). 240p. (Orig.). 1972. pap. text ed. 42.35x (ISBN 90-2792-322-1). Mouton.
Closed on Account of Death, Not Sam. Lee Boltin. 1977. pap. 2.95 o.p. (ISBN 0-345-27211-0). Ballantine.
Closed Ranks: An Experiment in Mental Health Education. Elaine Cumming & John H. Cumming. LC 57-9073. (Commonwealth Fund Publications Ser). 1957. 7.50x (ISBN 0-674-13600-4). Harvard U Pr.
Closed Shop in Britain. William E. McCarthy. 1964. 20.00x (ISBN 0-520-00837-5). U of Cal Pr.
Closely Watched Trains. Bohmil Hrabal. (Writers from the Other Europe Ser.). 1981. pap. 3.95 (ISBN 0-14-005808-7). Penguin.
Closeness & Creativity. Stanley Waldrop. LC 77-84984. 1977. 6.95 (ISBN 0-9603364-0-0). Waldrop Pubns.
Closeness of God. Ladislaus Boros. 1978. pap. 3.95 (ISBN 0-8164-2175-7). Crossroad NY.
Closer Look. Michael Godfrey. LC 75-8961. (Illus.). 160p. 1975. 14.95 o.p. (ISBN 0-87156-143-3). Sierra.
Closer Look at Ants. Valerie Pitt & David Cook. LC 75-4358. (Closer Look at Ser). (Illus.). 32p. (gr. 4 up). 1975. 2.95 (ISBN 0-531-02423-7); PLB 6.90 (ISBN 0-531-01098-8). Watts.
Closer Look at Arctic Lands. J. L. Hicks. LC 76-27971. (Closer Look at Ser.). (Illus.). (gr. 4-7). 1977. 2.95 (ISBN 0-531-02477-6); PLB 6.90 s&l (ISBN 0-531-00367-1). Watts.
Closer Look at Ariel. Nancy H. Steiner. 128p. 1974. pap. 1.50 o.p. (ISBN 0-445-03020-8). Popular Lib.
Closer Look at Birds. Jim Hicks. (Closer Look at Ser.). (Illus.). 32p. (gr. 5-8). 1976. 2.95 (ISBN 0-531-02433-4); PLB 6.90 (ISBN 0-531-01189-5). Watts.
Closer Look at Butterflies & Moths. Ralph Whitlock. (Closer Look at Ser.). (Illus.). (gr. 4-7). 1978. PLB 6.90 (ISBN 0-531-01425-8); pap. 1.95 (ISBN 0-531-02488-1). Watts.
Closer Look at Fish. Keith Banister. (gr. 5 up). 1980. PLB 6.90 (ISBN 0-531-03413-5). Watts.
Closer Look at Grasslands. Catherine Horton. (Closer Look at Ser.). (Illus.). (gr. 4 up). 1979. PLB 6.90 s&l (ISBN 0-531-03411-9). Watts.
Closer Look at Horses. Neil Thompson. (Closer Look at Ser.). (Illus.). (gr. 4 up). 1978. PLB 6.90 (ISBN 0-531-01428-2); pap. 1.95 (ISBN 0-531-02486-5). Watts.
Closer Look at Jungles. Joyce Pope. LC 78-4834. (Closer Look at Ser.). (Illus.). (gr. 5 up). 1978. PLB 6.90 s&l (ISBN 0-531-01485-1). Watts.
Closer Look at Oceans. Susannah Cook. (Closer Look at Ser.). (Illus.). 32p. (gr. 5-8). 1976. 2.95 (ISBN 0-531-02434-2); PLB 6.90 (ISBN 0-531-01190-9). Watts.
Closer Look at Plant Life. Bernard Stonehouse. (Closer Look at Ser.). (Illus.). (gr. 5-8). 1978. PLB 6.90 s&l (ISBN 0-531-01430-4). Watts.
Closer Look at Prehistoric Mammals. Beverly Halstead. (Closer Look at Ser.). (Illus.). 32p. (gr. 5-8). 1976. 2.95 (ISBN 0-531-02435-0); PLB 6.90 (ISBN 0-531-01191-7). Watts.
Closer Look at Reptiles. Bernard Stonehouse. LC 78-11539. (Closer Look at Ser.). (Illus.). (gr. 5-8). 1979. PLB 6.90 s&l (ISBN 0-531-03401-1). Watts.
Closer Look at the Dawn of Life. Beverly Halstead. (Closer Look at Ser.). (Illus.). (gr. 5-8). 1979. PLB 6.90 s&l (ISBN 0-531-03402-X). Watts.
Closer Look at Whales & Dolphins. Bernard Stonehouse. (Closer Look at Ser.). (Illus.). (gr. 4 up). 1978. PLB 6.90 s&l (ISBN 0-531-01484-3); pap. 1.95 (ISBN 0-531-02489-X). Watts.
Closeter Look at Hamburger. Jack King. 1981. 4.95 (ISBN 0-917530-12-8); pap. write for info. (ISBN 0-685-97205-4). Pig Iron Pr.
Closing Ceremonies. Harold King. 1980. pap. write for info. (ISBN 0-671-83396-0). PB.
Closing Correctional Institutions. Ed. by Yitzhak Bakal. LC 73-998. 275p. 1973. 16.95 (ISBN 0-669-86140-5). Lexington Bks.
Closing the Catalog: Proceedings of the LITA Institute. Library & Information Technology Association. Ed. by D. Kaye Gapen & Bonnie Juergens. 1980. lib. bdg. 18.50x (ISBN 0-912700-56-4). Oryx Pr.
Closing the Gap Between Technology & Application: Proceedings. EDUCOM Fall Conference, Oct. 1977. Ed. by James C. Emery. 1978. lib. bdg. 26.75x (ISBN 0-89158-167-7). Westview.
Closure in the Novel. Marianna Torgovnick. LC 80-8581. 272p. 1981. 16.50x (ISBN 0-691-06464-4). Princeton U Pr.
Clot. James L. Tullis. (Illus.). 592p. 1976. 54.50 (ISBN 0-398-03298-X). C C Thomas.
Cloth. Albert Knox. (Easy-Read Fact Book Ser.). (Illus.). 48p. (gr. 2-4). 1976. PLB 4.47 o.p. (ISBN 0-531-00353-1). Watts.
Cloth, from Fiber to Fabric. Walter Buehr. (Illus.). (gr. 5-9). 1965. PLB 6.96 (ISBN 0-688-31176-8). Morrow.
Clothes. Shirley Hughes. (Illus.). (ps). 1979. 1.25 (ISBN 0-370-02039-1, Pub. by Chatto Bodley Jonathan). Merrimack Bk Serv.
Clothes & Ornaments. Stephanie Thompson. LC 78-64657. (Fact Finders Ser.). (Illus.). 1979. lib. bdg. 3.96 (ISBN 0-686-51126-3). Silver.
Clothes & Your Appearance. Louise A. Liddell. LC 80-25167. (Illus.). 1981. text ed. 12.80 (ISBN 0-87006-311-1). Goodheart.
Clothes & Your Appearance. rev. ed. Louise A. Liddell. LC 80-25167. (Illus.). 352p. 1980. 13.20 (ISBN 0-87006-311-1). Good Heart.
Clothes & Your Appearance. rev. ed. Louise A. Liddell. LC 80-25167. (Illus.). 352p. 1981. text ed. 13.20 (ISBN 0-87006-311-1). Goodheart.
Clothes Make Magic. 2nd, rev. ed. Emmi Cotten. Ed. by Bargyla Rateaver & Gylver Rateaver. LC 79-55932. (Conservation Gardening & Farming Ser. C: The Home). (Illus.). 223p. (gr. 9-10). 1980. pap. 10.00 (ISBN 0-915966-00-X). Rateavers.
Clothes, on & off the Stage: A History of Dress from the Earliest Times to the Present Day. Helena Chalmers. LC 73-180965. (Illus.). xx, 292p. 1976. Repr. of 1928 ed. 22.00 (ISBN 0-8103-4033-X). Gale.
Clothes: Their Choosing, Making & Care. Margaret G. Butler. 1978. 25.50 (ISBN 0-7134-2700-0, Pub. by Batsford England); pap. 13.50 (ISBN 0-7134-3035-4). David & Charles.
Clothing Construction. 2nd ed. Evelyn A. Mansfield & Ethel G. Lucas. 454p. 1974. text ed. 18.95 (ISBN 0-395-16728-0). HM.
Clothing for the Handicapped, the Aged & Other People with Special Needs. Adeline M. Hoffman. (Illus.). 212p. 1979. text ed. 14.75 (ISBN 0-398-03860-0). C C Thomas.
Clothing for Young Men. D. Lyle. LC 78-135579. 1970. pap. 2.50 (ISBN 0-686-00148-6, 261-08302). Home Econ Educ.
Clothing Language. Jim Richey. (Survival Vocabulary Ser.). (Illus.). 48p. (gr. 7-12). 1979. pap. text ed. 2.45 (ISBN 0-915510-33-2). Janus Bks.
Clotilda. Jack Kent. LC 69-17438. (Illus.). (ps-2). 1978. 3.95 (ISBN 0-394-83911-0); PLB 4.99 (ISBN 0-394-93911-5). Random.
Clotilda's Magic. Kent. (ps-3). 1980. pap. 1.50 (ISBN 0-590-31247-2, Schol Pap). Schol Bk Serv.
Cloture of Notre-Dame & Its Role in the 14th Century Choir Program. Dorothy Gillerman. LC 76-23623. (Outstanding Dissertations in the Fine Arts - 2nd Series - Medieval). (Illus.). 1977. Repr. of 1973 ed. lib. bdg. 57.00 (ISBN 0-8240-2693-4). Garland Pub.
Cloud. G. A. Pottebaum. (Little People's Paperbacks Ser.). 1979. pap. 0.99 (ISBN 0-8164-2245-1). Crossroad NY.
Cloud Book. Julian May. Ed. by Publication Associates. LC 76-156056. (Investigating the Earth Ser). (Illus.). (gr. 4-6). 1972. PLB 5.95 o.p. (ISBN 0-87191-064-0). Creative Ed.
Cloud Catchers. Ursula Holden. 224p. 1981. pap. 2.25 (ISBN 0-523-41272-X). Pinnacle Bks.
Cloud Chamber. Howard Myers. 1977. pap. 1.50 o.p. (ISBN 0-445-03215-4). Popular Lib.
Cloud Messenger: Translated from the Sanskrit Meghaduta. bilingual ed. Kalidasa. Tr. by Franklin Edgerton & Eleanor Edgerton. (Sanskrit & Eng.). 1964. pap. 1.75 o.p. (ISBN 0-472-06087-2, 87, AA). U of Mich Pr.
Cloud of Unknowing. Ed. by James Walsh. (Classics of Western Spirituality Ser.). 1981. 11.95 (ISBN 0-8091-0314-1); pap. 7.95 (ISBN 0-8091-2332-0). Paulist Pr.
Cloud of Unknowing & the Book of Privy Counselling. Ed. by Johnston, William, S.J. LC 73-79737. 200p. 1973. pap. 2.95 (ISBN 0-385-03097-5, Im). Doubleday.
Cloudburst of Math Lab Experiments. Donald A. Buckeye et al. Incl. Vol. 1, Elementary. pap. o.p. (ISBN 0-910974-29-2); Vol. 2, Upper Elementary. pap. 6.95 (ISBN 0-910974-30-6); o.p. (ISBN 0-910974-60-8); Vol. 3, Junior High School. pap. 6.95 (ISBN 0-910974-61-6); o.p. (ISBN 0-910974-31-4); Vol. 4, High School. pap. 3.95 (ISBN 0-910974-32-2); card form o.p. 16.00 (ISBN 0-910974-62-4); Vol. 5, Lower College. pap. o.p. (ISBN 0-910974-40-3). tchrs. manual 3.50 (ISBN 0-910974-33-0). Midwest Pubns.
Cloudburst Two. Vic Marks. (Illus.). 1975. lib. bdg. 11.95 (ISBN 0-88930-009-7, Pub. by Cloudburst Canada); pap. 5.95 (ISBN 0-88930-010-0). Madrona Pubs.
Cloudcry. Sydney J. Van Scyoc. LC 76-49828. 1977. 7.95 o.p. (ISBN 0-399-11947-7, Pub. by Berkley Pub). Berkley Pub.
Clouded Lens: Persian Gulf Security & U.S. Policy. James H. Noyes. Ed. by Richard F. Staar. LC 78-70390. 1979. pap. 6.95 (ISBN 0-8179-7062-2). Hoover Inst Pr.
Clouds. Aristophanes. Ed. & tr. by Peter D. Arnott. Bd. with Pot of Gold. Plautus. LC 67-17194. (Crofts Classics Ser.). 1967. pap. text ed. 2.95x (ISBN 0-88295-005-3). AHM Pub.
Clouds & the Sea. Richard D. Cagg. (Illus.). 80p. 1980. pap. 4.00. Cagg.
Clouds & the Sea. Richard D. Cagg. 80p. 1980. pap. 4.00 (ISBN 0-9605636-0-1). Cagg.
Clouds & the Sea. Richard D. Cagg. LC 80-67080. Date not set. write for info. Cagg.
Clouds Blowing Away. James Grabill & Douglas Fiely. 1977. pap. 2.00 o.p. (ISBN 0-87711-093-X). Kayak.
Clouds of the World: A Complete Color Encyclopedia. Richard Scorer. 42.50 o.p. (ISBN 0-7153-5485-X). David & Charles.
Cloudy Day. Jane Stroschin. LC 79-65792. (Illus.). 56p. (ps-2). 1979. 7.95 (ISBN 0-89526-099-9). Regnery-Gateway.
Clough: The Critical Heritage. Ed. by Michael Thorpe. 1972. 34.00 (ISBN 0-7100-7156-6). Routledge & Kegan.
Clout. Don Gibbons. 1974. pap. 1.95 o.s.i. (ISBN 0-380-00005-9, 28126). Avon.
Clovis Crawfish & the Singing Cigales. Mary A. Fontenot. 48p. 1981. 6.95 (ISBN 0-88289-270-3). Pelican.
Clown. Heinrich Boll. 1975. pap. 2.25 (ISBN 0-380-00333-3, 37523, Bard). Avon.
Clown Book. Jeri S. Slevin. (Golden Book for Early Childhood Ser.). 24p. (ps-3). 1980. PLB 4.60 o.p. (ISBN 0-307-68993-X, Golden Pr). Western Pub.
Clown: For Circus & Stage. Mark Stolzenberg. LC 80-54337. (Illus.). 1981. 12.95 (ISBN 0-8069-7034-0); lib. bdg. 11.69 (ISBN 0-8069-7035-9). Sterling.
Clown in the Moonlight. James H. Kunstler. 256p. 1981. 10.95 (ISBN 0-312-14495-4). St Martin.
Clown Mania. Ed Radlauer & Ruth Radlauer. LC 80-21826. (Mania Bks). (Illus.). 32p. (gr. k-4). 1981. PLB 7.95g (ISBN 0-516-07783-X, Elk Grove Bks). Childrens.
Clown of God. DePaola. (Illus.). (gr. 2-3). Date not set. pap. cancelled (ISBN 0-590-30068-7, Schol Pap). Schol Bk Serv.
Clowns. John Towsen. LC 75-41793. (Illus.). 1978. pap. 6.95 (ISBN 0-8015-3963-3, Hawthorn). Dutton.
Clowns: The Fun Makers. Mel Boring. LC 80-17193. (Illus.). 128p. (gr. 7 up). 1980. PLB 8.29 (ISBN 0-671-33059-4). Messner.
Cloze Stories for Reading Success. Helen Shangold. (gr. k-3). 1981. 13.50 (ISBN 0-8027-9124-7). Walker & Co.
Club. Steven Gaines & Robert J. Cohen. 288p. 1980. pap. 2.50 (ISBN 0-553-13746-8). Bantam.
Club Foot. Association of Bone & Joint Surgeons. Ed. by Marshall R. Urist & Anthony F. De Palma. (Clinical Orthopaedics & Related Research Ser. No. 84). (Illus.). 1972. 12.00 o.p. (ISBN 0-685-24745-7); new subscribers 8.00 o.p. (ISBN 0-685-24746-5). Lippincott.
Club Foot. Vincent J. Turco. (Illus.). 1981. text ed. price not set (ISBN 0-443-08033-X). Churchill.
Club Management Operations. Club Managers Association & Horace G. Duncan. 320p. (Orig.). 1980. text ed. 19.95 (ISBN 0-8403-2188-0). Kendall-Hunt.
Club Motor Racing. Jim Gavin. 1977. 17.95 (ISBN 0-7134-0893-6, Pub. by Batsford England). David & Charles.
Club of Life. Jerome Ellison. LC 80-18444. 1980. pap. 7.95 (ISBN 0-8298-0410-2). Pilgrim NY.
Club Operations & Management. Ted White. LC 79-11864. (Illus.). 1979. text ed. 15.95 (ISBN 0-8436-0783-1). CBI Pub.
Club Woman As Feminist: True Womanhood Redefined, 1868 to 1914. Karen Blair. LC 79-26390. 1980. text ed. 29.50x (ISBN 0-8419-0538-X). Holmes & Meier.
Clubfoot. Wallace B. Lehman. (Illus.). 114p. 1980. 27.50 (ISBN 0-397-50457-8). Lippincott.
Clubs & Club Life in London with Anecodotes of Its Famous Coffee-Houses, Hostelries, & Taverns from the Seventeenth Century to the Present Time. John Timbs. LC 66-28045. 1967. Repr. of 1872 ed. 15.00 (ISBN 0-8103-3262-0). Gale.
Clubwoman's Manual. K. M. Monro & I. S. Monro. 1957. 5.95 o.s.i. (ISBN 0-02-585570-0). Macmillan.
Clue of the Old Sea Chest. Bernard Palmer. LC 80-65060. (Powell Family Ser.). 160p. (Orig.). (gr. 7-10). 1981. pap. 2.25 (ISBN 0-89636-051-2). Accent Bks.
Clue to Romance. Florence Faulkner. 192p. (YA) 1976. 4.95 o.p. (ISBN 0-685-59252-9, Avalon). Bouregy.
Clues & Clocks. (Reading Basics Plus Ser.). (gr. 3). 1976. 9.08 (ISBN 0-06-517014-8, SchDept); tchr's ed. 15.92 (ISBN 0-06-517212-4); 2.96 (ISBN 0-06-517309-0); tchr's wkbk. 6.60 (ISBN 0-06-517455-0). Har-Row.
Clues in the Woods. Peggy Parish. LC 68-20607. (Illus.). (gr. 2-4). 1968. 8.95g (ISBN 0-02-769880-7); pap. 1.25 (ISBN 0-02-769880-7). Macmillan.
Clues in the Woods. Peggy Parish. LC 68-20607. 128p. (gr. 2-4). 1972. pap. 1.25 o.s.i. (ISBN 0-02-044860-0, Collier). Macmillan.
Clues to Creativity, Vol. 2: J-P. M. Franklin & Maryann J. Dotts. (Orig.). 1975. pap. 4.50 (ISBN 0-377-00041-8). Friend Pr.
Clues to Suicide. Ed. by Edwin S. Shneidman & Norman L. Farberow. 1957. pap. 4.95 (ISBN 0-07-056981-9, SP). McGraw.
CLUG: Community Land Use Game. Allan Feldt. LC 78-190151. Orig. Title: Clug Players Manual. 1972. pap. text ed. 8.95 (ISBN 0-02-910090-9). Free Pr.
Clumpets Go Sailing. Jan Wahl. LC 73-23083. (Illus.). (ps-3). 1975. 5.95 o.s.i. (ISBN 0-8193-0770-X, Four Winds); PLB 5.41 o.s.i. (ISBN 0-8193-0771-8). Schol Bk Serv.
Clumsy Child. Sasson S. Gubbay. LC 75-12487. (MPN: Vol. 5). (Illus.). 275p. 1975. text ed. 20.00 (ISBN 0-7216-4340-X). Saunders.
Clumsy Child: A Program of Motor Therapy. 2nd ed. Daniel D. Arnheim & William A. Sinclair. LC 78-2. (Illus.). 1979. pap. 12.00 (ISBN 0-8016-0310-2). Mosby.
Cluster Analysis. 2nd ed. Brian Everitt. 136p. 1980. pap. 16.95x (ISBN 0-470-26991-X). Halsted Pr.
Cluster Analysis Algorithms: For Data Reduction & Classification of Objects. H. Spath. (Computers & Their Applications). 226p. 1980. 56.95x (ISBN 0-470-26946-4). Halsted Pr.
Cluster College. Jerry Gaff et al. LC 77-110641. (Higher Education Ser.). 1970. 12.95x o.p. (ISBN 0-87589-062-8). Jossey-Bass.
Cluster Headache: Mechanisms & Management. Lee Kudrow. (Illus.). 200p. 1980. text ed. 29.50x (ISBN 0-19-261169-0). Oxford U Pr.
Cluster Headache: Mechanisms & Management. Lee Kudrow. (Illus.). 200p. 1981. 29.50 (ISBN 0-19-261169-0). Oxford U Pr.

Clustering Algorithms. J. A. Hartigan. LC 74-14573. (Wiley Series in Probability & Mathematical Statistics). 368p. 1975. 28.50 (ISBN 0-471-35645-X, Pub. by Wiley-Interscience). Wiley.

Clustering Phenomena in Nuclei. (Illus., Orig.). 1969. pap. 20.00 (ISBN 92-0-130269-X, IAEA). Unipub.

Clutch of Constables. Ngaio Marsh. (Ngaio Marsh Mystery Ser.). 1981. pap. 2.25 (ISBN 0-515-06013-5). Jove Pubns.

Clutch of Fables. 4th ed. Teo Savory. LC 73-76686. (Illus.). 80p. 1976. 12.00 (ISBN 0-87775-043-2); pap. 4.00 (ISBN 0-87775-104-8). Unicorn Pr.

Clutch of Vipers. Jack S. Scott. 192p. 1981. pap. 1.95 (ISBN 0-445-04632-5). Popular Lib.

Clyde Baker's Modern Gunsmithing. John Traister. (Illus.). 544p. 1981. 19.95 (ISBN 0-8117-0983-3). Stackpole.

Clyde Company Papers. Ed. by Philip L. Brown. Incl. Vol. 2. 1836-40. 1952. 8.00x (ISBN 0-19-711411-3); Vol. 5. 1851-53. 1963. 11.25x (ISBN 0-19-711594-2); Vol. 6. 1854-58. 1968. 12.00x (ISBN 0-19-711627-2); Vol. 6. 1854-58. 1968. 12.00x (ISBN 0-19-711627-2). Oxford U Pr.

Clyde Puffer. Dan McDonald. LC 77-76092. 1977. 10.50 (ISBN 0-7153-7443-5). David & Charles.

Clyfford Still. Ed. by John P. O'Neill. (Illus.). 222p. 1979. text ed. 22.50 (ISBN 0-87099-213-9, MPL D1965); pap. write for info. (ISBN 0-87099-214-7). Metro Mus Art.

CM: The Construction Management Process. Adrian. (Illus.). 368p. 1981. text ed. 18.95 (ISBN 0-8359-0829-1). Reston.

CMA, 6 vols. Grant W. Newton. Incl. Vol. 1. Economics & Business. 177p. pap. text ed. 18.50 scp (ISBN 0-06-453723-4); Vol. 2. Organization & Behavior, Including Ethical Considerations. 123p. pap. text ed. 14.95 scp (ISBN 0-06-453729-3); Vol. 3. Public Reporting Standards & Auditing. 201p. pap. text ed. 18.50 scp (ISBN 0-06-453730-7); Vol. 4. Periodic Reporting for Internal & External Purposes. 260p. pap. text ed. 18.50 scp (ISBN 0-06-453731-5); Vol. 5. Decision Analysis, Including Modeling & Information Systems. 246p. pap. text ed. 19.50 scp (ISBN 0-06-453732-3); Vol. 6. Taxes Current Pronouncements, & Updated CMA Questions. 1980. pap. text ed. 18.50 scp (ISBN 0-06-453742-0). pap. (HarpC). Har-Row.

CME Casebook of Electrocardiographic Tracings. Jorge I. Martinez-Lopez. 1981. write for info. (ISBN 0-88416-307-5). PSG Pub.

CMOS Databook. William Hunter. (Illus.). 1978. 9.95 (ISBN 0-8306-7984-7); pap. 8.95 (ISBN 0-8306-6984-1, 984). TAB Bks.

Co-Determination in Business: Workers Representatives in the Boardroom. Robert J. Kuhne. LC 79-21415. (Praeger Special Study Ser.). (Illus.). 1980. 19.95 (ISBN 0-03-052386-9). Praeger.

Co-Financing for Development: Why Not More? Roger S. Leeds. LC 80-80117. (Development Papers Ser.: No. 92). 64p. 1980. pap. 3.00 (ISBN 0-686-28119-5). Overseas Dev Council.

Co-Ge-We-a, the Half-Blood: A Depiction of the Great Montana Cattle Range. Hum-Ishu-Ma. xviii, 320p. 1981. pap. 6.25 (ISBN 0-8032-8110-2, BB 754, Bison). U of Nebr Pr.

Co-Operation Between the Sexes: Writings on Women, Love & Marriage Sexuality, & Its Disorders. Ed. by Alfred Adler. LC 76-23804. 1978. pap. 3.95 (ISBN 0-385-09562-7, Anch). Doubleday.

Co-Operative Farmer & Welfare State: Economic Change in an Israeli Moshav. Jay S. Abarbanel. (Illus.). 231p. 1974. text ed. 18.25x (ISBN 0-7190-0573-6). Humanities.

Co-Operatives & Community. David H. Wright. 118p. 1979. pap. text ed. 8.75x (ISBN 0-7199-0952-X, Pub. by Bedford England). Renouf.

Coach Cabbage & Caboose. 34.95. Chatham Pub CA.

Coach Tom Cahill: Man for the Corps. Gordon White & Merv Hyman. (Illus.). (gr. 7 up). 1969. 5.95 o.s.i. (ISBN 0-02-626510-9). Macmillan.

Coach Trimming: Part One, 2 vols. Ed. by G. Mortimer et al. (Engineering Craftsmen: No. E3). (Illus.). 1969. Set. spiral bdg. 36.50x set (ISBN 0-85083-041-9). Intl Ideas.

Coach Trimming: Part Two. Ed. by G. Mortimer et al. (Engineering Craftsmen: No. E23). (Illus.). 1970. spiral bdg. 26.00x (ISBN 0-85083-124-5). Intl Ideas.

Coaches. Robert Armstrong. (Stars of the NBA Ser.). (Illus.). (gr. 4-12). 1977. PLB 7.95 (ISBN 0-87191-566-9). Creative Ed.

Coaches. Sam Hasegawa. LC 74-23422. (Stars of the NFL Ser.). (gr. 4-12). 1975. PLB 7.95 (ISBN 0-87191-421-2). Creative Ed.

Coaches' Collection of Soccer Drills. John A. Reeves & J. Malcolm Simon. LC 80-84212. (Illus.). 96p. (Orig.). 1981. pap. text ed. 4.95 (ISBN 0-918438-63-2). Leisure Pr.

Coaches' Guide to Offensive Line Fundamentals & Techniques. Mike Poff. LC 80-83977. (Illus.). 160p. (Orig.). 1981. pap. text ed. 5.95 (ISBN 0-918438-62-4). Leisure Pr.

Coaching: A Management Skill for Improving Individual Performance. Arthur X. Deegan, 2nd. LC 79-619. 1979. pap. text ed. 8.95 (ISBN 0-201-01266-9). A-W.

Coaching Basketball: Ten Winning Concepts. Maryalyce Jeremiah. LC 78-12292. 1979. text ed. 18.50 (ISBN 0-471-04090-8). Wiley.

Coaching Girls & Women: Psychological Perspectives. Patsy Neal & Thomas A. Tutko. 224p. 1975. text ed. 12.95x o.p. (ISBN 0-205-04693-2). Allyn.

Coaching: Ideas & Ideals. Arthur J. Gallon. 400p. 1974. pap. text ed. 9.50 o.p. (ISBN 0-395-17624-7). HM.

Coaching: Ideas & Ideals. 2nd ed. Arthur J. Gallon. LC 79-90061. (Illus.). 1980. text ed. 10.95 (ISBN 0-395-28693-X). HM.

Coaching Methods for Women. 2nd ed. Patsy Neal. LC 77-77737. (Physical Education Ser.). (Illus.). 1978. text ed. 14.95 (ISBN 0-201-05228-8). A-W.

Coaching Modern Soccer: Attack. Eric Batty. (Illus.). 128p. 1980. 15.95 (ISBN 0-571-09840-1, Pub. by Faber & Faber); pap. 6.95 (ISBN 0-571-11605-1, Pub. by Faber & Faber). Merrimack Bk Serv.

Coaching Track & Field. William J. Bowerman. 1974. text ed. 18.25 (ISBN 0-395-17834-7). HM.

Coaching Winning Baseball. Dell Bethel. 1979. 14.95 o.p. (ISBN 0-8092-7460-4); pap. 7.95 (ISBN 0-8092-7459-0). Contemp Bks.

Coaching Winning Soccer. Willy Roy & Jim Walker. 1979. 12.95 o.p. (ISBN 0-8092-7458-2); pap. 6.95 (ISBN 0-8092-7457-4). Contemp Bks.

Coachmakers. Ed. by Harold Nockolds. (Illus.). 26.25 (ISBN 0-85131-270-5, Dist. by Sporting Book Center). J A Allen.

Coactive Guidance: A Blueprint for the Future. Daniel L. Ballast & Ronald L. Shoemaker. 200p. 1980. 19.95 (ISBN 0-398-04089-3). C C Thomas.

Coagulation & Stability of Disperse Systems. H. Sonntag & K. Strenge. 139p. 1972. 27.95 (ISBN 0-470-81350-4). Halsted Pr.

Coagulation Disorders in Obstetrics: Pathobiochemistry-Pathophysiology-Diagnosis-Treatment. H. Graeff & W. Kuhn. Tr. by A. Davis from Ger. LC 79-48020. (Major Problems in Obstetrics & Gynecology Ser.: No. 13). 1980. write for info. (ISBN 0-7216-4192-X). Saunders.

Coagulation: The Essentials. David P. Fischbach & Richard P. Fogdall. (Illus.). 200p. 1981. write for info. softcover (ISBN 0-683-03312-3). Williams & Wilkins.

Coal. Betsy H. Kraft. (First Books Ser.). (Illus.). 72p. (gr. 4-6). 1977. PLB 6.45 (ISBN 0-531-00336-1). Watts.

Coal Age Empire: Pennsylvania Coal & Its Utilization to 1860. Frederick M. Binder. LC 75-621822. 184p. 1974. 8.50 (ISBN 0-911124-75-6). Pa Hist & Mus.

Coal Age Operating Handbook of Underground Mining, Vol. II. 2nd ed. Coal Age Magazine. (Coal Age Ser.). (Illus.). 430p. 1980. 19.50 (ISBN 0-07-011461-7, P&RB). McGraw.

Coal & Canada-U.S. Energy Relations. Richard L. Gordon. LC 76-20420. 76p. 1976. 3.00 (ISBN 0-88806-017-3). Natl Planning.

Coal & Crisis: The Political Dilemma of Energy Management. Walter A. Rosenbaum. LC 78-8606. (Praeger Special Studies). 1978. 20.95 (ISBN 0-03-042596-4). Praeger.

Coal & Energy: The Need to Exploit the World's Most Abundant Fossil Fuel. Derek Ezra. LC 78-5785. 1978. 19.95 (ISBN 0-470-26339-3). Halsted Pr.

Coal & Tobacco. J. V. Beckett. (Illus.). 280p. 1981. 47.50 (ISBN 0-521-23486-7). Cambridge U Pr.

Coal As an Energy Resource: Conflict & Consensus. Academy Forum. 1977. pap. 11.00 (ISBN 0-309-02728-4). Natl Acad Pr.

Coal Bridge to the Future, Vol. 1. Ed. by Carroll L. Wilson. (World Coal Study: Vol. 1). 1980. 12.95 (ISBN 0-88410-099-5). Ballinger Pub.

Coal Burning Issues. Ed. by A. E. Green. LC 79-25376. (Illus.). x, 390p. (Orig.). 1980. pap. 10.00 (ISBN 0-8130-0667-8). U Presses Fla.

Coal Burning with Clean Emissions: F.G.D.(Flue Gas Desulfurization. 1981. price not set. Inform.

Coal Cleaning: Rediscovered for the Eighties. 1981. price not set. Inform.

Coal Comfort: An Alternative Way to Heat Your House. Peter Hotton. (Illus.). 128p. (Orig.). 1980. pap. 7.95 (ISBN 0-316-37388-5). Little.

Coal Conversion Technology. Ed. by C. Y. Wen & E. Stanley Lee. LC 79-12975. (Energy Science & Technology: No. 2). (Illus.). 1979. text ed. 32.50 (ISBN 0-201-08300-0). A-W.

Coal, Gas & Electricity Industries. D. J. Harris et al. (Reviews of United Kingdom Statistical Sources Ser.: Vol. XI). 1979. 55.00 (ISBN 0-08-022461-X). Pergamon.

Coal Handbook. Meyers. Date not set. price not set (ISBN 0-8247-1270-6). Dekker.

Coal Heat. Schuler & Hull. (Illus.). 128p. 10.95 (ISBN 0-916838-34-X); pap. 5.95 (ISBN 0-916838-37-4). Schiffer.

Coal Hoppy. Joan Tate. pap. text ed. 1.95x o.p. (ISBN 0-435-11872-2). Heinemann Ed.

Coal in the U.S. Energy Market. Richard L. Gordon. LC 77-14625. (Illus.). 1978. 19.95 (ISBN 0-669-01987-9). Lexington Bks.

Coal Information Sources & Data Bases. Carolyn C. Bloch. LC 80-22344. 128p. 1981. 24.00 (ISBN 0-8155-0830-1). Noyes.

Coal: It's Role in Tomorrow's Technology. C. Simeons. 1978. text ed. 105.00 (ISBN 0-08-022712-0). Pergamon.

Coal Liquefaction Fundamentals. Ed. by D. D. Whitehurst. LC 80-20585. (ACS Symposium Ser.: No. 139). 1980. 38.00 (ISBN 0-8412-0587-6). Am Chemical.

Coal Liquefaction: The Chemistry & Technology of Thermal Process. D. D. Whitehurst et al. 1980. 19.50 (ISBN 0-12-747080-8). Acad Pr.

Coal Metropolis: Cardiff 1870-1914. M. J. Daunton. 1977. text ed. 31.25x (ISBN 0-7185-1139-5, Leicester). Humanities.

Coal Mine Ground Control. Syd S. Peng. LC 78-8965. 1978. 32.95 (ISBN 0-471-04121-1, Pub. by Wiley-Interscience). Wiley.

Coal Mine Health & Safety: The Case of West Virginia. J. Davitt McAteer. LC 72-92460. (Special Studies in U.S. Economic, Social & Political Issues). 1973. 28.50x (ISBN 0-275-28693-2). Irvington.

Coal Mine, Number Seven. Robert L. Nathan. 320p. 1981. 12.95 (ISBN 0-312-14499-7). St Martin.

Coal Miner's Daughter. Loretta Lynn & George Vecsey. Orig. Title: Loretta Lynn: Coal Miner's Daughter. (Illus.). 1977. pap. 2.50 (ISBN 0-446-91477-0). Warner Bks.

Coal Miners' Struggle for Industrial Status. Arthur E. Suffern. (Brookings Institution Reprint Ser). lib. bdg. 28.50x (ISBN 0-697-00170-9); pap. 9.95x (ISBN 0-89197-703-1). Irvington.

Coal-Mining Safety in the Progressive Period: The Political Economy of Reform. William Graebner. LC 75-38215. 256p. 1976. 18.00x (ISBN 0-8131-1339-3). U Pr of Ky.

Coal: Nineteen Eighty-Five & Beyond - A Perspective Study. United Nations Economic Commission for Europe. LC 77-30437. 1978. pap. text ed. 25.00 (ISBN 0-08-022409-1). Pergamon.

Coal on the Switchback: The Coal Industry Since Nationalisation. Israel Berkovitch. 1977. text ed. 25.00x (ISBN 0-04-622002-X). Allen Unwin.

Coal Preperation. 4th ed. Ed. by Joseph W. Leonard. LC 79-52245. (Illus.). 1204p. 1979. text ed. 42.00x (ISBN 0-89520-258-1). Soc Mining Eng.

Coal: Social, Economics, & Environmental Aspects. Ed. by Mones E. Hawley. (Benchmark Papers on Energy: Pt. 1). 1976. 47.00 (ISBN 0-12-786641-8); Set. 41.00. Acad Pr.

Coal: The New Energy Source. Robert V. Nelson. Ed. by Arthur F. Ide. LC 79-9940. (E Equals M C Squared Ser.). (Illus.). 70p. (Orig.). 1981. 12.00 (ISBN 0-86663-804-0); pap. 7.50 (ISBN 0-86663-805-9). Ide Hse.

Coal Viewer & Engine Builder's Practical Companion. John Curr. LC 74-96376. (Illus.). Repr. of 1797 ed. lib. bdg. 19.50x (ISBN 0-678-05104-6). Kelley.

Coal Workers' Pneumoconiosis-Medical Considerations, Some Social Implications: Mineral Resources & the Environment Supplementary Report. Committee on Mineral Resources & the Environment, National Research Council. LC 75-39531. 149p. 1976. pap. 6.00 (ISBN 0-309-02424-2). Natl Acad Pr.

Coalbrookdale & the Iron Revolution: Introduction to the History of Mankind. Christine Vialls. LC 77-94224. (Illus.). 3.95 (ISBN 0-521-21672-9). Cambridge U Pr.

Coalition & Connection in Games. S. Guiasu & M. Malitza. 1980. text ed. 33.00 (ISBN 0-08-023033-4). Pergamon.

Coalition Bargaining. Philip J. Schwartz. (Key Issues Ser.: No. 5). 1970. pap. 2.00 (ISBN 0-87546-241-3). NY Sch Indus Rel.

Coalition Statement: Vocational Home Economics Education. 1979. 1.00 (ISBN 0-686-26996-9, A261-08436). Home Econ Educ.

Coarse Fishing. Ed. by Kenneth Mansfield. (Angler's Library). 1978. 7.50 o.p. (ISBN 0-214-65253-X, 8001, Dist. by Arco). Barrie & Jenkins.

Coarse Fishing. Harvey Torbett. 10.00x (ISBN 0-392-06501-0, SpS). Soccer.

Coarse Fishing As a Pastime. Kenneth Mansfield. 10.00x (ISBN 0-392-06496-0, SpS). Soccer.

Coarticulation Manual for the Remediation of -S- Maria A. Naughton. LC 78-61748. 1979. pap. 2.95x (ISBN 0-8134-2051-2, 2051). Interstate.

Coast & Estuary: Archaeological Coast of New South Wales at Wombah & Schnapper Point. Isabel McBryde. (Australian Institute of Aboriginal Studies). 1981. pap. text ed. write for info. (ISBN 0-391-02194-X). Humanities.

Coast Defences of England & Wales: 1856-1956. Ian V. Hogg. 1974. 8.95 (ISBN 0-7153-6353-0). David & Charles.

Coast of England & Wales in Pictures. James A. Steers. 1960. 26.95 (ISBN 0-521-06549-6); pap. 13.95 (ISBN 0-521-29274-3). Cambridge U Pr.

Coast of Fear. Caroline Crane. LC 80-26819. 224p. 1980. 8.95 (ISBN 0-396-07950-4). Dodd.

Coast of Maine. rev ed. Louise D. Rich. LC 75-6662. (Illus.). 385p. 1975. 9.95 o.s.i. (ISBN 0-690-00698-5, TYC-T); pap. 6.95 o.s.i. (ISBN 0-690-00957-7, TYC-T). T Y Crowell.

Coast of Many Faces. Ulli Steltzer & Catherine Kerr. LC 79-4916. (Illus.). 224p. 1979. 27.50 (ISBN 0-295-95689-5). U of Wash Pr.

Coast of Trees. A. R. Ammons. 1981. 12.95 (ISBN 0-393-01447-9); pap. 4.95 (ISBN 0-393-00051-6). Norton.

Coast Salish & Western Washington Indians, Vol. 2. Incl. Ethnological Field Investigation & Analysis of the Puget Sound Indians. Carroll L. Riley; Influence of White Contact on Class Distinctions & Political Authority Among the Indians of Northern Puget Sound. June McC. Collins; The Quileute Indians of Puget Sound. Indian Claims Commission et al; Anthropological Investigation of the Medicine Creek Tribes. Herbert C. Taylor et al; Historical & Ethnological Study of the Snohomish Indian People. Colin E. Tweddell. (American Indian Ethnohistory Ser: Indians of the Northwest). (Illus.). lib. bdg. 42.00 (ISBN 0-8240-0784-0). Garland Pub.

Coast Salish & Western Washington Indians, Vol. 3. Incl. Anthropological Investigation of Makah Indians. Herbert C. Taylor; History of the Neah Bay Agency. Alix J. Gillis; Ethnographic Material on the Quileute Indians: Lapush & Hoh. Arthur Howeattle et al; Anthropological Investigation of the Chehalis Indians. Herbert C. Taylor. o.p. (ISBN 0-685-38385-7); John Work on the Chehalis Indians. Herbert C. Taylor; Territorial Distribution of the Aboriginal Population of Western Washington State & the Economic & Political Characteristics of Their Culture. Jacob Fried; Handbook of Cowlitz Indians. Verne F. Ray. (American Indian Ethnohistory Ser: Indians of the Northwest). (Illus.). lib. bdg. 42.00 (ISBN 0-8240-0785-9). Garland Pub.

Coast Salish & Western Washington Indians, Vol. 4. Incl. Structure of Twana Culture. William W. Elmendorf; A Study of Religious Change Among the Skagit Indians. June M. Collins. (American Indian Ethnohistory Ser.: Indians of the Northwest). (Illus.). lib. bdg. 42.00 (ISBN 0-8240-0786-7). Garland Pub.

Coast Salish & Western Washington Indians, Vol. 1: The Economic Life of the Coast Salish of Haro & Rosario Straits. Wayne P. Suttles. (American Indian Ethnohistory Ser.: Indians of the Northwest). (Illus.). lib. bdg. 42.00 (ISBN 0-8240-0783-2). Garland Pub.

Coast Salish & Western Washington Indians, Vol. 5: Findings of Fact, & Opinion. Indian Claims Commission. (American Indian Ethnohistory Ser: Indians of the Northwest). (Illus.). lib. bdg. 42.00 (ISBN 0-8240-0787-5). Garland Pub.

Coastal Almanac: For 1980--the Year of the Coast. Paul L. Ringold & John Clark. LC 80-22501. (Geology Ser.). (Illus.). 1980. 19.95x (ISBN 0-7167-1285-7); pap. 9.95x (ISBN 0-7167-1286-5). W H Freeman.

Coastal & Offshore Environmental Inventory: Cape Hatteras to Nantucket Shoals. Ed. by Saul B. Saila. LC 72-619712. (Marine Publications Ser.). 1973. No. 2. pap. 10.00 (ISBN 0-938412-04-3); No. 3. pap. 5.00, complementary vol. (ISBN 0-686-09595-2). URI MAS.

Coastal Aquaculture Law & Policy: A Case Study of California. Gerald Bowden. (Special Studies in Agricultural Science & Policy). 300p. 1981. lib. bdg. 25.00x (ISBN 0-86531-108-0). Westview.

Coastal Ecology: Bodega Head. Michael G. Barbour et al. (Illus.). 1974. 15.00x (ISBN 0-520-02147-9); pap. 6.95x (ISBN 0-520-03276-4). U of Cal Pr.

Coastal Ecosystem Management: A Technical Manual for the Conservation of Coastal Zone Resources. John R. Clark. LC 76-40125. 1977. 55.00 (ISBN 0-471-15854-2, Pub by Wiley-Interscience). Wiley.

Coastal Energy Impact Program in Texas. Ian Manners. (Research Monograph: 1980-1). 1980. pap. 5.00 (ISBN 0-87755-241-X). U of Tex Busn Res.

Coastal Engineering: An Introduction to Ocean Engineering. K. Horikawa. 1978. 42.95 (ISBN 0-470-26449-7). Halsted Pr.
Coastal Engineering: Proceedings. Coastal Engineering International Conference, 11th, London, Sept. 1968. Compiled By American Society of Civil Engineers. 1624p. 1969. pap. 39.50 (ISBN 0-87262-013-1). Am Soc Civil Eng.
Coastal Engineering: Proceedings. Coastal Engineering International Conference, 12th, September, 1970. Compiled By American Society of Civil Engineers. 2484p. 1971. pap. text ed. 59.00 o.p. (ISBN 0-87262-028-X). Am Soc Civil Eng.
Coastal Engineering: Proceedings, 3 vols. Coastal Engineering International Conference, 16th, Hamburg, Germany, Aug. 1978. Compiled By American Society of Civil Engineers. 3096p. 1979. pap. text ed. 110.00 (ISBN 0-87262-190-1). Am Soc Civil Eng.
Coastal Features of England & Wales: Eight Essays. J. Alfred Steers. (Illus.). 240p. 1980. 35.00 (ISBN 0-900891-70-X). Oleander Pr.
Coastal Fishing for Beginners. Joseph J. Cook & William L. Wisner. LC 77-6488. (Illus.). (gr. 5 up). 1977. PLB 5.95 (ISBN 0-396-07487-1). Dodd.
Coastal Geomorphology. Ed. by Donald Coates. (Binghamton Symposia in Geomorphology International Ser.: No. 3). (Illus.). 416p. 1980. text ed. 20.00x (ISBN 0-04-551038-5, 2506). Allen Unwin.
Coastal Lagoons. R. S. Barnes. LC 80-40041. (Cambridge Studies in Modern Biology: No. 1). (Illus.). 130p. 1980. 29.50 (ISBN 0-521-23422-0); pap. 11.95 (ISBN 0-521-29945-4). Cambridge U Pr.
Coastal Landforms of Cat Island, Bahamas: A Study of Holocene Accretionary Topography & Sea Level Change. Aulis O. Lind. LC 76-77892. (Research Papers Ser.: No. 122). 156p. 1969. pap. 8.00 (ISBN 0-89065-029-2). U Chicago Dept Geog.
Coastal Navigation for Beginners. Jeff Toghill. (Illus.). 1976. pap. 5.25 (ISBN 0-589-07191-2, Dist. by C. E. Tuttle). Reed.
Coastal Navigation for Beginners. Jeff Toghill. 1980. pap. 7.95x (ISBN 0-8464-1001-X). Beekman Pubs.
Coastal North Carolina Picture Book. Aerial Photo. Date not set. 2.00 (ISBN 0-936672-10-2). Aerial Photo.
Coastal Resources Management: Beyond Bureaucracy & the Market. Robert B. Ditton et al. (Lexington Books Studies in Marine Affairs). 1977. 21.00 (ISBN 0-669-00970-9). Lexington Bks.
Coastal Sediments: Proceedings. ASCE Waterway, Port Coastal & Ocean Division Conference, Charleston, Nov. 1977. Compiled By American Society of Civil Engineers. 1100p. 1977. pap. text ed. 47.00 (ISBN 0-87262-090-5). Am Soc Civil Eng.
Coastal Structures, 2 vols. ASCE Conference, Alexandria, Mar. 1979. Compiled By American Society of Civil Engineers. 1232p. 1979. pap. text ed. 75.00 (ISBN 0-87262-149-9). Am Soc Civil Eng.
Coastal Zone Management: Multiple Use with Conservation. J. Peel Brahtz. LC 74-178141. (University of California Engineering & Physical Sciences Extension Ser.). 384p. 1972. 34.00 o.p. (ISBN 0-471-09575-3, Pub. by Wiley-Interscience). Wiley.
Coastal Zone: Proceedings. ASCE Conference, San Francisco, May 1978. Compiled By American Society of Civil Engineers. 3180p. 1978. pap. text ed. 118.00 (ISBN 0-87262-134-0). Am Soc Civil Eng.
Coastal Zone '80, 3 vols. Ed. by Billy L. Edge. LC 80-69152. 2470p. 1980. pap. text ed. 110.00 (ISBN 0-87262-258-4). Am Soc Civil Eng.
Coastline of Scotland. J. A. Steers. LC 72-86419. (Illus.). 384p. 1973. 74.50 (ISBN 0-521-08696-5). Cambridge U Pr.
Coastwise & Offshore Cruising Wrinkles. Thomas E. Colvin. (Illus.). 1979. pap. 4.00 (ISBN 0-915160-14-5). McKay.
Coastwise Navigation. Frances W. Wright. (Illus.). 1980. pap. 7.50 (ISBN 0-87033-260-0). Cornell Maritime.
Coat & Skirtmaking: A Step-by-Step Approach. Samuel Heath. 1979. 12.95x (ISBN 0-8464-0047-2). Beekman Pubs.
Coat of Many Colors. Barrie Stavis. LC 68-11075. 1968. 7.95 o.p. (ISBN 0-498-06819-6). A S Barnes.
Coat of Varnish. C. P. Snow. 1981. 5.95 (ISBN 0-684-16949-5). Scribner.
Coates Brothers: A History, 1877-1977. J. B. Coates. (Illus.). 103p. 1980. 28.50 (ISBN 0-913720-12-7). Sandstone.
Coatings for Corrosion Prevention. 1979. 28.00 (ISBN 0-87170-083-2). ASM.
Coats & Clark's Sewing Book. new ed. (Illus.). 288p. 1976. 8.95 o.p. (ISBN 0-307-09865-6, Golden Pr). Western Pub.
Coats Book of Lacecrafts: Crochet, Tatting, Knitting. Jean Kinmond. (Illus.). 1980. 19.95 (ISBN 0-7134-0783-2, Pub. by Batsford England). David & Charles.
Cobalt, Vol. 6. Ed. by Ivan C. Smith & Bonnie L. Carson. LC 77-88486. (Trace Metals in the Environment Ser.). 1981. 49.50 (ISBN 0-250-40362-5). Ann Arbor Science.
Cobble Stone Gardens. William Burroughs. LC 76-40473. (Illus.). 1976. pap. 3.00x o.p. (ISBN 0-916156-14-1). Cherry Valley.
Cobbler in Congress: The Life of Henry Wilson, 1812-1875. Richard H. Abbott. LC 70-147856. (Illus.). 308p. 1972. 17.00x (ISBN 0-8131-1249-4). U Pr of Ky.
Cobbler's Reward. Barbara Reid & Ewa Reid. LC 78-4638. (Illus.). (gr. k-3). 1978. 8.95 (ISBN 0-02-775800-1, 77580). Macmillan.
Cobblestone Landmarks of New York State. Olaf W. Shelgren, Jr. et al. 1978. 12.95 o.p. (ISBN 0-8156-2201-5); pap. 7.95 o.p. (ISBN 0-8156-0149-2). Syracuse U Pr.
Cobol: A Self-Instructional Manual. 2nd ed. James A. Saxon. 1971. pap. 13.95 ref. ed. (ISBN 0-13-139469-X). P-H.
Cobol: A Simplified Approach. Seymour C. Hirsch. LC 73-13879. (Illus.). 160p. 1974. 8.95 (ISBN 0-87909-128-2). Reston.
Cobol: A Vehicle for Information Systems. R. Grauer. 1981. 18.95 (ISBN 0-13-139709-5). P-H.
Cobol: An Introduction. Thomas C. Richards. (Data Processing Ser.). 350p. 1981. pap. text ed. 12.95 (ISBN 0-675-08041-X). Merrill.
Cobol: An Introduction to Structured Logic & Modular Program Design. William S. Davis & Richard H. Fisher. 1979. pap. 13.95 (ISBN 0-201-01431-9); instrs'. manual 2.95 (ISBN 0-686-67461-8). A-W.
Cobol Book of Practice & Reference. Robert T. Grauer. (P-H Software Ser.). (Illus.). 352p. 1981. pap. text ed. 15.95 (ISBN 0-13-139717-6). P-H.
Cobol Demand Processing Manual. James D. Chappell. 80p. 1981. pap. text ed. 6.95 (ISBN 0-8403-2376-X). Kendall-Hunt.
Cobol for Beginners. Thomas Worth. (Illus.). 1977. pap. text ed. 13.95 (ISBN 0-13-139378-2). P-H.
Cobol for Small & Medium Sized Computers. Asad Khailany & Claude Duplissey. LC 75-23647. (Illus.). 400p. 1976. pap. text ed. 15.25 (ISBN 0-395-18921-7). HM.
Cobol Logic & Programming. 3rd ed. Fritz A. McCameron. 1974. pap. text ed. 10.95 (ISBN 0-256-01581-3). Irwin.
COBOL Programming & Applications. C. Joseph Sass. 1978. text ed. 15.95x (ISBN 0-205-06550-3); solutions man. avail. (ISBN 0-205-06552-X). Allyn.
COBOL with Style: Programming Proverbs. Henry F. Ledgard & Louis J. Chmura, Jr. (Computer Programming Ser.). 1976. pap. text ed. 8.35x (ISBN 0-8104-5781-4). Hayden.
Cobra in the Sky: The Supersonic Transport. Edward A. Herron. LC 68-22123. (World in the Making Ser). (Illus.). (gr. 7-10). 1968. 3.95g o.s.i. (ISBN 0-02-743690-X, CCPr). Macmillan.
Cobra in the Tub. Annie Mueser. (Pal Paperbacks, - Pal Skills II Ser.). (Illus.). (gr. 5-12). 1980. pap. 1.25 (ISBN 0-8374-6810-8). Xerox Ed Pubns.
Cobra Team. Robin Moore & Edward E. Mayer. 352p. 1981. pap. 2.75 (ISBN 0-441-11289-7). Charter Bks.
Cobweb Across the Moon. Catherine Darby. (The Moon Chalice Quest: No. 5). 1978. pap. 1.50 o.p. (ISBN 0-445-04143-9). Popular Lib.
Cobweb Attitudes: Essays on Educational & Cultural Mythology. Colin Greer. LC 76-94368. 1970. pap. text ed. 4.75x (ISBN 0-8077-1468-2). Tchrs Coll.
Cocaine & Blue Eyes. Fred Zachel. 1979. pap. 2.25 o.p. (ISBN 0-425-04456-4). Berkley Pub.
Cocaine Handbook. David Lee. 192p. 1981. price not set. And-or Pr.
Cocaine: Its History, Uses & Effects. Richard Ashley. 240p. 1976. pap. 2.75 (ISBN 0-446-95978-2). Warner Bks.
Cocaine: The Mystique & the Reality. Joel Phillips & Ronald D. Wynne. 1980. pap. 3.50 (ISBN 0-380-48678-4, 48678, Discus). Avon.
Cochin-China: Containing Many Admirable Rarities of That Countrey. Christoforo Borri. LC 71-25710. (English Experience Ser.: No. 223). 1970. Repr. of 1633 ed. 9.50 (ISBN 90-221-0223-8). Walter J Johnson.
Cochiti: New Mexico Pueblo, Past & Present. Charles H. Lange. LC 58-10852. (Illus.). 642p. 1968. lib. bdg. 14.95x (ISBN 0-8093-0295-0). S Ill U Pr.
Cochiti: New Mexico Pueblo, Past & Present. Charles H. Lange. LC 58-10852. (Arcturus Books Paperbacks). (Illus.). 642p. pap. 11.95 (ISBN 0-8093-0296-9). S Ill U Pr.
Cochran Family Book of Ski Racing. Mickey Cochran & Bill Bruns. LC 77-79914. (Illus.). 1977. 8.95 o.p. (ISBN 0-8015-1371-5). Dutton.
Cochran's German Review Grammar. 3rd ed. Jonathan B. Conant. LC 73-21535. 384p. 1974. text ed. 13.95 (ISBN 0-13-139501-7). P-H.
Cochran's Law Dictionary. Wesley Gilmer. LC 72-95860. 1978. pap. text ed. 6.00 (ISBN 0-87084-147-5). Anderson Pub Co.
Cock-A-Doodle-Doo. Berta Hader & Elmer Hader. (gr. 1-3). 1939. 5.95g o.s.i. (ISBN 0-02-738030-0). Macmillan.
Cock-a-Hoop. Ed. by David Chambers & Christopher Sandford. LC 76-10113. (Illus.). 128p. 1976. 15.00 o.p. (ISBN 0-498-01986-1); ltd. ed 50.00 o.p. (ISBN 0-498-01987-X). A S Barnes.
Cock & the Anchor: Being a Chronicle of Old Dublin City. Joseph S. Le Fanu. (Nineteenth Century Fiction Ser.: Ireland: Vol. 59). 1036p. 1979. lib. bdg. 46.00 (ISBN 0-8240-3508-9). Garland Pub.
Cockatiels. Nancy Curtis. (Orig.). pap. 2.50 (ISBN 0-87666-420-6, M517). TFH Pubns.
Cockatiels. Cyril H. Rogers. (Illus.). 80p. 1981. 3.95 (ISBN 0-903264-26-9, 5212-0, Pub. by K & R Bks England). Arco.
Cockatiels. Laura M. Tartak. (Illus.). 96p. 2.95 (ISBN 0-87666-885-6, KW-057). TFH Pubns.
Cockatoos, Taming & Training. Risa Teitler. (Illus.). 96p. 1980. 2.95 (ISBN 0-87666-888-0, KW-071). TFH Pubns.
Cocker Spaniel Guide. Hilary Harmar. 6.98 o.p. (ISBN 0-385-01653-0). Doubleday.
Cocker Spaniel Handbook. Ernest H. Hart. text ed. 9.95 (ISBN 0-87666-270-X, H923). TFH Pubns.
Cocker Spaniel: It's Care & Training. Kay Doxford. (Illus.). 100p. 1980. 3.95 (ISBN 0-903264-29-3, 4946-4, Pub. by K & R Bks England). Arco.
Cocker Spaniels. Bert King. (Illus.). 1979. 2.95 (ISBN 0-87666-692-6, KW-043). TFH Pubns.
Cockeyed Americana. Dick Hyman. LC 72-81526. 1972. 6.95 (ISBN 0-8289-0170-8). Greene.
Cockney Dialect. Peter Wright. 192p. 1981. 22.50 (ISBN 0-7134-2242-4, Pub. by Batsford England). David & Charles.
Cockney Past & Present: A Short History of the Dialect of London. William Matthews. LC 68-30638. 1970. Repr. of 1938 ed. 15.00 (ISBN 0-8103-3609-X). Gale.
Cockroach Combat Manual. Austin M. Frishman & Arthur P. Schwartz. LC 80-288. (Illus.). 1980. 9.95 (ISBN 0-688-03613-9, Quill); pap. 4.95 (ISBN 0-688-08613-6). Morrow.
Cockroaches: Here, There & Everywhere. Laurence Pringle. LC 79-132301. (Let's-Read & Find-Out Science Bk). (Illus.). (gr. k-3). 1971. PLB 7.89 (ISBN 0-690-19680-6, TYC-J). T Y Crowell.
Cocktail Book. Michael Walker. (Orig.). 1980. pap. 4.95 (ISBN 0-89586-069-4). H P Bks.
Cocktail Party Cookbook & Guide. Indiana University School of Medicine Faculty Women's Club. Ed. by Barbara Mealey. LC 76-12382. (Illus.). 256p. 1977. 7.95x (ISBN 0-253-11235-4). Ind U Pr.
Cocktails at Somoza's: A Reporter's Sketchbook of Events in Revolutionary Nicaragua. Richard Elman. 196p. 1981. 10.95 (ISBN 0-918222-28-1). Apple Wood.
Cocoa, Custom, & Socio-Economic Change in Rural Western Nigeria. Sara S. Berry. (Oxford Studies in African Affairs Ser). (Illus.). 256p. 1975. 37.50x (ISBN 0-19-821697-1). Oxford U Pr.
Cocoa Production: Economic & Botanical Perspectives. Ed. by John Simmons. LC 75-19821. (Special Studies). 1976. text ed. 44.50 (ISBN 0-275-56030-9). Praeger.
Coconut, the Tree of Life. Carolyn Meyer. LC 76-22673. (Illus.). 96p. (gr. 5-9). 1976. 7.25 (ISBN 0-688-22084-3); PLB 6.96 (ISBN 0-688-32084-8). Morrow.
Coconuts. 2nd ed. Reginald Child. (Tropical Agriculture Ser.). (Illus.). 1974. text ed. 33.00x o.p. (ISBN 0-582-46675-X). Longman.
Coconuts: Production, Processing, Products. 2nd ed. Jasper G. Woodroof. (Illus.). 1979. lib. bdg. 28.50 (ISBN 0-87055-276-7). AVI.
Cocoon. Cheryl A. Baxter. 90p. 1980. 4.95 (ISBN 0-87747-830-9). Deseret Bk.
Cocorrections: A Case Study of a Coed Federal Prison. rev. ed. John O. Smykla. LC 79-64719. 1979. pap. text ed. 5.75 (ISBN 0-8191-0767-0). U Pr of Amer.
Coco's Candy Shop. V. Gilbert Beers. 32p. (gr. 3-6). 1973. 4.95 (ISBN 0-8024-1586-5). Moody.
Cocteau: Five Plays. Jean Cocteau. Incl. Eagle with Two Heads; Antigone; Orphee; Intimate Relations; Holy Terrors. (Orig.). 1961. pap. 5.25 o.p. (ISBN 0-8090-0722-3, Mermaid). Hill & Wang.
Coda Alliance. Michael Brady. (Orig.). Date not set. pap. 2.50 (ISBN 0-440-11415-2). Dell.
CODASYL Approach to Data Base Management. T. W. Olle. 287p. 1978. 26.95 (ISBN 0-471-99579-7, 1-320). Wiley.
Code & Cipher Book. Jane Sarnoff & Reynold Ruffins. LC 74-24419. (Illus.). 40p. (gr. 1-5). 1975. reinforced bdg. 8.95 (ISBN 0-684-14246-5, ScribJ); pap. 2.95 (ISBN 0-684-16219-9, SL 869, ScribJ). Scribner.
Code Arrest: A Heart Stops. E. B. Dietrich & J. J. Fried. 1975. pap. 1.50 o.s.i. (ISBN 0-515-03797-4). Jove Pubns.
Code Cases Book: Boilers & Pressure Vessels. (Boiler & Pressure Vessel Code Ser.). 1977. pap. 70.00 loose-leaf o.p. (ISBN 0-685-76835-X, W00120). ASME.
Code Cases Book: Boilers & Pressure Vessels. (Boiler & Pressure Vessel Code Ser.). 1980. pap. 100.00 loose-leaf (V00120). ASME.
Code Cases Book: Boilers & Pressure Vessels. (Boilers & Pressure Vessel Code Ser.). 1980. pap. 100.00 loose-leaf (V00120). ASME.
Code Cases Book: Nuclear Components. (Boilers & Pressure Vessel Code Ser.). 1980. pap. 140.00 loose-leaf (V0012N). ASME.
Code Cases Book: Nuclear Components. (Boiler & Pressure Vessel Code Ser.). 1980. loose leaf 140.00 (V0012). ASME.
Code de la Communaute. Alexandre-Theodore Dezamy. (Fr.). 1977. lib. bdg. 31.25x o.p. (ISBN 0-8287-0274-8); pap. text ed. 21.25x o.p. (ISBN 0-685-75740-4). Clearwater Pub.
Code Du Mahayana En Chine: Amsterdam, 1892. J. J. De Groot. LC 78-74288. (Oriental Religions Ser.: Vol. 15). 281p. 1980. lib. bdg. 33.00 (ISBN 0-8240-3917-3). Garland Pub.
Code for the Construction & Equipment of Ships Carrying Dangerous Chemicals in Bulk. 86p. 1977. 11.00 (IMCO). Unipub.
Code in Context. D. Adlam. (Primary Socialization, Language & Education Ser.). 1977. 20.00x (ISBN 0-7100-8481-1). Routledge & Kegan.
Code Name Sebastian. James L. Johnson. 1978. pap. 2.95 (ISBN 0-310-37402-2). Zondervan.
Code Name Valkyrie: Count Claus von Stauffenberg & the Plot to Kill Hitler. James Forman. LC 72-12581. (Illus.). 256p. (gr. 9-12). 1973. PLB 10.95 (ISBN 0-87599-188-2). S G Phillips.
Code of Alabama 1975, 27 vols. Michie Editorial Staff. 1980. write for info. with 1979 cum suppl (ISBN 0-87215-126-3); write for info. 1980 cum. suppl (ISBN 0-87215-341-X). Michie.
Code of Life. Ernest Borek. LC 65-10944. 1965. 16.00x o.p. (ISBN 0-231-02634-X); pap. 5.00x o.p. (ISBN 0-231-08630-X). Columbia U Pr.
Code of Practice for Safe Use of Pesticides. 28p. 1980. pap. 5.00 (ISBN 0-643-00171-9, CO11, CSIRO). Unipub.
Code of Safe Practice for Bulk Cargoes. (Illus.). 137p. 1977. 15.25 (IMCO). Unipub.
Code of Safe Practice for Ships Carrying Timber Deck Cargoes. 31p. 1974. 7.00 (IMCO). Unipub.
Code of Safety for Fisherman & Fishing Vessels, 2 pts. Incl. Pt. A. Safety & Health Practice for Skippers & Crews. 108p. pap. 13.75 (ISBN 0-686-64932-X, IMCO 42); Pt. B. Safety & Health Requirements for the Construction & Equipment of Fishing Vessels. 158p. pap. 16.50 (ISBN 0-686-64933-8, IMCO 43). 1975 (IMCO). Unipub.
Code of Virginia, 1950, 23 vols. with 1980 cum. suppl. Michie Editorial Staff. Set. write for info. (ISBN 0-87215-137-9); write for info. 1980 suppl. (ISBN 0-87215-342-8). Michie.
Code Requirements for Nuclear Safety Related Concrete Structures: ACI 349-76. ACI Committee 349. 1976. 43.95 (ISBN 0-685-85087-0, 349-76) (ISBN 0-685-85088-9). ACI.
Code Seven. Lou Cameron. 1977. pap. 1.25 o.p. (ISBN 0-425-03296-5). Berkley Pub.
Code Switching & the Classroom Teacher. Guadalupe Valdes-Fallis. (Language in Education Ser.: No. 4). 1978. pap. 2.95 (ISBN 0-87281-080-1). Ctr Appl Ling.
Codebreakers. David Kahn. 1967. 29.95 (ISBN 0-02-560460-0). Macmillan.
Coded-Character Sets: History & Development. Charles E. Mackenzie. LC 77-90165. (IBM Ser.). 1980. text ed. 21.95 (ISBN 0-201-14460-3). A-W.
Codes & Ciphers. Alexander D'Agapeyeff. LC 73-19772. (Illus.). 1974. Repr. of 1939 ed. 18.00 (ISBN 0-8103-3716-9). Gale.
Codes & Ciphers: Amazing Ways to Scramble & Unscramble Secret Messages. Andrew Pennycook. 1978. 12.50 (ISBN 0-679-50856-2); pap. 7.95 (ISBN 0-679-50966-6). McKay.
Codes & Secret Writing. Herbert S. Zim. (Illus.). (gr. 5-9). 1948. PLB 6.48 (ISBN 0-688-31178-4). Morrow.
Codes, Ciphers, & Secret Writing. Martin Gardner. (gr. 5-7). 1973. pap. 1.25 (ISBN 0-671-29954-9). Archway.
Codes, Ciphers & Secret Writing. Martin Gardner. (gr. 5-7). 1979. pap. 1.25 (ISBN 0-671-29954-9). PB.
Codes for Kids. Burton Albert. LC 76-25456. (Activity Bks). (Illus.). (gr. 4-6). 1976. 6.50g (ISBN 0-8075-1239-7). A Whitman.

Codes for Reactor Computations. (Illus., Orig.). 1961. 17.25 (ISBN 92-0-050061-7, IAEA). Unipub.

Codetermination Movement in the West. Svetozar Pejovich. LC 77-18480. 1978. 21.00 (ISBN 0-669-02112-1). Lexington Bks.

Codex Atlanticus: A Facsimile of the Restored Manuscript, 12 vols. Leonardo Da Vinci. Set. 12000.00 (ISBN 0-685-32599-7). Johnson Repr.

Codex Fejervary-Mayer. Eduard Seler. Ed. by Karl Young. (Fourth Sun Ser.). (Illus.). lib. bdg. cancelled (ISBN 0-932282-40-7); pap. cancelled (ISBN 0-932282-39-3). Caledonia Pr.

Codification in Manufacturing & Materials Management. Hugh Mitchell. 1973. 13.95x o.p. (ISBN 0-8464-0252-1). Beekman Pubs.

Coding & Information Theory. Richard W. Hamming. (Illus.). 1980. text ed. 25.95 (ISBN 0-13-139139-9). P-H.

Coding the Therapeutic Process: Emblems of Encounter. Murray Cox. LC 77-30463. 1978. text ed. 18.00 (ISBN 0-08-021454-1); pap. text ed. 7.50 (ISBN 0-08-021453-3). Pergamon.

Coding the Universe. A. Beller et al. (London Mathematical Society Lecture Notes: No. 47). 300p. Date not set. price not set (ISBN 0-521-28040-0). Cambridge U Pr.

Coding Theorems of Information Theory. 2nd ed. Jacob Wolfowitz. (Ergebnisse der Mathematik und Ihrer Grenzgebiete: Vol. 31). 1964. 17.30 o.p. (ISBN 0-387-03124-3). Springer-Verlag.

Coding Theory. 2nd rev. ed. J. H. Van Lint. (Lecture Notes in Mathematics: Vol. 201). viii, 136p. 1973. pap. 9.20 o.p. (ISBN 0-387-06363-3). Springer-Verlag.

Codline's Child: The Autobiography of Wilbert Snow. Wilbert Snow. LC 73-15008. (Illus.). 504p. 1974. 20.00x (ISBN 0-8195-4069-2, Pub. by Wesleyan U Pr). Columbia U Pr.

Coed Killer. Margaret Cheney. LC 75-25196. 240p. 1976. 8.95 o.s.i. (ISBN 0-8027-0514-6). Walker & Co.

Coefficient Plane Models for Control System Analysis & Design. Denis R. Towill. (Mechanical Engineering Research Studies: Vol. 1). 260p. 1981. 44.50 (ISBN 0-471-27955-2, Pub. by Wiley-Interscience). Wiley.

Coefficient Regions for Schlicht Functions. A. C. Schaeffer & D. C. Spencer. Bd. with Region of Values of the Derivative of a Schlicht Function. Arthur Grad. LC 51-944. (Colloquium Pubns. Ser.: Vol. 35). 1950. 12.80 (ISBN 0-8218-1035-9, COLL-35). Am Math.

Coelomycetes. 694p. 1981. 115.00 (ISBN 0-85198-446-0, CAB 7, CAB). Unipub.

Coercion to Compliance. Harrell R. Rodgers, Jr. & Charles S. Bullock, 3rd. (Politics of Education Ser.). (Illus.). 1976. 17.95 (ISBN 0-669-00691-2); pap. 11.95 (ISBN 0-669-00965-2). Lexington Bks.

Coffee. Suzanne T. Moore. 144p. 1974. pap. 3.95 (ISBN 0-686-09052-7). MTM Pub Co.

Coffee. Joseph Philippe. (Q Books: Where Do Things Come from?). (Illus.). 1978. 3.95 (ISBN 0-8467-0443-9, Pub. by Two Continents). Hippocrene Bks.

Coffee: A Guide to Buying, Brewing & Enjoying. Kenneth Davids. LC 76-13003. (Illus.). 192p. 1976. 8.95 (ISBN 0-89286-103-7); pap. 5.95 (ISBN 0-685-66660-3). One Hund One Prods.

Coffee: A Revised Guide to Buying, Brewing & Enjoying. rev. ed. Kenneth Davids & M. L. Duniec. (Illus.). 192p. 1981. pap. 6.95 (ISBN 0-89286-186-X). One Hurd One Prods.

Coffee & the Ivory Coast: An Econometric Study. Theophilos Priovolos. LC 80-8630. (Wharton Econometric Studies). (Illus.). 240p. 1981. 24.95 (ISBN 0-669-04331-1). Lexington Bks.

Coffee Cookery. Ceil Dyer. LC 78-6188. (Illus.). 1978. 7.95 o.p. (ISBN 0-89586-010-4); pap. 4.95 (ISBN 0-89586-009-0). H P Bks.

Coffee in Colombia, Eighteen Hundred to Nineteen Hundred Seventy: An Economic, Social & Political History. Marco Palacios. LC 78-73251. (Cambridge Latin American Studies: No. 36). (Illus.). 1980. 34.50 (ISBN 0-521-22204-4). Cambridge U Pr.

Coffee Pulp: Composition, Technology & Utilization. 1979. pap. 8.50 (ISBN 0-88936-190-8, IDRC108, IDRC). Unipub.

Coffee Talk: Sharing Christ Through Friendly Gatherings. Barbara Ball. 80p. 1980. pap. 3.50 (ISBN 0-934396-08-6). Churches Alive.

Coffee Technology. Michael Sivetz & Norman W. Desrosier. (Illus.). 1979. lib. bdg. 56.00 (ISBN 0-87055-269-4). AVI.

Coffee Too. Suzanne T. Moore. 64p. (Orig.). 1975. pap. 1.95 (ISBN 0-686-10980-5). MTM Pub Co.

Cofferdams. 2nd rev & enl. ed. Ed. by Lazarus White & Edmund A. Prentis. LC 50-10778. 1956. 22.50x (ISBN 0-231-01777-4). Columbia U Pr.

Coffin for Dimitrios. Eric Ambler. 1977. pap. 1.75 o.p. (ISBN 0-345-25912-2). Ballantine.

Coffin's Overtones of Bel Canto: Phonetic Basis of Artistic Singing with One Hundred Chromatic Vowel-Chart Exercises. Berton Coffin. LC 80-21958. 254p. 1980. text ed. 20.00 (ISBN 0-8108-1370-X); Accompanying Chart. 7.50; Set. 27.50. Scarecrow.

Cog Railway to Pike's Peak. Morris W. Abbot. LC 73-9520. (Illus.). 48p. pap. 2.95 (ISBN 0-87095-052-5). Golden West.

Coge-we-a, the Half-Blood: A Depiction of the Great Montana Cattle Range. Hum-Ishu-ma. xvii, 320p. 1981. 17.95x (ISBN 0-8032-3069-9, BB 754, Bison); pap. 6.25 (ISBN 0-8032-8110-2). U of Nebr Pr.

Cognition & Figurative Language. Ed. by Richard P. Honeck & Robert R. Hoffman. LC 80-17225. 448p. 1980. text ed. 29.95 (ISBN 0-89859-047-7). L Erlbaum Assocs.

Cognition & Reality: Principles & Implications of Cognitive Psychology. Ulric Neisser. LC 76-24813. (Psychology Ser.). (Illus.). 1976. text ed. 16.00x o.p. (ISBN 0-7167-0478-1); pap. text ed. 8.95x (ISBN 0-7167-0477-3). W H Freeman.

Cognition & Social Behavior. Ed. by J. S. Carroll & John W. Payne. (Carnegie Mellon U. Cognition Studies). 1976. 16.50 o.p. (ISBN 0-470-99007-4). Halsted Pr.

Cognition & the Symbolic Processes, Vol. 2. Ed. by Walter B. Weimer & David Palermo. 426p. 1981. professional ref. text 24.95 (ISBN 0-89859-066-3). L Erlbaum Assocs.

Cognition, Convention, & Communication. Mark H. Bickhard. 210p. 1980. 24.95 (ISBN 0-03-056098-5). Praeger.

Cognition, Development & Instruction. Ed. by John R. Kirby & J. B. Biggs. LC 80-523. (Educational Psychology Ser.). 1980. 19.00 (ISBN 0-12-409550-X). Acad Pr.

Cognition in Human Motivation & Learning. Ed. by Gery D'Ydewalle & Willy Lens. LC 80-23715. 380p. 1981. text ed. 15.00 (ISBN 0-89859-067-1). L Erlbaum Assocs.

Cognition: Mental Structures & Processes. Dodd & White. 500p. 1980. text ed. 17.95 (ISBN 0-205-06930-4, 7969309). Allyn.

Cognition, Social Behavior, & the Environment. Ed. by John L. Harvey. 600p. 1981. ref. 29.95 (ISBN 0-89859-082-5). L Erlbaum Assocs.

Cognitive & Affective Growth: Developmental Interaction. Ed. by Edna K. Shapiro & Evelyn Weber. 240p. 1981. ref. 19.95 (ISBN 0-89859-092-2). L Erlbaum Assocs.

Cognitive Bases of Human Learning. Eli Saltz. 325p. 1971. pap. text ed. 17.95x (ISBN 0-256-01180-X). Dorsey.

Cognitive-Behavioral Approach Psychology: Implications for Practice, Research, & Training. Gerald L. Stone. LC 80-21344. 256p. 1980. 21.95 (ISBN 0-03-055926-X). Praeger.

Cognitive-Behavioral Reflections on Some Dimensions of Personality. Matt E. Jaremko. LC 79-6602. 1980. pap. text ed. 9.50 (ISBN 0-8191-0924-X). U Pr of Amer.

Cognitive Development. John H. Flavell. (Illus.). 1977. 14.95x (ISBN 0-13-139774-5); pap. 9.95 (ISBN 0-13-139766-4). P-H.

Cognitive Development: A Life-Span View. George E. Forman & Irving E. Sigel. Ed. by Freda Rabelsky & Lynn Dorman. LC 78-31176. (Life-Span Human Development Ser.). (Illus.). 1979. pap. text ed. 8.95 (ISBN 0-8185-0275-4). Brooks-Cole.

Cognitive Development & the Acquisition of Language. Ed. by Timothy E. Moore. 1973. 29.00 (ISBN 0-12-505850-0). Acad Pr.

Cognitive Development in the School Years. Ann Floyd. LC 78-9155. 1979. 24.95 (ISBN 0-470-26429-2). Halsted Pr.

Cognitive Development in Young Children. Nancy E. Jackson et al. Ed. by Larry Goulet. LC 77-1725. (Basic Concepts in Educational Psychology Ser.). 1977. pap. text ed. 5.95 o.p. (ISBN 0-8185-0225-8). Brooks-Cole.

Cognitive Paradigm. Marx De Mey. (Harvester Studies in Cognitive Science). 1980. text ed. write for info. (ISBN 0-391-01062-X). Humanities.

Cognitive Processes. Elizabeth Loftus et al. LC 78-16953. (P-H Ser. in Experimental Psychology). 1979. ref. ed. 19.95 (ISBN 0-13-139634-X). P-H.

Cognitive Processes in Choice & Decision Behavior. Ed. by Thomas S. Wallsten. LC 79-27553. (Illus.). 304p. 1980. text ed. 24.95 (ISBN 0-89859-054-X). L Erlbaum Assocs.

Cognitive Processes in Stereotyping & Intergroup Behavior. Ed. by David L. Hamilton. 384p. 1981. prof. - refer. 24.95 (ISBN 0-89859-081-7). L Erlbaum Assocs.

Cognitive Processes in Writing. Ed. by Lee W. Gregg & Erwin Steinberg. LC 80-18624. (Illus.). 208p. 1980. text ed. 19.95 (ISBN 0-89859-032-9). L Erlbaum Assocs.

Cognitive Processes of Nonhuman Primates. Ed. by Leonard E. Jarrard. 1971. 26.50 (ISBN 0-12-380850-2). Acad Pr.

Cognitive Psychoanalysis. Irving Bieber. LC 80-66921. 300p. 1980. 30.00 (ISBN 0-87668-419-3). Aronson.

Cognitive Psychology. Wayne A. Wickelgren. (Illus.). 1979. ref. ed. 19.95 (ISBN 0-13-139543-2). P-H.

Cognitive Psychology & Its Implications. John R. Anderson. LC 80-14354. (Psychology Ser.). (Illus.). 1980. text ed. 15.00x (ISBN 0-7167-1197-4). W H Freeman.

Cognitive Psychology: New Directions. Ed. by Guy Claxton. (International Library of Psychology). 1980. 35.00 (ISBN 0-7100-0485-0); pap. 17.50 (ISBN 0-7100-0486-9). Routledge & Kegan.

Cognitive Psychology: The Study of Knowing, Learning & Thinking. Barry F. Anderson. 1975. 16.95 (ISBN 0-12-057850-6). Acad Pr.

Cognitive Psychology: Thinking & Creating. John R. Hayes. 1978. pap. text ed. 16.95x (ISBN 0-256-02065-5). Dorsey.

Cognitive Psychophysiology: Principles of Covert Behavior. F. McGuigan. LC 78-18542. 1978. 31.95 (ISBN 0-13-139519-X). P-H.

Cognitive Responses in Persuasion. Ed. by Richard E. Petty et al. LC 80-26388. 512p. 1981. text ed. 29.95 (ISBN 0-89859-025-6). L Erlbaum Assocs.

Cognitive Skills & Their Acquisition. Ed. by John R. Anderson. (Carnegie Symposia on Cognition). 384p. 1981. ref. 24.95 (ISBN 0-89859-093-0). L Erlbaum Assocs.

Cognitive Skills Assessment Battery. Ann E. Boehm & Barbara R. Slater. 1974. complete kit 23.50 (ISBN 0-8077-5959-7); refill 8.25 (ISBN 0-8077-5960-0); interpretive manual 0.50 (ISBN 0-8077-5961-9); sampler 2.15 (ISBN 0-8077-5962-7). Tchrs Coll.

Cognitive Sociology. Aaron V. Cicourel. LC 73-18771. 1973. 10.95 (ISBN 0-02-905440-0); pap. text ed. 5.95 (ISBN 0-02-905450-8). Free Pr.

Cognitive Style: Five Approaches & Relevant Research. Kenneth M. Goldstein & Sheldon Blackman. LC 78-1378. 1978. 21.50 (ISBN 0-471-31275-4, Pub. by Wiley-Interscience). Wiley.

Cognitive Styles: Essence & Origins- Field Dependence & Field Independence. Herman A. Witkin & Donald R. Goodenough. (Psychological Issues Monograph: No. 51). (Illus.). 130p. 1981. text ed. 15.00x (ISBN 0-8236-1003-9, 00-1003). Intl Univs Pr.

Cognitive Unconscious: A Piagetian Approach to Psychotherapy. Melvin L. Weiner. LC 75-12937. (Illus.). 202p. 1975. 15.95x (ISBN 0-915662-01-9). Intl Psych Pr.

Coherence in a Fragmented World: Jonathan Edwards' Theology of the Holy Spirit. Patricia Wilson-Kastner. LC 78-62667. 1978. pap. text ed. 6.75 (ISBN 0-8191-0587-2). U Pr of Amer.

Coherence of Gothic Conventions. Eve K. Sedgwick. Ed. by Devendra P. Varma. LC 79-8462. (Gothic Studies & Dissertations Ser.). 1980. lib. bdg. 17.00x (ISBN 0-405-12650-6). Arno.

Coherent Communication with Applications to Pseudo-Noise Spread Spectrum Synchronization. Jack K. Holmes. 850p. 1981. 50.00 (ISBN 0-471-03301-4, Pub. by Wiley-Interscience). Wiley.

Coherent Nonlinear Optics: Recent Advances. Ed. by M. S. Feld & V. S. Letokhov. (Topics in Current Physics: Vol. 21). (Illus.). 377p. 1980. 44.50 (ISBN 0-387-10172-1). Springer-Verlag.

Coherent Raman Spectroscopy. G. L. Eesley. (Illus.). 150p. 1981. 41.00 (ISBN 0-08-025058-0). Pergamon.

Cohesion in English. M. A. Halliday & Ruqaiya Hasan. (English Language Ser.). (Illus.). 384p. 1976. text ed. 24.00x (ISBN 0-582-55031-9); pap. text ed. 14.50x (ISBN 0-582-55041-6). Longman.

Cohesion of Saudi Arabia: Evolution of Political Identity. Christine M. Helms. LC 80-8026. (Illus.). 320p. 1981. text ed. 28.00x (ISBN 0-8018-2475-3). Johns Hopkins.

Coil Slitting. J. W. Rogers & W. H. Millan. LC 73-7903. 127p. 1973. pap. text ed. 9.25 (ISBN 0-08-017696-8). Pergamon.

Coil Spring Making. 2nd ed. Ed. by E. T. Gross et al. (Engineering Craftsmen: No. H6). (Illus.). 1974. spiral bdg. 25.00x (ISBN 0-85083-172-5). Intl Ideas.

Coin Age of Northern India. P. C. Roy. 1980. 27.50x (ISBN 0-8364-0641-9, Pub. by Abhinav India). South Asia Bks.

Coin Collecting. Boy Scouts of America. LC 19-600. (Illus.). 32p. (gr. 6-12). 1975. pap. 0.70x (ISBN 0-8395-3390-X, 3390). BSA.

Coin Collecting As a Hobby. Burton H. Hobson. LC 67-27759. (Illus.). (gr. 3 up). 1977. 7.95 (ISBN 0-8069-6018-3); lib. bdg. 7.49 (ISBN 0-8069-6019-1). Sterling.

Coin Collecting As a Hobby. rev. ed. Burton H. Hobson. LC 67-27759. (Illus.). (gr. 6 up). 1980. 7.95 (ISBN 0-8069-6018-3); PLB 7.49 (ISBN 0-8069-6019-1). Sterling.

Coin Collecting for Beginners. Burton Hobson & Fred Reinfeld. pap. 3.00 (ISBN 0-87980-022-4). Wilshire.

Coin Collectors Fact Book. Walter J. Zimmerman. LC 73-77839. (Illus.). 192p. 1973. lib. bdg. 5.95 o. p. (ISBN 0-668-02991-9); pap. 3.95 (ISBN 0-668-02992-7). Arco.

Coin of Love. Barbara Cartland. pap. 1.75 (ISBN 0-515-05560-3). Jove Pubns.

Coinage of Ancient Africa: (Numismatique De L'Ancienne Afrique) L. Muller et al. (Illus.). 1977. 80.00 (ISBN 0-916710-35-1). Obol Intl.

Coinage of the Americas. Theodore V. Buttrey, Jr. (Illus.). 139p. 1973. pap. 8.50 o.p. (ISBN 0-685-48744-X). Interbk Inc.

Coinage of the Western Seleucid Mints. Edward T. Newall. (Illus.). 1977. pap. 35.00 o.p. (ISBN 0-89192-230-X). Interbk Inc.

Coinages of Lapsakos. A. Baldwin. (Illus.). 111p. 1980. 30.00 (ISBN 0-916710-70-X). Obol Intl.

Coins: An Illustrated Survey, 650 B.C. to the Present Day. Ed. by Martin J. Price. (Illus.). 320p. 1980. slipcased 50.00 (ISBN 0-416-00691-4). Methuen Inc.

Coins & All About Them: A Numismatic Quiz. Compiled by Brian Edge. 1973. 6.95 o.p. (ISBN 0-571-09984-X). Transatlantic.

Coins & Coinage in Viking-Age Norway. Kolbjorn Skaare. 1976. 36.00x (ISBN 8-200-01542-4, Dist. by Columbia U Pr). Universitet.

Coins & Tokens. Philip Leighton. (Junior Reference Ser.). (Illus.). 64p. (gr. 7 up). 1972. 7.95 (ISBN 0-7136-1238-X). Dufour.

Coins, Medals & Tokens of the Philippines. Aldo P. Basso. (Illus.). 144p. 1968. 5.95 (ISBN 0-912496-10-X). Shirjieh Pubs.

Coins of Canada. J. A. Haxby & R. C. Willey. (Whitman Coin Hobby Books). (Illus.). 1977. pap. 2.75 o.p. (ISBN 0-307-09058-2). Western Pub.

Coins of Mexico. Frank W. Grove. 1981. lib. bdg. 60.00 (ISBN 0-88000-123-2). Quarterman.

Coins of the Americas: A Catalogue of North, South, & Central American Coins Since 1525 & Their Valuations. Burton H. Hobson. LC 80-52323. (Illus.). 384p. 1980. cancelled o.p. (ISBN 0-8069-6072-8); lib. bdg. cancelled o.p. (ISBN 0-8069-6073-6). Sterling.

Coins of the Ancient Celts. Derek Allen & Dephne Nash. (Illus.). 250p. 1980. 25.00x (ISBN 0-85224-371-5, Pub. by Edinburgh U Pr Scotland). Columbia U Pr.

Coins of the World: Ancient, Medieval, Modern. R. A. Carson. (Illus.). 1962. 25.00x o.p. (ISBN 0-06-000750-8, HarpT). Har-Row.

Cojo que Camino de Nuevo. Mary Warren. Tr. by J. Alfonso Lockward from Eng. (Libros Arco). (Illus.). 32p. (Orig., Span.). (gr. 1-3). 1975. pap. 0.95 o.s.i. (ISBN 0-89922-037-1). Edit Caribe.

Coke of Norfolk: A Financial & Agricultural Study, 1707-1842. R. A. Parker. (Illus.). 232p. 1975. 37.50x (ISBN 0-19-822403-6). Oxford U Pr.

Cokesbury Worship Hymnal. 288p. 1976. 3.95 (ISBN 0-687-08863-1); pap. 1.95 (ISBN 0-687-08865-8); accompanist ed. 3.95 (ISBN 0-687-08866-6). Abingdon.

Colby Moves West. Sharon Miller. 132p. (gr. 6-12). 1981. pap. 2.25 (ISBN 0-88207-489-X). Victor Bks.

Cold Against Disease. Lucy Kavaler. LC 69-10810. (Wonders of Cold Ser). (Illus.). (gr. 7-9). 1971. 8.95 (ISBN 0-381-99773-1, A14760, JD-J). John Day.

Cold & Freezer Storage Manual. 2nd ed. Elliott R. Hallowell. (Illus.). 1980. text ed. 35.00 (ISBN 0-87055-366-6). AVI.

Cold & Freezer Storage Manual. Willis R. Woolrich & Elliot R. Hallowell. LC 76-115688. (Illus.). 1970. 28.00 o.p. (ISBN 0-87055-074-8). AVI.

Cold & Frost Injuries: Rewarming Damages. H. Killian. (Disaster Medicine: Vol. 3). (Illus.). 260p. 1981. pap. 49.60 (ISBN 0-387-08991-8). Springer-Verlag.

Cold Cash War. Robert Asprin. 1978. pap. 1.75 o.p. (ISBN 0-440-11364-4). Dell.

Cold Cathode Tubes. J. B. Dance. (Illus.). 1969. 10.00x (ISBN 0-685-20566-5). Transatlantic.

Cold Cuisine. Helen Hecht. LC 80-69374. 1981. 11.95 (ISBN 0-689-11130-4). Atheneum.

Cold Dawn: The Story of SALT. John Newhouse. LC 72-91556. 288p. 1973. 7.95 o.p. (ISBN 0-03-001631-2). HR&W.

Cold Feet. Gen LeRoy. (gr. 7 up). 1981. pap. 1.75 (ISBN 0-440-91336-5, LE). Dell.

Cold Hand in Mine. Robert Aickman. LC 77-3042. (gr. 5 up). 1977. 8.95 o.p. (ISBN 0-684-15132-4, ScribT). Scribner.

Cold Hands. Joseph Pintauro. 1980. pap. 2.50 (ISBN 0-451-09482-4, E9482, Sig). NAL.

Cold Harbors. C. W. Truesdale. 1973. 4.50 (ISBN 0-686-27598-5) (ISBN 0-686-27599-3). Latitudes Pr.

Cold Look at the Warm-Blooded Dinosaurs. Everett Olson & Roger D. Thomas. (American Association for the Advancement of Science Ser.). 1979. lib. bdg. 28.50x (ISBN 0-89158-350-5). Westview.

Cold Look at the Warm-Blooded Dinosaurs. Ed. by Roger D. K. Thomas & Everett C. Olson. (AAAS Selected Symposium: No. 28). (Illus.). 516p. 1980. lib. bdg. 28.50x (ISBN 0-89158-464-1). Westview.
Cold Platters-Cold Buffets. Gutta. 1981. 8.95 (ISBN 0-8120-5400-8). Barron.
Cold Room. Jeffrey Caine. 1977. 7.95 o.p. (ISBN 0-394-40903-5). Knopf.
Cold Spring Harbor Symposia on Quantitative Biology: Movable Genetic Elements, Vol. XLV. (Cold Spring Harbor Symposia on Quantitative Biology Ser.). 1981. price not set (ISBN 0-87969-044-5). Cold Spring Harbor.
Cold Spring Harbor Symposia on Quantitative Biology: Volume 19, the Mammalian Fetus. LC 34-8174. (Illus.). 237p. 1955. 30.00 o.p. (ISBN 0-87969-018-6). Cold Spring Harbor.
Cold Spring Harbor Symposia on Quantitative Biology: Vol. 41, Origins of Lymphocyte Diversity, 2 bk. set, Vol. 41. LC 34-8174. (Illus.). 1024p. 1977. Set. 85.00 (ISBN 0-87969-040-2). Cold Spring Harbor.
Cold War. Morrie Helitzer. (gr. 7 up). 1977. lib. bdg. 6.45 s&l (ISBN 0-531-02464-4). Watts.
Cold War. Alasdair Nicholson. Ed. by Malcolm Yapp et al. (World History Ser.). (Illus.). 32p. (gr. 10). 1980. Repr. of 1977 ed. 5.95 (ISBN 0-89908-236-X); pap. text ed. 1.95 (ISBN 0-89908-211-4). Greenhaven.
Cold War & Its Origins, 2 vols. D. F. Fleming. LC 61-9193. slipcased 17.95 (ISBN 0-385-02045-7). Doubleday.
Cold War of Kitty Pentecost: A Novel. Alexander Blackburn. LC 78-58533. (Writers West Book). 232p. 1979. 8.95 o.p. (ISBN 0-8040-9015-7); pap. 4.50 (ISBN 0-8040-9011-4). Swallow.
Cold War Political Justice: The Smith Act, the Communist Party, & American Civil Liberties. Michael R. Belknap. LC 77-4566. (Contributions in American History: No. 66). 1977. lib. bdg. 18.95x (ISBN 0-8371-9692-2, BCW/). Greenwood.
Cold Water. Lou Lipsitz. LC 67-15228. (Wesleyan Poetry Program: Vol. 34). (Orig.). 1967. 10.00x (ISBN 0-8195-2034-9, Pub. by Wesleyan U Pr); pap. 4.95 (ISBN 0-8195-1034-3). Columbia U Pr.
Cold Weather Catalog: Learning to Love Winter. Tree Communications. 1977. pap. 7.95 o.p. (ISBN 0-385-13494-0, Dolp). Doubleday.
Cold Wind River. Kent Nelson. LC 80-20013. 233p. 1981. 8.95 (ISBN 0-396-07835-4). Dodd.
Coldest War: The Russian Game in China. C. L. Sulzberger. LC 74-1466. 1974. 5.95 o.p. (ISBN 0-15-118979-X). HarBraceJ.
Coldest Winter in Peking: A Novel from Inside Red China. Hsia Chi-Yen. LC 77-26522. 1978. 10.00 o.p. (ISBN 0-385-13402-9). Doubleday.
Cole Weston: 18 Photographs. Ed. by Charis Wilson. (Illus.). 56p. 1981. pap. 19.95 (ISBN 0-87905-084-5). Peregrine Smith.
Colebrooke-Cameron Papers: Documents of British Colonial Policy in Ceylon, 1796-1833, 2 Vols. Ed. by G. C. Mendis. 1956. 22.85x o.p. (ISBN 0-19-635027-1). Oxford U Pr.
Coleccion Navidena, No. 1. J. W. Blair. 1980. Repr. of 1977 ed. pap. 1.30 (ISBN 0-311-08201-7). Casa Bautista.
Colecciones Botanicas de C. A. Purpus En Mexico Periodo 1898-1925. Mario Sousa Sanchez. (U. C. Publ. in Botany: Vol. 51). 1969. pap. 5.50x (ISBN 0-520-09024-1). U of Cal Pr.
Coleman's Drive. John Coleman. 1966. 4.95 (ISBN 0-685-52076-5). Transatlantic.
Coleridge. Richard Garnett. 111p. 1980. Repr. of 1904 ed. lib. bdg. 12.50 (ISBN 0-89987-307-3). Darby Bks.
Coleridge. Henry D. Traill. LC 67-23874. 1968. Repr. of 1884 ed. 18.00 (ISBN 0-8103-3052-0). Gale.
Coleridge: An Author Guide. Katharine Cooke. 1979. 19.00x (ISBN 0-7100-0141-X). Routledge & Kegan.
Coleridge & the Idea of Love. A. J. Harding. 1975. 42.00 (ISBN 0-521-20639-1). Cambridge U Pr.
Coleridge As Philosopher. John H. Muirhead. (Muirhead Library of Philosophy). 1970. Repr. of 1930 ed. text ed. 9.25x o.p. (ISBN 0-04-192025-2). Humanities.
Coleridge: Critic of Shakespeare. M. M. Badawi. LC 72-86417. 240p. 1973. 38.00 (ISBN 0-521-20040-7). Cambridge U Pr.
Coleridge on the Language of Verse. Emerson R. Marks. (Princeton Essays in Literature). 116p. 1981. 9.50x (ISBN 0-691-06458-X). Princeton U Pr.
Coleridge: The Clark Lectures, Nineteen Fifty-One to Nineteen Fifty-Two. Humphrey House. 1979. 14.95x (ISBN 0-8464-0086-3). Beekman Pubs.
Coleridge: The Critical Heritage. Ed. by J. R. Jackson. 1970. 40.00x (ISBN 0-7100-6594-9). Routledge & Kegan.
Coleridge's Decline As a Poet. L. D. Berkoben. (Studies in English Literature: No. 98). 171p. (Orig.). 1975. pap. text ed. 28.25x (ISBN 90-2793-226-3). Mouton.
Colette. Robert D. Cottrell. LC 73-84598. (Modern Literature Ser.). 1974. 10.95 (ISBN 0-8044-2130-7). Ungar.
Colin Archer & the Seaworthy Double-Ender. John Leather. LC 78-55782. (Illus.). 1979. 20.00 (ISBN 0-87742-086-6). Intl Marine.
Colin Wilson. John A. Weigel. LC 74-28137. (English Authors Ser.: No. 181). 1975. lib. bdg. 10.95 (ISBN 0-8057-1575-4). Twayne.
Coll & His White Pig. Lloyd Alexander. LC 65-21540. (Illus.). 32p. (gr. k-3). 1965. reinforced bdg. 5.95 o.p. (ISBN 0-03-089751-3). HR&W.
Collaboration: Artists & Architects. Barbaralee Diamonstein. 176p. (Orig.). 1981. 32.50 (Whitney Lib). Watson-Guptill.
Collaboration et Originalite Chez la Rochefoucauld. Susan R. Baker. LC 79-21085. (U. of Fla. Humanities Monographs: No. 48). 135p. (Orig.). 1980. pap. 9.00 (ISBN 0-8130-0657-0). U Presses Fla.
Collaboration in Organizations: Alternatives to Hierarchy. William A. Kraus. LC 80-11291. 274p. 1980. text ed. 19.95 (ISBN 0-87705-491-6). Human Sci Pr.
Collaboration One. Herbert Brun & Kenneth Gaburo. 24p. 1976. soft cover saddle-stitched 15.00. Lingua Pr.
Collage: An Intermediate French Program, 5 readers. Incl. Reader 1. Grammar. Lucia Baker. pap. text ed. 10.95 (ISBN 0-394-32643-1); Reader 2. Literary Reader. Laura Border. pap. text ed. 8.95 (ISBN 0-394-32644-X); Reader 3. Cultural Reader. Carmen Grace. pap. text ed. 7.95 (ISBN 0-394-32645-8); Reader 4. Activities Manual. Ester Zago. pap. text ed. 6.95 (ISBN 0-394-32646-6); Reader 5. Workbook. Ruth Bleuze. pap. text ed. 6.95 (ISBN 0-394-32647-4). 1981. Random.
Collage of Dreams: The Writings of Anais Nin. Sharon Spencer. LC 77-78781. 188p. 1977. 10.95 (ISBN 0-8040-0760-8). Swallow.
Collage of Dreams: The Writings of Anais Nin. Sharon Spencer. 1981. 5.95 (ISBN 0-15-618581-4, Harv). HarBraceJ.
Collage: The Art of Making Pictures from Odds & Ends. Janet Allen. 80p. 1981. pap. 7.95 (ISBN 0-8120-2289-0). Barron.
Collagenase in Normal & Pathological Connective Tissues. David E. Woolley & John M. Evanson. LC 79-19557. 1980. 46.00 (ISBN 0-471-27668-5, Pub. by Wiley-Interscience). Wiley.
Collagraph Printmaking. Donald Stoltenberg. LC 74-27699. (Illus.). 96p. 1975. 12.95 (ISBN 0-87192-067-0). Davis Mass.
Collagraph Printmaking. Mary A. Wenniger. (Illus.). 184p. 1980. pap. 10.95 (ISBN 0-8230-0666-2). Watson-Guptill.
Collapse of Democracy. Robert Moss. 1976. 9.95 o.p. (ISBN 0-87000-359-3). Arlington Hse.
Collapse of Gold & the Tragic Dilemma of the Swiss Banks. C. M. Flumiani. (Illus.). 205p. 1976. 39.50 (ISBN 0-918968-18-6). Am Classical Coll Pr.
Collapse of Liberal Empire: Science & the Revolution in the Twentieth Century. Paul N. Goldstene. (Political Science Ser.). 160p. 1980. pap. 5.95 (ISBN 0-88316-540-6). Chandler & Sharp.
Collapse of Orthodoxy: The Intellectual Ordeal of George Frederick Holmes. Neal C. Gillespie. LC 70-163978. 1972. 9.95x (ISBN 0-8139-0345-9). U Pr of Va.
Collapse of the Weimar Republic: Political Economy & Crisis. David Abraham. LC 80-8533. 550p. 1981. 30.00x (ISBN 0-691-05322-7); pap. 12.50x (ISBN 0-691-10118-3). Princeton U Pr.
Collapsing Spaces, Tilting Times. George Bailin. (Poetry Ser.: No. 11). 48p. (Orig.). 1981. pap. 4.50 (ISBN 0-930020-10-3). Stone Country.
Collateral Circulation in Clinical Surgery. D. E. Strandness, Jr. LC 68-23692. (Illus.). 1969. 18.50 o.p. (ISBN 0-7216-8610-9). Saunders.
Collation & Investigation of Manuscripts of Aeschylus. R. D. Dawe. 1964. 56.00 (ISBN 0-521-04800-1). Cambridge U Pr.
Colle, London & Blackmar Diemer Systems. T. D. Harding. 1979. 17.95 (ISBN 0-7134-2110-X, Pub. by Batsford England); pap. 12.50 (ISBN 0-7134-2111-8). David & Charles.
Colleagues in Organization: The Social Construction of Professional Work. Ed. by Ralph L. Blankenship. LC 80-18149. 442p. (Orig.). 1980. Repr. of 1977 ed. lib. bdg. 22.00 (ISBN 0-89874-233-1). Krieger.
Colleagues or Competitors. Margaret Martin. 103p. 1969. pap. text ed. 5.00x (ISBN 0-7135-1538-4, Pub. by Bedford England). Renouf.
Collect, Print & Paint from Nature. John Hawkinson. LC 63-13330. (Illus.). (gr. 3 up). 1963. 6.50g (ISBN 0-8075-1272-9). A Whitman.
Collectanea Juridica: Consisting of Tracts Relative to the Law & Constitution of England, 2 vols. Francis Hargrave. 1981. Repr. of 1791 ed. lib. bdg. 75.00x (ISBN 0-8377-0632-7). Rothman.
Collected Books of Jack Spicer. Jack Spicer. Ed. by Robin Blaser. 382p. (Orig.). 1975. 14.00 (ISBN 0-87685-242-8); pap. 7.50 (ISBN 0-87685-241-X). Black Sparrow.
Collected Dialogues of Plato. Ed. by H. Cairns & E. Hamilton. (Bollingen Ser.: No. 71). 1961. 16.95 (ISBN 0-691-09718-6). Princeton U Pr.
Collected Edition of the "Travaux Preparatoires of the European Convention on Human Rights" Vol. V Legal Committee-Ad Hoc Joint Committee-Committee of Ministers-Consultative Assembly 23 June - 28 August 1950. Ed. by Council of Europe. 356p. 1979. lib. bdg. 131.60 (ISBN 90-247-1970-4, Pub. by Martinus Nijhoff). Kluwer Boston.
Collected Essays, Journalism & Letters, Vol. 1: An Age Like This, 1920-1940. George Orwell. Ed. by Sonia Orwell & Ian Angus. LC 68-12591. 1971. pap. 6.95 (ISBN 0-15-618620-9, HB209, Harv). HarBraceJ.
Collected Essays, Journalism & Letters, Vol. 4: In Front of Your Nose, 1945-1950. George Orwell. Ed. by Sonia Orwell & Ian Angus. LC 68-12591. 1971. pap. 6.95 (ISBN 0-15-618623-3, HB212, Harv). HarBraceJ.
Collected Essays of J. V. Cunningham. J. V. Cunningham. LC 75-21800. xii, 463p. 1977. o.p 20.00 (ISBN 0-8040-0670-9); pap. 9.95 (ISBN 0-8040-0671-7). Swallow.
Collected Essays of John Peale Bishop. John Peale Bishop. Ed. by Edmund Wilson. 508p. 1975. Repr. of 1948 ed. lib. bdg. 25.00 (ISBN 0-374-90643-2). Octagon.
Collected Legal Papers. Oliver W. Holmes, Jr. 8.50 (ISBN 0-8446-1241-3). Peter Smith.
Collected Legislation of the U.S.S.R, Realeases 1 & 2. W. E. Butler. 1980. Set. looseleaf 300.00 (ISBN 0-379-20450-9). Oceana.
Collected Leters of Thomas & Jane Welsh Carlyle, Vols. 8 & 9. Ed. by Charles R. Sanders. 1980. 30.00 ea.; 59.75 set (ISBN 0-686-64383-6). Vol. 8 (ISBN 0-8223-0433-3). Vol. 9 (ISBN 0-8223-0434-1). Duke.
Collected Letters. Wilfred Owen. Ed. by Harold Owen & John Bell. 1967. 29.50x (ISBN 0-19-211180-9). Oxford U Pr.
Collected Letters of Antoni van Leeuwenhoek, 10 vols. Antoni Van Leeuwenhoek. Incl. Vol. 1. 454p. 1939; Vol. 2. 506p. 1941 (ISBN 90-265-0041-6); Vol. 3. 560p. 1948; Vol. 4. 383p. 1952 (ISBN 90-265-0043-2); Vol. 5. 457p. 1958 (ISBN 90-265-0044-0); Vol. 6. 425p. 1961 (ISBN 90-265-0045-9); Vol. 7. 427p. 1965 (ISBN 90-265-0046-7); Vol. 8. 383p. 1967 (ISBN 90-265-0047-5); Vol. 9. 482p. 1976 (ISBN 90-265-0220-6); Vol. 10. 362p. 1979 (ISBN 90-265-0285-0). (Illus., Dutch & Eng.). text ed. 105.00 ea. (Pub. by Swets Serv Holland). Swets North Am.
Collected Letters of Thomas & Jane Welsh Carlyle, Vols. 8-9. Ed. by Charles R. Sanders & Kenneth J. Fielding. LC 71-101132. (Illus., Consolidated Index in Vol. 9). 1981. Vol. 8, 1835-1836. 30.00 (ISBN 0-8223-0433-3); Vol. 9, 1836-1837. 30.00 (ISBN 0-8223-0434-1); Set. 59.75 (ISBN 0-686-69104-0). Duke.
Collected Letters of Thomas Hardy: Vol. 2 1893-1901. Ed. by Richard Little Purdy & Michael Millgate. (Illus.). 320p. 1980. 49.95 (ISBN 0-19-812619-0). Oxford U Pr.
Collected Lichenological Papers, 2 vols. E. Tuckerman. Ed. by W. L. Culberson. 1964. Vol. 1. 45.00 (ISBN 3-7682-0221-6); Vol. 2. 54.00 (ISBN 3-7682-0222-4); Set. 99.00 (ISBN 3-7682-0220-8). Lubrecht & Cramer.
Collected Lichenological Papers: Collected Lichenological Papers. W. Nylander. Incl. Vol. 4. Papers 1888-1900; Vol. 5. Synopsis Lichenum et Supplementum 1858-1869. (Illus.); Vol. 6. Prodromus Licherographiae Gallisae et Algeriae 1857. Lichens Scandinaviae sive Prodomus... 1861. Supplementum: Lichens Lapponicae orientalis 1866. (Illus.). Date not set. 75.00 ea. Lubrecht & Cramer. Postponed.
Collected Longer Poems. W. H. Auden. LC 69-16429. 1969. 7.95 o.p. (ISBN 0-394-40321-5). Random.
Collected Longer Poems (Giant) W. H. Auden. 1975. pap. 3.95 (ISBN 0-394-72014-8, V-2014, Vin). Random.
Collected Lyrics. Edna St. Vincent Millay. LC 43-51349. 1943. 10.95 o.p. (ISBN 0-06-012930-1, HarpT). Har-Row.
Collected Mathematical Papers, 2 Vols. Henry J. Smith. LC 65-11859. 60.00 (ISBN 0-8284-0187-X). Chelsea Pub.
Collected Mathematical Papers, 4 Vols. James J. Sylvester. LC 76-250188. 1973. Repr. of 1904 ed. text ed. 125.00 (ISBN 0-8284-0253-1). Chelsea Pub.
Collected Papers. A. M. Dale. Ed. by T. B. Webster & E. G. Turner. LC 69-10574. 1969. 48.00 (ISBN 0-521-04763-3). Cambridge U Pr.
Collected Papers. S. Ramanujan. LC 62-8326. 1962. 13.95 (ISBN 0-8284-0159-4). Chelsea Pub.
Collected Papers of Charles Darwin, 2 vol. set. Charles Darwin. Ed. by Paul H. Barrett. 886p. pap. 13.50. U of Chicago Pr.
Collected Papers of G. H. Hardy: Theory of Series, Vol. 6. Godfrey H. Hardy. Ed. by London Mathematical Society Committee. 1974. 49.00 (ISBN 0-19-853340-3). Oxford U Pr.
Collected Papers of P. L. Kapitza, 2 vols. P. L. Kapitza. Ed. by D. Ter Haar. Vol. 1. 1965. 42.35 o.p. (ISBN 0-08-010744-3); Vol. 2. 1965. o.p. (ISBN 0-08-010973-X). Pergamon.
Collected Papers on the History of Grammar in the Middle Ages. R. W. Hunt. Ed. by G. Bursill-Hall. (Studies in the History of Linguistics: No. 5). 1980. text ed. 31.50x (ISBN 0-391-01667-9). Humanities.
Collected Papers on the Paranormal. Theodore Besterman. LC 66-28500. (Illus.). 1968. 12.50 o.p. (ISBN 0-912326-21-2). Garrett-Helix.
Collected Plays of Euripides. Euripides. Tr. by Gilbert Murray. 1976. text ed. 14.95x o.p. (ISBN 0-04-882028-8); pap. text ed. 7.95x o.p. (ISBN 0-04-882056-3). Allen Unwin.
Collected Plays of Neil Simon, Vol. 2. Neil Simon. 744p. 1980. pap. 7.95 (ISBN 0-380-51904-6, 51094). Avon.
Collected Poems. Dannie Abse. LC 76-21049. (Pitt Poetry Ser.). 1977. pap. 4.95 (ISBN 0-685-75151-1). U of Pittsburgh Pr.
Collected Poems. 2nd ed. Conrad P. Aiken. LC 79-120179. 1970. 25.00 (ISBN 0-19-501258-5). Oxford U Pr.
Collected Poems. F. W. Allen. 1980. 5.95 (ISBN 0-533-04847-8). Vantage.
Collected Poems. Samuel Davies. Ed. by Richard B. Davis. LC 68-17019. 1968. 29.00x (ISBN 0-8201-1011-6). Schol Facsimiles.
Collected Poems. Edwin Denby. LC 75-23024. 1975. 14.95 (ISBN 0-916190-00-5); pap. 6.00 (ISBN 0-916190-01-3). Full Court NY.
Collected Poems. Austin Dobson. 567p. 1980. Repr. of 1907 ed. lib. bdg. 25.00 (ISBN 0-89984-151-1). Century Bookbindery.
Collected Poems. Lenna P. Duty. Date not set. 4.95 (ISBN 0-533-04771-4). Vantage.
Collected Poems. Padraic Fallon. 176p. 1974. text ed. 9.00x (ISBN 0-85105-232-0, Dolmen Pr). Humanities.
Collected Poems. rev. ed. Vachel Lindsay. (Illus.). 1925. 17.50 (ISBN 0-02-572530-0). Macmillan.
Collected Poems. Ed. by Louis MacNeice & E. R. Dodds (ISBN 0-571-04985-0, Pub. by Faber & Faber). pap. 11.50 (ISBN 0-571-11353-2). Merrimack Bk Serv.
Collected Poems. Marianne Moore. 1951. 8.95 (ISBN 0-02-586170-0). Macmillan.
Collected Poems. St. John Perse. Tr. by W. H. Auden. 1972. 27.50x o.p. (ISBN 0-691-09858-1). Princeton U Pr.
Collected Poems. Alexander Pope. Ed. by Bonamy Dobree. 1976. 7.50x (ISBN 0-460-00760-2, Evman); pap. 3.75 (ISBN 0-460-01760-8, Evman). Dutton.
Collected Poems. Kathleen Raine. 1966. 10.95 o.p. (ISBN 0-241-90115-4). Dufour.
Collected Poems. Edwin A. Robinson. 1937. 19.95 o.s.i. (ISBN 0-02-604080-8). Macmillan.
Collected Poems. Theodore Roethke. LC 65-23785. 288p. 1975. pap. 5.95 (ISBN 0-385-08601-6, Anch). Doubleday.
Collected Poems. Edith Sitwell. LC 67-31053. 1954. 15.00 (ISBN 0-8149-0203-0). Vanguard.
Collected Poems. Sydney G. Smith. (Scottish Library Ser). 269p. 1975. text ed. 22.25x (ISBN 0-7145-3511-7). Humanities.
Collected Poems. Dylan Thomas. LC 53-7766. 1971. pap. 4.95 (ISBN 0-8112-0205-4, NDP316). New Directions.
Collected Poems. Gilbert Thomas. 1969. text ed. 6.50x o.p. (ISBN 0-04-821023-4). Allen Unwin.
Collected Poems. Yvor Winters. 146p. 1960. pap. 4.95x (ISBN 0-8040-0047-6, 10). Swallow.
Collected Poems. James Wright. LC 70-142727. 1971. 15.00x (ISBN 0-8195-4031-5, Pub. by Wesleyan U Pr); pap. 6.95 (ISBN 0-8195-6022-7). Columbia U Pr.
Collected Poems. definitive 2nd ed. William B. Yeats. 1956. 14.95 (ISBN 0-02-632690-6). Macmillan.
Collected Poems and Epigrams. J. V. Cunningham. LC 71-132578. 142p. 1971. pap. 8.95 (ISBN 0-8040-0517-6). Swallow.
Collected Poems & Plays. Wyndham Lewis. Ed. by Alan Munton. (Poetry Ser.). 229p. 1979. 14.95 o.s.i. (ISBN 0-85635-171-7, Pub. by Carcanet New Pr England). Persea Bks.
Collected Poems & Plays. Rabindranath Tagore. 1966. 10.95 o.s.i. (ISBN 0-02-615920-1). Macmillan.
Collected Poems Nineteen Thirty-One to Nineteen Seventy-Four. Lawrence Durrell. Ed. by James A. Brigham. 352p. 1980. 22.95 (ISBN 0-670-22792-7). Viking Pr.

Collected Poems, Nineteen Twenty-Four to Nineteen Seventy-Four. John Beecher. LC 73-10560. 352p. 1974. 12.95 (ISBN 0-02-508310-4). Macmillan.

Collected Poems of E. L. Mayo. E. L. Mayo. Ed. by David Ray. LC 80-84519. (New Letters Bks.). 185p. (Orig.). 1981. pap. text ed. 6.00 (ISBN 0-938652-00-1). New Letters.

Collected Poems of Edward Thomas. Ed. by George R. Thomas. 240p. 1981. pap. 9.95 (ISBN 0-19-281288-2). Oxford U Pr.

Collected Poems of Elizabeth Barger Joseph. Harrison O. Joseph. 64p. 1981. 10.00 (ISBN 0-682-49674-X). Exposition.

Collected Poems of G. K. Chesterton. G. K. Chesterton. LC 80-16874. 1980. pap. 5.95 (ISBN 0-396-07896-6). Dodd.

Collected Poems of H. Phelps Putnam. H. Phelps Putnam. Ed. by Charles R. Walker. 232p. (Index of first lines). 1971. 10.00 o.p. (ISBN 0-374-12627-5). FS&G.

Collected Poems of Klara L. Kovacs: Eszmeles. Klara L. Kovacs. (Rainbow Bks.: No. 1). (Illus.). 1980. write for info. (ISBN 0-936398-01-9). Framo Pub.

Collected Poems of Malcolm MacDonald. Malcolm MacDonald. 1978. 4.75 o.p. (ISBN 0-533-02200-2). Vantage.

Collected Poems of Robert Service. Robert Service. LC 63-11542. 1944. 10.00 (ISBN 0-396-01356-2). Dodd.

Collected Poems of Rupert Brooke. Rupert Brooke. LC 80-16869. 1980. pap. 4.95 (ISBN 0-396-07894-X). Dodd.

Collected Poems of St. John Perse. Tr. by W. H. Auden. LC 70-100357. (Bollingen Ser., No. 87). 1972. 27.50x o.p. (ISBN 0-691-09858-1). Princeton U Pr.

Collected Poems of Sara Teasdale. Sara Teasdale. Ed. by Marya Zaturenska. 1967. 12.95 (ISBN 0-02-616890-1). Macmillan.

Collected Poems of Thomas Merton. Thomas Merton. LC 77-9902. 1088p. 1980. pap. 17.00 (ISBN 0-8112-0769-2, NDP504). New Directions.

Collected Poems of Weldon Kees. rev ed. Weldon Kees. Ed. by Donald Justice. LC 75-3567. xviii, 180p. 1975. 11.50x (ISBN 0-8032-0864-2); pap. 3.95 (ISBN 0-8032-5828-3, BB 609, Bison). U of Nebr Pr.

Collected Poems, Stories, & Collages: George Hitchcock. George Hitchcock. (Illus.). 340p. 1981. 12.95 (ISBN 0-937310-04-2); pap. 7.95 (ISBN 0-937310-05-0). Jazz Pr.

Collected Poems, 1835-1892. Christopher P. Cranch. Ed. by Joseph DeFalco. LC 70-161930. 1971. 65.00x (ISBN 0-8201-1091-4). Schol Facsimiles.

Collected Poems, 1909-1962. T. S. Eliot. LC 63-21424. 1963. 9.95 (ISBN 0-15-118978-1). HarBraceJ.

Collected Poems, 1915-1967. Kenneth Burke. 1968. 16.50x (ISBN 0-520-00195-8). U of Cal Pr.

Collected Poems, 1942-1968. William Hull. 20.00 (ISBN 0-89253-473-7); flexible cloth 10.00 (ISBN 0-89253-474-5). Ind-US Inc.

Collected Poems, 1944-1979. Kingsley Amis. 162p. 1980. 10.00 (ISBN 0-670-22910-5). Viking Pr.

Collected Poems, 1956-1976. David Wagoner. LC 75-28915. (Midland Bks.: No. 216). 320p. 1978. 12.50x (ISBN 0-253-11245-1); pap. 7.95x (ISBN 0-253-20216-7). Ind U Pr.

Collected Screenplays of Bernard Shaw. G. B. Shaw. Ed. by Bernard F. Dukore. LC 80-13320. (Illus.). 400p. 1980. 35.00 (ISBN 0-8203-0524-3). U of Ga Pr.

Collected Shorter Poems: 1927 to 1957. W. H. Auden. 352p. Date not set. pap. 3.95 (ISBN 0-394-72015-6, V-2015, Vin). Random.

Collected Shorter Poems 1927-1957. W. H. Auden. 1967. 15.95 (ISBN 0-394-40333-9). Random.

Collected Stories of Caroline Gordon. Caroline Gordon. 1981. 17.50 (ISBN 0-374-12630-5). FS&G.

Collected Stories of Elizabeth Bowen. Elizabeth Bowen. LC 80-8729. 784p. 1981. 17.95 (ISBN 0-394-51666-4). Knopf.

Collected Stories of Eudora Welty. Eudora Welty. LC 80-7947. 576p. 1980. 17.50 (ISBN 0-15-118994-3). HarBraceJ.

Collected Stories of Paul Bowles. Paul Bowles. 419p. 1980. 14.00 (ISBN 0-87685-397-1); pap. 7.50 (ISBN 0-87685-396-3). Black Sparrow.

Collected Stories, 1893-1897, 4 Vols. in One. Hubert Crackanthorpe. LC 74-75379. 1969. 75.00x (ISBN 0-8201-1056-6). Schol Facsimiles.

Collected Words. Barry Weaver. Date not set. 4.75 (ISBN 0-8062-1607-7). Carlton.

Collected Works. Antonin Artaud. Tr. by V. Corti & A. Hamilton. Incl. Vol. 1. Correspondence with J. Riviere-Umbilical Limbo-Nerve Scales- Art & Death-Cup & Ball-Seven Letters-Unpublished Prose & Poetry. 247p. 1968. 17.50x (ISBN 0-7145-0169-7); Vol. 2. The Alfred Jarry Theatre-Two Stage Scenarios & Two Production Plans-Reviews-On Literature & the Plastic Arts. (Illus.). 240p. 1971. 13.50x (ISBN 0-7145-0171-9); Vol. 3. Scenarios-On the Cinema-Interviews-Letters. (Illus.). 255p. 1972. 15.00x (ISBN 0-7145-0778-4); Vol. 4. The Theatre & Its Double-The Cenci-Documents. 1974. 15.00x (ISBN 0-7145-0622-2). LC 76-369595. (French Surrealism Ser.). Intl Pubns Serv.

Collected Works, 6 vols. John Von Neumann. Ed. by A. W. Taub. Incl. Vol. 1. Logic, Theory of Sets & Quantum Mechanics. 1961. 110.00 (ISBN 0-08-009567-4); Vol. 2. Operators, Ergodic Theory & Almost Periodic Functions in a Group. 1962. 110.00 (ISBN 0-08-009568-2); Vol. 3. Rings of Operators. 1962. 110.00 (ISBN 0-08-009569-0); Vol. 4. 1963. 110.00 (ISBN 0-08-009570-4); Vol. 5. 1963. 110.00 (ISBN 0-08-009571-2); Vol. 6. Theory of Games, Astrophysics, Hydrodynamics & Meteorology. 1963. 110.00 (ISBN 0-08-009572-0). 1963. Set. 660.00 (ISBN 0-08-009566-6). Pergamon.

Collected Works of Abraham Lincoln, 9 vols. Abraham Lincoln. Ed. by Roy P. Basler. 1953. Set. 275.00 (ISBN 0-8135-0172-5). Rutgers U Pr.

Collected Works of Buck Rogers. Dick Calkins & Phil Nowlan. Ed. by Robert C. Dille. LC 70-99585. (Illus.). 375p. 1981. pap. 12.50 (ISBN 0-87754-221-X). Chelsea Hse.

Collected Works of Carl G. Jung, Vols. 1-20. Carl G. Jung. Ed. by G. Adler et al. Tr. by R. F. Hull. Incl. Vol. 1. Psychiatric Studies. 2nd ed. 1970. 13.00 (ISBN 0-691-09768-2); Vol. 2. Experimental Researches. 1972. 21.00 (ISBN 0-691-09764-X); Vol. 3. Psychogenesis of Mental Disease. 1960. 16.00 (ISBN 0-691-09769-0); Vol. 4. Freud & Psychoanalysis. 1961. 18.00 (ISBN 0-691-09765-8); Vol. 5. Symbols of Transformation. 2nd ed. 1967. 24.00 (ISBN 0-691-09775-5); Vol. 6. Psychological Types. 25.00 (ISBN 0-691-09770-4); pap. 8.95; Vol. 7. Two Essays on Analytical Psychology. 1972. 16.00 (ISBN 0-691-09776-3); Vol. 8. Structure & Dynamics of the Psyche. 2nd ed. 1970. 21.00 (ISBN 0-691-09774-7); Vol. 9, Pt. 1. Archetypes & the Collective Unconscious. 2nd ed. 1969. 30.00 (ISBN 0-691-09761-5); Vol. 9, Pt. 2. Aion: Researches into the Phenomonology of the Self. 2nd ed. 1968. 18.00 (ISBN 0-691-09759-3); Vol. 10. Civilization in Transition. 2nd ed. 1964. 21.00 (ISBN 0-691-09762-3); Vol. 11. Psychology & Religion: East & West. 1970. 21.00 (ISBN 0-691-09772-0); Vol. 12. Psychology & Alchemy. 2nd ed. 1968. 24.00 (ISBN 0-691-09771-2); Vol. 13. Alchemical Studies. 1968. 20.00 (ISBN 0-691-09760-7); Vol. 14. Mysterium Coinunctionis. 2nd ed. 1970. 35.00 (ISBN 0-691-09766-6); Vol. 15. Spirit in Man, Art & Literature. 1971. 9.50 (ISBN 0-691-09773-9); Vol. 16. Practice of Psychotherapy. 2nd ed. 1966. 25.00 (ISBN 0-691-09767-4); Vol. 17. Development of Personality. 1954. 12.00 (ISBN 0-691-09763-1); Vol. 18. The Symbolic Life: Miscellaneous Writings. 1976. 30.00 (ISBN 0-691-09892-1); Vol. 19. General Bibliography. 1979. 17.50x (ISBN 0-691-09893-X); Vol.20. General Index. 1979. 25.00 (ISBN 0-691-09867-0). (Bollingen Ser.: No. 20). Princeton U Pr.

Collected Works of Isaac Rosenberg. Isaac Rosenberg. Ed. by Ian Parsons. (Illus.). 1979. 29.95 (ISBN 0-19-520143-4). Oxford U Pr.

Collected Works of Jane Austen. 1200p. Date not set. 9.95 (ISBN 0-7064-1150-1). Mayflower Bks.

Collected Works of Jane Bowles. Jane Bowles. 431p. 1966. 8.50 (ISBN 0-374-12576-7). FS&G.

Collected Works of Josiah Willard Gibbs, 2 vols. Josiah W. Gibbs. 1948. Set. 100.00x o.p. (ISBN 0-686-51355-X). Elliots Bks.

Collected Works of Mahatma Gandi: 04/01/1942 to 12/17/1942, Vol. 76. Mohandas K. Gahndi. LC 58-36286. (Illus.). 491p. 1979. 10.00x o.p. (ISBN 0-8002-2465-5). Intl Pubns Serv.

Collected Works of Mahatma Gandi: 12/17/1942 to 07/31/1944, Vol. 77. Mohanad K. Gandhi. LC 58-36286. (Illus.). 508p. 1979. 10.00x o.p. (ISBN 0-8002-2466-3). Intl Pubns Serv.

Collected Works of Paul Valery, Vol. 14. Analects. Paul Valery. Tr. by Stuart Gilbert. LC 56-9337. (Bollingen Ser.: Vol. 45). 1969. 21.50x o.p. (ISBN 0-691-09837-9). Princeton U Pr.

Collected Works of St. Teresa of Avila, Vol. 2. Tr. by Kieran Kavanaugh & Otilio Rodriguez. LC 75-31305. 560p. 1980. pap. 6.95x (ISBN 0-9600876-6-4). ICS Pubns.

Collected Works of Samuel Beckett, 23 vols. Samuel Beckett. LC 74-28586. 1981. Set. 125.00 (ISBN 0-394-49789-9). Grove.

Collected Works of Samuel Taylor Coleridge: Logic, Vol. 13. Samuel T. Coleridge. Ed. by J. R. Jackson. LC 68-10201. (Bollingen Ser.: No. LXXV). 1981. 30.00 (ISBN 0-691-09880-8). Princeton U Pr.

Collected Works: Vols. 1-77. Mohandas K. Gandhi. LC 58-36286. 1958-1979. Set. 10.00x ea. (ISBN 0-8002-0138-8). Intl Pubns Serv.

Collected Writings, 23 vols. John M. Keynes. Incl. Vol. 1. Indian Currency & Finance. 184p. 1971. Repr. of 1913 ed (ISBN 0-521-22093-9); Vol. 2. Economic Consequences of the Peace. LC 76-133449. 192p. 1971. Repr. of 1919 ed; Vol. 3. Revision of the Treaty. LC 76-133449. 158p. 1972 (ISBN 0-521-22095-5); Vol. 4. Tract on Monetary Reform. LC 76-133449. 172p. 1972 (ISBN 0-521-22096-3); Vol. 5. Pt. 1. Treatise on Money, the Pure Theory of Money. 336p. 1972 (ISBN 0-521-22097-1); Vol. 6, Pt.2. Treatise on Money, the Applied Theory of Money. 390p. 1972 (ISBN 0-521-22098-X); Vol. 7. General Theory of Employment, Interest, & Money. 428p. 1973 (ISBN 0-521-22099-8). pap. 5.95 (ISBN 0-521-29382-0); Vol. 8. Treatise on Probability. 514p. 1972 (ISBN 0-312-31885-5); Vol. 9. Essays & Persuasions. 451p. 1972 (ISBN 0-312-26355-4); Vol. 10. Essays in Biography. 460p. 1972 (ISBN 0-521-22102-1); Vol. 13. General Theory & After, Pt. One: Preparation. 653p. 1973 (ISBN 0-521-22103-X); Vol. 14. General Theory & After, Pt. Two: Defence & Development. 584p. 1973 (ISBN 0-521-22104-8); Vol. 15. Activities: Nineteen-Six to Nineteen-Fourteen: India & Cambridge. 312p. 1971 (ISBN 0-521-22105-6); Vol. 16. Activities, Nineteen-Fourteen to Nineteen-Nineteen: The Treasury & Versailles. 488p. 1971 (ISBN 0-521-22106-4); Vol. 17. Activities Nineteen Twenty to Twenty-Two: Treaty Revision & Reconstruction. 1978 (ISBN 0-521-21874-8); Vol. 18. Activities Nineteen Twenty-Two to Thirty-Two: The End of Reparations. 1978 (ISBN 0-521-21875-6); Vol. 19. Activities Nineteen Thirty-Nine to Forty-Five: Internal War Finance. 519p. 1978 (ISBN 0-521-21876-4); Vol. 20. Activities Nineteen Forty to Forty-Three: External War Finance. 330p. 1979 (ISBN 0-521-22016-5); Vol. 21. Activities Nineteen Forty-Four to Forty-Six: The Transition to Peace. 688p. 1979 (ISBN 0-521-22017-3); Vol. 22. Activities Nineteen Forty-Three to Forty-Six: Shaping the Post War World: the Clearing Union (ISBN 0-521-22018-1); Vol. 23. Activities Nineteen Forty-Three to Forty-Six: Shaping the Postwar World: Bretton Woods & Reparations. 368p. 1980 (ISBN 0-521-22934-0); Vol. 24. Activities Nineteen Forty to Forty-Six: Shaping the Post-War World: Employment & Commodities (ISBN 0-521-23074-8); General Theory & After: A Supplement. 309p. 1979 (ISBN 0-521-22949-9). 42.50 ea. Cambridge U Pr.

Collected Writings of Dougal Graham, Skellat Bellman of Glasgow, 2 Vols. Dougal Graham. LC 69-16478. 1968. Repr. of 1883 ed. Set. 18.00 (ISBN 0-8103-3535-2). Gale.

Collected Writings of H. P. Blavatsky. Helena P. Blavatsky. Incl. Vol. 1. 1874-1878. rev. ed (ISBN 0-8356-0082-3); Vol. 2. 1879-1880 (ISBN 0-8356-0091-2); Vol. 3. 1881-1882 (ISBN 0-8356-0099-8); Vol. 4. 1882-1883 (ISBN 0-8356-0106-4); Vol. 5. 1883 (ISBN 0-8356-0117-X); Vol. 6. 1883-1884-1885 (ISBN 0-8356-0125-0); Vol. 7. 1886-1887 (ISBN 0-8356-0222-2); Vol. 8. 1887 (ISBN 0-8356-7166-6); Vol. 9. 1888 (ISBN 0-8356-0217-6); Vol. 10. 1888-1889 (ISBN 0-8356-0218-4). (Illus.). 14.50 ea. Theos Pub Hse.

Collected Writings of John Maynard Keynes: The General Theory & After - A Supplement, Vol. 29. John M. Keynes. Ed. by D. Moggridge. LC 76-13349. 1980. 42.50 (ISBN 0-521-22949-9). Cambridge U Pr.

Collected Writings of John Maynard Keynes, Vol. 25, Activities 1940-44: Shaping the Postwar World: The Clearing Union. John M. Keynes. Ed. by D. Moggridge. LC 76-13349. 360p. 1980. 42.50 (ISBN 0-521-22018-1). Cambridge U Pr.

Collected Writings of John Maynard Keynes, Vol. 27, Activities 1940-46: Shaping the Postwar World: Employment & Commodities. John M. Keynes. Ed. by D. Moggridge. LC 76-13349. 424p. 1980. 42.50 (ISBN 0-521-23074-8). Cambridge U Pr.

Collected Writings of John Maynard Keynes, Vol. 26, Activities 1943-46: Shaping the Postwar World: Bretton Woods & Reparations. John M. Keynes. Ed. by D. Moggridge. LC 76-13349. 1980. 42.50 (ISBN 0-521-22939-1). Cambridge U Pr.

Collected Writings of John Murray: Lectures in Systematic Theology, Vol. 2. John Murray. 1978. 11.95 (ISBN 0-85151-242-9). Banner of Truth.

Collected Writings of John Murray: The Claims of Truth, Vol. 1. John Murray. 1976. 18.95 (ISBN 0-85151-241-0). Banner of Truth.

Collectible Chinese Art & Antiques. (Illus.). 1973. 7.95 o.p. (ISBN 0-685-33343-4). Warman.

Collectible Glass, 4 bks. Ted Logerberg & Vi. Logerberg. Incl. Bk. I. o.p. (ISBN 0-87069-232-1); Bk. II. o.p. (ISBN 0-87069-233-X); Bk. III. Durand Glass (ISBN 0-87069-234-8); Bk. IV. British Glass (ISBN 0-87069-235-6). (Illus.). 1978. ringbound 6.95 ea. Wallace-Homestead.

Collectible Locks. Richard Holiner. (Illus.). 1979. pap. 5.95 (ISBN 0-89145-115-3). Collector Bks.

Collectibles. James Mackay. (Illus.). 1979. 19.95x (ISBN 0-8464-0254-8). Beekman Pubs.

Collectibles: A Compendium. Marian Klamkin & Charles Klamkin. LC 77-37677. (Illus.). 288p. 1981. pap. 10.95 (ISBN 0-385-12176-8, Dolp). Doubleday.

Collectibles: The Nostalgia Collectors Bible. Bert R. Sugar. 1981. pap. 8.95 (ISBN 0-8256-3149-1, Quick Fox). Music Sales.

Collecting American Craft Antiques. William C. Ketchum. (Illus.). 160p. 1980. 12.95 (ISBN 0-525-93129-5); pap. 7.95 (ISBN 0-525-93130-9). Dutton.

Collecting & Care of Fine Art. Carl David. Ed. by Herbert Michelman. 160p. 1981. 10.00 (ISBN 0-517-54287-0, Michelman Books). Crown.

Collecting & Polishing Stones. Herbert Scarfe. (Illus.). 12.95 (ISBN 0-7134-2283-1). Dufour.

Collecting & Restoring Horse-Drawn Vehicles. D. J. Smith. (Illus.). 192p. 1981. 39.95 (ISBN 0-85059-429-4). Aztex.

Collecting & Restoring Horse-Drawn Vehicles. D. J. Smith. 120p. 1981. 39.95 (ISBN 0-85059-429-4). Aztex.

Collecting Antiques for the Future. Joan Bamford. (Illus.). 1976. 16.95x (ISBN 0-7188-7008-5). Intl Ideas.

Collecting Autographs. 96p. (gr. 4-7). 1981. price not set (ISBN 0-671-34025-5). Messner.

Collecting Autographs & Manuscripts. 2nd ed. Charles Hamilton. LC 61-9007. 1961. pap. 9.95 (ISBN 0-8061-1558-0). U of Okla Pr.

Collecting Chinese Export Porcelain. Elinor Gordon. LC 77-70474. (Illus.). 1977. 17.50x (ISBN 0-87663-295-9). Universe.

Collecting Chromos. Francine Kirsch. LC 80-26616. (Illus.). 288p. 1981. 25.00 (ISBN 0-498-02517-9). A S Barnes.

Collecting, Culturing, & Caring for Living Materials: A Guide for the Teacher, Student & Hobbyist. William E. Claflin. LC 80-69329. 110p. 1981. perfect bdg. 8.50 (ISBN 0-86548-026-5). Century Twenty One.

Collecting Decanters. June Hollingworth. (Christies International Collectors Ser.). (Illus.). 128p. 1980. 14.95 (ISBN 0-8317-2161-8). Mayflower Bks.

Collecting Fans. Susan Mayor. (Christies International Collectors Ser.). (Illus.). 128p. 1980. 14.95 (ISBN 0-8317-3199-0). Mayflower Bks.

Collecting for Fun... & Profit. Mel Lewis. (Illus.). 228p. (Orig.). 1981. pap. 9.95 (ISBN 0-906071-23-2). Proteus Pub NY.

Collecting for the City Naturalist. Lois J. Hussey & Catherine Pessino. LC 73-17293. (Illus.). 96p. (gr. 5 up). 1975. 7.95 (ISBN 0-690-00317-X, TYC-J). T Y Crowell.

Collecting for Tomorrow. Brian Jewell. (Illus.). 1979. 9.95 (ISBN 0-7137-0937-5, Pub by Blandford Pr England). Sterling.

Collecting from Nature. T. J. Jennings. (gr. 3 up). 1976. 8.10 o.p. (ISBN 0-08-016046-8). Pergamon.

Collecting Invertebrate Animals. R. J. Lincoln & J. G. Sheals. LC 79-14530. (Illus.). 1980. 22.50 (ISBN 0-521-22851-4); pap. 6.95 (ISBN 0-521-29677-3). Cambridge U Pr.

Collecting Marine Tropicals. Rodney Jonklaas. 1975. 17.50 o.p. (ISBN 0-87666-119-3, PS728). TFH Pubns.

Collecting Microscopes. Gerard L. Turner. (Christies International Collectors Ser.). (Illus.). 128p. 1980. 14.95 (ISBN 0-8317-5950-X). Mayflower Bks.

Collecting Military Antiques. Frederick Wilkinson. LC 74-15858. (Illus.). 192p. 1976. 14.95 o.s.i. (ISBN 0-06-014661-3, HarpT). Har-Row.

Collecting My Thoughts. William G. Carr. LC 80-82881. (Foundation Monograph Ser.). 101p. (Orig.). 1980. pap. 5.00 (ISBN 0-87367-424-3). Phi Delta Kappa.

Collecting Nostalgia. John Mebane. 1973. pap. 1.50 o.p. (ISBN 0-445-03008-9). Popular Lib.

Collecting Old Fishing Tackle. Art Kimball & Scott Kimball. LC 80-122941. (Illus.). 1980. 30.00 (ISBN 0-9604906-0-4); pap. 19.00 (ISBN 0-9604906-1-2). Aardvark Pubs.

Collecting Old Toy Soldiers. Ian Mackenzie. 1975. 30.00 (ISBN 0-7134-3036-2). David & Charles.

Collecting Original Prints. Rosemary Simons. (Christies International Collectors Ser.). (Illus.). 128p. 1980. 14.95 (ISBN 0-8317-1499-9). Mayflower Bks.
Collecting Paper Money & Bonds. Colin Narbeth et al. (Christies International Collectors Ser.). (Illus.). 128p. 1980. 14.95 (ISBN 0-8317-0940-5). Mayflower Bks.
Collecting People: Your Ancestors & Mine. Carolyn H. Ostler. (gr. 6 up). 1981. 10.00x (ISBN 0-686-08736-4). Genealog Inst.
Collecting Phonographs & Gramophones. Christopher Proudfoot. (Christies International Collectors Ser.). (Illus.). 128p. 1980. 14.95 (ISBN 0-8317-3952-5). Mayflower Bks.
Collecting Photographs: A Guide to the New Art Boom. Landt Dennis & Lisl Dennis. 1977. 12.95 (ISBN 0-87690-236-0); pap. 6.95 o.p. Dutton.
Collecting Postcards in Color 1894-1914. William Duval & Valerie Monahan. (Illus.). 1978. 10.95 (ISBN 0-7137-0823-9, Pub. by Blandford Pr England). Sterling.
Collecting Postcards in Color 1914-1930. Valerie Monahan. (Illus.). 176p. 1980. 12.95 (ISBN 0-7137-1002-0, Pub. by Blandford Pr England); pap. 6.95 (ISBN 0-7137-1080-2). Sterling.
Collecting Small Fossils. Lois J. Hussey & Catherine Pessino. LC 77-101932. (Illus.). (gr. 4-7). 1971. 7.95 (ISBN 0-690-19733-0, TYC-J). T Y Crowell.
Collecting Southwestern Native American Jewelry. Mark Bahti. (Illus.). 1980. pap. 8.95 (ISBN 0-679-50960-7). McKay.
Collecting Stamps. Paul Villiard. LC 73-10950. 208p. (gr. 5-7). 1974. PLB 7.95 (ISBN 0-385-08677-6). Doubleday.
Collecting the Edged Weapons of the Third Reich, Vol. 4. Thomas M. Johnson. Tr. by Wilfrid Bradach. LC 75-15486. (Illus.). 1981. 25.00 (ISBN 0-686-69390-6). T M Johnson.
Collecting Today for Tomorrow. David A. Herzog. LC 79-18557. (Illus.). 1981. 10.00 (ISBN 0-668-04717-8). Arco.
Collecting Today for Tomorrow. David A. Herzog. LC 79-18557. (Illus.). 192p. 1981. pap. 4.95 (ISBN 0-668-04883-2, 4883). Arco.
Collecting Victorian Ceramic Tiles. Julian Barnard. (Christies International Collectors Ser.). (Illus.). 128p. 1980. 14.95 (ISBN 0-8317-9168-3). Mayflower Bks.
Collection: Classic Community Cookbooks. 2nd ed. Hays, Rolfes & Associates. (Illus.). 1980. pap. 6.50 (ISBN 0-9602448-1-6). Hays Rolfes.
Collection Development Policy. (Orig.). 1976. pap. 10.00 o.p. (ISBN 0-930214-00-5). U TX Austin Gen Libs.
Collection: Literature of the Seventies. Gerald Messner & Nancy S. Messner. LC 79-162644. 915p. 1972. pap. text ed. 11.95x o.p. (ISBN 0-669-63636-3); tchrs. manual free o.p. (ISBN 0-669-75390-4). Heath.
Collection Litteraire, 6 vols. A. Lagarde & L. Michard. Incl. Vol. 1. Moyen Age. 9.60 (ISBN 0-685-58371-6); Vol. 2. Seizieme Siecle. 9.60 (ISBN 0-685-58372-4); Vol. 3. Dix-Septieme Siecle. 10.90 (ISBN 0-685-58373-2); Vol. 4. Dix-Huitieme Siecle. 12.25 (ISBN 0-685-58374-0); Vol. 5. Dix-Neuvieme Siecle. 13.65 (ISBN 0-685-58375-9); Vol. 6. Vingtieme Siecle. 17.25 (ISBN 0-685-58376-7). (Fr.). Schoenhof.
Collection: My Innermost Thoughts. Clayton L. Hannah. Date not set. 5.95 (ISBN 0-533-04703-X). Vantage.
Collection, Nineteen Seventy-Nine. Shirley G. Luthman. LC 79-92404. (Orig.). 1980. pap. 7.95 (ISBN 0-936094-02-8). Mehetabel & Co.
Collection of College Words & Customs. Benjamin H. Hall. LC 68-17995. 1968. Repr. of 1856 ed. 24.00 (ISBN 0-8103-3282-5). Gale.
Collection of Decisions of the Court of the King Bench Upon the Poor Laws. Edmund Bott. Ed. by David S. Berkowitz & Samuel E. Thorne. LC 77-89222. (Classics of English Legal History in the Modern Era: Vol. 67). 399p. 1979. lib. bdg. 40.00 (ISBN 0-8240-3166-0). Garland Pub.
Collection of Emblemes: Ancient & Moderne. George Wither. (Illus.). 303p. 1973. Repr. of 1633 ed. 30.00x (ISBN 0-85967-134-8, Pub. by Scolar Pr England). Biblio Dist.
Collection of Employer Contributions Institute, Las Vegas, Nevada, June 15 to 18, 1980: Proceedings. Ed. by Elizabeth A. Heib. 77p. (Orig.). 1980. pap. 8.00 (ISBN 0-89154-138-1). Intl Found Employ.
Collection of Essays. George Orwell. LC 54-7594. 1970. pap. 3.95 (ISBN 0-15-618600-4, HPL48, HPL). HarBraceJ.
Collection of Essays & Fugitiv Writings on Moral, Historical, Political, & Literary Subjects. Noah Webster. LC 77-22094. 1977. Repr. of 1790 ed. 45.00x (ISBN 0-8201-1297-6). Schol Facsimiles.
Collection of International Concessions & Related Instruments, Vols. 9-10. Fischer. 1980. 45.00 ea. Vol. 9 (ISBN 0-379-10084-3). Vol. 10 (ISBN 0-379-10085-1). Oceana.
Collection of Miscellanies. John Norris. Ed. by Rene Wellek. LC 75-11242. (British Philosophers & Theologians of the 17th & 18th Centuries Ser.). 1978. Repr. of 1687 ed. lib. bdg. 42.00 (ISBN 0-8240-1794-3). Garland Pub.
Collection of Models by John Flaxman at University College, London: A Catalogue & Introduction. Margaret Whinney & Rupert Gunnis. 1967. text ed. 11.50x (ISBN 0-485-11088-1, Athlone Pr). Humanities.
Collection of Outstanding Cases in Marketing Management. William Zikmund & William J. Lundstrom. (Illus.). 1979. pap. text ed. 12.95 (ISBN 0-8299-0234-1); instrs.' manual avail. (ISBN 0-8299-0585-5). West Pub.
Collection of Papers Relative to the Dispute Between Great Britain & America, 1764-1775. Ed. by John Almon. LC 70-146272. (Era of the American Revolution Ser). 1971. Repr. of 1777 ed. lib. bdg. 32.50 (ISBN 0-306-70127-8). Da Capo.
Collection of Poems. Charles P. McGovern. 1981. 5.95 (ISBN 0-533-04804-4). Vantage.
Collection of Problems in Classical Mechanics. G. I. Kotkin & V. G. Serbo. 1971. 18.00 (ISBN 0-08-015843-9). Pergamon.
Collection of Problems in Physical Chemistry. Jiri Bares et al. 1962. text ed. 27.00 (ISBN 0-08-009577-1). Pergamon.
Collection of Programming Problems & Techniques. H. A. Maurer & M. R. Williams. (Illus.). 256p. 1972. pap. 17.95x ref. ed. (ISBN 0-13-139592-0). P-H.
Collection of Seventy-Nine Black-Letter Ballads & Broadsides, Printed in the Reign of Queen Elizabeth, Between the Years 1559 & 1597. LC 68-20125. xxxvi, 319p. 1968. Repr. of 1867 ed. 20.00 (ISBN 0-8103-3410-0). Gale.
Collection of Several Pieces, 2 vols. John Toland. Ed. by Rene Wellek. LC 75-11258. (British Philosophers & Theologians of the 17th & 18th Centuries: Vol. 57). 1977. Repr. of 1726 ed. Set. lib. bdg. 76.00 (ISBN 0-8240-1808-7); lib. bdg. 42.00 ea. Garland Pub.
Collection of Solved Problems in Circuits, Electronics, & Signal Analysis, Vol. 1. Kendall L. Su. 96p. 1980. pap. text ed. 5.50 (ISBN 0-8403-2262-3). Kendall-Hunt.
Collection of Some of the Most Interesting Narratives of Indian Warfare in the West. Samuel L. Metcalf. LC 75-7060. (Indian Captivities Ser.: Vol. 38). 1977. Repr. of 1821 ed. lib. bdg. 44.00 (ISBN 0-8240-1662-9). Garland Pub.
Collection of Stuffed Dolls from a Fancy World. Kyoko Yoneyama. (Illus.). 1977. 11.50 (ISBN 0-87040-401-6). Japan Pubns.
Collection of Tales from Uji. D. E. Mills. LC 72-114604. (Cambridge Oriental Publications: No. 15). (Illus.). 1970. 49.50 (ISBN 0-521-07754-0). Cambridge U Pr.
Collection of the Moral & Instructive Sentiments, Maxims, Cautions, & Reflexions, Contained in the Histories of Pamela, Clarissa, & Sir Charles Grandison. Samuel Richardson. LC 80-22492. 1980. Repr. of 1755 ed. 45.00x (ISBN 0-8201-1357-3). Schol Facsimilies.
Collection of the Qur'an. J. Burton. LC 76-27899. 1977. 38.50 (ISBN 0-521-21439-4); pap. 12.95 (ISBN 0-521-29652-8). Cambridge U Pr.
Collections of the Massachusetts Historical Society, Vol. 3-4, 8. (Sixth Ser.). 25.00 (ISBN 0-686-27106-8). Mass Hist Soc.
Collective Bargaining. I. W. Abel. 84p. 1976. 8.50x (ISBN 0-915604-05-1). Columbia U Pr.
Collective Bargaining. Allan Flanders. 1967. 3.95 o.p. (ISBN 0-571-08232-7, Pub. by Faber & Faber). Merrimack Bk Serv.
Collective Bargaining & Government Policies in Ten OECD Countries: Austria, Canada, France, Germany, Italy, Japan, N. Zealand, Sweden, UK & US. OECD. (Illus.). 151p. (Orig.). 1980. pap. 9.00x (ISBN 92-64-12011-4). OECD.
Collective Bargaining & Industrial Relations. Thomas A. Kochan. 1980. 19.95x (ISBN 0-256-02353-0). Irwin.
Collective Bargaining & Labor Relations. E. Edward Herman. (Illus.). 576p. 1981. text ed. 19.95 (ISBN 0-13-140558-6). P-H.
Collective Bargaining & Productivity: The Longshore Mechanization Agreement. Paul T. Hartman. (Institute of Business & Economic Research, UC Berkeley). 1969. 21.00x (ISBN 0-520-01485-5). U of Cal Pr.
Collective Bargaining & Teacher Strikes. Judith Esmay. 1978. pap. text ed. 3.50 (ISBN 0-934460-07-8). NCCE.
Collective Bargaining & the Academic Librarian. John W. Weatherford. LC 76-45424. 1976. 10.00 (ISBN 0-8108-0983-4). Scarecrow.
Collective Bargaining Handbook for Hotels, Restaurants & Institutions. Arch Stokes. (Stokes Employee Relations Ser.). 352p. 1981. spiral bdg. 39.95 (ISBN 0-8436-2149-4). CBI Pub.
Collective Bargaining in Agriculture. Ewell P. Roy. LC 79-113823. 1970. pap. text ed. 7.50x (ISBN 0-8134-1161-0, 1161). Interstate.
Collective Bargaining in Government: Readings & Cases. J. Lowenberg & M. Moskow. (Illus.). 1972. pap. text ed. 12.95 (ISBN 0-13-140483-0). P-H.
Collective Bargaining in Law Enforcement. C. Maddox. (Illus.). 160p. 1975. 16.75 (ISBN 0-398-03192-4). C C Thomas.
Collective Bargaining in Public Employment: The TVA Experience. Michael L. Brookshire & Michael Rogers. LC 76-53867. (Illus.). 1977. 22.95 (ISBN 0-669-01291-2). Lexington Bks.
Collective Bargaining in the British Public Sector. A. W. J. Thomson & P. B. Beaumont. LC 78-71279. 1979. 25.95 (ISBN 0-03-050481-3). Praeger.
Collective Bargaining: New Dimensions in Labor Relations. Ed. by Franklin J. Havelick. (Westview Special Study). 1979. lib. bdg. 24.50x (ISBN 0-89158-386-6). Westview.
Collective Bargaining Procedures for Public Library Employees. Joseph A. Vignone. LC 79-160579. 1971. 10.00 (ISBN 0-8108-0412-3). Scarecrow.
Collective Bargaining: What You Always Wanted to Know About Trade Unions & Never Dared to Ask. Clive Jenkins & Barrie Sherman. 1977. 16.00 (ISBN 0-7100-8690-3); pap. 6.95 (ISBN 0-7100-8691-1). Routledge & Kegan.
Collective Behavior. 2nd ed. Ralph Turner & Lewis Killian. (Illus.). 480p. 1972. text ed. 18.95 (ISBN 0-13-140657-4). P-H.
Collective Definition of Deviance. Ed. by F. James Davis & Richard Stivers. LC 74-10138. 1975. pap. text ed. 9.95 (ISBN 0-02-907260-3). Free Pr.
Collective Memory. Maurice Halbwachs. Tr. by Francis J. Ditter, Jr. & Vida Y. Ditter. LC 74-18576. 256p. (Orig.). 1980. pap. 5.95 (ISBN 0-06-090800-9, CN 800, CN). Har-Row.
Collective Methods of Acceleration. Ed. by M. Reiser & N. Rostoker. (Accelerators & Storage Rings: Vol. 2). 752p. 1979. lib. bdg. 43.00 (ISBN 3-7186-0005-6). Harwood Academic.
Collective Negotiations: A Guide to School Board-Teacher Relations. Robert G. Andree. LC 74-121401. 1970. 29.50x (ISBN 0-89197-704-X). Irvington.
Collective Negotiations in Higher Education: A Reader. Ed. by Clarence R. Hughes et al. 226p. (Orig.). 1973. pap. 5.95 o.p. (ISBN 0-686-02465-6). Blackburn Coll.
Collective Oscillations in a Plasma. A. I. Akhiezer et al. 1967. 22.00 (ISBN 0-08-011894-1). Pergamon.
Collective Properties of Physical Systems: Proceedings. Ed. by Bengt Lundqvist & Stig Lundqvist. 1974. 43.50 (ISBN 0-12-460350-5). Acad Pr.
Collective Security in the 1930's: The Failure of Men or the Failure of Principle? G. Cohan. Ed. by Richard H. Brown & Van R. Halsey. (Amherst Ser.). (gr. 9-12). 1970. pap. text ed. 4.52 (ISBN 0-201-01161-1, Sch Div); tchr's. man. 1.92 (ISBN 0-201-01163-8). A-W.
Collective Self-Reliance of Developing Countries in the Fields of Science & Technology. 23p. 1981. pap. 6.75 (ISBN 92-808-0173-2, T*U*N*U 108, UNU). Unipub.
Collector's Book of Doll Poems. Ed. by Elaine Gilmore & Lachlan MacDonald. (Illus.). 1981. pap. 5.95 (ISBN 0-914598-37-6). Padre Prods.
Collector's Cabinet. Ruth Berges. LC 77-84560. (Illus.). 1980. 20.00 (ISBN 0-498-02117-3). A S Barnes.
Collector's Complete Dictionary of American Antiques. Frances Phipps. LC 72-97256. 656p. 1974. 15.95 (ISBN 0-385-03337-0). Doubleday.
Collector's Dicionary of Quilt Names & Patterns. Yvonne M. Khin. 1980. 29.50 (ISBN 0-87491-408-6); pap. 16.95 (ISBN 0-87491-409-4). Acropolis.
Collector's Dictionary. Henry Hainworth. (Illus.). 128p. 1981. pap. 14.95 (ISBN 0-7100-0745-0). Routledge & Kegan.
Collector's Encyclopedia of Fiesta. 4th rev. ed. Sharon Huxford & Bob Huxford. (Illus.). 1981. pap. 8.95 (ISBN 0-89145-168-4). Collector Bks.
Collector's Encyclopedia of Limoges Porcelain. Mary F. Gaston. (Illus.). 1980. 19.95 (ISBN 0-89145-132-3). Collector Bks.
Collector's Encyclopedia of Occupied Japan Collectibles II. Gene Florence. (Illus.). 1979. 12.95 (ISBN 0-89145-004-1). Collector Bks.
Collector's Encyclopedia of Roseville Pottery. Sharon Husford & Bob Husford. (2nd Ser.). (Illus.). 1980. 19.95 (ISBN 0-89145-139-0). Collector Bks.
Collector's Guide to Antique American Glass. Marvin D. Schwartz. LC 68-27138. 1969. 5.95 o.p. (ISBN 0-385-00889-9). Doubleday.
Collectors' Guide to Britains Model Soldiers. John Ruddle. (Illus.). 158p. 1980. 17.50x (ISBN 0-85242-568-6). Intl Pubns Serv.
Collector's Guide to Carnival Glass. Marian Klamkin. 224p. 1976. 21.50 (ISBN 0-8015-1396-0, Hawthorn); pap. 9.95 (ISBN 0-8015-1397-9, Hawthorn). Dutton.
Collector's Guide to Depression Glass. Marian Klamkin. (Illus.). 288p. 1973. pap. 12.95 (ISBN 0-8015-1399-5, Hawthorn). Dutton.
Collector's Guide to Dollhouses & Dollhouse Miniatures. Marian M. O'Brien. 1974. 16.95 (ISBN 0-8015-1404-5, Hawthorn); pap. 12.95 (ISBN 0-8015-1405-3, Hawthorn). Dutton.
Collector's Guide to European & American Art Pottery. Paulette Schwartzman. (Illus.). 1978. pap. 9.95 o.p. (ISBN 0-89145-072-6). Collector Bks.
Collector's Guide to Kitchen Antiques. Don Raycraft. (Illus.). 1980. 17.95 (ISBN 0-89145-140-4). Collector Bks.
Collector's Guide to Militaria. Derek E. Johnson. (Illus.). 1977. 8.95 o.p. (ISBN 0-8069-0110-1); lib. bdg. 8.29 o.p. (ISBN 0-8069-0111-X). Sterling.
Collector's Guide to Model Aero Engines. O. F. Fisher. (Illus.). 1977. 10.00x (ISBN 0-85242-492-2). Intl Pubns Serv.
Collector's Guide to Paperdolls. Mary Young. (Illus.). 1980. pap. 9.95 (ISBN 0-89145-133-1). Collector Bks.
Collectors Guide to Post Cards. Forrest Lyons, Jr. (Illus.). pap. 8.95 o.p. (ISBN 0-686-51578-1). Wallace-Homestead.
Collector's Guide to U.S. Auctions & Flea Markets. Andrea DiNoto. 320p. (Orig.). 1981. pap. 7.95 (ISBN 0-14-046481-6). Penguin.
Collector's History of the Teddy Bear. 1980. 19.95. Hobby Hse.
Collector's Index. Pearl Turner. (Useful Reference Ser. of Library Books: Vol. 115). 1980. 21.00 (ISBN 0-87305-119-X). Faxon.
Collectors' Paperweights-Price Guide & Catalogue. L. H. Selman. LC 79-87448. (Illus.). 1979. pap. 5.00 o.p. (ISBN 0-933756-00-3). Paperweight Pr.
Collectors' Paperweights-Price Guide & Catalogue. Lawrence H. Selman. (Illus.). 1981. pap. 5.00 (ISBN 0-933756-02-X). Paperweight Pr.
Collector's Twentieth-Century Music in the Western Hemisphere. Arthur Cohn. LC 74-167848. (Music Ser.). 1972. Repr. of 1961 ed. 25.00 (ISBN 0-306-70404-8). Da Capo.
Colleen. Michael Mannion. 1978. pap. 1.75 (ISBN 0-505-51274-2). Tower Bks.
College Accounting: An Introduction. Phebe M. Woltz & Richard T. Arlen. 1979. text ed. 12.95 (ISBN 0-07-071551-3, C); tests 7.95 (ISBN 0-07-071555-6); exams 7.95 (ISBN 0-07-071567-X); practice sets 1 4.95 (ISBN 0-07-071553-X); practice set 2 6.50 (ISBN 0-686-52289-3); transparencies, avail. (ISBN 0-07-074795-4) (ISBN 0-07-071552-1). working papers & solutions guide avail. (ISBN 0-07-071556-4). McGraw.
College Accounting Fundamentals: Principles & Procedures. rev. ed. James D. Edwards. 1981. 16.95x (ISBN 0-256-02460-X); study guides wkbks. 6.95x ea. Vol. 1 (ISBN 0-256-01961-4). Vol. 2 (ISBN 0-256-01962-2). practice sets 4.50x ea. Irwin.
College Administrator's Handbook. Rita Wolotkiewicz. 280p. 1980. text ed. 19.95 (ISBN 0-205-06873-1). Allyn.
College Admissions Data Service Handbook: National Edition, 1980-1981, 4 vols. rev. ed. Ed. by Susan Corderman & Jane McGarry. 2256p. 1980. Set. text ed. 110.00x looseleaf (ISBN 0-933510-12-8); Set. pap. text ed. 95.00x (ISBN 0-933510-11-X). Orchard Hse MA.
College Admissions Data Service Handbook, 1980-81: 1980-81 Edition. rev. ed. Ed. by Susan Corderman & Jane McGarry. Incl. Northeast Regional. 628p. pap. text ed. 30.00x (ISBN 0-933510-07-1); Southeast Regional. 602p. pap. text ed. 30.00x (ISBN 0-933510-08-X); Mid-West Regional. 520p. pap. text ed. 25.00x (ISBN 0-933510-09-8); West Regional. 502p. pap. text ed. 25.00x (ISBN 0-933510-10-1). 1980. Orchard Hse MA.
College Algebra. 2nd ed. Raymond A. Barnett. (Illus.). 1979. text ed. 14.95 (ISBN 0-07-003778-7, C); ans. manual 2.95 (ISBN 0-07-003779-5); tests 5.95 (ISBN 0-07-003784-1). McGraw.
College Algebra. 4th ed. Edwin Beckenbach et al. 1978. text ed. 18.95x (ISBN 0-534-00536-5); study guide 5.95x (ISBN 0-534-00537-3). Wadsworth Pub.
College Algebra. 2nd ed. Joseph L. Dorsett. 1977. pap. text ed. 11.95 o.p. (ISBN 0-8403-1690-9). Kendall-Hunt.
College Algebra. Irwin K. Feinstein & Kenneth H. Murphy. (Quality Paperback: No. 39). (Orig.). 1974. pap. 4.95 (ISBN 0-8226-0039-0). Littlefield.
College Algebra. Edward D. Gaughan. LC 73-81779. (Contemporary Undergraduate Mathematics Ser.). 1974. text ed. 16.95 o.p. (ISBN 0-8185-0097-2). Brooks-Cole.

College Algebra. 2nd ed. Edward D. Gaughan. LC 79-22247. 1980. text ed. 16.95 (ISBN 0-8185-0351-3). Brooks-Cole.
College Algebra. 6th ed. William L. Hart & Bert K. Waits. 1978. text ed. 16.95x (ISBN 0-669-01025-1); inst. manual free (ISBN 0-669-01026-X). Heath.
College Algebra. 3rd ed. Margaret L. Lial & Charles D. Miller. 1981. text ed. 16.95x (ISBN 0-673-15407-6); pap. text ed. 5.95x study guide (ISBN 0-673-15477-7). Scott F.
College Algebra. 2nd ed. Mustafa Munem et al. LC 78-65417. 1979. text ed. 16.95x (ISBN 0-87901-098-3); study guide 6.95x (ISBN 0-87901-099-1). Worth.
College Algebra. 8th, rev. ed. Paul K. Rees et al. (Illus.). 560p. 1981. text ed. 17.95 (ISBN 0-07-051733-9); write for info instr.' manual (ISBN 0-07-051734-7). McGraw.
College Algebra. 5th ed. Joseph B. Rosenbach et al. LC 79-135634. 1971. text ed. 18.95x (ISBN 0-471-00473-1); solutions manual avail. (ISBN 0-471-00474-X). Wiley.
College Algebra. Daniel Saltz & Steven Bryant. 1980. 17.95 (ISBN 0-87620-198-2); write for info. (ISBN 0-8302-1983-8). Goodyear.
College Algebra. Michael Sentlowitz & Margaret Trivisone. (Math - Remedial & Precalculus Ser.). 576p. 1981. text ed. 14.95 (ISBN 0-201-06626-2). A-W.
College Algebra. 3rd ed. Abraham Spitzbart. LC 77-81200. (Illus.). 1978. text ed. 15.95 (ISBN 0-201-07482-6). A-W.
College Algebra. Arnold R. Steffensen & L. Murphy Johnson. 1980. pap. text ed. 15.95x (ISBN 0-673-15370-3). Scott F.
College Algebra. Margaret F. Willerding & Stephen Hoffman. LC 72-165951. 1971. text ed. 18.50 o.p. (ISBN 0-471-94657-5). Wiley.
College Algebra: A Functions Approach. 2nd ed. Mervin L. Keedy & Marvin L. Bittinger. LC 77-79464. 1978. pap. text ed. 15.95 (ISBN 0-201-03866-8); special supplement 0.50 (ISBN 0-201-03861-7). A-W.
College Algebra: A Skills Approach. Nanney & Cable. 1978. pap. text ed. 16.75 (ISBN 0-205-05913-9); instr's manual (ISBN 0-205-05914-7). Allyn.
College Algebra: A Skills Approach, Lecture Version. Nanney & Cable. 320p. 1980. text ed. 16.75 (ISBN 0-205-06914-2, 5669146). Allyn.
College Algebra & Trigonometry. 2nd ed. William L. Hart & Bert K. Waits. 1978. text ed. 17.95x (ISBN 0-669-01460-5); inst. manual free (ISBN 0-669-01462-1). Heath.
College Algebra & Trigonometry. Michael Sentlowitz & Margaret Trivisone. (Math-Remedial & Precalculus Ser.). 576p. 1981. text ed. 14.95 (ISBN 0-201-06676-9). A-W.
College Algebra & Trigonometry. Ralph Steinlage. 1981. text ed. write for info. (ISBN 0-8302-1640-5). Goodyear.
College Algebra & Trigonometry. 2nd ed. Margaret F. Willerding. LC 74-22391. 613p. 1975. text ed. 20.95 (ISBN 0-471-94671-0). Wiley.
College Algebra & Trigonometry. Dennis G. Zill et al. 1979. text ed. 18.95x (ISBN 0-534-00612-4). Wadsworth Pub.
College Algebra & Trigonometry: A Functions Approach. Marshall Fraser. 1978. 18.95 (ISBN 0-8053-2590-5); instr's guide 5.95 (ISBN 0-8053-2591-3). Benjamin-Cummings.
College Algebra & Trigonometry: College Algebra. Lawrence Gilligan & Robert Nenno. 1981. text ed. write for info. (ISBN 0-8302-1996-X). Goodyear.
College Algebra & Trigonometry: Precalculus Math. Lawrence Gilligan & Robert Nenno. 1981. text ed. write for info. (ISBN 0-8302-1992-7). Goodyear.
College Algebra with Trigonometry. Joseph B. Rosenbach et al. LC 73-79572. (Illus.). 1963. text ed. 18.95x o.p. (ISBN 0-471-00476-6). Wiley.
College Alumni Publications. Richard Weiner & James F. Colasurdo. 190p. 1980. 20.00 (ISBN 0-913046-12-4). Public Relations.
College Alumni Publications. Richard Weiner & James F. Colasurdo. LC 80-81159. 1980. 20.00 (ISBN 0-913046-12-X). Public Relations.
College & Student: Selected Readings in the Social Psychology of Higher Education. Ed. by Kenneth A. Feldman. 502p. 1972. text ed. 27.00 (ISBN 0-08-016785-3); pap. text ed. 12.75 (ISBN 0-08-016788-8). Pergamon.
College & Universities Administrators Directory, 1980-1981. 2nd ed. 900p. 1981. 65.00 (ISBN 0-8103-1134-8). Gale.
College & University Administrators Directory 1979-1980. 1980. 65.00 (ISBN 0-8103-1133-X). Gale.
College & University Food Sevice Manual. Paul Fairbrook. LC 79-50956. (Illus.). 1979. pap. 17.50 (ISBN 0-9602456-0-X). Colman Pubs.
College & University Law. Kern Alexander & Erwin Solomon. 1972. incl. 1976 suppl. 17.00 (ISBN 0-87215-146-8); 1976 suppl 6.50 (ISBN 0-87215-298-7). Michie.
College & University Trustee. Louis H. Heilbron. LC 72-5888. (Higher Education Ser). 288p. 1973. 14.95x o.p. (ISBN 0-87589-196-9). Jossey-Bass.
College As a Training Ground for Jobs. Lewis C. Solmon et al. LC 77-2939. (Special Studies). 1977. text ed. 22.95 (ISBN 0-275-24450-4). Praeger.
College Board's Examination. Martin McDonough & Alvin J. Hansen. LC 75-21998. 416p. 1976. lib. bdg. 10.00 (ISBN 0-668-02624-3); pap. 6.00. Arco.
College-Bound Student's Almanac. William F. Shanahan. (Orig.). 1980. pap. 6.95 (ISBN 0-671-18431-8). Monarch Pr.
College Business English. 2nd ed. Jack S. Romine et al. (Illus.). 1972. pap. text ed. 13.95 (ISBN 0-13-141994-3). P-H.
College Business Mathematics. Harry D. Lewis. LC 76-19528. 1976. pap. 13.20 (ISBN 0-8273-0289-4); instructor's guide 2.75 (ISBN 0-8273-0290-8); test bklet 2.80 (ISBN 0-8273-0299-1). Delmar.
College Business Mathematics: An Audio Tutorial Approach. Stanleigh Ayres. 1977. pap. text ed. 13.95 (ISBN 0-675-08500-4); cassettes 95.00 (ISBN 0-675-08499-7). Merrill.
College Calculus with Analytic Geometry. 3rd ed. Murray H. Protter & Charles B. Morrey, Jr. LC 76-12800. (Mathematics Ser.). 1977. text ed. 25.95 (ISBN 0-201-06030-2). A-W.
College Chemistry. Bruce H. Mahan. 1966. text ed. 19.95 (ISBN 0-201-04404-8). A-W.
College Chemistry: An Introduction to Inorganic, Organic & Biochemistry. Morris Hein & Leo Best. LC 80-257. 1980. text ed. 19.95 (ISBN 0-8185-0349-1). Brooks-Cole.
College Chemistry in the Laboratory. Geno Zambotti et al. 1980. 7.25 (ISBN 0-8403-1888-X). Kendall-Hunt.
College Chemistry with Qualitative Analysis. 6th ed. William H. Nebergall et al. 1980. text ed. 21.95x (ISBN 0-669-02217-9); instrs.' manual avail. (ISBN 0-669-02475-9); study guide 7.95 (ISBN 0-669-02474-0); basic laboratory studies 8.95 (ISBN 0-669-02473-2); problems & solutions manual 6.95 (ISBN 0-669-02472-4). Heath.
College Cookbook. rev. ed. Geri Harrington. LC 72-11138. 1977. pap. 3.95 o.p. (ISBN 0-684-15269-X, SL740, ScribT). Scribner.
College Cost Book 1980-81. The College Scholarship Service of the College Board. 192p. (Orig.). 1980. pap. 7.50 (ISBN 0-87447-131-1, 001311). College Bd.
College Credit by Examination: A Systematic Guide to CLEP. Henry C. Allan, Jr. LC 74-6883. 144p. 1975. pap. 5.00 o.p. (ISBN 0-8092-8333-6). Contemp Bks.
College Degrees Through Independent Studies: An Alternative Approach. J. L. Holland. LC 78-67669. 1978. 5.98x (ISBN 0-932700-00-4). Centaur Pubn VA.
College English: Effective Usage Through Linguistics. rev. ed. Lois G. Johnson et al. LC 73-94293. (Illus.). 213p. 1980. pap. text ed. 10.15 (ISBN 0-913310-07-7). PAR Inc.
College English Workshop. Joseph Bellafiore. 1976. 8.17 (ISBN 0-87720-951-0). AMSCO Sch.
College Experience. Mervin B. Freedman. LC 67-13280. (Higher Education Ser.). 1967. 11.95x o.p. (ISBN 0-87589-004-0). Jossey-Bass.
College Experience: The Focus for Psychiatric Research, Vol. 4. GAP Committee on the College Student. (Report No. 52). 1962. pap. 2.00 (ISBN 0-87318-070-4). Adv Psychiatry.
College Geometry. Leslie H. Miller. LC 57-5574. (Century Mathematics Ser.). (Illus.). 1957. text ed. 14.95x (ISBN 0-89197-088-6). Irvington.
College Graduate Guide for Scoring High on Employment Tests. Solomon Wiener. 160p. (Orig.). 1981. pap. 4.95 (ISBN 0-686-69227-6). Monarch Pr.
College Graduates & Jobs: Adjusting to a New Labor Market Situation. Carnegie Commission on Higher Education. LC 73-3288. (Illus.). 264p. 1973. 8.50 o.p. (ISBN 0-07-010061-6, P&RB). McGraw.
College Hill: A Photographic Study of Brown University in Its Two Hundredth Year. William Gerold. LC 65-20874. (Illus.). 120p. 1965. 10.00 (ISBN 0-87057-089-7, Pub. by Brown U Pr). Univ Pr of New England.
College in Dispersion: Women at Bryn Mawr, 1896-1975. Ed. by Ann F. Miller. LC 76-2735. (Special Studies in Higher Education Ser). 1976. 23.50x (ISBN 0-89158-040-9). Westview.
College Instructor's Guide to Teaching & Academia. Roy Udolf. LC 76-7462. 172p. 1976. text ed. 13.95 (ISBN 0-88229-241-2). Nelson-Hall.
College Introductory Physical Science. Education Development Center Introductory Physical Science Group. 1969. pap. text ed. 13.95 (ISBN 0-13-145524-9); achievement tests 12.00 (ISBN 0-13-145540-0); ans. sheets (40 per pkg) 2.00 (ISBN 0-13-145557-5). P-H.
College Latin. Norman J. Dewitt et al. 1954. 16.95x (ISBN 0-673-05105-6). Scott F.
College Learning Resource Center. Dwight F. Burlingame et al. LC 78-13716. 1978. lib. bdg. 18.50x (ISBN 0-87287-189-4). Libs Unl.
College Librarianship. Ed. by William Miller & D. Stephen Rockwood. LC 80-25546. 290p. 1981. 15.00 (ISBN 0-8108-1383-1). Scarecrow.
College Library: A Collection of Essays. G. Jefferson & G. C. Smith-Burnett. 1978. 12.50 (ISBN 0-208-01665-1, Linnet). Shoe String.
College Matchmaker. Charles W. Blaker. LC 80-67604. (Illus.). 56p. (Orig.). (gr. 11-12). 1980. pap. text ed. 3.25 (ISBN 0-9604614-0-X). Rekalb Pr.
College Mathematics. Kaj L. Nielsen. (Orig.). 1958. pap. 3.95 (ISBN 0-06-460105-6, CO 105, COS). Har-Row.
College Mathematics for Business. 2nd ed. Flora M. Locke. LC 73-10090. 384p. 1974. text ed. 17.95x (ISBN 0-471-54321-7); wkbk. 7.95x (ISBN 0-471-54319-5). Wiley.
College Mathematics for Students of Business & the Social Sciences. Dennis G. Zill et al. 1977. text ed. 19.95x (ISBN 0-534-00467-9). Wadsworth Pub.
College Mathematics with Business Applications. 2nd ed. John E. Freund. (Illus.). 720p. 1975. ref. ed. 19.95 (ISBN 0-13-146464-7). P-H.
College Organic Chemistry. R. J. Cremlyn. 1970. text ed. 15.95x o.p. (ISBN 0-435-66192-2); pap. text ed. 9.95x o.p. (ISBN 0-435-66193-0). Heinemann Ed.
College Physical Science. 3rd ed. Wendell H. Slabaugh & Alfred B. Butler. (Illus.). 624p. 1973. text ed. 19.95 (ISBN 0-13-147371-9). P-H.
College Physics. 6th ed. Clarence E. Bennett. LC 67-16622. (Illus.). 1967. pap. 3.95 (ISBN 0-06-460021-1, CO 21, COS). Har-Row.
College Physics. John J. O'Dwyer. 752p. 1980. text ed. 22.95x (ISBN 0-534-00827-5). Wadsworth Pub.
College Physics. 5th ed. Francis W. Sears et al. LC 79-20729. (Physics Ser.). 1980. text ed. 22.95 (ISBN 0-201-07681-0). A-W.
College Placement Directory. 4th ed. O. T. Zimmerman & Mildred K. Zimmerman. 1965. 19.50 (ISBN 0-686-20567-7). Indus Res Serv.
College Planning - Search Book. 6th ed. The American College Testing Program. LC 75-28517. (Illus., Orig.). (gr. 9-12). pap. text ed. 6.00 (ISBN 0-937734-00-4). Am Coll Testing.
College Professoring: Or, Through Academia with Gun & Camera. Oliver P. Kolstoe. LC 75-1237. (Illus.). 159p. 1975. pap. 4.95 (ISBN 0-8093-0712-X). S Ill U Pr.
College Professors & Their Impact on Students. Robert C. Wilson et al. LC 74-26553. 256p. 1975. 18.95 (ISBN 0-471-94961-2, Pub. by Wiley-Interscience). Wiley.
College Reading Program, One. 1968. 270.00 (ISBN 0-574-17201-7, 13-0201); instr's guide avail. (ISBN 0-574-17215-7, 13-0215); student bk. 6.95 (ISBN 0-574-17214-9, 13-0214); specimen set 7.95 (ISBN 0-686-52752-6, 13-0222). SRA.
College Reading Program Two. 1969. 195.00 (ISBN 0-574-17230-0, 13-0230); instr's guide avail. (ISBN 0-574-17240-8, 13-0240); student bk. 6.95 (ISBN 0-574-17239-4); specimen set 7.95 (ISBN 0-686-52754-2). SRA.
College Reading Skills. Kathryn A. Blake. (Illus.). 304p. 1973. pap. text ed. 9.95 (ISBN 0-13-150003-1). P-H.
College Reading: Skills & Practice. Joel S. Weinberg. LC 77-78585. (Illus.). 1978. pap. text ed. 10.95 (ISBN 0-395-25319-5); inst. manual 0.45 (ISBN 0-395-25320-9). HM.
College Reading: Strategies for Success. Lee Kolzow & Jane Lehman. (Illus.). 352p. 1981. pap. text ed. 8.95 (ISBN 0-13-150052-X). P-H.
College Recruiting Report. Ed. by Steven Langer. 1979. pap. 50.00 o.p. (ISBN 0-916506-43-6). Abbott Langer Assocs.
College Recruiting Report: 1980. Ed. by Steven Langer. pap. 75.00 (ISBN 0-916506-57-6). Abbott Langer Assocs.
College Statistics. R. H. Clarke. 1969. pap. 13.95x (ISBN 0-17-741010-8). Intl Ideas.
College Student Introduction to the World of Wall Street. C. Flavian. (Illus.). 84p. 1974. text ed. 29.50 (ISBN 0-913314-31-5). Am Classical Coll Pr.
College Survival. 2nd ed. Elwood Chapman. 230p. 1980. pap. text ed. 6.95 (ISBN 0-574-20615-9, 13-3615); instr's. guide avail. (ISBN 0-574-20616-7, 13-3616). SRA.
College Survival: Find Yourself. Find a Career. Elwood N. Chapman. LC 73-93239. (Illus.). 168p. 1974. pap. text ed. 6.50 (ISBN 0-574-19108-9, 13-2108); instr's guide avail. (ISBN 0-574-20006-1, 13-3006). SRA.
College Survival Kit. Irv Brechner. 96p. 1980. pap. 2.95. Bantam.
College Teaching & College Learning. Ordway Tead. 1949. 16.50x (ISBN 0-685-69874-2). Elliots Bks.
College Trigonometry. Mustafa Munem & William Tschirhart. 1974. text ed. 16.95x (ISBN 0-87901-028-2); study guide 6.95x (ISBN 0-87901-029-0). Worth.
College Vacabulary Builder. Charles I. Freundlich. 256p. (Orig.). 1981. pap. 5.95 (ISBN 0-671-41337-6). Monarch Pr.
College Vocabulary Skills. James F. Shepherd. LC 78-69548. (Illus.). 1978. pap. text ed. 7.95 (ISBN 0-395-26851-6); inst. manual 0.30 (ISBN 0-395-26852-4). HM.
College Word Study. Raymond W. Hodges et al. LC 74-12551. (Illus.). 197p. 1980. pap. text ed. 10.15 (ISBN 0-913310-10-7). PAR Inc.
College Writer's Handbook. 2nd ed. Suzanne E. Jacobs & Roderick A. Jacobs. LC 75-28036. 288p. 1976. pap. text ed. 9.50x (ISBN 0-471-43591-0). Wiley.
College Writer's Workbook. Dorothy Sedley. 240p. 1981. pap. text ed. 7.95 (ISBN 0-675-08022-3); instr's. manual 3.95 (ISBN 0-686-69486-4). Merrill.
College Writing Skills. 2nd ed. Virginia Underwood & Merriellyn Kett. 320p. 1981. pap. text ed. 10.95 (ISBN 0-675-08046-0); test bank 3.95 (ISBN 0-686-69487-2); instr's. manual 3.95 (ISBN 0-686-69488-0); write for info 9 audiocassettes (ISBN 0-675-08031-2). Merrill.
College, Yes or No: The High School Student's Career Decision-Making Handbook. William F. Shanahan. LC 80-11608. 272p. 1980. lib. bdg. 9.95 (ISBN 0-668-04907-3, 4911-1); pap. 6.95 (ISBN 0-668-04911-1). Arco.
Collegefields: From Delinquency to Freedom. Harry N. Dubin. 176p. (Orig.). 1980. text ed. 16.95x (ISBN 0-8290-0273-1); pap. text ed. 8.95x (ISBN 0-8290-0274-X). Irvington.
Colleges & the Public 1787-1862. Ed. by Theodore R. Crane. LC 63-9583. (Orig.). 1963. text ed. 8.75 (ISBN 0-8077-1200-0); pap. text ed. 4.00x (ISBN 0-8077-1197-7). Tchrs Coll.
Colleges at the Crossroads. Ed. by William P. Lineberry. (Reference Shelf Ser: Vol. 37, No. 6). 1966. 6.25 (ISBN 0-8242-0088-8). Wilson.
Colleges of Education: Academic or Professional? T. W. Eason. (Higher Education Monograph: No. 2). 1970. pap. text ed. 6.25x (ISBN 0-685-23326-X, NFER). Humanities.
Colleges of Texas. June R. Welch. (Illus.). 230p. 1981. 17.95 (ISBN 0-912854-11-1). GLA Pr.
Colleges of the Forgotten Americans: A Profile of State Colleges & Regional Universities. Carnegie Commission on Higher Education. 1969. 8.95 o.p. (ISBN 0-07-010008-X, P&RB). McGraw.
Colleges Today & Tomorrow. Lewis B. Mayhew. LC 74-75939. (Higher Education Ser.). 1969. 13.95x o.p. (ISBN 0-87589-037-7). Jossey-Bass.
Collegians. Gerald Griffin. (Nineteenth Century Fiction Ser.: Ireland: Vol. 28). 1014p. 1979. lib. bdg. 46.00 (ISBN 0-8240-3477-5). Garland Pub.
Collegiate Business Mathematics. rev. ed. Hyman M. Berston & Paul Fisher. 1978. Repr. text ed. 12.95x (ISBN 0-256-01395-0). Irwin.
Collegiate Dictionary of Zoology. Robert W. Pennak. 1964. 21.50 (ISBN 0-8260-7100-7, Pub. by Wiley-Interscience). Wiley.
Collegiate Programs for Older Adults: A Summary Report on a 1976 Survey. Carol Florio. 52p. 1978. pap. 3.00 (ISBN 0-89192-241-5). Interbk Inc.
Collegium Internationale Neuro-Psychopharmacologicum, 10th Congress: Proceedings, 2 vols. Ed. by P. Deniker. 1977. Set. text ed. 255.00 (ISBN 0-08-021506-8). Pergamon.
Collie Guide. Anne Young. 6.98 o.p. (ISBN 0-385-01573-9). Doubleday.
Collier Tracts Seventeen Three to Seventeen Eight: Mr. Collier's Disuasive from the Playhouse. Jeremy Collier. Bd. with Farther Vindication of the Short View of the English Stage. Jeremy Collier; Person of Quality's Answer to Mr. Colliers Letters Being a Disswasive from the Playhouse. John Dennis; Representation of the Impiety & Immorality of the English Stage; Some Thoughts Concerning the Stage in a Letter to a Lady. Jeremy Collier; Stage-Beaux Toss'd in a Blanket. Charles Gildon. LC 70-170462. (English Stage Theory: Vol. 35). lib. bdg. 50.00 (ISBN 0-8240-0618-6). Garland Pub.
Collier Tracts 1698: Immorality of the English Pulpit. Bd. with Letter to A. H. Esq. Concerning the Stage. Charles Hopkins; Letter to Mr. Congreve on His Pretended Amendments; Occasional Paper. Richard Willis; Some Remarks Upon Mr. Collier's Defence of His Short View of the English Stage; Vindication of the Stage. LC 76-170453. (English Stage Ser.: Vol. 27). lib. bdg. 50.00 (ISBN 0-8240-0610-0). Garland Pub.

Colliery Spoil Tips-After Aberfan. G. McKecknie Thompson & S. Rodin. 98p. 1980. pap. 15.00x (ISBN 0-901948-59-4, Pub. by Telford England). State Mutual Bk.

Collies. Diane McCarty & Ted Kattell. (Illus.). 128p. 1980. 2.95 (ISBN 0-87666-684-5, KW-078). TFH Pubns.

Collies. Margaret Osborne. (Foyle's Handbks). 1973. 3.95 (ISBN 0-685-55800-2). Palmetto Pub.

Collin. Stefan Heym. 12.95 (ISBN 0-8184-0300-4). Lyle Stuart.

Collin's Illustrated Atlas of London. Henry G. Collins. (Victorian Library). 120p. 1973. Repr. of 1854 ed. text ed. 6.50x (ISBN 0-391-00156-6, Leicester). Humanities.

Collinsfield Guide to the Wild Flowers of Southeast Australia. Jean Galbraith. 450p. 1980. 13.95x (ISBN 0-00-219246-2, Pub. by W Collins Australia). Intl Schol Bk Serv.

Collision. Jack Pulman. 256p. 1981. pap. 2.25 (ISBN 0-449-24362-1, Crest). Fawcett.

Collision Course. Nigel Hinton. (YA) 1980. pap. 1.50 (ISBN 0-440-91367-5, LFL). Dell.

Collision Course. Del Storey. 1977. pap. 2.95 o.p. (ISBN 0-88270-230-0). Logos.

Collision Theory & Statistical Theory of Chemical Reactions. S. G. Christoph. (Lectures Notes in Chemistry: Vol. 18). (Illus.). 322p. 1980. pap. 27.70 (ISBN 0-387-10012-1). Springer-Verlag.

Colloid & Interface Science, Vols. 2-5. Ed. by Milton Kerker. Incl. Vol. 2. Aerosols, Emulsions & Surfactants. 35.00 (ISBN 0-12-404502-2); Vol. 3. Adsorption, Catalysis, Solid Surfaces, Wetting, Surface Tension & Water. 37.50 (ISBN 0-12-404503-0); Vol. 4. Hydrosols & Rheology. 36.50 (ISBN 0-12-404504-9); Vol. 5. Biocolloids, Polymers, Monolayers, Membranes & General Papers. 36.50 (ISBN 0-12-404505-7). 1976. Set. 122.00. Acad Pr.

Colloid & Surface Science: Proceedings of an International Conference, Budapest, 1975. Ed. by E. Wolfram. LC 76-44624. 1977. text ed. 34.00 (ISBN 0-08-021570-X). Pergamon.

Colloques Phytosociologiques VII: Lille 1978, le Vegetation Des Sois Tourbeux. Ed. by J. M. Gehu. 556p. (Fr.). 1981. lib. bdg. 75.00x (ISBN 3-7682-1260-2, Pub. by Cramer Germany). Lubrecht & Cramer.

Colloquial Arabic. 3rd ed. De Lacy O'Leary. (Trubner's Colloquial Manuals). 1963. pap. 7.95 (ISBN 0-7100-7909-5). Routledge & Kegan.

Colloquial Arabic: An Oral Approach. Raja Nasr. 1968. 10.95 (ISBN 0-685-77111-3). Intl Bk Ctr.

Colloquial Czech. 2nd ed. J. Schwartz. (Tribner's Colloquial Manuals). 1945. 15.00 (ISBN 0-7100-8346-7); pap. 9.75 (ISBN 0-7100-4335-X). Routledge & Kegan.

Colloquial English. Graham Coe. (Illus.). 192p. (Orig.). 1981. pap. 9.50 (ISBN 0-7100-0740-X). Routledge & Kegan.

Colloquial English. Harry Collis. 96p. 1981. pap. text ed. write for info. (ISBN 0-88345-428-9). Regents Pub.

Colloquial German. P. F. Doring. (Trubners Colloquial Manuals). 1975. 9.50 (ISBN 0-7100-8031-X); pap. 4.95 (ISBN 0-7100-8032-8). Routledge & Kegan.

Colloquial German. rev. ed. Inge Hubmann-Uhlich. (Colloquial Ser.). 1980. pap. 7.50 (ISBN 0-7100-8032-8). Routledge & Kegan.

Colloquial Greek. Katerina Harris. (Trubners Colloquial Manuals). 336p. 1975. 14.00 (ISBN 0-7100-8069-7); pap. 8.95 (ISBN 0-7100-8070-0). Routledge & Kegan.

Colloquial Hungarian. 2nd ed. Arthur H. Whitney. (Trubner's Colloquial Manuals). (Illus.). 1977. pap. 7.95 (ISBN 0-7100-8550-8). Routledge & Kegan.

Colloquial Japanese. H. D. Clarke & Motoko Hamamura. (Colloquial Ser.). (Orig.). 1981. pap. price not set (ISBN 0-7100-0595-4). Routledge & Kegan.

Colloquial Persian. L. P. Elwell-Sutton. (Trubner's Colloquial Manuals). 1975. pap. 6.95 (ISBN 0-7100-8083-2). Routledge & Kegan.

Colloquial Rumanian: Grammar, Exercises, Reader & Vocabulary. Grigore Nandris. (Tribner's Colloquial Manuals). 1967. 9.95 (ISBN 0-7100-4334-1). Routledge & Kegan.

Colloquial Russian. William Harrison et al. (Trubners Colloquial Manuals). 1973. 17.00 (ISBN 0-7100-7021-7); pap. 9.95 (ISBN 0-7100-7025-X). Routledge & Kegan.

Colloquial Spanish. 4th ed. W. R. Patterson. (Trubners Colloquial Manuals Ser.). 8.75 (ISBN 0-7100-4325-2); pap. 6.95 (ISBN 0-7100-6385-7). Routledge & Kegan.

Colloquial Turkish. Yusuf Mardin. (Trubner's Colloquial Manuals). 1961. pap. 8.95 (ISBN 0-7100-8415-3). Routledge & Kegan.

Colloquial Vietnamese. rev ed. Nguyen Dinh-Hoa. LC 74-5132. 400p. 1974. text ed. 14.95x (ISBN 0-8093-0685-9); pap. text ed. 10.95x (ISBN 0-8093-0686-7). S Ill U Pr.

Colloquium on the History of Landscape Architecture, 6 vols. Incl. Vol. 1. Italian Garden. Ed. by David Coffin. LC 72-93722. (Illus.). 114p. 1972..o.p. (ISBN 0-88402-044-4); Vol. 2. Picturesque Garden & Its Influence Outside the British Isles. Ed. by Nikolaus Pevsner. LC 74-196954. (Illus.). 1974. o. p. 10.00x (ISBN 0-88402-050-9); Vol. 3. French Formal Garden. Ed. by Elisabeth B. MacDougall & F. Hamilton Hazlehurst. LC 75-318945. (Illus.). 1974. 12.50x (ISBN 0-88402-052-5); Vol. 4. Islamic Garden. Ed. by Elisabeth B. MacDougall & Richard Ettinghausen. LC 76-468. (Illus.). 100p. 1976. o. p. 15.00x (ISBN 0-88402-064-9). Ctr Landscape Arch). Dumbarton Oaks.

Colloquium Spectroscopium, Internationale, 2. Ed. by J. P. Robin. 1977. text ed. 13.25 (ISBN 0-08-021569-6). Pergamon.

Collusion for Conformity. Andrew Slaby & Lawrence Tancredi. LC 75-5989. 1975. 20.00x (ISBN 0-87668-207-7). Aronson.

Colne Valley: Radicalism to Socialism. David Clark. (Illus.). 240p. text ed. 27.00 (ISBN 0-582-50293-4). Longman.

Cologne & Stockholm: Urban Planning & Land-Use Controls. Reuel Hemdahl. LC 77-167645. 1971. 12.00 (ISBN 0-8108-0421-2). Scarecrow.

Cologne Mani Codex. Tr. by Ron Cameron & Arthur J. Dewey. LC 79-14743. (Society of Biblical Literature Texts & Translations, 15. Early Christian Literature Ser.: No. 3). 1979. 10.50 (ISBN 0-89130-311-1, 060215); pap. 6.00 (ISBN 0-89130-312-X). Scholars Pr Ca.

Colombia: Armed Forces & Society. J. Mark Ruhl. LC 80-18762. (Latin American Ser.: Vol. 1). iv, 52p. (Orig.). 1980. pap. 4.50x (ISBN 0-915984-92-X). Syracuse U Foreign Comp.

Colombia, Republica De: Departemento Del Meta: Conservacion De los Recursos Naturales Renovables. (Span.). 1973. 5.50 (ISBN 0-8270-4030-X). OAS.

Colombian Penal Code. (American Series of Foreign Penal Codes: Vol. 14). 1967. 15.00x (ISBN 0-8377-0034-5). Rothman.

Colon & Rectal Surgery: Continuing Education Review. Ed. by Eric J. Lazaro. 1973. spiral bdg. 12.00 o.p. (ISBN 0-87488-338-5). Med Exam.

Colon, Rectum & Anus. 3rd ed. I. P. Todd. (Operative Surgery Ser.). 1977. 95.00 (ISBN 0-407-00606-0). Butterworths.

Colonel Jack: The History & Remarkable Life of the Truly Honorable Colonel Jacque, Commonly Called Colonel Jack. Daniel Defoe. Ed. by Samuel H. Monk. (Oxford English Novels Ser). 1965. pap. 3.95x (ISBN 0-19-281076-6, OPB). Oxford U Pr.

Colonel Stephens Railways. John Scott-Morgan. LC 77-91737. 1978. 17.95 (ISBN 0-7153-7544-X). David & Charles.

Colonial & Early American Lighting. 3rd ed. Arthur H. Hayward. 1962. pap. 4.50 (ISBN 0-486-20975-X). Dover.

Colonial Background of the American Revolution: Four Essays in American Colonial History. rev. ed. Charles M. Andrews. LC 31-2404. 1961. 16.00x (ISBN 0-300-00268-8); pap. 5.95x (ISBN 0-300-00004-9, Y44). Yale U Pr.

Colonial Bureaucracy & Creating Underdevelopment, Tanganyika, 1919-1940. D. M. McCarthy. 1981. 10.95 (ISBN 0-8138-1590-8). Iowa St U Pr.

Colonial Conquest of Africa. Robin McKown. LC 71-158424. (First Bks). (Illus.). (gr. 4-6). 1971. PLB 4.90 o.p. (ISBN 0-531-00743-X). Watts.

Colonial Conquest of Asia. John G. Roberts. LC 75-38165. (Impact Bks Ser). (Illus.). 96p. (gr. 7 up). 1976. PLB 6.90 (ISBN 0-531-01126-7). Watts.

Colonial Days in Old New York. Alice M. Earle. LC 68-21767. 1968. Repr. of 1896 ed. 15.00 (ISBN 0-8103-3428-3). Gale.

Colonial Delaware. Gardell D. Christensen & Eugenia Burney. LC 74-10265. (Colonial History Ser.). (Illus.). 160p. (gr. 5 up). 1975. 7.95 o.p. (ISBN 0-525-67118-8). Elsevier-Nelson.

Colonial Emancipation in the Pacific and the Caribbean: A Legal and Political Analysis. Arnold H. Leibowitz. LC 75-19801. (Prae Ger Special Studies Ser.). 240p. 1976. text ed. 23.95 (ISBN 0-275-56000-7). Praeger.

Colonial Eve: Sources on Women in Australia, 1788-1914. Ed. by Ruth Teale. 300p. 1978. 24.00x (ISBN 0-19-550545-X). Oxford U Pr.

Colonial Experience. David Hawke. LC 66-14829. 1966. 19.95 (ISBN 0-672-60688-7). Bobbs.

Colonial Furniture for Doll Houses & Miniature Rooms. Pat Midkiff. LC 76-27807. 1977. pap. 5.95 o.p. (ISBN 0-8069-8220-9). Sterling.

Colonial Governors from the Fifteenth Century to the Present. David P. Henige. LC 73-81320. 1970. 50.00x (ISBN 0-299-05440-3). U of Wis Pr.

Colonial History of Hartford. William D. Love. LC 73-85465. (Illus.). 416p. 1974. casebound 15.00 (ISBN 0-87106-133-3). Globe Pequot.

Colonial Image. Ed. by John C. Miller. LC 62-9930. (American Epochs Ser). 10.00 (ISBN 0-8076-0168-3); pap. 4.95 o.s.i. (ISBN 0-8076-0392-9). Braziller.

Colonial Keyboard Tunes. Ed. by J. S. Darling. LC 80-12691. 1980. pap. 1.50 (ISBN 0-87935-055-5). Williamsburg.

Colonial Kitchens, Their Furnishings & Their Gardens: The First Definitive Account Based on Settlers' Journals & Travelers' Diaries. Frances Phipps. LC 80-65251. (Illus.). 376p. 1980. pap. 8.95 (ISBN 0-8015-1435-5, Hawthorn). Dutton.

Colonial Living. Edwin Tunis. LC 75-29611. (Illus.). 160p. (gr. 7 up). 1976. 12.95 (ISBN 0-690-01063-X, TYC-J). T Y Crowell.

Colonial Manila: The Context of Hispanic Urbanism & Process of Morphogenesis. Robert R. Reed. (Publications in Geography Ser.: Vol. 22). 1978. pap. 12.00x (ISBN 0-520-09579-0). U of Cal Pr.

Colonial New York: A History. Michael Kammen. (Illus.). 1978. pap. 6.95 (ISBN 0-527-18725-9, Pub. by Two Continents). Hippocrene Bks.

Colonial Printer. Lawrence C. Wroth. (Illus.). 1964. pap. 3.95 (ISBN 0-8139-0250-9). U Pr of Va.

Colonial Records of North Carolina: Second Series, 5 vols. Ed. by Mattie E. Parker & William S. Price, Jr. Incl. Vol. 1. North Carolina Charters & Constitutions, 1578-1698. 247p. 1963. 10.00 (ISBN 0-86526-022-2); Vol. 2. North Carolina Higher-Court Records, 1670-1696. 533p. 1968. 11.00 (ISBN 0-86526-023-0); Vol. 3. North Carolina Higher Court Records, 1697-1701. 622p. 1971. 12.00 (ISBN 0-86526-024-9); Vol. 4. North Carolina Higher-Court Records, 1702-1708. 533p. 1974. 16.00 (ISBN 0-86526-025-7); Vol. 5. North Carolina Higher Court Minutes, 1709-1723. 1977. 21.00 (ISBN 0-86526-026-5). Set (ISBN 0-86526-020-6). NC Archives.

Colonial Revival. William B. Rhoads. LC 76-23695. (Outstanding Dissertations in the Fine Arts Ser.). 1977. lib. bdg. 133.00x (ISBN 0-8240-2722-1). Garland Pub.

Colonial Rhode Island. Carleton Beals. LC 73-99437. (Colonial History Ser). (Illus.). (gr. 5 up). 1970. PLB 6.75 o.p. (ISBN 0-8407-7107-X). Elsevier-Nelson.

Colonial Roots of Modern Brazil: Papers of the Newberry Library Conference. Ed. by Dauril Alden. LC 78-174458. 1973. 21.50x (ISBN 0-520-02140-1). U of Cal Pr.

Colonial Rule & Political Development in Tanzania: The Case of the Makonde. J. Gus Liebenow. LC 72-126898. 1971. 14.75x o.s.i. (ISBN 0-8101-0332-X). Northwestern U Pr.

Colonial Silversmiths, Masters & Apprentices. Kathryn C. Buhler. (Illus.). 1956. pap. 2.50 (ISBN 0-87846-160-4). Mus Fine Arts Boston.

Colonial Southern Bookshelf: Reading in the Eighteenth Century. Richard B. Davis. LC 78-3832. (Lamar Memorial Lectures: No. 21). 152p. 1979. 10.50x (ISBN 0-8203-0450-6). U of Ga Pr.

Colonial Spirit of '76. David C. Whitney. 1974. 39.00 (ISBN 0-87827-200-3). Ency Brit Ed.

Colonial Urban Development: Culture, Social Power & Environment. A. D. King. 1977. 27.50x (ISBN 0-7100-8404-8). Routledge & Kegan.

Colonial Virginia: Its People & Customs. Mary N. Stanard. LC 78-99055. (Social History Reference Ser.). (Illus.). 1970. Repr. of 1917 ed. 26.00 (ISBN 0-8103-0161-X). Gale.

Colonial Williamsburg Decorates for Christmas. Libbey H. Oliver. (Illus.). 80p. 1981. pap. 4.95 (ISBN 0-87935-056-3). Williamsburg.

Colonialism & Imperialism in Mozambique. Elisio Martins. 206p. 1974. pap. 4.95 (ISBN 0-88289-097-2). Pelican.

Colonialism & Underdevelopment: Processes of Political Economic Change in British Honduras. Norman Ashcraft. LC 72-92055. 1973. pap. text ed. 7.00x (ISBN 0-8077-2407-6). Tchrs Coll.

Colonies in Orbit: The Coming Age of Human Settlements in Space. David Knight. (gr. 5-9). 1977. 6.25 o.p. (ISBN 0-688-22096-7); PLB 6.96 (ISBN 0-688-32096-1). Morrow.

Colonies in Space. T. A. Heppenheimer. (Illus.). 1978. pap. 2.75 (ISBN 0-446-95559-0). Warner Bks.

Colonies into Nation. L. Kaplan. 1972. 14.95 (ISBN 0-02-560570-4). Macmillan.

Colonists for Sale: The Story of Indentured Servants in America. Clifford L. Alderman. 192p. (gr. 5-9). 1975. 8.95 (ISBN 0-02-700220-9, 70022). Macmillan.

Colonization of the Little Colorado. George S. Tanner & J. Morris Richards. LC 77-73890. 1977. 12.50 o.p. (ISBN 0-87358-163-6). Northland.

Colony: Earth. Richard E. Mooney. 320p. 1977. pap. 1.95 o.p. (ISBN 0-449-23243-3, Crest). Fawcett.

Colony of Connecticut. Clifford L. Alderman. LC 74-8893. (First Bks). (Illus.). 96p. (gr. 6 up). 1975. PLB 4.90 o.p. (ISBN 0-531-02773-2). Watts.

Colony of Delaware. Nanci A. Lyman. LC 74-26676. (First Bks). (Illus.). (gr. 5-8). 1975. PLB 6.45 (ISBN 0-531-00829-0). Watts.

Colony of Georgia. Harold C. Vaughan. LC 74-8790. (First Bks). (Illus.). 96p. (gr. 5-8). 1975. PLB 4.90 o.p. (ISBN 0-531-02774-0). Watts.

Colony of Maryland. Gene Gurney & Clare Gurney. LC 76-182897. (First Bks). (Illus.). 72p. (gr. 4-6). 1972. PLB 4.90 o.p. (ISBN 0-531-00757-X). Watts.

Colony of Massachusetts. rev ed. Alice Dickinson. LC 74-8744. (First Bks). (Illus.). 96p. (gr. 5-8). 1975. PLB 4.90 o.p. (ISBN 0-531-02775-9). Watts.

Colony of New Hampshire. Emil Lengyel. LC 74-12036. (First Bks). (Illus.). 72p. (gr. 5-8). 1975. PLB 4.90 o.p. (ISBN 0-531-02776-7). Watts.

Colony of New Jersey. Corinne J. Naden. LC 74-872. (First Bks). (Illus.). 96p. (gr. 4-7). 1974. PLB 4.90 o.p. (ISBN 0-531-02722-8). Watts.

Colony of New York. David Goodnough. LC 72-7087. (First Bks). (Illus.). 96p. (gr. 5-7). 1973. PLB 4.90 o.p. (ISBN 0-531-00783-9). Watts.

Colony of North Carolina. Dan Lacy. LC 74-22217. (First Bks). (Illus.). (gr. 5-8). 1975. PLB 4.90 o.p. (ISBN 0-531-00830-4). Watts.

Colony of Pennsylvania. Emil Lengyel. LC 74-846. (First Bks). (Illus.). 72p. (gr. 4-7). 1974. PLB 6.45 (ISBN 0-531-02721-X). Watts.

Colony of Rhode Island. Robert N. Webb. LC 70-189517. (First Bks). (Illus.). 96p. (gr. 5-8). 1972. PLB 6.45 (ISBN 0-531-00778-2). Watts.

Colony of South Carolina. Nanci A. Lyman. LC 74-22222. (First Bks). (Illus.). 96p. (gr. 5-8). 1975. PLB 4.90 o.p. (ISBN 0-531-00831-2). Watts.

Colony of Virginia. Dan Lacy. LC 72-10780. (First Bks). (Illus.). 72p. (gr. 6-8). 1973. PLB 4.90 o.p. (ISBN 0-531-00784-7). Watts.

Color. (Life Library of Photography). (Illus.). 1970. 14.95 (ISBN 0-8094-1019-2). Time-Life.

Color. J. M. Parramon. (Orig.). Date not set. pap. 4.95 (ISBN 0-89586-075-9). H P Bks. Postponed.

Color: A Complete Guide for Artists. Ralph Fabri. (Illus.). 1967. 19.50 (ISBN 0-8230-0700-6); pap. 9.95 o.p. (ISBN 0-8230-0651-4). Watson-Guptill.

Color Aerial Photography in the Pl Sc & Related Fields: Seventh Biennial Workshop. Intro. by William M. Ciesla. 255p. 1979. pap. 19.50 (ISBN 0-686-27663-9). ASP.

Color & Architecture. Konrad Gatz & Gerhard Achtenberg. Date not set. 22.50 o.p. (ISBN 0-8038-0039-8). Hastings.

Color & Design in Macrame. Virginia I. Harvey. (Illus.). 104p. 1980. pap. 9.95 (ISBN 0-914842-55-2). Madrona Pubs.

Color & Design in Macrame. Virginia I. Harvey. LC 80-25748. (Illus.). 104p. (gr. 11-12). 1980. pap. 9.95 (ISBN 0-914842-55-2). Madrona Pubs.

Color & Personality. Audrey Kargere. pap. 3.95 (ISBN 0-686-69317-5). Weiser.

Color & the Edgar Cayce Readings. Roger Lewis. 48p. 1973. pap. 1.95 (ISBN 0-87604-068-7). Are Pr.

Color Angle. L. Thomas. LC 79-64280. (Illus., Orig.). 1979. pap. 16.00 (ISBN 0-934190-00-3). Real Comp & Int.

Color Atlas & Textbook of Hematology: A Slide Presentation. William R. Platt. LC 75-733020. (Illus.). 48p. 1975. 185.00 o.p. (ISBN 0-397-50345-8). Lippincott.

Color Atlas of Cancer Cytology. 2nd ed. Masayoshi Takahashi. LC 80-85297. (Illus.). 550p. 1981. 125.00 (ISBN 0-89640-050-6). Igaku-Shoin.

Color Atlas of Colposcopy. Hanskurt Bauer. LC 78-62047. (Illus.). 1979. 45.00 (ISBN 0-89640-031-X). Igaku-Shoin.

Color Atlas of Gonioscopy. Ryozo Kimura. (Illus.). 1973. 35.00 (ISBN 0-89640-037-9). Igaku-Shoin.

Color Atlas of Intestinal Parasites. rev. ed. Francis M. Spencer & Lee S. Monroe. (Illus.). 176p. 1977. 23.50 (ISBN 0-398-03418-4). C C Thomas.

Color Atlas of Liver Biopsy: A Clinical Pathological Guide. Pedro J. Grases & Simon Beker G. Orig. Title: Guia Practica De Biopsia Hepatica En el Adulto. (Illus.). 125p. 1981. write for info. (ISBN 0-8451-0209-5). A R Liss.

Color Atlas of Oral Pathology. 3rd ed. Robert A. Colby et al. LC 73-147050. (Illus.). 200p. 1971. 27.50 (ISBN 0-397-50279-6). Lippincott.

Color Atlas of Pathology, Vol. 3. Charles F. Geschickter & Albert Cannon. LC 50-58214. 1963. 41.00 o.p. (ISBN 0-397-50091-2). Lippincott.

Color Atlas of Pathology of the Nervous System. Asao Hirano et al. LC 80-81620. (Illus.). 222p. 1980. 74.00 (ISBN 0-89640-045-X). Igaku Shoin.

Color Atlas of Sectional Anatomy: Chest, Abdomen, Pelvis. E. A. Lyons. LC 78-15746. 1978. text ed. 139.50 (ISBN 0-8016-3052-5). Mosby.

Color Atlas of the Diseases of Fishes, Amphibians, & Reptiles. E. Elkan & H. Reichenbach-Klinke. (Illus.). 256p. 1974. 20.00 (ISBN 0-87666-028-6, H-948). TFH Pubns.

Color Blindness: An Evolutionary Approach. Ricardo Cruz-Coke. (Amer. Lec. in Living Chemistry Ser.). (Illus.). 172p. 1970. text ed. 19.50 (ISBN 0-398-00375-0). C C Thomas.

Color Book. Wendon Blake. (Illus.). 256p. 25.00 (ISBN 0-8230-0694-8). Watson-Guptill.

Color-Change Mechanisms of Coldblooded Vertebrates. H. Waring. 1963. 31.50 (ISBN 0-12-735450-6). Acad Pr.

Color Drawing: A Marker-Colored-Pencil Approach. Michael E. Doyle. 320p. 1981. 35.00 (ISBN 0-442-22184-3). Van Nos Reinhold.

Color Film for Color Television. Rodger J. Ross. (Library of Image & Sound Technology). Date not set. 12.50 o.p. (ISBN 0-8038-1137-3). Hastings.

Color for Your Winter Yard & Garden. Helen Van Pelt Wilson. LC 77-13822. (Encore Edition). (Illus.). 1978. 4.95 (ISBN 0-684-16557-0, ScribT). Scribner.

Color: From Rainbows to Lasers. Franklyn M. Branley. LC 76-46304. (Illus.). (gr. 6 up). 1978. 8.95 o.p. (ISBN 0-690-01256-X, TYC-J); PLB 8.79 (ISBN 0-690-03847-X). T Y Crowell.

Color Handbook of House Plants. Ed. by Elvin McDonald et al. 1976. 9.95 o.p. (ISBN 0-8015-1441-X). Dutton.

Color in a Cage: The Personal Journey of an American of Color. Joseph C. Kennedy. (Illus.). 1981. 9.95 (ISBN 0-933184-19-0); pap. 4.95 (ISBN 0-933184-20-4). Flame Intl.

Color in Business, Science, & Industry. 3rd ed. Deane B. Judd & Gunter Wyszecki. LC 75-6590. (Pure & Applied Optics Ser.). 553p. 1975. 42.95 (ISBN 0-471-45212-2, Pub. by Wiley-Interscience). Wiley.

Color in Your Life. Irving Adler. LC 62-7784. (Illus.). (gr. 6 up). 1962. PLB 7.89 (ISBN 0-381-99995-5, A14860, JD-J). John Day.

Color It Home: A Builder's Guide to Interior Design & Merchandising. Beverly Trupp. (Illus.). 240p. 1981. 34.95 (ISBN 0-8436-0136-1). CBI Pub.

Color Kittens. Margaret W. Brown. (Illus.). (ps-3). 1949. PLB 7.62 (ISBN 0-307-60546-9, Golden Pr). Western Pub.

Color Me Beautiful. Carole Jackson. 216p. 1981. pap. 8.95 (ISBN 0-345-29015-1). Ballantine.

Color Me Beautiful: The Engagement & Beauty Calender for 1981. Carole Jackson. 1980. pap. 6.95 o.p. (ISBN 0-87491-410-8). Acropolis.

Color Me Greene. Illus. by Linda Tomcsanyi. (Illus.). 1980. 3.00 (ISBN 0-686-26237-9). E S Cunningham.

Color Metallography. E. Beraha & B. Shipigler. (TN 690.b47). 1977. 68.00 (ISBN 0-87170-045-X). ASM.

Color Observed. Enid Verity. 184p. 1980. 18.95 (ISBN 0-442-21906-7). Van Nos Reinhold.

Color of Dust. Michael Anania. LC 71-116681. (New Poetry Ser.: No. 40). 70p. 1970. 6.50 (ISBN 0-8040-0048-4); pap. 4.50 (ISBN 0-8040-0049-2). Swallow.

Color of Man. Robert Cohen. (gr. 5-9). 1968. pap. 1.95 o.p. (ISBN 0-394-82306-0, BYR). Random.

Color of Minerals. G. Rapp. (Earth Science Curriculum Project Pamphlet Ser). 1971. pap. 3.20 (ISBN 0-395-02620-2). HM.

Color Patterns of African Cichlids. J. Voss. Orig. Title: Livrees Ou Patrons De Coloration Chezles Poissons Chichlides Africains. (Illus.). 128p. 1980. 7.95 (ISBN 0-87666-503-2, PS-755). TFH Pubns.

Color Photo Book. Andreas Feininger. LC 69-12820. (Illus.). 1969. 12.95 o.p. (ISBN 0-13-152181-0). P-H.

Color Print Book: A Survey of Contemporary Photographic Printmaking Methods for the Creative Photographer. Arnold Gassan. (Extended Photo Media Ser.: No. 3). (Illus., Orig.). 1980. pap. 9.95 (ISBN 0-87992-023-8); 16.95 o.p. (ISBN 0-87992-024-6). Light Impressions.

Color Printing. Bob Mitchell. LC 75-8142. (Photography How-to Ser.). (Illus.). 1975. pap. 4.95 (ISBN 0-8227-0101-4). Petersen Pub.

Color Science & Dental Art. Jack D. Preston & Stephen F. Bergen. LC 80-17295. (Illus.). 88p. 1980. pap. 49.50 (ISBN 0-8016-4038-5). Mosby.

Color Seems. Ilma Haskins. LC 72-83356. (Illus.). 32p. (ps-3). 1974. 6.95 (ISBN 0-8149-0688-5). Vanguard.

Color Structure & Design. Richard G. Ellinger. 144p. 1980. pap. 9.95 (ISBN 0-442-23941-6). Van Nos Reinhold.

Color Symbolism, Eranos Excerpts: Eranos Excerpts. 1977. 9.00 o.p. (ISBN 0-88214-400-6). Spring Pubns.

Color the ABC's of What Should I Be When I Grow up? Illus. by Robyn Feld. 1980. pap. 1.35 (ISBN 0-931868-04-1). Beninda.

Color the Creatures. John J. Reichert. (Illus.). (gr. 4-12). 1979. pap. 2.50 (ISBN 0-930504-03-8). Polaris Pr.

Color Theory: A Guide to Information Sources. Ed. by Mary Buckley & David Baum. LC 73-17517. (Art & Architecture Information Guide Ser.: Vol. 2). x, 173p. 1975. 30.00 (ISBN 0-8103-1275-1). Gale.

Color TV: Principles & Servicing. Howard Bierman & Marvin Bierman. (Illus.). 1973. pap. 8.30 (ISBN 0-8104-5929-9). Hayden.

Color TV Training Manual. 4th ed. Howard W. Sams Editorial Staff. LC 77-76538. (Illus.). 1977. pap. 12.95 (ISBN 0-672-21412-1). Sams.

Color Vision. Committee on Vision. (Illus.). 1973. pap. 7.00 (ISBN 0-309-02105-7). Natl Acad Pr.

Color Vision. Leo M. Hurvich. LC 80-19077. (Illus.). 280p. 1981. text ed. 37.50 (ISBN 0-87893-336-0); pap. text ed. 25.00 (ISBN 0-87893-337-9). Sinauer Assoc.

Color Vision: An Historical Introduction. Gerald S. Wasserman. LC 78-5346. (Wiley Ser. in Behavior). 1978. 25.95 (ISBN 0-471-92128-9, Pub. by Wiley-Interscience). Wiley.

Color Woodcuts. Pierre Mornand. Tr. by Mira Intrator from Fr. (Illus.). 1972. pap. 6.00x (ISBN 0-933652-02-X). Domjan Studio.

Color Your Way into Black History Book. Adrienne V. Sealy. (Illus.). 78p. 1980. wkbk. 4.00 (ISBN 0-9602670-6-9). Assn Family Living.

Colorado. 28.00 (ISBN 0-89770-081-3). Curriculum Info Ctr.

Colorado: A Bicentennial History. Marshall Sprague. (States & the Nation Ser.). (Illus.). 1976. 12.95 (ISBN 0-393-05599-X). Norton.

Colorado & Southern Narrow Gauge. Mallory H. Ferrell. (Illus.). 1981. 34.95 (ISBN 0-87108-534-8). Pruett.

Colorado & Utah Industrial Minerals. 1974. 15.50. Minobras.

Colorado Bibliography. Ed. by Bohdan S. Wynar & Roberta J. Depp. LC 80-13752. 1980. lib. bdg. 60.00x (ISBN 0-87287-211-4). Libs Unl.

Colorado Crossing. Gene Curry. (Jim Saddler Ser.: No. 3). 1979. pap. 1.75 (ISBN 0-505-51418-4). Tower Bks.

Colorado Delta. Godfrey Sykes. LC 79-113298. 1970. Repr. of 1937 ed. 15.00 (ISBN 0-8046-1329-X). Kennikat.

Colorado Front Range Ski Tours. Tom Sudduth & Sanse Sudduth. LC 75-27837. (Illus.). 1975. pap. 6.95 o.p. (ISBN 0-911518-34-7). Touchstone Pr Ore.

Colorado Gem & Mineral Collecting Localities. Charles Baldwin. pap. 4.95 (ISBN 0-933472-08-0). Johnson Colo.

Colorado Gem Trails & Mineral Guide. rev., 3rd ed. Richard M. Pearl. LC 75-132587. (Illus.). 223p. 1972. 12.95 (ISBN 0-8040-0052-2, SB). Swallow.

Colorado Hi-Ways & By-Ways: A Comprehensive Guide to Picturesque Trails & Tours. Marian Talmadge & Iris Gilmore. LC 74-83023. 1975. pap. 4.95 o.p. (ISBN 0-87108-079-6). Pruett.

Colorado High Country. Margaret Lamb. LC 64-7814. (Illus., Orig.). 1965. pap. 2.95 (ISBN 0-8040-0053-0, CB6, SB). Swallow.

Colorado in the Great Depression. James F. Wickens. Ed. by Frank Freidel. LC 78-62518. (Modern American History Ser.: Vol. 20). 1979. lib. bdg. 30.00 (ISBN 0-8240-3643-3). Garland Pub.

Colorado Kill Zone. Don Pendleton. (Executioner Ser.: No. 25). 192p. (Orig.). 1976. pap. 1.95 (ISBN 0-523-40761-0). Pinnacle Bks.

Colorado Mining: A Photographic History. Duane A. Smith. LC 76-46583. (Illus.). 176p. 1979. Repr. of 1977 ed. 17.50 (ISBN 0-8263-0437-0). U of Nm Pr.

Colorado on Glass, Colorado's First Half Century As Seen by the Camera. Terry W. Mangan. Ed. by Russ Collman. (Illus.). 1975. 47.00 (ISBN 0-913582-13-1). Sundance.

Colorado on Glass: First 50 Years of Glass-Plate Photography in Colorado. Terry W. Mangan. (Illus.). 416p. 47.00 (ISBN 0-913582-13-1). Sundance.

Colorado Pass Book: A Guide to Colorado's Back Road Mountain Passes. Don Koch. (Illus.). 120p. (Orig.). 1980. 14.95 (ISBN 0-87108-566-6). Pruett.

Colorado Reader. Carl Ubbelohde. 6.50 o.p. (ISBN 0-87108-028-1). Pruett.

Colorado Real Estate: An Introduction to the Profession. Richard O. Jones & Bruce Harwood. LC 79-939. (Illus.). 1979. text ed. 15.95 (ISBN 0-8359-0883-6). Reston.

Colorado Report. Gerald A. Gyure. LC 80-83983. (Illus.). 144p. (Orig.). 1981. pap. 6.95 (ISBN 0-938354-01-9). Hi Country Pubs.

Colorado River Ghost Towns. Stanley W. Paher. (Illus.). 1976. 9.95 (ISBN 0-913814-08-3); pap. 5.95 (ISBN 0-913814-31-8). Nevada Pubns.

Colorado Ski & Winter Recreation Statistics, 1977: (1976-77 Season) C. R. Goeldner & Sally Courteney. 124p. 1977. 20.00 (ISBN 0-89478-036-0). U CO Busn Res Div.

Colorado Ski & Winter Recreation Statistics, 1978: (1977-78 Season) C. R. Goeldner & Karen Dicke. 117p. 1978. 20.00 (ISBN 0-89478-048-4). U CO Busn Res Div.

Colorado Ski & Winter Recreation Statistics, 1976: (1975-76 Season) C. R. Goeldner & Cheryl Fellhauer. 123p. 1977. 10.00 (ISBN 0-89478-030-1). U CO Busn Res Div.

Colorado Ski Industry Characteristics & Financial Analysis. Karen Dicke & C. R. Goeldner. 1981. 25.00 (ISBN 0-686-69386-8). U CO Busn Res Div.

Colorado Ski Industry Characteristics & Financial Analysis. C. R. Goeldner & Karen Dicke. 54p. 1979. 25.00 o.p. (ISBN 0-686-64150-7). U CO Busn Res Div.

Colorado Skier. C. R. Goeldner. 92p. 1978. 25.00 (ISBN 0-89478-044-1). U CO Busn Res Div.

Colorado's Highest: The Magestic Fourteeners. George Crouter. (Illus.). 144p. 16.50 (ISBN 0-913582-22-0). Sundance.

Colorado's Loneliest Railroads: The San Luis Southern. P. R. Griswold. (Illus.). 200p. 1980. 29.95 (ISBN 0-87108-554-2). Pruett.

Colorblind. Esther Taylor. Date not set. 12.95 (ISBN 0-87949-136-1). Ashley Bks.

Colorectal Cancer. Ed. by K. Welvaart et al. (Boerhaave Series for Postgraduate Medical Education: No. 18). (Illus.). 290p. 1981. PLB 58.00 (ISBN 90-6021-465-X, Pub. by Leiden U Pr). Kluwer Boston.

Colorectal Cancer: Prevention, Epidemiology, & Screening. Ed. by Sidney J. Winawer et al. (Progress in Cancer Research & Therapy). 432p. 1980. 39.50 (ISBN 0-89004-447-3). Raven.

Colored Glassware of the Depression Era 1970. H. M. Weatherman. (Illus.). 240p. 1981. 12.00 (ISBN 0-913074-00-4). Weatherman.

Colored Reading: The Graphic Art of Frances Butler. Frances Butler. (Lancaster-Miller Art Ser.). (Illus.). 1980. 8.95 (ISBN 0-89581-011-5). Lancaster-Miller.

Colored Symmetry. A. V. Shubnikov & N. V. Belov. 1964. 37.00 (ISBN 0-08-010505-X); pap. 22.00 (ISBN 0-08-013790-3). Pergamon.

Colorforms ABC Book. Colorforms Books. (Illus.). (ps-1). 1973. 2.95 (ISBN 0-394-82657-4, BYR). Random.

Colorful Britain. rev. ed. 126p. 1980. 22.00 (ISBN 0-85306-838-0, Pub. by B T A). Merrimack Bk Serv.

Colorful Cacti of the American Deserts. Edgar Lamb & Brian Lamb. LC 74-8615. (Pocket Encyclopedias in Color Ser). (Illus.). 208p. 1974. 9.95 (ISBN 0-02-567670-9). Macmillan.

Colorful California, Vol. II. Paul M. Lewis. Ed. by Robert D. Shangle. LC 78-12042. (Illus.). 72p. 1978. 14.95 (ISBN 0-915796-85-6); pap. 7.95 (ISBN 0-915796-84-8). Beautiful Am.

Colorful Glass Crafting. J. H. Eppens-Van Veen. (Illus.). 112p. (gr. 9 up). 1973. 9.95 o.p. (ISBN 0-8069-5226-1); PLB 9.29 o.p. (ISBN 0-8069-5227-X). Sterling.

Colorful Mineral Identifier. Anthony C. Tennissen. LC 72-151706. (Illus.). (gr. 10 up). 1971. 6.95 (ISBN 0-8069-3040-3); PLB 6.69 (ISBN 0-8069-3041-1). Sterling.

Colorful Northern California, Vol. II. William Curran. Ed. by Robert D. Shangle. LC 78-9901. (Illus.). 72p. 1978. 12.95 (ISBN 0-915796-32-5); pap. 7.95 (ISBN 0-915796-31-7). Beautiful Am.

Coloring, Finishing & Painting Wood. Adnah C. Newell. Ed. by Holtrop. (gr. 9-12). 1972. text ed. 18.00 (ISBN 0-87002-124-9). Bennett IL.

Coloring the Smithsonian. Margaret Brown. pap. 1.50 o.p. (ISBN 0-445-08302-6). Popular Lib.

Coloritto. J. C Le Blon. 98p. 1980. 12.50 (ISBN 0-442-24723-0). Van Nos Reinhold.

Colors. John J. Reiss. LC 69-13653. (Illus.). (ps-1). 1969. 8.95 (ISBN 0-87888-008-9). Bradbury Pr.

Colors. Gillian Youldon. (Picture Play Ser.). (Illus.). (ps-2). 1979. 2.95 (ISBN 0-531-02387-7); PLB 5.90 s&l (ISBN 0-531-00439-2). Watts.

Colors Are Nice. Adelaide Holl. (Illus.). (gr. k-2). 1962. PLB 5.00 (ISBN 0-307-60496-9, Golden Pr). Western Pub.

Colors from the Earth. Anne W. Thomas. 132p. 1980. 13.95 (ISBN 0-442-25786-4). Van Nos Reinhold.

Colors: I Colori. Dick Higgins. Tr. by Giulia Niccolai from Eng. Reggio Emilia. (Illus., It.). 1981. pap. 10.00 (ISBN 0-914162-32-2). Printed Edns.

Colors of My Days. Donald X. Burt. 175p. (Orig.). 1980. pap. 3.95 (ISBN 0-8146-1198-2). Liturgical Pr.

Colossal Sculpture of the Cinquecento. Virginia Bush. LC 75-23785. (Outstanding Dissertations in the Fine Arts - 16th Century). (Illus.). 1976. lib. bdg. 48.00 (ISBN 0-8240-1981-4). Garland Pub.

Colossian & Philemon Studies. H. C. G. Moule. Date not set. 10.50 (ISBN 0-86524-052-3). Klock & Klock.

Colossians. W. R. Nicholson. LC 73-81742. 1969. 6.95 (ISBN 0-8254-3301-0); pap. 4.95 (ISBN 0-8254-3300-2). Kregel.

Colossians. Patrick V. Rogers. (New Testament Message Ser.). 9.95 (ISBN 0-89453-138-7); pap. 4.95 (ISBN 0-89453-203-0). M Glazier.

Colossians - a Study Guide Commentary. Curtis Vaughan. 128p. 1973. pap. text ed. 3.50 (ISBN 0-310-33523-X). Zondervan.

Colossians & Philemon. Keith L. Brooks. (Teach Yourself the Bible Ser). 81p. (Orig.). 1961. pap. 1.75 (ISBN 0-8024-1525-3). Moody.

Colossians & Philemon. Eduard Lohse. Ed. by Helmut Koester. Tr. by William R. Poehlman & Robert J. Karris. LC 76-157550. (Hermeneia: A Critical & Historical Commentary on the Bible Ser). 256p. 1971. 14.95 (ISBN 0-8006-6001-3, 20-6001). Fortress.

Colossians & Philemon. Geoffrey B. Wilson. (Wilson's New Testament Commentaries). 111p. (Orig.). 1980. pap. 3.95 (ISBN 0-85151-313-1). Banner of Truth.

Colossians & Philemon: A Study Guide Commentary. Curtis Vaughan. (Study Guide Commentary Ser.). 144p. (Orig.). 1981. pap. 3.50 (ISBN 0-310-33583-3). Zondervan.

Colossians: The Mystery of Christ in Us. Gary Demarest. 1979. 7.95 (ISBN 0-8499-0120-0). Word Bks.

Colossus. D. F. Jones. pap. 1.95 (ISBN 0-425-04329-0). Berkley Pub.

Colour Atlas of Gynaecological Cytopathology. Chandra Grubb. (Illus.). 1977. text ed. 29.50 o.p. (ISBN 0-8016-8353-X). Mosby.

Colour Atlas of Ophthalmology. Arthur Lim & Ian J. Constable. (Illus.). 1979. 14.00x (ISBN 0-89289-409-1). HM Prof Med Div.

Colour Atlas of the Rat: Dissection Guide. R. J. Olds. LC 78-24742. 1979. text ed. 10.95 (ISBN 0-470-26647-3). Halsted Pr.

Colour Centres & Imperfections in Insulators & Semiconductors. P. D. Townsend & J. C. Kelley. LC 73-76960. 250p. 1973. 24.00x (ISBN 0-8448-0209-3). Crane-Russak Co.

Colour, Culture & Conflict: A Study of Pluralism in Fiji. Alexander F. Mamak. (Illus.). 1979. 29.00 (ISBN 0-08-023354-6); pap. 13.25 (ISBN 0-08-023353-8). Pergamon.

Colour for the Artist. Hans Schwarz. LC 79-56605. (Start to Paint Ser.). (Illus.). 104p. 1980. pap. 3.95 (ISBN 0-8008-1726-5, Pentalic). Taplinger.

Colour Guide to Clouds. R. S. Scorer & H. Wexler. 1976. 15.00 (ISBN 0-08-010375-8); pap. 7.00 (ISBN 0-08-010374-X). Pergamon.

Colour in Focus. Jorge Lewinski & Bob Clark. 1978. 16.95 o.p. (ISBN 0-85242-439-6, Pub. by Fountain). Morgan.

Colour: Its Principles & Their Applications. F. W. Clulow. 1972. 16.95 o.p. (ISBN 0-85242-098-6, Pub. by Fountain). Morgan.

Colour Printing & Colour Printers. Robert M. Burch. LC 78-74393. (Nineteenth Century Book Arts & Printing History Ser.: Vol. 8). 1980. lib. bdg. 33.00 (ISBN 0-8240-3882-7). Garland Pub.

Coloured Image. V. A. February. (Monographs from the African Studies Center,Leiden). 256p. 1981. price not set (ISBN 0-7103-0002-6). Routledge & Kegan.

Coloured Key to the Wildfowl of the World. rev. ed. P. Scott. (Illus.). 1972. 15.00 (ISBN 0-685-12001-5). Heinman.

Coloured Things: Stages 1 & 2. Sheila Parker. LC 77-83009. (Science 5-13 Ser.). (Illus.). 1977. pap. text ed. 9.30 (ISBN 0-356-04348-7). Raintree Child.

Colporteur Ministry. Ellen G. White. 1953. 3.25 (ISBN 0-8163-0110-7, 03431-4); pap. 2.25 (ISBN 0-8163-0111-5, 03430-6). Pacific Pr Pub Assn.

Colposcopy: A Scientific & Practical Approach to the Cervix in Health & Disease. 2nd ed. Malcolm Coppleson et al. (American Lecture in Gynecology & Obstetrics Ser.). (Illus.). 512p. 1978. 40.25 (ISBN 0-398-03761-2). C C Thomas.

Colt & Challenger Nineteen Seventy-One to Eighty. LC 80-70346. (Illus.). 242p. 1980. pap. 8.95. Chilton.

Colt Firearms from Eighteen Thirty-Six. James E. Serven. LC 54-8380. (Illus.). 416p. 1979. 29.95 (ISBN 0-8117-0400-9). Stackpole.

Colt-Packin' Parson. Edwin Booth. 192p. (YA) 1976. 5.95 (ISBN 0-685-57546-2, Avalon). Bouregy.

Colt's SAA: Post War Models. George Garton. 166p. 17.95 (ISBN 0-917714-23-7). Beinfeld Pub.

Columbella. Phyllis A. Whitney. 1978. pap. 1.75 o.p. (ISBN 0-449-22919-X, Crest). Fawcett.

Columbella. Phyllis A. Whitney. 256p. 1981. pap. 2.50 (ISBN 0-449-22919-X, Crest). Fawcett.

Columbia Bookkeeping Systems Double Entry. Russell H. McDermott. (Accounting-Bookkeeping Systems Ser.). (Illus.). 130p. 1980. text ed. 49.95 (ISBN 0-9604828-3-0). Columbia Bookkeeping.

Columbia Essays in International Affairs: The Dean's Papers, Vol. 2, 1966. Ed. by Andrew W. Cordier. LC 66-14078. 1967. 25.00x (ISBN 0-231-03047-9). Columbia U Pr.

Columbia Essays in International Affairs: The Dean's Papers, Vol. 3, 1967. Ed. by Andrew W. Cordier. LC 66-14078. 1968. 25.00x (ISBN 0-231-03156-4). Columbia U Pr.

Columbia Essays in International Affairs: The Dean's Papers, Vol. 4, 1968. Ed. by Andrew W. Cordier. LC 66-14078. 1969. 25.00x (ISBN 0-231-03270-6). Columbia U Pr.

Columbia Essays in International Affairs: The Dean's Papers, Vol. 5, 1969. Ed. by Andrew W. Cordier. LC 66-14078. 1970. 25.00x (ISBN 0-231-03487-3). Columbia U Pr.

Columbia Essays in International Affairs: The Dean's Papers, Vol. 6, 1970. Ed. by Andrew W. Cordier. LC 66-14078. 180p. 1971. 25.00x (ISBN 0-231-03550-0). Columbia U Pr.

Columbia Essays in International Affairs: The Dean's Papers, Vol. 7, 1971. Ed. by Andrew W. Cordier. LC 66-14078. 304p. 1972. 25.00x (ISBN 0-231-03667-1). Columbia U Pr.

Columbia Essays on Modern Writers, No. 74: Par Lagerkvist. Leif Sjoberg. 1976. pap. 2.00 (ISBN 0-231-03103-3). Columbia U Pr.

Columbia Essays on Modern Writers, No. 73: Sean O'Casey. John P. Frayne. 1976. pap. 2.00 (ISBN 0-231-03655-8). Columbia U Pr.

Columbia Montaigne Conference: Papers. Ed. by Donald M. Frame & Mary B. McKinley. (French Forum Monographs: No. 27). 120p. (Orig.). 1981. pap. 11.50 (ISBN 0-917058-26-7). French Forum.

Columbia River Estuary & Adjacent Ocean Waters: Bioenvironmental Studies. Ed. by A. T. Pruter & Dayton L. Alverson. LC 79-178705. (Illus.). 882p. 1972. 25.00 (ISBN 0-295-95177-X). U of Wash Pr.

Columbia River Salmon & Steelhead Trout: Their Fight for Survival. Anthony Netboy. LC 80-50866. (Illus.). 192p. 1980. 13.95 (ISBN 0-295-95768-9). U of Wash Pr.

Columbia University Oral History Collection: An Index to the Memoirs in Part 1 of the Microform Edition. Microfilming Corporation of America. 162p. 1979. 95.00 (ISBN 0-667-00612-5). Arno.

Columbine. Raymond Kennedy. 1981. pap. 3.95 (ISBN 0-14-005882-6). Penguin.

Columbo No. 1. Alfred Lawrence. 1975. pap. 1.25 o.p. (ISBN 0-445-08382-4). Popular Lib.

Columbus. (gr. 1). 1974. pap. text ed. 2.80 (ISBN 0-205-03867-0, 8038678); tchrs'. guide 12.00 (ISBN 0-205-03866-2, 803866X). Allyn.

Columbus. (MacDonald Educational Ser.). (Illus., Arabic.). 3.50 (ISBN 0-686-53090-X). Intl Bk Ctr.

Columbus. Matthew G. Grant. LC 73-13959. 1974. PLB 5.95 (ISBN 0-87191-286-4). Creative Ed.

Columbus. Desmond Painter. Ed. by Malcolm Yapp et al. (World History Ser.). (Illus.). 32p. (gr. 10). 1980. Repr. of 1977 ed. lib. bdg. 5.95 (ISBN 0-89908-042-1); pap. text ed. 1.95 (ISBN 0-89908-017-0). Greenhaven.

Columbus: America's Crossroads. Betty Garrett. Ed. by Ellen S. Blakey & Larry P. Silvey. LC 80-66337. (American Portrait Ser.). (Illus.). 256p. 1980. 24.95 (ISBN 0-932986-10-2). Continent Herit.

Columbus & Discovery of America. John Langdon-Davies. (Jackdaw Ser: No. 4). (gr. 7 up). 1972. 5.95 o.p. (ISBN 0-670-23092-8). Viking Pr.

Columbus Book of Euchre. Natty Bumppo. (Illus.). 64p. 1981. pap. price not set (ISBN 0-9604894-2-8). Borf Bks.

Columbus, Cortes, & Other Essays. Ramon Iglesia. Tr. by Lesley B. Simpson. LC 69-13727. 1969. 18.50x (ISBN 0-520-01469-3). U of Cal Pr.

Columbus Day. Paul Showers. LC 65-16186. (Holiday Ser.). (Illus.). (gr. k-3). 1965. 7.89 (ISBN 0-690-19982-1, TYC-J). T Y Crowell.

Columbus in the Arctic. Tornoe. 1965. text ed. 5.50x. Humanities.

Columnist Looks at Life. Calvin Rutstrum. 133p. (Orig.). 1981. pap. 5.95 (ISBN 0-931714-10-9). Nodin Pr.

Comanche. J. T. Edson. (J. T. Edson Ser.). 1978. pap. 1.50 o.p. (ISBN 0-425-03843-2, Medallion). Berkley Pub.

Comanches & Other Indians of Texas. Marian T. Place. LC 79-103829. (Curriculum Related Bks). (gr. 7 up). 1970. 5.50 o.p. (ISBN 0-15-219451-7, HJ). HarBraceJ.

Comanche's Woman. Jake Logan. LC 75-36298. (John Slocum Ser.: No. 5). 192p. 1975. pap. 1.75 (ISBN 0-87216-722-4, B16301). Playboy Pbks.

Combat Aircraft of World War II. Ed. by Elke C Weal & John A Weal. LC 77-961. 1977. 9.98 o.s.i. (ISBN 0-02-624660-0). Macmillan.

Combat Effectiveness: Cohesion, Stress, & the Volunteer Military. Ed. by Sam C. Sarkesian. LC 80-17486. (Sage Research Progress Ser. on War, Revolution, & Peacekeeping: Vol. 9). (Illus.). 305p. 1980. 20.00 (ISBN 0-8039-1440-7). Sage.

Combat Effectiveness: Cohesion, Stress, & the Volunteer Military. Ed. by Sam C. Sarkesian. LC 80-17486. (Sage Research Progress Ser. on War, Revolution, & Peacekeeping: Vol. 9). (Illus.). 305p. 1980. pap. 9.95 (ISBN 0-8039-1441-5). Sage.

Combat Films: American Realism, Nineteen Forty-Five to Nineteen Seventy. Steven J. Rubin. LC 80-17022. (Illus.). 245p. 1981. lib. bdg. 15.95x (ISBN 0-89950-013-7); pap. 11.95x (ISBN 0-89950-014-5). McFarland & Co.

Combat Fleets of the World Nineteen Eighty & Eighty-One: Their Ships, Aircraft, & Armament. Jean L. Couhat. LC 78-50192. (Illus.). 808p. 1980. 64.95x (ISBN 0-87021-123-4). Naval Inst Pr.

Combat Handgun Shooting. James D. Mason. (Illus.). 272p. 1980. 14.95 (ISBN 0-398-03461-3). C C Thomas.

Combat Handguns. George C. Nonte, Jr. Ed. by Lee F. Jurras. (Illus.). 354p. 1980. 19.95 (ISBN 0-8117-0409-2). Stackpole.

Combat History of the Second Infantry Division. (Divisional Ser.: No. 5). (Illus.). 1979. Repr. of 1946 ed. 25.00 o.p. (ISBN 0-89839-017-6). Battery Pr.

Combat Leader's Field Guide. (Illus.). 272p. 1973. pap. 6.95 (ISBN 0-8117-0395-9). Stackpole.

Combat Nurses of World War Two. Wyatt Blassingame. (Landmark Ser: No. 116). (gr. 4 up). 1967. PLB 5.99 o.p. (ISBN 0-394-90416-8). Random.

Combat of Shadows. Manohar Malgonkar. 292p. 1968. pap. 2.50 (ISBN 0-88253-056-9). Ind-US Inc.

Combat Reporter's Report. Sweeney. (gr. 6 up). 1980. PLB 7.90 (ISBN 0-531-04171-9, E20). Watts.

Combat Shooting for Police. 2nd ed. Paul B. Weston. (Police Science Ser.). (Illus.). 184p. 1978. 12.75 (ISBN 0-398-03747-7). C C Thomas.

Combat Support Equipment Nineteen Eighty to Nineteen Eighty-One. Foss. 1980. 125.00 (ISBN 0-531-03954-4). Watts.

Combat Without Weapons. E. Hartley Leather. (Illus.). 1975. pap. 3.00 (ISBN 0-87364-060-8). Paladin Ent.

Combating Crime Against Small Business. Ed. by Richards S. Post. 160p. 1972. 9.75 (ISBN 0-398-02383-2). C C Thomas.

Combating Managerial Obsolescence. Andrew N. Jones & Cary L. Cooper. LC 80-16307. 192p. 1980. lib. bdg. 19.95 (ISBN 0-86003-509-3, JCO/). Greenwood.

Combating Nutritional Blindness in Children: A Case Study of Technical Assistance in Indonesia. Carl Fritz. (Pergamon Policy Studies). 1980. 28.00 (ISBN 0-08-024636-2). Pergamon.

Combination Reference. Eldin Ricks. 3.95 o.p. (ISBN 0-87747-037-5); pocket ed. 2.50 (ISBN 0-87747-038-3). Deseret Bk.

Combinations in the Middle Game. I. Bonarevsky. (Chess Player Ser.). 1977. pap. 3.95 o.p. (ISBN 0-900928-93-X, H-1189). Hippocrene Bks.

Combinatorial Algorithms: Theory & Practice. Reingold et al. 1977. text ed. 23.95 (ISBN 0-13-152447-X). P-H.

Combinatorial Analysis: Proceedings, Vol. 10. Symposia in Applied Mathematics-New York-1958. Ed. by R. Bellman & M. Hall, Jr. LC 50-1183. 1979. Repr. of 1960 ed. 24.40 (ISBN 0-8218-1310-2, PSAPM-10). Am Math.

Combinatorial Introduction to Topology. Michael Henle. LC 78-14874. (Mathematical Sciences Ser.). (Illus.). 1979. text ed. 22.95x (ISBN 0-7167-0083-2). W H Freeman.

Combinatorial Mathematics VII: Proceedings. R. W. Robinson et al. (Lecture Notes in Mathematics Ser.: Vol. 829). (Illus.). 256p. 1981. pap. 16.80 (ISBN 0-387-10254-X). Springer-Verlag.

Combinatorics, Representation Theory & Statistical Methods in Groups: Young Day Proceedings. Nayrayana. 192p. 1980. 25.00 (ISBN 0-686-68601-2). Dekker.

Combined Catalog Anglo-American Law Collections University of California Law Libraries Berkeley & Davis with Library of Congress Class K Added, 9 vols. Ed. by Mortimer D. Schwartz & Dan F. Henke. 1970. text ed. 750.00x (ISBN 0-8377-0423-5). Rothman.

Combined Commercial Pilot Written Test Questions, Answers & Explanations Book. John King & Martha King. (Pilot Training Ser.). (Illus.). 210p. 1979. pap. 10.95 (ISBN 0-89100-167-0, EA-A C61-71 B-1). Aviation Maintenance.

Combined Effects of Alcohol & Other Drugs. Robert Forney & Francis Hughes. 132p. 1968. pap. 11.75 photocopy ed. spiral (ISBN 0-398-00597-4). C C Thomas.

Combined Effects of Radioactive Chemical & Thermal Releases to the Environment: Proceedings. Symposium, Stockholm, Sweden, June 2-5, 1975. (Illus.). 358p. 1976. pap. 32.75 (ISBN 92-0-020275-6, ISP404, IAEA). Unipub.

Combined Heat & Power Whole City Heating Planning: Tomorrows Energy Economy. W. R. Orchard & A. F. Sherratt. LC 80-41444. 234p. 1980. 59.95 (ISBN 0-470-27088-8). Halsted Pr.

Combined Heat, Ice & Water Balances at Selected Glacier Basins, Pt. 2: Specifications, Standards & Data Exchange. (Technical Papers in Hydrology Ser.). (Illus.). 32p. (Orig.). 1973. pap. 2.50 (ISBN 9-231-01050-6, #U738, UNESCO). Unipub.

Combined Membership List. (Miscellaneous Publications). 1980. 10.00 (ISBN 0-8218-0071-X). Am Math.

Combined Nonlinear & Linear (Micro & Macro) Fracture Mechanics: Applications to Modern Engineering Structures - Selected Papers, U.S.-Japan Seminar. Ed. by H. Liebowitz. 1976. pap. text ed. 46.00 (ISBN 0-08-019982-8). Pergamon.

Combined Payments & Constant Percent Tables: Quarterly Loan Schedules No. 188. 40.00 (ISBN 0-685-26871-3). Finan Pub.

Combined Proceedings: 1975, 2 vols. in 1. Ed. by Edward M. Mazze. LC 75-30572. 1975. pap. 15.00 o.p. (ISBN 0-87757-067-1). Am Mktg.

Combined Production of Electric Power & Heat: Proceedings of a Seminar Organized by the Committee on Electric Power of the United Nations Economic Commission for Europe, Hamburg, FR Germany, 6-9 November 1978. United Nations Economic Commission for Europe. LC 80-755. (Illus.). 150p. 32.00 (ISBN 0-08-025677-5). Pergamon.

Combined Retrospective Index to Book Reviews in Scholarly Humanities Journals, 1802-1974, 10 vols. Ed. by Evan I. Farber. 1981. 932.00 set (ISBN 0-8408-0238-2). Carrollton Pr.

Combined Retrospective Index to Book Reviews in Scholarly Journals, 1886-1974, 15 vols. Evan I. Farber. LC 79-89137. 1979. lib. bdg. 1232.00 (ISBN 0-8408-0157-2). Carrollton Pr.

Combined School - Public Libraries: A Survey with Conclusions & Recommendations. Wilma L. Woolard. LC 80-36742. 204p. 1980. 11.00 (ISBN 0-8108-1335-1). Scarecrow.

Combined Sewer Seperation Using Pressure Sewers. Compiled By American Society of Civil Engineers. 212p. 1969. pap. text ed. 12.00 (ISBN 0-87262-017-4). Am Soc Civil Eng.

Combing the Coast. Ruth Jackson. (Illus.). 160p. 1972. pap. 3.95 o.p. (ISBN 0-87701-014-5). Chronicle Bks.

Combing the Coast: San Francisco to Santa Cruz. Ruth A. Jackson. (Illus.). 116p. (Orig.). 1981. pap. 4.95 (ISBN 0-87701-140-0). Chronicle Bks.

Combining Sentences. George E. Sullivan & Warren Cox. Ed. by K. West & D. Johnston. (Writing Skills for Daily Living Ser.). (Illus.). 40p. (gr. 7-12). 1979. pap. text ed. 3.95x (ISBN 0-87453-098-9). Denoyer.

Combustion & Heat Transfer in Gas Turbine Systems. E. R. Norster. (Cranfield International Symposium Ser: Vol. 11). (Illus.). 1971. 58.00 o.p. (ISBN 0-08-016524-9). Pergamon.

Combustion Institute European Symposium: Papers Presented at Symposium Held at the University of Sheffield, Sept., 1973. Ed. by F. J. Weinberg. 1974. 94.50 (ISBN 0-12-742350-8). Acad Pr.

Combustion Modeling in Reciprocating Engines. Ed. by James N. Mattavi & Charles A. Amann. (General Motors Research Laboratories Ser.). 616p. 69.50 (ISBN 0-306-40431-1, Plenum Pr). Plenum Pub.

Combustion Stability. Karoly Remenyi. Tr. by E. Darabant. (Illus.). 175p. 1980. 20.00x (ISBN 963-05-2023-0). Intl Pubns Serv.

Combustion Theory. 2nd ed. Forman A. Williams. (Illus.). 1981. write for info. (ISBN 0-201-08652-2, Adv Bk Prog). A-W.

Comden & Green on Broadway. Betty Comden et al. LC 80-18531. (Illus.). 320p. 1981. 16.95 (ISBN 0-89676-042-1). Drama Bk.

Come Alive! Don Hawley. LC 75-21190. (Orig.). 1975. pap. 0.85 (ISBN 0-8280-0045-X). Review & Herald.

Come Alive. Frances Hunter. 1975. pap. 2.95 (ISBN 0-917726-34-0). Hunter Bks.

Come An' Get It: The Story of the Old Cowboy Cook. Ramon F. Adams. 171p. (Orig.). 1952. 7.95 (ISBN 0-8061-0254-3); pap. 3.95 (ISBN 0-8061-1013-9). U of Okla Pr.

Come & Follow. F. Washington Jarvis. pap. 3.95 (ISBN 0-8164-2072-6). Crossroad NY.

Come & Get It: A Natural Foods Cookbook for Children. 2nd ed. Kathleen M. Baxter. LC 78-73448. (Illus.). 128p. 1978. pap. 8.50 (ISBN 0-9603696-1-9). Children First.

Come Back, Lolly Ray. Beverly Lowry. 1978. pap. 1.95 o.p. (ISBN 0-445-04216-8). Popular Lib.

Come Back, Miranda. Anne Duffield. 1974. pap. 1.25 o.p. (ISBN 0-425-02971-9, Medallion). Berkley Pub.

Come Back to Love. Joyce Dingwell. (Harlequin Romances). 192p. 1981. pap. 1.25 (ISBN 0-373-02402-9, Pub. by Harlequin). PB.

Come Back, Wherever You Are. Lenora M. Weber. LC 69-13643. (Beany Malone Ser). (gr. 7 up). 1969. 10.95 (ISBN 0-690-20123-0, TYC-J). T Y Crowell.

Come by Here. Olivia Coolidge. LC 72-115451. (Illus.). (gr. 5 up). 1970. 6.95 (ISBN 0-395-10912-4). HM.

Come Clean. Charles W. Keysor. 128p. 1976. pap. 1.75 o.p. (ISBN 0-88207-732-5). Victor Bks.

Come Day, Go Day, God Send Sunday: The Songs & Life Story, Told in His Own Words, of John Maguire, Traditional Singer & Farmer from County Fermanagh, N. Ireland. Compiled by Robin Morton. (Illus.). 202p. 1973. 13.00 (ISBN 0-7100-7634-7). Routledge & Kegan.

Come Day, Go Day, God Send Sunday: The Songs & Life Story, Told in His Own Words, of John Maguire, Traditional Singer & Farmer from County Fermanagh, N. Ireland. Compiled by Robin Morton. (Illus.). 1976. pap. 6.95 (ISBN 0-7100-8388-2). Routledge & Kegan.

Come Die for Me. David Lyday. 1977. pap. 1.50 o.p. (ISBN 0-445-04110-2). Popular Lib.

Come Fight a Kite. Dinesh Bahadur. (Illus.). (gr. 5 up). 1978. PLB 6.79 (ISBN 0-8178-5928-4); pap. 3.95 (ISBN 0-8178-5927-6). Harvey.

Come, Follow Me. Rachel I. Scruggs. 1981. 7.95 (ISBN 0-533-04769-2). Vantage.

Come, Hear & See. Monica Stuart & Gill Soper. 1976. 8.95 o.p. (ISBN 0-571-10935-7, Pub. by Faber & Faber). Merrimack Bk Serv.

Come Here. Richard Kostelanetz. 1975. 2.50, signed & lettered A-Z 25.00 ea. (ISBN 0-685-56017-1). Assembling Pr.

Come Home, Dear. Lucy Walker. 192p. 1975. pap. 1.25 (ISBN 0-345-29556-0). Ballantine.

Come Home Wilma. Mitchell Sharmat. Ed. by Kathleen Tucker. LC 80-18991. (Concept Bks.). (Illus.). 32p. (ps-2). 1980. 6.95 (ISBN 0-8075-1278-8). A Whitman.

Come into My Kitchen. Celia Marks. 1969. spiral bd. 7.95. Plum Nelly.

Come, Let Us Celebrate. Blair Richards & Janice Sigmund. 160p. 1976. pap. 5.95 o.p. (ISBN 0-8015-1457-6). Dutton.

Come Let Us Eat: Preparing for First Communion. rev. ed. Sr. M. Charles Bryce. LC 70-183075. (Illus.). (gr. 1-2). 1972. pap. 1.45 (ISBN 0-8164-6076-0); first communion, parent-teacher manual 1.95 (ISBN 0-8164-6077-9). Crossroad NY.

Come, Let Us Reason Together. Beryl D. Cohon. LC 76-24330. 1977. 5.95x (ISBN 0-8197-0397-4). Bloch.

Come Like the Benediction. Clyde O. Jackson. (Illus.). 1981. 7.00 (ISBN 0-682-49723-1). Exposition.

Come Love with Me. Jonah Elaine. 1981. 4.95 (ISBN 0-8062-1646-8). Carlton.

Come Me Sacaras De Este Apuro, Senor? Ed. by Angela Whidden. (Span.). 1979. pap. 1.75 (ISBN 0-8297-0553-8). Vida Pubs.

C.O.M.E. Members Manual. Herbert Mayer. pap. 12.50 (ISBN 0-933350-24-4). Morse Pr.

Come Next Spring. Elizabeth Graham. (Harlequin Romances Ser.). (Orig.). 1980. pap. 1.25 o.p. (ISBN 0-373-02326-X, Pub. by Harlequin). PB.

Come Nineveh, Come Tyre. Allen Drury. LC 73-9347. 480p. 1973. 8.95 o.p. (ISBN 0-385-04392-9). Doubleday.

Come on Out, Daddy. Inger Sandberg. LC 70-122771. (Illus.). (ps-3). 1971. 4.95 (ISBN 0-440-01522-7, Sey Lawr); PLB 4.58 (ISBN 0-440-01523-5). Delacorte.

Come Out & Play. Gyo Fujikawa. (Gyo Fujikawa Tiny Board Books). (Illus.). 14p. (ps-k). 1981. 1.95 (ISBN 0-448-15115-4). G&D.

Come Out, Come Out, Wherever You Are. Donna L. Pape. LC 78-73528. (First Reader Ser.). (Illus.). (gr. k-3). Date not set. price not set (ISBN 0-89799-153-2); pap. price not set (ISBN 0-89799-071-4). Dandelion Pr. Postponed.

Come Out Smiling. Elizabeth Levy. LC 80-68734. 192p. (YA) (gr. 8-12). 1981. 8.95 (ISBN 0-440-01378-X). Delacorte.

Come Over, Red Rover. Stephen Marlowe. 1968. 4.95 o.s.i. (ISBN 0-02-579790-5). Macmillan.

Come Sea Fishing with Me. Richard Arnold. 9.95x (ISBN 0-392-06448-0, SpS). Soccer.

Come Sing with Me. Margaret C. McNeil. (ps). 1971. pap. 2.95 (ISBN 0-8170-0535-8); bk. & record o.p. 5.95 (ISBN 0-685-01111-9). Judson.

Come Slowly, Eden. Charlene Keel. 1978. pap. 1.75 (ISBN 0-505-51322-6). Tower Bks.
Come, Solitude, Speak to Me. Somesh Dasgupta. 8.00 (ISBN 0-89253-683-7); flexible cloth 4.80 (ISBN 0-89253-684-5). Ind-US Inc.
Come Songbook. Gary L. Johnson. 1980. pap. 1.95 (ISBN 0-87123-777-6, 280777). Bethany Fell.
Come Summer, Come Love. Isabel Cabot. (YA) 1977. 5.50 o.p. (ISBN 0-685-81422-X, Avalon). Bouregy.
Come Sweet Death. rev. ed. B. Davie Napier. 64p. 1981. pap. 4.95 (ISBN 0-8298-0422-6). Pilgrim NY.
Come Tell Me How You Live. Agatha Christie. 1980. pap. 2.50 (ISBN 0-671-43282-6). PB.
Come to Greenleaves. Kay Richardson. (YA) 1977. 4.95 o.p. (ISBN 0-685-75639-4, Avalon). Bouregy.
Come to the Doctor, Harry. Mary Chalmers. LC 80-7910. (Illus.). 32p. (ps-1). 1981. 5.95 (ISBN 0-06-021178-4, HarpJ); PLB 5.89g (ISBN 0-06-021179-2). Har-Row.
Come to Your Senses. B. Milbauer & K. K. Jacobson. (Getting in Touch Ser: Bk. 4). (gr. 5-8). 0.95 o.p. (ISBN 0-531-02090-8, Q28). Watts.
Come Under the Wings: A Midrash on Ruth. 2nd ed. Grace Goldin. LC 79-91327. 85p. 1980. pap. 4.95 (ISBN 0-8276-0171-9, 451). Jewish Pubn.
Come Unto These Yellow Sands. W. M. Von Heider. LC 79-55739. 1981. tchers & parents ed. 14.95 (ISBN 0-89742-031-4). Dawne-Leigh. Postponed.
Come Wade the River. limited ed. Roderick Haig-Brown & Ralph Wahl. LC 70-160188. 1971. 100.00 (ISBN 0-87564-006-0). Superior Pub.
Come Walk with Me. Nellie Beardmore. 1981. 5.95 (ISBN 0-533-04850-8). Vantage.
Come Walk with Me & Listen to the Wind. Pasquale J. Nunzio. (Illus.). 1978. pap. cancelled (ISBN 0-914090-51-8). Chicago Review.
Comeback Dog. Jane R. Thomas. (Illus.). 64p. (gr. 2-5). 1981. 7.95 (ISBN 0-395-29432-0, Clarion). HM.
Comecon Data Nineteen Seventy-Nine. Vienna Institute for Comparative Economic Studies. LC 80-17577. 436p. 1980. text ed. 45.50x (ISBN 0-8419-0607-6). Holmes & Meier.
COMECON Foreign Trade Data Nineteen Eighty. Ed. by Vienna Institute for Comparative Economic Studies. LC 80-28569. (Illus.). 509p. 1981. lib. bdg. 40.00 (ISBN 0-313-22988-0, VIC/). Greenwood.
Comecon Merchant Ships. 2nd ed. Ambrose Greenway. (Illus.). 150p. 1981. text ed. 20.00x (ISBN 0-911378-34-0). Sheridan.
Comedians. Graham Greene. 1981. 14.95 (ISBN 0-670-23208-4). Viking Pr.
Comedie Francaise Au XVIIIe: Etude Economique. Claude Alasseur. (Civilisation et Societes: No. 3). 1967. pap. 14.70x (ISBN 90-2796-074-7). Mouton.
Comedies of George Chapman: A Study in Development. Thomas M. Grant. (Salzburg Studies in English Literature, Jacobean Drama Studies: No. 5). 1972. pap. text ed. 25.00x (ISBN 0-391-01391-2). Humanities.
Comedies of Terence. Terence. Tr. by Frank O. Copley. Incl. The Brothers; The Eunuch; The Mother-in-Law; Phormio; The Self-Tormenter; The Woman of Andros. LC 67-20452. (Orig.). 1967. pap. 6.95 (ISBN 0-672-60279-2, LLA90). Bobbs.
Comedy: A Critical Anthology. Ed. by Robert W. Corrigan & Glenn M. Loney. LC 78-150137. (Orig.). 1971. pap. text ed. 9.75 (ISBN 0-395-04325-5). HM.
Comedy & America: The Lost World of Washington Irving. Martin Roth. (Literary Criticism Ser.). 1976. 15.00 (ISBN 0-8046-9132-0, Natl U). Kennikat.
Comedy & Conscience After the Restoration. rev. ed. Joseph W. Krutch. LC 24-28256. 1924. pap. 7.50x (ISBN 0-231-08516-8). Columbia U Pr.
Comedy & Tragedy: A Bibliography of Critical Studies. E. H. Mikhail. LC 75-183299. 1972. pap. 5.00x o.p. (ISBN 0-87875-019-3). Whitston Pub.
Comedy: Meaning & Form. 2nd ed. Robert W. Corrigan. 352p. 1980. pap. text ed. 10.95 scp (ISBN 0-06-041370-0, HarpC). Har-Row.
Comedy of Errors. rev. ed. William Shakespeare. Ed. by Arthur Quiller-Couch et al. (New Shakespeare Ser). 1968. 23.95 (ISBN 0-521-07528-9); pap. 4.50x (ISBN 0-521-09471-2). Cambridge U Pr.
Comedy of Errors. William Shakespeare. Ed. by Paul A. Jorgensen. (Shakespeare Ser.). 1964. pap. 2.50 (ISBN 0-14-071432-4, Pelican). Penguin.
Comedy of Language: Studies in Modern Comic Literature. Fred M. Robinson. LC 80-125. 200p. 1980. lib. bdg. 15.00x (ISBN 0-87023-297-5). U of Mass Pr.
Comedy of Manners. Kenneth Muir. 1970. pap. text ed. 2.50x (ISBN 0-09-100481-0, Hutchinson U Lib). Humanities.
Comedy of Manners from Sheridan to Maugham. Newell W. Sawyer. 1961. pap. 1.95 o.p. (ISBN 0-498-04057-7, Prpta). A S Barnes.
Comedy of Masks. Ernest Dowson & Arthur Moore. Ed. by Ian Fletcher & John Stokes. LC 76-20066. (Decadent Consciousness Ser.: Vol. 8). 1977. Repr. of 1896 ed. lib. bdg. 38.00 (ISBN 0-8240-2757-4). Garland Pub.
Comedy of Survival. Joseph W. Meeker. LC 79-54815. 1980. pap. 7.95 (ISBN 0-89615-048-8). Guild of Tutors.
Comely Frontispiece: The Emblematic Title-Page in England, 1550-1660. Margery Corbett & R. W. Lightbown. (Illus.). 1979. 35.00x (ISBN 0-7100-8554-0). Routledge & Kegan.
Comentario Arqueologica de la Biblia. Gonzalo Baez-Camargo. 339p. (Orig., Span.). 1979. pap. 7.25 (ISBN 0-89922-148-3). Edit Caribe.
Comentario Exegetico y Explicativo De la Biblia Tomo II. Jamieson-Fausett Brown. Tr. by Jaime C. Quarles & Lemuel C. Quarles. 1979. pap. 8.95 (ISBN 0-311-03005-X). Casa Bautista.
Comes the Blind Fury. John Saul. (Orig.). 1980. pap. 2.75 o.s.i. (ISBN 0-440-11428-4). Dell.
Comes Winter, the Sea Hunting. Norman Dubie. (Maguey Press Poetry Chapbook Ser.). (Orig.). Date not set. pap. 3.50 (ISBN 0-930778-08-1). Maguey Pr. Postponed.
Comet in Moominland. Tove Jansson. (gr. 3-5). 1975. pap. 1.95 (ISBN 0-380-00436-4, 52100, Camelot). Avon.
Comet Is Coming. Nigel Calder. 176p. 1981. 12.95 (ISBN 0-670-23216-5). Viking Pr.
Comets. David C. Knight. LC 68-16015. (First Bks). (Illus.). (gr. 4-6). 1968. PLB 4.90 o.p. (ISBN 0-531-00505-4). Watts.
Comets. Herbert S. Zim. (Illus.). (gr. 3-7). 1957. PLB 6.48 (ISBN 0-688-31180-6). Morrow.
Comets & Meteors. Isaac Asimov. LC 72-2499. (Beginning Science Ser.). (Illus.). 32p. (gr. 2-5). 1972. 2.50 o.p. (ISBN 0-695-80047-7); PLB 2.97 titan ed. o.p. (ISBN 0-695-40047-9). Follett.
Comets, Meteoroids & Asteroids: Mavericks of the Solar System. Franklyn M. Branley. LC 73-16043. (Exploring Our Universe Ser.). (Illus.). (gr. 7 up). 1974. 8.95 (ISBN 0-690-20176-1, TYC-J). T Y Crowell.
Comets, Meteors & Asteroids. Melvin Berger. (Illus.). 64p. (gr. 10 up). 1981. PLB 6.99 (ISBN 0-399-61148-7). Putnam.
Comfort Below Freezing. Robert McQuilkin. LC 79-28741. (Illus.). 176p. (Orig.). 1981. pap. 5.95 (ISBN 0-89037-184-9). Anderson World.
Comfort Clothes. Chris Rex. LC 80-69534. (Illus.). 80p. (Orig.). pap. 7.95 (ISBN 0-89087-312-7). Celestial Arts.
Comfort Clothes: How to Make & Wear West African Style Garments. Chris Rex. LC 80-69534. (Illus.). 80p. 1981. 7.95 (ISBN 0-89087-312-7). Celestial Arts.
Comfort for the Sick. rev. ed. B. P. Nommensen. 1976. pap. 5.00 (ISBN 0-8100-0011-3, 06N0553). Northwest Pub.
Comfort Heating. 2nd ed. Billy C. Langley. (Illus.). 1978. ref. 17.50 (ISBN 0-87909-091-X); instrs'. manual avail. Reston.
Comfort of Cats. Doreen Tovey. (Illus.). 181p. 1980. 9.95 (ISBN 0-312-15088-1). St Martin.
Comfort One Another with These Words. Harold Kesler. 1981. pap. 0.95 (ISBN 0-937396-11-7). Walterick Pubs.
Comfort to the Sick: A Recipe Book of Medicinal Herbs. Brother Aloysius. 416p. 1981. pap. 8.95 (ISBN 0-87728-525-X). Weiser.
Comfortable Quarters for Laboratory Animals. 7th ed. Animal Welfare Institute. (Illus.). 108p. 1979. pap. text ed. 3.00 (ISBN 0-938414-01-1). Animal Welfare.
Comforting the Wilderness. Robert Shaw. LC 77-74603. (Wesleyan Poetry Program: Vol. 87). 1977. pap. 4.95x (ISBN 0-8195-1087-4, Pub. by Wesleyan U Pr). Columbia U Pr.
Comforting Those Who Grieve. Cecil Murphey. LC 78-71052. 64p. 1979. pap. 2.50 (ISBN 0-8042-1099-3). John Knox.
Comfrey: Fodder, Food & Remedy. Lawrence D. Hills. LC 75-33485. (Illus.). 254p. 1976. 12.50x o.p. (ISBN 0-87663-273-8); pap. 5.95 (ISBN 0-87663-932-5). Universe.
Comfrey Report. Lawrence D. Hills. Ed. by Bargyla Rateaver & Gylver Rateaver. Bd. with Comfrey, the Herbal Healer. LC 75-23178. (Conservation Gardening & Farming Ser: Ser. C). 1975. pap. 6.00 (ISBN 0-9600698-9-5). Rateavers.
Comic Adventures of Old Mother Hubbard & Her Dog. Tomie De Paola. LC 80-19270. (Illus.). 32p. (ps-3). 1981. pap. 5.95 (ISBN 0-15-219542-4, VoyB). HarBraceJ.
Comic Adventures of Old Mother Hubbard & Her Dog. Tomie De Paola. LC 80-19270. (Illus.). 32p. (ps-3). 1981. 11.95 (ISBN 0-15-219541-6, HJ). HarBraceJ.
Comic Art & Caricature. Roy P. Nelson. 1978. 12.95 o.p. (ISBN 0-8092-7848-0); pap. 6.95 o.p. (ISBN 0-685-25108-X). Contemp Bks.
Comic Elements of Ben Jonson's Drama, 2 vols. Ingeborg Sturmberger. (Salzburg Studies in English Literature, Jacobean Drama Studies Ser.: Nos. 54-55). 548p. 1975. Set. pap. text ed. 50.25x (ISBN 0-391-01540-0). Humanities.
Comic Faith: The Great Tradition from Austen to Joyce. Robert M. Polhemus. LC 79-24856. 1980. 25.00 (ISBN 0-226-67320-0). U of Chicago Pr.
Comic Hero. Robert M. Torrance. LC 77-16316. 1978. 16.50x (ISBN 0-674-14431-7). Harvard U Pr.
Comic Imagination in American Literature. Ed. by Louis D. Rubin, Jr. (Illus.). 448p. 1973. 29.00 (ISBN 0-8135-0758-8). Rutgers U Pr.
Comic in Renaissance Comedy. David Farley-Hills. 1981. 26.50x (ISBN 0-389-20013-1). B&N.
Comic in Theory & Practice. Ed. by John J. Enck et al. (Orig.). 1960. pap. text ed. 10.50 (ISBN 0-13-152561-1). P-H.
Comic Justice in Shakespeare's Comedies, Vols. 1 & 2. Irene Makaryk. (Jacobean Drama Ser.: No. 91). 1980. pap. text ed. 25.00x ea. (ISBN 0-391-02143-5). Humanities.
Comic Justice in Shakespeare's Comedies, Vol. 2. Irene R. Makaryk. (Jacobean Drama Studies: No.91). 259p. 1980. pap. text ed. 25.00 (ISBN 0-391-02197-4). Humanities.
Comic Mark Twain Reader: The Most Humorous Selections from His Stories, Sketches, Novels, Travel Books & Speeches. Mark Twain. LC 76-23785. 1977. 10.95 (ISBN 0-385-11334-X). Doubleday.
Comic Mind: Comedy & the Movies. 2nd ed. Gerald Mast. LC 78-68546. (Illus.). 1979. lib. bdg. 24.00x (ISBN 0-226-50976-1); pap. 8.95 (ISBN 0-266-50978-9, P827, Phoen). U of Chicago Pr.
Comic Sense of Henry James: A Study of the Early Novels. Richard Poirer. 1967. pap. 4.95 (ISBN 0-19-500438-8, GB). Oxford U Pr.
Comic Spirit: Boccaccio to Thomas Mann. Bernard N. Schilling. LC 65-21652. (Waynebooks Ser: No. 26). 1965. 10.95x (ISBN 0-8143-1271-3); pap. 4.95x (ISBN 0-8143-1272-1). Wayne St U Pr.
Comic Spirit of Eighteenth Century Novels. Susan G. Auty. (National University Publications Literary Criticism Ser.). 200p. 1975. 15.00 (ISBN 0-8046-9120-7, Natl U.). Kennikat.
Comic Terror: The Novels of John Hawkes. rev. ed. Donald J. Greiner. LC 78-16886. 1978. pap. 6.95x (ISBN 0-87870-044-7). Memphis St Univ.
Comic Theatre: A Comedy in Three Acts. Carlo Goldoni. Tr. by John W. Miller. LC 69-14867. 1969. 7.50x (ISBN 0-8032-0056-0). U of Nebr Pr.
Comical Works of Don Francisco de Quevedo. 2nd ed. Francisco G. de Quevedo y Villegas. Tr. by John Stevens. LC 80-2494. 1981. Repr. of 1709 ed. 69.50 (ISBN 0-404-19128-2). AMS Pr.
Comicorum Graecorum Fragmenta in papyris reperta (1838-1971) Ed. by Colinus Austin. 1973. 197.00x (ISBN 3-11-004046-8). De Gruyter.
Comics of the American West. Maurice Horn. (Illus.). 1978. pap. 7.95 o.p. (ISBN 0-695-80954-7). Follett.
Coming Age of Psychosomatics: Proceedings of the 21st Annual Conference of the Society of Psychosomatic Research, November 21-22 1977, Royal College of Physicians. Annual Conference of the Society of Psychosomatic Research, 21st, Royal College of Physicians, London, November 21-22 1977 & P. Mellett. (Illus.). 163p. 1979. 29.50 (ISBN 0-08-023736-3). Pergamon.
Coming & Going of the Shaman: Eskimo Shamanism & Art. Jean Blodgett. (Illus.). 246p. 1981. pap. 17.50 (ISBN 0-88915-068-0, 08913-4, Pub. by Canadian Artic Producers Ltd). U of Chicago Pr.
Coming Apart. Jean Renvoize. LC 80-6202. 288p. 1981. 12.95 (ISBN 0-8128-2780-5). Stein & Day.
Coming Attractions. Fannie Flagg. 320p. 1981. 11.95 (ISBN 0-688-00472-5). Morrow.
Coming Back. Donald Honig. (Illus.). 48p. (gr. 3 up). 1974. PLB 6.45 (ISBN 0-531-02661-2); pap. 1.95 (ISBN 0-531-02369-9). Watts.
Coming Back: A Guide to Recovering from Heart Attack & Living Confidently. Cohn & Madrid. 10.95 (ISBN 0-201-04562-1). A-W.
Coming Back Alive. Dennis J. Reader. LC 79-5147. (Illus.). 256p. (gr. 7 up). 1981. 8.95 (ISBN 0-686-68070-7); PLB 8.99 (ISBN 0-686-68071-5). Random.
Coming Back...or Never Leaving: Instructional Programming for Handicapped Students in the Mainstream. Anne L. Pasanella & Cara B. Volkmor. 1977. pap. text ed. 13.95 (ISBN 0-675-08460-1); filmstrip & cassette 135.00 (ISBN 0-675-08459-8); 2-5 sets 85.00, 6 or more sets 65.00 (ISBN 0-685-75490-1); instructor's manual 3.95 (ISBN 0-686-67642-4). Merrill.
Coming Crisis of Western Sociology. Alvin W. Gouldner. 1971. pap. text ed. 5.45 o.s.i. (ISBN 0-380-01109-3, 22186). Avon.
Coming Currency Collapse & What to Do About It! Jerome F. Smith. LC 80-66785. (Illus.). 250p. 1980. 13.95 (ISBN 0-916728-41-2). Bks in Focus.
Coming Fury. Bruce Catton. LC 61-12502. (Centennial History of the Civil War: Vol. 1). 14.95 (ISBN 0-385-09813-8). Doubleday.
Coming Home. Shepard Ginandes. LC 76-8866. 1976. 7.95 o.s.i. (ISBN 0-440-01447-6, Sey Lawr). Delacorte.
Coming Home: The Experience of Enlightenment in Sacred Traditions. Lex Hixon. LC 77-77656. 1978. pap. 2.95 (ISBN 0-385-12907-6, Anch). Doubleday.
Coming Home to a Place You've Never Been Before. Bruce Clements & Hanna Clements. LC 75-26716. 192p. (gr. 7 up). 1975. 6.95 (ISBN 0-374-31530-2). FS&G.
Coming Matriarchy: How Women Will Gain the Balance of Power. Elizabeth Nickles & Laura Ashcraft. (Illus.). 352p. 1981. 13.95 (ISBN 0-87223-686-2). Seaview Bks.
Coming of Age. Simone De Beauvoir. 880p. 1973. pap. 2.95 o.s.i. (ISBN 0-446-83680-X). Warner Bks.
Coming of Age of American Business. Elisha P. Douglass. LC 78-132254. 1971. 24.00x (ISBN 0-8078-1170-X). U of NC Pr.
Coming of Age: Your Bar or Bat Mitzvah. Benjamin Efron & Alvan D. Rubin. LC 77-78031. (Illus.). 1977. 5.00 (ISBN 0-8074-0084-X, 142530). UAHC.
Coming of Grace: An Illustrated Biography of Zhou Enlai. Ed Hammond. 196p. 1980. 14.95 (ISBN 0-89581-455-2); pap. 8.95 (ISBN 0-89581-503-6). Lancaster-Miller.
Coming of the Civil War. Robert Goldston. LC 72-123139. (gr. 6 up). 1972. 8.95 (ISBN 0-02-736270-1). Macmillan.
Coming of the Cold War. Robert Goldston. LC 79-89585. (Illus.). (gr. 7 up). 1970. 4.50 o.s.i. (ISBN 0-02-736320-1). Macmillan.
Coming of the Horseclans. Robert Adams. 192p. (Orig.). 1980. pap. 1.95 o.p. (ISBN 0-523-40919-2). Pinnacle Bks.
Coming of the War, 1914, 2 Vols. Bernadotte E. Schmitt. 1968. Set. 48.50 (ISBN 0-86527-030-9). Fertig.
Coming of the Welfare State. Maurice Bruce. 1974. 33.00 (ISBN 0-7134-1351-4, Pub. by Batsford England); pap. 14.95 (ISBN 0-7134-1359-X). David & Charles.
Coming of War. Martin Gilbert. (Jackdaw Ser: No. 64). (Illus.). 1973. 5.95 o.p. (ISBN 0-670-23224-6, Grossman). Viking Pr.
Coming One. Kurt E. Koch. LC 72-85597. 1972. pap. 2.50 (ISBN 0-8254-3011-9). Kregel.
Coming Out. Pat Boone. 1978. pap. 2.50 (ISBN 0-89728-001-6, 693880). Omega Pubns OR.
Coming Out Stories. Ed. by Julia P. Stanley & Susan J. Wolfe. LC 79-27073. 286p. (Orig.). 1980. pap. text ed. 6.95 (ISBN 0-930436-03-2). Persephone.
Coming Real Estate Crash. Gray E. Cardiff & John W. English. 1980. pap. 2.50 (ISBN 0-446-91575-0). Warner Bks.
Coming Russian Invasion of Israel. Thomas S. McCall & Zola Levitt. 96p. 1976. 3.95 (ISBN 0-8024-1606-3). Moody.
Coming Through. William Sheldon & Nina C. Woessner. (Orig.). (RL 5). 1972. pap. text ed. 4.96 (ISBN 0-205-03096-3, 5230969); tchrs' guide 2.40 (ISBN 0-205-03094-7, 5230942); reading skills activities dupl. master 20.00 (ISBN 0-205-03095-5, 5230950). Allyn.
Coming to America. Josephine Hileman & Bruce Colman. (Newbury House Readers Ser.: Stage 3 - Intermediate). 48p. (Orig.). (gr. 7-12). 1981. pap. text ed. 1.95 (ISBN 0-88377-196-9). Newbury Hse.
Coming to America: Immigrants from the British Isles. Shirley Blumenthal & Jerome S. Ozer. LC 80-65841. 192p. (gr. 9-12). 1980. 9.95 (ISBN 0-440-01071-3). Delacorte.
Coming to America: Immigrants from the Far East. Linda Perrin. LC 80-65840. 160p. (gr. 9-12). 1980. 9.95 (ISBN 0-440-01072-1). Delacorte.
Coming to Crossroads, Level 15. Eldonna Evertts & Byron VanRoekel. (Design for Reading Ser). (Illus.). (gr. 5). 1972. text ed. 11.04 (ISBN 0-06-516008-8, SchDept); tchr's ed. 14.28 (ISBN 0-06-516206-4); wkbk. 3.20 (ISBN 0-06-516307-9); tchr's wkbk. 6.36 (ISBN 0-06-516407-5); dupl. masters 17.68 (ISBN 0-06-516838-0); mastery test pkg. 14.48 (ISBN 0-06-516616-7). Har-Row.

Coming to Know. Ed. by Phillida Salmon. 180p. 1980. pap. 17.50 (ISBN 0-686-65610-5). Routledge & Kegan.

Coming to My Senses. John Robben. 1977. pap. 1.75 o.p. (ISBN 0-345-24815-5). Ballantine.

Coming to Power: Critical Presidential Elections in American History. Ed. by Arthur M. Schlesinger, Jr. & Fred L. Israel. LC 70-39588. 570p. 1981. pap. 8.95 (ISBN 0-87754-217-1). Chelsea Hse.

Coming to Terms: A Lexicon for Science-Watchers. Wayne Biddle. 1981. 8.95 (ISBN 0-670-33092-2). Viking Pr.

Coming to Terms: Lexicon for the Science Watcher. Wayne Biddle. LC 80-54198. (Illus.). 128p. 1981. 8.95 (ISBN 0-670-33092-2). Viking Pr.

Coming to Terms with Death: How to Face the Inevitable with Wisdom & Dignity. Fred Cutter. LC 74-8397. 262p. 1974. 14.95 (ISBN 0-911012-29-X); pap. 7.95 (ISBN 0-88229-498-9). Nelson-Hall.

Coming Together: All Those Communities & What They're up to. Dave Jackson. LC 78-16123. 1978. pap. 3.95 (ISBN 0-87123-087-9, 210087). Bethany Fell.

Coming Together, Coming Apart. Jay Kuten. LC 73-1961. 212p. 1974. 5.95 o.s.i. (ISBN 0-02-567000-X). Macmillan.

Coming Together in the Spirit. Frederick H. Borsch. 1981. 1.75 (ISBN 0-8358-0426-7). Forward Movement.

Coming up for Air. George Orwell. LC 50-5002. 1969. pap. 4.95 (ISBN 0-15-619625-5, HPL44, HPL). HarBraceJ.

Coming Victory. Tom Rose & Robert Metcalf. (Coronation Ser.: No. 5). 206p. (Orig.). 1980. pap. 6.95x (ISBN 0-686-28757-6). Chr Stud Ctr.

Coming Victory: Proposals on How to Overcome the Troubles That Plague Us. Tom Rose & Robert Metcalf. LC 80-68679. 192p. 1980. pap. 6.95. American Ent Texas.

Coming World Dictator. John W. White. 144p. (Orig.). 1981. pap. 2.50 (ISBN 0-87123-042-9, 200042). Bethany Fell.

Coming World Earthquake. Joe Musser. 1981. pap. 2.25 (ISBN 0-8423-0405-3). Tyndale.

Comintern & Peasant in East Europe, 1919-1930. George D. Jackson, Jr. LC 66-15489. 1966. 20.00x (ISBN 0-231-02912-8). Columbia U Pr.

Command a King's Ship. Alexander Kent. pap. 2.25 (ISBN 0-515-05498-4). Jove Pubns.

Command Decision. William W. Haines. LC 80-15034. (Great Classic Stories of World War II Ser.). 1980. 8.95 (ISBN 0-396-07872-9); pap. 5.95 (ISBN 0-396-07873-7). Dodd.

Command Performance & Other Poems. Harry W. Nelson. LC 80-67066. (Illus.). 1980. pap. 3.95 (ISBN 0-915206-80-3). Blue Leaf.

Commanding Paragraphs. 2nd ed. Helen Mills. 1981. pap. text ed. 9.95x (ISBN 0-673-15442-4). Scott F.

Commandments, 2 Vols. Maimonides. Set. 35.00x (ISBN 0-685-01042-2). Bloch.

Commando: A Boer Journal Ofthe Boer War. Deneys Reitz. (Orig.). 1929. pap. 5.95 (ISBN 0-571-08778-7, Pub. by Faber & Faber). Merrimack Bk Serv.

Commando Force, No. 133. Bill Strutton. 224p. 1981. pap. 2.50 (ISBN 0-553-13581-3). Bantam.

Commandos. Elliot Arnold. 1979. pap. 1.75 (ISBN 0-505-51332-3). Tower Bks.

Commandos of World War II. Hodding Carter. LC 80-21142. (Landmark Bks.). (Illus.). 160p. (gr. 5-9). 1981. 2.95 (ISBN 0-394-84735-0, BYR); PLB 5.99 (ISBN 0-394-90561-X). Random.

Commemoration of the Centenary of the Birth of James Russell Lowell: Poet, Scholar, Diplomat. 88p. 1980. Repr. of 1919 ed. lib. bdg. 35.00 (ISBN 0-8495-3349-X). Arden Lib.

Commemorations. Hans Herlin. 320p. 1976. pap. 1.95 o.p. (ISBN 0-345-25223-3). Ballantine.

Commemorative Medal: Its Appreciation & Collection. Howard A. Linecar. LC 72-12989. (Illus.). 250p. 1974. 16.00 (ISBN 0-8103-2012-6). Gale.

Commencement Address: A Talk to University Freshmen & Other Heretical Essays. Harry L. Case. Date not set. 7.95 (ISBN 0-533-04579-7). Vantage.

Commendation und Huldigung Nach Frankischem Recht. Victor Ehrenberg. LC 80-2031. 1981. Repr. of 1877 ed. 22.00 (ISBN 0-404-18562-2). AMS Pr.

Comment & Controversy. Gerald A. Bryant, Jr. 1972. pap. text ed. 6.95x (ISBN 0-02-473350-4, 47335). Macmillan.

Comment on the Commentaries & a Fragment on Government. Jeremy Bentham. Ed. by J. H. Burns & H. L. Hart. (Collected Works of Jeremy Bentham Ser.). 1977. text ed. 69.00x (ISBN 0-485-13212-5, Athlone Pr). Humanities.

Comment Vaincre. Tr. by Harold Hill. (French Bks.). (Fr.). 1979. 1.75 (ISBN 0-8297-0814-6). Life Pubs Intl.

Commentaire D'alexandre D'aphrodise Aux "Seconds Analytiques" D'aristote. Paul Moraux. (Peripatoi Ser.). 1979. text ed. 43.50x (ISBN 3-11-007805-8). De Gruyter.

Commentar Zu Kants Kritik der Reinen Vernunft, 2 vols. Hans Vaihinger. Ed. by Lewis W. Beck. Incl. Vol. 1. Stuttgart 1881; Vol. 2. Stuttgart & Berlin 1892. LC 75-32048. (Philosophy of Immanual Kant Ser.: Vol. 8). 1976. Repr. of 1892 ed. Set. lib. bdg. 66.00 (ISBN 0-8240-2332-3). Garland Pub.

Commentaries in Plant Science. Ed. by Harry Smith. LC 76-7531. 272p. 1976. text ed. 46.00 (ISBN 0-08-019759-0). Pergamon.

Commentaries in Plant Science, Vol. 2. Ed. by H. Smith. LC 80-41007. (Illus.). 250p. Date not set. 41.01 (ISBN 0-08-025898-0). Pergamon.

Commentaries in the Neurosciences. A. D. Smith et al. (Illus.). 702p. 1980. 72.00 (ISBN 0-08-025501-9). Pergamon.

Commentaries of the Constitution of the United States with a Preliminary Review of the Constitutional History of the Colonies & States Before the Adoption of the Constitution. Joseph Story. LC 69-11327. (American Constitutional & Legal History Ser). 1970. Repr. of 1833 ed. Set. lib. bdg. 125.00 (ISBN 0-306-71179-6). Da Capo.

Commentaries on American Law, 4 Vols. J. Kent. LC 78-75290. (American Constitutional & Legal History Ser). 1971. Repr. of 1826 ed. Set. lib. bdg. 195.00 (ISBN 0-306-71293-8). Da Capo.

Commentaries on Research in Breast Disease, Vol. 2. Ed. by R. D. Bulbrook & D. Jane Taylor. 175p. 1981. price not set (ISBN 0-8451-1901-X). A R Liss.

Commentaries on the Bhagavad Gita. Sri Chinmoy. LC 78-189999. (Illus.). 192p. pap. 1.95 o.s.i. (ISBN 0-8334-1731-2). Steinerbks.

Commentaries on the Constitution of the Empire of Japan. Hirobumi Ito. (Studies in Japanese Law & Government). 310p. 1979. Repr. of 1906 ed. 25.00 (ISBN 0-89093-212-3). U Pubns Amer.

Commentaries on the Law of England. 4 vols. Sir William Blackstone. Ed. by David S. Berkowitz & Samuel E. Thorne. LC 77-86570. (Classics of English Legal History in the Modern Era Ser.: Vol. 10). 2025p. 1979. Set. lib. bdg. 160.00 (ISBN 0-8240-3059-1). Garland Pub.

Commentaries on the Liberty of the Subject & the Laws of England Relating to the Security of the Person, 2 vols. James Paterson. 1010p. 1980. Repr. of 1877 ed. Set. lib. bdg. 75.00x (ISBN 0-8377-1005-7). Rothman.

Commentaries on the Prophecies of Isaiah. 10th ed. Joseph A. Alexander. 1980. 19.95 (ISBN 0-310-20000-8, 6526). Zondervan.

Commentaries Upon Martial Law, with Special Reference to Its Regulation & Restraint: With an Introduction, Containing Comments Upon the Charge of the Lord Chief Justice in the Jamaica Case. W. F. Finlason. 287p. 1980. Repr. of 1867 ed. lib. bdg. 28.50x (ISBN 0-8377-0536-3). Rothman.

Commentarii, 2 Vols. Caesar. Ed. by R. L. Du Pontet. (O. C. T). 1900-1901. Vol. 1. 14.95x (ISBN 0-19-814602-7); Vol. 2. 14.95x (ISBN 0-19-814603-5). Oxford U Pr.

Commentary John's Gospel, 2 vols. in 1. Frederic L. Godet. LC 78-59145. (Kregel Reprint Library). 1979. 22.95 (ISBN 0-8254-2714-2). Kregel.

Commentary of Rabbi David Kimhi on Psalms 120-150. Ed. by J. Baker & E. W. Nicholson. (Cambridge Oriental Publications Ser.: No. 22). 34.50 (ISBN 0-521-08670-1). Cambridge U Pr.

Commentary of the Pastoral Epistles. J. N. Kelly. (Thornapple Commentaries Ser.). 272p. 1981. pap. 6.95 (ISBN 0-8010-5428-1). Baker Bk.

Commentary on Acts. McLaughlin. kivar 5.95 (ISBN 0-686-12858-3). Schmul Pub Co.

Commentary on Book One of the Epigrams of Martial. Peter Howell. 369p. 1980. text ed. 65.00x (Athlone Pr). Humanities.

Commentary on Building Code Requirements for Reinforced Concrete: ACI 318-77. ACI Committee 318. 1977. 20.75 (ISBN 0-685-03453-4, 318-77C) (ISBN 0-685-03454-2). ACI.

Commentary on Building Code Requirements for Reinforced Concrete: ACI 318-71. ACI Committee 318. 1971. 19.00 (ISBN 0-685-85077-3, 318-71C) (ISBN 0-685-85078-1). ACI.

Commentary on Catulus, Oxford, Eighteen Eighty-Nine. 2nd ed. Ellis Robinson. Ed. by Steele Commager. LC 77-70812. (Latin Poetry-Editions, Commentations Critical Works). 1979. lib. bdg. 55.00 (ISBN 0-8240-2953-4). Garland Pub.

Commentary on Daniel. Leon J. Wood. 320p. 1972. 12.95 (ISBN 0-310-34710-6). Zondervan.

Commentary on Epistle to the Hebrews. Brooke F. Westcott. (Gr). 1950. 9.95 (ISBN 0-8028-3289-X). Eerdmans.

Commentary on Exodus. J. P. Hyatt. Ed. by Ronald E. Clements. (New Century Bible Commentary Ser.). 1980. pap. 7.95 (ISBN 0-8028-1844-7). Eerdmans.

Commentary on First & Second Corinthians. F. F. Bruce. Ed. by Matthew Black. (New Century Bible Commentary Ser.). 224p. 1980. pap. 6.95 (ISBN 0-8028-1839-0). Eerdmans.

Commentary on First Corinthians. Frederick W. Grosheide. (New International Commentary on the New Testament). 1953. 12.95 (ISBN 0-8028-2185-5). Eerdmans.

Commentary on Genesis. W. Gunther Plaut. (Pardes Torah; Jewish Commentary on the Torah Ser.). 1974. 10.00 (ISBN 0-8074-0001-7, 381611); pap. 8.00 (ISBN 0-685-48959-0, 381601). UAHC.

Commentary on Genesis. Harold G. Stigers. 320p. 1975. 15.95 (ISBN 0-310-36800-6). Zondervan.

Commentary on Goethe's Faust. Dennis J. Enright. 158p. 1980. Repr. of 1949 ed. lib. bdg. 20.00 (ISBN 0-8414-1916-7). Folcroft.

Commentary on Hebrews. William Gouge. LC 79-2541. (Kregel Limited Edition Library). 1980. Repr. of 1866 ed. 29.95 (ISBN 0-686-52558-2). Kregel.

Commentary on Herodotus, 2 Vols. Ed. by Walter W. How & Joseph Wells. 1928. Vol. 1. 28.50x (ISBN 0-19-814128-9); Vol. 2. 23.50x (ISBN 0-19-814129-7). Oxford U Pr.

Commentary on Horace: Odes. Robin G. Nisbet & Margaret Hubbard. Bk. 1 1970. 55.00x (ISBN 0-19-814439-3); Bk. 2 1978. 39.00x (ISBN 0-19-814452-0). Oxford U Pr.

Commentary on Kant's Critick of Pure Reason. Kuno Fischer. Ed. by Lewis W. Beck. LC 75-32039. (Philosophy of Immanuel Kant Ser.: Vol. 3). 1977. Repr. of 1866 ed. lib. bdg. 26.00 (ISBN 0-8240-2327-7). Garland Pub.

Commentary on Leviticus. Bernard J. Bamberger. Ed. by W. Gunther Plaut. (Torah: a Modern Commentary Ser.). 1979. 17.50 (ISBN 0-8074-0011-4, 381608). UAHC.

Commentary on Livy, Bks 1-5. Robert M. Ogilvie. 1965. 59.00x (ISBN 0-19-814432-6). Oxford U Pr.

Commentary on Luke. Frederic L. Godet. LC 80-8068. 918p. 1981. 16.95 (ISBN 0-8254-2720-7). Kregel.

Commentary on Luke. McLaughlin. kivar 5.95 (ISBN 0-686-12859-1). Schmul Pub Co.

Commentary on Mark. McLaughlin. kivar 5.95 (ISBN 0-686-12860-5). Schmul Pub Co.

Commentary on Matthew. McLaughlin. kivar 5.95 (ISBN 0-686-12861-3). Schmul Pub Co.

Commentary on Personal Property Appraisal. LC 76-20415. (ASA Monograph Ser: No. 7). 1976. 5.00 (ISBN 0-937828-16-5). Am Soc Appraisers.

Commentary on Philippians. H. Leo Eddleman. 176p. (Orig.). 1981. pap. 4.75 (ISBN 0-682-49700-2). Exposition.

Commentary on Philippians. Ralph P. Martin. Ed. by Matthew Black. (New Century Bible Commentary Ser.). 192p. 1980. pap. 5.95 (ISBN 0-8028-1840-4). Eerdmans.

Commentary on Q. Curtius' Historiae Alexandri Magni. J. E. Atkinson. (London Studies in Classical Philology: No. 3). 1980. text ed. 68.50x (ISBN 90-70265-61-3). Humanities.

Commentary on Romans. Ernst Kasemann. Tr. by Geoffrey W. Bromiley. 1978. 22.50 (ISBN 0-8028-3499-X). Eerdmans.

Commentary on Romans. McLaughlin. kivar 5.95 (ISBN 0-686-12862-1). Schmul Pub Co.

Commentary on Romans. Anders Nygren. Tr. by Carl Rasmussen. LC 49-48317. 472p. 1949. pap. 5.50 (ISBN 0-8006-1684-7, 1-1684). Fortress.

Commentary on Saint Ignatius' Rules for the Discernment of Spirits: A Guide to the Principles & Practice. Jules J. Toner. LC 79-89606. 400p. Date not set. 14.00 (ISBN 0-912422-43-2); pap. 12.00 smyth sewn paper (ISBN 0-912422-42-4). Inst Jesuit. Postponed.

Commentary on St. John. McLaughlin. kivar 5.95 (ISBN 0-686-12863-X). Schmul Pub Co.

Commentary on St. Paul's Epistle to the Colossians & Philemon. Ed. by J. B. Lightfoot. 1957. 11.95 (ISBN 0-310-27630-6). Zondervan.

Commentary on St. Paul's Epistle to the Philippians. Ed. by J. B. Lightfoot. 1957. 14.95 (ISBN 0-310-27650-0). Zondervan.

Commentary on the Conflict of Laws. 2nd ed. Russell J. Weintraub. LC 80-10480. (University Textbook Ser.). 655p. 1980. write for info. (ISBN 0-88277-000-4). Foundation Pr.

Commentary on the Divine Liturgy. Nicholas Cabasilas. Tr. by J. M. Hussey & P. A. McNulty. LC 62-53410. 120p. 1977. pap. 4.95 (ISBN 0-913836-37-0). St Vladimirs.

Commentary on the Dream of Scipio. Tr. by W. H. Stahl. LC 52-1644. 1952. 20.00x (ISBN 0-231-01737-5). Columbia U Pr.

Commentary on the Epistle of Paul to the Hebrews. William S. Plumer. (Giant Summit Ser.). 560p. 1980. Repr. of 1872 ed. pap. 9.95 (ISBN 0-8010-7054-6). Baker Bk.

Commentary on the Epistle to the Hebrews, 2 vols. Franz Delitzsch. 1978. Set. 29.95 (ISBN 0-686-12950-4). Klock & Klock.

Commentary on the Epistle to the Seven Churches. Richard C. Trench. 1978. 8.50 (ISBN 0-686-12951-2). Klock & Klock.

Commentary on the First Six Books of Virgil's "Aeneid". Bernardus Silvestris. Tr. by E. G. Schreiber & Thomas E. Maresca. LC 79-9138. xxxvi, 129p. 1980. 11.50x (ISBN 0-8032-4108-9). U of Nebr Pr.

Commentary on the Gospel of John, 2 vols. E. W. Hengstenberg. Date not set. Set. 34.95 (ISBN 0-86524-047-7). Klock & Klock.

Commentary on the Gospel of John. Robert E. Obach & Albert Kirk. 288p. 1981. pap. 6.95 (ISBN 0-8091-2346-0). Paulist Pr.

Commentary on the Gospel of Matthew. Albert Kirk & Robert E. Obach. LC 78-65715. 1978. pap. 4.95 (ISBN 0-8091-2173-5). Paulist Pr.

Commentary on the Gospel of St. John, 2 pts. Thomas Aquinas. Ed. by James A. Weisheipl. Tr. by Fabian R. Larcher from Lat. LC 66-19306. (Aquinas Scripture Ser.: Vol. 4, Pt. 1). (Illus.). 512p. 1980. 35.00x (ISBN 0-87343-031-X). Magi Bks.

Commentary on the Gospel of Saint Luke, 2 vols. 5th ed. F. Godet. 920p. 1976. pap. text ed. 27.50x (ISBN 0-567-27446-2). Attic Pr.

Commentary on the Holy Bible. John R. Dummelow. 1909. 12.95 (ISBN 0-02-533770-X). Macmillan.

Commentary on the Holy Bible, 3 vols. Matthew Poole. 1979. Set. 79.95 (ISBN 0-85151-211-9); Vol. 1 Genesis-Job. 28.95 (ISBN 0-85151-054-X); Vol. 2 Psalms-Malachi. 28.95 (ISBN 0-85151-134-1); Vol. 3 Matthew-Revelation. 28.95 (ISBN 0-85151-135-X). Banner of Truth.

Commentary on the New Testament. John Trapp. 864p. 1981. Repr. of 1865 ed. 19.95 (ISBN 0-8010-8855-0). Baker Bk.

Commentary on the Psalms of David. Apostolos Makrakis. Ed. by Orthodox Christian Educational Society. Tr. by Denver Cummings from Hellenic. 990p. 1950. 10.00x (ISBN 0-938366-19-X). Orthodox Chr.

Commentary on the Satires of Juvenal. E. Courtney. 650p. 1981. text ed. 75.00x (ISBN 0-485-11190-X, Athlone Pr). Humanities.

Commentary on the Shorter Catechism. A. Whyte. (Handbook for Bible Classes Ser.). 213p. pap. text ed. 8.95 (ISBN 0-567-28144-2). Attic Pr.

Commentary on the Vita Hadriana in the Historia Augusta. Herbert W. Benario. LC 80-11953. (American Classical Studies: No. 7). 1980. 13.50x (ISBN 0-89130-391-X, 400407); pap. 9.00x. Scholars Pr CA.

Commentationes Mathematicae: Tomus Specialis in Honorem Ladislai Orlicz, 2 vols, Vol. I & Vol. II. Ed. by Julian Musielak. LC 78-326639. 1979. 27.50x ea. Vol. 1, 384 P (ISBN 0-8002-2271-7). Vol. 2, 347 P (ISBN 0-8002-2272-5). Intl Pubns Serv.

Commenting & Commentaries. (C. H. Spurgeon Library). 1981. pap. 3.95 (ISBN 0-8010-8194-7). Baker Bk.

Commerce & Conquest. C. Lestock Reid. LC 78-115328. 1971. Repr. of 1947 ed. 12.95 (ISBN 0-8046-1119-X). Kennikat.

Commerce & Social Standing in Ancient Rome. John H. D'Arms. LC 80-25956. (Illus.). 224p. 1981. text ed. 20.00 (ISBN 0-674-14475-9). Harvard U Pr.

Commerce of the Prairies. Josiah Gregg. Ed. by Milo M. Quaife. LC 27-1450. (Illus.). 1967. pap. 4.75 (ISBN 0-8032-5076-2, BB 324, Bison). U of Nebr Pr.

Commerce Power Versus States Rrights. Edward S. Corwin. 1959. write for info. (ISBN 0-8446-1130-1). Peter Smith.

Commercial Airline Industry: Managerial Practices & Policies. Nawal K. Taneja. LC 76-18052. 1976. 22.95x (ISBN 0-669-00129-5). Lexington Bks.

Commercial & Experimental Organic Insecticides. E. E. Kenaga & Robert W. Morgan. 1978. 6.70 (ISBN 0-686-18862-4). Entomol Soc.

Commercial & Industrial Condominiums. John C. Melaniphy, Jr. LC 76-27171. (Illus.). 80p. 1976. pap. text ed. 14.50 (ISBN 0-87420-572-7). Urban Land.

Commercial Banking. 2nd ed. E. Reed et al. 1980. 18.95 (ISBN 0-13-152785-1). P-H.

Commercial Banking in Mississippi, 1940-1975. Harvey S. Lewis & E. Nolan Waller. 1977. pap. 3.00 (ISBN 0-938004-07-7). U MS Bus Econ.

Commercial Banking in the Economy. rev. ed. Paul Nadler. 1973. pap. text ed. 3.95 o.p. (ISBN 0-394-31776-9). Random.

Commercial Banks & Economic Development: The Experience of Eastern Africa. Ali Issa Abdi. LC 77-12813. (Praeger Special Studies). 1978. 20.95 (ISBN 0-03-023031-4). Praeger.

Commercial Catfish Farming. Jasper S. Lee. LC 73-75382. (Illus.). 1973. 10.00 o.p. (ISBN 0-8134-1570-5, 1570). Interstate.

Commercial Catfish Farming. 2nd ed. Jasper S. Lee. (Illus.). 1981. 10.00 (ISBN 0-8134-2156-X, 2156). Interstate.

Commercial Chicken Production Manual. 2nd ed. Mack O. North. (Illus.). 1978. lib. bdg. 38.50 (ISBN 0-87055-259-7). AVI.

Commercial Dictionary, Spanish-English, English-Spanish. (El Secretario). 137p. 1975. 12.95 (ISBN 0-88332-135-1, 20974). Larousse.

Commercial Financing. M. R. Lazere. 310p. 1968. 23.95 (ISBN 0-471-06570-6). Wiley.

Commercial Financing. Ed. by Monroe R. Lazere. 1968. 23.95 (ISBN 0-8260-5300-9). Ronald Pr.

Commercial Fish Farming: With Special Reference to Fish Culture in Israel. Dalfour Hepher & Yoel Pruginin. 250p. 1981. 25.00 (ISBN 0-686-69368-X, Pub. by Wiley-Interscience). Wiley.

Commercial Fishing. Herbert S. Zim & Lucretia Krantz. LC 73-4931. (Illus.). 64p. (gr. 3-7). 1973. 6.75 (ISBN 0-688-20091-5); PLB 6.48 (ISBN 0-688-30091-X); pap. 1.25 (ISBN 0-688-05267-3). Morrow.

Commercial Fishing Methods: An Introduction to Vessels & Gear. John C. Sainsbury. (Illus.). 120p. 13.75 (ISBN 0-85238-076-3, FN). Unipub.

Commercial Food Patents, U. S. Nineteen Seventy-Nine. Hallie B. North. (Illus.). 1980. lib. bdg. 30.00 (ISBN 0-87055-358-5). AVI.

Commercial Food Patents, U.S. Nineteen-Eighty. Hallie B. North. (Illus.). 1981. lib. bdg. 30.00 (ISBN 0-87055-371-2). AVI.

Commercial Fruit & Vegetable Products. 4th ed. William V. Cruess. (Agricultural Sciences Ser). 1958. text ed. 26.00 o.p. (ISBN 0-07-014808-2, C). McGraw.

Commercial Fruit Processing. J. G. Woodroof & B. S. Luh. (Illus.). 710p. 1975. lib. bdg. 27.00 (ISBN 0-87055-178-7). AVI.

Commercial Future of Hong Kong. William F. Beazer. LC 76-24343. (Praeger Special Studies). 1978. 22.95 (ISBN 0-275-23670-6). Praeger.

Commercial Greenhouse. James W. Boodley. LC 78-74806. (Agriculture Ser.). 576p. 1981. 16.40 (ISBN 0-8273-1719-0); instr's. guide 1.45 (ISBN 0-8273-1718-2). Delmar.

Commercial Ice Makers. Ed. by A. Ross Sabin. (Illus.). 273p. (gr. 11). 1980. 20.00 (ISBN 0-938336-08-8). Whirlpool.

Commercial Law Information Sources. Julius J. Marke & Edward J. Bander. LC 73-120909. (Management Information Guide Ser.: No. 17). 1970. 30.00 (ISBN 0-8103-0817-7). Gale.

Commercial Marine Fish & Fisheries of Rhode Island. Stephen B. Olsen & David K. Stevenson. (Marine Technical Report Ser.: No. 34). 1975. pap. 3.50 o.p. (ISBN 0-686-18101-8). URI MAS.

Commercial Mauser 'ninety-Eight Sporting Rifle. Lester Womack. Ed. by Jay B. Angevine, Jr. (Illus.). 72p. 1981. 20.00x (ISBN 0-9605530-0-2). Womack Assoc.

Commercial Monomers & Polymers. (Plastics Studies). 1977. 525.00 (ISBN 0-89336-036-8, P-039). BCC.

Commercial Motor Transportation. 6th ed. Charles A. Taff. LC 80-12947. (Illus.). 1980. 20.00x (ISBN 0-87033-266-X). Cornell Maritime.

Commercial Oilfield Diving. nd ed. Nicholas B. Zinkowski. LC 78-7214. (Illus.). 1978. 19.00x (ISBN 0-87033-235-X). Cornell Maritime.

Commercial Pilot Flight Test Guide. 2nd ed. Federal Aviation Administration. (Pilot Training Ser.: Pilot Training Ser.). 70p. 1975. pap. 1.75 (ISBN 0-89100-172-7, E*A-A*C61-55A). Aviation Maintenance.

Commercial Pilot Written Test Guide. 3rd ed. Federal Aviation Administration. (Pilot Training Ser.). (Illus.). 141p. 1979. pap. 4.75 (ISBN 0-89100-110-7, E*A-A*C61-71B). Aviation Maintenance.

Commercial Portable Gauges for Radiometric Determination of the Density & Moisture Content of Building Materials. (Technical Reports Ser.: No. 130). (Illus.). 210p. (Orig.). 1972. pap. 13.50 (ISBN 92-0-165071-X, IAEA). Unipub.

Commercial Property Management. A. C. Grear & J. Oxborough. 1970. 24.00x o.p. (ISBN 0-8464-0258-0). Beekman Pubs.

Commercial Radiotelephone License: Question & Answer Study Guide. 3rd ed. Edward M. Noll. LC 75-16859. 1976. pap. 8.50 (ISBN 0-672-24033-5, 24033). Editors.

Commercial Radiotelephone License Question & Answer Study Guide. 3rd ed. Edward M. Noll. LC 75-16859. 1976. pap. 8.50 (ISBN 0-672-24033-5). Sams.

Commercial Real Estate Leases: Eleventh Course Handbook. (Real Estate Law & Practice Course Handbook Ser., 1979-80: Vol. 180). 1980. pap. 25.00 (ISBN 0-686-50954-4, N4-4351). PLI.

Commercial Relations Between British Overseas Territories & South America, 1806-1914. T. W. Keeble. (Institute of Latin American Studies Monographs: No. 3). 1970. text ed. 6.75x (ISBN 0-485-17703-X, Athlone Pr). Humanities.

Commercial Revolution of the Middle Ages, 950-1350. R. S. Lopez. LC 75-35453. (Illus.). 204p. 1976. 21.50 (ISBN 0-521-21111-5); pap. 7.95x (ISBN 0-521-29046-5). Cambridge U Pr.

Commercial Transactions: Text & Problems on Personalty, Realty & Services. Ellen A. Peters. 1971. text ed. 22.00 (ISBN 0-672-81703-9, Bobbs-Merrill Law). Michie.

Commercial Uses of Geothermal Heat. Ed. by Geothermal Resources Council. (Special Report: No. 9). (Illus.). 143p. 1980. pap. 3.50 (ISBN 0-934412-09-X). Geothermal.

Commercial Vegetable Processing. B. S. Luh & J. G. Woodroof. (Illus.). 1975. text ed. 27.00 (ISBN 0-87055-186-8); pap. text ed. 19.00 o.p. (ISBN 0-87055-282-1). AVI.

Commercial Vehicle Braking. T. P. Newcomb & R. T. Spurr. (Illus.). 1979. text ed. 15.95 (ISBN 0-408-00362-6). Butterworths.

Commercial Winemaking: Processing & Controls. Richard P. Vine. (Illus.). 1981. text ed. 19.50 (ISBN 0-87055-376-3). AVI.

Commerical Greenhouse Handbook. James W. Boodley. 544p. 1981. 24.95 (ISBN 0-442-23146-6). Van Nos Reinhold.

Commerical Handbook of China, 2 vols. Julean Arnold & Ramon H. Myers. LC 78-24800. (Modern Chinese Economy Ser.: Vol. 16). (Illus.). 1979. Set. lib. bdg. 110.00 (ISBN 0-8240-4264-6). Garland Pub.

Commerical Rabbit Raising. R. B. Casady & P. B. Jawin. (Illus.). 69p. pap. 3.00 (ISBN 0-8466-6054-7, SJU54). Shorey.

Commerically Available Chemical Agents for Paper & Board Manufacture. 3rd ed. Walter F. Reynolds. (TAPPI PRESS Reports). 74p. 1980. pap. 54.95 (ISBN 0-89852-383-4, 01-01-R083). TAPPI.

Commissariat of Enlightenment. Sheila Fitzpatrick. (Soviet & East European Studies). (Illus.). 1971. 47.95 (ISBN 0-521-07919-5). Cambridge U Pr.

Commission Book of Governor John Sevier, 1796-1801. John Sevier. Ed. by The Tennessee Historical Commission. 1957. 5.00x o.p. (ISBN 0-87402-008-5). U of Tenn Pr.

Commission for Agricultural Meteorology: Abridged Final Report of the Seventh Session. 65p. 1980. pap. 25.00 (ISBN 92-63-10546-4, W467, WMO). Unipub.

Commission on Critical Choices for Americans: Qualities of Life, Vol. VII. LC 75-44725. (Critical Choices for Americans Ser.). 1976. 23.95 (ISBN 0-669-00417-0). Lexington Bks.

Commissioned by the Lord Himself. J. Roy Legere. 168p. 1980. 7.95 (ISBN 0-935488-00-6); pap. 3.95 (ISBN 0-935488-01-4). Apostolic Formation.

Commissioned Spirits: The Shaping of Social Motion in Dickens, Carlyle, Melville, & Hawthorne. Jonathan Arac. 1979. 15.00 (ISBN 0-8135-0874-6). Rutgers U Pr.

Commissioners of Indian Affairs, 1824-1977. Ed. by Robert M. Kvasnicka & Herman J. Viola. LC 79-12336. 1979. 19.75x (ISBN 0-8032-2700-0). U of Nebr Pr.

Commissioning Procedures for Nuclear Plants. (Safety Ser.: No. 50-SG-04). pap. 9.00 (ISBN 0-686-69439-2, ISP 574, IAEA). Unipub.

Commissurotomy, Consciousness & Unity of Mind. Charles E. Marks. (Bradford Monograph Series in Cognitive & Neuro-Sciences). (Illus.). 64p. (Orig.). 1980. pap. 4.00 (ISBN 0-89706-003-2). Bradford Bks.

Commitment to Welfare. Richard M. Titmuss. 1976. text ed. 22.50x (ISBN 0-04-361020-X); pap. text ed. 8.95x (ISBN 0-04-361021-8). Allen Unwin.

Commitment Total. Alvin F. Coburn. LC 73-93939. 256p. 1975. 7.95 o.s.i. (ISBN 0-8027-0449-2). Walker & Co.

Committee. Hank Braxton. (Orig.). 1979. pap. 2.25 (ISBN 0-89083-484-9). Zebra.

Committee of One Million: China Lobby Politics, 1953-1971. Stanley D. Bachrack. LC 76-18117. 1976. 18.00x (ISBN 0-231-03933-6). Columbia U Pr.

Committee: The Extraordinary Career of the House Committee on un-American Activities. Walter Goodman. LC 68-13010. (Illus.). 564p. 1968. 15.00 (ISBN 0-374-12688-7). FS&G.

Committees & Commissions in India 1947-73: Vols. 1-10, 1947-73. Virendra Kumar. 1979. text ed. 25.00x ea. (ISBN 0-391-01934-1). Humanities.

Committees: How They Work & How to Work Them. Edgar Anstey. 1962. pap. 3.95 o.p. (ISBN 0-04-380001-7). Allen Unwin.

Commodities: A Chart Anthology. rev. ed. Edward D. Dobson. LC 79-112544. (Illus.). 1979. 3 ring looseleaf bdg 26.50 (ISBN 0-934380-00-7). Traders Pr.

Commodity Agreements & Price Stabilization. David L. McNichol. LC 77-75626. (Illus.). 1978. 16.95 (ISBN 0-669-01539-3). Lexington Bks.

Commodity Futures Markets & the Law of One Price. Arvind K. Jain. (Michigan International Business Studies: No. 16). (Illus.). 140p. 1980. pap. 6.00 (ISBN 0-87712-210-5). U Mich Busn Div Res.

Commodity Futures Trading & the Secrets to Make a Success of It. Edward R. Holman. (International Council for Excellence in Management Library). (Illus.). 107p. 1980. plastic spiral bdg. 28.95 (ISBN 0-89266-252-2). Am Classical Coll Pr.

Commodity Futures Trading: The Essential Knowledge Which Everybody, but Absolutely Everybody Ought to Possess About Speculating in Commodity Futures. Ronald Del Castillo. (Essential Knowledge Ser.). (Illus.). 1978. plastic spiral bdg. 28.95 (ISBN 0-89266-117-8). Am Classical Coll Pr.

Commodity Market Controls. Carmine Nappi. LC 78-24715. (Illus.). 224p. 1979. 23.95 (ISBN 0-669-02812-6). Lexington Bks.

Commodity Markets & Latin American Development: A Modeling Approach. Ed. by Walter C. Labys et al. LC 79-16533. 1980. 25.00 (ISBN 0-88410-481-8). Ballinger Pub.

Commodity Money Management Yearbook, 1980. Ed. by Leon Rose & Joy Rose. (Illus.). 1981. 39.50 (ISBN 0-936624-01-9). LJR Inc.

Commodity Prophecy & the Mastery of Commodity Futures Trading. Samuel Benner. (Illus.). 1979. Repr. of 1879 ed. deluxe ed. 69.75 (ISBN 0-918968-40-2). Inst Econ Finan.

Commodity Speculation for Beginners: A Guide to the Futures Market. Charles Huff & Barbara Marinacci. (Illus.). 224p. 1980. 11.95 (ISBN 0-02-555450-6). Macmillan.

Commodity Spreads: A Historical Chart Perspective, 2 vols. Edward D. Dobson. LC 79-112547. (Illus.). 1979. Set. 3 ring looseleaf bdg. 22.50 (ISBN 0-934380-00-7). Traders Pr.

Commodity Trade of the Third World. Ed. by Cheryl Payer. LC 75-23282. 1976. 34.95 (ISBN 0-470-67282-X). Halsted Pr.

Commodore Perry in Japan. Robert L. Reynolds & Douglas MacArthur, 2nd. LC 63-20168. (American Heritage Junior Library). (Illus.). 153p. (gr. 5 up). 1963. 9.95 (ISBN 0-8281-0396-8, J012-0); PLB 12.89 (ISBN 0-06-024951-X, Dist. by Har-Row). Am Heritage.

Common Afghan Street Games. Nico J. Van Oudenhoven. 78p. 1980. pap. 16.50 (ISBN 90-265-0293-1, Pub. by Swets Pub Serv Holland). Swets North Am.

Common Agricultural Policy of the European Community. Rosemary Fennell. LC 79-2961. 255p. 1980. text ed. 21.95 (ISBN 0-916672-29-8). Allanheld.

Common Background of Greek & Hebrew Civilizations. Cyrus H. Gordon. (Illus.). 1965. pap. 7.95 (ISBN 0-393-00293-4, Norton Lib). Norton.

Common Base of Social Work Practice. Harriett M. Bartlett. LC 72-116893. (Orig.). 1970. pap. 6.00x (ISBN 0-87101-054-2, CBO-054-C). Natl Assn Soc Wkrs.

Common Birds in New Zealand, 2 vols. Janet Marshall et al. (Mobil New Zealand Nature Ser.). (Illus.). 1973. Vol. 1. pap. 7.50 (ISBN 0-589-00730-0, Pub. by Reed Bks Australia); Vol. 2. pap. 7.50 (ISBN 0-589-00759-9). C E Tuttle.

Common Catechism: A Book of Christian Faith. Ed. by Johannes Feiner & Lukas Vischer. LC 75-1070. 690p. 1975. 10.95 (ISBN 0-8164-0283-3). Crossroad NY.

Common Clinical Perplexities. Carl Lyle & Raymond Bianchi. LC 78-71347. 1979. spiral 9.50 (ISBN 0-87488-958-8). Med Exam.

Common Continent of Men: Racial Equality in the Novels of Herman Melville. Edward S. Grejda. LC 74-80067. 1974. 12.00 (ISBN 0-8046-9073-1, Natl U). Kennikat.

Common Cures for Common Ailments: A Doctor's Guide to Nonprescription, Over-the-Counter Medicines & His Recommendations for Their Use. Albert Marchetti. LC 77-16114. 368p. 1981. pap. 8.95 (ISBN 0-8128-6107-8). Stein & Day.

Common Curriculum: Its Structure & Style in the Comprehensive School. Maurice Holt. (Education Bks.). 1978. 16.00x (ISBN 0-7100-8895-7). Routledge & Kegan.

Common Defense: Strategic Programs in National Politics. Samuel P. Huntington. LC 61-18197. 1961. 22.50x (ISBN 0-231-02518-1); pap. 7.50x (ISBN 0-231-08566-4). Columbia U Pr.

Common Differences. Gloria Joseph & Jill Lewis. LC 79-6885. 240p. 1981. pap. 7.95 (ISBN 0-385-14271-4, Anch). Doubleday.

Common Diseases. 2nd ed. John Fry. LC 79-88209. 1979. text ed. 24.00 (ISBN 0-397-58256-0). Lippincott.

Common Dormouse. Elaine Hurrell. (Mammel Society Ser.). (Illus.). 50p. 1980. 6.95 (ISBN 0-7137-0985-5, Pub. by Blandford Pr England). Sterling.

Common Edible Mushrooms. Clyde M. Christensen. (Illus.). 1969. 8.95x o.p. (ISBN 0-8166-0509-2); pap. 3.45 o.p. (ISBN 0-8166-0510-6, MP20). U of Minn Pr.

Common Efforts in the Development of Rural Sarawak, Malaysia. B. G. Grijpstra. (Studies of Developing Countries: No. 20). (Illus.). 1976. text ed. 28.25x (ISBN 90-232-1408-0). Humanities.

Common Elements in New Mathematics Programs: Their Origins & Evolution. Helene Sherman. LC 72-75560. (Illus.). 1972. pap. text ed. 7.25x (ISBN 0-8077-2151-4). Tchrs Coll.

Common Foot Disorders. Donald Neale. (Illus.). 224p. 1981. lib. bdg. 24.00 (ISBN 0-443-01938-X). Churchill.

Common Ground: A Naturalist's Cape Cod. Robert Finch. (Illus.). 1981. 12.50 (ISBN 0-87923-383-4); ltd. ed. 40.00 (ISBN 0-87923-384-2). Godine.

Common Human Needs. rev. ed. Charlotte Towle. LC 65-22393. 1965. pap. 4.00x (ISBN 0-87101-014-3, CBO-014-C). Natl Assn Soc Wkrs.

Common Indian Snakes: A Field Guide. Romulus Whitaker. (Illus.). 154p. (Orig.). 1979. pap. text ed. 4.00x (ISBN 0-333-90198-3). R Curtis Bks.

Common Insects of India. N. P. Kalyanam. 1967. pap. 4.50x (ISBN 0-210-27166-3). Asia.

Common Insects of North America. Lester A. Swan & Charles S. Papp. LC 75-138765. (Illus.). 752p. 1972. 17.50 o.p. (ISBN 0-06-014181-6, HarpT); lib. bdg. 13.27 (ISBN 0-06-014179-4). Har-Row.

Common Land & Inclosure. 2nd ed. Edward C. Gonner. (Illus.). Repr. of 1912 ed. 27.50 (ISBN 0-678-05050-3). Kelley.

Common Law. Oliver W. Holmes, Jr. 1964. 15.00 (ISBN 0-316-37131-9); pap. 4.95. Little.

Common Lot. Robert Herrick. 395p. 1980. Repr. of 1904 ed. lib. bdg. 25.00x (ISBN 0-89968-187-5). Lightyear.

Common Man: Poems. Bradley Hamilton. 1981. 6.50 (ISBN 0-8062-1554-2). Carlton.

Common Market. Paul Armitage. LC 78-61095. (Countries Ser.). (Illus.). 1978. lib. bdg. 7.95 (ISBN 0-686-51150-6). Silver.

Common Market. Ed. by Nancy L. Hoepli. (Reference Shelf Ser: Vol. 46, No. 5). 1975. 6.25 (ISBN 0-8242-0525-1). Wilson.

Common Market Law, Vol. 3. 2nd ed. A. Campbell. 1973. 65.00 (ISBN 0-379-16063-3). Oceana.

Common Market: Political Impacts. Ed. by Avrahm G. Mezerik. 1962. pap. 15.00 (ISBN 0-685-13191-2, 72). Intl Review.

Common Market: Uniting the European Community. Carol Rothkopf & David Rothkopf. (gr. 7 up). 1977. PLB 6.90 s&l (ISBN 0-531-01272-7). Watts.

Common Millionaire. Robert Heller. 384p. 1974. 8.95 o.p. (ISBN 0-440-03353-5). Delacorte.

Common Names of Insects & Related Organisms. Ed. by Douglas Sutherland. 1978. pap. 4.00 o.p. (ISBN 0-686-26208-5). Entomol Soc.

Common Orthopedic Problems in Pediatric Practice. Jacob Katz. 250p. 1981. 16.50 (ISBN 0-89004-273-X, 298). Raven.

Common People of Ancient Rome: Studies of Roman Life & Literature. Frank F. Abbott. LC 65-23487. (gr. 7 up). 1911. 11.00x (ISBN 0-8196-0157-8). Biblo.

Common People of the Old Testament. J. Stacey. 1976. pap. 4.30 (ISBN 0-08-018101-5). Pergamon.

Common Security Interests of Japan, the United States, & NATO. Ed. by U. Alexis Johnson & George R. Packard. 200p. 1981. professional reference 19.50x. Ballinger Pub.

Common Sense About Your Family Dollars. James C. Thomason. 1979. pap. 3.95 (ISBN 0-88207-636-1). Victor Bks.

Common Sense & Other Political Writings. Thomas Paine. Ed. by Nelson F. Adkins. LC 53-11326. 1953. pap. 5.50 (ISBN 0-672-60004-8, AHS5). Bobbs.

Common Sense & the Battle of the Sexes. Marie B. Hall. 2.50 (ISBN 0-938760-02-5). Veritas.

Common Sense & the Crisis. Thomas Paine. 1970. pap. 2.95 (ISBN 0-385-09527-9, Anch). Doubleday.

Common Sense Approach to Community Living Arrangements for the Mentally Retarded. John W. Fanning. (Illus.). 112p. 1975. 12.50 (ISBN 0-398-03300-5). C C Thomas.

Common Sense Composition: A Modern Approach to Improving Written Communication. Isabel L. Hawley. LC 73-83546. 140p. (Orig.). 1977. pap. 8.95x (ISBN 0-913636-04-5). Educ Res MA.

Common Sense Compost Making. Maye Bruce. (Illus., Orig.). 1973. pap. 3.95 (ISBN 0-571-09990-4, Pub. by Faber & Faber). Merrimack Bk Serv.

Common Sense for Hard Times. Jeremy Brechter & Tom Costello. 277p. 1979. 12.50 o.p. (ISBN 0-686-63874-3); pap. 5.00 (ISBN 0-89758-026-5). Inst Policy Stud.

Common-Sense Guide to Refinishing Antiques. rev. ed. Alfred Higgins. LC 76-8913. (Funk & W Bk.). (Illus.). 288p. 1976. 9.95 (ISBN 0-308-10252-5, TYC-T). T Y Crowell.

Common Sense in Music Teaching. William Lovelock. (Illus.). 1968. Repr. of 1965 ed. 6.95 (ISBN 0-7135-0682-2). Dufour.

Common Sense Industrial Relations. Dennis D. Hunt. LC 77-89384. 1978. 14.95 (ISBN 0-7153-7453-2). David & Charles.

Common Sense Medical Guide & Outdoor Reference. Newell D. Breyfogle. Ed. by Robert P. McGraw. (Illus.). 416p. 1981. text ed. 11.95 (ISBN 0-07-007672-3, HP); pap. text ed. 6.95 (ISBN 0-07-007673-1). McGraw.

Common Sense Self-Defense: A Practical Manual for Students & Teachers. Mary Conroy & Edward R. Ritvo. LC 76-28533. (Illus.). 1977. pap. text ed. 8.50 o.p. (ISBN 0-8016-1027-3). Mosby.

Common Weeds of the United States. U. S. Department Of Agriculture. 1970. pap. 6.50 (ISBN 0-486-20504-5). Dover.

Commonplace Book of Robert Reynes. Cameron Louis. LC 79-7933. (Medieval Texts Ser.: Vol. I). 630p. 1980. lib. bdg. 50.00 (ISBN 0-8240-9539-1). Garland Pub.

Commonplace Coastal Navigation. Hewitt Schlereth. (Illus.). 1981. 18.95 (ISBN 0-393-03224-8). Norton.

Commons in the Seventies. Ed. by S. A. Walkland & Michael Ryle. 285p. 1977. 25.50x (ISBN 0-85520-189-4, Pub. by Martin Robertson England). Biblio Dist.

Commonsense Approach to Coronary Care: A Program. 3rd ed. Marielle Vinsant & Martha I. Spence. LC 80-36795. 350p. 1980. pap. text ed. 13.95 (ISBN 0-8016-5235-9). Mosby.

Commonsense Design. Arnold Friedmann. LC 76-15179. (Encore Edition). (Illus.). 1976. encore ed. 5.95 o.p. (ISBN 0-684-16191-5, ScribT); pap. 6.95 o.p. (ISBN 0-684-14688-6, SL650, ScribT). Scribner.

Commonsense Grammar & Style. rev ed. Robert E. Morsberger. LC 78-78273. (Apollo Eds.). 400p. 1975. pap. 3.95 o.s.i. (ISBN 0-8152-0375-6, A-375, TYC-T). T Y Crowell.

Commonsense in Nuclear Energy. Fred Hoyle & Geoffrey Hoyle. LC 80-11811. (Illus.). 1980. text ed. 8.95x (ISBN 0-7167-1247-4); pap. text ed. 4.95x (ISBN 0-7167-1237-7). W H Freeman.

Commonsense Sailboat Buying. Hewitt Schlereth. LC 76-42443. 1977. 9.95 o.p. (ISBN 0-8092-8205-4). Contemp Bks.

Commonsense Statistics for Economists & Others. F. R. Jolliffe. (Students Library of Economics Ser.). 1974. 10.00x (ISBN 0-7100-7952-4); pap. 6.95 (ISBN 0-7100-7953-2). Routledge & Kegan.

Commonwealth at Work. D. Ingram. 1969. 12.25 (ISBN 0-08-013869-1); pap. 4.40 (ISBN 0-08-013868-3). Pergamon.

Commonwealth Bursars: Problems of Adjustment. Ed. by D. G. Burns. Orig. Title: Travelling Scholars. 1965. pap. text ed. 5.75x (ISBN 0-901225-64-9, NFER). Humanities.

Commonwealth Migration: Flows & Policies. T. E. Smith. 1980. text ed. 40.00x (ISBN 0-333-27898-4). Humanities.

Commonwealth of Music. Gustave Reese & R. Brandel. 1965. 7.50 o.s.i. (ISBN 0-02-926080-9). Free Pr.

Commonwealth or Anarchy: A Survey of Projects of Peace from the Sixteenth to the Twentieth Century. Sir John A. Marriott. LC 79-1636. 1981. Repr. of 1937 ed. 19.50 (ISBN 0-88355-939-0). Hyperion Conn.

Commonwealth Short Stories. Ed. by Anna Rutherford & Donald Hannah. 245p. 1980. text ed. 19.50x (ISBN 0-8419-5075-X); pap. text ed. 9.50x (ISBN 0-686-62972-8). Holmes & Meier.

Commonwealth Tracts 1625-1650: A Shorte Treatise Against Stage-Playes. Alexander Leighton. Bd. with Stage Players Complaint; Declaration...Also an Ordinance of Both Houses, for the Supression of Stage Playes; Actors Remonstrance; Two Ordinances; Ordinance for the Utter Suppression & Abolishing of All Stage-Playes & Interludes; Dagonizing of Bartholomew Fayre; Humble Petition of Diverse Poor & Distressed Men, Heretofore the Actors of Blackfriers & the Cock-Pit. LC 71-170417. (English Stage Ser.: Vol. 14). lib. bdg. 50.00 (ISBN 0-8240-0597-X). Garland Pub.

Communal Catholic: A Personal Manifesto. Andrew M. Greeley. 220p. 1976. 8.95 (ISBN 0-8164-0299-X). Crossroad NY.

Communal Dialogue Programs. rev. ed. Charlotte M. Stein. 1980. Vol. 1. 2.95 (ISBN 0-916634-21-3); Multi-volume Set. pap. write for info. (ISBN 0-916634-19-1). Double M Pr.

Communal Edge to Plural Societies: India & Malaysia. Ratna Naidu. 1978. text ed. 14.00x (ISBN 0-7069-0922-4). Humanities.

Commune De Paris, 1871, 13 vols. (Paris Commune Ser.). (Fr.). 1976. Set. lib. bdg. 200.00x o.p. (ISBN 0-8287-1349-9); Set. pap. text ed. 105.00x o.p. (ISBN 0-685-71495-0). Clearwater Pub.

Commune: Life in Rural China. Peggy Printz & Paul Steinle. LC 76-58427. (Illus.). 1977. 6.95 (ISBN 0-396-07420-0). Dodd.

Communes in Britain. Andrew Rigby. 1974. 13.50 (ISBN 0-7100-7906-0). Routledge & Kegan.

Communes, Sociology & Society. P. Abrams & A. McCulloch. LC 75-40985. (Themes in the Social Sciences Ser.: No. 3). 200p. 1976. 29.50 (ISBN 0-521-21188-3); pap. 7.95x (ISBN 0-521-29067-8). Cambridge U Pr.

Communicate! 2nd ed. Rudolph F. Verderber. 1978. pap. text ed. 9.95x o.p. (ISBN 0-534-00559-4). Wadsworth Pub.

Communicate. 3rd ed. Rudolph F. Verderber. 384p. 1980. pap. text ed. 10.95x (ISBN 0-534-00885-2). Wadsworth Pub.

Communicate One. K. Morrow & K. Johnson. (Cambridge English Language Learning Ser.). 1980. students' ed. 7.95 (ISBN 0-521-21850-0); tchr's. ed. 5.95 (ISBN 0-521-21849-7); cassette 13.95 (ISBN 0-521-21848-9). Cambridge U Pr.

Communicating. Churches Alive Inc. (Love One Another Bible Study). 1979. wkbk. 1.50 (ISBN 0-934396-06-X). Churches Alive.

Communicating. 2nd ed. Anita Taylor et al. (Ser.in Speech Communication). (Illus.). 1980. text ed. 14.95 (ISBN 0-13-153080-1). P-H.

Communicating: A Social & Career Focus. 2nd ed. Roy M. Berko & Andrew D. Wolvin. (Illus.). 432p. 1981. pap. text ed. 10.50 (ISBN 0-395-29170-4). HM.

Communicating: A Social & Career Focus. Roy M. Berko et al. LC 76-12008. (Illus.). 336p. 1977. pap. text ed. 12.95 (ISBN 0-395-24073-5); instructor's manual 2.10 (ISBN 0-395-24074-3). HM.

Communicating & Relating. Jacquelyn B. Carr. LC 78-58969. 1979. pap. text ed. 12.95 (ISBN 0-8053-1820-8); instr's guide 3.95 (ISBN 0-8053-1821-6). Benjamin-Cummings.

Communicating at the Top: What You Need to Know About Communicating to Run an Organization. George DeMare. LC 78-31951. 1979. 15.95 (ISBN 0-471-05681-2, Pub. by Wiley-Interscience). Wiley.

Communicating by Letter. Marilyn B. Gilbert. LC 72-11879. (Self-Teaching Guides Ser.). 192p. 1973. 6.95 (ISBN 0-471-29897-2). Wiley.

Communicating Clearly: The Effective Message. William H. Bonner. 384p. 1980. pap. text ed. 8.95 (ISBN 0-574-20605-1, 13-3605); instr's. guide avail. (ISBN 0-574-20606-X, 13-3606). SRA.

Communicating During Negotiations Strokes. J. William Jones. 1976. pap. 5.75 o.p. (ISBN 0-87545-007-5). Natl Sch Pr.

Communicating Effectively. Ann Huntsman & Jane Binger. LC 80-83694. (Management Anthology Ser.). 200p. 1981. pap. text ed. 10.95 (ISBN 0-913654-67-1). Nursing Res.

Communicating for Results. Thomas E. Anastasi, Jr. LC 72-82619. 200p. 1972. pap. text ed. 9.95 (ISBN 0-8465-0292-5). Benjamin-Cummings.

Communicating in Business. 2nd ed. Lindauer. 1979. 17.95 (ISBN 0-7216-5794-X). Dryden Pr.

Communicating in Business. Norman B. Sigband & David N. Bateman. 1981. text ed. 16.95x (ISBN 0-673-15175-1); study guide 6.95x (ISBN 0-673-15429-7). Scott F.

Communicating in Business: Key to Success, Vol. 1. rev. ed. William H. Bonner & Jean Voyles. LC 79-84832. (Illus.). 388p. 1980. text ed. 14.95x (ISBN 0-931920-07-8); study guide 4.95 (ISBN 0-686-63215-X); letter writing wkbk. 4.50 (ISBN 0-686-63216-8); report writing wkbk. 3.95 (ISBN 0-686-63217-6). Dame Pubns.

Communicating in Dentistry: Sources & Evaluation of Information & Preparation of Manuscripts, Oral Reports, & Proposals for Research. Ed. by Kenneth A. Easlick et al. (Illus.). 240p. 1974. pap. 24.50 photocopy ed. spiral (ISBN 0-398-02856-7). C C Thomas.

Communicating in Spanish for Medical Personnel. Julia J. Tabery et al. LC 73-17667. 600p. 1975. pap. text ed. 15.95 (ISBN 0-316-83101-8); tapes 25.00 (ISBN 0-316-83102-6); pap. text ed. 30.00 incl. text & tapes (ISBN 0-316-83103-4). Little.

Communicating in Spanish, Level I. Enrique E. Lamadrid et al. 800p. (Sp.). 1974. text ed. 18.25 (ISBN 0-686-57707-8); instructors' manual 12.10 (ISBN 0-395-17530-5); wkbk. 6.95 (ISBN 0-395-17531-3); tapes 158.76 (ISBN 0-395-17534-8). HM.

Communicating Information: Proceedings, Vol. 17. ASIS Annual Meeting, 43rd, 1980. Ed. by Alan R. Benenfeld. LC 64-8303. (Illus.). 417p. 1980. pap. text ed. 19.50 (ISBN 0-914236-73-3, American Society for Information Science). Knowledge Indus.

Communicating Love Through Prayer. Rosalind Rinker. 1966. pap. 1.75 (ISBN 0-310-32072-0). Zondervan.

Communicating on the Job: A Practical Guide for Supervisors. Charles R. Buening. 100p. 1974. text ed. 8.95 (ISBN 0-201-00855-6). A-W.

Communicating Personally: A Theory of Interpersonal Communication and Human Relationships. Charles M. Rossiter & W. B. Pearce, Jr. LC 74-23546. (SC Ser: No. 21). 286p. 1975. pap. 6.50 (ISBN 0-672-61352-2). Bobbs.

Communicating Technical Information. Robert R. Rathbone. LC 66-25632. (Engineering Ser). (Illus., Orig.). 1966. pap. 8.95 (ISBN 0-201-06305-0). A-W.

Communicating the Gospel God's Way. Charles H. Kraft. LC 80-53945. 60p. 1980. pap. 2.95x (ISBN 0-87808-742-7). William Carey Lib.

Communicating the Value of Comprehensive Pharmaceutical Services to the Consumer (Dichter Report) 1973. 12.00 (ISBN 0-917330-04-8). Am Pharm Assn.

Communicating Through Letters & Reports. 6th ed. J. H. Menning et al. 1976. text ed. 16.50x o.p. (ISBN 0-256-01819-7). Irwin.

Communicating Through Letters & Reports. 7th ed. C. W. Wilkinson & Peter B. Clarke. 1980. 17.95x (ISBN 0-256-02270-4). Irwin.

Communicating with a Computer. Albert B. Bolt & M. E. Wardle. LC 73-85713. (Illus.). 1970. 11.50 (ISBN 0-521-07633-1); pap. 5.75x (ISBN 0-521-09587-5). Cambridge U Pr.

Communicating with Consumers: The Information Processing Approach. Ed. by Michael L. Ray & Scott Ward. LC 75-32370. (Sage Contemporary Social Science Issues Ser.: Vol. 21). 1976. 4.95x (ISBN 0-8039-0579-3). Sage.

Communicating with Employees About Pension & Welfare Benefits. Jozetta H. Srb. (Key Issues Ser.: No. 8). 1971. pap. 2.00 (ISBN 0-87546-244-8). NY Sch Indus Rel.

Communicating with People: The Supervisor's Introduction to Verbal Communication & Decision-Making. Raymond J. Burby. LC 78-109507. (Supervision Ser). (Prog. Bk.). 1970. pap. text ed. 8.95 (ISBN 0-201-00735-5). A-W.

Communicating with the Computer: Introductory Experiences, Basic. Francis G. French & Zeney Jacobs. (Orig.). (gr. 9-12). 1975. pap. text ed. 10.96 (ISBN 0-205-04470-0, 2044706); tchrs'. guide 4.40 (ISBN 0-205-04471-9, 2044714). Allyn.

Communicating with the Computer: Introductory Experiences, Fortran IV. Zeney P. Jacobs et al. (gr. 9-12). 1973. text ed. 11.40 (ISBN 0-205-03819-0, 2038196); tchrs'. guide 4.40 (ISBN 0-205-03820-4, 203820X). Allyn.

Communicating with Twentieth Century Man. Jay Adams. 1979. pap. 1.95 (ISBN 0-87552-008-1). Presby & Reformed.

Communication. 2nd ed. Larry L. Barker. (Illus.). 448p. 1981. text ed. 13.95 (ISBN 0-13-153346-0); pap. 5.95 study guide (ISBN 0-13-153445-9). P-H.

Communication. Denis McQuail. LC 75-11683. (A.O.M.S. Social Processes Ser.). (Illus.). 240p. 1975. text ed. 13.95x (ISBN 0-582-48710-2); pap. text ed. 9.50x (ISBN 0-582-48711-0). Longman.

Communication. Eric N. Simons. LC 79-512663. (Pegasus Books: No. 28). (Illus.). 1970. 7.50x (ISBN 0-234-77317-0). Intl Pubns Serv.

Communication: A Guide to Information Sources. Ed. by A. George Gitter & Robert Grunin. LC 79-54692. (Psychology Information Guide Ser.: Vol. 3). 1980. 30.00 (ISBN 0-8103-1443-6). Gale.

Communication: A Scientific American Book. Scientific American Editors. LC 72-10100. (Illus.). 1972. text ed. 14.95x (ISBN 0-7167-0866-3); pap. text ed. 7.95x (ISBN 0-7167-0865-5). W H Freeman.

Communication, Action & Meaning: The Creation of Social Realities. W. Barnett Pearce & Vernon E. Cronen. 308p. 1980. 29.95 (ISBN 0-03-057611-3). Praeger.

Communication: An Introduction to the History of Writing, Printing, Books & Libraries. 4th ed. Elmer D. Johnson. LC 73-83. 1973. 11.00 (ISBN 0-8108-0588-X). Scarecrow.

Communication & Argument: Elements of Applied Semantics. Arne Naess. 1966. text ed. 17.00x (ISBN 8-200-02073-8, Dist. by Columbia U Pr). Universitet.

Communication & Behavior. Gerhard J. Hanneman & William J. McEwen. LC 74-19704. 464p. 1975. pap. text ed. 12.95 (ISBN 0-201-02745-3). A-W.

Communication & Communication Barriers in Sociology. Ed. by G. Boalt et al. LC 75-44623. 1976. 29.95 (ISBN 0-470-15016-5). Halsted Pr.

Communication & Culture: A Reading-Writing Text. Joan Gregg. (Orig.). 1980. pap. text ed. 8.95 (ISBN 0-442-23895-9); instr's. manual 2.95. D Van Nostrand.

Communication & Drug Abuse: Proceedings. Rutgers Symposium on Drug Abuse, 2nd. Ed. by J. R. Wittenborn et al. (Illus.). 556p. 1970. 29.50 o.p. (ISBN 0-398-02099-X). C C Thomas.

Communication & Learning in Small Groups. Barnes & Todd. (Direct Editions Ser.). (Orig.). 1977. pap. 9.75 (ISBN 0-7100-8512-5). Routledge & Kegan.

Communication & Learning in the Primary School. rev. ed. Leonard G. Sealey & Vivian Gibbon. 1963. text ed. 4.00x (ISBN 0-631-97120-3). Humanities.

Communication & Organizational Behavior. 4th ed. William V. Haney. 1979. text ed. 19.50 (ISBN 0-256-02244-5). Irwin.

Communication & Parapsychology: Proceedings of an International Conference Held in Vancouver, Canada; August 9-10, 1979. Ed. by Betty Shapin & Lisette Coly. LC 80-80486. 230p. 1980. 14.00 (ISBN 0-912328-32-0). Parapsych Foun.

Communication & Rural Development. (Illus.). 1977. pap. 7.00 (ISBN 92-3-101370-X, U77, UNESCO). Unipub.

Communication & Social Behavior: A Symbolic Interaction Perspective. Don F. Faules & Dennis C. Alexander. LC 76-46610. (Speech Communication Ser.). (Illus.). 1978. pap. text ed. 9.95 (ISBN 0-201-01982-5); instr's manual 3.00 (ISBN 0-201-01979-5). A-W.

Communication & Social Influence. Stephen W. King. 1975. text ed. 6.50 (ISBN 0-201-03720-3). A-W.

Communication & the Aging Process: Interaction Throughout the Life Cycle. Lois M. Tamir. (Pergamon General Psychology Ser.). 1980. 24.50 (ISBN 0-08-024621-4). Pergamon.

Communication & the Schools. C. W. Bending. LC 71-103930. 1970. 22.00 (ISBN 0-08-015663-0); pap. 10.75 (ISBN 0-08-015662-2). Pergamon.

Communication & the Small Group. 2nd ed. Gerald M. Phillips. LC 74-179366. (Speech Communication Ser.: No. 12). 180p. 1973. pap. text ed. 4.50 (ISBN 0-672-61302-6, SC12R). Bobbs.

Communication at Work. Susan K. Gilmore & Patrick W. Fraleigh. LC 80-69467. (Illus.). 150p. (Orig.). 1980. 6.95 (ISBN 0-938070-00-2). Friendly Pr.

Communication Behavior in Organizations. new ed. Aubrey Sanford et al. 1976. text ed. 16.95x (ISBN 0-675-08601-9). Merrill.

Communication Breakdown: Cause & Cure. David W. Shave. LC 73-377. 320p. 1975. 18.50 (ISBN 0-87527-125-1). Green.

Communication Circuits: Analysis & Design. Kenneth K. Clarke & Donald T. Hess. LC 78-125610. (Engineering Ser). 1971. text ed. 27.95 (ISBN 0-201-01040-2). A-W.

Communication: Concepts & Processes. rev. ed. Joseph A. De Vito. (Speech Communications Ser.). (Illus.). 352p. 1976. pap. text ed. 10.95x (ISBN 0-13-153023-2). P-H.

Communication: Concepts & Processes. 3rd ed. Joseph A. DeVito. (Illus.). 320p. 1981. pap. text ed. 10.95 (ISBN 0-13-153411-4). P-H.

Communication Contract. Susan B. Goldstein & Luther F. Sies. (Illus.). 384p. 1974. text ed. 18.75 (ISBN 0-685-49058-0). C C Thomas.

Communication Control in Computer Networks. Josef Puzman & Radoslav Porizek. (Wiley Series in Computing). 300p. 1981. 36.00 (ISBN 0-471-27894-7, Pub. by Wiley Interscience). Wiley.

Communication, Diffusion & Adoption of Innovations: A Bibliographical Update. Curtis W. Stofferahn & Peter F. Korsching. (Public Administration Ser.: Bibliography P-433). 50p. 1980. pap. 5.50. Vance Biblios.

Communication Disorders: Remedial Principles & Practices. Stanley Dickson et al. 520p. 1974. 17.95x (ISBN 0-673-07742-X). Scott F.

Communication: Everyday Encounters. Charles U. Larson. 240p. pap. text ed. 10.95 (ISBN 0-917974-60-3). Waveland Pr.

Communication for Business & the Professions. Malra Treece. 1978. text ed. 19.95 (ISBN 0-205-05956-2); instr's man. avail. (ISBN 0-205-05957-0). Allyn.

Communication for Business, Professional & Technical Students. 2nd ed. Doris W. Barr. 512p. 1980. pap. text ed. 18.95x (ISBN 0-534-00777-5). Wadsworth Pub.

Communication for Change with the Rural Disadvantaged. Agricultural Board. LC 72-186371. 1972. pap. 4.25 (ISBN 0-309-01942-7). Natl Acad Pr.

Communication for Management & Business. 2nd ed. Norman B. Sigband. 1976. 18.95x (ISBN 0-673-07884-1). Scott F.

Communication for Managers. P. Preston. 1979. 17.95 (ISBN 0-13-153957-4). P-H.

Communication for Nurses. Helen C. Morrin. (Quality Paperback: No. 302). (Orig.). 1965. pap. 2.95 (ISBN 0-8226-0302-0). Littlefield.

Communication for Supervisors & Managers. Lyle Sussman & Paul Krivonos. LC 78-22716. (Illus.). 1979. pap. text ed. 10.95x (ISBN 0-88284-077-0). Alfred Pub.

Communication for the Speechless. F. Silverman. 1980. 17.95 (ISBN 0-13-153361-4). P-H.

Communication Games. Don Byrne & Shelagh Rixon. (English Language Teaching Institute Ser.: No. 1). 96p. 1980. pap. text ed. 14.50x (ISBN 0-85633-189-9, NFER). Humanities.

Communication Games. Karen D. Krupar. LC 73-76074. (Orig.). 1973. pap. text ed. 6.95 (ISBN 0-02-917710-3). Free Pr.

Communication Guidelines for Technical Professionals. Ed. by Charlie Vervalin. 220p. (Orig.). 1981. pap. 15.95 (ISBN 0-87201-127-5). Gulf Pub.

Communication History. John D. Stevens & Hazel D. Garcia. LC 80-11132. (Sage Commtext Ser.: No. 2). (Illus.). 159p. 1980. 12.50x (ISBN 0-8039-1256-0); pap. 5.95 (ISBN 0-8039-1257-9). Sage.

Communication in Business. S. Bernard Rosenblatt et al. 1977. 16.95 (ISBN 0-13-153262-6). P-H.

Communication in Health Care. Norman Metzger & Harry Munn. 150p. 1981. text ed. price not set (ISBN 0-89443-356-3). Aspen Systems.

Communication in Health Care Organizations. Mary E. Lunz. 420p. 1981. text ed. price not set (ISBN 0-914904-69-8). Health Admin Pr.

Communication in Health Care: Understanding & Implementing Effective Human Relationships. Mattie Collins. (Illus.). 1977. pap. text ed. 10.00 (ISBN 0-8016-1021-4). Mosby.

Communication in Modern Organizations. George T. Vardaman & Patricia B. Vardaman. LC 72-7391. (Management & Administration Ser.). 516p. 1973. text ed. 21.95x (ISBN 0-471-90300-0); instr's manual o.p. (ISBN 0-471-90301-9); (ISBN 0-685-27917-0). Wiley.

Communication in Organizations. Dalmar Fisher. (Illus.). 480p. 1981. text ed. 16.95 (ISBN 0-8299-0374-7). West Pub.

Communication in Organizations. Everett M. Rogers & Rekha Agarwala-Rogers. LC 75-32368. (Illus.). 1976. pap. text ed. 7.95 (ISBN 0-02-926710-2). Free Pr.

Communication in Organizations: An Annotated Bibliography & Sourcebook. Ed. by Robert M. Carter. LC 73-161194. (Management Information Guide Ser.: No. 25). 1972. 30.00 (ISBN 0-8103-0825-8). Gale.

Communication in Social Work. Peter R. Day. LC 72-8466. 128p. 1973. text ed. 18.75 (ISBN 0-08-017064-1); pap. text ed. 9.25 (ISBN 0-08-017065-X). Pergamon.

Communication in the Church Concilium, Vol. III. Ed. by Gregory Baum & Andrew Greeley. 1978. pap. 4.95 (ISBN 0-8164-2170-6). Crossroad NY.

Communication in the Classroom. H. Thomas Hurt et al. LC 77-73960. (Education Ser.). (Illus.). 1978. pap. text ed. 7.95 (ISBN 0-201-03048-9). A-W.

Communication in the Dental Office: A Programmed Manual for the Dental Professional. Robert E. Froelich et al. (Illus.). 128p. 1976. pap. 10.95 (ISBN 0-8016-1698-0). Mosby.

Communication in the Human Services: A Guide to Therapeutic Journalism. Marcia S. Joslyn-Scherer. LC 79-28653. (Sage Human Services Guides: Vol. 13). 175p. 1980. pap. 8.00 (ISBN 0-8039-1418-0). Sage.

Communication in Writing. E. F. Pardoe. 1965. 8.50 (ISBN 0-08-011136-X); pap. 4.20 (ISBN 0-08-011135-1). Pergamon.

Communication Inquiry: A Perspective on a Process or, From Questions to Answers. G. R. Miller & H. E. Nicholson. 1976. 6.50 (ISBN 0-201-04746-2). A-W.

Communication Involvement: Personal Perspectives. William W. Wilmot & John R. Wenburg. LC 80-16247. 452p. 1981. Repr. of 1974 ed. lib. bdg. write for info. (ISBN 0-89874-185-8). Krieger.

Communication, Knowledge & the Librarian. Kevin McGarry. 207p. (Orig.). 1975. 12.50 o.p. (ISBN 0-208-01369-5, Linnet). Shoe String.

Communication Monitoring & Communications Projects. Robert B. Grove. 128p. 1979. pap. 5.95 (ISBN 0-8104-0894-5). Hayden.

Communication Networks: Towards a New Paradigm for Research. Everett M. Rogers & D. Lawrence Kincaid. LC 80-65202. (Illus.). 1981. 19.95 (ISBN 0-02-926740-4). Free Pr.

Communication of Ideas. Institute for Religious & Social Studies. Ed. by Lyman Bryson. (Religion & Civilization Ser). 1964. Repr. of 1948 ed. 28.50x (ISBN 0-8154-0035-7). Cooper Sq.

Communication of Ideas. Ed. by J. S. Yadava & Gautam Vinayshil. 256p. 1980. text ed. 15.75x (ISBN 0-391-02128-1). Humanities.

Communication of Innovations. 2nd ed. E. Rogers & F. Shoemaker. LC 78-122276. 1971. text ed. 14.95 (ISBN 0-02-926680-7). Free Pr.

Communication: Personal & Public. William I. Gorden. LC 76-30803. (Illus.). 325p. 1978. 11.50 (ISBN 0-88284-041-X). Alfred Pub.

Communication Policies in Brazil. (Communication Policy Ser.). 80p. 1976. pap. 6.00 (ISBN 9-2310-1296-7, U79, UNESCO). Unipub.

Communication Policies in Ireland. 73p. (Orig.). 1975. pap. 4.75 (ISBN 92-3-101145-6, U84, UNESCO). Unipub.

Communication Policies in Japan: Communication Policy Studies. 1978. pap. 4.75 (ISBN 92-3-101515-X, U826, UNESCO). Unipub.

Communication Policies in Kenya. 94p. 1980. pap. 7.50 (ISBN 92-3-101774-8, U1032, UNESCO). Unipub.

Communication Policies in Peru. (Illus.). 1977. pap. 6.00 (ISBN 92-3-101366-1, U85, UNESCO). Unipub.

Communication Policies in the Federal Republic of Germany. 86p. (Orig.). 1975. pap. 6.00 (ISBN 92-3-101184-7, U81, UNESCO). Unipub.

Communication Policies in Yugoslavia. Zdravko Lekovic & Mihalo Bjelica. 66p. 1977. pap. 4.75 (ISBN 92-3-101409-9, U88, UNESCO). Unipub.

Communication Policies in Zaire. 59p. 1980. pap. 5.25 (ISBN 92-3-101602-4, U1018, UNESCO). Unipub.

Communication Research & Drug Education. Ed. by Ronald E. Ostman. LC 75-11132. (International Yearbooks of Drug Addiction & Society: Vol. 3). 1976. 20.00x (ISBN 0-8039-0420-7); pap. 9.95x (ISBN 0-8039-0511-4). Sage.

Communication Skillbook Three: New Worlds in English. Dalene McClintock & Carolyn Holmes. (Communication Skillbooks). 64p. 1980. pap. text ed. 3.95 (ISBN 0-88499-223-3). Inst Mod Lang.

Communication Skills. Barbara Strain & Patricia Wysong. LC 78-64356. (Speech Communication Ser.). (Illus.). 1979. pap. text ed. 9.95 (ISBN 0-201-07318-8); instr. resource guide avail. 2.50 (ISBN 0-201-07333-1). A-W.

Communication Skills for the Human Services. K. Eriksen. 1978. 13.95 (ISBN 0-87909-100-2); pap. 7.95 (ISBN 0-87909-101-0). Reston.

Communication Skills in the Organization. Gary T. Hunt. (Illus.). 1980. text ed. 16.95 (ISBN 0-13-153296-0). P-H.

Communication Strategies for Family Planning. Everett M. Rogers. LC 73-1049. 1973. 17.95 (ISBN 0-02-926700-5). Free Pr.

Communication Strategies for Productivity Improvement. 236p. 1980. 24.50 (ISBN 92-833-1053-5, APO 86, APO). Unipub.

Communication Strategy: A Guide to Speech Preparation. Roselyn L. Schiff et al. 1980. pap. text ed. 6.95x (ISBN 0-673-15437-8). Scott F.

Communication System Principles. Peyton Z. Peebles. (Illus.). 1976. 27.50 (ISBN 0-201-05758-1, Adv Bk Prog); pap. 3.50 (ISBN 0-201-05759-X). A-W.

Communication Systems. Simon Haykin. LC 77-26752. 1978. text ed. 28.95 (ISBN 0-471-02977-7); tchrs. manual 10.00 (ISBN 0-471-03045-7). Wiley.

Communication Technologies & Information Flow. Ed. by Maxwell Lehman. (PPS on Science & Technology Ser.). (Illus.). 175p. 1981. 20.00 (ISBN 0-08-027169-3); pap. 12.50 (ISBN 0-08-027528-1). Pergamon.

Communication: The Essence of Science Facilitating Information Exchange Among Librarians, Scientists, Engineers, & Students. William D. Garvey. 1978. text ed. 49.00 (ISBN 0-08-022254-4); pap. text ed. 19.50 (ISBN 0-08-023344-9). Pergamon.

Communication: The Process of Organizing. Johnson. 1977. text ed. 17.95 (ISBN 0-205-05786-1); instructor's manual avail. (ISBN 0-205-05788-8). Allyn.

Communication: The Widening Circle. Estelle Zannes. LC 80-15150. (Speech Ser.). 324p. 1981. pap. text ed. 10.95 (ISBN 0-201-08997-1). A-W.

Communication Today. J. Michael Sproule. 1980. pap. text ed. 9.95x (ISBN 0-673-15168-9); wkbk. 4.95x (ISBN 0-673-15469-6). Scott F.

Communication, Transmission, & Transportation Networks. Howard Frank & Ivan T. Frisch. LC 78-119666. (Engineering Ser). 1971. text ed. 25.95 (ISBN 0-201-02081-5). A-W.

Communication Under Law: Vol. I, Free Speech. Joseph J. Hemmer, Jr. LC 79-19166. 307p. 1979. 16.50 (ISBN 0-8108-1248-7). Scarecrow.

Communication Variables of Cerebral Palsied & Mentally Retarded Children. Orvis C. Irwin. (Illus.). 400p. 1972. text ed. 29.75 (ISBN 0-398-02322-0). C C Thomas.

Communication Vibrations. Larry L. Barker. (Speech Communication Ser.). (Illus.). 160p. 1974. pap. text ed. 111.95 (ISBN 0-13-153007-0). P-H.

Communication with Extraterrestial Intelligence. Ed. by J. Billingham & R. Pesek. (Astronautica: Vol. 6, Nos. 1-2). 1979. 47.00 (ISBN 0-08-024727-X). Pergamon.

Communication with the Fatally Ill. Adriaan Verwoerdt. 196p. 1966. pap. 9.75 spiral (ISBN 0-398-01981-9). C C Thomas.

Communications. Boy Scouts of America. LC 19-600. (Illus.). 32p. (gr. 6-12). 1976. pap. 0.70x (ISBN 0-8395-3258-X, 3258). BSA.

Communications & Class Struggle: Capitalism, Imperialism, Vol. 1. Ed. by Armand Mattelart & Seth Siegelaub. 448p. 1979. pap. 16.95 (ISBN 0-88477-011-7). Intl General.

Communications & Data Management. Thomas F. Walton. Ed. by John W. Buckley. LC 76-10264. 1976. 33.50 (ISBN 0-471-91935-7, Pub. by Wiley-Interscience). Wiley.

Communications & National Integration in Communist China. Alan P. Liu. (Center for Chinese Studies, Univ. of Michigan). 1971. 20.00 (ISBN 0-520-01882-6); pap. 6.95x (ISBN 0-520-02901-1). U of Cal Pr.

Communications & Public Opinion: A Public Opinion Quarterly Reader. Ed. by Robert O. Carlson. LC 75-11687. 660p. 1975. text ed. 26.95 (ISBN 0-275-07510-9); pap. text ed. 11.95 (ISBN 0-275-89330-8). Praeger.

Communications & Relationships in Nursing. 2nd ed. Maureen O'Brien. LC 77-26260. (Illus.). 1978. pap. text ed. 9.50 (ISBN 0-8016-3700-7). Mosby.

Communications Architecture for Distributed Systems. R. J. Cypser. LC 76-52673. (Illus.). 1978. text ed. 21.95 (ISBN 0-201-14458-1). A-W.

Communications Eighty: Communications Equipment & Systems. (IEE Conference Publications Ser.: No. 184). (Illus.). 272p. 1980. softcover 41.50 (ISBN 0-85296-216-9). Inst Elect Eng.

Communications Electronics. James Hardy. 1981. text ed. 18.95 (ISBN 0-8359-0892-5); instr's. manual free (ISBN 0-8359-0893-3). Reston.

Communications for Tomorrow: Policy Perspectives for the 1980's. Ed. by Glen O. Robinson. 1978. 37.50 (ISBN 0-03-046546-X); pap. 12.95 student ed (ISBN 0-03-046541-9). Praeger.

Communications for Trade Unions. Austin H. Perlow. (Continuing Education-Labor Studies Ser.). 350p. (Orig.). 1980. write for info. BNA.

Communications from the Beginning. Alma Gilleo. LC 77-24211. (From the Beginning Ser.). (Illus.). (gr. 1-4). 1977. PLB 5.50 (ISBN 0-89565-003-7). Childs World.

Communications in Business. 2nd ed. Walter Wells. 1977. 18.95x (ISBN 0-534-00502-0). Wadsworth Pub.

Communications in Nursing Practice. Barba J. Edwards & John K. Brilhart. (Illus.). 240p. 1981. pap. text ed. 9.95 (ISBN 0-8016-0786-8). Mosby.

Communications in the Rural Third World: The Role of Information in Development. Ed. by Emile G. McAnany. LC 79-21406. (Praeger Special Studies). 1980. 23.95 (ISBN 0-03-052986-7). Praeger.

Communications Institute, Palm Springs Calif. April,12-15, 1977: Proceedings. Ed. by Elizabeth Hieb. 1977. spiral bdg. 7.00 (ISBN 0-89154-059-8). Intl Found Employ.

Communications Manual for Nonprofit Organizations. Lucille A. Maddalena. 286p. 1981. 17.95 (ISBN 0-8144-5606-5). Am Mgmt.

Communications Network Analysis. Howard Cravis. LC 75-39314. 1981. price not set (ISBN 0-669-00443-X). Lexington Bks.

Communications Policy for National Development: A Comparative Perspective. Ed. by Majid Teharanian et al. 1977. 25.00x (ISBN 0-7100-8597-4). Routledge & Kegan.

Communications Revolution. Elizabeth Wrangham. Ed. by Malcolm Yapp et al. (World History Ser.). (Illus.). 32p. (gr. 10). 1980. Repr. of 1977 ed. lib. bdg. 5.95 (ISBN 0-89908-134-7); pap. text ed. 1.95 (ISBN 0-89908-109-6). Greenhaven.

Communications Revolution & the Education of Americans. Change Magazine Editors. LC 80-66849. 64p. (Orig.). 1980. pap. 6.95 (ISBN 0-915390-24-8). Change Mag.

Communications Satellites: Message Centers in Space. Bernice Kohn. LC 74-26872. (Illus.). 64p. (gr. 2-5). 1975. 5.95 (ISBN 0-590-07356-7, Four Winds). Schol Bk Serv.

Communications Skill Book. Boys Scouts of America. 1976. pap. 0.50x (ISBN 0-8395-6582-8); tchr's guide 0.30 (ISBN 0-685-73153-7, 18-322). BSA.

Communications Small Group Discussions: A Case Study Approach. John F. Cragan & David W. Wright. (Illus.). 400p. 1980. text ed. 12.95 (ISBN 0-8299-0338-0); instrs.' manual avail. (ISBN 0-8299-0474-3). West Pub.

Communications Technology & Democratic Participation. Kenneth C. Laudon. LC 77-7471. (Special Studies). 1977. text ed. 21.95 (ISBN 0-03-021836-5). Praeger.

Communications Technology & Social Policy: Understanding the New Cultural Revolution. G. Gerbner et al. LC 73-7563. 1973. 34.00 (ISBN 0-471-29670-8, Pub. by Wiley-Interscience). Wiley.

Communications: The Transfer of Meaning. Don Fabun. 1968. pap. 2.95x (ISBN 0-02-477490-1, 47749). Macmillan.

Communicative Disorders: An Appraisal. Alan J. Weston. (Illus.). 432p. 1972. 19.75 (ISBN 0-398-02437-5). C C Thomas.

Communicative Disorders: Prevention & Early Intervention. 2nd ed. Curtis E. Weiss & Harold S. Lillywhite. (Illus.). 398p. 1981. pap. text ed. 12.50 (ISBN 0-8016-5389-4). Mosby.

Communicative Experience. Lawrence Rosenfield et al. 464p. 1976. text ed. 17.95x (ISBN 0-205-05419-6); instr's manual free (ISBN 0-205-05420-X). Allyn.

Communicative Grammar of English. Geoffrey Leech & Jan Svartvik. (Illus.). 368p. 1975. pap. text ed. 12.50x (ISBN 0-582-55238-9). Longman.

Communicator. Royce A. Coffin. LC 74-23481. (Illus.). 176p. 1975. 10.95 (ISBN 0-8144-5374-0). Am Mgmt.

Communicators & Society. D. Wilson. 1968. pap. 3.50 (ISBN 0-08-012977-3). Pergamon.

Communion & Intercommunion. K. Ware. 1980. pap. 1.95 (ISBN 0-937032-20-4). Light&Life Pub Co MN.

Communion of Possibility. Charles E. Winquist. LC 75-859. (Religions Quest Ser: Vol. 2). 160p. 1975. lib. bdg. 17.50x (ISBN 0-914914-05-7); pap. text ed. 6.95x (ISBN 0-914914-04-9). New Horizons.

Communion Under Both Kinds- an Ecumenical Surrender. Michael Davies. 1980. pap. 1.00 (ISBN 0-89555-141-1). Tan Bks Pubs.

Communion with God. large-type ed. Baha'U'Llah The Bab & Abdu'l-Baha. 1976. pap. 1.50 (ISBN 0-87743-110-8, 7-15-11). Baha'i.

Communism. 2nd ed. James D. Forman. (Studies in Contemporary Politics). (gr. 9 up). 1979. PLB 7.90 s&l (ISBN 0-531-02933-6). Watts.

Communism & Communist Systems. Robert G. Wesson. 1978. pap. 10.50 ref. (ISBN 0-13-153437-8). P-H.

Communism & Gita: A Philosophico-Ethical Study. H. S. Sinha. 1979. text ed. 15.50x (ISBN 0-391-01869-8). Humanities.

Communism & Human Values. Maurice Cornforth. LC 72-85924. 72p. 1972. pap. 1.00 o.p. (ISBN 0-7178-0378-3). Intl Pub Co.

Communism & Philosophy: Contemporary Dogmas & Revisions of Marxism. Maurice Cornforth. 1980. text ed. 23.25x (ISBN 0-85315-430-9). Humanities.

Communism & Political Systems in Western Europe. David E. Albright. (Westview Special Studies in West European Politics & Society). 1979. lib. bdg. 27.50x (ISBN 0-89158-308-4). Westview.

Communism & the Yugoslav National Question. Paul Shoup. LC 68-19759. (East Central European Studies). 1968. 20.00x (ISBN 0-231-03125-4). Columbia U Pr.

Communism, Anticommunism, & the CIO. Harvey Levenstein. LC 80-787. (Contributions in American History Ser.: No. 91). 360p. 1981. lib. bdg. 29.95 (ISBN 0-313-22072-7, LEC/). Greenwood.

Communism: End of the Monolith? Ed. by Evelyn Geller. (Reference Shelf Ser.: Vol. 50, No. 3). 1978. 6.25 (ISBN 0-8242-0624-X). Wilson.

Communism, Fascism, & Democracy. 2nd ed. Carl Cohen. 620p. 1972. pap. text ed. 8.95x (ISBN 0-394-31319-4, RanC). Random.

Communism in America: Liberty & Security in Conflict. G. Baker. Ed. by Richard H. Brown & Van R. Halsey. (Amherst Ser.). (gr. 9-12). 1970. pap. text ed. 4.52 o.p. (ISBN 0-201-00455-0, Sch Div); tchr's manual 1.72 o.p. (ISBN 0-201-00457-7). A-W.

Communism in China As Reported from Hankow in 1932. O. Edmund Clubb. LC 68-56634. (Illus.). 1968. 17.50x (ISBN 0-231-03209-9). Columbia U Pr.

Communism in Europe: Continuity, Change & the Sino-Soviet Dispute, 1 vol. Ed. by William E. Griffith. Incl. Vol. 2. East Germany, Czechoslovakia, Sweden, Norway, Finland. pap. 5.95x (ISBN 0-262-57009-2). 1967. MIT Pr.

Communism in Hungary from Kun to Kadar. Bennett Kovrig. Ed. by Richard F. Staar. LC 78-59863. (Publications Ser.: No. 211). (Illus.). 1979. pap. 10.95 (ISBN 0-8179-7112-2). Hoover Inst Pr.
Communism in Indian Politics. Bhabani Sen Gupta. LC 73-190190. (Southern Asian Inst. Ser). 390p. 1972. 22.50x (ISBN 0-231-03568-3). Columbia U Pr.
Communism in Korea, Vols. 1 & 2. Robert A. Scalapino & Chong-Sik Lee. Incl. Vol. 1. The Movement. 38.50x (ISBN 0-520-02080-4); Vol. 2. The Society. 40.00x (ISBN 0-520-02274-2). LC 79-165236. 1500p. 1973. U of Cal Pr.
Communism in Latin America. Robert J. Alexander. 1957. 22.50 (ISBN 0-8135-0268-3). Rutgers U Pr.
Communism in the Arab East. M. S. Agwani. 1970. 8.50x (ISBN 0-210-98157-1). Asia.
Communism Killed Kennedy but Did America Learn? James Bales. 3.95 (ISBN 0-89315-015-0). Lambert Bk.
Communism: Opposing Viewpoints. Ed. by Bruno Leone. (ISMS Ser.). (Illus.). (gr. 9-12). 8.95 (ISBN 0-912616-53-9); pap. 3.95 (ISBN 0-912616-52-0). Greenhaven.
Communist Cadre: The Social Background of the American Communist Party Elite. Harvey E. Klehr. LC 78-58488. (Publications 198). 168p. 9.95 (ISBN 0-8179-6981-0). Hoover Inst Pr.
Communist China & Arms Control: A Contingency Study, 1967-1976. Ed. by Yuan-li Wu. LC 68-54095. (Publications Ser.: No. 78). (Illus.). 1968. pap. 5.00 (ISBN 0-8179-1782-9). Hoover Inst Pr.
Communist China & Latin America. Cecil Johnson. LC 76-129054. 1970. 20.00x (ISBN 0-231-03309-5). Columbia U Pr.
Communist Conspiracy. Stephen King-Hall. LC 79-2907. 239p. 1981. Repr. of 1953 ed. 19.75 (ISBN 0-8305-0077-4). Hyperion Conn.
Communist Indochina & U. S. Foreign Policy: Forging New Relations. Joseph J. Zasloff & MacAlister Brown. LC 77-28462. 1978. lib. bdg. 24.00x (ISBN 0-89158-150-2). Westview.
Communist Insurrection in Malaya 1948-1960. Anthony Short. LC 73-93384. 513p. 1974. 32.50 (ISBN 0-8448-0306-5). Crane-Russak Co.
Communist Local Government: A Study of Poland. Jaroslaw Piekalkiewicz. LC 72-85539. xiv, 282p. 1975. 16.00x (ISBN 0-8214-0140-8). Ohio U Pr.
Communist Manifesto. Karl Marx & Friedrich Engels. Ed. by Joseph Katz. Tr. by Samuel Moore. (YA) (gr. 9-12). pap. 2.25 (ISBN 0-671-42218-9). WSP.
Communist Movement in Iran. Sepehr Zabih. 1966. 21.75x (ISBN 0-520-01377-8). U of Cal Pr.
Communist Parties of Italy France & Spain: Postwar Change & Continuity, a Casebook. Ed. by Peter Lange & Maurizio Vannicelli. (Casebook Series on European Politics & Society: No. 1). 392p. 1981. text ed. 42.00x (ISBN 0-04-329033-7, 2644-5); pap. text ed. 18.50 (ISBN 0-686-69601-8). Allen Unwin.
Communist Parties of Western Europe: A Comparative Study. R. Neal Tannahill. LC 77-94750. (Contributions in Political Science). 1978. lib. bdg. 19.95 (ISBN 0-313-20318-0, TCP/). Greenwood.
Communist Party & the Auto Workers Unions. Roger Keeran. LC 79-2599. 352p. 1980. 22.50x (ISBN 0-253-15754-4). Ind U Pr.
Communist Party of Indonesia, 1951-1963. Donald Hindley. 1964. 24.50x (ISBN 0-520-00561-9). U of Cal Pr.
Communist Party States: Comparative & International Studies. Ed. by Jan F. Triska. LC 69-15728. 1969. pap. 6.90 o.p. (ISBN 0-672-61254-2). Bobbs.
Communist Politics in North Korea. Ilpyong J. Kim. LC 72-92887. (Special Studies). 130p. 1975. text ed. 24.95 (ISBN 0-275-09190-2). Praeger.
Communist Power System. Ota Sik. (Praeger Special Studies). 170p. 1980. 21.95 (ISBN 0-03-044106-4). Praeger.
Communist Road to Power in Vietnam. William Duiker. (Westview Special Studies on South & Southeast Asia). 375p. 1981. lib. bdg. 32.50x (ISBN 0-89158-794-2). Westview.
Communist Subversion of Czechoslovakia, 1938-1948: The Failure of Coexistence. Josef Korbel. 1959. 16.50x o.p. (ISBN 0-691-08705-9); pap. 4.95 o.p. (ISBN 0-691-02502-9). Princeton U Pr.
Communist World: Marxist & Non-Marxist Views. Ed. by Harry G. Shaffer. LC 67-21993. (Illus.). 1967. 28.00x (ISBN 0-89197-093-2); pap. text ed. 12.95x (ISBN 0-89197-094-0). Irvington.
Communists & Peace. Jean-Paul Sartre. LC 68-17390. 1968. 6.95 o.s.i. (ISBN 0-8076-0451-8). Braziller.
Communists in Spain. Guy Hermet. 1974. 22.95 (ISBN 0-347-01032-6, 93492-5, Pub. by Saxon Hse England). Lexington Bks.
Communists of Poland: An Historical Outline. Jan B. De Weydenthal. Ed. by Richard F. Staar. LC 78-59465. (Publications Ser.: No. 202). (Illus.). 236p. 1979. pap. 7.95 (ISBN 0-8179-7022-3). Hoover Inst Pr.
Communities & Their Development: An Introductory Study with Special Reference to the Tropics. Thomas R. Batten. LC 80-14699. (Illus.). vi, 248p. 1980. Repr. of 1957 ed. lib. bdg. 22.50x (ISBN 0-313-22447-1, BACD). Greenwood.
Communities & Their Schools. Ed. by Don Davies. (Study of the Schooling in the United States Ser.). 352p. 1981. 16.95 (ISBN 0-07-015503-8, P&RB). McGraw.
Communities in Transition: Bedford & Lincoln, Massachusetts, Seventeen Twenty-Nine to Eighteen Fifty. Richard Holmes. Ed. by Robert Berkhofer. (Studies in American History & Culture III). 285p. 1980. 27.95 (ISBN 0-8357-1098-X, Pub by UMI Res Pr). Univ Microfilms.
Communities of Honor & Love in Henry James. Manfred MacKenzie. 292p. 1976. 12.50x (ISBN 0-674-15160-7). Harvard U Pr.
Community. Time-Life Editors. (Human Behavior Ser). 9.95 (ISBN 0-8094-1958-0). Time-Life.
Community Action & Local Government. Sean Baine. 96p. 1975. pap. text ed. 8.75x (ISBN 0-7135-1842-1, Pub. by Bedford England). Renouf.
Community-Action, Planning, Development: A Casebook. Ed. by Fred M. Cox et al. 250p. 1974. pap. text ed. 8.50 (ISBN 0-87581-158-2). Peacock Pubs.
Community Advisory Committees for the Representation of Socio-Economic Interest. Ed. by Economic & Social Committee of the European Communities - General Secretariat. 240p. 1980. text ed. 24.75x (ISBN 0-566-00328-7, Pub. by Gower Pub Co England). Renouf.
Community: An Introduction to a Social System. 3rd ed. I. T. Sanders. 1975. 19.95 (ISBN 0-8260-7821-4). Wiley.
Community & Environmental Simulations: Annotated Guide to Over 200 Games for College & Community Education. James D. Harrison. (Public Administration Ser.: Bibliographies: P-675). 138p. 1981. 15.00. Vance Biblios.
Community & Growth. Vean Vanier. Tr. by Ann Shearer from Fr. LC 79-91602. 214p. 1979. pap. 6.95 (ISBN 0-8091-2294-4). Paulist Pr.
Community & Liturgy: An Historical Overview. Gerald A. Largo. LC 80-1434. 151p. 1980. lib. bdg. 16.25 (ISBN 0-8191-1302-6); pap. text ed. 7.75 (ISBN 0-8191-1303-4). U Pr of Amer.
Community & Privacy: Toward a New Architecture of Humanism. Serge Chermayeff & Christopher Alexander. LC 63-10704. 1963. pap. 2.50 (ISBN 0-385-03476-8, A474, Anch). Doubleday.
Community & Regional Planning: Issues in Public Policy. 3rd ed. Melvin R. Levin. LC 76-12862. (Special Studies). 1977. text ed. 29.95 (ISBN 0-275-23690-0); pap. 11.95 (ISBN 0-275-85740-9). Praeger.
Community & Revolution in Modern Vietnam. Alexander B. Woodside. LC 75-18429. (Illus.). 418p. 1976. pap. text ed. 14.75 (ISBN 0-395-20367-8). HM.
Community & Social Change in America. Thomas Bender. (Sanford-Erpf Lecture Ser.). 1978. 10.50 (ISBN 0-8135-0858-4). Rutgers U Pr.
Community & Society. Ferdinand Tonnies. Tr. by Charles P. Loomis. LC 57-8428. 1977. pap. text ed. 3.95x o.p. (ISBN 0-06-131116-2, TB1116, Torch). Har-Row.
Community & the Police: Conflict or Cooperation? Joseph Fink & Lloyd G. Sealy. LC 74-1144. 216p. 1974. 18.95 (ISBN 0-471-25894-6, Pub. by Wiley-Interscience). Wiley.
Community: Approaches & Applications. Ed. by Marcia P. Effrat. LC 73-16604. (Illus.). 1974. pap. text ed. 8.95 (ISBN 0-02-909300-7). Free Pr.
Community Associations: A Guide for Public Officials. C. James Dowden. LC 79-57077. (Community Association Ser.). (Illus.). 88p. 1980. pap. text ed. 13.50 (ISBN 0-87420-590-5, C18). Urban Land.
Community Associations & Centres: A Comparative Study. A. C. Twelvetrees. 146p. 1976. text ed. 23.00 (ISBN 0-08-019938-0); pap. text ed. 12.75 (ISBN 0-08-019937-2). Pergamon.
Community-Based Corrections. V. Fox. 1977. 15.95 (ISBN 0-13-153254-5). P-H.
Community Builders. Edward P. Eichler & Marshall Kaplan. (California Studies in Urbanization & Environmental Design). 1967. 14.50x (ISBN 0-520-00380-2). U of Cal Pr.
Community Care for the Mentally Disabled. Ed. by J. K. Wing & Rolf Olsen. (Illus.). 1979. pap. text ed. 14.95x (ISBN 0-19-261146-1). Oxford U Pr.
Community Centers & Student Unions. Eugene Sternberg & Barbara Sternberg. LC 70-151719. 1976. 31.50x (Van Nos Reinhold). Westview.
Community, Character & Civilization. Don Martindale. LC 63-13540. 1963. 10.95 o.s.i. (ISBN 0-02-920140-3). Free Pr.
Community College: Values, Vision & Vitality. Edmund J. Gleazer, Jr. 1980. pap. 6.50 (ISBN 0-87117-097-3). Am Assn Comm J Coll.
Community Competencies for the Handicapped: School Graduation Requirements: A Basis for Curriculum & IEP Development. Jim Stewart et al. 208p. 1978. spiral bdg. 14.50 (ISBN 0-398-03765-5). C C Thomas.
Community Conflict & the Press. Philip J. Tichenor et al. LC 79-24401. (People & Communication Ser.: Vol. 8). 240p. 1980. 20.00x (ISBN 0-8039-1425-3); pap. 9.95x (ISBN 0-8039-1426-1). Sage.
Community Control of Economic Development: The Boards of Directors of Community Development Corporations. Rita M. Kelly. LC 77-7814. (Praeger Special Studies). 1977. text ed. 23.95 (ISBN 0-03-022351-2). Praeger.
Community Control of Schools. Ed. by Henry M. Levin et al. (Studies in Social Economics). 318p. 1970. 12.95 (ISBN 0-8157-5224-5). Brookings.
Community Control: The Black Demand for Participation in Large American Cities. Alan Altshuler. LC 72-110439. 1970. pap. 5.50 (ISBN 0-672-63517-8). Pegasus.
Community Corrections. Hassim M. Solomon. (Criminal Justice Ser.). 442p. 1976. text ed. 16.50 (ISBN 0-205-04996-6, 824996-2); instr's manual free (ISBN 0-205-04997-4, 824997-0). Allyn.
Community Corrections: A Reader. Ed. by Burt Galaway et al. (Illus.). 324p. 1976. 22.50 (ISBN 0-398-03533-4). C C Thomas.
Community Counseling: A Human Services Approach. Judith A. Lewis & Michael D. Lewis. LC 76-15274. (Wiley Series in Counseling & Human Development). 1977. text ed. 19.95 (ISBN 0-471-53203-7). Wiley.
Community, Culture & Care: A Cross-Cultural Guide for Health Workers. Ann T. Brownlee. LC 77-16253. (Illus.). 1978. pap. text ed. 12.95 (ISBN 0-8016-0829-5). Mosby.
Community Decision-Making for Social Welfare: Federalism, City Government, & the Poor. Robert S. Magill. LC 79-301. 1979. text ed. 19.95 (ISBN 0-87705-378-2); pap. text ed. 8.95 (ISBN 0-87705-398-7). Human Sci Pr.
Community Dentistry: Contributions to New Directions. Clifton O. Dummett. (American Lectures in Dentistry). (Illus.). 232p. 1974. 18.75- (ISBN 0-398-02882-6). C C Thomas.
Community Development & Human Reproductive Behavior. Sawon Hong. 196p. 1979. text ed. 10.00x (ISBN 0-8248-0685-9, Korea Devel Inst). U Pr of Hawaii.
Community Development in America. James A. Christenson & Jerry W. Robinson, Jr. (Illus.). 256p. 1980. text ed. 8.95 (ISBN 0-8138-1475-8). Iowa St U Pr.
Community Development: Learning & Action. Hayden Roberts. LC 78-12986. 1979. 15.00x (ISBN 0-8020-5437-4); pap. 6.50 (ISBN 0-8020-6351-9). U of Toronto Pr.
Community Development: Theory & Method of Planned Change. Ed. by Dan A. Chekki. LC 79-907884. xiv, 258p. 1980. text ed. 18.95x (ISBN 0-7069-0819-8, Pub. by Vikas India). Advent Bk.
Community Dynamics & Mental Health. D. C. Klein. LC 68-8105. 1968. 19.95 (ISBN 0-471-49050-4, Pub. by Wiley-Interscience). Wiley.
Community Education & Urban Schools. John Boyd. LC 77-5912. 1977. pap. text ed. 6.95x (ISBN 0-582-48945-8). Longman.
Community Elite & the Public Library: Uses of Information in Leadership. Pauline Wilson. LC 76-15336. (Contributions in Librarianship & Information Science: No. 18). 1977. lib. bdg. 16.95 (ISBN 0-8371-9031-2, WCE/). Greenwood.
Community Groups in Action. Hugh Butcher et al. 272p. 1980. 30.00x (ISBN 0-7100-0617-9); pap. 15.00 (ISBN 0-7100-0618-7). Routledge & Kegan.
Community Health. 3rd ed. C. L. Anderson & Richard R. Morton. LC 77-23864. (Illus.). 1978. text ed. 15.95 (ISBN 0-8016-0182-7). Mosby.
Community Health. Andrew J. Brown. 255p. (Orig.). 1981. pap. text ed. write for info. (ISBN 0-8087-4040-7). Burgess.
Community Health: A Systems Approach. Braden. 1976. pap. 11.00 (ISBN 0-8385-1184-8). ACC.
Community Health & Nursing Practices. 2nd ed. Evelyn P. Benson & Joan Q. DeVitt. (Illus.). 1980. text ed. 16.95 (ISBN 0-13-153171-9). P-H.
Community Health Nursing. 2nd ed. Martha M. Borlick et al. (Nursing Examination Bk.: Vol. 9). 1974. spiral bdg. 5.00 o.p. (ISBN 0-87488-509-4). Med Exam.
Community Health Nursing. Ilse R. Leeser et al. (Nursing Outline Ser.). 1975. spiral bdg. 6.00 o.p. (ISBN 0-87488-382-2). Med Exam.
Community Health Nursing. Judith Sullivan et al. (Illus.). 384p. 1981. text ed. 15.00 (ISBN 0-86542-004-1). Blackwell Sci.
Community Health Nursing: Concepts & Practice. Barbara W. Spradley. 1981. text ed. price not set (ISBN 0-316-80748-6). Little.
Community Health Nursing Continuing Education Review. Kathleen B. Blomquist et al. 1979. pap. 9.50 (ISBN 0-87488-401-2). Med Exam.
Community Health Nursing: Keeping the Public Healthy. Linda L. Jarvis. LC 80-16953. (Illus.). 896p. 1980. 22.00 (ISBN 0-8036-4925-8). Davis Co.
Community Health Nursing Practice. 2nd ed. Ruth B. Freeman & Janet Heinrich. (Illus.). 500p. 1981. text ed. price not set (ISBN 0-7216-3877-5). Saunders.
Community Health Services. 2nd ed. Harold Herman & Mary E. McKay. LC 61-15342. (Municipal Management Ser). 1969. 20.00 (ISBN 0-87326-007-4). Intl City Mgt.
Community Hospital & Rural Accessibility. R. M. Haynes & C. G. Bentham. 1979. text ed. 24.00x (ISBN 0-566-00271-X, Pub. by Gower Pub Co England). Renouf.
Community Idea in Canada. M. Vrieze. 1966. pap. 1.25 o.p. (ISBN 0-686-11995-9). Wedge Pub.
Community in the Lord. Paul Hinnebusch. LC 75-14741. 240p. 1975. pap. 3.50 o.p. (ISBN 0-87793-099-6). Ave Maria.
Community Information: What Libraries Can Do. Ed. by Library Association-the Working Party on Community Information. 1980. pap. 9.25x (ISBN 0-85365-872-2, Pub. by Lib Assn England). Oryx Pr.
Community, Junior, & Technical Colleges: A Public Relations Sourcebook. new ed. William A Harper. LC 77-1993. (Illus.). 1977. text ed. 19.95 (ISBN 0-89116-043-4). Hemisphere Pub.
Community Leaders & Noteworthy Americans. 10th ed. Ed. by J. S. Thomson. 609p. 1980. 44.95x (ISBN 0-934544-02-6, Pub. by Intl Biog). Biblio Dist.
Community Living Skill Book. Boy Scouts of America. 1976. pap. 0.50x (ISBN 0-8395-6583-6); tchr's guide 0.30 (ISBN 0-685-73154-5, 18-323). BSA.
Community Media Handbook. 2nd ed. A. C. Zelmer. LC 79-12989. (Illus.). 430p. 1979. 16.50 (ISBN 0-8108-1223-1). Scarecrow.
Community Medicine: Some New Perspectives. Rodney M. Coe & Max Pepper. (Illus.). 1978. pap. text ed. 10.95 (ISBN 0-07-011548-6, HP). McGraw.
Community Mental Health. A. W. Burgess & Lazare. LC 75-37561. 256p. 1976. 16.95x (ISBN 0-13-153148-4). P-H.
Community Mental Health: A Sourcebook for Professionals & Advisors. Wade H. Silverman. 450p. 1981. 39.95 (ISBN 0-03-057006-9). Praeger.
Community Mental Health & the Criminal Justice System. Ed. by John Monahan. 350p. 1976. pap. text ed. 12.75 (ISBN 0-08-018758-7). Pergamon.
Community Mental Health & the Law: An Annotated Bibliography. Steven J. Schwartz & Stephen F. Ferrarone. LC 80-18872. 256p. 1981. 22.50x (ISBN 0-8290-0239-1). Irvington.
Community Mental Health Center-an Interim Appraisal, 1969. R. M. Glasscote & J. N. Sussex. 156p. 1969. text ed. 8.00 (ISBN 0-685-31185-6, P206-0); pap. 5.00 (ISBN 0-685-31186-4, P206-1). Am Psychiatric.
Community Mental Health Centers. (Task Force Report: No. 4). 1972. 5.00 (ISBN 0-685-37537-4, P185-0). Am Psychiatric.
Community Mental Health Centers: A Decade Later. Naomi Naierman et al. LC 78-67184. 1978. 15.00x (ISBN 0-89011-510-9). Abt Assoc.
Community Mental Health Nursing: An Ecological Perspective. Ed. by Jeanette Lancaster. LC 79-26185. (Illus.). 1980. pap. text ed. 10.95 (ISBN 0-8016-2816-4). Mosby.
Community Newspaper: Front Office Worker. Larry Notman. (Illus.). 1978. pap. 4.00x (ISBN 0-918488-07-9). Newspaper Serv.
Community Newspaper Management: Starting Out. Larry Notman. 1981. pap. 10.00x (ISBN 0-918488-10-9). Newspaper Serv.
Community Nursing Manual: A Guide for Auxiliary Public Health Nurses. Elizabeth J. Leedam. (McGraw-Hill International Health Ser.). (Illus.). 1977. pap. text ed. 6.95 o.p. (ISBN 0-07-099412-9, C). McGraw.
Community Nutrition. Wright & Sims. 1981. pap. text ed. 11.95 (ISBN 0-686-69107-5). Duxbury Pr.
Community of Character: Toward a Constructive Christian Social Ethic. Stanley Hauerwas. LC 80-53072. 320p. 1981. text ed. 20.00 (ISBN 0-268-00733-0). U of Notre Dame Pr.
Community of Interest. Oscar Newman. (Illus.). 368p. 1981. pap. 8.95 (ISBN 0-385-11124-X, Anch). Doubleday.

Community of Scapegoats: The Segregation of Sex Offenders & Informers in Prisons. Philip Priestley. 150p. 1980. 24.00 (ISBN 0-08-025231-1). Pergamon.
Community on the American Frontier: Separate but Not Alone. Robert V. Hine. LC 80-5238. (Illus.). 300p. 1980. 12.50 (ISBN 0-8061-1678-1). U of Okla Pr.
Community Oral Health: A Systems Approach for the Dental Health Profession. Patricia P. Cormier & Joyce I. Levy. 240p. 1980. pap. 14.95x (ISBN 0-8385-1184-8). ACC.
Community Organization & Social Planning. Robert Perlman & Arnold Gurin. LC 71-177887. 1972. 17.95 (ISBN 0-471-68050-8). Wiley.
Community Organization in Religious Education. Hugh Hartshorne & J. Q. Miller. 1932. 37.50x (ISBN 0-686-51356-8). Elliots Bks.
Community Organizing. George Brager & Harry Specht. (Social Work & Social Issues Ser). 1973. 17.50x (ISBN 0-231-03393-1). Columbia U Pr.
Community Participation in Education. Carl A. Grant. 1978. text ed. 16.95x (ISBN 0-205-06052-8). Allyn.
Community Placement of the Mentally Retarded: A Handbook for Community Agencies and Social Work Practitioners. Richard A. Mamula & Nate Newman. (Illus.). 156p. 1973. 10.75 (ISBN 0-398-02704-8); pap. 6.75 (ISBN 0-398-02761-7). C C Thomas.
Community Police Administration. Peter C. Unsinger & Jack L. Kuykendall. LC 75-2119. (Nelson-Hall Law Enforcement Ser.). 475p. 1975. 19.95 (ISBN 0-88229-158-0). Nelson-Hall.
Community Policing. Evelyn B. Schaffer. 145p. 1980. 25.00x (ISBN 0-85664-939-2, Pub. by Croom Helm Ltd England). Biblio Dist.
Community Power & Decision Making: An International Handbook. Irving P. Leif. LC 74-4171. 1974. 10.00 (ISBN 0-8108-0717-3). Scarecrow.
Community Power Succession. Floyd Hunter. LC 79-305. 220p. 1980. 15.00x o.p. (ISBN 0-8078-1314-1); pap. 9.00x o.p. (ISBN 0-8078-4067-X). U of NC Pr.
Community Power Succession: Atlanta's Policy Makers Revisited. Floyd Hunter. 220p. 1980. 15.00x (ISBN 0-8078-1314-1); pap. 9.00x (ISBN 0-8078-4067-X). U of NC Pr.
Community Press in an Urban Setting: The Social Elements of Urbanism. 2nd ed. Morris Janowitz. LC 67-21391. 1967. 8.00x o.s.i. (ISBN 0-226-39312-7). U of Chicago Pr.
Community Property in the U. S. A Comparative Study by Cases, Materials & Problems. William A. Reppy & William Q. De Funiack. (Contemporary Legal Education Ser). 1975. 22.00 (ISBN 0-672-82067-6, Bobbs-Merrill Law); 1979 suppl. 4.00 (ISBN 0-672-83855-9). Michie.
Community Psychology. Philip A. Mann. LC 77-83164. 1978. text ed. 17.95 (ISBN 0-02-920000-8). Free Pr.
Community Psychology & Coordination. Penland & Williams. Date not set. price not set (ISBN 0-8247-6144-8). Dekker.
Community Psychology & Social Systems. Stanley Murrell. LC 73-8504. 228p. 1973. text ed. 14.95 (ISBN 0-87705-108-9). Human Sci Pr.
Community Psychology Concept: Integrating Theory, Education & Practice in Psychology, Social Work & Public Administration. Ernest R. Myers. 1977. pap. text ed. 9.00x (ISBN 0-8191-0291-1). U Pr of Amer.
Community Psychology: Theoretical & Empirical Approaches. Margaret S. Gibbs & Juliana R. Lachenmeyer. Ed. by Janet Sigal. LC 79-13755. 1980. 24.95x (ISBN 0-470-26787-9). Halsted Pr.
Community Relations & Criminal Justice. Charles P. McDowell. 500p. Date not set. text ed. price not set (ISBN 0-87084-558-6). Anderson Pub Co.
Community Relations & Riot Prevention. Raymond M. Momboisse. (Illus.). 272p. 1974. 13.75 (ISBN 0-398-01324-1). C C Thomas.
Community Relations & the Administration of Justice. 2nd ed. P. D. Mayhall & D. P. Geary. LC 78-135200. 1979. text ed. 17.50x (ISBN 0-471-04135-1); tchrs. manual avail. (ISBN 0-471-05311-2); study guide avail. (ISBN 0-471-05314-7). Wiley.
Community Resource Person's Guide for Experience-Based Learning. 1977. 1.75 (ISBN 0-89354-605-4). Northwest Regional.
Community Resources. Rulon K. Wood. Ed. by James E. Duane. LC 80-20963. (Instructional Media Library: Vol. 2). (Illus.). 96p. 1981. 13.95 (ISBN 0-87778-162-1). Educ Tech Pubns.
Community Revitalization. Ed. by Gerald F. Whittaker. 1979. pap. 5.00 o.p. (ISBN 0-87712-192-3). U Mich Busn Div Res.
Community School in Yugoslavia. Stevan Bezdanov. (Experiments & Innovations in Education Ser., No. 6). 40p. (Orig.). 1974. pap. 2.50 (ISBN 92-3-101130-8, U92, UNESCO). Unipub.
Community Services. Patience Barefoot. 1977. pap. 7.95 (ISBN 0-571-11052-5, Pub. by Faber & Faber). Merrimack Bk Serv.
Community Structure & Trade at Isthmus Cove: A Salvage Excavation on Catalina Island (Calif.) W. Patrick Finnerty et al. (Pacific Coast Archaeological Society Occasional Papers: No. 1). 81p. 1981. pap. 2.95. Acoma Bks.
Community, Technical, & Junior College in the United States. 96p. 1978. 3.50 (IIE). Unipub.
Community Technology. Karl Hess. LC 78-15828. 1979. pap. 3.50x (ISBN 0-06-090689-8, TB 1958, Torch). Har-Row.
Community Technology. Karl Hess. LC 78-15828. 1979. 7.95 o.p. (ISBN 0-06-011874-1, HarpT). Har-Row.
Community Treatment & Social Control: A Critical Analysis of Juvenile Correctional Policy. Paul Lerman. LC 74-11629. (Studies in Crime & Justice). xvi, 254p. 1975. 12.50x o.s.i. (ISBN 0-226-47307-4). U of Chicago Pr.
Community Work & Social Work. Peter Baldock. (Library of Social Work Ser.). 1974. 12.50x (ISBN 0-7100-8026-3); pap. 7.95 (ISBN 0-7100-8027-1). Routledge & Kegan.
Community Worker. James B. Taylor & Jerry Randolph. LC 74-34067. 148p. 1975. 17.50x (ISBN 0-87668-191-7). Aronson.
Community's Children. Ed. by Jessie Parfit. 1967. pap. text ed. 2.50x (ISBN 0-582-32417-3). Humanities.
Commutative Algebra. James T. Knight. LC 76-152625. (London Mathematical Society Lecture Notes Ser.: No. 5). (Illus.). 1971. pap. 14.50 (ISBN 0-521-08193-9). Cambridge U Pr.
Commutative Normed Rings. Israel M. Gelfand et al. LC 61-15024. 1964. 13.95 (ISBN 0-8284-0170-5). Chelsea Pub.
Como Aprovechar el Tiempo. Tr. by Ted W. Engstrom & R. A. McKenzie. (Spanish Bks.). (Span.). 1978. 1.50 (ISBN 0-8297-0518-X). Vida Pub.
Como Dominar la Tension Nerviosa. Clyde Narramore & Ruth Narramore. Tr. by Rhode Ward from Eng. 216p. (Orig., Span.). 1978. pap. 3.95 (ISBN 0-89922-129-7). Edit Caribe.
Como Fundar Iglesias. Tr. by Melvin Hodges. (Spanish Bks.). (Span.). 1978. 1.50 (ISBN 0-8297-0560-0). Life Pubs Intl.
Como Iniciar la Vida Cristiana. new ed. George Sweeting. Tr. by Alec Clifford from Eng. (Editorial Moody - Spanish Publications Ser.). 1977. pap. 1.95 (ISBN 0-8024-1615-2). Moody.
Como Leer Y Orar los Evangelios. Marilyn Norquist. Ed. by John McPhee. Tr. by Olimpia Diaz from Eng. (Handbook of the Bible Ser.). Orig. Title: Hand. 64p. 1980. pap. 1.50 (ISBN 0-89243-127-X). Liguori Pubns.
Como Leon Rugiente. Tr. by Jorge Otis. (Spanish Bks.). (Span.). 1978. 1.90 (ISBN 0-8297-0516-3). Life Pubs Intl.
Como los Ejecutivos Toman Decisiones. Alexander Hamilton Institute, Inc. Ed. by James M. Jenks. (Illus.). 79p. (Orig., Span.). 1976. pap. 43.75 (ISBN 0-86604-006-4). Hamilton Inst.
Como Mantener Tu Volkswagen Vivo. rev. ed. John Muir. Tr. by Virginia Holt from Eng. LC 75-21414. (Illus.). 1980. pap. 9.00 (ISBN 0-912528-21-4). John Muir.
Como Me Sacaras De Este Apuro, Senor? 1979. pap. 1.75 (ISBN 0-686-69350-7). Vida Pubs.
Como Obtener la Plenitud Del Poder. R. A. Torrey. Tr. by Jose G. Rivas from Eng. Orig. Title: How to Obtain Fullness of Power. 112p. (Span.). Date not set. pap. price not set (ISBN 0-311-46083-6). Casa Bautista.
Como Preparse Para la Prueba De Aptitud Academia y la Prueba De Aprovechamiento Academico, De Barron. Brownstein & Weiner. (Span. ed.). Date not set. pap. 4.95 (ISBN 0-8120-0593-7). Barron.
Como Se Dice. Ana C. Jarvis et al. 1976. text ed. 16.95x (ISBN 0-669-00192-9); instructor's manual free (ISBN 0-669-00357-3); wkbk. 5.95x (ISBN 0-669-00189-9); reels 70.00 (ISBN 0-669-00191-0); cassettes 70.00 (ISBN 0-669-00358-1). Heath.
Como Ser Encantadora (Para Alumna) Emily Hunter. Tr. by Wilma Mendoza De Mann & F. A. Mariotti. Orig. Title: Christian Charm Notebook. (Illus.). 56p. (Span.). Date not set. pap. price not set (ISBN 0-311-46054-2). Casa Bautista.
Como Ser Feliz En el Matrimonio. Elam J. Daniels. Orig. Title: How to Be Happily Married. 96p. 1979. pap. 1.65 (ISBN 0-311-46066-6). Casa Bautista.
Como Ser un Triunfador. Tr. by Harold Hill. (Spanish Bks.). (Span.). 1977. 1.90 (ISBN 0-8297-0750-6). Life Pubs Intl.
Como Servencedor. Tr. by Harold Hill. (Portuguese Bks.). 1979. 1.40 (ISBN 0-8297-0824-3). Life Pubs Intl.
Como Vencer a Depressao. Tr. by Tim LaHaye. (Portuguese Bks.). 1979. 1.50 (ISBN 0-8297-0648-8). Life Pubs Intl.
Como Vencer la Depresion. Tr. by Tim LaHaye. (Spanish Bks.). (Span.). 1978. 1.95 (ISBN 0-8297-0515-5). Life Pubs Intl.
Como Vivir Como un Hijo Del Rey. Tr. by Harold Hill. (Spanish Bks.). (Span.). 1978. 1.90 (ISBN 0-8297-0517-1). Life Pubs Intl.
Comodiae, 2 Vols. Aristophanes. Ed. by F. W. Hall & W. M. Geldart. (Oxford Classical Texts Ser). Vol. 1. 18.95x (ISBN 0-19-814504-7); Vol. 2. 16.95x (ISBN 0-19-814505-5). Oxford U Pr.
Comoediae, 2 Vols. Plautus. Ed. by W. M. Lindsay. 1905. Vol. 1. 24.00x (ISBN 0-19-814628-0); Vol. 2. 22.50x (ISBN 0-19-814629-9). Oxford U Pr.
Comoediae. 2nd ed. Terence. Ed. by R. Kauer & W. M. Lindsay. (Oxford Classical Texts Ser). 1926. 18.95x (ISBN 0-19-814636-1). Oxford U Pr.
COMP: Exercises in Comprehension & Composition. L. G. Alexander & E. T. Cornelius, Jr. (Illus.). 1978. pap. text ed. 2.95x (ISBN 0-582-79703-9). Longman.
Comp-Lab Exercises: Self-Teaching Exercises for Basic Writing. Mary Epes et al. 1980. pap. text ed. 11.95 (ISBN 0-13-153601-X). P-H.
Compact Anthology of Bartlett's Quotations. Theodore B. Backer. LC 74-1964. 1974. 8.95 o.p. (ISBN 0-685-50518-9). Jonathan David.
Compact Bible Reference Library, 4 vols. Incl. Cruden's Compact Concordance. Alexander Cruden; The New Compact Bible Dictionary. Thomas A. Bryant. (Illus.); Halley's Bible Handbook. H. H. Halley. (Illus.); Compact Topical Bible. Set. 32.80 (ISBN 0-310-35258-4). Zondervan.
Compact Convex Sets & Boundary Integrals. E. M. Alfsen. LC 72-136352. (Ergebnisse der Mathematik und Ihrer Grenzgebiete: Vol. 57). (Illus.). 1971. 27.60 (ISBN 0-387-05090-6). Springer-Verlag.
Compact Edition of the Handbook of the Birds of India & Pakistan, Together with Those of Bangladesh, Nepal, Bhutan & Sri Lanka. Salim Ali & Dillon Ripley. (Illus.). 816p. 1980. 96.95 (ISBN 0-19-561245-0). Oxford U Pr.
Compact Guide to Bible Based Beliefs. Thayer S. Warshaw. LC 80-19820. 49p. (Orig.). 1981. pap. 1.50 (ISBN 0-687-09254-X). Abingdon.
Compact Treasury of Inspiration. Compiled by Ken S. Giniger. (Orig.). pap. 1.95 (ISBN 0-89129-229-2). Jove Pubns.
Compadre Colonialism: Studies on the Philippines Under American Rule. Ed. by Norman G. Owen. LC 75-175623. (Michigan Papers on South & Southeast Asia: No. 3). (Illus.). 252p. 1971. pap. 4.00x o.p. (ISBN 0-89148-003-X). Ctr S&SE Asian.
Companies Holding Boiler & Pressure Vessel Certificates of Authorization for Use of Code Symbol Stamps: 1980 Edition, Three Issues. 1978. 675.00 (EX0052). ASME.
Companies Holding Boiler & Pressure Vessel Certificates of Authorization for Use of Code Symbol Stamps: 1980 Edition-Three Issues, No. EX0052. 1980. 75.00. ASME.
Companion Guide to London. David Piper. LC 77-72102. 1977. pap. 6.95 o.p. (ISBN 0-684-14954-0, ScribT). Scribner.
Companion Guide to Paris. Vincent Cronin. (Illus.). 1977. pap. 6.95 o.p. (ISBN 0-684-14952-4, SL 708, ScribT). Scribner.
Companion Guide to the South of France. Archibald Lyall. (Illus.). 1977. pap. 6.95 o.p. (ISBN 0-684-14955-9, SL705, ScribT). Scribner.
Companion Guide to Venice. Hugh Honour. LC 77-72101. (Encore Edition). 1977. pap. 2.95 (ISBN 0-684-16902-9, ScribT). Scribner.
Companion to Arber: Being a Calendar of Documents in Edward Arber's Transcript of the Registers of the Company of Stationers of London, 1554-1640. Ed. by Walter W. Greg. 1967. 20.50x o.p. (ISBN 0-19-818125-6). Oxford U Pr.
Companion to Biochemistry, Vol. 2. Ed. by Alan T. Bull et al. (Illus.). 1979. text ed. 35.00 (ISBN 0-582-46029-8). Longman.
Companion to Biochemistry: Selected Topics for Further Study, Vol. 1. Ed. by Alan T. Bull et al. J. R. Lagnado & J. O. Thomas. (Illus.). 432p. 1974. text ed. 26.00 (ISBN 0-582-46004-2). Longman.
Companion to California. James D. Hart. LC 76-57286. 1978. 27.50 (ISBN 0-19-502400-1). Oxford U Pr.
Companion to Cornucopia. John F. Froehlich. 1980. 6.50 (ISBN 0-8233-0321-7). Golden Quill.
Companion to Foreign Language Composition. Rose M. Alent. LC 73-75127. (German-English Guidebook to Literary Terms: Vol. 1). 143p. (Orig.). 1973. pap. text ed. 5.75x (ISBN 90-6203-337-7). Humanities.
Companion to Hymns of Faith & Life. Lawrence R. Schoenhals. (Orig.). 1980. pap. 9.95 (ISBN 0-89367-040-5). Light & Life.
Companion to Microbiology: Selected Topics for Further Study. Ed. by Alan T. Bull & Pauline M. Meadow. (Illus.). 1978. text ed. 33.00 (ISBN 0-582-46067-0). Longman.
Companion to Mozart's Piano Concertos. 2nd ed. Arthur Hutchings. 1950. 14.95x (ISBN 0-19-318404-4). Oxford U Pr.
Companion to Narnia. Paul Ford. LC 80-7734. (Illus.). 304p. 1980. 12.95 (ISBN 0-06-250340-5, HarpR). Har-Row.
Companion to Plato's Republic. Nicholas P. White. LC 78-70043. 1979. 16.50 (ISBN 0-915144-56-5); pap. text ed. 7.95 (ISBN 0-915144-92-1). Hackett Pub.
Companion to Shakespeare Studies. Harley Granville-Barker & George B. Harrison. 1934. 63.00 (ISBN 0-521-05132-0). Cambridge U Pr.
Companion to Shakespeare: The Non-Shakespearean Elizabethan Drama - An Introduction. Robert E. Adams. LC 78-58821. 1978. pap. text ed. 9.50 (ISBN 0-8191-0540-6). U Pr of Amer.
Companion to the Bible. Abraham J. Feldman. LC 64-20096. 3.00x (ISBN 0-8197-0078-9). Bloch.
Companion to The Cantos of Ezra Pound, Volume I, (Cantos 1-71) Carroll F. Terrell. 800p. 1980. 28.50x (ISBN 0-520-03687-5). U of Cal Pr.
Companion to the Good News: New Testament. Joseph Rhymer & Anthony Bullen. (Fount Religious Paperbacks Ser). 1976. pap. 1.95 (ISBN 0-00-624742-3, FA4742, Pub. by Collins Pubs). World Bible.
Companion to the Good News, Old Testament. Joseph Rhymer & Anthony Bullen. (Fount Religious Paperbacks Ser.). 1976. pap. 1.95 (ISBN 0-00-623354-6, FA3354, Pub. by Collins Pubs). World Bible.
Companion to the Hymnal. Fred D. Gealy et al. 1970. 14.95 (ISBN 0-687-09259-0). Abingdon.
Companion to the "Iliad". Malcolm M. Willcock. Tr. by Richmond Lattimore. LC 75-20894. (Illus.). 302p. 1976. 15.00x (ISBN 0-226-89854-7). U of Chicago Pr.
Companion to the "Iliad". Malcolm M. Willcock. LC 75-20894. 1976. pap. 6.95 (ISBN 0-226-89855-5, P677, Phoen). U of Chicago Pr.
Companion to the New Testament the Gospels. A. E. Harvey. 400p. 1972. pap. 7.95 (ISBN 0-521-09689-8). Cambridge U Pr.
Companion to William Carlos Williams' Paterson. Benjamin Sankey. LC 72-121193. (Illus.). 1971. 21.50x (ISBN 0-520-01742-0). U of Cal Pr.
Companions of Our Youth: Stories by Women for Young People's Magazines, 1865-1900. Ed. by Jane Benardete & Phyllis Moe. LC 80-5339. (Illus.). 1980. 12.95 (ISBN 0-8044-2043-2); pap. 5.95 (ISBN 0-8044-6047-7). Ungar.
Company. Samuel Beckett. LC 80-995. 64p. 1980. 8.95 (ISBN 0-394-51394-0, GP 833). Grove.
Company Accounts. 2nd ed. J. O.. Magee. 386p. 1978. pap. 12.95x (ISBN 0-7121-0384-8, Pub. by Macdonald & Evans England). Intl Ideas.
Company Administration Handbook. 4th ed. 832p. 1980. text ed. 69.75x (ISBN 0-566-02154-4, Pub. by Gower Pub Co England). Renouf.
Company Finance & the Capital Market. E. W. Davis & K. A. Yeomans. LC 74-16990. (Department of Applied Economics, Occasional Papers Ser.: No. 39). (Illus.). 200p. 1975. 25.50 (ISBN 0-521-20144-6); pap. 13.50x (ISBN 0-521-09792-4). Cambridge U Pr.
Company Financial Reporting: The Measurement & Communication of Accounting Information. T. A. Lee. 1976. text ed. 24.00x (ISBN 0-17-761041-7). Intl Ideas.
Company Financing in the U.K. A Flow of Funds Model. A. D. Bain et al. 1975. 28.00x (ISBN 0-85520-094-4, Pub by Martin Robertson England). Biblio Dist.
Company I've Kept: Essays in Autobiography. Hugh MacDiarmid. 1967. 17.50x (ISBN 0-520-00783-2). U of Cal Pr.
Company Law & Capitalism. 2nd ed. Tom Hadden. (Law in Context Ser.). 1977. 25.00x (ISBN 0-297-77334-8, Pub. by Weidenfeld & Nicolson). Rothman.
Company Law & Capitalism. 2nd ed. Tom Hadden. (Law in Context Ser.). 1977. 25.00x (ISBN 0-297-77334-8, Pub. by Weidenfeld & Nicolson England). Rothman.
Company Law in Europe. 1976. loose leaf 45.00 o.p. (ISBN 0-7161-0285-4, Gower). Unipub.
Company of the Committed. Elton Trueblood. LC 61-12834. 1961. 3.95 (ISBN 0-06-068551-4, RD 317, HarpR). Har-Row.
Company of Women. Mary Gordon. 1981. 12.95 (ISBN 0-394-50508-5). Random.
Company Organization: Theory & Practice. M. C. Barnes et al. (Unwin Professional Management Library). 1970. text ed. 10.95x o.p. (ISBN 0-04-658031-X). Allen Unwin.

Company Planning Meetings, Report No. 788. Rochelle O'Connor. (Illus.). v, 50p. (Orig.). 1980. pap. 15.00 (ISBN 0-8237-0224-3). Conference Bd.

Company Shops, North Carolina: The Town Built by a Railroad. Durward T. Stokes. 1981. 12.95 (ISBN 0-89587-016-9). Blair. Postponed.

Company's Comin' (Cookbook) George A. McKenzie & Sadie Gregory. (Lucas Text Ser). text ed. 3.95x (ISBN 0-87543-088-0). Lucas.

Comparability of Engineering Courses & Degrees: A Methodological Study. (Studies on International Equivalences of Degrees). 92p. (Orig.). 1975. pap. 6.00 (ISBN 92-3-101165-0, U95, UNESCO). Unipub.

Comparable Worth: Issues & Alternatives. Ed. by E. Robert Livernash. LC 80-67644. 260p. 1980. 21.00 (ISBN 0-937856-01-0). Equal Employ.

Comparation of a Vyrgin & a Martyr, 1537. Desiderius Erasmus. Tr. by Thomas Paynell from Latin. LC 70-101148. 1970. Repr. of 1537 ed. 20.00x (ISBN 0-8201-1072-8). Schol Facsimiles.

Comparative Accounting Theory. D. L. McDonald. 1972. pap. text ed. 6.50 (ISBN 0-201-04535-4). A-W.

Comparative Adult Education. W. J. Harris. (Illus.). 240p. 1981. pap. text ed. 14.95 (ISBN 0-582-29510-6). Longman.

Comparative Afro-American: An Historical-Comparative Study of English-Based Afro-American Dialects of the New World. Mervyne C. Alleyne. (Linguistica Extranea: Studia: No. 11). 220p. pap. 8.50 (ISBN 0-89720-032-2). Karoma.

Comparative Analysis of Complex Organizations. rev. ed. Amitai Etzioni. LC 74-21488. 1975. 19.95 (ISBN 0-02-909650-2); pap. text ed. 10.95 (ISBN 0-02-909620-0). Free Pr.

Comparative Analysis of the Italians & the Jews: The Two People Who Contributed the Most to the Civilization of Mankind with Strange & Unexpected Conclusions. Maxwell Kent. (Illus.). 1977. 47.75 (ISBN 0-89266-056-2). Am Classical Coll Pr.

Comparative Anatomy of Domestic Animals: A Guide. Bonnie Beaver. (Illus.). 180p. 1980. pap. 9.95 (ISBN 0-8138-1545-2). Iowa St U Pr.

Comparative Anatomy of Domestic Animals: A Guide. Bonnie V. Beaver. (Illus.). 209p. pap. 9.95 (ISBN 0-8138-1545-2). Iowa St U Pr.

Comparative Anatomy of the Male Genital Tube in Coleoptera. Sharp & Muir. (Illus.). 304p. 1969. 16.70 (ISBN 0-686-09300-3). Entomol Soc.

Comparative Anatomy of the Nervous System of Vertebrates Including Man, 3 vols. 2nd ed. C. U. Ariens et al. (Illus.). 1845p. 1936. 97.50 (ISBN 0-02-840400-9). Hafner.

Comparative Anatomy of the Vertebrates. 4th ed. George C. Kent. LC 77-13588. (Illus.). 1978. text ed. 21.95 (ISBN 0-8016-2650-1). Mosby.

Comparative Anatomy, Pathology, & Roentgenology of the Breast. Helen Ingleby & Jacob Gershon-Cohen. LC 59-8457. 1960. 10.00 o.p. (ISBN 0-8122-7279-X). U of Pa Pr.

Comparative & International Library Science. Ed. by John F. Harvey. LC 77-8923. 1977. 14.50 (ISBN 0-8108-1060-3). Scarecrow.

Comparative & Veterinary Medicine: A Bibliography of Resource Literature. Ed. by Ann E. Kerker & Henry T. Murphy. LC 72-7989. 224p. 1973. 29.50x (ISBN 0-299-06330-5). U of Wis Pr.

Comparative Animal Behavior. Richard A. Maier & Barbara M. Maier. LC 78-95056. (Core Bks. in Psychology Ser.). 1970. text ed. 14.95 o.p. (ISBN 0-685-07578-8). Brooks-Cole.

Comparative Anthology of Musical Forms, 2 vols. David Ward - Steinman & Susan L. Ward - Steinman. 1976. pap. text ed. 15.95x ea. (ISBN 0-685-69709-6); Vol. 1. (ISBN 0-534-00439-3); Vol. 2. (ISBN 0-534-00459-8). Wadsworth Pub.

Comparative Archeology of Early Mesopotamia. Ann L. Perkins. LC 49-10748. (Studies in Ancient Oriental Civilization: No. 25). (Illus.). xx, 201p. (Orig.). 1977. pap. text ed. 14.00x (ISBN 0-226-62396-3). Oriental Inst.

Comparative Aspects of Neuroendocrine Control of Behavior. Ed. by C. Valverde-Rodriguez & H. Arechiga. (Frontiers of Hormone Research: Vol. 6). (Illus.). 1980. 58.75 (ISBN 3-8055-0571-X). S Karger.

Comparative Behavior of Bees & Onagraceae. V. Camissonia & Oenothera Bees of Cismontane California. E. G. Linsley et al. (U. C. Publ. in Entomology: Vol. 71). 1973. pap. 8.50x (ISBN 0-520-09474-3). U of Cal Pr.

Comparative Biochemistry: A Comprehensive Treatise, 7 vols. Ed. by Marcel Florkin & Howard S. Mason. Incl. Vol. 1. Sources of Free Energy. 1960. 50.50 (ISBN 0-12-261001-6); Vol. 2. Free Energy & Biological Function. 1960. 50.50 (ISBN 0-12-261002-4); Vol. 3. Constituents of Life. 1962. 71.50 (ISBN 0-12-261003-2); Vol. 4. Constituents of Life. 1962. 66.25 (ISBN 0-12-261004-0); Vol. 5. Constituents of Life. 1963. 50.50 (ISBN 0-12-261005-9); Vol. 6. Cells & Organisms. 1963. 50.50 (ISBN 0-12-261006-7); Vol. 7. Supplementary Volume. 1964. 48.50 (ISBN 0-12-261007-5). LC 67-23158. Set. 315.00 (ISBN 0-685-23113-5). Acad Pr.

Comparative Clinical Haematology. Ed. by R. K. Archer & L. B. Jeffcott. 1977. 64.00x o.p. (ISBN 0-397-60454-8, Blackwell Scientific). Mosby.

Comparative Communism: The Soviet, Chinese, & Yugoslav Models. Ed. by Gary K. Bertsch & Thomas W. Ganschow. LC 75-20464. (Illus.). 1976. text ed. 21.95x (ISBN 0-7167-0733-0); pap. text ed. 10.95x (ISBN 0-7167-0732-2). W H Freeman.

Comparative Correlative Neuroanatomy of the Vertebrate Telencephalon. Ed. by Elizabeth C. Crosby & H. N. Schnitzlein. (Illus.). 1981. text ed. 65.00 (ISBN 0-02-325690-7). Macmillan.

Comparative Criminal Law in the United States. Gerhard O. Mueller. (New York University Criminal Law Education Research Center Monograph: No. 4). (Illus.). 72p. 1970. pap. text ed. 8.50x (ISBN 0-8377-0827-3). Rothman.

Comparative Criminology: A Text Book, 2 vols. Hermann Mannheim. (International Library of Sociology). 1970. Repr. of 1965 ed. 22.00x ea. Vol. 1 (ISBN 0-7100-3458-X). Vol. 2 (ISBN 0-7100-3483-0). Routledge & Kegan.

Comparative Criticism: A Yearbook, Vol. 1. Ed. by E. S. Shaffer. 1980. 32.50 (ISBN 0-521-22296-6). Cambridge U Pr.

Comparative Criticism: A Yearbook, Vol. 2. Ed. by E. S. Shaffer. 350p. 1980. 39.50 (ISBN 0-521-22756-9). Cambridge U Pr.

Comparative Development in Social Welfare. Ed. by E. W. Martin. 1972. text ed. 25.00x (ISBN 0-04-361014-5). Allen Unwin.

Comparative Dictionary of the Indo-Aryan Languages. Sir Ralph Turner. 862p. 1966. text ed. 69.00x (ISBN 0-19-713550-1). Oxford U Pr.

Comparative Ecology. 2nd ed. Y. Ito. Tr. by J. Kikkawa. LC 79-41581. (Illus.) 350p. Date not set. text ed. 54.00 (ISBN 0-521-22977-4); pap. text ed. 19.95 (ISBN 0-521-29845-8). Cambridge U Pr.

Comparative Economic History of Latin America, 1500-1914. Laura Randall. Incl. Vol. 2. Argentina. 18.75 (ISBN 0-8357-0272-3, SS-00043); Vol. 3. Brazil. 18.75 (ISBN 0-8357-0273-1, SS-00044); Vol. 4. Peru. 16.75 (ISBN 0-8357-0274-X, SS-00045). LC 77-81283. 1977. Univ Microfilms.

Comparative Economic Planning. Marvin E. Rozen. Ed. by David E. Novack. (Studies in Economics). 1967. pap. text ed. 2.95x o.p. (ISBN 0-669-46557-7). Heath.

Comparative Economic Systems. Paul Gregory & Robert Stuart. LC 79-87859. 1980. 17.75 (ISBN 0-395-28183-0); inst. manual 0.40 (ISBN 0-395-28184-9). HM.

Comparative Economic Systems: A Decision-Making Approach. Egon Neuberger & William J. Duffy. 384p. 1976. text ed. 20.95x (ISBN 0-205-04850-1). Allyn.

Comparative Economic Systems: Competing Ways to Stability, Growth & Welfare. 2nd ed. Allan G. Gruchy. LC 76-10899. (Illus.). 1977. text ed. 20.95 (ISBN 0-395-18606-4). HM.

Comparative Economic Systems: Models & Cases. 4th ed. Ed. by Morris Bornstein. 1979. text ed. 18.50x (ISBN 0-256-02152-X). Irwin.

Comparative Education: Some Considerations of Method. Brian Holmes. (Unwin Education Bks.). (Illus.). 1981. text ed. 22.50 (ISBN 0-04-370101-9, 2624/5); pap. text ed. 9.50 (ISBN 0-04-370102-7). Allen Unwin.

Comparative Educational Systems. Ed. by Edward Ignas & Raymond J. Corsini. LC 80-52449. 450p. 1981. text ed. 12.50 (ISBN 0-87581-260-0). Peacock Pubs.

Comparative Endocrinology, 2 vols. Ed. by U. S. Von Euler & H. Heller. Incl. Vol. 1. Glandular Hormones. 52.00 o.p. (ISBN 0-12-724901-X); Vol. 2. Invertebrate Hormones, Tissue Hormones. 36.00 o.s.i. (ISBN 0-12-724902-8). 1963. Acad Pr.

Comparative Epidemiology: A Tool for Better Disease Management. 122p. 1981. pap. 33.25 (ISBN 90-220-0721-9, PDC 212, Pudoc). Unipub.

Comparative Essays in Chinese Literature. Ed. by Marsha Wagner & James W. Miller. 1981. text ed. 20.00 (ISBN 0-89581-453-6, Asian Humanities). Lancaster-Miller.

Comparative Excellence & Obligation of Moral & Positive Duties, 1731. Thomas Chubb. Ed. by Rene Wellek. LC 75-11205. (British Philosophers & Theologians of the 17th & 18th Centuries Ser.). 1978. lib. bdg. 42.00 (ISBN 0-8240-1760-9). Garland Pub.

Comparative Frontiers: A Proposal for Studying the American West. Jerome O. Steffen. LC 79-20315. 128p. 1980. 10.95 (ISBN 0-8061-1617-X). U of Okla Pr.

Comparative Government & Politics. 2nd ed. Dell G. Hitchner & Carol Levine. 270p. 1980. pap. 11.50 scp (ISBN 0-06-042828-7, HarpC). Har-Row.

Comparative Government: Europe & Asia. Anthony T. Bouscaren. LC 79-64098. 1979. pap. text ed. 9.00 (ISBN 0-8191-0754-9). U Pr of Amer.

Comparative Government: Politics of Industrialized & Developing Nations. Karl W. Deutsch et al. (Illus.). 496p. 1981. text ed. 16.25 (ISBN 0-395-29759-1). HM.

Comparative Grammar of the Hittite Language. Edgar H. Sturtevant & E. A. Hahn. 1951. 45.00x (ISBN 0-686-51357-6). Elliots Bks.

Comparative Higher Education Abroad: Bibliography & Analysis. Ed. by Philip G. Altbach. LC 75-33872. (Special Studies). 288p. 1976. text ed. 19.95 o.p. (ISBN 0-275-55500-3). Praeger.

Comparative Histology: An Introduction to the Microscopic Structure of Animals. Lucy D. Leake. 1976. 97.50 (ISBN 0-12-441050-2). Acad Pr.

Comparative History of Civilization in Asia, Vols. 1 & 2. Edward L. Farmer et al. LC 75-12095. (History Ser). (Illus.). 1977. Vol. 1. text ed. 17.95 (ISBN 0-201-01998-1); Vol. 2. text ed. 15.95 (ISBN 0-201-01999-X). A-W.

Comparative Immunobiology. M. J. Manning & R. J. Turner. LC 75-42363. (Teritiary Level Biology Ser.). 1976. pap. 9.95 (ISBN 0-470-14995-7). Halsted Pr.

Comparative Immunology. Edward L. Cooper. (Foundations of Immunology Ser.). (Illus.). 480p. 1976. 23.95x (ISBN 0-13-153429-7). P-H.

Comparative Immunology. Ed. by J. J. Marchalonis. LC 76-18782. 1976. 49.95 (ISBN 0-470-15160-9). Halsted Pr.

Comparative Karyology of Primates. Ed. by Brunetto Chiarelli et al. (World Anthropology Ser.). text ed. 39.00x (ISBN 9-0279-7840-9). Mouton.

Comparative Law Cases-Text-Materials. 4th ed. Rudolph B. Schlesinger. LC 80-13375. (University Casebook Ser.). 894p. 1980. text ed. write for info. (ISBN 0-88277-007-1). Foundation Pr.

Comparative Law Yearbook, Vol. III. D. L. Campbell. 294p. 1980. 47.50x (ISBN 90-286-0340-9). Sijthoff & Noordhoff.

Comparative Legal Cultures. Henry W. Ehrmann. 176p. 1976. pap. text ed. 7.95 (ISBN 0-13-153858-6). P-H.

Comparative Legislative Systems. H. Hirsch & M. Hancock. LC 78-136612. 1971. 14.95 (ISBN 0-02-914720-4). Free Pr.

Comparative Legislatures. Jean Blondel. (Contemporary Comparative Politics Ser.). (Illus.). 176p. 1973. ref. ed. 7.95 (ISBN 0-13-153874-8); pap. text ed. 7.95 (ISBN 0-13-153866-7). P-H.

Comparative Mammalian Haematology: Cellular Components & Blood Coagulation in Captive Wild Animals. Christine M. Hawkey. 1975. 60.00x (ISBN 0-433-13390-2). Intl Ideas.

Comparative Marine Policy. Center for Ocean Management Studies. 288p. 1981. 24.95 (ISBN 0-03-058307-1). J F Bergin.

Comparative Marine Policy. Ed. by Center for Ocean Management Studies. 336p. 1980. 26.95 (ISBN 0-03-058307-1). Praeger.

Comparative Methods in Sociology: Essays on Trends & Applications. Ed. by Ivan Vallier. LC 76-121194. (Institute of International Studies, UC Berkeley). 1971. 22.75x (ISBN 0-520-01743-9); pap. 6.95x (ISBN 0-520-02488-5). U of Cal Pr.

Comparative Metropolitan Employment Complexes: New York, Chicago, Los Angeles, Houston, Atlanta. Dale L. Hiestand & Dean W. Morse. LC 77-84456. (Conservation of Human Resources Ser.: No. 7). 141p. 1979. text ed. 21.50x (ISBN 0-916672-82-4). Allanheld.

Comparative Modernization: A Reader. Ed. by Cyril E. Black. LC 75-16647. (Perspectives on Modernization Ser). 1976. 16.95 (ISBN 0-02-903530-9). Free Pr.

Comparative Morphology of Recent Crustacea. Patsy A. McLaughlin. LC 79-26066. (Illus.). 1980. text ed. 23.95x (ISBN 0-7167-1121-4). W H Freeman.

Comparative Morphology of the Life Stages of Cryptocellus pelaezi (Arachnida, Ricinulie) Kay Pittard & Robert W. Mitchell. (Graduate Studies: No. 1). (Illus., Orig.). 1972. pap. 4.00 (ISBN 0-89672-008-X). Tex Tech Pr.

Comparative Morphology of the Mammalian Ovary. Harland W. Mossman & Kenneth L. Duke. LC 72-143765. 320p. 1972. 35.00 (ISBN 0-299-05930-8, 593); pap. 12.50 (ISBN 0-299-05934-0). U of Wis Pr.

Comparative Morphology of Vascular Plants. 2nd ed. Adriance S. Foster & Ernest M. Gifford. LC 73-22459. (Illus.). 1974. text ed. 28.95x (ISBN 0-7167-0712-8). W H Freeman.

Comparative National Economic Policies: A Reader for Introductory Economics. William Moskoff. 1973. pap. text ed. 7.95x o.p. (ISBN 0-669-83188-3). Heath.

Comparative Organellography of the Cytoplasm. A. Frey-Wyssling. (Protoplasmatologia: Vol. 3g). (Illus.). vii, 106p. 1973. 31.30 o.p. (ISBN 0-387-81139-7). Springer-Verlag.

Comparative Organizations. Wolf Heydebrand. (General Sociology Ser.). (Illus.). 608p. 1973. text ed. 22.95 (ISBN 0-13-153932-9). P-H.

Comparative Pathogenic Bacteriology. Theodore T. Kramer. 32p. 1972. pap. 37.50, incl. film strips o.p. (ISBN 0-7216-9829-8). Saunders.

Comparative Pathology of the Tumors of Bone. Sheldon A. Jacobson. (Illus.). 500p. 1971. 39.75 (ISBN 0-398-02166-X). C C Thomas.

Comparative Pathology of Zoo Animals. Ed. by Richard J. Montali & George Migaki. LC 79-24354. (Symposia of the National Zoological Park Ser.: No. 6). (Illus.). 684p. 1980. text ed. 45.00x (ISBN 0-87474-642-6); pap. text ed. 25.00x (ISBN 0-87474-643-4). Smithsonian.

Comparative Perspectives of Third World Women: The Impact of Race, Sex, & Class. Ed. by Beverly Lindsay. LC 78-19793. (Praeger Special Studies). 334p. 1980. 24.95 (ISBN 0-03-046651-2). Praeger.

Comparative Perspectives on the Academic Profession. Ed. by Philip G. Altbach. LC 77-83481. (Comparative Education Ser.: Vol. 1). 1978. 22.95 (ISBN 0-03-040781-8). Praeger.

Comparative Pharmacology, 2 vols. Ed. by M. J. Michelson. 1008p. 1974. Set. text ed. 150.00 (ISBN 0-08-016389-0). Pergamon.

Comparative Philology & the Text of Job: A Study in Methodology. Lester L. Grabbe. LC 77-23489. (Society of Biblical Literature. Dissertation Ser.). 1977. pap. 7.50 (ISBN 0-89130-139-9, 060134). Scholars Pr Ca.

Comparative Physiology & Evolution of Vision in Invertebrates B: Invertebrate Visual Centers & Behavior I. Ed. by H. Autrum. (Handbook of Sensory Physiology: Vol. VII, Pt. 6B). (Illus.). 650p. 1980. 159.30 (ISBN 0-387-08703-6). Springer-Verlag.

Comparative Policy Process. T. Alexander Smith. LC 75-2373. (Studies in International & Comparative Politics: No. 8). 184p. 1975. 15.80 (ISBN 0-87436-210-5). ABC-Clio.

Comparative Political Analysis. Allan L. Larson. 1980. 14.95x (ISBN 0-88229-257-9); pap. 8.95 (ISBN 0-88229-729-5). Nelson-Hall.

Comparative Political Parties Data, Nineteen Fifty to Nineteen Sixty-Two. Kenneth Janda. LC 79-90467. 1980. 14.00 (ISBN 0-89138-966-0). ICPSR.

Comparative Politics: Introduction to the Politics of Britain, France, Germany, & the Soviet Union. Dan N. Jacobs et al. pap. 9.95 (ISBN 0-934540-05-5). Chatham Hse Pubs.

Comparative Politics: Introduction to the Politics of Britain, the United Kingdom, France, Germany, & the Soviet Union. Dan N. Jacobs et al. 320p. 1981. pap. text ed. 9.95x (ISBN 0-934540-05-5). Chatham Hse Pubs.

Comparative Politics: Notes & Readings. 5th ed. Ed. by Roy C. Macridis & Bernard E. Brown. 1977. pap. text ed. 12.95x (ISBN 0-256-01956-8). Dorsey.

Comparative Politics of North Africa: Algeria, Morocco, & Tunisia. John P. Entelis. (Illus.). 240p. 1980. pap. 8.95x (ISBN 0-8156-2214-7). Syracuse U Pr.

Comparative Politics of the Middle East: An Introduction. Bruce M. Borthwick. 1980. pap. text ed. 10.50 (ISBN 0-13-154088-2). P-H.

Comparative Psychology: An Evolutionary Analysis of Animal Behavior. M. Ray Denny. LC 79-21123. 1980. text ed. 22.95 (ISBN 0-471-70930-1). Wiley.

Comparative Public Policy & Citizen Participation: Energy, Education, Health & Local Governance in the U. S. A. & Germany. Ed. by Charles R. Foster. (Pergamon Policy Studies). 1980. 29.50 (ISBN 0-08-024624-9). Pergamon.

Comparative Recreation Needs & Services in New York Neighborhoods. Shirley Jenkins. 1963. 4.00 (ISBN 0-86671-000-0). Comm Coun Great NY.

Comparative Regional Systems: West & East Europe, North America, the Middle East & Developing Countries. Ed. by Werner Feld & Gavin Boyd. (Pergamon Policy Studies). 1980. 47.00 (ISBN 0-08-023358-9); pap. 13.50 (ISBN 0-08-023357-0). Pergamon.

Comparative Religion. Eric J. Sharpe. LC 75-44614. 1976. text ed. 13.95x (ISBN 0-684-14675-4, ScribC). Scribner.

Comparative Revolutionary Movements. Thomas H. Greene. LC 74-793. (Contemporary Comparative Politics Ser). (Illus.). 176p. 1974. pap. text ed. 7.95 (ISBN 0-13-154179-X). P-H.

Comparative Semitic Lexicon of the Phoenician & Punic Languages. Richard S. Tomback. LC 76-55377. (Society of Biblical Literature. Dissertation Ser.: No. 32). 1978. pap. 10.50 (ISBN 0-89130-126-7, 060132). Scholars Pr Ca.

Comparative Statement of Estimates & Statistics on Narcotic Drugs for 1978. 42p. 1980. pap. 4.00 (ISBN 0-686-68946-1, UN80/6/5, UN). Unipub.

Comparative Statistics on Health Facilities & Population: Metropolitan & Nonmetropolitan Areas. American Hospital Association. LC 78-7259. (Illus.). 1978. pap. 8.25 o.p. (ISBN 0-87258-222-1, 1802). Am Hospital.

Comparative Statutory Sources. 2nd ed. J. S. Schultz. LC 78-60176. 1978. 19.50 (ISBN 0-930342-62-3). W S Hein.

Comparative Structure & Function of Muscle. Henry Huddart. 1975. text ed. 56.00 (ISBN 0-08-017845-6). Pergamon.

Comparative Studies & Educational Decision. Edmund J. King. LC 67-29489. 1968. 9.50 (ISBN 0-672-60627-5). Bobbs.

Comparative Studies in Nursery Rhymes. Lina Eckenstein. LC 68-23469. 1968. Repr. of 1906 ed. 15.00 (ISBN 0-8103-3479-8). Gale.

Comparative Studies of Food & Environmental Contamination. (Illus.). 623p. (Orig.). 1974. pap. 47.25 (ISBN 92-0-010074-0, ISP348, IAEA). Unipub.

Comparative Studies on Fresh-Water Fisheries. (FAO Fisheries Technical Paper: No. 198). 54p. 1981. pap. 6.00 (ISBN 92-5-100952-X, FAO). Unipub.

Comparative Study of Political Elites. Robert D. Putnam. (Illus.). 256p. 1976. pap. 10.95x (ISBN 0-13-154195-1). P-H.

Comparative Study of Political Involvement in Three African States: Botswana, Ghana & Kenya. John D. Holm et al. LC 78-14731. (Foreign & Comparative Studies-African Ser.: No. XXX). 139p. 1979. pap. 6.50x (ISBN 0-915984-52-0). Syracuse U Foreign Comp.

Comparative Study of Public Policy. H. M. Leichter. LC 79-50625. (Illus.). 1979. 27.50 (ISBN 0-521-22648-1); pap. 8.95x (ISBN 0-521-29601-3). Cambridge U Pr.

Comparative Study of Religions. Joachim Wach & Joseph M. Kitagawa. LC 58-9237. (Lectures on the History of Religions: No. 4). 1958. pap. 6.00 (ISBN 0-231-08528-1). Columbia U Pr.

Comparative Study of Rural Relief & Non-Relief Households. Thomas C. McCormick. LC 70-165684. (FDR & the Era of the New Deal Ser.). 1971. Repr. of 1935 ed. lib. bdg. 17.50 (ISBN 0-306-70334-3). Da Capo.

Comparative Urban Desigh-Rare Engravings: 1830-1843. Melville C. Branch. 108p. 49.50 (ISBN 0-686-69145-8, Co Pub by U of Cal Pr). Arno.

Comparative Vertebrate Endocrinology. P. J. Bentley. LC 75-10235. (Illus.). 480p. 1976. 52.50 (ISBN 0-521-20726-6); pap. 17.50x (ISBN 0-521-09935-8). Cambridge U Pr.

Comparative Vertebrate Morphology. Douglas B. Webster & Molly Webster. 1974. text ed. 23.95 (ISBN 0-12-740850-9). Acad Pr.

Comparative World Literature: Seven Essays. John B. Alphonso-Karkala. 98p. 1976. lib. bdg. 9.95 (ISBN 0-89253-048-0). Ind-US Inc.

Comparing Adult Education Worldwide. Alexander N. Charters et al. LC 80-8911. (Higher Education Ser.). 1981. text ed. price not set (ISBN 0-87589-494-1). Jossey-Bass.

Comparing English & Spanish: Patterns in Phonology & Orthography. Rose Nash. 1977. pap. text ed. 8.95 (ISBN 0-88345-297-9); cassettes 25.00 (ISBN 0-685-79303-6). Regents Pub.

Comparing Political Systems: Power & Policy in Three Worlds. Gary K. Bertsch et al. LC 77-27575. 1978. text ed. 16.95 (ISBN 0-471-02674-3); tchrs. manual avail. (ISBN 0-471-04047-9). Wiley.

Comparing Political Thinkers. Ed. by Ross Fitzgerald. 320p. 1980. 29.00 (ISBN 0-08-024800-4); pap. 15.75 (ISBN 0-08-024799-7). Pergamon.

Comparing Public Policies: New Concepts & Methods. Ed. by Douglas E. Ashford. LC 77-79492. (Sage Yearbooks in Politics & Public Policy: Vol. 4). 1978. 20.00x (ISBN 0-8039-0904-7); pap. 9.95x (ISBN 0-8039-0905-5). Sage.

Comparing Public Policies: United States, Soviet Union & Europe. Richard L. Siegel & Leonard Weinberg. 1977. pap. 12.50x (ISBN 0-256-01935-5). Dorsey.

Comparing Theories of Child Development. R. Murray Thomas. 1978. text ed. 20.95x (ISBN 0-534-00591-8). Wadsworth Pub.

Comparison Advertising: A Worldwide Study. J. J. Boddewyn & Katherin Marton. (Illus.). 1978. pap. 9.50 (ISBN 0-8038-1249-3). Hastings.

Comparison Between the Two Stages: In Dialogue. LC 74-170466. (English Stage Ser.: Vol. 39). lib. bdg. 50.00 (ISBN 0-8240-0622-4). Garland Pub.

Comparison of Automatic & Oprations Research Techniques Applied to Large Systems Analysis. Ed. by M. J. Pelegrin et al. LC 80-40979. (Illus.). 240p. 40.00 (ISBN 0-08-024454-8). Pergamon.

Comparison of Box-Jenkins & Bonn Monetary Prediction Performance. M. N. Bhattacharyya. (Lecture Notes in Economics & Mathematical Systems: Vol. 178). (Illus.). 146p. 1980. pap. 15.00 (ISBN 0-387-10011-3). Springer-Verlag.

Comparison of Economic Systems: Theoretical & Methodological Approaches. Ed. by Alexander Eckstein. LC 79-118085. 1971. 25.00x (ISBN 0-520-01729-3); pap. 5.50x (ISBN 0-520-02489-3). U of Cal Pr.

Comparison of Formative Cultures in the Americas. James A. Ford. (Illus.). 211p. 1969. 45.00x (ISBN 0-87474-159-9). Smithsonian.

Comparison of Price Controls & Quantity Controls Under Uncertainty. Gary W. Yohe. LC 78-75060. (Outstanding Dissertations in Economics Ser.). 1979. lib. bdg. 28.00 (ISBN 0-8240-4137-2). Garland Pub.

Comparison of Sidney's Old & New Arcadia. Robert Levine. (Salzburg Studies in English Literature, Elizabethan & Renaissance Studies: No.13). 122p. 1976. pap. text ed. 25.00x (ISBN 0-391-01458-7). Humanities.

Comparison of the Chronic Miasms. Phyllis Speight. 56p. 1977. text ed. 15.50x (ISBN 0-8464-1002-8). Beekman Pubs.

Comparison of the Experimental Housing Allowance Program & Great Britain's Rent Allowance Program. John Trutko et al. (Institute Paper). 52p. 1978. pap. 5.00 (ISBN 0-87766-222-3, 22500). Urban Inst.

Comparison of Thermoregulation & Water Metabolism in the Kangaroo Rats Dypodomys agilis & Dipodomys merriami. R. E. Carpenter. (U. C. Publ. in Zoology: Vol. 78). 1966. pap. 4.50x (ISBN 0-520-09335-6). U of Cal Pr.

Comparison Shopping & Caring for Your Personal Possessions. Northwest Regional Educational Laboratory. (Lifeworks Ser.). (Illus.). 1980. pap. text ed. 4.00 (ISBN 0-07-047309-9). McGraw.

Comparisons. Diagram Group. (Illus.). 240p. 1980. 15.00 (ISBN 0-312-15484-4). St Martin.

Comparisons: A Short Story Anthology. Nicolaus Mills. 432p. 1972. text ed. 9.95 o.p. (ISBN 0-07-042370-9, C). McGraw.

Comparisons of the Performance of Swedish & U.K. Companies. C. F. Pratten. LC 76-19625. (Applied Economics Ser.: Occasional Papers, No. 47). (Illus.). 1976. pap. 16.95x (ISBN 0-521-29134-8). Cambridge U Pr.

Compartment East: Love & Adventure on the Orient Express. Pierre-Jean Remy. 1980. 13.95 (ISBN 0-688-03739-9). Morrow.

Compartment Saydromes & Volkmann's Contracture. Scott J. Mubarak et al. (Saunder's Monographs in Clinical Orthopedics: Vol. 3). (Illus.). 200p. 1981. text ed. price not set (ISBN 0-7216-6604-3). Saunders.

Compass Course 180 Degrees. Jack Conway. 1978. 7.50 (ISBN 0-8158-0367-2); pap. 4.95 (ISBN 0-686-68022-7). Chris Mass.

Compass Flower. W. S. Merwin. LC 76-27345. 1977. pap. 5.95 (ISBN 0-689-10768-4). Atheneum.

Compassion & Responsibility: Readings in the History of Social Welfare Policy in the United States. Ed. by Frank R. Breul & Steven J. Diner. LC 79-56040. 1980. pap. text ed. 9.95x (ISBN 0-226-07413-7). U of Chicago Pr.

Compassion & Self-Hate. Theodore I. Rubin. 228p. 1976. pap. 2.50 (ISBN 0-345-29475-0). Ballantine.

Compassionate Deathmakers. Denk Bobkins. (Orig.). 1980. pap. 2.25 (ISBN 0-532-23209-7). Manor Bks.

Compassionate Landscape. Humphrey Carver. LC 75-22280. (Illus.). 1975. pap. 6.00 (ISBN 0-8020-6269-5). U of Toronto Pr.

Compatibility & Testing of Electronic Components. C. E. Jowett. LC 72-7039. 345p. 1972. 32.95 (ISBN 0-470-45170-X). Halsted Pr.

Compelled by the Cross. J. Terry Young. LC 80-66768. 1981. 2.95 (ISBN 0-8054-5282-6). Broadman.

Compelling Selling. Philip R. Lund. (AMACOM Executive Bks). 1978. pap. 5.95 (ISBN 0-8144-7506-X). Am Mgmt.

Compendio De la Historia Cristiana. R. A. Baker. Tr. by Francisco G. Almanza. Orig. Title: Summary of Christian History. 372p. (Span.). Date not set. pap. price not set (ISBN 0-311-15032-2). Casa Bautista.

Compendio Manual De la Biblia. Henry H. Halley. Tr. by C. P. Denyer from Eng. (Illus.). Date not set. Repr. of 1977 ed. 9.95 (ISBN 0-311-03666-X). Casa Bautista.

Compendious History of English Literature. R. D. Trivedi. 866p. 1976. 15.00x (ISBN 0-7069-0427-3). Intl Pubns Serv.

Compendious History of the Cotton Manufacture. Richard Guest. LC 68-108209. (Illus.). Repr. of 1823 ed. 18.00x (ISBN 0-678-05170-4). Kelley.

Compendious Introduccion Unto the Pistle off Paul to the Romayns. William Tyndale. LC 74-28890. (English Experience Ser.: No. 767). 1975. Repr. 3.50 (ISBN 90-221-0767-1). Walter J Johnson.

Compendious Syriac Dictionary Founded Upon the Thesaurus Syriacus of R. Payne Smith. R. Payne Smith. Ed. by J. Payne Smith. 1903. 65.00x (ISBN 0-19-864307-1). Oxford U Pr.

Compendium for Literates: The Systematics of Writing. Karl Gerstner. Tr. by Dennis Q. Stephenson from Ger. LC 73-21246. 180p. 1974. 17.50 (ISBN 0-262-07061-8); pap. 10.00 (ISBN 0-262-57055-6). MIT Pr.

Compendium of Bunk or How to Spot a Con Artist: A Handbook for Fraud Investigators, Bankers & Other Custodians of the Public Trust. Mary Carey & George Sherman. 216p. 1976. 16.50 (ISBN 0-398-03498-2); pap. 11.50 (ISBN 0-398-03501-6). C C Thomas.

Compendium of Continuous Lattices. G. Gierz et al. 380p. 1980. 19.80 (ISBN 0-387-10111-X). Springer-Verlag.

Compendium of Corn Diseases. 2nd ed. M. C. Shurtleff. (Compendium Ser.: No. 1). (Illus.). 124p. 1980. 11.00 (ISBN 0-89054-029-2). Am Phytopathol Soc.

Compendium of Housing Statistics Nineteen Seventy-Five to Nineteen Seventy-Seven. 354p. 1980. pap. 31.00 (UN80/17/4, UN). Unipub.

Compendium of Information Relevant to Manpower Agencies. John C. Erfurt. 1973. pap. 7.00x (ISBN 0-87736-330-7). U of Mich Inst Labor.

Compendium of Legislative Authority: Vol. 1, Suppl. 1, 1978. 66p. 1979. pap. 7.50 (UNEP 39, UNEP). Unipub.

Compendium of Neutron Spectra in Critically Accident Dosimetry. (Technical Report Ser: No. 180). 1978. pap. 18.25 (ISBN 92-0-125178-5, IDC 180, IAEA). Unipub.

Compendium of Social Statistics, 1977. (Statistical Papers Series K: No. 4). 1325p. 1980. pap. 35.00 (UN80-17-6, UN). Unipub.

Compendium of Social Statistics 1977. (Statistical Papers K Ser.: No. 4). 1325p. 1980. pap. 35.00 (ISBN 0-686-68947-X, UN80/17/6, UN). Unipub.

Compendium of the Epilepsies. Ernst Niedermeyer. (Illus.). 352p. 1974. 19.75 (ISBN 0-398-02878-8). C C Thomas.

Compendium of Trends on General Social Survey Questions. Tom W. Smith & Guy J. Rich. (National Opinion Research Center (NORC): No. 129). (Orig.). 1980. pap. text ed. 7.50x (ISBN 0-932132-24-3). NORC.

Compendium of Trends on General Social Survey Questions. Tom W. Smith et al. 1980. pap. 7.50 (ISBN 0-932132-24-3). NORC.

Compendium of University Entrance Requirements: For First Degree Courses in the United Kingdom 1981-82. 18th ed. Association of Commmowealth Universities. LC 74-648109. 1980. pap. 12.50x (ISBN 0-85143-065-1). Intl Pubns Serv.

Compendium of University Entrance Requirements for First Degree Courses in the United Kingdom, 1981-82. 18th ed. Association of Commonwealth Universities. LC 74-648109. 347p. (Orig.). 1980. pap. 12.50x (ISBN 0-85143-065-1). Intl Pubns Serv.

Compendium: Questions & Suggested Solutions, Certified Internal Auditor Examinations, 1976 Through 1979. Institute of Internal Auditors, Inc. (Illus.). 152p. 1980. pap. text ed. 16.00 (ISBN 0-89413-083-8). Inst Inter Aud.

Compensation Administration. David W. Belcher. (Industrial Relations & Personnel Ser). (Illus.). 576p. 1974. ref. ed. 19.95 (ISBN 0-13-154161-7). P-H.

Compensation & Reward Perspectives. Thomas A. Mahoney. 1979. pap. 12.95 (ISBN 0-256-02229-1). Irwin.

Compensation for Incapacity: A Study of Law & Social Change in New Zealand & Australia. Geoffrey Palmer. 448p. 1980. 49.50x (ISBN 0-19-558045-1). Oxford U Pr.

Compensation in Human Resource Development. Ed. by Steven Langer. 1981. pap. 75.00 (ISBN 0-916506-59-2). Abbott Langer Assocs.

Compensation in Manufacturing: Engineers & Managers. 3rd ed. Ed. by Steven Langer. 1980. pap. 75.00 (ISBN 0-916506-56-8). Abbott Langer Assocs.

Compensation in Psychiatric Disability & Rehabilitation. Ed. by Jack J. Leedy. (Illus.). 384p. 1971. 36.75 (ISBN 0-398-02186-4). C C Thomas.

Compensation of Attorneys, Pt. I: Non-Law Firms. 2nd ed. Ed. by Steven Langer. 1980. pap. 50.00 (ISBN 0-916506-51-7). Abbott Langer Assocs.

Compensation of Industrial Engineering. 6th ed. Ed. by Steven Langer. 1981. 60.00 (ISBN 0-916506-63-0). Abbott Langer Assocs.

Compensation of Industrial Engineers. 5th ed. Steven Langer. 1980. pap. 50.00 (ISBN 0-916506-50-9). Abbott Langer Assocs.

Compensatory Adaptations, Reflex Activity & the Brain. E. A. Asratian. 1965. text ed. 37.00 (ISBN 0-08-010591-2). Pergamon.

Compensatory Education. Moses Ntuk-Idem. 164p. 1978. text ed. 19.00x (ISBN 0-566-00226-4, Pub. by Gower Pub Co England). Renouf.

Competence Game: How to Find, Use & Keep Competent Employees. Ruth W. Stidger. LC 80-17657. (Illus.). 160p. 1980. 12.95 (ISBN 0-444-00453-X, Thomond Pr). Elsevier.

Compete: A Dynamic Marketing Simulation. rev. ed. Anthony J. Faria et al. 1979. pap. 8.50x (ISBN 0-256-02077-9). Business Pubns.

Competence & Power in Managerial Decision-Making. Frank A. Heller. Ed. by Bernhard Wilpert. 256p. 1981. 34.50 (ISBN 0-471-27837-8, Pub. by Wiley-Interscience). Wiley.

Competence Process. Jay Hall. LC 80-51211. (Illus.). 1980. text ed. 17.95 (ISBN 0-937932-01-9). Teleometrics.

Competencies for Effective Teaching of the Severely & Profoundly Handicapped in Classroom Settings. L. Larsen. Date not set. 16.50 (ISBN 0-8391-1260-2). Univ Park. Postponed.

Competency & Creativity in Language Arts: A Multi-Ethnic Focus. Nancy Hansen-Krening. LC 78-18632. (Education Ser.). (Illus.). 1979. pap. text ed. 7.95 (ISBN 0-201-02802-6). A-W.

Competency-Based Education. Peggy Conder. 1978. pap. 9.50 o.p. (ISBN 0-685-87370-6). Natl Sch Pr.

Competency-Based Education: Beyond Minimum Competency Testing. Northwest Regional Educational Laboratory. Ed. by Ruth Nickes. Date not set. pap. price not set (ISBN 0-8077-2606-0). Tchrs Coll.

Competency-Based Education: Process for Improvement of Education. G. Hall & H. Jones. LC 75-17564. (Illus.). 384p. 1975. 18.95 (ISBN 0-13-154864-6). P-H.

Competency-Based Instruction for Exceptional Children. Stanley A. Winters & Eunice W. Cox. (Illus.). 160p. 1976. pap. 16.75 (ISBN 0-398-03402-8). C C Thomas.

Competency Based Teacher Education. James M. Cooper & M. Vere DeVault. LC 72-83478. 123p. 1973. 16.60x (ISBN 0-8211-0010-6); text ed. 15.00 in copies of 10 (ISBN 0-686-66847-2). McCutchan.

Competency in Teaching Reading. Carl J. Wallen. LC 72-190104. 1972. pap. text ed. 12.95 (ISBN 0-574-18500-3, 13-1500); instr's guide avail. (ISBN 0-574-18508-9, 13-1508). SRA.

Competency to Stand Trial. Ronald Roesch & Stephen L. Golding. LC 80-12456. 251p. 1981. 19.95 (ISBN 0-252-00825-1). U of Ill Pr.

Competency to Stand Trial & Mental Illness. Harvard Medical School, Laboratory of Community Psychiatry. LC 74-25406. 132p. 1975. 17.50x (ISBN 0-87668-190-9). Aronson.

Competent Ministry: A Guide to Effective Continuing Education. Mark Rouch. LC 73-22309. 192p. 1974. pap. 3.75 o.p. (ISBN 0-687-09318-X). Abingdon.

Competent Woman. Rosalind C. Barnett & Grace K. Baruch. LC 78-8380. (Irvington Social Relations Ser.). 1980. pap. text ed. 6.95x (ISBN 0-8290-0092-5). Irvington.

Competing in Cross-Country Skiing. B. H. Nilsson. LC 74-82340. (Illus.). 160p. (gr. 10 up). 1974. 9.95 (ISBN 0-8069-4076-X); PLB 9.29 (ISBN 0-8069-4077-8); pap. 4.95 (ISBN 0-8069-8866-5). Sterling.

Competing with Production Cars. Richard Hudson-Evans. (Illus.). 1978. 10.95 o.s.i. (ISBN 0-7134-0132-X). Hippocrene Bks.

Competing with the Sylph: Dancers & the Pursuit of the Ideal Body Form. L. M. Vincent. 143p. 1980. pap. 5.95 (ISBN 0-8362-2407-8). Andrews & McMeel.

Competition & Coercion: Blacks in the American Economy, 1865-1914. R. Higgs. LC 76-9178. (Illus.). 1977. 29.95 (ISBN 0-521-21120-4). Cambridge U Pr.

Competition & Controls in Banking: A Study of the Regulation of Bank Competition in Italy, France & England. David A. Alhadeff. (Institute of Business & Economic Research & Institute of Industrial Relations, UC Berkeley). 1968. 25.50x (ISBN 0-520-00011-0). U of Cal Pr.

Competition & Oligopsony in the Douglas-Fir Lumber Industry. Walter J. Mead. (Institute of Business & Economic Research, UC Berkeley). 1966. 21.50x (ISBN 0-520-00848-0). U of Cal Pr.

Competition & Playful Activities. James W. Keating. LC 78-62741. 1978. pap. text ed. 8.75 (ISBN 0-8191-0589-9). U Pr of Amer.

Competition in the General-Freight Motor-Carrier Industry. Annette M. LaMond. LC 79-3048. 1980. 16.95x (ISBN 0-669-03308-1). Lexington Bks.

Competition in the Health Care Sector: Past, Present & Future. Ed. by Warren Greenberg. LC 78-24573. 1978. text ed. 35.00 (ISBN 0-89443-081-5). Aspen Systems.

Competition Law of the European Economic Community. James P. Cunningham. LC 73-166765. 397p. 1973. pap. 30.00x (ISBN 0-85038-033-2). Intl Pubns Serv.

Competition Policy in Canada: Stage II, Bill C-13. J. W. Rowley & W. T. Stanbury. 311p. 1978. pap. text ed. 12.95x (ISBN 0-920380-02-6, Pub. by Inst Res Pub Canada). Renouf.

Competition Policy in Regulated Sectors with Special Reference to Energy, Transport Banking. 189p. 1979. 11.00 (ISBN 92-64-11975-2). OECD.

Competition Policy in the UK & EEC. K. D. George & Caroline Joll. LC 75-9285. 1975. 39.00 (ISBN 0-521-20943-9). Cambridge U Pr.

Competition-Substitution Between Plastics P-045R. 1981. 950.00 (ISBN 0-89336-258-1). BCC.

Competitive Behaviors of Olympic Gymnasts. J. H. Salmela. (Illus.). 164p. 1980. 19.75 (ISBN 0-398-04019-2); pap. 14.50 (ISBN 0-398-04021-4). C C Thomas.

Competitive Colleges: Who Are They? Compiled by Peterson's Guides Editors. 250p. 1981. pap. 6.95 (ISBN 0-87866-127-1). Petersons Guid.

Competitive Edge: The West Point Guide for the Weekend Athlete. James L. Anderson & Martin Cohen. (Illus.). 1981. 14.95. Morrow.

Competitive Edge: The West Point Guide for the Weekend Athlete. James L. Anderson & Martin Cohen. LC 80-23535. (Illus.). 352p. 1981. 14.95 (ISBN 0-688-00352-4). Morrow.

Competitive Employment: New Horizons for Severely Disabled Individuals. Paul Wehman. 210p. 1980. pap. 13.95 (ISBN 0-933716-12-5). P H Brookes.

Competitive Employment: New Horizons for Severely Disabled Individuals. Paul Wehman. LC 80-24926. (Illus.). 278p. (Orig.). 1981. pap. text ed. 13.95 (ISBN 0-933716-12-5). P H Brookes.

Competitive Karting. Gary Martin. LC 80-83189. (Illus.). 144p. 1980. pap. 9.95 (ISBN 0-9605068-0-2). Martin Motorsports.

Competitive Strategy: Techniques for Analyzing Industries & Competitors. Michael E. Porter. LC 80-65200. (Illus.). 400p. 1980. 14.95 (ISBN 0-02-925360-8). Free Pr.

Competitive Strategy: Techniques for Analyzing Industries & Competitors. Michael E. Porter. (Illus.). 1980. 15.95 (ISBN 0-02-925360-8). Macmillan.

Competitive Swimming. Hamilton Bland. (EP Sport Ser.). (Illus.). 1979. 12.95 (ISBN 0-8069-9108-9, Pub. by EP Publishing England). Sterling.

Competitive Weightlifting. Ronald V. Fodor. LC 77-93307. (Illus.). 1978. 9.95 (ISBN 0-8069-4124-3); lib. bdg. 9.29 (ISBN 0-8069-4125-1). Sterling.

Competitor's Handbook. Robert Kendal. 1978. 10.95 (ISBN 0-236-31083-6, Pub. by Paul Elek). Merrimack Bk Serv.

Compilation & Review of Financial Statements. (Statements on Standards for Accounting & Review Services Ser.: No. 1). 1978. pap. 1.50. Am Inst CPA.

Compilation on Sex. Alice A. Bailey & Djwhal Khul. 160p. (Orig.). pap. 5.00 (ISBN 0-85330-136-0). Lucis.

Compiler Construction: Theory & Practice. William A. Barrett & John D. Couch. LC 78-26183. 512p. 1979. text ed. 24.95 (ISBN 0-574-21160-8, 13-4335); inst. guide o.p. 2.00 (ISBN 0-574-18508-9, 13-4161). SRA.

Compiler Design Theory. Philip M. Lewis, 2nd et al. LC 75-9012. (Illus.). 672p. 1976. text ed. 21.95 (ISBN 0-201-14455-7). A-W.

Compiler Writing in PASCAL. Henry Davis. (Pascal Notebook Ser.: Vol. 3). 150p. 1981. pap. 9.95 (ISBN 0-918398-45-2). Dilithium Pr.

Complacent Wife. Barbara Cartland. (Barbara Cartland Ser.: No. 9). 272p. 1981. pap. 1.75 (ISBN 0-515-05568-9). Jove Pubns.

Complaint of Peace. Desiderius Erasmus. Incl. The Adages of Erasmus. Margaret M. Phillips. LC 71-147414. (Library of War & Peace; Proposals for Peace: a History). lib. bdg. 38.00 (ISBN 0-8240-0483-3). Garland Pub.

Complaint of the Poet: The Parnassus Plays. Paula Glatzer. (Salzburg Studies in English Literature: Elizabethan & Renaissance Studies: No. 60). 1977. pap. text ed. 25.00x (ISBN 0-391-01386-6). Humanities.

Complaintes. Jules Laforgue. Ed. by Michael Collie. (Athlone French Poets Ser). 192p. 1977. text ed. 30.00x (ISBN 0-485-14713-0, Athlone Pr); pap. text ed. 13.00x (ISBN 0-485-12713-X). Humanities.

Compleat Angler. Izaak Walton. 1953. 6.00x (ISBN 0-460-00070-5, Evman); pap. 3.95 (ISBN 0-460-01070-0). Dutton.

Compleat Angler. facsimile ed. Izaak Walton. 1976. Repr. 11.95x o.p. (ISBN 0-85417-459-1, Pub. by Scolar Pr England). Biblio Dist.

Compleat Angler. Izaak Walton & Charles Cotton. (World's Classics Ser: No. 430). 7.95 o.p. (ISBN 0-19-250430-4). Oxford U Pr.

Compleat Beatles Quiz Book. Edwin Goodgold & Dan Carlinsky. (Orig.). 1975. pap. 1.75 o.s.i. (ISBN 0-446-84644-9). Warner Bks.

Compleat Brown Trout. Cecil E. Heacox. 1974. 13.95 (ISBN 0-87691-129-7). Winchester Pr.

Compleat Computer. Dennis Van Tassel. LC 75-31760. (Illus.). 250p. 1976. pap. text ed. 8.95 (ISBN 0-574-21060-1, 13-4060). SRA.

Compleat Cruciverbalist: How to Solve & Compose Crossword Puzzles for Fun & Profit. Stan Kurzban et al. 156p. 1980. 9.95 (ISBN 0-442-25738-4). Van Nos Reinhold.

Compleat Cruiser. L. Francis Herreshoff. (Illus.). 372p. 1980. Repr. 14.50 (ISBN 0-911378-05-7). Sheridan.

Compleat Enchanter. L. Sprague De Camp & Fletcher Pratt. 416p. (Orig.). 1976. pap. 1.95 o.p. (ISBN 0-345-24638-1). Ballantine.

Compleat Herbal. Ed. by Ben C. Harris. LC 77-185615. 243p. (Orig.). 1972. pap. 1.75 (ISBN 0-915962-15-2). Larchmont Bks.

Compleat Memoirs of the Life of That Notorious Imposter Will Morrell, Alias Bowyer, Alias Wickham,Etc, Settle Elkanah. LC 80-2498. 1981. Repr. of 1694 ed. 47.50 (ISBN 0-404-19134-7). AMS Pr.

Compleat Motion Picture Quiz Book; or, Sixty Thousand Points About Motion Pictures. Harry D. Trigg & Yolanda L. Trigg. LC 74-27590. 384p. 1975. pap. 4.95 o.p. (ISBN 0-385-05185-9). Doubleday.

Compleat Oak Leaves. David Kraft. LC 80-23937. 192p. 1980. Repr. of 1979 ed. lib. bdg. 16.95x (ISBN 0-89370-092-4). Borgo Pr.

Compleat Parent. Nancy Van Pelt. LC 79-9946. (Orion Ser.). 160p. 1976. pap. 2.95 (ISBN 0-8127-0229-8). Southern Pub.

Compleat Plattmaker: Essays on Chart, Map, & Globe-Making in England in the 17th & 18th Centuries. Ed. by Norman J. Thrower. LC 77-78415. 1979. 18.50x (ISBN 0-520-03522-4). U of Cal Pr.

Compleat Politician: Political Strategy in Massachusetts. Murray B. Levin & George Blackwood. LC 62-18204. 1962. 24.50x (ISBN 0-672-51133-9); pap. text ed. 12.95x (ISBN 0-8290-0138-7). Irvington.

Compleat Practical Joker. rev. ed. H. Allen Smith. LC 80-20668. 288p. 1980. Repr. of 1953 ed. 12.95 (ISBN 0-688-03705-4). Morrow.

Complement: Mechanisms & Functions. A. Osler. 1976. 22.95 (ISBN 0-13-155226-0). P-H.

Complementary Variational Principles. 2nd ed. A. M. Arthurs. (Mathematical Monographs). 160p. 1980. 49.00 (ISBN 0-19-853532-5). Oxford U Pr.

Complete Actor. Stanley Glenn. 1977. text ed. 15.95 (ISBN 0-205-05580-X). Allyn.

Complete Adventures of the Borrowers, 4 bks. Mary Norton. Bd. with Bk 1. Borrowers; Bk. 2. Borrowers Afield; Bk. 3. Borrowers Afloat; Bk. 4. Borrowers Aloft. (Illus.). (gr. 8 up). 1975. pap. 7.25 boxed set (ISBN 0-15-613605-8, VoyB). HarBraceJ.

Complete Airbrush Techniques for Commercial, Technical, & Industrial Applications. Sol Dember. 1980. pap. 15.95 (ISBN 0-672-21783-X). Bobbs.

Complete All-in-the-Oven Cookbook: The Cookbook for Saving Time & Energy. Dolores Riccio & Joan Bingham. LC 80-5712. 300p. 1981. 12.95 (ISBN 0-8128-2699-X). Stein & Day.

Complete American Graffiti: The Novel. John Minahan. 1979. pap. 2.25 o.p. (ISBN 0-425-04249-9). Berkley Pub.

Complete Annals of Thomas Jefferson. Thomas Jefferson. Ed. by Franklin R. Sawvel. LC 70-75272. (Amer. Public Figures Ser.). 1970. Repr. of 1903 ed. lib. bdg. 32.50 (ISBN 0-306-71311-X). Da Capo.

Complete Annotated Resource Guide to Black American Art. Oakley Holmes, Jr. LC 78-112785. 275p. 1978. pap. text ed. 12.00 (ISBN 0-9604026-4-0). O N Holmes.

Complete Annotated Resource Guide to Black American Art. Oakley Holmes, Jr. (Orig.). pap. 12.00 (ISBN 0-686-27594-2, 0960426). O N Holmes.

Complete Assembling. Ed. by Richard Kostelanetz et al. (Orig.). 1979. pap. 60.00 (ISBN 0-915066-34-3). Assembling Pr.

Complete Ballooning Book. Will Hayes. LC 75-32444. (Illus.). 160p. 1977. Repr. of 1977 ed. handbk. 12.95 (ISBN 0-89037-111-3). Anderson World.

Complete Barbecue Cookbook. John Roberson & Marie Roberson. 1967. pap. 1.95 o.s.i. (ISBN 0-02-081240-X, Collier). Macmillan.

Complete Baseball Play Book. Jim Trainor. LC 77-165387. 352p. 1972. pap. 6.95 (ISBN 0-385-00075-8). Doubleday.

Complete Bed Building Book. HyDee Small. (Illus.). 1979. 12.95 o.p. (ISBN 0-8306-9822-1); pap. 7.95 (ISBN 0-8306-1124-X, 1124). TAB Bks.

Complete Beginner's Guide to Archery. Bernhard A. Roth. LC 75-26942. 192p. (gr. 6 up). 1976. PLB 7.95 (ISBN 0-385-07356-9). Doubleday.

Complete Beginner's Guide to Backpacking. Richard B. Lyttle. LC 74-18817. 160p. (gr. 4-9). 1975. PLB 4.95 (ISBN 0-385-06885-9). Doubleday.

Complete Beginner's Guide to Canoeing. Bernhard A. Roth. LC 76-42391. (gr. 7 up). 1977. PLB 7.95 (ISBN 0-385-07297-X). Doubleday.

Complete Beginners Guide to Everyday Italian Cooking. Betty L. Torre. LC 74-2527. (gr. 9 up). 1975. 5.95 o.p. (ISBN 0-385-08981-3). Doubleday.

Complete Beginner's Guide to Golf. Bill McCormick. LC 73-78770. 144p. (gr. 5-9). 1974. PLB 4.95 (ISBN 0-385-05529-3). Doubleday.

Complete Beginner's Guide to Horseback Riding. Gil Paust. LC 76-42380. 1977. 6.95 o.p. (ISBN 0-385-01747-2); PLB write for info. o.p. (ISBN 0-385-03347-8). Doubleday.

Complete Beginners Guide to Ice Skating. Edward F. Dolan, Jr. LC 73-10803. 192p. (gr. 5-9). 1974. 5.95 o.p. (ISBN 0-385-03779-1). Doubleday.

Complete Beginner's Guide to Judo. Stuart James. LC 76-56306. (gr. 6-12). 1978. PLB 6.95 (ISBN 0-385-06041-6). Doubleday.

Complete Beginner's Guide to Magic. Edward F. Dolan, Jr. LC 76-56281. (gr. 4-7). 1977. PLB 6.95 (ISBN 0-385-11555-5). Doubleday.

Complete Beginner's Guide to Microscopes & Telescopes. Aaron E. Klein. LC 78-22334. (Illus.). 224p. 1980. 9.95a (ISBN 0-385-14854-2); PLB (ISBN 0-385-14855-0). Doubleday.

Complete Beginner's Guide to Mountain Climbing. Howard E. Smith, Jr. LC 76-18366. (gr. 7 up). 1977. 6.95 o.p. (ISBN 0-385-11428-1); PLB write for info. o.p. (ISBN 0-385-11429-X). Doubleday.

Complete Beginner's Guide to Physical Fitness. Richard B. Lyttle. LC 77-80896. (gr. 1 up). 1978. 7.95a (ISBN 0-385-12773-1); PLB (ISBN 0-385-12774-X). Doubleday.

Complete Beginner's Guide to Sailing. new ed. A. H. Drummond, Jr. LC 70-103742. 192p. (YA) (gr. 7 up). 1975. 6.95 o.p. (ISBN 0-385-09356-X). Doubleday.

Complete Beginner's Guide to Skin Diving. Shaney Frey. LC 65-11061. (gr. 7-11). 5.95 o.p. (ISBN 0-385-04523-9). Doubleday.

Complete Beginner's Guide to Stereo. Richard B. Lyttle. LC 79-8564. (Illus.). 192p. 1981. 9.95a (ISBN 0-385-15532-8); lib. bdg. (ISBN 0-385-15533-6). Doubleday.

Complete Beginners Guide to Swimming. Shaney Frey. LC 74-9651. 208p. (gr. 5-9). 1975. PLB 5.95 (ISBN 0-385-00354-4). Doubleday.

Complete Beginnger's Guide to Making & Flying Kites. Edward F. Dolan, Jr. LC 75-36585. (gr. 4-7). 1977. PLB 6.95 (ISBN 0-385-04937-4). Doubleday.

Complete BioCycle Kit. Carol M. Spencer. (Illus.). 1974. 5.95 (ISBN 0-918882-01-X). PSI Rhythms.

Complete Birds of the World. Michael Walters. LC 79-56434. 256p. 1980. 38.00 (ISBN 0-7153-7666-7). David & Charles.

Complete Blender Cookbook. Zenja Carey & Virginia Habeeb. LC 78-52133. 1978. 9.95 (ISBN 0-87502-059-3); pap. 4.95 (ISBN 0-87502-060-7). Benjamin Co.

Complete Book of American Fish & Shellfish. John F. Nicolas. LC 80-16534. (Illus.). 384p. 1980. 29.95 (ISBN 0-8436-2191-5). CBI Pub.

Complete Book of American Surveys. Craig Norback. (Orig.). 1981. pap. 3.50 (ISBN 0-451-09571-5, E9571, Sig). NAL.

Complete Book of Autographing Collecting. George Sullivan. LC 75-37650. (gr. 4-7). 1971. 5.95 (ISBN 0-396-06385-3). Dodd.

Complete Book of Bacon. William J. Hogan. (Illus.). 1978. 22.50x (ISBN 0-7198-2627-6). Intl Ideas.

Complete Book of Baseball. The New York Times. LC 79-92320. (Sports Ser.). (Illus.). 224p. 1980. 14.95 (ISBN 0-686-61137-3). Bobbs.

Complete Book of Baskets & Basketry. Dorothy Wright. (Encore Edition). (Illus.). 1978. 3.95 (ISBN 0-684-16558-9, ScribT). Scribner.

Complete Book of Beans. Jacqueline Heriteau. LC 77-92314. 1978. 8.95 (ISBN 0-8015-1474-6, Hawthorn); pap. 5.95 (ISBN 0-8015-1475-4, Hawthorn). Dutton.

Complete Book of Bicycle Commuting. John S. Allen. (Illus.). 320p. 1980. 12.95 (ISBN 0-87857-342-9); pap. 9.95 (ISBN 0-87857-344-5). Rodale Pr Inc.

Complete Book of Bird Houses & Feeders. Monica Russo & Robert Dewire. LC 75-36155. (Illus.). 1976. pap. 5.95 (ISBN 0-8069-8224-1). Sterling.

Complete Book of Bow & Arrow. rev., 3rd ed. G. Howard Gillelan. (Illus.). 330p. 1981. pap. 9.95 (ISBN 0-8117-2118-3). Stackpole.

Complete Book of Breast Care. Robert E. Rothenberg. 228p. 1976. pap. 1.95 o.p. (ISBN 0-345-25114-8). Ballantine.

Complete Book of Bulbs. rev. ed. F. F. Rockwell & Esther C. Grayson. LC 77-4437. (Illus.). 1977. 10.00 o.p. (ISBN 0-397-01194-6). Lippincott.

Complete Book of Calligraphy. Emma M. Butterworth. LC 79-7642. (Illus.). 164p. 1980. 14.95 (ISBN 0-690-01852-5). Lippincott & Crowell.

Complete Book of Car Maintenance & Repair. John D. Hirsch. LC 77-3252. (Illus.). 1977. 14.95 o.p. (ISBN 0-684-14900-1, ScribT). Scribner.

Complete Book of Cat Care. rev. ed. Leon F. Whitney & George D. Whitney. LC 79-7216. (Illus.). 1980. 9.95 (ISBN 0-385-14707-4). Doubleday.

Complete Book of Cheerleading. Ed. by L. R. Herkimer & Phyllis Hollander. LC 73-81436. 288p. 1975. 9.95 (ISBN 0-385-08057-3); pap. 4.95 (ISBN 0-385-08059-X). Doubleday.

Complete Book of Chess. Israel A. Horowitz & P. L. Rothenberg. Orig. Title: Personality of Chess. (Illus.). 1969. pap. 2.95 o.s.i. (ISBN 0-02-028870-0, Collier). Macmillan.

Complete Book of Chess Openings. Fred Reinfeld. 1963. pap. 2.95 (ISBN 0-06-463274-1, EH 274, EH). Har-Row.

Complete Book of Children's Play. rev. ed. Ruth E. Hartley & Robert M. Goldenson. (Apollo Eds.). (Illus.). 1970. pap. 4.95 o.s.i. (ISBN 0-8152-0245-8, A245, TYC-T). T Y Crowell.

Complete Book of Children's Theater. Ed. by Vernon Howard. LC 69-10951. 1969. 9.95 o.p. (ISBN 0-385-03682-5). Doubleday.

Complete Book of Cooking Equipment. 2nd ed. Jule Wilkinson. LC 80-16554. 336p. 1980. 21.50 (ISBN 0-8436-2186-9). CBI Pub.

Complete Book of Corporate Forms. Ted Nicholas. LC 80-67502. 1980. 49.95 (ISBN 0-913864-54-4). Enterprise Del.

Complete Book of Country Swing & Western Dance. Peter Livingston et al. LC 80-70555. 1981. pap. 9.95 (ISBN 0-385-17601-5, Dolp). Doubleday.

Complete Book of Deer Hunting. Byron W. Dalrymple. 1973. 12.95 (ISBN 0-87691-108-4). Winchester Pr.

Complete Book of Dragons. E. Nesbit. LC 72-165245. (Illus.). 208p. (gr. 3 up). 1973. 5.95g o.s.i. (ISBN 0-02-768120-3). Macmillan.

Complete Book of Drawing & Painting. Hugh Laidman. (Handbooks Ser.). (Illus.). 1978. pap. 14.95 (ISBN 0-14-046349-6). Penguin.

Complete Book of Drills for Winning Soccer. James P. Mc Gettigan. 254p. 1980. 10.95 (ISBN 0-13-156356-4, Parker). P-H.

Complete Book of Duplicate Bridge. Norman Kay et al. LC 78-89862. (Orig.). 1969. pap. 4.95 (ISBN 0-06-463262-8, EH 262, EH). Har-Row.

Complete Book of Electric Vehicles. rev. ed. Sheldon R. Shacket. (Illus.). 224p. 1981. price not set (ISBN 0-89196-085-6, Domus Bks); pap. price not set (ISBN 0-89196-086-4). Quality Bks IL.

Complete Book of Entertaining. Elizabeth Post & Anthony Staffieri. LC 80-7879. (Illus.). 384p. 1981. 14.95 (ISBN 0-690-01970-X, HarpT). Har-Row.

Complete Book of Entertaining from the Emily Post Institute. Emily Post & Anthony Staffieri. LC 80-7879. 320p. 1981. 14.95. Lippincott & Crowell.

Complete Book of Fishing. A. C. Becker, Jr. LC 76-18477. (Illus.). 217p. 1981. Repr. of 1977 ed. 20.00 (ISBN 0-498-01973-X). A S Barnes.

Complete Book of Football: A New York Times Scrapbook History. The New York Times. LC 79-92321. (Sports Ser.). (Illus.). 224p. 1980. 14.95 (ISBN 0-672-52637-9). Bobbs.

Complete Book of Freezer Cookery. Ann Seranne. 7.95 o.p. (ISBN 0-385-03994-8). Doubleday.

Complete Book of Furniture Repair & Refinishing. Ed. by Family Handyman Magazine. (Illus.). 288p. 1981. 14.95 (ISBN 0-684-16839-1, ScribT). Scribner.

Complete Book of Furniture Repair & Refinishing. Ralph Kinney. LC 73-162743. (Illus.). 1971. 12.95 o.p. (ISBN 0-684-12437-8, ScribT). Scribner.

Complete Book of Furniture Repair & Refinishing. rev. ed. Ralph Kinney. LC 73-162743. (Illus.). 1981. 20.00x (ISBN 0-684-16839-1, ScribT). Scribner.

Complete Book of Games. Ed. by Clement Wood & Gloria Goddard. 1938. 8.95 o.p. (ISBN 0-385-00041-3). Doubleday.

Complete Book of Gardening. Ed. by Michael Wright. 1980. pap. 9.95 (ISBN 0-446-87239-3). Warner Bks.

Complete Book of Golf. The New York Times. LC 79-92319. (Sports Ser.). (Illus.). 224p. 1980. 14.95 (ISBN 0-672-52636-0). Bobbs.

Complete Book of Growing Plants. Haring. pap. 5.95 (ISBN 0-8015-1489-4, Hawthorn). Dutton.

Complete Book of Gymnastics. 3rd ed. Newton C. Loken & Robert J. Willoughby. (Illus.). 256p. 1977. text ed. 16.95 (ISBN 0-13-157172-9). P-H.

Complete Book of Handwriting Analysis. Mary Ruiz & Karen S. Amend. 1980. pap. 9.95 (ISBN 0-87877-050-X). Newcastle Pub.

Complete Book of Handwriting Analysis. Mary S. Ruiz & Karen Amend. LC 80-8672. (Illus.). 196p. 1980. Repr. of 1980 ed. lib. bdg. 17.95 (ISBN 0-89370-650-7). Borgo Pr.

Complete Book of Herbs. Roy Genders. LC 79-93206. (Illus.). 160p. 1980. 14.95 (ISBN 0-8069-3928-1); pap. 8.95 (ISBN 0-8069-3930-3). Sterling.

Complete Book of Herbs. Kay N. Sanecki. (Illus.). 252p. 1974. 12.95 (ISBN 0-02-606890-7). Macmillan.

Complete Book of High Altitude Baking. rev. ed. Donna M. Hamilton & Beverly A. Nemiro. LC 61-18656. 370p. 1967. 12.95 (ISBN 0-8040-0054-9, SB). Swallow.

Complete Book of High Protein Baking. Martha E. Katz. 1977. pap. 1.95 (ISBN 0-345-24186-X). Ballantine.

Complete Book of Home Buying: A Consumer's Guide to Housing in the 80's. rev. ed. Michael Sumichrast & Ronald G. Shafer. LC 80-11100. 366p. 1980. 14.95 (ISBN 0-87128-589-4). Dow Jones-Irwin.

Complete Book of Home Freezing. rev. ed. Hazel Meyer. (Illus.). 1970. 10.00 o.p. (ISBN 0-397-00639-X). Lippincott.

Complete Book of Home Improvement. Darrell Huff & Frances Huff. (Illus.). 1971. 14.95 o.s.i. (ISBN 0-06-011983-7, HarpT). Har-Row.

Complete Book of Home Inspection. Norman Becker. (McGraw Hill Paperbacks). (Illus., Orig.). 1980. 16.95 (ISBN 0-07-004181-4); pap. 8.95 (ISBN 0-07-004180-6). McGraw.

Complete Book of Home Preserving. Ann Seranne. 7.95 o.p. (ISBN 0-385-06608-2). Doubleday.

Complete Book of Home Workshops. David X. Manners. (Illus.). 1970. 12.95 o.p. (ISBN 0-06-012767-8, HarpT). Har-Row.

Complete Book of Houseplants. Charles M. Fitch. 1972. 10.95 o.p. (ISBN 0-8015-1650-1). Dutton.

Complete Book of Houseplants. Charles M. Fitch. (Illus.). 320p. 1980. pap. 7.95 (ISBN 0-8015-1660-9, Hawthorn). Dutton.

Complete Book of Hunting. Ed. by Robert Elman. (Illus.). 320p. 1981. 49.95 (ISBN 0-89659-174-3); pap. 16.95 (ISBN 0-89659-150-6). Abbeville Pr.

Complete Book of Inflatable Boats. Don Hubbard. LC 79-27460. (Illus.). 256p. (Orig.). 1980. pap. 7.95 (ISBN 0-930030-15-X). Western Marine Ent.

Complete Book of Jewish Observance. Leo Trepp. LC 79-1352. (Illus.). 1979. 14.95 (ISBN 0-87441-281-1). Behrman.

Complete Book of Jewish Observance. Leo Trepp. LC 79-1352. (Behrman House Book). (Illus.). 370p. 1980. 14.95 (ISBN 0-671-41797-5). Summit Bks.

Complete Book of Karting. Kart Magazine. Ed. by Dick Day. 1961. 14.95 (ISBN 0-13-157487-6). P-H.

Complete Book of Machine Quilting. Robbie Fanning & Tony Fanning. (Illus.). 224p. 1980. 15.95 (ISBN 0-8019-6802-X); pap. 9.95 (ISBN 0-8019-6803-8). Chilton.

Complete Book of Magic & Witchcraft. Kathryn Paulsen. (Orig.). 1970. pap. 1.25 o.p. (ISBN 0-451-05589-6, Y5589, Sig). NAL.

Complete Book of Masonary, Cement & Brickwork. LC 75-10974. (Drake Home Craftsman Ser.). (Illus.). 192p. 1975. pap. 4.95 o.p. (ISBN 0-8069-8232-2). Sterling.

Complete Book of Masonry, Cement & Brickwork. LC 80-52324. (Illus.). 192p. 1980. pap. 6.95 (ISBN 0-8069-8232-2). Sterling.

Complete Book of Mexican Cooking. Elisabeth L. Ortiz. LC 67-18534. (Illus.). 352p. 1967. 8.95 (ISBN 0-87131-074-0); 5.95 (ISBN 0-87131-333-2). M Evans.

Complete Book of Mexican Cooking. Elisabeth L. Ortiz. (Illus.). 352p. 1980. pap. 5.95 o.p. (ISBN 0-87131-333-2). M Evans.

Complete Book of Miniature Roses. Charles M. Fitch. (Illus.). 352p. 1980. pap. 10.95 (ISBN 0-8015-1507-6, Hawthorn). Dutton.

Complete Book of Minibikes & Minicycles. Lyle K. Engel. LC 72-88606. (Illus.). 160p. 1975. lib. bdg. 7.95 o.p. (ISBN 0-668-02733-9); pap. 3.95 o.p. (ISBN 0-668-03785-7). Arco.

Complete Book of Mobile Home Living. Lyle K. Engel. LC 73-85274. (Illus.). 160p. 1974. lib. bdg. 5.95 o.p. (ISBN 0-668-02896-3). Arco.

Complete Book of Mopeds. Ed. by Consumer Guide Editors. 1977. pap. 1.95 (ISBN 0-446-89475-3). Warner Bks.

Complete Book of Mopeds. Consumer's Guide Editors. 1977. pap. 1.95 o.s.i. (ISBN 0-446-89475-3). Warner Bks.

Complete Book of Mopeds. Laura Torbet & Jonathan Sternfield. (Funk & W Bk.). (Illus.). 1977. 9.95 o.s.i. (ISBN 0-308-10307-6, TYC-T); pap. 5.95 o.s.i. (ISBN 0-308-10308-4, TYC-T). T Y Crowell.

Complete Book of Mountain Sports. Curtis W. Casewit. LC 78-15901. (Illus.). (gr. 7 up). 1978. PLB 7.79 o.p. (ISBN 0-671-32902-2). Messner.

Complete Book of Movie Making. Tony Rose. 1972. 8.50 o.p. (ISBN 0-85242-083-8, Pub. by Fountain). Morgan.

Complete Book of Movie Making. Tony Rose. Date not set. 8.50 o.p. (ISBN 0-8038-1260-4). Hastings.

Complete Book of Natural Medicines. David Carroll. LC 80-11332. (Illus.). 416p. 1980. 17.95 (ISBN 0-671-24418-3); pap. 7.95 (ISBN 0-671-41623-5). Summit Bks.

Complete Book of Needlepoint. Carolyn Ambuter. LC 70-178814. (Illus.). 1972. 9.95 (ISBN 0-690-00337-4, TYC-T). T Y Crowell.

Complete Book of Outdoor Lore. Clyde Ormond. LC 64-13133. (Illus.). 1965. 9.95 o.p. (ISBN 0-06-071440-9, HarpT). Har-Row.

Complete Book of Pastry. Bernard Clayton. 17.95 (ISBN 0-671-24276-8). S&S.

Complete Book of Photographing People. Michael Busselle. 1980. 19.95 (ISBN 0-671-41257-4, Kenan Pr). S&S.

Complete Book of Pickup and Vans. 2nd ed. Spence Murray. LC 76-1545. (Petersen's Enthusiasts Ser.). (Illus.). 176p. 1976. pap. 3.95 o.p. (ISBN 0-8227-0667-9). Petersen Pub.

Complete Book of Pizza. 2nd ed. Louise Love. (Illus.). 1981. pap. write for info. Sassafras Pr.

Complete Book of Pleasure Boat Engines. Ernest A. Zadig. LC 79-24306. (Illus.). 320p. 1980. 17.95 (ISBN 0-13-157636-4). P-H.

Complete Book of Practical Handloading. John Wootters. (Illus.). 1976. 13.95 (ISBN 0-87691-215-3). Winchester Pr.

Complete Book of Prefabs, Kits & Manufactured Houses. Consumer Guide Editors. 160p. 1981. pap. 7.95 (ISBN 0-449-90051-7, Columbine). Fawcett.

Complete Book of Pregnancy & Childbirth. Sheila Kitzinger. LC 80-7650. (Illus.). 336p. 1980. 14.95 (ISBN 0-394-51349-5). Knopf.

Complete Book of Printing & Enlarging. O. R. Croy. Date not set. cancelled o.p. (ISBN 0-8038-1239-6). Hastings.

Complete Book of Puppets & Puppeteering. Robert T. Hanford. LC 80-54338. (Illus.). 160p. 1981. 12.95 (ISBN 0-8069-7032-4); lib. bdg. 11.69 (ISBN 0-8069-7033-2); pap. 7.95 (ISBN 0-8069-8970-X). Sterling.

Complete Book of Racquetball. Steve Keeley. pap. 8.95 (ISBN 0-695-80651-3). Follett.

Complete Book of Radio Transmitters. Joseph J. Carr. 350p. 1980. 8.95 o.p. (ISBN 0-8306-1224-6). Tab Bks.

Complete Book of Rifles & Shotguns. rev. ed. Jack O'Connor. LC 61-6454. (Illus.). 1966. 12.50 o.p. (ISBN 0-06-071351-8, HarpT). Har-Row.

Complete Book of Rug Hooking. Barbara Zarbock. LC 71-83216. (Illus.). 128p. 1972. pap. 5.95 o.p. (ISBN 0-8069-8630-1). Sterling.

Complete Book of Running. James F. Fixx. (Illus.). 1977. 10.00 (ISBN 0-394-41159-5). Random.

Complete Book of Sailing. Ed. by Peter Cook & Barbara Webb. LC 76-19620. 1977. 17.95 (ISBN 0-385-11531-8). Doubleday.

Complete Book of Salt-Water Aquariums: How to Equip & Maintain Your Marine Aquarium & Understand Its Ecology. Robert A. Stevenson. (Funk & W Bk.). 224p. 1974. 9.95 (ISBN 0-308-10090-5, TYC-T). T Y Crowell.

Complete Book of Shiatsu Therapy. Toru Namikoshi. LC 79-1963. (Illus.). 1980. pap. 9.95 (ISBN 0-87040-461-X). Japan Pubns.

Complete Book of Sports Medicine. Richard H. Dominguez. (Encore Editions). (Illus.). 1979. 4.95 (ISBN 0-684-16896-0, ScribT). Scribner.

Complete Book of Sports Medicine. Richard H. Dominguez. 1980. pap. 4.95 (ISBN 0-446-97213-4). Warner Bks.

Complete Book of Striped Bass Fishing. Henry Lyman & Frank Woolner. (Illus.). 1954. 6.95 o.p. (ISBN 0-498-08075-7). A S Barnes.

Complete Book of Swimming. James E. Counsilman. LC 72-82682. (Illus.). 1979. 9.95 (ISBN 0-689-10530-4); pap. 5.95 (ISBN 0-689-70583-2, 246). Atheneum.

Complete Book of Tennis: A New York Times Scrapbook History. New York Times. LC 79-56751. (Sports Ser.). (Illus.). 224p. 1980. 14.95 (ISBN 0-672-52638-7). Bobbs.

Complete Book of Terrarium Gardening. Jack Kramer. LC 73-17253. (Illus.). 160p. 1974. encore ed. 3.95 o.p. (ISBN 0-684-15707-1, ScribT). Scribner.

Complete Book of the American Musical Theater. rev. ed. David A. Ewen. (Illus.). 1970. 15.00 o.p. (ISBN 0-03-085060-6). HR&W.

Complete Book of the Appaloosa. Jan Haddle. LC 73-10521. (Illus.). 1977. pap. 7.95 o.p. (ISBN 0-498-02049-5). A S Barnes.

Complete Book of the Bow & Arrow. rev. ed. G. Howard Gillelan. LC 76-30484. (Illus.). 330p. 1981. 9.95 (ISBN 0-8117-2118-3). Stackpole.

Complete Book of Thirty-Five-mm Photography. Jerry Yulsman. LC 75-45425. (Illus.). 224p. (YA) 1976. 8.95 (ISBN 0-698-10734-9). Coward.

Complete Book of Trailering. Lyle K. Engel. LC 72-85679. (Illus.). 160p. 1974. lib. bdg. 5.95 o. p. (ISBN 0-668-02716-9); pap. 2.95 o.p. (ISBN 0-668-02715-0). Arco.

Complete Book of Trick & Fancy Shooting. Ernie Lind. (Illus.). 1972. 6.95 o.p. (ISBN 0-87691-045-2). Winchester Pr.

Complete Book of Video Games. Ed. by Consumer Guide Editors. 1977. pap. 1.95. Warner Bks.

Complete Book of Vitamins. Prevention Magazine. 1977. 16.95 (ISBN 0-87857-176-0). Rodale Pr Inc.

Complete Book of Walking. Ed. by Consumer Guide. 1980. 5.95 (ISBN 0-671-41286-8, Fireside). S&S.

Complete Book of Walking. Raymond Dreyfack. LC 80-26185. (Illus.). 288p. 1981. pap. 5.95 (ISBN 0-668-05167-1, 5167). Arco.

Complete Book of Walking. Charles T. Kuntzleman. 1980. lib. bdg. 14.95 (ISBN 0-8161-6768-0). G K Hall.

Complete Book of War Games. Consumer Guide & John Freeman. 1980. pap. 8.95 (ISBN 0-671-25375-1, Fireside). S&S.

Complete Book of Winemaking. H. E. Bravery. 160p. 1973. pap. 1.50 o.s.i. (ISBN 0-02-009250-4, Collier). Macmillan.

Complete Book of Women's Sports. Joann Lawless. LC 78-22816. (Illus.). 512p. 1981. 17.95 (ISBN 0-385-14175-0, Anchor Pr); pap. 10.95 (ISBN 0-385-17199-4). Doubleday.

Complete Book of Woodwork. rev. ed. Charles H. Hayward. LC 74-6079. (Drake Home Craftsman Ser.). (Illus.). 1974. pap. 5.95 (ISBN 0-8069-8248-9). Sterling.

Complete Book of Woodworking & Cabinetmaking. Byron Maguire. (Illus.). 1974. 16.95 (ISBN 0-87909-153-3); pap. text ed. 6.95 (ISBN 0-87909-182-7). Reston.

Complete Book on Hatching Egg Care & Sanitation. Al G. Horsting. 1981. write for info. Franklin Inst Pr.

Complete Bouvier Des Flandres. Claire McLean. LC 74-75115. (Other Dog Bks.). (Illus.). 1981. write for info. (ISBN 0-87714-077-4). Denlingers.

Complete British Clocks. Brian Loomes. LC 78-66804. (Illus.). 1978. 25.00 (ISBN 0-7153-7567-9). David & Charles.

Complete Building Construction. Ed. by John Phelps. LC 78-65477. 1978. 19.95 (ISBN 0-672-23323-1). Audel.

Complete Calorie Counter for Dining Out. K. F. Ernst. (Orig.). 1981. pap. 2.95 (ISBN 0-515-05500-X). Jove Pubns.

Complete Campers Cookbook: Nearly 200 Easy Recipes for Family Outdoor Cooking. Alberta G. Vigil. LC 80-83880. (Illus.). 104p. 1981. pap. 5.95 (ISBN 0-932906-09-5). Pan-Am Publishing Co.

Complete Camper's Cookbook: Nearly 200 Easy Recipes for Family Outdoor Cooking. Alberta G. Vigil. (Illus.). 104p. (Orig.). 1981. pap. 5.95 (ISBN 0-932906-09-5). Pan-Am Publishing Co.

Complete Candlelight Services for Christmas, No. 2. Arthur H. DeKruyter. 48p. 1980. pap. 2.95 (ISBN 0-310-42031-8, 10646P). Zondervan.

Complete Carbohydrate Counter for Dining Out. K. F. Ernst. 1981. pap. 2.95 (ISBN 0-515-05698-7). Jove Pubns.

Complete Care of Orphaned or Abandoned Baby Animals. C. E. Spaulding & Jackie Spaulding. (Illus.). 1979. 10.95 (ISBN 0-87857-266-X); pap. 7.95 (ISBN 0-87857-265-1). Rodale Pr Inc.

Complete Cat Guide. Grace Pond. 6.98 o.p. (ISBN 0-385-01607-7). Doubleday.

Complete Categorized Greek-English New Testament Vocabulary. David Holly. 1980. pap. 6.95 (ISBN 0-8010-4224-0). Baker Bk.

Complete Categorized Guide to Statistical Selection & Ranking Procedures. Edward J. Dudewicz & Joo Ok Koo. LC 80-68288. (American Sciences Press Ser. in Mathematical & Management Sciences: Vol. 6). 1981. text ed. write for info. (ISBN 0-935950-03-6). Am Sciences Pr.

Complete CB Radio Handbook. Len Buckwalter. LC 77-9300. (Illus.). 1977. 9.95 o.s.i. (ISBN 0-690-01442-2, TYC-T). T Y Crowell.

Complete Chamber Music for Strings. Franz Schubert. pap. 8.95 (ISBN 0-486-21463-X). Dover.

Complete Chesapeake Bay Retriever. Eloise H. Cherry. LC 80-25037. 1981. write for info. (ISBN 0-87605-074-7). Howell Bk.

Complete Chesapeake Bay Retriever. Eloise H. Cherry. LC 80-25037. (Illus.). 288p. 1981. 14.95 (ISBN 0-87605-074-7). Howell Bk.

Complete Chess Course. Fred Reinfeld. LC 59-13043. 1959. 12.95 (ISBN 0-385-00464-8). Doubleday.

Complete Chess Player. Fred Reinfeld. 1953. 6.95 o.p. (ISBN 0-13-159111-8). P-H.

Complete Chess Strategy: Play on the Wings, Vol. 3. Ludek Pachman. 176p. 1981. 3.95 (ISBN 0-346-12517-0). Cornerstone.

Complete Chessplayer. Fred Reinfeld. 1978. pap. 2.25 (ISBN 0-449-14101-2, GM). Fawcett.

Complete Christian. Larry Richards. 144p. 1975. pap. 2.50 (ISBN 0-88207-714-7). Victor Bks.

Complete Christmas Programs, No. 6. Grace Ramquist. 64p. 1980. pap. 1.95 (ISBN 0-310-31571-9, 10638P). Zondervan.

Complete Christmas Programs, No. 7. Grace Ramquist. 80p. 1980. pap. 1.95 (ISBN 0-310-31581-6, 10639P). Zondervan.

Complete Claudine. Colette. **Tr. by Antonia White from French. Incl. Claudine at School; Claudine & Annie; Claudine in Paris; Claudine Married. 1976. 20.00 (ISBN 0-374-12691-7); pap. 9.95 (ISBN 0-374-51379-1). FS&G.**

Complete Coalburning Stove & Furnace Guide. James W. Morrison. (Illus.). 288p. 1981. 11.95 (ISBN 0-668-05097-7, 5097-7). Arco.

Complete Collagraph: The Art & Technique of Printmaking from Collage Plates. Clare Romano & John Ross. LC 80-20685. (Illus.). 1980. 29.95 (ISBN 0-02-926770-6). Free Pr.

Complete Collagraph: The Art & Technique of Printmaking from Collage Plates. Clare Romano & John Ross. (Illus.). 1980. 29.95 (ISBN 0-02-926770-6). Macmillan.

Complete Cookie Book. Mike Thaler. 1980. pap. 1.95 (ISBN 0-380-76133-5, 76133, Camelot). Avon.

Complete Corvette Restoration & Technical Guide 1953 Through 1962, Vol. I. Noland Adams. LC 80-65894. (Illus.). 424p. 1980. 59.95 (ISBN 0-915038-14-5); leather edition 69.95 (ISBN 0-915038-22-6). Princeton Pub.

Complete Cotswolds. 2nd ed. J. Allan Cash. (History, People & Places Ser.). (Illus.). 1978. pap. 10.95 (ISBN 0-902875-45-0). Hippocrene Bks.

Complete Course in Electronic Piano Tuning. Floyd A. Stevens. LC 73-92238. (Illus.). 216p. 1974. 37.95 (ISBN 0-911012-24-9). Nelson-Hall.

Complete Course in Professional Locksmithing. Robert L. Robinson. LC 73-174584. (Illus.). 300p. 1973. 42.95 (ISBN 0-911012-15-X). Nelson-Hall.

Complete Course in Professional Piano Tuning, Repair & Rebuilding. Floyd A. Stevens. LC 74-173598. (Illus.). 1972. 37.95 (ISBN 0-911012-07-9). Nelson-Hall.

Complete Course in Short-Cut Mathematics: Combined with Simplified Mechanics for the Practical Man. B. A. Slade. 9.95 (ISBN 0-911012-11-7). Nelson-Hall.

Complete Course in Stained Glass. Pepe Mendez. 1977. 4.95 (ISBN 0-672-23287-1). Bobbs.

Complete Course in Super Ju Jitsu. Nelson Hall. pap. 13.95 (ISBN 0-911012-38-9). Nelson-Hall.

Complete Course of Lithography. Alois Senefelder. LC 68-27721. (Graphic Art Ser). (Illus.). 1968. Repr. of 1819 ed. lib. bdg. 35.00 (ISBN 0-306-71155-9). Da Capo.

Complete Credits & Collection Starter Success Kit. rev. ed. James V. Scalo. 150p. 1981. pap. 29.50 (ISBN 0-914306-55-3). Intl Wealth.

Complete Defence to 1d4: A Study of the Queen's Gambit Accepted. Bernard Cafferty & David Hooper. LC 79-41623. (Pergamon Chess Ser.). 160p. 1981. 15.75 (ISBN 0-08-024103-4); pap. 9.90 (ISBN 0-08-024102-6). Pergamon.

Complete Dentures: A Guide for Patient Treatment. Renner. (Monographs in Dentristy: Vol. 3). 1981. 32.50 (ISBN 0-89352-123-X). Masson Pub.

Complete Diabetic Cookbook. Mary Jane Finsand. LC 79-91382. (Illus.). 160p. 1980. 12.95 (ISBN 0-8069-5554-6); lib. bdg. 11.69 (ISBN 0-8069-5555-4); pap. 5.95 (ISBN 0-8069-8908-4). Sterling.

Complete Diabetic Exercise & Diet Guide. Robert C. Cantu & Hal Higdon. (Illus.). 224p. Date not set. 12.95 (ISBN 0-8027-0670-3) (ISBN 0-8027-7170-X). Walker & Co.

Complete Diamond Book. Louis A. Steiner. (Illus.). 296p. 1981. cancelled 10.95 (ISBN 0-89961-015-3). SBS Pub.

Complete Dictionary of Astrology. Alan Leo. 1978. pap. 6.95 (ISBN 0-685-62084-0). Weiser.

Complete Dictionary of Astrology. Alan Leo. (Astrologer's Library). 1978. pap. 6.95 (ISBN 0-89281-182-X). Inner Tradit.

Complete Dictionary of Buying & Merchandising. Murray Krieger. 125p. 1980. pap. text ed. 3.95 (ISBN 0-686-60189-0, M47780). Natl Ret Merch.

Complete Diet Guide: For Runners & Other Athletes. Ed. by Editors of Runner's World. LC 77-84521. (Illus.). 232p. 1978. pap. 4.95 (ISBN 0-89037-090-7); handbk. 7.95 (ISBN 0-89037-089-3). Anderson World.

Complete Dinner Party: The Dinner Party & Embroidering Our Heritage, 2 vols. Judy Chicago. 544p. 1981. pap. 28.90 boxed set (ISBN 0-385-17311-3, Anch). Doubleday.

Complete Doctor's Joke Book. Larry Wilde. 208p. (Orig.). 1981. pap. 1.95 (ISBN 0-553-14751-X). Bantam.

Complete Dog Guide. Frances Sefton. 6.98 o.p. (ISBN 0-385-01604-2). Doubleday.

Complete Dog Training Manual. Bruce Sessions. (Illus.). 1978. pap. 6.95 (ISBN 0-8306-7983-9, 983). TAB Bks.

Complete Dream Book. Edward F. Allen. 288p. 1973. pap. 2.75 (ISBN 0-446-95906-5). Warner Bks.

Complete Ecology Fact Book. Ed. by John Deedy & Philip Nobile. LC 73-175364. 408p. 1972. pap. 3.95 o.p. (ISBN 0-385-07803-X). Doubleday.

Complete Encyclopedia of Animated Cartoon Series. Jeff Lenburg. (Illus.). 192p. 1981. 24.95 (ISBN 0-87000-495-6). Arlington Hse.

Complete Encyclopedia of Commercial Vehicles. G. N. Georgano. 1979. 29.95 (ISBN 0-87341-024-6). Motorbooks Intl.

Complete Encyclopedia of Exercises. Diagram Group. 336p. 1981. pap. 9.95 (ISBN 0-442-23148-2). Van Nos Reinhold.

Complete Encyclopedia of Motorcars. rev. ed. G. N. Georgano. 1973. 30.00 o.p. (ISBN 0-525-08351-0). Dutton.

Complete Encyclopedia of Stitchery. Mildred G. Ryan. 1981. pap. 8.95 (ISBN 0-452-25264-4, Z5264, Plume). NAL.

Complete Encyclopedia of Stitchery: More Than 1400 Illustrations & 1000 Entries. Mildred G. Ryan. LC 77-16942. (Illus.). 1979. 14.95 (ISBN 0-385-12385-X). Doubleday.

Complete Encyclopedia of Television Programs, 2 vols. Vincent Terrace. LC 74-10022. 1976. Set. 29.95 o.p. (ISBN 0-498-01561-0). A S Barnes.

Complete Encyclopedia of Television Programs 1947-1979. 2nd rev. ed. Vincent Terrace. LC 79-87791. (Illus.). 1200p. 1981. 29.95 (ISBN 0-498-02177-7); pap. 10.95 (ISBN 0-498-02488-1). A S Barnes.

Complete Energy-Saving Home Improvement Guide. 4th ed. James W. Morrison. LC 80-23996. (Illus.). 1981. pap. 2.50 (ISBN 0-668-05085-3, 5085-3). Arco.

Complete England. Ed. by Reginald J. Hammond. (Ward Lock Red Guides Ser.). (Illus.). 1976. 12.95 o.p. (ISBN 0-7063-1192-2). Hippocrene Bks.

Complete English-Maori Dictionary. Ed. by Bruce Biggs. 250p. 1981. 34.00 (ISBN 0-19-647989-4). Oxford U Pr.

Complete Essays of Mark Twain. Mark Twain. LC 63-7714. 1963. 10.95 (ISBN 0-385-06590-6). Doubleday.

Complete Estate Planning Guide. rev. ed. Robert Brosterman. 1981. pap. 2.95 (ISBN 0-451-61962-5, ME1692, Ment). NAL.

Complete Estate Planning Guide: For Business & Professional Men & Women & Their Advisers. Robert Brosterman. 1964. 24.95 o.p. (ISBN 0-07-008123-9, P&RB). McGraw.

Complete Fairy Tales & Stories. Hans Christian Andersen. LC 73-83583. 1152p. (gr. 1 up). 1974. 17.95a (ISBN 0-385-01901-7); PLB (ISBN 0-385-05867-5). Doubleday.

Complete Family Guide to Living with High Blood Pressure. Michael K. Rees. LC 80-18767. 1980. 9.95 (ISBN 0-13-160432-5). P-H.

Complete Fencing. Albert Manley. LC 76-56319. 1979. 14.95 o.p. (ISBN 0-385-12075-3). Doubleday.

Complete Fisherman's Catalog: A Source Book of Information About Tackle & Accessories. Harmon Henkin. LC 76-56200. 1977. 14.95 o.s.i. (ISBN 0-397-01186-5); pap. 8.95 (ISBN 0-397-01205-5). Lippincott.

Complete Food Preservation Book: How to Can, Freeze, Preserve, Pickle, & Cure Edibles. Beverly Barbour. 1978. 12.95 o.p. (ISBN 0-679-50806-6); pap. 6.95 o.p. (ISBN 0-679-50825-2). McKay.

Complete Fortran, 3 vols. Jehosua Friedmann. Set. pap. text ed. 23.85 (ISBN 0-471-06452-1). Wiley.

Complete Games of Mikhail Tal, 1936-59. Hilary Thomas. LC 80-69576. 192p. 1981. 15.00 (ISBN 0-668-05187-6, 5187). Arco.

Complete Games of World Champion Karpov. K. J. O'Connell et al. 1976. pap. 18.95 (ISBN 0-7134-3141-5, Pub. by Batsford England). David & Charles.

Complete Guide & Cookbook for Raising Your Child As a Vegetarian. Michael Shandler & Nina Shandler. 384p. 1981. 15.50x (ISBN 0-8052-3758-5); pap. 8.95. Schocken.

Complete Guide for the Everyday Use of Gardeners, Fruit Growers, Poultrymen & Farmers on the Maketing of Their Products Directly to the Consumer. Gilbert S. Watts. (Illus.). 156p. Date not set. Repr. of 1926 ed. deluxe ed. 37.45 (ISBN 0-89901-013-X). Found Class Reprints.

Complete Guide to All Cats. Ernest H. Hart & Allan H. Hart. 1980. 14.95 (ISBN 0-684-16493-0). Scribner.

Complete Guide to American History. Robert Sobel. (Quick & Easy Ser). 1966. pap. 1.95 o.s.i. (ISBN 0-02-082060-7, Collier). Macmillan.

Complete Guide to American Pocket Watches 1981: Pocket Watches from 1809-1950. Cooksey Shugart. Ed. by Peter Schrieber. 1981. pap. 8.95 (ISBN 0-517-54378-8, Harmony). Crown.

Complete Guide to Better Golf. Bob Toski. (Illus.). 1977. 12.95 o.p. (ISBN 0-689-10722-6). Atheneum.

Complete Guide to Bowling Spares: The Encyclopedia of Spares. Dick Ritger & George Allen. LC 78-68659. (Illus.). 240p. 1979. 14.95 (ISBN 0-933554-04-4); pap. 9.95 (ISBN 0-933554-05-2). Ritger Sports.

Complete Guide to Bowling Strikes: The Encyclopedia of Strikes. George Allen & Dick Ritger. LC 80-53200. (Illus.). 240p. 1981. 14.95 (ISBN 0-933554-02-8); pap. 9.95 (ISBN 0-933554-03-6). Ritger Sports.

Complete Guide to Business Contracts. John C. Howell. 160p. 1980. pap. 5.95 (Spec). P-H.

Complete Guide to Card Conjuring. Ian Adair. LC 78-75281. (Illus.). 1979. 5.95 (ISBN 0-498-02099-1). A S Barnes.

Complete Guide to Careers in the Catholic Church for Religious & Laity. Moria B. Mathieson. 200p. (Orig.). 1980. pap. text ed. 15.00 (ISBN 0-8434-0759-X, Consortium). McGrath.

Complete Guide to Cibachrome Printing. Henry A. Shull & Peter Krause. LC 80-51937. (Illus.). 220p. 1980. 16.95 (ISBN 0-87165-057-6); pap. 11.95 (ISBN 0-87165-062-2). Ziff-Davis Pub.

Complete Guide to Co-Curricular Programs & Activities for the Middle Grades. John Frank. 1976. 11.95 o.p. (ISBN 0-13-160051-6). P-H.

Complete Guide to Communication with Deaf Blind Persons. Linda Kates & Jerome Schein. (Illus.). 108p. 1981. pap. text ed. 3.95 (ISBN 0-913072-40-0). Natl Assn Deaf.

Complete Guide to Cosmetic Facial Surgery. John W. McCurdy, Jr. LC 80-70945. (Illus.). 256p. 1981. 12.95 (ISBN 0-8119-0331-1). Fell.

Complete Guide to Demolition. D. M. Pledger. (Illus.). 1978. text ed. 18.00x (ISBN 0-904406-22-9). Longman.

Complete Guide to Disco Dancing. Karen Lustgarten. (Illus., Orig.). 1978. pap. 5.95 (ISBN 0-446-97245-2). Warner Bks.

Complete Guide to Effective Dictation. Jean Gonzalez. 1980. pap. text ed. 12.95 (ISBN 0-534-00811-9). Kent Pub Co.

Complete Guide to Electronic Games. Howard J. Blumenthal. 1981. pap. price not set (ISBN 0-452-25268-7, Z5268, Plume). NAL.

Complete Guide to Employee Benefit Plans. Ned A. Miller. LC 79-88343. 1977. 29.95 (ISBN 0-87863-149-6). Farnswth Pub.

Complete Guide to Everyday Law. rev. ed. 1977. 10.95 o.s.i. (ISBN 0-685-86168-6). Follett.

Complete Guide to Everyday Law. Samuel G. Kling. 1975. pap. 3.95 (ISBN 0-515-05824-6, Y3703). Jove Pubns.

Complete Guide to Eye Care, Eyeglasses & Contact Lenses. Herbert Solomon & Walter Zinn. LC 77-8753. 1977. 9.95 (ISBN 0-8119-0281-1). Fell.

Complete Guide to Fancy Paper Flowers. (Handicraft Ser.). (Illus.). 1979. pap. 5.50 (ISBN 0-87040-454-7). Japan Pubns.

Complete Guide to Furniture Styles. rev. ed. Louise Boger. LC 59-6239. (Encore Editions). (Illus.). 1969. 35.00 (ISBN 0-684-15020-4, ScribT). Scribner.

Complete Guide to Getting Yourself Out of Debt. Lewis M. Finley. LC 75-12716. 1975. 9.95 (ISBN 0-8119-0251-X). Fell.

Complete Guide to Hiking & Backpacking. Ed. by Andrew J. Carra. 1977. 10.95 (ISBN 0-87691-226-9). Winchester Pr.

Complete Guide to Home Appliance Repair. rev. ed. Evan Powell. LC 80-5262. (Popular Science Bk.). (Illus.). 464p. 1981. 15.95 (ISBN 0-06-013384-8, HarpT). Har-Row. Postponed.

Complete Guide to Houseboating. John W. Malo. LC 73-2122. (Illus.). 192p. 1974. 8.95 o.s.i. (ISBN 0-02-579300-4). Macmillan.

Complete Guide to Hunting. Arthur L. Cone, Jr. LC 70-119124. (Illus.). 1970. 6.95 o.s.i. (ISBN 0-02-527270-5). Macmillan.

Complete Guide to Kentucky Horse Country. William Strode. LC 80-67138. (Orig.). 1980. write for info. (ISBN 0-937222-00-3). Classic Pub.

Complete Guide to Legal Materials in Microforms: 1980 Supplement. Henry P. Tseng. 1980. perfect bdg. 25.00 (ISBN 0-686-68702-7). AMCO Intl.

Complete Guide to Modern Dance. Don McDonagh. 1977. pap. 2.50 o.p. (ISBN 0-445-08623-8). Popular Lib.

Complete Guide to Motorcycle Repair & Maintenance. Neil Schultz. LC 76-2820. 1977. pap. 4.95 o.p. (ISBN 0-385-11510-5). Doubleday.

Complete Guide to Organic Gardening West of the Cascades. Steve Solomon. 192p. 1981. pap. 9.95 (ISBN 0-914718-58-4). Pacific Search.

Complete Guide to Packaged Training Programs. Human Resource Development Press. Ed. by Leonard Nadler. 250p. (Orig.). 1981. book with periodic supplements 65.00x (ISBN 0-914234-52-8). Human Res Dev.

Complete Guide to Pest Control: With & Without Chemicals. George W. Ware. LC 80-52306. 1980. 18.50 (ISBN 0-913702-09-9). Thomson Pub CA.

Complete Guide to Prize Contests, Sweepstakes, & How to Win Them. new ed. Selma Glasser. LC 80-14523. 192p. 1980. 9.95 (ISBN 0-8119-0327-3). Fell.

Complete Guide to Researching & Writing the English Term Paper. Allan Blonde. LC 78-63036. (Orig.). 1978. pap. text ed. 3.95x (ISBN 0-87936-013-5). Scholium Intl.

Complete Guide to Riding People's Horses. Barbara Burn. (Illus.). 256p. 1981. pap. 5.95 (ISBN 0-312-15746-0). St Martin.

Complete Guide to Sea Angling. Ed. by Alan Wrangles. (Illus.). 16.95 (ISBN 0-7153-5886-3). David & Charles.

Complete Guide to Softball. George Sullivan. LC 65-14629. (Illus.). 1965. 6.95 (ISBN 0-8303-0002-3). Fleet.

Complete Guide to Successful Business Negotiation. K. H. Nothdurft. LC 73-77703. 224p. 1972. 9.00x (ISBN 0-900537-16-7, Dist. by Hippocrene Books Inc.). Leviathan Hse.

Complete Guide to Tennis Camps, Clinics & Reports in the U.S., with Special Listings for the Caribbean & Europe. Ed. by Sandra C. Friedman & Love Set, Inc. Staff. LC 78-6966. (All Seasons Travel Ser.). Date not set. pap. 5.95 o.p. (ISBN 0-87491-255-5). Acropolis.

Complete Guide to the Elementary Learning Center. Ann Piechowiak & Myra Cook. 252p. pap. 8.95 (ISBN 0-13-160309-4, Reward). P-H.

Complete Guide to the Soviet Union. Victor Louis & Jennifer Louis. 1980. pap. 9.95 o.p. (ISBN 0-312-15753-3). St Martin.

Complete Guide to Touch Dancing. Karen Lustgarten. (Illus., Orig.). 1979. pap. 5.95 (ISBN 0-446-97218-5). Warner Bks.

Complete Guide to U.S. Civil Service Jobs. 7th ed. David R. Turner. LC 72-148867. (Illus.). 1971. pap. 4.00 (ISBN 0-668-00537-8). Arco.

Complete Guide to Walleye Fishing. Art Moraski. 1980. pap. 9.95 (ISBN 0-932558-12-7). Willow Creek.

Complete Guide to Women's College Athletics. Carolyn Stanek. (Illus.). 1981. 14.95 (ISBN 0-8092-5986-9); pap. 7.95 (ISBN 0-8092-5985-0). Contemp Bks.

Complete Guide to Your Sinuses, Allergies, & Nasal Problems. John W. McCurdy, Jr. LC 80-70960. (Illus.). 256p. 1981. text ed. 12.95 (ISBN 0-8119-0429-6). Fell.

Complete Handbook of Baseball - 1981 Edition. Ed. by Zander Hollander. (Orig.). 1981. pap. 2.95 (ISBN 0-451-09682-7, Sig). NAL.

Complete Handbook of Baseball, 1980 Edition. Zander Hollander. (Orig.). (RL 7). 1980. pap. 2.50 (ISBN 0-451-09129-9, E9129, Sig). NAL.

Complete Handbook of College Basketball, 1981. Ed. by Zander Hollander. 1980. pap. 2.75 (ISBN 0-451-09497-2, E9487, Sig). NAL.

Complete Handbook of College Basketball: 1980 Edition. Ed. by Zander Hollander. (Illus.). (RL 7). 1979. pap. 2.50 (ISBN 0-451-08936-7, E8936, Sig). NAL.

Complete Handbook of Electrical & House Wiring. S. Blackwell Duncan. LC 77-1770. (Illus.). 1977. 10.95 o.p. (ISBN 0-8306-7913-8); pap. 6.95 (ISBN 0-8306-6913-2, 913). TAB Bks.

Complete Handbook of Electrical Principles & Applications. Samual T. Thornberg. 1980. 24.95 o.p. (ISBN 0-932812-02-3). Bradley CPA.

Complete Handbook of Electronics Principles & Applications. Phillip A. Johnson & Samual T. Thornberg. 1980. 29.95 o.p. (ISBN 0-932812-03-1). Bradley CPA.

Complete Handbook of Greek Verbs. N. Marinone & F. Guala. 353p. (YA) 1972. 9.95 (ISBN 0-685-20228-3). Schoenhof.

Complete Handbook of Home Painting. John L. Scherer. LC 74-33625. (Illus.). 210p. 1975. pap. 4.95 o.p. (ISBN 0-8306-4762-7, 762). TAB Bks.

Complete Handbook of Locks & Locksmithing. C. A. Roper. LC 76-43134. (Illus.). 1976. 12.95 (ISBN 0-8306-6920-5); pap. 7.95 (ISBN 0-8306-5920-X, 920). TAB Bks.

Complete Handbook of Magnetic Recording. Finn Jorgenson. (Illus.). 448p. (Orig.). 1980. 15.95 (ISBN 0-8306-9940-6); pap. text ed. 10.95 (ISBN 0-8306-1059-6, 1059). Tab Bks.

Complete Handbook of Maintenance Management. John Heintzelman. 336p. pap. 9.95 (ISBN 0-13-160986-6, Reward). P-H.

Complete Handbook of Orchid Growing. Peter M. Black. 160p. 1981. 19.95 (ISBN 0-8129-0951-8). Times Bks.

Complete Handbook of Plant Propagation. R. C. Wright & N. D. Hort. (Illus.). 192p. 1975. 14.95 (ISBN 0-02-631580-7). Macmillan.

Complete Handbook of Poultry Keeping. Stuart Banks. LC 79-14305. (Illus.). 216p. 1979. 14.95 (ISBN 0-442-23382-5); pap. 8.95 (ISBN 0-442-23383-3). Van Nos Reinhold.

Complete Handbook of Pro Basketball-1981. Ed. by Zander Hallander. pap. 2.75 (ISBN 0-451-09471-9, 9471, Sig). NAL.

Complete Handbook of Pro Football: 1980. Ed. by Zander Hollander. (Illus.). 275p. (Orig.). (YA) (RL 7). 1980. pap. 2.75 (ISBN 0-451-09359-3, E9359, Sig). NAL.

Complete Handbook of Pro Hockey, 1981. Ed. by Zander Hollander. 1980. pap. 2.75 (ISBN 0-451-09470-0, E9470, Sig). NAL.

Complete Handbook of Pruning. Ed. by Roger Grounds. LC 74-2865. (Illus.). 160p. 1975. 15.95 (ISBN 0-02-546000-5). Macmillan.

Complete Handbook of the Winter Olympic Games, Nineteen Eighty. Zander Hollander. (Illus., Orig.). 1979. pap. cancelled o.p. (ISBN 0-451-08904-9, E8904, Sig). NAL.

Complete Handbook of Videocassette Recorders. Harry Kybett. LC 77-79347. (Illus.). 1977. 9.95 o.p. (ISBN 0-8306-7811-5); pap. 5.95 o.p. (ISBN 0-8306-6811-X, 811). TAB Bks.

Complete Handyman Do-It-Yourself Encyclopedia, 26 vols. LC 74-21375. 1975. 155.48 (ISBN 0-87475-701-0). Stuttman.

Complete Hebrew-English, English-Hebrew Dictionary, 3 vols. Reuben Alcalay. 7180p. 1980. Repr. of 1965 ed. 62.00 set (ISBN 0-89961-017-X). Vol. 1 (ISBN 0-89961-003-X). Vol. 2 (ISBN 0-89961-007-2). Vol. 3 (ISBN 0-89961-008-0). SBS Pub.

Complete Home Carpenter. Ed. by George Daniels. LC 74-17659. (Illus.). 1978. pap. 9.95 (ISBN 0-672-52067-2). Bobbs.

Complete Home Guide to All the Vitamins. Ruth Adams. 432p. 1972. pap. 2.75 (ISBN 0-915962-05-5). Larchmont Bks.

Complete Home Insulation. Barry Wood. (Illus.). 1979. 14.95 (ISBN 0-7153-7799-X). David & Charles.

Complete Humorous Sketches & Tales of Mark Twain. Mark Twain. LC 61-6503. 1961. 12.95 (ISBN 0-385-01094-X). Doubleday.

Complete Hunter's Catalog. Norman Strung. LC 77-23867. (Illus.). 1977. 14.95 o.p. (ISBN 0-397-01217-9); pap. 8.95 o.s.i. (ISBN 0-397-01242-X). Lippincott.

Complete Illustrated Book of Card Games. George Hervey. LC 73-78145. 242p. 1973. 7.95 o.p. (ISBN 0-385-03251-X). Doubleday.

Complete Illustrated Book of Card Magic: The Principles & Techniques Fully Revealed in Text & Photographs. Walter B. Gibson. LC 69-10988. 1969. 15.95 o.p. (ISBN 0-385-06314-8). Doubleday.

Complete Illustrated Book of Dyes from Natural Sources. Arnold Krochmal & Connie Krochmal. LC 73-9167. 288p. 1974. pap. 4.95 o.p. (ISBN 0-385-05656-7). Doubleday.

Complete Illustrated Encyclopedia of the World's Motorcycles. Ed. by Erwin Tragatsch. LC 77-71370. (Illus.). 1977. 22.95 o.p. (ISBN 0-03-019296-X). HR&W.

Complete Illustrations from Delacroix's "Faust" & Manet's "Raven". Eugene Delacroix & Edouard Manet. (Illus.). 64p. (Orig.). 1981. pap. price not set (ISBN 0-486-24127-0). Dover.

Complete Index to P. E. & R. S. Nineteen Thirty-Foru to Nineteen Seventy-Nine. member 7.50; non-member 15.00. ASP.

Complete Index to the Gopher Historian, 1946-1972. Minnesota Historical Society. LC 68-51880. 73p. 1977. pap. 7.50 (ISBN 0-87351-113-1). Minn Hist.

Complete Indoor Exercise Book. Joyce Wilson. LC 79-642299. (Illus.). 160p. (Orig.). 1980. pap. cancelled (ISBN 0-89037-178-4). Anderson World.

Complete Indoor Gardener. rev. ed. Ed. by Dennis Brown. LC 79-4799. (Illus.). 1979. 19.95 (ISBN 0-394-50748-7); pap. 9.95 (ISBN 0-394-73813-6). Random.

Complete International Breakfast - Brunch Cookbook. Kay S. Nelson. LC 80-5714. 296p. 1981. 14.95 (ISBN 0-8128-2786-4). Stein & Day.
Complete International Salad Book. Kay S. Nelson. 304p. 1981. pap. 2.50 (ISBN 0-553-13557-0). Bantam.
Complete International Sandwich Cookbook. Sonia Uvezian. LC 80-5715. 288p. 1981. 14.95 (ISBN 0-8128-2787-2). Stein & Day.
Complete Job Book. Arnold R. Deutsch. 228p. (Orig.). 1980. pap. 6.95 (ISBN 0-346-12481-6). Cornerstone.
Complete Jogger. Jack Batten. (Illus.). 1978. pap. 1.95 (ISBN 0-515-04858-5). Jove Pubns.
Complete Junior Encyclopedia of Transportation. Ed. by A. M. Zehavi. LC 72-11310. (Illus.). 288p. (gr. 3 up). 1973. PLB 8.87 o.p. (ISBN 0-531-02596-9). Watts.
Complete L'amour, 9 bks. Louis L'Amour. Incl. To Tame a Land; Heller with a Gun; Tall Stranger; Last Stand at Papago Wells; Hondo; Kilkenny; Showdown at Yellow Butte; Utah Blaine; Crossfire Trail. (Western Fiction Ser.). 1981. Repr. of 1978 ed. Set. lib. bdg. 74.50 (ISBN 0-8398-2662-1). Gregg.
Complete Layman's Guide to the Law. J. Hanna. 1974. 15.95 o.p. (ISBN 0-13-161232-8, Spec). P-H.
Complete Layman's Guide to the Law. John P. Hanna. (Illus.). 544p. pap. 8.95 (ISBN 0-13-161224-7, Spec). P-H.
Complete Letters of Benjamin Disraeli, 1815 to 1834. Benjamin Disraeli. Ed. by John Matthews et al. 640p. 1981. 45.00x (ISBN 0-8020-5523-0). U of Toronto Pr.
Complete Letters of Lady Mary Wortley Montagu, 2 vols. Mary W. Montagu. Ed. by Robert Halsbard. Incl. Vol. 1. 1708-1720. 1965. 26.50x o.p. (ISBN 0-19-811446-X); Vol. 2. 1721-1751. 1966. 49.50x (ISBN 0-19-811455-9); Vol. 3. 1752-1762. 1967. 49.50x (ISBN 0-19-811456-7). Oxford U Pr.
Complete Letters of Vincent Van Gogh. Vincent Van Gogh. LC 78-7073. (Illus.). 1978. Repr. of 1958 ed. 75.00 (ISBN 0-8212-0735-0, 152846). NYGS.
Complete Limerick Book: The Origin, History & Achievements of the Limerick. Langford Reed. LC 78-175778. (Illus.). 147p. 1974. Repr. of 1925 ed. 15.00 (ISBN 0-8103-3974-9). Gale.
Complete List of IRS Tax Deductions. Rosalie Minkow & Howard Minkow. LC 80-82660. 272p. (Orig.). 1981. pap. 2.50 (ISBN 0-87216-775-5). Playboy Pbks.
Complete Manual of Criminal Forms, 2 vols. 2nd ed. F. Lee Bailey & Henry B. Rothblatt. LC 74-17692. (Criminal Law Library). 1974. 85.00 (ISBN 0-686-14486-4). Lawyers Co-Op.
Complete Manual of Skin Diving. A. P. Balder. LC 68-23060. (YA) 1968. 10.95 (ISBN 0-02-506410-X). Macmillan.
Complete Marriage. Nancy Van Pelt. LC 78-20770. (Orion Ser). 1979. pap. 2.95 (ISBN 0-8127-0218-2). Southern Pub.
Complete Medicine Book. Consumer Guide. 1980. 11.95 (ISBN 0-671-25501-0). S&S.
Complete Meditation. Steve Kravette. Tr. by Plunkett Dodge. (Illus.). 356p. (Orig.). 1981. pap. 9.95 (ISBN 0-914918-28-1). Para Res.
Complete Melancholick. Lewis Turco. 1981. price not set (ISBN 0-931460-12-3); pap. price not set (ISBN 0-931460-15-8). Bieler.
Complete Memoirs of George Sherston. Siegfried Sassoon. 320p. 1980. 23.95 (ISBN 0-571-06146-X, Pub by Faber & Faber); pap. 13.95 (ISBN 0-571-09913-0). Merrimack Bk Serv.
Complete MG Guide Model by Model. 2nd ed. John Christy & Karl Ludvigsen. (Illus.). 1979. cancelled (ISBN 0-8306-9783-7); pap. 4.95 (ISBN 0-8306-2056-7, 2056). TAB Bks.
Complete Mobile Home Book: The Guide to Manufactured Homes. Nicholas M. Raskhodoff. LC 80-5798. 240p. 1981. 19.95 (ISBN 0-8128-2781-3). Stein & Day.
Complete Money-Saving Book of Appliance Repairs. Harvey Morgan. (Illus.). 1980. 14.95 (ISBN 0-684-15290-8, ScribT). Scribner.
Complete Montana Travel Guide. Martin L. Peterson. LC 79-88126. (Illus.). 224p. 1980. pap. 5.95 (ISBN 0-686-28763-0). Lake County.
Complete Motorcycle Book. Lyle K. Engel. LC 73-88085. (Illus.). 208p. (YA) 1974. 8.95 o.s.i. (ISBN 0-590-17268-9, Four Winds). Schol Bk Serv.
Complete Movie Quizbook. Malcolm Vance. LC 76-16395. (Illus.). 1976. pap. 4.95 o.p. (ISBN 0-8473-1335-2). Sterling.
Complete Narrative Prose of Conrad Ferdinand Meyer, 2 vols. Tr. by George F. Folkers et al. 640p. 1976. Vol. 1, 1872-1879. 27.50 (ISBN 0-8387-1036-0); Vol. 2, 1881-1891. 27.50 (ISBN 0-8387-1547-8). Bucknell U Pr.
Complete New Encyclopedia of Little-Known, Highly Profitable Business Opportunities. rev. ed. Jack Payne. LC 74-75380. 256p. 1980. Repr. of 1971 ed. 10.95 (ISBN 0-8119-0345-1). Fell.
Complete New Guide to Preparing Baby Foods. rev. ed. Sue Castle. LC 79-6099. (Illus.). 336p. 1981. 12.95 (ISBN 0-385-15884-X). Doubleday.
Complete New Techniques in Printmaking. John Ross & Clare Romano. LC 74-2695. 1974. pap. text ed. 9.95 (ISBN 0-02-927410-9). Free Pr.
Complete Nineteen Eighty CB Handbook. Jethro K. Lieberman & Neil S. Rhodes. 1980. pap. 2.95 (ISBN 0-380-48587-7, 48587). Avon.
Complete Nonsense of Edward Lear. Edward Lear. Ed. by Holdrook Jackson. (Illus.). 7.50 (ISBN 0-8446-0722-3). Peter Smith.
Complete Novels of Guy De Maupassant. Guy De Maupassant. 756p. 1980. Repr. of 1928 ed. lib. bdg. 35.00 (ISBN 0-89987-564-5). Darby Bks.
Complete Novels of Jane Austen. Jane Austen. Incl. Vol. 1. Sense & Sensibility, Pride & Prejudice, Mansfield Park (ISBN 0-394-71891-7, V-891); Vol. 2. Emma, Northanger Abbey, Persuasion (ISBN 0-394-71892-5, V-892). 1976. pap. 4.95 ea. (Vin). Random.
Complete Official Austin-Healey 100-Six & 3000, 1956-1968. British Leyland Motors. LC 77-72588. (Illus.). 416p. 1977. pap. 25.00 (ISBN 0-8376-0133-9). Bentley.
Complete Official MGB, Model Years 1975-1980: Comprising the Official Driver's Handbook & Workshop Manual. British Leyland Motors. LC 80-65229. (Illus.). 304p. 1980. pap. 17.50 (ISBN 0-8376-0112-6). Bentley.
Complete Official Sprite-Midget 948 & 1098cc: Comprising the Official Driver's Handbook, Workshop Manual, Special Tuning Manual. British Leyland Motors. LC 67-28432. (Illus.). 384p. (Orig.). 1968. pap. 17.50 (ISBN 0-8376-0023-5). Bentley.
Complete Official Triumph GT6, GT6 Plus &GT6 Mk 3 1967-1973: Official Driver's Handbook & Official Workshop Manual. British Leyland Motors. LC 74-21353. (Illus.). 480p. 1975. pap. 25.00 (ISBN 0-8376-0120-7). Bentley.
Complete Official Triumph Spitfire MK III, MK IV & 1500, Model Years 1968-1974: Comprising the Official Driver's Handbook & Workshop Manual. British Leyland Motors. LC 74-20004. (Illus.). 480p. 1975. pap. 25.00 (ISBN 0-8376-0123-1). Bentley.
Complete Official Triumph Tr6 & Tr250, 1967-1976: Comprising the Official Driver's Handbook & Workshop Manual. British Leyland Motors. LC 77-91592. (Illus.). 608p. 1978. pap. 25.00 (ISBN 0-8376-0108-8). Bentley.
Complete Official Trump Spitfire Fifteen Hundred, Model Years 1975-1980: Comprising the Official Driver's Handbook & Workshop Manual. British Leyland Motors. LC 79-53184. (Illus.). 1980. pap. 17.50 (ISBN 0-8376-0122-3). Bentley.
Complete Official 1275 cc Sprite-Midget 1967-1974: Comprising the Official Driver's Handbook, Workshop Manual, Emission Control Supplement. British Leyland Motors. LC 75-37232. (Illus.). 400p. 1975. pap. 17.50 (ISBN 0-8376-0127-4). Bentley.
Complete Option Player. Kenneth R. Trester. (Illus.). 316p. 1977. 20.00 (ISBN 0-9604914-0-6). Investrek.
Complete Outdoor Cookbook. Dan Morris & Inez Morris. 1979. pap. 6.95 (ISBN 0-8015-1627-7, Hawthorn). Dutton.
Complete Outdoors Encyclopedia. Vin Sparano. LC 72-90934. 1980. 18.95 (ISBN 0-06-013955-2, HarpT). Har-Row.
Complete Outdoors Encyclopedia. rev. ed. Vin T. Sparano. LC 72-90934. (Outdoor Life Bk.). (Illus.). 634p. 1973. 16.95 (ISBN 0-06-013955-2, 0-06014033, HarpT). Har-Row.
Complete Outdoorsman's Guide to Edible Wild Plants. Berndt Berglund & Clare E. Bolsby. LC 78-162948. (Illus.). 1971. pap. 4.95 (ISBN 0-684-15481-1, SL278, ScribT). Scribner.
Complete Piano Sonatas, 2 vols. Ludwig Van Beethoven. Ed. by Heinrich Schenker. LC 74-83473. 1975. pap. 7.50 ea. Vol. 1 (ISBN 0-486-23134-8). Vol. 2 (ISBN 0-486-23135-6). Dover.
Complete Play Production Handbook. Carl Allensworth et al. LC 73-14814. (Illus.). 366p. 1973. 12.95 (ISBN 0-690-20752-2, TYC-T). T Y Crowell.
Complete Plays of Ben Johnson, Vol.1. Ed. by G. A. Wilkes. 428p. 1980. 89.00 (ISBN 0-19-812599-2). Oxford U Pr.
Complete Plays of Ben Jonson, Vol. 2. Ed. by G. A. Wilkes. 448p. 1981. 89.00 (ISBN 0-19-812601-8). Oxford U Pr.
Complete Plays of Christopher Marlowe. Christopher Marlowe. Ed. by Irving Ribner. LC 63-12619. 1963. pap. 9.50 (ISBN 0-672-63020-6). Odyssey Pr.
Complete Plays of Gilbert & Sullivan. W. S. Gilbert & Arthur Sullivan. (Illus.). 640p. 1976. pap. 8.95 (ISBN 0-393-00828-2, Norton Lib). Norton.
Complete Plays of T. S. Eliot. T. S. Eliot. LC 50-14646. 1969. 12.95 (ISBN 0-15-120755-0). HarBraceJ.
Complete Poems. Elizabeth Bishop. LC 69-15407. 216p. 1969. 10.00 (ISBN 0-374-12744-1); pap. 6.95 (ISBN 0-374-51516-6). FS&G.
Complete Poems. Emily J. Bronte. Ed. by C. W. Hatfield. LC 41-21750. 1941. 17.50x (ISBN 0-231-01222-5). Columbia U Pr.
Complete Poems. John Donne. Ed. by Roger Bennett. 1969. pap. 3.45 (ISBN 0-87532-103-8). Hendricks House.
Complete Poems. Randall Jarrell. 507p. 1969. 20.00 (ISBN 0-374-12716-6); pap. 10.95 (ISBN 0-374-51305-8). FS&G.
Complete Poems & Selected Letters. John Keats. Ed. by Clarence D. Thorpe. 1935. 13.95 (ISBN 0-672-63157-1). Odyssey Pr.
Complete Poems & Selected Letters & Prose of Hart Crane. Hart Crane. 1966. pap. 2.95 (ISBN 0-385-01531-3, A537, Anch). Doubleday.
Complete Poems & Selected Letters of Michelangelo. Tr. by Creighton Gilbert from It. LC 79-87767. 1980. 22.00x (ISBN 0-691-03925-9); pap. 5.95 (ISBN 0-691-00324-6). Princeton U Pr.
Complete Poems Nineteen-Thirteen to Nineteen Sixty-Two. E. E. Cummings. LC 80-14213. 1980. pap. 9.95 (ISBN 0-15-621062-2, Harv). HarBraceJ.
Complete Poems of Emily Jane Bronte. Ed. by C. W. Hatfield. LC 41-21750. 1941. 17.50x (ISBN 0-231-01222-5). Columbia U Pr.
Complete Poems of Marianne Moore. Marianne Moore. (Illus.). 320p. 1981. 16.95 (ISBN 0-670-23505-9). Viking Pr.
Complete Poems of Paul Laurence Dunbar. Paul L. Dunbar. LC 80-16651. 1980. pap. 4.95 (ISBN 0-396-07895-8). Dodd.
Complete Poems of Samar Sen. Samar Sen. Tr. by Pritish Nandy. (Writers Workshop Saffronbird Ser.). 1975. 11.00 (ISBN 0-88253-514-5); pap. text ed. 4.80 (ISBN 0-88253-513-7). Ind-US Inc.
Complete Poems of Thomas Hardy. Thomas Hardy. Ed. by James Gibson. LC 77-15579. 1978. 24.95 (ISBN 0-02-548150-9). Macmillan.
Complete Poetical Works of Percy Bysshe Shelley: 1814-1817, Vol. 2. Percy B. Shelley. (Oxford English Texts Ser.). 1974. 45.00x (ISBN 0-19-812707-3). Oxford U Pr.
Complete Poetical Works of Thomas Hood. Thomas Hood. Ed. by Walter Jerrold. LC 80-14589. (Illus.). xv, 773p. 1980. Repr. of 1920 ed. lib. bdg. 39.75x (ISBN 0-313-22486-2, HOCO). Greenwood.
Complete Poetical Works of William Wordsworth, 10 vols. Ed. by Andrew J. George. 1981. Repr. of 1919 ed. Set. lib. bdg. 350.00 (ISBN 0-89987-862-8). Darby Bks.
Complete Poetry & Selected Criticism of Edgar Allan Poe. Edgar A. Poe. Ed. by Allen Tate. 1981. pap. 5.95 (ISBN 0-452-00548-5, F548, Mer). NAL.
Complete Poetry of John Donne. Ed. by John T. Shawcross. LC 67-15386. pap. 5.95 (ISBN 0-385-05256-1, ACO11, Anch). Doubleday.
Complete Poetry of John Milton. Ed. by John T. Shawcross. LC 72-150934. 1971. pap. 5.95 (ISBN 0-385-02351-0, Anch). Doubleday.
Complete Postcards from the Americas: Poems of Road & Sea. Blaise Cendrars. LC 73-94445. 1976. 15.95x (ISBN 0-520-02716-7). U of Cal Pr.
Complete Practical Book of Country Crafts. Jack Hill. LC 79-51091. (Illus.). 1979. 22.50 (ISBN 0-7153-7706-X). David & Charles.
Complete Preludes & Etudes for Solo Piano. Frederic Chopin. Ed. by Ignacy J. Paderewski. 224p. 1980. pap. 6.50 (ISBN 0-486-24052-5). Dover.
Complete Problem Solver. John R. Hayes. 1981. write for info. Franklin Inst Pr.
Complete Professor Challenger Stories. Arthur Conan Doyle. 1952. 18.50 (ISBN 0-7195-0360-4). Transatlantic.
Complete Prose Works, 4 vols. Philip Sidney. Ed. by A. Feuillerat. Incl. Vol. 1. The Countesse of Pembroke's Arcadia. 65.00 (ISBN 0-521-06468-6); Vol. 2. The Last Part of Countesse of Pembroke's Arcadia & the Lady of May. 42.00 (ISBN 0-521-06469-4); Vol. 3. The Defence of Poesie, Political Discourses, Correspondence, Translations. 57.00 (ISBN 0-521-06470-8); Vol. 4. The Older Arcadia. 57.00 (ISBN 0-521-06471-6). 190.00 set (ISBN 0-521-08770-8). Cambridge U Pr.
Complete Published Poems of Nathaniel Tucker, Together with Columbinus: A Mask (1783) Nathaniel Tucker. LC 73-12391. 192p. 1973. lib. bdg. 25.00x (ISBN 0-8201-1121-X). Schol Facsimiles.
Complete Pun Book. 224p. 1980. pap. 1.95 (ISBN 0-345-28889-0). Ballantine.
Complete Puppy & Dog Book. rev. ed. Norman Johnson. LC 77-5685. (Illus.). 1977. 16.95 (ISBN 0-689-10808-7). Atheneum.
Complete Question & Answer Guide to Hairdressing & Cosmetology. Anthony B. Colletti. 1978. text ed. 16.00 (ISBN 0-912126-48-5, 1258-01); pap. text ed. 14.21 (ISBN 0-912126-49-3, 1258-00). Keystone Pubns.
Complete Reading Supervisor: Task & Roles. Leslie Burg et al. 1978. text ed. 15.95 (ISBN 0-675-08481-4); instr. manual 3.95 (ISBN 0-686-67972-5). Merrill.
Complete Real Estate Adviser. Daniel J. De Benedictis. 1977. pap. 4.95 (ISBN 0-346-12212-0). Cornerstone.
Complete Real Estate Investment Handbook. C. F. Sirmans & Austin J. Jaffe. (Illus.). 272p. 1981. 17.95 (ISBN 0-13-162321-4, Spectrum); pap. 8.95 (ISBN 0-13-162313-3). P-H.
Complete Real Estate Listings Handbook. Theodore Esau. 265p. 18.95 (ISBN 0-13-162404-0, Busn). P-H.
Complete Real Estate Math Book. Margie Sussex & John F. Stapleton. 320p. 1976. 14.95 (ISBN 0-13-162354-0). P-H.
Complete Relief Print. John Ross & Clare Romano. LC 74-2694. 1974. pap. text ed. 9.95 (ISBN 0-02-927390-0). Free Pr.
Complete Rhyming Dictionary. Ed. by Clement Wood. 1936. 8.95 (ISBN 0-385-00046-4). Doubleday.
Complete Rug Hooker: A Guide to the Craft. Joan Moshimer. LC 74-25357. (Illus.). 176p. 1975. 15.95 (ISBN 0-8212-0647-8, 152730); pap. 8.95 (ISBN 0-8212-0747-4, 152854). NYGS.
Complete Runner. Runner's World Magazine Editors. 1978. pap. 4.95 (ISBN 0-380-01885-3, 37127). Avon.
Complete Russian Course for Beginners. Michael Beresford. 1965. 14.50x (ISBN 0-19-815642-1). Oxford U Pr.
Complete Sayings of Hazrat Inayat Khan. Inayat Khan. LC 77-94684. (Collected Works of Hazrat Inayat Khan Ser.). 299p. 1978. 7.95 (ISBN 0-930872-02-9). Sufi Order Pubns.
Complete Scarsdale Medical Diet. Herman Tarnower & Samm S. Baker. 240p. 1981. pap. 2.95 (ISBN 0-553-14446-4). Bantam.
Complete Scotland. 13th ed. Reginald J. Hammond. Ed. by Kenneth E. Lowther. (Red Guide Ser.). (Illus.). 449p. 1980. 17.50x (ISBN 0-7063-5905-4). Intl Pubns Serv.
Complete Screen Print & the Lithograph. John Ross & Clare Romano. LC 74-2696. 1974. pap. text ed. 9.95 (ISBN 0-02-927380-3). Free Pr.
Complete Screenplays, Vol. I: A Prisoner Escaped. Robert Bresson. Ed. by Annette Michelson. Tr. by Noel Burch. 1981. 15.00 (ISBN 0-89396-033-0); pap. 7.95 (ISBN 0-89396-034-9). Urizen Bks. Postponed.
Complete Series 6 Study Book. Dennis Doyle. (Illus.). 350p. (Orig.). 1980. pap. text ed. 23.50 (ISBN 0-914234-14-5). Human Res Dev Pr.
Complete Set of Commentaries, 28 vols. H. A. Ironside. 170.00 (ISBN 0-87213-350-8). Loizeaux.
Complete Shellfisherman's Guide. David Tedone. (Illus.). 200p. 1981. pap. 7.95 (ISBN 0-933614-09-8). Peregrine Pr.
Complete Sherlock Holmes. Doyle, Arthur Conan, Sir. LC 65-6074. 11.95 (ISBN 0-385-00689-6); Two-volume edition 15.95 (ISBN 0-385-04591-3). Doubleday.
Complete Short Stories. H. G. Wells. LC 79-145813. 1971. 14.95 (ISBN 0-312-15855-6, C4000). St Martin.
Complete Short Stories of Mark Twain. Mark Twain. LC 57-5536. 1957. 10.95 (ISBN 0-385-01502-X). Doubleday.
Complete Shorter Works for Piano. Johannes Brahms. Ed. by Eusebius Mandyczewski. LC 70-116828. 1970. pap. 5.50 (ISBN 0-486-22651-4). Dover.
Complete Shortwave Listener's Handbook. 2nd ed. Hank Bennett & Harry L. Helms. (Illus.). 308p. 1980. 14.95 (ISBN 0-8306-9941-4); pap. 9.95 (ISBN 0-8306-1255-6, 1255). Tab Bks.
Complete Sing-for-Fun Book. Ray M. Cook. Ed. by Samuel Cook. (gr. 2-12). 1974. loose leaf 10.00 (ISBN 0-8074-0004-1, 583992). UAHC.
Complete Snooker. Joe Davis. (Illus.). 286p. 1975. 12.95 o.p. (ISBN 0-491-01521-6). Transatlantic.
Complete Song Cycles. Franz Schubert. Ed. by Euseblus Mandyczewski. Tr. by Henry S. Drinker. LC 74-116821. Orig. Title: Lieder & Gesange. 1970. pap. 6.00 (ISBN 0-486-22649-2). Dover.
Complete Songs of Rammohun Roy. Rammohun Roy. Tr. by Nikhiles Guha from Bengali. (Safronbird Book). 72p. (Eng.). 1975. 12.00 (ISBN 0-89253-544-X); pap. 4.80 (ISBN 0-88253-710-5). Ind-US Inc.
Complete Sprouting Cookbook. Karen C. Whyte. LC 72-92942. (Illus.). 120p. 1973. pap. 4.95 (ISBN 0-912300-28-0, 28-0). Troubador Pr.
Complete Stories. Flannery O'Connor. 555p. 1971. 17.50 (ISBN 0-374-12752-2); pap. 6.95 (ISBN 0-374-51536-0). FS&G.

Complete Stories & Poems of Edgar Allan Poe. Edgar Allan Poe. LC 66-24310. 9.95 (ISBN 0-385-07407-7). Doubleday.

Complete String Quartets Transcribed for Four-Hand Piano, 2 series. unabr. ed. C. F. Peters. Ser. 1, 320p. pap. 7.95 (ISBN 0-486-23974-8); Ser. 2, 256p. pap. 6.95 (ISBN 0-486-23975-6). Dover.

Complete String Quintets. Wolfgang A. Mozart. 181p. 1978. pap. 6.00 (ISBN 0-486-23603-X). Dover.

Complete Stylist & Handbook. 2nd ed. Sheridan Baker. 1980. text ed. 11.50 scp (ISBN 0-06-040452-3, HarpC); instructor's manual avail. (ISBN 0-685-95565-6). Har-Row.

Complete Sumi-E Techniques. Sadami Yamada. LC 66-24010. 1966. pap. 10.95 (ISBN 0-87040-361-3). Japan Pubns.

Complete Symphonies; in Full Orchestral Score. Johannes Brahms. Ed. by Hans Gal. LC 73-92635. 352p. 1974. pap. 8.95 (ISBN 0-486-23053-8). Dover.

Complete Symphonies in Full Score. Robert Schumann. 1980. pap. 11.95 (ISBN 0-486-24013-4). Dover.

Complete Tales of Uncle Remus. Joel C. Harris. Ed. by Richard Chase. (Illus.). (gr. 7 up). 1955. 24.50 (ISBN 0-395-06799-5). HM.

Complete Tap Dance Book. Anne S. Duggan. 1977. pap. text ed. 7.50x (ISBN 0-8191-0137-0). U Pr of Amer.

Complete Tent Book. Andrew Sugar. 1979. 12.95 o.p. (ISBN 0-8092-7522-8); pap. 5.95 o.p. (ISBN 0-8092-7520-1). Contemp Bks.

Complete Terrace Book. Stanley Schuler. 1974. pap. 5.95 o.s.i. (ISBN 0-02-063710-1, Collier). Macmillan.

Complete Terrace Book. Stanley Schuler. LC 73-22529. (Illus.). 256p. 1974. 8.95 o.s.i. (ISBN 0-02-607380-3). Macmillan.

Complete Text of the Equal Rights Amendment. Ed. by James K. Harris. 132p. 1981. 3.95 (ISBN 0-9605188-0-0). Ganis & Harris.

Complete Thames & Chilterns. Ed. by Reginald J. Hammond. LC 77-437537. (Red Guide Ser.). (Illus.). 1977. 11.25x (ISBN 0-7063-5502-4). Intl Pubns Serv.

Complete Treatise on the Art of Singing, Pt. 2. Manuel Garcia, II. Tr. & pref. by V. Paschke. LC 74-23382. xii, 261p. 1975. Repr. of 1972 ed. lib. bdg. 25.00 (ISBN 0-306-70660-1). Da Capo.

Complete Trout & Salmon Fisherman. Jack Thorndike. LC 78-60987. (Illus.). 1978. 17.95 (ISBN 0-7153-7717-5). David & Charles.

Complete Unabridged Super Trivia Encyclopedia. Fred L. Worth. 1978. pap. 3.50 (ISBN 0-446-96905-2). Warner Bks.

Complete Underwater Diving Manual. U. S. National Oceanic & Atmospheric Administration. (Nautical Ser.). (Illus.). 1977. 14.95 o.p. (ISBN 0-679-50774-4); pap. 8.95 (ISBN 0-679-50826-0). McKay.

Complete University Word Hunter. John T. Gause. (Apollo Eds.). (YA) (gr. 9-12). pap. 2.45 o.s.i. (ISBN 0-8152-0140-0, A140, TYC-T). T Y Crowell.

Complete Urban Farmer: How to Grow Your Own Fruits & Vegetables in Town. David Wickers. (Handbooks Ser). 1978. pap. 2.95 o.p. (ISBN 0-14-046288-0). Penguin.

Complete Van Gogh: Paintings, Drawings, Graphic Sketches. Jan Hulsker. (Illus.). 496p. 1980. 95.00 (ISBN 0-686-62711-3, 1701-7). Abrams.

Complete Vegetable Gardener. Peter Seabrook. (Illus.). 128p. 1981. 17.95 (ISBN 0-686-69382-5); pap. 7.95 (ISBN 0-686-69383-3). A & W Pubs.

Complete Vegetable Grower. W. E. Shewell-Cooper. 1973. pap. 5.50 (ISBN 0-571-04797-1, Pub. by Faber & Faber). Merrimack Bk Serv.

Complete Venus Equilateral. George O. Smith. 1976. pap. 1.95 o.p. (ISBN 0-345-25551-8). Ballantine.

Complete Visitor's Guide to Mesoamerican Ruins. Joyce Kelly. (Illus.). 480p. 1981. 35.00 (ISBN 0-8061-1566-1). U of Okla Pr.

Complete Welsh-English English-Welsh Dictionary: Y Geiriadur Mawr. 8th ed. H. Meurig Evans & W. O. Thomas. 1979. text ed. 27.50x (ISBN 0-391-01734-9). Humanities.

Complete Window Book. A Kirsch Company Publication. 1978. 5.95 o.p. (ISBN 0-385-14524-1). Doubleday.

Complete Woman. Patricia Gundry. LC 79-8928. 240p. 1981. 10.95 (ISBN 0-385-15521-2, Galilee). Doubleday.

Complete Women's Weight Training Guide. Edie Leen. LC 78-64384. (Illus.). 176p. 1980. pap. 6.95 (ISBN 0-89037-161-X). Anderson World.

Complete Woodworker. Bernard E. Jones. LC 80-634. (Illus.). 1980. pap. 7.95 (ISBN 0-89815-022-1). Ten Speed Pr.

Complete Word Game Finisher. John Griffiths. 1980. pap. 7.95 (ISBN 0-446-97582-6). Warner Bks.

Complete Works. Geoffrey Chaucer. Ed. by Walter W. Skeat. (Oxford Standard Authors). 1933. 27.50x (ISBN 0-19-254119-6). Oxford U Pr.

Complete Works, 2 vols. Anthony Holborne. Ed. by Masakata Kanazawa. Incl. Vol. 1. Music for Lute & Bandora. (Illus.). 1967. pap. 17.50x (ISBN 0-674-15500-9); Vol. 2. Music for Cittern. 1974. pap. 15.95x (ISBN 0-674-15512-2). LC 67-14341. (Publications in Music Ser: No. 1, 5). Harvard U Pr.

Complete Works for Pianoforte Solo, 2 vols. Felix Mendelssohn. 416p. 1975. pap. 6.00 ea. (ISBN 0-486-23136-4). Vol. 1. Vol. 2 (ISBN 0-486-23137-2). Dover.

Complete Works of Anne Bradstreet. Ed. by Joseph E. McElrath, Jr. (Critical Editions Program Ser.). 1981. lib. bdg. 35.00 (ISBN 0-8057-8533-7). Twayne.

Complete Works of Christopher Marlowe, 2 vols. Christopher Marlowe. Ed. by F. Bowers. 922p. 1973. Set. 144.00 (ISBN 0-521-07323-5); Vol. 1. 80.00 (ISBN 0-521-20031-8); Vol. 2. 84.00 (ISBN 0-521-20032-6). Cambridge U Pr.

Complete Works of Chuang Tzu. Chuang Tzu. Tr. by Burton Watson. LC 68-19000. (Translations from the Oriental Classics & Records of Civilization Ser.). 1968. 23.00x (ISBN 0-231-03147-5). Columbia U Pr.

Complete Works of Edgar Allen Poe, 10 vols. Edgar A. Poe. 1981. Repr. of 1908 ed. Set. lib. bdg. 400.00 (ISBN 0-89987-660-9). Darby Bks.

Complete Works of Flavius Josephus. Flavius Josephus. Tr. by William Whiston. LC 60-15405. (Orig.). 1974. 17.95 (ISBN 0-8254-2951-X); kivar 12.95 (ISBN 0-8254-2952-8). Kregel.

Complete Works of Lao Tzu: Tao Teh Ching & Hua Hu Ching. Master Ni Hua-Ching & Hua-Ching. LC 79-88745. 219p. 1979. pap. text ed. 7.50x (ISBN 0-937064-00-9). Wisdom Garden.

Complete Works of O. Henry. O. Henry. LC 53-6098. 1953. 14.95 (ISBN 0-385-00961-5). Doubleday.

Complete Works of Robert Browning: With Variant Readings & Annotations, Vol. V. Robert Browning. Ed. by Roma A. King, Jr. et al. LC 68-18389. (Illus.). 400p. 1981. 35.00x (ISBN 0-8214-0220-X). Ohio U Pr.

Complete Works of Shakespeare. 3rd ed. David Bevington. 1980. text ed. 21.95x (ISBN 0-673-15193-X). Scott F.

Complete Works of Shakespeare. 2nd ed. William Shakespeare. Ed. by Irving Ribner. 1971. 26.95 (ISBN 0-471-00553-3). Wiley.

Complete Works of Sister Nivedita, 4 vols. Sr. Nivedita. Incl. Vol. 1. Our Master & His Message, the Master As I Saw Him, Kali the Mother, Lectures & Articles (ISBN 0-87481-112-0); Vol. 2. Web of Indian Life, an Indian Study on Love & Death, Studies from an Eastern Home, Lectures & Articles (ISBN 0-87481-113-9); Vol. 3. Indian Art, Cradle Tales of Hinduism, Religion & Dharma (ISBN 0-87481-114-7); Vol. 4. Footfalls of Indian History, Bodh-Gaya, Civic Ideal & Indian Nationality, Hints on National Education in India (ISBN 0-87481-115-5). 32.00x set (ISBN 0-87481-150-3). Vedanta Pr.

Complete Works of Thomas Holley Chivers: Correspondence of Thomas Holley Chivers, 1838-1858, Vol. 1. Thomas H. Chivers. Ed. by Emma L. Chase & Lois F. Parks. LC 57-8677. 320p. 1957. 12.50x (ISBN 0-87057-047-1, Pub. by Brown U Pr). Univ Pr of New England.

Complete Works of Washington Irving: Letters, Eighteen Hundred Two to Eighteen Twenty-Three. Ed. by Ralph M. Aderman et al. (Twayne's Critical Editions Program: Vol. 1). 1978. lib. bdg. 30.00 (ISBN 0-8057-8522-1). G K Hall.

Complete Works of William Shakespeare. 1300p. Date not set. 19.98 (ISBN 0-7064-1400-4). Mayflower Bks.

Complete Works of William Shakespeare. William Shakespeare. 1946. 15.95 (ISBN 0-385-00049-9). Doubleday.

Complete Works with Selected Letters. Arthur Rimbaud. Tr. by Wallace Fowlie. LC 66-13885. (Fr & Eng). 1967. pap. 6.95 (ISBN 0-226-71973-1, P288, Phoen). U of Chicago Pr.

Complete Writings of William Blake, with Variant Readings. William Blake. Ed. by Geoffrey Keynes. (Oxford Standard Authors Ser.). 1966. 34.00 (ISBN 0-19-254157-9); pap. 9.95x (ISBN 0-19-281050-2). Oxford U Pr.

Complete Wye Valley, Hereford & Worchester. Ed. by Reginald J. Hammond & Kenneth Lowther. LC 77-351996. (Red Guide Ser.). (Illus.). 1976. 11.25x (ISBN 0-7063-5134-7). Intl Pubns Serv.

Complete Yogurt Cookbook. Karen C. Whyte. 160p. 1976. pap. 1.95 (ISBN 0-345-27725-2). Ballantine.

Completeness & Basis Properties of Sets of Special Functions. J. R. Higgins. LC 76-19630. (Cambridge Tracts in Mathematics Ser.: No. 72). (Illus.). 1977. 47.50 (ISBN 0-521-21376-2). Cambridge U Pr.

Complex Analysis. Serge R. Lang. LC 76-15463. (Illus.). 1977. text ed. 19.95 (ISBN 0-201-04137-5). A-W.

Complex Analysis & Its Applications, 3 vols. 1977. Set. pap. 80.25 (ISBN 0-685-79710-4, IAEA). Unipub.

Complex Analysis, Microbial Calculus & Relativistic Quantum Theory. Ed. by D. Iagolnitzer. (Lecture Notes in Physics: Vol. 126). 502p. 1980. pap. 33.60 (ISBN 0-387-09996-4). Springer-Verlag.

Complex Analytic Varieties. Hassler Whitney. 1972. 20.95 (ISBN 0-201-08653-0). A-W.

Complex Configuration: Modern Verse Drama. Donna Gerstenberger. (Salzburg Studies in English Literature, Poetic Drama & Poetic Theory: No. 5). 178p. 1973. pap. text ed. 25.00x (ISBN 0-391-01383-1). Humanities.

Complex Decision Problems: An Integrated Strategy for Resolution. K. J. Radford. (Illus.). 224p. 1977. text ed. 13.95 (ISBN 0-87909-171-1). Reston.

Complex Function Theory. Maurice Heins. (Pure & Applied Mathematics Ser.: Vol. 28). 1968. text ed. 24.95 (ISBN 0-12-337950-4). Acad Pr.

Complex Inheritance. Ed. by James G. Moseley. LC 75-8955. (American Academy of Religion. Dissertation Ser.). ix, 169p. 1975. pap. 7.50 (ISBN 0-89130-000-7, 010104). Scholars Pr Ca.

Complex Integration & Cauchy's Theorem. G. N. Watson. (Cambridge Tracts in Mathematics & Mathematical Physics Ser.: No. 15). 1960. Repr. of 1914 ed. 7.50 o.s.i. (ISBN 0-02-854490-0). Hafner.

Complex Numbers. Walter Ledermann. (Library of Mathematics). 1971. pap. 5.00 (ISBN 0-7100-4345-7). Routledge & Kegan.

Complex Numbers. J. Williams. (Problem Solvers Ser.). (Illus.). 1972. pap. text ed. 4.95x o.p. (ISBN 0-04-512019-6). Allen Unwin.

Complex Numbers in Geometry. I. M. Yaglom. 1967. 30.50 o.p. (ISBN 0-12-768150-7). Acad Pr.

Complex Organizations: A Critical Essay. 2nd ed. Charles Perrow. 1979. pap. text ed. 8.95x (ISBN 0-673-15205-7). Scott F.

Complex Organizations: Critical Perspectives. Mary Zey-Ferrell & Michael Aiken. pap. text ed. 11.95 (ISBN 0-673-15269-3). Scott F.

Complex Partial Seizures & Their Treatment. Ed. by J. K. Penry & D. D. Daly. LC 75-14584. (Advances in Neurology: Vol. 11). 480p. 1975. 32.00 (ISBN 0-89004-040-0). Raven.

Complex Scaling in the Spectral Theory of the Hamiltonian: Proceedings of the 1978 Sanibel Workshop. P. O. Lowdin. (International Journal of Quantum Chemistry Ser.: Vol. XIII, No. 4). 1978. pap. 33.50 (ISBN 0-471-05774-6, Pub. by Wiley-Interscience). Wiley.

Complex Variables. Robert B. Ash. 1971. text ed. 22.95 (ISBN 0-12-065250-1). Acad Pr.

Complex Variables. H. R. Chillingworth. LC 72-86178. 280p. 1973. text ed. 32.00 (ISBN 0-08-016938-4); pap. text ed. 18.75 (ISBN 0-08-016939-2). Pergamon.

Complex Variables. Norman Levinson & Raymond Redheffer. LC 76-113833. (Illus.). 1970. text ed. 24.95x (ISBN 0-8162-5104-5); sol. man. 2.95 (ISBN 0-8162-5114-2). Holden-Day.

Complex Variables. George Polya & Gordon Latta. LC 73-14882. 352p. 1974. text ed. 24.95 (ISBN 0-471-69330-8). Wiley.

Complex Variables. Herb Silverman. 1975. text ed. 21.50 (ISBN 0-395-18582-3). HM.

Complex Variables & the Laplace Transform for Engineers. Wilbur R. LePage. (Illus.). 1980. pap. text ed. 6.00 (ISBN 0-486-63926-6). Dover.

Compliance with Federal Election Campaign Requirements: A Guide for Candidates. 1978. 18.00 (ISBN 0-685-58494-1). Am Inst CPA.

Compliance with Revenue Sharing Auditing Requirements: The New York State Case. John T. Marlin. (Government Auditing Ser.). 67p. 1980. pap. 7.50 (ISBN 0-916450-31-7). Coun on Municipal.

Complications in Obstetric & Gynecologic Surgery. Ed. by George Schaefer & Edward A. Graber. (Illus.). 650p. 1981. text ed. write for info. (ISBN 0-06-142330-0, Harper Medical). Har-Row.

Complications in Opthalmic Surgery. Stephen R. Waltman & Theodore Krupin. (Illus.). 333p. 1980. text ed. 37.00 (ISBN 0-397-50441-1). Lippincott.

Complications in Vascular Surgery. Hugh G. Beebe. LC 73-7978. (Illus.). 402p. 1973. 37.50 (ISBN 0-397-50269-9). Lippincott.

Complications of Diagnostic Radiology. John F. Weigan & Sydney F. Thomas. (Illus.). 576p. 1973. 35.75 (ISBN 0-398-02501-0). C C Thomas.

Complications of External Skeletal Fixation: Causes, Prevention, & Treatment. Stuart A. Green. write for info. (ISBN 0-398-04482-1). C C Thomas.

Complications of Gastric Surgery. David Fromm. LC 77-9313. (Clinical Gastroenterology Monographs). 1977. 28.95 (ISBN 0-471-28291-X, Pub. by Wiley Medical). Wiley.

Complications of Nervous System Trauma. Ed. by Richard A. Thompson & John R. Green. LC 78-52425. (Advances in Neurology Ser.: Vol. 22). 1979. text ed. 34.50 (ISBN 0-89004-295-0). Raven.

Complicity & Conviction: An Architecture of Convention. William Q. Hubbard. (Illus.). 1980. text ed. 12.50 (ISBN 0-262-08106-7). MIT Pr.

Complying with Equal Employment Regulations for Handicapped Persons. 1979. pap. 3.00 (ISBN 0-917386-84-1). Exec Ent.

Component & Modular Techniques: A Builder's Handbook. Robert C. Reschke. Ed. by Virginia Case. (Illus.). 300p. 1981. 39.95 (ISBN 0-89999-016-9). Structures Pub.

Component Support Snubbers: Design, Application & Testing. Ed. by D. D. Reiff. (PVP: No. 42). 130p. 1980. 10.00 (H00169). ASME.

Component Units of Federal States & International Agreement. Luigi Di Marzo. LC 80-83265. 272p. 1980. 45.00x (ISBN 90-286-0330-1). Sijthoff & Noordhoff.

Componential Analysis of Lushai Phonology. Alfons Weidert. (Current Issues in Linguistics Theory: No. 2). 1979. text ed. 23.00x (ISBN 0-391-01640-7). Humanities.

Components & Finishes. Harold King & Alan Everett. (Mitchell's Building Construction Ser.). 1978. pap. 13.95 (ISBN 0-470-26351-2). Halsted Pr.

Components for Microcomputer System Design. Dave Bursky. 272p. 1980. pap. 11.95 (ISBN 0-8104-0975-5). Hayden.

Components of Synchronized Swimming. Joyce Lindeman & F. L. Jones. (Illus.). 336p. 1975. 15.95 (ISBN 0-13-164814-4). P-H.

Comportamento Do Crente. (Portuguese Bks.). 1979. write for info. (ISBN 0-8297-0650-X). Life Pubs Intl.

Comportement Du Croyant. Tr. by Morris Williams. (French Bks.). (Fr.). 1979. write for info. (ISBN 0-8297-0833-2). Life Pubs Intl.

Composer Reflects on His Art. Frank Martin. Tr. by Felix Aprahamian from Fr. LC 79-89940. (Illus.). Date not set. cancelled (ISBN 0-89793-015-0). Hunter Hse.

Composer's Advocate: A Radical Orthodoxy for Musicians. Erich Leinsdorf. LC 80-17614. (Illus.). 232p. 1981. 14.95 (ISBN 0-300-02427-4). Yale U Pr.

Composers in America. Claire R. Reis. LC 77-4158. (Music Reprint Ser., 1977). 1977. Repr. of 1947 ed. lib. bdg. 29.50 (ISBN 0-306-70893-0). Da Capo.

Composers of the Americas: Biographical Data & Catalog of Their Works, Vols. 7-10 & 13-14. Incl. Vol. 7. 104p. Repr. of 1961 ed (ISBN 0-8270-4410-0); Vol. 8. 158p. Repr. of 1962 ed; Vol. 9. 192p. Repr. of 1963 ed; Vol. 10. 123p. Repr. of 1964 ed; Vol. 13. 136p. Repr. of 1967 ed; Vol. 14. 172p. Repr. of 1968 ed. 1980. write for info. OAS.

Composer's Voice. Edward T. Cone. (Illus.). 1974. 16.95x (ISBN 0-520-02508-3). U of Cal Pr.

Composer's World: Horizons & Limitations. Paul Hindemith. 7.50 (ISBN 0-8446-0697-9). Peter Smith.

Composing: Writing As a Self-Creating Process. William E. Coles, Jr. 128p. (Orig.). 1974. pap. text ed. 5.95x (ISBN 0-8104-5838-1). Hayden.

Composite Construction Methods. John P. Cook. LC 76-26020. (Practical Construction Guides Ser.). 1977. 33.00 (ISBN 0-471-16905-6, Pub by Wiley-Interscience). Wiley.

Composite or Mixed Steel: Concrete Construction for Buildings. Compiled By American Society of Civil Engineers. 160p. 1977. pap. text ed. 11.50 (ISBN 0-87262-079-4). Am Soc Civil Eng.

Composite Reinforced Concrete. R. Taylor. 104p. 1980. 50.00x (ISBN 0-7277-0077-4, Pub. by Telford England). State Mutual Bk.

Composition. J. M. Parramon. (Orig.). 1981. pap. 4.95 (ISBN 0-89586-084-8). H P Bks.

Composition & Function of Body Fluids. 3rd ed. Shirley R. Burke. LC 80-17952. (Illus.). 208p. 1980. pap. text ed. 8.95 (ISBN 0-8016-0903-8). Mosby.

Composition: Guided - Free Kit Prog. 5-8. Gerald Dykstra et al. 1978. pap. text ed. 12.25x (ISBN 0-8077-2515-3). Tchrs Coll.

Composition: Guided-Free. Ed. by Gerald Dykstra et al. LC 73-76064. (gr. 1-6). 1974. Program 1. pap. text ed. 2.50x (ISBN 0-8077-2384-3); Program 2. pap. text ed. 2.50x (ISBN 0-8077-2385-1); Program 3. pap. text ed. 2.50x (ISBN 0-8077-2386-X); Program 4. pap. text ed. 2.50x (ISBN 0-8077-2387-8); tchrs. manual 2.50x (ISBN 0-8077-2383-5). Tchrs Coll.

Composition: Guided Free Manual. Gerald Dykstra et al. 1978. pap. text ed. 2.50 (ISBN 0-8077-2388-6). Tchrs Coll.

Composition: Guided Free Program 5. Gerald Dykstra et al. 1978. pap. text ed. 2.95x (ISBN 0-8077-2389-4). Tchrs Coll.

Composition: Guided Free Program 6. Gerald Dykstra et al. 1978. pap. text ed. 2.95x (ISBN 0-8077-2390-8). Tchrs Coll.

Composition: Guided Free Program 7. Gerald Dykstra et al. 1978. pap. text ed. 2.95x (ISBN 0-8077-2391-6). Tchrs Coll.

Composition: Guided Free Program 8. Gerald Dykstra et al. 1978. pap. text ed. 2.95x (ISBN 0-8077-2392-4). Tchrs Coll.

Composition of Scientific Words. Roland W. Brown. LC 78-14717. 882p. 1978. Repr. of 1956 ed. 15.00x (ISBN 0-87474-286-2). Smithsonian.

Composition, Reaction, & Equilibrium: Experiments in Chemistry. Norman C. Craig et al. LC 76-104966. 1970. pap. 11.95 (ISBN 0-201-01216-2); instructor's guide 2.50 (ISBN 0-201-01217-0). A-W.

Composition: Skills & Models. 2nd ed. Sidney T. Stovall et al. LC 77-77681. (Illus.). 1978. pap. text ed. 10.95 (ISBN 0-395-25749-2); inst. manual 0.25 (ISBN 0-395-25750-6). HM.

Composition Through Pictures. J. B. Heaton. 1975. pap. text ed. 3.25x (ISBN 0-582-52125-4). Longman.

Compositional Matrix. Allen Forte. LC 73-4337. 1974. Repr. of 1961 ed. lib. bdg. 14.00 (ISBN 0-306-70577-X). Da Capo.

Compositores De America, No. 8. rev. ed. OAS General Secretariat Technical Unit of Performing Arts. (Composers of the Americas Ser.). (Illus.). 157p. (Eng. -Span.). 1980. Repr. of 1962 ed. 7.00 (ISBN 0-8270-1085-0). OAS.

Compost Fruit Grower. W. E. Shewell-Cooper. 1975. 13.95 (ISBN 0-7207-0757-9, Pub. by Michael Joseph). Merrimack Bk Serv.

Compound Cinema: The Film Writings of Harry Alan Potamkin. Ed. by Lewis Jacobs. LC 76-55401. 1977. text ed. 26.50 (ISBN 0-8077-1559-X). Tchrs Coll.

Compound Eye & Vision of Insects. Ed. by G. A. Horridge. (Illus.). 614p. 1975. 74.00x (ISBN 0-19-857375-8). Oxford U Pr.

Compound Verb in Hindi. Peter Edwin Hook. LC 74-82629. (Michigan Series in South & Southeast Asian Languages & Linguistics: No. 1). 318p. 1974. pap. 7.50x (ISBN 0-89148-051-X). Ctr S&SE Asian.

Compounding & Discounting Tables for Project Evaluation. Ed. by J. Price Gittinger. LC 73-19353. (International Bank for Reconstruction & Development Ser.). (Illus.). 143p. 1973. pap. 5.50x (ISBN 0-8018-1604-1). Johns Hopkins.

Compounds from Marine Organisms, Vol. 2. Joseph T. Baker & Vreni Murphy. (Section B, Handbook of Marine Science). 192p. 1981. 39.95 (ISBN 0-8493-0214-5). CRC Pr.

Compounds of the Transition Elements Involving Metal-Metal Bonds. D. L. Kepert & K. Vrieze. (Pergamon Texts in Inorganic Chemistry: Vol. 27). 158p. 1975. text ed. 28.00 (ISBN 0-08-018880-X); pap. text ed. 17.50 (ISBN 0-08-018879-6). Pergamon.

Comprador in Nineteenth Century China: Bridge Between East & West. Hao Yen P'ing. LC 70-105372. (East Asian Ser: No. 45). (Illus.). 1970. 16.50x (ISBN 0-674-15525-4). Harvard U Pr.

Comprehending Technical Japanese. Edward E. Daub et al. LC 74-5900. 400p. 1975. 32.50x (ISBN 0-299-06680-0). U of Wis Pr.

Comprehensible Biochemistry. Michael Yudkin & Robin Offord. LC 73-85212. (Illus.). 576p. 1973. text ed. 23.00x (ISBN 0-582-44251-6). Longman.

Comprehension & Experimental Analysis in "A" Level Physics. Jean A. Pope. 1973. pap. text ed. 4.25x o.p. (ISBN 0-435-68725-5). Heinemann Ed.

Comprehension Approach to Foreign Language Instruction. Ed. by Harris Winitz. (Illus.). 352p. (Orig.). 1981. pap. text ed. 14.95 (ISBN 0-88377-181-0). Newbury Hse.

Comprehension Readers, 84 bks. Sullivan Assoc. pap. text ed. 1.00 ea. (ISBN 0-8449-3800-9). Learning Line.

Comprehensive. 3rd ed. Ed. by Nathaniel Wisch. (Medical Examination Review Books: Vol. 1). 1972. spiral bdg. 15.00 (ISBN 0-87488-101-3). Med Exam.

Comprehensive Arthroscopic Examination of the Knee. Lanny L. Johnson. LC 77-21646. (Illus.). 1977. 47.50 (ISBN 0-8016-2534-3). Mosby.

Comprehensive Bibliography for the Study of American Minorities, 2 vols. Compiled by Wayne Charles Miller. LC 74-21636. 1400p. 1976. 100.00x (ISBN 0-8147-5373-6). NYU Pr.

Comprehensive Bibliography of the Literary Works of Ivan (John) Molek. Compiled by Mary Molek. LC 76-50170. (Illus.). 82p. 1976. 3.50 (ISBN 0-9603142-0-2). M Molek Inc.

Comprehensive Bibliography on American Sign Language: A Resource Manual. Tom Federlin. LC 79-54021. 1979. pap. 6.95 (ISBN 0-9603136-0-5). Federlin.

Comprehensive Cardiac Care: A Text for Nurses, Physicians & Other Health Practitioners. 4th ed. Kathleen Andreoli et al. LC 78-9905. (Illus.). 1979. text ed. 14.95 (ISBN 0-8016-0256-4). Mosby.

Comprehensive Catalog & Encyclopedia of U.S. Morgan & Peace Silver Dollars. Leroy C. VanAllen & A. George Mallis. LC 76-18299. (Illus.). 1976. 25.00 (ISBN 0-668-04021-1). Arco.

Comprehensive Chicano Bibliography, 1960-1972. Edward Simmen et al. Ed. by Edward Simmen. LC 73-81559. 1973. 12.95 (ISBN 0-8363-0114-5). Jenkins.

Comprehensive Dental Hygiene Care. Irene R. Woodall. LC 80-15145. (Illus.). 506p. 1980. text ed. 19.95 (ISBN 0-8016-5624-9). Mosby.

Comprehensive Diabetic Cookbook. Dorothy Kaplan. 1977. pap. 5.95 (ISBN 0-8119-0360-5). Fell.

Comprehensive Dictionary of Psychological & Psychoanalytical Terms. Horace B. English & Ava C. English. LC 57-10524. 1958. pap. text ed. 17.95 (ISBN 0-679-30033-3, Pub. by MacKay). Longman.

Comprehensive Education in England & Wales. Ed. by T. G. Monks. (Research Reports Ser.). 1968. pap. text ed. 16.25x (ISBN 0-901225-28-2, NFER). Humanities.

Comprehensive Employment & Training Act: Impact on People, Places, & Programs: an Interim Report. William Mirengoff & Lester Rindler. LC 75-42971. 175p. 1976. pap. 6.00 (ISBN 0-309-02443-9). Natl Acad Pr.

Comprehensive English Review Text. 4th ed. Harold Levine. (Orig.). 1980. pap. text ed. 5.83 (ISBN 0-87720-390-3). AMSCO Sch.

Comprehensive Family & Community Health Nursing. Clemen & Eigsti. (Illus.). 544p. 1981. text ed. 19.95 (ISBN 0-07-011324-6, HP). McGraw.

Comprehensive Framework for Instructional Objectives: A Guide to Systematic Planning & Evaluation. Larry S. Hannah & John U. Michaelis. (Education Ser.). 1977. pap. text ed. 8.95 (ISBN 0-201-02757-7). A-W.

Comprehensive Graphic Arts. Erwin A. Dennis & John D. Jenkins. LC 72-92620. 1974. 20.95 (ISBN 0-672-97607-2); tchrs' manual 6.67 (ISBN 0-686-67512-6); students' manual 9.50 (ISBN 0-672-97608-0). Bobbs.

Comprehensive Group Psychotherapy. Harold I. Kaplan & Benjamin J. Sadock. 1971. 38.00 o.p. (ISBN 0-683-04518-0). Williams & Wilkins.

Comprehensive Guide to Children's Literature with a Jewish Theme. Enid Davis. LC 80-54139. 256p. 1981. 18.95x (ISBN 0-8052-3760-7). Schocken.

Comprehensive Guide to the Therapeutic Use of Cefsulodin. Ed. by L. D. Sabath & M. Finland. (Pharmanual: Vol. 1). (Illus.). vi, 94p. 1980. pap. 14.50 (ISBN 3-8055-1042-X). S Karger.

Comprehensive Handbook of Behavioral Medicine, 3 vols. Ed. by James Ferguson & Craig Taylor. Incl. Vol. 1. Systems Intervention. 364p. 1980 (ISBN 0-89335-078-8); Vol. 2. Syndromes & Special Areas. 308p. 1981 (ISBN 0-89335-111-3); Vol. 3. Extended Applications & Issues. 361p. 1980 (ISBN 0-89335-112-1). LC 79-24021. (Illus.). text ed. 30.00 ea. Spectrum Pub.

Comprehensive Hebrew Calendar. Arthur Spier. LC 75-32238. 1952. 14.95x (ISBN 0-87441-050-9). Behrman.

Comprehensive High School Reading Methods. 2nd ed. David L. Shepherd. Ed. by Arthur W. Heilman. (Secondary Education Ser.). 1978. text ed. 16.95 (ISBN 0-675-08426-1). Merrill.

Comprehensive History of the Church of Jesus Christ of Latter-Day-Saints, 6 vols. B. H. Roberts. 1978. pap. 9.95 set (ISBN 0-8425-1275-6). Brigham.

Comprehensive History of the Woollen & the Worsted Manufacturers, 2 vols. J. Bischoff. (Illus.). 1968. Repr. of 1842 ed. 75.00x (ISBN 0-7146-1387-8, F Cass). Biblio Dist.

Comprehensive History of the Woollen & Worsted Manufactures, 2 Vols. James Bischoff. LC 68-108156. (Illus.). 1842. 47.50x (ISBN 0-678-05155-0). Kelley.

Comprehensive Income Taxation. Joseph A. D. Pechman. LC 77-24246. (Studies of Government Finance). 1977. 14.95 (ISBN 0-8157-6982-2); pap. 5.95 (ISBN 0-8157-6981-4). Brookings.

Comprehensive Index to CPL Exchange Bibliographies, No. 1-1565: A Numerical Index. Jane Colokathis. (CPL Bibliographies: No. 3). 89p. 1979. pap. 9.00 (ISBN 0-86602-003-9). CPL Biblios.

Comprehensive Index to CPL Exchange Bibliographies, No. 1-1565: A Subject Index. Jane Colokathis. (CPL Bibliographies: No. 1). 119p. 1979. pap. 12.00 (ISBN 0-86602-001-2, Z5942). CPL Biblios.

Comprehensive Index to CPL Exchange Bibliographies, Nos. 1-1565: An Author Index. Jane Colokathis. (CPL Bibliographies: No. 2). 100p. 1979. pap. 10.00 (ISBN 0-86602-002-0). CPL Biblios.

Comprehensive Management of Epilepsy in Infancy, Childhood & Adolescence. Samuel Livingston. (Illus.). 672p. 1972. 39.75 (ISBN 0-398-02342-5). C C Thomas.

Comprehensive Management of Musculoskeletal Disorders in Hemophilia. Committee on Prosthetics Research & Development. (Illus.). 200p. 1973. pap. 8.75 (ISBN 0-309-02139-1). Natl Acad Pr.

Comprehensive Manual of Physical Education Activities for Men. George B. Dintiman & Loyd M. Barrow. (Illus., Orig.). 1970. pap. text ed. 11.00 (ISBN 0-13-165548-5). P-H.

Comprehensive Mental Health: The Challenge of Evaluation. Ed. by Leigh M. Roberts et al. (Illus.). 1968. 27.50x (ISBN 0-299-05000-9). U of Wis Pr.

Comprehensive Musicianship Through Band Performance: Zone 4, Book B. Brent Heisinger. (University of Hawaii Music Project). (gr. 7-8). 1976. 10.24 o.p. (ISBN 0-201-00849-1). A-W.

Comprehensive Musicianship Through Classroom Music: Zone 2, Hawaii. University of Hawaii Music Project & Leon Burton. (gr. 2-3). 1972. Bk. A. text ed. 4.88 (ISBN 0-201-00785-1, Sch Div); Bk. B. text ed. 6.20 (ISBN 0-201-00856-4); tchr's bk. for bk. A 11.48 (ISBN 0-201-00788-6); tchr's bk. for bk. B 11.48 (ISBN 0-201-00857-2). A-W.

Comprehensive Musicianship Through Classroom Music: Zone 3, Book A. Dorothy Gillett. Ed. by Leon Burton & William Thomson. (University of Hawaii Music Project). (gr. 3). 1974. pap. text ed. 6.84 (ISBN 0-201-00858-0, Sch Div); tchr's ed. 11.48 (ISBN 0-201-00859-9). A-W.

Comprehensive Pastoral Care: Enabling the Laity to Share in Pastoral Ministry. Samuel Southard. 128p. 1975. pap. 3.50 (ISBN 0-8170-0655-9); pap. 9.95 with casette (ISBN 0-8170-0692-3). Judson.

Comprehensive Pediatric Nursing. Gladys Scripien et al. (Illus.). 992p. 1975. text ed. 21.95 o.p. (ISBN 0-07-055787-X, HP). McGraw.

Comprehensive Persian-English Dictionary: Including the Arabic Words & Phrases to Be Met with in Persian Literature. F. Steingass. 1977. 65.00 (ISBN 0-7100-2152-6). Routledge & Kegan.

Comprehensive Persian-English Dictionary. F. Steingass. 1975. 60.00x (ISBN 0-685-77128-8). Intl Bk Ctr.

Comprehensive Psychotherapy. Paul Olsen. (Vol. 2). 1981. price not set. Gordon.

Comprehensive Psychotherapy, Vol. 2. Ed. by Paul Olsen. 1981. price not set. Gordon.

Comprehensive Qualitative Analysis for Advanced Level Chemistry. E. N. Lambert & M. J. Mohammed. 1978. pap. text ed. 5.95x (ISBN 0-435-65537-X). Heinemann Ed.

Comprehensive Rehabilitation Nursing. Martin et al. (Illus.). 816p. 1980. text ed. 22.95 (ISBN 0-07-040611-1, HP). McGraw.

Comprehensive Review for Dental Hygienists. 4th ed. Shailer Peterson. LC 79-28109. (Illus.). 1980. pap. text ed. 18.95 (ISBN 0-8016-3802-X). Mosby.

Comprehensive Review for Medical Technologists. 2nd ed. Alice Semrad. LC 78-31823. 1979. pap. text ed. 12.95 (ISBN 0-8016-4487-9). Mosby.

Comprehensive Review of Orthoptics & Ocular Motility: Theory, Therapy & Surgery. 2nd ed. Jane Hurtt et al. LC 77-8830. (Illus.). 1977. 26.50 o.p. (ISBN 0-8016-2316-2). Mosby.

Comprehensive Review of Respiratory Therapy. William V. Wojniechowski & Paula E. Neff. 400p. 1981. 15.95 (ISBN 0-471-08408-5, Pub. by Wiley Med). Wiley.

Comprehensive Russian Grammar of A.A. Barsov. Ed. by Lawrence W. Newman. lxxxvi, 382p. (Rus. & Eng.). 1980. 24.95 (ISBN 0-89357-072-9). Slavica.

Comprehensive School: Guidelines for the Reorganization of Secondary Education. rev ed. E. Halsall. LC 72-10107. 248p. 1975. 25.00 o.p. (ISBN 0-08-017068-4); pap. text ed. 17.50 (ISBN 0-08-018231-3). Pergamon.

Comprehensive Schools in Focus. J. M. Ross & G. Chanan. (Exploring Education Ser.). 1972. pap. text ed. 3.00x (ISBN 0-85633-014-0, NFER). Humanities.

Comprehensive Second Year Latin. William J. Buehner & John K. Colby. (Orig.). (gr. 9-10). 1977. pap. text ed. 5.50x (ISBN 0-88334-034-8). Ind Sch Pr.

Comprehensive Services to Rural Poor Families: An Evaluation of the Arizona Job College Program. Keith Baker et al. LC 75-36414. (Special Studies). (Illus.). 1976. text ed. 22.95 (ISBN 0-275-56310-3). Praeger.

Comprehensive Set: Purposeful Relaxation, Problem Solutions, Value Considerations & Communication, Set-A. rev. ed. Russell E. Mason. 1975. pap. 140.00x (ISBN 0-89533-021-0); 18 cassettes, notes, clinical applications 1979, relaxation training, feeling training, H.E.S.T. set incl. F I Comm.

Comprehensive Solved Problems in Organic Chemistry. Leonard S. Levitt & Barbara Levitt. LC 78-54189. Date not set. text ed. 12.95x (ISBN 0-8162-5151-7). Holden-Day.

Comprehensive Study of Egyptian Arabic: Lexicon, Vol. IV. Ernest T. Abdel-Massih et al. Incl. Pt. I. Egyptian Arabic - English: 34 Cultural Categories; Pt. II. English - Arabic: 34 Cultural Categories. LC 76-24957. 1979. pap. text ed. 8.00 (ISBN 0-932098-14-2). Ctr for NE & North African Stud.

Comprehensive Study of Music: Basic Principles of Music Theory, Vol. II. William Brandt et al. 1980. scp 16.50 (ISBN 0-06-040921-5, HarpC). Har-Row.

Comprehensive Textbook of Psychiatry. 3rd ed. Alfred M. Freedman & Harold I. Kaplan. (Illus.). 1975. 100.00 o.p. (ISBN 0-683-03357-3). Williams & Wilkins.

Comprehensive Transport Planning. G. R. Wells. 157p. 1975. 39.50x (ISBN 0-85264-233-4, Pub. by Griffin England). State Mutual Bk.

Comprehensive Treatise on Inorganic & Theoretical Chemistry. J. W. Mellor & G. D. Parkes. Incl. Vol. 1. 1922. o.p. (ISBN 0-471-59295-1); Vol. 3. 1922. o.p. (ISBN 0-471-59297-8); Vol. 4. 1923. o.p. (ISBN 0-471-59298-6); Vol. 5. 1924. o.p. (ISBN 0-471-59303-6); Vol. 6. 1929. o.p. (ISBN 0-471-59304-4); Vol. 7. 1930. o.p. (ISBN 0-471-59305-2); Vol. 8. 1930. o.p. (ISBN 0-471-59306-0); Vol. 9. 1930. 64.95 (ISBN 0-471-59307-9); Vol. 10. 1930. o.p. (ISBN 0-471-59308-7); Vol. 11. 1931. 69.95 (ISBN 0-471-59309-5); Vol. 12. 1932. o.p. (ISBN 0-471-59310-9); Vol. 13. 1934. o.p. (ISBN 0-471-59311-7); Vol. 14. 1935. o.p. (ISBN 0-471-59312-5); Vol. 15. 1936. o.p. (ISBN 0-471-59313-3); Vol. 16. 1937. o.p. (ISBN 0-471-59314-1). Halsted Pr.

Comprehensive Treatise on Inorganic & Theoretical Chemistry, Vol. 8. J. W. Mellor & G. D. Parkes. 1972. Suppl. 2. 69.95 o.p. (ISBN 0-471-59321-4); Suppl. 3. 114.95 o.p. (ISBN 0-471-59325-7). Halsted Pr.

Comprehensive Values. P. E. Daunt. (Organization in Schools Ser.). 1975. text ed. 15.95x (ISBN 0-435-80270-4). Heinemann Ed.

Comprehensive Verbal Graduate Record Exam Study Guide. Lee G. Boyajian. 1981. 6.95 (ISBN 0-533-04508-8). Vantage.

Comprehensive Virology: Methods Used in the Study of Viruses, Vol. 17. Ed. by Heinz F. Conrat & Robert Wagner. 425p. 1981. 39.50 (ISBN 0-306-40418-4). Plenum Pub.

Comprehensive Virology, Vol. 1: Descriptive Catalogue of Viruses. Ed. by H. Fraenkel-Conrat & R. R. Wagner. LC 74-5493. (Illus.). 200p. 1974. 22.50 (ISBN 0-306-35141-2, Plenum Pr). Plenum Pub.

Comprehensive Virology, Vol. 7: Reproduction-Bacterial DNA Viruses. Ed. by H. Fraenkel-Conrat & R. R. Wagner. (Illus.). 300p. 1977. 25.00 (ISBN 0-306-35147-1, Plenum Pr). Plenum Pub.

Comprehensive Virology, Vol. 8: Regulation & Genetics-Bacterial Dna Viruses. Ed. by H. Fraenkel-Conrat & R. R. Wagner. (Illus.). 350p. 1977. 29.50 (ISBN 0-306-35148-X, Plenum Pr). Plenum Pub.

Comprehensive Virology: Volume 16, Virus-Host Interactions. Ed. by Heinz Fraenkel-Conrat & Robert Wagner. 385p. 1980. 39.50 (ISBN 0-306-40488-5, Plenum Pr). Plenum Pub.

Compressible Flow. Stefan Schreier. 768p. 1981. 40.00 (ISBN 0-471-05691-X, Pub. by Wiley-Interscience). Wiley.

Compromise in Imperial China. Kung-Chuan Hsiao. 68p. 1979. pap. 3.00 (ISBN 0-295-95726-3). U of Wash Pr.

Compromised Love. Anne Hillary. (Candlelight Romance Ser.). (Orig.). 1981. pap. 1.50 (ISBN 0-440-11351-2). Dell.

Compromising Positions. Susan Isaacs. (Orig.). pap. 2.95 (ISBN 0-515-05976-5). Jove Pubns.

Compromiso y Mision. Orlando Costas. 159p. (Orig., Span.). 1979. pap. 3.50 (ISBN 0-89922-165-3). Edit Caribe.

Compton Effect. Leslie Horvitz & H. Harris Gerhard. 1980. pap. 2.25 (ISBN 0-451-09299-6, E9299, Sig). NAL.

Compton Mackenzie. D. J. Dooley. (English Authors Ser.: No. 173). 176p. 1974. lib. bdg. 9.95 (ISBN 0-8057-1361-1). Twayne.

Compton's Encyclopedia, 26 vols. LC 78-67841. (Illus.). 1980. 419.00 (ISBN 0-85229-350-X). Compton.

Compton's Encyclopedia, 1980, 26 vols. Ed. by Audrey Mitchell. 1980. write for info. (ISBN 0-85229-380-1). Ency Brit Ed.

Compulsion. Charlotte Lamb. (Harlequin Presents Ser.). 192p. 1981. pap. 1.50 (ISBN 0-373-10422-7, Pub. by Harlequin). PB.

Compulsion: The True Story of an Addictive Gambler. Robin Moore. LC 78-20028. 384p. 1981. 12.95 (ISBN 0-385-13322-7). Doubleday.
Compulsive Overeater. Bill B. 1981. 10.95 (ISBN 0-89638-046-7). CompCare.
Compulsive Overeater: Seven Steps to Thin Sanity. George F. Christians. LC 77-90808. 1978. 5.95 o.p. (ISBN 0-385-14038-X). Doubleday.
Compulsory Admissions to Mental Hospitals. Philip Bean. LC 79-41786. 1980. 46.00 (ISBN 0-471-27758-4, Pub. by Wiley-Interscience). Wiley.
Compulsory Arbitration & Government Intervention in Labor Disputes. Northrup. LC 66-22184. 7.00 (ISBN 0-910294-18-6). Brown Bk.
Compulsory Dancing. Da Free John. LC 80-80912. 1980. pap. 2.95 (ISBN 0-913922-50-1). Dawn Horse Pr.
Compulsory Jurisdiction of the International Court of Justice. R. P. Anand. 10.00x (ISBN 0-210-33826-1). Asia.
Computability. N. J. Cutland. LC 79-51823. (Illus.). 300p. 1980. 49.50 (ISBN 0-521-22384-9); pap. 16.50x (ISBN 0-521-29465-7). Cambridge U Pr.
Computability: An Introduction to Recursive Function Theory. N. J. Cutland. 1980. 49.50 (ISBN 0-521-22384-9); pap. 16.50 (ISBN 0-521-29465-7). Cambridge U Pr.
Computability & Logic. 2nd ed. G. S. Boolos & R. Jeffrey. LC 77-85710. (Illus.). 280p. 1981. 39.95 (ISBN 0-521-23479-4); pap. 13.95 (ISBN 0-521-29967-5). Cambridge U Pr.
Computability & Logic. G. S. Boolos & R. C. Jeffrey. LC 73-90811. 300p. 1974. 23.95x (ISBN 0-521-20402-X). Cambridge U Pr.
Computation & Theory in Ordinary Differential Equations. James W. Daniel & Ramon E. Moore. LC 71-117611. (Mathematics Ser.). (Illus.). 1970. text ed. 17.95x (ISBN 0-7167-0440-4). W H Freeman.
Computation & Theory of Optimal Control. P. Dyer & S. R. McReynolds. (Mathematics in Science & Engineering Ser., Vol. 65). 1970. 36.50 o.s.i. (ISBN 0-12-226250-6). Acad Pr.
Computation: Finite & Infinite Machines. Marvin Minsky. 1967. ref. ed. 23.95 (ISBN 0-13-165563-9). P-H.
Computation for Process Engineers. G. L. Wells & P. M. Robson. 1974. 19.95x (ISBN 0-249-44126-8). Intl Ideas.
Computation of Areas of Oriented Figures. A. M. Lopshits. (Topics in Mathematics Ser). 1963. pap. text ed. 2.95x o.p. (ISBN 0-669-19570-7). Heath.
Computation of Chemical Equilibria. F. Van Zeggeren & S. H. Storey. LC 78-92255. (Illus.). 1970. 35.50 (ISBN 0-521-07630-7). Cambridge U Pr.
Computation of Style: An Introduction to Statistics for Students & Readers of Literature. Anthony J. Kenny. Date not set. 30.01 (ISBN 0-08-024282-0); pap. 12.01 (ISBN 0-08-024281-2). Pergamon.
Computational Aspects for Large Chemical Systems. E. Clementi. (Lecture Notes in Chemistry: Vol. 19). (Illus.). 184p. 1980. pap. 17.50 (ISBN 0-387-10014-8). Springer-Verlag.
Computational Fluid Dynamics. R. M. Beam et al. Ed. by Herbert B. Keller. LC 78-9700. 1978. 17.60 (ISBN 0-8218-1331-5, SIAM-11). Am Math.
Computational Geometry for Designing & Manufacture. I. D. Faux & M. J. Pratt. LC 78-40637. 329p. 1980. pap. 22.95 (ISBN 0-470-27069-1). Halsted Pr.
Computational Grammar: An Artificial Intelligence Approach to Linguistic Description. Graeme D. Ritchie. (Harvester Studies in Cognitive Science: No. 15). 1980. 26.50x (ISBN 0-389-20048-4). B&N.
Computational Linear Algebra with Models. 2nd ed. Gareth Williams. 1978. text ed. 20.95 (ISBN 0-205-05998-8); write for info instr's man (ISBN 0-205-05999-6). Allyn.
Computational Linguistics & Computer Languages Eleven. Ed. by T. Frey & T. Vamos. 1979. pap. text ed. 24.00x (ISBN 0-686-58500-3). Humanities.
Computational Linguistics & Computer Languages Nine. Ed. by T. Frey. T. Vamos. (Orig.). 1979. pap. text ed. 24.00x (ISBN 0-391-01690-3). Humanities.
Computational Mathematics in Engineering. S. A. Hovanessian. 1976. 31.50 (ISBN 0-669-00733-1). Lexington Bks.
Computational Methods for Data Analysis. John M. Chambers. LC 77-9493. (Wiley Ser. in Probability & Mathematical Statistics: Applied Section). 1977. 21.50 (ISBN 0-471-02772-3, Pub. by Wiley-Interscience). Wiley.
Computational Methods for Offshore Structures. H. Armen & S. Stiansen. (AMD: Vol. 37). 154p. 1980. 24.00 (G00170). ASME.
Computational Methods for the Solution of Engineering Problems. C. A. Brebbia & A. J. Ferrante. LC 76-53093. 1977. 34.50x (ISBN 0-8448-1079-7). Crane-Russak Co.
Computational Methods in Linear Algebra. R. J. Goult et al. LC 75-19054. 201p. 1975. 16.95 (ISBN 0-470-31920-8). Halsted Pr.
Computational Methods in Nonlinear Mechanics: Selected Papers. International Conference on Computational Methods in Nonlinear Mechanics, 2nd, Univ. of Texas at Austin. Ed. by J. T. Oden. 160p. pap. 41.25 (ISBN 0-08-025068-8). Pergamon.
Computational Methods in Nonlinear Structural & Solid Mechanics: Papers Presented at the Symposium on Computational Methods in Nonlinear Structural & Solid Mechanics, 6-8 October 1980. Ed. by A. K. Noor & H. G. McComb. LC 80-41608. 70.00 (ISBN 0-08-027299-1). Pergamon.
Computational Methods in Optimal Control Problems. I. H. Mufti. LC 77-121990. (Lecture Notes in Operations Research & Mathematical Systems: Vol. 27). 1970. pap. 10.70 o.p. (ISBN 0-387-04951-7). Springer-Verlag.
Computational Methods in Structural Dynamics. Leonard Meirovitch. (Mechanics: Dynamical Systems Ser.: No. 4). 450p. 1980. 35.00x (ISBN 90-286-0580-0). Sijthoff & Noordhoff.
Computational Probability. Ed. by P. M. Kahn. LC 80-15014. 1980. 21.00 (ISBN 0-12-394680-8). Acad Pr.
Computational Probability & Simulation. Sidney J. Yakowitz. LC 77-3002. (Applied Mathematics & Computation Ser.: No. 12). 1977. text ed. 28.50 (ISBN 0-201-08892-4, Adv Bk Prog); pap. text ed. 16.50 (ISBN 0-201-08893-2). A-W.
Computational Problems in Abstract Algebra. J. Leech. 1970. 60.00 (ISBN 0-08-012975-7). Pergamon.
Computational Skills for College Students. Calman Goozner. 1976. pap. text ed. 7.58 (ISBN 0-87720-976-6). AMSCO Sch.
Computational Tools of Engineering. Michael M. Vartanian. (Advances in Modern Engineering Ser.). (Illus.). 125p. 1974. pap. text ed. 9.95 (ISBN 0-201-07985-2). A-W.
Computed Brain & Orbital Tomography: Technique & Interpretation. Carlos F. Gonzalez et al. LC 76-28530. (Wiley Series in Diagnostic & Therapeutic Radiology). 1976. 47.50 (ISBN 0-471-01692-6, Pub. by Wiley-Medical). Wiley.
Computed Tomographic Scanning: Institute of Medicine. 1977. pap. 5.00 (ISBN 0-309-02622-9). Natl Acad Pr.
Computed Tomography & Cerebral Infarctions. J. Valk. 190p. 1980. 29.50 (ISBN 0-89004-646-8). Raven.
Computed Tomography of Abdominal Abnormalities. John Haaga & Norbert E. Reich. LC 77-20661. (Illus.). 1978. 52.50 (ISBN 0-8016-2006-6). Mosby.
Computed Tomography of Congenital Malformations of the Brain. Mohammed Sarwar et al. (Illus.). 300p. 1981. 45.00 (ISBN 0-87527-231-2). Green.
Computed Tomography of the Brain Atlas of Normal Anatomy. G. Salamon & Y. P. Huang. (Illus.). 160p. 1980. 116.90 (ISBN 0-387-08825-3). Springer-Verlag.
Computed Tomography of the Larynx. Carol R. Archer. (Illus.). 200p. 1981. 19.75 (ISBN 0-87527-240-1). Green.
Computed Tomography, Ultrasound & X-Ray: An Integrated Approach, 1979. Ed. by Albert A. Moss. Henry I. Goldberg. (Illus.). 574p. 1979. 65.50 (ISBN 0-89352-055-1). Masson Pub.
Computer Age Copyfitting. Leslie Rasberry. (Art Direction Book). Date not set. pap. 8.95 o.p. (ISBN 0-8038-1250-7). Hastings.
Computer-Aided Analysis of Electronic Circuits: Algorathms & Computational Techniques. L. Chua & P. Lin. 1975. 32.95 (ISBN 0-13-165415-2). P-H.
Computer-Aided Circuit Design: Simulation & Optimization. Ed. by S. W. Director. LC 73-16060. (Benchmark Papers in Electrical Engineering). 400p. 1974. 37.50 (ISBN 0-12-786350-8). Acad Pr.
Computer-Aided Design & Manufacture. C. B. Besant. LC 79-40971. 1980. 42.95 (ISBN 0-470-26868-9). Halsted Pr.
Computer Aided Design Modelling, Systems Engineering, CAD Systems. J. Encarnacao. (Lecture Notes in Computer Science Ser.: Vol. 89). 459p. 1981. pap. 27.00 (ISBN 0-387-10242-6). Springer-Verlag.
Computer Aided Design of Control Systems: Proceedings. IFAC Symposium, Zurich, Switzerland, 29-31 Aug. 1979. Ed. by M. A. Cuenod. LC 79-42655. (IFAC Proceedings Ser.). (Illus.). 702p. 1980. 145.00 (ISBN 0-08-024488-2). Pergamon.
Computer Aided Design of Digital Systems. Douglas Lewin. LC 76-250. (Computer Systems Engineering Ser.). 1977. 27.50x (ISBN 0-8448-0918-7). Crane-Russak Co.
Computer-Aided Design of Electric Machinery. Cyril G. Veinott. Ed. by Alexander Kusko. (Monographs in Electric Technology). 182p. 1973. 16.50x o.p. (ISBN 0-262-22016-4). MIT Pr.
Computer-Aided Filter Design. Ed. by George Szentirmai. LC 73-85482. (IEEE Press Selected Reprint Ser.). 437p. 1973. 21.95 o.p. (ISBN 0-471-84301-6, Pub. by Wiley-Interscience). Wiley.
Computer-Aided Information Retrieval. Andrew E. Wessel. LC 74-32146. (Information Sciences Ser). 208p. 1975. text ed. 23.95 (ISBN 0-471-93376-7, Pub. by Wiley-Interscience). Wiley.
Computer-Aided Techniques for the Design of Multilayer Filters. Heather Liddell. 1981. 49.00 (ISBN 0-9960020-2-2, Pub. by a Hilger England). Heyden.
Computer Algorithms: Introduction to Design & Analysis. Sara Baase. LC 77-81197. 1978. text ed. 19.95 (ISBN 0-201-00327-9). A-W.
Computer & Africa: Applications, Problems & Potential. Ed. by D. R. Taylor & R. A. Obudho. LC 76-2910. (Special Studies). 1977. text ed. 37.95 (ISBN 0-275-56820-2). Praeger.
Computer & Chemistry: An Introduction to Programming & Numerical Methods. T. R. Dickson. LC 68-16758. (Illus.). 1968. text ed. 17.95x (ISBN 0-7167-0141-3). W H Freeman.
Computer & Medical Care. Donald A. Lindberg. (Illus.). 224p. 1971. 17.50 (ISBN 0-398-01131-1). C C Thomas.
Computer & the School of Business. Daniel Couger. 98p. 1967. 4.00 (ISBN 0-89478-006-9). U CO Busn Res Div.
Computer Application in Mental Health: A Source Book. Jeffrey L. Crawford et al. 1980. write for info. (ISBN 0-88410-712-4). Ballinger Pub.
Computer Applications in Architecture. Ed. by John S. Gero. (Illus.). 1977. 77.70x (ISBN 0-85334-737-9, Pub. by Applied Science). Burgess-Intl Ideas.
Computer Applications in Fermentation Technology, No. 9. Ed. by William B. Armiger. (Biotechnology & Bioengineering Symposium). 398p. 1980. pap. 28.00 (ISBN 0-471-05746-0, Pub. by Wiley-Interscience). Wiley.
Computer Applications in Large Scale Power Systems: Proceedings of the Symposium, New Delhi, India, 16-19 August 1979, 3 vols. Ed. by B. R. Subramanyam. (Illus.). 1100p. 1980. 205.00 (ISBN 0-08-024450-5). Pergamon.
Computer Applications in Reading. George E. Mason & Jay Blanchard. 106p. (Orig.). 1979. pap. text ed. 4.50 (ISBN 0-87207-936-8, 936). Intl Reading.
Computer Applications in the Private Security Business. Anne-Marie Sapse et al. LC 80-36754. (Praeger Special Studies). 154p. 1980. 18.95 (ISBN 0-03-057031-X). Praeger.
Computer Applications of Numerical Methods. Shan S. Kuo. LC 78-164654. 1972. text ed. 18.95 (ISBN 0-201-03956-7). A-W.
Computer Appreciation for the Majority. Ed. by National Computing Centre Ltd. LC 72-97128. 220p. 1973. pap. 27.50x (ISBN 0-85012-153-1). Intl Pubns Serv.
Computer Arithmetic. F. H. George. 1966. 17.25 (ISBN 0-08-011464-4); pap. 7.75 (ISBN 0-08-011463-6). Pergamon.
Computer Arithmetic in Theory & Practice. Ulrich W. Kulisch & Willard L. Miranker. LC 80-765. (Computer Science & Applied Mathematics Ser.). 1980. 25.00 (ISBN 0-12-428650-X). Acad Pr.
Computer Arithmetic: Principles, Architecture & Design. Kai Hwang. LC 78-18922. 1979. text ed. 27.95 (ISBN 0-471-03496-7); solutions manual (ISBN 0-471-05200-0). Wiley.
Computer-Assisted Analysis & Model Simplification. Ed. by John Maybee & Harvey Greenberg. 1981. price not set (ISBN 0-12-480720-8). Acad Pr.
Computer Assisted Audit Techniques. (Audit & Accounting Guide Ser.). 1979. pap. 5.00. Am Inst CPA.
Computer-Assisted Counseling. Donald E. Super et al. LC 71-137460. (Illus.). 1970. pap. 5.75x (ISBN 0-8077-2231-6). Tchrs Coll.
Computer-Assisted Human Resources Planning. Richard J. Niehaus. LC 78-27708. 338p. 1979. 29.95 (ISBN 0-471-04081-9, Pub. by Wiley-Interscience). Wiley.
Computer Assisted Mapping & Records Activity Manual. A P W A Research Foundation. (CAMRAS: Pt. 1). 1979. 25.00 (ISBN 0-917084-31-4). Am Public Works.
Computer-Assisted Mathematics of Finance. Jonathan C. Barron. LC 78-53421. 1978. pap. text ed. 11.25 (ISBN 0-8191-0496-5). U Pr of Amer.
Computer-Assisted Mineral Appraisal & Feasibility. Marvin P. Barnes. LC 79-52270. (Illus.). 167p. 1980. text ed. 30.00x (ISBN 0-89520-262-X). Soc Mining Eng.
Computer Assisted Research in the Humanities: A Directory of Scholars Active, 1966-1972. Joseph Raben. LC 75-16447. 1977. text ed. 69.50 (ISBN 0-08-019870-8). Pergamon.
Computer-Based Automation in Water Systems. American Water Works Association. (AWWA Handbooks-General Ser.). (Illus.). 104p. 1980. pap. text ed. 10.00 (ISBN 0-89867-230-9). Am Water Wks Assn.
Computer-Based Information Systems in Organizations. Henry C. Lucas. LC 72-92561. (Illus.). 292p. 1973. text ed. 16.95 (ISBN 0-574-18590-9, 13-1590); instr's guide avail. (ISBN 0-574-18591-7, 13-1591). SRA.
Computer-Based Instruction: A State-of-the-Art Assessment. Ed. by Harold F. O'Neil. (Educational Technology Ser.). 1981. price not set (ISBN 0-12-526760-6). Acad Pr.
Computer-Based Science Instruction. A. Jones & H. Weinstock. 376p. 1978. 37.50x (ISBN 90-286-0248-8). Sijthoff & Noordhoff.
Computer Basics for Managers. Ralph Morris. 241p. 1980. text ed. 23.50x (ISBN 0-09-141570-5, Pub. by Busn Bks England). Renouf.
Computer Buyer's Attorney. T. J. Sorger. (Illus., Orig.). pap. 39.95 (ISBN 0-9604072-0-0). Sorger Assocs.
Computer by the Tail: A User's Guide to Computer Management. H. Donaldson et al. 1976. text ed. 25.00x (ISBN 0-04-658220-7). Allen Unwin.
Computer Calculations for Multicomponent Vapor-Liquid & Liquid-Liquid Equilibrium. J. Prausnitz. 1980. 24.95 (ISBN 0-13-164962-0). P-H.
Computer Capers: Tales of Electronic Thievery, Embezzlement, & Fraud. Thomas Whiteside. LC 77-25184. 1978. 9.95 (ISBN 0-690-01743-X, TYC-T). T Y Crowell.
Computer Cartography. T. J. Peucker. LC 72-75261. (CCG Resource Papers Ser.: No. 17). 1972. pap. text ed. 4.00 (ISBN 0-89291-064-X). Assn Am Geographers.
Computer Cases in Accounting. Jonathan A. Cunitz. (Illus.). 96p. 1972. pap. 6.95 ref. ed. (ISBN 0-13-166140-X). P-H.
Computer Circuit Analysis: Theory & Application. Frank A. Ilardi. (Illus.). 416p. 1976. 21.95 (ISBN 0-13-165357-1). P-H.
Computer Clippings. Stephen J. Rogowski. 1976. 7.75 (ISBN 0-88488-083-4). Creative Pubns.
Computer Colorant Formulation. Rolf G. Kuehni. 128p. 1975. 17.95 (ISBN 0-669-03335-9). Lexington Bks.
Computer Compilation of Molecular Weights & Percentage Compositions for Organic Compounds. M. J. Dewar & R. Jones. 1969. 79.00 (ISBN 0-08-012707-X). Pergamon.
Computer Concepts. Marilyn Bohl. LC 75-101499. (Illus.). 1970. text ed. 17.95 (ISBN 0-574-16080-9, 13-0751); instr's guide avail. (ISBN 0-574-16082-5, 13-0753); problems & exercises 6.50 (ISBN 0-574-16081-7, 13-0752); transparency masters 33.00 (ISBN 0-574-16083-3, 13-0754); problem-set master tape 57.50 (ISBN 0-574-16084-1, 13-0755). SRA.
Computer Concepts, 2 vols. National Data Processing Institute, Inc. Incl. 1969. 3rd ed. Vol. 1 (ISBN 0-672-26021-2). Vol. 2 (ISBN 0-672-26023-9). pap. text ed. 13.95 ea.; tchr's manual 5.00 ea. (ISBN 0-672-96023-0). Bobbs.
Computer Concepts & Assembler Programming: 360-370 Systems. Richard Stark & Donald W. Dearholt. 1975. text ed. 20.95 (ISBN 0-12-664550-7); instr's manual 3.00 (ISBN 0-12-664552-3). Acad Pr.
Computer Connection. Alfred Bester. LC 74-30544. (YA) 1975. 6.95 o.p. (ISBN 0-399-11481-5). Berkley Pub.
Computer Connection. Alfred Bester. 1976. pap. 1.75 o.p. (ISBN 0-425-03039-3, Medallion). Berkley Pub.
Computer Control & Audit: A Total Systems Approach. John G. Burch, Jr. & Joseph L. Sardinas, Jr. 492p. 1978. 26.50 (ISBN 0-471-03491-6). Wiley.
Computer Crime. August Bequai. LC 77-3857. 1978. 17.95 (ISBN 0-669-01728-0). Lexington Bks.
Computer Data Base Organization. 2nd ed. J. Martin. 1977. 29.95 (ISBN 0-13-165423-3). P-H.
Computer Data Management & Data Base Technology. Harry Katzan, Jr. 347p. 1980. pap. 10.95 (ISBN 0-442-23896-7). Van Nos Reinhold.
Computer Diagnosis & Diagnostic Methods: The Proceedings of the Second Conference on the Diagnostic Process, University of Michigan. John A. Jacquez. (Illus.). 400p. 1972. 29.75 (ISBN 0-398-02521-5). C C Thomas.
Computer Dictionary. 3rd ed. Charles J. Sippl & Roger J. Sippl. LC 79-91696. 1980. pap. 12.95 (ISBN 0-672-21652-3, 21652). Sams.
Computer Dictionary & Handbook. 3rd ed. Charles J. Sippl & Roger J. Sippl. LC 79-67133. 1980. text ed. 29.95 (ISBN 0-672-21632-9, 21632). Sams.

Computer Dictionary for Everyone. rev. ed. Donald D. Spencer. 1980. 9.95 (ISBN 0-684-16946-0, ScribT). Scribner.

Computer Display of Curved Surfaces. Henri Gourand. LC 79-50558. (Outstanding Dissertations in the Computer Sciences). 1980. lib. bdg. 11.00 (ISBN 0-8240-4412-6). Garland Pub.

Computer Dissertations: First Supplement 1976-1978. Ed. by T. C. Hsiao. LC 78-59418. 400p. 1981. 25.00x (ISBN 0-686-60280-3). Sci & Tech Pr.

Computer Dissertations Nineteen Fifty to Nineteen Seventy-Five. Ed. by T. C. Hsiao. LC 78-59418. 450p. 1980. 35.00x (ISBN 0-686-09239-2). Sci & Tech Pr.

Computer Dissertations: Second Supplement, 1979-1980. Ed. by T. C. Hsiao. LC 78-59418. 300p. 1981. 25.00 (ISBN 0-686-28922-6). Sci & Tech Pr.

Computer Dump Debug Reference Guide. 1980. 5.75 (ISBN 0-8062-1556-9). Carlton.

Computer Engineering: A DEC View of Hardware Systems Design. C. Gordon Bell et al. LC 77-91677. (Illus.). 1978. 25.00 (ISBN 0-932376-00-2). Digital Pr.

Computer Faculty Directory (U. S. Edition) Ed. by T. C. Hsiao. 350p. 1981. 35.00 (ISBN 0-686-28923-4). Sci & Tech Pr.

Computer from Pascal to Von Neumann. Herman H. Goldstine. LC 70-173755. (Illus.). 400p. 1980. 22.50x (ISBN 0-691-08104-2); pap. 6.95 (ISBN 0-691-02367-0). Princeton U Pr.

Computer Glossary for Students & Teachers. Larry C. Schmalz & Charles J. Sippl. (Apollo Eds.). pap. 3.25 o.p. (ISBN 0-8152-0411-6, TYC-T). T Y Crowell.

Computer Graphics & Pictorial Information Processing. Theo Pavlidis. (Illus.). 1981. text ed. price not set (ISBN 0-914894-65-X). Computer Sci.

Computer Graphics Marketplace. Ed. by John Cosentino. 1981. pap. 22.50 (ISBN 0-912700-91-2). Oryx Pr.

Computer Guide for Pilots. Larry Reithmaier. LC 78-94966. (Pilot Guides). pap. 1.00 (ISBN 0-8168-7200-7). Aero.

Computer Handling of Geographical Data: An Examination of Selected Geographic Information Systems. (Natural Resources Research). (Illus.). 1976. pap. 17.50 (ISBN 92-3-101340-8, U97, UNESCO). Unipub.

Computer Hardware. 2nd ed. M. E. Sloan. 576p. Date not set. text ed. 19.95 (ISBN 0-686-63004-1); instr's guide avail. SRA. Postponed.

Computer Hardware & Organization. M. E. Sloan. LC 75-34109. (Illus.). 480p. 1976. text ed. 19.95 (ISBN 0-574-21065-2, 13-4065); instr's guide avail. (ISBN 0-574-21066-0, 13-4066). SRA.

Computer Hardware & Software: An Interdisciplinary Introduction. Marshall D. Abrams & Philip G. Stein. LC 72-3455. 1973. text ed. 18.95 (ISBN 0-201-00019-9). A-W.

Computer in Contemporary Cartography, Vol. 1. D. R. Taylor. LC 79-42727. (Progress in Contemporary Cartography Ser.). 256p. 1980. 41.25 (ISBN 0-471-27699-5). Wiley.

Computer in der Medizin. Dimitris N. Chorafas. (IS-Informations-Systeme). (Illus.). 127p. 1973. 29.50x (ISBN 3-11-004031-X). De Gruyter.

Computer in Literary & Linguistic Research. R. A. Wisbey. LC 70-152645. (Publications of the Literary & Linguistic Computing Centre: No. 1). 1971. 49.50 (ISBN 0-521-08146-7). Cambridge U Pr.

Computer in Optical Research: Methods & Applications. Ed. by B. R. Frieden. (Topics in Applied Physics: Vol. 41). (Illus.). 400p. 1980. 58.00 (ISBN 0-387-10119-5). Springer-Verlag.

Computer in the School: Tutor, Tutee, Tool. Ed. by Robert Taylor. 280p. (Orig.). 1980. pap. text ed. 14.95x (ISBN 0-8077-2611-7). Tchrs Coll.

Computer Industry: An Economic-Legal Analysis of Its Technology & Growth. John T. Soma. LC 76-2989. (Illus.). 1976. 21.50 (ISBN 0-669-00643-2). Lexington Bks.

Computer Interfacing & On-Line Operation. John C. Cluley. LC 74-16952. (Computer Systems Engineering Ser.). (Illus.). 190p. 1975. 19.50x (ISBN 0-8448-0567-X). Crane-Russak Co.

Computer Invasion. Craig T. Norback. 304p. 1981. text ed. 18.95 (ISBN 0-442-26121-7). Van Nos Reinhold.

Computer Law. Colin Tapper. (Business Data Processing Ser.). 1978. text ed. 19.95 (ISBN 0-582-45063-2). Longman.

Computer Law: Purchasing, Leasing, & Licensing Hardware, Software & Services. Ed. by Daniel T. Brooks. LC 80-82741. (Nineteen Eighty to Nineteen Eighty-One Commercial Law & Practice Course Handbook Ser.). 382p. 1981. pap. 25.00 (ISBN 0-686-69165-2, A4-3089). PLI.

Computer Literacy: Problem-Solving with Computers. Carin Horn & James Poirot. (Illus.). 215p. (Orig.). (gr. 7 up). 1981. pap. 10.95 (ISBN 0-88408-133-8). Sterling Swift.

Computer Logic, a Laboratory Workbook. H. V. Malmstadt & C. G. Enke. 1970. pap. 10.95 (ISBN 0-8053-6901-5). Benjamin-Cummings.

Computer Logic Design. M. Morris Mano. (Automatic Computation Ser.). (Illus.). 464p. 1972. 28.95 (ISBN 0-13-165472-1). P-H.

Computer Mapped Flora: A Study of the County of Warwickshire. Ed. by J. G. Hawkes et al. 1972. 60.00 (ISBN 0-12-333360-1). Acad Pr.

Computer Methods for Architects. R. A. Reynolds. (Illus.). 160p. 1980. text ed. 39.95 (ISBN 0-408-00476-2). Butterworths.

Computer Methods for Mathematical Computations. George E. Forsythe et al. (Illus.). 1977. ref. ed. 22.50x (ISBN 0-13-165332-6). P-H.

Computer Methods for Partial Differential Equations: Elliptical Equations & the Finite Element Method, Vol. 1. Robert Vichenevetsky. (Illus.). 400p. 1981. text ed. 28.00 (ISBN 0-686-69327-2). P-H.

Computer Methods in Structural Analysis. H. B. Harrison. (Civil Engineering & Engineering Mechanics Ser.). (Illus.). 400p. 1973. ref. ed. 25.95 (ISBN 0-13-166066-7). P-H.

Computer Methods in Tunnel Design. Ed. by Thomas Telford Editorial Staff, Ltd. 284p. 1980. 70.00x (ISBN 0-7277-0061-8, Pub. by Telford England). State Mutual Bk.

Computer Methods: The Fundamentals of Digital Nuclear Medicine. Ed. by David E. Lieberman. LC 77-10999. (Illus.). 1977. pap. 20.00 (ISBN 0-8016-3009-6). Mosby.

Computer Models & Application of the Sterile-Male Technique. (Illus.). 195p. (Orig.). 1973. pap. 13.50 (ISBN 92-0-111573-3, IAEA). Unipub.

Computer Models for Decision Analysis. Charles P. Bonini. (Illus.). 148p. (Orig.). 1980. pap. text ed. 13.50x (ISBN 0-89426-042-1); tchrs'. ed. 12.50x (ISBN 0-89426-043-X). Scientific Pr.

Computer Models in Management. Barbara B. Jackson. 1979. 19.95 (ISBN 0-256-02225-9). Irwin.

Computer Models of Thought & Language. Ed. by Roger C. Schank & Kenneth M. Colby. LC 73-11064. (Psychology Ser.). (Illus.). 1973. text ed. 29.95x (ISBN 0-7167-0834-5). W H Freeman.

Computer Networks & Communication. Ed. by Robert R. Korfhage. (Information Technology Ser.: Vol. IV). 150p. 1977. pap. 20.00 (ISBN 0-88283-017-1). AFIPS Pr.

Computer Networks & Distributed Processing: Software, Techniques, & Architecture. James Martin. (Illus.). 544p. 1981. text ed. 32.50 (ISBN 0-13-165258-3). P-H.

Computer Networks & Their Protocols. D. W. Davies et al. LC 78-21973. (Wiley Series in Computing). 487p. 1979. 53.25 (ISBN 0-471-99750-1, Pub. by Wiley Interscience). Wiley.

Computer Networks: Toward Distributed Processing Systems. Andrew S. Tanenbaum. (Illus.). 544p. 1981. text ed. 28.00 (ISBN 0-13-165183-8). P-H.

Computer Operating Systems. D. W. Barron. 135p. 1971. text ed. 10.95x o.p. (ISBN 0-412-09010-4, Pub. by Chapman & Hall). Methuen Inc.

Computer Operating Systems. D. W. Barron. 135p. 1971. 9.95 o.p. (ISBN 0-470-05426-3). Halsted Pr.

Computer Operations: Procedures & Management. Marjorie Leeson. LC 77-14204. 480p. 1978. pap. text ed. 15.95 (ISBN 0-574-21155-1, 13-4155); instr's guide avail. (ISBN 0-574-21156-X, 13-4156). SRA.

Computer Optimization Techniques. William Conley. 1980. 25.00 (ISBN 0-89433-111-6). Petrocelli.

Computer Organization & Assembly Language Programming. Ed. by James Peterson. (Computer Science & Applied Mathematics Ser.). 1978. 20.95 (ISBN 0-12-552250-9). Acad Pr.

Computer Organization & Microprogramming. Y. Chu. (Illus.). 528p. 1972. ref. ed. 24.95 (ISBN 0-13-166025-X). P-H.

Computer Organization: Hardware-Software. G. W. Gorsline. (Illus.). 1980. text ed. 21.95 (ISBN 0-13-165290-7). P-H.

Computer Oriented Production Exercise: An Experience in Understanding the Controlling the Behavior of a Productive System. George A. Johnson & Thomas E. Hendrick. 54p. 1977. 4.00 (ISBN 0-686-64181-7). U CO Busn Res Div.

Computer Peripherals for Minicomputers, Microprocessors & Personal Computers. C. Louis Hohenstein. (Illus.). 320p. 1980. 19.50 (ISBN 0-07-029451-8, P&RB). McGraw.

Computer Power & Human Reason: From Judgment to Calculation. Joseph Weizenbaum. LC 75-19305. (Illus.). 1976. 14.00x o.p. (ISBN 0-7167-0464-1); pap. text ed. 8.95x (ISBN 0-7167-0463-3). W H Freeman.

Computer Principles of Modeling & Simulation. Theodore Lewis & Brian J. Smith. LC 78-69604. (Illus.). 1979. text ed. 21.95 (ISBN 0-395-27143-6); instrs'. manual 0.65 (ISBN 0-395-27144-4). HM.

Computer Process Control: Modeling & Optimization. T. H. Lee et al. LC 67-30914. 1968. 29.95 o.p. (ISBN 0-471-52207-4, Pub. by Wiley-Interscience). Wiley.

Computer Programmer: Analyst Trainee. 4th ed. Milton Luftig. LC 74-82865. (Illus., Orig.). 1975. o. p. 10.00 (ISBN 0-668-01344-3); pap. 8.00 (ISBN 0-668-01232-3). Arco.

Computer Programmer Job Analysis Reference Text. Raymond M. Berger. (Illus.). 195p. 1974. pap. 10.00 (ISBN 0-88283-021-X). AFIPS Pr.

Computer Programming & Architecture: The VAX-11. Richard H. Eckhouse & Henry M. Levy. (Illus.). 432p. 1980. 26.00 (ISBN 0-932376-07-X). Digital Pr.

Computer Programming Assembler Language. Willard R. Jarchow. 1970. pap. text ed. 13.30 o.p. (ISBN 0-672-96100-8); tchrs'. manual 5.00 o.p. (ISBN 0-672-26101-4). Bobbs.

Computer Programming: Fortran Four. Decima M. Anderson. (Illus., Orig.). 1966. pap. 13.95 (ISBN 0-13-164822-5). P-H.

Computer Programming in the Basic Language. Zeney P. Jacobs et al. (gr. 9-12). 1978. pap. text ed. 11.60 (ISBN 0-205-05836-1, 2058367); tchrs.' guide 4.40 (ISBN 0-205-05837-X, 2058375). Allyn.

Computer Programming-RPG. 2nd ed. Willard R. Jarchow. LC 70-96931. 1969. pap. text ed. 15.50 (ISBN 0-672-96025-7); tchrs' manual 6.67 (ISBN 0-672-96026-5). Bobbs.

Computer Programming, Rpg II. Gary B. Shelly & Thomas J. Cashman. LC 76-19352. 1976. pap. text ed. 14.95x (ISBN 0-88236-226-7). Anaheim Pub Co.

Computer Programming: Techniques, Analyses & Mathematics. R. Andree et al. 1973. ref. ed. 21.95 (ISBN 0-13-166082-9). P-H.

Computer Programming Techniques: Fortran Language, Vol. 2. Robert J. Wimmert. 1978. pap. text ed. 9.95 o.p. (ISBN 0-8403-1282-2). Kendall-Hunt.

Computer Programming with Cobol. Marxer & Hartford. LC 73-2158. 216p. 1974. pap. 8.00 (ISBN 0-8273-0415-3); instrs'. guide 2.00 (ISBN 0-8273-0416-1). Delmar.

Computer Programs for Spelling Correction. J. L. Petersen. (Lecture Notes in Computer Science Ser.: Vol. 96). 213p. 1981. pap. 14.00 (ISBN 0-387-10259-0). Springer-Verlag.

Computer Programs for the Building Industry 1979: International Directory for the Building Industry. 2nd ed. Geoffrey Hutton & Michael Rostron. 312p. (Orig.). 1979. pap. 65.00x (ISBN 0-85139-312-8). Intl Pubns Serv.

Computer Proven Commodity Spreads. George Angell. 1981. write for info. Windsor.

Computer-Readable Data Bases: A Directory & Data Sourcebook. Ed. by Martha E. Williams. LC 66-46249. 1979. softcover 95.00 (ISBN 0-914236-45-8). Knowledge Indus.

Computer Revolution in Philosophy: Philosophy, Science & Models of Mind. Aaron Sloman. (Harvester Studies in Cognitive Science). 1978. text ed. 27.25x (ISBN 0-391-00830-7); pap. text ed. 15.50x (ISBN 0-391-00831-5). Humanities.

Computer Revolution: The Executive & the New Information Technology. Edward A. Tomeski. (Illus.). 1969. 6.95 o.s.i. (ISBN 0-02-619510-0). Macmillan.

Computer Science. 2nd ed. J. K. Atkin. (Illus.). 224p. (Orig.). 1980. pap. 12.95x (ISBN 0-7121-0396-1). Intl Ideas.

Computer Science. Alfonso F. Cardenas et al. LC 71-169162. 1972. 41.95 (ISBN 0-471-13468-6, Pub. by Wiley-Interscience). Wiley.

Computer Science. REA Staff. 960p. 1980. 22.85 (ISBN 0-87891-525-7). Res & Educ.

Computer Science: A First Course. 2nd ed. A. I. Forsythe et al. LC 74-34244. 876p. 1975. pap. text ed. 23.95 (ISBN 0-471-26681-7). Wiley.

Computer Science: A Primer. Alexandra I. Forsythe et al. LC 74-76053. 403p. 1969. 21.50 o.p. (ISBN 0-471-26680-9). Wiley.

Computer Science & Law. Ed. by Brian Niblett. LC 80-40071. 256p. 1980. 32.95 (ISBN 0-521-23451-4). Cambridge U Pr.

Computer Science Fundamentals: An Algorithmic Approach Via Structured Programming. E. A. Unger & Nasir Ahmed. 1979. text ed. 17.95 (ISBN 0-675-08301-X); instructor's manual 3.95 (ISBN 0-686-67287-9). Merrill.

Computer Science Mathematics. Donald D. Spencer. (Mathematics Ser.). 320p. 1976. text ed. 18.95 (ISBN 0-675-08650-7). Merrill.

Computer Science: Programming in BASIC. Alexander I. Forsythe et al. 1976. pap. 8.95 (ISBN 0-471-26684-1). Wiley.

Computer Security. John M. Carroll. LC 77-10615. (Illus.). 1977. 19.95 (ISBN 0-913708-28-3). Butterworths.

Computer Security: A Management Audit Approach. Norman L. Enger & Paul W. Howerton. 272p. 1980. 17.95 (ISBN 0-8144-5582-4). Am Mgmt.

Computer Security Management. Donn Parker. 304p. 1981. text ed. 21.95 (ISBN 0-8359-0905-0). Reston.

Computer Simulation Applications. Julian Reitman. 438p. 1981. Repr. lib. bdg. price not set (ISBN 0-89874-310-9). Krieger.

Computer Simulation Applications Discrete Event Simulation for Synthesis & Analysis of Complex Systems. Julian Reitman. LC 74-161138. (Systems Engineering & Analysis Ser.). 1971. 36.50 o.p. (ISBN 0-471-71625-1, Pub. by Wiley-Interscience). Wiley.

Computer Simulation in Business. Hugh J. Watson. 400p. 1981. text ed. 16.95 (ISBN 0-471-03638-2). Wiley.

Computer Simulation of Continous Systems. R. J. Ord-Smith & J. Stephenson. LC 74-12957. (Computer Science Texts Ser.: No. 3). (Illus.). 300p. 1975. pap. text ed. 16.95x (ISBN 0-521-09872-6). Cambridge U Pr.

Computer Simulation of Innovative Decision-Making in Organizations. Marcia W. Taylor. LC 78-56051. 1978. pap. text ed. 7.75 (ISBN 0-8191-0517-1). U Pr of Amer.

Computer Simulation Techniques. Thomas H. Naylor et al. LC 66-17622. 1966. 26.95 (ISBN 0-471-63060-8). Wiley.

Computer Simulation, 1951-1976: An Index to the Literature. Per Holst. 1979. 49.50 (ISBN 0-7201-0734-2, Pub. by Mansell England). Merrimack Bk Serv.

Computer Simulations of Voting Behavior. William R. Shaffer. (Studies in Behavioral Political Science Ser). 1972. text ed. 9.00x o.p. (ISBN 0-19-501536-3); pap. text ed. 4.95x (ISBN 0-19-501521-5). Oxford U Pr.

Computer Software Engineering: Symposium 24. Ed. by Jerome Fox. (Microwave Research Institute Symposia Ser.: Vol. 24). 1977. 44.95 o.p. (ISBN 0-470-98948-3). Halsted Pr.

Computer Software for Data Communications: An Introduction for Programmers. William D. Skees. LC 80-24266. 190p. 1981. text ed. 21.00 (ISBN 0-534-97979-3). Lifetime Learn.

Computer Software for the Geosciences: Proceedings of the Fifth Geochautauqua, 1976. Ed. by D. F. Merriam. LC 77-30468. 1977. pap. text ed. 41.25 (ISBN 0-08-022090-8). Pergamon.

Computer Solution of Linear Algebraic Systems. George E. Forsythe & C. Moler. 1967. ref. ed. 17.95 (ISBN 0-13-165779-8). P-H.

Computer Solution of Ordinary Differential Equations: The Initial Value Problem. Lawrence F. Shampine & Marilyn K. Gordon. LC 74-23246. (Illus.). 1975. text ed. 28.95x (ISBN 0-7167-0461-7). W H Freeman.

Computer Storage Systems & Technology. Richard E. Matick. LC 77-5812. 1977. 39.95 (ISBN 0-471-57629-8, Pub. by Wiley-Interscience). Wiley.

Computer System Architecture. M. Morris Mano. (Illus.). 528p. 1976. ref. ed. 24.95 (ISBN 0-13-166363-1). P-H.

Computer System Reliability. Roy Longbottom. LC 79-40649. (Wiley Ser. in Computing). 1980. 36.50 (ISBN 0-471-27634-0, Pub. by Wiley-Interscience). Wiley.

Computer System Selection. Jon D. Clark & Arnold Reisman. (Praeger Special Studies). 250p. 1980. 19.95 (ISBN 0-03-057888-4). Praeger.

Computer Systems in the Library: Handbook for Manager & Designer. Stanley J. Swihart & Beryl F. Hefley. LC 73-603. (Information Sciences Ser.). (Illus.). 336p. 1973. 29.95 (ISBN 0-471-83995-7, Pub. by Wiley-Interscience). Wiley.

Computer Systems in Work Design: The Ethnics Method: Effective Technical & Human Implementation of Computer Systems. Enid Mumford & Mary Weir. LC 78-32068. 1979. 34.95 (ISBN 0-470-26656-2). Halsted Pr.

Computer Systems Index. AASHTO Administrative Subcommittee on Computer Technology. 1980. 10.00 (ISBN 0-686-20962-1, CSI). AASHTO.

Computer Techniques for Electromagnetics. Ed. by R. A. J. Mittra. 416p. 1973. text ed. 75.00 (ISBN 0-08-016888-4). Pergamon.

Computer Techniques in Radiation Transport & Dosimetry. Ed. by Walter R. Nelson & T. M. Jenkins. (Ettore Majorana International Science Ser., Physical Sciences: Vol. 3). 530p. 1980. 55.00 (ISBN 0-306-40307-2, Plenum Pr). Plenum Pub.

Computer Technology in Neuroscience. Ed. by Paul B. Brown. LC 76-6884. 1976. 28.95 (ISBN 0-470-15061-0). Halsted Pr.

Computer Technology in the Health Sciences. David B. Shires. (Illus.). 160p. 1974. text ed. 14.75 (ISBN 0-398-03005-7). C C Thomas.

Computer Utility: Implications for Higher Education. Ed. by Michael A. Duggan et al. . LC 75-12104. 1969. 28.00x (ISBN 0-89197-708-2); pap. text ed. 14.95x (ISBN 0-89197-709-0). Irvington.

Computerist's Handy Manual. Clayton Hallmark. (Illus.). 1979. pap. 3.50 (ISBN 0-8306-1107-X, 1107). TAB Bks.

Computerization of Government Files: What Impact on the Individual? UCLA Law Review Staff. 124p. 1969. Repr. 3.00 o.p. (ISBN 0-685-22685-9). Am Bar Foun.

Computerization of Society. Simon Nora & Alain Minc. 1980. text ed. 12.50 (ISBN 0-262-14031-4). MIT Pr.

Computerized Accounting. Henry J. Beck & Roy J. Parrish, Jr. (Business Ser.). 1977. pap. text ed. 8.95 (ISBN 0-675-08449-0); card deck 3.95 (ISBN 0-685-79549-7); manual 3.95 (ISBN 0-686-67826-5); source dick 3.95 (ISBN 0-686-67827-3). Merrill.

Computerized Accounts Payable System: Manual & Source Code for Microcomputers. Jeffrey R. Weber. (International Data Management Computerized Accounting System Ser.). 144p. 1981. pap. 29.95 (ISBN 0-9604892-5-8). Five Arms Corp.

Computerized Accounts Receivable System: Manual & Source Code for Microcomputers. Jeffrey R. Weber. (International Data Management Computerized Accounting System Ser.). 144p. 1981. pap. 29.95 (ISBN 0-9604892-4-X). Five Arms Corp.

Computerized Business Systems: An Introduction to Data Processing. Irvine H. Forkner. LC 73-19. 501p. 1973. text ed. 21.95 (ISBN 0-471-26620-5); instructors' manual avail. (ISBN 0-471-26621-3). Wiley.

Computerized General Ledger System: Manual & Source Code for Microcomputers. Jeffrey R. Weber. (International Data Management Computerized Accounting System Ser.). 144p. 1981. pap. 29.95 (ISBN 0-9604892-6-6). Five Arms Corp.

Computerized Payroll System: Manual & Source Code for Microcomputers. Jeffrey R. Weber. (International Data Management Computerized Accouting System Ser.). 144p. 1981. pap. 29.95 (ISBN 0-9604892-3-1). Five Arms Corp.

Computerized Tomographic Scanners on Radiotheraopy in Europe. Ed. by R. J. Berry. 1980. 20.00x (Pub. by Brit Inst Radiology England). State Mutual Bk.

Computerized Tomography of the Orbit & Sella Turcica. Lawrence Jacobs et al. 1980. text ed. 92.00 (ISBN 0-685-95340-8). Raven.

Computerizing a Clinical Laboratory. Jerry K. Aikawa & Edward R. Pinfield. (Illus.). 112p. 1973. 12.75 (ISBN 0-398-02847-8). C C Thomas.

Computers. Boy Scouts Of America. LC 19-600. (Illus.). 64p. (gr. 6-12). 1973. pap. 0.70x (ISBN 0-8395-3338-1, 3338). BSA.

Computers. Linda O'Brien. (First Bks.). (Illus.). (gr. 4-6). 1978. PLB 6.45 s&l (ISBN 0-531-01486-X). Watts.

Computers. Jane J. Srivastava. LC 70-171009. (Young Math Ser.). (Illus.). (gr. 1-4). 1972. 7.95 (ISBN 0-690-20850-2, TYC-J); PLB 7.89 (ISBN 0-690-20851-0). T Y Crowell.

Computers & Banking: Electronic Fund Transfer Systems & Public Policy. Ed. by Kent W. Colton & Kenneth L. Kramer. (Applications of Modern Technology in Business Ser.). (Illus.). 325p. 1980. 25.00 (ISBN 0-306-40255-6, Plenum Pr). Plenum Pub.

Computers & Business Information Processing. William S. Davis. LC 80-10946. 448p. 1981. pap. text ed. 14.95 (ISBN 0-201-03161-2). A-W.

Computers & Common Sense: The Myth of Thinking Machines. Mortimer Taube. LC 61-17079. 1961. 15.50x (ISBN 0-231-02516-5). Columbia U Pr.

Computers & Communications: Proceedings. Federal Communications Commission Planning Conference November 8 & 9, 1976 & Lynn Hopewell. (Illus.). 197p. 1976. pap. 10.00 (ISBN 0-88283-022-8). AFIPS Pr.

Computers & Data Processing. David N. Groves & James L. Poirot. (Illus.). 1978. text ed. 14.95 (ISBN 0-88408-101-X); avail. tchrs. ed. Sterling Swift.

Computers & Data Processing: Concepts & Applications. Steven L. Mandell. (Data Processing & Information Systems Ser.). (Illus.). 1979. text ed. 17.95 (ISBN 0-8299-0198-1); study guide 6.95 (ISBN 0-8299-0254-6); study guide 6.95 (ISBN 0-8299-0254-6). West Pub.

Computers & Data Processing: Concepts & Applications with BASIC Appendix. Steven L. Mandell. (Data Processing & Information System Ser.). (Illus.). 1979. text ed. 18.95 (ISBN 0-8299-0247-3); instrs.' manual avail. (ISBN 0-8299-0633-9). West Pub.

Computers & Data Processing Information Sources. Chester Morrill, Jr. LC 70-85486. (Management Information Guide Ser.: No. 15). 1969. 30.00 (ISBN 0-8103-0815-0). Gale.

Computers & Data Processing Made Simple. Calvin A. Hofeditz. LC 78-22635. (Made Simple Books). (Illus.). 1979. pap. 3.50 (ISBN 0-385-14945-X, Made). Doubleday.

Computers & Economic Planning. Martin Cave. LC 79-7659. (Soviet & East European Studies). 1980. 27.50 (ISBN 0-521-22617-1). Cambridge U Pr.

Computers & Education. James L. Poirot. (Illus.). 96p. (Orig.). 1980. pap. 6.95 (ISBN 0-88408-137-0). Sterling Swift.

Computers & Human Communication: Problems & Prospects. Ed. by David L. Crowner & Laurence A. Marschall. LC 79-52964. 1979. pap. text ed. 9.75 (ISBN 0-8191-0787-5). U Pr of Amer.

Computers & Information Systems. Brabb. 1976. 17.50 o.p. (ISBN 0-395-20657-X); instrs'. manual 1.75 o.p. (ISBN 0-395-24065-4). HM.

Computers & Information Systems: An Introduction. E. W. Martin, Jr. & William C. Perkins. 1973. text ed. 18.95 (ISBN 0-256-01452-3). Irwin.

Computers & Information Systems in Business. 2nd ed. George Brabb. LC 79-88716. (Illus.). 1980. text ed. 18.50 (ISBN 0-395-28671-9); inst. manual .90 (ISBN 0-395-28670-0). HM.

Computers & Intractability: A Guide to the Theory of NP-Completeness. Michael R. Garey & David S. Johnson. LC 78-12361. (Mathematical Sciences Ser.). (Illus.). 1979. pap. text ed. 12.95x (ISBN 0-7167-1045-5). W H Freeman.

Computers & Local Government: A Manager's Guide, Vol. 1. Ed. by Kenneth L. Kraemer & John L. King. LC 77-23886. (Praeger Special Studies). 1977. 22.95 (ISBN 0-03-040846-6). Praeger.

Computers & Local Government: A Review of the Research, Vol. 2. Ed. by Kenneth L. Kraemer. John L. King. LC 77-23886. (Praeger Special Studies). 1978. 32.95 (ISBN 0-03-040761-3). Praeger.

Computers & Man. 2nd ed. Richard C. Dorf. 1978. pap. text ed. 11.95x (ISBN 0-87835-064-0). Boyd & Fraser.

Computers & Problem Solving. T. E. Hull & D. D. Day. 1969. pap. 8.95 o.p. (ISBN 0-201-03017-9). A-W.

Computers & Programming: A System 360-370 Assembler Language Approach. Reino Hannula. 400p. 1974. text ed. 22.50 (ISBN 0-395-16796-5). HM.

Computers & Security, Vol. III. Ed. by C. T. Dinardo. (Information Technology Ser.). (Illus.). 247p. 1977. pap. 20.00 (ISBN 0-88283-016-3). AFIPS Pr.

Computers & Social Change. Murray Laver. (Cambridge Computer Science Texts Ser.: No. 10). 128p. 1980. 10.95 (ISBN 0-521-23027-6); pap. 7.95x (ISBN 0-521-29771-0). Cambridge U Pr.

Computers & Social Controversy. Tom Logsdon. (Illus.). 123p. 1980. pap. text ed. write for info. wkbk (ISBN 0-914894-68-4). Computer Sci.

Computers & Society. George A. Nikolaieff. (Reference Shelf Ser: Vol. 41, No. 6). 1970. 6.25 (ISBN 0-8242-0111-6). Wilson.

Computers & Society. 2nd ed. Stanley Rothman & Charles Mosmann. LC 75-31622. (Illus.). 416p. 1976. text ed. 16.95 (ISBN 0-574-21055-5, 13-4055); instr's guide avail. (ISBN 0-574-21056-3, 13-4056). SRA.

Computers & the Accounting Process. R. F. Meigs. 1973. 6.95 o.p. (ISBN 0-07-041418-1, C). McGraw.

Computers & the Cybernetic Society. Michael Arbib. 494p. 1977. 16.95 (ISBN 0-12-059040-9); instrs'. manual 3.00 (ISBN 0-12-059042-5); avail. transparency masters (ISBN 0-12-059045-X). Acad Pr.

Computers & the Life Sciences. Theodor D. Sterling & Seymour V. Pollack. LC 65-27765. (Illus.). 1965. 20.00x (ISBN 0-231-02744-3). Columbia U Pr.

Computers & the Social Sciences. Alan Brier et al. 285p. 1974. 17.50x (ISBN 0-231-03914-X); pap. 7.50x (ISBN 0-231-03915-8). Columbia U Pr.

Computers & Thought. Edward A. Feigenbaum. LC 80-29508. 540p. 1981. Repr. of 1963 ed. lib. bdg. write for info. (ISBN 0-89874-199-8). Krieger.

Computers, Automation, & Society. Edward J. Laurie. 1979. pap. 13.95x (ISBN 0-256-02140-6). Irwin.

Computers, Communications, & Society. Murray Laver. (Science & Engineering Policy Ser.). (Illus.). 104p. 1975. 18.50x (ISBN 0-19-858323-0). Oxford U Pr.

Computers: Contracts & Law. 1979. pap. 53.00x (ISBN 0-903796-41-4, Pub. by Online Conferences England). Renouf.

Computers for Business: A Book of Readings. Ed. by Hugh J. Watson & Archie B. Carroll. 1980. pap. 10.50x (ISBN 0-256-02289-5). Business Pubns.

Computers for Everybody. Jerry Willis & Merl Miller. 140p. 1981. pap. 4.95 (ISBN 0-918398-49-5). Dilithium Pr.

Computers for Image-Making. David R. Clark. (Audio-Visual Media for Education & Research Ser.: Vol. 2). (Illus.). 166p. 1980. 29.00 (ISBN 0-08-024058-5); pap. 14.50 (ISBN 0-08-024059-3). Pergamon.

Computers for Pharmacy. Judith A. Lauer. LC 78-68406. (Illus.). 1978. 15.00 (ISBN 0-917330-21-8). Am Pharm Assn.

Computers for Spectroscopists. Carrington. LC 74-12526. 1975. 44.95 (ISBN 0-470-13581-6). Halsted Pr.

Computers for Technicians. Abraham Marcus & John D. Lenk. (Illus.). 400p. 1973. ref. ed. 18.95 (ISBN 0-13-166181-7). P-H.

Computers, Fortran IV, & Data-Processing Applications. John Keros. 1972. text ed. 6.95x o.p. (ISBN 0-205-03280-X, 1732803). Allyn.

Computers in Aerodynamics. Symposium on Computers in Aerodynamics at the Aerodynamics Laboratories Polytechnic Institute of New York, 1979. Ed. by S. G. Rubin & M. H. Bloom. 130p. 1980. 38.50 (ISBN 0-08-025426-8). Pergamon.

Computers in Algebra & Number Theory: Proceedings, Vol. 4. Society for Industrial & Applied Mathematics - American Mathematical Society Symposia - New York - March, 1971. Ed. by Garrett Birkhoff & Marshall Hall, Jr. LC 76-167685. 208p. 1980. Repr. of 1971 ed. 14.20 (ISBN 0-8218-1323-4, SIAMS-4). Am Math.

Computers in Biology. J. A. Nelder & R. D. Kime. (Wykeham Science Ser.: No. 32). 1974. 9.95x (ISBN 0-8448-1159-9). Crane Russak Co.

Computers in Biomedical Research, 4 vols. Ralph W. Stacy & Bruce Waxman. 1965-1964. Vol. 1. 51.00 (ISBN 0-12-662301-5); Vol. 2. 46.50 (ISBN 0-12-662302-3); Vol. 3. 46.50 (ISBN 0-12-662303-1); Vol. 4. 1974. 43.50 (ISBN 0-12-662304-X). Acad Pr.

Computers in Business. 2nd ed. M. Mackle. 80p. 1970. text ed. 3.40 (ISBN 0-7715-0724-0). Forkner.

Computers in Business Management: An Introduction. rev ed. James O'Brien. 1979. text ed. 18.50 (ISBN 0-256-02121-X). Irwin.

Computers in Critical Care & Pulmonary Medicine. Ed. by Sreedhar Nair et al. (Computers in Biology & Medicine Ser.). 418p. 1980. 39.50 (ISBN 0-306-40449-4, Plenum Pr). Plenum Pub.

Computers in Geography: A Practical Approach. Paul M. Mather. (Illus.). 1976. 21.95x (ISBN 0-631-16870-2, Pub. by Basil Blackwell). Biblio Dist.

Computers in Life Sciences. Ed. by R. Lewis. 128p. 1980. 25.00x (Pub. by Croom Helm England). State Mutual Bk.

Computers in Management & Business Studies. 2nd ed. Harold Lucas. (Illus., Orig.). 1979. pap. text ed. 19.95x (ISBN 0-7121-0390-2, Pub. by Macdonald & Evans England). Intl Ideas.

Computers in Medicine: An Introduction. Derek Enlander. LC 80-12221. (Illus.). 124p. 1980. pap. text ed. 12.95 (ISBN 0-8016-1525-9). Mosby.

Computers in Nursing. Rita Zielstorff. LC 80-80813. (Nursing Administration Ser.). 1980. pap. text ed. 10.95 (ISBN 0-913654-66-3). Nursing Res.

Computers in Psychiatry. 1969. pap. 0.75 o.p. (ISBN 0-685-77450-3, 201). Am Psychiatric.

Computers in Public Administration: An International Perspective. Ed. by Samuel J. Bernstein. 450p. 1976. text ed. 46.00 (ISBN 0-08-017869-3). Pergamon.

Computers in Radiotherapy: 1968 2nd International Conference. 1980. 9.00x (Pub. by Brit Inst Radiology England). State Mutual Bk.

Computers in Society. 3rd ed. Donald H. Sanders. 536p. 1981. text ed. 16.95 (ISBN 0-07-054672-X, C); instructor's manual 4.95 (ISBN 0-07-054673-8); study guide 7.95 (ISBN 0-07-054674-6); test bank 5.95 (ISBN 0-07-054675-4). McGraw.

Computers in Society: The Where's, Why's, & How's of Computer Use. Donald D. Spencer. (Illus.). 208p. 1974. 7.50 (ISBN 0-8104-5916-7); pap. 8.35 (ISBN 0-8104-5915-9). Hayden.

Computers in the Control of Treatment Units: Applications of Modern Technology in Radiotherapy. 1980. 10.00x (Pub. by Brit Inst Radiology England). State Mutual Bk.

Computers in the Home. C. C. Gotlieb. 65p. 1978. pap. text ed. 3.00x (ISBN 0-920380-10-7, Pub. by Inst Res Pub Canada). Renouf.

Computers in the Nineteen Eighties. Rein Turn. 224p. 1974. 17.50x (ISBN 0-231-03844-5); pap. 5.00x (ISBN 0-231-03845-3). Columbia U Pr.

Computers in the Service of Society. Ed. by Robert L. Chartrand. LC 73-112401. 256p. 1972. text ed. 27.00 (ISBN 0-08-016332-7). Pergamon.

Computers in the Teaching Process. Nicholas J. Rushby. LC 79-10138. 123p. 1979. 19.95 (ISBN 0-470-26699-6). Halsted Pr.

Computers, Language Reform, & Lexicography in China. Jim Mathias & Thomas L. Kennedy. 1980. pap. 5.00 (ISBN 0-87422-015-7). Bellman.

Computers, Law & Public Policy. Ed. by Stanley Winkler & William Wewer. LC 80-69245. (Executive Information Ser.). 400p. Date not set. price not set (ISBN 0-88283-030-9). AFIPS Pr.

Computers, Society & Law: The Role of Legal Education. Ed. by Joseph E. Leininger & Bruce Gilchrist. LC 73-93427. (Illus.). 264p. 1973. pap. 6.00 (ISBN 0-88283-001-5). AFIPS Pr.

Computers: Their Structure, Use, & Influence. Daniel L. Slotnick & Joan L. Slotnick. (Illus.). 1979. ref. 18.95 (ISBN 0-13-165068-8). P-H.

Computing: A Problem-Solving Approach Using FORTRAN Seventy-Seven. T. Ray Nanney. (Illus.). 432p. 1981. text ed. 17.95 (ISBN 0-13-165209-5). P-H.

Computing: An Introduction to Structured Problem Solving Using Pascal. Dyck et al. 1981. text ed. 18.95 (ISBN 0-8359-0902-6); instr's. manual free (ISBN 0-8359-0903-4). Reston.

Computing As a Language of Physics. (Illus.). 616p. (Orig.). 1973. pap. 37.50 (ISBN 92-0-130172-3, IAEA). Unipub.

Computing Fundamentals & Applications. Taylor L. Booth & Yi-Tzuu Chien. LC 73-20157. 1974. 22.95 (ISBN 0-471-08847-1). Wiley.

Computing in Civil Engineering: Proceedings. ASCE Technical Council on Computer Practices, June 1978. Compiled By American Society of Civil Engineers. 864p. 1978. pap. text ed. 42.00 (ISBN 0-87262-127-8). Am Soc Civil Eng.

Computing in Clinical Laboratories. Frederick Siemaszko. LC 77-94061. 1978. 31.95 (ISBN 0-471-04321-4, Pub. by Wiley Medical). Wiley.

Computing in Design. Patrick Purcell. 1981. text ed. price not set (ISBN 0-86103-045-1, Westbury Hse). Butterworth.

Computing in the Humanities. Ed. by Peter C. Patton & Renee A. Holoien. LC 79-3185. 1981. price not set (ISBN 0-669-03397-9). Lexington Bks.

Computing Mechanisms & Linkages. Antonin Svoboda & Hubert M. James. (Illus.). 1948. pap. text ed. 4.00 (ISBN 0-486-61404-2). Dover.

Computing Methods in Applied Sciences & Engineering, 2 pts. J. L. Lions & R. Glowinski. Incl. Pt. 1. (Lecture Notes in Computer Science: Vol. 10). 497p. pap. 17.60 o.p. (ISBN 0-387-06768-X); Pt. 2. (Lecture Notes in Computer Science: Vol. 11). 434p. (12 contributions in Fr., 8 in Eng.). pap. 17.60 o.p. (ISBN 0-387-06769-8). (Illus.). 1974. Springer-Verlag.

Computing System Fundamentals: An Approach Based on Microcomputers. Kenneth Danhof & Carol Smith. LC 79-14933. 1981. text ed. 21.95 (ISBN 0-201-01298-7). A-W.

Computing Systems Fundamentals: A Programmed Instruction Course. 1969. overview 6.95 (ISBN 0-574-16077-9, 15-0060); techniques 8.95 (ISBN 0-574-16078-7, 15-0061); wkbk. 1.95 (ISBN 0-574-16079-5, 15-0062). SRA.

Computing Systems Hardware. M. Wells. LC 75-27263. (Cambridge Computer Science Texts Ser.: No. 6). (Illus.). 225p. 1976. 16.95x (ISBN 0-521-29034-1). Cambridge U Pr.

Computing Systems Reliability. Ed. by T. Anderson & B. Randell. LC 78-75253. (Illus.). 1979. 41.95 (ISBN 0-521-22767-4). Cambridge U Pr.

Computing Today: An Introduction to Business Data Processing. Joseph L. Sardinias, Jr. 512p. 1981. text ed. 17.95 (ISBN 0-686-69273-X); pap. 5.95 student guide (ISBN 0-13-165100-5). P-H.

Computing with Mini Computers. Fred Gruenberger & David Babcock. LC 73-4793. 88p. 1973. 22.00 (ISBN 0-471-33005-1, Pub. by Wiley-Interscience). Wiley.

Computional Spherical Astronomy. Laurence G. Taff. LC 80-18834. 320p. 1981. 25.00 (ISBN 0-471-06257-X, Pub. by Wiley-Interscience). Wiley.

Comrade Editor: Letters to the People's Daily. 1980. pap. 4.95 (ISBN 0-8351-0734-5). China Bks.

Comrades & Christians. David I. Kertzer. LC 79-15313. (Illus.). 1980. 29.95 (ISBN 0-521-22879-4); pap. 7.95x (ISBN 0-521-29700-1). Cambridge U Pr.

COMSEARCH: Geographic. The Foundation Center. (COMSEARCH Printouts). (Orig.). 1980. write for info. (ISBN 0-87954-030-3); pap. write for info. (ISBN 0-87954-033-8). Foundation Ctr.

COMSEARCH: Special Topics. The Foundation Center. (COMSEARCH Printouts). (Orig.). 1980. pap. 12.00 (ISBN 0-87954-031-1); microfiche 4.00 (ISBN 0-87954-034-6). Foundation Ctr.

Comsearch: Subjects. The Foundation Center. (COMSEARCH Printouts). (Orig.). 1980. pap. 12.00 (ISBN 0-87954-029-X); microfiche 4.00 (ISBN 0-87954-032-X). Foundation Ctr.

Comstock Lode. Louis L'Amour. 384p. 1981. 14.95 (ISBN 0-553-05001-X); pap. 7.95 (ISBN 0-553-01307-6). Bantam.

Comstock Miners & Mining. Eliot Lord. (Illus.). 578p. Repr. of 1959 ed. 20.00 (ISBN 0-8310-7008-0). A S Barnes.

Comstock Miners & Mining. Eliot Lord. (Illus.). 578p. 1981. Repr. of 1959 ed. 20.00 (ISBN 0-8310-7008-0). Howell-North.

Comte Ory. Eugene Scribe & Charles-Gaspard Delestre-Poirson. Ed. by Philip Gossett & Charles Rosen. LC 76-49191. (Early Romantic Opera Ser.: Vol. 16). 1978. lib. bdg. 82.00 (ISBN 0-8240-2915-1). Garland Pub.

Comtesse. Joan Smith. (A Regency Romance Ser.). 1978. pap. 1.50 o.p. (ISBN 0-449-23490-8, Crest). Fawcett.

Comunicacion Cristiana. Alan Compton. Date not set. Repr. of 1979 ed. 2.75 (ISBN 0-311-13833-0). Casa Bautista.

Comunicacion Por Medio De la Predicacion. Orlando E. Costas. 255p. (Span.). 1978. pap. 4.75 (ISBN 0-89922-021-5). Edit Caribe.

Comunicando: A First Course in Spanish. David M. Stillman & Ronni L. Gordon. 1979. text ed. 16.95x (ISBN 0-669-01359-5); instrs'. manual free (ISBN 0-669-02404-X); wkbk.-lab. manual 5.25x (ISBN 0-669-01708-6); reel tapeset 60.00 (ISBN 0-669-01711-6); cassette tapeset 60.00 (ISBN 0-669-01710-8). Heath.

Con Quien Me Casare? Luis Palau. LC 76-42154. 127p. (Orig., Span.). 1975. pap. 2.25 (ISBN 0-89922-050-9). Edit Caribe.

Conan: No. 1. Robert E. Howard et al. 1977. pap. 2.25 (ISBN 0-441-11630-2). Ace Bks.

Conan of Cimmeria: No. 2. Robert E. Howard et al. 1977. pap. 2.25 (ISBN 0-441-11631-0). Ace Bks.

Conan of the Isles, No. 12. L. Sprague de Camp & Lin Carter. 1977. pap. 2.25 (ISBN 0-441-11641-8). Ace Bks.

Conan the Adventurer, No. 5. Robert E. Howard & L. Sprague de Camp. 1977. pap. 2.25 (ISBN 0-441-11634-5). Ace Bks.

Conan the Buccaneer, No. 6. L. Sprague de Camp & Lin Carter. 1977. pap. 2.25 (ISBN 0-441-11635-3). Ace Bks.

Conan the Conqueror, No. 9. Robert E. Howard. Ed. by L. Sprague de Camp. 1977. pap. 2.25 (ISBN 0-441-11638-8). Ace Bks.

Conan the Freebooter: No. 3. Robert E. Howard & L. Sprague De Camp. 1977. pap. 2.25 (ISBN 0-441-11632-9). Ace Bks.

Conan the Rebel, No. 5. Poul Anderson. 224p. (Orig.). 1980. pap. 2.25 (ISBN 0-553-13831-6). Bantam.

Conan the Usurper, No. 8. Robert E. Howard & L. Sprague de Camp. 1977. pap. 2.25 (ISBN 0-441-11637-X). Ace Bks.

Conan the Wanderer: No. 4. Robert E. Howard et al. 1977. pap. 2.25 (ISBN 0-441-11633-7). Ace Bks.

Conan the Warrior, No. 7. Robert E. Howard. Ed. by L. Sprague de Camp. 1977. pap. 2.25 (ISBN 0-441-11636-1). Ace Bks.

Concatenation: Enoch's Prophecy Fulfilling! Hebrew-Christian Metaphysics Supported by Modern Science. Evolyn B. Feiring. LC 72-96989. 3.00x (ISBN 0-9603386-0-8); pap. 2.00x (ISBN 0-9603386-1-6). Rocky Mtn Pr.

Concealed Tenancy & Its Implications for Economic Growth: A Case Study of Eastern Uttar Pradesh. Kripa Shankar. 144p. 1980. text ed. 9.50x (ISBN 0-391-02137-0). Humanities.

Conceited News of Sir Thomas Overbury & His Friends: With Sir Thomas Overbury His Wife. Thomas Overbury. Ed. by James E. Savage. LC 68-29084. 1968. 41.00x (ISBN 0-8201-1039-6). Schol Facsimiles.

Conceived in Liberty: American Individual Rights Today. Brad Sagstetter. LC 77-18506. 1978. pap. 6.95 (ISBN 0-87872-162-2). Duxbury Pr.

Concentration & Costs in Retailing. K. A. Tucker. 188p. 1978. 21.95x (ISBN 0-566-00165-9, Pub. by Saxon Hse England). Lexington Bks.

Concentration & Meditation. Christmas Humphries. 343p. 1981. pap. 10.00 (ISBN 0-89540-068-5). Sun Pub.

Concentration in British Industry 1935-1975. P. E. Hart & Roger Clarke. LC 79-41808. (Economic & Social Research Occasional Paper: No. 32). 163p. 1980. 29.50 (ISBN 0-521-23393-3). Cambridge U Pr.

Concentrations of Solutions. Charles B. Leonard, Jr. 120p. 1971. spiral bdg. 6.00 (ISBN 0-87488-602-3). Med Exam.

Concept Analysis: From Socrates to Wittgenstein. John Oastler. LC 78-52288. 1978. pap. text ed. 16.75x o.p. (ISBN 0-8191-0491-4). U Pr of Amer.

Concept & Logic of Classical Thermodynamics As a Theory of Heat Engines. Rigorously Constructed Upon Foundations Laid by S. Carnot & F. Reech. C. Truesdell & S. Bharatha. LC 76-48115. (Texts & Monographs in Physics). (Illus.). 1978. 28.70 (ISBN 0-387-07971-8). Springer-Verlag.

Concept & Measurement of Involuntary Unemployment. Ed. by G. David Worswick. LC 75-42385. 1976. 38.50x (ISBN 0-89158-527-3). Westview.

Concept Dictionary of English. Julius Laffal. LC 72-97927. 305p. 1973. 19.95 (ISBN 0-470-51160-5). Halsted Pr.

Concept Dictionary of English. Julius Laffal. LC 72-97927. 1973. text ed. 13.50 (ISBN 0-470-51160-5). Gallery Pr.

Concept Formalization in Nursing: Process & Product. 2nd ed. Nursing Development Conference Group. LC 79-88164. 313p. 1979. text ed. 12.95 (ISBN 0-316-61421-1). Little.

Concept Formation. Neil Bolton. 1977. text ed. 13.75 (ISBN 0-08-021493-2); pap. text ed. 8.25 (ISBN 0-08-021494-0). Pergamon.

Concept Formation & Personality. Zoltan P. Dienes. 1959. text ed. 3.50x (ISBN 0-7185-1019-4, Leicester). Humanities.

Concept Learning: An Information Processing Problem. Earl B. Hunt. LC 73-92140. 296p. 1974. Repr. of 1962 ed. 14.50 o.p. (ISBN 0-88275-152-2). Krieger.

Concept of a Legal System: An Introduction to the Theory of Legal System. Joseph Raz. 1970. 14.95x o.p. (ISBN 0-19-825189-0). Oxford U Pr.

Concept of a Legal System: An Introduction to the Theory of a Legal System. 2nd ed. Joseph Raz. 244p. 1980. 24.95x (ISBN 0-19-825362-1); pap. 11.95x (ISBN 0-19-825363-X). Oxford U Pr.

Concept of Activity in Soviet Psychology. Tr. by James V. Wertsch from Rus. 1981. 30.00 (ISBN 0-87332-158-8). M E Sharpe.

Concept of an Indian Literature: Six Essays by P. Lal. P. Lal. 49p. 1973. 10.00 (ISBN 0-88253-303-7). Ind-US Inc.

Concept of Art. Haig Khatchadourian. LC 70-145512. 1971. 17.50x (ISBN 0-8147-4553-9). NYU Pr.

Concept of Corporate Planning. R. L. Ackoff. LC 74-100318. 1969. 14.95 (ISBN 0-471-00290-9, Pub. by Wiley-Interscience). Wiley.

Concept of Corporate Strategy. rev. ed. Kenneth R. Andrews. 1980. pap. 8.95x (ISBN 0-256-02371-9). Irwin.

Concept of Correlation: Paul Tillich & the Possibility of a Mediating Theology. John P. Clayton. (Theologische Bibliothek Topelmann: No. 37). 427p. 1979. text ed. 51.25x (ISBN 3-11007-914-3). De Gruyter.

Concept of Cruel & Unusual Punishment. Larry C. Berkson. LC 75-16331. 272p. 1975. 22.95 (ISBN 0-669-00063-9). Lexington Bks.

Concept of Cultural Systems: A Key to Understanding Tribes & Nations. Leslie A. White. LC 75-33003. 192p. 1975. 15.00x (ISBN 0-231-03961-1). Columbia U Pr.

Concept of Culture. Leslie A. White & Beth Dillingham. LC 72-88749. (Basic Concepts in Anthropology Ser.). pap. 3.25 o.p. (ISBN 0-8087-2333-2). Burgess.

Concept of Education, Educational Conceptions, & Liberal Education. Tan Tai Wei. LC 77-18470. 1978. pap. text ed. 7.50x (ISBN 0-8191-0418-3). U Pr of Amer.

Concept of Empire in Western Europe from the Fifth to the Fourteenth Century. Robert Folz. Tr. by Sheila A. Ogilvie from French. LC 80-18796. xv, 250p. 1980. Repr. of 1969 ed. lib. bdg. 27.50x (ISBN 0-313-22453-6, FOCO). Greenwood.

Concept of Existence: A Study of Nonexistent Particulars. Dennis E. Bradford. LC 80-5526. 142p. 1980. lib. bdg. 16.75 (ISBN 0-8191-1124-4); pap. text ed. 7.50 (ISBN 0-8191-1127-9). U Pr of Amer.

Concept of Happiness in the Spanish Poetry of the Eighteenth Century. Robert McCormick. LC 80-68000. (Hispanic Studies Collection Ser.). 206p. (Orig.). 1980. pap. 19.95 (ISBN 0-89729-264-2). Ediciones.

Concept of Health. 3rd ed. Donald Read. 1978. 11.95 (ISBN 0-205-05686-5, 715686-3); instructor's manual free (ISBN 0-205-05687-3, 715687-1). Allyn.

Concept of Ideology. Jorge Larrain. LC 79-53386. 250p. 1980. 18.00x (ISBN 0-8203-0490-5). U of Ga Pr.

Concept of Ideology & Political Analysis: A Critical Examination of Its Usage by Marx, Lenin, & Mannheim. Walter Carlsnaes. LC 80-1202. (Contributions in Philosophy Ser.: No. 17). 280p. 1981. lib. bdg. 32.50 (ISBN 0-313-22267-3, CCI/). Greenwood.

Concept of Intentionality. Jitendra N. Mohanty. LC 70-176186. 213p. 1971. 12.50 (ISBN 0-87527-115-4). Fireside Bks.

Concept of Justice. N. M. Nathan. (New Studies in Practical Philosophy). (Illus.). 79p. 1972. text ed. 8.25x (ISBN 0-333-12398-0). Humanities.

Concept of Limits. 2nd ed. Donald W. Hight. LC 77-80029. 1978. pap. text ed. 3.25 (ISBN 0-486-63543-0). Dover.

Concept of Love in Sidney & Spenser; John Leanerd's the Rambling Justice, or the Jealous Husbands: A Restoration Plagiarism of Thomas Middletown's More Dissemblers Besides Women? Roswitha Mayr & James Hogg. (Salzburg Studies in English Literature, Elizabethan & Renaissance Studies: No. 70). 1978. pap. text ed. 25.00x (ISBN 0-391-01477-3). Humanities.

Concept of Mind. Gilbert Ryle. 1975. 22.00x (ISBN 0-06-496042-0); pap. 3.95 o.p. (ISBN 0-06-463251-2). B&N.

Concept of Morals. Walter T. Stace. 8.50 (ISBN 0-8446-2990-1). Peter Smith.

Concept of Motivation. 2nd ed. R. S. Peters. (Studies in Philosophical Psychology). 1969. pap. text ed. 6.50x (ISBN 0-391-00060-8). Humanities.

Concept of Nature. Alfred N. Whitehead. 32.95 (ISBN 0-521-06787-1); pap. 8.95x (ISBN 0-521-09245-0). Cambridge U Pr.

Concept of Race. Ed. by Ashley Montagu. LC 80-21682. xviii, 270p. 1980. Repr. of 1964 ed. lib. bdg. 27.50x (ISBN 0-313-22721-7, MOCR). Greenwood.

Concept of Representation. Hanna F. Pitkin. (Campus Ser.: No. 75). 1978. pap. 6.95x (ISBN 0-520-02156-8). U of Cal Pr.

Concept of Social Change: A Critique of the Functionalist Theory of Social Change. Anthony D. Smith. (Monographs in Social Theory). 208p. 1973. 18.50x (ISBN 0-7100-7607-X); pap. 8.95 (ISBN 0-7100-7697-5). Routledge & Kegan.

Concept of State & Law in Islam. Farooq Hassan. LC 80-69038. 321p. (Orig.). 1981. lib. bdg. 20.75 (ISBN 0-8191-1426-X); pap. text ed. 11.75 (ISBN 0-8191-1427-8). U Pr of Amer.

Concept of Structuralism: A Critical Analysis. Philip Pettit. LC 74-22971. 198p. 1975. 12.95x (ISBN 0-520-02882-1); pap. 2.95 (ISBN 0-520-03416-3). U of Cal Pr.

Concept of the Corporation. Peter F. Drucker. LC 72-74. (John Day Bk.). 352p. 1972. 11.95 (ISBN 0-381-98093-6, A16190, TYC-T). T Y Crowell.

Concept of the University. Kenneth R. Minogue. 1973. 16.50x (ISBN 0-520-02390-0, CAL 287). U of Cal Pr.

Concept of Truth. Leslie Armour. 1979. text ed. 29.50 (ISBN 90-232-0728-9). Humanities.

Concept Spelling Teacher's Manual. Ed. by Richard P. Archer. 132p. 1979. 50.00 (ISBN 0-935276-03-3). Am Spelling.

Conceptions of Ether: Studies in the History of Ether Theories 1740 to 1900. G. N. Cantor & M. J. Hodge. LC 80-21174. (Illus.). 350p. Date not set. price not set (ISBN 0-521-22430-6). Cambridge U Pr.

Conceptions of International Exhibitions. Hans Neuberg. Date not set. 37.50 o.p. (ISBN 0-8038-1138-1). Hastings.

Conceptions of Modern Psychiatry. Harry S. Sullivan. 1953. 8.50x (ISBN 0-393-01050-3, Norton Lib); pap. 4.95 (ISBN 0-393-00740-5, Norton Lib). Norton.

Conceptions of Space in Social Thought: A Geographic Perspective. Robert D. Sack. (Illus.). 240p. 1981. 27.50x (ISBN 0-8166-1012-6); pap. 9.95x (ISBN 0-8166-1015-0). U of Minn Pr.

Conceptography. Date not set. price not set. Creative Bks.

Conceptography. John Hicks & Regina Hicks. (Illus.). 52p. 1972. pap. 3.95 (ISBN 0-914606-00-X). Creative Bks.

Concepts & Applications of Finite Element Analysis. 2nd ed. Robert D. Cook. 576p. 1981. text ed. 31.95 (ISBN 0-471-03050-3); price not set tchr's ed (ISBN 0-471-08200-7). Wiley.

Concepts & Cases in Fashion Buying & Merchandising. Sidney Packard & Nathan Axelrod. LC 76-50439. 1977. text ed. 12.95 (ISBN 0-87005-182-2). Fairchild.

Concepts & Issues in American Government. R. Krinsky et al. 1976. pap. 6.95x (ISBN 0-02-475160-X). Macmillan.

Concepts & Mechanisms of Perception. R. L. Gregory. LC 74-7511. (Encore Edition). (Illus.). 712p. 1974. 14.95 o.p. (ISBN 0-684-15474-9, ScribT). Scribner.

Concepts & Methods of Social Work. 2nd ed. Friedlander et al. LC 75-45164. (Illus.). 288p. 1976. text ed. 15.95 (ISBN 0-13-166488-3). P-H.

Concepts & Models of Inorganic Chemistry. Bodie E. Douglas & D. H. McDaniel. 1965. text ed. 26.95 (ISBN 0-471-00129-5). Wiley.

Concepts & Practices of Intensive Care for Nurse Specialists. 2nd ed. L. E. Meltzer et al. LC 75-27692. 1976. 21.95 (ISBN 0-913486-48-5). Charles.

Concepts & Society. I. C. Jarvie. (International Library of Sociology). 230p. 1972. 20.00x (ISBN 0-7100-7265-1). Routledge & Kegan.

Concepts & Theories of Human Development. Richard M. Lerner. LC 75-12098. 1976. text ed. 14.95 (ISBN 0-201-04342-4). A-W.

Concepts & Values. Solomon Colodner. LC 68-58503. 140p. 1968. 5.95 (ISBN 0-88400-020-6). Shengold.

Concepts Basic to Nursing. 3rd ed. P. Mitchell. (Illus.). 720p. text ed. 18.95 (ISBN 0-07-042582-5). McGraw.

Concepts Concerning Dental Caries Prevention. John Gabrovsek. 200p. 1981. 16.50 (ISBN 0-87527-209-6). Green.

Concepts, Events, & History. L. B. Cebik. LC 78-64825. 1978. pap. text ed. 9.00 (ISBN 0-8191-0639-9). U Pr of Amer.

Concepts for Operations Management. Ray Wild. LC 77-7232. 1978. 46.25 (ISBN 0-471-99539-8, Pub. by Wiley-Interscience); pap. 20.75 (ISBN 0-471-99543-6). Wiley.

Concepts in Bioenergetics. Leonardo Peusner. (Concepts of Modern Biology Ser). (Illus.). 272p. 1974. pap. 11.95 reference ed. (ISBN 0-13-166264-3). P-H.

Concepts in Business Data Processing: A Student Guide. pap. 7.95 (ISBN 0-13-166413-1); pap. 7.95 issues (ISBN 0-13-093906-4). P-H.

Concepts in Cancer Care: A Practical Explanation of Radiotherapy & Chemotherapy for Primary Care Physicians. Jay S. Cooper & Donald J. Pizzarello. LC 80-10334. (Illus.). 273p. 1980. text ed. 16.50 (ISBN 0-8121-0716-0). Lea & Febiger.

Concepts in Cell Biology. William K. Stephenson. LC 77-16205. 1978. text ed. 12.95x (ISBN 0-471-03390-1). Wiley.

Concepts in Climatology. Crowe. 1979. pap. text ed. 16.95 o.p. (ISBN 0-582-30013-4). Longman.

Concepts in Context: Aspects of the Writer's Craft. Ray Kytle, Jr. LC 73-16245. 208p. 1974. 10.50 (ISBN 0-471-51127-7). Wiley.

Concepts in Drug Metabolism, Vol. 1. P. Jenner & B. Testa. (Drugs & the Pharmaceutical Sciences: Vol. 10). 424p. 1980. 49.50 (ISBN 0-8247-6906-6). Dekker.

Concepts in Leadership for the Licensed Practical Nurse. Elizabeth Smith & Barbara Huber. LC 73-4416. 1973. pap. text ed. 7.95 o.p. (ISBN 0-8016-4728-2). Mosby.

Concepts in Neurophysiology. William K. Stephenson. 1980. pap. text ed. 10.95x (ISBN 0-471-05585-9). Wiley.

Concepts in Physical Education with Laboratories & Experiments. 4th ed. Charles B. Corbin & J. Linus Dowell. 350p. 1981. pap. text ed. write for info. (ISBN 0-697-07177-4); instrs.' manual avail. (ISBN 0-697-07178-2). Wm C Brown.

Concepts in Physics. Robert Adair. 1969. 24.50 (ISBN 0-12-044050-4); tchrs' guide 4.95 (ISBN 0-12-044056-3). Acad Pr.

Concepts in Problem Solving. Moshe Rubinstein & Kenneth Pfeiffer. (Illus.). 1980. pap. text ed. 10.95 (ISBN 0-13-166603-7). P-H.

Concepts in Public Speaking: Consumer Responsibility. Clyde J. Faries. 112p. 1980. pap. text ed. 5.95 (ISBN 0-8403-2239-9). Kendall-Hunt.

Concepts in Quantum Mechanics. F. A. Kaempffer. (Pure & Applied Physics: Vol. 18). 1964. 33.00 (ISBN 0-12-394150-4). Acad Pr.

Concepts in Social Administration: A Framework for Analysis. Anthony Forder. 200p. 1974. 11.75x (ISBN 0-7100-7869-2); pap. 7.50 (ISBN 0-7100-7870-6). Routledge & Kegan.

Concepts in Theoretical Organic Chemistry. Jerry A. Hirsch. 320p. 1974. text ed. 24.95x o.p. (ISBN 0-205-03999-5). Allyn.

Concepts in Thermal Comfort. M. David Egan. (Illus.). 224p. 1975. 15.95 (ISBN 0-13-166447-6). P-H.

Concepts of Business. Richard H. Buskirk et al. LC 78-177981. text ed. 16.05 (ISBN 0-913310-45-X). Par Inc.

Concepts of Calculus with Applications to Business & Economics. David G. Crowdis et al. 1975. text ed. 14.95x (ISBN 0-02-473010-6); tchrs' manual free (ISBN 0-02-473020-3). Macmillan.

Concepts of Chemistry. William M. Porterfield. (Illus.). 1972. text ed. 18.95x (ISBN 0-393-09385-9). Norton.

Concepts of Classical Optics. John Strong. LC 57-6918. (Physics Ser.). (Illus.). 1958. 28.95x (ISBN 0-7167-0301-7). W H Freeman.

Concepts of Classical Thermodynamics. Hans A. Buchdahl. (Cambridge Monograph on Physics Ser). 1966. 35.50 (ISBN 0-521-04359-X). Cambridge U Pr.

Concepts of Communication: Reading, Ideas Module, Inferences Module. Mary Lou Conlin. LC 77-78895. (Illus.). 1977. pap. text ed. 9.95 (ISBN 0-395-25492-2); instrs'. guide 0.65 (ISBN 0-395-25493-0). HM.

Concepts of Communication: Reading Vocabulary Module. Mary Lou Conlin. LC 77-78866. (Illus.). 1977. pap. text ed. 7.75 (ISBN 0-395-25494-9). HM.

Concepts of Communication: Writing: Summary, Paragraph, Essay-Test, Theme Modules. 2nd ed. Mary Lou Conlin. LC 79-49830. 1980. pap. text ed. 9.95 (ISBN 0-395-28735-9); inst. man. 1.00 (ISBN 0-395-28485-6). HM.

Concepts of Communication: Writing: Writing Skills Module. 2nd ed. Mary Lou Conlin. LC 79-49830. 1980. pap. text ed. 10.95 (ISBN 0-395-28484-8); instrs'. manual avail. (ISBN 0-395-28485-6). HM.

Concepts of Criminal Law: Selected Readings. Robert W. Ferguson. (Criminal Justice Ser.). 1975. pap. text ed. 10.95 (ISBN 0-8299-0619-3). West Pub.

Concepts of Genetics. Rivian Lande & Marlys Knox. (Orig.). 1980. 5.95 (ISBN 0-8087-3826-7). Burgess.

Concepts of Health & Disease: Interdisciplinary Perspectives. A. L. Caplan et al. Ed. by J. J. McCartney. 1980. pap. write for info. o.p. (ISBN 0-201-00973-0). A-W.

Concepts of Health & Disease: Interdisciplinary Perspectives. Arthur L. Caplan et al. 608p. 1981. pap. text ed. write for info. (ISBN 0-201-00973-0). A-W.

Concepts of Illness, Disease & Morbus. F. K. Taylor. LC 78-15123. 1979. 18.95 (ISBN 0-521-22433-0). Cambridge U Pr.

Concepts of Indoctrination: Philosophical Essays. Ed. & intro. by I. A. Snook. (International Library of the Philosophy of Education). 224p. 1972. 15.00 (ISBN 0-7100-7279-1). Routledge & Kegan.

Concepts of Insanity in the United States, 1789-1865. Norman Dain. 1964. 18.50 (ISBN 0-8135-0443-0). Rutgers U Pr.

Concepts of International Politics: A Global Perspective. 3rd ed. Abdul A. Said & Charles Q. Lerche. 1979. text ed. 16.95 (ISBN 0-13-166033-0). P-H.

Concepts of Leisure. 2nd ed. James F. Murphy. (Illus.). 192p. 1981. text ed. 13.95 (ISBN 0-13-166512-X). P-H.

Concepts of Marketing Management. Joseph C. Seibert. Ed. by Jagdish Sheth. (Marketing Management Ser). (Illus.). 1973. text ed. 20.50 scp o.p. (ISBN 0-06-045878-X, HarpC); tchrs' manual avail. o.p. (ISBN 0-685-02864-X); scp study guide 6.50 o.p. (ISBN 0-06-044015-5). Har-Row.

Concepts of Membranes in Regulation & Excitation. Ed. by M. Rocha e Silva & G. Suarez-Kurtz. LC 74-21984. 1975. 22.50 (ISBN 0-89004-031-1). Raven.

Concepts of Mind in Indian Philosophy. Sarasvati Chennakesavan. 1980. 14.00x (ISBN 0-8364-0638-9). South Asia Bks.

Concepts of Modern Physics. 3rd ed. Arthur Beiser. (Illus.). 512p. 1981. text ed. 22.50 (ISBN 0-07-004382-5, C). McGraw.

Concepts of Neuroanatomy. Earl O. Butcher & E. D. Bueker. (Illus.). 1969. Repr. of 1949 ed. 12.00 o.s.i. (ISBN 0-02-842360-7). Hafner.

Concepts of Occupational Therapy. Kathlyn L. Reed & Sharon T. Sanderson. (Illus.). 29p. 1980. pap. 19.95 (ISBN 0-683-07200-5). Williams & Wilkins.

Concepts of Oncology Nursing. Donna L. Vredevoe et al. (Illus.). 400p. 1981. text ed. 18.95 (ISBN 0-13-166587-1). P-H.

Concepts of Physics. Amit Goswami. 1979. text ed. 19.95x (ISBN 0-669-01897-X). Heath.

Concepts of Programming Languages. Mark Elson. LC 72-94972. (Illus.). 333p. 1973. text ed. 19.95 (ISBN 0-574-17922-4, 13-0922); instr's guide avail. (ISBN 0-574-17923-2, 13-0923). SRA.

Concepts of Radiation Dosimetry. Kenneth R. Kase & Walter R. Nelson. LC 78-5705. (Illus.). 232p. 1978. 25.00 (ISBN 0-08-023162-4); pap. 12.50 (ISBN 0-08-023161-6). Pergamon.

Concepts of Structure. William Zuk. 80p. 1972. Repr. of 1963 ed. 7.50 o.p. (ISBN 0-88275-072-0). Krieger.

Concepts of Uranium Resources & Producibility. Board on Mineral Resources. 1978. pap. 7.25 (ISBN 0-309-02864-7). Natl Acad Pr.

Conceptual Approach to College Writing. 2nd ed. Edmund H. Buckley & Arnold Solkov. 112p. 1980. pap. text ed. 6.95 (ISBN 0-8403-2308-5). Kendall-Hunt.

Conceptual Approach to Moving & Learning. David L. Gallahue et al. LC 75-2369. 423p. 1975. text ed. 20.95 (ISBN 0-471-29043-2); tchrs' resource bk. avail. (ISBN 0-471-29039-4). Wiley.

Conceptual Approach to Teaching About Pennsylvania. Social Studies Division of the Pennsylvania Department of Education. LC 72-90894. 1973. pap. 7.50 (ISBN 0-931992-13-3). Penns Valley.

Conceptual Basis of the Classification of Knowledge: Proceedings of the Ottawa Conference. Ed. by Jercy A. Wojciechowski. 503p. 1978. text ed. 58.00 (ISBN 0-89664-016-7, Pub. by K G Saur). Gale.

Conceptual Blockbusting: A Guide to Better Ideas. 2nd ed. James L. Adams. (Illus.). 160p. 1980. 10.95 (ISBN 0-393-01223-9); pap. text ed. 3.95x (ISBN 0-393-95016-6). Norton.

Conceptual Design of an Automated National Library System. Norman R. Meise. (Illus.). 1969. 10.00 (ISBN 0-8108-0050-0). Scarecrow.

Conceptual Foundation of Genetics: Selected Readings. Harry O. Corwin & John B. Jenkins. LC 75-26092. (Illus.). 448p. 1976. pap. text ed. 11.50 (ISBN 0-395-24064-6). HM.

Conceptual Foundations of Business. 3rd ed. Richard Eells & Clarence Walton. 1974. 16.50x o.p. (ISBN 0-256-01559-7). Irwin.

Conceptual Foundations of Management Accounting. Ahmed Belkaoui. LC 80-16086. (A-W Paperback Series in Accounting). 125p. 1980. pap. 6.50 (ISBN 0-201-00097-0). A-W.

Conceptual Idealism. Nicholas Rescher. 1973. 25.00x (ISBN 0-631-14950-3, Pub. by Basil Blackwell). Biblio Dist.

Conceptual Issues in Operant Psychology. P. Harzem & T. R. Miles. LC 77-21280. 1978. 27.95 (ISBN 0-471-99603-3, Pub. by Wiley-Interscience). Wiley.

Conceptual Models for Psychopathology. C. Eisdorfer et al. 1981. text ed. write for info. (ISBN 0-89335-123-7). Spectrum Pub.

Conceptual Physics: A New Introduction to Your Environment. 4th ed. Hewitt. 1981. text ed. 16.95 (ISBN 0-316-35969-6); tchrs'. manual free (ISBN 0-316-35971-8); test bank avail. Little.

Conceptual Statistics for Beginners. Isadore Newman & Carole Newman. LC 79-64100. 1979. pap. text ed. 10.25 (ISBN 0-8191-0752-2). U Pr of Amer.

Conceptualization of the Inner Life: A Philosophical Exploration. Leslie Armour & Edward T. Bartlett, 3rd. 1981. text ed. 17.50 (ISBN 0-391-01759-4). Humanities.

Concern for the Church: Theological Investigations Vol. XX. Karl Rahner. (Theological Investigations Ser.). 272p. (Ger.). 1981. 12.95 (ISBN 0-8245-0027-X). Crossroad NY.

Concerned About the Planet: The Reporter Magazine & American Liberalism, 1949-1968. Martin K. Doudna. LC 77-10048. (Contributions in American Studies: No. 32). 1977. lib. bdg. 16.95 (ISBN 0-8371-9698-1, DCA/). Greenwood.

Concerning Death: A Practical Guide for the Living. Ed. by Earl A. Grollman. LC 73-17117. 384p. 1974. 9.95 o.p. (ISBN 0-8070-2764-2); pap. 5.95 (ISBN 0-8070-2765-0, BP484). Beacon Pr.

Concerning Justice. Lucilius A. Emery. 1914. 22.50x (ISBN 0-685-69818-1). Elliots Bks.

Concerning Our Duties to God. Apostolos Makrakis. Ed. by Orthodox Christian Educational Society. 170p. 1958. pap. text ed. 2.00x (ISBN 0-938366-13-0). Orthodox Chr.

Concerning Scandals. John Calvin. Tr. by John W. Fraser. LC 78-8675. 1978. 6.95 o.p. (ISBN 0-8028-3511-2). Eerdmans.

Concerning the Eternal Predestination of God. John Calvin. Ed. by J. K. Reid. 1961. 13.95 (ISBN 0-227-67438-3). Attic Pr.

Concerning the Force & Effect of Manuall Weapons of Fire. Humphrey Barwick. LC 74-80163. (English Experience Ser.: No. 643). 86p. 1974. Repr. of 1594 ed. 8.00 (ISBN 90-221-0643-8). Walter J Johnson.

Concerning the Spiritual in Art. Wassily Kandinsky. Tr. & intro. by M. T. Sadler. LC 76-23973. 160p. 1977. pap. text ed. 2.25 (ISBN 0-486-23411-8). Dover.

Concerning the Way of Color. Fritz Faiss. 12.50. Green Hut.

Concerning the Way of Color: An Artist's Approach. 2nd ed. Fritz W. Faiss. LC 76-23022. (Illus.). 120p. 1977. Wkbk. Incl. pap. text ed. 15.00 (ISBN 0-916678-02-4). Green Hut.

Concerns: Essays & Reviews 1972-76. Tom Montag. LC 75-1956. (Orig.). 1977. 18.50x (ISBN 0-915316-34-X); pap. 6.50x (ISBN 0-915316-09-9). Pentagram.

Concert of Europe. Ed. by Rene Albrecht-Carrie. LC 68-13327. (Documentary History of Western Civilization Ser.). 1968. 15.00x o.s.i. (ISBN 0-8027-2004-8). Walker & Co.

Concert of Hells. Beth A. Brombert. 205p. 1980. 17.95 (ISBN 0-241-10303-7, Pub. by Hamish Hamilton England). David & Charles.

Concert Piano Repertoire: A Manual of Solo Literature for Artists & Performers. Albert Faurot. LC 73-15567. 1974. 12.00 (ISBN 0-8108-0685-1). Scarecrow.

Concerto. Abraham Veinus. pap. 5.00 (ISBN 0-486-21178-9). Dover.

Concerto for Piano with Chamber Ensemble. Richard Swift. (U. C. Publ. in Contemporary Music: Vol. 3). (Illus., Orig.). 1968. pap. 9.50x (ISBN 0-520-01245-3). U of Cal Pr.

Concerto in the Key of Death. Barbara Fried. (Orig.). 1980. pap. 1.75 (ISBN 0-505-51508-3). Tower Bks.

Concerts en France Sous l'Ancien Regime. Michel Brenet. LC 68-16224. (Music Ser). 1970. Repr. of 1900 ed. lib. bdg. 35.00 (ISBN 0-306-71061-7). Da Capo.

Concession. Ann Ashton. LC 79-7484. (Romantic Suspense Ser.). 192p. 1981. 9.95 (ISBN 0-385-13210-7). Doubleday.

Concession et Leg. Petrolieres Pays Arabe. Salloum. (Fr.). 13.00x (ISBN 0-685-77134-2). Intl Bk Ctr.

Conchita: A Mother's Diary. M. M. Philipon. Tr. by Aloysius Owen. LC 78-1929. 1978. pap. 6.95 (ISBN 0-8189-0368-6). Alba.

Conchs, Tibias, & Harps. Jerry G. Walls. (Illus.). 192p. 1980. 9.95 (ISBN 0-87666-629-2, S-103). TFH Pubns.

Conciencia Intelectual De America: Antologia Del Ensayo Hispanoamericano. rev. 3rd ed. Carlos Ripoll. 1974. 9.50 (ISBN 0-88303-150-7). E Torres & Sons.

Conciencia Social De Miguel Delibes. Ramona F. Valle-Spinka. 1975. 12.95 (ISBN 0-88303-022-5); pap. 9.50 (ISBN 0-685-73223-1). E Torres & Sons.

Conciliation & Arbitration Procedures in Labour Disputes. 183p. 1980. pap. 16.00 (ISBN 92-2-102339-7, ILO 151, ILO). Unipub.

Concise Amharic Dictionary. Wolf Leslau. LC 73-90668. 1976. 65.00x (ISBN 0-520-02660-8). U of Cal Pr.

Concise Antibiotic Treatment. 2nd ed. W. H. Hughes & H. C. Stewart. 148p. 1973. text ed. 12.40 (ISBN 0-407-13881-1). Butterworths.

Concise Book of Orienteering. Terry Brown & Rob Hunter. 1979. pap. 2.95. Vanguard.

Concise Book of the Horse. Ed. by Candida Geddes. LC 76-1874. (Illus.). 1976. 9.95 o.p. (ISBN 0-668-03965-5). Arco.

Concise Cambridge Bibliography of English Literature, 600-1950. 2nd ed. George Watson. (Orig.). 1965. 45.00 (ISBN 0-521-04504-5); pap. 12.50x (ISBN 0-521-09265-5). Cambridge U Pr.

Concise Cambridge History of English Literature. rev. 3rd ed. George Sampson. LC 69-16287. 1970. 42.00 (ISBN 0-521-07385-5); pap. 17.95x (ISBN 0-521-09581-6). Cambridge U Pr.

Concise Cambridge Italian Dictionary. Barbara Reynolds. 1974. 42.00 (ISBN 0-521-07273-5). Cambridge U Pr.

Concise Color Encyclopedia of Nature. Michael Dempsey & Michael Chinery. LC 73-13688. (Illus.). 254p. 1972. 9.95 o.s.i. (ISBN 0-690-20859-6, TYC-T). T Y Crowell.

Concise Commentary on the Whole Bible. Matthew Henry & Thomas Scott. 18.95 (ISBN 0-8024-5190-X). Moody.

Concise Course in Embroidery. Carol Walker. (Illus.). 1979. pap. write for info. (ISBN 0-671-18391-5). Sovereign Bks.

Concise Dictionary of Business Terminology. Albert G. Giordano. 464p. 1981. text ed. 14.95 (ISBN 0-13-166553-7, Spec); pap. text ed. 5.95 (ISBN 0-13-166546-4). P-H.

Concise Dictionary of Cats. Janet Bloomfield. LC 76-51527. (Funk & W Bk.). (Illus.). 1977. 9.95 o.s.i. (ISBN 0-308-10278-9, TYC-T). T Y Crowell.

Concise Dictionary of Christian Ethics. Ed. by Bernard Stoeckle. 1979. 19.50 (ISBN 0-8164-0357-0). Crossroad NY.

Concise Dictionary of Correct English. Ed. by B. A. Phythian. (Littlefield, Adams Quality Paperback Ser.: No. 349). 1979. pap. 5.50 (ISBN 0-8226-0349-7). Littlefield.

Concise Dictionary of Military Biography: 200 Names in Land Warfare 10th-20th Centuries. Martin Windrow & F. K. Mason. 337p. 1975. 18.00x o.p. (ISBN 0-8464-0271-8). Beekman Pubs.

Concise Dictionary of Old Icelandic. Geir T. Zoega. 1910. 34.50x (ISBN 0-19-863108-1). Oxford U Pr.

Concise Economic History of Britain. William H. Court. pap. 11.95x (ISBN 0-521-09217-5). Cambridge U Pr.

Concise Encyclopedia of Industrial Relations. Ed. by A. I. Marsh. 1979. text ed. 41.00x (ISBN 0-566-02095-5, Pub. by Gower Pub Co England). Renouf.

Concise Encyclopedia of Management Techniques. Frank Finch. LC 76-5913. 1976. 24.50x (ISBN 0-8448-0963-2). Crane-Russak Co.

Concise Encyclopedia of Psychology & Psychiatry. Compiled by Alice Bregman. (Reference Collection Ser.). (Illus.). (gr. 6 up). 1977. PLB 9.90 s&l (ISBN 0-531-01332-4). Watts.

Concise Encyclopedia of the Sciences. John-David Yule. 1981. 29.95 (ISBN 0-87196-491-0). Facts on File.

Concise Encyclopedia of the Second World War. Alan Reid. (Illus.). 232p. 1974. 14.95x o.p. (ISBN 0-8464-0273-4). Beekman Pubs.

Concise English-Italian Italian-English Dictionary. Ed. by Giuseppe Ragazzini & Adele Biagi. LC 73-17088. 1214p. 1973. pap. 11.50 (ISBN 0-582-55505-1). Longman.

Concise Etymological Dictionary of the English Language. Ed. by Walter W. Skeat. 1911. 19.95x (ISBN 0-19-863105-7). Oxford U Pr.

Concise Gospel & the Acts. Christopher Christianson. 1973. 4.95 o.p. (ISBN 0-88270-042-1). Logos.

Concise Grammer of Polish. Oscar Swan. LC 77-18467. 1978. pap. text ed. 5.75x (ISBN 0-8191-0319-5). U Pr of Amer.

Concise Greek-English Dictionary of the New Testament. Barclay M. Newman. 1971. 3.50 (ISBN 3-438-06008-6, 56493). United Bible.

Concise Guide to Composition. 3rd ed. Louise E. Rorabacher. 304p. 1976. text ed. 8.95 scp (ISBN 0-06-045569-1, HarpC); scp practice pages 6.50 (ISBN 0-06-045568-3); answer manual avail. (ISBN 0-685-57572-1). Har-Row.

Concise Handbook for the Care of Patients with Abdominal Stomas. Jerome S. Abrams. (Illus.). 164p. 1981. 20.00 (ISBN 0-88416-292-3). PSG Pub.

Concise Handbook of English Composition. L. Hugh Moore & Karl F. Knight. (Illus.). 144p. 1972. pap. text ed. 5.95 (ISBN 0-13-166959-1). P-H.

Concise Handbook of Respiratory Diseases. Satter Farzan et al. (Illus.). 1978. text ed. 21.95 (ISBN 0-87909-180-0). Reston.

Concise Hebrew-English, English-Hebrew Dictionary. H. Danby & M. Segal. 15.00x o.p. (ISBN 0-686-00848-0). Colton Bk.

Concise Herbal Encyclopedia. Donald Law. LC 73-87589. (Illus.). 266p. 1974. 7.95 o.p. (ISBN 0-312-16135-2). St Martin.

Concise Herbal Encyclopedia. Donald Law. LC 73-87589. (Illus.). 1976. pap. 4.95 o.p. (ISBN 0-312-16170-0). St Martin.

Concise History of Avant Garde Music: From Debussy to Boulez. Paul Griffiths. LC 77-25056. (World of Art Ser.). (Illus.). 1978. pap. 9.95 (ISBN 0-19-520045-4). Oxford U Pr.

Concise History of Catholicism. Marian McKenna. (Quality Paperback: No. 143). 1962. pap. 2.95 (ISBN 0-8226-0143-5). Littlefield.

Concise History of Costume & Fashion. James Laver. LC 73-18802. (Illus.). 1974. pap. write for info. (ISBN 0-684-13522-1, SL477, ScribT). Scribner.

Concise History of French Painting. Edward Lucie-Smith. (World of Art Ser). (Illus.). 1978. pap. 9.95 (ISBN 0-19-520003-9). Oxford U Pr.

Concise History of Indian Art. Roy C. Craven. (World of Art Ser.). (Illus.). 1976. pap. 9.95 (ISBN 0-19-519944-8). Oxford U Pr.

Concise History of Irish Art. Bruce Arnold. LC 77-76835. (World of Art Ser.). (Illus.). 1977. 17.95 (ISBN 0-19-519962-6); pap. 9.95 (ISBN 0-19-519966-9). Oxford U Pr.

Concise History of London. Geoffrey Trease. LC 75-14077. (Encore Edition). (Illus.). 1975. 5.95 o.p. (ISBN 0-684-15466-8, ScribT). Scribner.

Concise History of Mathematics. 3rd rev. ed. Dirk J. Struik. (Illus.). (YA) (gr. 7-12). 1967. pap. text ed. 3.00 (ISBN 0-486-60255-9). Dover.

Concise History of Mexico from Hidalgo to Cardenas 1805-1940. J. Bazant. (Illus.). 1977. 26.95 (ISBN 0-521-21495-5); pap. 7.95x (ISBN 0-521-29173-9). Cambridge U Pr.

Concise History of Mining. Cedric E. Gregory. LC 80-13925. 1980. 30.00 (ISBN 0-08-023882-3). Pergamon.

Concise History of Modern Painting. Herbert Read. (World of Art Ser.). (Illus.). 1974. pap. 9.95 (ISBN 0-19-519940-5). Oxford U Pr.

Concise History of Modern Sculpture. Herbert Read. (World of Art Ser.). (Illus.). 1964. pap. 9.95 (ISBN 0-19-519941-3). Oxford U Pr.

Concise History of Painting: From Giotto to Cezanne. Michael Levey. (World of Art Ser.). (Illus.). 1962. pap. 9.95 (ISBN 0-19-519942-1). Oxford U Pr.

Concise History of Posters. John Barnicoat. LC 78-22019. (World of Art Ser.). (Illus.). 1979. pap. 9.95 (ISBN 0-19-520131-0). Oxford U Pr.

Concise History of Russian Art. Tamara T. Rice. (World of Art). (Illus.). 1963. pap. text ed. 9.95 (ISBN 0-19-520002-0). Oxford U Pr.

Concise History of Russian Literature, Vol. 1: From the Beginnings to Chekhov. Thais Lindstrom. LC 66-22218. (Gotham Library). (Orig.). 1966. 12.50x (ISBN 0-8147-0260-0); pap. 6.00x (ISBN 0-8147-0261-9). NYU Pr.

Concise History of Russian Literature, Vol. 2: 1900 to the Present. Thais S. Lindstrom. LC 77-14671. 1979. 17.50x (ISBN 0-8147-4980-1); pap. 8.00x (ISBN 0-8147-4981-X). NYU Pr.

Concise History of the Catholic Church. Thomas Bokenkotter. LC 78-20269. 1979. pap. 4.95 (ISBN 0-385-13015-5, Im). Doubleday.

Concise History of the Catholic Church. Thomas Bokenkotter. LC 77-75382. 1977. 10.00 o.p. (ISBN 0-385-13014-7). Doubleday.

Concise History of the Common Law. 5th ed. Theodore F. Plucknett. 802p. 1956. 21.50 (ISBN 0-316-71083-0). Little.

Concise History of the Middle East. Arthur Goldschmidt, Jr. 1979. lib. bdg. 28.50x (ISBN 0-89158-251-7); pap. text ed. 11.50x (ISBN 0-89158-289-4). Westview.

Concise History of the Mormon Battalion in the Mexican War, 1846-1848. Daniel Tyler. LC 64-15125. (Beautiful Rio Grande Classics Ser). Repr. of 1881 ed. lib. bdg. 12.00 (ISBN 0-87380-011-7). Rio Grande.

Concise History of the Theatre. Phyllis Hartnoll. 1973. pap. 8.95 (ISBN 0-684-13521-3, SL483, ScribT). Scribner.

Concise History of Watercolors. Graham Reynolds. (World of Art Ser.). (Illus.). 1978. pap. 9.95 (ISBN 0-19-520051-9). Oxford U Pr.

Concise History of Western Architecture. Robert Furneaux Jordan. LC 79-99555. 1970. 9.95 o.p. (ISBN 0-15-121275-9). HarBraceJ.

Concise Illustrated Russian-English Dictionary of Mechanical Engineering. V. V. Shvarts. (Illus.). 224p. 1981. pap. 30.00 (ISBN 0-08-027574-5). Pergamon.

Concise Introduction to Logic. Ian Hacking. (Orig.). 1971. pap. text ed. 8.95 (ISBN 0-394-31008-X). Random.

Concise Introduction to Music Listening. 2nd. ed. Charles Hoffer. 1979. pap. 12.95x (ISBN 0-534-00627-2); study guide 6.95x (ISBN 0-534-00705-8); records 16.95x (ISBN 0-534-00692-2). Wadsworth Pub.

Concise Introduction to Philosophy. 4th ed. William H. Halverson. 493p. 1981. text ed. 16.95 (ISBN 0-394-32533-8). Random.

Concise Introduction to the Philosophy of Nicholas of Cusa. 2nd ed. Jasper Hopkins. xii, 185p. 1980. 20.00x (ISBN 0-8166-1016-9). U of Minn Pr.

Concise Legal History of South-East Asia. M. B. Hooker. 1978. lib. bdg. 48.00x (ISBN 0-19-825344-3). Oxford U Pr.

Concise Manchu-English Lexicon. Jerry Norman. LC 77-14307. (Publications on Asia of the School for International Studies: No. 32). 336p. 1979. 22.50 (ISBN 0-295-95574-0). U of Wash Pr.

Concise Medical Parasitology. Lawrence J. Blecka. 1980. cancelled (ISBN 0-201-00756-8). A-W.

Concise Neurosurgery. E. Pasztor. (Illus.). 292p. 1980. 56.50 (ISBN 3-8055-1431-X). S Karger.

Concise Oxford Dictionary of Current English. 6th ed. Ed. by J. B. Sykes. 1976. 19.95 (ISBN 0-19-861121-8); thumb-indexed 22.50 (ISBN 0-19-861122-6). Oxford U Pr.

Concise Oxford Dictionary of English Place-Names. 4th ed. Eilert Ekwall. 1960. 29.00x (ISBN 0-19-869103-3). Oxford U Pr.

Concise Oxford Dictionary of Music. 3rd ed. Ed. by Michael Kennedy. (Out of Ser. K). (Illus.). 736p. 1981. 19.95 (ISBN 0-19-311315-5); pap. 9.95 (ISBN 0-19-311320-1). Oxford U Pr.

Concise Oxford Dictionary of Opera. 2nd ed. Ed. by Harold Rosenthal & John Warrack. (Out-of-Ser. Paperback). 576p. 1981. pap. 11.95 (ISBN 0-19-311321-X). Oxford U Pr.

Concise Oxford Dictionary of Quotations. abr. ed. 1964. pap. 5.95x (ISBN 0-19-281022-7). Oxford U Pr.

Concise Oxford Dictionary of the Christian Church. Ed. by E. A. Livingstone. 1978. 18.95 (ISBN 0-19-211549-9). Oxford U Pr.

Concise Oxford French Dictionary. Ed. by H. Ferrar et al. 912p. 1980. 22.50 (ISBN 0-19-864126-5). Oxford U Pr.

Concise Oxford Turkish Dictionary. Ed. by A. D. Alderson & Fahir Iz. 1959. 17.95x (ISBN 0-19-864109-5). Oxford U Pr.

Concise Readings in Philosophy. William H. Halverson. 447p. 1981. pap. text ed. 9.95 (ISBN 0-394-32551-6). Random.

Concise Russian Review Grammar with Exercises. Roger Phillips. 1974. pap. 3.95x (ISBN 0-299-06544-8). U of Wis Pr.

Concise Study Guide to the American Frontier. Nelson Klose. LC 64-15180. (Illus.). 1964. 13.95x (ISBN 0-8032-0093-5); pap. 2.75x (ISBN 0-8032-5110-6, BB 190, Bison). U of Nebr Pr.

Concise Text of Histology. William J. Krause & J. Jarry Cutts. (Illus.). 175p. 1981. write for info. soft cover (4784-1). Williams & Wilkins.

Concise Textbook for Midwives. 4th ed. Douglas G. Clyne. 1975. pap. text ed. 11.50 o.p. (ISBN 0-571-04845-5, Pub. by Faber & Faber). Merrimack Bk Serv.

Concise Textbook for Midwives. 5th ed. Douglas G. Clyne. (Illus.). 528p. 1980. pap. 17.95 (ISBN 0-571-18018-3, Pub. by Faber & Faber). Merrimack Bk Serv.

Concise Textbook of Organic Chemistry. C. G. Lyons et al. 1965. 14.50 (ISBN 0-08-010657-9); pap. 6.25 (ISBN 0-08-010656-0). Pergamon.

Concise Textbook of Physiology. Sarada Subrahmanyam & K. Madhaven Kutty. 332p. 1979. 15.00 (ISBN 0-86131-026-8, Pub. by Orient Longman India). State Mutual Bk.

Concise Textbook on Legal Capital. 2nd ed. Bayless Manning. (University Textbook Ser.). 180p. 1981. pap. text ed. write for info. (ISBN 0-88277-020-9). Foundation Pr.

Concise Usage & Abusage. Partridge. 4.95 o.p. (ISBN 0-8277-0094-6). British Bk Ctr.

Concise World Atlas of Geology & Mineral Deposits: Non-Metallic Minerals, Metallic Minerals & Energy Minerals. Duncan Derry. LC 80-675233. 110p. 1980. 61.95 (ISBN 0-470-26996-0). Halsted Pr.

Concluding Unscientific Postscript. Soren Kierkegaard. Tr. by D. F. Swenson & W. Lowrie. (American-Scandinavian Foundation). 1941. 25.00x (ISBN 0-691-07106-3); pap. 5.95 (ISBN 0-691-01960-6). Princeton U Pr.

Concomitant Learnings: Hidden Influences in the Classroom. S. Wallace. LC 78-68027. 1978. pap. 3.00 (ISBN 0-686-26202-6, 261-08432). Home Econ Educ.

Concord Notebook: Selections from the Critic, 1905-1906. Franklin B. Sanborn. LC 80-2514. 1981. 27.50 (ISBN 0-404-19062-6). AMS Pr.

Concord Saunterer. LC 80-2504. 1981. Repr. of 1940 ed. 19.50 (ISBN 0-404-19052-9). AMS Pr.

Concordance of the Septuagint. George Morrish. 14.95 (ISBN 0-310-20300-7). Zondervan.

Concordance to Baudelaire's les Fleurs Du Mal. 417p. 1965. 22.75 (ISBN 0-8173-9602-0). U of Ala Pr.

Concordance to Beowulf. Albert S. Cook. LC 68-23146. 1968. Repr. of 1911 ed. 18.00 (ISBN 0-8103-3169-1). Gale.

Concordance to Chu Hsi, "Ta Hsieh Chang Chu" And a Concordance to Chu Hsi, Chung Yung Chang Chu, Vol. 1. Ed. by Davdi Nivison. (Stanford Chinese Concordance Ser.). 1979. 20.00x (ISBN 0-89644-575-5, SCCS-1). Chinese Materials.

Concordance to Conrad's Nigger of the Narcissus. Todd K. Bender & James W. Parins. LC 79-8417. 150p. 1981. lib. bdg. 35.00 (ISBN 0-8240-9519-7). Garland Pub.

Concordance to Darwin's "Origin of Species". Ed. by Paul Barrett et al. 864p. 1981. 38.50x (ISBN 0-8014-1319-2). Cornell U Pr.

Concordance to F. Scott Fitzgerald's The Great Gatsby. Compiled by Andrew Crosland. LC 74-11607. (Bruccoli Clark Book). (Illus.). 425p. 1975. 52.00 (ISBN 0-8103-1005-8). Gale.

Concordance to Milton's English Poetry. Ed. by William Ingram & Kathleen M. Swain. 1972. 98.00x (ISBN 0-19-811138-X). Oxford U Pr.

Concordance to Pascal's "Les Provinciales". Pierre H. Dube & Hugh M. Davidson. LC 79-54323. (Garland Reference Library of the Humanities). 1000p. 1980. lib. bdg. 100.00 (ISBN 0-8240-9536-7). Garland Pub.

Concordance to Q. Richard A. Edwards. LC 75-6768. (Society of Biblical Literature. Sources for Biblical Study). iv, 186p. 1975. pap. 7.50 (ISBN 0-89130-056-2, 060307). Scholars Pr Ca.

Concordance to Tai Chen, "Yuan Shan". Ed. by David S. Nivison. Bd. with Concordance to Tai Chen, "Meng Tzu I Shu Cheng". (No. 6, Vol. 4). vi, 496p. (Stanford Chinese Concordance Ser.: No. 5, Vol. 4). xxviii, 152p. 1979. 35.00x. Chinese Materials.

Concordance to the Complete Nonsense of King Lear. Anne K. Lyons & Thomas R. Lyons. Ed. by Michael J. Preston. 341p. 1980. lib. bdg. 30.00 (ISBN 0-8482-1636-9). Norwood Edns.

Concordance to the Complete Poetry of Stephen Crane. Compiled by Andrew Crosland. LC 74-30426. (Bruccoli Clark Book). 1975. 60.00 (ISBN 0-8103-1006-6). Gale.

Concordance to the Essays of Francis Bacon. Ed. by David W. Davies & Elizabeth S. Wrigley. LC 73-8947. 392p. 1973. 48.00 (ISBN 0-8103-1004-X). Gale.

Concordance to the Greek Testament: According to the Texts of Westcott & Hort, Tischendorf & the English Revisers. 5th ed. W. F. Moulton et al. 1120p. 1978. text ed. 45.00x (ISBN 0-567-01021-X). Attic Pr.

Concordance to the Hidden Words of Baha'u'llah. Jalil Mahmoudi. (Orig.). 1980. pap. 5.00 (ISBN 0-87743-148-5, 7-68-52). Baha'i.

Concordance to the Pascal's Pensees. Ed. by Hugh M. Davidson & Pierre H. Dube. LC 75-16808. (Cornell Concordances Ser.). 1488p. 1975. 40.00x (ISBN 0-8014-0972-1). Cornell U Pr.

Concordance to the Poems of Alexander Pope, 2 vols. Ed. by Emmett G. Bedford & Robert J. Dilligan. LC 74-852. 1656p. 1974. Set. 125.00 (ISBN 0-8103-1008-2). Gale.

Concordance to the Poems of Dylan Thomas. Gary Lane. LC 76-18078. (Concordances Ser.: No. 5). 1976. 27.50 (ISBN 0-8108-0971-0). Scarecrow.

Concordance to the Poems of Edmund Spenser. Charles G. Osgood. 1963. 35.00 (ISBN 0-8446-1332-0). Peter Smith.

Concordance to the Poems of Hart Crane. Hilton Landry et al. LC 72-10663. (Concordances Ser.: No. 4). 1973. 16.50 (ISBN 0-8108-0564-2). Scarecrow.

Concordance to the Poems of John Keats. Dane L. Baldwin & L. N. Broughton. 1963. 35.00 (ISBN 0-8446-1044-5). Peter Smith.

Concordance to the Poems of Theodore Roethke. Gary Lane. (Concordances Ser.: No. 3). 1972. 20.50 (ISBN 0-8108-0514-6). Scarecrow.

Concordance to the Poetry of Thomas Traherne. George R. Guffey. 1974. 45.00x (ISBN 0-520-02449-4). U of Cal Pr.

Concordance to the Russian Poetry of Fedor I. Tiutchev. Borys Bilokur. LC 75-9419. 343p. 1975. 20.00x (ISBN 0-87057-145-1, Pub. by Brown U Pr). Univ Pr of New England.

Concordance to the Sonnet Sequences of Daniel, Drayton, Shakespeare, Sidney & Spenser. Herbert S. Donow. LC 72-76188. 1969. 17.50x o.p. (ISBN 0-8093-0400-7). S Ill U Pr.

Concordance to the Targum of Isaiah. J. B. Van Zijl. LC 78-25832. (Society of Biblical Literature. Aramaic Studies: No. 3). 1979. pap. 9.00 (ISBN 0-89130-273-5, 061303). Scholars Pr Ca.

Concordance to the Works of John Webster, Vol. 1 Pt. 2. Richard Corballis & J. M. Harding. (Salzburg Studies in English Literature, Jacobean Drama: No. 70-1). (Orig.). 1980. pap. text ed. 25.00x (ISBN 0-391-01316-5). Humanities.

Concordance to the Works of John Webster, Vol. 1 Pt. 3. Richard Corballis & J. M. Harding. (Salzburg Studies in English Literature, Jacobean Drama Ser.: 70). (Orig.). 1979. pap. text ed. 25.00x (ISBN 0-391-01723-3). Humanities.

Concordance to the Works of John Webster, Vol. 1 Pt. 4. Richard Corballis & J. M. Harding. (Salzburg Studies in English Literature, Jacobean Drama Ser.). (Orig.). 1979. pap. text ed. 25.00x (ISBN 0-391-01717-9). Humanities.

Concordance to the Works of John Webster, Vol. 2, Pt. 4. Richard Corballis & J. M. Harding. (Salzburg Studies in English Literature, Jacobean Drama: No. 70-2). 1979. pap. text ed. 25.00x (ISBN 0-391-01317-3). Humanities.

Concordance to the Works of John Webster, Vol. 2 Pt. 1. Richard Corballis & J. M. Harding. (Salzburg Studies in English Literature, Jacobean Drame Ser.: 70). (Orig.). 1979. pap. text ed. 25.00x (ISBN 0-391-01724-1). Humanities.

Concordance to the Works of John Webster, Vol. 2 Pt. 2. Richard Corballis & John Harding. (Salzburg Studies in English Literature, Jacobean Drama Ser.: 70). (Orig.). 1979. pap. text ed. 25.00x (ISBN 0-391-01737-3). Humanities.

Concordance to the Works of John Webster, Vol. 3 Pt. 1. Richard Corballis & J. M. Harding. (Salzburg Studies in English Literature, Jacobean Drama: No. 70-3). (Orig.). 1980. pap. text ed. 25.00x (ISBN 0-391-01318-1). Humanities.

Concordance to the Works of John Webster: Vol. 4, Appendix, Sir Thomas Wyatt. Richard Corballis & J. M. Harding. (Salzburg Studies in English Literature, Jacobean Drama Ser.: No. 70-4). (Orig.). 1979. pap. text ed. 25.00x (ISBN 0-391-01213-4). Humanities.

Concordance to Wang Yang-Ming, "Ch'uan Hsi Lu," Concordance. Ed. by David S. Nivison. Bd. with Concordance to Wang Yang-Ming, "Ta Hsueh Wen". (No. 4, Vol. 3). iv, 42p. (Stanford Chinese Concordance Ser.: No. 3.2, Vol. 3). xxvi, 510p. 1979. 30.00x (ISBN 0-89644-577-1). Chinese Materials.

Concordances to Conrad's Victory. Todd K. Bender. LC 79-8416. 150p. 1980. lib. bdg. 35.00 (ISBN 0-8240-9520-0). Garland Pub.

Concordancia Alfabetica De la Biblia. W. H. Sloan & A. Lerin. Date not set. pap. 9.95 (ISBN 0-311-42054-0). Casa Bautista.

Concordancia Breve De la Biblia. 280p. Date not set. pap. price not set (ISBN 0-311-42055-9, Edit Mundo). Casa Bautista.

Concordancia De la Biblia. (Spanish Bks.). (Span.). 1980. 1.25 (ISBN 0-8297-0775-1). Life Pubs Intl.

Concordancia De las Sagradas Escripturas. Carlos Denyer. LC 74-21722. 936p. (Span.). 1969. 24.95 (ISBN 0-89922-004-5); pap. 15.95 (ISBN 0-89922-121-1). Edit Caribe.

Concordancia Greco-Espanola. Hugo M. Petter. Ed. by Betty De Carroll. Date not set. Repr. of 1976 ed. 12.95 (ISBN 0-311-42047-8). Casa Bautista.

Concordant Greek Text. rev. ed. Ed. by A E. Knoch. 1975. lea. bdg. 20.00 (ISBN 0-910424-32-2). Concordant.

Concorde: Airport 79. Kerry Stewart. (Orig.). pap. 2.25 (ISBN 0-515-05348-1). Jove Pubns.

Concrete Afloat. Institute of Civil Engineers, UK. 208p. 1980. 55.00x (ISBN 0-7277-0048-0, Pub. by Telford England). State Mutual Bk.

Concrete & Cryogenics. F. H. Turner. (Viewpoint Publications Ser.). 1979. text ed. 27.50x (ISBN 0-7210-1124-1). Scholium Intl.

Concrete & Cryogenics. F. H. Turner. (Viewpoint Publication Ser.). (Illus.). 125p. 1979. pap. text ed. 27.50x (ISBN 0-7210-1124-1, Pub by C&CA London). Scholium Intl.

Concrete & Masonry. Tab Editional Staff. LC 76-1553. 392p. 1976. pap. 5.95 (ISBN 0-8306-5902-1, 902). TAB Bks.

Concrete Approach to Abstract Algebra. W. W. Sawyer. 1978. pap. text ed. 4.00 (ISBN 0-486-63647-X). Dover.

Concrete Box Girder Bridges. Oris H. Degenkolb. (Monograph No. 10). 1977. 19.00 (ISBN 0-685-85763-8) (ISBN 0-685-85764-6). ACI.

Concrete Bridge Design. R. E. Rowe. 1972. Repr. of 1966 ed. text ed. 52.20x (ISBN 0-85334-110-9, Pub. by Applied Science). Burgess-Intl Ideas.

Concrete Bridge Designer's Manual. Ernest Pennells. (Viewpoint Publication Ser.). (Illus.). 1978. text ed. 40.00 (ISBN 0-7210-1083-0). Scholium Intl.

Concrete Bridges: An Introduction to Structural Design. Derrick Beckett. (Illus.). 1973. 24.00x (ISBN 0-903384-01-9). Intl Ideas.

Concrete Christian Life. Christian Duquoc. LC 78-168653. (Concilium Ser.: Religion in the Seventies: Vol. 69). 1971. pap. 4.95 (ISBN 0-8164-2525-6). Crossroad NY.

Concrete Construction & Estimating. Portland Cement Association. Ed. by Craig Avery. LC 80-12349. (Illus.). 576p. 1980. pap. 14.00 (ISBN 0-910460-75-2). Craftsman.

Concrete Design: U. S. & European Practices. 1979. 29.50 (SP-59); 22.75. ACI.

Concrete for High Temperatures. 2nd ed. A. Petzold & M. Rohrs. Tr. by A. R. Phillips & F. H. Turner. (Illus.). 1970. text ed. 37.30x (ISBN 0-85334-033-1, Pub. by Applied Science). Burgess-Intl Ideas.

Concrete for Nuclear Reactors, 3 vols. 1972. Set. pap. 42.95 o.p. (ISBN 0-685-85110-9, SP-34); Set. pap. 28.50 members o.p. (ISBN 0-685-85111-7). ACI.

Concrete for Structural Engineers. Wilby. 1977. 29.95 (ISBN 0-408-00256-5). Butterworths.

Concrete in Highway Engineering. D. R. Sharp. LC 77-118319. 1970. 19.50 (ISBN 0-08-015845-5). Pergamon.

Concrete Inspection Procedures. Portland Cement Association. LC 74-28254. (National Concrete Technology Curriculum Project Ser). 146p. 1975. text ed. 17.95 (ISBN 0-471-67431-1). Wiley.

Concrete Liquid Retaining Structures. J. Keith Green & Philip H. Perkins. (Illus.). 1979. 55.00x (ISBN 0-85334-856-1, Pub. by Applied Science). Burgess-Intl Ideas.

Concrete Look at Nature. Eugene Kinkead. (Illus.). 242p. 1974. 8.00x (ISBN 0-8129-0471-0). E Kinkead.

Concrete, Masonry & Brickwork: A Practical Handbook for the Homeowner & Small Builder. U. S. Army. LC 75-12130. Orig. Title: Concrete & Masonry. (Illus.). 204p. 1975. pap. 5.00 (ISBN 0-486-23203-4). Dover.

Concrete Materials & Practices. 5th ed. L. J. Murdock & K. M. Brook. LC 78-27476. 1979. 54.95x (ISBN 0-470-26639-2). Halsted Pr.

Concrete Mix Design. F. D. Lydon. (Illus.). 1972. text ed. 26.00x (ISBN 0-85334-552-X, Pub. by Applied Science). Burgess-Intl Ideas.

Concrete Pressure Pipe-M9: AWWA Manuals. American Water Works Association. (Illus.). 1979. pap. text ed. 11.00 (ISBN 0-89867-067-5). Am Water Wks Assn.

Concrete Primer. 3rd ed. F. R. McMillan & Lewis H. Tuthill. 1973. 6.50 (ISBN 0-685-85094-3, SP-1) (ISBN 0-685-85095-1). ACI.

Concrete: Problems, Causes, & Cures. John C. Ropke. (Illus.). 192p. 1981. 21.50 (ISBN 0-07-053609-0). McGraw.

Concrete Shell Roofs. C. B. Wilby & I. Khwaja. LC 77-391. 1977. 59.95 (ISBN 0-470-99088-0). Halsted Pr.

Concrete Technology. 3rd ed. George R. White. LC 76-5304. 1977. pap. text ed. 6.00 (ISBN 0-8273-1095-1); instructor's guide 1.75 (ISBN 0-8273-1092-7). Delmar.

Concrete Technology, Vol. 2. rev. 3rd ed. D. F. Orchard. LC 72-13145. 1973. 39.95 (ISBN 0-470-65539-9). Halsted Pr.

Concrete Technology, Vol. 3. 3rd ed. D. F. Orchard. LC 72-13145. 1976. 44.95 (ISBN 0-470-65540-2). Halsted Pr.

Concrete Techology: Vol. 2, Practice. 4th ed. D. F. Orchard. 1979. 67.40 (ISBN 0-85334-837-5, Pub. by Applied Science). Burgess-Intl Ideas.

Concrete Work Simplified. Donald R. Brann. LC 66-24876. 1980. pap. 5.95 (ISBN 0-87733-617-2). Easi-Bild.

Concreteness in Generative Phonology: Evidence from French. Bernard Tranel. LC 80-51243. 400p. 1980. 29.50x (ISBN 0-520-04165-8). U of Cal Pr.

Concubine. Elechi Amadi. (African Writers Ser.). 1966. pap. text ed. 2.75 (ISBN 0-435-90025-0). Heinemann Ed.

Concubine. Norah Lofts. 336p. 1975. pap. 1.50 o.p. (ISBN 0-449-22405-8, Q2405, Crest). Fawcett.

Concurrent Jurisdiction of the Federal & State Courts. George C. Holt. xxvi, 237p. 1980. Repr. of 1888 ed. lib. bdg. 24.00x (ISBN 0-8377-0630-0). Rothman.

Conde Lucanor. Don J. Manuel. (Span.). 7.95 (ISBN 84-241-5615-3). E Torres & Sons.

Condemnation Appraisal Practice, Vol. 2. Ed. by American Institute of Real Estate Appraisers. 1973. 15.00 (ISBN 0-911780-32-7). Am Inst Real Estate Appraisers.

Condemned to Co-Exist: Road Maps to the Future. Bohdan Hawrylyshyn. (Illus.). 200p. 1980. 31.00 (ISBN 0-08-026115-9); pap. 11.00 (ISBN 0-08-026114-0). Pergamon.

Condemned to Life. Kenneth Hamilton & Alice Hamilton. 1976. pap. 5.50 o.p. (ISBN 0-8028-1655-X). Eerdmans.

Condemned to Life: The Plight of the Unwanted Child. Waldo Zimmerman. 260p. (Orig.). 1980. pap. 3.95 (ISBN 0-89260-181-7). Hwong Pub.

Condensation in Buildings. Ed. by D. J. Croome & A. F. Sherratt. (Illus.). 1972. text ed. 40.90x (ISBN 0-85334-548-1, Pub. by Applied Science). Burgess-Intl Ideas.

Condensation of Decimal & Metrical Systems: Jumelex Method. Marius F. Gagnadre. 1980. 5.95 (ISBN 0-533-04392-1). Vantage.

Condensed Geography & History of the Western States or the Mississippi Valley 1828, 2 Vols. Timothy Flint. LC 70-119865. 1970. Repr. of 1828 ed. 90.00x set (ISBN 0-8201-1076-0). Schol Facsimiles.

Condensed Gospel of Sri Ramakrishna. M, pseud. 1979. 10.50 o.s.i. (ISBN 0-87481-488-X); pap. 4.95 o.s.i. (ISBN 0-87481-489-8). Vedanta Pr.

Condensed History of the Apache & Comanche Indian Tribes. Jonathan H. Jones. LC 75-7129. (Indian Captivities Ser.: Vol. 102). 1976. Repr. of 1899 ed. lib. bdg. 44.00 (ISBN 0-8240-1726-9). Garland Pub.

Condition of Jewish Belief. Commentary Editors. (Orig.). 1967. 10.95 (ISBN 0-02-527260-8). Macmillan.

Conditioned Reflexes: An Investigation of the Physiological Activity of the Cerebral Cortex. Ivan P. Pavlov. Ed. by G. V. Anrep. 1927. pap. text ed. 4.50 (ISBN 0-486-60614-7). Dover.

Conditioning & Learning: Student Booklet. American Psychological Association. (Human Behavior Curriculum Project Ser.). 64p. (gr. 9-12). 1981. pap. text ed. 3.95 (ISBN 0-8077-2623-0). Tchrs Coll.

Conditioning & Learning: Teachers Handbook & Duplication Masters. American Psychological Association. (Human Behavior Curriculum Project Ser.). 48p. (gr. 9-12). 1981. 9.95 (ISBN 0-8077-2624-9). Tchrs Coll.

Conditioning for Baseball: Pre-Season, Regular Season & Off-Season. Robert R. Spackman, Jr. (Illus.). 100p. 1967. 10.75 (ISBN 0-398-01818-9). C C Thomas.

Conditioning for Distance Running: The Scientific Aspects. Jack Daniels et al. LC 77-22538. (American College of Sports Medicine Ser.). 1978. text ed. 13.95 (ISBN 0-471-19483-2). Wiley.

Conditioning for Football: Pre-Season, Regular Season & Off-Season. Robert R. Spackman, Jr. (Illus.). 112p. 1968. 11.50 (ISBN 0-398-01819-7). C C Thomas.

Conditioning for Gymnastics: Pre-Season, Regular Season & Off-Season. Robert R. Spackman, Jr. (Illus.). 120p. 1970. 12.75 (ISBN 0-398-01820-0). C C Thomas.

Conditioning for Sport. N. Whitehead. 128p. 1980. 12.95 (ISBN 0-8069-9110-0, Pub. by EP Publishing England); pap. 5.95 (ISBN 0-8069-9112-7). Sterling.

Conditioning Fundamentals. Olson. 1968. pap. text ed. 4.95 (ISBN 0-675-09684-7). Merrill.

Conditions & Consequences of Human Variability. Raymond Dodge. 1931. 32.50x (ISBN 0-685-69812-2). Elliots Bks.

Conditions & Needs of the Professional American Theatre. (Report Ser.: No. 11). 144p. 1980. pap. 4.50 (ISBN 0-89062-076-8, Pub. by Ctr for Arts Info). Pub Ctr Cult Res.

Conditions for Life: Readings from Scientific American. Intro. by Aharon Gibor. LC 76-22196. (Illus.). 1976. text ed. 19.95x (ISBN 0-7167-0480-3); pap. text ed. 9.95x (ISBN 0-7167-0479-X). W H Freeman.

Conditions for Success in Educational Planning. G. C. Ruscoe. 1969. pap. 6.00 (ISBN 92-803-1031-3, U116, UNESCO). Unipub.

Conditions of Agricultural Growth: The Economics of Agrarian Change Under Population Pressures. Ester Boserup. LC 65-19513. 1965. 12.95x (ISBN 0-202-07003-4). Aldine Pub.

Conditions of Learning & Instruction in Nursing: Modularized. Loucine M. Huckabay. LC 79-17015. 1979. text ed. 18.95 (ISBN 0-8016-2304-9). Mosby.

Conditions of the Black Worker. 298p. (Orig.). 1975. pap. text ed. 6.00 (ISBN 0-89192-067-6). Interbk Inc.

Conditions to Be Observed by British Undertakers of the Escheated Lands in Ulster. LC 74-38139. (English Experience Ser.: No. 490). 1972. Repr. of 1610 ed. 5.00 (ISBN 90-221-0490-7). Walter J Johnson.

Condominium. John D. Macdonald. LC 76-30593. 1977. 10.00 o.p. (ISBN 0-397-01203-9). Lippincott.

Condominium & Cooperative Conversions 1980: Course Handbook. Ed. by F. Scott Jackson & William J. Lippman. LC 80-81527. (Nineteen Seventy-Nine to Nineteen Eighty Real Estate Law & Practice Course Handbook Ser.). 549p. 1981. pap. 25.00 (ISBN 0-686-69166-0, N4-4352). PLI.

Condominium & Homeowners Associations That Work. David B. Wolfe. LC 78-67831. (Illus.). 136p. 1978. pap. text ed. 19.50 (ISBN 0-87420-583-2). Urban Land.

Condominium Book: A Guide to Getting the Most for Your Money. rev. ed. Lee Butcher. LC 80-10497. 150p. (Orig.). 1980. pap. 8.95 (ISBN 0-87128-588-6). Dow Jones-Irwin.

Condominium Buyer's Guide: What to Look for - and Look Out for - in Resort, Residential & Commercial Condominiums. James Karr. LC 72-97531. 1973. 9.95 (ISBN 0-8119-0219-6). Fell.

Condominium Community: A Guide for Owners, Boards, & Managers. Property Managers. 1978. 18.95 (ISBN 0-912104-22-8). Inst Real Estate.

Condominium Management. Jack R. Holeman. (Illus.). 1980. text ed. 18.95 (ISBN 0-13-167155-3). P-H.

Condominium Trap. Hugo Paul. LC 79-65558. 1981. 7.50 (ISBN 0-916620-36-0). Portals Pr.

Condominiums & Cooperatives. David Clurman & Edna L. Hebard. LC 73-106012. (Real Estate for Professional Practitioners Ser.). 1970. 31.50 (ISBN 0-471-16130-6, Pub. by Wiley-Interscience). Wiley.

Condominiums: The Effects of Conversion on a Community. John R. Dinkelspiel & Herbert Selesnick. 160p. 1981. 19.95 (ISBN 0-86569-059-6). Auburn Hse.

Condor. Glenn Pierce. (Orig.). 1980. pap. 1.95 (ISBN 0-505-51520-2). Tower Bks.

Condor Conspiracy. Charlotte Yarborough. (Orig.). 1980. pap. 1.75 (ISBN 0-8439-0739-8, Leisure Bks). Nordon Pubns.

Condorcet: Selected Writings. Ed. by Keith M. Baker. LC 75-38680. (Library of Liberal Arts No. 159). 1976. pap. 9.50 (ISBN 0-672-60381-0). Bobbs.

Condos. Robert G. Natelson. (Orig.). 1981. price not set. Cornerstone.

Conduct Disorders of Childhood & Adolescence: A Behavioral Approach to Assessment & Treatment. Martin Herbert. LC 77-9633. 1978. 36.50 (ISBN 0-471-99509-6, Pub. by Wiley-Interscience). Wiley.

Conduct of Soviet Foreign Policy. 2nd ed. Ed. by Erik P. Hoffman & Frederick J. Fleron, Jr. LC 80-68483. 1980. 34.95 (ISBN 0-202-24155-6); pap. 14.95 (ISBN 0-202-24156-4). Aldine Pub.

Conduct of the Earl of Nottingham: 1689-1694. Wm. A. Aiken. (Yale Historical Pubs., Manuscripts & Edited Texts: No. XVII). 1941. 47.50x (ISBN 0-685-69786-X). Elliots Bks.

Conduct of the Stage Consider'd. Bd. with Heydegger's Letter to the Bishop of London. John J. Heidegger; Seasonable Apology for Mr. H g r. LC 75-170485. (English Stage Ser.: Vol. 45). lib. bdg. 50.00 (ISBN 0-8240-0628-3). Garland Pub.

Conduct of United States Foreign Policy in the Nation's Third Century. Bayless Manning. (Headline Ser.: 231). 1976. pap. 2.00 (ISBN 0-87124-036-X, 76-9573). Foreign Policy.

Conducting an Amateur Orchestra. Malcolm H. Holmes. LC 51-10271. 1951. 6.95x (ISBN 0-674-16000-2). Harvard U Pr.

Conducting Evaluations: Three Perspectives. Marvin C. Alkin et al. LC 80-52791. 60p. (Orig.). 1980. pap. 2.95 (ISBN 0-87954-036-2). Foundation Ctr.

Conducting Guide to Selected Scores. 2nd ed. Emil Kahn. LC 75-30288. (Illus.). 1976. pap. text ed. 12.95 (ISBN 0-02-871030-4). Schirmer Bks.

Conducting Technique. William D. Clark. LC 78-66123. 1979. pap. text ed. 9.50 (ISBN 0-8191-0684-4). U Pr of Amer.

Conducting the Lawful Employment Interview. 1979. pap. 3.00 (ISBN 0-917386-87-6). Exec Ent.

Conducting the Small Group Experience. John M. Toothman. LC 78-59854. 1978. pap. 7.50 (ISBN 0-8191-0554-6). U Pr of Amer.

Conduction Heat Transfer. Vedat S. Arpaci. 1966. 23.95 (ISBN 0-201-00359-7). A-W.

Conduction of Electricity Through Gases. John Beynon. 1972. pap. text ed. 12.50x (ISBN 0-245-50580-6). Intl Ideas.

Conduction of Electricity Through Gases, 2 Vols. Joseph J. Thomson & George P. Thomson. LC 68-8881. (Illus.). 1969. pap. text ed. 4.50 ea.; Vol. 1. pap. text ed. (ISBN 0-486-62007-7); Vol. 2. pap. text ed. (ISBN 0-486-62008-5). Dover.

Conduction of Heat in Solids. 2nd ed. Horatio S. Carslaw & J. C. Jaeger. (Illus.). 1959. 39.50x (ISBN 0-19-853303-9). Oxford U Pr.

Conduction Velocity Distributions: A Population Approach to Electrophysiology of Nerve. Proceedings of a Workshop, Palo Alto, California, July 1979 et al. Ed. by Leslie J. Dorfman & Kenneth L. Cummins. (Progress in Clinical & Biological Research Ser.: No. 52). 338p. 1981. 30.00x (ISBN 0-8451-0052-1). A R Liss.

Conductor & His Score. Elizabeth Green & Nicolai Malko. LC 74-13718. (Illus.). 208p. 1975. 13.95 (ISBN 0-13-167312-2). P-H.

Conductor of the Dead. Subhas Kak. (Writers Workshop Redbird Ser.). 36p. 1975. 8.00 (ISBN 0-88253-516-1); pap. text ed. 4.80 (ISBN 0-88253-515-3). Ind-US Inc.

Cone-Gathers: A Novel. Robin Jenkins. LC 80-25757. 223p. 1981. 9.95 (ISBN 0-8008-1808-3). Taplinger.

Conejo de la Suerte. Kathleen Cowles. Tr. by Rene Sanchez. Orig. Title: Bugs Bunny Book. (Illus.). 24p. (Span.). (ps-3). 1977. PLB 5.92 o.p. (ISBN 0-307-68813-5, Golden Pr). Western Pub.

Conestoga Crossroads: Lancaster, Pennsylvania, 1730-1790. Jerome H. Wood, Jr. 1979. 11.00 (ISBN 0-911124-98-5). Pa Hist & Mus.

Coney Island Quickstep. George Gipe. 1979. pap. 2.25 o.p. (ISBN 0-345-27978-6). Ballantine.

Coney Island Quickstep. George Gipe. 1977. 8.95 o.s.i. (ISBN 0-690-01197-0, TYC-T). T Y Crowell.

Confabulario & Other Inventions. Juan J. Arreola. Tr. by George D. Schade. LC 64-13315. (Pan American Paperbacks Ser.). 264p. 1964. 9.95x (ISBN 0-292-73196-5); pap. 5.00x (ISBN 0-292-71030-5). U of Tex Pr.

Confederacy. Charles P. Roland. LC 60-12573. (History of American Civilization Ser.). (Illus.). 1960. 8.50x (ISBN 0-226-72450-6); pap. 5.95 (ISBN 0-226-72451-4, CHAC18). U of Chicago Pr.

Confederacy of Dunces. John K. Toole. LC 80-8922. 416p. 1981. pap. 3.50 (ISBN 0-394-17800-9, BC). Grove.

Confederate Death Roster at Gettysburg. Krick. 10.00. Pr of Morningside.

Confederate Finance & Purchasing in Great Britain. Richard I. Lester. LC 74-13916. (Illus.). 1975. 17.50x (ISBN 0-8139-0513-3). U Pr of Va.

Confederate General from Big Sur. Richard Brautigan. 1975. pap. 1.95 o.p. (ISBN 0-345-24213-0). Ballantine.

Confederate Longarms & Pistols: A Pictorial Study. Richard T. Hill & William E. Anthony. Ed. by Olivia R. Hill. (Illus.). 304p. 1978. 29.95 (ISBN 0-87833-309-6); lib. bdg. 26.95 (ISBN 0-686-28758-4). Confed Arms.

Confederate Nation Eighteen Sixty-One to Eighteen Sixty-Five. Emory M. Thomas. Ed. by Richard B. Morris & Henry S. Commager. LC 76-26255. (New American Nation Ser.). (Illus.). 1979. pap. 6.95 (ISBN 0-06-090703-7, CN-703, CN). Har-Row.

Confederate Navy: A Study in Organization. Tom H. Wells. LC 72-169496. 1971. 12.50 o.p. (ISBN 0-8173-5105-1). U of Ala Pr.

Confederate Negro: Virginia's Craftsmen & Military Laborers, 1861-1865. James H. Brewer. LC 75-86479. 1969. 9.75 o.p. (ISBN 0-8223-0204-7). Duke.

Confederate Postmaster Provisionals. Francis Crown, Jr. 1981. lib. bdg. 60.00 (ISBN 0-88000-124-0). Quarterman.

Confederate Quartermaster in the Trans-Mississippi. James L. Nichols. 1964. 9.95 (ISBN 0-292-73198-1). U of Tex Pr.

Confederate Reader. R. B. Harwell. LC 76-22465. 1976. 10.95 o.p. (ISBN 0-679-50675-6); pap. 5.95 o.p. (ISBN 0-679-50676-4). McKay.

Confederate State of Richmond: A Biography of the Capital. Emory M. Thomas. 1971. 15.00 (ISBN 0-292-70085-7). U of Tex Pr.

Confederation, 1867: Creating the Dominion of Canada. Michael Bliss. LC 75-9721. (World Focus Bks). (Illus.). 72p. (gr. 6 up). 1975. PLB 4.90 o.p. (ISBN 0-531-02173-4). Watts.

Conference About the Next Succession to the Crown of Ingland. Robert Parsons. LC 70-38217. (English Experience Ser.: No. 481). 1972. Repr. of 1594 ed. 32.50 (ISBN 90-221-0481-8). Walter J Johnson.

Conference on Community Development in Latin America & the U. S., October 15-17, 1970. Arpad Von Lazar. LC 74-150597. 1970. pap. 1.25 o.p. (ISBN 0-913456-79-9). Interbk Inc.

Conference on Integration, Topology and Geometry in Linear Spaces: Proceedings, Vol. 2. William H. Graves. LC 80-25417. (Contemporary Mathematics Ser.). 1980. 14.00 (ISBN 0-8218-5002-4). Am Math.

Conference on Power Thyristors & Their Applications. Institution of Electrical Engineers. LC 74-288481. (Illus.). 555p. 1970. pap. 50.00x (ISBN 0-85296-015-8). Intl Pubns Serv.

Conference on Practice & Procedure Under the Immigration & Nationality Act (McCarran-Walter Act) Held on June 13, 1953: Proceedings. New York University, Division of General Education. Ed. by Henry Sellin. LC 54-7877. xii, 145p. Repr. of 1954 ed. lib. bdg. 11.75x (ISBN 0-8371-7684-0, NYUP). Greenwood.

Conference on the Establishment of an International Compensation Fund for Oil Pollution Damage, 1971. 94p. 1972. 11.00 (IMCO). Unipub.

Conference on the Western Hemisphere. Ed. by N. A. Barletta et al. LC 76-175023. 1971. pap. 1.25 o.p. (ISBN 0-913456-80-2). Interbk Inc.

Conference Planning. 2nd ed. Ed. by W. Warner Burke & Richard Beckhard. LC 76-124090. 174p. 1962. pap. 10.00 (ISBN 0-88390-118-8). Univ Assocs.

Conference Proceedings in the IAEA Library. (Orig.). 1972. pap. 21.50 (ISBN 92-0-179072-4, IAEA). Unipub.

Conference Proceedings: Library Association National Conference, 1976. 1976. Scarborough. 5.50x (ISBN 0-85365-199-X, Pub. by Lib Assn England). Oryx Pr.

Conference Proceedings: Library Association National Conference, 1977. 1977. London Centenary. 7.75x (ISBN 0-85365-820-X, Pub. by Lib Assn England). Oryx Pr.

Conference Under the Tamarind Tree: Three Essays in Burmese History. Paul J. Bennett. (Monograph: No. 15). (Illus.). viii, 153p. 1971. 5.75 o.p. (ISBN 0-686-63727-5). Yale U Pr.

Conferences on Canadian-U. S. Economic Relations. Institute for Research on Public Policy, Canada & Brookings. 94p. 1978. pap. text ed. 3.00x (ISBN 0-920380-09-3, Pub. by Inst Res Pub Canada). Renouf.

Conferencing in California: A Guide to Affordable Retreats & Centers. Dawn Ungrue & Laurel Gillespie. LC 79-26005. 1980. pap. 6.95 (ISBN 0-915166-39-9). Impact Pubs Cal.

Confessing One Faith: A Joint Commentary on the Augsburg Confession by Lutheran & Catholic Theologians. George W. Forell & James F. McCue. LC 80-65557. 368p. 1981. pap. 15.00 (ISBN 0-8066-1802-7, 10-1637). Augsburg.

Confessio Amantis. John Gower. Ed. by Russell A. Peck. (Medieval Academy Reprints for Teaching Ser.). 570p. 1981. pap. 7.95x (ISBN 0-8020-6438-8). U of Toronto Pr.

Confession a Day Keeps the Devil Away. Frances Hunter. 1980. pap. 3.95 (ISBN 0-917726-37-5). Hunter Bks.

Confession & Forgiveness. Andrew Murray. pap. 2.50 (ISBN 0-310-29732-X). Zondervan.

Confession Can Change Your Life. David M. Knight. (Illus.). 40p. 1977. pap. 1.50 (ISBN 0-89570-102-2). Claretian Pubns.

Confession for Today's Catholic. Tad Guzie. (Illus.). 24p. 1977. pap. 0.25 o.p. (ISBN 0-89570-099-9). Claretian Pubns.

Confession of Faith. A. A. Hodge. 1978. 12.95 (ISBN 0-85151-275-5). Banner of Truth.

Confession of Faith Professit, & Belevit, Be the Protestantes Within the Realme of Scotland. LC 72-6029. (English Experience Ser.: No. 555). 1972. Repr. of 1561 ed. 7.00 (ISBN 90-221-0555-5). Walter J Johnson.

Confession of the Fayth of Certayne English People, Living in Exile in the Lowe Contreyes. LC 72-208. (English Experience Ser.: No. 346). 58p. Repr. of 1602 ed. 9.50 (ISBN 90-221-0346-3). Walter J Johnson.

Confession Writer's Handbook. rev. ed. Florence K. Palmer. LC 80-12270. 216p. 1980. 10.95 (ISBN 0-89879-032-8). Writers Digest.

Confessions. Enid Dame. Ed. by Stanley H. Barkan. (Cross-Cultural Review Chapbook 12). 16p. 1980. pap. 2.00 (ISBN 0-89304-811-9). Cross Cult.

Confessions, 2 vols. Jean-Jacques Rousseau. 1960. Vol. I. 5.00 ea. (ISBN 0-460-00859-5). Vol. II (ISBN 0-460-00860-9). Dutton.

Confessions of a Compulsive Eater. Diane Broughton. LC 78-1483. 1978. 8.95 o.p. (ISBN 0-525-66581-1). Elsevier-Nelson.

Confessions of a Crap Artist. Philip K. Dick. 184p. 1978. pap. 5.95 (ISBN 0-9601428-2-7). Entwhistle Bks.

Confessions of a Divorce Lawyer. Herbert A. Glieberman & Paul Neimark. 1977. pap. 1.75 o.p. (ISBN 0-345-25119-9). Ballantine.

Confessions of a Golf Duffer in Search of No Fault Insurance. Irving Gladstone. LC 77-10114. 1977. 6.95 (ISBN 0-8119-0286-2). Fell.

Confessions of a Happy Christian. Zig Ziglar. LC 78-6729. (gr. 6 up). 1978. 8.95 (ISBN 0-88289-196-0). Pelican.

Confessions of a Hollywood Columnist. Sheila Graham. 1969. 5.95 o.p. (ISBN 0-688-05017-4). Morrow.

Confessions of a Late Bloomer: Or, Wear Enough Eye Make-up & No One Will Notice Your Hips. P. R. Mecking. Ed. by K. Donnelly. (Illus., Orig.). 1979. pap. 4.95 (ISBN 0-935282-00-9). Quinn-Gallagher.

Confessions of a Muckraker. Jack Anderson & James Boyd. 416p. 1980. pap. 2.95 (ISBN 0-345-26025-2). Ballantine.

Confessions of a Poet. Paul Verlaine. Tr. by Ruth S. Wolf & Joanna Richardson. 192p. 1981. Repr. of 1950 ed. lib. bdg. 30.00 (ISBN 0-89987-876-8). Darby Bks.

Confessions of a Promiscuous Counterfeiter. Robert Baudin. LC 78-22243. 1979. 9.95 (ISBN 0-15-121853-6). HarBraceJ.

Confessions of a Psychic. Susy Smith. (Illus.). 1971. 10.95 (ISBN 0-02-612120-4). Macmillan.

Confessions of a Thug, 3vols.in 2. Phillip M. Taylor. LC 80-2500. 1981. Repr. of 1839 ed. 104.00 (ISBN 0-404-19136-3). AMS Pr.

Confessions of Aleister Crowley: An Autobiography. Ed. by John Symonds & Kenneth Grant. 1979. 37.00 (ISBN 0-7100-0175-4). Routledge & Kegan.

Confessions of an Advertising Man. David Ogilvy. LC 63-17855. 1963. 10.00 o.p. (ISBN 0-689-10215-1). Atheneum.

Confessions of an Advertising Man. David Ogilvy. LC 79-25505. 172p. 1980. pap. 5.95 (ISBN 0-689-70601-4, 260). Atheneum.

Confessions of an Arms Peddler. Donn R. Grand Pre. 1979. 9.95 (ISBN 0-912376-39-2). Chosen Bks Pub.

Confessions of an Ex-Fan Magazine Writer. Jane Wilkie. LC 80-780. (Illus.). 324p. 1981. 12.95 (ISBN 0-385-15921-8). Doubleday.

Confessions of an Immigrant's Daughter. Laura G. Salverson. (Social History of Canada Ser.). 400p. 1981. 30.00x (ISBN 0-8020-2424-6); pap. 15.00 (ISBN 0-8020-6434-5). U of Toronto Pr.

Confessions of an Ocelot. O. E. Middleton. Bd. with Not for a Seagull. LC 79-670341. (Orig.). 1979. pap. 8.50x (ISBN 0-908565-86-0). Intl Pubns Serv.

Confessions of Arsene Lupin. Maurice LeBlanc. 327p. 1980. Repr. of 1912 ed. lib. bdg. 15.50x (ISBN 0-89968-202-2). Lightyear.

Confessions of Augustine in Modern English. Sherwood Wirt. 1977. pap. 4.95 (ISBN 0-310-34641-X). Zondervan.

Confessions of Con Cregan, the Irish Gil Blas, 2 vols. in 1. Charles J. Lever. LC 80-2490. 1981. Repr. of 1877 ed. 98.50 (ISBN 0-404-19124-X). AMS Pr.

Confessions of O: Conversations with Pauline Reage. Regine Deforges. Tr. by Sabine D'Estree from Fr. (Richard Seaver Bk). 1979. 9.95 o.p. (ISBN 0-670-23720-5). Viking Pr.

Confessions of Phoebe Tyler. Ruth Warrick & Don Preston. LC 80-18272. 1980. 9.95 (ISBN 0-13-167403-X). P-H.

Confessions of Saint Augustine. Saint Saint Augustine. LC 60-13725. 4.50 (ISBN 0-385-02955-1, Im). Doubleday.

Confetti Man. Bonnie J Reynolds. 448p. 1976. pap. 1.95 o.p. (ISBN 0-345-25251-9). Ballantine.

Confidence in Fact. William J. Cook. 1969. pap. 3.40 (ISBN 0-89137-700-X). Quality Pubns.

Confidence in Public Speaking. Paul E. Nelson & Judy C. Pearson. 300p. 1981. pap. text ed. write for info. (ISBN 0-697-04179-4); instructor's manual avail. (ISBN 0-697-04183-2). Wm C Brown.

Confidence Man. Herman Melville. pap. 1.75 (ISBN 0-451-51367-3, CE1367, Sig Classics). NAL.

Confidence-Man: His Masquerade. Herman Melville. Ed. by H. Bruce Franklin. LC 66-30445. 1967. pap. 5.95 (ISBN 0-672-60986-X, LL13). Bobbs.

Confidence of British Philosophers: An Essay in Historical Narrative. Arthur Quinn. (Studies in the History of Christian Thought: No. XVII). 1977. text ed. 45.75x (ISBN 9-0040-5397-2). Humanities.

Confident Entertaining. Carolyn S. Self. LC 76-41764. 1976. 6.95 o.p. (ISBN 0-8407-4055-7). Nelson.

Confidential Agent. Graham Greene. 208p. 1981. pap. 2.95 (ISBN 0-14-001895-6). Penguin.

Confidential Information Sources: Public & Private. John M. Carroll. LC 74-20177. (Illus.). 320p. 1975. 18.95 (ISBN 0-913708-19-4). Butterworths.

Confidential Matter: The Letters of Richard Strauss & Stefan Zweig, 1931-1935. Richard Strauss & Stefan Zweig. Tr. by Max Knight from Ger. 1977. 11.95 (ISBN 0-520-03036-2). U of Cal Pr.

Confidential Report: Selected Poems. James Laughin. 1959. 3.95 (ISBN 0-8112-0781-1). New Directions.

Confidentiality & Third Parties. (Task Force Report: No. 9). 59p. 1975. pap. 5.00 (ISBN 0-685-63945-2, P218-0). Am Psychiatric.

Confidentiality in Social Work: Issues & Principles. Suanna J. Wilson. LC 77-18475. 1980. pap. text ed. 9.95 (ISBN 0-02-934850-1). Free Pr.

Confidentiality: Report of the Conference on Confidentiality of Health Records. Conference on Confidentiality of Health Records, Key Biscayne, Fla., Nov. 6-9, 1974. Ed. by Natalie D. Springarn. 58p. 1975. pap. 2.00 (ISBN 0-685-63944-4, P175-0). Am Psychiatric.

Configurations. Octavio Paz. LC 78-145932. (Span. & Eng.). 1971. pap. 4.95 (ISBN 0-8112-0150-3, NDP303). New Directions.

Configurations of Culture Growth. Alfred L. Kroeber. 1944. 22.75x (ISBN 0-520-00669-0). U of Cal Pr.

Configurations of Faust: Three Studies in the Gothic (1798-1820) Joseph A. Soldati. Ed. by Devendra P. Varma. LC 79-8482. (Gothic Studies & Dissertations Ser.). 1980. lib. bdg. 17.00x (ISBN 0-405-12662-X). Arno.

Configuring Distributed Computer Systems. 1981. pap. 5.00 (ISBN 0-918734-28-2). Reymont.

Confinement & Flight: An Essay on English Literature of the Eighteenth Century. W. B. Carnochan. 1977. 14.50x (ISBN 0-520-03188-1). U of Cal Pr.

Confinement in Maximum Custody: New Last-Resort Prisons in the United States & Western Europe. David A. Ward & Kenneth F. Schoen. LC 78-24630. 1981. write for info. (ISBN 0-669-02799-5). Lexington Bks.

Confirmation Issue: Celebrations of Maturity in Christ. Urban T. Holmes, 3rd. 112p. (Orig.). 1975. pap. 3.95 (ISBN 0-8164-2589-2). Crossroad NY.

Conflict. Rhodri Jones. pap. text ed. 2.95x o.p. (ISBN 0-435-14482-0); tchr's ed. 1.50 o.p. (ISBN 0-435-14486-3). Heinemann Ed.

Conflict. Olive H. Prouty. 224p. 1975. pap. 1.50 o.p. (ISBN 0-445-03069-0). Popular Lib.

Conflict & Change in Education. Francis A. Ianni et al. 470p. 1975. pap. 9.95x (ISBN 0-673-07750-0). Scott F.

Conflict & Change in Southern Africa: Papers from a Scandinavian-Canadian Conference. Ed. by Douglas G. Anglin et al. LC 78-70693. 1978. pap. text ed. 10.00 (ISBN 0-8191-0647-X). U Pr of Amer.

Conflict & Community: Europe Since 1750. J. D. Chambers. LC 68-107879. (Illus.). 492p. 1968. 8.75x (ISBN 0-540-00005-1). Intl Pubns Serv.

Conflict & Compromise in South Africa. Ed. by Robert I. Rotberg & John Barratt. LC 79-7712. 224p. 1980. 23.50 (ISBN 0-669-03205-0). Lexington Bks.

Conflict & Compromise: International Law & World Order in a Revolutionary Age. Edward McWhinney. LC 80-29045. 152p. 1981. text ed. 14.00x (ISBN 0-8419-0694-7); pap. text ed. 8.75x (ISBN 0-8419-0696-3). Holmes & Meier.

Conflict & Conflict Management. Joseph S. Himes. LC 78-32164. 342p. 1980. 23.00x (ISBN 0-8203-0473-5); pap. 9.00 (ISBN 0-8203-0509-X). U of Ga Pr.

Conflict & Consensus in Switzerland. Carol L. Schmid. 1981. 18.50x (ISBN 0-520-04079-1). U of Cal Pr.

Conflict & Control: Challenge to Legitimacy of Modern Governments. rev. ed. Ed. by Arthur J. Vidich & Ronald M. Glasman. LC 78-19653. (Saga Focus Editions: Vol. 7). (Illus.). 304p. 1979. 18.95 (ISBN 0-8039-0974-8). Sage.

Conflict & Control in Late Imperial China. Frederic Wakeman & Carolyn Grant. LC 73-87247. 400p. 1976. 23.75x (ISBN 0-520-02597-0). U of Cal Pr.

Conflict & Cooperation in the Persian Gulf. Ed. by Mohammed Mughisuddin. LC 77-11124. (Praeger Special Studies). 1977. 24.50 (ISBN 0-03-021851-9). Praeger.

Conflict & Democracy: Studies in Trade Union Government. John Hemingway. 1978. 16.95x o.p. (ISBN 0-19-827418-1). Oxford U Pr.

Conflict & Its Resolution in the Administration of Mineral Resources in Canada. R. M. Burns. 63p. (Orig.). 1976. pap. text ed. 3.50x (ISBN 0-88757-000-3, Pub. by Ctr Resource Stud Canada). Renouf.

Conflict & Stability in Fifteenth Century England. 3rd ed. J. R. Lander. 1977. pap. 5.75x (ISBN 0-09-095741-5, Hutchinson U Lib). Humanities.

Conflict & the Web of Group Affiliations. Georg Simmel. LC 54-10671. 1955. 12.95 (ISBN 0-02-928830-4); pap. text ed. 5.95 (ISBN 0-02-928840-1). Free Pr.

Conflict at Colossae: A Problem in the Interpretation of Early Christianity, Illustrated by Selected Modern Studies. Fred O. Francis. LC 75-15737. (Society of Biblical Literature. Sources for Biblical Study). 1975. pap. 7.50 (ISBN 0-89130-009-0, 060304). Scholars Pr Ca.

Conflict Between the California Indian & White Civilization. Sherburne F. Cook. LC 75-23860. 1976. 32.50x (ISBN 0-520-03142-3); pap. 6.95 (ISBN 0-520-03143-1, CAL332). U of Cal Pr.

Conflict in a Voluntary Association: A Case Study of a Classic Suburban Church Fight. Ed. by Perry D. LeFevre. LC 75-12388. (Studies in Ministry & Parish Life). 1975. 12.95x (ISBN 0-913552-03-8); pap. 5.00x (ISBN 0-913552-09-7). Exploration Pr.

Conflict in the Classroom. 4th ed. Nicholas J. Long et al. 464p. 1980. pap. text ed. 12.95x (ISBN 0-534-00791-0). Wadsworth Pub.

Conflict in the Classroom: The Education of Children with Problems. 3rd ed. Nicholas J. Long et al. 1976. pap. 11.95x o.p. (ISBN 0-534-00400-8). Wadsworth Pub.

Conflict in the Middle East. P. J. Vatikiotis. (Illus.). 1971. text ed. 27.50x (ISBN 0-04-327036-0). Allen Unwin.

Conflict in the North Country: A Study of the Implementation of Regional Land Use Controls by the Adirondack Park Agency. Richard A. Liroff & G. Gordon Davis. 1981. price not set (ISBN 0-88410-643-8). Ballinger Pub.

Conflict in Urban Transportation. Henry M. Steiner. LC 78-2070. (Illus.). 1978. 15.95 (ISBN 0-669-02268-3). Lexington Bks.

Conflict Intervention in Social-Domestic Violence. Carmen G. Warner. (Illus.). 256p. 1981. text ed. 14.95 (ISBN 0-87619-855-8); pap. text ed. 11.95 (ISBN 0-87619-854-X). R J Brady.

Conflict Ministry in the Church. Larry L. McSwain & William C. Treadwell, Jr. 1981. pap. 6.95 (ISBN 0-8054-2540-3). Broadman.

Conflict of European & Eastern Algonkian Cultures, 1504-1700: A Study in Canadian Civilization. 2nd ed. Alfred G. Bailey. LC 78-434310. 1969. pap. 6.50 (ISBN 0-8020-6310-1). U of Toronto Pr.

Conflict-of-Interest Regulation in the Federal Executive Branch. Robert G. Vaughn. (Illus.). 1979. 21.00 (ISBN 0-669-02776-6). Lexington Bks.

Conflict of Laws. 1981 ed. 200p. 1981. 10.50 (ISBN 0-87526-195-7). Gould.

Conflict of Laws: Cases & Materials. James A. Martin. 1978. text ed. 22.50 (ISBN 0-316-54851-0); write for info. suppl. Little.

Conflict of Nationality in Modern Ireland. Ed. by A. C. Hepburn. 1980. 19.95 (ISBN 0-312-16231-6). St Martin.

Conflict of the Ages. E. G. White. 1940. pap. 28.95 set (ISBN 0-8163-0293-6). Pacific Pr Pub Assn.

Conflict Over What Is to Be Learned in Schools: A History of Curriculum Politics in Africa. Stephen P. Heyneman. (Foreign & Comparative Studies-Eastern African Ser.: No. 2). 113p. 1971. pap. 4.50x (ISBN 0-915984-01-6). Syracuse U Foreign Comp.

Conflict Regulation. Paul Wehr. 1979. lib. bdg. 22.00x (ISBN 0-89158-351-3); pap. 8.50x (ISBN 0-89158-352-1). Westview.

Conflict Resolution & the Structure of the State System. Gregory A. Raymond. LC 79-53702. (Illus.). 122p. 1980. text ed. 22.50 (ISBN 0-916672-12-3). Allanheld.

Conflict: The Separation of the Church & State. Clayton L. Nuttall. LC 80-21267. 144p. 1980. pap. 4.95 (ISBN 0-87227-076-9, RBP5088). Reg Baptist.

Conflicting Conceptions of Curriculum. Elliot W. Eisner & Elizabeth Vallance. LC 73-17616. 1974. 15.50x (ISBN 0-8211-0411-X); text ed. 14.00x (ISBN 0-685-42630-0). McCutchan.

Conflicting Theories of Instruction: Conceptual Dimensions. Zvi Lamm. LC 76-9238. 1976. 17.50x (ISBN 0-8211-1112-4); text ed. 15.75x (ISBN 0-685-73826-4). McCutchan.

Conflicting Ways of Interpreting the Bible, Concilium 138. Ed. by Hans Kung & Jurgen Moltmann. (New Concilium 1980). 128p. 1981. pap. 5.95 (ISBN 0-8245-4771-3). Crossroad NY.

Conflicts About the Holy Spirit. Ed. by Hans Kung & Jurgen Moltmann. (New Concilium: Vol. 128). 120p. (Orig.). 1980. pap. 4.95 (ISBN 0-8164-2035-1). Crossroad NY.

Conflicts in Childhood Cancer: An Evaluation of Current Management Proceedings. Symposium, Roswell Park Memorial Institute, Buffalo, Sept. 1974. Ed. by Lucius F. Sinks & John O. Godden. LC 75-13857. (Progress in Clinical & Biological Research: Vol. 4). 452p. 1975. 30.00x (ISBN 0-8451-0004-1). A R Liss.

Conflicts in French Society: Anticlericalism, Education & Morals in the Nineteenth Century. Ed. by Theodore Zeldin. (St. Anthony's Publications). 1971. text ed. 17.95x o.p. (ISBN 0-04-301023-7). Allen Unwin.

Conflicts of Power in Modern Culture. Conference On Science - Philosophy And Religion - 7th Symposium. Ed. by L. Bryson et al. 703p. 1964. Repr. of 1947 ed. 35.00x (ISBN 0-8154-0037-3). Cooper Sq.

Conflicts of Religion in the Early Roman Empire. Terrot R. Glover. LC 74-20182. vii, 358p. 1975. Repr. of 1909 ed. lib. bdg. 32.50x (ISBN 0-8154-0510-3). Cooper Sq.

Conformal Mapping. Ludwig Bieberbach. LC 53-7209. 6.95 (ISBN 0-8284-0090-3); pap. 2.95 (ISBN 0-8284-0176-4). Chelsea Pub.

Conformal Mapping. Zeev Nehari. LC 74-27513. (Illus.). 416p. 1975. pap. text ed. 5.50 (ISBN 0-486-61137-X). Dover.

Conformal Mapping on Riemann Surfaces. Harvey Cohn. (Illus.). 352p. 1980. pap. text ed. 6.00 (ISBN 0-486-64025-6). Dover.

Conformity. Ed. by Charles A. Kiesler & Sara B. Kiesler. (Topics in Social Psychology Ser). (Orig.). 1969. pap. text ed. 6.95 (ISBN 0-201-03664-9). A-W.

Conformity & Conflict: Readings in Cultural Anthropology. 4th ed. 397p. 1980. pap. text ed. 7.95 (ISBN 0-316-80735-4); free instructors manual (ISBN 0-316-80749-4). Little.

Conformity: Standards & Change in Higher Education. Warren B. Martin. LC 72-92894. (Higher Education Ser.). 1969. 13.95x o.p. (ISBN 0-87589-045-8). Jossey-Bass.

Confront, Construct, Complete: A Comprehensive Approach to Writing, 2 bks. Jack Easterling & Jack Pasanen. (gr. 9-12). 1978. pap. text ed. 5.95x ea.; Bk. 1. pap. text ed. (ISBN 0-8104-6031-9); Bk. 2. pap. text ed. (ISBN 0-8104-6032-7); tchr's guide 1.50 (ISBN 0-8104-6029-7). Hayden.

Confront or Concede: The Alinsky Citizen-Action Organizations. Joan E. Lancourt. (Illus.). 1979. 19.50 (ISBN 0-669-02715-4). Lexington Bks.

Confrontation & Accomodation in Southern Africa. Kenneth W. Grundy. (Perspectives on Southern Africa Ser., No. 10). 1973. 22.50x (ISBN 0-520-02271-8). U of Cal Pr.

Confrontation at Winnipeg: Labour, Industrial Relations & the General Strike. David J. Bercuson. 224p. 1974. 10.00x o.p. (ISBN 0-7735-0215-7); pap. 9.95 (ISBN 0-7735-0226-2). McGill-Queens U Pr.

Confrontation Between the Young Deaf-Blind Child & the Outer World: How to Make the World Surveyable by Organized Structure? Mary R. Jurgens. 58p. 1977. text ed. 11.50 (ISBN 90-265-0261-3, Pub. by Swets Pub Serv Holland). Swets North Am.

Confrontation, Conflict & Dissent: A Bibliography of a Decade of Controversy, Nineteen Sixty to Nineteen Seventy. Albert J. Miller. LC 78-189440. 1972. 20.50 (ISBN 0-8108-0490-5). Scarecrow.

Confrontation for Better or Worse. Bernard G. Berenson & Kevin M. Mitchel. LC 74-75370. (Perspectives Ser.). (Illus.). 106p. 1974. pap. text ed. 10.95 (ISBN 0-914234-81-1). Human Res Dev Pr.

Confrontation in Adolescence. Jack L. Fadely & Virginia Hosler. LC 78-6709. (Illus.). 1979. pap. text ed. 10.50 (ISBN 0-8016-1553-4). Mosby.

Confrontation in Psychotherapy. Gerald Adler & Paul G. Meyerson. LC 72-93192. 1973. 25.00x (ISBN 0-87668-056-2). Aronson.

Confrontation: Politics & Protest. Michael Dorman. LC 72-7962. 256p. (gr. 7 up). 1974. 5.95 o.s.i. (ISBN 0-440-01628-2). Delacorte.

Confronting Crisis: Teachers in America. Ed. by Ernestine Sewell & Billi M. Rogers. (Illus.). 220p. 1980. 12.95 (ISBN 0-87706-111-4). U of Tex Arlington Pr.

Confronting Nonpromotability: How to Manage a Stalled Career. Edward Roseman. LC 77-8013. (Illus.). 1977. 14.95 (ISBN 0-8144-5441-0). Am Mgmt.

Confronting the Issues: Sex Roles, Marriage & the Family. 2nd ed. Kenneth Kammeyer. 372p. 1980. pap. text ed. 10.45 (ISBN 0-205-06996-7, 816996-9). Allyn.

Confronting the Issues: Sex Roles, Marriage & the Family. Kenneth C. Kammeyer. 1975. pap. text ed. 7.95x o.p. (ISBN 0-205-04813-7, 8148139). Allyn.

Confronting Youth Crime: Report of the Twentieth Century Fund Task Force on Sentencing Policy Toward Young Offenders. The Twentieth Century Fund. LC 78-3612. (Illus.). 1978. text ed. 14.95x (ISBN 0-8419-0381-6); pap. text ed. 5.75 o.p. (ISBN 0-8419-0382-4). Holmes & Meier.

Confronting Youth Unemployment in the Nineteen Eighties: Rhetoric Versus Reality. Ed. by Ray C. Rist. LC 80-19730. (Pergamon Policy Studies on Social Issues). 236p. 1980. 20.00 (ISBN 0-08-026077-2). Pergamon.

Confucian Analects. Ezra Pound. 1970. Repr. of 1956 ed. text ed. 18.25x (ISBN 0-7206-1850-9). Humanities.

Confucian China & Its Modern Fate: A Trilogy. Joseph R. Levenson. 1968. 21.50x (ISBN 0-520-00736-0); pap. 9.95x (ISBN 0-520-00737-9, CAMPUS12). U of Cal Pr.

Confucian Notebook. Edward H. Kenney. LC 79-2828. 89p. 1981. Repr. of 1950 ed. 12.00 (ISBN 0-8305-0008-1). Hyperion Conn.

Confucianism & Modern China. Reginald F. Johnston. LC 79-2830. (Illus.). 272p. 1981. Repr. of 1934 ed. 23.50 (ISBN 0-8305-0007-3). Hyperion Conn.

Confucius. D. H. Smith. (Encore Edition). (Illus.). 1973. 3.95 o.p. (ISBN 0-684-15706-3, ScribT). Scribner.

Confucius Enigma. Margaret Jones. 224p. 1981. 10.95 (ISBN 0-312-16238-3). St Martin.

Confucius: Moments in His Life. T. Nerbonne. (Illus.). 20.00 (ISBN 0-685-58449-6). Rogers Bk.

Confucius: The Great Digest, the Unwobbling Pivot, the Analects. Ezra Pound. 288p. 1951. 5.95 (ISBN 0-8112-0154-6, NDP-285). New Directions.

Confusing Collectibles: A Guide to the Identification of Contemporary Items. Dorothy Hammond. (Illus.). 19.95 (ISBN 0-87069-242-9). Wallace-Homestead.

Confusion: Prevention & Care. Mary O. Wolanin & Linda R. Phillips. (Illus.). 415p. 1980. pap. text ed. 18.95 (ISBN 0-8016-5629-X). Mosby.

Confutacion of That Treatise Which One John Standish Made Agaynst the Protestacion of D. Barnes. Myles Coverdale. LC 79-84096. (English Experience Ser.: No. 917). 212p. 1979. Repr. of 1541 ed. lib. bdg. 16.00 (ISBN 90-221-0917-8). Walter J Johnson.

Confutation of the Rhemists Translation, Glosses & Annotations on the New Testament. Thomas Cartwright. LC 71-171737. (English Experience Ser.: No. 364). 830p. 1971. Repr. of 1618 ed. 114.00 (ISBN 90-221-0364-1). Walter J Johnson.

Congenital & Acquired Cognitive Disorders. Ed. by Robert Katzman. LC 77-87458. (Association of Research in Nervous & Mental Disease Research Publication Ser.: Vol. 57). 1979. 29.00 (ISBN 0-89004-255-1). Raven.

Congenital Arteriovenous Aneurysms of the Carotid & Vertebral Arterial Systems. H. Olivecrona & J. Ladenheim. (Illus.). 1957. 69.70 o.p. (ISBN 0-387-02204-X). Springer-Verlag.

Congenital Clubfoot. Emil D. Hauser. (Illus.). 104p. 1966. 9.75 (ISBN 0-398-00796-9). C C Thomas.

Congenital Deformities of the Hand: An Atlas of Their Surgical Treatment. W. Blauth & F. R. Schneider-Sickert. (Illus.). 394p. 1980. 259.60 (ISBN 0-387-10084-9). Springer-Verlag.

Congenital Deformities of the Hand & Forearm. H. Kelikian. LC 73-89181. (Illus.). 1025p. 1974. text ed. 40.00 (ISBN 0-7216-5358-8). Saunders.

Congenital Deformities of the Testis & Epididymis. C. G. Scorer & G. H. Farrington. 1971. 16.20 (ISBN 0-407-13891-9). Butterworths.

Congenital Dislocation of the Hip. M. Tachdjian. Date not set. text ed. price not set (ISBN 0-443-08069-0). Churchill.

Congenital Dysplasia & Dislocation of the Hip. Sherman S. Coleman. LC 78-59669. 1978. 44.50 (ISBN 0-8016-1018-4). Mosby.

Congestion Pricing: A Research Summary. Damian J. Kulash. 33p. 1974. pap. 2.50 o.p. (ISBN 0-87766-125-1, 83000). Urban Inst.

Congestive Heart Failure. Pinneo. 1978. pap. 6.95 (ISBN 0-8385-1169-4). ACC.

Conglomerate Corporation: An Antitrust Law & Economics Symposium. Ed. by Roger D. Blair & Robert F. Lanzillotti. LC 80-22093. 288p. 1981. lib. bdg. 25.00 (ISBN 0-89946-051-8). Oelgeschlager.

Conglomerate Mergers & Market Competition. John C. Narver. (Institute of Business & Economic Research, UC Berkeley). 1967. 20.00x (ISBN 0-520-00915-0). U of Cal Pr.

Congo, Background of Conflict. Alan P. Merriam. (African Studies Ser.: No. 6). (Illus.). 1961. 14.95x o.s.i. (ISBN 0-8101-0169-6). Northwestern U Pr.

Congo Venus. Matthew Head. LC 75-44982. (Crime Fiction Ser). 1976. Repr. of 1950 ed. lib. bdg. 17.50 (ISBN 0-8240-2374-9). Garland Pub.

Congratulations - God Believes in You. Lloyd Ogilvie. 128p. 1980. 5.95 (ISBN 0-8499-0197-9). Word Bks.

Congratulations, You Made It... Again. Michael F. Jaress. (Illus.). 288p. (Orig.). 1981. pap. 6.95 (ISBN 0-938320-04-1). Comm Consultants.

Congratulations! You're Going to Be a Grandmother. Lanie Carter. LC 80-1345. 1980. PLB 5.95 (ISBN 0-916392-48-1); pap. 4.95 (ISBN 0-916392-53-8). Oak Tree Pubns.

Congregational Commonwealth: Connecticut, Sixteen Thirty-Six to Sixteen Sixty-Two. Mary J. Jones. LC 68-27543. (Illus.). 1968. 20.00x (ISBN 0-8195-3095-6, Pub. by Wesleyan U Pr). Columbia U Pr.

Congregational Readings. Cecil Ettinger. LC 75-8596. 1975. 4.00 o.p. (ISBN 0-8309-0145-0). Herald Hse.

Congregations Alive. Donald P. Smith. (Orig.). pap. write for info. (ISBN 0-664-24370-3). Westminster.

Congregations in Change. Elisa DesPortes. (Project Test Pattern Ser.). (Orig.). 1973. pap. 3.95 (ISBN 0-8164-2085-8). Crossroad NY.

Congres of Arras, Fourteen Thirty-Five. Joycelyne G. Dickinson. 1973. Repr. of 1955 ed. 15.00x (ISBN 0-8196-0281-7). Biblo.

Congress. Gerald W. Johnson. (Illus.). (gr. 5-9). 1963. PLB 7.44 (ISBN 0-688-31182-2). Morrow.

Congress. Dale Vinyard. (Orig.). 1968. pap. 2.45 o.p. (ISBN 0-684-12659-1, SL318, ScribT). Scribner.

Congress against Itself. Roger H. Davidson & Walter J. Oleszek. LC 76-12378. (Midland Bks.: No. 223). 320p. 1977. 15.00x (ISBN 0-253-31405-4); pap. 5.95x (ISBN 0-253-20223-X). Ind U Pr.

Congress Against the President. Ed. by Harvey C. Mansfield. LC 75-17154. (Special Studies). 208p. 1975. text ed. 24.95 (ISBN 0-275-56230-1); pap. text ed. 10.95 (ISBN 0-275-64420-0). Praeger.

Congress & Arms Control. Ed. by Alan Platt & Lawrence D. Weiler. LC 77-28307. (Westview Special Studies in International Relations & Foreign Policy Ser.). 1978. lib. bdg. 24.50 o.p. (ISBN 0-89158-157-X). Westview.

Congress & Conscience. Ed. by John B. Anderson et al. LC 77-120331. 1970. 4.95 o.p. (ISBN 0-397-10099-X). Lippincott.

Congress & Foreign Policy-Making: A Study in Legislative Influence & Initiative. James A. Robinson. LC 80-20372. x, 262p. 1980. Repr. of 1962 ed. lib. bdg. 27.50x (ISBN 0-313-22706-3, ROCF). Greenwood.

Congress & Higher Education in the Nineteenth Century. George N. Rainsford. LC 72-83343. 1972. 10.50x (ISBN 0-87049-140-7). U of Tenn Pr.

Congress & Money: Budgeting, Spending & Taxing. Allen Schick. LC 80-53322. 600p. 1980. 27.50 (ISBN 0-87766-278-9). Urban Inst.

Congress & the American People. William J. Keefe. (Illus.). 1980. pap. text ed. 8.50 (ISBN 0-13-167569-9). P-H.

Congress & the Colleges: The National Politics of Higher Education. Lawrence E. Gladieux & Thomas R. Wolanin. LC 75-22881. (Politics of Education Ser.). 288p. 1976. 21.95 (ISBN 0-669-00183-X). Lexington Bks.

Congress & the Politics of U. S. Foreign Economic Policy, 1929 to 1976. Robert A. Pastor. 416p. 1980. 24.50x (ISBN 0-520-03904-1). U of Cal Pr.

Congress & the Presidency. 3rd ed. Nelson Polsky. 192p. 1976. pap. text ed. 7.95 (ISBN 0-13-167692-X). P-H.

Congress & Urban Problems: A Casebook on the Legislative Process. Frederic N. Cleaveland et al. 405p. 1969. 14.95 (ISBN 0-8157-1474-2); pap. 5.95 (ISBN 0-8157-1473-4). Brookings.

Congress in Action: The Environmental Education Act. Dennis W. Brezina & Allen Overmyer. LC 73-6492. 1974. 10.95 (ISBN 0-02-904900-8). Free Pr.

Congress in the American System. Carl P. Chelf. LC 77-1084. 1978. text ed. 15.95 (ISBN 0-88229-210-2); pap. 8.95 (ISBN 0-88229-517-9). Nelson-Hall.

Congress Investigates: A Documented History, 1792-1974, 5 vols. Intro. by Arthur M. Schlesinger, Jr. & Roger Bruns. LC 74-34005. 1981. pap. 85.00 (ISBN 0-87754-132-9). Chelsea Hse.

Congress of Neurological Surgeons, Vol. 27. Peter W. Carmel. (CNS Ser.). (Illus.). 600p. 1981. lib. bdg. price not set (ISBN 0-683-02022-6). Williams & Wilkins.

Congress of Vienna: A Study in Allied Unity Eighteen Twelve to Eighteen Twenty-Two. Harold Nicolson. 8.00 (ISBN 0-8446-4053-0). Peter Smith.

Congress of Vienna, Eighteen-Fourteen to Eighteen-Fifteen: The Diplomacy Surrounding the End of the Napoleonic Era. Emil Lengyel. LC 73-12440. (World Focus Bks). (Illus.). 72p. (gr. 7 up). 1974. PLB 6.45 (ISBN 0-531-02169-6). Watts.

Congress on Microcirculation & Ischemic Vascular Diseases. Advances in Diagnosis & Therapy, Muenchen, November 1980. Ed. by K. Messmer & B. Fagrell. (Illus.). 240p. 1981. pap. 24.00 (ISBN 3-8055-2417-X). S Karger.

Congress Party in Rajasthan: Political Integration & Institution-Building in an Indian State. Richard Sisson. LC 70-129607. (Center for South & Southeast Asia Studies, UC Berkeley). 1972. 24.50x (ISBN 0-520-01808-7). U of Cal Pr.

Congress: Power & Purpose on Capitol Hill. Theis Lahr. (gr. 9-12). 1974. pap. text ed. 5.40 (ISBN 0-205-03972-3, 7639724). Allyn.

Congress-Testament, 2 vols. Incl. Vol. 1. American Heritage History of the Congress of the United States. Alvin M. Josephy, Jr. LC 75-22425. 416p. 1975 (ISBN 0-8281-0270-8); American Testament: Fifty Great Documents of American History, 2 vols. Ed. by Erwin Glusker & Richard M. Ketchum. LC 70-149728. 256p. 1971 (ISBN 0-8281-0256-2). (Illus.). Boxed Set. 32.50 o.p. (ISBN 0-8281-0255-4). Am Heritage.

Congress, the Bureaucracy & Public Policy. Randall B. Ripley & Grace A. Franklin. 1980. pap. text ed. 8.50x o.p. (ISBN 0-256-02256-9). Dorsey.

Congress, the Bureaucracy, & the Public Policy. rev. ed. Randall B. Ripley & Grace A. Franklin. 1980. pap. 9.50x (ISBN 0-256-02256-9). Dorsey.

Congress: The Electoral Connection. David R. Mayhew. LC 74-78471. (Studies in Political Science: No. 26). (Illus.). 192p. 1974. 12.00x (ISBN 0-300-01777-4, Y-277); pap. 3.95x (ISBN 0-300-01809-6). Yale U Pr.

Congress, the Presidency & American Foreign Policy. Ed. by John Spanier & Joe Nogee. (Pergamon Policy Studies). Date not set. price not set (ISBN 0-08-025575-2); pap. price not set (ISBN 0-08-025574-4). Pergamon.

Congressional Conservatism & the New Deal: The Growth of the Conservative Coalition in Congress, 1933-1939. James T. Patterson. LC 67-17845. (Illus.). 1967. pap. 6.50x (ISBN 0-8131-0123-9). U Pr of Ky.

Congressional Districting: The Issue of Equal Representation. rev. ed. Andrew Hacker. 1964. pap. 4.95 (ISBN 0-8157-3369-0). Brookings.

Congressional Ethics. 2nd ed. Congressional Quarterley Staff. 220p. (Orig.). 1980. pap. text ed. 7.95 (ISBN 0-87187-154-8). Congr Quarterly.

Congressional Ethics: The View from the House. Edmund Beard & Stephen Horn. LC 74-1434. 60p. 1975. pap. 3.95 (ISBN 0-8157-0855-6). Brookings.

Congressional Intent & Road User Payments. Kiran U. Bhatt et al. (Institute Paper). 97p. 1977. pap. 4.00 (ISBN 0-87766-189-8, 18500). Urban Inst.

Congressional Odyssey: The Saga of a Senate Bill. T. R. Reid. LC 80-10108. (Illus.). 1980. text ed. 10.95x (ISBN 0-7167-1171-0); pap. text ed. 5.95x (ISBN 0-7167-1172-9). W H Freeman.

Congressional Politics in the Second World War. Roland A. Young. LC 70-38757. (FDR & the Era of the New Deal Ser.). 282p. 1972. Repr. of 1956 ed. lib. bdg. 29.50 (ISBN 0-306-70442-0). Da Capo.

Congressional Quarterly Almanac, 1979. Congressional Quarterly Inc. (Almanac Ser.). 1980. 82.00 (ISBN 0-87187-192-0). Congr Quarterly.

Congressional Record: The Memoir of Bernie Sisk. B. F. Sisk. Ed. by A. I. Dickman. LC 80-84208. (Illus.). 280p. 1980. 20.00 (ISBN 0-914330-36-5). Panorama West.

Congressional Staff Directory. Ed. by Charles B. Brownson. LC 59-13987. 1981. Repr. of 1978 ed. 25.00. Congr Staff.

Congressional Staff Directory, Ltd. Ed. by Jerry R. Perrich. 272p. 1981. 69.95 (ISBN 0-8493-5693-8). CRC Pr.

Congressional Staff Directory, 1981. 23rd ed. Ed. by Charles B. Brownson. 1096p. 1981. pap. 25.00. Congr Staff.

Congressional Staffs: The Invisible Force in American Lawmaking. Harrison W. Fox, Jr. & Susan W. Hammond. LC 77-72041. (Illus.). 1979. pap. text ed. 7.95 (ISBN 0-02-910430-0). Free Pr.

Congressman Jerry L. Pettis. Miriam Wood. LC 77-80683. (Destiny Ser.). 1977. pap. 4.95 (ISBN 0-8163-0279-0). Pacific Pr Pub Assn.

Congressmen & the Electorate. Milton C. Cummings. LC 66-17692. 1966. 8.95 o.s.i. (ISBN 0-02-906920-3). Free Pr.

Congressmen's Voting Decisions. 2nd ed. John W. Kingdon. 313p. 1980. pap. text ed. 13.50 scp (ISBN 0-06-043657-3, HarpC). Har-Row.

Congresso Internazionale Di Linguistica E Filologia Romanza XIV: Atti Volume II: Comunicazione. Ed. by Alberto Varvaro. 1979. pap. text ed. 72.00x (ISBN 90-272-0943-X). Humanities.

Congresso Internazionale di Linguistica e Filologia Romanza, XIV, Napoli 15-20 Aprile 1974: Atti 1. Ed. by Alberto Varvaro. (Orig.). 1979. pap. text ed. 72.00x (ISBN 0-686-59701-X). Humanities.

Congruence of Sets, & Other Monographs, 4 vols. in 1. Waclaw Sierpinski et al. Incl. On the Congruence of Sets. Waclaw Sierpinski; Mathematical Theory of the Top. Felix Klein; Graphical Methods. Carl Runge; Algebraic Equations. Leonard E. Dickson. LC 67-17000. 14.95 (ISBN 0-8284-0209-4). Chelsea Pub.

Conhecendo As Doutrinas Da Biblia. Tr. by Myer Pearlman. (Portugese Bks.). (Port.). 1979. 2.95 (ISBN 0-8297-0647-X). Life Pubs Intl.

Conic Sections. 6th ed. George Salmon. LC 55-3390. 4.95 (ISBN 0-8284-0099-7); pap. 3.95 (ISBN 0-8284-0098-9). Chelsea Pub.

Conjectures & Refutations: The Growth of Scientific Knowledge. Karl R. Popper. 1968. pap. 7.50x (ISBN 0-06-131376-9, TB1376, Torch). Har-Row.

Conjectures of a Guilty Bystander. Thomas Merton. LC 66-24311. pap. 3.95 (ISBN 0-385-01018-4, Im). Doubleday.

Conjoint Marital Therapy. R. V. Fitzgerald. LC 73-81208. 256p. 1973. 25.00x (ISBN 0-87668-091-0). Aronson.

Conjugal Lewdness, or Matrimonial Whoredom. Daniel Defoe. LC 67-10178. 1967. Repr. of 1727 ed. 43.00x (ISBN 0-8201-1013-2). Schol Facsimiles.

Conjugal Visits in Prison: Psychological & Social Consequences. Jules Q. Burstein. LC 76-50485. (Illus.). 1977. 16.95 (ISBN 0-669-01287-4). Lexington Bks.

Conjunctions: An in Depth Delineation. Donald H. Yott. 1981. pap. 6.95 (ISBN 0-87728-524-1). Weiser.

Conjuror's Journal. Frances L. Shine. LC 78-17869. 1978. 8.95 (ISBN 0-396-07598-3). Dodd.

Connaissance du francais. Pierre Maubrey. 1973. text ed. 10.95x o.p. (ISBN 0-673-05112-9). Scott F.

Connally-Hicks Debate on Divorce & Remarriage. Andrew M. Connally & Olan Hicks. 1979. pap. 11.95 (ISBN 0-934916-31-4); pap. 8.95 (ISBN 0-686-23941-5). Natl Christian Pr.

Connecticut. 28.00 (ISBN 0-89770-082-1). Curriculum Info Ctr.

Connecticut Colony. Johanna Johnston. LC 69-19576. (Forge of Freedom Ser). (Illus.). (gr. 5-8). 1969. 8.95 (ISBN 0-02-747710-X, CCPr). Macmillan.

Connecticut River. Evan Hill & William Stekl. LC 72-3727. (Illus.). 144p. 1972. 15.00x (ISBN 0-8195-4051-X, Pub. by Wesleyan U Pr); pap. 7.95 o.p. (ISBN 0-8195-6042-1). Columbia U Pr.

Connecticut Sixteen Hundred-Seventy Census. Jay M. Holbrook. LC 77-152342. 1977. pap. 15.00 (ISBN 0-931248-04-3). Holbrook Res.

Connecticut Supplement. 2nd ed. Michael Galonska. 196p. 1980. pap. 7.95 (ISBN 0-695-81499-0). Follett.

Connecticut Supplement for Modern Real Estate Practice. 2nd ed. Michael L. Galonska. 184p. (Orig.). 1981. pap. 7.95 (ISBN 0-88462-319-X). Real Estate Ed Co.

Connecticut Town: Growth & Development, Sixteen Thirty-Five to Seventeen Ninety. Bruce C. Daniels. LC 79-65331. (Illus.). 1979. 17.50x (ISBN 0-8195-5036-1, Pub. by Wesleyan U Pr). Columbia U Pr.

Connecticut Yankee in King Arthur's Court. Mark Twain. (Literature Ser). (gr. 7-12). 1970. pap. text ed. 3.67 (ISBN 0-87720-723-2). AMSCO Sch.

Connecticut Yankee in King Arthur's Court. Mark Twain. pap. 1.50. Bantam.

Connecticut Yankee in King Arthur's Court: Student Activity Book. Marcia Sohl & Gerald Dackerman. (Now Age Illustrated Ser.). (Illus.). (gr. 4-12). 1976. 0.95 (ISBN 0-88301-287-1). Pendulum Pr.

Connection: Golf's Master Fundamental. Jim Ballard & Brennan Quinn. LC 80-66691. (Illus.). 176p. (Orig.). 1981. 12.95 (ISBN 0-914178-38-5). Golf Digest.

Connections. James Burke. LC 78-21662. 1979. 17.95 (ISBN 0-316-11685-8). Little.

Connections. James Burke. (Illus.). 312p. 1980. pap. 11.95 (ISBN 0-316-11685-8). Little.

Connections, Curvature, & Cohomology, 2 vols. Werner Greub et al. Incl. Vol. 1. De Rham Cohomology of Manifold & Vector Bundles. 1972. 48.50 (ISBN 0-12-302701-2); Vol. 2. Lie Groups, Principal Bundles & Characteristic Classes. 1973. 55.25 (ISBN 0-12-302702-0); Vol. 3. Cohomology of Principle Bundles & Homogeneous Spaces. 1976. 68.00 (ISBN 0-12-302703-9). (Pure & Applied Mathematics Ser.). Acad Pr.

Connective Bargaining: Communicating About Sex. Gail Andresen & Barry Weinhold. (Illus.). 224p. 1980. 13.95 (ISBN 0-13-167791-8, Spec); pap. 5.95 (ISBN 0-13-167783-7). P-H.

Connectivity in Graphs. William T. Tutte. LC 67-5800. 1967. 12.50x o.p. (ISBN 0-8020-1425-9). U of Toronto Pr.

Connie's New Eyes. Bernard Wolf. (Illus.). (YA) (gr. 7-9). 1978. pap. 1.25 (ISBN 0-671-29897-6). PB.
Connoisseur Illustrated Guide: Furniture. Edward Joy. (Illus.). 1975. pap. 5.95 o.s.i. (ISBN 0-380-01112-3, 26161). Avon.
Connoisseur's Guide to Chinese Ceramics. Cecile Beurdeley & Michel Beurdeley. Tr. by Katherine Watson from Fr. LC 74-1792. (Illus.). 320p. 1974. 75.00 o.s.i. (ISBN 0-06-010322-1, HarpT). Har-Row.
Connoisseurs' Handbook of California Wines. Charles Olken et al. LC 79-3476. 192p. 1980. pap. 4.95 (ISBN 0-394-73973-6). Knopf.
Conoce a Jesus. Sylvia Mandeville & Lance Pierson. Tr. by Edna L. Gutierrez from Eng. (Pointing Out Bk.). 1980. pap. 7.95 (ISBN 0-311-38531-1, Edit Mundo). Casa Bautista.
Conozcamos Al Alumno. C. H. Benson. Tr. by Fernando P. Villalobos from Eng. (Curso para Maestros Cristianos: No. 4). Orig. Title: Understanding Children & Youth. 128p. (Span.). 1972. pap. 2.50 (ISBN 0-89922-014-2); instr's manual 1.50 (ISBN 0-89922-015-0). Edit Caribe.
Conquer: The Story of the Ninth Army 1943-1945. LC 80-65182. (Combat Arms Ser.: No. 5). (Illus.). 1980. Repr. of 1947 ed. 22.50 (ISBN 0-89839-027-3). Battery Pr.
Conquered. Naomi Mitchison. 1959. 14.95 (ISBN 0-224-60496-1). Dufour.
Conquering Family. Thomas B. Costain. (Plantagenets Ser: No. 1). 1976. pap. 2.75 (ISBN 0-445-08511-8). Popular Lib.
Conquering Family Stress. J. Allan Petersen. 1978. pap. 3.95 (ISBN 0-88207-632-9). Victor Bks.
Conquering High Mountains. Marvin Moore. LC 79-84604. (+015). 1979. pap. 4.95 (ISBN 0-8163-0327-4, 03514-7). Pacific Pr Pub Assn.
Conquering Horse. Frederick Manfred. (Western Fiction Ser.). 1980. lib. bdg. 15.95 (ISBN 0-8398-2590-0). Gregg.
Conquering the Frontiers. James E. Serven. LC 74-75583. 1974. 19.95 (ISBN 0-910618-39-9). Foun Pubns.
Conquering Word Problems in Mathematics. Deborah A. Dryjanski. (gr. 6-8). 1979. incl. manual & cassettes 149.95 (ISBN 0-917792-02-5). Math Hse.
Conqueror of Smallpox: Dr. Edward Jenner. Israel E. Levine. LC 60-7817. (Biography Ser.). (gr. 7 up). 1960. 3.34 o.p. (ISBN 0-671-06900-4). Messner.
Conquerors & Confucians: Aspects of Political Change in Late Yuan China. John Dardess. (Studies in Oriental Culture Ser.). 240p. 1973. 20.00x (ISBN 0-231-03689-2). Columbia U Pr.
Conquerors & Slaves. K. Hopkins. LC 77-90209. (Illus.). 272p. 1981. pap. 12.50 (ISBN 0-521-28181-4). Cambridge U Pr.
Conquerors & Slaves: Sociological Studies in Roman History, Vol. 1. K. Hopkins. LC 77-90209. (Illus.). 1978. 32.50 (ISBN 0-521-21945-0). Cambridge U Pr.
Conquerors of the Dark Hills. Rufus M. Reed. 1978. 6.95 (ISBN 0-533-03701-8). Vantage.
Conquest. James M. Bryant. 1972. pap. 5.50 (ISBN 0-686-27963-8). J M Bryant.
Conquest & Colonisation. M. E. Collins. (History of Ireland Ser.: Vol. 2). (Illus.). 240p. 1969. pap. text ed. 8.50 (ISBN 0-7171-0256-4). Irish Bk Ctr.
Conquest & Overlord. Brian Jewell. (Illus.). 96p. 1981. 25.00 (ISBN 0-686-69381-7, 5209). Arco.
Conquest of Apacheria. Dan L. Thrapp. (Illus.). 1967. 16.95 (ISBN 0-8061-0751-0); pap. 7.95 (ISBN 0-8061-1286-7). U of Okla Pr.
Conquest of Brazil. Roy Nash. LC 67-29550. 1926. 14.00x (ISBN 0-8196-0207-8). Biblo.
Conquest of Bread. Peter Kropotkin. LC 75-188871. 235p. 1972. 12.00x (ISBN 0-8147-4554-7). NYU Pr.
Conquest of Cooper Mountain. Forbes Wilson. LC 80-69369. 1981. 14.95 (ISBN 0-689-11153-3). Atheneum.
Conquest of Frustration. Maxwell Maltz & Raymond C. Barker. 1979. pap. 2.50 (ISBN 0-345-27995-6). Ballantine.
Conquest of Gaul. Julius Caesar. Tr. by S. A. Handford. (Classics Ser). 1951. pap. 2.95 (ISBN 0-14-044021-6). Penguin.
Conquest of Mars. W. C. Chalk. 1971. pap. text ed. 2.75x o.p. (ISBN 0-435-11200-7). Heinemann Ed.
Conquest of Mexico & Peru. William H. Prescott. Ed. by Roger Howell. text ed. 20.00x (ISBN 0-8290-0220-0). Irvington.
Conquest of the North Atlantic. G. J. Marcus. (Illus.). 256p. 1981. 25.00 (ISBN 0-19-520252-X). Oxford U Pr.
Conquest of Violence: The Gandhian Philosophy of Conflict. rev. ed. Joan V. Bondurant. (gr. 9 up). 1965. 16.50x (ISBN 0-520-00143-5); pap. 4.95x (ISBN 0-520-00145-1, CAMPUS243). U of Cal Pr.
Conquista! Clyde R. Bulla & Michael Syson. LC 77-26585. (Illus.). (gr. 2-5). 1978. 7.95 (ISBN 0-690-03870-4, TYC-J); PLB 7.89 (ISBN 0-690-03871-2). T Y Crowell.
Conquistadores. Meridel Le Sueur. LC 72-6051. (First Bks). (Illus.). 96p. (gr. 5-7). 1973. PLB 4.90 o.p. (ISBN 0-531-00744-8). Watts.
Conquistadores, Aztecs & Incas: A Facasimile of 16th Century Engravings. Theodor De Bry. (Illus.). 108p. 1981. 60.00 (ISBN 0-8390-0257-2). Allanheld & Schram.
Conrad: "Almayer's Folly" to "Under Western Eyes". Daniel R. Schwarz. LC 79-48012. 1980. 23.50x (ISBN 0-8014-1311-7). Cornell U Pr.
Conrad & His World. Norman Sherry. LC 77-77381. (Illus.). 1977. 9.95 o.p. (ISBN 0-684-15300-9, ScribT). Scribner.
Conrad & the Congo. Alan Hall. (gr. 10-12). 1972. pap. text ed. 2.75x o.p. (ISBN 0-88334-047-X). Ind Sch Pr.
Conrad Ferdinand Meyer. Marianne Burkhard. (World Authors Ser.: No. 480 Spain). 1978. 11.95 (ISBN 0-8057-6321-X). Twayne.
Conrad in the Nineteenth Century. Ian Watt. 1980. 15.95 (ISBN 0-520-03683-2); pap. 7.95 (ISBN 0-520-04405-3). U of Cal Pr.
Conrad in the Nineteenth Century. Ian Watt. 1981. pap. 7.95 (ISBN 0-520-04405-3, CAL 507). U of Cal Pr.
Conrad: The Critical Heritage. Ed. by Norman Sherry. (Critical Heritage Ser.). 1973. 34.00x (ISBN 0-7100-7388-7). Routledge & Kegan.
Conrad, the Later Moralist. John E. Saveson. 129p. (Orig.). 1976. pap. text ed. 14.25x (ISBN 90-6203-248-6). Humanities.
Conrade Webb of Hampstead. William T. Hastings. LC 58-7622. (Illus.). 102p. 1958. 5.00x (ISBN 0-87057-050-1, Pub. by Brown U Pr). Univ Pr of New England.
Conrad's Eastern World. Norman Sherry. 1966. 49.50 (ISBN 0-521-06437-6); pap. 14.95x (ISBN 0-521-29120-8). Cambridge U Pr.
Conrad's Fossil Shells of the Tertiary Formations of North America: 1832-35. G. D. Harris. (Illus.). 1971. Repr. of 1893 ed. 5.00 (ISBN 0-87710-362-3). Paleo Res.
Conrad's Manifesto, Preface to a Career: The History of the Preface to "The Nigger of the 'Narcissus'". facsimile ed. Ed. by David Smith. (Illus.). 1966. 27.50 (ISBN 0-686-28306-6). Rosenbach Mus and Lib.
Conrad's Short Fiction. Lawrence Graver. LC 69-14302. 1968. 16.50x (ISBN 0-520-00513-9). U of Cal Pr.
Conrad's War. Andrew Davies. (gr. 5 up). 1980. 7.95 (ISBN 0-517-54007-X). Crown.
Conrad's Western World. Norman Sherry. LC 70-130910. (Illus.). 1971. 49.50 (ISBN 0-521-07972-1). Cambridge U Pr.
Conscience: A Structural Theory. Moshe Kroy. LC 74-10912. 1974. 32.50 (ISBN 0-470-50856-6). Halsted Pr.
Conscience & Convenience: The Asylum & Its Alternatives in Progressive America. Rothman. (Orig.). 1980. pap. text ed. 8.95 (ISBN 0-316-75775-6). Little.
Conscience & Convenience: The Asylum & Its Alternatives in Progressive America. David J. Rothman. 1980. 17.50 (ISBN 0-316-75774-8); pap. 8.95 (ISBN 0-316-75775-6). Little.
Conscience & Politics: British Government & the Conscientious Objector to Military Service, 1916-1919. John Rae. (Illus.). 1970. text ed. 11.25x o.p. (ISBN 0-19-215176-2). Oxford U Pr.
Conscience: Development & Self-Transcendence. Walter E. Conn. LC 80-24043. 280p. (Orig.). 1981. pap. 11.95 (ISBN 0-89135-025-X). Religious Educ.
Conscience Game. (Encounter Ser.). (gr. 3-7). 2.25 o.s.i. (ISBN 0-8198-0231-X). Dghtrs St Paul.
Conscience in Medieval Philosophy. T. C. Potts. 180p. 1980. 47.50 (ISBN 0-521-23287-2). Cambridge U Pr.
Conscience Malheureuse. Benjamin Fondane. LC 78-65073. (Phenomenology-Background, Foreground & Influences Ser.). 1980. lib. bdg. 33.55 (ISBN 0-8240-9565-0). Garland Pub.
Conscience of the Race: Sex & Religion in Irish & French Novels 1941-1973. Brian O'Rourke. 72p. 1981. 10.00x (ISBN 0-906127-22-X, Pub. by Irish Academic Pr Ireland). Biblio Dist.
Conscientious Evolution. Herbert F. Matare. 1981. 9.75 (ISBN 0-8062-1700-6). Carlton.
Conscientious Objector. Walter G. Kellogg. LC 77-107412. (Civil Liberties in American History Ser). 1970. Repr. of 1919 ed. lib. bdg. 15.00 (ISBN 0-306-71893-6). Da Capo.
Conscious Exercise & the Transcendental Sun. 3rd rev. ed. Da Free John. LC 77-83388. (Illus.). 55p. 1977. 10.95 (ISBN 0-913922-30-7); pap. 5.95. Dawn Horse Pr.
Conscious Lovers. Richard Steele. Ed. by Shirley S. Kenney. LC 68-11409. (Regents Restoration Drama Series). 1968. 8.95x (ISBN 0-8032-0369-1); pap. 2.25x (ISBN 0-8032-5369-9, BB 268, Bison). U of Nebr Pr.
Conscious Orientation. J. H. Van Der Hoop. Tr. by Luara Hutton. 352p. 1980. Repr. of 1930 ed. lib. bdg. 50.00 (ISBN 0-89987-875-X). Darby Bks.
Conscious Sedation in Dental Practice. 2nd ed. C. Richard Bennett. LC 78-4565. 1978. text ed. 26.50 (ISBN 0-8016-0612-8). Mosby.
Consciousness & Action Among the Western Working Class. Michael Mann. (Studies in Sociology). 80p. (Orig.). 1975. pap. 6.75x (ISBN 0-333-13773-6). Humanities.
Consciousness & Change: Symbolic Anthropology in Evolutionary Perspective. James L. Peacock. LC 75-1349. 264p. 1975. 20.95 (ISBN 0-470-67452-0). Halsted Pr.
Consciousness & Class Experience in 19th Century Europe. Ed. by John Merriman. LC 79-16032. 1980. text ed. 24.50x (ISBN 0-8419-0444-8); pap. 9.85x (ISBN 0-8419-0610-6). Holmes & Meier.
Consciousness & Reality. John B. Chethimattam. LC 73-164417. 1971. 5.95x o.p. (ISBN 0-88344-066-0). Orbis Bks.
Consciousness & the Physical World: Proceedings of an Interdisciplinary Symposium on Consciousness Held at the University of Cambridge, Jan. 1978. B. D. Josephson & V. S. Ramachandran. 1979. 25.00 (ISBN 0-08-024695-8). Pergamon.
Consciousness & the Ultimate. John J. Gleason, Jr. LC 80-21397. 192p. (Orig.). 1981. pap. 6.95 (ISBN 0-687-09470-4). Abingdon.
Consciousness in Advaita Vedanta. William M. Indich. 1980. 14.00x (ISBN 0-8364-0607-9). South Asia Bks.
Consciousness in Concord: The Text of Thoreau's Hitherto "Lost Journal," 1840-1841. Henry D. Thoreau. LC 80-2519. 1981. Repr. of 1958 ed. 29.50 (ISBN 0-404-19067-7). AMS Pr.
Consciousness of Christ. William G. Most. (Orig.). 1980. pap. text ed. 5.95 (ISBN 0-931888-03-4). Christendom Pubns.
Consciousness of Joyce. Richard Ellmann. 160p. 1981. pap. 3.95 (ISBN 0-19-502898-8, GB 636, OPB). Oxford U Pr.
Consciousness: Readings. Daniel Goleman & Richard Davidson. 1979. text ed. 6.95 scp (ISBN 0-06-383045-0, HarpC). Har-Row.
Consciousness Reformation. Robert Wuthnow. 1976. 18.95x (ISBN 0-520-03138-5). U of Cal Pr.
Consciousness: The End of Authority. Frank R. Wallace. 1980. pap. 2.00 (ISBN 0-911752-32-3). I & O Pub.
Conscription & Conflict in the Confederacy. Albert B. Moore. 1963. text ed. 15.00x (ISBN 0-391-00459-X). Humanities.
Consecrated Ingenuity: The Shakers & Their Inventions. John S. Williams. (Illus.). 1957. 1.00 (ISBN 0-937942-01-4). Shaker Mus.
Consejos a la Juventud. T. B. Maston. Tr. by H. F. Duffer, Jr. Orig. Title: Advice to Youth. 60p. (Span.). 1980. pap. 1.00 (ISBN 0-311-46005-4). Casa Bautista.
Consensus & Conflict in African Societies. Margaret Peil. (African Studies Ser). (Illus.). 1977. text ed. 21.00x (ISBN 0-582-64173-X); pap. text ed. 9.95x (ISBN 0-582-64174-8). Longman.
Consensus & Disunity: The Lloyd George Coalition Government, 1918 to 1922. Kenneth Morgan. 448p. 1979. text ed. 45.00x (ISBN 0-19-822497-4). Oxford U Pr.
Consensus & Peace. 231p. 1981. pap. 20.75 (ISBN 92-3-101851-5, U1055, UNESCO). Unipub.
Consensus, Conflict, & American Historians. Bernard Sternsher. LC 73-16531. (Illus.). 448p. 1975. 15.00x o.p. (ISBN 0-253-31410-0); pap. 8.95x (ISBN 0-253-28070-2). Ind U Pr.
Consent Manual: Policies, Laws, Procedures. Karen M. Engstrom. 100p. 1981. pap. 10.00 (ISBN 0-87125-062-4). Cath Health.
Consequences of Adolescent Childbearing for the Young Parent's Future Personal & Professional Life. Josefina Card. 1977. pap. 12.00 research report-paper (ISBN 0-89785-564-7). Am Inst Res.
Consequences, Truth and. Daniel Berrigan. LC 67-12794. 1967. 3.95 o.p. (ISBN 0-02-510220-6); pap. 1.45 (ISBN 0-02-083780-1). Macmillan.
Conservation & Development in Northern Thailand. 114p. 1980. pap. 15.00 (ISBN 92-808-0077-9, TUNU083, UNU). Unipub.
Conservation & Evolution. O. H. Frankel & M. E. Soule. LC 80-40528. (Illus.). 300p. Date not set. 49.50 (ISBN 0-521-23275-9); pap. 17.95 (ISBN 0-521-29889-X). Cambridge U Pr.
Conservation & Management of Whales. K. Radway Allen. LC 79-90505. (Washington Sea Grant). (Illus.). 120p. 1980. 12.50 (ISBN 0-295-95706-9). U of Wash Pr.
Conservation & Productivity of Natural Waters. Zoological Society of London - 29th Symposium. Ed. by R. W. Edwards & D. J. Garrod. 1972. 45.00 o.s.i. (ISBN 0-12-613329-8). Acad Pr.
Conservation & Restoration of Pictorial Art. N. S. Brommelle & P. Smith. LC 75-32570. 340p. 1976. 59.95 (ISBN 0-408-70712-7). Butterworths.
Conservation & the Changing Direction of Economic Growth. Ed. by Bernhard J. Abrahamsson. LC 77-28753. (Westview Special Studies in Natural Resources & Energy Management Ser.). 1978. lib. bdg. 22.00x (ISBN 0-89158-413-7). Westview.
Conservation & the Gospel of Efficiency: The Progressive Conservation Movement, 1890-1920. Samuel P. Hays. LC 59-9274. 1969. pap. text ed. 4.95x (ISBN 0-689-70091-1, 139). Atheneum.
Conservation & Utilization of Water & Energy Resources. Compiled By American Society of Civil Engineers. 544p. 1979. pap. text ed. 34.75 (ISBN 0-87262-189-8). Am Soc Civil Eng.
Conservation Archaeology in the Northeast: Toward a Research Orientation, No. 3. Ed. by A. E. Spiess. LC 78-56049. 1978. pap. 8.00 (ISBN 0-87365-953-8). Peabody Harvard.
Conservation Bibliography for Librarian, Archivists, & Administrators. Carolyn C. Morrow & Steven B. Schoenly. LC 79-64847. 271p. 1979. 18.50x (ISBN 0-87875-170-X). Whitston Pub.
Conservation Directory. Ed. by Jeannette Bryant. 301p. 1981. 6.00 (ISBN 0-912186-39-9). Natl Wildlife.
Conservation Directory 1980. rev. ed. Ed. by Jeannette Bryant. 1980. 4.00 (ISBN 0-912186-34-8). Natl Wildlife.
Conservation-Ecology: Resources for Environmental Education. David F. Harrah & Barbara K. Harrah. LC 74-23055. 1975. 14.50 (ISBN 0-8108-0780-7). Scarecrow.
Conservation, Equilibrium & Feedback Applied to Atmospheric & Fluvial Processes. J. N. Rayner. LC 77-189377. (CCG Resource Papers Ser.: No. 15). (Illus.). 1972. pap. text ed. 4.00 (ISBN 0-89291-062-3). Assn Am Geographers.
Conservation in the United States, 5 vols. Frank E. Smith. 1971. Set. 150.00x (ISBN 0-442-37775-4). Van Nos Reinhold.
Conservation of Antiquities & Works of Art: Treatment, Repair, & Restoration. 2nd ed. H. J. Plenderleith & A. E. Werner. 1971. 42.00x (ISBN 0-19-212960-0). Oxford U Pr.
Conservation of Coinage: Monetary Exploitation & Its Restraint in France, Catalonia, & Aragon C.1000-1225 A.D. Thomas N. Bisson. (Illus.). 1979. 45.00 (ISBN 0-19-828275-3). Oxford U Pr.
Conservation of Conservation: The Child's Acquisition of a Fundamental Concept. Adrien Pinard. Tr. by Helga Feider. LC 80-26339. (Chicago Originals Ser.). 200p. 1981. lib. bdg. 14.00x (ISBN 0-226-66834-7). U of Chicago Pr.
Conservation of Cultural Property with Special Reference to Tropical Conditions. (Museums & Monuments Ser., Vol. 11). (Illus.). 1968. 21.00 (ISBN 92-3-100717-3, U103, UNESCO). Unipub.
Conservation of Energy. Jane W. Watson. (First Books Ser.). (Illus.). (gr. 4 up). 1978. PLB 6.45 s&l (ISBN 0-531-01404-5). Watts.
Conservation of Germplasm Resources: An Imperative. Committee on Germplasm Resources. 1978. pap. 6.50 (ISBN 0-309-02744-6). Natl Acad Pr.
Conservation of Library Materials: A Manual & Bibliography on the Care, Repair, & Restoration of Library Materials, 2 vols. 2nd ed. George M. Cunha & Dorothy G. Cunha. LC 77-163871. Vol. 1, 1971. 15.00 (ISBN 0-8108-0760-2); Vol. 2, 1972. 15.00 (ISBN 0-8108-0525-1); Set. 27.50 (ISBN 0-686-60803-8). Scarecrow.
Conservation of Natural Resources. 4th ed. Ed. by Guy-Harold Smith. LC 71-129661. 1971. 21.95 (ISBN 0-471-80192-5). Wiley.
Conservation of Orbital Symmetry. R. B. Woodward & R. Hoffmann. LC 79-63636. (Illus.). 1970. 14.70 (ISBN 3-5272-5325-4); pap. 7.70 (ISBN 3-5272-5324-6). Verlag Chemie.
Conservation of Renewable Natural Resources. Pennsylvania University Bicentennial Conference. Ed. by Raphael Zon & William Cooper. LC 68-26200. Repr. of 1941 ed. 12.50 (ISBN 0-8046-0356-1). Kennikat.
Conservation of Water. Walter McCulloh. (Illus.). 1913. 47.50x (ISBN 0-686-51362-2). Elliots Bks.
Conservations. William A. Miller. 96p. 1980. pap. 2.95 (ISBN 0-934104-04-2). Woodland.
Conservatism in America: The Thankless Persuasion. 2nd, rev. ed. Clinton L. Rossiter. LC 80-27937. xii, 306p. 1981. Repr. of 1962 ed. lib. bdg. 27.50x (ISBN 0-313-22720-9, ROCN). Greenwood.
Conservatism in England. F. J. Hearnshaw. LC 67-24582. 1968. Repr. 17.00 (ISBN 0-86527-031-7). Fertig.

Conservative Crisis & the Rule of Law: Attitudes of Bar & Bench 1887-1895. Arnold M. Paul. 7.50 (ISBN 0-8446-0839-4). Peter Smith.

Conservative Investors Sleep Well. Philip A. Fisher. LC 74-20401. 188p. 1975. 10.00 o.s.i. (ISBN 0-06-011256-5, HarpT). Har-Row.

Conservative Looks at Cooperatives. Raymond W. Miller. LC 64-15585. 245p. 1964. 11.95 (ISBN 0-8214-0000-2). Ohio U Pr.

Conservative Millenarians: The Romantic Experience in Bavaria. Paul Gottfried. LC 74-20028. 1979. 22.50 (ISBN 0-8232-0982-2). Fordham.

Conservative Opportunity. Ed. by Robert Blake & John Patten. 1976. text ed. 20.75x (ISBN 0-333-19971-5); pap. text ed. 10.50x (ISBN 0-333-19972-3). Humanities.

Conservative Ordeal: Northern Democrats & Reconstruction, 1865 to 1868. Edward L. Gambill. 208p. 1981. text ed. 13.50 (ISBN 0-8138-1385-9). Iowa St U Pr.

Conservative Party from Heath to Thatcher: Policy & Politics 1974 to 1979. Robert Behrens. 152p. 15.95x (ISBN 0-566-00268-X, 03778-8, Pub. by Gower Pub Co England). Lexington Bks.

Conservatives in an Age of Change: The Nixon & Ford Administrations. A. James Reichley. 500p. 1981. 26.95 (ISBN 0-8157-7380-3); pap. 11.95 (ISBN 0-8157-7379-X). Brookings.

Conserve Neighborhoods Notebook. National Trust for Historic Preservation. (Illus.). 154p. 1980. 12.95 (ISBN 0-89133-092-5). Preservation Pr.

Conserver Solution. Lawrence Solomon. LC 78-19216. 1979. 12.50 o.p. (ISBN 0-385-14533-0); pap. 6.95 (ISBN 0-385-14534-9). Doubleday.

Conserving American Resources. 3rd ed. Ruben A. Parson et al. 640p. 1972. 20.95 (ISBN 0-13-167767-5). P-H.

Conserving Energy in Multifamily Housing: Alternatives to Master Metering. Inst. Real Estate & U. S. Department of Energy. Ed. by Nancye J. Kirk. 100p. (Orig.). pap. text ed. write for info. (ISBN 0-912104-50-3). Inst Real Estate.

Consider Him. 2nd ed. J. Oswald Sanders. 1979. pap. write for info. (ISBN 0-85363-123-9). OMF Bks.

Consider the Evidence, Stories of Mystery & Suspense. Compiled by Phyllis R. Fenner. LC 73-792. (Illus.). 192p. (gr. 7 up). 1973. 7.75 (ISBN 0-688-20080-X). Morrow.

Consider Your Call. English Benedictine Congregation Members & Daniel Rees. (Cistercian Studies Ser.: No. 20). 447p. 1980. 17.95 (ISBN 0-87907-820-0). Cistercian Pubns.

Consider Your Words. 3rd ed. Charles B. Jennings et al. 1980. pap. text ed. 10.50 scp (ISBN 0-06-043292-6, HarpC); instructor's manual free. Har-Row.

Considerations About the Use of Computers in Radiodiagnostic Departments. Ed. by G. H. DuBoulay. 1980. 45.00x (Pub. by Brit Inst Radiology England). State Mutual Bk.

Considerations on Painting. John La Farge. LC 70-9611. (Library of Amerrican Art Ser). 1969. Repr. of 1895 ed. lib. bdg. 35.00 (ISBN 0-306-71824-3). Da Capo.

Considerations on Representative Government. John S. Mill. Ed. by Currin V. Shields. LC 57-14632. 1958. pap. 6.25 o.p. (ISBN 0-672-60249-0, LLA71). Bobbs.

Considerations on the Nature of the French Revolution & on the Causes Which Prolong Its Duration. Jacques Mallet Du Pan. LC 74-13491. xxii, 114p. 1975. Repr. of 1793 ed. 13.50 (ISBN 0-86527-032-5). Fertig.

Considering the Victim: Readings in Restitution & Victim Compensation. Joe Hudson & Burton Galaway. 496p. 1975. 37.50 (ISBN 0-398-03216-5). C C Thomas.

Consistency of British Balance of Payments Policies. Dietrich K. Fausten. 1975. text ed. 32.50x (ISBN 0-8419-5008-3). Holmes & Meier.

Consistent Profits in Short Selling Speculation. Cornwall Dahl. (Illus.). 267p. 1976. 41.50 (ISBN 0-89266-011-2). Am Classical Coll Pr.

Consistent Profits in Tape Reading. Harold W. Mentelle. (New Stock Market Library Books). (Illus.). 1979. 37.50 (ISBN 0-89266-180-1); spiral bdg. 12.35 (ISBN 0-685-91838-6). Am Classical Coll Pr.

Consolation; a Poem Addressed to Lady Brydges, Repr. Of 1815 Ed. Edward Quillinan. Bd. with Monthermer; a Poem. Repr. of 1815 ed; Sacrifice of Isabel. A Poem. Repr. of 1816 ed; Elegiac Verses, Addressed to a Lady. Repr. of 1817 ed; Woodcuts & Verses. Repr. of 1820 ed; Carmina Brugensiana. Domestic Poems. Repr. of 1822 ed. LC 75-31249. (Romantic Context Ser.: Poetry 1789-1830: Vol. 98). 1978. lib. bdg. 47.00 (ISBN 0-8240-2197-5). Garland Pub.

Consolation in Samson Agonistes. Lynn V. Sadler. (Salzburg Institute for English Literature: No. 82). (Orig.). 1979. pap. text ed. 25.00x (ISBN 0-391-01707-1). Humanities.

Consolation of Philosophy. Boethius. Tr. by Richard H. Green. LC 62-11788. 1962. pap. 3.95 (ISBN 0-672-60273-3, LLA86). Bobbs.

Consolidated Financial Statements: Principles & Procedures. William H. Childs. 352p. 1949. 22.50x o.p. (ISBN 0-8014-0076-7). Cornell U Pr.

Consolidated List of Approved Common Names of Insecticides & Certain Other Pesticides. Ed. by Osborne. LC 52-44516. 1979. 3.35 (ISBN 0-686-18865-9). Entomol Soc.

Consolidation of Power in Central Arabia Under Ibn Saud, 1925-1928. Ibrahim A-Rashid. (Documents on the History of Saudi Arabia: Vol. 2). 60.00 (ISBN 0-89712-054-X). Documentary Pubns.

Consolidation of the South China Frontier. George V. Moseley, 3rd. (Center for Chinese Studies, UC Berkeley). 1973. 19.50x (ISBN 0-520-02102-9). U of Cal Pr.

Consolidations: A Simplified Approach. Ronald Fraser. LC 80-83431. 128p. 1981. pap. text ed. 9.15 (ISBN 0-8403-2303-4). Kendall-Hunt.

Consolidator or Memoirs of Sundry Transactions from the World in the Moon. Daniel De Foe. LC 75-170513. (Foundations of the Novel Ser.: Vol. 9). lib. bdg. 50.00 (ISBN 0-8240-0521-X). Garland Pub.

Consonant Articulation Drills. Lora L. Dumont. LC 71-187778. 268p. 1972. pap. text ed. 5.95x o.p. (ISBN 0-8134-1463-6, 1463). Interstate.

Consonant Articulation Drills. 2nd ed. Lora L. Dumont. 268p. 1980. pap. text ed. 5.95x (ISBN 0-8134-2129-2, 2129). Interstate.

Consonant Sounds. Virginia Polish. (Starting off with Phonics Ser.: Bk. 3). (gr. k). 1980. pap. text ed. 2.21 (ISBN 0-87895-053-2); tchrs. ed. 2.00 (ISBN 0-87895-063-X). Modern Curr.

Conspiracy. Anthony Summers. (Illus.). 656p. 1981. pap. 8.95 (ISBN 0-07-062400-3). McGraw.

Conspiracy Against Childhood. Eda J. LeShan. LC 67-28453. 1967. pap. 5.95 (ISBN 0-689-70276-0, 182). Atheneum.

Conspiracy & Civil Liberties. Robert Hazell. 128p. 1974. pap. text ed. 6.25x (ISBN 0-7135-1909-6, Pub. by Bedford England). Renouf.

Conspiracy at Matsukawa. Chalmers Johnson. LC 73-161998. (Illus.). 1972. 25.00x (ISBN 0-520-02063-4). U of Cal Pr.

Conspiracy at Mukden: The Rise of the Japanese Military. Takehiko Yoshihashi. LC 80-13747. (Yale Studies in Political Science: No. 9). (Illus.). xvi, 274p. 1980. Repr. of 1963 ed. lib. bdg. 22.50x (ISBN 0-313-22443-9, YOCO). Greenwood.

Conspiracy of God: The Holy Spirit in Men. Haughey, John C., S.J. LC 73-80730. 120p. 1976. pap. 1.95 (ISBN 0-385-11558-X, Im). Doubleday.

Conspiracy of Poisons. Jeffreys. 1977. 6.95 o.s.i. (ISBN 0-8027-5359-0). Walker & Co.

Conspirators. Alan Riefe. (Cage Ser.: No. 2). 176p. 1975. pap. 0.95 o.p. (ISBN 0-445-00650-1). Popular Lib.

Constable. John Walker. (Library of Great Painters). (Illus.). 1979. 35.00 (ISBN 0-8109-0752-6). Abrams.

Constance de Markievicz: In the Cause of Ireland. Jacqueline Van Voris. LC 67-11245. (Illus.). 1967. 15.00x (ISBN 0-87023-025-5); pap. 6.00 (ISBN 0-87023-058-1). U of Mass Pr.

Constance Howard Book of Stitches. Constance Howard. (Illus.). 1979. 15.50 o.s.i. (ISBN 0-7134-1005-1, Pub. by Batsford). Hippocrene Bks.

Constance Howard Book of Stitches. Constance Howard. (Illus.). 144p. 1980. 13.75 (ISBN 0-7134-1005-1). Branford.

Constant Companion. Marion Chesney. 224p. 1980. pap. 1.75 (ISBN 0-449-50114-0, Coventry). Fawcett.

Constant Companions: An Exhibition of Mythological Animals, Demons, & Monsters. Intro. by Dominique De Menil. (Illus.). 1964. pap. 6.00 (ISBN 0-914412-19-1). Inst for the Arts.

Constant Image. Marcia Davenport. 1979. pap. 2.25 o.p. (ISBN 0-445-00279-4). Popular Lib.

Constant Pest: A Short History of Crop Pests & Their Control. George Ordish. LC 75-35297. (Illus.). 1976. 12.95 o.p. (ISBN 0-684-14553-7, ScribT). Scribner.

Constantin Guys: Crimean War Drawings 1854-1856. Karen W. Smith. LC 78-14991. (Illus.). 84p. 1978. pap. 7.95x (ISBN 0-910386-43-9, Pub. by Cleveland Mus Art). Ind U Pr.

Constantine. Margaret Killingray. Ed. by Malcolm Yapp et al. (Greenhaven World History Ser.). (Illus.). 32p. (gr. 10). 1980. lib. bdg. 5.95 (ISBN 0-89908-040-5); pap. text ed. 1.95 (ISBN 0-89908-015-4). Greenhaven.

Constantine & Religious Liberty. Hermann Doerries. 1960. 29.50x (ISBN 0-686-51363-0). Elliots Bks.

Constantine Cavafy. Peter Bien. LC 64-22641. (Columbia Essays on Modern Writers Ser.: No. 5). (Orig.). 1964. pap. 1.50 o.p. (ISBN 0-231-02661-7, MW5). Columbia U Pr.

Constantine Cay. Catherine Dillon. 1976. pap. 1.95 o.p. (ISBN 0-451-08307-5, J8307, Sig). NAL.

Constantine Porphyrogenitus & His World. Arnold J. Toynbee. (Illus.). 792p. 1973. 45.00x (ISBN 0-19-215253-X). Oxford U Pr.

Constantinople, City on the Golden Horn. David Jacobs & Cyril A. Mango. LC 78-81403. (Horizon Caravel Bks). (Illus.). 153p. (gr. 6 up). 1969. 9.95 (ISBN 0-8281-5003-6, J037-0); PLB 6.89 (ISBN 0-06-022799-0, Dist. by Har-Row). Am Heritage.

Constantinople in the Age of Justinian. Glanville Downey. (Centers of Civilization Ser.: No. 3). 1980. Repr. of 1960 ed. 5.95 (ISBN 0-8061-0465-1). U of Okla Pr.

Constantinople in the Age of Justinian. Glanville Downey. LC 60-13473. (Centers of Civilization Ser.: Vol. 3). (Illus.). 181p. 1981. pap. 3.95 (ISBN 0-8061-1708-7). U of Okla Pr.

Constellation: A Shakespeare Anthology. Ed. by Margaret Hodges. LC 68-13677. (Index). (gr. 7 up). 1968. 4.95 o.p. (ISBN 0-374-31485-3). FS&G.

Constipation Control: An Exercise Program to Achieve Regularity. Richard R. Fuller. 64p. 1981. 5.00 (ISBN 0-682-49690-1). Exposition.

Constituency Politics. Frank Bealey. LC 65-27451. 1966. 9.95 o.s.i. (ISBN 0-02-902010-7). Free Pr.

Constitution & American Education. 2nd ed. Arval A. Morris. LC 79-28177. (American Casebook Ser.). 1034p. 1980. text ed. 19.95 (ISBN 0-8299-2080-3). West Pub.

Constitution & Socio-Economic Change. Henry Rottschaefer. LC 77-173667. (American Constitutional & Legal History Ser.). 253p. 1971. Repr. of 1948 ed. lib. bdg. 29.50 (ISBN 0-306-70410-2). Da Capo.

Constitution & Supplementary Laws & Documents of the Republic of China. (Studies in Chinese Government & Law). 198p. 1977. Repr. of 1924 ed. 21.00 (ISBN 0-89093-059-7). U Pubns Amer.

Constitution & the Budget. Ed. by W. S. Moore & Rudolph G. Penner. 1980. 13.25 (ISBN 0-8447-2179-4); pap. 7.25 (ISBN 0-8447-2180-8). Am Enterprise.

Constitution & the Common Law. Randall Bridwell & Ralph U. Whitten. LC 77-5281. 1977. 20.95 (ISBN 0-669-01601-2). Lexington Bks.

Constitution & the Conduct of Foreign Policy. Ed. by Francis O. Wilcox & Richard A. Frank. LC 75-23999. (Special Studies). 166p. 1976. text ed. 23.95 (ISBN 0-275-55860-6); pap. text ed. 8.95 (ISBN 0-275-89480-0). Praeger.

Constitution in Crisis Times, 1918-1969. Paul L. Murphy. LC 70-156570. (New American Nation Ser). (Illus.). 1972. 15.00x o.s.i. (ISBN 0-06-013118-7, HarpT). Har-Row.

Constitution-Making. Edward McWhinney. 240p. 1981. 20.00x (ISBN 0-8020-5553-2). U of Toronto Pr.

Constitution of Athens & Related Texts. Aristotle. (Library of Classics Ser.: No. 13). pap. text ed. 4.25 (ISBN 0-02-840420-3). Hafner.

Constitution of India for the Younger Reader. 1971. pap. 1.75 (ISBN 0-88253-410-6). Ind-US Inc.

Constitution of Japan & Criminal Statutes. Military of Justice, Japan. (Studies in Japanese Law & Government). 1979. Repr. of 1957 ed. 38.00 (ISBN 0-89093-221-2). U Pubns Amer.

Constitution of Malaysia: Its Development, Nineteen Fifty-Seven to Nineteen Seventy-Seven. Ed. by Tun M. Suffian et al. 1979. 29.00x (ISBN 0-19-580406-6). Oxford U Pr.

Constitution of Man Considered in Relation to External Objects. 2nd ed. George Combe. LC 74-16109. (Hist. of Psych. Ser.). 313p. 1974. Repr. of 1833 ed. 25.00x (ISBN 0-8201-1136-8). Schol Facsimiles.

Constitution of Nicaragua, 1974. 1976. pap. 2.00 (ISBN 0-8270-5425-4). OAS.

Constitution of Parliaments in England. Sir John Pettus. Ed. by David S. Berkowitz & Samuel E. Thorne. LC 77-89214. (Classics of English Legal History in the Modern Era Ser.: Vol. 63). 446p. 1979. lib. bdg. 40.00 (ISBN 0-8240-3162-8). Garland Pub.

Constitution of the People's Republic of China. 1978. 3.50 (ISBN 0-8351-0550-4); pap. 1.75 (ISBN 0-8351-0551-2). China Bks.

Constitution of the United States. Theodore E. Burton. 1923. 14.50x (ISBN 0-685-89744-3). Elliots Bks.

Constitution of the United States. 1978. 0.30. Lucas.

Constitution of the United States: With Case Summaries. 11th ed. Edward C. Smith. LC 75-21722. 1979. pap. 3.50 (ISBN 0-06-460184-6, CO 184, COS). Har-Row.

Constitutional Amendments. W. L. Katz & G. Bernard. LC 73-14794. 6.45 (ISBN 0-531-00813-4). Watts.

Constitutional Change: Amendment Politics & Supreme Court Litigation Since 1900. LC 72-1965. (Twentieth Century Fund Study). 1972. pap. 30.00 (ISBN 0-527-02785-5). Kraus Repr.

Constitutional Change & the Mining Industry in Canada. Wendy MacDonald. 73p. 1890. write for info. (Pub. by Ctr. Resource Stud Canada). Renouf.

Constitutional Convention. Harold C. Vaughan. LC 75-25726. (Focus Bks Ser). (Illus.). 96p. (gr. 7 up). 1976. PLB 4.90 o.p. (ISBN 0-531-01104-6). Watts.

Constitutional Crisis in the States in India. Meera Srivastava. 220p. 1980. text ed. 12.50x (ISBN 0-391-02135-4). Humanities.

Constitutional Decisions of John Marshall, 2 Vols. Ed. by Joseph P. Cotton. LC 67-25445. (Law, Politics & History Ser). 1969. Repr. of 1905 ed. 55.00 (ISBN 0-306-70947-3). Da Capo.

Constitutional Doctrines of Justice Harlan. Floyd B. Clark. LC 74-87560. (Law, Politics & History Ser). 1969. Repr. of 1915 ed. lib. bdg. 25.00 (ISBN 0-306-71391-8). Da Capo.

Constitutional Documents of the Reign of James 1, 1603-1625. Ed. by Joseph R. Tanner. 1930. pap. 14.50x (ISBN 0-521-09122-5). Cambridge U Pr.

Constitutional Faith. Hugo L. Black. 1968. 4.95 o.p. (ISBN 0-394-42020-9). Knopf.

Constitutional Free Speech Defined & Defended. Theodore A. Schroeder. LC 72-106497. (Civil Liberties in American History Ser). 1970. Repr. of 1919 ed. lib. bdg. 45.00 (ISBN 0-306-71872-3). Da Capo.

Constitutional Function of Presidential-Administrative Separation. Henry J. Merry. LC 78-53415. 1978. pap. text ed. 7.50x (ISBN 0-8191-0497-3). U Pr of Amer.

Constitutional Grounds for Impeachment. Impeachment Inquiry Staff of the House Judiciary Committee. 1.00 (ISBN 0-8183-0129-5). Pub Aff Pr.

Constitutional History of Australia. Winston G. McMinn. 228p. 1979. text ed. 29.95x (ISBN 0-19-550562-X). Oxford U Pr.

Constitutional History of England. Frederic W. Maitland. 1908. text ed. 59.95x (ISBN 0-521-05656-X); pap. text ed. 15.95x (ISBN 0-521-09137-3). Cambridge U Pr.

Constitutional History of England, from the Accession of Henry VII to the Death of George II, 2 vols, Vol. 83. Henry Hallam. Ed. by David Berkowitz & Samuel Thorne. LC 77-86590. (Classics of English Legal History in the Modern Era Ser.). 1979. lib. bdg. 110.00 (ISBN 0-8240-3070-2). Garland Pub.

Constitutional History of Habeas Corpus. William F. Duker. LC 79-6834. (Contributions in Legal Studies: No. 13). 349p. 1980. lib. bdg. 29.95 (ISBN 0-313-22264-9, DHC/). Greenwood.

Constitutional History of India: 1858-1919, 2 vols. A. C. Banerjee. 1978. Vol. 1. 20.00x o.p. (ISBN 0-8364-0286-3); Vol. 2. 22.50 o.p. (ISBN 0-685-81684-2). South Asia Bks.

Constitutional History of the Military Draft. John R. Graham. 5.95 (ISBN 0-87018-065-7); pap. 2.95 (ISBN 0-87018-070-3). Ross.

Constitutional History of the United States. Andrew C. McLaughlin. 1935. 29.50x (ISBN 0-89197-103-3); pap. text ed. 12.95x (ISBN 0-89197-104-1). Irvington.

Constitutional History of the United States, 3 Vols. Francis N. Thorpe. LC 76-124906. (American Constitutional & Legal History Ser). 1970. Repr. of 1901 ed. Set. lib. bdg. 175.00 (ISBN 0-306-71998-3). Da Capo.

Constitutional History of the United States: From Their Declaration of Independence to the Close of Their Civil War, 2 vols. George T. Curtis. (American Constitution & Legal History Ser.). 1100p. 1974. Repr. of 1896 ed. lib. bdg. 115.00 (ISBN 0-306-70611-3). Da Capo.

Constitutional Interpretation, Cases-Essays-Materials. 2nd ed. LC 79-14772. 1490p. 1979. text ed. 19.95 (ISBN 0-8299-2052-8). West Pub.

Constitutional Language: An Interpretation of Judicial Decision. John Brigham. LC 78-4020. (Contribution in Political Science: No. 17). 1978. lib. bdg. 17.50 (ISBN 0-313-20420-9, BCO/). Greenwood.

Constitutional Law. 4th ed. John C. Klotter & Jacqueline R. Kanovitz. (Justice Administration Legal Ser.). 900p. Date not set. price not set (ISBN 0-87084-492-X). Anderson Pub Co.

Constitutional Law: Cases & Comments. 2nd ed. James L. Maddex, Jr. (Criminal Justice Ser.). 1978. text ed. 18.95 (ISBN 0-8299-0185-X); instrs.' manual avail. (ISBN 0-8299-0598-7). West Pub.

Constitutional Law: Cases-Comments-Questions. 5th ed. William B. Lockhart et al. LC 80-21518. (American Casebook Ser.). 1829p. 1980. text ed. 23.95 (ISBN 0-8299-2110-9). West Pub.

Constitutional Law for Criminal Justice. George Felkenes. (Criminal Justice Ser.). 1978. ref. 17.95 (ISBN 0-13-167833-7). P-H.

Constitutional Law: Principles & Policy, Cases & Materials. Jerome A. Barron & C. Thomas Dienes. LC 74-2945. (Contemporary Legal Education Ser.). 1975. text ed. 24.00 (ISBN 0-672-81774-8, Bobbs-Merrill Law); 1980 cum. suppl. 8.00 (ISBN 0-672-83549-5). Michie.

Constitutional Limits to Union Power. Philip D. Bradley. 1976. pap. 10.00 (ISBN 0-685-79963-8). Coun Am Affairs.

Constitutional Powers: Cases on the Separation of Powers & Federalism. Howard Ball. LC 80-12820. 371p. 1980. pap. text ed. 11.95 (ISBN 0-8299-2090-0). West Pub.

Constitutional Problems in Church-State Relations: A Symposium. D. T. Mitzner et al. LC 75-155825. (Symposia on Law & Society Ser). 1971. Repr. of 1966 ed. lib. bdg. 14.50 (ISBN 0-306-70131-6). Da Capo.

Constitutional Reason of State: The Survival of the Constitutional Order. Carl J. Friedrich. LC 57-10150. 131p. 1957. 6.50x (ISBN 0-87057-046-3, Pub. by Brown U Pr). Univ Pr of New England.

Constitutional Revolution, Ltd. Edward S. Corwin. LC 77-805. 1977. Repr. of 1941 ed. lib. bdg. 15.00x (ISBN 0-8371-9498-9, COCO). Greenwood.

Constitutional Rights of College Students: A Study in Case Law. Richard C. Ratliff. LC 72-5729. 1972. 10.00 (ISBN 0-8108-0532-4). Scarecrow.

Constitutional Rights of the Accused: Post-Trial. new ed. Joseph G. Cook. LC 75-160369. (Criminal Law Library). 1976. 47.50 (ISBN 0-686-20646-0). Lawyers Co-Op.

Constitutional Rights of the Accused: Trial Rights. Joseph G. Cook. LC 75-160369. (Criminal Law Library). 1974. 47.50 (ISBN 0-686-14499-6). Lawyers Co-Op.

Constitutional Rights of the Accused: Pretrial Rights. Joseph G. Cook. LC 75-160369. 1972. 47.50 (ISBN 0-686-14498-8). Lawyers Co-Op.

Constitutional Rights of Women. Leslie F. Goldstein. 1979. pap. text ed. 10.95 (ISBN 0-582-28063-X). Longman.

Constitutional Studies: State & Federal. J. Schouler. LC 76-124894. (American Constitutional & Legal History Ser.). 1971. Repr. of 1897 ed. lib. bdg. 29.50 (ISBN 0-306-71993-2). Da Capo.

Constitutionalism & Resistance in the Sixteenth Century: Three Treatises by Heltman, Beza & Mornay. Ed. & tr. by Julian H. Franklin. LC 71-77131. (Orig.). 1969. 4.95 (ISBN 0-672-63519-4). Pegasus.

Constitutionalism & Resistance in the Sixteenth Century: Three Treatises by Holtman, Beza & Mornay. Ed. by Julian H. Franklin. LC 71-77131. 1969. 22.50x (ISBN 0-672-53519-X). Irvington.

Constitutionalism in Asia: Asian Views of the American Influence. Ed. by Lawrence W. Beer. 1979. 20.00x (ISBN 0-520-03701-4). U of Cal Pr.

Constitutions of the Society of Jesus. St. Ignatius Of Loyola. Tr. & commentary by George E. Ganss. LC 72-108258. (Jesuit Primary Sources in English Translation Ser.: No. 1). 432p. 1970. 11.00 (ISBN 0-912422-03-3); smyth sewn o.s.i. 6.00 (ISBN 0-912422-20-3); pap. 5.00 (ISBN 0-912422-06-8). Inst Jesuit.

Constraint & Innovation: The Content & Organization of Schooling. M. Bloomer & K. E. Shaw. 1979. 33.00 (ISBN 0-08-022994-8); pap. 15.75 (ISBN 0-08-022993-X). Pergamon.

Constraints to High Yields on Asian Rice Farms: An Interim Report. 235p. 1977. pap. 11.00 (R010, IRRI). Unipub.

Constructed Roman Alphabet. David L. Goines. 1981. 40.00 (ISBN 0-87923-391-5); ltd. ed. 140.00 (ISBN 0-87923-376-1). Godine.

Constructing a Life Philosophy: An Examination of Alternatives. rev.,3rd ed. Ed. by David L. Bender. (Opposing Viewpoints Ser.: Vol. 4). (Illus.). (gr. 9 up). 1976. lib. bdg. 10.60 o.p. (ISBN 0-912616-28-8); pap. text ed. 4.60 o.p. (ISBN 0-912616-18-0). Greenhaven.

Constructing a Life Philosophy: Opposing Viewpoints. David L. Bender. (Opposing Viewpoints Ser.). 144p. (gr. 12). 1980. lib. bdg. 8.95 (ISBN 0-89908-329-3); pap. text ed. 3.95 (ISBN 0-89908-304-8). Greenhaven.

Constructing Achievement Tests. 2nd ed. Norman E. Gronlund. 1977. pap. 8.95 ref. ed. (ISBN 0-13-169235-6). P-H.

Constructing & Manufacturing Wood Products. Wayne H. Zook. (Illus.). 434p. (gr. 9-12). 1974. 15.96 (ISBN 0-87345-048-5). McKnight.

Constructing Cross-Country Obstacles. Bill Thompson. (Illus.). 17.35 (ISBN 0-85131-140-7, Dist. by Sporting Book Center). J A Allen.

Constructing Modern Furniture. Victor J. Taylor. LC 79-91383. (Home Craftsman Bk.). (Illus.). 144p. 1980. pap. 5.95 (ISBN 0-8069-8888-6). Sterling.

Constructing Policy: Dialogues with Social Scientists in the National Political Arena. Ed. by Irving L. Horowitz. 1979. 25.95 (ISBN 0-03-046696-2). Praeger.

Constructing Social Problems. Malcom Spector & John Kitsuse. LC 76-29487. 1977. pap. text ed. 7.95 (ISBN 0-8465-6725-3). Benjamin-Cummings.

Construction. Jack M. Landers. LC 75-4032. (Illus.). 1976. text ed. 10.64 (ISBN 0-87006-291-3); lab manual 3.20 (ISBN 0-87006-214-X). Goodheart.

Construction & Design of Cable-Stayed Bridges. Walter Podolny, Jr. & John B. Scalzi. LC 75-46578. (Practical Construction Guides Ser.). 506p. 1976. 47.50 (ISBN 0-471-75625-3, Pub. by Wiley-Interscience). Wiley.

Construction & Maintenance for Farm & Home. E. W. Foss. 1960. text ed. 18.50x o.p. (ISBN 0-471-26763-5). Wiley.

Construction & the Related Professions. M. C. Fleming. (Illus.). 1980. 130.00 (ISBN 0-08-024034-8). Pergamon.

Construction & Use of Atomic & Molecular Models. H. Bassow. 1968. 19.50 (ISBN 0-08-012925-0); pap. 9.75 (ISBN 0-08-012924-2). Pergamon.

Construction Construed & Constitutions Vindicated. John Taylor. LC 77-117311. (American Constitutional & Legal History Ser). 1970. Repr. of 1820 ed. lib. bdg. 35.00 (ISBN 0-306-71983-5). Da Capo.

Construction Contract Claims. Ed. by B. C. Hart. LC 78-74032. (Professional Education Publications). 1979. 15.00 (ISBN 0-89707-002-X). Amer Bar Assn.

Construction Contracts. Keith Collier. (Illus.). 1979. ref. ed. 21.95 (ISBN 0-8359-0912-3); text ed. 16.95 (ISBN 0-8359-0912-3). Reston.

Construction Contracts & Specifications. Glenn M. Hardie. (Illus.). 1981. text ed. 21.95 (ISBN 0-8359-0923-9). Reston.

Construction Contracts in the Eighties. Jotham D. Pierce, Jr. LC 80-80760. (Real Estate Law & Practice Course Handbook Ser.). 896p. 1980. pap. text ed. 25.00 (ISBN 0-686-68821-X, N4-4348). PLI.

Construction Contracts 1979 Course Handbook. (Real Estate Law & Practice Course Handbook Ser., 1978-79: Vol. 166). 1979. pap. 20.00 o.p. (ISBN 0-686-50956-0, N4-4331). PLI.

Construction Cost Control. Compiled By American Society of Civil Engineers. 108p. 1979. pap. text ed. 10.00 (ISBN 0-87262-003-4). Am Soc Civil Eng.

Construction Delay: Responsibilities, Risks, and Litigation. James J. O'Brien. LC 76-19110. 1976. 19.50 o.p. (ISBN 0-8436-0162-0). CBI Pub.

Construction Dewatering: A Guide to Theory & Practice. J. Patrick Powers. LC 80-18851. (Wiley Ser. of Practical Construction Guides). 300p. 1981. 29.95 (ISBN 0-471-69591-2, Pub. by Wiley-Interscience). Wiley.

Construction Electrical Contracting. John E. Traister. LC 78-13441. (Wiley Series on Practical Construction Guides). 299p. 1978. 29.95 (ISBN 0-471-02986-6). Wiley.

Construction Engineer's Form Book. Edward R. Fisk. 256p. 1981. text ed. 40.00 (ISBN 0-471-06307-X). Wiley.

Construction Equipment Guide. David A. Day. LC 72-10163. (Practical Construction Guides Ser.). 563p. 1973. 47.50 (ISBN 0-471-19985-0, Pub. by Wiley-Interscience). Wiley.

Construction Estimating. R. Jones. 216p. 1967. pap. 14.00 (ISBN 0-8273-0108-1); instructor's guide 3.45 (ISBN 0-8273-0109-X). Delmar.

Construction Estimating. R. Petri. 1978. ref. ed. 20.95 (ISBN 0-87909-152-5); text ed. 18.95 (ISBN 0-87909-152-5). Reston.

Construction Failure. J. Feld. LC 68-30908. (Wiley Series of Practical Construction Guides). 1968. 29.95 (ISBN 0-471-25700-1, Pub. by Wiley-Interscience). Wiley.

Construction Financing 1977. (Real Estate Law & Practice Course Handbook Ser., 1976-77: Vol. 136). 1977. pap. 20.00 o.p. (ISBN 0-685-85332-2, N4-3394). PLI.

Construction for Profit. Ken Gooch & John Caroline. (Illus.). 240p. 1980. text ed. 21.95 (ISBN 0-8359-0938-7). Reston.

Construction Foreman - Supervisor - Inspector. 2nd ed. Arco Editorial Board. (Orig.). 1970. pap. 8.00 o.p. (ISBN 0-668-01085-1). Arco.

Construction Funding: Where the Money Comes from. Don A. Halperin. LC 74-11188. (Practical Construction Guides Ser). 256p. 1974. 22.95 (ISBN 0-471-34570-9, Pub. by Wiley-Interscience). Wiley.

Construction Guide for Soils & Foundations. Gordon A. Fletcher & Vernon A. Smoots. LC 73-21789. (Practical Construction Guides Ser). 420p. 1974. 32.50 (ISBN 0-471-26400-8, Pub. by Wiley-Interscience). Wiley.

Construction Industry: Balance-Wheel of the Economy. Julian E. Lange & Daniel Q. Mills. LC 79-1562. 256p. 1979. 18.95 (ISBN 0-669-02913-0). Lexington Bks.

Construction Industry Careers. Stephen Rudley. LC 77-3051. (Career Concise Guides Ser.). (gr. 6 up). 1977. PLB 6.45 (ISBN 0-531-01301-4). Watts.

Construction Industry Handbook. 2nd ed. Ed. by R. A. Burgess et al. 1973. 29.95 (ISBN 0-8436-0119-1). CBI Pub.

Construction Industry Labor Relations, 1979. (Litigation Course Handbook Ser., 1978-79: Vol. 138). 1979. pap. 20.00 (ISBN 0-686-50957-9, H4-3893). PLI.

Construction Management: An Effective Approach. Joseph M. Roberts, Sr. (Illus.). 368p. 1980. 21.95; text ed. 15.95 (ISBN 0-8359-0927-1). Reston.

Construction Management Practices. S. P. Volpe. 181p. 1972. 18.50 (ISBN 0-471-91010-4). Wiley.

Construction Management: Principles & Practices. Stanley Goldhaber et al. LC 76-58397. (Construction Management & Engineering Ser.). 450p. 1977. 28.95 (ISBN 0-471-44270-4, Pub. by Wiley-Interscience). Wiley.

Construction Manager in the Nineteen Eighties. King Royer. (Illus.). 496p. 1981. text ed. 32.00 (ISBN 0-13-168690-9). P-H.

Construction Manual for Highway Construction. 1980. 9.00. AASHTO.

Construction Materials. Byron W. Maguire. 375p. 1981. text ed. 19.95 (ISBN 0-8359-0935-2). Reston.

Construction Materials. W. Patton. 1976. 19.95 (ISBN 0-13-168724-7). P-H.

Construction Materials Evaluation & Selection: A Systematic Approach. Harold J. Rosen & Philip M. Bennett. LC 79-15885. (Wiley Series of Practical Construction Guides). 1979. 21.95 (ISBN 0-471-73565-5, Pub. by Wiley-Interscience). Wiley.

Construction Materials for Photographic Processing Equipment: Eastman Kodak Company Code No. K-12. (Illus.). 1980. pap. write for info. (ISBN 0-87985-250-X). Eastman Kodak.

Construction of a European Community: Achievements & Prospects for the Future. Pierre Maillet. LC 77-10605. (Praeger Special Studies). 1977. 22.95 (ISBN 0-03-022366-0). Praeger.

Construction of American Furniture Treasures. Lester Margon. (Illus.). 168p. 1975. pap. 5.00 (ISBN 0-486-23056-2). Dover.

Construction of Assemblages. new ed. Elizabeth Foy & John Schurer. Ed. by D. Steve Rahmas. (Handicraft Ser.: No. 7). (Illus.). 32p. (Orig.). (gr. 7-12). 1973. lib. bdg. 2.45 incl. catalog cards (ISBN 0-87157-907-3); pap. 1.25 vinyl laminated covers (ISBN 0-87157-407-1). SamHar Pr.

Construction of Buildings, 5 vols. R. Barry. (Illus.). 508p. 1971. Set. spiral bdg. 40.00x (ISBN 0-8464-0276-9). Beekman Pubs.

Construction of Gothic Cathedrals: A Study of Medieval Vault Erection. John Fitchen. (Midway Reprint Ser.). (Illus.). 1977. pap. text ed. 12.00x (ISBN 0-226-25202-7); pap. 9.95 (ISBN 0-226-25203-5). U of Chicago Pr.

Construction of Gothic Cathedrals: A Study of Medieval Vault Erection. John Fitchen. (Illus.). xxii, 344p. 1981. pap. 9.95 (ISBN 0-226-25203-5). U of Chicago Pr.

Construction of Hoover Dam. LC 77-79677. (Illus.). 1976. Repr. of 1936 ed. 1.00 (ISBN 0-916122-51-4). K C Pubns.

Construction of Lombard & Gothic Vaults. Kingsley A. Porter. 1911. 49.50x (ISBN 0-685-69851-3). Elliots Bks.

Construction of Madness: Emerging Conceptions & Interventions into Psychotic Process. Peter A. Magaro. 240p. 1976. text ed. 26.00 (ISBN 0-08-019904-6); pap. text ed. 12.00 (ISBN 0-08-019903-8). Pergamon.

Construction of Modern Science. R. S. Westfall. LC 77-84001. (History of Science Ser.). (Illus.). 1978. 21.95 (ISBN 0-521-21863-2); pap. 7.95x (ISBN 0-521-29295-6). Cambridge U Pr.

Construction of Prestressed Concrete Structures. Ben C. Gerwick. LC 71-140176. (Practical Construction Guides Ser). 1971. 28.95 (ISBN 0-471-29710-0, Pub. by Wiley-Interscience). Wiley.

Construction of Roads on Compressible Soils. Organization for Economic Cooperation & Development. (Road Research Ser.). (Illus.). 147p. (Orig.). 1980. pap. text ed. 13.50x (ISBN 92-64-12062-9, 7780021). OECD.

Construction Performance Control by Networks. H. N. Ahuja. LC 76-4774. (Construction Management & Engineering Ser.). 688p. 1976. 40.00 (ISBN 0-471-00960-1, Pub. by Wiley-Interscience). Wiley.

Construction Practices for Project Managers & Superintendents. W. J. Stillman. (Illus.). 1978. text ed. 18.95 (ISBN 0-87909-164-9). Reston.

Construction Principles. D. A. Reid. 1973. text ed. 17.50x (ISBN 0-7114-3305-4). Intl Ideas.

Construction: Principles, Materials & Methods. 4th ed. Harold Olin et al. 1980. text ed. 29.95 (ISBN 0-8134-2110-1). Interstate.

Construction Science & Materials for Technicians 2. Fincham Watkins. 1981. text ed. price not set (ISBN 0-408-00488-6). Butterworth.

Construction Specifications Writing Principles & Procedures. 2nd ed. Harold J. Rosen. 240p. 1981. 24.95 (ISBN 0-471-08328-3, Pub. by Wiley-Interscience). Wiley.

Construction Superintendent's Job Guide. Harvey V. Debo & Leo Diamant. LC 79-17979. (Ser. on Practical Construction Guides). 1980. 22.00 (ISBN 0-471-20457-9, Pub. by Wiley-Interscience). Wiley.

Construction Technology, Vol. 1. J. T. Grundy. (Illus.). 1977. pap. 12.95x (ISBN 0-7131-3387-2). Intl Ideas.

Construction Technology, Vol. 2. J. T. Grundy. (Illus.). 200p. 1979. pap. 13.95x (ISBN 0-7131-3403-8). Intl Ideas.

Construction Technology One: Checkbook. Chudley. 1981. text ed. price not set (ISBN 0-408-00602-1, Westbury Hse). Butterworth.

Constructional Geometry. Wallace Brunelle & Robert O'Neill. Ed. by Allan W. Gray. 1972. pap. text ed. 8.25 (ISBN 0-89420-077-1, 350299); cassette recordings 107.95 (ISBN 0-89420-201-4, 350300). Natl Book.

Constructional Mathematics, Vol. 1. Peter Horrobin. 1969. pap. 7.00 (ISBN 0-08-006890-1). Pergamon.

Constructive Criticism: A Handbook. rev. ed. Gracie Lyons. (Illus.). 112p. (Orig.). 1980. pap. 3.50 (ISBN 0-686-28724-X). IC&P.

Constructive Immigration Policy. Maurice R. Davie. 1923. pap. 12.50x (ISBN 0-685-69809-2). Elliots Bks.

Constructive Methods for Nonlinear Boundary Value Problems & Nonlinear Oscillations. Ed. by Lothar Collatz & Julius Albrecht. Tr. by K. Kirchgassner. (International Series of Numerical Mathematics: Vol. 48). 190p. 1979. pap. 19.50 (ISBN 3-7643-1098-7). Birkhauser.

Constructive Play: Applying Piaget in the Preschool. George E. Forman & D. Fleet Hill. LC 79-21316. 1980. pap. text ed. 10.95 (ISBN 0-8185-0391-2). Brooks-Cole.

Constructive Typology & Social Theory. John C. McKinney. LC 66-25454. (Century Sociology Ser.). 1966. 20.00x (ISBN 0-89197-105-X); pap. text ed. 6.95x (ISBN 0-89197-106-8). Irvington.

Constructivism. George Rickey. LC 67-27525. (Illus.). 1967. 25.00 o.s.i. (ISBN 0-8076-0426-7). Braziller.

Consuelo: A Romance of Venice. George Sand. 799p. 1979. pap. 8.95 (ISBN 0-686-68924-0). Da Capo.

Consuetudo, Vel Lex Mercatoria, or the Ancient Law-Merchant. Gerard De Malynes. LC 79-84121. (English Experience Ser.: No. 940). 524p. 1979. Repr. of 1622 ed. lib. bdg. 78.00 (ISBN 90-221-0940-2). Walter J Johnson.

Consulate of One. Louise Louis. (Illus.). 16p. 1977. lib. bdg. 1.99. Pen-Art.

Consultant. John McNeil. 1979. pap. 2.25 o.p. (ISBN 0-345-28108-X). Ballantine.

Consultant Connexion: Evaluation of the Federal Consulting Service. Mekki Mtewa. LC 80-8141. 238p. 1980. lib. bdg. 18.50 (ISBN 0-8191-1161-9); pap. text ed. 9.50 (ISBN 0-8191-1162-7). U Pr of Amer.

Consultants Can Help: The Use of Outside Experts in the U.S. Office of Child Development. Hanes D. Marver. LC 79-1557. 1979. 22.95 (ISBN 0-669-02904-1). Lexington Bks.

Consultant's Legal Guide. Nancy Pyeatt. (Consultant's Library). 1980. text ed. 30.00 (ISBN 0-930686-09-8). Bermont Bks.

Consultation: A Book of Readings. Don C. Dinkmeyer & Jon Carlson. LC 74-34048. 295p. 1975. text ed. 19.95 (ISBN 0-471-21562-7). Wiley.

Consultation Among the American Republics with Respect to the Argentine Situation. U. S. Dept. of State. LC 76-29632. (Latin America in the 20th Century Ser.). 1976. Repr. of 1946 ed. lib. bdg. 15.00 (ISBN 0-306-70838-8). Da Capo.

Consultation in Schools: Theory, Research Procedures. Ed. by Jane C. Conoley. LC 80-2329. (Educational Technology Ser.). 1981. price not set (ISBN 0-12-186020-5). Acad Pr.

Consultation in Social Work. Alfred Kadushin. LC 77-24345. 1977. 16.00x (ISBN 0-231-04124-1). Columbia U Pr.

Consultation: Strategy for Improving Education. new ed. Duane Brown et al. 1979. text ed. 18.95 (ISBN 0-685-96341-1). Allyn.

Consultation with a Cardiologist: Coronary Heart Disease & Heart Attacks: Management. Jacob I. Haft & Saretta Berlin. LC 78-21894. (Illus.). 1979. 15.95 (ISBN 0-88229-487-3). Nelson-Hall.

Consultation with a Cardiologist: Coronary Heart Disease & Heart Attacks: Prevention. Jacob I. Haft & Saretta Berlin. LC 78-26660. 1979. 19.95 (ISBN 0-88229-320-6). Nelson-Hall.

Consultation with a Plastic Surgeon. Ralph L. Dicker & Victor R. Syracuse. LC 74-30176. (Illus.). 384p. 1975. 14.95 (ISBN 0-88229-201-3). Nelson-Hall.

Consultations in Dermatology. Walter B. Shelley. LC 70-168599. (Illus.). 1972. 16.00 (ISBN 0-7216-8213-8). Saunders.

Consultations in Dermatology Two. Walter B. Shelley. LC 73-88979. (Illus.). 289p. 1974. 17.00 (ISBN 0-7216-8214-6). Saunders.

Consulting Engineering: A Guide to the Engagement of Engineering Services. Compiled By American Society of Civil Engineers. (Manual & Report on Engineering Practice Ser.: No. 45). 96p. 1972. pap. text ed. 3.00 (ISBN 0-87262-220-7). Am Soc Civil Eng.

Consulting Engineer's Who's Who & Yearbook 1979 (British Edition) Ed. by Northwood Publications,London. 1979. 25.00x (ISBN 0-7198-2780-9). Intl Ideas.

Consulting: Facilitating Human Potential & Change Processes. Don Dinkmeyer & Jon Carlson. LC 72-97006. 1973. text ed. 18.50 (ISBN 0-675-08958-1). Merrill.

Consulting Overseas: A Guide for Professionals in Construction. Reginald Bidgood. (Illus.). 1976. 18.95x (ISBN 0-7198-2640-3). Intl Ideas.

Consulting Process in Action. Gordon Lippitt & Ronald Lippitt. LC 77-15681. 130p. 1978. pap. 13.50 (ISBN 0-88390-141-2). Univ Assocs.

Consumer & Commercial Credit Management. 6th ed. Robert H. Cole. 1980. 20.95x (ISBN 0-256-02255-0). Irwin.

Consumer Approach to Community Psychology. James K. Morrison. LC 79-1172. 1979. 18.95 (ISBN 0-88229-458-X). Nelson-Hall.

Consumer Attitudes Toward Health Care & Medical Malpractice. Roger D. Blackwell & W. Wayne Talarzyk. LC 77-78191. 1977. pap. 9.95 o.p. (ISBN 0-88244-155-8). Grid Pub.

Consumer Banking in New York. David H. Rogers. 138p. 1975. 15.00x (ISBN 0-231-03935-2). Columbia U Pr.

Consumer Behavior. Dorothy Cohen. 504p. 1981. pap. text ed. 19.95 (ISBN 0-394-31160-4). Random.

Consumer Behavior. 3rd ed. Engel et al. 1978. 20.95 (ISBN 0-03-089673-8). Dryden Pr.

Consumer Behavior. 2nd ed. Runyon. (Marketing & Management Ser.). 504p. 1980. text ed. 19.95 (ISBN 0-675-08159-9). Merrill.

Consumer Behavior. Leon G. Schiffman et al. LC 77-25032. (Illus.). 1978. ref. 19.95x (ISBN 0-13-169201-1). P-H.

Consumer Behavior & Marketing Management. James H. Myers & William H. Reynolds. LC 68-1942. (Illus., Orig.). 1967. pap. 10.75 (ISBN 0-395-04987-3, 3-39771). HM.

Consumer Behavior: Basic Findings & Management Implications. G. Zaltman & M. Wallendorf. LC 78-23335. 1979. text ed. 23.95x (ISBN 0-471-98126-5); tchrs. manual avail. (ISBN 0-471-04862-3). Wiley.

Consumer Behavior: Concepts & Strategies. Terrell G. Williams. 600p. pap. text ed. 14.36 (ISBN 0-8299-0420-4). West Pub.

Consumer Behavior Dynamics: A Casebook. Wayne DeLozier. (Business Ser.). 1977. text ed. 12.95 (ISBN 0-675-08504-7); instructors manual 3.95 (ISBN 0-686-67643-2). Merrill.

Consumer Behavior: Implications for Marketing Strategy. Delbert I. Hawkins et al. 1980. 18.50 (ISBN 0-256-02290-9). Business Pubns.

Consumer Behavior in Latin America: Income & Spending of Families in Ten Andean Cities. Philip Musgrove. LC 77-1108. 1978. 18.95 (ISBN 0-8157-5914-2). Brookings.

Consumer Behavior: Learning Models of Purchasing. George H. Haines. LC 69-11164. (Illus.). 1969. 9.95 o.s.i. (ISBN 0-02-913390-4). Free Pr.

Consumer Behavior: Theoretical Sources. Ed. by Scott Ward & Thomas Robertson. (International Management Ser). (Illus.). 560p. 1973. ref. ed. 20.95 (ISBN 0-13-169391-3). P-H.

Consumer Behavior: Theory & Applications. Barbara J. Redman. (Illus.). 1979. pap. text ed. 12.50 (ISBN 0-87055-324-0). AVI.

Consumer Behavior, Theory & Practice. 3rd ed. C. Glenn Walters. 1978. text ed. 18.95 (ISBN 0-256-01999-1). Irwin.

Consumer Behaviour in India: An Econometric Study. B. N. Mahajan. 1980. text ed. 20.50x (ISBN 0-391-01834-5). Humanities.

Consumer Buying. Boy Scouts of America. LC 19-600. (Illus.). 64p. (gr. 6-12). 1975. pap. 0.70x (ISBN 0-8395-3387-X, 3387). BSA.

Consumer Complaint Guide. 8th ed. Joseph Rosenbloom. LC 73-182375. 1981. 12.50 (ISBN 0-02-469590-4). Macmillan.

Consumer Complete Buying Guide-Stereo Equipment. pap. 1.95 o.p. (ISBN 0-451-05814-3, J5814, Sig). NAL.

Consumer Complete Buying Guide to Camping & Backpacking. pap. 1.95 (ISBN 0-451-05848-8, J5848, Sig). NAL.

Consumer Credit. Elsie Fetterman & Jordan. (gr. 10-12). 1976. text ed. 10.60 (ISBN 0-87002-084-6); student guide 3.00 (ISBN 0-87002-183-4); tchr's guide 3.96 (ISBN 0-87002-191-5). Bennett IL.

Consumer Credit. Elsie Fetterman & Jordon. 1977. pap. 7.68 tchr's guide o.p. (ISBN 0-685-81853-5). Bennett IL.

Consumer Credit Compliance Manual. John R. Fonseca. LC 74-31560. (Commercial Law Library). 1975. 47.50 (ISBN 0-686-20647-9). Lawyers Co-Op.

Consumer Credit: 1980 Course Handbook. (Commercial Law & Practice Course Handbook Ser., 1979-80: Vol. 229). 1980. pap. 25.00 (ISBN 0-686-50958-7, A4-3072). PLI.

Consumer Demand: A New Approach. Kelvin Lancaster. LC 76-164502. (Study in Economics: No. 5). 1971. 17.50x (ISBN 0-231-03357-5). Columbia U Pr.

Consumer Demand for Cars in the U. S. A. R. P. Smith. LC 74-31802. (Department of Applied Economics, Occasional Papers Ser.: No. 44). (Illus.). 200p. 1975. 19.95 (ISBN 0-521-20770-3); pap. 12.95x (ISBN 0-521-09947-1). Cambridge U Pr.

Consumer Economics. Lewis Mandell. 448p. 1980. pap. text ed. 15.95 (ISBN 0-574-19290-5, 13-2290); instr's guide avail. (ISBN 0-574-19291-3, 13-2291). SRA.

Consumer Economics. James F. Niss & Melvin H. Smith. (Illus.). 224p. 1974. pap. 9.95 ref. ed. (ISBN 0-13-169441-3). P-H.

Consumer Education in Practice. Elsie Fetterman & Charles Klamkin. LC 75-38976. 1976. text ed. 12.00 o.p. (ISBN 0-471-25780-X); pap. text ed. 10.95 (ISBN 0-471-25781-8). Wiley.

Consumer Education in the Human Services. Gartner. (Pergamon Policy Studies). 1979. 25.00 (ISBN 0-08-023708-8). Pergamon.

Consumer Education Learning Activities. Jerry Forkner & Gail Schatz. 64p. (Orig.). 1981. pap. 10.95 (ISBN 0-89994-252-0). Soc Sci Ed.

Consumer Education Sourcebook. Dorothy Lungmus et al. LC 80-11872. (Orig.). 1980. pap. 9.95 (ISBN 0-89994-246-6). Soc Sci Ed.

Consumer Finance. Louis J. De Salvo. LC 76-46450. 1977. pap. text ed. 15.95 (ISBN 0-471-04391-5); tchr's manual avail. (ISBN 0-471-02418-X). Wiley.

Consumer Finance: The Consumer Experience. David J. Ward & Robert M. Niendorf. 1978. text ed. 17.95 (ISBN 0-256-02035-3). Irwin.

Consumer Food Selection & Nutrition Information. Fredrica Rudell. LC 79-10149. (Praeger Special Studies). 188p. 1979. 21.95 (ISBN 0-03-047596-1). Praeger.

Consumer Guide -- Complete Guide to Used Cars, 1981. 1981. pap. 3.50 (ISBN 0-451-09785-8, E9785, Sig). NAL.

Consumer Guide Body Fitness & Shaping Program. Ed. by Consumer Guide. (Illus.). 384p. 1981. pap. 8.95 (ISBN 0-89104-206-7). A & W Pubs.

Consumer Guide-Do It Yourself Product Test Report. pap. 1.95 (ISBN 0-451-05881-X, J5881, Sig). NAL.

Consumer Guide-How It Works & How to Fix It. pap. 2.50 (ISBN 0-451-08874-3, E8874, Sig). NAL.

Consumer Guide: Nineteen Eighty-One Buying Guide. Ed. by Consumer Guide. 1981. pap. 3.50 (ISBN 0-451-09623-1, E9623, Sig). NAL.

Consumer Guide: Nineteen Eighty-One Cars. Ed. by Consumer Guide. 1981. pap. 3.50 (ISBN 0-451-09625-8, Sig). NAL.

Consumer Guide-Sewing Machine & Fabric Buying. pap. 1.95 (ISBN 0-451-05880-1, J5880, Sig). NAL.

Consumer Health: A Guide to Intelligent Decisions. 2nd ed. Harold J. Cornacchia & Stephen Barrett. LC 80-11515. (Illus.). 1980. pap. text ed. 12.95 (ISBN 0-8016-1037-0). Mosby.

Consumer Health Education: A Guide to Hospital-Based Programs. OCHE & Myra E. Madnick. LC 79-90381. 1980. text ed. 17.95 (ISBN 0-913654-61-2). Nursing Res.

Consumer Health Guides Display, 30 bks. 1980. prepack 178.50 (ISBN 0-8385-0199-0). ACC.

Consumer Health Information Source Book. Alan M. Rees & Blanche A. Young. (Consumer Health Information Publications Program Ser.). 480p. 1981. 32.50 (ISBN 0-8352-1336-6). Bowker.

Consumer Incomes in the United States. United States National Resources Committee. LC 75-174476. (FDR & the Era of the New Deal Ser). 104p. 1972. Repr. of 1938 ed. lib. bdg. 20.00 (ISBN 0-306-70386-6). Da Capo.

Consumer Information Handbook: Europe & North America. Hans B. Thorelli & Sarah V. Thorelli. LC 73-10953. (Special Studies). 526p. 1974. 24.95 (ISBN 0-275-07890-6). Praeger.

Consumer Input for Marketing Decisions: A Study of Corporate Departments for Consumer Affairs. Claes Fornell. LC 76-14397. 1976. text ed. 21.95 (ISBN 0-275-23480-0). Praeger.

Consumer Law: Cases & Materials. John A. Spanogle, Jr. & Ralph J. Rohner. LC 79-12301. (American Casebook Ser.). 693p. 1979. text ed. 18.95 (ISBN 0-8299-2046-3). West Pub.

Consumer Law in a Nutshell. 2nd ed. David G. Epstin & Steve H. Nickles. (Nutshell Ser.). 400p. 1981. pap. text ed. 6.95 (ISBN 0-8299-2130-3). West Pub.

Consumer Market Developments. Fairchild Market Research Division. (Fact File Ser). (Orig.). 1978. pap. 9.50 o.p. (ISBN 0-87005-250-0). Fairchild.

Consumer Market Developments. Fairchild Market Research Division. (Fact File Ser.). (Illus.). 100p. 1980. pap. 10.00 (ISBN 0-87005-350-7). Fairchild.

Consumer Math Cassettes. Ed. by F. Lee McFadden. (Illus.). (gr. 8-10). 1979. manual & cassettes 169.95 (ISBN 0-917792-01-7). Math Hse.

Consumer Math Series, 7 bks. David H. Knowles. 1972. pap. 9.00 ea. (ISBN 0-8449-0200-4). Learning Line.

Consumer Mathematics. Charles A. Nickerson & Ingeborg A. Nickerson. (General Business Ser.). 325p. 1981. pap. text ed. 13.95 (ISBN 0-675-08071-1). Merrill.

Consumer Movement. James S. Haskins. LC 74-11351. 128p. (gr. 9 up). 1975. PLB 5.90 o.p. (ISBN 0-531-02794-5). Watts.

Consumer Product Safety Act Course Handbook. (Litigation & Administrative Practice Course Handbook Ser., 1977-78: Vol. 103). 1977. pap. 20.00 o.p. (ISBN 0-685-86092-2, H4-3852). PLI.

Consumer Protection: A Symposium. Ed. by Albert I. Clovis et al. LC 72-6757. 1972. Repr. of 1968 ed. lib. bdg. 15.00 (ISBN 0-306-70524-9). Da Capo.

Consumer Protection Experiments in Sweden. Donald B. King. LC 73-89036. iv, 116p. (Orig.). 1974. pap. text ed. 10.00x (ISBN 0-8377-0728-5). Rothman.

Consumer Protection for Boat Users. A. A. Painter. 104p. 1980. 12.00x (ISBN 0-245-53450-4, Pub. by Nautical England). State Mutual Bk.

Consumer Protection Guide, 1978. Joseph Rosenbloom. LC 77-84961. 1978. pap. 4.95 (ISBN 0-02-695740-X). Macmillan Info.

Consumer Protection: Implications for the International Trade, Report No. 789. Ed. by E. Patrick McGuire. (Illus.). vii, 63p. (Orig.). 1980. pap. 15.00 (ISBN 0-8237-0225-1). Conference Bd.

Consumer Protection Legislation & the Food Industry. Melvin J. Hinich & Richard Staelin. (Policy Studies). 1980. text ed. 16.25 (ISBN 0-08-025093-9). Pergamon.

Consumer Reports: The 1980 Buying Guide. Consumer Reports Editors. 1979. 3.50 o.p. (ISBN 0-385-15919-6). Doubleday.

Consumer Skills. Irene Oppenheim. 1977. 10.60 (ISBN 0-87002-184-2); tchr's guide 5.00 (ISBN 0-87002-186-9); student guide 4.40 (ISBN 0-87002-267-9). Bennett IL.

Consumer Sourcebook, 2 vols. 3rd ed. Ed. by Paul Wasserman & Jean Morgan. 1800p. 1981. Set. 78.00 (ISBN 0-8103-0383-3). Gale.

Consumer Sourcebook: A Directory & Guide, 2 vols. 2nd ed. Ed. by Paul Wasserman & Jean Morgan. LC 77-279. 1978. 68.00 set o.p. (ISBN 0-8103-0382-5). Gale.

Consumer Survival Notebook. Frieda Carrol. LC 80-70456. 1980. pap. 5.95 (ISBN 0-9605246-2-2). Biblio Pr GA.

Consumer Tactics Manual: How to Get Action on Your Complaints. John Dorfman. LC 80-65987. 1980. 9.95 (ISBN 0-689-11105-3); pap. 6.95 (ISBN 0-689-11115-0). Atheneum.

Consumer: The Art of Buying Wisely. John R. Wish et al. LC 77-13030. (Illus.). 1978. text ed. 15.95 (ISBN 0-13-169102-3). P-H.

Consumerism: A New Force in Society. Mary G. Jones & David M. Gardner. LC 76-10106. (Illus.). 1976. 18.95 (ISBN 0-669-00705-6). Lexington Bks.

Consumerism in the United States: An Inter-Industry Analysis. Ed. by Joel R. Evans. 31.95 (ISBN 0-03-056846-3). Praeger.

Consumerism: Search for the Consumer Interest. 3rd ed. Ed. by David A. Aaker & George S. Day. LC 77-83163. (Illus.). 1978. 17.95 (ISBN 0-02-900050-5); pap. text ed. 9.95 (ISBN 0-02-900040-8). Free Pr.

Consumers & the Market: An Introductory Analysis. Roger M. Swagler. 1979. pap. 8.95x (ISBN 0-669-01692-6). Heath.

Consumers & the Regulators. T. Gregory Kane. 123p. 1980. pap. text ed. 10.95x (ISBN 0-920380-60-3, Pub. by Inst Res Pub Canada). Renouf.

Consumer's Book of Health: Advice on Stretching Your Health Care Dollar. Jordan Braverman. LC 80-53186. 256p. (Orig.). 1981. 11.95 (ISBN 0-7216-1930-4); pap. 6.95 (ISBN 0-7216-1935-5). Saunders.

Consumer's Energy Handbook. Peter Norback & Craig Norback. 272p. 1981. 19.95 (ISBN 0-442-26066-0); pap. 14.95 (ISBN 0-442-26067-9). Van Nos Reinhold.

Consumer's Guide to Cosmetics. Science Action Coalition. LC 79-7193. (Illus.). 384p. 1980. pap. 3.95 (ISBN 0-385-13503-3, Anch). Doubleday.

Consumer's Guide to Fighting Back. Morris J. Bloomstein. LC 76-12428. 1976. 7.95 (ISBN 0-396-07321-2). Dodd.

Consumer's Guide to Life Insurance. J. Tracy Oehlbeck. (Orig.). 1975. pap. 1.75 o.s.i. (ISBN 0-515-03836-9). Jove Pubns.

Consumer's Guide to Personal Computing & Microcomputers. 2nd ed. Stephen Freiberger & Paul Chew, Jr. 208p. 1980. pap. 8.95 (ISBN 0-8104-5116-6). Hayden.

Consumers Index to Product Evaluations & Information Sources, 1980 Annual. 1981. 59.50 (ISBN 0-87650-130-7). Pierian.

Consumers Index to Product Evaluations & Information Sources: 1979 Annual. 1980. 59.50 (ISBN 0-87650-126-9). Pierian.

Consumers' Management. rev. ed. Margaret Raines. Orig. Title: Managing Livingtime. (Illus.). (gr. 9-12). 1973. text ed. 14.32 (ISBN 0-87002-123-0); tchr's guide avail. (ISBN 0-685-06849-8). Bennett IL.

Consumer's Nineteen Seventy-Eight Guide to Wholesale Prescription Drug Prices. Ed. by Kenwood Spriggle. LC 77-92884. (First annual suppl. 1980). 1978. spiral bdg. 8.95x (ISBN 0-938686-00-3). H Spriggle.

Consumer's Union Guide to Consumer Service. Consumer's Union. 1981. write for info. Little.

Consumers Union Report on Life Insurance: A Guide to Planning & Buying the Protection You Need. Consumer Reports Editors. 384p. 1981. 14.95 (ISBN 0-03-059109-0); pap. 7.95 (ISBN 0-03-059108-2). HR&W.

Consuming Public. Ed. by Grant S. McClellan. (Reference Shelf Ser: Vol. 40, No. 3). 1968. 6.25 (ISBN 0-8242-0102-7). Wilson.

Consumption Economics. M. C. Burk. 1968. prepub. 13.25 (ISBN 0-471-12370-6, Pub. by Wiley). Krieger.

Consumption Patterns in Eastern & Western Europe. Vera Cao-Pinna & Stanislav S. Shatalin. 1979. 37.00 (ISBN 0-08-021808-3). Pergamon.

Consumptive Use of Water. Compiled By American Society of Civil Engineers. 232p. 1974. pap. text ed. 10.75 (ISBN 0-87262-068-9). Am Soc Civil Eng.

Contact: A Guide to Writing Skills. Robert T. Mundhenk & William R. Siebenschuh. LC 77-73468. (Illus.). 1977. pap. text ed. 10.50 (ISBN 0-395-25110-9); inst. manual 0.25 (ISBN 0-395-25111-7). HM.

Contact: A Textbook in Applied Communications. 3rd ed. C. Howard et al. 1979. pap. 9.95 (ISBN 0-13-169052-3). P-H.

Contact & Discontinuity: Some Conventions of Speech & Action on the Greek Tragic Stage. Donald Mastronarde. (University of California Publications in Classical Studies: Vol. 21). 1979. pap. 14.50x (ISBN 0-520-09601-0). U of Cal Pr.

Contact Counseling. Len Sperry & Lee R. Hess. (Illus.). 240p. 1974. text ed. 11.95 (ISBN 0-201-07116-9). A-W.

Contact English: Contact 1. Colin Granger & Tony Hicks. 1977. 5.95x (ISBN 0-435-28371-5); tchr's manual 14.95x (ISBN 0-435-28370-7); three tapes 72.00 (ISBN 0-435-28372-3); three cassettes 60.00 (ISBN 0-435-28373-1). Heinemann Ed.

Contact Lens Design Tables. Janet Stone & Anthony Musset. 1981. text ed. price not set. Butterworth.

Contact Lens Practice: Hard & Flexible Lenses. 2nd ed. Robert B. Mandell. (Illus.). 840p. 1980. text ed. 33.75 (ISBN 0-398-03059-6). C C Thomas.

Contact Lenses, 2 vols. 2nd ed. J. Stone & A. Philips. LC 80-40981. 1980. Vol. I. 79.95 ea. (ISBN 0-407-93270-4). Vol.2 (ISBN 0-407-93271-2). Butterworths.

Contact Lenses: A Handbook for Patients. H. W. Roth & M. Roth-Wittig. Tr. by D. L. MacKeen. (Illus.). 75p. 1980. pap. text ed. 7.95 (ISBN 0-06-142301-7, Harper Medical). Har-Row.

Contact, Negotiation, & Conflict: An Ethnohistory of the Eastern Dakota, 1819-1839. John S. Wozniak. LC 78-62248. 1978. pap. text ed. 9.00 (ISBN 0-8191-0569-4). U Pr of Amer.

Contact Problems in the Classical Theory of Elasticity. G. M. Gladwell. (Mechanics of Elastic & Viscoelastic Solids Ser.). 716p. 1980. 60.00x (ISBN 9-0286-0440-5); pap. 35.00x (ISBN 9-0286-0760-9). Sijthoff & Noordhoff.

Contact: The First Four Minutes. Leonard Zunin & Natalie Zunin. 1972. 7.95 o.p. (ISBN 0-8402-1288-7). Nash Pub.

Contact: The First Four Minutes. Leonard Zunin & Natalie Zunin. 1975. pap. 2.50 (ISBN 0-345-28662-6). Ballantine.

Contacts: Langue et Culture Francaises. Jean-Paul Valette & Rebecca Valette. LC 75-32873. 1976. text ed. 17.35 (ISBN 0-395-20690-1); tchrs. ed. 18.40 (ISBN 0-395-20689-8); wkbk. cahier d'exercices 5.55 (ISBN 0-395-20692-8). HM.

Contacts: Langue et Culture Francaises. 2nd ed. Jean-Paul Valette & Rebecca Valette. (Illus.). 528p. 1981. text ed. 18.00 (ISBN 0-395-29328-6); tchrs. ed. 19.00 (ISBN 0-395-29329-4); wkbk 5.55 (ISBN 0-395-29330-8); reel-to-reel 250.00 (ISBN 0-395-29331-6); write for info. sample cassette (ISBN 0-395-29332-4). HM.

Container & Hanging Gardens. 96p. 1977. pap. 3.98 ea.; midwest-northeast ed. (ISBN 0-917102-15-0); pap. west ed. (ISBN 0-917102-14-2); pap. south ed. (ISBN 0-917102-16-9). Ortho.

Container Planting. (Countryside Outdoor Gardening Books Ser.). 1977. pap. 0.98 o.p. (ISBN 0-307-11914-9, Golden Pr). Western Pub.

Container Systems. Eric Rath. LC 72-13139. (Materials Handling & Packaging Ser.). 608p. 1973. 49.50 (ISBN 0-471-70921-2, Pub. by Wiley-Interscience). Wiley.

Containment & Change: Two Dissenting Views of American Society & Foreign Policy in the New Revolutionary Age. Carl Oglesby & Richard Shaull. Orig. Title: Third World Revolution, Orig. 1967. cloth o.p. 5.95 o.s.i. (ISBN 0-02-592610-1); pap. 1.45 o.s.i. (ISBN 0-02-088090-1). Macmillan.

Containment & Siting of Nuclear Power Plants. (Illus., Orig.). 1967. pap. 37.50 (ISBN 92-0-020167-9, IAEA). Unipub.

Containment: Documents on American Policy & Strategy 1945-1950. Thomas Etzold & John L. Gaddis. LC 77-20024. 1978. 27.50x (ISBN 0-231-04398-8); pap. 10.00x (ISBN 0-231-04399-6). Columbia U Pr.

Containment of Urban England. Peter Hall et al. (Political & Economic Planning Ser.). (Illus.). 1977. pap. text ed. 42.50x o.p. (ISBN 0-04-352066-9). Allen Unwin.

Contaminant. Leonard Reiffel. 1980. pap. 2.50 o.s.i. (ISBN 0-440-11473-X). Dell.

Contamination Control in Trace Element Analysis. Morris Zief & James W. Mitchell. LC 76-16837. (Chemical Analysis Ser.: Vol. 47). 336p. 1976. 37.50 (ISBN 0-471-61169-7, Pub. by Wiley-Interscience). Wiley.

Contando Para Divirtirme. Philip Mann. Tr. by Georgian Kreps from Eng. (Shape Board Play Books). Orig. Title: Counting for Fun. (Illus.). 14p. (Span.). (ps-3). 1981. bds. 3.50 plastic com bdg (ISBN 0-89828-203-9, 5003SP). Tuffy Bks.

Contemplation in a World of Action. Thomas Merton. 400p. 1973. pap. 3.95 (ISBN 0-385-02550-5, Im). Doubleday.

Contemplation of Sinners. LC 75-315474. (English Experience Ser.: No. 645). 200p. 1974. Repr. of 1499 ed. 17.50 (ISBN 90-221-0645-4). Walter J Johnson.

Contemplation: The Activity of Mystical Consciousness. 2nd ed. Helen Brungardt. 72p. 1980. pap. 3.00 (ISBN 0-87707-220-5). Red Earth.

Contemplative Christianity. Aelred Graham. 1975. 6.95 (ISBN 0-8164-0269-8). Crossroad NY.

Contemplative Man; or, the History of Christopher Crab, Esq., of North Wales, 1771, 2 vols. in 1. Herbert Lawrence. (Flowering of the Novel, 1740-1775 Ser: Vol. 96). 1974. lib. bdg. 50.00 (ISBN 0-8240-1195-3). Garland Pub.

Contemplative Prayer. Thomas Merton. 1971. pap. 1.95 (ISBN 0-385-09219-9, Im). Doubleday.

Contemporaries, from the Nineteenth Century to the Present. rev. ed. Alfred Kazin. 500p. 1981. 17.95 (ISBN 0-8180-1131-9); pap. 9.95 (ISBN 0-8180-1132-7). Horizon.

Contemporary Accounting Theory. E. S. Hendrickson & B. P. Budge. LC 73-81294. 1973. pap. 9.95 (ISBN 0-8221-0116-5). CBI Pub.

Contemporary Aesthetics. Ed. by Matthew Lipman. LC 73-76197. 1973. 28.50x (ISBN 0-89197-711-2); pap. text ed. 8.95x (ISBN 0-89197-712-0). Irvington.

Contemporary Africa: Geography & Change. C. Knight & J. Newman. 1976. 22.95 (ISBN 0-13-170035-9). P-H.

Contemporary African Art in South Africa. E. J. De Jager. (Illus.). 168p. 1973. text ed. 22.50x o.p. (ISBN 0-86977-025-X). Verry.

Contemporary African Arts. Maude Wahlman. LC 74-77117. (Illus.). 124p. 1974. pap. 5.00 (ISBN 0-914868-00-4, 25520-4). Field Mus.

Contemporary Agricultural Marketing. Ed. by Irving Dubov. LC 67-29414. 1968. 13.50x (ISBN 0-87049-082-6). U of Tenn Pr.

Contemporary American Criticism. James C. Bowman. 330p. 1980. Repr. of 1926 ed. lib. bdg. 35.00 (ISBN 0-8495-0457-0). Arden Lib.

Contemporary American Economic & Political Problems. Wesley M. Bagby. LC 80-22510. 296p. 1981. text ed. 19.95 (ISBN 0-88229-328-1); pap. text ed. 9.95 (ISBN 0-88229-765-1). Nelson-Hall.

Contemporary American Literature & Religion. Halford E. Luccock. 300p. 1980. Repr. of 1934 ed. lib. bdg. 30.00 (ISBN 0-89984-324-7). Century Bookbindery.

Contemporary American Novelists. Harry T. Moore. LC 64-20254. (Crosscurrents-Modern Critiques Ser.). 1966. pap. 7.95 (ISBN 0-8093-0195-4). S Ill U Pr.

Contemporary American Novelists. Ed. by Harry T. Moore. LC 64-20254. (Crosscurrents-Modern Critiques Ser.). 252p. 1964. 10.95 (ISBN 0-8093-0141-5). S Ill U Pr.

Contemporary American Poetry. 2nd ed. A. Poulin, Jr. 1975. pap. text ed. 9.95 o.p. (ISBN 0-395-18618-8). HM.

Contemporary American Poetry. Ed. by Miller Williams. (Illus.). 256p. 1972. pap. text ed. 7.95 (ISBN 0-394-31625-8). Random.

Contemporary American Poetry: A Checklist. Lloyd Davis & Robert Irwin. LC 75-19028. 1975. 10.00 (ISBN 0-8108-0832-3). Scarecrow.

Contemporary American Short Stories. Ed. by Douglas Angus & Sylvia Angus. 1978. pap. 2.50 (ISBN 0-449-30832-4, Prem). Fawcett.

Contemporary American Theatre Critics: A Dictionary & Anthology of Their Works. M. F. Comtois & Lynn F. Miller. LC 77-23063. 1977. 40.00 (ISBN 0-8108-1057-3). Scarecrow.

Contemporary Analytic Geometry. Thomas L. Wade & Howard E. Taylor. LC 79-22955. 338p. 1980. Repr. of 1969 ed. write for info (ISBN 0-89874-034-7). Krieger.

Contemporary Animal Learning Theory. A. Dickinson. (Problems in the Behavioral Sciences Ser.). (Illus.). 180p. 1981. 27.50 (ISBN 0-521-23469-7); pap. 9.95 (ISBN 0-521-29962-4). Cambridge U Pr.

Contemporary Anthropology: An Anthology. Daniel G. Bates & Susan H. Lees. 332p. 1981. pap. 8.95 (ISBN 0-394-32043-3). Knopf.

Contemporary Approach to the Middle Game. Aleksei Suetin. 1976. 18.95 (ISBN 0-7134-3123-7, Pub. by Batsford England). David & Charles.

Contemporary Approaches to Ibsen, Vol. II. Daniel Haakonsen. (Ibsen Yearbook). 210p. 1980. 22.00x (ISBN 82-00-01937-3). Universitet.

Contemporary Archaeology: A Guide to Theory & Contributions. Ed. by Mark P. Leone. LC 79-156779. 476p. 1972. pap. 12.95x (ISBN 0-8093-0534-8). S Ill U Pr.

Contemporary Architectural Drawing: Residential & Commercial. Frank R. Dagostino. 1977. 17.95 (ISBN 0-87909-132-0). Reston.

Contemporary Art in Europe. S. G. Benjamin. Ed. by H. Barbara Weinberg. LC 75-28868. (Art Experiences in Late 19th Century America Ser.: Vol. 4). (Illus.). 1976. Repr. of 1877 ed. lib. bdg. 60.00 (ISBN 0-8240-2228-9). Garland Pub.

Contemporary Art in Latin America. G. Chase. LC 70-78890. 1970. 9.95 o.s.i. (ISBN 0-02-905340-4). Free Pr.

Contemporary Art Nineteen Forty-Two to Seventy-Two: Collection of the Albright-Knox Art Gallery. Ed. by Ethel Moore. LC 70-189296. (Illus.). 1972. 18.00 (ISBN 0-914782-28-2, Pub. by Albright-Knox Art Gallery). C E Tuttle.

Contemporary Astronomy. Edward J. Devinney, Jr. et al. (Physical Science Ser). 288p. 1975. text ed. 19.95x (ISBN 0-675-08727-9). Merrill.

Contemporary Australian-American Relations. Dennis L. Cuddy. LC 80-65615. 155p. 1981. perfect bdg. 12.95 (ISBN 0-86548-027-3). Century Twenty One.

Contemporary Authors. Ann Evory. (New Revision Ser.: Vol. 2). 500p. 1981. 58.00 (ISBN 0-8103-1931-4). Gale.

Contemporary Authors. Ed. by Ann Evory. (New Revisions Ser.: No. 3). 500p. 1981. 58.00 (ISBN 0-8103-1932-2). Gale.

Contemporary Authors: A Bibliographical Guide to Current Writers in Fiction, General Nonfiction, Poetry, Journalism, Drama, Motion Pictures, Television, & Other Fields. Ed. by Frances C. Locher & Ann Evory. Incl. Vols. 1-4. rev. ed. 1967. (ISBN 0-8103-0000-1); Vols. 5-8. rev. ed. 1969. (ISBN 0-8103-0001-X); Vols. 9-12. rev. ed. 1974. (ISBN 0-8103-0002-8); Vols. 13-16. rev. ed. 1975. (ISBN 0-8103-0027-3); Vol. 17-20. rev. ed. 1976. (ISBN 0-8103-0032-X); Vols. 21-24. rev. ed. 1976. (ISBN 0-8103-0033-8); Vols. 25-28. rev. ed. 1977. (ISBN 0-8103-0034-6); Vols. 29-32. rev. ed. 1978. (ISBN 0-685-59670-2); Vols. 33-36. rev. ed. 1978. (ISBN 0-8103-0014-1); Vols. 37-40. rev. ed. 1979. (ISBN 0-8103-0016-8); Vols. 41-44. rev. ed. 1979. (ISBN 0-8103-0041-9); Vols. 45-48. 1974. (ISBN 0-8103-0020-6); Vols. 49-52. 1974. (ISBN 0-8103-0024-9); Vols. 53-56. 1975. (ISBN 0-8103-0022-2); Vols. 57-60. 1976. (ISBN 0-8103-0026-5); Vols. 61-64. 1976. (ISBN 0-8103-0028-1); Vols. 69-72. 1978. (ISBN 0-8103-0030-3); Vols. 73-76. (ISBN 0-8103-0031-1); Vol. 77-80. 1978 (ISBN 0-8103-0039-7); Vols. 81-84. 1979 (ISBN 0-8103-0046-X); Vols. 85-88. 1979 (ISBN 0-8103-0047-8); Vols. 89-92. 1980 (ISBN 0-8103-0048-6); Vols. 93-96. 1980 (ISBN 0-8103-0049-4). LC 62-52046. sold in 4 vol. units 58.00 ea. Gale.

Contemporary Authors: A Bio-Bibliographical Guide to Current Writers in Fiction, General Non-Fiction, Poetry, Journalism, Drama, Motion Pictures, Television & Other Fields. Ed. by Frances C. Locher. LC 62-52046. (Contemporary Author Ser.: Vols. 97-100). 900p. 1980. 58.00 (ISBN 0-8103-1900-4). Gale.

Contemporary Authors: A Bio-Bibliographical Guide to Current Writers in Fiction, General Non-Fiction, Poetry, Journalism, Drama, Motion Pictures, Television & Other Fields, Vol. 101. Ed. by Frances C. Locher. LC 62-52046. 900p. 1981. 58.00 (ISBN 0-8103-1901-2). Gale.

Contemporary Biology. 2nd ed. Mary E. Clark. LC 77-25553. (Illus.). 1979. 18.95 o.p. (ISBN 0-7216-2598-3). Saunders.

Contemporary Biology. Sebastian Haskel & David Sygoda. (gr. 9-12). 1977. pap. text ed. 6.00 (ISBN 0-87720-057-2). AMSCO Sch.

Contemporary Black Drama: Raisin in the Sun, Purlie Victorious, Funnyhouse of a Negro, Dutchman, Blues for Mister Charlie, Day of Absence, Happy Ending, Gentleman Caller, No Place to Be Somebody. Ed. by Clinton S. Oliver & Stephanie Sills. 1971. pap. text ed. 10.95x (ISBN 0-684-41432-5, ScribC). Scribner.

Contemporary Black Thought: Alternative Analyses in Social & Behavioral Science. Ed. by Molefi K. Asante & Abdulai S. Vandi. LC 80-15186. (Sage Focus Editions Ser.: Vol. 26). (Illus.). 302p. 1980. 18.95 (ISBN 0-8039-1500-4). Sage.

Contemporary Black Thought: Alternative Analyses in Social & Behavioral Science. Ed. by Molefi K. Asante & Abdulai S. Vandi. LC 80-15186. (Sage Focus Editions: Vol. 26). (Illus.). 302p. 1980. pap. 9.95 (ISBN 0-8039-1501-2). Sage.

Contemporary Brazil: Issues in Economic & Political Development. Ed. by H. Jon Rosenbaum & William G. Tyler. LC 73-180851. (Special Studies in International Economics & Development). 1972. 28.00x (ISBN 0-275-28285-9). Irvington.

Contemporary British Drama: An Outsider's View. A. D. Choudhuri. 1976. 10.50 o.p. (ISBN 0-8426-0883-4). Verry.

Contemporary British Novelists. Ed. by Charles Shapiro. LC 65-19772. (Crosscurrents-Modern Critiques Ser.). 182p. 1965. 10.95 (ISBN 0-8093-0176-8). S Ill U Pr.

Contemporary British Novelists. Ed. by Charles Shapiro. LC 65-19772. (Arcturus Books Paperbacks). 185p. 1969. pap. 5.95 (ISBN 0-8093-0353-1). S Ill U Pr.

Contemporary British Philosophy, Vol. 4. H. D. Lewis. (Muirhead Library of Philosophy). 1976. text ed. 24.75x (ISBN 0-391-00716-5). Humanities.

Contemporary British Philosophy Series One & Two, 2 Vols. in 1. Ed. by John H. Muirhead. (Muirhead Library of Philosophy). 1924. text ed. 41.75x (ISBN 0-04-192011-2). Humanities.

Contemporary Business. 2nd ed. Louis E. Boone & David L. Kurtz. 1979. 18.95 (ISBN 0-03-043646-X). Dryden Pr.

Contemporary Business: Challenges & Opportunities. Eddie Easley et al. (Illus.). 1978. pap. text ed. 13.95 (ISBN 0-8299-0166-3); study guide 6.50 (ISBN 0-8299-0218-X); instrs.' manual avail. (ISBN 0-8299-0476-X); transparency masters avail. (ISBN 0-8299-0477-8). West Pub.

Contemporary Business Law: Principles & Cases. Ralph Hoeber et al. Ed. by Gordon Severance. (Illus.). 1980. text ed. 19.95 (ISBN 0-07-029160-8); instr's manual 6.95 (ISBN 0-07-029161-6); test bank 13.95 (ISBN 0-07-029163-2); study guide 6.95 (ISBN 0-07-029162-4); student CPA examination suppl. 1.50 (ISBN 0-07-029164-0). McGraw.

Contemporary Business Writing. Michael E. Adelstein. 1971. text ed. 11.95 (ISBN 0-394-30373-3). Random.

Contemporary Cases Consumer Behavior. Blackwell et al. 1977. 10.95. Dryden Pr.

Contemporary Cases in Marketing. 2nd ed. 1979. 11.95 (ISBN 0-03-045436-0). Dryden Pr.

Contemporary Cash Management: Principles, Practices, Perspectives. Paul J. Beehler. LC 77-18998. (Systems & Controls for Financial Management Ser.). 1978. 27.95 (ISBN 0-471-06172-7). Ronald Pr.

Contemporary Ceramic Formulas. John W. Conrad. (Illus.). 256p. 1981. 17.95 (ISBN 0-686-65889-2). Macmillan.

Contemporary Ceramic Techniques. John W. Conrad. 1979. 17.95 (ISBN 0-13-169540-1). P-H.

Contemporary Chemistry. Saul L. Geffner & Gerard A. Kass. (Orig.). (gr. 10-12). 1981. pap. text ed. price not set (ISBN 0-87720-100-5). AMSCO Sch.

Contemporary Chemistry. John E. Hearst & James B. Ifft. LC 75-28230. (Illus.). 1976. text ed. 22.95x (ISBN 0-7167-0172-3). W H Freeman.

Contemporary Chicano Theatre. Roberto J. Garza. 1975. 16.95x (ISBN 0-268-00709-8); pap. 5.95x (ISBN 0-268-00710-1). U of Notre Dame Pr.

Contemporary Chinese Politics. James C. Wang. (Illus.). 1980. pap. text ed. 10.50 (ISBN 0-13-169987-3). P-H.

Contemporary Chinese Research Mathematics, Vol. 1: Bibliography of Mathematics Published in Communist China During the Period 1949-1960. Compiled by C. K. Tsao. 83p. 1961. 1.00 o.p. (ISBN 0-686-66979-7, CCBIB). Am Math.

Contemporary Chinese Research Mathematics, Vol. 2: A Report on Chinese-English Mathematical Dictionaries. S. H. Gould. 1964. 1.00 (ISBN 0-8218-0016-7, CED). Am Math.

Contemporary Christologies: A Jewish Response. Eugene B. Borowitz. LC 80-81051. 224p. (Orig.). 1980. pap. 7.95 (ISBN 0-8091-2305-3). Paulist Pr.

Contemporary Classics: Furniture of the Masters. Charles Gandy & Susan Zimmerman-Stidham. (Architectural Record Ser.). (Illus.). 160p. 1981. 19.75 (ISBN 0-07-022760-8, P&RB). McGraw.

Contemporary Collective Bargaining. 3rd ed. Harold W. Davey. LC 74-152315. 1972. ref. ed. 18.95 (ISBN 0-13-169607-6). P-H.

Contemporary College Physics. Donald E. Tilley. LC 78-57146. 1979. pap. text ed. 22.95 (ISBN 0-8053-9290-4); instr's guide 3.95 (ISBN 0-8053-9291-2). Benjamin-Cummings.

Contemporary College Reader. 2nd ed. Joyce S. Steward. 1981. pap. 7.95x (ISBN 0-673-15404-1). Scott F.

Contemporary College Speech. Albert E. Grzebien. LC 74-6010. (Illus.). 229p. 1974. pap. text ed. 10.15 (ISBN 0-913310-35-2). PAR Inc.

Contemporary Composers on Contemporary Music. Ed. by Elliot Schwartz & Barney Childs. (Music Reprint Ser., 1978). 1978. Repr. of 1967 ed. lib. bdg. 32.50 (ISBN 0-306-77587-5). Da Capo.

Contemporary Concert Music by Women: A Directory of the Composers & Their Works. Compiled by Judith L. Zaimont & Karen Famera. LC 80-39572. (Illus.). 320p. 1981. lib. bdg. 25.00 (ISBN 0-313-22921-X, ZCM/). Greenwood.

Contemporary Contrabass. Bertram Turetzky. (New Instrumentation Ser: Vol. 1). (Illus., Orig.). 1974. pap. 12.95x (ISBN 0-520-02291-2). U of Cal Pr.

Contemporary Corrections: A Concept in Search of Content. Ed. by Benjamin Frank. LC 73-20072. 272p. 1974. pap. 10.95 (ISBN 0-87909-151-7). Reston.

Contemporary Cost Accounting & Control. 2nd ed. George J. Benston. LC 76-27552. 1977. pap. 9.95 (ISBN 0-8221-0186-6). CBI Pub.

Contemporary Criticism. Ed. by Malcolm Bradbury & David Palmer. (Stratford-Upon-Avon Studies: No. 12). 219p. 1970. pap. text ed. 14.25x (ISBN 0-8419-5818-1). Holmes & Meier.

Contemporary Critiques of Religion. Kai Nielsen. Ed. by John Hick. LC 72-170200. (Philosophy of Religion Ser). 1972. 6.95 (ISBN 0-8164-1021-6). Crossroad NY.

Contemporary Decorative Arts. Philippe Garner. 224p. 1980. 27.50 (ISBN 0-87196-472-4). Facts on File.

Contemporary Developments in Nutrition. Bonnie S. Worthington-Roberts. LC 80-21557. (Illus.). 603p. 1980. pap. text ed. 17.95 (ISBN 0-8016-5627-3). Mosby.

Contemporary Drama & the Popular Dramatic Tradition in England. Peter Davison. LC 79-55526. 184p. 1981. text ed. 26.00x (ISBN 0-06-491617-0). B&N.

Contemporary Drama, Fifteen Plays. Ed. by E. Bradlee Watson & Benfield Pressey. Incl. Hedda Gabler. Henrik Ibsen; Importance of Being Earnest. Oscar Wilde; Uncle Vanya. Anton Chekhov; Dream Play. August Strindberg; Man & Superman. George B. Shaw; Riders to the Sea. John M. Synge; Henry Fourth. Luigi Pirandello; Ah, Wilderness. Eugene O'Neill; Blood Wedding. Federico Gracia Lorca; Murder in the Cathedral. T. S. Eliot; Purple Dust. Sean O'Casey; Skin of Our Teeth. Thornton Wilder; Come Back, Little Sheba. William Inge; Crucible. Arthur Miller; Look Homeward, Angel. Keti Frings. 577p. 1959. pap. text ed. 10.95x (ISBN 0-684-41478-3, ScribC). Scribner.

Contemporary Earth Science. Irving L. Horowitz. (Orig.). (gr. 10). 1976. pap. text ed. 6.00 (ISBN 0-87720-150-1). AMSCO Sch.

Contemporary Ecology of Arroyo Hondo, New Mexico. N. Edmund Kelley. (Arroyo Hondo Archaeological Ser.: Vol. 1). (Illus., Orig.). 1979. pap. 6.25 (ISBN 0-933452-01-2). Schol Am Res.

Contemporary Economic Analysis: Vol. 2, Papers Presented at the Conference of the Association of University Teachers of Economics 1978. Ed. by David Currie & Will Peters. 490p. 1980. 39.00x (ISBN 0-85664-803-5, Pub. by Croom Helm Ltd England). Biblio Dist.

Contemporary Economic Issues. rev. ed. Ed. by Neil W. Chamberlain. 1973. pap. text ed. 8.95x (ISBN 0-256-01427-2). Irwin.

Contemporary Economic Problems, 1979. Ed. by William J. Fellner. 1979. pap. 9.25 (ISBN 0-8447-1334-1). Am Enterprise.

Contemporary Economic Problems, 1980. Ed. by William Fellner. 1980. pap. 8.25 (ISBN 0-8447-3386-5). Am Enterprise.

Contemporary Economic Systems: A Comparative View. Gary M. Pickersgill & Joyce E. Pickersgill. (Illus.). 352p. 1974. ref. ed. 18.95x (ISBN 0-13-169342-5). P-H.

Contemporary Economics. 4th rev. ed. Milton H. Spencer. 1980. text ed. 18.95x (ISBN 0-87901-113-0); study guide 6.95 (ISBN 0-87901-109-2). Worth.

Contemporary Educational Psychology: Concepts, Issues & Applications. Robert C. Craig et al. LC 74-13462. 558p. 1975. pap. text ed. 23.50 (ISBN 0-471-18351-2). Wiley.

Contemporary England: 1914-1964. W. N. Medlicott. LC 67-26796. (Social & Economic History of England Ser.). 1976. pap. text ed. 12.95x (ISBN 0-582-48487-1). Longman.

Contemporary English in the Elementary School. 2nd ed. I. Tiedt & S. Tiedt. 1975. 17.95 (ISBN 0-13-169961-X). P-H.

Contemporary English Novel. Ed. by Malcolm Bradbury & David Palmer. LC 79-20447. (Stratford-Upon-Avon Studies: No. 18). 1980. text ed. 31.75x (ISBN 0-8419-0570-3); pap. text ed. 13.95x (ISBN 0-8419-0571-1). Holmes & Meier.

Contemporary Entrepreneurs: The Sociology of Residential Real Estate Agents. J. D. House. LC 76-52329. (Contributions in Sociology: No. 25). 1977. lib. bdg. 15.95x (ISBN 0-8371-9533-0, HCE/). Greenwood.

Contemporary Europe: A History. 4th ed. H. Stuart Hughes. (Illus.). 656p. 1976. Ref. Ed. 18.95 (ISBN 0-13-170019-7). P-H.

Contemporary Europe: Social Structures & Cultural Patterns. Ed. by Salvador Giner & Margaret S. Archer. (International Library of Sociology). 1978. 26.00x (ISBN 0-7100-8790-X); pap. 14.00 (ISBN 0-7100-8926-0). Routledge & Kegan.

Contemporary Explosion of Theology: Ecumenical Studies in Theology. Michael P. Ryan. LC 74-34125. 1975. 10.00 (ISBN 0-8108-0794-7). Scarecrow.

Contemporary Fiction in America & England, 1950-1970: A Guide to Information Sources. Ed. by Alfred F. Rosa & Paul A. Eschholz. LC 73-16990. (American Literature, English Literature, & World Literatures in English Information Guide Series: Vol. 10). 220p. 1976. 30.00 (ISBN 0-8103-1219-0). Gale.

Contemporary Financial Management. Charles R. Moyer & William Kretlow. (Illus.). 700p. 1981. text ed. 19.95 (ISBN 0-8299-0400-X). West Pub.

Contemporary French Literature: Essays by Justin O'Brien. Ed. by Leon S. Roudiez. LC 77-127052. 1971. 21.00 (ISBN 0-8135-0661-1). Rutgers U Pr.

Contemporary French Poetry. Tr. by Jethro Bithell. 227p. 1980. Repr. lib. bdg. 20.00 (ISBN 0-89760-041-X). Telegraph Bks.

Contemporary French Women Poets: A Bilingual Critical Anthology. Andree Chedid. Ed. by Carl W. Hermey. LC 76-3065. (Perivale Translation Series No. 4). 207p. 1977. pap. 6.95 (ISBN 0-912288-08-6). Perivale Pr.

Contemporary Games: a Directory & Bibliography Describing Play Situations or Simulations, Vol. 2. Ed. by Jean Belch. LC 72-6353. 1974. 65.00 (ISBN 0-8103-0969-6). Gale.

Contemporary German Philosophy, Vol. 1. Ed. by Darrel E. Christensen. 1980. text ed. 17.50x (ISBN 0-391-00983-4). Humanities.

Contemporary Greek Cinema. Mel Schuster. LC 78-20969. 1979. lib. bdg. 16.50 (ISBN 0-8108-1196-0). Scarecrow.

Contemporary Group Work. Charles D. Garvin. (P-H Ser. in Social Work Practice). (Illus.). 304p. 1981. text ed. 15.95 (ISBN 0-13-170233-5). P-H.

Contemporary Growth Therapies. Howard Clinebell. LC 80-24368. 304p. 1981. 10.95 (ISBN 0-687-09502-6). Abingdon.

Contemporary Gulf. Ed. by Surendra Bhutani. 1980. 12.00x (ISBN 0-8364-0667-2, Pub. by Academic India). South Asia Bks.

Contemporary Gymnastics. June Szypula & George Szypula. 1979. 6.95 o.p. (ISBN 0-8092-7702-6); pap. 3.95 (ISBN 0-8092-7701-8). Contemp Bks.

Contemporary Hindi Short Stories. Tr. by Jai Ratan. (Writers Workshop Saffronbird Ser.). 180p. 1975. 12.00 (ISBN 0-88253-518-8); pap. text ed. 4.80 (ISBN 0-88253-517-X). Ind-US Inc.

Contemporary Illusions People Live by. Hampton Starr. (Essential Knowledge Library). 1979. spiral bdg. 21.45 (ISBN 0-89266-170-4). Am Classical Coll Pr.

Contemporary Illustrators of Children's Books. Bertha Mahoney & Elinor Whitney. LC 79-185381. (Illus.). 1978. Repr. of 1930 ed. 34.00 (ISBN 0-8103-4308-8). Gale.

Contemporary Indian Philosophy. Basant K. Lal. 1979. 14.00x (ISBN 0-89684-012-3). South Asia Bks.

Contemporary Indian Philosophy. 2nd ed. Ed. by Sarvepelli Radhakrishnan & J. H. Muirhead. (Muirhead Library of Philosophy). 1963. Repr. of 1958 ed. text ed. 31.25x (ISBN 0-04-199004-8). Humanities.

Contemporary Indian Short Stories, 2 vols. Ed. by Bhabani Bhattacharya. 1967. Vol. 1. 2.50 (ISBN 0-88253-409-2); Vol. 2. 2.50 (ISBN 0-88253-327-4). Ind-US Inc.

Contemporary Indonesian-English Dictionary. A. Ed. Schmidgall-Tellings & Alan Stevens. LC 80-20994. 460p. 1981. 24.95x (ISBN 0-8214-0424-5); pap. 11.95 (ISBN 0-8214-0435-0). Ohio U Pr.

Contemporary Industrial Teaching. Ronald J. Baird. LC 78-185957. (Illus.). 200p. 1972. text ed. 9.28 (ISBN 0-87006-130-5). Goodheart.

Contemporary Industrialization: Spatial Analysis & Regional Analysis. Ed. by F. E. Hamilton. (Illus.). 1978. pap. text ed. 11.95 (ISBN 0-582-48592-4). Longman.

Contemporary International Law: A Concise Introduction. Werner Levi. 1978. lib. bdg. 28.50x (ISBN 0-89158-184-7); pap. text ed. 11.00x (ISBN 0-89158-187-1). Westview.

Contemporary Introduction to Logic with Applications. Codell K. Carter. 1977. text ed. 9.95 (ISBN 0-02-471500-X). Macmillan.

Contemporary Irish Poetry: An Anthology. Ed. by Anthony Bradley. 1980. 17.95 (ISBN 0-520-03389-2). U of Cal Pr.

Contemporary Issues in Accounting. Dhia Al Hashim & James W. Robertson. LC 79-9840. (ITT Key Issue Lecture Ser.). 296p. 1979. text ed. 12.50 (ISBN 0-672-97331-6); pap. text ed. 6.95 (ISBN 0-672-97332-4). Bobbs.

Contemporary Issues in Adolescent Development. John J. Conger. 522p. 1975. pap. text ed. 11.50 scp (ISBN 0-06-041363-8, HarpC). Harper-Row.

Contemporary Issues in American Democracy. 2nd ed. Eagleton Institute Of Politics. (gr. 11-12). 1969. text ed. 8.96 o.p. (ISBN 0-07-018717-7, W). McGraw.

Contemporary Issues in Bioethics. Tom L. Beauchamp & LeRoy Walters. 1978. 19.95x (ISBN 0-8221-0200-5). Dickenson.

Contemporary Issues in Canadian Personnel Administration. H. Jain. 1974. 14.95 o.p. (ISBN 0-13-170324-2); pap. 11.50 o.p. (ISBN 0-13-170316-1). P-H.

Contemporary Issues in Cost & Managerial Accounting: A Discipline in Transition. 3rd ed. Hector R. Anton et al. LC 77-74383. (Illus.). 1977. text ed. 18.95 (ISBN 0-395-25435-3). HM.

Contemporary Issues in Educational Psychology. 3rd ed. Harvey Clarizio et al. 1977. pap. text ed. 8.95x o.p. (ISBN 0-205-05627-X). Allyn.

Contemporary Issues in Educational Psychology. 4th ed. Harvey Clarizio et al. 1981. pap. text ed. 9.95 (ISBN 0-205-07331-X). Allyn.

Contemporary Issues in Human Resources Management. Fred E. Schuster. (Illus.). 496p. 1980. text ed. 21.95 (ISBN 0-8359-1005-9). Reston.

Contemporary Issues in Marketing Channels. Ed. by Robert F. Lusch & Paul H. Zinszer. 187p. 1979. 10.00 (ISBN 0-931880-00-9). U OK Ctr Econ.

Contemporary Issues in Political Theory. Robert B. Fowler & Jeffrey R. Orenstein. LC 76-7410. 288p. 1977. pap. text ed. 9.95x (ISBN 0-471-27032-6). Wiley.

Contemporary Italian Sociology: A Reader. Ed. by Diana Pinto. (Illus.). 224p. Date not set. price not set (ISBN 0-521-23738-6); pap. price not set (ISBN 0-521-28191-1). Cambridge U Pr.

Contemporary Japanese Budget Politics. John C. Campbell. 1977. 19.50x (ISBN 0-520-02573-3); pap. 6.95x (ISBN 0-520-04087-2, CAMPUS NO. 253). U of Cal Pr.

Contemporary Jogging. Jim Ferstle. LC 77-91153. 1978. 6.95 o.p. (ISBN 0-8092-7554-6); pap. 3.95 (ISBN 0-8092-7575-9). Contemp Bks.

Contemporary Labor Economics & Labor Relations. 2nd ed. Juanita M. Kreps et al. 496p. 1980. text ed. 21.95x (ISBN 0-534-00810-0). Wadsworth Pub.

Contemporary Labor Economics: Issues Analysis & Policies. 3rd ed. Juanita Kreps et al. 1974. 16.95x o.p. (ISBN 0-534-00303-6). Wadsworth Pub.

Contemporary Labor Relations. Philip Martin. 1979. pap. text ed. 8.95x (ISBN 0-534-00688-4). Wadsworth Pub.

Contemporary Lamps. Wallace W. Holbrook. (gr. 9 up). 1968. text ed. 13.28 (ISBN 0-87345-029-9). McKnight.

Contemporary Latin American Poetry. Ed. by Octavio Armand. 300p. (Orig.). 1981. price not set (ISBN 0-937406-09-0); pap. price not set (ISBN 0-937406-08-2); price not set limited ed. (ISBN 0-937406-10-4). Logbridge-Rhodes.

Contemporary Liquid Chromotography. Ed. by R. Scott. LC 74-15553. (Techniques of Chemistry Ser.: Vol. XI). 1976. 34.00 (ISBN 0-471-92900-X, Pub. by Wiley-Interscience). Wiley.

Contemporary Literary Criticism: Excerpts from Criticism of the Works of Today's Novelists, Poets, Playwrights, & Other Creative Writers. Ed. by Sharon Gunton. LC 76-38938. (Contemporary Literary Criticism Ser.: Vol. 17). 600p. 1981. 58.00 (ISBN 0-8103-0107-5). Gale.

Contemporary Literary Criticism: Excerpts from the Criticism of the Works of Today's Novelists, Poets,, Playwrights & Other Creative Writers, 15 vols. Ed. by Sharon Gunton. Incl. Vol. 1. 1973. (ISBN 0-8103-0100-8); Vol. 2. 1974. (ISBN 0-8103-0102-4); Vol. 3. 1975. (ISBN 0-8103-0104-0); Vol. 4. 1975. (ISBN 0-8103-0106-7); Vol. 5. 1976. (ISBN 0-8103-0108-3); Vol. 6. 1976. (ISBN 0-8103-0110-5); Vol. 7. 1977. (ISBN 0-8103-0112-1); Vol. 8. 1978. (ISBN 0-8103-0114-8); Vol. 9. 1978. (ISBN 0-685-92122-0); Vol. 10. 1979. (ISBN 0-8103-0118-0); Vol. 11. 1979 (ISBN 0-8103-0120-2); Vol. 12. 1979 (ISBN 0-8103-0122-9); Vol. 13. 1979 (ISBN 0-8103-0124-5); Vol. 14. 1980 (ISBN 0-8103-0101-6); Vol. 15. 1980 (ISBN 0-8103-0103-2). LC 76-38938. (Contemporary Literary Criticism Ser.). 58.00 ea. Gale.

Contemporary Literary Criticism, Vol. 16: Excerpts from Criticism of the Works of Today's Novelists, Poets, Playwrights & Other Creative Writers. Ed. by Sharon Gunton. LC 76-38938. (Contemporary Literary Criticism Ser.: Vol. 16). 600p. 1980. 58.00 (ISBN 0-8103-0105-9). Gale.

Contemporary Literary Criticism: Vol. 18, Excerpts from Criticism of the Works of Today's Novelists, Poets, Playwrights & Other Creative Writers. Ed. by Sharon Gunton. LC 76-38938. (Contemporary Literary Criticism Ser.: Vol. 17). 600p. 1981. 58.00 (ISBN 0-8103-0123-7). Gale.

Contemporary Living. Verdene Ryder. LC 78-23516. (Illus.). 1979. text ed. 13.20 (ISBN 0-87006-266-2); wkbk. 3.20 (ISBN 0-87006-280-8). Goodheart.

Contemporary Logic. Peter Longley. LC 80-1443. 178p. (Orig.). 1981. pap. text ed. 8.75 (ISBN 0-8191-1458-8). U Pr of Amer.

Contemporary Macroeconomics. 4th ed. Milton H. Spencer. (Illus.). text ed. 11.95x (ISBN 0-87901-114-9); study guide 4.95 (ISBN 0-87901-110-6). Worth.

Contemporary Management. 2nd ed. David R. Hampton. (Management Ser.). (Illus.). 528p. 1981. text ed. 19.95x (ISBN 0-07-025935-6); instructor's manual 7.95 (ISBN 0-07-025936-4); write for info study guide (ISBN 0-07-025937-2); test file 15.00 (ISBN 0-07-025938-0). McGraw.

Contemporary Management. F. T. Haner & James C. Ford. LC 72-95931. 1973. text ed. 17.95 (ISBN 0-675-08987-5). Merrill.

Contemporary Management Concepts. Bernard A. Deitzer et al. LC 79-11974. 1979. text ed. 18.50 (ISBN 0-88244-187-6). Grid Pub.

Contemporary Management Incidents. Bernard A. Deitzer & Karl A. Shilliff. LC 76-44998. (Management Ser.). 1977. pap. text ed. 9.95 (ISBN 0-88244-123-X). Grid Pub.

Contemporary Managerial Accounting: A Casebook. John K. Shank. (Illus.). 352p. 1981. 14.95 (ISBN 0-13-170357-9). P-H.

Contemporary Marketing. 3rd ed. Louis E. Boone & David L. Kurtz. 640p. 1980. 19.95 (ISBN 0-03-051391-X). Dryden Pr.

Contemporary Math. Frank Clark. LC 64-12131. (Illus.). (gr. 7 up). 1964. PLB 3.90 o.p. (ISBN 0-531-01650-1). Watts.

Contemporary Mathematics. 2nd ed. B. E. Meserve & Max A. Sobel. (Illus.). 1977. text ed. 18.95 (ISBN 0-13-170092-8). P-H.

Contemporary Mathematics. 3rd ed. Bruce E. Meserve & Max A. Sobel. (Illus.). 688p. 1981. text ed. 18.95 (ISBN 0-13-170076-6). P-H.

Contemporary Memoirs of Russia from the Year 1727 to 1744. Christof H. Von Manstein. (Russia Through European Eyes Ser). Repr. of 1856 ed. lib. bdg. 42.50 (ISBN 0-306-77027-X). Da Capo.

Contemporary Mexican Painting in a Time of Change. Shifra M. Goldman. LC 80-17107. 272p. 1981. text ed. 30.00x (ISBN 0-292-71061-5). U of Tex Pr.

Contemporary Mexico: Papers of the Fourth International Congress of Mexican History. Ed. by James W. Wilkie et al. 1976. 42.50x (ISBN 0-520-02798-1); pap. 16.75x (ISBN 0-520-02871-6, CAMPUS 144). U of Cal Pr.

Contemporary Microeconomics. 4th ed. Milton H. Spencer. 1980. text ed. 11.95x (ISBN 0-87901-115-7); study guide 4.95 (ISBN 0-87901-111-4). Worth.

Contemporary Military Strategy. 2nd ed. Morton H. Halperin. 1972. 8.95 o.p. (ISBN 0-571-04772-6, Pub. by Faber & Faber). Merrimack Bk Serv.

Contemporary Models of the Atomic Nucleus. P. E. Nemirovskii. 1963. 37.00 (ISBN 0-08-009840-1); pap. 22.00 (ISBN 0-08-013582-X). Pergamon.

Contemporary Monetary Economics Theory & Policy. Chaman L. Jain. LC 79-55682. (Illus.). 266p. (Orig.). 1981. text ed. 21.50 (ISBN 0-932126-02-2); pap. text ed. 17.50x (ISBN 0-932126-03-0). Graceway.

Contemporary Music & Music Cultures. Bruno Nettl et al. 304p. 1974. 14.95 (ISBN 0-13-170175-4). P-H.

Contemporary Music Education. Clifford K. Madsen & Terry L. Kuhn. LC 77-90672. (Illus.). 1978. pap. text ed. 7.50x (ISBN 0-88295-350-8). AHM Pub.

Contemporary Musician's Handbook & Dictionary. Larry Fotine. (Illus.). 1981. softcover 10.00 (ISBN 0-933830-03-3). Poly Tone.

Contemporary Native American Literature: A Selected & Partially Annotated Bibliography. Angeline Jacobson. LC 77-56114. 1977. lib. bdg. 13.50 (ISBN 0-8108-1031-X). Scarecrow.

Contemporary Newspaper Design: A Structural Approach. Mario R. Garcia. (Illus.). 240p. 1981. text ed. 25.95 (ISBN 0-13-170381-1); pap. text ed. 12.95 (ISBN 0-13-170373-0). P-H.

Contemporary Novel: A Checklist of Critical Literature on the British & American Novel Since 1945. Irving Adelman & Rita Dworkin. LC 72-4451. 1972. 20.50 (ISBN 0-8108-0517-0). Scarecrow.

Contemporary Obstetrics & Gynaecology. Geoffrey Chamberlin. (Illus.). 1977. 46.50x (ISBN 0-7198-2546-6). Intl Ideas.

Contemporary Oil Painters Handbook. Clifford Chieffo. LC 75-40302. (Illus.). 160p. 1976. 14.95 (ISBN 0-13-170167-3). P-H.

Contemporary Operations Management: Texts & Cases. Thomas M. Cook & Robert A. Russell. 1980. text ed. 21.95 (ISBN 0-13-170407-9). P-H.

Contemporary Operative Surgery. Ed. by Adrian Marston et al. (Illus.). 237p. 1979. text ed. 38.95x (ISBN 0-7198-2566-0). Intl Ideas.

Contemporary Optics for Scientists & Engineers. A. Nussbaum & R. Phillips. 1976. 27.95 (ISBN 0-13-170183-5). P-H.

Contemporary Perspectives in Organizational Behavior. Donald D. White. 500p. 1981. price not set (ISBN 0-205-07350-6); free (ISBN 0-205-07351-4). Allyn. Postponed.

Contemporary Perspectives in the Philosophy of Language. Ed. by Peter A. French et al. (Midwest Studies in Philosophy). 1977. 25.00x (ISBN 0-8166-0865-2); pap. 8.95x (ISBN 0-8166-0866-0). U of Minn Pr.

Contemporary Perspectives on European Integration: Attitudes, Nongovernmental Behavior & Collective Decision Making. Ed. by Leon Hurwitz. LC 79-6573. (Contributions in Political Science: No. 45). (Illus.). xx, 292p. 1980. lib. bdg. 27.50 (ISBN 0-313-21357-7, HEI/). Greenwood.

Contemporary Perspectives on the Medical Geography of South & Southeast Asia. Ed. by Ashok K. Dutt. (Illus.). 78p. 1980. pap. 20.00 (ISBN 0-08-026762-9). Pergamon.

Contemporary Pest Control Practices & Prospects: Report of the Executive Committee, 5 vols. Environmental Studies Board, National Research Council. LC 75-43468. (Pest Control Ser.: An Assessment of Present & Alternative Technologies, Vol. 1). 506p. 1975. pap. 11.75 (ISBN 0-309-02410-2). Natl Acad Pr.

Contemporary Philosophy. rev. ed. Frederick Copleston. Orig. Title: Contemporary Philosophy, Studies of Logical Positivism & Existentialism. 230p. 1972. pap. 4.95 (ISBN 0-8091-1757-6). Paulist Pr.

Contemporary Physics, 2 Vols. Trieste Symposium, 1968. (Illus., Orig.). 1969 (IAEA). Vol. 1. pap. 32.25 (ISBN 92-0-130069-7); Vol. 2. pap. 25.75 (ISBN 92-0-130169-3). Unipub.

Contemporary Poets. 3rd ed. Ed. by Jim Vinson & Daniel Kirkpatrick. (Contemporary Writers Ser.). 1900p. 1980. lib. bdg. 60.00x (ISBN 0-312-16765-2). St Martin.

Contemporary Poets in American Anthologies 1960-1977. Kirby Congdon. LC 78-13772. 1978. 12.00 (ISBN 0-8108-1168-5). Scarecrow.

Contemporary Poets of America 1980: A Dorrance Anthology. 100p. 1980. 7.50 (ISBN 0-8059-2770-0). Dorrance.

Contemporary Polish Sculpture. Andrzej Osek & Woljciech Skrodzki. Tr. by Krystyna Keplicz from Pol. LC 79-304319. Orig. Title: Wspolczesna Rzezba Polska. (Illus.). 160p. 1977. 15.00x (ISBN 0-8002-2296-2). Intl Pubns Serv.

Contemporary Political Analysis. Ed. by James C. Charlesworth. LC 67-14374. (Orig.). 1967. 9.95 (ISBN 0-02-905460-5); pap. text ed. 9.95 (ISBN 0-02-905470-2). Free Pr.

Contemporary Political Ideologies: A Comparative Analysis. 5th ed. Lyman T. Sargent. 1981. pap. text ed. 8.95x (ISBN 0-256-02545-2). Dorsey.

Contemporary Political Philosophers. Ed. by Anthony De Crespigny & Kenneth Minogue. LC 74-26158. 320p. (Orig.). 1975. pap. text ed. 11.50 scp (ISBN 0-06-041603-3, HarpC). Har-Row.

Contemporary Political Theory. Ed. by J. S. Bain & R. B. Jain. 300p. 1980. text ed. 13.25x (ISBN 0-391-01901-5). Humanities.

Contemporary Popular Music. Dean Tudor & Nancy Tudor. LC 78-32124. (American Popular Music on Elpee). 1979. lib. bdg. 22.50x (ISBN 0-87287-191-6). Libs Unl.

Contemporary Presidency. 2nd ed. Dorothy B. James. LC 73-19657. 350p. 1974. 9.85 o.p. (ISBN 0-672-53716-8); pap. 7.95 (ISBN 0-672-63716-2). Pegasus.

Contemporary Printed Sources for British & Irish Economic History, 1701-1750. Lawrence W. Hanson. 1964. 165.00 (ISBN 0-521-05196-7). Cambridge U Pr.

Contemporary Problems in Perception. Ed. by A. T. Welford & L. Houssiadas. 1970. 18.50x (ISBN 0-85066-039-4). Intl Ideas.

Contemporary Problems of Democracy. Marvin Zimmerman. 1972. text ed. 7.50x (ISBN 0-391-00223-6). Humanities.

Contemporary Psychology & Effective Behavior. 4th ed. James C. Coleman. 1979. text ed. 17.95x (ISBN 0-673-15202-2); student's guide 5.95x (ISBN 0-673-15203-0). Scott F.

Contemporary Psychology Experiments: Adaptations for Laboratory. 2nd ed. John Jung & Joan H. Bailey. LC 76-7896. 1976. text ed. 13.95x (ISBN 0-471-45327-7). Wiley.

Contemporary Psychotherapies. Ed. by Morris I. Stein. LC 61-13969. 1961. 14.95 (ISBN 0-02-930990-5). Free Pr.

Contemporary Public Administration: A Study in Emerging Realities. Thomas P. Murphy et al. LC 80-83377. 517p. 1981. text ed. 14.95 (ISBN 0-87581-269-4). Peacock Pubs.

Contemporary Public Budgeting. Ed. by Thomas Lynch. 250p. 1981. pap. text ed. 7.95 (ISBN 0-87855-722-9). Transaction Bks.

Contemporary Quantity Recipe File. John C. Birchfield et al. LC 75-12917. 346p. 1975. 21.50 (ISBN 0-8436-2065-X). CBI Pub.

Contemporary Reading of the Spiritual Exercises: A Companion to St. Ignatius' Text. 2nd ed. David L. Fleming. Ed. by George E. Ganss. LC 80-81812. (Study Aids on Jesuit Topics Ser.: No.2). 112p. 1980. pap. 3.00 (ISBN 0-912422-47-5); smyth sewn 4.00 (ISBN 0-912422-48-3). Inst Jesuit.

Contemporary Readings in American Government. Byron W. Daynes & Raymond Tatalovich. (Orig.). 1980. pap. text ed. 7.95 (ISBN 0-669-01163-0). Heath.

Contemporary Readings in Child Psychology. 2nd ed. Hetherington-Parke. Ed. by Patricia S. Nave. 448p. 1981. pap. text ed. 11.97 (ISBN 0-07-028426-1, C). McGraw.

Contemporary Readings in Organizational Behavior. 3rd ed. Fred Luthans & Kenneth R. Thompson. (Illus.). 512p. Date not set. text ed. 11.95x (ISBN 0-07-039148-3, C). McGraw.

Contemporary Real Estate Incidents. Michael P. Litka & Karl A. Shillif. LC 79-27028. (Real Estate Ser.). 189p. 1980. pap. text ed. 8.50 (ISBN 0-88244-222-8). Grid Pub.

Contemporary Relevance of Sri Aurobundo. Ed. by Kishore Gandhi. 1973. text ed. 10.50x (ISBN 0-391-00497-2). Humanities.

Contemporary Research in International Relations: A Perspective & a Critical Assessment. Dina A. Zinnes. LC 75-11290. (Illus.). 1976. 25.00 (ISBN 0-02-935730-6). Free Pr.

Contemporary Research in Operant Behavior. Charles A. Catania. 1968. pap. 11.95x (ISBN 0-673-05496-9). Scott F.

Contemporary Retailing. William H. Bolen. (Illus.). 1978. ref. ed. 18.95 (ISBN 0-13-170290-4). P-H.

Contemporary Rhetoric. 2nd ed. Maxine Hairston. LC 77-78916. (Illus.). 1977. text ed. 11.95 (ISBN 0-395-25450-7); inst. manual 0.45 (ISBN 0-395-25451-5). HM.

Contemporary Scenes for Student Actors. Ed. by Michael Schulman & Eva Mekler. (Orig.). 1980. pap. 3.95 (ISBN 0-14-048153-2). Penguin.

Contemporary School Psychology: Readings from Psychology in the Schools. 2nd ed. Ed. by James L. Carroll. 1981. pap. text ed. 12.95x (ISBN 0-88422-014-1). Clinical Psych.

Contemporary School Psychology: Readings from Psychology in the Schools. 2nd ed. Ed. by James L. Carroll. 1981. pap. 12.50x (ISBN 0-88422-014-1). Clinical Psych.

Contemporary Science Book 2. Milton Lesser et al. (gr. 6-10). 1977. pap. text ed. 7.33 (ISBN 0-87720-006-8). AMSCO Sch.

Contemporary Science Book 3. Milton Lesser et al. (gr. 6-10). 1978. pap. text ed. 8.33 (ISBN 0-87720-008-4). AMSCO Sch.

Contemporary Science Book,1. Milton Lesser et al. (gr. 6-10). 1977. pap. text ed. 7.33 (ISBN 0-87720-002-5). AMSCO Sch.

Contemporary Social Psychology: An Introduction. William S. Samuel. 512p. 1975. text ed. 19.95 (ISBN 0-13-170621-7). P-H.

Contemporary Social Psychology: Representative Readings. Thomas Blass. LC 75-17318. 1976. pap. text ed. 10.50 (ISBN 0-87581-190-6, 190). Peacock Pubs.

Contemporary Social Work: An Introduction to Social Work & Social Welfare. 2nd ed. Donald Brieland et al. Ed. by Eric M. Munson. (Illus.). Date not set. text ed. 16.95x (ISBN 0-07-007767-3); instr's manual 4.95 (ISBN 0-07-007768-1). McGraw.

Contemporary Society. Willard Sloshberg. (Illus.). 1978. pap. text ed. 12.50 (ISBN 0-8299-0140-X); wkbk. avail. (ISBN 0-8299-0574-X). West Pub.

Contemporary Sociological Theory. Ruth A. Wallace & Alison Wolf. LC 79-13971. (Sociology Ser.). (Illus.). 1980. text ed. 17.95 (ISBN 0-13-170506-7). P-H.

Contemporary Soviet Politics: An Introduction. Donald D. Barry & Carol B. Barry. LC 77-10871. (Illus.). 1978. pap. 11.50x ref. ed. (ISBN 0-13-170225-4). P-H.

Contemporary Soviet Society: Sociological Perspectives. Ed. by Jerry Pankhurst & Michael P. Sacks. 310p. 1980. 23.95 (ISBN 0-03-055916-2); pap. 9.95 (ISBN 0-03-055911-1). Praeger.

Contemporary Spanish-American Fiction. Jefferson R. Spell. LC 67-29553. 1968. Repr. of 1944 ed. 12.00x (ISBN 0-8196-0211-6). Biblo.

Contemporary Spanish Poetry: 1898-1963. Carl W. Cobb. LC 75-23016. (World Authors Ser.: Spain: No. 373). 1976. lib. bdg. 9.95 (ISBN 0-8057-6202-7). Twayne.

Contemporary Spanish Theater, 1949-1972. Marion P. Holt. (World Authors Ser.: Spain: No. 336). 1975. lib. bdg. 12.50 (ISBN 0-8057-2243-2). Twayne.

Contemporary Spirituality. Ed. by Robert W. Gleason. 1968. 9.95 o.s.i. (ISBN 0-02-544030-6). Macmillan.

Contemporary Stage Design - U.S.A. Ed. by Elizabeth B. Burdick. LC 74-26233. (Illus.). 1975. pap. 15.00x (ISBN 0-8195-8023-6, Pub. by Wesleyan U Pr). Columbia U Pr.

Contemporary Studies of Swift's Poetry. Ed. by Donald C. Mell et al. LC 79-21610. (Illus.). 216p. 1980. 18.50 (ISBN 0-87413-173-1, 173). U Delaware Pr.

Contemporary Suburban America. Peter O. Muller. (Illus.). 240p. 1981. pap. 9.95 (ISBN 0-13-170647-0). P-H.

Contemporary Swedish Poetry. Tr. by John Matthias & Goran Printz-Pahlson. LC 79-9655. 136p. 1980. 16.95x (ISBN 0-8040-0811-6); pap. 7.95 (ISBN 0-8040-0812-4). Swallow.

Contemporary Synagogue Art: Developments in the United States, 1945-1965. Avram Kampf. LC 65-25292. (Illus.). 1976. 15.00 o.p. (ISBN 0-8074-0085-8, 382630). UAHC.

Contemporary Systems Performance Modeling. Charles Sauer & Mani K. Chandy. (Illus.). 384p. 1981. text ed. 18.95 (ISBN 0-13-165175-7). P-H.

Contemporary Technical Mathematics with Calculus. Richard S. Paul & M. Leonard Shaevel. (Technical Mathematics Ser). 1970. text ed. 15.95 o.p. (ISBN 0-13-170654-3). P-H.

Contemporary Tennis. Roy Petty. LC 77-91165. 1978. 6.95 o.p. (ISBN 0-8092-7548-1); pap. 3.95 (ISBN 0-8092-7574-0). Contemp Bks.

Contemporary Theatre. Ed. by John R. Brown & Bernard Harris. (Stratford-Upon-Avon Studies: No. 4). 208p. 1962. pap. text ed. 15.00x (ISBN 0-8419-5811-4). Holmes & Meier.

Contemporary Theories & Systems in Psychology. rev., 2nd ed. Benjamin B. Wolman & Susan Knapp. 690p. 1981. 42.50 (ISBN 0-306-40515-6, Plenum Pr); pap. 17.95 (ISBN 0-306-40530-X). Plenum Pub.

Contemporary Theories in the Sociology of Education. Jack Demaine. 192p. 1980. text ed. 37.50x (ISBN 0-333-23448-0). Humanities.

Contemporary Theories of Schizophrenia: Review & Synthesis. Sue A. Shapiro. (Illus.). 1981. 18.95 (ISBN 0-07-056423-X). McGraw.

Contemporary Topics in Immunobiology, Vol. 11. Ed. by Noel L. Warner. (Illus.). 390p. 1980. 32.50 (ISBN 0-306-40419-2, Plenum Pr). Plenum Pub.

Contemporary Topics in Immunobiology: Volume 10, "in Situ" Expression of Tumor Immunity, Vol. 10. Ed. by Isaac Witz & M. G. Hanna. 330p. 1980. 32.50 (ISBN 0-306-40387-0, Plenum Pr). Plenum Pub.

Contemporary Topics in Immunobiology: Vol. 7, T Cells. Ed. by Osis Stutman. (Illus.). 386p. 1977. 35.00 (ISBN 0-306-37807-8, Plenum Pr). Plenum Pub.

Contemporary Topics in Immunobiology, Vol. 9: Self-Non Self Discrimination. Ed. by John J. Marchalonis & Nicholas Cohen. LC 79-179761. (Illus.). 309p. 1980. 29.50 (ISBN 0-306-40263-7, Plenum Pr). Plenum Pub.

Contemporary Transformations of Religion. Bryan Wilson. 1979. pap. text ed. 4.50x (ISBN 0-19-875045-5). Oxford U Pr.

Contemporary Transportation. Donald F. Wood & James C. Johnson. 641p. 1980. 18.95 (ISBN 0-87814-112-X). Pennwell Pub.

Contemporary Turkish Literature: Fiction & Poetry. Ed. & intro. by Talat S. Halman. LC 77-74391. 550p. 1981. 22.50 (ISBN 0-8386-1360-8). Fairleigh Dickinson.

Contemporary Venezuela & Its Role in International Affairs. Ed. by Robert D. Bond. LC 77-76055. (A Council on Foreign Relations Book). 267p. 1977. 15.00x (ISBN 0-8147-0991-5); pap. 7.00x (ISBN 0-8147-0992-3). NYU Pr.

Contemporary Views, Vol. 88. Association of Bone & Joint Surgeons. Ed. by Marshall Urist. (Clinical Orthopaedics & Related Research Ser.). 1972. 12.00 o.p. (ISBN 0-685-34609-9). Lippincott.

Contemporary Violence: A Multidisciplinary Examination. Charles G. Wilber. (Illus.). 176p. 1975. 14.75 (ISBN 0-398-03457-5). C C Thomas.

Contemporary Voices: The Short Story in Canada. Ed. by D. Stephens. 1973. pap. text ed. 6.95 o.p. (ISBN 0-13-171306-X). P-H.

Contemporary World Horoscopes, No. 1. Joseph Folino. Date not set. pap. cancelled (ISBN 0-88231-061-5). ASI Pubs Inc.

Contemporary World: Nineteen Fourteen to Present. rev. ed. William H. McNeill. 184p. 1975. pap. 7.95x (ISBN 0-673-07908-2). Scott F.

Contemporary Writer: Interviews with Sixteen Novelists & Poets. Ed. by L. S. Dembo & Cyrena N. Pondrom. LC 71-176410. 318p. 1972. 22.50 (ISBN 0-299-06141-8); pap. 7.95 (ISBN 0-299-06144-2). U of Wis Pr.

Contempt of Congress: A Study of the Prosecutions Initiated by the Committee on un-American Activities, 1945-1957. Carl Beck. LC 75-166090. (Studies in American History & Government Ser.). 264p. 1974. Repr. of 1959 ed. lib. bdg. 25.00 (ISBN 0-306-70229-0). Da Capo.

Contempt Power. Ronald L. Goldfarb. LC 63-20342. 1963. 22.50x (ISBN 0-231-02654-4). Columbia U Pr.

Contempt: Transcript of the Contempt Citations, Sentences & Responses of the Chicago Conspiracy 10. Intro. by H. Kalven, Jr. & R. Clark. LC 70-120687. 254p. (Orig.). 1970. 10.00 o.p. (ISBN 0-8040-0056-5); pap. 5.95 (ISBN 0-8040-0057-3). Swallow.

Contempts by Publication: The Law of Trial by Newspaper. Harold W. Sullivan. xiv, 230p. 1980. Repr. of 1941 ed. lib. bdg. 24.00x (ISBN 0-8377-1114-2). Rothman.

Contending with the Dark & Against That Time. Jeffrey Schwartz & Ron Schreiber. LC 77-93269. 88p. 1978. pap. 4.95 (ISBN 0-914086-22-7). Alicejamesbooks.

Content Analysis: An Introduction to Its Methodology. Klaus Krippendorff. LC 80-19166. (CommText Ser.: Vol. 5). (Illus.). 191p. 1980. 15.00 (ISBN 0-8039-1497-0); pap. 7.95 (ISBN 0-8039-1498-9). Sage.

Content Analysis for the Social Sciences & Humanities. O. R. Holsti. (Orig.). 1969. pap. text ed. 10.95 (ISBN 0-201-02940-5). A-W.

Content Analysis in Communications Research. Bernard Berelson. 1971. 20.00 (ISBN 0-02-841210-9). Hafner.

Content Analysis of Verbal Behavior: Further Studies. Ed. by Louis A. Gottschalk. 1979. 45.00 (ISBN 0-470-26367-9). Halsted Pr.

Content & Consciousness. D. C. Dennett. (International Library of Philosophy & Scientific Method). 1969. text ed. 16.25x (ISBN 0-391-01015-8). Humanities.

Content & Context: Essays on College Education. Carnegie Commission on Higher Education. Ed. by Carl Kaysen. LC 73-8858. (Illus.). 588p. 1973. 19.50 o.p. (ISBN 0-07-010048-9, P&RB). McGraw.

Content Area Reading. Richard T. Vacca. 1981. text ed. 14.95 (ISBN 0-316-89488-5). Little.

Content of Sixth-Form General Studies. R. A. Oliver & D. G. Lewis. 144p. 1974. 12.00x (ISBN 0-7190-0586-8, Pub. by Manchester U Pr England). State Mutual Bk.

Contention & Shakespeare's 2 Henry V. Charles T. Prouty. 1954. 32.50x (ISBN 0-685-69852-1). Elliots Bks.

Contents-Subject Index to General & Periodical Literature. Alfred Cotgreave. LC 74-31272. 1971. Repr. of 1900 ed. 42.00 (ISBN 0-8103-3778-9). Gale.

Contes Africains. Ed. by Mildred P. Mortimer. LC 71-168855. (Illus., Orig.). 1972. pap. text ed. 7.20 (ISBN 0-395-12078-0, 3-39210). HM.

Contes Choisis. Guy De Maupassant. Ed. by W. R. Price. 1930. 3.50 (ISBN 0-672-73238-6). Odyssey Pr.

Contes choisis. Charles Nodier. (Classiques Larousse). (Illus., Fr.). pap. 1.50 o.p. (ISBN 0-685-13841-0, 229). Larousse.

Contes d'Espagne et D'italie. Alfred De Musset. Ed. by Margaret Rees. (Athlone French Poets Ser.). 1973. text ed. 16.25x (ISBN 0-485-14703-3, Athlone Pr); pap. text ed. 5.50x (ISBN 0-485-12703-2, Athlone Pr). Humanities.

Contest. Nonny Hogrogian. LC 75-40389. (Illus.). (gr. k-3). 1976. 8.95 (ISBN 0-688-80042-4); PLB 8.59 (ISBN 0-688-84042-6). Greenwillow.

Contest Oratory: A Handbook for High School & College Contestants & Coaches. William Schrier. LC 71-171595. 1971. 10.00 (ISBN 0-8108-0416-6). Scarecrow.

Contest Over the Ratification of the Federal Constitution in the State of Massachusetts. Samuel B. Harding. LC 75-98687. (American Constitutional & Legal History Ser). 1970. Repr. of 1896 ed. lib. bdg. 25.00 (ISBN 0-306-71839-1). Da Capo.

Contestation in the Church. Ed. by Teodoro J. Urresti. LC 71-168654. (Concilium Ser.: Religion in the Seventies: Vol. 68). 1971. pap. 4.95 (ISBN 0-8164-2524-8). Crossroad NY.

Contested Terrain: The Transformation of the Workplace in America. Richard C. Edwards. LC 78-19942. 256p. 1980. pap. 4.95 (ISBN 0-465-01413-5). Basic.

Context-Free Grammars: Covers, Normal Forms, & Parsing. A. Nijholt. (Lecture Notes in Computer Science Ser.: Vol. 93). 253p. 1981. pap. 16.80 (ISBN 0-387-10245-0). Springer-Verlag.

Context of English Literature, Nineteen Hundred to Nineteen-Thirty. Ed. by Michael Bell. LC 80-7792. (Context of English Literature Ser.). 250p. 1980. text ed. 29.50x (ISBN 0-8419-0423-5); pap. text ed. 16.95x (ISBN 0-8419-0424-3). Holmes & Meier.

Context of Foreign Language Learning. Ed. by A. J. Van Essen & J. P. Menting. 200p. 1975. pap. text ed. 20.50x (ISBN 90-232-1250-9). Humanities.

Context of Self: A Phenomenological Inquiry Using Medicine As a Clue. Richard M. Zaner. LC 80-18500. (Continental Thought Ser.: Vol. 1). (Illus.). xiv, 282p. 1981. 16.95x (ISBN 0-8214-0443-1); pap. 8.95x (ISBN 0-8214-0600-0). Ohio U Pr.

Contextes: A College Reader. Jean Carduner & Sylvie Carduner. 1974. pap. text ed. 7.95x o.p. (ISBN 0-669-73627-9). Heath.

Contexts for Composition. 5th ed. David Spencer et al. 1979. pap. text ed. 9.95 (ISBN 0-13-171512-7). P-H.

Contextual Analysis: Concepts & Statistical Techniques. Lawrence H. Boyd & Gudmund R. Iversen. 1979. text ed. 25.95x (ISBN 0-534-00693-0). Wadsworth Pub.

Contextual Architecture: Responding to Existing Styles. Architectural Record Magazine. Ed. by Keith Ray. (Architecture Ser.). (Illus.). 1980. 27.50 (ISBN 0-07-002332-8). McGraw.

Contextualized Vocabulary Tests. L. A. Hill. 1975. Bk. 1. pap. text ed. 3.50x o.p. (ISBN 0-19-432564-4); Bk. 2. pap. text ed. 3.50x o.p. (ISBN 0-19-432565-2). Oxford U Pr.

Contigo Pan y Cebolla. Ed. by James C. Babcock et al. LC 49-8551. (Graded Spanish Readers, Bk. 3). (Span). (gr. 10-11). 1953. pap. text ed. 4.15 (ISBN 0-395-04126-0, 3-02255). HM.

Contiguity of Probability Measures: Some Applications in Statistics. G. G. Roussas. LC 71-171682. (Cambridge Tracts in Mathematics & Mathematical Physics: No. 63). 1972. 44.50 (ISBN 0-521-08354-0). Cambridge U Pr.

Continent of America: Its Discovery & Its Baptism. J. B. Thatcher. 1971. Repr. of 1896 ed. text ed. 42.50x (ISBN 90-6041-061-0). Humanities.

Continental Drift & Plate Tectonics. William Glen. (Physics & Physical Science Ser.). 192p. 1975. pap. text ed. 8.95 (ISBN 0-675-08799-6). Merrill.

Continental Handbook 1980. 41st ed. LC 51-34691. (Royal Automobile Club Ser.). (Illus.). 394p. 1980. pap. 15.00x (ISBN 0-902628-89-5). Intl Pubns Serv.

Continental Margins: Geological & Geophysical Research Needs. Ocean Sciences Board, National Research Council. pap. 16.25x (ISBN 0-309-02793-4). Natl Acad Pr.

Continental Op. Dashiell Hammett. LC 74-9050. 1974. 7.95 o.p. (ISBN 0-394-48704-4). Random.

Continental Police Practice: In the Formative Years. Sheldon Glueck. (Criminal Law Education and Research Center Ser.). 88p. 1974. 9.75 (ISBN 0-398-02880-X). C C Thomas.

Continental Renaissance, Fifteen Hundred to Sixteen Hundred. Ed. by A. J. Krailsheimer. (Pelican Guides to European Literature). 1978. Repr. of 1971 ed. text ed. 28.50x (ISBN 0-391-00816-1). Humanities.

Continental Scientific Drilling. Geophysics Research Board. 1979. pap. 5.50 (ISBN 0-309-02872-8). Natl Acad Pr.

Continental Short Stories. Ed. by Edward Mitchell & Rainer Schulte. 1969. 4.95x (ISBN 0-393-09797-8); study questions free (ISBN 0-393-09854-0). Norton.

Continental Short Story: An Existential Approach. Theodora L. West. LC 69-11184. (Orig.). 1969. pap. 7.70 o.p. (ISBN 0-672-63024-9). Odyssey Pr.

Continental Tectonics. 1980. 13.50 (ISBN 0-309-02928-7). Natl Acad Pr.

Continental Tectonics. Geophysics Research Board. (Studies in Geophysics). xii, 197p. 1980. pap. text ed. 13.50 (ISBN 0-309-02928-7). Natl Acad Pr.

Continents Adrift & Continents Aground: Readings from Scientific American. Intro. by J. Tuzo Wilson. LC 76-46564. (Illus.). 1976. pap. text ed. 9.95x (ISBN 0-7167-0280-0). W H Freeman.

Contingencies of Reinforcement: A Theoretical Analysis. B. F. Skinner. 1969. pap. 14.95 (ISBN 0-13-171728-6). P-H.

Contingency Management. Anne L. Langstaff & Cora B. Volkmor. (Educational Psychology Ser.). (Illus.). 96p. 1975. pap. text ed. 6.95x (ISBN 0-675-08708-2); instructor's manual 3.95 (ISBN 0-686-67123-6). Merrill.

Contingency Management in Education & Other Equally Exciting Places. 2nd ed. Richard Malott. (Illus.). 260p. 1972. pap. text ed. 10.00 (ISBN 0-914474-08-1); instr's. quiz manual avail. F Fournies.

Contingency Planning. Norwegina Petroleum Society. 223p. 1980. 75.00x (ISBN 8-27270-010-7, Pub. by Norwegian Info Norway). State Mutual Bk.

Contingency Plans for Chromium Utilization. Committee on Contingency Plans for Chromium Utilization, National Research Council. LC 77-95193. (Illus.). 1978. pap. text ed. 10.50 (ISBN 0-309-02737-3). Natl Acad Pr.

Contingency Table Analysis for Road Safety Studies. G. A. Fleischer. (NAtO Advanced Study Institute Ser.: Applied Science, No. 42). 300p. 1980. 32.50x (ISBN 90-286-0960-1). Sijthoff & Noordhoff.

Continous Transcutaneous Blood Gas Monitorin. Ed. by Albert Huch et al. LC 79-2586. (Alan R. Liss Ser.: Vol. 15, No. 4). 1979. 68.00 (ISBN 0-8451-1027-6). March of Dimes.

Continously Under Review. Rosemary Stewart. 70p. 1967. pap. text ed. 5.00x (Pub. by Bedford England). Renouf.

Continuation of Life. Gene Liberty. (Orig.). (gr. 7-10). 1975. pap. text ed. 6.42 (ISBN 0-87720-012-2). AMSCO Sch.

Continued Fractions: Analytic Theory & Applications. William B. Jones & W. J. Thron. (Encyclopedia of Mathematics & Applications Ser.: Vol. II). (Illus.). 450p. 1980. cancelled (ISBN 0-201-13510-8). A-W.

Continuing BASIC. P. E. Gosling. 160p. 1980. pap. 10.95 (ISBN 0-333-26286-7). Robotics Pr.

Continuing Care of Terminal Cancer Patients: Proceedings of an International Seminar on Continuing Care of Terminal Cancer Patients, 19-20 October 1979, Milan, Italy. R. G. Twycross & V. Ventafridda. 300p. 1980. 44.00 (ISBN 0-08-024943-4). Pergamon.

Continuing Challenge: The Past & the Future of Brown vs. Board of Education (A Symposium) LC 75-1552. 1975. 3.00 (ISBN 0-685-52791-3). Integrated Ed Assoc.

Continuing Conurbation: Change & Development in Greater Manchester. H. P. White. 224p. 1980. text ed. 30.75x (ISBN 0-566-00248-5, Pub. by Gower Pub Co England). Renouf.

Continuing Education & the Community College. Jack W. Fuller. LC 78-10905. 1979. 14.95 (ISBN 0-88229-371-0). Nelson-Hall.

Continuing Education in the Health Professions. Robert Boissoneau. LC 80-19748. 322p. 1980. text ed. 27.50 (ISBN 0-89443-325-3). Aspen Systems.

Continuing Evaluation of the Use of Fluorides. Ed. by Erling Johansen & Donald R. Taves. (AAAS Selected Symposium Ser.: No. 11). (Illus.). 1979. lib. bdg. 27.50x (ISBN 0-89158-439-0). Westview.

Continuing Language Skills. William F. Hunter et al. (Learning Skills Ser: Language Arts). (Illus.). 1978. pap. text ed. 4.52 (ISBN 0-07-031333-4, W); tchr's manual 6.32 (ISBN 0-07-031335-0). McGraw.

Continuing Medical Education in the Community Hospital. James J. Bergin & Geraldine C. Holmes. LC 79-55326. (Illus.). 1979. text ed. 22.00x (ISBN 0-935466-00-2); pap. text ed. 16.00x (ISBN 0-935466-01-0). Pierson Pubs.

Continuing Medical Education Syllabus & Scientific Proceedings in Summary Form. American Psychiatric Association. Annual Meeting, 131st, Atlanta, Ga., May 1978. (Scientific Proceedings of the APA). 1978. pap. 10.00 o.p. (ISBN 0-685-94002-0, 153-8). Am Psychiatric.

Continuing Medical Education Syllabus & Scientific Proceedings in Summary Form. new ed. American Psychiatric Association Annual Meeting, 132nd. (Scientific Proceedings of the APA Ser.). 1979. pap. text ed. 10.00x o.p. (ISBN 0-685-96759-X, 153-9). Am Psychiatric.

Continuing Quest: Large Scale Ocean Science for the Future. Ocean Sciences Board, National Research Council. (Orig.). 1979. pap. text ed. 7.25x (ISBN 0-309-02798-5). Natl Acad Pr.

Continuing Revolution: China Since 1894. 2nd, rev, enl. ed. Ann Trotter. (Illus.). 72p. 1975. pap. 4.50x o.p. (ISBN 0-8002-0677-0). Intl Pubns Sérv.

Continuing Revolution: China Since 1894. 2nd rev. & enl. ed. Ed. by Ann Trotter. (Illus.). 72p. 1975. pap. 4.50x (ISBN 0-686-65040-9). Intl Pubns Serv.

Continuing Story of Love of Chair. Tom Dunsmuir. (Electric Company Ser.). (Illus.). (gr. 1-5). 1973. PLB 5.38 (ISBN 0-307-64822-2, Golden Pr). Western Pub.

Continuing Struggle for Democracy in Latin America. Ed. by Howard J. Wiarda. LC 79-13551. (Westview Special Studies on Latin America). 26.50x (ISBN 0-89158-663-6). Westview.

Continuing Swing? Pupils' Reluctance to Study Science. Derek Duckworth. (General Ser.). (Illus.). 1979. pap. text ed. 7.00x (ISBN 0-85633-174-0, NFER). Humanities.

Continuities & Discontinuities in Political Thought. Ed. by D. Dodge & D. H. Baird. LC 74-16197. 1975. text ed. 14.95 (ISBN 0-470-21744-8); pap. text ed. 9.95x (ISBN 0-470-21745-6). Halsted Pr.

Continuities in Education: The Northern Ireland Schools Curriculum Project. Robert Crone & John Malone. 156p. 1980. pap. text ed. 16.50x (ISBN 0-85633-181-3, NFER). Humanities.

Continuities in Psychological Anthropology: A Historical Introduction. Philip K. Bock. LC 79-23200. (Illus.). 1980. text ed. 15.95x (ISBN 0-7167-1136-2); pap. text ed. 7.95x (ISBN 0-7167-1137-0). W H Freeman.

Continuities in the Language of Social Research. 2nd ed. Ed. by Paul Lazarsfeld et al. LC 77-143525. 1972. 19.95 (ISBN 0-02-918250-6). Free Pr.

Continuities in the Study of Social Conflict. Lewis A. Coser. LC 67-25330. 1970. pap. text ed. 3.50 o.s.i. (ISBN 0-02-906760-X). Free Pr.

Continuity & Change. Rita J. Simon. LC 77-15090. (ASA Rose Monograph Ser.: No. 6). (Illus.). 1978. 19.95 (ISBN 0-521-21938-8); pap. 6.95x (ISBN 0-521-29318-9). Cambridge U Pr.

Continuity & Change: Personnel & Administration of the Church in England, 1500-1642. Ed. by Rosemary O'Day & Felicity Heal. 300p. 1976. text ed. 21.00x (ISBN 0-7185-1138-7, Leicester). Humanities.

Continuity & Discontinuity: Higher Education & the Schools. Carnegie Commission on Higher Education. 1973. 3.95 o.p. (ISBN 0-07-010080-2, P&RB). McGraw.

Continuity & Innovation in Sean O'Casey's Drama. Ronald Ayling. (Salzburg Studies in English Literature Poetic Drama & Poetic Theory: No. 23). 1976. pap. 25.00x (ISBN 0-391-01304-1). Humanities.

Continuous Advancement Program 2: Individualized Mathematics Objectives & Self-Tests. Ellis A. Reeby et al. (Illus.). 207p. (Orig., Prog. Bk.). (gr. 8). 1973. pap. text ed. 3.50x o.p. (ISBN 0-686-66760-3). Ind Sch Pr.

Continuous Advancement Program 2: Individualized Mathematics Self-Learning Packet. Ellis A. Reeby et al. (Illus.). 315p. (Orig., Prog. Bk.). (gr. 8). 1973. pap. text ed. 4.50x o.p. (ISBN 0-686-66759-X). Ind Sch Pr.

Continuous Advancement Program 2: Individualized Mathematics Tests & Answers. Ellis A. Reeby et al. 345p. (Orig., Prog. Bk.). (gr. 8). 1973. pap. text ed. 15.00x o.p. (ISBN 0-88334-082-8). Ind Sch Pr.

Continuous City Planning: Integrating Municipal & City Planning. Melville C. Branch. 192p. 1980. 21.95 (ISBN 0-471-08943-5, Pub. by Wiley-Interscience). Wiley.

Continuous Compounding Savings Factor Tables No. 534. Financial Publishing Co. 15.00 (ISBN 0-685-02537-3). Finan Pub.

Continuous Crossed Products & Type 111 von Neumann Algebras. A. Van Daele. LC 77-91096. (London Mathematical Society Lecture Note Ser.: No. 31). 1978. limp bdg. 11.95x (ISBN 0-521-21975-2). Cambridge U Pr.

Continuous Culture: Applications & New Fields. Ed. by A. C. Dean et al. 1976. 42.95x (ISBN 0-470-98984-X). Halsted Pr.

Continuous Cultures of Cells, 2 vols. Peter H. Calcott. 1981. Vol. 1, 192p. 54.95 (ISBN 0-8493-5377-7); Vol. 2, 208p. 57.95 (ISBN 0-8493-5378-5). CRC Pr.

Continuous National Survey: A Compendium of Questionnaire Items, Articles 1 Through 12. James Murray. (Report Ser: No. 125). 1974. (ISBN 0-932132-18-9). NORC.

Continuous Progress in Spelling (Cps) Readiness. rev. ed. Ruel A. Allred et al. (Continuous Progress in Spelling Ser.). (gr. 1-3). 1977. pap. text ed. 2.85 (ISBN 0-87892-297-0); tchrs ed. 2.85 (ISBN 0-87892-298-9). Economy Co.

Continuous Progress in Spelling (CPS) 1. rev. ed. Edwin A. Read et al. (gr. 1-3). 1977. 2.97 (ISBN 0-87892-286-5); 2.97 (ISBN 0-87892-287-3); kit 124.50 (ISBN 0-87892-285-7). Economy Co.

Continuous Progress in Spelling (CPS) 2. rev. ed. Edwin A. Read et al. (gr. 4-6). 1977. 2.16 (ISBN 0-87892-289-X); tchrs' manual 2.16 (ISBN 0-87892-290-3); 124.50 (ISBN 0-87892-288-1). Economy Co.

Continuous Univariate Distribution: Distributions in Statistics, 2 vols. Norman L. Johnson & Samuel I. Kotz. (Wiley Series in Probability & Mathematical Statistics-Applied Probability & Statistics Section). 1970. Vol. 1. 31.95 (ISBN 0-471-44626-2, Pub. by Wiley-Interscience); Vol. 2. 31.95 (ISBN 0-471-44627-0). Wiley.

Continuum Electromechanics. James R. Melcher. (Illus.). 700p. 1981. text ed. 37.50x (ISBN 0-262-13165-X). MIT Pr.

Continuum Four. Roger Elwood. 1976. pap. 0.95 o.p. (ISBN 0-425-03077-6, Medallion). Berkley Pub.

Continuum Mechanics: Concise Theory & Problems. P. Chadwick. LC 75-26519. 1976. text ed. 16.95 o.p. (ISBN 0-470-14303-7). Halsted Pr.

Continuum Mechanics of Viscoelastic Liquids. R. R. Huilgol. LC 73-14413. (Illus.). 675p. 1975. 34.50 o.p. (ISBN 0-470-42043-X). Halsted Pr.

Continuum One. Ed. by Roger Elwood. LC 73-87184. 192p. (YA) 1974. 5.95 o.p. (ISBN 0-399-11283-9, Dist. by Putnam). Berkley Pub.

Continuum Spectra of Heavy-Ion Reactions. Ed. by T. Tamura & J. B. Natowitz. (Nuclear Science Research Conference Ser.: Vol. 2). 490p. 1980. 48.50 (ISBN 3-7186-0028-5). Harwood Academic.

Continuum Spectra of Heavy-Ion Reactions. T. Tamura et al. 590p. 1980. 48.50 (ISBN 3-7186-0028-5). Harwood Academic.

Continuum Three. Ed. by Roger Elwood. LC 73-87184. 160p. (YA) 1974. 5.95 o.p. (ISBN 0-399-11322-3, Dist. by Putnam). Berkley Pub.

Continuum Two. Ed. by Roger Elwood. 1975. pap. 1.25 o.p. (ISBN 0-425-03127-6, Medallion). Berkley Pub.

Contos do Brasil. Ed. by D. Lee Hamilton & Ned C. Fahs. LC 44-4280. (Port.). 1955. pap. text ed. 9.50x (ISBN 0-89197-108-4). Irvington.

Contours of a Christian Philosophy. L. Kalsbeek. 1975. 12.50x (ISBN 0-88906-000-2). Wedge Pub.

Contraband, A Romance of the North Atlantic. Randall Parrish. 1976. lib. bdg. 18.25x (ISBN 0-89968-085-2). Lightyear.

Contraception, Abortion, Pregnancy. Alice Fleming. LC 74-10268. 160p. 1974. 6.95 o.p. (ISBN 0-525-66396-7). Elsevier-Nelson.

Contraception: Science, Technology & Application. Division of Medical Sciences. 1979. pap. 16.00 (ISBN 0-309-02892-2). Natl Acad Pr.

Contraceptive Technology, Nineteen Eighty-Eighty-One. 10th, rev. ed. Robert A. Hatcher & Gary K. Stewart. (Illus., Orig.). 1980. 12.95 (ISBN 0-8290-0083-6); pap. text ed. 6.95x (ISBN 0-8290-0084-4). Irvington.

Contraceptives of the Future. R. V. Short & D. T. Baird. LC 77-371447. (Illus.). 1977. text ed. 22.50x (ISBN 0-85403-087-5). Scholium Intl.

Contract Bridge. Robert Ewen. LC 74-9620. (Illus.). 72p. 1975. PLB 4.47 o.p. (ISBN 0-531-02787-2). Watts.

Contract Bridge. Alan Truscott. LC 80-70959. 112p. 1982. pap. 2.95 (ISBN 0-8119-0422-9). Fell. Postponed.

Contract Food Service-Vending. Jerry G. Gardner. LC 73-76359. 1973. 16.95 (ISBN 0-8436-0568-5). CBI Pub.

Contract Labour in the Clothing Industry: Second Tripartite Technical Meeting for the Clothing Industry, Geneva, 1980, Report II. International Labour Office. ii, 75p. (Orig.). 1980. pap. 7.15 (ISBN 92-2-102432-6). Intl Labour Office.

Contract Law in America: A Social & Economic Case Study. Lawrence M. Friedman. 1965. 17.50x (ISBN 0-299-03570-0). U of Wis Pr.

Contract Law in Modern Society, Cases & Materials: Cases & Materials. 2nd ed. John H. Jackson & Lee C. Bollinger. LC 80-15562. (American Casebook Ser.). 1478p. 1980. text ed. 23.95 (ISBN 0-8299-2098-6). West Pub.

Contract Laws of U.S. 1981 ed. 112p. 1981. 10.00 (ISBN 0-87526-197-3). Gould.

Contract of Employment. Mark R. Freedland. 400p. 1975. 39.50x (ISBN 0-19-825306-0). Oxford U Pr.

Contract Rescue. Gayle Rivers & James Hudson. LC 80-1850. (Illus.). 240p. 1981. 11.95 (ISBN 0-385-17200-1). Doubleday.

Contractile Proteins & Muscle. Ed. by Kolomon Laki. 1971. 89.75 o.p. (ISBN 0-8247-1394-X). Dekker.

Contractors of Chartres. John James. (Illus.). 232p. 1980. 60.00 (ISBN 0-7099-0180-1, Pub. by Croom Held Ltd England). Biblio Dist.

Contracts & Taxation in the Norwegian North Sea. Norwegian Petroleum Society. 130p. 1980. 75.00x (Pub. by Norwegian Info Norway). State Mutual Bk.

Contracts: Cases & Materials. 2nd ed. Friedrich Kessler & Grant Gilmore. 1396p. 1976. 27.50 o.p. (ISBN 0-316-49016-4). Little.

Contracts for the Sale of Realty. Alexander Bicks. Rev. by Herman M. Glassner & William M. Kufeld. 1973. text ed. 10.00 o.p. (ISBN 0-685-85373-X, N1-0333). PLI.

Contractual Obligations in Ghana & Nigeria. U. U. Uche. 300p. 1971. 29.50x (ISBN 0-7146-2611-2, F Cass Co). Biblio Dist.

Contradictions of Socialist Construction. Ed. by Marlene Dixon & Susanne Jonas. 100p. (Orig.). 1979. pap. 4.00 (ISBN 0-89935-008-9). Synthesis Pubns.

Contrapuntal Harmonic Technique of the Eighteenth Century. Allen I. McHose. 1947. 19.95 (ISBN 0-13-171843-6). P-H.

Contraries: Essays. Joyce C. Oates. 192p. 1981. 15.00 (ISBN 0-19-502884-8). Oxford U Pr.

Contrary Pleasure. John D. MacDonald. 1979. pap. 1.75 o.p. (ISBN 0-449-14104-7, GM). Fawcett.

Contrary Pleasure. John D. MacDonald. 256p. 1981. pap. 2.50 (ISBN 0-449-14104-7, GM). Fawcett.

Contrast and Connection: Bicentennial Essays in Anglo-American History. Ed. by H. C. Allen & Roger Thompson. LC 76-7095. ix, 373p. 1976. 18.00x (ISBN 0-8214-0355-9). Ohio U Pr.

Contrast Arthography of the Synovial Joints. Ficat. 1981. price not set. Masson Pub.

Contrast, or the Evils of War, & the Blessings of Christianity Exemplified in the Life & Adventures of Paul Placid, Repr. Of 1830 Ed. Bd. with Short Biography of John Leeth, with a Brief Account of His Life Among the Indians. Repr. of 1831 ed; Or the Reward of Perseverance. William Weston. Repr. of 1832 ed. LC 75-7069. (Indian Captivities Ser.: Vol. 47). 1977. lib. bdg. 44.00 (ISBN 0-8240-1671-8). Garland Pub.

Contrastes. John G. Boucher & Robert L. Paris. (Fr.). (gr. 7-12). 1972. text ed. 14.80 (ISBN 0-205-03368-7, 3633683); tchrs'. guide 5.12 (ISBN 0-205-03369-5, 3633691); wkbk. 5.60 (ISBN 0-205-03370-9, 3633705); ans. bk. 2.40 (ISBN 0-205-03371-7, 3633713). Allyn.

Contrastes Culturales. David Suarez-Torrez. 336p. 1981. text ed. 11.95 case (ISBN 0-669-02662-X). Heath.

Contrasting Communities. Margaret Spufford. LC 73-83105. (Illus.). 1980. pap. 12.95 (ISBN 0-521-29748-6). Cambridge U Pr.
Contrasting Communities: English Villagers in the Sixteenth & Seventeenth Centuries. Margaret Spufford. LC 73-83105. (Illus.). 1974. 43.95 (ISBN 0-521-20323-6). Cambridge U Pr.
Contrastive Analysis. Carl James. (Applied Linguistics & Language Study). 1980. pap. text ed. 9.00 (ISBN 0-582-55370-9). Longman.
Contrasts in the Representation of Death by Sophocles, Webster, & Strindberg. Winifred K. Eaton. (Salzburg Studies in English Literature, Jacobean Drama Ser.: No. 17). 1975. pap. text ed. 25.00x (ISBN 0-391-01369-6). Humanities.
Contribucion Al Estudio De los Aphyllophorales Espanoles: With Key to Species in English. M. T. Telleria. (Bibliotheca Mycologica: No. 74). (Illus.). 474p. (Span.). 1981. lib. bdg. 50.00x (ISBN 3-7682-1274-2, Pub. by Cramer Germany). Lubrecht & Cramer.
Contributing. Churches Alive Inc. (Love One Another Bible Study). 1979. wkbk. 1.50 (ISBN 0-934396-05-1). Churches Alive.
Contributing to Family Living: A Guide to Household Management. Penny Stanaford. (Illus.). 99p. 1980. 7.95 (ISBN 0-9604850-1-5). Postscript.
Contribution a L'etude du Genre Colo-Lejeuna. Les Colclejeuniceas de Nouvelles Caledonie. P. Tixier. (Illus.). 1979. pap. text ed. 15.00x (ISBN 3-7682-1230-0). Lubrecht & Cramer.
Contribution of Behavior Modification to Education. Sidney W. Bijou & Roberto Ruiz. 352p. 1980. text ed. 24.95 (ISBN 0-89859-024-8). L Erlbaum Assocs.
Contribution of Behavior Modification to Education. Ed. by Sidney W. Bijou & Roberto Ruiz. 224p. 1981. 24.95 (ISBN 0-89859-051-5). L Erlbaum Assocs.
Contribution of French Historiography to French History. Paul Ricoeur. (Zaharoff Lectures Ser.). 56p. 1980. pap. 8.95x (ISBN 0-19-952249-9). Oxford U Pr.
Contribution of Irrigation & Drainage to World Food Supply. Compiled By American Society of Civil Engineers. 432p. 1975. pap. text ed. 22.00 (ISBN 0-87262-114-6). Am Soc Civil Eng.
Contribution of Varietal Tolerance for Problem Soils to Yield Stability in Rice. (IRRI Research Paper Ser.: No. 43). 15p. 1979. pap. 5.00 (R083, IRRI). Unipub.
Contribution to a Union Catalog of Sixteenth Century Imprints in Certain New England Libraries. Brown University Library. 466p. 1953. 15.00x (ISBN 0-87057-032-3, Pub. by Brown U Pr). Univ Pr of New England.
Contribution to Our Knowledge of Seedlings, 2 vols. Sir John Lubbock. (Landmark Reprints in Plant Science Ser.). 1978. Vol. 1 text ed. 29.50 (ISBN 0-86598-008-X); vol. 2. text ed. 29.50 (ISBN 0-86598-025-X). Allanheld.
Contribution to the Critique of Political Economy. Karl Marx. Ed. by Maurice Dobb. LC 69-20357. 1971. 7.50 o.p. (ISBN 0-7178-0042-3); pap. 3.25 (ISBN 0-7178-0041-5). Intl Pub Co.
Contribution to the Somatology of Periodic Catatonia. Lieve Gjessing. Tr. by H. Marshall. 1976. text ed. 75.00 (ISBN 0-08-015650-9). Pergamon.
Contribution to the Systematics of North American Species of Synhalonia (Hymenoptera, Apoidea) P. H. Timberlake. (U. C. Publ. in Entomology: Vol. 57). 1969. pap. 7.00x (ISBN 0-520-09130-2). U of Cal Pr.
Contribution to the Theory of the Trade Cycle. John R. Hicks. (Illus.). 1950. 11.50x (ISBN 0-19-828112-9). Oxford U Pr.
Contributions by Du Bois in Government Publications & Proceedings. Ed. by Herbert Aptheker. LC 80-13063. (Complete Published Works of W. E. Du Bois). 1981. lib. bdg. 70.00 (ISBN 0-527-25292-1). Kraus Intl.
Contributions of Faraday & Maxwell to Electrical Science. R. A. Tricker. 1966. 23.00 (ISBN 0-08-011977-8); pap. 11.25 (ISBN 0-08-011976-X). Pergamon.
Contributions of Four Accounting Pioneers: Kohler, Littleton, May, Paton. James D. Edwards & Roland F. Salmonson. LC 60-64043. 1961. 7.50 o.p. (ISBN 0-87744-016-6). Mich St U Busn.
Contributions of Joseph Ives to Connecticut Clock Technology, 1810-1862. Kenneth D. Roberts. LC 77-118414. 1970. 24.00 (ISBN 0-913602-00-0). K Roberts.
Contributions of Mussolini to the Civilization of Mankind. Warren S. Creighton. (Illus.). 137p. 1981. 51.55 (ISBN 0-89266-282-4). Am Classical Coll Pr.
Contributions of the Major Philosophers into the Problem of Body Resurrection & Personal Immortality. Richard T. Reesman. (Illus.). 117p. 1981. 41.85 (ISBN 0-89920-021-4). Am Inst Psych.
Contributions of Theology to Medical Ethics. James M. Gustafson. (Pere Marquette Theology Lectures). 1975. 6.95 (ISBN 0-87462-507-6). Marquette.
Contributions of Voice Research to Singing. Ed. by John Large. LC 79-57539. (Illus.). 432p. 1980. pap. text ed. 30.00 (ISBN 0-933014-53-8). College-Hill.
Contributions of Women: Art. Carol Fowler. LC 76-3479. (Contributions of Women Ser.). (Illus.). (gr. 6 up). 1976. PLB 8.95 (ISBN 0-87518-115-5). Dillon.
Contributions of Women: Aviation. Ann Genett. LC 74-19004. (Contributions of Women Ser.). (Illus.). (gr. 6 up). 1975. PLB 8.95 (ISBN 0-87518-089-2). Dillon.
Contributions of Women: Business. Nancy S. Levinson. LC 80-36667. (Contributions of Women Ser.). (Illus.). (gr. 6 up). 1981. PLB 8.95 (ISBN 0-87518-200-3). Dillon.
Contributions of Women: Dance. Carol Fowler. LC 78-10313. (Contributions of Women Ser.). (Illus.). (gr. 6 up). 1979. PLB 8.95 (ISBN 0-87518-169-4). Dillon.
Contributions of Women: Education. Mary W. Burgess. LC 74-32070. (Contributions of Women Ser.). (Illus.). (gr. 6 up). 1975. PLB 8.95 (ISBN 0-87518-080-9). Dillon.
Contributions of Women: Labor. Marcia M. Biddle. LC 78-23303. (Contributions of Women Ser.). (Illus.). (gr. 6 up). 1979. PLB 8.95 (ISBN 0-87518-167-8). Dillon.
Contributions of Women: Politics & Government. Louise G. Greenebaum. LC 77-9593. (Contributions of Women Ser.). (Illus.). (gr. 6 up). 1977. PLB 8.95 (ISBN 0-87518-144-9). Dillon.
Contributions of Women: Religion. Naomi Bloom. LC 77-20034. (Contributions of Women Ser.). (Illus.). (gr. 6 up). 1978. PLB 8.95 (ISBN 0-87518-123-6). Dillon.
Contributions of Women: Science. Diane D. Emberlin. LC 76-30621. (Contributions of Women Ser.). (Illus.). (gr. 6 up). 1977. PLB 8.95 (ISBN 0-87518-136-8). Dillon.
Contributions of Women: Social Reform. Ruth F. Brin. LC 77-9585. (Contributions of Women Ser.). (Illus.). (gr. 6 up). 1977. PLB 8.95 (ISBN 0-87518-145-7). Dillon.
Contributions of Women: Sports. Joan Ryan. LC 74-32058. (Contributions of Women Ser.). (Illus.). 135p. (gr. 6 up). 1975. PLB 8.95 (ISBN 0-87518-082-5). Dillon.
Contributions of Women: Theater. Cynthia Bix & Ann Dillon. LC 77-13094. (Contributions of Women Ser.). (Illus.). (gr. 6 up). 1978. PLB 8.95 (ISBN 0-87518-152-X). Dillon.
Contributions to Behavior - Genetic Analysis. Ed. by Gardner Lindzey & Delbert D. Thiessen. LC 73-92661. (Century Psychology Ser). 1970. 28.00x (ISBN 0-89197-109-2); pap. text ed. 8.95x (ISBN 0-89197-110-6). Irvington.
Contributions to Connecticut Cabinetmaking. Houghton Bulkeley. (Illus.). 1967. 7.50x (ISBN 0-686-26737-0). Conn Hist Soc.
Contributions to Mechanics. Ed. by David Abir. 1969. 67.00 (ISBN 0-08-012822-X). Pergamon.
Contributions to Medical Psychology, Vol. 2. Ed. by S. Rachman. (Illus.). 352p. 1980. 36.00 (ISBN 0-08-024684-2). Pergamon.
Contributions to Probability: A Collection of Papers Dedicated to Eugen Lukacs. Ed. by J. Gani & V. K. Rohatgi. LC 80-768. 1981. 40.00 (ISBN 0-12-274460-8). Acad Pr.
Contributions to Science. Ed. by Weymouth T. Jordan. (Illus.). 1954. pap. 2.00 o.p. (ISBN 0-8130-0461-6). U Presses Fla.
Contributions to Science. Ed. by William Randel et al. (Florida State U. Ser). (Illus.). 173p. 1950. pap. 2.50 o.p. (ISBN 0-8130-0451-9). U Presses Fla.
Contributions to Sensory Physiology, 5 vols. Ed. by William D. Neff. Incl. Vol. 1. 1965. 38.50 (ISBN 0-12-151801-9); Vol. 2. 1967 (ISBN 0-12-151802-7); Vol. 3. 1969 (ISBN 0-12-151803-5); Vol. 4. 1970 (ISBN 0-12-151804-3); Vol. 5. 1971 (ISBN 0-12-151805-1). 38.50 ea. Acad Pr.
Contributions to South Asian Studies I. Ed. by Gopal Krishna. (Illus.). 206p. 1979. text ed. 13.95x (ISBN 0-19-520252-X). Oxford U Pr.
Contributions to the Biology of Carapid Fishes (Paracanthopterygii, Gadiformes) Lamarr B. Trott. (U. C. Publ. in Zoology: Vol. 89). 1970. pap. 6.00x (ISBN 0-520-09346-1). U of Cal Pr.
Contributions to Thermal Physiology: Proceedings of a Satellite Symposium of the 28th International Congress of Physiological Sciences, Budapest, 1980. Z Szelenyi & M. Szekely. LC 80-41854. (Advances in Physiological Sciences Ser.: Vol. 32). (Illus.). 560p. 1981. 60.00 (ISBN 0-08-027354-8). Pergamon.
Contributors. Rowley S. Atterbury. (Illus.). 14.50 (ISBN 0-913720-03-8). Sandstone.
Control & Coordination in Hierarchical Systems. W. Findeisen et al. (IIASA International Ser. on Applied Systems Analysis: No. 9). 480p. 1980. 67.50 (ISBN 0-471-27742-8). Wiley.
Control & Dynamic Systems. Y. Takahashi et al. 1970. 27.95 (ISBN 0-201-07440-0). A-W.
Control & Dynamic Systems: Advances Theory & Application, Vol. 16. LC 64-8027. (Serial Publications Ser.). 1980. 27.50 (ISBN 0-12-012716-4). Acad Pr.
Control & Ideology in Organizations. Ed. by Graeme Salaman & Kenneth Thompson. 350p. (Orig.). 1980. pap. 12.50 (ISBN 0-262-69069-1). MIT Pr.
Control & Management of Capital Projects. John W. Hackney. LC 65-26846. 1965. 32.50 (ISBN 0-471-33846-X, Pub. by Wiley-Interscience). Wiley.
Control Language Summary. Ed. by Alan B. Forsythe. (BMDP Statistical Software). 56p. (Orig.). 1980. pap. 3.00 (ISBN 0-935386-01-7). UCLA Dept Biomath.
Control Mechanisms & Protein Synthesis. S. D. Wainwright. LC 72-2348. (Molecular Biology Ser). 528p. 1972. 30.00x (ISBN 0-231-03432-6). Columbia U Pr.
Control Mechanisms in Animal Cells: Specific Growth Factors. Ed. by L. Jimenez de Asua. 400p. 1980. text ed. 36.50 (ISBN 0-89004-509-7). Raven.
Control Mechanisms in Cancer. Ed. by Wayne E. Criss et al. LC 75-30234. (Progress in Cancer Research & Therapy Ser: Vol.1). 1976. 46.00 (ISBN 0-89004-083-4). Raven.
Control Mechanisms in Developmental Processes. Ed. by Michael Locke & Michael Locke. 1968. 37.50 (ISBN 0-12-612950-9); pap. 28.50 o.p. (ISBN 0-12-612956-8). Acad Pr.
Control Mechanisms in Plant Development. Arthur W. Galston & Peter J. Davies. (Foundations of Developmental Biology Ser). 1970. pap. 11.95x ref. ed. (ISBN 0-13-171801-0). P-H.
Control of Breathing During Sleep. Ed. by Colin E. Sullivan et al. (Sleep Ser.: Vol. 3, No. 3-4). 256p. 1981. text ed. 30.00 (ISBN 0-89004-652-2). Raven.
Control of Critical Points in Food Processing: A Systems Approach. Ed. by Edwin S. Doyle & Abe Mittler. (Illus.). 270p. 1977. text ed. 25.00 (ISBN 0-937774-04-9). Food Processors.
Control of DP Production. National Computing Centre. Ed. by G. S. Walker. LC 80-483613. (Illus.). 121p. 1980. pap. 27.50x (ISBN 0-85012-227-9). Intl Pubns Serv.
Control of Dynamic Systems: Advances in Theory & Application, Vols. 9, 10, 13 & 15. Ed. by C. T. Leondes. Incl. Vol. 9. 44.00 (ISBN 0-12-012709-1); Vol. 10. 44.00 (ISBN 0-12-012710-5); Vol. 13. 1977. 39.00 (ISBN 0-12-012713-X); Vol. 15. 1979. 22.50 (ISBN 0-12-012715-6). 1973. Acad Pr.
Control of Electric Machines. Irving L. Kosow. LC 72-5631. (Electronic Technology Ser). (Illus.). 368p. 1973. ref. ed. 21.95 (ISBN 0-13-171785-5). P-H.
Control of Engineering Projects. Ed. by S. H. Wearne. (Illus.). 1974. pap. 12.95x (ISBN 0-7131-3330-9). Intl Ideas.
Control of Feeding Behavior, & Biology of the Brain in Protein-Calorie Malnutrition. Ed. by Richard J. Wurtman & Judith J. Wurtman. LC 75-14593. (Nutrition & the Brain Ser: Vol. 2). 1977. 31.50 (ISBN 0-89004-046-X). Raven.
Control of Fish Quality. 222p. 1980. 21.25 (ISBN 0-85238-105-0, FN 83, FN). Unipub.
Control of Fluid Power. D. McCloy & H. R. Martin. LC 72-5349. 1973. 37.95 (ISBN 0-470-58195-6). Halsted Pr.
Control of Fluid Power: Analysis & Design. 2nd rev. ed. D. McCloy. LC 80-40027. 500p. 1980. 85.00 (ISBN 0-470-27012-8). Halsted Pr.
Control of Growth & Differentiation in Plants. 2nd ed. P. F. Wareing & I. D. Phillips. LC 78-30561. 1979. text ed. 45.00 (ISBN 0-08-021526-2); pap. text ed. 18.50 (ISBN 0-686-68007-3). Pergamon.
Control of Industry. Dennis Robertson & S. Dennison. (Cambridge Economic Handbook Ser). 1960. 10.95x (ISBN 0-521-08766-X). Cambridge U Pr.
Control of Iodine in the Nuclear Industry. (Technical Reports Ser.: No. 148). (Illus.). 101p. (Orig.). 1973. pap. 8.25 (ISBN 92-0-025073-4, IAEA). Unipub.
Control of Livestock Insect Pests by the Sterile Male Technique. (Illus., Orig.). 1968. pap. 6.50 (ISBN 92-0-011368-0, IAEA). Unipub.
Control of Long-Term International Capital Movements. Sir Alec Cairncross. 1973. pap. 3.95 (ISBN 0-8157-1237-5). Brookings.
Control of Natural Monopolies. Richard Schmalensee. LC 78-6061. 1979. 18.95 (ISBN 0-669-02322-1). Lexington Bks.
Control of Naval Armaments: Prospects & Possibilities. Barry M. B. Blechman. (Studies in Defense Policy). 1975. 3.95 (ISBN 0-8157-0987-0). Brookings.
Control of Neoplasia by Modulation of the Immune System. Ed. by Michael A. Chirigos. LC 76-5665. (Progress in Cancer Research & Therapy Ser.: Vol. 2). 1977. 43.50 (ISBN 0-89004-125-3). Raven.
Control of Oil. John Blair. 1978. pap. 4.95 (ISBN 0-394-72532-8, V-532, Vin). Random.
Control of Oil Pollution on the Sea & Inland Waters. Ed. by J. Wardley-Smith. 1976. 37.50x (ISBN 0-86010-021-9). Intl Pubns Serv.
Control of Oil Pollution on the Sea & Inland Waters. Ed. by J. Wardley-Smith. 251p. 1976. 26.00x (ISBN 0-686-64023-3, Pub. by Graham & Trotman England). State Mutual Bk.
Control of Ovulation. new ed. Ed. by D. B. Crighton et al. LC 78-40043. 1978. 74.95 (ISBN 0-408-70924-3). Butterworths.
Control of Ovulation. Ed. by C. A. Villee. 1961. pap. 16.00 (ISBN 0-08-013650-8). Pergamon.
Control of Reproductive Functions in Domestic Animals. Wolfgang Jochle & Ross Lamond. (Current Topics in Veterinary Medicine & Animal Science Ser.: No. 7). (Illus.). 1981. PLB 39.50 (ISBN 90-247-2400-7, Pub. by Martinus Nijhoff). Kluwer Boston.
Control of Technology. D. Elliot & R. Elliot. (Wykeham Science Ser.: Vol. 39). 1976. pap. 9.60 o.p. (ISBN 0-387-91130-8). Springer-Verlag.
Control of the Onset of Puberty. Ed. by Melvin M. Grumbach et al. LC 73-18091. (Clinical Pediatrics, Maternal & Child Health Ser.). 512p. 1974. 46.95 (ISBN 0-471-32265-2, Pub. by Wiley Medical). Wiley.
Control of the Upper-Extremity Prostheses & Orthoses. Ed. by Peter Herberts et al. (Illus.). 276p. 1974. 25.50 (ISBN 0-398-02869-9). C C Thomas.
Control of Urban Schools: Perspective on the Power of Educational Reformers. Joseph M. Cronin. LC 72-78608. 288p. 1973. 10.95 (ISBN 0-02-906910-6). Free Pr.
Control of Water Resource Systems: Proceedings of a IIASA Workshop, October, 1979. Ed. by E. F. Wood & A. Szollosi-Nagy. (IIASA Proceedings Ser: Vol. 8). 1980. 58.00 (ISBN 0-08-024486-6). Pergamon.
Control, Operation & Management of Activated Sludge Plants. W. W. Eckenfelder, Jr. et al. (Series I,Book 3). text ed. 40.00 (ISBN 0-937976-01-6). Enviro Pr.
Control Processes in Virus Multiplication. Ed. by D. C. Burke & W. C. Russell. (Society for General Microbiology Symposia Ser.: No. 25). (Illus.). 450p. 1975. 59.50 (ISBN 0-521-20728-2). Cambridge U Pr.
Control Programs of Nonlinear Programming: Proceedings of the IFAC Workshop, Denver, Colorado, USA, June 1979. Ed. by H. E. Rauch. (IFAC Proceedings). 130p. 1980. 35.00 (ISBN 0-08-024491-2). Pergamon.
Control System Design. 2nd ed. C. J. Savant, Jr. 1964. text ed. 25.50 o.p. (ISBN 0-07-054959-1, C). McGraw.
Control Systems Engineering. I. J. Nagrath & M. Gopal. 1977. pap. 12.95x (ISBN 0-470-99281-6). Halsted Pr.
Control Systems for Heating, Ventilating & Air Conditioning. R. W. Haines. LC 78-56751. 1978. pap. text ed. 8.00 (ISBN 0-8273-1804-9). Delmar.
Control Systems of Variable Structure. U. Itkis. LC 76-4870. 1976. 43.95 (ISBN 0-470-15072-6). Halsted Pr.
Control Theory & Biological Systems. Fred S. Grodins. LC 63-10521. 1963. 15.00x (ISBN 0-231-02517-3). Columbia U Pr.
Control Theory & Mathematical Economics: Proceedings of the Third Kingston Conference, Pt. B. P. T. Liu & J. G. Sutinen. 26.50 (ISBN 0-8247-6852-3). Dekker.
Control Theory & the Calculus of Variations. Ed. by A. V. Balakrishnan. LC 74-91431. 1969. 37.50 (ISBN 0-12-076953-0). Acad Pr.
Control Theory & Topics in Functional Analysis: Proceedings, 2 vols. International Seminar, Trieste. (Illus.). 1976. Vol. 2. pap. 26.75 (ISBN 92-0-130176-6, IAEA); Vol. 3. pap. 33.25 (ISBN 9-2013-0276-2). Unipub.
Control Theory & Topics in Functional Analysis: Proceedings, Vol. 1. (Illus.). 465p. 1976. pap. 37.50 (ISBN 92-0-130076-X, IAEA). Unipub.
Control Theory in Biology & Experimental Psychology. F. M. Toates. 1980. text ed. 21.00x (ISBN 0-09-119660-4, Hutchinson U Lib). Humanities.
Control Treatment & Rehabilitation of Juvenile Offenders. E. Eldefonso & W. Hartinger. 1976. 14.95x (ISBN 0-02-474160-4, 47416). Macmillan.
Control Yourself. David R. Wheeler. LC 75-15259. 180p. 1976. 12.95 (ISBN 0-88229-207-2). Nelson-Hall.
Controlled Environment Guidelines for Plant Research. Ed. by T. Tibbitts & T. K. Kozlowski. LC 79-23521. 1980. 25.00 (ISBN 0-12-690950-4). Acad Pr.
Controlled Environments for Plant Growth. Robert J. Downs. (Illus.). 200p. 1975. 17.50x (ISBN 0-231-03561-6). Columbia U Pr.

Controlled Nuclear Fusion: Current Research & Potential Progress. Committee on Nuclear & Alternative Energy Systems, National Research Council. 1978. pap. text ed. 4.75x (ISBN 0-309-02863-9). Natl Acad Pr.

Controlled Release of Bioactive Materials. Ed. by Richard Baker. 1980. 34.50 (ISBN 0-12-074450-3). Acad Pr.

Controlled Release Pharmaceuticals. Ed. by John Urquhart. LC 80-70561. 160p. 1981. pap. 27.00 (ISBN 0-917330-34-X). Am Pharm Assn.

Controlled Release Theologies, 2 vols. Agis F. Kydonieus. 1980. Vol. 1, 272p. 69.95 (ISBN 0-8493-5641-5); Vol. 2, 288p. 69.95 (ISBN 0-8493-5642-3). CRC Pr.

Controlled Storm Water Drainage. Louis Blendermann. LC 78-15080. (Illus.). 200p. 1979. 27.00 (ISBN 0-8311-1123-2). Indus Pr.

Controllership. 2nd ed. J. Brooks Heckert & J. D. Willson. (Illus.). 1963. 29.50 (ISBN 0-8260-4025-X, Pub. by Ronald Pr); instructors' manual avail. (ISBN 0-685-19872-3, Pub. by Ronald Pr). Ronald Pr.

Controllership: The Work of the Managerial Accountant. 3rd ed. James D. Willson & John B. Campbell. 800p. Date not set. write for info. (ISBN 0-471-05711-8). Wiley.

Controllership: The Work of the Managerial Accountant. 3rd ed. James D. Willson & John B. Campbell. 800p. 1981. 29.95 (ISBN 0-471-05711-8). Ronald Pr.

Controlling Airborne Particles. Committee on Particulate Control Technology, National Research Council. xi, 114p. (Orig.). 1980. pap. text ed. 8.00 (ISBN 0-309-03035-8). Natl Acad Pr.

Controlling Corrosion in Process Industry. Kenneth J. McNaughton et al. (Chemical Engineering Book Ser.). 288p. 1980. 24.50 (ISBN 0-07-010691-6). McGraw.

Controlling Diabetes with Diet. Annette Gormican. (Illus.). 232p. 1976. pap. 10.75 spiral (ISBN 0-398-00705-5). C C Thomas.

Controlling Discipline in Schools. Jim Docking. 1980. text ed. 18.35 (ISBN 0-06-318152-5, IntlDept); pap. text ed. 10.45 (ISBN 0-06-318153-3). Har-Row.

Controlling Drugs: International Handbook for Psychoactive Drug Classification. Richard H. Blum et al. LC 73-9070. (Social & Behavioral Science Ser.). 544p. 1974. 25.00x o.p. (ISBN 0-87589-203-5). Jossey-Bass.

Controlling Fruit Flies by the Sterile-Insect Technique. (Illus.). 175p. 1976. pap. 13.50 (ISBN 92-0-111575-X, IAEA). Unipub.

Controlling Infection. (Nursing Photobook Ser.). (Illus.). 160p. 1981. text ed. 12.95 (ISBN 0-916730-35-2). Intermed Comm.

Controlling Interest. Peter Engel. 384p. 1981. 13.95 (ISBN 0-312-16919-1). St Martin.

Controlling International Technology Transfer: Issues, Perspectives, & Policy Implications. Ed. by Tagi Sagafi-nejad et al. LC 80-28329. (PPS on International Development Ser.). 525p. 1981. 55.00. Pergamon.

Controlling International Violence Through International Institutions: Empirical Policy Analysis Materials. rev. ed. J. Martin Rochester & Jean Stern. Ed. by William D. Coplin. (Learning Packages in International Relations Ser.: No. 3). 88p. (Orig.). 1971. pap. text ed. 4.00x (ISBN 0-915984-73-3). Maxwell Schl Citizen.

Controlling London's Growth: Planning the Great Wen, 1940-1960. Donald L. Foley. (Illus.). 1963. 18.50x (ISBN 0-520-00424-8). U of Cal Pr.

Controlling Medicaid Utilization Patterns. John Holahan & Bruce Stuart. (Medicaid Cost Containment Ser.). 127p. 1977. pap. 4.00 (ISBN 0-87766-196-0, 17900). Urban Inst.

Controlling Strategic Nuclear Weapons. Walter Slocombe. (Headline Ser.: 226). (Illus.). 1975. pap. 2.00 (ISBN 0-87124-031-9, 75-9293). Foreign Policy.

Controlling Stress & Tension: A Holistic Approach. Daniel A. Girdano & George S. Everly, Jr. (Illus.). 1979. 12.95 (ISBN 0-13-172114-3); pap. 6.95 (ISBN 0-13-172106-2). P-H.

Controlling Technology: Genetic Engineering & the Law. Yvonne M. Cripps. 170p. 1980. 20.95 (ISBN 0-03-056806-4). Praeger.

Controlling the Spread of Infection: A Programmed Presentation. 2nd ed. Betty McInnes. LC 76-48945. (Illus.). 1977. pap. text ed. 8.00 (ISBN 0-8016-3334-6). Mosby.

Controlling the Supply of Hospital Beds. Institute of Medicine. LC 77-74651. 1977. pap. 6.00 (ISBN 0-309-02610-5). Natl Acad Pr.

Controlling the World with Your TRS-80. David A. Lieh. Ed. by David Gunzel. (Compusoft Learning Ser.). (Illus.). 300p. (gr. 7 up). 1981. pap. 19.95 (ISBN 0-932760-03-1). CompuSoft.

Controlling Tomorrow. LC 79-49831. 1980. 14.95 (ISBN 0-87863-202-6). Farnswth Pub.

Controlling Waste Anesthetic Gases. American Society for Hospital Engineering of the American Hospital Association. (Illus.). 52p. 1980. 10.75 (ISBN 0-87258-308-2, 1222). Am Hospital.

Controlling Your Weight. Barbara Benziger. (gr. 7-9). 1975. pap. 1.25 o.s.i. (ISBN 0-671-29735-X). Archway.

Controlling Your Weight. Barbara Benziger. (Illus.). (YA) (gr. 7-9). 1975. pap. 1.25 (ISBN 0-671-29735-X). PB.

Controlling Your Weight: A Concise Guide. Barbara Benziger. LC 73-5888. (Career Concise Guides Ser.). (gr. 5 up). 1973. PLB 4.90 o.p. (ISBN 0-531-02639-6). Watts.

Contrology: Beyond the New Criminology. Jason Ditton. (Illus.). 1979. text ed. 23.25x (ISBN 0-333-25965-3). Humanities.

Controls of Eating. Carl Thompson. LC 79-17853. (Monographs in Pharmacology & Physiology: Bol. 4). 296p. 1979. text ed. 40.00 (ISBN 0-89335-100-8). Spectrum Pub.

Controls on Health Care. Institute of Medicine. 1975. pap. 7.25 (ISBN 0-309-02330-0). Natl Acad Pr.

Controls Over Using & Changing Computer Programs. 1979. pap. 5.00. Am Inst CPA.

Controversial Horse. R. S. Summerhays & Stella A. Walker. (Illus.). 8.75 (ISBN 0-85131-075-3, Dist. by Sporting Book Center). J A Allen.

Controversial Issues in Gerontology. Harold J. Wershow. 1981. text ed. price not set (ISBN 0-8261-3100-X); pap. text ed. price not set (ISBN 0-8261-3101-8). Springer Pub.

Controversial Issues in Human Relations Training Groups. Kenneth T. Morris & Kenneth M. Cinnamon. 168p. 1975. 13.75 (ISBN 0-398-03456-7); pap. 8.50 (ISBN 0-398-03458-3). C C Thomas.

Controversial Issues in Our Schools. William Goldstein. LC 80-82679. (Fastback Ser.: No. 146). (Orig.). 1980. pap. 0.75 (ISBN 0-87367-146-5). Phi Delta Kappa.

Controversial Sholem Asch: An Introduction to His Fiction. Ben Siegel. LC 76-43446. 1976. 12.95 (ISBN 0-87972-076-X); pap. 7.95 (ISBN 0-87972-170-7). Bowling Green Univ.

Controversies in American Voting Behavior. Ed. by Richard G. Niemi & Herbert F. Weisberg. LC 76-13564. (Illus.). 1976. text ed. 21.95x (ISBN 0-7167-0536-2); pap. text ed. 10.95x (ISBN 0-7167-0535-4). W H Freeman.

Controversies in British Macroeconomics. K. A. Chrystal. 1979. 21.00x (ISBN 0-86003-022-9, Pub. by Allan Pubs England); pap. 10.50x (ISBN 0-86003-123-3). State Mutual Bk.

Controversies in Cancer: Design of Trials & Treatment. Ed. by Henri J. Tagnon & Maurice J. Staquet. LC 79-84480. (Illus.). 246p. 1979. 39.75 (ISBN 0-89352-049-7). Masson Pub.

Controversies in Child Health & Pediatrics. David H. Smith & Robert A. Hokelman. (Illus.). 480p. 1981. text ed. 29.95 (ISBN 0-07-058510-5, HP). McGraw.

Controversies in Nephrology. G. E. Schreiner. (Illus.). 722p. 1979. 49.50. Masson Pub.

Controversies in Nutrition. Leon Ellenbogen. (Contemporary Issues in Clinical Nutrition Ser.). (Illus.). 224p. 1981. lib. bdg. 20.00 (ISBN 0-443-08127-1). Churchill.

Controversies in Nutrition. Leon Ellenboren. (Contemporary Issues in Clinical Nutrition Ser.). 1981. text ed. price not set (ISBN 0-443-08127-1). Churchill.

Controversies in Patient Management. Ed. by V. Rosenoer & M. A. Rothschild. LC 80-21593. (Illus.). 312p. text ed. 30.00 (ISBN 0-89335-121-0). Spectrum Pub.

Controversies in Surgical Sepsis. Stephen Karran. 350p. 1980. 38.50. Praeger.

Controversy Advertising: How Advertisers Present Points of View in Public Affairs. Informational Advertising Association. (Illus.). 1977. pap. 9.50 (ISBN 0-8038-1215-9). Hastings.

Controversy & Dialogue in Marketing. Ross Goble & Roy Shaw. (Illus.). 480p. 1975. pap. text ed. 10.95 (ISBN 0-13-172320-0). P-H.

Controversy in Obstetrics & Gynecology Two. 2nd ed. Ed. by Duncan E. Reid & C. Donald Christian. LC 73-93432. (Illus.). 365p. 1974. text ed. 38.00 (ISBN 0-7216-7528-X). Saunders.

Controversy in Otolaryngology. Ed. by James B. Snow, Jr. LC 79-64601. (Illus.). 561p. 1980. text ed. 45.00 (ISBN 0-7216-8433-5). Saunders.

Controversy in Psychiatry. Ed. by John P. Brady & H. Keith Brodie. LC 77-77097. (Illus.). 1978. text ed. 19.50 (ISBN 0-7216-1912-6). Saunders.

Controversy: Politics of Technical Decisions. Dorothy Nelkin. LC 78-21339. (Focus Editions Ser.: Vol. 8). 256p. 1979. 18.95 (ISBN 0-8039-1209-9); pap. 9.95 (ISBN 0-8039-1210-2). Sage.

Controversy: Politics of Technical Decisions. Ed. by Dorothy Nelkin. LC 78-21339. (Sage Focus Editions: Vol. 8). 256p. 1979. 18.95 (ISBN 0-8039-1209-9); pap. 9.95 (ISBN 0-8039-1210-2). Sage.

Conures. Tony Silva & Barbara Kotlar. (Illus.). 96p. 1980. 2.95 (ISBN 0-87666-893-7, KW-121). TFH Pubns.

Convection Cookery. Caroline Kriz. LC 80-19915. (Illus.). 152p. (Orig.). 1980. pap. 5.95 (ISBN 0-89286-181-9). One Hund One Prods.

Convection Oven Cook Book. Sunset Editors. LC 80-81283. (Illus.). 96p. (Orig.). 1980. pap. 3.95 (ISBN 0-376-02311-2, Sunset Bks.). Sunset-Lane.

Convection Oven Cookbook. Consumer Guide Editors & Beatrice A. Ojakangas. (Illus.). 1980. pap. 6.95 (ISBN 0-449-90042-8, Columbine). Fawcett.

Convection Oven Cookbook. Carmel B. Reingold. LC 80-7859. 170p. 1980. 13.95; pap. 7.95. Lippincott & Crowell.

Convection Oven Cookbook. Carmel B. Reingold. 1980. 13.95 (ISBN 0-690-01980-7, HarpT); pap. 7.95 (ISBN 0-690-01982-3, HarpT). Har-Row.

Convection Oven Cooking. Linda A. Verkler & Edward N. Zempel. LC 79-63184. (Illus.). 1979. 10.95 o.p. (ISBN 0-930358-04-X); pap. 6.95 (ISBN 0-930358-03-1). Spoon River.

Convective Boiling & Condensation. 2nd ed. J. G. Collier. (Illus.). 460p. 1981. text ed. 59.50 (ISBN 0-07-011798-5). McGraw.

Convective Heat & Mass Transfer. 2nd ed. William M. Kays & Michael Crawford. (Mechanical Engineering Ser.). (Illus.). 1980. text ed. 27.95 (ISBN 0-07-033457-9); solutions manual 8.95 (ISBN 0-07-033458-7). McGraw.

Convective Stability of Incompressable Fluids. G. Z. Gershuni & E. M. Zhukovitskii. 1976. 41.95 o.p. (ISBN 0-470-98981-5). Halsted Pr.

Convencion Sobre Defensa Del Patrimonio Arqueologico, Historico y Artistico De las Naciones Americanas. (Treaty Ser.: No. 47). (Eng, Span, Port, Fr.). 1977. pap. text ed. 1.00 (ISBN 0-8270-0565-2). OAS.

Convenience & Fast Food Handbook. Marvin E. Thorner. (Illus.). 1973. text ed. 24.50 (ISBN 0-87055-134-5). AVI.

Convenience Foods & Microwave, GA-044: Directions. Business Communications Co. 1980. 725.00 (ISBN 0-89336-227-1). BCC.

Convention Decisions & Voting Records. rev. 2nd ed. Richard C. Bain & Judith H. Parris. (Studies in Presidential Selection). 500p. 1973. 15.95 (ISBN 0-8157-0768-1). Brookings.

Convention Hookers. 1976. pap. 1.50 (ISBN 0-685-91741-X). Tower Bks.

Convention on Territorial Asylum. (Treaty Ser.: No. 19). (Span., Fr., Eng. & Port.). 1954. pap. 1.00 (ISBN 0-8270-0365-X). OAS.

Convention on the Inter-Governmental Maritime Consultative Organization. 24p. 1979. 8.25 (IMCO). Unipub.

Convention Problem: Issues in Reform of Presidential Nominating Procedures. Judith H. Parris. (Studies in Presidential Selection). 176p. 1972. 10.95 (ISBN 0-8157-6928-8); pap. 4.95 (ISBN 0-8157-6927-X). Brookings.

Conventional & the Alternative in Education. new ed. Goodlad. LC 75-2780. 288p. 1975. 16.60x (ISBN 0-8211-0611-2); text ed. 15.00x (ISBN 0-685-53835-4). McCutchan.

Convergence of Probability Measures. P. Billingsley. (Probability & Mathematical Statistics Tracts: Probability & Statistics Section). 1968. 27.50 (ISBN 0-471-07242-7, Pub by Wiley-Interscience). Wiley.

Conversas Intimas. Tr. by Manoel A. Ribeiro. (Portugese Bks.). (Port.). 1979. 1.00 (ISBN 0-8297-0651-8). Life Pubs Intl.

Conversation Analysis: The Sociology of Talk. Donald Allen & Rebecca Guy. (Janua Linguarum, Ser. Minor: No. 200). 284p. 1978. pap. text ed. 31.75x (ISBN 90-279-3002-3). Mouton.

Conversation Book: English in Everyday Life, Bk. 1. Tina K. Carver & S. Douglas Fotinos. (Illus.). 1977. pap. text ed. 7.50 (ISBN 0-13-172239-5). P-H.

Conversation Book: English in Everyday Life, Bk. 2. Tina K. Carver & S. Douglas Fotinos. (Illus.). 1977. pap. text ed. 7.50 (ISBN 0-13-172247-6). P-H.

Conversation in English: Points of Departure. 2nd ed. Julia M. Dobson & Frank Sedwick. (Illus.). 112p. 1981. pap. text ed. 3.80 (ISBN 0-278-46430-0). Litton Educ Pub.

Conversation in English: Professional Careers. Julia M. Dobson & Gerald S. Hawkins. (Illus.). 108p. (gr. 9-12). 1978. pap. text ed. 3.96 (ISBN 0-278-46440-8). Litton Educ Pub.

Conversation in French: Points of Departure. 3rd ed. Peter Bonnell & Frank Sedwick. (Orig.). 1981. pap. text ed. write for info. (ISBN 0-442-24468-1). D Van Nostrand.

Conversation in German: Points of Departure. 3rd ed. Peter Bonnell & Frank Sedwick. (Orig.). 1981. pap. text ed. write for info. (ISBN 0-442-24466-5). D Van Nostrand.

Conversation in Italian: Points of Departure. 2nd ed. Paolozzi & Sedwick. (Illus., Orig.). 1981. pap. text ed. write for info. (ISBN 0-442-24474-6). D Van Nostrand.

Conversation in Portuguese: Points of Departure. rev 2nd ed. Neil Miller. LC 80-83025. (Illus.). 1980. pap. text ed. 5.95x (ISBN 0-9601444-2-0). N Miller.

Conversation in Spanish: Points of Departure. 3rd ed. Frank Sedwick. (Orig.). 1981. pap. text ed. write for info. (ISBN 0-442-24467-3). D Van Nostrand.

Conversation on Freemasonry. Henry W. Coil. 1980. Repr. soft cover 12.50 (ISBN 0-686-68272-6). Macoy Pub.

Conversation Starters for Speech & Language Therapy. 1981. pap. 2.75 (ISBN 0-8134-2186-1, 2186). Interstate.

Conversation Today. Albert B. Dahlquist. 14.95 (ISBN 0-911012-66-4). Nelson-Hall.

Conversational & Cultural French. Joseph Palmeri. (Fr.). 1966. text ed. 14.95 (ISBN 0-13-171900-9). P-H.

Conversational BASIC: A Dialogue Approach to Programming. Michael Mulcahy. LC 80-16705. 1980. pap. 11.95 (ISBN 0-8436-1600-8). CBI Pub.

Conversational Brazilian-Portuguese in 20 Lessons. The R. D. Cortina Company. 192p. 1980. pap. 3.95 (ISBN 0-06-463607-0, EH 607, EH). Har-Row.

Conversational English for the Non-English-Speaking Child. Nina Phillips. LC 68-23006. 1968. pap. text ed. 5.50x (ISBN 0-8077-1907-2). Tchrs Coll.

Conversational English in Ten Days. 1981. pap. 14.95 including tape (ISBN 0-686-69460-0). Plymouth Pr.

Conversational Japanese. rev. ed. (Cortina Method Language Ser). (Illus.). 6.95 o.p. (ISBN 0-385-00256-4). Doubleday.

Conversational Japanese in Twenty Lessons. The R. D. Cortina Company. 256p. 1980. pap. 4.95 (ISBN 0-06-463606-2, EH 606, EH). Har-Row.

Conversational Languages. I. Kupka & N. Wilsing. LC 80-40120. (Computing Ser.). 128p. 1980. text ed. 27.75 (ISBN 0-471-27778-9, Pub. by Wiley-Interscience). Wiley.

Conversational Modern Greek in Twenty Lessons. The R. D. Cortina Company. 288p. 1980. pap. 4.95 (ISBN 0-06-463604-6, EH 604, EH). Har-Row.

Conversational Prayer. Rosalind Rinker. 1976. pap. 1.75 (ISBN 0-89129-210-1). Jove Pubns.

Conversational Prayer. Rosalind Rinker. (Orig.). pap. 1.50 (ISBN 0-89129-210-1). Jove Pubns.

Conversational Routine. Ed. by Florian Coulmas. (Janua Linguarum, Ser. Maior-Rasmus Rask Studies in Pragmatic Linguistics: Vol. 2). 1980. text ed. 38.25x (ISBN 90-279-3098-8). Mouton.

Conversational Russian Twenty Lessons. 448p. 1980. pap. 5.95 (ISBN 0-06-463605-4, EH 605, EH). Har-Row.

Conversational Spanish for Medical Personnel. Rochelle Kelz. LC 76-55722. 1977. pap. text ed. 12.95 (ISBN 0-471-02154-7, Pub. by Wiley Medical). Wiley.

Conversational Spanish Review Grammar. R. J. Mondelli & Italo L. Ponterotto. (gr. 9-12). 1961. text ed. 5.25 o.p. (ISBN 0-8260-6185-0, Pub. by Ronald Pr). Wiley.

Conversational Statistics. Harry V. Roberts. (Data Analysis Series). 256p. 1974. pap. text ed. 15.95 (ISBN 0-07-053135-8, C). McGraw.

Conversationally Speaking: Tested New Ways to Increase Your Personal & Social Effectiveness. Alan Garner. 164p. (Orig.). 1980. pap. 4.95 (ISBN 0-938044-00-1). Psych Res Assoc.

Conversations. William A. Miller. LC 80-54283. 96p. 1980. pap. 3.95 (ISBN 0-934104-04-2). Woodland.

Conversations. The Mother. 1979. pap. 2.00 (ISBN 0-89744-935-5). Auromere.

Conversations at Little Gidding. Alvin M. Williams, Jr. LC 78-85741. (Illus.). 1970. 58.00 (ISBN 0-521-07680-3). Cambridge U Pr.

Conversations on the Principal Subjects of Political Economy. William Elder. (Neglected American Economists Ser.). 1974. lib. bdg. 50.00 (ISBN 0-8240-1021-3). Garland Pub.

Conversations: Reynolds Price & William Ray. Ed. by William Ray. (Mississippi Collection Bulletin, No. 9). (Illus.). 82p. 1976. pap. 5.95x (ISBN 0-87870-086-2). Memphis St Univ.

Conversations with a Corpse. Robert Dennis. 192p. 1976. pap. 1.50 o.p. (ISBN 0-345-25216-0). Ballantine.

Conversations with a Dancer. Kitty Cunningham. (Illus.). 192p. 1980. 12.95 (ISBN 0-312-16942-6). St Martin.

Conversations with an Executioner. Kazimierz Moczarski. (Illus.). 256p. 1981. 12.95 (ISBN 0-13-171918-1). P-H.

Conversations with Andre Gide. Claude Mauriac. LC 65-23178. 1965. 5.00 o.s.i. (ISBN 0-8076-0320-1). Braziller.

Conversations with Chester I. Barnard. William B. Wolf. LC 72-619666. (ILR Paperback Ser.: No. 12). 1973. pap. 6.25 special bdg. (ISBN 0-87546-280-4); pap. 3.25 (ISBN 0-87546-047-X). NY Sch Indus Rel.

Conversations with Frank Waters. Ed. & intro. by John Milton. LC 78-189195. 90p. 1971. 5.00 o.s.i. (ISBN 0-8040-0575-3); pap. 3.50 (ISBN 0-8040-0576-1). Swallow.

Conversations with Henry Moore. David Brewster. 1978. 2.50 (ISBN 0-686-63617-1). Jawbone Pr.

Conversations with Jazz Musicians. Ed. by Matthew J. Bruccoli et al. LC 77-9143. (Conversations Ser.: Vol. 2). 1977. 30.00 (ISBN 0-8103-0944-0, A Bruccoli Clark Book). Gale.

Conversations with Lukacs. Ed. by Theo Pinkus. LC 74-34021. 1975. 9.95x (ISBN 0-262-16062-5); pap. 4.95 (ISBN 0-262-66044-X). MIT Pr.

Conversations with Marilyn. W. J. Weatherby. 1977. pap. 1.75 o.p. (ISBN 0-345-25568-2). Ballantine.

Conversations with My Soul. Charles B. De La Fontein. (Intimate Life of Man Library). (Illus.). 1979. 37.50 (ISBN 0-89266-185-2). Am Classical Coll Pr.

Conversations with Seth, Vol. 1. Susan M. Watkins. LC 80-17760. 1980. 10.95 (ISBN 0-13-172007-4). P-H.

Conversations with the Dead: Photographs of Prison Life. Danny Lyon & Billy McCune. (Illus.). 1970. pap. 0.25 (ISBN 0-914412-00-0). Inst for the Arts.

Conversations with Toscanini. 2nd ed. B. H. Haggin. 1980. 11.95 (ISBN 0-8180-1244-7); pap. 5.95 (ISBN 0-8180-1220-X). Horizon.

Conversations with W. H. Auden. Howard Griffin. LC 80-24381. 128p. 1981. 12.95 (ISBN 0-912516-55-0); pap. 4.95 (ISBN 0-912516-56-9). Grey Fox.

Conversations with Wright Morris: Critical Views & Responses. Ed. by Robert E. Knoll. LC 76-25497. (Illus.). 1977. 10.95x (ISBN 0-8032-0904-5); pap. 3.95 (ISBN 0-8032-5854-2, BB 630, Bison). U of Nebr Pr.

Conversations with Writers. Ed. by Matthew J. Bruccoli et al. LC 77-9142. (Conversations Ser.: Vol. 1). 1977. 30.00 (ISBN 0-8103-0943-2, Bruccoli Clark Book). Gale.

Conversations with Writers II. Ed. by Matthew J. Bruccoli et al. LC 77-27992. (Conversations Ser.: Vol. 3). 1978. 30.00 (ISBN 0-8103-0945-9, Bruccoli Clark Book). Gale.

Conversion. Erik Routley. LC 77-20298. 64p. 1978. pap. 1.75 (ISBN 0-8006-1327-9, 1-1327). Fortress.

Conversion Factors & Tables. 3rd ed. O. T. Zimmerman & Irvin Lavine. 1961. 13.80 (ISBN 0-686-20568-5). Indus Res Serv.

Conversion Integrated Circuits. Ed. by D. J. Dooley. LC 80-10541. 1980. 26.95 (ISBN 0-87942-131-2). Inst Electrical.

Conversion of Grid-Point Data into Meteorological Maps with a Mini-Computer System. (World Weather Watch Report: No. 37). 27p. 1980. pap. 5.00 (ISBN 0-686-68191-6, W469, WMO). Unipub.

Conversion of Scripts: Its Nature, History, & Utilization. Hans H. Wellisch. LC 77-2205. 1978. 38.95 (ISBN 0-471-01620-9, Pub. by Wiley-Interscience). Wiley.

Conversion of Tropical Moist Forests. 1980. 12.50 (ISBN 0-309-02945-7). Natl Acad Pr.

Conversion: Perspectives on Personal & Social Transformation. Walter E. Conn. LC 78-19079. 1978. pap. 7.95 (ISBN 0-8189-0368-6). Alba.

Convert. Elizabeth Robins. 304p. 1980. pap. 5.95 (ISBN 0-912670-83-5). Feminist Pr.

Convert Your Oil Furnace to Wood. 2nd ed. Bill White. LC 76-58642. (Illus.). 1977. 3.50 (ISBN 0-9601794-1-0). FireBuilders.

Converter Cookbook. Walter G. Jung. LC 78-54453. 1978. pap. 13.95 (ISBN 0-672-21527-6). Sams.

Convexity. H. G. Eggleston. (Cambridge Tracts in Mathematics & Mathematical Physics: No. 47). 1958. 21.50 (ISBN 0-521-07734-6). Cambridge U Pr.

Convexity & Related Combinatorial Geometry. Breen. Date not set. price not set (ISBN 0-8247-1278-1). Dekker.

Convexity: Proceedings, Vol. 7. Symposia in Pure Mathematics-Seattle-1961. Ed. by V. Klee. LC 63-10760. 1979. Repr. of 1963 ed. 31.60 (ISBN 0-8218-1407-9, PSPUM-7). Am Math.

Conveys & Singles. Bob Gooch. LC 78-75306. (Illus.). 192p. 1980. 10.95 (ISBN 0-498-02342-7). A S Barnes.

Convict Guns. James Harvey. 1979. pap. 1.50 (ISBN 0-505-51366-8). Tower Bks.

Convicting the Innocent: Errors of Criminal Justice. Edwin M. Borchard. LC 74-107406. (Civil Liberties in American History Ser). 1970. Repr. of 1932 ed. lib. bdg. 29.50 (ISBN 0-306-71886-3). Da Capo.

Conviction. Peter D. Tattersall. LC 80-82368. (Illus.). 374p. 1980. 12.95 (ISBN 0-8119-0407-5, Pegasus Rex). Fell.

Conviction: The Law, the State & the Construction of Justice. Doreen McBarnet. (Oxford Sociolegal Studies). 1980. text ed. 50.00 (ISBN 0-333-25536-4). Humanities.

Convicts & Empire: A Naval Question, 1776-1811. Alan Frost. (Illus.). 280p. 1980. 45.00 (ISBN 0-19-554261-4). Oxford U Pr.

Convicts & Empire: A Naval Question Seventeen Seventy-Six-Eighteen Eleven. Alan Frost. (Illus.). 280p. 1980. 39.50 (ISBN 0-19-554261-4). Oxford U Pr.

Convicts and the Colonies. A. G. Shaw. (Illus.). 1966. 9.95 (ISBN 0-571-06663-1, Pub. by Faber & Faber). Merrimack Bk Serv.

Convicts, Clergymen & Churches. Allan M. Grocott. 356p. 1980. 27.50x (ISBN 0-424-00072-5, Pub. by Sydney U Pr Australia). Intl Schol Bk Serv.

Convolution & Fourier Transforms for Communications Engineers. D. Maurice. LC 75-34082. 1976. 24.95x (ISBN 0-470-57770-3). Halsted Pr.

Convolution Integral Equations with Special Function Kernals. H. M. Srivastava & R. G. Buschman. LC 76-52979. 1977. 12.95 (ISBN 0-470-99050-3). Halsted Pr.

Convulsive Therapy: Theory & Practice. Max Fink. LC 77-74618. 1979. text ed. 26.00 (ISBN 0-89004-221-7). Raven.

Conway Letters: Being the Correspondence of Anne, Viscountess Conway, Henry More & Their Friends. Anne Conway. Ed. by M. H. Nicolson. 1930. 47.50x (ISBN 0-685-89745-1). Elliots Bks.

Cook & Carry Book. Lynette Wenham. (Illus.). 160p. (Orig.). 1980. pap. 8.95 (ISBN 0-589-01275-4, Pub. by Reed Bks Australia). C E Tuttle.

Cook & Entertain the Burmese Way. Mi Mi Khaing. 12.95 (ISBN 0-89720-017-9). Green Hill.

Cook-Freeze Catering Systems. Brigid Boltman. (Illus.). 1978. text ed. 42.60x (ISBN 0-85334-768-9, Pub. by Applied Science). Burgess-Intl Ideas.

Cook Inlet Collection: Two Hundred Years of Selected Alaskan History. Ed. by Morgan Sherwood. LC 74-24638. (Illus.). 222p. (Orig.). 1974. 8.95 o.p. (ISBN 0-88240-051-7); pap. 4.95 o.p. (ISBN 0-88240-044-4). Alaska Northwest.

Cook Like a Peasant, Eat Like a King. Maria L. Scott & Jack D. Scott. 1927p. 1976. 7.95 o.p. (ISBN 0-695-80592-4). Follett.

Cook Now, Dine Later. Peter French-Hodges & Catherine Althaus. 1972. 9.50 (ISBN 0-571-08815-5, Pub. by Faber & Faber); pap. 4.95 (ISBN 0-571-09895-9). Merrimack Bk Serv.

Cook Out. Frances Kitchin. (Illus.). 1978. 6.95 (ISBN 0-7153-7610-1). David & Charles.

Cook to Your Heart's Content. Roslyn Nemet. 1981. pap. 1.75 (ISBN 0-8439-0870-X, Leisure Bks). Nordon Pubns.

Cook Voyage Artifacts in Leningrad, Berne, & Florence Museums. Ed. by Adrienne L. Kaeppler. LC 77-84835. (Bernice P. Bishop Museum Special Publications: No. 66). (Illus.). 196p. 1978. pap. 15.00 (ISBN 0-295-95728-X). U of Wash Pr.

Cookbook Decoder: or, Culinary Alchemy Explained. Arthur E. Grosser. 192p. 1981. 9.95 (ISBN 0-8253-0033-9). Beaufort Bks NY.

Cookbook: Favorite Recipes of French & American Residents of Paris. American Hospital of Paris. 1976. pap. 7.50 o.p. (ISBN 0-8415-0412-1). Dutton.

Cookbooks to Detective Fiction. Time-Life Books Editors. LC 77-99201. (Encyclopedia of Collectibles Ser.). (Illus.). 1978. lib. bdg. 10.98 (ISBN 0-686-50976-5). Silver.

Cookery for Entertaining. Marlene Sorosky. LC 78-71788. (Illus.). 1979. pap. 5.95 (ISBN 0-89586-019-8). H P Bks.

Cookery for One or Two. Barbara Swain. LC 78-60432. (Illus.). 1978. pap. 5.95 (ISBN 0-912656-95-6). H P Bks.

Cookery for Today. Joan Miller. 1974. pap. text ed. 4.95x o.p. (ISBN 0-435-42602-8). Heinemann Ed.

Cookie & Cracker Cookbook. Anne Lanigan. 1980. pap. 6.95 (ISBN 0-8256-3166-1). Music Sales.

Cookie & Cracker Cookbook. Anne Lanigan. (Illus.). 1980. cancelled (ISBN 0-8256-3188-2, Quick Fox). Music Sales.

Cookie & Cracker Technology. 2nd ed. Samuel A. Matz & Theresa D. Matz. (Illus.). 1978. lib. bdg. 36.50 (ISBN 0-87055-235-X). AVI.

Cookie Book. Ed. by Betty Crocker. 96p. 1980. 3.95 (ISBN 0-307-09930-X); lib. bdg. 5.95. Western Pub.

Cookie Book. Eva Moore. LC 76-190381. (gr. 1-4). 6.95 (ISBN 0-395-28866-5, Clarion). HM.

Cookie Monster & the Cookie Tree. David Korr. LC 79-10796. (Big Picture Bks.). (Illus.). (ps-k). 1979. 1.95 (ISBN 0-307-10821-X, Golden Pr); PLB 7.62 (ISBN 0-307-60821-2); PLB 5.00 Little Golden Reader (ISBN 0-307-60159-5). Western Pub.

Cookie Monster's Book of Cookie Shapes. Sesame Street. (Tell-a-Tale Reader Ser.). (gr. k-3). 1979. PLB 4.77 (ISBN 0-307-68403-2, Golden Pr). Western Pub.

Cookies. Lou S. Pappas. Ed. by Maureen Reynolds. LC 80-81247. (Illus.). 192p. 1980. pap. 4.95 (ISBN 0-911954-57-0). Nitty Gritty.

Cookies from Many Lands. Josephine Perry. (Dover Cook Book Ser). 160p. (gr. 6-12). 1972. pap. 2.50 (ISBN 0-486-22832-0). Dover.

Cooking. Boy Scouts Of America. LC 19-600. (Illus.). 80p. (gr. 6-12). 1967. pap. 0.70x (ISBN 0-8395-3257-1, 3257). BSA.

Cooking Across the South: A Collection & Recollection of Favorite Regional Recipes. Lillian B. Marshall. LC 80-80752. 280p. 1980. 12.95 (ISBN 0-8487-0505-X). Oxmoor Hse.

Cooking & Catering the Wholefood Way. Ursula M. Cavanagh. 1970. 6.95 o.p. (ISBN 0-571-09283-7). Transatlantic.

Cooking Down East. Marjorie Standish. 1979. 8.95 (ISBN 0-930096-00-2). G Gannett.

Cooking Down East. 12th ed. Marjorie Standish. (Illus.). 260p. 1980. 8.95 (ISBN 0-930096-14-2). G Gannett.

Cooking Fish & Wild Game. Francine Dufresne. LC 75-25760. (Illus.). 144p. 1975. 4.95 (ISBN 0-912238-75-5). One Hund One Prods.

Cooking for Absolute Beginners. Muriel Fitzsimmons. LC 75-35405. Orig. Title: You Can Cook If You Can Read. 380p. 1976. pap. 3.95 (ISBN 0-486-23311-1). Dover.

Cooking for Compliments. Knudsen Corporation. LC 77-88223. (Illus.). 1977. pap. 5.95 (ISBN 0-912656-91-3). H P Bks.

Cooking for Diabetics at Home & Away. Winnie B. Rhodes. 240p. 1976. pap. 16.75 (ISBN 0-398-03417-6). C C Thomas.

Cooking for Myself. Mirabelle Beaulieu. (Illus.). 1978. pap. 5.95 o.s.i. (ISBN 0-7715-9435-6, Pub. by Gage). Vanguard.

Cooking for One. 72p. 1980. 3.95 (ISBN 0-307-09924-5). Western Pub.

Cooking for One. 5th, rev. ed. Elinor Parker. LC 76-15365. 1976. 10.95 (ISBN 0-690-01176-8, TYC-T). T Y Crowell.

Cooking for One. Norah M. Wilmot. (Illus.). 1975. pap. 2.95 (ISBN 0-914842-03-X). Madrona Pubs.

Cooking for One or Two-or More. Amy G. Ireson & Shirley F. Lipscomb. LC 77-75156. (Illus.). 1978. spiral 8.75 (ISBN 0-395-25823-5). HM.

Cooking for the Eighties. Hermie Kranzdorf. (Illus.). 256p. 1980. 10.95 (ISBN 0-916838-31-5). Schiffer.

Cooking for the Freezer. Myra Waldo. 240p. 1975. pap. 1.95 (ISBN 0-385-06295-8, Dolp). Doubleday.

Cooking for the Professional Chef: A Structured Approach. Kenneth C. Wolfe. LC 76-5300. 1976. pap. text ed. 12.00 (ISBN 0-8273-0390-4); instructor's guide 1.60 (ISBN 0-8273-0391-2). Delmar.

Cooking for the Wayward Diabetic. Lily MacLeod. 1971. 6.25 o.p. (ISBN 0-571-04744-0). Transatlantic.

Cooking for Your Freezer. Audrey Ellis. (Leisure Plan Bks). pap. 2.95 (ISBN 0-600-01360-X). Transatlantic.

Cooking French the New Way. Sue Spitler & Culinary Arts Inst. Ed. by Edward G. Finnegan. LC 80-65527. (Adventures in Cooking Ser.). (Illus.). 1980. cloth cancelled (ISBN 0-8326-0610-3); pap. 3.95 (ISBN 0-8326-0609-X, 2519). Delair.

Cooking from Scratch: The Single Man's Guide to Making Out in the Kitchen. Willetta Warberg. 320p. (Orig.). 1976. pap. 1.95 o.p. (ISBN 0-345-25383-3). Ballantine.

Cooking Good Food with Grains & Vegetables. Yvette De Langre. Ed. by Jacques De Langre. LC 80-84991. (Illus.). 128p. (Orig.). 1980. spiral bdg 8.00 (ISBN 0-916508-11-0); pap. 6.00 (ISBN 0-916508-12-9). Happiness Pr.

Cooking in Season. Christine Brady. (Illus.). 1978. 16.95 (ISBN 0-241-89451-4, Pub. by Hamish Hamilton England). David & Charles.

Cooking in Style: Gourmet Recipes Without Meat or Fish. Sonia Allison. (Illus.). 176p. 1980. 19.95 (ISBN 0-241-10352-5, Pub. by Hamish Hamilton England). David & Charles.

Cooking in Ten Minutes. Edouard De Pomiane. (Illus.). 1967. pap. 4.95 (ISBN 0-571-08160-6, Pub. by Faber & Faber). Merrimack Bk Serv.

Cooking Irish Style Today. Noreen Kinney. 1977. pap. 4.50 (ISBN 0-85342-482-9). Irish Bk Ctr.

Cooking Kosher! The Natural Way. Jane Kinderlehrer. 1980. 12.50 (ISBN 0-8246-0240-4). Jonathan David.

Cooking Lite Feeling Right Cookbook. Hunt-Wesson Kitchens. 1980. 2.99 (ISBN 0-671-41778-9, Fireside). S&S.

Cooking: Making Things to Eat. McPhee Gribble. (Practical Puffins Ser.). 32p. (gr. 5 up). 1976. pap. 1.50 o.p. (ISBN 0-14-049142-2, Puffin). Penguin.

Cooking of China. Date not set. price not set. Time-Life.

Cooking of China. Emily Hahn. (Foods of the World Ser.). (Illus.). (gr. 9 up). 1968. 14.95 (ISBN 0-8094-0035-9). Time-Life.

Cooking of Germany. Nika S. Hazelton. LC 69-17198. (Foods of the World Ser). (Illus.). (gr. 6 up). 1969. PLB 14.94 (ISBN 0-8094-0064-2, Time-Life). Silver.

Cooking of Germany. Nika S. Hazelton. (Foods of the World Ser). (Illus.). 1969. 14.95 (ISBN 0-8094-0037-5). Time-Life.

Cooking of India. Santha Rama Rau. (Foods of the World Ser). (Illus.). 1969. 14.95 (ISBN 0-8094-0042-1). Time-Life.

Cooking of India. Santha R. Rau. LC 79-98164. (Foods of the World Ser). (Illus.). (gr. 6 up). 1969. PLB 14.94 (ISBN 0-8094-0069-3, Pub. by Time-Life). Silver.

Cooking of Italy. Waverley Root. LC 68-19230. (Foods of the World Ser). (Illus.). (gr. 6 up). 1968. PLB 14.94 (ISBN 0-8094-0057-X, Pub. by Time-Life). Silver.

Cooking of Italy. Waverley Root. (Foods of the World Ser). (Illus.). 1968. 14.95 (ISBN 0-8094-0030-8). Time-Life.

Cooking of Japan. Rafael Steinberg. LC 75-84632. (Foods of the World Ser.). (Illus.). (gr. 6 up). 1969. PLB 14.94 (ISBN 0-8094-0067-7, Pub. by Time-Life). Silver.

Cooking of Japan. Rafael Steinberg. (Foods of the World Ser.). (Illus.). 1969. 14.95 (ISBN 0-8094-0040-5). Time-Life.

Cooking of Provincial France. M. F. Fisher. (Foods of the World Ser). (Illus.). (gr. 6 up). 1968. PLB 14.94 (ISBN 0-8094-0056-1, Pub. by Time-Life). Silver.

Cooking of Provincial France. M. F. Fisher. (Foods of the World Ser). (Illus.). 1968. 14.95 (ISBN 0-8094-0029-4). Time-Life.

Cooking of Provincial Quebec. Mirabelle Beaulieu. (Illus.). 158p. 1976. 9.95 o.s.i. (ISBN 0-7715-9942-0). Vanguard.

Cooking of Scandinavia. Dale Brown. LC 68-21587. (Foods of the World Ser). (Illus.). (gr. 6 up). 1968. PLB 14.94 (ISBN 0-8094-0058-8, Pub. by Time-Life). Silver.

Cooking of Scandinavia. Dale Brown. (Foods of the World Ser). (Illus.). 1968. 14.95 (ISBN 0-8094-0031-6). Time-Life.

Cooking of Spain & Portugal. Peter S. Feibleman. LC 70-82142. (Foods of the World Ser.). (Illus.). (gr. 6 up). 1969. PLB 14.94 (ISBN 0-8094-0066-9, Pub. by Time-Life). Silver.

Cooking of Spain & Portugal. Peter S. Feibleman. (Foods of the World Ser). (Illus.). 1969. 14.95 (ISBN 0-8094-0039-1). Time-Life.

Cooking of the British Isles. Adrian Bailey. LC 69-19833. (Foods of the World Ser). (Illus.). (gr. 6 up). 1969. PLB 14.94 (ISBN 0-8094-0065-0, Pub. by Time-Life). Silver

Cooking of the British Isles. Adrian Bailey. (Foods of the World Ser). (Illus.). 1969. 14.95 (ISBN 0-8094-0038-3). Time-Life.

Cooking of the Caribbean Islands. Linda Wolfe. (Foods of the World Ser). (Illus.). 1970. 14.95 (ISBN 0-8094-0044-8). Time-Life.

Cooking of the Caribbean Islands. Linda Wolfe. LC 75-108615. (Foods of the World Ser.). (Illus.). (gr. 6 up). 1970. PLB 14.94 (ISBN 0-8094-0071-5, Pub. by Time-Life). Silver.

Cooking of Vienna's Empire. Joseph Wechsberg. LC 68-25883. (Foods of the World Ser). (Illus.). (gr. 6 up). 1968. PLB 14.94 (ISBN 0-8094-0059-6, Time-Life). Silver.

Cooking of Vienna's Empire. Joseph Wechsberg. (Foods of the World Ser). (Illus.). 1968. 14.95 (ISBN 0-8094-0032-4). Time-Life.

Cooking on a Woodburning Stove: 150 Down-Home Recipes. Andrew R. Addkison. LC 80-831192. 108p. (Orig.). 1980. pap. 7.95 (ISBN 0-915190-28-1). Jalmar Pr.

Cooking on the Go. rev. ed. Janet Groene. (Illus.). 1980. 13.95 (ISBN 0-393-03259-0). Norton.

Cooking Out-of-Doors: For Juniors, Brownies Cadettes, Seniors & Leaders. Girl Scouts of the USA. (Illus.). (gr. 1-12). 1960 spiral bdg. 4.00 (ISBN 0-88441-128-1, 19-984). GS.

Cooking Over Coals. Mel Marshall. 1971. 9.95 (ISBN 0-87691-033-9). Winchester Pr.

Cooking Skill Book. Boy Scouts of America. (Illus.). 32p. (gr. 6-12). 1975. pap. 0.50x (ISBN 0-8395-6585-2, 6585); cookings tchr's guide 0.30x (ISBN 0-685-53701-3, 18-325). BSA.

Cooking the British Way. Barbara Hill. (Easy Menu Ethnic Cookbooks). (Illus.). (YA) (gr. 5 up). 1981. PLB 4.95g (ISBN 0-8225-0903-2). Lerner Pubns.

Cooking the Chinese Way. Ling Yu. (Easy Menu Ethnic Cookooks). (Illus.). (YA) (gr. 5 up). 1981. PLB 4.95g (ISBN 0-8225-0902-4). Lerner Pubns.

Cooking the Dutch Oven Way. Leroy L. Woodruff. (Illus.). 144p. 1980. pap. 4.95 (ISBN 0-934802-01-7). Ind Camp Supply.

Cooking the French Way. Lynne M. Waldee. (Easy Menu Ethnic Cookbooks). (Illus.). (YA) (gr. 5 up). 1981. PLB 4.95g (ISBN 0-8225-0904-0). Lerner Pubns.

Cooking the Lebanese Way. Cedar Hashashe. (Illus.). 112p. (Orig.). 1979. pap. 7.50 (ISBN 0-589-01279-7, Pub. by Reed Books Australia). C E Tuttle.

Cooking the Norwegian Way. Sylvia Munsen. (Easy Menu Ethnic Cookbooks). (Illus.). (YA) (gr. 5 up). 1981. PLB 4.95g (ISBN 0-8225-0901-6). Lerner Pubns.

Cooking with Beer. Annette A. Stover & Culinary Arts Institute Staff. Ed. by Edward G. Finnegan. LC 80-65528. (Adventures in Cooking Ser). (Illus.). 1980. cloth cancelled (ISBN 0-8326-0614-6); pap. 3.95 (ISBN 0-8326-0613-8, 2521). Delair.

Cooking with Cheese. Mary Berry. (Illus.). 144p. 1980. 17.95 (ISBN 0-7134-1925-3, Pub. by Batsford England). David & Charles.

Cooking with Conscience. A. Benjamin. 1977. pap. 2.95 (ISBN 0-8164-0902-1). Crossroad NY.

Cooking with Exotic Fruit. Selma Payne & W. J. Payne. (Illus.). 144p. 1980. 19.95 (ISBN 0-7134-1192-9, Pub. by Batsford England). David & Charles.

Cooking with Flowers. Greet Buchner. (Illus.). 8.95 (ISBN 0-7225-0236-2). Dufour.

Cooking with Fructose. Anita Byrd. LC 80-25086. 128p. 1981. 8.95 (ISBN 0-668-05138-8); pap. 4.95 (ISBN 0-668-05142-6). Arco.

Cooking with Fruit. Mary Norwak. 1960. 6.50 (ISBN 0-685-20569-X). Transatlantic.

Cooking with Grass. George Vye & Stewart Grossman. LC 75-39089. (Illus.). 128p. (Orig.). 1976. pap. 3.95 (ISBN 0-8467-0151-0, Pub. by Two Continents). Hippocrene Bks.

Cooking with Love. Frwd. by Graham Kerr. 1977. pap. 2.95 (ISBN 0-89728-023-7, 677547). Omega Pubns OR.

Cooking with Love. L. Sellers. LC 77-99864. (Illus.). 1970. 11.25 (ISBN 0-08-006908-8); pap. 4.45 (ISBN 0-08-006907-X). Pergamon.

Cooking with Love & Cereal. Betty McMichael & Karen M. McDonald. LC 80-69312. 224p. 1981. spiral bdg. 9.95 (ISBN 0-915684-80-2). Christian Herald.

Cooking with Rice. Paul Eve. LC 74-4321. (Orig.). 1974. pap. 3.50 (ISBN 0-374-51132-2). FS&G.

Cooking with Vegetables. Marika H. Tenison. (Illus.). 284p. 1981. 16.95 (ISBN 0-224-01597-4, Pub. by Chatto-Bodley-Jonathan). Merrimack Bk Serv.

Cooking with Wholegrains. Mildred E. Orton. LC 77-148706. (Illus.). 72p. 1971. pap. 2.95 (ISBN 0-374-50936-0, N410). FS&G.

Cooking with Wild Plants: How to Recognize & Prepare Edible Wilderness Plants of the Rocky Mountains. Alan Briscoe. LC 78-52405. (Illus.). 1979. pap. 1.95 (ISBN 0-88290-091-9). Horizon Utah.

Cooking Without a Grain of Salt. Elma W. Bagg. LC 64-13870. 1964. 9.95 (ISBN 0-385-05432-7). Doubleday.

Cook's Guide. Macmillan. LC 77-7138. (Illus.). 1977. 8.95 o.s.i. (ISBN 0-02-578780-2). Macmillan.

Cook's Tour of Shreveport. 9th ed. Junior League of Shreveport, Inc. (Illus.). 336p. 1964. pap. 6.95x (ISBN 0-686-62767-9). Jr League Shreveport.

Cook's Tour of the Easton Shore. Memorial Hospital Junior Auxiliary Easton Maryland. LC 59-15724. (Illus.). 1959. pap. 8.50 (ISBN 0-87033-001-2, Pub. by Tidewater). Cornell Maritime.

Cool Cat. Frank Bonham. LC 77-133110. 160p. (gr. 7 up). 1971. PLB 7.95 o.p. (ISBN 0-525-28210-6). Dutton.

Cool Kids' Guide to Summer Camp. Bob Stine & Jane Stine. LC 80-24172. (Illus.). 80p. (gr. 3-7). 1981. 7.95 (ISBN 0-590-07704-X, Four Winds). Schol Bk Serv.

Cool World. Warren Miller. 1975. pap. 1.25 o.p. (ISBN 0-449-30751-4, P751, Prem). Fawcett.

Cooling. Lowell Ponte. LC 76-7963. 288p. 1976. 8.95 o.p. (ISBN 0-13-172312-X). P-H.

Cooling Techniques for Electronic Equipment. Dave S. Steinberg. LC 80-14141. 425p. 1980. 26.50 (ISBN 0-471-04403-2, Pub. by Wiley Interscience). Wiley.

Cooling Towers in Refrigeration. J. D. Gurney & I. A. Cotter. (Illus.). 1966. 20.50x (ISBN 0-85334-390-X, Pub. by Applied Science). Burgess-Intl Ideas.

Cooper, the McNallys' Big Black Dog. Nancy W. Parker. LC 80-21905. (Illus.). 32p. (gr. k-3). 1981. PLB 7.95 (ISBN 0-396-07914-8). Dodd.

Cooperation & Conflict in Southern Africa: Papers on a Regional Subsystem. Timothy M. Shaw & Kenneth A. Heard. 1976. pap. text ed. 14.55x o.p. (ISBN 0-8191-0005-6). U Pr of Amer.

Cooperation Between the Sexes: Writings on Women, Love, Marriage & Its Disorders. Alfred Adler. LC 76-23804. 480p. 1980. Repr. of 1978 ed. 25.00 (ISBN 0-87668-443-6). Aronson.

Cooperation in Education: Based on the Proceedings of the First International Conference on Cooperation in Education, Tel-Aviv, Israel. Ed. by Shlomo Sharan et al. LC 80-20192. (Illus.). 420p. (Orig.). 1980. pap. text ed. 14.95x (ISBN 0-8425-1836-3). Brigham.

Cooperation in Library Service to Children. Esther R. Dyer. LC 77-28190. 1978. 10.00 (ISBN 0-8108-1111-1). Scarecrow.

Cooperation in the European Market Economies. International Cooperative Alliance. Ed. by W. P. Watkins. 1967. pap. 4.50x (ISBN 0-210-22555-6). Asia.

Cooperativas Agricolas y Pecuarias. rev. ed. (Span.). 1967. pap. 1.00 o.p. (ISBN 0-8270-3225-0). OAS.

Cooperative & Commune: Group Farming in the Economic Development of Agriculture. Ed. by Peter Dorner. LC 76-53651. 1977. 25.00 (ISBN 0-299-07380-7). U of Wis Pr.

Cooperative Approaches to World Energy Problems. Tripartite report by fifteen experts from the European Community, Japan, & North America. 51p. 1974. pap. 2.00 (ISBN 0-8157-1555-2). Brookings.

Cooperative Education: Vocational, Occupational Career. Ronald Stadt & Bill Gooch. LC 75-36971. 1977. 11.95 (ISBN 0-672-97110-0). Bobbs.

Cooperative Education Workbook for Foodservice Hospitality. Jack E. Miller. LC 78-23193. (Illus.). (gr. 11-12). 1978. 9.95 (ISBN 0-8436-2117-6). CBI Pub.

Cooperative Leadership in South-East Asia. International Cooperative Alliance. 1963. 6.00x (ISBN 0-210-34055-X). Asia.

Cooperative Movements in Eastern Europe. Ed. by Aloysius Balawyder. LC 79-55001. (Illus.). 200p. 1980. text ed. 18.00 (ISBN 0-916672-45-X). Allanheld.

Cooperative Occupational Education & Work Experience in the Curriculum. Ralph E. Mason & Peter G. Haines. LC 72-76306. (Illus.). 1972. text ed. 11.75x o.p. (ISBN 0-8134-1779-1, 1779). Interstate.

Cooperative Occupational Education & Work Experience in the Curriculum. 3rd ed. Ralph E. Mason & Peter G. Haines. (Illus.). 1981. text ed. 11.75x (ISBN 0-8134-2150-0, 2150). Interstate.

Cooperative Phenomena in Biology. Ed. by George Karreman. LC 78-16572. 1980. 45.00 (ISBN 0-08-023186-1). Pergamon.

Cooperative School Television & Educational Change. John Middleton. 135p. 1979. pap. 6.95. NAEB.

Cooperative Sports & Games Book: Challenge Without Competition. Terry Orlick. LC 77-88771. 1978. 10.00 (ISBN 0-394-42215-5); pap. 3.95 (ISBN 0-394-73494-7). Pantheon.

Cooperative Vocational Education: Principles - Methods - Problems. new ed. E. F. Mitchell. 1977. text ed. 18.95 (ISBN 0-205-05768-3). Allyn.

Cooperatives: Development, Principles & Management. E. P. Roy. 1981. 11.95 o.p. (ISBN 0-8134-2143-8, 2143); pap. text ed. 8.95x o.p. (ISBN 0-685-73357-2). Interstate.

Cooperatives: Development, Principles & Management. 4th ed. Ewell P. Roy. 1981. 11.95 (ISBN 0-8134-2143-8, 2143); pap. text ed. 8.95x. Interstate.

Cooper's Landscapes: An Essay on the Picturesque Vision. Blake Nevius. LC 74-77730. (Quantum Bks). 1976. 14.50x (ISBN 0-520-02751-5). U of Cal Pr.

Coordinate Systems & Map Projections. D. H. Maling. LC 73-330722. (Illus.). 255p. 1973. 22.50x (ISBN 0-540-00974-1). Intl Pubns Serv.

Coordinated Cross Number Puzzle Books, 8 bks. Crouch. Incl. Bks. A1 & A2. (gr. 1-2). pap. 1.64 ea. worktexts; Bk. A1, Gr. 1. pap. (ISBN 0-8009-0722-1); Bk. A2, Gr. 2. pap. (ISBN 0-8009-0725-6); spirit masters 15.32 ea. Bk. A1 (ISBN 0-8009-0746-9). Bk. A2 (ISBN 0-8009-0748-5). ans. keys. Bk. A1 (ISBN 0-8009-0764-7). Bk. A2 (ISBN 0-8009-0766-3); Bks. A-F. (gr. 3-8). Bk. A, Gr. 3. pap. (ISBN 0-8009-0727-2); Bk. B, Gr. 4. pap. (ISBN 0-8009-0729-9); Bk. C, Gr. 5. pap. (ISBN 0-8009-0735-3); Bk. D, Gr. 6. pap. (ISBN 0-8009-0739-6); Bk. E, Gr. 7. pap. (ISBN 0-8009-0742-6); Bk. F, Gr. 8. pap. (ISBN 0-8009-0744-2). (gr. 1-8). 1979. Bks. A-F. pap. 1.76 ea. worktexts; spiritmasters for Bks. A-F 16.68 ea.; ans. keys for Bks. A1, A2, A-F 3.32 ea. McCormick-Mathers.

Coordinated Transportation: Problems & Requirements. Ed. by E. Grosvenor Plowman. LC 76-78376. 1968. pap. 7.50x (ISBN 0-87033-151-5). Cornell Maritime.

Coordinating Health Care. Edward W. Lehman. LC 75-691. (Sage Library of Social Research: Vol. 17). 1975. 18.00x (ISBN 0-8039-0442-8); pap. 7.95x o.p. (ISBN 0-8039-0512-2). Sage.

Coordinating Services to Handicapped Children: A Handbook for Interagency Collaboration. Ed. by Jerry O. Elder & Phyllis R. Magrab. 272p. 1980. pap. 13.95 (ISBN 0-933716-11-7). P H Brookes.

Coordinating Services to Handicapped Children: A Handbook for Interagency Collaboration. Ed. by Jerry O. Elder & Phyllis R. Magrab. LC 80-16033. (Illus.). 264p. (Orig.). 1980. pap. text ed. 13.95 (ISBN 0-933716-11-7). P H Brookes.

Coordination Chemistry. Ed. by Stanley Kirschner. LC 77-81522. 331p. 1969. 32.50 (ISBN 0-306-30402-3, Plenum Pr). Plenum Pub.

Coordination Chemistry: The Chemistry of Metal Complexes. F. Basolo & R. C. Johnson. 1964. pap. text ed. 8.95 (ISBN 0-8053-0651-X, 30651). Benjamin-Cummings.

Coordination Chemistry: Twentieth International Conference on Coordination Chemistry, Calcutta, India, 10-14 Dec. 1979. D. Banerjea. LC 80-41163. 286p. 1980. 75.00 (ISBN 0-08-023942-0). Pergamon.

Coordination Chemistry-Twenty One: Twenty First International Conference on Coodination Chemistry, Toulouse, France 7-11 July 1980. Ed. by J. P. Laurent. (IUPAC Symposium Ser.). 200p. 1981. 54.00 (ISBN 0-08-025300-8). Pergamon.

Coordination Compounds of Porphyrins & Phthalocyanine. E. D. Berezin. 256p. 1981. 52.00 (ISBN 0-471-27857-2, Pub. by Wiley-Interscience). Wiley.

Coordination: Concept or Reality? A Study of Libraries in a University System. William J. Myrick, Jr. LC 74-22456. 1975. 10.00 (ISBN 0-8108-0776-9). Scarecrow.

Coot Club. Arthur Ransome. (Illus.). 352p. (gr. 4-7). 1980. 9.95 (ISBN 0-224-60635-2, Pub. by Chatto Bodley Jonathan). Merrimack Bk Serv.

Cop Cade. Ed. by John Ball. LC 78-7750. 1978. 7.95 o.p. (ISBN 0-385-14374-5). Doubleday.

Cop Out. H. L. Lasher. 1978. pap. 1.75 (ISBN 0-505-51284-X). Tower Bks.

Copernican Achievement. Ed. by Robert S. Westman. 1976. 22.75x (ISBN 0-520-02877-5). U of Cal Pr.

Copie of a Letter Sent from Sea by a Gentleman. T. F. LC 72-5984. (English Experience Ser.: No. 511). 1973. Repr. of 1589 ed. 6.00 (ISBN 90-221-0511-3). Walter J Johnson.

Copie of a Letter Sent Out of England to don B. Mendoza. Richard Leigh. LC 72-6010. (English Experience Ser.: No. 536). 1973. Repr. of 1588 ed. 5.00 (ISBN 90-221-0536-9). Walter J Johnson.

Copies in Copyright. J. H. Spoor et al. Ed. by Herman C. Jehoram. LC 80-50456. (Monographs on Industrial Property & Copyright Law: Vol. IV). 187p. 1980. 37.50x (ISBN 90-286-0350-6). Sijthoff & Noordhoff.

Copies of Two Speeches in Parliament. The One by John Glanvill, Esquire. The Other by Sir Henry Martin, Knight. John Glanvill & Henry Martin. LC 74-28858. (English Experience Ser.: No. 739). 1975. Repr. of 1628 ed. 3.50 (ISBN 90-221-0739-6). Walter J Johnson.

Coping Alone. Elsa Ferri & Hilary Robinson. (Illus.). 80p. 1976. pap. text ed. 6.25x (ISBN 0-85633-086-8, NFER). Humanities.

Coping & Growth: A Theoretical & Empirical Study for Groups Under Moderate to Severe Stress. Edith E. Eger. (Holocaust Studies Ser.). 1980. text ed. 22.50x (ISBN 0-8290-0292-8). Irvington.

Coping in a Troubled Society. Marion Just et al. LC 74-13719. (Illus.). 1974. 14.95 (ISBN 0-669-95851-4). Lexington Bks.

Coping Successfully: A How-To Manual for Operational Improvement. Harry N. Dubin. 138p. (Orig.). 1980. pap. text ed. 16.95x (ISBN 0-8290-0262-6); pap. text ed. 9.95x (ISBN 0-8290-0270-7). Irvington.

Coping-When Your Family Falls Apart. Dianna D. Booher. LC 79-17342. 192p. (gr. 7 up). 1979. PLB 8.29 (ISBN 0-671-33083-7). Messner.

Coping with a Miscarriage. Hank Pizer & Christine O. Palinski. (Illus.). 1980. 10.95 (ISBN 0-8037-1380-0). Dial.

Coping with Children's Misbehavior. Rudolf Dreikurs. 1972. pap. 4.50 (ISBN 0-8015-1764-8, Hawthorn). Dutton.

Coping with Cliques. Shirley Schwarzrock & C. Gilbert Wrenn. (Coping with Ser.). (Illus.). 31p. (gr. 7-12). 1971. pap. text ed. 1.30 (ISBN 0-913476-30-7). Am Guidance.

Coping with Crisis. Gustave Simons. LC 72-81081. 288p. 1973. 7.95 o.s.i. (ISBN 0-02-611180-2). Macmillan.

Coping with Crisis. Christine Wood. 32p. 1980. 0.75 (ISBN 0-930756-52-5, 4240-CC). Women's Aglow.

Coping with Criticism. Jamie Buckingham. 1979. 6.95 (ISBN 0-88270-327-7). Logos.

Coping with Death & Dying. Elisabeth Kubler-Ross. (Illus.). 129p. 1980. 9.95 (ISBN 0-686-69030-3). Macmillan.

Coping with Difficult People. Robert M. Bramson. 240p. 1981. 11.95 (ISBN 0-385-17362-8, Anchor Pr). Doubleday.

Coping with Disruptive Behavior in Group Care. Eva M. Russo & Ann W. Shyne. LC 79-23739. (Orig.). 1980. 5.50 (ISBN 0-87868-137-X). Child Welfare.

Coping with Divorce. Jim Greteman. (Illus.). 80p. 1981. spiralbound 3.95 (ISBN 0-87793-226-3). Ave Maria.

Coping with Hunger: Toward a System of Food Security & Price Stabilization. David Bigman. 1981. write for info. (ISBN 0-88410-371-4). Ballinger Pub.

Coping with Illness. 2nd ed. Karen A. Noonan. LC 80-67825. (Practical Nursing Ser.). (Illus.). 288p. 1981. pap. text ed. 8.00 (ISBN 0-8273-1438-8); instr's. guide 1.25 (ISBN 0-8273-1922-3). Delmar.

Coping with Male Mid-Life: A Systematic Analysis Using Literature As a Data Source. Sharan B. Merriam. LC 80-5124. 137p. 1980. pap. text ed. 7.50 (ISBN 0-8191-1051-5). U Pr of Amer.

Coping with Prolonged Health Impairment in Your Child. Audrey T. McCollum. 242p. 1975. 12.95 (ISBN 0-316-54185-0). Little.

Coping with Proposition Thirteen. Roger L. Kemp. LC 80-8188. 1980. 21.95x (ISBN 0-669-03974-8). Lexington Bks.

Coping with Psychiatric & Psychological Testimony, 2 vols. 3rd ed. Jay Ziskin. Incl. Vol. 1. 429p. 50.00 (ISBN 0-9603630-2-5); Vol. 2. 577p. write for info. (ISBN 0-9603630-3-3). 1981. Set. 80.00 (ISBN 0-9603630-4-1). Law & Psych.

Coping with Psychiatric & Psychological Testimony. 2nd ed. Jay Ziskin. LC 75-1743. 1975. 30.00 o.p. (ISBN 0-9603630-0-9). Law & Psych.

Coping with Recurring Dreams & Nightmares. Elizabeth Lowe. 1980. 1.50 (ISBN 0-686-28864-5). Dreams Unltd.

Coping with Series. Shirley Schwarzrock & C. Gilbert Wrenn. (Illus., Orig.). (gr. 7-12). 1970-73. pap. text ed. 26.00 complete ref. set (ISBN 0-913476-10-2); manual 3.50 (ISBN 0-913476-11-0). Am Guidance.

Coping with Sexual Problems. Paul Gelinas. (Coping with Ser.). 140p. 1981. lib. bdg. 7.97 (ISBN 0-8239-0542-X). Rosen Pr.

Coping with Skin Care. May Annexton & Brent Schillinger. (Coping with Ser.). 1981. lib. bdg. 7.97 (ISBN 0-8239-0525-X). Rosen Pr.

Coping with Stroke. Helen Broida. LC 79-220. 136p. 1979. text ed. 14.95 (ISBN 0-933014-50-3). College-Hill.

Coping with Tension. Pauline E. Spray. (Direction Bks). 136p. 1981. pap. 2.95 (ISBN 0-8010-8189-0). Baker Bk.

Coping with Uncertainty Policy & Politics in the National Health Service. James Hunter. 320p. 1981. write for info. (ISBN 0-471-27906-4, Pub. by Wiley-Interscience). Wiley.

Copland on Music. Aaron Copland. LC 76-13512. 1976. Repr. of 1960 ed. lib. bdg. 25.00 (ISBN 0-306-70775-6). Da Capo.

Copper. Division of Medical Sciences, National Research Council. LC 76-57888. (Medical & Biologic Effects of Environmental Pollutants Ser.). 1977. pap. 7.00 (ISBN 0-309-02536-2). Natl Acad Pr.

Copper Base Powder Metallurgy. Pierre W. Taubenblat. LC 80-81464. (New Perspectives in Powder Metallurgy Ser.: Vol. 7). (Illus.). 232p. 1980. 42.00 (ISBN 0-918404-47-9). Metal Powder.

Copper Enameling. Jo Robert & Jean O'Hara. 2.95 (ISBN 0-934706-00-X). Prof Pubns Ohio.

Copper for America: The Hendricks Family & a National Industry, 1755-1939. Maxwell Whiteman. LC 79-153446. 1971. 23.00 (ISBN 0-8135-0687-5). Rutgers U Pr.

Copper Gold. Pauline Winslow. 1981. pap. 2.25 (ISBN 0-440-11130-7). Dell.

Copper: Its Geology & Economics. Robert Bowen & Ananda Gunatilaka. LC 77-5877. 1977. 99.95 (ISBN 0-470-99156-9). Halsted Pr.

Copper Proteins. Thomas G. Spiro. (Metal Ions in Biology Ser.: Vol. 3). 356p. 1981. 37.50 (ISBN 0-471-04400-8, Pub. by Wiley Interscience). Wiley.

Copper Red Filly & Her Enemy. Irene F. Hoatland. 1981. 3.95 (ISBN 0-8062-0854-6). Carlton.

Copper Spike. Lone E. Janson. LC 75-16446. (Illus.). 160p. 1975. pap. 9.95 (ISBN 0-88240-066-5). Alaska Northwest.

Copper: The Anatomy of an Industry. Sir Ronald Prain Mining Journal Books Ltd. 300p. 1980. 20.25x (ISBN 0-900117-07-9, Pub. by Mining Journal England). State Mutual Bk.

Cops & Dollars: The Economics of Criminal Law & Justice. Helen Reynolds. (Illus.). 256p. 1981. pap. 15.75 (ISBN 0-398-04115-6). C C Thomas.

Cops & Robbers. Allan Ahlberg. LC 78-5354. (Illus.). (gr. k-3). 1979. 7.75 (ISBN 0-688-80178-1); PLB 7.44 (ISBN 0-688-84178-3). Greenwillow.

Cops & Women. Micki Siegel. (Orig.). 1980. pap. 2.25 (ISBN 0-505-51524-5). Tower Bks.

Coptic Dictionary. Ed. by Walter E. Crum. 1939. 89.00x (ISBN 0-19-864404-3). Oxford U Pr.

Coptic Etymological Dictionary. Jaroslav Cerny. LC 69-10192. 350p. 1976. 160.00 (ISBN 0-521-07228-X). Cambridge U Pr.

Copy Preparation & Platemaking Using Kodak PMT Materials. Ed. by Eastman Kodak Company. (Illus.). 1980. pap. 4.50 (ISBN 0-87985-261-5, Q-71). Eastman Kodak.

Copycat. Barbara Samuels. LC 80-66640. 64p. 1980. 5.95 (ISBN 0-396-07862-1). Dodd.

Copying Other Nations' Policies: Two American Case Studies. Jerold Waltman. LC 80-12083. 110p. 1981. text ed. 11.25x (ISBN 0-87073-832-1). Schenkman.

Copyright Law in the Soviet Union. Michael A. Newcity. LC 76-12867. (Praeger Special Studies). 1978. 24.95 (ISBN 0-275-56450-9). Praeger.

Copyright Law Survey. 206p. 1980. binder 34.50 (ISBN 92-805-0011-2, WIPO62, WIPO). Unipub.

Copyright Law Symposium, No. 24. American Society of Composers, Authors & Publishers. 1980. 16.00x (ISBN 0-231-04864-5). Columbia U Pr.

Copyright, Patents & Trademarks. R. Wincor. 1980. 5.95 (ISBN 0-379-11138-1). Oceana.

Copyright Protection in the Americas. Organization of American States. 1979. looseleaf 150.00 (ISBN 0-379-20675-7). Oceana.

Copyright Protection in the Americas, Release 1, Vol. 2. Organization of American States. 1980. 75.00 (ISBN 0-379-20675-7). Oceana.

Cora. Daphne Athas. 1978. 10.95 o.p. (ISBN 0-670-24116-4). Viking Pr.

Cora Fry. Rosellen Brown. 1977. 9.95 (ISBN 0-393-04455-6); pap. 2.95 (ISBN 0-393-04461-0). Norton.

Coraje De Carol. 1980. pap. 1.30 (ISBN 0-686-69352-3). Vida Pubs.

Coral. Petra Leigh. 1979. pap. 2.50 (ISBN 0-446-91088-0). Warner Bks.

Coral Fishes. T. Ravensdale. (Encore Editions). (Illus.). 1973. 3.50 o.p. (ISBN 0-684-14995-8, ScribT). Scribner.

Coral Island. Robert Ballantyne. Ed. by Alison Lurie & Justin G. Schiller. LC 75-32167. (Classics of Children's Literature Ser.: 1621-1932). PLB 38.00 (ISBN 0-8240-2280-7). Garland Pub.

Coral Islanders. William Alkire. Ed. by Walter Goldschmidt. LC 77-90673. (World of Man Ser.). (Illus.). 1978. text ed. 11.50x (ISBN 0-88295-618-3); pap. text ed. 5.75x (ISBN 0-88295-619-1). AHM Pub.

Coral Reef. Jerry Greenberg. (Orig.). saddlestiched 4.95 (ISBN 0-913008-06-0). Seahawk Pr.

Coralline Algae: A First Synthesis. Ed. by H. William Johansen. 272p. 1981. 74.95 (ISBN 0-8493-5261-4). CRC Pr.

Corals. Warren E. Burgess. (Illus.). 1979. 2.95 (ISBN 0-87666-521-0, KW-053). TFH Pubns.

Corals. Lili Ronai. LC 75-6865. (Let's Read & Find Out Science Bk). (Illus.). 40p. (gr. k-3). 1976. 7.89 (ISBN 0-690-00921-6, TYC-J). T Y Crowell.

Corals. Herbert S. Zim. (Illus.). (gr. 3-7). 1966. PLB 6.48 (ISBN 0-688-31186-5). Morrow.

Coram's Children: The London Foundling Hospital in the Eighteenth Century. Ruth K. McClure. LC 80-21375. (Illus.). 336p. 1981. text ed. 27.50 (ISBN 0-300-02465-7). Yale U Pr.

Corazon Del Comunismo. Federico Schwartz. Tr. by Cecil Moore from English. 1977. pap. 0.60 o.p. (ISBN 0-311-14204-4, Edit Mundo). Casa Bautista.

Corbitt: The Story of Ted Corbitt, Long Distance Runner. John Chodes. LC 73-76246. (Illus.). 1974. 3.00 (ISBN 0-911520-45-7). Tafnews.

Corca Bascinn. James Liddy. 1977. pap. text ed. 6.50x (ISBN 0-85105-314-9, Dolmen Pr). Humanities.

Corded Shell: Reflections on Musical Expression. Peter Kivy. LC 80-7539. (Princeton Essays on the Arts: No. 9). 176p. 1980. 15.00 (ISBN 0-691-07258-2); pap. 5.95 (ISBN 0-691-02014-0). Princeton U Pr.

Corded Ware & Globular Amphora North-East of the Carpathians. T. Sulimirski. 1968. text ed. 41.00x (ISBN 0-485-11091-1, Athlone Pr). Humanities.

Cordilleran Metamorphic Core Complexes. Ed. by Max D. Crittenden, Jr. et al. George A. Davis & Peter J. Coney. (Memoir: No. 153). 1980. write for info. (ISBN 0-8137-1153-3). Geol Soc.

Corduroy Road, Glenn McCarthy: Texas Oil Field Saga. Wallace Davis. (Illus.). 1951. 15.00 (ISBN 0-685-04999-X). A Jones.

Cordwood Masonry Houses: A Practical Guide for the Owner-Builder. Robert L. Roy. LC 80-52325. (Illus.). 168p. 1980. 14.95 (ISBN 0-8069-5418-3); lib. bdg. 13.29 (ISBN 0-8069-5419-1); pap. 7.95 (ISBN 0-8069-8944-0). Sterling.

CORE: A Study in the Civil Rights Movement, 1942-1968. August Meier & Elliott Rudick. 448p. 1973. 24.95 (ISBN 0-19-501627-0). Oxford U Pr.

Core Mathematics. Dennis Bila et al. LC 74-82696. (Illus.). ix, 603p. (Prog. Bk.). 1975. text ed. 13.95x (ISBN 0-87901-035-5). Worth.

Core of Geriatric Medicine: A Guide for Students & Practitioners. Leslie S. Libow & Sherman. (Illus.). 354p. 1980. text ed. 22.95 (ISBN 0-8016-3096-7). Mosby.

Core Skills for the Health Occupations. E. Joy Hill. LC 71-176181. 320p. 1981. 24.50 (ISBN 0-87527-108-1). Green.

Core Studies in Obstetrics & Gynecology. 3rd ed. P. V. Dilts, Jr. et al. (Illus.). 248p. 1981. write for info. softcover (2572-4). Williams & Wilkins.

Corelli. Marc Pincherle. (Music Reprint Ser.). 1979. Repr. of 1956 ed. lib. bdg. 22.50 (ISBN 0-306-79576-0). Da Capo.

Coretta Scott King. Paula Taylor. LC 74-17360. (Illus.). (gr. 4-8). 1975. PLB 5.95 (ISBN 0-87191-410-7). Creative Ed.

Corey's Revenge. Harley Hess. (Orig.). 1980. pap. 1.75 (ISBN 0-532-23231-3). Manor Bks.

Corfu. Brian Dicks. LC 76-48823. (Islands Ser.). (Illus.). 1977. 14.95 (ISBN 0-7153-7311-0). David & Charles.

Corfu. Margaret Hopkins. 1977. 22.50 (ISBN 0-7134-0880-4). David & Charles.

Corgi Toys: The Ones with Windows. James Wieland & Edward Force. (Illus.). 1981. 8.95 (ISBN 0-87938-123-X). Motorbooks Intl.

Coring & Core Analysis Handbook. Gene Anderson. LC 74-33713. 1975. 23.00 (ISBN 0-87814-058-1). Pennwell Pub.

Corinthian Correspondence. Russell P. Spittler. (Radiant Life Ser). 128p. 1976. pap. 1.25 (ISBN 0-88243-892-1, 02-0892, Radiant Books); teachers ed. 2.50 (ISBN 0-88243-166-8, 32-0166). Gospel Pub.

Corinthians I. William F. Orr. (Anchor Bible Ser.: Vol. 32). 1976. 14.00 (ISBN 0-385-02853-9). Doubleday.

Corinthians I. A. Robertson & A. Plummer. (International Critical Commentary Ser.). 496p. Repr. of 1978 ed. write for info. (ISBN 0-567-05027-0). Attic Pr.

Corinthians I & II. William Baird. Ed. by John Hayes. LC 79-92064. (Knox Preaching Guides Ser.). 112p. (Orig.). 1980. pap. 4.50 (ISBN 0-8042-3239-3). John Knox.

Corinthians II. Alfred Plummer. LC 16-915. (International Critical Commentary Ser.). 462p. Repr. of 1916 ed. text ed. 23.00x (ISBN 0-567-05028-9). Attic Pr.

Corinthians 1 & 2. Charles Hodge. (Geneva Commentaries Ser.). 1978. 11.95 (ISBN 0-85151-185-6). Banner of Truth.

Coriolanus. William Shakespeare. Ed. by Arthur Quiller-Couch et al. (New Shakespeare Ser). 1969. 23.95 (ISBN 0-521-07529-7); pap. 4.50x (ISBN 0-521-09472-0). Cambridge U Pr.

Coriolanus. rev. ed. William Shakespeare. Ed. by Harry Levin. (Shakespeare Ser.). 1956. pap. 2.50 (ISBN 0-14-071402-2, Pelican). Penguin.

Coriolanus in Europe. David Daniell. 192p. 1981. text ed. 26.00x (ISBN 0-485-11192-6). Humanities.

Cork & Kerry. Sean Jennett. (Batsford Travel Ser.). (Illus.). 1977. 9.50 o.s.i. (ISBN 0-7134-0437-X). Hippocrene Bks.

Cork & Wood Crafts. Arden Newsome. LC 72-112370. (Illus.). 64p. (gr. k-3). 1971. PLB 7.21 (ISBN 0-87460-229-7). Lion.

Corkscrews: An Introduction to Their Appreciation. Manfred Heckmann. Ed. by Maurice Sullivan. (Illus.). 124p. 1981. 12.95 (ISBN 0-686-69566-6). Wine Appreciation.

Corky. Patricia Scarry. (Illus.). 24p. (gr. k-3). 1976. PLB 5.00 (ISBN 0-307-60086-6, Golden Pr). Western Pub.

Corky: Kel, Pt. 2. Mark Dunster. (Rin: Pt. 29). 82p. (Orig.). 1981. pap. 5.00 (ISBN 0-89642-072-8). Linden Pubs.

Corky's Brother. Jay Neugeboren. LC 78-87214. 1969. 5.95 o.p. (ISBN 0-374-12968-1). FS&G.

Corky's Hiccups. Nicolette Stack. (Illus.). 24p. (ps-4). 1968. PLB 5.00 (ISBN 0-307-60513-2, Golden Pr). Western Pub.

Corn: A Bibliography of the World Literature, 3 vols. International Maize & Wheat Improvement Center. LC 78-154562. 1971. Set. 67.50 (ISBN 0-8108-0378-X). Scarecrow.

Corn Among the Indians of the Upper Missouri. George F. Will & George E. Hyde. LC 64-63592. 323p. 1964. 14.50x (ISBN 0-8032-0892-8); pap. 3.95 (ISBN 0-8032-5846-1, BB 195, Bison). U of Nebr Pr.

Corn: Culture, Processing, Products. George E. Inglett. LC 77-126335. (Illus.). 1970. 29.50 (ISBN 0-87055-088-8). AVI.

Corn: Improvement, Seed Production, & Uses. Robert W. Jugenheimer. LC 75-32414. 1976. 49.95 (ISBN 0-471-45315-3, Pub. by Wiley-Interscience). Wiley.

Corn Is Maize: The Gift of the Indians. Aliki. LC 75-6928. (Let's-Read-&-Find-Out Science Bk). (Illus.). 40p. (gr. k-3). 1976. PLB 7.89 (ISBN 0-690-00975-5, TYC-J). T Y Crowell.

Corn-Soybeans Pest Control, 5 vols. Environmental Studies Board, Natl Research Council. (Pest Control Ser.: An Assessment of Present & Alternative Technologies, Vol. 2). 169p. 1975. pap. 5.50 (ISBN 0-309-02411-0). Natl Acad Pr.

Corncraft. Anna T. Connor. LC 78-69664. (Illus.). 1980. 9.95 (ISBN 0-498-02256-0). A S Barnes.

Cornea: Diseases. Charles I. Thomas. (Illus.). 1348p. 1956. 44.50 (ISBN 0-398-01914-2). C C Thomas.

Corneal Light Reflex: A Guide to Binocular Disorders. Emanuel Krimsky. (Illus.). 212p. 1972. 21.50 (ISBN 0-398-02596-7). C C Thomas.

Corneille: His Heroes & Their Worlds. Robert J. Nelson. LC 63-7859. 1963. 8.50x o.p. (ISBN 0-8122-7384-2). U of Pa Pr.

Cornelius Matthews. Allen F. Stein. (U. S. Authors Ser.: No. 221). 1974. lib. bdg. 10.95 (ISBN 0-8057-0478-7). Twayne.

Cornell Bread Book: Fifty-Four Recipes for Nutritious Loaves, Rolls & Coffee Cakes. rev ed. Clive M. McCay & Jeannette B. McCay. (Illus.). 52p. 1980. pap. 2.00 (ISBN 0-486-23995-0). Dover.

Cornell Conference on Women. Ed. by Sheila Tobias et al. 93p. 1969. pap. 3.00x o.p. (ISBN 0-912786-13-2). Know Inc.

Cornell Medical Update - 1. Lila A. Wallis. LC 78-51071. (Illus.). 1978. pap. 32.00 (ISBN 0-914316-14-1). Yorke Med.

Cornell Medical Update - 2. Ed. by Lila A. Wallis. LC 79-65407. (Illus.). 1979. pap. text ed. 38.00 (ISBN 0-914316-19-2). Yorke Med.

Corneo-plastic Surgery. Ed. by P. V. Rycroft. LC 68-58885. 1969. 97.00 (ISBN 0-08-013013-5). Pergamon.

Corner Restoration Circulars, 1883-1974. 1977. 18.00 (ISBN 0-686-23344-1, 507). CARBEN Survey.

Cornerstone Collector's Guide to Wicker. Jeffrey Weiss. 128p. 1981. 7.95 (ISBN 0-346-12535-9). Cornerstone.

Cornerstone's Collector's Guide to Glass. Jeffrey Weiss. 128p. 1981. 7.95 (ISBN 0-346-12534-0). Cornerstone.

Cornflakes. Lois H. Johnson. (Illus.). 80p. 1981. 6.00 (ISBN 0-682-49695-2). Exposition.

Cornish Clocks & Clockmakers. H. Miles Brown. (Illus.). 102p. 1980. Repr. 14.95 (ISBN 0-7153-4999-6). David & Charles.

Cornish Guernsey & Knit-Frocks. Mary Wright. 72p. 1980. 10.00x (ISBN 0-906720-05-2, Pub. by Hodge England). State Mutual Bk.

Cornish Ordinalia: A Critical Study. Jane A. Bakere. 191p. 1980. text ed. 50.00x (ISBN 0-7083-0745-0). Verry.

Cornrows. Camille Yarbrough. (Illus.). 48p. (Orig.). (gr. k-3). 1981. pap. 2.95 (ISBN 0-698-20529-4, Peppercorn). Coward.

Cornucopia: Homespun Philosophy. Noel F. Audley. 1981. 6.95 (ISBN 0-533-04631-9). Vantage.

Cornwall: A Shell Guide. John Betjeman. (Shell Guide Ser.). (Illus.). 1969. 8.95 o.p. (ISBN 0-571-05862-0, Pub. by Faber & Faber). Merrimack Bk Serv.

Cornwall: Its Mines & Miners. 2nd ed. J. R. Leifchild. LC 68-58855. Repr. of 1857 ed. 17.50x (ISBN 0-678-05064-3). Kelley.

Cornwall's Central Mines: The Northern District, 1810-1895. T. A. Morrison. 400p. 1980. 40.00x (ISBN 0-906720-10-9, Pub. by Hodge England). State Mutual Bk.

Cornzapoppin! Popcorn Recipes & Party Ideas for All Occasions. Barbara Williams. LC 75-28329. (Illus.). 160p. (gr. 6-12). 1976. 5.95 o.p. (ISBN 0-03-015166-X); pap. 2.95 (ISBN 0-03-053526-3). HR&W.

Corona & the Tin Frog. Russell Hoban. (Illus.). 30p. (gr. k-3). 1981. 8.95 (ISBN 0-224-01397-1, Pub. by Chatto-Bodley-Jonathan). Merrimack Bk Serv.

Corona De Amor Y Muerte. Alejandro Casona. Ed. by Jose Balseiro & J. Riis Owre. (Orig., Span). 1960. pap. 5.95x (ISBN 0-19-500844-8). Oxford U Pr.

Corona de Fuego: Primer Esquema Para una Tragedia Antihistorica Americana. Rodolfo Usigli. Ed. by Rex E. Ballinger. LC 72-167893. (Span.). 1972. pap. text ed. 6.95x (ISBN 0-672-63025-7). Irvington.

Coronado. Matthew G. Grant. LC 73-13957. 1974. PLB 5.95 (ISBN 0-87191-285-6). Creative Ed.

Coronado: Knight Pueblos & Plains. Herbert E. Bolton. LC 64-17854. 491p. 1974. Repr. of 1964 ed. 12.95. U of NM Pr.

Coronado's Children: Tales of Lost Mines & Buried Treasures of the Southwest. J. Frank Dobie. (Barker Texas History Center Ser.: No. 3). (Illus.). 1978. 9.95 (ISBN 0-292-71050-X). pap. 5.95 (ISBN 0-292-71052-6). U of Tex Pr.

Coronary Arteriography. 2nd ed. Ed. by Goffredo G. Gensini. 1981. write for info. (ISBN 0-87993-130-2). Futura Pub.

Coronary Artery Surgery: A Critical Review. Thomas A. Preston. LC 76-51977. 1977. 15.50 (ISBN 0-89004-165-2). Raven.

Coronary Care. Ed. by Joel Karliner & Gabriel Gregoratos. 1000p. 1980. text ed. 50.00x (ISBN 0-443-08061-5). Churchill.

Coronary Care Unit Nursing: A Workbook in Clinical Aspects. Harold A. Braun & Gerald A. Diettert. (Illus.). 1980. pap. text ed. 11.95 (ISBN 0-8359-1051-2). Reston.

Coronary Experience. 2nd ed. John R. Singh. LC 80-82823. (Illus.). 128p. (Orig.). 1980. text ed. 9.95 (ISBN 0-9604672-0-3); pap. text ed. 4.95 (ISBN 0-9604672-1-1). Mid Am Fr.

Coronary Heart Disease: A Twenty-Five Year Study in Retrospect. M. Gertler & P. D. White. 1976. 29.95 (ISBN 0-87489-093-4). Med Economics.

Coronary Heart Disease & the Mucopolysaccharides (Glycosaminoglycans) L. M. Morrison & O. A. Schjeide. (Illus.). 288p. 1974. 22.50 (ISBN 0-398-02903-2). C C Thomas.

Coronary: Prediction & Prevention. David T. Nash. LC 78-13099. (Illus.). 1979. 12.50 o.p. (ISBN 0-684-15820-5, ScribT). Scribner.

Coronation Everest. James Morris. (Illus.). 1958. 1.95 o.p. (ISBN 0-571-09649-2, Pub. by Faber & Faber). Merrimack Bk Serv.

Coronation of the Poet: Joachim Du Bellay's Debt to the Trivium. Robert Griffin. (U. C. Publ. in Modern Philology: Vol. 96). 1969. pap. 8.50x (ISBN 0-520-09291-0). U of Cal Pr.

Coronelismo. V. N. Leal. Tr. by J. Henfrey. LC 76-46044. (Cambridge Latin American Studies: No. 28). 1977. 29.95 (ISBN 0-521-21488-2). Cambridge U Pr.

Corot. (Selected Artist Art Ser). (Illus.). 1977. pap. 5.95 (ISBN 0-8120-0814-6). Barron.

Coroutines. C. D. Marlin. (Lecture Notes in Computer Science Ser.: Vol. 95). (Illus.). 246p. 1981. pap. 16.80 (ISBN 0-387-10256-6). Springer-Verlag.

Corporate Advertising: The What, the Why, & the How. Thomas Garbett. (Illus.). 224p. 1981. 24.95 (ISBN 0-07-022787-X, C). McGraw.

Corporate Affair. Mike Dolinsky. (Orig.). 1981. pap. 2.95 (ISBN 0-440-11435-7). Dell.

Corporate & Tax Aspects of Closely Held Corporations. William E. Painter. 670p. 1981. write for info (ISBN 0-316-68868-1). Little.

Corporate & Tax Aspects of Closely Held Corporations. William H. Painter. 1971. 40.00 (ISBN 0-316-68866-5); 1977 supplement 12.50 (ISBN 0-316-68864-9). Little.

Corporate Authorship: Its Role in Library Cataloging. Michael A. Carpenter. LC 80-1026. (Contributions in Librarianship & Information Science Ser.: No. 34). 248p. 1981. lib. bdg. 27.50 (ISBN 0-313-22065-4, CAU/). Greenwood.

Corporate Cash Management: Including Electronic Funds Transfer. Alfred L. Hunt. LC 78-16648. 1978. 19.95 (ISBN 0-8144-5464-X). Am Mgmt.

Corporate Collapse: The Causes & Symptoms. J. Argenti. LC 76-982. 1976. 19.95 (ISBN 0-470-15111-0). Halsted Pr.

Corporate Collections in Montgomery. Ed. by Diane J. Gingold. LC 76-15913. (Illus.). 1976. pap. cancelled (ISBN 0-89280-002-X). Montgomery Mus.

Corporate Competition Law in the European Communities. Ralph H. Folsom. LC 76-40404. (Illus.). 1978. 17.95 (ISBN 0-669-01043-X). Lexington Bks.

Corporate Control, Corporate Power. Edward S. Herman. LC 80-29447. (Illus.). 336p. 1981. 17.95 (ISBN 0-521-23996-6). Cambridge U Pr.

Corporate Crime. Marshall B. Clinard & Peter C. Yeager. LC 80-2156. (Illus.). 352p. 1980. 16.95 (ISBN 0-02-905710-8). Free Pr.

Corporate Crime. Marshall B. Clinard & Peter C. Yeager. 1980. 16.95 (ISBN 0-02-905710-8). Macmillan.

Corporate Crime in Canada: A Critical Analysis of Anti-Combines Legislation. C Goff & C. Reasons. 1978. pap. 8.50 (ISBN 0-13-173302-8). P-H.

Corporate Diagrams & Administrative Personnel of the Chemical Industry, Nineteen Seventy Nine to Nineteen Eighty. rev. 14th ed. Ed. by Kenneth R. Kern. LC 58-1742. 1979. binder 150.00 (ISBN 0-912060-16-6); without binder 137.50 (ISBN 0-912060-17-4). Chem Econ.

Corporate Dilemma: Traditional Values Versus Contemporary Problems. Dow Votaw & Prakash Sethi. (Illus.). 288p. 1973. pap. text ed. 9.95 (ISBN 0-13-174185-3). P-H.

Corporate Director. Arthur D. Little Inc. et al. LC 75-4838. 1975. 19.95 (ISBN 0-8436-0739-4). CBI Pub.

Corporate Dividend Policy. John A. Brittain. (Studies of Government Finance). (Orig.). 1966. 11.95 (ISBN 0-8157-1078-X); pap. 4.95 (ISBN 0-8157-1077-1). Brookings.

Corporate Executive's Legal Handbook. John C. Howell. 144p. 1980. pap. 5.95 (Spec). P-H.

Corporate Finance. 4th ed. Elvin F. Donaldson et al. 1975. 24.50 (ISBN 0-8260-2751-2); instrs'. manual avail. (ISBN 0-471-07459-4). Wiley.

Corporate Finance for Management. G. D. Bond. 1974. 19.95 (ISBN 0-408-70560-4). Butterworths.

Corporate Finance Sourcebook, 1979. Karen Zehring. 1979. 79.50 o.p. (ISBN 0-07-072775-9, P&RB). McGraw.

Corporate Financial Disclosure in the UK & the USA. George J. Benston. 1976. 21.95 (ISBN 0-347-01133-0, 00409-X, Pub. by Saxon Hse.). Lexington Bks.

Corporate Financial Planning Models. Henry I. Meyer. LC 77-24881. (Ser. on Systems & Controls for Financial Management). 1977. 29.95 (ISBN 0-471-59996-4, Pub. by Wiley-Interscience). Wiley.

Corporate Financial Reporting: Public or Private Control? Robert Chatov. LC 74-15368. 1975. 17.95 (ISBN 0-02-905410-9). Free Pr.

Corporate Financial Reporting: Text & Cases. rev ed. David F. Hawkins. 1977. text ed. 19.95x (ISBN 0-256-01643-7). Irwin.

Corporate Foundation Profiles. The Foundation Center. LC 80-69622. 512p. (Orig.). 1980. pap. 50.00 (ISBN 0-87954-038-9). Foundation Ctr.

Corporate Fund Raising: A Practical Plan of Action. W. Grant Brownrigg. LC 76-58748. (Illus.). 74p. (Orig.). 1978. pap. text ed. 12.50 (ISBN 0-915400-10-3). Am Council Arts.

Corporate Fund Raising a Practical Plan of Action. W. Grant Browrigg. 1978. pap. 12.50 o.p. (ISBN 0-915400-10-3). Interbk Inc.

Corporate Fund Raising Directory 1980-1981. 1980. 19.75 (ISBN 0-686-27210-2). Public Serv Materials.

Corporate Ideal in the Liberal State: 1900-1918. James Weinstein. LC 80-22211. xvii, 263p. 1981. Repr. of 1968 ed. lib. bdg. 25.00x (ISBN 0-313-22709-8, WECI). Greenwood.

Corporate Ideal in the Liberal State: Nineteen Hundred to Nineteen Eighteen. James Weinstein. 1969. pap. 5.95x (ISBN 0-8070-5457-7, BP327). Beacon Pr.

Corporate Imperialism: Conflict & Expropriation Transnational Corporations & Economic Nationalism in the Third World. Norman Girvan. LC 75-46112. 1976. 22.50 o.p. (ISBN 0-87332-073-5). M E Sharpe.

Corporate Manpower Planning. Ed. by A. R. Smith. 187p. 1980. text ed. 27.00x (ISBN 0-566-02167-6, Pub. by Gower Pub Co England). Renouf.

Corporate Marketing Planning. John M. Brion. LC 67-19446. (Marketing Ser.). 1967. 27.95 (ISBN 0-471-10440-X). Wiley.

Corporate Memory: A Profitable, Practical Approach to Information Management & Retention. Barbara N. Weaver & Wiley L. Bishop. LC 74-7410. (Systems & Controls for Financial Management Ser.). 257p. 1974. 29.50 (ISBN 0-471-92323-0, Pub. by Wiley-Interscience). Wiley.

Corporate Planner's Yearbook, 1974. Ed. by David E. Hussey. 1974. text ed. 17.05 o.p. (ISBN 0-08-017817-0). Pergamon.

Corporate Planners' Yearbook 1978-9. Ed. by David Hussey. (Illus.). 1979. 36.00 (ISBN 0-08-022255-2). Pergamon.

Corporate Planning: An Executive Viewpoint. Peter Lorange. (Illus.). 1980. text ed. 19.95 (ISBN 0-13-174755-X). P-H.

Corporate Planning & Modeling with Simplan. R. Britton Mayo & Social Systems, Inc. 1978. pap. text ed. 10.95 (ISBN 0-201-05227-X). A-W.

Corporate Planning & Policy Design. James M. Lyneis. 520p. 1980. text ed. 29.95x (ISBN 0-262-12083-6). MIT Pr.

Corporate Planning & Procurement. Ed. by David Farmer & Bernard Taylor. LC 74-19369. 1975. 27.95 (ISBN 0-470-25499-8). Halsted Pr.

Corporate Planning Models. Thomas H. Naylor. LC 77-93329. 1978. text ed. 20.50 (ISBN 0-201-05226-1). A-W.

Corporate Planning: Techniques & Applications. Malcom W. Pennington & Robert J. Allio. LC 78-25803. (Illus.). 1979. 21.95 (ISBN 0-8144-5497-6). Am Mgmt.

Corporate Planning: The Human Factor. David Hussey & M. J. Langham. 1978. text ed. 45.00 (ISBN 0-08-022464-4); pap. text ed. 19.50 (ISBN 0-08-022475-X). Pergamon.

Corporate Planning: Theory & Practice. David E. Hussey. LC 73-17304. 400p. 1974. text ed. 37.00 (ISBN 0-08-017748-4). Pergamon.

Corporate Policy: A Casebook. Jules J. Schwartz. (Illus.). 1978. 21.95 (ISBN 0-13-174813-0). P-H.

Corporate Power & Social Responsibility: A Blueprint for the Future. Neil H. Jacoby. LC 72-14073. (Studies of the Modern Corporation). 1977. pap. text ed. 7.95 (ISBN 0-02-915950-4). Free Pr.

Corporate Power & Social Responsibility. Neil H. Jacoby. (Studies of the Modern Corporation Ser.). 1973. 15.00 (ISBN 0-02-915940-7). Macmillan.

Corporate Power in an African State: The Political Impact of Multinational Mining Companies in Zambia. Richard L. Sklar. LC 74-81440. 1975. 24.50x (ISBN 0-520-02814-7). U of Cal Pr.

Corporate Power, Leadership, & Success: A Selective Bibliography to 1977. John J. Miletich. (Public Administration Ser.: Bibliography P-518). 49p. 1980. pap. 5.50. Vance Biblios.

Corporate Profits in Company Financial Reports, Tax Returns & the National Income & Product Accounts. Norman B. Ture. LC 77-95350. 1978. 1.50 (ISBN 0-685-91791-6). Finan Exec.

Corporate Real Estate Development: The Pursuit of America's Leading Corporations for Profit in Housing & Land Use. Robert A. Sigafoos. LC 76-3874. (Special Ser. in Real Estate & Urban Land Economics). (Illus.). 1976. 19.95 (ISBN 0-669-00644-0). Lexington Bks.

Corporate Responsibilities & Opportunities to 1990. Ellen T. Curtiss & Philip A. Untersee. (Arthur D. Little Books). (Illus.). 1979. 25.95 (ISBN 0-669-02848-7). Lexington Bks.

Corporate Risk Control. Donald L. MacDonald. 1966. 21.95 (ISBN 0-8260-5615-6). Wiley.

Corporate Role in Society. John D. Harper. LC 77-75047. 1977. 7.50x (ISBN 0-915604-11-6). Columbia U Pr.

Corporate Scriptwriting Book. Donna Matrazzo. LC 80-81823. (Illus.). 199p. (Orig.) 1980. pap. 14.95 (ISBN 0-935608-01-X). Media Concepts.

Corporate Social Accounting. R. W. Estes. 166p. 1976. 18.95 (ISBN 0-471-24592-5, Pub. by Wiley-Interscience). Wiley.

Corporate Social Challenge: Cases & Commentaries. rev. ed. Frederick Sturdivant & Larry M. Robinson. 1981. pap. 12.50x (ISBN 0-256-02518-5). Irwin.

Corporate Social Policy: Selections from Business & Society Review. R. L. Heilbroner & P. London. 1975. pap. 10.95 (ISBN 0-201-04360-2). A-W.

Corporate Social Responsibility. Richard N. Farmer & W. Dickerson Hogue. LC 72-96061. (Illus.). 223p. 1973. pap. text ed. 9.95 (ISBN 0-574-17930-5, 13-0930); instr's guide avail. (ISBN 0-574-17931-3, 13-0931). SRA.

Corporate Social Responsiveness: The Modern Dilemma. Robert W. Ackerman & Raymond A. Bauer. (Illus.). 472p. 1976. text ed. 24.95x (ISBN 0-87909-137-1); pap. text ed. 11.95 (ISBN 0-87909-136-3). Reston.

Corporate Society: Growth, Competition & Innovative Power. Ed. by Robin Marris. LC 73-14655. 1974. text ed. 32.95 (ISBN 0-470-57245-0). Halsted Pr.

Corporate Strategies for Social Performance. Melvin Anshen. LC 79-7888. (Studies of the Modern Corporation). 1980. 15.95 (ISBN 0-02-900730-5). Macmillan.

Corporate Strategies of the Automotive Manufacturers. John B. Schnapp. LC 79-2788. 224p. 1979. 22.95 (ISBN 0-669-03243-3). Lexington Bks.

Corporate Strategy & Functional Management. Yezdi M. Godiwalla et al. LC 79-65182. 1979. 20.95 (ISBN 0-03-049781-7). Praeger.

Corporate Strategy & Product Innovation. Ed. by Robert R. Rothberg. LC 75-32369. (Illus.). 1976. text ed. 17.75 o.s.i. (ISBN 0-02-927500-8). Free Pr.

Corporate Strategy & Product Innovation. 2nd ed. Ed. by Robert R. Rothberg. LC 80-1857. (Illus.). 1981. text ed. 17.95 (ISBN 0-02-927520-2). Free Pr.

Corporate Stress: How to Manage Stress & Make It Work for You. Rosalind Forbes. LC 78-55849. 1979. pap. 4.95 (ISBN 0-385-14440-7, Dolp). Doubleday.

Corporate Taxation & Taxation of Partnerships & Partners. Douglas A. Kahn & Pamela B. Gann. LC 78-26612. (American Casebook Ser.). 1979. text ed. 23.95 (ISBN 0-8299-2026-9). West Pub.

Corporate Taxation of the Netherlands Antilles. Francisco D. Leo & Antonio A. Amador. 1978. pap. 18.00x o.p. (ISBN 0-8464-0292-0). Beekman Pubs.

Corporate Turnaround: How Managers Turn Losers into Winners. Donald Bibeault. 416p. 1981. 22.95 (ISBN 0-07-005190-9). McGraw.

Corporate Views of the Public Interest: The Perceptions of the Forest Products Industry. Jeffrey A. Sonnenfeld. 200p. 1981. 19.95 (ISBN 0-86569-060-X). Auburn Hse.

Corporation As a Creative Environment. Don Fabun. 1972. pap. text ed. 2.50x (ISBN 0-02-475240-1, 47524). Macmillan.

Corporation Ethics: The Quest for Moral Authority. rev. ed. Ed. by George W. Forell & William H. Lazareth. LC 79-8899. (Justice Bks.). 1980. pap. 2.25 (ISBN 0-8006-1556-5, 1-1556). Fortress.

Corporation Finance: Policy, Planning, Administration. P. M. Van Arsdell. 1739p. 1968. 39.95. Wiley

Corporation Finance: Policy, Planning, Administration. Paul M. Van Arsdell. LC 68-13475. 1739p. 1968. 39.95 (ISBN 0-8260-8840-6, 90991). Ronald Pr.

Corporation Game. Jerry Kochler. LC 75-14061. 224p. 1975. 8.95 o.s.i. (ISBN 0-02-564950-7). Macmillan.

Corporation in Modern Society. Ed. by Edward S. Mason. LC 60-5392. 1966. pap. text ed. 4.95x (ISBN 0-689-70136-5, 86). Atheneum.

Corporation Income Tax in India. V. G. Rao. 240p. 1980. text ed. 13.50x (ISBN 0-391-02133-8). Humanities.

Corporations & Child Care: Profit-Making Day Care, Workplace Day Care & a Look at the Alternatives. Georgia Sassen & Cookie Avrin. LC 76-17319. (Illus.). 1974. pap. 3.50 (ISBN 0-685-85529-5). Womens Research Act.

Corporations & Information: Secrecy, Access & Disclosure. Russell B. Stevenson, Jr. LC 79-3683. 212p. 1980. text ed. 17.95x (ISBN 0-8018-2344-7). Johns Hopkins.

Corporations & Social Change. William Withers. Ed. & intro. by Mary E. Dillon. LC 73-189865. (Politics of Government Ser.). 155p. (Orig.). 1972. pap. 2.50 o.p. (ISBN 0-8120-0446-9). Barron.

Corporations & Their Critics. Thornton Bradshaw & David Vogel. 1980. 14.95 (ISBN 0-07-007075-X). McGraw.

Corporations in a Democratic Society. Ed. by Edward J. Bander. (Reference Shelf Ser: Vol. 46, No. 6). 1974. 6.25 (ISBN 0-8242-0526-X). Wilson.

Corporations in Recession: The Australian Agricultural Machinery Industry. D. A. Wadley. (Department of Human Geography Monograph: No. 13). 109p. (Orig.). 1980. pap. 5.95 (ISBN 0-908160-26-7, 0455). Bks Australia.

Corporatism & National Development in Latin America. Howard J. Wiarda. (Replica Edition Ser.). 325p. 1981. lib. bdg. 27.00x (ISBN 0-86531-031-9). Westview.

Corps Commander. Brian Horrocks et al. LC 77-7921. (Illus.). 1978. 14.95 o.p. (ISBN 0-684-15324-6, ScribT). Scribner.

Corpse for a Candidate. Michael Geller. (Bud Dugan Ser.: No. 2). 1980. pap. text ed. 1.75 (ISBN 0-505-51478-8). Tower Bks.

Corpus Delicti of Mystery Fiction: A Guide to the Body of the Case. Linda Herman & Beth Stiel. LC 74-16319. 1974. 10.00 (ISBN 0-8108-0770-X). Scarecrow.

Corpus of Cypriote Antiquities No. One: Early & Middle Bronze Age Pottery of the Cesnola Collection in the Stanford University Museum. Paola Villa. (Studies in Mediterranean Archaeology Ser.: No. XX, Pt. I). 1969. pap. text ed. 11.25x (ISBN 91-85058-21-1). Humanities.

Corpus of Early Arabic Sources for West African History. N. Levtzion & J. F. Hopkins. LC 78-67628. (Illus.). 448p. Date not set. 85.00 (ISBN 0-521-22422-5). Cambridge U Pr.

Corpus of Maya Hieroglyphic Inscriptions: Xultun, la Honradez, Vol. 5, No. 2. Ian Graham. 1981. pap. cancelled o.s.i. (ISBN 0-686-64360-7). Peabody Harvard.

Corpus of Maya Hieroglypic Inscriptions: Xultun, Vol. 5, Pt. 1. Eric Von Euw. Ed. by Lorna Condon. LC 78-50627. 1978. pap. text ed. 10.00 (ISBN 0-87365-184-7). Peabody Harvard.

Corpus of the Aramaic Incantation Bowls. Charles D. Isbell. LC 75-15949. (Society of Biblical Literature. Dissertation Ser.). xiv, 200p. 1975. pap. 7.50 (ISBN 0-89130-010-4, 060117). Scholars Pr Ca.

Corpus Signorium Imperii Romani: Hadrian's Wall, East of North Tyne, Vol. I, Fsc. I. E. J. Phillips. (British Academy Ser.). (Illus.). 1977. 69.00x (ISBN 0-19-725954-5). Oxford U Pr.

Corpus Vasorum Antiquorum. Pamela M. Packard & Paul A. Clement. (Los Angeles County Museum of Art. Ser. Fascicule 1, U.S.A., Fascicole 18). 1977. 49.50x (ISBN 0-520-02850-3). U of Cal Pr.

Corpus Vasorum Antiquorum Canada: Royal Ontario Museum, Ontario. Ed. by John Hayes. (Corpus Vasorum Antiquorum Ser.). (Illus.). 64p. 1980. 89.00 (ISBN 0-19-726000-4). Oxford U Pr.

Corpus Vasorum Antiquorum, Great Britain: Vol. 15: Castle Ashby. J. Boardman & C. M. Robertson. (Corpus Vasorum Antiquorum Ser.). (Illus.). 1979. 145.00 (ISBN 0-19-725981-2). Oxford U Pr.

Corre, Nicky, Corre. Tr. by Nicky Cruz. (Spanish Bks.). (Span.). 1978. 1.95 (ISBN 0-8297-0434-5). Life Pubs Intl.

Correct Language, Tojolabal: A Grammar with Ethnographic Notes. Louanna Furbee-Losee. LC 75-25115. (American Indian Linguistics Ser.). 1976. lib. bdg. 42.00 (ISBN 0-8240-1966-0). Garland Pub.

Correct Maid for Hotels & Motels. rev. 2nd ed. William B. Pfeiffer & Walter O. Voegele. (Illus., Orig.). 1965. pap. 2.99 (ISBN 0-8104-9456-6). Hayden.

Correct Planting Methods. (Countryside Outdoor Gardening Books Ser.). 1977. pap. 0.98 o.p. (ISBN 0-307-11918-1, Golden Pr). Western Pub.

Correct Waitress. 2nd ed. Susan Dietz. 1978. pap. 3.55 (ISBN 0-8104-9468-X). Hayden.

Correct Wrtiting, Form One. 2nd ed. Eugenia Butler et al. 384p. 1976. pap. text ed. 9.95x (ISBN 0-669-99655-6); answers free (ISBN 0-669-99663-7). Heath.

Corrected Age Data of the 1931 Indian Census. S. N. Aggarwala. 1967. 5.50x o.p. (ISBN 0-210-22722-2). Asia.

Correction Law of New York. (Supplemented annually). 1980. looseleaf 6.95 (ISBN 0-87526-198-1). Gould.

Correction of a Correctional Psychologist in Treatment of the Criminal Offender. Harold F. Uehling. (American Lectures in Behavioral Science & Law Ser.). 232p. 1973. 16.75 (ISBN 0-398-02615-7). C C Thomas.

Correctional Administration: The Management of Institutions, Probation, & Parole. Alan R. Coffey. (Illus.). 320p. 1975. 15.95 (ISBN 0-13-188284-8). P-H.

Correctional Counseling & Treatment. Kratcoski. (Illus.). 432p. 1980. pap. text ed. 10.95 (ISBN 0-686-65821-3). Duxbury Pr.

Correctional Facilities Planning. Ed. by M. Robert Montilla & Nora Harlow. LC 78-19930. 1979. 19.95 (ISBN 0-669-02437-6). Lexington Bks.

Correctional Intervention & Research: Current Issues & Future Prospects. Ted Palmer. LC 77-25777. (Illus.). 1978. 21.00 (ISBN 0-669-02166-0). Lexington Bks.

Correctional Management: Change & Control in Correctional Organizations. David E. Duffee. (Criminal Justice Ser.). (Illus.). 1980. text ed. 17.95 (ISBN 0-13-178400-5). P-H.

Corrections in America. 2nd ed. Harry E. Allen & Clifford E. Simonsen. 1978. text ed. 14.95 (ISBN 0-02-470830-5). Macmillan.

Corrections in the Community: Success Models in Correctional Reform. E. Eugene Miller & Robert Montilla. 1977. text ed. 14.95 (ISBN 0-87909-174-6); pap. text ed. 10.95 (ISBN 0-87909-173-8). Reston.

Corrections: Organization & Administration. Henry Burns. (Criminal Justice Ser.). 1975. text ed. 16.50 (ISBN 0-685-99574-7); pap. instrs. manual avail. (ISBN 0-8299-0610-X); instrs. manual avail. West Pub.

Corrections: Problems & Prospects. David M. Petersen & Charles W. Thomas. (Law Enforcement Ser.). 288p. 1975. pap. text ed. 10.95 o.p. (ISBN 0-13-178293-2). P-H.

Corrections: Problems & Prospects. 2nd ed. David M. Peterson & Charles W. Thomas. (Criminal Justice Ser.). 1980. pap. text ed. 13.95 (ISBN 0-13-178350-5). P-H.

Corrective & Reconstructive Rhinoplasty. H. J. Denecke & R. Meyer. Tr. by L. Oxtoby. (Plastic Surgery of Head & Neck: Vol. 1). (Illus.). 1967. 289.10 (ISBN 0-387-03757-8). Springer-Verlag.

Corrective & Remedial Teaching. 3rd ed. Wayne Otto & Richard J. Smith. LC 79-89740. (Illus.). 1980. text ed. 17.95 (ISBN 0-395-28355-8). HM.

Corrective & Remedial Teaching. 2nd ed. Wayne Otto et al. LC 72-4799. 500p. 1973. text ed. 17.95 o.p. (ISBN 0-395-12662-2, 3-42395). HM.

Corrective Reading. 4th ed. Miles V. Zintz. 470p. 1981. text ed. write for info. (ISBN 0-697-06187-6). Wm C Brown.

Corregidor. James H. Belote & William M. Belote. LC 80-80981. (World War Two Ser.). (Illus.). 272p. 1980. pap. 2.25 (ISBN 0-87216-696-1). Playboy Pbks.

Correlated Dictation & Transcription. 2nd. ed. Francis A. Brown & Hamden L. Forkner. (Forkner Shorthand). 1974. 12.80x (ISBN 0-912036-15-X); pap. 9.96x (ISBN 0-912036-16-8). Forkner.

Correlation & Causality. David A. Kenny. LC 79-4855. 1979. 24.50 (ISBN 0-471-02439-2, Pub. by Wiley-Interscience). Wiley.

Correlational Procedures for Research. R. M. Thorndike. LC 76-8462. 340p. 1978. 21.50 (ISBN 0-470-15090-4). Halsted Pr.

Correlations & Entropy in Classical Statistical Mechanics. J. Yvon. 1969. 26.00 (ISBN 0-08-012755-X). Pergamon.
Correlative Atlas of Adult Cardiac Disorders: Noninvasive Diagnostic Techniques. Michael V. Cohen. LC 80-66333. (Illus.). 428p. 1980. 48.50 (ISBN 0-87993-149-3). Futura Pub.
Correlative Neuroradiology. Ronald G. Quisling. LC 79-26947. 1980. 45.00 (ISBN 0-471-05737-1, Pub. by Wiley Medical). Wiley.
Correlative Neurosurgery, 2 vols. 3rd ed. R. C. Schneider. (Illus.). 1808p. 1981. Set. 190.00 (ISBN 0-398-04037-0). C C Thomas.
Correlative Sectional Anatomy of the Head & Neck: A Color Atlas, Vol. I. Joseph R. Thompson & Anton N. Hasso. LC 79-19978. (Illus.). 1979. text ed. 175.00 (ISBN 0-8016-4934-X). Mosby.
Correlative Study Guide for Neuroanatomy. 2nd ed. James L. Hall & Albert O. Humbertson, Jr. (Illus.). 1970. pap. 10.95x o.p. (ISBN 0-06-141076-4, Harper Medical). Har-Row.
Correspondance generale d'helvetius, Vol. I: 1737-1756. Ed. by D. W. Smith et al. (Romance Ser.). 384p. 1981. 35.00x (ISBN 0-8020-5517-6). U of Toronto Pr.
Correspondence, 5 vols. Walt Whitman. Ed. by Edwin H. Miller. Incl. Vol. 1. 1842-1867. 394p. 1961 (ISBN 0-8147-0435-2); Vol. 2. 1868-1875. 372p. 1961 (ISBN 0-8147-0436-0); Vol. 3. 1876-1885. 473p. 1964 (ISBN 0-8147-0437-9); Vol. 4. 1886-1889. 458p. 1969 (ISBN 0-8147-0438-7); Vol. 5. 1890-1892. 365p. 1969 (ISBN 0-8147-0439-5). LC 60-15980. (Illus.). 25.00x ea. NYU Pr.
Correspondence & Discourses of John Constable, R.A, 8 vols. John Constable. Ed. by R. B. Beckett. Incl. No. 1. The Family at East Bergholt, 1807-1837. (Illus.). 337p. 1976. Repr. 22.75x (ISBN 0-8476-1252-X); No. 2. Early Friends & Marie Bicknell (Mrs. Constable) (Illus.). 474p. 18.75x (ISBN 0-8476-1253-8); No. 3. The Correspendence with C.R. Leslie R.A. 12.50x (ISBN 0-8476-1254-6); No. 4. Patrons, Dealers & Fellow Artists. (Illus.). 481p. 18.75x (ISBN 0-8476-1255-4); No. 5. Various Friends with Charles Boner & the Artist's Children. (Illus.). 229p. 12.50x (ISBN 0-8476-1256-2); No. 6. The Fishers. Pref. by Geoffrey Grigson. (Illus.). 294p. 18.50x (ISBN 0-8476-1257-0); No. 7. Discourses. (Illus.). 109p. 12.50x (ISBN 0-8476-1258-9); No. 8. Further Correspondence & Documents. Ed. by Leslie Paris et al. (Illus.). 371p. 1976. 30.00x (ISBN 0-8476-1259-7). Set. 145.00x (ISBN 0-8476-1260-0). Rowman.
Correspondence & Public Papers of John Jay, 1763-1781. Ed. by H. P. Johnston. LC 69-16639. (American Public Figures Ser). 1971. Repr. of 1890 ed. lib. bdg. 65.00 (ISBN 0-306-71124-9). Da Capo.
Correspondence Between Henry Stephens Randall & Hugh Blair Grigsby 1856-1861. F. J. Klingberg & F. W. Klingberg. LC 73-37530. (American Scene Ser). 196p. 1972. Repr. of 1952 ed. lib. bdg. 22.50 (ISBN 0-306-70429-3). Da Capo.
Correspondence Between Prince A. M. Kurbsky & Tsar Ivan Fourth of Russia, 1564-1579. Tr. by J. L. Fennell. 1956. 48.00 (ISBN 0-521-05501-6). Cambridge U Pr.
Correspondence Between Richard Strauss & Hugo Von Hofmannsthal. Richard Strauss & Hugo Von Hofmannsthal. Tr. by Hanns Hammelmann & Ewald Osers. LC 80-40072. 576p. 1981. 67.50 (ISBN 0-521-23476-X); pap. 17.95 (ISBN 0-521-29911-X). Cambridge U Pr.
Correspondence Between Thomas Jefferson & Pierre Samuel Du Pont De Nemours, 1798-1817. Thomas Jefferson. Ed. by Dumas Malone. Tr. by Linwood Lehmann. LC 78-75282. (American Public Figures Ser). 1970. Repr. of 1930 ed. lib. bdg. 37.50 (ISBN 0-306-71301-2). Da Capo.
Correspondence of Adam Smith. Adam Smith. Ed. by Ernest C. Mossner & Ian S. Ross. 1977. 59.00x (ISBN 0-19-828185-4). Oxford U Pr.
Correspondence of Emerson & Carlyle. Ralph W. Emerson & Thomas Carlyle. Ed. by Joseph Slater. LC 63-17539. 1964. 22.50x (ISBN 0-231-02462-2). Columbia U Pr.
Correspondence of Erasmus, Vol. 6: Letters 842-992 (May 1518 - June 1519) Desiderius Erasmus. Tr. by R. A. Mynors & D. F. Thomson. (Collected Works of Erasmus). 1981. 30.00x (ISBN 0-8020-5500-1). U of Toronto Pr.
Correspondence of G. E. Morrison, 2 vols. Ed. by Hui-Min Lo. Set. 249.00 (ISBN 0-521-08779-1); Vol. 1 1895-1912. 119.00 (ISBN 0-521-20486-0); Vol. 2 1912-1920. 150.00 (ISBN 0-521-21561-7). Cambridge U Pr.
Correspondence of George, Prince of Wales, 1770-1812, 8 vols. George, Prince of Wales. Ed. by A. Aspinall. Incl. Vol. 1. 1770-1789. 1963. o.p. (ISBN 0-19-519464-0); Vol. 2. 1789-1794. 1964. 29.00x (ISBN 0-19-519465-9); Vol. 5. 1804-1806. 1968. 30.00x (ISBN 0-19-519468-3); Vol. 6. 1806-1809. 1969. 30.00x (ISBN 0-19-519469-1); Vol. 7. 1810-1811. 454p. 1970. 30.00x (ISBN 0-19-519516-7); Vol. 8. 1811-1812. 588p. 1971. 33.75 (ISBN 0-19-519517-5). Oxford U Pr.
Correspondence of Isaac Newton, 4 vols. Isaac Newton. Ed. by H. W. Turnbull & J. F. Scott. 1961. 72.50 ea.; Vol. 1. (ISBN 0-521-05812-0); Vol. 2. (ISBN 0-521-05813-9); Vol. 3. (ISBN 0-521-05814-7); Vol. 4. (ISBN 0-521-05815-5). Cambridge U Pr.
Correspondence of Jeremy Bentham, 3 vols. Jeremy Bentham. Ed. by T. L. Sprigge. Incl. Vols. 1-2. 1752-1780. 1968 (ISBN 0-485-13201-X); Vol. 3. January 1781-October 1788. 1971 (ISBN 0-485-13203-6). text ed. 74.00x ea. (Athlone Pr). Humanities.
Correspondence of John Locke: Vol. 5, Letters 1702-2198 Covering the Years 1694-1697. John Locke. Ed. by E. S. DeBeer. 808p. 1979. text ed. 89.00x (ISBN 0-19-824562-9). Oxford U Pr.
Correspondence of John Peale Bishop & Allen Tate. Ed. by Thomas D. Young & John J. Hindle. LC 80-5186. 1981. price not set (ISBN 0-8131-1443-8). U Pr of Ky.
Correspondence of Jonathan Swift, Vols. 4-5. Jonathan Swift. Ed. by Harold Williams. Incl. Vol. 4. 1732-1736; Vol. 5. 1737-1745; Appendixes & Indexes. 1965. Set. 55.00x (ISBN 0-19-811443-5). Oxford U Pr.
Correspondence of King George the Third with Lord North, 1768-1783. Ed. by W. B. Donne. LC 76-154697. (Era of the American Revolution Ser). 1971. Repr. of 1867 ed. lib. bdg. 75.00 (ISBN 0-306-70155-3). Da Capo.
Correspondence of Lord Overstone, 3 vols. Ed. by D. P. O'Brien. 1971. Vol. 1. 49.95 (ISBN 0-521-08097-5); Vol. 2. 49.95 (ISBN 0-521-08098-3); Vol. 3. 49.95 (ISBN 0-521-08099-1). Cambridge U Pr.
Correspondence of Lord William Bentinck, Governor General of India 1828-1835, 2 vols. William A. Bentinck. Ed. by Cyril H. Philips. 1977. 169.00x set (ISBN 0-19-713571-4). Oxford U Pr.
Correspondence of M. Tullius Cicero, 7 Vols. Cicero. Ed. by R. Y. Tyrell & L. C. Purser. Repr. Set. 350.00 (ISBN 3-4870-2445-4). Adler.
Correspondence of Richard Steele. Richard Steele. Ed. by Rae Blanchard. 1941. 49.00x o.p. (ISBN 0-19-811499-0). Oxford U Pr.
Correspondence of Robert M. T. Hunter, 1826-1876. Ed. by Charles H. Ambler. LC 76-75307. (American Scene Ser). 1971. Repr. of 1918 ed. lib. bdg. 39.50 (ISBN 0-306-71257-1). Da Capo.
Correspondence of Robert Toombs, Alexander H. Stephens, & Howell Cobb. U. B. Phillips. LC 68-54846. (American Scene Ser). 1970. Repr. of 1911 ed. lib. bdg. 79.50 (ISBN 0-306-71191-5). Da Capo.
Correspondence of the French Ministers to the United States, 1791-1797. Ed. by Frederick J. Turner. LC 75-75268. (American History, Politics & Law Ser). 1969. Repr. of 1904 ed. lib. bdg. 95.00 (ISBN 0-306-71315-2). Da Capo.
Correspondence of William Hickling Prescott, 1833-1847. W. H. Prescott. Ed. by Roger Wolcott. LC 76-112312. (American Public Figures Ser). 1970. Repr. of 1925 ed. lib. bdg. 42.50 (ISBN 0-306-71912-6). Da Capo.
Correspondence, Seventeen Hundred Nine to Seventeen Thirteen, Vol. 5. Isaac Newton. Ed. by A. R. Hall & Laura Tilling. 1975. 95.00 (ISBN 0-521-08721-X). Cambridge U Pr.
Correspondence, 1713-1718, Vols. 6 & 7. Isaac Newton. Ed. by A. R. Hall & Laura Tilling. (Correspondence of Isaac Newton Ser.). (Illus.). 500p. 1976. Vol. 6. 95.00 ea. (ISBN 0-521-08722-8). Vol. 7 (ISBN 0-521-08723-6). Cambridge U Pr.
Correspondences: A Family History in Letters. Anne Stevenson. LC 74-2871. 104p. 1974. 10.00x (ISBN 0-8195-4073-0, Pub. by Wesleyan U Pr). Columbia U Pr.
Corridors of Time: 1,700,000,000 Years of Earth. Ron Redfern. 200p. 1980. 50.00 (ISBN 0-8129-0922-4). Times Bks.
Corrie. Lorinda Hagen. 1978. pap. 1.95 (ISBN 0-505-51289-0). Tower Bks.
Corroboree. Kenneth Gangemi. LC 76-27241. 96p. 1977. pap. 2.95 (ISBN 0-685-56012-0). Assembling Pr.
Corrosion & Corrosion Control: An Introduction to Corrosion Science & Engineering. 2nd ed. Herbert H. Uhlig. LC 71-162425. 419p. 1971. 32.50 (ISBN 0-471-89563-6, Pub. by Wiley-Interscience). Wiley.
Corrosion & Encrustation in Water Wells. (FAO Irrigation & Drainage Paper Ser.: No. 34). 108p. 1981. pap. 5.75 (ISBN 92-5-100933-3, F2080, FAO). Unipub.
Corrosion Fatigue of Metals in Marine Environments. Carl E. Jaske et al. (Metals & Ceramics Information Center Ser.). (Illus.). 160p. 1981. 45.00 (ISBN 0-935470-07-7). Battelle.
Corrosion Handbook. Herbert H. Uhlig. 1948. 52.50 (ISBN 0-471-89562-8, Pub. by Wiley-Interscience). Wiley.
Corrosion in Civil Engineering. Thomas Telford Editorial Staff, Ltd. 172p. 1980. 40.00x (ISBN 0-7277-0079-0, Pub. by Telford England). State Mutual Bk.
Corrosion of Metals in Concrete. 1975. pap. 15.95 (ISBN 0-685-85130-3, SP-49) (ISBN 0-685-85131-1). ACI.
Corrosion of Pulp & Paper Mill Equipment. Vera Pollock & Jack Weiner. LC 76-21187. (Bibliographic Ser.: No. 269). 1976. pap. 40.00 (ISBN 0-87010-054-8). Inst Paper Chem.
Corrosion of Pulp & Paper Mill Equipment. Lillian Roth et al. LC 76-21187. (Bibliographic: No. 269, Supplement I, Part 2). 1980. pap. 45.00 (ISBN 0-87010-055-6). Inst Paper Chem.
Corrosion of Pulp & Paper Mill Equipment, Suppl. 1. Lillian Roth et al. LC 76-21187. (Bibliographic Ser.: No. 269, Suppl. 1). 1979. pap. 45.00 (ISBN 0-87010-056-4). Inst Paper Chem.
Corrosion of Steel & Aluminium Scuba Tanks. F. C. Cichy et al. (Marine Technical Report Ser.: No. 62). 2.00 (ISBN 0-938412-05-1). URI MAS.
Corrosion Prevention for Practicing Engineers. Joseph F. Bosich. LC 74-109530. 1970. pap. 10.95 (ISBN 0-8436-0325-9). CBI Pub.
Corrosion Prevention Practice. G. A. Balalaev. Tr. by I. Sapronova from Rus. 343p. 1972. text ed. 15.00x o.p. (ISBN 0-8464-0293-9). Beekman Pubs.
Corrosion Problems Related to Electrical, Instrumentation & Automation Components Offshore. Norwegian Petroleum Society. 152p. 1980. 75.00x (ISBN 82-7270-007-7, Pub. by Norwegian Info Norway). State Mutual Bk.
Corrosion Resistance of Alloys to Bleach Plant Environments. Arthur H. Tuthill et al. (TAPPI PRESS Reports). (Illus.). 99p. 1980. pap. 94.95 (ISBN 0-89852-384-2, 01-01-RO84). Tappi.
Corrugated Carton Crafting. Dick Van Voorst. LC 71-90803. (Little Craft Book Ser). (Illus.). (gr. 5 up). 1969. 5.95 (ISBN 0-8069-5138-9); PLB 6.69 (ISBN 0-8069-5139-7). Sterling.
Corrupt & Illegal Practices: A General Survey & a Case Study of an Election Petition. Leonard M. Helmore. (Library of Political Studies). (Orig.). 1967. text ed. 4.25x (ISBN 0-7100-5124-7); pap. text ed. 2.25x (ISBN 0-7100-5113-1). Humanities.
Corruptores. Tr. by Nicky Cruz. (Portuguese Bks.). 1979. 1.65 (ISBN 0-8297-0792-1). Life Pubs Intl.
Corsair Affair & Articles Related to the Writings. Soren Kierkegaard. Tr. by Howard V. Hong & Edna H. Hong. LC 80-7538. (Kierkegaards Writings: No. XIII). (Illus.). 380p. 1981. 25.00x (ISBN 0-691-07246-9). Princeton U Pr.
Corsair: The Life of J. Pierpont Morgan. Andrew Sinclair. 1981. 15.00 (ISBN 0-316-79240-3). Little.
Corsets & Crinolines. Norah Waugh. LC 69-11134. (Illus.). 1954. 11.95 o.s.i. (ISBN 0-87830-020-1); pap. 10.95 (ISBN 0-87830-526-2). Theatre Arts.
Corsica. Ian Thompson. (Islands Ser.). 1974. 14.95 (ISBN 0-7153-5329-2). David & Charles.
Corsica. Patrick Turnbull. 1976. 24.00 (ISBN 0-7134-3134-2). David & Charles.
Cortes & Montezuma. Maurice Collis. (Illus.). 1963. pap. 3.95 o.p. (ISBN 0-571-05626-1, Pub. by Faber & Faber). Merrimack Bk Serv.
Corticothalamic Projections & Sensorimotor Activities. Ed. by T. Frigyesi et al. LC 74-181303. (Illus.). 601p. 1972. 43.50 (ISBN 0-911216-35-9). Raven.
Cortisone. Edward C. Kendall. LC 72-123853. 1971. 7.95 o.p. (ISBN 0-684-31062-7, ScribT). Scribner.
Corvair Owners Handbook of Maintenance & Repair: 1960-1965. Ed. by Clymer Publications. (Illus.). 1965. pap. 7.95 (ISBN 0-89287-246-2, A140). Clymer Pubns.
Corvette: A Piece of the Action. Ed. by William L. Mitchell & Allan Girdler. LC 77-83506. 1977. 38.95 (ISBN 0-915038-11-0); leather ed. 58.95 (ISBN 0-915038-23-4). Princeton Pub.
Corvette Restoration Source Book, '68-'80. Date not set. 21.95 (ISBN 0-686-64613-4). Johnson VA. Postponed.
Corvette Service-Repair Handbook: All Models, 1966-1979. Eric Jorgensen. Ed. by Jeff Robinson. (Illus.). 1976. pap. text ed. 10.95 (ISBN 0-89287-082-6, A146). Clymer Pubns.
Corvette Stingray, Nineteen Sixty-Three to Nineteen Seventy-Nine. LC 78-20255. (Chilton's Repair & Tune-up Guides). (Illus.). 1979. pap. 8.95 (ISBN 0-8019-6843-7, 6843). Chilton.
Corvette V-Eight, Nineteen Fifty-Five to Nineteen Sixty-Two: Complete Owner's Handbook. Clymer Publications. (Illus.). 1961. pap. 7.95 (ISBN 0-89287-247-0, A141). Clymer Pubns.
Cosa: The Making of a Roman Town. Frank E. Brown. (Illus.). 150p. 1980. 20.00x (ISBN 0-472-04100-2). U of Mich Pr.
Cosas Que Hacer Para Navidad. (Editorial Mundo Hispano). (YA) 1980. 2.50 (ISBN 0-311-26607-X). Casa Bautista.
Cosgrove Report. G. J. O'Toole. 1981. pap. 2.95 (ISBN 0-440-11594-9). Dell.
Cosima Wagner. George R. Marek. LC 80-7591. (Illus.). 256p. 1981. 15.95 (ISBN 0-06-012704-X, HarpT). Har-Row.
Cosimo Tura: Paintings & Drawings. Eberhardt Ruhmer. (Illus.). 45.00 (ISBN 0-912158-47-6). Hennessey.
Cosmetic Ingredient: Their Safety Assessment. Ed. by Robert L. Elder. (Illus.). 1980. pap. text ed. 19.00 (ISBN 0-930376-19-6). Pathotox Pubs.
Cosmetic Science. Ed. by M. Breuer. Vol. 1, 1978. 49.00 (ISBN 0-12-133001-X); Vol. 2, 1980. 53.00 (ISBN 0-12-133002-8). Acad Pr.
Cosmetic Surgery: A Consumers Guide. Sylvia Rosenthal. LC 76-58921. (Illus.). 1977. 10.95 o.p. (ISBN 0-397-01211-X). Lippincott.
Cosmetic Surgery May Be for You. George Willeford. (Illus.). 1979. 7.95 (ISBN 0-88319-048-6); pap. 4.50 (ISBN 0-88319-049-4). Shoal Creek Pub.
Cosmetics: Science & Technology, 3 vols. 2nd ed. Ed. by M. S. Balsam & Edward Sagarin. LC 75-177888. Set. 145.75 (ISBN 0-471-04650-7); Vol. 1. 1972. 52.75 (ISBN 0-471-04646-9); Vol. 2. 1972. 52.75 (ISBN 0-471-04647-7); Vol. 3 1974. 58.25 (ISBN 0-471-04649-3, Pub. by Wiley-Interscience). Wiley.
Cosmetics: The Great American Skin Game. Toni Stabile. 1979. pap. 2.25 (ISBN 0-441-30246-7). Charter Bks.
Cosmetics: What the Ads Don't Tell You. Carol Rinzler. 256p. 1979. pap. 1.95 o.p. (ISBN 0-441-11750-3). Charter Bks.
Cosmetics: What the Ads Don't Tell You. Carol A. Rinzler. LC 77-4675. 1977. 9.95 o.s.i. (ISBN 0-690-01459-7, TYC-T). T Y Crowell.
Cosmetologia, la Guia Keystone Para Aprender el Arte De Embellecer. rev. ed. Anthony B. Colletti. (Span.). 1981. text ed. 16.78 (ISBN 0-912126-61-2, 1260-00); pap. text ed. 12.15 (ISBN 0-912126-62-0, 1261-00). Keystone Pubns.
Cosmetology. Anthony B. Colletti. (Illus.). 1980. 11.00x (ISBN 0-912126-29-9). Sheridan.
Cosmetology: A Professional Text. Sylvia Franco et al. (Illus.). 1980. text ed. 14.96 (ISBN 0-07-021791-2). McGraw.
Cosmetology Instructor's Guide, No. 1. Anthony B. Colletti. (Keystone Publications' Audio-Visual Program Ser.). 88p. 1976. 7.10 (ISBN 0-912126-16-7). Keystone Pubns.
Cosmetology Instructor's Guide, No. 2. Anthony B. Colletti. (Keystone Publications' Audio-Visual Program Ser.). 80p. 1976. 7 10311 (ISBN 0-912126-17-5). Keystone Pubns.
Cosmetology Instructor's Guide, No. 3. Anthony B. Colletti. (Keystone's Publications' Audio-Visual Program Ser.). 136p. 1976. 7.10 (ISBN 0-912126-18-3). Keystone Pubns.
Cosmetology Instructor's Guide, No. 4. Anthony B. Colletti. (Keystone Publications' Audio-Visual Program Ser.). 112p. 7.10 (ISBN 0-912126-19-1). Keystone Pubns.
Cosmetology Review Book. Anthony B. Colletti. 1981. pap. text ed. 5.00 (ISBN 0-912126-56-6, 1267-00). Keystone Pubns.
Cosmetology: The Keystone Guide to Beauty Culture. rev. ed. Anthony B. Colletti. 1981. text ed. 10.00 (ISBN 0-912126-59-0, 1248-00); pap. text ed. 7.14 (ISBN 0-912126-60-4, 1249-00). Keystone Pubns.
Cosmic Carnival of Stanislaw Lem: An Anthology of Entertaining Stories by the Modern Master of Science Fiction. Stanislaw Lem. Ed. by Michael Kandel. 256p. (Orig.). 1981. pap. 7.95 (ISBN 0-8264-0043-4). Continuum.
Cosmic Chase. Richard Hutton. 1981. pap. 3.50 (ISBN 0-451-61925-0, ME1925, Ment). NAL.
Cosmic Connection: An Extraterrestrial Perspective. Carl Sagan. LC 80-1857. (Illus.). 288p. 1980. pap. 5.95 (ISBN 0-385-17365-2, Anch). Doubleday.
Cosmic Crusaders. Pierre Barbet. (Science Fiction Ser.). 1980. pap. 2.25 (ISBN 0-87997-583-0, UE1583). DAW Bks.
Cosmic Dawn: The Origins of Matter & Life. Eric Chaisson. (Illus.). 320p. 1981. 14.95 (ISBN 0-316-13590-9, Pub. by Atlantic Monthly Pr). Little.

Cosmic Discovery: The Search, Scope, & Heritage of Astronomy. Martin Harwit. LC 80-68172. 70p. 1981. 25.00x (ISBN 0-465-01428-3). Basic.
Cosmic Doctrine. Dion Fortune. 5.95 (ISBN 0-87728-455-5). Weiser.
Cosmic Dust. P. G. Martin. (Studies in Physics). (Illus.). 1979. 24.95x (ISBN 0-19-851458-1). Oxford U Pr.
Cosmic Evolution: An Indroduction to Astronomy. George Field et al. LC 77-76420. (Illus.). 1978. text ed. 19.50 (ISBN 0-395-25321-7). HM.
Cosmic Factor: Bioastrology & You. James Vogh. LC 79-10628. 1979. 7.95 (ISBN 0-396-07685-8). Dodd.
Cosmic Fishing. Edgar J. Applewhite. 1977. 10.95 (ISBN 0-02-502710-7, 50271). Macmillan.
Cosmic Fragments. Heraclitus. Ed. by G. S. Kirk. 1954. 62.00 (ISBN 0-521-05245-9). Cambridge U Pr.
Cosmic Gas Dynamics. Evry Schatzman & Ludwig Biermann. LC 73-16025. 291p. 1974. 23.00 (ISBN 0-471-75720-9, Pub. by Wiley). Krieger.
Cosmic Harp: For Musicologist & Astrologer. Corinne Heline. 4.95 o.p. (ISBN 0-87613-005-8). New Age.
Cosmic Influences on Human Behavior. Michel Gauquelin. LC 77-28405. (Illus.). 1978. 8.95 (ISBN 0-88231-050-X). ASI Pubs Inc.
Cosmic Pulse of Life: The Revolutionary Biological Power Behind UFO's. Trevor J. Constable. LC 77-72046. (Illus.). 446p. 1977. pap. 7.95 (ISBN 0-8334-1777-0). Steinerbks.
Cosmic Rays. A. M. Hillas. 306p. 1972. text ed. 23.00 (ISBN 0-08-016724-1). Pergamon.
Cosmic Rays. J. G. Wilson & G. E. Perry. LC 75-38743. (Wykeham Science Ser.: No. 40). 1976. 8.60x (ISBN 0-8448-1167-X). Crane Russak Co.
Cosmic Reality Kill. Joseph Rosenberger. (Death Merchant Ser.: No. 36). (Orig.). 1979. pap. 1.95 (ISBN 0-523-41380-7). Pinnacle Bks.
Cosmic Satire in the Contemporary Novel. John W. Tilton. LC 75-18240. 150p. Date not set. cancelled o.p. (ISBN 0-8387-1801-9). Bucknell U Pr.
Cosmic View: The Universe in Forty Jumps. Kees Boeke. LC 57-14500. (Illus.). (gr. 5 up). 1957. 8.95 (ISBN 0-381-98016-2, A16260, JD-J). John Day.
Cosmic X-Ray Astronomy. Adams. 1980. 29.50 (ISBN 0-9960019-2-1, Pub. by a Hilger England). Heyden.
Cosmical Geophysics. Ed. by Alv Egeland et al. (Illus.). 360p. 1973. 33.50x (ISBN 8-200-02256-0, Dist. by Columbia U Pr). Universitet.
Cosmicomics. Italo Calvino. Tr. by William Weaver. LC 76-14795. 1976. pap. 2.95 (ISBN 0-15-622600-6). HarBraceJ.
Cosmographia of Bernardus Silvestris. Ed. & tr. by Winthrop Wetherbee. (Records of Civilization, Sources & Studies: Sources & Studies). 176p. 1973. 15.00x (ISBN 0-231-03673-6). Columbia U Pr.
Cosmological Argument: A Reassessment. Bruce R. Reichenbach. (Illus.). 160p. 1972. 14.50 (ISBN 0-398-02387-5). C C Thomas.
Cosmological Eye. Henry Miller. LC 75-88729. 1969. 10.95 (ISBN 0-8112-0319-0); pap. 7.95 (ISBN 0-8112-0110-4, NDP109). New Directions.
Cosmologies of Consciousness. E. C. Barksdale. 148p. 1980. text ed. 16.50x (ISBN 0-87073-969-7); pap. text ed. 11.25x (ISBN 0-87073-970-0). Schenkman.
Cosmology Plus One: Readings from Scientific American. Intro. by Owen Gingerich. LC 77-1448. (Illus.). 1977. text ed. 15.95x (ISBN 0-7167-0043-3); pap. text ed. 7.95x (ISBN 0-7167-0042-5). W H Freeman.
Cosmology: The Science of the Universe. Edward R. Harrison. LC 80-18703. (Illus.). 480p. Date not set. price not set (ISBN 0-521-22981-2). Cambridge U Pr.
Cosmonauts in Orbit: The Story of the Soviet Space Program. Gene Gurney & Clare Gurney. LC 76-189516. (Illus.). 192p. (gr. 7 up). 1972. PLB 8.87 o.p. (ISBN 0-531-02572-1). Watts.
Cosmopolitan Crimes: The Foreign Rivals of Sherlock Holmes. Ed. by Hugh Greene. 1972. pap. 1.95 o.p. (ISBN 0-14-003571-0). Penguin.
Cosmopolitan Girl. Rosalyn Drexler. 208p. 1976. pap. 1.75 o.s.i. (ISBN 0-446-59057-6). Warner Bks.
Cosmopolitan Tales. Peter Brook. 1980. pap. cancelled (ISBN 0-87881-087-0). Mojave Bks.
Cosmopolitan World Atlas. LC 62-20026. 1978. 35.00 (ISBN 0-528-83090-2); deluxe ed. 40.00 o.s.i. (ISBN 0-528-83063-5). Rand.
Cosmo's Restaurant. Harriet L. Sobol. LC 78-9685. (Illus.). (gr. 3-6). 1978. 8.95 (ISBN 0-02-785970-3, 78597). Macmillan.
Cost Accountability for Hospital Social Work. Society for Hospital Social Work Directors of the American Hospital Association. LC 80-12334. 48p. (Orig.). 1980. pap. 10.00 (ISBN 0-87258-278-7, 1330). Am Hospital.
Cost Accounting. James Cashin & Ralph S. Polimeni. 1981. write for info. oHT's (ISBN 0-07-010213-9, C); write for info. instrs.' manual (ISBN 0-07-010214-7); study guide 5.95 (ISBN 0-07-010257-0); price not set OHT's (ISBN 0-07-075018-1); job order costing practice set 6.95 (ISBN 0-07-010258-9); process costing practice set 6.95 (ISBN 0-07-010259-7); exam questions avail. (ISBN 0-07-010215-5). McGraw.
Cost Accounting: A Managerial Emphasis. 4th ed. Charles T. Horngren. LC 76-45816. (Illus.). 992p. 1977. pap. text ed. 22.95 (ISBN 0-13-179739-5); study guide 8.95 (ISBN 0-13-179705-0). P-H.
Cost Accounting: Accumulation, Analysis, & Control. Benny R. Copeland & Nelson G. Sullivan. 1977. text ed. 18.95 (ISBN 0-8299-0122-1); check figures bklt. avail. (ISBN 0-8299-0470-0); solutions manual avail. (ISBN 0-8299-0469-7). West Pub.
Cost Accounting & Financial Control Systems. John Dearden. LC 73-184160. 1973. text ed. 18.95 (ISBN 0-201-01507-2). A-W.
Cost Accounting for Management Application. Li. 1966. text ed. 18.95x (ISBN 0-675-09883-1); instructor's manual 3.95 (ISBN 0-686-66973-8). Merrill.
Cost Accounting for Managerial Decision Making. Larry N. Killough & Wayne F. Leininger. LC 76-52741. 1977. 15.95 (ISBN 0-8221-0191-2). CBI Pub.
Cost Accounting for Non-Accountants. John Myer. 1971. 7.95 o.p. (ISBN 0-8015-1776-1). Dutton.
Cost Accounting: Principles & Applications. 3rd ed. Horace Brock et al. (Accounting Instructional System). (Illus.). 1978. text ed. 11.95 (ISBN 0-07-008051-8, G); course management manual 9.95 (ISBN 0-07-008054-2); individualized performance guide 5.75 (ISBN 0-07-008052-6). McGraw.
Cost Accounting: Principles & Managerial Applications. 4th ed. Gerald Crowningshield & Kenneth A. Gorman. LC 78-69551. (Illus.). 1979. text ed. 20.95 (ISBN 0-395-26797-8); inst. manual 4.00 (ISBN 0-395-26798-6). HM.
Cost Accounting: Principles & Practice. 9th ed. John J. Neuner & Edward B. Deakin. 1977. pap. text ed. 18.95 (ISBN 0-256-01903-7); job order cost practice set 5.95x (ISBN 0-256-00377-7); study guide 4.95 (ISBN 0-256-01960-6). Irwin.
Cost Accounting: Processing, Evaluating, & Using Cost Data. Wayne J. Morse. (Illus.). 752p. 1981. text ed. 18.95 (ISBN 0-201-04677-6). A-W.
Cost & Financial Accounting in Forestry. K. Openshaw. 1977. text ed. 33.00 (ISBN 0-08-021456-8); pap. text ed. 15.00 (ISBN 0-08-021455-X). Pergamon.
Cost & Management Accountancy for Students. 2nd ed. Ed. by J. Batty. 1970. pap. text ed. 15.95x (ISBN 0-434-90112-1). Intl Ideas.
Cost Benefit Analysis. revised ed. E. J. Mishan. LC 76-1988. (Praeger Special Studies Ser.). 454p. 1976. text ed. 32.50 (ISBN 0-275-56530-0); pap. text ed. 11.95 (ISBN 0-275-85690-9). Praeger.
Cost Benefit Analysis & Environmental Problems. Peter Abelson. 1979. 19.50 (ISBN 0-566-00267-1, 02837-1, Saxon Hse). Lexington Bks.
Cost-Benefit Analysis & the Adult Educator. Sara Steele. 1971. 2.30 (ISBN 0-88379-002-5). Adult Ed.
Cost-Benefit Analysis in Administration. Trevor Newton. (Royal Institute of Public Administration). 1972. text ed. 21.00x o.p. (ISBN 0-04-336043-2). Allen Unwin.
Cost-Benefit Analysis in Educational Planning. Maureen Woodhall. (Fundamentals of Educational Planning Ser., No. 13). (Orig.). 1970. pap. 6.00 (ISBN 92-803-1038-0, U105, UNESCO). Unipub.
Cost Containment in Hospitals. Ephraim Turban et al. LC 80-13272. 648p. 1980. text ed. 39.75 (ISBN 0-89443-279-6). Aspen Systems.
Cost Containment Through Employee Incentives Program. Pat N. Groner. LC 77-72514. 1977. 22.00 (ISBN 0-912862-42-4). Aspen Systems.
Cost Containment Through Systems Engineering: A Guide for Hospitals. David F. Johannides. LC 79-15217. 1979. text ed. 31.00 (ISBN 0-89443-098-X). Aspen Systems.
Cost Control & Information Systems: A Complete Guide to Effective Design & Implementation. Pravin Shah. (Illus.). 608p. 1981. 24.95 (ISBN 0-07-056369-1, P&RB). McGraw.
Cost Control in Hospitals. John R. Griffith et al. 450p. 1976. 17.50 (ISBN 0-686-68582-2, 14916). Hospital Finan.
Cost Control in Hospitals. John R. Griffith et al. LC 75-28579. 375p. 1976. text ed. 17.50x (ISBN 0-914904-12-4). Health Admin Pr.
Cost Controls for the Hospitality Industry. Michael M. Coltman. 410p. 1980. text ed. 15.95 (ISBN 0-8436-2170-2). CBI Pub.
Cost Data for Landscape Construction: 1981 Edition. rev. ed. Kathleen W. Kerr et al. (Cost Data for Landscape Construction Ser.). (Illus.). 200p. 1981. pap. 24.95 (ISBN 0-937890-01-4). Kerr Assoc.
Cost-Effective Error Reduction in Data Processing. William Exton, Jr. 275p. 1981. 20.95 (ISBN 0-471-04682-5, Pub. by Wiley-Interscience). Wiley.
Cost-Effective Quality Food Service: An Institutional Guide. Judy F. Stokes. LC 78-25871. (Illus.). 1979. text ed. 29.75 (ISBN 0-89443-083-1). Aspen Systems.
Cost-Effective Self-Sufficiency: Middle Class Peasant. Terence McLaughlin & Eve McLaughlin. 1978. 17.95 (ISBN 0-7153-7474-5). David & Charles.
Cost Effectiveness: Economic Evaluation of Engineered Systems. J. M. English. LC 68-28500. 1968. 38.95 (ISBN 0-471-24170-9, Pub. by Wiley-Interscience). Wiley.
Cost Effectiveness in Training & Instruction. Alberto Pena & Ruth De Bliek. LC 80-82294. (Guideline Ser.). 60p. Date not set. pap. 6.95x (ISBN 0-931816-01-7). Kumarian Pr. Postponed.
Cost Effectiveness Notebook: Nineteen Eighty Update. Hospital Financial Management Association. 1980. write for info. (ISBN 0-930228-14-6). Hospital Finan.
Cost Effectiveness Notebook: Nineteen Seventy-Nine Update. Hospital Financial Management Association. 1979. looseleaf 4.00 (ISBN 0-930228-12-X). Hospital Finan.
Cost Engineering Analysis: A Guide to the Economic Evaluation of Engineering Projects. William R. Park. LC 72-10237. (Illus.). 373p. 1973. 29.50 (ISBN 0-471-65914-2, Pub. by Wiley-Interscience). Wiley.
Cost Factors in Planning Educational Technology Systems. Dean T. Jamison. (Fundamentals of Educational Planning Ser: No. 24). 1978. pap. 4.75 (ISBN 92-803-1076-3, U774, UNESCO). Unipub.
Cost Finding & Rate Setting for Hospitals. American Hospital Association. (Financial Management Ser.). (Illus.). 112p. 1968. pap. 15.00 (ISBN 0-87258-036-9, 1365). Am Hospital.
Cost Finding & Rate Setting for Hospitals. 103p. 1968. 9.25 (ISBN 0-686-68591-1, 1365). Hospital Finan.
Cost Improvement, Work Sampling & Short Interval Scheduling. W. J. Richardson. 1976. 18.95 (ISBN 0-87909-139-8). Reston.
Cost in Pentecost. Joseph Orsini. 1977. pap. 3.95 o.p. (ISBN 0-88270-243-2). Logos.
Cost of Catastrophic Illness. Howard Birnbaum. LC 77-9192. 1978. 14.95 (ISBN 0-669-01773-6). Lexington Bks.
Cost of Delay Due to Government Regulation in the Houston Housing Market. Rice Center. LC 79-65687. (ULI Research Report Ser.: No. 28). (Illus.). 92p. 1979. pap. text ed. 9.75 (ISBN 0-87420-328-7). Urban Land.
Cost of Discipleship. 2nd ed. Dietrich Bonhoeffer. 1967. 4.95 (ISBN 0-02-512920-1); pap. write for info. (ISBN 0-685-14934-X). Macmillan.
Cost of Disciplineship. Dietrich Bonhoeffer. 1963. pap. 3.95 (ISBN 0-02-083850-6, Collier). Macmillan.
Cost of Health Insurance Administration. Roger D. Blair & Ronald J. Vogel. 128p. 1975. 21.95 (ISBN 0-669-00165-1). Lexington Bks.
Cost of Implementing Federally Mandated Social Programs. Carol Van Alstyne & Sharon L. Coldren. 1976. pap. 3.50 o.p. (ISBN 0-685-83998-2). ACE.
Cost of Learning: The Policies of Primary Education in Kenya. L. Gray Cowan. LC 71-106991. 1970. pap. 5.75x (ISBN 0-8077-1193-4). Tchrs Coll.
Cost of Living Longer: National Health Insurance & the Elderly. Stephen M. Davidson et al. LC 79-2756. 160p. 1980. 19.95 (ISBN 0-669-03242-5). Lexington Bks.
Cost of Personal Borrowing in the United States. 9th ed. Financial Publishing Company Staff. Ed. by Charles H. Gushee. (Illus.). 1980. perfect bound 27.50 (ISBN 0-685-87665-9, 830). Finan Pub.
Cost of Silence. Margaret Yorke. LC 77-79964. 1977. 6.95 o.s.i. (ISBN 0-8027-5379-5). Walker & Co.
Cost of the War to Russia. S. Kohn & Alexander F. Meyendorff. 15.00 (ISBN 0-86527-034-1). Fertig.
Cost of Water from a Single-Purpose Multi-Stage Flash Plant with Vapour Recompression. (Technical Reports Ser.: No. 93). (Illus., Orig.). 1968. pap. 4.50 (ISBN 92-0-175268-7, IAEA). Unipub.
Cost-Sharing in Health Care: Proceedings. A. Brandt et al. (Illus.). 184p. 1981. pap. 22.50 (ISBN 0-387-10325-2). Springer-Verlag.
Cost Systems for Planning, Decisions & Controls: Concepts & Techniques. Felix P. Kollaritsch. LC 78-6799. (Accounting Ser.). 1979. text ed. 20.95 (ISBN 0-88244-172-8). Grid Pub.
Costing Matters for Managers. E. G. Wood. 199p. 1974. text ed. 24.50x (Pub. by Busn Bks England). Renouf.
Costing Methods for Nuclear Desalination. (Technical Reports Ser.: No. 69). (Orig.). 1966. pap. 2.75 (ISBN 92-0-145466-X, IAEA). Unipub.
Costs: Accounting, Analysis & Control. A. Wayne Corcoran. LC 77-18798. (Accounting & Information Systems Ser.). 1978. pap. text ed. 27.95 (ISBN 0-471-17251-0); solutions manual avail. (ISBN 0-471-03339-1). Wiley.
Costs & Benefits of Education. Robert D. Leiter. (Illus.). 215p. 1975. text ed. 15.00x (ISBN 0-8290-0398-3). Irvington.
Costs & Control in Further Education. John Pratt et al. (General Ser.). 1978. text ed. 36.75x (ISBN 0-85633-159-7, NFER). Humanities.
Costs and Resources of Legal Education: A Study in the Management of Educational Resources. new ed. Peter D. Swords & Frank K. Walwer. LC 74-22459. 345p. 1975. 17.50x (ISBN 0-915120-00-3). Columbia U Pr.
Costs at U. S. Educational Institutions. 156p. 1979. 20.00 (IIE). Unipub.
Costs at U. S. Educational Institutions. rev. ed. 212p. 1980. pap. 20.00 (ISBN 0-87206-105-1). Inst Intl Educ.
Costs of Crime. Ed. by Charles M. Gray. LC 79-18871. (Sage Criminal Jusice System Annuals: Vol. 12). (Illus.). 1979. 20.00x (ISBN 0-8039-1198-X); pap. 9.95x (ISBN 0-8039-1199-8). Sage.
Costs of Health Care Facilities. National Academy Of Engineering. 1968. pap. 7.75 (ISBN 0-309-01592-8). Natl Acad Pr.
Costs of Higher Education: How Much Do Colleges & Universities Spend Per Student & How Much Should They Spend? LC 80-8321. (Carnegie Council Ser.). 1980. text ed. 15.95x (ISBN 0-87589-485-2). Jossey-Bass.
Costs, Returns & Repayment Experience of Ujamaa Villages in Tanzania, Nineteen Seventy-Three to Nineteen Seventy-Six. Jean M. Due. LC 80-490. 167p. 1980. text ed. 17.25 (ISBN 0-8191-1019-1); pap. text ed. 8.75 (ISBN 0-8191-1020-5). U Pr of Amer.
Costume Book for Parties & Plays. Joseph Leeming. LC 38-27654. (Illus.). (gr. 7-9). 1938. PLB 8.95 o.p. (ISBN 0-397-30052-2). Lippincott.
Costume Design & Making. 2nd ed. Mary Fernald & Eileen Shenton. LC 67-14505. (Illus.). 1967. 13.25 (ISBN 0-87830-021-X). Theatre Arts.
Costume for Births, Marriages & Deaths. P. Cunnington. 1978. Repr. of 1972 ed. text ed. 22.75x (ISBN 0-7136-1192-8). Humanities.
Costume in England. 4th ed. Frederick W. Fairholt. LC 68-21769. 1968. Repr. of 1885 ed. 24.00 (ISBN 0-8103-3506-9). Gale.
Costume of Colonial Times. Alice M. Earle. LC 75-159946. xiv, 264p. 1975. Repr. of 1924 ed. 20.00 (ISBN 0-8103-3965-X). Gale.
Costume of the Classical World. Marion Sichel. (Illus.). 72p. 1980. 17.95 (ISBN 0-7134-1511-8, Pub. by Batsford England). David & Charles.
Costume of the Western World. Doreen Yarwood. 192p. 1980. 17.50x. St Martin.
Costume Patterns & Designs. Max Tilke. (Illus.). 1974. 65.00 o.s.i. (ISBN 0-8038-1191-8). Hastings.
Costume Reference Nine: Nineteen Thirty-Nine to Nineteen Fifty. Marion Sichel. 1979. 17.95 (ISBN 0-7134-1507-X, Pub. by Batsford England). David & Charles.
Costume Reference Ten: Nineteen Fifty to Present Day. Marion Sichel. 1979. 17.95 (ISBN 0-7134-1509-6, Pub. by Batsford England). David & Charles.
Costumes & Settings for Historical Plays: Volume Five, The Nineteenth Century. Jack Cassin-Scott. LC 79-56537. (Illus.). 96p. 1980. 14.95 (ISBN 0-7134-1710-2, Pub. by Batsford England). David & Charles.
Costumes & Uniforms. K. Wilson. 1980. pap. 3.95 (ISBN 0-931064-26-0). Starlog Pr.
Costumes for Children. Barbara Snook. 1970. 5.25 o.p. (ISBN 0-8231-1020-6). Branford.
Costumes for the Stage: A Complete Handbook for Every Kind of Play. Sheila Jackson. (Illus.). 1978. 12.95 (ISBN 0-87690-298-0). Dutton.
Costumes from Crepe Paper. Marie-Blanche Pointillart. (Little Craft Book Ser). (Illus.). 48p. (gr. 5 up). 1974. 4.95 o.p. (ISBN 0-8069-5302-0); PLB 5.89 o.p. (ISBN 0-8069-5303-9). Sterling.
Costumes of the Seventeenth & Eighteenth Century. Phillis Cunnington. LC 70-115950. (Illus.). 1971. 5.95 o.p. (ISBN 0-8238-0086-5). Plays.
Costumes to Make. Peggy Parish. LC 75-102969. (Illus.). 1970. 7.95 (ISBN 0-02-769950-1). Macmillan.
Cotorsion Modules. Eben Matlis. LC 52-42839. (Memoirs: No. 49). 1979. pap. 8.40 (ISBN 0-8218-1249-1, MEMO-49). Am Math.

Cotswolds. Brian Smith. 1979. 17.95 (ISBN 0-7134-3058-3, Pub. by Batsford England). David & Charles.

Cotswolds: A New Study. Charles Hadfield & Alice M. Hadfield. (Illus.). 1974. 22.95 (ISBN 0-7153-6224-0). David & Charles.

Cottage & Country Recipes. A Parker. (Illus.). 1975. 7.95 (ISBN 0-571-10500-9, Pub. by Faber & Faber). Merrimack Bk Serv.

Cottage Garden Flowers. Margery Fish. 1980. pap. 7.95 (ISBN 0-571-11462-8, Pub. by Faber& Faber). Merrimack Bk Serv.

Cottage Herbal. Elizabeth Cullum. LC 75-10563. (Illus.). 144p. 1976. 11.50 o.p. (ISBN 0-7153-7108-8). David & Charles.

Cottage Poems: A Miscellany of Descriptive Poems, Repr. Of 1811 Ed. Patrick Bronte. Bd. with Rural Minstrel: A Miscellany of Descriptive Poems. Repr. of 1813 ed. LC 75-31169. (Romantic Context Ser.: Poetry 1789-1830: Vol. 23). 1977. lib. bdg. 47.00 (ISBN 0-8240-2122-3). Garland Pub.

Cottagers of Glenburnie: A Tale for the Farmer's Ingle-Nook. Elizabeth Hamilton. LC 73-22147. (Feminist Controversy in England, 1788-1810 Ser.). 1974. lib. bdg. 50.00 (ISBN 0-8240-0864-2). Garland Pub.

Cotton. Joseph Philippe. (Q Books: Where Do Things Come from?). (Illus.). 1978. 3.95 (ISBN 0-8467-0444-7, Pub. by Two Continents). Hippocrene Bks.

Cotton & Cotton Goods in China. Richard Kraus. LC 78-22779. (Modern Chinese Economy Ser.). 500p. 1980. lib. bdg. 50.00 (ISBN 0-8240-4276-X). Garland Pub.

Cotton & Silk Making in Manchu China. Du Halde. LC 79-93005. (Illus.). 112p. 1980. pap. 12.50 (ISBN 0-8478-0306-6). Rizzoli Intl.

Cotton Belt Locomotives. 20.00 (ISBN 0-686-64894-3). Chatham Pub CA.

Cotton Candy on a Rainy Day. Nikki Giovanni. LC 78-16897. 1978. 5.95 (ISBN 0-688-03365-2); pap. 3.95 (ISBN 0-688-08365-X). Morrow.

Cotton Candy on a Rainy Day. Nikki Giovanni. LC 78-16897. 1980. pap. 3.95 (ISBN 0-688-08365-X, Quill). Morrow.

Cotton Mather. Babette M. Levy. (United States Authors Ser.: No. 328). 1979. lib. bdg. 9.95 (ISBN 0-8057-7261-8). Twayne.

Cotton Mather, Barrett Wendell. LC 80-23335. (American Men & Women of Letters). Orig. Title: Cotton Mather: the Puritan Priest. 328p. 1981. pap. 5.95 (ISBN 0-87754-166-3). Chelsea Hse.

Cotton Mather & American Science & Medicine: With Studies & Documents Concerning the Introduction of Inoculation or Variolation, 2 vols. Ed. by I. Bernard Cohen. LC 79-7974. (Three Centuries of Science in America Ser.). (Illus.). 1980. lib. bdg. 65.00x (ISBN 0-405-12556-9). Arno.

Cotton Pest Control, 5 vols. Environmental Studies Board, Natl Research Council. LC 75-37180. (Pest Control Ser.: An Assessment of Present & Alternative Technologies, Vol. 3). 139p. 1975. pap. 5.00 (ISBN 0-309-02412-9). Natl Acad Pr.

Cotton Trade of Great Britain. Thomas Ellison. LC 68-20034. Repr. of 1886 ed. 16.50x (ISBN 0-678-05044-9). Kelley.

Cotton Trade of Great Britain. James A. Mann. LC 72-354341. Repr. of 1860 ed. 21.00x (ISBN 0-678-05184-4). Kelley.

Cottonwood County. William Kloefkorn & Ted Kooser. 1980. pap. 3.00 (ISBN 0-931534-08-9). Windflower Pr.

Coturnix (Coturnix Coturnix Japonica) Standards & Guidelines for the Breeding, Care, & Management of Laboratory Animals. Institute Of Laboratory Animal Resources. LC 73-601933. (Illus., Orig.). 1969. pap. 4.00 (ISBN 0-309-01703-3). Natl Acad Pr.

Couch: Its Use & Meaning in Psychotherapy. Harold Stern. LC 77-15610. 1978. 19.95 (ISBN 0-87705-303-0). Human Sci Pr.

Couch on Insurance, 24 vols. 2nd ed. Ronald A. Anderson. LC 59-1915. 1971. 876.00 set (ISBN 0-686-14510-0). Lawyers Co-Op.

Couching: Decorative Laid Thread Embroidery. Gloria Ramsey. 1976. 19.94 o.p. (ISBN 0-7134-3130-X, Pub. by Batsford England). David & Charles.

Cougar. Kay McDearmon. LC 77-6086. (gr. 2-5). 1977. 4.95 (ISBN 0-396-07468-5). Dodd.

Could Anything Be Worse. Marilyn Hirsh. LC 73-17364. (Illus.). 32p. (gr. k-3). 1974. reinforced bdg. 8.95 (ISBN 0-8234-0239-8). Holiday.

Could Be Worse! James Stevenson. LC 76-28534. (gr. k-3). 1977. 8.25 (ISBN 0-688-80075-0); PLB 7.92 (ISBN 0-688-84075-2). Greenwillow.

Couldn't We Have a Turtle Instead. Judith Vigna. LC 75-8848. (Self Starter Ser). 32p. (gr. k-2). 1975. 6.50g (ISBN 0-8075-1312-1). A Whitman.

Coulomb's Memoir on Statics: An Essay in the History of Civil Engineering. Jacques Heyman. (Illus.). 240p. 1972. 44.50 (ISBN 0-521-08395-8). Cambridge U Pr.

Coulometric Analysis. Ed. by E. Pungor & L. Buzas. (Illus.). 301p. 1979. 32.50x (ISBN 963-05-2021-4). Intl Pubns Serv.

Coulometry in Analytical Chemistry. G. W. Milner & G. Phillips. 1967. text ed. 23.00 (ISBN 0-08-012439-9); pap. text ed. 11.25 (ISBN 0-08-012438-0). Pergamon.

Coulson's Valence. 3rd ed. Charles A. Coulson. Ed. by Roy McWeeny. (Illus.). 49.50x (ISBN 0-19-855144-4); pap. 23.00x (ISBN 0-19-855145-2). Oxford U Pr.

Coulter's Woman. Catherine Weber. (Orig.). 1980. pap. 1.95 (ISBN 0-532-23199-6). Manor Bks.

Council Fires: A Story of the Chippewa Indians in the Mid-1800s & the Treaties of the Great White Father. Bruce Calhoun. 158p. 1980. pap. 7.95 o.p. (ISBN 0-89404-004-9). Aztex.

Council Fires on the Upper Ohio. Randolph C. Downes. LC 40-34394. (Illus.). 1940. pap. 4.95 (ISBN 0-8229-5201-7). U of Pittsburgh Pr.

Councils & Assemblies. Ed. by G. J. Cuming & D. Baker. LC 70-132384. (Cambridge Studies in Church History: No. 7). 1971. 47.50 (ISBN 0-521-08038-X). Cambridge U Pr.

Councils, Committees & Boards: A Handbook of Advisory, Cunsultative, Executive & Similar Bodies in British Public Life. 4th ed. Ed. by I. G. Anderson. 409p. 1980. 100.00x (ISBN 0-900246-32-4). Intl Pubns Serv.

Councils of Governments: A Study of Political Incrementalism. Nelson Wikstrom. LC 76-28784. 1977. 14.95 (ISBN 0-88229-322-2). Nelson-Hall.

Counsel & Advise: A Political Biography of Samuel I. Rosenman. Samuel B. Hand. Ed. by Frank Freidel. LC 78-62383. (Modern American History Ser.: Vol. 8). 225p. 1979. lib. bdg. 30.00 (ISBN 0-8240-3632-8). Garland Pub.

Counsel for Christian Workers. Charles H. Spurgeon. (Charles H. Spurgeon Library). 124p. 1975. pap. 2.50 o.p. (ISBN 0-8010-8039-8). Baker Bk.

Counsel for the Poor: Criminal Defense in Urban America. Robert Hermann et al. LC 77-9151. 1977. 17.95 (ISBN 0-669-01810-4). Lexington Bks.

Counseling Across Cultures. rev. & expanded ed. Ed. by Paul B. Pedersen et al. 368p. (Orig.). 1981. pap. 10.00x (ISBN 0-8248-0725-1). U Pr of Hawaii.

Counseling & Accountability: Methods & Critique. H. D. Burck et al. 224p. 1973. text ed. 27.00 (ISBN 0-08-017029-3); pap. text ed. 10.00 (ISBN 0-08-017684-4). Pergamon.

Counseling & Psychology in Elementary Schools. Henry Kaczkowski & C. H. Patterson. (Illus.). 384p. 1975. photocopy ed., spiral 37.50 (ISBN 0-398-03218-1). C C Thomas.

Counseling & Psychotherapy. Carl R. Rogers. LC 42-24693. 1942. text ed. 18.95 (ISBN 0-395-05321-8). HM.

Counseling & Psychotherapy: A Behavioral Approach. E. Lakin Phillips. LC 77-1771. (Personality Processes Ser.). 1977. 25.95 (ISBN 0-471-01881-3, Pub. by Wiley-Interscience). Wiley.

Counseling & Psychotherapy: An Existential-Humanistic View. 3rd ed. Dugald S. Arbuckle. 500p. 1975. text ed. 17.95x o.p. (ISBN 0-205-04634-7, 2246341). Allyn.

Counseling & Psychotherapy: Skills, Theories & Practices. Allen E. Ivey. (Illus.). 1980. text ed. 18.95 (ISBN 0-13-183152-6). P-H.

Counseling & Rehabilitating the Cancer Patient. Ed. by Richard E. Hardy & John G. Cull. (American Lectures in Social & Rehabilitation Psychology Ser.). 164p. 1975. pap. 15.50 photocopy ed. spiral (ISBN 0-398-03297-1). C C Thomas.

Counseling & Rehabilitating the Diabetic. Ed. by John G. Cull & Richard E. Hardy. (American Lectures in Social & Rehabilitation Psychology Ser.). (Illus.). 164p. 1974. text ed. 12.95 (ISBN 0-398-02997-0). C C Thomas.

Counseling & Values: A Philosophical Examination. James A. Peterson. LC 74-117427. 1976. pap. text ed. 9.95 (ISBN 0-910328-24-2). Carroll Pr.

Counseling Children & Adolescents. new ed. William M. Walsh. LC 75-5097. 424p. 1976. 20.00x (ISBN 0-8211-2253-3); text ed. 18.00x (ISBN 0-685-61056-X). McCutchan.

Counseling Clients in the Entertainment Industry 1980, 2 vols. Martin E. Silfen. LC 80-80021. (Patents, Copyrights, Trademarks, & Literary Property Course Handbook Ser.). 1433p. 1980. pap. text ed. 25.00 (ISBN 0-686-68822-8, G6-3666). PLI.

Counseling Couples in Groups: A Manual for Improving Troubled Relationships. Robert L. Smith & Ann M. Alexander. (Illus.). 128p. 1974. 12.75 (ISBN 0-398-03191-6). C C Thomas.

Counseling for Career Development. 2nd ed. E. L. Tolbert. LC 79-89452. (Illus.). 1980. text ed. 16.95 o.p. (ISBN 0-686-65937-6); inst. manual 0.65 o.p. (ISBN 0-686-65938-4). HM.

Counseling: Group Theory & System. 2nd ed. Daniel W. Fullmer. LC 78-9058. 1978. 27.00 (ISBN 0-910328-12-9); pap. 16.50 (ISBN 0-686-52428-4). Carroll Pr.

Counseling High School Students: Special Problems & Approaches. Ed. by John G. Cull & Richard E. Hardy. (Amer. Lec. Social & Rehabilitation Psychology). (Illus.). 272p. 1974. 19.75 (ISBN 0-398-02913-X). C C Thomas.

Counseling in Medical Genetics. Ed. by Sheldon Reed. 246p. 1980. 26.00 (ISBN 0-8451-0208-7). A R Liss.

Counseling Manual in Astrology. Marc E. Jones. 200p. 1980. 13.50 o.p. (ISBN 0-87878-017-3, Sabian). Great Eastern.

Counseling Men. Ed. by Thomas M. Skovholt et al. LC 79-29722. (Counseling Psychology Ser.). (Orig.). 1980. pap. text ed. 9.95 (ISBN 0-8185-0372-6). Brooks-Cole.

Counseling Methods: Developing Counselors. John Eddy et al. LC 80-6315. 285p. 1981. lib. bdg. 19.25 (ISBN 0-8191-1474-X); pap. text ed. 10.25 (ISBN 0-8191-1475-8). U Pr of Amer.

Counseling Parents of Exceptional Children. Jack C. Stewart. (Special Education Ser.). 1978. pap. text ed. 7.50 (ISBN 0-675-08386-9). Merrill.

Counseling Parents of the Ill & the Handicapped. Ed. by Robert L. Noland. (Illus.). 628p. 1979. pap. 12.95 (ISBN 0-398-01404-3). C C Thomas.

Counseling Parents of the Mentally Retarded: A Sourcebook. Robert L. Noland. (Illus.). 420p. 1978. 16.75 (ISBN 0-398-01405-1). C C Thomas.

Counseling Psychology & Guidance: An Overview in Outline. Jerome A. Kroth. 272p. 1973. 12.75 (ISBN 0-398-02726-9). C C Thomas.

Counseling Skills for Church Leadership. Hyrum H. Huskey, Jr. 1980. pap. 5.75 (ISBN 0-8309-0295-3). Herald Hse.

Counseling Strategies & Intervention Techniques for the Human Services. Robert J. Wicks. LC 76-55408. 1977. pap. 6.50 scp (ISBN 0-397-47365-6, HarpC). Har-Row.

Counseling Strategies & Objectives. 2nd ed. Harold L. Hackney & Sherilyn N. Cormier. (P-H Series in Counseling & Human Development). 1979. ref. 13.95 (ISBN 0-13-183319-7); pap. 9.95 ref. (ISBN 0-13-183301-4). P-H.

Counseling Strategies with Special Populations. John G. Cull & Richard E. Hardy. (American Lectures in Social & Rehabilitation Psychology Ser.). (Illus.). 360p. 1975. 24.75 (ISBN 0-398-03284-X). C C Thomas.

Counseling the Disadvantaged Youth. William E. Amos & Jean D. Grambs. 1968. text ed. 18.95x (ISBN 0-13-183129-1). P-H.

Counseling the Dying. Margaretta Bowers et al. LC 74-33146. 192p. 1975. 17.50x (ISBN 0-87668-198-4). Aronson.

Counseling the Dying. Margaretta K. Bowers et al. LC 80-8903. (Harper's Ministers Paperback Library). 208p. 1981. pap. 4.95 (ISBN 0-06-061020-4). Har-Row.

Counseling the Elderly: A Systems Approach. James F. Keller & George Hughston. (Illus.). 192p. 1980. scp 14.50 (ISBN 0-06-453511-8, HarpC). Har-Row.

Counseling the Elderly: For Professional Helpers Who Work with the Aged. Garry L. Landreth & Robert C. Berg. (Illus.). 532p. 1980. 26.75 (ISBN 0-398-04058-3); pap. 19.75 (ISBN 0-398-04059-1). C C Thomas.

Counseling the Older Adult: A Training Manual. Patricia Alpaugh & Margaret Haney. LC 77-99241. 1978. 7.50 (ISBN 0-88474-043-9). USC Andrus Geron.

Counseling Theories: A Selective Examination for School Counselors. Louis Cunningham & Herman J. Peters. LC 72-83704. 1973. text ed. 15.95 (ISBN 0-675-09066-0). Merrill.

Counseling Theories & Techniques: Summarized & Critiqued. Lester N. Downing. LC 74-23725. 240p. 1975. 16.95 (ISBN 0-88229-203-X); pap. 9.95 (ISBN 0-88229-502-0). Nelson-Hall.

Counseling Theories: Developing Counselors. John Eddy et al. LC 80-6316. 138p. 1981. lib. bdg. 16.50 (ISBN 0-8191-1476-6); pap. text ed. 7.50 (ISBN 0-8191-1477-4). U Pr of Amer.

Counseling: Theory & Process. 2nd ed. James C. Hansen et al. 1977. text ed. 18.50x (ISBN 0-205-05626-1). Allyn.

Counseling with Confidence. William D. Barr. (Orig.). 1981. pap. 4.95 (ISBN 0-88270-492-3). Logos.

Counseling with Gay Men & Women: A Guide for Facilitating Positive Life-Styles. Natalie J. Woodman & Harry R. Lenna. LC 80-8002. (Social & Behavioral Science Ser.). 1980. text ed. 12.95x (ISBN 0-87589-468-2). Jossey-Bass.

Counseling with the Mind of Christ: The Dynamics of Spiritutherapy. Charles R. Solomon. 1977. pap. 4.95 (ISBN 0-8007-0889-X). Revell.

Counseling Women. Lenore Harmon et al. LC 77-22343. 1978. pap. text ed. 9.95 o.p. (ISBN 0-8185-0240-1). Brooks-Cole.

Counseling Youth. new ed. Clyde M. Narramore. 128p. (Orig.). 1974. pap. 3.95 (ISBN 0-310-29891-1). Zondervan.

Counselling & School Social Work: An Experimental Study. Gordon Rose & Tony M. Marshall. LC 74-1752. 345p. 1975. 27.95 (ISBN 0-471-73549-3, Pub. by Wiley-Interscience). Wiley.

Counselling at Work. A. G. Watts. 92p. 1977. text ed. 7.40x (ISBN 0-7199-0925-2, Pub. by Bedford England); pap. text ed. 4.40x (ISBN 0-7199-0924-4, Pub. by Bedford England). Renouf.

Counselling Older Persons: Careers, Retirement, Dying, Vol.4. Daniel Sinick. Ed. by Garry R. Walz & Libby Benjamin. LC 77-21963. (New Vistas in Counseling Ser.). 1977. 12.95 (ISBN 0-87705-312-X). Human Sci Pr.

Counselling the Intellectually Gifted Child. Avner Ziv. 1977. pap. text ed. 4.50x (ISBN 0-8077-8021-9). Tchrs Coll.

Counselor & Suicidal Crisis: Diagnosis & Intervention. John Hipple & Peter Cimbolic. 136p. 1979. text ed. 11.50 (ISBN 0-398-03872-4). C C Thomas.

Counselor Ayres' Memorial. Joaquim M. Machado de Assis. Tr. by Helen Caldwell from Port. LC 72-187876. 1973. 15.95x (ISBN 0-520-02227-0). U of Cal Pr.

Counselor Education & Supervision: Readings in Theory, Practice, & Research. Ed. by Milton Seligman & Norman F. Baldwin. (Illus.). 436p. 1972. 19.75 (ISBN 0-398-02406-5). C C Thomas.

Counselor-in-Training. Susan K. Gilmore. (Illus.). 1973. 15.95x (ISBN 0-13-183293-X). P-H.

Counselors-at-Law. Jerome Weidman. LC 78-14712. 408p. 1980. 12.95 (ISBN 0-385-12880-0). Doubleday.

Counselors' Comparative Guide to American Colleges, 1976. 2nd ed. James Cass & Max Birnbaum. LC 75-5789. 830p. 1975. pap. 12.50x o.s.i. (ISBN 0-06-010656-5, TD-225, HarpT). Har-Row.

Counselor's Handbook: Readings in Counseling, Student Aid & Rehabilitation. S. Norman Feingold. LC 79-190226. 288p. (gr. 9-12). 1972. text ed. 12.00x (ISBN 0-910328-05-6). Carroll Pr.

Counsels of Perfection: A Baha'i Guide to Mature Living. Genevieve Coy. 1979. 7.50 (ISBN 0-85398-079-9, 7-32-33, Pub by G Ronald England); pap. 2.50 (ISBN 0-85398-080-2, 7-32-34, Pub. by G Ronald England). Baha'i.

Counsels on Education. Ellen G. White. 1968. deluxe ed. 6.50 (ISBN 0-8163-0112-3, 03555-0); pap. 4.50 (ISBN 0-8163-0113-1, 035568). Pacific Pr Pub Assn.

Counsels on Health & Instruction to Medical Missionary Workers. Ellen G. White. 1951. deluxe ed. 7.50 (ISBN 0-8163-0114-X, 03561-8). Pacific Pr Pub Assn.

Counsels to Parents, Teachers & Students Regarding Christian Education. Ellen G. White. 1943. Repr. of 1913 ed. deluxe ed. 6.95 (ISBN 0-8163-0115-8, 03591-5). Pacific Pr Pub Assn.

Count & See. Tana Hoban. LC 72-175597. (Illus.). 40p. (ps-2). 1972. 8.95 (ISBN 0-02-744800-2). Macmillan.

Count Brass. Michael Morrcock. 1981. pap. 2.25 (ISBN 0-440-11541-8). Dell.

Count It All Joy! Phyllis Thompson. LC 78-64550. 1978. pap. 2.50 (ISBN 0-87788-103-0). Shaw Pubs.

Count Manfred. Miranda Seymour. 1979. pap. 1.95 o.p. (ISBN 0-445-04377-6). Popular Lib.

Count Morbida's Fang-Tastic Activity Book. (gr. 3-5). pap. 3.95 (ISBN 0-590-11813-7, Schol Pap). Schol Bk Serv.

Count of Monte Cristo. Alexandre Dumas. 1976. lib. bdg. 15.95x (ISBN 0-89968-147-6). Lightyear.

Count of Saint-Germain: The Secret of Kings. Isabel Cooper-Oakley. LC 70-137422. 256p. 1970. pap. 6.50 (ISBN 0-8334-1702-9). Steinerbks.

Count of Van Rheeden Castle. Scott Wright. 1976. pap. 1.25 o.p. (ISBN 0-445-08474-X). Popular Lib.

Count Presents Create a Creature. (Wipe off Bks.). 9p. (ps). Date not set. 2.39 (ISBN 0-307-01843-1, Golden Pr). Western Pub.

Count the Stars. Barbara Cartland. (Barbara Cartland Ser.: No. 10). 192p. (Orig.). 1981. pap. 1.75 (ISBN 0-515-05860-2). Jove Pubns.

Count to Ten. (Block Bk.). (Illus.). (ps). 1981. 2.50 (ISBN 0-686-69367-1, Golden Pr). Western Pub.

Count Vronsky's Daughter. Carola Salisbury. LC 80-2065. 312p. 1981. 12.95 (ISBN 0-385-15918-8). Doubleday.

Countdown: Skydiver, Rocket & Satellite Motion on Programmable Calculators. Robert Eisberg & Wendell Hyde. LC 78-24836. 107p. 1979. pap. 7.95 (ISBN 0-918398-26-6). Dilithium Pr.

Countdown to Space Fleet Landing. Ruth E. Norman. (Tesla Speaks Ser.: Vol. VII). (Illus.). 1974. pap. 4.95 (ISBN 0-932642-28-4). Unarius.

Countdown to Successful Reading. Barbara F. Oakman. (Illus., Orig.). (gr. 5-9). 1971. pap. text ed. 11.95 (ISBN 0-13-183616-1). P-H.

Counted Cross-Stitch Designs for Christmas. Danish Handcraft Guild. (Illus.). 1978. pap. 8.95 (ISBN 0-684-15975-9, SL821, ScribT). Scribner.

Counted Cross Stitch Patterns & Designs. Swedish Handcraft Guild. (Illus.). 72p. 1981. pap. 8.95 (ISBN 0-684-16950-9, ScsribT). Scribner.

Counter Culture: The Creation of an Alternative Society. Ed. by Joseph Berke. (Illus.). 19.95x (ISBN 0-8464-0295-5). Beekman Pubs.

Counter Current Extraction. S. Hartland. LC 69-17867. 1970. 25.00 (ISBN 0-08-012976-5). Pergamon.

Counter-Insurgency in Kenya, 1952-1960: A Study of Military Operations Against the Mau Mau. Anthony Clayton. (Transafrica Historical Papers: No. 4). (Illus.). 1976. pap. 5.00x (ISBN 0-8002-0203-1). Intl Pubns Serv.

Counter Point. large print ed. Isabelle Holland. LC 80-27954. 1981. Repr. of 1980 ed. 11.95 (ISBN 0-89621-262-9). Thorndike Pr.

Counter-Poyson..., to the Objections & Reproches, Wherewith the Aunswerer to the Abstract, Would Disgrace the Holy Discipline of Christ. Dudley Fenner. LC 74-28854. (English Experience Ser.: No. 735). 1975. Repr. of 1584 ed. 10.50 (ISBN 90-221-0735-3). Walter J Johnson.

Counter Reformation: Fifteen Fifty-Nine to Sixteen Ten. Marvin R. O'Connell. Ed. by William L. Langer. LC 73-14278. (Rise of Modern Europe Ser.). (Illus.). 408p. (YA) 1974. 15.00x o.s.i. (ISBN 0-06-013233-7, HarpT). Har-Row.

Counter-Revolution, Doctrine & Action, Seventeen Eighty-Nine to Eighteen Four. Jacques Godechot. LC 70-159820. 1971. 24.00 (ISBN 0-86527-035-X). Fertig.

Counter-Revolution in Pennsylvania: 1776-1790. Robert L. Brunhouse. LC 42-5025. (Illus.). 1971. 8.00 (ISBN 0-911124-65-9). Pa Hist & Mus.

Counter-Revolution of Science. LC 79-21045. 416p. 1980. 9.00 (ISBN 0-913966-66-5); pap. 4.00 (ISBN 0-913966-67-3). Liberty Fund.

Counter Service. Ser-Vol-Tel Institute. (Food Service Career Education Ser.). 1974. pap. 4.95 (ISBN 0-8436-2020-X). CBI Pub.

Counterdeterrence: A Report on Juvenile Sentencing & Effects of Prisonization. Gerald R. Wheeler. LC 77-26975. 1978. 15.95 (ISBN 0-88229-315-X). Nelson-Hall.

Counterfeit Kill. E. Howard Hunt. 160p. 1975. pap. 1.25 o.p. (ISBN 0-523-00589-X). Pinnacle Bks.

Counterfeit Lady Unveiled: Being a Full Account of the Birth, Life, Most Remarkable Actions, & Untimely Death of Mary Carleton, Known by the Name of the German Princess. Francis Kirkman. Bd. with Memoirs of Mary Carleton, Commonly Stiled, the German Princess: Being a Narrative of Her Life & Death. LC 80-2486. 1981. 74.50 (ISBN 0-404-19120-7). AMS Pr.

Counterfeit Miracles. B. B. Warfield. 1976. pap. 5.45 (ISBN 0-85151-166-X). Banner of Truth.

Counterforce Syndrome: A Guide to U. S. Nuclear Weapons & Strategic Doctrine. rev. ed. Robert C. Aldridge. (Illus.). 86p. 1979. pap. 4.95 (ISBN 0-89758-008-7). Inst Policy Stud.

Counterguerilla Operations: FM 1-16. Dept. of the Army, Washington D. C. (Illus.). 163p. 1967. pap. 8.00 (ISBN 0-87364-038-1). Paladin Ent.

Counterinsurgency Warfare. John S. Pustay. LC 65-11319. 1965. 9.95 o.s.i. (ISBN 0-02-925530-9). Free Pr.

Counterpoint. 2nd ed. Kent Kennan. LC 73-168625. (Illus.). 1972. ref. ed. 19.50 (ISBN 0-13-184291-9); wkbk. 4.25 (ISBN 0-13-184309-5). P-H.

Counterpoint: A Book of Poems. Clinton F. Larson. LC 73-15889. 111p. 1973. 6.95 o.p. (ISBN 0-8425-0449-4). Brigham.

Counterpoint: An Introduction to Polyphonic Composition. Hugo Kauder. (Music Reprint Ser.). 1979. Repr. of 1960 ed. lib. bdg. 19.50 (ISBN 0-306-79520-5). Da Capo.

Counterpoint: The Polyphonic Vocal Style of the Sixteenth Century. Knud Jeppesen. Tr. by G. Haydon. 1939. ref. ed. 19.95 (ISBN 0-13-183608-0). P-H.

Counterstroke. Andrew Garve. LC 78-378. 1978. 8.95 o.s.i. (ISBN 0-690-01748-0, TYC-T). T Y Crowell.

Countess. March Cost. LC 63-13789. 1963. 6.95 (ISBN 0-8149-0076-3). Vanguard.

Countesse of Lincolnes Nurserie. Elizabeth Clinton. LC 74-28838. (English Experience Ser.: No. 720). 1975. Repr. of 1622 ed. 3.50 (ISBN 90-221-0720-5). Walter J Johnson.

Countesthorpe Experience. Ed. by John Watts. (Unwin Education Bks). 1977. text ed. 19.50x (ISBN 0-04-373003-5). Allen Unwin.

Counting. Walt Disney Productions. 32p. (ps-1). 1979. PLB 6.08 (ISBN 0-307-61076-4, Golden Pr); pap. 1.95 o.p. (ISBN 0-307-11076-1, Golden Pr). Western Pub.

Counting. Gillian Youldos. (All a-Board Bks. Ser.). (ps-2). 1980. 3.50 (ISBN 0-531-02142-4). Watts.

Counting & Counters. R. M. Oberman. 192p. 1981. 29.95 (ISBN 0-470-27118-3). Halsted Pr.

Counting on You: The U. S. Census. Madelyn K. Anderson. 7.95 (ISBN 0-686-63972-3). Vanguard.

Counting Out Rhymes: A Dictionary. Tr. by Roger D. Abrahams & Lois Rankin. (Publications of the American Folklore Bibliographical & Special Ser.: Vol. 31). 288p. 1980. text ed. 17.50x (ISBN 0-292-71057-7). U of Tex Pr.

Counting-Out Rhymes of Children. Henry C. Bolton. LC 68-23139. 1969. Repr. of 1888 ed. 15.00 (ISBN 0-8103-3475-5). Gale.

Counting People: The Census in History. Hyman Alterman. LC 74-82635. (Illus.). (gr. 9-12). 1969. 7.50 o.p. (ISBN 0-15-220170-X, HJ). HarBraceJ.

Counting Rhymes. Illus. by Sharon Kane. (Illus.). 24p. (ps-4). 1960. PLB 4.57 o.p. (ISBN 0-307-60361-X, Golden Pr). Western Pub.

Counting Stars. William Coleman. LC 76-28973. 1976. 3.50 (ISBN 0-87123-055-0, 210055). Bethany Fell.

Counting the Grasses. Michael Mott. LC 80-67430. (Illus., Orig.). 1980. signed & numbered 25.00 (ISBN 0-938078-13-5); pap. 5.00 perfect bdg. (ISBN 0-938078-12-7). Anhinga Pr.

Counting the People in 1980: An Appraisal of Census Plans. Committee on National Statistics, National Research Council. 1978. pap. text ed. 10.50 (ISBN 0-309-02797-7). Natl Acad Pr.

Countrey Justice, Containing the Practise of the Justices of the Peace Out of Their Sessions. Michael Dalton. LC 74-28844. (English Experience Ser.: No. 725). 1975. Repr. of 1618 ed. 42.00 (ISBN 90-221-0725-6). Walter J Johnson.

Countries of the World & Their Leaders Yearbook 1981. (Illus.). 1000p. 1981. 48.00 (ISBN 0-8103-1052-X). Gale.

Country & Growing with Nature. Barbara Ford. Date not set. 4.95 (ISBN 0-8062-1134-2). Carlton.

Country Bed & Breakfast Places in Canada. John Thompson. 1979. pap. 5.95 o.p. (ISBN 0-88879-014-7). Berkshire Traveller.

Country Bed & Breakfast Places in Canada. rev ed. John Thompson. 1981. pap. 7.95 (ISBN 0-88879-045-7). Berkshire Traveller.

Country Blacksmithing. Charles McRaven. LC 80-7876. (Illus.). 208p. 1981. 14.95 (ISBN 0-06-014870-5, HarpT). Har-Row.

Country Blacksmithing. Charles McRaven. LC 80-7876. (Illus.). 208p. 1981. pap. 9.95 (ISBN 0-06-090870-X, CN870, CN). Har-Row.

Country Blues. Samuel B. Charters. LC 75-14122. (Roots of Jazz Ser.). (Illus.). 288p. 1975. lib. bdg. 22.50 (ISBN 0-306-70678-4); pap. 4.95 (ISBN 0-306-80014-4). Da Capo.

Country Book of the Year. Dennis L. Furnell. LC 79-56061. (Illus.). 192p. 1980. 22.50 (ISBN 0-7153-7878-3). David & Charles.

Country By-Ways. Sarah O. Jewett. 249p. 1980. Repr. of 1881 ed. lib. bdg. 20.00 (ISBN 0-89987-428-2). Darby Bks.

Country Camera, Eighteen Forty-Four to Nineteen Fourteen: Rural Life As Depicted in Photographs from the Early Days of Photography to the Outbreak of the First World War. Gordon Winter. LC 76-148407. (Illus.). 1971. Repr. of 1966 ed. 15.00 (ISBN 0-8103-3399-6). Gale.

Country Cat. Najaka. 111p. Date not set. 2.95 (ISBN 0-07-045859-6). McGraw.

Country Changes. Lee Rudolph. LC 78-60470. 72p. 1978. pap. 4.95 (ISBN 0-914086-23-5). Alicejamesbooks.

Country Chronicle. Gladys Taber. LC 73-19684. (Illus.). 1974. 6.95 o.s.i. (ISBN 0-397-01023-0). Lippincott.

Country Clocks & Their London Origins. Brian Loomes. LC 75-26361. (Illus.). 208p. 1976. 19.95 (ISBN 0-7153-7079-0). David & Charles.

Country Club People. Margaret C. Banning. 1976. lib. bdg. 14.85x (ISBN 0-89968-006-2). Lightyear.

Country, Colonial Themes. Jule Wilkinson. 1969. pap. 10.95 (ISBN 0-8436-0515-4). CBI Pub.

Country Comforts. Christian Bruyere & Robert Inwood. (Illus.). 224p. 1979. pap. 7.95 (ISBN 0-8069-8270-5). Sterling.

Country Cooking & Other Stories. Harry Mathews. (Burning Deck Fiction Ser.). (Illus.). 90p. 1980. 12.50 (ISBN 0-930900-81-2); pap. 3.50 (ISBN 0-930900-82-0). Burning Deck.

Country Cousin. Betty Cavanna. (gr. 7 up). 8.75 (ISBN 0-688-21189-5). Morrow.

Country Crafts. Peggy Mitchell. Ed. by P. Pringle. LC 70-468023. (Pegasus Bks.: No. 19). (Illus.). 1968. 10.50x (ISBN 0-234-77157-7). Intl Pubns Serv.

Country Crafts Today. John Manners. LC 74-4355. (Illus.). 208p. 1974. 26.00 (ISBN 0-8103-2013-4). Gale.

Country Cup: Old & New Recipes for Drinks of All Kinds Made from Wild Plants & Herbs. Wilma Paterson. (Illus.). 88p. (Orig.). 1981. 11.95 (ISBN 0-7207-1234-3). Merrimack Bk Serv.

Country Dance. Margiad Evans. 1980. 11.50 (ISBN 0-7145-3593-1); pap. 4.95 (ISBN 0-7145-3728-4). Riverrun NY.

Country Diary of an Edwardian Lady. Edith Holden. LC 77-71359. (Illus.). 1977. 16.95 (ISBN 0-03-021026-7). HR&W.

Country Dogs & City Cousins(the Care & Loving of All Puppies) Marion Damroth. LC 80-81371. (Illus.). 125p. Date not set. price not set (ISBN 0-937118-01-X). Home Frosted.

Country Editor. Henry B. Hough. 1980. pap. 3.95 (ISBN 0-85699-091-4). Devin.

Country Experts in the Federal Government. 1981. pap. 15.00 (ISBN 0-686-26069-4). Wash Res.

Country Gentleman in Politics: The Political Diaries of Sir Robert Sanders, First Lord of Bayford 1910-1935. Ed. by John Ramsen. 280p. 1980. text ed. 62.50x (ISBN 0-391-01778-0). Humanities.

Country Girl. Darrell Husted. 1978. pap. 1.75 o.p. (ISBN 0-445-04186-2). Popular Lib.

Country Herbal. Lesley Gordon. (Illus.). 208p. 1980. 19.95 (ISBN 0-8317-4446-4). Mayflower Bks.

Country Host Cookbook. Rona Deme. (Illus.). 288p. 1980. pap. 8.95 (ISBN 0-8256-3172-6, Quick Fox). Music Sales.

Country House Cookery from the West. Elizabeth Lothian. LC 77-85035. (Illus.). 1978. 11.95 (ISBN 0-7153-7476-1). David & Charles.

Country House in English Renaissance Poetry. William A. McClung. 1977. 17.50x (ISBN 0-520-03137-7). U of Cal Pr.

Country Houses. Ed. by Franco Magnani. (Illus.). 1981. 22.50 (ISBN 0-8230-7132-4). Watson-Guptill.

Country Housewife & Lady's Director. Richard Bradley. 500p. 1980. Repr. of 1736 ed. 37.50x (ISBN 0-907325-01-7, Pub. by Prospect England). U Pr of Va.

Country Inn Cookbook. rev. ed. Ed. by Berkshire Traveller. LC 75-2520. (Illus.). 1975. pap. 3.95 (ISBN 0-912944-18-8). Berkshire Traveller.

Country Inns & Back Roads, North America. 16th ed. Norman T. Simpson. (Illus.). 450p. (Orig.). 1981. pap. 8.95 (ISBN 0-912944-65-X). Berkshire Traveller.

Country Inns of the Great Lakes: A Guide to Inns, Lodges, & Historic Hostelries of the Upper Midwest. Robert Morris. 180p. (Orig.). 1981. pap. 4.95 (ISBN 0-89286-165-7). One Hund One Prods.

Country Kitchen Cookbook. Wes Bauman. 8.95 (ISBN 0-8423-0448-7). Tyndale.

Country Kitchen Cookbook: Eighteen Ninety-Four to Nineteen Seventy-Nine. Farmer Magazine. (Illus.). 1979. pap. 5.95 (ISBN 0-8015-1786-9, Hawthorn). Dutton.

Country Lawyer. Bellamy Partridge. (Illus.). 330p. 1979. pap. 6.95 (ISBN 0-89062-070-9, Pub. by Hughes Press). Pub Ctr Cult Res.

Country Life. Peter Quince. (Illus.). 1975. 10.95 o.p. (ISBN 0-04-630007-4). Allen Unwin.

Country Life Collector's Pocket Book. G. Bernard Hughes. 1976. 16.95 (ISBN 0-600-43055-3). Transatlantic.

Country Life Movement in America. William L. Bowers. LC 74-80587. 1974. 13.00 (ISBN 0-8046-9074-X, Natl U). Kennikat.

Country Living by Sea & Estuary. Suzanne Beedell. LC 79-91479. (Illus.). 1980. 22.50 (ISBN 0-7153-7796-5). David & Charles.

Country Lover's Guide to Wildlife. Kenneth A. Chambers. (Illus.). 1980. pap. 8.95 (ISBN 0-452-25239-3, Plume). NAL.

Country Music. Thomas A. Hill. (First Bks.). (Illus.). (gr. 4-6). 1978. PLB 6.45 (ISBN 0-531-01405-3). Watts.

Country Music. C. W. Smith. 304p. 1976. pap. 1.95 o.p. (ISBN 0-345-25068-0). Ballantine.

Country Music: The Poetry. Carol Offen. (Orig.). 1977. pap. 1.50 o.p. (ISBN 0-345-25606-9). Ballantine.

Country of Resemblances. Beth Bentley. LC 75-14549. 78p. 1976. 8.95 (ISBN 0-8214-0196-3); pap. 5.95 (ISBN 0-8214-0210-2). Ohio U Pr.

Country of the Pointed Firs. Sarah O. Jewett. (Keith Jennison Large Type Bks). (gr. 7 up). PLB 7.95 o.p. (ISBN 0-531-00177-6). Watts.

Country of Turkomans, an Anthology of Exploration. Royal Geographical Society. 1977. text ed. 32.50x (ISBN 0-905820-01-0). Humanities.

Country Operas, One: Romantic Intrigue & Deception with Southwark Fair, the Village Opera, the Chamber Maid, the Gentleman Gardiner, the Country Coquet, an Opera Called Westmeon Village. Ed. by Walter H. Rubsamen. (Ballad Opera Ser.). 1974. lib. bdg. 50.00 (ISBN 0-8240-0914-2). Garland Pub.

Country Operas, Three: Sentimental & Moral Comedies with Sylvia, the Jovial Crew, Lucinda, the Reapers. Ed. by Walter H. Rubsamen. (Ballad Opera Ser.). 1974. lib. bdg. 50.00 (ISBN 0-8240-0916-9). Garland Pub.

Country Operas, Two: Farcial Humor & Stratagem Wth Country Wedding, the Wedding (Hawker), Flora, a Sequel to Flora, the Livery Rake, the Whim, the Deceit, the Country-Wedding. Ed. by Walter H. Rubsamen. (Ballad Opera Ser.). 1974. lib. bdg. 50.00 (ISBN 0-8240-0915-0). Garland Pub.

Country Pie. Frank Asch. LC 78-14837. (Illus.). (gr. 1-3). 1979. 7.50 (ISBN 0-688-80188-9); PLB 7.20 (ISBN 0-688-84188-0). Greenwillow.

Country Railway. David Thomas. LC 76-20128. 1976. 14.95 (ISBN 0-7153-7285-8). David & Charles.

Country Rock Guitar. Green Note Music Publications Staff. Ed. by Straw Dog. (Contemporary Guitar Styles Ser.). (Illus.). 1978. pap. 8.95 (ISBN 0-912910-07-0). Green Note Music.

Country Rock Guitar, Vol. 2. Green Note Music Publications Staff. (Guitar Transcription Ser.). 1980. pap. 7.25 (ISBN 0-912910-10-0). Green Note Music.

Country Rose. Diana Lyndon. (Orig.). 1981. pap. 1.75 (ISBN 0-671-83448-7). PB.

Country Squire. Elizabeth Mansfield. 1980. pap. write for info. o.p. (ISBN 0-425-04677-X). Berkley Pub.

Country Squire in the White House. John Thomas Flynn. LC 77-167846. (FDR & the Era of the New Deal Ser.). 122p. 1972. Repr. of 1940 ed. lib. bdg. 17.50 (ISBN 0-306-70324-6). Da Capo.

Country Waif (Francois le Champi) George Sand. Tr. by Eirene Collis from Fr. LC 76-14125. 1977. 10.95x (ISBN 0-8032-0888-X); pap. 2.95 (ISBN 0-8032-5850-X, BB 627, Bison). U of Nebr Pr.

Country Wife. William Wycherley. Ed. by Thomas H. Fujimura. LC 65-10542. (Regents Restoration Drama Ser). 1965. 9.50x (ISBN 0-8032-0371-3); pap. 2.45x (ISBN 0-8032-5371-0, BB 250, Bison). U of Nebr Pr.

Country Woman's Scrapbook. Louisa V. Kyle. Ed. by Joseph Dunn. LC 80-84557. (Illus.). 120p. 1980. 10.95 (ISBN 0-938694-02-2). JCP Corp VA.

Country Women: A Handbook for the New Farmer. Jeanne Tetrault & Sherry Thomas. LC 75-32296. 8.95 (ISBN 0-385-03062-2, Anchor Pr). Doubleday.

Countryman Book of Village Trades & Crafts. Ed. by Elizabeth Seager. LC 77-91719. (Countryman Bks). (Illus.). 1978. 16.95 (ISBN 0-7153-7493-1). David & Charles.

Countryman's Britain. Ed. by Crispin Gill. LC 76-20122. (Countryman Books). 1976. 17.95 (ISBN 0-7153-7284-X). David & Charles.

Countryman's Britain in Pictures. Crispin Gill. (Countryman Books). 1977. 11.95 (ISBN 0-7153-7450-8). David & Charles.

Countryman's Flowers. Hal Borland. LC 80-2698. (Illus.). 208p. 1981. 22.50 (ISBN 0-394-51893-4). Knopf.

Countryside. J. C. Gagg. 7.50x (ISBN 0-392-07745-0, SpS). Soccer.

Countryside. Denys J. Watkins-Pitchford. LC 66-97721. (Pegasus Books: No. 1). (Illus.). 1964. 7.50x (ISBN 0-234-77773-7). Intl Pubns Serv.

Countryside: Planning & Change. Mark Blacksell & Andrew Gilg. (Resource Management Ser.: No. 2). (Illus.). 288p. (Orig.). 1981. text ed. 35.00x (ISBN 0-04-711008-2, 2599); pap. text ed. 17.50x (ISBN 0-04-711009-0, 2560). Allen Unwin.

Countryside Planning: The First Three Decades 1945-76. Andrew W. Gilg. LC 77-85036. (Illus.). 1978. 30.00 (ISBN 0-7153-7499-0). David & Charles.

Count's Number Parade. Norman Stiles. (Illus.). 24p. (ps-4). 1977. PLB 5.38 (ISBN 0-307-68876-3, Golden Pr). Western Pub.

Count's Poem. Ray Sipherd. (Illus.). (gr. k-1). 1978. PLB 4.77 (ISBN 0-307-68653-1, Whitman). Western Pub.

County & Court: Government & Politics in Norfolk 1558-1603. A. Hassell Smith. 392p. 1974. 48.00x (ISBN 0-19-822407-9). Oxford U Pr.

County Community in Peace & War: Sussex 1600-1660. Anthony Fletcher. (Illus.). 470p. 1976. text ed. 36.00x (ISBN 0-582-50024-9). Longman.

County Courts in Antebellum Kentucky. Robert M. Ireland. LC 71-160045. 208p. 1972. 12.00x (ISBN 0-8131-1257-5). U Pr of Ky.

County Durham: A Shell Guide. Henry Thorold. (Illus.). 192p. 1981. 14.95 (ISBN 0-571-11640-X, Pub. by Faber & Faber). Merrimack Bk Serv.

County Energy Plan Guidebook. 2nd ed. Alan Okagaki & Jim Benson. (Illus.). 200p. (Orig.). 1979. pap. text ed. 10.00x (ISBN 0-937786-01-2). Inst Ecologica.

County Funding of the Arts in New York State. Charles F. Chauncey. 24p. 1975. pap. 2.00x (ISBN 0-89062-033-4, Pub. by NYSCA). Pub Ctr Cult Res.

County Governing Bodies in New Jersey: Reorganization & Reform on Boards of Chosen Freeholders, 1798-1974. Harris I. Effross. 1976. 25.00x (ISBN 0-8135-0765-0). Rutgers U Pr.

County Government in England & Wales. Jeffrey Stanyer. (Library of Political Science). (Orig.). 1967. text ed. 6.00x (ISBN 0-7100-5116-6); pap. text ed. 2.75x (ISBN 0-391-01969-4). Humanities.

Coup De Grace. Marguerite Yourcenar. Tr. by Grace Frick from Fr. 151p. 1957. 15.00 (ISBN 0-374-13052-3). FS&G.

Coup De Grace. Marguerite Yourcenar. Tr. by Grace Frick from Fr. 1981. pap. 5.95 (ISBN 0-374-51631-6). FS&G.

Couple Communication I: Talking Together. Sherod Miller et al. (Couple Communication Ser.), 1979. pap. 8.95 (ISBN 0-917340-09-4). Interpersonal Comm.

Couple of Cooks. Patsy Swendson & Ole Swendson. (Illus.). 1980. 5.95. Corona Pub.

Couple Therapy. Frank Bockus. LC 80-66923. 300p. 1980. 27.50 (ISBN 0-87668-412-6). Aronson.

Couples in Conflict. Ed. by Alan S. Gurman & David G. Rice. LC 74-6951. 372p. 1975. 30.00x (ISBN 0-87668-150-X). Aronson.

Couples in the Bible. Daniel R. Seagren. (Contemporary Discussion Ser). 1972. pap. 2.50 (ISBN 0-8010-7971-3). Baker Bk.

Couple's Journey. Susan Campbell. LC 79-23836. 1980. pap. 5.95 (ISBN 0-915166-45-3). Impact Pubs Cal.

Couples: The Art of Staying Together. rev. ed. Anita Taylor & Robert Taylor. 1980. 4.95 (ISBN 0-87491-403-5). Acropolis.

Couples Therapy: A Nontraditional Approach. B. Wile. 240p. 1981. 22.50 (ISBN 0-471-07811-5, Pub. by Wiley Interscience). Wiley.

Coupling of External Electromagnetic Fields to Transmission Lines. Albert A. Smith, Jr. LC 76-49504. 1977. 22.50 (ISBN 0-471-01995-X, Pub. by Wiley-Interscience). Wiley.

Coupling to Shielded Cables. Edward F. Vance. LC 78-16186. 1978. 22.00 (ISBN 0-471-04107-6, Pub. by Wiley-Interscience). Wiley.

Couplings: A Book of Stories. Richard Hall. LC 80-26609. 160p. 1981. 12.00 (ISBN 0-912516-57-7); pap. 4.95 (ISBN 0-912516-58-5). Grey Fox.

Coupon Interest Calendar - 360-Day Basis No. 360. Financial Publishing Co. 20.00 (ISBN 0-685-02539-X). Finan Pub.

Coupon Interest Calendar - 365-Day Basis No. 365. Financial Publishing Co. 25.00 (ISBN 0-685-02538-1). Finan Pub.

Coupon Savers Cookbook. Beryl M. Marton. 224p. 1980. pap. 5.95 (ISBN 0-517-54203-X). Crown.

Coups & Earthquakes: Reporting the World to America. Mort Rosenblum. LC 79-1680. 240p. 1981. pap. 4.95 (ISBN 0-06-090856-4, CN 856, CN). Har-Row.

Courage. Jane B. Moncure. LC 80-14201. (What Does the Bible Say? Ser.). (Illus.). 32p. (ps-2). 1980. PLB 4.95 (ISBN 0-89565-168-8, 4930). Standard Pub.

Courage. rev. ed. Jane B. Moncure. LC 80-39515. (What Is It? Ser.). (Illus.). 32p. (gr. k-3). 1981. PLB 5.50 (ISBN 0-89565-202-1). Childs World.

Courage & Submission. 2nd ed. Stanley Collins. LC 74-32323. 1977. pap. 2.25 (ISBN 0-8307-0459-0, S292-1-22). Regal.

Courage in Darkness. Sarah Shears. 1974. 8.95 (ISBN 0-236-31066-6, Pub. by Paul Elek). Merrimack Bk Serv.

Courage to Believe. Craig Morton & Bob Burger. 1981. 9.95 (ISBN 0-13-184416-4). P-H.

Courage to Pray. Karl Rahner & Johann B. Metz. 112p. (Orig.). 1980. pap. 3.95 (ISBN 0-8245-2024-6). Crossroad NY.

Courageous Deaf Adults. Darlene Toole. 96p. 1980. 4.95 (ISBN 0-86575-132-3). Dormac.

Courageous Turk. Thomas Goffe. Ed. by Susan G. O'Malley & Stephen Orgel. LC 78-66772. (Renaissance Drama Ser.). 1979. lib. bdg. 33.00 (ISBN 0-8240-9737-8). Garland Pub.

Courante of Newes from the East India. LC 74-28848. (English Experience Ser.: No. 729). 1975. Repr. of 1662 ed. 3.50 (ISBN 90-221-0729-9). Walter J Johnson.

Courbet. Anthea Callen. (Oresko-Jupiter Art Bks). (Illus.). 96p. 1981. 17.95 (ISBN 0-933516-84-3, Pub. by Oresko-Jupiter England). Hippocrene Bks.

Courier's Fist. Harvey A. Eysman. LC 80-27338. 256p. 1981. 10.95 (ISBN 0-8253-0034-7). Beaufort Bks NY.

Cours De Langue et De Civilization Francaises, 4 Vols. Gaston Mauger. (Fr). Vol. 1. 7.00 (ISBN 0-685-20231-3); Vol. 2. 7.00 (ISBN 0-685-20232-1); Vol. 3. 7.50 (ISBN 0-685-20233-X); Vol. 4. 9.90 (ISBN 0-685-20234-8). Schoenhof.

Cours superieur de francais. Eli Blume. (Orig.). (gr. 11-12). 1970. pap. text ed. 5.75 (ISBN 0-87720-460-8); wkbk. 6.75 (ISBN 0-87720-462-4). AMSCO Sch.

Course Design: A Guide to Curriculum Development for Teachers. George J. Posner & Alan N. Rudnitsky. LC 77-17712. 1978. pap. text ed. 9.95x (ISBN 0-582-28038-9). Longman.

Course Guide for High School Theatre. 1975. 7.50, ATA members 6.00 (ISBN 0-686-05076-2). Am Theatre Assoc.

Course in APL with Applications. 2nd ed. Louis D. Grey. LC 76-5079. 300p. 1976. pap. text ed. 13.95 (ISBN 0-201-02563-9). A-W.

Course in Basic Scientific English. J. R. Ewer & G. Latorre. 1975. pap. text ed. 5.25x (ISBN 0-582-52009-6); teacher's bk. 2.75x (ISBN 0-582-52059-2). Longman.

Course in Biology. 3rd ed. Jeffrey J. Baker & Garland E. Allen. LC 78-67451. (Life Sciences Ser.). 1979. text ed. 18.95 (ISBN 0-201-00308-2). A-W.

Course in Colloquial Arabic. Leslie McLoughlin. 1974. 11.00 (ISBN 0-685-72032-2); with two cassettes 40.00 (ISBN 0-685-72033-0). Intl Bk Ctr.

Course in Computational Probability & Statistics. W. Freiberger & U. Grenander. LC 76-176272. (Applied Mathematical Sciences: Vol. 6). 168p. 1971. pap. 14.50 (ISBN 0-387-90029-2). Springer-Verlag.

Course in Diagnostics for Fusion Experiments: Proceedings, Varenna, Italy, 1978. Commission of the European Communities. Ed. by E. Sindoni & C. Wharton. (Commission of the European Communities, EUR, 6123). (Illus.). 1979. pap. 110.00 (ISBN 0-08-023429-1). Pergamon.

Course in General Linguistics. Ferdinand De Saussure. Tr. by Wade Baskin. 1966. pap. 4.95 (ISBN 0-07-016524-6, SP). McGraw.

Course in Intensive Therapy Nursing. Jack Tinker & Susan W. Porter. 294p. 1980. 30.00x (ISBN 0-7131-4347-9, Pub. by Arnold Pubs England). State Mutual Bk.

Course in Levantine Arabic. rev. ed. Ed. by Ernest McCarus et al. Hamdi Qafisheh & Raji Rammuny. (Orig.). 1978. pap. text ed. 6.00x (ISBN 0-916798-07-0, Pub. by U Mich Dept Near East Stud). Eisenbrauns.

Course in Modern Algebra. Peter Hilton & Yel-Chiang Wu. LC 73-18043. (Pure & Applied Mathematics Ser). 272p. 1974. 29.95 (ISBN 0-471-39967-1, Pub. by Wiley-Interscience). Wiley.

Course in Ordinary & Partial Differential Equations. Zalman Rubinstein. 1969. text ed. 22.95 (ISBN 0-12-601550-3). Acad Pr.

Course in Probability Theory. 2nd ed. Kai L. Chung. (Probability & Mathematical Statistics: A Series of Monographs & Textbooks). 1974. 23.95 (ISBN 0-12-174650-X). Acad Pr.

Course in Programming in FORTRAN IV. V. J. Calderbank. 88p. 1969. pap. text ed. 6.95x o.p. (ISBN 0-412-20640-4, Pub. by Chapman & Hall). Methuen Inc.

Course in Spoken Arabic. Shafi Shaikh. 136p. (Orig.). 1978. pap. text ed. 3.95x (ISBN 0-19-561067-9). Oxford U Pr.

Course in Standard Coral 66. J. D. Halliwell & T. A. Edwards. LC 77-367227. (Illus.). 1977. text ed. 12.50x (ISBN 0-85012-187-6). Intl Pubns Serv.

Course in the Openings, Vol. 1. Y. Estrin & V. Panov. (Pergamon Chess Series). 1980. 20.00 (ISBN 0-08-023103-9); pap. 12.95 (ISBN 0-08-023102-0). Pergamon.

Course in the Theoretical Statistics. N. A. Rahman. 1968. 14.25 o.s.i. (ISBN 0-02-850780-0). Hafner.

Course Making in Industrial Education. 3rd ed. John F. Friese & Williams. 1966. 11.96 (ISBN 0-87002-251-2). Bennett IL.

Course of Alcoholism: Four Years After Treatment. J. Michael Polich & David J. Armor. Ed. by Harriet B. Braiker. (Personality Processes Ser.). 312p. 1981. 25.00 (ISBN 0-471-08632-7, Pub. by Wiley-Interscience). Wiley.

Course of American Democratic Thought. 2nd ed. Ralph H. Gabriel. (gr. 10-12). 1956. text ed. 18.95 (ISBN 0-8260-3275-3). Wiley.

Course of Europe Since Waterloo, 2 vols. Hall & Davis. Ed. by Kurt R. Schmeller. Incl. Vol. 1. From Vienna to Sarajevo (ISBN 0-89197-203-X); Vol. 2. Twentieth Century (ISBN 0-8290-0379-7). LC 68-15856. (Illus.). 1980. pap. text ed. 14.50x ea. Irvington.

Course of Mathematics for Engineers & Scientists. B. Chirgwin & C. A. Plumpton. Vol. 1 2nd Ed. 1970. text ed. 34.00 (ISBN 0-08-006388-8); pap. text ed. 14.25 (ISBN 0-08-021678-1); Vol. 2. 2nd Ed. 1972. text ed. 16.50 (ISBN 0-08-015970-2); Vol. 3, 1st Ed. 1963. text ed. 34.00 (ISBN 0-08-009376-0); Vol. 3, 1978. pap. text ed. 14.00 (ISBN 0-08-023042-3); Vol. 4. 1st Ed. 1964. text ed. 12.00 (ISBN 0-08-009377-9); Vol. 4, 2nd Ed. pap. text ed. 11.25 (ISBN 0-08-021634-X); Vol. 5. 1st Ed. 1964. text ed. 9.00 (ISBN 0-08-009378-7); Vol. 6, 1st Ed. 1966. text ed. 18.00 (ISBN 0-08-009379-5). Pergamon.

Course of Mexican History. Michael C. Meyer & William L. Sherman. (Illus.). 1979. 29.95 (ISBN 0-19-502413-3); pap. text ed. 12.95x (ISBN 0-19-502414-1). Oxford U Pr.

Course of Modern Analysis. 4th ed. Edmund T. Whittaker & George N. Watson. 1927. 74.50 (ISBN 0-521-06794-4); pap. text ed. 19.95x (ISBN 0-521-09189-6). Cambridge U Pr.

Course on Group Theory. John S. Rose. LC 76-22984. (Illus.). 1978. 57.50 (ISBN 0-521-21409-2); pap. 18.50x (ISBN 0-521-29142-9). Cambridge U Pr.

Course on Plasma Diagnostics & Data Acquisition Systems. new ed. Ed. by H. Eubank & E. Sindoni. (Commission of the European Communities). (Illus.). 1979. pap. text ed. 65.00 o.p. (ISBN 0-08-024462-9). Pergamon.

Course on Programming in Fortran Four. V. J. Calderbank. 88p. 1969. pap. 8.95 o.p. (ISBN 0-470-12956-5). Halsted Pr.

Course on Reaction Mechanistics in Organic Chemistry. R. N. Usgaonkar. 320p. 1981. text ed. 18.95x (ISBN 0-7069-1236-5, Pub. by Vikas India). Advent Bk.

Course on Theoretical Physics: Statistical Physics, Vol. 5, Pt. 1. new ed. L. D. Landau & E. M. Lifshitz. (Illus.). 1980. text ed. 69.00 (ISBN 0-08-023039-3); pap. text ed. 22.00 (ISBN 0-08-023038-5). Pergamon.

Course Zero-Nine-Five to Eternity: The Saga of Destroyer Squadron Eleven. Elwyn E. Overshiner. LC 80-82005. (Illus.). 224p. (Orig.). 1981. pap. 4.95 (ISBN 0-937480-00-2). Overshiner.

Coursebook for Economics: Private & Public Choice. 2nd ed. James D. Gwartney et al. 1980. 7.95 (ISBN 0-12-311054-8). Acad Pr.

Courses, Components, & Exercises in Technical Communication. Ed. by Dwight W. Stevenson et al. 1981. pap. price not set (ISBN 0-8141-0877-6). NCTE.

Courses for Horses. new ed. C. Coldrey. 1978. 20.10 (ISBN 0-85131-305-1, Dist. by Sporting Book Center). J A Allen.

Court & City Vagaries, or Intrigues, of Both Sexes. Bd. with Tell-Tale or the Invisible Witness; Entertainments of Gallantry or Remedies of Love. LC 70-170525. (Foundations of the Novel Ser.: Vol. 18). lib. bdg. 50.00 (ISBN 0-8240-0530-9). Garland Pub.

Court Awarded Fees in "Public Interest" Litigation. (Litigation & Administrative Practice Course Handbook Series 1978-79: Vols. 123 & 124). 1978. pap. 20.00 o.p. (ISBN 0-685-90303-6, H6-3871). PLI.

Court, Church & Castle. Margaret W. Labarge. (Illus.). 112p. 1972. pap. 2.95 (ISBN 0-88884-431-X, 56310-3, Pub. by Natl Mus Canada). U of Chicago Pr.

Court Intrigue & Scandal, One: With Calista, Vanelia, the Humours of the Court, the Intriguing Courtiers. Ed. by Walter H. Rubsamen. (Ballad Opera Ser.). 1974. lib. bdg. 50.00 (ISBN 0-8240-0917-7). Garland Pub.

Court Intrigue & Scandal, Two: With the Fox Uncased, the Court Legacy, the Court Medley, the Fortunate Prince, the Wedding. Ed. by Walter A. Rubsamen. (Ballad Opera Ser.). 1974. lib. bdg. 50.00 (ISBN 0-8240-0918-5). Garland Pub.

Court Life Below Stairs: or London Under the Last Georges. J. Fitzgerald Molloy. 427p. 1980. Repr. of 1897 ed. lib. bdg. 50.00 (ISBN 0-89984-337-9). Century Bookbindery.

Court-Martial of George Armstrong Custer. Douglas C. Jones. 1977. pap. 2.25 o.s.i. (ISBN 0-446-82333-3). Warner Bks.

Court of Atalantis: A Four Years History of That Famous Island. LC 76-170532. (Foundations of the Novel Ser.: Vol. 21). lib. bdg. 50.00 (ISBN 0-8240-0533-3). Garland Pub.

Court of Elizabeth the First. Rachel A. Percival. (Illus.). 110p. 1976. 13.75x (ISBN 0-8476-6238-1). Rowman.

Court of Kings Bench Fourteen Fifty to Fifteen Fifty: A Study in Self-Help. Marjorie Blatcher. (University of London Legal Ser.: No. 12). 1978. text ed. 36.50x (ISBN 0-485-13412-8, Athlone Pr). Humanities.

Court of Orphans. Charles Carlton. 1974. text ed. 10.50x (ISBN 0-7185-1125-5, Leicester). Humanities.

Court of the Connectable: A Study of a French Administrative Tribunal During the Reign of Henry Iv. John H. Mitchell. 1947. 34.50x (ISBN 0-686-51365-7). Elliots Bks.

Court of the Palms: A Functional Interpretation of the Mari Palace. Yasin M. Al-Khalesi. Ed. by G. Buccellati. LC 77-94987. (Bibliotheca Mesopotamica Ser.: Vol. 8). (Illus.). 85p. 1978. 18.00 (ISBN 0-89003-029-4); pap. 14.50 (ISBN 0-89003-030-8). Undena Pubns.

Court of the Stone Children. Eleanor Cameron. 208p. (gr. 5 up). 1973. PLB 9.95 (ISBN 0-525-28350-1). Dutton.

Court of Virtue. Russell A. Fraser. 1961. 27.50 (ISBN 0-8135-0388-4). Rutgers U Pr.

Court on Court: A Life in Tennis. Margaret Court & McGann. LC 75-17650. (Illus.). 256p. 1975. 8.95 (ISBN 0-396-07210-0). Dodd.

Court Reform. Steven W. Hays. LC 77-10348. (Illus.). 1978. 16.95 (ISBN 0-669-01841-4). Lexington Bks.

Court Secret: A Melancholy Truth, 1741. George Lyttleton. Ed. by Michael F. Shugrue. Bd. with New Journey to the World in the Moon, 1741; Court Intrigue; or, the Statesman Detected, 1741. (Flowering of the Novel, 1740-1775 Ser: Vol. 5). 1974. lib. bdg. 50.00 (ISBN 0-8240-1104-X). Garland Pub.

Court Years: Nineteen Thirty-Nine to Nineteen Seventy-Five. William O. Douglas. (Illus.). 434p. 16.95 (ISBN 0-394-49240-4). Random.

Courtaulds: An Economic & Social History, 2 Vols. D. C. Coleman. 1969. Set. 45.00x o.p. (ISBN 0-19-920016-5). Oxford U Pr.

Courtaulds: An Economic & Social History Vol. III: Crisis & Change 1940-65. D. C. Coleman. (Illus.). 352p. 1980. 44.00x (ISBN 0-19-920111-0). Oxford U Pr.

Courtesan of Lucknow. Mirza Ruswa. Tr. by Khushwant Singh & M. A. Husaini 240p. 1970. pap. 4.00 (ISBN 0-88253-076-3). Ind-US Inc.

Courtesan: The Part She Has Played in Classical & Modern Literature & in Life. C. Hayward. Ed. by Charles Winick. LC 78-60872. (Prostitution Ser.: Vol. 7). (Illus.). 492p. 1979. lib. bdg. 40.00 (ISBN 0-8240-9721-1). Garland Pub.

Courthouse. Paul Hoffman. 1979. 12.50 (ISBN 0-8015-1790-7, Hawthorn). Dutton.

Courtier & Commoner in Ancient China: Selections from the History of Former Han by Pan Ku. Tr. by Burton Watson. LC 73-18003. 272p. 1974. 17.50x (ISBN 0-231-03765-1); pap. 6.50x (ISBN 0-231-08354-8). Columbia U Pr.

Courtier to the Crowd. Ray E. Hiebert. (Illus.). 1966. 8.95 o.p. (ISBN 0-8138-0355-1). Iowa St U Pr.

Courtis-Watters Illustrated Golden Dictionary for Young Readers. rev. ed. Stuart A. Courtis & Garnette Watters. (Illus.). 672p. (gr. 2-4). 1972. 6.95 (ISBN 0-307-15544-7, Golden Pr); PLB 13.77 (ISBN 0-307-66544-5). Western Pub.

Courtly Maker: An Essay on the Poetry of Wyatt & His Contemporaries. Raymond Southall. 1964. 16.50x o.p. (ISBN 0-631-08350-2, Pub. by Basil Blackwell). Biblio Dist.

Courtroom Testimony: A Policeman's Guide. Kevin Tierney. LC 75-98530. (Funk & W Bk.). 1970. 7.95 o.s.i. (ISBN 0-308-40087-9, TYC-T). T Y Crowell.

Courts: A Comparative & Political Analysis. Martin Shapiro. LC 80-18263. 1981. lib. bdg. 20.00x (ISBN 0-226-75042-6). U of Chicago Pr.

Courts & Diversion: Policy & Operations Studies. Ed. by Patricia L. Brantingham & Thomas G. Blomberg. (Sage Research Progress Ser. in Criminology: Vol. 14). (Illus.). 1979. 12.95x (ISBN 0-8039-1321-4); pap. 6.50x (ISBN 0-8039-1322-2). Sage.

Courts & Law in Early New York: Selected Essays. Ed. by Leo Hershkowitz & Milton M. Klein. (National University Pubns., Multi-Disciplinary Series in the Law). 1978. 12.50 (ISBN 0-8046-9206-8). Kennikat.

Courts & Social Policy. Donald L. Horowitz. LC 76-48944. 1977. 14.95 (ISBN 0-8157-3734-3); pap. 5.95 (ISBN 0-8157-3733-5). Brookings.

Courts & Trials: A Multidisciplinary Approach. Ed. by M. L. Friedland. LC 75-5672. 1975. pap. 4.95 (ISBN 0-8020-6273-3). U of Toronto Pr.

Courts & Tribunals: A Comparative Study. Attila Racz. Tr. by Miklos Zehery. 246p. 1980. 25.00x (ISBN 963-05-1799-X). Intl Pubns Serv.

Courts, Judges & Politics: An Introduction to the Judicial Process. 3rd ed. Ed. by Walter F. Murphy & Herman C. Pritchett. LC 78-24033. 1979. text ed. 17.95x (ISBN 0-394-32117-0). Random.

Courts, Judges & Politics: An Introduction to the Judicial Process. 2nd ed. Ed. by Walter F. Murphy & Herman C. Pritchett. 1974. 13.95 o.p. (ISBN 0-394-31809-9). Random.

Courts, Law & Judical Processes. Ed. by S. S. Ulmer. LC 80-1856. (Illus.). 1981. pap. text ed. 11.95 (ISBN 0-02-932970-1). Free Pr.

Courts of Appeals in the Federal Judicial System: A Study of the Second, Fifth, & District of Columbia. J. Woodford Howard, Jr. LC 80-7529. 408p. 1981. 32.50 (ISBN 0-691-07623-5); pap. 12.50 (ISBN 0-691-10100-0). Princeton U Pr.

Courts of Chaos. Roger Zelazny. 1979. pap. 1.75 (ISBN 0-380-47175-2, 47175). Avon.

Courts, the Constitution, & Capital Punishment. Hugo A. Bedau. LC 76-53666. 1977. 18.95 (ISBN 0-669-01290-4). Lexington Bks.

Courts, the Constitution & Parties. Andrew C. McLaughlin. LC 70-87405. (American Scene Ser.). 312p. 1972. Repr. of 1912 ed. lib. bdg. 32.50 (ISBN 0-306-71549-X). Da Capo.

Courtship of Birds. Hilda Simon. LC 77-3211. (Illus.). 1977. 12.95 (ISBN 0-396-07459-6). Dodd.

Cousin Beedie & Cousin Hot: My Life with the Carter Family of Plains, Georgia. Hugh Carter & F. Leighton. LC 78-4975. 1978. 12.50 o.p. (ISBN 0-13-185470-4). P-H.

Cousin Drewey & the Holy Twister. John L. Sinclair. LC 80-177530. 1980. 14.95 (ISBN 0-914366-18-1). Columbia Pub.

Cousin Kate. Georgette Heyer. 288p. 1978. pap. 2.25 (ISBN 0-449-23723-0, Crest). Fawcett.

Cousin Mercedes & the White Russian. A. G. Heinsohn, Jr. LC 74-18736. 1974. 4.00 (ISBN 0-88279-231-8). Western Islands.

Cousin Phillis & Other Tales. Elizabeth Gaskell. 1970. 5.00x o.p. (ISBN 0-460-00615-0, Evman). Dutton.

Cousinhood. C. Bermant. 1972. 10.95 o.s.i. (ISBN 0-02-510080-7). Macmillan.

Cousins Are Special. Susan Goldman. Ed. by Caroline Rubin. LC 75-11924. (Self-Starter Bks). (Illus.). (ps-2). 1978. 6.50g (ISBN 0-8075-1317-2). A Whitman.

Cousteau. (gr. 1). 1974. pap. text ed. 2.80 (ISBN 0-205-03874-3, 8038740); tchrs'. guide 12.00 (ISBN 0-205-03866-2, 803866X). Allyn.

Cousteau. (MacDonald Educational Ser.). (Illus., Arabic.). 3.50 (ISBN 0-686-53093-4). Intl Bk Ctr.

Cousteau Almanac of the Environment: An Inventory of Life on a Water Planet. Jacques-Yves Cousteau. 864p. 1981. 24.95 (ISBN 0-385-14875-5). Doubleday.

Cousteau Almanac of the Environment: An Inventory of Life on a Water Planet. Jacques-Yves Cousteau & Cousteau Society Staff. LC 79-7862. (Illus.). 864p. 1981. pap. 12.95 (ISBN 0-385-14876-3, Dolp). Doubleday.

Covenant. Larry Christenson. (Trinity Bible Ser.). 1973. pap. spiral wkbk. (ISBN 0-87123-551-X, 240551). Bethany Fell.

Covenant. James A. Michener. LC 80-5315. 1980. 35.00 (ISBN 0-394-50505-0); Limited Ed. 35.00 (ISBN 0-394-51400-9). Random.

Covenant Chain: Indian Ceremonial & Trade Silver. Jaye Frederickson & Sandra Gibb. (Illus.). 168p. 1980. 24.95 (ISBN 0-660-10347-8, 56313-8, Pub. by Natl Gallery Canada); pap. 19.95 (ISBN 0-660-10348-6, 56314-6). U of Chicago Pr.

Covent Garden. Harold Rosenthal. (Folio Miniature Ser.). 1979. 4.95 (ISBN 0-7181-1474-4, Pub. by Michael Joseph). Merrimack Bk Serv.

Coventry. Ed. by Reginald W. Ingram. (Records of Early English Drama Ser.). 700p. 1981. 47.50x (ISBN 0-8020-5542-7). U of Toronto Pr.

Cover Girls. Carole Conover. LC 78-15686. 1978. 10.95 o.p. (ISBN 0-13-188300-3). P-H.

Cover Girls. Maura Mara. (Illus.). 96p. (gr. 5 up). Date not set. PLB 9.55 (ISBN 0-688-51996-2); pap. 6.95 (ISBN 0-688-41996-8). Morrow. Postponed.

Cover to Cover. Michael Snow. LC 75-27116. 1975. 20.00x (ISBN 0-8147-7769-4); pap. 12.95x (ISBN 0-8147-7770-8). NYU Pr.

Cover-Up: Neckwear for the Laryngectomee & Other Neck Breathers. Dan H. Kelly & Peggy Welborn. LC 80-65470. (Illus.). 98p. 1980. pap. text ed. 14.95 (ISBN 0-933014-55-4). College-Hill.

Cover Up: What You Are Not Supposed to Know About Nuclear Power. Karl Grossman. 1980. 11.95 (ISBN 0-531-07405-6, Permanent Pr). Watts.

Coverage & Utilization of Care for Mental Conditions Under Health Insurance: Various Studies 1973-74. 80p. 1975. 5.00 (ISBN 0-685-77440-6). Am Psychiatric.

Covered Bridge House & Other Poems. Kaye Starbird. LC 79-11418. (Illus.). 64p. (gr. 3-7). 1979. 7.95 (ISBN 0-590-07544-6, Four Winds). Schol Bk Serv.

Covered Bridges Can Talk. Lewis A. Harlow. (Illus.). 1963. 4.95 o.p. (ISBN 0-87482-017-0). Wake-Brook.

Covered Bridges in Illinois, Iowa, & Wisconsin. rev. ed. Leslie C. Swanson. (Illus., Orig.). 1970. pap. 5.95 (ISBN 0-911466-14-2). Swanson.

Covered Bridges in Indiana. W. M. Weber. LC 77-84376. 14.95 o.p. (ISBN 0-87359-012-0). Northwood Inst.

Covered Bridges of the Northeast. Richard S. Allen. (Illus.). 128p. 1981. pap. 9.95 (ISBN 0-8289-0439-1). Greene.

Covering Islam: How the Media & the Experts Determine How We See the Rest of the World. Edward Said. 1981. 10.95 (ISBN 0-394-51319-3); pap. 3.95 (ISBN 0-394-74808-5). Pantheon.

Covering the Desegregation Story. Center for Equal Education. LC 76-45286. 1976. 3.00 (ISBN 0-912008-12-1). Integrated Ed Assoc.

Covering the Spread: How to Bet Pro Football. Gerry Strine & Neil Isaacs. 1978. 8.95 (ISBN 0-685-63568-6). Random.

Covert Conditioning. Ed. by Dennis Upper & Joseph R. Cautela. LC 79-61. (Pergamon General Psychology Ser.). (Illus.). 300p. 1980. 42.00 (ISBN 0-08-023347-3); pap. 12.95 (ISBN 0-08-023346-5). Pergamon.

Cove's End. Susan Hufford. 1977. pap. 1.50 o.p. (ISBN 0-445-04066-1). Popular Lib.

Cow Country. Edward E. Dale. (Western Frontier Library: Vol. 27). 258p. 1965. pap. 3.95 (ISBN 0-8061-1153-4). U of Okla Pr.

Cow Country. Will James. LC 27-22183. (Illus.). xii, 242p. 1973. pap. 4.25 (ISBN 0-8032-5774-0, BB 557, Bison). U of Nebr Pr.

Cow People. J. Frank Dobie. (Illus.). 317p. 1981. pap. 6.95 (ISBN 0-292-71060-7). U of Tex Pr.

Cow Went Over the Mountain. Jeanette Krinsley. (Illus.). (ps-2). 1963. PLB 5.00 (ISBN 0-307-60576-0, Golden Pr). Western Pub.

Cow Who Fell in the Canal. Phyllis Krasilovsky. (gr. k-3). 1950. pap. 1.49 (ISBN 0-385-08096-4, Zephyr). Doubleday.

Coward & the Hero of the Blue Dandenongs & Sonetone. Thomas O'Case. 4.50 o.p. (ISBN 0-685-58657-X). Vantage.

Coward's Almanac. Marvin Kitman. 128p. 1976. pap. 1.50 o.p. (ISBN 0-345-25051-6). Ballantine.

Cowboy. Aaron Fletcher. (Orig.). 1977. pap. 1.50 (ISBN 0-505-51152-5, BT51152). Tower Bks.

Cowboy. Don Hedgpeth. (Illus.). 1979. pap. 12.95 (ISBN 0-8032-6304-X, Buffalo Bill Hist. Ctr.). U of Nebr Pr.

Cowboy. Frank Roderus. LC 80-1866. (Double D Western Ser.). 192p. 1981. 9.95 (ISBN 0-385-17120-X). Doubleday.

Cowboy. Ross Santee. LC 77-7271. (Illus.). 1977. 11.95x (ISBN 0-8032-0931-2); pap. 3.50 (ISBN 0-8032-5867-4, BB 645, Bison). U of Nebr Pr.

Cowboy Artists of America: Fifteenth Annual Exhibition Catalog 1980. LC 73-162045. (Illus.). 72p. 1980. pap. 12.95 (ISBN 0-87358-272-1); ltd. ed. 150.00 (ISBN 0-87358-273-X). Northland.

Cowboy Artists of America, 1971: Sixth Annual Exhibition Catalog. LC 73-162045. (Illus.). 1971. pap. 4.95 o.p. (ISBN 0-87358-086-9). Northland.

Cowboy at Work. Fay E. Ward. Date not set. 14.95 (ISBN 0-8038-1204-3). Hastings.

Cowboy at Work: All About His Job & How He Does It. Fay E. Ward. (Illus.). 1976. Repr. 12.95 o.p. (ISBN 0-8038-1116-0). Hastings.

Cowboy Book. Mel Crawford. (Illus.). 24p. (gr. k-1). 1976. PLB 5.38 (ISBN 0-307-68981-6, Golden Pr). Western Pub.

Cowboy Catalog. Sandra Kaufmann. (Illus.). 192p. 1980. pap. 11.95 (ISBN 0-517-53950-0); pap. 10.95 (ISBN 0-517-54035-5). Potter.

Cowboy Cave. Jesse D. Jennings et al. (University of Utah Anthropological Papers: No. 104). (Illus.). 220p. (Orig.). 1981. pap. 20.00 (ISBN 0-87480-182-6). U of Utah Pr.

Cowboy Cookbook. Verne Carlson. LC 80-68342. (Illus.). 186p. 1981. 10.95 (ISBN 0-937844-00-4); pap. 6.95 (ISBN 0-937844-01-2). Caverne Pub.

Cowboy Culture. David Dary. LC 80-2699. (Illus.). 1981. 17.95 (ISBN 0-394-42605-3). Knopf.

Cowboy Fun. Frank Dean. LC 79-91384. (Illus.). 160p. 1980. 9.95 (ISBN 0-8069-4608-3); PLB 9.29 (ISBN 0-8069-4609-1). Sterling.

Cowboy Life: Reconstructing an American Myth. Ed. by William W. Savage, Jr. (Illus.). 1975. 10.95 (ISBN 0-8061-1218-2); pap. 6.95 (ISBN 0-8061-1592-0). U of Okla Pr.

Cowboy Reader. reissue ed. L. Tinkle & A. Maxwell. LC 76-16347. (gr. 7 up). 1976. 9.95 o.p. (ISBN 0-679-50677-2); pap. 4.95 o.p. (ISBN 0-679-50678-0). McKay.

Cowboy Slang. Edgar Potter. LC 70-170899. (Illus.). 1971. 6.95 o.p. (ISBN 0-87564-105-9). Superior Pub.

Cowboy Twins. Louis Slobodkin & Florence Slobodkin. LC 60-9731. (Illus.). (gr. 1-3). 1960. 5.95 (ISBN 0-8149-0393-2). Vanguard.

Cowboys. W. Forbis. LC 72-87680. (Old West Ser). (Illus.). (gr. 5 up). 1973. kivar 12.96 (ISBN 0-8094-1451-1, Pub. by Time-Life). Silver.

Cowboys. W. Forbis. (Old West Ser.). (Illus.). 1973. 12.95 (ISBN 0-8094-1450-3). Time-Life.

Cowboys. Marie Gorsline & Douglas Gorsline. LC 78-1131. (Picturebacks Ser.). (Illus.). 32p. (ps-2). 1980. PLB 4.99 o.p. (ISBN 0-394-93935-2, BYR); pap. 1.25 (ISBN 0-394-83935-8). Random.

Cowboys & Cattle Country. Don Ward & J. C. Dykes. LC 61-18251. (American Heritage Junior Library). (Illus.). 153p. (gr. 5 up). 1961. 9.95 (ISBN 0-8281-0389-5, J008-0). Am Heritage.

Cowboys & Cattle Kings: Life on the Range Today. Charles L. Sonnichsen. LC 80-12743. (Illus.). xviii, 316p. 1980. Repr. of 1950 ed. lib. bdg. 30.00x (ISBN 0-313-22472-2, SOCO). Greenwood.

Cowboys Under the Mogollon Rim. Slim Ellison. LC 68-9337. (Illus.). 240p. 1968. pap. 9.50 (ISBN 0-8165-0642-6). U of Ariz Pr.

Cowman Says It Salty. Ramon F. Adams. LC 73-174805. 1971. 5.95 o.p. (ISBN 0-8165-0311-7). U of Ariz Pr.

Cowpasture: The Every Day Life of an English Allotment. Roy Lacey. LC 79-56041. (Illus.). 1980. 17.95 (ISBN 0-7153-7916-X). David & Charles.

Cowslip. Betsy Haynes. LC 72-13251. 160p. (gr. 5-9). 1973. 6.95 o.p. (ISBN 0-525-66266-9). Elsevier-Nelson.

Coyote Gulch. Peter Field. 1976. lib. bdg. 13.50x (ISBN 0-89968-033-X). Lightyear.

Coyote Song. Clem Colt. 1978. pap. 1.50 (ISBN 0-505-51317-X). Tower Bks.

Coyote Was Going There: Indian Literature of the Oregon Country. Ed. by Jarold Ramsey. LC 76-49158. (Illus.). 336p. 1977. 14.95 (ISBN 0-295-95441-8); pap. 7.95 (ISBN 0-295-95731-X). U of Wash Pr.

CP-M User's Guide. Thom Hogan. 350p. (Orig.). 1981. pap. 12.99 (ISBN 0-931988-44-6). Osborne-McGraw.

CPA & the Computer Fraud. Charles R. Wagner. LC 77-90861. (Illus.). 1979. 16.95 (ISBN 0-669-02079-6). Lexington Bks.

C.P.A. Exam Booklet. 2nd ed. Sidney Davidson et al. 1981. pap. text ed. 6.95 (ISBN 0-686-69576-3). Dryden Pr.

CPA Exam Intermediate Acct. Davidsen et al. 1980. 5.95 (ISBN 0-03-058087-0). Dryden Pr.

CPA Examination: A Complete Review, Vol. II. Ed. by Belverd E. Needles, Jr. & Doyle Z. Williams. (Illus.). 768p. 1980. pap. text ed. 20.95 (ISBN 0-13-187815-8). P-H.

CPA Examination: A Complete Review, Vol. 1. Ed. by Belverd E. Needles, Jr. & Doyle Z. Williams. (Illus.). 1000p. 1980. text ed. 22.95 (ISBN 0-13-187807-7). P-H.

CPA Examination: A Comprehensive Review, Problems & Solutions. 3rd ed. Harold Q. Langenderfer & E. Ben Yager. (Business Ser.). 1979. text ed. 24.95 (ISBN 0-675-08298-6). Merrill.

CPA Firm Viability: A Study of Major Environmental Factors Affecting Firms of Various Sizes & Characteristics. Harold Arnett & Paul Danos. LC 79-18672. (Illus., Orig.). 1979. pap. 6.50 (ISBN 0-87712-199-0). U Mich Busn Div Res.

CPA Law Review. 5th ed. Joseph L. Frascona. 1977. text ed. 22.95 (ISBN 0-256-01891-X). Irwin.

CPA Problems & Approaches to Solutions, Vol. 2. 5th ed. Charles T. Horngren & J. Arthur Leer. 1979. 14.95 o.p. (ISBN 0-13-187906-5); text ed. 11.20 o.p. (ISBN 0-686-67265-8). P-H.

CPA Review Summary of APB Opinions & FASB Statements. 13th ed. CPA Study Aids, Inc. LC 79-55006. 1979. pap. 8.00 (ISBN 0-932788-12-2). Bradley CPA.

Crab Apple. Bob Reese. Ed. by Dan Wasserman. (Ten Word Bks.). (Illus.). (gr. k-1). 1979. PLB 4.50 (ISBN 0-89868-072-7); pap. 1.95 (ISBN 0-89868-083-2). ARO Pub.

Crab from Yesterday: The Life Cycle of a Horseshoe Crab. John F. Waters. LC 74-161067. (gr. 2-5). 1970. PLB 4.95 o.p. (ISBN 0-7232-6085-0). Warne.

Crab Nebula. Simon Mitton. (Illus.). 1979. 16.95 (ISBN 0-684-16077-3, ScribT). Scribner.

Crab Spiders of Canada & Alaska: Araneae; Philodromidae & Thomisidae. (Insects & Arachnids of Canada: Pt. 5). 254p. 1980. pap. 14.00 (ISBN 0-660-10104-1, SSC 142, SSC). Unipub.

Crabbe. Alfred Ainger. LC 72-78107. (Library of Lives & Letters). 1970. Repr. of 1903 ed. 15.00 (ISBN 0-8103-3600-6). Gale.

Crabbe: The Critical Heritage. Arthur Pollard. (Critical Heritage Ser.). 510p. 1972. 38.50 (ISBN 0-7100-7258-9). Routledge & Kegan.

Crabb's English Synonyms. George Crabb. 1966. Repr. of 1916 ed. 22.50 (ISBN 0-7100-1234-9). Routledge & Kegan.

Crabs. Herbert S. Zim & Lucretia Krantz. LC 73-16328. (Illus.). 64p. (gr. 3-7). 1974. 6.25 o.p. (ISBN 0-688-20114-8); PLB 6.48 (ISBN 0-688-30114-2). Morrow.

Crack Control in Concrete Masonry Unit Construction. Federal Construction Council - Building Research Advisory Board. 1964. pap. 3.00 (ISBN 0-309-01198-1). Natl Acad Pr.

Crack in the Sidewalk. Ruth Wolff. LC 65-23039. (John Day Bk.). (YA) 1965. 6.95 o.p. (ISBN 0-381-98201-7, A16460, TYC-T). T Y Crowell.

Crack in Time. Miesje Jolley. (Illus.). 48p. (Orig.). 1980. pap. 6.00 (ISBN 0-931122-20-1). West End.

Crack Shot. Glen Chase. 1976. pap. 1.25 o.p. (ISBN 0-685-72569-3, LB400ZK, Leisure Bks). Nordon Pubns.

Cracked Looking Glass: Stories of Other Realities. Ed. by L. M. Schulman. LC 78-138302. (gr. 9 up). 1971. 4.95 o.s.i. (ISBN 0-02-781400-9). Macmillan.

Cracker Factory. Joyce Rebeta-Burditt. 1977. 8.95 o.s.i. (ISBN 0-02-601250-2, 60125). Macmillan.

Crackerjacks. rev. ed. Grayce A. Ransom & Elaine Stowe. (Cornerstone Ser.). (gr. 4-5). 1978. pap. text ed. 4.52 (ISBN 0-201-41026-5, Sch Div); tchr's ed. 5.56 (ISBN 0-201-41027-3). A-W.

Crackle Gluck & the Sleeping Toad. Dick Gackenbach. LC 78-12635. (Illus.). (gr. 1-3). 1979. 7.95 (ISBN 0-395-28953-X, Clarion). HM.

Cracks in the Melting Pot. 2nd ed. M. Steinfield. 1973. pap. 7.95x (ISBN 0-02-478670-5, 47867). Macmillan.

Cradle of Civilization. Samuel N. Kramer. LC 67-29528. (Great Ages of Man). (Illus.). (gr. 6 up). 1967. PLB 11.97 (ISBN 0-8094-0378-1, Pub. by Time-Life). Silver.

Cradle of Civilization. Samuel N. Kramer. (Great Ages of Man Ser). (Illus.). 1967. 12.95 (ISBN 0-8094-0356-0); lib. bdg. avail. (ISBN 0-685-20547-9). Time-Life.

Cradle of Colonialism. George Masselman. 1963. 47.50x (ISBN 0-685-69840-8). Elliots Bks.

Cradle of the Middle Class: The Family in Oneida County, New York, 1780-1865. Mary P. Ryan. LC 80-18460. (Interdisciplinary Perspectives on Modern History Ser.). (Illus.). 336p. Date not set. price not set (ISBN 0-521-23200-7). Cambridge U Pr.

Cradle Tales of Hinduism. Sr. Nivedita. (Illus.). 329p. (gr. 3-12). 1972. 5.75 o.s.i. (ISBN 0-87481-170-8); pap. 3.95 (ISBN 0-87481-131-7). Vedanta Pr.

Cradle Will Fall. Mary H. Clark. 1981. pap. 3.50 (ISBN 0-440-11476-4). Dell.

Cradle Will Fall. Mary H. Clark. (Large Print Bks.). 1980. lib. bdg. 13.95 (ISBN 0-8161-3121-X). G K Hall.

Craft: A Handbook of Classroom Ideas to Motivate the Teaching of Intermediate Art. (Spice Ser.). 1977. 6.50 (ISBN 0-89273-124-9). Educ Serv.

Craft & Creation of Wood Sculpture. Cecil C. Carstenson. (Illus.). 192p. 1981. pap. price not set (ISBN 0-486-24094-0). Dover.

Craft Fun. Janet McCarty & Betty J. Paterson. (Golden Funtime Ser). (Illus.). (ps-6). 1975. PLB 7.62 o.p. (ISBN 0-307-66305-1, Golden Pr). Western Pub.

Craft Jewelery. Claude Geoffroy-Dechaume. (Illus.). 144p. 1980. 16.95 (ISBN 0-571-11486-5, Pub. by Faber & Faber); pap. 6.95 (ISBN 0-571-11309-5, Pub. by Faber & Faber). Merrimack Bk Serv.

Craft of Blackwork & Whitework. Erica Wilson. (Illus.). 96p. 1976. pap. 4.95 o.p. (ISBN 0-684-14496-4, SL617). Scribner.

Craft of Bookbinding: A Practical Guide. Eric Burdett. 1977. 38.00 (ISBN 0-7153-6656-4). David & Charles.

Craft of Comedy. Athene Seyler & Stephen Haggard. 1957. 5.95 (ISBN 0-87830-023-6). Theatre Arts.

Craft of Crewel Embroidery. Erica Wilson. LC 62-9637. (Illus.). 1971. pap. 5.95 (ISBN 0-684-12501-3, SL211, ScribT). Scribner.

Craft of Crocheted Afghans. Liz Blackwell. LC 73-5169. (Illus.). 96p. 1973. pap. 3.95 o.p. (ISBN 0-684-13574-4, SL472, ScribT). Scribner.

Craft of Furniture Making. David Johnston. 1979. 19.95 (ISBN 0-7134-1546-0, Pub. by Batsford England). David & Charles.

Craft of Modal Counterpoint: A Practice Approach. Thomas Benjamin. LC 77-90012. 1979. pap. text ed. 10.95 (ISBN 0-02-870480-0). Schirmer Bks.

Craft of Novel Writing. Dianne Doubtfire. 1981. pap. 5.95 (ISBN 0-8052-8087-1, Pub. by Allison & Busby England). Schocken.

Craft of Poetry. Ed. by William Packard. LC 74-2831. 240p. 1974. pap. 4.50 o.p. (ISBN 0-385-03468-7); pap. 4.50 Softbound o.p. (ISBN 0-385-03496-2). Doubleday.

Craft of Political Research. 2nd ed. W. Phillips Shively. (Contemporary Comparative Politics Ser.). (Illus.). 1980. pap. text ed. 8.95 (ISBN 0-13-188748-3). P-H.

Craft of Pottery. Frank Howell et al. LC 74-15859. (Illus.). 176p. 1975. 14.95 o.p. (ISBN 0-06-011966-7, HarpT); pap. 6.95 o.p. (ISBN 0-06-011959-4, TD-218, HarpT). Har-Row.

Craft of Programming. J. Reynolds. 1981. 22.95 (ISBN 0-13-188862-5). P-H.

Craft of Prose. 5th ed. Robert H. Woodward. 432p. 1979. pap. text ed. 7.95x (ISBN 0-534-00781-3). Wadsworth Pub.

Craft of Public Administration. 2nd ed. George E. Berkley. 1978. text ed. 16.95x o.p. (ISBN 0-205-06060-9). Allyn.

Craft of Public Administration. 3rd ed. George E. Berkley. 550p. 1980. text ed. 19.90 (ISBN 0-205-07211-9, 767211-X); tchrs'. ed. avail. (ISBN 0-205-07212-7). Allyn.

Craft of Ralph Ellison. Robert G. O'Meally. LC 80-12680. 1980. text ed. 14.00x (ISBN 0-674-17548-4). Harvard U Pr.

Craft of Silk & Gold Thread Embroidery & Stumpwork. Erica Wilson. (Illus.). 1977. pap. 4.95 o.p. (ISBN 0-684-15067-0, ScribT). Scribner.

Craft of Social Anthropology. Ed. by A. L. Epstein. 1979. 23.00 (ISBN 0-08-023693-6). Pergamon.

Craft of Surgery, 3 vols. 2nd ed. Philip Cooper. (Illus.). 1971. Set. 85.00 o.p. (ISBN 0-316-15554-3). Little.

Craft of Tatting. Bessie M. Attenborough. (Illus.). 1973. 5.25 o.p. (ISBN 0-8231-5039-9). Branford.

Craft of Wood Carving. Alan Bridgewater & Gill Bridgewater. LC 80-18562. (Illus.). 160p. 1981. 15.95 (ISBN 0-668-04985-5, 4985). Arco.

Craft of Writing. Thomas E. Berry. 1974. pap. text ed. 3.95 (ISBN 0-07-005051-1, SP). McGraw.

Craft of Writing. W. Brandt et al. 1969. pap. text ed. 7.95 (ISBN 0-13-188797-1). P-H.

Crafting Turquoise Jewelry. Bob Powers & Marc Barasch. LC 78-12277. (Illus.). 192p. 1978. 16.95 (ISBN 0-8117-1803-4). Stackpole.

Crafting with Nature's Materials. Chester J. Alkema. LC 72-81038. (Little Craft Book Ser.). (Illus.). 48p. (gr. 6 up). 1972. 5.95 (ISBN 0-8069-5214-8); PLB 6.69 (ISBN 0-8069-5215-6). Sterling.

Crafting with Newspapers. Vivien Eisner & William Shisler. LC 76-19771. (Little Craft Bk.). (gr. 5up). 1976. 5.95 (ISBN 0-8069-5368-3); PLB 6.69 (ISBN 0-8069-5369-1). Sterling.

Crafts & Hobbies. rev. ed. Ed. by Garry Winter. LC 64-21342. (Illus.). 1971. lib. bdg. 3.95 o.p. (ISBN 0-668-01212-9). Arco.

Crafts & Hobbies: A Step-by-Step Guide to Creative Skills. Reader's Digest. Date not set. 19.95 (ISBN 0-686-69221-7). Readers Digest Pr.

Crafts Careers. Patricia Brent. (Career Concise Guides Ser.). (Illus.). (gr. 7 up). 1977. PLB 6.45 s&l (ISBN 0-531-01304-9). Watts.

Crafts, Customs & Legends of Wales. Mary C Harris. LC 79-91477. (Illus.). 1980. 17.95 (ISBN 0-7153-7820-1). David & Charles.

Crafts for All Seasons. Lorraine Bodger & Delia Ephron. LC 79-6410. (Illus.). 112p. 1980. 9.95 o.s.i. (ISBN 0-87663-318-1); pap. 5.95 (ISBN 0-87663-996-1). Universe.

Crafts for Bible Discovery. Peggy Palmer. LC 79-55015. (Bible Discovery Books). 1979. pap. 4.25 (ISBN 0-8344-0111-8). Sweet.

Crafts for Christmas. Katherine N. Cutler & Kate Bogle. LC 74-8750. (Illus.). 128p. (gr. 3 up). 1974. PLB 7.44 (ISBN 0-688-51663-7). Lothrop.

Crafts for Cub Scouts. Boy Scouts Of America. (Illus.). 80p. 1963. pap. 1.25x (ISBN 0-8395-3843-X, 3843). BSA.

Crafts for Kids. Phyllis Guth. LC 75-4287. 182p. (gr. 4-8). 1975. 7.95 (ISBN 0-8306-5766-5); pap. 6.95 (ISBN 0-8306-4766-X, 766). TAB Bks.

Crafts for Preschoolers. Marie Frost. (Peter Panda Ser.). 1977. pap. 1.25 (ISBN 0-87239-144-2, 42036). Standard Pub.

Crafts for the Elderly. Elaine Gould & Loren Gould. (Illus.). 224p. 1976. 14.75 (ISBN 0-398-00710-1). C C Thomas.

Crafts for Today: Ceramics, Glasscrafting, Leather Working, Candlemaking & Other Popular Crafts. Rolly M. Harwell & Ann J. Harwell. LC 73-92979. (Spare Time Guides Ser.: No. 4). 220p. 1974. lib. bdg. 9.50 o.p. (ISBN 0-87287-067-7). Libs Unl.

Crafts Handbook for Children's Church: Graded Activities for Ages 3-7. Leslea Stringer & Lea Bowman. (Teaching Help Ser.). (Orig.). 1981. pap. 6.95 (ISBN 0-8010-8197-1). Baker Bk.

Crafts, Illustrated Designs & Techniques. Clois E. Kicklighter & Ronald J. Baird. LC 79-23955. (Illus.). 384p. 1980. text ed. 14.64 (ISBN 0-87006-298-0). Goodheart.

Crafts of China. Michael Carter. LC 76-51862. 1977. 9.95 o.p. (ISBN 0-385-13119-4). Doubleday.

Crafts of India. D. N. Saraf. (Illus.). 380p. 1980. 40.00x (ISBN 0-7069-0735-3, Pub. by Croom Helm Ltd England). Biblio Dist.

Crafts of Israel. Ruth Dayan & Willie Feinberg. LC 73-10787. (Illus.). 160p. 1974. 19.95 o.s.i. (ISBN 0-02-534420-X). Macmillan.

Crafts of the Highlands & Islands. John Manners. LC 77-91724. 1978. 11.95 (ISBN 0-7153-7485-0). David & Charles.

Craftsman's Survival Manual: Making a Full or Part-Time Living from Your Crafts. George Wettlaufer & Nancy Wettlaufer. (Creative Handcrafts Ser.). 1974. 9.95 o.p. (ISBN 0-13-188789-0, Spec); pap. 3.45 o.p. (ISBN 0-13-188771-8, Spec). P-H.

Craftsmanship in Competitive Industry. C. R. Ashbee. Ed. by Peter Stansky & Rodney Shewan. LC 76-17772. (Aesthetic Movement & the Arts & Crafts Movement Ser.). 1978. Repr. of 1908 ed. lib. bdg. 44.00x (ISBN 0-8240-2477-X). Garland Pub.

Craftsmen in Business: A Guide to Financial Management & Taxes. rev. ed. Howard W. Connaughton. LC 79-64530. 73p. 1979. 7.20 (ISBN 0-88321-032-0). Am Craft.

Craftworker's Market 1980. 2nd ed. Lynne Lapin. (Illus.). 1979. 11.95 o.p. (ISBN 0-89879-004-2). Writers Digest.

Crafty Ideas for the Home. Ed. by Millie Hines. (Illus.). 96p. (Orig.). 1980. pap. 2.00 (ISBN 0-918178-20-7). Simplicity.

Craghold Curse. Edwinna Noone. 1977. pap. 1.25 (ISBN 0-505-51156-8). Tower Bks.

Craig & Faust's Clinical Parasitology. 8th ed. Ernest C. Faust et al. LC 76-85841. (Illus.). 1970. text ed. 25.50 o.p. (ISBN 0-8121-0291-6). Lea & Febiger.

Craig Claiborne's Favorites, Vol. 3. Craig Claiborne. 1981. pap. 2.95 (ISBN 0-446-93808-4). Warner Bks.

Craig Claiborne's Favorites from The New York Times, 2 vols. Craig Claiborne. 1977. Vol. 1. pap. 2.95 (ISBN 0-446-93472-0); Vol. 2. pap. 2.95 (ISBN 0-446-93534-4). Warner Bks.

Craig Claiborne's Gourmet Diet. Craig Claiborne. 1981. pap. 2.95 (ISBN 0-345-29579-X). Ballantine.

Craig Claiborne's Gourmet Diet. Craig Claiborne & Pierre Franey. 288p. 1980. 10.95 (ISBN 0-8129-0914-3). Times Bks.

Craig Olson's Decorating with Plants. Craig Olson. Ed. by Kathe Grooms. (Illus.). 110p. 1981. pap. 2.95 (ISBN 0-915658-31-3). Meadowbrook Pr.

Cranberry Christmas. Wende Devlin & Harry Devlin. LC 80-16971. (Illus.). 40p. (ps-3). 1980. Repr. of 1976 ed. 8.95 (ISBN 0-590-07760-0, Four Winds). Schol Bk Serv.

Cranberry Mystery. Wende Devlin & Harry Devlin. LC 78-6219. (Illus.). 40p. (ps-3). 1978. 7.95 (ISBN 0-8193-0972-9, Four Winds); PLB 5.41 o.p. (ISBN 0-8193-0973-7). Schol Bk Serv.

Cranberry Thanksgiving. Wende Devlin & Harry Devlin. LC 80-17070. (Illus.). 48p. (ps-3). 1980. Repr. of 1971 ed. 8.95 (ISBN 0-590-07761-9, Four Winds). Schol Bk Serv.

Crane. Joan Tate. pap. text ed. 1.95x o.p. (ISBN 0-435-11873-0). Heinemann Ed.

Crane Design: Theory & Calculations of Reliability. Josef Kogan. LC 75-38664. 365p. 1976. 63.95 (ISBN 0-470-15224-9). Halsted Pr.

Crane Flies of California. C. P. Alexander. (Bulletin of the California Insect Survey: Vol. 8). 1967. pap. 10.00x (ISBN 0-520-09033-0). U of Cal Pr.

Crane Handbook. D. E. Dickie & Douglas Short. 1981. text ed. price not set (ISBN 0-408-00445-2, Newnes-Butterworth). Butterworths.

Crane Reading System, Practice Bks, A-J. Barbara J. Crane. Incl. Practice Book A (ISBN 0-89075-052-1); Practice Book B (ISBN 0-89075-054-8); Practice Book C (ISBN 0-89075-055-6); Practice Book D (ISBN 0-89075-056-4); Practice Book E (ISBN 0-89075-057-2); Practice Book F (ISBN 0-89075-058-0); Practice Book G (ISBN 0-89075-059-9); Practice Book H (ISBN 0-89075-060-2); Practice Book I (ISBN 0-89075-061-0); Practice Book J (ISBN 0-89075-062-9). (Illus.). (gr. k-2). 1977. pap. text ed. 2.55 ea. A-E; pap. 2.90 ea. F-J. Crane Pub Co.

Crane Reading System in Spanish, Levels A-e. Barbara J. Crane. Ed. by Lyneil L. Wasser & Louisa M. Gallegos. Tr. by Francisco Lasarte. Incl. Level A. Libro De Lectura. 2.85 (ISBN 0-89075-163-3); Libro De Ejercicios. 2.60 (ISBN 0-89075-158-7); Level B. Libro De Lectura. 2.85 (ISBN 0-89075-164-1); Libro De Ejercicios. 2.60 (ISBN 0-89075-159-5); Level C. Libro De Lectura. 2.85 (ISBN 0-89075-166-8); Libro De Ejercicios. pap. 2.60 (ISBN 0-89075-160-9); Level D. Libro De Lectura. 2.85 (ISBN 0-89075-167-6); Libro De Ejercicios. 2.60 (ISBN 0-89075-161-7); Level E. Libro De Lectura. 2.85 (ISBN 0-89075-168-4); Libro De Ejercicios. pap. 2.60 (ISBN 0-89075-162-5). (Illus.). (gr. k-6). 1978. levels A-E guidebook to system 20.35 (ISBN 0-89075-169-2). Crane Pub Co.

Crane Reading System in Spanish. Incl. Level F. Libro De Lectura. 4.25 (ISBN 0-89075-185-4); Libro De Ejercicios. 2.85 (ISBN 0-89075-175-7); Level G. Libro De Lectura. 4.25 (ISBN 0-89075-186-2); Libro De Ejercicios. 2.85 (ISBN 0-89075-176-5); Level H. Libro De Lectura. 5.40 (ISBN 0-686-53134-5); Libro De Ejercicios. 3.20 (ISBN 0-89075-177-3); Level I. Libro De Lectura. 5.40 (ISBN 0-89075-188-9); Libro De Ejercicios. 3.20 (ISBN 0-89075-178-1); Level J. Libro De Lectura. 6.50 (ISBN 0-89075-189-7); Libro De Ejercicios. 3.35 (ISBN 0-89075-180-3); Level K. Libro De Lectura. 6.50 (ISBN 0-89075-190-0); Libro De Ejercicios. 3.35 (ISBN 0-89075-181-1). Levels F-K Guidebook. 20.95 (ISBN 0-89075-202-8). Crane Pub Co.

Crane Reading System in Spanish: Libros de trabajo, Levels A-E. Barbara J. Crane. Incl. Level A-1 (ISBN 0-89075-152-8); Level A-2 (ISBN 0-89075-153-6); Level B-1 (ISBN 0-89075-154-4); Level C-1 (ISBN 0-89075-155-2); Level D-1 (ISBN 0-89075-156-0); Level E-1 (ISBN 0-89075-157-9). (Illus.). (gr. k-2). 1978. per 10 12.40 (ISBN 0-686-67205-4). Crane Pub Co.

Cranes in My Corral. Dayton Hyde. LC 70-153737. (Illus.). (gr. 4-6). 4.95 (ISBN 0-8037-1550-1); PLB 4.58 (ISBN 0-8037-1551-X). Dial.

Cranial Arteries of Mammals. George Du Boulay. (Illus.). 1973. 45.00x (ISBN 0-433-07850-2). Intl Ideas.

Cranial Manipulation Roots. 177p. pap. 9.00 (ISBN 0-917628-03-9). Coraco.

Cranial Variation in Man: A Study by Multivariate Analysis. W. W. Howells. LC 73-77203. (Peabody Museum Papers: Vol. 67). 1973. pap. text ed. 17.00 (ISBN 0-87365-189-8). Peabody Harvard.

Cranio Facial Growth in Man. R. E. Moyers & W. M. Krogman. 1971. 55.00 (ISBN 0-08-016331-9). Pergamon.

Craniofacial & Upper Cervical Arteries: Functional, Clinical & Angiographic Aspects. Pierre Lasjaunias. (Illus.). 220p. 1980. lib. bdg. write for info. (ISBN 0-683-04900-3). Williams & Wilkins.

Craniometry & Multivariate Analysis. W. W. Howells & J. M. Crichton. LC 66-4603. (Peabody Museum Papers Ser.: Vol. 57, No. 1). 1966. pap. text ed. 8.00 (ISBN 0-87365-167-7). Peabody Harvard.

Craniopathy: (Cranial Adjusting) 93 Technics in 10 Folios. 1975. 92.00 (ISBN 0-917628-01-2). Coraco.

Cranshaw Inheritance. Christina Etheridge. 1979. pap. 1.95 (ISBN 0-515-05148-9). Jove Pubns.

Craps by the Numbers. Allan Ackerman. (System Check Ser.). 1978. pap. 2.95 (ISBN 0-89650-655-X). Gamblers.

Craps Line Decisions. Huey Mahl. (System Check Ser.). 1978. pap. 2.95 (ISBN 0-89650-660-6). Gamblers.

Crash. J. G. Ballard. 1973. 6.95 o.p. (ISBN 0-374-13072-8). FS&G.

Crash Bang Boom. Peter Spier. LC 70-157625. (Illus.). (ps-1). 1972. 7.95a (ISBN 0-385-06780-1); PLB (ISBN 0-385-02496-7). Doubleday.

Crash Course in Composition. 3rd ed. Elizabeth McMahan. 272p. 1980. pap. text ed. 8.95 (ISBN 0-07-045458-2, C); instructor's manual 4.95 (ISBN 0-07-045459-0). McGraw.

Crash Dive. Lee Frederick. LC 78-15596. (Pacesetters Ser.). (Illus.). (gr. 4 up). 1978. PLB 7.95 (ISBN 0-516-02167-2). Childrens.

Crashing. Enid Harlow. 1981. pap. 2.75 (ISBN 0-553-14626-2). Bantam.

Crater. Richard Slotkin. LC 80-65988. 1980. 17.95 (ISBN 0-689-11107-X). Atheneum.

Craving for Superiority. Raymond Dodge & Eugen Kahn. 1931. 24.50 (ISBN 0-686-51366-5). Elliots Bks.

Crawfish-Man Rescues Ron Guidry. Timothy Edler. (Tim Edler's Tales from the Atchafalaya). (Illus.). (gr. k-8). 1980. lea. 5.00 (ISBN 0-931108-05-5). Little Cajun.

Crawlspace. Herbert Lieberman. 1981. pap. 2.50 (ISBN 0-671-43068-8). PB.

Crazy Car Book. Sloan Walker. LC 72-95805. (Illus.). 48p. (gr. 1 up). 1973. 4.95 o.s.i. (ISBN 0-8027-6147-X); PLB 8.85 (ISBN 0-8027-6148-8). Walker & Co.

Crazy Cat. Ron Reese. Ed. by Alton Jordan. (I Can Read Underwater Bks). (Illus.). (gr. k-3). 1974. PLB 3.50 (ISBN 0-89868-002-6, Read Res); pap. text ed. 1.75 (ISBN 0-89868-065-4). ARO Pub.

Crazy Cat's Bad Day. Ron Reese. Ed. by Alton Jordan. (Buppet Series). (Illus.). (gr. k-3). 1981. PLB 4.50 (ISBN 0-89868-090-5, Read Res); pap. text ed. 1.95 (ISBN 0-89868-101-4). ARO Pub.

Crazy Eights. Barbara Dana. 176p. (gr. 7-9). 1981. pap. 1.75 (ISBN 0-553-14435-9). Bantam.

Crazy Fox Remembers. Don Preston & Sue Preston. 224p. 11.95 (ISBN 0-13-188896-X). P-H.

Crazy Freddy's in Trouble Again & His Parents Are Going to... !! Dina Anastasio. (Write-It-Yourself Bks.). (Illus.). 48p. 1981. pap. 1.75 (ISBN 0-8431-0280-2). Price Stern.

Crazy Horse. Matthew G. Grant. LC 73-12403. 1974. PLB 5.95 (ISBN 0-87191-269-4). Creative Ed.

Crazy Horse. Mari Sandoz. 1975. Repr. 10.95 (ISBN 0-8038-1119-5). Hastings.

Crazy Horse, the Strange Man of the Oglalas. Mari Sandoz. LC 42-50340. (Illus.). 1961. pap. 4.50 (ISBN 0-8032-5171-8, BB 110, Bison). U of Nebr Pr.

Crazy in Love. Richard Kennedy. (Illus.). (gr. 3-7). 1980. PLB 7.95 (ISBN 0-525-28364-1). Dutton.

Crazy States: A Counterconventional Strategic Problem. Yehezkel Dror. LC 80-81613. 1980. Repr. lib. bdg. 18.00 (ISBN 0-527-25140-2). Kraus Repr.

Crazy Talk, Stupid Talk. Neil Postman. 1976. 8.95 o.s.i. (ISBN 0-440-01554-5). Delacorte.

Crazy to Be Alive in Such a Strange World. Ed. by Nancy Larrick. LC 76-49667. (Illus.). 192p. (gr. 5 up). 1977. 7.95 (ISBN 0-87131-225-5). M Evans.

Crazy to Fly. Martha O. Conn. LC 77-23871. (Illus.). (gr. 4-8). 1978. 8.95 (ISBN 0-689-30616-4). Atheneum.

Crazy Weather. Charles L. McNichols. LC 38-32977. 1967. pap. 2.95 (ISBN 0-8032-5132-7, BB 354, Bison). U of Nebr Pr.

Crazy Woman of Wales Hotel. Richard Dokey. (Short Story Discovery Ser.). pap. 5.00 (ISBN 0-933906-12-9). Gusto Pr.

CRC Handbook of Spectrophotometric Data of Drugs. Ed. by Irving Sunshine. 432p. 1981. 62.95 (ISBN 0-8493-3571-X). CRC Pr.

CRC Handbook of Tables of Commercial Thermal Processes for Low-Acid Canned Foods, 2 vols. C. R. Stumbo et al. Date not set. Vol. 1. 69.95 (ISBN 0-8493-2961-2); Vol. 2. 69.95 (ISBN 0-8493-2963-9). CRC Pr. Postponed.

Crc Handbook Series in Inorganic Electrochemistry. Louis Meites et al. 350p. 1980. 64.95 (ISBN 0-8493-0361-3). CRC Pr.

Creacion y Organizacion: Sintesis De Informes y Estudios Especiales Presentados, 1962-1971. Comision Especial De Consulta Sobre Seguridad. 140p. (Span.). 1971. pap. 1.00 o.p. (ISBN 0-8270-2925-X). OAS.

Creaciones y Creadores: A Basic Literary Reader. William F. Ratliff. 128p. 1981. pap. text ed. 7.95 (ISBN 0-394-32654-7). Random.

Cream... Contains Jack of All Trades, a Matter-of-Fact Romance, & the Autobiography of a Thief. Charles Reade. LC 80-2495. 1981. Repr. of 1858 ed. 35.00 (ISBN 0-404-19129-0). AMS Pr.

Creamware. Donald Towner. LC 78-320727. (Illus.). 1978. 43.00 (ISBN 0-571-04964-8, Pub. by Faber & Faber). Merrimack Bk Serv.

Create-A-Cookbook: Guide to Easy Meal Planning. Penny Stanaford. (Illus.). 68p. 1980. 10.95 (ISBN 0-9604850-0-7). Postscript.

Create: A Handbook of Classroom Ideas to Motivate the Teaching of Primary Art. (Spice Ser). 1977. 6.50 (ISBN 0-89273-105-2). Educ Serv.

Create, One. Regina R. Barnett. 31p. (Orig.). (ps). 1978. pap. text ed. 4.95 student work pad (ISBN 0-697-01678-1); tchr's manual 10.75 (ISBN 0-697-01677-3). Wm C Brown.

Create, Two. Regina R. Barnett. 31p. (Orig.). (ps). 1979. pap. text ed. 4.95 student work pad (ISBN 0-697-01705-2); tchr's manual 10.75 (ISBN 0-697-01706-0). Wm C Brown.

Created, the Destroyer. Warren Murphy. (Destroyer Ser.: No. 1). 1976. pap. 1.95 (ISBN 0-523-41216-9). Pinnacle Bks.

Created to Praise. Derek Prime. 128p. (Orig.). 1981. pap. 2.95 (ISBN 0-87784-825-4). Inter-Varsity.

Createurs de l'Opera-Comique Francais. Georges Cucuel. LC 80-2271. 1981. Repr. of 1914 ed. 29.50 (ISBN 0-404-18834-6). AMS Pr.

Createurs De l'Opera Francais. Lionel de La Laurencie. LC 80-2287. 1981. Repr. of 1921 ed. 26.00 (ISBN 0-404-18854-0). AMS Pr.

Creating a Community Association: The Developer's Role in Condominium & Homeowners Association. Community Associations Institute. LC 76-56982. 1976. 12.00 (ISBN 0-87420-574-3). Urban Land.

Creating a School Media Program. John T. Gillespie & Diana L. Spirt. LC 77-164032. (Illus.). 236p. 1973. 16.25 o.p. (ISBN 0-8352-0484-7). Bowker.

Creating a Successful Christian Marriage. Cleveland McDonald. LC 74-20202. 1975. 10.95 (ISBN 0-87227-038-6). Reg Baptist.

Creating a Tailored Garment. rev ed. Lenore L. Landry & Emma M. Jorde. (Illus.). 1977. pap. text ed. 3.95 o.s.i. (ISBN 0-89534-005-4). Am Pub Co WI.

Creating an Early Learning Center in an Unused Building. 55p. 1972. 2.00. Natl Cath Educ.

Creating Change in Mental Health Organizations. George W. Fairweather et al. 200p. 1974. text ed. 19.75 (ISBN 0-08-017833-2); pap. text ed. 10.75 (ISBN 0-08-017832-4). Pergamon.

Creating Community Acceptance for Handicapped People. Roberta Nelson. (Illus.). 240p. 1978. 17.50 (ISBN 0-398-03788-4). C C Thomas.

Creating Community Services for Widows: A Pilot Project. Starr R. Hiltz. LC 76-18292. 1977. 12.95 (ISBN 0-8046-9157-6). Kennikat.

Creating Compositions. 3rd ed. Harvey S. Wiener. Ed. by Phillip A. Butcher. (Illus.). 448p. 1981. pap. text ed. 9.95x (ISBN 0-07-070160-1, C); instructor's manual 3.95x (ISBN 0-07-070161-X). McGraw.

Creating Contexts: A Practical Approach to Writing. Domenick Caruso & Stephen Weidenborner. LC 76-55159. (Illus.). 1977. pap. text ed. 6.95x (ISBN 0-393-09101-5); tchrs manual gratis (ISBN 0-393-09107-4). Norton.

Creating Fiction from Experience. rev. ed. Peggy S. Curry. 1975. 8.95 (ISBN 0-87116-089-7). Writer.

Creating for Ourselves. Peter Abbs. (Approacher Ser.: No. 4). 1974. pap. text ed. 2.95x o.p. (ISBN 0-435-10024-6). Heinemann Ed.

Creating from Remnants: Stitchery with Imperfect Fabrics. Ethel J. Beitler. LC 74-82325. (Little Craft Bk.). (Illus.). 48p. (gr. 6 up). 1974. 5.95 (ISBN 0-8069-5306-3); PLB 6.69 (ISBN 0-8069-5307-1). Sterling.

Creating Groups. Harvey J. Bertcher & Frank F. Maple. LC 77-22401. (Sage Human Services Guides: Vol. 2). 1977. pap. 6.00x (ISBN 0-8039-0881-4). Sage.

Creating Historical Drama: A Guide for the Community & the Interested Individual. George McCalmon & Christian Moe. LC 65-12501. (Illus.). 1965. 15.00x o.p. (ISBN 0-8093-0189-X). S Ill U Pr.

Creating in Cloth. Judith S. Kalina. LC 76-16601. (Illus.). 1976. pap. 4.95 o.p. (ISBN 0-915684-09-8). Christian Herald.

Creating Instructional Materials. 2nd ed. Robert V. Bullough. (Elementary Education Ser.). 1978. pap. text ed. 12.95x (ISBN 0-675-08361-3). Merrill.

Creating Jobs: Public Employment Programs & Wage Subsidies. Ed. by John L. Palmer. (Studies in Social Economics). 1978. 17.95 (ISBN 0-8157-6892-3); pap. 6.95 (ISBN 0-8157-6891-5). Brookings.

Creating Reality: How TV News Distorts Events. David L. Altheide. LC 76-22602. (Sage Library of Social Research: Vol. 33). 1976. 18.00x (ISBN 0-8039-0671-4); pap. 8.95x (ISBN 0-8039-0672-2). Sage.

Creating Silver Jewelry with Beads. Marianne Seitz. LC 75-180455. (Little Craft Bk.). (Illus.). 48p. (gr. 9 up). 1972. 4.95 o.p. (ISBN 0-8069-5196-6); PLB 5.89 o.p. (ISBN 0-8069-5197-4). Sterling.

Creating the Entangling Alliance: The Origins of the North Atlantic Treaty Organization. Timothy P. Ireland. LC 80-655. (Contributions in Political Science: No. 50). 264p. 1981. lib. bdg. 27.50 (ISBN 0-313-22094-8, IRC/). Greenwood.

Creating the Welfare State: The Political Economy of Twentieth Century Reform. Edward Berkowitz & Kim McQuaid. LC 79-22524. 1980. 22.95 (ISBN 0-03-056243-0). Praeger.

Creating Things That Move, Fun with Kinetic Art. Harry Helfman. LC 75-11719. (Illus.). 48p. (gr. 4-6). 1975. PLB 6.48 (ISBN 0-688-32038-4). Morrow.

Creating with Flexible Foam. A. De Brouwer. LC 71-167657. (Little Craft Bk.). (Illus.). (gr. 4 up). 1971. 5.95 (ISBN 0-8069-5182-6); PLB 6.69 (ISBN 0-8069-5183-4). Sterling.

Creating with Paper. Pauline Johnson. LC 58-6007. (Illus.). 224p. (gr. 3 up). 1975. 12.50 (ISBN 0-295-95408-6). U of Wash Pr.

Creating with Puppets. Lothar Kampmann. Date not set. 9.95 (ISBN 0-8238-0248-5). Plays. Postponed.

Creating with Sheet Plastic. Gregg LeFevre. LC 74-82326. (Little Craft Bk.). (Illus.). 48p. (gr. 10 up). 1974. 4.95 o.p. (ISBN 0-8069-5314-4); PLB 5.89 o.p. (ISBN 0-8069-5315-2). Sterling.

Creating Your Own Restaurant. John Herbert. (Herman's Foodservice Guide Ser.). (Illus., Prof. ed.). 1981. price not set (ISBN 0-89047-040-5). Herman Pub.

Creation. Gordon Lindsay. (Old Testament Ser.). 1.25 (ISBN 0-89985-123-1). Christ Nations.

Creation. Claus Westermann. Tr. by John J. Scullion from Ger. LC 74-75730. 144p. (Orig.). 1974. pap. 3.25 o.p. (ISBN 0-8006-1072-5, 1-1072). Fortress.

Creation: A Scientist's Choice. Zola Levitt. 132p. 1976. pap. 2.95 o.p. (ISBN 0-88207-629-9). Victor Bks.

Creation & Gospel: The New Situation of European Theology. Gustaf Wingren. LC 78-78183. (Toronto Studies in Theology: Vol. 2). lii, 189p. 1979. soft cover 19.95x (ISBN 0-88946-994-6). E Mellen.

Creation, Christ & Culture: Studies in Honor of T. F. Torrance. Ed. by W. A. McKinney. 336p. Repr. of 1976 ed. text ed. 17.95x (ISBN 0-567-01019-8). Attic Pr.

Creation of Deviance: Interpersonal & Organizational Determinants. new ed. Richard Hawkins & Gary Tiedman. (Sociology Ser). 320p. 1975. text ed. 17.95x (ISBN 0-675-08693-0). Merrill.

Creation of Purchasing Power: A Study in the Problem of Economic Stabilization. David M. Wright. xiv, 251p. 1980. Repr. of 1942 ed. lib. bdg. 17.50x (ISBN 0-87991-072-0). Porcupine Pr.

Creation of States in International Law. James Crawford. 1979. 49.95x (ISBN 0-19-825347-8). Oxford U Pr.

Creation of the National Health Service. Arthur J. Willcocks. (Orig.). 1967. text ed. 6.00x (ISBN 0-7100-4021-0); pap. 2.75x (ISBN 0-7100-4024-5). Humanities.

Creation of the Presidency, Seventeen Seventy-Five to Seventeen Eighty-Nine. Charles C. Thach. LC 74-87710. (American History, Politics & Law Ser). 1969. Repr. of 1922 ed. lib. bdg. 14.50 (ISBN 0-306-71680-1). Da Capo.

Creation of Tomorrow: Fifty Years of Magazine Science Fiction. Paul A. Carter. LC 77-5606. (Illus.). 1977. 16.00x (ISBN 0-231-04210-8). Columbia U Pr.

Creation of Tomorrow: Fifty Years of Magazine Science Fiction. Paul A. Carter. (Illus.). 330p. 1980. pap. 6.95 (ISBN 0-231-04211-6). Columbia U Pr.

Creation of Woman: A Psychoanalytic Inquiry into the Myth of Eve. Theodor Reik. LC 60-5613. 160p. 1973. Repr. of 1960 ed. pap. 1.95 o.p. (ISBN 0-07-051813-0, SP). McGraw.

Creation of Yugoslavia, Nineteen Fourteen to Nineteen Eighteen. Ed. by Dimitrije Djordjevic. LC 79-22331. 256p. 1980. text ed. 19.50 (ISBN 0-87436-253-9). ABC-Clio.

Creation, Science, & Theology: Essays in Response to Karl Barth. W. A. Whitehouse. 272p. (Orig.). 1981. pap. 10.95 (ISBN 0-8028-1870-6). Eerdmans.

Creation Vs. Evolution Handbook. Thomas F. Heinze. (Direction Books). 1973. pap. 2.25 (ISBN 0-8010-4002-7). Baker Bk.

Creational Theory of Man & of the Universe. Timothy R. McDaniel. (Illus.). 141p. 1980. deluxe ed. 36.35 (ISBN 0-89266-242-5). Am Classical Coll Pr.

Creationism: Its Basis, Its Essence, & Its Interwoven Relation to All Life. Reuben L. Katter. Date not set. pap. price not set (ISBN 0-685-96812-X). Theotes.

Creative Academic Bargaining: Managing Conflict in the Unionized College & University. Robert Birnbaum. 288p. 1981. text ed. 19.95x (ISBN 0-8077-2631-1). Tchrs Coll.

Creative Activities for Young Children. Mayesky et al. LC 78-52620. 1980. pap. 10.60 (ISBN 0-8273-1571-6); instructor's guide 1.50 (ISBN 0-8273-1572-4). Delmar.

Creative Activities Resource Book for Elementary School Teachers. Thomas Turner. (Illus.). 1978. pap. text ed. 13.95 (ISBN 0-87909-205-X). Reston.

Creative Administration in Physical Education & Athletics. Robert A. Pestolesi & William A. Sinclair. LC 77-7075. (Illus.). 1978. 16.95 (ISBN 0-13-188987-7). P-H.

Creative Administration in Recreation & Parks. 2nd ed. Richard G. Kraus & Joseph E. Curtis. LC 76-29696. (Illus.). 1977. text ed. 16.95 (ISBN 0-8016-2739-7). Mosby.

Creative Alternatives to Communism: Guidelines for the Future. Donald Wilhelm. 188p. 1980. 12.95x (ISBN 0-8290-0298-7); pap. 6.95x (ISBN 0-8290-0299-5). Irvington.

Creative Alternatives to Communism: Guidelines for Tomorrow's World. Donald Wilhelm. 1977. text ed. 13.00x (ISBN 0-333-21852-3); pap. text ed. 4.00x (ISBN 0-333-21856-6). Humanities.

Creative Art, Elementary Grades. rev. ed. Fran Trucksess. (Illus.). 1962. pap. 4.95x o.p. (ISBN 0-87108-169-5). Pruett.

Creative Art: Junior High Grades. Verle Mickish. (Illus.). 1962. pap. 4.95x o.p. (ISBN 0-87108-133-4). Pruett.

Creative Art Through Photography. Alan Kay. LC 72-8378. (Illus.). 128p. (gr. 5 up). 1973. 9.25 o.p. (ISBN 0-8231-1023-0). Branford.

Creative Arts. Malcolm Ross. LC 78-324078. (Organization in Schools Ser.). 1978. text ed. 27.95x (ISBN 0-435-80780-3); pap. text ed. 14.95x (ISBN 0-435-80781-1). Heinemann Ed.

Creative Bible Study. Lawrence O. Richards. 1979. pap. 5.95 (ISBN 0-310-31911-0). Zondervan.

Creative Bible Teaching. Lawrence O. Richards. 1970. 8.95 (ISBN 0-8024-1640-3). Moody.

Creative Bird Carving. William I. Tawes. LC 79-107781. (Illus.). 1969. 8.50 (ISBN 0-87033-141-8, Pub. by Tidewater). Cornell Maritime.

Creative Bookbinding. Pauline Johnson. LC 63-10798. (Illus.). 275p. 1973. pap. 12.95 (ISBN 0-295-95267-9). U of Wash Pr.

Creative Camera Collection: No. 5. Ed. by Colin Osman & Peter Turner. (Illus.). 1978. 27.50 (ISBN 0-685-67248-4, Pub. by Two Continents). Hippocrene Bks.

Creative Camera Techniques. Axel Bruck. LC 80-41402. (Illus.). 144p. 1981. 19.95 (ISBN 0-240-51106-9). Focal Pr.

Creative Cash: How to Sell Your Crafts, Needlework, Designs, & Know-How. Barbara Brabec. LC 79-64792. (Illus.). 1979. pap. 9.95 (ISBN 0-88453-017-5). Barrington.

Creative Christmas: Simple Crafts from Many Lands. Kathryn Shoemaker. 1978. pap. 7.95 (ISBN 0-03-045716-5). Winston Pr.

Creative Classroom. Kathryn Shoemaker. 1980. pap. 7.95 (ISBN 0-03-053441-0). Winston Pr.

Creative College Student: An Unmet Challenge. Ed. by Paul Heist. LC 68-21316. (Higher Education Ser.). 1968. 13.95x o.p. (ISBN 0-87589-015-6). Jossey-Bass.

Creative Color: A Practical Guide for Oil Painters. Wendon Blake. LC 79-1905. (Illus.). 176p. 1972. 21.95 o.p. (ISBN 0-8230-1035-X). Watson-Guptill.

Creative Coloring I. Dianne Draze. (Illus.). (gr. 1-6). 1978. wkbk 1.50 o.p. (ISBN 0-931724-05-8). Dandy Lion.

Creative Coloring II. Dianne Draze. (Illus.). (gr. 1-6). 1978. wkbk 1.50 o.p. (ISBN 0-931724-06-6). Dandy Lion.

Creative Communication. Fran A. Tanner. 402p. 1979. lib. bdg. 7.85 (ISBN 0-931054-01-X). Clark Pub.

Creative Conflict in Religious Education & Church Administration. Donald E. Bossart. LC 80-12704. 284p. (Orig.). 1980. pap. 9.95 (ISBN 0-89135-048-9). Religious Educ.

Creative Conflict: Learning to Love with Total Honesty. Christopher Hills. Ed. by Deborah Rozman & Ann Ray. LC 80-5562. (Illus.). 324p. (Orig.). 1980. pap. 5.95 (ISBN 0-916438-36-8). Univ of Trees.

Creative Cooking Sugar Free. Caroline Weiss et al. (Illus.). 1979. pap. 2.50 (ISBN 0-686-65551-6). Budlong.

Creative Cooking without Wheat, Milk & Eggs. Ruth R. Shattuck. LC 72-6392. 152p. 1973. 8.95 (ISBN 0-498-01157-7); large type o.p. 8.95 (ISBN 0-498-01856-3); pap. 5.95 (ISBN 0-498-02047-9). A S Barnes.

Creative Cost Improvement for Managers. Louis E. Tagliaferri. (Self-Teaching Guide Ser.). 208p. 1981. pap. text ed. 8.95 (ISBN 0-471-08708-4). Wiley.

Creative Craft Ideas for All Ages. Ed. by Shirley Beegle. (Illus., Orig.). (gr. k up). 1966. pap. 5.50 (ISBN 0-87239-321-6, 2795). Standard Pub.

Creative Crafts. Linda Hetzer. LC 77-28864. (Illustrated Crafts for Beginners). (Illus.). (gr. 3-7). Date not set. PLB cancelled (ISBN 0-8172-1194-2). Raintree Pubs.

Creative Crafts. Ed. by Angela Jeffs. (Illus.). 1977. 35.00 (ISBN 0-8069-5378-0); lib. bdg. 32.99 (ISBN 0-8069-5379-9). Sterling.

Creative Crafts in Education. Seonaid M. Robertson. (Illus.). 1967. Repr. of 1952 ed. 20.00 (ISBN 0-7100-2045-7). Routledge & Kegan.

Creative Crepe Cookery. William I. Kaufman. (Orig.). pap. 1.50 o.s.i. (ISBN 0-515-04259-5). Jove Pubns.

Creative Customizing. Ed. by Spence Murray. LC 78-50827. (Illus.). 176p. (Orig.). 1978. pap. 6.95 (ISBN 0-8227-5026-0). Petersen Pub.

Creative Design. Time Life Bks Editors. LC 74-29449. (Art of Sewing Ser.). (Illus.). 208p. (gr. 6 up). 1975. lib. bdg. 11.97 (ISBN 0-8094-1743-X). Silver.

Creative Design in Wall Hangings. Lili Blumenau. 1967. 16.00 o.p. (ISBN 0-87245-035-X). Textile Bk.

Creative Designs with Children at Worship. A. Roger Gobbel & Phillip C. Huber. LC 80-82225. 96p. (Orig.). 1981. pap. 4.95 (ISBN 0-8042-1526-X). John Knox.

Creative Dislocation: The Movement of Grace. Robert M. Brown. LC 80-16433. (Journey in Faith Ser.). 144p. 1980. 7.95 (ISBN 0-687-09826-2). Abingdon.

Creative Divorce: A New Opportunity for Personal Growth. Mel Krantzler. LC 73-82863. 268p. 1974. 8.95 (ISBN 0-87131-131-3). M Evans.

Creative Drama in the Classroom. 3rd ed. Nellie McCaslin. 1980. text ed. 10.95 (ISBN 0-582-28139-3). Longman.

Creative Dramatics for the Classroom Teacher. Ruth B. Heinig & Lyda Stillwell. LC 73-21875. 240p. 1974. 13.95 (ISBN 0-13-189407-2). P-H.

Creative Dramatics in the Classroom. 2nd ed. Nellie McCaslin. LC 73-88681. 1977. pap. 6.95x o.p. (ISBN 0-582-28007-9). Longman.

Creative Dreaming. Patricia Garfield. 256p. 1976. pap. 2.50 (ISBN 0-345-28468-2). Ballantine.

Creative Editing & Writing Workbook. Ed. by Emily P. Flint. 279p. 1979. 40.00 (ISBN 0-89964-038-9). CASE.

Creative Enamelling & Jewelry-Making. Katharina Zechlin. Tr. by Paul Kuttner. LC 65-20877. (gr. 10 up). 1965. 6.95 (ISBN 0-8069-5062-5); PLB 6.69 (ISBN 0-8069-5063-3). Sterling.

Creative Encounter. David B. Lutyens. 200p. 1980. Repr. of 1960 ed. lib. bdg. 30.00 (ISBN 0-89987-506-8). Darby Bks.

Creative Engineer: The Art of Inventing. new ed. Ed. by Winston E. Kock. (Illus.). 399p. 1978. 25.00 (ISBN 0-306-30987-4, Plenum Pr). Plenum Pub.

Creative Escapes. Barbara Christian. LC 80-65477. 1980. pap. 5.50 (ISBN 0-8224-1631-X). Pitman Learning.

Creative Experience. Mary P. Follett. 8.00 (ISBN 0-8446-1186-7). Peter Smith.

Creative Exploration in Crafts. Gretchen Andersen. (Illus.). 368p. 1976. 14.95 (ISBN 0-87909-169-X); pap. 9.95 (ISBN 0-87909-168-1). Reston.

Creative Expression in the Primary School. Peter Dixon. (Practical Guides for Teachers Ser.). (Illus.). 1974. pap. 5.95x (ISBN 0-631-94120-7, Pub. by Basil Blackwell). Biblio Dist.

Creative Firing: Why Management Firings Happen & How to Reduce Them. Chester Burger. Orig. Title: Walking the Executive Plank. 112p. 1973. pap. 1.50 o.s.i. (ISBN 0-02-008150-2, Collier). Macmillan.

Creative Fly Tying & Fishing. Rex Gerlach. 1974. 13.95 (ISBN 0-87691-122-X). Winchester Pr.

Creative Food Experiences for Children. rev. ed. Mary T. Goodwin & Gerry Pollen. (Illus.). 256p. 1980. text ed. 12.95 (ISBN 0-89329-028-9). Ctr Sci Public.

Creative Glass Blowing: Scientific & Ornamental. James E. Hammesfahr & Clair L. Stong. LC 68-14225. (Illus.). 1978. pap. text ed. 11.95x (ISBN 0-7167-0088-3). W H Freeman.

Creative Growth Games. Eugene Raudsepp & George P. Hough. LC 77-2522. (Illus.). 1977. pap. 3.95 o.p. (ISBN 0-15-622735-5, Harv). HarBraceJ.

Creative Growth with Handwriting. Walter B. Barbe et al. Incl. Readiness (ISBN 0-88309-233-6); Grade One. tchrs.' manual 9.95 (ISBN 0-88309-245-X); consumable (ISBN 0-88309-234-4); non-consumable (ISBN 0-88309-256-5); Grade Two. tchrs.' manual 9.95 (ISBN 0-88309-246-8); consumable (ISBN 0-88309-235-2); non-consumable; Book 2T. tchrs.' manual 9.95 (ISBN 0-88309-247-6); consumable (ISBN 0-88309-236-0); non-consumable (ISBN 0-88309-236-0); Grade 3T. tchrs.' manual 9.95 (ISBN 0-88309-248-4); consumable (ISBN 0-88309-259-X); non-consumable (ISBN 0-88309-237-9); Grade 4. tchrs.' manual 9.95 (ISBN 0-88309-250-6); consumable (ISBN 0-88309-239-5); non-consumable; Grade 5. tchrs.' manual 9.95 (ISBN 0-88309-251-4); consumable (ISBN 0-88309-262-X); non-consumable (ISBN 0-88309-240-9); Grade 6. tchrs.' manual 9.95 (ISBN 0-88309-252-2); consumable (ISBN 0-88309-263-8); non-consumable (ISBN 0-88309-241-7); Grade 7. tchrs.' manual 6.96 (ISBN 0-88309-253-0); consumable (ISBN 0-88309-264-6); non-consumable (ISBN 0-88309-242-5); Grade 8. tchrs.' manual 6.95 (ISBN 0-88309-254-9); consumable; non-consumable. (Illus.). 1979. pupil bk., consumable or non-consumable 1.97 ea. Zaner-Bloser.

Creative Guide for Preschool Teachers. Joanne Wylie. 1966. pap. 10.50 (ISBN 0-685-93229-X). Bobbs.

Creative Harmony & Musicianship: An Introduction to the Structure of Music. Howard A. Murphy & E. J. Stringham. 1951. pap. 16.95 (ISBN 0-13-189704-7). P-H.

Creative Home Decorating. Annette Stramesi. 7.95 (ISBN 0-916752-14-3). Green Hill.

Creative Home Economics Instruction. 2nd ed. Valerie Chamberlain & Joan Kelly. Ed. by Martha O'Neill. (Illus.). 256p. 1980. pap. text ed. 10.95 (ISBN 0-07-010424-7, W). McGraw.

Creative Home Economics Instruction. Valerie M. Chamberlain & Joan Kelly. (Illus.). 272p. 1974. pap. text ed. 10.95 (ISBN 0-07-010423-9, W). McGraw.

Creative Home Remodeling. Stanley Myers & Richard Figiel. (Illus.). 240p. 1981. text ed. 16.95 (ISBN 0-13-189613-X, Spec); pap. text ed. 7.95 (ISBN 0-13-189605-9, Spec). P-H.

Creative Homemaker. Mary L. Bouma. LC 73-17234. 1973. pap. 2.45 (ISBN 0-87123-078-X, 210508); study guide 0.95 (ISBN 0-87123-508-0). Bethany Fell.

Creative Ideas. Ernest Holmes. 1964. pap. 3.50 (ISBN 0-911336-00-1). Sci of Mind.
Creative Ideas for Bible Discovery. Monte Corley & Roy Nichols. LC 79-67509. (Bible Discovery Bks.). 1979. pap. 4.25 (ISBN 0-8344-0109-6). Sweet.
Creative Imagination: Enlightenment to Romanticism. James Engell. 1981. write for info. Harvard U Pr.
Creative Imagination in the Sufism of Ibn 'arabi. Henry Corbin. LC 68-20869. (Bollingen Ser.: XCI). (Illus.). 420p. 1980. pap. 6.95 (ISBN 0-691-01828-6). Princeton U Pr.
Creative Imagination: Your Key to High Accomplishment. Jona Lewis. (Illus.). 1980. pap. 12.95 o.p. (ISBN 0-930490-27-4). Future Shop.
Creative Imitation & Latin Literature. Ed. by D. West & T. Woodman. LC 79-1181. 1980. 36.00 (ISBN 0-521-22668-6). Cambridge U Pr.
Creative Intention. Earl Hubbard. 192p. 1974. 8.75 o.p. (ISBN 0-913456-67-5); pap. 3.95 (ISBN 0-913456-68-3). Interbk Inc.
Creative Interviewing: The Writer's Guide to Gathering Information by Asking Questions. K. Metzler. 1977. 12.95 (ISBN 0-13-189720-9); pap. 7.95 (ISBN 0-13-189712-8). P-H.
Creative Intimacy. Jerry Greenwald. 1977. pap. 2.75 (ISBN 0-515-05971-4). Jove Pubns.
Creative Jewelry. Patti Clarke. LC 77-90127. 1978. 13.95 (ISBN 0-8008-1995-0). Taplinger.
Creative Journal: The Art of Finding Yourself. Lucia Capacchione. LC 78-51590. (Illus.). 180p. 1980. pap. 9.95 (ISBN 0-8040-0798-5). Swallow.
Creative Lace-Making with Thread & Yarn. Harriet U. Fish. LC 72-81039. (Little Craft Book Ser.). (Illus.). 50p. 1972. 5.95 (ISBN 0-8069-5216-4); lib. bdg. 6.69 (ISBN 0-8069-5217-2). Sterling.
Creative Leadership in Elementary Schools. Dale L. Brubaker. LC 76-15719. 1976. pap. text ed. 6.95 (ISBN 0-8403-1494-9). Kendall-Hunt.
Creative Learning & Teaching. E. Paul Torrance & R. E. Myers. (Illus.). 1970. text ed. 11.95x scp (ISBN 0-06-046633-2, HarpC). Har-Row.
Creative Learning in Perspective. T. P. Jones. LC 72-8705. 112p. 1972. 7.95 o.p. (ISBN 0-470-44885-7). Halsted Pr.
Creative Life. Sarvepalli Radhakrishnan. 146p. 1976. pap. 2.40 (ISBN 0-89253-049-9). Ind-US Inc.
Creative Living. Ernest Holmes. Ed. by Willis Kinnear. 96p. 1975. pap. 4.50 (ISBN 0-911336-63-X). Sci of Mind.
Creative Living. National Federation of Community Assoc. 76p. 1974. pap. text ed. 3.75x (ISBN 0-7199-0896-5, Pub. by Bedford England). Renouf.
Creative Love. Louis H. Evans, Jr. 1979. pap. 1.75 o.p. (ISBN 0-449-14021-0, GM). Fawcett.
Creative Malady. George Pickering. 1974. 13.95 (ISBN 0-19-519800-X). Oxford U Pr.
Creative Management Techniques in Interscholastic Athletics. D. E. Fuoss & R. J. Troppman. LC 76-46500. 1977. 19.95 (ISBN 0-471-28815-2). Wiley.
Creative Marriage: The Middle Years. Clayton D. Barbeau. 160p. 1976. 6.95 (ISBN 0-8164-0284-1). Crossroad NY.
Creative Mental Health Services for the Elderly. R. M. Glasscote et al. 189p. 1977. 10.00 (ISBN 0-685-86111-2). Am Psychiatric.
Creative Music Education. Murray Schafer. LC 75-30286. (Illus.). 1976. pap. text ed. 9.95 (ISBN 0-02-872330-9). Schirmer Bks.
Creative Music Theory. Mildred N. Landecker. (gr. 8-12). 1972. pap. text ed. 13.20 o.p. (ISBN 0-205-02775-X, 5827752); tchr's guide 2.00 o.p. (ISBN 0-205-02776-8, 5827760). Allyn.
Creative Newsletter Graphics. Charles M. Helmken. 1976. 40.00 (ISBN 0-89964-014-1). CASE.
Creative Origami. Kunihiko Kasahara. LC 67-87040. (Illus.). 1977. pap. 12.95 (ISBN 0-87040-411-3). Japan Pubns.
Creative Package: A Working Text for Advertising Copy & Layout. Sandra B. Ernst. 1979. pap. text ed. 10.50 (ISBN 0-88244-185-X). Grid Pub.
Creative Paper Craft. Ernst Rottger. 1973. pap. 11.95 (ISBN 0-7134-2805-8, Pub. by Batsford England). David & Charles.
Creative Papercraft. Stuart Grainger. (Illus.). 128p. 1980. 12.95 (ISBN 0-7137-1008-X, Pub. by Blandford Pr England). Sterling.
Creative Pencil Drawing. Paul Hogarth. (Illus.). 1964. 14.95 o.p. (ISBN 0-8230-1100-3); pap. 9.95 o.p. (ISBN 0-8230-1101-1). Watson-Guptill.
Creative Perspective. Robert W. Gill. (Illus.). 1980. pap. 5.95 (ISBN 0-500-27056-2). Thames Hudson.
Creative Philanthropy: Carnegie Corporation in Africa, 1953-74. E. Jefferson Murphy. LC 76-14886. 1976. text ed. 19.90 (ISBN 0-8077-2473-4); pap. text ed. 9.95 (ISBN 0-8077-2479-3). Tchrs Coll.
Creative Piano: A Modular Approach for Adult Beginners. Lily Owyang & Linda Ostrander. LC 77-78909. (Illus.). 1978. pap. text ed. 14.50 (ISBN 0-395-25569-4). HM.
Creative Picture Framing. William J. Cantore & Virginia B. Cantore. (Illus.). 128p. 1981. 12.95 (ISBN 0-13-190645-3, Spec); pap. 6.95 (ISBN 0-13-190637-2). P-H.
Creative Play Acting: Learning Through Drama. 2nd ed. Isabel B. Burger. (Illus.). 1966. 10.50 o.p. (ISBN 0-8260-1535-2). Wiley.
Creative Play Direction. Robert Cohen & John Harrop. (Theater & Drama Ser). (Illus.). 304p. 1974. ref. ed. 14.95 (ISBN 0-13-190918-5). P-H.
Creative Plays & Programs for Girls & Boys. Claire Boiko. (gr. 3-6). 1972. 9.95 (ISBN 0-8238-0134-9). Plays.
Creative Power of Mind. Ed. by Willis Kinnear. 1966. pap. 7.95 (ISBN 0-911336-01-X). Sci of Mind.
Creative Procedures for Adult Groups. Ed. by Harold D. Minor. LC 68-17624. (Orig.). 1968. pap. 2.50 o.p. (ISBN 0-687-09833-5). Abingdon.
Creative Procrastination. Frieda Porat. LC 80-7750. 192p. (Orig.). 1980. pap. text ed. 4.95 (ISBN 0-06-250690-0, BN3003, HarpR). Har-Row.
Creative Recreation for the Mentally Retarded. Issam B. Amary. 128p. 1975. 14.75 (ISBN 0-398-03292-0). C C Thomas.
Creative Retirement. J. Donovan. 1977. 110.00 o.p. (ISBN 0-201-01059-3); 5 pack wkbks. 55.00 o.p. (ISBN 0-201-01060-7). A-W.
Creative Rhetoric. Francine Hardaway. 304p. 1976. pap. text ed. 9.95 (ISBN 0-13-191072-8). P-H.
Creative Rubbings. H. E. Andrew. 1972. 16.95 (ISBN 0-7134-2257-2, Pub. by Batsford England). David & Charles.
Creative Sales Counseling: Using Psychology to Sell Real Estate. James E. Lumley. 1981. pap. 24.95 (ISBN 0-933928-04-1). Realvest Pub Co.
Creative Sculpture. William I. Tawes. LC 76-10862. (Illus.). 1976. 10.00 (ISBN 0-87033-219-8, Pub. by Tidewater). Cornell Maritime.
Creative Seascape Painting. Edward Betts. 160p. 1981. 19.15. Watson-Guptill.
Creative Selling. Ben Feldman. LC 79-88528. (Illus.). 1979. 9.95 (ISBN 0-87863-054-6). Farnswth Pub.
Creative Shellcraft. Katherine N. Cutler. LC 73-148484. 1971. PLB 7.44 (ISBN 0-688-50988-6); pap. 2.95 (ISBN 0-688-45011-3). Lothrop.
Creative Social Work. Ed. by David Brandon & Bill Jordan. 1979. 29.50x (ISBN 0-631-11831-4, Pub. by Basil Blackwell); pap. 10.00x (ISBN 0-631-11841-1). Biblio Dist.
Creative Strategy & Tactics in Advertising: A Managerial Approach to Copywriting & Production. Sherilyn Zeigler & J. Douglas Johnson. LC 80-23899. (Advertising Ser.). 360p. 1981. text ed. 19.95 (ISBN 0-88244-229-5). Grid Pub.
Creative Sunprinting. Peter Frederick. (Illus.). 192p. 1980. 35.00 (ISBN 0-240-51045-3). Focal Pr.
Creative Survival in Education Bureaucracies. Dale L. Brubaker & Roland H. Nelson, Jr. LC 73-17608. 1974. 16.00 (ISBN 0-8211-0125-0); text ed. 14.50x (ISBN 0-685-42627-0). McCutchan.
Creative Teachers: Who Wants Them? Robert Hahn. LC 73-6592. 272p. 1973. 16.50 (ISBN 0-471-33905-9, Pub. by Wiley). Krieger.
Creative Teaching. Audrey Nicholls & Howard Nicholls. (Unwin Education Books). 1975. text ed. 13.50x (ISBN 0-04-371039-5); pap. text ed. 6.95x (ISBN 0-04-371040-9). Allen Unwin.
Creative Teaching in Clinical Nursing. 3rd ed. Jean E. Schweer. LC 75-31627. (Illus.). 316p. 1976. pap. 10.95 (ISBN 0-8016-4377-5). Mosby.
Creative Teaching of Language Arts in the Elementary School, 2. 2nd ed. James A. Smith. 384p. 1973. pap. text ed. 10.95x (ISBN 0-205-03834-4, 2238349). Allyn.
Creative Teaching of Mathematics in the Elementary School. 2nd ed. Alvin M. Westcott & James A. Smith. 1978. pap. text ed. 11.50 (ISBN 0-205-06051-X). Allyn.
Creative Teaching of Reading in the Elementary School. 2nd ed. James A. Smith. (Series in Creative Teaching in the Elementary School). 350p. 1975. text ed. 14.95x (ISBN 0-205-04688-6); pap. text ed. 10.45x (ISBN 0-205-04687-8, 2246880). Allyn.
Creative Teaching of Science in the Elementary School. 2nd ed. Albert Piltz & Robert Sund. 320p. 1974. pap. text ed. 11.95x (ISBN 0-205-04278-3). Allyn.
Creative Teaching of the Social Studies in the Elementary School. James A. Smith. (Orig.). 1967. pap. text ed. 10.95x o.p. (ISBN 0-205-00089-4, 2200899). Allyn.
Creative Techniques in Landscape Photography. Gerald Woods & John Williams. LC 80-8396. (Illus.). 200p. 1981. 18.95 (ISBN 0-06-014835-7, HarpT). Har-Row.
Creative Themes. Henry Pluckrose. (Illus.). 1969. 5.25x o.p. (ISBN 0-237-28647-5). Intl Pubns Serv.
Creative Thinking & Brainstorming. J. Geoffrey Rawlinson. LC 80-22724. 144p. 1981. 14.95 (ISBN 0-470-27091-8). Halsted Pr.
Creative Thread Design. Mair Morris. LC 73-17334. (Illus.). 88p. 1974. 9.95 (ISBN 0-8231-7033-0). Branford.
Creative Use of Clay: In First & Middle Schools. Michael B. Moulder. (Practical Guides for Teachers Ser.). (Illus.). 1973. pap. 3.50x o.p. (ISBN 0-631-14060-3, Pub. by Basil Blackwell). Biblio Dist.
Creative Vision: A Longitudinal Study of Problem Finding in Art. Jacob W. Getzels & Mihaly Csikszentmihalyi. LC 76-16862. 304p. 1976. 24.95 (ISBN 0-471-01486-9, Pub. by Wiley-Interscience). Wiley.
Creative Watercolor Techniques. Zoltan Szabo. (Illus.). 176p. 1974. 18.95 (ISBN 0-8230-1119-4). Watson-Guptill.
Creative Watercolour Techniques. John Blockley. (Leisure Arts Painting Ser.). (Illus.). 1980. pap. 2.50 (ISBN 0-8008-2005-3, Pentalic). Taplinger.
Creative Way to Finding the Best Job for You. Arthur C. Simon. (Illus.). 1980. pap. 12.95 o.p. (ISBN 0-930490-22-3). Future Shop.
Creative Ways with Acrylic Painting. Ed. by Walter Brooks. 1974. pap. 1.25 o.p. (ISBN 0-307-40054-9, Golden Pr). Western Pub.
Creative Ways with Drawing. Ed. by Walter Brooks. 1974. pap. 1.25 o.p. (ISBN 0-307-40052-2, Golden Pr). Western Pub.
Creative Ways with Drawing Dogs & Cats. Ed. by Walter Brooks. 1974. pap. 1.25 o.p. (ISBN 0-307-40053-0, Golden Pr). Western Pub.
Creative Ways with Flower Painting. Ed. by Walter Brooks. 1974. pap. 1.25 o.p. (ISBN 0-307-40055-7, Golden Pr). Western Pub.
Creative Ways with Oil Painting. Ed. by Walter Brooks. 1974. pap. 1.25 o.p. (ISBN 0-307-40051-4, Golden Pr). Western Pub.
Creative Ways with Watercolor Painting. Ed. by Walter Brooks. 1974. pap. 1.25 o.p. (ISBN 0-307-40050-6, Golden Pr). Western Pub.
Creative Woodwork. P. F. Lye. (Illus.). 1974. cloth 15.95x (ISBN 0-245-53168-8); pap. 9.95x. Intl Ideas.
Creative Worklife. Don N. Scobel. 1980. 12.95x (ISBN 0-87201-905-5). Gulf Pub.
Creative Writing. John Freeman. (gr. 9-12). pap. 3.95 (ISBN 0-584-62006-3). Transatlantic.
Creative Writing. Gary Grimm & Don Mitchell. (gr. 3-8). 1976. 7.95 (ISBN 0-916456-04-8, GA61). Good Apple.
Creative Writing Activities, 2-6. Constance McAllister. (gr. 2-6). 1980. write for info. (ISBN 0-87534-176-4). Highlights.
Creative Writing for Juniors. Barry Maybury. 1972. pap. 16.95 (ISBN 0-7134-3175-X, Pub. by Batsford England). David & Charles.
Creative Writing: From Thought to Action. Holly Hickler & C. Lowell May. 1979. pap. text ed. 5.32 (ISBN 0-205-06187-7, 4961870); wkbk. 5.36 (ISBN 0-685-99030-3). Allyn.
Creative Years. Reuel L. Howe. (Orig.). pap. 3.95 (ISBN 0-8164-2012-2, SP8). Crossroad NY.
Creatively Gifted: Recognising & Developing the Creative Personality. David Willings. 184p. 30.00x (ISBN 0-85941-120-6, Pub. by Woodhead-Faulkner England). State Mutual Bk.
Creativite lexicale. Louis Guilbert. (Collection langue et langage). 285p. (Fr.). 1975. pap. 23.95 (ISBN 2-03-070340-0). Larousse.
Creativity & God: A Challenge to Process Theology. Robert C. Neville. 192p. 1980. 9.95 (ISBN 0-8164-0120-9). Crossroad NY.
Creativity & Imagination. Jacolyn Mott. LC 73-610. (Illus.). (gr. 5-12). 1973. PLB 7.50 o.p. (ISBN 0-87191-249-X). Creative Ed.
Creativity & Innovation in Engineering. S. A. Gregory. 313p. 1973. 19.50x o.p. (ISBN 0-408-70339-3). Transatlantic.
Creativity & Innovation in Organizations. Dean C. Dauw. 380p. 1980. pap. text ed. 12.95x (ISBN 0-917974-42-5). Waveland Pr.
Creativity & Psychopathology: A Neurocognitive Perspective. Robert A. Prentky. 282p. 1980. 27.95 (ISBN 0-03-053376-7). Praeger.
Creativity in Henry Nelson Wieman. William S. Minor. LC 77-8087. (ATLA Monograph Ser.: No. 11). 250p. 1977. lib. bdg. 12.00 (ISBN 0-8108-1041-7). Scarecrow.
Creativity in Human Development: An Interpretive & Annotated Bibliography. A. R. Arasteh & J. D. Arasteh. 1976. 12.95 (ISBN 0-470-98933-5). Halsted Pr.
Creativity in Orthopaedics: Marius N. Smith-Peterson Commemoration. Association of Bone & Joint Surgeons. Ed. by Marshall R. Urist. (Clinical Orthopaedics Ser., Vol. 66). 1969. 15.00 (ISBN 0-685-22847-9). Lippincott.
Creativity: Road to Self Discovery. Irwin DiCyan. 1978. pap. 1.95 o.s.i. (ISBN 0-515-04234-X). Jove Pubns.
Creativity: Theoretical & Socio-Cosmic Reflections. Ignacio L. Gotz. LC 78-59126. 1978. pap. text ed. 7.75 (ISBN 0-8191-0548-1). U Pr of Amer.
Creativity: What Is It? Daniel Cohen. LC 77-23481. (Illus.). 160p. (gr. 7 up). 1977. 5.95 (ISBN 0-87131-245-X). M Evans.
Creator & Man. Warren B. Blumenthal. LC 80-5843. 139p. 1980. lib. bdg. 15.75 (ISBN 0-8191-1340-9); pap. text ed. 7.50 (ISBN 0-8191-1341-7). U Pr of Amer.
Creature! A Chrestomathy of "Monstery". Bill Pronzini. LC 80-70221. 304p. 1981. 12.95 (ISBN 0-87795-310-4); pap. 5.95 (ISBN 0-87795-321-X). Arbor Hse.
Creature from the Black Lagoon. 1977. pap. 1.25 o.p. (ISBN 0-425-03464-X, Medallion). Berkley Pub.
Creature of Creatures: Selected Poems. Danilo Dolci. Ed. by Justin Vitiello. (Stanford French & Italian Studies: Col. 22). Orig. Title: Creatura Di Creature, Poseie, 1949-1978. 136p. 1980. pap. 20.00 (ISBN 0-915838-17-6). Anma Libri.
Creature Teachers. Hiriam Alexander et al. (Illus.). (gr. 1-3). 1974. student's book 3.99 (ISBN 0-87892-871-5); tchr's handbook 3.99 (ISBN 0-87892-875-8); tapes 167.25 (ISBN 0-87892-876-6). Economy Co.
Creatures from Lost Worlds. Seymour Simon. LC 78-25875. (Eerie Ser.). (Illus.). (gr. 2-4). 1979. 7.95 (ISBN 0-397-31834-0); PLB 7.89 (ISBN 0-397-31852-9). Lippincott.
Creatures from the UFO's. Daniel Cohen. LC 78-7730. (High Interest-Low Vocabulary Book). (Illus.). (gr. 4 up). 1978. 5.95 (ISBN 0-396-07582-7). Dodd.
Creatures from UFO's. Daniel Cohen. (gr. 4 up). 1979. pap. 1.50 (ISBN 0-671-29951-4). Archway.
Creatures of Darkness. John F. Waters. LC 74-78113. (Illus.). 128p. (gr. 3-7). 1975. 5.95 o.p. (ISBN 0-8027-6199-2); PLB 5.83 (ISBN 0-8027-6200-X). Walker & Co.
Creatures of Light & Darkness. Roger Zelazny. 1976. pap. 1.50 (ISBN 0-380-01122-0, 35956). Avon.
Creatures of Mystery. Jan Fortman. LC 77-24705. (Great Unsolved Mysteries Ser.). (Illus.). (gr. 4-5). 1977. PLB 9.65 (ISBN 0-8172-1063-6). Raintree Pubs.
Creatures of Paradise: Pictures to Grow Up With. Bryan Holme. (Illus.). 96p. (gr. 4 up). 1980. 12.95 (ISBN 0-19-520205-8). Oxford U Pr.
Creatures of the Outer Edge. Jerome Clark & Loren Coleman. 1978. pap. 1.95 o.s.i. (ISBN 0-446-89150-9). Warner Bks.
Creatures That Help Each Other. Ernest Prescott. (Easy-Read Wildlife Bk.). (Illus.). 31p. (gr. 2-4). 1976. PLB 4.90 o.p. (ISBN 0-531-00354-X). Watts.
Creatures That Look Alike. Susan Harris. (Easy-Read Wildlife Bks.). (Illus.). (gr. 2 up). 1979. PLB 6.45 s&l (ISBN 0-531-01375-8). Watts.
Crecimiento De la Iglesia. Tr. by Melvin Hodges. (Spanish Bks.). (Span.). 1979. 1.50 (ISBN 0-8297-0905-3). Life Pubs Intl.
Credential Society: A Historical Sociology of Education & Stratification. Randall Collins. LC 78-20042. 1979. 13.50 (ISBN 0-12-181360-6). Acad Pr.
Credentials: A Guide to Business Designations. Mona A. Milbrath. LC 80-66740. 221p. (Orig.). 1980. pap. 9.95 (ISBN 0-936324-01-5). Blue River.
Credit & Borrowing in Illinois. William R. Wishard. LC 79-13022. 1981. pap. 6.95 (ISBN 0-89666-005-2, Dist. by Caroline Hse.). Cragmont Pubns.
Credit & Borrowing in New York. William R. Wishard. LC 79-12957. 1981. pap. 6.95 (ISBN 0-89666-004-4, Dist. by Caroline Hse.). Cragmont Pubns.
Credit & Borrowing in Texas: Consumers' Rights & Duties. William R. Wishard & Frederick E. Felder. LC 78-15355. 1978. pap. 6.95 (ISBN 0-89666-001-X). Cragmont Pubns.
Credit & Collection Letters. 2nd ed. Ed. by Nacm. 324p. 1971. loose-leaf 23.00 (ISBN 0-934914-01-X). NACM.
Credit & Collections: A Practical Guide. Rick S. Hayes. LC 77-20141. (Illus.). 1978. 22.50 (ISBN 0-8436-0753-X). CBI Pub.
Credit & Collections for Small Business. Donald Kitzing. Ed. by William R. Newton. (Illus.). 192p. 1981. 15.95 (ISBN 0-07-034915-0, P&RB). McGraw.
Credit & Free Enterprise: A Chance to Survive. Joseph P. Krug. 1977. pap. 5.50 (ISBN 0-934914-04-4). NACM.
Credit Clues in Financial Statements. Ed. by Nacm. 1975. pap. 3.95 (ISBN 0-934914-20-6). NACM.

Credit Department Management. Margaret A. Hoffman & Gerald C. Fischer. LC 80-65026. (Illus.). 264p. 1980. 23.00 (ISBN 0-936742-00-3). R Morris Assocs.

Credit in Early America. Sol Barzman. 1975. pap. 2.95 (ISBN 0-934914-11-7). NACM.

Credit Language. Jim Richey. (Survival Vocabulary Ser.). (Illus.). 48p. (gr. 7-12). 1980. pap. text ed. 2.45 (ISBN 0-915510-36-7). Janus Bks.

Credit Management: How to Manage Credit Effectively. R. M. Bass. 352p. 1979. pap. 14.75x (ISBN 0-220-67029-3, Pub. by Busn Bks England). Renouf.

Credit Manual of Commercial Laws. Ed. by NACM Publications. 1980. 30.00 o.p. (ISBN 0-934914-33-8). NACM.

Credit Manual of Commercial Laws, 1981 Ed. 1980. 32.00 (ISBN 0-934914-37-0). NACM.

Credits & Collections. 5th ed. Richard P. Ettinger & D. E. Golieb. 1962. text ed. 18.95 (ISBN 0-13-192641-1). P-H.

Credulities Past & Present. William Jones. LC 67-24355. 1968. Repr. of 1880 ed. 22.00 (ISBN 0-8103-3447-X). Gale.

Cree Life: The Art of Allen Sapp. Allen Sapp. (Illus.). 1977. 24.95 (ISBN 0-295-95684-4, Pub. by Douglas & McIntyre Canada). U of Wash Pr.

Creed & Catechetics. Eugene Kevane. 1978. lib. bdg. 12.50 o.p. (ISBN 0-87061-007-4); pap. text ed. 7.95 o.p. (ISBN 0-685-03667-7). Chr Classics.

Creed & Personal Identity: The Meaning of the Apostles' Creed. David B. Harned. LC 80-3056. 120p. 1981. 6.95 (ISBN 0-8006-0645-0, 1-645). Fortress.

Creed Country. Jenny Overton. (gr. 7 up). 1970. 4.95g o.s.i. (ISBN 0-02-769000-8). Macmillan.

Creed for a Young Catholic. Richard Chilson. 128p. (Orig.). (gr. 5-9). pap. 2.45 (ISBN 0-529-05780-8). Collins Pubs.

Creed for a Young Catholic. Richard Chilson. LC 80-2073. 128p. 1981. pap. 2.75 (ISBN 0-385-17436-5, Im). Doubleday.

Creeds & Platforms of Congregationalism. Ed. by Williston Walker. LC 60-14698. 1960. 10.95 (ISBN 0-8298-0034-4). Pilgrim NY.

Creeds of the Churches: A Reader in Christian Doctrine from the Bible to the Present. rev. ed. Ed. by John H. Leith. LC 73-5346. 608p. 1973. pap. 5.95 (ISBN 0-8042-0515-9). John Knox.

Creek. Victor Depta. LC 72-85541. 1973. 7.95 (ISBN 0-8214-0121-1). Ohio U Pr.

Creek Called Wounded Knee. Douglas C. Jones. 1979. pap. 2.50 (ISBN 0-446-91121-6). Warner Bks.

Creek Called Wounded Knee. Douglas C. Jones. LC 78-16660. 1978. 8.95 o.p. (ISBN 0-684-15822-1, ScribT). Scribner.

Creek Indians. James F. Doster. Ed. by David A. Horr. (American Indian Ethnohistory Ser.). 1978. lib. bdg. 42.00 (ISBN 0-8240-0788-3). Garland Pub.

Creek Mary's Blood. Dee Brown. 1981. pap. 3.50 (ISBN 0-671-42028-3). PB.

Creeks: A Critical Bibliography. Michael D. Green. LC 79-2166. (Newberry Library Center for the History of the American Indian Bibliographical Ser.). 132p. (Orig.). 1980. pap. 4.95x (ISBN 0-253-31776-2). Ind U Pr.

Creel Report. U. S. Committee on Public Information. LC 75-37319. (Civil Liberties in American History Ser). 290p. 1972. Repr. of 1920 ed. lib. bdg. 32.50 (ISBN 0-306-70241-X). Da Capo.

Creencias Basicas. (Aglow Bible Study: Bk. 5). 64p. (Sp.). 1.95 (ISBN 0-930756-29-0, 4220-5(S)). Women's Aglow.

Creep. Susan Dodson. LC 79-1102. 224p. (gr. 7 up). 1979. 7.95 (ISBN 0-590-07599-3, Four Winds). Schol Bk Serv.

Creep Analysis. Harry Kraus. LC 80-15242. 250p. 1980. 28.75 (ISBN 0-471-06255-3, Pub. by Wiley-Interscience). Wiley.

Creep, Viscoelasticity & Creep Fracture in Solids. John Gittus. LC 74-26524. 725p. 1975. 98.95 (ISBN 0-470-30265-8). Halsted Pr.

Creepies, Creepies, Creepies. Ed. by Helen Hoke. (Terrific Triple Titles Ser.). (Illus.). (gr. 7 up). 1977. s&l 7.90 (ISBN 0-531-01323-5). Watts.

Cremation Cemeteries in Eastern Massachusetts. Dena F. Dincauze. LC 68-2247. (Peabody Museum Papers Ser.: Vol. 59, No.1). 1968. pap. text ed. 10.00 (ISBN 0-87365-171-5). Peabody Harvard.

Creo en el Espiritu Santo. Michael Green. Tr. by Ernesto S. Vilela from Eng. LC 77-164. (Serie Creo). 267p. (Orig., Span.). 1977. pap. 3.95 (ISBN 0-89922-090-8). Edit Caribe.

Creo en la Evangelizacion. David Watson. Tr. by Elsa S. Schwieters from Eng. (Serie Creo). 235p. (Orig., Span.). 1979. pap. 3.95 (ISBN 0-89922-133-5). Edit Caribe.

Creo en la Gran Comision. Max Warren. Tr. by Edwin Sipowicz from Eng. LC 78-54272. (Serie Creo). 205p. (Orig., Span.). 1978. pap. 3.95 (ISBN 0-89922-112-2). Edit Caribe.

Creo en la Resurreccion de Jesus. George E. Ladd. Tr. by Miguel Blanch from Eng. LC 77-79934. (Serie Creo). 204p. (Orig., Span.). 1977. pap. 3.95 (ISBN 0-89922-091-6). Edit Caribe.

Creo en la Revalacion. Leon Morris. Tr. by Miguel Blanch from Eng. (Serie Creo). 223p. (Orig., Span.). 1979. pap. 3.95 (ISBN 0-89922-140-8). Edit Caribe.

Creole. Stephen Cosgrove. (Serendipity Bks). (Illus.). (gr. k-4). 1978. PLB 6.95 (ISBN 0-87191-655-X). Creative Ed.

Creole Cajun Cooking Cards from an Old New Orleans Bag. Terry Flettrich & Jan Carr. 1973. 2.95 (ISBN 0-88289-014-X). Pelican.

Creole Phonology. Henri Tinelli. (Janua Linguarum, Ser. Practica: No. 117). 1980. pap. text ed. 40.00x (ISBN 90-279-3048-1). Mouton.

Creoles of Sierra Leone: Responses to Colonialism, 1870-1945. Leo Spitzer. LC 74-5908. 304p. 1974. 25.00x (ISBN 0-299-06590-1). U of Wis Pr.

Crepe & Pancake Cookbook. Cecilia Norman. (Illus.). 1979. 9.95 o.p. (ISBN 0-214-20577-0, ADON 8074-4, Dist by Arco). Barrie & Jenkins.

Crepe Cookery. Mable Hoffman. LC 76-3230. (Illus.). 1976. pap. 5.95 (ISBN 0-912656-50-6). H P Bks.

Crepes. Fayal Greene. 1977. pap. 1.25 o.p. (ISBN 0-445-08560-6). Popular Lib.

Crescent & the Cross: The Early Crusades. Daniel Theis. LC 78-2385. (gr. 6 up). 1978. 8.95 o.p. (ISBN 0-525-66596-X). Elsevier-Nelson.

Crescent City Silver. Carey T. Mackie et al. (Illus.). vi, 130p. 1980. pap. 15.00x (ISBN 0-917860-05-5). Historic New Orleans.

Crescent Dictionary of American Politics. Eugene J. McCarthy. 1962. 5.95 o.s.i. (ISBN 0-02-582810-X). Macmillan.

Crescent Dictionary of Mathematics. William Karush. 1962. 7.50 o.s.i. (ISBN 0-02-560690-5). Macmillan.

Crestwood Heights: A North American Suburb. John R. Seeley et al. LC 56-9099. (Illus.). 1956. pap. 7.50 (ISBN 0-8020-6021-8). U of Toronto Pr.

Cretaceous of Llano Estacado of Texas. J. P. Brand. (Illus.). 59p. 1953. 0.70 (RI 20). Bur Econ Geology.

Cretan Runner. George Psychoudakis. Tr. by Patrick L. Fermor. (Illus.). 1978. pap. 8.50 (ISBN 0-7195-3475-5). Transatlantic.

Crete. Robin Mead. (Illus.). 144p. 1980. 24.00 (ISBN 0-7134-1331-X, Pub. by Batsford England). David & Charles.

Crewel Embroidery. Eleanor Young. (Career Concise Guides Ser.). (Illus.). 96p. (gr. 6 up). 1976. PLB 6.45 (ISBN 0-531-00341-8). Watts.

Crib Quilts: And Other Small Wonders. Thomas K. Woodard & Blanche Greenstein. Ed. by Cyril T. Nelson. (Illus.). 144p. 1981. 27.95 (ISBN 0-525-20565-9); pap. 15.95 (ISBN 0-525-47628-8). Dutton.

Cribbage Is the Name of the Game. Richard E. Lowder. (Everday Handbook Ser.). (Illus.). 96p. 1975. pap. 2.50 (ISBN 0-06-463402-7, EH 402, Eh). Har-Row.

Cricket. Nathaniel Lande. 1981. 12.95 (ISBN 0-453-00392-3, H392). NAL.

Cricket Beneath the Waterfall & Other Stories. Miroslav Krleza. Ed. by Branko Lenski. LC 72-83354. 256p. 1972. 8.95 (ISBN 0-8149-0699-0). Vanguard.

Cricket Boy: A Chinese Tale Retold. Feenie Ziner & Ed Young. LC 76-51999. (gr. 3 up). 1977. PLB 6.95 (ISBN 0-385-12507-0); PLB (ISBN 0-385-12507-0). Doubleday.

Cricket in a Thicket. Aileen Fisher. (Illus.). (gr. k-3). 1963. reinforced bdg. 4.95 o.p. (ISBN 0-684-13456-X); pap. 0.95 o.p. (ISBN 0-684-12784-9, SBF15, ScribJ). Scribner.

Cricket in the Grass. Philip Van Soelen. LC 79-4108. (Sierra Club-Scribner's Juvenile Ser.). (Illus.). 128p. 1979. 9.95 (ISBN 0-684-16110-9). Scribner.

Cricket in the Thorn Tree: Helen Suzman & the Progressive Party of South Africa. Joanna Strangwayes-Booth. LC 76-486. 320p. 1976. 12.50x (ISBN 0-253-31483-6). Ind U Pr.

Cricket in Times Square. George Selden. (Illus.). (gr. 2-7). 1970. pap. 1.50 (ISBN 0-440-41563-2, YB). Dell.

Cricket Sings. Federico G. Lorca. Tr. by Will Kirkland. LC 80-15560. (Illus.). 64p. (Orig.). 1980. pap. 4.95 (ISBN 0-8112-0734-X, NDP506). New Directions.

Cricket Term. Antonia Forest. (gr. 5 up). 1974. 9.95 (ISBN 0-571-10632-3, Pub. by Faber & Faber). Merrimack Bk Serv.

Cricket's Cookery. Pauline Watson & Cricket Magazine Editors. LC 77-3637. (Illus.). (gr. 1-6). 1977. 2.95 (ISBN 0-394-83540-9, BYR); PLB 3.99 (ISBN 0-394-93540-3). Random.

Cricket's Expeditions: Outdoor & Indoor Activities. Kathleen Leverich & Cricket Magazine Editors. LC 77-3231. (Illus.). (gr. 1-6). 1977. 2.95 (ISBN 0-394-83543-3, BYR); PLB 3.99 (ISBN 0-394-93543-8). Random.

Cricket's Jokes, Riddles & Other Stuff. Marcia Leonard & Cricket Magazine Editors. LC 77-3164. (Illus.). (gr. 1-6). 1977. 2.95 (ISBN 0-394-83545-X); PLB 3.99 (ISBN 0-394-93545-4). Random.

Cries - but Silent. Andrew Costello. 180p. 1981. 8.95 (ISBN 0-88347-126-4). Thomas More.

Cries of London. F. Newbery. Ed. by Alison Lurie & Justin G. Schiller. Incl. Cries of New York. Samuel Wood. LC 75-32142. (Classics of Children's Literature 1621-1932 Ser.). PLB 38.00 (ISBN 0-8240-2258-0). Garland Pub.

Crime. Virginia Adams. (Human Behavior Ser.). 1976. 9.95 (ISBN 0-8094-1962-9). Time-Life.

Crime. Nagrib Mahfouz. pap. 5.50 arabic (ISBN 0-685-82818-2). Intl Bk Ctr.

Crime. Ed. by Time Life Books. LC 76-29184. (Human Behavior). (Illus.). (gr. 5 up). 1976. PLB 9.99 o.p. (ISBN 0-8094-1963-7, Pub. by Time-Life). Silver.

Crime, Abnormal Minds & the Law. Ernest B. Hoag & Edward H. Williams. (Historical Foundations of Forensic Psychiatry & Psychology Ser.). 405p. 1980. Repr. of 1923 ed. lib. bdg. 35.00 (ISBN 0-306-76060-6). Da Capo.

Crime & Capital Punishment. Robert Loeb. (Impact Books Ser.). (Illus.). (gr. 7 up). 1978. PLB 6.90 s&l (ISBN 0-531-01453-3). Watts.

Crime & Class: Essays in Marxist Criminology. Ed. by David F. Greenberg. 350p. (Orig.). 1981. write for info (ISBN 0-87484-505-X). Mayfield Pub.

Crime & Criminal Justice in a Declining Economy. Ed. by Kevin N. Wright. LC 80-26623. 128p. 1981. lib. bdg. 20.00 (ISBN 0-89946-046-1). Oelgeschlager.

Crime & Criminal Responsibility. David A. Jones. LC 77-25906. (Nelson-Hall Law Enforcement Ser.). 1978. 20.95 (ISBN 0-911012-84-2). Nelson-Hall.

Crime & Criminals: Opposing Viewpoints. Ed. by David L. Bender & Gary E. McCuen. (Opposing Viewpoints Ser: Vol. 13). (Illus.). 1977. lib. bdg. 8.95 (ISBN 0-912616-39-3); pap. text ed. 3.95 (ISBN 0-912616-20-2). Greenhaven.

Crime & Custom in Savage Society. Bronislaw Malinowski. (Quality Paperback: No. 210). 1976. pap. 3.50 (ISBN 0-8226-0210-5). Littlefield.

Crime & Deviance: A Comparative Perspective. Ed. by Graeme R Newman. LC 80-11629. (Sage Annual Reviews of Studies in Deviance: Vol. 4). (Illus.). 335p. 1980. 20.00x (ISBN 0-8039-1076-2); pap. 9.95x (ISBN 0-8039-1077-0). Sage.

Crime & Deviance in America. Sheila Balkan & Ronald Berger. 416p. 1980. pap. text ed. 12.95x (ISBN 0-534-00803-8). Wadsworth Pub.

Crime & Gerontology. Alan A. Malinchak. (Ser. in Criminal Justice). (Illus.). 1980. text ed. 15.95 (ISBN 0-13-192815-5); pap. text ed. 13.95 (ISBN 0-13-192807-4). P-H.

Crime & Immorality in the Catholic Church. Emmett McLoughlin. LC 62-7778. 1962. 4.95 (ISBN 0-910294-19-4). Brown Bk.

Crime & Its Correction: An International Survey of Attitudes & Practices. John P. Conrad. 1976. 16.50x o.p. (ISBN 0-520-03057-5). U of Cal Pr.

Crime & Its Modification: A Social Learning Perspective. Michael Nietzel. LC 78-23984. (Pergamon General Psychology Ser.: Vol. 77). (Illus.). 1979. 33.00 (ISBN 0-08-023878-5); pap. 10.95 (ISBN 0-08-023877-7). Pergamon.

Crime & Its Prevention. Ed. by Stephen Lewin. LC 68-17131. (Reference Shelf Ser: Vol. 40, No. 4). 1968. 6.25 (ISBN 0-8242-0103-5). Wilson.

Crime & Justice, 2 vols. Ed. by Jackwell Susman. (AMS Anthology). 1972-1974. Set. lib. bdg. 60.00 (ISBN 0-404-10200-X); Vol. 1. lib. bdg. 30.00 (ISBN 0-404-10201-8); Vol. 2. lib. bdg. 30.00 (ISBN 0-404-10202-6); Vol. 2. pap. 5.95 (ISBN 0-404-10252-2). AMS Pr.

Crime & Justice: An Annual Review of Criminal Justice Research, Vol. II. Norval Morris. Ed. by Michael Tonry. 1981. lib. bdg. 19.50x (ISBN 0-226-53957-1). U of Chicago Pr.

Crime & Justice: An Annual Review of Research. Norval Morris & Michael Tonry. (Vol. II). 480p. 1981. pap. 7.95 (ISBN 0-226-53959-8). U of Chicago Pr.

Crime & Justice: An Annual Review of Research. Ed. by Norval Morris & Michael Tonry. (Vol. 1). xii, 348p. 1980. pap. 6.95 (ISBN 0-226-53956-3, P903, Phoen). U of Chicago Pr.

Crime & Justice in America. Ed. by John T. O'Brien. LC 79-182. (Pergamon Policy Studies). (Illus.). 1979. 39.00 (ISBN 0-08-023857-2). Pergamon.

Crime & Justice in Our Time. Margaret O. Hyde. (gr. 7 up). 1980. PLB 7.90 (ISBN 0-531-04116-6, A34). Watts.

Crime & Juvenile Delinquency: A Bibliographic Guide to the 1978 Documents Update. 1980. pap. write for info. (ISBN 0-667-00571-4). Microfilming Corp.

Crime & Juvenile Delinquency: A Bibliographic Guide to the 1979 Documents Update. 1980. pap. write for info. (ISBN 0-667-00588-9). Microfilming Corp.

Crime & Law in Nineteeth Century Britain. W. R. Cornish et al. (Government & Society in 19th Century Britain Ser.). 232p. 1978. 25.00x (ISBN 0-7165-2213-6, Pub. by Irish Academic Pr Ireland). Biblio Dist.

Crime & Modernization: The Impact of Industrialization & Urbanization on Crime. Louise I. Shelley. LC 80-24044. (Science & International Affairs Ser.). 216p. 1981. 22.50x (ISBN 0-8093-0983-1). S Ill U Pr.

Crime & Penal Policy. Barbara Wootton. 1978. text ed. 25.00x (ISBN 0-04-364011-7); pap. text ed. 9.95x (ISBN 0-04-364013-3). Allen Unwin.

Crime & Punishment. Fedor Dostoyevsky. Tr. by Constance Garnett. 1955. 12.95x (ISBN 0-460-00501-4, Evman); pap. 4.50 (ISBN 0-460-01501-X). Dutton.

Crime & Punishment. Fedor Dostoyevsky. Tr. by David Magarshack. (Classics Ser.). (Orig.). 1952. pap. 3.95 (ISBN 0-14-044023-2). Penguin.

Crime & Punishment. Feodor Dostoyevsky. (Literature Ser). (gr. 9-12). 1969. pap. text ed. 3.83 (ISBN 0-87720-705-4). AMSCO Sch.

Crime & Punishment. Fyodor Dostoyevsky. (Now Age Illustrated V Ser.). (Illus.). 64p. (gr. 4-12). 1979. text ed. 4.50 (ISBN 0-686-26918-7); pap. text ed. 1.45 (ISBN 0-88301-386-X); student activity bk. 0.95 (ISBN 0-88301-410-6). Pendulum Pr.

Crime & Punishment: A Novel in 6 Pts. & Epilogue. Fedor M. Dostoyevsky. Tr. by Jessie Coulson. (World Classics Ser). Set. 9.95 (ISBN 0-19-250619-6). Oxford U Pr.

Crime & Punishment: An Introduction to Criminology. Harry E. Allen et al. LC 80-69715. (Illus.). 464p. 1981. text ed. 14.95 (ISBN 0-02-900460-8). Free Pr.

Crime & Punishment: Changing Attitudes in America. Arthur L. Stinchcombe et al. LC 80-8004. (Social & Behavioral Science Ser.). 1980. text ed. 15.95x (ISBN 0-87589-472-0). Jossey-Bass.

Crime & Punishment in Revolutionary Paris. Antoinette Wills. LC 80-654. (Contributions in Legal Studies: No. 15). (Illus.). xxi, 227p. 1981. lib. bdg. 32.50 (ISBN 0-313-21494-8, WCP/). Greenwood.

Crime & Punishment in the Caribbean. Ed. by Rosemary Brana-Shute & Gary Brana-Shute. LC 80-21078. (Illus.). x, 146p. 1980. pap. 6.00 (ISBN 0-8130-0685-6). U Presses Fla.

Crime & Punishment with Reader's Guide. Feodor Dostoyevsky. (Amsco Literature Program). (gr. 10-12). 1970. pap. text ed. 4.50 (ISBN 0-87720-805-0); tchr's ed. 2.95 (ISBN 0-87720-905-7). AMSCO Sch.

Crime & Society. Ed. by Eric F. Oatman. (Reference Shelf Ser.). 1979. 6.25 (ISBN 0-8242-0632-0). Wilson.

Crime & Society in Early Modern Seville. Mary E. Perry. LC 79-66452. (Illus.). 310p. 1980. text ed. 14.00x (ISBN 0-87451-177-1). U Pr of New Eng.

Crime & Suicide in the Nation's Capital: Toward Macro-Historical Perspectives. Gloria Count-van Manen. LC 76-24347. (Praeger Special Studies). 1977. text ed. 25.95 (ISBN 0-275-56860-1). Praeger.

Crime & the Community. Paul R. Wilson & J. W. Brown. 1973. pap. 6.00x (ISBN 0-7022-0839-6). U of Queensland Pr.

Crime & the Elderly. Jack Goldsmith & Sharon Goldsmith. (Illus.). 1976. 19.95 (ISBN 0-669-00561-4). Lexington Bks.

Crime & the Responsible Community. Ed. by John Scott & Nicholas Miller. 160p. 1980. pap. 6.95 (ISBN 0-8028-1831-5). Eerdmans.

Crime & the Sexual Psychopath. J. Paul De River. (Illus.). 384p. 1958. 27.50 (ISBN 0-398-00436-6). C C Thomas.

Crime As Work. Peter Letkemann. LC 73-12071. (Illus.). 192p. 1973. pap. 2.95 o.p. (ISBN 0-13-192922-4, S308, Spec). P-H.

Crime Codes of Pennsylvania. Gould Editorial Staff. 400p. (Supplemented annually). 1980. looseleaf 13.00 (ISBN 0-87526-216-3). Gould.

Crime Control by the National Government. Arthur Chester Millspaugh. LC 70-168678. (American Constitutional Legal History Ser). 306p. 1972. Repr. of 1937 ed. lib. bdg. 29.50 (ISBN 0-306-70418-8). Da Capo.

Crime Control in Japan. William Clifford. LC 75-22883. 224p. 1976. 19.95 (ISBN 0-669-00184-8). Lexington Bks.

Crime, Correction, & Society. 4th ed. Elmer H. Johnson. 1978. text ed. 17.95x (ISBN 0-256-02063-9). Dorsey.

Crime, Detective, Espionage, Mystery, & Thriller Fiction & Film: A Comprehensive Bibliography of Critical Writing Through 1979. David Skene Melvin & Ann Skene Melvin. LC 80-1194. 384p. 1980. lib. bdg. 29.95 (ISBN 0-313-22062-X, MCD/). Greenwood.

Crime Fiction Criticism: An Annotated Bibliography. Timothy W. Johnson et al. LC 80-8497. 450p. 1981. lib. bdg. 40.00 (ISBN 0-8240-9490-5). Garland Pub.

Crime in a Free Society. 3rd ed. Robert W. Winslow. 1977. pap. text ed. 13.95x (ISBN 0-8221-0192-0). Dickenson.

Crime in Developing Countries: A Comparative Perspective. Marshall B. Clinard & Daniel J. Abbott. LC 73-4031. 319p. 1973. 25.95 (ISBN 0-471-16060-1, Pub. by Wiley-Interscience). Wiley.

Crime in Society. Leonard D. Savitz & Norman Johnston. LC 78-806. 1978. pap. text ed. 19.95 (ISBN 0-471-03385-5). Wiley.

Crime Investigation. 2nd ed. Paul L. Kirk et al. LC 73-19854. 1974. text ed. 23.95 (ISBN 0-471-48247-1). Wiley.

Crime Laboratory: Organization & Operation. Paul L. Kirk & Lowell W. Bradford. (August Vollmer Criminalistics Ser). (Illus.). 132p. 1972. 9.50 (ISBN 0-398-01022-6). C C Thomas.

Crime Labs: The Science of Forensic Medicine. John F. Waters. (Impact Ser.). (Illus.). (gr. 7 up). 1979. PLB 6.90 s&l (ISBN 0-531-02286-2). Watts.

Crime, Law & Corrections. Ralph Slovenko. (Illus.). 1966. 76.75 (ISBN 0-398-01774-3). C C Thomas.

Crime, Law & Social Science. Jerome Michael & Mortimer J. Adler. (Social Science Classics Ser.). 440p. 1982. 19.95 (ISBN 0-87855-362-2); text ed. 19.95 (ISBN 0-686-68056-1); pap. 7.95 (ISBN 0-87855-786-5); pap. text ed. 7.95 (ISBN 0-686-68057-X). Transaction Bks. Postponed.

Crime, Law & Society. J. Goldstein & A. Goldstein. LC 77-136009. 1971. 14.50 (ISBN 0-02-912270-8); pap. text ed. 10.95 (ISBN 0-02-912260-0). Free Pr.

Crime News & the Public. Doris Graber. LC 80-16032. 256p. 1980. 24.95 (ISBN 0-03-055756-9). Praeger.

Crime of Martin Coverly. Leonard Wibberley. LC 79-28538. 184p. (gr. 4 up). 1980. 8.95 (ISBN 0-374-31656-2). FS&G.

Crime of Moscow in Vynnytsia. 2nd new ed. Ed. by John F. Stewart. (Illus.). 48p. 1980. pap. 3.00 (ISBN 0-911038-90-6, 357). Noontide.

Crime of Passion: Murder & the Murderer. David Lester & Gene Lester. LC 74-20788. 1975. 15.95 (ISBN 0-88229-139-4). Nelson-Hall.

Crime Prevention. Paul M. Whisenand. (Criminal Justice Ser.). 419p. 1977. text ed. 16.50 (ISBN 0-205-05548-6, 825595-4); instructor's manual free (ISBN 0-205-05596-6). Allyn.

Crime Scene Investigation. K. Goddard. 1977. 13.00 (ISBN 0-87909-172-X); students manual avail. Reston.

Crime Scene Investigation. Donald Schultz & Samuel Scheer. LC 76-7559. (Criminal Justice Ser.). (Illus.). 1977. 15.95x (ISBN 0-13-192864-3). P-H.

Crime Story. Jay R. Nash. 1981. 10,95 (ISBN 0-440-01534-0). Delacorte.

Crime That Never Was. Carl A. Coppolino. LC 80-81163. (Illus.). 309p. 1980. 13.95 (ISBN 0-936802-00-6). Justice Pr.

Crime Wave. John Wynne. 1981. 12.95. Riverrun NY.

Crime Without Punishment. David A. Jones. LC 78-19538. 1979. 22.95 (ISBN 0-669-02512-7). Lexington Bks.

Crimean Tartars & Volga Germans. Ann Sheehey. (Minority Rights Group: No. 6). 1971. pap. 2.50 (ISBN 0-89192-095-1). Interbk Inc.

Crimean War. John Langdon-Davies. (Jackdaw Ser: No. 11). (Illus.). 1968. 5.95 o.p. (ISBN 0-670-24748-0, Grossman). Viking Pr.

Crimes Against Internationally Protected Persons: Prevention & Punishment - an Analysis of the UN Convention. Louis M. Bloomfield & Gerald F. FitzGerald. LC 74-33031. 296p. 1975. text ed. 28.95 (ISBN 0-275-05350-4). Praeger.

Crimes of Violence: Homicide & Assault. F. Lee Bailey & Henry B. Rothblatt. LC 72-97625. (Criminal Law Library). 543p. 1973. 47.50 (ISBN 0-686-05455-5). Lawyers Co-Op.

Crimes of Violence: Rape & Other Sex Crimes. F. Lee Bailey & Henry B. Rothblatt. LC 72-97625. (Criminal Law Library). 1973. 47.50 (ISBN 0-686-14500-3). Lawyers Co-Op.

Crimes Without Victims: Deviance & the Criminal Law. Robert M. Rich. LC 78-63258. 1978. pap. text ed. 10.25 (ISBN 0-8191-0618-6). U Pr of Amer.

Criminal & Civil Investigation Handbook. Joseph J. Grau. (Illus.). 1088p. 1982. 39.50 (ISBN 0-07-024130-9). McGraw.

Criminal Aspects of Tax Fraud Cases. 3rd ed. 288p. 1980. text ed. 35.00 (ISBN 0-686-28652-9, T057B). ALI ABA.

Criminal Behavior: A Psychosocial Approach. Curt R. Bartol. (Criminal Justice Ser.). (Illus.). 1980. text ed. 17.95 (ISBN 0-13-193169-5). P-H.

Criminal Behaviour: A Psychological Analysis. M. Philip Feldman. LC 76-13229. 1977. 36.50 (ISBN 0-471-99401-4, Pub. by Wiley-Interscience). Wiley.

Criminal Behaviour: An Introduction to Its Causes & Treatment. Herschel Prins. 240p. 1974. pap. 6.95x o.p. (ISBN 0-8464-0299-8). Beekman Pubs.

Criminal Court. Roberta Rovner-Pieczník. LC 76-42854. (Illus.). 1978. 14.95 (ISBN 0-669-01056-1). Lexington Bks.

Criminal Evidence. Edward J. Imwinkelried et al. (Criminal Justice Ser.). 1979. pap. text ed. 16.95 (ISBN 0-8299-0221-X); tchrs.' manual avail. (ISBN 0-8299-0591-X). West Pub.

Criminal Evidence. 3rd rev. ed. John C. Klotter. LC 79-55201. (Criminal Justice Studies). 500p. 1980. text ed. 18.95 (ISBN 0-87084-500-4). Anderson Pub Co.

Criminal Evidence. Lawrence C. Waddington. 1978. text ed. 13.95x (ISBN 0-02-479510-0). Macmillan.

Criminal Evidence. Jon R. Waltz. LC 74-12398. (Law Enforcement Ser). 448p. 1975. 21.95 (ISBN 0-88229-130-0); pap. text ed. 13.95 (ISBN 0-88229-586-1). Nelson Hall.

Criminal Evidence for Police. 2nd ed. John C Klotter & Carl L. Meier. 1975. text ed. 16.95 o.p. (ISBN 0-87084-499-7). Anderson Pub Co.

Criminal Evidence: Principles, Cases & Readings. Thomas J. Gardner. (Criminal Justice Ser.). (Illus.). 1978. text ed. 17.95 (ISBN 0-8299-0148-5); instrs.' maual avail. (ISBN 0-8299-0589-8). West Pub.

Criminal Interrogation. 3rd ed. Arthur S. Aubry, Jr. & Rudolph R. Caputo. 464p. 1980. 18.75 (ISBN 0-398-03978-X). C C Thomas.

Criminal Investigation. Wayne W. Bennett & Karen M. Hess. (Criminal Justice Ser.). 450p. 1980. text ed. 15.95 (ISBN 0-8299-0342-9). West Pub.

Criminal Investigation. Charles M. Bozza. LC 77-9896. (Nelson-Hall Law Enforcement Ser.). 1977. 21.95 (ISBN 0-88229-183-1). Nelson-Hall.

Criminal Investigation. Gilbert. (Public Service Technology Ser.). 496p. 1980. text ed. 17.95 (ISBN 0-675-08186-6). Merrill.

Criminal Investigation. George B. Mettler. 1977. text ed. 16.50 (ISBN 0-205-05761-6, 825761-2); instructor's manual free (ISBN 0-205-05762-4, 825762-0). Allyn.

Criminal Investigation. 2nd ed. C. R. Swanson et al. Tr. by Leonard Territo. 1980. text ed. write for info. (ISBN 0-8302-2060-7). Goodyear.

Criminal Investigation & Identification. V. A. Leonard. (Illus.). 160p. 1971. 10.75 (ISBN 0-398-01098-6). C C Thomas.

Criminal Investigation & Presentation of Evidence. Arnold Markle. (Criminal Justice Ser.). 1976. 12.95; instrs.' manual avail. (ISBN 0-8299-0370-4); pap. write for info. West Pub.

Criminal Justice Administration. Remington et al. (Contemporary Legal Education Ser.). 1969. 20.00 (ISBN 0-672-80989-3, Bobbs-Merrill Law). Michie.

Criminal Justice & the American Constitution. H. Frank Way. 1980. text ed. 17.95 (ISBN 0-87872-238-6). Duxbury Pr.

Criminal Justice & the Community. Robert Trojanowicz & Samuel Dixon. (Illus.). 464p. 1974. ref. ed. 17.95x (ISBN 0-13-193557-7). P-H.

Criminal Justice & the Victim. Ed. by William F. McDonald. LC 75-42754. (Sage Criminal Justice System Annuals Ser.: Vol. 6). 1976. 20.00x (ISBN 0-8039-0508-4); pap. 9.95x (ISBN 0-8039-0509-2). Sage.

Criminal Justice Education: The End of the Beginning. Richard Pearson et al. 220p. (Orig.). 1980. pap. 5.50x (ISBN 0-89444-030-6). John Jay Pr.

Criminal Justice Game. Ralph Baker & Fred Meyer, Jr. 1980. pap. text ed. 8.95 (ISBN 0-87872-240-8). Duxbury Pr.

Criminal Justice History: An International Annual, 1980, Vol. I. Ed. by Henry Cohen. (Criminal Justice History Ser.). (Illus.). 294p. 1980. lib. bdg. 20.00x (ISBN 0-686-28890-4). Crime & Justice Hist.

Criminal Justice in America. Roscoe Pound. LC 79-37841. (American Constitutional & Legal History Ser). 224p. 1972. Repr. of 1930 ed. lib. bdg. 22.50 (ISBN 0-306-70435-8). Da Capo.

Criminal Justice in America: Process & Issues. Peter C. Kratcoski & Donald B. Walker. 1978. 16.95x (ISBN 0-673-15051-8). Scott F.

Criminal Justice in Eighteenth Century Mexico: A Study of the Tribunal of the Acordada. Colin M. MacLachlan. LC 72-97737. 1975. 18.50x (ISBN 0-520-02416-8). U of Cal Pr.

Criminal Justice in Metropolitan Court. Harry I. Subin. LC 72-172177. (American Constitutional & Legal History Ser). 234p. 1973. Repr. of 1966 ed. lib. bdg. 22.50 (ISBN 0-306-70239-8). Da Capo.

Criminal Justice Instructional Techniques. John C. Klotter & Joseph Rosenfeld. (Illus.). 216p. 1979. text ed. 16.75 (ISBN 0-398-03887-2); pap. text ed. 7.50 student workbook, 80p. (ISBN 0-398-03892-9). C C Thomas.

Criminal Justice: Its Transdisciplinary Nature. Gordon E. Misner. 1981. pap. text ed. 14.95 (ISBN 0-8016-3457-1). Mosby.

Criminal Justice Management: A Text & Readings. Harry W. More. (Criminal Justice Ser.). 1977. pap. text ed. 12.95; pap. write for info. (ISBN 0-8299-0625-8). West Pub.

Criminal Justice: Opposing Viewpoints. Ed. by David L. Bender. (Opposing Viewpoints Ser.). (gr. 12). 1981. lib. bdg. 8.95 (ISBN 0-89908-332-3); pap. text ed. 3.95 (ISBN 0-89908-307-2). Greenhaven.

Criminal Justice: Organization, Structure & Analysis. David Duffee et al. (Criminal Justice Ser.). 1978. ref. 17.95 (ISBN 0-13-193490-2). P-H.

Criminal Justice Planning. Ed. by Joseph E. Scott & Simon Dinitz. LC 76-14129. (Praeger Special Studies). 1977. 22.95 (ISBN 0-03-040896-2). Praeger.

Criminal Justice Planning. Shanahan & Whisenand. 444p. 1980. text ed. 16.95 (ISBN 0-205-06668-2, 8266689). Allyn.

Criminal Justice Planning: An Introduction. Don C. Gibbons et al. (Illus.). 192p. 1977. text ed. 15.95x (ISBN 0-13-193037-0). P-H.

Criminal Justice Planning & Development. Ed. by Alvin W. Cohn. LC 77-81154. (Sage Research Progress Series in Criminology: Vol. 4). 1977. 12.95x (ISBN 0-8039-0918-7); pap. 6.50x (ISBN 0-8039-0913-6). Sage.

Criminal Justice Research: New Models & Findings. Ed. by Barbara R. Price & Phyllis J. Baunach. LC 80-20145. (Illus.). 143p. 1980. 12.95 (ISBN 0-8039-1509-8); pap. 6.50 (ISBN 0-8039-1510-1). Sage.

Criminal Justice: Selected Readings. Ed. by John Baldwin & A. Keith Bottomley. 311p. 1978. 36.00x (ISBN 0-85520-234-3, Pub by Martin Robertson England); pap. 12.50x (ISBN 0-85520-233-5). Biblio Dist.

Criminal Justice Studies: Their Trans-Disciplinary Nature. Gordon E. Misner & D. Crim. (Illus.). 350p. 1981. pap. text ed. 14.95 (ISBN 0-8016-3457-1). Mosby.

Criminal Justice System: An Introduction. 2nd ed. Ronald J. Waldron et al. LC 79-65288. (Illus.). 1980. text ed. 17.95 (ISBN 0-395-28669-7); inst. manual 0.65 (ISBN 0-395-28668-9); study guide 4.95 (ISBN 0-395-29304-9). HM.

Criminal Justice System: An Introduction. Ronald J. Waldron et al. LC 75-26098. (Illus.). 480p. 1976. pap. text ed. 15.75 o.p. (ISBN 0-395-18592-0); instr. manual o.p. 1.25 o.p. (ISBN 0-395-18785-0). HM.

Criminal Justice System of the USSR. M. Cherif Bassiouni & V. M. Savitski. 296p. 1979. text ed. 27.50 (ISBN 0-398-03868-6). C C Thomas.

Criminal Justice Vocabulary. J. A. Martin & N. A. Astone. 312p. 1980. lexotone 29.50 (ISBN 0-398-03987-9). C C Thomas.

Criminal Law & Court Procedures. M. B. Hutnick. 176p. 1974. pap. 8.00 o.p. (ISBN 0-8273-1429-9); instructor's guide 1.45 o.p. (ISBN 0-8273-1430-2). Delmar.

Criminal Law & Its Administration: The Ditchley Papers. W. C. Warren et al. LC 70-152650. (Symposia on Law & Society Ser). 1971. Repr. of 1966 ed. lib. bdg. 15.00 (ISBN 0-306-70130-8). Da Capo.

Criminal Law, Cases, Comment & Questions. 3rd ed. Lloyd L. Weinreb. LC 80-14620. (University Casebook Ser.). 894p. 1980. text ed. write for info. (ISBN 0-88277-008-X). Foundation Pr.

Criminal Law, Cases, Materials & Text on the Substantive Criminal Law in Its Procedural Context. 2nd ed. Phillip E. Johnson. LC 80-14283. (American Casebook Ser.). 993p. 1980. text ed. 21.95 (ISBN 0-8299-2093-5). West Pub.

Criminal Law: History, Philosophy, & Enforcement. Edward Eldefonso & Alan R. Coffey. (Illus.). 304p. 1980. text ed. 17.50 scp (ISBN 0-06-041879-6, HarpC); avail. Har-Row.

Criminal Law in a Nutshell. Arnold H. Loewy. (Nutshell Ser.). 302p. 1980. pap. text ed. 6.95 (ISBN 0-8299-2067-6). West Pub.

Criminal Law in Action. William J. Chambliss. LC 74-32149. 480p. 1975. text ed. 17.95 (ISBN 0-471-14474-6). Wiley.

Criminal Law in the United States. Eugene Smith. (Russell Sage Foundation Reprint Ser). Repr. of 1910 ed. lib. bdg. 24.50x (ISBN 0-697-00208-X). Irvington.

Criminal Law New York Questions & Answers. 1979 ed. 250p. 1981. 8.50 (ISBN 0-87526-203-1). Gould.

Criminal Law of New York. Eugene R. Canudo. 660p. (Supplemented annually). 1980. looseleaf 15.00 (ISBN 0-87526-201-5). Gould.

Criminal Law Outline. William A. Grimes. (Ser. 1050). 1980. pap. 8.00 (ISBN 0-686-08768-2). Natl Judicial Coll.

Criminal Law: Theory & Process. 2nd ed. Joseph Goldstein et al. LC 73-22533. (Illus.). 1974. text ed. 45.00 (ISBN 0-02-912310-0). Free Pr.

Criminal Laws of Illinois. Gould Editorial Staff. (Annual). 1981. text ed. 9.95x (ISBN 0-87526-199-X). Gould.

Criminal Laws of Ohio. Gould Editorial Staff. (Annual). 1981. looseleaf 10.50x (ISBN 0-87526-202-3). Gould.

Criminal Life: Views from the Inside. Ed. by Marcello Truzzi & David M. Petersen. 240p. 1972. pap. text ed. 9.95 (ISBN 0-13-192955-0). P-H.

Criminal Prisons of London. Henry Mayhew & J. Binny. LC 68-18227. (Illus.). Repr. of 1862 ed. 22.50x (ISBN 0-678-05072-4). Kelley.

Criminal Procedure: An Analysis of Constitutional Cases & Concepts. Charles H. Whitebread. LC 80-14619. (University Textbook Ser.). 644p. 1980. text ed. write for info. (ISBN 0-88277-006-3). Foundation Pr.

Criminal Procedure in a Nutshell: Constitutional Limitations. 3rd ed. Jerold H. Israel & Wayne R. LaFave. LC 80-23164. (Nutshell Ser.). 438p. 1980. pap. text ed. 6.95 (ISBN 0-8299-2107-9). West Pub.

Criminal Procedure Law (N.Y.) (Supplemented annually). 1980. looseleaf 5.95 (ISBN 0-87526-138-8); pap. 5.50 (ISBN 0-87526-260-0). Gould.

Criminal Procedure Law of New York Quizzer, 1978-79. Gould Editorial Staff. 1978. looseleaf 5.50x o.p. (ISBN 0-685-80905-6). Gould.

Criminal Procedure: The Supreme Court's View Cases. Peter W. Lewis. (Criminal Justice Ser.). (Illus.). 1979. pap. text ed. 14.95 (ISBN 0-8299-0236-8); resource manual avail. (ISBN 0-8299-0597-9). West Pub.

Criminal Procedure: The Supreme Court's View - Cases. Lewis. (Criminal Justice Ser.). 131p. 1980. pap. text ed. write for info. (ISBN 0-8299-0321-6); 1980 supplement avail. West Pub.

Criminal Procedure Under the Federal Rules, 7 vols. Lester B. Orfield. LC 66-17952. 1968. Set. 297.50 (ISBN 0-686-14508-9). Lawyers Co-Op.

Criminal Prosecution in England. Patrick Devlin. 1958. 24.50x (ISBN 0-685-69811-4). Elliots Bks.

Criminal Recidivism in New York City: An Evaluation of the Impact of Rehabilitation & Diversion Services. Robert Fishman. LC 76-12850. (Special Studies). 1977. text ed. 24.95 (ISBN 0-275-23580-7). Praeger.

Criminal Rehabilitation - Within & Without the Walls: With Contributions from Experts Within the Field. Ed. by Edward M. Scott & Kathryn L. Scott. 236p. 1973. 11.75 (ISBN 0-398-02730-7). C C Thomas.

Criminal Responsibility. Charles Mercier. (Historical Foundations of Forensic Psychiatry & Psychology Ser.). 256p. 1980. Repr. of 1931 ed. lib. bdg. 25.00 (ISBN 0-306-76064-9). Da Capo.

Criminal Sentences: Law Without Order. Marvin E. Frankel. LC 72-95111. 144p. 1973. 5.95 (ISBN 0-8090-3709-2, AmCen); pap. 5.25 (ISBN 0-8090-1374-6, AmCen). Hill & Wang.

Criminal Violence, Criminal Justice. Charles E. Silberman. LC 79-2318. 1980. pap. 3.75 (ISBN 0-394-74147-1, Vin). Random.

Criminalistics: An Introduction to Forensic Science. 2nd ed. Richard Saferstein. (Criminal Justice Ser.). 1981. 18.95 (ISBN 0-686-63386-5). P-H.

Criminality & Psychiatric Disorders. Samuel B. Guze. 176p. 1976. text ed. 10.95x (ISBN 0-19-501973-3). Oxford U Pr.

Criminals. David Kranes. 256p. (Orig.). pap. 2.50 (ISBN 0-441-12174-8). Charter Bks.

Criminal's Image of the City. rev. ed. Ronald L. Carter & Kim Q. Hill. (Illus.). 1979. 13.75 (ISBN 0-08-024633-8). Pergamon.

Criminological Enterprise: Theories & Perspectives. Don Gibbons. (P-H Series in Sociology). 1979. pap. text ed. 9.95 (ISBN 0-13-193615-8). P-H.

Criminological Theory. Ed. by Stephen Schafer & Richard D. Knudten. LC 76-18488. 1977. 22.95 (ISBN 0-669-00795-1). Lexington Bks.

Criminology. 2nd ed. Robert G. Caldwell. 1965. 18.95 (ISBN 0-8260-1655-3). Wiley.

Criminology. Stephan Hurwitz & Karl O. Christiansen. LC 74-7977. (Illus.). 400p. 1981. 30.00 (ISBN 0-8386-1477-9). Fairleigh Dickinson.

Criminology & Criminal Justice in America: A Guide to the Literature. rev. ed. J. Kinton. (Specialized Bibliography Ser.: No. 2). 1981. 3.95 (ISBN 0-685-53690-4). Soc Sci & Soc Res.

Criminology in Literature. Ed. by Paul E. Dow. (Longman English & Humanities Ser.). 1980. pap. text ed. 8.95 (ISBN 0-582-28164-4). Longman.

Criminology in Perspective: Essays in Honor of Israel Drapkin. Simha F. Landau & Leslie Sebba. LC 76-50437. 1978. 19.95 (ISBN 0-669-01281-5). Lexington Bks.

Criminology, Law Enforcement & Offender Treatment: A Sourcebook. rev. ed. Ed. by J. Kinton. 1981. write for info. (ISBN 0-685-96247-4). Soc Sci & Soc Res.

Criminology: New Concerns. Ed. by Edward Sagarin. LC 79-14116. (Focus Editions Ser.: Vol. 10). (Illus.). 1979. 18.95x (ISBN 0-8039-1275-7); pap. 9.95x (ISBN 0-8039-1276-5). Sage.

Criminology of Deviant Women. Freda Adler & Rita J. Simon. LC 78-69555. (Illus.). 1979. pap. text ed. 8.95 (ISBN 0-395-26719-6). HM.

Criminology: Perspectives on Crime & Criminality. Peter Wickman et al. 1980. text ed. 17.95 (ISBN 0-669-01600-4); instr's guide free (ISBN 0-669-01922-4). Heath.

Criminology: Power, Crime & Criminal Law. John F. Galliher & James McCartney. 1977. 15.50x (ISBN 0-256-01942-8). Dorsey.

Criminology Review Yearbook, Vol. 2. Ed. by Egon Bittner & Sheldon L. Messinger. (Illus.). 733p. 1980. 35.00 (ISBN 0-8039-1309-5). Sage.

Crimson Cage. Margaret W. Tuttle. (Orig.). (gr. 8-12). 1978. pap. 4.50 (ISBN 0-932384-01-3). Tashmoo.

Crimson Chalice. Victor Canning. 1979. pap. 2.50 (ISBN 0-441-12190-X). Charter Bks.

Crimson Glory. Theresa Conway. 1979. pap. 2.25 o.p. (ISBN 0-449-14112-8, GM). Fawcett.

Crimson Intrigue. Devon Lindsay. (Orig.). 1981. pap. write for info. (ISBN 0-671-41781-9). PB.

Crimson Kisses. Asa Drake. 304p. 1981. pap. 2.50 (ISBN 0-380-77131-4, 77131). Avon.

Crimson Roses, No. 10. Grace L. Hill. 192p. 1981. pap. 1.95 (ISBN 0-553-14510-X). Bantam.

Crinolines & Crimping Irons: Victorian Clothes, How They Were Cleaned & Cared for. Christina Walkley & V. Foster. (Illus.). 1978. text ed. 22.50x (ISBN 0-7206-0500-8). Humanities.

Crippled Eagles. Robin Moore. Ed. by A. Bradley Harris. 375p. 13.95 (ISBN 0-89975-005-2, Hippocrene Book Co). World Authors.

Crises & Special Problems in Psychoanalysis & Psychotherapy. Leopold Bellak & Peri E. Faithorn. 264p. 1981. 17.50 (ISBN 0-87630-257-6). Brunner-Mazel.

Crises in Campus Management: Case Studies in the Administration of Colleges & Universities. Ed. by George J. Mauer. LC 75-23981. (Special Studies). 1976. text ed. 19.95 o.p. (ISBN 0-275-55710-3). Praeger.

Crises in Myasthenia Gravis. A. Szobor. Tr. by P. Fenyo. 1970. 12.00 o.s.i. (ISBN 0-02-853150-7). Hafner.

Crises of Power: Foreign Policy in the Kissinger Years. Seyom Brown. LC 79-15796. 1979. 12.50 (ISBN 0-231-04264-7). Columbia U Pr.

Crises Youth Face Today. Shirley Schwarzrock & C. Gilbert Wrenn. (Coping with Ser.). (Illus.). 64p. (gr. 7-12). 1973. pap. text ed. 1.30 (ISBN 0-913476-28-5). Am Guidance.

Crisis & Consciousness. Ed. by Ralph Faris. (Philosophical Currents Ser.: 20). 1977. pap. text ed. 23.00x (ISBN 90-6032-093-X). Humanities.

Crisis & Contention in Sociology. Ed. by Tom Bottomore. LC 75-24787. (Sage Studies in International Sociology: Vol. 1). 1976. 18.00x (ISBN 0-8039-9955-0); pap. 9.95x (ISBN 0-8039-9962-3). Sage.

Crisis & Development. V. Skipp. LC 77-71426. (Illus.). 1978. 21.95 (ISBN 0-521-21660-5). Cambridge U Pr.

Crisis & Legitimacy. James O. Freedman. LC 78-5183. 1978. 27.50 (ISBN 0-521-22063-7); pap. 9.95 (ISBN 0-521-29380-4). Cambridge U Pr.

Crisis & Legitimacy. James O. Freedman. LC 78-51683. 352p. 1980. pap. 9.95 (ISBN 0-521-29380-4). Cambridge U Pr.

Crisis & the "Crash" Soviet Studies of the West (1917-1939) Richard B. Day. 320p. 1981. 22.50 (Pub. by NLB England). Schocken.

Crisis at the Twenty-Third Hour. Walter E. Adams. 175p. 1981. pap. 4.50 (ISBN 0-937408-03-4). Gospel Pubns FL.

Crisis, Cambios y Conflictos. 1980. pap. 1.40 (ISBN 0-686-69360-4). Vida Pubs.

Crisis Center Hotline: A Guidebook to Beginning & Operating. Ed. by Ursula Delworth et al. (Illus.). 160p. 1972. photocopy ed. spiral 14.75 (ISBN 0-398-02561-4). C C Thomas.

Crisis Counseling: The Essential Guide for Non-Professional Counselors. Eugene Kennedy. 208p. 1981. 12.95 (ISBN 0-8264-0038-8). Continuum.

Crisis Experiences in the Lives of Noted Christians. V. Raymond Edman. 1970. pap. 1.95 (ISBN 0-87123-065-8, 200065). Bethany Fell.

Crisis in Buganda 1953 to 1955: The Story of the Exile & Return of the Kaboka, Mutesa II. Paulo Kavuma. 112p. 1979. 12.50x (ISBN 0-8476-3280-6). Rowman.

Crisis in Child Mental Health: Critical Assessment, Vol. 8. GAP Ad Hoc Committee. LC 72-184968. (Report No. 82). 1972. pap. 2.00 (ISBN 0-87318-115-8). Adv Psychiatry.

Crisis in Communication: The Functions & Future of Medical Journals. Theodore Fox. (Heath Clark Lectures 1963). 1965. text ed. 2.50x (ISBN 0-485-26316-5, Athlone Pr). Humanities.

Crisis in Consciousness. Robert Powell. 11.50 (ISBN 0-227-67426-X). Attic Pr.

Crisis in Costa Rica: The Nineteen Forty-Eight Revolution. John P. Bell. LC 77-165920. (Latin American Monographs Ser.: No. 24). 192p. 1971. 9.95x (ISBN 0-292-70147-0). U of Tex Pr.

Crisis in Democracy: A Policy Analysis of American Government. Harrell R. Rodgers, Jr. LC 77-79458. (Political Science Ser.). 1978. pap. text ed. 8.95 (ISBN 0-201-06468-5). A-W.

Crisis in Economic Theory. Ed. by Daniel Bell & Irving Kristol. LC 80-70392. 242p. 1981. 13.95 (ISBN 0-465-01476-3); pap. 4.95. Basic.

Crisis in English Poetry, Eighteen Eighty to Nineteen Forty. Vivian De Sola Pinto. (Repr. of 1951 ed). 1967. text ed. 6.25x (ISBN 0-09-024411-7, Hutchinson U Lib); pap. text ed. 3.00x (ISBN 0-09-024412-5, Hutchinson U Lib). Humanities.

Crisis in Forecasting & the Emergence of the "Prospective" Approach: With Case Studies in Energy & Air Transport. Michel Godet. LC 78-10548. (Pergamon Policy Studies). 1979. 16.50 (ISBN 0-08-022487-3). Pergamon.

Crisis in Lutheran Theology, 2 vols. in one. John W. Montgomery. 1973. pap. 6.95 (ISBN 0-87123-050-X, 210050). Bethany Fell.

Crisis in Marxism. Jack Lindsay. 1981. 22.50x (ISBN 0-389-20185-5). B&N.

Crisis in Psychiatric Hospitalization, Vol. 7. GAP Committee on Therapeutic Care. LC 62-2872. (Report No. 72). 1969. pap. 2.00 (ISBN 0-87318-101-8). Adv Psychiatry.

Crisis in Rhodesia. Nathan Shamuyarira. 1965. 9.95 (ISBN 0-685-20570-3). Transatlantic.

Crisis in Socialist Planning: Eastern Europe & the USSR. Jan Marczewski. Tr. by Noel Lindsay from Fr. LC 73-15190. (Special Studies). (Illus.). 365p. 1974. text ed. 29.95 (ISBN 0-275-08140-0). Praeger.

Crisis in Sociology: Problems of Sociological Epistemology. Raymond Boudon. (European Perspectives Ser.). 272p. 1981. 25.00x (ISBN 0-231-05178-6). Columbia U Pr.

Crisis in the Congo: A U.N. Force in Action. Ernest W. Lefever. 1965. 11.95 (ISBN 0-8157-5198-2); pap. 4.95 (ISBN 0-8157-5197-4). Brookings.

Crisis in the Health Service: The Politics of Management. Stuart Haywood & Andy Alaszewski. 154p. 1980. 30.00x (ISBN 0-7099-0013-9, Pub. by Croom Helm Ltd England). Biblio Dist.

Crisis in the Making: The Political Economy of New York State Since Nineteen Forty-Five. Peter D. McClelland & Alan L. Magdovitz. LC 80-24167. (Studies in Economic History & Policy: the United States in the Twentieth Century). (Illus.). 512p. Date not set. price not set (ISBN 0-521-23807-2). Cambridge U Pr.

Crisis in the Public Sector: A Reader. Ed. by Union for Radical Political Enconomics (URPE) LC 80-8936. 1981. pap. 7.50 (ISBN 0-85345-575-9). Monthly Rev.

Crisis: In the Third World. Andre G. Frank. LC 80-239444. 1981. text ed. 29.50x (ISBN 0-8419-0584-3); pap. text ed. 9.75x (ISBN 0-8419-0597-5). Holmes & Meier.

Crisis: In the World Economy. Andre G. Frank. LC 80-14540. 1980. text ed. 28.50x (ISBN 0-8419-0583-5); pap. text ed. 9.75x (ISBN 0-8419-0596-7). Holmes & Meier.

Crisis in Urban Housing. Ed. by Grant S. McClellan. (Reference Shelf Ser.). 1974. 6.25 (ISBN 0-8242-0509-X). Wilson.

Crisis in Urban Recreational Services. Jay S. Shivers & Joseph W. Halper. LC 79-17414. 384p. 1981. 27.50 (ISBN 0-8386-3006-5, 3006). Fairleigh Dickinson.

Crisis Intervention. Ed. by Gerald Specter & William Claiborn. LC 73-4360. (Continuing Series in Community-Clinical Psychology: Vol. 2). 224p. 1973. text ed. 19.95 (ISBN 0-87705-118-6); pap. write for info. (ISBN 0-87705-124-0). Human Sci Pr.

Crisis Intervention & Counseling by Telephone. David Lester & Gene W. Brockopp. (Illus.). 336p. 1976. pap. 29.50 photocopy ed., spiral (ISBN 0-398-02641-6). C C Thomas.

Crisis Intervention & How It Works. Romaine V. Edwards. (Illus.). 88p. 1979. 11.50 (ISBN 0-398-03580-6). C C Thomas.

Crisis Intervention As Psychotherapy. Charles P. Ewing. 1978. pap. 4.95x (ISBN 0-19-502271-8). Oxford U Pr.

Crisis Intervention: Case Histories. J. K. Morrice. Ed. by J. H. Kahn. 117p. 1976. text ed. 16.50 (ISBN 0-08-019742-6); pap. text ed. 7.75 (ISBN 0-08-019741-8). Pergamon.

Crisis Intervention Theory & Practice: A Clinical Guide. Ann W. Burgess & Bruce Baldwin. (Illus.). 288p. 1981. text ed. 14.95 (ISBN 0-13-193466-X); pap. text ed. 11.95 (ISBN 0-686-69274-8). P-H.

Crisis Intervention Theory & Practice: A Source Book. Larry L. Smith. 1976. pap. text ed. 10.50x (ISBN 0-8191-0077-3). U Pr of Amer.

Crisis Management & the Super-Powers in the Middle East. Ed. by Gregory Traverton. LC 80-67837. (Adelphi Library: Vol. 5). 172p. 1981. text ed. 29.50 (ISBN 0-916672-73-5). Allanheld.

Crisis Management: Confrontation & Diplomacy in the Nuclear Age. Philip Williams. 1976. 24.95 (ISBN 0-470-98899-1). Halsted Pr.

Crisis of Capitalism in America. M. J. Bonn. Tr. by Winifred Ray. Date not set. Repr. of 1932 ed. lib. bdg. 25.00 (ISBN 0-89760-030-4). Telegraph Bks.

Crisis of Chinese Consciousness: Radical Antitraditionalism in the May Fourth Era. Yu-Sheng Lin. LC 77-91057. 1978. 20.00 (ISBN 0-299-07410-2). U of Wis Pr.

Crisis of Civilization. Hilaire Belloc. LC 73-114465. 245p. 1973. Repr. of 1937 ed. lib. bdg. 19.75x (ISBN 0-8371-4761-1, BECC). Greenwood.

Crisis of Democracy: Report on the Governability of Democracies to the Trilateral Commission. Michel Crozier et al. LC 75-27167. 1975. 12.00x (ISBN 0-8147-1364-5); pap. 5.00x (ISBN 0-8147-1365-3). NYU Pr.

Crisis of Democratic Theory: Scientific Naturalism & the Problem of Value. Edward A. Purcell, Jr. LC 72-91669. 344p. 1979. pap. 7.50x (ISBN 0-8131-0141-7). U Pr of Ky.

Crisis of France's East Central European Diplomacy, 1933-1938. Anthony T. Komjathy. (East European Monographs: No. 21). 1977. 14.50x o.p. (ISBN 0-914710-14-1, Dist. by Columbia U Pr). East Eur Quarterly.

Crisis of German Ideology: Intellectual Origins of the Third Reich. George L. Mosse. 1979. Repr. 22.50 o.p. (ISBN 0-86527-036-8). Fertig.

Crisis of German Ideology: Intellectual Origins of the Third Reich. George L. Mosse. LC 78-19126. vill, 373p. 1981. Repr. of 1964 ed. 27.50x (ISBN 0-86527-036-8). Fertig.

Crisis of Germany Ideology: Intellectual Origins of the Third Reich. George L. Mosse. 384p. 1981. Repr. of 1964 ed. pap. text ed. 7.95 (ISBN 0-8052-0669-8). Schocken.

Crisis of Human Rights. Niels C. Nielsen, Jr. LC 78-4056. 1978. pap. 3.95 o.p. (ISBN 0-8407-5644-5). Nelson.

Crisis of Indian Unity, 1917-1940. R. J. Moore. 280p. 1974. 24.95x (ISBN 0-19-821560-6). Oxford U Pr.

Crisis of Industrial Society. Norman Birnbaum. 1969. pap. 4.95 (ISBN 0-19-500794-8, 295, GB). Oxford U Pr.

Crisis of Psychoanalysis. Erich Fromm. 1977. pap. 1.50 o.p. (ISBN 0-449-30792-1, Prem). Fawcett.

Crisis of Religious Language. Ed. by J. B. Metz & J. P. Jossua. (Concilium Ser.: Religion in the Seventies: Vol. 85). 156p. 1973. pap. 4.95 (ISBN 0-8164-2541-8). Crossroad NY.

Crisis of Russian Populism. Richard Wortman. 1967. 26.95 (ISBN 0-521-06913-0). Cambridge U Pr.

Crisis of the Aristocracy, 1558-1641. Lawrence Stone. 1965. 49.00x (ISBN 0-19-821314-X). Oxford U Pr.

Crisis of the Early Italian Renaissance: Civic Humanism & Republican Liberty in an Age of Classicism & Tyranny. rev. ed. Hans Baron. 1966. 25.00 (ISBN 0-691-05114-3); pap. 5.95 (ISBN 0-691-00752-7). Princeton U Pr.

Crisis of the Union, 1841-1877, Vol. 3. D. Malone & B. Rauch. 1964. 14.95 (ISBN 0-13-193573-9). P-H.

Crisis: Psychological First Aid for Recovery & Growth. Ann S. Kliman. LC 77-133353. 1978. 8.95 o.p. (ISBN 0-03-019461-X). HR&W.

Crisis Resolution: Presidential Decision Making in the Mayaguez & Korean Confrontations. Richard G. Head et al. (Westview Special Study). 1978. lib. bdg. 26.00x (ISBN 0-89158-163-4). Westview.

Crisis Services for Campus & Community: A Handbook for the Volunteer. E. Robert Sinnett. 260p. 1976. 17.50 (ISBN 0-398-03467-2). C C Thomas.

Crisis: Ten Original Stories of Science Fiction. Ed. by Roger Elwood. LC 73-19901. 224p. (gr. 6 up). 1974. 7.95 o.p. (ISBN 0-525-66374-6). Elsevier-Nelson.

Crisis Therapy. Joseph B. France. LC 80-83967. 1980. pap. text ed. 8.75x (ISBN 0-918970-28-8). Intl Gen Semantics.

Crisp County, Georgia: Historical Sketches. W. P. Fleming. LC 80-13477. (Illus.). 288p. 1980. Repr. of 1932 ed. 20.00 (ISBN 0-87152-319-1). Reprint.

Crispan Magicker. Mark M. Lowenthal. 1978. pap. 1.95 (ISBN 0-380-42333-2, 42333). Avon.

Crispin's Castle. Kathleen M. Duncan. (Pathfinder Ser.). (Illus.). (gr. 2-6). 1979. pap. 2.95 (ISBN 0-310-37821-4). Zondervan.

Crispus Attucks. (Black History Illustrated: No. 3). (Illus.). 1967. pap. 0.59 o.p. (ISBN 0-685-78148-8). Guild Bks.

Crisscross: Structured Writing in Context. Gregory Barnes. (Illus.). 208p. 1981. pap. text ed. 8.95 (ISBN 0-13-193920-3). P-H.

Cristero Rebellion. J. A. Meyer. LC 75-35455. (Cambridge Latin American Studies: No. 24). (Illus.). 1976. 32.95 (ISBN 0-521-21031-3). Cambridge U Pr.

Cristianismo y Otras Religiones. E. L. Copeland. Tr. by Abdias A. Mora. Orig. Title: Christianity & World Religious. (Illus.). 192p. (Span.). Date not set. pap. price not set (ISBN 0-311-05760-8, Edit Mundo). Casa Bautista.

Cristo y el Comunismo. E. Stanley Jones. Tr. by C. T. Gattinoni from Eng. Orig. Title: Christ's Alternative to Communism. 96p. (Span.). Date not set. pap. price not set (ISBN 0-311-05040-9, Edit Mundo). Casa Bautista.

Cristobal Colon. (Span.). 7.95 (ISBN 84-241-5406-1). E Torres & Sons.

Cristobal de Villalon. Joseph J. Kincaid. (World Authors Ser.: Spain: No. 264). 1971. lib. bdg. 10.95 (ISBN 0-8057-2963-1). Twayne.

Cristobal De Virues. John G. Weiger. (World Authors Ser.: No. 497 (Spain)). 1978. 12.95 (ISBN 0-8057-6338-4). Twayne.

Criteria & Standards of Quality, Vol. II. Avedis Donabedian. (Explorations in Quality Assessment & Monitoring Ser.). (Illus.). 420p. 1981. text ed. price not set (ISBN 0-914904-67-1); pap. text ed. price not set. Health Admin Pr.

Criteria (Dose-Effect Relationships) for Radium. Commission of the European Communities. LC 77-30193. 1977. text ed. 28.00 (ISBN 0-08-022024-X). Pergamon.

Criteria for Awarding School Leaving Certificates, an International Discussion: Proceedings. International Association for Educational Assessment, Third Annual Conference Narrobi, May 23, 1977. Ed. by Frances M. Ottobre. 1979. 30.00 (ISBN 0-08-024685-0). Pergamon.

Criteria for Compacted Fills. Building Research Advisory Board - Federal Housing Administration. 1965. pap. 3.00 (ISBN 0-309-01281-3). Natl Acad Pr.

Criteria for Energy Storage R&D. Energy Engineering Board, Assembly of Engineering, National Research Council. LC 76-47080. 1976. pap. 6.25 (ISBN 0-309-02530-3). Natl Acad Pr.

Criteria for Hydraulic Fills. Federal Housing Administration - Building Research Advisory Board. 1962. pap. 3.75 (ISBN 0-309-01076-4). Natl Acad Pr.

Criteria for Nuclear Safety Related Piping & Component Support Snubbers. M. N. Bressler et al. (PVP: No. 45). 40p. 1980. 6.00 (H00173). ASME.

Criteria for Quality of Petroleum Products. Ed. by J. R. Allinson. LC 73-7958. 286p. 1973. 29.95 (ISBN 0-470-02500-X). Halsted Pr.

Criteria for Selecting Appropriate Technologies Under Different Cultural, Technical & Social Conditions: IFAC Symposium, Bari, Italy, May 21-22, 1979. Ed. by A. De Giorgio. (IFAC Proceedings Ser.). (Illus.). 320p. 1980. 66.00 (ISBN 0-08-024455-6). Pergamon.

Criteria for the Acceptance of Cast Iron Soil Pipe. Building Research Advisory Board - Federal Construction Council. 1960. pap. 3.00 (ISBN 0-309-00836-0). Natl Acad Pr.

Criteria for Transport Pricing. Ed. by James R. Nelson. LC 73-4373. 1973. pap. 10.00x (ISBN 0-87033-176-0). Cornell Maritime.

Criteria for Underground Heat Distribution Systems. Building Research Advisory Board. LC 74-32581. 1975. pap. 4.75 (ISBN 0-309-02320-3). Natl Acad Pr.

Criterion-Referenced Measurement. W. James Popham. (Illus.). 1978. pap. 12.95 (ISBN 0-13-193607-7). P-H.

Criterion-Referenced Measurement & Criterion-Referenced Tests: Some Published Work Reviewed. R. Sumner & T. S. Robertson. (General Ser.). 1977. pap. text ed. 15.75x (ISBN 0-85633-116-3, NFER). Humanities.

Criterion-Referenced Testing for the Social Studies, No. 64. Ed. by Paul L. Williams & Jerry R. Moore. LC 80-84889. (Bulletin Ser.). 1980. pap. write for info. (ISBN 0-87986-034-0). Coun Soc Studies.

Critic of Civilization: Georges Duhamel & His Writings. L. Clark Keating. LC 65-12103. 288p. 1965. 11.00x (ISBN 0-8131-1104-8). U Pr of Ky.

Critical. John Somerville. 4.50 o.p. (ISBN 0-8062-1230-6). Carlton.

Critical Affairs: A Composer's Journal. Ned Rorem. LC 70-128574. 1970. 5.95 o.s.i. (ISBN 0-8076-0569-7). Braziller.

Critical Analysis of Radical Economics, the New Left, in Relationship to Karl Marx's Economic Theories: Radical Effects Upon Orthodox & Marxian Economic Doctrines. Dennis Phelps & Patricia Phelps. 1976. pap. text ed. 10.25x (ISBN 0-8191-0036-6). U Pr of Amer.

Critical & Biographical Notes on Early Spanish Music. J. F. Riano. LC 79-158958. (Music Ser). 1971. Repr. of 1887 ed. lib. bdg. 19.50 (ISBN 0-306-70193-6). Da Capo.

Critical & Doctrinal Commentary on Romans. William G. T. Shedd. 1978. 15.75 (ISBN 0-686-12955-5). Klock & Klock.

Critical & Historical Essays. 2nd ed. Edward MacDowell. LC 69-11289. 1969. Repr. of 1912 ed. lib. bdg. 19.50 (ISBN 0-306-71098-6). Da Capo.

Critical Appraisal of Comprehensive Education. J. M. Ross et al. (Research Reports Ser). 240p. (Orig.). 1972. pap. text ed. 18.25x (ISBN 0-901225-95-9, NFER). Humanities.

Critical Approaches to Literature. Daiches. 1979. pap. text ed. 11.50x (ISBN 0-582-48411-1). Longman.

Critical Approaches to Mark Twain's Short Stories. Ed. by Elizabeth McMahan. (National University Publications, Literary Criticism Ser.). 160p. 1981. 15.00 (ISBN 0-8046-9274-2). Kennikat.

Critical Approaches to Medieval Literature: Selected English Institute Papers 1958-1959. Ed. by Dorothy Bethurum. LC 60-13104. 1960. 15.00x (ISBN 0-231-02417-7). Columbia U Pr.

Critical Assumptions. K. K. Ruthven. LC 78-57760. 1979. 28.50 (ISBN 0-521-22257-5). Cambridge U Pr.

Critical Behaviors in Psychiatric-Mental Health Nursing: Monograph, 2 vols. Angeline M. Jacobs et al. Incl. Vol. 1. Survey of Mental Health Nursing Practices. 119p. pap. 4.00 (ISBN 0-89785-546-9); Vol. 3. Behavior of Attendants. 525p. pap. 8.50 (ISBN 0-89785-547-7). 1973. Am Inst Res.

Critical Bibliography of French Literature, Vol. 1: The Medieval Period. Ed. by David C. Cabeen & Urban T. Holmes. LC 47-3282. 1952. 25.00x (ISBN 0-8156-2005-5). Syracuse U Pr.

Critical Bibliography of French Literature, Vol. 2: The Sixteenth Century. Ed. by David C. Cabeen & Alexander H. Schutz. LC 47-3282. 1956. 25.00x (ISBN 0-8156-2006-3). Syracuse U Pr.

Critical Bibliography of French Literature, Vol. 3: The Seventeenth Century. Ed. by David C. Cabeen & Jules Brody. LC 47-3282. 1961. 25.00x (ISBN 0-8156-2007-1). Syracuse U Pr.

Critical Bibliography of German Literature in English Translation, 1481-1927. 2nd ed. Bayard Q. Morgan. LC 65-13549. 1965. Repr. of 1938 ed. 13.50 (ISBN 0-8108-0032-2). Scarecrow.

Critical Care. 3rd ed. Zeb Burrell, Jr. & Lennette O. Burrell. LC 76-53564. (Illus.). 1977. lib. bdg. 15.95 (ISBN 0-8016-0914-3). Mosby.

Critical Care Cardiology. Charles E. Rackley. Ed. by Albert N. Brest. (Cardiovascular Clinics Ser.: Vol. 11, No. 3). (Illus.). 245p. 1981. text ed. 40.00 (ISBN 0-8036-7242-X). Davis Co.

Critical Care Manual: A Systems Approach Method. 2nd ed. Burton A. Waisbren. 1977. pap. 16.00 (ISBN 0-87488-983-9). Med Exam.

Critical Care Medicine. I. William Goldfarb & Anthony P. Yates. 1980. Repr. of 1977 ed. write for info. (ISBN 0-935170-01-4). Synapse Pubns.

Critical Care Nursing. Mary E. Hazzard. (Nursing Outline Ser.). 1978. spiral bdg. 9.50 (ISBN 0-87488-384-9). Med Exam.

Critical Care Nursing: Body - Mind - Spirit. Cornelia V. Kenner et al. 1981. text ed. price not set (ISBN 0-316-48910-7). Little.

Critical Care Nursing of Children & Adolescents. American Assoc. of Critical-Care Nurses. Ed. by Annalee Oakes. (Illus.). 750p. 1981. pap. write for info. (ISBN 0-7216-1003-X). Saunders.

Critical Care Nursing of the Multi-Injured Patient. American Association of Critical Care Nurses. Ed. by James K. Mann & Annalee R Oakes. LC 79-67787. (Illus.). 168p. 1980. pap. 10.95 (ISBN 0-7216-1002-1). Saunders.

Critical Care Nursing Skills. Ardith J. Hamilton. 256p. 1981. pap. 12.95 (ISBN 0-8385-1242-9). ACC.

Critical Care of Neurologic & Neurosurgical Emergencies. Ed. by Richard A. Thompson & John R. Green. 1979. text ed. 22.50 (ISBN 0-89004-401-5). Raven.

Critical Circle: Literature & History in Contemporary Hermeneutics. David C. Hoy. 1978. 15.75x (ISBN 0-520-03434-1). U of Cal Pr.

Critical Criminology. Ian Taylor et al. (International Library of Sociology). 1975. 22.50x (ISBN 0-7100-8023-9); pap. 10.95 (ISBN 0-7100-8024-7). Routledge & Kegan.

Critical Dictionary of Composers & Their Music. Percy M. Young. LC 78-66927. (Encore Music Editions Ser.). 1981. Repr. of 1954 ed. 27.50 (ISBN 0-88355-771-1). Hyperion Conn.

Critical Dictionary of English Literature & British & American Authors, 3 Vols. S. Austin Allibone. LC 67-295. 1965. Repr. of 1872 ed. Set. 130.00 (ISBN 0-8103-3017-2). Gale.

Critical Difference: Essays in the Contemporary Rhetoric of Reading. Barbara Johnson. LC 80-21533. 176p. 1981. text ed. 12.00x (ISBN 0-8018-2458-3). Johns Hopkins.

Critical Edition of Ford's "Perkin Warbeck". Mildred C. Struble. (Publications in Language & Literature: No. 3). (Illus.). 214p. 1926. pap. 5.00 (ISBN 0-295-73760-3). U of Wash Pr.

Critical Edition of Robert Browning's "Bishop Blougram's Apology". Frank C. Allen. (Salzburg Studies in English Literature: Romantic Reassessment: No. 60). 243p. (Orig.). 1976. pap. 25.00x (ISBN 0-391-01296-7). Humanities.

Critical Edition of Tirso De Molina's Marta la Piadosa. Elvira F. Garcia. (Salzburg Studies in English Literature: Elizabethan & Renaissance Studies: No. 78). 1978. pap. text ed. 25.00x (ISBN 0-391-01380-7). Humanities.

Critical Edition of Wit's Triumvirate, or the Philosopher, 2 vols. Ed. by Cathryn A. Nelson. (Salzburg Studies in English Literature, Jacobean Drama Studies Ser.: Nos. 57-58). 422p. 1975. Set. pap. text ed. 50.25x (ISBN 0-391-01490-0). Humanities.

Critical Edition of Yeats' A Vision. Harper. 1980. text ed. 42.50x (ISBN 0-333-21299-1). Humanities.

Critical Elections & the Mainsprings of American Politics. Walter D. Burnham. (Illus.). 1971. pap. 5.95x (ISBN 0-393-09397-2). Norton.

Critical Encounters: Writers & Themes in Science Fiction. Ed. by Dick Riley. LC 78-4300. (Recognitions Ser.). 1978. 10.95 (ISBN 0-8044-2713-5); pap. 3.95 (ISBN 0-8044-6732-3). Ungar.

Critical Essays. Roland Barthes. Tr. by Richard Howard. xxi, 279p. 1972. 15.95x (ISBN 0-8101-0370-2); pap. 6.95x (ISBN 0-8101-0589-6). Northwestern U Pr.

Critical Essays from The Spectator. Joseph Addison. Ed. by Donald F. Bond. (Orig.). 1970. pap. 4.95x (ISBN 0-19-501359-X). Oxford U Pr.

Critical Essays of the Seventeenth Century, 3 vols. Ed. by Joel E. Spingarn. Incl. Vol. 1. 364p. 12.50x (ISBN 0-253-31551-4); Vol. 2. 368p. 12.50x (ISBN 0-253-31552-2); Vol. 3. 384p. 12.50x (ISBN 0-253-31553-0). LC 57-10727. 1957. Set. 32.50x (ISBN 0-253-31554-9). Ind U Pr.

Critical Essays on Charles Brockden Brown. Bernard Rosenthal. (Critical Essays on American Literature). 1981. lib. bdg. 25.00 (ISBN 0-8161-8255-8). Twayne.

Critical Essays on Erskine Caldwell. Scott MacDonald. (Critical Essays on American Literature). 1981. lib. bdg. 25.00 (ISBN 0-8161-8299-X). Twayne.

Critical Essays on Indo-Anglian Themes. Murli D. Melwani. (Greybird Bk.). 1976. 9.00 (ISBN 0-89253-595-4); flexible bdg. 5.00 (ISBN 0-89253-128-2). Ind-US Inc.

Critical Essays on Jane Austen. Ed. by B. C. Southam. 1968. 14.00x (ISBN 0-7100-6243-5); pap. 6.50 (ISBN 0-7100-6904-9). Routledge & Kegan.

Critical Essays on Psychoanalysis. S. Rachman. 1963. 19.25 o.p. (ISBN 0-08-010181-X). Pergamon.

Critical Essays on the Poetry of Tennyson. Ed. by John Killham. 1960. pap. 10.00 (ISBN 0-7100-4669-3). Routledge & Kegan.

Critical Essays on the Western American Novel. William T. Pilkington. (Reference Bks). 1980. lib. bdg. 25.00 (ISBN 0-8161-8351-1). G K Hall.

Critical Essays on Theodore Dreiser. Donald Pizer. (Critical Essays on American Literature). 1981. lib. bdg. 25.00 (ISBN 0-8161-8257-4). Twayne.

Critical Evaluation of Chemical & Physical Structural Information. Division of Chemistry & Chemical Technology. LC 74-4164. (Illus.). 624p. 1974. pap. 36.50 (ISBN 0-309-02146-4). Natl Acad Pr.

Critical Evaluation of Equilibrium Constants Involving Hydroxyquinoline & Its Metal Chelates: Critical Evaluation of Equilibrium Constants in Solutions: Pt. A: Stability Constants of Metal Complexes. Ed. by J. Stary et al. (Chemical Data Ser.: Vol. 24). (Illus.). 1979. text ed. 16.50 (ISBN 0-08-023929-3). Pergamon.

Critical Evaluation of Tumor Markers. Ed. by Sabine Von Kleist & H. Breuer. (Beitraege zur Onkologie (Contributions to Oncology): Vol. 7). (Illus.). x, 144p. 1981. pap. 28.75 (ISBN 3-8055-2353-X). S Karger.

Critical Examination of Our Financial Policy During the Southern Rebellion. Simon Newcomb. (Neglected American Economists Ser.). 1974. lib. bdg. 50.00 (ISBN 0-8240-1016-7). Garland Pub.

Critical Examination of the Belief in a Life After Death. C. J. Ducasse. (American Lecture Philosophy Ser). 336p. 1974. pap. 12.75 (ISBN 0-398-03037-5). C C Thomas.

Critical Examination of the Belief in a Life After Death. C. J. Ducasse. (American Lectures of Philosophy). 336p. 1974. pap. text ed. 9.75 o.p. (ISBN 0-398-02772-2). C C Thomas.

Critical Existentialism. Nicola Abbagnano. Ed. by Nino Langiulli. 6.75 (ISBN 0-8446-0450-X). Peter Smith.

Critical Food Issues of the Nineteen Eighties. Marylin Chou & David P. Harmon, Jr. LC 79-14718. (Pergamon Policy Studies). (Illus.). 1979. 44.00 (ISBN 0-08-024611-7); pap. 9.95 (ISBN 0-08-024639-7). Pergamon.

Critical Hermeneutics: A Study in the Thought of Paul Ricoeur & Jurgen Habermas. J. B. Thompson. LC 80-41935. 238p. Date not set. price not set (ISBN 0-521-23932-X). Cambridge U Pr.

Critical History of Children's Literature. rev. ed. Cornelia Meigs et al. LC 67-10271. (Illus.). 1969. 17.95 (ISBN 0-02-583900-4). Macmillan.

Critical History of English Literature, 2 vols. 2nd ed. D. Daiches. 1970. Set. 30.00 (ISBN 0-471-06962-0). Wiley.

Critical History of Modern Philosophy, Bacon to Kant: Hegal to Bradley. Y. Masih. 471p. 1976. text ed. 19.50x (ISBN 0-8426-0803-6). Verry.

Critical History of Police Reform. Samuel Walker. LC 76-53866. 1977. 21.95x (ISBN 0-669-01292-0). Lexington Bks.

Critical History of Western Philosophy. Ed. by Daniel J. O'Connor. LC 64-13242. 1964. text ed. 19.95 (ISBN 0-02-923260-0). Free Pr.

Critical Incident in Growth Groups: A Manual for Group Leaders. Arthur M. Cohen & R. Douglas Smith. LC 75-18139. 262p. 1976. 12.50 (ISBN 0-88390-107-2). Univ Assocs.

Critical Incident in Growth Groups: Theory & Technique. Arthur M. Cohen & R. Douglas Smith. LC 75-22510. 286p. 1976. pap. 14.95 (ISBN 0-88390-102-1). Univ Assocs.

Critical Incident Technique: A Bibliography. 2nd ed. Ed. by Grace Fivars. 1980. pap. 7.50 (ISBN 0-89785-662-7). Am Inst Res.

Critical Incidents in Management. 3rd ed. John M. Champion & John H. James. (Ser. in Management). (Orig.). 1975. pap. text ed. 7.95x o.p. (ISBN 0-256-01557-0). Irwin.

Critical Incidents in Management. 4th ed. John M. Champion & John H. James. 1980. pap. 10.95x (ISBN 0-256-02269-0). Irwin.

Critical Incidents in Organizational Behavior & Administration: With Selected Readings. James E. Chapman & F. J. Bridges. (Illus.). 1977. pap. text ed. 12.95 (ISBN 0-13-193896-7). P-H.

Critical Index: A Bibliography of Articles on Film in English, 1946-1973 - Arranged by Names & Topics. John Gerlach & Lana Gerlach. Ed. by Louis T. Milic. LC 74-1959. 1974. text ed. 20.00 o.p. (ISBN 0-8077-2442-4); pap. text ed. 9.25x (ISBN 0-8077-2438-6). Tchrs Coll.

Critical Introduction to Modern Arabic Poetry. M. M. Badawi. LC 75-9279. 275p. 1976. 48.00 (ISBN 0-521-20699-5); pap. 16.95x (ISBN 0-521-29023-6). Cambridge U Pr.

Critical Issues in Coal Transportation Systems. Maritime Transportation Research Board, National Research Council. 1979. pap. text ed. 9.75 (ISBN 0-309-02869-8). Natl Acad Pr.

Critical Issues in Corrections: Problems, Trends, & Prospects. Roy R. Roberg & Vincent J. Webb. 300p. 1981. pap. text ed. 10.95 (ISBN 0-8299-0405-0). West Pub.

Critical Issues in Criminal Justice. Donald O. Schultz. (Illus.). 304p. 1975. 18.75 (ISBN 0-398-03331-5). C C Thomas.

Critical Issues in Educational Policy: An Administrator's Overview. Louis J. Rubin. 492p. 1980. text ed. 19.95 (ISBN 0-205-06815-4). Allyn.

Critical Issues in Law Enforcement. 3d ed. Ed. by Harry More. LC 79-55205. 352p. 1981. pap. text ed. price not set (ISBN 0-87084-582-9). Anderson Pub Co.

Critical Issues in Modern Religion. R. Johnson et al. 1973. pap. 12.95 (ISBN 0-13-193979-3). P-H.

Critical Issues in Psychiatric Diagnosis. Ed. by Robert L. Spitzer & Donald F. Klein. LC 77-72812. (American Psychopathological Association Ser.). 1978. 31.50 (ISBN 0-89004-213-6). Raven.

Critical Issues of Skin Colour: A Treatise on the Sociological, Economic & Political Reality of Blacks in a White Society. Mphahlele K. Lukman. 125p. 1980. text ed. 10.50 (ISBN 0-9602660-0-3). M Lukman.

Critical Look at "Urban Dynamics". Harvey A. Garn & Robert H. Wilson. 38p. 1970. pap. 2.00 o.p. (ISBN 0-87766-096-4, 30009). Urban Inst.

Critical Moments: Reflecting on Theater & Society. Robert Brustein. 1980. 10.00 (ISBN 0-394-51093-3). Random.

Critical Neurological Assessment & Management. Nikas. 1981. text ed. price not set. Churchill.

Critical Neurological Surgical Assessment & Management: Contemporary Issues in Critical Care Nursing. Diana L. Nikas. (Vol. 2). (Illus.). 224p. 1981. lib. bdg. 20.00 (ISBN 0-443-08158-1). Churchill.

Critical Ninth Assembling. Ed. by Richard Kostelanetz. LC 78-72282. (Illus.). 1979. pap. text ed. 10.00 (ISBN 0-915066-33-5). Assembling Pr.

Critical Path. R. Buckminster Fuller. 448p. 1981. 15.95 (ISBN 0-312-17488-8). St Martin.

Critical Path: An Essay on the Social Context of Literary Criticism. Northrop Frye. LC 70-143246. (Midland Bks.: No. 158). 176p. 1971. 8.95x (ISBN 0-253-31568-9); pap. 3.50x (ISBN 0-253-20158-6). Ind U Pr.

Critical Path: Construction & Analysis. L. W. Morris. 1967. text ed. 25.00 (ISBN 0-08-012472-0); pap. text ed. 12.75 (ISBN 0-08-012471-2). Pergamon.

Critical Path: Network Analysis & Resource Scheduling. 2nd ed. C. B. Reynaud. 1970. text ed. 17.50x (ISBN 0-7121-3301-1). Intl Ideas.

Critical Perspectives & Issues in Health Policy. Ed. by Ralph Straetz et al. (Orig.). 1980. pap. 5.00 (ISBN 0-918592-42-9). Policy Studies.

Critical Perspectives on Amos Tutuola. Ed. by Bernth Lindfors. LC 75-13706. 318p. (Orig.). 1975. 20.00 (ISBN 0-914478-05-2); pap. 9.00 (ISBN 0-914478-06-0). Three Continents.

Critical Perspectives on Child Abuse. Ed. by Richard Bourne & Eli H. Newberger. LC 77-18565. (Illus.). 1978. 19.95 (ISBN 0-669-02109-1). Lexington Bks.

Critical Perspectives on Modern Arabic Literature. Ed. by Issa Boullata. LC 78-13851. (Orig.). 1980. 22.00x (ISBN 0-89410-007-6); pap. 10.00x (ISBN 0-89410-008-4). Three Continents.

Critical Perspectives on Nigerian Literatures. Ed. by Bernth Lindfors. 1976. cased 20.00 (ISBN 0-914478-27-3); pap. 9.00 (ISBN 0-914478-28-1). Three Continents.

Critical Perspectives on the "Decameron". Ed. by Robert S. Dombroski. LC 76-24068. 1977. text ed. 16.50x o.p. (ISBN 0-06-491735-5). B&N.

Critical Perspectives on V. S. Naipaul. Robert D. Hamner. LC 77-71683. (Illus., Orig.). 1977. 20.00x (ISBN 0-914478-17-6); pap. 9.00x (ISBN 0-914478-18-4). Three Continents.

Critical Perspectives on Wole Soyinka. Ed. by James Gibbs. LC 79-89931. (Critical Perspectives Ser.). (Illus.). 274p. (Orig.). 1980. 20.00 (ISBN 0-914478-49-4); pap. 9.00 (ISBN 0-914478-50-8). Three Continents.

Critical Phenomena. Ed. by M. S. Green. (Italian Physical Society: Course 51). 1973. 56.00 (ISBN 0-12-368851-5). Acad Pr.

Critical Practice. Catherine Belsey. 176p. 1980. 17.00 (ISBN 0-416-72940-1, 2022); pap. 7.95 (ISBN 0-416-72950-9, 2021). Methuen Inc.

Critical Problems in the History of Science. Ed. by Marshall Clagett. 1959. 25.00x (ISBN 0-299-01870-9); pap. 9.95x (ISBN 0-299-01874-1). U of Wis Pr.

Critical Psychiatry: The Politics of Mental Health. Ed. by David Ingleby. 1980. 11.95 (ISBN 0-394-42622-3); pap. 5.95 (ISBN 0-394-73560-9). Pantheon.

Critical Reading: Workbook A Reusable Edition. George F. Lowerre & Alice M. Scandure. (gr. 3-8). 1973. 4.50 (ISBN 0-89039-070-3); tchrs' manual 2.00 (ISBN 0-686-67915-6). Ann Arbor Pubs.

Critical Reading, Workbook B: Reusable Edition. George F. Lowerre. (gr. 3-8). 1973. wkbk. 5.00 (ISBN 0-89039-072-X). Ann Arbor Pubs.

Critical Reading: Workbook C Reusable Edition. George F. Lowerre. (gr. 3-8). 1973. wkbk. 5.50 (ISBN 0-89039-074-6). Ann Arbor Pubs.

Critical Reading: Workbook D, Reusable Edition. George F. Lowerre & Alice M. Scandure. (gr. 3-8). 1973. wkbk. 5.00 (ISBN 0-89039-076-2). Ann Arbor Pubs.

Critical Reception of Browning's The Ring & the Book, 1868-89,1951-68. Ezzat A. Khattab. (Salzburg Studies in English Literature: Romantic Reassessment Ser.: No. 66). (Orig.). 1977. pap. text ed. 25.00x (ISBN 0-391-01444-7). Humanities.

Critical Reception of Howard Nemerov: A Selection of Essays & a Bibliography. Bowie Duncan. LC 70-154299. 1971. 10.00 (ISBN 0-8108-0400-X). Scarecrow.

Critical Reception of Shakespeare's "Antony & Cleopatra" from 1607 to 1905. Michael Von Steppat. (Bochum Studies in English: No. 9). 619p. 1980. text ed. 45.75x (ISBN 90-6032-188-X). Humanities.

Critical Reflections on Transformational Grammar. rev. ed. Claude Hagege. Tr. by Valerie B. Makkai from Fr. Orig. Title: Grammaire Generative: Reflexions Critiques. 1981. pap. 12.00 (ISBN 0-933104-09-X). Jupiter Pr.

Critical Reputation of Byron's Don Juan. Jay A. Ward. (Salzburg Institute for English Literature Jacobean Drama Studies). (Orig.). 1979. pap. text ed. 25.00x (ISBN 0-391-01722-5). Humanities.

Critical Reputation of Restoration Comedy in Modern Times up to 1950, 2 vols, Vols. 1 & 2. Steven Van der Weele. (Salzburg Studies in English Literature, Poetic Drama & Poetic Theory: No. 36). 1978. pap. text ed. 25.00x ea. Vol. 1 (ISBN 0-391-01560-5). Vol. 2 (ISBN 0-391-01561-3). Humanities.

Critical Response: Selected Essays on the American, Commonwealth, Indian & British Traditions in Literature. D. V. Raghavacharyulu. 1980. 13.50x (ISBN 0-8364-0632-X, Pub. by Macmillan India). South Asia Bks.

Critical Review of Equilibrium Data for Proton- and Metal Complexes of 1,10-Phenanthroline, 2,2'-Bipyridyl & Related Compounds: Critical Evaluation of Equilibrium Const. in Solution; Part A: Stability Const. of Metal Complexes, Vol. 17. Ed. by W. A. McBryde. 1978. pap. text ed. 18.75 (ISBN 0-08-022344-3). Pergamon.

Critical Review of Recent Literature on Toxicity of Cyanides to Fish. Peter Doudoroff. LC 80-68588. 71p. (Orig.). 1980. pap. 3.60 (ISBN 0-89364-039-5, API 847-87000). Am Petroleum.

Critical Stability Constants, Vols.1-4. Ed. by Arthur E. Martell & Robert M. Smith. Incl. Vol. 1. Amino Acids. 469p. 1974. 35.00 (ISBN 0-306-35211-7); Vol. 2. Amines. 415p. 1975. 45.00 (ISBN 0-306-35212-5); Vol. 3. Other Organic Ligands. 495p. 1977. 49.50 (ISBN 0-306-35213-3); Vol. 4. Inorganic Complexes. 257p. 1976. 35.00 (ISBN 0-306-35214-1). LC 74-10610. (Illus., Plenum Pr). Plenum Pub.

Critical Studies in Indian Grammarians I, Theory of Homogeneity: Savarnya. Madhav Deshpande. LC 75-36896. (Michigan Series in South & Southeast Asian Languages & Linguistics: No. 2). 223p. 1975. pap. 6.00x (ISBN 0-89148-052-8). Ctr S&SE Asian.

Critical Study of Freud's Concept of Unconscious Mental Processes with Special Reference to Gestalt Psychology. Allan R. Strauss, Jr. (Illus.). 1980. 12.50 (ISBN 0-682-49602-2, University). Exposition.

Critical Study of Hinduism. Sarasvati Chennakesvan. 1980. 12.50x (ISBN 0-8364-0614-1). South Asia Bks.

Critical Study of Sacred Texts. Ed. by Wendy D. O'Flaherty. 1980. 16.00 (ISBN 0-89581-101-4). Lancaster-Miller.

Critical Study of the Malindapanha: Critique of Buddhist Philosophy. Rabindranath Basu. 1978. 7.50x o.p. (ISBN 0-8364-0141-7). South Asia Bks.

Critical Surgical Illness. 2nd ed. James D. Hardy. (Illus.). 750p. 1980. text ed. 42.50 (ISBN 0-7216-4511-9). Saunders.

Critical Survey of Indian Philosophy. Chandradhar D. Sharma. 1964. 7.50x o.p. (ISBN 0-8426-1517-2). Verry.

Critical Survey of Stability Constants & Related Thermodynamic Data of Flouride Complexes in Aqueous Solution. Ed. by A. M. Bond & G. T. Hefter. (Chemical Data Ser.: No. 27). 80p. 1980. 29.00 (ISBN 0-08-022377-X). Pergamon.

Critical Survey of Western Philosophy. Barlingay & Kulkarni. 1980. write for info (ISBN 0-391-01767-5). Humanities.

Critical Theory. Max Horkheimer. Tr. by Matthew J. O'Connell et al from Ger. LC 72-5309. 300p. 1972. pap. 3.50 (ISBN 0-8164-9226-3); o.p. (ISBN 0-8164-9272-7, Continuum). Continuum.

Critical Theory of Literature. Costanzo Di Girolamo. 1981. 15.00 (ISBN 0-299-08120-6). U of Wis Pr.

Critical Theory of Society. Albrecht Wellmer. LC 70-150309. 1971. pap. 3.50 (ISBN 0-8164-9189-5); o.p. (ISBN 0-8164-9189-5, Continuum). Continuum.

Critical Thinking. 2nd ed. Max Black. 1952. text ed. 16.50 (ISBN 0-13-194092-9). P-H.

Critical Twilight: Explorations in the Ideology of Anglo-American Literary Theory from Eliot to McLuhan. John Fekete. (International Library of Phenomenology & Moral Sciences). 1978. 22.50x (ISBN 0-7100-8618-0). Routledge & Kegan.

Critical Way in Religion. Duncan Howlett. LC 80-7460. 360p. 1980. 14.95 (ISBN 0-87975-133-9). Prometheus Bks.

Critical Writings of Adrian Stokes. Adrian Stokes. Ed. by Lawrence Gowing. 1978. 24.95 ea. (ISBN 0-685-87325-0); Vol. I. (ISBN 0-500-01175-3); Vol. II. (ISBN 0-500-01176-1); Vol. III. (ISBN 0-500-01177-X). Thames Hudson.

Critical Writings of Ford Madox Ford. Ford M. Ford. Ed. by Frank MacShane. LC 64-11356. (Regents Critics Ser). 1964. 9.75x (ISBN 0-8032-0455-8); pap. 2.65x (ISBN 0-8032-5454-7, B*B 401, Bison). U of Nebr Pr.

Criticality Control of Fissile Materials. (Illus., Orig.). 1966. pap. 39.75 (ISBN 92-0-020066-4, IAEA). Unipub.

Criticism As Dialogue. Walter Stein. LC 69-12929. 1969. 42.00 (ISBN 0-521-07439-8). Cambridge U Pr.

Criticism of Henry Fielding. Ioan Williams. 1970. 30.00 (ISBN 0-7100-6596-5). Routledge & Kegan.

Criticizing the Critics. John W. English. (Humanistic Studies in the Communication Arts). Date not set. 14.95 (ISBN 0-8038-1270-1); pap. text ed. 7.95 (ISBN 0-8038-1272-8). Hastings.

Critics. Lehman Engel. 1976. 14.95 o.s.i. (ISBN 0-02-536060-4). Macmillan.

Critics & Criticism. A. G. George. 1971. lib. bdg. 8.75x (ISBN 0-210-22347-2). Asia.

Critics of Abstract Expressionism. Stephen C. Foster. Ed. by Donald B. Kuspit. (Studies in Fine Arts: Criticism: No. 13). 130p. 1980. 21.95 (ISBN 0-8357-1088-2, Pub. by UMI Res Pr). Univ Microfilms.

Critics of Consciousness: The Existential Structures of Literature. Sarah N. Lawall. LC 68-25614. 1968. 15.00x (ISBN 0-674-17750-9). Harvard U Pr.

Critics on Shakespeare. Ed. by W. T. Andrews. (Readings in Literary Criticism). 1973. pap. text ed. 6.75x (ISBN 0-04-821034-X). Allen Unwin.

Critics on Wordsworth. Ed. by Raymond Cowell. (Readings in Literary Criticism). 1973. pap. text ed. 6.75x (ISBN 0-04-801015-4). Allen Unwin.

Critique of Film Theory. Brian Henderson. 224p. 1980. 15.95 (ISBN 0-525-08740-0); pap. 8.95 (ISBN 0-525-47526-5). Dutton.

Critique of Hegel's "Philosophy of Right". Karl Marx. Ed. by J. O'Malley. LC 74-112471. (Cambridge Studies in the History & Theory of Politics). 1970. 23.95 o.p. (ISBN 0-521-07836-9); pap. 8.50x (ISBN 0-521-29211-5). Cambridge U Pr.

Critique of Instrumental Reason. Max Horkheimer et al. LC 74-8450. 160p. 1974. 7.95 (ISBN 0-8164-9221-2); pap. 4.95 (ISBN 0-8164-9336-7). Continuum.

Critique of Practical Reason. Immanuel Kant. Tr. by Lewis W. Beck. LC 56-2993. 1956. pap. 4.95 (ISBN 0-672-60223-7, LLA52). Bobbs.

Critique of Practical Reason & Other Writings in Moral Philosophy. Immanuel Kant. Tr. by Lewis W. Beck. LC 75-32038. (Philosophy of Immanuel Kant Ser.: Vol. 1). 1977. Repr. of 1949 ed. lib. bdg. 35.00 (ISBN 0-8240-2325-0). Garland Pub.

Critique of Pure Reason. Immanuel Kant. pap. 3.95 (ISBN 0-385-07534-0, A551, Anch). Doubleday.

Critique of Religion & Philosophy. Walter Kaufmann. 1978. 17.50x (ISBN 0-691-07230-2); pap. 5.95 (ISBN 0-691-02001-9). Princeton U Pr.

Critique of Soviet Economics. Mao Tse Tung. Tr. by Moss Roberts from Chinese. LC 77-70971. 1977. 10.00 o.p. (ISBN 0-85345-412-4, CL4124). Monthly Rev.

Critique of the Gotha Program. Marx. pap. 1.25 (ISBN 0-8351-0059-6). China Bks.

Critiques & Essays on Modern Fiction, 1920-1951: Representing the Achievement of Modern American & British Critics. Ed. by John W. Aldridge. LC 52-6180. 1952. 13.95 (ISBN 0-8260-0275-7). Wiley.

Critiques of Confucius in Contemporary China. Kamm Louie. LC 80-214. 210p. 1980. 22.50 (ISBN 0-312-17645-7). St Martin.

Critiques of God. Ed. by Peter Angeles. LC 76-43520. (Skeptic's Bookshelf Ser.). 371p. 1976. 13.95 (ISBN 0-87975-077-4); pap. 8.95 (ISBN 0-87975-078-2). Prometheus Bks.

Critiques of God. Ed. by Peter Angeles. pap. 7.00 (ISBN 0-87980-349-5). Wilshire.

Crito. Plato. Ed. by James Adam. (Gr). text ed. 6.50x with vocab. (ISBN 0-521-05959-3). Cambridge U Pr.

Crittenden: A Kentucky Story of Love & War. John Fox. 1976. lib. bdg. 12.95x (ISBN 0-89968-035-6). Lightyear.

Critter Chronicles: Tales for Next Tuesday. John Barnetson. LC 80-66262. (Illus.). 96p. 1981. 12.95 (ISBN 0-89742-037-3). Dawne-Leigh. Postponed.

Cro-Magnon Man. Tom Prideaux. LC 73-79435. (Emergence of Man Ser). (Illus.). (gr. 6 up). 1973. lib. bdg. 11.56 o.p. (ISBN 0-8094-1272-1, Pub. by Time-Life). Silver.

Cro-Magnon Man. Tom Prideaux. (Emergence of Man Ser.). (Illus.). 1973. 9.95 (ISBN 0-8094-1271-3); lib. bdg. avail. (ISBN 0-685-41617-8). Time-Life.

Croatian-English, English-Croatian Pocket Dictionary. R. Filipovic. 1977. pap. 7.50 o.p. (ISBN 0-686-22671-1, Y-726). Vanous.

Crochet. Rita Van Der Klip. (Illus.). 1977. 6.95 (ISBN 0-8467-0240-1, Pub. by Two Continents). Hippocrene Bks.

Crochet Designs from Simple Motifs. Maggie Jo Norton. 1978. 19.95 (ISBN 0-7134-1238-0). David & Charles.

Crochet for Beginners. Jessie Rubenstone. LC 74-4462. (Illus.). 64p. (gr. 3-4). 1974. 7.95 (ISBN 0-397-31547-3); pap. 2.95 o.p. (ISBN 0-397-31548-1). Lippincott.

Crochet for the Connoisseur. Rosemarie Anderson. (Illus.). 120p. 1980. 22.50 (ISBN 0-7134-1144-9, Pub. by Batsford England). David & Charles.

Crochet Lace with Complete Diagrams. Ondori Staff. (Ondori Needlecraft Ser.). (Illus.). 1978. pap. 6.95 (ISBN 0-87040-415-6). Japan Pubns.

Crochet: Pretty & Practical. Caroline Horne. (Illus.). 120p. 1975. 11.50 (ISBN 0-263-05151-X). Transatlantic.

Crochet, Step by Step. Emily Wildman. (Step by Step Craft Ser). 1972. PLB 9.15 o.p. (ISBN 0-307-62009-3, Golden Pr); pap. 2.95 (ISBN 0-307-42009-4). Western Pub.

Crocheting Afgans. Rita Weiss. (Illus.). 1979. pap. 1.50 (ISBN 0-486-23883-0). Dover.

Crocheting Doilies. Ed. by Rita Weiss. LC 76-24565. (Illus.). 48p. 1976. pap. 1.75 (ISBN 0-486-23424-X). Dover.

Crocheting Edgings. Rita Weiss. (Illus.). 48p. 1980. pap. 1.75 (ISBN 0-486-24031-2). Dover.

Crocheting Storybook Hand Puppets. Susan Verkest. 1980. pap. 1.50 (ISBN 0-486-23887-3). Dover.

Crocheting Tablecloths & Placemats. Ed. & intro. by Florence Weinstein. LC 74-21221. (Illus.). 160p. 1975. pap. 4.00 (ISBN 0-486-20659-9). Dover.

Crochets & Quavers: Or Revelations of an Opera Manager in America. 2nd ed. Max Maretzek. LC 65-23397. (Music Ser). 1966. Repr. of 1855 ed. lib. bdg. 27.50 (ISBN 0-306-70915-5). Da Capo.

Crociato in Egitto, 2 vols. Giacomo Meyerbeer. Ed. by Philip Gossett & Charles Rosen. LC 76-49193. (Early Romantic Opera Ser.: Vol. 18). 1980. Set. lib. bdg. 164.00 (ISBN 0-8240-2917-8). Garland Pub.

Crock of Gold. James Stephens. (Illus.). 1960. 5.95 o.p. (ISBN 0-02-614120-5). Macmillan.

Crockery Cookery. Mable Hoffman. LC 74-30823. 192p. 1975. pap. 5.95 (ISBN 0-912656-43-3). H P Bks.

Crockery Pot Cookbook. Carmel B. Reingold. (Orig.). 1975. pap. 1.50 (ISBN 0-515-03950-0). Jove Pubns.

Crockett: Brand of Fear. Brad Lang. 1976. pap. 1.25 o.p. (ISBN 0-685-69159-4, LB367ZK, Leisure Bks). Nordon Pubns.

Crockett on the Loose. Brad Lang. (Crockett Ser). (Orig.). 1975. pap. 1.25 o.p. (ISBN 0-685-53900-8, LB283ZK, Leisure Bks). Nordon Pubns.

Crockford's Clerical Directory, 1975-76: A Reference Book of the Clergy of the Provinces of Canterbury & York of Other Anglican Provinces & Dioceses, Eighty-Sixth Issue. (Illus.). 1976. 49.50x o.p. (ISBN 0-19-200008-X). Oxford U Pr.

Crockford's Clerical Directory, 1977-1979. 1550p. 1980. 98.00x (ISBN 0-19-200009-8). Oxford U Pr.

Crocodile on the Sandbank. Elizabeth Peters. LC 74-31490. 1975. 7.95 (ISBN 0-396-07080-9). Dodd.

Crocodile on the Sandbank. Elizabeth Peters. 1978. pap. 1.75 o.p. (ISBN 0-449-23713-3, Crest). Fawcett.

Crocodile Under Louis Finneberg's Bed. Nancy W. Parker. LC 77-16875. (ps-4). 1978. 5.50 (ISBN 0-396-07542-8). Dodd.

Crocodiles & Alligators. Susan Harris. (gr. 2-4). 1980. PLB 6.45 (ISBN 0-531-00443-0). Watts.

Crohn's Disease. James Kyle. (Illus.). 1972. 17.50x (ISBN 0-433-18900-2). Intl Ideas.

Crohn's Disease of the Gastrointestinal Tract. Howard Schachter & Joseph B. Kirsner. LC 80-10339. (Clinical Gastroenterology Monographs). 1980. 28.50 (ISBN 0-471-48896-8, Pub. by Wiley Medical). Wiley.

Cromwell & Communism. Eduard Bernstein. LC 63-18392. 1930. 21.00x (ISBN 0-678-05153-4). Kelley.

Cromwell & the New Model Foreign Policy. Charles P. Korr. 1975. 19.50x (ISBN 0-520-02281-5). U of Cal Pr.

Cromwellian Ireland: English Government & Reform in Ireland 1649-1660. T. C. Barnard. (Oxford Historical Monographs). 352p. 1975. text ed. 45.00x (ISBN 0-19-821858-3). Oxford U Pr.

Cronaca Familiare. Vasco Pratolini. Ed. by Ilene T. Olken. LC 73-130788. (Orig., Ital.). 1971. pap. text ed. 8.95x (ISBN 0-89197-117-3). Irvington.

Cronicas Brasileiras: A Portuguese Reader. Ed. by Alfred Hower & Richard A. Preto-Rodas. LC 77-634081. 1971. pap. 7.00x (ISBN 0-8130-0325-3). U Presses Fla.

Cronistoria, 5 vols. Ed. by Giselda Capetti. 400p. (Orig.). 1980. Set. pap. write for info. (ISBN 0-89944-043-6); Vol. 1. pap. (ISBN 0-89944-044-4); Vol. 2. pap. (ISBN 0-89944-045-2); Vol. 3. pap. (ISBN 0-89944-046-0); Vol. 4. pap. (ISBN 0-89944-047-9); Vol. 5. pap. (ISBN 0-89944-048-7). D Bosco Pubns.

Cronopios & Famas. Julio Cortazar. Tr. by Paul Blackburn from Span. LC 69-15477. (Illus.). 1978. pap. 2.95 (ISBN 0-394-73616-8). Pantheon.

Crooked & Narrow Streets of the Town of Boston, 1630-1822. Annie H. Thwing. LC 74-129974. (Illus.). 1970. Repr. of 1920 ed. 18.00 (ISBN 0-8103-3538-7). Gale.

Crooked Colt. Clarence W. Anderson. (Illus.). (gr. k-3). 1966. 7.95 (ISBN 0-02-703410-0). Macmillan.

Crooked Hinge. John D. Carr. 1964. pap. 2.95 (ISBN 0-02-018510-3, Collier). Macmillan.

Crooked House. Agatha Christie. 1980. pap. 2.50 (ISBN 0-671-83319-7). PB.

Crooked Letter. Linda DuBreuil. 1979. pap. 1.75 (ISBN 0-505-51385-4). Tower Bks.

Crooked Paths: Reflections on Socialism, Conservatism & the Welfare State. Peter Clecak. LC 76-5118. 1977. 10.95 o.s.i. (ISBN 0-06-010838-X, HarpT). Har-Row.

Crooked Road: A History of the Alaska Highway. David A. Remley. LC 75-23239. (Illus.). 1976. 10.95 o.p. (ISBN 0-07-051872-6, GB). McGraw.

Crooked Tree. Robert C. Wilson. 1981. pap. 2.75 (ISBN 0-425-04842-X). Berkley Pub.

Crop Genetic Resources for Today & Tomorrow. Ed. by O. H. Frankel & J. G. Hawkes. LC 74-82586. (International Biological Programme Ser.: Vol. 2). (Illus.). 544p. 1975. 75.00 (ISBN 0-521-20575-1). Cambridge U Pr.

Crop Husbandry. 2nd ed. R. D. Park & Maurice Eddowes. (Illus.). 332p. 1975. 36.00x (ISBN 0-19-859443-7). Oxford U Pr.

Crop Physiology. Ed. by L. T. Evans. LC 73-91816. (Illus.). 384p. 1975. 47.50 (ISBN 0-521-20422-4); pap. 17.50x (ISBN 0-521-29390-1). Cambridge U Pr.

Crop Production in Europe. Maurice Eddowes. (Illus.). 1977. 36.00x (ISBN 0-19-859444-5). Oxford U Pr.

Crop Production: Principles & Practices. Stephen R. Chapman & Lark P. Carter. LC 75-40318. (Illus.). 1976. text ed. 23.95x (ISBN 0-7167-0581-8). W H Freeman.

Crop Reactions to Water & Temperature Stresses in Humid, Temperate Climates. C. David Raper & Paul J. Kramer. (Special Studies in Agricultural Science & Policy). 425p. 1981. lib. bdg. 30.00x (ISBN 0-686-69585-2). Westview.

Crop Science: Laboratory Manual. 2nd ed. Richard P. Waldren & Stanley W. Ehler. 1981. write for info. (ISBN 0-8087-3717-1). Burgess.

Croppy: A Tale of 1798, 3 vols. John Banim & Michael Banim. Ed. by Robert L. Wolff. (Ireland Nineteenth Century Fiction Ser. Two: Vol. 19). 948p. 1979. Set. lib. bdg. 96.00 (ISBN 0-8240-3468-6). Garland Pub.

Crops on a Few Acres. (Country Home Ser.). 96p. 2.95 (ISBN 0-88453-010-8). Berkshire Traveller.

Crops on a Few Acres. Hollis Lee. (Country Home & Small Farm Guides Ser.). (Illus.). 1978. pap. 2.95 (ISBN 0-88453-010-8). Barrington.

Croquet. Jim Charlton & Bill Thompson. LC 76-56089. (Encore Edition). (Illus.). 1977. 9.95 o.p. (ISBN 0-916844-01-3, ScribT); pap. 2.45 o.p. (ISBN 0-684-16369-1, ScribT). Scribner.

Cross. Morton T. Kelsey. LC 80-82086. 118p. 1980. pap. 2.95 (ISBN 0-8091-2337-1). Paulist Pr.

Cross & Common Man. H. Gockel. 1980. 5.95 (ISBN 0-8100-0119-5). Northwest Pub.

Cross & Santification. T. A. Hegre. LC 51-7866. Orig. Title: Three Aspects of the Cross. 1960. pap. 3.50 (ISBN 0-87123-067-4, 210067). Bethany Fell.

Cross & the Church. James D. Bales. pap. 1.95 (ISBN 0-89315-011-8). Lambert Bk.

Cross & the Ensign: A Naval History of Malta 1798-1978. Peter R. Elliott. LC 79-93365. (Illus.). 192p. 1980. 16.95 (ISBN 0-87021-926-X). Naval Inst Pr.

Cross & the Switchblade. David Wilkerson. 1976. pap. 1.50 (ISBN 0-89129-197-0). Jove Pubns.

Cross & the Switchblade. David Wilkerson et al. 1970. pap. 2.25 (ISBN 0-515-05844-0). Jove Pubns.

Cross-Country. Herbert Kastle. 336p. 1975. 8.95 o.p. (ISBN 0-440-03383-7). Delacorte.

Cross-Country Cat. Mary Calhoun. (Illus.). (gr. k-3). 1979. 7.50 (ISBN 0-688-22186-6); PLB 7.20 (ISBN 0-688-32186-0). Morrow.

Cross-Country Flying. Paul Garrison. (Illus.). 192p. 1980. 9.95 (ISBN 0-8306-9966-X); pap. 5.95 (ISBN 0-8306-2284-5, 2284). TAB Bks.

Cross-Country Running. Marc Bloom. LC 77-84523. 193p. 1978. pap. 3.95 (ISBN 0-89037-092-3); write for info. handbk. (ISBN 0-89037-091-5). Anderson World.

Cross-Country Ski Trails in the Rockies. John Williams. 1978. 11.95 o.p. (ISBN 0-8092-7573-2); pap. 5.95 (ISBN 0-8092-7572-4). Contemp Bks.

Cross Country Skiing. Toni Reiter & Siegfried Maier. (Illus.). 1980. pap. 4.95 (ISBN 0-8120-2040-5). Barron.

Cross-Country Skiing & Snowshoeing. Erwin A. Bauer. (Illus.). 256p. 1975. 11.95 (ISBN 0-87691-200-5). Winchester Pr.

Cross-Country Skiing Handbook. rev. ed. Edward Baldwin. 1973. pap. 4.95 o.p. (ISBN 0-684-13420-9, SL397, ScribT). Scribner.

Cross Creek Cookery. Marjorie K. Rawlings. LC 42-25465. (Illus.). 1942. 12.95 (ISBN 0-684-10487-3, ScribT). Scribner.

Cross-Cultural Broadcasting. (Reports & Papers on Mass Communication: No. 77). 1976. pap. 2.50 (ISBN 9-2310-1353-X, U107, UNESCO). Unipub.

Cross-Cultural Contributions to Psychology: Selected Papers from the 4th International Conference of the International Association for Cross-Cultural Psychology, Munich, July 28-August 5, 1978. Ed. by Lutz H. Eckensberger et al. 442p. 1979. pap. text ed. 31.75 (ISBN 90-265-0300-8, Pub. by Swets Pub Serv Holland). Swets North Am.

Cross-Cultural Counseling & Psychotherapy. Anthony Marsella & Paul B. Pedersen. (General Psychology Ser.). Date not set. price not set (ISBN 0-08-025545-0). Pergamon. Postponed.

Cross Cultural Perspectives on Learning. Ed. by R. W. Brislin et al. LC 73-91353. 366p. 1975. 18.95 (ISBN 0-470-10471-6). Halsted Pr.

Cross-Cultural Psychiatry. Ed. by Albert Gaw. 475p. 1981. text ed. 37.50 (ISBN 0-88416-338-5). PSG Pub.

Cross-Cultural Research Methods. Richard W. Brislin et al. LC 73-772. (Comparative Studies in Behavioral Sciences). 1973. 18.95 (ISBN 0-471-10470-1, Pub. by Wiley-Interscience). Wiley.

Cross-Cultural Review Chapbook Series of World Literature & Art, 14 bks. Incl. Chapbook 1. Raccomandazione. Wat Scammacca. Ed. by Stanley H. Barkan. pap. 2.50 saddlestitched (ISBN 0-89304-800-3); Chapbook 2. Man Who Fell in Love with a Chicken. David B. Axelrod. Ed. by Stanley H. Barkan. pap. 2.00 saddlestitched (ISBN 0-89304-801-1); Chapbook 3. Gentle Spears. Arthur Dobrin. Ed. by Stanley H. Barkan. pap. 2.00 saddlestitched (ISBN 0-89304-802-X); Chapbook 4. Bird & I. Frazil H. Daglarca. Ed. by Stanley H. Barkan. Tr. by Talat S. Halman. pap. 2.00 saddlestitched (ISBN 0-89304-803-8); Chapbook 5. You & I & the World. Werner Aspenstrom. Ed. by Stanley H. Barkan. Tr. by Siv Cedering. pap. 3.50 saddlestitched (ISBN 0-89304-804-6); Chapbook 6. Unfinished Sequence. Edward Butscher. Ed. by Stanley H. Barkan. pap. 2.00 saddlestitched (ISBN 0-89304-805-4); Chapbook 7. Satyr. Susan Hartman. Ed. by Stanley H. Barkan. (Illus.). pap. 2.00 saddlestitched (ISBN 0-89304-806-2); Chapbook 8. Strangled Cries. Julius Balbin. Ed. by Stanley H. Barkan. Tr. by Charles Rizzuto. pap. 2.50 saddlestitched (ISBN 0-89304-807-0); Chapbook 9. What Poetry Is. Harry Mulisch. Ed. by Stanley H. Barkan. Tr. by Claire N. White. pap. 3.50 saddlestitched (ISBN 0-89304-808-9); Chapbook 10. Translator's Son. Joseph Bruchac. Ed. by Stanley H. Barkan. (Illus.). pap. 3.50 saddlestitched (ISBN 0-89304-809-7); Chapbook 11. Footnotes. Donald Lev. Ed. by Stanley H. Barkan. pap. 2.00 saddlestitched (ISBN 0-89304-810-0); Chapbook 12. Confessions. Enid Dame. Ed. by Stanley H. Barkan. pap. 2.00 saddlestitched (ISBN 0-89304-811-9); Chapbook 13. Blue Apple. Nina Cassian. Tr. by Eve Feiler. pap. 2.00 saddlestitched (ISBN 0-89304-812-7); Chapbook 14. When Sorrow-Song Descends on You. Vinoko Akpalu. Tr. by Kofi Awoonor. pap. 2.00 saddlestitched (ISBN 0-89304-813-5). Cross Cult.

Cross-Cultural Review: Five Contemporary Flemish Poets, No. 3. Compiled by Hans Van de Warsenburg. Tr. by James S. Holmes et al. Ed. by Stanley H. Barkan. 48p. 10.00 (ISBN 0-89304-604-3); pap. 4.00 (ISBN 0-89304-605-1). Cross Cult.

Cross-Cultural Review: Five Contemporary Turkish Poets, No. 6. Compiled by Talat S. Halman & Stanley H. Barkan. 48p. 10.00 (ISBN 0-89304-610-8); pap. 4.00 (ISBN 0-89304-611-6). Cross Cult.

Cross-Cultural Review: Four Contemporary Swedish Poets, No. 5. Compiled by Gunnar Harding & Stanley H. Barkan. Tr. by Robin Fulton & Anselm Hollo. 48p. 10.00 (ISBN 0-89304-608-6); pap. 4.00 (ISBN 0-89304-609-4). Cross Cult.

Cross-Cultural Study of a Multinational Company: Attitudinal Responses to Participative Management. Dietrich L. Schaupp. LC 78-8453. (Praeger Special Studies). 1978. 21.95 (ISBN 0-03-022871-9). Praeger.

Cross Currents in the South. Keith F. McKean. LC 60-14586. 50p. 1960. pap. 1.00 (ISBN 0-8040-0058-1). Swallow.

Cross-Examination in Criminal Trials, Vol. 1. F. Lee Bailey & Henry Rothblatt. LC 78-18628. 1978. 47.50. Lawyers Co-Op.

Cross-Fertilization: The Human Spirit As Place. Intro. by Morty Sklar. (Contemporary Anthology Ser.: No. 3). (Illus.). 64p. 1980. pap. 2.50 (ISBN 0-930370-10-4) (ISBN 0-930370-10-4). Spirit That Moves.

Cross Fire. Ole Anthony. LC 75-38198. 1976. pap. 2.95 o.p. (ISBN 0-88270-157-6). Logos.

Cross Fox. Jane Scott. LC 80-13515. 144p. (gr. 4-7). 1980. 8.95 (ISBN 0-689-50183-8, McElderry Bk). Atheneum.

Cross-National Perspectives, United States & Canada. Ed. by Robert Presthus. (International Studies in Sociology & Social Anthropology: No.XXIV). 1977. text ed. 32.00x (ISBN 90-04-05238-0). Humanities.

Cross National Study of Health Systems by Countries & World Region, & Special Problems: A Guide to Information Sources. Ed. by Ray H. Elling. LC 79-26099. (Health Affairs Information Guide Ser.: Vol. 3). 1980. 30.00 (ISBN 0-8103-1453-3). Gale.

Cross National Study of Health Systems; Concepts, Methods, & Data Sources: a Guide to Information Sources. Ed. by Ray H. Elling. LC 79-24028. (Health Affairs Information Guide Ser.: Vol. 2). 1980. 30.00 (ISBN 0-8103-1449-5). Gale.

Cross of Christ, the Throne of God. F. J. Huegel. 1965. pap. 2.50 (ISBN 0-87123-068-2, 210068). Bethany Fell.

Cross or a Ladder? Ruth J. Buntain. (Uplook Ser.). 31p. 1970. pap. 0.75 (ISBN 0-8163-0069-0, 03654-1). Pacific Pr Pub Assn.

Cross-Polity Time-Series Data. Arthur S. Banks. 328p. 1971. 50.00 (ISBN 0-262-02071-8). MIT Pr.

Cross-Reacting Antigens & Neoantigens. J. J. Trentin. 138p. 1967. 10.25 o.p. (ISBN 0-685-54441-9). Krieger.

Cross-Sectional Approach to Anatomy. Roy R. Peterson. (Illus.). 1980. 49.95 (ISBN 0-8151-6668-0). Year Bk Med.

Cross Stitch Designs. Ondori Publishing Co. Staff. (Ondori Handicraft Er). (Illus.). 96p. 1976. pap. 5.95 (ISBN 0-87040-366-4). Japan Pubns.

Cross Stitch Patterns. Irmgard Gierl. LC 77-75315. (Illus.). 1977. encore ed. o.p. 2.95 (ISBN 0-684-16192-3, ScribT); pap. 3.95 (ISBN 0-684-15232-0, ScribT). Scribner.

Cross Stitch Patterns. Ondori Publishing Co. Staff & Misako Murayama. (Ondori Handicraft Ser.). (Illus.). 64p. 1976. pap. 3.95 (ISBN 0-87040-374-5). Japan Pubns.

Cross Stitch Patterns Two. new ed. Misako Murayama. (Ondori Needlework Ser.). (Illus.). 1978. pap. 4.50 (ISBN 0-87040-427-X). Japan Pubns.

Cross Through the Scriptures. F. J. Huegel. LC 65-25948. 1969. pap. 3.50 (ISBN 0-87123-069-0, 210069). Bethany Fell.

Cross: Tradition & Interpretation of the Crucifixion of Jesus in the World of the New Testament. Hans-Ruedi Weber. 1978. pap. 6.95 o.p. (ISBN 0-8028-1739-4). Eerdmans.

Cross Your Fingers, Spit in Your Hat. Alvin Schwartz. LC 73-21912. (Illus.). 160p. (gr. 4 up). 1974. 8.95 (ISBN 0-397-31530-9); pap. 2.95 (ISBN 0-397-31531-7). Lippincott.

Crossbet Two. Huey Mahl. (Gambler's Book Shelf). 64p. 1975. pap. 2.95 (ISBN 0-89650-551-0). Gamblers.

Crosscultural Encounters: Face-to-Face Interaction. Richard W. Brislin. LC 80-20202. (Pergamon General Psychology Ser.: No. 94). 350p. 1981. 35.01 (ISBN 0-08-026313-5); pap. 12.91 (ISBN 0-08-026312-7). Pergamon.

Crosscurrents Along the Colorado: The Impact of Government Policy on the Quechan Indians. Robert L. Bee. 1981. text ed. 20.00x (ISBN 0-8165-0558-6); pap. 9.50x (ISBN 0-686-69385-X). U of Ariz Pr.

Crosscurrents: Children, Families, & Religion. Evelyn Kaye. 224p. 1980. 11.95 (ISBN 0-517-53292-1). Potter.

Crosscurrents in College Admissions. Humphrey Doermann. LC 68-54672. 1970. text ed. 10.25x (ISBN 0-8077-1249-3). Tchrs Coll.

Crosscurrents in Leadership. Ed. by James G. Hunt & Lars L. Larson. LC 79-13576. (Southern Illinois Leadership Symposium Ser.). 316p. 1979. 18.95x (ISBN 0-8093-0932-7). S Ill U Pr.

Crosscurrents of Criticism: Horn Book Essays, 1968-1977. Ed. by Paul Heins. LC 77-24256. 1977. 14.50 (ISBN 0-87675-034-X). Horn Bk.

Crossfire. Edwin Booth. 1977. pap. 1.75 (ISBN 0-441-12270-1). Ace Bks.

Crossfire. Joseph Califano. 15.95 (ISBN 0-671-25428-6). S&S.

Crossfire in Professional Education. Bruno A. Boley. LC 76-47033. 1977. 14.00 (ISBN 0-08-021429-0). Pergamon.

Crossfire Trail. Louis L'Amour. 1978. pap. 1.95 (ISBN 0-449-14276-0, GM). Fawcett.

Crossing. Aiain Albert. LC 64-12397. 1964. 4.00 o.s.i. (ISBN 0-8076-0257-4). Braziller.

Crossing. Clay Fisher. 288p. (Orig.). 1980. pap. 1.75 (ISBN 0-553-14178-3). Bantam.

Crossing Jordan at Flood Tide. R. H. Nightingale. LC 75-16541. 1975. pap. 2.95 o.p. (ISBN 0-8163-0172-7, 03648-3). Pacific Pr Pub Assn.

Crossing of the Suez. Saad El Shazly. Ed. by Susan Benson. (Illus.). 333p. 1980. 14.00 (ISBN 0-9604562-0-1, 80-67107). Am Mideast.

Crossing Point: Selected Talks & Writings. Mary C. Richards. LC 73-6010. (Illus.). 1973. 15.00x (ISBN 0-8195-4060-9, Pub. by Wesleyan U Pr); pap. 6.95 (ISBN 0-8195-6029-4). Columbia U Pr.

Crossing the Border. Joyce C. Oates. LC 76-7148. 256p. 1976. 10.95 (ISBN 0-8149-0774-1). Vanguard.

Crossing the Cultural Divide: Indians & New Englanders, 1605-1763. Alden T. Vaughan & Daniel K. Richter. 76p. 1980. pap. write for info. (ISBN 0-912296-48-8). Am Antiquarian.

Crossing the Rubicon: The Story of a Chinese Refugee Family. Nathan S. Yuan. 115p. 1980. 5.95 (ISBN 0-8059-2731-X). Dorrance.

Crossing the Water. Sylvia Plath. LC 71-138756. 1971. 8.95 (ISBN 0-06-013366-X, HarpT); pap. 3.95 (ISBN 0-06-013374-0, TD230, HarpT). Har-Row.

Crossnumber Puzzle Books, 2 bks. Diana Hestwood & Edward Huseby. 1972. Bk. 1. pap. 4.95 wkbk. (ISBN 0-88488-013-3); Bk. 2. pap. 4.95 wkbk. (ISBN 0-88488-014-1). Creative Pubns.

Crossroads. John D. MacDonald. 1978. pap. 1.75 o.p. (ISBN 0-449-14033-4, GM). Fawcett.

Crossroads in Korea. T. R. Fehrenbach. (gr. 9-12). 1968. 8.95 (ISBN 0-02-734380-4). Macmillan.

Crossroads of Death: The Story of the Malmedy Massacre & Trial. James J. Weingartner. LC 77-91771. 1979. 16.95x (ISBN 0-520-03623-9). U of Cal Pr.

Crossroads of the Labyrinth. Cornelius Castoriadis. Tr. by Kate Sozu & Martin Ryle. Date not set. 35.00 (ISBN 0-89396-032-2). Urizen Bks.

Crossroads to Israel 1917-1948. Christopher Sykes. LC 72-93912. (Midland Bks.: No. 165). 416p. 1973. pap. 3.95x (ISBN 0-253-20165-9). Ind U Pr.

Crosswinds: An Airman's Memoir. Najeeb E. Halaby. LC 78-8210. 1978. 10.95 o.p. (ISBN 0-385-04963-3). Doubleday.

Crosswinds One. Ed. by Dolly Hasinbiller & Mel Cebulash. (Illus.). 320p. (gr. 7). 1979. text ed. 8.70 (ISBN 0-8372-3582-0); wkbk 2.52 (ISBN 0-8372-3583-9); tchrs' guide 2.52 (ISBN 0-8372-3584-7). Bowmar-Noble.

Crosswinds, Two. Ed. by Dolly Hasinbiller & Mel Cebulash. (Illus.). 320p. (gr. 8). 1979. text ed. 8.70 (ISBN 0-8372-3585-5); wkbk 2.52 (ISBN 0-8372-3586-3); tchrs' guide 2.52 (ISBN 0-8372-3587-1). Bowmar-Noble.

Crossword Puzzle Dictionary. 4th, rev, new ed. Andrew Swanfeldt. LC 76-57994. 1977. 12.50 (ISBN 0-690-00426-5, TYC-T); thumb-indexed 13.95 (ISBN 0-690-01198-9). T Y Crowell.

Crossword Puzzle Mastery, Level 1. Enid L. Huelsbergd. (Michigan Progrrammed Spelling Ser.). (gr. 1-3). 1975. wkbk. 2.50 (ISBN 0-89039-090-8). Ann Arbor Pubs.

Crossword Puzzle Mastery: Level 2. Enid L. Huelsberrg. (gr. 4-7). 1975. wkbk. 2.50 (ISBN 0-89039-092-4). Ann Arbor Pubs.

Crossword Puzzles: Their History & Their Cult. Roger Millington. LC 75-9505. (Illus.). 190p. (gr. 7 up). 1975. 7.95 o.p. (ISBN 0-525-66471-8). Elsevier-Nelson.

Crosswords for Reading Success. Helen Shangold. (gr. k-3). 1981. 13.60 (ISBN 0-8027-9125-5). Walker & Co.

Crow & the Pitcher. Ed. by Denise Guynn. (Aesop's Fables Bk). (Illus.). 16p. (ps). 1980. pap. 22.00 ten bks. & one cass. (ISBN 0-89290-077-6, BC14-5). Soc for Visual.

Crow Indians. Incl. The Crow Tribe of Indians. Norman B. Plummer; Findings of Fact, & Opinion. Indian Claims Commission. (American Indian Ethnohistory Ser: Plains Indians). (Illus.). lib. bdg. 42.00 (ISBN 0-8240-0756-5). Garland Pub.

Crow Who Came to Stay. Judy Varga. (Illus.). (ps-3). 1967. 8.25 (ISBN 0-688-21203-4); PLB 7.92 (ISBN 0-688-31203-9). Morrow.

Crowd & Mass Behavior. Sociological Resources for the Social Studies. (Readings in Sociology Ser.). (gr. 9-12). 1972. pap. text ed. 4.96 (ISBN 0-205-02578-1, 8125783). Allyn.

Crowd Pleasers. Rosemary Rogers. 1978. pap. 3.95 (ISBN 0-380-38927-4, 38927). Avon.

Crowd Pleasers. rev. ed. Rosemary Rogers. 528p. 1980. pap. 2.75 (ISBN 0-380-75622-6, 75622). Avon.

Crowding & Behavior. Jonathan Freedman. LC 75-20217. (Psychology Ser.). 1975. pap. text ed. 7.95x (ISBN 0-7167-0750-0). W H Freeman.

Crowding in Real Environments. Ed. by Susan Saegart. LC 75-42756. (Sage Contemporary Social Science Issues: Vol. 25). 1976. 4.95x (ISBN 0-8039-0583-1). Sage.

Crowding: Theoretical & Research Implications for Population - Environment Psychology. Ed. by Larry Severy. LC 78-61527. 1979. pap. 6.95x (ISBN 0-87705-376-6). Human Sci Pr.

Crowell College Reader. S. Baker. 1974. pap. text ed. 10.50 scp (ISBN 0-690-00170-3, HarpC); instructor's manual avail. (ISBN 0-685-99798-7). Har-Row.

Crowell's Handbook of Classical Literature: A Modern Guide to the Drama, Poetry, & Prose of Greece & Rome, with Biographies of Their Authors. Lillian Feder. LC 64-18162. 1980. pap. 7.95 (ISBN 0-06-090802-5, CN 802, CN). Har-Row.

Crowell's Handbook of Classical Literature. Lillian Feder. 1964. 12.95 o.p. (ISBN 0-690-22537-7, TYC-T). T Y Crowell.

Crowell's Handbook of Classical Mythology. Edward Tripp. LC 74-127614. (Illus.). 1970. 17.50 o.s.i. (ISBN 0-690-22608-X, TYC-T). T Y Crowell.

Crowell's Handbook of Contemporary American Poetry. Karl Malkoff. LC 73-14787. 338p. 1973. 10.95 o.s.i. (ISBN 0-690-22625-X, TYC-T). T Y Crowell.

Crowell's Handbook of Elizabethan & Stuart Literature. James E. Ruoff. LC 73-22097. 576p. 1975. 14.95 o.s.i. (ISBN 0-690-22661-6, TYC-T). T Y Crowell.

Crown & Castle: British Rule in Ireland 1800-1830. Edward Brynn. (Illus.). 1978. text ed. 32.00x (ISBN 0-7705-1496-0). Humanities.

Crown & Charter: The Early Years of the British South Africa Company. John S. Galbraith. LC 73-93050. (Perspectives on Southern Africa Ser.). 1974. 21.50x (ISBN 0-520-02693-4). U of Cal Pr.

Crown & the Loincloth: A Novel. Chaman Lal. 432p. 1981. 22.50x (ISBN 0-7069-1285-3, Pub. by Vikas India). Advent Bk.

Crown Court. James Follett. LC 77-24773. 1978. 7.95 o.p. (ISBN 0-312-17737-2). St Martin.

Crown for Azora. Jackson Cole. 1976. pap. 0.95 o.p. (ISBN 0-445-00695-1). Popular Lib.

Crown of Aloes. Norah Lofts. 1977. pap. 1.75 o.p. (ISBN 0-449-23030-9, Crest). Fawcett.

Crown of Feathers. Isaac B. Singer. 1979. pap. 2.95 (ISBN 0-449-23465-7, Crest). Fawcett.

Crown of Feathers. Isaac B. Singer. 1981. pap. 6.95 (ISBN 0-374-51622-7). FS&G.

Crown of Glory: Life of J. J. Strang, Moses, of the Mormons. O. U. Riegel. 1935. 45.00x (ISBN 0-685-69857-2). Elliots Bks.

Crown of Gold. Lauretta J. Ngcobo. (Sun-Lit Ser.). 250p. (Orig.). 1981. 10.00x (ISBN 0-89410-170-6); pap. 6.00x (ISBN 0-89410-171-4). Three Continents.

Crown of Life. Roe Halper. LC 80-19465. (Illus.). 1980. 15.00 (ISBN 0-916326-02-0). Bloch.

Crown of Passion. Jocelyn Carew. 416p. (Orig.). 1980. pap. 2.75 (ISBN 0-380-76414-8, 76414). Avon.

Crowned Cannibals: Writings on Repression in Iran. Reza Baraheni. 1977. pap. 3.95 (ISBN 0-394-72357-0, V-357, Vin). Random.

Crowned Knot of Tree. Elizabeth A. Eliot. LC 79-67045. 1980. 8.95 (ISBN 0-533-04425-1). Vantage.

Crowning Phase of the Critical Philosophy: A Study in Kant's Critique of Judgment. R. A. Macmillan. Ed. by Lewis W. Beck. LC 75-32041. (Philosophy of Immanuel Kant Ser.: Vol. 4). 1977. Repr. of 1912 ed. lib. bdg. 33.00 (ISBN 0-8240-2328-5). Garland Pub.

Crowns & Coronations, a History of Regalia. William Jones. LC 67-24356. (Illus.). 1968. Repr. of 1902 ed. 26.00 (ISBN 0-8103-3448-8). Gale.

Crows: A Study of the Corvids of Europe. Franklin Coombs. 1978. 38.00 (ISBN 0-7134-1327-1, Pub. by Batsford England). David & Charles.

Crows, Jays, Ravens (& Their Relatives) Sylvia B. Wilmore. (Illus.). 1979. 6.95 (ISBN 0-87666-878-3, PS-779). TFH Pubns.
Crows of the World. Derek Goodwin. LC 76-20194. (Illus.). 352p. 1976. 32.50x (ISBN 0-8014-1057-6). Comstock.
Croy's Camera Trickery. O. R. Croy. Date not set. cancelled o.p. (ISBN 0-8038-1216-7). Hastings.
CRT Controller Handbook. Gerry Kane. 250p. (Orig.). 1980. pap. 6.99 (ISBN 0-931988-45-4). Osborne-McGraw.
CRT Typesetting Handbook. Stanley Rice. 415p. 1981. 35.00 (ISBN 0-442-23889-4). Van Nos Reinhold.
Crucial Experiments in Modern Physics. Ed. by George L. Trigg. LC 75-21567. 1975. pap. 4.95x (ISBN 0-8448-0765-6). Crane-Russak Co.
Crucial Hours. William Lauterbach. 1977. pap. 4.95 (ISBN 0-8100-0050-4, 15-0358). Northwest Pub.
Crucial Issues in Psychotherapy. Herbert S. Strean. LC 76-14907. 1976. 13.50 (ISBN 0-8108-0968-0). Scarecrow.
Crucial Issues in Testing. Ralph W. Tyler & Richard M. Wolf. LC 73-20855. 1974. 15.25x (ISBN 0-8211-1714-9); text ed. 13.75x (ISBN 0-685-42643-2). McCutchan.
Crucial Years: Nineteen Thirty-Nine to Nineteen Forty-One. Hanson W. Baldwin. LC 74-15808. (Illus.). 516p. 1976. 20.00 o.s.i. (ISBN 0-06-010186-5, HarpT). Har-Row.
Crucible of Europe: The Ninth & Tenth Centuries in European History. Geoffrey Barraclough. LC 75-21934. (Illus.). 180p. 1976. 22.50x (ISBN 0-520-03105-9); pap. 6.95 (ISBN 0-520-03118-0, CAL 362). U of Cal Pr.
Crucible: Text & Criticism. Arthur Miller. Ed. by Gerald Weales. LC 73-119776. (Critical Library: No. 7). 1977. pap. 5.50 (ISBN 0-14-015507-4). Penguin.
Crucibles: The Story of Chemistry from Ancient Alchemy to Nuclear Fission. Bernard Jaffe. (Illus.). 1976. pap. text ed. 5.00 (ISBN 0-486-23342-1). Dover.
Crucibles: The Story of Chemistry from Ancient Alchemy to Nuclear Fission. 4th rev. ed. Bernard Jaffe. 9.00 (ISBN 0-8446-5486-8). Peter Smith.
Crucified God. Jurgen Moltmann. LC 73-18694. 352p. 1974. 15.95 (ISBN 0-06-065901-7, HarpR). Har-Row.
Crucified Jesus Is No Stranger. Sebastian Moore. 1977. 6.95 (ISBN 0-8164-0341-4). Crossroad NY.
Crucifixions. Sujatha Modayil. (Redbird Ser). 1975. 8.00 (ISBN 0-88253-725-3); flexible bdg. 4.80 (ISBN 0-89253-543-1). Ind-US Inc.
Crude Black Molasses. Cyril Scott. 1980. pap. 1.95 (ISBN 0-87904-010-6). Lust.
Cruden's Concordance. Alexander Cruden. handy reference ed. 7.50 (ISBN 0-8010-2341-6). Baker Bk.
Cruden's Unabridged Concordance. Alexander Cruden. 14.95 (ISBN 0-8010-2316-5). Baker Bk.
Cruel & Unusual Punishments: From the Here & the Hereafter. Golem N. Sadist. (Odd Books for Odd Moments Ser.). (Illus.). 72p. (Orig.). 1980. pap. 3.95 (ISBN 0-938338-03-X). Winds World Pr.
Cruel Flame. Charlotte Lamb. (Harlequin Presents Ser.). 192p. 1980. pap. 1.50 (ISBN 0-373-10387-5, Pub. by Harlequin). PB.
Cruel Shoes. Steve Martin. 1980. pap. 2.25 (ISBN 0-446-92070-3). Warner Bks.
Cruelly Murdered. Bernard Taylor. 384p. 1980. 17.95 (ISBN 0-285-62387-7, Pub. by Souvenir Pr England). Intl Schol Bk Serv.
Cruise Missile: Bargaining Chip or Defense Bargain? Robert L. Pfaltzgraff, Jr. & Jacquelyn K. Davis. LC 76-51854. (Special Reports Ser.). 1977. 3.00 (ISBN 0-89549-002-1). Inst Foreign Policy Anal.
Cruise of the Kate. E. D. Middleton. (Mariners Library). 1953. Repr. of 1870 ed. text ed. 4.75x o.p. (ISBN 0-246-63543-6). Humanities.
Cruise of the Lanikai. Kemp Tolley. LC 73-82484. (Illus.). 356p. 1973. 13.50 o.p. (ISBN 0-87021-132-3). Naval Inst Pr.
Cruiser. Warren Tute. 1981. pap. 2.75 (ISBN 0-345-29573-0). Ballantine.
Cruisers. A. Preston. LC 79-89592. 192p. 1980. 16.95 (ISBN 0-13-194902-0). P-H.
Cruising. (Library of Boating Ser.). (Illus.). 1976. 14.95 (ISBN 0-8094-2120-8). Time-Life.
Cruising. Ed. by Time Life Books. LC 75-27445. (Library of Boating Ser.). (gr. 6 up). 1975. PLB 13.95 (ISBN 0-8094-2121-6, Pub. by Time-Life). Silver.
Cruising: A Manual for the Small Sailing Boat Owner. J. D. Sleightholme. (Illus.). 238p. 1977. 21.95x (ISBN 0-8464-0305-6). Beekman Pubs.
Cruising for Fun. Tom Bottomley. (Illus.). 1977. 8.95 o.p. (ISBN 0-8096-1913-X, Assn Pr); pap. 4.95 o.p. (ISBN 0-8096-1908-3). Follett.
Cruising Grounds. (Library of Boating Ser.). (Illus.). 1976. 14.95 (ISBN 0-8094-2132-1). Time-Life.
Cruising Grounds. Ed. by Time Life Books. LC 76-9629. (Library of Boating Ser.). (Illus.). (gr. 6 up). 1976. PLB 13.95 (ISBN 0-8094-2133-X, Pub. by Time-Life). Silver.
Cruising Guide to the Abacos & the Northern Bahamas. rev. 2nd ed. Julius M. Wilensky. Ed. by Carol Weber. LC 80-50792. (Illus.). 220p. 1980. pap. 17.25 (ISBN 0-918752-03-5). Wescott Cove.
Cruising Guide to the Caribbean & the Bahamas. Jerrems C. Hart & William T. Stone. LC 75-43577. (Illus.). 1979. 20.00 (ISBN 0-396-07774-9). Dodd.
Cruising Guide to the Channel Islands. Brian M. Fagan & Graham Pomeroy. (Illus.). 276p. pap. 16.95 (ISBN 0-88496-093-5). Western Marine Ent.
Cruising Guide to the New England Coast. rev. ed. Roger F. Duncan & John P. Ware. LC 78-22734. (Illus.). 1979. 19.95 (ISBN 0-396-07629-7). Dodd.
Cruising into Measurements. Ed. by Runelle Konsler & Lauren Mirabella. 1980. pap. text ed. 8.95 (ISBN 0-8302-2140-9). Goodyear.
Cruising Life. Ross Norgrove. LC 79-53764. (Illus.). 1980. pap. 19.95 (ISBN 0-87742-114-5). Intl Marine.
Cruising Nova Scotia. Wayne Clarke et al. LC 79-11352. 1979. 12.95 (ISBN 0-396-07671-8). Dodd.
Cruising: The Boats & the Places. Bill Robinson. (Illus.). 1981. 17.95 (ISBN 0-393-03258-2). Norton.
Cruising the Columbia & Snake Rivers: Eleven Cruises in the Inland Waterway. Sharlene Nelson & Joan LeMieux. 192p. 1981. pap. 8.95 (ISBN 0-914718-57-6). Pacific Search.
Cruising Under Sail. rev. ed. Eric Hiscock. (Illus.). 544p. 1981. 35.00 (ISBN 0-19-217599-8). Oxford U Pr.
Cruising Yacht Maintenance. James Morrison. (Illus.). 144p. Date not set. 10.95 (ISBN 0-668-04993-6, 4993-6). Arco.
Cruising Yachtsman's Troubleshooter. Richard Simpkin. 1979. 11.95 o.p. (ISBN 0-214-20384-0, 8028, Dist. by Arco). Barrie & Jenkins.
Crumb. Jean S. Doty. LC 75-33648. 128p. (gr. 5-9). 1976. PLB 6.96 (ISBN 0-688-84035-3). Greenwillow.
Crunchy Bananas & Other Great Recipes Kids Can Cook. Barbara Wilms. LC 74-31139. (Illus.). 112p. (ps-3). 1975. pap. 4.95 o.s.i. (ISBN 0-87905-507-3). Sagamore Bks.
Crusade Against Ignorance: Thomas Jefferson on Education. Ed. by Gordon C. Lee. LC 61-10961. (Orig.). 1961. text ed. 8.75 (ISBN 0-8077-1671-5); pap. text ed. 4.00x (ISBN 0-8077-1668-5). Tchrs Coll.
Crusade Against Radicalism; New York During the Red Scare, Nineteen Fourteen to Nineteen Twenty Four. Julian F. Jaffe. LC 75-189556. (National University Publications). 1972. 17.50 (ISBN 0-8046-9026-X). Kennikat.
Crusade in Spain. Jason Gurney. (Illus.). 1974. 7.95 o.p. (ISBN 0-571-10310-3, Pub. by Faber & Faber). Merrimack Bk Serv.
Crusader for Christ (Billy Graham) Jean Wilson. (gr. 6-9). 1973. pap. 1.95 (ISBN 0-87508-602-0). Chr Lit.
Crusader in Pink. Henry Cloud. (Illus.). 176p. (Orig.). 1981. pap. 2.50 (ISBN 0-553-14996-2). Bantam.
Crusader Institutions. Joshua Prawer. (Illus.). 536p. 1980. 89.00x (ISBN 0-19-822536-9). Oxford U Pr.
Crusader No. 1: The Accursed Tower. John Cleve. 1974. pap. 1.50 o.p. (ISBN 0-685-47910-2, D3444, Dist. by Dell). Grove.
Crusader No. 2: The Passionate Princess. John Cleve. 1974. pap. 1.50 o.p. (ISBN 0-685-47911-0, D6039, Dist. by Dell). Grove.
Crusader No. 3: Julanar the Lioness. John Cleve. 1975. pap. 1.50 o.p. (ISBN 0-685-56547-5, D4731, Dist. by Dell). Grove.
Crusader No. 4: My Lady Queen. John Cleve. 1975. pap. 1.50 o.p. (ISBN 0-685-56548-3, D5749, Dist. by Dell). Grove.
Crusader: The Accursed Tower the Passionate Princess, Bks. 1 & 2. John Cleve. LC 80-1000. 1980. pap. 2.95 (ISBN 0-394-17735-5, B440, BC). Grove.
Crusaders in the East. W. B. Stevenson. 16.00x (ISBN 0-686-53119-1). Intl Bk Ctr.
Crusades. Hans E. Mayer. Tr. by John Gillingham from Ger. (Illus.). 336p. 1973. pap. text ed. 8.95x (ISBN 0-19-873016-0). Oxford U Pr.
Crusades. T. Newhall. 146p. 1963. pap. 6.50 (ISBN 0-03-082837-6, Pub. by HR&W). Krieger.
Crusading Warfare, 1097-1193: A Contribution to Medieval Military History. R. C. Smail. LC 67-26956. (Cambridge Studies in Medieval Life & Thought Ser). (Cambridge U Pr Library Editions). 1967. 35.50 (ISBN 0-521-21315-0); pap. 11.50 (ISBN 0-521-09730-4). Cambridge U Pr.
Crushing. Ronald McKie. LC 78-21981. 1979. 8.95 o.p. (ISBN 0-684-15919-8, ScribT). Scribner.
Crustaceans. Waldo L. Schmitt. 4.95 (ISBN 0-472-05014-1). U of Mich Pr.
Crustal Evolution in Northwestern Britain & Adjacent Regions: Geological Journal Special Issue, No. 10. D. R. Bowes & B. E. Leake. (Liverpool Geological Society & the Manchester Geological Association). 508p. 1980. 97.50 (ISBN 0-471-27757-6, Pub. by Wiley-Interscience). Wiley.
Cruz y el Punal. Tr. by David Wilkerson. (Spanish Bks.). 1979. 1.90 (ISBN 0-8297-0522-8). Life Pubs Intl.
Cry Comanche. Harold B. Simpson. (Illus.). 1979. lib. bdg. 10.50 o.p. (ISBN 0-912172-25-8). Hill Jr. Coll.
Cry for Help. Gordon Carlson. Ed. by Thomas J. Mooney. (Beginning Pal Paperbacks Ser.). (Illus., Orig.). (gr. 7-12). 1977. pap. text ed. 1.25 (ISBN 0-8374-3452-1). Xerox Ed Pubns.
Cry for Help. Norman L. Farberow & Edwin S. Shneidman. 1961. pap. 4.95 o.p. (ISBN 0-07-019943-4, SP). McGraw.
Cry for Mercy: Prayers from the Genesee. Henri J. Nouwen. LC 80-2563. 144p. 1981. 9.95 (ISBN 0-385-17507-8). Doubleday.
Cry for the Demon. Julia Grice. 400p. (Orig.). 1980. pap. 2.75 (ISBN 0-446-95497-7). Warner Bks.
Cry for the World. Lucille Oliver. 1981. pap. price not set (ISBN 0-8309-0307-0). Herald Hse.
Cry from the Earth: Music of the North American Indians. John Bierhorst. LC 78-21538. (Illus.). 128p. (gr. 5 up). 1979. 9.95 (ISBN 0-590-07533-0, Four Winds). Schol Bk Serv.
Cry Guilty. Sara Woods. 192p. 1981. 9.95 (ISBN 0-312-17802-6). St Martin.
Cry Hard, Cry Fast. John D. MacDonald. 1978. pap. 1.50 o.p. (ISBN 0-449-13969-7, GM). Fawcett.
Cry Justice: The Bible on Hunger & Poverty. Ronald J. Sider. LC 80-82133. 192p. 1980. pap. 2.45 (ISBN 0-8091-2308-8). Paulist Pr.
Cry Justice: The Bible on Hunger & Poverty. Ronald J. Sider. 192p. (Orig.). 1980. pap. 2.95 (ISBN 0-87784-495-X). Inter-Varsity.
Cry Macho. N. Richard Nash. 1975. 7.95 o.p. (ISBN 0-440-04996-2). Delacorte.
Cry of Home: Cultural Nationalism & the Modern Writer. Ed. by H. Ernest Lewald. LC 76-173656. 412p. 1972. 15.50x (ISBN 0-87049-135-0). U of Tenn Pr.
Cry of My People. Esther Arias & Mortimer Arias. (Orig.). 1980. pap. 2.95 (ISBN 0-377-00095-7). Friend Pr.
Cry of the Human Heart. Juan Carlos Ortiz. LC 76-24099. 1977. pap. 3.95 (ISBN 0-88419-010-2). Creation Hse.
Cry, the Beloved Country. Alan Paton. (Lib. Rep. Ed.). (YA) 1961. 15.00x (ISBN 0-684-15559-1, ScribT); pap. 3.95 (ISBN 0-684-71863-4, SL7, ScribT); pap. text ed. 4.96 (ISBN 0-684-51544-X, SSP7, ScribC). Scribner.
Cry Viva! William Hopson. 1978. pap. 1.25 (ISBN 0-505-51256-4). Tower Bks.
Cry Within, Yours Is the Goal. 2.00 o.p. (ISBN 0-685-61399-2). Aum Pubns.
Crying for the Carolines. Bruce Bastin. (Paul Oliver Blues Ser.). pap. 2.95 (ISBN 0-913714-31-3). Legacy Bks.
Crying Heart. Clara B. Miller. 1965. pap. 3.50 (ISBN 0-8024-3813-X). Moody.
Crying of Lot Forty-Nine. Thomas Pynchon. LC 66-12340. 1966. 5.95 o.p. (ISBN 0-397-00418-4). Lippincott.
Crying Wind. LC 80-3843. 192p. 1981. pap. 2.95 (ISBN 0-89081-263-2). Harvest Hse.
Cryogenic Preservation of Cell Cultures. Commission on Sociotechnical Systems. 1975. pap. 5.75 (ISBN 0-309-02344-0). Natl Acad Pr.
Cryogenic Processes & Equipment in Energy Systems. W. M. Toscano et al. 193p. 1980. 40.00 (H00164). ASME.
Cryogenic Recycling & Processing. Norman R. Braton. 272p. 1980. 67.95 (ISBN 0-8493-5779-9). CRC Pr.
Cryogenics Handbook. Ed. by Beverly Law. 1980. text ed. 39.00 (ISBN 0-86103-021-4). Butterworths.
Cryptanalysis: A Study of Ciphers & Their Solutions. Helen F. Gaines. (Illus.). 1939. pap. text ed. 4.00 (ISBN 0-486-20097-3). Dover.
Cryptanalysis of an Enciphered Code Problem: Where an "Additive" Method of Encipherement Has Been Used. Wayne G. Barker. (Cryptographic Ser.). (Orig.). 1979. pap. 22.40 (ISBN 0-89412-037-9). Aegean Park Pr.
Cryptodiplomacy: CIA & the Third World. Satish Kumar. 210p. 1981. text ed. 22.50x (ISBN 0-7069-1292-6, Pub by Vikas India). Advent Bk.
Cryptograms & Spygrams. Norma Gleason. 128p. (Orig.). 1981. pap. price not set. Dover.
Cryptograms: Cyanobacteria, Algae, Fungi, Lichens, Textbook & Practical Guide. Karl Esser. Tr. by Michael G. Hackston & John Webster. LC 80-41070. 624p. Date not set. text ed. price not set (ISBN 0-521-23621-5); pap. text ed. price not set (ISBN 0-521-28080-X). Cambridge U Pr.
Crystal, Bk. VII. Helen Luster. 1980. pap. 5.00 (ISBN 0-686-28713-4). Man-Root.
Crystal Ball. Sibyl Ferguson. 1980. pap. 1.00 (ISBN 0-87728-483-0). Weiser.
Crystal Bucket. Clive James. 192p. 1981. 11.95 (ISBN 0-224-01890-6, Pub. by Chatto-Bodley-Jonathan). Merrimack Bk Serv.
Crystal Cabinet. Horace Gregory & Marya Zaturenska. 1967. pap. 1.50 o.s.i. (ISBN 0-02-069540-3, Collier). Macmillan.
Crystal Chemistry & Physics of Metals & Alloys. William B. Pearson. LC 70-176284. (Series on the Science & Technology of Materials). 1972. 58.00 o.p. (ISBN 0-471-67540-7, Pub. by Wiley-Interscience). Wiley.
Crystal Growth. Brian R. Pamplin. LC 73-21909. 1975. text ed. 82.00 (ISBN 0-08-017003-X); pap. text ed. 32.00 (ISBN 0-08-021310-3). Pergamon.
Crystal Land: Patterns of Artifice in Vladimir Nabokov's English Novels. Julia Bader. 1973. 18.50x (ISBN 0-520-02167-3). U of Cal Pr.
Crystal Lee: A Woman of Inheritance. Henry P. Leifermann. LC 75-14118. 192p. 1975. 8.95 o.s.i. (ISBN 0-02-570220-3). Macmillan.
Crystal Nights. Michele Murray. LC 72-93807. 320p. (gr. 6 up). 1973. 7.95 (ISBN 0-395-28920-3, Clarion). HM.
Crystal Palace. Maye Barrett. 1978. pap. 1.95 o.p. (ISBN 0-425-03677-4, Medallion). Berkley Pub.
Crystal Physics. G. S. Zhdanov. 1966. 48.00 (ISBN 0-12-779650-9). Acad Pr.
Crystal River Pictorial. Dell McCoy. (Illus.). 224p. 27.00 (ISBN 0-913582-04-2). Sundance.
Crystal Ship: Three Original Novellas of Science Fiction. Vonda N. McIntyre et al. Ed. by Robert Silverberg. LC 76-26902. (Nelson's Science Fiction Ser.). (gr. 8 up). 1976. 7.95 o.p. (ISBN 0-525-66527-7). Elsevier-Nelson.
Crystal Spring, 2 vols. Ed. by Maud Karples & Pat Shaw. 1975. Vol. 1. pap. 7.50 (ISBN 0-19-330516-X); Vol. 2. pap. 7.50 (ISBN 0-19-330517-8). Oxford U Pr.
Crystal Stopper. Maurice LeBlanc. 287p. 1980. Repr. of 1913 ed. lib. bdg. 14.25x (ISBN 0-89968-201-4). Lightyear.
Crystal Structure Analysis: A Primer. Jenny P. Glusker & Kenneth N. Trueblood. (Illus.). 1972. 12.95x (ISBN 0-19-501425-1); pap. 6.95x (ISBN 0-19-501426-X). Oxford U Pr.
Crystal Structure at High Pressure. Ed. by Mowhan. pap. 5.00 (ISBN 0-686-60376-1). Polycrystal Bk Serv.
Crystal Structures, 5 vols, Vols. 1-2, 4-6. 2nd ed. Ralph W. Wyckoff. LC 48-9169. 1963-71. Vol. 1. 33.00x o.p. (ISBN 0-470-96860-5); Vol. 2. 47.00 o.p. (ISBN 0-470-96862-1); Vol. 4. 48.95x o.p. (ISBN 0-470-96866-4); Vol. 5. 62.95x (ISBN 0-470-96868-0); Vol. 6, Pt. 1. 43.50x o.p. (ISBN 0-471-96869-2); Vol. 6, Pt. 2. 65.00x o.p. (ISBN 0-471-96870-6, Pub. by Wiley-Interscience). Wiley.
Crystal Structures, Vol. 3. Ralph W. Wyckoff. 989p. 1981. Repr. of 1951 ed. lib. bdg. write for info. (ISBN 0-88275-800-4). Krieger.
Crystal Technology. W. L. Bond. LC 75-23364. (Pure & Applied Optics Ser). 342p. 1976. 32.95 (ISBN 0-471-08765-3, Pub. by Wiley-Interscience). Wiley.
Crystalline Basement of the Antarctic Platform. M. G. Ravich & E. N. Kamenev. Ed. by R. Bogosh. Tr. by N. Kaner from Rus. LC 74-13646. 582p. 1975. 79.95 (ISBN 0-470-70990-1). Halsted Pr.
Crystalline Electric Fields & Structural Effects in f-Electron Systems. Ed. by Jack E. Crow et al. 650p. 1980. 69.50 (ISBN 0-306-40443-5, Plenum Pr). Plenum Pub.
Crystalline Solids. Duncan McKie & Christine McKie. LC 73-34. 628p. 1974. text ed. 24.95 (ISBN 0-470-58455-6). Halsted Pr.
Crystallographic Groups of Four-Dimensional Space. Harold Brown et al. (Wiley Monographs in Crystallography). 1978. 55.50 (ISBN 0-471-03095-3, Pub. by Wiley-Interscience). Wiley.
Crystallography: An Introduction for Earth Science (and Other Solid State) Students. E. J. Whittaker. LC 80-41188. (Illus.). 240p. 1981. 33.00 (ISBN 0-686-69443-0); pap. 19.50 (ISBN 0-08-023804-1). Pergamon.
Crystallography & Crystal Defects. Anthony Kelly & G. W. Groves. (Engineering Ser). (Illus.). 1970. text ed. 25.95 (ISBN 0-201-03696-7). A-W.
Crystallography & Practical Crystal Measurement, 2 vols. 2nd ed. A. E. Tutton. Incl. Vol. 1. Form & Structure; Vol. 2. Physical & Chemical. 1964. Set. 25.00 (ISBN 0-934454-27-2). Lubrecht & Cramer.

Crystals & Crystal Growing. Alan Holden & Phyllis Singer. LC 60-5932. pap. 2.95 (ISBN 0-385-09430-2, S7, Anch). Doubleday.

Crystals and Light: An Introduction to Optical Crystallography. Elizabeth A. Wood. LC 76-27458. (Illus.). 156p. 1977. pap. text ed. 3.00 (ISBN 0-486-23431-2). Dover.

Crystals & X-Rays. H. Lipson & R. M. Lee. (Wykeham Science Ser.: No. 13). 1970. 9.95x (ISBN 0-8448-1115-7). Crane Russak Co.

Crystals, X-Rays, & Protein. Dennis H. Sherwood. LC 73-7098. 1976. 44.95 (ISBN 0-470-78590-X). Halsted Pr.

Crytography: A Primer. Alan G. Konheim. 450p. 1981. 25.00 (ISBN 0-471-08132-9, Pub. by Wiley-Interscience). Wiley.

C.S. Lewis & the Church of Rome. Christopher Derrick. LC 80-83049. (Orig.). 1981. pap. price not set (ISBN 0-89870-009-4). Ignatius Pr.

CS 1 Skill Booklet. Barbara J. Crane. (Crane Reading System - English Ser.). (Illus.). (gr. k-2). 1977. pap. text ed. 12.20 per 10 (ISBN 0-89075-032-7). Crane Pub Co.

Csardas. Diane Pearson. LC 75-5880. 1975. 10.00 o.p. (ISBN 0-397-01085-0). Lippincott.

CT Scanners: A Technical Report. American Hospital Association. LC 77-509. 1977. pap. 12.00 o.p. (ISBN 0-87258-188-8, 1100). Am Hospital.

Cuaderno de Espanol Practico Comercial. Paul Rivers. 231p. 1980. pap. text ed. 7.95 (ISBN 0-686-64979-6, HC). HarBraceJ.

Cual Camino? (Spanish Bks.). 1977. 2.25 (ISBN 0-8297-0523-6). Life Pubs Intl.

Cuando Me Enojo. Norma Simon. Ed. by Caroline Rubin. Tr. by Alma F. Ada from Eng. LC 76-4932. (Concept Bks). (Illus.). 40p. (Span.). (gr. k-3). 1976. 6.50 (ISBN 0-8075-1371-7). A Whitman.

Cuatro Comedias (in Spanish) Alarcon. 3.75x o.s.i. (ISBN 0-686-12052-3). Colton Bk.

Cuatro Dramas De Navidad. E. W. Watson & Miquel A. Blanco. 1977. pap. 0.65 (ISBN 0-311-08224-6). Casa Bautista.

Cub Scout at Last. Henry G. Felsen. (Illus.). (gr. 2-5). 1952. pap. 0.95 o.p. (ISBN 0-684-12785-7, ScribT, SBF14). Scribner.

Cub Scout Family Book. Boy Scouts of America. (Illus.). 32p. (gr. 6-12). 1975. pap. 0.50x (ISBN 0-8395-3846-4, 3846). BSA.

Cub Scout Fun Book. Boy Scouts Of America. LC 67-23384. (Illus.). 96p. (gr. 3-5). 1967. pap. 2.45x (ISBN 0-8395-3215-6, 3215). BSA.

Cub Scout Magic. Boy Scouts Of America. LC 68-9493. (Illus.). 152p. (gr. 3-5). 1960. pap. 3.75x (ISBN 0-8395-3219-9, 3219). BSA.

Cub Scout Songbook. Boy Scouts Of America. (Illus.). (gr. 3-5). 1969. pap. 0.85x (ISBN 0-8395-3222-9, 3222). BSA.

Cuba. Edmund Lindon. (gr. 4 up). 1980. PLB 6.90 (ISBN 0-531-04101-8). Watts.

Cuba. Herbert L. Matthews. (Illus.). (gr. 7 up). 1964. 6.95g (ISBN 0-02-765280-7). Macmillan.

Cuba & the United States: Long Range Perspectives. Ed. by John N. Plank et al. 1967. 11.95 (ISBN 0-8157-7100-2). Brookings.

Cuba: Dictatorship or Democracy? Marta Harnecker. 288p. 1980. 15.95 (ISBN 0-88208-100-4); pap. 7.95 (ISBN 0-88208-101-2). Lawrence Hill.

Cuba: From Columbus to Castro. Jaime Suchlicki. LC 73-1325. 256p. 1974. 7.95 o.p. (ISBN 0-684-13715-1, ScribC); pap. text ed. 4.95x o.p. (ISBN 0-684-13762-3, ScribC). Scribner.

Cuba Today. Lee Chadwick. LC 75-43185. (Illus.). 224p. 1976. 7.95 (ISBN 0-88208-065-2); pap. 5.95 (ISBN 0-88208-066-0). Lawrence Hill.

Cuban Communism. Irving L. Horowitz. 550p. 1981. pap. 9.95 (ISBN 0-87855-838-1). Transaction Bks.

Cuban Death Lift. (Dusky MacMorgan Ser.: No. 3). (Orig.). 1981. pap. 1.95 (ISBN 0-451-09768-8, 9768, Sig). NAL.

Cuban Missile Crisis, October 1962: The U. S. & Russia Face a Nuclear Showdown. Fred J. Cook. LC 76-39813. (World Focus Books). (Illus.). 72p. (gr. 7-12). 1972. PLB 4.90 o.p. (ISBN 0-531-02159-9). Watts.

Cuban Revolutionary War, 1953-1958: A Bibliography. Louis A. Perez, Jr. LC 76-18742. 1976. 11.00 (ISBN 0-8108-0954-0). Scarecrow.

Cuba's Policy in Africa, Nineteen Fifty-Nine to Nineteen Eighty. William M. LeoGrande. (Policy Papers in International Affairs: No. 13). vi, 80p. 1980. pap. 3.25x (ISBN 0-87725-513-X). U of Cal Intl St.

Cube-O-Gram Math Teacher Lesson Plan & Activity Book. James Pearson et al. (Cube-O-Math Ser.). (Illus.). 194p. (gr. k-3). 1979. pap. 9.95 (ISBN 0-933358-57-1). Enrich.

Cubical City: A Novel. Janet Flanner. LC 74-8655. (Lost American Fiction Ser). 440p. 1974. Repr. of 1926 ed. 13.95 (ISBN 0-8093-0700-6). S Ill U Pr.

Cubism. Edward F. Fry. (World of Art Ser.). (Illus.). 1978. pap. 9.95 (ISBN 0-19-520069-1). Oxford U Pr.

Cubism: A History & an Analysis, 1907-1914. rev. ed. John Golding. (Icon Edition Ser). (Illus.). 1972. pap. 5.95x o.s.i. (ISBN 0-06-430008-0, IN-8, HarpT). Har-Row.

Cubism & Twentieth Century Art. Robert Rosenblum. 1976. pap. 13.95 (ISBN 0-13-195065-7). P-H.

Cubism, Futurism & Constructivism. J. Nash. LC 77-76770. (Modern Movements in Art Ser.). 1978. pap. 1.95 (ISBN 0-8120-0881-2). Barron.

Cubism in Architecture & the Applied Arts. Ivan Margolius. LC 79-56251. (Illus.). 128p. 1980. 28.00 (ISBN 0-7153-7673-X). David & Charles.

Cubist Cinema. Standish D. Lawder. LC 72-96466. 1975. 20.00x (ISBN 0-8147-4956-9); pap. 12.00 (ISBN 0-8147-4957-7). NYU Pr.

Cubist Criticism. Lynn Gamwell. Ed. by Donald B. Kuspit. (Studies in Fine Arts - Criticism). 229p. 1980. 24.95 (ISBN 0-8357-1089-0, Pub. by UMI Res Pr). Univ Microfilms.

Cubmaster's Packbook. Boy Scouts Of America. LC 67-26305. (Illus.). 352p. 1967. pap. 3.45x (ISBN 0-8395-3210-5, 3210). BSA.

Cuchilo. J. T. Edson. (Orig.). 1981. pap. 1.95 (ISBN 0-425-04836-5). Berkley Pub.

Cuchulain Plays of W. B. Yeats: A Study. Reg Skene. 264p. 1974. 17.50x (ISBN 0-231-03930-1). Columbia U Pr.

Cucina Magra, Cucina Sana: Slim & Healthy Italian Cooking. Marina Polvay. (Illus.). 192p. 1981. 13.95 (ISBN 0-13-195081-9, Spec); pap. 6.95 (ISBN 0-13-195073-8). P-H.

Cuckoo Clock, Repr. Of 1877 Ed. Mary L. Molesworth. Bd. with Tapestry Room. Repr. of 1879 ed. LC 75-32182. (Classics of Children's Literature, 1621-1932: Vol. 45). (Illus.). 1976. PLB 38.00 (ISBN 0-8240-2294-7). Garland Pub.

Cuckoo Clock Castle of Shir. Michoel Muchnik. LC 79-55560. (Illus.). (ps-3). 1980. 5.95 (ISBN 0-8197-0476-8). Bloch.

Cuckoo in Spring. Elizabeth Cadell. 214p. 1976. Repr. of 1954 ed. lib. bdg. 13.95x (ISBN 0-89244-067-8). Queens Hse.

Cucumber Princess. Jan Wahl. (Illus.). 40p. (gr. 2 up). 1981. 9.95 (ISBN 0-916144-76-3); pap. 5.95 (ISBN 0-916144-77-1). Stemmer Hse.

Cuenca Del Rio De la Plata: Estudio Para Su Planificacion y Desarrollo Inventario y Analisis de la Informacion Basica Sobre Recursos Naturales. (Illus., Span. & Port.). 1971. incl. maps & report 35.00 (ISBN 0-8270-3915-8). OAS.

Cuentecitos. Johnm. Pittaro. 128p. (gr. 8-10). 1968. pap. text ed. 2.75 (ISBN 0-88345-034-8, 17444); cassettes 25.00 (ISBN 0-686-67013-2). Regents Pub.

Cuentistas de Hoy. Mario B. Rodriguez. LC 52-14409. (Span). 1952. pap. text ed. 7.50 (ISBN 0-395-05317-X). HM.

Cuento De un Cocodrilo. Jose Aruego & Ariane Aruego. Tr. by Agentina Palacios from Span. (gr. k-3). 1979. pap. 1.95 (ISBN 0-590-10310-5, Schol Pap). Schol Bk Serv.

Cuento Mexicano Index. Compiled by Herbert H. Hoffman. LC 79-127156. (Humanitas Books). 600p. 1978. 22.00x (ISBN 0-89537-007-7). Headway Pubns.

Cuentos. Ignacio Aldecoa. (Easy Readers). (Illus.). 1977. pap. text ed. 3.75 (ISBN 0-88436-283-3). EMC.

Cuentos. Angus MacLean. 205p. 1979. pap. 9.95 (ISBN 0-914330-26-8); pap. write for info. (ISBN 0-914330-26-8). Western Tanager.

Cuentos Americanos. 3rd ed. Ed. by Donald Walsh & L. B. Kiddle. (Illus., Span.). 1970. pap. 5.95x (ISBN 0-393-09907-5, NortonC). Norton.

Cuentos Contemporaneos. Ed. by Doris K. Arjona & Edith F. Helman. (Orig., Span.). 1935. pap. 6.95x (ISBN 0-393-09432-4, NortonC). Norton.

Cuentos De Ambos Mundos. J. G. Babcock, Jr. et al. (Graded Spanish Readers: Bk. 2). 1950. pap. text ed. 3.90 (ISBN 0-395-04125-2). HM.

Cuentos de Andersen. (Span.). 7.95 (ISBN 84-241-5629-3). E Torres & Sons.

Cuentos Faciles De Hoy y Ayer. John M. Pittaro. (Illus.). 128p. (gr. 8). 1973. pap. text ed. 2.75x (ISBN 0-88334-059-3). Ind Sch Pr.

Cuentos: Tales from the Hispanic Southwest. Jose Griego & Maestas. Tr. by Rudolfo Anaya from Sp. (Illus.). 1980. 12.95 (ISBN 0-89013-110-4); pap. 6.95 (ISBN 0-89013-111-2). Museum NM Pr.

Cues & Comprehension: Level 1. Kitty Wehrli. (Ann Arbor Tracking Program Ser.). (gr. 2). 1976. wkbk. 5.00 (ISBN 0-89039-168-8). Ann Arbor Pubs.

Cues & Comprehension: Level 2. Kitty Wehrli. (Ann Arbor Tracking Program Ser.). (gr. 2). 1976. wkbk. 5.00 (ISBN 0-89039-169-6). Ann Arbor Pubs.

Cues & Comprehension: Level 3. Kitty Wehrli. (Ann Arbor Tracking Progam Ser.). (gr. 2). 1976. wkbk. 5.00 (ISBN 0-89039-170-X). Ann Arbor Pubs.

Cues & Comprehension: Level 4. Kitty Wehrli. (gr. 2). 1976. wkbk. 5.00 (ISBN 0-89039-171-8). Ann Arbor Pubs.

Cues & Signals 1: A Self-Instruction Workbook for Visual Accuracy. reusable ed. Ed. by B. Steele. (gr. 4). 1971. wkbk. 5.00 (ISBN 0-89039-023-1). Ann Arbor Pubs.

Cues & Signals 2: A Self-Instruction Workbook for Visual Accuracy. reusable ed. Ed. by B. Steele & K. Wehrli. (gr. 4). 1971. wkbk. 5.00 (ISBN 0-89039-025-8). Ann Arbor Pubs.

Cues & Signals 3: A Self-Instruction Workbook for Visual Accuracy. reusable ed. Ed. by B. Steele & K. Wehrli. (gr. 4). 1971. wkbk. 5.00 (ISBN 0-89039-027-4). Ann Arbor Pubs.

Cues & Signals 4: A Self-Instruction Workbook for Visual Accuracy. reusable ed. Ed. by B. Steele & K. Wehrli. (gr. 4). 1971. wkbk. 5.00 (ISBN 0-89039-029-0). Ann Arbor Pubs.

Cuestionario Demografico Basico: Recoleccion de Patos y Analysis en Encuestas por Muestro. POPLAB Staff. (Manual Ser.: No. 7). (Span.). 1980. pap. 3.50 (ISBN 0-89383-068-2). Intl Program Labs.

CUFC: Educational Film Locator 1980. 2nd ed. 1980. 50.00 (ISBN 0-8352-1295-5). Bowker.

Cuidado De Dios. Maria S. De Eudaly. Tr. by Emma Z. Villasenor. (gr. 1-3). Date not set. pap. 0.80 (ISBN 0-311-03662-7). Casa Bautista.

Cuidado Pastoral De la Iglesia. C. W. Brister. Tr. by D. Tinao et al. Orig. Title: Pastoral Care in the Church. 226p. (Span.). 1980. pap. 4.75 (ISBN 0-311-42040-0). Casa Bautista.

Cuisinart Food Processor Cookbook. Carmel B. Reingold. 1981. pap. price not set (Delta). Dell.

Cuisine of China. Chen et al. 1981. 15.95 (ISBN 0-8120-5361-3). Barron.

Cuisine of France. Danielle Ancelet. (Illus.). 184p. 1981. 15.95 (ISBN 0-312-17834-4). St Martin.

Culinary Arts Institute Encyclopedic Cookbook. Ed. by Ruth Berolzheimer. 1980. 8.95 (ISBN 0-671-41408-9, Fireside). S&S.

Culinary Design & Decoration. William Emery. 135p. 1980. 26.95 (ISBN 0-8436-2187-7). CBI Pub.

Culinary Olympics Cookbook. Ferdinand Metz. LC 78-23567. 1979. 24.95 (ISBN 0-8436-2151-6). CBI Pub.

Culpeper's Complete Herbal. Nicholas Culpeper. (Illus.). 1959. 12.95 (ISBN 0-8069-3900-1); lib. bdg. 10.79 (ISBN 0-8069-3901-X). Sterling.

Culpeper's Herbal Remedies. Nicholas Culpeper. pap. 3.00 (ISBN 0-87980-025-9). Wilshire.

Cult of Assur. G. Van Driel. (Studia Semitica Neerlandica: No. 13). 1969. text ed. 24.50x (ISBN 0-685-12390-1). Humanities.

Cult of Killers. Donald Macivers. 1976. pap. 1.50 o.p. (ISBN 0-685-69156-X, LB364DK, Leisure Bks). Nordon Pubns.

Cult of Kingship in Anglo-Saxon England: The Transition from Paganism to Christianity. William A. Chaney. LC 72-79041. 1970. 18.50x (ISBN 0-520-01401-4). U of Cal Pr.

Cult of the Saints: Its Rise & Function in Latin Christianity. Peter Brown. LC 80-11210. 1980. lib. bdg. 15.00x (ISBN 0-226-07621-0). U of Chicago Pr.

Cult of the Seer in the Ancient Middle East: A Contribution to Current Research on Hallucinations Drawn from Coptic & Other Texts. Violet MacDermot. LC 79-152047. (Wellcome Institute of the History of Medicine). 1971. 55.00x (ISBN 0-520-02030-8). U of Cal Pr.

Cult of the Wild. Boyce Rensberger. LC 76-53415. 1977. 7.95 o.p. (ISBN 0-385-09962-2); pap. 2.95 o.p. (ISBN 0-385-09963-0). Doubleday.

Cult of Violence: Sorel & the Sorelians. Jack J. Roth. 1980. 27.50x (ISBN 0-520-03772-3). U of Cal Pr.

Cult of Youth in Middle-Class America. Ed. by Richard L. Rapson. LC 74-146876. (Problems in American Civilization Ser.). 118p. pap. text ed. 4.95x o.p. (ISBN 0-669-73387-3). Heath.

Culte et Loix D'une Societe D'hommes Sans Dieu. Sylvain Marechal. 64p. (Fr.). 1977. lib. bdg. 16.25x o.p. (ISBN 0-8287-0577-1); pap. text ed. 6.25x o.p. (ISBN 0-685-75625-4). Clearwater Pub.

Cultivated Conifers in North America: Comprising the Pine Family & the Taxads. L. H. Bailey. (Landmark Reprints in Plant Science). 1933. text ed. 27.00 (ISBN 0-86598-007-1). Allanheld.

Cultivated Flowers. Frank J. Anderson. (Abbeville Library of Art Ser.). (Illus.). 112p. (Orig.). 1981. pap. 4.95 (ISBN 0-89659-182-4). Abbeville Pr.

Cultivated Plants & Domesticated Animals in Their Migration from Asia to Europe: Historico-Linguistic Studies. Victor Hehn. (Amsterdam Classics in Linguistics Ser.: No. 7). 1979. text ed. 71.25x (ISBN 90-272-0871-9). Humanities.

Cultivating Leadership: An Approach. Don Betz. LC 80-69039. 120p. (Orig.). 1981. pap. text ed. 4.95 (ISBN 0-8191-1441-3). U Pr of Amer.

Cultivating the Presence. T. Sampson. 1977. 8.95 o.p. (ISBN 0-690-01205-5, TYC-T); pap. 3.95 o.p. (ISBN 0-690-01206-3, TYC-T). T Y Crowell.

Cultivation of Harmatopoetic Stem Cells & of Comitted Leucocyte Progenitor Cells. Ed. by W. D. Gassel. (Vol. 62, No. 5-6). (Illus.). 58p. 1980. pap. cancelled o.p. (ISBN 3-8055-0697-X). S Karger.

Cultivation of Marine Organisms & Its Importance for Marine Biology. O. Kinne & H. P. Bulnheim. (International Symposium Helgoland 1969 Ser.). (Illus.). 722p. 1973. pap. text ed. 93.60x (ISBN 3-87429-059-X). Lubrecht & Cramer.

Culto a Satanas. Richard DeHaan. Tr. by Rodolfo De la Cerda from Eng. 136p. (Orig., Span.). 1975. pap. 2.25 (ISBN 0-89922-059-2). Edit Caribe.

Cults & Beliefs at Edessa. H. J. Drijvers. 1980. text ed. 54.75x (ISBN 90-04-06050-2). Humanities.

Cults & Beliefs at Edessa. H. J. W. Drijvers. (Illus.). 204p. 1980. text ed. 54.75 (ISBN 90-04-06050-2). Humanities.

Cults & Cons: The Exploitation of the Emotional Growth Consumer. Kenneth Cinnamon & Dave Farson. 1979. 10.95 (ISBN 0-88229-456-3); pap. 6.95 (ISBN 0-88229-671-X). Nelson-Hall.

Cults & the Occult. rev. ed. Edmund C. Gruss. pap. 2.95 (ISBN 0-87552-308-0). Presby & Reformed.

Cults in America. David Hanna. 1979. pap. 2.25 (ISBN 0-505-51447-8). Tower Bks.

Cults of the Greek States, 5 vols. Lewis R. Farnell. Incl. Vol. 1. Cronos, Zeus, Hera, Athena. 45.00 (ISBN 0-89241-029-9); Vol. 2. Artemis, Aphrodite. 45.00 (ISBN 0-89241-030-2); Vol. 3. Cults of the Mother of the Gods, Reah, Cybele. 45.00 (ISBN 0-89241-031-0); Vol. 4. Poseidon, Apollo. 55.00 (ISBN 0-89241-032-9); Vol. 5. Minor Cults. 55.00 (ISBN 0-89241-033-7). (Illus.). 1977. Repr. 200.00 set (ISBN 0-89241-049-3). Caratzas Bros.

Cults, World Religions, & You. Kenneth Boa. 1977. pap. 3.95 (ISBN 0-88207-752-X). Victor Bks.

Cultura Hispanica: Dentro y Fuera de los Estados Unidos. Michael H. Handelsman & William H. Heslin, Jr. 128p. 1981. pap. text ed. 7.95 (ISBN 0-394-32653-9). Random.

Cultural Accumulation in Latin America. Paul E. Zopf, Jr. LC 79-48091. 393p. 1980. text ed. 20.00 (ISBN 0-8191-1012-4); pap. text ed. 12.25 (ISBN 0-8191-1013-2). U Pr of Amer.

Cultural Adaptation Within Modern Africa. Ed. by S. H. Irvine & J. T. Sanders. LC 79-171692. 1972. text ed. 9.25x (ISBN 0-8077-1550-6). Tchrs Coll.

Cultural Anthropology. Joseph B. Aceves & H. Gill King. 1978. pap. text ed. 11.95x (ISBN 0-673-15305-3); study guide 4.95x (ISBN 0-673-15292-8). Scott F.

Cultural Anthropology. Daniel Bates & Fred Plog. 1979. pap. text ed. 12.95 (ISBN 0-394-32094-8). Knopf.

Cultural Anthropology. 3rd ed. Carol R. Ember & Melvin Ember. (Illus.). 416p. 1981. pap. text ed. 13.95 (ISBN 0-13-195230-7). P-H.

Cultural Anthropology. 2nd ed. M. Ember & C. Ember. 1977. pap. text ed. 13.95 (ISBN 0-13-195198-X). P-H.

Cultural Anthropology. 2nd ed. Conrad P. Kottak. LC 78-15704. (Illus.). 1978. pap. text ed. 10.95x (ISBN 0-394-32221-5). Random.

Cultural Anthropology. Henry Selby & Lucy Garretson. 432p. 1981. pap. text ed. write for info. (ISBN 0-697-07562-1); instr's manual avail. (ISBN 0-697-07563-X). Wm C Brown.

Cultural Anthropology: A Christian Perspective. Stephen A. Grunlan & Marvin K. Mayers. 1979. 8.95 (ISBN 0-310-36321-7). Zondervan.

Cultural Appraisal of Development Projects. D. Glynn Cochrane. LC 78-31130. 1979. 20.95 (ISBN 0-03-047586-4). Praeger.

Cultural Arts of Africa. Benedict Donahue. LC 79-66646. (Illus.). 1979. pap. text ed. 9.50 (ISBN 0-8191-0845-6). U Pr of Amer.

Cultural Awareness for Young Children at the Learning Tree. rev. ed. Earldene McNeill et al. LC 75-34504. (Illus.). 252p. (Orig.). (gr. 2). 1976. pap. 11.95 (ISBN 0-686-28415-1). CAYC Learning Tree.

Cultural Background of Personality. Ralph Linton. LC 80-29240. xix, 157p. 1981. Repr. of 1945 ed. lib. bdg. 17.50x (ISBN 0-313-22783-7, LICU). Greenwood.

Cultural Co-operation: Studies & Experiences in the Cultural Content of Education. (Joint Study: No. 9). 100p. 1980. pap. 7.50 (ISBN 0-686-68809-0, U1023, UNESCO). Unipub.

Cultural Conceptions & Mental Illness: A Comparison of Germany & America. John M. Townsend. LC 77-22342. (Illus.). 1978. lib. bdg. 11.00x (ISBN 0-226-81098-4). U of Chicago Pr.

Cultural Conformity in Books for Children: Further Readings in Racism. Ed. by Donnarae MacCann & Gloria Woodard. LC 77-22174. 1977. 10.00 (ISBN 0-8108-1064-6). Scarecrow.

Cultural Congress of Havana. Special Consultative Committee On Security. (Eng. & Span.). 1968. 2.00 ea. o.p. OAS.

Cultural Context: An Introduction to Cultural Anthropology. Robert Anderson. LC 75-16796. 1976. pap. text ed. 12.95 (ISBN 0-8087-0126-6). Burgess.

Cultural Context of Childhood. new ed. Ronald W. Henderson & John R. Bergan. 1976. text ed. 17.95 (ISBN 0-675-08599-3); instructor's manual 3.95 (ISBN 0-686-67315-8). Merrill.

Cultural Context of Thinking: A Comparative Study of Punjabi & English Boys. Paul A. Ghuman. (General Ser.). 139p. 1975. pap. text ed. 13.25x (ISBN 0-85633-078-7, NFER). Humanities.

Cultural Contexts: An Introduction to the Anthropological Perspective. Dubbs & Whitney. 320p. 1980. pap. text ed. 10.45 (ISBN 0-205-06871-5, 6668712). Allyn.

Cultural Creation in Modern Society. Lucien Goldmann. Tr. by Bart Grahl from Fr. LC 75-46394. 150p. 1976. 9.50 (ISBN 0-914386-08-5); pap. 3.00 (ISBN 0-914386-09-3). Telos Pr.

Cultural Dialogue: An Introduction to Intercultural Communication. Michael H. Prosser. LC 77-89049. (Illus.). 1978. text ed. 13.95 (ISBN 0-395-24448-X). HM.

Cultural Diversity in Health & Illness. Rachel E. Spector. (Illus.). 1979. pap. 13.85 (ISBN 0-8385-1394-8). ACC.

Cultural Economics. Richard L. Brinkman. LC 78-62056. 450p. 1981. pap. text ed. 15.95 (ISBN 0-913244-15-5). Hapi Pr.

Cultural Factors in Alcohol Research & Treatment. Ed. by D. W. Heath et al. (Journal of Studies on Alcohol: Suppl. No. 9). 1981. 10.00x (ISBN 0-911290-08-7). Rutgers Ctr Alcohol.

Cultural Geography of the United States. Wilbur Zelinsky. LC 72-4503. (Illus.). 176p. 1973. pap. 6.95 ref. ed. (ISBN 0-13-195495-4). P-H.

Cultural Heritage of India, 4 vols. Ed. by Bhattacharyya et al. Incl. Vol. 1. Early Phases. Intro. by S. Radhakrishnan (ISBN 0-87481-560-6); Vol. 2. Itihasas, Puranas, Dharma & Other Shastras (ISBN 0-87481-561-4); Vol. 3. The Philosophies (ISBN 0-87481-562-2); Vol. 4. The Religions (ISBN 0-87481-563-0). (Illus.). 30.00x ea.; Set. 150.00x (ISBN 0-87481-558-4). Vedanta Pr.

Cultural Heritage of Ladakh, Vol. 1. David L. Snellgrove & Tadeusz Skorupski. (Illus.). 1977. 30.00 (ISBN 0-87773-700-2, Prajna). Great Eastern.

Cultural Heritage of Malaya. 2nd ed. N. J. Ryan. Orig. Title: The Cultural Background of the Peoples of Malaya. (Illus.). 184p. 1971. pap. text ed. 3.25x (ISBN 0-582-72417-1). Humanities.

Cultural History of India. Ed. by A. L. Basham. (Illus.). 642p. 1975. 34.00x (ISBN 0-19-821914-8). Oxford U Pr.

Cultural History of Spanish America: From Conquest to Independence. Mariano Picon-Salas. Tr. by Irving A. Leonard. 1962. pap. 4.95x (ISBN 0-520-01012-4, CAMPUS15). U of Cal Pr.

Cultural History of Tibet. David L. Snellgrove & Hugh E. Richardson. LC 78-13032. (Illus.). 1980. pap. 12.50 (ISBN 0-87773-740-1, Prajna). Great Eastern.

Cultural Life of the American Colonies. Ed. by Louis B. Wright. (New American Nation Ser.). pap. 5.95x (ISBN 0-06-133005-1, TB3005, Torch). Har-Row.

Cultural Patterns in Urban Schools: A Manual for Teachers, Counselors, & Administrators. Joseph D. Lohman. (Orig.). 1967. pap. 5.95x (ISBN 0-520-01424-3, CAMPUS24). U of Cal Pr.

Cultural Pluralism. Edgar G. Epps. LC 73-17617. 1974. 15.50x (ISBN 0-8211-0412-8); text ed. 14.00x (ISBN 0-685-42631-9). McCutchan.

Cultural Pluralism & the American Idea: An Essay in Social Philosophy. Horace M. Kallen. LC 56-11801. 1956. 9.00x o.p. (ISBN 0-8122-7030-4). U of Pa Pr.

Cultural Pluralism in Education: A Mandate for Change. new ed. Madelon D. Stent. Ed. by William R. Hazard & Harry N. Rivlin. LC 72-92109. 1973. 12.95 (ISBN 0-13-195461-X). P-H.

Cultural Policy in Australia. 86p. 1980. pap. 6.25 (ISBN 92-3-101778-0, U1031, UNESCO). Unipub.

Cultural Policy in Colombia. (Studies & Documents on Cultural Policy). 1978. pap. 7.00 (ISBN 92-3-101417-X, U809, UNESCO). Unipub.

Cultural Policy in Cuba. Lisandro Otero. (Studies & Documents on Cultural Policies). 55p. (Orig.). 1972. pap. 4.75 (ISBN 92-3-100967-2, U114, UNESCO). Unipub.

Cultural Policy in Ghana. (Studies & Documents on Cultural Policies Ser.). (Illus.). 50p. 1976. pap. 2.50 (ISBN 92-3-101328-9, U121, UNESCO). Unipub.

Cultural Policy in Indonesia. (Studies & Documents on Cultural Policies). (Illus.). 46p. (Orig.). 1974. pap. 2.50 (ISBN 92-3-101128-6, U124, UNESCO). Unipub.

Cultural Policy in Romania. (Illus.). 70p. 1975. pap. 4.00 (ISBN 92-3-101188-X, U136, UNESCO). Unipub.

Cultural Policy in Senegal. Mamadou S. M'Bengue. (Studies & Documents on Cultural Policies). (Illus.). 61p. (Orig.). 1974. pap. 2.50 (ISBN 92-3-101118-9, U137, UNESCO). Unipub.

Cultural Policy in the Phillippines. (Studies & Documents on Cultural Policies). (Illus.). 40p. (Orig.). 1974. pap. 2.50 (ISBN 92-3-101133-2, U134, UNESCO). Unipub.

Cultural Relics Unearthed During the Great Cultural Revolution. (Illus.). 1972. linen bdg. 30.00 (ISBN 0-8351-0060-X). China Bks.

Cultural Relics Unearthed in Kwangsi. 1978. 50.00 (ISBN 0-8351-0573-3). China Bks.

Cultural Relics Unearthed in Sinkiang. (Illus.). 1975. 50.00 (ISBN 0-8351-0061-8). China Bks.

Cultural Resource Development: Planning Survey & Analysis. LC 75-19790. 245p. 1976. pap. 5.00x (ISBN 0-275-55640-9, Pub. by NYSCA). Pub Ctr Cult Res.

Cultural Resources in Lebanon. Nassar Foundation for Lebanese Std. (Arab Background Ser.). 12.00x (ISBN 0-685-72034-9). Intl Bk Ctr.

Cultural Resources: Planning & Management. Roy S. Dickens & Carole E. Hill. 1978. lib. bdg. 21.50x (ISBN 0-89158-254-1). Westview.

Cultural Revolution in China. Ed. by Thomas W. Robinson. LC 77-129609. 1971. 25.00x (ISBN 0-520-01811-7). U of Cal Pr.

Cultural Roots of National Socialism. Herman Glaser. Tr. by Ernest A. Menze. LC 77-89144. Orig. Title: Spiesser-ideologie. 1978. 15.00x (ISBN 0-292-71044-5). U of Tex Pr.

Cultural Significance of Accounts. D. R. Scott. (Lucas Text Ser). 1978. Repr. text ed. 5.95x perfect bdg. (ISBN 0-87543-041-4). Lucas.

Cultural Transmission & Evolution: A Quantitative Approach. L. L. Cavalli-Sforza & M. W. Feldman. Ed. by Robert M. May. LC 80-8539. (Monographs in Population Biology: No. 16). (Illus.). 368p. 1981. 20.00x (ISBN 0-691-08280-4); pap. 8.95x (ISBN 0-691-08283-9). Princeton U Pr.

Cultural Ways: A Concise Edition of "Introduction to Cultural Anthropology". 2nd ed. Robert B. Taylor & Dickinson. 383p. 1976. pap. text ed. 6.95x o.p. (ISBN 0-205-04878-1); instr's manual free o.p. (ISBN 0-205-05495-1). Allyn.

Culture - an Introduction. B. S. Sanyal. 1962. 10.00x (ISBN 0-210-34097-5). Asia.

Culture & Anarchy. Matthew Arnold. 1932. 36.50 (ISBN 0-521-04061-2); pap. 7.95 (ISBN 0-521-09103-9, 103). Cambridge U Pr.

Culture & Anarchy: An Essay in Political & Social Criticism. Matthew Arnold. Ed. by Ian Gregor. LC 79-95714. (Library of Literature Ser). 1971. pap. 6.95 (ISBN 0-672-60994-0, LL17). Bobbs.

Culture & Anarchy in Ireland Eighteen Nineteen to Nineteen Thirty-Nine: The Ford Lectures 1978. F. S. Lyons. 1979. 14.95x (ISBN 0-19-822493-1). Oxford U Pr.

Culture & Behavior of the Sebei: A Study in Continuity & Adaptation. Walter Goldschmidt. LC 74-82848. 1976. 34.50x (ISBN 0-520-02828-7). U of Cal Pr.

Culture & Childrearing. Ann L. Clark. LC 80-19481. (Illus.). 255p. 1980. 24.00 (ISBN 0-8036-1836-0). Davis Co.

Culture & Commitment. rev. ed. Margaret Mead. 1978. 12.50x (ISBN 0-231-04632-4). Columbia U Pr.

Culture & Commitment-the New Relationships Between the Generations in the 1970s. Margaret Mead. 1978. pap. 2.95 (ISBN 0-385-13387-1, Anch). Doubleday.

Culture & Communication. E. Leach. LC 75-30439. (Themes in the Social Sciences Ser.). (Illus.). 120p. 1976. 16.95 (ISBN 0-521-21131-X); pap. 5.95x (ISBN 0-521-29052-X). Cambridge U Pr.

Culture & Communication: The Problem of Penetrating National & Cultural Boundaries. Robert Oliver. 184p. 1962. pap. 8.25 spiral (ISBN 0-398-01422-1). C C Thomas.

Culture & Conduct in the Novels of Henry James. A. Berland. 225p. Date not set. 39.95 (ISBN 0-521-23343-7). Cambridge U Pr.

Culture & Consciousness: Perspectives in the Social Sciences. Ed. by G. B. Levitas. LC 67-24209. (Science Ser). 1967. 7.50 (ISBN 0-8076-0431-3). Braziller.

Culture & Controversy: An Investigation of the Tongues of Pentecost. R. Clyde McCone. 136p. 1978. 6.95 (ISBN 0-8059-2532-5). Dorrance.

Culture & Cosmology: Essays on the Birth of World View. Harry C. Stafford. LC 80-5642. 371p. 1981. lib. bdg. 21.25 (ISBN 0-8191-1371-9); pap. text ed. 12.50 (ISBN 0-8191-1372-7). U Pr of Amer.

Culture & Crisis in Britain in the Thirties. Ed. by Jon Clark et al. 1980. text ed. 19.50x (ISBN 0-85315-491-0). Humanities.

Culture & Diplomacy: The American Experience. Morrell Heald & Lawrence S. Kaplan. LC 77-71863. (Contributions in American History: No. 63). 1977. lib. bdg. 22.50 (ISBN 0-8371-9541-1, HEA/). Greenwood.

Culture & Diseases of Game Fishes. H. S. Davis. (Illus.). 1953. 18.50x (ISBN 0-520-00293-8). U of Cal Pr.

Culture & Early Interactions. Ed. by Tiffany Field. 300p. 1981. ref. ed. 19.95 (ISBN 0-89859-097-3). L Erlbaum Assocs.

Culture & History of the Spanish. Alfonso Lowe. 1977. pap. 5.95 o.p. (ISBN 0-86033-050-8). Gordon-Cremonesi.

Culture & Human Development: Insights into Growing Human. Ed. by Ashley Montagu. LC 74-18338. 192p. 1974. 8.95 (ISBN 0-13-195578-0, Spec); pap. 2.95 o.p. (ISBN 0-13-195560-8, Spec). P-H.

Culture & Human Values: Christian Intervention in Anthropological Perspective. Jacob A. Loewen. Ed. by William A. Smalley. LC 75-12653. (Applied Cultural Anthropology Ser.). 443p. (Orig.). 1975. pap. 6.95x (ISBN 0-87808-722-2). William Carey Lib.

Culture & Inference: A Trobriand Case Study. Edwin Hutchins. LC 80-13280. (Cognitive Science Ser,: No. 2). 1980. text ed. 14.00x (ISBN 0-674-17970-6). Harvard U Pr.

Culture & Personality. 3rd ed. Victor Barnouw. 1979. text ed. 19.50x (ISBN 0-256-02193-7). Dorsey.

Culture & Personality. Ed. by S. Stansfeld Sargent & Marion Smith. LC 73-76142. (Illus.). 219p. 1975. Repr. of 1949 ed. lib. bdg. 11.50x (ISBN 0-8154-0488-3). Cooper Sq.

Culture & Personality: Contemporary Readings. Ed. by Robert A. LeVine. LC 79-16915. 1974. lib. bdg. 22.95x (ISBN 0-202-01121-6); pap. text ed. 13.95x (ISBN 0-202-01122-4). Aldine Pub.

Culture & Population: A Collection of Current Studies. Ed. by Steven Polgar. LC 80-20070. (Carolina Population Center, Monograph: 9). vi, 195p. 1980. Repr. of 1971 ed. lib. bdg. 19.75x (ISBN 0-313-22620-2, POCP). Greenwood.

Culture & Practical Reason. Marshall Sahlins. LC 75-27899. (Illus.). 1978. pap. 5.95 (ISBN 0-226-73361-0, P773, Phoen). U of Chicago Pr.

Culture & Society in France: Eighteen Forty-Eight to Eighteen Ninety-Eight. D. W. Hemmings. 1971. 40.00 (ISBN 0-7134-1522-3, Pub. by Batsford England). David & Charles.

Culture & Society in Italy: Twelve Ninety to Fourteen Twenty. John Larner. 1971. 38.00 (ISBN 0-7134-1521-5, Pub. by Batsford England). David & Charles.

Culture & Society in Renaissance Italy, 1420-1540. Peter Burke. LC 70-110682. (Illus.). 1972. 14.95 o.p. (ISBN 0-684-12576-5, ScribT). Scribner.

Culture & Society in Seventeenth Century France. David Maland. 1970. 40.00 (ISBN 0-7134-1520-7, Pub. by Batsford England). David & Charles.

Culture & the Bilingual Classroom: Studies in Classroom Ethnography. Ed. by Henry T. Trueba et al. (Bilingual Multicultural Education Ser.). 288p. (Orig.). 1981. pap. text ed. 15.95 (ISBN 0-88377-182-9). Newbury Hse.

Culture & the City: Cultural Philanthropy in Chicago from the 1880's to 1917. Helen L. Horowitz. LC 75-3546. 302p. 1976. 17.50x (ISBN 0-8131-1344-X). U Pr of Ky.

Culture & the Educative Process. Kimball. LC 73-21760. 285p. 1974. text ed. 10.25x (ISBN 0-8077-2422-X); pap. text ed. 6.50x (ISBN 0-8077-2434-3). Tchrs Coll.

Culture & the Evolution of Man. Ashley Montagu. (Illus., Orig.). 1962. pap. 4.95 (ISBN 0-19-500701-8, GB88, GB). Oxford U Pr.

Culture & Thought: A Psychological Introduction. M. Cole & S. Scribner. LC 73-16360. 1974. pap. 11.95 (ISBN 0-471-16477-1). Wiley.

Culture & Value. Ludwig Wittgenstein. Ed. by G. H. Von Wright. Tr. by Peter Winch. LC 80-15234. 1980. 20.00x (ISBN 0-226-90432-6). U of Chicago Pr.

Culture As Praxis. Zygmunt Bauman. (Monographs in Social Theory). 204p. 1973. 15.95x (ISBN 0-7100-7606-1). Routledge & Kegan.

Culture, Behavior & Education: A Study of Hawaiian-Americans. Ronald Gallimore et al. LC 74-75863. (Sage Library of Social Research: Vol. 11). 1974. 18.00x (ISBN 0-8039-0380-4); pap. 8.95x (ISBN 0-8039-0446-0). Sage.

Culture, Behavior, & Personality. 2nd ed. 320p. 1981. 22.95x (ISBN 0-686-69599-2); pap. text ed. 11.95x (ISBN 0-686-69600-X). Aldine Pub.

Culture, Behavior & Personality. 2nd ed. Ed. by Robert A. LeVine. LC 75-169514. 320p. 1979. text ed. 17.95x (ISBN 0-202-01085-6). Aldine Pub.

Culture Change in an Inter-Tribal Market. D. P. Sinha. 7.50x (ISBN 0-210-27031-4). Asia.

Culture, Communication, & Dependency: The Tradition of H. A. Innis. William H. Melody et al. 288p. 1980. text ed. write for info. (ISBN 0-89391-065-1). Ablex Pub.

Culture Contact & Culture Change. P. S. Wells. LC 80-40212. (New Studies in Archaeology). (Illus.). 195p. 1981. 24.95 (ISBN 0-521-22808-5). Cambridge U Pr.

Culture, Curers, & Contagion. Ed. by Norman Klein. LC 79-10888. (Anthropology Ser.). 256p. 1979. pap. text ed. 6.95x (ISBN 0-88316-531-7). Chandler & Sharp.

Culture Factory: Boston Public Schools, 1789-1860. Stanley K. Schultz. (Illus.). 352p. 1973. 17.95 (ISBN 0-19-501668-8). Oxford U Pr.

Culture Groups & Language Groups in Native North America. Ed. by Harold E. Driver. 1975. pap. text ed. 1.00x (ISBN 90-316-0065-2). Humanities.

Culture Gulch: Notes on Art & Its Public in the 1960's. John Canaday. 1969. 5.95 o.p. (ISBN 0-374-13332-8). FS&G.

Culture in Context: Selected Writings of Weston La Barre. Weston La Barre. LC 78-74728. (Illus.). viii, 338p. 1980. 19.75 (ISBN 0-8223-0424-4). Duke.

Culture in History: Essays in Honor of Paul Radin. Stanley Diamond. 1980. Repr. of 1960 ed. lib. bdg. 70.00x (ISBN 0-374-92155-5). Octagon.

Culture in Language & Learning. Ed. by G. Reginald Bishop, Jr. Incl. Anthropological Concept of Culture. Ernestine Friedl; Language As Culture. William E. Welmers; Teaching of Classical Cultures. Doris E. Kibbe; Teaching of Western European Cultures. Ira Wade; Teaching of Slavic Cultures. Leon I. Twarog. 1960. pap. 7.95x (ISBN 0-915432-60-9). NE Conf Teach Foreign.

Culture, Industrialization & Education. Geoffrey H. Bantock. (Students Library of Education). 1968. text ed. 5.50x (ISBN 0-7100-6132-3); pap. text ed. 2.00x (ISBN 0-7100-6133-1). Humanities.

Culture, Language, & Personality: Selected Essays. Edward Sapir. Ed. by David G. Mandelbaum. 1949. pap. 5.95x (ISBN 0-520-01116-3, CAL5). U of Cal Pr.

Culture, Language & Society. Ward Goodenough. 1981. 9.95; pap. 5.95. Benjamin-Cummings.

Culture, Literature, & Articulation. Ed. by Germaine Bree. Incl. Classical & Modern Foreign Languages: Common Areas & Problems. Barbara P. McCarthy; Foreign Language Instruction in Elementary Schools. Mary P. Thompson; Foreign Language Instruction in the Secondary School. Robert G. Mead, Jr; Place of Culture & Civilization in Foreign Language Teaching. Laurence Wylie; Preparation of Foreign Language Teachers. Alonzo G. Grace; Role of Foreign Languages in American Life. Wilmarth H. Starr; Role of Literature in Language Teaching. Archibald T. MacAllister; Teaching Aids & Techniques: Principle Demonstrations. Jeanne V. Pleasants; Tests: All Skills, Speaking Test. Nelson Brooks. 188p. 1955. pap. 7.95x (ISBN 0-915432-55-2). NE Conf Teach Foreign.

Culture of a Community College. Howard B. London. LC 78-8697. (Praeger Special Studies). 1978. 22.95 (ISBN 0-03-044701-1). Praeger.

Culture of Bivalve Molluscs: Fifty Years' Experience at Conwy. Peter R. Walne. (Illus.). 190p. 16.25 (ISBN 0-85238-063-1, FN). Unipub.

Culture of Ceylon in Mediaeval Times. Wilhelm Geiger. LC 60-39625. (Illus.). 309p. 1960. 42.50x (ISBN 3-447-00278-6). Intl Pubns Serv.

Culture of Childhood: Child's-Eye Views of Society & Culture. Mary E. Goodman. LC 75-106992. 1970. pap. 6.50x (ISBN 0-8077-1444-5). Tchrs Coll.

Culture of Cities. Lewis Mumford. LC 80-23130. (Illus.). xviii, 586p. 1981. Repr. of 1970 ed. lib. bdg. 45.00x (ISBN 0-313-22746-2, MUCC). Greenwood.

Culture of Consent: Mass Organization of Leisure in Fascist Italy. Victoria De Grazia. LC 80-24361. (Illus.). 304p. Date not set. price not set (ISBN 0-521-23705-X). Cambridge U Pr.

Culture of Experience: Philosophical Essays in the American Grain. John J. McDermott. LC 76-5962. 237p. 1976. 15.00x (ISBN 0-8147-5406-6); pap. 6.00x (ISBN 0-8147-5424-4). NYU Pr.

Culture of Narcissism. Christopher Lasch. 1979. pap. 3.50 (ISBN 0-446-93264-7); pap. 6.95 (ISBN 0-446-97495-1). Warner Bks.

Culture of Public Problems: Drinking-Driving & the Symbolic Order. Joseph R. Gusfield. LC 80-17007. 1981. lib. bdg. 20.00x (ISBN 0-226-31093-0). U of Chicago Pr.

Culture of the School & the Problem of Change. Seymour Sarason. 1971. pap. text ed. 9.95x (ISBN 0-205-02840-3, 2228408). Allyn.

Culture of the Twenties. Ed. by Loren Baritz. LC 69-14821. (American Heritage Ser). (Illus.). 1970. 9.50 (ISBN 0-672-60138-9, AHS83). Bobbs.

Culture of the University: Governance & Education. Caleb Foote & Henry Meyer. LC 68-54947. (Higher Education Ser). 1968. 13.95x o.p. (ISBN 0-87589-027-X). Jossey-Bass.

Culture of Unbelief: Studies & Proceedings from the First International Symposium on Belief, Held in Rome, March 22-27, 1969. Ed. by Rocco Caporale & Antonio Grumelli. LC 75-138513. 1971. 20.00x (ISBN 0-520-01856-7). U of Cal Pr.

Culture Populaire et Litteratures Au Quebec. Ed. by Rene Bouchard. (Stanford French & Italian Studies: Vol. 19). 308p. (Fr.). 1980. pap. 20.00 (ISBN 0-915838-20-6). Anma Libri.

Culture-Protestantism: German Liberal Theology at the Turn of the Twentieth Century. George Rupp. LC 77-13763. (American Academy of Religion. Studies in Religion: No. 15). 1977. pap. 7.50 (ISBN 0-89130-197-6, 010015). Scholars Pr Ca.

Culture: The Anthropological Perspective. Marc J. Swartz & David K. Jordan. LC 79-9211. 1980. pap. text ed. 15.95x (ISBN 0-471-03333-2). Wiley.

Culture Theory. David Kaplan & Robert Manners. 224p. 1972. pap. 6.95 ref. ed. (ISBN 0-13-195511-X). P-H.

Culture, Tradition & Society in the West African Novel. E. Obiechina. LC 74-80358. (African Studies: No. 14). 300p. 1975. 45.00 (ISBN 0-521-20525-5); pap. 12.50x (ISBN 0-521-09876-9). Cambridge U Pr.

Culture Watch: Essays on Theatre & Society, 1969-1974. Robert Brustein. 1975. 7.95 o.p. (ISBN 0-394-49814-3). Knopf.

Culture's Consequences: International Differences in Work-Related Values. Geert Hofstede. LC 80-16327. (Sage Ser. on Cross-Cultural Research & Methodology: Vol. 5). (Illus.). 475p. 1980. 29.95 (ISBN 0-8039-1444-X). Sage.

Cultures in Conflict: The Four Faces of Indian Bureaucracy. Stanley J. Heginbotham. LC 74-31206. 352p. 1975. 17.50x (ISBN 0-231-03888-7). Columbia U Pr.

Cultures in Crisis. 2nd ed. James F. Downs. 1975. pap. text ed. 5.95x (ISBN 0-02-472300-2, 47230). Macmillan.

Cultures of Management. Robert H. Roy. LC 76-47385. (Illus.). 512p. 1977. 19.95x (ISBN 0-8018-1875-3); pap. text ed. 9.95 (ISBN 0-8018-2524-5). Johns Hopkins.

Cultures of Prehistoric Egypt. Elise J. Baumgartel. LC 80-24186. (Illus.). 268p. 1981. Repr. of 1955 ed. lib. bdg. 60.00x (ISBN 0-313-22524-9, BACU). Greenwood.

Cultures of Prehistoric Egypt, 2 vols. in one. Elise J. Baumgartel. LC 80-24186. (Illus.). xxiii, 286p. 1981. Repr. of 1960 ed. lib. bdg. 63.33 (ISBN 0-313-22524-9, BAUC). Greenwoodd.

Cultures of the Islamic Middle East. John W. Bagnole. (America-Mideast Educational & Training Servies, Inc. - Occasional Paper: No. 4). 86p. (Orig.). 1978. pap. text ed. 4.00 (ISBN 0-89192-296-2). Interbk Inc.

Cultures of the North Pacific Coast. Philip Drucker. (Culture Area Studies Ser.). (Illus., Orig.). 1965. pap. text ed. 10.95 scp (HarpC). Har-Row.

Cultures of the Pacific. T. Harding & B. Wallace. LC 70-91883. 1970. 17.95 (ISBN 0-02-913810-8); pap. text ed. 10.95 (ISBN 0-02-913800-0). Free Pr.

Cumberland County. Ava H. Chadbourne. (Maine County Place - Name Ser.). Date not set. pap. 4.95 (ISBN 0-87027-115-6). Wheelwright. Postponed.

Cummulative Index to Public Administration: Journal of the Royal Institute of Public Administration, Vols. 1-55, 1928-1977, Mohinder Singh & R. N. Sharma. 1979. text ed. 17.50x (ISBN 0-391-01871-X). Humanities.

Cumulated Index to the U. S. State Department Papers Relating to the Foreign Relations of the United States, 1939-1945, 2 vols. 1981. Set. lib. bdg. 180.00 (ISBN 0-527-20744-6). Kraus Intl.

Cumulated Indexes to the Public Papers of the Presidents of the United States: Gerald R. Ford, 1974-1977. 1980. lib. bdg. 30.00 (ISBN 0-527-20756-X). Kraus Intl.

Cumulative Index of Hospital Literature: 1965-1969. American Hospital Association. 864p. 1970. 62.50 (ISBN 0-87258-055-5, 1384). Am Hospital.

Cumulative Index of Hospital Literature. American Hospital Association. Incl. 1955-1959. 460p. 1960. casebound 31.25 (ISBN 0-87258-329-5, 1381); 1950-1954. 540p. 1955. 31.25 (ISBN 0-87258-328-7, 1380). Am Hospital.

Cumulative Index of SAE Technical Papers, 1965-1978. Society of Automotive Engineers. 1979. 39.95. Soc Auto Engineers.

Cumulative Index of the Southwestern Historical Quarterly, Vols. 1-40. LC 12-20299. 1950. 12.50 (ISBN 0-87611-009-X). Tex St Hist Assn.

Cumulative Index of the Southwestern Historical Quarterly, Vols. 41-60. LC 12-20299. 1960. 17.50 (ISBN 0-87611-010-3). Tex St Hist Assn.

Cumulative Index of the Southwestern Historical Quarterly, Vols. 61-70. LC 12-20299. 1980. 20.00 (ISBN 0-87611-046-4); pap. 12.50 (ISBN 0-87611-049-9). Tex St Hist As.

Cumulative Index to Journal of Chemical Education, 3 vols. Ed. by W. F. Kieffer & Rakestraw. index 7.50 ea. Vol. 1 (ISBN 0-910362-10-6, 1924-1949). Vol. 2 (ISBN 0-910362-11-4, 1949-1958). Vol. 3 (ISBN 0-910362-12-2, 1958-1968). Chem Educ.

Cumulative Index to Nursing & Allied Health Literature, Vol. 22. Ed. by Mildred Grandbois. LC 78-643434. 1977. 50.00 (ISBN 0-910478-13-9). Glendale Advent Med.

Cumulative Index to Nursing & Allied Health Literature, Vol. 23. Ed. by Virginia Inman. LC 78-643434. 1978. 50.00 (ISBN 0-910478-14-7). Glendale Advent Med.

Cumulative Index to Nursing & Allied Health Literature, Vol. 24. Ed. by Ferne Fanin. LC 78-643434. 1979. 50.00 (ISBN 0-910478-15-5). Glendale Advent Med.

Cumulative Index to the American Journal of Public Health, Vols. 60-69: 1970-1979. Date not set. lib. bdg. 34.50 (ISBN 0-88471-042-4). Numarc Bk Corp.

Cumulative Index to the Proceedings of the British Academy, 1903-1968. K. Balasundara Gupta. 1971. 8.00 o.p. (ISBN 0-8108-0383-6). Scarecrow.

Cumulative Personal Author Indexes for the Monthly Catalog of U.S. Government Publications, 1941-1975, 5 vols. Ed. by Edward Przebienda. Incl. Decennial Cumulative Personal Author Index, 1941-50. 1971. 35.00 (ISBN 0-87650-007-6); Decennial Cumulative Personal Author Index, 1951-60. 1971. 35.00 (ISBN 0-87650-008-4); Quinquennial Cumulative Personal Author Index, 1961-65. 1971. 35.00 (ISBN 0-87650-009-2); Quinquennial Cumulative Personal Author Index, 1966-70. 1971. 35.00 (ISBN 0-87650-016-5); Quinquennnial Cumulative Personal Author Index, 1971-75. 1979. 35.00 (ISBN 0-87650-097-1). LC 4-18088. (Cumulative Author Index Ser.: No. 2). Set. 150.00. Pierian.

Cumulative Record: A Selection of Papers. 3rd ed. Ed. by B. F. Skinner. (Century Psychology Ser). (Illus.). 450p. 1961. 19.95 (ISBN 0-13-195305-2). P-H.

Cumulative Title Index to the Classified Collections of the Library of Congress, 132 vols. 1980. Set. 11,432.00 (ISBN 0-8408-0350-8). Carrollton Pr.

Cunning Intelligence in Greek Culture & Society. Marcel Detienne & Jean-Pierre Vernant. Tr. by J. Lloyd from Greek. (European Philosophy & the Human Sciences Ser.). 1978. text ed. 33.75x (ISBN 0-391-00740-8). Humanities.

Cunning of History. Richard Rubenstein. 1978. pap. 3.50 (ISBN 0-06-090597-2, CN 597, CN). Har-Row.

Cunningham: The Commander. S. W. Pack. (Illus.). 1975. 21.00 o.s.i. (ISBN 0-7134-2788-4). Hippocrene Bks.

Cunninghame Graham. C. T. Watts & L. Davies. LC 78-18107. (Illus.). 1979. 32.50 (ISBN 0-521-22467-5). Cambridge U Pr.

Cunningham's Manual of Practical Anatomy: Head & Neck & Brain, Vol. 3. 14th ed. Ed. by G. J. Romanes. (Illus.). 1979. pap. text ed. 10.95x (ISBN 0-19-263205-1). Oxford U Pr.

Cunningham's Manual of Practical Anatomy: Thorax and Abdomen, Vol. 2. 14th ed. G. J. Romanes. (Illus.). 1977. pap. text ed. 10.95x (ISBN 0-19-263135-7). Oxford U Pr.

Cunningham's Manual of Practical Anatomy: Upper & Lower Limbs, Vol. 1. 14th ed. Cunningham. Ed. by G. J. Romanes. (Illus.). 270p. 1976. pap. text ed. 10.95x (ISBN 0-19-263129-2). Oxford U Pr.

Cunningham's Rooster. Barbara Brenner. LC 74-12285. (Illus.). 1975. 5.95 o.s.i. (ISBN 0-8193-0783-1, Four Winds); PLB 5.41 o.s.i. (ISBN 0-8193-0784-X). Schol Bk Serv.

Cunningham's Textbook of Anatomy. 12th ed. Ed. by G. J. Romanes. (Illus.). 1080p. 1981. text ed. 39.50x (ISBN 0-19-263134-9). Oxford U Pr.

Cupboard. John Burningham. LC 76-17797. (Illus.). (ps-1). 1976. 2.50 (ISBN 0-690-01300-0, TYC-J); PLB 4.89 (ISBN 0-690-01301-9). T Y Crowell.

Cupboard Love. Roberta Leigh. (Alpha Books). 78p. 1979. pap. text ed. 2.25x (ISBN 0-19-424165-3). Oxford U Pr.

Cupid & Psyche. Walter Pater. (Illus.). 1978. 9.95 (ISBN 0-571-11115-7, Pub. by Faber & Faber). Merrimack Bk Serv.

Cupid & Psyche: A Love Story. Edna Barth. LC 76-8821. (Illus.). (gr. 3-6). 1976. 7.95 (ISBN 0-395-28840-1, Clarion). HM.

Curative Factors in Dynamic Psychotherapy. Samuel Slipp. (Illus.). 448p. 1981. 22.95 (ISBN 0-07-058190-8). McGraw.

Curators' Choice: From the Collections of the Art Museums of the U. S. (Midwestern Edition) Babbette B. Fromme. Ed. by Brandt Aymar. (Illus.). 160p. 1981. pap. 6.95 (ISBN 0-517-54199-8). Crown.

Curators' Choice: From the Collections of the Art Museums of the U. S. (Northeastern Edition) Babbette B. Fromme. Ed. by Brandt Aymar. (Illus.). 288p. 1981. pap. 8.95 (ISBN 0-517-54197-1). Crown.

Curators' Choice: From the Collections of the Art Museums of the U. S. (Southern Edition) Babbette B. Fromme. Ed. by Brandt Aymar. (Illus.). 160p. 1981. pap. 6.95 (ISBN 0-686-69482-1). Crown.

Curators' Choice: From the Collections of the Art Museums of the U. S. (Western Edition) Babbette B. Fromme. (Illus.). 160p. 1981. pap. 6.95 (ISBN 0-517-54200-5). Crown.

Curator's Choice: Western Edition. Babette Brandt. Ed. by Brant Aymar. 1981. pap. 6.95 (ISBN 0-517-54200-5). Crown.

Curds & Whey. Susan Ogilvy. LC 79-56445. (Illus.). 120p. 1980. 19.95 (ISBN 0-7134-1990-3, Pub. by Batsford England). David & Charles.

Cure & Care of Neuroses: Theory & Practice of Behavioral Psychotherapy. Isaac Marks. 272p. 1981. 22.50 (ISBN 0-471-08808-0, Pub. by Wiley-Interscience). Wiley.

Cure & Recognize Aquarium Fish Diseases. Gottfried Schubert. (Illus.). 128p. 1974. pap. 4.95 (ISBN 0-87666-033-2, PS-210). TFH Pubns.

Cure Your Nerves Yourself. rev. ed. Ed. by Louis E. Bisch. 1977. pap. 1.75 o.p. (ISBN 0-449-23433-9, Crest). Fawcett.

Cures: The Story of Cures That Failed. James J. Walsh. LC 70-137343. 1971. Repr. of 1923 ed. 20.00 (ISBN 0-8103-3773-8). Gale.

Curfew on Olympus: The Last Days of British Rule in India. G. N. Molesworth. 12.50x (ISBN 0-210-27143-4). Asia.

Curia & Cortes in Leon & Castille, Ten Seventy-Two to Twelve Ninety-Five. Evelyn S. Procter. LC 79-51750. (Cambridge Iberian & Latin American Studies). (Illus.). 350p. 1980. 42.50 (ISBN 0-521-22639-2). Cambridge U Pr.

Curiculum Development for the Gifted. June Maker. 375p. 1981. text ed. price not set (ISBN 0-89443-347-4). Aspen Systems.

Curing & Caring: A Review of the Factors Affecting the Quality & Acceptability of Health Care. Ed. by Allen D. Spiegel & Bernard Backhaut. (Health Systems Management Ser.: Vol. 13). 205p. 1980. text ed. 30.00 (ISBN 0-89335-099-0). Spectrum Pub.

Curing Chronic Inflation. Ed. by Arthur M. Okun & George L. Perry. 1978. 14.95 (ISBN 0-8157-6474-X); pap. 5.95 (ISBN 0-8157-6473-1). Brookings.

Curing the Mischiefs of Faction: Party Reform in America. Austin Ranney. (Jefferson Memorial Lectures). 1975. 16.95x (ISBN 0-520-02650-0); pap. 3.25 (ISBN 0-520-03215-2, CAL 335). U of Cal Pr.

Curiosities of Civilization. Andrew Wynter. LC 67-23949. (Social History Reference Ser.: No. 11). 1968. Repr. of 1860 ed. 15.00 (ISBN 0-8103-3264-7). Gale.

Curiosities of Clocks & Watches from the Earliest Times. Edward J. Wood. LC 70-174149. (Illus.). x, 443p. 1974. Repr. of 1866 ed. 20.00 (ISBN 0-8103-3984-6). Gale.

Curiosities of Indo-European Tradition & Folk-Lore. Walter K. Kelly. LC 68-22032. 1969. Repr. of 1863 ed. 18.00 (ISBN 0-8103-3837-8). Gale.

Curiosities of London. rev. ed. John Timbs. LC 68-22056. 1968. Repr. of 1867 ed. 26.00 (ISBN 0-8103-3497-6). Gale.

Curiosities of Medical Experience. J. G. Millingen. LC 72-83373. 1969. Repr. of 1839 ed. 20.00 (ISBN 0-8103-3487-9). Gale.

Curiosities of Popular Customs. William S. Walsh. LC 66-23951. 1966. Repr. of 1898 ed. 40.00 (ISBN 0-8103-3008-3). Gale.

Curiosities of Superstition. William H. D. Adams. LC 76-155434. 1971. 20.00 (ISBN 0-8103-3383-X). Gale.

Curiosities of the Search-Room. Julia Byrne. LC 70-78117. 1969. Repr. of 1880 ed. 18.00 (ISBN 0-8103-3573-5). Gale.

Curious Affair of the Third Dog. Patricia Moyes. 208p. 1976. pap. 1.95 o.p. (ISBN 0-14-004027-7). Penguin.

Curious Book: Fascinating Facts About People, Places & Things. Arkady Leokum. LC 76-19772. (Illus.). (gr. 10 up). 1976. 7.95 o.p. (ISBN 0-8069-0100-4); PLB 7.49 o.p. (ISBN 0-8069-0101-2). Sterling.

Curious Creatures. Helen Oxenbury. LC 79-2980. (Heads, Bodies, Legs Ser.). (Illus.). 9p. (ps-3). 1980. 3.95 (ISBN 0-06-024597-2, HarpJ). Har-Row.

Curious Creatures in Zoology. John Ashton. LC 68-57297. 1968. Repr. of 1890 ed. 20.00 (ISBN 0-8103-3525-5). Gale.

Curious Eye. W. Leecing & J. L. Armstrong. 1970. text ed. 10.50 o.p. (ISBN 0-07-037006-0, C); instructor's guide 3.95 o.p. (ISBN 0-07-037007-9). McGraw.

Curious George. H. A. Rey. (Illus.). 48p. (gr. k-3). 1973. pap. 2.50 (ISBN 0-395-15023-X, Sandpiper). HM.

Curious George Gets a Medal. H. A. Rey. (Illus.). (gr. k-3). 1957. reinforced bdg. 8.95 (ISBN 0-395-16973-9). HM.

Curious George Learns the Alphabet. H. A. Rey. LC 62-12261. (Illus.). 72p. (gr. k-3). 1973. pap. 2.95 (ISBN 0-395-13718-7, Sandpiper). HM.

Curious Knotted Garden: The Form, Themes & Contexts of Shakespeare's Love's Labour's Lost. Louis A. Montrose. (Salzburg Studies in English Literature: Elizabethan & Renaissance Studies: No. 56). (Orig.). 1977. pap. text ed. 25.00x (ISBN 0-391-01483-8). Humanities.

Curious Little Kitten. Linday Hayward. (Golden Storytime Bks.). 1981. 1.95 (ISBN 0-307-11952-1, Golden Pr). Western Pub.

Curious Magic. Elizabeth Beresford. (gr. 4-8). 1980. 7.95 (ISBN 0-525-66682-6). Elsevier-Nelson.

Curious Missie. Virginia Sorensen. LC 53-7872. (Illus.). (gr. 3-6). 1963. 5.50 o.p. (ISBN 0-15-221085-7, HJ). HarBraceJ.

Curious Mollusks. Marie M. Jenkins. LC 72-75597. (Illus.). (gr. 7 up). 1972. 7.95 o.p. (ISBN 0-8234-0209-6). Holiday.

Curious Punishments of Bygone Days. Alice M. Earle. LC 68-31516. (Illus.). 1968. Repr. of 1896 ed. 15.00 (ISBN 0-8103-3504-2). Gale.

Curious Questions in History, Literature, Art, & Social Life, 3 Vols. Sarah H. Killikelly. LC 68-26581. 1968. Repr. of 1900 ed. Set. 58.00 (ISBN 0-8103-3091-1). Gale.

Curious Rogue. Joan Vincent. (Orig.). 1981. pap. 1.50 (ISBN 0-440-11186-2). Dell.

Curious Sofa. Edward Gorey. LC 61-12368. 64p. 1980. 5.95 (ISBN 0-396-07861-3). Dodd.

Curious Sofa, Ogdred Weary. Edward Gorey. (Illus.). 1961. pap. 3.50 (ISBN 0-8392-1020-5). Astor-Honor.

Curious Tales. Milos Macourek. 96p. (gr. 4 up). 1980. 11.95 (ISBN 0-19-271427-9). Oxford U Pr.

Curious What You Might Find When You Go Out to Look for Elephants. Mary Macur. LC 48-29. pap. 5.00 (ISBN 0-686-28865-3). First Amend.

Curity Baby Book. Susan Aukema & Marilyn Kostick. 7.95 (ISBN 0-916752-06-2). Green Hill.

Curlers & Camping. Betty Tucker. (Illus.). 1971. 1.00 (ISBN 0-910856-42-7). La Siesta.

Currency & Financial System of Mainland China. Tadao Miyashita. (China in the 20th Century Ser.). 1976. Repr. of 1966 ed. lib. bdg. 22.50 (ISBN 0-306-70758-6). Da Capo.

Currency Management. Richard Lassen. 168p. 1980. 40.00x (ISBN 0-85941-154-0, Pub. by Woodhead-Faulkner England). State Mutual Bk.

Currency Translation & Performance Evaluation in Multinationals. Helen G. Morsicato. Ed. by Gunter Dufey. (Research for Business Decisions). 176p. 1980. 24.95 (ISBN 0-8357-1104-8, Pub. by UMI Res Pr). Univ Microfilms.

Current Advances in Mechanical Design & Production: Proceedings of the First International Conference, Cairo University, 27-29 December 1979. Ed. by G. S. A. Shawki & S. M. Metwalli. LC 80-41666. (Illus.). 500p. 1981. 75.00 (ISBN 0-08-027294-0). Pergamon.

Current Advances in Oral Surgery, Vols. 2-3. Ed. by William B. Irby. LC 74-8602. (Illus.). Vol. 2, 1977. 49.95 (ISBN 0-8016-2341-3); Vol. 3, 1980. 49.95 (ISBN 0-8016-2342-1). Mosby.

Current African Directories. 200p. 1972. 38.00x (ISBN 0-900246-11-1). Intl Pubns Serv.

Current Algebras & Their Applications. B. Renner. 1968. 34.00 (ISBN 0-08-012504-2). Pergamon.

Current American Usage: How Americans Say It & Write It. Ed. by Margaret M. Bryant. LC 62-9735. (Funk & W Bk.). 1965. 6.00 (ISBN 0-308-40056-9, TYC-T). T Y Crowell.

Current Antique Furniture Style & Price Guide. George Grotz. LC 77-27673. 1979. 9.95 (ISBN 0-385-13165-8, Dolp). Doubleday.

Current Approaches to the Teaching of Grammar in ESL. David M. Davidson. (Language in Education Ser.: No. 5). 1978. pap. 2.95 (ISBN 0-87281-081-X). Ctr Appl Ling.

Current Argument on Early Man: Nobel Symposium "Current Argument on Early Man" Royal Swedish Academy of Sciences & the Nobel Foundation, Karlskoga, Sweden, May 21-27, 1978. Ed. by Lars-Konig Konigsson & Stephan Sundstrom. (Illus.). 1980. 69.00 (ISBN 0-08-024956-6). Pergamon.

Current Asian & Australian Directories. Ed. by I. G. Anderson. 264p. 1978. 85.00x (ISBN 0-900246-25-1). Intl Pubns Serv.

Current Aspects of Biochemical Energetics. Ed. by Nathan O. Kaplan & Eugene P. Kennedy. 1967. 48.00 (ISBN 0-12-397350-3). Acad Pr.

Current Awareness Services. Alasdair Kemp. (Outlines of Modern Librarianship Ser.). 181p. 1979. text ed. 12.00 (ISBN 0-89664-420-0, Pub. by K G Saur). Shoe String.

Current British Directories. 9th ed. Ed. by I. G. Anderson. LC 53-26894. 1979. 105.00x (ISBN 0-900246-31-6). Intl Pubns Serv.

Current British Directories: A Guide to the Directories Published in Great Britain, Ireland, British Commonwealth & South Africa. 9th ed. Ed. by I. G. Anderson. 369p. 1979. 120.00 (ISBN 0-900246-31-6). Gale.

Current Cardiology, Vol. 1. Ed. by M. Irene Ferrer. (Current Ser.). 1979. 30.00x (ISBN 0-89289-104-1). HM Prof Med Div.

Current Cardiology, Vol. 2. Ed. by Kenneth M. Rosen. (Current Ser). (Illus.). 500p. 1980. 35.00x (ISBN 0-89289-109-2). HM Prof Med Div.

Current Career & Occupational Literature,1973-1977. Ed. by Leonard H. Goodman. 1978. 12.00 (ISBN 0-8242-0616-9). Wilson.

Current Career & Occupational Literature, 1977-1979. Ed. by Leonard H. Goodman. 1980. 15.00. Wilson.

Current Chemotherapy & Infectious Disease: Proceedings, 2 vols. International Congress of Chemotherapy, 11th & Interscience Conference on Antimicrobial Agents & Chemotherapy, 19th. Ed. by John D. Nelson & Carlo Grassi. (Illus.). 1980. Set. 75.00 (ISBN 0-914826-22-0). Am Soc Microbio.

Current Clinical Dental Terminology: A Glossary of Accepted Terms in All Disciplines of Dentistry. 2nd ed. Ed. by Carl O. Boucher. LC 73-4651. 1974. 27.50 (ISBN 0-8016-0719-1). Mosby.

Current Clinical Topics in Infectious Diseases, No. 1. Jack S. Remington & Morton N. Swartz. (Illus.). 1980. text ed. 30.00 (ISBN 0-07-051850-5). McGraw.

Current Clinical Topics in Infectious Diseases, No. 2. Jack S. Remington & Morton N. Swartz. (Illus.). 304p. 1981. text ed. 30.00 (ISBN 0-07-051851-3, HP). McGraw.

Current Concept in the Therapy of Hypertension with Beta-Blockers. S. Chaithiraphan. (Journal: Cardiology Ser.: Vol. 66, Suppl. 1). (Illus.). vi, 62p. 1980. pap. 19.50 (ISBN 3-8055-0912-X). S Karger.

Current Concepts in Cataract Surgery: Selected Proceedings of the Sixth Biennial Cataract Surgical & Intraocular Lens Congress. Jared M. Emery & Adrienne C. Jacobson. LC 80-24694. (Illus.). 466p. 1980. text ed. 64.50 (ISBN 0-8016-1527-5). Mosby.

Current Concepts in Cataract Surgery: Selected Proceedings of the Fifth Biennial Cataract Surgical Congress. 5th ed. Ed. by Jared M. Emery. LC 78-23408. (Illus.). 1978. text ed. 66.50 (ISBN 0-8016-1524-0). Mosby.

Current Concepts in Cerebravascular Disease. Ed. by Fletcher H. McDowell. (Progress in Cardiovascular Disease Ser.). 1980. write for info. (ISBN 0-8089-1353-0). Grune.

Current Concepts in Clinical Cardiology. Ed. by J. H. Vogel. (Advances in Cardiology Ser.: Vol. 27). (Illus.). viii, 360p. 1980. 118.75 (ISBN 3-8055-0098-X). S Karger.

Current Concepts in Clinical Nursing, Vol. 2. Ed. by Betty Bergersen et al. LC 67-30797. (Illus.). 1969. 15.50 o.p. (ISBN 0-8016-0636-5). Mosby.

Current Concepts in Dental Hygiene, Vol. 2. Suzanne S. Boundy & Nancy J Reynolds. LC 76-40164. (Illus.). 1979. pap. text ed. 17.95 (ISBN 0-8016-0747-7). Mosby.

Current Concepts in Emergency Medicines: Vol. 1, Management of the Unconscious Patient. Ed. by William R. Darmody. LC 75-37770. (Illus.). 120p. 1976. 13.50 (ISBN 0-8016-2748-6). Mosby.

Current Concepts in Library Management. Ed. by Martha Boaz. LC 79-20734. 1979. lib. bdg. 25.00x (ISBN 0-87287-204-1). Libs Unl.

Current Concepts in Migraine Research. Ed. by Raymond Greene. LC 77-83690. 1978. 22.50 (ISBN 0-89004-199-7). Raven.

Current Concepts in Ophthalmology, Vol. 5. Ed. by Kaufman & Zimmerman. LC 67-14718. (Illus.). 1976. 36.50 o.p. (ISBN 0-8016-2627-7). Mosby.

Current Concepts in the Treatment of Parkinsonism. Ed. by M. D. Yahr. LC 74-79191. 1974. 24.50 (ISBN 0-911216-83-9). Raven.

Current Concepts of Infectious Diseases. Ed. by Edward W. Hook et al. LC 77-4458. 1977. 35.95 (ISBN 0-471-01598-9, Pub. by Wiley Medical). Wiley.

Current Concepts of Myopathies. W. King Engel. (Clinical Orthopaedics & Related Research Ser, Vol. 39). (Illus.). 4.00 o.p. (ISBN 0-685-14227-2). Lippincott.

Current Concerns in Mineral Policy. 75p. (Orig.). 1978. pap. text ed. 3.00x (ISBN 0-88757-010-0, Pub. by Ctr Resource Stud Canada). Renouf.

Current Concerns in Occupational Stress. Cary L. Cooper & Roy Payne. LC 79-40641. (Wiley Ser. on Studies in Occupational Stress). 1980. 39.75 (ISBN 0-471-27624-3, Pub. by Wiley-Interscience). Wiley.

Current Constitutional Issues: A Symposium. C. J. Antieau et al. LC 77-153885. (Symposia on Law & Society Ser.). 1971. Repr. of 1967 ed. lib. bdg. 19.50 (ISBN 0-306-70154-5). Da Capo.

Current Contents of Academic Journals in Japan, 1978. 18th ed. Ed. by Center for Academic Publications Japan. LC 72-623679. 392p. (Orig.). 1980. pap. 55.00x (ISBN 0-8002-2740-9). Intl Pubns Serv.

Current Contents of Academic Journals in Japan, 1977: The Humanities & Social Sciences. Center for Academic Publications Japan. LC 72-623679. 344p. (Orig.). 1979. pap. 50.00x (ISBN 0-8002-2322-5). Intl Pubns Serv.

Current Contents of Academic Journals in Japan 1974-75. Center for Academic Publications, Japan. LC 72-623679. 1973. pap. 45.00x (ISBN 0-8002-0311-9). Intl Pubns Serv.

Current Controversies & Issues in Personality. Lawrence A. Pervin. LC 78-15361. 1978. pap. text ed. 10.95 (ISBN 0-471-02035-4). Wiley.

Current Controversies in Urologic Management. Ed. by Russell Scott, Jr. et al. LC 70-173342. (Illus.). 391p. 1972. 20.00 (ISBN 0-7216-8043-7). Saunders.

Current Conventions Made Clear. Ben Cohen & Rhoda Lederer. 1973. 9.50 o.p. (ISBN 0-04-793020-9). Allen Unwin.

Current Dermatologic Management. 2nd ed. Ed. by Stuart Maddin. LC 74-3001. 480p. 1975. 45.00 o.p. (ISBN 0-8016-3061-4). Mosby.

Current Development of the World Economy. 74p. 1980. pap. 5.00 (ISBN 92-808-0150-3, TUNU096, UNU). Unipub.

Current Developments in Anthropological Genetics: Vol. 1, Theory & Methods, Vol. 1. Ed. by James H. Mielke & Michael H. Crawford. 450p. 1980. 45.00 (ISBN 0-306-40390-0, Plenum Pr). Plenum Pub.

Current Developments in Bankruptcy, Reorganization & Arrangements: Proceedings, 1978. (Corporate Law & Practice Course Handbook Ser. 1977-78: Vol. 274). 1978. 20.00 o.p. (ISBN 0-685-63704-2, B4-5565). PLI.

Current Developments in Patent Law 1980 Course Handbook. (Patents, Copyrights, Trademarks & Literary Property Course Handbook Ser., 1979-80: Vol. 116). 1980. pap. 25.00 (ISBN 0-685-59697-4, G4-3667). PLI.

Current Developments in Psychopharmacology, Vol. VI. Ed. by W. Essman & L. Valzelli. (Illus.). 339p. 1981. text ed. 50.00 (ISBN 0-89335-090-7). Spectrum Pub.

Current Developments in Trademark Law & Unfair Competition, 1980. (Patents, Copyrights, Trademarks & Literary Property Course Handbook Ser. 1979-80: Vol. 121). 1980. 25.00 (ISBN 0-685-63711-5, G4-3677). PLI.

Current Diagnosis - 5. Ed. by Howard F. Conn & Rex B. Conn. LC 66-15617. (Illus.). 1977. text ed. 35.00 (ISBN 0-7216-2674-2). Saunders.

Current Diagnosis & Management of Chorioretinal Diseases. Ed. by Francis A. L'Esperance, Jr. (Illus.). 1977. text ed. 67.50 o.p. (ISBN 0-8016-2949-7). Mosby.

Current Diagnosis Six. Howard F. Conn & Rex B. Conn, Jr. (Illus.). 1424p. 1980. text ed. 48.00 (ISBN 0-7216-2707-2). Saunders.

Current Economic Problems. Ed. by J. M. Parkin & A. R. Nobay. 1975. 52.50 (ISBN 0-521-20818-1). Cambridge U Pr.

Current Economic Problems: A Book of Readings. Ed. by Royall Brandis & Steven R. Cox. 1972. pap. text ed. 8.50x o.p. (ISBN 0-256-00239-8). Irwin.

Current Estimates from the Health Interview Survey: United States-1979. Susan S. Jack & Peter W. Ries. Ed. by Klaudia Cox. (Ser. 10: No. 136). 55p. 1981. pap. text ed. 1.75 (ISBN 0-8406-0219-7). Natl Ctr Health Stats.

Current Gastroenterology, Vol. 1. Ed. by Gary L. Gitnick. (Current Ser). (Illus.). 464p. 1980. 35.00 (ISBN 0-89289-115-7). HM Prof Med Div.

Current Gastroenterology & Hepatology. Ed. by Gary L. Gitnick. (Illus.). 1979. 35.00 (ISBN 0-89289-108-4). HM Prof Med Div.

Current Genetical, Clinical & Morphological Problems. Ed. by W. Straub. (Developments in Ophthalmology: Vol. 3). (Illus.). 1981. 66.00 (ISBN 3-8055-2000-X). S Karger.

Current Geotechnical Practice in Mine Waste Disposal. Compiled By American Society of Civil Engineers. 272p. 1979. pap. text ed. 19.25 (ISBN 0-87262-141-3). Am Soc Civil Eng.

Current Hepatology, Vol. 1. Ed. by Gary L. Gitnick. (Current Ser). (Illus.). 384p. 1980. 35.00x (ISBN 0-89289-114-9). HM Prof Med Div.

Current History Encyclopedia of Developing Nations. Ed. by Carol L. Thompson et al. (Illus.). 384p. 1981. 34.95 (ISBN 0-07-064387-3, P&RB). McGraw.

Current Index to Journals in Education, Annual Cumulation 1970. Educational Resources Information Center. 1971. 75.00 o.s.i. (ISBN 0-02-469880-6). Macmillan Info.

Current Index to Journals in Education, Annual Cumulation 1969. Educational Resources Information Center. 1970. 75.00 o.s.i. (ISBN 0-02-469870-9). Macmillan Info.

Current Index to Journals in Education: Annual Cumulation 1971. Educational Resources Information Center. 1972. 75.00 o.s.i. (ISBN 0-02-469890-3). Macmillan Info.

Current Index to Journals in Education: Semi-Annual Cumulation, January-June, 1977. ERIC (Educational Information Center) LC 75-7532. 1977. 37.50 (ISBN 0-02-693050-1). Macmillan Info.

Current Index to Journals in Education: Semi-Annual Cumulation, July-December, 1977. ERIC (Educational Resources Information Center) LC 75-7532. 1978. 37.50 (ISBN 0-02-693060-9). Macmillan Info.

Current Index to Journals in Education: Semi-Annual Cumulation, January-June, 1978. ERIC (Educational Resources Information Center) LC 75-7532. 1978. 37.50 (ISBN 0-02-693120-6). Macmillan Info.

Current Index to Journals in Education: Semi-Annual Cumulation, July-December, 1978. ERIC (Educational Resources Information Center) LC 75-7532. 1979. 37.50 (ISBN 0-02-693130-3). Macmillan Info.

Current Induced Reactions. Ed. by J. G. Korner et al. (Lecture Notes in Physics: Vol. 56). 1976. soft cover 22.00 (ISBN 3-540-07866-5). Springer-Verlag.

Current Interruption in High-Voltage Networks. Ed. by Klaus Ragaller. LC 78-6057. (Brown Boveri Symposia Ser.). 380p. 1978. 37.50 (ISBN 0-306-40007-3, Plenum Pr). Plenum Pub.

Current Issues & Research in Advertising, 1980. Ed. by James H. Leigh & Claude R. Martin, Jr. (Illus.). 250p. 1980. pap. 7.00 (ISBN 0-87712-209-1). U Mich Busn Div Res.

Current Issues & Strategies in Organization Development. W. Warner Burke. LC 76-28755. 448p. 1977. 24.95 (ISBN 0-87705-270-0). Human Sci Pr.

Current Issues in Accounting. Bryan Carsberg. Ed. by Tony Hope. 304p. 1977. 34.50x (ISBN 0-86003-503-4, Pub. by Allan Pubs England); pap. 17.25x (ISBN 0-86003-603-0). State Mutual Bk.

Current Issues in American Democracy. Gerson Antell & Walter Harris. (Orig.). (gr. 10-12). 1975. pap. text ed. 6.75 (ISBN 0-87720-605-8). AMSCO Sch.

Current Issues in American Economy, 1980-1981. Ed. by Robert C. Puth. (Orig.). 1980. pap. text ed. 7.95 (ISBN 0-669-02479-1). Heath.

Current Issues in Clinical Geriatrics. Michael B. Miller. LC 77-95435. 1979. casebound 13.50 (ISBN 0-685-85789-1). Tiresias Pr.

Current Issues in Community Work. Community Work Group. 1973. 14.95 o.s.i. (ISBN 0-7100-7687-8); pap. 5.75 o.s.i. (ISBN 0-7100-7688-6). Routledge & Kegan.

Current Issues in Economic Policy. R. M. Grant & G. K. Shaw. 320p. 28.50x (ISBN 0-86003-029-6, Pub. by Allan Pubs England); pap. 14.25x (ISBN 0-86003-128-4). State Mutual Bk.

Current Issues in Energy. C. Starr. 1979. text ed. 28.00 (ISBN 0-08-023243-4); pap. text ed. 12.75 (ISBN 0-08-023244-2). Pergamon.

Current Issues in Fiscal Policy. Ed. by S. T. Cook & P. M. Jackson. 230p. 1981. pap. 13.50x (ISBN 0-85520-352-8, Pub. by Martin Robertson England). Biblio Dist.

Current Issues in Language Teaching. Ed. by William F. Bottiglia. Incl. Linguistics & Language Teaching. Robert A. Hall, Jr; Programmed Learning. Alfred S. Hayes; A Survey of FLES Practices. Nancy V. Alkons & Mary A. Biophy. 1962. 7.95x (ISBN 0-915432-62-5). NE Conf Teach Foreign.

Current Issues in Linguistic Theory. Ed. by Roger W. Cole. LC 76-26427. (Illus.). 312p. 1977. 17.50x (ISBN 0-253-31608-1); pap. 9.95x (ISBN 0-253-11262-1). Ind U Pr.

Current Issues in Monetary Theory & Policy. 2nd ed. Ed. by Thomas M. Havrilesky & John T. Boorman. LC 79-55733. (Illus.). 1980. pap. text ed. 14.95x (ISBN 0-88295-406-7). AHM Pub.

Current Issues in Nursing. Ed. by Lisbeth Hockey. (Recent Advances in Nursing Ser.). 200p. 1981. pap. text ed. 14.00 (ISBN 0-443-02186-4). Churchill.

Current Issues in Nursing. Joanne C. McCloskey et al. (Illus.). 480p. (Orig.). 1981. pap. text ed. 14.95 (ISBN 0-86542-005-X). Blackwell Sci.

Current Issues in Transportation Policies. Ed. by Alan Altshuler. LC 78-19631. (Policy Studies Organization Ser.). (Illus.). 224p. 1979. 19.95 (ISBN 0-669-02623-9). Lexington Bks.

Current Issues of Economic Policy. Lloyd G. Reynolds et al. 1973. pap. text ed. 9.95 (ISBN 0-256-01441-8). Irwin.

Current Legal Concepts in Education. Ed. by Lee O. Garber. LC 65-22382. 1966. 9.00x o.p. (ISBN 0-8122-7497-0). U of Pa Pr.

Current Literary Terms. Ed. by A. F. Scott. 324p. Repr. of 1980 ed. lib. bdg. 14.95x (ISBN 0-312-17956-1). St Martin.

Current Mathematics: A Work-Text. I Sidore Dressler. (gr. 7 up). 1977. Bk. I. wkbk 8.67 (ISBN 0-87720-239-7). AMSCO Sch.

Current Medical Diagnosis & Treatment. rev. ed. Ed. by Marcus A. Krupp & Milton J. Chatton. LC 74-641062. (Illus.). 1100p. 1981. lexotone cover 21.00 (ISBN 0-87041-251-5). Lange.

Current Medical Diagnosis & Treatment. rev. ed. Ed. by Marcus A. Krupp & Milton J. Chatton. LC 74-641062. 1116p. 1980. lexotone cover 19.00 (ISBN 0-87041-250-7). Lange.

Current Methodology. Ed. by Brooker et al. LC 78-55806. (Advances in Cyclic Nucleotide Research Ser.: Vol. 10). 1979. 38.00 (ISBN 0-89004-265-9). Raven.

Current Nephrology. Incl. Vol. 3 (ISBN 0-89289-106-8); Vol. 4 (ISBN 0-89289-110-6). (Current Ser.). (Illus.). 500p. 1980. 48.00x o.p. HM Prof Med Div.

Current Nephrology, Vol. 1. Ed. by Harvey C. Gonick. (Illus.). 1977. 48.00 (ISBN 0-89289-013-4). HM Prof Med Div.

Current Nephrology, Vol. 2. Ed. by Harvey C. Gonick. 1978. 48.00 (ISBN 0-89289-103-3). HM Prof Med Div.

Current Nephrology, Vol. 3. Ed. by Harvey C. Gonick. 1979. 48.00 (ISBN 0-89289-106-8). HM Prof Med Div.

Current Nephrology, Vol. 4. Ed. by Harvey C. Gonick. (Current Ser.). (Illus.). 500p. 1980. text ed. 48.00 (ISBN 0-89289-110-6). HM Prof Med Div.

Current Neurology, Vol. 1. Ed. by H. Richard Tyler & David Dawson. (Illus.). 1978. 29.00x o.p. (ISBN 0-89289-101-7). HM Prof Med Div.

Current Neurology, Vol. 2. Ed. by H. Richard Tyler & David Dawson. (Illus.). 1979. 34.00x (ISBN 0-89289-105-X). HM Prof Med Div.

Current Neurology, Vol. 3. Ed. by Stanley H. Appel. LC 78-68042. (Current Ser.). (Illus.). 545p. 1981. text ed. price not set (ISBN 0-89289-112-2). HM Prof Med Div.

Current Ocular Therapy. F. T. Fraunfelder & F. Hampton Roy. 600p. 1980. text ed. 42.50 (ISBN 0-7216-3860-0). Saunders.

Current of Spirituality. Hubert Van Zeller. pap. 3.95 (ISBN 0-87243-048-0). Templegate.

Current Personality Theories. Ed. by Raymond J. Corsini. 1977. text ed. 15.95 (ISBN 0-87581-204-X, 204). Peacock Pubs.

Current Perspectives. Arthur Blumberg. 1974. text ed. 10.95 (ISBN 0-394-31123-X, RanC). Knopf.

Current Perspectives in Banking: Operations, Managements & Regulation. 2nd ed. Thomas M. Havrilesky & John T. Boorman. LC 79-55734. (Illus.). 1980. pap. text ed. 14.95 (ISBN 0-88295-405-9). AHM Pub.

Current Perspectives in Latin American Urban Research. Ed. by Alejandro Portes & Harley L. Browning. LC 75-620107. (Institute of Latin American Studies Special Pubn. Ser.). 176p. 1976. 9.95x (ISBN 0-292-71036-4); pap. 4.95 (ISBN 0-292-71037-2). U of Tex Pr.

Current Perspectives in Nursing Education, Vol. 2. Janet A. Williamson. LC 75-32544. (Current Perspectives Ser.). (Illus.). 1978. 11.95 (ISBN 0-8016-5578-1); pap. 9.50 (ISBN 0-8016-5579-X). Mosby.

Current Perspectives in Nursing Management, Vol. I. Ann Marriner. LC 78-31446. (Illus.). 1979. text ed. 12.50 (ISBN 0-8016-3119-X); pap. text ed. 9.50 (ISBN 0-8016-3120-3). Mosby.

Current Perspectives in Nursing: Social Issues & Trends. Ed. by Michael H. Miller & Beverly Flynn. LC 76-57746. (Current Perspectives Ser.). (Illus.). 1979. 12.50 (ISBN 0-8016-3461-X); pap. 9.50 (ISBN 0-8016-3464-4). Mosby.

Current Perspectives in Nursing: Social Issues & Trends, Vol. 2. Beverly Flynn. LC 76-57746. (Current Perspectives Ser.). (Illus.). 1979. pap. text ed. 10.50 (ISBN 0-8016-3466-0). Mosby.

Current Perspectives in Oncologic Nursing, Vol. II. Ed. by Carolyn J. Kellogg & Barbara P. Sullivan. LC 78-492. (Current Perspectives Ser.). (Illus.). 1978. 11.95 (ISBN 0-8016-3794-5); pap. 8.95 (ISBN 0-8016-3795-3). Mosby.

Current Perspectives in Psychiatric Nursing: Issues & Trends, Vol. 1. Carol R. Kneisl. 228p. 1976. case bound 11.95 o.p. (ISBN 0-8016-2714-1); pap. 8.95 o.p. (ISBN 0-8016-2713-3). Mosby.

Current Perspectives in Rehabilitation Nursing. Rosemary Murray & Jean C. Kijek. (Illus.). 1979. text ed. 12.50 (ISBN 0-8016-3605-1); pap. text ed. 10.50 (ISBN 0-8016-3606-X). Mosby.

Current Perspectives on Criminal Behavior. 2nd ed. Abraham S. Blumberg. 442p. 1981. pap. text ed. 10.95 (ISBN 0-394-32156-1). Knopf.

Current Practice in Family-Centered Community Nursing. Ed. by Adina M. Reinhardt & Mildred D. Quinn. LC 76-26006. (Illus.). 1977. 11.95 o.p. (ISBN 0-8016-4114-4); pap. 8.95 o.p. (ISBN 0-8016-4107-1). Mosby.

Current Practice in Family-Centered Community Nursing: A Sociocultural Framework, Vol. II. Adina M. Reinhardt & Mildred D. Quinn. LC 73-8681. (Current Practice Ser.). (Illus.). 1980. pap. text ed. 12.95 (ISBN 0-8016-4121-7). Mosby.

Current Practice in Gerontological Nursing. Adina M. Reinhardt & Mildred D. Quinn. LC 78-31424. (Current Practice Ser.). 1979. text ed. 12.50 (ISBN 0-8016-4122-5); pap. text ed. 10.95 (ISBN 0-8016-4113-6). Mosby.

Current Practice in Obstetric & Gynecologic Nursing, Vol. 1. Leota K. McNall. LC 75-2940. (Illus.). 224p. 1976. case bound 11.95 o.p. (ISBN 0-8016-3328-1); pap. text ed. 8.95 case bound o.p. (ISBN 0-8016-3329-X). Mosby.

Current Practice in Obstetric & Gynecologic Nursing, Vol. 2. Ed. by Leota K. McNall. Janet Galeener. LC 75-29240. (Current Practice Ser.). (Illus.). 1978. 12.50 (ISBN 0-8016-3326-5); pap. 9.50 (ISBN 0-8016-3327-3). Mosby.

Current Practice in Obstetric & Gynecologic Nursing, Vol. 3. Lee McNall. (Current Practice Ser.). 1980. pap. 12.95 (ISBN 0-8016-3325-7). Mosby.

Current Practice in Oncologic Nursing, Vol. 1. Barbara H. Peterson & Carolyn J. Kellogg. LC 75-31734. 232p. 1976. case bound 11.95 o.p. (ISBN 0-8016-3791-0); pap. 8.95 o.p. (ISBN 0-8016-3792-9). Mosby.

Current Practice in Orthopaedic Surgery, Vol. 6. Ed. by James P. Ahstrom, Jr. LC 63-18841. (Illus.). 264p. 1975. text ed. 34.50 o.p. (ISBN 0-8016-0097-9). Mosby.

Current Practice in Orthopaedic Surgery, Vol. 7. James P. Ahstrom. LC 63-18841. (Illus.). 1977. 34.50 o.p. (ISBN 0-8016-0095-2). Mosby.

Current Practice in Pediatric Nursing, Vol. 1. Patricia A. Brandt & Peggy L. Chinn. LC 75-22183. (Illus.). 242p. 1976. 11.95 o.p. (ISBN 0-8016-0962-3); pap. 8.95 o.p. (ISBN 0-8016-0745-0). Mosby.

Current Practice in Pediatric Nursing, Vol. 2. Patricia Brandt et al. LC 75-22183. (Current Practice Ser.). 1978. 12.50 (ISBN 0-8016-0750-7); pap. 9.50 (ISBN 0-8016-0751-5). Mosby.

Current Practice in Pediatric Nursing, Vol. 3. Peggy L. Chinn. LC 75-22183. (Current Practice Ser.). (Illus.). 1980. pap. 12.95 (ISBN 0-8016-1111-3). Mosby.

Current Practice, Issues, & Concepts: Nursing Care of the Ill Adult. Maureen O. Kennedy & Gail Molnar. LC 79-12298. (Current Practice Ser.). (Illus.). 1979. text ed. 12.50 (ISBN 0-8016-2646-3); pap. text ed. 9.50 (ISBN 0-8016-2635-8). Mosby.

Current Practice of Clinical Electroencephalography. Ed. by Donald W. Klass & David D. Daly. LC 75-32088. 1979. text ed. 52.00 (ISBN 0-89004-088-5). Raven.

Current Problems in Partnership Investment, Management & Control. (Tax Law & Estate Planning Course Handbook Ser. 1977-78: Vol. 115). 1977. 20.00 o.p. (ISBN 0-686-00431-0, J4-3446). PLI.

Current Problems of Teacher Education. Ed. by Alfred Yates. (International Studies in Education). (Orig.). 1971. pap. 9.25 (ISBN 0-685-02838-0, U145, UNESCO). Unipub.

Current Psychiatric Therapies, Vol. XIX. Ed. by Jules H. Masserman. 1980. 29.50 (ISBN 0-8089-1300-X). Grune.

Current Psychotherapies. 2nd ed. Raymond J. Corsini. LC 78-61880. 1979. pap. text ed. 13.95 (ISBN 0-87581-240-6). Peacock Pubs.

Current Pulmonology, Vol. 1. Ed. by Daniel H. Simmons. (Illus.). 1979. 40.00 (ISBN 0-89289-102-5). HM Prof Med Div.

Current Pulmonology, Vol. 2. Daniel E. Simmons. (Current Pulmonology Ser.). (Illus.). 1980. text ed. 40.00 (ISBN 0-89289-113-0). HM Prof Med Div.

Current Radiology, Vol. 1. Ed. by Gabriel H. Wilson. (Illus.). 1978. 35.00x (ISBN 0-89289-100-9). HM Prof Med Div.

Current Radiology, Vol. 2. Ed. by Gabriel H. Wilson. 1979. 40.00x (ISBN 0-89289-107-6). HM Prof Med Div.

Current Research in British Studies. 8th ed. Ed. by Robert K. Donovan. 1980. pap. write for info. (ISBN 0-89126-084-6). Military Aff Aero.

Current Research in Comparative Communism: An Analysis & Bibliographic Guide to the Soviet System. Lawrence L. Whetten. LC 76-19553. 1976. text ed. 22.95 (ISBN 0-275-23550-5). Praeger.

Current Research in Earthquake Prediction, Vol. 1. Ed. by Tsuneji Rikitake. (Developments in Earth & Planetary Sciences Ser.: No. 2). 400p. 1981. PLB 37.00 (ISBN 0-686-28846-7, Pub. by D. Reidel). Kluwer Boston.

Current Research in Ophthalmic Electron Microscopy, 3. Ed. by W. R. Lee. (Illus.). 160p. 1980. 28.40 (ISBN 0-686-62616-8). Springer-Verlag.

Current Research in Sociology: Published on the Occasion of the 8th World Congress of Sociology. Ed. by M. S. Archer. (Current Sociology, Supplementary Ser: Vol. 1). 430p. 1974. pap. text ed. 37.05x (ISBN 90-2797-325-3). Mouton.

Current Research on Tall Buildings. Compiled By American Society of Civil Engineers. 144p. 1972. pap. text ed. 5.50 (ISBN 0-87262-039-5). Am Soc Civil Eng.

Current Researches in Education & Educational Psychology: 1968-69. A. E. Sanderson. (General Ser.). 1970. text ed. 20.00x (ISBN 0-901225-29-0, NFER). Humanities.

Current Reviews. Ed. by W. Friedlander. LC 75-14572. (Advances in Neurology Ser.: Vol. 13). 415p. 1975. 36.00 (ISBN 0-89004-000-1). Raven.

Current Reviews of Higher Nervous System Dysfunction. Ed. by Walter J. Friedlander. LC 74-15667. (Advances in Neurology Ser.: Vol. 7). 1975. 24.50 (ISBN 0-911216-78-2). Raven.

Current Status of Lithium Therapy: Report of the APA Task Force. 1975. Repr. pap. 0.50 o.p. (ISBN 0-685-77452-X, 132). Am Psychiatric.

Current Status of Modular Coordination. National Academy Of Sciences. 1960. 2.50 o.p. (ISBN 0-309-00782-8). Natl Acad Pr.

Current Status of Some Major Problems in Developmental Biology: Proceedings. Society For The Study Of Developmental Biology - 25th Symposium. Ed. by Michael Locke. 1967. 46.50 (ISBN 0-12-454162-3). Acad Pr.

Current Studies in Urology. Martin I. Resnick. (Illus.). 190p. 1981. write for info. (7216-1). Williams & Wilkins.

Current Surgical Diagnosis & Treatment. 4th ed. Ed. by J. Englebert Dunphy & Lawrence W. Way. LC 79-88082. (Illus.). 1162p. 1979. lexotone cover 19.00 (ISBN 0-87041-193-4). Lange.

Current Techniques in Architectural Practice. Ed. by Robert A. Class & Robert E. Koehler. (Illus.). 1976. 27.50 o.p. (ISBN 0-07-002324-7, Architectural Res Bks). McGraw.

Current Therapy in Dentistry, Vols. 4-6. Ed. by Henry M. Goldman et al. (Illus.). Vol. 4, 1970. 37.50 (ISBN 0-8016-1193-8); Vol. 5, 1974. 39.50 (ISBN 0-8016-1194-6); Vol. 6, 1977. 43.50 (ISBN 0-8016-1195-4). Mosby.

Current Therapy in Dentistry, Vol. 7. William C. Hurt. LC 78-31587. (Current Therapy Ser.). 1980. text ed. 47.50 (ISBN 0-8016-1189-X). Mosby.

Current Therapy in Obstetrics & Gynecology. Edward J. Quilligan. LC 79-65461. (Illus.). 224p. 1980. text ed. 22.50 (ISBN 0-7216-7414-3). Saunders.

Current Therapy in Theriogenology: Diagnosis, Treatment & Prevention of Reproductive Diseases in Animal. David A. Morrow. LC 77-84675. (Illus.). 1287p. 1980. text ed. 69.50 (ISBN 0-7216-6564-0). Saunders.

Current Therapy of Allergy. 2nd ed. Ed. by Claude A. Frazier. 1978. spiral bdg. 21.00 (ISBN 0-87488-745-3). Med Exam.

Current Therapy 1981. Ed. by Howard Conn. (Illus.). 1100p. 1981. pap. write for info. (ISBN 0-7216-2709-9). Saunders.

Current Thinking & Writing. Ralph L. Henry & Rachel Salisbury. (Seventh Ser.). 1976. pap. 9.95 (ISBN 0-13-195693-0). P-H.

Current Topics in Bioenergetics, Vol. XI. Ed. by D. Rao Sanadi. (Serial Publications). 1981. write for info. (ISBN 0-12-152511-2). Acad Pr.

Current Topics in Bioenergetics, Vol. 10. S. Rao Sanadi. LC 66-28678. (Serial Pub). 1980. 34.50 (ISBN 0-12-152510-4). Acad Pr.

Current Topics in Cellular Regulation: Biological Cycles, Vol. 18. Ed. by Bernard Horecker & Ronald Estabrook. (Serial Publication Ser.). 1981. write for info. (ISBN 0-12-152818-9); lib ed. (ISBN 0-12-152892-8); microfiche ed. (ISBN 0-12-152893-6). Acad Pr.

Current Topics in Cellular Regulation, 016 vols. Ed. by Bernard L. Hoercker & Earl R. Stadtman. Incl. Vol. 1. 1969. 41.00 (ISBN 0-12-152801-4); Vol. 2. 1970. 41.00 (ISBN 0-12-152802-2); Vol. 3. 1971. 41.00 (ISBN 0-12-152803-0); Vol. 4. 1971. 41.00 (ISBN 0-12-152804-9); Vol. 5. 1972. 41.00 (ISBN 0-12-152805-7); Vol. 6. 1973. 41.00 (ISBN 0-12-152806-5); Vol. 7. 1973. 37.50 (ISBN 0-12-152807-3); Vol. 8. 1974. 48.00 (ISBN 0-12-152808-1); Vol. 9. 1976. 41.00 (ISBN 0-12-152811-1); lib ed. 52.50 (ISBN 0-12-152878-2); microfiche 29.50 (ISBN 0-686-66776-X); Vol. 10. 1974. 48.00 (ISBN 0-12-152810-3); lib ed. 59.50 (ISBN 0-12-152876-6); 36.50 (ISBN 0-12-152877-4); Vol. 11. 1974. 44.50 (ISBN 0-12-152811-1); Vol. 12. 1977. 44.00 (ISBN 0-12-152812-X); lib. ed. 56.00 (ISBN 0-12-152880-4); microfiche 33.00 (ISBN 0-12-152881-2); Vol. 13. 1978. 40.00 (ISBN 0-12-152813-8); lib ed. 51.00 (ISBN 0-12-152882-0); microfiche 29.00 (ISBN 0-12-152883-9); Vol. 14. 1978. 37.00 (ISBN 0-12-152814-6); lib ed. 47.50 (ISBN 0-12-152884-7); microfiche 27.00 (ISBN 0-12-152885-5); Vol. 15. 1979. 36.50 (ISBN 0-12-152815-4); lib. bdg. 43.50 (ISBN 0-12-152886-3); microfiche 23.50 (ISBN 0-12-152887-1); Vol. 16. 1980. 36.00 (ISBN 0-12-152816-2); lib. bdg. 44.00 (ISBN 0-12-152888-X); microfiche 24.00 (ISBN 0-12-152889-8); Vol. 17. 1980. 35.00 (ISBN 0-12-152817-0); lib. bdg. 45.50 (ISBN 0-12-152890-1); microfiche 24.50 (ISBN 0-12-152891-X). Acad Pr.

Current Topics in Developmental Biology: Emergence of Specificity in Neural Histogenesis, Vol. 15. Ed. by R. Kevin Hunt. LC 66-28604. (Serial Publication). 1980. 34.00 (ISBN 0-12-153115-5). Acad Pr.

Current Topics in Developmental Biology, Vols. 1-12. Ed. by Alberto Monroy & A. A. Moscona. Incl. Vol. 1. 1966. 38.50 (ISBN 0-12-153101-5); Vol. 2. 1967. 38.50 (ISBN 0-12-153102-3); Vol. 3. 1968. 38.50 (ISBN 0-12-153103-1); Vol. 4. 1969. 38.50 (ISBN 0-12-153104-X); Vol. 5. 1970. 44.50 (ISBN 0-12-153105-8); Vol. 6. 1971. 38.50 (ISBN 0-12-153106-6); Vol. 7. 1972. 38.50 (ISBN 0-12-153107-4); Vol. 8. 1974. 38.50 (ISBN 0-12-153108-2); Vol. 9. 1975. 33.00 (ISBN 0-12-153109-0); Vol. 10. 1975. 33.00 (ISBN 0-12-153110-4); Vol. 11. 1977. 30.50 (ISBN 0-12-153111-2); Vol. 12. 1978. 30.50 (ISBN 0-12-153112-0). Acad Pr.

Current Topics in Developmental Biology: Vol. 16, Neural Development in Model Systems. Ed. by R. Kevin Hunt. LC 66-28604. 1980. 34.00 (ISBN 0-12-153116-3). Acad Pr.

Current Topics in Early Childhood Education, Vol. 3. Ed. by Lilian G. Katz. 304p. 1980. text ed. 17.50 (ISBN 0-89391-057-0); pap. 13.50 (ISBN 0-89391-066-X). Ablex Pub.

Current Topics in Extrapyramidal Disorders. Ed. by A. Carlsson et al. (Journal of Neural Transmission Supplementum: No. 16). (Illus.). 240p. 1980. 57.90 (ISBN 0-387-81570-8). Springer-Verlag.

Current Topics in Eye Research, Vol. 2. Ed. by Jose A. Zadunaisky & Hugh Davson. (Serial Publication). 1980. 35.00 (ISBN 0-12-153002-7). Acad Pr.

Current Topics in Hematology, Vol. 1. Sergio Piomelli & Stanley Yachnin. LC 78-19681. 247p. 1978. 28.00x (ISBN 0-8451-0350-4). A R Liss.

Current Topics in Hematology, Vol. 3, Ed. by Sergio Piomelli & Stanley Yachnin. LC 78-19681. 280p. 1980. 30.00x (ISBN 0-8451-0352-0). A R Liss.

Current Topics in Management of Respiratory Diseases, Vol. 1. Brody & Snider. 1981. pap. text ed. price not set (ISBN 0-443-08104-2). Churchill.

Current Topics in Management of Respiratory Diseases, Vol. 2. Brody & Snider. 1981. pap. text ed. price not set (ISBN 0-443-08103-4). Churchill.

Current Topics in Membranes & Transport, Vol. 14. Ed. by Felix Bronner et al. 1980. 49.50 (ISBN 0-12-153314-X). Acad Pr.

Current Topics in Microbiology & Immunology, Vols. 40-55. Ed. by W. Arber et al. Incl. Vol. 40. Chronic Infections Neuropathic Agents & Other Slow Virsus Infections. Ed. by J. A. Brody et al. (Illus.). vii, 74p. 1967. 22.90 (ISBN 0-387-03754-3); Vol. 41. (Illus.). iv, 183p. 1967. 49.00 (ISBN 0-387-03755-1); Vol. 42. Insect Viruses. Ed. by K. Maramorosch. (Illus.). viii, 192p. 1968. 25.40 (ISBN 0-387-04071-4); Vol. 43. (Illus.). iii, 233p. (Incl. 32 pp. in German). 1968. 52.00 (ISBN 0-387-04072-2); Vol. 44. (Illus.). iii, 175p. 1968. 52.00 (ISBN 0-387-04073-0); Vol. 45. (Illus.). iii, 237p. (Incl. 61 pp. in German). 1968. 52.00 (ISBN 0-387-04074-9); Vol. 46. (Illus.). iii, 203p. (Incl. 90 pp. in German). 1968. 57.90 (ISBN 0-387-04075-7); Vol. 47. (Illus.). iii, 222p. (Incl. 29 pp. in German). 1969. 55.50 (ISBN 0-387-04445-0); Vol. 48. (Illus.). iii, 206p. 1969. 55.50 (ISBN 0-387-04446-9); Vol. 49. (Illus.). iii, 250p. 1969. 55.50 (ISBN 0-387-04447-7); Vol. 50. (Illus.). iii, 238p. 1969. 55.50 (ISBN 0-387-04448-5); Vol.52. (Illus.). iv, 197p. 1970. 55.50 (ISBN 0-387-04787-5); Vol. 53. (Illus.). 236p. 1970. 58.50 (ISBN 0-387-05069-8); Vol. 54. (Illus.). 230p. 1971. 58.50 (ISBN 0-387-05289-5); Vol. 55. Arthropod Cell Cultures & Their Application to the Study of Viruses. Ed. by E. Weiss. (Illus.). 340p. 1971. 49.10 (ISBN 0-387-05451-0). (Illus., Eng. & Ger.). Springer-Verlag.

Current Topics in Microbiology & Immunology, Vol. 77. Ed. by W. Arber et al. LC 15-12910. (Illus.). 1977. 41.50 (ISBN 0-387-08401-0). Springer-Verlag.

Current Topics in Microbiology & Immunology, Vols. 86-87. Ed. by W. Arber et al. (Illus.). 1980. Vol. 86. 37.40 (ISBN 0-387-09432-6); Vol. 87. 37.40 (ISBN 0-387-09433-4). Springer-Verlag.

Current Topics in Microbiology & Immunology, Vol. 90. Ed. by W. Arber et al. (Illus.). 147p. 1980. 51.90 (ISBN 0-387-10181-0). Springer-Verlag.

Current Topics in Microbiology & Immunology: Vol. 88. (Illus.). 142p. 1980. 35.20 (ISBN 0-387-09415-6). Springer-Verlag.

Current Topics in Nerve & Muscle Research. Ed. by A. G. Aguayo & G. Karpati. LC 79-13037. (International Congress Ser.: No. 455). 328p. 1979. 58.75 (ISBN 0-444-90057-8, North Holland). Elsevier.

Current Topics in Pathology, Vol. 51-57. Ed. by K. W. Altmann et al. Incl. Vol. 51. 219p. 1970. 52.00 (ISBN 0-387-04788-3); Vol. 52. 244p. 1970. 52.00 (ISBN 0-387-04789-1); Vol. 53. 253p. 1970. 57.90 (ISBN 0-387-05070-1); Vol. 54. 191p. 1971. 62.60 (ISBN 0-387-05071-X); Vol. 55. 214p. 1971. 62.60 (ISBN 0-387-05428-6); Vol. 56. 236p. 1972. 62.60 (ISBN 0-387-05709-9); Vol. 57. 206p. 1973. 70.80 (ISBN 0-387-06000-6). (Illus.). Springer-Verlag.

Current Topics in Pediatrics: Abstracts of Papers from the International Congress of Pediatrics, New Delhi, India, Oct 23-29 1977. O. P. Ghai & P. N. Taneja. 350p. 1980. pap. 12.50x (ISBN 0-89955-324-9, Pub. by Interprint India). Intl Schol Bk Serv.

Current Topics in the Management of Respiratory Disease, Vol II. Ed. by Jerome S. Brody & Gordon Snider. (Illus.). 200p. 1981. pap. text ed. 12.50 (ISBN 0-443-08103-4). Churchill.

Current Topics in the Management of Respiratory Diseases. Ed. by Jerome S. Brody & Gordon Snider. (Illus.). 200p. 1981. pap. text ed. 12.50 (ISBN 0-443-08104-2). Churchill.

Current Topics in Thyroid Research. Ed. by C. Cassano & M. Andreoli. 1966. 88.00 (ISBN 0-12-163750-6). Acad Pr.

Current Trends in Design & Construction of Embankment Dams. Stanley D. Wilson & Raul Marsal. 136p. 1979. pap. text ed. 11.75 (ISBN 0-87262-197-9). Am Soc Civil Eng.

Current Trends in European Pre-School Research. Karl-Gustaf Stukat. (Council of Europe Trend Reports). (Orig.). 1976. pap. text ed. 10.50x (ISBN 0-85633-091-4, NFER). Humanities.

Current Trends in Histocompatability, 2 vols. Ed. by Ralph A. Reisfeld & Soldano Ferrone. Incl. Vol. 1. Immunogenetic & Molecular Profiles. 565p. 49.50 (ISBN 0-306-40480-X); Vol. 2. Biological & Clinical Concepts. 310p. 2.50 (ISBN 0-306-40481-8). 1981 (Plenum Pr). Plenum Pub.

Current Trends in Immunology. Ed. by Soldano Ferrone et al. LC 78-31911. (Illus.). 400p. 1979. lib. bdg. 42.50 (ISBN 0-8240-7065-8). Garland Pub.

Current Trends in Programming Methodology: Program Validation, Vol. 2. Ed. by R. Yeh. 1977. 21.95x (ISBN 0-13-195719-8). P-H.

Current Trends in Programming Methodology: Software Modeling, Vol. 3. Ed. by K. Chandy & Raymond T. Yeh. (Illus.). 1978. ref. 21.95 (ISBN 0-13-195727-9). P-H.

Current Trends in Social Psychology. 299p. 1980. Repr. of 1948 ed. lib. bdg. 35.00 (ISBN 0-89984-108-2). Century Bookbindery.
Current Trends in Truck Suspensions. Society of Automotive Engineers. 1980. 15.00 (ISBN 0-89883-246-2). Soc Auto Engineers.
Current Veterinary Therapy: Food Animal Practice. Ed. by Jimmy L. Howard et al. (Illus.). 800p. 1981. text ed. write for info. (ISBN 0-7216-4778-2). Saunders.
Currents: Concerns & Composition. Thomas E. Sanders. 1971. pap. text ed. 9.95x (ISBN 0-02-477600-9, 47760). Macmillan.
Currents in Alcoholism: Treatment, Rehabilitation & Epidemiology, Vol. 6. Ed. by Marc Galanter. 1979. 33.50 (ISBN 0-8089-1201-1). Grune.
Currents in Anthropology: Essays in Honor of Sol Tax. Ed. by Robert Hinshaw. 1979. text ed. 88.25x (ISBN 90-279-7758-5). Mouton.
Currents of Change. Robert Garretson. 83p. 1980. 5.95 (ISBN 0-8059-2758-1). Dorrance.
Currents of Space. Isaac Asimov. 1978. pap. 1.95 (ISBN 0-449-23829-6, Crest). Fawcett.
Currents of Unrest: An Introduction to Collective Behavior. Orrin E. Klapp. LC 76-189252. 1972. 24.00x (ISBN 0-03-085305-2); pap. text ed. 12.95x (ISBN 0-89197-717-1). Irvington.
Curriculum: A Comprehensive Approach. 2nd ed. John D. McNeil. 1981. text ed. 14.95 (ISBN 0-316-56308-0). Little.
Curriculum: An Introduction to the Field. Ed. by James R. Gress & David E. Purpel. LC 77-23651. (National Society for the Study of Education Series on Contemporary Educ. Issues). 1978. 17.90 (ISBN 0-8211-0613-9); text ed. 16.20 ten copies (ISBN 0-686-52368-7). McCutchan.
Curriculum & Evaluation. Ed. by Arno A. Bellack & Herbert E. Kliebard. LC 76-18040. (Readings in Educational Research Ser.). 1977. 25.00 (ISBN 0-8211-0129-3); text ed. 22.50 10 or more copies (ISBN 0-686-67488-X). McCutchan.
Curriculum & Instruction: Alternatives in Education. Ed. by Henry A. Giroux et al. LC 80-84142. 1981. price not set (ISBN 0-8211-0615-5); text ed. price not set. McCutchan.
Curriculum & the Cultural Revolutions: A Book of Essays & Readings. David Purpel & Maurice Belanger. LC 76-183259. 300p. 1972. 20.00x (ISBN 0-685-23647-1); text ed. 18.00x (ISBN 0-8211-1509-X). McCutchan.
Curriculum & the Disciplines of Knowledge. A. R. King, Jr. & J. A. Brownell. LC 74-13124. 240p. 1976. Repr. of 1966 ed. 12.50 o.p. (ISBN 0-88275-211-1). Krieger.
Curriculum Building for Adult Learning. John R. Verduin, Jr. LC 79-23111. 192p. 1980. 11.95x (ISBN 0-8093-0960-2). S Ill U Pr.
Curriculum Building in Nursing: A Process. 2nd ed. Em Olivia Bevis. LC 77-13045. (Illus.). 1978. pap. text ed. 12.95 (ISBN 0-8016-0668-3). Mosby.
Curriculum Change. Ed. by Maurice Galton. 120p. 1980. pap. text ed. 10.50x (ISBN 0-7185-1183-2, Leicester). Humanities.
Curriculum Change in the 19th & 20th Centuries. Peter Gordon & Denis Lawton. LC 78-23803. 1979. pap. 18.00x (ISBN 0-8419-6216-2). Holmes & Meier.
Curriculum: Content & Change. Ed. by Alice M. Kirby. 128p. (Orig.). 1980. pap. 4.95 (ISBN 0-88200-141-8, C2883). Alexander Graham.
Curriculum Context. A. V. Kelly. 1980. 18.50 (IntlDept). Har-Row.
Curriculum, Culture & Classroom: Trends in Curriculum Studies. Ed. by P. H. Taylor & W. A. Reid. (General Ser.). 1980. pap. text ed. cancelled (ISBN 0-85633-163-5, NFER). Humanities.
Curriculum Design. Curriculum Design & Development Course Team. LC 75-20255. 1975. pap. 19.95 (ISBN 0-470-99202-6). Halsted Pr.
Curriculum: Design for Learning. Donald F. Cay. LC 63-16939. 1965. text ed. 7.50 (ISBN 0-672-60630-5). Bobbs.
Curriculum Design for Severely & Profoundly Handicapped. Paul H. Wehman. LC 78-23704. 1979. text ed. 14.95x (ISBN 0-87705-365-0). Human Sci Pr.
Curriculum Development. Ed. by P. Taylor & M. Johnson. (General Ser.). 200p. 1974. pap. text ed. 16.00x (ISBN 0-85633-035-3, NFER). Humanities.
Curriculum Development: A Guide to Practice Elementary Education. Jon Wiles & Joseph Bondi. 1979. text ed. 16.95 (ISBN 0-675-08315-X). Merrill.
Curriculum Development: A Humanized Systems Approach. Robert S. Gilchrist & Bernice R. Roberts. LC 72-93705. 1974. pap. 3.95 (ISBN 0-8224-1687-5). Pitman Learning.
Curriculum Development for Public Management Innovation. Samuel Doctors et al. LC 80-39481. 160p. 1981. text ed. 20.00 (ISBN 0-89946-079-8). Oelgeschlager.
Curriculum Development in Mathematics. A. G. Howson et al. 200p. Date not set. price not set (ISBN 0-521-23767-X). Cambridge U Pr.
Curriculum Development in Trade, Industrial, & Technical Education. Gordon McMahon. LC 74-187804. 160p. 1972. pap. text ed. 12.95 (ISBN 0-675-09117-9). Merrill.
Curriculum Development in Vocational & Technical Education: Planning Content & Implementation. new ed. Curtis R. Finch & John R. Crunkilton. 1978. text ed. 17.95 (ISBN 0-205-06148-6). Allyn.
Curriculum Development: Program Planning & Improvement. Francis P. Hunkins. (Elementary Education Ser.: No. C22). 410p. 1980. text ed. 16.95 (ISBN 0-675-08177-7). Merrill.
Curriculum Evaluation for Lifelong Education. R. Skager & Ravindra H. Dave. 1977. text ed. 19.50 (ISBN 0-08-021816-4); pap. 9.00 o.p. (ISBN 0-08-021817-2). Pergamon.
Curriculum for Preschools. 2nd ed. Carol Seefeldt. (Early Childhood Education Ser.: No. C24). 368p. 1980. text ed. 14.95 (ISBN 0-675-08137-8); instructor's manual 3.95 (ISBN 0-686-63183-8). Merrill.
Curriculum for Teaching the Visually Impaired. Jane M. Rhyne. 320p. 1981. text ed. 27.50 (ISBN 0-398-04161-X); pap. text ed. 27.50 spiral bdg. (ISBN 0-398-04161-X). C C Thomas.
Curriculum for the Mentally Retarded Young Adult. William F. Sniff. 180p. 1973. 10.75 (ISBN 0-398-01804-9). C C Thomas.
Curriculum for the Preschool-Primary Child: A Review of the Research. new ed. Ed. by Carol Seefeldt. (Elementary Education Ser.). 352p. 1976. text ed. 15.95x (ISBN 0-675-08678-7). Merrill.
Curriculum Guide for Health Education: Nutrition. 112p. 1975. 12.50. Natl Cath Educ.
Curriculum Guide for Plastics Education. Plasitics Education Foundation. LC 77-4080. 1977. pap. 12.95 (ISBN 0-672-97113-5). Bobbs.
Curriculum Guides in Art Education. 64p. 1980. 4.50 (ISBN 0-686-27495-4). Natl Art Ed.
Curriculum Handbook: The Disciplines, Current Movements, Instructional Methodology, Administration & Theory. abr. ed. Louis Rubin. 1977. pap. 13.95 (ISBN 0-205-05910-4). Allyn.
Curriculum Improvement: Decision Making & Process. 4th ed. Ronald C. Doll. 1978. text ed. 18.95 (ISBN 0-205-06046-3). Allyn.
Curriculum in Physical Education. 3rd ed. Carol Willgoose. (Illus.). 1979. ref. ed. 17.95 (ISBN 0-13-196303-1). P-H.
Curriculum Innovation. Curriculum Design & Development Course Team. LC 75-22488. 1975. pap. 17.95 (ISBN 0-470-26333-4). Halsted Pr.
Curriculum Integration & Lifelong Education. J. B. Ingram. (Advances in Lifelong Education: Vol 6). 1979. 15.00 (ISBN 0-08-024301-0); pap. 9.00 (ISBN 0-08-024300-2). Pergamon.
Curriculum Material Useful for the Hearing Impaired. McCarr & Wisser. 204p. 1980. 12.95 (ISBN 0-86575-131-5). Dormac.
Curriculum on Conflict Management. Uvaldo Palomares & Ben Logan. 1975. 5.95 (ISBN 0-86584-014-8). Human Dev Train.
Curriculum Planning: A New Approach. 3rd ed. Hass. 540p. 1980. pap. text ed. 12.95 (ISBN 0-205-06869-3, 2368692). Allyn.
Curriculum Planning & Some Current Health Problems. (Educational Studies & Documents, No. 13). 10p. (Orig.). 1974. pap. 2.50 (ISBN 92-3-101129-4, U753, UNESCO). Unipub.
Curriculum Planning for Social Studies & Teaching Cultural Approach. Craig Kissock. 125p. 1981. 28.00 (ISBN 0-471-27868-8, Pub. by Wiley Interscience). Wiley.
Curriculum Planning in Geography. Norman Graves. 1979. text ed. 29.95 (ISBN 0-435-35313-6); pap. text ed. 10.50 (ISBN 0-435-35312-8). Heinemann Ed.
Curriculum: Quest for Relevance. 2nd ed. William Van Til. LC 79-144319. 400p. 1974. pap. text ed. 12.95 (ISBN 0-395-17787-1, 3-57530). HM.
Curriculum, School & Society: An Introduction to Curriculum Studies. Ed. by Philip H. Taylor & Kenneth Tye. 1975. pap. text ed. 22.00x (ISBN 0-85633-065-5, NFER). Humanities.
Curriculum Targets in the Elementary School. Daisy M. Jones. 1977. text ed. 17.95 (ISBN 0-13-196337-6). P-H.
Curriculum: Teaching the What, How, and Why of Living. Louise M. Berman & Jessie A. Roderick. (Elementary Education Ser.). 1977. text ed. 15.95 (ISBN 0-675-08480-6). Merrill.
Curriculum Theorizing: The Reconceptualists. Ed. by William Pinar. LC 74-12821. 472p. 1974. 15.75 o.p. (ISBN 0-8211-1513-8); text ed. 14.15 o.p. (ISBN 0-685-52300-4). McCutchan.
Curriculum Theory. 3rd ed. George A. Beauchamp. 1975. cancelled 5.75 (ISBN 0-912200-05-7). Kagg Pr.
Curriculum Theory. 4th ed. George A. Beauchamp. LC 80-84104. 225p. 1981. pap. text ed. 8.50 (ISBN 0-87581-270-8). Peacock Pubs.
Curriculum Theory & Design in Physical Education. Anthony A. Annarino et al. LC 80-282. (Illus.). 1980. text ed. 15.95 (ISBN 0-8016-0297-1). Mosby.
Curriculum: U. S. Capacities, Developing Countries' Needs. 244p. 1979. 14.00 (IIE). Unipub.
Currier & Ives. Albert K. Baragwanath. LC 79-57412. (Abbeville Library of Art: No. 6). (Illus.). 112p. (Orig.). 1980. pap. 4.95 (ISBN 0-89659-092-5). Abbeville Pr.
Curries from the Sultan's Kitchen. rev. ed. Doris M. Ady. (Illus.). 126p. 1980. pap. 8.25 (ISBN 0-589-50188-7, Pub. by Reed Books Australia). C E Tuttle.
Curse: A Cultural History of Menstruation. Janice Delaney et al. 1977. pap. 1.95 o.p. (ISBN 0-451-61560-3, MJ1560, Ment). NAL.
Curse of Black Charlie. Marilyn Ross. (Stewarts of Stormhaven Ser.: No. 1). 256p. 1976. pap. 1.25 o.p. (ISBN 0-445-00396-0). Popular Lib.
Curse of Camp Gray Owl. Patricia E. Clyne. LC 80-2783. 176p. (gr. 5 up). 1981. PLB 7.95 (ISBN 0-396-07922-9). Dodd.
Curse of King Tut. Elizabeth Hogan. Ed. by Richard Uhlich. (Bluejeans Paperbacks Ser.). (Illus., Orig.). (gr. 7-12). 1978. pap. text ed. 1.25 (ISBN 0-8374-5007-1). Xerox Ed Pubns.
Curse of the Cobra. Gary Paulsen. LC 76-54275. (Mallard Mystery Ser.). (Illus.). (gr. 3-6). 1977. 7.75 (ISBN 0-8172-0928-X). Raintree Pubs.
Curse of the Cobra-CB Radio Caper. Paulsen. (gr. 3-5). pap. 1.25 (ISBN 0-590-12081-6, Schol Pap). Schol Bk Serv.
Curse of the Concullens. Florence Stevenson. pap. 1.50 (ISBN 0-451-07228-6, W7228, Sig). NAL.
Curse of the Factory System. John Fielden. LC 68-23399. Repr. of 1836 ed. 15.00x (ISBN 0-678-05010-4). Kelley.
Curse of the Factory System. 2nd rev. ed. John Fielden. 74p. 1969. 25.00x (ISBN 0-7146-1394-0, F Cass Co). Biblio Dist.
Curse of the Kings. Victoria Holt. 1978. pap. 2.50 (ISBN 0-449-23284-0, Crest). Fawcett.
Curse of the Pennsylvania Dutch. Patricia Knarr. 1980. 4.50 o.p. (ISBN 0-8062-1226-8). Carlton.
Curse of the Pharaohs. Philipp Vandenberg. Tr. by Tom Weyr. LC 75-830. (Illus.). 1975. 9.95 (ISBN 0-397-01035-4). Lippincott.
Curse of the Pharoahs. Elizabeth Peters. LC 80-27945. 320p. 1981. 9.95 (ISBN 0-396-07963-6). Dodd.
Curse of the Rebellars. Georgia M. Shewmake. 192p. (YA) 1975. 5.95 (ISBN 0-685-52654-2, Avalon). Bouregy.
Curse of the Vampires. Ronan. (gr. 7-12). 1980. pap. 1.25 (ISBN 0-590-30062-8, Schol Pap). Schol Bk Serv.
Curses, & Songs & Poems. Lee Rudolph. LC 74-81380. 72p. 1974. pap. 4.95 (ISBN 0-914086-04-9). Alicejamesbooks.
Curses, Lucks & Talismans. John G. Lockhart. LC 70-132016. (Illus.). 1971. Repr. of 1938 ed. 20.00 (ISBN 0-8103-3376-7). Gale.
Cursive Tracking: Reusable Edition. Ed. by W. Edwards & S. Edwards. (gr. 3). 1972. wkbk. 5.00 (ISBN 0-89039-021-5). Ann Arbor Pubs.
Cursive Writing: Words: Reusable Edition, Book 1. Ed. by W. Edwards & S. Edwards. (gr. 1-3). 1975. wkbk. 5.00 (ISBN 0-89039-135-1). Ann Arbor Pubs.
Cursive Writing: Words: Reusable Edition, Book 2. Ed. by W. Edwards & S. Edwards. (gr. 3-6). 1975. wkbk. 5.00 (ISBN 0-89039-136-X). Ann Arbor Pubs.
Cursive Writing 2: Reusable Edition. Ed. by W. Edwards & S. Edwards. (gr. 1). 1972. wkbk. 5.00 (ISBN 0-89039-051-7). Ann Arbor Pubs.
Curso basico de Ciencias Sociales: Con especial interes para Puerto Rico. Jose J. Santa Pinter. LC 79-15841. (Illus.). 500p. (Sp.). 1980. pap. text ed. write for info. (ISBN 0-8477-2449-2). U of PR Pr.
Curso Biblico Elemental, 3 vols. Incl. Vol. 1. Nueva Vida En Cristo - Nuestra Biblia. Luisa J. Walker. 1.95 (ISBN 0-8297-0526-0); tchr's guide 1.50 (ISBN 0-686-28834-3); Vol. 2. Poder Divino-Preguntas y Respuestas-Administradores Fieles. M. David Grams et al. 1.95 (ISBN 0-686-28835-1); tchr's guide 2.00 (ISBN 0-686-28836-X); Vol. 3. Iglesia En Marcha-Nuestros Cantos-Nuestra Salud. Melvin Hodges et al. 1.95 (ISBN 0-8297-0530-9); tchr's guide 2.00 (ISBN 0-686-28837-8). 1977. Set. 5.20 (ISBN 0-686-28832-7); Set. tchr's guide 5.00 (ISBN 0-686-28833-5). Life Pubs Intl.
Curso De Fisica General. Beatriz Alvarenga & Maximo Alvarenga. 1976. text ed. 8.50 (ISBN 0-06-310012-6, IntlDept). Har-Row.
Curso de Mercadotecnica. Frederick E. Webster, Jr. (Span.). 1977. pap. text ed. 9.00 (ISBN 0-06-317070-1, IntlDept). Har-Row.
Curso Moderno de Taquigrafia Pitman. 1978. pap. 5.28 (ISBN 0-8224-1721-9); key 2.00 (ISBN 0-8224-1723-5). Pitman Learning.
Curso Practico De Pronunciacion Del Ingles. M. Elizabeth Clarey & Robert J. Dixson. Ed. by Julio I. Andujar. (gr. 10 up). 1967. pap. text ed. 2.95 (ISBN 0-88345-039-9, 17377); with 3 records 18.00 (ISBN 0-685-04773-3). Regents Pub.
Curso Primero. Marvin Wasserman & Carol Wasserman. (gr. 8-10). 1979. 5.42 (ISBN 0-87720-521-3). AMSCO Sch.
Curso Superior De Sinaxtis Espanola. S. D. Gili Gaya. 12.50x (ISBN 0-686-00849-9). Colton Bk.
Curtain Raisers for Evangelism. Ruth Vaughn. LC 76-11486. 1976. pap. 2.25 (ISBN 0-87239-110-8, 2768). Standard Pub.
Curtaine-Drawer of the World: Or, Chamberlaine of That Inne of Iniquity. William Parkes. LC 79-84130. (English Experience Ser.: No.934). 76p. 1979. Repr. of 1612 ed. lib. bdg. 9.00 (ISBN 90-221-0948-8). Walter J Johnson.
Curtains, Draperies & Shades. Sunset Editors. LC 78-70270. (Illus.). 104p. 1979. pap. 4.95 (ISBN 0-376-01733-3, Sunset Bks). Sunset-Lane.
Curtis Park. Don Etter. LC 78-73982. 1980. 15.00 (ISBN 0-87081-077-4). Colo Assoc.
Curtis' Western Indians: Life & Worksof Edw. C. Curtis. encore ed. R. W. Andrews. LC 62-14491. (Illus.). 1962. encore ed. 9.95 (ISBN 0-87564-336-1). Superior Pub.
Curve of Binding Energy. John McPhee. 224p. 1974. 10.95 (ISBN 0-374-13373-5); pap. 5.95 (ISBN 0-374-51598-0). FS&G.
Curve of Binding Energy: A Journey into the Awesome & Alarming World of Theodore B. Taylor. John McPhee. 160p. 1976. pap. 2.25 (ISBN 0-345-28000-8). Ballantine.
Curve Tracing. 5th ed. Percival Frost. LC 60-10348. 9.95 (ISBN 0-8284-0140-3). Chelsea Pub.
Curves & Their Jacobians. David Mumford. LC 75-14899. (Ziwet Lectures Ser: 1974). 1975. pap. 6.95x (ISBN 0-472-66000-4). U of Mich Pr.
Cushla & Her Books. Dorothy Butler. LC 79-25695. (Illus.). 128p. 1980. Repr. 13.50 (ISBN 0-87675-279-2). Horn Bk.
Custard & Company. Ogden Nash. (Illus.). 128p. 1980. 8.95 (ISBN 0-316-59834-8). Little.
Custer & the Great Controversy. (Illus.). 1980. 8.50 (ISBN 0-87026-053-7). Westernlore.
Custer & the Little Big Horn: A Psychobiographical Inquiry. Charles K. Hofling. 152p. 1981. 15.95 (ISBN 0-8143-1668-9). Wayne St U Pr.
Custer Died for Your Sins: An Indian Manifesto. Vine Deloria, Jr. 1969. 12.95 o.s.i. (ISBN 0-02-530650-2). Macmillan.
Custer on the Little Bighorn. Thomas B. Marquis & Anne R. Heil. (Illus.). 1967. pap. 3.50 (ISBN 0-686-51606-0); tchr's ed. 2.10 (ISBN 0-686-51607-9). Custer.
Custer: The Life of General George Armstrong Custer. Jay Monaghan. LC 59-5937. (Illus.). 1971. 16.95x (ISBN 0-8032-3056-7); pap. 5.25 (ISBN 0-8032-5732-5, BB 530, Bison). U of Nebr Pr.
Custer's Gold: The United States Cavalry Expedition of 1874. Donald Jackson. LC 66-21521. (Illus.). 1972. pap. 2.25 (ISBN 0-8032-5750-3, BB 543, Bison). U of Nebr Pr.
Custer's Last Battle. Richard A. Roberts. (Custer Monograph: No. 4). 60p. 1978. pap. 8.00x (ISBN 0-686-26878-4). Monroe County Lib.
Custer's Luck. Edgar I. Stewart. (Illus.). 522p. 1955. 17.95 (ISBN 0-8061-0321-3); pap. 12.50 (ISBN 0-8061-1632-3). U of Okla Pr.
Custody Handbook. Persia Woolley. LC 79-10862. 1980. pap. 5.95 (ISBN 0-671-44841-2). Summit Bks.
Custody Trap: Helping Children of Divorce. June Noble & William Noble. LC 78-64642. Date not set. pap. 4.50 cancelled (ISBN 0-931328-03-9). Timely Bks.
Custom & Politics in Urban Africa: A Study of Hausa Migrants in Yoruba Towns. Abner Cohen. 1969. 18.50x (ISBN 0-520-01571-1); pap. 6.95x (ISBN 0-520-01836-2, CAMPUS43). U of Cal Pr.
Custom Bicycle: Buying, Setting Up & Riding the Quality Bicycle. Michael J. Kolin & Denise M. De La Rosa. 12.95 (ISBN 0-87857-254-6); pap. 8.95 (ISBN 0-87857-255-4). Rodale Pr Inc.
Custom Cars & Trucks. Mark Rich. (On the Move Ser.). (Illus.). 48p. (gr. 3-6). 1981. PLB 9.25 (ISBN 0-516-03886-9). Childrens.
Custom Cycles. Mark Rich. LC 80-26659. (On the Move Ser.). (Illus.). 48p. (gr. 3-6). 1981. PLB 9.25 (ISBN 0-516-03887-7). Childrens.
Custom Look. Editors of Time-Life Books. LC 73-87766. (Art of Sewing). (Illus.). (gr. 6 up). 1973. PLB 11.97 (ISBN 0-8094-1707-3, Pub. by Time-Life). Silver.

Custom-Made Child? Women-Centered Perspectives. Ed. by Helen B. Holmes et al. (Contemporary Issues in Biomedicine, Ethics, & Society Ser.). 384p. 1981. 14.95 (ISBN 0-89603-024-5); pap. 7.95 (ISBN 0-89603-025-3). Humana.

Custom of Living. Margery Cavanagh. LC 80-5487. 72p. (Orig.). 1980. pap. 3.95 (ISBN 0-931694-08-6). Wampeter Pr.

Custom of the Country. Edith Wharton. 1976. lib.rep.ed. 17.50x (ISBN 0-684-14655-X, ScribT); pap. 5.95 (ISBN 0-684-71926-6, SL 62, ScribT). Scribner.

Custom Tailoring for Homemakers. Doris M. Beck. (Illus.). (gr. 10-12). 1972. text ed. 8.80 (ISBN 0-87002-122-2). Bennett IL.

Custom Vans. Mark Rich. LC 80-25792. (On the Move Ser.). (Illus.). 48p. (gr. 3-6). 1981. PLB 9.25 (ISBN 0-516-03885-0). Childrens.

Customer-Employee Relationship. Ser-Vol-Tel Institute. (Foodservice Career Education Ser.). 1974. pap. 4.95 (ISBN 0-8436-2013-7). CBI Pub.

Customer Satisfaction in the Postal Services. Santha Gopinath. 105p. 1980. text ed. 10.25x (ISBN 0-391-02125-7). Humanities.

Customer Service & Distribution Strategy. Martin Christopher et al. LC 79-24121. 191p. 1980. 34.95x (ISBN 0-470-26890-5). Halsted Pr.

Customer Service Manual with Model Letters & Forms. Benjamin I. French, Jr. 1976. 17.95 o.p. (ISBN 0-13-196568-9). P-H.

Customer Services. L. M. Buckner. (Occupational Manuals & Projects in Marketing). 1971. 5.96 o.p. (ISBN 0-07-008821-7, G); tchr's manual & key 3.00 o.p. (ISBN 0-07-008822-5). McGraw.

Customizing Cars. Colin Burnham. LC 79-24124. (Illus.). 1980. 15.00 (ISBN 0-668-04888-3); pap. 7.95 (ISBN 0-668-04892-1). Arco.

Customs. Lisa Zeidner. LC 80-21478. 288p. 11.95 (ISBN 0-394-51475-0). Knopf.

Customs & Cultures: Anthropology for Christian Missions. 2nd ed. Eugene A. Nida. LC 54-8976. (Applied Cultural Anthropology Ser.). 306p. 1975. Repr. of 1954 ed. 5.95x (ISBN 0-87808-723-0). William Carey Lib.

Customs & Fashions in Old New England. Alice M. Earle. LC 68-17959. 1968. Repr. of 1893 ed. 15.00 (ISBN 0-8103-0155-5). Gale.

Customs & Festivals in Germany. Jennifer Russ. (Illus.). 1980. text ed. write for info. (ISBN 0-85496-365-0). Humanities.

Customs & Habits of the Sicilian Peasants. Salvatore Salomone-Marino. Ed. & tr. by Rosalie N. Norris. LC 80-65583. (Illus.). 256p. 1981. 19.50 (ISBN 0-8386-3010-3). Fairleigh Dickinson.

Customs Dictionary: German-English-French-Italian. Wilhelm Muller. LC 72-311634. 277p. 1971. 17.50x (ISBN 3-8029-8565-6). Intl Pubns Serv.

Customs Law Digest, 1960, 5 Vols. Set. text ed. 300.00 with 1980 suppl (ISBN 0-672-83709-9, Bobbs-Merrill Law); 1980 suppl 133.35 (ISBN 0-672-84308-0). Michie.

Cut & Assemble the Emerald City of Oz. Dick Martin. (Illus.). 48p. (Orig.). (gr. 1-5). 1981. pap. 3.95 (ISBN 0-486-24053-3). Dover.

Cut & Assemble the Pretty Village. McLoulin Bros. 1980. pap. 4.00 (ISBN 0-486-23938-1). Dover.

Cut & Color Paper Masks. Michael Grater. (Dover Coloring Book Ser.). 32p. (Orig.). 1975. pap. 1.75 (ISBN 0-486-23171-2). Dover.

Cut & Fold Paper Spaceships That Fly. Michael Grater. (Illus.). 48p. (Orig.). (gr. 1-5). Date not set. pap. price not set (ISBN 0-486-23978-0). Dover. Postponed.

Cut Glass Handbook & Price Guide. John F. Hotchkiss. LC 76-131428. (Illus.). 1970. pap. 4.75 o.p. (ISBN 0-8015-1878-4, Pub. by Hotchkiss House). Dutton.

Cut of Men's Clothes: 1600-1900. Norah Waugh. LC 64-21658. (Illus.). 1964. 19.95 (ISBN 0-87830-025-2). Theatre Arts.

Cut of Women's Clothes: 1600-1930. Norah Waugh. LC 68-13408. (Illus.). 1968. 32.45 (ISBN 0-87830-026-0). Theatre Arts.

Cut-Out. Colin Smith. 1981. 10.95 (ISBN 0-670-25192-5). Viking Pr.

Cutaneous Immunopathology. J. Thivolet & D. Schmitt. (Illus.). 506p. 1978. pap. 19.50 (ISBN 2-85598-175-1). Masson Pub.

Cutaneous Lesions of the Lower Extremities. M. H. Samitz & Alan S. Dana, Jr. LC 75-152141. (Illus.). 1971. 30.00 o.p. (ISBN 0-397-50280-X). Lippincott.

Cutaneous Vasculitides: Immunologic & Histologic Correlations. Richard J. Reed. LC 77-22502. (Illus.). 1978. text ed. 16.00 (ISBN 0-89189-033-5, 16-1-028-00); slides 58.00 (ISBN 0-89189-097-1, 15-1-028-00). Am Soc Clinical.

Cuticle Techniques in Arthropods. T. A. Miller. (Springer Series in Experimental Entomology). (Illus.). 410p. 1981. 59.80 (ISBN 0-387-90475-1). Springer-Verlag.

Cutlass: Nineteen Sixty Seven to Eighty Repair & Tune-up Guide. (New Automotive Bks.). 224p. 1980. 8.95 (ISBN 0-8019-6933-6). Chilton.

Cutler No. 4: Yellowstone. H. V. Elkin. (Orig.). 1980. pap. 1.75 (ISBN 0-505-51512-1). Tower Bks.

Cutting a Record in Nashville, No. 3. Lani Van Ryzin. (Hi Lo Ser.). 96p. (YA) (gr. 6 up). 1981. pap. 1.50 (ISBN 0-553-14620-3). Bantam.

Cutting & Grinding Fluids: Selection & Application. Ed. by R. K. Springborn. LC 67-17077. (Manufacturing Data Ser). 1967. pap. 8.75 (ISBN 0-87263-001-3). SME.

Cutting & Polishing of Electro-Optic Materials. G. W. Fynn & W. J. Powell. LC 78-21139. 1979. 74.95 (ISBN 0-470-26607-4). Halsted Pr.

Cutting & Setting Stones. Herbert Scarfe. 1972. 17.95 (ISBN 0-7134-2302-1, Pub. by Batsford England). David & Charles.

Cutting Back City Hall. Robert Poole, Jr. LC 79-6411. 224p. 1981. pap. 5.95 (ISBN 0-87663-557-5). Universe.

Cutting Back City Hall. Robert Poole, Jr. LC 79-6411. (Free Life Editions Bk.). 224p. 1980. 12.50x (ISBN 0-87663-266-5). Universe.

Cutting Cost. Peggy Gonder. 1977. pap. 8.00 (ISBN 0-87545-008-3). Natl Sch Pr.

Cutting Edge, Vol. 2. LC 79-52420. (Steps to Maturity Ser.). 1975. student's manual 12.50 (ISBN 0-86508-003-8); tchr's. manual 14.95 (ISBN 0-86508-004-6). BCM Inc.

Cutting for Construction: A Handbook of Methods & Applications of Hard Cutting & Breaking on Site. David Lazenby & Paul Phillips. LC 78-40610. 1978. 24.95 (ISBN 0-470-26437-3). Halsted Pr.

Cutting Library Costs: Increasing Productivity & Raising Revenues. Eleanor F. Brown. LC 79-19448. 274p. 1979. 13.50 (ISBN 0-8108-1250-9). Scarecrow.

Cutting Our Losses. Steven Kowit. 60p. (Orig.). 1981. pap. 3.00 (ISBN 0-686-69322-1). Contact Two.

Cutting the Cost of Energy: A Practical Guide for the Householder. Michael Clayton. LC 80-67579. (Illus.). 160p. 1981. 16.95 (ISBN 0-7153-7927-5). David & Charles.

Cutting Tool Material Selection. Ed. by Haldon J. Swinehart. LC 68-27332. (Manufacturing Data Ser). (Illus., Orig.). 1968. pap. 8.25x (ISBN 0-87263-010-2). SME.

Cuttings: The Pick of "Country Life" from Punch. Compiled by Guy Pierce. (Illus.). 64p. 1981. pap. 4.50 (ISBN 0-241-10496-3, Pub. by Hamish Hamilton England). David & Charles.

Cuzco Circle. Leopoldo Castedo. LC 76-381383. (Illus.). 144p. 1980. 16.50 (ISBN 0-295-95738-7); pap. 9.95 (ISBN 0-295-95739-5). U of Wash Pr.

CV: Carrier Aviation. Peter Garrison. (Illus.). 1980. cancelled (ISBN 0-89141-117-8); pap. 8.95 (ISBN 0-89141-074-0). Presidio Pr.

CVR Fitness: A Basic Guide for Cardio-Vascular-Respiratory Exercise. 2nd ed. J. Boyce Davis & E. Leslie Knight. (Illus.). 1978. pap. text ed. 6.95 (ISBN 0-8403-1442-6). Kendall-Hunt.

CWLA Directory of Member Agencies & Associates Listing. LC 78-646558. (Orig.). 1981. pap. text ed. 10.00 (ISBN 0-87868-201-5). Child Welfare.

Cyanophycees des Cotes d'Europe. Pierre Fremy. (Memoires of the National Society of Natural Sciences & Mathematics of Cherborg Ser.). (Illus.). 1972. 49.00 (ISBN 90-6123-274-0). Lubrecht & Cramer.

Cybele. Joyce Carol Oates. 200p. 1979. 14.00 (ISBN 0-87685-425-0); pap. 5.00 (ISBN 0-87685-424-2). Black Sparrow.

Cybernetic Approach to the Assessment of Children: Toward a More Humane Use of Human Beings. Ed. by Mark N. Ozer. (Westview Special Study). 1979. lib. bdg. 25.00x (ISBN 0-89158-466-8). Westview.

Cybernetic Revolution: Thought & Control in Man & Machine. Milton A. Rothman. LC 70-185691. (International Library). (Illus.). 128p. (gr. 7-12). 1972. text ed. 6.90 o.p. (ISBN 0-531-02106-8). Watts.

Cybernetic Society. R. Parkman. 400p. 1972. text ed. 27.00 (ISBN 0-08-016949-X); pap. text ed. 12.75 (ISBN 0-08-017185-0). Pergamon.

Cybernetics: A Sourcebook. Ed. by Robert Trappl. 1982. text ed. 39.50 (ISBN 0-89116-128-7). Hemisphere Pub. Postponed.

Cybernetics A to Z. V. Pekelis. (Illus.). 310p. 1975. 10.00x o.p. (ISBN 0-8464-0310-2). Beekman Pubs.

Cybernetics & the Philosophy of Mind. Kenneth M. Sayre. (International Library of Philosophy & Scientific Method). 350p. 1976. text ed. 18.25x (ISBN 0-391-00594-4). Humanities.

Cybernetics: Or Control & Communication in the Animal & the Machine. 2nd ed. Norbert Wiener. (Illus., Orig.). 1961. 17.50x (ISBN 0-262-23007-0); pap. 5.95 (ISBN 0-262-73009-X). MIT Pr.

Cybil War. Betsy Byars. LC 80-26912. (Illus.). 144p. (gr. 8-12). 1981. 8.95 (ISBN 0-670-25248-4). Viking Pr.

Cycle of American Literature. Robert E. Spiller. LC 68-7396. 1967. pap. 6.95 (ISBN 0-02-930420-2). Free Pr.

Cycle of American Literature: An Essay in Historical Criticism. Robert E. Spiller. 1967. 5.95 o.s.i. (ISBN 0-02-613040-8). Macmillan.

Cycle of Erosion in Different Climates. Pierre Birot. 1968. 16.50x (ISBN 0-520-00121-4). U of Cal Pr.

Cycle of Fire. Hal Clement. 192p. 1981. pap. 2.25 (ISBN 0-345-29172-7, Del Rey). Ballantine.

Cycle of Frescoes of the Chapel of Le Liget. Voichita Munteanu. LC 77-94712. (Outstanding Dissertations in the Fine Arts Ser.). 1978. lib. bdg. 31.00x (ISBN 0-8240-3244-6). Garland Pub.

Cycle of Life. Donna Ewy & Rodger Ewy. (Illus.). 384p. 1981. 17.95 (ISBN 0-525-93181-3). Dutton.

Cycle of Power: The Career of Jersey City Mayor Frank Hague. Richard J. Connors. LC 71-168603. 1971. 10.00 (ISBN 0-8108-0435-2). Scarecrow.

Cycle of the Seasons. William White, Jr. LC 76-51172. (Living Nature Ser.). (gr. 4 up). 1977. 7.95 (ISBN 0-8069-3580-4); PLB 7.49 (ISBN 0-8069-3581-2). Sterling.

Cycle of Violence: Assertive, Aggressive, & Abusive Family Interation. Suzanne K. Steinmetz. LC 77-24411. (Praeger Special Studies). 1977. text ed. 21.95 (ISBN 0-03-022876-X); pap. 9.95 (ISBN 0-03-046806-X). Praeger.

Cycle Racing: Training to Win. Les Woodland. (Illus.). 144p. 1976. 12.50 (ISBN 0-7207-0788-9). Transatlantic.

Cycles in Color. Robert Wilkinson-Latham. (Illus.). 1978. 11.95 (ISBN 0-7137-0853-0, Pub. by Blandford Pr England). Sterling.

Cycles of Becoming: The Planetary Pattern of Growth. Alexander Ruperti. LC 77-84029. 1978. pap. 7.95 (ISBN 0-916360-07-5). CRCS Pubns NV.

Cycles of Heaven. Guy L. Playfair & Scott Hill. 1979. pap. 2.75 (ISBN 0-380-45419-X, 45419). Avon.

Cycles of War: The Next Six Years. R. E. McMaster, Jr. 11.00 (ISBN 0-9604348-0-1). L McMaster.

Cycles: The Mysterious Forces That Trigger Events. Edward R. Dewey & Og Mandino. 1976. pap. 4.95 o.p. (ISBN 0-8015-1880-6). Dutton.

Cyclic Hope, Cyclic Pain. Uma Parameswaran. (Writers Workshop Redbird Ser.). 23p. 1975. 8.00 (ISBN 0-88253-520-X); pap. text ed. 4.00 (ISBN 0-88253-519-6). Ind-US Inc.

Cyclic Neofields & Combinatorial Designs. D. F. Hsu. (Lecture Notes in Mathematics Ser.: Vol. 824). (Illus.). 230p. 1981. pap. 14.00 (ISBN 0-387-10243-4). Springer-Verlag.

Cyclic Nucleotides, Phosphorylated Proteins, & Neuronal Function. Paul Greengard. LC 78-66349. (Distinguished Lecture Series of the Society of General Physiologists). 1978. 15.00 (ISBN 0-89004-281-0). Raven.

Cyclic Phenomena in Marine Plants & Animals. Ed. by E. Naylor & E. G. Hartnoll. 1979. 6.80 (ISBN 0-08-023217-5). Pergamon.

Cyclical Indicators for the Post War British Economy. D. J. O'Dea. LC 75-2738. (National Institute of Economic & Social Research, Occasional Papers Ser.: No. 28). (Illus.). 180p. 1975. 19.95x (ISBN 0-521-09963-3). Cambridge U Pr.

Cyclical Theories of Stock Market Action. Newton Roberts. (Illus.). 1978. deluxe binder 49.75 (ISBN 0-918968-02-X). Inst Econ Finan.

Cycling. Boy Scouts Of America. LC 19-600. (Illus.). 40p. (gr. 6-12). 1971. pap. 0.70x (ISBN 0-8395-3277-6, 3277). BSA.

Cycling Female: Her Menstrual Rhythm. Allen Lein. LC 78-23675. (Illus.). 1979. pap. text ed. 7.95x (ISBN 0-7167-1038-2). W H Freeman.

Cycling on Dizzy Duncan. Suzy Siddons. (Illus.). 24p. (gr. 6 up) 1980. pap. 1.60 ea. (Pub. by Dinosaur Pubns); pap. in 5 pk. avail. (ISBN 0-85122-199-8). Merrimack Bk Serv.

Cyclist's Manual. Dick Teresi & Doug Colligan. LC 76-1344. (Illus.). 1981. 14.95 (ISBN 0-8069-5562-7); lib. bdg. 13.29 (ISBN 0-8069-5563-5). Sterling.

Cyclone, South by Southwest. Will Howard. LC 79-52113. 247p. 1979. 9.95 (ISBN 0-686-69222-5). Red Feather.

Cyclopaedia of American Literature, 2 vols. Evert A. Duyckinck & George L. Duyckinck. Ed. by M. Laird Simons. LC 66-31801. 1965. Repr. of 1875 ed. Set. 68.00 (ISBN 0-8103-3021-0). Gale.

Cyclopaedia of Commerical and Business Anecdotes: Comprising Interesting Reminiscences & Facts, Remarkable Traits & Humors, & Notable Sayings, Dealings, Experiences & Witticisms of Merchants, Etc, 2 vols. Frazar Kirkland. LC 73-95777. (Illus.). 1969. Repr. of 1864 ed. 38.00 (ISBN 0-8103-3131-4). Gale.

Cyclopaedia of Fraternities. 2nd rev. ed. Albert C. Stevens. LC 66-20332. 1966. Repr. of 1907 ed. 20.00 (ISBN 0-8103-3084-9). Gale.

Cyclopaedia of India & of Eastern & Southern Asia: Commercial, Industrial & Scientific; Products of Mineral, Vegetable & Animal Kindoms, Useful Arts & Manufactures, 3 vols. 3rd ed. Edward G. Balfour. LC 5-12913. 3632p. 1968. Repr. of 1885 ed. Set. 387.50x (ISBN 3-201-00028-0). Intl Pubns Serv.

Cyclopaedia of Literary & Scientific Anecdote: Illustrative of the Characters, Habits, & Conversation of Men of Letters & Science. Ed. by William Keddie. LC 74-156925. 1971. Repr. of 1859 ed. 26.00 (ISBN 0-8103-3730-4). Gale.

Cyclopaedic Dictionary of Music. Ralph Dunstan. LC 72-14060. 642p. 1973. Repr. of 1925 ed. lib. bdg. 52.50 (ISBN 0-306-70559-1). Da Capo.

Cyclopedia of Anecdotes of Literature. Kazlitt Arvine. LC 67-14020. 1967. Repr. of 1851 ed. 22.00 (ISBN 0-8103-3296-5). Gale.

Cyclopedia of Biblical, Theological, & Ecclesiastical Literature, 12 vols. John McClintock & James Strong. 12400p. 1961. text ed. 395.00 (ISBN 0-8010-6123-7). Baker Bk.

Cyclopedia of Classified Dates, with Exhaustive Index. Charles E. Little. LC 66-27839. 1967. Repr. of 1900 ed. 56.00 (ISBN 0-8103-3334-1). Gale.

Cyclopedia of Education, 5 vols. Ed. by Paul Monroe. LC 68-56361. (Illus.). 1968. Repr. of 1911 ed. Set. 260.00 (ISBN 0-8103-3537-9). Gale.

Cyclopedia of English Literature: A History, Critical & Biographical, of British Authors, from the Earliest to the Present Times, 3 vols. Robert Chambers. (Illus.). 1979. Repr. of 1938 ed. Set. 130.00 (ISBN 0-8103-4213-8). Gale.

Cyclopedia of Literary Characters. Ed. by Frank N. Magill. 1964. 22.50 (ISBN 0-06-003990-6, HarpT); PLB 19.79 o.p (ISBN 0-06-003991-4, HarpT). Har-Row.

Cyclopedia of Trial Practice, 10 vols. 2nd ed. Sidney C. Schweitzer. Incl. Vols 1-4. 1970. 240.00 (ISBN 0-686-14519-4, 745A); Vols. 5 & 5a. Dollar Verdicts. 1968. 80.00 (ISBN 0-686-14520-8); Vols. 6-10. Proof of Traumatic Injuries. 1972. 160.00 (ISBN 0-686-14521-6). LC 70-123204. Set. 375.00 (ISBN 0-686-14518-6). Lawyers Co-Op.

Cyclopedia of United States Postmarks & Postal History. Ed. by Delf Norona. LC 75-1788. (Illus.). 416p. 1975. Repr. 35.00x (ISBN 0-88000-063-5). Quarterman.

Cyclopedia of World Authors. Ed. by Frank N. Magill. 1958. lib. bdg. 19.79 o.s.i. (ISBN 0-06-003960-4, HarpT). Har-Row.

Cyclops. Euripides. Ed. by D. M. Simmonds & R. R. Timberlake. text ed. 5.75x (ISBN 0-521-04946-6). Cambridge U Pr.

Cylindrical Shell Roof Design. Z. M. Elias. 1972. pap. 11.95x (ISBN 0-8156-6036-7, Am U Beirut). Syracuse U Pr.

Cymbeline. William Shakespeare. Ed. by Arthur Quiller-Couch et al. (New Shakespeare Ser). 1968. 23.95 (ISBN 0-521-07530-0); pap. 4.50x (ISBN 0-521-09473-9). Cambridge U Pr.

Cymbidium List: Species, Hybirds & Awards 1799-1976, Vol. 1. Arthur R. Koester. LC 79-84474. (Orig.). 1979. pap. 11.00x (ISBN 0-9602558-0-X). A R Koester Bks.

Cynic Epistles: A Study Edition. Abraham J. Malherbe. LC 77-21619. (Society of Biblical Literature. Sources for Biblical Studies: No. 12). 1977. pap. 9.00 (ISBN 0-89130-151-8, 060312). Scholars Pr Ca.

Cypress Chest-Kiparisovy Larets. Innokenty Annensky. Tr. by R. Morrison. (Rus & Eng.). 1981. pap. 7.50 (ISBN 0-88233-474-3). Ardis Pubs.

Cyprian Norwid. George Gomori. LC 73-17341. (World Author's Ser.: Poland: No. 305). 168p. 1974. lib. bdg. 10.95 o.p. (ISBN 0-8057-2656-X). Twayne.

Cyprus. Vassos Karageorghis. (Archaeologia Mundi Ser.). (Illus.). 272p. 1968. 29.50 o.p. (ISBN 0-88254-149-8). Hippocrene Bks.

Cyprus. Michael Lee & Hanka Lee. (Islands Ser.). 1974. 14.95 (ISBN 0-7153-5980-0). David & Charles.

Cyprus. Franz G. Maier. 1968. 11.95 (ISBN 0-236-17602-1, Pub. by Paul Elek). Merrimack Bk Serv.

Cyprus & the War of Greek Independence 1821-1829. John T. Koumoulides. (Bibliothea Historica Cyprica). (Illus.). 1977. text ed. 13.00x (ISBN 0-900834-81-1); pap. text ed. 8.00x (ISBN 0-900834-82-X). Humanities.

Cyprus: Conflict & Negotiation 1960-1980. Polyvios G. Polyviou. 246p. 1981. text ed. 40.00x (ISBN 0-8419-0683-1). Holmes & Meier.

Cyprus, Nineteen Fifty-Eight to Nineteen Sixty-Seven. Thomas Ehrlich. (International Crises & the Role of Law Ser.). 160p. 1974. pap. text ed. 3.95x (ISBN 0-19-825321-4). Oxford U Pr.

Cyprus Under British Rule. C. W. Orr. (Bibliotheca Historica Cyprica). (Illus.). 1972. text ed. 11.75x (ISBN 0-900834-19-6). Humanities.

Cyrano de Bergerac. 18th ed. Edmond Rostand. (French Texts Ser.). 1976. pap. text ed. 9.95x (ISBN 0-631-00550-1, Pub. by Basil Blackwell). Biblio Dist.

Cyrano De Bergerac & the Polemics of Modernity. Erica Harth. LC 73-9786. 1970. 20.00x (ISBN 0-231-03301-X). Columbia U Pr.

Cyril Ray's Book of Wine. Cyril Ray. (Illus.). 1978. 12.95 o.p. (ISBN 0-688-03333-4). Morrow.

Cyril Tourneur. Samuel Schuman. (English Author Ser.: No. 221). 1977. lib. bdg. 12.50 (ISBN 0-8057-6690-1). Twayne.

Cyrus Hall Maccormick, 2 Vols. 2nd ed. William T. Hutchinson. LC 68-8127. (American Scene Ser). 1969. Repr. of 1935 ed. lib. bdg. 69.50 (ISBN 0-306-71162-1). Da Capo.

Cystic Diseases of the Kidney. Ed. by Kenneth D. Gardner, Jr. LC 75-31626. (Perspectives in Nephrology & Hypertension Ser.). 1976. 43.50 (ISBN 0-471-29146-3, Pub. by Wiley Medical). Wiley.

Cystitis. Peter Evans. 1979. 9.95x (ISBN 0-8464-0053-7). Beekman Pubs.

Cystitis: The Complete Self-Help Guide. Angela Kilmartin. LC 79-26425. (Illus.). 256p. 1980. 9.95 (ISBN 0-446-51203-6); pap. 5.95 (ISBN 0-446-97720-9). Warner Bks.

Cytherea's Breath. Sarah Aldridge. 1980. 6.50 (ISBN 0-930044-02-9). Naiad Pr.

Cytochemical Bioassay of Polypeptide Hormones. J. Chayen. (Monographs on Endocrinology: Vol. 17). (Illus.). 230p. 1980. 46.00 (ISBN 0-387-10040-7). Springer-Verlag.

Cytodifferentiation in Plants. L. W. Roberts. LC 75-10041. (Developmental & Cell Biology Ser.: No. 2). (Illus.). 250p. 1976. 32.50 (ISBN 0-521-20804-1). Cambridge U Pr.

Cytogenetic Testing of Environmental Mutagens. Ed. by T. C. Hsu. LC 79-88262. 430p. 1981. text ed. 35.00 (ISBN 0-916672-56-5). Allanheld.

Cytogenetics. Carl P. Swanson et al. (Illus., Orig.). 1967. pap. 10.95x ref. ed. (ISBN 0-13-196634-0). P-H.

Cytogenetics in Animal Reproduction. (Illus.). 96p. 1981. 45.00 (ISBN 0-85198-444-4, CAB 8, CAB). Unipub.

Cytogenetics of Cells in Culture. International Society For Cell Biology. Ed. by R. J. Harris. (Proceedings: Vol. 3). 1964. 49.00 (ISBN 0-12-611903-1). Acad Pr.

Cytogenetics: Plant Breeding & Evolution. U. Sinha & Sunita Sinha. 1980. text ed. 25.00x (ISBN 0-7069-0469-9, Pub. by Vikas Indig). Advent Bk.

Cytogenetics: Plants, Animals, Humans. J. Schulz-Schaeffer. (Illus.). 460p. 1980. 32.80 (ISBN 0-387-90467-0). Springer-Verlag.

Cytogenetics: The Chromosome in Division, Inheritance, & Evolution. 2nd ed. Carl B. Swanson et al. (Biology Ser.). (Illus.). 1980. text ed. 23.95 (ISBN 0-13-196618-9). P-H.

Cytogentics, Environment, & Malformation Syndromes: Proceedings. Birth Defects Conference, 1975, Kansas City, Missouri. Ed. by Daniel Bergsma & R. Neil Schimke. LC 76-20510. (Birth Defects Original Article Ser.: Vol. 12, No. 5). 364p. 1976. 35.00x (ISBN 0-8451-1004-7). A R Liss.

Cytology. Edmund J. Messina. LC 74-79836. (Allied Health Ser). 1975. pap. 7.65 (ISBN 0-672-61382-4). Bobbs.

Cytology & Evolution. rev. ed. Edward N. Willmer. 1970. 55.00 o.s.i. (ISBN 0-12-757652-5). Acad Pr.

Cytology Examination Review Book, Vol. 1. 2nd ed. Ed. by Zuther M. Naib & Dean Willis. 1978. spiral bdg. 9.50 (ISBN 0-87488-454-3). Med Exam.

Cytology Examination Review Book, Essay Questions & Answers, Vol. 2. Emmerich Von Haam. 1975. spiral bdg. 9.50 (ISBN 0-87488-367-9). Med Exam.

Cytology of Non-Gynaecological Sites. G. Riotton & W. M. Christopherson. (World Health Organization: International Histological Classification of Tumours Ser.). (Illus.). 1977. text ed. 66.00 (ISBN 92-4-176017-6, 70-1-017-20); with slides 195.00 (ISBN 92-4-176017-6, 70-1-017-00). Am Soc Clinical.

Cytology of the Female Genital Tract. C. Riotton & William Christopherson. (World Health Organization: International Histological Classification of Tumours Ser.). 1977. 66.00 (ISBN 0-685-77240-3, 70-0-008-20); incl. slides 160.50 (ISBN 0-685-77241-1, 70-0-008-00). Am Soc Clinical.

Cytopathology of Sarcomas & Other Non-Epithelial Malignant Tumors. Steven I. Hajdu & Eva O. Hajdu. LC 75-12488. (Illus.). 415p. 1976. text ed. 35.00 (ISBN 0-7216-4451-1). Saunders.

Cytopharmacology of Secretion: Proceedings. Nato Advanced Study Institution et al. Ed. by B. Ceccarelli et al. LC 74-76090. (Advances in Cytopharmacology Ser: Vol. 2). 400p. 1974. 58.50 (ISBN 0-911216-58-8). Raven.

Cytoplasmic Genetics and Evolution. Paul Grun. (Illus.). 384p. 1976. 30.00x (ISBN 0-231-03975-1). Columbia U Pr.

Cytotaxonomical Atlas of the Arctic Flora. A. Love & D. Love. (Cytotaxonomical Atlases: Vol. 2). (Illus.). 598p. 1975. lib. bdg. 100.00x (ISBN 3-7682-0976-8). Lubrecht & Cramer.

Cytotoxic & Complement Mediated Reactions. Ed. by P. Dukor et al. (Par Pseudo-Allergic Reactions. Involvement of Drugs & Chemicals: Vol. 2). (Illus.). viii, 144p. 1980. 39.00 (ISBN 3-8055-0666-X). S Karger.

C.Z. & Elvin's Week-by-Week Garden Guide. C. Z. Guest & Elvin McDonald. LC 80-67097. (Illus.). 180p. (Orig.). 1980. pap. 5.95 (ISBN 0-87754-137-X). Chelsea Hse.

CZ Service-Repair Handbook: Single Exhaust Models-Through 1978. Mike Bishop. Ed. by Jeff Robinson. (Illus.). 1976. pap. text ed. 9.95 (ISBN 0-89287-102-4, M425). Clymer Pubns.

CZ: The Story of the California Zephyr. Karl R. Zimmermann. (Illus.). 1975. 10.95 o.s.i. (ISBN 0-931726-01-8). Delford Pr.

Czartoryski & European Unity: 1770-1861. Marian Kukiel. LC 80-22899. (Poland's Millenium Ser. of the Kosciuszko Foundation). (Illus.). xvii, 354p. 1981. Repr. of 1955 ed. lib. bdg. 35.00x (ISBN 0-313-22511-7, KUCZ). Greenwood.

Czech-English-Czech Dictionary. V. Kolafova & D. Slaba. (For Travel Ser.). 394p. 1979. text ed. write for info. (ISBN 0-89918-302-6). Vanous.

Czech-English-Czech Dictionary. new ed. J. Poldauf. 1980. text ed. 13.50x (ISBN 0-89918-253-4, C253). Vanous.

Czech-English, English-Czech Pocket Dictionary. 1223p. 1980. 16.95 (ISBN 0-88254-542-6, Pub. by Artia Czechoslovakia). Hippocrene Bks.

Czech Prose & Verse: A Selection with an Introductory Essay. Ed. by R. Pynsent. (London East European). 1979. pap. text ed. 26.25x (ISBN 0-485-17519-3, Athlone Pr). Humanities.

Czechoslovak Armoured Fighting Vehicles, 1918-1945. H. C. Doyle & C. K. Kliment. (Illus.). 139p. (Orig.). pap. 11.25x (ISBN 0-85242-628-3). Intl Pubns Serv.

Czechoslovak Experiment, 1968-1969. Ivan Svitak. LC 74-141888. (Illus.). 1971. 22.50x (ISBN 0-231-03462-8). Columbia U Pr.

Czechoslovak Reform Movement, 1963-1968: A Study in the Theory of Socialism. Benjamin B. Page. (Philosophical Currents Ser: No. 4). 127p. 1973. pap. text ed. 15.00x (ISBN 90-6032-007-7). Humanities.

Czechoslovakia. John Burke. 1976. 22.50 (ISBN 0-7134-3222-5). David & Charles.

Czechoslovakia. Carol Z. Rothkopf. LC 73-14703. (First Bks). (Illus.). 72p. (gr. 5-8). 1974. PLB 4.90 o.p. (ISBN 0-531-00814-2). Watts.

Czechoslovakia. W. V. Wallace. LC 76-4494. (Nations of the Modern World Ser). 1977. 32.50x (ISBN 0-89158-027-1). Westview.

Czechoslovakia Before Munich: The German Minority Problem & British Appeasement Policy. J. W. Bruegel. 41.95 (ISBN 0-521-08687-6). Cambridge U Pr.

Czechoslovakia, Nineteen Sixty-Eight. Philip Windsor & Adam Roberts. LC 70-79086. 1969. 20.00 (ISBN 0-231-03306-0); pap. 3.50 (ISBN 0-686-63930-8). Columbia U Pr.

Czechoslovakia: Profile of a Binational Socialist Country. David W. Paul. (Nations of Contemporary Eastern Europe Ser.). 128p. 1981. lib. bdg. 16.50x (ISBN 0-89158-861-2). Westview.

Czechoslovakia Since World War Two. Tad Szulc. LC 70-83248. 1971. 14.00 o.p. (ISBN 0-670-25332-4). Viking Pr.

Czechoslovakia's Role in Soviet Strategy. Josef Kalvoda. LC 77-18499. 1978. pap. text ed. 12.25x (ISBN 0-8191-0413-2). U Pr of Amer.

Czechs Under Nazi Rule: The Failure of National Resistance, 1939-42. Vojtech Mastny. LC 72-132065. (East Central European Studies of the Russian Institute). 1971. 17.50x (ISBN 0-231-03303-6). Columbia U Pr.

D

D & D Standard Oil Abbreviator. 2nd ed. Association of Desk & Derrick Clubs of America. LC 72-96172. 256p. 9.50 (ISBN 0-87814-017-4). Pennwell Pub.

D C Super Heroes Super Healthy Cookbook. D. C. Comics. (Illus., Orig.). 1981. pap. 8.95 (ISBN 0-446-51227-3). Warner Bks.

D-Day. C. B. S. News Staff. Ed. by William E. Shapiro. (Illus.). (gr. 7 up). 1968. PLB 3.90 o.p. (ISBN 0-531-01136-4). Watts.

D-Day. Warren Tute. 1974. pap. 9.95 (ISBN 0-02-038090-9, Collier). Macmillan.

D-Day Seers Speak. Michael X. 1969. pap. 5.95 (ISBN 0-685-20195-3). Saucerian.

D-Day with the Screaming Eagles. George E. Kosimaki. (Illus.). 1977. 10.00 (ISBN 0-686-22784-0). One Hund First Air.

D. H. Lawrence. George J. Becker. LC 79-48075. (Modern Literature Ser.). 160p. 1980. 10.95 (ISBN 0-8044-2029-7); pap. 4.95 (ISBN 0-8044-6033-7). Ungar.

D. H. Lawrence. Ronald P. Draper. (English Authors Ser.: No. 7). 1964. lib. bdg. 9.95 (ISBN 0-8057-1320-4). Twayne.

D. H. Lawrence. Niven. 1980. 9.95 (ISBN 0-684-16666-6, ScribT). Scribner.

D. H. Lawrence: A Composite Biography, 3 vols. Ed. by Edward H. Nehls. 1957-59. 30.00 ea.; Vol. 1. (ISBN 0-299-81501-3); Vol. 2. (ISBN 0-299-81502-1); Vol. 3. (ISBN 0-299-81503-X). U of Wis Pr.

D. H. Lawrence: A Personal Record, by E. T. Jessie Chambers. LC 80-40254. 223p. 1980. pap. 8.95 (ISBN 0-521-29919-5). Cambridge U Pr.

D. H. Lawrence: An Eastern View. Chaman Nahal. LC 72-120066. 1970. 12.00 o.p. (ISBN 0-498-07720-9). A S Barnes.

D. H. Lawrence: An Unprofessional Study. Anais Nin. LC 64-16109. 110p. (Orig.). 1964. pap. 4.95 (ISBN 0-8040-0067-0, 58). Swallow.

D. H. Lawrence & the Psychology of Rhythm: The Meaning of Form in the Rainbow. Peter Balbert. (Studies in English Literature: No. 99). 1974. pap. 20.00x (ISBN 0-686-22634-8). Mouton.

D. H. Lawrence: Apocalypse & Other Writings on Revelation. Ed. by Mara Kalnins. (Cambridge Edition of the Letters & Works of D. H. Lawrence Ser.). 200p. 1980. 27.50 (ISBN 0-521-22407-1); pap. cancelled (ISBN 0-521-29478-9). Cambridge U Pr.

D. H. Lawrence: Future Primitive. Dolores LaChapelle. LC 80-67900. 1981. 12.95 (ISBN 0-89615-027-5); pap. 7.95 (ISBN 0-89615-028-3). Guild of Tutors.

D. H. Lawrence: His Life & Works. Harry T. Moore. (Illus.). 330p. 1964. 24.50x (ISBN 0-8290-0164-6). Irvington.

D. H. Lawrence in Italy. Leo Hamalian. 224p. 1981. 10.95 (ISBN 0-8008-4572-2). Taplinger.

D. H. Lawrence: Interviews & Recollections, 2 vols. Ed. by Norman Page. 1981. Vol. 1, 160p. 26.50x (ISBN 0-389-20070-0); Vol. 2, 160p. 26.50x (ISBN 0-686-62941-8). B&N.

D. H. Lawrence: Novelist, Poet, Prophet. Ed. by Stephen Spender. LC 73-2000. (Illus.). 288p. 1973. 17.50 o.s.i. (ISBN 0-06-013956-0, HarpT). Har-Row.

D. H. Lawrence: Sons & Lovers. Ed. by Gamini Saigado. (Casebook Ser.). 1970. 2.50 o.s.i. (ISBN 0-87695-041-1). Aurora Pubs.

D. H. Lawrence: The Critical Heritage. Ed. by R. P. Draper. (Critical Heritage Ser.). 1970. 35.00x (ISBN 0-7100-6591-4). Routledge & Kegan.

D. H. Lawrence, the Man Who Lived: Papers. Ed. by Robert B. Partlow. LC 80-15262. 320p. 1980. 18.95 (ISBN 0-8093-0981-5). S Ill U Pr.

D. H. Lawrence: The Novels. A. Niven. LC 77-8475. (British Authors Ser.). 1978. 26.50 (ISBN 0-521-21744-X); pap. 7.95 (ISBN 0-521-29272-7). Cambridge U Pr.

D. H. Lawrence: The Rainbow & Women in Love. Ed. by Colin Clarke. (Casebook Ser.). 1970. 2.50 o.s.i. (ISBN 0-685-59923-X). Aurora Pubs.

D Is for Donald. (Wipe off Bks.). 9p. (ps). Date not set. 2.39 (ISBN 0-307-01842-3, Golden Pr). Western Pub.

D. J. Enright: Poet of Humanism. William Walsh. LC 73-90814. 120p. 1974. 18.95 (ISBN 0-521-20383-X). Cambridge U Pr.

D. L. Moody. Faith C. Bailey. 1959. pap. 2.50 (ISBN 0-8024-0039-6). Moody.

D. L. Moody. Faith C. Bailey. 160p. 1980. pap. 2.50 o.p. (ISBN 0-686-62771-7). Moody.

D. W. Griffith: His Biograph Films in Perspective. Kemp R. Niver. LC 74-81838. (Illus.). 1974. 15.00 (ISBN 0-913986-06-2). Locare.

D. W. Griffith: The Years at Biograph. Robert M. Henderson. (Illus.). 1970. pap. 2.95 (ISBN 0-374-50958-1). FS&G.

D. W. Griffith's "the Battle at Elderbush Gulch". Kemp R. Niver. LC 72-85599. (Illus.). 1972. 7.50 (ISBN 0-913986-04-6). Locare.

Da Vinci. Ernest Raboff. LC 78-139054. (gr. 3-7). PLB 6.95 (ISBN 0-385-07738-6). Doubleday.

Da Vinci Machine: Tales of the Population Explosion. Earl Conrad. LC 66-25986. 1969. 6.95 (ISBN 0-8303-0067-8). Fleet.

Da Vinci's Bicycle: Ten Stories by Guy Davenport. Guy Davenport. LC 78-22513. 1979. 12.95 o.p. (ISBN 0-8018-2208-4); pap. 4.95 (ISBN 0-8018-2220-3). Johns Hopkins.

Dachshund Guide. Hans Brunotte. 6.98 o.p. (ISBN 0-385-01574-7). Doubleday.

Dachshunds. Edita Van Der Lyn. (Illus.). 128p. 1980. 2.95 (ISBN 0-87666-704-3, KW-085). TFH Pubns.

Dad. William Wharton. LC 80-2725. 416p. 1981. 12.95 (ISBN 0-394-51097-6). Knopf.

Dada & Surrealism. D. Ades. LC 77-76765. (Modern Movements in Art Ser.). 1978. pap. 1.95 (ISBN 0-8120-0877-4). Barron.

Dada: Art & Anti-Art. Hans Richter. (World of Art Ser.). (Illus.). 1978. pap. 9.95 (ISBN 0-19-520071-3). Oxford U Pr.

Dada Caper. Ross H. Spencer. 1977. pap. 1.75 (ISBN 0-380-01839-X, 36293). Avon.

Dada Painters & Poets: An Anthology. Ed. by Robert Motherwell. LC 79-91825. (Documents of Modern Art Ser.). (Illus.). 388p. 1981. Repr. of 1951 ed. lib. bdg. 40.00 (ISBN 0-87817-266-1). Hacker. Postponed.

Daddy Doesn't Live Here Anymore. Rita Turow. LC 78-7771. 1978. pap. 3.50 (ISBN 0-385-14512-8, Anch). Doubleday.

Daddy Isn't Coming Home. Matilda Norvedt. (Pathfinder Ser.). 96p. (Orig.). (gr. 3-6). 1981. pap. 2.95 (ISBN 0-310-43941-8). Zondervan.

Daddy King. Martin L. King, Sr. & Clayton Riley. 1981. lib. bdg. 13.95 (ISBN 0-8161-3157-0, Large Print Bks). G K Hall.

Daddy Long Ears. Robert Kraus. (Illus.). 32p. (ps-2). Date not set. pap. 1.95 (ISBN 0-671-42582-X, Pub. by Windmill). S&S.

Daddy Long Legs. Jean Webster. (gr. 7 up). 1980. pap. 1.95 (ISBN 0-448-17147-3, Tempo). G&D.

Daddy Was a Numbers Runner. Louise Meriwether. 1976. pap. 1.95 (ISBN 0-515-05456-9). Jove Pubns.

Daddyji. Ved Mehta. 224p. 1972. 6.95 o.p. (ISBN 0-374-13438-3). FS&G.

Dads Are God's Idea. Roy Lessin. (God's Idea Books Ser.). (Illus.). 32p. (ps-4). 1981. pap. 1.25 (ISBN 0-87123-176-X, 210176). Bethany Fell.

Daffodil Affair. Michael Innes. LC 75-44986. (Crime Fiction Ser). 1976. Repr. of 1942 ed. lib. bdg. 17.50 (ISBN 0-8240-2378-1). Garland Pub.

Daffy Definitions of Medical Terms. Angela. Date not set. 5.95 (ISBN 0-533-04834-6). Vantage.

Daffy Dictionary: Funabridged Definitions from Aardvark to Zuider Zee. Joseph Rosenbloom. LC 76-51173. (Illus.). (gr. 3 up). 1977. 7.95 (ISBN 0-8069-4542-7); PLB 8.29 (ISBN 0-8069-4543-5). Sterling.

Daffynitions. Compiled by Charles Keller. LC 75-34280. (Illus.). (gr. 3 up). 1976. PLB 5.95 (ISBN 0-13-196584-0); pap. 1.95 (ISBN 0-13-196576-X). P-H.

Dag Hammarskjold. Ann M. Mayer. LC 74-1498. (Personal Closeups Ser). 40p. 1974. 5.75 o.p. (ISBN 0-87191-322-4). Creative Ed.

Dag Hammarskjold's United Nations. Mark W. Zacher. LC 71-101593. (International Organization Ser.: No. 7). 1969. 20.00x (ISBN 0-231-03275-7). Columbia U Pr.

Dagda's Harp. Sharon Newman. LC 76-10559. (YA) 1977. 7.50 o.p. (ISBN 0-312-18200-7). St Martin.

Dagger of Islam. John Laffin. 224p. 1981. pap. 2.95 (ISBN 0-553-14287-9). Bantam.

Daguerreotype in America. Beaumont Newhall. (Illus.). 176p. 1976. pap. 7.95 (ISBN 0-486-23322-7). Dover.

Daguerreotype in America. 3rd rev. ed. Beaumont Newhall. (Illus.). 12.50 (ISBN 0-8446-5461-2). Peter Smith.

Daguerreotypes of Southworth & Hawes. Robert A. Sobieszek & Odette M. Appel. (Illus.). 1980. pap. text ed. 6.95 (ISBN 0-486-23841-5). Dover.

Dahl's Russian Dictionary, 4 vols. Vladimir I. Dahl. LC 79-40161. (Illus.). 3000p. 1981. Set. 255.00 (ISBN 0-08-023573-5). Pergamon.

Dai Greatcoat: A Self-Portrait of David Jones in His Letters. Rene Hague. LC 80-670267. (Illus.). 320p. 1980. 37.50 (ISBN 0-571-11540-3, Pub. by Faber & Faber). Merrimack Bk Serv.

Dai-San. Eric Van Lustbader. 272p. 1981. pap. 2.50 (ISBN 0-425-04454-8). Berkley Pub.

Daily Biographer. J. P. Shawcross. 388p. 1980. Repr. of 1915 ed. lib. bdg. 50.00 (ISBN 0-8492-8118-0). R West.

Daily Bread Cookbook. pap. 5.95 (ISBN 0-686-12670-X, BE-141). Evangel Indiana.

Daily Compounding Growth Tables. 10.00 o.p. (ISBN 0-685-59984-1, 732). Finan Pub.

Daily Experience in Residential Life. Juliet Berry. (Library of Social Work). 1975. 16.95x (ISBN 0-7100-8115-4); pap. 7.95 (ISBN 0-7100-8116-2). Routledge & Kegan.

Daily Help. Charles H. Spurgeon. (Summit Ser.). 296p. 1981. pap. 3.95 (ISBN 0-8010-8195-5). Baker Bk.

Daily Lessons Received at 'Akka January 1908. rev. ed. Helen S. Goodall & Ella G. Cooper. LC 79-19806. 1979. pap. 5.00 (ISBN 0-87743-135-3, 7-32-41). Baha'i.

Daily Life in Ancient India. J. Auboyer. 1965. 6.95 o.s.i. (ISBN 0-02-504420-6). Macmillan.

Daily Life in Carthage at the Time of Hannibal. Gilbert Charles-Picard & Colette Charles-Picard. (Illus.). 1961. 10.95 (ISBN 0-02-523970-8). Macmillan.

Daily Life in China in the Thirteenth Century. Jacques Gernet. 1962. 4.95 o.s.i. (ISBN 0-02-543060-2). Macmillan.

Daily Life in Peru Under the Last Incas. Louis Baudin. Tr. by Winifred Bradford. (Illus.). 1962. 10.95 (ISBN 0-02-507870-4). Macmillan.

Daily Life in Spain in the Golden Age. Mercelin Defourneaux. Tr. by Newton Branch. (Illus.). 1971. 12.50x (ISBN 0-8047-1036-8); pap. 4.95 (ISBN 0-8047-1029-5, SP-153). Stanford U Pr.

Daily Life in the Time of Homer. Emile Mireaux. Tr. by Iris Sells. 1959. 9.95 (ISBN 0-02-585090-3). Macmillan.

Daily Life in the Time of Jesus. Henri - Daniel-Rops. Tr. by Patrick O'Brian from Fr. (Illus.). 518p. 1981. pap. 7.95 (ISBN 0-89283-085-9). Servant.

Daily Light on the Daily Path. blue bdg. 7.95 (ISBN 0-310-23060-8); pap. 4.95 (ISBN 0-310-23061-6). Zondervan.

Daily Light on the Daily Path (NIV) 384p. 1981. 8.95 (ISBN 0-310-23110-8); pap. 4.95 (ISBN 0-310-23111-6). Zondervan.

Daily Living in the Twelfth Century: Based on the Observations of Alexander Neckam in London & Paris. Urban T. Holmes, Jr. (Illus.). 1952. pap. 7.95x (ISBN 0-299-00854-1). U of Wis Pr.

Daily Living in the Twelfth Century: Based on the Observations of Alexander Neckam in London & Paris. Urban T. Holmes, Jr. LC 80-19991. (Illus.). ix, 337p. 1980. Repr. of 1973 ed. lib. bdg. 29.50x (ISBN 0-313-22796-9, HODL). Greenwood.

Daily Management of Youth - Onset Diabetes Mellitus: An Integrated Guide for Patients & Physicians. Richard Sandler & Michael Sandler. (Illus.). 102p. 1977. 12.25 (ISBN 0-398-03631-4). C C Thomas.

Daily Meditations with F. B. Meyer. Al Bryant. 1979. 8.95 (ISBN 0-8499-0148-0). Word Bks.

Daily Needs & Interests of Older People. Adeline M. Hoffman. (Illus.). 528p. 1976. 24.75 (ISBN 0-398-00852-3). C C Thomas.

Daily Power Thoughts. Robert H. Schuller. LC 77-68012. 1978. 8.95 (ISBN 0-89081-131-8); kivar 5.95 (ISBN 0-89081-123-7). Harvest Hse.

Daily Pursuits & Timeless Values: A Woman's View. Seunghi Lee-Chon. LC 78-729955. 1978. 6.30 (ISBN 0-930878-11-6). Hollym Intl.

Daily Round: New Poems. Phillip Lopate. LC 76-7709. 1976. 10.00 (ISBN 0-915342-15-4); pap. 4.00 (ISBN 0-915342-14-6). SUN.

Daily Secrets of Christian Living. Andrew Murray. LC 77-17187. 1978. pap. 4.95 (ISBN 0-87123-500-5, 210500). Bethany Fell.

Daily Study Bible, 18 vols. rev. ed. William Barclay. Incl. The Gospel of Matthew. (ISBN 0-664-21300-6); softcover (ISBN 0-664-24100-X); The Gospel of Matthew. (ISBN 0-664-21301-4); softcover (ISBN 0-664-24101-8); The Gospel of Mark. (ISBN 0-664-21302-2); softcover (ISBN 0-664-24102-6); The Gospel of Luke. (ISBN 0-664-21303-0); softcover (ISBN 0-664-24103-4); The Gospel of John. (ISBN 0-664-21304-9); softcover (ISBN 0-664-24104-2); The Gospel of John. (ISBN 0-664-21305-7); softcover (ISBN 0-664-24105-0); The Acts of the Apostles. (ISBN 0-664-21306-5); softcover (ISBN 0-664-24106-9); The Letter to the Romans. (ISBN 0-664-21307-3); softcover (ISBN 0-664-24107-7); The Letters to the Corinthians. (ISBN 0-664-21308-1); softcover (ISBN 0-664-24108-5); The Letters to the Galatians & Ephesians. (ISBN 0-664-21309-X); softcover (ISBN 0-664-24109-3); The Letters to the Philippians, Colossians & Thessalonians. (ISBN 0-664-21310-3); softcover (ISBN 0-664-24110-7); The Letters to Timothy, Titus & Philemon. (ISBN 0-664-21311-1); softcover (ISBN 0-664-24111-5); The Letter to the Hebrews. (ISBN 0-664-21312-X); softcover (ISBN 0-664-24112-3); The Letters of James & Peter. (ISBN 0-664-21313-8); softcover (ISBN 0-664-24113-1); The Letters of John & Jude. (ISBN 0-664-21314-6); softcover (ISBN 0-664-24114-X); Vol. 1. The Revelation of John. (ISBN 0-664-21315-4); softcover (ISBN 0-664-24115-8); Vol. 2. The Revelation of John. (ISBN 0-664-21316-2); softcover (ISBN 0-664-24116-6). 1977. Set. deluxe ed. 150.00 (ISBN 0-664-21318-9); Set. softcover 76.00 (ISBN 0-664-24098-4); deluxe ed. 8.95 ea.; softcover 4.50 ea.; index vol. (ISBN 0-664-21370-7); softcover (ISBN 0-664-24215-4). Westminster.

Daily Telegraph: The Peterborough Book. Ed. by Michael Green. LC 80-69341. 64p. 1981. 8.95 (ISBN 0-7153-8082-6). David & Charles.

Daily Thoughts for Disciples. Oswald Chambers. 251p. 1976. 6.95. Chr Lit.

Daily with the King. W. Glyn Evans. 1979. pap. 4.50 (ISBN 0-8024-1739-6). Moody.

Daimon: An Adventure Story for First Year Latin Students. (Illus.). (gr. 7-10). 1977. pap. text ed. 2.25x (ISBN 0-88334-095-X). Ind Sch Pr.

Dain Curse. Dashiell Hammett. 213p. Date not set. pap. 1.50 (ISBN 0-686-68486-9, Vin). Random.

Dairy Cattle Feeding & Management. 6th ed. William M. Etgen & Paul M. Reaves. LC 63-20646. 1978. text ed. 28.50 (ISBN 0-471-71199-3). Wiley.

Dairy Cattle: Judging Techniques. 2nd ed. George W. Trimberger. LC 76-2672. (Illus.). 1977. 18.95 (ISBN 0-13-197020-8). P-H.

Dairy Cattle Science. 2nd ed. M. E. Ensminger. LC 78-78193. (Illus.). 640p. 1980. 29.95 (ISBN 0-8134-2079-2, 2079); text ed. 22.95x (ISBN 0-685-25894-7). Interstate.

Dairy Farm Management. Thomas Quinn. LC 77-90330. 1980. pap. text ed. 13.80 (ISBN 0-8273-1679-8); instructor's guide 1.75 (ISBN 0-8273-1679-8). Delmar.

Dairy Goats. Diana Gregory. LC 76-235. 1976. o. p. 7.95 (ISBN 0-668-03938-8); pap. 3.95 (ISBN 0-668-03941-8). Arco.

Dairy Goats: Breeding-Feeding Management. Date not set. 1.75 (ISBN 0-686-26685-4). Dairy Goat.

Dairy Industry in America. Ralph Selitzer. LC 76-21921. 1976. 45.00 (ISBN 0-89451-001-0). Mag Indus.

Dairy Technology & Engineering. W. J. Harper & Carl W. Hall. (Illus.). 1976. pap. text ed. 26.00 (ISBN 0-87055-296-1). AVI.

Daisy. Fritzi Ketcher. 1977. 4.00 o.p. (ISBN 0-682-48806-2). Exposition.

Daisy Chain. Charlotte Yonge. LC 75-32169. (Classics of Children's Literature, 1621-1932: Vol. 33). (Illus.). 1977. Repr. of 1868 ed. PLB 38.00 (ISBN 0-8240-2282-3). Garland Pub.

Daisy, Daisy: A Journey Across America on a Bicycle. Christian Miller. LC 80-2946. 192p. 1981. 11.95 (ISBN 0-385-17475-6). Doubleday.

Daisy Dog's Wake-Up Book. Ilse-Margret Vogel. (Young Reader Ser.). (Illus.). 24p. (gr. k-3). 1979. PLB 5.00 (ISBN 0-307-60102-1, Golden Pr). Western Pub.

Dakar & West African Economic Development. R. J. Peterec. LC 67-19651. 1967. 20.00x (ISBN 0-231-03016-9). Columbia U Pr.

Dakota Badlands. John Benteen. (Fargo Ser.). 1977. pap. 1.50 (ISBN 0-505-51173-8). Tower Bks.

Dakota Boomtown. Frank Castle. 1979. pap. 1.50 o.p. (ISBN 0-449-14180-2, GM). Fawcett.

Dakota Cowboy: My Life in the Old Days. Ike Blasingame. LC 58-11667. (Illus.). 1964. 12.95x (ISBN 0-8032-0906-1); pap. 3.45 (ISBN 0-8032-5015-0, BB 191, Bison). U of Nebr Pr.

Dakota Death Trap. Lauran Paine. 1979. pap. 1.50 (ISBN 0-505-51421-4). Tower Bks.

Dakota Image. Bill Scneider. LC 80-83707. (Illus.). 96p. 1980. 20.00 (ISBN 0-934318-02-6). Falcon Pr MT.

Dakota Territory. John Benteen. (Sundance: No. 3). 1979. pap. 1.75 (ISBN 0-8439-0708-8, Leisure Bks). Nordon Pubns.

Dakota War Whoop; or Indian Massacres & War in Minnesota. Harriet E. Bishop. Ed. by Wilcomb E. Washburn. LC 75-7103. (Narratives of North American Indian Captivities Ser.: Vol. 78). 1978. Repr. of 1863 ed. lib. bdg. 44.00x (ISBN 0-8240-1702-1). Garland Pub.

Dakota Wild. Jon Sharpe. (Trailsman: No. 6). (Orig.). 1981. pap. 1.95 (ISBN 0-451-09777-7, J9777, Sig). NAL.

Daktar. Viggo Olsen. 1976. pap. 1.75 (ISBN 0-89129-166-0). Jove Pubns.

Dale Loves Sophie to Death. Robb F. Dew. 1981. 12.95 (ISBN 0-374-13450-2). FS&G.

Dali. Robert Descharnes. LC 74-4257. (Library of Great Painters Ser.). (Illus.). 176p. 1976. 35.00 (ISBN 0-8109-0222-2). Abrams.

Dali: The Wines of Gala. Max Gerard & Louis Orizet. LC 77-8625. (Illus.). 1978. 50.00 o.p. (ISBN 0-8109-0802-6). Abrams.

Dallas. Clayton Matthews. pap. 2.50 (ISBN 0-686-68322-6). PB.

Dallas. Lee Raintree. 1980. pap. 2.50 (ISBN 0-440-11752-6). Dell.

Dallas Cowboys. Julian May. LC 74-3241. (Superbowl Champions Ser). 48p. 1974. PLB 6.45 (ISBN 0-87191-327-5); pap. 2.95 (ISBN 0-89812-085-3). Creative Ed.

Dallas Cowboys. Julian May. (NFL Today Ser.). (gr. 4-8). 1980. PLB 6.45 (ISBN 0-87191-730-0); pap. 2.95 (ISBN 0-89812-233-3). Creative Ed.

Dallas: The Deciding Years - a Historical Portrait. A. C. Greene. (Illus.). 192p. 1974. 12.50 o.p. (ISBN 0-88426-034-8). Encino Pr.

Dalmatian: Coach Dog-Firehouse Dog. Alfred Treen & Esmeralda Treen. LC 80-10650. (Complete Breed Bk.). (Illus.). 288p. 1980. 14.95 (ISBN 0-87605-109-3). Howell Bk.

Dalmatians. Catherine Gore. Ed. by Christina Foyle. (Foyle's Handbks). (Illus.). 1973. 3.95 (ISBN 0-685-55792-8). Palmetto Pub.

Dalmatians. Catherine Gore. LC 76-11029. (Illus.). 1976. bds. 2.25 o.p. (ISBN 0-668-03983-3). Arco.

Dalton's Directory: Business & Industry. 18th ed. 500p. Date not set. 57.00x. Dalton.

Dam. Robert Byrne. LC 80-22109. 1981. 12.95 (ISBN 0-689-11123-1). Atheneum.

Damaged Parents: An Anatomy of Child Neglect. Norman A. Polansky et al. LC 80-22793. (Illus.). 288p. 1981. 15.00 (ISBN 0-226-67221-2). U of Chicago Pr.

Damages. Richard Howard. LC 67-24112. (Wesleyan Poetry Program: Vol. 35). (Orig.). 1967. 10.00x (ISBN 0-8195-2035-7, Pub. by Wesleyan U Pr); pap. 4.95x (ISBN 0-8195-1035-1). Columbia U Pr.

Damages & Recovery: Personal Injury & Death Actions. Jacob A. Stein. LC 72-91244. 1972. 47.50 (ISBN 0-686-14531-3). Lawyers Co-Op.

Damaris. Jane Sheridan. 1980. pap. 2.75 (ISBN 0-425-04482-3). Berkley Pub.

Damascus Cover. Howard Kaplan. 1978. pap. 1.75 o.p. (ISBN 0-449-23412-6, Crest). Fawcett.

Dames of the Theatre. Eric Johns. (Illus.). 1975. 8.95 o.p. (ISBN 0-87000-310-0). Arlington Hse.

Damien the Leper. John Farrow. 1954. pap. 2.95 (ISBN 0-385-02918-7, D3, Im). Doubleday.

Damned. John D. Macdonald. 1978. pap. 1.95 (ISBN 0-449-13997-2, GM). Fawcett.

Damned & the Beautiful: American Youth in the 1920's. Paula S. Fass. LC 76-42644. 1979. pap. 6.95 (ISBN 0-19-502492-3, GB567, GB). Oxford U Pr.

Damned Art: Essays in the Literature of Witchcraft. Ed. by Sydney Anglo. 1977. 25.00 (ISBN 0-7100-8589-3). Routledge & Kegan.

Damned Through the Church. John W. Montgomery. 1970. 1.25 (ISBN 0-87123-090-9, 200090). Bethany Fell.

Damning Owl Tree. Robert Bowie. LC 78-63430. (Orig.). 1980. pap. cancelled o.p. (ISBN 0-930138-05-8). Harold Hse.

Damocles Effect. Martin Caidin. Date not set. 12.95 (ISBN 0-525-08851-2). Dutton. Postponed.

Damocles Syndrome: Psychosocial Consequences of Surviving Childhood Cancer. Gerald P. Koocher & John E. O'Malley. 1981. 15.95 (ISBN 0-07-035340-9). McGraw.

Damon. C. Terry Cline, Jr. 320p. 1978. pap. 2.25 (ISBN 0-449-22702-2, Crest). Fawcett.

Damp Diffusion & Buildings. Karl Seiffert. Tr. by A. B. Phillips & F. H. Turner. (Illus.). 1970. text ed. 37.30x (ISBN 0-444-20073-8, Pub. by Applied Science). Burgess-Intl Ideas.

Damping Applications for Vibration Control. Ed. by P. J. Torvik. (AMD: Vol. 38). 160p. 1980. 24.00 (G00171). ASME.

Dams in Africa. Ed. by Neville Rubin & William M. Warren. LC 68-19216. 1968. 25.00x (ISBN 0-678-05196-8). Kelley.

Dams of National Hunt Winners, 1955-60. Ed. by E. Buckle. pap. 3.60 (ISBN 0-85131-076-1, Dist. by Sporting Book Center). J A Allen.

Dams of National Hunt Winners, 1963-64, Compiled by E. Buckle. pap. 3.60 (ISBN 0-85131-077-X, Dist. by Sporting Book Center). J A Allen.

Dams of National Hunt Winners, 1966-73. Compiled by E. Buckle. (Illus.). pap. 18.35 (ISBN 0-85131-237-3, Dist. by Sporting Book Center). J A Allen.

Dams of National Hunt Winners: 1973-1975. Esme Buckle. 17.50 (ISBN 0-85131-340-X). J A Allen.

Dams, Parks & Politics: Resource Development & Preservation in the Truman-Eisenhower Era. Elmo Richardson. LC 72-91670. (Illus.). 256p. 1973. 14.00x (ISBN 0-8131-1284-2). U Pr of Ky.

Damselfishes. Gerald R. Allen. (Illus.). 240p. 1975. 9.95 (ISBN 0-87666-034-0, H-950). TFH Pubns.

Dan. Barbara Fisher. (Illus.). 20p. (Orig.). (gr. k-5). 1981. pap. 2.00 (ISBN 0-934830-19-3). Ten Penny.

Dan Barry's Daughter. Max Brand. 256p. 1976. pap. 1.95 (ISBN 0-446-90665-4). Warner Bks.

Dan Emmett & the Rise of Early Negro Minstrelsy. Hans Nathan. (Illus.). 1962. 22.50 (ISBN 0-8061-0540-2); pap. 9.95 (ISBN 0-8061-1423-1). U of Okla Pr.

Dan Freeman. Dan Jaffe. LC 67-13150. (Illus.). 1967. pap. 1.65 (ISBN 0-8032-5101-7, BB 371, Bison). U of Nebr Pr.

Dan Graham Video-Architecture-Television: Works, Propositions & Projects, Writings 1970-1978. Benjamin H. Buchloh. LC 79-89645. (Illus.). 89p. 1979. 17.50x (ISBN 0-8147-1025-5); pap. 9.95x (ISBN 0-8147-1026-3). NYU Pr.

Dan Moves up. Paul J. Deegan. LC 74-17069. (Dan Murphy Sports Ser.). 40p. (gr. 3-6). 1975. PLB 5.95 (ISBN 0-87191-406-9); pap. 2.95 (ISBN 0-89812-153-1). Creative Ed.

Dan Rather. Ellen Erlanger. (Achievers Ser.). (Illus.). (gr. 4-9). 1981. PLB 5.95 (ISBN 0-8225-0487-1). Lerner Pubns.

Danby & George. Betty Baker. LC 80-15707. (Illus.). 64p. (gr. 3-5). 1981. 7.95 (ISBN 0-688-80289-3); PLB 7.63 (ISBN 0-688-84289-5). Greenwillow.

Dance: A Creative Art Experience. 2nd ed. Margaret N. H'Doubler. (Illus.). 1957. 17.50 (ISBN 0-299-01520-3); pap. 6.45 (ISBN 0-299-01524-6). U of Wis Pr.

Dance Aerobics. Maxine Polley. LC 80-23906. (Illus.). 160p. (Orig.). 1981. pap. 5.95 (ISBN 0-89037-186-5). Anderson World.

Dance & Magic Drama in Ceylon. Beryl De Zoete. (Illus.). 1957. 4.95 (ISBN 0-87830-032-5). Theatre Arts.

Dance & Mime Film & Videotape Catalog. rev. ed. Ed. by Jessie Kitching & Susan Braun. (Orig.). 1980. pap. 10.95 (ISBN 0-914438-00-X). Dance Films.

Dance & Society in Eastern Africa 1890-1970: The Beni Ngoma. T. O. Ranger. LC 74-76389. 1974. 20.00x (ISBN 0-520-02729-9). U of Cal Pr.

Dance Around the Sun: The Life of Mary Little Bear Inkanish: Cheyenne. Alice Marriott & Carol K. Rachlin. LC 77-1859. (Illus.). 1977. 12.95 o.s.i. (ISBN 0-690-01450-3, TYC-T). T Y Crowell.

Dance As Life. Franklin Stevens. 1977. pap. 2.95 (ISBN 0-380-01711-3, 33860, Discus). Avon.

Dance Beat: Selected Views & Reviews Nineteen Sixty-Seven to Nineteen Seventy-Six. D. Jowitt. 1977. 9.95 o.p. (ISBN 0-8247-6506-0). Dekker.

Dance Card. John Feegel. 352p. 1981. 11.95 (ISBN 0-8037-1593-5). Dial.

Dance Composition: A Practical Guide for Teachers. Jacqueline M. Smith. (Illus.). 1978. 14.00 (ISBN 0-86019-016-1). Transatlantic.

Dance Composition & Production. Elizabeth R. Hayes. LC 80-69958. (Illus.). 210p. 1981. pap. 8.95 (ISBN 0-87127-121-4). Dance Horiz.

Dance for Life: Ballet in South Africa. Montgomery Cooper & Jane Allyn. (Illus.). 160p. 1981. 22.00x (ISBN 0-8476-3286-5). Rowman.

Dance Hall of the Dead. Tony Hillerman. 1975. pap. 1.75 (ISBN 0-380-49494-9, 49494). Avon.

Dance Has Many Faces. 2nd ed. Ed. by Walter Sorell. LC 66-25457. (Illus.). (YA) (gr. 9 up). 1966. 17.50x (ISBN 0-231-02968-3). Columbia U Pr.

Dance in America. Walter Terry. (Dance Ser.). (Illus.). xiv, 274p. 1981. Repr. of 1971 ed. lib. bdg. 25.00 (ISBN 0-306-76059-2). Da Capo.

Dance in Christianity. Marilyn Daniels. (Illus.). 112p. (Orig.). 1981. pap. 4.95 (ISBN 0-8091-2381-9). Paulist Pr.

Dance in India. 3rd ed. Enakshi Bhavnani. 261p. 1979. 45.00x (ISBN 0-8002-0696-7). Intl Pubns Serv.

Dance in India: An Annotated Guide to Source Materials. rev. ed. Judy A. Van Zile. LC 73-90410. (A (Bibliographies), No. 3). xi, 129p. 1973. pap. text ed. 7.50x (ISBN 0-913360-06-6). Asian Music Pub.

Dance in Its Time. Walter Sorell. LC 80-913. (Illus.). 480p. 1981. 19.95 (ISBN 0-385-13418-5). Doubleday.

Dance in the Desert. Madeleine L'Engle. LC 68-29465. (Illus.). (gr. 4 up). 1969. 8.95 (ISBN 0-374-31684-8). FS&G.

Dance Injuries: Their Prevention & Care. 2nd ed. Daniel D. Arnheim. LC 79-24524. (Illus.). 1980. pap. text ed. 12.00 (ISBN 0-8016-0311-0). Mosby.

Dance Injuries: Their Prevention & Care. Daniel D. Arnheim & Joan Schlaich. LC 74-22491. 1975. pap. text ed. 10.50 o.p. (ISBN 0-8016-0313-7). Mosby.

Dance Makers: Conversations with American Choreographers. Elinor Rogosin. (Illus.). 192p. 1980. 14.95 (ISBN 0-8027-0648-7). Walker & Co.

Dance Now. Jan Murray. 1979. pap. 3.95 o.p. (ISBN 0-14-005307-7). Penguin.

Dance of Court & Theatre: The French Noble Style 1690-1725. Wendy Hilton. LC 78-70248. (Illus.). 1981. 35.00 (ISBN 0-916622-09-6). Princeton Bk Co.

Dance of Creation. James Boulden. (Illus.). 96p. (Orig.). 1981. pap. cancelled (ISBN 0-87516-416-1). De Vorss.

Dance of Love: My Life with Meher Baba. Margaret Craske. LC 80-53859. 180p. 1980. pap. 6.95 (ISBN 0-913078-40-9). Sheriar Pr.

Dance of the Money Bees: A Professional Speaks Frankly on Investing. John Train. LC 74-5796. 256p. 1974. 10.95 o.p. (ISBN 0-06-014349-5, HarpT). Har-Row.

Dance of the Tiger: A Novel of the Ice Age. Bjorn Kurten. 1980. 10.95 (ISBN 0-394-51267-7). Pantheon.

Dance Sequence. John Unterecker. (Illus.). 1975. pap. 2.00 o.p. (ISBN 0-87711-056-5). Kayak.

Dance, Snake! Dance! Pampatti. Tr. by David C. Buck. (Translated from Tamil). 12.00 (ISBN 0-89253-797-3); flexible cloth 8.00 (ISBN 0-89253-798-1). Ind-US Inc.

Dance Technique of Doris Humphrey & Its Creative Potential. Ernestine Stodelle. LC 78-5124. (Illus.). 279p. 1978. 14.95 o.p. (ISBN 0-916622-07-X). Princeton Bk Co.

Dance: The Art of Production. Ed. by Joan Schlaich & Betty Dupont. LC 76-26583. (Illus.). 1977. pap. text ed. 7.75 o.p. (ISBN 0-8016-4346-5). Mosby.

Dance Therapy: Narrative Case Histories of Therapy Sessions with Six Patients. Helene Lefco. LC 73-88511. 1974. 13.95 (ISBN 0-911012-93-1). Nelson-Hall.

Dance Therapy: Theory & Application. Liljan Espenak. (Illus.). 210p. 1981. text ed. 19.75 (ISBN 0-398-04110-5). C C Thomas.

Dance Time. Beverly Jablons. 1981. pap. 2.25 (ISBN 0-425-04797-0). Berkley Pub.

Dance Toward Wholeness: Moving Methods to Heal Individuals & Groups. Barbara Lyon. Ed. by Doug Adams. (Illus.). 112p. 1981. pap. text ed. 5.95 (ISBN 0-686-28737-1). Sharing Co.

Dance with Who Brung Us. new ed. Ed. by Robert Heard. LC 76-20276. 158p. 1976. 8.95 o.p. (ISBN 0-8363-0142-0). Jenkins.

Dance Writing, Sutton Movement Shorthand, the Classical Ballet Key: Key One. Valerie J. Sutton. (Illus.). 1979. text ed. 20.00 (ISBN 0-914336-04-5); 8 hr. audio cassettes 35.00 (ISBN 0-685-91352-X); book & cassette 50.00x (ISBN 0-914336-05-3). Move Short Soc.

Dancer. Leland Cooley. 1979. pap. 2.75 (ISBN 0-451-08651-1, E8651, Sig). NAL.

Dancer & Other Aesthetic Objects: San Francisco: Balletmonographs, 1980. James M. Friedman. LC 80-65960. (Illus.). xii, 144p. (Orig.). 1980. pap. 5.95 (ISBN 0-9604232-0-6). J M Friedman.

Dancer & the Ring. M. P. Bhaskaran. 8.00 (ISBN 0-89253-459-1); flexible cloth 4.00 (ISBN 0-89253-460-5). Ind-US Inc.

Dancer in the Shadows. Linda Wisdom. 192p. (Orig.). 1980. pap. 1.50 (ISBN 0-671-57049-8). S&S.

Dancer Prepares: Modern Dance for Beginners. 2nd, rev. ed. James Penrod & Janice Plastino. LC 79-91836. (Illus.). 77p. 1980. pap. text ed. 3.95 (ISBN 0-87484-340-5). Mayfield Pub.

Dancer to Dancer: Advice for Today's Dancer. Melissa Hayden. LC 80-940. (Illus.). 192p. 1981. 19.95 (ISBN 0-385-15582-4, Anchor Pr). Doubleday.

Dancer to Dancer: Advice for Today's Dancer. Melissa Hayden. LC 80-940. (Illus.). 192p. 1981. 19.95 (ISBN 0-385-15550-6, Anch). Doubleday.

Dancer's Choice: The Ballet in Music & Pictures. Vera Zorina. Date not set. 27.00 (ISBN 0-03-057982-1, HarpT). Har-Row.

Dancer's Death. Phil Davis. 176p. 1981. pap. 2.25 (ISBN 0-380-76612-4, 76612). Avon.

Dancer's Dream. Richard C. Downer. 1981. 9.95 (ISBN 0-8062-1620-4). Carlton.

Dancers of Arun. Elizabeth A. Lynn. 1979. 10.95 o.p. (ISBN 0-399-12329-6). Berkley Pub.

Dancers on Dancing. Cynthia Lyle. LC 76-16375. 1976. pap. 4.95 o.p. (ISBN 0-8473-1313-1). Sterling.

Dances & Stories of the American Indian. Bernard S. Mason. (Illus.). 1944. 11.95 o.p. (ISBN 0-8260-5735-7). Wiley.

Dancing: A Handbook of the Terpsichorean Arts in Diverse Places & Times, Savage & Civilized. Lilly Grove. LC 76-76138. (Illus.). xviii, 454p. 1969. Repr. of 1895 ed. 18.00 (ISBN 0-8103-3469-0). Gale.

Dancing All the Way: (How to Dance Your Way to Success) Bonnie Powers. (Illus.). 1980. pap. 12.95 o.p. (ISBN 0-930490-24-X). Future Shop.

Dancing As a Career for Men. Glasstone Richard. LC 80-54339. (Illus.). 120p. (gr. 10 up). 1981. 8.95 (ISBN 0-8069-4640-7); lib. bdg. 9.29 (ISBN 0-8069-4641-5). Sterling.

Dancing at My Funeral. Maxie D. Dunnam. (Illus.). 1973. pap. 2.95x (ISBN 0-8358-0297-3). Upper Room.

Dancing Dodo. John Gardner. LC 77-80888. 1978. 8.95 o.p. (ISBN 0-385-12462-7). Doubleday.

Dancing Dodo. John Gardner. 336p. 1980. pap. 2.25. Bantam.

Dancing Games for Children of All Ages. Esther L. Nelson. LC 78-83456. (Illus.). 72p. (gr. 2 up). 1973. 8.95 (ISBN 0-8069-4522-2); PLB 8.29 (ISBN 0-8069-4523-0). Sterling.

Dancing in the Shadows. (Aston Hall Ser.: No. 119). 192p. (Orig.). 1981. pap. 1.75 (ISBN 0-523-41135-9). Pinnacle Bks.

Dancing in Your Ear: Poems of Protest, Humor & Love. Dean W. Golden & A. J. Wright. (Doctor Jazz Press Chapbook Ser.: No. 1). (Illus.). 40p. (Orig.). 1980. pap. 2.50 (ISBN 0-934002-00-2). Doctor Jazz.

Dancing Man. Ruth Bornstein. LC 77-29124. (Illus.). (gr. 1-4). 1978. 6.95 (ISBN 0-395-28770-7, Clarion). HM.

Dancing Palm Tree & Other Nigerian Folktales. Barbara K. Walker. LC 68-21085. (Illus.). (gr. 3-7). 1968. 5.95 o.s.i. (ISBN 0-8193-0329-1, Four Winds); PLB 5.41 o.s.i. (ISBN 0-8193-0330-5). Schol Bk Serv.

Dancing Princess. Jean Bothwell. LC 65-18726. (gr. 7 up). 4.50 o.p. (ISBN 0-15-221637-5, HJ). HarBraceJ.

Dancing Shoes. Noel Streatfeild. (gr. k-6). 1980. pap. 1.75 (ISBN 0-440-42289-2, YB). Dell.

Dancing Tigers. Russell Hoban. (Illus.). 32p. (gr. k-3). 1981. 8.95 (ISBN 0-224-01374-2, Pub. by Chatto-Bodley-Jonathan). Merrimack Bk Serv.

Dancing Tom. Elizabeth Coatsworth. (Illus.). (gr. 3-8). 1967. 4.25g o.s.i. (ISBN 0-02-720100-7). Macmillan.

Dancing Turtle. Maggie Duff. LC 80-24683. (Illus.). 32p. (gr. k-3). 1981. PLB 7.95 (ISBN 0-02-733010-9). Macmillan.

Dancing Without Music: Deafness in America. Beryl L. Benderly. LC 79-6092. 312p. 1980. 11.95 (ISBN 0-385-14703-1, Anchor Pr). Doubleday.

Dancing Wu Li Masters: An Overview of the New Physics. Gary Zukav. LC 78-25827. (Illus.). 1979. 12.95 (ISBN 0-688-03402-0); pap. 6.95 (ISBN 0-688-08402-8). Morrow.

Danda. Nkem Nwankwo. (African Writers Ser.). 1970. pap. text ed. 5.25 (ISBN 0-435-90067-6). Heinemann Ed.

Dandelion. Don Freeman. LC 64-21472. (Illus.). (ps-2). 1977. pap. 2.50 (ISBN 0-14-050218-1, VS4, Puffin). Penguin.

Dandelion. Paula Z. Hogan. LC 78-21155. (Life Cycles Ser.). (Illus.). (gr. k-3). 1979. PLB 9.95 (ISBN 0-8172-1250-7). Raintree Pubs.

Dandelion. Jay Morgenstern. 1980. 6.95 o.p. (ISBN 0-934256-00-4). Caroline Hse.

Dandelion. Ladislav Svatos. LC 73-20911. 32p. (gr. 1-3). 1976. PLB 5.95 (ISBN 0-385-04629-4). Doubleday.

Dandelion Cottage. 4th ed. Carroll W. Rankin. 1977. Repr. of 1904 ed. 4.95 (ISBN 0-938746-00-6). Marquette Cnty Hist.

Dandelion Year. Ron McTrusty. LC 74-83424. (Bks Without Words). (Illus.). 32p. (ps-5). 1974. PLB 4.95 (ISBN 0-8178-5292-1). Harvey.

Dandy. Peter S. Gethers. 1978. 8.95 o.p. (ISBN 0-525-08852-0). Dutton.

Dandy & the Mystery of the Locked Room. Cena C. Draper. (Illus.). (gr. 6 up). 1974. 7.50 o.p. (ISBN 0-8309-0114-0, 15-0118-6). Independence Pr.

Dandy: Brummell to Beerbohm. Ellen Moers. LC 78-8915. (Illus.). 1978. 15.00x (ISBN 0-8032-3052-4); pap. 4.95 (ISBN 0-8032-8101-3, BB 674, Bison). U of Nebr Pr.

Dandy-Walker Syndrome. Anthony J. Raimondi et al. (Illus.). vi, 80p. 1981. 34.75 (ISBN 3-8055-1722-X). S Karger.

Dandylions Never Roar Book. Gary Grimm & Don Mitchell. (gr. k-8). 1976. 5.95 (ISBN 0-916456-03-X, GA53). Good Apple.

Danes in Wisconsin. Frederick Hale. LC 80-26088. (Illus., Orig.). 1981. pap. 2.00 (ISBN 0-87020-205-7). State Hist Soc Wis.

Danger Angels. Jay Schleifer. Ed. by Thomas J. Mooney. (Pal Paperbacks, Pal Skills Ser.). (Illus., Orig.). (gr. 7-12). 1978. pap. text ed. 1.25 (ISBN 0-8374-6706-3). Xerox Ed Pubns.

Danger at Black Dyke. Winifred Finlay. LC 68-31174. (Illus.). (gr. 7-10). 1968. 9.95 (ISBN 0-87599-150-5). S G Phillips.

Danger at Dahlkari. Edwina Marlow. 256p. (YA) 1975. 7.95 o.p. (ISBN 0-399-11607-9, Dist. by Putnam). Berkley Pub.

Danger at Dahlkari. Edwina Marlow. 1977. pap. 1.95 o.p. (ISBN 0-425-03448-8). Berkley Pub.

Danger at Sneaker Hill. Jane Little. (Illus.). (gr. 3-5). 1975. pap. 1.25 (ISBN 0-671-29734-1). PB.

Danger Feeds My Fear. Michael Strong. 192p. 1980. 9.95 o.s.i. (ISBN 0-686-60241-2) (ISBN 0-8027-5419-8). Walker & Co.

Danger! Fire Fighters at Work Safety One. National Fire Protection Association. LC 79-720640. (Illus.). 1979. pap. text ed. 60.00 (ISBN 0-87765-163-9, SL-53). Natl Fire Prot.

Danger from Below: Earthquakes - Past, Present, & Future. Seymour Simon. LC 78-22283. (Illus.). 96p. (gr. 3-7). 1979. 7.95 (ISBN 0-590-07514-4, Four Winds). Schol Bk Serv.

Danger in Paradise. Suzanne Roberts. (YA) 5.95 (ISBN 0-685-07427-7, Avalon). Bouregy.

Danger Money. Mignon G. Eberhart. 192p. 1976. pap. 1.25 o.p. (ISBN 0-445-00343-X). Popular Lib.

Danger of Democracy: The Presidential Nominating Process. Terry Sanford. 160p. 1981. 15.00 (ISBN 0-86531-159-5). Westview.

Danger of Masquerades & Raree-Shows: As Being the Ground & Occasion of the Late Decay of Wit in the Island of Great-Britain. Bd. with Dancing Devils or the Roaring Dragon: A Dumb Farce; Letter to My Lord...on the Present Diversions of the Town. (English Stage Ser.: Vol. 46). lib. bdg. 50.00 (ISBN 0-8240-0629-1). Garland Pub.

Danger on Broken Arrow Trail. Alex B. Allen. LC 74-19499. (Springboard Sports Ser.). (Illus.). 64p. (gr. 3-6). 1974. 5.75g (ISBN 0-8075-1455-1). A Whitman.

Danger on Shadow Mountain. Marian Rumsey. (Illus.). (gr. 5-9). 1970. 7.25 o.p. (ISBN 0-688-21208-5). Morrow.

Danger Rides the Forest. Dorothy Guck. LC 68-30261. (Illus.). (gr. 6-8). 1968. 5.95 (ISBN 0-8149-0312-6). Vanguard.

Danger Song. Bryant Rollins. (African American Library). 1971. pap. 1.95 o.s.i. (ISBN 0-02-053500-7, Collier). Macmillan.

Danger UXB. Michael Book. 1981. pap. 2.95 (ISBN 0-14-005852-4). Penguin.

Danger Wherein the Kingdome Now Standeth, & the Remedie. Sir Robert B. Cotton. LC 74-28839. (No. 721). 1975. Repr. of 1628 ed. 3.50 (ISBN 90-221-0721-3). Walter J Johnson.

Danger Zone. J. M. Flynn. 1977. pap. 1.50 (ISBN 0-505-51171-1). Tower Bks.

Dangerford. Deirdre Stiles. 1977. pap. 1.75 (ISBN 0-505-51212-2). Tower Bks.

Dangerous Air. Lucy Kavaler. LC 67-10819. (Illus.). (gr. 8 up). 1967. 8.95 (ISBN 0-381-99772-3, A17060, JD-J). John Day.

Dangerous Engagement. Caroline Courtney. 1980. lib. bdg. 12.95 (ISBN 0-8161-3094-9, Large Print Bks). G K Hall.

Dangerous Funeral. large print ed. Mary McMullen. 1981. Repr. of 1977 ed. 9.95 (ISBN 0-89621-269-6). Thorndike Pr.

Dangerous Game. Milton Dank. (YA) (gr. 7-12). 1980. pap. 1.50 (ISBN 0-440-91765-4, LFL). Dell.

Dangerous Game. Milton Dank. LC 77-23453. (gr. 5-9). 1977. 8.95 (ISBN 0-397-31753-0). Lippincott.

Dangerous Games. Marta Randall. (Orig.). 1980. pap. write for info. (ISBN 0-671-82417-1). PB.

Dangerous Journey: Symbolic Aspects of Boys' Initiation Among the Wagenia of Kisangani, Zaire. Andre Droogers. (Change & Continuity in Africa Ser.). 1979. pap. text ed. 34.75x (ISBN 90-279-3357-X). Mouton.

Dangerous Lives. Glassman. (gr. 7-12). 1980. pap. 1.25 (ISBN 0-590-30875-0, Schol Pap). Schol Bk Serv.

Dangerous Magic. Frances Lynch. LC 77-17766. 1978. 8.95 o.p. (ISBN 0-312-18218-X). St Martin.

Dangerous Man. Mary Wibberley. (Harlequin Romances Ser.). (Orig.). 1980. pap. text ed. 1.25 o.p. (ISBN 0-373-02340-5, Pub. by Harlequin). PB.

Dangerous Marine Animals: That Bite, Sting, Shock, Are Non-Edible. 2nd ed. Bruce W. Halstead. LC 80-15475. (Illus.). 1980. 15.00 (ISBN 0-87033-268-6). Cornell Maritime.

Dangerous Marriage. Mary Wibberley. (Harlequin Romances Ser.). 192p. 1980. pap. 1.25 o.p. (ISBN 0-373-02364-2, Pub. by Harlequin). PB.

Dangerous Masquerade-a World of Love. Hermina Black. 1977. pap. 1.75 o.p. (ISBN 0-451-07703-2, E7703, Sig). NAL.

Dangerous Memory. Lorena Ann Olmsted. 192p. (YA) 1974. 5.95 (ISBN 0-685-39471-9, Avalon). Bouregy.

Dangerous Men: The Sociology of Parole. Richard McCleary. LC 78-19859. (Sage Library of Social Research: Vol. 71). 1978. 18.00x (ISBN 0-8039-1094-0); pap. 8.95x (ISBN 0-8039-1095-9). Sage.

Dangerous Music. Jessica T. Hagedorn. LC 75-32698. 1975. 10.00x o.p. (ISBN 0-917672-04-6); pap. 4.95x (ISBN 0-917672-03-8). Momos.

Dangerous Paradise. Louise Bergstrom. 192p. (YA) 1975. 5.95 (ISBN 0-685-52655-0, Avalon). Bouregy.

Dangerous Plants. John Tampion. LC 76-55116. (Illus.). 1977. 12.50x o.s.i. (ISBN 0-87663-280-0). Universe.

Dangerous Plants Snakes Anthropods & Marine Life-Toxicity & Treatment. Ed. by Michael D. Ellis. LC 78-50198. 1978. 18.00 (ISBN 0-914768-32-8). Drug Intl Pubns.

Dangerous Pleasure. Geraldine Youcha. LC 78-53486. 1978. 10.95 o.p. (ISBN 0-8015-1922-5). Dutton.

Dangerous Positions & Proceedings. Richard Bancroft. LC 74-38147. (English Experience Ser.: No. 427). 192p. 1972. Repr. of 1593 ed. 28.50 (ISBN 90-221-0427-3). Walter J Johnson.

Dangerous Sea Creatures. (Wild, Wild World of Animal Ser.). (Illus.). 1976. 10.95 (ISBN 0-913948-04-7). Time-Life.

Dangerous Sea Creatures. LC 75-45283. (Wild, Wild World of Animals). (Illus.). (gr. 5 up). 1976. lib. bdg. 11.97 (ISBN 0-685-73291-6, Pub. by Time-Life Television). Silver.

Dangerous to Know. Marian Babson. 1981. 9.95 (ISBN 0-8027-5442-2). Walker & Co.

Dangers of Noise. Lucy Kavaler. LC 77-26588. (Illus.). (gr. 4-7). 1978. 8.95 (ISBN 0-690-03905-0, TYC-J); PLB 8.79 (ISBN 0-690-03906-9). T Y Crowell.

Dangers of Nuclear War. Ed. by Franklyn Griffiths & John C. Polanyi. LC 79-18825. 1979. 15.00 (ISBN 0-8020-2356-8); pap. 5.95 (ISBN 0-8020-6389-6). U of Toronto Pr.

Dangling Witness: A Mystery. Jay Bennett. LC 74-5502. 160p. (gr. 7 up). 1974. 5.95 o.s.i. (ISBN 0-440-03483-3). Delacorte.

Daniel. Paul Butler. (Bible Study Textbook Ser.). (Illus.). 1971. 13.50 (ISBN 0-89900-025-8). College Pr Pub.

Daniel. Desmond Ford. LC 78-8172. (Anvil Ser.). 1978. pap. 6.95 (ISBN 0-8127-0174-7). Southern Pub.

Daniel. Hersh Goldwurm. (Art Scroll Tanach Ser.). 352p. 1979. 12.95 (ISBN 0-89906-079-X); pap. 9.95 (ISBN 0-89906-080-3). Mesorah Pubns.

Daniel. A. Montgomery. LC 27-14200. (International Critical Commentary Ser.). 520p. Repr. of 1927 ed. 23.00x (ISBN 0-567-05017-3). Attic Pr.

Daniel & His Prophecy. Frederick Tatford. Date not set. 8.25 (ISBN 0-86524-045-0). Klock & Klock.

Daniel & the Lions. (Tell-a-Bible Story Ser.). (Illus.). 28p. bds. 0.69 (ISBN 0-686-68640-3, 3684). Standard Pub.

Daniel Boone. Matthew G. Grant. LC 73-10070. 1974. PLB 5.95 (ISBN 0-87191-256-2). Creative Ed.

Daniel Boone: Wilderness Scout. Stewart E. White. 1976. lib. bdg. 14.75x (ISBN 0-89968-125-5). Lightyear.

Daniel Boone's Echo. William O. Steele. LC 57-9741. (Illus.). (gr. k-3). 1957. 5.95 o.p. (ISBN 0-15-221980-3, HJ). HarBraceJ.

Daniel: Decoder of Dreams. Donald K. Campbell. 1977. pap. 2.95 (ISBN 0-88207-747-3). Victor Bks.

Daniel Defoe & the Status of Women. Shirlene Mason. LC 78-59369. 1978. 12.95 (ISBN 0-88831-025-0). EPWP.

Daniel Defoe's Many Voices: A Rhetorical Study of Prose Style & Literary Method. E. Anthony James. 269p. (Orig.). 1972. pap. text ed. 27.50x (ISBN 9-0620-3317-2). Humanities.

Daniel Fuchs. Gabriel Miller. (United States Authors Ser.: No. 333). 1979. lib. bdg. 14.95 (ISBN 0-8057-7240-5). Twayne.

Daniel H. Burnham: Architect Planner of Cities. Charles Moore. LC 68-27726. (Architecture & Decorative Art Ser). (Illus.). 1968. Repr. of 1921 ed. lib. bdg. 45.00 (ISBN 0-306-71151-6). Da Capo.

Daniel Heinsius. Baerbel Becker-Cantarino. (World Author Ser.: No. 477). 1978. lib. bdg. 12.50 (ISBN 0-8057-6318-X). Twayne.

Daniel Inouye. Jane Goodsell. LC 77-1405. (Biography Ser.). (Illus.). (gr. 1-4). 1977. PLB 7.89 (ISBN 0-690-01358-2, TYC-J). T Y Crowell.

Daniel O'Connell & His World. Dudley Edwards. LC 77-77380. (Illus.). 1977. 9.95 o.p. (ISBN 0-684-15302-5, ScribT). Scribner.

Daniel O'Connell & the Repeal Year. Lawrence J. McCaffrey. LC 65-27011. 272p. 1966. 10.00x (ISBN 0-8131-1115-3). U Pr of Ky.

Daniel Ricketson & His Friends: Letter, Poems, Sketches, Etc. Ed. by Anna Ricketson & Walton Ricketson. LC 80-2513. 1981. Repr. of 1902 ed. 60.00 (ISBN 0-404-19061-8). AMS Pr.

Daniel: The Man & His Visions. Charles L. Feinberg. LC 80-70117. 212p. 1981. 8.95 (ISBN 0-915684-86-1). Christian Herald.

Daniel the Prophet. Martin R. De Haan. 1947. 10.95 (ISBN 0-310-23320-8). Zondervan.

Daniel the Prophet. H. A. Ironside. Date not set. with chart 6.75 (ISBN 0-87213-357-5); chart only 0.15 (ISBN 0-87213-358-3). Loizeaux.

Daniel the Prophet. Edward B. Pusey. 1978. 19.50 (ISBN 0-686-12942-3). Klock & Klock.

Daniel Webster, 2 Vols. 2nd ed. Claude M. Fuess. LC 68-8722. (American Scene Ser). (Illus.). 1968. Repr. of 1930 ed. lib. bdg. 65.00 (ISBN 0-306-71186-9). Da Capo.

Daniel Webster. Henry C. Lodge. LC 80-24628. (American Statesmen Ser.). 370p. 1981. pap. 5.95 (ISBN 0-87754-184-1). Chelsea Hse.

Daniele Manin & the Venetian Revolution of 1848-49. Paul Ginsborg. LC 78-56180. (Illus.). 1979. 41.50 (ISBN 0-521-22077-7). Cambridge U Pr.

Daniil Kharms: Izbrannoe. Ed. by George Gibian. (Colloquium Shavicum: No. 5). (Eng & Rus.). 1974. pap. text ed. 16.50x (ISBN 3-7778-0115-1). Humanities.

Danish: An Elementary Grammar & Reader. Elias Bredsdorff. 1959. 17.50x (ISBN 0-521-09821-1). Cambridge U Pr.

Danish Communes: An Analysis of Collective Families in Contemporary Danish & American Society. Thomas H. Shey. LC 78-60793. (Illus.). 1978. pap. text ed. 8.50 o.p. (ISBN 0-8191-0322-5). U Pr of Amer.

Danish Cross-Stitched Zodiac Samplers: Charted Designs for the Astrological Year. Jana Hauschild. (Illus.). 1980. pap. 2.25 daddlewire (ISBN 0-486-24032-0). Dover.

Danish-English, English-Danish Dictionary, 2 vols. 8th & 10th ed. Ed. by H. Vinterberg & J. Axelsen. 1979. Set. 50.00 (ISBN 0-685-36173-X). Vol. 1, Danish-English (ISBN 8-7001-1282-8). Vol. 2, English-Danish (ISBN 8-7013-3451-4). Heinman.

Danish Languague: Way to. 3rd ed. E. Norlev & H. Koefoed. 1979. text ed. 20.00x (ISBN 8-7160-0998-3, D-727). Vanous.

Danish Modern for Udlaendinge. I. Steimann & M. Njssen. 1974. pap. 18.50x (ISBN 8-7008-1281-1, D-728). Vanous.

Danish National Child Care System: A Successful System As Model for the Reconstruction of American Child Care. Marsden Wagner & Mary Wagner. LC 75-33183. 200p. 1976. 19.00x (ISBN 0-89158-008-5). Westview.

Danish Pocket Dictionary. Host. (English-Danish-English., Dan). 1978. pap. text ed. 7.00x (ISBN 8-7146-1178-3, D711). Vanous.

Danish Settlements in West Africa, 1658-1850. Georg Norregard. LC 66-21611. (Pub. by Boston U Pr). 1966. 11.50x (ISBN 0-8419-8708-4, Africana). Holmes & Meier.

Danny Dunn & the Anti-Gravity Paint, No. 7. Jay Williams & Raymond Abrashkin. (Illus.). (gr. 4-6). 1979. pap. 1.75 (ISBN 0-671-42060-7). Archway.

Danny Dunn & the Automatic House. Jay Williams & Raymond Abrashkin. (gr. 4-7). 1965. PLB 6.95 o.p. (ISBN 0-07-070533-X, GB). McGraw.

Danny Dunn & the Automatic House: No. 12. Jay Williams & Raymond Abrashkin. (Illus.). (gr. 4-6). 1979. pap. 1.75 (ISBN 0-671-29977-8). PB.

Danny Dunn & the Heat Ray: No. 14. Jay Williams & Raymond Abrashkin. (Illus.). (gr. 4-6). pap. 1.75 (ISBN 0-671-29969-7). PB.

Danny Dunn & the Smallifying Machine, No. 1. Jay Williams & Raymond Abrashkin. (Danny Dunn Ser.: No. 1). (Illus.). (gr. 4-6). 1979. pap. 1.75 (ISBN 0-671-41496-8). Archway.

Danny Dunn & the Voice from Space, No. 12. Jay Williams & Raymond Abrashkin. (Illus.). (gr. 4-6). 1979. pap. 1.95 (ISBN 0-671-42684-2). Archway.

Danny Dunn & the Weather Machine, No. 10. Jay Williams & Raymond Abrashkin. (Illus.). (gr. 4-6). 1979. pap. 1.75 (ISBN 0-671-42888-8). Archway.

Danny Dunn on a Desert Islanda: No. 15. Jay Williams & Raymond Abrashkin. (gr. 4-6). 1979. pap. 1.75 (ISBN 0-671-29976-X). PB.

Danny Dunn on the Ocean Floor. Jay Williams & Raymond Abrashkin. (gr. 4-7). 1964. PLB 6.95 o.p. (ISBN 0-07-070524-0, GB). McGraw.

Danny Dunn on the Ocean Floor, No. 9. Jay Williams & Raymond Abrashkin. (Illus.). (gr. 4-6). 1979. pap. 1.75 (ISBN 0-671-41855-6). Archway.

Danny Dunn, Time Traveler, No. 8. Jay Williams & Raymond Abrashkin. (gr. 4-6). 1979. pap. 1.75 (ISBN 0-671-42451-3). Archway.

Danny Loves a Holiday. Sydney Taylor. (Illus.). 80p. (gr. 1-3). 1980. 7.95g (ISBN 0-525-28510-5). Dutton.

Danny Lyon. Danny Lyon. 144p. 1981. 35.00 (ISBN 0-89381-073-8). Aperture.

Dante. Francis Ferguson. 1966. 4.95 o.s.i. (ISBN 0-02-537300-5). Macmillan.

Dante. Francis Ferguson. Ed. by Louis Kronenberger. LC 75-14006. (Masters of World Literature Ser.). (Illus.). 224p. 1975. pap. 3.95 o.s.i. (ISBN 0-02-069350-8, 06935, Collier). Macmillan.

Dante Alighieri. Ricardo Quinones. (World Authors Ser.: No. 563). 1979. lib. bdg. 13.50 (ISBN 0-8057-6405-4). Twayne.

Dante Commentaries: Eight Studies of the Divine Comedy. Ed. by David Nolan. 184p. 1977. 21.50x (ISBN 0-87471-966-6). Rowman.

Dante Gabriel Rossetti. Oswald Doughty. Ed. by Bonamy Dobree et al. Bd. with William Morris. Philip Henderson; Algernon Charles Swinburne. H. J. Grierson. LC 63-63096. (British Writers & Their Work Ser: Vol. 7). 1965. pap. 1.60x (ISBN 0-8032-5657-4, BB 456, Bison). U of Nebr Pr.

Dante Gabriel Rossetti: An Alien Victorian. Brian Dobbs & Judy Dobbs. 1977. text ed. 20.75x (ISBN 0-685-02497-0). Humanities.

Dante Gabriel Rossetti's Versecraft. Joseph F. Vogel. LC 76-150655. (U of Fla. Humanities Monographs: No. 34). 1971. pap. 3.50 (ISBN 0-8130-0324-5). U Presses Fla.

Dante His Times & His Work. Arthur J. Butler. 201p. 1980. Repr. of 1895 ed. lib. bdg. 30.00 (ISBN 0-8495-0475-9). Arden Lib.

Dante: Philomythes & Philosopher. P. Boyde. LC 80-40551. (Illus.). 520p. Date not set. 55.00 (ISBN 0-521-23598-7). Cambridge U Pr.

Dante, Poet of the Secular World. Erich Auerbach. Ed. by Theodore Silverstein. Tr. by Ralph Manheim. 1961. 6.00x (ISBN 0-226-03207-8). U of Chicago Pr.

Dante Soundings. Ed. by David Nolan. 1981. 22.50x (ISBN 0-8476-3633-X). Rowman.

Dante's Paradiso & the Limitations of Modern Criticism. R. Kirkpatrick. LC 77-80839. 1978. 36.00 (ISBN 0-521-21785-7). Cambridge U Pr.

Dante's Vita Nuova: A Translation & an Essay. new ed. Dante Alighieri. Tr. by Mark Musa from It. LC 72-79905. (Midland Bks.: No. 162). 224p. 1973. 8.50x (ISBN 0-253-31620-0); pap. 4.50x (ISBN 0-253-20162-4). Ind U Pr.

Danton's Tod & Woyzeck. G. Buchner. Ed. by M. Jacobs. 220p. 1954. 9.00x (ISBN 0-7190-0456-X, Pub. by Manchester U Pr England). State Mutual Bk.

Danube. Car Hills. LC 78-62988. (Rivers of the World Ser.). (Illus.). 1978. lib. bdg. 7.95 (ISBN 0-686-50005-9). Silver.

Danzantes of Monte Alban, 2 vols. John F. Scott. LC 79-63725. (Studies in Pre-Columbian Art & Archaeology: No. 19). (Illus.). 238p. 1978. pap. 10.00 (ISBN 0-88402-079-7, Ctr Pre-Columbian). Dumbarton Oaks.

Danzig Trilogy of Gunter Grass: A Study of The Tin Drum, Cat & Mouse, & Dog Years. John Reddick. 1974. 13.50 o.p. (ISBN 0-15-123815-4). HarBraceJ.

Darconville's Cat. Alexander Theroux. LC 80-629. 624p. 1981. 15.95 (ISBN 0-385-15951-X). Doubleday.

Darcourt. Isabelle Holland. 1977. pap. 1.75 o.p. (ISBN 0-449-23224-7, Crest). Fawcett.

D'Arcy Cresswell. Roderick Finlayson. (World Authors Ser.: New Zealand: No. 205). lib. bdg. 10.95 (ISBN 0-8057-2248-3). Twayne.

Dare. Philip J. Farmer. (Science Fiction Ser.). 1980. lib. bdg. 11.95 (ISBN 0-8398-2621-4). Gregg.

Dare. William D. Koller. (Pal Paperbacks, - Pal Skills II Ser.). (Illus.). (gr. 5-12). 1980. pap. 1.25 (ISBN 0-8374-6805-1). Xerox Ed Pubns.

Dare County. David Stick. (Illus.). 1975. pap. 2.00 (ISBN 0-86526-125-3). NC Archives.

DARE Information Management System: A Condensed System Description (Computer Design Version 2) (Reports and Papers in the Social Sciences: No. 31). (Illus.). 23p. 1976. pap. 2.50 (ISBN 9-2310-1256-8, U148, UNESCO). Unipub.

Dare the School Build a New Social Order? George S. Counts. LC 78-18895. (Arcturus Books Paperbacks). 64p. 1978. pap. 4.95 (ISBN 0-8093-0878-9). S Ill U Pr.

Dare to Be Different. Fred Hartley. 1980. pap. 3.95 (ISBN 0-8007-5041-1). Revell.

Dare to Be Different: A Biography of Louis H. Levin of Baltimore. Alexandra L. Levin. 1972. 7.50x (ISBN 0-8197-0280-3). Bloch.

Dare to Be You. James R. Dolby. Orig. Title: I, Too, Am Man. 1977. pap. 1.50 (ISBN 0-89129-207-1). Jove Pubns.

Dare to Defy: Challenging Sterotypes & Looking at Relationships in a Christian Context. Kenneth W. Chalker. LC 80-54478. 144p. 1981. pap. 4.50x (ISBN 0-8358-0418-6). Upper Room.

Dare to Lead. Timothy D. Foster. LC 76-57013. 1977. pap. 3.25 o.p. (ISBN 0-8307-0519-8, 54-054-08); study guide 1.39 o.p. (ISBN 0-8307-0530-9, 61-006-00). Regal.

Dare to Live Now. Bruce Larson. 1967. pap. 1.75 (ISBN 0-310-27202-5). Zondervan.

Dare to Live: The Taize Youth Experience. Roger Schutz. LC 73-17912. 1974. pap. 2.95 (ISBN 0-8164-2582-5). Crossroad NY.

Daredevils of Sassoun: The Armenian National Epic. Leon Surmelian. LC 64-66183. 1964. 8.95 o.p. (ISBN 0-8040-0061-1). Swallow.

Darien: The Death & Rebirth of a Southern Town. Spencer B. King, Jr. LC 80-83662. (Illus.). 100p. 1981. 13.95x (ISBN 0-86554-003-9). Mercer Univ Pr.

Darien Venture. Frank Slaughter. 1976. Repr. of 1955 ed. lib. bdg. 12.45 (ISBN 0-89190-532-4). Am Repr-Rivercity Pr.

Darjeeling Tea? Asif Currimbhoy. (Writers Workshop Bluebird Ser.). 64p. 1975. 8.00 (ISBN 0-88253-522-6); pap. text ed. 4.80 (ISBN 0-88253-521-8). Ind-US Inc.

Dark. Max Franklin. (Illus., Orig.). 1978. pap. 1.75 o.p. (ISBN 0-451-08242-7, E8242, Sig). NAL.

Dark Age of Greece. A. M. Snodgrass. 1972. 26.50x (ISBN 0-85224-089-9, Pub. by Edinburgh U Pr Scotland). Columbia U Pr.

Dark Ages. Colin McEvedy & Sarah McEvedy. LC 72-178600. (Atlas of World History Ser). (Illus.). 64p. (gr. 6-12). 1972. 9.95 (ISBN 0-02-765540-7, CCPr). Macmillan.

Dark Ages. Paul Titley. (Let's Make History Ser.). (Orig.). 1980. pap. 3.50 (ISBN 0-263-06337-2). Transatlantic.

Dark & Secret Place. Margaret Summerton. 1978. pap. 1.75 (ISBN 0-380-41301-9, 41301). Avon.

Dark & the Feeling. Clarence Major. LC 73-83162. 5.95 (ISBN 0-89388-119-8). Okpaku Communications.

Dark Backward. Marie Buchanan. 1976. pap. 1.75 o.p. (ISBN 0-345-25067-2). Ballantine.

Dark Beginnings. Katrinka Blickle. LC 77-80877. 1978. 8.95 o.p. (ISBN 0-385-12750-2). Doubleday.

Dark Brown Is the River. John Maxtone-Graham. LC 75-42365. 375p. 1976. 9.95 o.s.i. (ISBN 0-02-582360-4, 58236). Macmillan.

Dark Comedy: The Development of Modern Comic Tragedy. 2nd ed. J. L. Styan. LC 68-23185. 42.00 (ISBN 0-521-06572-0); pap. 10.50x (ISBN 0-521-09529-8). Cambridge U Pr.

Dark Conceit: The Making of Allegory. Edwin Honig. LC 72-2452. 210p. 1972. Repr. of 1959 ed. 7.50 (ISBN 0-87057-138-9, Pub. by Brown U Pr). Univ Pr of New England.

Dark Design. Philip J. Farmer. LC 77-5138. (Riverworld Ser.). (YA) 1977. pap. 2.25 (ISBN 0-425-03831-9, Dist. by Putnam). Berkley Pub.

Dark Dove. A. C. Stewart. LC 74-14814. 192p. (gr. 6-9). 1974. 9.95 (ISBN 0-87599-203-X). S G Phillips.

Dark Drums. Wenzell Brown. (Orig.). 1977. pap. 1.95 o.s.i. (ISBN 0-446-89292-0). Warner Bks.

Dark Eagle: The Story of Benedict Arnold. Clifford L. Alderman. LC 75-40087. 160p. (gr. 5-9). 1976. 8.95 (ISBN 0-02-700210-1, 70021). Macmillan.

Dark Eyes of the Soul. Laura Kwong. (Illus.). 1979. pap. cancelled (ISBN 0-9601428-6-X). Entwhistle Bks.

Dark Fire. Linda Murray. LC 76-58848. 1977. 11.95 o.p. (ISBN 0-688-03198-6). Morrow.

Dark Fires. Rosemary Rogers. 1975. pap. write for info. (ISBN 0-380-00425-9, 76570). Avon.

Dark Flight. John Rossiter. LC 80-69380. 1981. 9.95 (ISBN 0-686-69530-5). Atheneum.

Dark Frigate. rev. ed. Charles B. Hawes. (Illus.). (gr. 7 up). 1971. 7.95 (ISBN 0-316-35096-6, Pub. by Atlantic Monthly Pr). Little.

Dark Gator. Timothy Edler. (Tim Edler's New Swamp Wars Ser.). (Illus.). (gr. k-8). 1980. lea. 5.00 (ISBN 0-931108-06-3). Little Cajun.

Dark Ghetto. Kenneth B. Clark. LC 64-7834. 1965. 10.00 o.p. (ISBN 0-06-031470-2, HarpT). Har-Row.

Dark Glass: Vision & Technique in the Poetry of Dante Gabriel Rossetti. Ronnalie R. Howard. LC 70-158176. xiii, 218p. 1972. 12.00x (ISBN 0-8214-0099-1). Ohio U Pr.

Dark Goddess. Marvin H. Albert. LC 77-76219. 1978. 10.00 o.p. (ISBN 0-385-12182-2). Doubleday.

Dark Horse Barnaby. Marjorie Reynolds. (Illus.). (gr. 4-6). 1967. 3.95g o.s.i. (ISBN 0-02-776060-X). Macmillan.

Dark Horseman. Marianne Harvey. 1981. pap. 3.25 (ISBN 0-440-11758-5). Dell.

Dark Horses Leaping into Flames. Ira Herman. 1979. 10.95 (ISBN 0-89002-122-8); pap. 3.50 (ISBN 0-89002-121-X). Northwoods Pr.

Dark Inheritance. Carola Salisbury. 1979. pap. 1.75 o.p. (ISBN 0-449-23888-1, Crest). Fawcett.

Dark Interval: Towards a Theology of Story. John D. Crossan. 1975. pap. 2.75 (ISBN 0-913592-52-8). Argus Comm.

Dark Island. Dorothy Daniels. 272p. (Orig.). 1972. pap. 1.75 (ISBN 0-446-84801-8). Warner Bks.

Dark Knight. Margaret Shauers. 192p. (YA) 1976. 5.95 (ISBN 0-685-61052-7, Avalon). Bouregy.

Dark Lord of Pengersick. Richard Carlyon. LC 80-13360. (Illus.). (gr. 4 up). 1980. 10.95 (ISBN 0-374-31700-3). FS&G.

Dark Moon. J. H. Brennan. LC 80-20034. 264p. 1981. 13.95 (ISBN 0-03-058013-7). HR&W.

Dark Nantucket Noon. Jane Langton. LC 74-5799. (Harper Novel of Suspense). (Illus.). 302p. (YA) 1975. 8.95 o.p. (ISBN 0-06-012502-0, HarpT). Har-Row.

Dark Oasis. Margaret Pargeter. (Harlequin Presents Ser.). 192p. 1981. pap. 1.50 (ISBN 0-373-10431-6, Pub. by Harlequin). PB.

Dark of the Moon. Howard Richardson & William Berney. LC 56-9611. (Orig.). 1966. pap. 2.65x (ISBN 0-87830-517-3). Theatre Arts.

Dark of the Screen. Sidney Peterson. (Anthology Film Archives Ser.: No. 4). (Illus.). 220p. 1980. 22.50x (ISBN 0-8147-6581-5); pap. 9.00x (ISBN 0-8147-6582-3). NYU Pr.

Dark Palazzo. Virginia Coffman. 1978. pap. 1.75 o.p. (ISBN 0-449-23545-9, Crest). Fawcett.

Dark Pasture. Jessica Stirling. LC 77-15325. 1978. 8.95 o.p. (ISBN 0-312-18257-0). St Martin.

Dark Peninsula: Logging History, Upper Peninsula, Mich. 2nd ed. LC 75-42923. (Illus.). 3.95 o.s.i. (ISBN 0-932212-04-2). Avery Color.

Dark Places, Deep Regions & Other Stories. Margaret Sutherland. LC 80-17008. 1980. 9.95 (ISBN 0-916144-53-4). Stemmer Hse.

Dark Priestess. Juanita Coulson. (Orig.). 1977. pap. 1.95 o.p. (ISBN 0-345-24958-5). Ballantine.

Dark Room. R. K. Narayan. iv, 210p. 1981. lib. bdg. 15.00x (ISBN 0-226-56836-9); pap. 4.95 (ISBN 0-226-56837-7). U of Chicago Pr.

Dark Room. John Weisman. 1981. pap. 2.50 (E9724, Sig). NAL.

Dark Room. Junnosuke Yoshiyuki. Tr. by John Bester from Japanese. LC 75-11390. 170p. 1980. pap. 3.95 (ISBN 0-87011-361-5). Kodansha.

Dark Season at Aerie. Juanita T. Osborne. (YA) 1977. 5.95 (ISBN 0-685-81423-8, Avalon). Bouregy.

Dark Shore. Susan Howatch. 192p. 1978. pap. 2.25 (ISBN 0-449-24241-2, Q2845, Crest). Fawcett.

Dark Side of Paradise. Jo Anne Creighton. 256p. 1976. pap. 1.25 o.p. (ISBN 0-445-00390-1). Popular Lib.

Dark Side of the Millennium: The Problem of Evil in Revelation 20: 1-10. Arthur H. Lewis. 96p. (Orig.). 1980. pap. 4.95 (ISBN 0-8010-5596-2). Baker Bk.

Dark Side of the Moon. William Corlett. LC 76-57890. (gr. 6-9). 1977. 6.95 (ISBN 0-87888-118-2). Bradbury Pr.

Dark Side of the Screen: Film Noir. Foster Hirsh. LC 80-28955. (Illus.). 192p. 1981. 14.95 (ISBN 0-498-02234-X). A S Barnes.

Dark Side of the Sun. Terry Pratchett. LC 75-29644. 1976. 7.95 o.p. (ISBN 0-312-18270-8). St Martin.

Dark Sins, Dark Dreams. Ed. by Barry N. Malzberg & Bill Pronzini. LC 77-76247. 1978. 7.95 o.p. (ISBN 0-385-12832-0). Doubleday.

Dark Soliloquy: The Selected Poems of Gertrud Kolmar. Gertrud Kolmar. Tr. by Henry A. Smith from Ger, LC 75-2239. 192p. 1975. 9.95 o.p. (ISBN 0-8164-9199-2). Continuum.

Dark Stage. Dorothy Daniels. 160p. 1970. pap. 0.95 (ISBN 0-446-75553-2). Warner Bks.

Dark Star. Alan D. Foster. 1978. pap. 1.95 (ISBN 0-345-28871-8, Del Rey Bks). Ballantine.

Dark Stars & Other Illuminations. Tom Monteleone. LC 79-6872. (Double D Science Fiction Ser.). 192p. 1981. 9.95 (ISBN 0-385-15769-X). Doubleday.

Dark Sweet Wanton. Sheila Lancaster. (Historical Romance). 256p. (Orig.). 1981. pap. 2.50 (ISBN 0-515-05759-2). Jove Pubns.

Dark Symphony: Negro Literature in America. Ed. by James A. Emanuel & Theodore L. Gross. LC 68-54984. 1968. 15.95 o.s.i. (ISBN 0-02-909550-6); pap. text ed. 9.95 (ISBN 0-02-909540-9). Free Pr.

Dark Threshold. Grace Corren. 1977. pap. 1.50 o.p. (ISBN 0-445-03227-8). Popular Lib.

Dark Triangle. Hugh Walters. 128p. (gr. 5-12). 1981. 13.95 (ISBN 0-571-11584-5, Pub. by Faber & Faber). Merrimack Bk Serv.

Dark Water. Ralph Hayes. 1978. pap. 1.95 (ISBN 0-505-51320-X). Tower Bks.

Darkening Chamber: The Growth of Tragic Consciousness in Keats. Jacob Wigod. (Salzburg Studies in English Literature, Romantic Reassessment: No. 22). 231p. 1972. pap. text ed. 25.00x (ISBN 0-391-01567-2). Humanities.

Darkening Green. Elizabeth Clarke. (Illus.). 1964. 8.95 (ISBN 0-571-05680-6, Pub. by Faber & Faber). Merrimack Bk Serv.

Darker Ends, Poems by Robert Nye. Robert Nye. LC 69-16840. 1969. pap. 1.75 o.p. (ISBN 0-8090-1348-7). Hill & Wang.

Darker Reaches of Government: Access to Information About Public Administration in the United States, Britain & South Africa. Anthony S. Mathews. LC 78-64475. (Perspectives on Southern Africa Ser.: No. 27). 1979. 27.50x (ISBN 0-520-03803-7). U of Cal Pr.

Darker Side of Love. Anna James. (Orig.). 1979. pap. 2.50 (ISBN 0-515-05096-2). Jove Pubns.

Darker Than Amber. John D. MacDonald. (Travis McGee Ser.). 1979. pap. 2.25 (ISBN 0-449-14162-4, GM). Fawcett.

Darker Than Amber: A Travis McGee Story. John D. MacDonald. (Orig.). 1970. Repr. 5.95 o.s.i. (ISBN 0-397-00642-X). Lippincott.

Darker Vision of the Renaissance: Beyond the Fields of Reason. Robert S. Kinsman. 1975. 20.00x (ISBN 0-520-02259-9). U of Cal Pr.

Darkest Hours: A Narrative Encyclopedia of World Wide Disasters from Ancient Times to the Present. Jay R. Nash. LC 76-7390. (Illus.). 1976. 49.95 (ISBN 0-88229-140-8). Nelson-Hall.

Darkhaven. Dorothy Daniels. 160p. 1965. pap. 0.95 (ISBN 0-446-75564-8). Warner Bks.

Darkling Plain: A Bibliography of Books About World War I. Jill M. Phillips. (Bibliographies for Librarians Ser.). 1980. lib. bdg. 69.95 (ISBN 0-8490-3207-5). Gordon Pr.

Darkness & Daylight: Or, Lights & Shadows of New York Life: A Pictorial Record of Personal Experiences by Day & Night in the Great Metropolis with Hundreds of Thrilling Anecdotes & Incidents. Helen Campbell. LC 76-81511. 1969. Repr. of 1895 ed. 24.00 (ISBN 0-8103-3566-2). Gale.

Darkness & the Light. Robert Coles. LC 74-76878. (Illus.). 112p. 1974. 20.00 (ISBN 0-912334-60-6); pap. 12.50 (ISBN 0-912334-64-9). Aperture.

Darkness at Each Elbow. Harley Elliott. 1981. pap. 4.00 (ISBN 0-914610-21-X). Hanging Loose.

Darkness at Noon. A. Koestler. 1941. 12.95 (ISBN 0-02-565200-1). Macmillan.

Darkness at Pemberley. T. H. White. LC 77-20549. 1978. pap. 3.75 (ISBN 0-486-23613-7). Dover.

Darkness at the Dawning: Race & Reform in the Progressive South. Jack T. Kirby. LC 77-161416. (Critical Periods of History Ser). 220p. 1972. 6.95 o.p. (ISBN 0-397-47225-0); pap. text ed. 2.95 o.p. (ISBN 0-397-47209-9). Lippincott.

Darkness by the River & Other Stories. Adapted by Lewis Jones. (Readers Ser.: Stage 2). 1981. pap. text ed. 1.95 (ISBN 0-88377-142-X). Newbury Hse.

Darkness in Summer. Takeshi Kaiko. Tr. by Cecilia S. Seigle from Japanese. 212p. 1972. pap. 5.75 (ISBN 0-8048-1375-2). C E Tuttle.

Darkness of Love. Sonda T. Robinson. 1977. pap. 1.25 o.s.i. (ISBN 0-515-04195-5). Jove Pubns.

Darkness Over the Valley. Wendelgard Von Staden. Tr. by Mollie C. Peters from Ger. LC 80-15579. Orig. Title: Nacht Uber dem Tal. 1981. 9.95 (ISBN 0-89919-009-X). Ticknor & Fields.

Darkness Under the Hills. Bill Scott. (Illus.). 149p. (gr. 7 up). 1980. 9.95 (ISBN 0-19-554275-4). Oxford U Pr.

Darkness Visible. William Golding. 265p. 1979. 10.95 (ISBN 0-374-13502-9). FS&G.

Darkness Visible: A Study of Vergil's Aeneid. W. R. Johnson. LC 74-82845. 1976. 16.60x (ISBN 0-520-02942-9); pap. 5.95x (ISBN 0-520-03848-7). U of Cal Pr.

Darkroom. Eleanor Lewis. (Illus., Orig.). 1979. pap. 17.50 (ISBN 0-912810-19-X). Lustrum Pr.

Darkroom Dynamics: An Introduction to Creative Printing. Ed. by Jim Stone. 208p. 1981. pap. 12.95 (ISBN 0-442-27927-2). Van Nos Reinhold.

Darkroom Guide. Kalton C. Lahue. (Petersen's Photographic Library). (Illus.). 160p. 1980. pap. 8.95 o.p. (ISBN 0-8227-4039-7). Petersen Pub.

Darkroom Handbook. Michael Langford. LC 80-2703. (Illus.). 352p. 1981. 25.00 (ISBN 0-394-51370-3). Knopf.

Darkroom Techniques. Ronald Spillman. 1976. 12.95 o.p. (ISBN 0-85242-367-5, Pub. by Fountain). Morgan.

Darkroom Techniques, Vol. 2: Enlarging & Contact Printing. Andreas Feininger. LC 73-82108. (Illus.). 304p. 1973. 8.95 (ISBN 0-13-197533-1). P-H.

Darkroom Two. Jain Kelley. (Illus., Orig.). 1979. pap. 17.50 (ISBN 0-912810-21-1). Lustrum Pr.

Darkwater. Dorothy Eden. 1978. pap. 2.25 (ISBN 0-449-23544-0, Crest). Fawcett.

Darlin' Bill. Jerome Charyn. 1980. 11.95 (ISBN 0-87795-283-3). Arbor Hse.

Darling Daughters. Elizabeth Troop. 224p. 1981. 9.95 (ISBN 0-312-18281-3). St Martin.

Darnley's Bride. Vivian Stuart. 1976. pap. 1.25 o.s.i. (ISBN 0-515-04066-5). Jove Pubns.

Darrington & Index Rock Climbing Guide. Fred Beckey. LC 76-8296. (Illus.). 64p. (Orig.). 1976. pap. 2.95 (ISBN 0-916890-41-4). Mountaineers.

Darstellung der Landschaft in der griechischen Dichtung: Untersuchungen Zur Antiken Literatur und Geschicht, Vol.15. Winfried Elliger. LC 73-93160. (Ger.). 1975. 103.00x (ISBN 3-11-004794-2). De Gruyter.

Dartmoor: A New Study. Fish. 1978. 25.00 (ISBN 0-7153-5041-2). David & Charles.

Dartmouth College Causes & the Supreme Court of the United States. John. M. Shirley. LC 79-124904. (American Constitutional & Legal History Ser). (Illus.). 1971. Repr. of 1895 ed. lib. bdg. 45.00 (ISBN 0-306-71995-9). Da Capo.

Dartmouth Experience: Convocation Addresses..., Valedictories..., & Honorary-Degree Citations. John S. Dickey. Ed. by Edward C. Lathem. (Illus.). 322p. 1977. text ed. 15.00x (ISBN 0-87451-154-2). U Pr of New Eng.

Dartmouth: The Royal Naval College, Seventy-Five Years in Pictures. E. L. Davies & E. J. Grove. (Illus.). 96p. 1980. 14.95 (ISBN 0-85997-462-6). McCartan & Root.

Dartmouth Time-Sharing System. G. M. Bull. LC 80-41327. (Computers & Their Applications Ser.). 240p. 1980. 65.00 (ISBN 0-470-27082-9). Halsted Pr.

Darts. Keith Turner. LC 79-56063. (Illus.). 128p. 1980. 14.95 (ISBN 0-7153-7943-7). David & Charles.

Darts: Fifty Ways to Play the Game. Jabez Gotobed. (Illus.). 1979. 9.95 (ISBN 0-900891-71-8); pap. 4.95 (ISBN 0-900891-72-6). Oleander Pr.

Darwin. 2nd ed. Ed. by Philip Appleman. (Norton Critical Edition). 1979. 24.95 (ISBN 0-393-01192-5); pap. 6.95x (ISBN 0-393-95009-3). Norton.

Darwin. (Clarendon Biography). (Illus.). 1975. pap. 3.50 (ISBN 0-912728-91-4). Newbury Bks. Inc.

Darwin. Edmund O'Connor. Ed. by Malcolm Yapp et al. (World History Ser.). (Illus.). 32p. (gr. 10). 1980. Repr. of 1977 ed. lib. bdg. 5.95 (ISBN 0-89908-047-2); pap. text ed. 1.95 (ISBN 0-89908-022-7). Greenhaven.

Darwin & Henslow: The Growth of an Idea, Letters 1831-1860. Ed. by Nora Barlow. 1967. 20.00x (ISBN 0-520-00080-3). U of Cal Pr.

Darwin & the Beagle. Alan Moorehead. LC 69-17879. (Illus.). 1969. 20.00 o.p. (ISBN 0-06-013016-4, HarpT); pap. 8.95 o.s.i. (ISBN 0-06-013017-2, TD-120, HarpT). Har-Row.

Darwin, Marx, & Wagner: Critique of a Heritage. rev. ed. Jacques Barzun. LC 58-2647. 1958. pap. 2.95 (ISBN 0-385-09341-1, A127, Anch). Doubleday.

Darwin on Humus & the Earthworm: The Formation of Vegetable Mould. 4th ed. Charles Darwin. 1966. text ed. 5.00x (ISBN 0-571-06778-6). Humanities.

Darwin on Man: A Psychological Study of Scientific Creativity. 2nd ed. Howard E. Gruber. LC 80-28453. 1981. lib. bdg. price not set (ISBN 0-226-31008-6); pap. price not set (ISBN 0-226-31007-8). U of Chicago Pr.

Darwin to Double Helix: The Biological Theme in Science Fiction. Isaacs. 1977. 3.95 (ISBN 0-408-71302-X). Butterworths.

Darwin to Einstein: Historical Studies in Science & Belief. Colin Chant & John Fauvel. (Illus.). 352p. 1981. text ed. 25.00 (ISBN 0-582-49156-8). Longman.

Darwin to Einstein: Primary Sources on Science & Belief. Ed. by Noel Coley & Vance Hall. (Illus.). 368p. 1981. text ed. 25.00 (ISBN 0-582-49158-4). Longman.

Darwinian Impacts. David R. Oldroyd. 1980. pap. text ed. 13.50x (ISBN 0-391-02091-9). Humanities.

Darwinism. J. R. Angell et al. Bd. with Natural Inheritance. Francis Galton. (Contributions to the History of Psychology Ser., Vol. IV, Pt. D: Comparative Psychology). 1978. 30.00 (ISBN 0-89093-173-9). U Pubns Amer.

Darwin's Century: Evolution & the Men Who Discovered It. Loren Eiseley. LC 58-6638. 1958. pap. 3.50 (ISBN 0-385-08141-3, A244, Anch). Doubleday.

Darwin's Finches: An Essay on the General Biological Theory of Evolution. David Lack. (Illus.). 7.75 (ISBN 0-8446-1275-8). Peter Smith.

Darwin's Forgotten World. Darwwin. 9.98 (ISBN 0-517-29559-8). Bonanza.

Das Energi. Paul Williams. LC 73-80135. 160p. 1980. pap. 4.95 (ISBN 0-934558-00-0). Entwhistle Bks.

Dasavatara & Other Poems. R. Rabindranath Menon. (Redbird Bk.). 1976. lib. bdg. 5.00 (ISBN 0-89253-118-5); flexible bdg. 4.00 (ISBN 0-89253-148-7). Ind-US Inc.

Dasher, the Roots & the Rising of Jimmy Carter. James Wooten. LC 77-25272. 1978. 11.95 (ISBN 0-671-40004-5). Summit Bks.

Dashiel & the Night. Larry Callen. LC 80-10948. (Illus.). (gr. 1-5). 1981. PLB 8.95 (ISBN 0-525-28540-7). Dutton.

Dastanbuy: A Diary of the Indian Revolt of 1857 by Mirza Asadullah Ghalib. Khwaja A. Fariqi. 1971. 7.95x (ISBN 0-210-22338-3). Asia.

Data Acquisitions for Signal Analysis. K. G. Beauchamp & C. K. Yuen. (Illus.). 288p. 1980. text ed. 50.00x (ISBN 0-04-621028-8, 2530). Allen Unwin.

Data Analysis for Politics & Policy. Edward R. Tufte. (Illus.). 192p. 1974. pap. text ed. 7.95 (ISBN 0-13-197525-0). P-H.

Data Analysis for Scientists & Engineers. Stuart L. Meyer. LC 74-8873. (Illus.). 448p. 1975. text ed. 28.95 (ISBN 0-471-59995-6). Wiley.

Data & Formulae for Engineering Students. 2nd ed. J. C. Anderson et al. 1969. text ed. 8.50 (ISBN 0-08-013989-2); pap. text ed. 3.50 (ISBN 0-08-013988-4). Pergamon.

Data Archives for the Social Sciences: Purposes, Operations, & Problems. David Nasatir. LC 72-96443. 126p. (Orig.). 1973. pap. 4.75 (ISBN 92-3-101052-2, U150, UNESCO). Unipub.

Data Bank Applications in Archaeology. Sylvia W. Gaines. 1980. pap. write for info. (ISBN 0-8165-0686-8). U of Ariz Pr.

Data Base Design Methodology. M. Vetter & R. Maddison. 1980. 28.00 (ISBN 0-13-196535-2). P-H.

Data Base Management Systems. Dennis C. Tsichritzis & F. H. Lochovsky. 1977. text ed. 20.95 (ISBN 0-12-701740-2). Acad Pr.

Data Base Selection: Design & Administration. Jon D. Clark. LC 80-607121. 250p. 1980. 23.95 (ISBN 0-03-055891-3). Praeger.

Data Base Structured Techniques to Designing Performance & Management: A Case Study Approach. Shakuntala Atre. LC 80-14808. (Business Data Processing Wiley Ser.). 500p. 1980. 27.95 (ISBN 0-471-05267-1, Pub. by Wiley-Interscience). Wiley.

Data Base Systems. Ed. by H. Hasselmeier & W. C. Spruth. (Lecture Notes in Computer Science: Vol. 39). 390p. 1976. pap. 16.80 o.p. (ISBN 0-387-07612-3). Springer-Verlag.

Data Book for Civil Engineers, 3 vols. E. Seelye. Incl. Vol. 1. Design. 3rd ed. 670p. 1960. 57.95 (ISBN 0-471-77286-0); Vol. 2. Specifications & Costs. 3rd ed. 566p. 1957. 55.00 (ISBN 0-471-77319-0); Vol. 3. Field Practice. 2nd ed. 394p. 1954. 29.95 (ISBN 0-471-77352-2). LC 57-5932 (Pub. by Wiley-Interscience). Wiley.

Data Book for Residential Contractors & Estimators. Alonzo Wass. (Illus.). 1979. 19.95 (ISBN 0-87909-177-0). Reston.

Data Book for Welfare-Employment Programs. Demetra S. Nightingale & John J. Mitchell. (Institute Paper). 187p. 1978. pap. 9.50 (ISBN 0-87766-239-8, 24200). Urban Inst.

Data Book of Social Studies Materials & Resources, Vol. 6. Ed. by Laurel R. Singleton. (Data Bk.). (Orig.). 1981. pap. 10.00 (ISBN 0-89994-254-7). Soc Sci Ed.

Data Collection in Developing Countries. D. J. Casley & D. A. Lury. (Illus.). 1981. 45.00 (ISBN 0-19-877123-1); pap. 14.95 (ISBN 0-19-877124-X). Oxford U Pr.

Data Communication for Distributed Information Systems. Dimitris Chorafas. (Illus.). 235p. 1980. 24.00 (ISBN 0-07-091061-8). McGraw.

Data Communications. Graham Stephens. 1981. text ed. price not set (ISBN 0-86103-046-X, Westbury Hse). Butterworth.

Data Communications: An Introduction to Concepts & Design. Robert Techo. (Applications of Modern Technology in Business Ser.). 300p. 1980. 24.50 (ISBN 0-306-40398-6, Plenum Pr). Plenum Pub.

Data Communications & Teleprocessing Systems. Trevor Housley. (P-H Data Processing Management Ser.). (Illus.). 1979. text ed. 25.95 (ISBN 0-13-197368-1). P-H.

Data Communications & the Systems Designer. Francis G. Smith. Ed. by Gunter Dufey. (Research for Business Decisions). 207p. 1980. 24.95 (ISBN 0-8357-1127-7, Pub. by UMI Res Pr). Univ Microfilms.

Data Communications Via Fading Channels. K. Brayer. LC 74-33060. (IEEE Press Selected Reprint Ser.). 1975. 23.95 o.p. (ISBN 0-471-09815-9, Pub. by Wiley-Interscience); pap. text ed. 11.95x (ISBN 0-471-09816-7). Wiley.

Data-Conversion Integrated Circuits. Daniel J. Dooley. (IEEE Press Selected Reprint Ser.). 298p. 1980. 26.95 (ISBN 0-471-08154-X, Pub. by Wiley-Interscience); pap. 17.50 (ISBN 0-471-08155-8). Wiley.

Data Definition Facility for Programming Languages. Thomas A. Standish. LC 79-7307. (Outstanding Dissertations in the Computer Sciences). 1980. lib. bdg. 30.00 (ISBN 0-8240-4422-3). Garland Pub.

Data Dictionaries & Data Administration: Concepts & Practices for Data Resource Management. Ronald G. Ross. 549p. 1981. 25.95 (ISBN 0-8144-5596-4). Am Mgmt.

Data Entry: Concepts & Applications. Beth Buzby. 480p. 1980. pap. text ed. 14.95 (ISBN 0-574-21255-8, 13-4255); instructor's guide avail. (ISBN 0-574-21256-6, 13-4256). SRA.

Data File Programming in Basic. Leroy Finkel & Jerald R. Brown. (Self-Teaching Guide Ser.). 320p. 1981. pap. text ed. 9.95 (ISBN 0-471-08333-X). Wiley.

Data Files in Basic. L. Finkel & J. Brown. (Wiley Self Teaching Guide Ser.). 320p. 1981. write for info. (ISBN 0-471-08333-X). Wiley.

Data Files in BASIC. L. Finkel & J. Brown. (Wiley Self-Teaching Guides). 320p. 1981. write for info. (ISBN 0-471-08333-X). Wiley.

Data Handbook for Clay Materials & Other Non-Metallic Minerals. Ed. by H. Van Olphen & J. J. Fripiat. (Illus.). 1979. text ed. 76.00 (ISBN 0-08-022850-X). Pergamon.

Data Management & Analysis Using SPSS. William S. Pooler. (Learning Packages in the Policy Sciences: No. 16). 68p. (Orig.). 1978. pap. text ed. 3.50 (ISBN 0-936826-05-3). Pol Stud Assocs.

Data Management Systems. Carl Cagan. LC 73-11036. 141p. 1973. 26.95 (ISBN 0-471-12915-1, Pub. by Wiley-Interscience). Wiley.

Data Networks: Development & Uses. Ed. by Derek Barber. 690p. 1980. pap. text ed. 160.00x (ISBN 0-903796-59-7, Pub. by Online Conferences England). Renouf.

Data of Jurisprudence. William G. Miller. xiv, 477p. 1980. Repr. of 1903 ed. lib. bdg. 42.50x (ISBN 0-8377-0835-4). Rothman.

Data Processing: An Introduction. Donald D. Spencer. (Business C11 Ser.). 1978. pap. text ed. 15.95 (ISBN 0-675-08416-4); instructor's manual 3.95 (ISBN 0-686-67973-3); transparencies 3.95 (ISBN 0-686-67974-1). Merrill.

Data Processing & Computer Programming: A Modular Approach. Thomas J. Cashman & William J. Keys. (Illus.). 1971. text ed. 20.50 scp o.p. (ISBN 0-06-382360-8, HarpC). Har-Row.

Data Processing & Computers: An Introduction. Robert Fleck & C. Brian Honess. (Business C11 Ser.). 1978. pap. text ed. 15.95 (ISBN 0-675-08412-1); media pkg. 595.00 (ISBN 0-675-08413-X); 350.00, 2-4 sets; 250.00, 5-9 sets (ISBN 0-685-86832-X); 200.00, 10-14 sets (ISBN 0-685-86833-8); 15 or more sets 165.00. Merrill.

Data Processing & Management Information Systems. 3rd ed. R. G. Anderson. (Illus.). 480p. 1980. pap. text ed. 15.95x (ISBN 0-7121-0417-8). Intl Ideas.

Data Processing: Computers in Action. Perry Edwards & Bruce Broadwell. 1979. pap. text ed. 18.95x (ISBN 0-534-00615-9); wkbk. 7.95x (ISBN 0-534-00723-6). Wadsworth Pub.

Data Processing: Computers in Action with Fortran. Perry Edwards & Bruce Broadwell. 496p. 1980. text ed. 18.95x (ISBN 0-534-00805-4); wkbk. 7.95x (ISBN 0-534-00879-8). Wadsworth Pub.

Data Processing Documentation: Standards, Procedures & Applications. William Harper. 1973. 27.95 o.p. (ISBN 0-13-196782-7). P-H.

Data Processing in Electroencephalography: Medical Computing, Vol. 2. C. D. Binnie. 1979. 14.95 o.p. (ISBN 0-89355-003-5). Res Stud Pr.

Data Processing Programming: Datenerfassung Programmiering. Ed. by Ing E. Buerger. (English-german-french-russian). 1978. 55.00 (ISBN 3-87144-264-X). Adler.

Data Processing Security Game: Fundamentals of Data Processing Security. R. S. Becker. 1977. text ed. 8.25 (ISBN 0-08-021790-7). Pergamon.

Data Processing Self-Study Kit. General Electric Company. Incl. Introduction to Electronic Data Processing. 256p. (ISBN 0-932078-38-9); Introduction to Magnetic Discs. 98p. (ISBN 0-932078-39-7); Introduction to Integrated Data Store. 97p. (ISBN 0-932078-40-0); Time-Sharing's BASIC Language. 250p. (ISBN 0-932078-41-9). 1970. pap. 8.50 ea. GE Tech Prom & Train.

Data Processing Systems Analysis & Design. 2nd ed. Robert J. Condon. (Illus.). 1978. ref. ed. 17.95 (ISBN 0-8359-1251-5); instrs'. manual avail. Reston.

Data Processing Technology & Economics. Montgomery Phister, Jr. LC 76-24121. (Illus.). 1977. text ed. 29.95 o.p. (ISBN 0-917640-01-2); pap. text ed. 19.95x o.p. (ISBN 0-917640-02-0). Santa Monica Pub.

Data Processing Technology & Economics. 2nd ed. Montgomery Phister, Jr. (Illus.). 1979. 45.00 (ISBN 0-932376-03-7, Co-Pub. by Santa Monica Pub); pap. 30.00 (ISBN 0-932376-04-5). Digital Pr.

Data Processing Technology & Economics: 1975-1978 Supplement. Montgomery Phister, Jr. (Illus.). 1979. pap. 10.00x (ISBN 0-917640-03-9). Santa Monica Pub.

Data Processing with Applications. abr. ed. Robert Condon. 1981. pap. text ed. 12.95 (ISBN 0-8359-1259-0); instr's. manual free (ISBN 0-8359-1260-4). Reston.

Data Processing with Applications. Robert J. Condon. (Illus.). 1978. text ed. 15.95 (ISBN 0-87909-181-9); students manual avail. Reston.

Data Profile on Mercury. (IRPTC Data Profile Ser.: No. 3). 198p. 1981. pap. 20.00 (ISBN 0-686-69541-0, UNEP 42, UNEP). Unipub.

Data Response Questions in A Level Economics. J. M. Oliver. 1976. pap. text ed. 3.50x o.p. (ISBN 0-435-84529-2). Heinemann Ed.

Data Structure & Management. 2nd ed. Ivan Flores. 1977. 23.95 (ISBN 0-13-197335-5). P-H.

Data Structures & Computer Architecture. Kenneth J. Thurber & Peter C. Patton. LC 76-12688. 1977. 19.95 (ISBN 0-669-00723-4). Lexington Bks.

Data Structures & PL-1 Programming. Moshe Augenstein & Aaron Tenenbaum. (Illus.). 1979. text ed. 25.95 (ISBN 0-13-197731-8); exercise manual 6.95 (ISBN 0-13-197756-3). P-H.

Data Structures: Theory & Practice. 2nd ed. A. T. Berztiss. (Computer Science & Applied Mathematics Ser.). 586p. 1975. 21.95 (ISBN 0-12-093552-X). Acad Pr.

Data Structures Using PASCAL. Moshe Augenstein & Aaron M. Tenenbaum. (Illus.). 528p. 1981. text ed. 23.95 (ISBN 0-13-196501-8). P-H.

Data Systems & Management. 2nd ed. Alton R. Kindred. (Illus.). 1980. text ed. 18.95 (ISBN 0-13-196402-X). P-H.

Data Systems & Management: An Introduction to Systems Analysis & Design. Alton R. Kindred. (Illus.). 368p. 1973. text ed. 15.95 o.p. (ISBN 0-13-196766-5); 5.95 o.p. study guide & wkbk. (ISBN 0-13-196865-3). P-H.

Data Systems Dictionary: English-German & German-English. Karl-Heinz Brinkman & Rudolf Schmidt. 1974. pap. 40.00x (ISBN 3-87097-095-2). Intl Learn Syst.

Data-Telecommunications Progress Report. BCC Staff. 1981. 850.00 (ISBN 0-89336-241-7, G-009R). BCC.

Data-Text Primer. D. J. Armor & A. S. Couch. LC 78-165564. 1972. pap. text ed. 10.95 (ISBN 0-02-901020-9). Free Pr.

Data Transmission: Analysis; Design; Applications. Dogan Tugal & Osman Tugal. (Illus.). 384p. 1982. 19.50 (ISBN 0-07-065427-1). McGraw.

Data Types & Structures. C. C. Gotlieb & Leo R. Gotlieb. (Illus.). 1978. ref. ed. 22.95 (ISBN 0-13-197095-X). P-H.

Database: A Bibliography of the Nineteen Seventy's, Vol. I. Yahiko Kambayashi. 1980. text ed. price not set o.p. (ISBN 0-914894-64-1). Computer Sci.

Database Administrator. John K. Lyon. LC 75-42442. (Business Data Processing Ser). 240p. 1976. 23.50 (ISBN 0-471-55741-2, Pub. by Wiley-Interscience). Wiley.

Database Design. Gio Wiederhold. (Computer Science Ser.). 1977. text ed. 25.95 (ISBN 0-07-070130-X, C); write for info. instructor's manual (ISBN 0-07-070131-8). McGraw.

Database Management Systems. Ed. by Ben Shneiderman. LC 76-41070. (Information Technology Ser.: Vol. I). (Illus.). 137p. 1976. pap. 15.00 (ISBN 0-88283-014-7). AFIPS Pr.

Database Processing: Fundamentals, Modeling, Applications. David M. Kroenke. LC 76-41803. 416p. 1977. text ed. 20.95 (ISBN 0-574-21100-4, 13-4100); instr's guide avail. (ISBN 0-574-21101-2, 13-4101). SRA.

Database Security & Integrity. Eduardo B. Fernandez et al. LC 80-15153. (IBM Systems Programming Ser.). (Illus.). 288p. 1981. text ed. 18.95 (ISBN 0-201-14467-0). A-W.

Date & Composition of Ezekiel. Carl G. Howie. (Society of Biblical Literature, Monographs). 1950. pap. 7.50 (ISBN 0-89130-174-7, 060004). Scholars Pr Ca.

Date Palm. Hilda Simon. LC 77-14244. (gr. 7 up). 1978. 8.95 (ISBN 0-396-07523-1). Dodd.

Date with Sandburg. Norman Corwin. (Santa Susana Press Ser.). 1981. 17.50 (ISBN 0-937048-30-5). CSUN.

Dated Greek Manuscripts of the Thirteenth & Fourteenth Centuries in the Libraries of Great Britian. Alexander Turyn. LC 80-81547. (Dumbarton Oaks Studies: Vol. 17). (Illus.). 198p. 1980. 65.00 (ISBN 0-88402-077-0, Ctr Byzantine). Dumbarton Oaks.

Dateline: White House. Helen Thomas. (Illus.). 320p. 1975. 9.95 o.s.i. (ISBN 0-02-617620-3). Macmillan.

Dating. Jean C. Lipke. LC 79-104893. (Being Together Books). (Illus.). (gr. 5-11). 1971. PLB 4.95 o.p. (ISBN 0-8225-0592-4). Lerner Pubns.

Dating & Hanging Out. Eisner. (gr. 7-12). Date not set. pap. cancelled (ISBN 0-590-30031-8, Schol Pap). Schol Bk Serv.

Datsun F Ten & Three Hundred Ten: Nineteen Seventy-Six to Seventy-Nine Shop Manual. Eric Ahlstrand. (Illus.). 186p. (Orig.). 1980. pap. text ed. 10.95 (ISBN 0-89287-318-3, A202). Clymer Pubns.

Datsun Five-Ten 1978-1979 Shop Manual. Alan Ahlstrand. Ed. by Eric Jorgensen. (Illus.). 313p. (Orig.). 1979. pap. text ed. 10.95 (ISBN 0-89287-244-6, A201). Clymer Pubns.

Datsun Nineteen Seventy-Three to Eighty. (Illus.). 288p. 1979. pap. 8.95. Chilton.

Datsun Nineteen Seventy-Three to Nineteen Eighty. Chilton's Automotive Editorial Dept. (Illus.). 1980. pap. 8.95 (ISBN 0-8019-6960-3). Chilton.

Datsun Service-Repair Handbook L521, P1521, P1620 Pickups, 1968-1980. new ed. Alan Ahlstrand. Ed. by Jeff Robinson. (Illus.). 1977. pap. 10.95 (ISBN 0-89287-151-2, A-148). Clymer Pubns.

Datsun Service Repair Handbook 510, 610, & 710, 1968-1977. 3rd ed. Alan Ahlstrand. Ed. by Jeff Robinson. (Illus.). 1979. pap. text ed. 10.95 (ISBN 0-89287-281-0, A149). Clymer Pubns.

Datsun Sports Car Handbook: 1600 & 2000cc. Ed. by Clymer Publications. (Illus.). 1970. pap. 11.00 o.p. (ISBN 0-89287-248-9, A150). Clymer Pubns.

Datsun Tune-up & Repair. Ed. by Al Hall. LC 79-64834. (Tune-up & Repair Ser.). (Illus.). 198p. (Orig.). 1979. pap. 4.95 (ISBN 0-8227-5050-3). Petersen Pub.

Datsun Tune-up for Everybody. Paul Young. (Illus.). 1980. pap. 7.95 (ISBN 0-89815-026-4). Ten Speed Pr.

Datsun Twelve Hundred & B-Two Ten: 1971-78 Service-Repair Handbook. Alan Ahlstrand. Ed. by Jeff Robinson. (Illus.). 1978. pap. 10.95 (ISBN 0-89287-284-5, A151). Clymer Pubns.

Datsun Two-Forty, Two-Sixty & Two-Eighty-Z & ZX: 1970-79 Service-Repair Handbook. 4th ed. Alan Ahlstrand. Ed. by Eric Jorgensen. (Illus.). 1978. pap. 10.95 (ISBN 0-89287-290-X, A152). Clymer Pubns.

Datsun Two Hundred SX 1977-1979 Shop Manual. Alan Ahlstrand. Ed. by Eric Jorgensen. (Illus.). 184p. (Orig.). 1979. pap. text ed. 10.95 (ISBN 0-89287-294-2, A200). Clymer Pubns.

Datsun Two Hundred Ten: Nineteen Seventy-Nine to Nineteen Eighty Shop Manual. Alan Ahlstrand. Ed. by Eric Jorgensen. (Illus.). 336p. (Orig.). 1980. pap. text ed. 11.95 (ISBN 0-89287-322-1, A 203). Clymer Pubns.

Datsun Z Cars: Nineteen Seventy to Eighty Repair & Tune-up Guide. (New Automotive Bks.). 208p. 1980. 8.95 (ISBN 0-8019-6932-8). Chilton.

Datsun 810: 1977-1980 Shop Manual. Alan Ahlstrand. Ed. by Eric Jorgensen. (Illus.). 296p. 1980. pap. 10.95 (ISBN 0-89287-334-5). Clymer Pubns.

Daughter & Shadow. James B. Johnson. (Science Fiction Ser.). 1981. pap. 1.95 (ISBN 0-87997-605-5, UJ1605). DAW Bks.

Daughter of Anderson Crow. George B. McCutcheon. 1976. lib. bdg. 15.75x (ISBN 0-89968-060-7). Lightyear.

Daughter of Destiny. Jamie Buckingham. 1978. 7.95 o.p. (ISBN 0-88270-078-2); pap. 2.95 pocket ed. (ISBN 0-88270-318-8). Logos.

Daughter of Discontent. Hila Colman. LC 74-155995. (gr. 7 up). 1971. PLB 6.48 o.p. (ISBN 0-688-31215-2). Morrow.

Daughter of Earth. Agnes Smedley. 416p. 1973. 10.00 (ISBN 0-912670-87-8); pap. 4.95 (ISBN 0-912670-10-X). Feminist Pr.

Daughter of Night: A Tale of Three Worlds. Lydia Obukhova. Tr. by Mirra Ginsburg from Rus. LC 73-22621. 176p. (gr. 9 up). 1974. 5.95g o.s.i. (ISBN 0-02-768500-4, 76850). Macmillan.

Daughter of the Moon. Gregory Maguire. LC 79-25683. 257p. (gr. 3 up). 1980. 9.95 (ISBN 0-374-31705-4). FS&G.

Daughter of the Plain Folk. S. Earl Dubbel. 192p. 1975. pap. 2.25 (ISBN 0-8024-1762-0). Moody.

Daughter of the Sacred Mountain. Mozelle Richardson. LC 76-46415. 1977. 7.95 o.p. (ISBN 0-688-03145-5). Morrow.

Daughter of the Waves: Memories of Growing up in Pre-War Palestine. Ruth Jordan. LC 80-39526. 224p. 1981. 10.95 (ISBN 0-8008-2120-3). Taplinger.

Daughters of Columbia: Women, Intellect, & Ideology in Revolutionary America. Linda K. Kerber. 320p. 1980. 19.50 o.p. (ISBN 0-8078-1440-7); pap. 9.00 o.p. (ISBN 0-8078-4065-3). U of NC Pr.

Daughters of Erin. Elizabeth Coxhead. (Orig.). pap. text ed. 7.25x (ISBN 0-901072-60-5). Humanities.

Daughters of Eve. Lois Duncan. (YA) (gr. 7-12). 1980. pap. 1.75 (ISBN 0-440-91864-2, LFL). Dell.

Daughters of Rachel: Women in Israel. Natalie Rein. 1980. pap. 4.95 (ISBN 0-14-005731-5). Penguin.

Daughters of the Far Islands. Aola Vandergriff. (Orig.). 1979. pap. 2.95 (ISBN 0-446-93910-2). Warner Bks.

Daughters of the Law. Sandy Asher. LC 80-20400. 160p. (gr. 7 up). 1980. 7.95 (ISBN 0-8253-0006-1). Beaufort Bks NY.

Daughters of the Opal Skies. Aola Vandergriff. (Orig.). 1980. pap. 2.50 (ISBN 0-446-81930-1). Warner Bks.

Daughters of the Southwind. Aola Vandergriff. (Orig.). 1977. pap. 2.95 (ISBN 0-446-93909-9). Warner Bks.

Daughters of the Wild Country. Aola Vandergriff. (Orig.). 1978. pap. 2.95 (ISBN 0-446-93908-0). Warner Bks.

D'Aulaires' Book of Greek Myths. Ingri D'Aulaire & Edgar Parin D'Aulaire. LC 62-15877. 1962. 10.95a (ISBN 0-385-01583-6); PLB (ISBN 0-385-07108-6). Doubleday.

D'Aulaires' Trolls. Ingri D'Aulaire & Edgar P. D'Aulaire. LC 76-158897. 64p. (gr. 1-3). 1972. 6.95a (ISBN 0-385-08255-X); limited ed. 50.00 (ISBN 0-385-04343-0); PLB (ISBN 0-385-01275-6). Doubleday.

Daumier. Sarah Symmons. (Oresko-Jupiter Art Bks). (Illus.). 104p. 1980. 17.95 (ISBN 0-905368-42-8, Pub. by Oresko-Jupiter England). Hippocrene Bks.

Daumier & Music. Honore Daumier. (Music Ser.). 1981. 25.00 (ISBN 0-306-76054-1). Da Capo.

Dave Berg Looks Around. Dave Berg. (Mad Ser.). (Illus.). 192p. 1975. pap. 1.75 (ISBN 0-446-94399-1). Warner Bks.

Dave Berg Looks at Living. Dave Berg. (Mad Ser.). (Illus.). 192p. (Orig.). 1973. pap. 1.50 (ISBN 0-446-88735-8). Warner Bks.

Dave Berg Looks at Modern Thinking. Dave Berg. (Mad Ser.). (Illus.). 192p. 1976. pap. 1.75 (ISBN 0-446-94401-7). Warner Bks.

Dave Berg Looks at Things. Dave Berg. (Mad Ser.). (Illus.). 192p. 1974. pap. 1.75 (ISBN 0-446-94403-3). Warner Bks.

Dave Berg: Our Sick World. Dave Berg. (Mad Ser.). (Illus.). 1978. pap. 1.75 (ISBN 0-446-94404-1). Warner Bks.

Dave Cowens. Robert Armstrong. (Sports Superstars Ser.). (Illus.). (gr. 3-9). 1978. PLB 5.95 (ISBN 0-87191-668-1); pap. 2.95 (ISBN 0-89812-182-5). Creative Ed.

Dave Cowens: A Biography. George Sullivan. LC 76-50795. (gr. 3-7). 1977. PLB 5.95 (ISBN 0-385-11524-5). Doubleday.

Dave Maynard's Tried & True All-Night Radio Secret Family Recipe Cookbook. Dave Maynard. (Illus.). 256p. pap. 6.95 (ISBN 0-201-05008-0). A-W.

Dave Sulkin Cares! Fletcher Knebel. LC 77-25600. 1978. 8.95 o.p. (ISBN 0-385-13693-5). Doubleday.

David. Maud Petersham & Miska Petersham. (Illus.). (gr. 4-6). 1967. 4.95g o.s.i. (ISBN 0-02-771900-6). Macmillan.

David & Charles Book of Castles. Plantagenet S. Fry. LC 80-69352. (Illus.). 496p. 1981. 33.00 (ISBN 0-7153-7976-3). David & Charles.

David & Goliath. (Tell-a-Bible Story Ser.). (Illus.). 28p. bds. 0.69 (ISBN 0-686-68639-X, 3683). Standard Pub.

David & Goliath. Illus. by Alan Howard. (Illus.). 1977. 5.95 (ISBN 0-571-08413-3, Pub. by Faber & Faber). Merrimack Bk Serv.

David & His Alien Friend, Bks. I & II. Dagmar M. Meier. (Illus.). Date not set. 8.00 (ISBN 0-682-49505-0). Exposition.

David C. Broderick: A Political Portrait. David A. Williams. LC 79-85342. 1969. 10.00 (ISBN 0-87328-035-0). Huntington Lib.

David Comes into the Kingdom. Gordon Lindsay. (Old Testament Ser.). 1.25 (ISBN 0-89985-142-8). Christ Nations.

David Copperfield. Charles Dickens. (Macmillan Classics). (gr. 7 up). 1962. 5.95g o.s.i. (ISBN 0-02-730440-X). Macmillan.

David Copperfield. Charles Dickens. Ed. by Nina Burgis. (Clarendon Dickens Ser.). (Illus.). 948p. 1981. 115.00 (ISBN 0-19-812492-9). Oxford U Pr.

David Elginbrod, 1863. George MacDonald. Ed. by Robert L. Wolff. LC 75-1502. (Victorian Fiction Ser). 1975. lib. bdg. 66.00 (ISBN 0-8240-1577-0). Garland Pub.

David G. Burnett, First President of Texas. M. W. Clarke. LC 77-79108. (Illus.). 12.50 (ISBN 0-8363-0024-6); limited ed. 85.00 (ISBN 0-685-13270-6). Jenkins.

David Garrick: A Critical Biography. George W. Stone, Jr. & George M. Kahrl. LC 79-9476. (Illus.). 791p. 1979. 60.00x (ISBN 0-8093-0931-9). S Ill U Pr.

David Garrick: Director. Kalman A. Burnim. LC 72-11834. (Arcturus Books Paperbacks). 250p. 1973. pap. 6.95 (ISBN 0-8093-0625-5). S Ill U Pr.

David Garrick, Dramatist. Elizabeth P. Stein. 315p. 1980. Repr. of 1937 ed. lib. bdg. 40.00 (ISBN 0-89760-827-5). Telegraph Bks.

David Hamilton's Private Collection. Photos by David Hamilton. LC 80-83281. (Illus.). 128p. 1980. pap. 10.95 (ISBN 0-688-00402-4, Quill). Morrow.

David Hicks on Living with Taste. David Hicks. 1969. 12.95 o.s.i. (ISBN 0-02-551370-2). Macmillan.

David Hume. Nicholas Capaldi. LC 74-20931. (World Leaders Ser.: No. 48). 1975. lib. bdg. 9.95 (ISBN 0-8057-3685-9). Twayne.

David Hume. John V. Price. LC 68-24287. (English Authors Ser.: No. 77). 1969. lib. bdg. 10.95 (ISBN 0-8057-1280-1). Twayne.

David Hume: Bicentenary Papers. Ed. by G. P. Morice. LC 77-81915. 1978. 12.50 (ISBN 0-292-71515-3). U of Tex Pr.

David Hume: Writings on Economics. Ed. by Eugene Rotwein. LC 55-12064. 1970. pap. 7.95 (ISBN 0-299-01324-3). U of Wis Pr.

David Jones. Samuel Rees. (English Authors Ser.: No. 246). 1978. 12.50 (ISBN 0-8057-6726-6). Twayne.

David, King of Israel. William G. Blaikie. Date not set. 14.50 (ISBN 0-86524-054-X). Klock & Klock.

David Kopay Story. David Kopay & Perry D. Young. 1980. pap. 5.95 (ISBN 0-87795-290-6). Arbor Hse.

David Lean: A Guide to References & Resources. Louis Castelli & Caryn L. Cleeland. 1980. lib. bdg. 18.50 (ISBN 0-8161-7933-6). G K Hall.

David Livingstone. (Ladybird Ser.). 1.49. Chr Lit.

David Livingstone. J. H. Worcester, Jr. pap. 2.25 (ISBN 0-8024-4782-1). Moody.

David Lloyd, Colonial Lawmaker. Roy N. Lokken. LC 59-13419. (Publications in History). (Illus.). 319p. 1959. 9.50 (ISBN 0-295-73762-X). U of Wash Pr.

David Lloyd George: A Biography. Peter Rowland. (Illus.). 896p. 1976. 20.00 o.s.i. (ISBN 0-02-605590-2). Macmillan.

David McCheever's Twenty-Nine Dogs. (Read-by-Yourself Bks.). (gr. 1-2). 1980. pap. 2.95 o.p. (ISBN 0-395-29928-4). HM.

David McCutchion: Shraddanjali. P. Lal. 15.00 (ISBN 0-89253-671-3); flexible cloth 6.75 (ISBN 0-89253-672-1). Ind-US Inc.

David: Man After God's Own Heart, 2 vols. Robbie Castleman. (Fisherman Bible Studyguide Ser.). 72p. 1981. saddle stitched 2.25 ea. Vol. 1 (ISBN 0-87788-164-2). Vol. 2 (ISBN 0-87788-165-0). Shaw Pubs.

David Meyer Is a Mother. Gail Parent. LC 74-15885. 256p. 1976. 7.95 o.s.i. (ISBN 0-06-013274-4, HarpT). Har-Row.

David Newsom, the Western Observer, 1805-1882. David Newsom. LC 72-92062. (Illus.). 1972. pap. 7.95 (ISBN 0-87595-040-X). Oreg Hist Soc.

David O. Selznick's Hollywood. Ronald Haver. LC 79-2224. (Illus.). 400p. 1980. 85.00 (ISBN 0-394-42595-2). Knopf.

David Popper: Violoncello Virtuoso & Composer. Stephen De'ak. (Illus.). 320p. 1980. 14.95 (ISBN 0-87666-621-7, Z-32). Paganiniana Pubns.

David Reaping the Whirlwind. Gordon Lindsay. (Old Testament Ser.). 1.25 (ISBN 0-89985-143-6). Christ Nations.

David Ricardo. Michael J. Gootzeit. (Essays on the Great Economists Ser). 96p. 1975. 12.50x (ISBN 0-231-03524-1); pap. 5.00x (ISBN 0-231-03916-6). Columbia U Pr.

David Snedden & Education for Social Efficiency. Walter H. Drost. (Illus.). 1967. 22.50x (ISBN 0-299-04460-2). U of Wis Pr.

David, the Shepherd Boy. Scripture Union. (New Owl Ser.). 1978. pap. 0.49 (ISBN 0-87508-928-3). Chr Lit.

David Wynne. Richard E. Jones. (Composers of Wales Ser.: No. 3). 1979. pap. text ed. 6.00 (ISBN 0-7083-0714-0). Verry.

Davids Asks, "Why?". Linda S. Chandler. (gr. 3-7). 1981. 4.95 (ISBN 0-8054-4266-9). Broadman.

David's Cookies Cookie Cookbook. David Leiderman & Susan V. Liederman. (Illus.). 128p. 1981. 8.95 (ISBN 0-89480-151-1); pap. 4.95 (ISBN 0-89480-149-X). Workman Pub.

David's Real World. Ruth R. Stornetta. (Illus.). 1980. 6.00 (ISBN 0-682-49624-3). Exposition.

Davie: A Love Story. Donald McDougall. 1978. pap. 1.95 o.p. (ISBN 0-445-04293-1). Popular Lib.

Davie County: A Brief History. James W. Wall. (Illus.). 1976. pap. 2.00 (ISBN 0-86526-126-1). NC Archives.

Davis Family: A Personal Recordkeeping Practice Set. 2nd ed. Merle Wood. (Illus.). (gr. 10-12). 1981. 6.28 (ISBN 0-07-071623-4, G). McGraw.

Davis, Mangan, Ferguson: Tradition & the Irish Writer. William B. Yeats & T. Kinsella. (Tower Ser. of Anglo Irish Studies). 1970. pap. text ed. 1.75 (ISBN 0-85105-166-9, Dolmen Pr). Humanities.

Davison's Knit Goods Trade. 1981. 40.00 (ISBN 0-686-67904-0). Davison.

Davison's Salesman's Book. 1981. 25.00 (ISBN 0-686-67905-9). Davison.

Davison's Textile Bluebook. 1981. 60.00 (ISBN 0-686-67903-2). Davison.

Davison's Textile Buyers Guide. 1981. 25.00 (ISBN 0-686-67906-7). Davison.

Davy. Edgar Pangborn. 288p. 1976. pap. 1.50 o.p. (ISBN 0-345-24968-2). Ballantine.

Davy Crockett. Matthew G. Grant. LC 73-10072. 1974. PLB 5.95 (ISBN 0-87191-258-9). Creative Ed.

Davy Crockett. Stewart Holbrook. (Landmark Ser.: No. 57). (Illus.). (gr. 4-6). 1955. 2.95 o.p. (ISBN 0-685-19688-7, BYR); PLB 5.99 (ISBN 0-394-90357-9). Random.

Dawes Act & the Allotment of Indian Land. D. S. Otis. (Civilization of the American Indian Ser.: Vol. 123). 215p. 1973. 9.95x (ISBN 0-8061-1039-2). U of Okla Pr.

Dawn. Uri Shulevitz. LC 74-9761. (Illus.). 32p. (ps-3). 1974. 8.95 (ISBN 0-374-31707-0). FS&G.

Dawn. Elie Wiesel. 1973. pap. 1.95 (ISBN 0-380-01132-8, 42663, Bard). Avon.

Dawn & the Darkest Hour: A Study of Aldous Huxley. George Woodcock. 1972. 9.95 (ISBN 0-571-08939-9, Pub. by Faber & Faber). Merrimack Bk Serv.

Dawn Blossoms Plucked at Dusk-Lu Hsun. 1.95 (ISBN 0-8351-0064-2). China Bks.

Dawn-Breakers. Nabil-i-A'zam. Ed. & tr. by Shoghi Effendi. LC 32-8946. (Illus.). 1932. 18.00 (ISBN 0-87743-010-1, 7-31-53); pap. 8.00 (ISBN 0-87743-092-6, 7-31-54). Baha'i.

Dawn Is Always New: Seleeted Poetry of Rocco Scotellaro. Tr. by Ruth Feldman & Brian Swann. LC 79-3229. (Lockert Libary of Poetry in Translation). (Ital. & Eng.). 1980. 14.50x (ISBN 0-691-06423-7); pap. 6.95 (ISBN 0-691-01370-5). Princeton U Pr.

Dawn of a New Day: The New York World's Fair, 1939-1940. Ed. by Helen A. Harrison. (Illus.). 128p. 1980. 24.95x (ISBN 0-8147-3407-3); pap. 12.95x (ISBN 0-8147-3408-1). NYU Pr.

Dawn of a New Era: 1250-1453. Edward P. Cheyney. (Rise of Modern Europe Ser). (Illus.). 1936. 15.00x o.s.i. (ISBN 0-06-010760-X, HarpT). Har-Row.

Dawn of a New Era: 1250-1453. Edward P. Cheyney. (Rise of Modern Europe Ser). pap. 4.95x o.p. (ISBN 0-06-133002-7, TB3002, Torch). Har-Row.

Dawn of African History. 2nd ed. Ed. by Roland Oliver. (Illus., Orig.). (gr. 9-12). 1968. pap. 3.95x (ISBN 0-19-500355-1). Oxford U Pr.

Dawn of British Trade to the East Indies. Henry Stevens. 331p. Repr. of 1967 ed. 27.50x (ISBN 0-7146-1105-0, F Cass Co). Biblio Dist.

Dawn of Empire: Rome's Rise to World Power. R. M. Errington. LC 75-176296. (Illus.). 330p. 1972. 20.00x (ISBN 0-8014-0689-7); pap. 5.95 452p., 1973 (ISBN 0-8014-9128-2, CP128). Cornell U Pr.

Dawn of Love: No. 125. Barbara Cartland. 192p. (Orig.). 1980. pap. 1.75 o.p. (ISBN 0-553-13830-8). Bantam.

Dawn of the Apocalyptic: The Historical & Sociological Roots of Jewish Apocalyptic Eschatology. rev. ed. Paul D. Hanson. LC 79-17099. 464p. 1979. 14.95 (ISBN 0-8006-0285-4, 1-285). Fortress.

Dawn of the Nineteenth Century in England. John Ashton. LC 67-23941. (Social History Reference Ser). 1968. Repr. of 1886 ed. 18.000 (ISBN 0-8103-3247-7). Gale.

Dawn of World Railways 1800-1850. O. S. Nock & Clifford Meadway. LC 76-152282. (Illus.). 192p. 1972. 8.95 (ISBN 0-02-589730-6). Macmillan.

Dawn Over Chungking. Lin Adet. LC 74-31239. (China in the 20th Century Ser). 240p. 1975. Repr. of 1941 ed. lib. bdg. 22.50 (ISBN 0-306-70692-X). Da Capo.

Dawn Over Mount Hira & Other Essays. Marzieh Gail. 1976. 9.50 (ISBN 0-85398-063-2, 7-32-18, Pub. by G Ronald England); pap. 5.50 (ISBN 0-85398-064-0, 7-32-19, Pub. by G Ronald England). Baha'i.

Dawn: Portrait of a Teenage Runaway. Julia Sorel. (Orig.). 1971. pap. 1.95 (ISBN 0-345-29610-9). Ballantine.

Dawn Song: Choral Music. Baha'i Committee on Music. 1969. pap. 5.00 (ISBN 0-87743-061-6, 7-58-03). Baha'i.

Dawn Steals Softly. Anne Hampson. 192p. (Orig.). 1980. pap. 1.50 (ISBN 0-671-57027-7). S&S.

Dawn Wind. David Pickard. 1980. pap. 2.50 (ISBN 0-85363-133-6). OMF Bks.

Dawn Wind. Christina Savage. (Orig.). 1980. pap. 2.50 o.s.i. (ISBN 0-440-11792-5). Dell.

Dawning of America. John Schutz. LC 80-68812. (Orig.). 1981. pap. text ed. 7.95x (ISBN 0-88273-109-2). Forum Pr MO.

Dawning of Music in Kentucky, The Western Minstrel. Anthony P. Heinrich. LC 79-39732. (Earlier American Music Ser: Vol. 10). 297p. 1973. Repr. of 1820 ed. lib. bdg. 29.50 (ISBN 0-306-77310-4). Da Capo.

Dawn's Early Light. Elswyth Thane. 1943. unabridged ed. 10.00 (ISBN 0-8015-1957-8, Hawthorn). Dutton.

Dawn's Early Light. Elswyth Thane. (Williamsburg Ser.: No. 1). 1981. lib. bdg. 16.95 (ISBN 0-8161-3167-8, Large Print Bks). G K Hall.

Daws: The Story of Dawson Trotman, Founder of the Navigators. Betty L. Skinner. 392p. 1975. pap. 6.95 (ISBN 0-310-32801-2). Zondervan.

Day After Christmas. D. Alyce Davidge. (Illus.). 30p. (Orig.). (gr. k-4). 1981. pap. 4.00 (ISBN 0-9604780-1-9). Soup to Nuts.

Day After Tomorrow in the Pacific Region, Nineteen Seventy-Eight. Norman Macrae et al. (Worldview Symposium Ser.). 1978. pap. 2.00 o.p. (ISBN 0-685-99241-1). Asia Soc.

Day After Yesterday. Geraldine Kaye. (Illus.). 96p. (gr. 2-6). 1981. 8.95 (ISBN 0-233-97344-3). Andre Deutsch.

Day & a Night in a Forest. Mary Adrian. (Illus.). Date not set. 4.95 (ISBN 0-8038-1513-1). Hastings.

Day & Night in the Wynds of Edinburgh. George Bell. Incl. Blackfriars' Wynd Analysed. 1973. Repr. of 1850 ed. text ed. 12.50 (ISBN 0-8277-1536-6). British Bk Ctr.

Day at the Beach. Mircea Vasiliu. LC 76-24169. (Picturebacks Ser). (Illus.). (ps-1). 1977. pap. 1.25 (ISBN 0-394-83475-5, BYR). Random.

Day by Day. Andrew Murray. 1969. pap. 2.25 (ISBN 0-87123-092-5, 200092). Bethany Fell.

Day by Day: Three Hundred Calendar-Related Activities, Crafts, & Bulletin Board Ideas for the Elementary Grades. Ed. by Bonnie Bernstein. LC 80-81680. (Learning Ideabooks Ser.). 1980. pap. 12.95 (ISBN 0-8224-4252-3). Pitman Learning.

Day by Day with D. L. Moody. D. L. Moody. 1977. pap. 2.25 (ISBN 0-8024-1759-0). Moody.

Day by Night. Tanith Lee. (Science Fiction Ser.). 1980. pap. 2.25 (ISBN 0-87997-576-8, UE1576). DAW Bks.

Day Care: Curriculum Considerations. Michael Langenbach & Teanna W. Neskora. (Elementary Education Ser.). 1977. text ed. 16.95 (ISBN 0-675-08544-6). Merrill.

Day Care in Context. Greta G. Fein & K. Alison Clarke-Stewart. LC 72-8588. 359p. 1973. 28.95 (ISBN 0-471-25695-1, Pub. by Wiley - Interscience). Wiley.

Day Care: Problems, Process, Prospects. Donald A. Peters. LC 75-34609. 1975. 11.95 (ISBN 0-87705-279-4); pap. 6.95 (ISBN 0-87705-290-5). Human Sci Pr.

Day Christ Died. Jim Bishop. LC 57-6125. 1978. pap. 2.95 (ISBN 0-06-060786-6, HJ 38, HarpR). Har-Row.

Day Daddy Died. Alan Burns. (Illus.). 192p. 1981. 13.95 (ISBN 0-8052-8086-3, Pub. by Allison & Busby England); pap. 5.95 (ISBN 0-8052-8085-5). Schocken.

Day Daddy Stayed Home. Ethel Kessler & Leonard Kessler. LC 59-5898. (gr. k-3). Softbound 1.95 (ISBN 0-385-01073-7, Zephyr). Doubleday.

Day God Laughed: Sayings, Fables & Entertainments of the Jewish Sages. Tr. by Hyam Maccoby from Heb. LC 78-53502. 1978. 10.00 o.p. (ISBN 0-312-18403-4). St Martin.

Day Hiker's Guide to Southern California. John McKinney. 160p. (Orig.). 1981. pap. 8.85 (ISBN 0-88496-163-X). Capra Pr.

Day Hospital: Organization & Management. Charlotte M. Hamill. LC 80-607802. 192p. 1981. text ed. write for info. (ISBN 0-8261-3040-2). Springer Pub.

Day I Was Born. Marjorie W. Weinman & Mitchell Sharmat. (Illus.). (ps-2). 1980. PLB 7.95 (ISBN 0-525-28560-1). Dutton.

Day in Autumn: A Poem, Repr. Of 1820 Ed. Bernard Barton. Bd. with Napoleon, & Other Poems. Repr. of 1822 ed; Verses on the Death of Percy Bysshe Shelley. Repr. of 1822 ed. LC 75-31153. (Romantic Context: Poetry 1789-1830 Ser.: Vol. 9). 1977. lib. bdg. 47.00 (ISBN 0-8240-2108-8). Garland Pub.

Day in Day Out. Dorothy Michener & Beverly Muschlitz. LC 80-82304. (Illus.). 160p. 1980. pap. text ed. 8.95 (ISBN 0-913916-71-4). Incentive Pubns.

Day in Old Athens. William S. Davis. LC 60-16707. (Illus.). (gr. 7 up). 10.00x (ISBN 0-8196-0111-X). Biblo.

Day in Old Rome. William S. Davis. LC 61-24993. (Illus.). (gr. 7 up). 10.00x (ISBN 0-8196-0106-3). Biblo.

Day in the Life. Ed. by Gardner Dozois. LC 78-160655. 1972. 7.95 o.s.i. (ISBN 0-06-011076-7, HarpT). Har-Row.

Day in the Life of a Firefighter. Betsy Smith. LC 80-54099. (Illus.). 32p. (gr. 4 up). 1980. PLB 5.89 (ISBN 0-89375-444-7); pap. 2.50 (ISBN 0-89375-445-5). Troll Assocs.

Day in the Life of a Marine Biologist. David Paige. LC 80-54097. (Illus.). 32p. (gr. 4 up). 1980. PLB 5.89 (ISBN 0-89375-446-3); pap. 2.50 (ISBN 0-89375-447-1). Troll Assocs.

Day in the Life of a Meteorologist. Margot Witty & Ken Witty. LC 80-54098. (Illus.). 32p. (gr. 4 up). 1980. PLB 5.89 (ISBN 0-89375-450-1); pap. 2.50 (ISBN 0-89375-451-X). Troll Assocs.

Day in the Life of a Police Detective. David Paige. LC 80-54102. (Illus.). 32p. (gr. 4 up). 1980. PLB 5.89 (ISBN 0-89375-442-0); pap. 2.50. Troll Assocs.

Day in the Life of a School Basketball Coach. David Paige. LC 80-54101. (Illus.). 32p. (gr. 4 up). 1980. PLB 5.89 (ISBN 0-686-63461-6); pap. 2.50 (ISBN 0-89375-453-6). Troll Assocs.

Day in the Life of a Television News Reporter. William Jaspersohn. (Illus.). 96p. (gr. 5 up). 1981. 9.95 (ISBN 0-316-45813-9). Little.

Day in the Life of a Victorian Domestic Servant. Leonore Davidoff & Ruth Hawthorn. (Victorian Day Ser.). 1976. text ed. 10.95x o.p. (ISBN 0-04-942142-5); pap. text ed. 5.95x (ISBN 0-04-942143-3). Allen Unwin.

Day in the Life of a Victorian Factory Worker. Frank E. Huggett. (Victorian Day Ser.). 1973. pap. text ed. 5.95x (ISBN 0-04-942113-1). Allen Unwin.

Day in the Life of a Victorian Farm Worker. Frank E. Huggett. (Victorian Day Ser.). (Illus.). 1972. text ed. 12.50x (ISBN 0-04-942099-2); pap. text ed. 5.95x (ISBN 0-04-942100-X). Allen Unwin.

Day in the Life of a Victorian Policeman. John Garforth. (Victorian Day Ser.). 1974. pap. text ed. 5.95x (ISBN 0-04-942123-9). Allen Unwin.

Day in the Life of an Illustrator. Ken Witty. LC 80-54100. (Illus.). 32p. (gr. 4 up). 1980. PLB 5.89 (ISBN 0-89375-448-X); pap. 2.50 (ISBN 0-89375-449-8). Troll Assocs.

Day in the Life: The Beatles Day-by-Day 1960-1970. Tom Schultheiss. LC 79-91185. 1980. 11.95 (ISBN 0-87650-120-X). Pierian.

Day in the Zoo. LC 79-93050. (Illus.). 1980. 8.95 (ISBN 0-670-25919-5). Viking Pr.

Day Kennedy Was Shot. 2nd ed. Jim Bishop. LC 68-31633. (Funk & W Bk.). (Illus.). 1972. 9.95 o.s.i. (ISBN 0-308-70271-9, 770530, TYC-T). T Y Crowell.

Day Lincoln Was Shot. Jim Bishop. 1964. pap. 2.25 (ISBN 0-06-080005-4, P5, PL). Har-Row.

Day Man Lost: Hiroshima, 6 August 1945. Pacific War Research Society. LC 76-174219. (Illus.). 312p. 1972. 10.00x (ISBN 0-87011-174-4). Kodansha.

Day of Fate. Theodore A. Cheney. 288p. (Orig.). 1981. pap. 2.50 (ISBN 0-441-13908-6). Charter Bks.

Day of Fear. John Creasy. LC 77-73867. 1978. 6.95x o.p. (ISBN 0-03-022396-2). HR&W.

Day of Humiliation: Times of Affliction & Disaster. Cotton Mather. LC 68-24211. 1970. 41.00x (ISBN 0-8201-1067-1). Schol Facsimiles.

Day of San Jacinto. 2nd ed. Frank X. Tolbert. (Texas Heritage Ser). (Illus.). 1969. 12.95 (ISBN 0-8363-0025-4). Jenkins.

Day of Shining Red. Gilbert Lewis. LC 78-68354. (Studies in Social Anthropology: No. 27). 1980. 24.95 (ISBN 0-521-22278-8). Cambridge U Pr.

Day of Surprises. Sylvia R. Tester. LC 78-23263. (Illus.). (ps-3). 1979. PLB 5.95 (ISBN 0-89565-022-3). Childs World.

Day of the Blizzard. Moskin. (gr. 5). Date not set. pap. cancelled (ISBN 0-590-30092-X, Schol Pap). Schol Bk Serv.

Day of the Butterfly. Norah Lofts. 320p. 1981. pap. 2.95 (ISBN 0-449-24359-1, Crest). Fawcett.

Day of the Buzzard. T. V. Olsen. 1979. pap. 1.50 o.p. (ISBN 0-449-14161-6, GM). Fawcett.

Day of the Dolphin. Robert Merle. 1977. pap. 1.95 o.p. (ISBN 0-449-23240-9, Crest). Fawcett.

Day of the Drag Race. Philip Harkins. (gr. 7 up). 1960. 7.25 (ISBN 0-688-21223-9). Morrow.

Day of the Drag Race. Philip Harkins. (gr. 5-9). pap. 1.25 o.p. (ISBN 0-425-03705-3, Highland). Berkley Pub.

Day of the Earthlings. Eve Bunting. (Science Fiction Ser.). (Illus.). 32p. (gr. 3-9). 1978. PLB 5.95 (ISBN 0-87191-621-5); pap. 2.95 (ISBN 0-89812-054-3). Creative Ed.

Day of the Guns. Mickey Spillane. pap. 1.50 (ISBN 0-451-07512-9, W9092, Sig). NAL.

Day of the Guns. Mickey Spillane. Bd. with Death Dealers. 1981. pap. 2.95 (ISBN 0-451-09733-5, 9733, Sig). NAL.

Day of the Halfbreeds. Peter McCurtin. (Sundance Ser.: No. 29). 1979. pap. 1.75 (ISBN 0-8439-0693-6, Leisure Bks). Nordon Pubns.

Day of the Horse. Bernard Garbutt. (Illus.). 67p. 1976. 10.50 o.p. (ISBN 0-87358-145-8). Northland.

Day of the Ness. Andre Norton & Michael Gilbert. LC 74-78111. (Illus.). 128p. (gr. 3-7). 1975. 5.95 o.s.i. (ISBN 0-8027-6195-X). Walker & Co.

Day of the Pigeons. Roy Brown. LC 72-78079. (gr. 4-7). 1969. 4.50g o.s.i. (ISBN 0-02-714910-2). Macmillan.

Day of the Storm. Rosamunde Pilcher. LC 75-26190. 1976. 7.95 o.p. (ISBN 0-312-18445-X). St Martin.

Day of the Triffids. John Wyndham. 192p. 1981. pap. 2.50 (ISBN 0-449-23721-4, Crest). Fawcett.

Day of Their Return. Paul Anderson. pap. 1.50 (ISBN 0-451-07941-8, W7941, Sig). NAL.

Day Our TV Broke Down. Betty R. Wright. LC 80-14434. (Life & Living from a Child's Point of View Ser.). (Illus.). 32p. (gr. k-5). 1980. PLB 9.65 (ISBN 0-8172-1365-1). Raintree Pubs.

Day Outings. Colourmaster. (Travel in England Ser.). (Illus.). 96p. 1975. 7.95 (ISBN 0-85936-004-0). Transatlantic.

Day Richmond Died. A. A. Hoehling & Mary Hoehling. (Illus.). 272p. 1981. 12.95 (ISBN 0-498-02313-3). A S Barnes.

Day Services for Adults Somewhere to Go. Jan Carter. (National Institute Social Services Library: No. 40). 352p. 1981. text ed. 35.00x (ISBN 0-04-262035-X, 2620). Allen Unwin.

Day the Bubble Burst: A Social History of the Wall Street Crash of 1929. Gordon Thomas & Max Morgan-Witts. 1980. pap. 5.95 (ISBN 0-14-005640-8). Penguin.

Day the Circus Came to Lone Tree. Glen Rounds. LC 73-78458. (Illus.). (gr. k-3). 1973. reinforced bdg. 6.95 (ISBN 0-8234-0232-0). Holiday.

Day the Circus Came to Lone Tree. Glen Rounds. (gr. k-6). 1980. pap. 1.25 (ISBN 0-440-41769-4, YB). Dell.

Day the Cowboys Quit. Elmer Kelton. 1980. pap. 1.95 (ISBN 0-441-13907-8). Ace Bks.

Day the Dollar Dies: Biblical Prophecy of a New World System in the End Times. Willard Cantelon. LC 72-94186. 190p. 1973. 4.95 o.p. (ISBN 0-912106-92-1); pap. 2.50 (ISBN 0-88270-170-3). Logos.

Day the Laughter Stopped. David Yallop. LC 75-40810. (Illus.). 1976. 12.50 o.p. (ISBN 0-312-18410-7). St Martin.

Day the Music Died. Joseph C. Smith. LC 80-8914. 464p. 1981. 12.95 (ISBN 0-394-51951-5). Grove.

Day the Perfect Speakers Left. Leonard Nathan. LC 69-17791. (Wesleyan Poetry Program: Vol. 45). 1969. 10.00x (ISBN 0-8195-2045-4, Pub. by Wesleyan U Pr); pap. 4.95 (ISBN 0-8195-1045-9). Columbia U Pr.

Day the Sea Rolled by. Mickey Spillane. 128p. 1981. pap. 1.75 (ISBN 0-553-14597-5). Bantam.

Day the Sparrow Died. William K. Esler. (Orig.). 1980. pap. 2.25 (ISBN 0-532-23313-1). Manor Bks.

Day the Sun Fell. Robert L. Duncan. 1979. pap. 2.25 o.p. (ISBN 0-345-27167-X). Ballantine.

Day the Sun Stood Still - Three Original Novellas of Science Fiction. Poul Anderson et al. LC 77-38748. 1972. 7.95 o.p. (ISBN 0-525-66206-5). Elsevier-Nelson.

Day the Whores Came Out to Play Tennis & Other Plays. Arthur Kopit. Incl. Chamber Music; The Questioning of Nick; Sing to Me Through Open Windows; The Hero; The Conquest of Everest. 140p. (Orig.). 1965. pap. 3.95 (ISBN 0-8090-0736-3, Mermaid). Hill & Wang.

Day the World Ended. Sax Rohmer. 1976. Repr. of 1930 ed. lib. bdg. 13.10 (ISBN 0-89190-804-8). Am Repr-Rivercity Pr.

Day They Kidnapped Queen Victoria. H. K. Fleming. LC 77-18383. 1978. 7.95 o.p. (ISBN 0-312-18457-3). St Martin.

Day They Stole the Mona Lisa. Seymour V. Reit. 1981. 11.95 (ISBN 0-671-25056-6). Summit Bks.

Day Treatment & Other Partial Hospitals: A Comprehensive Guide. Geoffrey A. Di Bella et al. 450p. 1981. 30.00 (ISBN 0-87630-270-3). Brunner-Mazel.

Day Treatment Center: Principles, Application & Evaluation. 252p. 1966. pap. 11.25 spiral (ISBN 0-398-01284-9). C C Thomas.

Day with Charlotte Bronte. May C. Byron. 50p. 1980. Repr. lib. bdg. 8.50 (ISBN 0-8495-0462-7). Arden Lib.

Day X. Kurt E. Koch. LC 70-160688. 1969. pap. 2.50 (ISBN 0-8254-3005-4). Kregel.

Dayananda Sarasvati: His Life & Ideas. Jordans. 1979. 15.50x (ISBN 0-19-560995-6). Oxford U Pr.

Daydreams & Night. Elisabeth Nardine. LC 76-15240. (Moods & Emotions Ser.). (Illus.). 32p. (gr. k-3). 1976. PLB 8.95 (ISBN 0-8172-0014-2). Raintree Pubs.

Daykeeper: The Life & Discourse of As IXII Deliver. Benjamin N. Colby & Lore M. Colby. (Illus.). 352p. 1981. text ed. 25.00 (ISBN 0-674-19409-8). Harvard U Pr.

Daylight & Its Spectrum. 2nd ed. S. T. Henderson. LC 77-88254. 1978. 36.95 (ISBN 0-470-99328-6). Halsted Pr.

Daylight Must Come. Alan Burgess. (Illus.). 288p. 1975. 8.95 o.p. (ISBN 0-440-03365-9). Delacorte.

Daylight Must Come. Alan Burgess. 1978. pap. 2.50 (ISBN 0-87123-107-7, 200107). Bethany Fell.

Days & Nights at Costello's. Joe P. McCarthy. 288p. 1980. 12.95 (ISBN 0-316-55373-5). Little.

Day's End for Gunmen. Marion Chrisomalis. 1979. pap. 1.50 (ISBN 0-505-51450-8). Tower Bks.

Days of Augusta. Ed. by Jean E. Speare. LC 75-13479. (Illus.). 1977. pap. 5.95 sewn binding (ISBN 0-914842-04-8). Madrona Pubs.

Days of Blood. Charles R. Pike. LC 80-69749. (Jubal Cade Westerns Ser.). 125p. 1981. pap. 2.95 (ISBN 0-87754-238-4). Chelsea Hse.

Days of Commerce. Ed. by Bill Bradley. (Special Ser.: No.X-8). 1981. pap. write for info. (ISBN 0-916374-45-9). Interurban.

Days of Heaven & Earth. A. B. Simpson. 371p. 1945. pap. 1.50 o.p. (ISBN 0-686-65444-7). Chr Pubns.

Days of His Grace. Eyvind Johnson. LC 77-134666. 1970. 10.00 (ISBN 0-8149-0681-8). Vanguard.

Days of Sorrow & Pain: Leo Baeck & the Berlin Jews. Leonard Baker. (Illus.). 412p. 1980. pap. 7.95 (ISBN 0-19-502800-7, GB 611). Oxford U Pr.

Days of the Beloved. Harriet R. Lynton & Mohini Rajan. 1974. 15.75 (ISBN 0-520-02442-7); pap. 5.95 (ISBN 0-520-03939-4). U of Cal Pr.

Days of the Year. Joyce McLellan. (gr. 2-6). 1976. 3.15 (ISBN 0-08-006799-9). Pergamon.

Days on Sea, Loch & River. Muriel Foster. (Illus.). 124p. 1981. 4.95 (ISBN 0-7181-1788-3). Merrimack Bk Serv.

Days on the Wing: Being the War Memoirs of Major the Chevalier Willy Coppens De Houthulst D.S.O., M.C., Etc., Etc. Willy Coppens de Houthulst. Ed. by James Gilbert. Tr. by A. J. Insall. LC 79-7242. (Flight: Its First Seventy-Five Years Ser.). (Illus.). 1979. Repr. of 1931 ed. 22.00x (ISBN 0-405-12157-1). Arno.

Days Run Away Like Wild Horses Over the Hills. Charles Bukowski. 156p. (Orig.). 1979. 10.00 (ISBN 0-87685-006-9); pap. 5.00 (ISBN 0-87685-005-0). Black Sparrow.

Days That We Have Seen. George E. Evans. 1975. 12.95 (ISBN 0-571-10726-5, Pub. by Faber & Faber). Merrimack Bk Serv.

Days with Ulanova. Albert E. Kahn. LC 79-7770. (Dance Ser.). (Illus.). 1980. Repr. of 1962 ed. lib. bdg. 43.00x (ISBN 0-8369-9297-0). Arno.

Days Without Beginnings. Steven Shuecraft. 1981. 4.50 (ISBN 0-8062-1619-0). Carlton.

Dayspring. Ruth Archer. 1981. pap. 2.95 (ISBN 0-935236-18-X). Nurseco.

Dayspring: Words of Personal Prophecy for Daily Devotions. Anne White. LC 71-160700. 180p. 1971. pap. 4.95 (ISBN 0-912106-21-2). Logos.

Daystar & Shadow. James B. Johnson. (Science Fiction Ser.). 1981. pap. 1.95 (ISBN 0-87997-605-5, UJ1605, Daw Bks). DAW Bks.

Daytime Star: The Story of Our Sun. Simon Mitton. (Illus.). 192p. 1981. 14.95 (ISBN 0-684-16840-5, ScribT). Scribner.

Daytime TV's Star Directory. Paul Denis. 1976. pap. 1.50 o.p. (ISBN 0-445-03161-1). Popular Lib.

Daytona Five-Hundred. Julian May. LC 76-8443. (Sports Classics Ser.). (Illus.). (gr. 4-12). 1976. PLB 8.95 o.p. (ISBN 0-87191-522-7). Creative Ed.

Dazzle. Dora Landey & Elinor Klein. 416p. 1981. pap. 2.95 (ISBN 0-446-93476-3). Warner Bks.

Dazzled by Diamonds. Phyllis Kuhn. (Orig.). 1981. pap. 1.50 o.s.i. (ISBN 0-440-11710-0). Dell.

Dazzling Twenties. Edmund Lindop. LC 75-94767. (Modern America Ser). (Illus.). (gr. 7 up). 1970. PLB 4.33 o.p. (ISBN 0-531-01840-7). Watts.

DC Motors, Speed Controls, Servo Systems: An Engineering Handbook. 3rd, expanded ed. Electro-Craft Corp. LC 76-56647. 1977. text ed. 38.00 (ISBN 0-08-021714-1); pap. text ed. 16.50 (ISBN 0-08-021715-X). Pergamon.

DC Power Supplies: Application & Theory. Robert J. Traister. (Illus.). 1979. text ed. 16.95 (ISBN 0-8359-1275-2). Reston.

DC Super Heroes Super Healthy Cookbook. D. C. Comics. (Illus., Orig.). 1981. 8.95 (ISBN 0-446-51227-3). Warner Bks.

DDT: Scientists, Citizens, & Public Policy. Thomas R. Dunlap. LC 80-8546. 304p. 1981. 18.50x (ISBN 0-691-04680-8). Princeton U Pr.

De Abajo: Novela De la Revolucion Mexicana. rev. ed. Ed. by M. Azuela et al. 1971. pap. write for info. (ISBN 0-13-540690-0). P-H.

De-Addiction Process: Studies in the De-Addiction of Confirmed Heroin Addicts. Leon Brill. 180p. 1972. 18.75 (ISBN 0-398-02532-0). C C Thomas.

De Anima. Aristotle. Ed. by W. David Ross. (Oxford Classical Texts Ser). 1956. 14.95x (ISBN 0-19-814508-X). Oxford U Pr.

De Anima, Bks. 2 & 3. Aristotle. Tr. & intro. by D. W. Hamlyn. (Clarendon Aristotle Ser). 184p. (With certain passages from bk. 1). 1975. pap. 13.50x (ISBN 0-19-872076-9). Oxford U Pr.

De Anima of Alexander of Aphrodisias: A Translation & Commentary. Athanasios P. Fotinis. LC 80-5062. 362p. 1980. text ed. 20.00 (ISBN 0-8191-1032-9); pap. text ed. 12.00 (ISBN 0-8191-1033-7). U Pr of Amer.

De Arta Poetica of Marco Girolamo Vida. Ed. & tr. by Ralph G. Williams. 288p. 1976. 22.50x (ISBN 0-231-03959-X). Columbia U Pr.

De Arte Poetica. Aristotle. Ed. by Rudolf V. Kassel. (Oxford Classical Texts Ser.). 1965. 10.50x (ISBN 0-19-814564-0). Oxford U Pr.

De Bever Hall. Rosemary Folliott. (Illus.). 75p. 1976. 8.95 (ISBN 0-7156-1018-X, Pub. by Duckworth England). Biblio Dist.

De Canibus: Dog & Hound in Antiquity. R. H. Merlen. (Illus.). 8.75 (ISBN 0-85131-054-0, Dist. by Sporting Book Center). J A Allen.

De Canibus: Dog & Hound in Antiquity. Rene Merlin. 1972. 10.95 o.p. (ISBN 0-8277-1033-X). British Bk Ctr.

De Casibus Illustrium Virorum. Giovanni Boccaccio. LC 62-7017. 1962. Repr. of 1520 ed. 26.00x (ISBN 0-8201-1005-1). Schol Facsimiles.

De Coracao Para Coracao. Tr. by Willard Cantelon. (Portuguese Bks.). 1979. 1.00 (ISBN 0-8297-0657-7). Life Pubs Intl.

De Cristoforo's House Building Illustrated. R. J. De Cristoforo. LC 77-6659. (Popular Science Bk.). (Illus.). 1978. 18.95 (ISBN 0-06-010987-4, HarpT). Har-Row.

De Deis Gentium. Lilio G. Giraldi. LC 75-27850. (Renaissance & the Gods Ser.: Vol. 8). (Illus.). 1976. Repr. of 1548 ed. lib. bdg. 73.00 (ISBN 0-8240-2057-X). Garland Pub.

De-Gaming Teaching & Learning: How to Motivate Learners & Invite OKness. Richard J. Stapleton. LC 78-73696. (Illus., Orig.). 1979. pap. 15.00 (ISBN 0-933594-00-3). Effect Learning GA.

De Gaulle & European Unity. H. S. Chopra. LC 75-900442. 1974. 12.50 o.p. (ISBN 0-88386-551-3). South Asia Bks.

De la poesie dramatique. new ed. Denis Diderot. (Nouveaux Classiques Larousse). (Illus.). 1976. pap. 2.95 (ISBN 0-685-66282-9, 86). Larousse.

De la Prision a la Alabanza. Tr. by Merlin Carothers. (Spanish Bks.). (Span.). 1979. 1.60 (ISBN 0-8297-0447-7). Life Pubs Intl.

De la Propriete Ou la Cause Du Pauvre Plaidee Au Tribunal De la Raison, De la Justice et De la Verite. Antoine De Cournand. (Fr.). 1977. lib. bdg. 18.75x o.p. (ISBN 0-8287-0231-4); pap. text ed. 8.75x o.p. (ISBN 0-685-74922-3). Clearwater Pub.

De la Salle: A Pioneer of Modern Education. W. J. Battersby. 236p. 1981. Repr. of 1949 ed. lib. bdg. 40.00 (ISBN 0-89987-065-1). Darby Bks.

De la Terre a la Lune. Verne. (Easy Reader, C). pap. 3.75 (ISBN 0-88436-048-2, FRA201053). EMC.

De Lapsis & De Ecclesiae Catholicae Unitate. Cyprian. Ed. by Maurice Benevot. (Oxford Early Christian Texts Ser). 151p. 1971. 22.50x (ISBN 0-19-826804-1). Oxford U Pr.

De Laudibus Legum Anglie. John Fortescue. Intro. by S. B. Chrimes. LC 78-62331. 1979. Repr. of 1942 ed. 26.50 (ISBN 0-88355-793-2). Hyperion Conn.

De Levis Hours & the Bedford Workshop. Millard Meiss. 73p. 1981. text ed. 10.00x (ISBN 0-300-03507-1). Yale U Pr.

De l'Opera En France, 2 vols. Francois H. Blaze. LC 80-2259. 1981. Repr. of 1820 ed. Set. 82.50 (ISBN 0-404-18810-9). AMS Pr.

De Miseria Condicionis Humane. Ed. by Robert E. Lewis. LC 75-26119. 310p. 1978. 25.00 (ISBN 0-8203-0395-X). U of Ga Pr.

De Motu Cordis: Anatomical Studies on the Motion of the Heart & Blood. 5th ed. William Harvey. Tr. by Chauncey D. Leake. (Illus.). 186p. 1978. pap. 6.75 (ISBN 0-398-00793-4). C C Thomas.

De Pace Regis et Regni. Ferdinand Pulton. Ed. by David S. Berkowitz & Samuel E. Thorne. LC 77-86638. (Classics of English Legal History in the Modern Era Ser.: Vol.29). 574p. 1979. lib. bdg. 40.00 (ISBN 0-8240-3078-8). Garland Pub.

De Profundis: Grand Motet for Soloists, Chorus, Woodwinds, Strings, & Continuo. Michel-Richard Delalande. Ed. by James R. Anthony. LC 79-29740. viii, 173p. 1981. write for info. (ISBN 0-8078-1439-3). U of NC Pr.

De Que Hablamos? George E. Starnes & Oscar Fernandez. (Orig., Span.). 1981. Repr. of 1952 ed. pap. text ed. 9.50x. Irvington.

De re aedificatoria. Leon B. Alberti. (Documents of Art & Architectural History Series 2: Vol. 1). 420p. (Latin.). 1981. Repr. of 1485 ed. 45.00x (ISBN 0-89371-201-9). Broude Intl Edns

De Republica Anglorum: A Discourse on the Commonwealth of England. Thomas Smith. 210p. 1972. Repr. of 1583 ed. 23.00x (ISBN 0-686-28335-X, Pub. by Irish Academic Pr). Biblio Dist.

De Rerum Natura. Lucretius. Ed. by Ed Kenney. (Cambridge Greek & Latin Classics Ser.: Bk. 3). 34.50 (ISBN 0-521-08142-4); pap. 11.95x (ISBN 0-521-29177-1). Cambridge U Pr.

De Rerum Natura, Bk. 5. Lucretius. Ed. by James D. Duff. text ed. 4.50x (ISBN 0-521-05610-1). Cambridge U Pr.

De-Romanization of the American Catholic Church. Wakin & Scheuer. 3.95 o.p. (ISBN 0-452-25009-9, Z5009, Plume). NAL.

De Sade: A Critical Biography. Ronald Hayman. LC 78-3170. 1978. 12.95 o.s.i. (ISBN 0-690-01416-3, TYC-T). T Y Crowell.

De Sapientia Veterum, Repr. Of 1609 Ed. Francis Bacon. Bd. with Wisedome of the Ancients. Tr. by Arthur Gorges. Repr. of 1619 ed. LC 75-27863. (Renaissance & the Gods Ser.: Vol. 20). (Illus.). 1976. lib. bdg. 73.00 (ISBN 0-8240-2068-5). Garland Pub.

De-Schooling Society. Ivan Illich. Ed. by Ruth N. Anshen. LC 74-138738. (World Perspectives). 1971. 8.95 o.s.i. (ISBN 0-06-012139-4, HarpT). Har-Row.

De sculptura. Pomponio Gaurico. (Documents of Art & Architectural History Series 2: Vol. 2). 104p. (Latin.). 1981. Repr. of 1504 ed. 25.00x (ISBN 0-89371-202-7). Broude Intl Edns.

De Soto. (gr. 1). 1974. pap. text ed. 2.80 (ISBN 0-205-03875-1, 8038759); tchrs'. guide 12.00 (ISBN 0-205-03866-2, 803866X). Allyn.

De Soto: Finder of the Mississippi. Ronald Syme. (Illus.). (gr. 3-7). 1957. PLB 6.96 (ISBN 0-688-31224-1). Morrow.

De Stael - Du Pont Letters: Correspondence of Madame De Stael & Pierre Samuel Du Pont De Nemours, & of Other Members of the Necker & Du Pont Families. Tr. by James F. Marshall. (Illus.). 1968. 35.00 (ISBN 0-299-05061-0). U of Wis Pr.

De Theologia Gentili, 3 vols. Gerardus Vossius. LC 75-27872. (Renaissance & the Gods Ser.: Vol. 28). (Illus.). 1977. Repr. of 1641 ed. Set. lib. bdg. 219.00 (ISBN 0-8240-2077-4). Garland Pub.

De Vita Agricolae. 2nd ed. Tacitus. Ed. by R. M. Ogilvie et al. (Illus.). 1967. 17.50x (ISBN 0-19-814438-5). Oxford U Pr.

De Witt Colony of Texas. Edward A. Lukes. LC 76-14583. (Illus.). 1976. 14.95 (ISBN 0-8363-0148-X). Jenkins.

Deacon & His Work. James D. Bales. pap. 1.95 (ISBN 0-89315-025-8). Lambert Bk.

Deacon & the Jewess: Adventures in Heresy. Samuel Meyer. LC 80-84734. 1981. 10.00 (ISBN 0-8022-2379-6). Philos Lib.

Deacon at Work. Frederick A. Agar. 1923. 3.25 (ISBN 0-8170-0783-0). Judson.

Deacon in the Church. Edward P. Echlin. LC 75-158571. 1971. 4.95 (ISBN 0-8189-0213-2). Alba.

Deacon of Dobbinsville. John A. Morrison. 64p. pap. 0.60. Faith Pub Hse.

Dead. Hank Harrison. LC 79-56661. (Illus.). 336p. (Orig.). 1980. 14.95 (ISBN 0-89087-282-1); pap. 9.95 (ISBN 0-89087-300-3). Celestial Arts.

Dead & Buried. Chelsea Q. Yarbro. (Orig.). 1980. pap. 2.75 (ISBN 0-446-95886-7). Warner Bks.

Dead As the Dodo. Lynne Edwards. LC 72-6957. (Illus.). 40p. (ps-3). 1973. 5.95 o.s.i. (ISBN 0-8193-0640-1, Four Winds); PLB 5.41 o.s.i. (ISBN 0-8193-0641-X). Schol Bk Serv.

Dead Color. Charles Wright. (Fine Press Poetry Ser.). (Illus.). 20p. 1980. fabriano covers, signed 45.00 (ISBN 0-931356-04-0). Seluzicki Poetry.

Dead Fingers. Elisabeth Sutton. 295p. 1980. Repr. lib. bdg. 15.25x (ISBN 0-89968-208-1). Lightyear.

Dead Freight for Piute. Luke Short. 160p. (Orig.). 1981. pap. 1.95 (ISBN 0-553-13553-8). Bantam.

Dead Heat. Raymond Obstfeld. 224p. (Orig.). 1981. pap. 2.25 (ISBN 0-441-14110-2). Charter Bks.

Dead in the Water. Brock Yates. 224p. 1975. 7.95 o.p. (ISBN 0-374-13544-4). FS&G.

Dead Man's Canyon. John Benteen. (Sundance: No. 2). 1979. pap. 1.75 (ISBN 0-8439-0709-6, Leisure Bks). Nordon Pubns.

Dead Man's Noose. Morgan Hill. (Orig.). 1980. pap. 1.95 (ISBN 0-440-12073-X). Dell.

Dead Man's Tears. Joel Newman. LC 80-27171. 192p. 1981. 9.95 (ISBN 0-8253-0035-5). Beaufort Bks NY.

Dead Men's Plans. Mignon G. Eberhart. 176p. 1974. pap. 0.95 o.p. (ISBN 0-445-00549-1). Popular Lib.

Dead Moon. Leo P. Kelley. LC 78-68228. (Galaxy Five Ser.). (Illus.). 64p. (gr. 4 up). 1980. PLB 7.95 (ISBN 0-516-02251-2). Childrens.

Dead Piano. Henry Van Dyke. 182p. 1971. 5.95 o.p. (ISBN 0-374-13550-9). FS&G.

Dead Reckoning. C. Northcote Parkinson. LC 80-81631. 272p. 1980. pap. 2.25 (ISBN 0-87216-728-3). Playboy Pbks.

Dead Runner. Frank Ross. 1978. pap. 1.75 o.p. (ISBN 0-449-23454-1, Crest). Fawcett.

Dead Sea Scrolls. J. M. Allegro. 1956. pap. 3.50 (ISBN 0-14-020376-1, Pelican). Penguin.

Dead Sea Scrolls. Menahem Mansoor. 1964. Repr. 4.95 o.p. (ISBN 0-8028-3181-8). Eerdmans.

Dead Sea Scrolls & the Bible. rev. & enl. ed. Charles F. Pfeiffer. Ed. by Charles F. Pfeiffer. (Baker Studies in Biblical Archaeology). (Illus.). 1969. pap. 3.95 (ISBN 0-8010-6898-3). Baker Bk.

Dead Sea Scrolls in English. Geza Vermes. (Orig.). 1962. pap. 3.50 (ISBN 0-14-020551-9, Pelican). Penguin.

Dead Sea Scrolls: Major Publications & Tools for Study. Joseph A. Fitzmyer. LC 75-5987. (Society of Biblical Literature. Sources for Biblical Study). xiv, 171p. 1975. pap. 7.50 (ISBN 0-88414-053-9, 060308). Scholars Pr Ca.

Dead Sea Scrolls: Qumran in Perspective. Geza Vermes. LC 80-2382. 240p. 1981. pap. 8.50 (ISBN 0-8006-1435-6, 1-1435). Fortress.

Dead Side of the Mike. Simon Brett. 1980. 8.95 (ISBN 0-684-16729-8, ScribT). Scribner.

Dead Skip. Joe Gores. 1981. pap. 2.25 (ISBN 0-345-29206-5). Ballantine.

Dead Tree. Alvin Tresselt. LC 72-174601. (gr. k-4). 1972. PLB 5.41 o.s.i. (ISBN 0-8193-0564-2, Four Winds). Schol Bk Serv.

Dead Wrong. William Doxey. 1980. pap. 1.75 (ISBN 0-505-51455-9). Tower Bks.

Dead Zone. Stephen King. 1980. pap. 3.50 (ISBN 0-451-09338-0, E9338, Sig). NAL.

Deadfall. Jane MacLean. 1979. 9.95 o.p. (ISBN 0-525-10585-9, Thomas Congdon Book). Dutton.

Deadlier Than the Male. J. C. Conaway. 1977. pap. 1.50 (ISBN 0-505-51160-6). Tower Bks.

Deadliest Game. Mike Jahn. (Rockford Ser.: No. 2). 192p. 1976. pap. 1.25 o.p. (ISBN 0-445-00354-5). Popular Lib.

Deadliest Profession. Tiny Boyles & Hank Nuwer. LC 80-83561. 224p. (Orig.). 1981. pap. 2.50 (ISBN 0-87216-804-2). Playboy Pbks.

Deadline. John Dunning. 224p. (Orig.). 1981. pap. 2.50 (ISBN 0-449-14398-8, GM). Fawcett.

Deadline for McGurk. E. W. Hildick. LC 74-20616. (Illus.). 112p. (gr. 4-6). 1975. 5.95g o.s.i. (ISBN 0-02-743800-7). Macmillan.

Deadline for McGurk: A McGurk Mystery, No. 1. E. W. Hildick. (Illus.). (gr. 3-5). 1978. pap. 1.50 (ISBN 0-671-56107-3). PB.

Deadly Amigos: Two Graves for a Gunman. Barry Cord. 1979. pap. 2.25 (ISBN 0-505-51419-2). Tower Bks.

Deadly Bugs & Killer Insects. Hal Hellman. LC 78-17403. 192p. (gr. 5 up). 1978. 6.95 (ISBN 0-87131-269-7). M Evans.

Deadly Companions. Bob Sang & Dusty Sang. 1978. pap. 1.50 (ISBN 0-505-51243-2). Tower Bks.

Deadly Diamonds. Laurence Swinburne & Irene Swinburne. LC 77-10764. (Great Unsolved Mysteries Ser.). (Illus.). (gr. 4-5). 1977. PLB 9.65 (ISBN 0-8172-1064-4). Raintree Pubs.

Deadly Dinner. J. A. Senn. Ed. by Mary Verdick. (Pal Paperbacks, Pal Skills Ser.). (Illus., Orig.). (gr. 7-12). 1978. pap. text ed. 1.25 (ISBN 0-8374-6711-X). Xerox Ed Pubns.

Deadly Document. Michael Bar Zohar. 1981. pap. 2.50 (ISBN 0-440-12165-5). Dell.

Deadly Duo: The B25-B26 in World War Two. Charles A. Mendenhall. (Illus.). 200p. 1981. write for info. (ISBN 0-933424-22-1). Specialty Pr.

Deadly Element: The Story of Uranium. Lennard Bickel. LC 78-66243. (Illus.). 320p. 1980. pap. 7.95 (ISBN 0-8128-6089-6). Stein & Day.

Deadly Encounter. Richard Woodley. 192p. (Orig.). 1980. pap. 1.95 (ISBN 0-515-04844-5). Jove Pubns.

Deadly Frost. Terrence Moon. 1980. pap. 2.75 (ISBN 0-345-28947-1). Ballantine.

Deadly Game at Stoney Creek. Peter Z. Cohen. (Orig.). (gr. 6-12). 1980. pap. 1.25 (ISBN 0-440-91288-1, LFL). Dell.

Deadly Gold. John Rossiter. 1977. pap. 1.25 o.p. (ISBN 0-445-04077-7). Popular Lib.

Deadly Hoax. Scott Corbett. LC 80-26552. (gr. 5 up). 1981. PLB 9.95 (ISBN 0-525-28585-7). Dutton.

Deadly Legacy. Yvonne MacManus. 256p. 1981. pap. 2.25 (ISBN 0-523-41259-2). Pinnacle Bks.

Deadly Magic. Edward Van Der Rhoer. LC 78-17120. (Illus.). 1978. 9.95 o.p. (ISBN 0-684-15873-6, ScribT). Scribner.

Deadly Party. Linda DuBreuil. 1979. pap. 1.50 (ISBN 0-505-51374-9). Tower Bks.

Deadly Prey. Ralph Hayes. (Hunter Ser). (Orig.). 1975. pap. 1.25 o.p. (ISBN 0-685-53130-9, LB277ZK, Leisure Bks). Nordon Pubns.

Deadly Pursuit. Marcia Miller. 192p. (YA) 1976. 5.95 (ISBN 0-685-66477-5, Avalon). Bouregy.

Deadly Quarrels: Lewis F. Richardson & the Statistical Study of War. David Wilkinson. 1980. 18.50 (ISBN 0-520-03829-0). U of Cal Pr.

Deadly Routine. Jack Morris. LC 80-82429. (Illus.). 210p. 1980. wkbk 8.95 (ISBN 0-686-28036-9). Palmer Pub CA.

Deadly Seeds. Warren Murphy. (Destroyer Ser.: No. 21). 192p. (Orig.). 1975. pap. 1.50 (ISBN 0-523-40295-3). Pinnacle Bks.

Deadly Shade of Gold. John D. MacDonald. LC 73-20286. 1974. 7.50 o.s.i. (ISBN 0-397-01032-X). Lippincott.

Deadly Silents. Lee Killogh. 256p. (Orig.). 1981. pap. 2.25 (ISBN 0-345-28780-0, Del Rey). Ballantine.

Deadly Spring. Jim Conaway. 1976. pap. 1.50 o.p. (ISBN 0-685-72567-7, LB395). Nordon Pubns.

Deadly State of Mind. Lee Hays. (Columbo: No. 6). 1976. pap. 1.50 o.p. (ISBN 0-445-03118-2). Popular Lib.

Deadly Words. Jeanne Favret-Saada. Tr. by Catherine Cullen from Fr. LC 79-41607. (Illus.). 1981. 45.00 (ISBN 0-521-22317-2); pap. text ed. 12.95 (ISBN 0-521-29787-7). Cambridge U Pr.

Deadman's Cocktail. Bruce Crowther. 1978. 7.95 o.s.i. (ISBN 0-8027-5385-X). Walker & Co.

Deadwood City. Edward Packard. (Choose Your Own Adventure Ser.: No. 8). 128p. 1980. pap. 1.50 (ISBN 0-553-13994-0). Bantam.

Deadwood: The Golden Years. Watson Parker. LC 80-24100. (Illus.). xiv, 293p. 1981. 17.50 (ISBN 0-8032-0973-8). U of Nebr Pr.

Deaf Adult Speaks Out. 2nd, rev. ed. Leo M. Jacobs. xiv, 192p. 1981. 7.95 (ISBN 0-913580-63-5); pap. 5.95 (ISBN 0-913580-71-6). Gallaudet Coll.

Deaf-Blind Children & Their Education: Proceedings. International Conference, St. Michielsgestel, Netherlands, August 25-29, 1968. (Modern Approaches to the Diagnosis & Instruction of Multi-Handicapped Children Ser.: Vol. 2). 150p. 1971. text ed. 21.50 (ISBN 90-237-4102-1, Pub. by Swets Pub Serv Holland). Swets North Am.

Deaf Child & His Family. Susan Gregory. LC 75-39523. 1976. 19.95 (ISBN 0-470-32662-X). Halsted Pr.

Deaf Heritage: A Narrative History of Deaf America. Jack Gannon. 1981. text ed. 19.00x (ISBN 0-913072-38-9); pap. text ed. 12.00x (ISBN 0-913072-39-7). Natl Assn Deaf.

Deafness. June Hyman. (gr. 4 up). 1980. PLB 6.45 (ISBN 0-531-02940-9). Watts.

Deafness & Child Development. Kathryn P. Meadow. LC 74-81435. 1980. 12.95 (ISBN 0-520-02819-8). U of Cal Pr.

Deafness & Learning: A Psycho-Social Approach. Hans G. Furth. 140p. 1973. pap. 7.95x (ISBN 0-534-00231-5). Wadsworth Pub.

Deafness & Mental Health. Laszlo K. Stein et al. 1981. write for info. (ISBN 0-8089-1347-6). Grune.

Deafness & Public Responsibility. Peter Gregory. 56p. 1964. pap. text ed. 3.75x (Pub. by Bedford England). Renouf.

Deafness in Infancy & Early Childhood. Ed. by Peter J. Fine. LC 73-17327. 250p. 1974. 13.95 o.p. (ISBN 0-683-03208-9). Williams & Wilkins.

Dealer's Choice. Adrienne Palmer. 1978. pap. 1.75 (ISBN 0-505-51323-4). Tower Bks.

Dealer's Special. Mike Newman. 1979. pap. 2.95 (ISBN 0-89650-672-X, Gambler's Book Shelf). Gamblers.

Dealing on the London Metal Exchange & Commodity Markets. Ed. by M. C. Brackenbury et al. 1976. 22.50 (ISBN 0-9504936-0-0, Pub. by Kogan Pg). Nichols Pub.

Dealing with Alcoholism in the Workplace, Report No. 784. Richard M. Weiss. (Illus.). vii, 59p. (Orig.). 1980. pap. 15.00 (ISBN 0-8237-0220-0). Conference Bd.

Dealing with Crisis: A Guide to Critical Life Problems. Lawrence G. Calhoun. 1976. 14.95 (ISBN 0-13-197723-7, Spec); pap. 4.95 (ISBN 0-13-197715-6). P-H.

Dealing with Data. A. J. Lyon. LC 76-92111. 1970. text ed. 28.00 (ISBN 0-08-006398-5); pap. text ed. 17.00 (ISBN 0-08-006397-7). Pergamon.

Dealing with Death. 1973. pap. 3.00 (ISBN 0-88474-025-0). USC Andrus Geron.

Dealing with Hunger. Lord Walston. 1977. 10.00 (ISBN 0-370-10464-1). Transatlantic.

Dealing with Problem People. A. Sunier. 84p. 1980. pap. text ed. 8.50x (ISBN 90-232-1761-6). Humanities.

Dealing with Violence: The Challenge Faced by Police & Other Peacekeepers. Karl L. Schonborn. (Illus.). 376p. 1975. 22.75 (ISBN 0-398-03333-1); pap. 16.75 (ISBN 0-398-03334-X). C C Thomas.

Dealmakers. Charles Dennis. (Orig.). 1981. pap. 2.95 (ISBN 0-440-11852-2). Dell.

Dean Acheson: The State Department Years. David S. McLellan. LC 76-8482. (Illus.). 1976. 17.50 (ISBN 0-396-07313-1). Dodd.

Dean Rusk. Warren I. Cohen. (American Secretaries of State & Their Diplomacy: Vol. XIX). 375p. 1980. 22.50x (ISBN 0-8154-0519-7). Cooper Sq.

Dean Tucker & Eighteenth Century Economic & Political Thought. W. G. Shelton. LC 79-29742. 1980. write for info. (ISBN 0-312-18538-3). St Martin.

Deane's Doctrine of Naval Architecture 1670. Brian Lavery. 192p. 1980. 69.50x (ISBN 0-85177-180-7, Pub. by Conway Maritime England). State Mutual Bk.

Dean's Death. Jan Hartman. (Columbo: No. 2). 1975. pap. 1.25 o.p. (ISBN 0-445-00265-4). Popular Lib.

Dean's List. Roy Dean. (Illus.). 1980. write for info. Rho-Delta Pr.

Dear America. Ed. by Seymour Connor. LC 70-172388. 1971. 8.50 (ISBN 0-685-02299-4). Jenkins.

Dear & Glorious Physician. Taylor Caldwell. LC 58-12032. 1959. 9.95 o.p. (ISBN 0-385-05215-4). Doubleday.

Dear & Glorious Physician. Taylor Caldwell. 608p. 1981. pap. 3.50 (ISBN 0-553-14246-1). Bantam.

Dear Angie: Your Family Is Getting a Divorce. Carol Nelson. LC 79-57210. (gr. 5-8). 1980. pap. 2.50 (ISBN 0-89191-246-0). Cook.

Dear Boris: The Life of William Henry Pratt, a.k.a. Boris Karloff. Cynthia Lindsay. 1975. 12.50 o.p. (ISBN 0-394-47579-8). Knopf.

Dear-Bought Heritage. Eugenie A. Leonard. LC 64-24496. (Illus.). 1965. 15.00x o.p. (ISBN 0-8122-7436-9). U of Pa Pr.

Dear Bruce Lee. Ohara Publications. (Series 407). pap. 7.95 (ISBN 0-89750-069-5). Ohara Pubns.

Dear Dad, Love, Jane. Jane A. Frees. (Illus.). 1980. 9.95 (ISBN 0-8323-0361-5). Binford.

Dear Dark Faces. Ed. by Helen E. Simcox. (Illus.). 110p. (Orig.). 1980. pap. 6.00 perf. bound (ISBN 0-916418-23-5). Lotus.

Dear Dr. Salk: Answers to Your Questions About Your Family. Lee Salk. 1980. pap. 2.50 (ISBN 0-446-91486-X). Warner Bks.

Dear Ellen: Two Mormon Women & Their Letters. S. George Ellsworth. (Utah, the Mormons, & the West: No. 3). 1974. 12.00 (ISBN 0-87480-159-1, Tanner). U of Utah Pr.

Dear Georgia. Beulah F. Stevens. LC 78-13546. 1979. pap. 0.65 (ISBN 0-8127-0204-2). Southern Pub.

Dear Heavenly Father: Letters from an Adopted Son. T. T. Martin. 1978. 4.50 o.p. (ISBN 0-682-49049-0). Exposition.

Dear Hildegarde. Bernard Waber. (gr. 3 up). 1980. 4.95 (ISBN 0-395-29745-1). HM.

Dear Jeffie: Being the Letters from Jeffries Wyman to His Son Jeffries Wyman, Jr. Ed. by George E. Gifford. LC 78-58830. (gr. 6 up). 1978. 10.00 (ISBN 0-87365-796-9). Peabody Harvard.

Dear Liberty: Connecticut's Mobilization for the Revolutionary War. Richard Buel, Jr. 432p. 1980. 22.50x (ISBN 0-8195-5047-7). Wesleyan U Pr.

Dear Lola: Or How to Build Your Own Family: a Tale. Judie Angell. LC 80-15111. 160p. (gr. 4-6). 8.95 (ISBN 0-87888-170-0). Bradbury Pr.

Dear Me. Edita Morris. LC 67-27522. 1967. 5.00 o.s.i. (ISBN 0-8076-0425-9). Braziller.

Dear Once. Zelda Popkin. LC 75-11870. 384p. 1975. 8.95 o.s.i. (ISBN 0-397-01053-2). Lippincott.

Dear Osborne. John A. Matson. (Illus.). 1978. 17.95 (ISBN 0-241-89870-6, Pub. by Hamish Hamilton England). David & Charles.

Dear Papa. Thyre F. Bjorn. 1976. pap. 1.75 (ISBN 0-89129-138-5). Jove Pubns.

Dear Parrot. John Phillips. (Illus.). 1979. 5.95 (ISBN 0-517-53868-7). Potter.

Dear Rat. Julia Cunningham. (gr. 2-5). 1976. pap. 1.50 (ISBN 0-380-00908-0, 46615, Camelot). Avon.

Dear Russell-Dear Jourdain. Ed. by I. Grattan-Guinness. LC 77-9431. 1977. 22.50x (ISBN 0-231-04460-7). Columbia U Pr.

Dear Sarah. Elisabeth Borchers. Tr. by Elisabeth Shub from Ger. LC 80-14512. (Illus.). 32p. (gr. k-3). 1981. 9.95 (ISBN 0-688-80277-X); PLB 9.55 (ISBN 0-688-84277-1). Greenwillow.

Dear Teacher. Diana Lize & Emile Lize. (Illus.). 75p. 1980. pap. 3.95 o.p. (ISBN 0-919676-22-7, 1657). Caroline Hse.

Dear Theo: The Autobiography of Vincent Van Gogh. Ed. by Irving Stone. LC 46-4152. (Illus.). 12.95 (ISBN 0-385-17197-8). Doubleday.

Dear World: A Collection of Form Letters for You to Use & Enjoy. Sally Minnick. 1981. 7.95. Green Hill.

Dear Worried Brown Eyes. Rosemary Ratcliff. 1969. 10.00 (ISBN 0-08-007041-8). Pergamon.

Dearest Debbie. Dale E. Rogers. 1966. pap. 1.25 o.s.i. (ISBN 0-89129-073-7). Jove Pubns.

Death. Lydia Anderson. (gr. 4 up). 1980. PLB 6.45 (ISBN 0-531-04107-7). Watts.

Death: A Bibliographical Guide. Albert J. Miller & Michael J. Acri. LC 77-1205. 1977. 19.50 (ISBN 0-8108-1025-5). Scarecrow.

Death After Breakfast. Hugh Pentecost. 1980. pap. 2.25 (ISBN 0-440-11687-2). Dell.

Death & After Death. George E. Barker. LC 78-65349. 1978. pap. text ed. 7.25 (ISBN 0-8191-0653-4). U Pr of Amer.

Death & Bereavement. Austin H. Kutscher. 392p. 1974. 16.75 (ISBN 0-398-01070-6); pap. 12.50 (ISBN 0-398-03293-9). C C Thomas.

Death & Beyond. Andrew Greeley. 1976. pap. 5.95 (ISBN 0-88347-062-4). Thomas More.

Death & Burial in the Roman World. J. M. Toynbee. Ed. by H. H. Scullard. LC 77-120603. (Aspects of Greek & Roman Life Ser). (Illus.). 336p. 1971. 19.50x (ISBN 0-8014-0593-9); pap. 4.95 o.p. (ISBN 0-8014-9165-7). Cornell U Pr.

Death & Dying A to Z. LC 80-65302. 1980. 69.00 (ISBN 0-87514-007-6). Croner.

Death & Dying: Challenge & Change. Ed. by Robert Fulton. (Illus.). 1978. lib. bdg. 12.00 o.p. (ISBN 0-201-07724-8); pap. 5.95 o.p. (ISBN 0-201-07723-X); pap. text ed. 9.95 o.p. (ISBN 0-201-07722-1); tchr's ed. 1.95 o.p. (ISBN 0-201-07727-2). A-W.

Death & Dying: Opposing Viewpoints. Ed. by David L. Bender. (Opposing Viewpoints Ser.). (gr. 12). 1980. lib. bdg. 8.95 (ISBN 0-89908-331-5); pap. text ed. 3.95 (ISBN 0-89908-306-4). Greenhaven.

Death & Eternal Life. John H. Hick. LC 76-9965. 1977. 15.00 o.p. (ISBN 0-06-063901-6, HarpR). Har-Row.

Death & Eternal Life. John H. Hick. LC 76-9965. 496p. 1980. pap. text ed. 9.95 (ISBN 0-06-063904-0, RD 332, HarpR). Har-Row.

Death & I Ching: A/Mystery Novel. Lulla Rosenfeld. Ed. by Carol Southern. 192p. 1981. 9.95 (ISBN 0-517-54029-0). Potter.

Death & Letters. Elizabeth Daly. 1981. pap. 2.25 (ISBN 0-440-11791-7). Dell.

Death & Letters of Alice James: Selected Correspondence. Ed. by Ruth B. Yeazell. (Illus.). 200p. 1980. 12.95 (ISBN 0-520-03745-6). U of Cal Pr.

Death & Life. Otto Kaiser & Eduard Lohse. Tr. by John E. Steely. LC 80-21265. (Biblical Encounter Ser.). 176p. 1981. pap. 6.95 (ISBN 0-687-10332-0). Abingdon.

Death & Life in the Tenth Century. Eleanor S. Duckett. (Illus.). 1971. pap. 3.45 o.p. (ISBN 0-472-06172-0, 172, AA). U of Mich Pr.

Death & Ministry: Pastoral Care of the Dying & Bereaved. Donald Bane & Austin H. Kutscher. 196p. 1975. 10.95 (ISBN 0-8164-0260-4). Crossroad NY.

Death & Nachiketas. M. Sivaram. 192p. 1981. text ed. 15.00x (ISBN 0-7069-1284-5, Pub by Vikas India). Advent Bk.

Death & the Caring Community. Larry Richards & Paul Johnson. LC 80-19752. (Critical Concern Bks.). 1981. 8.95 (ISBN 0-930014-45-6). Multnomah.

Death & the Creative Life. Lisl M. Goodman. 1981. text ed. price not set (ISBN 0-8261-3500-5). Springer Pub.

Death & the Dancing Footman. Ngaio Marsh. (Ngaio Marsh Mysteries Ser.). pap. 1.95 (ISBN 0-515-05409-7). Jove Pubns.

Death & the Devil. Adolf Holl. 1976. 9.95 (ISBN 0-8164-0313-9). Crossroad NY.

Death & the Family. Lily Pincus. 1976. pap. 2.95 (ISBN 0-394-71900-X, Vin). Random.

Death & the Good Life. Richard Hugo. 192p. 1981. 10.95 (ISBN 0-312-18588-X). St Martin.

Death & the Magician. Raymund FitzSimons. LC 80-21071. 1981. 10.95 (ISBN 0-689-11122-3). Atheneum.

Death & Variations. Ivon Baker. LC 77-157. Date not set. cancelled (ISBN 0-312-18880-3). St Martin.

Death & Western Thought. Jacques Choron. LC 62-17575. 320p. 1973. 6.95 o.s.i. (ISBN 0-02-525200-3). Macmillan.

Death Anxiety: The Loss of the Self. James B. McCarthy. 1980. 19.95 (ISBN 0-470-26508-6). Halsted Pr.

Death As a Fact of Life. David Hendin. 224p. 1974. pap. 2.25 o.s.i. (ISBN 0-446-92241-2). Warner Bks.

Death As in Matador. L. V. Roper. 176p. (Orig.). 1975. pap. 0.95 o.p. (ISBN 0-445-00644-7). Popular Lib.

Death As the Curtain Rises. Philips Judson. 192p. 1981. 8.95 (ISBN 0-396-07954-7). Dodd.

Death at the Bar. Ngaio Marsh. 1979. pap. 1.75 o.p. (ISBN 0-425-04082-8). Berkley Pub.

Death at the Bar. Ngaio Marsh. (Ngaio Marsh Mysteries Ser.). pap. 1.95 (ISBN 0-515-05641-3). Jove Pubns.

Death Bed. Stephen Greenleaf. 306p. 1980. 10.95 (ISBN 0-686-69082-6). Dial.

Death Before Bedtime. Edgar Box. LC 79-10248. 1979. pap. 1.95 (ISBN 0-394-74053-X, V-53, Vin). Random.

Death Before Birth. Harold O. Brown. LC 77-13884. 1977. 5.95 o.p. (ISBN -08407-5119-2). Nelson.

Death by Dreaming. Jon M. White. 160p. 1981. 10.95 (ISBN 0-918222-27-3). Apple Wood.

Death by Narration. Debby Knight. 48p. 1981. 5.95 (ISBN 0-89962-051-5). Todd & Honeywell.

Death Check. Warren Murphy. (Destroyer Ser.: No. 2). 192p. 1980. pap. 1.95 (ISBN 0-523-41217-7). Pinnacle Bks.

Death Comes As the End. Agatha Christie. 1977. pap. 2.50 (ISBN 0-671-43283-4). PB.

Death Comes Dancing: Celebrating Life with Bhagwan Shree Rajneesh. Ma Satya Bharti. 200p. 1981. pap. 9.95 (ISBN 0-7100-0705-1). Routledge & Kegan.

Death Cry of an Eagle: The Rise and Fall of Christian Values in the United States. Rene Noorbergen. 192p. 1980. pap. 5.95 (ISBN 0-310-30431-8). Zondervan.

Death: Current Perspectives. Ed. by Edwin S. Shneidman. LC 75-21075. 1976. pap. 10.95 o.p. (ISBN 0-87484-332-4). Mayfield Pub.

Death: Current Perspectives. 2nd ed. Ed. by Edwin S. Shneidman. LC 80-81360. 557p. 1980. pap. text ed. 12.95 (ISBN 0-87484-508-4). Mayfield Pub.

Death Customs: An Analytical Study of Burial Rites. Effie Bendann. 1971. 20.00 (ISBN 0-8103-3733-9). Gale.

Death Dance. Peter McCurtin. (Sundance Ser.: No. 27). 1979. pap. 1.75 (ISBN 0-8439-0669-3, Leisure Bks). Nordon Pubns.

Death Dealers. Ed. by Robert Weinberg. LC 80-8667. 80p. 1980. lib. bdg. 11.95 (ISBN 0-89370-099-1); pap. 5.95 (ISBN 0-89370-097-5). Borgo Pr.

Death Drive. George Gilman. (Edge Ser.: No. 27). 1978. pap. 1.75 (ISBN 0-523-41309-2, Dist. by Independent News Co.). Pinnacle Bks.

Death, Dying, & Euthanasia. Ed. by Dennis J. Horan & David Mall. 1977. 24.00 (ISBN 0-89093-139-9); pap. 10.00 (ISBN 0-89093-140-2). U Pubns Amer.

Death, Dying, & the Biological Revolution: Our Last Quest for Responsibility. Robert M. Veatch. LC 75-43337. 1976. 17.50x (ISBN 0-300-01949-1); pap. 6.95x (ISBN 0-300-02290-5). Yale U Pr.

Death Educators Directory. Caren Elin & Death Education Directory Staff. 70p. 1981. pap. 7.95 (ISBN 0-930194-06-3). Highly Specialized.

Death, Fate & the Gods: The Development of a Religious Idea in Greek Popular Belief & in Homer. B. C. Dietrich. 1967. text ed. 21.50x (ISBN 0-485-13703-8, Athlone Pr). Humanities.

Death Files for Congress. Theda O. Henle. LC 72-134670. 1970. 6.95 (ISBN 0-8149-0687-7). Vanguard.

Death Flight. Domini Wiles. 1978. pap. 1.95 o.s.i. (ISBN 0-515-04719-8). Jove Pubns.

Death Freak. Clifford Irving & Herbert Buckholz. 1979. pap. 2.50 o.p. (ISBN 0-345-28155-1). Ballantine.

Death Fuse. Martin Russell. 196p. 1981. 9.95 (ISBN 0-312-18698-3). St Martin.

Death Games. Dinah Brooke. LC 75-37524. 180p. 1976. 6.95 o.p. (ISBN 0-15-124093-0). HarBraceJ.

Death Giver: Shadow No. 23. Maxwell Grant. 1978. pap. 1.25 o.s.i. (ISBN 0-515-04282-X). Jove Pubns.

Death, Grief & Caring Relationships. Richard A. Kalish. LC 80-18938. 350p. 1980. text ed. 13.95 (ISBN 0-8185-0417-X). Brooks-Cole.

Death in a Cold Climate. Robert Barnard. 196p. 1981. 8.95 (ISBN 0-684-16795-6, ScribT). Scribner.

Death in a Tenured Position. Amanda Cross. 1981. 9.95 (ISBN 0-525-08935-7). Dutton.

Death in a White Tie. Ngaio Marsh. (Ngaio Marsh Mysteries Ser.). pap. 2.25 (ISBN 0-515-05896-3). Jove Pubns.

Death in America. Ed. by David E. Stannard. LC 75-10124. 1975. 13.95 (ISBN 0-8122-7695-7); pap. 5.95x (ISBN 0-8122-1084-0, Pa Paperbks). U of Pa Pr.

Death in Beirut. Tawfiq Y. Awwad. Tr. by Leslie McLoughlin from Arabic. 1978. 9.00 (ISBN 0-914478-86-9); pap. 5.00 (ISBN 0-914478-87-7). Three Continents.

Death in Delhi: Modern Hindi Short Stories. Ed. & tr. by Gordon Roadarmel. LC 74-187871. 1973. 12.95x (ISBN 0-520-02220-3). U of Cal Pr.

Death in Early America: History & Folklore of Customs & Superstitions of Early Medicine, Funerals, Burial & Mourning. Margaret M. Coffin. LC 76-7513. (Illus.). 224p. (gr. 8 up). 1976. Repr. 8.95 o.p. (ISBN 0-525-66482-3). Elsevier-Nelson.

Death in Ecstasy. Ngaio Marsh. 256p. 1980. pap. 1.95 (ISBN 0-515-05499-2). Jove Pubns.

Death in Five Boxes. Carter Dickson. 1977. pap. 1.50 (ISBN 0-505-51203-3). Tower Bks.

Death in Florence. George Alec Effinger. LC 77-80883. 1978. 6.95 o.p. (ISBN 0-385-11190-8). Doubleday.

Death in Life & Life in Death: Cuchulain Comforted & News for the Delphic Oracle. Kathleen Raine. (New Yeats Papers Ser: No. 8). 62p. 1974. pap. text ed. 7.50x (ISBN 0-85105-245-2, Dolmen Pr). Humanities.

Death in Literature. Ed. by Robert F. Weir. 432p. 1980. 25.00x (ISBN 0-231-04936-6); pap. 10.00x (ISBN 0-231-04937-4). Columbia U Pr.

Death in Paris, 1795-1801: The Records of the Basse-Geole De la Seine. Richard C. Cobb. 1978. 19.50x (ISBN 0-19-215843-0). Oxford U Pr.

Death in the Afternoon. Ernest Hemingway. (Illus.). 1932. lib. rep. ed. 27.50x (ISBN 0-684-15750-0, ScribT); pap. 6.95 (ISBN 0-684-71796-4, SL175, ScribT). Scribner.

Death in the Family. James Agee. (Literature Ser). (gr. 10-12). 1970. pap. text ed. 4.25 (ISBN 0-87720-750-X). AMSCO Sch.

Death in the Forest: The Story of the Katyn Forest Massacre. J. K. Zawodny. LC 62-16639. (Illus.). 235p. 1980. text ed. 14.00 (ISBN 0-268-00849-3); pap. text ed. 7.95 (ISBN 0-268-00850-7). U of Notre Dame Pr.

Death in the Lava. John Benteen. (Sundance: No. 4). 1979. pap. 1.75 (ISBN 0-8439-0707-X, Leisure Bks). Nordon Pubns.

Death in the Long Grass. Peter H. Capstick. LC 77-9224. (Illus.). 1978. 10.95 (ISBN 0-312-18613-4). St Martin.

Death in the Morning. Sheila Radley. 1981. lib. bdg. 13.95 (ISBN 0-8161-3199-6, Large Print Bks). G K Hall.

Death in the Silent Places. Peter Capstick. 320p. 1981. 13.95 (ISBN 0-312-18618-5). St Martin.

Death in Washington: The Murder of Orlando Letelier. Donald Freed & Fred S. Landis. 256p. 1980. 12.95 (ISBN 0-88208-123-3); pap. 6.95 (ISBN 0-88208-124-1). Lawrence Hill.

Death Is a Dirty Trick. Judson Philips. LC 79-27738. (Peter Styles Mystery Novel Ser.). 192p. 1980. 7.95 (ISBN 0-396-07820-6). Dodd.

Death Is, & Approaches to the Edge. William J. Higginson. (Xtras Ser.: No. 9). (Orig.). 1980. pap. 2.00 (ISBN 0-89120-019-3). From Here.

Death Is Natural. Laurence Pringle. LC 76-48923. (Illus.). 64p. (gr. 1-5). 1977. 6.95 (ISBN 0-590-07440-7, Four Winds). Schol Bk Serv.

Death Jag. Albert C. Ellis & Jeff Slaten. (Orig.). 1980. pap. 1.95 (ISBN 0-532-23312-3). Manor Bks.

Death Mask. Hugh Pentecost. LC 80-15717. (Julian Quist Mystery Novel Ser.). 224p. 1980. 8.95 (ISBN 0-396-07883-4). Dodd.

Death Merchant, No. 44. Joseph Rosenberger. 192p. (Orig.). 1981. pap. 1.95 (ISBN 0-523-41325-4). Pinnacle Bks.

Death Merchant: No. 1. Joseph N. Rosenberger. 1972. pap. 1.95 (ISBN 0-523-41345-9). Pinnacle Bks.

Death Merchant No. 34: Operation Mind-Murder. Joseph Rosenberger. 1979. pap. 1.95 (ISBN 0-523-41378-5). Pinnacle Bks.

Death Merchant: The Devil's Trashcan, No. 45. Joseph Rosenberger. 192p. (Orig.). 1981. pap. 1.95 (ISBN 0-523-41021-2). Pinnacle Bks.

Death Notices of Ontario. William D. Reid. 417p. 1980. PLB 20.00 (ISBN 0-912606-06-1). Hunterdon Hse.

Death of a Big Man. John Wainright. 1979. pap. 1.95 o.p. (ISBN 0-425-04131-X). Berkley Pub.

Death of a Division. Charles Whiting. LC 80-5717. (Illus.). 176p. 1981. 11.95 (ISBN 0-8128-2760-0). Stein & Day.

Death of a Fool. Ngaio Marsh. 1978. pap. 1.50 o.p. (ISBN 0-515-04478-4). Jove Pubns.

Death of a Fool. Ngaio Marsh. (Ngaio Marsh Mystery Ser.). 288p. 1981. pap. 1.95 (ISBN 0-515-05762-2). Jove Pubns.

Death of a Low Handicap Man. Brian Ball. 1978. 8.95 o.s.i. (ISBN 0-8027-5403-1). Walker & Co.

Death of a Naturalist. Seamus Heaney. 1969. 4.95 o.p. (ISBN 0-571-06665-8, Pub. by Faber & Faber); pap. 4.95 (ISBN 0-571-09024-9). Merrimack Bk Serv.

Death of a Peer. Ngaio Marsh. pap. 1.95 (ISBN 0-515-05413-5). Jove Pubns.

Death of a President: November 20-25, 1963. William Manchester. 1977. pap. 4.95 o.p. (ISBN 0-14-004801-4). Penguin.

Death of a Rebel: Phil Ochs & a Small Circle of Friends. Marc Eliot. LC 77-25586. 1979. pap. 4.95 (ISBN 0-385-13610-2, Anch). Doubleday.

Death of a Riverkeeper: And Other Stories. Ernest Schwiebert. (Illus.). 288p. 1981. 14.95 (ISBN 0-525-08947-0). Dutton.

Death of a Salesman. Arthur Miller. (Illus.). 1949. 10.00 (ISBN 0-670-26154-8). Viking Pr.

Death of a Salesman: Special Illustrated Edition. Arthur Miller. LC 80-53290. (Illus.). 144p. 1981. 15.00 (ISBN 0-670-26156-4) (ISBN 0-670-26157-2). Viking Pr.

Death of a Scavenger. Keith Spore. 1980. pap. 1.95 (ISBN 0-505-51465-6). Tower Bks.

Death of a Shipowner. Thomas Henege. LC 80-26917. 224p. 1981. 8.95 (ISBN 0-396-07952-0). Dodd.

Death of a Simple Giant & Other Modern Yugoslav Stories. Ed. by Branko Lenski. LC 64-23319. 1964. 7.95 (ISBN 0-8149-0143-3). Vanguard.

Death of a Song & Other Stories. Kartar S. Duggal. (Indian Short Stories Ser.). 186p. 1974. 4.95 (ISBN 0-88253-458-0). Ind-US Inc.

Death of a Thin-Skinned Animal. Patrick Alexander. 1979. pap. 1.75 o.s.i. (ISBN 0-685-63661-5, 04679-5). Jove Pubns.

Death of a Wedding Guest. Anne Morice. LC 75-26187. 1976. 7.95 o.p. (ISBN 0-312-18830-7). St Martin.

Death of a Woman. Jane Wheelwright. 288p. 1981. 12.95 (ISBN 0-312-18744-0). St Martin.

Death of a Wombat. Ivan Smith. 1972. 14.95 (ISBN 0-85885-009-5). David & Charles.

Death of Abbe Didier. Richard Grayson. 180p. 1981. 9.95 (ISBN 0-312-18648-7). St Martin.

Death of Adolph Hitler. Lev Bezymenski. 1978. pap. 1.75 o.s.i. (ISBN 0-515-04594-2). Jove Pubns.

Death of an Expert Witness. P. D. James. 1980. pap. write for info. (ISBN 0-445-04301-6). Popular Lib.

Death of an Oil Rig. Arthur Catherall. LC 70-77310. (Illus.). (gr. 5-8). 1969. 9.95 (ISBN 0-87599-159-9). S G Phillips.

Death of an Old Goat. Robert Barnard. 1977. 6.95 o.s.i. (ISBN 0-8027-5365-5). Walker & Co.

Death of Bragg. Janet Langmuir. LC 80-27109. (Prime Time Adventures Ser.). (Illus.). 64p. (gr. 4 up). 1981. PLB 7.95 (ISBN 0-516-02103-6). Childrens.

Death of Classical Paganism. John H. Smith. 1977. 12.95 o.p. (ISBN 0-684-14449-2, ScribT). Scribner.

Death of Gandhi: January 30, 1948: India's Spiritual Leader Helps His Nation Win Independence. Robert C. Goldston. LC 72-6074. (World Focus Bks.). (Illus.). 96p. 1973. PLB 6.45 (ISBN 0-531-02160-2). Watts.

Death of God. Gabriel Vahanian. LC 61-9962. 1961. 6.95 (ISBN 0-8076-0144-6); pap. 2.95 o.p. (ISBN 0-8076-0360-0). Braziller.

Death of Grass. John Christopher. (Alpha Books). 96p. (Orig.). 1979. pap. text ed. 2.25x (ISBN 0-19-424232-3). Oxford U Pr.

Death of Gurdjieff in the Foothills of Georgia: Secret Papers of an American Work Group. Jan. 316p. 1980. 9.00 (ISBN 0-936380-03-9). Chan Shal Imi.

Death of Horn & Hardart: Special Issue 15. Edward Zuckrow. pap. 1.00 o.p. (ISBN 0-685-78396-0). The Smith.

Death of Ivan Ilyich. Leo Tolstoy. pap. 1.95. Bantam.

Death of Jim Loney. James Welch. LC 79-1712. 192p. 1981. pap. 2.25 (ISBN 0-06-080538-2, P 538, PL). Har-Row.

Death of King Arthur. Tr. by James Cable from Fr. (Classics Ser.). 1972. pap. 2.95 (ISBN 0-14-044255-3). Penguin.

Death of Nobody. Jules Romains. Tr. by D. Maccarthy & S. Waterlow. LC 74-23525. 1977. Repr. of 1944 ed. 13.75 (ISBN 0-86527-233-6). Fertig.

Death of Odysseus. Ben H. Brown. LC 77-74291. 1977. 5.95 o.p. (ISBN 0-533-02426-9). Vantage.

Death of Satan. Antonin Artaud. 1980. pap. 3.95 (ISBN 0-7145-1085-8). Riverrun NY.

Death of Satan. Antonin Artaud. Tr. by Alastair Hamilton. 1980. pap. 3.95 (ISBN 0-7145-1085-8). Riverrun NY.

Death of Schooner Integrity. Frank Mulville. Ed. by Dennis Campbell. (Illus.). 169p. Date not set. 12.95 (ISBN 0-89182-032-9); pap. 7.95 (ISBN 0-89182-033-7). Charles River Bks.

Death of Socrates: Living, Dying & Immortality--the Theater of Ideas in Plato's Phaedo. Jerome Eckstein. 288p. 1981. 18.00 (ISBN 0-914366-19-X). Columbia Pub.

Death of the American Republic. Peter J. Riga. LC 80-67050. (Scholarly Monographs). 250p. 1980. pap. 20.00 (ISBN 0-8408-0511-X). Carrollton Pr.

Death of the Detective. Mark Smith. 1975. pap. 2.25 (ISBN 0-380-00549-2, 36897). Avon.

Death of the Heart. Elizabeth Bowen. 352p. Date not set. pap. 2.45 (ISBN 0-394-70021-X, Vin). Random.

Death of the Other Self. Peter Packer. 1979. pap. 1.75 (ISBN 0-505-51356-0). Tower Bks.

Death of the Past. J. H. Plumb. 152p. 1978. text ed. 12.50x (ISBN 0-333-06050-4). Humanities.

Death of the Sun. John Gribbin. 1981. pap. price not set (ISBN 0-440-51854-7, Delta). Dell.

Death of Tragedy. George Steiner. 1963. 13.95 (ISBN 0-571-05467-6, Pub. by Faber & Faber); pap. 8.95 (ISBN 0-571-05658-X). Merrimack Bk Serv.

Death of Virgil. Hermann Broch. 8.75 (ISBN 0-8446-1742-3). Peter Smith.

Death of White Sociology. Ed. by Joyce Ladner. 1973. 12.50 o.p. (ISBN 0-394-48208-5). Random.

Death on a Birthday Morning. Stephen E. Lindstrom. 1977. 8.95 o.p. (ISBN 0-533-02709-8). Vantage.

Death on the High C's. Robert Barnard. 1978. 7.95 o.s.i. (ISBN 0-8027-5398-1). Walker & Co.

Death on the High C's. Robert Barnard. 1981. pap. 2.25 (ISBN 0-440-11900-6). Dell.

Death on the Job. Daniel M. Berman. LC 78-13914. 1979. 12.95 o.p. (ISBN 0-85345-462-0, CL-4620). Monthly Rev.

Death on the Nile. Agatha Christie. 288p. 1981. pap. 2.50 (ISBN 0-553-14847-8). Bantam.

Death on Wheels. Steve Otfinoski. Ed. by Mary Verdick. (Pal Paperbacks, Pal Skills Ser.). (Illus., Orig.). (gr. 7-12). 1978. pap. text ed. 1.25 (ISBN 0-8374-6708-X). Xerox Ed Pubns.

Death Penalty. Ed. by Irwin Isenberg. (Reference Shelf Ser.). 1977. 6.25 (ISBN 0-8242-0604-5). Wilson.

Death Penalty & Crime: Empirical Studies. Kilman Shin. LC 77-84025. 1978. text ed. 20.00 (ISBN 0-686-12042-6). Ctr Econ Analysis.

Death Penalty & Torture. Ed. by Franz Bockle & Jacques Pohier. (Concilium: Vol. 120). (Orig.). 1978. pap. 4.95 (ISBN 0-8164-2200-1). Crossroad NY.

Death Penalty in America: An Anthology. 2nd ed. Ed. by Hugo A. Bedau. LC 68-19886. 1967. 29.95x (ISBN 0-202-24000-2). Aldine Pub.

Death Raid. Jon Hart. LC 81-65241. (Mercenaries Ser.). 128p. 1981. pap. 2.95 (ISBN 0-87754-244-9). Chelsea Hse.

Death Rides the Rails. Jim Hopwood. (Orig.). 1980. pap. 1.95 (ISBN 0-532-23126-0). Manor Bks.

Death Row. Bruce Jackson & Diane Christian. LC 79-53752. (Illus.). 312p. 1981. pap. 6.95 (ISBN 0-8070-3203-4). Beacon Pr.

Death Sentence. Leo P. Kelley. LC 79-51081. (Space Police Bks.). (Illus.). 64p. (gr. 4 up). 1980. PLB 7.95 (ISBN 0-516-02232-6). Childrens.

Death Set to Music. Mark Hebden. 1979. 16.95 (ISBN 0-241-10085-2, Pub. by Hamish Hamilton England). David & Charles.

Death Shall Have No Dominion. Alfred McBride. 208p. 1979. pap. 4.25 (ISBN 0-697-01700-1); tchrs'. manual 3.00 (ISBN 0-697-01707-9); pap. text ed. 4.25. Wm C Brown.

Death Shall Overcome. Emma Lathen. 1981. pap. 2.50 (ISBN 0-671-83675-7). PB.

Death Squadron. Grover C. Hall, Jr. (World at War Ser.: No. 20). 432p. 1980. pap. 2.75 (ISBN 0-89083-636-1). Zebra.

Death Stalk. Bob Langley. (Penguin Crime Monthly). 1980. pap. 2.75 (ISBN 0-14-005328-X). Penguin.

Death Stalks the Punjab. Melvin A. Casberg. LC 80-23558. (Illus.). 240p. (Orig.). 1981. pap. 6.95 (ISBN 0-89407-045-2). Strawberry Hill.

Death Sty: A Pig's Tale. Raymond Cousse. LC 79-2349. Orig. Title: Strategie Pour Deux Jambons. 1980. 5.95 (ISBN 0-394-17573-5, E747, Ever). Grove.

Death Style. J. C. Conway. 1977. pap. text ed. 1.50 (ISBN 0-505-51160-6, BT51160). Tower Bks.

Death Switch. Henry Henn. (Orig.). 1980. pap. 2.25 (ISBN 0-532-23221-6). Manor Bks.

Death: The Final Frontier. Dale V. Hardt. (Illus.). 1979. 12.50 (ISBN 0-13-197772-5); pap. 7.50 (ISBN 0-13-197780-6). P-H.

Death: The Final Stage of Growth. Ed. by Elisabeth Kubler-Ross. (Human Development Ser.). (Illus.). 192p. 1975. 13.95 (ISBN 0-13-197012-7, Spec); pap. 2.95 (ISBN 0-13-196998-6, Spec). P-H.

Death Tide. Warren Norville. 1979. pap. 1.95 o.s.i. (ISBN 0-515-05146-2). Jove Pubns.

Death Toll. William E. Chambers. 1976. pap. 1.25 o.p. (ISBN 0-445-00385-5). Popular Lib.

Death, Too, for The-Heavy-Runner. Ben Bennett. (Illus.). 192p. 1981. 15.95 (ISBN 0-87842-131-9); pap. 7.95 (ISBN 0-87842-132-7). Mountain Pr.

Death Trap. John D. MacDonald. 1981. pap. 1.95 (ISBN 0-449-14323-6, GM). Fawcett.

Death Under Sail. C. P. Snow. 256p. 1981. 9.95 (ISBN 0-684-16735-2, ScribT). Scribner.

Death Valley: Geology, Ecology, Archaeology. Charles B. Hunt. LC 74-2460. 256p. 1975. 14.95 (ISBN 0-520-02460-5); CAL 315. pap. 7.95 (ISBN 0-520-03013-3). U of Cal Pr.

Death Valley in '49. William L. Manly. 1977. 13.95 (ISBN 0-686-60853-4); pap. 9.95x (ISBN 0-912494-23-9). Chalfant Pr.

Death Valley Teamsters. Stanley W. Paher. (Illus.). 1973. pap. 1.00 (ISBN 0-913814-07-5). Nevada Pubns.

Death Valley: The Story Behind the Scenery. rev. ed. William D. Clark. Ed. by Gweneth R. Dendooven. LC 79-91050. (Illus.). 1980. 7.95 (ISBN 0-916122-37-9); pap. 3.00 (ISBN 0-686-60733-3). K C Pubns.

Death Walks in Eastrepps. Francis Beeding. 272p. 1980. pap. 4.00 (ISBN 0-486-24014-2). Dover.

Death Wears a Red Hat. William Kienzle. 288p. 1981. pap. 2.75 (ISBN 0-553-14429-4). Bantam.

Death Wears Grey. Charles R. Pike. LC 80-69221. (Jubal Cade Westerns Ser.). 144p. 1981. pap. 2.95 (ISBN 0-87754-237-6). Chelsea Hse.

Death Wishes? The Understanding & Management of Deliberate Self-Harm. H. G. Morgan. LC 79-1044. 1980. 36.00 (ISBN 0-471-27591-3, Pub. by Wiley-Interscience). Wiley.

Deathbeast. David Gerrold. 1978. pap. 1.75 o.p. (ISBN 0-445-04245-1). Popular Lib.

Deathbed Observations by Physicians & Nurses. 3rd ed. Karlis Osis. LC 61-18247. (Parapsychological Monograph No. 3). 1961. pap. 2.50 (ISBN 0-912328-06-1). Parapsych Foun.

Deathbird Stories. Harlan Ellison. LC 73-18663. 352p. (YA) 1975. 12.50 o.s.i. (ISBN 0-06-011176-3, HarpT). Har-Row.

Deathbite. Michael Maryk & Brent Monahan. 1979. 8.95 o.p. (ISBN 0-8362-6104-6). Andrews & McMeel.

Deathless Train: The Life & Work of Robert Smith Surtees. D. R. Johnston-Jones. (Salzburg Studies in English Literature, Romantic Reassessment: No. 36). 183p. 1974. pap. text ed. 25.00x (ISBN 0-391-01439-0). Humanities.

Deathman, Do Not Follow Me. Jay Bennett. (gr. 7 up). 1968. 6.95 o.p. (ISBN 0-8015-1998-5). Dutton.

Death's Angel. Kathleen Sky. (Star Trek Ser.). 192p. (Orig.). 1981. pap. 2.25 (ISBN 0-553-14703-X). Bantam.

Death's Bounty. George G. Gilman. (Edge Ser.: No. 12). 1974. pap. 1.75 (ISBN 0-523-41290-8). Pinnacle Bks.

Death's Dark Music. Marilyn Ross. (Stewarts of Stormhaven Ser.: No. 4). 1977. pap. 1.50 o.p. (ISBN 0-445-03182-4). Popular Lib.

Death's Epicure. Suresh Kohli. 5.00 (ISBN 0-89253-695-0). Ind-US Inc.

Death's-Head Trail. Jory Sherman. (Gunn Ser.: No. 3). 240p. (Orig.). 1980. pap. 1.95 (ISBN 0-89083-648-5). Zebra.

Death's Pale Flag. Edward Wiley. 1981. pap. 1.95 (ISBN 0-8439-0859-9, Leisure Bks). Nordon Pubns.

Deathtrek. Jeffery M. Wallman. (Orig.). 1980. pap. 1.75 (ISBN 0-505-51528-8). Tower Bks.

Deathwatch. Robb White. LC 75-157637. (gr. 9-12). 1972. 6.95a o.p. (ISBN 0-385-02510-6); PLB (ISBN 0-385-02612-9). Doubleday.

Deathwing Over Veynaa. Douglas Hill. LC 80-20262. (Illus.). 132p. (gr. 7 up). 1981. 7.95 (ISBN 0-689-50192-7, McElderry Book). Atheneum.

Deathwork. James McLendon. LC 77-4774. 1977. 8.95 o.p. (ISBN 0-397-01193-8). Lippincott.

Deathworld Trilogy. Harry Harrison. pap. 2.50 (ISBN 0-425-04859-4). Berkley Pub.

Debacle: The American Failure in Iran. Michael Ledeen & William Lewis. LC 80-27149. 320p. 12.95 (ISBN 0-686-69414-7). Knopf.

Debajo del Sol. LC 75-17687. 62p. (Orig., Sp.). 1975. pap. 1.50 (ISBN 0-89922-051-7). Edit Caribe.

Debate on Soviet Power: Minutes of the All-Russian Central Executive Committee of Soviets, October 1917-January 1918. Ed. by John L. H. Keep. 1979. 49.50x (ISBN 0-19-822554-7). Oxford U Pr.

Debate Over Detente. Charles Gati & Toby T. Gati. (Headline Ser.: 234). (Illus.). 1977. pap. 2.00 (ISBN 0-87124-039-4, 76-55300). Foreign Policy.

Debater's Guide. James J. Murphy & Jon M. Ericson. LC 61-17897. (Orig.). 1961. pap. 3.95 (ISBN 0-685-07188-X). Bobbs.

Debating Consumer Protection Policy 1980-81: High School Debate Analysis. 1980. pap. 3.75 (ISBN 0-8447-1831-9). Am Enterprise.

Debating the Direction of U. S. Foreign Policy 1979-80: High School Debate Analysis. 1979. pap. 3.25 (ISBN 0-8447-1830-0). Am Enterprise.

Debbie in Dreamland. Dorothy K. Kripke. (gr. 2-5). 1960. 3.95x (ISBN 0-685-06929-X). Bloch.

Debby Boone. Patricia M. Eldred. (gr. 4-12). 1979. PLB 5.95 (ISBN 0-87191-696-7); pap. 2.95 (ISBN 0-89812-096-9). Creative Ed.

Deborah. new ed. Margit S. Heppenstall. LC 67-19497. (Crown Ser.). (gr. 5-8). 1977. pap. 4.50 (ISBN 0-8127-0169-0). Southern Pub.

Deborah: A Wilderness Narrative. David Roberts. LC 76-134663. (Illus.). (gr. 7-12). 8.95 (ISBN 0-8149-0677-X). Vanguard.

Deborah Sampson, Soldier of the Revolution. Harold W. Felton. LC 76-13438. (gr. 4 up). 1976. 5.95 (ISBN 0-396-07343-3). Dodd.

Debrett's Peerage & Baronetage. Ed. by Patrick Montaigne-Smith. LC 42-17925. 2336p. 1980. 112.50x (ISBN 0-905649-20-6). Intl Pubns Serv.

Debrett's Peerage & Baronetage Nineteen Eighty: Comprises Information Concerning the Royal Family, the Peerage, Privy Counsellors, Scottish Lords of Session, Baronets, & Chiefs of Names & Clans in Scotland. Ed. by Patrick Montague-Smith. (Illus.). 1979. 135.00 (ISBN 0-8103-0949-1, Debretts Peerage Ltd). Gale.

Debriefing. Robert Littell. 1981. pap. 2.75 (ISBN 0-440-11873-5). Dell.

Debs. Ed. by Ronald Radosh. (Great Lives Observed Ser). 1971. pap. 2.45 o.p. (ISBN 0-13-197673-7, S728, Spec). P-H.

Debt & the Developing Countries: New Problems & New Actors. Paul M. Watson. LC 78-57185. (Development Papers: No. 26). 88p. 1978. pap. 1.50 (ISBN 0-686-28673-1). Overseas Dev Council.

Debt & the Less Developed Countries. Ed. by Jonathan D. Aronson. (Special Studies in National Security & Defense Policy). 1979. lib. bdg. 28.50x (ISBN 0-89158-370-X). Westview.

Debt of Dishonour. Mary Wibberley. (Harlequin Presents Ser.). 192p. 1980. pap. 1.50 (ISBN 0-373-10390-5, Pub. by Harlequin). PB.

Debt of Honor. Adam Kennedy. 1981. 12.95 (ISBN 0-440-00012-2). Delacorte.

Debt of Honor: No. 16. Barbara Cartland. 1978. pap. 1.50 o.s.i. (ISBN 0-515-04831-3). Jove Pubns.

Debt Trap: The IMF & the Third World. Cheryl Payer. LC 74-24794. 256p. 1975. 11.50 o.p. (ISBN 0-85345-375-6, CL3756); pap. 5.00 (ISBN 0-85345-376-4, PB3764). Monthly Rev.

Debtor-Creditor Law in a Nutshell. 2nd ed. David G. Epstein. LC 79-25091. (Nutshell Ser.). 324p. 1980. pap. 6.95 (ISBN 0-8299-2072-2). West Pub.

Deburring Capabilities & Limitations. Ed. by Laroux K. Gillespie. LC 76-47179. (Illus.). text ed. 15.95 (ISBN 0-87263-038-2). SME.

Debussy. Roger Nichols. (Oxford Studies of Composers Ser: No. 10). (Illus.). 86p. 1973. pap. 7.95x (ISBN 0-19-315426-9). Oxford U Pr.

Debussy & the Crisis of Tonality. Roland L. Nadeau. 1981. cancelled (ISBN 0-930350-11-1). NE U Pr.

Debussy: His Life & Mind. E. Lockspeiser. LC 78-51668. (Illus.). 1979. Vol. 1. 39.50 (ISBN 0-521-22053-X); pap. 10.50 (ISBN 0-521-29341-3); Vol. 2. 49.50 (ISBN 0-521-22054-8); pap. 12.50 (ISBN 0-521-29342-1). Cambridge U Pr.

Debussy, His Life & Mind, 2 Vols. Edward Lockspeiser. 8.00 ea. o.s.i. Macmillan.

Debussy: Man & Artist. Oscar Thompson. (Illus.). 1937. pap. 6.00 (ISBN 0-486-21783-3). Dover.

Debussy Man & Artist. Oscar Thompson. 395p. 1980. Repr. of 1940 ed. lib. bdg. 30.00 (ISBN 0-89984-474-X). Century Bookbindery.

Debut. Anita Brookner. 1981. 11.95 (ISBN 0-671-42626-5, Linden). S&S.

Debuts. John Boucher & Robert L. Paris. (Orig.). (gr. 10-12). 1975. text ed. 14.80 (ISBN 0-205-04148-5, 3641481); tchrs'. guide 5.12 (ISBN 0-205-04149-3, 364149X); workbook 4.92 (ISBN 0-205-04150-7, 3641503); cassettes 280.00 (ISBN 0-205-04151-5, 3641511); tests-dup masters 38.00 (ISBN 0-205-05402-1, 3654028). Allyn.

Decade of Censorship in America: The Threat to Classrooms & Libraries, 1966-1975. L. B. Woods. LC 79-20960. 195p. 1979. 11.00 (ISBN 0-8108-1260-6). Scarecrow.

Decade of Champions: The Greatest Years in the History of Thoroughbred Racing, 1970-1980. Richard S. Reeves & Patrick Robinson. LC 79-92604. (Illus.). 192p. 1980. 75.00 (ISBN 0-8487-0508-4). Oxmoor Hse.

Decade of Computers & Law. Jon Bing & Knut S. Selmer. 480p. 1980. pap. 35.00x (ISBN 82-0005-376-8). Universitet.

Decade of D & H. Karl R. Zimmermann. (Illus.). 1978. pap. 6.95 o.s.i. (ISBN 0-931726-02-6). Delford Pr.

Decade of Decision. Michael Harrington. 1981. pap. 6.95 (ISBN 0-671-42808-X, Touchstone). S&S.

Decade of Decision: The Crisis of the American System. Michael Harrington. 354p. 11.95. S&S.

Decade of Decisions: American Policy Toward the Arab-Israeli Conflict, 1967-1976. William B. Quandt. 1977. 14.95 o.p. (ISBN 0-520-03469-4); pap. 5.95x (ISBN 0-520-03536-4). U of Cal Pr.

Decade of Euphoria: Western Literature in Post-Stalin Russia, 1954-1964. Maurice Friedberg. LC 76-11932. 384p. 1977. 17.50x (ISBN 0-253-31675-8). Ind U Pr.

Decade of the Trains: The 1940s. Don Ball, Jr. & Rogers E. M. Whitaker. LC 75-37282. (Illus.). 1977. 24.95 (ISBN 0-8212-0706-7, 178853); pap. 12.95 (ISBN 0-8212-0759-8, 178861). NYGS.

Decade of Women: A Ms. History of the Seventies in Words & Pictures. Suzanne Levine et al. 17.95 (ISBN 0-399-12490-X). Putnam.

Decadence & the Eighteen Nineties. Ed. by Ian Fletcher. LC 79-20174. (Stratford-Upon-Avon Studies: Vol. 17). 1980. text ed. 32.95x (ISBN 0-8419-0568-1); pap. text ed. 15.95x (ISBN 0-8419-0569-X). Holmes & Meier.

Decadence of Judaism in Our Time. Moshe Menuhin. 7.00 o.p. (ISBN 0-911026-00-2); pap. 5.00 o.p. (ISBN 0-685-18877-9). New World Press NY.

Decadence of Judaism in Our Time. Moshe Menuhin. 585p. 1969. 13.00x (ISBN 0-911038-88-4, Inst Hist Rev). Noontide.

Decadence: The Strange Life of an Epithet. Richard Gilman. 192p. 1979. 8.95 (ISBN 0-374-13567-3); pap. 4.95 (ISBN 0-374-51553-0). FS&G.

Decadent Poetry of the Eighteen Nineties. Ed. by John M. Munro. (Illus.). 1967. 10.00x (ISBN 0-8156-6018-9, Am U Beirut). Syracuse U Pr.

Decades: Lifestyle Changes in Career Expectations. Edith M. Lynch. 160p. 1980. 11.95 (ISBN 0-8144-5603-0). Am Mgmt.

Decalogue & the Gospel. Sotirios D. Philaretos. Ed. by Orthodox Christian Educational Society. Tr. by D. Cummings from Hellenic. 62p. (Orig.). Date not set. pap. 1.50x (ISBN 0-938366-43-2). Orthodox Chr.

Decameron, 2 vols. Giovanni Boccaccio. 1953. 10.50x ea. (Evman). Vol. 1 (ISBN 0-460-00845-5). Vol. 2 (ISBN 0-460-00846-3). pap. 1.95 o.p.; Vol. 1. pap. o.p.; Vol. 2. pap. o.p. Dutton.

Decameron. Giovanni Boccaccio. Ed. by Mark Musa & Peter Bondanella. LC 77-5664. (Norton Critical Editions). 1977. pap. 4.95x (ISBN 0-393-04458-0); pap. 4.95 (ISBN 0-393-09132-5). Norton.

Decay Heat Removal & Natural Convection in Fast Breeder Reactors. Ed. by Ashok K. Agrawal & James G. Guppy. LC 81-329. 500p. 1981. text ed. 55.00 (ISBN 0-89116-196-1). Hemisphere Pub.

Decayed, Missing & Filled Teeth Among Persons One to Seventy-Four: United States, 1971-74, No. 11-223. Clair Harvey & James E. Kelly. Ed. by Audrey Shipp. 50p. Date not set. pap. text ed. price not set (ISBN 0-8406-0209-X). Natl Ctr Health Stats.

Deccan Nursery Tales; or, Fairy Tales from the South. Charles A. Kincaid. LC 76-78183. xiv, 135p. 1972. Repr. of 1914 ed. 18.00 (ISBN 0-8103-3815-7). Gale.

Decedent Hair Styling: Desairology Manual. Noella. LC 82-330. (Illus.). 100p. 1980. 17.95x (ISBN 0-9604610-0-0); pap. 11.95x (ISBN 0-9604610-1-9). JJ Pub FL.

Deceit of the New Economics. Hyppolite La Grande. (Illus.). 150p. 1975. 37.50 (ISBN 0-913314-50-1). Am Classical Coll Pr.

Deceived: The Story of the Donner Party. Peter R. Limburg. (Illus.). 256p. (gr. 7 up). Date not set. PLB 7.95 (ISBN 0-396-07942-3). Dodd. Postponed.

Deceivers. John D. MacDonald. 1978. pap. 1.75 o.p. (ISBN 0-449-14016-4, GM). Fawcett.

Deceivers & Deceived: Observations on Confidence Men & Their Victims, Informants & Their Quarry, Political & Industrial Spies & Ordinary Citizens. Richard H. Blum. (Illus.). 340p. 1972. 24.50 (ISBN 0-398-02235-6). C C Thomas.

December Decorations. Peggy Parish. LC 75-14285. (Illus.). 64p. (gr. 1-4). 1975. 7.95 (ISBN 0-02-769920-X, 76992). Macmillan.

December Nineteen Seventy-Five. Rod Tulloss. (Xtras Ser.: No. 7). 20p. (Orig.). 1978. pap. 1.50 (ISBN 0-89120-037-1). From Here.

December Tale. Marilyn Sachs. LC 76-7697. (gr. 5-9). 1976. PLB 5.95a (ISBN 0-385-12315-9). Doubleday.

Decennial Cumulative Index 1941-1950 to United States Government Publications Monthly Catalog, 2 Vols. United States Superintendent of Documents. LC 77-84611. 1972. Repr. of 1953 ed. 56.00 (ISBN 0-8103-3361-9). Gale.

Decennium Luctuosum. an History of...the Long War, Which New England Hath Had with the Indian Savages. Cotten Mather. LC 75-7022. (Indian Captivities Ser.: Vol. 3). 1976. Repr. of 1698 ed. lib. bdg. 44.00 (ISBN 0-8240-1627-0). Garland Pub.

Decentralization & School Effectiveness. Melvin Zimet. LC 73-78731. 1973. text ed. 9.25x (ISBN 0-8077-2399-1); pap. text ed. 6.50x (ISBN 0-8077-2420-3). Tchrs Coll.

Decentralizing City Government. Allen Barton et al. (Illus.). 1977. 22.95 (ISBN 0-669-01098-7). Lexington Bks.

Decentralizing Hospital Management: A Manual for Supervisors. Joseph Bean, Jr. & Rene Laliberty. 1980. pap. text ed. 8.95 (ISBN 0-201-00556-5). A-W.

Deceptive Ash: Bilingualism & Canadian Policy in Africa, 1957-1971. John P. Schlegel. LC 78-64827. 1978. pap. text ed. 15.00 (ISBN 0-8191-0637-2). U Pr of Amer.

Deceptive Hands of Wing Chu. Douglas L. Wong. LC 76-55613. (Illus.). 112p. 1977. pap. 4.95 (ISBN 0-86568-027-2). Unique Pubns.

Decibel Notation. V. V. Rao. 7.50x (ISBN 0-210-33831-8). Asia.

Decidability Questions for Petri Nets. Michel Hack. LC 79-7310. (Outstanding Dissertations in the Computer Sciences Ser.: Vol. 8). 1980. lib. bdg. 21.00 (ISBN 0-8240-4424-X). Garland Pub.

Decide: A Managerial Decision Game to Accompany Principles of Management by Kurtz & Boone. Thomas Pray & Daniel Strong. 120p. 1981. pap. text ed. 6.95 (ISBN 0-394-32698-9). Random.

Decide to Love. Anthony L. Ash. LC 80-80294. (Journey Books). 140p. (Orig.). 1980. pap. 2.35 (ISBN 0-8344-0116-9). Sweet.

Deciding. Michele McCarty. (Orig.). (gr. 11-12). 1981. pap. text ed. 4.25 (ISBN 0-697-01778-8); tchrs' manual 5.00 (ISBN 0-697-01779-6). Wm C Brown.

Deciding on Divorce: Personal & Family Considerations. Ed. by John G. Cull & Richard E. Hardy. (American Lectures in Social & Rehabilitation Psychology Ser.). 172p. 1974. 12.75 (ISBN 0-398-03035-9). C C Thomas.

Deciduous Garden Trees and Shrubs: A Macmillan Color-Identification Guide. Anthony Huxley. Tr. by Alan R. Toogood & Denis Hardwicke. (Illus.). 192p. 1973. 7.95 o.s.i. (ISBN 0-02-557970-3). Macmillan.

Decima Primeira Reunino Do Conselho Interamericano De Educacao, Ciencia E Cultura: Relatorio Final. OAS General Secretariat. 206p. (Port., 27 de julho a 2 de agosto de 1980, Bogota, Colombia). 1980. pap. text ed. 19.00 (ISBN 0-8270-1199-7). OAS.

Decimal Computation. Hermann Schmid. LC 74-10798. 304p. 1974. 27.50 o.p. (ISBN 0-471-76180-X, Pub. by Wiley-Interscience). Wiley.

Decimal Computation. Hermann Schmid. 280p. 1981. Repr. of 1974 ed. lib. bdg. write for info. (ISBN 0-89874-318-4). Krieger.

Decimals. P. Driscoll et al. Ed. by K. West & D. Johnston. (Math Skills for Daily Living Ser.). (Illus.). 32p. (gr. 7-12). 1979. pap. text ed. 3.95x (ISBN 0-87453-093-8, 82093). Denoyer.

Decimals. Marjorie Fineberg & John Shaw. LC 79-730043. (Illus.). 1978. pap. text ed. 99.00 (ISBN 0-89290-095-4, A511-SATC). Soc for Visual.

Decimals, Percent & Money: Measurement & Transportation. Learning Achievement Corp. Ed. by Therese A. Zak. (MATCH Ser.). (Illus.). 144p. 1981. text ed. 5.28 (ISBN 0-07-037114-8, G). McGraw.

Deciphering the Learning Domains: A Second Generation Classification Model for Educational Objectives. Walter D. Pierce & Charles E. Gray. LC 79-66225. 1979. pap. text ed. 10.50 (ISBN 0-8191-0816-2). U Pr of Amer.

Decipherment of Linear B. John Chadwick. (Illus.). 1970. 29.95 (ISBN 0-521-04599-1); pap. 7.50x (ISBN 0-521-09596-4, 596). Cambridge U Pr.

Decision According to Law: Nineteen Seventy-Nine Holmes Lectures. Charles L. Black, Jr. 1981. 12.95 (ISBN 0-393-01452-5). Norton.

Decision Analysis. William T. Morris. LC 76-15720. 1977. pap. 10.95 (ISBN 0-88244-131-0). Grid Pub.

Decision Analysis for Petroleum Exploration. Paul D. Newendorp. LC 75-10936. 1976. 39.50 (ISBN 0-87814-064-6). Pennwell Pub.

Decision & Responsibility: A Wrinkle in Time. H. Ganse Little, Jr. LC 74-24729. (American Academy of Religion. Studies in Religion). 1974. pap. 7.50 (ISBN 0-88420-122-8, 010008). Scholars Pr Ca.

Decision & Stress. D. E. Broadbent. 1971. 46.00 o.s.i. (ISBN 0-12-135550-0). Acad Pr.

Decision at Delphi. Helen MacInnes. 1979. pap. 2.50 (ISBN 0-449-24015-0, Crest). Fawcett.

Decision at Doona. Anne McCaffrey. 256p. 1975. pap. 2.25 (ISBN 0-345-28506-9). Ballantine.

Decision at Sea. Ruby C. Tolliver. LC 80-65972. (gr. 9-12). 1980. pap. 4.95 (ISBN 0-8054-7314-9). Broadman.

Decision Making: A Case Study of the Decision to Raise the Bank Rate in September 1957. R. A. Chapman. (Library of Political Studies). 1969. text ed. 5.75x (ISBN 0-7100-6302-4). Humanities.

Decision Making: A Psychological Analysis of Conflict, Choice & Commitment. Irving L. Janis & Leon Mann. LC 76-19643. (Illus.). 1979. pap. text ed. 9.95 (ISBN 0-02-916190-8). Free Pr.

Decision Making: A Psychological Analysis of Conflict, Choice, & Commitment. Irving L. Janis & Leon Mann. LC 76-19643. 1977. 17.95 (ISBN 0-02-916160-6). Free Pr.

Decision Making & Age. A. T. Welford & James E. Birren. Ed. by Leon Stein. LC 79-8699. (Growing Old Ser.). (Illus.). 1980. Repr. of 1969 ed. lib. bdg. 14.00x (ISBN 0-405-12810-X). Arno.

Decision-Making & Agriculture. Ed. by Theodor Dams & Kenneth E. Hunt. LC 77-93962. 1978. pap. 21.50x o.p. (ISBN 0-8032-7201-4). U of Nebr Pr.

Decision Making & Planning for the Corporate Treasurer. H. Bierman. 195p. 1977. 27.95 (ISBN 0-471-07238-9). Wiley.

Decision Making & Planning for the Corporate Treasurer. Harold Bierman, Jr. LC 76-58435. (Systems & Controls for Financial Management Ser.). 1977. 27.95 (ISBN 0-471-07238-9). Ronald Pr.

Decision Making & the Defective Newborn. Chester A. Swinyard. (Illus.). 672p. 1978. 32.75 (ISBN 0-398-03662-4). C C Thomas.

Decision Making & the Will of God. Garry Friesen & J. Robin Maxson. LC 80-24592. (Critical Concern Bks.). 1981. 9.95 (ISBN 0-930014-47-2). Multnomah.

Decision Making Chicago-Style: The Genesis of a University of Illinois Campus. George Rosen. LC 79-25643. (Illus.). 224p. 1980. 15.00 (ISBN 0-252-00803-0). U of Ill Pr.

Decision Making for Energy Futures: A Case Study on the Windscale Inquiry into the Reprocessing of Spent Oxide Fuels. D. W. Pearce et al. 1979. text ed. 26.00x (ISBN 0-333-27438-5). Humanities.

Decision Making for Regulating Chemicals in the Environment. Environmental Studies Board Commission on Natural Resources, National Research Council. 288p. 1975. pap. 12.75 (ISBN 0-309-02401-3). Natl Acad Pr.

Decision-Making for Schools & Colleges. Dean F. Juniper. 324p. 1976. text ed. 41.00 (ISBN 0-08-019885-6); pap. text ed. 17.25 (ISBN 0-08-019884-8). Pergamon.

Decision Making for Small Business Management. Jerrald F. Young. LC 76-25970. 1977. text ed. 16.95 (ISBN 0-471-97938-4); instrs'. manual avail. (ISBN 0-471-02426-0). Wiley.

Decision Making for Small Business Management. Jerrald F. Young. 256p. 1981. Repr. of 1977 ed. lib. bdg. price not set (ISBN 0-89874-346-X). Krieger.

Decision-Making in American Government. Jack R. Fraenkel et al. (gr. 9-12). 1980. text ed. 16.40 (ISBN 0-205-06845-6, 7668457); tchrs'. guide 6.12 (ISBN 0-205-06852-9, 766852-X). Allyn.

Decision Making in Criminal Justice: Toward the Rational Exercise of Discretion. Michael R. Gottfredson & Don M. Gottfredson. 424p. 1980. 28.50 (ISBN 0-88410-234-3). Ballinger Pub.

Decision Making in Developing Countries: Multiobjective Formulation & Evaluation Methods. Alfredo Sfeir-Younis & Daniel W. Bromley. LC 77-9636. (Praeger Special Studies). 1977. text ed. 23.95 (ISBN 0-03-022286-9). Praeger.

Decision Making in Multinational Corporations. Donna G Goehle. Ed. by Gunter Dufey. (Research for Business Decisions). 237p. 1980. 26.95 (ISBN 0-8357-1102-1, Pub. by UMI Res Pr). Univ Microfilms.

Decision Making in Nursing: Tools for Change. June T. Bailey & Karen E. Claus. LC 74-28268. 168p. 1975. pap. text ed. 10.50 (ISBN 0-8016-0422-2). Mosby.

Decision Making in Small Groups: The Search for Alternatives. Kowitz & Knutson. 1980. text ed. 16.95 (ISBN 0-205-06650-X, 486650-9). Allyn.

Decision Making in the Coronary Care Unit. 2nd ed. William P. Hamilton & Mary A. Lavin. LC 75-30994. (Illus.). 184p. 1976. pap. text ed. 9.50 (ISBN 0-8016-2026-0). Mosby.

Decision Making in the European Community. Christoph Sasse et al. LC 77-1258. (Special Studies). 1977. text ed. 37.95 (ISBN 0-275-23900-4). Praeger.

Decision-Making in the White House: The Olive Branch or the Olives. Theodore C. Sorensen. LC 63-20465. 1963. 12.50x (ISBN 0-231-02673-0); pap. 5.00x (ISBN 0-231-08550-8). Columbia U Pr.

Decision Making Through Operations Research. 2nd ed. Robert J. Thierauf & Robert C. Klekamp. LC 74-19473. (Management & Administration Ser). 640p. 1975. 25.95 (ISBN 0-471-85861-7); instructors manual avail. (ISBN 0-471-85856-0); Wiley.

Decision Mathematics. Dennis E. Grawoig. (Accounting Ser.). 1967. text ed. 18.95 (ISBN 0-07-024177-5, C); solutions manual 3.00 (ISBN 0-07-024178-3). McGraw.

Decision of Destiny. Walter S. Schoenberger. LC 70-81452. viii, 330p. 1969. 14.00x (ISBN 0-8214-0068-1). Ohio U Pr.

Decision on Palestine: How the U. S. Came to Recognize Israel. Evan M. Wilson. LC 78-59867. (Publications Ser.: 218). (Illus.). 244p. 1979. 14.95 (ISBN 0-8179-7181-5). Hoover Inst Pr.

Decision Order & Time in Human Affairs. 2nd ed. George L. Shackle. 1970. 38.50 (ISBN 0-521-07711-7). Cambridge U Pr.

Decision-Oriented Manual of Retinoscopy. Stephen M. Weinstock & Jonathan D. Wirtschafter. (Illus.). 116p. 1976. 16.50 (ISBN 0-398-03397-8); pap. 10.75 (ISBN 0-398-03406-0). C C Thomas.

Decision-Related Research on the Organization of Service Delivery Systems in Metropolitan Areas: Fire Protection. Lois MacGillivray. LC 79-83819. 1979. codebook 34.00 (ISBN 0-89138-985-7). ICPSR.

Decision-Related Research on the Organization of Service Delivery Systems in Metropolitan Areas: Public Health. Patrick O'Donoghue. LC 79-83820. 1979. codebook 14.00 (ISBN 0-89138-984-9). ICPSR.

Decision-Related Research on the Organization of Service Delivery Systems in Metropolitan Areas: Police Protection. Elinor Ostrom. LC 79-83821. 1979. codebook 26.00 (ISBN 0-89138-983-0). ICPSR.

Decision-Related Research on the Organization of Service Delivery Systems in Metropolitan Areas: Solid Waste Management. Steven E. Savas. LC 79-83822. 1979. codebook 30.00 (ISBN 0-89138-982-2). ICPSR.

Decision Science Process. Thaddeus B. Green & Sang M. Lee. (Illus.). 1979. text ed. 23.00 (ISBN 0-89433-060-8). Petrocelli.

Decision Styles & Organizational Effectiveness. B. L. Maheshwari. 240p. 1980. text ed. 22.50 (ISBN 0-7069-1032-X, Pub. by Vikas India). Advent Bk.

Decision Support Systems--Issues & Challenges: Proceedings of an International Task Foce Meeting, June 23-25, 1980. Ed. by G. Fick & R. H. Sprague, Jr. (IIASA Proceedings: Vol. 11). (Illus.). 190p. 1980. pap. 29.50 (ISBN 0-08-027321-1). Pergamon.

Decision Support Systems: An Organizational Perspective. Peter F. Keen & Michael S. Scott-Morton. 1978. text ed. 17.95 (ISBN 0-201-03667-3). A-W.

Decision Systems for Inventory Management & Production Planning. Rein Peterson & Edward A. Silver. LC 78-4980. (Ser. in Management Administration). 1979. text ed. 27.95 (ISBN 0-471-68327-2). Wiley.

Decision Tables: Program Structure, Data Structure. Mike Montalbano. LC 73-92630. (Illus.). 210p. 1974. pap. text ed. 10.95 (ISBN 0-574-19040-6, 13-2040). SRA.

Decision Theory & the Legal Process. Stuart S. Nagel & Marion Neef. LC 78-20348. 1979. 24.95 (ISBN 0-669-02742-1). Lexington Bks.

Decision to Parent: A Teaching Guide. Jerelyn Schultz & Penny Ralston. 164p. (gr. 7-12). 1980. pap. 7.95 (ISBN 0-8138-1595-9). Iowa St U Pr.

Decision to Prosecute: Organization & Public Policy in the Antitrust Division. Suzanne Weaver. 208p. 1980. 17.50 (ISBN 0-262-23085-2); pap. 5.95 (ISBN 0-262-73053-7). MIT Pr.

Decisions. John Brunt. LC 79-16158. (Horizon Ser.). 1979. pap. 4.50 (ISBN 0-8127-0235-2). Southern Pub.

Decisions: A Study of Christian Ethics. Jack Roeda. LC 80-189628. (Orig.). 1980. pap. text ed. 2.45 (ISBN 0-933140-14-2); tchr's manual 3.85 (ISBN 0-933140-15-0). Bd of Pubns CRC.

Decisions About the Teaching of English. John S. Simmons et al. 324p. 1976. text ed. 17.95x (ISBN 0-205-04542-1). Allyn.

Decisions & Decision-Makers in the Modern State. 1967. pap. 11.50 (ISBN 92-3-100679-7, U151, UNESCO). Unipub.

Decisions for Sale: Corruption & Reform in Localland-Use & Building Regulation. John A. Gardiner & Theodore R. Lyman. LC 78-19758. 1978. 23.95 (ISBN 0-03-044691-0). Praeger.

Decisions of the International Court of Justice, a Digest. J. Syatauw. 1963. 12.00 (ISBN 0-379-00187-X). Oceana.

Decisions of the United States Supreme Court: 1963-64, 1964-65, 1965-66, 1966-67, 1967-68, 1968-69, 1969-70, 1970-71, 1971-72, 1972-73, 1973-74, 1974-75, 1975-76, 1976-77, 1977-78, 1978-79, 1979-80, 1980-81, 18 vols. Lawyers Co-Operative Publishing Company Staff. 25.00 ea.; 376.00 set (ISBN 0-686-28514-X). Lawyers Co-Op.

Decisions, Politics & Change: A Study of Norwegian Urban Budgeting. Andrew T. Cowart & Karl E. Brofoss. 1979. pap. 15.00x (ISBN 82-00-01882-2, Dist. by Columbia U. Pr.). Universitet.

Decisions, Strategies & New Ventures: Modern Tools for Top Management. W. G. Byrnes & B. K. Chesterton. LC 73-18321. 195p. 1973. 14.95 o.p. (ISBN 0-470-12899-2). Halsted Pr.

Decisions: What to Eat. Lynn Blinn. (Home Economics Ser.). (Illus.). 300p. (Orig.). 1981. pap. text ed. price not set (ISBN 0-8273-1853-7); price not set instr's guide (ISBN 0-8273-1854-5). Delmar.

Decisive Battles of the American Revolution. Joseph B. Mitchell. 1976. pap. 2.25 (ISBN 0-449-30745-X, Q745, Prem). Fawcett.

Decisive Writing: An Improvement Program. Linda Driskill & Margaret Simpson. (Illus.). 1977. pap. text ed. 6.95x (ISBN 0-19-502121-5). Oxford U Pr.

Deck Machinery. Percy D. Smith. LC 73-12704. (Illus.). 1973. 7.00x (ISBN 0-87033-185-X, Pub. by Tidewater). Cornell Maritime.

Decks: How to Build. Sunset Editors. LC 79-90331. (Illus.). 96p. 1980. pap. 4.95 (ISBN 0-376-01076-2, Sunset Bks). Sunset-Lane.

Declaration of Independence: A Study in the History of Political Ideas. Carl L. Becker. 1958. pap. 2.45 (ISBN 0-394-70060-0, V-60, Vin). Random.

Declaration of Independence: An Interpretation & an Analysis. Herbert Friedenwald. LC 77-166325. (American Constitutional & Legal History Ser.). xii, 299p. 1974. Repr. of 1904 ed. lib. bdg. 29.50 (ISBN 0-306-70230-4). Da Capo.

Declaration of Independence-Constitution of the U. S, 2 vols. Date not set. deluxe ed. 24.95 deluxe miniature, boxed (ISBN 0-686-63049-1); vinyl miniature, boxed 12.95 (ISBN 0-686-63050-5). Lion.

Declaration of Independence: Its History. John H. Hazelton. LC 79-124892. (American Constitutional & Legal History Ser). (Illus.). 1970. Repr. of 1906 ed. lib. bdg. 39.50 (ISBN 0-306-71987-8). Da Capo.

Declaration of Independence: The Constitution of the United States. 1976. pap. text ed. 0.60 (ISBN 0-685-62914-7). Lion.

Declaration of Legal Faith. Wiley Rutledge. LC 74-114563. (American Constitutional & Legal History Ser). 1970. Repr. of 1947 ed. lib. bdg. 14.95 (ISBN 0-306-71921-5). Da Capo.

Declaration of the Causes Mouing the Queenes Maiestie to Send a Navy to the Seas. LC 72-5979. (English Experience Ser.: No. 507). 1973. Repr. of 1596 ed. 6.00 (ISBN 90-221-0507-5). Walter J Johnson.

Declaration of the Fauourable Dealing of Her Maiesties Commissioners Appointed for the Examination of Certaine Traitours. William Cecil. LC 73-25637. (English Experience Ser.: No. 113). 1969. Repr. of 1583 ed. 7.00 (ISBN 90-221-0113-4). Walter J Johnson.

Declaration of the People's Natural Right to a Share in the Legislature. Granville Sharp. LC 74-119046. (Era of the American Revolution Ser). 1971. Repr. of 1774 ed. lib. bdg. 27.50 (ISBN 0-306-71955-X). Da Capo.

Declaration of the State of the Colonie & Affaires of Virginia: By His Majesties Counseil for Virginia. LC 72-6037. (English Experience Ser.: No. 563). 1973. Repr. of 1620 ed. 11.50 (ISBN 90-221-0563-6). Walter J Johnson.

Declaration on the Juridical Personality of Foreign Companies. (Treaty Ser.: No. 26). 16p. (Eng., Span., Port. & Fr.). 1936. pap. 1.00 (ISBN 0-8270-0405-2). OAS.

Declaration Solennelle des Droits De l'Homme Dans l'Etat Social. Jean-Francois Varlet. (Fr.). 1977. lib. bdg. 13.75x o.p. (ISBN 0-8287-0854-1); pap. text ed. 3.75x o.p. (ISBN 0-685-75742-0). Clearwater Pub.

Declarations. Lalitha Venkateswaran. 4.80 (ISBN 0-89253-760-4); flexible cloth 4.00 (ISBN 0-89253-761-2). Ind-US Inc.

Declare Yourself: Discovering the Me in Relationships. David Burkett & John Narcisco. LC 75-11802. (Illus.). 1975. 9.95 (ISBN 0-13-197582-X, Spec); pap. 3.95 (ISBN 0-13-197574-9, Spec). P-H.

Declassified Documents Reference System. Ed. by Elizabeth Jones. (Nineteen Eighty Annual Collection). 1980. 685.00 (ISBN 0-8408-0330-3). Carrollton Pr.

Declassified Documents Reference System: 1979 Annual Collection. Ed. by Elizabeth Jones. 1979. 685.00 (ISBN 0-8408-0329-X). Carrollton Pr.

Declassified Eisenhower: A Divided Legacy. Blanche W. Cook. LC 80-699. 360p. 1981. 15.95 (ISBN 0-385-05456-4). Doubleday.

Declination: A Study of the Linguistic Theory of Marcus Terrentius Varro. Daniel Taylor. (Studies in the History of Linguistics: No. 2). 1979. text ed. 25.75x (ISBN 0-391-01642-3). Humanities.

Decline & Decay of American Education. C. M. Flumiani. (Illus.). 200p. 1976. 37.50 (ISBN 0-913314-79-X). Am Classical Coll Pr.

Decline & Fall of Israel & Judah. Gordon Lindsay. (Old Testament Ser.). 1.25 (ISBN 0-89985-153-3). Christ Nations.

Decline & Fall of the Roman Empire, 6 vols. Edward Gibbon. 1954 (Evman). Vol. 1. 5.00x (ISBN 0-460-00434-4); Vol. 2. 12.95x (ISBN 0-460-00435-2); Vol. 3. 12.95x (ISBN 0-460-00436-0); Vol. 4. 9.00x (ISBN 0-460-00474-3); Vol. 5. 10.00x (ISBN 0-460-00475-1); Vol. 6. 10.00x (ISBN 0-460-00476-X). Dutton.

Decline of American Gentility. Stow Persons. LC 73-534. 352p. 1973. 20.00x (ISBN 0-231-03015-0); pap. 7.50x (ISBN 0-231-08347-5). Columbia U Pr.

Decline of an Empire: The Soviet Socialist Republic in Revolt. Helene C. D'Encausse. LC 80-8402. (Illus.). 304p. 1981. pap. 4.95 (ISBN 0-06-090844-0, CN 844, CN). Harper-Row.

Decline of Antwerp Under Philip of Spain. Jervis Wegg. LC 78-20500. 1981. Repr. of 1924 ed. 26.50 (ISBN 0-88355-876-9). Hyperion Conn.

Decline of Bismarck's European Order: Franco-Russian Relations, 1875-1890. George F. Kennan. LC 79-83997. (Illus.). 1979. 25.00 (ISBN 0-691-05282-4); pap. 6.95 (ISBN 0-691-00784-5). Princeton U Pr.

Decline of Bismarck's European Order: Franco-Russian Relations, 1875-1890. George F. Kennan. LC 79-83997. (Illus.). 478p. (Orig.). 1981. pap. 6.95 (ISBN 0-691-00784-5). Princeton U Pr.

Decline of British Economic Power Since Eighteen Seventy. M. W. Kirby. 216p. 1981. text ed. 24.95x (ISBN 0-04-942169-7, 2614). Allen Unwin.

Decline of Inland Bills of Exchange in the London Money Market, 1855-1913. Shizuya Nishimura. LC 70-134613. (Illus.). 1971. 41.00 (ISBN 0-521-08055-X). Cambridge U Pr.

Decline of Liberalism As an Ideology. John H. Hallowell. LC 75-80554. 1971. Repr. 13.75 (ISBN 0-86527-038-4). Fertig.

Decline of the Ancient World. A. H. Jones. (General History of Europe Ser.). 1975. pap. text ed. 11.95x (ISBN 0-582-48309-3). Longman.

Decline of the Californios: A Social History of the Spanish-Speaking Californians, 1846-1890. Leonard Pitt. 1966. 11.95 (ISBN 0-520-01019-1); pap. 5.95 (ISBN 0-520-01637-8, CAL186). U of Cal Pr.

Decline of the Rehabilitative Ideal: Penal Policy & Social Purpose. Francis A. Allen. LC 80-25098. (Storrs Lectures). 160p. 1981. 15.00x (ISBN 0-300-02565-3). Yale U Pr.

Decline of the West? George Kennan & His Critics. Ed. by Martin F. Herz. 189p. 1978. 9.50 (ISBN 0-89633-036-2); pap. 5.00 (ISBN 0-89633-018-4). Ethics & Public Policy.

Decline of U. S. Power: & What We Can Do About It. Business Week. 1980. 9.95 (ISBN 0-395-29248-4). HM.

Declining Enrollments. Carol Epstein. 1976. pap. 8.00 (ISBN 0-87545-005-9). Natl Sch Pr.

Declining Enrollments--Implications for Citizen Action & Building Use. Date not set. pap. write for info. (ISBN 0-934460-12-4). NCCE.

Declining Enrollments, Declining Resources. Ed. by Sara Lake. (Special Interest Resource Guides in Education Ser.). (Orig.). 1981. pap. text ed. 9.50x (ISBN 0-912700-86-6). Oryx Pr.

Declining Liberty & Other Papers. John Augustine Ryan. LC 73-159802. (Civil Liberties in American History Ser). 350p. 1972. Repr. of 1927 ed. lib. bdg. 35.00 (ISBN 0-306-70253-3). Da Capo.

Declining Northeast: Demographic & Economic Analyses. Benjamin Chinitz. LC 78-6137. (Praeger Special Studies). 1978. 22.95 (ISBN 0-03-043476-9). Praeger.

Declining Population Growth Revisited. Joseph J. Spengler. LC 80-23714. (Carolina Population Center Monograph: No. 14). (Illus.). 60p. 1980. Repr. of 1971 ed. lib. bdg. 13.75x (ISBN 0-313-22621-0, SPDE). Greenwood.

Declining Significance of Race: Blacks & Changing American Institutions. 2nd ed. William J. Wilson. 1980. pap. 5.95 (ISBN 0-226-90129-7, P900, Phoen). U of Chicago Pr.

Decoded New Testament, Authorized Version: An Authoritative Translations of the Sacred Teachings of Light As Contained in the Encoded Writings of the Gospels, Acts, & Epistles. Gene Savoy. LC 73-90340. (Sacred Teachings of Light, Codex II: Vol. 1). xix, 118p. 1975. text ed. 39.50 (ISBN 0-936202-01-7). Intl Comm Christ.

Decoding Corporate Camouflage: U. S. Business Support for Apartheid. Elizabeth Schmidt. 127p. 1980. pap. 4.95 (ISBN 0-89758-022-2). Inst Policy Stud.

Decoding Keys for Reading Success. Philip McInnis. (gr. k-9). 1981. 298.00 (ISBN 0-8027-9129-8); Primary Level. 98.00 (ISBN 0-8027-9130-1); Intermediate Level. 96.00 (ISBN 0-8027-9131-X); Advanced Level. 108.00 (ISBN 0-8027-9132-8); 4.50 (ISBN 0-8027-9133-6). Walker & Co.

Decolonisation & After: The British & French Experience. Ed. by W. H. Morris-Jones & Georges Fischer. (Studies in Commonwealth Politics & History: No. 7). 369p. 1980. 29.50x (ISBN 0-7146-3095-0, F Cass Co). Biblio Dist.

Decolonization of the British, French, Dutch & Belgian Empires: 1919-1963. Henri Grimal. LC 77-922. 1978. lib. bdg. 33.50x (ISBN 0-89158-732-2). Westview.

Decolonization: The Administration & Future of the Colonies, Nineteen Nineteen to Nineteen Sixty. Rudolf Von Albertini. Tr. by Francisca Gravie from Ger. 680p. 1981. text ed. 29.50x (ISBN 0-8419-0603-3); pap. 11.50x (ISBN 0-8419-0654-8). Holmes & Meier.

Decolonizing Theology: A Caribbean Perspective. Noel L. Erskine. LC 80-21784. 160p. (Orig.). 1981. pap. 6.95 (ISBN 0-88344-087-3). Orbis Bks.

Decommissioning of Nuclear Facilities. 694p. 1980. pap. 81.75 (ISBN 92-0-020179-2, ISP500, IAEA). Unipub.

Decomposition of Superpositions of Density Functions & Discrete Distributions. Pal Medgyessy. LC 75-46231. 1977. 39.95x (ISBN 0-470-15017-3). Halsted Pr.

Decomposition of Walsh & Fourier Series. I. I. Hirschman. LC 52-42839. (Memoirs: No. 15). 1980. pap. 4.40 (ISBN 0-8218-1215-7, MEMO-15). Am Math.

Decompression Sickness: The Biophysical Basis of Prevention & Treatment, Vol. 1. B. A. Hills. LC 76-55806. 1977. 49.00 (ISBN 0-471-99457-X, Pub. by Wiley-Interscience). Wiley.

Decontamination & Decommissioning of Nuclear Facilities. Ed. by Marilyn M. Osterhout. 820p. 1980. 75.00 (ISBN 0-306-40429-X, Plenum Pr). Plenum Pub.

Decontamination of Animal Feeds by Irridation. 1979. pap. 18.75 (ISBN 92-0-111079-0, ISP508, IAEA). Unipub.

Decontamination of Nuclear Reactors & Equipment. Ed. by J. A. Ayres. (Illus.). 815p. 1970. 50.00 (ISBN 0-471-06687-7, Pub. by Wiley-Interscience). Wiley.

Decorated Gourds in North-Eastern Nigeria. T. J. Chappel. 1977. text ed. 55.00x (ISBN 0-905788-02-8). Humanities.

Decorated Gun. Carson I. Ritchie. LC 78-75331. (Illus.). Date not set. 15.00 o.p. (ISBN 0-498-02203-X). A S Barnes. Postponed.

Decorated Letter. Ed. by J. J. Alexander. (Magnificent Paperback Ser.). 1978. 22.95 (ISBN 0-8076-0894-7); pap. 10.95 (ISBN 0-8076-0895-5). Braziller.

Decorated Tumbler "PriceGuy". Hazel M. Weatherman. 128p. 1979. pap. 3.75 (ISBN 0-913074-13-6). Weatherman.

Decorating Made Simple. Mary Jean Alexander. LC 64-13823. 1964. pap. 3.50 (ISBN 0-385-01695-6, Made). Doubleday.

Decorating Pottery. F. Carlton Ball. 3.95 (ISBN 0-934706-05-0). Prof Pubns Ohio.

Decorating with Fabric: An Idea Book. rev. ed. Judy Lindahl. 128p. 1980. pap. 4.95 (ISBN 0-9603032-1-9). Lindahl.

Decorating with Flowers. Denise Otis & Ronaldo Maia. (Illus.). 1978. 40.00 (ISBN 0-8109-0808-5). Abrams.

Decorating with Plants. James U. Crockett & Oliver E. Allen. LC 77-95146. (Time-Life Encyclopedia of Gardening Ser.). (Illus.). 1978. lib. bdg. 10.98 (ISBN 0-686-51058-5). Silver.

Decorating with Plants. Ed. by Time-Life Books & Time Life Books Editors. (Encyclopedia of Gardening Ser.). (Illus.). 1978. 9.95 (ISBN 0-8094-2579-3). Time-Life.

Decorating with Stitches. L. Denne & M. Johnson. 104p. 1975. 13.95 (ISBN 0-8231-5047-X). Branford.

Decorating Your Room: A Do-It-Yourself Guide. Ellen Liman & Carol Panter. LC 73-9999. (Illus.). 128p. (gr. 5 up). 1974. 9.90 o.p. (ISBN 0-531-02651-5). Watts.

Decorative Art & Modern Interiors: Environments for People. Ed. by Maria Schofield. LC 80-81603. (Decorative Art & Modern Interiors, Theme Changes Annually). (Illus.). 192p. 1980. 35.00 (ISBN 0-688-03480-2). Morrow.

Decorative Art of Leon Bakst. Leon Bakst. Tr. by Harry Melvill. LC 73-187844. (Illus.). 144p. 1973. pap. 6.00 (ISBN 0-486-22871-1). Dover.

Decorative Arts of Japan. Ed. by C. F. Yamada. LC 63-22011. (Illus.). 1963. 85.00 (ISBN 0-87011-006-3). Kodansha.

Decorative Braiding & Weaving. June Barker. (Illus.). 112p. 1973. 9.95 (ISBN 0-8231-7031-4). Branford.

Decorative Crafts. Linda Hetzer. LC 77-28702. (Illustrated Crafts for Beginners). (Illus.). (gr. 3-7). 1978. PLB 9.95 (ISBN 0-8172-1178-0). Raintree Pubs.

Decorative Design in Mexican Homes. V. C. Shipway & W. Shipway. Date not set. 18.95 (ISBN 0-8038-0058-4). Hastings.

Decorative Design in Mexican Homes. Verna C. Shipway & Warren Shipway. (Illus.). 1966. 16.95 (ISBN 0-8038-0058-4). Architectural.

Decorative Frames & Borders: 396 Examples from the Renaissance to the Present Day. Edmund V. Gillon, Jr. LC 72-96186. (Illus.). 224p. (Orig.). 1973. pap. 5.00 (ISBN 0-486-22928-9). Dover.

Decorative Gardening in Containers. Elvin McDonald. LC 77-92224. 1978. 8.95 o.p. (ISBN 0-385-09590-2). Doubleday.

Decorative Napkin Folding: A Lost Art Revived & Made Simple. Jean-Jacques R. Paimblanc. (Foodservice Guides Ser.). (Illus.). 128p. 1981. 19.95 (ISBN 0-89046-072-8). Herman Pub.

Decorative Napkin Folding for Beginners. Lillian Oppenheimer & Natalie Epstein. (Illus.). 1980. pap. 1.75 (ISBN 0-486-23797-4). Dover.

Decorative Techniques. Ed. by Time-Life Books. LC 75-29597. (Art of Sewing). (Illus.). (gr. 6 up). 1976. PLB 11.97 (ISBN 0-8094-1763-4, Pub. by Time-Life). Silver.
Decorative Thirties. Martin Battersfy. 208p. 1975. pap. 7.95 o.s.i. (ISBN 0-02-000210-6, Collier). Macmillan.
Decorative Tile: An Illustrated History of English Tile-Making & Design. Jill Austwick & Brian Austwick. (Illus.). 1981. 30.00 (ISBN 0-684-16761-1). Scribner.
Decorative Touch: How to Decorate, Glaze, & Fire Your Pots. Carl E. Peak. (Creative Handicrafts Ser.). (Illus.). 160p. 1981. 17.95 (ISBN 0-13-198085-8, Spec); pap. 8.95 (ISBN 0-13-198077-7). P-H.
Decorative Twenties. Martin Battersfy. 216p. 1975. pap. 7.95 o.s.i. (ISBN 0-02-000200-9, Collier). Macmillan.
Decorative Work in Wrought Iron & Other Metals. Fritz Kuhn. Date not set. 24.95 (ISBN 0-8038-0060-6). Hastings.
Decorative Work of John la Farge. H. Barbara Weinberg. LC 76-23654. (Outstanding Dissertations in the Fine Arts - 2nd Series - American). (Illus.). 1977. Repr. of 1972 ed. lib. bdg. 84.00 (ISBN 0-8240-2736-1). Garland Pub.
Decorative Work of Robert Adam. Damie Stillman. 20.00 (ISBN 0-85458-160-X). Transatlantic.
Decorattivo 1. (Illus.). 1977. 29.95 o.p. (ISBN 0-8120-5223-4). Barron.
Decoupage. Patricia E. Nimocks. LC 68-11372. (Encore Ed.). (Illus.). 1968. 3.95 o.p. (ISBN 0-684-15430-7, ScribT). Scribner.
Decoupage: A New Look at an Old Craft. Leslie Linsley. LC 73-168290. (Illus.). 160p. 1972. pap. 3.95 o.p. (ISBN 0-385-08863-9). Doubleday.
Decoupage Crafts. Florence Temko. LC 74-33666. 64p. (gr. 3-7). 1976. PLB 5.95 o.p. (ISBN 0-385-07791-2). Doubleday.
Decoupage for Young Crafters. Leslie Linsley. (Illus.). (gr. 1-5). 1977. PLB 7.95 (ISBN 0-525-28614-4). Dutton.
Decoupage: Simple & Sophisticated. Joan Priolo. LC 73-93597. (Little Craft Book Ser). (Illus.). 48p. (gr. 4 up). 1974. 5.95 (ISBN 0-8069-5300-4); PLB 6.69 (ISBN 0-8069-5301-2). Sterling.
Decoupage, Step by Step. Dee Davis. (Step by Step Craft Ser.). (Illus.). 1976. PLB 9.15 o.p. (ISBN 0-307-62017-4, Golden Pr); pap. 2.95 (ISBN 0-307-42017-5). Western Pub.
Decoupage, the Ancient Art of Surface Finishing & Antiquing. new ed. Elizabeth Foy. LC 73-185673. (Handicraft Ser.). (Illus.). 32p. (Orig.). (gr. 7-12). 1971. lib. bdg. 2.45 incl. catalog cards (ISBN 0-87157-905-7); pap. 1.25 vinyl laminated covers (ISBN 0-87157-405-5). SamHar Pr.
Decouvrir la France, 7 vols. Ed. by Roger Brunet. Incl. Vol. 1. Bretagne, Normandie, Poitou, Vendee, Charentes (ISBN 2-03-013351-5, 3578); Vol. 2. Paris, Bassin parisien, Pays de Loire (3579); Vol. 3. Nord, Alsace, Lorraine, Bourgogne (3581); Vol. 4. Franche-Comte, Auvergne, Lyonnais, Alpes (3582); Vol. 5. Languedoc, Provence, Cote d'azur, Corse (3583); Vol. 6. Limousin, Bassin aquitain, Pyrenees, Pays basque et catalan (3584); Vol. 7. France d'outre-Mer, la France maintenant (3585). (Illus.). 336p. 1972. 78.25 ea. Larousse.
Decouvrir la France, 4 vols, Vols. 6-9. Incl. Vol. 6. Pays de Loire; Vol. 7. Le Nord; Vol. 8. L'Alsace; Vol. 9. Les Vosges et la Lorraine. 22.50 ea. Larousse.
Decouvrir la France, 18 vols, Vols. 1-5 & 10-22. Ed. by Roger Brunet. Incl. Vol. 1. Bretagne (ISBN 2-03-013801-0); Vol. 2. Maine et la Normandie; Vol. 3. Poitou, Charentes, Vendee; Vol. 4. Paris (ISBN 2-03-013804-5); Vol. 5. Champagne, Picardie, Ile de France; Vol. 10. Bourgogne et Franche Comte; Vol. 11. Auvergne et le Boubonnais; Vol. 12. En Pays lyonnais (ISBN 2-03-013812-6); Vol. 13. Les Alpes (ISBN 2-03-013813-4); Vol. 14. Bas Languedoc, Cevennes, Causses, Languedoc (ISBN 2-03-013814-2); Vol. 15. La Provence; Vol. 16. Cote d'azur, la Corse (ISBN 2-03-013816-9); Vol. 17. Limousin, Perigord, Quercy, Bouergue; Vol. 18. Aquitaine (ISBN 2-03-013818-5); Vol. 19. Midi toulousain; Vol. 20. Pyrenees du Pays Basque au Pays Catalan; Vol. 21. France d'outre-mer; Vol. 22. France maintenant (ISBN 2-03-013822-3). (Illus.). 1972. 22.50 ea. Larousse.
Decoys & Decoy Carvers of Illinois. Paul W. Parmalee & Forrest D. Loomis. LC 69-19824. (Illus.). 408p. 1969. pap. 25.00 (ISBN 0-87580-524-8). N Ill U Pr.
Decree & Establishment of the Kingsmaiestie, Upon a Controversie of Precedence, Betweene the Yonger Sonnes of Viscounts & Barons, & the Baronets. LC 74-28850. (English Experience Ser.: No. 731). 1975. Repr. of 1612 ed. 3.50 (ISBN 90-221-0731-0). Walter J Johnson.
Dedicacion Valiente. Louise H. Farrior. Tr. by Justo L. Gonzalez from Eng. 123p. (Orig., Span.). 1979. pap. 2.25 (ISBN 0-89922-134-3). Edit Caribe.
Dedication of Books to Patron & Friend. Henry B. Wheatley. LC 68-30615. 1968. Repr. of 1887 ed. 15.00 (ISBN 0-8103-3316-3). Gale.
Dedication: What It's All About. Marjorie A. Collins. 1976. pap. 3.50 (ISBN 0-87123-103-4, 210103). Bethany Fell.
Deduction & Analysis. rev. ed. Richard Butrick. LC 80-6177. 121p. 1981. lib. bdg. 15.75 (ISBN 0-8191-1410-3); pap. text ed. 6.75 (ISBN 0-8191-1411-1). U Pr of Amer.
Deduction Transcendentale Dans L'oueuvre De Kant, 3 vols. H. J. De Vleeschauwer. Ed. by Lewis W. Beck. LC 75-32049. (Philosophy of Immanuel Kant Ser.). 1976. Set. lib. bdg. 100.00 (ISBN 0-8240-2326-9). Garland Pub.
Deductive Logic. 2nd ed. Hugues Leblanc & William Wisdom. 354p. 1976. text ed. 19.95 (ISBN 0-205-05496-X). Allyn.
Deductive Transformation Geometry. R. P. Burn. LC 74-82223. (Illus.). 152p. 1975. 19.95 (ISBN 0-521-20565-4). Cambridge U Pr.
Deed. Gerold Frank. 1979. pap. 2.25 o.p. (ISBN 0-425-03913-7). Berkley Pub.
Deenie. Judy Blume. LC 73-80197. 192p. (gr. 6-8). 1973. 8.95 (ISBN 0-87888-061-5). Bradbury Pr.
Deep Blue Good-by. John D. Macdonald. LC 75-1092. 204p. 1975. Repr. of 1964 ed. 6.95 o.s.i. (ISBN 0-397-01090-7). Lippincott.
Deep Blues. Robert Palmer. LC 80-52000. (Illus.). 1981. 13.95 (ISBN 0-670-49511-5). Viking Pr.
Deep Cover. Brian Garfield. 1978. pap. 1.95 o.p. (ISBN 0-449-23601-3, Crest). Fawcett.
Deep Down in the Jungle: Negro Narrative Folklore from the Streets of Philadelphia. Roger D. Abrahams. LC 78-124404. 1970. 16.95 (ISBN 0-202-00109-1); pap. 7.50 (ISBN 0-686-66359-4). Aldine Pub.
Deep Dyslexia. Ed. by Max Coltheart et al. (International Library of Psychology). 1980. 45.00x (ISBN 0-7100-0456-7). Routledge & Kegan.
Deep Foundations. Frank Fuller. LC 80-69155. 540p. 1981. pap. text ed. 25.00 (ISBN 0-87262-256-8). Am Soc Civil Eng.
Deep Freezing. 2nd ed. Pat M. Cox. (Illus.). 1979. 32.00 o.p. (ISBN 0-571-04954-0, Pub. by Faber & Faber). Merrimack Bk Serv.
Deep in Debt Valley. Cass Thurner. LC 78-74744. 1979. 6.00 (ISBN 0-915854-12-0); pap. 3.00 (ISBN 0-915854-16-3). Friend Freedom.
Deep River. Howard Thurman. Bd. with Negro Spiritual Speaks of Life & Death. LC 75-27041. 136p. 1975. pap. 2.95 (ISBN 0-913408-20-4). Friends United.
Deep Roots. Murli D. Melwani. (Writers Workshop Bluebird Ser.). 56p. 1975. 8.00 (ISBN 0-88253-524-2); pap. text ed. 4.80 (ISBN 0-88253-523-4). Ind-US Inc.
Deep-Sea Canoe: The Story of Third World Missionaries in the South Pacific. Alan R. Tippett. LC 77-8660. (Illus.). 1977. pap. 3.95x (ISBN 0-87808-158-5). William Carey Lib.
Deep Sea Diver: Yesterday, Today & Tomorrow. R. C. Martin. LC 77-19076. (Illus.). 1978. 10.00 (ISBN 0-87033-238-4). Cornell Maritime.
Deep Seabed Resources: Politics & Technology. Jack N. Barkenbus. LC 78-73024. 1979. 17.95 (ISBN 0-02-901830-7). Free Pr.
Deep Six. Randy Striker. (Dusky MacMorgan Ser.: No. 2). (Orig.). 1981. pap. 1.95 (ISBN 0-451-09568-5, J9568, Sig). NAL.
Deep South: Memory & Observation. Erskine Caldwell. LC 80-16013. (Brown Thrasher Ser.). 270p. 1980. pap. 5.95 (ISBN 0-8203-0525-1). U of Ga Pr.
Deep South Natural Foods Cookbook. May Lou McCracken. 1977. pap. 1.75 (ISBN 0-515-03661-7). Jove Pubns.
Deep South Piano. Karl Gert zur Heide. (Paul Oliver Blues Ser.). pap. 2.95 (ISBN 0-913714-32-1). Legacy Bks.
Deep Summer. Gwen Bristow. LC 37-1118. 1964. 10.95 (ISBN 0-690-23318-3, TYC-T). T Y Crowell.
Deep Water Cruising. 1980. 17.95 (ISBN 0-679-50976-3). McKay.
Deep-Water Fishes of California. John E. Fitch & Robert J. Lavenberg. LC 68-64172. (California Natural History Guides: No. 25). (Illus.). 1968. pap. 2.25 o.p. (ISBN 0-520-00421-3). U of Cal Pr.
Deep Well at Noon. Jessica Stirling. 1980. 12.95 o.p. (ISBN 0-312-19090-5). St Martin.
Deepening Crisis of U.S. Capitalism: Essays by Harry Magdoff & Paul M. Sweezy. Harry Magdoff & Paul M. Sweezy. LC 80-8935. 256p. 1981. 16.00 (ISBN 0-85345-573-2); pap. 6.50 (ISBN 0-85345-574-0). Monthly Rev.
Deepening Stream. Francena H. Arnold. pap. 2.50 (ISBN 0-310-20212-4). Zondervan.
Deeper into Movies. Pauline Kael. 1980. pap. 2.95 (ISBN 0-446-93525-5). Warner Bks.
Deeper Self: A Meditation on Christian Mysticism. Louis Dupre. 128p. (Orig.). 1981. pap. 4.50 (ISBN 0-8245-0007-5). Crossroad NY.
Deeper Than Shame. Esther E. Pearl. 384p. (Orig.). 1980. pap. 2.50 (ISBN 0-515-05533-6). Jove Pubns.
Deeper Than Speech: Frontiers of Language & Communication. Michael Chester. LC 75-14167. (Illus.). 96p. (gr. 6 up). 1975. 5.95 o.s.i. (ISBN 0-02-718310-6, 71831). Macmillan.
Deepwater Ports in the United States: An Economic & Environmental Impact Study. Tobey L. Winters. LC 76-12885. (Special Studies). 1977. text ed. 27.50 (ISBN 0-275-23250-6). Praeger.
Deepwood. Walter S. Swanson. 1981. 10.95 (ISBN 0-316-82476-3). Little.
Deer. Raymond E. Chaplin. (Illus.). 1978. 17.50 (ISBN 0-7137-0796-8, Pub by Blandford Pr England). Sterling.
Deer Hunter. E. M. Corder. 1979. pap. 1.95 (ISBN 0-515-05321-X). Jove Pubns.
Deer Hunter's Bible. rev. ed. George Laycock. LC 76-50875. 1971. softbound 3.50 (ISBN 0-385-12896-7). Doubleday.
Deer Hunting. rev. ed. Richard P. Smith. (Illus.). 256p. 1981. pap. 9.95 (ISBN 0-8117-2132-9). Stackpole.
Deer in the Pasture. Donald Carrick. LC 75-23193. (Illus.). 32p. (gr. k-3). 1976. PLB 7.92 (ISBN 0-688-84023-X). Greenwillow.
Deer Park. Norman Mailer. 384p. 1981. pap. 4.95 (ISBN 0-399-50531-8, Perigee). Putnam.
Deer Park. Norman Mailer. LC 79-20163. 375p. 1980. Repr. of 1955 ed. 15.95 (ISBN 0-86527-235-2). Fertig.
Deer Range: Management & Improvement. 2nd ed. William Dasmann. LC 80-28280. Orig. Title: If Deer Are to Survive. (Illus.). 175p. 1981. lib. bdg. write for info (ISBN 0-89950-027-7). McFarland & Co.
Deer Rifle. L. R. Wallack. (Illus.). 1978. 12.95 (ISBN 0-87691-269-2). Winchester Pr.
Deer Stalking: The Whys & Wherefores. Edmund Luxmoore. (Illus.). 160p. 1980. 22.50 (ISBN 0-7153-8063-X). David & Charles.
Deerslayer. (Classics Illus. Ser.). (Illus.). pap. 0.59 o.p. (ISBN 0-685-74087-0, 17). Guild Bks.
Deerstalker! Holmes & Watson on the Screen. Ron Haydock. LC 77-24465. 1978. 15.00 (ISBN 0-8108-1061-1). Scarecrow.
Defeat in the East. Juergen Thorwald. 304p. 1980. pap. 2.50 (ISBN 0-553-13469-8). Bantam.
Defeat of the Bird God. C. Peter Wagner. LC 67-11615. (Illus.). 256p. 1975. Repr. of 1967 ed. 5.95 (ISBN 0-87808-721-4). William Carey Lib.
Defeating Depression. Gary Emery. 12.95 (ISBN 0-671-24866-9). S&S.
Defects & Radiation Damage in Metals. M. W. Thompson. LC 69-10434. (Cambridge Monographs on Physics). (Illus.). 1969. 60.50 (ISBN 0-521-07068-6); pap. 18.50x (ISBN 0-521-09865-3). Cambridge U Pr.
Defects & Surfaces in Semiconducting Materials & Devices. David B. Holt & Dan Haneman. (International Series in the Science of the Solid State: Vol. 12). Date not set. cancelled (ISBN 0-08-020620-4). Pergamon.
Defects in the Alkaline Earth Oxides: With Applications to Radiation Damage & Catalysis. B. Henderson & J. E. Wertz. LC 77-23366. 1977. 27.95 (ISBN 0-470-99205-0). Halsted Pr.
Defence by Ministry. Franklyn Johnson. LC 79-28587. 234p. 1980. text ed. 42.50x (ISBN 0-8419-0598-3). Holmes & Meier.
Defence in Animals. Malcolm Edmunds. LC 73-92246. (Illus.). 288p. 1975. pap. text ed. 16.95x (ISBN 0-582-44132-3). Longman.
Defence Mechanisms of Plants. B. J. Deverall. LC 76-12917. (Monographs in Experimental Biology Ser.: No. 19). (Illus.). 1977. 21.50 (ISBN 0-521-21335-5). Cambridge U Pr.
Defence of Contraries. Tr. by A. Munday from Fr. LC 72-188. (English Experience Ser.: No. 175). 1969. Repr. of 1593 ed. 13.00 (ISBN 90-221-0175-4). Walter J Johnson.
Defence of Dramatick Poetry. Elkanah Settle. Incl. Farther Defence of Dramatick Poetry. LC 79-170450. (English Stage Ser.: Vol. 25). lib. bdg. 50.00 (ISBN 0-8240-0608-9). Garland Pub.
Defence of Human Rights in Latin America (16th to 18th Centuries) Silvio Zavala. 1964. pap. 2.50 (ISBN 92-3-100571-5, U152, UNESCO). Unipub.
Defence of Plays: The Stage Vindicated from...Mr. Collier's Short View. Edward Filmer. LC 70-170449. (English Stage Ser.: Vol. 36). lib. bdg. 50.00 (ISBN 0-8240-0619-4). Garland Pub.
Defence of Tabacco: With a Friendly Answer to Worke for Chimnysweepers. Roger Marbecke. LC 68-54636. (English Experience Ser.: No. 33). 1968. Repr. of 1602 ed. 11.50 (ISBN 90-221-0033-2). Walter J Johnson.
Defence of the Short View off the Profaneness & Immorality of the English Stage. Jeremy Collier. LC 72-170444. (English Stage Ser.: Vol. 30). lib. bdg. 50.00 (ISBN 0-8240-0613-5). Garland Pub.
Defence of True Liberty from Ante-Cedent & Extrinsical Necessity. an Answer to Hobbes' a Treatise of Liberty & Necessity. John Bramhall. Ed. by Rene Wellek. LC 75-11200. (British Philosophers & Theologians of the 17th & 18th Centuries: Vol. 7). 1976. Repr. of 1655 ed. lib. bdg. 42.00 (ISBN 0-8240-1756-0). Garland Pub.
Defence of Truth. A. D. Bedford. 271p. 1979. 51.00x (ISBN 0-7190-0740-2, Pub. by Manchester U Pr England). State Mutual Bk.
Defence Yearbook 1980. 90th ed. Ed. by Royal United Services Institute for Defence Studies, London. LC 75-614843. (Illus.). 355p. 1979. 40.00x (ISBN 0-904609-37-5). Intl Pubns Serv.
Defences of Philadelphia in 1777. Ed. by W. C. Ford. LC 71-146145. (Era of the American Revolution Ser). 1971. Repr. of 1897 ed. lib. bdg. 32.50 (ISBN 0-306-70140-5). Da Capo.
Defend Yourself: Scientific Personal Defense. Armond Seidler. LC 77-79405. (Illus.). 1978. pap. text ed. 8.25 (ISBN 0-395-25822-7). HM.
Defendants in the Criminal Process. A. E. Bottoms & J. D. McClean. (International Library of Social Policy). 250p. 1975. 27.75x (ISBN 0-7100-8274-6). Routledge & Kegan.
Defendant's Rights Today. David Fellman. 1977. 25.00 (ISBN 0-299-07200-2); pap. 8.95 (ISBN 0-299-07204-5). U of Wis Pr.
Defender of Angels. J. Kimbrough. 1969. 6.95 o.s.i. (ISBN 0-02-563030-X). Macmillan.
Defending Business & White Collar Crimes. F. Lee Bailey & Henry B. Rothblatt. LC 77-83168. (Criminal Law Library). 1969. 47.50 (ISBN 0-686-14487-2). Lawyers Co-Op.
Defending Intellectual Freedom: The Library & the Censor. Eli M. Oboler. LC 79-8585. (Contributions in Librarianship & Information Science: No. 32). xix, 246p. 1980. lib. bdg. 22.95 (ISBN 0-313-21472-7, ODF/). Greenwood.
Defending the Undefendables: The Pimp, Prostitute, Scab, Usurer, Libeler, & Other Scapegoats in the Rogue's Gallery of American Society. new ed. Walter Block. LC 74-21359. 1976. 9.95 (ISBN 0-8303-0136-4); pap. 5.95 (ISBN 0-8303-0183-6). Fleet.
Defensa De Naturaliza. (Eng & Span.). 1973. pap. 1.00 (ISBN 0-8270-3960-3). OAS.
Defense & Foreign Affairs Handbook 1980. 1980. 70.00 (ISBN 0-531-03917-X). Watts.
Defense at Bridge. Victor Mollo & Aksel J. Nielson. 1976. 15.95 (ISBN 0-571-10891-1, Pub. by Faber & Faber). Merrimack Bk Serv.
Defense Attorney & Basic Defense Tactics. Welcome D. Pierson. 1956. incl. 1966 suppl. 15.00 (ISBN 0-672-80022-5, Bobbs-Merrill Law); 1966 suppl. 6.00 (ISBN 0-672-80024-1). Michie.
Defense in-Plant Quality Assurance Program. Dept. of Defense-Defense Supply Agency. 1976. 9.50x (ISBN 0-912702-08-7). Global Eng.
Defense Industry. Jacques S. Gansler. 432p. 1980. text ed. 19.95 (ISBN 0-262-07078-2). MIT Pr.
Defense Mechanisms of the Modern State. Nagendra Singh. 1964. 30.00x (ISBN 0-210-33832-6). Asia.
Defense Never Rests. F. Lee Bailey. pap. 2.50 (ISBN 0-451-08236-2, E9236, Sig). NAL.
Defense of the Constitutions of Government of the United States of America, 3 Vols. John A. Adams. LC 69-11328. (American Constitutional & Legal History Ser). 1971. Repr. of 1788 ed. lib. bdg. 125.00 (ISBN 0-306-71176-1). Da Capo.
Defense of the Homeland & the End of the War: Japanese Military Studies 1937-1949. Ed. by Donald S. Detwiler & Charles B. Burdick. (War in Asia & the Pacific Ser., 1937 to 1949: Vol. 12). 1980. lib. bdg. 60.50 (ISBN 0-8240-3296-9); lib. bdg. 650.00 set of 15 vols. (ISBN 0-686-60101-7). Garland Pub.
Defense of the Realm: British Strategy in the Nuclear Epoch. Richard N. Rosecrance. LC 67-26368. 1968. 20.00x (ISBN 0-231-03065-7). Columbia U Pr.
Defense Policy. 2nd ed. Ed. by Congressional Quarterly. 200p. 1980. pap. text ed. 7.95 (ISBN 0-87187-158-0). Congr Quarterly.
Defense Policy & the Presidency, Carter's First Years. Ed. by Sam C. Sarkesian. (Special Studies in National Security & Defense Policy). 1979. lib. bdg. 26.50x (ISBN 0-89158-273-8). Westview.
Defense Politics of the Atlantic Alliance. Ed. by Edwin H. Fedder. 180p. 1980. 21.95 (ISBN 0-03-058018-8). Praeger.
Defense Tactics for Law Enforcement: Weaponless Defense & Control & Baton Techniques. rev. ed. Bruce Tegner. LC 77-28136. (Illus.). 1978. pap. 4.95 (ISBN 0-87407-028-7, T-28). Thor.

Defense Technology & the Atlantic Alliance: Competition or Collaboration? Frank T. Bray & Michael Moodie. LC 77-80297. (Foreign Policy Report Ser.). 5.00 (ISBN 0-89549-000-5). Inst Foreign Policy Anal.

Defenses of Narragansett Bay in World War II. Walter K. Schroder. (Illus.). 133p. (Orig.). 1980. pap. 5.95 (ISBN 0-917012-22-4, 80-51763). RI Pubns Soc.

Defensive Linemen. Jay H. Smith. LC 74-23193. (Stars of the NFL Ser.). (gr. 4-12). 1975. PLB 7.95 (ISBN 0-87191-420-4). Creative Ed.

Defensive Play in Bridge: Featuring the Distribution Signal. Helge Vinje. Ed. by Terence Reese. LC 79-57451. (Illus.). 192p. 1980. 7.95 o.p. (ISBN 0-8069-4938-4); lib. bdg. 7.49 o.p. (ISBN 0-8069-4939-2). Sterling.

Defensor Pacis. Marsilius Of Padua. Tr. by Alan Gewirth. (Medieval Academy Reprints for Teaching Ser.). 1980. pap. 6.00x (ISBN 0-8020-6412-4). U of Toronto Pr.

Defiance Mountain. Frank Bonham. 1979. pap. 1.50 o.p. (ISBN 0-425-03955-2). Berkley Pub.

Defiance Mountain. rev. ed. Frank Bonham. 1981. pap. 1.95 (ISBN 0-425-04932-9). Berkley Pub.

Defiant Desire. Kaye W. Klem. 1977. pap. 1.75 o.p. (ISBN 0-449-13741-4, GM). Fawcett.

Defiant Ones: A Screen Adaptation of the Story of "The Long Road". Nathan Douglas et al. Ed. by George Garrett et al. LC 71-135273. (Film Scripts Ser.). 1971. pap. text ed. 5.95x (ISBN 0-89197-725-2). Irvington.

Defining America's Social Problems. J. Douglas. 1974. pap. 11.95 (ISBN 0-13-197624-9). P-H.

Defining Crime. Sarah McCabe & Frank Sutcliffe. 1978. pap. 6.00x o.p. (ISBN 0-631-14300-9, Pub. by Basil Blackwell England). Biblio Dist.

Defining the Laboratory Animal. Institute Of Laboratory Animal Resources. LC 72-609048. (Illus.). 1971. 19.25 (ISBN 0-309-01862-5). Natl Acad Pr.

Defining the Situation: The Organization of Meaning in Social Interaction. Peter McHugh. LC 68-2800. 1968. 7.50 o.p. (ISBN 0-672-51135-5); pap. 5.50 (ISBN 0-672-60812-X). Bobbs.

Definitely Maybe. Arkady Strugatsky & Boris Strugatsky. LC 77-16550. (Best of Soviet Science Fiction). 1978. 10.95 (ISBN 0-02-615180-4); pap. 1.95 (ISBN 0-02-025590-X). Macmillan.

Definition & Measurement of Poverty: Annotated Bibliography, Vol. 2. Ed. by Sharon M. Oster et al. LC 77-5233. (Westview Special Studies in Applied Social Research Ser.). 1978. lib. bdg. 37.50x (ISBN 0-89158-246-0). Westview.

Definition & Measurement of Poverty: A Review, Vol. 1. S. M. Oster et al. LC 77-5233. 1977. lib. bdg. 26.50x (ISBN 0-89158-245-2). Westview.

Definition of Programming Languages. Andrew McGettrick. LC 79-21635. (Cambridge Computer Science Texts). 1980. 29.95 (ISBN 0-521-22631-7); pap. 12.95 (ISBN 0-521-29585-8). Cambridge U Pr.

Definition of Psychology. 2nd ed. Fred S. Keller. LC 72-94282. 128p. 1973. 8.95 (ISBN 0-13-197616-8). P-H.

Definition of Quality & Approaches to Its Assessment, Vol. 1. Avedis Donabedian. (Explorations in Quality Assessment & Monitoring Ser.). (Illus.). 180p. 1980. text ed. 17.95 (ISBN 0-914904-47-7); pap. text ed. 12.95 (ISBN 0-914904-48-5). Health Admin Pr.

Definitions & Criteria. Marcella M. DuPont. LC 65-16526. 1965. 3.50 (ISBN 0-8040-0065-4). Swallow.

Definitions & Measurement of Detente: East & West Perspectives. Ed. by Daniel Frei. LC 80-27960. 256p. 1981. lib. bdg. 22.50 (ISBN 0-89946-080-1). Oelgeschlager.

Definitions of Nonviolence. Lanza Del Vasto. Tr. by Jean Sidgwick. Orig. Title: Fr. 27p. (Orig.). 1972. pap. 1.00 (ISBN 0-934676-06-2). Greenlf Bks.

Defoe: The Critical Heritage. Ed. by Pat Rogers. (Critical Heritage Ser). 1972. 25.00 (ISBN 0-7100-7259-7). Routledge & Kegan.

Defoe's Early Life. F. Bastian. (Illus.). 456p. 1981. 36.00x (ISBN 0-389-20094-8). B&N.

Deformation & Flow of Solids: Proceedings. International Union of Theoretical & Applied Mechanics Colloquium, Madrid, 1955. Ed. by Richard Grammel. (Illus., Eng, Ger, Fr. & Span.). 1956. 34.30 (ISBN 0-387-02095-0). Springer-Verlag.

Deformation & Fracture of Solids. Robert M. Caddell. (Illus.). 1980. text ed. 26.95 (ISBN 0-13-198309-1). P-H.

Deformation Geometry for Material Scientists. C. N. Reid. LC 73-4716. 220p. 1973. text ed. 25.00 (ISBN 0-08-017237-7); pap. text ed. 13.25 (ISBN 0-08-017745-X). Pergamon.

Deformation Kinetics. A. S. Krausz & H. Eyring. LC 75-12554. 398p. 1975. 39.95 (ISBN 0-471-24983-1, Pub. by Wiley-Interscience). Wiley.

Deformation Processing. Walter A. Backofen. LC 71-132054. (Engineering Science Ser). 1972. text ed. 21.95 (ISBN 0-201-00388-0). A-W.

Deformations of Fibre-Reinforced Materials. A. J. Spencer. (Oxford Science Research Papers). (Illus.). 140p. 1972. pap. 19.95x (ISBN 0-19-851939-7). Oxford U Pr.

Defrosting of Minnesota. Helen J. Cichy. LC 77-86170. 1977. 7.00 (ISBN 0-9601852-1-6); pap. 4.75 (ISBN 0-685-89498-3). H J Cichy.

Defrosting of Minnesota. Helen J. Cichy. LC 77-86170. 1977. 8.00 (ISBN 0-9601852-0-8); pap. 4.75 (ISBN 0-9601852-1-6). H J Cichy.

Defy & Endure: Great Sieges of Modern History. Eversley Belfield. LC 68-21302. Orig. Title: Great Sieges. (Illus.). (gr. 7-10). 1968. 4.50g o.s.i. (ISBN 0-02-709030-2, CCPr). Macmillan.

Defy the Savage Winds. June L. Shiplett. (Orig.). 1980. pap. 2.50 (ISBN 0-451-09337-2, E9337, Sig). NAL.

Defy the Storm. Diana Haviland. 352p. 1981. pap. 2.75 (ISBN 0-449-14379-1, GM). Fawcett.

Degas. Daniel C. Rich. (Library Great Painters Ser). (Illus., Orig.). 1951. 35.00 (ISBN 0-8109-0067-X). Abrams.

Degas' Drawings. Degas. (Illus.). 10.00 (ISBN 0-8446-5022-6). Peter Smith.

Degas Letters. Edgar G. Degas. Ed. by Marcel Guerin. Tr. by Marguerite Kay. (Illus.). 12.95 (ISBN 0-912158-53-0). Hennessey.

Degas Pastels. Alfred Werner. (Illus.). 1977. pap. 8.95 o.p. (ISBN 0-8230-1276-X). Watson-Guptill.

Degeneration in the Leadership in the United States As the Primary Cause for the Moral, Economic & Political Collapse of the World. Robert Mosby. (Illus.). 243p. 1976. 25.00 (ISBN 0-913314-67-6); lib. bdg. 39.50 (ISBN 0-685-66467-8). Am Classical Coll Pr.

Degeneration of the Female of the Species & the Decay of the Human Society. enl. ed. Cosmo Galante. (Illus.). 68p. 1973. 39.45 (ISBN 0-913314-18-8). Am Classical Coll Pr.

Degradation of Synthetic Organic Molecules in the Biosphere. Division of Biology & Agriculture. (Illus.). 352p. pap. 19.50 (ISBN 0-309-02046-8). Natl Acad Pr.

Degree & What Else? Correlates & Consequences of a College Education. Carnegie Commission on Higher Education. 1971. 9.95 o.p. (ISBN 0-07-010035-7, P&RB). McGraw.

Degree of Difference. George B. Ford. 1969. 5.95 o.p. (ISBN 0-374-13640-8). FS&G.

Degree of Difference: The Open Uninversity of the United Kingdom. Naomi E. McIntosh et al. LC 77-23034. (Praeger Special Studies). 1977. 29.95 (ISBN 0-03-040341-3). Praeger.

Degree Problems in Soil Mechanics & Foundation Engineering. 1977. pap. 5.95 (ISBN 0-408-00296-4). Butterworths.

Degree Theory. N. G. Lloyd. LC 77-3205. (Tracts in Mathematics Ser.: No. 73). (Illus.). 1978. 35.50 (ISBN 0-521-21614-1). Cambridge U Pr.

Degree Words. Dwight Bolinger. (Janua Linguarum, Ser. Major: No. 53). 1972. text ed. 51.75x (ISBN 0-686-22528-7). Mouton.

Deidre of the Sorrows: And the Tinker's Wedding & the Shadow of the Glen. John M. Synge. (Unwin Book). 1967. pap. 2.95 (ISBN 0-04-822033-7). Allen Unwin.

Deification of Man: Its Methods & Stages According to the Yoga Vasistha Including a Translation of the Essence of Vasistha's Teachings. B. L. Atreya. 116p. 1980. pap. 4.50 (ISBN 0-935548-02-5). Santarasa Pubns.

Deinstitutionalization & Institutional Reform. R. C. Scheerenberger. (Illus.). 272p. 1976. 23.75 (ISBN 0-398-03552-0). C C Thomas.

Deirdre. James Stephens. LC 23-12751. (Illus.). (gr. 7 up). 1970. 8.95 (ISBN 0-02-788020-6). Macmillan.

Deirdre: A Celtic Legend. David Guard. LC 77-23492. (Illus.). (gr. k-12). 1977. pap. 4.95 o.p. (ISBN 0-89087-201-5). Celestial Arts.

Deirdre: A Celtic Legend. David Guard. LC 80-69774. (Illus.). 118p. (gr. 6). 1981. Repr. of 1977 ed. 9.95 (ISBN 0-89742-047-0). Dawne-Leigh.

Deist's Manual; or a Rational Enquiry into the Christian Religion. Charles Gildon. Ed. by Rene Wellek. LC 75-11220. (British Philosophers & Theologians of the 17th & 18th Centuries: Vol. 23). 1976. Repr. of 1705 ed. lib. bdg. 42.00 (ISBN 0-8240-1774-9). Garland Pub.

Deja-Vu. Dominique Saint-Alban. LC 77-15341. 1978. 7.95 o.p. (ISBN 0-312-19183-9). St Martin.

Dejango Reinhardt (Jazz) Charles Delavnay. 247p. 22.50 (ISBN 0-306-76057-6). Da Capo.

Dejeuner De Sousceyrac. Benoit. (Easy Readers Ser.). 1978. pap. text ed. 3.75 (ISBN 0-88436-293-0). EMC.

Del Corazon de una Mujer. Carole Mayhall. Tr. by Juan Rojas from Eng. 111p. (Orig., Span.). 1978. pap. 2.25 (ISBN 0-89922-130-0). Edit Caribe.

Del Odio Al Amor. Francisco Ordonez. 1980. pap. 1.20 (ISBN 0-311-08223-8). Casa Bautista.

Delacroix. (Selected Artists Art Ser). (Illus.). 1977. pap. 5.95 (ISBN 0-8120-0816-2). Barron.

Delacroix. Claude Roger-Marx & Sabine Cotte. LC 70-132366. (Great Draughtsmen Ser). (Illus.). 1971. 7.95 o.s.i. (ISBN 0-8076-0586-7). Braziller.

Delacroix & Raphael. Sara Lichtenstein. Ed. by Sydney J. Freedberg. LC 78-74970. (Outstanding Dissertations in the Fine Arts Ser.). (Illus.). 1979. lib. bdg. 44.00 (ISBN 0-8240-3972-6). Garland Pub.

DeLange Syndrome. J. M. Berg et al. LC 72-124065. 1970. 22.00 (ISBN 0-08-016125-1). Pergamon.

Delaware. 23.00 (ISBN 0-89770-083-X). Curriculum Info Ctr.

Delaware, a Bicentennial History. Carol E. Hoffecker. (States & the Nation Ser.). (Illus.). 1977. 12.95 (ISBN 0-393-05620-1). Norton.

Delaware Colony. H. Clay Reed. LC 77-95297. (Forge of Freedom Ser). (Illus.). (gr. 5-8). 1970. 8.95 (ISBN 0-02-775730-7, CCPr). Macmillan.

Delaware in Word & Pictures. Dennis Fradin. LC 80-5842. (Young Peoples Stories of Our States Ser.). (Illus.). 48p. (gr. 2-5). 1980. PLB 8.95 (ISBN 0-516-03908-3). Childrens.

Delaware Indian Symposium. Ed. by Herbert C. Kraft. (Pennsylvania Historical & Museum Comm. Anthropological Ser., No. 4). (Illus.). 160p. 1974. 7.00 (ISBN 0-911124-77-2); pap. 4.00 (ISBN 0-911124-76-4). Pa Hist & Mus.

Delaware Indians: A History. C. A. Weslager. (Illus.). 576p. 1972. 35.00 (ISBN 0-8135-0702-2). Rutgers U Pr.

Delaware Indians: Eastern Fishermen & Farmers. Sonia Bleeker. (Illus.). (gr. 3-6). 1953. PLB 6.67 (ISBN 0-688-31230-6). Morrow.

Delaware State Industrial Directory, 1980. State Industrial Directories Corp. 1980. pap. 20.00 (ISBN 0-89910-032-5). State Indus Dir.

Delaware Valley Rails. John R. Pawson. (Illus.). 1979. pap. 11.50 (ISBN 0-9602080-0-3). Pawson.

Delaware Verbal Morphology: A Descriptive & Comparative Study. Ives Goddard. Ed. by Jorge Hankamer. LC 78-66556. (Outstanding Dissertations in Linguistics Ser.). 1979. lib. bdg. 26.50 (ISBN 0-8240-9685-1). Garland Pub.

Delawares: A Critical Bibliography. C. A. Weslager. LC 78-3250. (Newberry Library Center for the History of the American Indian Bibliographical Ser.). 96p. 1978. pap. 4.95x (ISBN 0-253-31680-4). Ind U Pr.

Delayed Fission Neutrons. (Illus., Orig.). 1968. pap. text ed. 14.50 (ISBN 92-0-031068-0, IAEA). Unipub.

Deleatur. Herbert Gall. (Suhrkamp Taschenbuecher: St 639). 244p. (Orig.). 1980. pap. text ed. 5.20 (ISBN 3-518-37139-8, Pub. by Insel Verlag Germany). Suhrkamp.

Delectable Vegetable. Kay S. Nelson. (John Day Bk.). 1976. 8.95 o.p. (ISBN 0-381-98292-0, TYC-T). T Y Crowell.

Delegate from New Jersey: The Journal of John Fell. John Fell. Ed. by Donald W. Whisenhunt. LC 73-83264. 222p. 1974. 13.50 (ISBN 0-8046-9041-3). Kennikat.

Delegate from New York. John R. Lansing. Ed. by J. R. Strayer. LC 67-27618. 1967. Repr. of 1939 ed. 12.00 (ISBN 0-8046-0262-X). Kennikat.

Delegation & Autonomy. Arthur W. Macmahon. 1962. 4.50x o.p. (ISBN 0-210-33833-4). Asia.

Deletion in Coordinate Structures. Ed. by Jorge Hankamer. LC 78-67738. (Outstanding Dissertations in Linguistics Ser.). 1979. lib. bdg. 41.00 (ISBN 0-8240-9669-X). Garland Pub.

Delicate Arrangement: The Strange Case of Charles Darwin & Alfred Russel Wallace. 384p. 1980. 14.95 (ISBN 0-8129-0883-X). Times Bks.

Delicate Art of Nursing Supervision & Leadership. Ed. by Barbara Stevens. LC 77-85309. 1977. pap. 6.95 o.s.i. (ISBN 0-913654-41-8). Nursing Res.

Delicate Mission. Conrad O'Brien-ffrench. 250p. 1980. 29.75x (ISBN 0-7050-0062-1, Pub. by Skilton & Shaw England). State Mutual Bk.

Delicate Prey. Paul Bowles. LC 72-80780. 307p. 1981. pap. 7.95 (ISBN 0-912946-01-6). Ecco Pr.

Delicate Wear. Time Life Bks Editors. LC 74-21557. (Art of Sewing Ser.). (Illus.). 208p. (gr. 6 up). 1975. lib. bdg. 11.97 (ISBN 0-8094-1739-1). Silver.

Delicious & Easy Rice Flour Recipes: A Sequel to Gourmet Food on a Wheat-Free Diet. Marion N. Wood. 160p. 1972. pap. 8.50 (ISBN 0-398-02441-3). C C Thomas.

Delicious Diet Cookbook: The Sensible Way to Slim. Lois Levine. (Illus.). 192p. 1974. 6.95 o.s.i. (ISBN 0-02-570400-1). Macmillan.

Delie. Maurice Sceve. Ed. by I. D. McFarlane. 1966. 75.00 (ISBN 0-521-05628-4). Cambridge U Pr.

Delight of Being His Daughter. Dotty Schmitt. 1981. pap. 4.95 (ISBN 0-88270-509-1). Logos.

Delightful Journey: Down the Green & Colorado Rivers. Barry M. Goldwater. LC 77-94876. 1970. 15.00 (ISBN 0-685-67965-9). AZ Hist Foun.

Delights & Prejudices. James Beard. (Illus.). 1964. 6.95 (ISBN 0-689-00007-3); pap. 7.95 (ISBN 0-689-70605-7). Atheneum.

Delights of Anna. John Colleton. (Orig.). 1980. pap. 2.75 (ISBN 0-451-09453-0, E9453, Sig). NAL.

Delights of Olding. Frederick Kohner. LC 77-74004. (Illus.). 1979. 7.00 o.p. (ISBN 0-89430-012-1). Morgan-Pacific.

Delinquency & Opportunity: A Theory of Delinquent Gangs. Richard A. Cloward & Lloyd E. Ohlin. LC 60-10892. 1966. 17.95 (ISBN 0-02-905600-4); pap. text ed. 5.95 (ISBN 0-02-905590-3). Free Pr.

Delinquency & Puberty Examination of a Juvenile Delinquency Fad. Gerhard O. Mueller et al. (New York University Criminal Law Education & Research Center Monograph: No. 5). (Illus.). 123p. (Orig.). 1971. pap. text ed. 8.50x (ISBN 0-8377-0830-3). Rothman.

Delinquency, Crime & Social Process. Ed. by Donald R. Cressey & David A. Ward. 1969. text ed. write for info. o.p. (ISBN 0-06-041414-6, HarpC). Har-Row.

Delinquency in Three Cultures. Carl M. Rosenquist & Edwin I. Megargee. (Hogg Foundation Research Ser). (Illus.). 1969. 17.50 (ISBN 0-292-78415-5). U of Tex Pr.

Delinquent Behavior. 2nd ed. Don C. Gibbons. (Illus.). 1976. text ed. 17.95 (ISBN 0-13-197939-6). P-H.

Delinquent Behavior. 3rd ed. Don C. Gibbons. (Illus.). 1980. text ed. 17.95 (ISBN 0-13-197962-0). P-H.

Delinquent Boys. A. K. Cohen. LC 55-7337. 1955. 14.95 (ISBN 0-02-905760-4); pap. text ed. 4.95 (ISBN 0-02-905770-1). Free Pr.

Delinquent Children in Juvenile Correctional Institutions: State Administered Reception & Diagnostic Centers. Ed. by William E. Amos & Raymond L. Manella. (Illus.). 176p. 1973. pap. 14.75 (ISBN 0-398-00040-9). C C Thomas.

Delinquent Fantasies. Patricia Morgan. LC 78-309292. 1979. 18.50 (ISBN 0-85117-116-8). Transatlantic.

Delinquent Way of Life. D. J. West & D. P. Farrington. LC 76-41090. 1977. 18.00x (ISBN 0-8448-1033-9). Crane-Russak Co.

Delinquents in the Making. Sheldon Glueck & Eleanor Glueck. LC 51-11917. 1952. 7.95x o.p. (ISBN 0-06-032370-1, HarpT). Har-Row.

Deliquency & Drift. D. Matza. LC 64-18135. 1964. pap. text ed. 8.95x (ISBN 0-471-57708-1). Wiley.

Delirious New York: A Retroactive Manifesto for Manhattan. Rem Koolhaas. LC 77-17418. (Illus.). 1978. 39.95 (ISBN 0-19-520035-7). Oxford U Pr.

Delirium. Barbara Alberti. Tr. by Lawrence Venuti from It. 1981. 15.00 (ISBN 0-374-13744-7). FS&G.

Delirium. Z. J. Lipowski. 1980. 39.75 o.p. (ISBN 0-398-03909-7). C C Thomas.

Delirium: Acute Brain Failure in Man. Z. J. Lipowski. (American Lecture in Living Chemistry Ser.). 576p. 1980. text ed. 39.75 (ISBN 0-398-03909-7). C C Thomas.

Delius. Alan Jefferson. (Master Musicians Ser). (Illus.). 189p. 1972. 7.95x (ISBN 0-460-03131-7, Pub. by J. M. Dent England). Biblio Dist.

Delius Companion: A 70th Birthday Tribute to Eric Fenby. Ed. by Christopher Redwood. LC 76-57756. (Music Reprint Ser.). (Illus.). 1977. Repr. of 1976 ed. lib. bdg. 25.00 (ISBN 0-306-77532-8). Da Capo.

Deliver Us from Evil. Don Basham. 1972. 4.95 (ISBN 0-912376-06-6); pap. 2.95 o.p. (ISBN 0-685-56346-4). Chosen Bks Pub.

Deliver Us from Evil: The Prayer of Our Lord. John B. Coburn. 1976. pap. 4.95 (ISBN 0-8164-2124-2). Crossroad NY.

Deliver Us from Love. Suzanne Brogger. 1976. 8.95 o.p. (ISBN 0-440-01851-X, Sey Lawr). Delacorte.

Deliverance Book. Kent Philpott & R. L. Hymers. pap. cancelled o.s.i. (ISBN 0-89728-024-5, 677389). Omega Pubns OR.

Delivering Educational Services. David Goodwin. LC 76-54166. 1977. pap. text ed. 8.25x (ISBN 0-8077-2507-2). Tchrs Coll.

Delivering Mental Health Services: Needs, Priorities & Strategies. 1975. 5.00 o.p. (ISBN 0-685-77441-4, 176). Am Psychiatric.

Delivery. Carolyn Bell. (Outlaws Ser.: Vol. 3). 1980. pap. 4.50x (ISBN 0-917624-19-X). Lame Johnny.

Delivery. Georges Simenon. Ed. by Eileen Ellenbogen. LC 80-8759. (Helen & Kurt Wolff Bk.). 1981. 10.95 (ISBN 0-15-124655-6). HarBraceJ.
Dell Crossword Dictionary. Kathleen Rafferty. 1981. pap. 2.95 (ISBN 0-440-16314-5). Dell.
Dell Encyclopedia of Dogs. Lou S. Ashworth et al. (Illus.). 240p. 1974. 8.95 o.s.i. (ISBN 0-440-01784-X). Delacorte.
Dell Word Search, No. 20. Kathleen Rafferty. 1981. pap. 1.95 (ISBN 0-440-12071-3). Dell.
Deller's Walker on Patents: 1964-76. 2nd ed. Anthony W. Deller. LC 64-6861. 1976. Vols. 1-9. 42.50 ea.; Set. 382.50 (ISBN 0-686-14533-X). Lawyers Co-Op.
Dell'Opera in Musica. Antonio Planelli. LC 80-2292. 1981. Repr. of 1772 ed. 31.50 (ISBN 0-404-18861-3). AMS Pr.
Delos. Veronica Robinson. LC 80-65667. (Illus.). 128p. (gr. 6 up). 1980. 8.95 (ISBN 0-233-97259-5). Andre Deutsch.
Delphi Method: Techniques & Applications. Ed. by Harold A. Linstone & Murray Turoff. LC 75-25650. 672p. 1975. text ed. 35.50 (ISBN 0-201-04294-0, Adv Bk Prog); pap. text ed. 21.50 (ISBN 0-201-04293-2, Adv Bk Prog). A-W.
Delphic Oracle: Its Responses & Operations. Joseph Fontenrose. LC 76-47969. 1978. 30.00x (ISBN 0-520-03360-4). U of Cal Pr.
Delphic Oracle: Its Responses & Operations. Joseph Fontenrose. 1981. pap. 10.95 (ISBN 0-520-04359-6, CAL 490). U of Cal Pr.
Delphinid (Mammalia: Cetacea) from the Miocene of Palos Verdes Hills, California. Leslie E. Wilson. (U. C. Publ. in Geological Sciences: Vol. 103). 1973. pap. 7.00x (ISBN 0-520-09458-1). U of Cal Pr.
Delta Decision. Wilbur Smith. LC 79-6660. 408p. 1981. 12.95 (ISBN 0-385-13604-8). Doubleday.
Delta Flame. Marilyn Ross. 1978. pap. 1.95 o.p. (ISBN 0-445-04157-9). Popular Lib.
Delta Ladies. Fern Michaels. 1980. pap. 2.75 (ISBN 0-671-83337-5). PB.
Delta Modulation Systems. R. Steele. LC 74-11299. 379p. 1975. 42.95 (ISBN 0-470-82104-3). Halsted Pr.
Delta Products Case Study. Marjorie Leeson. 112p. 1980. pap. text ed. 6.95t (ISBN 0-574-21288-4, 13-4288); solutions manual avail. (ISBN 0-574-21289-2, 13-4289). SRA.
Delta's Effective English As a Second Language for the 21st Century Laotian Supplement. Tr. by Souksomboun Sayasithsena. 104p. (Orig.). 1980. pap. 4.95 (ISBN 0-937354-02-3). Delta Systems.
Deltoid Pumpkin Seed. John McPhee. 192p. 1973. 12.95 (ISBN 0-374-13781-1). FS&G.
Deltoid Pumpkin Seed. John McPhee. 160p. 1976. pap. 2.25 (ISBN 0-345-27999-9). Ballantine.
Deltoid Pumpkin Seed. John McPhee. 1981. pap. 5.95 (ISBN 0-374-51635-9). FS&G.
Deluge. Gerald W. Wheeler. LC 78-8404. (Flame Ser.). 1978. pap. 0.95 (ISBN 0-8127-0191-7). Southern Pub.
Deluge Story in Stone. Byron C. Nelson. (Illus.). 1968. Repr. of 1931 ed. 4.95 (ISBN 0-87123-095-X, 210095). Bethany Fell.
Delusions & Discoveries: Studies on India in the British Imagination 1880-1930. Benita Parry. 1972. 24.50x (ISBN 0-520-02215-7). U of Cal Pr.
Delux Designs for Coloring Transfers. Ruth Heller. Incl. Bk. 1. (Illus.). 48p. pap. 2.95 (ISBN 0-448-14759-9); Bk. 2. (Illus.). 48p. pap. 2.95 (ISBN 0-448-14760-2). 1981. G&D.
Demand Analysis & Inventory Control. Colin D. Lewis. 1974. 23.50 (ISBN 0-347-01038-5, 93518-2, Pub. by Saxon Hse England). Lexington Bks.
Demand Analysis for Marketing Decisions. G. David Hughes. 1973. text ed. 18.95x (ISBN 0-256-01479-5). Irwin.
Demand & Supply. 2nd ed. Ralph Turvey. (Illus.). 128p. 1980. text ed. 17.95x (ISBN 0-04-330302-1, 2479); pap. text ed. 4.95 (ISBN 0-04-330303-X, 2480). Allen Unwin.
Demand & Supply in U. S. Higher Education. Carnegie Commission on Higher Educaion. Ed. by K. Radner & L. S. Miller. 1975. 22.95 o.p. (ISBN 0-07-010113-2, P&RB). McGraw.
Demand for Energy in North-West India. Prithvi N. Dhar & D. U. Sastry. 1967. 5.50 o.p. (ISBN 0-210-22506-8). Asia.
Demand for Financial Assets. D. K. Bhattacharyya. 1978. text ed. 25.25x (ISBN 0-566-00228-0, Pub. by Gower Pub Co England). Renouf.
Demand for Financial Assets. D. K. Bhattacharyya. 200p. 1978. text ed. 25.25x (ISBN 0-566-00228-0, Pub. by Gower Pub Co England). Renouf.
Demand for Food: An Exercise in Household Budget Analysis. Ed. & intro. by W. J. Thomas. (Illus.). 136p. 1972. text ed. 11.50x (ISBN 0-7190-0512-4). Humanities.
Demand for Money in Norway. Arne Isachsen. 1976. pap. text ed. 6.00x (ISBN 8-200-01569-6, Dist. by Columbia U Pr). Universitet.
Demand for Natural Gas in the United States. Pietro Balestra. (Contributions to Economic Analysis Ser.: No. 46). 1967. text ed. 16.50x (ISBN 0-7204-3142-5, Pub. by North Holland). Humanities.
Demand for Residential Telephone Service. Gary P. Mahan. LC 79-620020. 1979. pap. 6.00 (ISBN 0-87744-158-8). Mich St U Busn.
Demand Revelation & the Provision of Public Goods. Edward H. Clarke. 1980. 26.50 (ISBN 0-88410-686-1). Ballinger Pub.
Demands of Art. Max Raphael. Tr. by Norbert Guterman. LC 65-10431. (Bollingen Ser.: Vol. 78). (Illus.). 1968. 30.00 o.p. (ISBN 0-691-09722-4). Princeton U Pr.
Demaundes of Holy Scripture, with Answeres to the Same. Thomas Becon. LC 79-84087. (English Experience Ser.: No.907). 116p. 1979. Repr. of 1577 ed. lib. bdg. 9.00 (ISBN 90-221-0907-0). Walter J Johnson.
Demelza No.2. (Poldark Ser.). 1977. pap. 2.25 (ISBN 0-345-27732-5). Ballantine.
Dementia in the Presenium. Andrew E. Slaby & Richard J. Wyatt. (Illus.). 244p. 1974. 18.50 (ISBN 0-398-02946-6). C C Thomas.
Demetrius "On Style" A New Edition with Commentary. C. Anagnostou. (London Studies in Classical Philology). 1980. pap. text ed. write for info. (ISBN 0-391-01158-8). Humanities.
Demise of a Rural Economy: From Subsistence to Capitalism in a Latin American Village. Stephen Gudeman. (International Library of Anthropology). 1978. 21.00x (ISBN 0-7100-8835-3); pap. 8.95 (ISBN 0-7100-8836-1). Routledge & Kegan.
Democracy. Carl Cohen. LC 77-142911. 1973. pap. text ed. 3.95 (ISBN 0-02-906100-8). Free Pr.
Democracy. Don Lawson. LC 78-1860. (First Bks). (Illus.). (gr. 4-6). 1978. PLB 6.45 s&l (ISBN 0-531-01487-8). Watts.
Democracy, an American Novel. Henry Adams. (Classics Ser). (YA) (gr. 9 up). pap. 1.50 (ISBN 0-8049-0164-3, CL-164). Airmont.
Democracy: Ancient & Modern. M. I. Finley. 112p. 1973. 8.00 o.p. (ISBN 0-8135-0751-0). Rutgers U Pr.
Democracy & Classical Greece. J. K. Davies. (Fontana History of the Ancient World Ser.). 1978. text ed. 22.25x (ISBN 0-391-00766-1). Humanities.
Democracy & Complexity: Who Governs the Governors. Ed. by Fred Krinsky. (Insight Series: Studies in Contemporary Issues). 128p. 1968. pap. text ed. 4.95x (ISBN 0-02-476030-7, 47603). Macmillan.
Democracy & Development in Turkey. C. H. Dodd. 1980. text ed. 27.50 (ISBN 0-906719-01-1); pap. text ed. 13.75x (ISBN 0-906719-00-3). Humanities.
Democracy & Disobedience. Peter Singer. 150p. 1974. pap. text ed. 3.95x (ISBN 0-19-519803-4). Oxford U Pr.
Democracy & Economic Change in India. rev. ed. George Rosen. 1966. 20.00x (ISBN 0-520-01089-2). U of Cal Pr.
Democracy & Illusion: An Examination of Certain Aspects of Modern Democratic Theory. John Plamenatz. 1977. pap. text ed. 10.50x (ISBN 0-582-48575-4). Longman.
Democracy & Its Discontents: Reflections on Everyday America. Daniel J. Boorstin. LC 74-20812. pap. 2.45 (ISBN 0-394-71501-2, V-501, Vin). Random.
Democracy & Liberty. William E. Lecky. LC 80-82371. 1981. Set. 18.00 (ISBN 0-913966-80-0); Vol. I, 520p. (ISBN 0-913966-82-7); Vol. II 528p. (ISBN 0-913966-83-5); Set. pap. 6.00 (ISBN 0-913966-81-9). Vol. I (ISBN 0-913966-84-3). Vol. II. (ISBN 0-913966-85-1). Liberty Fund.
Democracy & Mediating Structures: A Theological Inquiry. Ed. by Michael Novak. 1980. 13.25 (ISBN 0-8447-2175-1); pap. 7.25 (ISBN 0-8447-2176-X). Am Enterprise.
Democracy & Poetry. Robert P. Warren. LC 74-31993. 102p. 1975. 6.95 (ISBN 0-674-19625-2); pap. 2.95 (ISBN 0-674-19626-0). Harvard U Pr.
Democracy & the Amendments to the Constitution. Alan P. Grimes. LC 78-4342. (Illus.). 1978. 19.95 (ISBN 0-669-02344-2). Lexington Bks.
Democracy & the Novel: Popular Resistance to Classic American Writers. Henry N. Smith. (Galaxy Book: No. 633). 214p. 1981. pap. 5.95 (ISBN 0-19-502896-1). Oxford U Pr.
Democracy & the Novel: Popular Resistance to Classic American Writers. Henry N. Smith. 214p. 1981. pap. 5.95 (ISBN 0-19-502896-1, GB 633, OPB). Oxford U Pr.
Democracy & the Party Movement in Pre-War Japan: The Failure of the First Attempt. Robert A. Scalapino. (California Library Repr. Ser). 1975. Repr. of 1953 ed. 30.00x (ISBN 0-520-02914-3). U of Cal Pr.
Democracy & the Public Service. Frederick C. Mosher. (Public Administration & Democracy Ser). (Orig.). 1968. 12.95 (ISBN 0-19-500031-5); pap. 5.95x (ISBN 0-19-501000-0). Oxford U Pr.
Democracy & Welfare Economics. H. Van Den Doel. LC 78-21160. 1979. 29.50 (ISBN 0-521-22568-X); pap. 9.95x (ISBN 0-521-29555-6). Cambridge U Pr.
Democracy & World Conflict, 1868-1965: A History of Modern Britain. T. L. Jarman. (History of England Ser). 1968. text ed. 5.50x o.p. (ISBN 0-7137-0315-6). Humanities.
Democracy, Authority, & Alienation in Work: Workers' Participation in an American Corporation. John F. Witte. LC 80-16241. (Illus.). 1980. lib. bdg. 20.00x (ISBN 0-226-90420-2). U of Chicago Pr.
Democracy, Bureaucracy & Technocracy. M. A. Muttalib. 144p. 1980. text ed. 11.25x (ISBN 0-391-02120-6). Humanities.
Democracy in Alberta: Social Credit & the Party System. C. B. Macpherson. LC 54-4046. (Canadian University Paperbooks). 1953. pap. 6.95 (ISBN 0-8020-6009-9). U of Toronto Pr.
Democracy in America. abr. ed. Alexis De Tocqueville. Ed. by Richard D. Heffner. pap. 2.75 (ISBN 0-451-61620-0, ME1888, Ment). NAL.
Democracy in America. Alexis de Tocqueville. Ed. by J. P. Mayer & A. P. Kerr. 1969. pap. 7.95 (ISBN 0-385-08170-7, A05, Anch). Doubleday.
Democracy in France. Francois P. Guizot. LC 74-19357. v, 82p. 1974. Repr. of 1849 ed. 10.00 (ISBN 0-86527-040-6). Fertig.
Democracy in France Since Eighteen Seventy. 5th ed. David Thomson. (Royal Institute of Int'l Affairs Ser.). (Orig.). 1969. pap. 7.95x (ISBN 0-19-285036-9). Oxford U Pr.
Democracy, Militarism, & Nationalism in Argentina, 1930-1966: An Interpretation. Marvin Goldwert. (Latin American Monographs: No. 25). 286p. 1972. 10.00 (ISBN 0-292-71500-5). U of Tex Pr.
Democracy Reborn. Henry A. Wallace. Ed. by Russell Lord. LC 72-2387. (FDR & the Era of the New Deal Ser.). 280p. Repr. of 1944 ed. lib. bdg. 27.50 (ISBN 0-306-70487-0). Da Capo.
Democracy, Technology, Collision. Al P. Klose. (ITT Key Issues Lecture Ser.). 1980. pap. 4.95 (ISBN 0-672-97676-5). Bobbs.
Democracy's Railroads: Public Enterprise in Jacksonian Michigan. Robert J. Parks. LC 79-189557. (National University Publications). 1972. 17.50 (ISBN 0-8046-9027-8). Kennikat.
Democracy's Stepchildren: A Study of Need & Belief. Elizabeth L. Simpson. LC 73-146735. (Social & Behavioral Science Ser.). 1971. 12.95x o.p. (ISBN 0-87589-089-X). Jossey-Bass.
Democratic Art: An Exhibition on the History of Chromolithography in America, 1840-1900. Peter C. Mmarzio. 1979. pap. 9.95 (ISBN 0-88360-034-X). Amon Carter.
Democratic Dictatorship: The Emergent Constitution of Control. Arthur S. Miller. LC 80-25424. (Contributions in American Studies: No. 54). 312p. 1981. lib. bdg. 29.95 (ISBN 0-313-22836-1, MDD/). Greenwood.
Democratic Experience, 2 vols. 5th ed. Carl N. Degler et al. 1981. pap. text ed. 14.95x (ISBN 0-673-15450-5); Vol. 1. pap. text ed. 9.95x (ISBN 0-673-15451-3); Vol. 2. pap. text ed. 9.95x (ISBN 0-673-15452-1). Scott F.
Democratic Polity & Social Change in India: Crisis & Opportunities. Ranji Kothari. LC 76-904213. 1976. text ed. 7.50x o.p. (ISBN 0-88386-881-4); pap. text ed. 4.00x o.p. (ISBN 0-685-74909-6). South Asia Bks.
Democratic Process & Administrative Law. rev. ed. Robert S. Lorch. LC 69-10420. (Waynebooks Ser: No. 39). 1973. pap. 6.50x (ISBN 0-8143-1513-5). Wayne St U Pr.
Democratic Republic, 1801-1815. Marshal L. Smelser. Ed. by Henry S. Commager & Richard S. Morris. LC 68-28218. (New American Nation Series). (Illus.). 1968. 15.00 o.s.i. (ISBN 0-06-013927-7, HarpT). Har-Row.
Democratic Socialism & the Cost of Defence: The Report & Papers of the Labour Party Defence Study Group. Ed. by Mary Kaldor et al. Dan Smith & Steve Vines. 1979. 45.00x (ISBN 0-85664-886-8, Pub. by Croom Helm Ltd England). Biblio Dist.
Democratic Socialism: The Mass Left in Advanced Industrial Societies. Ed. by Bogdan Denitch. 220p. 1981. text ed. 26.00 (ISBN 0-86598-015-2). Allanheld.
Democratic Theory & Local Government. Dilys M. Hill. (New Local Government Ser.). 1974. pap. text ed. 9.95x (ISBN 0-04-352053-7). Allen Unwin.
Democratic Values & the Rights of Management. Eli Ginzberg et al. LC 63-20227. 1963. 20.00x (ISBN 0-231-02664-1). Columbia U Pr.
Democratization of Clothing in America: Student Syllabus. Barbara H. Salser. (gr. 10-12). 1979. pap. text ed. 6.95 (ISBN 0-89420-062-3, 165021); cassette recordings 88.10 (ISBN 0-89420-204-9, 165000). Natl Book.
Democratization of the Church. Alois Muller. LC 73-147026. (Concilium Ser.: Religion in the Seventies: Vol. 63). 1971. pap. 4.95 (ISBN 0-8164-2519-1). Crossroad NY.
Democrats & Labor in Rhode Island, 1952-1962: Changes in the Old Alliance. Jay S. Goodman. LC 67-26817. (Illus.). 154p. 1967. 7.50 (ISBN 0-87057-104-4, Pub. by Brown U Pr). Univ Pr of New England.
Democrats & Progressives: The 1948 Presidential Election As a Test of Postwar Liberalism. Allen Yarnell. 1974. 16.95x (ISBN 0-520-02539-3). U of Cal Pr.
Democrats, Dinners, & Dollars: A History of the Democratic Party, Its Dinners, Its Ritual. Ronald F. Stinnett. 1967. 8.95 o.p. (ISBN 0-685-99404-X). Iowa St U Pr.
Democrats: The Years After FDR. Herbert S. Parmet. LC 75-25990. (Illus.). 384p. 1976. 14.95 (ISBN 0-02-594770-2, 59477). Macmillan.
Demographic Analysis. Bernard Benjamin. (Studies in Sociology Ser.). 1969. text ed. 14.95x (ISBN 0-04-519002-X); pap. text ed. 6.50x o.p. (ISBN 0-04-519003-8). Allen Unwin.
Demographic Analysis: Methods, Results & Applications. Roland Pressat. LC 69-11228. 1972. 26.95x (ISBN 0-202-30093-5). Aldine Pub.
Demographic Analysis of East Africa: A Sociological Interpretation. Mette Monsted & Parve Walii. (Scandinavian Institute of African Studies, Uppsala). 1978. pap. text ed. 14.50x (ISBN 0-8419-9728-4). Holmes & Meier.
Demographic Aspects of Educational Planning. Ta N. Chau. (Fundamentals of Educational Planning Ser., No. 9). (Illus., Orig.). 1969. pap. 6.00 (ISBN 92-803-1028-3, U153, UNESCO). Unipub.
Demographic Behavior: Interdisciplinary Perspectives on Decision Making. Ed. by Thomas K. Burch. (AAAS Selected Symposium: No. 45). 45p. 1980. lib. bdg. 22.00x (ISBN 0-89158-785-3). Westview.
Demographic Developments in Eastern Europe. Ed. by Leszek A. Kosinski. LC 76-12858. (Special Studies). 1977. text ed. 32.50 (ISBN 0-275-56180-1). Praeger.
Demographic Dynamics in America. Wilbur J. Cohen & Charles F. Westoff. LC 77-80227. 1977. 12.95 (ISBN 0-02-905780-9). Free Pr.
Demographic Patterns in Developed Societies. Hiorns. (Symposia Ser.: Vol. 12). 216p. 1980. text ed. 26.00x (ISBN 0-85066-173-0). Humanities.
Demographic Problems: Controversy Over Population Control. 2nd ed. Ralph Thomlinson. (Contemporary Social Problems Ser.). 1975. pap. text ed. 7.95x (ISBN 0-8221-0166-1). Dickenson.
Demographic, Social, Educational & Economic Data for France, 1833-1925: Historical Population, Economic & Social Data: France,1901-1921. 1979. codebook 20.00 (ISBN 0-89138-978-4). ICPSR.
Demographic, Social, Educational & Economic Data for France, 1833-1925: Vital Statistics for France, 1836-1925. LC 79-63207. 1979. codebook 20.00 (ISBN 0-89138-979-2). ICPSR.
Demographic Techniques. A. H. Pollard et al. 161p. 1974. 17.75 (ISBN 0-08-017378-0). Pergamon.
Demographic Transition & Socio-Economic Development. (Population Studies: No. 65). 153p. 1979. pap. 10.00 (ISBN 0-686-68948-8, UN79/13/2, UN). Unipub.
Demographic Yearbook 1978. 30th ed. United Nations. Incl. 1962. 25.00 (ISBN 0-685-60085-8). LC 50-641. 1980. 36.00x (ISBN 0-8002-1051-4). Intl Pubns Serv.
Demography. 5th ed. Ed. by Peter R. Cox. LC 70-92245. (Illus.). 1976. 49.50 (ISBN 0-521-21003-8); pap. 15.95x (ISBN 0-521-29020-1). Cambridge U Pr.
Demography. O. S. Shrivastava. 500p. 1980. text ed. 25.00 (ISBN 0-7069-1109-1, Pub. by Vikas India). Advent Bk.
Demography & Evolution in Plant Populations. Ed. by Otto T. Solbrig. (Botanical Monographs Ser.: Vol. 15). 1980. monograph 32.50x (ISBN 0-520-03931-9). U of Cal Pr.
Demography: Principles & Methods. 2nd ed. T. Lynn Smith & Paul E. Zopf, Jr. LC 75-23243. (Illus.). 600p. 1976. text ed. 13.50x (ISBN 0-88284-033-9). Alfred Pub.
Demon Device. Robert Saffron. 288p. 1981. pap. 2.50 (ISBN 0-441-14255-9). Charter Bks.
Demon Letting. Gayle Feyrer. 1976. 30.00x o.p. (ISBN 0-931460-05-0). Bieler.
Demon Lover. Dion Fortune. pap. 6.00 (ISBN 0-87728-173-4). Weiser.

Demon of Padeng. Olive Bohner. LC 77-20928. (Nova Ser.). 1977. pap. 5.95 (ISBN 0-8127-0150-X). Southern Pub.
Demon Possession. John W. Montgomery. LC 75-19313. 1967. pap. 6.95 (ISBN 0-87123-102-6, 210102). Bethany Fell.
Demon Samurai. Clay Grant. 1978. pap. 1.50 (ISBN 0-505-51244-0). Tower Bks.
Demon Stalking. Debra Thrall. (Orig.). 1979. pap. 1.95 (ISBN 0-532-23116-3). Manor Bks.
Demonic Mnemonics. Murray Suid. LC 80-82982. 1981. pap. 5.50 (ISBN 0-8224-6464-0). Pitman Learning.
Demonic Possession. Hans Holzer. (Orig.). 1980. pap. 2.25 (ISBN 0-532-23128-7). Manor Bks.
Demonologist: The Extraordinary Career of Ed & Lorraine Warren. Gerald Brittle. LC 80-21065. (Illus.). 216p. 1981. 10.95 (ISBN 0-13-198333-4). P-H.
Demonology, Past & Present. Kurt E. Koch. LC 72-93353. 1973. pap. 2.95 (ISBN 0-8254-3013-5). Kregel.
Demons at My Door. Barbara Morgenroth. LC 80-12053. 168p. (gr. 5-10). 1980. 8.95 (ISBN 0-689-30781-0). Atheneum.
Demons by Daylight. Ramsey Campbell. pap. 1.75 o.s.i. (ISBN 0-515-04737-6). Jove Pubns.
Demons, Demons, Demons. Newport. LC 78-189503. 4.95 (ISBN 0-8054-5518-3). Broadman.
Demons, Dreamers, & Madmen: The Defense of Reason in Descartes Meditations. Harry Frankfurt. LC 70-75142. 1970. 10.95 (ISBN 0-672-51136-3). Bobbs.
Demons Have Had It. Charles Scriven. LC 76-2926. 128p. 1976. pap. 4.95 (ISBN 0-8127-0111-9). Southern Pub.
Demons of Rajpur. Betsy Bang. LC 80-10467. (Illus.). 96p. (gr. 3-6). 1980. 7.95 (ISBN 0-688-80263-X); PLB 7.63 (ISBN 0-688-84263-1). Greenwillow.
Demonstration of the First Visible Wave-Length Direct Nuclear Pumped Laser. M. Alfred Akerman. LC 78-75011. (Outstanding Dissertations on Energy Ser.). 1979. lib. bdg. 11.00 (ISBN 0-8240-3984-X). Garland Pub.
Demophoon. Maria L. Cherubini. Ed. by Philip Gossett & Charles Rosen. LC 76-49213. (Early Romantic Opera Ser.: Vol. 32). 1979. lib. bdg. 82.00 (ISBN 0-8240-2931-3). Garland Pub.
Demotic Mathematical Papyri. Richard A. Parker. LC 77-177501. (Brown University Studies: No. 7). (Illus.). 86p. 1972. 25.00x (ISBN 0-87057-132-X, Pub. by Brown U Pr). Univ Pr of New England.
Demotic Ostraca from Medinet Habu. Miriam Lichtheim. LC 57-9105. (Oriental Institute Pubns. Ser: No. 80). (Illus.). 1957. 25.00x o.s.i. (ISBN 0-226-62181-2). U of Chicago Pr.
Dempsey. Jack Dempsey & Barbara P. Dempsey. LC 76-26220. (Illus.). 1977. 12.50 o.s.i. (ISBN 0-06-011054-6, HarpT). Har-Row.
Demu Trilogy. F. M. Busby. (gr. 10-12). 1980. pap. 3.50 (ISBN 0-671-43288-5). PB.
Demurrer; or, Proofs of Error in the Decision of the Supreme Court of the State of New York Requiring Faith in a Particular Religious Doctrine As a Legal Qualification of Witnesses. Thomas Herttell. LC 70-122160. (Civil Liberties in American History Ser). 154p. 1972. Repr. of 1828 ed. lib. bdg. 15.00 (ISBN 0-306-71971-1). Da Capo.
Demystifying Parole. Janet Schmidt. LC 76-48375. (Illus.). 1977. 21.95 (ISBN 0-669-01145-2). Lexington Bks.
Den Chief Handbook. Boy Scouts Of America. LC 33-3848. (Illus.). 128p. (gr. 6-12). 1968. flexible bdg. 1.50 o.p. (ISBN 0-8395-3211-3, 3211). BSA.
Den Chief Handbook. Boy Scouts, of America. LC 79-55446. (Illus.). 128p. (gr. 6-12). 1980. flexible bdg. 1.75x. BSA.
Den Leader's Book. Boy Scouts Of America. LC 38-16321. (Illus.). 208p. 1967. pap. 1.75x (ISBN 0-8395-3212-1, 3212). BSA.
Deneki: An Alaskan Moose. William D. Berry. (gr. 4-6). 1965. 4.50g o.s.i. (ISBN 0-02-709510-X). Macmillan.
Deni of Western Brazil. Gordon Koop et al. (Museum of Anthropology Ser.: No. 7). 200p. 1980. write for info. (ISBN 0-88312-156-5); price not set microfiche (ISBN 0-88312-243-X). Summer Inst Ling.
Denial of Death. Ernest Becker. LC 73-1860. 1973. 12.95 (ISBN 0-02-902150-2); pap. 3.95 (ISBN 0-02-902310-6). Free Pr.
Denial of Justice: Criminal Process in the United States. Lloyd L. Weinreb. LC 76-27222. 1979. pap. text ed. 6.95 (ISBN 0-02-934870-6). Free Pr.
Denial of Stress. Shlomo Breznitz. 1981. write for info. (ISBN 0-8236-1185-X). Intl Univs Pr.
Denials of Doubt: An Interpretation of American History. Richard L. Rapson. LC 78-58595. 1978. pap. text ed. 13.50 (ISBN 0-8191-0541-4). U Pr of Amer.
Denigration of Capitalism. Ed. by Michael Novak. 1979. pap. 4.25 (ISBN 0-8447-3364-4). Am Enterprise.
Denim & Dogwood. Bob Logan. (Illus.). 96p. 1981. 5.95 (ISBN 0-89962-049-3). Todd & Honeywell.
Denim Book. Sharon Rosenberg & Joan W. Bordow. LC 78-1984. (Creative Handcraft Ser.). (Illus.). 1978. 15.95 o.p.- (ISBN 0-13-198424-1, Spec); pap. 8.95 (ISBN 0-13-198416-0). P-H.
Denis Fonvizin. Charles A. Moser. (World Authors Ser.: No. 560). 1979. lib. bdg. 14.95 (ISBN 0-8057-6402-X). Twayne.
Denis Johnston. Gene A. Barnett. (English Author Ser.: No. 230). 1978. 12.50 (ISBN 0-8057-6701-0). Twayne.
Denis Johnston's Irish Theatre. Harold Ferrar. (Irish Theatre Ser.: No.5). 144p. (Orig.). 1973. pap. text ed. 5.25x (ISBN 0-85105-208-8, Dolmen Pr). Humanities.
Denitrification Loss of Fertilizer Nitrogen in Paddy Soils - Its Recognition & Impact. (IRRI Research Paper Ser.: No. 37). 10p. 1979. pap. 5.00 (R077, IRRI). Unipub.
Denitrifigation, Nitrification, & Atmospheric Nitrous Oxide. C. C. Delwiche. LC 80-22698. 260p. 1981. 27.50 (ISBN 0-471-04896-8, Pub. by Wiley-Interscience). Wiley.
Denmark: An Archaeological Guide. Elisabeth Munksgaard. (Illus.). 1974. 5.50 (ISBN 0-571-09196-2, Pub. by Faber & Faber). Merrimack Bk Serv.
Denmark, Hamlet & Shakespeare, 2 vols. Cay Dollerup. (Salzburg Studies in English Literature, Elizabethan & Renaissance Studies Ser.: No. 47). 347p. (Orig.). 1975. Set. pap. text ed. 50.25x (ISBN 0-391-01363-7). Humanities.
Denmark in Pictures. Sterling Publishing Company Editors. LC 61-10396. (Visual Geography Ser). (gr. 5 up). PLB 4.99 (ISBN 0-8069-1003-8); pap. 2.95 (ISBN 0-8069-1002-X). Sterling.
Denmark Vesey: The Slave Conspiracy of 1822. Ed. by Robert S. Starobin. (Great Lives Observed Ser). 1970. pap. 1.95 o.p. (ISBN 0-13-198432-2, Spec). P-H.
Dennis the Menace: All American Kid. Hank Ketcham. (Dennis the Menace Ser.). (Illus.). 1977. pap. 1.50 (ISBN 0-449-13779-1, GM). Fawcett.
Dennis the Menace & His Pal Joey. Hank Ketcham. (Dennis the Menace Ser.). (Illus.). 1978. pap. 1.50 (ISBN 0-449-13822-4, GM). Fawcett.
Dennis the Menace & Poor Ol' Mr. Wilson. Hank Ketcham. (Dennis the Menace Ser.). (Illus.). 1978. pap. 1.50 (ISBN 0-449-13837-2, GM). Fawcett.
Dennis the Menace: Busy Body. Hank Ketcham. (Dennis the Menace Ser.). (Illus.). 128p. 1977. pap. 1.50 (ISBN 0-449-13658-2, GM). Fawcett.
Dennis the Menace: Good Intenshuns. Hank Ketchum. 128p. 1981. pap. 1.50 (ISBN 0-449-14395-3, GM). Fawcett.
Dennis the Menace: Happy Half-Pint. Hank Ketcham. (Dennis the Menace Ser). (Illus.). 1977. pap. 1.50 (ISBN 0-449-13649-3, GM). Fawcett.
Dennis the Menace: Here Comes Trouble. Hank Ketcham. (Dennis the Menace Ser.). (Illus.). 1978. pap. 1.50 (ISBN 0-449-13634-5, GM). Fawcett.
Dennis the Menace: Household Hurricane. Hank Ketcham. (Dennis the Menace Ser.). (Illus.). 1977. pap. 1.50 (ISBN 0-449-13679-5, GM). Fawcett.
Dennis the Menace: I Done It My Way. Hank Ketchum. (Dennis the Menace Ser.). 1979. pap. 1.50 (ISBN 0-449-14095-4, GM). Fawcett.
Dennis the Menace: Little Man in a Big Hurry. Hank Ketcham. (Dennis the Menace Ser.). (Illus.). 128p. 1978. pap. 1.50 (ISBN 0-449-13630-2, Gm). Fawcett.
Dennis the Menace: Make-Believe Angel. Hank Ketcham. (Dennis the Menace Ser.). (Illus.). 1977. pap. 1.50 (ISBN 0-449-13902-6, GM). Fawcett.
Dennis the Menace: The Kid Next Door. Hank Ketcham. (Dennis the Menace Ser.). (Illus.). 128p. 1977. pap. 1.50 (ISBN 0-449-13656-6, GM). Fawcett.
Dennis the Menace to the Core. Hank Ketcham. (Dennis the Menace Ser.). (Illus.). 128p. 1978. pap. 1.50 (ISBN 0-449-13873-9, GM). Fawcett.
Dennis the Menace Versus Everybody. Hank Ketcham. (Dennis the Menace Ser). (Illus.). 1978. pap. 1.50 (ISBN 0-449-13750-3, GM). Fawcett.
Denny Laine: How to Play the Guitar. Denny Laine. (Illus.). 110p. 1980. 10.95 (ISBN 0-517-54207-2, Harmony); pap. 6.95 (ISBN 0-517-54208-0, Harmony). Crown.
Denny's Knoll: A History of the Metropolitan Tract of the University of Washington. Neal O. Hines. LC 79-6760. (Illus.). 480p. 1980. 14.95 (ISBN 0-295-95718-2). U of Wash Pr.
Denominationalism. Ed. by Russell E. Richey. LC 74-49103. 1977. 15.95 o.p. (ISBN 0-687-10469-6); pap. 6.95 o.p. (ISBN 0-687-10470-X). Abingdon.
Denounced, 3 vols. John Banim & Michael Banim. Ed. by Robert L. Wolff. (Ireland Nineteenth Century Fiction Ser. Two: Vol. 21). 1979. Set. lib. bdg. 138.00 (ISBN 0-8240-3470-8). Garland Pub.
Densening & Chilling in Foundary Work. E. Longden. 178p. 1954. 10.95x (ISBN 0-85264-040-4, Pub. by Griffin England). State Mutual Bk.
Density: Five Perspectives. LC 72-79134. (Special Report Ser.). (Illus.). 1972. pap. 4.75 (ISBN 0-87420-556-5). Urban Land.
Dental Amalgam. M. Vrijhoef et al. (Illus.). 114p. 1980. 46.00 (ISBN 0-931386-16-0). Quint Pub Co.
Dental Analgesia. Ed. by Gerald D. Allen et al. LC 78-55278. (Postgraduate Dental Handbook Ser.: Vol. 6). (Illus.). 258p. 1979. casebound 25.00 (ISBN 0-685-47639-1). PSG Pub.
Dental & Oral Tissues: An Introduction for Paraprofessionals in Dentistry. Letty Moss-Salentijn & Marlene Klyvert. LC 80-10516. (Illus.). 326p. 1980. text ed. 16.50 (ISBN 0-8121-0701-2). Lea & Febiger.
Dental Assistant. 3rd ed. P. C. Anderson. 372p. 1974. pap. 11.00 (ISBN 0-8273-1339-X); instructor's guide 1.60 (ISBN 0-8273-1340-3). Delmar.
Dental Assistant. 3rd ed. Pauline C. Anderson. 372p. 1981. text ed. 14.95 (ISBN 0-442-21873-7). Nos Van Reinhold.
Dental Assistant: Syllabus. E. A. Jacobson & Alma Jacobson. 1978. pap. text ed. 9.75 (ISBN 0-89420-046-1, 198040); cassette recordings 228.60 (ISBN 0-89420-139-5, 198000). Natl Book.
Dental Assistant Techniques. Betty Lorenzen. LC 74-18674. (Allied Health Ser). 1975. pap. 10.25 (ISBN 0-672-61395-6). Bobbs.
Dental Assistant's Manual. Claude E. Norman & Elizabeth Livingstone. (Illus.). 1971. 16.95x (ISBN 0-685-83745-9). Intl Ideas.
Dental Assisting Manuals. Incl. No. I. Professionalism, Legal Considerations, & Office Management. Ethel M. Earl. (Illus.). 110p. 1980. pap. text ed. 6.00x (ISBN 0-8078-1375-3); No. II. Basic Sciences. E. Jeff Burkes, Jr. & Matthew T. Wood. (Illus.). 120p. 1980. pap. text ed. 7.00x (ISBN 0-8078-1376-1); No. III. Preclinical Sciences. Matthew T. Wood & E. Jeff Burkes, Jr. (Illus.). 130p. 1980. pap. text ed. 7.00x (ISBN 0-8078-1377-X); No. IV. Communication, Psychology, Nutrition, & Preventive Dentistry. Mary C. George et al. (Illus.). 160p. 1980. pap. text ed. 8.00x (ISBN 0-8078-1378-8); No. V. Dental Radiology. Stephen R. Matteson et al. (Illus.). 130p. 1980. pap. text ed. 8.00x (ISBN 0-8078-1379-6); No. VI. Dental Materials & Technical Application. Karl E. Leinfelder et al. (Illus.). 150p. 1980. pap. text ed. 10.00x (ISBN 0-8078-1380-X); No. VII. Clinical Sciences. William D. Strickland & Aldridge D. Wilder, Jr. (Illus.). 140p. 1980. pap. text ed. 10.00x (ISBN 0-8078-1381-8); No. VIII. Clinical Chairside Assisting. William D. Strickland & Aldridge D. Wilder, Jr. (Illus.). 160p. 1980. pap. text ed. 10.00x (ISBN 0-8078-1382-6). U of NC Pr.
Dental Auxiliary Practice. Martin J. Dunn. Incl. Module 2. Dentofacial Growth & Development - Orthodontics. pap. 8.95 (ISBN 0-683-02688-7); Module 3. Oral Pathology. pap. 8.95 (ISBN 0-685-59330-4); Module 4. Internal Med. pap. 8.95 (ISBN 0-683-02690-9); Module 5. Pharmacology, Pain Control, Sterile Technique, & Oral Surgery. pap. 10.95 (ISBN 0-683-02691-7); Module 6. Periodontics. pap. 10.95 (ISBN 0-683-02692-5). 1975. Williams & Wilkins.
Dental Care in Society: The Sociology of Dental Health. Marcel A. Fredericks et al. LC 80-15985. (Illus.). 194p. 1980. text ed. 15.95x (ISBN 0-89950-001-3). McFarland & Co.
Dental Examination Review Book. Ed. by Alvin F. Gardner. Vol. 1, 5th Ed. 1977. spiral bdg. 14.50 (ISBN 0-87488-431-4); Vol. 2, 4th Ed. 1978. spiral bdg. 14.50 (ISBN 0-87488-432-2); Vol. 3, 3rd Ed. 1978. spiral bdg. 14.50 (ISBN 0-87488-433-0). Med Exam.
Dental Fluoride Chemistry. Alan F. Berndt & Robert I. Stearns. (Illus.). 144p. 1978. 14.75 (ISBN 0-398-03753-1). C C Thomas.
Dental Health. Refna Wilkin. LC 76-9871. (First Books Ser.). (Illus.). 72p. (gr. 4-6). 1976. PLB 4.90 o.p. (ISBN 0-531-00321-3). Watts.
Dental Hygiene Examination Review Book, Vol. 1. 3rd ed. Theodore E. Bolden et al. 1973. spiral bdg. 9.50 (ISBN 0-87488-461-6). Med Exam.
Dental Hygienist "Mock" National Board. Ed. by E. E. Levy. (Illus.). 128p. 1976. 13.75 (ISBN 0-398-03176-2); pap. 9.25 (ISBN 0-398-03177-0). C C Thomas.
Dental Implantology & Prostheses. Morton L. Perel. LC 76-2596. 226p. 1977. 44.75 o.p. (ISBN 0-397-50347-4). Lippincott.
Dental Laboratory Procedures, Complete Dentures, Vol. 1. Morrow et al. LC 79-16785. (Illus.). 1979. text ed. 37.50 (ISBN 0-8016-3513-6). Mosby.
Dental Laboratory Procedures: Fixed Partial Dentures, Vol. 2. Harold F. Eissmann et al. LC 79-16785. (Illus.). 367p. 1980. text ed. 37.50 (ISBN 0-8016-3517-9). Mosby.
Dental Laboratory Procedures: Removable Partial Dentures, Vol. III. Kenneth D. Rudd et al. (Illus.). 612p. 1981. text ed. 37.50 (ISBN 0-8016-3516-0). Mosby.
Dental Laboratory Prosthodontics. Morris Hudis. LC 76-8578. (Illus.). 1977. text ed. 25.00 (ISBN 0-7216-4794-4). Saunders.
Dental Management of the Medically Compromised Patient. James W. Little & Falace. LC 80-15164. (Illus.). 300p. 1980. pap. text ed. 14.95 (ISBN 0-8016-3045-2). Mosby.
Dental Manifestations of Systemic Disease. D. H. Trapnell & J. E. Bowerman. (Radiology in Clinical Diagnosis Ser.,). 1973. 24.95 (ISBN 0-407-14400-5). Butterworths.
Dental Materials: A Problem Oriented Approach. Ed. by Robert G. Craig et al. LC 77-18734. (Illus.). 1978. text ed. 15.95 (ISBN 0-8016-1064-8). Mosby.
Dental Materials in Clinical Dentistry, Vol. 11. Ed. by M. H. Reisbick. LC 79-21849. (Post Graduate Dental Handbook Ser.). (Illus.). 350p. 1981. text ed. 29.50 (ISBN 0-88416-166-8). PSG Pub.
Dental Materials: Properties & Manipulation. 2nd ed. Robert G. Craig et al. LC 78-16677. (Illus.). 1979. pap. text ed. 12.95 (ISBN 0-8016-1072-9); wkbk. 6.95. Mosby.
Dental Organization Management. G. E. Robinson & M. G. Newport. (Illus.). 196p. 1974. 14.75 (ISBN 0-398-03045-6). C C Thomas.
Dental Planning for the Adult Patient. Laurence I. Barsh. (Illus.). 376p. 1981. text ed. price not set (ISBN 0-7216-1533-3). Saunders.
Dental Practice Management: Concepts & Application. Larry R. Domer et al. LC 80-15309. (Illus.). 376p. 1980. text ed. 32.50 (ISBN 0-8016-1422-8). Mosby.
Dental Problems in Medical Practice. J. R. Cooper. 1976. pap. text ed. 21.00x (ISBN 0-433-06425-0). Intl Ideas.
Dental Public Health & Community Dentistry. Anthony Jong. (Illus.). 300p. Date not set. pap. text ed. 12.95 (ISBN 0-8016-2575-0). Mosby.
Dental Pulp. 2nd ed. Samuel Seltzer & I. B. Bender. LC 75-22039. (Illus.). 356p. 1975. text ed. 25.95 (ISBN 0-397-52068-9). Lippincott.
Dental Radiology. Pauline Anderson. 96p. 1974. pap. 5.80 (ISBN 0-8273-0341-6); instructor's guide 1.60 (ISBN 0-8273-0342-4). Delmar.
Dental Radiology. 3rd ed. Stephen R. Matteson et al. (Dental Assisting Manuals: No. 5). 130p. 1980. 8.00 (ISBN 0-8078-1379-6). U of NC Pr.
Dental Radiology. 5th ed. Arthur H. Wuehrmann & Lincoln R. Manson-Hing. (Illus.). 500p. 1981. text ed. 27.50 (ISBN 0-8016-5643-5). Mosby.
Dental Specialties in General Practice. Ed. by Alvin L. Morris. Harry M. Bohannan. LC 68-23689. (Illus.). 1969. 26.50 o.p. (ISBN 0-7216-6560-8). Saunders.
Dental Teamwork Strategies: Interpersonal & Organizational Approaches. Judy C. Morton et al. LC 79-20229. 1979. pap. 11.95 (ISBN 0-8016-0979-8). Mosby.
Dental Technology: Theory & Practice. Richard Blakeslee et al. LC 80-157. (Illus.). 1980. text ed. 24.95 (ISBN 0-8016-0695-0). Mosby.
Dentist & Me. Joy Schaleben-Lewis. LC 76-46533. (Moods & Emotions Ser.). (Illus.). (gr. k-3). 1977. PLB 8.95 (ISBN 0-8172-0064-9). Raintree Pubs.
Dentistry. Boy Scouts of America. LC 19-600. (Illus.). 32p. (gr. 6-12). 1975. pap. 0.70x (ISBN 0-8395-3394-2, 3394). BSA.
Dentistry & Its Victims. Marvin Schissel. 336p. 1981. 11.95 (ISBN 0-312-19391-2). St Martin.
Dentistry & the Allergic Patient. Ed. by Claude A. Frazier. (Illus.). 456p. 1973. text ed. 28.75 (ISBN 0-398-02585-1). C C Thomas.
Dentistry for the Adolescent Patient. new ed. C. R. Castaldi & George A. Brass. LC 77-88308. (Illus.). 1979. text ed. 40.00 (ISBN 0-7216-2445-6). Saunders.
Dentistry for the Child & Adolescent. 3rd ed. Ralph E. McDonald & David R. Avery. LC 73-11347. (Illus.). 1978. text ed. 32.50 (ISBN 0-8016-3276-5). Mosby.
Dentistry in Cerebral Palsy & Related Handicapping Conditions. Solomon N. Rosenstein. (American Lecture in Cerebral Palsy Ser.). (Illus.). 184p. 1978. 18.50 (ISBN 0-398-03710-8). C C Thomas.

Dentistry in the Interdisciplinary Treatment of Genetic Diseases. Ed. by Carlos F. Salinas & Ronald J. Jorgenson. (Birth Defects: Original Article Ser.: Vol. XVI, No. 5). 216p. 1980. 26.00 (ISBN 0-8451-1039-X). A R Liss.

Dentist's Desk Reference: Materials, Instruments & Equipment. (Illus.). 1981. 13.95 (ISBN 0-686-69611-5). Am Dental.

Dentist's Manual of Emergency Medical Treatment. Robert J. Braun. (Illus.). 1979. text ed. 13.95 (ISBN 0-8359-1263-9). Reston.

Dentofacial Deformities: Surgical-Orthodontic Correction. Bruce N. Epker. LC 80-12405. (Illus.). 400p. 1980. text ed. 59.50 (ISBN 0-8016-1606-9). Mosby.

Denton Welch. Robert Phillips. (English Authors Ser.: No. 163). 1974. lib. bdg. 12.50 (ISBN 0-8057-1567-3). Twayne.

Denton's Army. Ralph Cross. 1979. pap. 1.75 (ISBN 0-505-51388-9). Tower Bks.

Dentro del Circulo. Rosalind Rinker. Tr. by James R. Cochrane from Eng. 110p. (Orig., Span.). 1976. pap. 2.25 (ISBN 0-89922-075-4). Edit Caribe.

Denver: A Pictorial History. William Jones. (Illus., Orig.). Date not set. pap. 10.95 (ISBN 0-87108-575-5). Pruett.

Denver & Rio Grande Western Railroad: Rebel of the Rockies. Robert G. Athearn. LC 76-30296. (Illus.). 1977. 18.50x (ISBN 0-8032-0920-7); pap. 8.95 (ISBN 0-8032-5861-5, 641, Bison). U of Nebr Pr.

Denver Auditory Phoneme Sequencing Test. James Aten. LC 79-651. (Illus.). 310p. 1979. clinical test 59.95 (ISBN 0-933014-51-1). College-Hill.

Denver Broncos. Julian May. (NFL Today Ser.). (gr. 4-8). 1980. lib. bdg. 6.45 (ISBN 0-87191-732-7); pap. 2.95 (ISBN 0-89812-235-X). Creative Ed.

Denver Crossroads. Marion Kelleran & John M. Krumm. 1979. 1.60 (ISBN 0-686-28775-4). Forward Movement.

Denver: Rocky Mountain Gold. Thomas Noel. Ed. by Ellen S. Blakey & Larry P. Silvey. LC 80-66339. (American Portrait Ser.). (Illus.). 240p. 1980. 24.95 (ISBN 0-932986-12-9). Continent Herit.

Deoband School & the Demand for Pakistan. Ziya-Ul-Hasan Faruqi. 7.00x (ISBN 0-210-33835-0). Asia.

Deontic Logic: A Comprehensive Appraisal & a View Proposal. Azizah Al-Hibri. LC 78-66422. 1978. pap. text ed. 8.75 (ISBN 0-8191-0303-9). U Pr of Amer.

DePalma's the Management of Fractures & Dislocations: An Atlas, 2 vols. 3rd ed. Ed. by John F. Connolly. (Illus.). 2000p. Date not set. Set. text ed. price not set (ISBN 0-7216-2666-1); Vol. 1. price not set (ISBN 0-7216-2702-1); Vol. 2. price not set (ISBN 0-7216-2703-X). Saunders.

Department of Death. John Creasey. 1979. pap. 1.75 o.p. (ISBN 0-445-04371-7). Popular Lib.

Department of Justice of the United States. Albert Langeluttig. (Brookings Institution Reprint Ser). Repr. of 1927 ed. lib. bdg. 28.50x (ISBN 0-697-00161-X). Irvington.

Department of War, Seventeen Eighty-One to Seventeen Ninety-Five. Harry M. Ward. LC 80-28410. xi, 287p. 1981. Repr. of 1962 ed. lib. bdg. 29.75x (ISBN 0-313-22895-7, WADW). Greenwood.

Department Store Sales. Fairchild Market Research Division. (Fairchild Fact File Ser.). 1979. pap. 10.00 (ISBN 0-87005-327-2). Fairchild.

Department Store Sales, Pt. 1. Fairchild Market Research Division. (Fact File Ser). 1978. pap. 10.00 (ISBN 0-87005-220-9). Fairchild.

Department Store Sales, Pt. 2. Fairchild Market Research Division. (Fact File Ser). 1978. pap. 10.00 (ISBN 0-87005-254-3). Fairchild.

Department Store Sales, 1980. Fairchild Market Research Division. (Fairchild Fact Files Ser.). (Illus.). 80p. 1980. pap. 10.00 (ISBN 0-87005-355-8). Fairchild.

Departmental Method Handbook. Hospital Financial Management Association. LC 79-88945. 70p. 1979. pap. 10.00 (ISBN 0-930228-11-1, 14411). Hospital Finan.

Departure & Other Stories. Howard Fast. LC 80-23584. 197p. 1980. pap. 7.95 (ISBN 0-915238-37-3). Peace Pr.

Departures. Jane Bernstein. 304p. 1981. pap. 2.50 (ISBN 0-380-53736-2). Avon.

Dependence & Exploitation in Work & Marriage. Ed. by D. L. Barker & S. Allen. LC 75-43517. 1976. text ed. 20.00x (ISBN 0-582-48673-4); pap. text ed. 10.95x (ISBN 0-582-48674-2). Longman.

Dependence & Transformation: The Economics of the Transition. Clive Thomas. LC 73-90081. 228p. 1974. 10.95 o.p. (ISBN 0-85345-317-9, CL3179). Monthly Rev.

Dependency & Development in Latin America. Fernando E. Cardoso & Enzo Faletto. Tr. by Marjory M. Urquidi. (Campus Ser.: No. 203). 1979. 22.75x (ISBN 0-520-03193-8); pap. 4.95x (ISBN 0-520-03527-5). U of Cal Pr.

Dependency Road: Communications, Capitalism, Consciousness & Canada. Dallas W. Smythe. 300p. 1981. text ed. price not set (ISBN 0-89391-067-8). Ablex Pub.

Dependent Capitalism in Crisis: Sri Lanka 1948-1978. Satchi Ponnambalam. 256p. 1981. 16.95 (ISBN 0-905762-85-1, Pub. by Zed Pr). Lawrence Hill.

Dependent Development & Industrial Order. Fredric C. Deyo. (Fraeger Special Studies). 1980. 19.95 (ISBN 0-03-047386-1). Praeger.

Dependent Development in United Kingdom Regions with Particular Reference to Wales. Philip Cooke. (Progress on Planning Ser.: Vol. 15, Part 1). 90p. 1980. pap. 13.50 (ISBN 0-08-026809-9). Pergamon.

Dependent Industrialization in Latin America: The Automotive Industry in Argentina, Chile, & Mexico. Rhys O. Jenkins. LC 76-25352. (Illus.). 1976. text ed. 29.95 (ISBN 0-275-23220-4). Praeger.

Depletion Myth: A History of Railroad Use of Timber. Sherry H. Olson. LC 70-148940. 1971. 11.00x (ISBN 0-674-19820-4). Harvard U Pr.

Deplorable Scarcity: The Failure of Industrialization in the Slave Economy. Fred Bateman & Thomas Weiss. LC 80-13238. xii, 237p. 1981. 19.00x (ISBN 0-8078-1447-4). U of NC Pr.

Depois De a Cruz E O Punhal. Tr. by David Wilkerson. (Portuguese Bks.). 1979. 1.40 (ISBN 0-8297-0731-X). Life Pubs Intl.

Deportation Cases of Nineteen-Nineteen to Nineteen-Twenty. Constantine M. Panunzio. LC 77-109547. (Civil Liberties in American History Ser). 1970. Repr. of 1921 ed. lib. bdg. 14.50 (ISBN 0-306-71901-0). Da Capo.

Deportations Delirium of Nineteen-Twenty. Louis F. Post. LC 73-114343. (Civil Liberties in American History Ser). 1970. Repr. of 1923 ed. lib. bdg. 32.50 (ISBN 0-306-71882-0). Da Capo.

Deportes En Puerto Rico. Huyre. 1968. 19.95 (ISBN 0-87751-013-X, Pub by Troutman Press). E Torres & Sons.

Deposition & Corrosion in Gas Turbines. Ed. by A. B. Hart & A. J. Cutler. LC 73-8187. 425p. 1973. 59.95 (ISBN 0-470-35639-1). Halsted Pr.

Depositional Sedimentary Environments-with Reference to Terrigenous Classics. H. E. Reineck & I. B. Singh. (Illus.). 439p. 1974. 50.00 o.p. (ISBN 0-387-06115-0). Springer-Verlag.

Depositional Sedimentary Environments with Reference to Terrigenous Clastics. 2nd rev. ed. H. E. Reineck & I. B. Singh. (Illus.). 549p. 1980. pap. 29.80 (ISBN 0-387-10189-6). Springer-Verlag.

Depositional Systems in the Paluxy Formation (Lower Cretaceous) Northeast Texas-Oil, Gas, & Ground-Water Resources. C. A. Caughey. (Illus.). 59p. 1977. 2.00 (GC 77-8). Bur Econ Geology.

Depostional Systems in the Wilcox Group of Texas & Their Relationship to Occurrence of Oil & Gas. W. L. Fisher & J. H. McGowen. 125p. 1967. Repr. 1.00 (GC 67-4). Bur Econ Geology.

Depression. Dominian. 1976. pap. 2.95 o.p. (ISBN 0-531-06071-3, Fontana Pap). Watts.

Depression. Wina Sturgeon. 256p. 1981. pap. 5.95 (ISBN 0-346-12514-6). Cornerstone.

Depression--What It Is & What to Do About It. Roger K. Barrett. 1979. pap. 3.95 (ISBN 0-89191-179-0). Cook.

Depression After Childbirth: How to Recognize & Treat Postnatal Illness. Katharina Dalton. (Illus.). 192p. 1981. 13.95 (ISBN 0-19-217701-X); pap. 6.95 (ISBN 0-19-286008-9). Oxford U Pr.

Depression: Causes & Treatment. Aaron T. Beck. LC 67-23826. 1972. 15.00x (ISBN 0-8122-7652-3); pap. 8.50x (ISBN 0-8122-1032-8, Pa Paperbks). U of Pa Pr.

Depression, Fragmentation, & the Void. James Park. (Existential Freedom Ser.: No. 9). 1976. pap. 2.00x (ISBN 0-89231-009-X). Existential Bks.

Depression Glass Book Three in Colors. Sandra M. Stout. (Illus.). 6.95 (ISBN 0-87069-181-3); price guide 1.50 (ISBN 0-87069-182-1). Wallace-Homestead.

Depression Glass Collector's Price Guide. Marian Klamkin. (Illus.). 96p. 1974. pap. 4.50 (ISBN 0-8015-2018-5, Hawthorn). Dutton.

Depression Glass in Color. Sandra Stout. No. 1. plastic bdg. 6.95 (ISBN 0-87069-022-1); No. 2. plastic bdg. 6.95 (ISBN 0-87069-023-X). Wallace-Homestead.

Depression in Childhood: Diagnosis, Treatment & Conceptual Models. Ed. by Joy G. Schulterbrandt & Allen Raskin. LC 76-47122. 1977. 15.50 (ISBN 0-89004-147-4); pap. 11.00 (ISBN 0-685-74515-5). Raven.

Depression in Children & Adolescents. Alfred French & Irving Berlin. 300p. 1979. text ed. 29.95 (ISBN 0-87705-390-1). Human Sci Pr.

Depression Modern: The Thirties Style in America. Martin Greif. LC 75-11140. (Illus.). 1977. pap. 7.95 o.s.i. (ISBN 0-87663-925-2). Universe.

Deprivation & School Progress, Vol. 1. Maurice Chazan et al. (Studies in Infant School Children). 1976. 65.00x o.p. (ISBN 0-631-17050-2, Pub. by Basil Blackwell England). Biblio Dist.

Deprivation in America. Victor Ficker & Herbert S. Graves. (Studies in Contemporary Issues). 1971. pap. text ed. 4.95x (ISBN 0-02-474680-0, 47468). Macmillan.

Dept. of Nursing Staff Education Manual. Massachusetts General Hospital. Ed. by Cheryl B. Stetler et al. 1981. text ed. 34.95 (ISBN 0-8359-1281-7). Reston.

Depth Psychology & the New Ethic. Erich Neumann. Tr. by Eugene Rolfe from Ger. 160p. 1973. pap. 3.95 (ISBN 0-06-131777-2, TB1777, Torch). Har-Row.

Depth Psychology & Vocation: A Psycho-Social Perspective. Luigi M. Rulla. LC 70-146938. 1971. 12.50 o.p. (ISBN 0-8294-0210-1). Loyola.

Deputy Marshall. Charles N. Heckelmann. 1977. pap. 1.25 o.p. (ISBN 0-445-04124-2). Popular Lib.

Deputy of San Riano. Lawrence A. Keating & Al P. Nelson. 1981. pap. 1.95 (ISBN 0-8439-0908-0, Leisure Bks). Nordon Pubns.

Deputyes & Libertyes: The Origins of Representative Government in Colonial America. Michael Kammen. 1969. 6.95 o.p. (ISBN 0-394-42207-4). Knopf.

Derain, No. 111. (Maeght Gallery: Derriere le Miroir Ser.). (Fr.). 1977. pap. 19.95 (ISBN 0-8120-0915-0). Barron.

Derain, Nos. 94 & 95. (Maeght Gallery: Derriere le Miroir Ser.). 1977. pap. 19.95 (ISBN 0-8120-0914-2). Barron.

Derby: A Celebration of the World's Most Famous Horse Race. Michael W. Jones. (Illus.). 204p. 1980. 21.00x (ISBN 0-85664-884-1, Pub. by Croom Helm Ltd England). Biblio Dist.

Derby Day. David Holloway. (Folio Miniature Ser.). 1975. 4.95 (ISBN 0-7181-1303-9, Pub. by Michael Joseph). Merrimack Bk Serv.

Derby Porcelain, 1750-1848. Franklin A. Barrett & Arthur L. Thorpe. 1971. 43.00 (ISBN 0-571-09577-1, Pub. by Faber & Faber). Merrimack Bk Serv.

Derby: The Life & Times of the 12th Earl of. Millard Cox. (Illus.). 31.50 (ISBN 0-85131-199-7, Dist. by Sporting Book Center). J A Allen.

Derbyshire. Roy Christian. 27.00 (ISBN 0-7134-1295-X, Pub. by Batsford England). David & Charles.

Deregulating American Industry: Legal & Economic Problems. Ed. by Donald L. Martin & Warren C. Schwartz. LC 77-5273. (Illus.). 1977. 15.95 (ISBN 0-669-01603-9). Lexington Bks.

Deregulation of the Banking & Securities Industries. Lawrence G. Goldberg & Lawrence J. White. LC 78-19705. 1979. 23.95 (ISBN 0-669-02720-0). Lexington Bks.

Derelicts of Company K: A Sociological Study of Demoralization. Tamotsu Shibutani. LC 77-79237. 1978. 17.95 (ISBN 0-520-03524-0). U of Cal Pr.

Derld. L. M. Pickett. (Chess Player Ser.). 1977. pap. 5.95 o.p. (ISBN 0-900928-52-2, H-1160). Hippocrene Bks.

Dermatoglyphics Fifty Years Later. Ed. by Wladimir Wertelecki & Chris C. Plato. LC 79-2595. (Alan R. Liss Ser.: Vol. 15, No. 6). 1979. 76.00 (ISBN 0-8451-1031-4). March of Dimes.

Dermatoglypics: An International Perspective. Jamshed Mavalwala. (World Anthropology Ser.). 1978. text ed. 47.00x (ISBN 90-279-7590-6). Mouton.

Dermatology. R. Feinstein. (Illus.). 1975. pap. 7.95 (ISBN 0-87618-066-7). R J Brady.

Dermatology. 4th ed. Ed. by Dennis A. Weigand. (Medical Examination Review Book: Vol. 21). 1980. pap. 18.00 (ISBN 0-87488-127-7). Med Exam.

Dermatology - a Practitioner's Guide. Ray O. Noojin et al. 1977. spiral bdg. 14.50 (ISBN 0-87488-720-8). Med Exam.

Dermatology: An Illustrated Guide. 2nd ed. Lionel Fry. (Illus.). 1978. text ed. 19.00x (ISBN 0-906141-02-8, Pub. by Update Pubns England). Kluwer Boston.

Dermatology Continuing Education Review. 2nd. ed. Dennis A. Weigand. Ed. by Robert L. Olson. 1980. pap. 14.50 (ISBN 0-87488-341-5). Med Exam.

Dermatology: Diagnosis & Treatment of Cutaneous Disorders. 4th ed. William D. Stewart et al. LC 78-12789. (Illus.). 1978. text ed. 38.50 (ISBN 0-8016-4809-2). Mosby.

Dermatology for Students. Ray O. Noojin. (Illus.). 320p. 1961. 13.75 (ISBN 0-398-01407-8). C C Thomas.

Dermatology for the House Officer: Problem Oriented Approach. Peter J. Lynch. 225p. 1981. write for info. softcover (5250-0). Williams & Wilkins.

Dermatology in Internal Medicine. Sam Shuster. 1979. pap. 11.95x (ISBN 0-19-261142-9). Oxford U Pr.

Dermatology Specialty Board Review. 3rd ed. Victor J. Selmanowitz & Frederick A. Pereira. 1978. spiral bdg. 16.50 (ISBN 0-87488-311-3). Med Exam.

Dermatopathology. John M. Budinger. LC 77-95399. (Slide Seminar Ser.). (Illus.). 1978. text & slides 55.00 (ISBN 0-89189-049-1, 15-1-025-00); slides 5.50 (ISBN 0-89189-024-6, 50-1-041-00). Am Soc Clinical.

Dermatophytes in Human Skin, Hair & Nails. James T. Sinski. (American Lectures in Clinical Microbiology Ser.). (Illus.). 64p. 1974. text ed. 10.75 (ISBN 0-398-03102-9). C C Thomas.

Derrick Henry Lehmer Dedication: Dedication Issue on His 70th Birthday. (Mathematics of Computation Ser.: Vol. 29, No. 129). 1975. 14.00 (ISBN 0-8218-0061-2, MCOM 29-129, DHL). Am Math.

Derrotando O Desespero E Depressao. Tr. by Matilda Norvedt. (Portuguese Bks.). 1979. 1.25 (ISBN 0-8297-0828-6). Life Pubs Intl.

Dervish Dance. Louise Louis. 40p. 1971. Repr. of 1958 ed. text ed. 4.95. Pen-Art.

Deryni Checkmate. Katherine Kurtz. 1976. pap. 2.25 (ISBN 0-345-29224-3). Ballantine.

Deryni Rising. Katherine Kurtz. 1976. pap. 2.25 (ISBN 0-345-29105-0). Ballantine.

Des Feldpredigers Schmelzle Reise Nach Flatz. Jean Paul. Ed. by J. W. Smeed. (Clarendon German Ser). (Ger.). 1966. 3.25x o.p. (ISBN 0-19-832450-2). Oxford U Pr.

Des Moines Festival of the Avant-Garde Invites You to a Show Without Really Being There. Ed. by Fred Truck. (Orig.). pap. text ed. 7.50 (ISBN 0-938236-02-4). Cookie Pr.

Desairology: Hairdressing for Decedents. Papagno et al. LC 80-82330. (The Family, the Funeral & the Hairdresser). (Illus.). 104p. (Orig.). 1980. 17.95x (ISBN 0-9604610-0-0); lib. bdg. 15.50 (ISBN 0-686-27695-7); pap. 12.95 (ISBN 0-9604610-1-9). JJ Pub Fl.

Desalination of Seawater by Reverse Osmosis. Ed. by Jeanette Scott. LC 80-26421. (Pollution Tech. Rev. Ser.: No. 75). 431p. 1981. 39.00 (ISBN 0-8155-0837-9). Noyes.

Desalination of Water Using Conventional & Nuclear Energy. (Technical Reports Ser.: No. 24). (Illus., Orig.). 1964. pap. 2.75 (ISBN 92-0-145164-4, IAEA). Unipub.

Desarollo Del Nino. Helen Bee. (Span.). 1977. pap. text ed. 8.00 (ISBN 0-06-310061-4, IntlDept). Har-Row.

Desarrollando Destrezas En Preparacion Para el Examen de Equivalencia De Escuela Superior En Espanol: El Escribir. Paul M. Lloyd. (Span.). (gr. 9-12). Date not set. pap. text ed. 3.75 (ISBN 0-8120-0559-7). Barron.

Desarrollando Destrezas En Preparacion Para el Examen Equivalencia De Escuela Superior En Espanol: Mathematicas: Developing Skills in Math for High School Equivalency Test in Spanish. Zoila De Zayas. (gr. 10-12). Date not set. pap. text ed. 3.75 (ISBN 0-8120-0560-0). Barron.

Desarrollando Destrezas En Preparacion Para el Examen Equivalencia De Escuela Superior En Espanol: Ciencia. Sallese & Dominicis. Date not set. pap. 2.75 (ISBN 0-8120-0989-4). Barron.

Desarrollando Destrezas En Preparacion Para el Examen Equivalencia De Escuela Superior En Espanol: Estudios Sociales. Sallese & Dominicis. Date not set. pap. 2.75 (ISBN 0-8120-0988-6). Barron.

Desarrollando Destrezas En Preparacion Para el Examen Equivalencia De Escuela Superior En Espanol: Lectura: Developing Skills in Reading for the H.S. Equivalency Test in Spanish. Nicolas F. Sallese et al. (gr. 11-12). Date not set. pap. text ed. 2.75 (ISBN 0-8120-0990-8). Barron.

Desarrollo Del Varon De Dios. Tr. by Melvin Hodges. (Spanish Bks.). (Span.). 1978. 0.80 (ISBN 0-8297-0528-7). Life Pubs Intl.

Descartes. Leon Pearl. (World Leaders Ser.: No. 63). 1977. lib. bdg. 10.95 (ISBN 0-8057-7714-8). Twayne.

Descartes. Paul Valery. 133p. 1980. Repr. lib. bdg. 10.00 (ISBN 0-89984-477-4). Century Bookbindery.

Descartes & Hume. Ezra Talmor. LC 79-41748. 188p. 1980. 19.75 (ISBN 0-08-024274-X). Pergamon.

Descartes & Medicine. G. A. Lindeboom. (Nieuwe Nederlandse Bijdragen Tot De Geschiedenis der Geneekundem: No. 1). (Illus.). 1978. pap. text ed. 17.25x (ISBN 90-6203-882-4). Humanities.

Descartes: Critical & Interpretive Essays. Ed. by Michael Hooker. 1978. text ed. 22.50 (ISBN 0-8018-2111-8); pap. text ed. 4.95 (ISBN 0-8018-2122-3). Johns Hopkins.

Descartes: Philosophy, Mathematics & Physics. Ed. by Stephen Gaukroger. (Harvester Readings in the History of Science & Philosophy Ser.: No. 1). 329p. 1980. 30.00x (ISBN 0-389-20084-0). B&N.

Descendants. Kamala Das. (Writers Workshop Redbird Ser.). 35p. 1975. 8.00 (ISBN 0-88253-526-9); pap. text ed. 4.00 (ISBN 0-88253-525-0). Ind-US Inc.

Descendants of Hugh Mosher & Rebecca Maxson Through Seven Generations. Mildred Chamberlain & Laura Clarenbach. LC 80-51754. 808p. 1980. 22.50 (ISBN 0-9604142-0-7). M M Chamberlain.

Descendants of Jacob Young of Shelby County, Kentucky: Including President Harry S. Truman. Elsie S. Davis. LC 80-70981. (Illus.). 171p. (Orig.). 1980. 16.00 (ISBN 0-9605618-1-1); pap. 9.00 (ISBN 0-9605618-0-3). E S Davis.

Descensus As Terram: The Acquisition & Reception of the Elgin Marbles. Jacob Rothenberg. LC 76-23716. (Outstanding Dissertations in the Fine Arts Ser.). 1977. lib. bdg. 70.00x (ISBN 0-8240-2726-4). Garland Pub.

Descent from the Cross: Its Relation to the Extra-Liturgical Depositio Drama. Elizabeth C. Parker. LC 77-94713. (Outstanding Dissertations in the Fine Arts Ser.). 1978. lib. bdg. 34.00 (ISBN 0-8240-3245-4). Garland Pub.

Descent into Words: Jakob Bohme's Transcendental Linguistics. Steven A. Konopacki. (Linguistica Extranea: Studia: No. 7). 201p. 1979. pap. 7.50 (ISBN 0-89720-019-5). Karoma.

Descent of Darwin: The Popularization of Darwinism in Germany, 1860-1914. Alfred Kelly. LC 80-19445. 200p. 1981. 18.50x (ISBN 0-8078-1460-1). U of NC Pr.

Descent of Man. Fred Merkel. 36p. 1975. pap. 1.00 o.p. (ISBN 0-686-20749-1). Samisdat.

Descent of Man & Other Stories. T. Coraghessan Boyle. 228p. 1980. pap. 3.95 (ISBN 0-07-006956-5, SB). McGraw.

Descent of Man & Selection in Relation to Sex. Charles Darwin. LC 73-20158. (Illus.). 672p. 1974. Repr. of 1874 ed. 35.00 (ISBN 0-8103-3963-3). Gale.

Descent of Man & Selection in Relation to Sex. Charles Darwin. LC 80-8679. (Illus.). 935p. 1981. 30.00x (ISBN 0-691-08278-2); pap. 8.95 (ISBN 0-691-02369-7). Princeton U Pr.

Descent of the Doves: Camus's Journey to the Spirit. Alfred Cordes. LC 79-3811. 1980. text ed. 18.50 (ISBN 0-8191-0931-2); pap. text ed. 10.25 (ISBN 0-8191-0932-0). U Pr of Amer.

Descent of the Gods: Mystical Writings of A. E. Raghavan Iyer & Nandini Iyer. Raghavan Iyer. (Collected Edition of the Writings of G.W. Russell III). 1980. text ed. write for info. (ISBN 0-391-01143-X). Humanities.

Describing Bilingual Education Classrooms: The Role of the Teacher in Evaluation. Andrew D. Cohen. LC 80-80307. 64p. (Orig.). 1980. pap. 3.00 (ISBN 0-89763-050-5). Natl Clearinghse Bilingual.

Describing Data Statistically. Charles D. Hopkins. LC 73-92000. (Psychology & Educational Psychology Ser.). 128p. 1974. pap. text ed. 7.95 (ISBN 0-675-08820-8). Merrill.

Description & Comparison in Cultural Anthropology. Ward H. Goodenough. LC 80-67925. (Lewis Henry Morgan Lectures). 192p. 1981. 22.50 (ISBN 0-521-23740-8); pap. 6.95 (ISBN 0-521-28196-2). Cambridge U Pr.

Description & First Procreation & Increase of the Towne of Great Yarmouth. Thomas Nash. Incl. Of the Praise of the Red Herring. 1975. text ed. 8.50 (ISBN 0-8277-3928-1); pap. text ed. 4.95 (ISBN 0-8277-2390-3). British Bk Ctr.

Description Generale Des Monnaies Des Rois Wisigoths d'Espagne. Aloiss Heiss. (Illus.). iv, 185p. (Fr.). 1980. Repr. 30.00 (ISBN 0-916710-64-5). Obol Intl.

Description of British Guiana. Robert H. Schomburgk. LC 67-16358. Repr. of 1840 ed. 17.50x (ISBN 0-678-05002-3). Kelley.

Description of Greece, 6 Vols. 2nd ed. Pausanias. Tr. by J. G. Frazer. LC 65-13634. (Illus.). 1897. Set. 95.00x (ISBN 0-8196-0144-6). Biblo.

Description of Louisiana by Thomas Jefferys: From His "Natural & Civil History of the French Dominions in North & South America". Ed. by C. Edward Skeen. (Mississippi Valley Collection Bulletin, No. 6). (Illus.). 50p. 1973. pap. 5.95x facsimile ed. (ISBN 0-87870-082-X). Memphis St Univ.

Description of Millenium Hall, & the Country Adjacent, 1762. Sarah Scott. (Flowering of the Novel, 1740-1775 Ser: Vol. 62). 1974. lib. bdg. 50.00 (ISBN 0-8240-1161-9). Garland Pub.

Description: Sign, Self, Desire. Marc E. Blanchard. (Approaches to Semiotics Ser.: No. 43). 1979. text ed. 40.00x (ISBN 0-686-27019-3). Mouton.

Descriptive Analysis of Einai. Lane C. McGaughy. LC 72-88437. (Society of Biblical Literature, Dissertation Ser.). 1972. pap. 9.00 (ISBN 0-89130-162-3, 060106). Scholars Pr Ca.

Descriptive & Illustrated Catalogue of the Malcolm Macdonald Collection of Chinese Ceramics. Irenus Legeza. Orig. Title: Laszlo. (Illus.). 1972. pap. 65.00 (ISBN 0-19-713135-2). Oxford U Pr.

Descriptive & Inferential Statistics: A Contemporary Approach. Richard P. Runyon. LC 76-52668. (Statistiics Ser.). 1977. 13.95 (ISBN 0-201-06655-6). A-W.

Descriptive & Inferential Statistics: An Introduction. 2nd ed. Loether & McTavish. 624p. 1980. text ed. 20.95 (ISBN 0-205-06905-3, 8169055). Allyn.

Descriptive & Inferential Statistics: An Introduction. Herman J. Loether & Donald G. McTavish. 640p. 1976. text ed. 14.95x o.p. (ISBN 0-205-05476-5). Allyn.

Descriptive & Interpretive Studies of South American Platyrrhine Fossils: 1891-1952. LC 78-72716. 1980. 41.50 (ISBN 0-404-18291-7). AMS Pr.

Descriptive Cataloging in a New Light: Polemical Chapters for Librarians. Herbert H. Hoffman. LC 76-380445. 171p. 1976. pap. 6.00x (ISBN 0-89537-000-X). Headway Pubns.

Descriptive Catalogue of Printing in Spain & Portugal, 1501-1520. F. J. Norton. LC 76-11062. 1978. 240.00 (ISBN 0-521-21136-0). Cambridge U Pr.

Descriptive Catalogue of the Milton Collection in the Alexander Turnbull Library, Wellington, New Zealand. K. A. Coleridge. (Illus.). 544p. 1980. 98.00x (ISBN 0-19-920110-2). Oxford U Pr.

Descriptive Cataloguing: A Student's Introduction to the Anglo-American Cataloguins Rules, 1967. 2nd ed. James A. Tait & F. Douglas Anderson. 1971. 10.50 o.p. (ISBN 0-208-01077-7, Linnet). Shoe String.

Descriptive Checklist of Book Catalogues Separately Printed America. Robert B. Winans. 1981. 35.00 (ISBN 0-912296-47-X, Dist. by U Pr of Va). Am Antiquarian.

Descriptive Directory of Psychiatric Training Programs in the U. S., 1972-1973. Ed. by Lee Gurel. 144p. 1973. 3.25 o.p. (ISBN 0-685-38354-7, 186). Am Psychiatric.

Descriptive English Grammar. 2nd ed. Susan E. Harman & H. House. 1950. text ed. 14.95 (ISBN 0-13-199083-7). P-H.

Descriptive Flora of the Maltese Islands Including the Ferns & Flowering Plants. John Borg. 846p. 1976. pap. text ed. 108.90 (ISBN 3-87429-104-9). Lubrecht & Cramer.

Descriptive Geometry. 2nd ed. James H. Earle. LC 76-55640. (Illus.). 384p. 1978. text ed. 17.95 (ISBN 0-201-01776-8). A-W.

Descriptive Index to Shakespeare's Characters, in Shakespeare's Words. Walter C. Jerrold. LC 74-23634. xvi, 176p. 1975. Repr. of 1905 ed. 25.00 (ISBN 0-8103-4097-6). Gale.

Descriptive Inventory of the English Collection. Arlene H. Eakle et al. (Finding Aids to the Microfilmed Manuscript Collection of the Genealogical Society of Utah). 1979. pap. 12.00x (ISBN 0-87480-154-0). U of Utah Pr.

Descriptive Inventory of the New York Collection. Arlene H. Eakle & L. Ray Gunn. (Finding Aids to the Microfilmed Manuscript Collection of the Genealogical Society of Utah). (Orig.). 1980. pap. 15.00x (ISBN 0-87480-170-2). U of Utah Pr.

Descriptive List of the Map Collection in the Pennsylvania State Archives. Martha L. Simonett. Ed. by Donald H. Kent & Harry E. Whipkey. 1976. 8.00 (ISBN 0-911124-83-7). Pa Hist & Mus.

Descriptive Phonetics. Donald Calvert. 1980. 16.00. Thieme Stratton.

Descriptive Physical Oceanography. 2nd ed. G. L. Pickard. 220p. 1976. text ed. 12.10 o.p. (ISBN 0-08-018159-7); pap. text ed. 7.00 o.p. (ISBN 0-08-018158-9). Pergamon.

Descriptive Physical Oceanography. 3rd ed. G. L. Pickard. (International Series in Geophysics). (Illus.). 1979. text ed. 35.00 (ISBN 0-08-023824-6); pap. text ed. 11.50 (ISBN 0-08-023825-4). Pergamon.

Descriptive Regional Oceanography. P. Tchernia. Tr. by D. Densmore. (Pergamon Marine Ser.: Vol. 3). (Illus.). 256p. 1980. 45.00 (ISBN 0-08-020925-4); pap. 19.50 (ISBN 0-08-020919-X). Pergamon.

Descriptive Set Theory. Y. N. Moschovakis. (Studies in Logic & the Foundations of Mathematics: Vol. 100). 640p. 1979. 73.25 (ISBN 0-444-85305-7, North Holland). Elsevier.

Descriptive Statistics: A Contemporary Approach. Richard P. Runyon. LC 76-15467. (Statistics Ser.). 1977. pap. text ed. 9.95 (ISBN 0-201-06652-1); test book avail. 2.75 (ISBN 0-201-06635-1). A-W.

Descriptive Statistics for Public Policy Analysis. Gary Hammerstrom & Amy M. Kafton. (Learning Packages in the Policy Sciences: No. 20). (Illus.). 110p. (Orig.). 1980. pap. text ed. 4.50 (ISBN 0-936826-09-6). Pol Stud Assocs.

Descriptive Statistics for Sociologists: An Introduction. Herman J. Loether & Donald G. McTavish. 368p. 1974. pap. text ed. 13.60x (ISBN 0-205-04435-2). Allyn.

Descriptors for Rice Oryza Sativa1. 21p. 1981. pap. 5.00 (ISBN 0-686-69533-X, R 121, IRRI). Unipub.

Descryston of Chinese Poetry & Porcelain. Stephen W. Bushell. (Oxford in Asia Studies in Ceramics). 1978. 24.95x (ISBN 0-19-580372-8). Oxford U Pr.

Descubramos Como Orar. Hope McDonald. Tr. by F. G. Coleman from Eng. (Span.). 1980. pap. 2.50 (ISBN 0-311-40040-X). Casa Bautista.

Descubrimiento De Harry Stottlemeier. Matthew Lipman. Tr. by Oscar R. Marti from Eng. (Philosophy for Children). 190p. (Orig., Eng. & Span.). (gr. 5-6). pap. 10.00 (ISBN 0-916834-16-6). Inst Adv Philo.

Descubrir y Crear. 2nd ed. Jose Almeida et al. (Illus.). 402p. (Span.). 1981. text ed. 18.95 scp (ISBN 0-06-040224-5, HarpC). Har-Row.

Desde el Siglo XVI hasta el Siglo XX. Kenneth S. Latourette. Tr. by Jaime C. Quarles & Lemuel C. Quarles. (Historia del Cristianismo: Tomo II). Orig. Title: History of the Expansion of Christianity. 968p. 1980. pap. 10.80 (ISBN 0-311-15012-8). Casa Bautista.

Desecration of Susan Browning. Russell Martin. LC 80-83567. 256p. 1981. pap. 2.50 (ISBN 0-87216-802-6). Playboy Pbks.

Desegregation & Hispanic Students: A Community Perspective. Tony Baez et al. LC 80-80311. 84p. (Orig.). 1980. pap. 3.50 (ISBN 0-89763-023-8). Natl Clearinghse Bilingual Ed.

Desegregation Law: An Introduction. Ed. by Integrated Education Associates Editorial Staff. pap. 1.00 o.p. (ISBN 0-912008-05-9). Integrated Ed Assoc.

Desegregation Works: A Primer for Parents & Teachers. Lillian S. Calhoun. 1968. pap. 0.90 (ISBN 0-685-38478-0). Integrated Ed Assoc.

Desert. A. Starker Leopold. LC 61-18379. (Life Nature Library). (Illus.). (gr. 5 up). 1961. PLB 8.97 o.p. (ISBN 0-8094-0615-2, Pub. by Time-Life). Silver.

Desert. A. Starker Leopold. (Young Readers Library). (Illus.). 1977. lib. bdg. 7.95 (ISBN 0-686-51086-0). Silver.

Desert Adventure. Dorothy Spicer. (YA) 1968. 5.95 (ISBN 0-685-07428-5, Avalon). Bouregy.

Desert Animals. Ro Tate. LC 79-185645. (Animal Life Ser.). (Illus.). 152p. 1972. pap. 2.95 o.p. (ISBN 0-06-014222-7, TD-121, HarpT). Har-Row.

Desert Bighorn: Its Life History, Ecology, & Management. Ed. by Gale Monson & Lowell Sumner. LC 80-18889. 1980. text ed. 27.50x (ISBN 0-8165-0689-2); pap. 14.95 (ISBN 0-8165-0713-9). U of Ariz Pr.

Desert Biology, 2 vols. Brown. 102.00 set; Vol. 1, 1968. 63.00 (ISBN 0-12-135901-8); Vol. 2. 63.00 (ISBN 0-12-135902-6). Acad Pr.

Desert Captive. Elliott Tokson. 288p. 1977. pap. 1.75 o.p. (ISBN 0-449-13722-8, GM). Fawcett.

Desert Crossing. Luke Short. 160p. (Orig.). 1980. pap. 1.75 (ISBN 0-553-13760-3). Bantam.

Desert Doctor. H. G. Gunther. (H. G. Gunther Ser.). pap. 1.95 (ISBN 0-515-05675-8). Jove Pubns.

Desert Dream. Rosemary Carter. (Harlequin Presents Ser.). 192p. 1980. pap. 1.50 (ISBN 0-373-10397-2, Pub. by Harlequin). PB.

Desert Fire. Brooke Hastings. 192p. (Orig.). 1980. pap. 1.50 (ISBN 0-671-57044-7). S&S.

Desert Gardening. Sunset Editors. LC 67-27445. (Illus.). 96p. 1967. pap. 2.95 (ISBN 0-376-03132-8, Sunset Bks). Sunset-Lane.

Desert Immigrants: The Mexican of El Paso, 1880-1920. Mario T. Gracia. LC 80-36862. (Western Americana Ser.: No. 32). (Illus.). 328p. 1981. text ed. 23.00x (ISBN 0-300-02520-3). Yale U Pr.

Desert Is Fertile. Dom H. Camara. 1976. pap. 1.50 (ISBN 0-89129-060-5). Jove Pubns.

Desert Is Theirs. Byrd Baylor. (Illus.). 32p. (gr. 1-5). pap. 2.95 (ISBN 0-689-70481-X, A-108, Aladdin). Atheneum.

Desert King: The Life of Ibn Saud. David Howarth. 14.00 (ISBN 0-685-89875-X). Intl Bk Ctr.

Desert Notes: Reflections in the Eye of the Raven. Barry H. Lopez. 96p. pap. 2.25 (ISBN 0-380-53819-9, 53819, Bard). Avon.

Desert Peaks Guide One. rev. ed. Ed. by Walt Wheelock. (Illus.). 1964. wrappers 1.95 (ISBN 0-910856-03-6). La Siesta.

Desert Rapture. Denise Robins. 1978. pap. 1.75 (ISBN 0-380-42416-9, 42416). Avon.

Desert Rats at War: Europe. George Forty. (Illus.). 1977. 16.95 o.p. (ISBN 0-7110-0733-0). Hippocrene Bks.

Desert Rose...English Moon. Claudette Williams. 256p. (Orig.). 1981. pap. 2.50 (ISBN 0-449-24388-5, Crest). Fawcett.

Desert Solitaire. rev. ed. Edward Abbey. (Literature of the American Wilderness). (Illus.). 296p. 1981. Repr. of 1968 ed. 12.50 (ISBN 0-87905-070-5). Peregrine Smith.

Desert Solitaire: A Season in the Wilderness. Edward Abbey. 320p. 1977. pap. 2.50 (ISBN 0-345-27866-6). Ballantine.

Desert Voices. Byrd Baylor. (Illus.). 32p. (gr. 1-5). 1981. 9.95 (ISBN 0-684-16712-3). Scribner.

Desert Wife. Hilda Faunce. LC 80-22163. (Illus.). xiv, 305p. 1981. 17.95x (ISBN 0-8032-1957-1); pap. 5.95 (ISBN 0-8032-6853-X, BB 761, Bison). U of Nebr Pr.

Desert World. David F. Costello. LC 77-184973. (Illus.). 256p. 1972. 9.95 (ISBN 0-690-23513-5, TYC-T). T Y Crowell.

Deserted Stage: The Search for Dramatic Form in Nineteenth-Century England. Terry Otten. LC 74-181685. 200p. 1972. 9.50x o.p. (ISBN 0-8214-0102-5). Ohio U Pr.

Desertification. Michael Glantz. LC 77-3901. (Westview Special Studies in Natural Resources & Energy Management). 1977. lib. bdg. 28.00x (ISBN 0-89158-115-4). Westview.

Desertification: Associated Case Studies Prepared for the United Nations Conference on Desertification. Margaret R. Biswas & Asit K. Biswas. LC 80-40024. (Environmental Sciences & Applications: Vol. 12). (Illus.). 532p. 1980. 87.00 (ISBN 0-08-023581-6). Pergamon.

Desertification: Its Causes & Consequences. United Nations, Secretariat. Conference on Desertification, Nairobi 1977. LC 77-81423. 1977. text ed. 82.00 (ISBN 0-08-022023-1); pap. text ed. 42.00 (ISBN 0-08-022395-8). Pergamon.

Deserts. Maurice Burton. (Illus.). 119p. (gr. 4 up). 1975. 8.50 (ISBN 0-584-62047-0). Transatlantic.

Deserts. Delia Goetz. (Illus.). (gr. 3-7). 1956. PLB 6.48 (ISBN 0-688-31232-2). Morrow.

Deserts. Carroll R. Norden. LC 77-27090. (Read About Sciences Ser.). (Illus.). (gr. k-3). 1978. PLB 9.95 (ISBN 0-8393-0082-4). Raintree Child.

Deserts: Hot & Cold. Julian May. Ed. by Publication Associates. LC 71-156052. (Investigating the Earth Ser). (Illus.). (gr. 4-6). 1971. PLB 5.95 o.p. (ISBN 0-87191-056-X). Creative Ed.

Deserts of the World. M. P. Petrov. LC 75-12921. 1977. 87.95 (ISBN 0-470-68447-X). Halsted Pr.

Deserts of the World: Future Threat or Promise? Jane W. Watson. (Illus.). 136p. (gr. 10-12). 1981. 12.95 (ISBN 0-399-20785-6). Philomel.

Desiderius Erasmus. J. Kelley Soward. LC 74-23864. (World Authors Ser.: Netherlands: No. 353). 1975. lib. bdg. 12.50 (ISBN 0-8057-2302-1). Twayne.

Desiderius Erasmus Concerning the Aim & Method of Education. Ed. by William H. Woodward. LC 64-18613. (Orig.). 1964. text ed. 9.75 (ISBN 0-8077-2350-9); pap. text ed. 4.25x (ISBN 0-8077-2347-9). Tchrs Coll.

Design, Bk. 2. The Editors of Fine Woodworking Magazine. LC 78-68950. (Illus.). 1979. 15.95 (ISBN 0-918804-08-6, Dist. by Van Nostrand Reinhold); pap. 11.95 (ISBN 0-918804-07-8). Taunton.

Design & Analysis: A Researcher's Handbook. Geoffrey Keppel. LC 72-6434. (Illus.). 640p. 1973. ref. ed. 21.95 (ISBN 0-13-200030-X). P-H.

Design & Analysis of Cold Formed Sections. Ed. by A. C. Walker. LC 75-1315. 190p. 1975. 18.95 o.p. (ISBN 0-470-91809-8). Halsted Pr.

Design & Analysis of Computer Algorithms. Alfred Aho & John Hopcroft. 480p. 1974. text ed. 21.95 (ISBN 0-201-00029-6). A-W.

Design & Analysis of Experiments. Douglas C. Montgomery. 1976. text ed. 25.95x (ISBN 0-471-61421-1). Wiley.

Design & Analysis of Experiments in the Animal & Medical Sciences, Vol. 1. John L. Gill. (Illus.). 1978. text ed. 16.50 (ISBN 0-8138-0020-X). Iowa St U Pr.

Design & Art Direction Nineteen Seventy-Nine. 17th ed. Ed. by Edward Booth-Clibborn. Date not set. 42.50 o.p. (ISBN 0-8038-1567-0). Hastings.

Design & Art Direction One Hundred Eighty: The 18th Annual of British Graphics, Advertising, Television & Editorial Design. Ed. by Edward Booth-Clibborn. (Visual Communications Bks.). (Illus.). 440p. 1980. cancelled o.p. (ISBN 0-8038-1574-3). Hastings.

Design & Build a Patio or Terrace. Geoff Hamilton. 4.50. David & Charles.

Design & Build a Rockery. Geoff Hamilton. 4.50. David & Charles.

Design & Chart Your Own Needlepoint. Rita Weiss. (Dover Needlework Ser.). (Illus.). 48p. (Orig.). 1976. pap. 2.95 (ISBN 0-486-23301-4). Dover.

Design & Consruction of Dry Docks. B. K. Mazurkiewicz. (Illus.). 500p. 68.00x (ISBN 0-87849-028-0); pap. 38.00x (ISBN 0-87849-036-1). Trans Tech.

Design & Construction of Flexible & Efficent Interactive Programming Systems. James G. Mitchell. LC 79-50563. (Outstanding Dissertations in the Computer Sciences Ser.: Vol.12). 1980. lib. bdg. 15.50 (ISBN 0-8240-4414-2). Garland Pub.

Design & Construction of Offshore Structures. Thomas Telford Editorial Staff, Ltd. 184p. 1980. 60.00x (ISBN 0-7277-0041-3, Pub. by Telford England). State Mutual Bk.

Design & Construction of Sanitary & Storm Sewers. Compiled by American Society of Civil Engineers. 352p. 1969. text ed. 17.00 (ISBN 0-87262-214-2). Am Soc Civil Eng.

Design & Construction of Stables. Peter C. Smith. (Illus.). 18.35 (ISBN 0-85131-000-1, Dist. by Sporting Book Center). J A Allen.

Design & Construction of Steel Chimney Liners. Compiled By American Society of Civil Engineers. 232p. pap. text ed. 9.00 (ISBN 0-87262-111-1). Am Soc Civil Eng.

Design & Estimating for Heating, Ventilating, & Air Conditioning. Ennio A. Rizzi. 480p. 1980. text ed. 27.95 (ISBN 0-442-26952-8). Van Nos Reinhold.

Design & Evaluation of Reliable Computing Structures. Daniel Siewiorek & Robert Swarz. 520p. Date not set. 35.00 (ISBN 0-932376-13-4). Digital Pr.

Design & Function at the Threshold of Life: The Viruses. Heinz Fraenkel-Conrat. (Orig.). 1962. o. p. 20.50 (ISBN 0-12-265162-6); pap. 10.50 (ISBN 0-12-265168-5). Acad Pr.

Design & Implementation of Computer-Based Information Systems. Ed. by N. Szperski & E. Grochla. 383p. 1979. 47.50x (ISBN 90-286-0519-3). Sijthoff & Noordhoff.

Design & Implementation of Low Cost Automation. F. P. Bernardo, Jr. LC 72-86487. 116p. 1972. 7.75 (ISBN 92-833-1020-9, APO17, APO). Unipub.

Design & Installation Manual for Thermal Storage. 2nd ed. Solar Energy Group, Argonne National Laboratory. 1981. 39.95 (ISBN 0-89934-009-1); pap. 24.95 (ISBN 0-89934-010-5). Solar Energy Info.

Design & Manufacture of Plastic Injection Moulds. (Productivity Ser.: No. 13). 70p. 1979. pap. 8.25 (ISBN 92-833-1703-3, APO 93, APO). Unipub.

Design & Marketing of New Products. Glen Urban & John R. Hauser. (Illus.). 1980. 28.00 (ISBN 0-13-201269-3); text ed. 24.00 (ISBN 0-686-66020-X). P-H.

Design & Operation of Small Sewage Works. D. Barnes & F. Wilson. LC 76-48093. 1977. 19.95 o.p. (ISBN 0-470-99015-5). Halsted Pr.

Design & Planning of Engineering Systems. Dale D. Meredith et al. (Civil Engineering & Engineering Mechanics Ser). (Illus.). 384p. 1973. ref. ed. 26.95 (ISBN 0-13-200196-9). P-H.

Design & Planning of Swimming Pools. John Dawes. LC 79-40059. 276p. 1979. 52.50 (ISBN 0-8436-0169-8). CBI Pub.

Design & Purpose: A Study in the Drama of Evolution. Henry T. Edge. (Study Ser.: No. 4). 1980. 1.25 (ISBN 0-686-59832-6, 913004-37). Point Loma Pub.

Design & Sew Children's Clothes. Bomie Halpern & Kathryn Larson. 1979. pap. 5.95 o.p. (ISBN 0-385-14923-9, Dolp). Doubleday.

Design & Strategy for Distributed Data Processing. James Martin. (Illus.). 672p. 1981. text ed. 37.50 (ISBN 0-13-201657-5). P-H.

Design Automation of Digital Systems: Theory & Techniques, Vol. 1. Melvin A. Breuer. (Illus.). 1972. ref. ed. 25.95 (ISBN 0-13-199893-5). P-H.

Design by Photography. rev. ed. O. R. Croy. Date not set. 15.95 o.p. (ISBN 0-8038-1548-4). Hastings.

Design Charts for Water Retaining Structures: BS 5337. A. J. Threlfall. (Viewpoint Publication Ser). (Illus.). 1978. pap. text ed. 17.50 (ISBN 0-7210-1104-7). Scholium Intl.

Design Connection: Energy & Technology in Architecture. Ed. by Ralph W. Crump. Martin J. Harms. (Preston Thomas Memorial Series in Architecture). 144p. 1981. text ed. 19.95 (ISBN 0-442-23125-3). Van Nos Reinhold.

Design Construction & Operating Experience of Demonstration LMFBRs. (Illus.). 1979. pap. 79.25 (ISBN 92-0-050278-4, ISP490, IAEA). Unipub.

Design Cost File, Nineteen Seventy-Eight. Berger & Associated Cost Consultants, Inc. 299p. 1980. pap. text ed. 29.95 (ISBN 0-442-12217-9). Van Nos Reinhold.

Design Crochet. Ed. by Mark Dittrick. LC 78-53411. 1979. 14.95 (ISBN 0-8015-2019-3, Hawthorn). Dutton.

Design Drafting. J. H. Earle. (gr. 7-12). 1972. text ed. 16.95 o.p. (ISBN 0-201-01677-X, Sch Div). A-W.

Design Drawing. 2nd rev. ed. William K. Lockard. LC 79-65405. (Illus.). 1981. pap. 15.00x (ISBN 0-914468-06-5). Pepper Pub.

Design Drawing. William K. Lockard. LC 74-16003. (Illus.). 1974. pap. text ed. 12.50x (ISBN 0-914468-01-4). Pepper Pub.

Design Drawing Experiences. 4th. rev. ed. William K. Lockard. LC 79-65404. (Illus.). 1979. pap. text ed. 12.50x (ISBN 0-914468-07-3). Pepper Pub.

Design Education. Peter Green. (Illus.). 137p. 1974. 12.50x (ISBN 0-7134-2321-8). Intl Pubns Serv.

Design Education in Crafts & Technology: Proceedings. Northampton Craft Conference 1976. 1976. pap. 13.50 (ISBN 0-7134-3177-6, Pub. by Batsford England). David & Charles.

Design Education: Problem Solving & Visual Experience. Peter Green. 1974. pap. 17.95 (ISBN 0-7134-2325-0, Pub. by Batsford England). David & Charles.

Design for Change: A Guide to New Careers. Marie Kisiel. (New Viewpoints Vision Bks.). 352p. 1980. 12.95 (ISBN 0-531-02374-5, EE40); pap. 8.95 (ISBN 0-531-06754-8). Watts.

Design for Decision. Irwin D. Bross. 1965. pap. text ed. 5.95 (ISBN 0-02-904740-4). Free Pr.

Design for Desegregation Evaluation. William M. Harris. 1976. pap. text ed. 5.75x (ISBN 0-8191-0006-4). U Pr of Amer.

Design for Fire Safety. Marchant. 1981. text ed. price not set (ISBN 0-408-00487-8). Butterworth.

Design for Good Acoustics & Noise Control. J. E. Moore. 1979. text ed. 26.50x (ISBN 0-333-24292-0); pap. 15.95x (ISBN 0-333-24293-9). Scholium Intl.

Design for Health. Anthony Cox & Philip Groves. (Newnes-Butterworth Design Ser.). 1981. text ed. price not set (ISBN 0-408-00389-8, Newnes-Butterworth). Butterworth.

Design for Human Affairs. C. M. Deasy. LC 74-5198. 250p. 1974. text ed. 10.95 o.p. (ISBN 0-470-20454-0). Halsted Pr.

Design for Industry. E. Mills. (Illus.). Date not set. text ed. cancelled (ISBN 0-408-00342-1). Butterworths.

Design for Love. Kristin Michaels. (Orig.). 1981. pap. price not set (Signet Bks). NAL.

Design for Love. Nora Powers. 192p. (Orig.). 1980. pap. 1.50 (ISBN 0-671-57042-0). S&S.

Design for Movement. Lyn Oxenford. 1951. pap. 5.95 (ISBN 0-87830-561-0). Theatre Arts.

Design for Music Learning. Douglas Greer. LC 79-21117. 1980. pap. text ed. 12.95x (ISBN 0-8077-2573-0). Tchrs Coll.

Design for Need. Ed. by J. Bicknell & L. McQuiston. 1977. pap. 19.25 o.p. (ISBN 0-08-021500-9). Pergamon.

Design for Passenger Transport. new ed. Ed. by Frank Height. (Illus.). 1979. text ed. 32.00 (ISBN 0-08-023735-5). Pergamon.

Design for Reliability in Deepwater Floating Drilling Operations. L. M. Harris. 320p. 1980. 35.00 (ISBN 0-87814-082-4). Pennwell Pub.

Design for Religion - Toward Ecumenical Education. Gabriel Moran. LC 78-130860. 1971. pap. 1.95 (ISBN 0-8164-2544-2). Crossroad NY.

Design for Safety of Nuclear Power Plants. (IAEA Safety Ser.: No. 50-C-D). 43p. 1979. pap. 6.50 (ISBN 92-0-123778-2, ISP516, IAEA). Unipub.

Design for Security. R. J. Healy. LC 61-21179. 1968. 28.50 (ISBN 0-471-36664-1, Pub. by Wiley-Interscience). Wiley.

Design for Social Work Practice. Ed. by Felice D. Perlmutter. LC 74-1200. 1974. 15.00x (ISBN 0-231-03808-9). Columbia U Pr.

Design for Structural Stability. P. A. Kirby & D. A. Nethercot. LC 79-754. 1979. 43.95 (ISBN 0-470-26691-0). Halsted Pr.

Design for the Eighties. (Illus.). 1981. text ed. 40.00 (ISBN 0-937976-05-9). Enviro Pr.

Design for Tourism: An I.C.S.I.D. Interdesign Report. Ed. by Michael Gorman & Frank Height. 64p. 1977. text ed. 15.00 (ISBN 0-08-021481-9). Pergamon.

Design for Writing Workbook. Janet F. Egleson. 1970. pap. text ed. 4.95x (ISBN 0-02-474140-X, 47414). Macmillan.

Design Graphs for Concrete Shell Roofs. C. B. Wilby. (Illus.). xii, 148p. 1980. 37.50x (ISBN 0-85334-899-5). Burgess-Intl Ideas.

Design Guide & Commentary on Wood Structures. Compiled By American Society of Civil Engineers. 432p. 1975. pap. text ed. 16.00 (ISBN 0-87262-109-X). Am Soc Civil Eng.

Design Guide for Local Roads & Streets: Rural & Urban. 1971. 1.00. AASHTO.

Design Guide Plant Cast Precast & Prestressed Concrete. softcover 17.50 (ISBN 0-937040-17-7). Prestressed Concrete.

Design Handbook in Accordance with the Strength Design Method of ACI 318-71, Vol. 1. ACI Committee 340. 1973. 7-ring bnd. 43.75 (ISBN 0-685-85091-9, SP-17(73)) (ISBN 0-685-85092-7). ACI.

Design Handbook in Accordance with the Strength Design Method of ACI 318-77: Columns, Vol. 2. ACI Committee 340. 1978. binder 37.25 (ISBN 0-685-85093-5, SP-17A78). ACI.

Design, Implementation & Evaluation of Mathematical Modeling Procedures for Decisioning Among Educational Alternatives. Brent E. Wholebep. LC 80-5437. 474p. 1980. lib. bdg. 24.50 (ISBN 0-8191-1093-0); pap. text ed. 15.50 (ISBN 0-8191-1094-9). U Pr of Amer.

Design in Blockwork. 3rd ed. Ed. by Michael Gage & T. Kirkbridge. (Illus.). 1980. 25.00 (ISBN 0-686-60663-9, Pub. by Architectural Pr). Nichols Pub.

Design in Embroidery. Kay Whyte. (Illus.). 240p. 1969. 14.75 (ISBN 0-8231-4008-3). Branford.

Design in Liberal Learning. Maxwell H. Goldberg. LC 71-110645. (Higher Education Ser.). 1971. 11.95x o.p. (ISBN 0-87589-102-0). Jossey-Bass.

Design in Structural Steel. 3rd ed. John E. Lothers. LC 71-160254. (Civil Engineering & Engineering Mechanics Ser). (Illus.). 1972. 26.95 (ISBN 0-13-201921-3). P-H.

Design, Installation & Operation of Small, Stand-Alone Photovoltaic Powersystems. PRC Energy Analysis Co. 300p. 1981. pap. 34.50 (ISBN 0-89934-092-X). Solar Energy Info.

Design Knitting. Ed. by Mark Dittrick. LC 78-53411. 1979. 14.95 (ISBN 0-8015-2021-5, Hawthorn). Dutton.

Design Methods in Rock Mechanics: Proceedings. Rock Mechanics International Society & the U. S. National Committee, 16th. Compiled By American Society of Civil Engineers et al. 432p. 1977. text ed. 31.00 (ISBN 0-87262-080-8). Am Soc Civil Eng.

Design Methods: Seeds of Human Factors. J. Christopher Jones. LC 77-122347. 1971. 25.75 (ISBN 0-471-44790-0, Pub. by Wiley-Interscience). Wiley.

Design Methods: Seeds of Human Futures 1980 Edition a Review of New Topics. J. Christopher Jones. 440p. 1981. 22.50 (Pub. by Wiley Interscience). Wiley.

Design of a Housing Allowance. Frank De Leeuw et al. 42p. 1970. pap. 2.75 o.p. (ISBN 0-87766-049-2, 30005). Urban Inst.

Design of a Maintainance System. (Productivity Ser.: No. 14). 50p. 1979. pap. 8.25 (ISBN 92-833-1704-1, APO92, APO). Unipub.

Design of Advertising. 4th ed. Roy P. Nelson. 1980. text ed. 16.95x (ISBN 0-697-04348-7). Wm C Brown.

Design of & Equipment for Hot Laboratories. (STI-PUB-436). (Illus.). 1977. pap. 54.25 (ISBN 92-0-020476-7, ISP436, IAEA). Unipub.

Design of Biological Monitoring Systems for Pest Management. S. M. Welch & B. A. Croft. LC 79-10960. 1980. pap. 19.95x (ISBN 0-470-26632-5). Halsted Pr.

Design of Biopharmaceutical Properties Through Prodrugs & Analogs. LC 77-81663. 1977. 30.00 (ISBN 0-917330-16-1). Am Pharm Assn.

Design of Building Frames. John S. Gero & H. J. Cowan. LC 75-28388. 1976. 57.95 (ISBN 0-470-29683-6). Halsted Pr.

Design of Cities. rev ed. Edmund N. Bacon. (Illus.). 336p. 1976. pap. 18.95 (ISBN 0-14-004236-9). Penguin.

Design of Construction & Process Operations. Daniel W. Halpin & Ronald W. Woodhead. LC 76-9784. 424p. 1976. 29.95 (ISBN 0-471-34565-2). Wiley.

Design of Counting Systems for Dynamic Studies & Uptake Measurements. 1980. 10.00 (Pub. by Brit Inst Radiology England). State Mutual Bk.

Design of Cutting Tools: Use of Metal Cutting Theory. Inyong Ham & Amitabha Bhattacharyya. LC 68-29237. (Manufacturing Data Ser). (Illus.). 1969. 11.00x (ISBN 0-87263-014-5). SME.

Design of Cylindrical Concrete Shell Roofs. Compiled By American Society of Civil Engineers. (Manual & Report on Engineering Practice Ser.: No. 31). 192p. 1953. pap. 6.75 (ISBN 0-87262-209-6). Am Soc Civil Eng.

Design of Design. Gordon L. Glegg. LC 69-12432. (Cambridge Engineering Pubns.). (Illus.). 1969. 14.50 (ISBN 0-521-07447-9). Cambridge U Pr.

Design of Earthquake Resistant Structures. Ed. by Emilio Rosenblueth. LC 79-9499. 295p. 1980. 47.95x (ISBN 0-470-26839-5). Halsted Pr.

Design of English Elementary & Primary Schools: A Select Annotated Bibliography. John McNicholas. (Select Bibliographies Ser.). (Illus.). 36p. 1974. pap. text ed. 3.75x (ISBN 0-85633-044-2, NFER). Humanities.

Design of Executive Protection Systems. Joe B. Flynn. (Illus.). 100p. 1979. text ed. 12.75 (ISBN 0-398-03894-5). C C Thomas.

Design of Foundations to Control Settlements. Compiled By American Society of Civil Engineers. 602p. 1966. pap. text ed. 29.50 (ISBN 0-87262-007-7). Am Soc Civil Eng.

Design of High Pressure Steam & High Temperature Water Plants. William J. Scullhorpe. 128p. 1972. 25.00 o.p. (ISBN 0-8311-1075-9). Indus Pr.

Design of Library Areas & Buildings. Ina J. Weis. (Architecture Ser.: Bibliography: A-413). 80p. 1981. pap. 12.00. Vance Biblios.

Design of Liquid-Retaining Concrete Structures. R. D. Anchor. 176p. 1981. 49.95 (ISBN 0-470-27123-X). Halsted Pr.

Design of Machine Elements. 5th ed. M. F. Spotts. (Illus.). 1978. ref. ed. 27.95 (ISBN 0-13-200576-X). P-H.

Design of Machine Members. 4th ed. Venton L. Doughtie & A. Vallance. 1964. text ed. 22.50 o.p. (ISBN 0-07-017635-3, C). McGraw.

Design of Man-Computer Dialogues. James Martin. (Illus.). 496p. 1973. ref. ed. 29.00 (ISBN 0-13-201251-0). P-H.

Design of Medical Environments for Children & Adolescents: An Annotated Bibliography. Wendy Sarkissian et al. (Archtecture Ser.: Bibliography A-261). 65p. 1980. pap. 7.00. Vance Biblios.

Design of Modern Transistor Circuits. Maurice Yunik. (Illus.). 384p. 1973. 18.95x o.p. (ISBN 0-13-201285-5). P-H.

Design of on-Line Computer Systems. Edward Yourdon. (Illus.). 576p. 1972. ref. ed. 24.95 (ISBN 0-13-201301-0). P-H.

Design of Op-Amp Circuits, with Experiments. Howard M. Berlin. LC 78-56606. 1978. pap. 8.95 (ISBN 0-672-21537-3). Sams.

Design of Phase-Locked Loop Circuits, with Experiments. Howard M. Berlin. LC 78-57203. 1978. pap. 9.95 (ISBN 0-672-21545-4). Sams.

Design of Piled Foundations. 2nd ed. Thomas Whitaker. 224p. 1976. text ed. 27.00 (ISBN 0-08-019706-X); pap. text ed. 14.75 (ISBN 0-08-019705-1). Pergamon.

Design of Piping Systems. rev. 2nd ed. Kellogg Company. 1964. 37.50 (ISBN 0-471-46795-2, Pub. by Wiley-Interscience). Wiley.

Design of Plumbing & Drainage Systems. 2nd ed. Louis Blendermann. (Illus.). 1963. 20.00 (ISBN 0-8311-3004-0). Indus Pr.

Design of Poetry. Charles B. Wheeler. 1967. 6.50x (ISBN 0-393-04256-1); pap. 6.95x (ISBN 0-393-09707-2, NortonC). Norton.

Design of Polytechnic Institute Buildings. (Illus.). 96p. (Orig.). 1972. pap. 11.50 (ISBN 92-3-100963-X, U155, UNESCO). Unipub.

Design of Precast Concrete: An Introduction to Practical Design. Robert Hartland. LC 75-23528. 1976. 17.95 (ISBN 0-470-35654-5). Halsted Pr.

Design of Prestressed Concrete Structures. 3rd ed. T. Y. Lin & Ned H. Burns. 752p. 1981. text ed. 28.95 (ISBN 0-471-01898-8); tchrs.' ed. avail. (ISBN 0-471-08788-2). Wiley.

Design of Racing Sports Cars. Colin Campbell. LC 73-85158. (Illus.). 268p. 1973. 12.50 (ISBN 0-8376-0081-2). Bentley.

Design of Radiotracer Experiments in Marine Biology Studies. (Technical Report Ser.: No. 167). (Illus.). 289p. 1975. pap. 22.50 (ISBN 92-0-125175-0, IAEA). Unipub.

Design of Real Time Computer Systems. J. Martin. 1967. ref. ed. 25.95 (ISBN 0-13-201400-9). P-H.

Design of Sewage Sludge Incineration Systems. Calvin Brunner. LC 80-21916. (Pollution Technology Review: No. 71). (Illus.). 380p. 1981. 48.00 (ISBN 0-8155-0825-5). Noyes.

Design of Social Policy Research. K. Mayer & Ernest Greenwood. (Illus.). 1980. text ed. 18.95 (ISBN 0-13-201558-7). P-H.

Design of Steel Structures. 2nd ed. B. Bresler et al. 1968. 34.50 (ISBN 0-471-10297-0). Wiley.

Design of Structural Steelwork. Peter Knowles. (Illus.). 1977. 24.95x (ISBN 0-903384-16-7). Intl Ideas.

Design of Textiles for Industrial Applications. P. W. Harrison. 218p. 1977. 60.00x (ISBN 0-686-63759-3). State Mutual Bk.

Design of the Industrial Classroom. Kenniston W. Lord, Jr. LC 76-46605. (Illus.). 1977. text ed. 10.95 (ISBN 0-201-04357-2). A-W.

Design of Thermal Systems. 2nd ed. W. F. Stoecker. (Illus.). 1980. 29.95 (ISBN 0-07-061618-3). McGraw.

Design of Urban Space: A GLC Manual. Richard M. Cartwright. 208p. 1981. 44.95 (ISBN 0-470-27066-7). Halsted Pr.

Design of VMOS Circuits, with Experiments. Robert T. Stone & Howard M. Berlin. LC 79-5617. 1980. pap. 8.95 (ISBN 0-672-21686-8). Sams.

Design of Well-Structured & Correct Programs. S. Alagic & M. A. Arbib. LC 77-27087. (Texts & Monographs in Computer Science). 1978. 14.80 (ISBN 0-387-90299-6). Springer-Verlag.

Design of Wood Structures. Donald E. Breyer & John A. Ank. (Illus.). 1980. 27.50 (ISBN 0-07-007671-5). McGraw.

Design on Fabrics. 2nd ed. Meda P. Johnston & Glen Kaufman. 188p. 1981. 14.95 (ISBN 0-442-26339-2); pap. 9.95 (ISBN 0-442-23145-8). Van Nos Reinhold.

Design, Operation & Testing of Synchronous Machines. Gian C. Jain. 1966. 20.00x o.p. (ISBN 0-210-33836-9). Asia.

Design Production Safety Systems. William C. Boyle. 276p. 1979. 30.00 (ISBN 0-87814-096-4). Pennwell Pub.

Design Review in Historic Districts. Alice M. Bowsher. LC 78-61513. (Illus.). 138p. 1978. pap. 6.95 (ISBN 0-89133-080-1). Preservation Pr.

Design: Science-Method. 1980. pap. text ed. 46.80. Butterworths.

Design Tables for Beams on Elastic Foundations & Related Structural Problems. K. T. Iyengar & S. Anantha Ramu. (Illus.). 1979. 38.90x (ISBN 0-85334-841-3, Pub. by Applied Science). Burgess-Intl Ideas.

Design Techniques for Electronics Engineers. Electronics Magazine. LC 77-8323. (Illus.). 370p. pap. text ed. 15.95 (ISBN 0-07-099711-X, R-726). McGraw.

Design Your Own Stuffed Toys. Anne Dyer. LC 75-105680. (Illus.). 1970. 8.50 (ISBN 0-8231-5021-6). Branford.

Designation. Michael Devitt. LC 80-26471. 304p. 1981. 22.50x (ISBN 0-231-05126-3). Columbia U Pr.

Designed to Be Like Him. Dwight Pentecost. 1981. pap. 5.95 (ISBN 0-8024-2132-6). Moody.

Designed to Win. Roger Marshall. (Illus.). 1981. 28.50 (ISBN 0-393-03229-9). Norton.

Designer Crafts. Linda Hetzer. LC 77-28784. (Illustrated Crafts for Beginners). (Illus.). (gr. 3-7). PLB 9.95 (ISBN 0-8172-1188-8). Raintree Pubs.

Designer's Choice: The Best Products, Graphics & Environments of 1980. Industrial Design Magazine. Ed. by George Finley. 120p. 1980. pap. 7.95 (ISBN 0-07-031710-0, P&RB). McGraw.

Designers Design for Themselves. Patricia Corbin. (Illus.). 96p. 1981. 19.95 (ISBN 0-525-93135-X). Dutton.

Designer's Guide to Text Type. Ed. by Jean C. King & Tony Esposito. 320p. 1980. pap. 24.95 (ISBN 0-442-25425-3). Van Nos Reinhold.

Designing a Distributed Processing System. Hamish Donaldson. LC 79-22523. 233p. 1980. 34.95x (ISBN 0-470-26889-1). Halsted Pr.

Designing a National Scientific & Technological Communication System. Ed. by Russell L. Ackoff. LC 76-20150. 1976. 19.50x (ISBN 0-8122-7716-3). U of Pa Pr.

Designing & Building Your Own Home. Kay Crowdis & David Crowdis. (Illus.). 240p. 1980. text ed. 14.95 (ISBN 0-8359-1272-8). Reston.

Designing & Drafting for Handweavers. Berta Frey. 240p. 1975. 10.95 (ISBN 0-02-541460-7). Macmillan.

Designing & Making Dolls. Ilse Gray. LC 72-1449. (Illus.). 96p. 1972. 9.95 o.p. (ISBN 0-8230-2991-3). Watson-Guptill.

Designing Apparel Through the Flat Pattern. 4th ed. Ernestine Kopp et al. LC 73-132040. 1971. 13.50 o.p. (ISBN 0-87005-094-X). Fairchild.

Designing Apparel Through the Flat Pattern. 5th, new ed. Ernestine Kopp et al. (Illus.). 250p. 1980. pap. text ed. 18.95 (ISBN 0-87005-258-6). Fairchild.

Designing Architectural Facades: An Ideas File for Architects. Kurt Hoffmann et al. (Illus.). 168p. 1975. 29.95x (ISBN 0-7114-3408-5). Intl Ideas.

Designing Complex Organizations. Jay Galbraith. LC 72-11887. 1973. pap. text ed. 6.50 (ISBN 0-201-02559-0). A-W.

Designing Dress Patterns. rev. ed. Helen N. Tanous. (Illus.). (gr. 10-12). 1971. text ed. 13.28 (ISBN 0-87002-112-5). Bennett IL.

Designing for Aging: Patterns of Use. Sandra C. Howell. (Illus.). 345p. 1980. text ed. 25.00x (ISBN 0-262-08107-5). MIT Pr.

Designing for Industry: The Architecture of Albert Kahn. Grant Hildebrand. 224p. 1974. pap. 8.95x (ISBN 0-262-58040-3). MIT Pr.

Designing for Needlepoint & Embroidery from Ancient & Primitive Sources. Jan Messent. LC 76-7589. 128p. 1976. 14.95 o.s.i. (ISBN 0-02-584431-8, 58443). Macmillan.

Designing Hospital Training Programs. Reba D. Grubb & Carolyn J. Mueller. (Illus.). 216p. 1975. 20.50 (ISBN 0-398-03316-1). C C Thomas.

Designing Houses: An Illustrated Guide. Les Walker & Jeffrey Milstein. LC 75-7684. (Illus.). 1979. pap. 5.95 (ISBN 0-87951-096-X). Overlook Pr.

Designing Learning Environments. Ed. by Phillip Sleeman & D. M. Rockwell. (Professional Books Ser.). (Illus.). 288p. 1980. lib. bdg. 22.50 (ISBN 0-582-28077-X). Longman.

Designing Library Buildings for Activity. J. M. Orr. (Grafton Books on Library Science). 1977. lib. bdg. 16.00x (ISBN 0-233-96230-1). Westview.

Designing Microcomputer Systems. U. Pooch & R. Chattergy. (Microcomputer Ser.). 224p. 1979. pap. 9.95 (ISBN 0-8104-5679-6). Hayden.

Designing Organisations for Satisfaction & Efficiency. K. Legge & E. Mugford. 1978. text ed. 24.00x (ISBN 0-566-02102-1, Pub. by Gower Pub Co England). Renouf.

Designing Organisations for Satisfaction & Efficiency. K. Legge & E. Mugford. 160p. 1978. text ed. 24.00x (ISBN 0-566-02102-1, Pub. by Gower Pub Co England). Renouf.

Designing Schools & Schooling for the Handicapped. Jack W. Birch & B. Kenneth Johnstone. (Illus.). 244p. 1975. 22.50 (ISBN 0-398-03362-5). C C Thomas.

Designing Sensible Surveys. Donald C. Orlich. (Orig.). 1979. pap. 11.90 (ISBN 0-913178-50-0, Pub. by Two Continents). Hippocrene Bks.

Designing Technical Reports: Writing for Audiences in Organizations. J. C. Mathes & Dwight W. Stevenson. LC 75-44249. 1976. text ed. 19.95 (ISBN 0-672-61367-0); tchr's manual 2.50 (ISBN 0-672-61405-7). Bobbs.

Designing the Sermon: Order & Movement in Preaching. James E. Massey. LC 80-17920. (Abingdon Preacher's Library). 128p. (Orig.). 1980. pap. 4.95 (ISBN 0-687-10490-4). Abingdon.

Designing Today's Manufactured Products. John R. Lindbeck. LC 72-79110. 225p. (gr. 10-12). 1972. text ed. 17.16 (ISBN 0-87345-440-5). McKnight.

Designing with Field Effect Transistors. Siliconix, Inc. (Illus.). 352p. 1981. 24.50 (ISBN 0-07-057449-9). McGraw.

Designing with Glass Reinforced Cement. John Young. 1979. 12.50x (ISBN 0-85139-017-X, Pub. by Architectural Pr). Nichols Pub.

Designing with Type. James Craig. Ed. by Susan E. Meyer. 1971. 15.95 o.p. (ISBN 0-8230-1320-0). Watson-Guptill.

Designing with Type. rev. ed. James Craig. Ed. by Susan Meyer. (Illus.). 1980. 15.95 (ISBN 0-8230-1321-9). Watson-Guptill.

Designing Your Own Room. Mary J. Alexander. (Career Concise Guides Ser.). (Illus.). (gr. 7 up). 1977. PLB 4.90 o.p. (ISBN 0-531-00091-5). Watts.

Designs. Ruth Heller. (Creative Coloring Activity Pandabacks). (Illus.). 32p. 1981. pap. 1.25 (ISBN 0-448-49621-6). G&D.

Designs. Richard Horn. 350p. 1980. 10.95 (ISBN 0-87131-329-4). M Evans.

Designs & Pattern Cutting for Children's Clothes. Peter Morgan. 1977. 24.00 (ISBN 0-7134-2712-4, Pub. by Batsford England). David & Charles.

Designs & Patterns from Historic Ornaments. W. Audsley & G. Audsley. Orig. Title: Outlines of Ornament in the Leading Styles. (Illus.). 9.00 (ISBN 0-8446-1565-X). Peter Smith.

Designs by Erte: Fashion Drawings & Illustrations from Harper's Bazaar. Erte. Ed. by S. Blum. (Illus.). 13.50 (ISBN 0-8446-5571-6). Peter Smith.

Designs for Evaluating Social Programs. Lawrence P. Clark. (Learning Packages in the Policy Sciences: No. 11). vi, 44p. (Orig.). 1979. pap. text ed. 3.00 (ISBN 0-936826-00-2). Pol Stud Assocs.

Designs for Glued Trusses. 4th ed. Midwest Plan Service Engineers. Ed. by Midwest Plan Service Staff. LC 80-39547. (Illus., 4#80). 1981. pap. 3.00 (ISBN 0-89373-051-3, MWPS-9). Midwest Plan Serv.

Designs for Glued Trusses. 3rd ed. Midwest Plan Service Personnel. LC 78-4488. (Illus.). 1978. pap. 2.50 o.p. (ISBN 0-89373-033-5, MWPS-9). Midwest Plan Serv.

Designs for the Dream King: The Castles & Palaces of Ludwig II of Bavaria. Simon Jervis & Gerhard Hojer. (Illus.). 1979. 17.50 o.p. (ISBN 0-670-26892-5, Debrett's Peerage, Ltd.). Viking Pr.

Designs for the Woodcarver. Richard A. Dabrowski. LC 76-1141. (Illus.). 1979. Repr. of 1976 ed. spiral bdg. 9.50 (ISBN 0-918036-02-X). Woodcraft Supply.

Designs to Color, 6 bks. Betty Schaffner. (ps-2). 1968. 2.50; Bk. 1. 1.95 (ISBN 0-8431-0005-2); Bk. 2. 2.50 (ISBN 0-8431-0006-0); Bk. 3. 1.95 (ISBN 0-8431-0007-9); Bk. 4. 1.95 (ISBN 0-8431-0008-7); Bk. 5. 2.50 (ISBN 0-8431-0104-0); Bk. 6. 1.95 (ISBN 0-8431-0218-7). Price Stern.

Designs Upon the Trestleboard. Arthur R. Herrmann. 1980. Repr. softcover 6.00 (ISBN 0-686-68267-X). Macoy Pub.

Desirability of a Correctional Ombudsman. Timothy L. Fitzharris. LC 72-13057. 114p. (Orig.). 1973. pap. 4.00x (ISBN 0-87772-155-6). Inst Gov Stud Berk.

Desirable Aliens: Stories. John Bovey. LC 80-18596. (Illinois Short Fiction Ser.). 147p. 1980. 10.00 (ISBN 0-252-00837-5); pap. 3.95 (ISBN 0-252-00838-3). U of Ill Pr.

Desire. Christine Dunn & Eileen McMahon. (Orig.). 1980. pap. 2.50 (ISBN 0-446-91174-7). Warner Bks.

Desire. Ed. by William Packard. 176p. 1980. 12.95 (ISBN 0-312-19469-2). St Martin.

Desire in Language: A Semoitic Approach to Literature & Art. Julia Kristeva. Ed. by Leon S. Roudiez. Tr. by Alice Jardine & Thomas Gora. LC 80-10689. (European Perspectives Ser.). (Illus.). 336p. 1980. 16.95 (ISBN 0-231-04806-8). Columbia U Pr.

Desire of Ages. Ellen G. White. 1940. 5.95 (ISBN 0-8163-0029-1, 04259-8); pap. 0.95 newsprint ed. (ISBN 0-8163-0030-5, 04261-4); pap. 3.50 (ISBN 0-8163-0031-3, 04254-9); deluxe ed. 9.50 (ISBN 0-8163-0032-1, 04257-2). Pacific Pr Pub Assn.

Desire of the Heart. Barbara Cartland. 224p. 1980. pap. 1.75 (ISBN 0-515-05497-6). Jove Pubns.

Desires. John L'Heureux. LC 80-20228. 1981. 11.95 (ISBN 0-03-058902-9). HR&W.

Desk-Book of Errors in English. Frank H. Vizetelly. LC 74-3021. 1974. Repr. of 1920 ed. 18.00 (ISBN 0-8103-3637-5). Gale.

Desk-Book of Idioms & Idiomatic Phrases in English Speech & Literature. Frank H. Vizetelly & Leander J. De Bekker. LC 73-121208. 1970. Repr. of 1923 ed. 24.00 (ISBN 0-8103-3291-4). Gale.

Desk Reference Library. (Orig.). 1981. pap. 9.95 (ISBN 0-8326-0203-5, 6465). Delair.

Desk Reference of Legal Terms for School Psychologists & Special Educators. D. P. Hanson & D. A. Penrod. 224p. 1980. 19.75 (ISBN 0-398-04015-X). C C Thomas.

Desmidiales, Sarccodermae, Mesotaeniaceae. G. W. Prescott et al. LC 70-183418. (North American Flora, Ser. II: Part 6). 1972. pap. 5.75 (ISBN 0-89327-018-0). NY Botanical.

Desmond: A Novel, 3 vols. Charlotte Smith. Ed. by Gina Luria. LC 73-22133. (Feminist Controversy in England, 1788-1810 Ser.). 1974. lib. bdg. 50.00 ea. (ISBN 0-8240-0879-0). Garland Pub.

Desmosomatidae (Isopoda: Asellota) of the Gay Head Bermuda Transect. Robert R. Hessler. (Bulletin of the Scripps Institution of Oceanography: Vol. 15). 1970. pap. 10.00x (ISBN 0-520-09320-8). U of Cal Pr.

Desolation Wilderness. 2nd rev. ed. Robert S. Wood. (Illus.). 256p. 1975. pap. 4.95 (ISBN 0-89815-044-2). Ten Speed Pr.

DeSoto. Matthew G. Grant. LC 73-13917. 1974. PLB 5.95 (ISBN 0-87191-283-X). Creative Ed.

Desperado's Gold. L. L. Foreman. 1979. pap. 1.50 (ISBN 0-505-51431-1). Tower Bks.

Desperate Alternatives of the Soviet Leaders in the Face of the Incipient Break-up of the Communist Empire. Douglas Wittikoff. (Major Currents in Contemporary World History Library Ser.). (Illus.). 143p. 1981. 69.85 (ISBN 0-930008-81-2). Inst Econ Pol.

Desperate Diplomacy: William H. Seward's Foreign Policy, 1861. Norman B. Ferris. LC 75-5509. 1976. 14.50x (ISBN 0-87049-170-9). U of Tenn Pr.

Desperate Dragons. Norris Lloyd. (Illus.). (gr. 2-4). 1966. PLB 3.99 o.s.i. (ISBN 0-8038-1522-0). Hastings.

Desperate Longings. Frances Flores. (Candlelight Romance Ser.). (Orig.). Date not set. pap. 1.50 (ISBN 0-440-12015-2). Dell.

Desperate Season. Diana Davenport. 1978. pap. 1.95 o.p. (ISBN 0-449-13981-6, GM). Fawcett.

Desperate Siege. Ted Ferguson. LC 78-20071. (Illus.). 240p. 1980. 11.95 (ISBN 0-385-14694-9). Doubleday.

Desperate Voyagers. Marvin Tokayer & Mary Swartz. 1980. pap. 2.75 (ISBN 0-440-12223-6). Dell.

Despierta, Continente Mio. Hugo Gasco. LC 78-50624. 159p. (Orig., Span.). 1978. pap. 3.50 (ISBN 0-89922-108-4). Edit Caribe.

Despised & the Damned: The Russian Peasant Through the Ages. Jules Koslow. (Russia Old & New Ser.). (Illus.). 192p. 1972. 5.95 o.s.i. (ISBN 0-02-566500-6). Macmillan.

Despues De la Cruz y el Punal. Tr. by David Wilkerson. (Spanish Bks.). (Span.). 1978. 1.75 (ISBN 0-8297-0537-6). Life Pubs Intl.

Desserts. Sunset Editors. LC 69-14150. (Illus.). 96p. 1968. pap. 3.95 (ISBN 0-376-02344-9, Sunset Bks). Sunset-Lane.

Destinada a Viver. Tr. by Johanna R. Dobschiner. (Portugese Bks.). (Port.). 1979. 1.60 (ISBN 0-8297-0655-0). Life Pubs Intl.

Destination Peace: Three Decades of Israeli Foreign Policy. Gideon Rafael. LC 80-9060. 400p. 1981. 16.95 (ISBN 0-8128-2812-7). Stein & Day.

Destination Saturn. Grinnell & Carter. (YA) 4.95 o.p. (ISBN 0-685-07429-3, Avalon). Bouregy.

Destination: Void. Frank Herbert. 1978. pap. 2.25 (ISBN 0-425-04366-5, Dist. by Putnam). Berkley Pub.

Destined. Joanna Warren. (Belle Meade Ser.: No. 3). 432p. (Orig.). 1980. pap. 2.50 (ISBN 0-89083-693-0). Zebra.

Destiny His Choice: The Loyalism of Andrew Marvell. John M. Wallace. LC 68-10334. 1968. 44.00 (ISBN 0-521-06725-1). Cambridge U Pr.

Destiny His Choice: The Loyalism of Andrew Marvell. John M. Wallace. 266p. 1981. pap. 13.50 (ISBN 0-521-28042-7). Cambridge U Pr.

Destiny of America. Charles R. Taylor. pap. cancelled o.s.i. (ISBN 0-89728-025-3, 532831). Omega Pubns OR.

Destiny of Civilization. Radhakamal Mukerjee. 1964. 10.00x (ISBN 0-210-31185-1). Asia.

Destiny Times Three & Riding the Torch. Fritz Leiber & Norman Spinrad. (Binary Star: No. 1). 1978. pap. 1.75 o.s.i. (ISBN 0-440-10564-1). Dell.

Destiny's Bride. Diane Stuart. 1978. pap. 1.95 o.p. (ISBN 0-425-03996-X). Berkley Pub.

Destiny's Daughter. Frances Noble. 1980. pap. 2.25 (ISBN 0-505-51462-1). Tower Bks.

Destitutes & Development. Nirmal Sengupta. 1979. text ed. 9.00x (ISBN 0-391-01864-7). Humanities.

Destroyer: Midnight Man, No. 43. Warren Murphy. 192p. (Orig.). 1981. pap. 1.95 (ISBN 0-523-40717-3). Pinnacle Bks.

Destroyer, No. 10: Terror Squad. Warren Murphy. (Orig.). 1974. pap. 1.50 (ISBN 0-523-40284-8). Pinnacle Bks.

Destroyer, No. 11: Kill or Cure. Richard Sapir & Warren Murphy. (Orig.). 1974. pap. 1.95 (ISBN 0-523-41226-6). Pinnacle Bks.

Destroyer, No. 12: Slave Safari. Warren Murphy. 1974. pap. 1.75 (ISBN 0-523-40888-9). Pinnacle Bks.

Destroyer, No. 13: Acid Rock. Warren Murphy. (Orig.). 1973. pap. 1.50 (ISBN 0-523-40287-2). Pinnacle Bks.

Destroyer, No. 14: Judgement Day. Warren Murphy. 192p. (Orig.). 1974. pap. 1.75 (ISBN 0-523-40890-0). Pinnacle Bks.

Destroyer, No. 16: Oil Slick. Warren Murphy. 192p. (Orig.). 1974. pap. 1.50 (ISBN 0-523-40290-2). Pinnacle Bks.

Destroyer, No. 17: Last War Dance. Warren Murphy. 192p. (Orig.). 1974. pap. 1.50 (ISBN 0-523-40291-0). Pinnacle Bks.

Destroyer, No. 18: Funny Money. Warren Murphy. 192p. (Orig.). 1975. pap. 1.75 (ISBN 0-523-40894-3). Pinnacle Bks.

Destroyer, No. 19: Holy Terror. Warren Murphy. 192p. (Orig.). 1975. pap. 1.75 (ISBN 0-523-40895-1). Pinnacle Bks.

Destroyer, No. 2: Death Check. Warren Murphy. (Destroyer Ser.). 1977. pap. 1.95 (ISBN 0-523-41217-7). Pinnacle Bks.

Destroyer, No. 27: The Last Temple. Warren Murphy. (Destroyer Ser.). (Orig.). 1977. pap. 1.95 (ISBN 0-523-41242-8). Pinnacle Bks.

Destroyer, No. 28: Ship of Death. Warren Murphy. (The Destroyer Ser.). 192p. 1977. pap. 1.95 (ISBN 0-523-41243-6). Pinnacle Bks.

Destroyer, No. 3: Chinese Puzzle. Warren Murphy. (Orig.). 1974. pap. 1.75 (ISBN 0-523-40879-X). Pinnacle Bks.

Destroyer: No. 37, Bottom Line. Warren Murphy. 1979. pap. 1.95 (ISBN 0-523-41252-5). Pinnacle Bks.

Destroyer, No. 4: Mafia Fix. Warren Murphy. (Orig.). 1974. pap. 1.75 (ISBN 0-523-40880-3). Pinnacle Bks.

Destroyer, No. 5: Dr. Quake. Warren Murphy. (Orig.). 1974. pap. 1.75 (ISBN 0-523-40881-1). Pinnacle Bks.

Destroyer, No. 6: Death Therapy. Warren Murphy. (Orig.). 1974. pap. 1.75 (ISBN 0-523-40882-X). Pinnacle Bks.

Destroyer, No. 7: Union Bust. Warren Murphy. (Orig.). 1974. pap. 1.95 (ISBN 0-523-41222-3). Pinnacle Bks.

Destroyer No. 8: Summit Chase. Warren Murphy. (Orig.). 1974. pap. 1.75 (ISBN 0-523-40884-6). Pinnacle Bks.

Destroyer, No. 9: Murder's Shield. Warren Murphy. (Orig.). 1974. pap. 1.95 (ISBN 0-523-41224-X). Pinnacle Bks.

Destroyer, Number Forty-Four: Balance of Power. Warren Murphy. 192p. (Orig.). 1981. pap. 1.95 (ISBN 0-523-40718-1). Pinnacle Bks.

Destroyers. A. W. Miller. (Orig.). 1980. pap. 1.75 (ISBN 0-8439-0738-X, Leisure Bks). Nordon Pubns.

Destruction-Decouverte: Le Fontionnement de la Rhetorique dans les Essais de Montaigne. Lawrence D. Kritzman. LC 80-66329. (French Forum Monographs: No. 21). 187p. (Orig.). 1980. pap. 11.50 (ISBN 0-917058-20-8). French Forum.

Destruction of Brazilian Slavery, 1850-1888. Robert Conrad. 1972. pap. 6.50x (ISBN 0-520-02371-4, CAMPUS89). U of Cal Pr.

Destruction of California. Raymond F. Dasmann. 1966. pap. 2.95 (ISBN 0-02-072800-X, Collier). Macmillan.

Destruction of Nature in the Soviet Union. Boris Komarov. Tr. by Michel Vale from Rus. Orig. Title: Unichtozhenie Prioroda Obostrenie Ekologicheskogo Krizi Sa V SSSR. 192p. 1980. 15.00 (ISBN 0-87332-157-X). M E Sharpe.

Destruction of the Natural Vegetation of North-Central Chile. Conrad J. Bahre. LC 78-50836. (Publications in Geography Ser.: Vol. 23). 1979. 10.50x (ISBN 0-520-09594-4). U of Cal Pr.

Destructive Poetics: Heidegger & Modern American Poetry. Paul A. Bove. 1980. text ed. 17.50x (ISBN 0-231-04690-1). Columbia U Pr.

Desultory Thoughts in London; Titus & Gisippus; with Other Poems. 1821. Charles Lloyd. Ed. by Donald H. Reiman. LC 75-31227. (Romantic Context Ser.: Poetry 1789-1830). 1978. lib. bdg. 47.00 (ISBN 0-8240-2177-0). Garland Pub.

Detailed Reports on the Salzburger Emigrants Who Settled in America, Vol. 6. Ed. by George F. Jones & Renate Wilson. LC 67-27137. (Wormsloe Foundation Publication Ser.: No. 15). 360p. 1981. 20.00 (ISBN 0-8203-0512-X). U of Ga Pr.

Details of a Sunset & Other Stories. Vladimir Nabokov. (McGraw-Hill Paperback Ser.). 180p. 1980. pap. 4.95 (ISBN 0-07-045721-2). McGraw.

Detecting & Controlling Hypertension. 1976. 3.00 (ISBN 0-917330-13-7). Am Pharm Assn.

Detection & Estimation: Applications to Radar. Ed. by S. S. Haykin. LC 75-33340. (Benchmark Papers in Electrical Engineering & Computer Science Ser.: Vol. 13). 1976. 41.00 (ISBN 0-12-786648-5). Acad Pr.

Detection & Location of Failed Fuel Elements. (Illus., Orig.). 1968. pap. 12.50 (ISBN 92-0-051168-6, IAEA). Unipub.

Detection & Spectronomy of Faint Light. John Meaburn. (Astrophysics & Space Science Library: No. 56). 270p. 1980. pap. 14.95 (ISBN 90-277-1198-4, Pub. by D. Reidel). Kluwer Boston.

Detection of Fish. D. H. Cushing. 220p. 1973. text ed. 42.00 (ISBN 0-08-017123-0). Pergamon.

Detection of Hearing Loss & Ear Disease in Children. K. S. Gerwin & A. Glorig. (Illus.). 208p. 1974. 16.75 (ISBN 0-398-03175-4). C C Thomas.

Detectionary. Mill Roseman. Ed. by Otto Penzler et al. LC 75-27326. (Illus.). 320p. 1980. pap. 5.95 (ISBN 0-87951-114-1). Overlook Pr.

Detective Arthur, Master Sleuth. Mary J. Fulton. 1974. PLB 9.15 o.p. (ISBN 0-307-65790-6, Golden Pr). Western Pub.

Detective Arthur on the Scent. Mary J. Fulton. (Scratch & Sniff Ser.). (Illus.). (ps-3). 1971. 4.95 o.p. (ISBN 0-307-13535-7, Golden Pr); PLB 9.92 (ISBN 0-307-64535-5). Western Pub.

Detective Bob & the Great Ape Escape. David L. Harrison. LC 80-10584. (Illus.). 48p. (ps-3). 1981. 4.95 (ISBN 0-8193-1031-X); PLB 5.95 (ISBN 0-8193-1032-8). Parents.

Detective Mole & the Halloween Mystery. Robert Quackenbush. LC 80-20784. (Illus.). 32p. (gr. 1-3). 1981. 7.95 (ISBN 0-688-41988-7); PLB 7.63 (ISBN 0-688-51988-1). Morrow.

Detective Novel of Manners: Hedonism, Morality, & the Life of Reason. Hanna Charney. LC 79-17634. 160p. 1981. 16.50 (ISBN 0-8386-3004-9). Fairleigh Dickinson.

Detective Short Story: A Bibliography. Ellery Queen. LC 73-79517. 1969. 17.00x (ISBN 0-8196-0237-X); signed 30.00x (ISBN 0-685-06922-2). Biblo.

Detective Work: A Study of Criminal Investigations. William B. Sanders. LC 77-72687. (Illus.). 1977. 15.95 (ISBN 0-02-927660-8). Free Pr.

Detective Work: A Study of Criminal Investigations. William B. Sanders. LC 77-72687. (Illus.). 1979. pap. text ed. 7.95 (ISBN 0-02-927590-3). Free Pr.

Detectives. Jean McConnell. 160p. 1976. 5.95 (ISBN 0-7153-7140-1). David & Charles.

Detectives: Crime & Detection in Fact & Fiction. Frank Smyth & Myles Ludwig. (Illus.). 1978. 12.50 o.p. (ISBN 0-397-01253-5); pap. 7.95 o.p. (ISBN 0-397-01252-7). Lippincott.

Detectives of the Sky: Investigating Aviation Tragedies. Michael Dorman. LC 74-858. (Illus.). 128p. (gr. 6 up). 1976. PLB 6.90 (ISBN 0-531-00342-6). Watts.

Detente: A Documentary Record. Charles E. Timberlake. LC 78-19465. 1978. 26.50 (ISBN 0-03-046666-0). Praeger.

Detente & Papal-Communist Relations, 1962-1978. Dennis J. Dunn. (Westview Replica Edition). 1979. lib. bdg. 23.50x (ISBN 0-89158-197-9). Westview.

Detente & the Democratic Movement in the USSR. Frederick C. Barghoorn. LC 76-4425. 1976. 15.95 (ISBN 0-02-901850-1). Free Pr.

Detente: Promises & Pitfalls. Gerald L. Steibel. LC 74-33205. 1975. pap. 2.95x (ISBN 0-8448-0661-7). Crane-Russak Co.

Detergency, Pt. III. Cutler & Davis. 384p. Date not set. 47.50 (ISBN 0-8247-6982-1). Dekker.

Determinacion De Prioridades Del Desarrallo Cientifico Tecnologico a Nivel Nacional. (Span.). 1975. pap. 1.50 o.p. (ISBN 0-685-65423-0). OAS.

Determinantentheorie. 3rd ed. Gerhard Kowalewski. LC 49-22682. (Ger). 14.95 (ISBN 0-8284-0039-3). Chelsea Pub.

Determinants & Effects of Mergers: An International Comparison. Ed. by Dennis C. Mueller. 416p. 1980. text ed. 27.50 (ISBN 0-89946-045-3). Oelgeschlager.

Determinants of Fertility in Advanced Societies. Rudolf Andorka. LC 78-62993. 431p. 1978. Repr. 25.00 (ISBN 0-02-900780-1). Free Pr.

Determinants of Human Migration. Richard J. Cebula. LC 79-2271. 160p. 1979. 18.95 (ISBN 0-669-03096-1). Lexington Bks.

Determinants of Large Bank Dividend Policy. William F. Kennedy. Ed. by Gunter Dufey. (Research for Business Decisions). 185p. 1980. 24.95 (ISBN 0-8357-1128-5, Pub. by UMI Res Pr). Univ Microfilms.

Determinants of Law Enforcement Policies. Ed. by Fred Meyer & Ralph Baker. LC 79-1540. (Policy Studies Organization Bk.). 240p. 1979. 19.95 (ISBN 0-669-02900-9). Lexington Bks.

Determinants of the Availability of Nutrients to the Brain. Ed. by Richard J. Wurtman & Judith J. Wurtman. LC 75-14593. (Nutrition & the Brain Ser: Vol. 1). 1977. 31.50 (ISBN 0-89004-045-1). Raven.

Determinants of Travel Choice. David Hensher & Quasin Dalvi. LC 78-58818. 1978. 37.95 (ISBN 0-03-046236-3). Praeger.

Determination & Interpretaion of Molecular Wave Functions. E. Steiner. LC 75-78120. (Monographs in Physical Chemistry: No. 3). 250p. 1976. 44.50 (ISBN 0-521-21037-2). Cambridge U Pr.

Determination of Absorbed Dose in Reactors. (Technical Reports Ser.: No. 127). (Illus.). 251p. (Orig.). 1972. pap. 14.50 (ISBN 92-0-157071-6, IAEA). Unipub.

Determination of Carboxylic Functional Groups. R. D. Tiwari & J. P. Sharma. LC 73-104121. 1970. 21.00 (ISBN 0-08-015516-2). Pergamon.

Determination of Dynamic Properties of Polymers & Composites. B. E. Read & G. D. Dean. LC 78-12690. 1979. 60.95 (ISBN 0-470-26543-4). Halsted Pr.

Determination of Epoxide Groups. B. Dobinson et al. 1969. 19.50 (ISBN 0-08-012788-6). Pergamon.

Determination of Food Carbohydrates. D. A. Southgate. (Illus.). 1976. 40.90x (ISBN 0-85334-693-3, Pub. by Applied Science). Burgess-Intl Ideas.

Determination of Hydrazine-Hydrazide Groups. H. E. Malone. 1970. 46.00 (ISBN 0-08-015871-4). Pergamon.

Determination of Impurities in Nuclear Grade Sodium Metal & Related Sodium Compounds. Louis Silverman. 156p. 1971. 26.00 (ISBN 0-08-016165-0). Pergamon.

Determination of Molecular Structure. 2nd, rev. ed. P. J. Wheatley. 264p. 1981. pap. 5.00 (ISBN 0-486-64068-X). Dover.

Determination of Organic Peroxides. R. M. Johnson & I. W. Siddiqi. LC 75-104884. 1970. 22.00 (ISBN 0-08-015586-3). Pergamon.

Determination of Units in Real Cyclic Sextic Fields. S. Maeki. (Lecture Notes in Mathematics: Vol. 797). 1980. pap. 14.00 (ISBN 0-387-09984-0). Springer-Verlag.

Determinations of the Moste Famous Universities of Italy & Fraunce. LC 72-189. (English Experience Ser.: No. 329). 308p. Repr. of 1531 ed. 22.00 (ISBN 90-221-0329-3). Walter J Johnson.

Determinative Team. Andrew P. Swanson. 1979. pap. 6.00 o.p. (ISBN 0-682-49248-5). Exposition.

Determined Bachelor. Judith Harkness. (Orig.). 1981. pap. 1.95 (ISBN 0-451-09609-6, J9609, Sig). NAL.

Determining & Exploiting the Long-Term of the Market. Richard D. Wyckoff. (New Stock Market Library). (Illus.). 1979. 59.75 (ISBN 0-89266-196-8). Am Classical Coll Pr.

Determining Effectiveness of Teaching Home Ec. H. Chadderdon. LC 74-78396. 1971. pap. 2.50 (ISBN 0-686-00147-8, 261-08408). Home Econ Educ.

Determining Superior Cropping Patterns for Small Farms in a Dryland Rice Environment: Test of Methodology. (IRRI Research Paper Ser.: No. 33). 15p. 1979. pap. 5.00 (R073, IRRI). Unipub.

Determinism. Bernard Berofsky. LC 70-112994. 1971. 16.50 (ISBN 0-691-07169-1). Princeton U Pr.

Deterrence & Defense in Korea: The Role of U. S. Forces. Ralph N. Clough. (Studies in Defense Policy). 1976. pap. 3.95 (ISBN 0-8157-1481-5). Brookings.

Deterrence & Defense: Toward a Theory of National Security. Glenn H. Snyder. LC 75-18405. (Illus.). 294p. 1975. Repr. of 1961 ed. lib. bdg. 22.25x (ISBN 0-8371-8333-2, SNDD). Greenwood.

Deterrence & Incapacitation: Estimating the Effects of Criminal Sanctions on Crime Rates. Assembly of Behavioral & Social Sciences. 1977. pap. 15.25 (ISBN 0-309-02649-0). Natl Acad Pr.

Deterrence in American Foreign Policy: Theory & Practice. Alexander George et al. LC 74-7120. 656p. 1974. 25.00x (ISBN 0-231-03837-2); pap. 10.00x (ISBN 0-231-03838-0). Columbia U Pr.

Deterrent Diplomacy: Japan, Germany, & the USSR, 1935-1940. Ed. by James W. Morley. LC 75-25524. (Japan's Road to the Pacific War Ser.). 376p. 1976. 20.00x (ISBN 0-231-08969-4). Columbia U Pr.

Deterring Criminals: Policy Making & the American Political Tradition. Jeffery L. Sedgwick. 1980. pap. 4.25 (ISBN 0-8447-3385-7). Am Enterprise.

Detonation. Wildon Fickett & William C. Davis. LC 77-85760. (Los Alamos Ser. in Basic & Applied Sciences). 1979. 30.00x (ISBN 0-520-03587-9). U of Cal Pr.

Detour for Meg. Helen D. Olds. (gr. 6-9). 1967. pap. 1.25 o.p. (ISBN 0-671-29836-4). Archway.

Detour for Meg. Helen D. Olds. (gr. 6-9). 1967. pap. 1.25 (ISBN 0-671-29836-4). PB.

Detroit & the Problem of Order, 1830-1880. John C. Schneider. LC 79-16492. xvi, 171p. 1980. 13.50x (ISBN 0-8032-4113-5). U of Nebr Pr.

Detroit Institute of Arts Illustrated Handbook. Ed. by Frederick J. Cummings & Charles H. Elam. LC 76-168631. (Illus.). 1971. 8.95x (ISBN 0-8143-1457-0); pap. 3.95 (ISBN 0-8143-1458-9). Wayne St U Pr.

Detroit Race Riot. Robert Shogan & Tom Craig. LC 76-1011. (Fdr & the Era of the New Deal). 1976. Repr. of 1964 ed. lib. bdg. 22.50 (ISBN 0-306-70808-6). Da Capo.

Deus Destroyed: The Image of Christianity in Early Modern Japan. George Elison. LC 72-97833. (East Asian Ser: No. 72). 704p. 1974. 30.00x (ISBN 0-674-19961-8). Harvard U Pr.

Deutche Oper: Grundzuge Ihres Werdens & Wesens. Ludwig Schiedermair. LC 80-2299. 1981. Repr. of 1930 ed. 38.50 (ISBN 0-404-18868-0). AMS Pr.

Deuteronomic History. Martin Noth. (Journal for the Study of the Old Testament, Supplement Ser.: No. 15). 1980. 19.95 (ISBN 0-905774-25-6, Pub. by JSOT Pr England). Eisenbrauns.

Deuteronomistische Pentateuchredaktion in Exodus 3-17. Werner Fuss. (Beiheft 126 zur Zeitschrift fuer die alttestamentliche Wissenschaft). xii, 406p. 1972. 60.60x (ISBN 3-11-003854-4). De Gruyter.

Deuteronomy. 3rd ed. S. R. Driver. LC 2-25926. (International Critical Commentary Ser.). 556p. 20.00x (ISBN 0-567-05003-3). Attic Pr.

Deuteronomy. A. D. Mayes. Ed. by Ronald E. Clements. (New Century Bible Commentary Ser.). (Orig.). 1981. pap. 8.95 (ISBN 0-8028-1882-X). Eerdmans.

Deuteronomy. A. D. Mayes. (New Century Bible Ser.). 352p. Repr. of 1979 ed. 19.50x (ISBN 0-551-00804-0). Attic Pr.

Deuteronomy. Bruce Oberst. LC 70-1070. (Bible Study Textbook Ser.). 1968. 13.50 (ISBN 0-89900-009-6). College Pr Pub.

Deuteronomy, Joshua. Edward P. Blair. LC 59-10454. (Layman's Bible Commentary Ser: Vol. 5). 1964. pap. 4.25 (ISBN 0-8042-3005-6). John Knox.

Deutsch: Aktuell 1. Wolfgang S. Kraft. LC 78-11445. 1979. 8.95 (ISBN 0-88436-539-5); pap. 5.95 (ISBN 0-88436-537-9). EMC.

Deutsch: Aktuell 2. Wolfgang S. Kraft. LC 79-12315. (Illus.). 1980. 9.50 (ISBN 0-88436-542-5); pap. 6.50 (ISBN 0-88436-540-9, GEA 132021). EMC.

Deutsch Als Fremdsprache: Ein Unterrichtswerk Fuer Auslaender. K. Braun et al. Incl. Pt. 1. **Grundkurs. text ed. 9.25x lehrbuch (ISBN 3-12-554100-X); strukturuebungen und tests 7.55x (ISBN 3-12-554150-6); dialogische uebungen 8.20x (ISBN 3-12-554160-3); glossar deutsch-englisch 2.10x (ISBN 3-12-556110-8); sprechuebungen fuer das elektronische klassenzimmer, textband. 8.60x, 8 tonbaender, 9.5 cm/s, tapes, 405.00x (ISBN 3-12-554120-4); 4 schallplatten, lektion 1-19 des grundkurses, 17 cm, 33 1/3 rpm, records 16.95x (ISBN 3-12-554110-7); compact-cassette, lektion 1-19 des grundkurses 16.65x (ISBN 0-685-47448-8); 16 tonba 200.00x (ISBN 0-685-47449-6); Pt. 1B. Ergaenzungskurs. text ed. 9.25x lehrbuch (ISBN 3-12-554500-5); glossar deutsch-englisch 2.20x (ISBN 3-12-556510-3); schallplatten, records 16.65x (ISBN 0-685-47450-X); Pt. 2. Aufbaukurs. text ed. 9.25x lehrbuch (ISBN 3-12-554200-6); strukturuebungen und tests 7.25x (ISBN 0-686-66995-9); dialogische uebungen 8.60x (ISBN 0-686-66996-7); glossar deutsch-englisch 2.20x (ISBN 3-12-556210-4); 3 schallplatten, lektion 1-17 des aufbaukurses,17 cm, 33 1/3 rpm, records 16.65x (ISBN 3-12-554210-3); compact-cassette, lektion 1-17 des aufbaukurses 16.65x (ISBN 0-685-47451-8); 12 tonbaender, dialoge und hoer-sprechuebungen, 9.5 cm/s, tapes 221.00x (ISBN 3-12-990430-1). Schoenhof.**

Deutsch: Erleben Wir Es! 2nd ed. Edda Weiss. Ed. by Joan Saslow. LC 80-16484. (Illus.). 344p. (Ger.). (gr. 10). 1980. text ed. 14.64 (ISBN 0-07-069215-7, W); tchrs. ed. 15.96 (ISBN 0-07-069216-5); wkbk. 4.26 (ISBN 0-07-069217-3); tests 69.00 (ISBN 0-07-069218-1); tapes 404.00 (ISBN 0-07-097815-8); cassettes 381.80 (ISBN 0-07-097816-6); filmstrips 113.36 (ISBN 0-07-097817-4). McGraw.

Deutsch Fuer Auslaender: Grundstufe. Hermann Kessler. Incl. Pt. 1. Leichter Anfang (Lehrbuch) pap. text ed. 9.10x (ISBN 0-685-47452-6); Pt. 1a. Leichte Aufgaben (Arbeitsheft) pap. text ed. 4.55x (ISBN 0-685-47453-4); Part 1 & Part 1a in One Volume. text ed. 8.50x (ISBN 0-685-47454-2); Pt. 1b. Leichte Erzaelungen (Leseband) pap. text ed. 3.60x (ISBN 0-685-47455-0); Pt. 1c. Sprachlaboruebungen. 4.25x (ISBN 0-685-47456-9); Tonbaender fuer das Sprachlabor. 11 tapes, 9.5 cm/s 260.00x (ISBN 0-685-47457-7); Tonband mit Lehrbuchtexten. tape, 9.5 cm/s 29.25 (ISBN 0-685-47458-5). Schoenhof.

Deutsch Fuer Auslaender: Mittelstufe. Hermann Kessler. Incl. Pt. 2. Schneller Fortgang (Lehrbuch) pap. text ed. 9.10x (ISBN 0-685-47459-3); Pt. 2a. Kurze Uebungen (Arbeitsheft) 4.55x (ISBN 0-685-47460-7); Part 2 & Part 2a in One Volume. text ed. 8.50x (ISBN 0-685-47461-5); Pt. 2b. Kurze Geschichten (Leseband) pap. text ed. 3.60x (ISBN 0-685-47462-3); Pt. 2c. Sprachlaboruebungen. 4.25x (ISBN 0-685-47463-1); Tonbaender fuer das Sprachlabor. 10 tapes, 9.5 cm/s 260.00x (ISBN 0-685-47464-X); Tonband mit Lehrbuchtexten. tape 29.25x (ISBN 0-685-47465-8). Schoenhof.

Deutsch Fuer Auslaender: Oberstufe. Hermann Kessler. Incl. Pt. 3. Deutschlandkunde (Lehrbuch) pap. text ed. 11.70 (ISBN 0-685-47466-6); Pt. 3b. Moderne Dichtungen (Leseband) pap. text ed. 4.25x (ISBN 0-685-47467-4); tonband 29.25x, tape, 9.5 cm/s (ISBN 0-685-47468-2); Pt. 3d. Dichter unserer Zeit. pap. text ed. 4.25x (ISBN 0-685-47469-0); tonband 29.25x, tape, 9.5 cm/s (ISBN 0-685-47470-4). Schoenhof.

Deutsch Fur Alle: Beginning College German: a Comprehensive Approach. Werner Haas & Gustave B. Mathieu. LC 79-21295. 1980. text ed. 17.95 (ISBN 0-471-02210-1); tchrs. manual avail. (ISBN 0-471-04192-0); wkbk. avail. (ISBN 0-471-02211-X); tapes avail. (ISBN 0-471-05513-1). Wiley.

Deutsch Fur Anfanger. Erna K. Neuse. LC 77-135899. (Orig., Ger.). 1971. text ed. 13.95 (ISBN 0-13-203356-9); audiotape 150.00 (ISBN 0-13-203372-0). P-H.

Deutsch Heute: Grundstufe. 2nd ed. Jack Moeller & Helmut Liedloff. LC 78-52718. (Illus.). 1979. text ed. 17.15 (ISBN 0-395-27175-4); inst. annot. ed. 18.25 (ISBN 0-395-27174-6); wkbk. 5.50 (ISBN 0-395-27173-8); recordings 114.68 (ISBN 0-395-27171-1). HM.

Deutsch Macht Spass. Marilyn B. Rey & Katherine Maloof. (gr. 8-11). 1979. wkbk. 4.50 (ISBN 0-87720-582-5). AMSCO Sch.

Deutsch Mit Emil. Ed. by Helga Tilton. 1980. pap. text ed. 5.95x (ISBN 0-393-95111-1). Norton.

Deutsch und Deutschland Heute. 2nd ed. Albert Lloyd. 1981. text ed. price not set (ISBN 0-442-24461-4). D Van Nostrand.

Deutsche Drama, Vol. 2. Ed. by Harry Steinhauer. 1939. 6.95x (ISBN 0-393-09435-9, NortonC). Norton.
Deutsche Drama Von Kleist Bis Hauptmann. Ed. by A. Peter Foulkes & Edgar Lohner. LC 76-185793. 680p. 1973. text ed. 21.80 (ISBN 0-395-12742-4). HM.
Deutsche Gedichte: Von Den Anfaengen Bis Zur Gegenwart. Ed. by B. Von Wiese. (Ger). 1972. 10.95 (ISBN 0-685-20235-6). Schoenhof.
Deutsche Heldensagen. (Insel Taschenbuecher: It 345). 414p. pap. text ed. 6.50 (ISBN 3-458-32045-8, Pub. by Insel Verlag Germany). Suhrkamp.
Deutsche Lyrik. Ed. by Konrad Schaum. (Orig., Ger.). 1963. pap. 2.95x (ISBN 0-393-09612-2, NortonC). Norton.
Deutsche Novelle, 1880-1950. expanded ed. Ed. by Harry Steinhauer. 1958. 7.50x o.p. (ISBN 0-393-09515-0, NortonC). Norton.
Deutsche Revue: Herausgegeben Von Karl Gutzkow & Ludolf Weinbarg, No. 1. Bd. with Nos. 1 & 2. Deutsche Blatter Leben, Kunst Wissenschaft: Herausgegeben Von Karl Gutzkow. (Unpublished). Repr. of 1835 ed. (Unpublished). 1973. Repr. of 1835 ed. 19.00 (ISBN 0-384-11535-7); unbound 14.50 (ISBN 0-685-30624-0). Johnson Repr.
Deutsche Sprach und Landeskunde. John E. Crean et al. Incl. Joanna Ratyck. wkbk. 6.95 (ISBN 0-394-32649-0); John E. Crean. lab manual 6.95 (ISBN 0-394-32650-4). 608p. 1981. text ed. 17.95 (ISBN 0-394-32648-2). Random.
Deutsche Sprachlehre Amerikaner. Dora Schulz et al. LC 77-96479. 1970. pap. text ed. 14.95 (ISBN 0-684-41465-1, Scribner-C). Scribner.
Deutsche Sprachlehre Fuer Auslaender. Dora Schulz & Heinz Griesbach. Incl. Grundstufe in einem Band. 5.80x o.p. (ISBN 0-685-47471-2); pap. text ed. 7.80x (ISBN 0-685-47472-0); glossar deutsch-englisch 4.10x (ISBN 0-685-47473-9); leseheft 1, by roland hils. 3.25x (ISBN 0-685-47474-7); grammar german-english 4.55xschuelerheft.contrasfive (ISBN 0-685-47475-5); Grundstufe. Ausgabe in zwei Baenden. pap. text ed. 4.00xGrundstufe 1. teil (ISBN 0-685-47476-3); pap. text ed. 7.15x grundstufe 2. teil (ISBN 0-685-47477-1); teaching supplement-phraseological glossary-key 5.20x (ISBN 0-685-47478-X); 2 tonbaender, aufnahme der lesetexte des buches und von uebungen, 9.5 cm/s, tapes 52.00x (ISBN 0-685-47479-8); Mittelstufe; Moderner Deutscher Sprachgebrauch.Ein Lehrgang Fuer Fortgeschrittene. pap. text ed. 12.25x (ISBN 0-685-47480-1); lehrerheft 4.90x (ISBN 0-685-47481-X); schuelerheft mit schluessel zuden uebungen 7.15x (ISBN 0-685-47482-8); 1 tonband, aufnahme von 28 lesetexten des lehrbuchs, 9.5 cm/s, tapes 31.20x (ISBN 0-685-47483-6). Schoenhof.
Deutsche Texte und Wortschatzuebungen. M. Skilton. LC 76-93127. pap. 3.20 o.p. (ISBN 0-08-006462-0); pap. 3.20 o.p. (ISBN 0-08-006461-2); tchr's. ed. 4.40 o.p. (ISBN 0-08-015811-0). Pergamon.
Deutsches Dichterjubilaum: A Facsimile in Color & Halftone of the Special Hand-Colored Edition of 1923. Arno Holz. 1977. 15.00 (ISBN 0-88233-279-1). Kylix Pr.
Deutsches Literaturlesebuch. 4th ed. Otto S. Fleissner & E. M. Fleissner. (Ger.). 1968. pap. text ed. 8.50 (ISBN 0-13-203364-X). P-H.
Deux Journees. Maria L. Cherubini. Ed. by Phillip Gossett & Charles Rosen. LC 76-49214. (Early Romantic Opera Ser.: No. 35). 1980. lib. bdg. 82.00 (ISBN 0-8240-2934-8). Garland Pub.
Deva. Michael Tobias. 260p. (Orig.). 1981. pap. text ed. 6.95 (ISBN 0-932238-10-6). Word Shop.
Devalino Caper. A. J. Russell. 1977. pap. 1.75 o.p. (ISBN 0-345-25106-7). Ballantine.
Devastating Eighties. Stanley J. Goodwin. 80p. 1980. pap. 2.40 (ISBN 0-686-27500-4). Northland Pubns WA.
Devastators. Donald Hamilton. (Matt Helm Ser.). 1978. pap. 1.95 (ISBN 0-449-14084-9, GM). Fawcett.
Developers Dictionary & Handbook. Collison. 160p. 1974. 17.95 (ISBN 0-669-92882-8). Lexington Bks.
Developing a Commanding Personality. C. R. Coates. LC 79-23634. 180p. 1981. 14.95 (ISBN 0-88229-414-8). Nelson-Hall.
Developing a Curriculum for Modern Living. 2nd ed. Florence Stratemeyer et al. LC 57-11371. 1957. text ed. 12.95x (ISBN 0-8077-2221-9). Tchrs Coll.
Developing a Tough-Minded Climate for Results. J. D. Batten. LC 65-16483. 1965. 14.95 (ISBN 0-8144-5101-2). Am Mgmt.
Developing a Unit-Credit Scheme of Adult Language Learning. J. L. Trim. LC 80-40756. (Council of Europe Modern Languages Project). 96p. 1980. pap. 10.00 (ISBN 0-08-024596-X). Pergamon.
Developing, Administering, & Evaluating Adult Education. Alan B. Knox et al. LC 80-7998. (Higher Education Ser.). 1980. text ed. 15.95x (ISBN 0-87589-467-4). Jossey-Bass.
Developing Agriculture of the Middle East: Opportunities & Prospects. Ed. by K. S. McLackhlan. 74p. 1976. 43.00x (ISBN 0-86010-046-4, Pub. by Graham & Trotman England). State Mutual Bk.
Developing an Adult Education Program Through Community Linkages. Harold Beder & Franceska Smith. 1977. 5.75 (ISBN 0-685-82348-2). Adult Ed.
Developing an Educationally Accountable Program. Lesley H. Browder et al. LC 72-83476. (Illus.). 350p. 1973. 16.25x o.p. (ISBN 0-8211-0121-8); text ed. 14.60x o.p. (ISBN 0-685-26755-5). McCutchan.
Developing & Administering a Child Care Center. Dorothy J. Sciarra & Anne G. Dorsey. LC 78-69564. (Illus.). 1978. 15.95 (ISBN 0-395-26263-1). HM.
Developing & Administering an Industrial Training Program. Robert P. Drolet & John R. Dowling. LC 79-10713. (Illus.). 1979. pap. 11.95 (ISBN 0-8436-0777-7). CBI Pub.
Developing & Diseased Muscle: A Histochemical Study, Vol. 2. Victor Dubowitz. (Clinics in Developmental Medicine Research Monographs). 1968. 7.50 o.p. (ISBN 0-685-34619-6). Lippincott.
Developing & Managing Open Organizations. Oscar G. Mink. LC 79-10195. 1979. text ed. 17.95 (ISBN 0-89384-045-9). Learning Concepts.
Developing Assessment Programs for the Multi-Handicapped Child. Joseph N. Murray. (Illus.). 304p. 1980. 17.50 (ISBN 0-398-04052-4); pap. 11.75 (ISBN 0-398-04076-1). C C Thomas.
Developing Attitude Toward Learning. Robert F. Mager. LC 68-54250. 1968. pap. 4.50 (ISBN 0-8224-2000-7). Pitman Learning.
Developing Bookkeeping Skills. Wallace W. Kravitz. (gr. 10-11). 1978. wkbk 9.42 (ISBN 0-87720-404-7). AMSCO Sch.
Developing British Colonial Resources Nineteen Forty-Five to Nineteen Fifty-One, Vol. 2. D. J. Morgan. 1980. text ed. cancelled (ISBN 0-391-01685-7). Humanities.
Developing Career Information Centers in Libraries: A Guide to Collection Building & Counseling. Sara Fine. LC 80-11634. 175p. 1980. pap. 17.95x (ISBN 0-918212-19-7). Neal-Schuman.
Developing Casework Skills. James A. Pippin. LC 80-18799. (Sage Human Services Guides: No. 15). 160p. 1980. pap. 8.00 (ISBN 0-8039-1503-9). Sage.
Developing Child. 2nd ed. Helen Bee. (Illus.). 1978. text ed. 19.50 scp (ISBN 0-06-040583-X, HarpC); inst. manual free (ISBN 0-06-360560-0); study guide scp 6.50 (ISBN 0-06-040864-2). Har-Row.
Developing Child. rev. ed. Brisbane. (gr. 9-12). 1980. text ed. 13.72 (ISBN 0-87002-312-8); tchr's guide avail. (ISBN 0-87002-324-1); student guide 3.20 (ISBN 0-87002-325-X). Bennett IL.
Developing Child. rev. ed. Holly E. Brisbane. (Illus.). (gr. 9-12). 1980. text ed. 11.96 (ISBN 0-87002-312-8); tchr guide avail. (ISBN 0-685-03307-4). Bennett IL.
Developing Children's Thinking Through Science. R. Anderson et al. 1970. ref. ed. 17.95 (ISBN 0-13-204214-2). P-H.
Developing Competencies in Teaching Reading: A Modular Program for Preservice & Inservice Elementary & Middle School Teachers. Charles T. Mangrum & Harry W. Forgan. Ed. by Arthur W. Heilman. (Elementary Education Ser.). 1979. pap. text ed. 15.95 (ISBN 0-675-08367-2); instructor's manual 3.95 (ISBN 0-685-86834-6). Merrill.
Developing Computer-Based Library Systems. John Corbin. (Neal-Schuman Professional Bk). 1981. lib. bdg. 18.50 (ISBN 0-912700-10-6). Oryx Pr.
Developing Countries & the World Economic Order. Lars Anell & Birgitta Nygren. 208p. 1980. pap. 8.95 (ISBN 0-416-74630-6, 2002). Methuen Inc.
Developing Country Debt. Lawrence G. Franko & Marilyn J. Seiber. 1979. text ed. 44.00 (ISBN 0-08-023864-5). Pergamon.
Developing Effective Managers. Tom Roberts. LC 75-318208. (Management in Perspective Ser.). 168p. 1974. pap. 7.50x (ISBN 0-85292-100-4). Intl Pubns Serv.
Developing Employee Relations. Peter Warr et al. 216p. 1978. text ed. 21.75x (ISBN 0-566-00209-4, Pub. by Gower Pub Co England). Renouf.
Developing Human Brain: Growth & Epidemiologic Neuropathology. Floyd H. Giles et al. Date not set. write for info. (ISBN 0-88416-254-0). PSG Pub.
Developing Human Potential: A Handbook of Activities for Personal & Social Growth. Robert C. Hawley & Isabel L. Hawley. LC 75-2963. 128p. (Orig.). 1975. pap. 6.95 (ISBN 0-913636-06-1). Educ Res MA.
Developing Human Potential: More Activities for Person & Social Growth, Vol. 2. Robert C. Hawley & Isabel L. Hawley. LC 76-51467. 1977. pap. 6.95 (ISBN 0-913636-09-6). Educ Res MA.
Developing Human Resources. 2nd ed. Leonard Nadler. LC 79-4147. 1979. text ed. 17.95 (ISBN 0-89384-044-0). Learning Concepts.
Developing Human Rights. Ed. by Ned P. Nanda et al. (Westview Special Study Ser.). 285p. 1981. lib. bdg. 28.50x (ISBN 0-89158-858-2). Westview.
Developing Individualized Instructional Material. Stuart R. Johnson & Rita B. Johnson. 1970. text ed. 4.44 (ISBN 0-88250-403-7). Westinghouse Learn.
Developing Instructional Units: For the Regular & Special Teacher. 3rd ed. Edward L. Meyen. 325p. 1981. pap. text ed. 7.95x (ISBN 0-697-06245-7); instructor's manual avail. (ISBN 0-697-06228-7). Wm C Brown.
Developing Language Programs for Young Disadvantaged Children. Margaret Yonemura. LC 79-75451. 1969. pap. 4.50x (ISBN 0-8077-2364-9). Tchrs Coll.
Developing Language Skills in the Elementary Schools. 5th ed. Harry A. Greene & Walter T. Petty. 480p. 1975. text ed. 15.95x o.p. (ISBN 0-205-04670-3, 2246708); student guide 5.95x o.p. (ISBN 0-205-04672-X); instr's manual free o.p. (ISBN 0-205-04671-1). Allyn.
Developing Leadership. new ed. Burton L. Fischman. LC 76-25925. (Illus.). 1976. pap. text ed. 7.90 o.p. (ISBN 0-913310-43-3). Par Inc.
Developing Leadership for Parent-Citizen Groups. Crystal Kuykendall. 1976. pap. 3.50 (ISBN 0-934460-02-7). NCCE.
Developing Libraries in Brazil: with a Chapter on Paraguay. Cavan McCarthy. LC 74-23681. 1975. 10.00 (ISBN 0-8108-0750-5). Scarecrow.
Developing Library Collections. G. Edward Evans. LC 78-27303. (Library Science Text Ser.). 1979. lib. bdg. 19.50x (ISBN 0-87287-145-2); pap. text ed. 13.50x. Libs Unl.
Developing Linebackers the Penn State Way. Jerry Sandusky. LC 80-84214. (Fitness America Ser.). (Illus.). 160p. (Orig.). 1981. pap. text ed. 5.95 (ISBN 0-918438-64-0). Leisure Pr.
Developing Listening Comprehension for ESL Students: The Kingdom of Kochen. T. Plaister. 1976. pap. 8.50 (ISBN 0-13-204479-X); tapes 125.00 (ISBN 0-13-204495-1). P-H.
Developing Managerial Information Systems. Andrew McCosh et al. 1980. 29.95x (ISBN 0-470-26913-8). Halsted Pr.
Developing Managers for the Nineteen Eighties. Cary Cooper. LC 80-15212. 160p. 1981. text ed. 36.00x (ISBN 0-8419-0649-1). Holmes & Meier.
Developing Mathematical Skills. Arthur Whimbey & Jack Lochhead. (Illus.). 448p. 1981. text ed. 11.95 (ISBN 0-07-069517-2, C). McGraw.
Developing Methods of Inquiry: A Source Book for Elementary Media Personnel. Nancy Polette. LC 72-11992. 1973. 10.00 (ISBN 0-8108-0575-8). Scarecrow.
Developing Nations. Ed. by Irwin Isenberg. (Reference Shelf Ser: Vol. 41, No. 1). 1968. 6.25 (ISBN 0-8242-0106-X). Wilson.
Developing Nations: A Comparative Perspective. Robert E. Gamer. 651p. 1976. pap. text ed. 12.95x (ISBN 0-205-05418-8). Allyn.
Developing Nations: A Guide to Information Sources. Ed. by Eloise ReQua & Jane Statham. LC 65-17576. (Management Information Guide Ser.: No. 5). 1965. 30.00 (ISBN 0-8103-0805-3). Gale.
Developing New Products & Repositing Mature Brands: A Risk-Reduction System That Produces Investment Alternatives. Eugene J. Cafarelli. (Marketing Management Ser.). 1980. 21.95 (ISBN 0-471-04634-5, Pub by Ronald Pr). Wiley.
Developing Organizations: Diagnosis & Action. Paul R. Lawrence & Jay W. Lorsch. LC 78-93985. (Organization Development Ser). (Orig.). 1969. pap. text ed. 6.50 (ISBN 0-201-04204-5). A-W.
Developing Person. 3rd ed. Helen Bee & Sandra Mitchell. 1980. text ed. 19.50 scp (ISBN 0-06-040579-1, HarpC); scp study guide 6.50 (ISBN 0-06-040586-4); instr's. manual free (ISBN 0-06-360561-9). Har-Row.
Developing Person. Kathleen S. Berger. (Illus.). 1980. 17.95x (ISBN 0-87901-117-3); study guide 5.95x (ISBN 0-87901-118-1). Worth.
Developing Programs for the Educationally Disadvantaged. Ed. by A. Harry Passow. LC 67-19026. 1968. text ed. 13.75 (ISBN 0-8077-1885-8); pap. text ed. 7.50x (ISBN 0-8077-1884-X). Tchrs Coll.
Developing Reading Efficiency. Karen M. Hess et al. LC 74-26850. 288p. 1975. text ed. 10.50x (ISBN 0-471-37452-0). Wiley.
Developing Reading Skills for Business & Industry. Richard P. Santeusanio. LC 80-23463. 330p. 1980. pap. 9.95 (ISBN 0-8436-0792-0). CBI Pub.
Developing Reading Skills for the High School Equivalency Examination (Ged) in Social Studies, Science, & Literature: In 26 Lessons. Eugene J. Farley & Alice R. Farley. LC 72-84413. 1972. pap. text ed. 5.75 (ISBN 0-8120-0487-6). Barron.
Developing Self-Control. Carol Foster. 136p. 1980. pap. text ed. 7.00 (ISBN 0-917472-02-0). F Fournies.
Developing Skills for Human Interaction. 2nd ed. Linda Heun & Richard Heun. (Speech & Drama Ser.). 1978. pap. text ed. 13.50x (ISBN 0-675-08396-6); instructor's manual 3.95 (ISBN 0-686-67976-8). Merrill.
Developing Skills for the High School Equivalency Examination in Grammar, Usage, Spelling & Vocabulary. Murray Rockowitz. 1972. pap. text ed. 5.50 (ISBN 0-8120-0485-X). Barron.
Developing Skills in Algebra: A Lecture Worktext, 2 vols. 2nd ed. Louis Nanney & John Cable. 1976. Vol. 1. pap. text ed. 8.50x o.p. (ISBN 0-205-05417-X); Vol. 2. pap. text ed. 9.50x o.p. (ISBN 0-205-05472-2); pap. text ed. 14.95x combined ed. o.p. (ISBN 0-205-05493-5). Allyn.
Developing Skills in Algebra: A Lecture Worktext, 2 vols. 3rd ed. Louis Nanney & John Cable. 1978. pap. text ed. 17.80 set; Vol. I. 13.25 (ISBN 0-205-06507-4); Vol. II. 12.55 (ISBN 0-205-06508-2); Combined Ed. pap. text ed. 15.95x (ISBN 0-205-06509-0); instr's. manual avail. (ISBN 0-205-06534-1). Allyn.
Developing Skills in Mathematics for the High School Equivalency Exam (GED) in Spanish. Zoila E. DeZayas. Date not set. pap. 3.75 (ISBN 0-8120-0560-0). Barron.
Developing Skills in Statistics. Neal R. Townsend & Grayson Wheatley. 1978. text ed. 17.80 (ISBN 0-205-05994-5); instr's man. avail. (ISBN 0-205-05995-3). Allyn.
Developing Social Policies in Conditions of Rapid Change. National Conference on Social Welfare. 1973. 20.00x (ISBN 0-231-03790-2). Columbia U Pr.
Developing Social Skills in Managers: Advances in Group Training. Ed. by Cary L. Cooper. LC 75-30510. 140p. 1976. 18.95 o.p. (ISBN 0-470-17121-9). Halsted Pr.
Developing Spiritually Sensitive Children. Olive Alexander. LC 80-23603. 132p. (Orig.). 1980. pap. 3.95 (ISBN 0-87123-111-5, 210111). Bethany Fell.
Developing Structured Systems: A Methodology Using Structured Techniques. Brian Dickinson. LC 80-54609. (Illus.). 392p. 1981. 45.00 (ISBN 0-917072-23-5). Yourdon.
Developing Support Groups: A Manual for Facilitators & Participants. Howard Kirschenbaum & Barbara Glaser. LC 78-60280. 82p. 1978. pap. 8.50 (ISBN 0-88390-145-5). Univ Assocs.
Developing Teacher Competencies. Ed. by James E. Weigand. LC 70-149972. (Illus.). 1971. pap. text ed. 11.95 (ISBN 0-13-205278-4). P-H.
Developing Teacher Skills in Physical Education. Daryl Siedentop. LC 75-26084. (Illus.). 352p. 1976. pap. text ed. 12.25 (ISBN 0-395-20616-2). HM.
Developing Teaching Competencies. James De Lee et al. LC 79-9910. 72p. 1979. pap. 3.95 (ISBN 0-88289-215-0). Pelican.
Developing Teams & Organizations: A Practical Handbook for Managers & Consultants. Uri Merry & Melvin E. Allerhand. LC 76-17719. (Illus.). 1977. text ed. 18.95 (ISBN 0-201-04531-1). A-W.
Developing the Afro-American Economy: Building on Strength. Richard F. America. LC 76-54557. (Illus.). 1977. 15.95 (ISBN 0-669-01304-8). Lexington Bks.
Developing the Competencies of the Religion Teacher. 162p. 1974. 3.00. Natl Cath Educ.
Developing the ICBM: A Study in Bureaucratic Politics. Edmund Beard. (Institute of War & Peace Studies). 288p. 1976. 17.50x (ISBN 0-231-04012-1). Columbia U Pr.
Developing the Library Collection in Political Science. Robert B. Harmon. LC 75-44396. 1976. 10.00 (ISBN 0-8108-0898-6). Scarecrow.
Developing the Multicultural Process in Classroom Instruction: Competencies for Teachers. H. Prentice Baptiste, Jr. & Mira L. Baptiste. LC 79-89993. 1979. pap. text ed. 11.75 (ISBN 0-8191-0855-3). U Pr of Amer.
Developing the Municipal Organization. Ed. by Stanley P. Powers et al. LC 74-79125. (Municipal Management Ser.). 1974. text ed. 22.00 (ISBN 0-87326-001-5). Intl City Mgt.
Developing Values with Exceptional Children. Sidney B. Simon & Robert O'Rourke. (Illus.). 160p. 1977. pap. text ed. 9.95 (ISBN 0-13-205310-1). P-H.

Developing Vocal Skills. 2nd ed. Theodore O. Hanley & Wayne L. Thurman. LC 79-97849. (Illus.). 1970. 29.50x (ISBN 0-03-083992-0); pap. text ed. 18.95x (ISBN 0-89197-726-0). Irvington.

Developing Writer: A Guide to Basic Skills. Martin M. McKoski & Lynne C. Hahn. LC 80-21912. 250p. 1981. text ed. 8.95 (ISBN 0-471-05812-2). Wiley.

Development. 2nd ed. Gerald Karp & N. J. Berrill. (Illus.). 640p. 1981. text ed. 21.95 (ISBN 0-07-033340-8, C). McGraw.

Development, Growth & Aging. Ed. by Nicholas Carter. 169p. 1980. 27.50x (ISBN 0-85664-861-2, Pub. by Croom Helm Ltd England). Biblio Dist.

Development Administration in Latin America. Clarence E. Thurber & Lawrence S. Graham. LC 72-96986. (Comparative Adminstration Group of the American Society for Public Administration Ser.). 550p. 1973. 19.75 (ISBN 0-8223-0292-6). Duke.

Development Administration: The Kenyon Experience. Goran Hyden et al. (Illus.). 384p. 1970. text ed. 12.95x. Oxford U Pr.

Development & Dependency: The Political Economy of Papua New Guinea. Azeem Amarshu et al. (Illus.). 306p. 1979. text ed. 28.00x (ISBN 0-19-550582-4). Oxford U Pr.

Development & Differentiation, Vol. III. Margaret E. Buckingham. (Biochemistry of Cellular Regulation Ser.). 240p. 1980. 59.95 (ISBN 0-8493-5456-0). CRC Pr.

Development & Disorders of Speech in Childhood. Isaac W. Karlin et al. (American Lecture Speech & Hearing Ser). (Illus.). 324p. 1977. 17.75 (ISBN 0-398-00973-2). C C Thomas.

Development & Evolution of Behavior, Essays in Memory of T. C. Schneirla. Ed. by Lester R. Aronson et al. LC 76-84600. (Illus.). 1970. text ed. 31.95x (ISBN 0-7167-0921-X). W H Freeman.

Development & Implement Individualized Education Program. Turnbull. 1978. 12.95 (ISBN 0-675-08318-4). Merrill.

Development & Implementation of a Patient's Bill of Rights in Hospitals. Alexandra B. Gekas & Kathleen M. Countryman. LC 80-11366. 24p. 1980. pap. 7.50 (ISBN 0-87258-306-6, 1580). Am Hospital.

Development & Participation: Operational Implications for Social Welfare. International Council on Social Welfare. 404p. 1975. 23.00x (ISBN 0-231-03972-7). Columbia U Pr.

Development & Scope of Higher Education in the United States. Richard Hofstadter & C. De Witt Hardy. LC 52-14741. 1952. 20.00x (ISBN 0-231-01956-4). Columbia U Pr.

Development & Socio-Economic Impact of Transportation in Tanzania Eighteen Eighty-Four - Present. Frank M. Chiteji. LC 80-5092. 151p. 1980. pap. text ed. 7.75 (ISBN 0-8191-1041-8). U Pr of Amer.

Development & Specialisation of Skeletal Muscle. Ed. by D. F. Goldspink. (Society for Experimental Biology Seminar Ser.: No. 7). (Illus.). 200p. Date not set. 45.00 (ISBN 0-521-23317-8); pap. 19.95 (ISBN 0-521-29907-1). Cambridge U Pr.

Development & Structure of the Furniture Industry. J. L. Oliver. 1965. 13.75 (ISBN 0-08-011460-1). Pergamon.

Development & Use of the Outdoor Classroom: An Annotated Bibliography. Wynnlee Crisp. LC 75-15537. 145p. 1975. 10.00 (ISBN 0-8108-0831-5). Scarecrow.

Development As If Women Mattered: An Annotated Bibliography with a Third World Focus. May Rihani. LC 78-57205. (Occasional Papers: No. 10). 144p. 1978. pap. 3.00 (ISBN 0-686-28694-4). Overseas Dev Council.

Development Assistance in the Seventies: Alternatives for the United States. Robert E. Asher et al. 1970. 11.95 (ISBN 0-8157-0542-5). Brookings.

Development Banking. Joseph A. Kane. LC 74-25071. 1975. 22.50 (ISBN 0-669-97402-1). Lexington Bks.

Development Co-Operation, 1976 Review: Efforts & Policies. Members of the Development Assistance Committee. 1976. 16.25 o.p. (ISBN 92-64-11589-7). OECD.

Development Economics. Subrata Ghatak. (Modern Economics). (Illus.). 1978. pap. text ed. 12.95 (ISBN 0-582-44874-3). Longman.

Development Economics & Policy Readings. Ed. by Ian Livingstone. (Illus.). 368p. (Orig.). 1981. text ed. 38.95x (ISBN 0-04-382025-5, 2581); pap. text ed. 15.00x (ISBN 0-04-382026-3, 2582). Allen Unwin.

Development Economics: Theory and Findings. S. K. Singh. LC 72-1966. (Illus.). 320p. 1975. 23.95 (ISBN 0-669-83626-5). Lexington Bks.

Development Education & Guidance of Talented Learners. Robert A. Male & Philip Perrone. 350p. 1981. text ed. price not set (ISBN 0-89443-359-8). Aspen Systems.

Development, Environment & Technology: Towards a Technology for Self-Reliance. 51p. 1978. pap. 6.00 (ISBN 0-686-68949-6, UN78/2D11, UN). Unipub.

Development from Above or Below? A Radical Reappraisal of Spatial Planning in Developing. Walter Stohr & D. R. Taylor. 448p. 1981. 47.85 (ISBN 0-471-27823-8, Pub.by Wiley-Interscience). Wiley.

Development from Below: Local Government & Finance in Developing Countries of the Commonwealth. Ursula K. Hicks. 1961. 24.95x o.p. (ISBN 0-19-828139-0). Oxford U Pr.

Development from Kant to Hegel, with Chapters on the Philosophy of Religion. Andrew Seth. Ed. by Lewis W. Beck. LC 75-32044. (Philosophy of Immanuel Kant Ser.: Vol. 7). 1977. Repr. of 1882 ed. lib. bdg. 20.00 (ISBN 0-8240-2331-5). Garland Pub.

Development Gap: A Spatial Analysis of World Poverty & Inequality. J. P. Cole. LC 80-40284. 1981. write for info. (ISBN 0-471-16477-1). Wiley.

Development Gap: A Spatial Analysis of World Poverty & Inequality. J. P. Cole. 416p. 1981. write for info. (ISBN 0-471-27796-7, Pub. by Wiley-Interscience). Wiley.

Development Group Work with Adolescents. Leslie Button. LC 74-26787. 208p. 1975. 15.95 (ISBN 0-470-12775-9). Halsted Pr.

Development, Growth, & Aging. Ed. by Nicholas Carter. 176p. 1980. 25.00x (ISBN 0-85664-861-2, Pub. by Croom Helm England). State Mutual Bk.

Development in an Inflationary World. Ed. by M. June Flanders & Assaf Razin. (Economic Theory, Econometrics & Mathematical Economics Ser.). 1981. price not set (ISBN 0-12-259750-8). Acad Pr.

Development in Infancy. T. G. R. Bower. LC 73-19995. (Psychology Ser.). (Illus.). 1974. text ed. 20.95x (ISBN 0-7167-0777-2); pap. text ed. 10.95x (ISBN 0-7167-0776-4). W H Freeman.

Development in the People's Republic of China: A Selected Bibliography. Ed. by Patricia Blair. LC 76-53149. (Occasional Papers: No. 8). 94p. 1976. 2.50 (ISBN 0-686-28696-0). Overseas Dev Council.

Development, Income Distribution & Social Change in Rural Egypt 1952-1970. M. Abdel-Fadil. LC 75-17114. (Department of Applied Economics, Occasional Papers Ser.: No. 45). 1976. pap. 14.95x (ISBN 0-521-29019-8). Cambridge U Pr.

Development of a Prototype Equation for Public Housing Operating Expenses. Robert Sadacca et al. (Institute Paper). 111p. 1975. pap. 3.00 (ISBN 0-87766-144-8, 11900). Urban Inst.

Development of Adaptive Intelligence: A Cross-Cultural Study. Carol F. Feldman et al. LC 73-22557. (Social & Behavioral Science Ser.). 1974. 13.95x o.p. (ISBN 0-87589-224-8). Jossey-Bass.

Development of Admiralty, Jurisdiction & Practice Since 1800. F. L. Wiswall. LC 77-108113. (Illus.). 1971. 35.50 (ISBN 0-521-07751-6). Cambridge U Pr.

Development of Aircraft Engines & Fuels. R. Schlaifer & S. D. Heron. 1970. Repr. of 1950 ed. 54.00 (ISBN 0-08-018740-4). Pergamon.

Development of American Political Science: From Burgess to Behavioralism. enl. ed. Albert Somit & Joseph Tanenhaus. 1981. 21.00x (ISBN 0-8290-0122-0); pap. text ed. 10.95x (ISBN 0-8290-0123-9). Irvington.

Development of American Romance: The Sacrifice of Relation. Michael D. Bell. LC 80-12241. 272p. 1981. lib. bdg. 22.50x (ISBN 0-226-04211-1). U of Chicago Pr.

Development of an African Working Class. Richard Sandbrook & Robin Cohen. 1976. pap. 9.00. U of Toronto Pr.

Development of an Education Service: The West Riding, 1889-1974. P. H. Gosden & P. R. Sharp. 273p. 1978. 36.00x (ISBN 0-85520-150-9, Pub by Martin Robertson England). Biblio Dist.

Development of Anthropological Ideas. John J. Honigman. 1976. 18.95x (ISBN 0-256-01803-0). Dorsey.

Development of Behavior: A Synthesis of Developmental & Comparative Psychology. Bill M. Seay & Nathan Gottfried. LC 78-50639. (Illus.). 1978. text ed. 19.95 (ISBN 0-395-24747-0); inst. manual 0.65 (ISBN 0-395-24746-2). HM.

Development of Capitalism in Colonial Indochina. Martin J. Murray. 1981. 29.50x (ISBN 0-520-04000-7). U of Cal Pr.

Development of Capitalistic Enterprise in India. Daniel H. Buchannan. LC 66-9611. Repr. of 1934 ed. 27.50x (ISBN 0-678-05032-5). Kelley.

Development of Chemical Principles. Cooper H. Langford & Ralph A. Beebe. 1969. text ed. 16.95 (ISBN 0-201-04207-X). A-W.

Development of Children's Friendships. Ed. by Steven Asher & John Gottman. LC 80-25920. (Illus.). 336p. Date not set. price not set (ISBN 0-521-23103-5); pap. price not set (ISBN 0-521-29806-7). Cambridge U Pr.

Development of Computer-Based Production Systems. A. K. Kochhar. LC 79-902. 274p. 1979. 38.95 (ISBN 0-470-26693-7). Halsted Pr.

Development of Conscience. Geoffrey M. Stephenson. (International Library of Sociology & Social Reconstruction). 1966. text ed. 8.50x (ISBN 0-7100-3460-1). Humanities.

Development of Constitutional Guarantees of Liberty. Roscoe Pound. LC 75-14600. 207p. 1975. Repr. of 1957 ed. lib. bdg. 18.50x (ISBN 0-8371-8225-5, PODC). Greenwood.

Development of Corporate Capitalism in Kenya, Nineteen Eighteen to Nineteen Seventy-Seven. Nicola Swainson. 1980. 20.00 (ISBN 0-686-65115-4, CAMPUS 258); pap. 8.50 (ISBN 0-520-04019-8). U of Cal Pr.

Development of Creative Ability. Eileen Pickard. (Orig.). 1979. pap. text ed. 20.75x (ISBN 0-85633-178-3, NEFR). Humanities.

Development of Design & Operational Criteria for Wastewater Treatment. Carl E. Adams et al. LC 80-69077. (Illus.). 550p. 1980. text ed. 40.00 (ISBN 0-937976-00-8). Enviro Pr.

Development of Economic Analysis. 3rd ed. I. H. Rima. 1978. text ed. 18.95 (ISBN 0-256-02030-2). Irwin.

Development of Economic Doctrine. A. Gray & A. E. Thompson. 496p. 1980. pap. text ed. 17.95 (ISBN 0-582-44871-9). Longman.

Development of Education in East Africa. John Cameron. LC 68-9320. (Illus.). 1970. pap. text ed. 5.75x (ISBN 0-8077-1137-3). Tchrs Coll.

Development of English Biography. Harold Nicolson. 1928. text ed. 3.50x (ISBN 0-7012-0176-2). Humanities.

Development of English Building Construction (1916) C. F. Innocent. (Illus.). 320p. 1971. 32.00 (ISBN 0-7153-5299-7). David & Charles.

Development of English Thought: A Study in the Economic Interpretation of History. Simon Patten. (Neglected American Economists Ser.). 1974. lib. bdg. 50.00 (ISBN 0-8240-1026-4). Garland Pub.

Development of European Society: 1770-1870. John R. Gillis. LC 76-10891. (Illus.). 1977. pap. text ed. 14.25 (ISBN 0-395-24482-X). HM.

Development of Farm Buildings. J. E. Peters. 298p. 1969. 35.00x (ISBN 0-7190-0386-5). State Mutual Bk.

Development of Franz Brentano's Ethics. Linda McAlister. 170p. 1980. pap. text ed. 14.25x (ISBN 0-391-01954-6). Humanities.

Development of Garden Flowers. Richard Gorer. 1970. 12.25 o.p. (ISBN 0-8231-6036-X). Branford.

Development of Governmental Forest Control in the United States. Jenks Cameron. LC 79-38096. (Law, Politics, & History Ser). 484p. 1972. Repr. of 1928 ed. lib. bdg. 45.00 (ISBN 0-306-70440-4). Da Capo.

Development of Handwriting Skills: A Book of Resources for Teachers. Christopher Jarman. 150p. 1980. 17.95x (ISBN 0-631-19240-9, Pub. by Basil Blackwell); pap. 9.95x (ISBN 0-631-19230-1). Biblio Dist.

Development of Hearing. Sybil Yeates. (Studies in Developmental Pediatrics Ser.: Vol. 2). 240p. 1981. text ed. 17.50 (ISBN 0-88416-378-4). PSG Pub.

Development of Heavy Current Electricity in the United Kingdom. Lord Hinton Of Bankside. 1978. text ed. 15.00 (ISBN 0-08-023246-9); pap. text ed. 7.00 (ISBN 0-08-023247-7). Pergamon.

Development of Higher Education in Africa. 1963. pap. 11.50 (ISBN 92-3-100535-9, U158, UNESCO). Unipub.

Development of Host Defenses. Ed. by Max D. Cooper & Delbert H. Dayton. LC 76-51866. 1977. 31.50 (ISBN 0-89004-117-2). Raven.

Development of Housing in Scotland. Douglas Niven. (Illus.). 136p. 1979. 19.00x (ISBN 0-7099-0159-3, Pub. by Croom Helm Lgtd England). Biblio Dist.

Development of Human Resources. Eli Ginzberg. 1966. 13.95 o.p. (ISBN 0-07-023277-6, C); pap. 9.95 o.p. (ISBN 0-07-023276-8). McGraw.

Development of Ideologies in Quebec. Denis Moniere. Tr. by Richard Howard from Fr. Orig. Title: Developpement Des Ideologies Du Quebec. 320p. 1981. 27.50x (ISBN 0-8020-5452-8); pap. 10.00 (ISBN 0-8020-6358-6). U of Toronto Pr.

Development of Integrated Data Bases for Social, Economic & Demographic Statistics. (Studies in Methods Ser. F: No. 27). 62p. 1979. pap. 6.00 (ISBN 0-686-68950-X, UN79/17/14, UN). Unipub.

Development of Iron & Steel Technology in China. J. Needham. LC 75-22549. (Illus.). 76p. 1975. 19.95 (ISBN 0-521-21045-3). Cambridge U Pr.

Development of Japanese Business, 1600-1973. Johannes Hirschmeier & Tsunehiko Yui. LC 74-82190. 350p. 1975. 16.50x (ISBN 0-674-20045-4). Harvard U Pr.

Development of Job Design Theories & Techniques. David A. Buchanan. LC 79-83808. (Praeger Special Studies). 180p. 1979. 22.95 (ISBN 0-03-052376-1). Praeger.

Development of Kamakura Rule, 1180-1250: A History with Documents. Jeffrey P. Mass. LC 78-62271. 1979. 18.50x (ISBN 0-8047-1003-1). Stanford U Pr.

Development of Language & Reading in the Young Child. 2nd ed. Susanna Pflaum-Connor. Ed. by Arthur W. Heilman. (Early Childhood Education Ser.). 1978. text ed. 9.95 (ISBN 0-675-08392-3). Merrill.

Development of Linguistic System in English Speaking American Children, Vol. 2. Joe E. Pierce. 185p. (Orig.). 1981. pap. 8.95 (ISBN 0-913244-51-1). Hapi Pr.

Development of Mathematics in China & Japan. 2nd ed. Y. Mikami. LC 74-6716. 383p. 1974. text ed. 12.95 (ISBN 0-8284-0149-7). Chelsea Pub.

Development of Meaning: A Study of Children's Use of Language. Joan Tough. 1977. pap. text ed. 17.95 (ISBN 0-470-15178-1). Halsted Pr.

Development of Medical Bibliography. Estelle Brodman. 226p. 1981. Repr. of 1954 ed. 8.25 (ISBN 0-912176-00-8). Med Lib Assn.

Development of Memory in Children. Robert Kail. LC 79-12262. (Psychology Ser.). (Illus.). 1979. text ed. 14.95x (ISBN 0-7167-1097-8); pap. text ed. 7.95x (ISBN 0-7167-1098-6). W H Freeman.

Development of Metalinguistic Abilities in Children. D. T. Hakes. (Springer Series in Language & Communication: Vol. 9). (Illus.). 119p. 1980. 22.50 (ISBN 0-387-10295-7). Springer-Verlag.

Development of Metaphysics in Persia: A Contribution to the History of Philosophy. Muhammad Iqbal. (Studies in Islamic History: No. 19). 195p. 1980. Repr. of 1908 ed. lib. bdg. 15.00x (ISBN 0-686-63157-9). Porcupine Pr.

Development of Modal Reasoning: Genesis of Necessity & Probability Notions. Gilbert Pieraut-Le Bonniec. LC 79-24969. (Developmental Psychology Ser.). 1980. 16.50 (ISBN 0-12-554650-5). Acad Pr.

Development of Modern English. 2nd ed. Robertson & Cassidy. 1953. 16.95 (ISBN 0-13-208330-2). P-H.

Development of Modern Italy. Cecil J. Sprigge. 1969. 14.00 (ISBN 0-86527-043-0). Fertig.

Development of Modern Mathematics. J. M. Dubbey. LC 72-88125. 153p. 1975. pap. 9.50x (ISBN 0-8448-0656-0). Crane-Russak Co.

Development of Moral Reasoning: Practical Approaches. Ed. by Don Cochrane & Michael Manley-Casimir. LC 80-17141. 352p. 1980. 27.95 (ISBN 0-03-056209-0). Praeger.

Development of Ornamental Art in the International Exhibition. Christopher Dresser. Ed. by Peter Stansky & Rodney Shewan. LC 76-17750. (Aesthetic Movement & the Arts & Crafts Movement Ser.). 1978. Repr. of 1862 ed. lib. bdg. 44.00x (ISBN 0-8240-2452-4). Garland Pub.

Development of Personality. T. A. Ratcliffe. 1967. text ed. 5.50x (ISBN 0-04-150013-X). Humanities.

Development of Physical Theory in the Middle Ages. James A. Weisheipl. 1971. 5.95 o.p. (ISBN 0-472-09181-6). U of Mich Pr.

Development of Rates of Postage. A. D. Smith. LC 77-77433. 1979. Repr. of 1917 ed. lib. bdg. 65.00x (ISBN 0-88000-110-0). Quarterman.

Development of Reading Skills: A Book of Resources for Teachers. Frances Ball. 1977. 18.00x (ISBN 0-631-17660-8, Pub. by Basil Blackwell); pap. 9.50x (ISBN 0-631-18290-X, Pub. by Basil Blackwell). Biblio Dist.

Development of Regulatory Procedures for the Disposal of Solid Radioactive Waste in Deep, Continental Formations. (Safety Ser.: No. 51). 26p. 1980. pap. 4.50 (ISBN 92-0-123080-X, ISP-540, IAEA). Unipub.

Development of Religion & Thought in Ancient Egypt. James H. Breasted. LC 58-7111. 406p. 1972. pap. 6.95x (ISBN 0-8122-1045-X, Pa Paperbks). U of Pa Pr.

Development of Religious Liberty in Connecticut. M. Louise Greene. LC 74-99858. (Civil Liberties in American History Ser). 1970. Repr. of 1905 ed. lib. bdg. 49.50 (ISBN 0-306-71861-8). Da Capo.

Development of Responsiveness to Steroid Hormones: Bat-Sheva Seminar on the Development of Responsiveness to Steroid Hormones Weizmann Institute of Science, Israel 18-26 Oct., 1978. Ed. by A. M. Kaye & Myra Kaye. LC 79-42938. (Advances in the Biosciences: Vol. 25). (Illus.). 494p. 1980. 68.00 (ISBN 0-08-024940-X). Pergamon.

Development of Retinotectal Projection in the Chicken. G. Rager. (Advances in Anatomy, Embryology & Cell Biology: Vol. 63). (Illus.). 92p. 1980. pap. 30.70 (ISBN 0-387-10121-7). Springer-Verlag.

Development of Self-Regulation Through Private Speech. Gail Zivin. LC 78-27615. (Origins of Behavior Ser.). 1980. 29.50 (ISBN 0-471-98380-2, Pub by Wiley-Interscience). Wiley.

Development of Sensory Systems. Ed. by M. Jacobson. (Handbook of Sensory Physiology: Vol. 9). (Illus.). 1978. 120.80 (ISBN 0-387-08632-3). Springer-Verlag.

Development of Settlement Systems. Ed. by Gyorgy Enyedi & Julia Meszaros. (Studies in Geography in Hungary: 15). (Illus.). 265p. 1980. 27.50x (ISBN 963-05-1898-8). Intl Pubns Serv.

Development of Social Maturity. Ed. by David C. McClelland. 1981. text ed. 18.50x (ISBN 0-8290-0089-5). Irvington.

Development of Social Sensitivity. P. Light. LC 78-12415. (Illus.). 1979. 17.95 (ISBN 0-521-22372-5). Cambridge U Pr.

Development of Social Theory. James P. Lichtenberger. 482p. 1980. Repr. of 1925 ed. lib. bdg. 45.00 (ISBN 0-89987-508-4). Darby Bks.

Development of Socio-Medical Care in the Netherlands. Arie Querido. (Library of Social Policy & Administration). 1968. text ed. 4.75x (ISBN 0-7100-4032-6). Humanities.

Development of Southern French & Catalan Society Seven Eighteen to Ten Fifty. Archibald R. Lewis. LC 80-2019. 1981. Repr. of 1965 ed. 47.50 (ISBN 0-404-18575-4). AMS Pr.

Development of Speech. Paula Menyuk. LC 74-173981. (Studies in Communicative Disorders Ser). 1972. pap. text ed. 2.15 o.p. (ISBN 0-672-61276-3). Bobbs.

Development of Standards & Accreditation in Collegiate Nursing Education. Gwendoline MacDonald. (Nursing Education Monograph Series No. 8). 1965. pap. 3.75 o.p. (ISBN 0-397-54039-6). Lippincott.

Development of State-Chartered Banking in Texas from Predecessor Systems Until 1970. Joseph M. Grant & Lawrence L. Crum. (Studies in Banking & Finance: No. 11). 1978. 10.00 (ISBN 0-87755-219-3); pap. 6.00 (ISBN 0-87755-238-X). U of Tex Busn Res.

Development of State Legislation Concerning the Free Negro. Franklin Johnson. LC 78-118. 1979. Repr. of 1919 ed. lib. bdg. 19.25x (ISBN 0-8371-5844-3, JOD&). Greenwood.

Development of Sumerian Art. Charles L. Woolley. LC 80-24292. (Illus.). 140p. 1981. Repr. of 1935 ed. lib. bdg. 35.00x (ISBN 0-8371-4373-X, WOSA). Greenwood.

Development of the Agrarian Movement & Agrarian Legislation in China. Jefferson D. Lamb. LC 78-74319. (Modern Chinese Economy Ser.: Vol. 12). 254p. 1980. lib. bdg. 33.00 (ISBN 0-8240-4261-1). Garland Pub.

Development of the American Economy. 2nd ed. Bolino. LC 66-20200. 1966. text ed. 13.95 (ISBN 0-675-09974-9). Merrill.

Development of the American Short Story. Fred L. Pattee. LC 66-13477. 1923. 15.00x (ISBN 0-8196-0175-6). Biblo.

Development of the Child. David Elkind & Irving B. Weiner. LC 77-14214. 1978. text ed. 21.95 (ISBN 0-471-23785-X); tchrs. manual avail. (ISBN 0-471-04049-5); study guide 7.50 (ISBN 0-471-03435-5). Wiley.

Development of the Child. Henri Wallon. Ed. by Gilbert Voyat. LC 80-69666. 260p. 1981. 30.00 (ISBN 0-87668-434-7). Aronson.

Development of the Chinese Collection in the Library of Congress. Shu Chao Hu. LC 79-1741. (Westview Replica Edition Ser.). (Illus.). 1979. lib. bdg. 25.50x (ISBN 0-89158-552-4). Westview.

Development of the Communist Bloc. Ed. by Roger Pethybridge. (History & Politics Ser.). 1965. pap. text ed. 2.95x o.p. (ISBN 0-669-23267-X). Heath.

Development of the Emerging Countries: An Agenda for Research. Robert E. Asher et al. 239p. 1962. pap. 3.95 (ISBN 0-8157-0539-5). Brookings.

Development of the English Law of Conspiracy. J. W. Bryan. LC 72-77737. (Law, Politics, & History Ser). 1970. Repr. of 1909 ed. lib. bdg. 20.00 (ISBN 0-306-71375-6). Da Capo.

Development of the Facing Head Motif on Greek Coins & Its Relation to Classical Art. Katherine P. Erhart. Ed. by Sydney J. Freedberg. LC 78-74366. (Outstanding Disserations in the Fine Arts Ser.). (Illus.). 1979. lib. bdg. 50.00 (ISBN 0-8240-3954-8). Garland Pub.

Development of the Human Communication & Joint Regulation of Behavior. E. Tronick. 1981. 18.00 (ISBN 0-8391-1510-5). Univ Park.

Development of the Infant: The First Year of Life in Photographs. Mark Van Blank. (Illus.). 1975. pap. 11.95x (ISBN 0-433-03235-9). Intl Ideas.

Development of the Iranian Oil Industry: International & Domestic Aspects. Fereidun Fesharaki. LC 75-19782. (Special Studies). (Illus.). 300p. 1976. text ed. 31.95 (ISBN 0-275-55600-X). Praeger.

Development of the Locomotive Engine. Angus Sinclair. 1970. 6.95 o.p. (ISBN 0-262-19068-0). MIT Pr.

Development of the London Livery Companies. William F. Kahl. (Kress Library of Business & Economics: No. 15). (Illus.). 1960. pap. 5.00x (ISBN 0-678-09910-3, Baker Lib). Kelley.

Development of the Minkowski Geometry of Numbers, 2 vols. Harris Hancock. pap. text ed. 3.50 ea. Vol. 1 (ISBN 0-486-61203-1). Vol. 2 (ISBN 0-486-61204-X). Dover.

Development of the Monist View of History. George V. Plekhanov. 1982. 19.95 (ISBN 0-87855-322-3); pap. 4.95 (ISBN 0-87855-704-0). Transaction Bks.

Development of the Playhouse: A Survey of Theatre Architecture from the Renaissance to the Present. Donald C. Mullin. LC 77-84532. (Illus.). 1970. 25.00x (ISBN 0-520-01391-3). U of Cal Pr.

Development of the Proto-Indo-European Laryngeals in Greek. R. S. Beekes. (Janua Linguarum, Ser. Practica: No. 42). 1969. pap. text ed. 68.25x (ISBN 90-2790-693-9). Mouton.

Development of the Social Security Act. Edwin E. Witte. 1962. 25.00x (ISBN 0-299-02540-3); pap. 7.95x (ISBN 0-299-02544-6). U of Wis Pr.

Development of the Sociology of Knowledge. S. Lukes. (Studies in Sociology). 1980. pap. text ed. write for info. (ISBN 0-391-01130-8). Humanities.

Development of Theraputic Skills. Mary Jo Bulbrook. 1979. text ed. 12.95 (ISBN 0-316-11472-3, Little Med Div). Little.

Development of Transportation in Modern England. William T. Jackman. LC 67-40294. Repr. of 1916 ed. 30.00x (ISBN 0-678-05178-X). Kelley.

Development of Underdevelopment in China: A Symposium. Ed. by Philip C. Huang. LC 80-51203. 1980. text ed. 15.00 (ISBN 0-87332-164-2). M E Sharpe.

Development of Universities in Nigeria: A Study of the Influence of Political & Other Factors on University Development in Nigeria, 1868-1967. Nduka Okafor. (Illus.). 1971. pap. text ed. 5.75x (ISBN 0-582-64060-1). Humanities.

Development of Urban Systems in Africa. Ed. by R. A. Obudho & Salah S. El-Shakhs. LC 78-19766. 432p. 1979. 32.50 (ISBN 0-03-047066-8). Praeger.

Development of Vertebrate Anatomy. Joy B. Phillips. LC 74-14876. 1975. text ed. 17.95 (ISBN 0-8016-3927-1). Mosby.

Development of Vision, Vol.4. P. A. Gardiner. 240p. 1981. 17.50 (ISBN 0-88416-379-2). PSG Pub.

Development of Walden: A Genetic Text. Ronald Clapper. LC 80-2503. 1981. 75.00 (ISBN 0-686-28931-5). AMS Pr.

Development of Welfare States in Europe & America. Ed. by Peter Flora & Arnold J. Heidenheimer. 264p. 1981. 16.95 (ISBN 0-87855-357-6). Transaction Bks.

Development of Writing. Carol Donoughue. (Jackdaw Ser: No. 47). (Illus.). 1969. 5.95 o.s.i. (ISBN 0-670-27074-1, Grossman). Viking Pr.

Development Paths in Africa & China. Ukandi G Damachi et al. LC 75-45447. 1976. 26.25x (ISBN 0-89158-541-9). Westview.

Development Perspectives. Paul Streeten. 35.00 (ISBN 0-312-19690-3). St Martin.

Development Perspectives: Problems, Strategies & Policies. V. V. Bhatt. (Illus.). 352p. 1980. 50.00 (ISBN 0-08-025774-7). Pergamon.

Development Planning. W. Arthur Lewis. 1966. pap. text ed. 11.50 (ISBN 0-04-330049-9). Allen Unwin.

Development Planning: Lessons from the Japanese Model. V. S. Mahajan. LC 76-52207. 1977. 8.50x (ISBN 0-88386-805-9). South Asia Bks.

Development Planning: The Essentials of Economic Policy. W. Arthur Lewis. LC 66-10655. 1966. 10.95x o.p. (ISBN 0-06-033615-3, HarpT). Har-Row.

Development Policy in Guyana: Planning, Finance, & Administration. Kempe R. Hope. LC 79-5229. (Westview Replica Editions). lib. bdg. 26.50x (ISBN 0-89158-583-4). Westview.

Development Problems in Latin America: An Analysis by the United Nations Economic Commission for Latin America. Economic Commission for Latin America. (ECLA). 318p. 1970. 15.00x (ISBN 0-292-70042-3). U of Tex Pr.

Development Projects Observed. Albert O. Hirschman. 1967. 11.95 (ISBN 0-8157-3650-9); pap. 4.95 (ISBN 0-8157-3649-5). Brookings.

Development Regions in the Soviet Union, Eastern Europe, & Canada. Andrew F. Burghardt. LC 74-31502. (Illus.). 175p. 1975. text ed. 24.95 (ISBN 0-275-09810-9). Praeger.

Development Strategy of Bangladesh. Nural Islam. 1977. text ed. 19.00 (ISBN 0-08-021840-7). Pergamon.

Development Through Cooperation Between the Scandinavian & Oapec Countries. Norwegian Petroleum Society. 296p. 1980. 75.00x (Pub. by Norwegian Info Norway). State Mutual Bk.

Development Through Drama. Brian Way. (Orig.). 1967. pap. text ed. 4.95x (ISBN 0-391-00296-1). Humanities.

Development Through Life: A Case Study Approach. Ed. by Barbara M. Newman & Phillip R. Newman. 1976. pap. 9.50x (ISBN 0-256-01779-4). Dorsey.

Development Through Life: A Psychosocial Approach, Revised Edition: Study Guide. Barbara M. Newman & Philip R. Newman. 1979. pap. text ed. 4.00x (ISBN 0-256-02240-2). Dorsey.

Development Through Life: A Psychosocial Approach. rev. ed. Barbara M. Newman & Philip R. Newman. 1979. pap. text ed. 18.95x (ISBN 0-256-02198-8). Dorsey.

Development Without Dependence. Pierre Uri. LC 75-19829. (Praeger Special Studies). 160p. 1976. text ed. 18.95 o.p. (ISBN 0-275-55830-4); pap. text ed. 11.95 (ISBN 0-275-89470-3). Praeger.

Developmental & Adapted Physical Education. 2nd ed. H. Harrison Clarke & David H. Clarke. (Illus.). 1978. ref. ed. 15.95 (ISBN 0-13-208421-X). P-H.

Developmental & Cellular Skeletal Biology. Brian K. Hall. 1978. 27.50 (ISBN 0-12-318950-0). Acad Pr.

Developmental & Comparative Immunology I: First Congress of Developmental & Comparative Immunology, 27 July-1 August 1980, Aberdeen. Ed. by J. B. Soloman. (Illus.). 580p. 1980. 90.00 (ISBN 0-08-025922-7). Pergamon.

Developmental & Growth Studies of the Euphausiid Nematoscelis Difficilis (Crustacea) Based on Rearing. K. Gopalakrishnan. (Bulletin of the Scripps Institution of Oceanography: Vol. 20). 1973. pap. 7.00x (ISBN 0-520-09463-8). U of Cal Pr.

Developmental & Physiological Correlates of Cardiac Muscle: Perspectives in Cardiovascular Research, Vol. 1. Ed. by M. Lieberman & T. Sano. LC 74-21979. 336p. 1976. 34.50 (ISBN 0-89004-027-3). Raven.

Developmental & Remedial Reading in the Middle Grades. new ed. Mark W. Aulls. 1978. text ed. 19.95 (ISBN 0-205-06092-7). Allyn.

Developmental & Remedial Reading in the Middle Grades. abr. ed. Mark W. Aulls. 1978. pap. text ed. 10.95 (ISBN 0-205-06081-1). Allyn.

Developmental Arts...Hands-on Enrichment Activities for Young Children. 2nd rev. ed. Diane J. Munini. LC 80-70128. 68p. 1980. pap. 6.50 (ISBN 0-9605372-0-1). Developmental Arts.

Developmental Aspects of Antibody Formation & Structure: Proceedings, Vols. 1 & 2. Ed. by J. Sterzl & I. Riha. 1971. Vol. 1. 51.75 (ISBN 0-12-667901-0); Vol. 2. 51.75 (ISBN 0-12-667902-9). Acad Pr.

Developmental Aspects of Craniofacial Dysmorphology. Ed. by Michael Melnick & Ronald Jorgenson. LC 79-2487. (Alan R. Liss Ser.: Vol. 15, No. 8). 1979. 16.00 (ISBN 0-8451-1033-0). March of Dimes.

Developmental Aspects of the Cell Cycle. Ed. by Ivan L. Cameron & George M. Padilla. (Cell Biology Ser). 1971. 52.50 o.s.i. (ISBN 0-12-156960-8). Acad Pr.

Developmental Biology of Prokaryotes. Ed. by J. H. Parish. (Studies in Microbiology: Vol. 1). 1980. 52.50x (ISBN 0-520-04016-3). U of Cal Pr.

Developmental Change: An Annotated Bibliography. Allan A. Spitz. LC 69-19766. 328p. 1969. 16.00x (ISBN 0-8131-1179-X). U Pr of Ky.

Developmental Conditioning for Women & Men. 2nd ed. Anthony A. Annarino. LC 75-9879. (Illus.). 262p. 1976. pap. text ed. 8.95 o.p. (ISBN 0-8016-0249-1). Mosby.

Developmental Counseling. 2nd ed. D. H. Blocher. 320p. 1974. 17.50 (ISBN 0-471-06894-2). Wiley.

Developmental Counseling. 2nd ed. Donald H. Blocher. (Illus.). 371p. 1974. 17.50 (ISBN 0-8260-1131-4). Ronald Pr.

Developmental Counseling & Guidance in the Elementary School. D. Dinkmeyer & E. Caldwell. (Guidance Counseling & Student Personnel in Education). 1970. 16.95 o.p. (ISBN 0-07-017003-7, C). McGraw.

Developmental Cybernetics of Handwriting & Graphic Behavior: An Experimental System Analysis of Writing Readiness & Instruction. Nils Sovik. 1975. pap. text ed. 30.00x (ISBN 8-200-01476-2, Dist. by Columbia U Pr). Universitet.

Developmental Cycle in Domestic Groups. Jack Goody. LC 78-160087. (Papers in Social Anthropology: No. 1). (Illus.). 1972. 19.95 (ISBN 0-521-05116-9); pap. 9.95x (ISBN 0-521-09660-X). Cambridge U Pr.

Developmental Disabilities: A Training Guide. Henri Deutsch & Sheldon M. Bustow. (American Health Care Association Ser.). 192p. 1981. 15.95 (ISBN 0-8436-0851-X). CBI Pub.

Developmental Disabilities Handbook. David H. Fils. LC 79-57296. (Professional Handbook Ser.). 50p. 1980. pap. 7.50x (ISBN 0-87424-139-1). Western Psych.

Developmental Disabilities: Psychologic & Social Implications; Proceedings of a Symposium Sponsored by the National Foundation March of Dimes & the Johns Hopkins University School of Hygiene & Public Health, Baltimore, Md., Ed. by Daniel Bergsma & Ann E. Pulver. LC 76-44446. (Birth Defects - Original Article Ser.: Vol. 12, No. 4.). 204p. 1976. 21.00 (ISBN 0-8451-1007-1). A R Liss.

Developmental Disabilities: The DD Movement. Ed. by Ronald Wiegerink & John W. Pelosi. LC 79-15516. 184p. (Orig.). 1979. pap. text ed. 10.50 (ISBN 0-933716-02-8). P H Brookes.

Developmental Disabilities: The DD Movement. Ed. by Ronald Wiegerink & John W. Pelosi. 182p. 1979. pap. 10.50 (ISBN 0-933716-02-8). P H Brookes.

Developmental Economics. Subrata Ghatak. 1979. text ed. 21.00x (ISBN 0-582-44873-5). Longman.

Developmental Games Rhythms for Children. A. M. Farina. (Illus.). 800p. 1980. 48.75 (ISBN 0-398-04022-2). C C Thomas.

Developmental Groups for Children. J. A. Duncan & J. Gumaer. (Illus.). 440p. 1980. 29.75 (ISBN 0-398-04025-7). C C Thomas.

Developmental Handicaps in Babies & Young Children: A Guide for Parents. Diana L. Brown. 100p. 1972. 11.75 (ISBN 0-398-02534-7). C C Thomas.

Developmental Horizons in Human Embryos: Age Groups XI to XXIII. (Illus.). 194p. 1951. 9.50 (ISBN 0-87279-949-2). Carnegie Inst.

Developmental Human Behavior Genetics: Nature-Nurture Redefined. Warner K. Schaie et al. LC 75-733. 320p. 1975. 21.50 (ISBN 0-669-99515-0). Lexington Bks.

Developmental Immunology. Ed. by Matteo Adinolfi. (Clinics in Developmental Medicine Ser.: Vol. 34). 187p. 1969. 19.50 (ISBN 0-685-59041-0). Lippincott.

Developmental Intervention with Young Physically Handicapped Children. Philip L. Safford & Dena C. Arbitman. (Illus.). 336p. 1975. 28.75 (ISBN 0-398-03326-9). C C Thomas.

Developmental Journey: A Guide to the Development of Logical & Moral Reasoning & Social Perspective. Mary M. Wilcox. LC 79-1340. 1979. 10.95 (ISBN 0-687-10510-2). Abingdon.

Developmental Kindergarten: Individualized Instruction Through Diagnostic Grouping. Fred R. Petrone. (Illus.). 240p. 1976. 18.75 (ISBN 0-398-03506-7). C C Thomas.

Developmental Language Intervention: Psycholinguistic Application. Ruder. Date not set. 16.50 (ISBN 0-8391-1632-2). Univ Park.

Developmental Language Programming for the Retarded. new ed. Rolland J. Van Hattum. 1978. text ed. 18.95 (ISBN 0-205-06452-3). Allyn.

Developmental Mathematics: Basic Arithmetic with a Brief Introduction to Algebra. Ronald Staszkow. 384p. 1980. pap. text ed. 14.95 (ISBN 0-8403-2213-5). Kendall-Hunt.

Developmental Microbiology. John F. Peberdy. LC 80-14825. (Tertiary Level Biology Ser.). 230p. 1980. pap. 29.95x (ISBN 0-470-26989-8). Halsted Pr.

Developmental Neurobiology of Arthropods. Ed. by D. Young. (Illus.). 200p. 1973. 47.50 (ISBN 0-521-20229-9). Cambridge U Pr.

Developmental Nutrition. Lucille Hurley. (Illus.). 1979. text ed. 16.95 (ISBN 0-13-207639-X). P-H.

Developmental Pediatrics. Kenneth S. Holt. (Postgraduate Pediatric Ser.). 304p. 1977. 14.95 (ISBN 0-407-00065-8). Butterworths.

Developmental Physiology & Aging. P. S. Timiras. (Illus.). 692p. 1972. text ed. 25.95 (ISBN 0-02-420840-X). Macmillan.

Developmental Plasticity: Behavioral & Biological Aspects of Variations in Development. Ed. by Eugene S. Gollin. (Developmental Psychology Ser.). 1981. write for info. (ISBN 0-12-289620-3). Acad Pr.

Developmental Psychology. Theron Alexander et al. (Illus.). 532p. 1980. text ed. 16.95 (ISBN 0-442-25212-9). Van Nos Reinhold.

Developmental Psychology. John Dworetzky. (Illus.). 550p. 1981. pap. text ed. 12.76 (ISBN 0-8299-0368-2). West Pub.

Developmental Psychology. 3rd ed. Robert M. Liebert & Wickes Pelson. (Illus.). 640p. 1981. text ed. 18.95 (ISBN 0-13-208256-X). P-H.

Developmental Psychology. 2nd ed. Robert M. Liebert et al. (Illus.). 1977. text ed. 18.95 (ISBN 0-13-208231-4). P-H.

Developmental Psychology: A Life-Span Approach. James E. Birren et al. LC 80-82839. (Illus.). 736p. 1981. write for info. (ISBN 0-395-29717-6); price not set instr's manual (ISBN 0-395-29718-4); price not set test-bank (ISBN 0-395-29720-6). HM.

Developmental Psychology: A Psychobiological Approach. 2nd ed. John Nash. LC 77-27813. (Illus.). 1978. ref. ed. 19.95 (ISBN 0-13-208272-1). P-H.

Developmental Psychology for the Health Care Professions: Prenatal Through Adolescent Development, Pt. 1. Katherine A. Billingham. (Behavioral Sciences for Health Care Professionals Ser.). 128p. (Orig.). 1981. lib. bdg. 15.00x (ISBN 0-86531-000-9); pap. text ed. 6.00x (ISBN 0-86531-001-7). Westview.

Developmental Psychology for the Health Care Professions: Young Adult Through Late Aging, Pt. II. Alfred W. Kaszniak. (Behavioral Sciences for Health Care Professionals Ser.). 128p. (Orig.). 1981. lib. bdg. 15.00x (ISBN 0-86531-012-2); pap. text ed. 6.00x (ISBN 0-86531-013-0). Westview.

Developmental Psychology: Studies in Human Development. rev. ed. Ed. by Hiram E. Fitzgerald & John P. McKinney. 1977. pap. 10.95x (ISBN 0-256-01937-1). Dorsey.

Developmental Psychology: The Adolescent & Young Adult. John P. McKinney et al. 1977. pap. 8.95x (ISBN 0-256-01940-1). Dorsey.

Developmental Psychology: The Infant & Young Child. Hiram E. Fitzgerald et al. 1977. pap. 8.95x (ISBN 0-256-01888-X). Dorsey.

Developmental Psychology: The Problems of Disordered Mental Development. Ed. by Alaine Lane. (Special Education Ser.). (Illus., Orig.). 1979. pap. text ed. 9.95 o.p. (ISBN 0-89568-108-0). Spec Learn Corp.

Developmental Psychology: The School-Aged Child. Ellen A. Strommen et al. 1977. pap. 8.95x (ISBN 0-256-01939-8). Dorsey.

Developmental Psychometrics: A Resource Book for Mental Health Workers & Educators. Jack L. Fadely & Virginia N. Hosler. (Illus.). 168p. 1980. 13.75 (ISBN 0-398-04056-7); pap. 9.75 (ISBN 0-398-04057-5). C C Thomas.

Developmental Psychopathology. Thomas M. Achenbach. (Illus.). 726p. 1974. 24.95 (ISBN 0-8260-0210-2). Wiley.

Developmental Psychophysiology of Mental Retardation: Concepts & Studies. Rathe Karrer. (Illus.). 528p. 1976. 35.50 (ISBN 0-398-03414-1). C C Thomas.

Developmental Reading Ser, One, Two, Three. Anne E. Hughes & Hazel C. Hart. Incl. Forward in Reading. (gr. 7). o.p. (ISBN 0-672-70573-7); Onward in Reading. (gr. 8) (ISBN 0-672-70575-3); Upward in Reading. (gr. 9) (ISBN 0-672-70577-X). (gr. 7-9). 1970. text ed. 3.48 ea.; annot. tchr's ed. 3.48 ea. Bobbs.

Developmental Reading Text Workbooks. William H. Burton et al. Incl. Ready to Read. (readiness). text ed. 1.60 o.p. (ISBN 0-672-70588-5); Play Time. (primer). text ed. o.p. (ISBN 0-672-71285-7); Up & Away. (gr. 1). text ed. 2.00 (ISBN 0-672-71287-3); Animal Parade. (gr. 2). text ed. 2.00 (ISBN 0-672-71289-X); Picnic Basket. (gr. 3). text ed. 2.00 (ISBN 0-672-71291-1); Blazing New Trails. (gr. 6). text ed. 2.24 (ISBN 0-672-71293-8); Flying High. (gr. 5). text ed. 2.24 (ISBN 0-672-71295-4); Shooting Stars. (gr. 6). text ed. 2.24 (ISBN 0-672-71297-0). (readiness-6). 1975. tchrs' ed. 2.40 ea. Bobbs.

Developmental Screening 0-5 Years. Ed. by D. F. Egan et al. (Clinics in Developmental Medicine Ser. No. 30). 64p. 1969. 17.00 (ISBN 0-685-24738-4). Lippincott.

Developmental Sequence of the Marine Red Alga Pseudogloiophloea in Culture. J. Ramus. (U. C. Publ. in Botany: Vol. 52). 1969. pap. 6.50x (ISBN 0-520-09026-8). U of Cal Pr.

Developmental Social Psychology: Theory & Research. Ed. by Sharon S. Brehm et al. (Illus.). 352p. 1981. text ed. 19.95x (ISBN 0-19-502840-6); pap. text ed. 11.95x (ISBN 0-19-502841-4). Oxford U Pr.

Developmental Tasks Resource Guide for Elementary School Children. Charles M. Harris & Nancy D. Gardenhour. LC 75-21740. 1976. 15.00 (ISBN 0-8108-0877-3). Scarecrow.

Developmental Toxicity. Ed. by Carole A. Kimmel & Judith Buelke-Sam. (Target Organ Toxicity Ser.). 1981. price not set. Raven.

Developmental Understanding of the Child. Humberto Nagera. LC 80-69668. 378p. 1981. 30.00 (ISBN 0-87668-432-0). Aronson.

Developments in Art Teaching. Terence Wooff. (Changing Classroom). (Illus.). 1976. text ed. 9.75x (ISBN 0-7291-0039-1); pap. text ed. 4.75x (ISBN 0-7291-0034-0). Humanities.

Developments in Biodegradation of Hydrocarbons, Vol. 1. Ed. by R. J. Watkinson. (Illus.). 1978. text ed. 45.50x (ISBN 0-85334-751-4, Pub. by Applied Science). Burgess-Intl Ideas.

Developments in Boundary Element Methods, Vol. 1. Ed. by P. K. Banerjee & R. Butterfield. (Illus.). 1979. 69.90 (ISBN 0-85334-845-6, Pub. by Applied Science). Burgess-Intl Ideas.

Developments in Building Maintenance, Vol. 1. Ed. by E. J. Gibson. (Illus.). 1979. 38.90x (ISBN 0-85334-801-4, Pub. by Applied Science). Burgess-Intl Ideas.

Developments in Close Range Photogrammetry - One. Ed. by K. B. Atkinson. (Illus.). xii, 220p. 1980. 45.00x (ISBN 0-85334-882-0). Burgess-Intl Ideas.

Developments in Collection Building in University Libraries in Western Europe. Willeur R. Koops & Johannes Stellingwerf. 109p. 1977. text ed. 17.00 (ISBN 3-7940-7020-8, Pub. by K G Saur). Shoe String.

Developments in Composite Materials, Vol. 1. Ed. by G. S. Holister. (Illus.). 1977. 43.50x (ISBN 0-85334-740-9, Pub. by Applied Science). Burgess-Intl Ideas.

Developments in Concrete Technology, Vol. 1. Ed. by F. D. Lydon. (Illus.). 1979. 60.95x (ISBN 0-85334-855-3, Pub. by Applied Science). Burgess-Intl Ideas.

Developments in Design Education. John Eggleston. (Changing Classroom). (Illus.). 1976. text ed. 10.25x (ISBN 0-7291-0097-9); pap. text ed. 4.75x (ISBN 0-7291-0092-8). Humanities.

Developments in Digestive Diseases, Vol. 3. Ed. by J. Edward Berk. (Illus.). 258p. 1980. text ed. 24.00 (ISBN 0-8121-0754-3). Lea & Febiger.

Developments in Drama Teaching. Lynn McGregor. (Changing Classroom). 1976. text ed. 11.25 o.p. (ISBN 0-7291-0007-3); pap. text ed. 4.00x (ISBN 0-7291-0002-2). Humanities.

Developments in Early Childhood Education. Janet Lancaster & Joan Gaunt. (Changing Classroom). 1976. text ed. 11.75x (ISBN 0-7291-0027-8); pap. text ed. 4.75x (ISBN 0-7291-0022-7). Humanities.

Developments in Electronics for Offshore Fields, Vol. 1. Ed. by C. Bedwell. (Illus.). 1978. text ed. 42.60x (ISBN 0-85334-753-0, Pub. by Applied Science). Burgess-Intl Ideas.

Developments in Environmental Control & Public Health, Vol. 1. Ed. by A. Porteus. (Illus.). 1979. 51.80x (ISBN 0-85334-834-0, Pub. by Applied Science). Burgess-Intl Ideas.

Developments in Fire Protection of Offshore Platforms, Vol. 1. Ed. by R. G. Gowar. (Illus.). 1978. text ed. 42.80 (ISBN 0-85334-792-1, Pub. by Applied Science). Burgess-Intl Ideas.

Developments in Food Analysis Techniques-2. Ed. by R. D. King. (Illus.). ix, 268p. 1981. 46.00x (ISBN 0-85334-921-5). Burgess-Intl Ideas.

Developments in Food Analysis Techniques, Vol. 1. Ed. by R. D. King. (Illus.). 1978. text ed. 71.00x (ISBN 0-85334-755-7, Pub. by Applied Science). Burgess-Intl Ideas.

Developments in Food Carbohydrate, Vol. 1. Ed. by G. G. Birch & R. S. Shallenberger. (Illus.). 1977. text ed. 43.50x (ISBN 0-85334-733-6, Pub. by Applied Science). Burgess-Intl Ideas.

Developments in Food Carbohydrate, Vol. 2. Ed. by C. K. Lee. (Illus.). 402p. 1980. 75.00x (ISBN 0-85334-857-X, Pub. by Applied Science). Burgess-Intl Ideas.

Developments in Food Colour - One. Ed. by J. Walford. (Illus.). ix, 259p. 1980. 45.00x (ISBN 0-85334-881-2, Pub. by Applied Science). Burgess-Intl Ideas.

Developments in Food Packaging - One. Ed. by S. J. Palling. (Illus.). xv, 192p. 1980. 45.00x (ISBN 0-85334-917-7). Burgess-Intl Ideas.

Developments in Food Preservatives, No. 1. Ed. by R. H. Tilbury. x, 168p. 1981. 34.00x (ISBN 0-85334-918-5). Intl Ideas.

Developments in Fracture Mechanics-1. Ed. by G. G. Chell. (Illus.). 1979. 57.00x (ISBN 0-85334-858-8, Pub. by Applied Science). Burgess-Intl Ideas.

Developments in Geophysical Exploration Methods, Vol. 1. Ed. by A. A. Fitch. (Illus.). 1979. 51.80x (ISBN 0-85334-835-9, Pub. by Applied Science). Burgess-Intl Ideas.

Developments in Heat Exchanger Technology - One. Ed. by D. Chisholm. (Illus.). x, 288p. 1980. 65.00x (ISBN 0-85334-913-4). Burgess-Intl Ideas.

Developments in Highway-Pavement Engineering, Vol. 1. Ed. by P. S. Pell. (Illus.). 1978. 54.00x (ISBN 0-85334-781-6, Pub. by Applied Science). Burgess-Intl Ideas.

Developments in Highway Pavement Engineering, Vol. 2. Ed. by P. S. Pell. (Illus.). 1978. 36.80x (ISBN 0-85334-804-9, Pub. by Applied Science). Burgess-Intl Ideas.

Developments in Industrial Microbiology, 11 vols. Society for Industrial Microbiology. LC 60-13953. Vols. 5-15. 25.00 ea. Lubrecht & Cramer.

Developments in Industrial Microbiology, Vols. 16 & 17. 1975-76. Vol. 16. 25.00 (ISBN 0-934454-82-5); Vol. 17. 25.00 (ISBN 0-686-21617-2). Vol.18. 29.95 (ISBN 0-934454-83-3). Lubrecht & Cramer.

Developments in Injection Molding, Vol. 1. Ed. by A. Whelan & J. L. Craft. (Illus.). 1978. text ed. 51.40x (ISBN 0-85334-798-0, Pub. by Applied Science). Burgess-Intl Ideas.

Developments in Lighting, Vol. 1. Ed. by J. A. Lynes. (Illus.). 1978. text ed. 48.30x (ISBN 0-85334-774-3, Pub. by Applied Science). Burgess-Intl Ideas.

Developments in Management Thought. Harold R. Pollard. LC 72-84394. 288p. 1975. pap. 14.50x (ISBN 0-8448-0772-9). Crane-Russak Co.

Developments in Mathematical Education. Ed. by A. G. Howson. (Illus.). 250p. 1973. 35.50 (ISBN 0-521-20190-X); pap. 13.95 (ISBN 0-521-09803-3). Cambridge U Pr.

Developments in Mathematics Teaching. F. R. Watson. (Changing Classroom). 1976. text ed. 9.75x (ISBN 0-7291-0085-5); pap. text ed. 4.75x (ISBN 0-7291-0080-4). Humanities.

Developments in Occupational Medicine. Ed. by Carl Zenz. (Illus.). 448p. 1980. 45.75. Year Bk Med.

Developments in Ophthalmology, Vol. 2. Ed. by C. Gailloud. (Illus.). viii, 492p. 1981. 180.00 (ISBN 3-8055-1672-X). S Karger.

Developments in Petroleum Geology, Vol. 1. Ed. by G. D. Hobson. (Illus.). 1977. 77.70x (ISBN 0-85334-745-X, Pub. by Applied Science). Burgess-Intl Ideas.

Developments in Petroleum Geology - Two. Ed. by G. D. Hobson. (Illus.). 345p. 1980. 70.00x (ISBN 0-85334-907-X). Burgess-Intl Ideas.

Developments in Polymer Characterisation - Two. Ed. by J. V. Dawkins. (Illus.). x, 240p. 1980. 55.00x (ISBN 0-85334-909-6). Burgess-Intl Ideas.

Developments in Polymer Degradation, Vol. 2. Ed. by N. Grassie. (Illus.). 1979. 50.00x (ISBN 0-85334-854-5, Pub. by Applied Science). Burgess-Intl Ideas.

Developments in Polymer Fracture, Vol. 1. Ed. by E. H. Andrews. (Illus.). 1979. 59.60x (ISBN 0-85334-819-7, Pub. by Applied Science). Burgess-Intl Ideas.

Developments in Polymer Photochemistry - One. Ed. by N. S. Allen. (Illus.). x, 222p. 1980. 42.50x (ISBN 0-85334-911-8). Burgess-Intl Ideas.

Developments in Polymer Stabilisation - Two. Ed. by Gerald Scott. (Illus.). x, 245p. 1980. 45.00x (ISBN 0-85334-885-5). Burgess-Intl Ideas.

Developments in Polymer Stabilisation, Vol. 1. Ed. by Gerald Scott. (Illus.). 1979. 70.00x (ISBN 0-85334-838-3, Pub. by Applied Science). Burgess-Intl Ideas.

Developments in Polymer Stabilisation, No. 3. Ed. by Gerald Scott. (Illus.). ix, 195p. 1981. 38.00x (ISBN 0-85334-890-1). Intl Ideas.

Developments in Polymerisation, Vol. 2. Ed. by R. N. Haward. (Illus.). 1979. 64.60x (ISBN 0-85334-821-9, Pub. by Applied Science). Burgess-Intl Ideas.

Developments in Polymerisation, Vol. 1: Ionic & Ring-Opening Polymerisation & Polymerisation of Conjugated Dienes. Ed. by R. N. Haward. (Illus.). 1979. 51.80x (ISBN 0-85334-822-7, Pub. by Applied Science). Burgess-Intl Ideas.

Developments in Pressure Vessel Technology: Materials & Fabrication, No. 3. Ed. by R. W. Nichols. (Illus.). xii, 364p. 1981. 68.00x (ISBN 0-686-69032-X). Intl Ideas.

Developments in Pressure Vessel Technology Vol. 1: Flaw Analysis. Ed. by R. W. Nichols. (Illus.). 1979. 46.70x (ISBN 0-85334-802-2, Pub. by Applied Science). Burgess-Intl Ideas.

Developments in Pressure Vessel Technology, Vol. 2: Inspection & Testing. Ed. by R. W. Nichols. (Illus.). 1979. 37.50x (ISBN 0-85334-806-5, Pub. by Applied Science). Burgess-Intl Ideas.

Developments in Prestressed Concrete, Vol. 1. Ed. by F. Sawko. (Illus.). 1978. text ed. 45.50x (ISBN 0-85334-790-5, Pub. by Applied Science). Burgess-Intl Ideas.

Developments in Prestressed Concrete, Vol. 2. Ed. by F. Sawko. (Illus.). 1978. text ed. 28.50x (ISBN 0-85334-811-1, Pub. by Applied Science). Burgess-Intl Ideas.

Developments in Reinforced Plastics, No. 1. Ed. by G. Pritchard. (Illus.). xii, 283p. 1981. 62.00x (ISBN 0-85334-919-3). Intl Ideas.

Developments in Rubber & Rubber Composites - One. Ed. by Colin W. Evans. (Illus.). ix, 184p. 1980. 35.00x (ISBN 0-85334-892-8). Burgess-Intl Ideas.

Developments in Sewerage, Vol. 1. Ed. by R. E. Bartlett. (Illus.). 1979. 31.00x (ISBN 0-85334-831-6, Pub. by Applied Science). Burgess-Intl Ideas.

Developments in Social Studies Teaching. Denis Gleeson & Geoff Whitty. (Changing Classroom). 1976. text ed. 11.75x (ISBN 0-7291-0099-5); pap. text ed. 4.75x (ISBN 0-7291-0094-4). Humanities.

Developments in Soft Drinks Technology, Vol. 1. Ed. by L. F. Green. (Illus.). 1978. text ed. 51.30x (ISBN 0-85334-767-0, Pub. by Applied Science). Burgess-Intl Ideas.

Developments in Soil Mechanics, Vol. 1. Ed. by C. R. Scott. (Illus.). 1978. text ed. 79.80x (ISBN 0-85334-771-9, Pub. by Applied Science). Burgess-Intl Ideas.

Developments in Statistics, Vol. 3. Ed. by P. R. Krishnaiah. 1980. 35.00 (ISBN 0-12-426603-7). Acad Pr.

Developments in Stress Analysis, Vol. 1. Ed. by G. S. Holister. (Illus.). 1979. 41.40x (ISBN 0-85334-812-X, Pub. by Applied Science). Burgess-Intl Ideas.

Developments in Stress Analysis for Pressured Components. Ed. by R. W. Nichols. (Illus.). 1977. 49.70x (ISBN 0-85334-724-7, Pub. by Applied Science). Burgess-Intl Ideas.

Developments in Sweeteners, Vol. 1. Ed. by C. A. Hough et al. (Illus.). 1979. 38.90x (ISBN 0-85334-820-0, Pub. by Applied Science). Burgess-Intl Ideas.

Developments in the Clothing Industry. D. L. Munden & C. M. Dorkin. 56p. 1973. 70.00x (ISBN 0-686-63760-7). State Mutual Bk.

Developments in the Organization of Non-Book Materials: Proceedings of a Joint Aslib-CET-LS Conference. 1977. pap. 3.50x (ISBN 0-686-64056-X, Pub. by Lib Assn England). Oryx Pr.

Developments in the Physics of Nuclear Power Reactors. (Technical Reports Ser.: No. 143). (Illus.). 291p. (Orig.). 1973. pap. 18.75 (ISBN 92-0-135073-2, IAEA). Unipub.

Developments in the Theory of Turbulence. D. C. Leslie. (Illus.). 368p. 1973. 38.50x o.p. (ISBN 0-19-856318-3). Oxford U Pr.

Developments in Theoretical & Applied Mechanics, Vols. 2-4. Vol. 2. 1965. 35.75 o.p. (ISBN 0-08-011024-X); Vol. 3. 1968. 82.00 (ISBN 0-08-012211-6); Vol. 4, 1970. 75.00 (ISBN 0-08-006513-9). Pergamon.

Developments in Water Treatment - One. Ed. by W. M. Lewis. (Illus.). xii, 195p. 1980. 42.50x (ISBN 0-85334-902-9). Burgess-Intl Ideas.

Developments in Water Treatment-2. Ed. by W. M. Lewis. (Illus.). xii, 225p. 1981. 39.00x (ISBN 0-85334-903-7). Burgess-Intl Ideas.

Developments of Cancer Chemotherapy. Ed. by K. Lapis. (Journal: Oncology: Suppl. 1, Vol. 37). (Illus.). iv, 120p. 1980. pap. 19.75 (ISBN 3-8055-1588-X). S Karger.

Developments with Natural Rubber. Ed. by J. A. Brydson. (Illus.). 1967. 22.30x (ISBN 0-85334-062-5). Intl Ideas.

Developments with Thermosetting Plastics. Ed. by A. Whelan & J. A. Brydson. LC 74-34013. 198p. 1975. 29.95 (ISBN 0-470-93772-6). Halsted Pr.

Deviance. Douglas & Waksler. 1981. text ed. 16.95 (ISBN 0-316-19111-6); tchrs'. manual free (ISBN 0-316-19112-4). Little.

Deviance: A Cross-Cultural Perspective. new ed. Robert B. Edgerton. LC 75-28641. (Cummings Modular Program in Anthropology). 1976. pap. text ed. 6.95 (ISBN 0-8465-1301-3). Benjamin-Cummings.

Deviance-Action, Reaction, Interaction: Studies in Positive & Negative Deviance. Frank R. Scarpitti & Paul T. McFarlane. LC 74-4719. 1975. text ed. 9.95 (ISBN 0-201-06721-8). A-W.

Deviance & Control. Terence Morris. 1980. pap. text ed. 9.25x (ISBN 0-09-126871-0, Hutchinson U Lib). Humanities.

Deviance & Decency: The Ethics of Research with Human Subjects. Ed. by Carl B. Klockars & Finbarr W. O'Connor. LC 79-18034. (Sage Annual Reviews of Studies in Deviance: Vol. 3). (Illus.). 1979. 20.00x (ISBN 0-8039-1359-1); pap. 9.95x (ISBN 0-8039-1360-5). Sage.

Deviance & Identity. John Lofland. 1969. pap. text ed. 12.95 (ISBN 0-13-208413-9). P-H.

Deviance & Mass Media. Ed. by Charles Winick. LC 78-16024. (Sage Annual Reviews of Studies in Deviance: Vol. 2). 1978. 20.00x (ISBN 0-8039-1040-1); pap. 9.95x (ISBN 0-8039-1041-X). Sage.

Deviance & Medicalization: From Badness to Sickness. Peter Conrad & Joseph W. Schneider. LC 79-20333. 1980. pap. text ed. 11.50 (ISBN 0-8016-1025-7). Mosby.

Deviance & Social Control in Chinese Society. Amy A. Wilson et al. LC 76-12886. (Special Studies). 1977. text ed. 26.95 (ISBN 0-275-56470-3); pap. 11.95 (ISBN 0-275-89650-1). Praeger.
Deviance in Classrooms. David H. Hargreaves et al. 280p. 1975. 20.00x (ISBN 0-7100-8275-4); pap. 8.00 (ISBN 0-7100-8490-0). Routledge & Kegan.
Deviance in Soviet Society: Crime, Delinquency, Alcoholism. Walter D. Connor. LC 71-180044. 1972. 22.50x (ISBN 0-231-03439-3). Columbia U Pr.
Deviance, Reality, & Change: Sex, Dope, & Cheap Thrills. H. Taylor Buckner. 1971. text ed. 14.95 (ISBN 0-394-31002-0). Random.
Deviancy & the Family. Clifton D. Bryant. LC 72-77588. pap. 10.95x (ISBN 0-88295-201-3). AHM Pub.
Deviant Behavior. Paul Rock. 1976. text ed. 9.50x (ISBN 0-09-115440-5, Hutchinson U Lib); pap. text ed. 4.75x (ISBN 0-09-115441-3). Humanities.
Deviant Behavior. Alex Thio. LC 77-90439. (Illus.). 1978. text ed. 18.50 (ISBN 0-395-25323-3); inst. manual 0.65 (ISBN 0-395-25324-1). HM.
Deviant Behavior: An Interactionist Approach. Erich Goode. LC 77-20487. (P-H Ser. in Sociology). (Illus.). 1978. 17.95 (ISBN 0-13-208306-X). P-H.
Deviant Behavior in Defense of Self. Howard B. Kaplan. LC 79-6795. 1980. 22.00 (ISBN 0-12-396850-X). Acad Pr.
Deviant Imagination: Psychiatry, Social Work & Social Change. Geoffrey Pearson. LC 75-9815. 252p. 1980. text ed. 27.50x (ISBN 0-8419-0209-7); pap. text ed. 11.50x (ISBN 0-8419-0616-5). Holmes & Meier.
Deviant Logic. Susan Haack. LC 74-76949. 208p. 1975. 23.95 (ISBN 0-521-20500-X). Cambridge U Pr.
Deviant Reality: Alternative World Views. 2nd ed. Lowney & Winslow. 420p. 1980. pap. text ed. 10.95 (ISBN 0-205-07243-7, 8172439). Allyn.
Deviant Street Networks: Prostitution in New York. Bernard Cohen. LC 80-8039. 1980. 19.95 (ISBN 0-669-03949-7). Lexington Bks.
Devil & Commodity Fetishism in South America. Michael Taussig. LC 79-17685. xiii, 264p. 1980. 19.50x (ISBN 0-8078-1412-1). U of NC Pr.
Devil & Daniel Webster & Other Stories. Stephen V. Benet. (gr. 7-9). 1972. pap. 1.75 (ISBN 0-671-42889-6). Archway.
Devil & Daniel Webster & Other Stories. Stephen V. Benet. (Illus.). (YA) (gr. 7-9). 1967. pap. 1.50 (ISBN 0-671-29943-3). PB.
Devil & John Webster. Muriel West. (Salzburg Studies in English Literature, Jacobean Drama Studies: No. 11). 319p. 1974. pap. text ed. 25.00x (ISBN 0-391-01563-X). Humanities.
Devil & W. Kaspar. Benjamin Appel. 1977. pap. 1.50 o.p. (ISBN 0-445-03190-5). Popular Lib.
Devil at the Wheel. Gordon McLean & Ken Pestana. LC 74-28547. 144p. (Orig.). (YA) 1975. pap. 1.95 (ISBN 0-87123-101-8, 200101). Bethany Fell.
Devil Dances for Gold. Regina Ross. 1977. pap. 1.95 o.p. (ISBN 0-345-25256-X). Ballantine.
Devil Fire, Love's Revenge. Barbara Paul. 1977. pap. 1.95 o.p. (ISBN 0-345-25950-5). Ballantine.
Devil Gun. William Syers. 1978. pap. 1.75 o.p. (ISBN 0-445-04163-3). Popular Lib.
Devil Horse. Max Brand. 1974. pap. 1.75 (ISBN 0-446-94289-8). Warner Bks.
Devil in a Forest. Gene Wolfe. LC 76-5318. 224p. (gr. 7 up). 1976. 6.95 o.p. (ISBN 0-695-80667-X); PLB 6.99 o.p. (ISBN 0-695-40667-1). Follett.
Devil in Britain & America. John Ashton. LC 73-18391. Repr. of 1896 ed. 26.00 (ISBN 0-8103-3626-X). Gale.
Devil in Britain & America. John Ashton. LC 80-19692. 363p. 1980. Repr. of 1972 ed. lib. bdg. 10.95x (ISBN 0-89370-608-6). Borgo Pr.
Devil in Command. Helen Bianchin. (Harlequin Presents Ser.). 192p. (Orig.). 1981. pap. 1.50 (ISBN 0-373-10409-X, Pub. by Harlequin). PB.
Devil in Crystal. Erica Lindley. 1977. pap. 1.95 (ISBN 0-451-07643-5, E7643, Sig). NAL.
Devil in Massachusetts: A Modern Enquiry into the Salem Witch Trials. Marion L. Starkey. LC 49-10395. 1969. pap. 2.95 (ISBN 0-385-03509-8, Anch). Doubleday.
Devil in Vienna. Doris Ohgel. (gr. 7-12). 1980. pap. 1.50 (ISBN 0-440-91777-8, LFL). Dell.
Devil Is a Mean Man. Walter E. Adams. 140p. (Orig.). 1981. pap. 3.95 (ISBN 0-937408-01-8). Gospel Pubns Fl.
Devil Lover. Carole Mortimer. (Harlequin Presents Ser.). 192p. 1981. pap. 1.50 (ISBN 0-373-10430-8, Pub. by Harlequin). PB.
Devil-May-Care. Elizabeth Peters. 1977. 7.95 o.p. (ISBN 0-396-07413-8). Dodd.
Devil-May-Care. Elizabeth Peters. 1978. pap. 1.75 o.p. (ISBN 0-449-23581-5, Crest). Fawcett.
Devil on the Road. Robert Westall. LC 79-10427. (gr. 6 up). 1979. 7.95 (ISBN 0-688-80227-3); lib. bdg. 7.63 (ISBN 0-688-84227-5). Greenwillow.
Devil Take All. Alice Brennan. 256p. (Orig.). 1974. pap. 0.95 o.p. (ISBN 0-445-00612-9). Popular Lib.
Devil Take Her: A Study of the Rebellious Lover in English Poetry. Louis B. Salomon. pap. 1.95 o.p. (ISBN 0-498-04058-5, Prpta). A S Barnes.
Devil Take You, Barnabas Beane! Mary B. Christian. LC 79-7891. (Illus.). (ps-3). 1980. 6.95 (ISBN 0-690-03997-2, TYC-J); PLB 6.89 (ISBN 0-690-03998-0). T Y Crowell.
Devil Tree. Jerzy Kosinski. 256p. 1981. 11.95 (ISBN 0-312-19794-2). St Martin.
Devil, You Say: Man & His Personal Devils & Angels. Andrew M. Greeley. 200p. 1976. pap. 1.45 o.p. (ISBN 0-385-12069-9, Im). Doubleday.
Devils. J. Charles Wall. LC 69-16798. 1969. Repr. of 1904 ed. 18.00 (ISBN 0-8103-3541-7). Gale.
Devil's Advocate. Taylor Caldwell. pap. 3.75 (ISBN 0-515-05092-X). Jove Pubns.
Devil's Alphabet. Kurt E. Koch. LC 76-160692. 1972. pap. 2.95 (ISBN 0-8254-3004-6). Kregel.
Devil's Apple Corps. Raymond Barrio. (Illus.). 50p. 1976. pap. 1.50 (ISBN 0-917438-06-X). Ventura Pr.
Devil's Backbone: The Story of the Natchez Trace. Jonathan Daniels. (American Trails Library Ser). (Illus.). 1962. 9.95 o.p. (ISBN 0-07-015302-7, GB). McGraw.
Devil's Canyon. E. E. Halleran. 160p. 1981. pap. 1.75 (ISBN 0-345-29433-5, 01866). Ballantine.
Devil's Charter (1607) Barnabe Barnes. Ed. by Jim C. Pogue & Stephen Orgel. LC 79-54358. (Renaissance Drama Second Ser.). 225p. 1980. lib. bdg. 25.00 (ISBN 0-8240-4474-6). Garland Pub.
Devil's Children. Ed. by Michel Parry. pap. 1.50 o.p. (ISBN 0-425-03202-7). Berkley Pub.
Devils, Devils, Devils. Helen Hoke. LC 75-38035. (Terrific Triple Titles Ser). (Illus.). 224p. (gr. 4 up). 1976. PLB 6.90 o.p. (ISBN 0-531-01140-2). Watts.
Devil's Dictionary. Ambrose Bierce. 6.75 (ISBN 0-8446-0492-5). Peter Smith.
Devil's Dictionary. Ambrose Bierce. LC 78-13294. (Illus.). 1978. 14.95 (ISBN 0-916144-34-8); pap. 7.95 (ISBN 0-916144-35-6). Stemmer Hse.
Devil's Disciple. George B. Shaw. Ed. by Robert F. Whitman. LC 79-56706. (Bernard Shaw Early Texts: Play Manuscripts in Facsimile). 1981. lib. bdg. 45.00 (ISBN 0-8240-4581-5). Garland Pub.
Devil's Ditties: Being Stories of the Kentucky Mountain People, Told by Jean Thomas, with the Songs They Sing. Jean Thomas. LC 75-16369. (Illus.). viii, 180p. 1976. Repr. of 1931 ed. 22.00 (ISBN 0-8103-3999-4). Gale.
Devil's Donkey. Bill Brittain. LC 80-7907. (Illus.). 128p. (gr. 3-7). 1981. 8.95 (ISBN 0-06-020682-9, HarpJ); PLB 8.79g (ISBN 0-06-020683-7). Har-Row.
Devil's Doorstep. Marian Rumsey. (Illus.). (gr. 3-7). 1966. 7.25 (ISBN 0-688-21235-2). Morrow.
Devil's DP Dictionary. Stan Kelly-Bootle. (Illus.). 160p. 1981. 5.95 (ISBN 0-07-034022-6, P&RB). McGraw.
Devils, Drugs & Doctors. H. W. Haggard. (Illus.). 1976. Repr. 25.00x o.p. (ISBN 0-7158-1117-7). Charles River Bks.
Devil's Elixirs. E. T. Hoffman. 1980. 10.95 (ISBN 0-7145-0194-8). Riverrun NY.
Devil's Footsteps. John Burke. 1978. pap. 1.75 o.p. (ISBN 0-445-04204-4). Popular Lib.
Devil's Game. Paul Anderson. 1980. pap. write for info. (ISBN 0-671-83689-7). PB.
Devil's Garden: Facts & Folklore of Perilous Plants. Edward R. Ricciuti. LC 77-79624. (Illus.). 1978. 10.95 o.s.i. (ISBN 0-8027-0581-2). Walker & Co.
Devil's Gate. Arlene Fitzgerald. 1977. pap. 1.50 o.p. (ISBN 0-445-03178-6). Popular Lib.
Devil's Gold. Chet Cunningham. (Orig.). 1980. pap. 1.95 (ISBN 0-505-51510-5). Tower Bks.
Devil's Island. Brian Peachment. 1976. pap. 1.55 (ISBN 0-08-017613-5). Pergamon.
Devils Island: Revelations of the French Penal Settlements in Guiana. William Allison-Booth. LC 71-162504. (Illus.). 1971. Repr. of 1931 ed. 18.00 (ISBN 0-8103-3761-4). Gale.
Devil's Love. Lane Harris. (Orig.). 1981. pap. 2.95 (ISBN 0-440-11915-4). Dell.
Devil's Nob. Philip Turner. LC 72-8918. 190p. (gr. 6-9). 1973. 6.95 o.p. (ISBN 0-525-66270-7). Elsevier-Nelson.
Devils of Loudun. Aldous Huxley. 1979. pap. 5.95 (ISBN 0-06-090210-8, CN-210, CN). Har-Row.
Devil's Son-in-Law. Paul Garon. (Paul Oliver Blues Ser.). pap. 2.95 (ISBN 0-913714-34-8). Legacy Bks.
Devil's Sonata. Susan Hufford. 256p. 1976. pap. 1.25 o.p. (ISBN 0-445-00340-5). Popular Lib.
Devil's Tramping Ground & Other North Carolina Mystery Stories. John Harden. 1949. 7.95 (ISBN 0-8078-0561-0). U of NC Pr.
Devil's Tramping Ground & Other North Carolina Mystery Stories. John Harden. 178p. 1980. pap. 4.95 o.p. (ISBN 0-8078-4070-X). U of NC Pr.
Devil's Triangle. Elwood D. Baumann. LC 75-22020. (Illus.). 160p. (gr. 7 up). 1976. PLB 7.45 (ISBN 0-531-01094-5). Watts.
Devil's Voyage. Jack L. Chalker. LC 79-7841. 336p. 1981. 11.95 (ISBN 0-385-15284-1). Doubleday.
Devils' Wine. Martin Booth. 112p. 1980. text ed. 16.25x (ISBN 0-86140-044-5); pap. text ed. 8.50x (ISBN 0-86140-044-5). Humanities.
Devil's Wine. Sue Scalf. LC 76-41420. 1978. 5.95 (ISBN 0-916624-04-8). TSU Pr.
Devil's Wine. Susan Scalf. LC 76-41420. 1976. pap. 3.95 (ISBN 0-916624-05-6). TSU Pr.
Devocionario Biblico Guadalupano. Jose L. Ortega. 64p. 1980. pap. 1.50 (ISBN 0-89243-130-X). Liguori Pubns.
Devolution at Work. D. G. Kermode. 1979. text ed. 24.50x (ISBN 0-566-00237-X, Pub. by Gower Pub Co England). Renouf.
Devon. W. G. Hoskins. (Illus.). 624p. 1972. 25.00 (ISBN 0-7153-5577-5). David & Charles.
Devon: A Shell Guide. Ann Jellicoe & Roger Mayne. (Shell Guide Ser.). (Illus.). 1975. 12.95 (ISBN 0-571-04836-6, Pub. by Faber & Faber). Merrimack Bk Serv.
Devon: A Thematic Study. Brian Chugg. LC 79-56459. (Illus.). 208p. 1980. 27.00 (ISBN 0-7134-0417-5, Pub. by Batsford England). David & Charles.
Devon Shipwrecks. Richard Larn. LC 74-76178. 1974. 14.95 (ISBN 0-7153-6337-9). David & Charles.
Devotion for Every Day, 1981-1982: Fourteenth Annual. 384p. (Orig.). 1981. pap. 2.95 (ISBN 0-87239-433-6, 3082). Standard Pub.
Devotion for Every Day, 1981-1982: Third Annual. Ed. by J. David Lang. 384p. (Orig.). 1981. pap. 5.50 large type ed. (ISBN 0-87239-434-4, 4082). Standard Pub.
Devotion for Everyday: 1980-1981. J. David Lang. 1980. pap. 2.95 (ISBN 0-87239-399-2, 4081); pap. 4.95 large print ed. (ISBN 0-87239-400-X). Standard Pub.
Devotion to the Sacred Heart: Objects, Ends, Practice, Motives. Louis Verheylezoon. LC 78-74569. 1979. pap. 6.00 (ISBN 0-89555-083-0, 129). TAN Bks Pubs.
Devotional Commentary on Exodus. F. B. Meyer. LC 78-9530. 1978. 10.95 (ISBN 0-8254-3225-1). Kregel.
Devotional Guide to John. John Killinger. 144p. 1981. 7.95 (ISBN 0-8499-0256-8). Word Bks.
Devotional Poems of Mirabai. A. J. Alston. 144p. 1980. text ed. 13.50 (ISBN 0-8426-1643-8). Verry.
Devotional Poems of Mirabai. Tr. by Shreeprakash Kurl. (Writers Workshop Saffronbird Ser.). 87p. 1975. 15.00 (ISBN 0-88253-722-9); pap. 6.75 (ISBN 0-89253-539-3). Ind-US Inc.
Devotional Poetry in France, Fifteen Seventy to Sixteen Thirteen. Terence C. Cave. LC 68-23177. 1969. 58.00 (ISBN 0-521-07145-3). Cambridge U Pr.
Devotions for Christian Workers. Leroy Koopman. (Good Morning Lord Ser.). 96p. 1980. 3.95 (ISBN 0-8010-5418-4). Baker Bk.
Devotions for Early Teens, Vol. 4. Ruth I. Johnson. 128p. (gr. 7-12). 1974. pap. 1.50 (ISBN 0-8024-2184-9). Moody.
Devotions Upon Emergent Occasions: A Critical Edition with an Introduction & Commentary, 2 vols. Sr. John Donne. Ed. by Elizabeth Savage. (Salzburg Studies in English Literature, Elizabethan & Renaissance Studies Ser.: No. 21). 392p. (Orig.). 1975. Set. pap. text ed. 50.25 (ISBN 0-391-01364-5). Humanities.
Dewdrops. Victoria Ullman. 1981. 5.50 (ISBN 0-8062-1683-2). Carlton.
Dewey & His Critics. Ed. by Sidney Morgenbesser. LC 77-94488. 1977. lib. bdg. 30.00 (ISBN 0-931206-00-6); pap. text ed. 12.50 (ISBN 0-931206-01-4). Hackett Pub.
Dewey Decimal & Sears Update: Supplement to How to Classify, Catalog, & Maintain Media. Jacqulyn Anderson. 1981. Repr. saddle wire 2.25 (ISBN 0-8054-3705-3). Broadman.
Dewey Decimal Classification & Relative Index. 11th abridged ed. Melvil Dewey. LC 78-12514. 1979. 24.00x (ISBN 0-910608-22-9). Forest Pr.
Dewey Decimal Classification & Relative Index, 3 vols. 19th ed. Dewey Melvil. LC 77-27967. 1979. Set. 90.00x (ISBN 0-910608-23-7); Vol 1, Introduction & Tables. 30.00x (ISBN 0-910608-19-9); Vol. 2, Schedules. 30.00x (ISBN 0-910608-20-2); Vol. 3, Index. 30.00x (ISBN 0-910608-21-0). Forest Pr.
Dewey Decimal Classification & Subject Index for Arranging the Books & Pamphlets of a Library (1876) facsimile ed. Melvil Dewey. 1975. 5.00x (ISBN 0-910608-16-4). Forest Pr.
Dewey Decimal Classification for British Schools: Introduction. 3rd ed. B. A. J. Winslade & Dewey Melvil. 1977. 5.50x (ISBN 0-910608-18-0). Forest Pr.
Dewey Decimal Classification: Proposed Revision of 780 Music. Melvil Dewey. Ed. by Russell Sweeney et al. LC 80-16730. 1980. pap. text ed. 5.00x (ISBN 0-910608-25-3). Forest Pr.
Dewey International: Papers Given at the European Centenary Seminar, Banbury, 1976. Ed. by J. C. Downing & M. Yelland. 1977. pap. 9.95x (ISBN 0-85365-469-7, Pub. by Lib Assn England). Oryx Pr.
Dewey on Education: Selections, with an Introduction & Notes. Ed. by Martin Dwork. LC 59-15893. (Illus.). 1959. text ed. 8.50 (ISBN 0-8077-1266-3); pap. text ed. 3.95x (ISBN 0-8077-1263-9). Tchrs Coll.
Dewitt's Strike. Greg Hunt. 1980. pap. 1.95 (ISBN 0-440-12024-1). Dell.
Dextran & Its Use in Colloidal Infusion Solutions. Anders Gronwall. (Illus.). 1957. 23.50 (ISBN 0-12-304050-7). Acad Pr.
Dezoito, Nao Ha Tempo Que Perder. Tr. by Margaret Johnson. (Portuguese Bks.). 1979. 1.30 (ISBN 0-8297-0656-9). Life Pubs Intl.
Dhamma: Western Academic & Sinhalese Buddhist Interpretations: A Study of a Religious Concept. John R. Carter. 1978. 32.50 (ISBN 0-89346-014-1, Pub. by Hokuseido Pr.). Heian Intl.
Dhammapada. ix, 139p. 1955. 3.00 (ISBN 0-938998-16-1). Cunningham Pr.
Dhammapada. Tr. by Juan Mascaro. (Classics Ser.). 1973. pap. 2.25 (ISBN 0-14-044284-7). Penguin.
Dhammapada & Sutta-Nipata, Vol. 10. Ed. by F. Max Mueller. Tr. by Rhys Davids. (Sacred Books of the East Ser.). 15.00x (ISBN 0-8426-1397-8). Verry.
Dhammapada, Wisdom of the Buddha. Harishchandra Kaviratna. 1980. 8.50 (ISBN 0-911500-39-1); softcover 5.00 (ISBN 0-911500-40-5). Theos U Pr.
Dharma Bums. Jack Kerouac. 1971. pap. 4.95 (ISBN 0-14-004252-0). Penguin.
Dharma of Faith: An Introduction to Classical Pure Land Buddhism. Paul O. Ingram. 1978. pap. text ed. 7.75x (ISBN 0-8191-0373-X). U Pr of Amer.
Dhikra al Babbaga, al Suri & al Nami. Al Tha'alibi. Tr. by Arthur Wormhoudt. (Arab Translation Ser.: No. 24). 1976. pap. 6.50 (ISBN 0-916358-74-7). Wormhoudt.
Dhikra Al Tanisi. Tr. by Arthur Wormhoudt from Classical Arabic. (Arab Translation Ser.: No. 53). (Illus.). 1981. pap. 6.50x (ISBN 0-916358-09-7). Wormhoudt.
Dhikra Ibn Al Hajjaj. Tr. by Arthur Wormhoudt. (Arab Translation Ser.: No. 55). (Illus.). 160p. pap. 6.50x (ISBN 0-916358-04-6). Wormhoudt.
Dhow. Clifford W. Hawkins. 144p. 1980. 57.00x (ISBN 0-245-52655-2, Pub. by Nautical England). State Mutual Bk.
Dhows to Deltas. Renato S. Levi. 255p. 1980. 15.00x (ISBN 0-245-59956-8, Pub. by Nautical England). State Mutual Bk.
Dhrupada: A Study of Its Origin, Historical Development, Structure & Present State. I. P. Srivastava. (Illus.). 176p. 1980. text ed. 15.00x (ISBN 0-8426-1648-9). Verry.
Di las Cosas Como Son. Tr. by Fritz Ridenour. (Spanish Bks.). (Span.). 1978. 1.90 (ISBN 0-8297-0862-6). Life Pubs Intl.
Dia De las Madres. 1980. pap. 0.85 (ISBN 0-311-07301-8). Casa Bautista.
Dia-Tras-Dia Con Billy Graham. Compiled by Joan W Brown. Orig. Title: Day by Day with Billy Graham. 1978. 2.70 (ISBN 0-311-40039-6). Casa Bautista.
Dia-Tras-Dia Con Billy Graham. Compiled by Joan W. Brown. Orig. Title: Day by Day with Billy Graham. 1978. 2.70 (ISBN 0-311-40039-6, Edit Mundo). Casa Bautista.
Dia y una Vida. Fernando Salaz. (Span. & Eng.). (gr. 7-8). 1977. pap. text ed. 3.00x o.p. (ISBN 0-87108-201-2). Pruett.
Diabetes. Sarah R. Riedman. (gr. 4 up). 1980. PLB 6.45 (ISBN 0-531-04107-7). Watts.
Diabetes - A Clinical Guide. 2nd ed. Jeanne R. Bonar. 1980. pap. 19.50 (ISBN 0-87488-710-0). Med Exam.
Diabetes: A Guide for Patient Education. Allene Van Son. 288p. 1981. pap. 9.50 (ISBN 0-8385-1596-7). ACC.
Diabetes: A Guide to Self-Management for Patients & Their Families. Terri Kivelowitz. (Illus.). 224p. 1981. 12.95 (ISBN 0-13-208637-9, Spec); pap. 5.95 (ISBN 0-13-208629-8). P-H.
Diabetes & Metabolic Disorders Continuing Education Review. John A. Colwell & German Lizarralde. 1975. 12.00 o.p. (ISBN 0-87488-362-8). Med Exam.

Diabetes & Other Endocrine Disorders During Pregnancy & in the Newborn: Proceedings. Nat'l Foundation-March of Dimes Symposium, April, 1976, New York City. Ed. by Maria I. New & Robert H. Fiser, Jr. LC 76-21204. (Progress in Clinical & Biological Research: Vol. 10). 262p. 1976. 30.00x (ISBN 0-8451-0010-6). A R Liss.

Diabetes & the Heart. Samuel Zoneraich. (Illus.). 320p. 1978. 35.75 (ISBN 0-398-03644-6). C C Thomas.

Diabetes Dictionary & Guide. Joseph F. Brown. LC 77-92938. (Illus.). 1978. 13.95 (ISBN 0-9601484-1-8). Press West.

Diabetes Mellitus. Ed. by Jay S. Skyler & George F. Cahill. (Illus.). 400p. 1981. text ed. write for info. (ISBN 0-914316-23-0). Yorke Med.

Diabetes Mellitus, Vol. 5. new ed. Ed. by Harold Rifkin & Philip Raskin. (Illus.). 391p. 1980. text ed. 22.95 (ISBN 0-87619-747-0). R J Brady.

Diabetes Mellitus Case Studies. Buris R. Boshell. 1976. spiral bdg. 14.00 (ISBN 0-87488-031-9). Med Exam.

Diabetes Outpatient Care Through Physician Assistants: A Model for Health Maintenance Organizations. Lawrence Power et al. (Illus.). 116p. 1973. text ed. 9.75 (ISBN 0-398-02676-9). C C Thomas.

Diabetes: Reach for Health & Freedom. Dorothea S. Sims. LC 80-16065. (Illus.). 145p. 1980. pap. 5.95 (ISBN 0-8016-4657-X). Mosby.

Diabetes: The Glucograph Method for Normalizing Blood Sugar. Richard K. Bernstein. Ed. by Marion Behrman. (Illus.). 320p. 1981. 14.95 (ISBN 0-517-54155-6). Crown.

Diabetes: The Sugar Disease. Alvin Silverstein & Virginia B. Silverstein. LC 78-11631. 1979. 7.95 (ISBN 0-397-31844-8). Lippincott.

Diabetes Without Fear. Joseph I. Goodman & W. Watts Biggers. 1980. pap. 5.95 (ISBN 0-87795-294-9). Arbor Hse.

Diabetic Angiopathy in Children. Ed. by B. Weber. (Pediatric & Adolescent Endocrinology Ser.: Vol. 9). (Illus.). viii, 422p. 1981. 114.00 (ISBN 3-8055-1574-X). S Karger.

Diabetic Child. James W. Farquhar. (Patient Handbook Ser.). (Illus.). 96p. 1981. pap. 2.95 (ISBN 0-443-02193-7). Churchill.

Diabetic Diet Exchange Lists for Low Sodium Diets. Margaret B. Salmon. (Illus.). 1979. pap. 1.50 (ISBN 0-918662-06-0). Techkits.

Diabetic Diet Handbook. Margaret B. Salmon. (Illus.). 1977. pap. 1.50 (ISBN 0-918662-02-8). Techkits.

Diabetic Macro- & Microahgiopathy. Julian Mincu. LC 73-82434. 1975. 73.00x (ISBN 3-11-004533-8). De Gruyter.

Diabetic Menus, Meals & Recipes. Betty M. West. LC 76-53412. 1978. 8.95 (ISBN 0-385-04651-0). Doubleday.

Diabetic Renal-Retinal Syndrome. Ed. by Eli A. Friedman & Frances L'Esperance. 1980. 39.50 (ISBN 0-8089-1302-6). Grune.

Diabetic Retinopathy. A. Urrets-Zavalia. 125p. 1977. 24.75 (ISBN 0-89352-003-9). Masson Pub.

Diabetic's Sports & Exercise Book. June Bierman & Barbara Toohey. 1978. pap. 2.25 (ISBN 0-515-04513-6). Jove Pubns.

Diabetic's Sports & Exercise Book: How to Play Your Way to Better Health. June Biermann & Barbara Toohey. LC 76-17894. (Illus.). 1977. 10.95 o.s.i. (ISBN 0-397-01115-6); pap. 5.95 (ISBN 0-397-01202-0). Lippincott.

Diable, a Dog. Jack London. Ed. by Walter Pauk & Raymond Harris. (Classics Ser). (Illus.). (gr. 6-12). 1976. pap. text ed. 1.60x (ISBN 0-89061-046-0, 513); tchrs. ed. 3.00 (ISBN 0-89061-047-9, 515). Jamestown Pubs.

Diable au Corps. Radiguet. (Easy Reader, B). pap. 3.75 (ISBN 0-88436-059-8, FRA201057). EMC.

Diable Boiteux, or the Devil Upon Two Sticks. Alain R. Le Sage. LC 73-170518. (Foundations of the Novel Ser.: Vol. 13). lib. bdg. 50.00 (ISBN 0-8240-0525-2). Garland Pub.

Diabolus Amans. John Davidson. Ed. by Ian Fletcher. Bd. with North Wall. LC 76-20055. (Decadent Consciousness Ser.: Vol. 6). 1978. Repr. of 1885 ed. lib. bdg. 38.00 (ISBN 0-8240-2755-8). Garland Pub.

Diagnose und Differentialdiagnose in der Schaedelroentgenologie. E. G. Mayer. (Ger, Eng, Span, Fr.). 1959. 147.50 (ISBN 0-387-80517-6). Springer-Verlag.

Diagnosing & Correcting Reading Disabilities. George D. Spache. 416p. 1976. pap. text ed. 15.95x o.s.i. (ISBN 0-205-04916-8). Allyn.

Diagnosing & Correcting Reading Disabilities. 2nd ed. George D. Spache. 480p. 1980. text ed. 18.95 (ISBN 0-205-07175-9, 2371758). Allyn.

Diagnosing Learning Disabilities. Wilma J. Bush & Kenneth Waugh. (Illus.). 300p. 1976. text ed. 16.95 (ISBN 0-675-08612-4). Merrill.

Diagnosing Mathematical Difficulties. Richard G. Underhill et al. (Elementary Education Ser.: No. C22). 408p. 1980. text ed. 15.95 (ISBN 0-675-08195-5). Merrill.

Diagnosis & Early Management of Trauma Emergencies: A Manual for the Emergency Service. Ed. by Robert J. Touloukian & Thomas J. Krizek. (Illus.). 160p. 1974. text ed. 15.75 (ISBN 0-398-03133-9); pap. text ed. 9.75 (ISBN 0-398-03134-7). C C Thomas.

Diagnosis & Genetics of Defective Color Vision. Hans Kalmus. 1965. 25.00 (ISBN 0-08-011119-X). Pergamon.

Diagnosis & Interpretations of Changing Patterns in Multiple Disease States. Branwood. 1981. price not set (ISBN 0-89352-025-X). Masson Pub.

Diagnosis & Management of Acute Respiratory Failure. Farokh E. Udwadia. (Illus.). 1979. text ed. 29.95x (ISBN 0-19-561072-5). Oxford U Pr.

Diagnosis & Management of Depression. Aaron T. Beck. LC 73-83290. 160p. 1973. 11.95x (ISBN 0-8122-7674-4, Pa Paperbks). U of Pa Pr.

Diagnosis & Management of the Fetus & Neonate at Risk: A Guide for Team Care. 4th ed. S. Gorham Babson et al. LC 79-16957. (Illus.). 1979. text ed. 21.95 (ISBN 0-8016-0415-X). Mosby.

Diagnosis & Nonsurgical Management of Chronic Pain. Ed. by Nelson Hendler. LC 78-51277. 1980. 25.00 (ISBN 0-89004-289-6). Raven.

Diagnosis & Remediation of Reading Problems. Jack Rudman. (College Proficiency Examination Ser: CLEP-38). (Cloth bdg. avail. on request). pap. 9.95 (ISBN 0-8373-5438-2). Natl Learning.

Diagnosis & Remediation of the Disabled Reader. Eldon E. Ekwall. 512p. 1976. text ed. 17.95x (ISBN 0-205-05416-1). Allyn.

Diagnosis & Treatment in Clinical Child Psychiatry. Eva A. Frommer. (Illus.). 1972. 24.00x (ISBN 0-433-10910-6). Intl Ideas.

Diagnosis & Treatment of Alcoholism. 2nd ed. Gary G. Forrest. 364p. 1978. 22.50 (ISBN 0-398-03779-5); pap. 15.75 (ISBN 0-398-03780-9). C C Thomas.

Diagnosis & Treatment of Brain Ischemia, Vol. 30. Ed. by Andrew L. Carney & Evelyn M. Anderson. (Advances in Neurology). 450p. 1981. 43.00 (ISBN 0-89004-529-1). Raven.

Diagnosis & Treatment of Breast Cancer: International Clinical Congress. Edward F. Lewison & Albert C. Montague. (Illus.). 268p. 1981. write for info. (4954-2). Williams & Wilkins.

Diagnosis & Treatment of Cardiac Arrhythmias: Proceedings. International Symposium on Diagnosis & Treatment of Cardiac Arrhythmias, Barcelona, Spain, 5-8 October 1977. Ed. by A. J. Bayes De Luna. (Illus.). 1980. 220.00 (ISBN 0-08-024426-2). Pergamon.

Diagnosis & Treatment of Dento-Facial Abnormalities. Viken Sassouni & George C. Sotereanos. (Illus.). 512p. 1974. 39.75 (ISBN 0-398-02888-5). C C Thomas.

Diagnosis & Treatment of Fungal Infections: A Symposium. Harry M. Robinson, Jr. (Illus.). 580p. 1974. 41.75 (ISBN 0-398-02789-7). C C Thomas.

Diagnosis & Treatment of Incorporated Radionuclides. (Proceedings Ser.). (Illus.). 1976. pap. 62.25 (ISBN 92-0-020176-8, ISP411, IAEA). Unipub.

Diagnosis & Treatment of Radioactive Poisoning. (Illus.). 1963. 17.25 (ISBN 92-0-020163-6, IAEA). Unipub.

Diagnosis of Acute Abdominal Pain. F. T. De Dombal. (Illus.). 192p. 1981. pap. text ed. 12.50 (ISBN 0-443-01901-0). Churchill.

Diagnosis of Bone & Joint Disorders with Emphasis on Articlar Abnormalities. Donald Resnick & Gen Niwayama. (Illus.). 2200p. Date not set. price not set (ISBN 0-7216-7561-1). Saunders. Postponed.

Diagnosis of Learning Disabilities. Clark Johnson. 400p. 1981. text ed. 15.00x (ISBN 0-87108-236-5). Pruett.

Diagnosis of the Brazilian Crisis. Celso Furtado. Tr. by Suzette Macedo. 1965. 16.50x (ISBN 0-520-00444-2). U of Cal Pr.

Diagnosti Approaches to Malformed Fetus, Abortus, Stillborn & Deceased Newborn. Ed. by Mitchell S. Golbus & Bryan D. Hall. LC 79-2369. (Alan R. Liss Ser.: Vol. 15, No. 5a). 1979. 22.00 (ISBN 0-8451-1028-4). March of Dimes.

Diagnostic & Corrective Procedure in Teaching Reading. Selma E. Herr. spiral bdg. 2.95x (ISBN 0-87543-507-6). Lucas.

Diagnostic & Prescriptive Reading Instruction: A Guide for Classroom Teachers. Martha C. Cheek & Earl H. Cheek, Jr. 1980. text ed. 13.95x (ISBN 0-697-06019-5); inst. manual avail. (ISBN 0-697-06028-4). Wm C Brown.

Diagnostic & Remedial Reading for Classroom & Clinic. 4th ed. Robert M. Wilson. (Illus.). 448p. 1981. text ed. 17.95 (ISBN 0-675-08048-7); instr's. manual 3.95 (ISBN 0-686-69489-9). Merrill.

Diagnostic & Statistical Manual of Mental Disorders. 2nd ed. American Psychiatric Association, Committee on Nomenclature & Statistics. 1968. pap. 3.50 o.p. (ISBN 0-685-24852-6, 145). Am Psychiatric.

Diagnostic Electron Microscopy of Tumors. F. N. Ghadially. LC 79-42839. 1980. text ed. 98.95 (ISBN 0-407-00156-5). Butterworths.

Diagnostic Imaging in Pulmonary Disease. Charles E. Putman. 1981. 32.50 (ISBN 0-8385-1682-3). ACC.

Diagnostic Immunohistochemistry of Tumor Markers. Delellis. 1981. write for info. Masson Pub.

Diagnostic Immunology & Serology: A Clinician's Guide. J. D. Wilson. Ed. by Sandra I. Simpson. 161p. 1980. pap. text ed. 14.95 (ISBN 0-909337-01-2). ADIS Pr.

Diagnostic-Language Development Approach to Individualized Reading Instruction. Roger L. Rouch & Shirley Birr. 1976. 11.95 o.p. (ISBN 0-13-208553-4). P-H.

Diagnostic Methods in Viral Hepatitis: Proceedings. Symposium Held by European Group for Rapid Virus Diagnosis, London, Jan. 1978. Ed. by Colin R. Howard & P. S. Gardner. LC 78-20364. (Laboratory & Research Methods in Biology & Medicine: Vol. 2). 1978. 14.00x (ISBN 0-8451-1651-7). A R Liss.

Diagnostic Microbiology: A Textbook for the Isolation & Identification of Pathogenic Microorganisms. 5th ed. Sydney M. Finegold et al. LC 77-28251. (Illus.). 1978. text ed. 24.95 (ISBN 0-8016-0421-4). Mosby.

Diagnostic Neuropathology. Garcia. 1981. price not set. Masson Pub.

Diagnostic Parasitology: Clinical Laboratory Manual. 2nd ed. Lynne S. Garcia & Lawrence R. Ash. LC 78-31497. (Illus.). 1979. pap. text ed. 14.95 (ISBN 0-8016-1741-3). Mosby.

Diagnostic Pathways in Clinical Medicine. B. J. Essex. (Medicine in the Tropics Ser.). (Illus.). 208p. 1981. pap. text ed. 17.00 (ISBN 0-443-02059-0). Churchill.

Diagnostic Pathways in Clinical Medicine. 2nd ed. Benjamin J. Essex. (Medicine in the Tropics Ser.). (Illus.). Date not set. pap. text ed. 19.00 (ISBN 0-443-02059-0). Churchill.

Diagnostic Pointers in Electrocardiology, Vol. 2. Leo Schamroth. LC 79-51385. (Cardiology & Critical Care Ser.). (Illus.). 248p. 1979. text ed. 24.95 (ISBN 0-89303-004-X). Charles.

Diagnostic Procedures. Ed. by Ralph C. Scott. (Clinical Cardiology & Diabetes: Vol. I, Part II). (Illus.). 352p. 1981. 32.00 (ISBN 0-87993-142-6). Futura Pub.

Diagnostic Procedures in Veterinary Bacteriology & Mycology. 3rd. ed. G. R. Carter. (Illus.). 496p. 1979. 32.75 (ISBN 0-398-03792-2). C C Thomas.

Diagnostic Process in Child Psychiatry, Vol. 3. GAP Committee on Child Psychiatry. (Report No. 38). 1957. pap. 2.00 (ISBN 0-87318-048-8). Adv Psychiatry.

Diagnostic Pulmonary Cytology. Geno Saccomanno. LC 78-8285. (Illus.). 1978. text ed. 45.00 (ISBN 0-89189-050-5, 16-3-003-00). Am Soc Clinical.

Diagnostic Radiology, 1979. Ed. by Alexander R. Margulis & Charles A. Gooding. (Illus.). 125p. 1979. 96.25 (ISBN 0-89352-056-X). Masson Pub.

Diagnostic Respiratory Cytopathology. William W. Johnston & William J. Frable. LC 79-84478. (Masson Monographs in Diagnostic Cytopathology). 328p. 1979. 41.25 (ISBN 0-89352-047-0). Masson Pub.

Diagnostic Studies. Walter R. Mahler. (Illus.). 224p. 1974. text ed. 16.95 (ISBN 0-201-04437-4). A-W.

Diagnostic Teaching of the Language Arts. Marie Marcus. LC 76-52400. 1977. text ed. 21.95x (ISBN 0-471-56854-6). Wiley.

Diagnostic Techniques in Pulmonary Disease, Pt. 1. Sackner. 746p. 1980. 49.50 (ISBN 0-8247-1059-2). Dekker.

Diagnostic Transmission Electron Miscroscopy. Erlandson. 1981. write for info. Masson Pub.

Diagnostic Ultrasonics: Principles & Use of Instruments. 2nd ed. W. N. McDicken. LC 80-20750. 360p. 1981. 39.50 (ISBN 0-471-05740-1, Pub. by Wiley Med). Wiley.

Diagnostic Ultrasound. Ed. by G. Kossoff. 1980. with 400 slides 609.75 (ISBN 0-444-90056-X, Excerpta Medica). Elsevier.

Diagnostic Ultrasound in Clinical Obstetrics & Gynecology. H. E. Thompson & R. L. Bernstine. 192p. 1978. 34.95 (ISBN 0-471-86080-8, 1-322). Wiley.

Diagnostico Enzimatico en las Enfermedades de Corazon, Higado y Pancreas. L. Adolph & Rita Lorenz. (Illus.). 126p. 1980. soft cover 13.25 (ISBN 3-8055-0506-X). S Karger.

Diagnostics. Ed. by Intermed Communications. (Nurse's Reference Library). (Illus.). 1200p. 1981. text ed. 19.95 (ISBN 0-916730-29-8). Intermed Comm.

Diagnostik und Therapie des Prostatakarzinoms. Ed. by H. Goettinger. (Beitraece zur Urologie: Vol. 1). 1979. soft cover 24.00 (ISBN 3-8055-0294-X). S Karger.

Diagram Group. Diagram Group. Date not set. 19.95 (ISBN 0-686-69378-7). Facts on File.

Diagram of Synoptic Relationships. Allan Barr. Repr. of 1938 ed. text ed. 9.50x (ISBN 0-567-02021-5). Attic Pr.

Diagrams for Faceting. Glenn Vargas & Martha Vargas. LC 75-21404. (Illus.). 190p. 1975. 12.00 (ISBN 0-917646-02-9). Glenn Vargas.

Diakoptics & Networks. H. H. Happ. (Mathematics in Science & Engineering Ser.: Vol. 69). 1971. 46.50 (ISBN 0-12-324150-2). Acad Pr.

Dial-a-Word from the Bible. Gordon DeYoung. (Quiz & Puzzle Bks). 1977. pap. 0.95 (ISBN 0-8010-2862-0). Baker Bk.

Dial Leroi Rupert, DJ. Jamie Gilson. 1981. pap. 1.75 (ISBN 0-671-56099-9). Archway.

Dial Nine One Nine. Dave Jackson. 160p. 1981. pap. text ed. 5.95 (ISBN 0-8361-1952-5). Herald Pr.

Dial Nine One One: Modern Emergency Communications Networks. George Leon & Leo G. Sands. (Illus.). 128p. 1975. pap. 3.95 o.p. (ISBN 0-8104-0343-9). Hayden.

Dialect Clash in America: Issues & Answers. Paul D. Brandes & Jeutonne Brewer. LC 76-41248. 1977. 25.00 o.p. (ISBN 0-8108-0936-2). Scarecrow.

Dialect of the English Gypsies. 2nd ed. Bath C. Smart & H. T. Crofton. LC 68-22050. 1968. Repr. of 1875 ed. 18.00 (ISBN 0-8103-3292-2). Gale.

Dialectic of Common Sense: The Master Thinkers. Ivan Svitak. LC 78-65849. 1979. pap. text ed. 9.75 (ISBN 0-8191-0675-5). U Pr of Amer.

Dialectic of Revolution. Chris Arthur. (Philosophy Now Ser.). 1980. text ed. write for info. (ISBN 0-391-00841-2); pap. text ed. write for info. (ISBN 0-391-00842-0). Humanities.

Dialectic of World Politics. Silviu Brucan. LC 77-85349. 1978. 19.95 (ISBN 0-02-904680-7). Free Pr.

Dialectical Criticism & Renaissance Literature. Michael McCanles. 1975. 23.75x (ISBN 0-520-02694-2). U of Cal Pr.

Dialectical Materialism, 3 vols. new ed. Maurice Cornforth. Incl. Vol. 1. Materialism & the Dialectical Method. pap. 1.45 (ISBN 0-7178-0326-0); Vol. 2. Historical Materialism. pap. 1.65 (ISBN 0-7178-0327-9); Vol. 3. The Theory of Knowledge. pap. 2.75 (ISBN 0-7178-0328-7). 1971. Intl Pub Co.

Dialectical Phenomenology: Marx's Method. Roslyn W. Bologh. (International Library of Phenomenology & Moral Sciences). 1979. 23.50x (ISBN 0-7100-0335-8). Routledge & Kegan.

Dialectical Transformation: A Study of "Dialogue" As a Method for Research & Development in a Rural Milieu. 10p. 1981. pap. 10.00 (ISBN 92-808-0162-7, TUNU 105, UNU). Unipub.

Dialectics & Revolution. David Degrood. (Philosophical Currents Ser.: No. 25). 1980. pap. text ed. 27.50x (ISBN 9-0603-2154-5). Humanities.

Dialectics & Revolution, Vol. 1. David H. Degrood. (Philosophical Currents Ser.: No. 21). 1978. pap. text ed. 23.00x (ISBN 90-6032-097-2). Humanities.

Dialectics & Revolution, Vol. 2. David H. Degrood. (Philosophical Currents Ser.: No. 25). (Orig.). 1978. pap. text ed. 28.50x (ISBN 90-6032-154-5). Humanities.

Dialectics of Social Life: Alarms & Escursions in Anthropological Theory. Robert Murphy. (Morningside Book). 272p. 1980. pap. 6.00x (ISBN 0-231-05069-0). Columbia U Pr.

Dialectics of Third World Development. Ed. by Ingolf Vogeler & Anthony De Souza. LC 79-53704. (Illus.). 366p. 1980. text ed. 20.50 (ISBN 0-916672-33-6); pap. text ed. 9.50 (ISBN 0-916672-35-2). Allanheld.

Dialectologia Hispanoamericana: Estudios Actuales. Gary E. Scavnicky. 127p. (Orig., Span.). 1980. pap. text ed. 6.95 (ISBN 0-87840-080-X). Georgetown U Pr.

Dialectology. J. K. Chambers & P. Trudgill. LC 79-41604. (Cambridge Textbooks in Linguistics). (Illus.). 210p. 1980. 34.50 (ISBN 0-521-22401-2); pap. 11.95 (ISBN 0-521-29473-8). Cambridge U Pr.

Dialects for the Actor. Robert Westrom. 69p. (Orig.). 1978. pap. 2.95 (ISBN 0-938230-01-8). Westrom.

Dialects for the Stage. Evangeline Machlin. LC 75-7880. 1975. 39.95; tapes incl. (ISBN 0-87830-040-6). Theatre Arts.

Dialogic Imagination: Four Essays. M. M. Bakhtin. Ed. by Michael Holquist. Tr. by Caryl Emerson from Rus. LC 80-15450. (No. 1). 480p. 1981. text ed. 25.00x (ISBN 0-292-71527-7). U of Tex Pr.
Dialogue & Discourse: A Socio-Linguistic Approach to Modern Drama Dialogue & Naturally-Occurring Conversation. Deirdre Burton. 220p. 1980. 30.00 (ISBN 0-7100-0560-1). Routledge & Kegan.
Dialogue Concerning the Two Chief World Systems- Ptolemaic & Copernican. 3rd ed. Galileo Galilei. Tr. & intro. by Stillman Drake. 1980. 30.00x (ISBN 0-520-04104-6). U of Cal Pr.
Dialogue Concerning the Two Chief World Systems-Ptolemaic & Copernican. 2nd rev. ed. Galileo Galilei. Tr. by Stillman Drake. 1967. 25.00x (ISBN 0-520-00449-3); pap. 7.95x (ISBN 0-520-00450-7, CAL66). U of Cal Pr.
Dialogue for Christmas Eve. Mary Edwardine. 2.00 (ISBN 0-8283-1569-8). Branden.
Dialogue in Art: Japan & the West. Ed. by Chisaburoh F. Yamada. LC 73-79772. (Illus.). 334p. 1976. 60.00 (ISBN 0-87011-214-7). Kodansha.
Dialogue: In Search of Jewish-Christian Understanding. John S. Spong & Jack D. Spiro. LC 75-2192. 109p. 1975. pap. 3.50 (ISBN 0-8164-2115-3). Crossroad NY.
Dialogue of Religions. Ninian Smart. LC 79-8730. (Library of Philosophy & Theology). 142p. 1981. Repr. of 1960 ed. lib. bdg. 17.50x (ISBN 0-313-22187-1, SMDR). Greenwood.
Dialogue of St. Catherine of Siena. St. Catherine Of Siena. Tr. & intro. by Algar Thorold. 1976. pap. 4.00 (ISBN 0-89555-037-7, 150). TAN Bks Pubs.
Dialogue on Dialects. Walt Wolfram & Donna Christian. (Dialects & Educational Equity Ser.: No. 1). 1979. pap. 2.50 (ISBN 0-87281-120-4). Ctr Appl Ling.
Dialogue on George Santayana. Ed. by Corliss Lamont. 115p. (Orig.). 1981. pap. 4.95 (ISBN 0-8180-1327-3). Horizon.
Dialogue on John Dewey. Ed. by Corliss Lamont. 155p. (Orig.). 1981. pap. 4.95 (ISBN 0-8180-1328-1). Horizon.
Dialogue on the Soul. Aelred Of Rievaulx. (Cistercian Fathers Ser.: No. 22). Orig. Title: De Anima. 1981. price not set (ISBN 0-87907-222-9). Cistercian Pubns.
Dialogue on Wealth & Welfare: An Alternative View of World Capital Formation, a Report to the Club of Rome. Orio Giarini. (Illus.). 368p. 1980. 48.00 (ISBN 0-08-026088-8); pap. 24.00 (ISBN 0-08-026087-X). Pergamon.
Dialogue with Death: The Spiritual Psychology of the Katha Upanishad. Eknath Easwaran. 288p. (Orig.). 1981. pap. 6.00 (ISBN 0-915132-24-9). Nilgiri Pr.
Dialogue with Photography. Thomas Cooper & Paul Hill. (Illus.). 448p. 1980. 12.95 (ISBN 0-374-13893-1); pap. 6.95 (ISBN 0-374-51544-1). FS&G.
Dialogues. St. Gregory The Great. (Fathers of the Church Ser.: Vol. 39). 15.00 (ISBN 0-8132-0039-3). Cath U Pr.
Dialogues. Jean-Jacques Rousseau. Bd. with Reveries. (Documentation thematique). pap. 2.95 (ISBN 0-685-24456-3, 292). Larousse.
Dialogues Concerning Natural Religion. David Hume. Ed. by Norman K. Smith. 1947. pap. 5.95 (ISBN 0-672-60404-3, LLA174). Bobbs.
Dialogues Concerning Natural Religion: Text & Critical Essays. David Hume. Ed. by Nelson Pike. LC 77-132933. (Text & Critical Essays Ser). (Orig.). 1970. pap. 6.50 (ISBN 0-672-61119-8, TC6). Bobbs.
Dialogues Concerning Two New Sciences. Galileo Galilei. (Illus.). 1914. pap. text ed. 4.00 (ISBN 0-486-60099-8). Dover.
Dialogues Concerning Two New Sciences. Galilei Galileo. (Illus.). 8.50 (ISBN 0-8446-0636-7). Peter Smith.
Dialogues et Situations. 2nd ed. Stefan Max. 1979. cassettes 35.00 (ISBN 0-669-01788-4); cahier de travaux practiques 4.95 (ISBN 0-669-01788-4); cahier de travaux practiques 4.95 (ISBN 0-669-01907-0); cassettes 30.00 (ISBN 0-669-01908-9). Heath.
Dialogues in Metapsychiatry. Thomas Hora. LC 77-8268. 1977. 12.95 (ISBN 0-8164-0352-X). Crossroad NY.
Dialogues in the English & Malaiane Languages. Gothard Arthus. Tr. by A. Spalding. LC 74-80160. (English Experience Ser.: No. 640). 1974. Repr. of 1614 ed. 8.00 (ISBN 90-221-0640-3). Walter J Johnson.
Dialogue's in Turgenev's Novels: Speech Introductory Devices. Ludmila Hellgren. (Stockholm Studies in Russian Literature: No. 12). 148p. 1980. pap. 15.00x (ISBN 91-22-00369-X). Humanities.
Dialogues of Alfred North Whitehead. Alfred N. Whitehead. LC 76-49903. (Illus.). 1977. Repr. of 1954 ed. lib. bdg. 27.75x (ISBN 0-8371-9341-9, WHDI). Greenwood.
Dialogues of G. De Purucker, 3 vols. G. De Purucker. Ed. by Arthur L. Conger. LC 79-65630. 1948. Set. 20.00 (ISBN 0-911500-59-6). Theos U Pr.
Dialogues of Gurdjieff: An Allegorical Work Adventure, Vol. 1. rev., enl. ed. Jan. 314p. 1980. 9.00 (ISBN 0-936380-02-0). Chan Shal Imi.
Dialogues of Modern Philosophy. Philip E. Davis. 1977. pap. text ed. 12.95x o.p. (ISBN 0-205-05511-7). Allyn.
Dialogues of Plato. Plato. Ed. by William C. Greene. Tr. by B. Jowett. 1954. 7.95x o.p. (ISBN 0-87140-858-9). Liveright.
Dialogues of Plato. Plato. Ed. by Justin E. Kaplan. Tr. by Benjamin E. Jowett. pap. 2.95 (ISBN 0-671-42137-9). WSP.
Dialogues on American Politics. Irving L. Horowitz & Seymour M. Lipset. 1978. 12.95 (ISBN 0-19-502449-4). Oxford U Pr.
Dialogues on Art. Edouard Roditi. LC 79-91612. 250p. 1980. pap. 6.95 (ISBN 0-915520-21-4). Ross-Erikson.
Dialogues on the Usefulness of Ancient Medals. Joseph Addison. LC 75-27883. (Renaissance & the Gods Ser.: Vol. 38). (Illus.). 1976. Repr. of 1726 ed. lib. bdg. 73.00 (ISBN 0-8240-2087-1). Garland Pub.
Dialogues with Mothers. Bruno Bettelheim. LC 62-10583. 1962. text ed. 14.95 (ISBN 0-02-903120-6). Free Pr.
Dialoque Philosophique Dans la Litterature Francaise Du Seizieme Siecle. Mustapha K. Benouis. (De Proprietatibus Litterarum, Series Maior: No. 31). 1976. text ed. 48.25x (ISBN 90-2793-201-8). Mouton.
Diamond Book: The Investors Guide to Value, Price & Liquidity. Michael Freedman. LC 80-70145. 222p. 1981. 14.95 (ISBN 0-87094-223-9). Dow Jones-Irwin.
Diamond Exchange. Thomas Chastain. LC 80-1118. 240p. 1981. 10.95 (ISBN 0-385-14438-5). Doubleday.
Diamond Flush. Zeke Masters. 192p. 1980. pap. 1.75 (ISBN 0-671-83435-5). PB.
Diamond Healing: Tibetan Buddhist Medicine & Psychiatry. Terry Clifford. 196p. 1981. pap. 7.95 (ISBN 0-87728-528-4). Weiser.
Diamond Magnates. Brian Roberts. (Illus.). 1973. 8.95 o.p. (ISBN 0-684-14661-4, ScribT). Scribner.
Diamond People. Muarry Schumach. (Illus.). 1981. 12.95 (ISBN 0-393-01404-5). Norton.
Diamond Range. James Wesley. 192p. (YA) 1975. 5.95 (ISBN 0-685-52911-8, Avalon). Bouregy.
Diamond Sutra: Three Mongolian Versions of the Vajracchedika Prajnaparamita. Nicholas Poppe. 1971. 52.50x (ISBN 3-447-00594-7). Intl Pubns Serv.
Diamondola. Mildred Olson. 1980. pap. 3.25 (ISBN 0-8280-0046-8, 04305-9). Review & Herald.
Diamonds. Herbert S. Zim. (Illus.). (gr. 3-7). 1959. PLB 6.48 (ISBN 0-688-31236-5). Morrow.
Diamonds Are Forever. Ian Fleming. 224p. 1980. pap. 1.95 (ISBN 0-515-05516-6). Jove Pubns.
Diamonds Are Trouble. Scott Corbett. LC 67-17998. 1967. reinforced bdg. 4.95 o.p. (ISBN 0-03-089822-6). HR&W.
Diamonds at the Bottom of the Sea & Other Stories. Desmond Hogan. 1980. 8.95 (ISBN 0-8076-0934-X). Braziller.
Diamonds Wild. Alan Caillou. 1979. pap. 2.25 (ISBN 0-380-43588-8, 43588). Avon.
Diana & Nikon: Essays on the Aesthetic of Photography. Janet Malcolm. (Illus.). 176p. 1980. pap. 8.95 (ISBN 0-87923-387-7). Godine.
Diana Ross. Patricia M. Eldred. (Rock 'n Pop Stars Ser.). (Illus.). (gr. 4-12). 1975. PLB 5.95 (ISBN 0-87191-462-X); pap. 2.75 o. p. (ISBN 0-89812-112-4). Creative Ed.
Diana Ross - Supreme Lady. Connie Berman. 1978. pap. 1.75 o.p. (ISBN 0-445-04283-4). Popular Lib.
Diana Show, Pictures Through a Plastic Lens. David Featherstone. LC 80-80296. (Untitled 21 Ser.). (Illus., Orig.). 1980. pap. 7.95 (ISBN 0-933286-17-1). Friends Photography.
Diane Clark's Microwave Cookbook. Diane Clark. 1981. 14.95 (ISBN 0-8015-2023-1, Hawthorn). Dutton.
Diaphragm Walls & Anchorages. Institute of Civil Engineers. 234p. 1980. 79.00x (ISBN 0-7277-0005-7, Pub. by Telford England). State Mutual Bk.
Diaries of a Cabinet Minister, III. Ed. by Richard Crossman. LC 76-30680. (Illus.). 1978. 22.95 o.p. (ISBN 0-03-040871-7). HR&W.
Diaries of George Washington: January 1790 to December1799, Vol. 6. George Washington. Ed. by Donald Jackson. 1980. 30.00x (ISBN 0-8139-0807-8). U Pr of Va.
Diaries of Julia Cowles. Julia Cowles. Ed. by Mosely. 1931. 24.50x (ISBN 0-685-89746-X). Elliots Bks.
Diaries of Lewis Carroll, 2 vols. Charles L. Dodgson. Ed. & suppl. by Roger L. Green. LC 74-110268. (Illus.). Repr. of 1954 ed. lib. bdg. 33.00x (ISBN 0-8371-4494-9, DOLC). Greenwood.
Diaries of Lord Lugard: East Africa 1889-92, 3 vols. Lord Lugard et al. Ed. by Perham & Bull. (Illus.). 1959. 39.00 set o.p. (ISBN 0-571-03632-5, Pub. by Faber & Faber). Vol. 1 (ISBN 0-571-03634-1). Vol. 2 (ISBN 0-571-03633-3). Vol. 3 (ISBN 0-571-03632-5). Merrimack Bk Serv.
Diaries of Private Horace Bruckshaw, Royal Marine Light Infantry, Nineteen Fifteen to Nineteen Sixteen. Ed. by Martin Middlebrook. (Illus.). xxiii, 229p. 1980. 18.50 (ISBN 0-208-01879-4, Archon). Shoe String.
Diaries of Tchaikovsky. Petr I. Tchaikovsky. Tr. by Wladimir Lakond. LC 79-138104. (Illus.). 365p. 1973. Repr. of 1945 ed. lib. bdg. 28.50x (ISBN 0-8371-5680-7, CHDI). Greenwood.
Diaries of the Popish Plot. Ed. by Douglas Greene. LC 77-938. 1977. 40.00 (ISBN 0-8201-1288-7). Schol Facsimilies.
Diario. Bernardo De Galvez. 52p. 1966. pap. 5.00. South Pass Pr.
Diary. Philip Henslowe. Ed. by R. A. Foakes & R. T. Rickert. 1961. 80.00 (ISBN 0-521-05244-0). Cambridge U Pr.
Diary, 3 Vols. Samuel Pepys. 1953. Vol. 1. 8.50x (ISBN 0-460-00053-5, Evman); Vol. 2. 12.95x (ISBN 0-460-00054-3); Vol. 3. 12.95 (ISBN 0-460-00055-1). Dutton.
Diary After Death. Franklin Loehr. 1976. pap. 1.50 (ISBN 0-89129-057-5). Jove Pubns.
Diary & Correspondence of Salmon P. Chase. Salmon P. Chase. LC 74-75301. (Law, Politics, & History Ser). 1971. Repr. of 1903 ed. lib. bdg. 49.50 (ISBN 0-306-71264-4). Da Capo.
Diary & Letters of Gouverneur Morris, 2 Vols. Gouverneur Morris. Ed. by Anne C. Morris. LC 70-98691. (American Public Figures Ser). 1969. Repr. of 1888 ed. lib. bdg. 95.00 (ISBN 0-306-71835-9). Da Capo.
Diary by E. B. B. Ed. by Philip Kelley & Ronald Hudson. LC 68-18390. 1969. 17.50x (ISBN 0-8214-0047-9). Ohio U Pr.
Diary for Teachers of Young Children. Freda Cliff & Philip Cliff. pap. 1.95x (ISBN 0-8192-4036-2). Morehouse.
Diary of a Cotswold Parson. F. E. Witts. Ed. by David Verey. (Illus.). 192p. 1980. text ed. 19.25x (ISBN 0-686-64329-1). Humanities.
Diary of a Country Priest. Georges Bernanos. 240p. 1974. pap. 2.95 (ISBN 0-385-09600-3, Im). Doubleday.
Diary of a Dead Man, Eighteen Sixty-Two to Eighteen Sixty-Four. Ed. by J. P. Ray. (Illus.). 430p. (Orig.). 1979. pap. 4.00 (ISBN 0-686-27871-2, Pub. by Eastern Natl Park). Eastern Acorn.
Diary of a Deaf Mute. David Chagall. 1971. pap. 3.50 (ISBN 0-916538-01-X). Millenium Hse.
Diary of a Delinquent Episode. Jane Sparrow. (Orig.). 1976. pap. 7.95 (ISBN 0-7100-8340-8). Routledge & Kegan.
Diary of a Divorce. Valerie Cooper. (Orig.). 1981. pap. 3.95 (ISBN 0-88449-054-8). Vision Hse.
Diary of a Divorced Mother. Marilyn M. Willison. 192p. 1981. pap. 2.50 (ISBN 0-553-14501-0). Bantam.
Diary of a Frantic Kid Sister. Hila Colman. (gr. 4-6). 1975. pap. 1.75 (ISBN 0-671-42452-1, 29625-6). Archway.
Diary of a Frantic Kid Sister. Hila Colman. (gr. 4-6). 1975. pap. 1.50 (ISBN 0-671-29986-7). PB.
Diary of a Lover. Richard K. Sharon. 272p. (Orig.). 1975. pap. 2.50 (ISBN 0-446-91703-6). Warner Bks.
Diary of a Man in Despair. Friedrich P. Reck-Malleczewen. Tr. by Paul Rubens. LC 74-85783. 1970. 6.95 o.s.i. (ISBN 0-02-601400-9). Macmillan.
Diary of a Nobody. George Grossmith & Weedon Grossmith. 1962. 8.00x o.p. (ISBN 0-460-00963-X, Evman); pap. 3.50 (ISBN 0-460-01963-5). Dutton.
Diary of a Novel: The Story of Writing Margaret's Story. Eugenia Price. LC 80-7869. 160p. 1980. 9.95 (ISBN 0-690-01937-8). Lippincott & Crowell.
Diary of a Russian Priest. Alexander Elchaninov. Tr. by Iswolsky. (Illus.). 1967. 12.95 (ISBN 0-571-08029-4, Pub. by Faber & Faber). Merrimack Bk Serv.
Diary of a Sea Captain's Wife: Tales of Santa Cruz Island. Margaret H. Eaton & Vera E. Amey. Ed. by Janice Timbrook. (Illus.). 272p. 1980. 16.50 (ISBN 0-87461-032-X); pap. 9.50 (ISBN 0-87461-033-8). McNally.
Diary of a Student Social Worker. Jane Sparrow. 1978. 14.00 (ISBN 0-7100-8857-4). Routledge & Kegan.
Diary of a Yankee-Hater. Bob Marshall. 256p. (Orig.). 1981. pap. 7.95 (ISBN 0-531-09945-8). Watts.
Diary of Adolf Hitler. 225p. 1980. 14.95 (ISBN 0-9605224-1-7); pap. 8.88 (ISBN 0-9605224-0-9). Ancient Age.
Diary of an Artist. Raphael Soyer. LC 77-4798. (Illus.). 1977. 15.95 o.p. (ISBN 0-915220-29-6); deluxe ed. 200.00 o.p. (ISBN 0-915220-33-4). New Republic.
Diary of an Early American Boy. Eric Sloane. LC 62-18313. 1977. pap. 4.95 (ISBN 0-345-29451-3). Ballantine.
Diary of an Old Man. Junichiro Tanizaki. Tr. by Howard Hibbett from Jap. (Perigee Japanese Library). 320p. Date not set. pap. 5.95 (ISBN 0-399-50524-5, Perigee). Putnam.
Diary of Anais Nin, 7 vols. Anais Nin. 1978. Set. pap. 22.50 (ISBN 0-15-626034-4, Harv). HarBraceJ.
Diary of Anna Green Winslow, a Boston Schoolgirl of 1771. Anna G. Winslow. Ed. by Allic M. Earle. LC 71-124586. (Illus.). 1970. Repr. of 1894 ed. 15.00 (ISBN 0-8103-3586-7). Gale.
Diary of Anne Frank. Adapted by Linda A. Cadrain. (Contemporary Motivators Ser.). (Illus.). 32p. (Orig.). (gr. 4-12). 1979. pap. text ed. 1.25 (ISBN 0-88301-308-8) (ISBN 0-686-65677-6). Pendulum Pr.
Diary of Brigham Young, 1857. Ed. by Everett L. Cooley. (Utah, the Mormons, & the West Ser). 132p. 1981. 17.50 (ISBN 0-87480-195-8, Tanner). U of Utah Pr.
Diary of Ebenezer Parkman 1703-1782: 1719-1755, Pt. 1. Ed. by Francis G. Walett. LC 68-30686. 316p. 1974. 22.50x (ISBN 0-912296-04-6, Dist. by U. Pr. of Va.). Am Antiquarian.
Diary of Evil. Violet Hawthorne. 1976. pap. 1.25 o.p. (ISBN 0-685-69153-5, LB352ZK, Leisure Bks). Nordon Pubns.
Diary of Gathorne Hardy, Later Lord Cranbook, 1866-1892: Political Selections. Ed. by Nancy E. Johnson. 650p. 1981. 144.00 (ISBN 0-19-822622-5). Oxford U Pr.
Diary of His Excellency Ching-Shan: Being a Chinese Account of the Boxer Trouble. Ching-Shan. Tr. by Jan J. Duyvendak from Chinese. (Studies in Chinese History & Civilization). 134p. 1977. Repr. of 1924 ed. 14.50 (ISBN 0-89093-074-0). U Pubns Amer.
Diary of Humphrey O'Sullivan 1827-1835. Humphrey O'Sullivan. Tr. by Tomas De Bhaldraithe from Irish. Orig. Title: Cin Lae Amhlaoibh. (Illus.). 139p. 1979. pap. 5.50 (ISBN 0-85342-588-4). Irish Bk Ctr.
Diary of Isaac Backus, 3 vols. Isaac Backus. Ed. by William G. McLoughlin. LC 76-12018. (Illus.). 1780p. 1980. Set. 120.00x (ISBN 0-87057-148-6, Pub. by Brown U Pr). Univ Pr of New England.
Diary of John Manningham of the Middle Temple, 1602-1603. John Manningham. Ed. by Robert P. Sorlien. LC 74-22553. 481p. 1976. text ed. 27.50x (ISBN 0-87451-113-5). U Pr of New Eng.
Diary of Joseph Farington, R.A, 2 vols. Ed. by Kenneth Garlick & Angus MacIntyre. (Studies in British Art Ser.). 1979. Set. 60.00x (ISBN 0-300-02314-6); Vol 1. write for info. (ISBN 0-300-02294-8); Vol. 2. write for info. (ISBN 0-300-02295-6). Yale U Pr.
Diary of Kenneth Macrae. Ed. by Iain H. Murray. (Illus.). 535p. 1980. 16.95 (ISBN 0-85151-297-6). Banner of Truth.
Diary of Marquis Kido, Nineteen Thirty-One to Nineteen Forty-Five: Selected Translation Selected Translations into English. Marquis K. Koichi. 500p. 1980. 34.00 (ISBN 0-89093-273-5). U Pubns Amer.
Diary of Michael Floy Jr., Bowery Village, Eighteen Thirty-Three to Eighteen Thirty-Seven. Michael Floy. Ed. by R. A. Brooks. 1941. 47.50 (ISBN 0-686-51371-1). Elliots Bks.
Diary of My Travels in America. Louis Philippe. Tr. by Stephen Becker. (Illus.). 1977. 14.95 o.p. (ISBN 0-440-01844-7). Delacorte.
Diary of One of Garibaldi's Thousand. Giuseppe C. Abba. Tr. by E. R. Vincent from Ital. LC 80-24181. (Oxford Library of Italian Classics). (Illus.). xxi, 166p. 1981. Repr. of 1962 ed. lib. bdg. 18.75x (ISBN 0-313-22446-3, ABDO). Greenwood.
Diary of Prayer: Daily Meditations on the Parables of Jesus. J. Barrie Shepherd. (Orig.). 1981. pap. 5.95 (ISBN 0-664-24352-5). Westminster.
Diary of Private Prayer. John Baillie. 1949. pap. 5.95 (ISBN 0-684-30997-1, ScribT). Scribner.
Diary of Ralph Josselin, 1616-1683. Ralph Josselin. Ed. by Alan Macffarlane. (British Academy Ser.). (Illus.). 1976. 95.00x (ISBN 0-19-725955-3). Oxford U Pr.
Diary of Roger Lowe of Ashton-in-Makerfield, Lancashire Sixteen Sixty-Three to Sixteen Seventy-Four. Roger Lowe. Ed. by W. L. Sachse. 1938. 27.50 (ISBN 0-686-51372-X). Elliots Bks.
Diary of Samuel Pepys. Samuel Pepys. Ed. by O. F. Morshead. (Illus.). 1960. 8.50 (ISBN 0-8446-2727-5). Peter Smith.

Diary of Samuel Pepys, 9 vols. Samuel Pepys. Ed. by Robert Latham & William Matthews. Incl. Vol. 1. 1660. 1970. 27.50 (ISBN 0-520-01575-4); Vol. 2. 1661. 22.75 (ISBN 0-520-01576-2); Vol. 3. 1662. 22.75 (ISBN 0-520-01577-0); Vol. 4. 1663. 22.75 (ISBN 0-520-01857-5); Vol. 5. 1664. 21.50 (ISBN 0-520-01858-3); Vol. 6. 1665. 21.50 (ISBN 0-520-01859-1); Vol. 7. 1666. 22.75 (ISBN 0-520-02094-4); Vol. 8. 1667. 24.50 (ISBN 0-520-02095-2); Vol. 9. 1668-1669. 24.50 (ISBN 0-520-02096-0). U of Cal Pr.

Diary of Sir David Hamilton. David Hamilton. Ed. by Philip Roberts. 220p. 1975. 36.00x (ISBN 0-19-822364-1). Oxford U Pr.

Diary of Sir Edward Walter Hamilton, Eighteen-Eighty to Eighteen-Eighty Five, 2. Edward W. Hamilton. Ed. by Dudley W. Bahlman. 1972. 54.00x (ISBN 0-19-822324-2). Oxford U Pr.

Diary of the Discovery Expedition to the Antarctic Regions, 1901-1904. Edward Wilson. 1967. text ed. 25.00x (ISBN 0-7137-0431-4). Humanities.

Diary of Trilby Frost. Dianne Glaser. LC 75-37080. 192p. (gr. 6 up). 1976. 8.95 (ISBN 0-8234-0277-0). Holiday.

Diary of Valery Bryusov (1893-1905) With Reminiscences by V. F. Khodasevich & Marina Tsvetaeva. Ed. by Joan D. Grossman. (Documentary Studies in Modern Russian Poetry). 200p. 1980. 15.75x (ISBN 0-520-03858-4). U of Cal Pr.

Diary of Virginia Woolf: Vol. 2, 1920-1924. Virginia Woolf. LC 78-23882. 1980. pap. 5.95 (ISBN 0-15-626037-9, Harv). HarBraceJ.

Diary of Virginia Woolf: Volume Four 1931-1935. Virginia Woolf. Pref. by Ann O. Bell & Andrew McNeillie. 1981. price not set. HarBraceJ.

Diary with Ingmar Bergman. Vilgot Sjoman. 243p. 1978. 9.95 (ISBN 0-89720-015-2, L136); pap. 5.50 (ISBN 0-89720-016-0). Karoma.

Dias Sin Gloria. Jose R. Estrada. 64p. (Span.). 1980. pap. 1.45 (ISBN 0-311-08213-0, Edit Mundo). Casa Bautista.

Diatomic Interaction Potential Theory, 2 vols. Jerry Goodisman. Incl. Vol. 1. Fundamentals. 1973. 47.00 (ISBN 0-12-290201-7); Vol. 2. Applications. 1973. 52.25 (ISBN 0-12-290202-5). (Physical Chemistry Ser.). Set. 80.00 (ISBN 0-12-290202-5). Acad Pr.

Diatoms in New Zealand, the North Island. N. Foged. (Bibliotheca Phycologica: No. 47). (Illus.). 1979. pap. text ed. 30.00x (ISBN 3-7682-1253-X). Lubrecht & Cramer.

Diatoms of North America. 2nd ed. William C. Vinyard. (Illus.). 1979. pap. 5.95x (ISBN 0-916422-15-1). Mad River.

Diatoms of the Tittabawassee River, Michigan. E. D. Wujek & R. F. Rupp. (Bibliotheca Phycologica: No. 50). (Illus.). 160p. 1981. pap. text ed. 25.00x (ISBN 3-7682-1271-8, Pub. by Cramer Germany). Lubrecht & Cramer.

Dibble & the Great Blob: A Parable for Children Over & Under 21. Jim Ballard. LC 75-25393. (Mandala Ser. in Education). 1975. pap. text ed. 2.50 (ISBN 0-916250-06-7). Irvington.

Dibs: In Search of Self. Virginia M. Axline. 224p. 1976. pap. 2.50 (ISBN 0-345-29536-6). Ballantine.

Diccionario Biblico. Tr. by Merill E. Tenney. (Spanish Bks.). (Span.). 1979. 3.50 (ISBN 0-8297-0540-6); pap. 2.50 (ISBN 0-686-28811-4). Life Pubs Intl.

Diccionario Conciso Griego-Espanol Del Nuevo Testamento. E. Tamez De Foulkes & I. W. De Foulkes. 1978. vinyl 3.50 (ISBN 3-438-06005-1, 56530). United Bible.

Diccionario De Especialidades Farmaceuticas. 26th mexican ed. Ed. by E. Rosenstein. (Span.). 1980. pap. 35.00 (ISBN 0-914768-37-9). Drug Intl Pubns.

Diccionario De la Lengua Espanola. (Span.). 1970. 70.00 (ISBN 0-8277-3007-1). Maxwell Sci Intl.

Diccionario De la Santa Biblia. W. W. Rand. Orig. Title: Dictionary of the Holy Bible. (Illus.). 768p. (Span.). 1969. pap. 10.95 (ISBN 0-89922-003-7). Edit Caribe.

Diccionario de Terminos Filologicos. 3rd ed. Fernando L. Carreter. 444p. (Espn.). 1977. 22.25 (ISBN 84-249-1112-1, S-50129, French & Eur). French & Eur.

Diccionario de 201 Verbos Ingleses. Ruth P. Craig. LC 77-184894. 1972. pap. text ed. 7.95 (ISBN 0-8120-0417-5). Barron.

Diccionario Del Ingles Americano. Gladys Lipton & Olivia Munoz. (Illus.). 368p. (gr. 10-12). 1981. pap. 2.95 (ISBN 0-8120-2319-6). Barron.

Diccionario Enciclopedico Abreviado, 7 vols. & 2 vol supplement. 7th ed. (Span.). 1954. 240.00 (ISBN 0-8277-3008-X). Maxwell Sci Intl.

Diccionario Enciclopedico Espasa, 12 vols. (Span.). 1978. Set. 165.00. Pergamon.

Diccionario Enciclopedico Illustrado Sopena, 5 vols. (Span.). 1978. Set. 425.00. Pergamon.

Diccionario Enciclopedico Labor, 8 vols. & 2 supplements. (Span.). 1975. 485.00 (ISBN 0-8277-3009-8). Maxwell Sci Intl.

Diccionario Enciclopedico Salvat, 20 vols. new ed. (Span.). 1972-1976. 675.00 (ISBN 0-8277-3010-1). Maxwell Sci Intl.

Diccionario Enciclopedico Uteha, 13 vols. Date not set. price not set o.p. (ISBN 0-8277-3011-X). Maxwell Sci Intl.

Diccionario Everest Punto English-Spanish Spanish-English. 2.95 (ISBN 84-241-1211-3, 22882). Larousse.

Diccionario General de Bibliografia Espanola, 7 vols. D. Hidalgo. Repr. of 1881 ed. Set. 279.50 (ISBN 3-4870-4678-4). Adler.

Diccionario Ideologico. Casares. (Span). 47.50x (ISBN 0-686-00066-8). Colton Bk.

Diccionario Ilustrado de la Biblia. Ed. by Wilton M. Nelson. (Illus.). 735p. (Span.). 1974. 24.95 (ISBN 0-89922-033-9); pap. 15.95 (ISBN 0-89922-099-1). Edit Caribe.

Diccionario Porrua De Historia, Biografia Y Geographia De Mexico, 2 Vols. 2nd ed. 75.00x o.s.i. (ISBN 0-686-00856-1). Colton Bk.

Dice Cup: Selected Prose Poems. Max Jacob. Ed. by Michael Brownstein. Tr. by John Ashbery et al. LC 79-26610. 122p. (Orig.). 1980. pap. 5.00 (ISBN 0-915342-32-4). SUN.

Dice Games. John Belton & Joella Cramblit. LC 75-43625. (Games & Activities Ser.). (Illus.). 48p. (gr. k-3). 1976. 9.30 (ISBN 0-8172-0024-X); PLB 6.60 (ISBN 0-8172-0023-1). Raintree Pubs.

Dice Games New & Old. William E. Tredd. (Oleander Games & Pastimes Ser.: Vol. 3). (Illus.). 64p. 1981. 9.95 (ISBN 0-906672-00-7); pap. 4.75 (ISBN 0-906672-01-5). Oleander Pr.

Dicho y Hecho: Beginning Spanish: A Simplified Approach. Albert C. Dawson & Laila M. Dawson. LC 80-19506. 352p. 1981. text ed. 13.95 (ISBN 0-471-06476-9); tchr's ed. 7.00 (ISBN 0-471-08577-4); wkbk. avail. (ISBN 0-471-06103-4); tapes 1.00 (ISBN 0-471-06475-0). Wiley.

Dick & Jane As Victims: Sex Stereotyping in Children's Readers. 2nd ed. LC 74-77374. 1975. pap. 3.00 (ISBN 0-9600724-1-1). Women on Words.

Dick Walker's Angling: Theory & Practice, Past, Present & to Come. Richard Walker. LC 79-51097. (Illus.). 1979. 19.95 (ISBN 0-7153-7814-7). David & Charles.

Dick Whittington. (Illus.). Arabic 2.50x (ISBN 0-685-82820-4). Intl Bk Ctr.

Dick Whittington & His Amazing Cat. Pat Hume. (Orig.). 1980. playscript 2.00 (ISBN 0-87602-230-1). Anchorage.

Dickens & Charity. Norris Pope, Jr. 1978. 18.00x (ISBN 0-231-04478-X). Columbia U Pr.

Dickens & Dickensiana: A Catalogue of the Richard Gimbel Collection in the Yale University Library. John B Podeschi. LC 79-66938. 594p. 1981. text ed. 65.00x (ISBN 0-300-03506-3). Yale U Pr.

Dickens & Ellen Ternan. Ada Nisbet. 1952. 15.00x (ISBN 0-520-00946-0). U of Cal Pr.

Dickens & Kafka; a Mutual Interpretation. Mark Spilka. 7.50 (ISBN 0-8446-0928-5). Peter Smith.

Dickens & Melville in Their Time. Pearl C. Solomon. LC 74-13307. 1975. 12.50x (ISBN 0-231-03889-5). Columbia U Pr.

Dickens & Reality. John Romano. LC 77-10745. 1978. 15.00x (ISBN 0-231-04246-9). Columbia U Pr.

Dickens at Play. S. J. Newman. 1981. 14.95 (ISBN 0-312-19980-5). St Martin.

Dickens Centennial Essays. Ed. by Ada Nisbet & Blake Nevius. 1971. 18.50x (ISBN 0-520-01874-5). U of Cal Pr.

Dicken's Doctors. David Smithers. 1979. text ed. 17.25 (ISBN 0-08-023386-4). Pergamon.

Dickens, Money & Society. Grahame Smith. 1968. 19.50x (ISBN 0-520-01190-2). U of Cal Pr.

Dickens on the Romantic Side of Familiar Things: Bleak House & the Novel Tradition. Robert Newsom. LC 77-23476. 1977. 20.00x (ISBN 0-231-04244-2). Columbia U Pr.

Dickens: The Critical Heritage. Philip Collins. (Critical Heritage Ser.). 1971. 27.00x (ISBN 0-7100-6907-3). Routledge & Kegan.

Dickins & the Suspended Quotation. Mark Lambert. LC 80-22072. 208p. 1981. 16.50 (ISBN 0-300-02555-6). Yale U Pr.

Dickinson: The Modern Idiom. David Porter. LC 80-24322. 336p. 1981. text ed. 20.00 (ISBN 0-674-20444-1). Harvard U Pr.

Dickinson's American Historical Fiction. 4th ed. Virginia B. Gerhardstein. LC 80-23450. 328p. 1981. 15.00 (ISBN 0-8108-1362-9). Scarecrow.

Dicta-Typing: A Short Course. Farmer & Brown. 72p. 1974. text ed. 4.60 wkbk. (ISBN 0-7715-0861-1); tchr's. manual, 136p. 28.33 (ISBN 0-7715-0862-X). Forkner.

Dictating Effectively: A Time Saving Manual. Jefferson D. Bates. (Illus.). 1980. 12.50 (ISBN 0-87491-411-6); pap. 5.95 (ISBN 0-87491-414-0). Acropolis.

Dictation Book. rev. ed. Auren Uris. 113p. pap. text ed. 8.95 (ISBN 0-935220-05-4). Intl Word Process.

Dictionaire De Literature Contemporaire. Claude Bonnefoy et al. 22.50 (ISBN 2-7113-0077-3). Gaylord Prof Pubns.

Dictionaire Des Termes Economiques et Commerciaux: Francais-Arabe. Mustapha Henni. 20.00x. Intl Bk Ctr.

Dictionaire Francais-Arabe. Louis Saisse. 1980. pap. 7.95x. Intl Bk Ctr.

Dictionaries, Encyclopedias & Other Word-Related Books, 2 vols. 2nd ed. Ed. by Annie M. Brewer. LC 78-31449. 1979. Set. 70.00 (ISBN 0-8103-1131-3); Vol. 1. 92.00 (ISBN 0-8103-1129-1); Vol. 2. 84.00 (ISBN 0-8103-1130-5). Gale.

Dictionarium Historicum, Geographicum, Poeticum. Charles Stephanus. LC 75-27859. (Renaissance & the Gods Ser.: Vol. 16). (Illus.). 1976. Repr. of 1596 ed. lib. bdg. 73.00 (ISBN 0-8240-2065-0). Garland Pub.

Dictionary. Brooke M. Beebe & Ruth Y. Rosenblatt. LC 77-730283. (Illus.). (gr. 3-5). 1977. pap. text ed. 64.00 (ISBN 0-89290-121-7, A151-SAR). Soc for Visual.

Dictionary & Encyclopaedia of Paper & Paper-Making. 2nd, rev. ed. E. J. Labarre. 500p. 1952. text ed. 71.50 (ISBN 90-265-0037-8, Pub. by Swets Pub Serv Holland). Swets North Am.

Dictionary & Glossary of the Koran. John Penrice. 17.00 (ISBN 0-686-63545-0). Intl Bk Ctr.

Dictionary & Glossary of the Koran, with Copious Grammatical References & Explanations. John Penrice. LC 70-90039. 1969. Repr. of 1873 ed. 17.50x (ISBN 0-8196-0252-3). Biblo.

Dictionary & Glossary of the Koran: With Copious Grammatical References & Explanations of the Text. John Penrice. 176p. 1976. Repr. of 1971 ed. 12.50x o.p. (ISBN 0-87471-787-6). Rowman.

Dictionary & Thesaurus of the Hebrew Language, 8 Vols. Ed. by Eliezer Ben-Yehuda. Set. 150.00 (ISBN 0-498-07038-7, Yoseloff); lea. bd. set o.p. 250.00 (ISBN 0-498-08915-0). A S Barnes.

Dictionary Catalog of the Library of the Pontifical Institute of Mediaeval Studies: First Supplement. Pontifical Institute of Mediaeval Studies, Toronto. (Library Catalogs-Bib. Guides). 1979. lib. bdg. 125.00 (ISBN 0-8161-1061-1). G K Hall.

Dictionary Catalog of the Water Resources Center: Sixth Supplement, 2 vols. Water Resources Center, University at Berkeley, Calif. 1978. Set. lib. bdg. 250.00 (ISBN 0-8161-0244-9). G K Hall.

Dictionary Catalog of the Whitney M. Young, Jr., Memorial Library of Social Work. School of Social Work, Columbia University. (Library Catalogs & Supplements Ser.). 1980. lib. bdg. 1275.00 (ISBN 0-8161-0307-0). G K Hall.

Dictionary-Catalogue of Operas & Operettas, 2 Vols. John Towers. LC 67-25996. (Music Ser). 1967. Repr. of 1910 ed. lib. bdg. 59.50 (ISBN 0-306-70962-7). Da Capo.

Dictionary Catalogue of the Library of the Pontifical Institute of Mediaeval Studies: First Supplement, 5 vols. Pontifical Institute of Mediaeval Studies, Ontario. 1979. Set. lib. bdg. 125.00 (ISBN 0-8161-1061-1). G K Hall.

Dictionary Drills. Edward B. Fry. 128p. (gr. 9 up). 1980. pap. text ed. 4.00x (ISBN 0-89061-206-4, 752). Jamestown Pubs.

Dictionary for Law. L. B. Curzon. 384p. 1979. pap. 14.95x (ISBN 0-7121-0380-5, Pub. by Macdonald & Evans England). Intl Ideas.

Dictionary for the Health Professional: English-Spanish-Spanish-English. Dorothy H. Mills & Jorge C. Martinez. LC 79-90820. (Illus.). 250p. 1981. pap. 21.20 (ISBN 0-935356-03-7). Mills Pub Co.

Dictionary Hebrew Verbs. M. Debahy. 1974. 12.00x (ISBN 0-685-77115-6). Intl Bk Ctr.

Dictionary Noms de Vetements Chez Arabes. Dozy. 16.00x (ISBN 0-685-85422-1). Intl Bk Ctr.

Dictionary of Abbreviations. Walter T. Rogers. LC 68-30662. 1969. Repr. of 1913 ed. 20.00 (ISBN 0-8103-3338-4). Gale.

Dictionary of Abbreviations in Medicine & the Health Sciences. Harold K. Hughes. 1977. 25.95 (ISBN 0-669-00688-2). Lexington Bks.

Dictionary of Accounting. Ralph W. Estes. 300p. 1981. text ed. 15.00x (ISBN 0-262-05024-2); pap. text ed. 4.95x (ISBN 0-262-55009-1). MIT Pr.

Dictionary of Afro-Latin American Civilization. Benjamin Nunez. LC 79-7731. (Illus.). xxxv, 525p. 1980. lib. bdg. 45.00 (ISBN 0-313-21138-8, NAL/). Greenwood.

Dictionary of American Authors. 5th ed. Oscar F. Adams. LC 68-2175. 1969. Repr. of 1904 ed. 26.00 (ISBN 0-8103-3148-9). Gale.

Dictionary of American Biography Including Men of the Time. Francis S. Drake. LC 73-11061. 1974. Repr. of 1872 ed. 56.00 (ISBN 0-8103-3731-2). Gale.

Dictionary of American English on Historical Principles, 4 Vols. Ed. by William A. Craigie & James R. Hulbert. LC 36-21500. 1938-1944. Set. 200.00 (ISBN 0-226-11741-3); 40.00 o.s.i.; Vol. 1. o.s.i. (ISBN 0-226-11737-5); Vol. 2. o.s.i. (ISBN 0-226-11738-3); Vol. 3. o.s.i. (ISBN 0-226-11739-1); Vol. 4. o.s.i. (ISBN 0-226-11740-5). U of Chicago Pr.

Dictionary of American Idioms in Chinese. Adam Makkai. Ed. by Gates & Boatner. 396p. 1981. pap. 10.95 (ISBN 0-8120-2386-2). Barron.

Dictionary of American Library Biography. Ed. by Bohdan S. Wynar et al. LC 77-28791. 1978. lib. bdg. 85.00x (ISBN 0-87287-180-0). Libs Unl.

Dictionary of American Politics. 2nd ed. Edward C. Smith & Arnold J. Zurcher. LC 67-28530. (Orig., Maps). 1968. pap. 4.95 (ISBN 0-06-463261-X, EH 261, EH). Har-Row.

Dictionary of American Politics. 2nd ed. Edward C. Smith & Arnold J. Zurcher. (Illus.). 1968. pap. text ed. 12.50x (ISBN 0-06-480803-3). B&N.

Dictionary of American Sign Language on Linguistic Principles. William C. Stokoe. LC 65-28740. 1965. 9.00x (ISBN 0-932130-00-3). Linstok Pr.

Dictionary of American Slang. 2nd ed. Harold Wentworth & Stuart B. Flexner. LC 75-8644. 766p. 1975. 14.95 (ISBN 0-690-00670-5, TYC-T). T Y Crowell.

Dictionary of Angels: Including the Fallen Angels. Gustov Davidson. LC 66-19757. (Illus.). 1967. 17.00 (ISBN 0-02-906940-8); pap. 9.95 (ISBN 0-02-907050-3). Free Pr.

Dictionary of Arabic-Persian Quotes. Claud Fielo. 16.00x (ISBN 0-686-53121-3). Intl Bk Ctr.

Dictionary of Archaeology. Cozens & Goodslall. 3.75 o.p. (ISBN 0-685-28352-6). Philos Lib.

Dictionary of Archaic & Provincial Words, Obsolete Phrases, Proverbs, & Ancient Customs, from the Fourteenth Century, 2 vols. James O. Halliwell-Phillipps. LC 66-27837. 1968. Repr. of 1847 ed. Set. 58.00 (ISBN 0-8103-3283-3). Gale.

Dictionary of Architectural Science. Henry J. Cowan. LC 73-15839. (Illus.). 300p. 1973. pap. 14.95 (ISBN 0-470-18070-6). Halsted Pr.

Dictionary of Architecture. Nikolaus Pevsner et al. LC 75-27325. (Illus.). 554p. 1976. 22.50 (ISBN 0-87951-040-4). Overlook Pr.

Dictionary of Architecture & Building, Biographical & Descriptive, 3 Vols. Russell Sturgis. LC 66-26997. (Illus.). 1966. Repr. of 1902 ed. Set. 50.00 (ISBN 0-8103-3075-X). Gale.

Dictionary of Art Terms & Techniques. Ralph Mayer. (Illus.). 1969. 12.95 (ISBN 0-690-23673-5, TYC-T). T Y Crowell.

Dictionary of Art Terms & Techniques. Ralph Mayer. LC 69-15414. (Apollo Eds.). (Illus.). 464p. 1975. pap. 6.95 o.s.i. (ISBN 0-8152-0371-3, A-371, TYC-T). T Y Crowell.

Dictionary of Art Terms & Techniques. Ralph Mayer. LC 80-8854. (Illus.). 464p. 1981. pap. 6.95 (ISBN 0-06-463531-7, EH 531, EH). Har-Row.

Dictionary of Aviation. David Wragg. LC 74-75382. 1974. 9.95 (ISBN 0-8119-0236-6). Fell.

Dictionary of Banking. F. E. Perry. 304p. 1979. text ed. 19.95x (ISBN 0-7121-0428-3, Pub. by Macdonald & Evans England). Intl Ideas.

Dictionary of Banking & Finance. Lewis E. Davids. 229p. 1980. 15.00x (ISBN 0-8476-6132-6). Rowman.

Dictionary of Battles. David Eggenberger. (Illus.). 1967. 16.95 o.s.i. (ISBN 0-690-23744-8, TYC-T). T Y Crowell.

Dictionary of Battles. Thomas B. Harbottle. LC 66-22672. 1966. Repr. of 1905 ed. 19.00 (ISBN 0-8103-3004-0). Gale.

Dictionary of Biblical Theology. new ed. Ed. by Xavier Leon-Dufour. Tr. by P. Joseph Cahill from Fr. LC 73-6437. 710p. 1973. Repr. 22.50 (ISBN 0-8164-1146-8). Crossroad NY.

Dictionary of Biochemistry. J. Stenesh. LC 75-23037. 344p. 1975. 33.50 (ISBN 0-471-82105-5, Pub. by Wiley-Interscience). Wiley.

Dictionary of Biographies of Authors Represented in the Authors Digest Series: With a Supplemental List of Later Titles & a Supplementary Biographical Section. Ed. by Rossiter Johnson. LC 71-167011. 476p. 1974. Repr. of 1927 ed. 28.00 (ISBN 0-8103-3876-9). Gale.

Dictionary of Biography: Past & Present, Containing the Chief Events in the Lives of Eminent Persons of All Ages & Nations. Benjamin Vincent. LC 77-174132. 641p. 1974. Repr. of 1877 ed. 42.00 (ISBN 0-8103-3983-8). Gale.

Dictionary of Black Culture. Wade Baskin & Richard N. Runes. LC 72-78162. 400p. 1973. 15.00 o.p. (ISBN 0-8022-2090-8). Philos Lib.

Dictionary of Book Illustrators, 1800-1970. Brigid Peppin. (Illus.). 544p. Date not set. 30.00 (ISBN 0-668-04366-0). Arco.

Dictionary of Book Publishing. Ulrich Stiehl. 538p. (Eng. & Ger.). 1977. text ed. 55.00 (ISBN 3-7940-4147-X, Pub. by K G Saur). Gale.

Dictionary of Books Relating to America, 29 Vols. in 2. Joseph Sabin. LC 66-31865. 1966. Repr. Set. 147.50 (ISBN 0-8108-0033-0). Scarecrow.

Dictionary of British Book Illustrators & Caricaturists, Eighteen Hundred to Nineteen Fourteen. Ed. by Simon Houfe. (Illus.). 520p. 1978. 94.00 (ISBN 0-902028-73-1, Pub. by Antique Collectors Club England). Gale.

Dictionary of British Landscape Painters: From the 16th to the 20th Century. Maurice H. Grant. (Illus.). 236p. 1970. 40.00x (ISBN 0-85317-250-1). Intl Pubns Serv.

Dictionary of British Miniature Painters, 2 vols. Daphne Foskett. 1972. Set. 145.00 o.p. (ISBN 0-686-16376-1, Pub. by Faber & Faber); Vol. 1. (ISBN 0-571-08295-5); Vol. 2. (ISBN 0-571-09746-4). Merrimack Bk Serv.

Dictionary of British Surnames. 2nd ed. P. H. Reaney. 1976. 42.00 (ISBN 0-7100-8106-5). Routledge & Kegan.

Dictionary of Business and Economics. Christine Ammer & Dean S. Ammer. LC 76-41625. 1977. 22.50 (ISBN 0-02-900590-6). Free Pr.

Dictionary of Business & Management. Jerry M. Rosenberg. LC 78-7796. 1978. 27.95 (ISBN 0-471-01681-0, Pub. by Wiley-Interscience). Wiley.

Dictionary of Business Terms. Peron. 29.95 (ISBN 2-03-020609-1). Larousse.

Dictionary of Canadian Biography. Ed. by Francess Halpenny. Incl. Vol. I. 1000-1700. Ed. by G. W. Brown & Marcel Trudel. xxiii, 755p. 1966. 35.00 (ISBN 0-8020-3142-0); Laurentian ed. 75.00 (ISBN 0-8020-3139-0); Vol. II. 1701-1740. Ed. by David Hayne & Andre Vachon. xli, 759p. 1969. 35.00 (ISBN 0-8020-3240-0); Laurentian ed. 75.00 (ISBN 0-8020-3249-4); Vol. III. 1741-1770. Ed. by Marc La Terreur. 1974. 35.00 (ISBN 0-8020-3314-8); Laurentian ed. 75.00 (ISBN 0-8020-3315-6); Vol. IV. 1771-1800. Ed. by Frances Halpenny. 1979. 35.00 (ISBN 0-8020-3351-2); laurentian ed. 100.00 (ISBN 0-8020-3352-0); Vol. IX. 1861-1870. Ed. by Jean Hamelin. 1976. 35.00 (ISBN 0-8020-3319-9); Laurentian ed. 75.00 (ISBN 0-8020-3320-2); Vol. X. 1871-1880. Ed. by Marc La Terreur. 1972. 35.00 (ISBN 0-8020-3287-7); laurentian ed. 75.00 (ISBN 0-8020-3288-5). LC 66-31909. U of Toronto Pr.

Dictionary of Chemistry & Chemical Technology in Six Languages. rev. ed. Ed. by Z. Sobecka et al. 1966. 120.00 (ISBN 0-08-011600-0). Pergamon.

Dictionary of Chess Openings. M. R. Carter. (Illus.). 320p. 1979. 15.00 o.p. (ISBN 0-498-01655-2). A S Barnes.

Dictionary of Chinese Law & Government: Chinese-English. Phillip R. Bilancia. LC 73-80618. 832p. 1981. 45.00x (ISBN 0-8047-0864-9). Stanford U Pr.

Dictionary of Civil Engineering. 3rd ed. John S. Scott. LC 80-24419. 308p. 1980. 19.95 (ISBN 0-470-27087-X). Halsted Pr.

Dictionary of Civil Engineering & Construction Machinery & Equipment, 2 vols. 4th ed. 1180p. 1978. plastic bdg. 90.00x ea. o.p. Vol. 1, Ger-Eng (ISBN 3-7625-0502-0). Vol. 2, Eng.-Ger (ISBN 3-7625-0950-6). Intl Pubns Serv.

Dictionary of Classical Mythology: Symbols, Attributes, & Associations. Robert E. Bell. Ed. by Gail Schlachter. (No. 1). 1981. write for info. (ISBN 0-87436-305-5). ABC Clio.

Dictionary of Collective Nouns & Group Terms. Ed. by Ivan G. Sparkes. LC 75-4117. 213p. 1975. 28.00 (ISBN 0-8103-2016-9, Pub. by White Lion Publishers). Gale.

Dictionary of Colonial American Printer's Ornaments & Illustrations. Elizabeth C. Reilly. (Illus.). xxxvi, 514p. 1975. 45.00x (ISBN 0-912296-06-2, Dist. by U Pr of Va). Am Antiquarian.

Dictionary of Commercial, Economic, & Legal Terms; Woerterbuch der Wirschafts-, Rechts-, und Handelssprache: Including the Terminology of the European Community, 2 vols. Clara-Erika Dietl. Incl. Vol. 1. English-German. 1971 (ISBN 0-8002-1256-8); Vol. 2. German-English. 1974. LC 72-326078. 25.00x ea. Intl Pubns Serv.

Dictionary of Commercial, Financial & Legal Terms, 3 Vols. R. Herbst. (Eng, Fr. & Ger.). 93.50 ea. Adler.

Dictionary of Commodities Carried by Ship. Pierre Garoche. 1952. pap. 6.00x (ISBN 0-87033-019-5). Cornell Maritime.

Dictionary of Common Fallacies. Philip Ward. (Oleander Reference Books Ser.). 1978. 16.50 o.p. (ISBN 0-900891-14-9). Oleander Pr.

Dictionary of Common Language Errors & Their Corrections: Arabic-Arabic. Muhammad Adnani. 16.00x (ISBN 0-685-72039-X). Intl Bk Ctr.

Dictionary of Concepts. James B. Whisker. LC 80-15591. 285p. 1980. pap. 7.95 (ISBN 0-471-07716-X). Wiley.

Dictionary of Contemporary Music. Ed. by John Vinton. 1974. 25.00 o.p. (ISBN 0-525-09125-4). Dutton.

Dictionary of Correct English Usage. Ed. by Leo Lieberman. LC 63-15604. 1963. 4.75 o.p. (ISBN 0-8022-0973-4). Philos Lib.

Dictionary of Cosmetology & Related Services. Anthony B. Colletti. Ed. by Gary Chiranky. 1981. text ed. 23.57 (ISBN 0-912126-58-2, 1275-00). Keystone Pubns.

Dictionary of Costume. R. Wilcox. 1979. 45.00 (ISBN 0-7134-0856-1, Pub. by Batsford England). David & Charles.

Dictionary of Criminal Justice. George E. Rush. (Criminal Justice Ser.). 1977. text ed. 13.95 o.p. (ISBN 0-205-05815-9, 825814-7); pap. text ed. 9.50 (ISBN 0-686-68522-9, 825815-5). Allyn.

Dictionary of Data Processing: Hardware-Software. Carl Amkreutz. 905p. (Ger, Eng, Fr.). 1972. 32.50x (ISBN 0-8002-1258-4). Intl Pubns Serv.

Dictionary of Dinosaurs. Joseph Rosenbloom. LC 80-18525. (Illus.). 96p. (gr. 4 up). 1980. PLB 8.29 (ISBN 0-671-34038-7). Messner.

Dictionary of Diseased English. Kenneth Hudson. LC 77-11529. 1978. 12.95 o.p. (ISBN 0-06-011955-1, HarpT). Har-Row.

Dictionary of Earth Science: French-English & English-French. Jean-Pierre Michel & Rhodes W. Fairbridge. 340p. 1980. 14.50 (ISBN 0-89352-076-4). Masson Pub.

Dictionary of Ecclesiastical Terms: Being a History & Explanation of Certain Terms Used in Architecture, Ecclesiology, Liturgiology, Music, Ritual, Cathedral, Constitution, Etc. John S. Bumpus. LC 68-30653. 1969. Repr. of 1910 ed. 15.00 (ISBN 0-8103-3321-X). Gale.

Dictionary of Economic Terms. rev. ed. P. A. Taylor. 1968. pap. 1.95 o.s.i. (ISBN 0-7100-6100-5). Routledge & Kegan.

Dictionary of Economics & Commerce. Ed. by J. L. Hanson. 1965. 10.00 o.p. (ISBN 0-8022-0675-1). Philos Lib.

Dictionary of Electrical & Electronic Engineering: German-English & English-German. 2nd ed. Hans F. Schwenkhagen. LC 67-74452. 909p. 1967. 105.00x (ISBN 3-7736-5072-8). Intl Pubns Serv.

Dictionary of Electrical Engineering. 2nd ed. K. G. Jackson & R. Feinberg. 1981. text ed. price not set (ISBN 0-408-00450-9, Newnes-Butterworth). Butterworth.

Dictionary of Electrochemistry. C. W. Davies & A. M. James. LC 76-4876. 525p. 1976. 29.95 (ISBN 0-470-15064-5). Halsted Pr.

Dictionary of Electronics. S. W. Amos. 1981. text ed. price not set (ISBN 0-408-00331-6, Newnes-Butterworth). Butterworth.

Dictionary of Electronics: English-German. Ed. by Alfred Oppermann. 692p. 1980. 120.00 (ISBN 3-598-10312-3, Dist. by Gale Research Co.). K G Saur.

Dictionary of English & Folk-Names of British Birds. Harry K. Swann. LC 68-30664. 1968. Repr. of 1913 ed. 15.00 (ISBN 0-8103-3340-6). Gale.

Dictionary of English & Sanskrit. M. Monier Williams. LC 73-495007. 1971. Repr. of 1851 ed. 17.50x (ISBN 0-8002-0172-8). Intl Pubns Serv.

Dictionary of English Authors: Biographical & Bibliographical. Ed. by R. Farquharson Sharp. LC 75-35577. 1978. Repr. of 1904 ed. 26.00 (ISBN 0-8103-4281-2). Gale.

Dictionary of English Literature. William D. Adams. LC 66-25162. 1966. Repr. of 1880 ed. 34.00 (ISBN 0-8103-0150-4). Gale.

Dictionary of English Phrases: Phraseological Allusions, Catchwords, Stereotyped Modes of Speech & Metaphors, Nicknames, Sobriquets, Derivations from Personal Names. Albert M. Hyamson. LC 66-22673. 1970. Repr. of 1922 ed. 20.00 (ISBN 0-8103-3852-1). Gale.

Dictionary of English Phrases with Illustrative Sentences. Kwong Ki Chaou. LC 74-136559. (Illus.). 1971. Repr. of 1881 ed. 38.00 (ISBN 0-8103-3386-4). Gale.

Dictionary of English Weights & Measures from Anglo-Saxon Times to the Nineteenth Century. Ronald E. Zupko. LC 68-14038. 1968. 25.00x (ISBN 0-299-04870-5). U of Wis Pr.

Dictionary of Entomology. A. W. Leftwich. LC 75-27143. 1976. 27.50x (ISBN 0-8448-0820-2). Crane-Russak Co.

Dictionary of European Literature, Designed As a Companion to English Studies. rev. ed. Laurie Magnus. LC 74-6269. xii, 605p. 1975. Repr. of 1927 ed. 32.00 (ISBN 0-8103-4014-3). Gale.

Dictionary of Famous Names in Fiction, Drama, Poetry, History & Art. Ed. by Rossiter Johnson. LC 75-167012. 1974. Repr. of 1908 ed. 28.00 (ISBN 0-8103-3875-0). Gale.

Dictionary of Fantastic Art. Jorg Krichbaum & Rein Zondergeld. (Pocket Art Ser.). (Illus.). 1981. pap. 5.95 (ISBN 0-8120-2110-X). Barron.

Dictionary of Ferrous Metals. Eric N. Simons. (Illus.). 1971. 14.00 (ISBN 0-584-10059-0). Transatlantic.

Dictionary of Film Makers. Georges Sadoul. Tr. by Peter Morris from Fr. LC 78-136028. 1972. 22.95x (ISBN 0-520-01862-1); pap. 5.95 (ISBN 0-520-02151-7, CAL241). U of Cal Pr.

Dictionary of Films. Georges Sadoul. Tr. by Peter Morris from Fr. LC 78-136028. 1972. 22.95x (ISBN 0-520-01864-8); pap. 8.95 (ISBN 0-520-02152-5, CAL240). U of Cal Pr.

Dictionary of Food & What's in It for You. Barbara L. Gelb. 1979. pap. 3.50 (ISBN 0-345-29479-3). Ballantine.

Dictionary of Foreign Quotations. Robert Collison & Mary Collison. 1980. 29.95 (ISBN 0-87196-428-7). Facts on File.

Dictionary of Foreign Terms. rev. 2nd ed. C. O. Mawson. Ed. by Charles Berlitz. LC 74-12492. 384p. 1974. 9.95 o.s.i. (ISBN 0-690-00171-1, TYC-T). T Y Crowell.

Dictionary of Foreign Terms in the English Language. David Carroll. 1979. pap. 4.95 (ISBN 0-8015-2053-3, Hawthorn). Dutton.

Dictionary of Freshman Composition. Forrest G. Smith. LC 70-78633. (Quality Paperback: No. 239). (Orig.). 1969. pap. 3.95 (ISBN 0-8226-0239-3). Littlefield.

Dictionary of Gardening: A Practical & Scientific Encyclopedia of Horticulture, 4 Vols. 2nd ed. Ed. by F. J. Chittenden & P. M. Synge. 1956. 195.00x (ISBN 0-19-869106-8). Oxford U Pr.

Dictionary of Gastronomy. 2nd ed. Andre L. Simon & Robin Howe. LC 78-16260. (Illus.). 400p. 1979. 25.00 (ISBN 0-87951-081-1). Overlook Pr.

Dictionary of Geological Terms. rev. ed. American Geological Institute. LC 73-9004. 600p. 1976. pap. 4.50 (ISBN 0-385-08452-8, Anch). Doubleday.

Dictionary of German Synonyms. 3rd ed. R. B. Farrell. LC 75-36175. 1977. 45.00 (ISBN 0-521-21189-1); pap. 12.95 (ISBN 0-521-29068-6). Cambridge U Pr.

Dictionary of Gestures. Betty J. Bauml & Franz H. Bauml. LC 75-3144. 1975. 12.00 (ISBN 0-8108-0863-3). Scarecrow.

Dictionary of Hammond Organ Stops. 4th rev. ed. Stevens Irwin. 1970. pap. 8.95 (ISBN 0-02-871110-6). Schirmer Bks.

Dictionary of Historical Allusions. Thomas B. Harbottle. LC 68-23163. 1968. Repr. of 1904 ed. 18.00 (ISBN 0-8103-3088-1). Gale.

Dictionary of History. R. J. Unstead. (Illus.). (gr. 4-8). 1977. 12.95 (ISBN 0-8467-0230-4, Pub. by Two Continents). Hippocrene Bks.

Dictionary of Human Behavior. D. Statt. 1981. text ed. 15.70 (ISBN 0-686-69149-0, Pub. by Har-Row Ltd England). Har-Row.

Dictionary of Idioms French-English: Dictionnaire des locutions. 32.95 (ISBN 2-03-021101-X, 3681). Larousse.

Dictionary of Imaginary Places. Ed. by Alberto Manguel & Gianni Guadalupi. (Illus.). 416p. 1980. 24.95 (ISBN 0-02-579310-1). Macmillan.

Dictionary of Indian Biography. Charles E. Buckland. LC 68-23140. 1968. Repr. of 1906 ed. 34.00 (ISBN 0-8103-3156-X). Gale.

Dictionary of Indian Tribes of the Americas, 4 vols. Ed. by American Indian Publishers. (Illus.). 1980. Set. lib. bdg. 225.00 (ISBN 0-937862-25-8). Am Hist Pubs.

Dictionary of Industrial Pollution, Ecology & Environment. David F. Tver. (Illus.). 1981. price not set (ISBN 0-8311-1060-0). Indus Pr.

Dictionary of Industrial Property, Legal & Related Terms: English, Spanish, French & German. Ed. by Francis J. Kase. 232p. 1980. 50.00x (ISBN 90-286-0619-X). Sijthoff & Noordhoff.

Dictionary of Industrial Techniques: English-French-German-Portuguese-Spanish. Ed. by Michel Feutry et al. 1312p. 1979. 80.00 (ISBN 2-85608-000-6). Heinman.

Dictionary of Initials. Betsy M. Parks. 1981. 12.95 (ISBN 0-8065-0750-0). Lyle Stuart.

Dictionary of International Biography, 1978, 2 pts, Vol. 14. 967p. 1978. Set, A-K & L-Z. 75.00x (ISBN 0-8476-6027-3). Rowman.

Dictionary of International Biography, 1980, Vol. 16. 948p. 1980. 59.50x (ISBN 0-900332-52-2, Pub. by Intl Biog). Biblio Dist.

Dictionary of Inventions and Discoveries. rev. 2nd ed. E. F. Carter. LC 75-37058. 214p. 1976. 14.50x (ISBN 0-8448-0867-9). Crane-Russak Co.

Dictionary of Iraqi Arabic: Arabic-English. Ed. by Daniel Woodhead & Wayne Beene. (Richard Slade Harrell Arabic Ser). 509p. 1967. pap. 8.50 (ISBN 0-87840-003-6). Georgetown U Pr.

Dictionary of Irish Artists, 2 vols. Walter G. Strickland. (Illus.). 1358p. 1968. Repr. of 1913 ed. 90.00x set (ISBN 0-7165-0602-5, Pub. by Irish Academic Pr Ireland). Biblio Dist.

Dictionary of Irish History Since 1800. Denis Hickey & James Doherty. 615p. 1980. 38.50x (ISBN 0-389-20160-X). B&N.

Dictionary of Islam. Thomas P. Hughes. 1976. Repr. 35.00x (ISBN 0-8364-0395-9). South Asia Bks.

Dictionary of Jamaican English. 2nd ed. Ed. by F. G. Cassidy & R. B. Le Page. LC 78-17799. 1980. 75.00 (ISBN 0-521-22165-X). Cambridge U Pr.

Dictionary of Japanese & English Idiomatic Equivalents. Charles Corwin et al. LC 68-11818. 302p. 1980. 15.00 (ISBN 0-87011-111-6). Kodansha.

Dictionary of Khotan Saka. H. W. Bailey. LC 77-80825. 1979. 210.00 (ISBN 0-521-21737-7). Cambridge U Pr.

Dictionary of Labour Biography, 5 vols. Ed. by Joyce M. Bellamy & John Saville. LC 78-185417. 414p. 1972. Vol. 1. lib. bdg. 37.50x (ISBN 0-678-07008-3); Vol. 2. lib. bdg. 47.50x (ISBN 0-678-07018-0); Vols. 3. lib. bdg. 37.50x (ISBN 0-333-14415-5); Vol. 4. lib. bdg. 37.50x (ISBN 0-333-19704-6); Vol. 5. lib. bdg. 37.50x (ISBN 0-333-22015-3). Kelley.

Dictionary of Language & Linguistics. Ed. by R. R. Hartmann & F. C. Stork. LC 72-6251. 1976. 32.95 (ISBN 0-470-35667-7); pap. 24.95 (ISBN 0-470-15200-1). Halsted Pr.

Dictionary of Late Egyptian, 2 vols. Ed. by Leonard H. Lesko. 1980. lib. bdg. write for info. (ISBN 0-930548-03-5); pap. text ed. write for info. (ISBN 0-930548-04-3). B C Scribe.

Dictionary of Legal Abbreviations Used in American Law Books. Doris M. Bieber. LC 78-60173. 1979. lib. bdg. 19.50 (ISBN 0-930342-61-5); pap. text ed. 7.50 (ISBN 0-930342-96-8). W S Hein.

Dictionary of Legal Quotations. James W. Norton-Kyshe. LC 68-30648. 1968. Repr. of 1904 ed. 18.00 (ISBN 0-8103-3189-6). Gale.

Dictionary of Legal Terms. Steven H. Gifis. 1981. pap. 2.95 (ISBN 0-8120-2013-8). Barron. Postponed.

Dictionary of Legal Terms & Maxims, Vol. 58. 2nd ed. Edward J. Bander. 1979. 5.95 (ISBN 0-379-11119-5). Oceana.

Dictionary of Legal Words & Phrases. 1981 ed. 1981. 10.00 (ISBN 0-87526-205-8). Gould.

Dictionary of Linguistics. Mario Pei & Frank Gaynor. (Quality Paperback: No. 177). 1980. pap. 4.95 (ISBN 0-8226-0177-X). Littlefield.

Dictionary of Literary & Linguistic Terms: Arabic-Arabic. Magdi Wahba. 25.00x. Intl Bk Ctr.

Dictionary of Literary Terms (English-French-Arabic) Magdi Wahba. 1974. 30.00 (ISBN 0-685-72035-7). Intl Bk Ctr.

Dictionary of Literature in the English Language, 2 vols. Robin Myers. LC 68-18529. Vol. 1. 52.50 (ISBN 0-08-012079-2); Vol. 2. 37.50 (ISBN 0-08-016142-1); Set. 85.00 (ISBN 0-08-016143-X). Pergamon.

Dictionary of Literature in the English Language. Robin Myers. 1978. 85.00 (ISBN 0-08-018050-7). Pergamon.

Dictionary of Marketing & Communication. Frank Jefkins. 1973. text ed. 16.50x (ISBN 0-7002-0218-8). Intl Ideas.

Dictionary of Marketing Terms. 4th ed. Irving J. Shapiro. (Littlefield, Adams Quality Paperback Ser.: No. 363). 276p. (Orig.). 1981. pap. 7.95 (ISBN 0-8226-0363-2). Littlefield.

Dictionary of Marketing Terms. 4th ed. Irving J. Shapiro. 276p. 1981. 19.50x (ISBN 0-8476-6967-X). Rowman.

Dictionary of Marks. Margaret MacDonald-Taylor. (Illus.). 1962. 7.95 o.p. (ISBN 0-8015-2088-6, Hawthorn); pap. 4.95 (ISBN 0-8015-2089-4, Hawthorn). Dutton.

Dictionary of Mathematics. William Millington & T. Alaric Millington. 1971. pap. 3.95 (ISBN 0-06-463311-X, EH 311, EH). Har-Row.

Dictionary of Mechanical Engineering. 8th rev. ed. Henry G. Freeman. LC 72-347328. (Eng. Ger.). 1971. 45.00x (ISBN 3-7736-5031-0). Intl Pubns Serv.

Dictionary of Medical Ethics. Ed. by A. S. Duncan et al. 1977. pap. text ed. 15.50x (ISBN 0-232-51302-3). Humanities.

Dictionary of Medical Ethics. Ed. by A. S. Duncan et al. 496p. 1981. 24.50 (ISBN 0-8245-0038-5). Crossroad NY.

Dictionary of Medieval Latin from British Sources: Fascicule I, A-B. Compiled by R. E. Latham. 280p. 1975. pap. 49.00x (ISBN 0-19-725948-0). Oxford U Pr.

Dictionary of Microbial Taxonmix Usage. S. T. Cowan. 1968. 7.50 (ISBN 0-934454-28-0). Lubrecht & Cramer.

Dictionary of Microbial Taxonomy. S. T. Cowan. Ed. by L. R. Hill. LC 77-85705. (Illus.). 1978. 42.50 (ISBN 0-521-21890-X). Cambridge U Pr.

Dictionary of Military Terms: Chinese-English, English-Chinese. Joseph D. Lowe. LC 76-7063. 1977. 50.00x (ISBN 0-89158-032-8). Westview.

Dictionary of Miracles, Imitative, Realistic, & Dogmatic. E. Cobham Brewer. LC 66-29783. 1966. Repr. of 1885 ed. 24.00 (ISBN 0-8103-3000-8). Gale.
Dictionary of Misinformation. Tom Burnam. 1977. pap. 2.50 (ISBN 0-345-29534-X). Ballantine.
Dictionary of Misinformation. Tom Burnham. LC 75-15651. 352p. 1975. 12.95 (ISBN 0-690-00147-9, TYC-T). T Y Crowell.
Dictionary of Modern American Usage. 2nd ed. Herbert W. Horwill. 1944. 19.50x (ISBN 0-19-869109-2). Oxford U Pr.
Dictionary of Modern Business. Louis Robb. (Span. -Eng. & Eng. -Span.). 1960. 25.00 (ISBN 0-685-06098-5) Anderson Kramer.
Dictionary of Modern Engineering, 2 vols. 3rd ed. Ed. by Alfred Oppermann. Incl. Vol. 1. English-German. 912p. 1972. 80.00 (ISBN 3-7940-6001-6); Vol. 2. German-English. 952p. 1974. 80.00 (ISBN 3-7940-6002-4). 160.00 set (ISBN 3-7940-6003-2). Gale.
Dictionary of Modern German Prose Usage. H. F. Eggeling. 1961. 26.00x (ISBN 0-19-864110-9). Oxford U Pr.
Dictionary of Modern Italian. Ed. by John Purves. 1953. 12.00 (ISBN 0-7100-1977-7). Routledge & Kegan.
Dictionary of Modern Lebanese Proverbs. Anis Freyha. (Arabic-Eng.). 1974. 23.00x (ISBN 0-685-77118-0). Intl Bk Ctr.
Dictionary of Modern Music & Musicians. Ed. by A. Eaglefield-Hull. LC 78-139192. (Music Ser). 1971. Repr. of 1924 ed. lib. bdg. 27.00 (ISBN 0-306-70086-7). Da Capo.
Dictionary of Modern War. Edward Luttwak. LC 77-159574. (Illus.). 1971. 12.50 o.p. (ISBN 0-06-012732-5, HarpT). Har-Row.
Dictionary of Motion Picture & Video Terms. John Quick & Tom LaBau. (Illus.). 1981. 14.95 (ISBN 0-89046-067-1). Herman Pub.
Dictionary of Music. Hugo Riemann. LC 75-125060. (Music Ser). 1970. Repr. of 1908 ed. lib. bdg. 65.00 (ISBN 0-306-70025-5). Da Capo.
Dictionary of Musical Terms. Theodore Baker. 1923. 7.95 (ISBN 0-02-870200-X). Schirmer Bks.
Dictionary of Mythology, Folklore & Symbols, 2 Vols. Gertrude Jobes. LC 61-860. 1961. Set. 50.00 (ISBN 0-8108-0034-9). Scarecrow.
Dictionary of Names & Titles in Poe's Collected Works. Burton R. Pollin. LC 68-28982. (Paperback Ser.). 1968. lib. bdg. 19.50 (ISBN 0-306-71154-0). Da Capo.
Dictionary of Names, Nicknames, & Surnames. Edward Latham. LC 66-22674. 1966. Repr. of 1904 ed. 22.00 (ISBN 0-8103-0157-1). Gale.
Dictionary of National Biography, 22 vols. George Smith. Ed. by Leslie Stephen & Sidney Lee. 1882-1953. suppl. 1. 695.00x (ISBN 0-19-865101-5); suppl. 2. 65.00x (ISBN 0-19-865201-1); suppl. 3 65.00x (ISBN 0-19-865202-X); suppl. 4 65.00x (ISBN 0-19-865203-8); suppl. 5 65.00x (ISBN 0-19-865204-6); suppl. 6 65.00x (ISBN 0-19-865205-4). Oxford U Pr.
Dictionary of National Biography, Concise Dictionary Pt. 1: From the Beginning to 1900. 1953. 49.95x (ISBN 0-19-865301-8). Oxford U Pr.
Dictionary of National Biography, Concise Dictionary Pt. 2: 1900-1950. 1961. 43.00x (ISBN 0-19-865302-6). Oxford U Pr.
Dictionary of National Biography: The Compact Edition, 2 vols. 3000p. (Reading glass supplied). 1975. 165.00x (ISBN 0-19-865102-3). Oxford U Pr.
Dictionary of National Biography, 1951-1960. 7th suppl ed. Ed. by E. T. Williams & Helen M. Palmer. 1176p. 1971. 65.00x (ISBN 0-19-865206-2). Oxford U Pr.
Dictionary of Natural Environment with English-Arabic Glossary. F. Monkhouse. 16.00x (ISBN 0-686-65472-2). Intl Bk Ctr.
Dictionary of Needlework. Sophia F. Caulfield & Blanche C. Saward. LC 75-172439. (Illus.). 1971. Repr. of 1882 ed. 54.00 (ISBN 0-8103-3404-6). Gale.
Dictionary of New Testament Greek Synonyms. George R. Berry. 1979. 5.95 (ISBN 0-310-21160-3). Zondervan.
Dictionary of Nineteenth-Century American Artists in Italy, 1760-1914. Regina Soria. LC 74-4986. 600p. 1981. 27.50 (ISBN 0-8386-1310-1). Fairleigh Dickinson.
Dictionary of Non-Classical Vocables in Spoken Arabic. Anis Freyha. 1973. 14.00x (ISBN 0-685-77117-2). Intl Bk Ctr.
Dictionary of North American Authors Deceased Before 1950. William S. Wallace. LC 68-19955. 1968. Repr. of 1951 ed. 22.00 (ISBN 0-8103-3153-5). Gale.
Dictionary of Occult, Hermetic & Alchemical Sigils. Fred Gettings. 1981. 34.95 (ISBN 0-7100-0095-2). Routledge & Kegan. Postponed.
Dictionary of Oregon History. Ed. by Howard M. Corning. 15.00 (ISBN 0-8323-0099-3). Binford.
Dictionary of Oriental Quotations. Claud H. Field. LC 68-23157. 1969. Repr. of 1911 ed. 21.00 (ISBN 0-8103-3183-7). Gale.
Dictionary of Oto-Rhino-Laryngology in Five Languages: English-French-Spanish-German-Italian. A. Larrauri. LC 71-501781. 1008p. 1971. 48.00x (ISBN 0-8002-0197-3). Intl Pubns Serv.
Dictionary of Painting & Decorating. J. H. Goodier. 308p. 1974. 39.50x (ISBN 0-85264-224-5, Pub. by Griffin England). State Mutual Bk.
Dictionary of Participants. International Congress of Pediatrics, Fifteenth, New Delhi, India, Oct 23-29, 1977. 148p. 1980. pap. 15.00x (ISBN 0-89955-327-3, Pub. by Interprint India). Intl Schol Bk Serv.
Dictionary of Persian Loan Words in the Arabic Language. Al-Sayyid Addi. 1980. 15.00x. Intl Bk Ctr.
Dictionary of Petroleum Technology-Dictionnaire Dechnique Du Petrol: English-French - French-English. rev. ed. Ed. by Magdaleine Moureau & Gerald Brace. LC 64-56944. (Collection Des Dictionnaires Techniques: No. 1). 975p. 1979. 100.00x (ISBN 2-7108-0361-5). Intl Pubns Serv.
Dictionary of Philosophy. A. R. Lacey. 1976. 16.00x (ISBN 0-7100-8361-0). Routledge & Kegan.
Dictionary of Philosophy. rev., enl. ed. Ed. by Dagobert D. Runes. 1981. Repr. 25.00 (ISBN 0-8022-2388-5). Philos Lib.
Dictionary of Pipe Organ Stops. rev. ed. Stevens Irwin. 1965. pap. 10.95 (ISBN 0-02-871130-0). Schirmer Bks.
Dictionary of Plants Used by Man. George Usher. LC 74-2707. 1974. 15.95 o.s.i. (ISBN 0-02-853800-5). Hafner.
Dictionary of Plastics. J. A. Wordingham & P. Reboul. (Quality Paperback: No. 174). 1967. pap. 2.95 (ISBN 0-8226-0174-5). Littlefield.
Dictionary of Platitudes. Gustave Flaubert. (Illus.). 1961. pap. 1.45 o.p. (ISBN 0-498-04024-0, Prpta). A S Barnes.
Dictionary of Political Economy, 3 vols. Robert H. Palgrave. LC 74-31358. 1976. Repr. of 1910 ed. Set. 130.00 (ISBN 0-8103-4210-3). Gale.
Dictionary of Political Phrases & Allusions with a Short Bibliography. Hugh Montgomery. LC 68-28333. 1968. Repr. of 1906 ed. 18.00 (ISBN 0-8103-3092-X). Gale.
Dictionary of Political Terminology. Compiled by M. B. Khopkar. 1970. pap. 2.75 (ISBN 0-88253-149-2). Ind-US Inc.
Dictionary of Politics. rev. ed. Walter Laqueur. LC 74-9232. 1974. 17.95 (ISBN 0-02-917950-5). Free Pr.
Dictionary of Politics. Walter J. Raymond. LC 78-50189. (Illus.). deluxe ed. 24.95x (ISBN 0-931494-00-1). Brunswick Pub.
Dictionary of Practical Materia Medica, 3 vols. 2585p. 1980. text ed. 119.95x (ISBN 0-8464-1004-4). Beekman Pubs.
Dictionary of Pronunciation of Artists' Names. 2nd ed. G. E. Kaltenbach. 74p. 1935. pap. text ed. 0.75 (ISBN 0-86559-000-1). Art Inst Chi.
Dictionary of Proper Names & Notable Matters in the Works of Dante. 2nd ed. Paget J. Toynbee. Ed. by Charles S. Singleton. 1968. 63.00x (ISBN 0-19-815356-2). Oxford U Pr.
Dictionary of Protestant Church Music. James R. Davidson. LC 74-30101. 1975. 15.00 (ISBN 0-8108-0788-2). Scarecrow.
Dictionary of Psychology: With Thesaurus. William Verplanck. Date not set. postponed 35.00x (ISBN 0-89197-729-5). Irvington. Postponed.
Dictionary of Puns in Milton's English Poetry. Edward Le Comte. 240p. 1981. text ed. 25.00x (ISBN 0-231-05102-6). Columbia U Pr.
Dictionary of Races or Peoples. United States Immigration Commission. LC 68-30665. 1969. Repr. of 1911 ed. 15.00 (ISBN 0-8103-3364-3). Gale.
Dictionary of Radio, TV & Audio. R. S. Roberts. 1981. text ed. price not set (ISBN 0-408-00339-1, Newnes-Butterworth). Butterworth.
Dictionary of Radiological Engineering. Gustav F. Neuder & Heinz M. Ullrich. 1979. pap. text ed. 36.50 (ISBN 3-11-007807-4). De Gruyter.
Dictionary of Reading & Learning Disabilities. Clifford L. Bush & Robert C. Andrews. LC 79-57293. 179p. 1978. pap. 8.00x (ISBN 0-87424-153-7). Western Psych.
Dictionary of Recent American History. Stanley Hochman. LC 79-12265. 1979. 19.95 (ISBN 0-07-029103-9, P&RB). McGraw.
Dictionary of Refrigeration & Air Conditioning. K. M. Booth. 1970. 29.90x (ISBN 0-444-20069-X, Pub. by Applied Science). Burgess-Intl Ideas.
Dictionary of Religion & Ethics. Ed. by Shailer Mathews & Gerald B. Smith. LC 70-145713. 1971. Repr. of 1921 ed. 22.00 o.p. (ISBN 0-8103-3196-9). Gale.
Dictionary of Reprography: Terms & Definitions. Ed. by Deutsches Kommitee Fur Reprographie. 273p. (Ger. & Fr.). 1976. pap. text ed. 34.00 (ISBN 3-7940-3186-5, Pub. by K G Saur). Gale.
Dictionary of Rubber. K. F. Heinisch. Ed. by K. S. Lee & D. A. Smith. Tr. by J. Ford-Smith from Ger. LC 74-932. 545p. 1974. 54.95 (ISBN 0-470-36897-7). Halsted Pr.
Dictionary of Russian Obscenities. 24p. 1971. pap. 2.50x (ISBN 0-685-47489-5). Schoenhof.
Dictionary of Russian Obscenities. David A. Drummond & G. Perkins. (Orig., Eng. & Rus.). 1979. pap. 2.95 o.p. (ISBN 0-933884-06-0). Berkeley Slavic.
Dictionary of Russian Obscenities. rev. ed. David A. Drummond & G. Perkins. 79p. (Rus. & Eng.). 1980. pap. text ed. 3.50 (ISBN 0-933884-17-6). Berkeley Slavic.
Dictionary of Russian Personal Names. Ed. by Morton Benson. LC 64-19386. 1964. 12.00x (ISBN 0-8122-7452-0). U of Pa Pr.
Dictionary of Saints. John J. Delaney. LC 79-7783. (Illus.). 648p. 1980. 22.50 (ISBN 0-385-13594-7). Doubleday.
Dictionary of Scientific Biography. American Council Of Learned Societies. 1970. 55.00x ea. o.p.; Vol. 1. (ISBN 0-684-10112-2); Vol. 2. (ISBN 0-684-10113-0); Vol. 3. (ISBN 0-684-10114-9); Vol. 4. (ISBN 0-684-10115-7); Vol. 5. (ISBN 0-684-10116-5); Vol. 6. (ISBN 0-684-10117-3); lib. bdg. 36.00 o.p. (ISBN 0-685-20283-6). Scribner.
Dictionary of Scientific Biography, 8 vols. Ed. by Charles C. Gillispie. 1981. lib. bdg. 595.00 set (ISBN 0-684-16962-2); lib. bdg. 80.00 ea. Scribner.
Dictionary of Scientific Biography, Vol. 11. American Council of Learned Societies. LC 69-18090. 1975. 44.00 o.p. (ISBN 0-684-10122-X); lib. bdg. 36.00 o.p. (ISBN 0-685-63862-6). Scribner.
Dictionary of Scientific Biography, Vol. 12. American Council of Learned Societies. LC 69-18090. 1975. 44.00 o.p. (ISBN 0-684-12924-8); lib. bdg. 36.00 o.p. (ISBN 0-685-63863-4). Scribner.
Dictionary of Scientific Biography, Vol. 13. American Council of Learned Societies. 1976. 44.00 o.p. (ISBN 0-685-63864-2); lib. bdg. 36.00 o.p. (ISBN 0-684-12925-6). Scribner.
Dictionary of Scientific Biography, Vol. 14. American Council of Learned Societies. LC 69-18090. 1976. 44.00 o.p. (ISBN 0-684-12926-4); lib. bdg. 36.00 o.p. (ISBN 0-685-63865-0). Scribner.
Dictionary of Scientific Biography: Compact Edition, 8 vols. Ed. by Charles C. Gillispie. LC 69-18090. 1970-1980. Set. text ed. 695.00 (ISBN 0-684-16962-2, ScribR). Scribner.
Dictionary of Secret & Other Societies. Ed. by Arthur Preuss. LC 66-21186. 1966. Repr. of 1924 ed. 26.00 (ISBN 0-8103-3083-0). Gale.
Dictionary of Sects, Heresies, Ecclesiastical Parties & Schools of Religious Thought. John H. Blunt. LC 74-9653. 1974. Repr. of 1874 ed. 42.00 (ISBN 0-8103-3751-7). Gale.
Dictionary of Slang & Its Analogues, 2 Vols. John S. Farmer & W. E. Henley. 1965. Vol. 1. (ISBN 0-8216-0068-0); 15.00 o.p. (ISBN 0-685-20856-7); Vol. 8. 10.00 o.p. (ISBN 0-685-20857-5). Univ Bks.
Dictionary of Slang & Unconventional English. 7th ed. Eric Partridge. 1970. 39.95 (ISBN 0-02-594970-5). Macmillan.
Dictionary of Slang, Jargon & Cant, 2 Vols. Albert Barrere. Ed. by Charles G. Leland. LC 66-27828. 1967. Repr. of 1889 ed. Set. 52.00 (ISBN 0-8103-3242-6). Gale.
Dictionary of Social Behavior & Social Research Methods. David J. Stang & Lawrence S. Wrightman. LC 80-21511. 250p. 1980. pap. text ed. 6.95 (ISBN 0-8185-0243-6). Brooks-Cole.
Dictionary of Social Sciences: English-French-Arabic. A. Badawi. 25.00x (ISBN 0-686-63544-2). Intl Bk Ctr.
Dictionary of Social Services- Policy & Practice. Joan Clegg. 147p. 1977. text ed. 12.50x (ISBN 0-7199-0932-5, Pub. by Bedford England). Renouf.
Dictionary of Sociology. Ed. by G. Duncan Mitchell. LC 67-30870. 1967. 15.95x (ISBN 0-202-30079-X). Aldine Pub.
Dictionary of Special Education Terms. B. C. Moore et al. 128p. 1980. lexotone 12.75 (ISBN 0-398-04009-5). C C Thomas.
Dictionary of Special Libraries & Information Centers, 3 vols. 6th ed. Ed. by Margaret L. Young & Harold C. Young. Incl. Vol. 1. Special Libraries & Information Centers in the United States & Canada (ISBN 0-8103-0258-6); Vol. 2. Geographic-Personnel Index (ISBN 0-8103-0259-4); Vol. 3. New Special Libraries (ISBN 0-8103-0260-8). 1000p. 1981. price not set. Gale.
Dictionary of Spoken Russian: Russian-English: English-Russian. U. S. War Department. 1959. pap. 7.50 (ISBN 0-486-20496-0). Dover.
Dictionary of Spoken Spanish: Spanish-English, English-Spanish. U. S. War Department. pap. 4.95 (ISBN 0-486-20495-2). Dover.
Dictionary of Spoken Spanish Words, Phrases, Sentences. U. S. Armed Forces. LC 30-900. pap. 5.95 (ISBN 0-385-00976-3). Doubleday.
Dictionary of Sri Aurobindo's Yoga. Sri Aurobindo. Ed. by Sri M. Pandit. 1979. Repr. of 1966 ed. 7.50 (ISBN 0-89744-905-3). Auromere.
Dictionary of Statistics. Michael G. Mulhall. LC 68-18013. 1969. Repr. of 1899 ed. 44.00 (ISBN 0-8103-3887-4). Gale.
Dictionary of Subjects & Symbols in Art. 2nd, rev. ed. James Hall. LC 74-6578. (Icon Editions). (Illus.). 1979. 15.95 (ISBN 0-06-433316-7, HarpT); pap. 7.95 (ISBN 0-06-430100-1, IN-100, HarpT). Har-Row.
Dictionary of Superstitions & Mythology. Biren Bonnerjea. LC 69-17755. 1969. Repr. of 1927 ed. 20.00 (ISBN 0-8103-3572-7). Gale.
Dictionary of Telecommunication. Aries. 1981. text ed. price not set (ISBN 0-408-00328-6). Butterworth.
Dictionary of Terms & Techniques in Archeology. Sara Champion. 1980. 15.95 (ISBN 0-87196-445-7). Facts on File.
Dictionary of Terms in Art. Ed. by Frederick W. Fairholt. LC 68-30630. (Illus.). 1969. Repr. of 1854 ed. 20.00 (ISBN 0-8103-3071-7). Gale.
Dictionary of the Bible. Ed. by James Hastings. 1963. lib. rep. ed. 45.00x (ISBN 0-684-15556-7, ScribT). Scribner.
Dictionary of the Characters & Proper Names in the Works of Shakespeare. Francis G. Stokes. Repr. of 1960 ed. 49.00 (ISBN 0-403-04029-9). Somerset Pub.
Dictionary of the Characters in the Waverley Novels of Sir Walter Scott. M. F. Husband. 1962. Repr. of 1910 ed. text ed. 15.00x (ISBN 0-391-00626-6). Humanities.
Dictionary of the English Language. 1966. 49.95 Random.
Dictionary of the English Language, 2 vols. 4th ed. Samuel Johnson. 1980. 230.00 (ISBN 0-686-63570-1). Intl Bk Ctr.
Dictionary of the English Language: In Which the Words Are Deduced from Their Originals & Illustrated in Their Different Significations by Examples from the Best Writers, 2 Vols. Samuel Johnson. 1968. Repr. of 1755 ed. Set. 283.25 (ISBN 3-4870-1935-3). Adler.
Dictionary of the First or Oldest Words in the English Language: From the Semi-Saxon Period of Ad 1250 to 1300, Consisting of an Alphabetical Inventory of Every Word Found in the Printed English Literature of the 13th Century. Herbert Coleridge. LC 74-19205. 103p. 1975. Repr. of 1863 ed. 20.00 (ISBN 0-8103-4119-0). Gale.
Dictionary of the Flowering Plants & Ferns Vol. 1: Generie & Family Names. 8th ed. J. C. Willis. LC 72-83581. 1300p. 1973. 90.00 (ISBN 0-521-08699-X). Cambridge U Pr.
Dictionary of the Hawaiian Language. Lorrin Andrews. LC 72-89745. 1973. 17.50 (ISBN 0-8048-1087-7). C E Tuttle.
Dictionary of the History of Ideas. Ed. by Philip P. Wiener. 1980. pap. 100.00 5-volume boxed edition (ISBN 0-686-61145-4). Scribner.
Dictionary of the History of the American Brewing & Distilling Industries. William L. Downard. LC 79-6826.1980. lib. bdg. 35.00 (ISBN 0-313-21330-5,DOD/). Greenwood.
Dictionary of the Jewish Religion. Ben Isaacson. Ed. by David C. Gross. 208p. 1980. 12.95 (ISBN 0-89961-002-1). SBS Pub.
Dictionary of the Natural Environment: English-Arabic. Ahmad Khatib. 1979. pap. 5.95. Intl BkCtr.
Dictionary of the Natural Environment. rev. ed. F. J. Monkhouse. Ed. by John Small. 1977. 29.95 (ISBN 0-470-99333-2); pap. 9.95 (ISBN 0-470-99334-0). Halsted Pr.
Dictionary of the New Testament. Xavier Leon-Dufour. Tr. by Terrence Prendergast. LC 79-3004. (Illus.). 448p. (Fr.). 1980. 19.95 (ISBN 0-06-062100-1, HarpR). Har-Row.
Dictionary of the Occult. Ed. by Julian Franklyn. Repr. of 1935 ed. 18.00 (ISBN 0-685-32596-2). Gale.
Dictionary of the Older Scottish Tongue: From the Twelfth Century to the End of the Seventeenth, Founded on the Collections of Sir Wm Craigie, Pt. 30. Ed. by A. J. Aitken et al. 1981. pap. price not set (ISBN 0-226-11721-9, Copub with Oxford). U of Chicago Pr.
Dictionary of the Older Scottish Tongue, 4 vols. 29 pts. Sir William Craigie. 1967. Vol. I A-C. 70.00x o.s.i. (ISBN 0-226-11674-3); Vol. II D-G. 60.00x o.s.i. (ISBN 0-226-11675-1); Vol. III H-L. 80.00x o.s.i. (ISBN 0-226-11677-8); Vol. IV M-N. 50.00x o.s.i. (ISBN 0-226-11678-6); Pts. 5-8, 26, 27-29. vols. I-IV 260.00 o.s.i. (ISBN 0-226-11679-4); Pts. 8-29. 16.00 ea. o.s.i. U of Chicago Pr.
Dictionary of the Social Sciences. Hugo F. Reading. 1977. 14.00 (ISBN 0-7100-8642-3); pap. 6.95 (ISBN 0-7100-8650-4). Routledge & Kegan.

Dictionary of the Welsh Language, Vol. 1. A-ffysvr. Wales University. 1950. Pts. 1-21. 90.00 (ISBN 0-7083-0504-0); Pts. 22-29. pap. 8.00x ea. Verry.
Dictionary of Theology. 2nd ed. Karl Rahner & Herbert Vorgrimler. 500p. (Ger.). 1981. 24.50 (ISBN 0-8245-0040-7). Crossroad NY.
Dictionary of Theoretical Concepts in Biology. Keith E. Roe & Richard G. Frederick. LC 80-19889. 312p. 1981. 17.50 (ISBN 0-8108-1353-X). Scarecrow.
Dictionary of Thermodynamics. Arthur M. James. LC 76-5472. 1976. 19.95 (ISBN 0-470-15035-1). Halsted Pr.
Dictionary of Tools. Salaman. 1974. 47.50 (ISBN 0-87002-912-6). Bennett IL.
Dictionary of Tourism. Ed. by Charles J. Metelka. 1981. 14.95 (ISBN 0-916032-10-8). Merton Hse.
Dictionary of Tropical American Crops & Their Diseases. Frederick L. Wellman. LC 77-8558. 1977. 24.00 (ISBN 0-8108-1071-9). Scarecrow.
Dictionary of Tropical Fish. 12.95 o.p. (ISBN 0-87666-157-6, H904). TFH Pubns.
Dictionary of Twentieth Century Italian Violin Makers & Import Dealers Scrapbook. Marlin Brinser. 1978. pap. 12.50 (ISBN 0-9602298-1-7). M Brinser.
Dictionary of United States History: Alphabetical, Chronological, Statistical. rev. ed. J. Franklin Jameson. Ed. by Albert E. McKinley. LC 68-30658. (Illus.). 1971. Repr. of 1931 ed. 34.00 (ISBN 0-8103-3332-5). Gale.
Dictionary of Universal Biography of All Ages & of All People. 2nd ed. Albert M. Hyamson. 1976. Repr. of 1916 ed. 46.00 (ISBN 0-7100-1580-1). Routledge & Kegan.
Dictionary of Urdu, Classical Hindi, & English. John T. Platts. 1930. 74.00x (ISBN 0-19-864309-8). Oxford U Pr.
Dictionary of Useful & Everyday Plants & Their Common Names. F. N. Howes. LC 73-91701. 300p. 1974. 32.95 (ISBN 0-521-08520-9). Cambridge U Pr.
Dictionary of Vedic Rituals. Chitrabhanu Sen. 1978. 22.50x o.p. (ISBN 0-8364-0278-2). South Asia Bks.
Dictionary of Victorian Painters. 2nd ed. Ed. by Christopher Wood. (Illus.). 764p. 1978. 95.00 (ISBN 0-902028-72-3, Pub. by Antique Collectors Club England). Gale.
Dictionary of Visual Language. Compiled by Philip Thompson & Peter Davenport. (Illus.). 288p. 1981. 30.00x (ISBN 0-312-20108-7). St Martin.
Dictionary of Waste & Water Treatment. Scott & Smith. 1981. text ed. price not set (ISBN 0-408-00495-9). Butterworth.
Dictionary of Western Kamchadal. Dean S. Worth. (U. C. Publ. in Linguistics: Vol. 59). 1969. pap. 10.00x (ISBN 0-520-09256-2). U of Cal Pr.
Dictionary of Wine Terms. 19th ed. Irving H. Marcus. 72p. 1979. pap. 1.25 (ISBN 0-686-64866-8). Wine Pubns.
Dictionary of Zoology. 3rd ed. A. W. Leftwich. 487p. 1973. 27.50x (ISBN 0-8448-0845-8). Crane-Russak Co.
Dictionary Skills. (Elementary Skills Ser.). (gr. 3-6). 1977. 1.35 ea. Bk. C (ISBN 0-8372-3510-3). Bk. D (ISBN 0-8372-3511-1). Bk. E. Bk. F (ISBN 0-8372-3513-8). tchr's ed. avail. Bowmar-Noble.
Dictionary Studies Duplicating Masters, 4 vols. (Spice Duplicating Masters Ser). 1974. Vol. 1, Grades K-2, Single Letters. 5.95 (ISBN 0-89273-527-9); Vol. 2, Grades K-2, Letter Combinations. 5.95 (ISBN 0-89273-528-7); Vol. 3, Grades 3-6. 5.95 (ISBN 0-89273-529-5); Vol. 4, Grades 7-9. 5.95 (ISBN 0-89273-530-9). Educ Serv.
Dictionnaire analogique. G. Niobey. (Fr). 26.50 (ISBN 0-685-13850-X, 3608). Larousse.
Dictionnaire art contemporain. Raymond Charmet. (Illus., Fr.). pap. 8.50 (ISBN 0-685-13851-8, 3704). Larousse.
Dictionnaire bilingue francais-russe et russe-francais. 10.50 (ISBN 2-03-020904-X, 2715, Apollo). Larousse.
Dictionnaire bilingue Larousse, francais-anglais, anglais-francais. L. Chaffurin & J. Mergault. (Apollo). (Fr. & Eng.). 10.50 (ISBN 0-685-13856-9, 3767). Larousse.
Dictionnaire bilingue Larousse, francais-alemand et allemand-francais. A. Pinloche & A. Jolivet. (Apollo). (Fr. & Ger.). 10.50 (ISBN 0-685-13853-4, 3779). Larousse.
Dictionnaire bilingue Larousse, francais-espagnol, espanol-frances. M. De Toro & Gisbert. (Apollo). (Fr. & Span.). 10.50 (ISBN 0-685-13857-7, 3774). Larousse.
Dictionnaire bilingue Larousse, francais-italien et italien-francais. G. Padovani & R. Silvestri. (Apollo). (Fr.). 10.50 (ISBN 0-685-13854-2, 3784). Larousse.
Dictionnaire bilingue Larousse, francais-portugais et portugais-francais. F. Peixoto Da Fonseca. (Apollo). (Fr. & Port.). 10.50 (ISBN 2-03-020909-0, 3791). Larousse.
Dictionnaire chasse. Tony Burnand. (Dictionnaires de l'homme du vingtieme siecle). (Fr). 1970. 8.50 (ISBN 0-685-13859-3, 3711). Larousse.
Dictionnaire chateaux de France. (Illus., Fr.). pap. 8.50 (ISBN 0-685-13860-7, 3712). Larousse.
Dictionnaire civilisation grecque. G. Rachet & M. F. Rachet. (Illus., Fr.). pap. 8.50 (ISBN 0-685-13861-5, 3715). Larousse.
Dictionnaire civilisation romaine. Jean C. Fredoville. (Dictionnaires de l'homme du vingtieme siecle). (Illus., Fr.). 1968. 8.50 (ISBN 0-685-13862-3, 3716). Larousse.
Dictionnaire complet des mots croises. Larousse And Co. (Fr). 27.50 (ISBN 2-03-020294-0, 3617). Larousse.
Dictionnaire d'anglais. F. Dubois-Charlier et al. 868p. (Fr.). 1975. pap. text ed. 11.50 (ISBN 2-03-040531-0). Larousse.
Dictionnaire De Bibliographie Haitienne: Premier Supplement. Max Bissainthe. LC 51-12164. 1973. 10.00 (ISBN 0-8108-0667-3). Scarecrow.
Dictionnaire de linguistique. J. Dubois & M. Giacomo. 516p. (Fr.). 1974. 27.50 (ISBN 2-03-020299-1, 1002). Larousse.
Dictionnaire De Plain-Chant et De Musique D'eglise. M. J. D'Ortigue. LC 79-155353. (Music Ser). 1971. Repr. of 1854 ed. lib. bdg. 65.00 (ISBN 0-306-70165-0). Da Capo.
Dictionnaire De Two Hundred One Verbes Anglais Conjugues Completement a Tous les Temps et a Toutes les Personnes. Kendris. Date not set. pap. 3.95 (ISBN 0-8120-0550-3). Barron.
Dictionnaire De Two Hundred One Verbes Allemandes. Date not set. 6.95 (ISBN 0-8120-2118-5). Barron.
Dictionnaire de Victor Hugo. Philippe Van Tieghem. (Dictionnaires de l'homme du vingtieme siecle). (Orig., Fr). 1970. pap. 8.50 (ISBN 0-685-13864-X, 3722). Larousse.
Dictionnaire Des Arts Du Spectacle. Cecile Giteau. LC 79-499699. 455p. (Fr, Eng. & Ger.). 1970. 25.00x (ISBN 0-8002-1364-5). Intl Pubns Serv.
Dictionnaire des Communes de France (Guide to French Townships) Michelin Guides & Maps. 1979. 45.00 (ISBN 2-06-007500-9). Michelin.
Dictionnaire des difficultes de la langue francaise. A. V. Thomas. (Fr). 23.50 (ISBN 0-685-13865-8, 3611). Larousse.
Dictionnaire des fromages. Robert J. Courtine. 255p. (Fr.). 1972. pap. 8.50 (ISBN 2-03-075473-0, 3792). Larousse.
Dictionnaire Des Idees Dans L'oeuvre De Simone de Beauvoir. Christian van den Berghe. (Collection Dictionnaires Des Idees, Litterature Francaise: No. 1). 1966. 20.50x (ISBN 0-686-20917-6). Mouton.
Dictionnaire des locutions francaises. M. Rat. (Fr). 23.50 (ISBN 0-685-13866-6, 3613). Larousse.
Dictionnaire des noms de famille et prenoms de France. A. Dauzat. (Fr). 23.50 (ISBN 2-03-020260-6, 3615). Larousse.
Dictionnaire Des Operas, 2 Vols. Felix Clement & Pierre Larousse. LC 69-15617. (Music Reprint Ser). 1969. Repr. of 1905 ed. 95.00 (ISBN 0-306-71197-4). Da Capo.
Dictionnaire des proverbes, sentences et maximes. M. Maloux. (Fr). 23.50 (ISBN 2-03-020291-6, 3618). Larousse.
Dictionnaire des rimes orales et ecrites. new ed. Leon Warnant. 553p. (Fr.). 1972. 23.50 (ISBN 2-03-020271-1, 3546). Larousse.
Dictionnaire des synonymes. R. Bailly. (Fr). 23.50 (ISBN 0-685-13870-4, 3621). Larousse.
Dictionnaire Des Techniques Aerospatiales. LC 72-315260. 406p. (Eng. & Fr.). 1971. 32.50x (ISBN 0-8002-1216-9). Intl Pubns Serv.
Dictionnaire Des Terms Juridiques et Commerciaux (Francais-Arabe) Mamdouh Hakki. 1973. 20.00x (ISBN 0-685-72038-1). Intl Bk Ctr.
Dictionnaire des verbes francais. J. P. Caput & J. Caput. (Fr). 27.50 (ISBN 0-685-13871-2, 3622). Larousse.
Dictionnaire du francais contemporain: Manuel et travaux pratique. (Fr.). 17.95 (ISBN 0-685-92177-8, 4078). Larousse.
Dictionnaire du francais contemporain. Jean Dubois et al. 940p. (Fr.). 1975. pap. 16.50 (ISBN 2-03-029325-3, 3935). Larousse.
Dictionnaire du francais contemporain. Larousse And Co. (Fr). 27.50 (ISBN 0-685-13872-0, 3745). Larousse.
Dictionnaire du vocabulaire essentiel. Larousse And Co. (Illus., Fr.). pap. 12.25 (ISBN 0-685-13873-9, 3753). Larousse.
Dictionnaire Encyclopedique Quillet, 10 vols. (Fr.). 1977. 545.00 (ISBN 0-8277-3013-6). Maxwell Sci Intl.
Dictionnaire francais-anglais, anglais-francais des affaires: A French-English English-French Dictionary of Business Terms. rev. ed. Michel Peron et al. 512p. 1974. 29.95 (ISBN 2-03-020609-1, 3764). Larousse.
Dictionnaire francais-hebreu. M. M. Cohn. (Fr. & Heb.). 29.00 (ISBN 0-685-13874-7). Larousse.
Dictionnaire General, 5 vols. Emile B. De La Chavignerie & Louis Auvray. Ed. by Robert Rosenblum. LC 78-68412. 1979. Repr. of 1885 ed. lib. bdg. 275.00 (ISBN 0-8240-3539-9). Garland Pub.
Dictionnaire mathematiques modernes. L. Chambadal. (Illus., Fr.). pap. 7.75 o.p. (ISBN 0-685-13875-5). Larousse.
Dictionnaire moderne Larousse, francais-allemand et allemand-francais. P. Grappin. (Fr. & Ger.). 39.95 (ISBN 2-03-020603-2, 3778). Larousse.
Dictionnaire moderne Larousse, francais-espagnol et espagnol-francais. R. Garcia-Pelayo & J. Testas. (Span. & Fr.). 39.95 (ISBN 2-03-020601-6, 3773). Larousse.
Dictionnaire mythologie grecque et romaine. J. Schmidt. (Illus., Fr.). pap. 8.50 (ISBN 2-03-075408-0, 3728). Larousse.
Dictionnaire oiseaux. Michel Cuisin. (Illus., Fr.). pap. 8.50 (ISBN 0-685-13879-8, 3729). Larousse.
Dictionnaire philosophie. D. Julia. (Illus., Fr.). pap. 8.50 (ISBN 0-685-13881-X). Larousse.
Dictionnaire prehistoire. (Illus., Fr.). pap. 8.50 (ISBN 0-685-13882-8). Larousse.
Dictionnaire psychologie. N. Sillamy. (Illus., Fr.). pap. 8.50 (ISBN 0-685-13883-6). Larousse.
Dictionnaire russe-francais. P. Pauliat. 11.95 (ISBN 0-685-13884-4, 3790). Larousse.
Dictionnaire theatre francais contemporain. Alfred Simon. (Dict. de l'Homme du Vingtieme Siecle). (Illus., Fr.). 1970. 8.50 (ISBN 0-685-13885-2, 3740). Larousse.
Dictionnaire vins. Gerard Debuigne. (Illus., Fr.). pap. 8.50 (ISBN 0-03-075459-3, 3742). Larousse.
Did Adam Name the Vinegarron? X. J. Kennedy. (Illus.). 32p. 1980. 10.00 (ISBN 0-87923-389-3). Godine.
Did Genesis Man Conquer Space? Emil Gaverluk. LC 74-1262. (Illus.). 192p. 1974. pap. 2.95 o.p. (ISBN 0-8407-5553-8). Nelson.
Did I Have a Good Time? Teenage Drinking. Marion Howard. 192p. 1980. 10.95 (ISBN 0-8264-0017-5). Continuum.
Did I Say That? (Editing Your First Draft) Sidney R. Wilson & Eugene H. Soules. 1976. pap. 3.25 (ISBN 0-86589-005-6). Individual Learn.
Did Jesus Exist? G. A. Wells. (Skeptic's Bookshelf Ser.). 241p. 1975. 13.95 (ISBN 0-87975-086-3). Prometheus Bks.
Did We Save the Earth at Stockholm? Peter B. Stone. (Earth Island Ser). 1973. 5.95x o.p. (ISBN 0-85644-017-5); pap. 3.95 o.p. (ISBN 0-85644-023-X). Friends Earth.
Did You Ever. Paula Goldsmid. (Illus.). 30p. (ps-k). 1971. pap. 2.50 (ISBN 0-914996-01-0). Lollipop Power.
Did You Ever. Doris H. Lund. LC 64-19768. (Illus.). (gr. k-2). 1965. 5.95 o.s.i. (ISBN 0-8193-0088-8, Four Winds); PLB 5.41 o.s.i. (ISBN 0-8193-0089-6). Schol Bk Serv.
Did You Ever? Traditional Verse. Gwen Fulton. 24p. (gr. k up). 1981. 8.95 (ISBN 0-224-01740-3, Pub. by Chatto-Bodley-Jonathan). Merrimack Bk Serv.
Did You Hear What Happened to Andrea? Gloria D. Miklowitz. (YA) (gr. 7-12). pap. 1.75 (ISBN 0-440-91853-7, LE). Dell.
Did You Whittinghill This Morning? The Madcap Adventures of a Hollywood Disc Jockey. Dick Whittinghill & Don Page. LC 76-6294. (Illus.). 1976. 7.95 o.p. (ISBN 0-8092-8064-7). Contemp Bks.
Didactics & Mathematics. University of Oregon. 1978. 12.00 (ISBN 0-88488-088-5). Creative Pubns.
Diddie, Dumps & Tot. Louise-Clarke Pyrnelle. 1963. 8.95 (ISBN 0-911116-17-6). Pelican.
Diderot. Otis Fellows. (World Authors Ser.: France: No. 425). 1977. lib. bdg. 10.95 (ISBN 0-8057-6265-5). Twayne.
Diderot & the Encyclopaedists, 2 vols. John Morley. LC 74-145521. 1971. Repr. of 1923 ed. 24.00 (ISBN 0-8103-3987-0). Gale.
Diderot & the Jews. Leon Schwartz. LC 78-73304. 220p. 1981. 14.50 (ISBN 0-8386-2377-8). Fairleigh Dickinson.
Diderot, Interpreter of Nature: Selected Writings. Denis Diderot. Ed. by Jonathon Kemp. Tr. by Jean Stewart & Jonathon Kemp. LC 78-65607. 1981. Repr. of 1937 ed. 26.50 (ISBN 0-88355-841-6). Hyperion Conn.
Dido, Queen of Infinite Literary Variety: The English Renaissance Borrowings & Influences. Adrianne Roberts-Baytop. (Salzburg Studies in English Literature, Elizabethan & Renaissance Studies: No. 25). 154p. 1974. pap. text ed. 25.00x (ISBN 0-391-01511-7). Humanities.
Die & Mould Making. Ed. by L. R. Brazier et al. (Engineering Craftsmen: No. H22). (Illus.). 1970. spiral bdg. 18.50x (ISBN 0-85083-126-1). Intl Ideas.
Die Design Fundamentals. J. R. Paquin. (Illus.). (gr. 11-12). 1962. 19.00 (ISBN 0-8311-1010-4); wkbk. 7.00 (ISBN 0-8311-1011-2). Indus Pr.
Die Laughing. Lawrence Kane et al. LC 79-7498. (Illus.). 1980. pap. 4.95 (ISBN 0-385-15071-7, Dolp). Doubleday.
Die Methods: Design, Frabrication, Maintainance & Application, Bk. 1. Ed. by Paul B. Schubert. LC 66-19984. (Illus.). 464p. 1966. 18.00 (ISBN 0-8311-1013-9). Indus Pr.
Die of Gold. Chet Cunningham. 1980. pap. 1.50 (ISBN 0-505-51471-0). Tower Bks.
Die Song. Donald T. Lunde & Jefferson Morgan. LC 80-83566. 288p. 1981. pap. 2.95 (ISBN 0-87216-803-4). Playboy Pbks.
Die Varieties of Early United States Coins. Robert Hilt. 208p. 1980. 75.00x (ISBN 0-934904-08-1). J & L Lee.
Dieciocho, No Hay Tiempo Que Perder. Tr. by Margaret Johnson. (Spanish Bks.). (Span.). 1978. 1.65 (ISBN 0-8297-0533-3). Life Pubs Intl.
Died on a Rainy Sunday. Joan Aiken. LC 72-182777. 160p. (gr. 7 up). 1972. reinforced bdg. 4.95 o.p. (ISBN 0-03-089491-3). HR&W.
Died on the Fourth of July: A Jewish Unitarian Psychologist Flees a Fascist Fellowship. Albert Eglash. LC 80-53581. (Illus.). 100p. (Orig.). 1981. pap. 20.00 (ISBN 0-935320-22-9). Quest Pr.
Diego De Saavedra Fajardo. John Dowling. (World Authors Ser.: No. 437). 1977. lib. bdg. 12.50 (ISBN 0-8057-6200-0). Twayne.
Diego De Torres Villarroel. I. L. McClelland. (World Authos Ser.: Spain: No. 395). 1976. lib. bdg. 12.50 (ISBN 0-8057-6237-X). Twayne.
Dieguenо Indians. A. L. Kroeber et al. 1975. pap. 2.00 (ISBN 0-916552-02-0). Acoma Bks.
Dielectric Behaviour of Biological Molecules in Solution. E. H. Grant et al. (Monographs on Physical Biochemistry). (Illus.). 1978. 39.95x (ISBN 0-19-854621-1). Oxford U Pr.
Dielectric Phenomena & the Double Layer in Disperse Systems & Polyelectrolytes. S. S. Dukhin & V. N. Shilov. Ed. by P. Greenberg. Tr. by D. Lederman from Rus. LC 74-13579. 200p. 1974. 34.95 (ISBN 0-470-22415-0). Halsted Pr.
Dielectric Properties of Binary Solutions: A Data Handbook. Ya Y. Akhadov. 400p. Date not set. 112.50 (ISBN 0-08-023600-6). Pergamon.
Dielectric Solids. A. A. Zaky & R. Hawley. (Solid-State Physics Ser.). 1970. pap. 5.00 (ISBN 0-7100-6604-X). Routledge & Kegan.
Dielectric Spectroscopy of Polymers. Peter Hedvig. LC 75-9653. 1977. 59.95 (ISBN 0-470-36747-4). Halsted Pr.
Dielectrics. P. J. Harrop. 1972. 12.95 (ISBN 0-408-70387-3); pap. 7.95 (ISBN 0-408-70388-1). Butterworths.
Dielectrophoresis. H. A. Pohl. LC 77-71421. (Cambridge Monographs on Physics). (Illus.). 1978. 99.50 (ISBN 0-521-21657-5). Cambridge U Pr.
Dien Bien Phu, 1954: The Battle That Ended the First Indochina War. Phillip Poole. LC 79-185286. (World Focus Bks). (Illus.). 96p. (gr. 7 up). 1972. PLB 4.90 o.p. (ISBN 0-531-02156-4). Watts.
Dieppe. Harold Calin. 1978. pap. 1.75 (ISBN 0-505-51231-9). Tower Bks.
Diesel Car Book. Roger Barlow. LC 80-8913. (Illus.). 288p. (Orig.). 1981. pap. 7.95 (ISBN 0-394-17895-5, Ever). Grove.
Diesel Combustion & Emissions. Society of Automotive Engineers. 1980. 30.00 (ISBN 0-89883-055-9). Soc Auto Engineers.
Diesel Engine Manual. 3rd ed. Perry O. Black. LC 64-23154. (Illus.). 480p. 1964. 10.95 (ISBN 0-672-23199-9, 23199). Audel.
Diesel Engineers, Combustion & Emissions Research in Japan. Society of Automotive Engineers. 1980. 25.00 (ISBN 0-89883-239-X). Soc Auto Engineers.
Diesel Engines for Automobiles & Small Trucks. Tom Weathers & Claud Hunter. 300p. 1981. text ed. 16.95 (ISBN 0-8359-1288-4); instr's. manual free (ISBN 0-8359-1289-2). Reston.
Diesel Engines Noise Conference: Proceedings. Society of Automotive Engineers. 1979. 29.95 (ISBN 0-89883-050-8). Soc Auto Engineers.
Diesel Engines Thermal Loading. Society of Automotive Engineers. 1979. 22.00 (ISBN 0-89883-220-9). Soc Auto Engineers.
Diesel Equipment I, Workbook: Lubrication, Hydraulics, Brakes, Wheels, Tires. Erich J. Schulz. Ed. by D. E. Gilmore. (Illus.). 56p. 1980. 5.95 (ISBN 0-07-055716-0, G); intructor's guide avail. (ISBN 0-07-055718-7); wkbk. avail. (ISBN 0-07-055717-9). McGraw.

Diesel Equipment II, Workbook: Design, Electronic Controls, Frames, Suspensions, Steering, Transmissions, Drive Lines, Air Conditioning. Erich J. Schulz. Ed. by D. E. Gilmore. (Illus.). 64p. 1980. 5.95 (ISBN 0-07-055708-X, G); instructor's guide avail. (ISBN 0-07-055711-X); wkbk. avail. (ISBN 0-07-055709-8). McGraw.

Diesel Fuel Systems. Robert N. Brady. (Illus.). 640p. 1981. text ed. 21.95 (ISBN 0-8359-1293-0). soln. manual avail. (ISBN 0-8359-1294-9). Reston.

Diesel Hydraulic Locomotives of the Western Region: England. Brian Reed. LC 74-81059. (Locomotive Studies). (Illus.). 112p. 1981. 16.95 (ISBN 0-7153-6769-2). David & Charles.

Diesel Years. Robert Olmsted. LC 75-17721. (Illus.). 1975. 19.95 (ISBN 0-87095-054-1). Golden West.

Diet & Drug in Atherosclerosis. Ed. by Giorgio Noseda et al. 352p. 1980. text ed. 26.00 (ISBN 0-89004-491-0). Raven.

Diet & Exercise Diary. James Wagenvoord. (Illus.). 160p. 1981. 6.95 (ISBN 0-312-20996-7). St Martin.

Diet & Menu Guide for Hospitals. American Hospital Association. (Illus.). 64p. 1969. pap. 10.25 o.p. (ISBN 0-87258-046-6, 1411). Am Hospital.

Diet Chef's Gourmet Cookbook. Myles Omel. LC 80-70958. 288p. 1981. 14.95 (ISBN 0-8119-0328-1). Fell.

Diet Diary. William I. Kaufman. (Watch Your Diet Ser.). (Orig.). 1981. pap. 1.75 (ISBN 0-515-05915-3). Jove Pubns.

Diet for a Happy Heart: A Low-Cholesterol, Low-Saturated Fat, Low Calorie Cookbook. rev. ed. Jeanne Jones. (Illus.). 192p. 1981. pap. 6.95 (ISBN 0-89286-183-5). One Hurd One Prods.

Diet for a Small Planet. rev ed. Frances M. Lappe. 432p. 1975. spiral bdg. 7.95 (ISBN 0-345-28919-6); pap. 2.75 (ISBN 0-345-29515-3). Ballantine.

Diet for Life. Francine Prince. 1981. pap. 4.95 (ISBN 0-346-12496-4). Cornerstone.

Diet for One Hundred Healthy, Happy Years. Morvyth McQueen-Williams & Barbara Appisson. 1978. pap. 1.95 (ISBN 0-515-04523-3). Jove Pubns.

Diet in Health & Disease: Rationale & Practice. R. S. Dickie. 296p. 1975. 24.75 (ISBN 0-398-02899-0); pap. 18.50 (ISBN 0-398-02919-9). C C Thomas.

Diet in Pregnancy: A Randomized Controlled Trail of Nutritional Supplements. Ed. by David Rush et al. LC 79-3846. (Alan R. Liss Ser.: Vol. 16, No. 3). 1980. 26.00 (ISBN 0-8451-1037-3). March of Dimes.

Diet in Pregnancy: A Randomized Controlled Trial of Nutritional Supplements, Vol.xvi,no.3. David Rush et al. LC 79-3846. (Birth Defects: Original Article Series: Vol. XVI, No. 3). 188p. 1980. 26.00x (ISBN 0-8451-1037-3). A R Liss.

Diet Management for Ulcerative Colitis: Menus, Recipes & Methods of Food Preparation for Anti-Inflammatory Treatment. Map Hanson. 80p. 1971. pap. 10.50 spiral (ISBN 0-398-02307-7). C C Thomas.

Diet, Nutrition & Dentistry. Patricia M. Randolph. (Illus.). 358p. 1980. pap. text ed. 14.95 (ISBN 0-8016-4088-1). Mosby.

Diet of Man: Needs & Wants. Ed. by John Yudkin. (Illus.). 1978. text ed. 57.00x (ISBN 0-85334-750-6, Pub. by Applied Science). Burgess-Intl Ideas.

Diet the Natural Way. Eydie May & Arn Hunsberger. LC 77-75938. (Orig.). 1980. pap. cancelled (ISBN 0-89081-067-2). Harvest Hse.

Diet Training for Sportsmen. Rosewall & Wilson. pap. 1.00x (ISBN 0-392-07230-0, SpS). Soccer.

Diet with Vitamins. David P. Rubincam & John Rubincam. LC 77-73140. 1977. 8.95 o.p. (ISBN 0-89479-007-2). A & W Pubs.

Diet Without Hunger. Doris M. Townsend. LC 77-11603. 1978. pap. 2.95 (ISBN 0-87469-016-1, 8084). Larousse.

Dieta Siabetica Para Buena Salud. Margaret B. Salmon. (Illus.). 1979. pap. 1.50 (ISBN 0-918662-06-0). Techkits.

Dietary Lipids & Postnatal Development. Ed. by C. Galli et al. LC 73-79580. (Illus.). 286p. 1973. 27.00 (ISBN 0-911216-50-2). Raven.

Dietary Nutrient Guide. Jean A. Pennington. (Illus.). 1976. pap. text ed. 21.50 (ISBN 0-87055-196-5). AVI.

Dieter's Complete Guide to Calories, Carbohydrates, Sodium, Fats & Cholesterol. Consumer Guide Editors. 192p. (Orig.). 1981. pap. 5.95 (ISBN 0-449-90050-9, Columbine). Fawcett.

Dietetic Com Pak Student Guide. Loretta Hoover & Aimee Moore. 1978. text ed. 6.50x (ISBN 0-87543-094-5). Lucas.

Dieting Gourmet. Eileen Reece. 1976. 10.50 o.p. (ISBN 0-04-641028-7). Allen Unwin.

Dietrich Bonhoeffer. Edwin H. Robertson. LC 66-15514. (Makers of Contemporary Theology Ser). (Orig.). 1966. pap. 3.45 (ISBN 0-8042-0535-3). John Knox.

Diets for Birds in Captivity. Kenton C. Lint & Alice M. Lint. (Illus.). 192p. 1981. 50.00 (ISBN 0-7137-1087-X, Pub. by Blandford Pr England). Sterling.

Diets for Sick Children. 3rd ed. Dorothy Francis & Daphne Dixon. 432p. 1975. 25.00 (ISBN 0-397-60319-3, Blackwell). Mosby.

Dieu Repond-Problemes-Hommes. Tr. by D. Pentecost. (French Bks.). (Fr.). 1979. write for info. Life Pubs Intl.

Diez Comedias Atribuidas a Lope De Vega: Estudio Do Su Autenticidad. Augusto A. Portuondo. 1980. pap. 17.00 (ISBN 84-499-3788-4). Biblio Siglo.

Diez Cuentos Hispanoamericanos. Alejandro Arratia & Carlos D. Hamilton. (Span). 1958. pap. 5.95x (ISBN 0-19-500818-9). Oxford U Pr.

Diez Pasos Para Alcanzar la Victoria. Tr. by Harold Hill. (Spanish Bks.). (Span.). 1978. 1.90 (ISBN 0-8297-0864-2). Life Pubs Intl.

Difference Between the Fichtean & Schellingian Systems of Philosophy. G. W. Hegel. Tr. by Jere P. Surber from Ger. 1978. pap. text ed. 6.50x (ISBN 0-917930-12-6); lib. bdg. 21.00 (ISBN 0-917930-32-0). Ridgeview.

Difference in the Family: Life with a Disabled Child. Helen Featherstone. LC 79-56668. 262p. 1980. 13.95 (ISBN 0-465-01654-5). Basic.

Difference Methods for Initial-Value Problems. 2nd ed. Robert D. Richtmyer & K. W. Morton. LC 67-13959. (Pure & Applied Mathematics Ser.). (Illus.). 1967. 37.95 (ISBN 0-470-72040-9, Pub. by Wiley-Interscience). Wiley.

Differences Between States in Arid Law Administration. M. D. Young. 1980. 13.00x (ISBN 0-643-00336-3, Pub. by CSJRO Australia). State Mutual Bk.

Different Dream. Donna Vitek. 192p. (Orig.). 1980. pap. 1.50 (ISBN 0-671-57033-1). S&S.

Different Drummer. William Melvin Kelley. LC 62-11453. 1969. pap. 2.50 (ISBN 0-385-01079-6, A678, Anch). Doubleday.

Different Face. Joan Mellows. (Regency Romance Ser.). 1979. pap. 1.75 o.p. (ISBN 0-449-24046-0, Crest). Fawcett.

Different Flame. Marjorie M. Bitker. 1976. pap. 1.50 o.p. (ISBN 0-445-03126-3). Popular Lib.

Different Kind of Gold. Cecily Stern. LC 80-8452. (Illus.). 128p. (gr. 5 up). 1981. 9.95 (ISBN 0-06-025770-9, HarpJ); PLB 9.89g (ISBN 0-06-025771-7). Har-Row.

Different Light. Elizabeth A. Lynn. 1980. pap. 2.25 (ISBN 0-425-04824-1). Berkley Pub.

Different Story: A Black History of Fredericksburg, Stafford & Spotsylvania, Virginia. Ruth C. Fitzgerald. LC 79-67534. (Illus.). 336p. 1980. 9.95 (ISBN 0-9604564-2-2); pap. 4.95 (ISBN 0-9604564-3-0). Unicorn VA.

Different Strokes: Pathways to Maturity in the Boston Ghetto. Robert Rosenthal et al. LC 76-7952. 1976. 27.50x (ISBN 0-89158-036-0); pap. 11.00x (ISBN 0-89158-047-6). Westview.

Different War Story. Laurel Speer. (Novella Discovery Ser.). 150p. (Orig.). pap. 5.00 (ISBN 0-933906-11-0). Gusto Pr.

Differentiable Dynamics: An Introduction to the Orbit Structure of Diffeomorphisms. Zbigniew Nitecki. 1971. pap. 10.00x (ISBN 0-262-64011-2). MIT Pr.

Differentiable Germs & Catastrophes. T. H. Brocker. Tr. by L. Lander from Ger. LC 74-17000. (London Mathematical Society Lecture Note Ser.: No. 17). 160p. (Eng.). 1975. pap. text ed. 19.95 (ISBN 0-521-20681-2). Cambridge U Pr.

Differential Analysis. T. M. Flett. Ed. by J. S. Pym. LC 78-67303. (Illus.). 1980. 47.50 (ISBN 0-521-22420-9). Cambridge U Pr.

Differential & Integral Calculus, 2 vols. R. Courant. Incl. Vol. 1. 630p. 1937. 26.95 (ISBN 0-471-17820-9); Vol. 2. 692p. 1936. 26.95 (ISBN 0-471-17853-5). Pub. by Wiley-Interscience). Wiley.

Differential & Integral Calculus. F. Erwe. Tr. by B. Fishel. (Illus.). 1967. 14.25 o.s.i. (ISBN 0-02-844300-4). Hafner.

Differential & Riemannian Geometry. D. Laugwitz. Tr. by F. Steinhardt. 1965. 33.50 (ISBN 0-12-437750-5). Acad Pr.

Differential Calculus. P. J. Hilton. (Library of Mathematics). 1968. pap. 5.00 (ISBN 0-7100-4341-4). Routledge & Kegan.

Differential-Delay Equations with Two Time Lags. Roger D. Nussbaum. LC 78-16320. (Memoirs: No. 205). 1978. 6.80 (ISBN 0-8218-2205-5, MEMO-205). Am Math.

Differential Diagnosis: An Integrated Handbook. Harold T. Hyman. 1965. 14.00 o.p. (ISBN 0-397-50136-6). Lippincott.

Differential Diagnosis & Treatment in Social Work. 2nd ed. Francis J. Turner. LC 75-26054. 1976. text ed. 18.95 (ISBN 0-02-932730-X). Free Pr.

Differential Diagnosis & Treatment of Hoarseness. D. P. Bryce. (Illus.). 88p. 1974. 11.75 (ISBN 0-398-03166-5). C C Thomas.

Differential Diagnosis & Treatment of Pediatric Allergy. Bernard A. Berman & Kenneth F. MacDonnell. 1981. text ed. write for info (ISBN 0-316-09182-0). Little.

Differential Diagnosis in Dermatopathology. A. Bernard Ackerman et al. (Illus.). 200p. 1981. text ed. 86.00 (ISBN 0-8121-0800-0). Lea & Febiger.

Differential Diagnosis in Pediatrics. H. Ewerbeck. 470p. 1980. spiral bdg. 19.00 (ISBN 0-387-90474-3). Springer-Verlag.

Differential Diagnosis of Chest Pain & Other Cardiac Symptoms. Ed. by Jacob I. Haft. LC 80-68061. (Advances in the Management of Clinical Heart Disease Monograph: Vol. 4). (Illus.). 230p. 1980. 26.50 (ISBN 0-87993-150-7). Futura Pub.

Differential Diagnosis of Intraocular Tumors: A Stereoscopic Presentation. J. Donald Gass. (Illus.). 1974. text ed. 79.50 o.p. (ISBN 0-8016-1750-2). Mosby.

Differential Diagnostisches Kompendium. 2nd ed. J. Horny. (Illus.). xvi, 260p. 1980. pap. text ed. 17.00 (ISBN 3-8055-0585-X). S Karger.

Differential Equations. Harry Bateman. LC 66-23754. 1967. 11.95 (ISBN 0-8284-0190-X). Chelsea Pub.

Differential Equations. 2nd ed. Kaj L. Nielsen. (Orig.). 1969. pap. 4.95 (ISBN 0-06-460072-6, CO 72, COS). Har-Row.

Differential Equations. 2nd ed. Shepley L. Ross. LC 73-84447. 1974. text ed. 21.95 (ISBN 0-471-00930-X). Wiley.

Differential Equations. John A. Tierney. 1978. text ed. 20.95x (ISBN 0-205-06167-2). Allyn.

Differential Equations: A Modern Approach. Harry Hochstadt. LC 75-2569. (Illus.). 320p. 1975. pap. text ed. 5.00 (ISBN 0-486-61941-9). Dover.

Differential Equations & Their Applications: An Introduction to Applied Mathematics. M. Braun. LC 74-31123. (Applied Mathematics Sciences Ser.: Vol. 15). (Illus.). xiv, 718p. 1975. pap. 15.60 o.p. (ISBN 0-387-90114-0). Springer-Verlag.

Differential Equations, Dynamical Systems & Linear Algebra. Morris Hirsch & Stephen Smale. 1974. text ed. 21.95 (ISBN 0-12-349550-4). Acad Pr.

Differential Equations of Applied Mathematics. George F. Duff & D. Naylor. 1966. 27.95 o.p. (ISBN 0-471-22367-0). Wiley.

Differential Equations Problem Solver: A Supplement to Any Class Text. LC 78-63609. 1978. pap. text ed. 22.85 (ISBN 0-87891-513-3). Res & Educ.

Differential Equations: Theory & Use in Time & Motion. Alice B. Dickinson. LC 77-136120. (Mathematics Ser). 1972. text ed. 18.95 (ISBN 0-201-01515-3). A-W.

Differential Equations with Small Parameters & Relaxation Oscillations. E. F. Mishchenko & B. Kh Rozov. (Mathematical Concepts & Methods in Science & Engineering Ser.: Vol. 13). (Illus.). 251p. 1980. 29.50 (ISBN 0-306-39253-4, Plenum Pr). Plenum Pub.

Differential Forms: With Applications to the Physical Sciences. Harley Flanders. (Mathematics in Science & Engineering Ser.). 203p. 1963. text ed. 18.95 (ISBN 0-12-259650-1). Acad Pr.

Differential Games. Avner Friedman. LC 75-155119. (Pure & Applied Mathematics Ser.). 1971. 38.95 (ISBN 0-471-28049-6, Pub. by Wiley-Interscience). Wiley.

Differential Geometric Structures. Walter A. Poor. (Illus.). 320p. 1981. text ed. 44.95 (ISBN 0-07-050435-0, C). McGraw.

Differential Geometry. Heinrich Guggenheimer. pap. text ed. 6.00 (ISBN 0-486-63433-7). Dover.

Differential Geometry. James Stoker. (Pure & Applied Mathematics Ser.). 1969. 32.50 (ISBN 0-471-82825-4, Pub. by Wiley-Interscience). Wiley.

Differential Manifolds. Serge A. Lang. LC 71-161227. (Mathematics Ser). 1972. text ed. 17.95 (ISBN 0-201-04166-9). A-W.

Differential Response of Rice Varieties to the Brown Plant-Hopper in International Screening Tests. (IRRI Research Paper Ser.: No. 52). 13p. 1980. pap. 5.00 (R132, IRRI). Unipub.

Differential Social Program Evaluation. Tony Tripodi et al. LC 77-83401. 1978. pap. text ed. 6.50 (ISBN 0-87581-227-9). Peacock Pubs.

Differential Thermal Analysis, Vol. 1: Fundamental Aspects. R. C. MacKenzie. 1970. 99.00 (ISBN 0-12-464401-5). Acad Pr.

Differential Topology. Victor Guillemin & Alan Pollack. (Math. Ser). (Illus.). 324p. 1974. 21.95x (ISBN 0-13-212605-2). P-H.

Differential Use of Social Work Manpower. Robert L. Barker & Thomas L. Briggs. LC 68-27158. 1968. 5.00x o.p. (ISBN 0-87101-049-6, CHO-049-C). Natl Assn Soc Wkrs.

Differentialgeometrie, 2 Vols. in 1. Wilhelm Blaschke. LC 62-11596. (Ger). 24.95 (ISBN 0-8284-0202-7). Chelsea Pub.

Differentialgleichungen: Loesungsmethoden und Loesungen, Vol. 2: Partielle Differentialgleichungen Erster Ordnung Fuer eine Gesuchte Funktion. Erich Kamke. LC 49-5862. 243p. 1974. Repr. of 1967 ed. text ed. 11.95 (ISBN 0-8284-0277-9). Chelsea Pub.

Differentialgleichungen, Vol. 1: Loesungsmethoden und Loesungen. Erich Kamke. LC 49-5862. (Ger). text ed. 24.95 (ISBN 0-8284-0044-X). Chelsea Pub.

Differentiated Lymphocyte Functions & Their Ontogeny. Ed. by A. L. De Weck. (Progress in Allergy Ser.: Vol. 28). (Illus.). 250p. 1981. 90.00 (ISBN 3-8055-1834-X). S Karger.

Differentiated Patterns of Education in Catholic Elementary Schools. 74p. 1973. 2.95. Natl Cath Educ.

Differentiating the Media. Ed. by Lester Asheim & Sara I. Fenwick. (Studies in Library Science). vi, 74p. 1975. 10.00x (ISBN 0-226-02964-6). U of Chicago Pr.

Differentiation & Carcinogenesis in Liver Cell Cultures. new ed. Ed. by Carmia Borek & Gary M. Williams. LC 80-20918. (Vol. 349). 429p. 1980. 83.00 (ISBN 0-89766-087-0). NY Acad Sci.

Differentiation & Co-Operation in an Israeli Veteran Moshav. E. Baldwin. 1972. text ed. 14.00x (ISBN 0-7190-0438-1). Humanities.

Differentiation & Immunology. International Society for Cell Biology. Ed. by Katherine B. Warren. (Proceedings: Vol. 7). 1969. 49.00 (ISBN 0-12-611907-4). Acad Pr.

Differentiation & Neoplasia. Ed. by R. G. McKinnell. (Results & Problems in Cell Differentiation: Vol. 11). (Illus.). 350p. 1980. 76.20 (ISBN 0-387-10177-2). Springer-Verlag.

Differentiation of Human Oral Stratified Epithelia. H. E. Schroeder. (Illus.). 310p. 1980. 90.00 (ISBN 3-8055-1462-X). S Karger.

Differentiation of Local Populations of Sockeye Salmon Oncorhynchus Nerka. S. M. Konovalov. Tr. by Leda V. Sagen from Rus. LC 75-14733. (Publications in Fisheries, Ser.: No. 6). (Illus.). 256p. (Orig.). 1975. pap. text ed. 12.50 (ISBN 0-295-95406-X). U of Wash Pr.

Differentiation of Normal & Neoplastic Hematopoietic Cells: Cold Spring Harbor Conferences on Cell Proliferation, 2 bks, Vol. 5. Ed. by Bayard Clarkson et al. LC 78-60391. (Illus.). 994p. 1978. Set. text ed. 95.00 (ISBN 0-87969-121-2). Cold Spring Harbor.

Differenzenrechung. Niels H. Noerlund. LC 56-1592. (Ger). 19.50 (ISBN 0-8284-0100-4). Chelsea Pub.

Differing Eye: An Introduction to Literature. William C. Doster. LC 74-85767. 350p. (Orig.). 1970. pap. 6.95x (ISBN 0-02-473980-4, 47398); teachers' manual free (ISBN 0-685-11740-5, 47397). Macmillan.

Differential Geometry and the Calculus of Variations. 2nd ed. Robert Hermann. LC 68-14664. (Intermath Ser.: No. 17). 1977. 42.00 (ISBN 0-915692-24-4). Math Sci Pr.

Difficult Act to Follow. Henry J. Korn. LC 79-57461. 80p. 1981. 15.00 (ISBN 0-686-69412-0); pap. 5.95 (ISBN 0-686-69413-9). Assembling Pr.

Difficult Decision. Janet Dailey. (Harlequin Presents Ser.). 192p. 1980. pap. 1.50 (ISBN 0-373-10386-7, Pub. by Harlequin). PB.

Difficult Orthopedic Diagnosis. Lewis Cozen. (Illus.). 104p. 1972. text ed. 14.75 (ISBN 0-398-02212-7). C C Thomas.

Difficult Soul: Zinaida Gippius. Vladimir Zlobin. Ed. by Simon Karlinsky. (Documentary Studies in Modern Russian Poetry). 200p. 1980. 14.50x (ISBN 0-520-03867-3). U of Cal Pr.

Difficulties in the Analytic Encounter. John Klauber. LC 80-69670. 200p. 1981. 25.00 (ISBN 0-87668-430-4). Aronson.

Difficulty of Being. Jean Cocteau. Tr. by Elizabeth Sprigge from Fr. (Illus.). 160p. 1980. text ed. 17.25x (ISBN 0-7206-2518-1). Humanities.

Difficulty of Being Christian. Soren Kierkegaard. Ed. by Jacques Collette. Tr. by M. McInery & L. Turcotte. 1968. 24.50x (ISBN 0-89197-730-9). Irvington.

Diffraction Theory & Antennas. R. H. Clarke & John Brown. 320p. 1980. 97.50x (ISBN 0-470-27003-9). Halsted Pr.

Diffuse Pulmonary Disease: A Radiologic Approach. Irwin M. Freundlich. LC 77-27745. (Illus.). 1979. pap. text ed. 15.95 o.p. (ISBN 0-7216-3866-X). Saunders.

Diffusion & Adoption of Genetic Materials Among Rice Breeding Programs in Asia. (IRRI Research Paper Ser.: No. 18). 25p. 1978. pap. 5.00 (R058, IRRI). Unipub.

Diffusion Chamber Culture: Hemopoiesis, Cloning of Tumors, Cytogenetic & Carinogenic Assays. E. P. Cronkite & A. L. Carstens. (Illus.). 270p. 1980. pap. 46.00 (ISBN 0-387-10064-4). Springer-Verlag.

Diffusion of Material Culture. Ed. by H. H. E. Loofs-Wissowa. (Asian & Pacific Archaeology Ser.: No.9). (Illus.). 393p. (Orig.). 1980. pap. 10.00x (ISBN 0-8248-0744-8). U Pr of Hawaii.

Diffusion of New Technology. L. Nabseth & G. F. Ray. (National Institute of Economic & Social Research Economic & Social Studies: No. 29). (Illus.). 300p. 1974. 35.50 (ISBN 0-521-20430-5). Cambridge U Pr.

Diffusion of Process Innovations. S. Davies. LC 78-15143. 1979. 32.95 (ISBN 0-521-22193-5). Cambridge U Pr.

Diffusion Problems & Partial Differential Equations. S. R. S. Varadhan. (Tate Institute Lectures on Mathematics Ser.). 315p. 1981. pap. 10.70 (ISBN 0-387-08773-7). Springer-Verlag.

Diffusional Mass Transfer. A. H. Skelland. LC 73-12976. 510p. 1974. 45.00 (ISBN 0-471-79374-4, Pub. by Wiley-Interscience). Wiley.

Dig, Drill, Dump, Fill. Tana Hoban. LC 75-11987. (Illus.). 32p. (ps-3). 1975. PLB 6.96 (ISBN 0-688-84016-7). Greenwillow.

Diga! Diga! Louis Cabat & Robert Cabat. (gr. 7-12). 1974. pap. text ed. 4.08 (ISBN 0-87720-510-8). AMSCO Sch.

Digenis Akritas: The Two Blood Border Lord. Tr. by Denison B. Hull from Medieval Greek. LC 79-141384. (Illus.). xlviii, 148p. 1972. 10.00x (ISBN 0-8214-0097-5). Ohio U Pr.

Digest Book of Horse Care. Jack Lewis. (Sports & Leisure Library). (Illus.). 96p. 1979. pap. 2.95 (ISBN 0-695-81325-0). Follett.

Digest Book of Upland Game Shooting. Bob Bell. (Sports & Leisure Library). (Illus.). 96p. 1979. pap. 2.95 (ISBN 0-686-66063-3). Follett.

Digest Des Briefes Originals, et Des Choses Concernant Eux. Simon Theloall. Ed. by David S. Berkowitz & Samuel E. Thorne. LC 77-89257. (Classics of English Legal History in the Modern Era: Vol. 145). 1979. lib. bdg. 55.00 (ISBN 0-8240-3182-2). Garland Pub.

Digest of All the Laws at Present in Existence Respecting Masters & Work People. George White. Ed. by David S. Berkowitz & Samuel E. Thorne. LC 77-89205. (Classics of English Legal History in the Modern Era Ser.: Vol. 59). 159p. 1979. lib. bdg. 40.00 (ISBN 0-8240-3158-X). Garland Pub.

Digest of Hospital Cost Containment Projects. 3rd ed. American Hospital Assn. LC 79-27674. (Orig.). 1980. pap. 6.25 (ISBN 0-87258-299-X, 1020). Am Hospital.

Digest of Investigations in the Teaching of Sciences in the Elementary & Secondary Schools. Francis D. Curtis. LC 74-153694. 1971. Repr. of 1926 ed. text ed. 12.25x (ISBN 0-8077-1223-X). Tchrs Coll.

Digest of Legal Activities of International & Other Institutions, Release 1. 4th ed. International Institute for the Unification of Private Law. 1980. 85.00 (ISBN 0-379-00545-X). Oceana.

Digest of Literature on Dielectrics, Vols. 11-13, 18-42. Conference on Electrical Insulation & Dielectric Phenomena. Incl. Vol. 11. 1947. 5.00 (ISBN 0-309-00013-0); Vol. 12. 1948. 5.00 (ISBN 0-309-00014-9); Vol. 13. 1949. 5.00 (ISBN 0-309-00015-7); Vol. 18. 1954. 5.00 (ISBN 0-309-00383-0); Vol. 19. 1955. 5.00 (ISBN 0-309-00503-5); Vol. 20. 1956. 5.00 (ISBN 0-309-00562-0); Vol. 21. 1957. 5.00 (ISBN 0-309-00599-X); Vol. 22. 1958. 5.00 (ISBN 0-309-00713-5); Vol. 24. 1960. 10.00 (ISBN 0-309-00917-0); Vol. 25. 1961. 15.00 (ISBN 0-309-01034-9); Vol. 26. 1962. 15.00 (ISBN 0-309-01139-6); Vol. 27. 1963. 15.00 (ISBN 0-309-01230-9); Vol. 28. 1964. 27.00 (ISBN 0-309-01342-9); Vol. 29. 1965. 27.00 (ISBN 0-309-01461-1); Vol. 30. 1966. 27.00 (ISBN 0-309-01496-4); Vol. 31. 1967. 27.00 (ISBN 0-309-01595-2); Vol. 32. 1968. 35.00 (ISBN 0-309-01732-7); Vol. 33. 1969. 35.00 (ISBN 0-309-01856-0); Vol. 34. 1970. 35.00 (ISBN 0-309-01920-6); Vol. 35. 1971. 40.00 (ISBN 0-309-02049-2); Vol. 36. 1972. 40.00 (ISBN 0-309-02316-5); Vol. 37. 1973. 40.00 (ISBN 0-309-02437-4); Vol. 38, 1974. 40.00 (ISBN 0-686-66646-1); Vol. 39, 1975. 45.00 (ISBN 0-309-02748-9); Vol. 40, 1976. 45.00 (ISBN 0-309-02787-X); Vol. 41, 1979. 45.00 (ISBN 0-309-02886-8); Vol. 42, 1979. 45.00 (ISBN 0-309-02934-1). Natl Acad Pr.

Digest of Literature on Dielectrics, Vols. 38-42. Conference on Electrical Insulation & Dielectric Phenomena. 1977. Vol. 38, 1977. 40.00 (ISBN 0-309-02643-1); Vol. 39. 1978 45.00 (ISBN 0-309-02748-9); Vol. 40. 1978. 45.00 (ISBN 0-309-02787-X); Vol. 41, 1979. 45.00 (ISBN 0-309-02886-8); Vol. 42, 1979. 45.00 (ISBN 0-309-02934-1). Natl Acad Pr.

Digest of Reports of the Carnegie Commission on Higher Education. Carnegie Commission on Higher Education. LC 73-22231. (Illus.). 416p. 1974. 19.50 o.p. (ISBN 0-07-010103-5, P&RB). McGraw.

Digestive Physiology & Metabolism in Ruminants. Y. Ruckebusch & P. Thivend. (Illus., American ed.). 1980. pap. text ed. 54.00 (ISBN 0-87055-359-3). AVI.

Digestive Physiology & Nutrition of Ruminants: Practical Nutrition, Vol. 3. 2nd ed. Ed. by D. C. Church. 1980. text ed. 25.00 (ISBN 0-9601586-7-7). O & B Bks.

Digestive System. Kathleen Elgin. LC 73-4417. (Human Body Ser). (gr. 4 up). 1973. PLB 6.90 (ISBN 0-531-01183-6). Watts.

Digestive System Basic Sciences. Ed. by Myron E. Tracht et al. (Basic Science Review Bks.). 1973. spiral bdg. 8.00 o.p. (ISBN 0-87488-215-X). Med Exam.

Digestive System: Disease, Diagnosis, Treatment. P. Toskes. (Clinical Monographs Ser.). (Illus.). 1975. pap. 7.95 (ISBN 0-87618-063-2). R J Brady.

Digger. Peter Burchard. 128p. (gr. 5-12). 1980. 8.95 (ISBN 0-399-20717-1). Putnam.

Digger's Game. George V. Higgins. 224p. 1974. pap. 1.75 o.p. (ISBN 0-445-08256-9). Popular Lib.

Digger's Game. George V. Higgins. 176p. 1981. pap. 2.25 (ISBN 0-345-28970-6). Ballantine.

Digging. George Cecil. (Easy-Read Fact Book Ser.). (Illus.). 48p. (gr. 2-4). 1976. PLB 4.47 o.p. (ISBN 0-531-01218-2). Watts.

Digging for Gold: A Story of California. Horatio Alger. 1968. pap. 1.95 o.s.i. (ISBN 0-02-030230-4, Collier). Macmillan.

Digging in Assyria. Ed. by Shirley Glubok. LC 79-103679. (Illus.). (gr. 7 up). 1970. 7.95g o.s.i. (ISBN 0-02-736110-1). Macmillan.

Digging into South Texas Prehistory. Thomas R. Hester. (Illus.). 202p. 1980. 14.00 (ISBN 0-931722-05-5); pap. 8.95 (ISBN 0-931722-04-7). Corona Pub.

Digging up the Past. 2nd ed. Charles L. Woolley. LC 77-13325. (Illus.). 1977. Repr. of 1954 ed. lib. bdg. 17.50x (ISBN 0-8371-9853-4, WODU). Greenwood.

Diggs. Bob Chase. 1981. 10.00 (ISBN 0-533-04670-X). Vantage.

Diggstown Ringers. Leonard Wise. LC 77-27722. 1978. 10.00 o.p. (ISBN 0-385-13126-7). Doubleday.

Digital & Analog Communication Systems. K. Sam Shanmugam. LC 78-26191. 1979. text ed. 26.95 (ISBN 0-471-03090-2); solutions manual (ISBN 0-471-07832-8). Wiley.

Digital & Microprocessor Technology. Frank Cave & David Terrell. 448p. 1981. text ed. 18.95 (ISBN 0-8359-1326-0); instrs. manual avail. (ISBN 0-8359-1327-9). Reston.

Digital Circuits: A Preparation for Microprocessors. Charles W. McKay. LC 77-13058. (Illus.). 1978. ref. 19.95 (ISBN 0-13-212175-1). P-H.

Digital Circuits & Microcomputers. David E. Johnson et al. LC 78-13244. (Illus.). 1979. ref. ed. 23.95 (ISBN 0-13-214015-2). P-H.

Digital Circuits & Microprocessors. Herbert Taub. (Electrical Engineering Ser.). (Illus.). 608p. 1981. text ed. 26.95x (ISBN 0-07-062945-5, C); solutions manual 12.95 (ISBN 0-07-062946-3). McGraw.

Digital Circuits & Systems. Richard L. Castellucis. 356p. 1981. text ed. 18.95 (ISBN 0-8359-1297-3); instrs. manual avail. (ISBN 0-8359-1298-1). Reston.

Digital Circuits for Binary Arithmetic. R. M. Oberman. 340p. 1979. 39.95x (ISBN 0-470-26373-3). Halsted Pr.

Digital Communication by Satellite. J. Spilker, Jr. 1976. 39.95 (ISBN 0-13-214155-8). P-H.

Digital Computer Applications to Process Control: Proceedings of the Sixth IFAC-IFIP Conference, Dusseldorf, Federal Republic of Germany, 14-17 October 1980. R. Isermann & H. Kaltenecker. LC 80-41343. (IFAC Proceedings). 550p. 1981. 100.00 (ISBN 0-08-026749-1). Pergamon.

Digital Computer Circuits & Concepts. 3rd ed. Bill Deem et al. (Illus.). 1980. text ed. 18.95 (ISBN 0-8359-1299-X); free instrs'. manual. Reston.

Digital Computer Design. Raymond M. Kline. (Illus.). 1977. 27.95 (ISBN 0-13-214205-8). P-H.

Digital Computer Fundamentals. 5th ed. Thomas Bartee. (Illus.). 576p. 1981. text ed. 22.95 (ISBN 0-07-003894-5, C); instr's manual 4.95 (ISBN 0-07-003895-3). McGraw.

Digital Computer Fundamentals. Jefferson C. Boyce. LC 76-11768. (Illus.). 1977. 19.95 (ISBN 0-13-214114-0). P-H.

Digital Computer Programming: Principles, Techniques, & Applications. Bing H. Lieu. (Illus., Orig.). 1974. pap. text ed. 4.00 (ISBN 0-486-22948-3). Dover.

Digital Computer Simulation. Fred J. Maryanski. 336p. 1980. 15.95 (ISBN 0-8104-5118-2). Hayden.

Digital Computer Treatment of Partial Differential Equations. V. Vemuri & Walter Karplus. (Illus.). 480p. 1981. text ed. 26.50 (ISBN 0-13-212407-6). P-H.

Digital Computers & Logic Circuits. Frank P. Tedeschi & John A. Scigiano. LC 78-11983. (Illus., Orig.). 1971. text ed. 6.95x (ISBN 0-02-478780-9, 47878); wkbk. 5.50x (ISBN 0-02-478830-9, 47883). Macmillan.

Digital Computers in the Behavioral Laboratory. Bernard Weiss. (Century Psychology Ser.). (Illus.). 1979. Repr. of 1973 ed. text ed. 22.50x o.p. (ISBN 0-8290-0058-5). Irvington.

Digital Computers' Memory Technology. D. Dutta-Majumdar & J. Das. 424p. 1980. 19.95x (ISBN 0-470-26932-4). Halsted Pr.

Digital Continuous System Simulation. Granino A. Korn & John V. Wait. (Illus.). 1978. ref. ed. 21.95 (ISBN 0-13-212274-X). P-H.

Digital Electronics: A Hands-on Learning Approach. George Young. (gr. 12). 1980. pap. 8.95 (ISBN 0-8104-5668-0). Hayden.

Digital Electronics: An Introduction to Theory & Practice. William H. Gothmann. LC 76-18258. (Illus.). 1977. 19.95 (ISBN 0-13-212217-0). P-H.

Digital Electronics for Works Electricians. Noel M. Morris. (Illus.). 148p. 1980. pap. 14.50 (ISBN 0-07-084523-9). McGraw.

Digital Electronics: Fundamental Concepts & Applications. Christopher E. Strangio. (Illus.). 1980. text ed. 25.95 (ISBN 0-13-212100-X). P-H.

Digital Electronics with Engineering Applications. Thomas P. Sifferlen & Vartan Vartanian. (Electrical Engineering Ser). 1970. ref. ed. 22.95 (ISBN 0-13-214304-6). P-H.

Digital Filter Design Handbook. Taylor. Date not set. price not set (ISBN 0-8247-1357-5). Dekker.

Digital Filters. R. W. Hamming. (Illus.). 256p. 1977. text ed. 23.95x (ISBN 0-13-212571-4). P-H.

Digital Image Processing. Kenneth R. Castleman. LC 78-27578. (Illus.). 1979. text ed. 32.95 (ISBN 0-13-212365-7). P-H.

Digital Image Processing. William K. Pratt. LC 77-20888. 1978. 42.50 (ISBN 0-471-01888-0, Pub. by Wiley-Interscience). Wiley.

Digital Image Processing & Recognition. Rafael C. Gonzalez & Paul Wintz. LC 77-10317. (Applied Mathematics & Computation Ser.: No. 13). 1977. text ed. 33.50 (ISBN 0-201-02596-5, Adv Bk Prog); pap. text ed. 19.50 (ISBN 0-201-02597-3). A-W.

Digital Image Processing for Remote Sensing. Bernstein. LC 77-94520. (IEEE Reprint Ser.). 1978. 35.95 (ISBN 0-471-04939-5); pap. 23.50 (ISBN 0-471-04938-7, Pub. by Wiley-Interscience). Wiley.

Digital Image Restoration. Harry C. Andrews & B. R. Hunt. (Signal Processing Ser.). (Illus.). 1977. 28.95 (ISBN 0-13-214213-9). P-H.

Digital Logic & Computer Design. M. Mano. 1979. 27.95 (ISBN 0-13-214510-3). P-H.

Digital Logic Design. Holdsworth. 1981. text ed. price not set (ISBN 0-408-00404-5); pap. text ed. price not set (ISBN 0-408-00566-1). Butterworth.

Digital-Logic Electronics Handbook. William Hunter. LC 75-29681. (Illus.). 308p. 1975. 9.95 o.p. (ISBN 0-8306-5774-6); pap. 6.95 (ISBN 0-8306-4774-0, 774). TAB Bks.

Digital Logic Fundamentals. Thomas L. Floyd. (Electronics Technology Ser.). 1977. text ed. 20.95 (ISBN 0-675-08495-4); instructor's manual 3.95 (ISBN 0-685-74279-2). Merrill.

Digital Network & Computer Systems. 2nd ed. Taylor L. Booth. LC 77-10832. 1978. text ed. 26.95 (ISBN 0-471-08842-0); tchrs. manual avail. (ISBN 0-471-03049-X). Wiley.

Digital Networks. J. A. Brzozowski & M. Yoeli. (Illus.). 416p. 1976. ref. ed. 24.00 (ISBN 0-13-214189-2). P-H.

Digital Pattern Recognition. 2nd ed. Ed. by K. S. Fu. (Communication & Cybernetics: Vol. 10). (Illus.). 234p. 1980. pap. 29.80 (ISBN 0-387-10207-8). Springer-Verlag.

Digital Processing of Speech Signals. Lawrence R. Rabiner & Ronald W. Schafer. (P-H Signal Processing Ser.). 1978. ref. ed. 29.95 (ISBN 0-13-213603-1). P-H.

Digital Signal Analysis. Sam D. Stearns. 288p. 1975. text ed. 23.95x (ISBN 0-8104-5828-4). Hayden.

Digital Signal Processing. Alan V. Oppenheim & Ronald W. Schafer. LC 74-17280. (Illus.). 608p. 1975. text ed. 27.95 (ISBN 0-13-214635-5). P-H.

Digital Signal Processing in Fortran. Fred I. Taylor & Steve L. Smith. LC 75-28940. 192p. 1976. 27.95 (ISBN 0-669-00330-1). Lexington Bks.

Digital Signal Processing: Theory, Design & Implemetation. Abraham Peled & Bede Liu. LC 76-17326. 1976. text ed. 24.95 (ISBN 0-471-01941-0); avail. solutions manual (ISBN 0-471-03634-X). Wiley.

Digital System Implementation. Gerritt A. Blaauw. (Illus.). 1976. 25.95 (ISBN 0-13-212241-3). P-H.

Digital Systems: Hardware Organization & Design. 2nd ed. Frederick J. Hill & Gerald R. Peterson. LC 78-7209. 1978. text ed. 29.95 (ISBN 0-471-39608-7); tchrs. ed. avail. (ISBN 0-471-03694-3). Wiley.

Digital Systems: Principles & Applications. rev. & enl. ed. Ronald J. Tocci. (Illus.). 1980. text ed. 14.95 (ISBN 0-13-212290-1). P-H.

Digital Technology. Gerald Williams. LC 76-47660. 1977. text ed. 18.95 (ISBN 0-574-21500-X, 13-4500); instr's guide avail. (ISBN 0-574-21501-8, 13-4501); lab. manual 4.95 (ISBN 0-574-21502-6, 13-4502). SRA.

Digital Television: Bandwidth Reduction & Communication Aspects. R. H. Stafford. LC 80-17542. 400p. 1980. 34.95 (ISBN 0-471-07857-3, Pub. by Wiley-Interscience). Wiley.

Digital Theory & Experimentation Using Integrated Circuits. M. Levine. LC 73-12863. 1974. pap. 14.95 ref. ed. (ISBN 0-13-212258-8). P-H.

Digital Theory & Practice Using Integrated Circuits. Morris E. Levine. 1978. ref. 19.95 (ISBN 0-13-212613-3). P-H.

Digital Time Series Analysis. Robert K. Otnes & Loren Enochson. LC 72-637. (Wiley Series in Probability & Mathematical Statistics: Applied Probability & Statistics Section). 552p. 1972. 32.95 (ISBN 0-471-65719-0, Pub. by Wiley-Interscience). Wiley.

Digital Transmission Systems. rev. ed. P. Bylanski & D. G. Ingram. (IEE Telecommunications Ser.). 431p. pap. write for info. (ISBN 0-906048-37-0, Pub. by Peregrinus England). Inst Electrical.

Digital Troubleshooting: Practical Digital Theory & Troubleshooting Tips. Riechard E. Gasperini. 1976. pap. 10.95x (ISBN 0-8104-5708-3). Hayden.

Dignita Cavalleresca Nel Comune Di Firenze. Gaetano Salvemini. LC 80-2005. 1981. Repr. of 1896 ed. 22.00 (ISBN 0-404-18589-4). AMS Pr.

Dignity of the Despised on Earth. Ed. by Jacques Pohier & Dietmar Mieth. (New Concilium: Vol. 130). 120p. (Orig.). 1980. pap. 4.95 (ISBN 0-8164-2038-6). Crossroad NY.

Dilation of the Uterine Cervix: Connective Tissue Biology & Clinical Management. Ed. by Frederick Naftolin & Phillip G. Stubblefield. 1979. text ed. 38.50 (ISBN 0-89004-300-0). Raven.

Dilema. Tr. by Robert McAlister. (Spanish Bks.). 1978. 1.50 (ISBN 0-8297-0888-X). Life Pubs Intl.

Dilema. Tr. by Robert McAlister. (Portuguese Bks.). 1979. write for info. (ISBN 0-8297-0654-2). Life Pubs Intl.

Dilemma: A Nurse's Guide for Making Ethical Decisions. Judith A. Shelly. (Orig.). 1980. pap. text ed. 4.95 (ISBN 0-87784-666-9). Inter-Varsity.

Dilemma in Duet. Margaret SeBastian. (Regency Love Story). 1979. pap. 1.75 (ISBN 0-449-50003-9, Coventry). Fawcett.

Dilemma in the Congressional Power to Enforce the Fourteenth Amendment. Frederick P. Lewis. 110p. 1980. text ed. 15.50 (ISBN 0-8191-1045-0); pap. text ed. 7.50 (ISBN 0-8191-1046-9). U Pr of Amer.

Dilemma of a Ghost. Illus. by Ama A. Aidoo. (African-American Lib). 1971. pap. 1.25 o.s.i. (ISBN 0-02-012020-6, Collier). Macmillan.

Dilemma of Deanship. Ed. by Daniel E. Griffiths & Donald J. McCarty. LC 78-61237. 1980. 11.95x (ISBN 0-8134-2041-5, 2041). Interstate.

Dilemma of Freight Transport Regulation. Ann F. Friedlaender. LC 69-18820. (Studies in the Regulation of Economic Activity). 216p. 1969. 11.95 (ISBN 0-8157-2936-7). Brookings.

Dilemma of Local Government: Discrimination in the Provision of Public Services. Paul R. Dimond. LC 78-57187. (Illus.). 1978. 21.95 (ISBN 0-669-02372-8). Lexington Bks.

Dilemma of Our Society: A Proposal for Moral Maturity. Errol A. Gibbs. (Illus.). 336p. 1980. 15.00 (ISBN 0-682-49650-2). Exposition.

Dilemma of the Talented Heroine: A Study in Nineteenth Century Fiction. Susan S. Siefert. 1978. 14.95 (ISBN 0-88831-018-8). EPWP.

Dilemmas. Gilbert Ryle. 1954-1960. 19.95 (ISBN 0-521-06177-6); pap. 6.95x (ISBN 0-521-09115-2). Cambridge U Pr.

Dilemmas of Administrative Behavior. John D. Aram. 144p. 1976. Ref. Ed. 9.95 (ISBN 0-13-214247-3). P-H.

Dilemmas of Correction. Rick J. Carlson. LC 75-32223. 1976. 19.95 (ISBN 0-669-00346-8). Lexington Bks.

Dilemmas of Euthanasia. Ed. by John A. Behnke & Sissela Bok. LC 75-5267. 200p. 1975. pap. 2.95 (ISBN 0-385-09730-1, Anch). Doubleday.

Dilemmas of Freedom. Eva Ancsel. 1978. 9.00x (ISBN 9-6305-1694-2). Intl Pubns Serv.

Dilemmas of Political Development. 2nd ed. Monte Palmer. LC 79-91100. 291p. 1980. pap. text ed. 7.95 (ISBN 0-87581-255-4). Peacock Pubs.

Dilemmas of the Atlantic Alliance: Two Germanys, Scandinavia, Canada, Nato & the EEC. Peter C. Ludz et al. LC 75-25737. (Atlantic Institute Studies: No. 1). 1975. text ed. 25.95 (ISBN 0-275-01490-8). Praeger.

Dilemmas of the Curriculum. G. H. Bantock. LC 80-11764. 146p. 1980. 15.95x (ISBN 0-470-26920-0). Halsted Pr.

Dilemme. Tr. by Robert McAlister. (French Bks.). (Fr.). 1979. wirte for info. (ISBN 0-8297-0934-7). Life Pubs Intl.

Diller, a Dollar: Rhymes & Sayings for the Ten O'Clock Scholar. Ed. by Lillian Morrison. LC 55-9213. (Illus.). (gr. 4 up). 1955. 8.95 (ISBN 0-690-23957-2, TYC-J). T Y Crowell.

Dilly Dally. William Stobbs. (Illus.). 1975. 3.95 (ISBN 0-7207-0767-6, Pub. by Michael Joseph). Merrimack Bk Serv.

Diltheys Erlebnisbegriff: Entstehung, Glanzzeit und Verkuemmerung eines literaturhistorischen Begriffs. Karol Sauerland. 182p. 1972. 39.45x (ISBN 3-11-003599-5). De Gruyter.

Dime Store Dreams. Lester Glassner & Brownie Harris. 128p. 1981. write for info. (ISBN 0-670-27279-5, Studio). Viking Pr.

Dime Store Dreams. Lester Glassner & Brownie Harris. 1981. pap. 12.95 (ISBN 0-14-005668-8). Penguin. Postponed.

Dimension: A Reader of German Literature Since Nineteen Sixty-Eight. Ed. by A. L. Willson. 320p. 1981. 9.95 (ISBN 0-8264-0042-6). Continuum.

Dimension & Tolerances (an Interpretation of ANSI y14.5) Ed. by Jerome H. Lieblich. 1973. pap. 3.75x (ISBN 0-912702-05-2). Global Eng.

Dimension Theory. Keio Nagami. (Pure & Applied Mathematics Ser.: Vol. 37). 1970. 38.00 (ISBN 0-12-513650-1). Acad Pr.

Dimensional Analysis & Group Theory in Astrophysics. Rudolf Kurth. 249p. 1972. text ed. 55.00 (ISBN 0-08-016616-4). Pergamon.

Dimensional Analysis & Hydraulic Model Testing. H. M. Raghunath. 1968. 5.50x o.p. (ISBN 0-210-22655-2). Asia.

Dimensional Analysis for Engineers. Edward S. Taylor. (Illus.). 174p. 1974. text ed. 29.95x (ISBN 0-19-856122-9). Oxford U Pr.

Dimensional Analysis in the Biomedical Sciences. B. Schepartz. (Illus.). 184p. 1980. 19.75 (ISBN 0-398-03991-7). C C Thomas.

Dimensional Methods in Physics: Reference Sets & Their Extensions. E. Isaacson & M. Isaacson. LC 75-8311. 1975. 27.95 (ISBN 0-470-42866-X). Halsted Pr.

Dimensional Tolerances for Cast-In-Place Concrete. Building Research Advisory Board For The Federal Construction Council. 1964. pap. 3.00 (ISBN 0-309-01227-9). Natl Acad Pr.

Dimensionless Parameters: Theory & Methodology. H. A. Becker. LC 76-1570. 128p. 1976. 24.95 (ISBN 0-470-15048-3). Halsted Pr.

Dimensions Beyond the Known. Bhagwan Sri Rajneesh. (Orig.). 1979. pap. 6.95 (ISBN 0-914794-35-3). Wisdom Garden.

Dimensions for Happening. Lois H. Young. LC 76-144081. 1971. pap. 2.50 o.p. (ISBN 0-8170-0506-4). Judson.

Dimensions in Modern Management. 2nd ed. Patrick E. Connor. LC 77-75692. (Illus.). 1977. pap. text ed. 10.95 (ISBN 0-395-25515-5). HM.

Dimensions in Wholistic Healing: New Frontiers in the Treatment of the Whole Person. Ed. by Herbert A. Otto & James W. Knight. LC 78-27071. 1979. 23.95 (ISBN 0-88229-513-6); pap. text ed. 13.95 (ISBN 0-88229-697-3). Nelson-Hall.

Dimensions of American Education. Theodore R. Crane. 1974. pap. text ed. 8.50 (ISBN 0-201-01212-X). A-W.

Dimensions of an Anthropology of Aging. Ed. by Christine L. Fry. LC 79-13198. (Illus.). 1980. 23.95 (ISBN 0-03-052971-9). Praeger.

Dimensions of Belief & Unbelief. John R. Connolly. LC 80-67241. 373p. 1981. lib. bdg. 21.75 (ISBN 0-8191-1389-1); pap. text ed. 12.75 (ISBN 0-8191-1390-5). U Pr of Amer.

Dimensions of Change. Don Fabun. 1971. text ed. 6.95x (ISBN 0-02-475500-1, 47550). Macmillan.

Dimensions of Change: Problems & Issues of American Colonial History. Lawrence H. Leder. LC 72-75882. 1972. pap. text ed. 6.95 o.p. (ISBN 0-8087-1220-9). Burgess.

Dimensions of China's Foreign Relations. Ed. by Chun-Tu Hsueh. LC 76-24354. 1977. text ed. 32.50 (ISBN 0-275-56780-X). Praeger.

Dimensions of Communication. Ed. by S. Lee Richardson. (Illus., Orig.). 1969. pap. text ed. 14.95 (ISBN 0-13-214494-8). P-H.

Dimensions of Community Psychiatry, Vol. 6. GAP Committee on Preventive Psychiatry. LC 62-2872. (Report No. 69). 1968. pap. 2.00 (ISBN 0-87318-094-1). Adv Psychiatry.

Dimensions of Detente. Ed. by Della Sheldon. LC 78-6041. (Praegerspecial Studies). 1978. 24.95 (ISBN 0-03-044246-X). Praeger.

Dimensions of Dying & Rebirth. Stanislav Grof & Hugh L. Cayce. 1977. pap. 2.50 o.p. (ISBN 0-87604-099-7). ARE Pr.

Dimensions of Evil & Transcendence: A Sociological Perspective. Natalia R. Moehle. LC 78-59124. 1978. pap. text ed. 10.50 (ISBN 0-8191-0550-3). U Pr of Amer.

Dimensions of Family Therapy. Ed. by Maurizio Andolfi. Israel Zwerling. 280p. 1980. text ed. 20.00 (ISBN 0-89862-602-1). Guilford Pr.

Dimensions of His Literary Art: A Collection of Critical Essays. Ed. by David D. Anderson. 141p. 1976. 9.50x (ISBN 0-87013-204-0). Mich St U Pr.

Dimensions of Intervention for Student Development. Ed. by Weston H. Morrill & James C. Hurst. Tr. by E. R. Oetting. LC 80-16939. (Counseling & Human Development Ser.). 360p. 1980. text ed. 26.50 (ISBN 0-471-05249-3, Pub. by Wiley-Interscience). Wiley.

Dimensions of Meaning. Ed. by S. I. Hayakawa & William Dresser. LC 68-24164. (Composition & Rhetoric Ser). (Orig.). 1970. pap. 2.95 (ISBN 0-672-60902-9, CR16). Bobbs.

Dimensions of Midnight: Poetry & Prose. Cecil Hemley. Ed. by E. Gottlieb. LC 66-25957. xv, 233p. 1966. 10.95 (ISBN 0-8214-0023-1). Ohio U Pr.

Dimensions of Nations, Vol. 1. R. J. Rummel. LC 72-84054. 416p. 1972. 25.00x (ISBN 0-8039-0170-4). Sage.

Dimensions of Parking. George A. Devlin et al. LC 79-64130. (Illus.). 120p. 1979. pap. text ed. 18.00 (ISBN 0-87420-585-9). Urban Land.

Dimensions of Personality. Harvey London & John E. Exner, Jr. LC 77-25328. (Wiley Series on Personality Processes). 1978. 28.95 (ISBN 0-471-54392-6, Pub. by Wiley-Interscience). Wiley.

Dimensions of Personality: Essays in Honour of H. J. Eysenck. Ed. by R. Lynn. (Illus.). 490p. 1981. 95.00 (ISBN 0-08-024294-4). Pergamon.

Dimensions of Physical Education. 2nd ed. Ed. by Charles A. Bucher. LC 73-18169. (Illus.). 1974. pap. text ed. 8.95 o.p. (ISBN 0-8016-0879-1). Mosby.

Dimensions of Psychology: Introductory Readings. Ed. by Gale B. Bishop & Winfred Hill. LC 79-155877. 400p. 1972. pap. text ed. 5.95 o.p. (ISBN 0-397-47210-2). Lippincott.

Dimensions of Psychotherapy: An Experimental & Clinical Approach. Donald R. Stieper & Daniel N. Wiener. LC 65-22494. 1965. 24.50x (ISBN 0-89197-622-1). Irvington.

Dimensions of Public Administration. 3rd ed. Joseph A. Uveges, Jr. 1978. pap. text ed. 13.95x (ISBN 0-205-06510-4). Allyn.

Dimensions of Public Communication. John Wilson & Carroll Arnold. 272p. 1976. pap. text ed. 10.95x (ISBN 0-205-04917-6, 4849175); instructor's manual free (ISBN 0-205-04918-4). Allyn.

Dimensions of Quantitative Research in History. Ed. by William O. Aydelotte et al. LC 72-736. (Quantitative Studies in History Ser). 420p. 1972. 19.50x (ISBN 0-691-07544-1); pap. 7.50 (ISBN 0-691-10045-4, 45). Princeton U Pr.

Dimensions of Radionics. David V. Tansley. 224p. 1977. 18.95x (ISBN 0-8464-1005-2). Beekman Pubs.

Dimensions of Reading Difficulties. A. T. Ravenette. 1968. 11.25 (ISBN 0-08-012956-0); pap. 5.75 (ISBN 0-08-012955-2). Pergamon.

Dimensions of School Health. Victor Eisner & Laurence B. Callan. 192p. 1974. 14.75 (ISBN 0-398-02948-2). C C Thomas.

Dimensions of Sight Singing: An Anthology. Paul Cooper. (Longman Music Ser.). (Orig.). 1981. pap. text ed. 12.95 (ISBN 0-582-28159-8). Longman.

Dimensions of Social Welfare Policy. Neil Gilbert & Harry Specht. (Illus.). 208p. 1974. 15.95 (ISBN 0-13-214486-7). P-H.

Dimensions of Spirituality. Ed. by Christian Duquoc. (Concilium Ser.: Religion in the Seventies: Vol. 59). 1970. pap. 4.95 (ISBN 0-8164-2515-9). Crossroad NY.

Dimensions of States' Education & Public Health Policies. Kant Patel. LC 78-64563. 1978. pap. text ed. 7.75 (ISBN 0-8191-0636-4). U Pr of Amer.

Dimensions of the Holocaust: Perpetrators, Victims, Bystanders & Resisters--Then & Now; Papers of the 1979 Bernhard E. Olson Scholar's Conference on the Church Struggle & the Holocaust Sponsored by the National Conference of Christians & Jews. Ed. by Michael D. Ryan. (Texts & Studies in Religion: Vol. 9). 300p. 1981. soft cover 24.95x (ISBN 0-88946-902-4). E Mellen.

Dimensions of the Modern Presidency. Edward Kearny. LC 80-68461. (Orig.). 1981. pap. text ed. 7.95x (ISBN 0-88273-268-4). Forum Pr MO.

Dimensions of the New Identity: Jefferson Lectures 1973. Erik H. Erikson. LC 73-22289. 125p. 1974. 10.95 (ISBN 0-393-05515-9). Norton.

Dimensions of the Short Story: A Critical Anthology. 2nd ed. James E. Miller, Jr. & Bernice Slote. 598p. 1980. pap. text ed. 8.95 scp (ISBN 0-06-044457-6, HarpC); avail. Harrow.

Dimethyl Sulphoxide. D. Martin & H. Hauthal. LC 75-1600. 1976. 64.95 (ISBN 0-470-57362-7). Halsted Pr.

Diminishing Returns to Technology: An Essay on the Crisis in Economic Growth. Orio Giarini & Henri Louberge. 1978. text ed. 23.00 (ISBN 0-08-023338-4); pap. text ed. 8.50 (ISBN 0-08-023337-6). Pergamon.

Diminutive, Augumentative & Pejorative Suffixes in Modern Spanish. 2nd ed. A. Gooch. 1970. 21.00 (ISBN 0-08-015808-0); pap. text ed. 3.50 (ISBN 0-08-011960-3). Pergamon.

Dimitrov of Bulgaria. Charles Moser. 14.95. Green Hill.

Dimity Convictions: The American Woman in the Nineteenth Century. Barbara Welter. LC 76-8305. 230p. 1976. 12.95x (ISBN 0-8214-0352-4); pap. 5.95x (ISBN 0-8214-0358-3). Ohio U Pr.

Din Dan Don It's Christmas. Janina Domanska. LC 75-8509. (Illus.). 32p. (ps-3). 1975. 8.25 (ISBN 0-688-80003-3); PLB 7.92 (ISBN 0-688-84003-5). Greenwillow.

Din-Katalog Nineteen Seventy Eight - Catalogue Nineteen Seventy Eight of Din Standards & Drafts. 1978. cancelled (ISBN 0-8002-1368-8). Intl Pubns Serv.

Dina. Richard Calhoun. 1978. pap. 1.95 o.p. (ISBN 0-425-03805-X, Medallion). Berkley Pub.

Dinah & the Fat Green Kingdom. Isabelle Holland. LC 78-8612. (gr. 5-12). 1978. 8.95 (ISBN 0-397-31818-9). Lippincott.

Dinah & the Green Kingdom. Isabelle Holland. (gr. 7 up). 1981. pap. 1.75 (ISBN 0-440-91918-5, LE). Dell.

Dine System: For Better Nutrition & Health. Darwin Dennison. 96p. 1981. pap. text ed. 7.95 (ISBN 0-8403-2371-9). Kendall-Hunt.

Dinero of Doom. Jackson Cole. 1975. pap. 0.95 o.p. (ISBN 0-445-00674-9). Popular Lib.

Diner's Dictionary: French Regional & Specialty Dishes. Dawn Nelson & Douglas Nelson. (The Diner's Dictionaries Ser.). (Illus.). 128p. 1981. 4.95 (ISBN 0-906071-52-6). Proteus Pub NY.

Diner's Dictionary: German & Austrian. Dawn Nelson & Douglas Nelson. (Diner's Dictionaries Ser.). (Illus.). 128p. 1981. 4.95 (ISBN 0-906071-44-5). Proteus Pub NY.

Diner's Dictionary: Italian. Dawn Nelson & Douglas Nelson. (Illus.). 128p. 1981. 4.95 (ISBN 0-906071-33-X). Proteus Pub NY.

Diner's Guide to Wine. Howard Hillman. LC 77-70119. Orig. Title: Art of Serving Wine with Food. (Illus.). 1978. pap. 5.95 o.p. (ISBN 0-8015-0416-3). Dutton.

Diners of the Northeast. Donald Kaplan & Alan Billink. (Illus., Orig.). Date not set. pap. 7.95 (ISBN 0-690-01880-0). Lippincott. Postponed.

Ding Hao: America's Air War in China, 1937-1945. Wanda Cornelius & Thayne Short. LC 80-19337. (Illus.). 502p. 1980. 19.95 (ISBN 0-88289-253-3). Pelican.

Dinghies for All Waters: Safe Family Cruising & Day Sailing. Eric Coleman. (Illus.). 176p. 1976. 12.00 (ISBN 0-370-10459-5); pap. 9.95 (ISBN 0-685-69467-4). Transatlantic.

Dinghy-Owner's Handbook. Dave Jenkins. (Illus.). 224p. 1976. 14.00 (ISBN 0-370-10243-6); pap. 9.95 (ISBN 0-370-10346-7). Transatlantic.

Dinghy Racing. Ron Riachardson. 11.95 (ISBN 0-7134-0319-5, SpS). Soccer.

Dinghy Sailing Illustrated: The Dinghy Sailor's Bible. Pat Royce. (Illus.). 1974. pap. 2.50 o.p. (ISBN 0-930030-07-9). Western Marine Ent.

Dingle Ridge Fox & Other Stories. Sam Savitt. LC 78-7739. (Illus.). (gr. 5 up). 1978. 5.95 (ISBN 0-396-07614-9). Dodd.

Dingley Falls. Michael Malone. 1981. pap. price not set (ISBN 0-671-42264-2). PB.

Dining in-Cincinnati. Valerie Beeler. (Dining in Ser.). 1981. pap. 7.95 (ISBN 0-89716-079-7). Peanut Butter.

Dining in Houston, Vol. II. Ann Criswell. (Dining in Ser.). 200p. 1980. pap. 7.95 (ISBN 0-89716-065-7). Peanut Butter.

Dining in Philadelphia. Parke Rouse. (Dining in-Ser.). 200p. 1981. pap. 7.95 (ISBN 0-89716-039-8). Peanut Butter.

Dining in-Sun Valley. Muffet Hemingway & Russ Armstrong. (Dining in Ser.). 1981. pap. 7.95 (ISBN 0-89716-078-9). Peanut Butter.

Dining in-Vail. (Dining in Ser.). 1981. pap. 7.95 (ISBN 0-89716-059-2). Peanut Butter.

Dining Out & Dining in: Memorable Menus & Recipes from Washington's Finest Restaurants. Sheilah Geoghegan. 128p. 1981. 10.00 (ISBN 0-914440-47-0). EPM Pubns.

Dining Room & the Drawing Room & the Bedroom & the Boudoir. M. J. Loftie et al. Ed. by Peter Stansky & Rodney Shewan. LC 76-18321. (Aesthetic Movement & the Arts & Crafts Movement Ser.). 1978. lib. bdg. 44.00x (ISBN 0-8240-2461-3). Garland Pub.

Dining Room Service. Lewis Lehrman. LC 70-142510. 1971. text ed. 14.50 (ISBN 0-672-96065-6); tchr's manual 5.90 (ISBN 0-672-96067-2); wkbk. 6.50 (ISBN 0-672-96066-4). Bobbs.

Dink. Sloan Rankin. LC 80-81545. (Illus.). 96p. 1980. 6.95 (ISBN 0-396-07837-0). Dodd.

Dinka & Their Songs. Francis M. Deng. (Oxford Library of African Literature Ser). 308p. 1973. 24.95x (ISBN 0-19-815138-1). Oxford U Pr.

Dinky & Sam: And the Long Way Home. Alice. (Illus.). 1981. 4.95 (ISBN 0-533-04711-0). Vantage.

Dinner at Alberta's. (gr. k-6). 1980. pap. 1.25 (ISBN 0-440-41864-X, YB). Dell.

Dinner at Alberta's. Russell Hoban. LC 73-94796. (Illus.). 40p. (gr. 1-3). 1975. 8.95 (ISBN 0-690-23992-0, TYC-J); PLB 8.79 (ISBN 0-690-23993-9). T Y Crowell.

Dinner Can Be a Picnic All Year Round. Sharon A. Elliot. LC 80-70050. 1981. pap. 5.95 (ISBN 0-9601398-4-2). Fresh Pr.

Dinner in Town. Claude Mauriac. Tr. by Richard Howard. 1980. pap. 4.95 (ISBN 0-7145-0199-9). Riverrun NY.

Dinny & the Witches: Two Plays. William Gibson. Bd. with Miracle Worker. LC 60-7778. 1960. 4.50 (ISBN 0-689-10095-7). Atheneum.

Dinny Gordon: Sophomore. Anne Emery. (gr. 7-10). pap. 0.95 o.p. (ISBN 0-425-03028-8, Highland). Berkley Pub.

Dino-Mite Foozles. Pat Fortunato. (YA) (gr. 6 up). 1979. pap. 1.25 (ISBN 0-440-91950-9, LFL). Dell.

Dino's Happy & Sad Book. Leslie Max. (Play & Learn Shape Board Bks). 14p. (gr. k-3). 1981. bds. 2.95 comb bdg. (ISBN 0-89828-103-2, 6004, Ottenheimer Pubs Inc). Tuffy Bks.

Dinosaur Coloring Book. Anthony Rao. (Illus.). 48p. (Orig.). (gr. 1-4). 1980. pap. 2.00 (ISBN 0-486-24022-3). Dover.

Dinosaur Cooler. Randy Fingland & Andrea Schneider. (Illus.). 1980. pap. 2.25 (ISBN 0-931020-13-1). Crosscut Saw.

Dinosaur Do's & Don't's. Syd Hoff. LC 80-13729. (Illus.). 48p. (ps-2). 1980. pap. 2.95 (ISBN 0-671-41200-0, Pub. by Windmill). S&S.

Dinosaur Fun Book. William Johnson. (Illus.). 48p. (gr. k-12). 1979. pap. 2.25 (ISBN 0-89844-007-6, 007-6). Troubador Pr.

Dinosaur Funny Bones. J. Polhamus & M. Funai. 1974. 4.95 (ISBN 0-13-214536-7); pap. 1.95 (ISBN 0-13-214585-5). P-H.

Dinosaur Hunt. George O. Whitaker & Joan Meyers. LC 65-12614. (Illus.). (gr. 5-8). 1965. 5.95 o.p. (ISBN 0-15-223501-9, HJ). HarBraceJ.

Dinosaur Is Too Big. Elizabeth Bram. LC 76-22669. (Illus.). (gr. k-3). 1977. PLB 6.00 (ISBN 0-688-84071-X). Greenwillow.

Dinosaur Mysteries. Mary Elting & Ann Goodman. LC 79-55035. (Bronto Bks). (Illus.). 64p. (gr. 3-8). 1980. 4.95 (ISBN 0-448-13617-1); PLB 9.30 (ISBN 0-686-64320-8). Platt.

Dinosaur Planet. Anne McCaffrey. (Del Rey Bks). 1978. 2.25 (ISBN 0-345-29593-5); pap. 1.95 (ISBN 0-345-28509-3). Ballantine.

Dinosaur Scrapbook. Donald F. Glut. 1980. 19.95 (ISBN 0-8065-0671-7). Lyle Stuart.

Dinosaur Story. Joanna Cole. LC 74-5931. (Illus.). 32p. (gr. k-3). 1974. PLB 6.48 (ISBN 0-688-31826-6). Morrow.

Dinosaur: The Story Behind the Scenery. Allen Hagood. LC 75-157460. (Illus.). 1972. 7.95 (ISBN 0-916122-35-2); pap. 2.50 (ISBN 0-916122-10-7). K C Pubns.

Dinosaur World. Edwin H. Colbert. LC 76-16586. (Illus.). 1977. 8.95 (ISBN 0-87396-081-5). Stravon.

Dinosaurios Gigantes (Giant Dinosaurs) Rowe. (ps-3). 1980. pap. 1.95 (ISBN 0-590-30928-5, Schol Pap). Schol Bk Serv.

Dinosaurs. Kathleen Daly. (Look-Look Ser.). (Illus.). 1977. PLB 5.38 (ISBN 0-307-61835-8, Golden Pr); pap. 0.95 (ISBN 0-307-11835-5). Western Pub.

Dinosaurs. (MacDonald Educational Ser.). (Illus., Arabic.). 3.50 (ISBN 0-686-53078-0). Intl Bk Ctr.

Dinosaurs. Nora Sullivan. (Easy-Read Fact Book Ser.). (Illus.). 48p. (gr. 2-4). 1976. PLB 6.45 (ISBN 0-531-00365-5). Watts.

Dinosaurs. Jane Watson. (ps-3). 1959. PLB 5.00 (ISBN 0-307-60355-5, Golden Pr). Western Pub.

Dinosaurs. Ruth Wheeler & Harold G. Coffin. LC 78-50443. (Panda Ser.). 1978. pap. 4.95 (ISBN 0-8163-0195-6, 04340-6). Pacific Pr Pub Assn.

Dinosaurs. Herbert S. Zim. (Illus.). (gr. 3-7). 1954. PLB 6.48 (ISBN 0-688-31239-X). Morrow.

Dinosaurs & More Dinosaurs. 2nd ed. M. Jean Craig. LC 68-27276. (Illus.). 96p. (gr. 1-4). 1968. 9.95 (ISBN 0-590-07028-2, Four Winds). Schol Bk Serv.

Dinosaurs & Other First Animals. Dean Morris. LC 77-23398. (Read About Animals Ser.). (Illus.). (gr. k-3). 1977. PLB 9.95 (ISBN 0-8393-0000-X). Raintree Child.

Dinosaurs & Other Reptiles from the Beginning. Alma Gilleo. LC 77-24957. (From the Beginning Ser.). (Illus.). (gr. 1-4). 1977. PLB 5.50 (ISBN 0-89565-004-5). Childs World.

Dinosaurs & Their Living Relatives. British Museum Natural History. LC 79-14504. 1980. 17.95 (ISBN 0-521-22887-5); pap. 6.95 (ISBN 0-521-29698-6). Cambridge U Pr.

Dinosaurs Discovered. John Gilbert. LC 80-82756. (Illus.). 96p. 1981. 8.95 (ISBN 0-88332-252-8). Larousse.

Dinosaurs, Giants of the Past. Kathleen Daly. (gr. 4-7). 1974. 1.95 (ISBN 0-307-10501-6, Golden Pr); PLB 7.62 (ISBN 0-307-60501-9). Western Pub.

Dinosaurs of North America. Helen R. Sattler. (Illus.). 160p. (gr. 2 up). 1981. 10.95 (ISBN 0-688-51952-0); pap. 5.95 o.p. (ISBN 0-688-41952-6). Morrow.

Dinosaurs of the Southwest. Ronald P. Ratkevich. LC 75-40837. (Illus.). 115p. 1977. pap. 4.95 (ISBN 0-8263-0406-0). U of NM Pr.

Dinwiddie County, "the Country of the Apamatica.". Writers Program, Virginia. LC 73-3659. (American Guide Ser.). 1942. Repr. 16.00 (ISBN 0-404-57955-8). AMS Pr.

Dion Boucicault: A Biography. Richard Fawkes. 274p. 1980. 21.95 (ISBN 0-7043-2221-8, Pub. by Quartet England). Horizon.

Dionysios Solomos. M. Byron Raizis. (World Authors Ser.: Greece: No. 193). lib. bdg. 10.95 (ISBN 0-8057-2846-5). Twayne.

Dionysius of Halicarnassus: On Thucydides. W. Kendrick Pritchett. 1975. 14.50x (ISBN 0-520-02922-4); pap. 7.95x (ISBN 0-520-02959-3). U of Cal Pr.

Dionysius Von Alexandrien Zur Frage Des Originismus. Wolfgang Bienert. (Patristische Texte und Studien, 21). 1978. 51.75x (ISBN 3-11-007442-7). De Gruyter.

Dionysus in Sixty-Nine. Ed. by Richard Schechner. 114p. 1970. 10.00 (ISBN 0-374-14004-9). FS&G.

Dionysus: Myth & Cult. Walter F. Otto. Tr. by Robert B. Palmer. LC 65-11792. (Midland Bks.: No. 95). (Illus.). 1965. pap. 2.95x o.p. (ISBN 0-253-20095-4). Ind U Pr.

Diophantische Approximationen. Hermann Minkowski. LC 56-13056. (Ger). 11.95 (ISBN 0-8284-0118-7). Chelsea Pub.

Diophantische Gleichungen. Thoralf Skolem. LC 51-6891. (Ger). 8.95 (ISBN 0-8284-0075-X). Chelsea Pub.

Dios de Nuestros Libertadores. Luis Salem. LC 77-165. (Illus.). 172p. (Orig., Span.). 1977. pap. 2.75 (ISBN 0-89922-093-2). Edit Caribe.

Dios, el Atomo, y el Universo. James Reid. Tr. by Julio Orozco from Eng. LC 76-55491. 240p. (Orig., Span.). 1977. pap. 3.50 (ISBN 0-89922-083-5). Edit Caribe.

Dios Guia Tu Futuro. Tr. by Roger C. Palms. (Spanish Bks.). (Span.). 1977. 1.60 (ISBN 0-8297-0767-0). Life Pubs Intl.

Dios Quiere Sanarte y Revolucionar Tu Vida. Tr. by Kathryn Kuhlman. (Spanish Bks.). (Span.). 1977. 2.25 (ISBN 0-8297-0751-4). Life Pubs Intl.

Dios, Tu y Tu Familia. Tr. by Betty M. De Poor. (Dios, Tu y la Vida). Orig. Title: Deus, Voce E Sua Familia. 1978. 0.75 (ISBN 0-311-46202-2). Casa Bautista.

Dios y Sus Ayudantes. (Illus.). 48p. (Span.). Date not set. pap. price not set (ISBN 0-311-38548-6). Casa Bautista.

Dioxin: Toxicological & Chemical Aspects. Ed. by Caball Cattabeni et al. (Monographs of the Giovanni Lorenzini Foundation). 1978. 20.00 (ISBN 0-470-26361-X). Halsted Pr.

Diploids. Katherine Maclean. (Science Fiction Ser.). 1981. PLB 13.95 (ISBN 0-8398-2510-2). Gregg.

Diploma Disease: Education, Qualification, & Development. Ronald P. Dore. 1976. 20.00x (ISBN 0-520-03107-5); CAMPUS 181. pap. 6.95x (ISBN 0-520-03270-5). U of Cal Pr.

Diplomacy & Its Discontents. James Eayrs. LC 73-163811. 198p. 1971. pap. 3.50 (ISBN 0-8020-6121-4). U of Toronto Pr.

Diplomacy & Revolution: The Franco-American Alliance of 1778. Ed. by Ronald Hoffman & Peter J. Albert. LC 80-13931. 1981. write for info. (ISBN 0-8139-0864-7). U Pr of Va.

Diplomacy of Frustration: The Manchurian Crisis of 1931-1933 As Revealed in the Paper of Stanley K. Hornbeck. Compiled by Justus D. Doenecke. (Publication Ser.: No. 231). 1981. 22.95 (ISBN 0-8179-7311-7). Hoover Inst Pr.

Diplomacy of Ideas: U. S. Foreign Policy & Cultural Relations, 1938-1950. F. A. Ninkovich. 256p. Date not set. 24.95 (ISBN 0-521-23241-4). Cambridge U Pr.

Diplomacy of Power: Soviet Armed Forces As a Political Instrument. Stephen S. Kaplan. 600p. 1980. 29.95 (ISBN 0-8157-4824-8); pap. 14.95 (ISBN 0-8157-4823-X). Brookings.

Diplomacy of the American Revolution. Samuel F. Bemis. LC 57-7878. (Midland Bks.: No. 6). 1957. pap. 2.95x o.p. (ISBN 0-253-20006-7). Ind U Pr.

Diplomas of King Aethelred 'the Unready' 978 to 1016. Simon Keynes. LC 79-7651. (Studies in Medieval Life & Thought Ser.: No. 13). (Illus.). 1980. 42.50 (ISBN 0-521-22718-6). Cambridge U Pr.

Diplomat in Berlin, 1933-1939: Papers & Memoris of Jozef Lipski, Ambassador of Poland. Ed. by Waclaw Jedrzejewicz. LC 67-25871. (Illus.). 1968. 22.50x (ISBN 0-231-03070-3). Columbia U Pr.

Diplomat in Paris, 1936-1939: Memoirs of Juliusz Lukasiewicz, Ambassador of Poland. Ed. by Waclaw Jedrzejewicz. LC 79-83535. 1969. 22.50x (ISBN 0-231-03308-7). Columbia U Pr.

Diplomatic Ceremonial & Protocol. John R. Wood & Jean Serres. 1970. 30.00x (ISBN 0-231-03138-6). Columbia U Pr.

Diplomatic Prelude, 1938-1939. L. B. Namier. 19.50 o.p. (ISBN 0-86527-044-9). Fertig.

Diplomats in Buckskins: A History of Indian Delegations in Washington City. Herman J. Viola. LC 80-607804. (Illus.). 1981. 17.50 (ISBN 0-87474-944-1). Smithsonian.

Diplomats in Crisis: United States-Chinese-Japanese Relations, 1919-1941. Ed. by Richard D. Burns & Edward M. Bennett. LC 74-76444. 346p. 1974. text ed. 10.65 (ISBN 0-87436-135-4). ABC-Clio.

Dips in Learning. Ed. by Thomas G. Bever. 300p. 1981. prof. - refer. 19.95 (ISBN 0-89859-096-5). L Erlbaum Assocs.

Diptera: Asilidae Insecta II, Vol. 2. Oskar Theodor. (Fauna Palaestina). (Illus.). 458p. 1981. text ed. 30.00x (ISBN 0-87474-910-7). Smithsonian.

Dire Tel Quel. Tr. by Fritz Ridenour. (French Bks.). (Fr.). 1979. 2.05 (ISBN 0-686-28822-X). Life Pubs Intl.

Direct Action & Liberal Democracy. April Carter. 1974. pap. 2.95x (ISBN 0-06-131816-7, TB1816, Torch). Har-Row.

Direct Broadcast Satellites & the United Nations. K. M. Queeney. 344p. 1978. 41.00x (ISBN 90-286-0069-8). Sijthoff & Noordhoff.

Direct Characterization of Fine Particles. Brian H. Kaye. (Chemical Analysis Ser.). 500p. 1981. 50.00 (ISBN 0-471-46150-4, Pub. by Wiley-Interscience). Wiley.

Direct Cost & Contribution Accounting: An Integrated Management Accounting System. Germain B. Boer. LC 73-17324. (Systems & Controls for Financial Managment Ser). 256p. 1974. 26.95 (ISBN 0-471-08505-7, Pub. by Wiley-Interscience). Wiley.

Direct Current Fundamentals. Loper. LC 70-153729. 352p. 1978. 13.60 (ISBN 0-8273-1143-5); pap. 10.40 (ISBN 0-8273-1147-8); instructor's guide 2.00 (ISBN 0-8273-1145-1). Delmar.

Direct Current Machines. M. G. Say & E. O. Taylor. LC 79-19519. 1980. pap. text ed. 19.95x (ISBN 0-470-26838-7). Halsted Pr.

Direct Current Motors: Characteristics & Applications. Peter Walker. (Illus.). 1978. 15.95 (ISBN 0-8306-8931-1, 931). TAB Bks.

Direct Decision Therapy. Harold Greenwald. LC 73-75565. 1973. text ed. 10.95 (ISBN 0-912736-15-1). EDITS Pubs.

Direct Energy Conversion. 3rd ed. Stanley W. Angrist. 1976. text ed. 26.95x (ISBN 0-205-05581-8). Allyn.

Direct Energy Conversion. M. Ali Kettani. (Electrical Engineering Ser). 1970. text ed. 25.95 (ISBN 0-201-03663-0). A-W.

Direct Foreign Investment: A Japanese Model of Multinational Business Operations. Kiyoshi Kojima. LC 78-61337. (Praeger Special Studies). 1979. 27.95 (ISBN 0-03-047471-X). Praeger.

Direct Instruction Mathematics. Jerry Silbert et al. (Illus., Orig.). 1981. pap. text ed. write for info. (ISBN 0-675-08047-9). Merrill.

Direct Integrel Theory. Nielsen. 184p. 1980. 23.50 (ISBN 0-8247-6971-6). Dekker.

Direct Investment & Development in the U.S. A Guide to Incentive Programs, Laws & Restrictions, 1980-81. rev. ed. Raymond J. Waldmann. LC 80-51673. 453p. 1980. pap. text ed. 75.00 (ISBN 0-933678-01-0). Transnatl Invest.

Direct Mail Databook. 3rd ed. 288p. 1980. text ed. 65.00x (ISBN 0-566-02177-3, Pub. by Pub Co England). Renouf.

Direct Marketing. LC 80-67813. (Marketing Ser.). 1980. pap. 4.95 (ISBN 0-87251-052-2). Crain Bks.

Direct Marketing Business, GB-060: New Perspectives. Business Communications Co. 1980. cancelled (ISBN 0-89336-276-X). BCC.

Direct Marketing Market Place Nineteen Eighty. Ed. & intro. by Edward L. Stern. 1979. pap. 25.00 o.p. (ISBN 0-934464-01-4). Hilary Hse Pubs.

Direct Marketing Market Place 1981. Pamela Hemingway. 375p. 1981. pap. 40.00 (ISBN 0-934464-02-2). Hilary House Pubs.

Direct Measures of Writing Skills: Issues & Applications. 1980. pap. 3.75 (ISBN 0-89354-829-4). Northwest Regional.

Direct Observation & Measurement of Behavior. S. J. Hutt & Corrine Hutt. (American Lecture Living Chemistry Ser). (Illus.). 240p. 1978. 18.50 (ISBN 0-398-00892-2). C C Thomas.

Direct Participation in Action: The New Bureaucracy. David Pace & John Hunter. 1978. 17.95 (ISBN 0-566-00205-1, 02012-5, Pub. by Saxon Hse England). Lexington Bks.

Direct Perception. Claire F. Michaels & Claudia A. Carello. (Illus.). 224p. 1981. text ed. 18.00 (ISBN 0-13-214791-2). P-H.

Direct Physical Measurement of Mass Yields in Thermal Fission of Uranium. Gino J. DiIorio. LC 78-75005. (Outstanding Disserations on Energy Ser.). 1979. lib. bdg. 11.00 (ISBN 0-8240-3985-8). Garland Pub.

Direct Silkscreen Printing & Painting: New Directions - Versatile Approaches. Ted Jones. Ed. by Evelyn Jones. (Illus.). 1980. pap. write for info. (ISBN 0-916928-05-5). New Dimen Studio.

Direct Use of the Sun's Energy. Farrington Daniels. 1974. pap. 2.50 (ISBN 0-345-29226-X). Ballantine.

Direct Utilization of Geothermal Energy: A Symposium, January 31-February 2, 1978, San Diego, California. Ed. by Geothermal Resources Council. (Illus., Orig.). pap. 2.50 o.p. (ISBN 0-934412-74-X). Geothermal.

Directed-Energy Weapons: A Juridical Analysis. Edward A. Fessler. LC 79-65950. (Praeger Special Studies). 204p. 1979. 20.95 (ISBN 0-03-053511-5). Praeger.

Directed Readings: Introduction to Psychology. 2nd ed. A. Bond Woodruff. 144p. 1980. pap. text ed. 5.95 (ISBN 0-8403-2243-7). Kendall-Hunt.

Directing Arithmetic Skills. 2nd ed. W. F. Hunter et al. (gr. 8-12). 1976. 5.60 (ISBN 0-07-031324-5, W); tchr's manual 6.64 (ISBN 0-07-031325-3). McGraw.

Directing Drama. John Miles-Brown. (Illus.). 176p. 1980. text ed. 24.75x (ISBN 0-7206-0557-1). Humanities.

Directing in the Theatre: A Casebook. J. Robert Wills. LC 80-19432. 149p. 1980. 10.00 (ISBN 0-8108-1348-3); instr's manual avail. Scarecrow.

Directing Language Skills. William F. Hunter et al. (Learning Skill Ser: Lanugage Arts). (Illus.). 1978. pap. text ed. 4.52 (ISBN 0-07-031334-2, W); tchr's manual 6.32 (ISBN 0-07-031335-0). McGraw.

Directing the Television Commercial. Ben Gradus. (Communication Arts Books). 228p. 1981. 16.95x (ISBN 0-8038-1575-1, Communications Arts); pap. 9.95x (ISBN 0-8038-1577-8). Hastings.

Direction for the English Traveller. Jacob Van Langeren. LC 72-211. (English Experience Ser.: No. 197). 1969. Repr. of 1635 ed. 8.00 (ISBN 90-221-0197-5). Walter J Johnson.

Direction or Preparative to the Study of the Lawe: London, 1600. William Fulbecke. (Classics of English Legal History in the Modern Era Ser.: Vol. 3). 99p. 1980. lib. bdg. 60.50 (ISBN 0-8240-4602-1). Garland Pub.

Directions. Howard N. Fox. LC 79-14499. (Illus.). 103p. 1979. 17.50 (ISBN 0-87474-434-2). Smithsonian.

Directions: A Guide to Career Planning. Thomas D. Bachhuber & Richard K. Harwood. LC 77-78015. (Illus.). 1978. pap. text ed. 9.50 (ISBN 0-395-25385-3). HM.

Directions: A Look at the Paths of Life. Walter R. Scragg. LC 77-78101. (Horizon Ser.). 1977. pap. 4.50 (ISBN 0-8127-0136-4). Southern Pub.

Directions & Angles. Irving Adler & Ruth Adler. LC 69-10489. (Reason Why Ser). (Illus.). (gr. 3-6). 1969. PLB 6.89 o.p. (ISBN 0-381-99615-8, A18860, JD-J). John Day.

Directions for Criticism: Structuralism & Its Alternatives. Ed. by Murray Krieger & L. S. Dembo. 1977. 17.50 (ISBN 0-299-07390-4, 739); pap. text ed. 5.95 (ISBN 0-299-07394-7). U of Wis Pr.

Directions for Data Buoy Technology, 1978-1983. 112p. 1974. pap. 3.50 (ISBN 0-309-02230-4). Natl Acad Pr.

Directions for House & Ship Painting. Hezekiah Reynolds. (AAS Facsimiles: No. 1). (Illus., Orig.). 1978. pap. 2.95 (ISBN 0-912296-16-X, Dist. by U Pr of Va). Am Antiquarian.

Directions for the Decade: Library Instruction in the 1980's. Ed. by Carolyn A. Kirkendall. (Library Orientation Ser.: No. 12). 1980. 10.00. Pierian.

Directions in Energy Policy: A Comprehensive Approach to Energy Resource Decision-Making. Ed. by Behram Kursunoglu & Arnold Perlmutter. LC 79-21524. 736p. reference 38.00 (ISBN 0-88410-089-8). Ballinger Pub.

Directions in Managing Construction: A Critical Look at Present & Future Industry Practices, Problems & Policies. Donald S. Barrie. (Construction Management & Engineering Ser.). 500p. 1981. 34.95 (ISBN 0-471-04642-6, Pub. by Wiley-Interscience). Wiley.

Directions in Physics: Lectures Delivered During a Visit to Australia & New Zealand, August & September, 1975. Pam Dirac et al. LC 77-24892. 1978. 17.50 (ISBN 0-471-02997-1, Pub. by Wiley-Interscience). Wiley.

Directions in Safety: A Selection of Safety Readings. Ted S. Ferry & D. A. Weaver. (Illus.). 498p. 1976. 34.75 (ISBN 0-398-03365-X). C C Thomas.

Directive Teaching of Children with Learning & Behavioral Handicaps. 2nd ed. Thomas M. Stephens. 272p. 1976. pap. text ed. 9.95 (ISBN 0-675-08590-X). Merrill.

Director of Maintenance. Jack Rudman. (Career Examination Ser.: C-2812). (Cloth bdg. avail. on request). 1980. pap. 14.00 (ISBN 0-8373-2812-8). Natl Learning.

Director's & Company Secretary's Handbook of Draft Legal Letters. 2nd ed. Ewan Mitchell. 596p. 1979. text ed. 43.00x (ISBN 0-220-67001-3, Pub. by Busn Bks England). Renouf.

Director's Lawyer & the Company Secretary's Legal Guide. 4th ed. Ewan Mitchell. 645p. 1978. text ed. 43.00x (ISBN 0-220-66346-7, Pub. by Busn Bks England). Renouf.

Directors on Directing. rev. ed. Ed. by Toby Cole & Helen K. Chinoy. LC 62-20686. Orig. Title: Directing the Play. 1963. pap. 8.95 (ISBN 0-672-60622-4). Bobbs.

Directory-Department of Chief Administrators of Catholic Education. 62p. 3.00. Natl Cath Educ.

Directory for Exceptional Children. 9th ed. Ed. by Porter Sargent Staff. LC 54-4975. (Special Education Ser.). (Illus.). 1384p. 1981. 30.00 (ISBN 0-87558-097-1). Porter Sargent.

Directory for the Arts. Center for Arts Information. LC 78-18486. 1978. 10.00 (ISBN 0-89062-048-2, Pub. by Ctr for Arts Info); pap. 6.00 (ISBN 0-89062-061-X). Pub Ctr Cult Res.

Directory for the Disabled: A Handbook of Information & Opportunities for Disabled & Handicapped People. 2nd ed. Ann Darnbrough & Derek Kinrade. 208p. 1980. 27.00x (ISBN 0-85941-106-0, Pub. by Woodhead-Faulkner England); pap. 12.00x (ISBN 0-85941-108-7). State Mutual Bk.

Directory of Agencies. LC 78-51890. 1978. pap. 5.00x o.p. (ISBN 0-87101-077-1, CBD-077-C). Natl Assn Soc Wkrs.

Directory of Agencies Serving the Visually Handicapped in the U. S. 21st ed. American Foundation for the Blind. Ed. by Mary E. Mulholland. 450p. Date not set. pap. 16.00 (ISBN 0-89128-100-2). Am Foun Blind.

Directory of Agencies: U. S. Voluntary, International Voluntary, Intergovernmental. rev. ed. LC 80-81981. 104p. 1980. pap. 5.00x (ISBN 0-87101-085-2, CBD-085-C). Natl Assn Soc Wkrs.

Directory of American Book Workers. Compiled by Renee Roff. 1981. 19.95 (ISBN 0-935164-05-7). N T Smith.

Directory of American Fiction Writers, 1976 Edition. Poets & Writers, Inc. LC 75-25710. 104p. 1976. 10.00 o.p. (ISBN 0-913734-04-7); pap. 5.00 o.p. (ISBN 0-913734-05-5). Poets & Writers.

Directory of American Poets & Fiction Writers 1980-81 Edition. LC 80-7449. 224p. 1980. 18.00 (ISBN 0-913734-11-X); pap. 10.00 (ISBN 0-913734-12-8). Poets & Writers.

Directory of American Savings & Loan Associations. 1979. 37.50 o.p. (ISBN 0-686-23693-9). T K Sanderson.

Directory of American Savings & Loan Associations. 1978. case bound 35.00 o.p. (ISBN 0-686-20511-1); supplementary regional pocket directories 15.50 ea. o.p. T K Sanderson.

Directory of American Savings & Loan Associations. 1981. case bound 40.00 (ISBN 0-686-26949-7); pap. 15.50 regional pocket directory (ISBN 0-686-26950-0). T K Sanderson.

Directory of Antique Radio Collectors & Suppliers. 5th ed. Hartford Beitman. (Orig.). 1980. pap. 3.00x (ISBN 0-938630-00-8); notebook 4.00x (ISBN 0-938630-01-6). Antique Radio.

Directory of Antique Radio Collectors & Suppliers. pap. 3.00 (ISBN 0-686-27838-0). Antique Radio.

Directory of Artists Slide Registries. Suzy Ticho. 65p. (Orig.). 1980. pap. 6.95 (ISBN 0-915400-25-1). Am Council Arts.

Directory of Associations in Canada. 3rd ed. Ed. by Brian Land. 696p. cancelled o.s.i. (ISBN 0-8020-4531-6, Pub.by U. of Toronto Pr). Bowker.

Directory of Athletic Scholarships: Where They Are & How to Get Them. Barry Green & Alan Green. 312p. 1981. 14.95 (ISBN 0-399-12620-1, Perigee); pap. 6.95 (ISBN 0-399-50533-4). Putnam.

Directory of Blacks in the Performing Arts. Edward Mapp. LC 78-2436. 1978. 21.00 (ISBN 0-8108-1126-X). Scarecrow.

Directory of British Alternative Periodicals Nineteen Sixty-Five to Nineteen Seventy-Four. John Noyce. 1978. text ed. 52.00x (ISBN 0-391-00898-6). Humanities.

Directory of British Associations & Associations in Ireland. 6th ed. Ed. by G. P. Henderson & S. P. Henderson. 1980. 125.00 (ISBN 0-900246-34-0, Pub. by CBD Research). Gale.

Directory of Business Archives in the United States & Canada. 56p. (Orig.). 1980. pap. 6.00 (ISBN 0-931828-24-4). Soc Am Archivists.

Directory of Buyers. 2nd ed. Francis Hulme. 1981. pap. 7.95x (ISBN 0-936588-01-2). Buyer's Directory.

Directory of Catholic Residential Schools. 1978. 2.00. Natl Cath Educ.

Directory of Children's Theatre in the United States. Ed. by Gayle Cornelison. 1980. pap. 9.00; ATA members 7.00. Am Theatre Assoc.

Directory of Chinese American Librarians. Tze-Chung Li & Roy Chang. LC 77-373584. 1977. pap. 5.00 (ISBN 0-686-24156-8). CHCUS Inc.

Directory of Clothing Research. M. S. Davies et al. 136p. 1968. 35.00x (ISBN 0-686-63762-3). State Mutual Bk.

Directory of College & University Archives in the United States & Canada. Ed. by College & University Archives Committee. LC 80-50627. 80p. 1980. pap. 10.00 (ISBN 0-931828-21-X). Soc Am Archivists.

Directory of Community Services Organizations in Greater Los Angeles. Ed. by Paul Bullock. 255p. 1980. 6.50 (ISBN 0-89215-106-4). U Cal LA Indus Rel.

Directory of Computer Education & Research. Tr. by T. C. Hsiao. 1100p. 1981. 120.00. Sci & Tech Pr.

Directory of Conservative & Libertarian Serials, Publishers, & Freelance Markets. Dennis D. Murphy. LC 78-65733. 1979. pap. 4.95x o.p. (ISBN 0-918788-02-1). D D Murphy.

Directory of Construction Associations. 2nd ed. Professional Publications. Ed. by Joseph A. MacDonald. (Orig.). 1980. pap. 19.95 (ISBN 0-932836-01-1). Prof Pubns NY.

Directory of Contemporary Musical Instrument Makers. Susan C. Farrell. LC 80-24924. 320p. 1981. text ed. 24.00x (ISBN 0-8262-0322-1). U of Mo Pr.

Directory of Continuing Education Opportunities for Library, Information, Media Personnel. 2nd ed. Ed. by Continuing Library Education Network & Exchange. 292p. 1979. text ed. 30.00 (ISBN 0-89664-064-7, Pub. by K G Saur). Gale.

Directory of Convenience Store Companies, 1981. 1981. 60.00 (ISBN 0-911790-42-X). Prog Grocer.

Directory of Conventions: With Supplement. Sales Meeting Magazine Research Staff. (Annual). Date not set. pap. 60.00x (ISBN 0-89047-045-6). Herman Pub.

Directory of Corporate Affiliations. National Register Publishing Co. LC 67-22770. 1981. 140.00 (ISBN 0-87217-002-0). Natl Register.

Directory of Defense Electronic Products & Services: U. S. Suppliers, 1981. rev. 7th ed. 228p. pap. write for info. (ISBN 0-931634-06-7). Info Clearing House.

Directory of Directories: An Annotated Guide to Business & Industrial Directories, Professional & Scientific Rosters, & Other Lists & Guides of All Kinds. Ed. by James M. Ethridge. 1980. 60.00 (ISBN 0-8103-0270-5, Pub. by Information Ent). Gale.

Directory of Directors in the City of New York & Surburbs, 1980. rev. ed. Ed. by A. M. Dahl & Joan E. Joseph. 680p. 1980. 115.00 (ISBN 0-936612-01-0). DODC.

Directory of Dividend Reinvestment Plans. Dickie L. Fox. LC 80-19078. 240p. (Orig.). 1980. pap. 15.00 (ISBN 0-930256-06-9). Almar.

Directory of Engineering Document Sources. 2nd ed. Dave Simonton. 436p. 1974. perfect bnd. 39.95x (ISBN 0-912702-06-0). Global Eng.

Directory of Engineering Societies & Related Organizations. Engineers Joint Council Editors. 1976. pap. 18.00 o.p. (ISBN 0-685-47812-2). AAES.

Directory of English Studies in Brazil. 185p. 1980. 50.00x (ISBN 0-901618-21-7, Pub. by Brit Coun England). State Mutual Bk.

Directory of European Associations: National Industrial, Trade & Professional Associations, Pt. One. 3rd ed. Ed. by I. G. Anderson. 500p. 1981. 125.00. Gale.

Directory of European Associations: Part 1 - National Industrial, Trade & Professional Associations. 2nd ed. Ed. by I. G. Anderson. LC 76-11697. 1976. 125.00 (ISBN 0-685-67342-1, Pub. by CBD Research). Gale.

Directory of European Associations: Part 2- National Learned, Scientific & Technical Societies. 2nd ed. Ed. by I. G. Anderson. LC 76-11697. 1979. 130.00 (ISBN 0-900246-29-4, Pub. by CBD Research). Gale.

Directory of European Information. Ed. by Irene Kingston & William A. Benjamin. 590p. 1979. 85.00 (ISBN 2-85993-001-9). Ballinger Pub.

Directory of Evaluation Consultants. Ed. by Richard Johnson. LC 80-67499. (Orig.). 1981. pap. 8.95 (ISBN 0-87954-035-4). Foundation Ctr.

Directory of Fee-Based Information Services 1980-81. Ed. by Kelly Warnken. LC 76-55469. 1980. pap. 6.95 (ISBN 0-936288-00-0). Info Alternative.

Directory of Financial Aids for Women. Gail A. Schlachter. LC 77-78149. 16.95 (ISBN 0-918276-02-0). Ref Serv Pr.

Directory of Fire Research. 8th ed. Committee on Fire Research, National Research Council. 1978. pap. text ed. 9.50x (ISBN 0-309-02799-3). Natl Acad Pr.

Directory of Fire Research in the United States, 1967-1969. 5th ed. Committee on Fire Research. LC 68-60084. 1970. pap. text ed. 14.25 (ISBN 0-309-01763-7). Natl Acad Pr.

Directory of Fire Research in the U. S. 1969-1971. 6th ed. Committee on Fire Research. LC 68-60084. 800p. 1972. pap. 16.00 (ISBN 0-309-02033-6). Natl Acad Pr.

Directory of Fire Research in the United States: 1971-1973. 7th ed. LC 74-32544. 1975. pap. 12.75 (ISBN 0-309-02327-0). Natl Acad Pr.

Directory of Franchising Organizations 1981. Samuel Small & Pilot Books Staff. LC 62-39831. 1981. pap. 3.50 (ISBN 0-87576-000-7). Pilot Bks.

Directory of Geoscience Departments. 19th ed. 180p. 1980. 12.00 (ISBN 0-913312-51-7). Am Geol.

Directory of Geoscience Departments: 1979-1980. 18th ed. American Geological Institute. 180p. (Orig.). 1979. pap. 12.00 (ISBN 0-913312-23-1). Am Geol.

Directory of Health Sciences Libraries in the United States. Ed. by Alan M. Rees & Susan Crawford. LC 80-65893. 356p. 1980. 25.00. Med Lib Assn.

Directory of High-Discount Merchandise & Product Sources for Distributors & Mail-Order Wealth Builders. 2nd ed. Tyler G. Hicks. 150p. 1981. pap. 17.50 (ISBN 0-914306-58-8). Intl Wealth.

Directory of High-Energy Radio Therapy Centres. (STI-PUB: No. 448). (Illus., Orig.). 1976. pap. 24.25 (ISBN 92-0-112076-1, ISP448; IAEA). Unipub.

Directory of Historical Societies & Agencies in the United States & Canada. 11th ed. American Association for State & Local History. Ed. by Donna McDonald. LC 56-4164. (Illus.). 1978. pap. 24.00x (ISBN 0-910050-36-8). AASLH.

Directory of Industrial Heat Processing & Combustion Equipment, U. S. Manufactures: 1979-1980. 2nd ed. 1979. pap. text ed. 20.00 o.s.i. (ISBN 0-931634-01-6). Info Clearing House.

Directory of Industrial Heat Processing & Combustion Equipment: U. S. Manufacturers, 1981-1982. 3rd biennial ed. Industrial Heating Equipment Assn. 224p. (Orig.). 1981. pap. write for info. (ISBN 0-931634-05-9). Info Clearing House.

Directory of Inland Waterway Facilities. Mike Harper. (Illus.). 1979. pap. 5.95 o.s.i. (ISBN 0-7134-1292-5). Hippocrene Bks.

Directory of Inland Waterway Facilities. Mike Harper. 1978. pap. 10.50 (ISBN 0-7134-1292-5, Pub. by Batsford England). David & Charles.

Directory of Institutions & Individuals Active in Environmentally Sound & Appropriate Technologies. (UNEP Reference Ser.: Vol. 1). 152p. 1979. pap. 20.00 (ISBN 0-08-025658-9, PERG20, UNEP). Unipub.

Directory of International Business Travel & Relocation. 1st ed. (Illus.). 900p. 1980. 95.00 (ISBN 0-8103-0997-1). Gale.

Directory of International Schools. 204p. 1977. pap. 7.00 o.p. (ISBN 0-89192-062-5). Interbk Inc.

Directory of Italian & Italian American Organizations & Community Services in the Metropolitan Area of Greater New York: in the Metropolitan Area of Greater New York, Vol. II. rev. ed. Compiled by Andrew Brizzolara. 1980. 9.95x (ISBN 0-913256-44-7). Ctr Migration.

Directory of Libraries & Special Collections on Latin America & the West Indies. Ed. by Bernard Naylor et al. (Institute of Latin American Studies Monographs: No. 5). 100p. 1975. text ed. 16.25x (ISBN 0-485-17705-6, Athlone Pr). Humanities.

Directory of Management Education Programs. Ed. by Fred E. Voss. LC 77-82267. (Annual). 1977. 125.00 (ISBN 0-8144-5525-5). Am Mgmt.

Directory of Management Resources for Community Based Organizations: Third Annual. Marvin L. Peebles. 100p. 1981. spiral bdg. 12.00 (ISBN 0-939020-03-3). MLP Ent.

Directory of Management Training Opportunities for Nonprofit Executives. Ed. by Jean Brodsky. 1976. 35.00 o.s.i. (ISBN 0-914756-13-3). Taft Corp.

Directory of Medical Libraries in the British Isles. 4th ed. 1976. pap. 8.75x (ISBN 0-85365-049-7, Pub. by Lib Assn England). Oryx Pr.

Directory of Medical Specialists 1974-75, 2 vols. 16th ed. LC 40-9671. 4000p. 1974. Set. 59.50 (ISBN 0-8379-0517-6). Marquis.

Directory of Modeling Schools & Agencies U.S.A. & Canada. 125p. 1980. 15.00 (ISBN 0-87314-053-2). Peter Glenn.

Directory of Multihospital Systems. American Hospital Association. LC 80-363. 80p. 1980. pap. 30.00 (ISBN 0-87258-285-X, 1209). Am Hospital.

Directory of Music Companies: United States & Foreign. J. W. Worrel. pap. 4.50 o.p. (ISBN 0-686-15898-9). Instrumental Co.

Directory of National Organizations Concerned with School Health. 8th ed. write for info. o.s.i. (ISBN 0-917160-02-9). Am Sch Health.

Directory of NCTM Individual Members. National Council of Teachers of Mathematics. 1980. 20.00 (ISBN 0-87353-168-X). NCTM.

Directory of Newspaper Libraries in the U. S. & Canada. 2nd ed. Ed. by Elizabeth Anderson. LC 76-9751. 1980. write for info. (ISBN 0-87111-265-5). SLA.

Directory of Non-Governmental Agricultural Organizations. 6th ed. 1980. pap. 40.00 (ISBN 3-598-10147-3, Dist by Gale Research Co.). K G Saur.

Directory of North & South American Universities, Vol. 24. Ed. by Michael Zils. 1978. 58.00 (ISBN 0-89664-001-9, Pub. by K G Saur). Gale.

Directory of Nuclear Reactors. Incl. Vol. 2. Research, Text & Experimental Reactors: Power Reactors. 1959. pap. 11.25 (ISBN 92-0-152159-6, ISP397); Vol. 3. Research, Test & Experimental Reactors, Supplement. 378p. 1960. pap. 12.50 (ISBN 92-0-152060-3); Vol. 4. Power Reactors, Supplement. 324p. 1962. pap. 15.75 (ISBN 92-0-152062-X). (Technical Directories Ser., IAEA). Unipub.

Directory of Nuclear Reactors. Incl. Vol. 5. Research, Test & Experimental Reactors, Supplement. 1964. 16.25 (ISBN 92-0-152064-6, ISP397); Vol. 6. Research, Test & Experimental Reactors, Supplement. 1966. 13.50 (ISBN 92-0-152066-2); Vol. 7. Power Reactors, Supplement. 1967. 20.50 (ISBN 92-0-152067-0); Vol. 8. Research, Test & Experimental Reactors, Supplement. 1970. 17.75 (ISBN 92-0-152170-7); Vol. 9. Power Reactors, Supplement. 1971. 17.25 (ISBN 92-0-152171-5). IAEA). Unipub.

Directory of Nuclear Reactors: Power & Research Reactors, Vol. 10. (Directories of Nuclear Reactors). (Illus.). 1976. 41.25 (ISBN 92-0-152076-X, ISP397-10, IAEA). Unipub.

Directory of Official Architecture & Planning (United Kingdon) 1978. 25.00x (ISBN 0-7114-5503-1). Nichols Pub.

Directory of Online Information Resources: Semi-Annual. 6th ed. Janet Kubalak. Orig. Title: Directory of on-Line Bibliographic Services. 55p. pap. 12.00 (ISBN 0-686-28098-9); four issue subscription 38.00 (ISBN 0-686-28099-7). CSG Pr.

Directory of Patent Attorneys & Agents. LC 80-23400. 328p. 1980. pap. 11.00 (ISBN 0-08-026343-7). Pergamon.

Directory of Planning & Urban Affairs Libraries in the United States & Canada. 4th ed. Ed. by Jean S. Gottlieb. 112p. 1980. pap. 15.00 (ISBN 0-86602-000-4). CPL Biblios.

Directory of Preachers. 1959. 0.75 o.p. (ISBN 0-89225-077-1). Gospel Advocate.

Directory of Publishing & Bookselling in Brazil. 179p. 1980. 50.00x (ISBN 0-901618-22-5, Pub. by Brit Coun England). State Mutual Bk.

Directory of Recycable Waste, Bk. 2. Ed. by Billy Mason. (Orig.). 1981. pap. 9.95 (ISBN 0-686-28908-0). Kelso.

Directory of Religious Organizations, No. 2. 2nd ed. 500p. 1980. 75.00 (ISBN 0-8434-0757-3, Consortium). McGrath.

Directory of Research Grants, 1981. Ed. by William K. Wilson & Betty L. Wilson. 360p. 1981. pap. 37.50 (ISBN 0-912700-92-0). Oryx Pr.

Directory of Sexual Advisory Services (in Great Britain) Ann Darnbrough & Derek Kinrade. 128p. 1980. 24.00x (ISBN 0-85941-162-1, Pub. by Woodhead-Faulkner England); pap. 9.00. State Mutual Bk.

Directory of Shared Services Organizations for Health Care Institutions. American Hospital Association. LC 79-18493. 444p. 1979. pap. 40.00 (ISBN 0-87258-286-8, 1202). Am Hospital.

Directory of Sheffield. LC 69-18826. (Architecture & Decorative Art Ser.). 1969. Repr. of 1707 ed. 19.50 (ISBN 0-306-71251-2). Da Capo.

Directory of Shipowners, Shipbuilders & Marine Engineers 1980. 78th ed. Ed. by Simon Timm. LC 25-4199. 1514p. 1980. 55.00x (ISBN 0-617-00301-7). Intl Pubns Serv.

Directory of Shop-by-Mail Bargain Sources. rev. ed. Margaret A. Boyd & Sue Scott-Martin. LC 77-17778. 1981. pap. 3.50 (ISBN 0-87576-063-5). Pilot Bks.

Directory of Social & Health Agencies of New York City. 1979. 24.00 (ISBN 0-231-04650-2, Pub. by Columbia U Pr). Comm Coun Great NY.

Directory of Social & Health Agencies of New York City, 1981 to 1982. 32.50 (ISBN 0-686-28925-0); pap. 24.00 (ISBN 0-686-28926-9). Comm Coun Great NY.

Directory of Social & Health Agencies of New York City: 1981-1982. Ed. by William P. Germano & Nancy Lecyn. 576p. 1981. 32.50x (ISBN 0-231-05134-4); pap. text ed. 24.00x (ISBN 0-231-05135-2). Columbia U Pr.

Directory of Speakers. Ed. by Howard J. Langer. 1981. lib. bdg. 32.00x (ISBN 0-912700-26-2). Oryx Pr.

Directory of Special Libraries & Information Centers: Vol. 2-Geographic & Personnel Indexes. 5th ed. Ed. by Margaret L. Young et al. LC 79-16788. 1979. 92.00 (ISBN 0-8103-0298-5). Gale.

Directory of Special Libraries & Information Centers: Vol. 3-New Special Libraries. 5th ed. Ed. by Margaret L. Young et al. 1979. pap. text ed. 110.00 (ISBN 0-8103-0281-0). Gale.

Directory of Special Libraries in Alaska. Ed. by Alan E. Schorr. LC 75-29043. 1975. 5.00 o.p. (ISBN 0-87111-239-6). SLA.

Directory of Specialized American Bookdealers 1981-1982. Staff of American Book Collector. 256p. 1981. lib. bdg. 19.95 (ISBN 0-668-05203-1). Arco.

Directory of State Archives in the United States. Compiled by Frank R. Levstik. 66p. (Orig.). 1980. pap. 8.00 (ISBN 0-931828-26-0). Soc Am Archivists.

Directory of the American Right. Laird M. Wilcox. 1980. pap. 12.95 (ISBN 0-933592-06-X). Edit Res Serv.

Directory of the Furnishing Trade 1979. (Benn Directories Ser.). 1979. 70.00 (ISBN 0-686-60655-8, Pub by Benn Pubns). Nichols Pub.

Directory of the Geologic Division, U. S. Geological Survey. American Geological Institute. (Illus.). 144p. 1980. pap. 6.00 (ISBN 0-913312-45-2). Am Geol.

Directory of the West German Chemical Industry-Firmenhandbuch Chemische Industrie, 1979 to 1981, 2 vols. 10th ed. Intro. by Dietrich Wunder. 512p. 1979. 115.00x (ISBN 3-430-12758-0). Intl Pubns Serv.

Directory of U.S. & Canadian Marketing Surveys & Services. 3rd ed. Ed. by Joan E. Huber. 1979. loose-leaf 125.00 (ISBN 0-917148-75-4). Kline.

Directory of Vermont Foundations. rev. 2nd ed. Ed. by John P. Huber. 24p. 1975. pap. 3.00 o.p. (ISBN 0-915884-07-0). Eastern CT St Coll Fdn.

Directory of Washington Representtatives of American Associations & Industry. 264p. 1979. 32.00 (ISBN 0-686-62452-1). B Klein Pubns.

Directory of Wetlands of International Importance in the Western Paleartic. 506p. 1981. pap. 27.50 (IUCN 87, IUCN). Unipub.

Directory of Whole-Body Radioactivity Monitors. (Technical Directories). (Illus., Orig.). 1970. pap. 59.00 (ISBN 92-0-112070-2, IAEA). Unipub.

Directory of Women Mathematicians. (Supplemented yearly through 1977). 1973. 2.00 o.p. (ISBN 0-8218-0057-4, DWM). Am Math.

Directory of World Museums. Kenneth Hudson & Ann Nicholl. 900p. 1981. 75.00 (ISBN 0-87196-468-6). Facts on File.

Directory of Zoological & Entomological Specimen Collections of Tropical Institutions. 1962. pap. 2.50 (ISBN 92-3-100493-X, U164, UNESCO). Unipub.

Directory Technology. R. Johnston & P. Gummett. 240p. 1980. 30.00x (ISBN 0-85664-740-3, Pub. by Croom Helm England). State Mutual Bk.

Dirks Escape. C. Brandon Rimmer. LC 79-88496. (Orig.). 1979. pap. 2.50 (ISBN 0-87123-108-5, 200108). Bethany Fell.

Dirt. Carolyn Downs. (Illus.). 1980. pap. 9.95 o.p. (ISBN 0-930490-31-2). Future Shop.
Dirt Cheap: Evolution of Renewable Resource Management. Hallie Black. LC 79-11353. (Illus.). (gr. 4-6). 1979. 8.50 (ISBN 0-688-22184-X); PLB 8.16 (ISBN 0-688-32184-4). Morrow.
Dirt Road. Carol Carrick. LC 73-116758. (Illus.). (gr. k-2). 1970. 4.95g o.s.i. (ISBN 0-02-717300-3). Macmillan.
Dirt Track Summer. William C. Gault. (gr. 7-9). 1961. PLB 6.95 o.p. (ISBN 0-525-28752-3). Dutton.
Dirty Feet. Steven Kroll. LC 80-17570. (Illus.). 48p. (ps-3). 1981. 4.95 (ISBN 0-8193-1035-2); PLB 5.95 (ISBN 0-8193-1036-0). Parents.
Dirty Filthy Book: The Writings of Charles Knowlton & Annie Besant. Sripati Chandrasekhar. 1981. 12.50 (ISBN 0-520-04168-2). U of Cal Pr.
Dirty Money Can't Wash Both Hands at Once. Joseph M. Glazner. (Orig.). 1980. pap. 1.95 (ISBN 0-446-90165-2). Warner Bks.
Dirty Old Mad. Mad Magazine Editors. (Mad Ser: No. 30). (Illus.). 1971. pap. 1.75 (ISBN 0-446-94362-2). Warner Bks.
Dirty Rotten Truth. Roy Sparkia. 1973. pap. 1.25 (ISBN 0-451-07721-0, Y7721, Sig). NAL.
Dirty Way to Die. Gene Curry. (Saddler Ser.: No. 1). 1979. pap. 1.75 (ISBN 0-505-51398-6). Tower Bks.
Dirty Way to Die. Bruno Rossi. (Sharpshooter Ser). (Orig.). 1975. pap. 1.25 o.p. (ISBN 0-685-53129-5, LB276ZK, Leisure Bks). Nordon Pubns.
Disability in Childhood & Youth. Peter Henderson. 208p. 1974. pap. text ed. 6.95x o.p. (ISBN 0-19-264168-9). Oxford U Pr.
Disability Policies & Government Programs. LC 79-10074. 1979. 22.95 (ISBN 0-03-051431-2). Praeger.
Disabled Homemaker. Hoyt Anderson. (Illus.). 328p. 1980. 19.50 (ISBN 0-398-04077-X); pap. 12.75 (ISBN 0-398-04078-8). C C Thomas.
Disabled Learner, Early Detection & Intervention. Ed. by Paul Satz & J. L. Ross. (Modern Approaches to the Diagnosis & Instruction of Multi-Handicapped Children Ser.: Vol. 8). 298p. 1973. text ed. 34.25 (ISBN 90-237-4107-2, Pub. by Swets Pub Serv Holland). Swets North Am.
Disabling Professions. Ivan Illich et al. (Ideas in Progress Ser.). 1978. 11.95 (ISBN 0-7145-2509-X, Pub. by M Boyars); pap. 5.95 (ISBN 0-7145-2510-3). Merrimack Bk Serv.
Disadvantaged Child: Issues & Innovations. 2nd ed. Joe L. Frost & Glenn R. Hawkes. LC 70-16422. (Illus., Orig.). 1970. pap. text ed. 12.95 (ISBN 0-395-04475-8). HM.
Disadvantaged Consumer. Alan R. Andreasen. LC 75-2805. (Illus.). 1975. 16.95 (ISBN 0-02-900690-2). Free Pr.
Disadvantaged Families & Playgroups. Elsa Ferri & Rosalind Niblett. 1977. pap. text ed. 9.75x (ISBN 0-85633-133-3, NFER). Humanities.
Disadvantaged Preschool Children: A Source Book for Teachers. Michael Bender & Rosmary K. Bender. LC 79-12001. (Illus.). 308p. (Orig.). 1979. pap. text ed. 14.95 (ISBN 0-933716-00-1). P H Brookes.
Disappearance. Philip Wylie. 1978. pap. 2.25 o.s.i. (ISBN 0-446-82837-8). Warner Bks.
Disappearance of Flight Nineteen. Larry Kusche. (Illus.). 224p. 1981. 3.95 (ISBN 0-06-464044-2, BN4044, BN). Har-Row.
Disappearance of God: Five Nineteenth Century Writers. J. Hillis Miller. 392p. 1976. text ed. 17.50x (ISBN 0-674-21101-4). Harvard U Pr.
Disappearance of Mr. Allan. Foster Kennedy. (gr. 4-6). 1977. pap. 1.50 o.p. (ISBN 0-590-11841-2, Schol Pap). Schol Bk Serv.
Disappearance of the Small Landowner. A. H. Johnson. LC 79-14625. (Illus.). xiii, 164p. 1979. Repr. of 1909 ed. lib. bdg. 13.50x (ISBN 0-678-08077-1). Kelley.
Disappearances. William Wiser. LC 79-55616. 1980. 11.95 (ISBN 0-689-11062-6). Atheneum.
Disappearing ABC Game Book. Hazel S. Gamec. (Illus.). 12p. write for info. (ISBN 0-938042-02-5). Printek.
Disappearing Grandad. Lynn Hall. 64p. 1980. lib. bdg. 5.39 (ISBN 0-695-41467-4). Follett.
Disappointing Marriage: A Study of the Gains from Merger. G. Meeks. LC 77-73287. (Department of Applied Economics, Occasional Paper: No. 51). (Illus.). 1977. 14.95 o.p. (ISBN 0-521-21691-5); pap. 15.95x (ISBN 0-521-29234-4). Cambridge U Pr.
Disarmament & Security Since Locarno, 1925-1931. John W. Wheeler-Bennett. 22.00 (ISBN 0-86527-045-7). Fertig.
Disarmament & World Development. new ed. Ed. by Richard Jolly. 1978. text ed. 23.00 (ISBN 0-08-023019-9); pap. text ed. 8.50 (ISBN 0-08-023018-0). Pergamon.
Disarmament Education. M. Haavelsrud. 1981. text ed. write for info. (ISBN 0-86103-043-5, Westbury Hse). Butterworth.
Disarmament: The Human Factor: Pproceedings of a Colloquium on the Societal Context for Disarmament. Ed. by Ervin Laszlo & Donald Keys. 200p. 1981. 25.00 (ISBN 0-08-024703-2). Pergamon.
Disaster. 1981. 7.95 (ISBN 0-679-20954-9). McKay.
Disaster. Donald Sobol. (Orig.). (YA) (gr. 7-9). 1979. pap. 1.50 (ISBN 0-671-29939-5). PB.
Disaster & Deliverance. Larry Armstrong. LC 79-88400. 1979. pap. 4.25 (ISBN 0-933350-22-8). Morse Pr.
Disaster & Fiction: The Impact of the Asia Minor Disaster of 1922 on Modern Greek Fiction. Thomas Doulis. 1977. 17.50x (ISBN 0-520-03112-1). U of Cal Pr.
Disaster at Bari. Glenn Infield. (Illus.). 1971. 7.95 o.s.i. (ISBN 0-02-558150-3). Macmillan.
Disaster at Moscow: Von Bock's Campaigns, 1941-1942. Alfred W. Turney. LC 74-107098. 1970. 6.95 o.p. (ISBN 0-8263-0167-3). U of NM Pr.
Disaster Creek. Dwight Bennett. LC 80-1061. (Double D Western Ser.). 192p. 1981. 9.95 (ISBN 0-385-15629-4). Doubleday.
Disaster Detectives. Louis Wolfe. (Illus.). 160p. (gr. 8-12). 1981. PLB price not set (ISBN 0-671-34042-5). Messner.
Disaster in the Desert: Failures of International Relief in the West African Drought. Hal Sheets & Roger Morris. LC 74-76361. 1974. pap. 2.00 (ISBN 0-87003-027-2). Carnegie Endow.
Disaster Insurance Protection: Public Policy Lessons. Howard Kunreuther. LC 77-179. 1978. 34.95 (ISBN 0-471-03259-X, Pub. by Wiley-Interscience). Wiley.
Disaster Planning: The Preservation of Life & Property. H. D. Foster. (Springer Series on Environmental Management). (Illus.). 275p. 1981. 29.80 (ISBN 0-387-90498-0). Springer-Verlag.
Disaster Preparedness & the United Nations: Advance Planning for Disaster Relief. Barbara Brown. LC 79-179. (Pergamon Policy Studies). 120p. 1979. 17.75 (ISBN 0-08-022486-5). Pergamon.
Disaster Survival: How to Choose Secure Sites & Make Practical Escape Plans. H. McKinley Conway. LC 80-68816. (Illus.). 1980. 48.00 (ISBN 0-910436-17-7). Conway Pubns.
Disaster Technology: An Annotated Bibliography. D. Manning. 300p. 1976. text ed. 40.00 (ISBN 0-08-019984-4); pap. text ed. 25.00 (ISBN 0-08-019983-6). Pergamon.
Disasters & the Mass Media. 1980. 9.75 (ISBN 0-309-03024-2). Natl Acad Pr.
Disasters & the Small Dwelling. Ed. by I. Davis. 220p. 1981. 30.00 (ISBN 0-08-024753-9). Pergamon.
Disasters: Hospital Planning. P. E. Savage. 1979. 28.00 (ISBN 0-08-024914-0); pap. 12.75 (ISBN 0-08-024913-2). Pergamon.
Disasters: Medical Organization. Ed. by Jan De Boer & Thomas W. Baillie. (Illus.). 112p. 1980. 16.75 (ISBN 0-08-025491-8). Pergamon.
Disasters of War. Leighton Rollins. LC 80-69430. 1981. signed limited ed. 20.00 (ISBN 0-932274-16-1); pap. 4.00 (ISBN 0-932274-15-3). Cadmus Eds.
Disasters: The Anatomy of Environmental Hazards. John Whittow. LC 79-5236. (Illus.). 405p. 1981. pap. 9.95 (ISBN 0-8203-0542-1). U of Ga Pr.
Disasters: Theory & Research. Ed. by E. L. Quarantelli. LC 76-52786. (Sage Studies in International Sociology: Vol. 13). 1978. 18.00x (ISBN 0-8039-9851-1); pap. 9.95x (ISBN 0-8039-9852-X). Sage.
Discarded Image. Clive S. Lewis. LC 64-21555. (Orig.). 1968. 29.95 (ISBN 0-521-05551-2); pap. 7.50 (ISBN 0-521-09450-X). Cambridge U Pr.
Discerning the Way: A Theology of the Jewish-Christian Reality. Paul M. Van Buren. 192p. 1980. 12.95 (ISBN 0-8164-0124-1). Crossroad NY.
Discernment of the Spirit & the Spirits. Ed. by Christian Duquoc & Casiano Floristan. (Concilium Ser.: Vol. 119). (Orig.). 1978. pap. 4.95 (ISBN 0-8164-2199-4). Crossroad NY.
Discharge from Nursing Homes: 1977 National Nursing Home Survey. Aurora Zappolo. Ed. by Klaudia Cox. (Ser. 13: No. 54). 60p. 1981. pap. 1.75 (ISBN 0-8406-0216-2). Natl Ctr Health Stats.
Disciple. Paul Bourget. (Classiques Larousse). (Illus., Fr.). pap. 1.95 o.p. (ISBN 0-685-13888-7, 36). Larousse.
Disciple. Paul Bourget. xvii, 341p. 1976. Repr. of 1901 ed. 17.50 (ISBN 0-86527-238-7). Fertig.
Disciples & Prophets. F. J. Moloney. 240p. 1981. 9.95 (ISBN 0-8245-0049-0). Crossroad NY.
Disciples Are Made-Not Born. Walter A. Henrichsen. LC 74-79162. 160p. 1974. pap. 2.95 (ISBN 0-88207-706-6). Victor Bks.
Disciples in Action. LeRoy Eims. (Orig.). 1981. pap. price not set (ISBN 0-89109-477-6). NavPress.
Disciples in Action. Leroy Eims. 324p. 1981. pap. 5.95 (ISBN 0-88207-343-5). Victor Bks.
Disciple's Religion. W. H. Hutton. (Scholar As Preacher Ser.). 246p. Repr. of 1911 ed. 7.75 (ISBN 0-567-04410-6). Attic Pr.
Discipleship. G. Campbell Morgan. (Morgan Library). 1973. pap. 3.45 (ISBN 0-8010-5920-8). Baker Bk.
Discipleship Evangelism. Ken Stephens. LC 81-80258. 1981. pap. 6.95 (ISBN 0-89081-283-7). Harvest Hse.
Discipleship, Shepherding, Commitment. Derek Prince. 1.50 (ISBN 0-934920-15-X, B-27). Derek Prince.
Disciplina Clericalis of Petrus Alfonsi. Petrus Alfonsi. Ed. by Eberhard Hermes. Tr. by P. R. Quarrie. LC 73-94434. (Islamic World Ser.). 250p. 1977. 18.00x (ISBN 0-520-02704-3). U of Cal Pr.
Discipline & Classroom Control. Compiled by Sara Lake. (Special Interest Resource Guides in Education). 1980. pap. text ed. 7.50x (ISBN 0-912700-71-8). Oryx Pr.
Discipline & Discovery. rev. ed. Albert E. Day. 1977. pap. 2.95x (ISBN 0-8358-0354-6). Upper Room.
Discipline Book: A Complete Guide to School & Classroom Management. Richard Curwin & Allen Mendler. (Illus.). 1979. text ed. 13.95 (ISBN 0-8359-1338-4). Reston.
Discipline-Causes & Remedies of Problem Behaviors in School. Ed. by Fred Streit & Donald L. Halsted. 1977. pap. 10.00 o.p. (ISBN 0-686-00904-5, D-103). Essence Pubns.
Discipline Crisis in Schools: The Problem, Causes, & the Search for Solutions. J. William Jones & National School Public Relations Association. 1973. 5.75 o.p. (ISBN 0-685-36732-0, 411-13445). Natl Sch PR.
Discipline in the Classroom: Solving the Teaching Puzzle. Robert G. Howell, Jr. & Patricia L. Howell. (Illus.). 1980. text ed. 13.95 (ISBN 0-8359-1344-9). Reston.
Discipline: Negotiating Conflict with Today's Kids. James P. Raffini. 160p. 1980. 10.95 (ISBN 0-13-215731-4, Spec); pap. 3.95 (ISBN 0-13-215723-3). P-H.
Discipline: Negotiating Conflicts with Today's Kids. James P. Raffini. 192p. 1980. 10.95 (Spec); pap. 3.95. P-H.
Discipline of Programming. Edward W. Dijkstra. (Illus.). 240p. 1976. 22.95x (ISBN 0-13-215871-X). P-H.
Discipline of the Cave. John N. Findlay. (Muirhead Library of Philosophy Ser.). 1966. text ed. 9.00x o.p. (ISBN 0-04-111001-3). Humanities.
Discipline Without Tears. Rudolph Dreikurs. 1974. pap. 3.95 (ISBN 0-8015-2132-7, Hawthorn). Dutton.
Disciplined Life. Richard S. Taylor. LC 62-7123. 110p. 1974. pap. 1.75 (ISBN 0-87123-098-4, 200098). Bethany Fell.
Disciplines in Transformation: A Guide to Theology & the Behavioral Sciences. William W. Everett & T. J. Bachmeyer. LC 78-68570. 1979. pap. text ed. 9.75 (ISBN 0-8191-0692-5). U Pr of Amer.
Disciplines of the Holy Quest. 4th ed. Flower A. Newhouse. LC 59-15553. (Illus.). 1959. 9.00 (ISBN 0-910378-05-3). Christward.
Discipling the Children of Black America: A Discussion of Christian Black Education for Black Youth. Walter A. McCray. 50p. (Orig.). 1981. pap. 4.00 (ISBN 0-933176-02-3). Black Light Fellow.
Disclosure of Corporate Social Performance: Survey, Evaluation, & Prospects. Harold L. Johnson. LC 78-10594. (Praeger Special Studies). 1979. 20.95 (ISBN 0-03-047206-7). Praeger.
Disclosure of the Ultimate: Fundamental Theology Reconsidered. Richard W. Rousseau. LC 80-8259. 399p. 1980. lib. bdg. 21.50 (ISBN 0-8191-1284-4); pap. 13.25 (ISBN 0-8191-1285-2). U Pr of Amer.
Disclosure Whether It May Be Lawful to Take Use for Money. Sir Robert Filmer. Ed. by David S. Berkowitz & Samuel E. Thorne. LC 77-89250. (Classics of English Legal History in the Modern Era Ser.: Vol. 79). 166p. 1979. lib. bdg. 40.00 (ISBN 0-8240-3179-2). Garland Pub.
Disco. Lani Van Ryzin. (Concise Guides). (Illus.). (gr. 6 up). 1979. PLB 6.45 s&l (ISBN 0-531-02891-7). Watts.
Disco Dancing. Jerolyn Nentl. Ed. by Howard Schroeder. LC 79-27801. (Funseekers Ser.). (Illus.). (gr. 3-5). 1980. lib. bdg. 5.95 (ISBN 0-89686-073-6); pap. 2.95 (ISBN 0-89686-077-9). Crestwood Hse.
Disco Handbook. Pollack. (gr. 7-12). 1980. pap. 1.50 (ISBN 0-590-30003-2, Schol Pap). Schol Bk Serv.
Disco Kid No. 1. Curtis Gathje. (Hi Lo Ser.). 96p. (gr. 6 up). 1981. pap. 1.50 (ISBN 0-553-14618-1). Bantam.
Disco Text: The Complete Book of Disco Dance Instruction. Jan Jasek. LC 78-70439. (Illus.). 1978. pap. 4.95 o.p. (ISBN 0-932846-01-7). And Bks.
Disconnected. P. Kimball. LC 72-6349. 1972. 17.50x (ISBN 0-231-03696-5). Columbia U Pr.
Discordia Concors: The Wit of Metaphysical Poetry. Melissa C. Wanamaker. 239p. 1975. 12.00 (ISBN 0-8046-9089-8, Natl U). Kennikat.
Discorso Sopra la Mascherata Della Genealogia Delg'Iddei, Repr. Of 1565 Ed. Baccio Baldini. Bd. with Discorso Sopra Li Dei De'Gentili. Jacopo Zucchi. Repr. of 1602 ed. LC 75-27852. (Renaissance & the Gods Ser.: Vol. 10). (Illus.). 1976. lib. bdg. 73.00 (ISBN 0-8240-2059-6). Garland Pub.
Discount & Equivalent Interest Tables No. 948. Financial Publishing Co. 42.50 (ISBN 0-685-02540-3). Finan Pub.
Discount Guide for Travelers Over Fifty-Five. Caroline Weintz & Walter Weintz. 1981. pap. 5.95 (ISBN 0-525-93175-9). Dutton.
Discours Communiste. Dominique Labbe. 1977. lib. bdg. 27.50x o.p. (ISBN 2-7246-0380-X); pap. 20.00x o.p. (ISBN 0-685-86514-2). Clearwater Pub.
Discours De la Religion Des Anciens Romains Illustre. Guillaume Du Choul. LC 75-27851. (Renaissance & the Gods Ser.: Vol. 9). (Illus.). 1976. Repr. of 1556 ed. lib. bdg. 73.00 (ISBN 0-8240-2058-8). Garland Pub.
Discours Sur la Polysynodie... Castel de Sainte-Pierre & Abbe Charles-Irenee. (Utopias Ser.). 1976. Repr. of 1719 ed. lib. bdg. 34.00x o.p. (ISBN 0-8287-0165-2). Clearwater Pub.
Discours Sur les Moyens De Sauver la France et la Liberte. Jacques Roux. 49p. (Fr.). 1977. lib. bdg. 15.00x o.p. (ISBN 0-8287-0742-1); pap. text ed. 5.00x o.p. (ISBN 0-685-75622-X). Clearwater Pub.
Discourse About the State of True Happinesse. Robert Bolton. LC 79-84089. (English Experience Ser.: No. 909). 184p. 1979. Repr. of 1611 ed. lib. bdg. 14.00 (ISBN 90-221-0909-7). Walter J Johnson.
Discourse Analysis in Second Language Research. Ed. by Diane Larsen-Freeman. 283p. (Orig.). 1980. pap. text ed. 11.95 (ISBN 0-88377-163-2). Newbury Hse.
Discourse Cameos. Compiled by Albert Zobell, Jr. 67p. 1973. 0.75 o.p. (ISBN 0-87747-497-4). Deseret Bk.
Discourse Concerning Treasons & Bills of Attainder. Richard West et al. Ed. by David S. Berkowitz & Samuel E. Thorne. LC 77-89246. (Classics of English Legal History in the Modern Era Ser.: Vol. 77). 273p. 1979. lib. bdg. 40.00 (ISBN 0-8240-3176-8). Garland Pub.
Discourse Concerning Unlimited Submission. Jonathan Mayhew. Ed. by Norman E. Tanis. (American Classics Facsimile Ser.: Pt. III). 1976. pap. 10.00 (ISBN 0-937048-02-X). CSUN.
Discourse: Essay on English & American Literature. John W. Crawford. (Costerus New Ser.: No. XIV). 1978. pap. text ed. 25.00x (ISBN 90-6203-672-4). Humanities.
Discourse Intonation & Language Teaching. Malcolm Coulthard et al. (Applied Linguistics & Language Study). 1980. pap. text ed. 9.00 (ISBN 0-582-55366-0); cassette 15.00 (ISBN 0-582-55367-9). Longman.
Discourse of the Civile Warres in Fraunce, Drawn into Englishe by G. Fenton. Tr. by Geoffrey Fenton. LC 76-26510. (English Experience Ser.: No. 248). 1970. Repr. of 1570 ed. 20.00 (ISBN 90-221-0248-3). Walter J Johnson.
Discourse on Colonialism. Aime Cesaire. Tr. by Joan Pinkham. LC 72-178714. 96p. 1972. 4.95 o.p. (ISBN 0-85345-205-9, CL-2059); pap. 2.95 (ISBN 0-685-23743-5, PB-2266). Monthly Rev.
Discourse on Fourier Series. C. Lanczos. 1966. 16.25 o.s.i. (ISBN 0-02-848310-3). Hafner.
Discourse on Method. 2nd ed. Rene Descartes. Tr. by Laurence J. Lafleur. LC 60-13395. (Orig.). 1956. pap. 2.50 (ISBN 0-672-60180-X, LLA19). Bobbs.
Discourse on Method & Meditations. Descartes. Tr. by Laurence J. Lafleur. LC 60-13395. 1960. pap. 3.95 (ISBN 0-672-60278-4, LLA 89). Bobbs.
Discourse on the Grounds & Reasons of the Christian Religion. Anthony Collins. Ed. by Rene Wellek. LC 75-11212. (British Philosophers & Theologians of the 17th & 18th Centuries: Vol. 15). 1976. Repr. of 1724 ed. lib. bdg. 41.00 (ISBN 0-8240-1766-8). Garland Pub.
Discourse on the Real Nature of Self. Sankaracarya. Tr. by Deb K. Das from Sanskrit. (Writers Workshop Redbird Ser.). 1977. flexible bdg. 4.80 (ISBN 0-89253-618-7); lib. bdg. 8.00 (ISBN 0-89253-617-9). Ind-US Inc.

Discourse on the Studies of the University. Adam Sedgwick. (Victorian Library). 1969. Repr. of 1833 ed. text ed. 8.00x (ISBN 0-7185-5004-8, Leicester). Humanities.

Discourse on Usury. Thomas Wilson. Ed. by R. H. Tawney. LC 65-31641. Repr. of 1925 ed. 25.00x (ISBN 0-678-05095-3). Kelley.

Discourse Production Model for Twenty Questions. Michael D. Fortescue. (Pragmatics & Beyond Ser.: No.2). 145p. 1980. pap. text ed. 17.25x (ISBN 90-272-2505-2). Humanities.

Discourse, Tendered to the High Court of Parliament. LC 74-28870. (English Experience Ser.: No. 749). 1975. Repr. of 1629 ed. 3.50 (ISBN 90-221-0749-3). Walter J Johnson.

Discourses, 2 vols. Niccolo Machiavelli. Tr. by Leslie J. Walker. 1975. Set. 65.00x (ISBN 0-7100-8076-X); 24.50x ea. Routledge & Kegan.

Discourses & Sayings of Our Lord Jesus Christ, 3 vols. John Brown. Date not set. Set. 45.00 (ISBN 0-88469-142-X). BMH Bks.

Discourses Mixed Congregations. John H. Newman. 1966. 10.50 o.p. (ISBN 0-87061-029-5). Chr Classics.

Discourses of Brigham Young. John A. Widtsoe. 497p. pap. 2.50 (ISBN 0-87747-788-4). Deseret Bk.

Discourses on Davila. John Adams. LC 70-87665. (American Constitutional & Legal History Ser.). 260p. 1973. Repr. of 1805 ed. lib. bdg. 25.00 (ISBN 0-306-71761-1). Da Capo.

Discourses on Ethics & Business. Jack N. Behrman. LC 80-23626. 192p. 1981. lib. bdg. 20.00 (ISBN 0-89946-064-X). Oelgeschlager.

Discourses on the Heroic Poem. Torquato Tasso. Ed. by Mariella Cavalchini & Irene Samuel. 1973. 29.95x (ISBN 0-19-815714-2). Oxford U Pr.

Discourses on the Miracles of Our Savior. Thomas Woolston. Ed. by Rene Wellek. LC 75-11268. (British Philosophers & Theologians of the 17th & 18th Centuries Ser.: Vol. 67). 565p. 1979. lib. bdg. 42.00 (ISBN 0-8240-1778-1); lib. bdg. 2700.00 set of 101 vols. (ISBN 0-686-60102-5). Garland Pub.

Discover a Richer Life. Ernest Holmes. 1961. pap. 3.50 (ISBN 0-911336-27-3). Sci of Mind.

Discover Archaelogy. George Sullivan. LC 79-7223. (Illus.). 1980. 10.95 (ISBN 0-385-14522-5). Doubleday.

Discover Archaeology. Ed. by George Sullivan. 288p. 1981. pap. 4.95 (ISBN 0-14-046491-3). Penguin.

Discover Courage to Face Your Future. Robert H. Schuller. (Orig.). 1978. pap. 1.25 (ISBN 0-89081-156-3). Harvest Hse.

Discover Data Communications. Brian Warrington. (Illus.). 128p. 1980. 14.95x (ISBN 0-7198-2581-4). Intl Ideas.

Discover Denver: A Pennywise Survival Handbook. Kay Kane & Louise Gold. (Illus.). 184p. (Orig.). 1980. pap. 5.95 (ISBN 0-9604430-0-2). Gold-Kane Ent.

Discover English. Red Bolitho & Brian Tomlinson. (Illus.). 168p. (Orig.). 1980. pap. text ed. 9.95x (ISBN 0-04-371076-X, 2586). Allen Unwin.

Discover Freedom. Robert H. Schuller. (Orig.). 1978. pap. 1.25 (ISBN 0-89081-155-5). Harvest Hse.

Discover Health & Happiness. Robert H. Schuller. (Orig.). 1978. pap. 1.25 (ISBN 0-89081-143-1). Harvest Hse.

Discover How Life Can Be Beautiful. Robert H. Schuller. (Orig.). 1978. pap. 1.25 (ISBN 0-89081-153-9). Harvest Hse.

Discover How to Bloom Where You Are Planted. Robert H. Schuller. 1978. pap. 1.25 (ISBN 0-89081-154-7). Harvest Hse.

Discover How to Get Your Priorities Straight. Robert H. Schuller. (Orig.). 1978. pap. 1.25 (ISBN 0-89081-137-7). Harvest Hse.

Discover How to Turn Activity into Energy. Robert H. Schuller. (Orig.). 1978. pap. 1.25 (ISBN 0-89081-135-0). Harvest Hse.

Discover Self-Love. Robert H. Schuller. (Orig.). 1978. pap. 1.25 (ISBN 0-89081-134-2). Harvest Hse.

Discover Swaging. David R. Corbin. LC 78-22085. (Illus.). 288p. 1979. 16.95 (ISBN 0-8117-0497-1). Stackpole.

Discover the Miracles in Your Life. Robert H. Schuller. (Orig.). 1978. pap. 1.25 (ISBN 0-89081-136-9). Harvest Hse.

Discover the Power for Overcoming Defeat. Robert H. Schuller. (Orig.). 1978. pap. 1.25 (ISBN 0-89081-141-5). Harvest Hse.

Discover the Power Within You. Eric Butterworth. LC 68-17583. 1968. 9.95 (ISBN 0-06-061266-5, HarpR). Har-Row.

Discover the Trees. Jerry Cowle. LC 76-51174. (Illus.). (gr. 5 up). 1977. 7.95 (ISBN 0-8069-3734-3); PLB 7.49 (ISBN 0-8069-3735-1). Sterling.

Discover Unexpected London. Andrew Lawson. LC 77-82736. (Illus.). 1978. 8.95 (ISBN 0-8467-0369-6, Pub. by Two Continents). Hippocrene Bks.

Discover Wildlife in Your Backyard. Leah Bendavid-Val et al. Ed. by John C. Stone. (Illus.). 1977. 24.95 (ISBN 0-912186-25-9). Natl Wildlife.

Discover Your Fountain of Health. N. W. Walker. 60p. 1979. pap. 0.95 (ISBN 0-89019-070-4). O'Sullivan Woodside.

Discover Your Opportunities. Robert H. Schuller. (Orig.). 1978. pap. 1.25 (ISBN 0-89081-142-3). Harvest Hse.

Discover Your Possibilities. Robert H. Schuller. 1979. pap. 2.25 (ISBN 0-345-29455-6). Ballantine.

Discover Your Possibilities. Robert H. Schuller. (Orig.). 1980. pap. 2.25 (ISBN 0-89081-214-4). Harvest Hse.

Discover Your Self-Confidence. Robert H. Schuller. (Orig.). 1978. pap. 1.25 (ISBN 0-89081-144-X). Harvest Hse.

Discoverers of the New World. Josef Berger & Lawrence C. Wroth. LC 60-10300. (American Heritage Junior Library). (Illus.). 153p. (gr. 5 up). 1960. 9.95 (ISBN 0-8281-0353-4, J002-0). Am Heritage.

Discoveries & Opinions of Galileo. Galileo. LC 57-6305. 1957. pap. 2.95 (ISBN 0-385-09239-3, A94, Anch). Doubleday.

Discoveries at Karatepe: A Phoenician Royal Inscription from Cilicia. Julian Obermann. (Supplements: 9). (Illus.). 1948. pap. 1.00 (ISBN 0-686-00045-5). Am Orient Soc.

Discoveries of the Hidden Things of God. Erma Mestinsek. 64p. 1980. 12.50 (ISBN 0-682-49635-9). Exposition.

Discovering American Seventeen Hundred to Eighteen Seventy-Five. Henry Savage, Jr. LC 78-20113. (New American Nation Ser.). (Illus.). 1980. pap. 6.95 (ISBN 0-06-090740-1, CN 740, CN). Har-Row.

Discovering Antiques. Jane Toller. LC 75-24713. (Illus.). 176p. 1976. 7.95 o.p. (ISBN 0-498-01844-X). A S Barnes.

Discovering Art History. Gerald F. Brommer. LC 79-57018. (Illus.). 384p. 1981. 24.95 (ISBN 0-87192-121-9). Davis Mass.

Discovering Astronomy. Robert D. Chapman. LC 77-16024. (Illus.). 1978. text ed. 26.95x (ISBN 0-7167-0034-4); pap. text ed. 16.95x (ISBN 0-7167-0033-6); instructors' guide avail. W H Freeman.

Discovering Balanchine. B. H. Haggin. (Illus.). 196p. 1981. 19.95 (ISBN 0-8180-0404-5). Horizon.

Discovering BASIC: A Problem Solving Approach. Robert E. Smith. (Illus.). (gr. 10 up). 1970. pap. 8.25x (ISBN 0-8104-5783-0). Hayden.

Discovering Books & Libraries. 2nd ed. Florence D. Cleary. 1977. pap. 4.00 (ISBN 0-8242-0594-4). Wilson.

Discovering (British) Surnames. 72p. 1980. pap. 2.95 (ISBN 0-85263-007-7, Pub. by B T A). Merrimack Bk Serv.

Discovering Cake Decorating. Bernice Vercoe & Dorothy Evans. 1974. 4.75 o.p. (ISBN 0-600-07243-6). Exposition.

Discovering Cathedrals. British Tourist Authority. (Illus.). 80p. 1981. pap. write for info. (ISBN 0-85263-472-2, Pub. by Auto Assn-British Tourist Authority England). Merrimack Bk Serv.

Discovering Chemistry. Elizabeth K. Cooper. LC 59-7281. (Illus.). (gr. 7-9). 1959. 5.50 o.p. (ISBN 0-15-223591-4, HJ). HarBraceJ.

Discovering Chess. Raymond Bott & Stanley Morrison. 1975. 10.00 (ISBN 0-571-04834-X). Transatlantic.

Discovering Discipleship: A Resource for Home Bible Studies. Thomas A. Smith. (Illus.). 64p. (Orig.). 1981. pap. 2.75 (ISBN 0-87239-438-7, 88570). Standard Pub.

Discovering Discourse. H. G. Widdowson. (Orig.). 1979. pap. text ed. 5.95x (ISBN 0-19-451355-6); ed. 8.95xtchr's (ISBN 0-19-451356-4). Oxford U Pr.

Discovering English Customs & Traditions. British Tourist Authority. (Illus.). 80p. Date not set. pap. price not set (Pub. by Auto Assn-British Tourist Authority). Merrimack Bk Serv.

Discovering Food. Helen Kowtaluk. (gr. 9-12). 1978. 8.64 (ISBN 0-87002-270-9); pap. 5.96 (ISBN 0-87002-272-5); student guide 3.96 (ISBN 0-87002-278-4); tchrs. guide 7.36 (ISBN 0-87002-280-6). Bennett IL.

Discovering Food. Connie R. Sasse. 1978. pap. 3.84 student guide o.p. (ISBN 0-87002-278-4). Bennett IL.

Discovering Food Teacher's Guide: Discovering Food. Connie R. Sasse. 1978. pap. 7.36 tchr's guide o.p. (ISBN 0-87002-280-6). Bennett IL.

Discovering Foods. Kowtaluk. (gr. 9-12). 1978. pap. 5.80 o.p. (ISBN 0-87002-272-5). Bennett IL.

Discovering Free Will & Personal Responsibility. Joseph F. Rychlak. LC 78-31709. 1979. 13.95 (ISBN 0-19-502687-X); pap. text ed. 5.95x (ISBN 0-686-66190-7). Oxford U Pr.

Discovering Gardens in Britain. British Tourist Authority. (Illus.). 80p. Date not set. pap. price not set (ISBN 0-85263-456-0, Pub. by Auto Assn-British Tourist Authority England). Merrimack Bk Serv.

Discovering God's Presence. Robert F. Morneau. 175p. (Orig.). 1980. pap. 5.95 (ISBN 0-8146-1197-4). Liturgical Pr.

Discovering Indian Sculpture. Charles Fabri. (Illus.). 84p. 1970. 10.00 (ISBN 0-88253-798-9); pap. 5.00 (ISBN 0-88253-037-2). Ind-US Inc.

Discovering Israel: A Popular Guide to the Holy Land. Jack Finegan. LC 80-26952. (Illus.). 176p. 1981. pap. 7.95 (ISBN 0-8028-1869-2). Eerdmans.

Discovering Kings & Queens. British Tourist Authority. (Illus.). 88p. 1981. pap. write for info. (ISBN 0-85263-439-0, Pub. by Auto Assn-British Tourist Authority England). Merrimack Bk Serv.

Discovering Language with Children. Ed. by Gay S. Pinnell. LC 80-24795. 132p. (Orig.). 1980. pap. 5.50 (ISBN 0-8141-1210-2, 12102). NCTE.

Discovering Lapidary Work. John Wainwright. (Illus.). 216p. 1973. 12.75 o.p. (ISBN 0-263-51531-1). Transatlantic.

Discovering London for Children. 88p. 1980. pap. 2.95 (ISBN 0-85263-429-3, Pub. by B T A). Merrimack Bk Serv.

Discovering London's Inns & Taverns. 64p. 1980. pap. 2.95 (ISBN 0-85263-433-1, Pub. by B T A). Merrimack Bk Serv.

Discovering London's Villages. British Tourist Authority. (Illus.). 72p. 1981. pap. write for info. (ISBN 0-85263-451-X, Pub. by Auto Assn-British Tourist Authority England). Merrimack Bk Serv.

Discovering Mayaland. Allen R. Ellis & Phyllis T. Ellis. (Illus.). 1965. 8.00 o.p. (ISBN 0-87062-013-4). A H Clark.

Discovering Nature. Ed. by Angela Sheehan. LC 77-6206. (Illus.). (gr. 3-12). 1977. PLB 15.95 (ISBN 0-8393-0025-5). Raintree Child.

Discovering Nutrition. Helen Kowtaluk. (gr. 7-12). 1980. text ed. 9.28 o.p. (ISBN 0-87002-310-1); tchr's guide avail. o.p.; student guide avail. o.p. Bennett IL.

Discovering Nutrition. Helen Kowtaluk. 1980. text ed. 9.28 (ISBN 0-87002-310-1); tchr's guide 6.00 (ISBN 0-87002-318-7); student guide 2.64 (ISBN 0-87002-317-9). Bennett IL.

Discovering Philosophy. Matthew Lipman. 1981. Repr. of 1969 ed. text ed. 14.95x (ISBN 0-8290-0049-6). Irvington.

Discovering Preserved Railways. British Tourist Authority. (Illus.). 72p. Date not set. pap. price not set (ISBN 0-85263-515-X, Pub. by Auto Assn-British Tourist Authority England). Merrimack Bk Serv.

Discovering Provence. Patrick Turnbull. 1973. 24.00 (ISBN 0-7134-2860-0, Pub. by Batsford England). David & Charles.

Discovering Relativity for Yourself. S. Lilley. LC 80-40263. (Illus.). 425p. Date not set. 49.50; pap. 19.95 (ISBN 0-521-29780-X). Cambridge U Pr.

Discovering Sociology: Studies in Sociological Theory & Method. John Rex. 288p. 1973. 24.00 (ISBN 0-7100-7411-5). Routledge & Kegan.

Discovering Spanish Wine. John Reay-Smith. (Illus.). 1977. 14.00 (ISBN 0-7091-5464-X). Transatlantic.

Discovering the Bible, Bk. 2. John Tickle. 96p. (Orig.). 1980. pap. 3.95 (ISBN 0-89243-133-4). Liguori Pubns.

Discovering the Bible: 8 Simple Keys for Learning & Praying. John Tickle. 1978. pap. 3.95 (ISBN 0-89243-074-5). Liguori Pubns.

Discovering the Biblical World. Harry T. Frank. LC 74-25082. (Illus.). 288p. 1975. 19.95 o.p. (ISBN 0-06-063014-0, HarpR). Har-Row.

Discovering the Biblical World. Harry T. Frank. LC 74-7044. (Illus.). 1977. pap. 11.95 (ISBN 0-8437-3625-9). Hammond Inc.

Discovering the Desert: The Legacy of the Carnegie Desert Botanical Laboratory. William G. McGinnies. 1981. text ed. 21.95x (ISBN 0-8165-0719-8); pap. text ed. 9.50x (ISBN 0-8165-0728-7). U of Ariz Pr.

Discovering the Human Body: How Pioneers of Modern Medicine Solved the Mysteries of the Body's Structure & Surface & Function. Bernard Knight. LC 80-7886. (Illus.). 192p. 1980. 17.95 (ISBN 0-690-01928-9). Lippincott & Crowell.

Discovering the Intimate Marriage. R. C. Sproul. LC 75-23494. 1975. pap. 2.45 (ISBN 0-87123-249-9, 210249). Bethany Fell.

Discovering the Intimate Marriage. R. C. Sproul. 160p. 1981. pap. 2.95 (ISBN 0-87123-118-2, 200118). Bethany Fell.

Discovering the Mind, Vol. 2: Nietzsche, Heidegger & Buber. Walter Kaufmann. LC 79-25209. (Discovering the Mind Ser.). 336p. 1980. 14.95 (ISBN 0-07-033312-2). McGraw.

Discovering the News: A Social History of American Newspapers. Michael Schudson. LC 78-54997. 288p. 1981. pap. 5.95 (ISBN 0-465-01666-9). Basic.

Discovering the Old Testament. John E. Eggleton. 306p. 1980. Repr. pap. text ed. 7.95 (ISBN 0-933656-07-6). Trinity Pub Hse.

Discovering the Present. Harold Rosenberg. 1973. pap. 3.95 o.s.i. (ISBN 0-226-72681-9, P691, Phoen). U of Chicago Pr.

Discovering the Present: Three Decades in Art, Culture, & Politics. Harold Rosenberg. 1973. 7.00x (ISBN 0-226-72680-0). U of Chicago Pr.

Discovering the Royal Tombs at Ur. Ed. by Shirley Glubok. LC 76-78088. (Illus.). (gr. 7 up). 1969. 7.95g o.s.i. (ISBN 0-02-736050-4). Macmillan.

Discovering, the Word of God. Dean Guest. 64p. (Orig.). 1980. Repr. pap. 1.95 (ISBN 0-89841-011-8). Zoe Pubns.

Discovering the World of the Three-Toed Sloth. John Hoke. (Illus.). 96p. (gr. 4 up). 1976. PLB 4.33 o.p. (ISBN 0-531-00339-6). Watts.

Discovering Tut-Ankh-Amen's Tomb. Ed. by Shirley Glubok. LC 68-12069. (Illus.). (gr. 5 up). 1968. 14.95 (ISBN 0-02-736030-X). Macmillan.

Discovering What Crickets Do. Seymour Simon. LC 72-10078. (Illus.). 48p. (gr. 3-6). 1973. PLB 6.95 o.p. (ISBN 0-07-057438-3, GB). McGraw.

Discovering Your Family Tree. rev. ed. 64p. 1980. pap. 2.95 (ISBN 0-85263-404-8, Pub. by B T A). Merrimack Bk Serv.

Discovering Your Teaching Self: Humanistic Approaches to Effective Teaching. Richard Curwin & Barbara Fuhrmann. LC 74-11371. (Curriculum & Teaching Ser.). (Illus.). 256p. 1975. pap. text ed. 10.95 (ISBN 0-13-216077-3). P-H.

Discovery. James Parry. LC 77-1904. 1978. 10.95 o.s.i. (ISBN 0-690-01166-0, TYC-T). T Y Crowell.

Discovery & Conquest of Mexico. Diaz Del Castillo & Bernal. 478p. 1956. pap. 8.95 (ISBN 0-374-50384-2). FS&G.

Discovery & Recognition. Ed. by James Alinder. (Untitled Ser.: No. 25). 56p. (Orig.). 1981. pap. 9.95 (ISBN 0-933286-24-4). Friends Photography.

Discovery Book of Inside & Outside. Judith Conaway. LC 76-46347. (Discovery Ser.). (Illus.). (gr. k-3). 1977. PLB 8.65 (ISBN 0-8172-0250-1). Raintree Pubs.

Discovery Book of Size. Judith Conaway. LC 76-46471. (Discovery Ser.). (Illus.). (gr. k-3). 1977. PLB 8.65 (ISBN 0-8172-0252-8). Raintree Pubs.

Discovery Book of Time. Judith Conaway. LC 76-44236. (Discovery Ser). (Illus.). (gr. k-3). 1977. PLB 8.65 (ISBN 0-8172-0253-6). Raintree Pubs.

Discovery Book of Up & Down. Judith Conaway. LC 76-46470. (Discovery Ser.). (Illus.). (gr. k-3). 1977. PLB 8.65 (ISBN 0-8172-0251-X). Raintree Pubs.

Discovery, Expansion & Empire. W. D. Hussey. text ed. 4.95x (ISBN 0-521-05352-8). Cambridge U Pr.

Discovery II. Campus Crusade for Christ Staff. 1980. pap. 2.25 saddlestitched (ISBN 0-918956-63-3). Campus Crusade.

Discovery in Russian & Siberian Waters. L. H. Neatby. LC 72-85535. (Illus.). 226p. 1973. 12.95x (ISBN 0-8214-0124-6). Ohio U Pr.

Discovery of a New World (Mundus Alter et Idem) Joseph Hall. Tr. by J. Healey. LC 72-6935. (English Experience Ser.: No. 119). 1969. Repr. of 1609 ed. 46.00 (ISBN 90-221-0119-3). Walter J Johnson.

Discovery of Dura-Europos. Hopkins. 1979. 19.95x (ISBN 0-300-02288-3). Yale U Pr.

Discovery of Grounded Theory: Strategies for Qualitative Research. Barney G. Glaser & Anselm L. Straus. LC 66-28314. 1967. text ed. 18.95x (ISBN 0-202-30028-5); pap. text ed. 7.50x (ISBN 0-202-30260-1). Aldine Pub.

Discovery of Humanity: An Introduction to Anthropology. Chad Oliver. (Illus.). 1980. text ed. 17.50 scp (ISBN 0-397-47407-5, HarpC); instrs'. manual free. Har-Row.

Discovery of Illusion: Flaubert's Early Works, 1835-1837. Eric L. Gans. (U. C. Publ. in Modern Philology: Vol. 100). 1971. pap. 8.50x (ISBN 0-520-09371-2). U of Cal Pr.

Discovery of Lost Worlds. Joseph J. Thorndike, Jr. LC 79-15881. (Illus.). 352p. 1980. 14.95 (ISBN 0-8281-0312-7, Dist by Scribner); pap. 9.95 (ISBN 0-686-65846-9). Scribner.

Discovery of Lost Worlds. Ed. by Joseph J. Thorndike, Jr. LC 79-15881. (Illus.). 352p. 1979. 34.95 (ISBN 0-8281-0308-9, Dist. by Scribner); deluxe ed. 39.95 (ISBN 0-8281-0309-7, Dist. by Scribner). Am Heritage.

Discovery of New Mexico by the Franciscan Monk Friar Marcos de Niza in 1539. Adolph F. Bandelier. Tr. by Madeleine T. Rodack from Fr. LC 80-25083. 1981. 10.95x (ISBN 0-8165-0717-1). U of Ariz Pr.

Discovery of the Child. Maria Montessori. 1972. pap. 2.75 (ISBN 0-345-29390-8). Ballantine.

Discovery of the Great Subtiltie & Wonderful Wisdom of the Italians. G. B. A. F. LC 74-80221. (English Experience Ser.: No. 656). 1974. Repr. of 1591 ed. 10.50 (ISBN 90-221-0656-X). Walter J Johnson.

Discovery of the Individual, 1050-1200. Colin Morris. LC 72-84235. 208p. 1973. 4.50x (ISBN 0-06-131718-7, TB1718, Torch). Har-Row.

Discovery of the Mississippi. Intro. by Dorman H. Winfrey. LC 74-19562. 208p. 1975. Repr. of 1844 ed. 1.50 o.p. (ISBN 0-88319-020-6). Shoal Creek Pub.

Discovery of Yellowstone Park: Journal of the Washburn Expedition to the Yellowstone & Firehole Rivers in the Year 1870. Nathaniel P. Langford. LC 78-93106. (Illus.). 1972. 9.75x (ISBN 0-8032-0710-7); pap. 3.95 (ISBN 0-8032-5705-8, BB 508, Bison). U of Nebr Pr.

Discovery Our Family Covenant. Danny Morris. 1981. pap. 2.25x (ISBN 0-8358-0419-4). Upper Room.

Discovery: The Story of the Second Byrd Antarctic Expedition. Richard E. Byrd. LC 76-159906. (Tower Bks). (Illus.). 1971. Repr. of 1935 ed. 28.00 (ISBN 0-8103-3904-8). Gale.

Discovery Under the Southern Cross. Roselyn Poignant. (International Library). (Illus.). 128p. (gr. 7 up). 1976. PLB 6.90 o.p. (ISBN 0-531-02121-1). Watts.

Discrepancy Evaluation: For Educational Program Improvement & Assessment. Malcolm M. Provus. LC 75-146312. 1971. 19.00 (ISBN 0-8211-1509-X); text ed. 17.00 (ISBN 0-685-04199-9). McCutchan.

Discrete Distributions: Distributions in Statistics. N. L. Johnson & S. I. Kotz. (Wiley Series in Math & Statistics). 1970. 31.95 (ISBN 0-471-44360-3, Pub. by Wiley-Interscience). Wiley.

Discrete Groups and Automorphic Functions. Ed. by W. J. Harvey. 1978. 56.00 (ISBN 0-12-329950-0). Acad Pr.

Discrete Linear Control: The Polynomial Equation Approach. Vladimir Kucera. LC 78-12956. 1980. 40.95 (ISBN 0-471-99726-9, Pub. by Wiley-Interscience). Wiley.

Discrete Mathematical Models with Applications to Social Biological & Environmental Problems. Fred S. Roberts. (Illus.). 560p. 1976. Ref. Ed. 22.95 (ISBN 0-13-214171-X). P-H.

Discrete Mathematical Structures for Computer Science. Ronald E. Prather. LC 75-25014. (Illus.). 680p. 1976. text ed. 20.95 (ISBN 0-395-20622-7); solutions manual 1.50 (ISBN 0-395-20623-5). HM.

Discrete Mathematics: Applied Algebra for Computer & Information Science. Leonard S. Bobrow & Michael A. Arbib. LC 73-77936. (Illus.). 1974. 24.50 (ISBN 0-7216-1768-9). Hemisphere Pub.

Discrete Multivariate Analysis: Theory & Practice. Yvonne Bishop et al. 1977. text ed. 40.00x (ISBN 0-262-02113-7); pap. 15.00 (ISBN 0-262-52040-0). MIT Pr.

Discrete Structures of Computer Science. Leon S. Levy. LC 79-11218. 1980. text ed. 20.95 (ISBN 0-471-03208-5). Wiley.

Discrete Time & Computer Control Systems. James A. Cadzow & Hinrich R. Martens. (Electrical Engineering Ser). 1970. ref. ed. 26.95 (ISBN 0-13-216036-6). P-H.

Discrete-Time Systems. Herbert Freeman. LC 80-15357. 256p. 1980. Repr. of 1965 ed. lib. bdg. 19.25 (ISBN 0-89874-228-5). Krieger.

Discrete Time Systems: An Introduction with Interdisciplinary Applications. James A. Cadzow. (Computer Applications in Electrical Engineering Ser.). (Illus.). 448p. 1973. ref. ed. 26.95 (ISBN 0-13-215996-1). P-H.

Discrete-Transistor Circuit Sourcemaster. Kendall Webster Sessions. LC 78-6774. 1978. text ed. 33.95 (ISBN 0-471-02626-3). Wiley.

Discrete Variable Methods in Ordinary Differential Equations. Peter Henrici. LC 61-17359. 1962. 27.50 (ISBN 0-471-37224-2, Pub. by Wiley-Interscience). Wiley.

Discretion & Lawlessness: Compliance in Juvenile Court. James T. Sprowls. LC 79-6735. 144p. 1980. 14.95x (ISBN 0-669-03540-8). Lexington Bks.

Discretionary Justice. Paul E. Dow. 1981. price not set reference (ISBN 0-88410-835-X). Ballinger Pub.

Discretionary Justice: A Preliminary Inquiry. Kenneth C. Davis. LC 80-16898. xii, 233p. 1980. Repr. of 1969 ed. lib. bdg. 21.25x (ISBN 0-313-22503-6, DADC). Greenwood.

Discretions. Mary De Rachewiltz. (Illus.). 1971. 9.95 o.p. (ISBN 0-571-09623-9, Pub. by Faber & Faber). Merrimack Bk Serv.

Discriminant Analysis. William R. Klecka. LC 80-50927. (Quantitative Applications in the Social Sciences Ser.: No. 19). (Illus.). 71p. 1980. pap. 3.50 (ISBN 0-8039-1491-1). Sage.

Discriminating Against Discrimination: Preferential Admissions & the DeFunis Case. Robert M. O'Neil. LC 75-3888. 288p. 1976. 10.95x (ISBN 0-253-31800-9). Ind U Pr.

Discrimination in Mass Transit. Damian J. Kulash & William Silverman. 1974. pap. 2.25 o.p. (ISBN 0-87766-112-X, 64000). Urban Inst.

Discrimination in Private Employment in Puerto Rico (Color, Sex & National Origin) Center for Environmental & Consumer Justice. LC 79-16965. 450p. 1980. pap. write for info. (ISBN 0-8477-2454-9). U of PR Pr.

Discrimination in Reverse: Is Turn-About Fair Play? Barry R. Gross. LC 77-14672. 1978. pap. 5.00x (ISBN 0-8147-2967-3); pap. 4.95x (ISBN 0-8147-2970-3). NYU Pr.

Discrimination Process & Development. B. J. Fellows. 1968. 32.00 (ISBN 0-08-012521-2). Pergamon.

Discriminative Properties of Reinforcement Schedules. Ed. by Michael Commons & John A. Nevin. (Quantitative Analysis of Behavior Ser.). 1981. price not set professional reference (ISBN 0-88410-377-3). Ballinger Pub.

Discurso Del Metodo. billingual ed. Rinaldo Descartes. (Biblioteca De Cultura Basica). pap. 2.50 o.p. (ISBN 0-8477-0704-0); pap. 2.50 (ISBN 0-8477-0705-9). U of PR Pr.

Discurso Retorico y Mundo Pastoral en la "Egloga Segunda" de Garcilaso. Ines Azar. (Purdue Univ. Monographs in Romance Languages: No. 5). 160p. (Span.). 1980. text ed. 23.00x (ISBN 90-272-1715-7). Humanities.

Discursos a Mis Estudiantes. Carlos M. Spurgeon. 1980. pap. 4.50 (ISBN 0-311-42006-0). Casa Bautista.

Discursos Selectos De Jose Marti. Jose Marti. LC 77-90959. 1977. pap. 4.95 (ISBN 0-685-95270-3). Ediciones.

Discus. Gunter Keller. (Illus., Orig.). 1976. pap. 2.95 (ISBN 0-87666-457-5, PS-314). TFH Pubns.

Discus. Tony Silva & Barbara Kotlar. (Illus.). 98p. 1980. 2.95 (ISBN 0-87666-535-0, KW-097). TFH Pubns.

Discussion. Ed. by Annina N. Weber. LC 78-19533. (Illus.). 1980. pap. 14.95 (ISBN 0-915570-13-0). Oolp Pr.

Discussion & Conference. 2nd ed. William M. Sattler & W. Miller. 1968. text ed. 16.95 (ISBN 0-13-216135-4). P-H.

Discussion in Small Groups. 3rd ed. David Potter & Martin P. Anderson. 1976. pap. text ed. 9.95x (ISBN 0-534-00426-1). Wadsworth Pub.

Discussion Manual for Student Relationships, Vol. 3. Dawson McAllister. 1979. pap. 7.95 (ISBN 0-8024-2240-3). Moody.

Discussion on Civil & Religious Liberty. John Hughes & John Breckinridge. LC 76-122167. (Civil Liberties in American History Ser). 1970. Repr. of 1836 ed. lib. bdg. 55.00 (ISBN 0-306-71979-7). Da Capo.

Discussion Starters for Youth Groups: Series 1. Ann Billups. (Orig.). 1966. pap. 7.95 (ISBN 0-8170-0351-7). Judson.

Discussion Starters for Youth Groups: Series 2. Ann Billups. LC 70-75185. 1969. pap. 7.95 (ISBN 0-8170-0443-2). Judson.

Discussion Starters for Youth Groups, Series 3. Ann Billups. LC 70-75185. 224p. 1976. pap. 7.95 (ISBN 0-8170-0687-7). Judson.

Discussion Topics for Oldsters in Nursing Homes: 365 Things to Talk About. Toni Merrill. 256p. 1974. pap. 24.75 (ISBN 0-398-03129-0). C C Thomas.

Discussions of the Uranium Geology Working Groups, IGC, Sydney. (Technical Reports Ser: No. 183). 1978. pap. 10.25 (ISBN 92-0-145078-8, IDC 183, IAEA). Unipub.

Disease & Economic Development: The Impact of Parasitic Diseases in St. Lucia. Burton A. Weisbrod et al. LC 72-7997. 224p. 1973. 27.50x (ISBN 0-299-06340-2). U of Wis Pr.

Disease & Social Behavior: An Elementary Exposition. Horatio Fabrega, Jr. 1974. pap. 9.95x (ISBN 0-262-56020-8). MIT Pr.

Disease & Urbanization. Ed. by E. J. Clegg & J. P. Garlick. (Symposia of the Society for the Study of Human Biology: Vol. 20). 1980. text ed. 22.25x (ISBN 0-85066-190-0). Humanities.

Disease Detectives. Melvin Berger. LC 77-26589. (Scientists at Work Ser.). (Illus.). (gr. 4 up). 1978. 8.95 (ISBN 0-690-03907-7, TYC-J); PLB 8.79 (ISBN 0-690-03908-5). T Y Crowell.

Disease Detectives. Louis Wolfe. (Illus.). (gr. 4-6). 1979. PLB 6.90 s&l (ISBN 0-531-02921-2). Watts.

Disease of the Oral Mucosa: A Color Atlas. M. Strassburg & G. Knolie. (Illus.). 270p. 1972. 58.00. Quint Pub Co.

Disease of the Temporomandibular Apparatus: A Multidisciplinary Approach. Douglas Morgan & William Hall. LC 77-3904. (Illus.). 1977. 49.50 (ISBN 0-8016-3487-3). Mosby.

Diseases. Intro. by Lillian Brunner. (Reference Library). (Illus.). 1980. 19.95 (ISBN 0-916730-19-0). InterMed Comm.

Diseases & Parasites of Livestock in the Tropics. H. Hall. (Intermediate Tropical Agriculture Ser.). 1977. pap. text ed. 7.95x (ISBN 0-582-60618-7). Longman.

Diseases in Antiquity: A Survey of the Diseases, Injuries & Surgery of Early Populations. Don Brothwell & A. T. Sandison. (Illus.). 792p. 1967. 74.50 (ISBN 0-398-00233-9). C C Thomas.

Diseases of Cage & Aviary Birds. 2nd ed. Ed. by Margaret L. Petrak. (Illus.). 540p. 1981. text ed. price not set (ISBN 0-8121-0692-X). Lea & Febiger.

Diseases of Children. 3rd ed. Hugh Jolly. (Illus.). 1976. 21.75 (ISBN 0-632-00396-0, Blackwell). Mosby.

Diseases of Children in the Subtropics & Tropics. 3rd ed. D. B. Jelliffe & J. Paget Stanfield. (Illus.). 1978. 80.00x (ISBN 0-7131-4277-4). Intl Ideas.

Diseases of Cocoa. C. A. Thorold. (Illus.). 438p. 1975. text ed. 54.00x (ISBN 0-19-854507-X). Oxford U Pr.

Diseases of Dogs. H. J. Christoph. LC 71-163386. 279p. 1974. text ed. 115.00 (ISBN 0-08-015800-5). Pergamon.

Diseases of Fish. Zoological Society of London - 30th Symposium. Ed. by Lionel E. Mawdesley-Thomas. 1972. 50.50 o.s.i. (ISBN 0-12-613330-1). Acad Pr.

Diseases of Fishes: Bacteria. S. Sniezko et al. (Illus.). 12.95 (ISBN 0-87666-038-3, PS202). TFH Pubns.

Diseases of Hematopoietic System. Ed. by Philip H. Lieberman & Robert A. Good. (Anatomic Pathology Slide Seminar Ser.). (Illus.). 137p. 1981. pap. text ed. 18.00 (ISBN 0-89189-085-8); slides 85.00 (ISBN 0-686-69528-3). Am Soc Clinical.

Diseases of Marine Animals: Bivalvia to Arthopoda, Vol. 2. O. Kinne. 1980. write for info. (ISBN 0-471-99585-1, Pub. by Wiley-Interscience). Wiley.

Diseases of Memory. Theodule A. Ribot. Tr. by W. H. Smith & M. M. Snell. Bd. with Diseases of Personality. Repr. of 1891 ed; Diseases of the Will. Repr. of 1894 ed. (Contributions to the History of Psychology, Vol. I, Pt. C: Medical Psychology). 1978. Repr. of 1882 ed. 30.00 (ISBN 0-89093-165-8). U Pubns Amer.

Diseases of Swine. 5th ed. Ed. by A. Leman et al. (Illus.). 1981. 60.00 (ISBN 0-8138-0440-X). Iowa St U Pr.

Diseases of the Chest. 4th ed. H. Corwin Hinshaw & Johhn F. Murray. LC 77-16975. (Illus.). 1044p. 1980. text ed. 46.00 (ISBN 0-7216-4697-2). Saunders.

Diseases of the Chest. Raman Viswanathan. 1968. 15.95x o.p. (ISBN 0-210-31243-2). Asia.

Diseases of the Cornea. Grayson. LC 79-16021. 1979. 79.50 (ISBN 0-8016-1964-5). Mosby.

Diseases of the Fundus Oculi. A. Sorsby. 1976. 54.95 (ISBN 0-407-00023-2). Butterworths.

Diseases of the Gallbladder & Biliary System. Leslie J. Schoenfield. LC 77-5695. (Clinical Gastroenterology Monographs). 1977. 41.50 (ISBN 0-471-76246-6, Pub. by Wiley Medical). Wiley.

Diseases of the Liver. 4th ed. Ed. by Leon Schiff. LC 75-20047. (Illus.). 1450p. 1975. text ed. 87.50 (ISBN 0-397-50319-9). Lippincott.

Diseases of the Motor Unit. Donald L. Schotland. (Illus.). 1981. price not set (ISBN 0-89289-410-5). HM.

Diseases of the Oral Mucosa. 2nd ed. Philip L. McCarthy & Gerald Shklar. LC 80-10335. (Illus.). 579p. 1980. text ed. 47.50 (ISBN 0-8121-0641-5). Lea & Febiger.

Diseases of the Thyroid. David Evered. LC 76-20230. 1976. 15.95 o.p. (ISBN 0-471-02216-0, Pub. by Wiley Medical). Wiley.

Diseases, Pests & Weeds in Tropical Crops. Ed. by J. Kranz et al. LC 78-6212. 1978. 79.25 (ISBN 0-471-99667-X, Pub. by Wiley-Interscience). Wiley.

Diseases Transmitted from Animals to Man. 6th ed. Ed. by William T. Hubbert et al. (Illus.). 1236p. 1975. text ed. 79.75 (ISBN 0-398-03056-1). C C Thomas.

Disembodied Laughter: Troilus & the Apotheosis Tradition. John M. Steadman. 1972. 17.50x (ISBN 0-520-02047-2). U of Cal Pr.

Disenchanted Images: A Literary Iconology. Theodore Ziolkowski. 1977. text ed. 16.50 (ISBN 0-691-06334-6). Princeton U Pr.

Disequalibrium of the Labour Market. R. S. Lenderink & J. C. Siebrand. 1979. text ed. 17.00x (ISBN 90-237-2277-9, Pub. by Gower Pub Co England). Renouf.

Disequilibrium Economics. J. Van Doorn. LC 75-19139. 96p. 1976. pap. text ed. 8.95x (ISBN 0-470-89902-6). Halsted Pr.

Disequilibrium Model in a Controlled Economy. David H. Howard. LC 78-24828. (Illus.). 128p. 1979. 14.95 (ISBN 0-669-02851-7). Lexington Bks.

Disestablishment in Ireland: Implications for Catholic Objectives in Higher Education, 1869-1879. S. Macpherson Pemberton. LC 79-64245. 1979. pap. text ed. 7.75 (ISBN 0-8191-0759-X). U Pr of Amer.

Disguise & Role-Playing in Ben Jonson's Drama. Peter Hyland. (Salzburg Studies in English Literature, Jacobean Drama Studies: No. 69). (Orig.). 1977. pap. text ed. 25.00x (ISBN 0-391-01432-3). Humanities.

Dish Ran Away with the Spoon. Elizabeth Benoist. 212p. 1980. pap. 5.95 (ISBN 0-86629-007-9). Sunrise MO.

Dishes for Special Occasions. Eulalia Blair. LC 75-4684. (Foodservice Menu Planning Ser.). 1975. 16.50 (ISBN 0-8436-2058-7). CBI Pub.

Dishes from Indonesia. Yohani Johns. (Illus.). 1978. 17.95 (ISBN 0-241-89943-5, Pub. by Hamish Hamilton England). David & Charles.

Dishwashing Procedures. Ser-Vo-Tel Institute. (Foodservice Career Education Ser.). 1975. pap. 4.95 (ISBN 0-8436-2026-9). CBI Pub.

Disinfection Chemistry & Biology. Ed. by J. Donald Johnson. LC 79-55143. Date not set. 39.95 (ISBN 0-250-40267-X). Ann Arbor Science. Postponed.

Disinfestation of Fruit by Irradiation. (Illus.). 180p. (Orig.). 1972. pap. 10.75 (ISBN 92-0-111571-7, IAEA). Unipub.

Disinherited. Jack Conroy. 1963. pap. 5.95 o.p. (ISBN 0-8090-0060-1, AmCen). Hill & Wang.

Disinherited: The Lost Birthright of the American Indian. Dale Van Every. 1967. pap. 2.95 (ISBN 0-380-01141-7, 51326, Discus). Avon.

Disinvestment of Foreign Subsidiaries. Brent D. Wilson. Ed. by Gunter Dufey. (Research for Business Decisions). 112p. 1980. 19.95 (ISBN 0-8357-1132-3, Pub. by UMI Res Pr). Univ Microfilms.

Disjoined Partners: Austria & Germany Since 1815. Peter Katzenstein. LC 74-30526. 1976. 21.50x (ISBN 0-520-02945-3). U of Cal Pr.

Dislocations & Plastic Deformations. T. Kovacs & L. Zsoldos. LC 73-6995. 364p. 1974. 23.00 (ISBN 0-08-017062-5). Pergamon.

Dismemberment of Orpheus: Toward a Postmodern Literature. Ihab Hassan. 1971. 14.95 (ISBN 0-19-501393-X). Oxford U Pr.

Disney's Children's Adventure Travel Guide to California. (Fodor's Modern Travel Guides Ser.). 1980. 3.95 (ISBN 0-679-00577-3). McKay.

Disney's Children's Adventure Travel Guide to Florida. (Fodor's Modern Travel Guides Ser.). 1980. 3.95 (ISBN 0-679-00575-7). McKay.

Disorder & Progress: Bandits, Police, & Mexican Development. Paul J. Vanderwood. LC 80-22345. (Illus.). xx, 269p. 1981. 19.95x (ISBN 0-8032-4651-X, Bison); pap. 7.95 (ISBN 0-8032-9600-2, BB 767). U of Nebr Pr.

Disordered Thought in Schizophrenia. L. Chapman. 1974. 19.95 (ISBN 0-13-216192-3). P-H.

Disorderly Girl. Bruce Stewart. 294p. 1981. 11.95 (ISBN 0-312-21265-8). St Martin.

Disorderly Houses. Alan Ansen. LC 61-14240. (Wesleyan Poetry Program: Vol. 11). (Orig.). 1962. 10.00x (ISBN 0-8195-2011-X, Pub. by Wesleyan U Pr); pap. 5.00 (ISBN 0-8195-1011-4). Columbia U Pr.

Disorderly Knights. Dorothy Dunnett. 576p. 1980. pap. 2.75 (ISBN 0-445-08497-9). Popular Lib.

Disorders in the Kingdom. Malcom K. Burton. 1981. 11.95 (ISBN 0-533-04751-X). Vantage.

Disorders of Articulation. John Irwin. LC 79-186626. (Studies in Communicative Disorders Ser). 1972. pap. 2.95 (ISBN 0-672-61278-X). Bobbs.

Disorders of Blood & Blood-Forming Organs in Childhood. H. S. Baar & E. Stransky. (Illus.). 1963. 71.50 o.s.i. (ISBN 0-02-840710-5). Hafner.

Disorders of Calcium & Phosphate Metabolism in Childhood & Adolescence. Harold E. Harrison & Helen C. Harrison. LC 78-64712. (MPCP Ser.: Mpcp Ser. XX). (Illus.). 314p. 1979. text ed. 35.00 (ISBN 0-7216-4537-2). Saunders.

Disorders of Communication: Proceedings, Vol. 42. Association For Research In Nervous And Mental Disease. 1969. Repr. 30.25 o.s.i. (ISBN 0-02-846430-3). Hafner.

Disorders of Hemostasis. Philip D. Zieve & Jack Levin. LC 76-1252. (Major Problems in Internal Medicine Ser.: Vol. 10). 1976. text ed. 14.50 (ISBN 0-7216-9685-6). Saunders.

Disorders of Personality: DSMIII; AXIS II. Theodore Millon. 352p. 1981. 27.50 (ISBN 0-471-06403-3, Pub. by Wiley-Interscience). Wiley.

Disorders of the Cerebellum. Ed. by Sid Gilman et al. LC 80-23393. (Contemporary Neurology Ser.: No. 21). (Illus.). 415p. 1981. text ed. 40.00 (ISBN 0-8036-4150-8). Davis Co.

Disorders of the Foot. Arthur J. Helfet et al. 1980. text ed. 27.50 (ISBN 0-397-50430-6). Lippincott.

Disorders of Voice. Margaret Greene. LC 77-183113. (Studies in Communicative Disorders Ser.). 1972. pap. 2.95 (ISBN 0-672-61279-8). Bobbs.

Disorders of Written Language: Methods & Programming for Redemiation. Diana Phelps-Terasaki & Trisha Phelps. 350p. 1981. text ed. price not set (ISBN 0-89443-360-1). Aspen Systems.

Disparity Reduction Rates in Social Indicators: A Proposal for Measuring & Targeting Progress in Meeting Basic Needs. James P. Grant. LC 78-61153. (Monographs: No. 11). 88p. 1978. 3.00 (ISBN 0-686-28684-7). Overseas Dev Council.

Dispassionate Justice: A Synthesis of the Judicial Opinions of Robert H. Jackson. Glendon Schubert. LC 69-13634. 1969. 28.50x (ISBN 0-672-51138-X). Irvington.

Dispatch from Cadiz. Bruce Weiser. (Chenevix Ser.: No. 2). 1981. pap. 2.25 (ISBN 0-8439-0826-2, Leisure Bks). Nordon Pubns.

Dispatches. Michael Herr. 288p. 1980. pap. 2.50 (ISBN 0-380-01976-0, 52639). Avon.

Dispatches from Washington, 1941 to 1945: Weekly Political Reports from the British Embassy. Ed. by H. G. Nicholas. 748p. 1981. 40.00 (ISBN 0-226-58004-0). U of Chicago Pr.

Dispatches, with Related Documents, of Milanese Ambassadors in France & Burgundy, 1450-1483. Ed. by Paul M. Kendall & Vincent Ilardi. LC 68-20933. 1970. Vol. 1, lvi 390p. 15.00x (ISBN 0-8214-0067-3); Vol. 2, 486p. 15.00x (ISBN 0-8214-0082-7). Ohio U Pr.

Dispatches with Related Documents of Milanese Ambassadors in France, (Mar. 11- June 29 1466, Vol. 3. Ed. by Vincent Ilardi. Tr. by Frank J. Fata. LC 68-20933. 444p. 1980. 35.00 (ISBN 0-87580-069-6). N Ill U Pr.

Dispensary: With a Short Account of the Proceedings of the College of Physicians, London, in Relation to the Sick Poor (1697) & Claremont (1715) Samuel Garth. LC 74-23391. 160p. 1975. Repr. lib. bdg. 20.00x (ISBN 0-8201-1145-7). Schol Facsimiles.

Dispensation of Baha'u'llah. Shoghi Effendi. 1934. pap. 3.00 (ISBN 0-87743-050-0, 7-08-08). Baha'i.

Dispersing Population: What America Can Learn from Europe. James L. Sundquist. 290p. 1975. 14.95 (ISBN 0-8157-8214-4); pap. 5.95 (ISBN 0-8157-8213-6). Brookings.

Dispersion Method in Binary Additive Problems. Ju. V. Linnik. LC 63-15660. (Translations of Mathematical Monographs: Vol. 4). 1979. Repr. of 1963 ed. 17.60 (ISBN 0-8218-1554-7, MMONO-4). Am Math.

Dispersion of Nuclear Weapons: Strategy & Politics. Ed. by Richard N. Rosecrance. LC 64-17019. 1964. 20.00x (ISBN 0-231-02709-5). Columbia U Pr.

Displaced Homemakers: Organizing for a New Life. Laurie Shields. (McGraw-Hill Paperback Ser.). 256p. (Orig.). 1980. pap. 5.95 (ISBN 0-07-056802-2). McGraw.

Displaced Persons. John Morressy. 224p. 1976. pap. 1.50 o.p. (ISBN 0-445-03130-1). Popular Lib.

Display: A Handbook of Bulletin Board Ideas. (The Spice Ser.). 1975. 6.50 (ISBN 0-89273-117-6). Educ Serv.

Display & Merchandising Idea Book. 2nd ed. Progressive Grocer's Marketing Guidebook Staff. (Illus.). 1981. 19.95 (ISBN 0-911790-55-1). Prog Grocer.

Display Boards. Sr. Robert V. Bullough. Ed. by James E. Duane. LC 80-21332. (Instructional Media Library: Vol. 3). (Illus.). 112p. 1981. 13.95 (ISBN 0-87778-163-X). Educ Tech Pubns.

Display Devices. Ed. by J. I. Pankove. (Topics in Applied Physics Ser.: Vol. 40). (Illus.). 300p. 1980. 49.80 (ISBN 0-387-09868-2). Springer-Verlag.

Display of Heraldrie. John Guillim. LC 79-84115. (English Experience Ser.: No. 934). 308p. 1979. Repr. of 1611 ed. lib. bdg. 46.00 (ISBN 90-221-0934-8). Walter J Johnson.

Disposable Patients. Daryl B. Matthews. LC 77-25778. 1980. 14.95 (ISBN 0-669-02164-4). Lexington Bks.

Disposable People. Heron A. Sam. LC 79-66268. 133p. 1980. 7.95 (ISBN 0-533-04374-3). Vantage.

Disposal in the Marine Environment: An Oceanographic Assessment. Ocean Affairs Board, Natl. Research Council. LC 76-1319. 1976. pap. 5.00 (ISBN 0-309-02446-3). Natl Acad Pr.

Disposal of Dredged Material in Rhode Island: An Evaluation of Past Practices & Future Options. George R. Seavey & S. D. Pratt. (Marine Technical Report Ser.: No. 72). write for info. (ISBN 0-938412-06-X). URI MAS.

Disposal of Radioactive Wastes into Rivers, Lakes & Estuaries. (Safety Ser.: No. 36). (Orig.). 1971. pap. 6.50 (ISBN 92-0-123171-7, ISP283, IAEA). Unipub.

Disposal of Radioactive Wastes into Seas, Oceans & Surface Waters. (Illus., Orig.). 1966. pap. 47.75 (ISBN 92-0-020266-7, ISP126, IAEA). Unipub.

Disposal of Radioactive Wastes into the Ground. (Illus., Orig.). 1967. pap. 38.00 (ISBN 92-0-020267-5, IAEA). Unipub.

Dispossessed. Ursula Le Guin. 1975. pap. 2.50 (ISBN 0-380-00382-1, 51284). Avon.

Disputation & Dialogue: Readings in the Jewish Christian Encounter. Frank Talmage. pap. 9.95x (ISBN 0-685-56218-2). Ktav.

Disputation of Nachmanides: With Introduction & Commentaries. Tr. by B. Haskelevich from Hebrew. (Rus.). 1981. pap. 3.75 (ISBN 0-938666-00-2). CHAMH.

Dispute & Conflict Resolution in Plymouth County, Massachusetts, 1725 - 1825. William E. Nelson. LC 80-17403. (Studies in Legal History). 240p. 1980. 19.50x (ISBN 0-8078-1454-7). U of NC Pr.

Disputed Lands. Alexander B. Adams. 480p. 1981. 17.95 (ISBN 0-399-12530-2). Putnam.

Disputed Paternity. Neville Bryant. 1980. 24.00. Thieme Stratton.

Disputed Questions in Philosophy. James F. Keleher. LC 65-21757. 1966. 3.50 o.p. (ISBN 0-8022-0840-1). Philos Lib.

Disputes Procedure in Action. R. Hyman. 1972. text ed. 6.95x o.p. (ISBN 0-435-85320-1). Heinemann Ed.

Disputing Process in Ten Societies. Ed. by Laura Nader & Harry F. Todd, Jr. 1978. 22.50x (ISBN 0-231-04536-0); pap. 10.00x (ISBN 0-231-04537-9). Columbia U Pr.

Disquisition on Government. John C. Calhoun. 1958. 6.00 (ISBN 0-8446-1099-2). Peter Smith.

Disquisition on Government & Selections from the Discourse. John C. A. Calhoun. Ed. by C. Gordon Post. 1953. pap. 4.95 (ISBN 0-672-60014-5, AHS10). Bobbs.

Disquisitions Relating Matter & Spirit, 2 vols. in 1. Joseph Priestley. Ed. by Rene Wellek. Bd. with Doctrine of Philosophical Necessity Illustrated: Being an Appendix to the Disquestions Relating to Matter & Spirit. LC 75-11248. (British Philosophers & Theologians of the 17th & 18th Centuries: Vol. 47). 1977. Repr. of 1777 ed. lib. bdg. 42.00 (ISBN 0-8240-1799-4). Garland Pub.

Disraeli: Portrait of a Romantic. David Butler. (Orig.). 1980. pap. 2.75 (ISBN 0-446-85776-9). Warner Bks.

Disraeli's Fiction. Daniel R. Schwarz. 1979. text ed. 24.00x (ISBN 0-06-496124-9). B&N.

Disraeli's Novels Reviewed, Eighteen Twenty-Six to Nineteen Sixty-Eight. R. W. Stewart. LC 74-28454. 1975. 12.00 (ISBN 0-8108-0759-9). Scarecrow.

Disrupting the Spectacle: Five Years of Experience & Fringe Theatre in Britain. Peter Ansorge. 1975. pap. 10.00x (ISBN 0-273-00351-8, Pub. by Wesleyan U Pr); pap. 5.00x (ISBN 0-273-00255-4). Columbia U Pr.

Disruption of the Pennsylvania Democracy, 1848-1860. John F. Coleman. LC 75-623874. (Illus.). 184p. 1975. 8.00 (ISBN 0-911124-82-9). Pa Hist & Mus.

Disruptive Behavior in Group Care: Problems & Solutions. Ann W. Shyne & Eva M. Russo. LC 79-23739. 80p. (Orig.). 1980. pap. text ed. write for info. o.p. (ISBN 0-87868-137-X). Child Welfare.

Dissection of the Cat & Comparisons with Man: A Laboratory Manual on Felis Domestica. 7th ed. Bruce M. Harrison. (Illus.). 1976. pap. text ed. 7.50 (ISBN 0-8016-2075-9). Mosby.

Dissection of the Fetal Pig. 2nd ed. Warren F. Walker, Jr. (Illus.). 1974. pap. text ed. 3.25x o.p. (ISBN 0-7167-0587-7); tchr's guide avail. o.p.; individual exercises 0.50 ea. o.p. W H Freeman.

Dissector's Guide: A Detailed Investigation of Musculoskeletal Anatomy. Claudette Finley. (Illus.). 176p. 1975. vinyl cover 16.50 (ISBN 0-398-03084-7). C C Thomas.

Dissemination of Curriculum Development. J. Rudduck & P. Kelly. Ed. by Jack Wrigley & Freddie Sparrow. (Council of Europe Trend Reports). (Orig.). 1976. pap. text ed. 13.75 (ISBN 0-85633-092-2, NFER). Humanities.

Dissemination of Information. J. E. Rowley & C. M. Turner. LC 78-6138. (Grafton Library of Information Science). 1978. lib. bdg. 29.50x (ISBN 0-89158-830-2). Westview.

Dissension in the House of Commons: Nineteen Seventy-Four to Nineteen Seventy-Nine. Philip Norton. (Illus.). 560p. 1980. text ed. 79.00x (ISBN 0-19-827430-0). Oxford U Pr.

Dissent & Disruption: Proposals for Consideration by the Campus. Carnegie Commission on Higher Education. 1971. 5.95 o.p. (ISBN 0-07-010031-4, P&RB). McGraw.

Dissent & Parliamentary Politics in England 1661-1689: A Study in the Perpetuation & Tempering of Parliamentarianism. Douglas R. Lacey. 1969. 35.00 (ISBN 0-8135-0594-1). Rutgers U Pr.

Dissent in Ukraine: Ukranian Herald Issue Six. LC 75-39367. 1976. 6.95 (ISBN 0-685-79368-0); pap. 3.95 o.p. (ISBN 0-685-79369-9). Cataract Pr.

Dissent Without Opinion: The Behavior of Justice William O. Douglas in Federal Tax Cases. Bernard Wolfman et al. LC 74-16827. 224p. 1975. 14.00x (ISBN 0-8122-7682-5). U of Pa Pr.

Dissenters: From the Reformation to the French Revolution, Vol. 1. Michael R. Watts. (Illus.). 1978. 49.00x (ISBN 0-19-822460-5). Oxford U Pr.

Dissenting Tradition: Essays for Leland H. Carlson. Ed. by C. Robert Cole & Michael E. Moody. LC 74-27706. xxiii, 272p. 1975. 15.00x (ISBN 0-8214-0176-9). Ohio U Pr.

Dissertation. R. M. Koster. LC 80-20066. 438p. 1981. pap. 7.95 (ISBN 0-688-00043-6, Quill). Morrow.

Dissertation on Musical Taste. Thomas Hastings. LC 68-16237. (Music Ser.). 228p. 1974. Repr. of 1822 ed. lib. bdg. 22.50 (ISBN 0-306-71085-4). Da Capo.

Dissertation on Natural Phonology. David Stampe. Ed. by Jorge Hankamer. LC 78-66538. (Outstanding Dissertations in Linguistics Ser.). 1979. lib. bdg. 16.50 (ISBN 0-8240-9674-6). Garland Pub.

Dissertation on the Functions of the Nervous System. Georg Prochaska. Tr. by T. Laycock. Bd. with On the Study of Character. (Contributions to the History of Psychology Ser., Vol. XIV, Pt. A: Orientations). 1980. Repr. of 1851 ed. 30.00 (ISBN 0-89093-316-2). U Pubns Amer.

Dissertation on the Law of Nature, the Law of Nations, & the Civil Law in General. Together with Some Observations on the Roman Civil Law in Particular: To Which Is Added, by Way of Appendix, a Curious Catalogue of Books, Very Useful to the Students of These Several Laws, Together with the Canon Law. 132p. 1980. Repr. of 1723 ed. lib. bdg. 20.00x (ISBN 0-8377-0510-X). Rothman.

Dissertation on the Poor Laws: By a Well-Wisher to Mankind. Joseph Townsend. 1971. 15.75x (ISBN 0-520-01700-5). U of Cal Pr.

Dissertation on the Sanskrit Language. Paulinus S. Bartholomaeo. Ed. by L. Rocher. (Studies in the History of Linguistics: No. 12). 1979. text ed. 37.00x (ISBN 0-391-01675-X). Humanities.

Dissertation Proposal Guidebook: How to Prepare a Research Proposal & Get It Accepted. David C. Gardner & Grace J. Beatty. (Illus.). 112p. 1980. 9.50 (ISBN 0-398-04086-9); pap. 5.75 (ISBN 0-398-04087-7). C C Thomas.

Dissertations in English & American Literature: Theses Accepted in American, British & German Universities, 1865-1964. Ed. by Lawrence McNamee. LC 68-27446. 1124p. 1968. 23.50 o.p. (ISBN 0-8352-0043-4). Bowker.

Dissertations in Hispanic Languages & Literatures: 1876-1966. James R. Chatham & Enrique Ruiz-Fornells. LC 70-80093. 136p. 1970. 15.50x (ISBN 0-8131-1183-8). U Pr of Ky.

Dissertations on British History, 1815-1914: An Index to British & American Theses. S. Peter Bell. LC 75-15489. 1974. 8.50 o.p. (ISBN 0-8108-0733-5). Scarecrow.

Dissertations on Pennsylvania History, 1886-1976: A Bibliography. Ed. by Roland M. Baumann. 1978. pap. 3.00 (ISBN 0-911124-93-4). Pa Hist & Mus.

Dissident M. L. A. Asif Currimbhoy. (Bluebird Bk.). 56p. 1975. 8.00 (ISBN 0-88253-841-1); pap. 4.80 (ISBN 0-88253-842-X). Ind-US Inc.

Dissipative Structures & Spatiotemporal Organization Studies in Biomedical Research. George P. Scott & J. M. McMillin. (Illus.). 271p. 1980. pap. text ed. 9.95. Iowa St U Pr.

Dissipative Structures in Biomedical Research. Ed. by George P. Scott & J. Michael McMillan. 1980. 9.95 (ISBN 0-8138-1620-3). Iowa St U Pr.

Dissolution of Character: Changing Perspectives in La Bruyere's Caracteres. Michael S. Koppisch. (French Forum Monographs: No.24). 120p. (Orig.). 1981. pap. 10.50 (ISBN 0-917058-23-2). French Forum.

Dissolution of the Medieval Outlook. Gordon Leff. (Orig.). 1976. pap. 4.95x o.p. (ISBN 0-06-131897-3, TB1897, Torch). Har-Row.

Dissolution of the Medieval Outlook: An Essay on Intellectual & Spiritual Change in the Fourteenth Century. Gordon Leff. LC 76-48865. 154p. 1976. 10.00x (ISBN 0-8147-4974-7). NYU Pr.

Dissolution of the Monasteries. Joyce Youings. (Historical Problems: Studies & Documents). 1971. pap. text ed. 9.95x (ISBN 0-04-942090-9). Allen Unwin.

Dissolution of the Religious Orders in Ireland Under Henry Eighth. B. Bradshaw. LC 73-83104. (Illus.). 248p. 1974. 41.50 (ISBN 0-521-20342-2). Cambridge U Pr.

Dissolution Technology. Lewis J. Leeson & J. Thuro Carstenpen. 1974. 21.00 (ISBN 0-917330-15-3). Am Pharm Assn.

Distaff Diplomacy: The Empress Eugenie & the Foreign Policy of the Second Empire. Nancy N. Barker. 1967. 12.50x (ISBN 0-292-73694-0). U of Tex Pr.

Distance & Development: Transport & Communications in India. Wilfred Owen. LC 67-30599. (Transport Research Program). 1968. 10.95 (ISBN 0-8157-6768-4). Brookings.

Distance Teaching. Ed. by Anthony Kay & Greville Rumble. 350p. 1981. 37.50x (ISBN 0-89397-099-9). Nichols Pub.

Distances. Charles Levendosky. 24p. 1980. pap. 4.50 (ISBN 0-937160-01-6). Dooryard.

Distant Drum. Alice L. Covert. 256p. (YA) 1974. 5.95 (ISBN 0-685-49584-1, Avalon). Bouregy.

Distant Grief. F. Kefa Sempangi. LC 79-50394. 1979. pap. 4.95 (ISBN 0-8307-0684-4, 5411807). Regal.

Distant Hunger: Agriculture, Food & Human Values. Heather J. Nicholson & Ralph L. Nicholson. LC 78-60761. (Science & Society: a Purdue University Series in Science Technology, & Human Values: Vol. 3.). (Illus.). 240p. 1979. pap. 3.95 (ISBN 0-931682-00-2). Purdue Univ Bks.

Distant Mirror. Barbara Tuchman. 1980. pap. 8.95 (ISBN 0-345-29542-0). Ballantine.

Distant Trumpet. Paul Horgan. 1960. 12.95 o.p. (ISBN 0-374-14089-8). FS&G.

Distillation Control: For Productivity & Energy Conservation. F. Greg Shinskey. 1976. 23.95 (ISBN 0-07-056893-6, P&RB). McGraw.

Distinction of Stories: The Medieval Unity of Chaucer's Fair Chain of Narratives for Canterbury. Judson B. Allen & Theresa A. Moritz. 280p. 1981. write for info. (ISBN 0-8142-0310-8). Ohio St U Pr.

Distinctive Black College: Talladega, Tuskegee, & Morehouse. Addie J. Butler. LC 77-22756. 1977. 10.00 (ISBN 0-8108-1055-7). Scarecrow.

Distinctive Elements in Christianity. Karl Holl. Tr. by Norman V. Hope. LC 38-24885. 79p. pap. text ed. 3.50. Attic Pr.

Distinctive Homes. Hiawatha T. Estes. (Illus.). 1981. 2.00 (ISBN 0-911008-18-7). H Estes.

Distinguishing Moral Education, Values Clarification & Religion-Studies: Proceedings. N. Piediscalzi et al. Ed. by B. Swyhart. LC 76-26670. (American Academy of Religion. Section Papers). 1976. pap. 4.50 (ISBN 0-89130-082-1, 010918). Scholars Pr Ca.

Distortion or Development? Contending Perspectives on the Multinational Corporation. Thomas J. Biersteker. 1979. text ed. 20.00x (ISBN 0-262-02133-1). MIT Pr.

Distortions in Body Image in Illness & Disability. Ed. by Fay L. Bower. LC 77-4429. (Nursing Concept Modules Ser.). 1977. pap. 10.95 (ISBN 0-471-02169-5, Pub. by Wiley Medical). Wiley.

Distress Property: How to Buy It in California. 323p. 1981. 55.00 (ISBN 0-934668-07-8). B Greene.

Distributed Computer Control Systems: Proceedings of the IFAC Workshop, Tampa, Fla., 2-4 Oct. 1979. T. J. Harrison. (IFAC Proceedings). (Illus.). 240p. 1980. 64.00 (ISBN 0-08-024490-4). Pergamon.

Distributed Data Bases. Ed. by I. W. Draffan & F. Poole. LC 80-40399. 400p. Date not set. 29.95 (ISBN 0-521-23091-8). Cambridge U Pr.

Distributed Energy Systems in California's Future. U. S. Department of Energy. 359p. 1980. pap. 19.95 cancelled (ISBN 0-89934-011-3). Solar Energy Info.

Distributed Micro Minicomputer Systems: Structure, Implementation & Application. Cay Weitzman. (Illus.). 1980. text ed. 24.95 (ISBN 0-13-216481-7). P-H.

Distributed Processing, G-051. Ed. by Business Communications. 1980. 700.00 (ISBN 0-89336-217-4). BCC.

Distributed Processor Communication Architecture. Kenneth J. Thurber & G. M. Masson. LC 79-1563. (Illus.). 288p. 1979. 23.95 (ISBN 0-669-02914-9). Lexington Bks.

Distributed System Environment. Grayce M. Booth. (Illus.). 288p. 1980. 21.95 (ISBN 0-07-006507-1, P&RB). McGraw.

Distribution, Allocation, Social Structure & Spatial Form: Elements of Planning Theory. Juval Portugali. (Progress in Planning: Vol. 14, Part 3). (Illus.). 83p. 1980. pap. 13.50 (ISBN 0-08-026808-0). Pergamon.

Distribution & Biogeography of Mammals of Iowa. John B. Bowles. (Special Publications: No. 9). (Illus., Orig.). 1975. pap. 8.00 (ISBN 0-89672-034-9). Tex Tech Pr.

Distribution & Ecology of Radiolaria in the Central Pacific-Plankton & Surface Sediments. G. W. Renz. (Bulletin of the Scripps Institution of Oceanography: Vol. 22). 1976. pap. 14.00x (ISBN 0-520-09533-2). U of Cal Pr.

Distribution & Transportation Handbook. Harry J. Bruce. LC 76-132669. (Illus.). 1971. 17.50 (ISBN 0-8436-1400-5). CBI Pub.

Distribution of Consumer Goods. T. S. Ward. LC 73-84321. (Dept. of Applied Economics, Occasional Papers: No. 38). (Illus.). 250p. 1973. 32.95 (ISBN 0-521-20145-4); pap. 14.95 (ISBN 0-521-09791-6). Cambridge U Pr.

Distribution of Farm Subsidies: Who Gets the Benefits? Charles L. Schultze. 1971. pap. 2.00 (ISBN 0-8157-7753-1). Brookings.

Distribution of Income & Wealth: Theory & Evidence for Ontario. Charles M. Beach et al. (Ontario Economic Council Research Studies). 1981. pap. 17.50 (ISBN 0-8020-3369-5). U of Toronto Pr.

Distribution of Income Between Persons. D. G. Champernowne. LC 73-75859. (Illus.). 316p. 1973. 47.50 (ISBN 0-521-08546-2). Cambridge U Pr.

Distribution of Personal Income in the United Kingdom, 1949-1963. Thomas Stark. LC 72-160099. (Illus.). 1972. 34.50 (ISBN 0-521-08258-7). Cambridge U Pr.

Distribution of Personal Wealth in Britain. A. B. Atkinson & A. J. Harrison. LC 77-2715. 1978. 41.50 (ISBN 0-521-21735-0). Cambridge U Pr.

Distribution of Prime Numbers: Large Sieves & Zero-Density Theorems. M. N. Huxley. (Oxford Mathematical Monographs). (Illus.). 145p. 1972. text ed. 37.50x (ISBN 0-19-853518-X). Oxford U Pr.

Distribution of Rural Incomes in China: A Comparison of the 1930's & 1950's. Charles R. Roll, Jr. LC 78-74301. (Modern Chinese Economy Ser.: Vol. 13). 223p. 1980. lib. bdg. 22.00 (ISBN 0-8240-4288-3). Garland Pub.

Distribution of the Human Immunoglobulin Allotypes. Arthur G. Steinberg & Charles E. Cook. (Illus.). 272p. 1981. text ed. 65.00x (ISBN 0-19-261181-X). Oxford U Pr.

Distribution of the Size of the Maximum Cluster of Points on a Line. Norman D. Neff & Joseph I. Naus. LC 74-6283. (Selected Tables in Mathematical Statistics: Vol. 6). 1980. 12.80 (ISBN 0-8218-1906-2). Am Math.

Distribution of the Tax Burden. Edgar K. Browning & William R. Johnson. 1979. pap. 4.25 (ISBN 0-8447-3349-0). Am Enterprise.

Distribution of Zeros of Entire Functions. rev. ed. Boris J. Levin. LC 63-15661. (Translations of Mathematical Monographs: Vol. 5). 1980. 27.60 (ISBN 0-8218-4505-5, MMONO-5). Am Math.

Distribution Planning & Control. Martin Christopher et al. LC 77-378813. 1979. 19.95 (ISBN 0-566-02013-0, 00314-X, Pub. by Saxon Hse England). Lexington Bks.

Distribution Research. Tim Cannon. 1973. pap. text ed. 11.00x (ISBN 0-7002-0232-3). Intl Ideas.

Distribution Sampling for Computer Simulation. Theodore G. Lewis. LC 74-25058. 128p. 1975. 19.95 (ISBN 0-669-97139-1). Lexington Bks.

Distribution Systems: Actions & Innovations. American Water Works Association. (General Handbooks). (Illus.). 256p. 1980. pap. text ed. 20.00 (ISBN 0-89867-246-5). Am Water Wks Assn.

Distributional Effects of Public Expenditure. Vera Morris. 176p. 1980. 21.50x (ISBN 0-86003-030-X, Pub. by Allan Pubs England); pap. 10.50x (ISBN 0-86003-129-2). State Mutual Bk.

Distributional History of the Biota of the Southern Appalachians, 3 vols. Ed. by Perry C. Holt et al. Incl. Pt. 1. Invertebrates. 1969. pap. 4.95x (ISBN 0-8139-0538-9); Pt 2. Flora. 1970. pap. 5.95x (ISBN 0-8139-0539-7); Pt 3. Vertebrates. 1971. pap. 5.95x o.p. (ISBN 0-8139-0540-0); Pt. 4, Algae & Fungi. Ed. by Bruce C. Parker & Martha K. Roane. LC 75-636021. 1977. 20.00x (ISBN 0-8139-0660-1). Set, Pt. I-III. 15.00x o.p. (ISBN 0-685-56113-5). U Pr of Va.

Distributions in Statistics: Continuous Multivariate Distributions. Norman L. Johnson & Samuel Kotz. LC 72-1342. (Probability & Statistics Ser.). 368p. 1972. 33.95 (ISBN 0-471-44370-0, Pub. by Wiley-Interscience). Wiley.

Distributive Education Teacher-Coordinators' Handbook. Ed. by Carroll B. Coakley. LC 77-190664. 190p. 1972. pap. text ed. 4.25x o.p. (ISBN 0-8134-1467-9, 1467). Interstate.

Distributive Justice: A Constructive Critique of the Utilitarian Theory of Distribution. Nicholas Rescher. LC 66-29532. 1966. 18.50x (ISBN 0-672-60711-5); pap. text ed. 8.95x (ISBN 0-89197-733-3). Irvington.

Distributive System. S. R. Hill. 1966. 15.00 (ISBN 0-08-011738-4); pap. 7.00 (ISBN 0-08-011737-6). Pergamon.

District Administration in Metropolitan Calcutta. Frank J. Tysen. 3.25x o.p. (ISBN 0-210-27116-7). Asia.

District Heating Thermal Generation & Distribution. MacKenzie. 1979. text ed. 37.00 (ISBN 0-08-022711-2). Pergamon.

District Magistrate in Late Imperial China. John R. Watt. LC 79-187299. (East Asian Institute Ser). 384p. 1972. 20.00x (ISBN 0-231-03535-7). Columbia U Pr.

District of Columbia. 23.00 (ISBN 0-89770-084-8). Curriculum Info Ctr.

District of Columbia. Kay Lumley. (Young People's Stories of Our States Ser.). (Illus.). 48p. (gr. 2-5). 1981. PLB 8.65g (ISBN 0-516-03951-2, Time Line). Childrens.

District of Columbia: A Bicentennial History. David L. Lewis. (States & the Nation Ser.). (Illus.). 1976. 12.95 (ISBN 0-393-05601-5, Co-Pub by AASLH). Norton.

Distrust & Democracy. Vivien Hart. LC 77-84803. (Illus.). 1978. 27.50 (ISBN 0-521-21857-8). Cambridge U Pr.

Disturb Not the Dream. Paula Trachtman. Ed. by Brandt Aymar. 320p. 1981. 11.95 (ISBN 0-517-54322-2). Crown.

Disturbances in Lipid & Lipoprotein Metabolism. American Physiological Society. Ed. by John M. Dietschy. (American Physiological Society Monograph Ser.). 1978. 25.00 (ISBN 0-683-02557-0). Williams & Wilkins.

Disturbances of Amino Acid Metabolism: Clinical Chemistry & Diagnosis. Hans J. Bremer et al. LC 78-31995. (Illus.). 430p. 1981. text ed. 54.00 (ISBN 0-8067-0251-6). Urban & S.

Disturbances of Water & Electrolyte Metabolism. Ed. by J. Bahlmann & J. Brod. (Contributions to Nephrology Ser.: Vol. 21). (Illus.). 1980. soft cover 45.00 (ISBN 3-8055-0215-X). S Karger.

Disturbed Child: Recognition & Psychoeducational Therapy in the Classroom. Pearl H. Berkowitz & Esther P. Rothman. LC 60-6418. 1960. 12.00x (ISBN 0-8147-0040-3). NYU Pr.

Disturbed Communication. Jurgen Ruesch. 1972. pap. 4.95 o.p. (ISBN 0-393-00634-4, Norton Lib). Norton.

Disturbing the Universe. Freeman Dyson. LC 78-20665. 304p. 1981. pap. 4.95 (ISBN 0-06-090771-1, CN 771, CN). Har-Row.

Ditado. Ildazio Tavares. (Bi-Lingual Port. -Eng.). 1981. pap. 1.50. Ghost Dance.

Ditch Diggers. Jacinta Reid. 1979. 6.95 o.p. (ISBN 0-533-03777-8). Vantage.

Dittersdorfiana. Carl Krebs. LC 72-166092. (Music Ser.). 1972. Repr. of 1900 ed. lib. bdg. 19.50 (ISBN 0-306-70259-2). Da Capo.

Div, Grad, Curl & All That: An Informal Text on Vector Calculus. Harry M. Schey. (Illus.). 150p. 1973. pap. text ed. 5.95x (ISBN 0-393-09367-0). Norton.

Diva: The Life & Death of Maria Callas. Steven Linakis. LC 80-18919. 1980. 10.95 (ISBN 0-13-216572-4). P-H.

Divan & Other Writings. Federico G. Lorca & Edward Honig. (Illus.). 1977. pap. 4.50 (ISBN 0-914278-14-2). Copper Beech.

Divan of Manuchihri Damghani: A Critical Study. Jerome W. Clinton. LC 72-87873. (Studies in Middle Eastern Literatures Ser: No. 1). 1972. pap. 15.00x (ISBN 0-88297-001-1). Bibliotheca.

Divani Nurbakhsh: Sufi Poetry. Javad Nurbaksh. Ed. by Jeffrey Rothschild & Paul Weber. Tr. by Alan Godlas & Leonard Lewisohn. 280p. 1980. 9.95 (ISBN 0-933546-04-1). Khaniqahi-Nimatullahi.

Dive In. Mike Neigoff. LC 65-23885. (Pilot Book Ser). (Illus.). (gr. 3-5). 1965. 6.95g (ISBN 0-8075-1644-9). A Whitman.

Dive in the Sun. Douglas Reeman. 240p. 1981. pap. 2.50 (ISBN 0-515-05876-9). Jove Pubns.

Dive: The Complete Book of Skin Diving. rev. ed. Rick Carrier & Barbara Carrier. Ed. by Charles Berlitz. LC 73-4513. (Funk & W Bk.). (Illus.). 304p. 1973. 7.95 o.s.i. (ISBN 0-308-10056-5, TYC-T). T Y Crowell.

Divergent Series. Godfrey H. Hardy. 1949. 42.00x (ISBN 0-19-853309-8). Oxford U Pr.

Divergent Series; Asymptotic Series, 2 Vols. in 1. Walter B. Ford. LC 60-16836. 14.95 (ISBN 0-8284-0143-8). Chelsea Pub.

Divergent Views in Psychiatry. Maurice Dongier & Eric D. Wittkower. (Illus.). Date not set. text ed. price not set (ISBN 0-06-140695-3, Harper Medical). Har-Row.

Diverging Parallels: A Comparison of American & European Thought & Actions. Ed. by A. Den Hollander. 222p. 1971. text ed. 28.00x (ISBN 90-0402-635-5). Humanities.

Divers & Diving. Reginald Vallintine. (Illus.). 176p. 1981. 12.95 (ISBN 0-7137-0855-7, Pub. by Blandford Pr England); pap. 6.95 (ISBN 0-7137-1128-0). Sterling.

Diver's Handbook of Underwater Calculations. Wayne C. Tucker. (Illus.). 1980. pap. 10.00x (ISBN 0-87033-254-6, 2546). Cornell Maritime.

Diversification & Competition. M. A. Utton. LC 79-11664. (NIESR, Occasional Papers Ser.: No. 31). 1979. 18.95 (ISBN 0-521-22725-9). Cambridge U Pr.

Diversions by the Wayside. K. D. Katrak. 23p. 1975. 8.00 (ISBN 0-88253-528-5); pap. text ed. 4.80 (ISBN 0-88253-527-7). Ind-US Inc.

Diversions of a Westerner: With Emphasis Upon Owen Wister's & Frederic Remington's Books & Libraries. N. Orwin Rush. LC 78-53134. (Illus.). 224p. 1979. 10.00 (ISBN 0-932068-05-7). South Pass Pr.

Diversity, Accessibility & Quality: A Brief Introduction to American Education for Non-Americans. Clifford F. Sjogren. (Illus., Orig.). 1977. pap. 2.00 o.p. (ISBN 0-87447-036-6, 221620). College Bd.

Diversity & Choice in Higher Education. A. G. Watts. 1972. 22.50x (ISBN 0-7100-7400-X). Routledge & Kegan.

Diversity & Unity in Education. Ed. by Brian Holmes. 176p. 1980. text ed. 25.00 (ISBN 0-04-370094-2). Allen Unwin.

Diversity in International Communism: A Documentary Record. Ed. by Alexander Dallin et al. LC 62-21515. (Orig.). 1963. pap. 15.00x (ISBN 0-231-08611-3). Columbia U Pr.

Diversity of Bacterial Respiratory Systems, 2 vols. Christopher J. Knowles. (Vol. 1-256pp., vol. 2-240pp.). 1980. 59.95 ea. Vol. 1 (ISBN 0-8493-5399-8). Vol. 2 (ISBN 0-8493-5400-5). CRC Pr.

Diversity of Insect Faunas: Symposium. Royal Entomological Society of London, Ninth. Ed. by L. A. Mound & N. Waloff. 1979. 43.95 (ISBN 0-470-26544-2). Halsted Pr.

Diverticular Disease of the Colon. Bentley P. Colcock. LC 79-158398. (Major Problems in Clinical Surgery: Vol. 11). (Illus.). 1971. 12.50 (ISBN 0-7216-2636-X). Saunders.

Diverting Adventures of Tom Thumb. Barry Wilkinson. LC 74-140867. (Illus.). (gr. 3-6). 1969. 4.95 o.p. (ISBN 0-15-201620-1, HJ). HarBraceJ.

Dives & Pauper, Vol. I, Pt. 2. Ed. by Priscilla H. Barnum. (Early English Text Society Original Ser.). (Illus.). 400p. 1980. 29.50 (ISBN 0-19-722282-X). Oxford U Pr.

Divide. William Overgard. pap. 2.50 (ISBN 0-515-05492-5). Jove Pubns.

Divide & Conquer or Life Among the Left Overs. Marjory V. Maud. (Illus.). 1981. 9.95 (ISBN 0-938562-00-2). Single Impressionns.

Divided Academy: Professors & Politics. Carnegie Commission on Higher Education & Everett C. Ladd. LC 74-17247. (Illus.). 407p. 1975. 19.95 o.p. (ISBN 0-07-010112-4, P&RB). McGraw.

Divided Children. Ed. by Michael Wheeler. 223p. 1981. pap. 4.95 (ISBN 0-14-005777-3). Penguin.

Divided Consciousness: Multiple Controls in Human Thought & Action. Ernest R. Hilgard. LC 77-7925. (Wiley Ser. in Behavior). 1977. 24.95 (ISBN 0-471-39602-8, Pub. by Wiley-Interscience). Wiley.

Divided Loyalties: British Regional Assertion & European Integration. Ed. by Martin Kolinsky & D. S. Bell. 1978. text ed. 33.50x (ISBN 0-7190-0694-5). Humanities.

Divided Mind: Studies in Defoe & Richardson. Sudesh Vaid. 1979. text ed. 17.50x (ISBN 0-210-40619-4). Asia.

Divided Nation: The Roots of a Bourgeois Thinker, G. W. F. Hegel. Jose-Maria Ripalda. (Dialectic & Society: No. 3). 1977. text ed. 31.25x (ISBN 90-232-1514-1). Humanities.

Divided School. Peter E. Woods. (Education Bks). 1979. 25.00x (ISBN 0-7100-0124-X). Routledge & Kegan.

Divided We Fall. James E. Smith. LC 79-67439. 96p. (Orig.). 1980. pap. 1.95 (ISBN 0-87239-381-X, 40086). Standard Pub.

Divided We Stand: The Crisis of a Frontierless Democracy. Walter P. Webb. LC 79-1598. 1981. Repr. of 1944 ed. 16.00 (ISBN 0-88355-903-X). Hyperion Conn.

Dividing & Reuniting of America. George McJimsey. LC 80-68811. (Orig.). 1981. pap. text ed. 7.95x (ISBN 0-88273-108-4). Forum Pr MO.

Dividing Head & Deluxe Accessories. David J. Gingery. LC 80-66142. (Build Your Own Metal Working Shop from Scrap: Bk. 6). (Illus.). 112p. (Orig.). 1981. pap. 7.95 (ISBN 0-9604330-5-8). D J Gingery.

Dividing the Waters: A Century of Controversy Between the United States & Mexico. Norris Hundley, Jr. 1966. 18.50x (ISBN 0-520-00586-4). U of Cal Pr.

Dividing the Wealth. Howard E. Kershner. 1980. pap. 4.95 (ISBN 0-8159-5308-9). Devin.

Divinas Palabras. Inclan Del Valle. Tr. by T. Faulkner from Span. (National Theatre Plays Ser.). 1977. pap. text ed. 5.75 o.p. (ISBN 0-435-23425-0). Heinemann Ed.

Divination of Disease. H. Tomlinson. 1980. 9.50x (ISBN 0-8464-1006-0). Beekman Pubs.

Divine Analogy: A Study of the Creation Motif in Blake & Coleridge. Warren Stevenson. (Salzburg Studies in English Literature, Romantic Reassessment: No. 25). 403p. 1972. pap. text ed. 25.00x (ISBN 0-391-01534-6). Humanities.

Divine & Sacred Catechism. Apostolos Makrakis. Ed. by Orthodox Christian Educational Society. 224p. 1946. 4.00x (ISBN 0-938366-15-7). Orthodox Chr.

Divine Art of Living: Selections from Writings of Baha'u'llah & Abdu'l-Baha. 4th rev. ed. Baha'u'llah & Abdu'l-Baha. LC 77-27001. 1979. pap. 3.00 (ISBN 0-87743-123-X, 7-15-23). Baha'i.

Divine Banquet of the Brain. Macdonald Critchley. LC 78-24621. 1979. text ed. 19.50 (ISBN 0-89004-348-5). Raven.

Divine Comedy. Dante Alighieri. Tr. by J. B. Fletcher. 1951. 27.50x (ISBN 0-231-01806-1, A51-9849). Columbia U Pr.

Divine Comedy. rev. ed. Dante Alighieri. Tr. by Geoffrey Bickersteth from It. 805p. 1972. 22.50x (ISBN 0-87471-295-5). Rowman.

Divine Comedy: The Inferno, Vol. 1. Dante Aligieri. Tr. by Charles S. Singleton from Italian. LC 68-57090. (Bollingen Ser: Lxxx). (Illus.). 1088p. (Bilingual ed.). 1980. pap. 12.50 (ISBN 0-691-01832-4). Princeton U Pr.

Divine Command Morality: Historical & Contemporary Readings. Janine Marie Idziak. (Texts & Studies in Religion: Vol. 5). 1980. soft cover 24.95x (ISBN 0-88946-969-5). E Mellen.

Divine Commands & Morality. Ed. by Paul Helm. (Readings in Philosophy Ser.). 192p. 1981. pap. 11.50 (ISBN 0-19-875049-8). Oxford U Pr.

Divine Consolation of the Blessed Angela Da Foligno. Angela Da Foligno. Tr. by M. G. Steegman. LC 66-30731. (Medieval Library). (Illus.). 265p. 1966. Repr. of 1926 ed. 22.50x (ISBN 0-8154-0072-1). Cooper Sq.

Divine Cordial. Thomas Watson. (Summit Ser.). 96p. 1981. pap. 2.45 (ISBN 0-8010-9646-4). Baker Bk.

Divine Dancer: Abiography of Ruth St. Denis. Suzanne Shelton. LC 80-2442. (Illus.). 312p. 1981. 14.95 (ISBN 0-385-14159-9). Doubleday.

Divine Hierarchy: Popular Hinduism in Central India. Lawrence A. Babb. (Illus.). 272p. 1975. 17.50x (ISBN 0-231-03882-8). Columbia U Pr.

Divine-Human Encounter: A Study of Abraham Joshua Heschel. Harold Kasimow. LC 79-63562. 1979. pap. text ed. 7.75 (ISBN 0-8191-0731-X). U Pr of Amer.

Divine Imagination: William Blake's Major Prophetic Visions. Ronald L. Grimes. LC 72-6437. (ATLA Monograph: No. 1). 1972. 10.00 (ISBN 0-8108-0539-1). Scarecrow.

Divine Legation of Moses, 4 vols. 2nd ed. Ed. by Rene Wellek. LC 75-11264. (British Philosophers & Theologians of the 17th & 18th Centuries Ser.: Vol. 62). 1978. Set. lib. bdg. 168.00 (ISBN 0-8240-1813-3); lib. bdg. 42.00 ea. Garland Pub.

Divine Life. Swami Yatiswarananda. 1935. 2.25 o.p. (ISBN 0-87481-442-1). Vedanta Pr.

Divine Luminous Wisdom That Dispels the Darkness God-Man Man-God. rev. ed. M. R. Bawa Muhaiyaddeen. (Illus.). 288p. 1977. pap. 5.95 (ISBN 0-914390-12-0). Fellowship Pr PA.

Divine Milieu: An Essay on the Interior Life. Pierre Teilhard De Chardin. pap. 3.95 (ISBN 0-06-090487-9, CN487, CN). Har-Row.

Divine Origin of the Craft of the Herbalist. E. A. Wallis Budge. LC 78-174013. (Illus.). 1971. Repr. of 1928 ed. 18.00 (ISBN 0-8103-3794-0). Gale.

Divine Overruling. W. Sanday. 112p. Repr. of 1920 ed. 2.95 (ISBN 0-567-02225-0). Attic Pr.

Divine Pastime: Theatre Essays. Harold Clurman. LC 73-10561. 352p. 1974. 7.95 o.s.i. (ISBN 0-02-526150-9). Macmillan.

Divine Physical Healing, Past & Present. 272p. pap. 2.50. Faith Pub Hse.

Divine Physician. rev. ed. William B. Ward. LC 53-11762. (Orig.). 1957. pap. 2.95 (ISBN 0-8042-2316-5). John Knox.

Divine Plan: Commentary on the Secret Doctrine. 3rd ed. Geoffrey Barborka. 1972. 11.95 (ISBN 0-8356-7167-4). Theos Pub Hse.

Divine Poems. 2nd ed. John Donne. Ed. by Helen Gardner. (Oxford English Texts). 1979. 37.50x (ISBN 0-19-812745-6). Oxford U Pr.

Divine Poetry & Drama in Sixteenth-Century England. Lily B. Campbell. LC 59-3609. 1972. 16.75xx o.p. (ISBN 0-520-02108-8). U of Cal Pr.

Divine Proportion: A Study in Mathematical Beauty. H. E. Huntley. LC 70-93195. (Orig.). 1970. pap. text ed. 3.00 (ISBN 0-486-22254-3). Dover.

Divine Rebel: The Life of Anne Marbury Hutchinson. Selma R. Williams. LC 80-20109. 256p. 1981. 12.95 (ISBN 0-03-055846-8). HR&W.

Divine Sovereignty & Human Responsibility: Biblical Perspectives in Tension. D. A. Carson. Ed. by Peter Toon & Ralph Martin. LC 79-27589. (New Foundations Theological Library). 228p. 1981. 18.50 (ISBN 0-8042-3707-7); pap. 9.95 (ISBN 0-8042-3727-1). John Knox.

Divine Struggle for Human Salvation: Biblical Convictions in Their Historical Settings. Andrew C Tunyogi. LC 78-65852. 1979. pap. text ed. 15.50 (ISBN 0-8191-0676-3). U Pr of Amer.

Divine Trap: Background on the Parables, Ser. A. Richard C. Hoefler. 168p. (Orig.). 1980. pap. 5.70 (ISBN 0-89536-445-X). CSS Pub.

Divine Weeks & Works of Guillaume de Saluste, Sieur du Bartas, 2 vols. Guillaume De Saluste & Sieur Du Bartas. Ed. by Susan Synder. Tr. by Joshua Sylvester. (Oxford English Texts Ser.). (Illus.). 964p. 1979. text ed. 98.00x (ISBN 0-19-812717-0). Oxford U Pr.

Divine Woman: Dragon Ladies & Rain Maidens in T'ang Literature. Edward H. Schafer. 250p. 1980. pap. 7.50 (ISBN 0-86547-009-X). N Point Pr.

Divine Yes. E. Stanley Jones. 1976. pap. 1.50 (ISBN 0-89129-154-7). Jove Pubns.

Diving Companions: Sea Lion-Elephant Seal-Walrus. Jacques Y. Cousteau & Philippe Diole. LC 73-20508. (Undersea Discoveries of Jacques-Yves Cousteau). (Illus.). 1977. pap. 8.95 (ISBN 0-89104-078-1). A & W Pubs.

Diving Companions: Sea-Lion-Elephant Seal-Walrus. Jacques-Yves Cousteau & Philippe Diole. LC 73-20508. 304p. 1974. 12.95 o.p. (ISBN 0-385-00031-6). Doubleday.

Diving Complete. George Rackham. (Illus.). 232p. 1976. 18.00 (ISBN 0-571-10342-1). Transatlantic.

Diving, Cutting & Welding in Underwater Salvage Operations. Frank E. Thompson, Jr. LC 70-92687. (Illus.). 1944. pap. 4.00x (ISBN 0-87033-139-6). Cornell Maritime.

Diving Deep & Surfacing: Women Writers on Spiritual Quest. Carol P. Christ. LC 79-51153. 176p. 1980. pap. 4.95 (ISBN 0-8070-6363-0, BP 609). Beacon Pr.

Diving for Sunken Treasure. Jacques-Yves Cousteau & Philippe Diole. LC 76-158349. 1972. 12.95 o.p. (ISBN 0-385-06894-8). Doubleday.

Diving for Sunken Treasure. Jacques-Yves Cousteau & Philippe Diole. (Underseas Discoveries of Jacques-Yves Cousteau). (Illus.). 1978. pap. 8.95 (ISBN 0-89104-110-9). A & W Pubs.

Diving West. rev. ed. John A. Fulton & Steven M. Gordon. (Updated Every 2 to 4 Years Ser.). (Illus.). 96p. (Orig.). 1980. pap. 4.95 (ISBN 0-938206-01-X). ChartGuide.

Divinity & Experience: The Religion of the Dinka. Godfrey Lienhardt. 1961. 37.50x (ISBN 0-19-823119-9). Oxford U Pr.

Divinity of Marriage. D. Coffey Parker. 1980. 5.00. D C Parker.

Divinity of Our Lord. Henry P. Liddon. 1978. 20.25 (ISBN 0-686-12948-2). Klock & Klock.

Division. K. Wehrli. (Michigan Arithmetric Program Ser.). (gr. 4). 1976. wkbk. 7.00 (ISBN 0-89039-180-7). Ann Arbor Pubs.

Division & the Stresses of Reunion: 1845-1876. David M. Potter. 240p. 1973. pap. 7.95x (ISBN 0-673-05786-0). Scott F.

Division of Labor in Society. Emile Durkheim. 1947. 14.95 (ISBN 0-02-907840-7); pap. text ed. 7.95 (ISBN 0-02-907850-4). Free Pr.

Division of Labour: The Labour Process & Class-Struggle in Modern Capitalism. Ed. by Andre Gorz. Tr. by John Mepham et al from Fr. (Marxist Theory & Contemporary Capitalism 2 Ser.). 208p. 1976. 12.50x (ISBN 0-85527-124-8); pap. text ed. 10.00x (ISBN 0-85527-781-5). Humanities.

Division Officer's Guide. 7th ed. John V. Noel, Jr. LC 75-39931. 224p. 1976. 9.95x (ISBN 0-87021-160-9). Naval Inst Pr.

Division 1 - Nuclear Power Plant Components: General Reguirements. (Boiler & Pressure Vessel Code Ser.: Sec. 3). 1977. 45.00 o.p. (ISBN 0-685-76798-1, R0003R); pap. 70.00 loose-leaf o.p. (ISBN 0-685-76799-X, W0003R). ASME.

Division 1 - Nuclear Power Plant Components: General Requirements. (Boiler & Pressure Vessel Code Ser.: Sec. 3). 1980. 55.00 (P0003R); pap. 80.00 loose-leaf (V0003R). ASME.

Division 1: Appendices. (Boiler & Pressure Vessel Code Ser.: Sec. 3). 1977. 100.00 o.p. (ISBN 0-685-76812-0, R0003A); pap. 75.00 loose-leaf o.p. (ISBN 0-685-76813-9, W0003A). ASME.

Division 1: Appendices. (Boiler & Pressure Vessel Code Ser.: Sec. 3). 1980. 100.00 (P0003A); pap. 125.00 loose-leaf (V0003A). ASME.

Division 1: Subsection NB-Class 1 Components. (Boiler & Pressure Vessel Code Ser.: Sec. 3). 1977. 60.00 o.p. (ISBN 0-685-76800-7, R0003B); pap. 90.00 loose-leaf o.p. (ISBN 0-685-76801-5, W0003B). ASME.

Division 1: Subsection NB-Class 1 Components. (Boiler & Pressure Vessel Code Ser.: Sec. 3). 1980. 70.00 (P0003B); pap. 100.00 loose-leaf (V0003B). ASME.

Division 1: Subsection NC-Class 2 Components. (Boiler & Pressure Vessel Code Ser.: Sec. 3). 1977. 60.00 o.p. (ISBN 0-685-76802-3, R0003C); pap. 90.00 loose-leaf o.p. (ISBN 0-685-76803-1, W0003C). ASME.

Division 1: Subsection NC-Class 2 Components. (Boiler & Pressure Vessel Code Ser.: Sec. 3). 1980. 70.00 (P0003C); pap. 100.00 loose-leaf (V0003C). ASME.

Division 1: Subsection ND-Class 3 Components. (Boiler & Pressure Vessel Code Ser.: Sec. 3). 1977. 60.00 o.p. (ISBN 0-685-76804-X, R0003D); pap. 90.00 loose-leaf o.p. (ISBN 0-685-76805-8, W0003D). ASME.

Division 1: Subsection ND-Class 3 Components. (Boiler & Pressure Vessel Code Ser.: Sec. 3). 1980. 70.00 (P0003D); pap. 100.00 loose-leaf (V0003D). ASME.

Division 1: Subsection NE-Class MC Components. (Boiler & Pressure Vessel Code Ser.: Sec. 3). 1977. bound-edition 60.00 o.p. (ISBN 0-685-76806-6, R0003E); pap. 90.00 loose-leaf o.p. (ISBN 0-685-76807-4, W0003E). ASME.

Division 1: Subsection NE Class MC Components. (Boiler & Pressure Vessel Code Ser.: Sec. 3). 1980. bound edition 70.00 (P0003E); pap. 100.00 loose-leaf (P0003E). ASME.

Division 1: Subsection NF-Component Supports. (Boiler & Pressure Vessel Code Ser.: Sec. 3). 1977. 35.00 o.p. (ISBN 0-685-76808-2, R0003F); pap. 45.00 loose-leaf o.p. (ISBN 0-685-76809-0, W0003F). ASME.

Division 1: Subsection NF-Component Supports. (Boiler & Pressure Vessel Code Ser.: Sec. 3). 1980. 55.00 (P0003F); pap. 65.00 loose-leaf (V0003F). ASME.

Division 1: Subsection NG-Core Support Structures. (Boiler & Pressure Vessel Code Ser.: Sec. 3). 1977. 45.00 o.p. (ISBN 0-685-76810-4, R0003G); pap. 75.00 loose-leaf o.p. (ISBN 0-685-76811-2, W0003G). ASME.

Division 1: Subsection NG-Core Support Structures. (Boiler & Pressure Vessel Code Ser.: Sec. 3). 1980. 55.00 (P0003G); pap. 65.00 loose-leaf (V0003G). ASME.

Division 2-Code for Concrete Reactor Vessels & Containments. (Boiler & Pressure Vessel Code Ser.: Sec. 3). 1977. 80.00 o.p. (ISBN 0-685-76814-7, R00032); pap. 110.00 loose-leaf o.p. (ISBN 0-685-76815-5, W00032). ASME.

Division 2-Code for Concrete Reactor Vessels & Containments. (Boiler & Pressure Vessel Code Ser.: Sec. 3). 1980. 90.00 (P00032); pap. 125.00 loose-leaf (V00032). ASME.

Divisional Performance: Measurement & Control. David Solomons. 1968. pap. text ed. 10.50 (ISBN 0-256-00529-X). Irwin.

Divisions-Two. Martin J. Rosenblum. LC 77-95158. (Orig.). 1981. pap. 8.00 (ISBN 0-89018-006-7). Lionhead Pub.

Divorce. Ann S. Smith. LC 78-10464. (First Bks.). (gr. 4 up). 1979. PLB 6.45 s&l (ISBN 0-531-02254-4). Watts.

Divorce: A Selected Annotated Bibliography. Mary McKenney. LC 74-22423. 1974. 10.00 (ISBN 0-8108-0777-7). Scarecrow.

Divorce & Annulment in the Fifty States. rev. ed. Michael F. Mayer. LC 74-24800. (Know Your Law Bks.). 1975. pap. 1.45 o.p. (ISBN 0-668-01437-7). Arc Bks.

Divorce & Remarriage. Guy Duty. LC 96-2485. 1967. 6.95 (ISBN 0-87123-097-6, 230097). Bethany Fell.

Divorce & Remarriage: Are Non-Christians Amenable to the Law of Christ? Thomas B. Warren. 1977. pap. 3.95 (ISBN 0-934916-30-6). Natl Christian Pr.

Divorce & Remarriage for Catholics. Stephen J. Kelleher. LC 75-17075. 160p. 1976. pap. 1.75 o.p. (ISBN 0-385-11371-4, Im). Doubleday.

Divorce & Remarriage in the Church. Stanley A. Ellison. 160p. 1980. pap. 3.95 (ISBN 0-310-35561-3). Zondervan.

Divorce & the American Family. Jan Andrew. (gr. 7 up). 1978. PLB 7.45 (ISBN 0-531-01470-3). Watts.

Divorce & the Roman Doctrine of Nullity. R. H. Charles. 100p. 1927. text ed. 2.95 (ISBN 0-567-22067-2). Attic Pr.

Divorce & You. W. T. Winter. 1963. 2.50 o.s.i. (ISBN 0-02-630540-2). Macmillan.

Divorce, Child Custody & the Family, Vol. 10. Gap Committee on the Family. LC 80-25935. (Publications Ser.: No. 106). 1980. pap. 12.95 (ISBN 0-910958-10-6, 106, Mental Health Materials Center). Adv Psychiatry.

Divorce Dirty Tricks. R. H. Morrison. 248p. 1980. 9.95 (ISBN 0-8119-0408-3, Pegasus Rex). Fell.

Divorce Dirty Tricks. R. H. Morrison. 265p. 1980. 9.95 (ISBN 0-937484-03-2). Pegasus Rex NJ.

Divorce: How & When to Let Go. J. & N. Adam. 9.95 (ISBN 0-13-216416-7); pap. 4.95 (ISBN 0-13-216408-6). P-H.

Divorce in the Parsonage. Mary La Grand Bouma. LC 79-16157. 1979. pap. 3.95 (ISBN 0-87123-109-3, 210109). Bethany Fell.

Divorce in the United States, Canada, & Great Britain: A Guide to Information Sources. Ed. by Kenneth D. Sell & Betty Sell. LC 78-15894. (Social Issues & Social Problems Information Guide Ser.: Vol. 1). 1978. 30.00 (ISBN 0-8103-1396-0). Gale.

Divorce Is a Grown up Problem. Janet Sinberg. 1978. pap. 2.95 (ISBN 0-380-01901-9, 37333). Avon.

Divorce Is a Kid's Coloring Book. Ken Magid & Walt Schreibman. LC 80-80436. (Illus.). 62p. 1980. pap. 4.95 (ISBN 0-88289-276-2). Pelican.

Divorce Mediation. Howard I. Irving. LC 80-54399. 216p. 1981. 11.95 (ISBN 0-87663-351-3). Universe.

Divorce Mediation: A/Practical Guide for Therapists & Counselors. John M. Haynes. LC 80-25065. 1981. text ed. 17.95 (ISBN 0-8261-2590-5); pap. text ed. price not set (ISBN 0-8261-2591-3). Springer Pub.

Divorce or Marriage: A Legal Guide. Howard L. Bass & M. L. Rein. 1976. 9.95 o.p. (ISBN 0-685-67125-9, Spec). P-H.

Divorce-Texas Style. Elayne S. Tatar. Date not set. price not set (ISBN 0-89896-060-6). Larksdale.

Divorce Won't Help. Edmund Bergler. 1978. 12.95 (ISBN 0-87140-635-7); pap. 3.95 (ISBN 0-87140-124-X). Liveright.

Divry's English-To-Greek Phrase & Conversation Pronouncing Manual. George C. Divry. 1966. flexible bdg. 5.00 (ISBN 0-685-09027-2). Divry.

Divry's Greek-English Dialogues. D. C. Divry. 1947. pocket ed. 5.00 (ISBN 0-685-09028-0). Divry.

Divry's New Self Taught English Method for Greeks. George C. Divry. 1956. 5.00 (ISBN 0-685-09032-9). Divry.

Divus Julius Caesar. Suetonius. Ed. by H. E. Butler & M. Cary. 1927. 13.95x (ISBN 0-19-814418-0). Oxford U Pr.

Diwan 'Abdallah ibn al Mu'tazz. Tr. by Arthur Wormhoudt from Arabic. (Arab Translation Ser.: No. 38). 1978. pap. 6.50 (ISBN 0-916358-88-7). Wormhoudt.

Diwan Al Gazal: Love Poems by Abu Nuwas & Abu Tammam. Tr. by Arthur Wormhoudt from Arabic. (Arab Translation Ser.: No. 48). 180p. 1980. pap. 6.50 (ISBN 0-916358-98-4). Wormhoudt.

Diwan al Mutanabbi, Farsiyyat. Tr. by Arthur Wormhoudt from Arabic. (Arab Translation Ser.: No. 37). 1978. pap. 6.50 (ISBN 0-916358-87-9). Wormhoudt.

Diwan al Mutanabbi, Misriyyat. Tr. by Arthur Wormhoudt from Arabic. (Arab Translation Ser.: No. 36). 1978. pap. 6.50 (ISBN 0-916358-86-0). Wormhoudt.

Diwan al Mutanabbi: Selections. Tr. by Arthur Wormhoudt from Arabic. (Arab Translation Ser.: No. 1). 1968. pap. 2.50 (ISBN 0-916358-51-8). Wormhoudt.

Diwan al Mutanabbi, Shawmiyyat, 3 pts. Tr. by Arthur Wormhoudt from Arabic. (Arab Translation Ser.: No. 31-33). 1978. pap. 6.50 ea. Pt. 1 (ISBN 0-916358-81-X). Pt. 2 (ISBN 0-916358-82-8). Pt. 3 (ISBN 0-916358-83-6). Wormhoudt.

Diwan al Mutanabbi, Shawmiyyat, 2 pts. Tr. by Arthur Wormhoudt from Arabic. (Arab Translation Ser.: No. 34-35). 1978. pap. 6.50 ea. Pt. 1 (ISBN 0-916358-84-4). Pt. 2 (ISBN 0-916358-85-2). Wormhoudt.

Diwan Ibn al Rumi. (Arab Translation Ser.: No. 26). 1977. pap. 6.50 (ISBN 0-916358-76-3). Wormhoudt.

Diwan Jarwal Ibn Malik Ibn Makhzum Al 'absi Called Al Hutaia. Tr. by Arthur Wormhoudt from Arabic. (Arab Translation Ser.: No. 46). 175p. pap. 6.50x (ISBN 0-916358-96-8). Wormhoudt.

Diwan Ka'b ibn Zuhair & Akhbar Majnun. Tr. by Arthur Wormhoudt from Arabic. (Arab Translation Ser.: No. 18). 1975. pap. 6.50 (ISBN 0-916358-68-2). Wormhoudt.

Diwan of Abu Tayyib Al Mutanabbi: Complete with Comments. Tr. by Arthur Wormhoudt from Classical Arabic. (Arab Translation Ser.: No. 52). 200p. 1981. pap. 6.50x (ISBN 0-916358-07-0). Wormhoudt.

Diwan of Muslim ibn al Walid. Tr. by Arthur Wormhoudt from Classical Arabic. (Arab Translation Ser.: No. 54). (Illus.). 175p. 1980. pap. 6.50 (ISBN 0-916358-02-X). Wormhoudt.

Dixiana Moon. William P. Fox. LC 80-51770. 256p. 1981. 11.95 (ISBN 0-670-27453-4). Viking Pr.

Dixie. Beth Hill & Norma Youngberg. LC 67-28841. 1967. pap. 4.50 o.p. (ISBN 0-8163-0094-1, 04375-2). Pacific Pr Pub Assn.

Dixie After the War: An Exposition of Social Conditions Existing in the South, During the 12 Years Succeeding the Fall of Richmond. Myrta L. Avary. LC 79-77701. (American Scene Ser). (Illus.). 1970. Repr. of 1937 ed. 35.00 (ISBN 0-306-71339-X). Da Capo.

Dixie Gun Works Antique Arms Catalog. 1.50 (ISBN 0-913150-40-1). Pioneer Pr.

Dixiecrats & Democrats: Alabama Politics 1942-1950. William D. Barnard. LC 73-22711. 1974. 13.95 (ISBN 0-8173-4820-4). U of Ala Pr.

Dizionario Comleto Italiano-Portoghese (Brasiliano)--Portoghese (Brasiliano)-Italiano: Con L'etimologia Delle Voci Itaiane e Portoghesi (Brasiliane), la Loro Esatta Traduzione, Frasi e Modi Di Dire, 2 vols. 1978. Set. 82.00; Vol. 1, 920 Pp. (ISBN 88-203-1010-4); Vol. 2, 1052pp. (ISBN 88-203-0216-0). S F Vanni.

Dizionario Commerciale Inglese-Italiano--Italiano-Inglese: Economia, Legge, Finanza, Banca, Etc. Giuseppe Motta. 1051p. 1978. 40.00x (ISBN 0-913298-50-6). S F Vanni.

Dizionario Enciclopedico Italiano, 12 Vols. (Ital.). 1955. 1050.00 (ISBN 0-8277-3014-4). Maxwell Sci Intl.

Dizionario Medico Ragionato Inglese-Italiano: Termini, Abbreviazioni, Sigle, Eponimi e Sinonimi Medici, Medico-Biologici e Delle Specializzazioni Mediche. Mario Lucchesi. 1490p. 1978. 98.00x (ISBN 0-913298-52-2). S F Vanni.

Dizionario Moderno Spagnuolo-Italiano--Italiano-Spagnuolo, 2 vols. Gaetano Frisoni. 1865p. Set. 44.00x (ISBN 0-913298-51-4). S F Vanni.

Dizionario Tecnico Italiano-Inglese--Inglese-Italiano. 9th rev. ed. Renzo Denti. 1811p. 1979. 44.00x (ISBN 88-203-1052-X). S F Vanni.

Djinn. Graham Masterton. 192p. 1977. pap. 1.75 o.p. (ISBN 0-685-75677-7, 40-523-0). Pinnacle Bks.

Djuka Society & Social Change: History of an Attempt to Develop a Bush Negro Community in Surinam, 1917-1926. Silvia W. De Groot. 1969. text ed. 19.25x (ISBN 90-232-0108-6). Humanities.

Dmitri. Jamey Cohen. 1981. pap. 2.25 (ISBN 0-451-09663-0, E9663, Sig). NAL.

DNA Action Model. Robert F. Clarke et al. 1968. 2.95 o.p. (ISBN 0-8087-0324-2). Burgess.

DNA Molecule: Structure & Properties. David Freifelder. LC 77-2768. (Illus.). 1978. text ed. 27.95x (ISBN 0-7167-0287-8); pap. text ed. 16.95x (ISBN 0-7167-0286-X). W H Freeman.

DNA: Recombination, Interactions & Repair. FEBS Symposium on DNA, Liblice, 24-29 September, 1979. Ed. by S. Zadrazil & J. Sponar. (Vol. 63). (Illus.). 600p. 1980. 92.00 (ISBN 0-08-025494-2). Pergamon.

DNA Repair, Pt. 1A. Freidberg & Hanawalt. 312p. 1981. 29.75 (ISBN 0-8247-6848-5). Dekker.

DNA Replication. Arthur Kornberg. LC 79-19543. (Illus.). 1980. text ed. 34.95x (ISBN 0-7167-1102-8). W H Freeman.

DNA Synthesis. Arthur Kornberg. LC 74-3005. (Illus.). 1974. text ed. 30.95x (ISBN 0-7167-0586-9). W H Freeman.

DNA Tumor Viruses: Molecular Biology of Tumor Viruses, Vol. 10b. 2nd ed. Ed. by John Tooze. LC 79-19882. (Cold Spring Harbor Monograph Series). 945p. 1980. 65.00 (ISBN 0-87969-126-3). Cold Spring Harbor.

Do-Anything Wagon. Rebecca S. Fazio. 32p. (gr. 3-5). 1978. 2.95 (ISBN 0-8059-2593-7). Dorrance.

Do Bananas Chew Gum? Jamie Gilson. LC 80-11414. 160p. (gr. 5-9). 1980. 6.95 (ISBN 0-688-41960-7); PLB 6.67 (ISBN 0-688-51960-1). Lothrop.

Do Cats Think? Paul Corey. 1978. pap. 1.75 (ISBN 0-515-04484-9). Jove Pubns.

Do Dzherel: Istorychno-Literaturni Ta Krytychni Statti. Mykola Zerov. LC 68-53064. (Ukra.). 1967. text ed. 15.00 (ISBN 0-918884-15-2). Slavia Lib.

Do I Have a Girl for You? Bill Wenzel. 1978. pap. 1.50 (ISBN 0-505-51232-7). Tower Bks.

Do I Have to? Stacy Quigley. LC 79-23890. (Life & Living from a Child's Point of View Ser.). (Illus.). (gr. k-5). 1980. PLB 9.65 (ISBN 0-8172-1352-X). Raintree Child.

Do I Know the "Me" Others See? Shirley Schwarzrock & C. Gilbert Wrenn. (Coping with Ser.). (Illus.). 55p. (gr. 7-12). 1973. pap. text ed. 1.30 (ISBN 0-913476-27-7). Am Guidance.

Do-in Two: A Most Complete Work on the Ancient Art of Self-Massage. 4th rev. ed. 156p. 1981. 10.50 (ISBN 0-916508-02-1); lib. bdg. 13.50 (ISBN 0-916508-00-5). Happiness Pr.

Do-It-Better Book. Shari Lewis. LC 79-3839. (Kids-Only Club Bks.). (Illus.). 96p. (Orig.). (gr. 3-6). 1981. 6.95 (ISBN 0-03-049721-3); pap. 3.95 (ISBN 0-03-049726-4). HR&W.

Do-It-Quick but Do-It Right Home Repair Hints. Al Carrell. LC 80-24659. 1981. 9.95 (ISBN 0-13-875906-5). P-H.

Do It up Brown. Patty Newman. pap. 3.95 (ISBN 0-686-05784-8). Prod Hse.

Do-It-Yourself Conveyancing. R. Steele. LC 78-62481. 1978. 14.95 (ISBN 0-7153-7676-4). David & Charles.

Do-It-Yourself Guide to Natural Stonework. J. A. Harrison. (Illus.). 1979. 17.95 (ISBN 0-7153-7840-6). David & Charles.

Do It Yourself Hebrew & Greek: Everybody's Guide to the Language Tools. Edward W. Goodrick. 256p. (Orig.). 1980. pap. 9.95 (ISBN 0-310-41741-4). Zondervan.

Do-It-Yourself Home Projects. Tony Wilkins. (Illus.). 1971. 5.75 o.p. (ISBN 0-258-96782-X). Transatlantic.

Do-It-Yourself Housebuilding Step-by-Step. Charles D. Neal. LC 72-91256. 1977. pap. 10.95 (ISBN 0-8128-2188-2). Stein & Day.

Do-It-Yourself Moving. George Sullivan. (Illus.). 192p. 1973. pap. 3.95 o.s.i. (ISBN 0-02-082090-9, Collier). Macmillan.

Do-It-Yourself Psychotherapy Book. Martin Shepard. LC 76-11881. 1976. pap. 3.95 o.p. (ISBN 0-8415-0447-4). Dutton.

Do-It-Yourself Roofing & Siding. Max Alth. LC 76-56515. (Illus.). 1978. 9.95 o.p. (ISBN 0-8015-2150-5, Hawthorn); pap. 4.95 (ISBN 0-8015-2151-3, Hawthorn). Dutton.

Do-It-Yourself Safety Inspective Manual. rev. ed. Arnold Naidich. 1978. 59.95 (ISBN 0-686-26874-1). Busn Res Pubns.

Do-It-Yourself Super Spa Home Weekend. Prudence McCullough. (Illus., Orig.). 1981. pap. 6.95 (ISBN 0-8092-7083-8). Contemp Bks.

Do-It-Yourselfer's Guide to Chainsaw Use & Repair. Charles R. Self. LC 77-1731. (Illus.). 1977. pap. 5.95 (ISBN 0-8306-6892-6, 892). TAB Bks.

Do-It Yourselfer's Guide to Home Planning & Construction. William Clarneau. LC 76-24781. 1976. 8.95 o.p. (ISBN 0-8306-6888-8); pap. 4.95 o.p. (ISBN 0-8306-5888-2, 888). TAB Bks.

Do-It-Yourselfer's Guide to Van Conversion. Van World Editors. (Illus.). 1977. 8.95 o.p. (ISBN 0-8306-7992-8); pap. 6.95 (ISBN 0-8306-6992-2, 992). TAB Bks.

Do Not Annoy the Indians. Betty Baker. (Illus.). (gr. 4-6). 1968. 4.95g o.s.i. (ISBN 0-02-708300-4). Macmillan.

Do Not Defuse. Valery Oisteanu. 1980. pap. 2.50 (ISBN 0-9601870-2-2). Pass.

Do Not Go Gentle. Ed. by William Packard. 128p. 1981. 9.95 (ISBN 0-312-21469-3). St Martin.

Do of Cooking Ryorido: Winter. Cornellia Aihara. 1973. pap. 2.95 o.p. (ISBN 0-918860-15-6). G Ohsawa.

Do Parties Make a Difference? Richard Rose. pap. 8.95 (ISBN 0-934540-08-X). Chatham Hse Pubs.

Do People Like Me Have Any Control Over Politics? A Study of the Locus of Political Control As Perceived by Mexican-American Adolescents of South Texas. James A. Davis. LC 80-65614. 140p. 1981. perfect bdg. 11.50 (ISBN 0-86548-029-X). Century Twenty One.

Do Polar Bears Experience Religious Ecstasy? Ian Warden. (Illus.). 217p. (Orig.). 1981. pap. 7.25x (ISBN 0-7022-1519-8). U of Queensland Pr.

Do Something Special on Your Birthday. Drawson. (ps-3). pap. 1.25 (ISBN 0-590-05799-5, Schol Pap). Schol Bk Serv.

Do the Poor Want to Work? A Social-Psychological Study of Work Orientations. Leonard Goodwin. 170p. 1972. 11.95 (ISBN 0-8157-3206-6); pap. 4.95 (ISBN 0-8157-3205-8). Brookings.

Do They Understand You? Wesley Wiksell. 1960. 4.95 o.s.i. (ISBN 0-02-628480-4). Macmillan.

Do with Me What You Will. Joyce C. Oates. LC 73-83039. 579p. 1973. 10.95 (ISBN 0-8149-0751-2). Vanguard.

Do With Me What You Will. Joyce C. Oates. 544p. 1978. pap. 2.95 (ISBN 0-449-23610-2, Crest). Fawcett.

Do You Have the Time Lydia. Evaline Ness. (Illus.). (gr. k-3). 1971. 7.95 o.p. (ISBN 0-525-28790-6). Dutton.

Do You Have the Time Lydia? Evaline Ness. (gr. k-3). 1974. pap. 1.25 o.p. (ISBN 0-525-45024-6, Anytime Bks). Dutton.

Do You Hear Them? Nathalie Sarraute. Tr. by Maria Jolas from Fr. LC 72-86680. 178p. 1973. 5.95 o.p. (ISBN 0-8076-0663-4); pap. 2.95 o.p. (ISBN 0-8076-0739-8). Braziller.

Do You Know. Lilian Lee Schalet. (Illus.). 39p. 1979. 4.50 o.p. (ISBN 0-533-03765-4). Vantage.

Do You Know About Stars. Mae B. Freeman. LC 70-123070. (Illus.). (gr. k-3). 1970. PLB 3.99 (ISBN 0-394-90620-9). Random.

Do You Know? One Hundred Fascinating Facts. B. G. Ford. LC 78-62132. (Picture Ser.). (Illus.). (ps-1). 1979. PLB 3.99 (ISBN 0-394-94070-9, BYR); pap. 1.25 (ISBN 0-394-84070-4). Random.

Do You Know What Day Tomorrow Is? A Teacher's Almanac. Lee Bennett Hopkins & Misha Arenstein. LC 75-23145. 240p. 1975. pap. text ed. 4.75 (ISBN 0-590-09604-4, Citation). Schol Bk Serv.

Do You Love Me? Dick Gackenbach. LC 74-34104. (Illus.). 48p. (ps-4). 1975. 6.95 (ISBN 0-395-28794-4, Clarion). HM.

Do You Need a Lawyer? Philip J. Hermann. (Illus.). 160p. 1980. 12.95 (ISBN 0-13-216721-2, Spec); pap. 4.95 (ISBN 0-13-216713-1). P-H.

Do You Not See: Sixteen Chinese Poems. Sally Nichols. LC 79-3833. (Illus., Orig.). 1980. pap. 6.95 (ISBN 0-06-090772-X, CN 772, CN). Har-Row.

Do You Really Need Eye Surgery? 2nd ed. William Lh. Havener. 1977. pap. 4.50 o.p. (ISBN 0-398-03800-7). C C Thomas.

Do You Really Need Eyeglasses? Marilyn Rosanes-Berrett. 1978. pap. 1.95 (ISBN 0-445-04154-4). Popular Lib.

Do You Want to See Something? Eve Merriam. (Illus.). (gr. 2-3). 1969. pap. 1.25 o.p. (ISBN 0-590-00103-5, Schol Pap). Schol Bk Serv.

Do Your Own Horse. Derrick Parsons. (Illus.). 12.25 (ISBN 0-85131-280-2). J A Allen.

Do Your Own Thing. Nina Howard. (Illus.). 96p. (ps-6). 1980. 9.90 (ISBN 0-917206-12-6). Children Learn Ctr.

Doane's Farm Management Guide. 14th ed. Ed. by Irving D. Smith. LC 79-56892. (Illus.). 1980. pap. 8.95 (ISBN 0-932250-09-2). Doane Agricultural.

Dobzhansky's Genetics of Natural Populations: I-XLIII. Theodosius Dobzhansky. Ed. by R. C. Lewontin et al. 1024p. 1981. 42.50x (ISBN 0-231-05132-8). Columbia U Pr.

Doc Holliday. John M. Myers. LC 55-5528. 224p. 1973. pap. 3.95 (ISBN 0-8032-5781-3, BB 570, Bison). U of Nebr Pr.

Doc Middleton: Life & Legends of the Notorious Plains Outlaw. Harold Hutton. LC 67-14260. (Illus.). 290p. 1980. 14.95 (ISBN 0-8040-0532-X, SB). Swallow.

Doc Savage. Philip J. Farmer. LC 81-80083. 288p. 1981. pap. 2.50 (ISBN 0-87216-854-9). Playboy Pbks.

Doce Cestas De Mendrugos. Tr. by Elizabeth Elliot. (Spanish Bks.). (Span.). 1977. 1.90 (ISBN 0-8297-0804-9). Life Pubs Intl.

Docere Verbo et Exemplo. Caroline W. Bynum. LC 78-14025. (Harvard Theological Studies: No. 31). 1979. 15.00 (ISBN 0-89130-267-0, 020031); pap. 10.50 (ISBN 0-89130-298-0). Scholars Pr Ca.

Dock & Harbour Engineering: The Design of Docks, Vol. 1. H. F. Cornick. 338p. 80.00x (ISBN 0-85264-037-4, Pub. by Griffin England). State Mutual Bk.

Dock & Harbour Engineering: The Design of Harbours, Vol. 2. 352p. 1969. 80.00x (ISBN 0-85264-041-2, Pub. by Griffin England). State Mutual Bk.

Docker. Gardner Patterson. LC 80-13514. 156p. (gr. 7 up). 1980. 8.95 (ISBN 0-689-50182-X, McElderry Bk). Atheneum.

Docks After Devlin. Michael Mellish. Ed. by Hugh Clegg & George Bain. 1972. pap. text ed. 6.95x o.p. (ISBN 0-435-85605-7). Heinemann Ed.

Docto Schiff's One-Day-at-a-Time Weight-Loss Plan. Martin M. Schiff. 1980. 9.95 (ISBN 0-8128-2692-2). Stein & Day.

Doctor: A Tale of the Rockies. Ralph Connor. 1976. lib. bdg. 17.25x (ISBN 0-89968-015-1). Lighthouse Pr NY.

Doctor & Annie. Ida S. Panther. 1981. 5.75 (ISBN 0-8062-1628-X). Carlton.

Doctor & His Patient: A Sociological Interpretation. Samuel W. Bloom. LC 66-1994. 1965. pap. text ed. 4.95 (ISBN 0-02-903890-1). Free Pr.

Doctor & Patient in the Teaching Hospital: A Tale of Two Life-Worlds. Cecilia M. Roberts. LC 75-40629. 1977. 16.95 (ISBN 0-669-00453-7). Lexington Bks.

Doctor as Judge of Who Shall Live & Who Shall Die. Helmut Thielicke. Tr. by Edward A. Cooperrider from Ger. LC 75-42836. 48p. (Orig.). 1976. pap. 1.00 (ISBN 0-8006-1228-0, 1-1228). Fortress.

Doctor at Calvary. Barbet, Pierre, M.D. pap. 2.95 (ISBN 0-385-06687-2, D155, Im). Doubleday.

Dr. Atkins Diet Revolution. Robert Atkins. 336p. 1981. pap. 2.95 (ISBN 0-553-14736-6). Bantam.

Dr. Barnes of Merion. Henry Hart. 1963. 4.95 o.p. (ISBN 0-374-14285-8). FS&G.

Doctor Bombard Goes to Sea. Alain Bombard. LC 57-7890. (gr. 7 up). 3.95 (ISBN 0-8149-0272-3). Vanguard.

Dr. Church's "Hoax". Richard E. Huss. LC 75-44946. (Illus.). 1976. 12.00 (ISBN 0-9605622-0-6). Graphic Crafts.

Doctor Copernicus. John Banville. 1977. 8.95 o.p. (ISBN 0-393-08757-3). Norton.

Doctor Death: Twelve Must Die. Harold W. Zorro. LC 80-8666. 80p. 1980. lib. bdg. 11.95 (ISBN 0-89370-083-5); pap. 5.95 (ISBN 0-89370-082-7). Borgo Pr.

Doctor Discuss Headaches. Shideler Harpe & Jose L. Salazar. (Illus.). 1979. pap. 2.50 (ISBN 0-686-65548-6). Budlong.

Doctor Discusses a Man's Sexual Health. Robert E. Dunbar. (Illus.). 1979. pap. 2.50 (ISBN 0-685-64313-1). Budlong.

Doctor Discusses Allergy Fact & Fallacies. Lou Joseph & Alice S. Mills. (Illus., Orig.). 1980. pap. 2.50 (ISBN 0-685-35676-0). Budlong.

Doctor Discusses Breast Feeding. Marie P. Warner & Miriam Gilbert. (Illus.). 1980. pap. 2.50 (ISBN 0-685-03351-1). Budlong.

Doctor Discusses Cancer. Tom Maher & Malcolm Schwartz. (Illus.). 1981. pap. 2.50 (ISBN 0-686-69338-8). Budlong.

Doctor Discusses Care of the Back. Paul Neimark & Gerald Berkowitz. 1980. pap. 2.50 (ISBN 0-910304-04-1). Budlong.

Doctor Discusses Care of the Feet. Sue Berkman et al. (Illus.). 110p. 1979. pap. 2.50 (ISBN 0-685-46330-3). Budlong.

Doctor Discusses Care of the Skin. Richard G. Mills & John M. Weiss. (Doctor Discusses...Ser.). (Illus.). 112p. pap. cancelled o.s.i. (ISBN 0-686-63407-1). Budlong.

Doctor Discusses Children's Colds. Lou Joseph & Oscar Novick. (Illus.). 1979. pap. 2.50 (ISBN 0-686-65549-4). Budlong.

Doctor Discusses Diabetes. Lou Joseph & John J. Lynch. (Illus.). 1980. pap. 2.50 (ISBN 0-685-46339-7). Budlong.

Doctor Discusses Family Problems. Robert Rutherford & Jean Rutherford. (Illus.). 1969. pap. 2.50 (ISBN 0-910304-17-3). Budlong.

Doctor Discusses Female Surgery. Paul Neimark & Samuel Matlin. (Illus.). 1979. pap. 2.50 (ISBN 0-686-65550-8). Budlong.

Doctor Discusses How to Get a Good Nights Sleep. James Kepler & Charles K. Wolfe, Jr. (Doctor Discusses...Ser.). (Illus., Orig.). 1980. pap. 2.50 (ISBN 0-686-63406-3). Budlong.

Doctor Discusses How to Stay Young & Live Longer. Paul G. Neimark & Jay Schmidt. (Illus.). 1977. pap. 2.50 (ISBN 0-685-46340-0). Budlong.

Doctor Discusses Hypertension. Arthur J. Snider & Suzanne Oparil. (Illus.). 1981. pap. 2.50 (ISBN 0-685-79070-3). Budlong.

Doctor Discusses Learning How to Live with Nervous Tension. Arthur J. Snider & I. J. Adatto. (Illus.). 1980. pap. 2.50 (ISBN 0-685-58312-0). Budlong.

Doctor Discusses Learning to Cope with Arthritis Rheumatism & Govt. Robert E. Dunbar & Harold F. Segall. (Illus., Orig.). 1973. pap. 2.50 (ISBN 0-685-35675-2). Budlong.

Doctor Discusses Learning to Live with Heart Trouble. Arthur J. Snider & I. J. Adatto. (Illus.). 1980. pap. 2.50 (ISBN 0-685-35677-9). Budlong.

Doctor Discusses Menopause & Estrogens. M. Edward Davis & Dona Meilach. (Illus.). 1980. pap. 2.50 (ISBN 0-910304-26-2). Budlong.

Doctor Discusses Pregnancy. William G. Birch & Dona Z. Meilach. (Illus.). 1980. pap. 2.50 (ISBN 0-910304-00-9). Budlong.

Doctor Discusses Prepared Childbirth. Lou Joseph & Ulisse Cucco. 1980. pap. 2.50 (ISBN 0-910304-21-1). Budlong.

Doctor Discusses Talking with Your Child About Sex. Arlene Uslander & Lee D. Weiss. (Illus.). 1978. pap. 2.50 (ISBN 0-685-46343-5). Budlong.

Doctor Discusses the Care & Development of Your Baby. May Guy & Miriam Gilbert. (Illus.). 1979. pap. 2.50 (ISBN 0-685-56949-7). Budlong.

Doctor Discusses Your New Baby & Your New Life. Paul Neimark et al. (Illus.). 1980. pap. 2.50 (ISBN 0-685-46338-9). Budlong.

Doctor Discussses Making the Mid-Years the Prime of Life. Kathleen Newton & Gerald Looney. (Illus.). 1978. pap. 2.50 (ISBN 0-685-46333-8). Budlong.

Dr. Dobb's Journal of Computer Calisthenics & Orthodontia, Vol. 1. Ed. by Jim Warren. 1977. pap. 18.95 (ISBN 0-8104-5475-0). Peoples Computer.

Dr. Dobb's Journal of Computer Calesthenics & Orthodontia: Running Light Without Overbyte, 3 vols. People's Computer Company. 1980. pap. 18.95 ea.; Vol. 1. pap. (ISBN 0-8104-5475-0); Vol. 2. pap. (ISBN 0-8104-5484-X); Vol. 3. pap. (ISBN 0-8104-5490-4). Hayden.

Dr. Dobson Fala Sobre Amor, Ira. Tr. by James Dobson. (Portugese Bks.). (Port.). 1979. write for info. (ISBN 0-8297-0674-7). Life Pubs Intl.

Doctor Dolittle: A Treasury. Hugh Lofting. LC 67-19270. (Illus.). (gr. 4-6). 1967. 8.95 o.p. (ISBN 0-397-30937-6). Lippincott.

Doctor Dolittle & His Friends. Adapted by Polly Berrien. (Illus.). (gr. k-4). 1967. PLB 3.99 o.p. (ISBN 0-394-90739-6, BYR). Random.

Doctor Dolittle & the Green Canary. Hugh Lofting. (Illus.). (gr. 4-6). 1950. 10.95 (ISBN 0-397-30166-9). Lippincott.

Doctor Dolittle & the Secret Lake. Hugh Lofting. (Illus.). (gr. 4-6). 1948. 10.95 (ISBN 0-397-30135-9). Lippincott.

Doctor Dolittle's Birthday Book. Hugh Lofting. LC 68-8923. (Illus.). (gr. 4-6). 1968. 7.95 (ISBN 0-397-30996-1). Lippincott.

Doctor Dolittle's Caravan. Hugh Lofting. (Illus.). (gr. 4-6). 1926. 10.95 (ISBN 0-397-30011-5). Lippincott.

Doctor Dolittle's Circus. Hugh Lofting. (Illus.). (gr. 4-6). 1924. 6.50 o.p. (ISBN 0-397-30008-5). Lippincott.

Doctor Dolittle's Garden. Hugh Lofting. (Illus.). (gr. 4-6). 1927. 5.50 o.p. (ISBN 0-397-30012-3). Lippincott.

Doctor Dolittle's Zoo. Hugh Lofting. (Illus.). (gr. 4-6). 1925. 10.95 (ISBN 0-397-30009-3). Lippincott.

Dr. Doom Superstar. Ernesto T. Bethancourt. 128p. (gr. 6-9). 1980. pap. 1.75 (ISBN 0-553-13929-0). Bantam.

Dr. Doom: Superstar. T. Ernesto Bethancourt. LC 78-6315. (YA) 1978. 8.95 (ISBN 0-8234-0333-5). Holiday.

Dr. Drummond's Spirited Guide to Health Care in a Dying Empire. Hugh Drummond. LC 80-994. 288p. 1980. pap. 2.95 (ISBN 0-394-17674-X, BC-447, BC). Grove.

Doctor Durant & His Iron Horse. Harold K. Hochschild. (Illus.). 15p. 1962. pap. 3.50 (ISBN 0-8156-8019-8, Pub. by Adirondack Museum). Syracuse U Pr.

Dr. Eden's Diet & Nutrition Program for Children. Alvin N. Eden & Joan Heilman. 1980. 9.95 (ISBN 0-8015-3180-2, Hawthorn); pap. 6.95 (ISBN 0-8015-3181-0). Dutton.

Dr. Erica Werner. H. G. Gunther. (H. G. Gunther Ser.: No. 4). 224p. 1981. pap. 1.95 (ISBN 0-515-05673-1). Jove Pubns.

Doctor Faustus. Christopher Marlowe. Ed. by John Jump. LC 72-127572. (Casebook Ser). 1970. pap. text ed. 2.50 o.s.i. (ISBN 0-87695-043-8). Aurora Pubs.

Doctor Faustus: Text & Major Criticism. Christopher Marlowe. Ed. by Irving Ribner. LC 65-26778. 1966. pap. 5.55 (ISBN 0-672-63058-3). Odyssey Pr.

Doctor for the People: 2000 Years of General Practice in Britain. John Cule. (Illus.). 1981. PLB 38.70 (ISBN 0-906141-29-X, Pub. by Update Books Ltd). Kluwer Boston.

Doctor from Lhasa. T. Rampa. pap. 2.50 (ISBN 0-685-88124-5). Weiser.

Doctor Fromme's Book on Sex & Marriage. Allan Fromme. 1950. pap. 2.25 (ISBN 0-06-463264-4, EH 264, EH). Har-Row.

Dr. Galen's Dilemma. Ruth Burnett. 192p. (YA) 1976. 5.95 (ISBN 0-685-59253-7, Avalon). Bouregy.

Doctor Game. Howard A. Olgin. 1979. pap. 2.50 o.s.i. (ISBN 0-440-12006-3). Dell.

Doctor Game. Howard A. Olgin. LC 77-20032. 1978. 8.95 o.p. (ISBN 0-397-01246-2). Lippincott.

Dr. Gardner's Fables for Our Times, Vol. 1. Richard A. Gardner. LC 80-26098. (Illus.). 125p. (gr. k-6). 10.95 (ISBN 0-933812-06-X). Creative Therapeutics.

Dr. Gardner's Stories About the Real World, Vol. II. Richard A. Gardner. (Illus.). 110p. (gr. k-6). write for info. Creative Therapeutics.

Dr. George Wasington Carver: Scientist. Graham & Lipscomb. (gr. 7-9). pap. 1.25 o.p. (ISBN 0-686-68475-3, 29796). Archway.

Dr. Gloom's Monster Jokes & Puzzles. Susan Whitney. (Dr. Gloom Activity Ser.). (Illus.). 64p. (gr. 4-6). pap. 1.95 (ISBN 0-15-224223-6, VoyB). HarBraceJ.

Dr. Gloom's Outer Space Jokes & Puzzles. Susan Whitney. (Dr. Gloom's Activity Ser.). (Illus.). 64p. (gr. 4-6). pap. 1.95 (ISBN 0-15-224225-2, VoyB). HarBraceJ.

Dr. Harmful Food Additives: The Eat-Safe Guide. Milton Houben & William Kropf. 8.95 (ISBN 0-87949-161-2). Ashley Bks.

Doctor in History, Literature, Folklore. William Andrews. LC 74-99779. 1970. Repr. of 1896 ed. 18.00 (ISBN 0-8103-3595-6). Gale.

Doctor in the Zoo. Bruce Buchenholz. (Illus.). 192p. 1976. pap. 3.95 o.p. (ISBN 0-14-004238-5). Penguin.

Doctor Ironside's Bible. H. A. Ironside. (Illus.). Date not set. pap. 2.50 (ISBN 0-87213-393-1). Loizeaux.

Doctor J: A Biography of Julius Erving. James S. Haskins. LC 74-33645. (Illus.). 96p. (gr. 8-9). 1975. 4.95 o.p. (ISBN 0-385-09905-3); PLB write for info. o.p. (ISBN 0-385-09906-1). Doubleday.

Dr. Jekyl & Mr. Hyde. Robert L. Stevenson. Incl. Merrymen & Other Tales. 1954. 10.50x (ISBN 0-460-00767-X, Evman); pap. 4.50 (ISBN 0-460-01767-5). Dutton.

Dr. Jekyll & Mr. Hyde & Other Stories. Robert L. Stevenson. Ed. by Jenni Calder. 1981. pap. 2.95 (ISBN 0-14-005776-5). Penguin.
Dr. Jekyll & Mr. Mad. Mad Magazine Editors. (Mad Ser.: No. 38). (Illus.). 1975. pap. 1.75 (ISBN 0-446-94363-0). Warner Bks.
Dr. Jesus Christ & the Sick World. Money Alian Kirby. 1980. 4.50 o.p. (ISBN 0-682-49101-2). Exposition.
Dr. Jimmy: Some Reminiscences by James Fowler Fraser 1893-1979. James F. Fraser. 150p. 1980. pap. 10.90 (ISBN 0-08-025737-2). Pergamon.
Dr. John Arbuthnot. Robert C. Steensma. (English Authors Ser.: No. 256). 1979. lib. bdg. 13.95 (ISBN 0-8057-6749-5). Twayne.
Doctor John Bull 1562-1628. Leigh Henry. LC 68-15589. (Music Ser). (Illus.). 1968. Repr. of 1937 ed. lib. bdg. 29.50 (ISBN 0-306-70982-1). Da Capo.
Dr. John Ebenezer Esslemont. Moojan Momen. (Illus.). 1979. pap. 2.50 (ISBN 0-900125-30-6, 7-31-06). Baha'i.
Dr. Johnson & Chinese Culture. Ts'Un-Chung Fan. 50p. 1980. Repr. of 1945 ed. lib. bdg. 8.50 (ISBN 0-8495-1714-1). Arden Lib.
Doctor, Lawyer. Collin Wilcox. (Mystery Ser.). 192p. 1981. pap. 1.95 (ISBN 0-515-05194-2). Jove Pubns.
Dr. Luke Examines Jesus. Bill Meyers. 1979. pap. 2.50 (ISBN 0-88207-768-6). Victor Bks.
Dr. Mandell's Five-Day Allergy Relief System. Marshall Mandell & Lynne W. Scanlon. LC 78-3309. (Illus.). 1979. 10.95 (ISBN 0-690-01471-6, TYC-T). T Y Crowell.
Dr. Marchetti's Walking Book. Albert Marchetti. LC 78-66258. 142p. 1981. pap. 6.95 (ISBN 0-8128-6114-0). Stein & Day.
Dr. Marshall's Lifelong Weight Control Program. Edward Marshall. 132p. 1981. 7.95 (ISBN 0-395-29476-2). HM.
Doctor Migration & World Health. Oscar Gish. 151p. 1971. pap. text ed. 6.90x (ISBN 0-7135-1611-9, Pub. by Bedford England). Renouf.
Dr. Monte Cristo. Irwin Philip Sobel. LC 77-82773. 1978. 8.95 o.p. (ISBN 0-385-12085-0). Doubleday.
Dr. Nikola Returns. Guy Boothby. LC 80-22358. (Dr. Nikola, Master of Occult Mystery: No. 2). 256p. 1980. Repr. of 1976 ed. lib. bdg. 9.95x (ISBN 0-89370-634-5). Borgo Pr.
Doctor No. Ian Fleming. 240p. 1980. pap. 1.95 (ISBN 0-515-05517-4). Jove Pubns.
Doctor of the Hills. Mary S. Burk. (YA) 1977. 4.95 o.p. (ISBN 0-685-71794-1, Avalon). Bouregy.
Doctor on the Stage: Medicine & Medical Men in Seventeenth-Century England. Herbert Silvette. Ed. by Francelia Butler. LC 66-14775. 1967. 14.50x (ISBN 0-87049-074-5). U of Tenn Pr.
Doctor Ox's Experiment. Jules Verne. 1963. 8.95 (ISBN 0-02-621810-0). Macmillan.
Doctor Proctor & Mrs. Merriweather. Irma S. Black. LC 78-150800. (Concept Bks). (Illus.). (gr. k-2). 1971. 5.75g o.p. (ISBN 0-8075-1654-6). A Whitman.
Dr. Rader's "No-Diet Program for Permanent Weight Control". William Rader. LC 79-66688. 239p. 1981. 9.95 (ISBN 0-87477-139-0). J P Tarcher.
Dr. Revien's Eye Exercise Program for Athletes: How to Direct Your Eyes to Win in 15 Minutes a Day. Leon Revien & Mark Gabor. LC 80-54623. (Illus.). 192p. 1981. pap. 4.95 (ISBN 0-89480-152-X). Workman Pub.
Dr. Sara's Vigil. Ruth McCarthy Sears. (YA) 1978. 5.95 (ISBN 0-685-84746-2, Avalon). Bouregy.
Doctor Solomon's Easy, No Risk Diet. Neil Solomon & Mary Knudson. 240p. 1976. pap. 1.95 o.s.i. (ISBN 0-446-89012-X). Warner Bks.
Dr. Spaulding's Veterinary Answer Book. Clark Spaulding & Jackie Spaulding. (Illus.). 1978. lib. bdg. 13.50 (ISBN 0-88930-026-7, Pub. by Cloudburst Canada); pap. 6.95 (ISBN 0-88930-025-9). Madrona Pubs.
Doctor Speaks on Sexual Expression in Marriage. 2nd ed. Donald W. Hastings. 190p. 1971. 12.95 (ISBN 0-316-35017-6). Little.
Dr. Strang: Marvel Comics. (YA) pap. 2.25 (ISBN 0-671-82582-8). PB.
Doctor Talks to Five to Eight Year Olds. Dona Z. Meilach & Elias Mandel. (Illus.). 1980. pap. 2.50 (ISBN 0-910304-14-9). Budlong.
Doctor Talks to Nine to Twelve Year Olds. Marion O. Lerrigo & Michael Cassidy. (Illus.). 1980. pap. 2.50 (ISBN 0-910304-03-3). Budlong.
Doctor Tennis: A Complete Guide to Conditioning & Injury Prevention for All Ages. George B. Dintiman et al. LC 80-65623. (Illus.). 106p. (Orig.). 1980. text ed. 4.95 (ISBN 0-938074-00-8). Champion Athlete.
Dr. Thomas Sydenham (1624-1689) His Life & Original Writings. Kenneth Dewhurst. (Wellcome Institute of the History of Medicine). 1966. 18.50x (ISBN 0-520-00320-9). U of Cal Pr.
Dr. Thompson's New Way for You to Cure Your Aching Back. Jess Stearn. LC 72-96260. 216p. 1973. 7.95 o.p. (ISBN 0-385-00473-7). Doubleday.
Dr. Thorndyke's Dilemma. John H. Dirckx. (Illus.). 95p. (Orig.). 1974. pap. 5.00 o.p. (ISBN 0-915230-04-6). Rue Morgue.
Dr. Thorne. Anthony Trollope. 1953. 12.95x (ISBN 0-460-00360-7, Evman). Dutton.
Dr. Thorne. Anthony Trollope. (Zodiac Press Ser.). 1978. 9.95 (ISBN 0-7011-1251-4, Pub. by Chatto Bodley Jonathan). Merrimack Bk Serv.
Doctor to Basuto, Boer & Briton, 1877-1906: Memoirs of Dr. Henry Taylor. Henry Taylor. Ed. by Peter Hadley. (Illus.). 213p. 1972. 10.50x (ISBN 0-8476-2394-7). Rowman.
Doctor to the Stars. Murray Leinster. 1977. pap. 1.50 o.s.i. (ISBN 0-515-04482-2). Jove Pubns.
Doctor Upstairs. T. R. Torkelson. LC 70-103126. (Stories That Win Ser.). 64p. 1960. pap. 0.95 o.p. (ISBN 0-8163-0052-6, 04423-0). Pacific Pr Pub Assn.
Doctor W. C. Rontgen. 2nd ed. Otto Glasser. (Illus.). 192p. 1972. 10.75 (ISBN 0-398-02196-1). C C Thomas.
Doctor, What Can I Do? Helen Rhodes. (Horizon Ser.). 128p. 1981. pap. price not set (ISBN 0-8127-0327-8). Southern Pub.
Dr. Wigder's Guide to Over-the-Counter Drugs. H. Neil Wigder. 1979. 8.95 o.p. (ISBN 0-312-90489-4). St Martin.
Dr. William Beaumont: The Mackinac Years. Keith R. Widder. (Illus.). 40p. (Orig.). 1975. pap. 1.50 (ISBN 0-911872-15-9). Mackinac Island.
Doctor Within. Hal Z. Bennett. (Illus.). 160p. 1981. 11.95 (ISBN 0-517-54178-5); pap. 5.95 (ISBN 0-517-54299-4). Potter.
Dr. Woodward's Shield: History, Science, & Satire in Augustan England. Joseph M. Levine. 1977. 28.50x (ISBN 0-520-03132-6). U of Cal Pr.
Dr. Zed's Brilliant Book of Science Experiments. Gordon Penrose. LC 77-88864. (Illus.). (gr. 3-6). 1977. pap. 3.75 (ISBN 0-8120-0892-8). Barron.
Dr. Zhivago. Boris Pasternak. 576p. 1981. pap. 3.50 (ISBN 0-345-29310-X). Ballantine.
Doctoral Dissertation As an Information Source: A Study of Scientific Information Flow. Calvin J. Boyer. 1973. 8.00 o.p. (ISBN 0-8108-0623-1). Scarecrow.
Doctoral Dissertations on Catholic Education 1968-1975. 67p. 1975. 3.00. Natl Cath Educ.
Doctoral Dissertations on South Asia, 1966-1970: An Annotated Bibliography Covering North America, Europe, & Australia. Frank J. Shulman. LC 78-186256. (Michigan Papers on South & Southeast Asia: No. 4). 223p. 1971. pap. 6.00x (ISBN 0-89148-004-8). Ctr S&SE Asian.
Doctoral Programs in Marketing: Proceedings of the Educational Workshop on Doctoral Education in Marketing, Univ. of N. C., Spring, 1976. Ed. by James E. Littlefield & Donald L. Shawver. LC 77-6724. 1977. pap. text ed. 7.00 o.p. (ISBN 0-87757-096-5). Am Mktg.
Doctorate Production in United States Universities, 1920-1962, with Baccalaureate Origins of Doctorates in Sciences, Arts & Professions. Office Of Scientific Personnel. (Illus.). 1963. pap. 6.00 (ISBN 0-309-01142-6). Natl Acad Pr.
Doctorate Recipients from United States Universities, 1958-1966. Office Of Scientific Personnel. 1967. pap. 9.75 (ISBN 0-309-01489-1). Natl Acad Pr.
Doctoring Together: A Study of Professional Social Control. Eliot Freidson. LC 80-15513. 312p. 1980. pap. 7.95 (ISBN 0-226-26222-7, P911, Phoen). U of Chicago Pr.
Doctors. Leonard E. Fisher. LC 68-24610. (Colonial Americans Ser). (Illus.). (gr. 4-6). 1968. PLB 4.90 o.p. (ISBN 0-531-01027-9). Watts.
Doctor's Administrative Program, 6 vols. A. Ziegler. Incl. **Dap 1. Patient Contract & Public Relations (ISBN 0-87489-150-7); Dap 2. Bookkeeping & Tax Reports (ISBN 0-87489-151-5); Dap 3. Insurance & Third-Party-Payable Claims (ISBN 0-87489-152-3); Dap 4. Correspondence (ISBN 0-87489-153-1); Billing & Collections; Dap 6. Patient Records Control (ISBN 0-87489-155-8). 1978. Set. write for info. (ISBN 0-87489-158-2); Ea. Vol. write for info.**
Doctor's Amazing Speed Reducing Diet. Rex Adams. LC 79-11343. 1979. 10.95 (ISBN 0-13-216275-X, Parker). P-H.
Doctors & Patients Handbook of Medicines & Drugs. Peter Parish. 1977. 12.95 o.p. (ISBN 0-394-49407-5); pap. 6.95 o.p. (ISBN 0-394-73337-1). Knopf.
Doctors & Their Workshops: Economic Models of Physician Behavior. Mark V. Pauly. LC 80-16112. (National Bureau of Economic Research Ser.). (Illus.). 144p. 1980. lib. bdg. 17.00x (ISBN 0-226-65044-8). U of Chicago Pr.
Doctors & Wives. Ann Pinchot. 352p. 1981. pap. 2.75 (ISBN 0-553-14804-4). Bantam.
Doctor's Calories-Plus Diet: The New Food IQ Way to Weight Loss. Henry A. Jordan & Theodore Berland. 1981. 10.95 (ISBN 0-8092-5939-7). Contemp Bks.
Doctor's Carbohydrate Diet List. Sylvan R. Lewis. 128p. 1981. pap. 1.95 (ISBN 0-936320-12-5). Compact Pubns.
Doctors' Case Against the Pill. Barbara Seaman. 264p. 1980. pap. 6.50 (ISBN 0-385-14575-6, Dolp). Doubleday.
Doctor's Diet & Fitness Guide. Sylvan Lewis. 1979. pap. cancelled (ISBN 0-686-26708-7). Haldon Pubns.
Doctor's Dilemma. Bernard Shaw. (Play Ser). 1975. pap. 2.95 (ISBN 0-14-048001-3). Penguin.
Doctor's Dilemma. George B. Shaw. Ed. by Margery M. Morgan. LC 79-56709. (Bernard Shaw Early Texts: Play Manuscripts in Facsimile). 1981. lib. bdg. 55.00 (ISBN 0-8240-4584-X). Garland Pub.
Doctor's Guide to Tennis Elbow. Leon Root & Thomas Kiernan. 1980. 8.95 (ISBN 0-679-50460-5); pap. 4.95 (ISBN 0-679-50977-1). McKay.
Doctors in Elizabethan Drama. Percival M. Yearsley. 128p. 1980. Repr. of 1933 ed. lib. bdg. 20.00 (ISBN 0-8495-6101-9). Arden Lib.
Doctors in Gray: The Confederate Medical Service. H. H. Cunningham. (Illus.). 8.50 (ISBN 0-8446-0566-2). Peter Smith.
Doctor's Lawyer: A Legal Handbook for Doctors. Marc J. Lane. (Illus.). 112p. 1974. text ed. 17.50 (ISBN 0-398-02988-1). C C Thomas.
Doctor's Overnight Beauty Program. Bedford Shelmire. (Illus.). 192p. 1981. 12.95 (ISBN 0-312-21489-8). St Martin.
Doctors, Patients, & Health Insurance: The Organization & Financing of Medical Care. Herman M. Somers & Anne R. Somers. 1961. 15.95 (ISBN 0-8157-8036-2). Brookings.
Doctors, Patients & Pathology. Hilarly Rose. 79p. 1972. pap. text ed. 5.00x (ISBN 0-7135-1741-7, Pub. by Bedford England). Renouf.
Doctor's Quick Teenage Diet. Samm S. Baker & Irwin M. Stillman. 256p. 1972. pap. 1.25 o.s.i. (ISBN 0-446-76808-1). Warner Bks.
Doctor's Secret Journal. George May. (Illus.). 1960. pap. 1.50 (ISBN 0-911872-30-2). Mackinac Island.
Doctor's Sensible Approach to Alcohol & Alcoholism. Gene Mariken & Eugene Scheimann. (Illus.). 1969. pap. 2.50 (ISBN 0-685-56948-9). Budlong.
Doctor's Sensible Approach to Dieting & Weight Control. Eugene Scheimann & Paul Neimark. (Illus.). 1976. pap. 2.50 (ISBN 0-910304-19-X). Budlong.
Doctor's Sex Guide for Patients. Bernard S. Greenblatt. (Illus.). 1976. pap. 2.50 (ISBN 0-685-07679-2). Budlong.
Doctor's Walking Book. Fred A. Stutman & Lillian Africano. (Orig.). 1980. pap. 6.95 (ISBN 0-345-28764-9). Ballantine.
Doctrina Cristiana. T. Conner. Tr. by Adolfo Robleto. Orig. Title: Christian Doctrine. 408p. (Span.). Date not set. pap. price not set (ISBN 0-311-09012-5). Casa Bautista.
Doctrina de la Trinidad. Eberhard Jungel. Tr. by Arnoldo Canclini from Eng. 152p. (Orig., Span.). 1980. pap. 3.95 (ISBN 0-89922-153-X). Edit Caribe.
Doctrinas Biblicas. Tr. by P. C. Nelson. (Spanish Bks.). (Span.). 1979. pap. 1.75 (ISBN 0-8297-0539-2). Life Pubs Intl.
Doctrinas Claves. Edwin H. Palmer. 2.50 (ISBN 0-686-12552-5). Banner of Truth.
Doctrine & Covenants. Ed. by Board of Publication of the Reorganized Church of Jesus Christ of Latter Day Saints. LC 78-134922. 1978. 9.00 (ISBN 0-8309-0204-X). Herald Hse.
Doctrine & Covenants & Pearl of Great Price. missionary ed. 2.95 o.p. (ISBN 0-87747-573-3). Deseret Bk.
Doctrine of Atonement & the Shorter Road. Ed. by Michael Agerskov. LC 79-9595. Orig. Title: Forsoningslaeren Og Genvejen. 1979. pap. 2.95 (ISBN 87-87871-56-4). Toward the Light.
Doctrine of Chances: Including Treatise on Annuities. 3rd ed. Abraham De Moivre. LC 66-23756. 1967. 15.95 (ISBN 0-8284-0200-0). Chelsea Pub.
Doctrine of God. Herman Bavinck. Tr. by W. Hendricksen. (Student's Reformed Theological Library Ser.). 1977. 14.95 (ISBN 0-85151-255-0). Banner of Truth
Doctrine of God. Herman Bavinck. (Twin Brooks Ser.). 1977. pap. 7.95 (ISBN 0-8010-0723-2). Baker Bk.
Doctrine of Man. H. D. McDonald. (Foundations for Faith Ser.). 5.95 (ISBN 0-89107-217-9). Good News.
Doctrine of St. John Damascene on the Procession of the Holy Spirit. N. Bogorodskii. LC 80-2351. 1981. Repr. of 1879 ed. 28.50 (ISBN 0-404-18903-2). AMS Pr.
Doctrine of Scripture: Locus 2 of Institutio Theologiae Elencticae. Francis Turretin. Ed. by John W. Beardslee, III. 200p. (Orig.). 1981. 12.95 (ISBN 0-8010-8858-5); pap. 7.95 (ISBN 0-8010-8857-7). Baker Bk.
Doctrine of the Atonement. John K. Mozley. (Studies in Theology: No. 19). 1915. 6.00x o.p. (ISBN 0-8401-6019-4). Allenson.
Doctrine of the Atonement According to the Apostles. George Smeaton. Date not set. 17.95 (ISBN 0-88469-136-5). BMH Bks.
Doctrine of the Holy Spirit. Hendrikus Berkhof. LC 64-16279. 1976. pap. 3.95 (ISBN 0-8042-0551-5). John Knox.
Doctrine of the Holy Spirit. George Smeaton. 1980. 12.95 (ISBN 0-85151-187-2). Banner of Truth.
Doctrine of the Jainas. Walther Schubring. Tr. by Wolfgang Buerlen. 1978. Repr. 12.50 (ISBN 0-89684-005-0, Pub. by Motilal Banarsidass India). Orient Bk Dist.
Doctrine of the Nerves: Chapters in the History of Neurology. John D. Spillane. (Illus.). 500p. 1981. text ed. 50.00x (ISBN 0-19-261135-6). Oxford U Pr.
Doctrine of the New Testament in Ten Great Subjects. G. W. Lane. 127p. 1964. pap. 1.50 (ISBN 0-87148-250-9). Pathway Pr.
Doctrine of the Person of Jesus Christ. 2nd ed. (International Theological Library). 560p. Repr. of 1913 ed. pap. text ed. 14.50. Attic Pr.
Doctrine of the Sufis. A. J. Arberry. LC 76-58075. 1977. 32.50 (ISBN 0-521-21647-8); pap. 8.95x (ISBN 0-521-29218-2). Cambridge U Pr.
Document A-777. (Santa Susana Press Ser.). 1981. 38.00 (ISBN 0-937048-31-3). CSUN.
Document Mark (Blip) Used in Image Mark Retrieval Systems: ANSI-NMA MS8-1979. National Micrographics Assn. 1980. 4.50 (ISBN 0-89258-060-7). Natl Micrograph.
Documentary: A History of the Non-Fiction Film. Erik Barnouw. LC 74-79618. (Illus.). 336p. 1976. pap. 5.95 (ISBN 0-19-502005-7, 451, GB). Oxford U Pr.
Documentary Conscience: A Casebook in Film-Making. Alan Rosenthal. (Illus.). 1980. 19.50 (ISBN 0-520-03932-7); pap. 8.95 (ISBN 0-520-04022-8, CAL. NO. 436). U of Cal Pr.
Documentary Expression & Thirties America. William Stott. LC 73-82676. (Illus.). 441p. 1976. pap. 6.95 (ISBN 0-19-502099-5, 474, GB). Oxford U Pr.
Documentary History of American Interiors. Edgar D. Mayhew & Minor Myers. (Illus.). 1980. 45.00 (ISBN 0-684-16293-8, ScribT). Scribner.
Documentary History of Art, Vol. 1. Ed. by Elizabeth G. Holt. pap. 3.50 ea. (Anch); Vol. 1. pap. (ISBN 0-385-09320-9); Vol. 2. pap. (ISBN 0-385-09366-7). Doubleday.
Documentary History of Banking & Currency in the U. S, 4 vols. Ed. by Herman E. Krooss. LC 69-16011. 3300p. 1981. Set. pap. 67.50 (ISBN 0-87754-209-0). Chelsea Hse.
Documentary History of Slavery in North America. Willie L. Rose. LC 75-16906. 544p. 1976. 29.95x (ISBN 0-19-501976-8); pap. text ed. 8.95x (ISBN 0-19-501978-4). Oxford U Pr.
Documentary History of the First Federal Elections, Vol. 1. Ed. by Merrill Jensen & Robert A. Becker. LC 74-5903. 800p. 1976. 50.00x (ISBN 0-299-06690-8). U of Wis Pr.
Documentary History of the Struggle for Religious Liberty in Virginia. Charles F. James. LC 70-121101. (Civil Liberties in American History Ser). 1971. Repr. of 1900 ed. lib. bdg. 27.50 (ISBN 0-306-71977-0). Da Capo.
Documentary Photography. (Life Library of Photography). (Illus.). 1972. 14.95 (ISBN 0-8094-1046-X). Time-Life.
Documentary Problems in Canadian History, 2 Vols. Ed. by J. M. Bumsted. 1969. pap. text ed. 8.95x ea.; Vol. I. pap. Pre-Confederation (ISBN 0-256-01061-7); Vol. II. pap. Post-Confederation (ISBN 0-256-01066-8). Dorsey.
Documentary Supplement to Financial & Economic Journalism: Analysis, Interpretation & Reporting. Donald Kirsch. LC 78-55415. 1978. pap. 8.00x (ISBN 0-8147-4572-5). NYU Pr.
Documentation by Social Workers in Medical Records. Society for Hospital Social Work Directors of the American Hospital Association. 1978. pap. 6.00 (ISBN 0-87258-256-6, 1085). Am Hospital.
Documentation in Education. Arvid J. Burke & Mary A. Burke. LC 67-17818. 1967. text ed. 14.95x (ISBN 0-8077-1134-9). Tchrs Coll.

Documentation in the O. E. D. Shakespeare & Nashe As Test Cases. Jurgen Schafer. (Illus.). 186p. 1980. text ed. 29.50x (ISBN 0-19-811938-0). Oxford U Pr.

Documentation of Building Science Literature. National Academy Of Sciences. 1960. pap. 2.00 (ISBN 0-309-00791-7). Natl Acad Pr.

Documentation of Collections. Compiled by Rosemary S. Reese & Frederick L. Rath, Jr. (Bibliography on Historical Organization Practices: Vol. 4). 1979. text ed. 12.50x (ISBN 0-910050-38-4). AASLH.

Documentation of Intergovernmental Organizations: Proceedings of the Workshop, Indiana U., 24-26 May 1978. Carolyn Kohler & Gloria Westfall. 70p. 1980. 29.90 (ISBN 0-08-024670-2). Pergamon.

Documentation of the United Nations System: Co-Ordination in Its Bibliographic Control. Luciana Marulli. LC 79-17510. 235p. 1979. 16.50 (ISBN 0-8108-1233-9). Scarecrow.

Documentation Source Book. Gertrude Schutze. LC 65-13551. 1965. 18.50 (ISBN 0-8108-0271-6). Scarecrow.

Documents & Notes on Privileges & Immunities with Special Reference to the Organization of American States. 1968. pap. 2.50 Eng. ed. (ISBN 0-8270-5220-0); pap. 2.50 Span. ed. (ISBN 0-8270-5215-4). OAS.

Documents for the History of the Russian-American Company. Ed. by Richard A. Pierce. Tr. by Marina Ramsay. (Materials for the Study of Alaska History Ser.: No. 7). (Illus.). 1976. 10.00x (ISBN 0-919642-56-X). Limestone Pr.

Documents for the Study of the Gospels. David R. Cartlidge & David L. Dungan. LC 79-21341. 300p. (Orig.). 1980. 14.95 (1-640); pap. 8.95 (ISBN -08006-1640-5, 1-1640). Fortress.

Documents Illustrating the Crisis of 1297-98 in England. Ed. by Michael Prestwich. (Royal Historical Society: Camden Society Fourth Ser.: Vol. 24). 216p. 1980. 20.00x (ISBN 0-8476-3307-1). Rowman.

Documents in Early Christian Thought. Ed. by M. Wiles & M. Santer. LC 74-31807. 304p. 1976. 36.00 (ISBN 0-521-20669-3); pap. 8.50x (ISBN 0-521-09915-3). Cambridge U Pr.

Documents in English History: Early Times to the Present. Brian L. Blakeley & Jacquelin Collins. LC 74-18264. 448p. 1975. pap. text ed. 12.95 (ISBN 0-471-07946-4). Wiley.

Documents in International Court Justice. 2nd ed. S. Rosenne. 1979. 50.00 (ISBN 0-379-20460-6). Oceana.

Documents in Mycenaen Greek. 2nd ed. M. Ventris & J. Chadwick. (Illus.). 600p. 1973. 110.00 (ISBN 0-521-08558-6). Cambridge U Pr.

Documents in the History of American Philosophy: From Jonathan Edward to John Dewey. Ed. by Morton White. 1972. text ed. 10.95x (ISBN 0-19-501556-8); pap. text ed. 8.95x (ISBN 0-19-501555-X). Oxford U Pr.

Documents of American Broadcasting. 3rd ed. Ed. by F. Kahn. 1978. 19.50 (ISBN 0-13-217067-1). P-H.

Documents of American History, 2 vols. 9th ed. Ed. by A. Commager. 1974. Vol. 1. pap. 13.95 (ISBN 0-13-216994-0); Vol. 2. pap. 14.95 (ISBN 0-13-217000-0). P-H.

Documents of Dissent: Chinese Political Thought Since Mao. Tr. by J. Chester Cheng. (Publication Ser.: No. 230). 120p. (Orig.). 1980. pap. 7.95 (ISBN 0-8179-7302-8). Hoover Inst Pr.

Documents of Milanese Ambassadors in France & Burgundy, 1450-1483, Vol. 3. Ed. by Caterina Santoro. LC 68-20933. 508p. 1980. 50.00x o.p. (ISBN 0-87580-069-6). N Ill U Pr.

Documents of the American Revolution, 1770-1783, Vols. 8 & 9. K. G. Davies. Incl. Vol. 8. Transcript 1774. 244p (ISBN 0-7165-2093-1); Vol. 9. Transcript Jan.-June, 1775. 244p (ISBN 0-7165-2094-X). 1976. 50.00x ea. (Pub. by Irish Academic Pr Ireland). Biblio Dist.

Documents of the American Revolution: Calendar 1777-1778, Vol. 13. Ed. by K. G. Davies. (Colonial Office Ser.). 1976. 60.00x (ISBN 0-7165-2098-2, Pub. by Irish Academic Pr Ireland). Biblio Dist.

Documents of the American Revolution 1770-1783: Calender 1781-1783 with Addenda 1770-1780. Ed. by K. G. Davies. (Colonial Office Ser: Vol. 19). 550p. 1978. 60.00x (ISBN 0-7165-2104-0, Pub by Irish Academic Pr Ireland). Biblio Dist.

Documents of the American Revolution 1770-1783: Calendar 1779-1780, Vol. 16. Ed. by K. G. Davies. (Colonial Office Ser.). 556p. 1977. 60.00x (ISBN 0-7165-2101-6, Pub. by Irish Academic Pr Ireland). Biblio Dist.

Documents of the American Revolution, 1770-1783: Transcripts 1781, Vol. 20. Ed. by K. G. Davies. (Colonial Office Ser.). 309p. 1980. 50.00x (ISBN 0-7165-2105-9, Pub. by Irish Academic Pr Ireland). Biblio Dist.

Documents of the American Revolution 1770-1783: Transcripts 1776, Vol. 12. K. G. Davies. (Colonial Office Ser.). 308p. 1976. 50.00x (ISBN 0-7165-2097-4, Pub. by Irish Academic Pr Ireland). Biblio Dist.

Documents of the American Revolution 1770-1783: Transcripts 1777, Vol. 14. Ed. by K. G. Davies. (Colonial Office Ser.). 1977. 50.00x (ISBN 0-7165-2099-0, Pub. by Irish Academic Pr Ireland). Biblio Dist.

Documents of the American Revolution 1770-1783: Transcripts 1778, Vol. 15. Ed. by K. G. Davies. (Colonial Office Ser.). 1977. 50.00x (ISBN 0-7165-2100-8, Pub. by Irish Academic Pr Ireland). Biblio Dist.

Documents of the American Revolution 1770-1783: Transcripts 1779, Vol. 17. Ed. by K. G. Davies. (Colonial Office Ser.). 296p. 1977. 50.00x (ISBN 0-7165-2102-4, Pub. by Irish Academic Pr Ireland). Biblio Dist.

Documents of the American Revolution 1770-1783, Vol. 21, Transcripts & Addenda: 1782-1783, Vol. 21. Ed. by K. G. Davies. (Colonial Offices Ser.). 1981. 50.00x (ISBN 0-7165-2106-7, Pub. by Irish Academic Pr Ireland). Biblio Dist.

Documents of the Chilean Road to Socialism. Ed. by Ben Hahm. Incl. Vol. 1. El Primer Ano del Gobierno Popular. 224p; Vol. 2. El Segundo Ano del Gobierno Popular. 400p. LC 77-26450. 1977. Set. 29.50x (ISBN 0-915980-36-3). Inst Study Human.

Documents of the Chilean Road to Socialism, Vol. 3. Chile 1971: Habla Fidel Castro. Intro. by Ben Hahm. (Illus.). 1981. Repr. of 1971 ed. text ed. 16.75x (ISBN 0-915980-31-2). Inst Study Human.

Documents of the Christian Church. 2nd ed. Ed. by Henry Bettenson. 1970. pap. 5.95 (ISBN 0-19-501293-3, GB). Oxford U Pr.

Documents of the History of the Communist Party of India, Vol. 1. G. Adhikari. LC 71-925316. 1971. 12.50x o.p. (ISBN 0-8364-0396-7). South Asia Bks.

Documents of the History of the Communist Party of India, Vol. 2. G. Adhikari. 756p. 1974. 15.00x o.p. (ISBN 0-88386-560-2). South Asia Bks.

Documents of the History of the Communist Party of India, Vol. 3 (1927) Ed. by G. Adhikari. 1978. 11.50x o.p. (ISBN 0-8364-0213-8). South Asia Bks.

Documents of United States Indian Policy. Ed. by Francis P. Prucha. LC 74-14081. x, 278p. 1975. 14.95x (ISBN 0-8032-0852-9); pap. 4.95x (ISBN 0-8032-5814-3, BB 599, Bison). U of Nebr Pr.

Documents on Indian Affairs: 1960. Girja Kumar & V. K. Aurora. 1965. 20.00x o.p. (ISBN 0-210-22619-6). Asia.

Documents on Medical Anthropology: Untrodden Fields of Anthropology, 2 vols. X. Jacobus. LC 73-185239. 906p. 1972. Repr. of 1898 ed. 35.00 o.p. (ISBN 0-88275-028-3). Krieger.

Documents on the History of Saudi Arabia, 3 vols. Ed. by Ibrahim Al-Rashid. Incl. Vol. I. Unification of Central Arabia Under Ibn Saud, 1909-1925 (ISBN 0-89712-053-1); Vol. 2. Consolidation of Power in Central Arabia Under Ibn Saud, 1925-1928 (ISBN 0-89712-054-X); Vol. 3. Establishment of the Kingdom of Saudi Arabia Under Ibn Saud, 1928-1935 (ISBN 0-89712-055-8). 1976. Set. lib. bdg. 60.00 (ISBN 0-89712-052-3). Documentary Pubns.

Documents on the State-Wide Initiative, Referendum & Recall. Charles A. Beard & Birl E. Schultz. LC 70-120853. (Law, Politics & History Ser). 1970. Repr. of 1912 ed. lib. bdg. 39.50 (ISBN 0-306-71958-4). Da Capo.

Documents Relating to the Commercial Policy of Spain with Florida. limited ed. Arthur P. Whitaker. 1921. 85.00x o.p. (ISBN 0-685-69882-3). Elliots Bks.

Dodge & Plymouth Vans, 1971-1979: Shop Manual. Jim Combs. Ed. by Eric Jorgensen. (Illus.). 420p. (Orig.). 1980. pap. text ed. 10.95 (ISBN 0-89287-314-0, A244). Clymer Pubns.

Dodge Aspen: 1976-1979 Shop Manual. Jim Combs. Ed. by Eric Jorgensen. (Illus.). 328p. (Orig.). 1980. pap. text ed. 10.95 (ISBN 0-89287-311-6, A199). Clymer Pubns.

Dodge Construction Systems Costs, 1980. Dodge Cost Information Systems Division. 262p. 1979. pap. 39.80 (ISBN 0-07-017331-1, P&RB). McGraw.

Dodge Construction Systems Costs, 1981. 262p. 1981. 43.80 (ISBN 0-07-017327-3). McGraw.

Dodge Guide to Public Works & Heavy Construction Costs, 1981. Dodge Cost Information Systems Division. 232p. 1981. 31.80 (ISBN 0-07-017326-5). McGraw.

Dodge Guide to Public Works & Heavy Construction Costs, 1980. Dodge Cost Information Systems Division. 232p. 1979. pap. 28.80 o.p. (ISBN 0-07-017332-X, P&RB). McGraw.

Dodge Manual for Building Construction Pricing & Scheduling, 1981. Dodge Cost Information Systems Division. 292p. 1981. 29.80 (ISBN 0-07-017328-1). McGraw.

Dodge Manual for Building Construction Pricing & Scheduling, 1980. Dodge Cost Information Systems Division. 292p. 1979. pap. 39.80 (ISBN 0-07-017330-3, P&RB). McGraw.

Dodge Omni: 1978-1980 Shop Manual. Jim Combs. Ed. by Eric Jorgensen. (Illus.). 1979. pap. 10.95 (ISBN 0-89287-297-7, A155). Clymer Pubns.

Dodge Pickups: 1971-1979 Shop Manual. Jim Combs. Ed. by Eric Jorgensen. (Illus.). 400p. (Orig.). 1980. pap. text ed. 10.95 (ISBN 0-89287-313-2, A243). Clymer Pubns.

Dodge Plymouth Ramcharger, Trail Duster & Pickups: 4-Wheel Drive Maintenance, 1965-1978. Mike Bishop. Ed. by Eric Jorgensen. (Illus.). 1978. pap. 7.95 (ISBN 0-89287-289-6, A231). Clymer Pubns.

Dodge Plymouth Tune-up Maintenance: Vans & Pickups, 1965-1978. Mike Bishop: Ed. by Eric Jorgensen. (Illus.). 1978. pap. 7.00 o.p. (ISBN 0-89287-239-X, A241). Clymer Pubns.

Dodge-Plymouth Vans: Nineteen Sixty Seven to Eighty Repair & Tune-up Guide. (New Automotive Bks.). 1980. 8.95 (ISBN 0-8019-6934-4). Chilton.

Dodge Service - Repair Handbook: Colt; 1971-1979. Ray Hoy. Ed. by Jeff Robinson. (Illus.). 1978. pap. 10.95 (ISBN 0-89287-162-8, A154). Clymer Pubns.

Dodge Tune-up & Maintenance, Nineteen Sixty-Seven to Nineteen Seventy-Nine. new ed. Jim Combs. Ed. by Jeff Robinson. (Illus.). 1977. pap. 7.95 (ISBN 0-89287-143-1, A-153). Clymer Pubns.

Dodo. E. F. Benson. LC 78-19214. 1978. 14.95 o.s.i. (ISBN 0-690-01782-0, TYC-T). T Y Crowell.

Dodos & Dinosaurs Are Extinct. Julian May. Ed. by Publication Associates. LC 73-104925. (gr. 2-4). 1970. PLB 6.95 o.p. (ISBN 0-87191-038-1). Creative Ed.

Dod's Parliamentary (Pocket) Companion. 161st ed. Intro. by J. Berwick Smith. LC 6-7438. (Illus.). 653p. 1980. 57.50x (ISBN 0-905702-04-2). Intl Pubns Serv.

Doers of the Word. John V. Apczynski. LC 76-51640. (American Academy of Religion. Dissertation Ser.). 1977. pap. 7.50 (ISBN 0-89130-128-3, 010118). Scholars Pr Ca.

Does Anyone Care About Lou Emma Miller? Alberta W. Constant. LC 78-4774. (gr. 3-7). 1979. 7.95 (ISBN 0-690-01335-3, TYC-J); PLB 8.79 (ISBN 0-690-03890-9). T Y Crowell.

Does Anyone Care How I Feel? Mildred Tengbom. 128p. (gr. 4 up). 1981. pap. 3.95 (ISBN 0-87123-142-5, 210142). Bethany Fell.

Does Christianity Make Sense? Mike Phillips. 1978. pap. 1.95 (ISBN 0-88207-513-6). Victor Bks.

Does God Exist? An Answer for Today. Hans Kung. Tr. by Edward Quinn. LC 79-6576. 864p. 1980. 17.50 (ISBN 0-385-13592-0). Doubleday.

Does God Have a Body? Rosalyn Kendrick. 1979. pap. 3.95 (ISBN 0-8192-1257-1). Morehouse.

Does He Really Care: In Search of an Intimate God. Ruth Vaughn. (Orig.). 1981. pap. 3.95 (ISBN 0-88449-011-4). Vision Hse.

Does Jesus Make a Difference? Ed. by Thomas R. McFadden. LC 73-17902. 1974. 7.95 (ISBN 0-8164-1151-4). Crossroad NY.

Does Mass Communication Change Public Opinion, After All? A New Approach to Effects Analysis. James B. Lemert. LC 80-23826. 260p. 1981. text ed. 17.95 (ISBN 0-88229-474-1); pap. text ed. 8.95 (ISBN 0-88229-764-3). Nelson-Hall.

Does Prayer Make a Difference? Dan D. Whitsett. (Prayers in My Life Ser.: Ser. I). 1974. pap. 1.00x (ISBN 0-8358-0312-0). Upper Room.

Does She Know She's There? Nicola Schaefer. LC 78-52115. 1978. 7.95 o.p. (ISBN 0-385-14413-X). Doubleday.

Does the Bible Teach Millennialism. L. R. Thomas. pap. 2.25 (ISBN 0-685-36796-7). Reiner.

Does the Wet Suit You? The Confessions of a Kayak Bum. Whit Deschner. LC 80-70510. (Illus.). 96p. 1981. pap. 6.45 (ISBN 0-9605388-0-1). Tern Pr.

Does This School Have Capital Punishment? Nat Hentoff. LC 80-68733. 160p. (YA) (gr. 8-12). 1981. 8.95 (ISBN 0-440-02051-4). Delacorte.

Does Your Child Have a Learning Disability? Questions Answered for Parents. Stephen W. Freeman. 128p. 1974. pap. 7.50 (ISBN 0-398-03073-1). C C Thomas.

Doesn't Everyone...? Suzanne Topper. (Orig.). 1976. pap. 1.50 o.p. (ISBN 0-685-64270-4, LB338DK, Leisure Bks). Nordon Pubns.

Dog. John Burningham. LC 76-17626. (Illus.). (ps-1). 1976. 2.50 (ISBN 0-690-01271-3, TYC-J); PLB 4.89 (ISBN 0-690-01272-1). T Y Crowell.

Dog: An Owner's Maintenance Manual. David Taylor. (Illus.). 96p. (Orig.). 1980. pap. 3.50 (ISBN 0-04-636012-3, 2505). Allen Unwin.

Dog & Cat Owner's & Consumer Handbook. Shimon De Alcantara. Ed. by Lay C. Fox. (Pet Owners Ser.). (Orig.). 1980. pap. write for info. North Am Consumer.

Dog Book. Jan Pfloog. (ps-2). 1964. PLB 5.38 (ISBN 0-307-68900-X, Golden Pr). Western Pub.

Dog Breeding. E. Fitch Daglish. Ed. by Christina Foyle. 1973. 3.95 (ISBN 0-685-55810-X). Palmetto Pub.

Dog Called Houdini. C. Everard Palmer. (Illus.). (gr. 2-7). 1979. PLB 6.50 (ISBN 0-233-96985-3). Andre Deutsch.

Dog Care. Boy Scouts Of America. LC 19-600. (Illus.). 64p. (gr. 6-12). 1972. pap. 0.70x (ISBN 0-8395-3289-X, 3289). BSA.

Dog Catalog. Don Myrus. 1978. 19.95 (ISBN 0-02-588230-9). Macmillan.

Dog Crisis. Iris Nowell. LC 78-221402. 1979. 8.95 o.p. (ISBN 0-312-21613-0). St Martin.

Dog Crusoe. R. M. Ballantyne. (Childrens Illustrated Classics Ser). (Illus.). 1972. Repr. of 1966 ed. 9.00x o.p. (ISBN 0-460-05070-2, Pub. by J. M. Dent England). Biblio Dist.

Dog Days & Cat Naps. Gene Kemp. (Illus.). 110p. (gr. 2-5). 1981. 11.95 (ISBN 0-571-11595-0, Pub. by Faber & Faber). Merrimack Bk Serv.

Dog Days at the White House: The Outrageous Memoirs of the Presidential Kennel-Keeper Truman to Nixon. Traphes L. Bryant & Frances S. Leighton. (Illus.). 288p. 1975. 9.95 o.s.i. (ISBN 0-02-517990-X). Macmillan.

Dog Days of Arthur Cane. T. Ernesto Bethancourt. LC 76-15033. (gr. 7 up). 1976. 8.95 (ISBN 0-8234-0286-X). Holiday.

Dog Days of Arthur Cane. T. Ernesto Bethancourt. 160p. 1981. pap. 1.75 (ISBN 0-553-14835-4). Bantam.

Dog Horoscope Book: Your Dog Needs a Birthday. Robin. (Illus.). 1972. pap. 2.00 o.p. (ISBN 0-87666-317-X, PS-684). TFH Pubns.

Dog Judge's Handbook. Sari B. Tietjen. LC 80-36820. (Illus.). 224p. 1980. 10.95 (ISBN 0-87605-512-9). Howell Bk.

Dog Kill. Al Dempsey. LC 75-46552. 1976. 7.95 o.p. (ISBN 0-13-217257-7). P-H.

Dog Light. William Clipman. (Wesleyan Poetry Program Ser.: No. 102). 72p. 1981. 8.00; pap. 3.95. Wesleyan U Pr.

Dog Named Sam. Melvin T. Chambers. 1978. 6.00 o.p. (ISBN 0-682-49064-4). Exposition.

Dog Obedience Training. Gust Kessopulos. LC 73-10524. (Illus.). 160p. 1975. 7.95 o.p. (ISBN 0-498-01415-0). A S Barnes.

Dog Obedience Training. rev. ed. Milo Pearsall & Charles G. Leedham. (Illus.). 1978. 12.95 o.p. (ISBN 0-684-16158-3, ScribT). Scribner.

Dog Problems. Carol L. Benjamin. LC 80-1082. 192p. 1981. 10.95 (ISBN 0-385-15710-X). Doubleday.

Dog Sense. C. R. Acton. 12.50x (ISBN 0-392-06322-0, SpS). Soccer.

Dog Soldiers. Robert Stone. 352p. 1975. pap. 2.75 (ISBN 0-345-27574-8). Ballantine.

Dog Tags. Stephen Becker. 1978. pap. 1.95 o.p. (ISBN 0-425-03664-2, Medallion). Berkley Pub.

Dog Training. Date not set. price not set. TFH Pubns. Postponed.

Dog Training Guide. Jack Kenworthy. 6.98 o.p. (ISBN 0-385-01562-3). Doubleday.

Dog Training My Way. Barbara Woodhouse. LC 72-82833. (Illus.). 128p. 1981. pap. 5.95 (ISBN 0-8128-6082-9). Stein & Day.

Dog Tricks: Teaching Your Dog to Be Useful, Fun & Entertaining. Haggerty, Arthur J., Capt. LC 77-16919. 1978. pap. 4.95 (ISBN 0-385-13493-2, Dolp). Doubleday.

Dog Who Came to Dinner. Sydney Taylor. (Beginning-to-Read Ser.). (Illus.). (gr. 1-3). 1966. 2.50 o.p. (ISBN 0-695-82086-9); lib. ed. 2.97 o.p. (ISBN 0-695-42086-0). Follett.

Dog Who Thought He Was a Boy. Cora Annett. (Illus.). (gr. k-3). 1965. reinforced bdg. 8.95 (ISBN 0-395-18471-1). HM.

Dog Who Wouldn't Be. Farley Mowat. (gr. 6-10). 1970. pap. 1.50 (ISBN 0-515-05617-0, N2333). Jove Pubns.

Dog Who Wouldn't Be. Farley Mowat. 208p. 1981. pap. 1.95 (ISBN 0-553-14354-9). Bantam.

Dogfight & More Games Calculators Play. Wallace Judd. 1977. pap. 1.75 o.s.i. (ISBN 0-446-84398-9). Warner Bks.

Doggone Mystery. Mary B. Christian. Ed. by Ann Fay. LC 80-10448. (First Read-Alone Mystery Bk.). (Illus.). (gr. 1-3). 1980. 5.50g (ISBN 0-8075-1656-2). A Whitman.

Dogma & Pluralism. Ed. by Edward Schillebeeckx. (Concilium Ser.: Religion in the Seventies: Vol. 51). pap. 4.95 (ISBN 0-8164-2507-8). Crossroad NY.

Dogma, Depression, and the New Deal: The Debate of Political Leaders Over Economic Recovery. Theodore Rosenof. 1975. 13.50 (ISBN 0-8046-9113-4, Natl U). Kennikat.

Dogma of Christ & Other Essays. Erich Fromm. 1974. pap. 1.25 o.p. (ISBN 0-449-30715-8, P715, Prem). Fawcett.

Dogma of Immaculate Perception: A Critique of Positivistic Thought. Howard A. Slaatte. LC 79-66858. 1979. pap. text ed. 7.50 (ISBN 0-8191-0849-9). U Pr of Amer.

Dogmatic Canons & Decrees of the Council of Trent, Vatican Council I, Plus the Decree on the Immaculate Conception & the Syllabus of Errors. Devin-Adair Staff. LC 79-112469. (Eng.). 1977. pap. 4.00 (ISBN 0-89555-018-0, 197). TAN Bks Pubs.

Dogmatic Theology, 4 vols. William G. Shedd. 1979. Repr. of 1889 ed. 49.50 (ISBN 0-686-25156-3); text ed. 44.95 (ISBN 0-686-25157-1). Klock & Klock.

Dogmatic Theology for the Laity. Mattias Premm. LC 67-21425. 1977. pap. 10.00 (ISBN 0-89555-022-9, 183). TAN Bks Pubs.

Dogs. rev. ed. Beth Brown. LC 68-9405. (Illus.). (gr. 3 up). 1981. PLB 6.87 (ISBN 0-87460-095-2). Lion.

Dogs. Robert Calder. 1976. 7.95 o.s.i. (ISBN 0-440-02050-6). Delacorte.

Dogs. Fiora Henrie. (gr. 2-5). 1980. PLB 5.90 (ISBN 0-531-04120-4, E30). Watts.

Dogs. Michael Holman. LC 76-13877. (Easy-Read Fact Book Ser.). (Illus.). 48p. (gr. 2-4). 1976. PLB 6.45 (ISBN 0-531-01213-1). Watts.

Dogs - in Fact & Legend. Adele Millard. (gr. 5 up). 1977. 5.95 o.p. (ISBN 0-8069-3736-X); PLB 5.89 o.p. (ISBN 0-8069-3737-8). Sterling.

Dogs & Dragons, Trees & Dreams: A Collection of Poems. Karla Kuskin. LC 79-2814. (Illus.). 96p. (gr. 1-6). 1980. 8.95 (ISBN 0-06-023543-8, HarpJ); PLB 8.79 (ISBN 0-06-023544-6). Har-Row.

Dogs & Puppies. Jane Rockwell. LC 75-25750. (First Bks. Ser). (Illus.). 96p. (gr. 5 up). 1976. PLB 6.45 (ISBN 0-531-00840-1). Watts.

Dogs & Puppies. Jane Rockwell. (Illus.). (gr. 4-6). 1979. pap. 1.50 (ISBN 0-671-56038-7). PB.

Dogs & Puppies Coloring Album. Illus. by Rita Warner. (Illus.). 1977. pap. 3.50 (ISBN 0-912300-81-7, 87-7). Troubador Pr.

Dogs Bodies. Ralph Steadman. 1971. pap. 1.95 o.p. (ISBN 0-200-71727-8). Transatlantic.

Dogs for Police Service: Programming & Training. Sam D. Watson, Jr. (Illus.). 100p. 1972. 12.75 (ISBN 0-398-02025-6). C C Thomas.

Dogs in Shakespeare. John A. Donovan. 9.95 (ISBN 0-87714-074-X). Green Hill.

Dog's Life: Stories of Champions, Hunters, & Faithful Friends. Compiled by Phyllis R. Fenner. (Illus.). (gr. 7-9). 1978. 7.95 (ISBN 0-688-22156-4); PLB 7.63 (ISBN 0-688-32156-9). Morrow.

Dogs of Dewsbury. Cliff Ashby. (Poetry Ser.). 1979. 5.95 o.s.i. (ISBN 0-685-96487-6, Pub. by Carcanet New Pr England). Persea Bks.

Dogs of the World in Color. Ivan Swedrup. Tr. by Rosamund Oldfield. LC 70-77364. (Illus.). 1969. 3.50 o.p. (ISBN 0-668-01940-9). Arco.

Dogs: Standards & Guidelines for the Breeding, Care, & Management of Laboratory Animals. Institute of Laboratory Animal Resources. (Illus.). 60p. 1973. pap. 3.75 (ISBN 0-309-02102-2). Natl Acad Pr.

Dogs to Fishing Tackle. Time-Life Books Editors. (Encyclopedia of Collectibles Ser.). (Illus.). 1978. lib. bdg. 10.98 (ISBN 0-686-50977-3). Silver.

Dogsbody. Diana W. Jones. LC 76-28715. (gr. 5-9). 1977. 8.25 (ISBN 0-688-80074-2); PLB 7.92 (ISBN 0-688-84074-4). Greenwillow.

Dogsled. Slim Randles. 1978. pap. 3.95 (ISBN 0-87691-261-7). Winchester Pr.

Dogwatch. Ted Jones. (Illus.). 1981. 14.95 (ISBN 0-393-03252-3). Norton.

Doing Better & Feeling Worse. Ed. by John H. Knowles. 1977. 9.95 (ISBN 0-393-06419-0); pap. text ed. 5.95 (ISBN 0-393-06423-9). Norton.

Doing Business in Egypt. Nicholas A. Abraham. Ed. by Karl E. Prinz. (Doing Business in the Middle East: Vol. 2). (Illus.). 280p. (Orig.). 1979. pap. text ed. 79.95x (ISBN 0-934592-00-4). Trade Ship Pub Co.

Doing Business in Saudi Arabia. Nicholas A. Abraham. Ed. by Christine A. Hanna. (Doing Business in the Middle East: Vol. 1). (Illus.). 336p. (Orig.). 1980. pap. text ed. 79.95x (ISBN 0-934592-01-2). Trade Ship Pub Co.

Doing Business in Saudi Arabia. Hasan Kabir. 350p. 1980. 49.95 (ISBN 0-89260-187-6). Hwong Pub.

Doing Business in Saudi Arabia & the Arab Gulf States. N. A. Shilling. LC 75-37251. (Doing Business in the Middle East Ser.). 185.00 (ISBN 0-916400-01-8); supplement 65.00 (ISBN 0-685-83461-1); 40.00 (ISBN 0-916400-01-8); 55.00 (ISBN 0-916400-01-8). Inter-Crescent.

Doing Business in the European Community. Jon S. Drew. (Illus.). 1979. text ed. 28.95 (ISBN 0-408-10631-X). Butterworths.

Doing Business in Washington: How to Win Friends & Influence Governemnt. Harrison W. Fox, Jr. & Martin Schnitzer. LC 80-2313. (Illus.). 1981. 14.95 (ISBN 0-02-910460-2). Free Pr.

Doing Business with Japan. William Duncan. 1976. 27.50 o.s.i. (ISBN 0-7161-0303-6). Herman Pub.

Doing Business with the Russians. Westshore, Inc. (Praeger Special Studies). 1979. 20.95 (ISBN 0-03-048456-1). Praeger.

Doing Feminist Research. Ed. by Helen Roberts. 224p. (Orig.). 1981. pap. price not set (ISBN 0-7100-0772-8). Routledge & Kegam.

Doing Field Research. John M. Johnson. LC 74-27599. 1975. 12.95 (ISBN 0-02-916600-4). Free Pr.

Doing Field Research. John M. Johnson. LC 74-27599. 1978. pap. text ed. 7.95 (ISBN 0-02-916610-1). Free Pr.

Doing Good by Doing Little: Race & Schooling in Britain. David L. Kirp. 1979. 12.95x (ISBN 0-520-03740-5). U of Cal Pr.

Doing Library Research: An Introduction for Community College Students. Robert K. Baker. (Westview Guides to Library Research Ser.). 260p. 27.50x (ISBN 0-89158-778-0). Westview.

Doing Philosophy. Thomas E. Katen. (Illus.). 368p. 1973. text ed. 15.95 (ISBN 0-13-217570-3). P-H.

Doing Sociological Research. Ed. by Colin Bell & Howard Newby. LC 77-84959. 1978. 16.95 (ISBN 0-02-902350-5). Free Pr.

Doing Something Nice, Inc. & Other Short Plays for Kids. Donald Arneson. (Illus.). 72p. (Orig.). (gr. 3-6). 1978. write for info. (ISBN 0-934778-00-0); pap. write for info. Bookmaker.

Doing Their Thing. Stanley L. Weinberg & Herbert J. Stoltze. (Action Biology Ser). (gr. 9-12). 1974. pap. text ed. 3.20 (ISBN 0-205-04146-9, 6741460). Allyn.

Doing Theology in a Revolutionary Situation. Jose M. Bonino. Ed. by William H. Lazareth. LC 74-80424. (Confrontation Bks). 208p. 1975. pap. 4.50 (ISBN 0-8006-1451-8, 1-1451). Fortress.

Doing Theology in New Places. J. P. Jossua & J. B. Metz. (Concilium Ser.: Religion in the Seventies Vol. 115). 1979. pap. 4.95 (ISBN 0-8164-2611-2). Crossroad NY.

Doing Things Together. Carol Barkin & Elizabeth James. LC 75-20083. (Moods & Emotions Ser.). (Illus.). 32p. (gr. k-2). 1975. PLB 8.95 (ISBN 0-8172-0036-3). Raintree Pubs.

Doing Time: A Look at Crime & Prisons. new ed. Robert Lehrman & Phyllis E. Clark. (Illus.). 160p. 1980. 10.95 (ISBN 0-8038-1566-2). Hastings.

Doings of Raffles Haw. A. Conan Doyle. LC 80-67702. (Conan Doyle Centennial Ser.). (Illus.). 147p. 1981. 11.95 (ISBN 0-934468-43-5). Gaslight.

Doktor Zhivago. Boris Pasternak. LC 60-15772. 1959. 19.95 (ISBN 0-472-71796-0). U of Mich Pr.

Dolce Cucina: The Italian Dessert Cookbook. Anna Seldis. (Illus.). 256p. 1974. pap. 2.95 o.s.i. (ISBN 0-02-010300-X, Collier). Macmillan.

Doll Book. Delores Draper. (Illus.). (gr. k-2). 1977. PLB 5.38 (ISBN 0-307-68917-4, Golden Pr). Western Pub.

Doll: Bottle-Nosed Dolphin. Sally Glendinning. LC 80-13660. (Young Animal Adventures Ser.). 40p. (gr. 2). 1980. PLB 5.88 (ISBN 0-8116-7501-7). Garrard.

Doll Catalog, Nineteen Eighty. 1980. pap. 6.95 (ISBN 0-87588-163-7). Hobby Hse.

Doll Collectors' Manual, 1973, Vol. 8. Dorothy S. Coleman et al. LC 65-29362. 1978. 8.50 (ISBN 0-9603210-0-4). Doll Collect Am.

Doll Crochet of Yesterday. (Illus.). 1978. pap. 1.50 (ISBN 0-87588-145-9). Hobby Hse.

Doll Modes: Doll Fashions with Patterns. Eleanor-Jean Carter. 105p. 1972. pap. 10.00x o.p. (ISBN 0-685-27933-2). Hobby Hse.

Doll Named Moses. Arthur A. Crawford. 1981. 12.50 (ISBN 0-682-49729-0). Exposition.

Doll Repair. Evelyn Gaylin. 1976. 11.95 o.p. (ISBN 0-87588-121-1); pap. 7.95 o.p. (ISBN 0-87588-122-X). Hobby Hse.

Doll Who Ate His Mother. Ramsey Campbell. 1978. pap. 1.75 o.s.i. (ISBN 0-515-04483-0). Jove Pubns.

Doll Who Came Alive. rev. ed. Enys Tregarthen. Ed. by Elizabeth Yates. LC 70-179780. (Illus.). 80p. (gr. 1-4). 1972. Repr. of 1942 ed. 6.95 (ISBN 0-381-99683-2, A19760, JD-J). John Day.

Doll with the Opal Eyes. Jean De Weese. 1977. pap. 1.95 o.p. (ISBN 0-445-04197-8). Popular Lib.

Dollar Drain & American Forces in Germany: Managing the Political Economics of Alliance. Gregory F. Treverton. LC 76-51689. xvi, 226p. 1978. 14.00x (ISBN 0-8214-0368-0). Ohio U Pr.

Dollar Making Tips for Survival in the Eighties. Billy Mason. 50p. (Orig.). 1981. lib. bdg. 9.95 (ISBN 0-686-28909-9). Kelso.

Dollar Princesses. Ruth Brandon. LC 80-7627. (Illus.). 224p. 1980. 12.95 (ISBN 0-394-50403-8). Knopf.

Dollar Squeeze - & How to Beat It. George Sullivan. LC 79-113937. 1970. 5.95 o.s.i. (ISBN 0-02-615340-8). Macmillan.

Dollars & Cents of Shopping Centers: A Study of Receipts & Expenditures, 1972. 5th ed. Ed. by J. Ross McKeever. LC 70-81240. (Special Publications Ser.). (Illus.). 1972. pap. 24.25 (ISBN 0-87420-906-4); pap. 16.25 o.p. (ISBN 0-686-66562-7). Urban Land.

Dollars & Cents of Shopping Centers-1975. 6th ed. Ed. by J. Ross McKeever. LC 75-799. (Special Publication Ser). (Illus.). 1975. pap. 42.00 (ISBN 0-87420-563-8). Urban Land.

Dollars & Cents of Shopping Centers: 1978. 7th ed. Frank H. Spink, Jr. LC 78-50885. (Triennial Report Ser.). (Illus.). 300p. 1978. pap. 55.00 (ISBN 0-87420-581-6). Urban Land.

Dollars & Deficits: Inflation, Monetary Policy & the Balance of Payments. M. Friedman. 1968. pap. 10.95 (ISBN 0-13-218289-0). P-H.

Dollars & Diplomacy: Ambassador David Rowland Francis & the Fall of Tsarism, 1916-17. Ed. by Jamie H. Cockfield. LC 80-19786. ix, 149p. 1981. 12.75 (ISBN 0-8223-2445-8). Duke.

Dollars & Sense. Joseph Bensman. 1967. 9.95 (ISBN 0-02-509000-3). Macmillan.

Dollars & Sense. Elizabeth McGough. LC 75-19109. (Illus.). 160p. (gr. 7 up). 1975. PLB 6.96 (ISBN 0-688-32046-5). Morrow.

Dollars & Sense: An Introduction to Economics. 2nd ed. Marilu H. McCarty. 1979. pap. text ed. 11.95x (ISBN 0-673-15230-8); study guide 4.95x (ISBN 0-673-15238-3). Scott F.

Dollars & Sense of Honesty: Stories from the Business World. George D. Armerding & Phil Landrum. LC 77-7854. 1979. 6.95 o.p. (ISBN 0-06-060301-1, HarpR). Har-Row.

Dollars & Sense of Hospital Malpractice Insurance. Michael Sumner. LC 78-67846. 1979. text ed. 22.50 (ISBN 0-89011-517-6). Abt Assoc.

Dollars, Dependents, & Dogma: Overseas Chinese Remittances to Communist China. Chun-hsi Wu. LC 67-24368. (Publications Ser.: No. 55). 1967. 10.00 (ISBN 0-8179-1551-6). Hoover Inst Pr.

Dollars for Reform: The OEO Neighborhood Health Center Experience. Isabel Marcus. LC 78-2198. 1981. 22.95x (ISBN 0-669-03092-9). Lexington Bks.

Dollars for the Duke. Barbara Cartland. 160p. (Orig.). 1981. pap. 1.95 (ISBN 0-553-14650-5). Bantam.

Dollars from Washington: An Individual's. Charles F. Lasure. 64p. 1980. 5.00 (ISBN 0-682-49647-2). Exposition.

Dollarwise Guide to California & Las Vegas, 1979-80. 312p. pap. 4.95 (ISBN 0-671-24897-9). Frommer-Pasmantier.

Dollarwise Guide to California & Las Vegas: 1981-82. pap. 5.95 (ISBN 0-671-41426-7). Frommer-Pasmantier.

Dollarwise Guide to Canada, 1980-81. 672p. pap. 6.95 (ISBN 0-671-25179-1). Frommer-Pasmantier.

Dollarwise Guide to Egypt, 1980-81. 256p. pap. 4.95 (ISBN 0-671-25488-X). Frommer-Pasmantier.

Dollarwise Guide to England & Scotland 1981-82. 608p. 1981. pap. 6.95 (ISBN 0-671-41424-0). Frommer-Pasmantier.

Dollarwise Guide to France, 1981-82. 496p. 1981. pap. 6.95 (ISBN 0-671-41425-9). Frommer-Pasmantier.

Dollarwise Guide to Germany: 1980-81 Edition. 1981. pap. 4.95 (ISBN 0-671-25487-1). Frommer-Pasmantier.

Dollarwise Guide to Italy, 1981-82. 300p. 1981. pap. 5.95 (ISBN 0-671-43033-5). Frommer-Pasmantier.

Dollarwise Guide to New England, 1980-81. 400p. pap. 4.95 (ISBN 0-671-25486-3). Frommer-Pasmantier.

Dollarwise Guide to Portugal: 1980-81 Edition. 1981. pap. 4.95 (ISBN 0-671-25177-5). Frommer-Pasmantier.

Dollarwise Guide to the Caribbean, 1980-81. 688p. pap. 6.95 (ISBN 0-671-25178-3). Frommer-Pasmantier.

Dollarwise Guide to the Southeast & New Orleans, 1980-81. 300p. pap. 4.95 (ISBN 0-671-25175-9). Frommer-Pasmantier.

Dolley Madison. Matthew G. Grant. LC 73-15848. 1974. PLB 5.95 (ISBN 0-87191-308-9). Creative Ed.

Dollhouse Idea Book. Pauline Flick & Valerie Jackson. 1976. pap. 3.50 o.p. (ISBN 0-8015-2152-1). Dutton.

Dollmaker. H. S. Arnow. 1962. pap. 1.50 o.s.i. (ISBN 0-02-016310-X, Collier). Macmillan.

Dollmaker. Harriet Arnow. (YA) 1972. pap. 2.95 (ISBN 0-380-00947-1, 53926, Bard). Avon.

Dollmaker. Harriette S. Arnow. 1967. 9.95 o.s.i. (ISBN 0-02-503360-3); large print ed 8.95 o.s.i. (ISBN 0-02-489370-6). Macmillan.

Dollmaker's Ghost. Larry Levis. 1981. 9.95 (ISBN 0-525-09450-4); pap. 5.95 (ISBN 0-525-47662-8). Dutton.

Dolls: A New Guide for Collectors. Clara H. Fawcett. 282p. 1964. 15.50 (ISBN 0-8231-3021-5). Branford.

Dolls & Puppets. Mary Cockett. LC 74-76185. (David & Charles Children's Books). (Illus.). 80p. (gr. 3-8). 1974. 4.95 o.p. (ISBN 0-7153-6311-5). David & Charles.

Dolls & Puppets. Max Von Boehn. Tr. by Josephine Nicoll. (Illus.). 1966. Repr. of 1932 ed. 25.00x (ISBN 0-8154-0026-8). Cooper Sq.

Dolls' Christmas. Tasha Tudor. LC 59-12744. (Illus.). (gr. k-3). 1950. 5.95g (ISBN 0-8098-1026-3); pap. 2.50 (ISBN 0-8098-2912-6). Walck.

Dolls for Children to Make. Suzy Ives. 1975. 14.95 (ISBN 0-7134-2991-7, Pub. by Batsford England). David & Charles.

Dolls for Sale. Valerie Janitch. (Illus.). 1980. 15.95 (ISBN 0-571-11535-7, Pub. by Faber & Faber); pap. 6.95 (ISBN 0-571-11536-5, Pub. by Faber & Faber). Merrimack Bk Serv.

Doll's House & Other Plays. Henrik Ibsen. Tr. by Peter Watts. Incl. League of Youth; Lady from the Sea. (Classics Ser.). 1965. pap. 2.95 (ISBN 0-14-044146-8). Penguin.

Doll's House, The Wild Duck & Lady from the Sea. Henrik Ibsen. 1979. 7.00x (ISBN 0-460-00494-8, Evman); pap. 3.75 (ISBN 0-460-01494-3, Evman). Dutton.

Dolls' Houses in America: Historic Preservation in Miniature. Flora G. Jacobs. LC 73-1100. (Encore Edition). (Illus.). 1978. pap. 6.95 (ISBN 0-684-16905-3). Scribner.

Dolls in Color. Faith Eaton. LC 75-17668. (Illus.). 176p. 1976. 6.95 o.s.i. (ISBN 0-02-534710-1, 53471). Macmillan.

Dolls in National & Folk Costume. Jean Greenhowe. (Illus.). 112p. 1978. 11.75 (ISBN 0-8231-3033-9). Branford.

Dolls in National Costume. Iola Barlow. (gr. 6 up). 6.50 (ISBN 0-8231-3023-1). Branford.

Dolls of the Nineteen Thirties Paper Dolls. Janet Nason. 8p. (gr. 8-12). 1978. pap. 3.50 (ISBN 0-914510-08-8). Evergreen.

Dolls Through the Ages. Nancie Swanberg. (Illus.). (gr. 1-12). 1979. pap. 3.50 (ISBN 0-89844-005-X). Troubador Pr.

Dolly Parton. John Keely. (Rock 'n Pop Stars). (Illus.). (gr. 4-12). 1979. PLB 5.95 (ISBN 0-87191-695-9); pap. 2.95 (ISBN 0-89812-095-0). Creative Ed.

Dolly Parton. Robert K. Krishef. LC 79-28247. (Country Music Bks.). (Illus.). (YA) (gr. 4 up). 1980. PLB 5.95g (ISBN 0-8225-1411-7). Lerner Pubns.

Dolly Parton: A Photo-Bio. Otis James. (Orig.). pap. 1.95 (ISBN 0-515-05157-8). Jove Pubns.

Dolly Purdo. M. M. Walsh. 1977. pap. 1.50 o.p. (ISBN 0-425-03299-X). Berkley Pub.

Dolmen Press XXV Years: Illustrated Bibliography of the Dolmen Press 1951-1976. Compiled by Liam Miller. (Dolmen Editions Ser.: No. XxV). 1976. text ed. 39.00x (ISBN 0-85105-309-2, Dolmen Pr). Humanities.

Dolores: A River Running Guide. M. Stanislaus McCaffrey. 96p. (Orig.). 1981. pap. 4.95 (ISBN 0-87108-578-X). Pruett.

Dolores Medio. Margaret E. Jones. (World Authors Ser.: Spain: No. 281). 1974. lib. bdg. 10.95 (ISBN 0-8057-2610-1). Twayne.

Dolphin. Morris. (Illus.). (gr. 2-3). Date not set. pap. cancelled (ISBN 0-590-30026-1, Schol Pap). Schol Bk Serv.

Dolphin Guide to San Francisco & the Bay Area. rev. ed. Curt Gentry. LC 69-11017. 1969. pap. 2.50 (ISBN 0-385-05489-0, C205, Dolp). Doubleday.

Dolphin Island. Arthur C. Clarke. 1971. pap. 1.75 (ISBN 0-425-04302-9, Medallion). Berkley Pub.

Dolphin Summer. Carola Salisbury. 1978. pap. 1.75 o.p. (ISBN 0-449-23415-0, Crest). Fawcett.

Dolphins. Jacques Y. Cousteau & Philippe Diole. LC 74-9481. (Undersea Discoveries of Jacques-Yves Cousteau). (Illus.). 1977. pap. 8.95 (ISBN 0-89104-076-5). A & W Pubs.

Dolphins. Martha Moffett & Robert Moffett. LC 76-134497. (First Bks). (Illus.). (gr. 4-6). 1971. PLB 4.90 o.p. (ISBN 0-531-00723-5). Watts.

Dolphins. George Shea. LC 80-18259. (Creatures Wild & Free Ser.). (gr. 1-6). 1981. 5.95 (ISBN 0-88436-770-3). EMC.

Dolphins at Cochin. Tom Buchan. LC 69-20017. 1969. 3.50 o.p. (ISBN 0-8090-3950-8). Hill & Wang.

Dolphins in the City. Bo Carpelan. Tr. by Sheila Lafarge from Swedish. LC 75-8001. 128p. 1976. 5.95 o.s.i. (ISBN 0-440-05073-1, Sey Lawr). Delacorte.

Dom & Va. John Christopher. 176p. (gr. 5-8). 1973. 7.95 (ISBN 0-02-718320-3). Macmillan.

Dom Casmurro. Machado De Assis. 1980. pap. 2.95 (ISBN 0-380-49668-2, 49668, Bard). Avon.

Dom Juan Ou le Festin De Pierre. Moliere. Ed. by W. D. Howarth. (French Texts Ser.). 1975. pap. text ed. 9.95x (ISBN 0-631-00580-3, Pub. by Basil Blackwell). Biblio Dist.

Dom Sebastien, Gaetano Donizetti, 2 vols. Gaetano Donizetti. Ed. by Charles Rosen & Philip Gossett. LC 76-49210. (Early Romantic Opera Ser.: Vol. 29). 1980. lib. bdg. 82.00 (ISBN 0-8240-2928-3). Garland Pub.

Domain Referenced Testing in Special Education. Maynard Reynolds & Wells Hively. 1975. pap. text ed. 4.00x o.p. (ISBN 0-86586-022-X). Coun Exc Child.

Domaine Royal Sous les Premiers Capetiens (987-1180) William M. Newman. LC 80-2014. 1981. Repr. of 1937 ed. 36.00 (ISBN 0-404-18581-9). AMS Pr.

Dombey & Son. Charles Dickens. Ed. by Alan Horsman. (Illus.). 931p. 1974. 74.00x (ISBN 0-19-812491-0). Oxford U Pr.

Domenico Gnoli. Luigi Carluccio. LC 74-82606. (Illus.). 168p. 1975. 40.00 (ISBN 0-87951-026-9). Overlook Pr.

Domes: "The Frank O'Hara Award Series". John Koethe. (Full Court Rebound Bk.). 1978. 14.95 (ISBN 0-231-03743-0); pap. 66.00 (ISBN 0-231-03744-9). Full Court NY.

Domesday Book: A Guide. Rex W. Finn. 109p. 1973. 12.50x (ISBN 0-87471-640-3). Rowman.

Domesday Book in the Classroom. John Fines. 48p. 1981. pap. 7.50x (ISBN 0-8476-3165-6). Rowman.

Domesday Book: Its Place in Administrative History. Vivian H. Galbraith. 232p. 1975. 24.50x (ISBN 0-19-822424-9). Oxford U Pr.

Domesday England. Ed. by H. C. Darby. LC 76-11485. (Domesday Geography of England Ser.). (Illus.). 1977. 77.50 (ISBN 0-521-21307-X). Cambridge U Pr.

Domesday of Crown Lands. Sidney J. Madge. LC 67-31560. (Illus.). Repr. of 1938 ed. 26.00x (ISBN 0-678-05071-6). Kelley.

Domesday Studies: The Eastern Countries. Reginald A. Finn. LC 80-2231. (Illus.). 1981. Repr. of 1967 ed. 34.50 (ISBN 0-404-18759-5). AMS Pr.

Domesday Studies: The Liber Exoniensis. Reginald A. Finn. LC 80-2239. 1981. Repr. of 1964 ed. 29.50 (ISBN 0-404-18760-9). AMS Pr.

Domestic Affections, & Other Poems. 1812. Felicia D. Hemans. Ed. by Donald H. Reiman. LC 75-31214. (Romantic Context Ser.: Poetry 1789-1830). 1978. lib. bdg. 47.00 (ISBN 0-8240-2164-9). Garland Pub.

Domestic Air Transportation Network of the United States. Walter F. Wacht. LC 73-92651. (Research Papers Ser.: No. 154). (Illus.). 98p. 1974. pap. 8.00 (ISBN 0-89065-061-6). U Chicago Dept Geog.

Domestic Airline Industry. D. Daryl Wyckoff & David H. Maister. LC 76-54612. (Lexington Casebook Series in Industry Analysis). 1977. 18.95 (ISBN 0-669-01307-2); instructors manual free (ISBN 0-669-01843-0). Lexington Bks.

Domestic & Artistic Life of John Singleton Cop. Martha B. Amory. LC 71-77698. (Library of American Art Ser). 1882. Repr. of 1969 ed. lib. bdg. 39.50 (ISBN 0-306-71336-5). Da Capo.

Domestic & Heroic in Tennyson's Poetry. Donald S. Hair. 272p. 1981. 25.00x (ISBN 0-8020-5530-3). U of Toronto Pr.

Domestic Animal Behavior: Causes & Implications for Animal Care & Management. James V. Craig. (Illus.). 400p. 1981. text ed. 19.95 (ISBN 0-13-218339-0). P-H.

Domestic Animal Behavior for Veterinarians & Animal Scientists. Katherine A. Houpt & Thomas R. Wolski. text ed. 16.50 (ISBN 0-8138-1060-4). Iowa St U Pr.

Domestic Architecture in Rural France. Samuel Chamberlain. (Illus.). 64p. (Orig.). 1981. pap. 7.95 (ISBN 0-8038-1578-6). Hastings.

Domestic Arrangements. Norma Klein. Ed. by Herbert M. Katz. 224p. 1981. 11.95 (ISBN 0-87131-343-X). M Evans.

Domestic Capital Formation in the United Kingdom. C. H. Feinstein. (Publications of the National Institute of Economic & Social Research & Cambridge Department of Applied Economics: No. 4). 45.00 (ISBN 0-521-04986-5, Q). Cambridge U Pr.

Domestic Context of American Foreign Policy. Barry B. Hughes. LC 77-17472. (Illus.). 1978. text ed. 18.95x (ISBN 0-7167-0040-9); pap. text ed. 9.95x (ISBN 0-7167-0039-5). W H Freeman.

Domestic Context of Soviet Foreign Policy. Ed. by Seweryn Bialer. 500p. 1980. lib. bdg. 35.00x (ISBN 0-89158-783-7); pap. text ed. 15.00x (ISBN 0-89158-891-4). Westview.

Domestic Descendants. (Wild, Wild World of Animals Ser.). (Illus.). 1979. lib. bdg. 11.97 (ISBN 0-686-51178-6). Silver.

Domestic Economic Policies in the Industrial Countries. Tripartite report by fourteen economists from Japan, Europe, & North America. 1978. pap. 2.00 (ISBN 0-8157-1893-4). Brookings.

Domestic Goals in an Interdependent World: The Frankfurt Dialogue. Hinshaw. Date not set. 25.00 (ISBN 0-8247-6999-6). Dekker.

Domestic Goddess Planning Notebook, 1981. 1980. 8.95 (ISBN 0-911094-11-3). Pacific Santa Barbara.

Domestic Influences on Soviet Foreign Policy. Dina R. Spechler. LC 78-61396. 1978. pap. text ed. 6.75 (ISBN 0-8191-0596-1). U Pr of Amer.

Domestic Intelligence: Monitoring Dissent in America. Richard E. Morgan. LC 80-13254. 204p. 1980. text ed. 13.95x (ISBN 0-292-76463-4); pap. 6.95x (ISBN 0-292-71529-3). U of Tex Pr.

Domestic Policy Review of Solar Energy. U. S. Dept. of Energy. 153p. 1980. 29.50 (ISBN 0-89934-061-X, V953-PP); pap. 14.50. Solar Energy Info.

Domestic Political Realities of European Unification: A Study of Mass Public & Elites in the European Community Countries. new ed. Werner J. Feld & John K. Wilgen. LC 76-28703. (Westview Replica Editions). 1977. PLB 21.00x (ISBN 0-89158-149-9). Westview.

Domestic Potential of Solar & Other Renewable Energy Sources. Committee on Nuclear & Alternative Energy Systems. 1979. pap. 8.00 (ISBN 0-309-02927-9). Natl Acad Pr.

Domestic Rabbit. 3rd ed. J. C. Sandford. LC 78-11915. 1979. 17.95 (ISBN 0-470-26526-4). Halsted Pr.

Domestic Relations: Law & Skills. William P. Statsky. LC 78-7303. (Paralegal Ser.). 537p. 1978. text ed. 18.95 (ISBN 0-8299-2007-2). West Pub.

Domestic Satellite Policy: An FCC Giant Step Toward Competitive Telecommunications Policy. Robert S. Magnant. LC 76-30840. (Illus.). 1977. PLB 27.50x (ISBN 0-89158-226-6). Westview.

Domestic Servant Class in Eighteenth Century England. J. Jean Hecht. LC 79-2938. 240p. 1981. Repr. of 1956 ed. 19.50 (ISBN 0-8305-0104-5). Hyperion Conn.

Domestic Service, London, Nineteen Sixteen. C. V. Butler. LC 79-56953. (English Working Class Ser.). 1980. lib. bdg. 15.00 (ISBN 0-8240-0107-9). Garland Pub.

Domestic Sources of Foreign Policy. James N. Rosenau. LC 67-10347. 1967. 17.95 (ISBN 0-02-927000-6). Free Pr.

Domestic Taxation & Foreign Trade: The United States-European Border Tax Dispute. Michael Von Steinaecker. LC 72-83010. (Special Studies in International Economics & Development). 1973. 28.00x (ISBN 0-275-28652-5). Irvington.

Domestic Transportation: Practice, Theory, & Policy. 4th ed. Roy Sampson & Martin T. Farris. LC 78-69576. (Illus.). 1978. text ed. 19.50 (ISBN 0-395-26793-5); inst. manual 0.65 (ISBN 0-395-26794-3). HM.

Domesticating the Clergy: The Inception of the Reformation in Strasbourg 1522-1524. William S. Stafford. LC 76-15567. (American Academy of Religion, Dissertation Ser.). 1976. pap. 9.00 (ISBN 0-89130-109-7, 010117). Scholars Pr Ca.

Dominance & Diversity: The International Hierarchy. Steven L. Spiegel. LC 80-8295. 317p. 1980. lib. bdg. 19.00 (ISBN 0-8191-1331-X); pap. text ed. 10.50 (ISBN 0-8191-1332-8). U Pr of Amer.

Dominance Signals. Gerald Kaminski. LC 80-12997. 200p. Date not set. pap. price not set (ISBN 0-914974-25-4). Holmgangers. Postponed.

Dominant & Alternative Life Styles in Poland: An Outline. 41p. 1980. pap. 5.00 (ISBN 92-808-0139-2, TUNU 067, UNU). Unipub.

Dominant Ideology Thesis. Nicholas Abercrombie et al. 240p. 1980. text ed. 28.50x (ISBN 0-04-301117-9, 2531). Allen Unwin.

Dominant Issues in Medical Sociology. Howard D. Schwartz & Cary S. Kart. LC 77-76118. (Sociology Ser.). 1978. pap. text ed. 14.95 (ISBN 0-201-06781-1). A-W.

Dominant Ways of Life in Denmark--Alternative Ways of Life in Denmark. 77p. 1980. pap. 5.00 (ISBN 92-808-0140-6, TUNU095, UNU). Unipub.

Domination, Legitimation, & Resistance: The Incorporation of the Nineteenth-Century English Working Class. Francis Hearn. LC 77-84753. (Contributions in Labor History: No. 3). 1978. lib. bdg. 19.95 (ISBN 0-8371-9847-X, HDL/). Greenwood.

Dominations & Powers: Reflections on Liberty, Society & Government. George Santayana. LC 75-158153. Repr. of 1954 ed. lib. bdg. 19.50x (ISBN 0-678-02775-7). Kelley.

Domingo Faustino Sarmiento. Frances G. Crowley. (World Authors Ser.: No. 156). lib. bdg. 10.95 (ISBN 0-8057-2798-1). Twayne.

Dominic Savio: Teenage Saint. Peter Lappin. LC 54-11044. (gr. 5-10). 1954. 2.75 (ISBN 0-89944-034-7); pap. 1.25 (ISBN 0-89944-033-9). D Bosco Pubns.

Dominican Diaspora: From the Dominican Republic to New York City, Villagers in Transition. Glenn Hendricks. LC 74-4203. 1974. text ed. 10.50x (ISBN 0-8077-2426-2); pap. text ed. 7.95x (ISBN 0-8077-2459-9). Tchrs Coll.

Dominican Republic. Ian Bell. LC 80-13968. (Nations of the Modern World Ser.). (Illus.). 360p. 1981. lib. bdg. 26.50x (ISBN 0-89158-780-2). Westview.

Dominion of Ceylon, the Development of Its Laws & Constitution. William I. Jennings & Henry W. Tambiah. Repr. of 1952 ed. lib. bdg. 19.75x (ISBN 0-8371-3023-9, JEDC). Greenwood.

Dominique. R. Chetwynd-Hayes. 1979. pap. 1.50 (ISBN 0-505-51345-5). Tower Bks.

Dominique. Eugene Fromentin. Ed. by Barbara Wright. (French Texts Ser.). 1965. pap. text ed. 7.00x o.p. (ISBN 0-631-00650-8, Pub. by Basil Blackwell). Biblio Dist.

Dominique & the Dragon. Jurgen Tamchina. LC 68-59618. (Illus.). (gr. 3-6). 1969. 6.50 o.p. (ISBN 0-15-223972-3, HJ). HarBraceJ.

Dominique's Famous Fish, Game & Meat Recipes. Dominique D'Ermo. 1981. 12.95 (ISBN 0-87491-083-8); pap. 6.95 (ISBN 0-87491-080-3); ltd. edition hidebound 50.00 (ISBN 0-87491-082-X). Acropolis.

Domino. Phyllis A. Whitney. 1980. pap. 2.75 (ISBN 0-449-24350-8, Crest). Fawcett.

Domino Games. John Belton & Joella Cramblit. LC 76-8864. (Games & Activities Ser.). (Illus.). 48p. (gr. 4-9). 1976. PLB 8.95 (ISBN 0-8172-0625-6). Raintree Pubs.

Dominoes: Popular Games, Rules & Strategy. Dominic C. Armanino. LC 77-93308. (Illus.). 1978. 7.95 (ISBN 0-8069-4948-1); lib. bdg. 7.49 (ISBN 0-8069-4949-X). Sterling.

Don Bolles: An Investigation into His Murder. Martin Tallberg. 1978. pap. 1.95 o.p. (ISBN 0-445-04122-6). Popular Lib.

Don Bosco & the Spiritual Life. Francis Desramaut. Tr. by Roger M. Luna from Fr. LC 79-52674. (Orig.). 1979. pap. text ed. 8.95 (ISBN 0-89944-022-3). D Bosco Pubns.

Don Camillo. Guareschi. (Easy Reader, B). pap. 3.75 (ISBN 0-88436-121-7, ITA201052). EMC.

Don Camillo Omnibus. Giovanni Guareschi. 1981. 20.00 (ISBN 0-374-29290-6); pap. 12.95 (ISBN 0-374-51646-4). FS&G.

Don Carlos & Other Stories. James A. Fitzgerald. 168p. 1981. 9.95. Bond Pub Co.

Don Goyo. Demetrio Aguilera-Malta. Tr. by John Brushwood & Carolyn Brushwood. LC 80-81656. (Contemporary Literature Ser.). (Illus.). 208p. 1980. 9.95 (ISBN 0-89603-019-9). Humana.

Don Juan De Moliere: Une Dramaturgie De Rupture. R. Horville. (Collection Themes & Textes Ser.). 288p. (Orig., Fr.). 1972. pap. 6.75 (ISBN 2-03-035011-7, 2690). Larousse.

Don Juan in Tulsa. Richard Power. 1981. 12.50 (ISBN 0-916620-54-9). Portals Pr.

Don Juan McQueen. Eugenia Price. LC 74-8941. 1974. 8.95 o.s.i. (ISBN 0-397-01057-5). Lippincott.

Don Juan Manuel. H. Tracy Sturcken. (World Authors Ser.: Spain: No. 303). 1974. lib. bdg. 10.95 (ISBN 0-8057-2590-3). Twayne.

Don Juan, Mescalito & Modern Magic: The Mythology of Inner Space. Nevill Drury. 1978. pap. 7.95 (ISBN 0-7100-8582-6). Routledge & Kegan.

Don Juan: Or, the Continuum of the Libido. Paul Goodman. Ed. by Taylor Stoehr. 225p. 1979. 14.00 (ISBN 0-87685-422-6); deluxe ed. 25.00 (ISBN 0-87685-423-4); pap. 5.00 (ISBN 0-87685-421-8). Black Sparrow.

Don Juan Papers: Further Castaneda Controversies. Ed. by Richard De Mille. LC 80-10158. 520p. 1980. 15.95 (ISBN 0-915520-25-7); pap. 8.95 (ISBN 0-915520-24-9). Ross-Erikson.

Don Marquis. Lynn Lee. (United States Authors Ser: No. 393). 1981. lib. bdg. 11.95 (ISBN 0-8057-7282-0). Twayne.

Don Martin Cooks up More Tales. Don Martin. (Mad Ser.). (Illus.). 192p. 1976. pap. 1.75 (ISBN 0-446-94413-0). Warner Bks.

Don Martin Drops 13 Stories. Don Martin. (Mad Ser.). (Illus.). 1973. pap. 1.75 (ISBN 0-446-94414-9). Warner Bks.

Don Martin Forges Ahead. Don Martin. (Mad Ser.). (Illus., Orig.). 1977. pap. 1.75 (ISBN 0-446-94415-7). Warner Bks.

Don Martin Steps Out. Don Martin. (Mad Ser.). (Illus.). 1975. pap. 1.75 (ISBN 0-446-94416-5). Warner Bks.

Don Quijote. Miguel De Cervantes. (Span). 6.00x (ISBN 0-686-00858-8). Colton Bk.

Don Quijote De la Mancha, Pt. 2. Miguel De Cervantes Saavedra. (Illus., Span.). (gr. 11-12). 1971. pap. 3.95 (ISBN 0-88345-138-7); manual, filmstrips, & cassettes o.p. 145.00 (ISBN 0-685-69627-8). Regents Pub.

Don Quixote. Cervantes. (Easy Reader, D). pap. 3.75 (ISBN 0-88436-056-3, SPA301051). EMC.

Don Quixote. Miguel De Cervantes. (Oxford Progressive English Readers Ser.). (Illus.). 1973. pap. text ed. 2.95x (ISBN 0-19-638224-6). Oxford U Pr.

Don Quixote. Miguel De Cervantes. Tr. by John M. Cohen. (Classics Ser.). (Orig.). (YA) (gr. 9 up). 1951. pap. 4.95 (ISBN 0-14-044010-0). Penguin.

Don Quixote. Miguel De Cervantes. Ed. by Joseph R. Jones & Kenneth Douglas. (Critical Editions Ser.). 1980. 29.95x (ISBN 0-393-04514-5); pap. text ed. 8.95x (ISBN 0-393-09018-3). Norton.

Don Quixote: The Knight of La Mancha. Margaret Church. LC 70-172419. 1971. 12.00x (ISBN 0-8147-1352-1). NYU Pr.

Don: The Life & Death of Sam Giancana. William Brashler. LC 76-5113. 1977. 10.95 o.p. (ISBN 0-06-010447-3, HarpT). Har-Row.

Dona Flor & Her Two Husbands. Jorge Amado. 1977. pap. 3.95 (ISBN 0-380-01796-2, 35402, Bard). Avon.

Dona Luz. Juan Valera. Tr. by M. J. Serrano from Span. LC 75-1185. 284p. 1975. Repr. of 1891 ed. 16.50 (ISBN 0-86527-239-5). Fertig.

Donahue: My Own Story. Phil Donahue et al. 288p. 1981. pap. 2.95 (ISBN 0-449-24358-3, Crest). Fawcett.

Donald Blumberg. Buffalo Fine Arts Academy & Cranbook Academy of Art-Museum. LC 79-50455. (Illus.). Date not set. pap. 8.95 (ISBN 0-914782-24-X). Buffalo Acad.

Donald Davidson. Thomas D. Young & M. Thomas Inge. (U. S. Authors Ser.: No. 190). lib. bdg. 10.95 (ISBN 0-8057-0188-5). Twayne.

Donald Duck. Illus. by Carl Barks. LC 78-14844. (Walt Disney Best Comics Ser.). (Illus.). 1978. 17.95 (ISBN 0-89659-006-2). Abbeville Pr.

Donald Duck & the Golden Helmet. Illus. by Carl Barks. (Illus.). 36p. 1981. 3.95 (ISBN 0-89659-178-6). Abbeville Pr.

Donald Duck & the Magic Hourglass. Illus. by Carl Barks. (Illus.). 36p. 1981. 3.95 (ISBN 0-89659-177-8). Abbeville Pr.

Donald Duck & the Magic Mailbox. Walt Disney Studios. (Golden Look-Look Bks.). (ps-3). 1978. PLB 5.38 (ISBN 0-307-61851-X, Golden Pr); pap. 0.95 (ISBN 0-307-11851-7). Western Pub.

Donald Duck & the One Bear. Walt Disney. (Illus.). (ps-3). 1977. PLB 5.00 (ISBN 0-307-60039-4, Golden Pr). Western Pub.

Donald Duck & the Super-Sticky Secret. Walt Disney Productions. (Tell-a-Tale Reader). 32p. (ps-3). 1980. PLB 4.77 (ISBN 0-307-68425-3, Golden Pr). Western Pub.

Donald Duck & the Witch Next Door. Walt Disney Studio. (Illus.). (ps-3). 1976. PLB 5.00 (ISBN 0-307-60217-6, Golden Pr). Western Pub.

Donald Duck Book. Daphne Davis. (ps-1). 1964. PLB 5.38 (ISBN 0-307-68911-5, Golden Pr). Western Pub.

Donald Duck Goes Camping. Walt Disney Productions. (Tell-a-Tale Readers). (Illus.). (gr. k-3). 1979. PLB 4.77 (ISBN 0-307-68609-4, Whitman). Western Pub.

Donald Duck: Instant Millionaire. Walt Disney. (Young Reader Ser.). (Illus.). (gr. k-3). 1979. PLB 5.00 (ISBN 0-307-60140-4, Golden Pr). Western Pub.

Donald Duck, It's Play Time! Walt Disney Studios. (Big Picture Bks.). 24p. (gr. k-3). PLB 7.62 (ISBN 0-307-60828-X, Golden Pr); pap. 1.95 (ISBN 0-307-10828-7). Western Pub.

Donald Duck on Tom Sawyer's Island. Dorothea Snow. (Tell-a-Tale Readers). (Illus.). (gr. k-3). 1978. PLB 4.77 (ISBN 0-307-68409-1, Whitman). Western Pub.

Donald Judd. Brydon Smith. (Illus.). 1975. 20.00 o.s.i. (ISBN 0-88884-277-5, 56317-0, Pub. by Natl Gallery Canada). U of Chicago Pr.

Donald Judd: Complete Writings 1959-1975. Donald Judd. LC 75-13761. (Nova Scotia Ser.). (Illus.). 229p. 1975. 25.00x, c (ISBN 0-8147-4155-X); pap. 14.95, c (ISBN 0-8147-4156-8). NYU Pr.

Donald Judd: Drawings 1956-1976. Donald Judd. LC 76-11429. (Nova Scotia Ser.). (Illus.). 110p. 1976. 20.00x, C (ISBN 0-8147-4157-6); pap. 12.95, c (ISBN 0-8147-4158-4). NYU Pr.

Donatello. G. Gaeta Bertela. (Scala Art Book). (Illus., Orig.). 1978. pap. 5.95 (ISBN 0-8467-0471-4, Pub. by Two Continents). Hippocrene Bks.

Donavan's Delight. Carter Brown. 1979. pap. 1.50 (ISBN 0-505-51382-X). Tower Bks.

Donegal Fairy Stories. Ed. by Seumas MacManus. (Illus.). (gr. 4-6). 1968. pap. 3.50 (ISBN 0-486-21971-2). Dover.

Dongolese Nubian: A Grammar. C. H. Armbruster. 1965. text ed. 170.00 (ISBN 0-521-04050-7). Cambridge U Pr.

Dongolese Nubian, a Lexicon. C. H. Armbruster. 1965. text ed. 145.00 (ISBN 0-521-04051-5). Cambridge U Pr.

Donkey-Cart Kids. Bobbie Montgomery. LC 80-15656. (Orion Ser.). 128p. (gr. 1-6). 1980. pap. 2.50 (ISBN 0-8127-0286-7). Southern Pub.

Donkey-Donkey. Roger Duvoisin. LC 68-11655. (Illus.). (gr. k-3). 1968. 5.95 o.s.i. (ISBN 0-8193-0209-0, Four Winds); PLB 5.41 o.s.i. (ISBN 0-8193-0210-4). Schol Bk Serv.

Donkey Tales. Doris Rust. (Illus.). (ps-5). 1972. 6.50 (ISBN 0-571-09867-3, Pub. by Faber & Faber). Merrimack Bk Serv.

Donkey Wrinkles & Tales. Marjorie Dunkels. (Illus.). pap. 4.35 (ISBN 0-85131-274-8). J A Allen.

Donkey Ysabel. Dorothy O. Van Woerkom. LC 78-5140. (Ready-to-Read Ser.). (Illus.). (gr. 1-4). 1978. 7.95 (ISBN 0-02-791280-9, 79128). Macmillan.

Donkeys Galore. Averil Swinfen. LC 76-2883. 1976. 11.95 (ISBN 0-7153-7150-9). David & Charles.

Donkeys: Their Care & Management. M. R. De Wesselow. 5.00 (ISBN 0-8283-1369-5). Branden.

Donna Rae Easy Exercise Program. Donna Rae. 160p. (Orig.). 1980. pap. cancelled (ISBN 0-346-12459-X). Cornerstone.

Donnie's Dangers. Aleda Renken. (Haley Adventures Ser.). 1981. pap. 2.50 (ISBN 0-570-07235-2, 39-1070). Concordia.

Donny & Marie. Partricia M. Eldred. (Rock 'n Pop Stars Ser.). (Illus.). (gr. 4-12). 1978. PLB 5.95 (ISBN 0-87191-618-5); pap. 2.75 o. p. (ISBN 0-89812-121-3). Creative Ed.

Donor-Acceptor Bond. E. N. Gur'Yanova et al. Ed. by D. Slutzkin. Tr. by R. Kondor from Rus. LC 75-12804. 366p. 1975. 57.95 (ISBN 0-470-33680-3). Halsted Pr.

Donovan, a Novel, 1882. Ada E. Bayley. Ed. by Robert L. Wolff. LC 75-1529. (Victorian Fiction Series). 1975. lib. bdg. 66.00 (ISBN 0-8240-1601-7). Garland Pub.

Dons Do Espirito Santo. Tr. by Harold Horton. (Portuguese Bks.). 1979. 1.35 (ISBN 0-8297-0837-5). Life Pubs Intl.

Dons Spirituels. Tr. by Aril Edvarsen. (French Bks.). (Fr.). 1979. 2.10 (ISBN 0-686-28819-X). Life Pubs Intl.

Don't Ask Me How the Time Goes by. Jose E. Pacheco. Tr. by Alastair Reid from Span. 1978. 15.00x (ISBN 0-231-04284-1); pap. 5.95 (ISBN 0-231-04285-X). Columbia U Pr.

Don't Ask Miranda. Lila Perl. LC 78-23835. (gr. 3-6). 1979. 7.50 (ISBN 0-395-28961-0, Clarion). HM.

Don't Bank on It! Martin J. Meyer. LC 79-3156. 1979. 9.95 (ISBN 0-87863-174-7). Farnswth Pub.

Don't Bank on It. Martin J. Meyer. 240p. pap. 2.50 (ISBN 0-671-41606-5). PB.

Don't Be Afraid: A Program for Overcoming Your Fears & Phobias. Gerald Rosen. 1976. text ed. 8.95 o.p. (ISBN 0-13-218412-5, Spec); pap. text ed. 2.95 o.p. (ISBN 0-13-218404-4). P-H.

Don't Be Scared Book. Isle-Margret Vogel. (Illus.). (ps-1). 1974. pap. 2.95 (ISBN 0-689-70307-4, Aladdin). Atheneum.

Don't Become the Victim. Marcus W. Ratledge. 120p. 1981. pap. 6.00 (ISBN 0-87364-211-2). Paladin Ent.

Don't Blame God. Kenneth E. Hagin. 1979. mini bk. .50 (ISBN 0-89276-056-7). Hagin Ministries.

Don't Blame the Fish. Robert Warner. (Illus.). 1974. 8.95 o.p. (ISBN 0-87691-127-0). Winchester Pr.

Don't Call Me Fatso. Barbara Philips. LC 79-23888. (Life & Living from a Child's Point of View Ser.). (Illus.). (gr. k-5). 1980. PLB 9.65 (ISBN 0-8172-1350-3). Raintree Child.

Don't Call Me Katie Rose. Lenora M. Weber. LC 64-13909. (gr. 5 up). 1964. 10.95 (ISBN 0-690-24241-7, TYC-J). T Y Crowell.

Don't Call Me Ma. Sam Churchill. LC 77-70895. 1977. 7.95 o.p. (ISBN 0-385-08481-1). Doubleday.

Don't Count Your Chicks. Ingri D'Aulaire & Edgar Parin D'Aulaire. (ps-1). 1973. pap. 1.95 (ISBN 0-385-05233-2, Zephyr). Doubleday.

Don't Die Baby. Jo A. Bacon. Ed. by Patricia McCarthy. (Pal Paperbacks Ser., Kit A). (Illus., Orig.). (gr. 7-12). 1974. pap. text ed. 1.25 (ISBN 0-8374-3468-8). Xerox Ed Pubns.

Don't Die Broke! A Guide to Secure Retirement. Melvin J. Swartz. 252p. 1975. 8.95 o.s.i. (ISBN 0-02-615560-5). Macmillan.

Don't Ever Change, Boopsie. Gary Trudeau. (Doonesbury Ser). (Illus.). 1981. pap. 1.75 (ISBN 0-445-00608-0). Popular Lib.

Don't Forget, Don't Forgive, Don't Hate. Kent O. W. Wahle. 1981. 6.95 (ISBN 0-533-04495-2). Vantage.

Don't Forget, Matilda. Ronda Armitage. (Illus.). (ps-2). 1979. PLB 8.95 (ISBN 0-233-97075-4). Andre Deutsch.

Don't Forget the Bacon! Pat Hutchins. LC 75-17935. (Illus.). 32p. (gr. k-3). 1976. 8.25 (ISBN 0-688-80019-X); PLB 7.92 (ISBN 0-688-84019-1). Greenwillow.

Don't Forget Tom. Hanne Larsen. LC 77-20953. (John Day Bk.). (Illus.). (gr. k-4). 1978. PLB 7.89 (ISBN 0-381-99554-2, TYC-J). T Y Crowell.

Don't Give up. Norman Brisoff. LC 72-75126. (Mystery & Adventure Ser.). (gr. 2-4). 1973. PLB 6.75 (ISBN 0-87191-207-4). Creative Ed.

Don't Go Dancing Mother. Rose Safran. LC 79-64288. (Illus.). 1979. pap. 4.95 (ISBN 0-9602786-1-3). Tide Bk Pub Co.

Don't Go Overseas Until You've Read This Book. Neil Gallagher. LC 77-2643. 1977. pap. 3.50 (ISBN 0-87123-105-0, 210105). Bethany Fell.

Don't Hurt Laurie! Willo D. Roberts. LC 76-46569. (Illus.). (gr. 4-6). 1977. 8.95 (ISBN 0-689-30571-0). Atheneum.

Don't Hurt Laurie! Willo D. Roberts. (gr. 3-7). pap. 2.95 (ISBN 0-689-70496-8, A-123, Aladdin). Atheneum.

Don't Just Sit There Reading: A Fun-To-Do Book on the Americas. Myra Scovel & Phillda Ragland. (Orig.). (gr. 1-4). 1970. pap. 2.25 o.p. (ISBN 0-377-10751-4). Friend Pr.

Don't Lick the Chopsticks: The Creative, Harmonious Ma Family Chinese Cookbook. Nancy Chih Ma et al. LC 73-79770. (Illus.). 156p. 1973. 9.95 o.p. (ISBN 0-87011-201-5). Kodansha.

Don't Look Now. Ethel Barrett. LC 68-25807. (Illus., Orig.). 1968. pap. 2.25 o.p. (ISBN 0-8307-0019-6, 5000602). Regal.

Don't Look Now. Daphne DuMaurier. 1977. pap. 2.50 (ISBN 0-380-01144-1, 45252). Avon.

Don't Mention Moon to Me. Beatrice S. Smith. 1974. 6.95 o.p. (ISBN 0-525-66397-5). Elsevier-Nelson.

Don't Open This Box. James Razzi. LC 72-10219. (Illus.). 48p. (ps-2). 1973. 5.95 o.s.i. (ISBN 0-8193-0669-X, Four Winds); PLB 5.41 o.s.i. (ISBN 0-8193-0670-3). Schol Bk Serv.

Don't Put Your Cart Before the Horse Race. Thomas Van Aarle. (gr. k-3). 1980. reinforced bdg. 8.95 (ISBN 0-395-29095-3). HM.

Don't Raise Your Child to Be a Fat Adult. J. F. Wilkinson. 1981. Repr. pap. 2.50 (ISBN 0-451-09902-8, E9902, Sig). NAL.

Don't Run: An Illustrated Poem of Juan Ramon Jimenez. Hide Oshiro. (Illus.). 1981. 2.00 (ISBN 0-934834-21-0). White Pine.

Don't Say Yes Until I Finish Talking. Mel Gussow. (Illus.). 318p. Date not set. pap. 7.95 (ISBN 0-306-80132-9). Da Capo.

Don't Sit in the Draft. R. Charles Johnson & Charles E. Sherman. 240p. (Orig.). 1980. pap. 6.95 (ISBN 0-917316-32-0). Nolo Pr.

Don't Sit Under the Apple Tree. Robin F. Brancato. 128p. 1980. pap. 1.75 (ISBN 0-553-12966-X). Bantam.

Don't Speak Now. Eric Green. 121p. 1981. 6.95 (ISBN 0-533-04650-5). Vantage.

Don't Talk to Me About Death. Charles R. Murrah. LC 77-75935. 1977. text ed. 3.95 (ISBN 0-87863-147-X). Farnswth Pub.

Don't Talk to Strangers. Beverly Hastings. 224p. 1981. pap. 2.50 (ISBN 0-515-06001-1). Jove Pubns.

Don't Teach Let Me Learn About Aerodynamics, Robots & Computers, Science Fiction & Astronomy. Nina E. Crosby & Elizabeth H. Marten. (Illus.). 80p. (Orig.). 1979. pap. 4.95 (ISBN 0-914634-60-7). DOK Pubs.

Don't Tell Me. Richard Mullin. 1976. pap. 1.50 (ISBN 0-8024-1781-7). Moody.

Don't Tell Your Name. Hollis Hodges. 192p. 1981. pap. 2.25 (ISBN 0-380-53751-6, 53751). Avon.

Don't Touch That Dial. Fred J. MacDonald. LC 79-87700. 1979. 16.95 (ISBN 0-88229-528-4); pap. 8.95 (ISBN 0-88229-673-6). Nelson-Hall.

Don't Use a Resume. Richard Lathrop. 1980. pap. 1.95 (ISBN 0-89815-027-2). Ten Speed Pr.

Don't Worry. Janice A. Henderson. 250p. 1981. 8.95 (ISBN 0-396-07901-6). Dodd.

Don't You Remember? Lucille Clifton. (Illus.). 32p. (ps-2). 1973. PLB 8.50 (ISBN 0-525-28840-6). Dutton.

Doobled-up. Rhoda Butler. 120p. 1980. pap. 11.95 (ISBN 0-906191-25-4, Pub. by Thule Pr England). Intl Schol Bk Serv.

Doodle Book. Norman B. Uris. (Illus.). 1970. pap. 1.25 o.s.i. (ISBN 0-02-078120-2, Collier). Macmillan.

Doolittle's Tokyo Raiders. Carroll V. Glines. 464p. 1981. pap. 7.95 (ISBN 0-442-21925-3). Van Nos Reinhold.

Doom Platoon. Nick Brady. 1978. pap. 1.75 (ISBN 0-505-51302-1). Tower Bks.

Doomfarers of Coramonde. Brian Daley. (Del Rey Bk.). (Orig.). 1977. pap. 2.25 (ISBN 0-345-29180-8). Ballantine.

Doomsday Bullet. Ray Hogan. LC 80-2839. 192p. 1981. 9.95 (ISBN 0-385-17554-X). Doubleday.

Doomsday Cult: A Study of Conversion, Proselytization, & Maintenance of Faith. enl. ed. John Lofland. LC 77-23028. 1981. pap. text ed. 9.50x (ISBN 0-8290-0095-X). Irvington.

Doomsday Gang. Kin Platt. LC 77-18864. (gr. 7-9). 1978. 7.95 (ISBN 0-688-80143-9); PLB 7.63 (ISBN 0-688-84143-0). Greenwillow.

Doomsday Nineteen Ninety-Nine A.D. Charles Berlitz. LC 80-1084. (Illus.). 240p. 1981. 11.95 (ISBN 0-385-15982-X). Doubleday.

Doomsday Scroll. Barbara Rogers. LC 79-7101. 1979. 8.95 (ISBN 0-396-07655-6). Dodd.

Doomstar. Jack Downey. LC 79-66398. 97p. 1980. 6.95 (ISBN 0-533-04388-3). Vantage.

Doomstar. Edmond Hamilton. 1979. pap. 1.25 (ISBN 0-505-51336-6). Tower Bks.

Doomtime. Doris Pirserchia. (Science Fiction Ser.). 1981. pap. 2.25 (ISBN 0-87997-619-5, UE1619). DAW Bks.

Doon De la Roche, Chanson De Geste. 1921. 28.00 (ISBN 0-384-12360-0); pap. 23.00 (ISBN 0-384-12361-9). Johnson Repr.

Door in the Hedge. Robin McKinley. LC 80-21903. 224p. (gr. 7 up). 1981. 8.95 (ISBN 0-688-00312-5). Greenwillow.

Door in the Wall: Story of Medieval London. Marguerite De Angeli. LC 64-7025. (gr. 3-6). 7.95a (ISBN 0-385-07283-X); PLB (ISBN 0-385-05743-1); pap. 1.95 (ISBN 0-385-07909-5). Doubleday.

Door into the Dark. Seamus Heaney. 1972. pap. 4.95 (ISBN 0-571-08998-4, Pub. by Faber & Faber). Merrimack Bk Serv.

Door to Door. Maureen Roffey & Bernard Lodge. LC 80-50229. (Illus.). 32p. (gr. k-1). 1980. 7.95 (ISBN 0-688-41966-6). Lothrop.

Door Way. Norbert Blei. 240p. 1980. 16.95 (ISBN 0-933180-22-5). Ellis Pr.

Doorman. Jack Libert. (Orig.). 1966. 6.00 (ISBN 0-911732-50-0); pap. 4.00 (ISBN 0-911732-51-9). Irego.

Doors. Val Clery. (Illus.). 144p. 1979. 14.95 o.p. (ISBN 0-670-28039-9, Studio). Viking Pr.

Doors. Ezra Hannon. 256p. 1976. pap. write for info. (ISBN 0-446-79730-8). Warner Bks.

Doors & Windows. LC 78-1384. (Home Repair & Improvement Ser.). (Illus.). 1978. lib. bdg. 11.97 (ISBN 0-686-51036-4). Silver.

Doors & Windows. Time-Life Books. (Home Repair & Improvement). (Illus.). 1978. 10.95 (ISBN 0-8094-2406-1). Time-Life.

Doors: Excellence in International Design. Gretl Hoffmann. (Illus.). 144p. 1977. 35.00x (ISBN 0-8230-7135-9). Intl Ideas.

Doors into Poetry. 2nd ed. Chad Walsh. 1970. pap. text ed. 9.50 (ISBN 0-13-218727-2). P-H.

Doors of the Universe. Sylvia Engdahl. LC 80-18804. 276p. (gr. 7 up). 1981. PLB 11.95 (ISBN 0-689-30807-8, Argo). Atheneum.

Doors: Poems-1981. Peter-Paul Zahl et al. 128p. 1981. 8.95 (ISBN 0-87376-037-9). Red Dust.

Doors to More Mature Reading: Detailed Notes on Adult Books for Use with Young People. American Library Association - Young Adult Services Division. LC 64-8298. 1964. pap. 5.00 o.p. (ISBN 0-8389-3029-8). ALA.

Doors to the Sacred. Joseph Martos. LC 80-626. 552p. 1981. 15.95 (ISBN 0-385-15738-X). Doubleday.

Doorway to Meditation. Avery Brooke. 1976. pap. 4.95 (ISBN 0-8164-0903-X). Crossroad NY.

Doorways to Discipleship. Winkie Pratney. LC 77-80008. 1977. pap. 3.95 (ISBN 0-87123-106-9, 210106). Bethany Fell.

Dopamine. Ed. by Peter J. Roberts et al. LC 78-4355. (Advances in Biochemical Psychopharmacology Ser.: Vol. 19). 1978. 31.50 (ISBN 0-89004-239-X). Raven.

Dopaminergic Ergot Derivatives & Motor Function: Proceedings of an International Symposium, Stockholm, 1978. Ed. by K. Fuxe. (Wenner-Gren Center International Symposium Series: Vol. 31). (Illus.). 1979. 75.00 (ISBN 0-08-024408-4). Pergamon.

Dopaminergic Mechanisms. Ed. by D. B. Calne et al. LC 74-13904. (Advances in Neurology Ser: Vol. 9). 1975. 41.50 (ISBN 0-911216-93-6). Raven.

Dope Chronicles: Eighteen Fifty to Nineteen Fifty. Gary T. Silver. LC 78-15835. (Illus., Orig.). 1979. pap. 7.95 o.p. (ISBN 0-06-250790-7, RD 231, HarpR). Har-Row.

Dope: The Use of Drugs in Sport. Les Woodland. LC 80-66086. (Illus.). 164p. 1980. 22.50 (ISBN 0-7153-7894-5). David & Charles.

Dopple Gang. rev. ed. Theodore L. Harris et al. (Keys to Reading Ser.). (Illus.). 160p. (gr. 6). 1975. pap. text ed. 2.97 (ISBN 0-87892-456-6); tchrs'. ed. 2.97 (ISBN 0-87892-457-4); 15.51 (ISBN 0-87892-051-X). Economy Co.

Dorando: A Spanish Tale, 1767. James Boswell. Ed. by Michael F. Shugrue. Bd. with History of Nourjahad, 1767. Frances Sheridan. LC 74-17301. (Flowering of the Novel, 1740-1775 Ser: Vol. 78). 1974. lib. bdg. 50.00 (ISBN 0-8240-1177-5). Garland Pub.

Dorcas. Gordon Stowell. Tr. by S. D. de Lerin from English. (Libros Pescaditos Sobre Personajes Biblicos). (Illus.). 1978. pap. 0.40 (ISBN 0-311-38517-6, Edit Mundo). Casa Bautista.

Dordogne. Patrick Turnbull. (Illus.). 155p. 1980. 24.00 (ISBN 0-7134-1335-2, Pub. by Batsford England). David & Charles.

Dore Bible Illustrations. Gustave Dore. (Illus.). 256p. 1974. pap. 6.00 (ISBN 0-486-23004-X). Dover.

Dore Gallery. Gustave Dore. LC 73-91686. 15.00 o.p. (ISBN 0-668-03444-0). Arco.

Doris Fein: Phantom of the Casino. T. Ernesto Bethancourt. LC 80-8814. 160p. (YA) 1981. 8.95 (ISBN 0-8234-0391-2). Holiday.

Doris Fein: Quartz Boyar. T. Ernesto Bethancourt. LC 80-15920. 160p. (YA) (gr. 9 up). 1980. 8.95 (ISBN 0-8234-0378-5). Holiday.

Doris Fein: Superspy. T. Ernesto Bethancourt. LC 79-23339. 160p. (YA) (gr. 9 up). 1980. 8.95 (ISBN 0-8234-0407-2). Holiday.

Doris Lessing: An Annotated Bibliography of Criticism. Compiled by Dee Seligman. LC 80-24540. 160p. 1981. lib. bdg. 25.00 (ISBN 0-313-21270-8, SDL/). Greenwood.

Doris Lessing's Africa. Michael Thorpe. LC 79-15676. 1979. text ed. 17.50x (ISBN 0-8419-6000-3); pap. text ed. 8.50x (ISBN 0-8419-6001-1). Holmes & Meier.

Dorita, la Nina Que Nadie Amaba. 1980. pap. 1.60 (ISBN 0-686-69359-0). Vida Pubs.

Dorland's Illustrated Medical Dictionary. 25th ed. (Illus.). 1748p. 1974. deluxe ed. 40.00 (ISBN 0-7216-3149-5); text ed. 29.00 (ISBN 0-7216-3148-7). Saunders.

Dorland's Medical Dictionary: Shorter Edition. LC 79-67113. (Illus.). 768p. 1980. 14.95 (ISBN 0-7216-3142-8). Saunders.

Dorothea Lange: Farm Security Administration Photographs, 1935 - 1939, 2 vols. LC 80-24201. (Illus., Vol. 1 236pp.; vol. 2 176 pp.). 1980. Vol.1, 732 Photos & Maps On 9 Black & White Fiche, Captions In Text,236 Pages. 34.50 (ISBN 0-89969-000-9); Vol. 2, 622 Photos & Maps On 8 Black & White Fiche, Caption In Text, 176 Pages. 32.50 (ISBN 0-89969-001-7); Set. 67.00 (ISBN 0-89969-002-5). Text-Fiche.

Dorothea Lynde Dix. Francis Tiffany. LC 70-145702. 1971. Repr. of 1918 ed. 24.00 (ISBN 0-8103-3655-3). Gale.

Dorothy Allison: A Psychic Story. Dorothy Allison & Scott Jacobson. (Orig.). 1980. pap. 2.50 (ISBN 0-515-05304-X). Jove Pubns.

Dorothy & the Lizard of Oz. Richard A. Gardner. LC 80-12787. (Illus.). 108p. (gr. 1-6). 1980. 9.95 (ISBN 0-933812-03-5). Creative Therapeutics.

Dorothy & William Wordsworth: The Heart of a Circle of Friends. Seon Manley. LC 70-188693. (gr. 6-12). 1974. 7.95 (ISBN 0-8149-0710-5). Vanguard.

Dorothy Day: Friend of the Poor. Carol B. Church. Ed. by David L. Bender & Gary E. Mc Cuen. (Focus on Famous Women Ser). (Illus.). (gr. 3-9). 1976. 6.95 (ISBN 0-912616-45-8); read-along cassette 9.95 (ISBN 0-89908-244-0). Greenhaven.

Dorothy Hamill. Miranda Smith. (Sports Superstars Ser.). (Illus.). (gr. 3-9). 1977. PLB 5.95 (ISBN 0-87191-546-4); pap. 2.95 (ISBN 0-89812-194-9). Creative Ed.

Dorothy Hamill: Skate to Victory. Dorothy C. Schmitz. LC 77-70888. (Pros Ser.). (Illus.). (gr. 2). 1977. PLB 6.45 (ISBN 0-913940-62-3). Crestwood Hse.

Dorothy Huang's Chinese Cooking. Dorothy Huang. Ed. by Lorry B. Harju. 200p. 1980. 12.95. Pinewood.

Dorothy L. Sayers: A Biography. James Brabazon. (Illus.). 320p. 1981. 15.95 (ISBN 0-684-16864-2, ScribT). Scribner.

Dorothy L. Sayers: A Literary Biography. Ralph E. Hone. LC 79-9783. (Illus.). 1979. 15.00x (ISBN 0-87338-228-5); pap. 7.00 (ISBN 0-87338-253-6). Kent St U Pr.

Dorothy L. Sayers: A Pilgrim Soul. Nancy M. Tischler. LC 79-87739. 1980. 8.95 (ISBN 0-8042-0882-4). John Knox.

Dorothy L. Sayers: Nine Literary Studies. Trevor H. Hall. (Illus.). 132p. 1980. 19.50 (ISBN 0-208-01877-8, Archon). Shoe String.

Dorothy Parker. Arthur F. Kinney. (United States Authors Ser.: No. 315). 1978. 9.95 (ISBN 0-8057-7241-3). Twayne.

Dorothy Richardson. Thomas F. Staley. (English Authors Ser.: No. 187). 1976. lib. bdg. 12.50 (ISBN 0-8057-6662-6). Twayne.

Dorothy Richardson: The Genius They Forgot. John Rosenberg. 1979. pap. 10.95x o.p. (ISBN 0-7156-0655-7, Pub. by Duckworth England). Biblio Dist.

Dorp Dead. Julia Cunningham. (Illus.). (gr. 3-7). 1974. pap. 1.95 (ISBN 0-380-00709-6, 51458, Camelot). Avon.

Dorr Rebellion: A Study in American Radicalism: 1833-1849. Marvin E. Gettleman. LC 79-1205. 296p. 1980. Repr. of 1973 ed. lib. bdg. 11.50 (ISBN 0-88275-894-2). Krieger.

Dorrie & the Witchville Fair. Patricia Coombs. LC 80-10189. (Illus.). 48p. (gr. 1-4). 1980. 6.95 (ISBN 0-688-41957-7); PLB 6.67 (ISBN 0-688-51957-1). Lothrop.

Dorset: A Shell Guide. Michael Pitt-Rivers. (Shell Guide Ser.). (Illus.). 1969. 7.95 (ISBN 0-686-24603-9, Pub. by Faber & Faber). Merrimack Bk Serv.

Dos Amigos--Viajando por Hispanoamerica. Rogelio A. Castro-Amaya & Jorge Kattan-Zablah. Ed. by Mildred Buchsbaum. (Illus., Span.). Date not set. pap. text ed. 5.95 (ISBN 0-910286-66-3). Boxwood. Postponed.

Do's & Don'ts of Yesterday. Eric Sloane. (Illus.). 1975. pap. 3.45 o.p. (ISBN 0-380-00429-1, 25858). Avon.

Dos Ensayos En Microeconomica: La Industria Mundial Del Cobre la I.T.T. y la Puerto Rico Telephone Company. LC 77-1432. (Planning Ser.: No. E-1). 1976. pap. write for info. o.p. (ISBN 0-8477-2438-7). U of PR Pr.

Dos Passos: A Collection of Critical Essays. Ed. by Andrew Hook. LC 73-21561. 192p. 1974. pap. 2.45 (ISBN 0-13-218859-7, STC114, Spec). P-H.

Dos Passos & the Fiction of Despair. Iain Colley. 170p. 1978. 25.00x (ISBN 0-8476-6020-6). Rowman.

Dosadi Experiment. Frank Herbert. LC 77-3653. (YA) 1977. 2.25 (ISBN 0-425-03834-3, Dist. by Putnam). Berkley Pub.

Dosimetry in Agriculture, Industry, Biology & Medicine. (Illus.). 685p. (Orig.). 1973. pap. 45.00 (ISBN 92-0-010073-2, IAEA). Unipub.

Dossier of Flaubert's un Coeur Simple. George A. Willebrink. 1976. pap. text ed. 37.25x (ISBN 90-6203-409-8). Humanities.

Dostoevski the Adapter. Charles E. Passage. (Studies in Comp. Lit.: No. 10). lib. bdg. 12.50x (ISBN 0-8078-7010-2); pap. text ed. 6.50x (ISBN 0-8078-7010-2). U of NC Pr.

Dostoevsky. Nicholas Berdyaev. pap. 2.95 o.p. (ISBN 0-452-00415-2, F415, Mer). NAL.

Dostoevsky: A Collection of Critical Essays. Ed. by Rene Wellek. 1962. pap. 2.95 o.p. (ISBN 0-13-218784-1, Spec). P-H.

Dostoevsky & Dickens: A Study of Literary Influence. N. M. Lary. 188p. 1973. 17.00 (ISBN 0-7100-7554-5). Routledge & Kegan.

Dostoevsky: The Literary Artist. Erik Krag. 1976. pap. text ed. 26.00x (ISBN 8-200-01450-9, Dist. by Columbia U Pr). Universitet.

Dostoevsky, Tolstoy & Nietzsche. Lev Shestov. Tr. by Bernard Martin & Spencer E. Roberts. LC 74-78504. xxx, 322p. 1969. 16.00x (ISBN 0-8214-0053-3). Ohio U Pr.

Dostoevsky's Crime & Punishment: Murder As Philosonic Experiment. A. D. Nuttall. (Text & Context Ser.). 1978. pap. 9.25x (ISBN 0-85621-071-4). Humanities.

Dostoevsky's Dickens: A Study of Literary Influence. Loralee MacPike. 270p. 1980. 19.50x (ISBN 0-389-20062-X). B&N.

Dostoyevsky. Richard A. Peace. LC 77-116838. 1971. 48.00 (ISBN 0-521-07911-X); text ed. 10.95x (ISBN 0-521-09994-3). Cambridge U Pr.

Dostoyevsky & the Jews, Vol. 3, Vol 3. David I. Goldstein. (University of Texas Press Slavic Ser: Vol. 3). 224p. 1980. 17.50x (ISBN 0-292-71528-5). U of Tex Pr.

Dot Book for Visual Perception Training. Katherine H. O'Connor. (Illus.). 28p. (gr. k-2). 1972. wkbk 0.60 (ISBN 0-910812-08-X). Johnny Reads.

Dot for Short. Frieda Friedman. (Illus.). (gr. 4-6). 1947. 8.25 (ISBN 0-688-21242-5). Morrow.

Dot Town. Dave Morice. (Illus.). 36p. (Orig.). (gr. 2-4). 1981. pap. 5.00 (ISBN 0-915124-38-6). Toothpaste.

Dotty's Suitcase. Constance C. Greene. 168p. (gr. 5-9). 1980. 8.95 (ISBN 0-670-28050-X). Viking Pr.

Douay-Rheims Bible. LC 77-80633. 1407p. 1980. pap. text ed. 23.00 (ISBN 0-89555-000-8). Tan Bks Pubs.

Douay-Rheims New Testament. Tr. by St. Jerome. LC 77-80634. 1977. pap. 5.50 (ISBN 0-89555-001-6). TAN Bks Pubs.

Double-Agent Fugitive. Max Ross. 1978. 10.00 o.p. (ISBN 0-682-48972-7). Exposition.

Double Bed Was Not for Two. Samuel B. Fielding. 1981. 8.95 (ISBN 0-533-04848-6). Vantage.

Double Bill. Alec McCowen. LC 80-66018. 1981. 10.95 (ISBN 0-689-11070-7). Atheneum.

Double Cross. Charles R. Pike. LC 80-68160. (Jubal Cade Westerns Ser.). 128p. 1980. pap. 2.95 (ISBN 0-87754-231-7). Chelsea Hse.

Double-Cross Ranch. Stuart Brock. 256p. (YA) 1974. 5.95 (ISBN 0-685-49064-5, Avalon). Bouregy.

Double Cross System. J. C. Masterman. 4.95 (ISBN 0-686-28851-3). Academy Chi Ltd.

Double Crown Club. James Moran. (Illus.). 128p. 1980. 85.00 (ISBN 0-913720-16-X). Sandstone.

Double Cure, or Redemption Twofold. D. O. Teasley. 160p. pap. 1.50 large print. Faith Pub Hse.

Double Date. Rosamond Du Jardin. (gr. 4-9). 1952. 9.89 (ISBN 0-397-30208-8). Lippincott.

Double Disappearance of Walter Fozbek. new ed. Steve Senn. 128p. (gr. 8-12). 1980. 8.95 (ISBN 0-8038-1571-9). Hastings.

Double Discovery. Jessamyn West. LC 80-7948. 1980. 11.95 (ISBN 0-15-126402-3). HarBraceJ.

Double-Dog-Dare. Ray Prather. LC 74-13316. (Ready-to-Read Ser.). (Illus.). 40p. (gr. 1-3). 1975. 4.95g o.s.i. (ISBN 0-02-775040-X). Macmillan.

Double, Double. Ellery Queen. 1976. pap. 1.75 (ISBN 0-345-28289-2). Ballantine.

Double Dying: Reflections on Holocaust Literature. Alvin H. Rosenfeld. LC 79-3006. 224p. 1980. 17.50x (ISBN 0-253-13337-8). Ind U Pr.

Double E. Percival Goodman. LC 76-50873. 1977. pap. 3.50 (ISBN 0-385-12868-1, Anch). Doubleday.

Double-Edged Secrets. W. J. Holmes. 1981. pap. 2.95 (ISBN 0-425-04714-8). Berkley Pub.

Double Ellery Queen. Ellery Queen. 1978. pap. 1.75 (ISBN 0-451-08025-4, E8025, Sig). NAL.

Double Exile: African & West Indian Writing Between Two Cultures. Gareth Griffiths. (Critical Appraisals). 1978. text ed. 18.25x (ISBN 0-7145-2622-3). Humanities.

Double Feature. Rosamond Du Jardin. LC 53-8910. (gr. 4-9). 1953. 8.95 o.p. (ISBN 0-397-31599-6). Lippincott.

Double Feature. Rosamond Du Jardin. (gr. 7-10). pap. 0.75 o.p. (ISBN 0-425-02666-3, Highland). Berkley Pub.

Double for Death. Rex Stout. 1979. pap. 1.75 (ISBN 0-515-05277-9). Jove Pubns.

Double for Death. Rex Stout. 1973. pap. 0.95 o.s.i. (ISBN 0-515-03119-4, N3119). Jove Pubns.

Double Helix: A Norton Critical Edition. James D. Watson. Ed. by Gunther S. Stent. 1981. write for info. (ISBN 0-393-01245-X); pap. text ed. 5.95x (ISBN 0-393-95075-1). Norton.

Double Helix: Being a Personal Account of the Discovery of the Structure of DNA. James D. Watson. LC 68-11211. (Illus.). 1968. 7.95 (ISBN 0-689-10285-2); pap. 5.95 (ISBN 0-689-70602-2, 261). Atheneum.

Double Image of the Double Helix: The Recombinant-DNA Debate. Clifford Grobstein. LC 78-26093. (Biology Ser.). (Illus.). 1979. text ed. 16.95x (ISBN 0-7167-1056-0); pap. text ed. 8.95x (ISBN 0-7167-1057-9). W H Freeman.

Double Invention of Komo. Jay Wright. (U. T. Poetry Ser.: No. 5). (Illus.). 120p. 1980. 10.95 (ISBN 0-292-71525-0); pap. 6.95 (ISBN 0-292-71526-9). U of Tex Pr.

Double Leverage: The Whole Truth. Ray H. Dittmore. 1979. 5.95 (ISBN 0-685-66731-6). Vantage.

Double Life. Karolina Pavlova. Tr. by Barbara H. Monter from Russian. 1978. 12.00 (ISBN 0-88233-223-6); pap. 3.95 o.p. (ISBN 0-88233-224-4). Ardis Pubs.

Double List Word Book. Ethel C. Sherard. 306p. (Orig.). 1981. pap. 9.95 (ISBN 0-9605288-0-6). Gwethine Pub Co.

Double Lives. Jane Barnes. LC 79-7795. 264p. 1981. 11.95 (ISBN 0-385-15647-2). Doubleday.

Double Masquerade. Karen Lynn. LC 80-2944. 192p. 1981. 9.95 (ISBN 0-385-17467-5). Doubleday.

Double Negative. David Carkeet. 246p. 1980. 9.95 (ISBN 0-8037-1777-6). Dial.

Double Shadow. Frederick Turner. (YA) 1978. 7.95 o.p. (ISBN 0-399-12150-1). Berkley Pub.

Double Shadow. Frederick Turner. 1979. pap. 1.75 o.p. (ISBN 0-425-03951-X). Berkley Pub.

Double Takes: Notes & Afterthoughts on the Movies, 1956-1976. Alexander Walker. 1978. 17.95 (ISBN 0-241-89395-X, Pub. by Hamish Hamilton England). David & Charles.

Double Witness: Poems. Ben Belitt. LC 77-2534. (Princeton Series of Contemporary Poets). 1977. 9.00 (ISBN 0-691-06346-X); pap. 3.75 (ISBN 0-691-01341-1). Princeton U Pr.

Double Your Money Every Three Years. Gerald Appel. 1974. 25.00 o.p. (ISBN 0-87000-896-X). Arlington Hse.

Double Your Money in Real Estate Every Two Years. Dave Glubetich. Ed. by Judy Moretz. (Illus.). 232p. 1980. 12.95 (ISBN 0-9601530-4-7). Impact Pub.

Doubleday Cookbook: Complete Contemporary Cooking. Jean Anderson & Elaine Hanna. LC 75-1000. 1344p. 1975. 15.95 (ISBN 0-385-09088-9). Doubleday.

Doubleday Devotional Classics, Vol. 1. Ed. by E. Glenn Hinson. LC 77-16923. 1978. pap. 4.95 o.p. (ISBN 0-385-13424-X, Galilee). Doubleday.

Doubleday Devotional Classics, Vol. 2. Ed. by E. Glenn Hinson. LC 77-16923. 1978. pap. 5.95 o.p. (ISBN 0-385-13425-8). Doubleday.

Doubleday Devotional Classics, Vol. 3. Ed. by E. Glenn Hinson. LC 77-16923. 1978. pap. 3.95 o.p. (ISBN 0-385-13426-6, Galilee). Doubleday.

Doubleday Dictionary: For Home, School & Office. Ed. by Sidney Landau & Ronald Bogus. LC 74-3543. 936p. 1975. 5.95 (ISBN 0-385-04099-7); thumb-indexed 7.95 (ISBN 0-385-03368-0). Doubleday.

Doubleday Roget's Thesaurus in Dictionary Form. Ed. by Sidney Landau & Ronald Bogus. LC 76-7696. 564p. 1977. 6.95 (ISBN 0-385-01236-5); thumb-indexed 7.95 (ISBN 0-385-12379-5). Doubleday.

Doubletalk: The Story of the First Strategic Arms Limitation Talks. Gerard Smith. LC 76-50788. (Illus.). 576p. 1980. 17.95 (ISBN 0-385-11444-3). Doubleday.

Doubling and Incest Repetition and Revenge: A Speculative Reading of Faulkner. John T. Irwin. LC 75-11341. 192p. 1975. 12.50x (ISBN 0-8018-1722-6); pap. text ed. 4.95 (ISBN 0-8018-2564-4). Johns Hopkins.

Doubt & Dogmatism: Studies in Hellenistic Epistemology. Ed. by Malcolm Schofield et al. 354p. 1980. text ed. 37.50x (ISBN 0-19-824601-3). Oxford U Pr.

Doubtfire. Robert Nye. 1968. 4.95 o.p. (ISBN 0-8090-3960-5). Hill & Wang.

Doubtful Guest. Edward Gorey. LC 57-10200. (Illus.). 1978. 5.95 (ISBN 0-396-07628-9). Dodd.

Doubting Kind. Alison Prince. (gr. 7 up). 1977. 8.25 (ISBN 0-688-22126-2); PLB 7.92 (ISBN 0-688-32126-7). Morrow.

Doubting Kind. Alison Prince. 228p. 1981. pap. 1.95 (ISBN 0-448-16499-X, Tempo). G&D.

Doubting Thomas. Yvonne Patterson. (Arch Bk.: No. 18). 1981. pap. 0.79 (ISBN 0-570-06144-X, 59-1261). Concordia.

Doughnut Dropout. E. Wallace Hildick. LC 70-180081. (gr. 4-7). 1972. PLB 4.50 o.p. (ISBN 0-385-09113-3). Doubleday.

Doughty's English. Walt Taylor et al. Ed. by Steele Commager. Incl. Adjectives from Proper Names; On the Diction of Tennyson; Split Infinitive & a System of Clauses; Slang; Growth of American English One; Growth of American English Two; Completing the Record of English; Some Anomalies of Spelling; Index to Tracts XLI-LIX. (Society for Pure English Ser.: Vol. 6). 1979. lib. bdg. 42.00 (ISBN 0-8240-3670-0). Garland Pub.

Douglas C. McMurtrie: Bibliographer & Historian of Printing. Scott Bruntjen & Melissa L. Young. LC 78-25682. (Great Bibliographers Ser.: No. 4). 1979. lib. bdg. 10.00 (ISBN 0-8108-1188-X). Scarecrow.

Douglas DC-3. Len Morgan. LC 64-7851. 1980. pap. 4.95 (ISBN 0-8168-5650-8). Aero.

Douglas Jerrold. Richard M. Kelly. LC 79-187615. (English Authors Ser.: No. 146). lib. bdg. 10.95 (ISBN 0-8057-1292-5). Twayne.

Douglas McHenry International Symposium on Concrete & Concrete Structures. 1978. 28.95 (SP-55). ACI.

Douglas of the Forests: The North American Journals of David Douglas. David Douglas. Ed. by John Davies. LC 80-12535. (Illus.). 194p. 1980. 14.95 (ISBN 0-295-95707-7). U of Wash Pr.

Douglas Sirk. Edinburgh Festival. (EIFF Ser.). 1978. pap. 3.50 o.p. (ISBN 0-918432-14-6). NY Zoetrope.

Douglas Sirk. Michael Stern. (Theatrical Arts Ser.). 1979. lib. bdg. 10.95 (ISBN 0-8057-9269-4). Twayne.

Douglas Stewart. Clement Semmler. LC 74-7389. (World Authors Ser.: Australia: No. 327). 176p. 1974. lib. bdg. 12.50 (ISBN 0-8057-2863-5). Twayne.

Doukai: A Contribution to Byzantine Prosopography. D. I. Polemis. (Univ. of London Historical Studies: No. 22). 1968. text ed. 30.00x (ISBN 0-485-13122-6, Athlone Pr). Humanities.

Doukhobors of British Columbia. Doukhobor Research Committee. Ed. by Harry B. Hawthorn. LC 79-8711. (Illus.). xii, 288p. 1980. Repr. of 1955 ed. lib. bdg. 28.50x (ISBN 0-313-20652-X, DOBC). Greenwood.

Doutrinas Biblicas. Tr. by P. C. Nelson. (Portuguese Bks.). 1979. 1.25 (ISBN 0-8297-0658-5). Life Pubs Intl.

Douze Contes De Maupassant. Eli Blume. (Fr.). (gr. 10-12). 1973. pap. text ed. 5.17 (ISBN 0-87720-468-3). AMSCO Sch.

Dove of the East. Mark Helprin. 1981. pap. 5.95 (ISBN 0-440-52151-3, Delta). Dell.

Dove Shooter's Handbook. Dan M. Russell. 1974. 9.95 (ISBN 0-87691-135-1). Winchester Pr.

Doves & Diplomats: Foreign Offices & Peace Movements in Europe & America in the 20th Century. Ed. by Solomon Wank. LC 77-20278. (Contributions in Political Science: No. 4). (Illus.). 1978. lib. bdg. 19.95 (ISBN 0-313-20027-0, WDD/). Greenwood.

Doves & Pomegranates. Christina Rossetti. Ed. by David Powell. LC 74-146624. (Illus.). (gr. 5 up). 1971. 5.95 (ISBN 0-02-777760-X). Macmillan.

D'Ovid a Racine. Georges May. (Yale Romanic Studies). 1949. pap. 27.50x (ISBN 0-685-69841-6). Elliots Bks.

Dow Is Dead: How to Profit in Uncommon Stocks. James D. Nisbet. Ed. by Betty Folts. LC 79-54885. (Illus.). 1979. 14.95 (ISBN 0-686-26329-4). Capital Tech.

Dow Jones Crosswords for the Serious. 1980. pap. 3.50 ea. Bk. I (ISBN 0-87128-585-1). Bk. 2 (ISBN 0-87128-586-X). Dow Jones-Irwin.

Dow Jones Crosswords for the Serious, Bk. 3. Charles Preston. 60p. 1981. pap. 3.50 (ISBN 0-87094-238-7). Dow Jones-Irwin.

Dow Jones Crosswords for the Serious, Bk. 4. Charles Preston. 60p. 1981. pap. 3.50 (ISBN 0-87094-239-5). Dow Jones-Irwin.

Dow Jones-Irwin Business Almanac, Nineteen Eighty-One. Ed. by Sumner N. Levine. LC 76-53629. 800p. 1981. 16.95 (ISBN 0-87094-225-5). Dow Jones-Irwin.

Dow Jones-Irwin Guide to Common Stocks. Chris Mader & Robert W. Hagin. LC 75-43167. 300p. 1976. 12.95 o.p. (ISBN 0-87094-108-9). Dow Jones-Irwin.

Dow-Jones Irwin Guide to Estate Planning. 3rd ed. William C. Clay. 176p. 1981. pap. 2.50 (ISBN 0-553-14913-X). Bantam.

Dow Jones-Irwin Guide to Estate Planning. rev. ed. William C. Clay, Jr. LC 76-2113. 1977. 9.95 o.p. (ISBN 0-87094-138-0). Dow Jones-Irwin.

Dow Jones-Irwin Guide to Interest. Lawrence R. Rosen. LC 73-89120. (Illus.). 180p. 1974. 9.95 o.p. (ISBN 0-87094-067-8). Dow Jones-Irwin.

Dow Jones-Irwin Guide to Real Estate Investing. Chris Mader. LC 74-25812. 206p. 1975. 12.95 o.p. (ISBN 0-87094-095-3). Dow Jones-Irwin.

Dow Jones-Irwin Guide to Real Estate Investing. rev. ed. Chris Mader. 1981. 14.95 (ISBN 0-87094-214-X). Dow Jones-Irwin.

Dow Jones-Irwin Guide to Stock Market Cycles. Michael Hayes. LC 76-28903. 1977. 25.00 (ISBN 0-87094-134-8). Dow Jones-Irwin.

Dow Jones-Irwin Guide to Tax Planning. rev. ed. Ray M. Sommerfeld. LC 77-83537. 1978. 17.50 o.p. (ISBN 0-87094-155-0). Dow Jones-Irwin.

Dow Jones-Irwin Guide to Tax Planning. 3rd ed. Ray M. Sommerfeld. 364p. 1981. pap. 9.95 (ISBN 0-87094-233-6). Dow Jones-Irwin.

Dowbeaters: How to Buy Stocks That Go up. Ira Cobleigh & Bruce Dorfman. (Illus.). 1979. 10.95 (ISBN 0-02-526500-8). Macmillan.

Down Among the Dead Men. Brian Peachment. 1976. pap. 1.55 (ISBN 0-08-017615-1). Pergamon.

Down Among the Jocks. Ralph Dennis. (Hardman Ser.: No. 5). 176p. 1974. pap. 0.95 o.p. (ISBN 0-445-00605-6). Popular Lib.

Down & Country. Glenn Myles. (Bebop Drawing Club Book). (Illus.). 58p. 1974. pap. 2.00 (ISBN 0-9605468-0-4). Artmans Pr.

Down & Out. Lee Toomey. LC 73-173720. (New Citizen Books). (Illus.). 80p. 1973. 7.50x (ISBN 0-85340-237-X). Intl Pubns Serv.

Down & Out in Britain. Jeremy Sandford. (Illus.). 1971. text ed. 9.25x (ISBN 0-7206-0341-2). Humanities.

Down & Out in the USA: A History of Social Welfare. updated ed. Lucy Komisar. 256p. (gr. 6 up). 1977. PLB 7.45 (ISBN 0-531-02647-7). Watts.

Down Below: Aboard the World's Classic Yachts. Matthew Walker. LC 80-12327. (Illus.). 136p. 1980. 16.95 (ISBN 0-87701-137-0). Chronicle Bks.

Down by the Creek Bank. Dottie Rambo. (Creek Bank Kids Ser.: Vol. 1). (ps-8). 1979. 3.95 (ISBN 0-914850-50-4). Impact Tenn.

Down, Down the Mountain. Ellis Credle. (Illus.). (gr. k-3). 1934. 6.95 (ISBN 0-525-66020-8). Elsevier-Nelson.

Down-East Spirituals & Others: Three Hundred Songs Supplementary to the Author's "Spiritual Folk-Songs of Early America". Ed. by George P. Jackson. LC 74-34317. (Music Reprint Ser). (Illus.). 296p. 1975. Repr. of 1943 ed. lib. bdg. 27.50 (ISBN 0-306-70666-0). Da Capo.

Down from the Hills. Orval E. Faubus. (Illus.). 528p. 1980. text ed. 25.00. Faubus.

Down Half the World. Elizabeth Coatsworth. (Illus.). (gr. 7 up). 1968. 4.50g o.s.i. (ISBN 0-02-721470-2). Macmillan.

Down Home. George Mettler. 352p. (Orig.). 1981. pap. 2.95 (ISBN 0-449-14403-8, GM). Fawcett.

Down-Home Gallery of American Wildlife. Ralph J. McDonald. (Illus.). 101p. 1980. 39.95 (ISBN 0-9605428-1-7); signed numbered ed. 95.00 (ISBN 0-9605428-0-9). Countryside Studio.
Down Illinois Rivers. George W. May. (Illus.). 400p. 1981. 16.00 (ISBN 0-9605566-5-6). G W May.
Down in the Boondocks. Wilson Gage. (gr. k-6). 1980. pap. 0.95 (ISBN 0-440-41745-7, YB). Dell.
Down Second Avenue: Growing up in a South African Ghetto. Ezekiel Mphahlele. 7.50 (ISBN 0-8446-4451-X). Peter Smith.
Down the Mississippi. Clyde R. Bulla. LC 54-5614. (Illus.). (gr. 2-5). 1954. 8.95 (ISBN 0-690-24383-9, TYC-J). T Y Crowell.
Down the Santa Fe Trail & into Mexico: The Diary of Susan Shelby Magoffin, 1846-1847. Susan S. Magoffin. Ed. by Stella M. Drumm. LC 75-31417. (Illus.). 344p. 1975. Repr. of 1962 ed. 25.00 o.p. (ISBN 0-88307-518-0). Gannon.
Down the Silent Night Road. Subhas C. Saha. (Writers Workshop Redbird Book Ser.). 72p. 1975. 12.00 (ISBN 0-88253-530-7); pap. text ed. 4.80 (ISBN 0-88253-529-3). Ind-US Inc.
Down the Spanish Coast. Philip Bristow. 196p. 1980. 12.00x (ISBN 0-245-52935-7, Pub. by Nautical England). State Mutual Bk.
Down to a Sunless Sea. David Graham. 1981. 13.95 (ISBN 0-671-41217-5). S&S.
Down to Earth: An Introduction to Geology. Carey G. Croneis & William C. Krumbein. LC 36-10420. (Illus.). 1961. pap. 3.50 o.s.i. (ISBN 0-226-12099-6, P501, Phoen). U of Chicago Pr.
Down to Earth at Walden. Marilynne Roach. (gr. 5 up). 1980. 7.95 (ISBN 0-395-29647-1). HM.
Down to Earth Cookbook. rev. ed. Anita Borghese. LC 80-21483. (Illus.). 128p. (gr. 3 up). 1980. 8.95 (ISBN 0-684-16618-6). Scribner.
Down to Earth Sociology. 2nd ed. James M. Henslin. LC 75-36108. 1976. pap. text ed. 6.95 (ISBN 0-02-914620-8). Free Pr.
Down to Earth Sociology: Society, Structure, & Everyday Life. 3rd ed. Ed. by James M. Henslin. LC 80-2315. 1981. pap. text ed. 9.95 (ISBN 0-02-914660-7). Free Pr.
Down Under & Dirty. Dan Streib. (Hawk Ser.: No. 9). (Orig.). 1981. pap. 1.95 (ISBN 0-515-05874-2). Jove Pubns.
Downbelow Station. C. J. Cherryh. (Science Fiction Ser.). 1981. pap. 2.75 (ISBN 0-87997-594-6, UE1594). Daw Bks.
Downfall. (Classics Illus. Ser.). (Illus.). pap. 0.59 o.p. (ISBN 0-685-74108-7, 126). Guild Bks.
Downfall of the Gold Standard. Gustav Cassel. LC 66-52921. Repr. of 1936 ed. 19.50x (ISBN 0-678-05160-7). Kelley.
Downhill, Hotdogging, & Cross-Country--If the Snow Isn't Sticky. Gary Paulsen. LC 78-26256. (Sports on the Light Side Ser.). (Illus.). (gr. 4-6). 1979. PLB 9.65 (ISBN 0-8172-0187-4). Raintree Pubs.
Downhill Lies & Other Falsehoods; or, How to Play Dirty Golf. Rex Lardner. (Illus.). 192p. 1973. pap. 3.50 (ISBN 0-8015-2198-X, Hawthorn). Dutton.
Downhill to Uphill. Robert L. Nelson. LC 79-6756. 76p. 1980. pap. text ed. 5.75 (ISBN 0-8191-0946-0). U Pr of Amer.
Downhole Operations. Philip F. Lynch. (Basic Petroleum Production Operations Ser.: Vol. 3). (Illus.). 128p. (Orig.). 1981. pap. text ed. 14.95 (ISBN 0-87201-225-5). Gulf Pub.
Down's Syndrome: Growing & Learning. Siegfried M. Pueschel et al. 1978. 8.95 (ISBN 0-8362-2804-9); pap. 5.95 (ISBN 0-8362-2805-7). Andrews & McMeel.
Down's Syndrome: The Psychology of Mongolism. D. Gibson. LC 77-87381. 1979. 45.00 (ISBN 0-521-21914-0). Cambridge U Pr.
Downshire Estates in Ireland 1801-1845: The Management of Irish Landed Estates in the Early Nineteenth Century. W. A. Maguire. (Illus.). 282p. 1972. text ed. 34.50x (ISBN 0-19-822357-9). Oxford U Pr.
Downtown Development Handbook. Ralph J. Basile et al. LC 80-50928. (Community Builder Handbook Ser.). (Illus.). 278p. 1980. 34.00 (ISBN 0-87420-591-3, D12). Urban Land.
Dowser's Primer. Robert E. Steffy. 60p. 1980. pap. 4.50 (ISBN 0-935648-04-6). Halldin Pub.
Dowsing for Everyone. Harvey Howells. LC 78-26713. (Illus.). 1979. 8.95 o.p. (ISBN 0-8289-0341-7); pap. 5.95 (ISBN 0-8289-0342-5). Greene.
Dowst Revisited. Ron Thacker. (Gambler's Book Shelf). 1976. pap. 2.95 (ISBN 0-89650-572-3). Gamblers.
Doxorubicin. Federico Arcamone. LC 80-1106. (Medicinal Chemistry Ser.). 1981. price not set (ISBN 0-12-059280-0). Acad Pr.
Dozen Daring Christians. William L. Coleman. LC 79-50813. 1979. pap. 2.95 (ISBN 0-89636-023-7). Accent Bks.
Drabble. Kevin Fagan. 132p. (Orig.). 1981. pap. 3.95 (ISBN 0-449-90052-5, Columbine). Fawcett.
Dracula. Bram Stoker. pap. 2.50 (ISBN 0-515-05347-3). Jove Pubns.
Dracula. Bram Stoker. Adapted by Alice Schick & Joel Schick. LC 80-13619. (Illus.). 48p. (gr. 3 up). 1980. PLB 8.44 (ISBN 0-440-01349-6); pap. 4.95 (ISBN 0-440-01348-8). Delacorte.
Dracula Book. Donald F. Glut. LC 75-4917. (Illus.). 410p. 1975. 15.00 (ISBN 0-8108-0804-8). Scarecrow.
Dracula Book of Great Vampire Stories. Ed. by Leslie Shepard. 1978. pap. 1.95 o.s.i. (ISBN 0-515-04506-3). Jove Pubns.
Dracula, Frankenstein, Dr. Jekyll & Mr. Hyde. Bram Stoker & Mary Shelley. 672p. (RL 7). Date not set. pap. 2.50 (ISBN 0-451-51290-1, CE1290, Sig Classics). NAL.
Dracula, Go Home. Kin Platt. (gr. 7-12). 1981. pap. 1.25 (ISBN 0-440-92022-1, LE). Dell.
Dracula's Cat. Jan Wahl. LC 77-27051. (Illus.). (gr. 1-3). 1978. 6.95 (ISBN 0-13-218933-X). P-H.
Dracula's Children. Richard Lertz. 208p. 1981. 12.95 (ISBN 0-932966-15-2). Permanent Pr.
Draft International Code of Conduct on the Transfer of Technology. Wolfgang Fikentscher. (IIC Studies: Vol. 4). 211p. (Orig.). 1980. pap. text ed. 23.80 (ISBN 0-89573-030-8). Verlag Chemie.
Draft of Shadows & Other Poems. Octavio Paz. Tr. by Eliot Weinberger from Sp. LC 79-15588. 1979. 11.95 (ISBN 0-8112-0737-4); pap. 4.95 (ISBN 0-8112-0738-2, NDP489). New Directions.
Drafting. Boy Scouts Of America. LC 19-600. (Illus.). 32p. (gr. 6-12). 1965. pap. 0.70x (ISBN 0-8395-3273-3, 3273). BSA.
Drafting. Walter C. Brown. (Illus.). 1978. text ed. 4.80 (ISBN 0-87006-256-5). Goodheart.
Drafting. Los Angeles Unified School District. Ed. by Richard A. Vorndran. LC 77-73291. 64p. (gr. 7-9). 1978. pap. text ed. 3.64 (ISBN 0-02-820410-7). Glencoe.
Drafting. Wilbur R. Miller. LC 78-53388. (Basic Industrial Arts Ser.). (Illus.). 1978. 6.00 (ISBN 0-87345-793-5); softbound 4.48 (ISBN 0-87345-785-4). McKnight.
Drafting for Industry: 1978 Ed. Walter C. Brown. LC 77-25196. (Illus.). 616p. 1980. 16.56 (ISBN 0-87006-247-6); wkbk. 4.80 (ISBN 0-87006-306-5). Goodheart.
Drafting Made Simple. Yonny Segel. LC 61-9550. pap. 3.50 (ISBN 0-385-01348-5, Made). Doubleday.
Drafting Projects for Today. Bruce A. Renton. 1975. pap. 8.80 (ISBN 0-8273-1926-6). Delmar.
Drafting Technology & Practice. rev ed. Spence. (gr. 9-12). 1980. text ed. 22.60 (ISBN 0-87002-303-9); worksheets 10.00 (ISBN 0-87002-130-3). Bennett IL.
Drafting Technology & Practice. William Spence. (gr. 9-12). 1973. text ed. 19.96 o.p. (ISBN 0-87002-129-X); wksheets 8.68 o.p. (ISBN 0-87002-130-3). Bennett IL.
Drafting Technology Problems. 2nd ed. Lawrence E. Gerevas. 1981. pap. write for info. (ISBN 0-672-97701-X); write for info. answer bk. (ISBN 0-672-97864-4). Bobbs.
Drag Boat Racing: The National Championships. Al Jackson & Gene Tardy. (Sports Action Ser). (Illus.). 48p. (gr. 3-12). 1973. PLB 5.51 (ISBN 0-914844-05-9); pap. 3.95 (ISBN 0-914844-06-7). J Alden.
Drag Hunting. Jane Kidd. 1978. 5.25 (ISBN 0-85131-285-3, Dist. by Sporting Book Center). J A Allen.
Drag Racing. Charles Coombs. (Illus.). (gr. 5-9). 1970. PLB 6.96 (ISBN 0-688-31243-8). Morrow.
Drag Reduction by Additives: Review & Bibliography. Ed. by J. A. G. Hemmings & A. White. 1976. pap. 50.00 (ISBN 0-900983-58-2, Dist. by Air Science Co.). BHRA Fluid.
Drag Strip. William C. Gault. (gr. 5-8). pap. 0.95 o.p. (ISBN 0-425-03014-8, Highland). Berkley Pub.
Draggermen: Fishing on Georges Bank. George Matteson. LC 78-21767. (Illus.). 144p. (gr. 5 up). 1979. 8.95 (ISBN 0-590-07534-9, Four Winds). Schol Bk Serv.
Dragon. Eugene Schwarz. Tr. by Elizabeth R. Hapgood. (Orig.). 1969. pap. 1.65x (ISBN 0-87830-512-2, 12). Theatre Arts.
Dragon & Monster Tales. new ed. Corinne Denan. LC 79-66329. (Illus.). 48p. (gr. 2-6). 1980. PLB 4.89 (ISBN 0-89375-326-2); pap. 1.50 (ISBN 0-89375-325-4). Troll Assocs.
Dragon & the George. Gordon R. Dickson. 1978. pap. 2.25 (ISBN 0-345-29514-5). Ballantine.
Dragon & the Rose. Roberta Gellis. LC 76-43400. 1977. pap. 1.95 o.p. (ISBN 0-87216-364-4). Playboy Pbks.
Dragon Bound: Revelation Speaks to Our Times. Ernest L. Stoffel. 120p. (Orig.). 1981. pap. 4.50 (ISBN 0-8042-0227-3). John Knox.
Dragon Circle. Krensky. (gr. 3-5). 1980. pap. 1.25 (ISBN 0-590-30069-5, Schol Pap). Schol Bk Serv.
Dragon Don & John: Dragon Donaldo y Juan. Lee Mountain. Tr. by Monica Gunning. (Storybooks for Beginners Ser.). (Illus.). 15p. (Eng. & Span.). 1980. pap. 12.50 set (ISBN 0-89061-213-7). Jamestown Pubs.
Dragon Don: Dragon Donaldo, Bk. 1. Lee Mountain. Tr. by Monica Gunning. (Storybooks for Beginners Ser.). (Illus.). 15p. 1980. pap. 12.50 set (ISBN 0-89061-212-9). Jamestown Pubs.
Dragon Franz. Ursula Konopka & Josef Guggenmos. LC 76-40986. (Illus.). (gr. k-3). 1977. 8.25 (ISBN 0-688-80077-7); PLB 7.92 (ISBN 0-688-84077-9). Greenwillow.
Dragon Horses: The Edwardian Ideal. Roderick Gradidge. LC 80-17866. 272p. 30.00 (ISBN 0-8076-0988-9). Braziller.
Dragon in the Gate: Studies in the Poetry of G. M. Hopkins. Elisabeth Schneider. LC 68-31434. (Perspectives in Criticism: No. 20). 1968. 19.50x (ISBN 0-520-01150-3). U of Cal Pr.
Dragon in the Sea. Frank Herbert. (Science Fiction Ser.). 1980. lib. bdg. 13.95 (ISBN 0-8398-2646-X). Gregg.
Dragon Knight: A Poem in Twelve Cantos. James B. Burges. Ed. by Donald H. Reiman. LC 75-31174. (Romantic Context Ser.: Poetry 1789-1830). 1977. lib. bdg. 47.00 (ISBN 0-8240-2126-6). Garland Pub.
Dragon Lord. David Drake. 1979. 8.95 o.p. (ISBN 0-399-12380-6). Berkley Pub.
Dragon Net. Silas Hong. 1976. 4.95 o.p. (ISBN 0-8007-0775-3). Revell.
Dragon Stirs: An Intimate Sketchbook of China's Kuomintang Revolution. Henry F. Misselwitz. LC 79-2835. (Illus.). 296p. 1981. Repr. of 1941 ed. 22.50 (ISBN 0-8305-0012-X). Hyperion Conn.
Dragon Tree. Victor Canning. 1980. pap. 2.25 (ISBN 0-441-16659-8). Charter Bks.
Dragon Winter. Niel Hancock. 1978. pap. 2.50 (ISBN 0-445-04191-9). Popular Lib.
Dragonflame & Other Bedtime Nightmares. Don McGregor. LC 77-17761. (Illus.). 1978. pap. 5.00 (ISBN 0-934882-02-9). Fictioneer Bks.
Dragonflame, & Other Bedtime Nightmares. Don McGregor. LC 80-197751. 128p. 1980. Repr. of 1977 ed. lib. bdg. 12.95 (ISBN 0-89370-093-2). Borgo Pr.
Dragonflies. Oxford Scientific Films. (Illus.). 32p. 1980. 7.95 (ISBN 0-399-20731-7). Putnam.
Dragonflies Draw Flame. Monika Varma. 4.80 (ISBN 0-89253-745-0); flexible cloth 4.00 (ISBN 0-89253-746-9). Ind-US Inc.
Dragonflies of Great Britain & Ireland. C. O. Hammond. 116p. 1980. 36.00x (ISBN 0-902068-06-7, Pub. by Curwen England). State Mutual Bk.
Dragonflight. Anne McCaffrey. 1975. pap. 2.50 (ISBN 0-345-29568-4). Ballantine.
Dragonmede. Rona Randall. 320p. 1975. pap. 1.75 o.p. (ISBN 0-345-24351-X). Ballantine.
Dragonquest. Anne McCaffrey. 1975. pap. 2.50 (ISBN 0-345-29666-4). Ballantine.
Dragons. Peter Hogarth & Val Clery. LC 79-4530. (Illus.). 1979. 16.95 o.p. (ISBN 0-670-28176-X, Studio). Viking Pr.
Dragons & Other Creatures: Chinese Embrodiery of Katherine Westphal. Katherine Westphal. (Lancaster-Miller Art Ser.). (Illus.). 1980. 8.95 (ISBN 0-89581-012-3). Lancaster-Miller.
Dragon's Breath. Frank Smith. LC 80-21818. 368p. 1980. 12.95 (ISBN 0-8253-0007-X). Beaufort Bks NY.
Dragon's Delight. Lynn Hall. (Dragon Ser.). 112p. 1980. lib. bdg. 5.97 (ISBN 0-695-41366-X). Follett.
Dragons, Dragons, Dragons. Ed. by Helen Hoke. LC 74-182300. (Terrific Triple Titles Ser). (Illus.). 256p. (gr. 1 up). 1972. PLB 6.90 o.p. (ISBN 0-531-02036-3). Watts.
Dragons of Eden. Carl Sagan. 1978. pap. 2.50 (ISBN 0-345-28153-5). Ballantine.
Dragons of Peking. Wesley Poter. (Illus.). (gr. k-3). 1979. 2.95 (ISBN 0-531-02500-4); PLB 6.90 s&l o.p. (ISBN 0-531-04079-8). Watts.
Dragon's Tail: America's Continuing Nuclear Experiment. Corinne Browne & Robert Munroe. (Illus.). 288p. 1981. 10.95 (ISBN 0-688-03691-0). Morrow.
Dragon's Village. Yuan-Tsung Chen. 1981. pap. 4.95 (ISBN 0-14-005811-7). Penguin.
Dragonslayer. Wayland Drew. (Orig.). 1981. pap. 2.75 (ISBN 0-345-29694-X, Del Ray). Ballantine.
Dragonwyck. Anya Seton. 1977. pap. 1.95 o.p. (ISBN 0-449-23341-3, Crest). Fawcett.
Drainage Basin Form & Process: A Geomorphological Approach. K. J. Gregory & D. E. Walling. 1976. pap. text ed. 16.95 (ISBN 0-470-15198-6). Halsted Pr.
Drainage Details in SI Metric. Leslie Woolley. (Illus.). 1978. 13.50x (ISBN 0-7198-2520-2). Intl Ideas.
Drainage in Homoeopathy. E. A. Maury. 1980. text ed. 4.00x (ISBN 0-8464-1007-9). Beekman Pubs.
Draining of the Somerset Levels. Michael Williams. LC 73-75830. (Illus.). 1970. 57.50 (ISBN 0-521-07486-X). Cambridge U Pr.
Drake Family of New Hampshire: Robert, of Hampton, & Some of His Descendants, A Geneology. Compiled by Alice Smith Thompson. LC 63-62916. (Illus.). 1962. text ed. 15.00x (ISBN 0-915916-03-7). U Pr of New Eng.
Drake in England. rev. ed. Anthony Wagner. (Illus.). 119p. 1970. text ed. 10.00x (ISBN 0-915916-04-5). U Pr of New Eng.
Drakov Memoranda. Jon Winters. 1977. pap. 2.25 (ISBN 0-380-47563-4, 47563). Avon.
Drama & Art: An Introduction to the Use of Evidence from the Visual Arts for the Study of Early Drama. Clifford Davidson. (Early Drama, Art, & Music Ser.). (Illus.). 1977. pap. 4.95 (ISBN 0-918720-00-1). Medieval Inst.
Drama & Reality: The European Theatre Since Ibsen. Ronald Gaskell. 1972. 12.75x (ISBN 0-7100-7145-0); pap. 6.95 (ISBN 0-7100-7146-9). Routledge & Kegan.
Drama & Revolution. Ed. by Bernard F. Dukore. LC 71-130652. 1971. pap. text ed. 10.95x (ISBN 0-03-083569-0). Irvington.
Drama & the Theatre: With Radio, Film & Television; an Outline for the Student. Ed. by John R. Brown. (Outlines Ser). 1971. 14.00x (ISBN 0-7100-6971-5); pap. 7.95 (ISBN 0-7100-7053-5). Routledge & Kegan.
Drama & Theatre. Jack Rudman. (Undergraduate Program Field Test Ser.: UPFT-5). (Cloth bdg. avail. on request). pap. 9.95 (ISBN 0-8373-6005-6). Natl Learning.
Drama As Literature. Jiri Veltrusky. (Pdr Press Publications in Semiotics of Literature: No. 2). (Orig.). 1977. pap. text ed. 8.00x (ISBN 90-316-0127-6). Humanities.
Drama As Propaganda: A Study of The Troublesome Reign of King John. Virginia M. Carr. (Salzburg Studies in English Literature, Elizabethan & Renaissance Studies: No. 28). 185p. 1974. pap. text ed. 25.00x (ISBN 0-391-01341-6). Humanities.
Drama Criticism, 2 vols. Arthur Coleman & Gary R. Tyler. Incl. Vol. 1. A Checklist of Interpretation Since 1940 of English & American Plays. LC 66-30426. 1966. 18.00x (ISBN 0-8040-0069-7); Vol. 2. A Checklist of Interpretation Since 1940 of Classical & Continental Plays. LC 75-115031. 446p. 1970. 18.00x (ISBN 0-8040-0500-1). Swallow.
Drama, Dance & Music. J. Redmond. (Themes in Drama Ser.: No. 3). (Illus.). 260p. Date not set. 36.00 (ISBN 0-521-22180-3). Cambridge U Pr.
Drama for Classroom & Stage. Albert Johnson & Bertha Johnson. LC 68-27249. (Illus.). 1969. 12.00 o.p. (ISBN 0-498-06711-4). A S Barnes.
Drama for Middle & Upper Schools. Christopher Day. 1975. 19.95 o.p. (ISBN 0-7134-2969-0, Pub. by Batsford England); pap. 13.50 (ISBN 0-7134-2980-1). David & Charles.
Drama in Real Life. 1980. pap. 2.50 (ISBN 0-425-04723-7). Berkley Pub.
Drama in Therapy, 2 vols. Ed. by Gertrud Schattner & Richard Courtney. Incl. Vol. I. Drama in Therapy for Children. 1981. text ed. 15.00x (ISBN 0-89676-013-8); Vol. II. Drama in Therapy for Adults. 1981. text ed. 15.00x (ISBN 0-89676-014-6). LC 80-15680. Drama Bk.
Drama in Worship. Lawrence Waddy. LC 78-58952. 1978. pap. 8.95 (ISBN 0-8091-2107-7). Paulist Pr.
Drama of Incarnation. 3rd ed. Flower A. Newhouse. 1948. 6.50 (ISBN 0-910378-04-5). Christward.
Drama of Power: Studies in Shakespeare's History Plays. Moody E. Prior. 1973. 16.75x o.s.i. (ISBN 0-8101-0421-0). Northwestern U Pr.
Drama of Revolt: A Critical Study of Georg Buchner. M. B. Benn. LC 75-3974. (Anglica Germanica Ser.: No. 2). (Illus.). 300p. 1976. 49.50 (ISBN 0-521-20828-9); pap. 13.95x (ISBN 0-521-29415-0). Cambridge U Pr.
Drama of Salvation. Rosemary Haughton. 154p. 1975. 6.95 (ISBN 0-8164-1201-4). Crossroad NY.
Drama of Speech Acts: Shakespeare's Lancastrian Tetralogy. J. A. Porter. 1979. 14.50x (ISBN 0-520-03702-2). U of Cal Pr.
Drama of the Renaissance: Essays for Leicester Bradner. Ed. by Elmer M. Blistein. LC 72-91653. 199p. 1970. 8.50x (ISBN 0-87057-117-6, Pub. by Brown U Pr). Univ Pr of New England.
Drama of Thought: An Inquiry into the Place of Philosophy in Human Experience. David A. Sprintzen. LC 78-64821. 1978. pap. text ed. 9.00 (ISBN 0-8191-0640-2). U Pr of Amer.
Drama of W. B. Yeats: Irish Myth & the Japanese No. Richard Taylor. LC 75-43336. 1976. 20.00x (ISBN 0-300-01904-1). Yale U Pr.

Drama: Principles & Plays. 2nd ed. Theodore W. Hatlen. (Illus.). 768p. 1975. pap. text ed. 13.95 (ISBN 0-13-218982-8). P-H.

Drama Reader: Full-Length Plays for the Secondary School. S. Perry Congdon, 2nd. LC 62-13409. 1962. text ed. 4.40 o.p. (ISBN 0-672-73248-3); pap. text ed. 4.95 (ISBN 0-672-73220-3). Odyssey Pr.

Drama Scholars Index to Plays & Filmscripts. Gordon Samples. LC 73-22165. 1974. 15.00 (ISBN 0-8108-0699-1). Scarecrow.

Drama, Stage & Audience. J. L. Styan. LC 74-76948. 260p. 1975. 32.00 (ISBN 0-521-20504-2); pap. 8.50 (ISBN 0-521-09869-6). Cambridge U Pr.

Drama, Theatre & the Handicapped. Ed. by Ann M. Shaw & C. J. Stevens. 121p. 1979. 6.95; ATA members 4.95. Am Theatre Assoc.

Drama Through Performance. Mark Auburn & Katherine Burkman. LC 76-19458. (Illus.). 1977. pap. text ed. 12.95 (ISBN 0-395-24548-6); inst. manual 1.25 (ISBN 0-395-24550-8). HM.

Dramas, Fields, & Metaphors: Symbolic Action in Human Society. Victor Turner. LC 73-16968. (Symbol, Myth & Ritual Ser.). (Illus.). 312p. 1975. pap. 5.95 o.p. (ISBN 0-8014-9151-7). Cornell U Pr.

Dramas of Political Life. James N. Rosenau. LC 79-17804. (Illus.). 1980. pap. text ed. 7.95 (ISBN 0-87872-246-7). Duxbury Pr.

Dramas y Poemas Para Dias Especiales, No. 1. Adolfo Robleto. 94p. (Span.). 1980. pap. 1.95 (ISBN 0-311-07004-3, Edit Mundo). Casa Bautista.

Dramas y Poemas Para Dias Especiales, No. 2. Adolfo Robleto. 1979. Repr. of 1977 ed. 1.95 (ISBN 0-311-07008-6, Edit Mundo). Casa Bautista.

Dramatic & Poetical Works of the Late Lieut. Gen. J. Burgoyne. John Burgoyne. LC 77-2932. 1977. Repr. of 1808 ed. 52.00x (ISBN 0-8201-1285-2). Schol Facsimiles.

Dramatic Criticism Index: Bibliography of Commentaries on Playwrights from Ibsen to the Avant-Garde. Paul F. Breed & Florence M. Sniderman. LC 79-127598. 1972. 40.00 (ISBN 0-8103-1090-2). Gale.

Dramatic Criticism: 1895-98; a Selection by John F. Matthews. George B. Shaw. LC 77-136084. 1971. Repr. of 1959 ed. lib. bdg. 23.00x (ISBN 0-8371-5234-8, S*H*D*R). Greenwood.

Dramatic Curriculum. Richard Courtney. 130p. 1980. text ed. 10.00x (ISBN 0-89676-061-8); pap. text ed. 6.95x (ISBN 0-89676-063-4). Drama Bk.

Dramatic Experience. J. L. Styan. 1965. 23.95 (ISBN 0-521-06573-9); pap. 8.95 (ISBN 0-521-09984-6). Cambridge U Pr.

Dramatic Imagery in the Plays of John Webster. Susan H. McLeod. (Salzburg Studies in English Literature: Jacobean Drama Studies: No. 68). 1977. pap. text ed. 25.00x (ISBN 0-391-01481-1). Humanities.

Dramatic Imagination. Robert E. Jones. 1941. 5.95 (ISBN 0-87830-035-X). Theatre Arts.

Dramatic Imagination: A Handbook for Teachers. 1975. pap. 6.00x. Jenfred Pr.

Dramatic Irony in Chaucer. Germaine Dempster. 1959. text ed. 8.50x (ISBN 0-391-00492-1). Humanities.

Dramatic Literature for Children: A Century in Review. Roger L. Bedard. Date not set. text ed. price not set (ISBN 0-87602-019-8); pap. text ed. price not set (ISBN 0-87602-020-1). Anchorage.

Dramatic Monologue: Vox Humana. Frances B. Carleton. (Salzburg Studies in English Literature: Romantic Reassessment: 64). 1977. pap. text ed. 25.00x (ISBN 0-391-01340-8). Humanities.

Dramatic Music: Catalogue of Full Scores. Oscar G. Sonneck. LC 69-12619. (Music Ser). 1969. Repr. of 1908 ed. lib. bdg. 25.00 (ISBN 0-306-71229-6). Da Capo.

Dramatic Quicklyisms: Malapropic Wordplay Technique in Shakespeare's Henriad, 2 vols. Barbara Hardy. (SSEL Poetic Drama Studies: No. 85, Vols. 1 & 2). 382p. 1979. Vol. 1. pap. text ed. 25.00x (ISBN 0-391-01748-9); Vol. 2. pap. text ed. 25.00x (ISBN 0-391-01749-7). Humanities.

Dramatic Scenes & Other Poems 1819; Marcian Colonna, 1820: Proctor Bryan Waller ("Barry Cornwall") (1787-1874) Ed. by Donald H. Reiman. LC 75-31246. (Romantic Context Ser.: Poetry 1789-1830). 1978. lib. bdg. 47.00 (ISBN 0-8240-2194-0). Garland Pub.

Dramatic Scenes from Real Life, 2vols. Lady Morgan S. Owenson. Ed. by Robert L. Wolff. (Ireland-Nineteenth Century Fiction, Ser. Two: Vol. 10). 1979. lib. bdg. 92.00 (ISBN 0-8240-3459-7). Garland Pub.

Dramatic Structure: The Shaping of Experience. Jackson G. Barry. LC 78-100607. 1970. 20.00x (ISBN 0-520-01624-6). U of Cal Pr.

Dramatic Technique. George P. Baker. LC 77-77706. (Theatre, Film & the Performing Arts Ser). 532p. 1971. Repr. of 1919 ed. lib. bdg. 35.00 (ISBN 0-306-71344-6). Da Capo.

Dramatic Works. Jean De La Taille. Ed. by Kathleen M. Hall & C. N. Smith. 1972. text ed. 15.00x (ISBN 0-485-13804-2, Athlone Pr); pap. text ed. 6.50x (ISBN 0-485-12804-7, Athlone Pr). Humanities.

Dramatic Works of Denis Johnston, 2 vols. Denis Johnston. Incl. Vol. 1. 1977. text ed. 35.00x (ISBN 0-685-51837-X); Vol. 2. 1978. text ed. 36.50x (ISBN 0-901072-53-2). Humanities.

Dramatic Works of Thomas Dekker, 4 vols. Thomas Dekker. Ed. by Fredson Bowers. 1953-61. Vol. 1. 72.00 (ISBN 0-521-04808-7); Vol. 2. 72.00 (ISBN 0-521-04809-5); Vol. 3. 72.00 (ISBN 0-521-04810-9); Vol. 4. 72.00 (ISBN 0-521-04811-7). Cambridge U Pr.

Dramatics for the Elderly: A Guide for Directors of Dramatics Groups in Senior Centers & Residential Care Settings. Paula G. Gray. LC 74-3185. 1974. pap. text ed. 3.50x (ISBN 0-8077-2400-9). Tchrs Coll.

Dramatist & the Received Idea. Wilbur Sanders. 1968. 58.00 (ISBN 0-521-06924-6). Cambridge U Pr.

Dramatizaciones Infantiles Para Dias Especiales. Norma H. C. De Deiros. 1978. pap. 1.95 (ISBN 0-311-07606-8). Casa Bautista.

Draughtsmanship: Architectural & Building Graphics. 3rd ed. Fraser Reekie. (Illus.). 248p. 1976. pap. 12.95x (ISBN 0-7131-3368-6). Intl Ideas.

Draupadi & Jayadratha & Other Poems. P. Lal. 18p. 1973. 5.00 (ISBN 0-88253-271-5); bdg. 4.00flexible (ISBN 0-89253-540-7). Ind-US Inc.

Dravidian Etymological Dictionary. Thomas Burrow & Murray B. Emeneau. 1961. 49.95x (ISBN 0-19-864310-1). Oxford U Pr.

Dravidian Kinship. Thomas R. Trautmann. LC 80-24214. (Cambridge Studies in Social Anthropology: No. 36). (Illus.). 704p. Date not set. price not set (ISBN 0-521-23703-3). Cambridge U Pr.

Draw a Dark Circle. Iona Charles. 1977. pap. 1.50 o.p. (ISBN 0-445-03191-3). Popular Lib.

Draw! A Visual Approach to Thinking, Learning & Communicating. Kurt Hanks & Larry Belliston. LC 77-6328. (Illus.). 242p. 1977. 19.75 o.p. (ISBN 0-913232-45-9); pap. 9.75 (ISBN 0-913232-46-7). W Kaufmann.

Draw Fifty Dogs. Lee J. Ames. LC 79-6853. (Illus.). 64p. (gr. 4-6). 1981. 6.95a (ISBN 0-385-15686-3); PLB (ISBN 0-385-15687-1). Doubleday.

Draw Fifty Vehicles. Lee J. Ames. LC 77-94862. (gr. 1 up). 1978. pap. 2.95 (ISBN 0-385-14154-8). Doubleday.

Draw Horses with Sam Savitt. Sam Savitt. LC 80-21812. (Illus.). 96p. 1981. 14.95 (ISBN 0-670-28259-6, Studio). Viking Pr.

Draw or Drag. Wayne D. Overholser. 1981. pap. 1.95 (ISBN 0-440-13263-0). Dell.

Draw up Your Own Will Without a Lawyer, or Else... Why You Can't Afford to Live--or Die--Without One! Benji O. Anosike. LC 80-966444. 84p. (Orig.). 1980. pap. text ed. 5.95x (ISBN 0-932704-05-0). Do-It-Yourself Pubns.

Draw with Dots. Isobel R. Beard. (Activity Fun Books). (Illus., Orig.). (ps-3). 0.99 o.p. (ISBN 0-695-90180-X). Follett.

Draw Your Own Zoo & Color It Too. James Dickie. 1973. pap. 4.95 (ISBN 0-8224-2400-2). Pitman Learning.

Drawin Fabric Embroidery. Edna Wark. 1979. 24.00 (ISBN 0-7134-1476-6). David & Charles.

Drawing. Alberto Martinez-Juarez. 1981. 5.95 (ISBN 0-8062-1590-9). Carlton.

Drawing. Daniel M. Mendelowitz. LC 80-50905. (Illus.). xvi, 464p. 1980. Repr. of 1967 ed. 29.50 (ISBN 0-8047-1089-9). Stanford U Pr.

Drawing. J. M. Parramon. (Orig.). 1980. pap. 4.95 (ISBN 0-89586-072-4). H P Bks.

Drawing. R. Smith. (Teach Yourself Ser.). 1975. pap. 2.95 o.p. (ISBN 0-679-10422-4). McKay.

Drawing a Conclusion: Advanced Level. James A. Giroux. Ed. by Edward Spargo. (Comprehension Skills Ser). (Illus.). (gr. 9-12). 1974. pap. text ed. 2.40x (ISBN 0-89061-015-0). Jamestown Pubs.

Drawing a Conclusion: Middle Level. Glenn R. Williston. (Comprehension Skills Ser.). (Illus.). 64p. (gr. 6-8). 1976. pap. text ed. 2.40x (ISBN 0-89061-067-3, CB-4M). Jamestown Pubs.

Drawing: A Studio Guide. Lu Bro. (Illus.). 1978. pap. text ed. 8.95x (ISBN 0-393-95018-2). Norton.

Drawing All Animals. Arthur Zaidenberg. (Funk & W Bk.). (Illus.). 176p. 1974. pap. 6.95 (ISBN 0-308-10108-1, F99, TYC-T). T Y Crowell.

Drawing & Designing Children's & Teenage Fashions. Patrick J. Ireland. LC 79-1265. 1979. 13.95x (ISBN 0-470-26592-2). Halsted Pr.

Drawing & Materials. 2nd ed. V. E. Boxall. (Illus.). 1975. pap. 16.50x (ISBN 0-7131-3320-1). Intl Ideas.

Drawing & Painting Faces & Figures. Adrian Hill. (Illus.). 79p. 1973. 6.50 (ISBN 0-7137-0026-2). Transatlantic.

Drawing & Painting from Imagination. Don Stacy. (Illus.). 224p. 1980. 14.95 (ISBN 0-87396-083-1). Stravon.

Drawing & Planning for the Industrial Arts. new ed. John L. Feirer & Lindbeck. (Illus.). (gr. 7-12). 1975. text ed. 11.64 (ISBN 0-87002-159-1); tchr's guide, charts & worksheets 5.60 (ISBN 0-87002-162-1). Bennett IL.

Drawing Dogs & Puppies. Paul Frame. (How to Draw Ser.). (Illus.). (gr. 4-6). 1978. PLB 6.90 s&l (ISBN 0-531-01452-5). Watts.

Drawing for Product Planning. George E. Stephenson. (gr. 7-12). 1970. text ed. 7.96 (ISBN 0-87002-037-4); student guide 1.80 (ISBN 0-87002-087-0). Bennett IL.

Drawing from Memory. R. Smith Catterson. (Illus.). 1979. deluxe ed. 34.45 (ISBN 0-930582-44-6). Gloucester Art.

Drawing Home Plans: A Simplified Drafting System for Planning & Design. June Curran. Ed. by Nancy Giumarra & Ruth Weine. LC 78-72188. (Illus.). 1979. 19.95 (ISBN 0-932370-01-2); pap. 12.95 (ISBN 0-932370-02-0). Brooks Pub Co.

Drawing Horses & Foals. Don Bolognese. (How to Draw Ser.). (gr. 4-6). 1977. PLB 6.90 (ISBN 0-531-00379-5). Watts.

Drawing on the Right Side of the Brain. Betty Edwards. LC 78-62794. (Illus.). 1979. 12.50 o.p. (ISBN 0-312-90491-6); pap. 7.50 o.p. (ISBN 0-312-90492-4). St Martin.

Drawing on the Right Side of the Brain. Betty Edwards. 1980. cloth. 13.95 (ISBN 0-87477-087-4); pap. 8.95 (ISBN 0-87477-088-2). HM.

Drawing on the Walls. Jay Meek. LC 79-51607. (Poetry Ser.). 1980. 9.95 (ISBN 0-915604-31-0); pap. 4.95 (ISBN 0-915604-32-9). Carnegie-Mellon.

Drawing People. Elliott Ivenbaum. (gr. 4 up). 1980. PLB 6.90 (ISBN 0-531-02283-8, A46). Watts.

Drawing Pets. Carol Nicklaus. (gr. 1-3). 1980. PLB 7.90 (ISBN 0-531-04138-7). Watts.

Drawing Requirement Manual. 4th ed. Ed. by Jerome H. Lieblich. 624p. 1981. lib. bdg. 21.95x perfect bdg (ISBN 0-912702-02-8). Global Eng.

Drawing Requirements Manual. 3rd ed. Ed. by Jerome H. Lieblich. (Illus.). 1979. pap. text ed. 19.95 o.p. (ISBN 0-685-96581-3). Global Eng.

Drawing Sharp Focus Still Lifes. Robert Zappalorti. 192p. 1981. 18.95 (ISBN 0-8230-1435-5). Watson-Guptill.

Drawing the Figure from Top to Toe. Arthur Zaidenberg. (Funk & W Bk.). (Illus.). 176p. 1974. pap. 6.95 (ISBN 0-308-10107-3, F98, TYC-T). T Y Crowell.

Drawing Your Family & Friends. Carol Nicklaus. (gr. 1-3). 1980. PLB 7.90 (ISBN 0-531-04139-5). Watts.

Drawings. Hilaire G. Degas. (Illus.). 1974. pap. 4.50 (ISBN 0-486-21233-5). Dover.

Drawings. William Steig. 192p. 1979. 19.95 (ISBN 0-374-29031-8). FS&G.

Drawings & Watercolours by Peter De Wint. Fitzwilliam Museum. LC 79-4652. (Illus.). 32.50 (ISBN 0-521-22745-3); pap. 8.95 (ISBN 0-521-29631-5). Cambridge U Pr.

Drawings by American Architects. Alfred M. Kemper. LC 72-13428. 621p. 1973. 55.00 (ISBN 0-471-46845-2, Pub. by Wiley-Interscience). Wiley.

Drawings into Sculpture. Ed. by Colin Eisler. (Illus.). 108p. (Orig.). 1981. pap. 12.50 (ISBN 0-9601068-7-1). Agrinde Bks.

Drawings of Albrecht Durer: Selected. Albert Durer. (Illus.). 8.75 (ISBN 0-8446-0593-X). Peter Smith.

Drawings of Alfred Pellan. Reesa Geenenberg. (National Gallery of Canada Ser.). (Illus.). 192p. 1981. pap. 15.95 (ISBN 0-88884-458-1, 56319-7, Pub. by Natl Mus Canada). U of Chicago Pr.

Drawings of British Plants, 8 vols. Stella Ross-Craig. Incl. Vol. 1 (ISBN 0-7135-1137-0); Vol. 2 (ISBN 0-7135-1138-9); Vol. 3 (ISBN 0-7135-1139-7); Vol. 4; Vol. 5 (ISBN 0-7135-1141-9); Vol. 6 (ISBN 0-7135-1142-7); Vol. 7 (ISBN 0-7135-1143-5); Vol. 8. (Illus.). 1980. 256.25 set (ISBN 0-7135-1110-9); 32.50 ea. Lubrecht & Cramer.

Drawings of Edouard Manet. Alain De Leiris. (Studies in the History of Art: No. 10). 1969. 52.50x (ISBN 0-520-01547-9). U of Cal Pr.

Drawings of Henry Moore. Tate Gallery. Date not set. pap. 15.95 (ISBN 0-8120-2063-4). Barron.

Drawings of Leonardo da Vinci. A. E. Popham. (Illus.). 320p. 1981. 15.95 (ISBN 0-224-00909-5, Pub. by Chatto-Bodley-Jonathan). Merrimack Bk Serv.

Drawings of Pontormo, 2 vols. rev. ed. Janet Cox-Rearick. LC 79-93167. (Illus.). 880p. 1980. Repr. of 1964 ed. Set. lib. bdg. 90.00 (ISBN 0-87817-272-6). Hacker.

Drawings of Rosso Fiorentino, 2 vols. Eugene A. Carroll. LC 75-23786. (Outstanding Dissertations in the Fine Arts - 16th Century). (Illus.). 1976. Set. lib. bdg. 121.00 (ISBN 0-8240-1982-2). Garland Pub.

Drawings of Salvator Rosa, 2 vols. Michael Mahoney. LC 76-23637. (Outstanding Dissertations in the Fine Arts - 17th Century). (Illus.). 1977. Repr. of 1965 ed. Set. lib. bdg. 133.00 (ISBN 0-8240-2707-8). Garland Pub.

Drawings: The Pluralist Decade. Nancy Foote et al. LC 80-83653. (Illus.). 1979. pap. 8.00 (ISBN 0-88454-057-X). U of Pa Contemp Art.

Drayton Hall: An Annotated Bibliography. William Bynum. LC 78-59288. (Research on Historic Properties Occasional Papers). (Illus.). 1978. 5.00 o.p. (ISBN 0-89133-068-2). Preservation Pr.

DRE Reader: A Sourcebook in Education & Ministry. Ed. by Maria Harris. LC 80-52059. 192p. (Orig.). 1980. pap. 6.95 (ISBN 0-88489-124-0). St Marys.

Dread & the Love of Nature. Avebury. (Illus.). 1980. Repr. of 1909 ed. deluxe ed. 29.75 deluxe binding (ISBN 0-89901-012-1). Found Class Reprints.

Dread Diseases. Marianne Tully. (First Bks). (Illus.). (gr. 4-6). 1978. PLB 6.45 s&l (ISBN 0-531-01406-1). Watts.

Dreadful Hollow. Nicholas Blake. LC 53-7730. 1979. pap. 1.95 (ISBN 0-06-080493-9, P 493, PL). Har-Row.

Dreadful Lemon Sky. John D. MacDonald. LC 74-23085. (Travis McGee Ser). 1975. 6.95 o.p. (ISBN 0-397-01074-5). Lippincott.

Dreadful Lemon Sky. John D. MacDonald. (Travis McGee Ser.). 272p. 1978. pap. 2.25 (ISBN 0-449-14148-9, GM). Fawcett.

Dreadful Summit. Stanley Ellin. (Foul Play Press Ser.). 192p. pap. 4.95 (ISBN 0-914378-66-X). Countryman.

Dreadnoughts. David P. Howarth. (Seafarers Ser.). (Illus.). 1979. lib. bdg. 11.97 (ISBN 0-8094-2712-5); kivar bdg. 9.93 (ISBN 0-8094-2713-3). Silver.

Dream & Human Societies. Ed. by Gustave E. Von Grunebaum & Roger Caillois. (Near Eastern Center, UCLA). 1966. 29.75x (ISBN 0-520-01305-0). U of Cal Pr.

Dream & the Underworld. James Hillman. LC 78-4733. 1979. 10.95 o.p. (ISBN 0-06-011902-0, HarpT). Har-Row.

Dream Apart. Lesley Egan. LC 77-82756. 1978. 6.95 o.p. (ISBN 0-385-13412-6). Doubleday.

Dream Below the Sun: Selected Poems of Antonio Machado. rev., enl ed. Tr. by Willis Barnstone from Span. (Illus.). 176p. (Span., Eng.). 1981. 12.95 (ISBN 0-89594-048-5); pap. 6.95 (ISBN 0-89594-047-7). Crossing Pr.

Dream Collector. Arthur Tress & John Minahan. LC 72-88362. (Illus.). 1973. pap. 4.45 o.p. (ISBN 0-380-01149-2, 17392). Avon.

Dream Come True. Mary Verdick. Ed. by Thomas J. Mooney. (Beginning Pal Paperbacks Ser.). (Illus., Orig.). (gr. 7-12). 1977. pap. text ed. 1.25 (ISBN 0-8374-3451-3). Xerox Ed Pubns.

Dream Come True: Great Houses of Los Angeles. Brendan Gill. 1980. 40.00 (ISBN 0-690-01893-2); ltd. ed 100.00 (ISBN 0-690-01961-0). Har-Row.

Dream Dancer. Evelyn Bolton. LC 74-9571. (Evelyn Bolton's Horse Stories Ser). (Illus.). 32p. (gr. 3-7). 1974. PLB 5.95 (ISBN 0-87191-371-2); pap. 2.95 (ISBN 0-89812-128-0). Creative Ed.

Dream Dancer. Janet Morris. 312p. 1981. 12.95 (ISBN 0-399-12591-4). Putnam.

Dream Days. Kenneth Grahame. (Illus.). 1975. pap. 4.95 o.p. (ISBN 0-380-00288-4, 23994). Avon.

Dream Days. Kenneth Grahame. LC 75-32201. (Classics of Children's Literature, 1621-1932: Vol. 62). (Illus.). 1976. Repr. of 1902 ed. PLB 38.00 (ISBN 0-8240-2311-0). Garland Pub.

Dream Dictionary. Wallace Yancy. 1981. 6.95 (ISBN 0-8062-1685-9). Carlton.

Dream Eater. Christian Garrison. LC 78-55213. (Illus.). (ps-2). 1978. 9.95 (ISBN 0-87888-134-4). Bradbury Pr.

Dream for America. John Lapp. Orig. Title: Bicentennial. 1976. pap. 1.50 (ISBN 0-89129-159-8). Jove Pubns.

Dream for Sale. Dorothy W. Ball. (YA) 1969. 4.95 o.p. (ISBN 0-685-07430-7, Avalon). Bouregy.

Dream Is Deadly. Carter Brown. Bd. with Savage Salome. 1981. pap. price not set (ISBN 0-451-09776-9, Sig). NAL.

Dream Journey. James Hanley. 1978. pap. 2.25 o.p. (ISBN 0-445-04279-6). Popular Lib.

Dream Lake. Marietta D. Moskin. LC 80-18999. 156p. (gr. 5-9). 1981. PLB 8.95 (ISBN 0-689-30821-3). Atheneum.

Dream Life of Balso Snell. Nathanael West. Bd. with Cool Million. 179p. 1963. pap. 4.95 (ISBN 0-374-50292-7, N244). FS&G.

Dream Makers: Discovering Your Breakthrough Dreams. Richard Corriere & Joseph Hart. LC 76-47680. (Funk & W Bk.). 1977. 8.95 o.s.i. (ISBN 0-308-10276-2, TYC-T). T Y Crowell.

Dream Master. Roger Zelazny. 192p. 1975. pap. 1.95 (ISBN 0-441-16705-5). Ace Bks.

Dream Master. Roger Zelazny. (Science Fiction Ser.). 1976. Repr. of 1966 ed. lib. bdg. 10.00 (ISBN 0-8398-2345-2). Gregg.

Dream Merchants. Harold Robbins. 1980. pap. 3.50 (ISBN 0-671-83455-X). PB.

Dream, Mirror of Conscience: A History of Dream Interpretation from 2000 B.C. & a New Theory of Dream Synthesis. Werner Wolff. LC 70-152618. (Illus.). 348p. 1972. Repr. of 1952 ed. lib. bdg. 27.50x (ISBN 0-8371-6053-7, WODR). Greenwood.

Dream Museum. Seymour Epstein. 1973. pap. 1.25 o.p. (ISBN 0-380-01150-6, 15222). Avon.

Dream of an Outcaste: Patrick F. Healy. Albert S. Foley. 1981. 12.50 (ISBN 0-916620-31-X). Portals Pr.

Dream of Chief Crazy Horse. David Pownall. (gr. 5 up). 1975. 6.95 (ISBN 0-571-10672-2, Pub. by Faber & Faber); pap. 2.95 (ISBN 0-571-10673-0). Merrimack Bk Serv.

Dream of Dracula. Leonard Wolf. 1977. pap. 1.95 o.p. (ISBN 0-445-08567-3). Popular Lib.

Dream of Dragon Flies. Noel Langley. Ed. by Alick Bartholomew. 1971. 4.95 o.s.i. (ISBN 0-02-567900-7). Macmillan.

Dream of Empire: German Colonialism, 1919-1945. Wolfe W. Schmokel. LC 80-15400. (Yale Historical Publications: Miscellany 78). xiv, 204p. 1980. Repr. of 1964 ed. lib. bdg. 22.50x (ISBN 0-313-22437-4, SCDE). Greenwood.

Dream of Feet. David B. Axelrod. LC 76-21123. (Poetry Ser.). (Illus.). 1976. o. p. 8.95x (ISBN 0-89304-004-5, CCC105); signed ltd. ed. 15.00 (ISBN 0-89304-042-8); pap. 3.95x (ISBN 0-89304-007-X); pap. 3.95x signed ltd. ed. o.p. (ISBN 0-89304-043-6). Cross Cult.

Dream of Ghosts. Frank Bonham. 160p. (gr. 3-6). 1973. PLB 7.95 o.p. (ISBN 0-525-28923-2). Dutton.

Dream of Governors. Louis Simpson. LC 59-12480. (Wesleyan Poetry Program: Vol. 3). (Orig.). 1959. 10.00x (ISBN 0-8195-2003-9, Pub. by Wesleyan U Pr). Columbia U Pr.

Dream of Icarus. Kenneth Coutts-Smith. LC 74-104700. 1970. 5.95 o.s.i. (ISBN 0-8076-0533-6). Braziller.

Dream of Springtime. Alicia Ostriker. LC 78-59769. (Illus., Orig.). 1979. pap. 3.50 (ISBN 0-912292-52-0). The Smith.

Dream of Success: A Study of the Modern American Imagination. Kenneth S. Lynn. LC 73-176134. 269p. 1972. Repr. of 1955 ed. lib. bdg. 19.75x (ISBN 0-8371-6269-6, LYDS). Greenwood.

Dream of the Blue Heron. Victor Barnouw. LC 66-20995. (Illus.). (gr. 4-6). 1966. 4.50 o.s.i. (ISBN 0-440-02150-2, Sey Lawr). Delacorte.

Dream of the Dinosaurs. Blake Hodgetts. LC 77-82949. (gr. k-3). 1978. PLB 6.95 (ISBN 0-385-12139-3). Doubleday.

Dream of the Little Elephant. Ruth Bornstein. LC 76-27748. (Illus.). (ps-3). 6.95 (ISBN 0-395-28771-5, Clarion). HM.

Dream of the Red Chamber: A Critical Study. Jeanne Knoerle. LC 72-183609. (East Asian Ser). 170p. 1973. 8.95x (ISBN 0-253-39102-4). Ind U Pr.

Dream of Thee. Mary Wibberley. (Harlequin Presents Ser.). 192p. 1981. pap. 1.50 (ISBN 0-373-10419-7, Pub. by Harlequin). PB.

Dream of Wings: Americans & the Airplane, Eighteen Seventy-Five to Nineteen Hundred Five. Tom D. Crouch. (Illus.). 1981. 15.95 (ISBN 0-393-01385-5). Norton.

Dream of Zorel. Jokob Lorber. Tr. by Violet Ozols from Ger. 124p. Date not set. pap. 5.00 (ISBN 0-934616-17-5). Valkyrie Pr.

Dream on Monkey Mountain & Other Plays. Derek Walcott. 326p. 1970. pap. 5.95 (ISBN 0-374-50860-7, N390). FS&G.

Dream on Monkey Mountain & Other Plays. Derek Walcott. 1970. 15.00 (ISBN 0-685-77062-1). Univ Place.

Dream Power. Ann Faraday. 1981. pap. 2.50 (ISBN 0-425-04863-2). Berkley Pub.

Dream Psychology. Maurice Nicoll. 1979. pap. 4.95 (ISBN 0-87728-475-X). Weiser.

Dream Road. Xavier Herbert. 108p. 1980. 20.95x (ISBN 0-00-221593-4, Pub. by W Collins Australia). Intl Schol Bk Serv.

Dream Sellers: Perspectives on Drug Dealers. Richard H. Blum et al. LC 79-184960. (Social & Behavioral Science Ser.). 1972. 16.95x o.p. (ISBN 0-87589-119-5). Jossey-Bass.

Dream Ships. Maurice Griffiths. 290p. 1980. 29.95x (ISBN 0-85177-076-2, Pub. by Cornell England). State Mutual Bk.

Dream Studies & Telepathy. Montague Ullman & Stanley Krippner. LC 71-113639. (Parapsychological Monograph No. 12). 1970. pap. 4.00 (ISBN 0-912328-16-9). Parapsych Foun.

Dream Tree. Steve Cosgrove. (Serendipity Bks). (Illus.). (gr. k-4). 1978. PLB 6.95 (ISBN 0-87191-665-7). Creative Ed.

Dream Tree. (gr. 1-6). 1974. pap. 1.50 (ISBN 0-8431-0553-4). Serendipity Pr.

Dream Within, No. 62. Barbara Cartland. 1978. pap. 1.50 o.s.i. (ISBN 0-515-04593-4). Jove Pubns.

Dream Within a Dream: A Thematic Approach to Scott's Vision of Fictional Reality. Lars Hartveit. 1974. pap. text ed. 23.00x (ISBN 8-200-01361-8, Dist. by Columbia U Pr). Universitet.

Dreambook for Our Time. Tadeusz Konwicki. Tr. by David Welsh. 1970. 17.50x o.p. (ISBN 0-262-11035-0). MIT Pr.

Dreamer & Other Stories. Krishan Chander. Tr. by Jai Ratan. 160p. 1970. pap. 2.50 (ISBN 0-88253-025-9). InterCulture.

Dreamer Beware. Ruth Wissman. 1978. pap. 1.50 o.p. (ISBN 0-445-04167-6). Popular Lib.

Dreamer, Lost in Terror. Alison King. 256p. 1976. pap. 1.25 o.p. (ISBN 0-445-00356-1). Popular Lib.

Dreamer of the Vine: A Novel About Nostramus. Liz Greene. 1981. 12.95 (ISBN 0-393-01434-7). Norton.

Dreamers. James Gunn. 1981. 10.95 (ISBN 0-671-25280-1). S&S.

Dreamer's Dictionary. Stearn Robinson. 1975. pap. 2.95 (ISBN 0-446-93917-X). Warner Bks.

Dreamers of the American Dream. Stewart H. Holbrook. LC 57-11424. 6.95 o.p. (ISBN 0-385-04889-0). Doubleday.

Dreaming. Norman Malcolm. 1962. text ed. 10.00x (ISBN 0-7100-3836-4); pap. text ed. 6.25x (ISBN 0-7100-8434-X). Humanities.

Dreaming & Waking. Richard Corriere et al. LC 80-21876. 226p. 1980. pap. 6.95 (ISBN 0-915238-41-1). Peace Pr.

Dreaming in Color. Ruth Lepson. LC 79-54882. 72p. 1980. pap. 4.95 (ISBN 0-914086-27-8). Alicejamesbooks.

Dreaming of Babylon. Richard Brautigan. 1977. 7.95 o.s.i. (ISBN 0-440-02146-4, Sey Lawr). Delacorte.

Dreaming Swimmer. Elisabeth Ogilvie. 1979. pap. 1.75 (ISBN 0-380-01878-0, 37051). Avon.

Dreaming Witness. Jean Davison. 1978. pap. 1.75 o.p. (ISBN 0-425-03667-7, Medallion). Berkley Pub.

Dreamland & Other Poems & Tecumseh: A Drama. Charles Mair. LC 73-82586. (Literature of Canada Ser). 1974. pap. 5.00 (ISBN 0-8020-6203-2). U of Toronto Pr.

Dreams. Ezra J. Keats. LC 73-15857. (Illus.). 32p. (ps-2). 1974. 8.95g (ISBN 0-02-749610-4). Macmillan.

Dreams. Larry Kettelkamp. (Illus.). (gr. 5-9). 1968. PLB 6.96 (ISBN 0-688-31245-4). Morrow.

Dreams: A Portrait of the Psyche. Stuart R. McLeod. LC 80-65607. 170p. 1981. perfect bdg. 14.95 (ISBN 0-86548-046-X). Century Twenty One.

Dreams: A Way to Listen to God. Morton Kelsey. LC 77-83583. 1978. pap. 2.95 (ISBN 0-8091-2046-1). Paulist Pr.

Dreams & Dreaming. Norman MacKenzie. LC 65-26071. (Illus.). 1965. 15.00 (ISBN 0-8149-0151-4). Vanguard.

Dreams & Drummers. Doris B. Smith. LC 77-26590. (gr. 6 up). 1978. 6.95 (ISBN 0-690-01381-7, TYC-J); PLB 7.89 (ISBN 0-690-03843-7). T Y Crowell.

Dreams & Spiritual Experiences. Elizabeth Lowe. 1980. 1.50 (ISBN 0-686-28863-7). Dreams Unltd.

Dreams & the Growth of Personality: Expanding Awareness in Psychotherapy. Ernest L. Rossi. 232p. 1972. text ed. 19.00 (ISBN 0-08-016787-X). Pergamon.

Dreams and What They Mean. Migene Wippler. pap. 2.25. Merit Pubns.

Dreams Beyond Dreaming. Jean Campbell. LC 79-26131. 1980. pap. 5.95 (ISBN 0-89865-015-1, Unilaw). Donning Co.

Dreams, Culture & the Individual. Carl W. O'Nell. LC 76-513. (Cross-Cultural Themes Ser.). 96p. 1976. pap. text ed. 3.00 o.s.i. (ISBN 0-88316-523-6). Chandler & Sharp.

Dreams Do Come True, No. 141. Barbara Cartland. (Orig.). 1981. pap. 1.95 (ISBN 0-553-14750-1). Bantam.

Dream's Edge: Science Fiction Stories About the Future of Planet Earth. Ed. by Terry Carr. LC 80-13389. 320p. 1980. 14.95 (ISBN 0-87156-232-4); pap. 5.95 (ISBN 0-87156-238-3). Sierra.

Dreams: God's Forgotten Language. John A. Sanford. LC 60-29727. 1968. 9.95 (ISBN 0-397-10056-6). Lippincott.

Dreams in a Wasteland. Franklin Camuti. 156p. 1980. 7.95 (ISBN 0-8059-2733-6). Dorrance.

Dreams in Greek Tragedy: An Ethno-Psycho-Analytic Study. George Devereux. 400p. 1976. 25.00x (ISBN 0-520-02921-6). U of Cal Pr.

Dreams in Harrisson Railroad Park. 2 nd ed. Nellie Wong et al. Ed. by Brodine & LaPalma. (Illus.). 1978. 3.75 o.p. (ISBN 0-932716-09-1). Kelsey St Pr.

Dreams in Old Norse Literature & Their Affinities in Folklore. Georgia D. Kelchner. 154p. 1980. Repr. of 1935 ed. lib. bdg. 30.00 (ISBN 0-8492-1496-3). R West.

Dreams of Donald Roller Wilson. Donald R. Wilson. (Illus.). 1979. pap. 9.95 (ISBN 0-8015-0353-1, Hawthorn). Dutton.

Dreams of France. Georges Blond. (Illus.). 120p. 1969. 13.50x (ISBN 0-8002-0756-4). Intl Pubns Serv.

Dreams of Leaving. David Hare. 48p. (Orig.). 1980. pap. 6.95 (ISBN 0-571-11568-3, Pub. by Faber & Faber). Merrimack Bk Serv.

Dreams of Natural Places: A New England Schooner Odyssey. Herbert Smith. LC 80-69529. (Illus.). 102p. 1981. 15.95 (ISBN 0-89272-107-3). Down East.

Dreams of Paris. Illus. by P. Molinard. LC 75-465802. (Illus.). 1967. 13.50x (ISBN 0-8002-0754-8). Intl Pubns Serv.

Dreams of Passion: The Theater of Luigi Pirandello. Roger W. Oliver. LC 79-2179. 1979. 16.00x (ISBN 0-8147-6157-7); pap. 7.00x (ISBN 0-8147-6158-5). NYU Pr.

Dreams of Reason. Xavier Domingo. Tr. by L. Kemp. LC 65-10198. 1966. 5.00 o.s.i. (ISBN 0-8076-0344-9). Braziller.

Dreams of Reason: Science & Utopias. Rene J. Dubos. (George B. Pegram Lecture Ser.). 1961. 12.00x (ISBN 0-231-02493-2); pap. 3.00 (ISBN 0-231-08544-3). Columbia U Pr.

Dreams of Sex. (Illus.). 4.95 (ISBN 0-910550-32-8). Centurion Pr.

Dreams of the Chateaux of the Loire. Ed. by Armand Lanoux. (Illus.). 92p. 1967. 13.50x (ISBN 0-8002-0758-0). Intl Pubns Serv.

Dreams of Victory. Ellen Conford. (Illus.). 144p. (gr. 4-6). 1973. 7.95 (ISBN 0-316-15294-3). Little.

Dreams to Come. Melanie Ward & Richard Curtis. 1978. pap. 2.25 o.s.i. (ISBN 0-515-04474-1). Jove Pubns.

Dreams, Visions & Drugs: A Search for Other Realities. Daniel Cohen. LC 75-33694. 160p. (gr. 7 up). 1976. PLB 7.45 (ISBN 0-531-01141-0). Watts.

Dreams Your Magic Mirror: With Interpretations of Edgar Cayce. Elsie Sechrist. 256p. 1974. pap. 2.25 (ISBN 0-446-92688-4, 9508-3). Warner Bks.

Dreamstalkers. rev. ed. Theodore L. Harris et al. (Keys to Reading Ser.). (Illus.). 192p. (gr. 8). 1975. pap. text ed. 3.48 (ISBN 0-87892-466-3); resource bk. 9.90 (ISBN 0-87892-467-1); datalog student guide 3.96 (ISBN 0-87892-468-X); tchr's ed. 3.96 (ISBN 0-87892-469-8); 19.53 (ISBN 0-87892-499-X). Economy Co.

Dreamtime. Katherine Kent. (Orig.). 1981. pap. 2.75 (ISBN 0-671-41783-5). PB.

Dred Scott Decision, March 6, 1857: Slavery & the Supreme Court's Self-Inflicted Wound. Frank B. Latham. LC 68-25729. (Focus Bks). (Illus.). (gr. 7 up). 1968. PLB 4.90 o.p. (ISBN 0-531-01000-7); pap. 1.25 o.p. (ISBN 0-531-02329-X). Watts.

Dredging. Institute of Civil Engineers, UK. 124p. 1980. 70.00x (ISBN 0-901948-40-3, Pub. by Telford England). State Mutual Bk.

Dredging: A Handbook for Engineers. R. N. Bray. (Illus.). 276p. 1979. 75.00x (ISBN 0-7131-3412-7). Intl Ideas.

Dredging & Its Environmental Effects. Compiled By American Society of Civil Engineers. 1048p. 1976. pap. text ed. 30.00 (ISBN 0-87262-165-0). Am Soc Civil Eng.

Drei Horspiele. Friedrich Durrenmatt. Ed. by Henry Regensteiner. LC 79-22768. (Ger.). 1980. pap. text ed. 7.95x (ISBN 0-8290-0116-6). Irvington.

Drei Manner Im Schnee. Kaestner. (Easy Reader, C). pap. 3.75 (ISBN 0-88436-038-5, GEA201051). EMC.

Dreiser. W. A. Swanberg. (Illus.). 1965. lib. rep. ed. 25.00x (ISBN 0-684-14552-9, ScribT). Scribner.

Dress. rev. ed. Eleanor Gawne & Oerke. 672p. (gr. 9-12). 1975. 17.96 (ISBN 0-87002-069-2); tchr's guide 3.80 (ISBN 0-87002-900-2). Bennett IL.

Dress, Adornment, & the Social Order. Ed. by Mary Ellen Roach & Joanne B. Eicher. LC 65-19482. 1965. pap. text ed. 14.95x (ISBN 0-471-72476-9). Wiley.

Dress Design: Draping & Flat Pattern Making. Marion S. Hillhouse & E. A. Mansfield. LC 48-7554. 1948. text ed. 19.50 (ISBN 0-395-04627-0, 3-25310). HM.

Dress for Health: The New Clothes Consciousness. Maggie Nussdorf & Steve Nussdorf. (Illus.). 224p. 1980. 14.95 (ISBN 0-8117-0524-2). Stackpole.

Dress for Less: One Thousand & One for Saving Money on Clothes. Vicki Audette. Ed. by Kathe Grooms. (Consumer-Aid Bk.). (Illus.). 160p. 1981. pap. 3.95 (ISBN 0-915658-33-X). Meadowbrook Pr.

Dress for Success. John T. Molloy. (Illus.). 1978. pap. 3.95 (ISBN 0-446-97529-X). Warner Bks.

Dress for Success. John T. Molloy. (Illus.). 248p. 1976. pap. 2.50 (ISBN 0-446-93706-1). Warner Bks.

Dress Her in Indigo. John D. MacDonald. 1971. 8.95 (ISBN 0-397-00697-7). Lippincott.

Dress Thin, Look Thin. Bonnie August & Ellen Count. LC 80-51245. (Illus.). 304p. 1981. 13.95 (ISBN 0-89256-137-8). Rawson Wade.

Dressage: Begin the Right Way. Lockie Richards. LC 75-6. (Illus.). 96p. 1975. 12.95 (ISBN 0-7153-6926-1). David & Charles.

Dressage Riding. Richard L. Watjen. (Illus.). 1978. Repr. 10.35 (ISBN 0-85131-275-6, Dist. by Sporting Book Center). J A Allen.

Dresses Cut-to-Fit. Ruth Oblander. Ed. by Mary Leppert. LC 76-53237. 1976. 3.80 (ISBN 0-933956-02-9); tchrs ed. 3.04. Sew-Fit.

Dressing. Helen Oxenbury. (Baby Board Bks.). (Illus.). 12p. (ps-k). Date not set. boards 3.50 (ISBN 0-671-42113-1, Little Simon). S&S.

Dressing Dolls. Audrey Johnson. (Illus.). 1969. 16.95 (ISBN 0-8231-3025-8). Branford.

Dressing of Diamond. Nicolas Freeling. LC 73-18710. (Harper Novel of Suspense). 256p. 1974. 7.95 o.p. (ISBN 0-06-011352-9, HarpT). Har-Row.

Dressing Our Wounds in Warm Clothes. Donna Henes. LC 81-65197. (Illus.). 72p. (Orig.). 1981. pap. 9.00 (ISBN 0-937122-02-5). Astro Artz.

Dressing Sexy. Molly Cochran. (Orig.). 1980. pap. (ISBN 0-671-41529-8, Fireside). S&S.

Dressing Thin. Dale Goday. 1980. 3.95 (ISBN 0-671-25471-5, 25471, Fireside). S&S.

Dressmaking & Fashion. Eileen Corderoy. LC 68-95775. (Pegasus Books: No. 8). (Illus.). 1967. 10.50x (ISBN 0-234-77940-3). Intl Pubns Serv.

Dressmaking with Basic Patterns. Ann Ladbury. 1976. pap. 8.95 (ISBN 0-7134-3226-8). David & Charles.

Dressmaking with Leather. Maureen Goldsworthy. 1977. 17.95 (ISBN 0-7134-3240-3, Pub. by Batsford England). David & Charles.

DRI-McGraw-Hill Readings in Macroeconomics. Ed. by Allen R. Sanderson. (Illus.). 480p. 1981. pap. text ed. 7.95 (ISBN 0-07-054659-2). McGraw.

Dribbling, Shooting, & Scoring Sometimes. Gary Paulsen. LC 76-12614. (Sports on the Light Side Ser.). (Illus.). 32p. (gr. 3-6). 1976. PLB 9.65 (ISBN 0-8172-0179-3). Raintree Pubs.

Driblets from the Pen of E. G. W. Elvera G. Wright. LC 80-52185. (Illus.). 65p. 1981. 5.95 (ISBN 0-533-04747-1). Vantage.

Dried Flowers from Antiquity to the Present: A History & Practical Guide to Flower Drying. Leonard Karel. LC 72-10909. 1973. 10.00 (ISBN 0-8108-0512-X). Scarecrow.

Dried Grasses, Grains, Gourds, Pods & Cones. Leonard Karel. LC 74-31178. (Illus.). 1975. 10.00 (ISBN 0-8108-0792-0). Scarecrow.

Drieu la Rochelle & the Fiction of Testimony. Frederic J. Grover. 1958. 17.50x (ISBN 0-520-00526-0). U of Cal Pr.

Drift Fence. Walt Coburn. Orig. Title: Rope Law. 1978. pap. 1.25 (ISBN 0-505-51236-X). Tower Bks.

Drifters. B. Miller. 1972. pap. 1.95 o.s.i. (ISBN 0-02-061320-2, Collier). Macmillan.

Drifting. Stephen Jones. LC 75-122294. (Illus.). 1971. 12.50 o.s.i. (ISBN 0-02-559830-9). Macmillan.

Drifting Cities. Stratis Tsirkas. Tr. by Kay Cicellis. 1974. 10.00 o.p. (ISBN 0-394-46971-2). Knopf.

Drifting Continents, Shifting Seas: An Introduction to Plate Tectonics. Patrick Young. (Impact Bks). (Illus.). 96p. (gr. 7 up). 1976. PLB 4.90 o.p. (ISBN 0-531-00848-7). Watts.

Driftwood Prayers Passions & Permissions. Don Kimball. LC 77-82766. 1978. Softbound 4.95 o.p. (ISBN 0-385-13369-3). Doubleday.

Drill for Skill. C. C. Rickett. (Illus., Orig.). (gr. 9-10). 1946. pap. text ed. 3.92 (ISBN 0-87720-327-X). AMSCO Sch.

Drill Press. David J. Gingery. LC 80-66142. (Build Your Own Metal Working Shop from Scrap Ser.: Bk. 5). (Illus.). 72p. (Orig.). 1981. pap. 6.95 (ISBN 0-9604330-4-X). D J Gingery.

Drill Press Work. David L. Taylor. LC 79-50536. (Metalworking Ser.). (gr. 8). 1980. pap. text ed. 5.08 (ISBN 0-8273-1823-5); instr's manual 1.50 (ISBN 0-8273-1824-3). Delmar.

Drilling Ahead. William Rintoul. (Illus.). 300p. 1981. 16.95 (ISBN 0-934136-09-2, Valley Pub). Western Tanager.

Drilling Data Handbook. Ed. by Institut du Petrole Francaise. (Illus.). 420p. 1980. 39.95x (ISBN 0-87201-204-2). Gulf Pub.

Drilling Practices Manual. Preston L. Moore. LC 74-80812. 600p. 1974. 37.50 (ISBN 0-87814-057-3). Pennwell Pub.

Drilling Technology. S. F. Krar & J. W. Oswald. LC 73-13486. 1977. pap. text ed. 7.40 (ISBN 0-8273-0210-X). Delmar.

Drina Dances in Italy. Jean Estoril. LC 61-15484. (gr. 3-6). 1961. 5.95 (ISBN 0-8149-0300-2). Vanguard.
Drink This. Eileen Dewhurst. LC 80-2320. 192p. 1981. 9.95 (ISBN 0-385-17457-8). Doubleday.
Drink Your Troubles Away. John B. Lust. LC 66-28198. 1976. pap. 2.25 (ISBN 0-87904-006-8). Lust.
Drinker's Addiction: Its Nature & Practical Treatment. Francis T. Chambers, Jr. 164p. 1968. pap. 14.75 photocopy ed. spiral (ISBN 0-398-00301-7). C C Thomas.
Drinking & Damage: Theoretical Advances & Implications for Prevention. B. G. Frankel & P. C. Whitehead. (Rutgers Center for Alcohol Studies Monograph: No. 14). 1981. 10.00x (ISBN 0-911290-09-5). Rutgers Ctr Alcohol.
Drinking Beer at Twenty-Two Below. Kirk Robertson. 1980. 2.00 (ISBN 0-917554-04-3). Maelstrom.
Drinking Driver. Barent F. Landstreet. 128p. 1977. 14.75 (ISBN 0-398-03560-1). C C Thomas.
Drinking: Everything You Want to Know. John A. Ewing. 130p. 1981. 10.95 (ISBN 0-8359-1474-7); pap. 6.95 (ISBN 0-8359-1473-9). Reston.
Drinking Man. David C. McClelland et al. LC 79-143504. 1972. 15.95 (ISBN 0-02-920460-7). Free Pr.
Drinking Problem. John E. Keller. Ed. by William E. Hulme. LC 75-133036. (Pocket Counsel Bks.). 64p. 1971. pap. 1.95 (ISBN 0-8006-0155-6, 1-155). Fortress.
Drinking Water & Health. Incl. Vol. I. 1977. 20.75 (ISBN 0-309-02619-9); Vol. II. 1980. 17.00 (ISBN 0-686-64937-0); Vol. III. 1980. 15.00 (ISBN 0-309-02932-5). Natl Acad Pr.
Drinking Water & Health, Vol. 1. Committee on Drinking Water, National Research Committee. LC 77-89284. (Illus.). 1978. pap. text ed. 20.75 (ISBN 0-309-02619-9). Natl Acad Pr.
Drinks, Drugs, & Do-Gooders. Charles E. Goshen. LC 72-93309. (Illus.). 1973. 10.95 (ISBN 0-02-912620-7). Free Pr.
Drinks of the World. James Mew & John Ashton. LC 70-78207. (Illus.). 1971. Repr. of 1892 ed. 20.00 (ISBN 0-8103-3772-X). Gale.
Drip, Drop. Donald Carrick. LC 73-4056. (Illus.). 32p. (ps-2). 1973. 5.95g o.s.i. (ISBN 0-02-717340-2). Macmillan.
Driscoll's Diamonds. Ian MacAlister. 208p. 1977. pap. 1.50 o.p. (ISBN 0-449-13600-0, Gm). Fawcett.
Drive Against Illiteracy. Ed. by Irwin Isenberg. (Reference Shelf Ser.: Vol. 36, No. 5). 1964. 6.25 (ISBN 0-8242-0082-9). Wilson.
Drive America. Reader's Digest. (Illus.). 1981. 22.95 (ISBN 0-89577-085-7, Pub. by Reader's Digest). Norton.
Drive for Power. Arnold A. Hutschnecker. LC 74-79982. 360p. 1974. 9.95 (ISBN 0-87131-165-8). M Evans.
Driven Magnetic Fusion Reactors: Proceedings. B. Brunelli. (Commission of the European Communities Ser.: EUR 6146). (Illus.). pap. 82.00 (ISBN 0-08-024459-9). Pergamon.
Driven to Win: A. J. Foyt. Mike Kupper. LC 75-19276. (Sports Profiles Ser.). (Illus.). 48p. (gr. 4-11). 1975. PLB 8.50 (ISBN 0-8172-0120-3). Raintree Pubs.
Driver. Clyde B. Phillips. 1978. pap. 1.95 (ISBN 0-345-27295-1). Ballantine.
Driver, Give a Soldier a Lift. Susan Berman. 1977. pap. 1.50 o.p. (ISBN 0-425-03500-X, Medallion). Berkley Pub.
Drivers License Guide Nineteen Eighty-One. Drivers License Guide Co. (Illus.). 96p. 1981. pap. 9.45. Drivers License.
Drivers License Language. Jim Richey. (Survival Vocabulary Ser.). (Illus.). 48p. (Orig.). (gr. 7 up). 1980. pap. 2.45 (ISBN 0-915510-49-9). Janus Bks.
Drives & Reinforcements: Behavioral Studies of Hypothalamic Functions. James Olds. LC 75-31480. 1977. pap. 10.50 (ISBN 0-89004-087-7). Raven.
Driving Book. H. Faudel-Phillips. pap. 5.25 (ISBN 0-85131-032-X, Dist. by Sporting Book Center). J A Allen.
Driving: How to Get a License (and Keep It!) Ross R. Olney. LC 73-23003. (Career Concise Guides Ser.). (Illus.). 72p. (gr. 9 up). 1974. PLB 4.90 o.p. (ISBN 0-531-02718-X). Watts.
Driving Safely. Edward A. McInroy. (Quick & Easy Ser). (Orig.). 1967. pap. 1.95 o.s.i. (ISBN 0-02-080850-X, Collier). Macmillan.
Driving Through the Clouds & Other Stories. Jo Stanchfield. LC 72-92846. (Highway Holidays Ser). 1973. pap. text ed. 3.54 (ISBN 0-8372-0798-3). Bowmar-Noble.
Driving to Win. Bob Holbert & Al Holbert. (Illus.). 1981. pap. 7.95 (ISBN 0-89404-024-3). Aztex.
Drogen & Alkohol. Ed. by D. Ladewig. (Illus.). xii, 220p. 1980. pap. 23.50 (ISBN 3-8055-1624-X). S Karger.
Droit Des Fiefs Dans la Coutume De Hainaut Au Moyen Age. Noel Didier. LC 80-2032. 1981. Repr. of 1945 ed. 29.50 (ISBN 0-404-18561-4). AMS Pr.
Droits de l'Homme et du Citoyen ou la Cause des Journaliers, Ouvriers et Artisans. Abbe de Favre. (Fr.). 1977. lib. bdg. 16.25x o.p. (ISBN 0-8287-0334-5); pap. text ed. 6.25x o.p. (ISBN 0-685-75744-7). Clearwater Pub.
Drole d'alphabet. A. Rosenstiehl. (Illus.). 1978. 14.75 (ISBN 2-03-051423-3, 3804). Larousse.
Droles De Journal. Carl Rakosi. LC 80-28307. 1981. 25.00 (ISBN 0-915124-43-2, Bookslinger); pap. 5.00 (ISBN 0-915124-44-0). Toothpaste.
Drop of Blood. Paul Showers. LC 67-23672. (Let's-Read-&-Find-Out Science Bk). (Illus.). (gr. k-3). 1967. PLB 7.89 (ISBN 0-690-24526-2, TYC-J); filmstrip with record 11.95 (ISBN 0-690-24527-0); film with cassette 14.95 (ISBN 0-690-24529-7). T Y Crowell.
Drop-Out. Jeannette Eyerly. (gr. 7-10). 1969. pap. 1.95 (ISBN 0-425-04420-3). Berkley Pub.
Drop-Outs: A Treatment Study of Intellectually Capable Students Who Drop Out of High School. Solomon O. Lichter et al. LC 62-11853. 1962. 12.95 (ISBN 0-02-918900-4). Free Pr.
Drop Your Blood Pressure. Lloyd Rosenvold. 176p. (Orig.). 1980. pap. 2.50 (ISBN 0-515-05721-5). Jove Pubns.
Dropout. Ernst Wenk & Nora Harlow. LC 79-66854. (Dialogue Bks). 128p. (Orig.). 1980. pap. 5.75 (ISBN 0-89881-007-8). Intl Dialogue Pr.
Drosophila. B. Shorrocks. (Illus.). 144p. 1980. 12.00 (ISBN 0-08-025941-3). Pergamon.
Drosophila Guide: Introduction to the Genetics & Cytology of Drosophila melanogaster. rev. ed. M. Demerec & B. P. Kaufmann. (Illus.). 47p. 1969. lab manual 2.50 (ISBN 0-87279-950-6). Carnegie Inst.
Drought & Irrigation in North-East Brazil. A. Hall. LC 77-82497. (Latin American Studies: No. 29). (Illus.). 1978. 23.95 (ISBN 0-521-21811-X). Cambridge U Pr.
Drought & Rice Improvement in Perspective. (IRRI Research Paper Ser.: No. 14). 27p. 1978. pap. 5.00 (R054, IRRI). Unipub.
Drought, Famine & Population Movement in Africa. Ed. by James L. Newman. LC 74-25877. (Foreign & Comparative Studies-Eastern African Ser.: No. 17). 144p. 1975. pap. 4.50x (ISBN 0-915984-14-8). Syracuse U Foreign Comp.
Drought in the Great Plains: Research on Impacts & Strategies. Ed. by Norman J. Rosenberg. 1980. 16.50 (ISBN 0-918334-34-9). WRP.
Drowner. John D. MacDonald. 160p. 1977. pap. 1.75 o.p. (ISBN 0-449-13582-9, GM). Fawcett.
Drowning from the Inside Out. Seaborn Jones. LC 80-20642. 88p. 1981. 9.50x (ISBN 0-916156-53-2); pap. 4.00x (ISBN 0-916156-52-4). Cherry Valley.
Drowning of an Old Cat & Other Stories. Hwang Chun-ming. Tr. by Howard Goldblatt. LC 80-7494. (Chinese Literature in Translation Ser.). 320p. 1980. 27.50x (ISBN 0-253-32452-1); pap. 9.95 (ISBN 0-253-20253-1). Ind U Pr.
Drowning Season. Alice Hoffman. 1980. pap. 2.50 (ISBN 0-449-24352-4, Crest). Fawcett.
Drowning with Others. James Dickey. LC 62-10570. (Wesleyan Poetry Program: Vol. 14). (Orig.). 1962. 10.00x (ISBN 0-8195-2014-4, Pub. by Wesleyan U Pr); pap. 3.95 o.p. (ISBN 0-8195-1014-9). Columbia U Pr.
Drownproofing Techniques for Floating, Swimming & Open Water Survival. Reagh Wetmore. (Illus., Orig.). 1981. pap. 7.95 (ISBN 0-8289-0410-3). Greene.
Drucker: The Man Who Invented the Corporate Society. John J. Tarrant LC 75-44263. 300p. 1976. 10.95 o.p. (ISBN 0-8436-0744-0). CBI Pub.
Drucker: The Man Who Invented the Corporate Society. John J. Tarrant. 1977. pap. 6.95 (ISBN 0-446-97702-0). Warner Bks.
Drudgerie Divine: The Rhetoric of God & Man in George Herbert. Edmund Miller. (SSEL Elizabethan Studies: No. 84). 1980. pap. text ed. 25.00x (ISBN 0-391-01904-X). Humanities.
Drug Abuse. Ed. by Sara Lake. (Special Interest Resource Guides in Education). 1980. pap. text ed. 8.50 (ISBN 0-912700-72-6). Oryx Pr.
Drug Abuse: A Criminal Justice Primer. Jerome Platt & Robert Wicks. 1977. pap. text ed. 6.95x (ISBN 0-02-477200-3). Macmillan.
Drug Abuse & Alcoholism: Current Critical Issues. Ed. by Sidney Cohen. LC 79-25648. (Collected Essay Ser.). 1981. pap. text ed. 6.95 (ISBN 0-917724-10-0). Haworth Pr.
Drug Abuse & What We Can Do About It. James C. Bennett & George D. Demos. 148p. 1972. 14.75 (ISBN 0-398-00132-4). C C Thomas.
Drug Abuse Bibliography for 1977. 730p. 1980. 42.50x (ISBN 0-87875-176-9). Whitston Pub.
Drug Abuse: Current Concepts & Research. Ed. by Wolfram Keup. (Illus.). 496p. 1972. 27.50 (ISBN 0-398-02331-X). C C Thomas.
Drug Abuse: Data & Debate. Ed. by Paul H. Blachly. (Illus.). 340p. 1973. 21.50 (ISBN 0-398-00159-6). C C Thomas.
Drug Abuse in Industry: Growing Corporate Dilemma. Jordan M. Scher. (Illus.). 336p. 1973. 16.50 (ISBN 0-398-02809-5). C C Thomas.
Drug Abuse in the Modern World: a Perspective for the Eighties: Proceedings of a Symposium Held at the College of Physicians & Surgeons of Columbia University, New York, N.Y. Ed. by Gabriel G. Nahas & Henry C. Frick, II. (Illus.). 320p. 40.00 (ISBN 0-08-026300-3). Pergamon.
Drug Abuse: What Can We Do? Loyd V. Allen, Jr. LC 79-92950. 144p. (Orig.). 1981. pap. text ed. 2.50 (ISBN 0-8307-0744-1, 5016702). Regal.
Drug Action & Design. Mechanism Based on Enzyme Inhibitors: Proceedings. Medicinal Chemistry Symposium, 20th, New York, May 1979. Ed. by T. I. Kalman. LC 79-17370. (Developments in Biochemistry: Vol. 6). 1979. 40.00 (ISBN 0-444-00345-2, North Holland). Elsevier.
Drug Adulteration: Detection & Control in Nineteenth-Century Britain. Ernst W. Stieb & Glenn Sonnedecker. (Illus.). 1966. 29.50x (ISBN 0-299-04150-6). U of Wis Pr.
Drug & Alcohol Emergencies. Brent Hoben. 1980. pap. 4.95. Hazelden.
Drug & Chemical Risks to the Fetus & Newborn. Ed. by Richard A. Schwarz & Sumner J. Yaffe. LC 79-26191. (Progress in Clinical & Biological Research Ser.: Vol. 36). 166p. 1980. 20.00 (ISBN 0-8451-0036-X). A R Liss.
Drug Assay. 2nd ed. Kalman. 1981. price not set. Masson Pub.
Drug Assay: The Strategy of Therapeutic Drug Monitoring. Sumner M. Kalman & Dennis R. Clark. LC 79-63201. 210p. 1979. 22.50 (ISBN 0-89352-053-5). Masson Pub.
Drug Control in the Americas. William O. Walker, III. (Illus.). 328p. 1981. price not set (ISBN 0-8263-0579-2). U of NM Pr.
Drug Dealers - Taking Action: Options for International Respc .se. Richard H. Blum et al. LC 76-187065. (Social & Behavioral Science Ser.). 1973. 15.95x o.p. (ISBN 0-87589-166-7). Jossey-Bass.
Drug Delivery Systems: Characteristics & Biomedical Applications. Ed. by R. L. Juliano. (Illus.). 336p. 1980. text ed. 27.50x (ISBN 0-19-502700-0). Oxford U Pr.
Drug Dependence. 2nd ed. J. H. Willis. (Illus.). 1974. 7.95 (ISBN 0-571-04861-7, Pub. by Faber & Faber); pap. 3.95 (ISBN 0-571-04862-5). Merrimack Bk Serv.
Drug Dependence & Alcohol, 2 vols. Ed. by Arnold J. Schecter. Incl. Biomedical Issues. 1350p (ISBN 0-306-40323-4); Vol. 2. Social & Behavioral Issues. 996p (ISBN 0-306-40324-2). 1981. 47.50 ea. (Plenum Pr). Plenum Pub.
Drug Dependence & Rehabilitation Approaches. Richard E. Hardy & John G. Cull. (Illus.). 252p. 1973. pap. 22.75 photocopy ed. spiral (ISBN 0-398-02690-4). C C Thomas.
Drug Dependence: Aspects of Ego Functions. Henry Krystal & Herbert A. Raskin. LC 76-121920. 1970. text ed. 8.95x (ISBN 0-8143-1419-8). Wayne St U Pr.
Drug Design. E. J. Ariens. (Medicinal Chemistry Ser.: Vol. 11). Vol. 1 1971. 56.00 (ISBN 0-12-060301-2); Vol. 2 1972. 56.00, by subscription 48.00 (ISBN 0-12-060302-0); Vol.3 1972. 53.00 (ISBN 0-12-060303-9); Vol 4. 1973. 54.00 (ISBN 0-12-060304-7); Vol. 5 1975. 52.50, by subscription 43.00 (ISBN 0-12-060305-5); Vol. 6 1975. 52.50, by subscription 45.00 (ISBN 0-12-060306-3); Vol. 7 1976. 50.50, by subscription 43.50 (ISBN 0-686-66291-1); Vol. 8, 1978. 51.50, by subscription 44.00 (ISBN 0-12-060308-X). Acad Pr.
Drug Dosage & Solutions Workbook. Mary F. Norville. (Illus.). 128p. (Orig.). 1981. pap. text ed. 9.95 (ISBN 0-87619-920-1). R J Brady.
Drug Dosage in Laboratory Animals: A Handbook. 2nd rev. & enl. ed. C. D. Barnes & L. G. Eltherington. 1973. 26.75x (ISBN 0-520-02273-4). U of Cal Pr.
Drug Education. alt. ed. D. A. Girdano & D. D. Girdano. 1972. pap. 5.95 o.p. (ISBN 0-201-02372-5). A-W.
Drug Education: Content & Methods. 3rd ed. Daniel A. Girdano & Dorothy Dusek. LC 79-21100. (Health Education Ser.). (Illus.). 1980. text ed. 9.50 (ISBN 0-201-02963-4); overlay masters 6.50 (ISBN 0-201-02389-X). A-W.
Drug Education: Content & Methods. 2nd ed. Daniel A. Girdano & Dorothy D. Girdano. LC 75-20986. (Health Education Ser.). 224p. 1976. pap. text ed. 10.75 o.p. (ISBN 0-201-02381-4); overlay masters 6.50 o.p. (ISBN 0-201-02389-X). A-W.
Drug Education: Results & Recommendations. Richard H. Blum et al. LC 75-45821. (Illus.). 1976. 21.50 (ISBN 0-669-00575-4). Lexington Bks.
Drug Effects in Hospitalized Patients: Experiences of the Boston Collaborative Drug Surveillance Program, 1966-1975. Russell R. Miller & David J. Greenblatt. LC 75-28124. 368p. 1976. 35.95 (ISBN 0-471-60372-4, Pub. by Wiley Medical). Wiley.
Drug Effects on Laboratory Test Results. Ed. by G. Siest. (Developments in Clinical Biochemistry: No. 2). (Illus.). 338p. 1981. PLB 49.50 (ISBN 0-686-28843-2, Pub. by Martinus Nijhoff). Kluwer Boston.
Drug Effects on the Fetus. M. Tuchmann-Depleiss. (Illus.). 267p. 1975. text ed. 21.50 (ISBN 0-9599827-4-4). ADIS Pr.
Drug Experiments on Prisoners. Peter B. Meyer. LC 75-13307. 144p. 1976. 16.95 (ISBN 0-669-00047-7). Lexington Bks.
Drug Fate & Metabolism, Vol. 2. Ed. by Jean L. Hirtz & E. R. Garrett. 1978. 49.50 (ISBN 0-8247-6603-2). Dekker.
Drug-Free Therapeutic Community. Robert Brook & Paul Whitehead. 158p. 1980. 14.95 (ISBN 0-87705-383-9). Human Sci Pr.
Drug Hang-up: America's Fifty Year Folly. Rufus King. 398p. 1974. pap. 12.75 (ISBN 0-398-03071-5). C C Thomas.
Drug Identification Guide. 1977. pap. text ed. 4.95 o.s.i. (ISBN 0-8273-1716-6). Delmar.
Drug Induced Nutritional Deficiencies. Daphne A. Roe. (Illus.). 1976. lib. bdg. 22.50 (ISBN 0-87055-205-8). AVI.
Drug Induced Pathology. Ed. by E. Grundmann. (Current Topics in Phathology Ser.: Vol. 69). (Illus.). 384p. 1981. 70.00 (ISBN 0-387-10415-1). Springer-Verlag.
Drug Information for Patients. H. Winter Griffith. LC 76-58602. 1978. 39.00 (ISBN 0-7216-4275-6). Saunders.
Drug Interactions. Joseph R. Dipalma. 1976. pap. text ed. 4.95 o.p. (ISBN 0-8273-1313-6). Delmar.
Drug Interactions. Ed. by P. L. Morselli et al. LC 74-77802. (Monograph of the Mario Negri Institute for Pharmacological Research). 1974. 37.50 (ISBN 0-911216-59-6). Raven.
Drug Interactions in Anesthesia. Ed. by N. Ty Smith et al. LC 80-17454. (Illus.). 351p. 1981. text ed. write for info. (ISBN 0-8121-0683-0). Lea & Febiger.
Drug Issues in Geropsychiatry. William E. Fann & George L. Maddox. 122p. 1974. pap. 9.50 (ISBN 0-683-03002-7). Krieger.
Drug Language & Lore. Ed. by Richard E. Hardy & John G. Cull. (American Lectures in Social & Rehabilitation Psychology Ser.). (Illus.). 182p. 1975. pap. 11.75 (ISBN 0-398-03245-9). C C Thomas.
Drug Laws & the Rights That Protect You. Kenneth L. Weiss & David J. Kurland. (Orig.). 1980. pap. (ISBN 0-671-41362-7, Fireside). S&S.
Drug Level Monitoring: Analytical Techniques, Metabolism, & Pharmacokinetics. Wolfgang Sadee & Geertruida C. Beelen. LC 79-22652. 1980. 35.00 (ISBN 0-471-04881-X, Pub. by Wiley-Interscience). Wiley.
Drug Metabolism: From Microbe to Man. D. V. Parke & R. L. Smith. 1977. 57.50x o.p. (ISBN 0-8448-1127-0). Crane-Russak Co.
Drug Misuse: a Psychiatric View of a Modern Dilemma, Vol. 7. GAP Committee on Mental Health Services. LC 62-2872. (Report No. 80). 1970. pap. 2.00 (ISBN 0-87318-112-3). Adv Psychiatry.
Drug Monitoring & Pharmacokinetic Date. Ed. by George Morrell et al. LC 79-90657. 1980. 19.50 (ISBN 0-930376-10-2). Pathotox Pubs.
Drug Phenomenon: Social Aspects of Drug Taking. Erich Goode. LC 73-920. (Studies in Sociology Ser.). 66p. 1973. pap. text ed. 3.50 (ISBN 0-672-61326-3). Bobbs.
Drug Receptors in the Central Nervous System - Based on a Workshop Sponsored by the European Molecular Biology Organization: Proceedings. Weizman Institute of Science, Rehovot, Israel, Feb. 1980 & U. Z. Littauer. 350p. 1980. 43.00 (ISBN 0-471-27893-9, Pub. by Wiley-Interscience). Wiley.
Drug-Resistance Factors & Other Bacterial Plasmids. G. G. Meynell. 1973. 18.00 (ISBN 0-262-13085-8). MIT Pr.
Drug Resistance in Antimicrobial Therapy. E. J. Lowbury & G. A. Ayliffe. (American Lectures in Living Chemistry Ser.). (Illus.). 168p. 1974. 22.50 (ISBN 0-398-02966-0). C C Thomas.
Drug Screening: Fundamentals of Drug Evaluation Techniques in Pharmacology. Emmanuel B. Thompson. LC 80-83409. (Illus.). 325p. (Orig.). 1981. text ed. 23.00x (ISBN 0-932126-06-5); pap. text ed. 18.00x (ISBN 0-932126-07-3). Graceway.
Drug Therapy for the Elderly. Rubin Bressler & Kenneth Conrad. (Illus.). 300p. 1981. pap. text ed. 13.95 (ISBN 0-8016-0782-5). Mosby.

Drug Therapy Reviews. Russell R. Miller & David J. Greenblatt. LC 76-54569. 272p. 1977. 33.00 (ISBN 0-89352-001-2). Masson Pub.

Drug Treatment in Psychiatry. rev. ed. Trevor Silverstone & Paul Turner. (Social & Psychological Aspects of Medical Practice Ser.). 1978. 22.00 (ISBN 0-7100-8933-3); pap. 9.75 (ISBN 0-7100-8934-1). Routledge & Kegan.

Drug Treatment of Mental Disorders. Ed. by L. L. Simpson. LC 74-14480. 400p. 1976. 22.00 (ISBN 0-89004-007-9). Raven.

Drug Treatment of Respiratory Disease. R. B. Cole. (Monographs in Clinical Pharmacology). (Illus.). Date not set. text ed. price not set (ISBN 0-443-08012-7). Churchill. Postponed.

Drug Treatment of Sexual Dysfunction. Ed. by T. A. Ban & F. A. Freyhan. (Modern Problems of Pharmacopsychiatry: Vol. 15). (Illus.). viii, 196p. 1980. 58.75 (ISBN 3-8055-2906-6). S Karger.

Drug Use & Abuse. Terri D. Vacalis. 1975. wire coil bdg. 2.95 o.p. (ISBN 0-88252-101-2). Paladin Hse.

Drug Use & Drug Abuse. Geraldine Woods. (First Bks.). (Illus.). (gr. 4 up). 1979. s&l 6.45 (ISBN 0-531-02941-7). Watts.

Drugging of the Americas: How Multinational Drug Companies Say One Thing About Their Products to Physicians in the United States, & Another Thing to Physicians in Latin America. Milton Silverman. LC 75-27935. 1976. 14.95x (ISBN 0-520-03122-9). U of Cal Pr.

Drugs. Walter Modell & Alfred Lansing. LC 67-25859. (Life Science Library). (Illus.). (gr. 5 up). 1967. PLB 8.97 o.p. (ISBN 0-8094-0482-6, Pub. by Time-Life). Silver.

Drugs - A Factual Account. 2nd ed. Dorothy D. Girdano & Daniel A. Girdano. LC 75-18154. (Health Education Ser.). 224p. 1976. pap. text ed. 9.95 o.p. (ISBN 0-201-02379-2). A-W.

Drugs: A Factual Account. 3rd ed. Dorothy Dusek & Daniel Girdano. LC 79-21381. 1980. text ed. 8.95 (ISBN 0-201-02962-6). A-W.

Drugs: A Multimedia Sourcebook for Young Adults. Sari Feldman & Charles Feldman. (Selection Guide Ser.: No. 4). 256p. 1980. 14.95 (ISBN 0-87436-281-4, Co-Pub. by Neal-Schuman). ABC-Clio.

Drugs: Action, Reactions. G. E. Demaree. (Clinical Monographs Ser.). (Illus.). 1973. pap. 7.95 (ISBN 0-87618-057-8). R J Brady.

Drugs & American Youth. Lloyd Johnston. LC 71-190022. 287p. 1973. cloth 10.00 (ISBN 0-87944-133-X); pap. 6.50 (ISBN 0-87944-120-8). U of Mich Soc Res.

Drugs & Athletic Peformance. Melvin H. Williams. 212p. 1974. 14.75 (ISBN 0-398-03064-2). C C Thomas.

Drugs & Behavior: A Primer in Neuropsychopharmacology. Ernest L. Abel. LC 80-11313. 240p. 1981. Repr. of 1974 ed. lib. bdg. write for info. (ISBN 0-89874-137-8). Krieger.

Drugs & Dissent. Burl Hogins & Gerald Bryant, Jr. 1970. pap. text ed. 3.95x (ISBN 0-02-474960-5, 47496). Macmillan.

Drugs & Drug Dependence. Griffith Edwards et al. LC 75-30136. 264p. 1976. 23.95 (ISBN 0-347-01126-8, 00369-7, Pub. by Saxon Hse). Lexington Bks.

Drugs & Nursing Implications. 3rd ed. Laura E. Govoni & Janice E. Hayes. 1978. 25.00 (ISBN 0-8385-1785-4); pap. 14.95 (ISBN 0-8385-1784-6). ACC.

Drugs & People. Donald A. Read. (gr. 6-12). 1972. pap. text ed. 3.80 (ISBN 0-205-03381-4, 7133812); tchr's guide 2.40 (ISBN 0-205-02613-3, 7126131). Allyn.

Drugs & the Elderly. rev. ed. Ed. by Ronald C. Kayne. LC 78-52886. 1978. 5.00 (ISBN 0-88474-045-5). USC Andrus Geron.

Drugs & the Eye. J. Vale & B. Cox. 1978. 19.95 (ISBN 0-407-00128-X). Butterworths.

Drugs & the Youth Culture. Ed. by Frank R. Scarpitti & Susan K. Datesman. LC 80-11613. (Sage Annual Reviews of Drug & Alcohol Abuse: Vol. 4). (Illus.). 320p. 1980. 20.00x (ISBN 0-8039-1103-3); pap. 9.95x (ISBN 0-8039-1104-1). Sage.

Drugs & Youth: Proceedings. Rutgers Symposium on Drug Abuse. Ed. by J. R. Wittenborn et al. (Illus.). 500p. 1969. text ed. 29.00 o.p. (ISBN 0-398-02097-3). C C Thomas.

Drugs & Youth: The Challenge of Today. Ed. by E. Harms. 1973. text ed. 21.00 (ISBN 0-08-017063-3). Pergamon.

Drugs, Crime, & Politics. Ed. by Arnold S. Trebach. LC 78-5735. (Praeger Special Studies). 1978. 23.95 (ISBN 0-03-042286-8). Praeger.

Drugs, Daydreaming, & Personality: A Study of College Youth. Bernard Segal et al. LC 80-10094. 256p. 1980. 19.95 (ISBN 0-89859-042-6). L Erlbaum Assocs.

Drugs Demystified: Drug Education. 92p. 1975. pap. 2.50 (ISBN 92-3-101231-2, U172, UNESCO). Unipub.

Drugs, Development, & Cerebral Function. Ed. by W. Lynn Smith. (Illus.). 424p. 1972. 31.75 (ISBN 0-398-02417-0). C C Thomas.

Drugs, Doctors, Demons & Disease. Perry A. Sperber. LC 70-111808. 294p. 1973. 15.50 (ISBN 0-87527-127-8). Fireside Bks.

Drugs for Young People: Their Use & Misuse. 2nd ed. Kenneth Leech & Brenda Jordan. 1974. 3.85 (ISBN 0-08-017938-X). Pergamon.

Drugs from A to Z: A Dictionary. 2nd ed. Richard R. Lingeman. (McGraw-Hill Paperbacks). 320p. (Orig.). 1974. text ed. 4.95 (ISBN 0-07-037913-0, SP); pap. 3.95 (ISBN 0-07-037912-2). McGraw.

Drugs Handbook. Paul Turner & Glyn Volans. 1978. text ed. 20.75x (ISBN 0-333-21612-1). Humanities.

Drugs in American Life. Ed. by Morrow Wilson & Suzanne Wilson. (Reference Shelf Ser: Vol. 47, No. 1). 1975. 6.25 (ISBN 0-8242-0569-3). Wilson.

Drugs in Anesthetic Practice. 5th ed. M. D. Vickers & F. G. Wood-Smith. (Illus.). 1978. text ed. 39.95 (ISBN 0-407-15503-1). Butterworths.

Drugs in Cerebral Palsy. Ed. by Eric Denhoff. (Clinics in Developmental Medicine Ser. No. 16). 88p. 1964. 4.50 o.p. (ISBN 0-685-24718-X). Lippincott.

Drugs in Current Use & New Drugs 1981. Ed. by Walter Modell. 1981. pap. text ed. 8.95 (ISBN 0-8261-0159-3). Springer Pub.

Drugs in Reast Miilk. 110p. 1980. 17.50 (ISBN 0-909337-34-9). ADIS Pr.

Drugs in the Classroom: A Conceptual Model for School Programs. 2nd ed. Harold J. Cornacchia et al. LC 77-22968. (Illus.). 1978. pap. text ed. 13.95 (ISBN 0-8016-1043-5). Mosby.

Drugs in Veterinary Practice. Joseph S. Spinelli & L. Reed Enos. LC 78-7046. 1978. pap. text ed. 26.50 (ISBN 0-8016-4749-5). Mosby.

Drugs, Kids & Schools: Practical Strategies for Educators & Other Concerned Adults. Diane J. Tessler. LC 80-17294. 1980. pap. 8.95 (ISBN 0-8302-2224-3). Goodyear.

Drugs of Choice, Nineteen Eighty to Nineteen Eighty-One. Walter Modell. LC 58-6889. (Illus.). 1980. text ed. 44.50 (ISBN 0-8016-3444-X). Mosby.

Drugs, Society & Human Behavior. 2nd ed. Oakley S. Ray. LC 77-20660. (Illus.). 1978. pap. text ed. 14.50 (ISBN 0-8016-4094-6). Mosby.

Drugs, Society & the Law. Harvey Teff. (Illus.). 219p. 1975. 23.95 (ISBN 0-347-01079-2, 97790-0, Pub. by Saxon Hse). Lexington Bks.

Drugs: Substance Abuse. 2nd ed. Kenneth Jones et al. LC 75-1400. Orig. Title: Drugs, Alcohol & Tobacco. 196p. 1975. pap. text ed. 6.50 scp o.p. (ISBN 0-06-384361-7, HarpC). Har-Row.

Drugs, the Drug Industry & Prices. John Adriani. LC 70-176187. 192p. 1981. 10.50 (ISBN 0-87527-196-0). Green.

Drugs Useful Vs Infectious Diseases. Maxwell Finland. LC 74-21394. (Principles & Techniques of Human Research & Therapeutics Ser: Vol. 7). (Illus.). 132p. 1975. 13.50 (ISBN 0-87993-051-9). Futura Pub.

Drugs, What They Are- How They Look- What They Do. Frank Gannon. LC 70-148361. 1971. 8.95 (ISBN 0-89388-005-1). Okpaku Communications.

Druid. Leonard Mosley. LC 80-69367. 1981. 12.95 (ISBN 0-689-11106-1). Atheneum.

Druid's Retreat. Kathryn Kent. 1979. pap. 1.75 o.p. (ISBN 0-523-40404-2). Pinnacle Bks.

Drum: An Introduction to the Instrument. Thomas A. Hill. LC 74-10694. (Keynote Bks). (Illus.). 28p. (gr. 6 up). 1975. PLB 5.90 (ISBN 0-531-02789-9). Watts.

Drum & the Hoe: Life & Lore of the Haitian People. Harold Courlander. (California Library Reprint Series: No. 31). (Illus.). 1973. 22.95x o.p. (ISBN 0-520-00273-3). U of Cal Pr.

Drum & the Hoe: Life & Lore of the Haitian People. Harold Courlander. (California Library Reprint Ser.: No. 31). (Illus.). 436p. 1981. Repr. of 1973 ed. 25.00x (ISBN 0-520-02364-1). U of Cal Pr.

Drum Major for a Dream: Poetic Tributes to Martin Luther King, Jr. Ed. by Ira G. Zepp, Jr. & Melvyn D. Palmer. 1976. 12.00 (ISBN 0-89253-801-5); flexible cloth 8.00 (ISBN 0-89253-802-3). Ind-US Inc.

Drumbeats. rev. ed. Grayce A. Ransom & Elaine Stowe. (Cornerstone Ser.). (gr. 4-5). 1978. pap. text ed. 4.52 (ISBN 0-201-41028-1, Sch Div); tchr's ed. 5.56 (ISBN 0-201-41029-X). A-W.

Drummer Boy. Cyprian O. Ekwensi. 1960. text ed. 2.95x (ISBN 0-521-04882-6). Cambridge U Pr.

Drummer Hoff. Barbara Emberley. (Illus.). (ps-1). 1967. PLB 8.95 (ISBN 0-13-220822-9); pap. 2.95 (ISBN 0-13-220855-5). P-H.

Drummer in the Dark. Francis Clifford. 1977. pap. 1.50 o.p. (ISBN 0-345-25609-3). Ballantine.

Drummer in the Woods. Burton Spiller. (Illus.). 240p. 1980. Repr. of 1962 ed. text ed. 13.95 (ISBN 0-8117-0528-5). Stackpole.

Drummond Greyhounds of the LSWR. D. L. Bradley. 1977. 14.95 (ISBN 0-7153-7329-3). David & Charles.

Drummond on Hawthornden: The Story of His Life & Writings. David Masson. 490p. 1980. Repr. of 1873 ed. lib. bdg. 50.00 (ISBN 0-8492-6834-6). R West.

Drums & Trumpets: The House of Stuart. Kirsty McLeod. LC 77-1496. (gr. 6 up). 1977. 8.95 (ISBN 0-395-28918-1, Clarion). HM.

Drums in the Forest. Allan Dwight. (Illus.). (gr. 7 up). 1936. 8.95 (ISBN 0-02-732960-7). Macmillan.

Drums of Darkness. Elizabeth Lane. 304p. (Orig.). 1981. pap. 2.75 (ISBN 0-515-05664-2). Jove Pubns.

Drums of Darkness (Leo) Marion Bradley. (Zodiac Ser.). (Orig.). 1976. pap. 1.25 o.p. (ISBN 0-345-25108-3). Ballantine.

Drums, Rattles, & Bells. Larry Kettelkamp. (Illus.). (gr. 3-7). 1960. PLB 7.44 (ISBN 0-688-31247-0). Morrow.

Drums, Tomtoms & Rattles: Primitive Percussion Instruments for Modern Use. Bernard S. Mason. (Illus.). 7.50 (ISBN 0-8446-5063-3). Peter Smith.

Drunken Comportment: A Social Explanation. Craig MacAndrew & Robert B. Edgerton. LC 68-8154. 1969. 16.50x (ISBN 0-202-30095-1). Aldine Pub.

Drury's Guide to Best Plays. 3rd ed. James M. Salem. LC 77-18139. 1978. 19.50 (ISBN 0-8108-1097-2). Scarecrow.

Drusilla. Emma Brock. (Illus.). (gr. 4-6). 1937. 3.95g o.s.i. (ISBN 0-02-714440-2). Macmillan.

Druzes in Israel: A Political Study: Political Innovation & Integration in a Middle Eastern Minority. Gabriel Ben-Dor. 287p. 1980. lib. bdg. 30.00x (ISBN 0-686-64555-3, Pub. by Magnes Pr). Westview.

Dry Fly Trouting for Beginners. Richard Barder. 1976. 5.95 (ISBN 0-7153-7055-3). David & Charles.

Dry Gultch Town. Harry Whittington. 128p. (gr. 7 up). Date not set. pap. 1.50 (ISBN 0-686-26923-3, Tempo). G&D.

Dry It, You'll Like It. Gen MacManiman. (Illus.). 1973. pap. 3.95 (ISBN 0-685-52952-5, Pub. by MacManiman). Madrona Pubs.

Dry Kiln Handbook. Jack L. Bachrich. (Illus.). 400p. 1980. 50.00 (ISBN 0-87930-087-6, Pub. by H a Simons Intl Canada). Miller Freeman.

Dry Land Log Handling & Sorting. Charles M. Hampton. LC 80-80437. (Forest Industries Bk). (Illus.). 216p. 1981. pap. 45.00 (ISBN 0-87930-081-7). Miller Freeman.

Dry Martini. John Thomas. (Lost American Fiction Ser.). 1975. pap. 1.50 o.p. (ISBN 0-445-03093-3). Popular Lib.

Dry Strength Additives. Walter F. Reynolds. LC 79-67261. (TAPPI PRESS Bks.). 1980. 34.95 (ISBN 0-89855-204-4, 01-02-B044). TAPPI.

Dryden. William Myers. 1973. text ed. 9.00x (ISBN 0-09-116540-7, Hutchinson U Lib); pap. text ed. 5.50x (ISBN 0-09-116451-6). Humanities.

Dryden. George E. Saintsbury. LC 67-23875. 1968. Repr. of 1881 ed. 20.00 (ISBN 0-8103-3053-9). Gale.

Dryden & Pope in the Early 19th Century. Upali Amarasinghe. 1962. 42.00 (ISBN 0-521-04026-4). Cambridge U Pr.

Dryden & the Conservative Myth. Bernard M. Schilling. 1961. 37.50x (ISBN 0-685-69862-9). Elliots Bks.

Dryden & the Tradition of Panegyric. James D. Garrison. LC 73-91676. 1975. 16.50x (ISBN 0-520-02682-9). U of Cal Pr.

Dryden As Propagandist: Absalom & Architophel & Its Background. James Hogg. (Salzburger Studien Anglistik & Amerikanistik). 1979. pap. text ed. 25.00x (ISBN 0-391-01426-9). Humanities.

Dryden: Poetry & Prose. Ed. by Douglas Grant & Douglas Grant. 1979. 10.95x (ISBN 0-8464-0085-5). Beekman Pubs.

Dryden: The Critical Heritage. Ed. by James Kinsley & Helen Kinsley. 1971. 38.00x (ISBN 0-7100-6977-4). Routledge & Kegan.

Drydeniana, 14 vols. Incl. Vol. 1. Early Career, 1668-1671 (ISBN 0-8240-1225-9); Vol. 2. On Heroic Love, One (ISBN 0-8240-1226-7); Vol. 3. On Heroic Love, Two (ISBN 0-8240-1227-5); Vol. 4. On Heroic Love 3 (ISBN 0-8240-1228-3); Vol. 5. Censure of the Rota: Elkanah Settle (ISBN 0-8240-1229-1); Vol. 6. On Absalom & Achitophel (ISBN 0-8240-1230-5); Vol. 7. On the Duke of Guise (ISBN 0-8240-1231-3); Vol. 8. Hind & the Panther, & Other Works (ISBN 0-8240-1232-1); Vol. 9. Mr. Bays & His Religion (ISBN 0-8240-1233-X); Vol. 10. Late Criticism (ISBN 0-8240-1234-8); Vol. 11. Blount on Poetry. Thomas P. Blount (ISBN 0-8240-1235-6); Vol. 12. On Dryden's Virgil. Luke Milbourne (ISBN 0-8240-1236-4); Vol. 13. Folio Verse Relating to Dryden (ISBN 0-8240-1237-2); Vol. 14. On the Death of Dryden: Folio Verse (ISBN 0-8240-1238-0). (Life & Times of Seven Major British Writers Ser). 1974. lib. bdg. 47.00 ea. Garland Pub.

Dryden's Aeneid & Its Seventeenth Century Predecessors. L. Proutfoot. 278p. 1980. Repr. of 1960 ed. text ed. 30.00 (ISBN 0-8495-2173-4). R West.

Dryden's Political Poetry: The Typology of King & Nation. Steven N. Zwicker. LC 70-188832. 154p. 1972. 8.00x (ISBN 0-87057-134-6, Pub. by Brown U Pr). Univ Pr of New England.

Dryden's Rhymed Heroic Tragedies: A Critical Study of the Plays & of Their Place in Dryden's Poetry, 2 vols. Michael W. Alssid. (Salzburg Studies in English Literature, Poetic Drama & Poetic Theory: No. 7). 429p. 1974. Set. pap. text ed. 50.25x (ISBN 0-391-01298-3). Humanities.

Drying & Preserving Flowers. Winifrede Morrison. 1973. 17.95 (ISBN 0-7134-2324-2, Pub. by Batsford England). David & Charles.

Drying & Storage of Agricultural Crops. Carl W. Hall. (Illus.). 1980. pap. text ed. 21.50 (ISBN 0-87055-364-X). AVI.

Drying Cereal Grains. Donald B. Brooker et al. (Illus.). 1974. text ed. 26.00 (ISBN 0-87055-161-2); pap. 17.50 (ISBN 0-87055-303-8). AVI.

Drying Foods Naturally: A Handbook for Preserving Foods & Using Them Later. Pamela G. Wubben. 80p. 1980. pap. 4.50 (ISBN 0-935442-01-4). One Percent.

Drying of Milk & Milk Products. 2nd ed. Carl W. Hall & T. I. Hedrick. (Illus.). 1971. text ed. 29.50 (ISBN 0-87055-107-8). AVI.

Drying: Principles & Practice. R. B. Keey. 1973. text ed. 67.00 (ISBN 0-08-016903-1). Pergamon.

DS 1 Skill booklet. Barbara J. Crane. (Crane Reading System - English Ser.). (Illus.). (gr. k-2). 1977. pap. text ed. 12.20 per 10 (ISBN 0-89075-034-3). Crane Pub Co.

Du Contrat Social. Jean-Jacques Rousseau. Ed. by Ronald Grimsley. 264p. (Fr.). 1972. 22.50x (ISBN 0-19-815710-X). Oxford U Pr.

Du Magnetisme Animal: Considere Dans Ses Rapports Avec Diverses Brances De la Physique Generale. A. M. Chastenet de Puysegur. 483p. (Fr.). Repr. of 1807 ed. text ed. 32.00x (ISBN 0-8290-0285-5). Irvington.

Du Pont De Nemours on the Dangers of Inflation. Tr. by Edmond E. Lincoln. (Kress Library of Business & Economics: No. 7). 1949. pap. 5.00x (ISBN 0-678-09902-2, Baker Lib). Kelley.

Du Pont Family. John D. Gates. LC 78-7753. 1979. 11.95 o.p. (ISBN 0-385-13043-0). Doubleday.

Du Regime Des Fiefs En Normandie Au Moyen Age. Maurice Rabasse. LC 80-2006. 1981. Repr. of 1905 ed. 29.50 (ISBN 0-404-18588-6). AMS Pr.

Dual Career Couples. Ed. by Fran Pepitone-Rockwell. LC 80-15747. (Sage Focus Editions Ser.: Vol. 24). (Illus.). 294p. 1980. 18.95 (ISBN 0-8039-1436-9); pap. 9.95x (ISBN 0-8039-1437-7). Sage.

Dual-Career Families Re-Examined: New Integrations of Work & Family. 2nd ed. Rhona Rapoport & Robert N. Rapoport. 382p. 1976. 25.50x (ISBN 0-85520-125-8, Pub. by Martin Robertson England); pap. 10.95x (ISBN 0-85520-124-X). Biblio Dist.

Dual Purpose Labrador. Mary R. Williams. 1969. 8.95 (ISBN 0-7207-0242-9, Pub. by Michael Joseph). Merrimack Bk Serv.

Dualism & Discontinuity in Industrial Societies. Suzanne Berger & Michael Piore. LC 79-25172. (Illus.). 176p. 1980. 17.95 (ISBN 0-521-23134-5). Cambridge U Pr.

Dubin's Lives. Bernard Malamud. 432p. 1979. pap. 2.50 (ISBN 0-380-48413-7, 48413). Avon.

Dubious Specter: A Skeptical Look at the Soviet Nuclear Threat. rev. ed. Fred Kaplan. LC 80-50894. 93p. 1980. pap. 4.95 (ISBN 0-89758-023-0). Inst Policy Stud.

Duble Weave: Theory & Practice. Laya Brostoff. LC 79-91202. (Illus.). 54p. 1979. 4.95 (ISBN 0-934026-01-7). Interweave.

Dublin. Desmond Clarke. 1977. 19.95 (ISBN 0-7134-0146-X). David & Charles.

Dublin. B. Lehane. Ed. by Time-Life Books. (Great Cities Ser.). (Illus.). 1979. 14.95 (ISBN 0-8094-2343-X). Time-Life.

Dublin. B. Lehane. (Great Cities Ser.). (Illus.). 1978. lib. bdg. 14.94 (ISBN 0-686-51002-X). Silver.

Dublin: A City in Crisis. Royal Institute of the Architects of Ireland. LC 76-369270. 108p. 1975. pap. 10.50x o.p. (ISBN 0-9504628-0-2). Intl Pubns Serv.

Dublin Castle & the 1916 Rising. Leon O'Broin. LC 78-138554. 1971. 12.00 (ISBN 0-8147-6150-X). NYU Pr.

Dublin Decorative Plasterwork. C. P. Durran. 1967. 25.00 (ISBN 0-693-01112-2). Transatlantic.

Dublin Divided City: Portrait of Dublin 1913. Curriculum Development Unit. 1978. text ed. 10.50x (ISBN 0-905140-50-8). Humanities.

Dublin Drama League. Harold Ferrar & Brenna K. Clarke. (Irish Theatre Ser.: No. 9). 1979. pap. text ed. 5.25x (ISBN 0-85105-316-5, Dolmen Pr). Humanities.

Dublin from Old Photographs. Ed. by Maurice Gorham. (Illus.). 1975. 11.50 o.s.i. (ISBN 0-7134-0122-2). Hippocrene Bks.

Dublin Pawn. John Keckhut. 1977. 8.95 o.p. (ISBN 0-393-08761-1). Norton.

Dublin Sixteen Sixty - Eighteen Sixty. Maurice Craig. (Illus.). 1969. pap. 3.00 o.p. (ISBN 0-686-12064-7). Irish Bk Ctr.

Dubliners: A Facsimile of Drafts & Manuscripts. James Joyce. Ed. by Michael Groden. LC 78-16029. (The James Joyce Archive Ser.). 1978. lib. bdg. 73.00 (ISBN 0-8240-2803-1). Garland Pub.

Dubliners: A Facsimile of Proofs for the 1910 Edition. James Joyce. Ed. by Michael Groden. LC 77-22832. (James Joyce Archive Ser.). 1977. lib. bdg. 73.00 (ISBN 0-8240-2804-X). Garland Pub.

Dubliners: A Facsimile of Proofs for the 1914 Edition. James Joyce. Ed. by Michael Groden. LC 77-22835. (James Joyce Archive Ser.). 1977. lib. bdg. 73.00 (ISBN 0-8240-2805-8). Garland Pub.

Dubrovnik in the Fourteenth & Fifteenth Centuries: A City Between East & West. Barisa Krekic. LC 76-177340. (Center of Civilization Ser.: Vol. 30). 188p. 1972. 5.95 o.p. (ISBN 0-8061-0999-8). U of Okla Pr.

Dubrovnik, Italy & the Balkans in the Late Middle Ages. Barisa Krekic. 332p. 1980. 75.00x (ISBN 0-86078-070-8, Pub. by Variorum England). State Mutual Bk.

Ducati Service-Repair Handbook: 160, 250,350, 450cc, Through 1974. Clymer Publications Staff. (Illus.). 136p. 1974. pap. text ed. 9.95 (ISBN 0-89287-004-4, M306). Clymer Pubns.

Duchess of Asherwood. Mary A. Garratt. (Orig.). 1981. pap. 2.95 o.s.i. (ISBN 0-440-12157-4). Dell.

Duchess of Malfi. John Webster. Ed. by Vincent F. Hopper & Gerald B. Lahey. (gr. 9 up). 1962. 4.75 (ISBN 0-8120-5030-4); pap. text ed. 2.95 (ISBN 0-8120-0058-7). Barron.

Duchess of Windsor. Diana Mosley. LC 80-20793. (Illus.). 224p. 1980. 14.95 (ISBN 0-8128-2759-7). Stein & Day.

Duchess Polly. David Telfair. (Orig.). 1979. pap. text ed. 2.50 o.p. (ISBN 0-425-04152-2). Berkley Pub.

Duck. Angela Sheehan. (First Look at Nature Bks). (Illus.). (gr. 2-4). 1979. 2.50 (ISBN 0-531-09098-1); PLB 6.45 s&l (ISBN 0-531-09074-4). Watts.

Duck Decoys & How to Rig Them. Ralf Coykendall. (Illus.). 1965. 7.95 o.p. (ISBN 0-03-026910-5). HR&W.

Duck Hunter's Handbook. Bob Hinman. 1974. 11.95 (ISBN 0-87691-146-7). Winchester Pr.

Duck-Huntingest Gentleman. Keith C. Russell. (Illus.). 312p. 1980. 14.95 (ISBN 0-87691-328-1). Winchester Pr.

Duck with Squeaky Feet. Denys Cazet. LC 80-18018. (Illus.). 32p. (ps-2). 7.95 (ISBN 0-87888-171-9). Bradbury Pr.

Ducks & Dragons: Poems for Children. Ed. by Gene Kemp. LC 80-670271. 128p. (gr. 2-5). 1980. 8.95 (ISBN 0-571-11523-3, Pub. by Faber & Faber). Merrimack Bk Serv.

Ducks Don't Get Wet. Augusta Goldin. LC 65-11647. (Let's-Read-&-Find-Out Science Bk). (Illus.). (gr. k-3). PLB 7.89 (ISBN 0-690-24668-4, TYC-J); filmstrip with cassette 14.95 (ISBN 0-690-24671-4); filmstrip with record 11.95 (ISBN 0-690-24669-2). T Y Crowell.

Ducks, Geese & Swans of North America. rev. ed. E. H. Kortright. Rev. by Frank C. Bellrose. LC 75-33962. (Illus.). 568p. 1981. 24.95 (ISBN 0-8117-0535-8). Stackpole.

Ducks on the Pond: A Little League Lexicon. Mary Remmers. (Illus.). (gr. 1-6). 1981. pap. price not set (ISBN 0-88319-056-7). Shoal Creek Pub.

Ducky, Ucky & Mucky. Robert Oechsle. (Illus.). 40p. (ps). 1975. pap. 4.25 (ISBN 0-9603376-0-1). Flourtown Pub.

Ductor in Linguas: The Guide into Tongues. John Minsheu. LC 78-14754. 600p. 1978. Repr. of 1617 ed. lib. bdg. 120.00x (ISBN 0-8201-1321-2). Schol Facsimiles.

Ductus Arteriosus. Donald E. Cassels. (Illus.). 356p. 1973. text ed. 32.50 (ISBN 0-398-02720-X). C C Thomas.

Dude Ranger. Zane Grey. 1981. pap. 1.95 (ISBN 0-671-83591-2). PB.

Dudley Carleton to John Chamberlain 1603-1624: Jacobean Letters. Ed. by Maurice Lee, Jr. LC 76-185391. 1972. 22.50 (ISBN 0-8135-0723-5). Rutgers U Pr.

Due Process in Teacher Evaluation. Ed. by Donovan Peterson & Annie Ward. LC 80-5233. 223p. 1980. lib. bdg. 17.00 (ISBN 0-8191-1063-9); pap. text ed. 9.50 (ISBN 0-8191-1064-7). U Pr of Amer.

Due Process of Law. Rodney L. Mott. LC 72-165604. (American Constitutional & Legal History Ser.). 702p. 1973. Repr. of 1926 ed. lib. bdg. 65.00 (ISBN 0-306-70225-8). Da Capo.

Due Process of Law Under the Federal Constitution. Lucius P. McGehee. (Studies in Constitutional Law). x, 452p. 1981. Repr. of 1906 ed. lib. bdg. 37.50x (ISBN 0-8377-0837-0). Rothman.

Duel. Donald Seaman. 220p. 1981. pap. 2.50 (ISBN 0-445-04601-5). Popular Lib.

Duel & the Oath. Henry C. Lea. (Middle Ages Ser). Orig. Title: Superstition & Force. 1974. 12.00x (ISBN 0-8122-7681-7); pap. 4.95x (ISBN 0-8122-1080-8). U of Pa Pr.

Duel to the Death: Eyewitness Accounts of Great Battles at Sea. Ed. by John Slinkman & Navy Times Editors. LC 69-13779. (Illus.). (gr. 4-7). 1969. 5.50 o.p. (ISBN 0-15-224290-2, HJ). HarBraceJ.

Duet for Two Voices. Hugh Carey. LC 78-62115. (Illus.). 1980. 24.95 (ISBN 0-521-22312-1). Cambridge U Pr.

Duet with an Occasional Chorus. A. Conan Doyle. LC 80-67707. (Conan Doyle Centennial Ser.). (Illus.). 1982. price not set (ISBN 0-934468-48-6). Gaslight.

Duetti Facili per Flauti in Do: Twenty Nine Duets for Recorder & Flute. pap. 1.95 (ISBN 0-916786-45-5). St George Bk Serv.

Duffer's Guide to Bogey Golf. Brian Swarbrick. LC 72-6539. (Illus.). 160p. 1973. 5.95 o.p. (ISBN 0-13-220939-X); pap. 2.95 o.p. (ISBN 0-13-220897-0). P-H.

Dugan the Duck. Gale Brennan. (Illus.). 1980. 5.95g (ISBN 0-516-09101-8). Childrens.

Dugout Tycoon. Jackson Scholz. (gr. 7 up). 1963. 6.75 o.p. (ISBN 0-688-21248-4). Morrow.

Duke Ellington. Pamela Barclay. LC 74-8211. (Illus.). 40p. (gr. 4-8). 1975. PLB 5.75 o.p. (ISBN 0-87191-367-4). Creative Ed.

Duke Ellington: His Life & Music. Ed. by Peter Gammond. LC 77-1927. (The Roots of Jazz Ser.). 1977. Repr. of 1958 ed. lib. bdg. 22.50 (ISBN 0-306-70874-4). Da Capo.

Duke Ellington in Person. Mercer Ellington & Stanley Dance. 236p. pap. 5.95 (ISBN 0-306-80104-3). Da Capo.

Duke of Rivas. Gabriel Lovett. (World Authors Ser.: No. 452). 1977. lib. bdg. 12.50 (ISBN 0-8057-6289-2). Twayne.

Duke University Guide to Manuscripts. Ed. by Richard C. Davis & Linda A. Miller. LC 79-28688. 1005p. 1980. lib. bdg. 32.50 (ISBN 0-87436-299-7). Abc-Clio.

Dukes. Malcolm Ross. Date not set. 13.95 (ISBN 0-671-25111-2). S&S.

Duke's Command. Phyllis L. Berk. (Illus.). (gr. 2-5). 4.25 o.p. (ISBN 0-8313-0005-1); FLB 6.19 (ISBN 0-685-13772-4). Lantern.

Duke's Mistress. F. W. Kenyon. 1978. pap. 1.95 (ISBN 0-505-51299-8). Tower Bks.

DUKW: Two & One Half Ton Six by Six Amphibian. Jeff Woods. (MV - Ser.: No. 2). (Illus., Orig.). 1978. pap. 3.95 o.s.i. (ISBN 0-686-53150-7). Beachcomber Bks. Postponed.

Dulac. Ed. by David Larkin. (Encore Ed.). (Illus.). 1975. 3.95 o.p. (ISBN 0-684-16161-3, ScribT). Scribner.

Dulcimer Street. Norman Collins. 1977. pap. 2.50 o.p. (ISBN 0-445-08588-6). Popular Lib.

Dulwich Picture Gallery: A Catalogue. Peter Murray. (Illus.). 312p. 1980. 85.00x (ISBN 0-85667-071-5, Pub. by Sotheby Parke Bernet England). Biblio Dist.

Dumb Like Me, Olivia Potts. Lila Perl. LC 76-7986. (gr. 5 up). 1976. 7.95 (ISBN 0-395-28870-3, Clarion). HM.

Dumbarton Castle. 2nd ed. I. M. Macphail. 215p. 1980. text ed. 26.00x (ISBN 0-85976-051-0). Humanities.

Dumbarton Oaks Conference on the Olmec: October 28 & 29, 1967. Ed. by Elizabeth P. Benson. LC 68-58523. (Illus.). 186p. 1968. 7.50 (ISBN 0-88402-027-4, Ctr Pre-Columbian). Dumbarton Oaks.

Dummy up & Deal. Lee Solkey. 160p. (Orig.). 1980. pap. 3.95 (ISBN 0-89650-677-0). Gamblers.

Dun & Bradstreet's Guide to Your Investment, Nineteen Seventy-Nine to Nineteen Eighty. 24th ed. C. Colburn Hardy. LC 73-18050. (Illus.). 1979. 14.95 o.s.i. (ISBN 0-690-01768-5, TYC-T); pap. 8.95 o.s.i. (ISBN 0-690-01769-3, TYC-T). T Y Crowell.

Dun & Bradstreet's Guide to Your Investments 1981. C. Colburn Hardy. LC 73-18050. (Illus.). 192p. 1981. 12.95 (ISBN 0-690-01956-4); pap. 8.95 (ISBN 0-690-01958-0). Lippincott & Crowell.

Dun & Bradstreet's Guide to Your Investments 1980-1981. 25th, rev. ed. C. Colburn Hardy. (Illus.). 1980. 14.95 o.s.i. (ISBN 0-690-01853-3, TYC-T); pap. 8.95 o.s.i. (ISBN 0-690-01854-1). T Y Crowell.

Dun & Bradstreet's Handbook of Executive Tax Management. Robert S. Holzman. 512p. 1974. 25.00 o.p. (ISBN 0-690-00309-9, TYC-T). T Y Crowell.

Dun & Bradstreet's Handbook of Modern Factoring & Commercial Finance. Louis Moskowitz. LC 76-26628. 1977. 18.95 o.s.i. (ISBN 0-690-01203-9, TYC-T). T Y Crowell.

Dun Emer Press Later the Cuala Press. Liam Miller. (New Yeats Papers Ser.: Vol. 7). 1973. pap. text ed. 7.50x (ISBN 0-85105-246-0, Dolmen Pr). Humanities.

Dunaire, Sixteen Hundred to Nineteen Hundred: Poems of the Dispossessed. Sean O'Tuama & Thomas Kinsella. (Illus.). 432p. 1980. text ed. 30.00x (ISBN 0-85105-363-7, Dolmen Pr); pap. text ed. 11.75x (ISBN 0-85105-364-5, Dolmen Pr). Humanities.

Duncan Dancer. Irma Duncan. LC 79-7759. (Dance Ser.). 1980. Repr. of 1966 ed. lib. bdg. 33.00x (ISBN 0-8369-9288-1). Arno.

Duncan, Son of Malcolm. Lois Parker. LC 77-12724. (Crown Ser.). 1977. pap. 4.50 (ISBN 0-8127-0156-9). Southern Pub.

Duncton Wood. William Horwood. 736p. 1981. pap. 3.50 (ISBN 0-345-29113-1). Ballantine.

Dune Buggy Mystery. Laura Lee Hope. Ed. by Wendy Barish. (Bobbsey Twins Ser.). (Illus.). 128p. (gr. 2-5). 1981. price not set (ISBN 0-671-42293-6); pap. price not set (ISBN 0-671-42294-4). Wanderer Bks.

Dune Country: A Guide for Hikers & Naturalists. Glenda Daniel. LC 77-78782. (Illus.). 167p. 1977. pap. 5.95 (ISBN 0-8040-0757-8). Swallow.

Dune Master: A Pictorial Frank Herbert Bibliography. Compiled by Daniel J. Levack. (Illus.). 96p. 1980. 17.50 (ISBN 0-934438-38-2); pap. 6.95 (ISBN 0-934438-37-4). Underwood-Miller.

Dunhill Golf Yearbook, Nineteen Seventy-Nine. Mark McCormack. (Illus.). 1979. 17.95 o.p. (ISBN 0-385-14940-9); pap. 9.95 o.p. (ISBN 0-385-14941-7). Doubleday.

Dunhill Golf Yearbook 1980. Mark H. McCormack. 448p. 1980. 18.95 (ISBN 0-385-14942-5); pap. 10.95 (ISBN 0-385-14943-3). Doubleday.

Dunkirk. Basil Collier. (Jackdaw Ser: No. 130). 1974. 5.95 o.p. (ISBN 0-670-28628-1, Grossman). Viking Pr.

Dunkirk. Robert Jackson. LC 79-89323. (World War II Ser.). 1980. pap. 2.25 (ISBN 0-87216-597-3). Playboy Pbks.

Dunkirk Directive. Donald Richmond. LC 79-65119. 1980. 12.95 (ISBN 0-8128-2687-6). Stein & Day.

Dunkirk: The Storms of War. John Harris. 1980. 19.95 (ISBN 0-7153-7857-0). David & Charles.

Dunlan & Clotilda. Giovanni Guaresch. Tr. by L. K. Conrad. 1968. 4.95 o.p. (ISBN 0-686-63532-9). FS&G.

Dunninger's Monument to Magic. Joseph Dunninger. LC 73-76824. 224p. 1974. 14.95 (ISBN 0-8184-0160-5). Lyle Stuart.

Dunstaple. Margaret Bent. (Studies of Composers: No. 17). 96p. 1981. pap. 14.95 (ISBN 0-19-315225-8). Oxford U Pr.

Dunsun: A North Borneo Society. Thomas R. Williams. Ed. by George Spindler & Louise Spindler. (Case Studies in Cultural Anthropology). 114p. pap. text ed. 6.95x (ISBN 0-8290-0310-X). Irvington.

Dunwich Horror & Others. H. P. Lovecraft. 1978. pap. 1.75 o.s.i. (ISBN 0-685-86424-3). Jove Pubns.

Duo Concertante for Violin & Piano. Roy Travis. (U.C. Publ. in Contemporary Music: Vol. 4). 1970. pap. 11.00x (ISBN 0-520-09055-1). U of Cal Pr.

Duodenal Ulcer, Vol. 1. K. G. Wormsley. 1977. 14.40 (ISBN 0-904406-53-9). Eden Med Res.

Duping of the American: Dishonesty & Deception in Presidential Television Advertising. Robert Spero. 1980. 12.95 (ISBN 0-690-01884-3). Lippincott.

Duplicate Bridge. Alfred Sheinwold. pap. 2.50 (ISBN 0-486-22741-3). Dover.

Duplicate Partners. Anna L. Hendershot. 1975. pap. text ed. 2.25 (ISBN 0-911832-08-4). Hendershot.

Duplications. Kenneth Koch. 1977. 6.95 o.p. (ISBN 0-394-40614-1); pap. 3.95 (ISBN 0-394-73368-1). Random.

Dura-Europos Synagogue: A Re-Evaluation 1932-1972. Ed. by Joseph Gutmann. LC 73-85879. (American Academy of Religion & Society of Biblical Literature. Religion & the Arts Ser.). (Illus.). 1973. 9.00 (ISBN 0-89130-329-4, 090101). Scholars Pr Ca.

Durability in Concrete Construction. Hubert Woods. (Monograph: No. 4). 1968. 13.25 (ISBN 0-685-85138-9, M-4) (ISBN 0-685-85139-7). ACI.

Durability of Adhesive Bonded Structures: Journal of Applied Polymer Science. M. J. Bodnar. (Applied Polymer Symposium: No. 32). 1977. 33.50 (ISBN 0-471-04564-0, Pub. by Wiley-Interscience). Wiley.

Durability of Concrete. 1975. pap. 23.25 (ISBN 0-685-85126-5, SP-47) (ISBN 0-685-85127-3). ACI.

Durable Desert Tortoise. Colleen S. Bare. LC 79-12806. (Skylight Bk.). (Illus.). (gr. 2-5). 1979. 4.95 (ISBN 0-396-07706-4). Dodd.

Durable Fig Leaf: A Historical, Cultural, Medical, Social, Literary, & Iconographic Account of Man's Relations with His Penis. Mark Strage. 1979. 14.95 (ISBN 0-688-03582-5); pap. 7.95 (ISBN 0-688-08582-2, Quill). Morrow.

Durable Group: Thoughts on Human Identity. Frederick Samuels. 1977. pap. text ed. 7.50x (ISBN 0-8191-0087-0). U Pr of Amer.

Durango South Project: Archaeological Salvage of Two Basketmaker III Sites in the Durango District. John D. Gooding. (Anthropological Papers Ser.: No. 34). 1980. write for info. (ISBN 0-8165-0705-8). U of Ariz Pr.

Durango Street. Frank Bonham. (gr. 7 up). 1967. PLB 7.95 (ISBN 0-525-28950-X). Dutton.

Duration of Marriage to Divorce United States. Alexander A. Plateris & Audrey Shipp. (Ser. 21: No. 38). 50p. 1981. pap. text ed. 1.75 (ISBN 0-8406-0217-0). Natl Ctr Health Stats.

Durer. (Selected Artist Art Ser). (Illus.). 1977. pap. 5.95 (ISBN 0-8120-0763-8). Barron.

Durer-Katalog. J. Meder & Ein Handbuck. LC 75-87642. (Graphic Art Ser.: Vol. 12). (Illus.). 358p. 1971. Repr. of 1932 ed. lib. bdg. 59.50 (ISBN 0-306-71788-3). Da Capo.

Durer: Paintings. Tofani. (The Jewel Ser.). Date not set. 4.95 (ISBN 0-8120-5346-X). Barron.

Durgnat on Film. Raymond Durgnat. (Illus.). 1976. pap. 7.95 (ISBN 0-571-10656-0, Pub. by Faber & Faber). Merrimack Bk Serv.

Durham Book: Being the First Draft of the Revision of the Book of Common Prayer in 1661. Church of England. Ed. by G. J. Cuming. LC 79-12674. 1979. Repr. of 1961 ed. lib. bdg. 27.50x (ISBN 0-313-21481-6, CEBC). Greenwood.

Durham Priory, Fourteen Hundred to Fourteen Fifty. R. B. Dobson. LC 72-89809. (Studies in Medieval Life & Thought). 390p. 1973. 53.95 (ISBN 0-521-20140-3). Cambridge U Pr.

Duricrusts in Tropical & Sub-Tropical Landscapes. Andrew S. Goudie. (Oxford Research Studies in Geography). (Illus.). 192p. 1973. 19.95x o.p. (ISBN 0-19-823212-8). Oxford U Pr.

During Water Peaches. Laurel Trivelpiece. LC 78-14393. 1979. 8.95 (ISBN 0-397-31831-6). Lippincott.

Durkheim, Bernard & Epistemology. Paul Q. Hirst. 1975. 18.50 (ISBN 0-7100-8071-9). Routledge & Kegan.

Durkheim on Religion. Ed. by W. S. Pickering. 1975. 28.00x (ISBN 0-7100-8108-1). Routledge & Kegan.

Dusky & Swallow-Tailed Gulls of the Galapagos Islands. Alfred M. Bailey. (Museum Pictorial: No. 15). 1961. pap. 1.10 o.p. (ISBN 0-916278-42-5). Denver Mus Natl Hist.

Dusky-Footed Wood Rat: A Record of Observations Made on the Hastings Natural History Reservation. Jean M. Linsdale & Lloyd P. Tevis, Jr. (Illus.). 1951. 25.00x (ISBN 0-520-00754-9). U of Cal Pr.

Dusky Rose. Joanna Scott. 192p. (Orig.). 1980. pap. 1.50 (ISBN 0-671-57050-1). S&S.

Dust Bowl: The Southern Plains in the 1930's. Donald Worster. (Illus.). 1979. 16.95 (ISBN 0-19-502550-4). Oxford U Pr.

Dust in the Lion's Paw. Freya Stark. 1975. 22.00 (ISBN 0-7195-1334-0). Transatlantic.

Dust of Death. Os Guinness. LC 72-94670. 430p. 1973. pap. 8.95 (ISBN 0-87784-911-0). Inter-Varsity.

Dust of Far Suns. Jack Vance. (Science Fiction Ser.). 1981. pap. 1.75 (ISBN 0-87997-588-1, UE1588). Daw Bks.

Dust of Life. Liz Thomas. (Illus.). 1978. 8.95 o.p. (ISBN 0-525-09580-2). Dutton.

Dust of Old Adobe. Wallace H. Fuller. 40p. 1980. 3.50 (ISBN 0-8059-2765-4). Dorrance.

Dust on a Precipice. Evelyn Ames. LC 80-26142. 1981. 8.95 (ISBN 0-87233-055-9); pap. 4.95 (ISBN 0-686-69211-X). Bauhan.

Dustbin Who Wanted to Be a General. Jeremy Kingston. (Illus.). (ps-5). 1970. 6.95 (ISBN 0-571-09517-8, Pub. by Faber & Faber). Merrimack Bk Serv.

Dusty Dawn. Anne Duffield. 1975. pap. 1.25 o.p. (ISBN 0-425-02714-7, Medallion). Berkley Pub.

Dutch. Holloway Staff. (Harper Phrase Books for the Traveler Ser.). (Orig.). 1977. pap. 1.00 o.p. (ISBN 0-8467-0308-4, Pub. by Two Continents). Hippocrene Bks.

Dutch Americans: A Guide to Information Sources. Ed. by Linda P. Doezema. LC 79-13030. (Ethnic Studies Information Guide Ser.: Vol. 3). 1979. 30.00 (ISBN 0-8103-1407-X). Gale.

Dutch Anabaptism. Cornelius Krahn. 320p. 1981. pap. 18.00 (ISBN 0-8361-1243-1). Herald Pr.

Dutch Baking & Pastry. H. Menkveld. (Illus.). viii, 156p. 1980. 15.00x (ISBN 0-85334-839-1, Pub. by Applied Science). Burgess-Intl Ideas.

Dutch Cooking. H. Halverhout. 1975. pap. 11.00 (ISBN 0-911268-20-0). Rogers Bk.

Dutch Costumes. E. M. Valeton. (Illus.). 15.00 (ISBN 0-685-47296-5). Heinman.

Dutch Courtesan. John Marston. Ed. by M. L. Wine. LC 65-11519. (Regents Renaissance Drama Ser). 1965. 8.75x (ISBN 0-8032-0274-1); pap. 2.35x (ISBN 0-8032-5274-9, BB 210, Bison). U of Nebr Pr.

Dutch-English & English-Dutch Dictionary. Ed. by F. G. Renier. 1949. 12.00 (ISBN 0-7100-2023-6). Routledge & Kegan.

Dutch Explorers, Traders & Settlers in the Delaware Valley. Clinton A Weslager. LC 61-5543. 1964. 10.00x o.p. (ISBN 0-8122-7262-5). U of Pa Pr.

Dutch Foreign Policy Since Eighteen Fifteen: A Study in Small Power Politics. Amry Vandenbosch. LC 79-2292. 1981. Repr. of 1959 ed. 23.50 (ISBN 0-88355-968-4). Hyperion Conn.

Dutch Genre Drawings. Peter Schatborn & Carlos Van Hasselt. LC 72-86013. (Illus.). 162p. (Orig.). 1972. pap. 7.50. Intl Exhibit Foun.

Dutch Genre Paintings. 2nd rev ed. Miklos Mojzer. Tr. by Evz Racz from Hungarian. (Illus.). 1977. 25.00 (ISBN 0-8283-1727-5). Branden.

Dutch Homesteader on the Prairies: Letters of William De Gelder, 1910-1913. Willem De Gelder. Tr. by Herman Ganzevoort. LC 73-85658. (Social History of Canada Ser.). (Illus.). 1973. pap. 4.50x (ISBN 0-8020-6192-3). U of Toronto Pr.

Dutch in America, 1609-1974. Gerald F. De Jong. (Immigrant Heritage of America Ser). 1975. lib. bdg. 12.50 (ISBN 0-8057-3214-4). Twayne.

Dutch Landscape Etchers of the Seventeenth Century. William A. Bradley. (Illus.). 1919. 27.50x (ISBN 0-685-89748-6). Elliots Bks.

Dutch Landscape Painting of the Seventeenth Century. Wolfgang Stechow. LC 79-91824. (Illus.). 494p. 1980. Repr. of 1966 ed. lib. bdg. 60.00 (ISBN 0-87817-268-8). Hacker.

Dutch Morphology: A Study of Word Formation in Generative Grammar. G. E. Booij. (PdR Press Dutch: No. 2). (Illus.). 1977. pap. text ed. 14.25x (ISBN 90-316-0150-0). Humanities.

Dutch Oven Cooking. John G. Ragsdale. LC 73-75475. (Illus.). 61p. (Orig.). 1973. pap. 2.50 (ISBN 0-88415-200-6). Pacesetter Pr.

Dutch Painters: One Hundred Seventeenth Century Masters. Christopher Wright. LC 77-21988. (Illus.). 1978. 14.95 (ISBN 0-8120-5163-7). Barron.

Dutch Painting. R. H. Fuchs. (World of Art Ser.). (Illus.). 1978. 17.95 (ISBN 0-19-520060-8); pap. 9.95 (ISBN 0-19-520061-6). Oxford U Pr.

Dutch Paintings. Herwig Guratzsch. (Alpine Fine Arts Collection). (Illus.). 304p. 1981. 50.00 (ISBN 0-933516-09-6, Pub by Alpine Fine Arts). Hippocrene Bks.

Dutch Revolt. Geoffrey Parker. 320p. 1977. 20.00 (ISBN 0-8014-1136-X). Cornell U Pr.

Dutch Seaborne Empire, Sixteen Hundred to Eighteen Hundred. C. R. Boxer. 1980. pap. text ed. 11.75x (ISBN 0-09-131051-2, Hutchinson U Lib). Humanities.

Dutch Theses Nineteen Seventy-Seven. Ed. by Bibliotheek der Rijksuniversiteit Utrecht, Department of Classification. 132p. 1980. text ed. 30.95 (ISBN 90-265-0330-X, Pub. by Swets Pub Serv Holland). Swets North Am.

Dutch Treat. Tristan Jones. 1979. 9.95 o.p. (ISBN 0-8362-6107-0). Andrews & McMeel.

Dutch Uncle's Guidebook to School Law. Karl J. Vander Horck. 194p. (Orig.). 1980. pap. 6.95 (ISBN 0-87839-035-9). North Star.

Dutchman Bound for Paradise. Albertine J. Tilstra. Ed. by Bobbie J. Van Dolson. 128p. 1980. pap. write for info. (ISBN 0-8280-0021-2). Review & Herald.

Duties Beyond Borders: On the Limits & Possibilities of Ethical International Politics. Stanley Hoffman. 288p. 1981. 18.00 (ISBN 0-8156-0167-0); pap. 9.95 (ISBN 0-8156-0168-9). Syracuse U Pr.

Duties of Administrators in High Education. S. Salmen. (Studies of the Modern Corporation Ser.). 1971. 9.95 o.s.i. (ISBN 0-02-927760-4). Macmillan.

Duties of Constables, Borsholders, Tithing-Men, & Such Other Low Ministers of the Peace. William Lambard. LC 70-25853. (English Experience Ser.: No. 176). 1969. Repr. of 1583 ed. 8.00 (ISBN 90-221-0176-2). Walter J Johnson.

Duties of Man & Other Essays. Joseph Mazzini. 327p. 1980. lib. bdg. 15.00 (ISBN 0-89760-546-2). Telegraph Bks.

DuVries' Surgery of the Foot. 4th ed. Roger A. Mann. LC 78-10829. (Illus.). 1978. text ed. 44.50 (ISBN 0-8016-2333-2). Mosby.

Dvorak. Hans-Hubert Schonzeler. 192p. Date not set. 13.95 (ISBN 0-7145-2575-8, Pub. by M. Boyars). Merrimack Bk Serv.

Dvorak: His Life & Times. Neil Butterworth. (Life & Times of the Composers Ser.). (Illus.). 1981. 16.95 (ISBN 0-8467-0583-4, Pub. by Midas Bks); pap. 7.95 cancelled (ISBN 0-8467-0584-2, Pub. by Midas Bks). Hippocrene Bks.

Dvorak Symphonies & Concertos. Robert Layton. LC 77-82650. (BBC Music Guides: No. 38). (Illus.). 64p. (Orig.). 1978. pap. 2.95 (ISBN 0-295-95505-8). U of Wash Pr.

Dwarf. Par Lagerkvist. Tr. by Alexandra Dick. 228p. (Orig.). 1958. pap. 4.25 (ISBN 0-8090-1303-7). Hill & Wang.

Dwarf Bulbs. Brian Mathew. 1973. 30.00 (ISBN 0-7134-0403-5, Pub. by Batsford England). David & Charles.

Dwarf Rhododendrons. Peter Cox. (Illus.). 288p. 1973. 14.95 (ISBN 0-02-528560-2). Macmillan.

Dwarf Shrubs: Maintenance-Free Woody Plants for Today's Gardens. Donald Wyman. (Illus.). 160p. 1975. 9.95 o.s.i. (ISBN 0-02-632040-1). Macmillan.

Dwarfed Fruit Trees. Harold B. Tukey. LC 77-12289. (Illus.). 576p. 1978. 32.50x (ISBN 0-8014-1126-2). Comstock.

Dwasuparna: A Novel in Two Parts, 2 vols, Vol. 1. Nishi Khanolkar. (Greenbird Bk.). 1976. Set. text ed. 24.00 (ISBN 0-89253-120-7); flexible bdg. 13.50 (ISBN 0-89253-136-3). Ind-US Inc.

Dweller on Two Planets. Phylos The Tibetan. (Illus.). 450p. 1974. pap. 3.95 (ISBN 0-8334-1753-3). Steinerbks.

Dweller on Two Planets: The Dividing of the Way-Phylos the Thibetan. Frederick S. Oliver. LC 80-8896. (Harper Library of Spiritual Wisdom Ser.). (Illus.). 432p. 1981. pap. 6.95 (ISBN 0-06-066565-3). Har-Row.

Dwellers of the Tundra: Life in an Alaskan Eskimo Village. Aylette Jenness. LC 74-93716. (gr. 7 up). 1970. 9.95 o.s.i. (ISBN 0-02-747720-7, CCPr). Macmillan.

Dwellings. Suzanne Delehanty & Lucy Lippard. (Illus.). 1978. pap. 4.00 (ISBN 0-88454-050-2). U of Pa Contemp Art.

Dwight D. Eisenhower. Sue Hendrix. LC 74-19176. (Illus.). 40p. (gr. 4-8). 1975. PLB 5.95 (ISBN 0-87191-409-3). Creative Ed.

Dyaloge Descrybyng the Orygynall Ground of These Lutheran Saccyons, That Is, Faccyons. William Barlow. LC 74-80161. (English Experience Ser.: No. 641). 200p. 1974. Repr. of 1531 ed. 13.00 (ISBN 90-221-0641-1). Walter J Johnson.

Dyaloge of Syr T. More...Wherein Be Treatyd Dyvers Maters, As of the Veneration & Worshyp of Ymagys. Sir Thomas More. LC 74-28873. (English Experience Ser.: No. 752). 1975. Repr. of 1529 ed. 26.50 (ISBN 90-221-0752-3). Walter J Johnson.

Dye Lasers. Ed. by F. P. Schaefer. LC 73-11593. (Topics in Applied Physics: Vol. 1). (Illus.). xi, 285p. 1974. 37.80 o.p. (ISBN 0-387-06438-9). Springer-Verlag.

Dyed for Death. Warrick W. Rider. (Orig.). 1980. pap. 1.95 (ISBN 0-505-51497-4). Tower Bks.

Dyer's Hand & Other Essays. W. H. Auden. 1968. pap. 3.95 (ISBN 0-394-70418-5, V-418, Vin). Random.

Dyes from Natural Sources. Anne Dyer. 88p. 1976. 7.50 (ISBN 0-8231-5049-6). Branford.

Dyes from the Kitchen. David Green & Jenni Ashburner. 1979. 17.95 (ISBN 0-7134-1565-7, Pub. by Batsford England). David & Charles.

Dying. Miriam Dyak. LC 78-70873. 1978. pap. 3.00 (ISBN 0-934678-00-6). New Victoria Pubs.

Dying. rev. ed. John Hinton. (Orig.). 1967. pap. 2.95 o.p. (ISBN 0-14-020866-6, Pelican). Penguin.

Dying & Death. David Barton. 1977. pap. text ed. 15.95 (ISBN 0-683-00440-9). Williams & Wilkins.

Dying & Death: An Annotated Bibliography. Irene L. Sell. LC 76-58052. 1977. casebound 9.00 o.s.i. (ISBN 0-913292-36-2). Tiresias Pr.

Dying & Dignity: The Meaning & Control of a Personal Death. Melvin J. Krant. 164p. 1974. 11.75 (ISBN 0-398-02995-4); pap. 8.50 (ISBN 0-398-02996-2). C C Thomas.

Dying at Home with Dignity. Deborah Duda. (Illus., Orig.). 1981. pap. 7.00 (ISBN 0-686-69339-6). John Muir.

Dying Child: The Management of the Child or Adolescent Who Is Dying. William M. Easson. (Illus.). 112p. 1977. pap. 8.50 (ISBN 0-398-03676-4). C C Thomas.

Dying, Death, & Grief: A Critically Annotated Bibliography & Source Book of Thanatology & Terminal Care. Ed. by M. A. Simpson. LC 78-27273. 300p. 1979. 21.95 (ISBN 0-306-40147-9, Plenum Pr). Plenum Pub.

Dying in the Sun. K. Palangyo. (African Writers Ser.). 1968. pap. text ed. 3.95 (ISBN 0-435-90053-6). Heinemann Ed.

Dying Patient. Orville G. Brim, Jr. et al. 390p. (Orig.). 1981. pap. 7.95 (ISBN 0-87855-684-2). Transaction Bks.

Dying Self. Charles M. Fair. LC 77-82538. 1969. 15.00x (ISBN 0-8195-4004-8, Pub. by Wesleyan U Pr). Columbia U Pr.

Dyirbal Language of North Queensland: Studies in Linguistics. R. M. Dixon. LC 78-190415. (No. 9). (Illus.). 448p. 1973. 57.50 (ISBN 0-521-08510-1); pap. 15.95x (ISBN 0-521-09748-7). Cambridge U Pr.

Dylan: Druid of the Broken Body. Aneirin T. Davies. 1977. text ed. 11.25x (ISBN 0-7154-0347-8). Humanities.

Dylan Thomas. Jacob Korg. (English Authors Ser.: No. 20). 1964. lib. bdg. 10.95 (ISBN 0-8057-1548-7). Twayne.

Dylan Thomas' New York. Tryntje V. Seymour. LC 78-13286. (Illus.). 1978. pap. 5.95 (ISBN 0-916144-32-1). Stemmer Hse.

Dylan Thomas: The Code of Night. David Holbrook. 1972. text ed. 25.00x (ISBN 0-391-00261-9, Athlone Pr). Humanities.

Dymaxion World of Buckminster Fuller. R. Buckminster Fuller & Robert W. Marks. LC 74-164727. 256p. 1973. pap. 5.95 (ISBN 0-385-01804-5, Anch). Doubleday.

Dynamic Aikido. Gozo Shioda. Tr. by Geoffrey Hamilton. LC 68-31356. (Illus.). 1968. 9.95 o.p. (ISBN 0-87011-096-9). Kodansha.

Dynamic & Inspirational Sermons for Today. Ralph L. Greene. 128p. 1980. 7.95 (ISBN 0-89962-021-3). Todd & Honeywell.

Dynamic Aspects of Cells. M. A. Tribe et al. LC 75-46198. (Basic Biology Course: Bk.3). (Illus.). 112p. 1976. 29.95 (ISBN 0-521-21175-1); pap. 9.75x (ISBN 0-521-21176-X). Cambridge U Pr.

Dynamic Aspects of Host Parasite Relationships, Vol.1. Ed. by Avivah Zuckerman & David W. Weiss. 1973. 31.00 (ISBN 0-12-782001-9). Acad Pr.

Dynamic Aspects of Host-Parasite Relationships, Vol. 2. Ed. by A. Zuckerman. LC 70-189940. 225p. 1976. 41.95 (ISBN 0-470-98430-9). Halsted Pr.

Dynamic Astronomy. 2nd ed. R. Dixon. 1975. pap. 13.95 o.p. (ISBN 0-13-221234-X). P-H.

Dynamic Astronomy. 3rd ed. Robert Dixon. (Illus.). 1980. pap. text ed. 16.95 (ISBN 0-13-221267-6). P-H.

Dynamic Auscultation & Phonocardiography. Joseph Baragan et al. Ed. by Morton E. Tavel & Morton E. Tavel. (Illus.). 314p. 1979. 31.95 (ISBN 0-87619-458-7). Charles.

Dynamic Breaking Techniques. Pu Gill Gwon. LC 77-89191. (Ser. 128). 1977. pap. 6.95 (ISBN 0-89750-023-7). Ohara Pubns.

Dynamic Bronchoscopy. M. A. De Kock. 1977. 59.60 (ISBN 0-387-08109-7). Springer-Verlag.

Dynamic Cardiac Auscultation & Phonocardiography. Abner Delman & Emanuel Stein. LC 77-16990. (Illus.). 1979. text ed. 55.00 o.p. (ISBN 0-7216-3022-7). Saunders.

Dynamic Changes in Terrestrial Ecosystems: Patterns of Change, Techniques for Study & Applications to Management. (MAB Technical Notes: No. 4). 30p. 1977. pap. 2.50 (ISBN 92-3-101458-7, U173, UNESCO). Unipub.

Dynamic Chess: The Modern Style of Aggressive Play. rev. & enl. ed. Richard N. Coles. (Illus.). 1966. pap. 3.50 (ISBN 0-486-21676-4). Dover.

Dynamic Cost Reduction. Irving Dlugatch. LC 78-21078. (Systems & Controls for Financial Management Ser.). 1979. 29.50 (ISBN 0-471-03565-3, Pub. by Wiley-Interscience). Wiley.

Dynamic Discipleship. Kenneth C. Kinghorn. 160p. 1975. pap. 3.95 (ISBN 0-8010-5357-9). Baker Bk.

Dynamic Earth: Textbook in Geosciences. Peter J. Wyllie. LC 73-155909. (Illus.). 1971. 31.95 (ISBN 0-471-96889-7, Pub. by Wiley-Interscience). Wiley.

Dynamic Educational Change: Models, Strategies, Tactics, & Management. Gerald Zaltman & Linda Sikorski. LC 76-19645. (Illus.). 1977. 17.95 (ISBN 0-02-935750-0). Free Pr.

Dynamic Environment of the Ocean Floor. Kent A. Fanning & Frank T. Manheim. LC 78-24651. 1981. write for info. (ISBN 0-669-02809-6). Lexington Bks.

Dynamic Fields & the Structure of Language. Uhlan Slagle & Raimo Anttila. (Current Issues in Linguistic Theory: No. 6). 1980. text ed. 37.25x (ISBN 0-391-01644-X). Humanities.

Dynamic Information & Library Processing. Gerard Salton. (Illus.). 416p. 1975. ref. ed. 26.95 (ISBN 0-13-221325-7). P-H.

Dynamic Investing: The System for Automatic Profits – No Matter Which Way the Market Goes. Jerome Tuccille. 1981. pap. 9.95 (H398). NAL.

Dynamic Islanders: From Cellar to Stanley Cup. Tim Moriarty & Joe Bereswell. (Illus.). 144p. 1981. pap. 9.95 (ISBN 0-385-17489-6). Doubleday.

Dynamic Karate. M. Nakayama. Tr. by Herman Kauz. LC 66-28954. (Illus.). 308p. 1966. 22.50 (ISBN 0-87011-037-3). Kodansha.

Dynamic Kicks: Essentials for Free Fighting. Chong Lee. Ed. by Gilbert Johnson. LC 75-36052. (Ser. 122). (Illus.). 1975. pap. text ed. 5.95 (ISBN 0-89750-017-2). Ohara Pubns.

Dynamic Leadership. Bernard Lall & Geeta Lall. 1979. pap. 6.95 o.p. (ISBN 0-8163-0323-1, 04900-7). Pacific Pr Pub Assn.

Dynamic Light Scattering: With Applications to Chemistry, Biology & Physics. Bruce J. Berne & Robert Pecora. LC 75-19140. 376p. 1976. 40.95 (ISBN 0-471-07100-5, Pub. by Wiley-Interscience). Wiley.

Dynamic Management Communications. Robert D. Breth. (Orig.). 1969. pap. 8.95 (ISBN 0-201-00702-9). A-W.

Dynamic Management Education. 2nd ed. Allen A. Zoll, 3rd. 1969. 21.95 (ISBN 0-201-08800-2). A-W.

Dynamic Managing: Principles, Process, Practice. Mervin Kohn. LC 76-14002. 1977. pap. text ed. 18.95 (ISBN 0-8465-3676-5); instr's guide 3.50 (ISBN 0-8465-3677-3). Benjamin-Cummings.

Dynamic Movement Experiences for Elementary School Children: Combining the Traditional Approach with Movement Education to Produce a Physical Education That Enhances & Complements Intellectual Growth. Louis E. Means & Harry A. Applequist. (Illus.). 536p. 1974. 29.75 (ISBN 0-398-03148-7); pap. 21.75 (ISBN 0-398-03151-7). C C Thomas.

Dynamic Optimization & Economic Applications. Ronald E. Miller. (Illus.). 1980. text ed. 32.95 (ISBN 0-07-042180-3); solutions manual 3.95 (ISBN 0-07-042181-1). McGraw.

Dynamic Optimization & Mathematical Economics. Ed. by Pon-Tai Liu. (Mathematical Concepts & Methods in Science & Engineering Ser.: Vol. 19). (Illus.). 280p. 1980. 29.50 (ISBN 0-306-40245-9, Plenum Pr). Plenum Pub.

Dynamic Personal Adjustment. Herbert L. Sachs. LC 74-8053. 364p. 1975. 9.95 (ISBN 0-87705-165-8). Human Sci Pr.

Dynamic Planning for Environmental Quality in the Eighties. Compiled By American Society of Civil Engineers. 288p. 1978. pap. text ed. 19.75 (ISBN 0-87262-098-0). Am Soc Civil Eng.

Dynamic Power of Self-Love. Francois De La Rochefoucauld. (Illus.). 1980. Repr. of 1899 ed. 33.45 (ISBN 0-89901-006-7). Found Class Reprints.

Dynamic Principle of Historical Growth. George Dickinson. (Illus.). 1978. 39.95 (ISBN 0-89266-089-9). Am Classical Coll Pr.

Dynamic Programming with Management Applications. N. A. Hastings. 177p. 1973. 11.75x o.p. (ISBN 0-8448-1035-5). Crane-Russak Co.

Dynamic Properties of Forest Ecosystems. Ed. by D. E. Reichle. LC 78-72093. (International Biological Programme Ser.: No. 23). (Illus.). 850p. Date not set. 95.00 (ISBN 0-521-22508-6). Cambridge U Pr.

Dynamic Properties of Glia Cells: An Interdisciplinary Approach to Their Study in the Central & Peripheral Nervous System. Ed. by E. Schoffeniels et al. LC 78-40218. 1978. text ed. 69.00 (ISBN 0-08-021555-6). Pergamon.

Dynamic Regression: Theory & Algorithms. M. H. Pesaran & L. J. Slater. LC 79-41652. (Computers & Their Applications Ser.). 363p. 1980. 74.95 (ISBN 0-470-26939-1). Halsted Pr.

Dynamic Response of Pile Foundations: Analytical Aspects. Ed. by Michael W. O'Neill & Ricardo Dobry. LC 80-69151. 112p. 1980. pap. text ed. 12.00 (ISBN 0-87262-257-6). Am Soc Civil Eng.

Dynamic Response of Structures. Gary Hart. LC 80-70135. 992p. 1981. pap. text ed. 65.00 (ISBN 0-87262-261-4). Am Soc Civil Eng.

Dynamic Response of Structures. Ed. by G. Herrmann & N. Perrone. 1972. 51.00 (ISBN 0-08-016850-7). Pergamon.

Dynamic Response of Structures to Wind & Earthquake Loading. Phillip L. Gould & S. H. Abu-Sitta. LC 79-23741. 175p. 1980. 39.95x (ISBN 0-470-26905-7). Halsted Pr.

Dynamic Retailing. Elwood Chapman. 416p. 1980. pap. text ed. 15.50 (ISBN 0-574-20610-8, 13-3610); instr's. guide avail. (ISBN 0-574-20611-6, 13-3611). SRA.

Dynamic Stability: The Soviet Economy Today. Ellen Perlo & Victor Perlo. (Illus.). 365p. (Orig.). 1981. pap. 4.75 (ISBN 0-7178-0577-8). Intl Pub Co.

Dynamic State of Body Constituents. R. Schoenheimer. 1964. Repr. of 1942 ed. 5.25 o.s.i. (ISBN 0-02-851800-4). Hafner.

Dynamic Stock Option Trading. Joseph T. Stewart. 184p. 1981. 31.95 (ISBN 0-471-08670-3). Ronald Pr.

Dynamic Stratigraphy: An Introduction to Sedimentation & Stratigraphy. Robley K. Matthews. 1974. 20.95 (ISBN 0-13-222273-6). P-H.

Dynamic Stratigraphy of the British Isles. R. Anderton et al. (Illus.). 1979. text ed. 35.00x (ISBN 0-04-551027-X); pap. text ed. 19.95x (ISBN 0-04-551028-8). Allen Unwin.

Dynamic Studies with Radioisotopes in Medicine 1974, Vol. II: Proceedings. Symposium, Knoxville, July 15-19, 1974. (Illus.). 443p. 1975. pap. 38.75 (ISBN 92-0-010175-5, ISP376-2, IAEA). Unipub.

Dynamic Studies with Radioisotopes in Medicine. (Illus., Orig.). 1971. pap. 53.50 (ISBN 92-0-010071-6, IAEA). Unipub.

Dynamic Studies with Radioisotopes in Medicine, Vol. 1. (Illus.). 489p. 1975. pap. 41.75 (ISBN 92-0-010075-9, ISP376-1, IAEA). Unipub.

Dynamic Synthesis, Analysis, & Design of Modeled Cam Systems. Delbert Tesar & Gary K. Matthew. LC 75-24655. 1976. 28.95 (ISBN 0-669-00226-7). Lexington Bks.

Dynamic Tension. Harry Wong. LC 80-53545. (Illus.). 144p. 1980. pap. 5.95 (ISBN 0-86568-013-2). Unique Pubns.

Dynamic Track & Field. Jim Bush & Donald C. Weiskopf. 1978. text ed. 19.95 (ISBN 0-205-06004-8). Allyn.

Dynamic University. Zakir Husain. 1965. 5.00x o.p. (ISBN 0-210-27053-5). Asia.

Dynamic Word: New Testament Insights for Contemporary Christians. Karl P. Donfried. LC 80-8905. 244p. 1981. 12.95 (ISBN 0-06-061945-7). Har-Row.

Dynamical Behaviour of Structures. 2nd ed. Ed. by Geoffrey B. Warburton. 1977. text ed. 50.00 (ISBN 0-08-020364-7); pap. text ed. 22.00 (ISBN 0-08-020363-9). Pergamon.

Dynamical Systems: An International Symposium, Vol. 2. Ed. by Lamberto Cesari et al. 1975. 51.50 (ISBN 0-12-164902-4); Set. 84.50 (ISBN 0-685-99221-7). Acad Pr.

Dynamical Systems & Evolution Equations - Theory & Applications. J. A. Walker. (Mathematical Concepts & Methods in Science & Engineering Ser.: Vol. 20). 240p. 1980. 29.50 (ISBN 0-306-40362-5, Plenum Pr). Plenum Pub.

Dynamical Systems & Microphysics. Ed. by A. Blaquiere et al. (CISM - International Centre for Mechanical Sciences Courses & Lectures: Vol. 261). (Illus.). ix, 412p. 1980. pap. 39.00 (ISBN 0-387-81533-3). Springer-Verlag.

Dynamical Systems, Theory & Applications. J. Moser. LC 75-14488. (Lecture Notes in Physics Ser.). vi, 624p. 1975. pap. 23.90 o.p. (ISBN 0-387-07171-7). Springer-Verlag.

Dynamical Systems Theory in Biology: Stability Theory & Its Applications, Vol. 1. Robert Rosen. LC 74-126231. (Biomedical Engineering Ser.). 1970. 40.95 (ISBN 0-471-73550-7, Pub. by Wiley-Interscience). Wiley.

Dynamics. 2nd ed. J. L. Meriam. LC 74-30017. 480p. (SI version). 1975. text ed. 20.95x (ISBN 0-471-59607-8); solutions manual avail. (ISBN 0-471-59610-8). Wiley.

Dynamics. 2nd ed. James L. Meriam. LC 71-142138. 1971. text ed. 20.95x (ISBN 0-471-59601-9). Wiley.

Dynamics & Modeling of Reactive Systems. Ed. by Warren E. Stewart et al. (Mathematics Research Center Ser.). 1980. 17.50 (ISBN 0-12-669550-4). Acad Pr.

Dynamics & Thermodynamics of Compressible Fluid Flow, 2 Vols. Ascher H. Shapiro. (Illus.). 1953-54. Vol. 1. 25.95 (ISBN 0-471-06845-4); Vol. 2. 23.95 (ISBN 0-8260-8075-8). Wiley.

Dynamics in Metazoan Evolution: The Origin of the Coelom & Segments. Robert B. Clark. 1964. 29.95x (ISBN 0-19-854353-0). Oxford U Pr.

Dynamics of Academic Reform. JB Lon Hefferlin. LC 76-92895. (Higher Education Ser.). 1969. 13.95x o.p. (ISBN 0-87589-048-2). Jossey-Bass.

Dynamics of Achievement: A Radical Perspective. H. Dieter Seibel. LC 73-13502. (Studies in Sociology Ser). 1974. pap. text ed. 2.50 (ISBN 0-672-61335-2). Bobbs.

Dynamics of Administrative Reform. Richard A. Chapman & J. R. Greenaway. 249p. 1980. 37.50x (ISBN 0-85664-107-3, Pub. by Croom Helm Ltd England). Biblio Dist.

Dynamics of Aging: Original Essays on the Process & Experience of Growing Old. Forrest J. Berghorn et al. 542p. 1980. lib. bdg. 32.50x (ISBN 0-89158-781-0); pap. text ed. 13.50x (ISBN 0-89158-782-9). Westview.

Dynamics of Agricultural Development in India. Ali Mohammad. 1978. 24.00x o.p. (ISBN 0-8364-0314-2). South Asia Bks.

Dynamics of Agricultural Development in India. Ed. by Ali Mohammad. 1979. text ed. 19.50x (ISBN 0-391-01859-0). Humanities.

Dynamics of Alaska Native Self-Government. Gerald A. McBeath & Thomas A. Morehouse. LC 80-8166. 141p. 1980. lib. bdg. 16.75 (ISBN 0-8191-1171-6); pap. text ed. 7.50 (ISBN 0-8191-1172-4). U Pr of Amer.

Dynamics of American Politics. R. E. Wolfinger et al. 1976. text ed. 16.95 (ISBN 0-13-221168-8); pap. 4.95 study guide & wkbk. (ISBN 0-13-221176-9). P-H.

Dynamics of American Politics. 2nd ed. Raymond Wolfinger et al. (Illus.). 1980. text ed. 17.95 (ISBN 0-13-221143-2); study guide & wkbk. 4.95 (ISBN 0-13-221127-0). P-H.

Dynamics of Anxiety & Hysteria: An Experimental Application of Modern Learning Theory to Psychiatry. H. J. Eysenck. (Illus.). 1967. Repr. of 1957 ed. 22.00x (ISBN 0-7100-1354-X). Routledge & Kegan.

Dynamics of Bureacracy. 2nd. rev. ed. Peter M. Blau. LC 63-22822. xiv, 322p. 1973. text ed. 6.95 (ISBN 0-226-05726-7, P500, Phoen). U of Chicago Pr.

Dynamics of Business Cycles. Jan Tinbergen. Tr. by J. J. Polak from Dutch. (Midway Reprint Ser). x, 366p. 1975. pap. 15.00x o.s.i. (ISBN 0-226-80418-6). U of Chicago Pr.

Dynamics of Canine Gait. Leon Hollenbeck. (Other Dog Bk.). (Illus.). 240p. 1981. write for info. (ISBN 0-87714-081-2). Denlingers.

Dynamics of Chromatography, Pt. 1: Principles & Theory. J. C. Giddings. (Chromatographic Science Ser.: Vol. 1). 1965. 39.75 o.p. (ISBN 0-8247-1225-0). Dekker.

Dynamics of Classroom Structure. Charles J. Nier. LC 80-69330. 140p. 1981. perfect bdg. 11.50 (ISBN 0-86548-052-4). Century Twenty One.

Dynamics of Clinical Dietetics. Marion Mason et al. LC 77-21936. 1977. pap. text ed. 15.95 (ISBN 0-471-02172-5, Pub. by Wiley Medical). Wiley.

Dynamics of Color & Light: How They Affect Human Health & Behavior. John N. Ott. (Illus.). 256p. 1981. 10.00 (ISBN 0-8159-5314-3). Devin.

Dynamics of Communism in Eastern Europe. Richard V. Burks. LC 73-17027. (Illus.). 1976. Repr. of 1961 ed. lib. bdg. 20.25x (ISBN 0-8371-8961-6, BUDY). Greenwood.

Dynamics of Community Development. Jack D. Mezirow. LC 63-7458. 1963. 10.00 (ISBN 0-8108-0038-1). Scarecrow.

Dynamics of Corrections Administration. John O. Truitt & Donald D. Brewer. (Illus.). 125p. 1981. pap. text ed. price not set (ISBN 0-87084-854-2). Anderson Pub Co.

Dynamics of Degeneration & Growth in Neurons. Ed. by K. Fuxe et al. 1974. text ed. 115.00 (ISBN 0-08-017917-7). Pergamon.

Dynamics of Dental Practice Administration: A Guide for Efficient Dental Health Care Delivery. Douglas L. Roberts et al. LC 77-84139. 1977. spiral bdg. 18.00 (ISBN 0-87488-974-X). Med Exam.

Dynamics of Discussion: Communication in Small Groups. 2nd ed. Stanley E. Jones et al. (Illus.). 1980. pap. text ed. 10.95 scp (ISBN 0-06-380438-7, HarpC). Har-Row.

Dynamics of Drama. Bernard Beckerman. LC 79-65301. 1979. pap. text ed. 7.95x (ISBN 0-89676-019-7). Drama Bk.

Dynamics of Education: A Methodology of Progressive Educational Thought. Hilda Taba. 278p. 1980. Repr. of 1932 ed. lib. bdg. 35.00 (ISBN 0-89760-880-1). Telegraph Bks.

Dynamics of Electrical Energy Supply & Demand: An Economic Analysis. R. K. Pachauri. LC 75-19806. (Special Studies). (Illus.). 202p. 1975. text ed. 24.95 (ISBN 0-275-01530-0). Praeger.

Dynamics of Evangelism. Gerald L. Borchert. LC 76-2866. 1976. 5.95 o.p. (ISBN 0-87680-468-7, 80468). Word Bks.

Dynamics of Feedback Systems. A. I. Mees. LC 80-40501. 212p. 1981. 35.75 (ISBN 0-471-27822-X, Pub. by Wiley-Interscience). Wiley.

Dynamics of Folklore. Barre Toelken. LC 78-69536. (Illus.). 1978. text ed. 14.50 (ISBN 0-395-27068-5); inst. manual 0.40 (ISBN 0-395-27069-3). HM.

Dynamics of Group Decisions. Ed. by Hermann Brandstatter et al. LC 78-19143. (Sage Focus Editions: Vol. 5). 1978. 18.95x (ISBN 0-8039-0872-5); pap. 9.95x (ISBN 0-8039-0873-3). Sage.

Dynamics of Health & Disease. Marshall. 1972. 12.50 o.p. (ISBN 0-8385-1873-7). ACC.

Dynamics of Human Communication. 3rd ed. Gail Meyers & Michele Myers. (Illus.). 1980. pap. text ed. 13.95 (ISBN 0-07-044218-5); instrs'. manual 4.95 (ISBN 0-07-044219-3). McGraw.

Dynamics of Human Communication: A Laboratory Approach. 2nd ed. Gail E. Myers & Michele T. Myers. (Illus.). 416p. 1975. pap. text ed. 11.95 o.p. (ISBN 0-07-044212-6, C); instructor's manual 3.95 o.p. (ISBN 0-07-044213-4). McGraw.

Dynamics of Human Relations in Vocational Education: The Development of Self-Confidence & a Sense of Mastery. Duane L. Blake. LC 77-9416. 152p. 1979. pap. 10.00 (ISBN 0-910328-26-9). Carroll Pr.

Dynamics of Human Rights in U. S. Foreign Policy. Ed. by Natalie K. Hevener. 305p. 1981. 19.95 (ISBN 0-87855-347-9). Transaction Bks.

Dynamics of Idealism: White Activists in a Black Movement. N. J. Demerath et al. LC 75-148656. (Social & Behavioral Science Ser.). 1971. 13.95x o.p. (ISBN 0-87589-100-4). Jossey-Bass.

Dynamics of Instructional Groups. Ed. by Gale E. Jensen. LC 60-1494. (National Society for the Study of Education Yearbooks Ser: No. 59, Pt. 2). 1960. 6.00x o.s.i. (ISBN 0-226-60057-2). U of Chicago Pr.

Dynamics of Interviewing: Theory, Technique & Cases. R. L. Kahn & C. F. Cannell. 1957. 24.95 (ISBN 0-471-45441-9). Wiley.

Dynamics of Large Mammal Populations. Charles W. Fowler & Tim D. Smith. 525p. 1981. 40.00 (ISBN 0-471-05160-8, Pub.by Wiley Interscience). Wiley.

Dynamics of Making a Fortune in Mail Order. Raymond J. Brandell & Raymond E. Brandell. (Illus.). 360p. 1980. 19.95 (ISBN 0-8119-0325-7). Fell.

Dynamics of Marine Vehicles. Rameswar Bhattacharya. LC 78-950. (Ocean Engineering Ser.). 1978. text ed. 50.00 (ISBN 0-471-07206-0, Pub. by Wiley-Interscience). Wiley.

Dynamics of Mechanical Systems. 2nd ed. J. M. Prentice. LC 79-41460. 486p. 1980. 59.95x (ISBN 0-470-26938-3). Halsted Pr.

Dynamics of Modernization: A Study in Comparative History. Cyril E. Black. 1967. pap. 4.95x (ISBN 0-06-131321-1, TB1321, Torch). Har-Row.

Dynamics of Motor-Skill Acquisition. Margaret D. Robb. (Illus.). 192p. 1972. pap. text ed. 8.95 (ISBN 0-13-222059-8). P-H.

Dynamics of Nazism: Leadership, Ideology & the Holocaust. Fred Weinstein. LC 80-514. (Studies in Social Discontinuity Ser.). 1980. 13.50 (ISBN 0-12-742480-6). Acad Pr.

Dynamics of Organization Theory: Gaining a Macro Perspective. John F. Veiga & John N. Yanouzas. (Illus.). 1979. text ed. 14.95 (ISBN 0-8299-0182-5); insts.' manual avail. (ISBN 0-8299-0578-2). West Pub.

Dynamics of Party Support. Philip E. Converse. LC 76-40523. (Sage Library of Social Research: Vol. 35). 1976. 18.00x (ISBN 0-8039-0727-3); pap. 8.95x (ISBN 0-8039-0728-1). Sage.

Dynamics of Personal Adjustment. 3rd ed. Harold W. Bernard & Wesley C. Huckins. 476p. 1978. text ed. 16.95 (ISBN 0-205-06032-3, 7960328); instr's manual o.p. (ISBN 0-205-06033-1). Allyn.

Dynamics of Personal Adjustment. 3rd ed. Harold W. Bernard & Wesley C. Huckins. 1978. text ed. 18.95 (ISBN 0-205-06032-3, 7960328). Allyn.

Dynamics of Planned Educational Change: Case Studies & Analyses. Ed. by Robert E. Herriott & Neal Gross. LC 78-61456. 1979. 17.00 (ISBN 0-8211-0761-5); text ed. 15.25 ten or more copies (ISBN 0-685-59768-7). McCutchan.

Dynamics of Planning. E. P. Ward. 1970. 25.00 (ISBN 0-08-015512-X); pap. 12.75 (ISBN 0-08-015513-8). Pergamon.

Dynamics of Polymeric Liquids, 2 vols. Byron R. Bird et al. Incl. Vol. 1. Fluid Mechanics. 43.95 (ISBN 0-471-07375-X); Vol. 2. Kinetic Theory. 41.95 (ISBN 0-471-01596-2). LC 76-15408. 1977. Wiley.

Dynamics of Public Bureaucracy: An Introduction to Public Management. 2nd ed. (Illus.). 480p. 1981. pap. text ed. 16.95 (ISBN 0-87626-199-3). Winthrop.

Dynamics of Public Policy: A Comparative Analysis. Ed. by Richard Rose. LC 75-31293. 1976. 18.50x (ISBN 0-8039-9965-8); pap. 8.95x (ISBN 0-8039-9966-6). Sage.

Dynamics of Racism in Social Work Practice. Ed. by James A. Goodman. LC 73-88446. 388p. 1973. pap. 10.00 (ISBN 0-87101-068-2, CBA-068-C). Natl Assn Soc Wkrs.

Dynamics of Riots. Barbara Salert & John Sprague. Ed. by Michael Hannan. LC 80-18546. (Methodology Monograph Ser.). (Illus.). 126p. (Orig.). 1980. pap. 9.25 (ISBN 0-89138-956-3, IS-00114, Pub. by ICPSR). Univ Microfilms.

Dynamics of Rotors: Selected Papers. Indian Society of Theoretical & Applied Mechanics, 20th Congress, India, 1975. Ed. by J. S. Rao. 1977. pap. text ed. 29.00 (ISBN 0-08-022124-6). Pergamon.

Dynamics of Small Group Communication. Edward A. Mabry & Richard E. Barnes. (Illus.). 1980. text ed. 15.95 (ISBN 0-13-222000-8). P-H.

Dynamics of Social Change: A Reader in Marxist Social Science. Ed. by Howard Selsam et al. LC 77-120820. 1970. 10.00 (ISBN 0-7178-0242-6); pap. 4.50 (ISBN 0-7178-0264-7). Intl Pub Co.

Dynamics of Spectroscopic Transitions Illustrated by Magnetic Resonance & Laser Effects. James Macomber. LC 75-25852. (Monographs in Chemical Physics Ser). 332p. 1976. 29.95 o.p. (ISBN 0-471-56300-5, Pub. by Wiley-Interscience). Wiley.

Dynamics of Stellar Systems. K. F. Ogorodnikov. 1965. 46.00 (ISBN 0-08-010163-1); pap. 26.00 (ISBN 0-08-013772-5). Pergamon.

Dynamics of Structures. Walter C. Hurty & M. F. Rubinstein. (Illus.). 1964. ref. ed. 27.95 (ISBN 0-13-222075-X). P-H.

Dynamics of Structures & Machinery: Problems & Solutions. Gregory Szuladzinski. 700p. 1981. 50.00 (ISBN 0-471-09027-1, Pub. by Wiley Interscience). Wiley.

Dynamics of Teaching Secondary Mathematics. Thomas J. Cooney et al. 1975. 17.95 (ISBN 0-395-18617-X). HM.

Dynamics of Technical Controversy. Allan C. Mazur. (Illus.). 175p. 1981. text ed. 11.95x (ISBN 0-89461-033-3); pap. text ed. 5.95x (ISBN 0-89461-034-1). Comm Pr Inc.

Dynamics of Television. J. P. Baggaley & Steve Duck. 1977. 21.95 (ISBN 0-347-01124-1, 00255-0, Pub. by Saxon Hse). Lexington Bks.

Dynamics of the Arms Race. Ed. by David Carlton & Carlo Schaerf. LC 74-20106. 244p. 1975. 26.95 (ISBN 0-470-13480-1). Halsted Pr.

Dynamics of the Civil Aviation Industry. A. P. Ellison & E. M. Stafford. 1974. 23.95 (ISBN 0-347-01019-9, 91249-2, Pub. by Saxon Hse England). Lexington Bks.

Dynamics of the Party System: Alignment & Realignment of Political Parties in the United States. James L. Sundquist. 1973. 14.95 (ISBN 0-8157-8216-0); pap. 7.95 (ISBN 0-8157-8215-2). Brookings.

Dynamics of the Upper Atmosphere. Ed. by Susumo Kato. (Developments in Earth & Planetary Sciences Ser.: No. 1). 233p. 1980. PLB 29.95 (ISBN 90-277-1132-1, Pub. by D. Reidel). Kluwer Boston.

Dynamics of the Upper Ocean. 2nd ed. O. M. Phillips. LC 76-26371. (Monographs on Mechanics & Applied Mathematics). (Illus.). 1977. 59.95 (ISBN 0-521-21421-1). Cambridge U Pr.

Dynamics of the Upper Ocean. O. M. Phillips. LC 76-26371. (Cambridge Monographs on Mechanics & Applied Mathematics). 344p. 1980. pap. 21.50x (ISBN 0-521-29801-6). Cambridge U Pr.

Dynamics of Therapy in a Controlled Relationship. Jessie Taft. 7.50 (ISBN 0-8446-3045-4). Peter Smith.

Dynamics of University Protest. Ed. by Donald Light, Jr. & John D. Spiegel. LC 77-2364. 1977. 14.95 (ISBN 0-88229-164-5). Nelson-Hall.

Dynamics of Vehicles on Roads & on Railway Tracks: Proceedings. IUTAM Symposium Held at the Delft University of Technology, Department of Mechanical Engineering, Delft, August 1975. Ed. by Hans B. Pacejka. 586p. 1976. pap. text ed. 50.75 (ISBN 90-265-0234-6, Pub. by Swets Pub Serv Holland). Swets North Am.

Dynamics of Vehicles on Roads & on Tracks: Proceedings. IAVSD-Symposium Held at the Technical University Berlin, 6th, September 1979. Ed. by H. P. Willumeit. 522p. 1980. pap. text ed. 46.00 (ISBN 90-265-0327-X, Pub. by Swets Pub Serv Holland). Swets North Am.

Dynamics of Vehicles on Roads & on Tracks: Proceedings. IUTAM Symposium 5th, VSD-2nd, Held at Technical University, Vienna, Austria, Sept. 19-23, 1977. Ed. by A. Slibar & H. Springer. 530p. 1978. pap. text ed. 46.00 (ISBN 90-265-0270-2, Pub. by Swets Pub Serv Holland). Swets North Am.

Dynamics of War & Revolution. 2nd ed. Lawrence Dennis & James J. Martin. 259p. 1941. pap. 10.00 (ISBN 0-911038-91-4, Inst Hist Rev). Noontide.

Dynamics of World History. Christopher Dawson. 12.95 (ISBN 0-89385-009-8). Green Hill.

Dynamics of World Power: A Documentary History of U. S. Foreign Policy, 1945-73. Ed. by Arthur M. Schlesinger, Jr. LC 78-150208. 5075p. 1981. pap. 80.00 (ISBN 0-87754-259-7). Chelsea Hse.

Dynamics of Yoga, 3 vols. M. P. Pandit. 1979. Vol. I. 8.00 (ISBN 0-89744-961-4); Vol. II. 8.00 (ISBN 0-89744-962-2); Vol. III. 9.00 (ISBN 0-89744-963-0). Auromere.

Dynamique Spirituelle. Tr. by G. R. Carlson. (French Bks.). (Fr.). 1979. 1.80 (ISBN 0-8297-0777-8). Life Pubs Intl.

Dynamite Book of Bummers. (gr. 3-5). pap. 1.50 (ISBN 0-590-11805-6, Schol Pap). Schol Bk Serv.

Dynamite Book of Top Secret Information. (gr. 3-5). pap. 1.50 (ISBN 0-590-11804-8, Schol Pap). Schol Bk Serv.

Dynamite Monster Hall of Fame. (gr. 3-5). pap. 1.50 (ISBN 0-590-11806-4, Schol Pap). Schol Bk Serv.

Dynamite War: Irish-American Bombers in Victorian Britain. Kenneth Short. (Illus.). 1979. text ed. 23.25x (ISBN 0-391-00964-8). Humanities.

Dynamite 3-D Poster Book. (gr. 3-5). pap. 3.95 (ISBN 0-590-11816-1, Schol Pap). Schol Bk Serv.

Dynamos & Virgins Revisited: Women & Technological Change in History: an Anthology. Ed. by Martha M. Trescott. LC 79-21404. 235p. 1979. 15.00 (ISBN 0-8108-1263-0). Scarecrow.

Dynast. Paul Erikson. LC 78-12194. 1979. 8.95 (ISBN 0-688-03418-7). Morrow.

Dynastic Arts of the Kushans. John M. Rosenfield. (California Studies in the History of Art: No. V). 1967. 60.00x (ISBN 0-520-01091-4). U of Cal Pr.

Dynasty of Death. Taylor Caldwell. 1979. pap. 3.50 (ISBN 0-515-05981-1). Jove Pubns.

Dynasty of Love. Robert J. Shaw & Thom Racina. (Orig.). 1979. pap. 2.25 o.s.i. (ISBN 0-515-05180-2). Jove Pubns.

Dynasty of Raghu. Kalidasa. Tr. by Robert Antoine from Sanskrit. (Writers Workshop Saffronbird Book Ser.). 217p. 1975. 15.00 (ISBN 0-88253-532-3); pap. text ed. 6.75 (ISBN 0-88253-531-5). Ind-US Inc.

Dynasty of Spies. Dan Sherman. LC 79-54012. 1980. 11.95 (ISBN 0-87795-255-8). Arbor Hse.

Dysfunctional Alliance Emotion & Reason in Justice Administration. Daniel B. Kennedy. LC 77-73529. 1977. pap. text ed. 10.95 (ISBN 0-87084-483-0). Anderson Pub Co.

Dyslexia: An Appraisal of Current Knowledge. Ed. by Arthur L. Benton. (Illus.). 1978. 19.50x o.p. (ISBN 0-19-502384-6). Oxford U Pr.

Dyslexia Defined. Macdonald Critchley & Eileen A. Critchley. (Illus.). 172p. 1978. 17.00 (ISBN 0-398-03885-6). C C Thomas.

Dyslexia in the Classroom. 2nd ed. Dale R. Jordan. (Elementary Education Ser.). 1977. pap. text ed. 9.95 (ISBN 0-675-08466-0). Merrill.

Dyslexia Research & Its Applications to Education. George Pavlidis & Timothy R. Miles. 264p. 1981. 29.75 (ISBN 0-471-27841-6, Pub. by Wiley Interscience). Wiley.

Dyslexia Screening Survey. 1980. pap. write for info. o.p. (ISBN 0-8224-2502-5). Pitman Learning.

Dystonia. Ed. by Roswell Eldridge & Stanley Fahn. LC 75-25112. (Advances in Neurology Ser: Vol. 14). 1976. 48.00 (ISBN 0-89004-070-2). Raven.

Dziga Vertov: A Guide to References & Resources. Seth R. Feldman. 1979. lib. bdg. 30.00 (ISBN 0-8161-8085-7). G K Hall.

E

E. A. Baratynsky. Benjamin Dees. (World Authors Ser.: Russia: No. 202). 1972. lib. bdg. 10.95 (ISBN 0-8057-2092-8). Twayne.

E. B. The Story of Elias Boudinot IV. Barbara L. Clark. (Illus.). 1977. 10.00 (ISBN 0-8059-2246-6). Dorrance.

E. B. White. Edward C. Sampson. (U. S. Authors Ser.: No. 232). 1974. lib. bdg. 10.95 (ISBN 0-8057-0787-5). Twayne.

E. B. White: A Bibliographic Catalogue of Printed Materials in the Department of Rare Books, Cornell University Library. Katherine R. Hall. (Garland Reference Library of the Humanities Ser.). 550p. 1979. lib. bdg. 40.00 (ISBN 0-8240-9549-9). Garland Pub.

E. B. White: A Bibliography. A. J. Anderson. LC 78-2783. (Author Bibliographies Ser.: No. 37). 1978. 10.00 (ISBN 0-8108-1121-9). Scarecrow.

E-Boat Threat. Bryan Cooper. 1980. 12.95 (ISBN 0-356-08144-3, Pub. by MacDonald & Jane's England). Hippocrene Bks.

E-Boats & Coastal Craft. Paul Beaver. (Worldwar Two Photo Album: No. 17). (Illus.). 96p. 1981. pap. 5.95 (ISBN 0-89404-045-6). Aztex.

E. E. Cummings. Barry A. Marks. (U. S. Authors Ser.: No. 46). 1963. lib. bdg. 9.95 (ISBN 0-8057-0176-1). Twayne.

E. E. Cummings: An Introduction to the Poetry. Rushworth M. Kidder. LC 79-772. (Columbia Introductions to Twentieth-Century American Poetry Ser.). 1979. 15.95 (ISBN 0-231-04044-X). Columbia U Pr.

E. E. Cummings: The Growth of a Writer. Norman Friedman. LC 80-17081. (Arcturus Books Paperbacks Ser.). 208p. 1980. pap. 5.95 (ISBN 0-8093-0978-5). S Ill U Pr.

E Ele Concedeu Uns Para Mestres. Tr. by D. V. Hurst. (Portuguese Bks.). 1979. 2.35 (ISBN 0-8297-0838-3). Life Pubs Intl.

E Equals M C Squared: Energy - Management, Conservation & Communication, 17 vols. Robert V. Nelson & Rosalie K. Nelson. Ed. by Arthur F. Ide. (Illus., Orig.). 1981. write for info. (ISBN 0-86663-800-8); pap. write for info. (ISBN 0-86663-801-6). Ide Hse.

E Is for Everybody: A Manual for Bringing Fine Picture Books into the Hands & Hearts of Children. Nancy Polette. LC 76-16199. (Illus.). 165p. 1976. 10.00 (ISBN 0-8108-0966-4). Scarecrow.

E. K.'s Commentary on The Shepheardes Calendar. Patsy S. Cornelius. (Salzburg Studies in English Literature, Elizabethan & Renaissance Studies: No. 31). 111p. 1974. pap. text ed. 25.00x (ISBN 0-391-01350-5). Humanities.

E. M. Forster. Frederick P. McDowell. (English Authors Ser.: No. 89). lib. bdg. 10.95 (ISBN 0-8057-1208-9). Twayne.

E. M. Forster: A Critical Study. Ed. by Laurence Brander. 1979. 16.95x (ISBN 0-8464-0080-4); pap. 9.95 (ISBN 0-8464-0081-2). Beekman Pubs.

E. M. Forster: An Annotated Bibliography of Secondary Materials. Alfred Borrello. LC 73-7990. (Author Bibliographies Ser.: No. 11). 1973. 10.00 (ISBN 0-8108-0668-1). Scarecrow.

E. M. Forster Dictionary. Alfred Borrello. LC 72-151091. 1971. 8.00 o.p. (ISBN 0-8108-0392-5). Scarecrow.

E. M. Forster Glossary. Alfred Borrello. LC 74-188548. 1972. 12.00 (ISBN 0-8108-0475-1). Scarecrow.

E. M. Forster: The Critical Heritage. Ed. by Philip Gardner. (Critical Heritage Ser). 518p. 1973. 38.50x (ISBN 0-7100-7641-X). Routledge & Kegan.

E. M. Forster, the Endless Journey. J. S. Martin. LC 76-4755. (British Authors Ser). 1976. 26.50 (ISBN 0-521-21272-3); pap. 7.95x (ISBN 0-521-29082-1). Cambridge U Pr.

E. M. Forster: The Religious Dimension. Chaman L. Sahni. 160p. 1981. text ed. write for info. (ISBN 0-391-02201-6). Humanities.

E. M. Forster's Letters to Donald Windham. E. M. Forster. 1975. wrappers, ltd. ed. 35.00x (ISBN 0-917366-04-2). S Campbell.

E. M. Forster's Passages to India. Robin J. Lewis. LC 79-843. 1979. 17.50x (ISBN 0-231-04508-5). Columbia U Pr.

E N D C & the Press. Loyal N. Gould. (Stockholm International Peace Research Institute: No. 3). (Orig.). 1969. pap. text ed. 4.50x (ISBN 0-391-00028-4). Humanities.

E P R of Free Radicals in Radiation Chemistry. S. Ya. Pshezhetsky et al. Ed. by D. Slutzkin. Tr. by P. Shelnitz. LC 74-8760. 446p. 1974. 54.95 (ISBN 0-470-70154-4). Halsted Pr.

E R C's President's Guide. E R C Editorial Staff. 1970. 97.50 (ISBN 0-13-925438-2). P-H.

E. Y. Mullins Lectures on Preaching with Reference to the Aristotelian Triad. Don M. Aycock. LC 79-6080. 113p. 1980. text ed. 15.75 (ISBN 0-8191-0981-9); pap. text ed. 7.50 (ISBN 0-8191-0982-7). U Pr of Amer.

Each Man in His Time. Raoul Walsh. 1974. 10.00 o.p. (ISBN 0-374-14553-9). FS&G.

Eagle & the Dove. Ruth F. Solomon. 512p. 1980. pap. 2.75 (ISBN 0-515-05248-5). Jove Pubns.

Eagle & the Phoenix. M. V. Sarma. 108p. 1980. pap. text ed. 3.00x (ISBN 0-391-01914-7). Humanities.

Eagle & the Serpent. Martin L. Guzman. Tr. by Harriet De Onis. 6.50 (ISBN 0-8446-0668-5). Peter Smith.

Eagle & the Sword. Harvey K. Schreiber. 1979. pap. 1.75 o.p. (ISBN 0-445-04346-6). Popular Lib.

Eagle at the Gate. Rona Randall. 1978. pap. 2.25 (ISBN 0-380-42846-6, 42846). Avon.

Eagle Book of Modern Adventures. 5.00 o.p. (ISBN 0-392-02738-0, SpS). Soccer.

Eagle Claw Fish Cookbook. Kenneth N. Anderson. LC 77-89549. (Illus.). 1978. 6.95 (ISBN 0-916752-17-8). Dorison Hse.

Eagle Entangled. Ed. by Kenneth A. Oye et al. (Illus.). 1978. 19.95 (ISBN 0-582-29003-1); pap. text ed. 10.95 (ISBN 0-582-29002-3). Longman.

Eagle in the Sky. Wilbur Smith. 1981. pap. 2.75 (ISBN 0-440-14592-9). Dell.

Eagle Man. H. V. Elkin. (Cutler Ser.: No. 1). 1978. pap. 1.50 (ISBN 0-505-51295-5). Tower Bks.

Eagle Mask: A West Coast Indian Tale. James Houston. LC 66-10074. (Illus.). (gr. 2-6). 1966. 5.50 (ISBN 0-15-224444-1, HJ); pap. 5.50 o.p. (ISBN 0-15-224445-X). HarBraceJ.

Eagle Pine. Dirk Gringhuis. LC 58-7206. (Illus., Orig.). (gr. 5-8). 1969. pap. text ed. 2.75 (ISBN 0-910726-81-7). Hillsdale Educ.

Eagle: The Autobiography of Santa Anna. Ed. by Ann Crawford & William D. Wittliff. LC 68-5896. (Illus.). 12.50 o.p. (ISBN 0-8363-0026-2); limited ed 45.00 o.p. (ISBN 0-685-13271-4). Jenkins.

Eagles. Maggie Davis. LC 80-14471. 384p. 1980. 13.95 (ISBN 0-688-03727-5). Morrow.

Eagles. John Swenson. (Headliners Ser.). 192p. (Orig.). (gr. 4 up). 1981. pap. 2.25 (ISBN 0-448-17174-0, Tempo). G&D.

Eagles Gather. Taylor Caldwell. 1979. pap. 2.75 (ISBN 0-515-05093-8). Jove Pubns.

Eagle's Nest. John Carter. 1978. pap. 1.50 o.p. (ISBN 0-425-03994-3, Dist. by Putnam). Berkley Pub.

Eagles of the Pacific: Consairways Service During WW-II. Edwin Spight & Jeanne Spight. (Illus.). 1980. 12.95 (ISBN 0-911852-88-3, Pub. by Hist Avn. Album). Aviation.

Eagles Over Big Sur. Jack Curtis. 144p. (Orig.). 1981. pap. 6.95 (ISBN 0-88496-160-5). Capra Pr.

Eagle's Trees & Shrubs of New Zealand in Colour. Audrey Eagle. LC 76-361038. (Illus.). 311p. 1975. 75.00x (ISBN 0-685-61095-0). Intl Pubns Serv.

Ear. J. Ballantyne. Ed. by Rob & Smith. (Operative Surgery Ser). 1976. text ed. 45.00 (ISBN 0-407-00097-6). Butterworths.

Ear. Kathleen Elgin. LC 67-10136. (Human Body Ser). (Illus.). (gr. 4-6). 1967. PLB 6.90 (ISBN 0-531-01171-2). Watts.

Ear & Temporal Bone. Michel Portmann et al. LC 78-61476. (Illus.). 464p. 1979. 71.50 (ISBN 0-89352-034-9). Masson Pub.

Ear, Nose, & Throat Book: A Doctor's Guide to Better Health. Stanley N. Farb. (Appleton Consumer Health Guides). (Illus.). 158p. 1980. 12.95 (ISBN 0-8385-2021-9); pap. 5.95 (ISBN 0-8385-2020-0). ACC.

Ear, Nose and Throat Disorders: A Practitioners Guide. Ed. by John R. Ausband. 1974. spiral bdg. 12.00 o.p. (ISBN 0-87488-705-4). Med Exam.

Ear, Nose, Throat: Surgery & Nursing. R. Pracy et al. LC 77-84317. 1977. 14.50 (ISBN 0-471-03918-7). Wiley.

Ear Training & Sight-Singing: An Integrated Approach, Book 1. Allen R. Trubitt & Robert S. Hines. LC 77-5214. 1979. pap. text ed. 12.95 (ISBN 0-02-870810-5); tapes 49.50 (ISBN 0-02-870770-2). Schirmer Bks.

Ear Training & Sight-Singing: Book II, an Integrated Approach. Allen R. Trubitt & Robert S. Hines. LC 77-5214. 1980. pap. text ed. 14.95 (ISBN 0-02-870820-2); tapes 49.50 (ISBN 0-02-872670-7). Schirmer Bks.

Earl Campbell: The Driving Force. Sam Blair. 1980. 8.95 (ISBN 0-8499-0259-2). Word Bks.

Earl of Gowries Conspiracie Against the Kings Maiestie of Scotland. John Ruthven. LC 76-26080. (English Experience Ser.: No. 182). 1969. Repr. of 1600 ed. 7.00 (ISBN 90-221-0182-7). Walter J Johnson.

Earless Ho-Ichi. Lafcadio Hearn. LC 66-12171. (Illus.). 1966. 8.95x (ISBN 0-87011-021-7). Kodansha.

Earlier History of English Bookselling. William Roberts. LC 66-28043. 1967. Repr. of 1889 ed. 15.00 (ISBN 0-8103-3314-7). Gale.

Earlier Philosophical Writings: The Cartesian Principles & Thoughts on Metaphysics. Baruch Spinoza. Tr. by Frank A. Hayes from Latin. LC 63-12199. 1973. 29.50x (ISBN 0-672-51071-5); pap. text ed. 4.95x (ISBN 0-672-60389-6). Irvington.

Earlier Renaissance. G. Saintsbury. LC 68-9660. 1968. Repr. of 1901 ed. 16.00 (ISBN 0-86527-047-3). Fertig.

Earlier Stone Age Settlement of Scandanavia. Grahame Clark. LC 73-94358. (Illus.). 304p. 1975. 42.50 (ISBN 0-521-20446-1). Cambridge U Pr.

Earlier Than You Think: A Personal View of Man in America. George F. Carter. LC 79-5280. (4#368). 1980. 19.95 (ISBN 0-89096-091-7). Tex A&M Univ Pr.

Earlier Tudors, 1485-1558. John D. Mackie. (Oxford History of England Ser.). (Illus.). 1952. 34.00x (ISBN 0-19-821706-4). Oxford U Pr.

Earliest European Helmets: Bronze Age or Early Iron Age. Hugh Hencken. LC 78-152525. (ASPR Bulletin: No. 28). 1971. pap. text ed. 17.00 (ISBN 0-87365-530-3). Peabody Harvard.

Earliest Farmers & the First Cities. Charles Higham. LC 78-179166. (Cambridge Introduction to the History of Mankind). 1972. 3.95 (ISBN 0-521-08440-7). Cambridge U Pr.

Earliest Round Coins of China. Arthur B. Coole. (Encyclopedia of Chinese Coins Ser.: Vol. 7). 325p. Date not set. lib. bdg. 35.00 (ISBN 0-88000-122-4). Quarterman.

Earlihee the Turtle. Bruce Stringer. 4.95 (ISBN 0-932298-06-0). Green Hill.

Earls & Girls. Madeline Bingham. (Illus.). 150p. 1980. 27.00 (ISBN 0-241-10270-7, Pub. by Hamish Hamilton England). David & Charles.

Early Abbasid Caliphate: A Political History. Hugh Kennedy. 238p. 1981. 27.50x (ISBN 0-389-20018-2). B&N.

Early Aircraft. John E. Allen. LC 78-64653. (Fact Finders Ser.). (Illus.). 1979. lib. bdg. 3.96 (ISBN 0-686-51127-1). Silver.

Early American Architecture: From the First Colonial Settlement to the National Period. Hugh Morrison. 1952. text ed. 19.95x (ISBN 0-19-500999-1). Oxford U Pr.

Early American Books & Printing. John T. Winterich. LC 74-3022. 1974. Repr. of 1935 ed. 22.00 (ISBN 0-8103-3661-8). Gale.

Early American Butter Prints. (Americana Books Ser.). (Illus.). 1968. 1.50 o.p. (ISBN 0-911410-17-1). Applied Arts.

Early American Clocks, Vol. 1. 5.95 o.p. (ISBN 0-685-00922-X). Warman.

Early American Clocks, Vol. 2. (Illus.). 6.95 o.p. (ISBN 0-685-26804-7). Warman.

Early American Clocks, Vol. 3. (Illus.). 6.95 o.p. (ISBN 0-685-48561-7). Warman.

Early American Dramatists: From the Beginnings to 1900. Jack A. Vaughn. LC 80-53703. (World Dramatists Ser.). (Illus.). 224p. 1981. 13.95 (ISBN 0-8044-2940-5). Ungar.

Early American Furniture. Kevin Callahan. LC 76-4519. (Illus.). 200p. 1976. pap. 5.95x (ISBN 0-8069-8290-X). Sterling.

Early American Furniture. James M. O'Neill. (gr. 7 up). 1963. text ed. 14.00 (ISBN 0-87345-045-0). McKnight.

Early American Furniture. Don Raycraft & Carol Raycraft. 6.95 o.p. (ISBN 0-87069-026-4). Wallace-Homestead.

Early American Furniture Maker's Manual. A. W. Marlow. (Illus.). 160p. 1973. 12.95 (ISBN 0-02-579810-3). Macmillan.

Early American Houses & a Glossary of Colonial Architectural Terms, 2 vols. Norman M. Isham. LC 67-27458. (Architecture & Decorative Art Ser). 1967. Repr. of 1939 ed. lib. bdg. 17.50 (ISBN 0-306-70973-2). Da Capo.

Early American Imprints, 2 vols. John Jenkins. (Illus.). Date not set. Vol. 1. 15.00 (ISBN 0-8363-0158-7). Vol. 2 (ISBN 0-8363-0163-3). Jenkins.

Early American Iron-on Transfer Patterns for Crewel & Embroidery. Rita Weiss. (Needlework Ser.). pap. 1.75 (ISBN 0-486-23162-3). Dover.

Early American Locomotives. John H. White, Jr. LC 79-188951. (Illus.). 142p. (Orig.). 1972. pap. 5.00 (ISBN 0-486-22772-3). Dover.

Early American Metal Projects. Joseph W. Daniele. LC 75-130495. 14.00 (ISBN 0-87345-142-2). McKnight.

Early American Music. Harold Gleason & Warren Becker. (Music Literature Outlines Ser. III). 1980. write for info. (ISBN 0-89917-265-2, Frangipani Pr). TIS Inc.

Early American-Philippine Trade: The Journal of Nathaniel Bowditch in Manila, 1796. Thomas R. McHale & Mary C. McHale. (Monograph: No. 2). viii, 63p. 1962. 3.25 o.p. (ISBN 0-686-63729-1). Yale U Pr.

Early American Poetry: Bradstreet, Taylor, Dwight, Freneau & Bryant. Jane D. Eberwein. LC 77-91051. 1978. 25.00 (ISBN 0-299-07440-4); pap. 7.95 (ISBN 0-299-07444-7). U of Wis Pr.

Early American Portrait Draughtsmen in Crayons. Theodore Bolton. LC 74-77724. (Library of American Art Ser). (Illus.). 1970. Repr. of 1923 ed. lib. bdg. 25.00 (ISBN 0-306-71362-4). Da Capo.

Early American Song Book. A. Lansburg. LC 74-76864. 1974. 12.95 o.p. (ISBN 0-13-222778-9). P-H.

Early American Stencils on Walls & Furniture. Janet Waring. (Illus.). 12.50 (ISBN 0-685-22719-7). Peter Smith.

Early American Wall Paintings, 1710-1850. Edward B. Allen. LC 77-77694. (Library of American Art Ser.). 1971. Repr. of 1926 ed. lib. bdg. 27.50 (ISBN 0-306-71332-2). Da Capo.

Early American Women Printers & Publishers, 1639-1820. Leona M. Hudak. LC 78-825. 1978. 35.00 (ISBN 0-8108-1119-7). Scarecrow.

Early Americans. Carl Bridenbaugh. (Illus.). 256p. 1981. 19.95 (ISBN 0-19-502788-4). Oxford U Pr.

Early & Middle Childhood: Parenthood in a Free Nation, Vol. 2. Ethel Kawin. (Illus.). 1969. pap. 2.75 (ISBN 0-931682-06-1). Purdue Univ Bks.

Early Anthropology in the Sixteenth & Seventeenth Centuries. Margaret T. Hodgen. LC 62-11265. (Illus.). 1971. pap. text ed. 6.95x (ISBN 0-8122-1014-X, Pa Paperbks). U of Pa Pr.

Early Architecture in New Mexico. Bainbridge Bunting. LC 76-21511. (Illus.). 122p. 1976. 12.95 o.p. (ISBN 0-8263-0424-9); pap. 7.95 o.p. (ISBN 0-8263-0435-4). U of NM Pr.

Early Auden. Edward Mendelson. 1981. 16.95 (ISBN 0-670-28712-1). Viking Pr.

Early Autum. Robert B. Parker. 1981. 10.95 (ISBN 0-440-02248-7, Sey Lawr). Delacorte.

Early Babylonian Letters from Larsa. Henry F. Lutz. (Yale Oriental Babylon Texts Ser.: No. II). 1917. 27.50x (ISBN 0-685-69839-4). Elliots Bks.

Early Ballads, Illustrative of History, Traditions, & Customs. Ed. by Robert Bell. LC 67-23928. 1968. Repr. of 1877 ed. 20.00 (ISBN 0-8103-3408-9). Gale.

Early Barrow Diggers. Barry M. Marsden. LC 74-76137. (Illus.). 126p. 1974. 9.95 (ISBN 0-8155-5027-8, NP). Noyes.

Early Bird. Richard Scarry. (Illus.). (ps-1). 1968. 2.95 (ISBN 0-394-81138-0); PLB 3.99 (ISBN 0-394-91138-5). Random.

Early Birds: An Informal Account of the Birth of Aviation. John Halpern. (Illus.). 96p. 1981. 19.95 (ISBN 0-525-93134-1). Dutton.

Early Blazon: Heraldic Terminology in the Twelfth & Thirteenth Centuries; with Special Reference to Arthurian Literature. Gerard J. Brault. (Illus.). 328p. 1972. text ed. 45.00x (ISBN 0-19-822337-4). Oxford U Pr.

Early Britain: The Celts, Romans, & Anglo-Saxons. Norman W. Pittenger. LC 72-256. (First Bks). (Illus.). 96p. (gr. 5-8). 1972. PLB 4.90 o.p. (ISBN 0-531-00742-1). Watts.

Early British Computers. Simon Lavington. (History of Computing). (Illus.). 140p. 1980. pap. 8.00 (ISBN 0-932376-08-8). Digital Pr.

Early Buddhist Architecture in Japan. Kakichi Suzuki. Tr. by Nancy Shatzman from Japanese. LC 79-7342. (Japanese Arts Library: Vol. 9). (Illus.). 1980. 16.95 (ISBN 0-87011-386-0). Kodansha.

Early Buddhist Philosophy in Light of the Four Noble Truths. Alfonso Verdu. LC 79-66172. 1979. pap. text ed. 9.50 (ISBN 0-8191-0189-3). U Pr of Amer.

Early California Costumes: 1769-1850. Margaret G. Mackey & Louise P. Sooy. (Illus.). 1932. 9.50x (ISBN 0-8047-0994-7). Stanford U Pr.

Early Cambridgestive. A. Taylor et al. (Cambridge Town, Gown & Country Ser.: Vol. 28). 192p. 1977. 20.00 (ISBN 0-900891-08-4). Oleander Pr.

Early Care of the Injured Patient. 2nd ed. American College of Surgeons. LC 76-8566. (Illus.). 1976. text ed. 17.00 (ISBN 0-7216-1161-3). Saunders.

Early Care of the Stroke Patient: A Positive Approach. rev. ed. Janet Carr & Roberta Shepherd. (Illus.). 1979. pap. 10.00 (ISBN 0-433-30140-6). Heinman.

Early Celtic Art in North Britain: A Study of the Decorative Metalwork from the Third Century BC to the Third Century AD, 2 vols. Morna MacGregor. Incl. Vol. 1. (Illus.). 240p; Vol. 2. (Illus.). 322p. 1975. text ed. 57.50x (ISBN 0-7185-1135-2, Leicester). Humanities.

Early Celtic Art in the British Isles, 2 vols. E. M. Jope & P. Jacobsthal. (Illus.). 392p. 1980. text ed. 99.00x (ISBN 0-19-817318-0). Oxford U Pr.

Early Chamber Music. 2nd ed. Ruth H. Rowen. LC 68-8144. (Music Reprint Ser). 1969. Repr. of 1949 ed. lib. bdg. 22.50 (ISBN 0-306-71160-5). Da Capo.

Early Ch'an in China & Tibet. Ed. by Lewis Lancaster & Whalen Lai. 1981. 22.50 (ISBN 0-89581-152-9). Lancaster-Miller.

Early Charters of Northern England & the North Midlands. C. R. Hart. (Studies in Early English History Ser: No. 6). 424p. 1975. text ed. 36.50x (ISBN 0-7185-1131-X, Leicester). Humanities.

Early Charters of the Thames Valley. Margaret Gelling. (Studies in Early English History). (Illus.). 208p. 1980. text ed. 35.00x (ISBN 0-7185-1132-8, Leicester). Humanities.

Early Childhood. Merle B. Karnes & Richard C. Lee. 1978. pap. text ed. 5.50 (ISBN 0-86586-023-8). Coun Exc Child.

Early Childhood. Donald L. Peters & Sherry L. Willis. LC 77-12237. (Brooks-Cole Life-Span Developmental Psychology Ser.). (Illus.). 1978. pap. text ed. 6.95 (ISBN 0-8185-0248-7). Brooks-Cole.

Early Childhood Achievement Units. Robert L. Doan. Incl. Language Development Achievement Activities: Bk. 1. (ISBN 0-87628-281-8); Arts & Crafts Achievement Activities: Bk. 2. (ISBN 0-87628-282-6); Number Readiness Achievement Activities: Bk. 3. (ISBN 0-87628-283-4); Body Management Achievement Activities: Bk. 4. (ISBN 0-87628-284-2); Science Discovery Achievement Activities: Bk. 5. (ISBN 0-87628-285-0); Social Development Achievement Activities: Bk. 6. (ISBN 0-87628-286-9). 1979. 5.95x ea. Ctr Appl Res.

Early Childhood Autism. 2nd ed. Ed. by Lorna Wing. 314p. 1976. text ed. 30.00 (ISBN 0-08-017177-X); pap. text ed. 12.75 (ISBN 0-08-017178-8). Pergamon.

Early Childhood Autism: An Ethological Approach. E. A. Tinbergen & N. Tinbergen. (Advances in Ethology Ser.: Vol. 10). (Illus.). 53p. (Orig.). 1972. pap. text ed. 14.00 (ISBN 3-489-78036-1). Parey Sci Pubs.

Early Childhood Curriculum Materials: An Annotated Bibliography: Early Education for the Handicapped. Ed. by Gloria Harbin et al. (First Chance Ser). 1976. pap. 6.95 o.s.i. (ISBN 0-8027-9040-2). Walker & Co.

Early Childhood: Development & Education. Jeanne M. Gilley et al. LC 78-73823. 1980. pap. 12.20 (ISBN 0-8273-1579-1); instructor's guide 1.50 (ISBN 0-8273-1580-5). Delmar.

Early Childhood Education. Bernard Spodek. (Viewpoint & Alternatives Ser.). (Illus.). 288p. 1973. pap. text ed. 11.95 (ISBN 0-13-222414-3). P-H.

Early Childhood Education: A Guide for Observation & Participation. 2nd ed. Lucile Lindberg & Rita Swedlow. LC 23-67203. 1980. pap. text ed. 10.50 (ISBN 0-205-06720-4, 2367203). Allyn.

Early Childhood Education: A Guide for Observation & Participation. Lucile Lindberg & Rita Swedlow. 320p. 1976. pap. text ed. 7.95x o.s.i. (ISBN 0-205-05442-0). Allyn.

Early Childhood Education: A Methods & Materials Book. Harold D. Love & W. H. Osborne. 160p. 1971. 9.75 (ISBN 0-398-02344-1). C C Thomas.

Early Childhood Education: A Perceptual Models Curriculum. Doris P. Fromberg. LC 76-45390. 1977. text ed. 18.95x (ISBN 0-471-28286-3). Wiley.

Early Childhood Education (a Report Sponsored by the Social Science Research Council) Barbara Tizard. 160p. 1975. pap. text ed. 12.00x (ISBN 0-85633-076-0, NFER). Humanities.

Early Childhood Education & the Waldorf School Plan. Elizabeth M. Grunelius. 1974. pap. 2.95 o.p. (ISBN 0-916786-06-4, Pub by Waldorf School Monographs). St George Bk Serv.

Early Childhood Education in Historical Perspective. rev. ed. D. Keith Osbon. 1980. 11.95 (ISBN 0-918772-08-7); pap. 5.95 (ISBN 0-918772-07-9). Ed Assocs.

Early Childhood Education in Historical Perspective. D. Keith Osborn. LC 75-30492. 1977. pap. 4.95 o.p. (ISBN 0-918772-01-X). Ed Assocs.

Early Childhood Education in the Home. Elinor T. Massoglia. LC 76-14091. (gr. 9-12). 1977. pap. text ed. 9.20 (ISBN 0-8273-0589-3); instructor's guide 1.60 (ISBN 0-8273-0590-7). Delmar.

Early Childhood Education: Issues & Insights. Ed. by Bernard Spodek & Herbert J. Walberg. LC 76-62804. 1977. 15.25 (ISBN 0-8211-1856-0); text ed. 13.75x 10 or more copies (ISBN 0-685-74999-1). McCutchan.

Early Childhood Education Today. 2nd ed. George S. Morrison. (Early Childhood Education Ser.: No. C24). 456p. 1980. text ed. 16.95 (ISBN 0-675-08133-5); instructor's manual 3.95 (ISBN 0-686-63337-7). Merrill.

Early Childhood Environment Rating Scale. Thelma Harms & Richard M. Clifford. (Orig.). 1980. pap. 5.95x (ISBN 0-8077-2632-X); 30 scoring sheets 4.95 (ISBN 0-8077-2635-4). Tchrs Coll.

Early Childhood Experiences in Language Arts. Jeanne Machado. LC 78-55972. 1980. pap. 9.80 (ISBN 0-8273-1573-2); instructor's guide 1.50 (ISBN 0-8273-1574-0). Delmar.

Early Childhood Programs: Developmental Objectives & Their Uses. new ed. Annie L. Butler et al. (Elementary Education Ser). 224p. 1975. text ed. 14.95 (ISBN 0-675-08725-2). Merrill.

Early Childhood Series, 28 vols, Vols. 1-24. large type ed. Photos by Harvey Mandlin. Incl. Apple Is Red. Nancy Curry. LC 67-31186 (ISBN 0-8372-0252-3); Beautiful Day for a Picnic. Nancy Curry. LC 67-31187 (ISBN 0-8372-0255-8); Benny's Four Hats. Ruth M. Jaynes. Ed. by Nancy Curry. LC 67-26370 (ISBN 0-8372-0243-4); The Biggest House. Ruth M. Jaynes. Ed. by Nancy Curry. LC 67-31188; Box Tied with a Red Ribbon. Ruth M. Jaynes. Ed. by Nancy Curry. LC 68-17034 (ISBN 0-8372-0261-2); Colors. Ruth Radlauer & Ed Radlauer. Ed. by Nancy Curry. LC 68-17026. o.p. (ISBN 0-8372-0259-0); Do You Know What. Ruth M. Jaynes. Ed. by Nancy Curry. LC 67-31189 (ISBN 0-8372-0253-1); Do You Suppose Miss Riley Knows. Nancy Curry. LC 67-31327 (ISBN 0-8372-0263-9); Evening. Ruth Radlauer & Ed Radlauer. Ed. by Nancy Curry. LC 68-17033 (ISBN 0-8372-0269-8); Father Is Big. Ruth Radlauer & Ed Radlauer; Follow the Leader. Marion W. Crume (ISBN 0-8372-0242-6); Friends, Friends, Friends. Ruth M. Jaynes. Ed. by Nancy Curry. LC 67-26371 (ISBN 0-8372-0245-0); Funny Mr. Clown. Marion W. Crume. Ed. by Nancy Curry. LC 67-27124 (ISBN 0-8372-0248-5); Furry Boy. Marion W. Crume. Ed. by Nancy Curry. LC 67-31474 (ISBN 0-8372-0264-7); I Like Cats. Marion W. Crume. Ed. by Nancy Curry. LC 67-31475 (ISBN 0-8372-0260-4); Let Me See You Try. Marion W. Crume. Ed. by Nancy Curry. LC 67-31185 (ISBN 0-8372-0256-6); Listen. Marion W. Crume. LC 68-54580 (ISBN 0-8372-0251-5); The Littlest House. Nancy Curry. LC 68-17032 (ISBN 0-8372-0258-2); Melinda's Christmas Stocking. Ruth M. Jaynes. Ed. by Nancy Curry. LC 68-17031. o.p. (ISBN 0-8372-0265-5); Morning. Marion W. Crume. Ed. by Nancy Curry. LC 68-17030; My Friend Is Mrs. Jones. Nancy Curry. LC 67-26369 (ISBN 0-8372-0244-2); My Tricycle & I. Ruth M. Jaynes (ISBN 0-8372-0266-3); Tell Me, Please, What's That. Ruth M. Jaynes. Ed. by Nancy Curry. LC 68-17028 (ISBN 0-8372-0267-1); That's What It Is. Ruth M. Jaynes. Ed. by Nancy Curry. LC 67-31543 (ISBN 0-8372-0250-7). (ps-3). 1967-68. 5.97 ea.; 7 inch records avail. 3.39 ea. Bowmar-Noble.

Early Childrearing by Young Mothers: A Research Study. CWLA Research Center & Lucille Grow. LC 79-53504. 1979. pap. text ed. 8.95 o.p. (ISBN 0-87868-138-8). Child Welfare.

Early China. Wendy Boase. (Civilization Library). (Illus.). (gr. 5-8). 1978. PLB 6.90 s&l (ISBN 0-531-01426-6). Watts.

Early China, No. 5. Ed. by David Keightley et al. 131p. 1980. pap. 7.00 (ISBN 0-912966-26-2). IEAS Ctr Chinese Stud.

Early China & the Wall. P. Nancarrow. LC 76-51411. (Cambridge Introduction to the History of Mankind). 1978. pap. 3.95 (ISBN 0-521-20880-7). Cambridge U Pr.

Early Chinese Literature. Burton Watson. LC 62-17552. (Companions to Asian Studies). 1962. 20.00x (ISBN 0-231-02579-3); pap. 4.95 (ISBN 0-231-08671-7). Columbia U Pr.

Early Ch'ing Imperial Printing. Shiow-Jyu L. Shaw. (Asian Library Ser.: No. 20). (Illus.). 1980. write for info. (ISBN 0-89644-621-2). Chinese Materials.

Early Christian Art. Andre Grabar. LC 68-10414. (Arts of Mankind Ser). 30.00 o.s.i. (ISBN 0-8076-0506-9). Braziller.

Early Christian Creeds. 3rd ed. J. N. Kelly. 446p. 1979. text ed. 25.00x (ISBN 0-582-48931-8). Longman.

Early Christian Fathers: A Selection from the Writings of the Fathers from St. Clement of Rome to St. Athanasius. Tr. by Henry Bettenson. (Oxford Paperbacks Ser). 1969. pap. 5.95x (ISBN 0-19-283009-0, 174). Oxford U Pr.

Early Church. D. R. Norbie. 1981. pap. 10.00 (ISBN 0-937396-13-3). Walterick Pubs.

Early Church Fathers As Educators. E. Matsagouras. 1977. pap. 3.95 (ISBN 0-937032-10-7). Light & Life Pub Co MN.

Early Churches of Washington State. Esther Pearson. LC 79-57216. (Illus.). 182p. 1980. 22.50 (ISBN 0-295-95713-1). U of Wash Pr.

Early Cognitive Development. Ed. by John Oates. LC 78-17694. 1979. 24.95 (ISBN 0-470-26431-4). Halsted Pr.

Early Cognitive Instruction for the Moderately & Severely Handicapped: Teaching Sequences. James E. McCormack & Amanda J. Chalmers. LC 78-62903. (Illus.). 1978. loose-leaf 34.95 (ISBN 0-87822-188-3). Res Press.

Early Coins of the Chou Dynasty. Arthur B. Coole. LC 72-86804. (Encyclopedia of Chinese Coins: Vol. 2). (Illus.). 550p. 1973. 35.00x (ISBN 0-88000-010-4). Quarterman.

Early Cola Architecture & Sculpture, 866-1014 A.D. Douglas Barrett. 1974. 52.00 o.p. (ISBN 0-571-10507-6, Pub. by Faber & Faber). Merrimack Bk Serv.

Early Community at Bedford Park: The Pursuit of "Corporate Happiness" in the First Garden Suburb. Margaret J. Bolsterli. LC 76-8299. (Illus.). xii, 133p. 1977. 14.00x (ISBN 0-8214-0224-2). Ohio U Pr.

Early Concert-Life in America: 1731-1800. O. G. Sonneck. LC 78-2580. (Music Reprint, 1978 Ser.). 1978. Repr. of 1907 ed. lib. bdg. 29.50 (ISBN 0-306-77591-3). Da Capo.

Early Connecticut Meeting Houses, 2 Vols. J. F. Kelly. (Illus.). 1948. Set. 75.00 (ISBN 0-685-02489-X). Kelly.

Early Cretaceous Forminifera from the Budden Canyon Formation, Northwestern Sacramento Valley, California. Donald H. Dailey. (U. C. Publ. in Geological Sciences: Vol. 106). 1975. pap. 12.00x (ISBN 0-520-09486-7). U of Cal Pr.

Early Day History of Wilbarger County. Charles P. Ross & T. L. Rouse. 7.95 o.p. (ISBN 0-685-48811-X). Nortex Pr.

Early Days Among the Cheyenne & Arapahoe Indians. John H. Seger. Ed. by Stanley Vestal. (Illus.). 1934. 8.95 (ISBN 0-8061-0344-2); pap. 4.95 (ISBN 0-8061-1533-5). U of Okla Pr.

Early Days in Detroit: Papers Written by General Friend Palmer, of Detroit, Being His Personal Reminiscences of Important Events & Descriptions of the City for Over Eighty Years. Friend Palmer. LC 74-13871. (Illus.). 1032p. 1979. Repr. of 1906 ed. 29.00 (ISBN 0-8103-4068-2). Gale.

Early Days in Jackson Hole. Virginia Huidekoper. LC 78-60201. (Illus.). 1979. 19.50 (ISBN 0-87081-118-5); pap. 8.95 (ISBN 0-87081-119-3). Colo Assoc.

Early Days-in Photographs. 2nd ed. Al Whattam. (Illus.). 16p. (Orig.). 1981. pap. 2.29 (ISBN 0-918146-01-1). Peninsula WA.

Early Days of Automobiles. Elizabeth Janeway. (Landmark Ser). (Illus.). (gr. 4-6). 1956. PLB 5.99 (ISBN 0-394-90368-4, BYR). Random.

Early Days on the Upper Willamette. 2nd, rev ed. Veryl M. Jensen-Worth. (Illus.). 142p. 1981. 17.50; pap. 9.95. Worth Co.

Early Del Rey, 2 vols. Lester Del Rey. 352p. 1976. Vol. 1. pap. 1.95 o.p. (ISBN 0-345-25063-X); Vol. 2. pap. 1.95 o.p. (ISBN 0-345-25111-3). Ballantine.

Early Detection of Potential Diabetes: The Problems & the Promise. Ed. by Gilman Grave. 1979. 28.00 (ISBN 0-89004-301-9). Raven.

Early Development & Education of the Child. Willi Hoffer. LC 76-5230. 196p. 1980. 10.00 (ISBN 0-686-64206-6). Aronson.

Early Development of Mammals. Ed. by M. Balls & A. E. Wild. (British Society for Developmental Biology Symposium Ser), (Illus.). 500p. 1975. 92.00 (ISBN 0-521-20771-1). Cambridge U Pr.

Early Developmental Hazards: Predictors & Precautions. Ed. by Frances D. Horowitz. LC 78-352. (AAAS Selected Symposium Ser.: No. 19). 1978. lib. bdg. 16.00x (ISBN 0-89158-084-0). Westview.

Early Developments in Mathematical Economics. rev. ed. Reghinos D. Theocharis. LC 80-16638. 1980. lib. bdg. 32.50x (ISBN 0-87991-808-X). Porcupine Pr.

Early Diagenesis: A Theoretical Approach. Robert A. Berner. LC 80-7510. (Princeton Series in Geochemistry: No. 1). (Illus.). 256p. 1980. 25.00x (ISBN 0-691-08258-8); pap. 9.50 (ISBN 0-691-08260-X). Princeton U Pr.

Early Disorder. Rebecca Josephs. 1980. 10.95 (ISBN 0-374-14579-2). FS&G.

Early Domestic Architecture of Connecticut. John F. Kelly. (Illus.). 13.50 (ISBN 0-8446-2363-6). Peter Smith.

Early Draft of John Stuart Mill's "Autobiography". Ed. by Jack Stillinger. LC 61-62769. 1961. 10.00 o.p. (ISBN 0-252-72386-4). U of Ill Pr.

Early Drawings of Charles Edouard Jeanneret le Corbusier 1902-1908. Mary P. Sekler. LC 76-23726. (Outstanding Dissertations in the Fine Arts Ser.). 1978. lib. bdg. 80.00x (ISBN 0-8240-2728-0). Garland Pub.

Early Earth. John C. Whitcomb. 1972. pap. 3.95 (ISBN 0-8010-9524-7). Baker Bk.

Early Eighteenth Century English Glass. Frank Davis. (Country Life Collectors Guides Ser). 1972. 4.95 (ISBN 0-600-43601-2). Transatlantic.

Early Electrodynamics. R. A. Tricker. 1965. 15.00 (ISBN 0-08-010794-X); pap. 7.50 (ISBN 0-08-010793-1). Pergamon.

Early English Carols. 2nd ed. Ed. by Richard L. Greene. 1977. 85.00x (ISBN 0-19-812715-4). Oxford U Pr.

Early English Christian Poetry. Tr. by Charles W. Kennedy. 1963. pap. 5.95 (ISBN 0-19-500246-6, GB94, GB). Oxford U Pr.

Early English Meals & Manners. Ed. by Frederick J. Furnival. LC 73-81154. 1969. Repr. of 1868 ed. 32.00 (ISBN 0-8103-3853-X). Gale.

Early English Stages, Vol. III: Plays & Their Makers to 1576. Glynne Wickham. (Early English Stages Ser.). 1980. 22.50x o.p. (ISBN 0-231-08938-4). Columbia U Pr.

Early English Stages: 1300 to 1660, 2 vols. Glynne W. Wickham. Incl. 1300 to 1576. Vol. 1. 20.00x o.p. (ISBN 0-231-08935-X); 1576 to 1660. Vol. 2, Pt. 1. 30.00x (ISBN 0-231-08936-8); Vol. 2, Pt. 2. 30.00x (ISBN 0-231-08937-6). (Illus.). 1959. Columbia U Pr.

Early English Travellers in India. 2nd rev. ed. R. C. Prasad. 391p. 1980. text ed. 27.00 (ISBN 0-8426-1649-7). Verry.

Early Experience & Visual Information Processing Perceptual & Reading Disorders. Brain Sciences Committee - Division Of Medical Sciences. LC 72-605763. (Illus.). 1970. text ed. 10.75 o.p. (ISBN 0-309-01765-3). Natl Acad Pr.

Early Experience: Myth & Evidence. Ed. by Ann M. Clarke & A. D. Clarke. LC 76-21992. 1979. pap. text ed. 7.95 (ISBN 0-02-905690-X). Free Pr.

Early Experience: Myth & Evidence. Ed. by Ann M. Clarke & A. D. Clarke. LC 76-21992. 1977. 13.95 o.s.i. (ISBN 0-02-905630-6). Free Pr.

Early Experiences. Roy Richards. LC 77-82994. (Science 5-13 Ser.). (Illus.). 1977. pap. text ed. 9.30 (ISBN 0-356-04005-4). Raintree Child.

Early Explorations. Margaret Collis. LC 77-83012. (Using the Environment Ser.). (Illus.). 1977. pap. text ed. 9.30 (ISBN 0-356-04353-3). Raintree Child.

Early Feature Films: A Pictorial Survey of Fifty American Classics, Nineteen Twelve to Nineteen Twenty. Anthony Slide & Edward Wagenknecht. (Illus.). 176p. (Orig.). 1980. pap. 6.95 (ISBN 0-486-23985-3). Dover.

Early Feminine Development: Current Psychoanalytic Views. Dale Mandell. 1981. text ed. write for info. (ISBN 0-89335-135-0). Spectrum Pub.

Early Flemish Painters: Notices of Their Lives & Works. J. A. Crowe & G. B. Cavalcaselle. Ed. by Sydney J. Freedberg. LC 77-18679. (Connoisseurship, Criticism, & Art History Ser.: Vol. 6). 383p. 1979. lib. bdg. 38.00 (ISBN 0-8240-3263-2). Garland Pub.

Early Floral Engravings. Emmanuel Sweerts. Ed. by E. F. Bleiler. LC 73-76963. (Illus.). 256p. 1976. pap. 6.95 (ISBN 0-486-23038-4). Dover.

Early Foundations for Japan's Twentieth Century Economic Emergence. Soji Mizuno. Date not set. 8.95 (ISBN 0-533-04541-X). Vantage.

Early French Parody Noel. Adrienne F. Block. Ed. by George Buelow. (Studies in Musicology). 430p. 1981. 39.95 (ISBN 0-8357-1123-4, Pub. by UMI Res Pr). Univ Microfilms.

Early Georgian Portraits, 2 vols. John Kerslake. (Illus.). 800p. Set. 160.00 (ISBN 0-312-22476-1). St. Martin.

Early German Epigram: A Study in Baroque Poetry. R. K. Angress. LC 70-111501. (Studies in Germanic Languages & Literatures: No. 2). 136p. 1971. 9.00x (ISBN 0-8131-1231-1). U Pr of Ky.

Early German Music in Philadelphia. Robert R. Drummond. LC 74-125068. (Music Ser). 1970. Repr. of 1910 ed. lib. bdg. 14.50 (ISBN 0-306-70005-0). Da Capo.

Early Germanic Kingship in England & on the Continent. J. M. Wallace-Hadrill. (Oxford Lectures Ser). 1971. 22.50x (ISBN 0-19-821491-X). Oxford U Pr.

Early Greek Philosophy. 4th ed. John Burnet. 1963. Repr. of 1930 ed. 19.50x (ISBN 0-06-490783-X). B&N.

Early Greek Warfare. P. A. Greenhalgh. LC 72-87437. 228p. 1973. 32.50 (ISBN 0-521-20056-3). Cambridge U Pr.

Early Growth of Logic in the Child: Classification & Seriation. Barbel Inhelder & Jean Piaget. Orig. Title: Genesedes Structures Logiques Elementaires. 1970. text ed. 16.25x (ISBN 0-391-00124-8). Humanities.

Early Guitar: A History & Handbook. James Tyler. (Early Music Ser.). (Illus.). 176p. (Orig.). 1980. pap. text ed. 22.95x (ISBN 0-19-323182-4). Oxford U Pr.

Early Hanoverian Age: 1714-1760 Commentaries of an Era. A. F. Scott. (Illus.). 175p. 1980. 20.00x (ISBN 0-7099-0145-3, Pub. by Croom Helm Ltd England). Biblio Dist.

Early Hawaiians: An Initial Study of Skeletal Remains from Mokapu, Oahu. Charles E. Snow. LC 72-81317. (Illus.). 192p. 1974. 17.50x (ISBN 0-8131-1277-X). U Pr of Ky.

Early Hebrew Orthography: A Study of the Epigraphic Evidence. Frank M. Cross, Jr. & David N. Freedman. (American Oriental Ser.: Vol. 36). 1952. pap. 9.00x (ISBN 0-686-00019-6). Am Orient Soc.

Early Helpers of God. Maureen Curley. (Children of the Kingdom Activities Ser.). (gr. 1-4). 1975. 7.95 (ISBN 0-686-13685-3). Pflaum Pr.

Early Histological Diagnosis of Cervical Cancer. Erich Burghardt. LC 79-176203. (Major Problem in Obstetrics & Gynecology Ser.: Vol. 6). (Illus.). 1973. text ed. 27.00 (ISBN 0-7216-2175-9). Saunders.

Early History & Growth of Calcutta. rev. ed. K. Deb. 1978. 12.00x o.p. (ISBN 0-8364-0252-9). South Asia Bks.

Early History of French Painting. Maurice De Fontenelle. (Illus.). 121p. 1981. 39.55 (ISBN 0-930582-93-4). Gloucester Art.

Early History of Motley County. Harry H. Campbell. 6.95 (ISBN 0-685-48802-0). Nortex Pr.

Early History of Panna Maria, Texas. T. Lindsay Baker. (Graduate Studies: No. 9). (Illus., Orig.). 1975. pap. 4.00 (ISBN 0-89672-016-0). Tex Tech Pr.

Early History of Planck's Radiation Law. Hans Kangro. LC 76-40534. 1976. 39.50x (ISBN 0-8448-1029-0). Crane-Russak Co.

Early History of Rome. Livy. Tr. by Aubrey DeSelincourt. lib. bdg. 10.50x (ISBN 0-88307-393-5). Gannon.

Early History of Syria & Palestine. Lewis B. Paton. LC 79-2878. (Illus.). 302p. 1981. Repr. of 1901 ed. 26.50 (ISBN 0-8305-0046-4). Hyperion Conn.

Early History of the Dekkan. R. Bhandarkar. 1975. Repr. 8.50x o.p. (ISBN 0-88386-670-6). South Asia Bks.

Early History of the Rumanian Language. Andre Du Nay. LC 79-115770. (Edward Sapir Monograph Series in Language, Culture, & Cognition: No. 3). (Illus.). xii, 275p. 1977. pap. 7.00x (ISBN 0-933104-03-0). Jupiter Pr.

Early History of Veterinary Literature & Its British Development. limited ed. Frederick Smith. (Illus.). 140.00 (ISBN 0-85131-026-5, Dist. by Sporting Book Center). J A Allen.

Early Identification of Emotionally Handicapped Children in School. 2nd ed. Eli M. Bower. (American Lecture in Psychology). (Illus.). 276p. 1974. pap. 14.75 photocopy ed., spiral (ISBN 0-398-00202-9). C C Thomas.

Early Illustrations & Views of American Architecture. Edmund V. Gillon, Jr. (Illus.). 1971. pap. 8.95 (ISBN 0-486-22750-2). Dover.

Early Industrial Revolution. Eric Pawson. 1979. 29.95 o.p. (ISBN 0-7134-1625-4, Pub. by Batsford England); pap. 16.95 o.p. (ISBN 0-7134-1626-2). David & Charles.

Early Ionians. G. L. Huxley. 1966. pap. text ed. 8.50x (ISBN 0-7165-2065-6). Humanities.

Early Irish Lyrics: Eighth to Twelfth Century. Ed. by Gerard Murphy. 1956. 24.00x (ISBN 0-19-815207-8). Oxford U Pr.

Early Islam. Desmond Stewart. LC 67-27863. (Great Ages of Man Ser.). (gr. 6 up). 1967. PLB 11.97 (ISBN 0-8094-0377-3, Pub. by Time-Life). Silver.

Early Islamic Ceramics. Helen Philon. (Catalogue of Islamic Art in the Benaki Museum: Vol. 1). (Illus.). 376p. 1981. 147.50x (ISBN 0-85667-098-7, Pub. by Sotheby Parke Bernet England). Biblio Dist.

Early Italina Love Stories Taken from the Originals. Una Taylor. 144p. 1980. Repr. of 1899 ed. lib. bdg. 50.00 (ISBN 0-89760-882-8). Telegraph Bks.

Early Japan. Jonathan N. Leonard. (Great Ages of Man Ser). (Illus.). 1968. 12.95 (ISBN 0-8094-0360-9). Time-Life.

Early Japan. Jonathan N. Leonard. LC 68-27297. (Great Ages of Man). (Illus.). (gr. 6 up). 1968. PLB 11.97 (ISBN 0-8094-0382-X, Pub. by Time-Life). Silver.

Early Japanese History (40 B. C.-A. D. 1167, 2 vols. Robert K. Reischauer & Jean Reischauer. 19.00 (ISBN 0-8446-1381-9). Peter Smith.

Early Jewish Hermeneutic in Palestine. Daniel Patte. LC 75-22225. (Society of Biblical Literature. Dissertation Ser.). 350p. 1975. pap. 9.00 (ISBN 0-89130-015-5, 060122). Scholars Pr Ca.

Early Kings of Israel. Gordon Lindsay. (Old Testament Ser.). 1.25 (ISBN 0-89985-147-9). Christ Nations.

Early Kings of Judah. Gordon Lindsay. (Old Testament Ser.). 1.25 (ISBN 0-89985-146-0). Christ Nations.

Early Life History of Marine Fish: The Egg Stage. Gotthilf Hempel. LC 79-14549. (Washington Sea Grant). 86p. 1980. pap. 7.50 (ISBN 0-295-95672-0). U of Wash Pr.

Early Life of David. Gordon Lindsay. (Old Testament Ser.). 1.25 (ISBN 0-89985-141-X). Christ Nations.

Early Life of George Eliot. Mary H. Deakin. 188p. 1980. Repr. of 1913 ed. lib. bdg. 30.00 (ISBN 0-8495-1121-6). Arden Lib.

Early Liturgy, to the Time of Gregory the Great. Josef A. Jungmann. Tr. by Francis A. Brunner. (Liturgical Studies Ser.: No. 7). 1959. 10.95 (ISBN 0-268-00083-2). U of Notre Dame Pr.

Early Lives of Melville: Nineteenth-Century Biographical Sketches & Their Authors. Merton M. Sealts, Jr. LC 74-5906. 320p. 1975. 25.00x (ISBN 0-299-06570-7). U of Wis Pr.

Early Madhyamika in India & China. Richard H. Robinson. 1977. text ed. 13.50x o.p. (ISBN 0-8426-0904-0). Verry.

Early Man. rev. ed. F. Clark Howell. LC 65-20165. (Life Nature Library). (Illus.). (gr. 5 up). 1973. PLB 8.97 o.p. (ISBN 0-8094-0636-5, Pub. by Time-Life). Silver.

Early Man. F. Clark Howell. (Young Readers Library). (Illus.). 1977. lib. bdg. 7.95 (ISBN 0-686-51087-9). Silver.

Early Man in America: Readings from Scientific American. Intro. by Richard S. MacNeish. LC 72-12251. (Illus.). 1973. text ed. 15.95x (ISBN 0-7167-0864-7); pap. text ed. 7.95x (ISBN 0-7167-0863-9). W H Freeman.

Early Man in Britain & Ireland. Alex Morrison. 1980. write for info. (ISBN 0-312-22463-X). St Martin.

Early Management of Hearing Loss. George T. Mencher & Sanford Gerber. 1980. write for info. (ISBN 0-8089-1346-8). Grune.

Early Medieval Art. John Beckwith. (World of Art Ser.). (Illus.). 1964. pap. 9.95 (ISBN 0-19-519922-7). Oxford U Pr.

Early Medieval Sequence. Richard L. Crocker. LC 74-84143. 1977. 38.50x (ISBN 0-520-02847-3). U of Cal Pr.

Early Meisterlieder of Hans Sachs. Frances H. Ellis. LC 73-81163. (Illus.). 340p. 1974. 20.00x (ISBN 0-253-31853-X). Ind U Pr.

Early Middle Ages. Robert Brentano. LC 64-21204. 1964. pap. text ed. 6.95 (ISBN 0-02-904670-X). Free Pr.

Early Middle English Verse & Prose. 2nd ed. Ed. by J. A. Bennett & G. V. Smithers. 1968. text ed. 22.50x (ISBN 0-19-811493-1). Oxford U Pr.

Early Middle Eocene Flora from the Yellowstone-Absaroka Volcanic Province North-Western Wind River Basin, Wyoming. Harry D. MacGinitie. (Publications in Geological Sciences, Vol. 108). 1974. pap. 10.75x (ISBN 0-520-09496-4). U of Cal Pr.

Early Modern Town. Ed. by Peter Clark. LC 76-7041. (Open University set book). 1976. text ed. 18.95x (ISBN 0-582-48404-9); pap. text ed. 8.95x (ISBN 0-582-48405-7). Longman.

Early Morning Rounds: A Portrait of a Hospital. Burnham Holmes. LC 80-69995. (Illus.). 128p. (gr. 7 up). 1981. 9.95 (ISBN 0-590-07611-6, Four Winds). Schol Bk Serv.

Early Muslim Dogma. M. Cook. 256p. Date not set. 49.50 (ISBN 0-521-23379-8). Cambridge U Pr.

Early Native Americans. Ed. by D. L. Browman. (World Anthropology Ser.). 1979. text ed. 48.25x (ISBN 90-279-7940-5). Mouton.

Early Near Eastern Seals in the Yale Babylonian Collection. Briggs Buchanan. Ed. by Ulla Kasten. LC 75-43309. (Illus.). 520p. 1981. text ed. 65.00 (ISBN 0-300-01852-5). Yale U Pr.

Early Neo-Classicism in France. Svend Eriksen. 1974. 98.00 (ISBN 0-571-08717-5, Pub. by Faber & Faber). Merrimack Bk Serv.

Early Netherlandish Painting, 2 vols, Vols. 1 & 2. Erwin Panofsky. (Icon Edition). (Illus.). 1971. Vol. 1. pap. 11.95x (ISBN 0-06-430002-1, IN-2, HarpT); Vol. 2. pap. 8.95x (ISBN 0-06-430003-X, IN-3). Har-Row.

Early Netherlandish Triptychs: A Study in Patronage. Shirley N. Blum. LC 68-10902. (California Studies in the History of Art: No. XIII). (Illus.). 1969. 65.00x (ISBN 0-520-01444-8). U of Cal Pr.

Early Nevada: The Period of Exploraton Seventeen Seventy-Six to Eighteen Forty-Eight. F. N. Fletcher. LC 80-19035. (Vintage Nevada Ser). (Illus.). xi, 195p. 1980. pap. 5.25 (ISBN 0-87417-061-3). U of Nev Pr.

Early New England Catechisms. Wilberforce Eames. LC 68-31081. 1969. Repr. of 1898 ed. 15.00 (ISBN 0-8103-3478-X). Gale.

Early New England Psalmody: An Historical Appreciation, 1620-1820. Hamilton C. MacDougall. LC 79-87398. (Music Reprint Ser). 1969. Repr. of 1940 ed. lib. bdg. 19.50 (ISBN 0-306-71542-2). Da Capo.

Early Pennsylvania Hardware. Herbert F. Schiffer. (Illus.). 64p. 1966. pap. 3.75 (ISBN 0-916838-42-0). Schiffer.

Early Physicians of the West. Frederick Eberson. LC 79-63659. 1979. 6.95 (ISBN 0-912760-92-3). Valkyrie Pr.

Early Piano. C. F. Colt & Anthony Miall. (Illus.). 160p. 1981. 75.00x (ISBN 0-389-20187-1). B&N.

Early Pliocene Marine Climate Environment of the Eastern Ventura Basin, Southern California. John Philip Kern. (U. C. Publ. in Geological Sciences: Vol. 96). pap. 10.00x (ISBN 0-520-09424-7). U of Cal Pr.

Early Poems & the Fiction. Walt Whitman. Ed. by Thomas L. Brasher. LC 60-15980. (Illus.). 1963. 25.00x (ISBN 0-8147-0441-7). NYU Pr.

Early Poems of Yvor Winters Nineteen-Twenty to Nineteen-Twenty-Eight. Yvor Winters. LC 66-25962. 148p. 1966. 4.95x (ISBN 0-8040-0072-7). Swallow.

Early Poems 1935-1955. Octavio Paz. Tr. by Muriel Rukeyser et al from Span. LC 72-93981. (Poetry Ser.). Orig. Title: Selected Poems. 160p. 1973. 7.95x (ISBN 0-253-31867-X). Ind U Pr.

Early Poetry of W. B. Yeats: The Poetic Quest. Thomas L. Byrd, Jr. (National University Pubns. Literary Criticism Ser.). 1978. 12.00 (ISBN 0-8046-9184-3). Kennikat.

Early Political Caricature in America & the History of the United States. William R. Garrett. (Illus.). 1979. 31.45 (ISBN 0-89266-164-X). Am Classical Coll Pr.

Early Political Machinery in the United States. G. D. Luetscher. LC 70-155356. (Studies in American History & Government Ser.). 1971. Repr. of 1903 ed. lib. bdg. 20.00 (ISBN 0-306-70187-1). Da Capo.

Early Portland Or, Stumptown Triumphant. Eugene E. Snyder. (Illus.). 1970. 7.95 (ISBN 0-8323-0218-X); pap. 4.85 o.p. (ISBN 0-685-06924-9). Binford.

Early Printed Books to the End of the Sixteenth Century: A Bibliography of Bibliographies. 2nd rev. & enl. ed. Theodore Besterman. 344p. 1969. 21.50x (ISBN 0-87471-008-1). Rowman.

Early Reading & Writing. Ramin Minovi. (Classroom Close-Ups Ser.). 1976. text ed. 10.50x o.p. (ISBN 0-04-372016-1); pap. text ed. 4.95x o.p. (ISBN 0-04-372017-X). Allen Unwin.

Early Reading Development. Janet Friedlander & Elizabeth H. Grunden. 1981. text ed. 52.80 (ISBN 0-06-318161-4, IntlDept). Har-Row.

Early Recollections & Life of Dr. James Still, 1812-1885. James Still. (Illus.). 288p. 1973. Repr. 19.50 (ISBN 0-8135-0769-3). Rutgers U Pr.

Early Recollections: Their Use in Diagnosis & Psychotherapy. Harry A. Olson. (Illus.). 416p. 1979. text ed. 29.75 (ISBN 0-398-03826-0). C C Thomas.

Early Reform in American Higher Education. Ed. by David N. Portman. LC 72-186982. 1972. 16.95x (ISBN 0-911012-41-9). Nelson-Hall.

Early Reminiscences, 1834-1864. Sabine Baring-Gould. LC 67-23868. 1967. Repr. of 1923 ed. 15.00 (ISBN 0-8103-3049-0). Gale.

Early Retirement: Boon or Bane. Dean Morse & Susan Gray. LC 79-54970. (Conservation of Human Resources Ser.: No. 14). (Illus.). 180p. 1980. text ed. 23.00 (ISBN 0-916672-44-1). Allanheld.

Early Returns: Poems. David Long. 55p. 1981. 15.00 (ISBN 0-918116-21-X); pap. 5.00 (ISBN 0-918116-20-1). Jawbone Pr.

Early Routines. William Burroughs. Ed. by James Grauerholz & Jeffrey Miller. LC 79-54919. 1981. signed limited ed. 40.00 (ISBN 0-932274-03-X); pap. 10.00 (ISBN 0-932274-02-1). Cadmus Eds.

Early Russian Literature. John Fennell & Antony Stokes. 1974. 26.75x (ISBN 0-520-02343-9). U of Cal Pr.

Early Scottish Limited Companies, Eighteen Fifty-Six to Eighteen Ninety-Five. Peter L. Payne. 144p. 1981. 22.00x (Pub. by Scottish Academic Pr Scotland). Columbia U Pr.

Early Sculpture of Bartolomeo Ammanati. Peter Kinney. LC 75-23798. (Outstanding Dissertations in the Fine Arts - 16th Century). (Illus.). 1976. lib. bdg. 41.00 (ISBN 0-8240-1993-8). Garland Pub.

Early Sculpture of Picasso, 1901-1914. Ron Johnson. LC 75-23795. (Outstanding Dissertations in the Fine Arts - 20th Century). (Illus.). 1976. lib. bdg. 41.00 (ISBN 0-8240-1990-3). Garland Pub.

Early Settlers of Nantucket: Sixteen Fifty-Nine to Eighteen Fifty. Compiled by Lydia S. Hinchman. LC 80-54078. (Illus.). 346p. 1981. Repr. of 1926 ed. 35.00 (ISBN 0-8048-1354-X). C E Tuttle.

Early Sino-American Relations (1841-1912) The Collected Articles of Earl Swisher. Ed. by Kenneth Rea. LC 77-13252. 1977. lib. bdg. 21.00 o.p. (ISBN 0-89158-305-X). Westview.

Early Solar Physics. A. J. Meadows. LC 74-103021. 1970. 35.00 (ISBN 0-08-006653-4); pap. 11.75 (ISBN 0-08-006654-2). Pergamon.

Early Spanish Ballad. David W. Foster. (World Authors Ser.: Spain: No. 185). lib. bdg. 10.95 (ISBN 0-8057-2288-2). Twayne.

Early Spanish Main. Carl O. Sauer. 1969. pap. 8.95 (ISBN 0-520-01415-4, CAL182). U of Cal Pr.

Early Sparta. G. L. Huxley. 164p. 1970. Repr. of 1962 ed. 17.00x (ISBN 0-7165-0596-7, Pub. by Irish Academic Pr Ireland). Biblio Dist.

Early Supports for Family Life: A Social Work Experiment. Ludwig L. Geismar et al. LC 70-188665. 1972. 10.00 (ISBN 0-8108-0476-X). Scarecrow.

Early Syntactic Development: A Cross Linguistic Study with Special Reference to Finnish. Melissa Bowerman. (Cambridge Studies in Linguistics: No. 11). 42.50 (ISBN 0-521-20019-9); pap. 10.95x (ISBN 0-521-09797-5). Cambridge U Pr.

Early Tahiti As the Explorers Saw It. Edwin N. Ferdon. LC 80-26469. 1981. text ed. 19.50x (ISBN 0-8165-0708-2); pap. 12.50 (ISBN 0-8165-0720-1). U of Ariz Pr.
Early Theological Writings. G. W. Hegel. Tr. by T. M. Knox & R. Kroner. (Works in Continental Philosophy Ser). 1971. pap. 6.50x (ISBN 0-8122-1022-0, Pa. Paperbacks). U of Pa Pr.
Early Tin Plate Model Railways. Udo Becher. (Illus.). 180p. 1980. 33.95 (ISBN 0-8038-1964-1). Hastings.
Early to Rise: A Suffolk Morning. Hugh Barrett. 1967. 6.95 (ISBN 0-571-08140-1, Pub. by Faber & Faber). Merrimack Bk Serv.
Early Town on the Deh Luran Plain: Excavations at Tepe Farukhabad. Henry T. Wright, III. (Memoirs Ser.: No. 13). 1980. pap. write for info. (ISBN 0-932206-87-5). U Mich Mus Anthro.
Early Traveiers in Mexico (1534 to 1816) William Mayer. (Illus.). 20.00 (ISBN 0-911268-31-6). Rogers Bk.
Early Twentieth Century Lighting Fixtures. (Illus.). 1980. pap. 11.95 (ISBN 0-89145-143-9). Collector Bks.
Early Vasas. Michael Roberts. (Illus.). 1968. 59.95 (ISBN 0-521-06930-0). Cambridge U Pr.
Early Victorian & Other Papers. E S. Haynes. 78p. 1980. Repr. lib. bdg. 25.00 (ISBN 0-89984-287-9). Century Bookbindery.
Early Victorian Architecture in Britain, 2 vols. Henry-Russell Hitchcock. LC 72-151765. (Architecture & Decorative Art Ser.). 658p. 1972. Repr. of 1954 ed. Set. lib. bdg. 65.00 (ISBN 0-306-70195-2). Da Capo.
Early Victorian Portraits, 2 vol. Richard Ormond. (Illus.). 900p. 1980. Set. 160.00 (ISBN 0-312-22480-X). St Martin.
Early Views of India: The Picturesque Journeys of Thomas & William Daniell 1788-1793. Mildred Archer. (Illus.). 240p. 1980. 37.50 (ISBN 0-500-01238-5). Thames Hudson.
Early Virgil. William Berg. 198p. 1974. text ed. 20.75x (ISBN 0-485-11145-4, Athlone Pr). Humanities.
Early Warning. Christopher Fitzsimons. 256p. 1981. pap. 2.25 (ISBN 0-380-50179-1, 50179). Avon.
Early Washington Atlas. Ralph N. Preston. LC 78-57006. (Illus.). 1980. pap. 6.50 (ISBN 0-8323-0311-9). Binford.
Early Window: the Effect of Television on Children & Youth. R. M. Liebert et al. 1976. 21.00 (ISBN 0-08-017091-9); pap. 8.75 (ISBN 0-08-017780-8). Pergamon.
Early Work of Signorelli: 1465-1490. Gloria Kury. LC 77-94701. (Outstanding Dissertations in the Fine Arts Ser.). (Illus.). 1978. lib. bdg. 45.00 (ISBN 0-8240-3233-0). Garland Pub.
Early Works of John Dewey, 1882-1898, 5 vols. MLA-CEAA textual ed. John Dewey. Ed. by Jo Ann Boydston. Incl. Vol. 1 (1882-1888): Collected Essays & Leibniz's New Essays Concerning the Human Understanding. Intro. by Lewis E. Hahn. 493p. 1969 (ISBN 0-8093-0349-3). pap. (ISBN 0-8093-0722-7); Vol. 2 (1887): Psychology. Intro. by Herbert W. Schneider. 420p. 1967 (ISBN 0-8093-0282-9). pap. (ISBN 0-8093-0723-5); Vol. 3 (1889-1892): Collected Essays & Outline of a Critical Theory of Ethics. Intro. by S. Morris Eames. 495p. 1969 (ISBN 0-8093-0402-3). pap. (ISBN 0-8093-0724-3); Vol. 4 (1893-1894): Collected Essays & the Study of Ethics. Intro. by Wayne A. Leys. 463p. 1971 (ISBN 0-8093-0496-1). pap. (ISBN 0-8093-0725-1); Vol. 5 (1895-1898): Collected Essays. Intro. by William R. McKenzie. 670p. 1972. (ISBN 0-8093-0540-2); pap. (ISBN 0-8093-0726-X). LC 67-13938. Vols. 1,3,4. 17.50x (ISBN 0-686-57468-0); Vol. 5. 18.95x (ISBN 0-686-57469-9); Vol. 2. 19.95x; pap. 7.95; pap. 6.95; Vol. 5. pap. 8.95. S Ill U Pr.
Early Writing, 1946-1951. Frank O'Hara. Ed. by Donald Allen. LC 77-652. 1977. 12.00 (ISBN 0-912516-16-X); pap. 4.00 (ISBN 0-912516-17-8). Grey Fox.
Early Writings. Karl Marx. 1963. pap. 3.95 (ISBN 0-07-040671-5, SP). McGraw.
Early Writings in Science & Science Fiction. H. G. Wells. Ed. by Robert M. Philmus & David Hughes. LC 73-91673. 1975. 18.50x (ISBN 0-520-02679-9). U of Cal Pr.
Early Years of Lenin. Nikolay Valentinov. Tr. by Rolf H. Theen from Rus. 1980. cancelled (ISBN 0-915042-05-3). Lib Soc Sci.
Early Years of Modern Civil Engineering. R. S. Kirby. 1932. 47.50x (ISBN 0-685-69833-5). Elliots Bks.
Early Years: Twenty Thousand B.C. to Seventeen Sixty-Three A. D. The Educational Research Council. (American Adventure Concepts & Inquiry Ser.). (gr. 8). 1975. pap. text ed. 8.96 (ISBN 0-205-04628-2, 804628X). Allyn.
Earned Income Tax Credit: Welfare Reform or Tax Relief? an Analysis of Alternative Proposals. Wayne L. Hoffman. (Welfare Reform Policy Analysis Ser.: No. 5). 52p. 1978. pap. 3.50 (ISBN 0-87766-235-5, 23300). Urban Inst.
Earning & Learning. Robert L. Bennett. LC 80-65003. (Illus.). 256p. (Orig.). 1980. pap. 7.95 (ISBN 0-936148-01-2). Action Link.
Earning One's Livelihood in Mahuva. D. P. Pandit. 5.25x o.p. (ISBN 0-210-22622-6). Asia.
Earning Your Living with Animals. Jeremy Mallinson. LC 74-81067. 176p. 1975. 10.50 (ISBN 0-7153-6760-9). David & Charles.
Earp Brothers of Tombstone: The Story of Mrs. Virgil Earp. Frank Waters. LC 75-38611. (Illus.). viii, 247p. 1976. 14.95x (ISBN 0-8032-0873-1); pap. 3.75 (ISBN 0-8032-5838-0, BB 618, Bison). U of Nebr Pr.
Earps Talk. Ed. by Alford E. Turner. LC 80-65456. (Illus.). 193p. 1979. 15.50 (ISBN 0-932702-05-8); collector's edition 75.00 (ISBN 0-932702-06-6). Creative Texas.
EARS. William Liddle. (Illus., Orig.). (gr. k-3). 1974. student's bk. 3.60 (ISBN 0-87892-854-5); tchr's handbook 3.60 (ISBN 0-87892-856-1); tapes 84.90 (ISBN 0-87892-857-X). Economy Co.
Ears of the Jungle. Pierre Boulle. LC 72-83350. 230p. 1972. 8.95 (ISBN 0-8149-0720-2). Vanguard.
Earth. Arthur Beiser. (Young Readers Library). (Illus.). 1977. lib. bdg. 7.95 (ISBN 0-686-51088-7). Silver.
Earth. Arthur Beiser. LC 62-16141. (Life Nature Library). 1970. lib. bdg. 8.97 o.p. (ISBN 0-8094-0618-7). Silver.
Earth. 6th ed. Harold Jeffreys. LC 74-19527. (Illus.). 600p. 1976. 83.50 (ISBN 0-521-20648-0). Cambridge U Pr.
Earth. 2nd ed. Frank Press & Raymond Siever. LC 77-25209. (Illus.). 1978. text ed. 21.95x (ISBN 0-7167-0289-4); instr' guide avail. W H Freeman.
Earth. Emile Zola. 1960. 13.95 (ISBN 0-236-30863-7, Pub. by Paul Elek). Merrimack Bk Serv.
Earth: A Topical Geography. 2nd ed. H. J. De Blij. LC 79-18051. 1980. text ed. 21.95 (ISBN 0-471-05169-1); tchr's manual (ISBN 0-471-06358-4). Wiley.
Earth & Cosmos. Robert S. Kandel. (Illus.). 1980. 35.00 (ISBN 0-08-025016-5); pap. 16.75 (ISBN 0-08-023086-5). Pergamon.
Earth & Earth-Rock Dams: Engineering Problems of Design & Construction. James L. Sherard et al. LC 63-14068. 1963. 49.95 (ISBN 0-471-78547-4, Pub. by Wiley-Interscience). Wiley.
Earth & Its Environment. Walter H. Hesse & Robert L. McDonald. 1974. text ed. 18.95x (ISBN 0-8221-0115-7). Dickenson.
Earth & Its Oceans. A. Duxbury. LC 73-131202. (Earth Science Ser.). 1971. 19.95 (ISBN 0-201-01616-8). A-W.
Earth Angels. Susan Cahill. 1978. pap. 1.95 o.p. (ISBN 0-445-04205-2). Popular Lib.
Earth Changes Update. Hugh L. Cayce. 134p. (Orig.). 1980. pap. 4.95 (ISBN 0-87604-121-7). ARE Pr.
Earth Dancing. Daniela Gioseffi. (Illus.). 224p. 1980. pap. 13.95 o.p. (ISBN 0-8117-2116-7). Stackpole.
Earth Dancing: Mother Nature's Oldest Rite. Daniela Gioseffi. 224p. 1980. pap. 13.95 (ISBN 0-8117-2116-7). Stackpole.
Earth Day Reconsidered. John Baden. LC 80-81670. 1980. 4.00 (ISBN 0-89195-028-1). Heritage Found.
Earth Environment. John J. Fagan, Jr. (Illus.). 288p. 1974. pap. 8.95 ref. ed. o.p. (ISBN 0-13-222752-5). P-H.
Earth Father-Sky Father: The Changing Concept of Fathering. Arthur Colman & Libby Colman. (Illus.). 224p. 1981. 12.95t (ISBN 0-13-223032-1, Spec); pap. 5.95b (ISBN 0-13-223024-0). P-H.
Earth in Crisis: An Introduction to the Earth Sciences. Thomas L. Burrus & Herbert J. Spiegel. LC 75-22029. (Illus.). 440p. 1976. 15.95 o.p. (ISBN 0-8016-0918-6). Mosby.
Earth in Crisis: An Introduction to the Earth Sciences. 2nd ed. Thomas L. Burrus & Herbert J. Spiegel. LC 79-19596. (Illus.). 1980. 19.95 (ISBN 0-8016-0902-X). Mosby.
Earth in Motion: The Concept of Plate Tectonics. R. V. Fodor. LC 77-12568. (Illus.). (gr. 3-7). 1978. 6.95 (ISBN 0-688-22135-1); PLB 6.67 (ISBN 0-688-32135-6). Morrow.
Earth in Space. John Polgreen & Cathleen Polgreen. 1963. 2.95 o.p. (ISBN 0-394-80127-X, BYR). Random.
Earth in the Heavens. L. Edward Johndro. 1979. pap. 6.95 (ISBN 0-87728-486-5). Weiser.
Earth, Inc. R. Buckminster Fuller. LC 73-75587. 192p. 1973. pap. 2.95 (ISBN 0-385-01825-8, Anch). Doubleday.
Earth Is but One Country. John Huddleston. (Illus.). 1978. 15.00 (ISBN 0-900125-31-4, 7-32-31, Pub. by British Baha'i Pub Trust). Baha'i.
Earth Is Sore: Native Americans on Nature. Aline Amon. LC 80-36854. (Illus.). 96p. 1981. PLB 9.95 (ISBN 0-689-30798-5). Atheneum.
Earth Is the Lord's. Taylor Caldwell. 1979. pap. 2.75 (ISBN 0-515-05094-6). Jove Pubns.
Earth Is the Lord's. Abraham J. Heschel. 109p. 1978. 7.50 o.p. (ISBN 0-374-50958-1). FS&G.
Earth Is the Strangest Planet. Ed. by Robert Silverberg. LC 76-55728. (Nelson's Science Fiction Ser.). (gr. 8 up). 1977. 7.95 o.p. (ISBN 0-525-66401-7). Elsevier-Nelson.
Earth: Its Birth & Growth. Minoru Ozima. Tr. by J. F. Wakabayashi. (Illus.). 180p. Date not set. price not set (ISBN 0-521-23500-6); pap. price not set (ISBN 0-521-28005-2). Cambridge U Pr.
Earth Might Be Fair: Reflections on Ethics, Religion & Ecology. Ian Barbour. LC 73-167916. 1972. pap. text ed. 7.95 (ISBN 0-13-222679-0). P-H.
Earth Movers. David Grinstead. 1980. 10.95 (ISBN 0-316-32892-8, Pub. by Atlantic Little Brown). Little.
Earth Moving Machines. William D. Stone. LC 78-26947. (Machine World Ser.). (Illus.). (gr. 2-4). 1979. PLB 9.95 (ISBN 0-8172-1329-5). Raintree Pubs.
Earth: Our Physical Environment. William Donn. LC 79-37431. 621p. 1972. 26.95 (ISBN 0-471-21785-9). Wiley.
Earth: Planet Number Three. Franklyn M. Branley. LC 66-12668. (Exploring Our Universe Ser.). (Illus.). (gr. 7 up). 1966. 8.95 (ISBN 0-690-25022-3, TYC-J). T Y Crowell.
Earth Power: The Story of Geothermal Energy. Madeleine Yates. LC 79-25155. (Illus.). 64p. (gr. 4-7). 1980. 7.95g (ISBN 0-687-11450-0). Abingdon.
Earth Resources. 2nd ed. B. Skinner. 1976. pap. 7.95 (ISBN 0-13-223008-9). P-H.
Earth Resources, Energy & the Environment. Douglas G. Brookins. (Illus.). 160p. (Orig.). 1981. pap. text ed. 6.95 (ISBN 0-675-08113-0). Merrill.
Earth Science. David Berey. LC 57-58736. (High School Regents Exams & Answer Ser.). (gr. 9-12). 1976. pap. 3.95 (ISBN 0-8120-0194-X). Barron.
Earth Science. 3rd ed. John F. Lounsbury & Lawrence Ogden. LC 78-21130. 1979. text ed. 19.50 scp (ISBN 0-06-044059-7, HarpC); inst. manual avail. Har-Row.
Earth Science. 2nd ed. Edward Tarbuck & Fred Lutgens. 1979. text ed. 19.95 (ISBN 0-675-08303-6); instructor's manual 3.95 (ISBN 0-686-67288-7). Merrill.
Earth Science: Intermediate Level. Constantine Constant. (gr. 7-10). 1972. wkbk. ed. 7.08 (ISBN 0-87720-154-4). AMSCO Sch.
Earth Science Investigations. Irving L. Horowitz. (gr. 9-12). 1973. pap. text ed. 7.08 (ISBN 0-87720-155-2). AMSCO Sch.
Earth Sciences, 3 vols. Royal Institution Library of Science. Ed. by W. L. Bragg & S. K. Runcorn. LC 74-169065. 1592p. 1971. Set. 79.95 (ISBN 0-470-74389-1). Halsted Pr.
Earth, Sea & Air: A Survey of the Geophysical Sciences. 2nd ed. J. Spar. (gr. 9-12). 1965. pap. 8.50 (ISBN 0-201-07093-6). A-W.
Earth Shelters: The New Way to Live. David Martindale. (Illus.). 160p. 1981. 18.95 (ISBN 0-525-93199-6); pap. 10.95 (ISBN 0-525-93200-3). Dutton.
Earth Ship & Star Song. Ethan I. Shedley. 224p. 1981. pap. 1.95 (ISBN 0-445-04639-2). Popular Lib.
Earth Shook, the Sky Burned. William Bronson. LC 59-6893. 1959. 14.95 (ISBN 0-385-05379-7). Doubleday.
Earth, Space, & Time: An Introduction to Earth Science. John G. Navarra. LC 79-14000. 1980. text ed. 22.95x (ISBN 0-471-63061-6). Wiley.
Earth Surface Sediment Transport. Ian Statham. (Contemporary Problems in Geography Ser.). (Illus.). 1977. 29.95x (ISBN 0-19-874076-X); pap. 6.95x (ISBN 0-19-874077-8). Oxford U Pr.
Earth: The Living Planet. Michael J. Bradshaw. LC 77-946. 1977. text ed. 19.95x (ISBN 0-470-99107-0). Halsted Pr.
Earth, the Stars, & the Bible. Paul M. Steidl. 1979. pap. 5.95 (ISBN 0-8010-8169-6). Baker Bk.
Earth Two. Leo P. Kelley. LC 79-51077. (Space Police Bks.). (Illus.). 64p. (gr. 4 up). 1980. PLB 7.95 (ISBN 0-516-02233-4). Childrens.
Earth Watch. Roger Borsheim. 64p. 1980. 8.00 (ISBN 0-682-49634-0). Exposition.
Earth Will Be Invaded from Outer Space. Arthur Longley. (Orig.). 1981. pap. 4.95 (ISBN 0-88270-505-9). Logos.
Earth Witch. Louise Lawrence. LC 80-8431. 224p. (YA) (gr. 7 up). 1981. 9.95 (ISBN 0-06-023751-1, HarpJ); PLB 9.89g (ISBN 0-06-023752-X). Har-Row.
Earthbreakers. Ernest Haycox. 1976. Repr. of 1952 ed. lib. bdg. 9.95 o.p. (ISBN 0-89190-977-X). Am Repr-Rivercity Pr.
Earthcare: Global Protection of Natural Areas; Proceedings of the Fourteenth Biennial Walderness Conference. Ed. by Edmund Schofield. LC 76-29358. (14th Biennial Wilderness Conference). 1978. 40.00x (ISBN 0-89158-034-4). Westview.
Earthdivers: Tribal Narratives on Mixed Descent. Gerald Vizenor. (Illus.). 195p. 1981. 14.95 (ISBN 0-8166-1048-7). U of Minn Pr.
Earthfasts. William Mayne. (gr. 5 up). 1967. PLB 7.95 o.p. (ISBN 0-525-29008-7). Dutton.
Earthkeeping: Christian Stewardship of Natural Resources. 2nd ed. Ed. by Loren Wilkinson. (Orig.). 1980. pap. 10.95 (ISBN 0-8028-1834-X). Eerdmans.
Earthlight. Arthur C. Clarke. 1975. pap. 1.75 (ISBN 0-345-27273-0). Ballantine.
Earthlike Planets: Surfaces of Mercury, Venus, Earth, Moon, Mars. Bruce Murray et al. LC 80-19608. (Illus.). 1981. text ed. 24.95x (ISBN 0-7167-1148-6); pap. text ed. 14.95x (ISBN 0-7167-1149-4). W H Freeman.
Earthly Paradise: An Autobiography of Colette Drawn from Her Lifetime Writings. Colette. Ed. by Robert Phelps. pap. 9.95 (ISBN 0-685-83818-8). FS&G.
Earthly Pleasures. Roger Swain. (Illus.). 192p. 1981. 10.00 (ISBN 0-684-16657-7, ScribT). Scribner.
Earthly Powers. Anthony Burgess. 1980. 13.95 (ISBN 0-671-41490-9). Bobbs.
Earthly Powers: A Novel. Anthony Burgess. 1980. 15.95 (ISBN 0-671-41490-9). S&S.
Earthly Republic: Italian Humanists on Government & Society. Benjamin G. Kohl & Ronald G. Witt. LC 78-53335. 1978. 22.00x (ISBN 0-8122-7752-X); pap. 9.50x (ISBN 0-8122-1097-2). U of Pa Pr.
Earthman's Burden. Poul Anderson & Gordon R. Dickson. 1979. pap. 1.75 (ISBN 0-380-47993-1, 47993, Camelot). Avon.
Earthquake. John G. Navarra. LC 79-8938. (Illus.). 96p. (gr. 6-7). 1980. 7.95a (ISBN 0-385-15080-6); PLB (ISBN 0-385-15081-4). Doubleday.
Earthquake. Harold Richards. LC 79-13559. (Flame Ser.). 1979. pap. 0.95 (ISBN 0-8127-0240-9). Southern Pub.
Earthquake: Are You Prepared? William G. Obermeyer, Jr. & Pauline M. Jue-Obermeyer. LC 80-50463. (Illus.). 68p. (Orig.). 1980. pap. 2.95 (ISBN 0-936706-01-5). CERA.
Earthquake Country: California. Ed. by Robert Iacopi. LC 78-163736. (Illus.). 160p. 1971. pap. 5.95 (ISBN 0-376-06144-8, Sunset Bks.). Sunset-Lane.
Earthquake Engineering. Robert L. Wiegel et al. (Civil Engineering Ser). 1969. ref. ed. 34.95 (ISBN 0-13-222646-4). P-H.
Earthquake Engineering & Hazards Reduction in China. 1980. 11.50 (ISBN 0-309-02937-6). Natl Acad Pr.
Earthquake Guidelines for Reactor Siting. (Technical Reports Ser.: No. 139). 53p. (Orig.). 1973. pap. 3.25 (ISBN 92-0-125272-2, IDC139, IAEA). Unipub.
Earthquake Man. W. L. Heath. LC 80-20270. 96p. (gr. 6 up). 1980. 7.95 (ISBN 0-8253-0008-8). Beaufort Bks NY.
Earthquake Prediction & Public Policy. Panel on the Public Policy Implications of Earthquake Prediction, Advisory Committee on Emergency Planning, Natl Research Council. LC 75-31953. ix, 142p. 1975. pap. 8.00 (ISBN 0-309-02404-8). Natl Acad Pr.
Earthquake Prediction & Rock Mechanics. Ed. by Max Wyss. (Contributions to Current Research in Geophysics: Vol. 1). 1975. text ed. 60.00x (ISBN 3-7643-0809-5). Renouf.
Earthquake Protection of Essential Building Equipment: Design, Engineering, Installation. Gary L. McGavin. 496p. 1981. 25.00 (ISBN 0-471-06270-7, Pub. by Wiley-Interscience). Wiley.
Earthquake Ready. Virginia Kimball. LC 80-8997. (Illus.). 128p. (Orig.). (gr. 6 up). 1981. pap. 5.95 (ISBN 0-915238-46-2). Peace Pr.
Earthquake Research for the Safer Siting of Critical Facilities. Earthquake Problems Related to the Siting of Critical Facilities, Committee on Seismology. LC 80-82030. 1980. pap. text ed. 5.50 (ISBN 0-309-03082-X). Natl Acad Pr.
Earthquake Risk & Damage Functions: Applications to New Madrid. Ben-Chieh Liu et al. (Special Studies in Earth Sciences). 300p. 1981. lib. bdg. 24.50x (ISBN 0-86531-144-7). Westview.
Earthquakes. Charles Cazeau. LC 73-93549. (Beginning Science Ser.). (Illus.). 32p. (gr. 2-4). 1974. 2.50 o.p. (ISBN 0-695-80474-X); lib. bdg. 2.97 o.p. (ISBN 0-695-40474-1). Follett.
Earthquakes. G. A. Eiby. 209p. 1980. 14.95 (ISBN 0-442-25191-2). Van Nos Reinhold.
Earthquakes: A Natural History. D. S. Halacy, Jr. LC 73-13227. (Illus.). 160p. 1974. 8.50 o.p. (ISBN 0-672-51803-1). Bobbs.

Earthquakes: A Primer. Bruce A. Bolt. LC 77-12908. (Geology Ser.). (Illus.). 1978. pap. text ed. 9.95x (ISBN 0-7167-0057-3). W H Freeman.

Earthquakes & Associated Topics in Relation to Nuclear Power Plant Siting. (Safety Ser.: No. 50-SG-S1). 1979. pap. 10.25 (ISBN 92-0-123879-7, ISP 537, IAEA). Unipub.

Earthquakes & Earth Structure. John H. Hodgson. (Illus.). 1964. text ed. 10.95 (ISBN 0-13-222455-0). P-H.

Earthquakes & the Urban Environment, 3 vols. G. Lennis Berlin. 1980. Vol. 1. 59.95 (ISBN 0-8493-5173-1); Vol. 2. 69.95 (ISBN 0-8493-5174-X); Vol. 3. 78.95 (ISBN 0-8493-5175-8). CRC Pr.

Earthquakes & Volcanoes: Readings from Scientific American. Intro. by Bruce A. Bolt. LC 79-21684. (Illus.). 1980. text ed. 16.95x (ISBN 0-7167-1163-X); pap. text ed. 8.95x (ISBN 0-7167-1164-8). W H Freeman.

Earthquakes: Our Restless Planet. Margaret Reuter. LC 76-45653. (Science Information Ser.). (Illus.). (gr. 4-6). 1977. PLB 8.65 (ISBN 0-8172-0352-4). Raintree Pubs.

Earthrise. Theodore L. Harris et al. (Keys to Reading Ser.). (gr. 6). 1974. pap. text ed. 3.60 (ISBN 0-87892-541-4); resource book 8.85 (ISBN 0-87892-544-9); Master Key (student guide) 3.96 (ISBN 0-87892-545-7); duplicating masters 19.53 (ISBN 0-87892-547-3). Economy Co.

Earth's Age & Geochronology. D. York & R. M. Farquhar. 1972. pap. 14.50 (ISBN 0-08-016387-4). Pergamon.

Earth's Answer: Exploring Planetary Culture at the Lindisfarne Conferences. Ed. by Lindisfarne Association. LC 76-26240. (Illus.). 1977. pap. 6.95 o.s.i. (ISBN 0-06-012632-9, TD276, HarpT). Har-Row.

Earth's Changing Surface. Michael J. Bradshaw et al. LC 77-25024. 1978. pap. text ed. 18.95 (ISBN 0-470-99365-0). Halsted Pr.

Earth's Core. J. A. Jacobs. (International Geophysics Ser.). 1976. 25.00 (ISBN 0-12-378950-8). Acad Pr.

Earth's Crust. Irving Adler & Ruth Adler. LC 63-10011. (Reason Why Ser.). (Illus.). (gr. 3-6). 1963. PLB 7.89 (ISBN 0-381-99971-8, JD-J). John Day.

Earth's Crust. William H. Matthews, 3rd. LC 76-134367. (First Bks). (Illus.). (gr. 4-6). 1971. PLB 4.90 o.p. (ISBN 0-531-00724-3). Watts.

Earth's Earliest Ages. G. H. Pember. LC 75-13928. 1975. 8.95 (ISBN 0-8254-3508-0). Kregel.

Earth's Energy & Mineral Resources. Ed. by Brian J. Skinner. (Earth & Its Inhabitants: Selected Readings from American Scientist Ser.). (Illus.). 200p. 1980. pap. 8.95 (ISBN 0-913232-90-4). W Kaufmann.

Earth's Hidden Mysteries. Carl Cohen. Ed. by Pat McCarthy. (Pal Paperbacks Ser., Kit B). (Illus., Orig.). (gr. 7-12). 1974. pap. text ed. 1.25 (ISBN 0-8374-3506-4). Xerox Ed Pubns.

Earth's History, Structure, & Materials. Ed. by Brian J. Skinner. (Earth & Its Inhabitants: Selected Readings from American Scientist Ser.). (Illus.). 184p. (Orig.). 1980. pap. 8.95 (ISBN 0-913232-89-0). W Kaufmann.

Earth's Shape & Gravity. G. D. Garland. 1965. 21.00 (ISBN 0-08-010823-7); pap. 9.75 (ISBN 0-08-010822-9). Pergamon.

Earth's Story. Gerald Ames & Rose Wyler. LC 66-30640. (Creative Science Ser.). (gr. 4-9). 1967. PLB 7.95 (ISBN 0-87191-012-8). Creative Ed.

Earth's Surface. Walter A. Turber & Robert E. Kilburn. (Exploring Earth Science Program Ser.). (gr. 7-12). 1976. pap. text ed. 5.12 (ISBN 0-205-04742-4, 6947426). Allyn.

Earth's Variable Rotation. K. Lambeck. LC 79-7653. (Cambridge Monographs on Mechanics & Applied Mathematics). (Illus.). 400p. 1980. 92.50 (ISBN 0-521-22769-0). Cambridge U Pr.

Earthwalk. Philip Slater. LC 73-83671. 240p. 1974. pap. 3.95 (ISBN 0-385-03286-2, Anch). Doubleday.

Earthworks. Brian Aldiss. 1980. pap. 1.95 (ISBN 0-686-69267-5, 52159). Avon.

Earthworks: Land Reclamation As Sculture. Ed. by Robert Morris & King County Arts Commision. 71p. 1980. pap. text ed. 5.95 (ISBN 0-932216-04-8). Seattle Art.

Earthworks: Ten Years on the Environmental Front. Friends of the Earth Staff. Ed. by Mary Lou Vander Vender. LC 79-56910. (Orig.). 1980. pap. 8.95 (ISBN 0-913890-39-1). Friends Earth.

Earthworm Is Born. William White, Jr. LC 75-14512. (Nature Ser.). (Illus.). 96p. (gr. 5 up). 1975. 7.95 (ISBN 0-8069-3530-8); PLB 7.49 (ISBN 0-8069-3531-6). Sterling.

Easier Way: A Handbook for the Elderly & Handicapped. Jean V. Sargent. (Illus.). 216p. 1981. pap. 9.95 (ISBN 0-686-69403-1). Iowa St U Pr.

Easing the Scene. Shirley Schwarzrock & C. Gilbert Wrenn. (Coping with Ser.). (Illus.). (gr. 7-12). 1970. pap. text ed. 1.30 (ISBN 0-913476-23-4). Am Guidance.

East Across the Pacific. Ed. by Hilary Conroy & T. Scott Miyakawa. LC 72-77825. 322p. 1972. pap. 2.85 (ISBN 0-87436-087-0). ABC-Clio.

East Africa. Lawrence Fellows. LC 76-165108. (Nations Today Bks). (gr. 7 up). 1972. 7.95 (ISBN 0-02-734450-9). Macmillan.

East Africa. Ed. by William P. Lineberry. (Reference Shelf Ser: Vol. 40, No. 2). 1968. 6.25 (ISBN 0-8242-0101-9). Wilson.

East Africa. Helen O'Clery. (Pegasus Books: No. 32). (Illus.). 184p. 1972. 10.50x (ISBN 0-234-77680-3). Intl Pubns Serv.

East Africa: A Travel Guide. Alan Magary & Kerstin F. Magary. LC 74-1836. (Illus.). 736p. 1975. 15.00 o.s.i. (ISBN 0-06-012792-9, HarpT); pap. 7.95 o.p. (ISBN 0-06-012808-9, TD-237, HarpT). Har-Row.

East Africa: Kenya, Tanzania, Uganda. Lila Perl. 160p. (gr. 5-9). 1973. PLB 7.44 (ISBN 0-688-30088-X). Morrow.

East African Culture History. Ed. by Joseph Gallagher. LC 76-50927. (Foreign & Comparative Studies-Eastern Africa Ser.: No. 25). 93p. 1976. pap. text ed. 4.50x (ISBN 0-915984-22-9). Syracuse U Foreign Comp.

East African Societies. Aylward Shorter. (Library of Man). 1974. 12.50x (ISBN 0-7100-7957-5); pap. 6.95 (ISBN 0-7100-7958-3). Routledge & Kegan.

East & Central Africa to the Late Nineteenth Century. Basil Davidson. LC 68-104173. 1967. 8.00x (ISBN 0-582-60245-9). Intl Pubns Serv.

East & Other Plays. Steven Berkoff. 1980. pap. 4.95 (ISBN 0-7145-3637-7). Riverrun NY.

East & West. Nuber Kazanjian. 1981. 8.95 (ISBN 0-533-04669-6). Vantage.

East & West: The Nobel Lecture on Literature, a World Split Apart, Letter to the Soviet Leaders, & a BBC Interview with Aleksandr I. Solzhenitsyn. Aleksandr I. Solzhenitsyn. LC 79-5222. 1980. pap. 1.95 (ISBN 0-06-080508-0, P 508, PL). Har-Row.

East Anglia. rev. ed. British Tourist Authority. (Illus.). 114p. Date not set. pap. price not set (ISBN 0-86143-044-1, Pub. by Auto Assn-British Tourist Authority England). Merrimack Bk Serv.

East Anglian Pubs. Vincent Jones. (Illus.). 1965. 3.50 o.p. (ISBN 0-8038-1874-2). Hastings.

East Asia: Tradition & Transformation. 2nd ed. John K. Fairbank et al. LC 77-77994. (Illus.). 1977. text ed. 19.95 (ISBN 0-395-25812-X). HM.

East Asian Cooking. Sozuki. 1981. 8.95 (ISBN 0-8120-5401-6). Barron.

East Asian Economies: A Guide to Information Sources. Ed. by Molly K. Lee. LC 78-13114. (Economics Information Guide Ser.: Vol. 1). 1979. 30.00 (ISBN 0-8103-1427-4). Gale.

East Asian Medicine in Urban Japan: Varieties of Medical Experience. Margaret M. Lock. 1980. 20.00x (ISBN 0-520-03820-7). U of Cal Pr.

East Asia's Turbulent Century: With American Diplomatic Documents. Ed. by Young H. Kim. LC 66-10328. (Orig.). 1966. pap. text ed. 7.95x (ISBN 0-89197-513-6). Irvington.

East Bay Trails. 4th, rev. ed. Bob Newey. LC 80-69075. (Illus.). 144p. 1981. pap. 4.95 (ISBN 0-9605186-0-6). Footloose Pr.

East Bay Trails - a Hiker's Guide. 3rd ed. Bob Newey. (Illus.). 1976. pap. 3.50 o.p. (ISBN 0-686-21246-0). Footloose Pr.

East Broad Top. Krause & Grenard. (Carstens Hobby Bks: No. C40). 1980. pap. 9.95 (ISBN 0-911868-40-2). Carstens Pubns.

East Burlap Parables. Richard N. Rinker. LC 69-11775. (Illus.). xiv, 169p. 1969. 9.95x (ISBN 0-8032-0154-0); pap. 1.95 (ISBN 0-8032-5161-0, BB 394, Bison). U of Nebr Pr.

East Coast Floods. Dorothy Summers. LC 78-62498. (Illus.). 1978. 16.95 (ISBN 0-7153-7456-7). David & Charles.

East End Underworld, Vol. 2: The Life of Arthur Harding. Ed. by Raphael Samuel. (History Workshop Ser.). (Illus.). 400p. 1981. price not set (ISBN 0-7100-0725-6); pap. price not set (ISBN 0-7100-0726-4). Routledge & Kegan.

East Europe. Carol Z. Rothkopf. LC 78-184357. (First Bks). (Illus.). 96p. (gr. 7-9). 1972. PLB 4.90 o.p. (ISBN 0-531-00758-8). Watts.

East European and Soviet Economic Affairs: A Bibliography (1965-1973) Alexander S. Birkos & Lewis A. Tambs. LC 74-28495. 170p. 1975. lib. bdg. 13.50x o.p. (ISBN 0-87287-097-9). Libs Unl.

East European Cooperation: The Role of Money & Finance. Jozef M. Van Brabant. LC 76-2911. (Illus.). 1976. text ed. 34.50 (ISBN 0-275-56650-1). Praeger.

East European Integration & East-West Trade. Ed. by Paul Marer & John M. Montias. LC 79-3181. 416p. 1980. 32.50x (ISBN 0-253-16865-1). Ind U Pr.

East European Languages & Literatures: A Subject & Name Index to Articles in English-Language Journals, 1900-1977. Garth M. Terry. 275p. 1978. 47.50. ABC-Clio.

East European Presantries: Social Reflections-an Annotated Bibliography of Periodical Articles, Vol.2. Irwin Sanders et al. (Reference Books Ser.). 1981. 16.00 (ISBN 0-8161-8488-7). G K Hall.

East Florida As a British Province, 1763-1784. Charles L. Mowat. LC 64-66326. (Floridia Facsimile && Reprint Ser.). 1964. Repr. of 1943 ed. 9.50 (ISBN 0-8130-0167-6). U Presses Fla.

East Germany. Barthold Fles. (First Bks). (gr. 7-12). 1973. PLB 4.90 o.p. (ISBN 0-531-00807-X). Watts.

East Germany & the Warsaw Alliance: The Politics of Detente. N. Edwina Moreton. (Westview Replica Edition). 1978. lib. bdg. 24.50x (ISBN 0-89158-265-7). Westview.

East India Slavery. George Saintsbury. 52p. 1972. Repr. of 1829 ed. text ed. 5.75x (ISBN 0-7165-1816-3). Humanities.

East India Slavery. George Saintsbury. 52p. 1972. Repr. of 1929 ed. 15.00x (ISBN 0-7165-1816-3, Pub. by Irish Academic Pr Ireland). Biblio Dist.

East Indiamen. Russell Miller. Ed. by Time-Life Books. (Seafarers Ser.). (Illus.). 176p. 1981. 14.95 (ISBN 0-8094-2689-7). Time-Life.

East Indian Company in Eighteenth Century Politics. Lucy S. Sutherland. LC 79-1593. 1981. Repr. of 1952 ed. 29.50 (ISBN 0-88355-898-X). Hyperion Conn.

East Indian Fortunes: The British in Bengal in the Eighteenth Century. P. J. Marshall. (Illus.). 1976. 37.50x (ISBN 0-19-821566-5). Oxford U Pr.

East Indians of Guyana & Trinidad. Malcolm Cross. (Minority Rights Group: No. 13). 1972. 2.50 (ISBN 0-89192-114-1). Interbk Inc.

East Is West. Freya Stark. (Illus.). 19.50 (ISBN 0-7195-1324-3). Transatlantic.

East London: London, Nineteen One. Walter Besant. LC 79-56945. (English Working Class Ser.). 1980. lib. bdg. 32.00 (ISBN 0-8240-0100-1). Garland Pub.

East Meets West: The Transpersonal Approach. Ed. by Rosemarie Stewart. LC 80-53952. 202p. 1981. pap. 5.25 (ISBN 0-8356-0544-2). Theos Pub Hse.

East Midlands. rev. ed. British Tourist Authority. (Illus.). 66p. Date not set. pap. price not set (ISBN 0-86143-042-5, Pub. by Auto Assn-British Tourist Authority England). Merrimack Bk Serv.

East of Malta West of Suez. L. R. Pratt. LC 75-23534. (Illus.). 224p. 1975. 31.95 (ISBN 0-521-20869-6). Cambridge U Pr.

East of Midnight. Tanith Lee. LC 77-15867. 1978. 7.95 o.p. (ISBN 0-312-22494-X). St Martin.

East of the Gabilans. Marjorie Pierce. LC 76-56566. 190p. 1981. 17.95 (ISBN 0-934136-14-9); pap. 9.95 (ISBN 0-934136-11-4). Western Tanager.

East of the Sun & West of the Moon. Kathleen Hague & Michael Hague. LC 80-13499. (Illus.). 48p. (gr. k-3). 1980. pap. 3.95 (ISBN 0-15-224703-3, VoyB). HarBraceJ.

East of the Sun & West of the Moon. Mercer Mayer. LC 80-11496. (Illus.). 48p. 1980. 10.95 (ISBN 0-590-07538-1, Four Winds). Schol Bk Serv.

East of the Sun & West of the Moon & Other Tales. P. C. Asbjornsen & Jorgen E. Moe. (Illus.). (gr. k-3). 1953. 3.95g o.s.i. (ISBN 0-02-705740-2). Macmillan.

East Side West Side. Margaret Maitland. 1977. pap. 1.75 (ISBN 0-505-51210-6). Tower Bks.

East Sussex: A Shell Guide. William S. Mitchell. 1978. 14.95 (ISBN 0-571-10751-6, Pub. by Faber & Faber). Merrimack Bk Serv.

East to the Azores: A Guide to Offshore Passage-Making. Richard Henderson. LC 77-91878. (Illus.). 1978. 12.50 (ISBN 0-87742-097-1). Intl Marine.

East-West Dialogues: Foundations & Problems of Revolutionary Praxis. P. K. Crosser et al. (Philosophical Currents Ser: No. 5). 180p. 1973. pap. text ed. 20.50x (ISBN 90-6032-008-5). Humanities.

East-West Economic Cooperation: Problems & Solution. Albert Masnata. 1974. 17.95 (ISBN 0-347-01036-9, 93534-4, Pub. by Saxon Hse England). Lexington Bks.

East-West In Art. Ed. by Theodore Bowie. LC 66-12723. (Illus.). 192p. (Orig.). 1966. pap. 6.50x (ISBN 0-253-11901-4). Ind U Pr.

East-West Industrial Co-Operation. 122p. 1979. pap. 10.00 (ISBN 0-686-68951-8, UN79/2E25, UN). Unipub.

East-West Technology Transfer: European Perspectives. Angela S. Yergin. LC 80-80363. (Washington Papers: No. 75). (Illus.). 88p. 1980. pap. 3.50x (ISBN 0-8039-1463-6). Sage.

East-West Technology Transfers: Japan & the Communist Bloc. Stephen Sternheimer. LC 80-50901. (Washington Papers: No. 76). (Illus.). 88p. 1980. pap. 3.50 (ISBN 0-8039-1485-7). Sage.

East-West Trade in Chemicals. Organization for Economic Cooperation & Development. (Document Ser.). (Illus.). 78p. (Orig.). 1980. pap. text ed. 4.50x (ISBN 92-64-12034-3, 22 80 01 1). OECD.

East-West Trade: Managing Encounter & Accomodation. Atlantic Council Committee on East-West Trade. LC 76-39928. 1977. pap. text ed. 8.25 o.p. (ISBN 0-89158-216-9). Westview.

East-West Trade: Theory & Evidence. Pref. by Josef C. Brada & V. S. Somanath. LC 78-16941. (Studies in East European & Soviet Planning, Development & Trade Ser.: No. 27). (Illus.). 1978. pap. text ed. 10.00 o.p. (ISBN 0-89249-025-X). Intl Development.

East-West Trade 1975: International Yearbook. Ed. by Z. Zeman & J. Zoubek. 170p. 1976. text ed. 140.00 (ISBN 0-08-019504-0). Pergamon.

East Wind: West Wind. Pearl S. Buck. (John Day Bk.). 1930. 9.95 (ISBN 0-381-98026-X, A21660, TYC-T). T Y Crowell.

Easter. Aileen Fisher. LC 67-23666. (Holiday Ser.). (Illus.). (gr. k-3). 1968. PLB 7.89 (ISBN 0-690-25236-6, TYC-J). T Y Crowell.

Easter. Howard G. Hageman & J. C. Beker. LC 73-88346. (Proclamation 1: Aids for Interpreting the Lessons of the Church Year, Ser. B). 64p. 1974. pap. 1.95 (ISBN 0-8006-4055-1, 1-4055). Fortress.

Easter. Edgar Krentz & Arthur A. Vogel. Ed. by Elizabeth Achtemeier et al. LC 79-7377. (Proclamation 2: Aids for Interpreting the Lessons of the Church Year, Ser. C). 64p. 1980. pap. 2.50 (ISBN 0-8006-4080-2, 1-4080). Fortress.

Easter. Bob Reese. Ed. by Alton Jordan. (Holidays Ser.). (Illus.). (gr. k-3). 1977. PLB 3.50 (ISBN 0-89868-032-8, Read Res); pap. text ed. 1.75 (ISBN 0-89868-065-4). ARO Pub.

Easter. Charles Rice & J. Louis Martyn. LC 74-24958. (Proclamation 1: Aids for Interpreting the Lessons of the Church Year, Ser. B). 64p. 1975. pap. 1.95 (ISBN 0-8006-4075-6, 1-4075). Fortress.

Easter. Theodore E. Saleske. (Living Values Ser.). (Illus.). 64p. (Orig.). 1980. pap. 3.95 (ISBN 0-89107-206-3). Good News.

Easter. Cass R. Sandak. (gr. 2-4). 1980. PLB 7.90 (ISBN 0-531-04148-4). Watts.

Easter. John H. Snow & Victor P. Furnish. LC 74-76927. (Proclamation 1: Aids for Interpreting the Lessons of the Church Year, Ser. A). 64p. 1975. pap. 2.50 (ISBN 0-8006-4065-9, 1-4065). Fortress.

Easter. Bruce Vawter & William J. Carl, III. LC 79-7377. (Proclamation 2: Aids for Interpreting the Lessons of the Church Year, Ser. A). 64p. (Orig.). 1981. pap. 6.95 (ISBN 0-8006-4095-0, 1-4095). Fortress.

Easter Book. Jenny Vaughan. LC 80-83362. (Illus.). 48p. (gr. 1-6). 1981. 4.95 (ISBN 0-448-11541-7); lib. bdg. 10.15 (ISBN 0-448-13492-6). G&D.

Easter Bunny's Lost Egg. Sharon Gordon. (Illus.). 32p. (gr. k-3). 1980. PLB 2.96 (ISBN 0-89375-375-0); pap. 0.95 (ISBN 0-89375-275-4). Troll Assocs.

Easter Cat. Meindert De Jong. LC 78-141933. (Illus.). (gr. 4-6). 1971. 5.95g o.s.i. (ISBN 0-02-726550-1). Macmillan.

Easter Egg Artists. Adrienne Adams. (Illus.). 32p. (gr. k-3). pap. 2.95 (ISBN 0-689-70479-8, A-106, Aladdin). Atheneum.

Easter Hill Village: Some Social Implications of Design. Clare C. Cooper. LC 74-10311. (Illus.). 1975. 17.95 (ISBN 0-02-906670-0). Free Pr.

Easter Island. Bob Putigny. LC 75-39804. (Island Ser.). (Illus.). 128p. 1976. pap. 7.95 (ISBN 0-8467-0164-2, Pub. by Two Continents). Hippocrene Bks.

Easter Lamb. G. A. Pottebaum. (Little People's Paperbacks Ser.). 1979. pap. 0.99 (ISBN 0-8164-2247-8). Crossroad NY.

Easter Moment. John S. Spong. 176p. 1980. 9.95 (ISBN 0-8164-0133-0). Crossroad NY.

Easter Proclamation of the Irish Republic, 1916. 1975. pap. text ed. 2.25x (ISBN 0-85105-289-4, Dolmen Pr). Humanities.

Easter Proclamation: Remembrance & Renewal. C. Welton Gaddy. LC 73-87065. pap. 1.95 (ISBN 0-8054-1921-7). Broadman.

Easter Programs for the Church, No. 6. Ed. by Jacqueline Westers. 1977. pap. 2.75 (ISBN 0-87239-159-0, 8718). Standard Pub.

Easter Rising: Dublin, 1916. Neil Grant. LC 72-3532. (World Focus Bks). (Illus.). 96p. (gr. 7-12). 1972. PLB 6.45 (ISBN 0-531-02161-0). Watts.

Easter Rising: Revolution & Irish Nationalism. Alan J. Ward. LC 79-55729. (AHM Europe Since 1500 Ser.). (Illus., Orig.). 1980. pap. text ed. 5.95x (ISBN 0-88295-803-8). AHM Pub.

Easter Story. Jenny Robertson. (Ladybird Bible Ser.). (Illus.). 32p. (ps-4). 1980. Repr. 1.95 (ISBN 0-310-42860-2). Zondervan.

Easter Story for Children. Ralph W. Sockman. (Illus.). (gr. 2-5). 1966. 6.95 (ISBN 0-687-11507-8). Abingdon.

Eastern Arabian Frontiers. J. B. Kelly. (Illus.). 1964. 5.95 o.p. (ISBN 0-571-06963-0, Pub. by Faber & Faber). Merrimack Bk Serv.

Eastern Arabic: An Introduction to the Spoken Arabic of Palestine, Syria & Lebanon. Frank A. Rice. 1977. pap. 7.95x (ISBN 0-686-63542-6). Intl Bk Ctr.

Eastern Association in the English Civil War. C. Holmes. LC 73-91616. (Illus.). 320p. 1974. 35.50 (ISBN 0-521-20400-3). Cambridge U Pr.

Eastern Churches Review: An Index to Volumes One Through Ten, 1966-1978. Boden Clarke & Mary A. Burgess. LC 80-2550. (Borgo Reference Library: Vol. 6). 64p. 1981. lib. bdg. 8.95x (ISBN 0-89370-812-7); pap. text ed. 2.95x (ISBN 0-89370-912-3). Borgo Pr.

Eastern Civilizations. 2nd ed. G. Robina Quale. (Illus., Orig.). 1975. 19.95 (ISBN 0-13-222976-5); pap. text ed. 15.95 (ISBN 0-13-222992-7). P-H.

Eastern Definitions: A Short Encyclopedia of Religions of the Orient. Edward Rice. LC 77-19359. 1978. 10.00 (ISBN 0-385-08563-X). Doubleday.

Eastern Europe: A Geography of the Comecon Countries. Roy E. Mellor. 1975. 20.00x (ISBN 0-231-03940-9); pap. 12.50x (ISBN 0-231-03945-X). Columbia U Pr.

Eastern Europe & the New International Economic Order: A Review of Four Representative Samples of Socialist Perspectives. Ed. by Ervin Laszlo & Joel Kurtzman. LC 79-20028. (Pergamon Policy Studies). 110p. 1980. 16.50 (ISBN 0-08-025115-3). Pergamon.

Eastern Europe in the Nineteen Eighties. Ed. by Stephen Fischer-Galati. 384p. (Orig.). 1981. lib. bdg. 25.00x (ISBN 0-89158-198-7); pap. 11.50x (ISBN 0-686-69586-0). Westview.

Eastern Europe in the 1970's. Ed. by Sylva Sinanian et al. LC 72-85944. (Special Studies in International Politics & Government). 1972. 28.00x (ISBN 0-275-28632-0); pap. text ed. 12.50x (ISBN 0-89197-740-6). Irvington.

Eastern European Academies of Sciences: A Directory. Office Of The Foreign Secretary. 1963. pap. 3.50 (ISBN 0-309-01090-X). Natl Acad Pr.

Eastern European Transportation: Systems & Modes. Ed. by Bogdan Mieczkowski. (Developments in Transportation Studies: No. 2). 366p. 1980. lib. bdg. 44.75 (ISBN 90-247-2390-6). Kluwer Boston.

Eastern Europe's Uncertain Future: A Selection of Radio Free Europe Research Reports. Ed. by Robert R. King & James F. Brown. LC 77-10666. (Praeger Special Studies). 1977. 37.50 (ISBN 0-03-040861-X). Praeger.

Eastern Hemisphere. Harold D. Drummond & James W. Hughes. (Our World Today Ser.). (gr. 7-12). 1980. text ed. 16.20 (ISBN 0-205-06627-5, 7766270); 18.00 (ISBN 0-205-06628-3); wkbk 5.12 (ISBN 0-205-06629-1). Allyn.

Eastern Hemlock & Its Variations. John C. Swartley. LC 79-18983. 272p. 1980. lib. bdg. 25.00 (ISBN 0-686-63240-0). Garland Pub.

Eastern Lacustrine Bantu. Margaret C. Fallers. LC 70-407857. 1968. 8.50x (ISBN 0-8002-0567-7). Intl Pubns Serv.

Eastern North America's Wildflowers: A Full-Color Guide of 373 Life-Size Paintings for Easy Flower Identification. Louis C. Linn. 1978. pap. 9.95 o.p. (ISBN 0-87690-262-X). Dutton.

Eastern Politics of the Vatican, 1917-1979. Hansjakob Stehle. Tr. by Sandra Smith from Ger. LC 80-15236. Orig. Title: Ostpolitik Des Vatikans, 1917-1975. (Illus.). 1981. 20.00x (ISBN 0-8214-0367-2, 0367E); pap. 10.00 (ISBN 0-8214-0564-0, 0564E). Ohio U Pr.

Eastern Question: An Historical Study in European Diplomacy. 4th ed. John A. Marriott. (Histories of Nations Ser). (Illus.). 1940. 37.50x (ISBN 0-19-821508-8). Oxford U Pr.

Eastern Question in the Eighteenth Century: The Partition of Poland & the Treaty of Kainardji. Albert Sorel. LC 68-9661. 1969. Repr. of 1898 ed. 15.75 (ISBN 0-86527-048-1). Fertig.

Eastern Religions & Western Thought. 2nd ed. S. Radhakrishnan. 396p. 1975. pap. text ed. 6.95x (ISBN 0-19-560604-3). Oxford U Pr.

Eastern Rhythms. Drachen Theaker. LC 79-89945. (Orig.). Date not set. pap. cancelled (ISBN 0-89793-017-7). Hunter Hse.

Eastern Sudanic Languages, Vol. 1. A. N. Tucker. (African Language & Linguistics Series). (Illus.). 1967. 30.00x (ISBN 0-7129-0203-1). Intl Pubns Serv.

Eastern Texas History: Selections from East Texas Historical Journal. Ed. by Archie P. McDonald. 12.50 (ISBN 0-8363-0159-5). Jenkins.

Eastlake-Influenced American Furniture, 1870-1890. Intro. by Mary Jean S. Madigan. LC 73-90034. (Illus.). 68p. 1974. pap. 5.00 (ISBN 0-87100-043-1, Pub. by Hudson River Mus). Pub Ctr Cult Res.

Easy ABC Shorthand. Rose Sargant. 1964. pap. 3.00 o.s.i. (ISBN 0-910458-00-6). Select Bks.

Easy Art of Smoking Food. Chris Dubbs & Dave Heberle. 1978. pap. 7.95 (ISBN 0-87691-264-1). Winchester Pr.

Easy Baseball Book. Jonah Kalb. LC 75-44085. (Illus.). 64p. (gr. 2-5). 1976. 6.95 (ISBN 0-395-24385-8). HM.

Easy Bazaar Crafts. Ed. by Better Homes & Gardens Books Editors. (Illus.). 96p. 1981. 4.95 (ISBN 0-696-00665-0). Meredith Corp.

Easy Bible Talks from Common Objects. Bettie Stubbs. Ed. by Olga Packard. (Standard Ideas Ser.). (Illus.). 1978. pap. 1.75 (ISBN 0-87239-217-1, 2818). Standard Pub.

Easy Book of Fractions. David C. Whitney. LC 70-100093. (First Steps to Math Ser). (Illus.). (gr. 4-6). 1970. PLB 4.47 o.p. (ISBN 0-531-01842-3). Watts.

Easy Book of Numbers & Numerals. David C. Whitney. LC 73-6695. (First Steps to Math Ser). (Illus.). (gr. 2-4). 1973. PLB 6.45 (ISBN 0-531-02597-7). Watts.

Easy Book of Sets. David C. Whitney. LC 70-39841. (First Steps to Math Ser). (Illus.). 48p. (gr. 3-5). 1972. PLB 6.45 (ISBN 0-531-02554-3). Watts.

Easy Bulletin Boards - Number 2. Melvyn K. Bowers. LC 73-21798. (Illus.). 1974. 10.00 (ISBN 0-8108-0695-9). Scarecrow.

Easy Car Care. 2nd ed. Chilton Staff. LC 78-7152. 384p. Date not set. 12.95 (ISBN 0-8019-6887-9); pap. 9.95 (ISBN 0-8019-6888-7). Chilton.

Easy Company & the Big Medicine. John W. Howard. (Easy Company Ser.: No. 6). (Orig.). 1981. pap. 1.95 (ISBN 0-515-05947-1). Jove Pubns.

Easy Company & the Green Arrows. John W. Howard. (Easy Company Ser.: No. 3). 192p. (Orig.). 1981. pap. 1.95 (ISBN 0-515-05887-4). Jove Pubns.

Easy Company & the Longhorns. John W. Howard. (Easy Company Ser.: No. 5). (Orig.). 1981. pap. 1.95 (ISBN 0-515-05946-3). Jove Pubns.

Easy Company & the Medicine Gun. John W. Howard. (Easy Company Ser.: No. 2). 240p. (Orig.). 1981. pap. 1.95 (ISBN 0-515-05804-1). Jove Pubns.

Easy Company & the Suicide Boys. John W. Howard. (Easy Company Ser.: No. 1). 224p. (Orig.). 1981. pap. 1.95 (ISBN 0-515-05761-4). Jove Pubns.

Easy Company & the White Man's Path. John W. Howard. (Easy Company Ser.: No. 4). 192p. (Orig.). 1981. pap. 1.95 (ISBN 0-515-05945-5). Jove Pubns.

Easy Cooking for One or Two. Louise Davies. (Handbook Ser). 1981. pap. 2.95 (ISBN 0-14-046379-8). Penguin.

Easy Cooking, Simple Recipes for Beginning Cooks. Ann Beebe. (Illus.). 48p. (gr. 4-6). 1972. PLB 6.96 (ISBN 0-688-30039-1). Morrow.

Easy Costumes You Don't Have to Sew. Goldie T. Chernoff. LC 76-46428. (Illus.). 48p. (gr. 1-5). 1977. 6.95 (ISBN 0-590-07491-1, Four Winds). Schol Bk Serv.

Easy Crafts Book. Sterling Editors. LC 75-14517. (Illus.). 112p. (gr. 4 up). 1975. 9.95 (ISBN 0-8069-5328-4); PLB 9.29 (ISBN 0-8069-5329-2). Sterling.

Easy Devotions to Give. Amy Bolding. (Paperback Program Ser.). 96p. (Orig.). 1981. pap. 2.95 (ISBN 0-8010-0794-1). Baker Bk.

Easy Does It. Ester Wier. LC 65-17375. (Illus.). (gr. 4-7). 1965. 5.95 (ISBN 0-8149-0438-6). Vanguard.

Easy, Elegant Luncheon Menus. Beverly Barbour. (Illus.). 1980. 14.95 (ISBN 0-8019-6831-3). Chilton.

Easy Embroidery. Ondori Publishing Company Staff. (Ondori Embroidery Ser.: Vol. 1). (Illus.). 81p. 1974. pap. 3.95 (ISBN 0-87040-356-7). Japan Pubns.

Easy Expert in American Antiques: Knowing, Finding, Buying & Restoring Early American Furniture. rev. ed. Moreton Marsh. LC 78-9050. Orig. Title: The Easy Expert in Collecting & Restoring American Antiques. 1978. 12.95 (ISBN 0-397-01287-X); pap. 7.95 (ISBN 0-397-01288-8). Lippincott.

Easy Field Guide to Interesting Birds of Glacier National Park. Dick Nelson & Sharon Nelson. (Illus.). 32p. (Orig.). (gr. 1-12). 1978. pap. 1.00 (ISBN 0-915030-17-9). Tecolote Pr.

Easy Field Guide to Mammals of Glacier National Park. Dick Nelson & Sharon Nelson. (Illus.). 32p. (Orig.). (gr. 1-12). 1978. pap. 1.00 (ISBN 0-915030-15-2). Tecolote Pr.

Easy Field Guide to Trees of Glacier National Park. Dick Nelson & Sharon Nelson. (Illus.). 32p. (Orig.). (gr. 1-12). 1978. pap. 1.00 (ISBN 0-915030-16-0). Tecolote Pr.

Easy Games for Young Children. Compiled by Patricia Shely. (Standard Ideas Ser.). (Illus.). 1978. pap. 1.75 (ISBN 0-87239-213-9, 2814). Standard Pub.

Easy Gardens. James U. Crockett & C. Prendergast. (Time-Life Encyclopedia of Gardening Ser.). (Illus.). 1979. lib. bdg. 11.97 (ISBN 0-686-51065-8). Silver.

Easy Gardens. Elvin McDonald. 1981. 8.95 (ISBN 0-916752-20-8). Green Hill.

Easy Gardens. Curtis Prendergast. Ed. by Time-Life Books. (Encyclopedia of Gardening Ser.). (Illus.). 1979. 11.95 (ISBN 0-8094-2637-4). Time-Life.

Easy Gardens: A Weed Eater Book. Elvin McDonald. (Berkley-Dorison House Bks.). (Illus.). (YA) 1978. 6.95 o.p. (ISBN 0-685-85770-0, Dist. by Putnam). Berkley Pub.

Easy Glamour. Barbara Walden & Vicki Lindner. (Illus.). 224p. 1981. 9.95 (ISBN 0-688-00416-4). Morrow.

Easy Going: A Guide to Good Health & Good Spirits on Your Journey Away from Home. Mel London. (Illus.). 320p. (Orig.). 1981. 12.95 (ISBN 0-87857-331-3); pap. 9.95 (ISBN 0-87857-345-3). Rodale Pr Inc.

Easy Guide to Meditation. Roy E. Davis. 1978. 3.95x (ISBN 0-87707-208-6). CSA Pr.

Easy Identification Guide to North American Snakes. Hilda Simon. LC 79-55263. (Illus.). 1979. flex. cover 8.95 (ISBN 0-396-07771-4). Dodd.

Easy Journey to Other Planets. A. C. Bhaktivedanta. 96p. 1972. pap. 1.25 o.s.i. (ISBN 0-02-083590-6, Collier). Macmillan.

Easy Journey to Other Planets. Swami A. C. Bhaktivedanta. LC 70-118080. (Illus.). 1970. pap. 1.50 (ISBN 0-912776-10-2). Bhaktivedanta.

Easy Magic: Good Tricks & How to Present Them. Roy Holmes. (Illus.). 144p. pap. 2.25 o.p. (ISBN 0-06-463412-4, 412, EH). Har-Row.

Easy Metric Cookbook. Illus. by Mary A. McAllister. (Illus.). 1977. pap. 3.98x o.p. (ISBN 0-685-81817-9). Nature Bks Pubs.

Easy Models You Can Make. S. Simon. LC 75-134660. (Science at Work). (gr. 4-6). 1971. 4.90 o.p. (ISBN 0-531-01972-1, G-49). Watts.

Easy Money. S. M. Fiederer. LC 80-54016. 1981. pap. 14.95 (ISBN 0-938584-00-6, 123058). United Pub NY.

Easy Money. Frank Roderus. LC 78-52121. 1978. 7.95 o.p. (ISBN 0-385-14423-7). Doubleday.

Easy Motorcycle Riding. rev. enlarged ed. Theresa Wallach. LC 78-57787. (Illus.). 1978. 7.95 (ISBN 0-8069-4134-0); lib. bdg. 7.49 (ISBN 0-8069-4135-9). Sterling.

Easy Natural Breads Even a Kid Can Bake. Lisa Pack-Miller et al. Ed. by Catherine J. Frompovich. (Illus.). 14p. (gr. 3 up). 1980. pap. 1.50 (ISBN 0-935322-07-8). C J Frompovich.

Easy Plants for Difficult Places. Jack Kramer. 1977. pap. 1.50 o.p. (ISBN 0-345-24865-1). Ballantine.

Easy Quillery: Projects with Paper Coils & Scrolls. Eva V. Amidon. (Illus.). (gr. 3-8). 1977. 7.25 (ISBN 0-688-22130-0); PLB 6.96 (ISBN 0-688-32130-5). Morrow.

Easy Reading Selections in English. rev. ed. Robert J. Dixson. (Illus., Orig., Sequel to Elementary Reader in English). (gr. 7-9). 1971. pap. text ed. 2.75 (ISBN 0-88345-043-7, 17976); cassettes 40.00 (ISBN 0-685-19788-3); tapes o.p. 40.00 (ISBN 0-685-19789-1). Regents Pub.

Easy Recipes of California Winemakers. Wine Advisory Board. Ed. by Marjorie K. Jacobs. (Illus.). 1970. 5.95 (ISBN 0-932664-05-9). Wine Appreciation.

Easy Suppers. Pat Jester. (Orig.). 1980. pap. 5.95 (ISBN 0-89586-064-3). H P Bks.

Easy Things to Make with Concrete & Masonry. Richard Day. LC 72-85574. (Illus.). 112p. 1972. lib. bdg. 4.95 o.p. (ISBN 0-668-02698-7); pap. 2.50 o.p. (ISBN 0-668-04130-7). Arco.

Easy Time: The Experiences of Female Inmates on Temporary Release. Belinda R. McCarthy. LC 78-13819. 1979. 22.50 (ISBN 0-669-02669-7). Lexington Bks.

Easy to Make Candles. Gary V. Guy. (Illus.). 1980. pap. 2.00 (ISBN 0-486-23881-4). Dover.

Easy-to-Make Children's Furniture. David Stiles. (Illus.). 1980. 7.95 (ISBN 0-394-73871-3). Pantheon.

Easy to Make Electric Gadgets. Leon R. Stanley. LC 80-82003. (Easy to Make Ser.). (Illus.). 64p. (gr. 3-6). 1981. PLB 5.79 (ISBN 0-8178-0011-5). Harvey.

Easy-to-Make Felt Bean Bag Toys. Jane Ethe. (Illus., Orig.). Date not set. pap. 2.50 (ISBN 0-486-23884-9). Dover. Postponed.

Easy-to-Make Felt Ornaments for Christmas and Other Occasions. Betty Deems. (Dover Needlework Ser). (Illus., Orig.). 1976. pap. 3.00 (ISBN 0-486-23389-8). Dover.

Easy-to-Make Patchwork Skirts. Nancy A. Pfeiffer-Dennis. (Illus., Orig.). 1980. pap. 3.50 (ISBN 0-486-23888-1). Dover.

Easy to Make Puppets & How to Use Them. Fran Rottman. Incl. Children & Youth. pap. 4.95 (ISBN 0-8307-0560-0, 52-022-05); Early Childhood. pap. 3.95 (ISBN 0-8307-0559-7, 52-021-08). 1978. Regal.

Easy-to-Make Slotted Furniture. Larry Buckley. (Illus.). 52p. (Orig.). 1980. pap. 2.25 (ISBN 0-486-23983-7). Dover.

Easy-to-Make Stained Glass Lightcatchers: Sixty-Seven Designs for Small Ornaments, with Full-Size Templates. Ed Sibbett, Jr. (Illus., Orig.). 1981. pap. price not set (ISBN 0-486-24081-9). Dover.

Easy to Make Wooden Sundials: Instructions & Plans for Five Projects. Milton Stoneman. (Illus.). 64p. (Orig.). 1981. pap. price not set (ISBN 0-486-24141-6). Dover.

Easy-to-Use Sermon Outlines. Russell E. Spray. (Sermon Outline Ser.). 1978. pap. 1.95 (ISBN 0-8010-8143-2). Baker Bk.

Easy Vegetable Growing. Martyn T. Hall. (Penny Pinchers Ser.). 1978. 2.95 (ISBN 0-7153-7547-4). David & Charles.

Easy Vietnamese. rev. ed. Nguyen-Dinh-Hoa. LC 66-17558. (Orig.). (gr. 7 up). 1966. pap. 3.75 (ISBN 0-8048-0160-6). C E Tuttle.

Easy Way to Good Looks. Shirley Lord. LC 75-20216. (Illus.). 224p. 1976. 10.00 o.s.i. (ISBN 0-690-00763-9, TYC-T). T y Crowell.

Easy Way to Service Radio Receivers. Leo G. Sands. LC 68-16049. 1968. 7.95 o.p. (ISBN 0-8306-8429-8, 429). TAB Bks.

Easy Ways to Decorate Your Kitchen. Ed. by Millie Hines. (Illus.). 96p. (Orig.). 1981. pap. 2.00 (ISBN 0-918178-24-X). Simplicity.

Easy Whole-Food Recipes. Elinor Wunderlich. LC 80-81655. (Orig.). 1980. pap. 3.95 (ISBN 0-910812-26-8). Johnny Reads.

Easy Woodstuff for Kids. David T. Thompson. LC 80-84599. (Illus.). 130p. 1981. pap. 7.95 (ISBN 0-87659-101-2). Gryphon Hse.

Eat - & - Reduce. Victor H. Lindlahr. LC 80-19206. 194p. 1980. Repr. of 1972 ed. lib. bdg. 9.95x (ISBN 0-89370-615-9). Borgo Pr.

Eat & Run: Your 1980 Diet, Exercise & Engagement Calendar. Jan F. Koltun. (Illus., Orig.). 1979. pap. 6.95 o.p. (ISBN 0-03-044571-X). HR&W.

Eat, Drink & Be Healthy. Agnes Toms. 1968. pap. 1.50 (ISBN 0-515-04606-X). Jove Pubns.

Eat, Drink & Be Slim. Anne Skimming. 1972. 4.95 o.p. (ISBN 0-571-09646-8, Pub. by Faber & Faber). Merrimack Bk Serv.

Eat Not This Flesh: Food Avoidances in the Old World. Frederick J. Simoons. LC 80-22232. (Illus.). xiii, 241p. 1981. Repr. of 1967 ed. lib. bdg. 29.75x (ISBN 0-313-22772-1, SIEN). Greenwood.

Eat, Think & Be Thinner: The Weigh of Life Way. Ruth Maislen et al. LC 76-19810. 1976. 8.95 (ISBN 0-8069-0150-0); lib. bdg. 8.29 (ISBN 0-8069-0151-9). Sterling.

Eat to Live. Joyce Flaum. LC 72-88600. 144p. 1973. pap. 1.45 o.p. (ISBN 0-668-02739-8). Arc Bks.

Eat Well to Keep Well. Max Warmbrand. 1970. pap. 1.25 o.s.i. (ISBN 0-515-02173-3, V2173). Jove Pubns.

Eat Your House: Art Eco Guide to Self Sufficiency. Fredric Hobbs. (Illus.). 120p. (Orig.). 1980. pap. 9.95 (ISBN 0-686-28070-9). VA City Rest.

Eat Yourself Thin: Secrets of the Harbor Island Spas. Barbie Fillian & Lida Livingston. LC 77-84426. 1977. 9.95 (ISBN 0-8119-0284-6). Fell.

Eater. Peter Michelson. LC 78-189187. (New Poetry Ser.: No. 45). 119p. 1972. 7.95 (ISBN 0-8040-0586-9). Swallow.

Eater's Digest: The Consumer's Factbook of Food Additives. Michael F. Jacobson. LC 75-186030. pap. 3.50 (ISBN 0-385-05341-X). Doubleday.

Eater's Guide: Nutrition Basics for Busy People. Candy Cumming & Vicky Newman. (Illus.). 192p. 1981. 11.95 (ISBN 0-13-223057-7); pap. 5.95 (ISBN 0-13-223040-2). P-H.

Eating & Allergy. Robert Eagle. LC 80-1860. 216p. 1981. pap. 5.95 (ISBN 0-385-17361-X, Dolp). Doubleday.

Eating, Drinking, & Thinking: A Gourmet Perspective. Phylis Magida. LC 73-86024. 1973. 14.95 (ISBN 0-911012-91-5). Nelson-Hall.

Eating for Life. Nathaniel Altman. LC 73-1950. (Illus.). 1977. pap. 3.25 o.p. (ISBN 0-8356-0496-9, Quest). Theos Pub Hse.

Eating for the Eighties. Janie C. Hartbarger & Neil J. Hartbarger. LC 80-53187. 256p. 1981. 12.95 (ISBN 0-03-059077-9); pap. 6.95 (ISBN 0-03-059076-0). HR&W.

Eating for the Eighties: A Complete Guide to Vegetarian Nutrition. Janie C. Hartbarger & Neil J. Hartbarger. LC 80-53187. 320p. 12.95 (ISBN 0-7216-4550-X); pap. 6.95 (ISBN 0-7216-4549-6). Saunders.

Eating in America: A History. Waverley Root & Richard De Rochement. LC 76-16145. 1976. 16.95 o.p. (ISBN 0-688-03096-3). Morrow.

Eating in Eden. Ruth Adams. 196p. (Orig.). 1976. pap. 1.75 (ISBN 0-915962-16-0). Larchmont Bks.

Eating in the Open. Beryl Gould-Marks. 1974. 9.95 (ISBN 0-571-09299-3, Pub. by Faber & Faber). Merrimack Bk Serv.

Eating Is Okay: A Radical Approach to Weight Loss. Henry Jordan et al. Ed. by Steve Gelman. 1978. pap. 1.75 (ISBN 0-451-09305-4, E9305, Sig). NAL.

Eating May Be Hazardous to Your Health. Jacqueline Verrett & Jean Carper. 240p. 1975. pap. 2.95 (ISBN 0-385-11193-2, Anchor Pr). Doubleday.

Eating Naturally: Recipes for Food with Fibre. Maggie Black & Pat Howard. 148p. 1981. 21.00 (ISBN 0-571-11602-7, Pub. by Faber & Faber); pap. 9.50 (ISBN 0-571-11603-5). Merrimack Bk Serv.

Eating Oil: Energy Use in Food Production. Maurice B. Green. 1978. lib. bdg. 22.50x (ISBN 0-89158-244-4). Westview.

Eating Places. Herbert S. Zim & James R. Skelly. LC 74-14949. (Illus.). 64p. (gr. 3-7). 1975. 6.00 o.p. (ISBN 0-688-22011-8); PLB 6.00 (ISBN 0-688-32011-2). Morrow.

Eating Rich Cookbook. Leonard L. Levinson. LC 73-12700. 1977. pap. 7.95 o.p. (ISBN 0-8128-2257-9). Stein & Day.

Eating Scientifically. L. Bijlani. 188p. 1979. 10.00x (ISBN 0-86125-049-4, Pub. by Orient Longman India). State Mutual Bk.

Eating the Vegetarian Way: Good Food from the Earth. Lila Perl. LC 80-18416. (Illus.). 96p. (gr. 4-6). 1980. 7.95 (ISBN 0-688-22248-X); PLB 7.63 (ISBN 0-688-32248-4). Morrow.

Eating to Win. Frances S. Goulart. LC 77-8756. 1978. 25.00x (ISBN 0-8128-2322-2); pap. 6.95 (ISBN 0-686-67964-4). Stein & Day.

Eating What Comes Naturally: A Guide to Vegetarian Restaurants in New York City. Linell P. Hunter. (Illus.). 130p. (Orig.). 1980. pap. 4.95 (ISBN 0-934700-00-1). Old Mill.

Eating What Grows Naturally. Kathleen Gay. LC 80-68745. (Illus.). 120p. 1980. pap. 5.95 (ISBN 0-89708-031-9). And Bks.

Eating with Wine. Guirne Van Zuylen. (Illus.). 1972. 8.95 (ISBN 0-571-09958-0). Transatlantic.

Eating Your Way Through Life. Judith J. Wurtman. LC 77-84121. 1979. text ed. 14.50 (ISBN 0-89004-280-2); pap. text ed. 10.50 (ISBN 0-685-99040-0). Raven.

Eating Your Way to Health. Ruth Bircher. 1961. 10.95 (ISBN 0-571-06984-3, Pub. by Faber & Faber). Merrimack Bk Serv.

Eau. Harlan Wade. Tr. by Claude Potvin & Rose-Ella Potvin. (Book About Ser.). Orig. Title: Water. (Illus., Fr.). (gr. k-3). 1979. PLB 7.30 (ISBN 0-8172-1465-8). Raintree Pubs.

Eau Trouble. Lucette Lafitte. 1963. text ed. 2.95x (ISBN 0-521-05506-7). Cambridge U Pr.

Eavesdroppers. Samuel Dash et al. LC 71-136498. (Civil Liberties in American History Ser). (Illus.). 1970. Repr. of 1959 ed. lib. bdg. 25.00 (ISBN 0-306-70074-3). Da Capo.

Eavesdropping on Space: The Quest of Radio Astronomy. David Knight. LC 74-19285. (Illus.). 96p. (gr. 5-9). 1975. PLB 6.96 (ISBN 0-688-32019-8). Morrow.

Ebbie. Eve Rice. LC 75-11688. (Illus.). 32p. (ps-3). 1975. 7.25 (ISBN 0-688-80017-3); PLB 6.96 (ISBN 0-688-84017-5). Greenwillow.

Ebenezer Kinnersley: Franklin's Friend. J. Leo Lemay. LC 64-10894. 1964. 9.00x o.p. (ISBN 0-8122-7425-3). U of Pa Pr.

EBLA: An Empire Rediscovered. Paolo Matthiae. LC 77-80898. (Illus.). 240p. 1981. 14.95 (ISBN 0-385-12904-1). Doubleday.

Ebony Brass. Jesse J. Johnson. 1976. 8.00 (ISBN 0-915044-01-3); pap. 2.00 (ISBN 0-915044-02-1); pap. 1.50 pocketbook (ISBN 0-915044-03-X). Carver Pub.

Ebony Image. Earl Zentmyer. Date not set. 12.95 (ISBN 0-87949-133-7). Ashley Bks.

Eca De Queiros & European Realism. Alexander Coleman. LC 79-3011. (Gotham Library). 1980. 17.50x (ISBN 0-8147-1378-5); pap. 9.00x (ISBN 0-8147-1379-3). NYU Pr.

Ecce Homo: A Lexicon of Man. Luigi Romeo. 1980. text ed. 20.00x (ISBN 90-272-2006-9). Humanities.

Ecce Mundus Industrial Ideals, the Book Beautiful, Repr. Of 1902. T. J. Cobden-Sanderson. Ed. by Peter Stansky & Rodney Shewan. Incl. The Arts & Crafts Movement. Repr. of 1905 ed. LC 76-18325. (Aesthetic Movement & the Arts & Crafts Movement Ser.). 1977. lib. bdg. 44.00x (ISBN 0-8240-2479-6). Garland Pub.

Eccentric Design: Form in the Classic American Novel. Marius Bewley. LC 59-13769. 1959. pap. 10.00x (ISBN 0-231-08542-7, 42). Columbia U Pr.

Eccentric Spaces. Robert Harbison. 192p. 1979. pap. 2.50 (ISBN 0-380-49122-2, 49122, Discus). Avon.

Ecclesial Cybernetics: A Study of Democracy in the Church. Patrick Granfield. LC 72-87158. 320p. 1973. 8.95 o.s.i. (ISBN 0-02-545030-1). Macmillan.

Ecclesiastes. G. A. Barton. LC 8-15777. (International Critical Commentary Ser.). 236p. Repr. of 1908 ed. 17.50x (ISBN 0-567-05014-9). Attic Pr.

Ecclesiastes - Song of Solomon. R. J. Kidwell & Don DeWelt. LC 78-301088. (Bible Study Textbook Ser.). 1977. 13.50 (ISBN 0-89900-019-3). College Pr Pub.

Ecclesiastes & the Song of Solomon. Irving L. Jensen. (Bible Self Study Guide Ser.). 1974. pap. 2.25 (ISBN 0-8024-1021-9). Moody.

Ecclesiastical Authority & Spiritual Power in the Church of the First Three Centuries. Hans Von Campenhausen. Tr. by J. A. Baker. 1969. 12.95x (ISBN 0-8047-0665-4). Stanford U Pr.

Ecclesiastical History. Eusebius. (Twin Brooks Ser). pap. 7.95 (ISBN 0-8010-3306-3). Baker Bk.

Ecclesiastical History of England. Bede. Repr. 45.00 o.p. (ISBN 0-686-12351-4). Church History.

Ecclesiastical History of New England. George Burgess. 55.00 (ISBN 0-686-12406-5). Church History.

Ecclesiastical History of Orderic Vitalis, Vol. 1. Ed. by Marjorie Chibnall. (Oxford Medieval Texts Ser.). (Illus.). 416p. 1980. 79.00 (ISBN 0-19-822243-2). Oxford U Pr.

Ecclesiastical History of the English Nation. Bede. Tr. by John Stevens. 1973. 12.95x (ISBN 0-460-00479-4, Evman). Dutton.

Ecclesiastical Office & the Primacy of Rome: An Evaluation of Recent Theological Discussion of 1 Clement. John Fuellenbach. (Studies in Christian Antiquity: Vol. 20). 278p. 25.00x (ISBN 0-8132-0551-4, Pub. by Cath U of America Pr). Intl Schol Bk Serv.

Ecclesiazusae. Aristophanes. Ed. by Roland G. Ussher. 300p. 1973. 14.50x o.p. (ISBN 0-19-814191-2). Oxford U Pr.

ECFMG Examination Review, Pt. 1. 4th ed. Warner F. Bowers et al. LC 76-9880. 1976. Pt. 1. pap. 11.75 (ISBN 0-87488-120-X); Pt. 2. pap. 11.75 (ISBN 0-87488-121-8). Med Exam.

ECG Case Studies. 2nd ed. Julian Frieden & Ira Rubin. LC 77-94387. 1974. pap. 9.50 (ISBN 0-87488-003-3). Med Exam.

Echelle: Structures Essentielles du Francais. R. L. Politzer et al. 1966. 18.95 (ISBN 0-471-00432-4); wkbk. 7.95x (ISBN 0-471-00433-2). Wiley.

Echerichia coli Infections in Domestic Animals. Ed. by Herman Willinger & Albert Weber. (Advances in Veterinary Medicine Ser.: Vol. 29). (Illus.). 86p. (Orig.). 1979. pap. text ed. 25.90 (ISBN 3-489-77916-9). Parey Sci Pubs.

Echidnas. M. Griffiths. LC 68-21385. 1968. 42.00 (ISBN 0-08-012650-2). Pergamon.

Echinoderm Biology. Zoological Society Of London - 20th Symposium. Ed. by N. Millot. 1968. 34.00 (ISBN 0-12-613320-4). Acad Pr.

Echinoderms. David Nichols. (Orig.). 1966. text ed. 5.25x (ISBN 0-09-065994-5, Hutchinson U Lib); pap. text ed. 5.00x (ISBN 0-09-065993-7, Hutchinson U Lib). Humanities.

Echo. Kenneth Jupp. 228p. 1981. 10.95 (ISBN 0-316-47703-6). Little.

Echo. Giles Lutz. 160p. 1981. pap. 1.75 (ISBN 0-345-29100-X). Ballantine.

Echo Sounding & Sonar for Fishing. 102p. 1980. pap. 22.50 (ISBN 0-85238-110-7, FN86, FN). Unipub.

Echocardiographic Interpretation. Abdul S. Abbasi. (Illus.). 448p. 1981. text ed. price not set (ISBN 0-398-04153-9). C C Thomas.

Echocardiography. 3rd. ed. Harvey Feigenbaum. LC 80-20682. (Illus.). 580p. 1981. text ed. 35.00 (ISBN 0-8121-0758-6). Lea & Febiger.

Echocardiography - A Manual for Technicians. Christine Miskovits. 1977. spiral bdg. 15.00 (ISBN 0-87488-987-1). Med Exam.

Echocardiography Case Studies. Jack J. Kleid & Nelson B. Schiller. 1974. spiral bdg. 12.00 o.p. (ISBN 0-87488-040-8). Med Exam.

Echoes from Old Calcutta. H. E. Busteed. (Illus.). 454p. 1972. Repr. of 1908 ed. 31.00x (ISBN 0-7165-2115-6, Pub. by Irish Academic Pr Ireland). Biblio Dist.

Echoes from the Past. LC 79-90484. (Illus.). 128p. 1979. 25.00 (ISBN 0-934586-03-9). Plan Parent.

Echoes from the Past. Planned Parenthood Federation of America, Inc. (Illus.). 128p. 1979. 25.00 (ISBN 0-934586-03-9). Plan Parent.

Echoes in an Empty Room. Carolyn Lane. LC 80-20278. 160p. (gr. 4-7). 1981. 8.95 (ISBN 0-03-057477-3). HR&W.

Echoes in My Mind. Howard Gardner. Date not set. 7.95 (ISBN 0-533-04727-7). Vantage.

Echoes of a Summer. William Johnston. 1976. pap. 1.50 o.p. (ISBN 0-345-25633-6). Ballantine.

Echoes of Marching Feet. Mary B. Runyon. Ed. by Joseph Lawrence. LC 79-64729. 1979. 9.95 (ISBN 0-89144-083-6); pap. 4.95 (ISBN 0-686-68514-8). Crescent Pubns.

Echoes of Puget Sound: Fifty Years of Logging & Steamboating. Torger Birkeland. (Illus.). 252p. pap. 10.00 (ISBN 0-8466-0315-2). Shorey.

Echoes of the Wordless "Word". Ed. by Daniel C. Noel. LC 73-88582. (American Academy of Religion & Society of Biblical Literature. Religion & the Arts Ser.). 1973. 9.00 (ISBN 0-88414-033-4, 090102). Scholars Pr Ca.

Echoes of Their Voices. Carl R. Baldwin. 400p. 1978. 10.95 (ISBN 0-86629-003-6). Sunrise MO.

Echoes of Thunder. Harry L. Green. LC 80-66322. 167p. 1980. 10.95 (ISBN 0-936958-00-6); pap. 5.95 (ISBN 0-936958-01-4). Emerald Hse.

Echoes of Yesterday. Nomi Berger. LC 80-82848. 384p. (Orig.). 1981. pap. 2.95 (ISBN 0-87216-777-1). Playboy Pbks.

Ecidujerp-Prejudice: Either Way It Doesn't Make Sense. Irene Gersten & Betsy Bliss. LC 73-10371. (Illus.). 96p. (gr. 4-7). 1974. PLB 3.90 o.p. (ISBN 0-531-02669-8). Watts.

Eclipse. Alan Riddel. 1980. pap. 3.95 (ISBN 0-7145-0908-6). Riverrun NY.

Eclipse. Natalie Robins. 64p. 1981. 8.95 (ISBN 0-8040-0367-X); pap. 4.95 (ISBN 0-8040-0368-8). Swallow.

Eclipse. Dirk Wittenborn. LC 77-24285. 1977. 8.95 (ISBN 0-396-07383-2). Dodd.

Eclipse: Darkness in Daytime. Franklyn M. Branley. LC 73-3492. (Let's-Read-&-Find-Out Science Bk). (Illus.). (gr. k-3). 1973. PLB 7.89 (ISBN 0-690-25414-8, TYC-J). T Y Crowell.

Eclipse of Christianity in Asia. Lawrence E. Browne. 1967. Repr. 15.75 (ISBN 0-86527-049-X). Fertig.

Eclipse of Excellence. Steven M. Cahn. 1.00 (ISBN 0-8183-0142-2). Pub Aff Pr.

Eclipse of God: Studies in the Relation Between Religion & Philosophy. Martin Buber. 1979. pap. text ed. 3.95x (ISBN 0-391-00902-8). Humanities.

Eclipse of the Self: The Development of Heidegger's Concept of Authenticity. Michael Zimmerman. LC 80-19042. xxx, 331p. 1981. 18.95x (ISBN 0-8214-0570-5); pap. 9.95 (ISBN 0-8214-0601-9). Ohio U Pr.

ECMT: 25th Annual Report, Vol. II. Resolutions of the Council of Ministers of Transport & Reports Approved in 1978. (4#149). 1979. 12.50 (ISBN 92-821-1054-0). OECD.

Eco: A Handbook of Classroom Ideas to Motivate the Teaching of Elementary Ecology. (Spice Ser). 1974. 6.50 (ISBN 0-89273-114-1). Educ Serv.

Eco-Philosophy. Henryk Skolimowsky. LC 79-56846. (Ideas in Progress Ser.). 1980. 12.00 (ISBN 0-7145-2677-0, Pub. by M Boyars); pap. 6.95 (ISBN 0-7145-2676-2, Pub. by M. Boyars). Merrimack Bk Serv.

Eco-Tech: The Whole-Earther's Guide to the Alternate Society. Robert S. De Ropp. 352p. 1975. 10.00 o.p. (ISBN 0-440-02233-9, Sey Lawr). Delacorte.

Ecodevelopment. Robert Riddell. 1980. 27.50 (ISBN 0-312-22585-7). St Martin.

Ecole des Femmes & la Critique de L'ecole des Femmes. Moliere. Ed. by W. D. Howarth. (Blackwell's French Text Ser.). 1968. pap. text ed. 9.95x (ISBN 0-631-00630-3, Pub. by Basil Blackwell). Biblio Dist.

Ecologic Economic Analysis for Regional Development. Walter Isard. LC 75-134313. 1972. 25.00 (ISBN 0-02-915810-9). Free Pr.

Ecological & Evolutionary Ethic. Ed. by Daniel G. Kozlovsky. (Illus.). 128p. 1974. pap. 10.95 (ISBN 0-13-222935-8). P-H.

Ecological & Nutritional Approach to Behavioral Medicine. Dan R. O'Banion. (Illus.). 248p. 1981. price not set (ISBN 0-398-04457-0). C C Thomas.

Ecological & Nutritional Treatment of Health Disorders. Dan R. O'Bannon. (Illus.). 240p. 1981. price not set (ISBN 0-398-04455-4). C C Thomas.

Ecological Animal Parasitology. C. R. Kennedy. LC 75-5760. 1975. 13.95 o.p. (ISBN 0-470-46910-2). Halsted Pr.

Ecological Anthropology. D. L. Hardesty. 1977. 19.95x (ISBN 0-471-35144-X). Wiley.

Ecological Approach to Visual Perception. James J. Gibson. LC 78-69585. (Illus.). 1979. text ed. 29.95 (ISBN 0-395-27049-9). HM.

Ecological Aspects of Toxicity Testing of Oils & Dispersants. Ed. by L. R. Beynon & E. B. Cowell. 1974. 22.95 (ISBN 0-470-07190-7). Halsted Pr.

Ecological Assessment of Child Problem Behavior. Robert G. Wahler et al. 1976. pap. text ed. 7.25 (ISBN 0-08-019586-5). Pergamon.

Ecological Atlas of Soils of the World. Philippe Duchaufour. Tr. by C. R. De Kimpe from Fr. LC 77-94822. (Illus.). 178p. 1978. 35.75 (ISBN 0-89352-012-8). Masson Pub.

Ecological Basis for Subsistence Change Among the Sandawe of Tanzania. James Newman. LC 75-607171. (Foreign Field Research Program Ser). (Illus., Orig.). 1970. pap. 11.75 (ISBN 0-309-01851-X). Natl Acad Pr.

Ecological Consciousness: Essays from the Earthday X Colloquium. Earthday X Colloquium, University of Denver, April 21-24, 1980. Ed. by Robert C. Schultz & J. Donald Hughes. LC 80-6084. 510p. 1981. lib. bdg. 26.50 (ISBN 0-8191-1496-0); pap. text ed. 16.75 (ISBN 0-8191-1497-9). U Pr of Amer.

Ecological Data in Comparative Research. Jerome M. Clubb. (Reports & Papers in the Social Sciences Ser., No. 25). (Orig). 1970. pap. 2.50 (ISBN 92-3-100845-5, U174, UNESCO). Unipub.

Ecological Diversity. Evelyn C. Pielou. LC 75-9663. 165p. 1975. 21.95 (ISBN 0-471-68925-4, Pub. by Wiley-Interscience). Wiley.

Ecological Eclair. Francis S. Goulart. 1975. pap. 3.50 o.s.i. (ISBN 0-02-009650-X, Collier). Macmillan.

Ecological Eclair: And Other Sugarless Treats. Frances S. Goulart. 144p. 1975. 9.50 o.s.i. (ISBN 0-02-544910-9). Macmillan.

Ecological Effects of Agricultural Chemistry. Newman. 1981. text ed. price not set. Butterworth.

Ecological Effects of Biological & Chemical Control of Undesirable Plants & Animals. 118p. 1961. pap. 7.50 (ISBN 0-686-68189-4, IUCN85, IUCN). Unipub.

Ecological Effects of Waste Water. E. B. Welch. LC 78-11371. 1980. 32.50 (ISBN 0-521-22495-0); pap. 9.95x (ISBN 0-521-29525-4). Cambridge U Pr.

Ecological Garden. Catharine O. Foster. Tr. by Erick Ingraham. (Illus.). 188p. (Orig.). 1981. 12.50 (ISBN 0-8159-5407-7); pap. 6.95 (ISBN 0-8159-5408-5). Devin.

Ecological Genetics. David J. Merrell. (Illus.). 570p. 1981. 25.00x (ISBN 0-8166-1019-3). U of Minn Pr.

Ecological Guidelines for Balanced Land Use: Conservation & Development in High Mountains. 40p. 1980. pap. 7.50 (ISBN 2-88032-100-X, IUCN77, IUCN). Unipub.

Ecological House. Robert B. Butler. 256p. 1981. pap. 9.95 (ISBN 0-87100-175-6). Morgan.

Ecological Impact Assessment: Principles & Applications. Paul A. Erickson. 1979. 29.00 (ISBN 0-12-241550-7). Acad Pr.

Ecological Management of Arid & Semi-Arid Rangelands of Africa, the Near & Middle East. Emarar - Phase II: Vol. VII, Near East Grassland Education & Training. 55p. 1979. pap. 6.00 (ISBN 92-5-100680-6, F1619, FAO). Unipub.

Ecological Politics: The Rise of the Green Movement. J. F. Pilat. LC 80-52547. (Washington Papers: No. 77). 96p. 1980. pap. 3.50 (ISBN 0-8039-1535-7). Sage.

Ecological Principles, No. 4. M. A. Tribe et al. LC 75-6285. (Basic Biology Course Ser). (Illus.). 160p. (Prog. Bk.). 1975. 35.95 (ISBN 0-521-20658-8); pap. 13.95x (ISBN 0-521-20638-3). Cambridge U Pr.

Ecological Processes in Coastal Environments: Nineteenth Symposium of the British Ecological Society. Ed. by R. L. Jefferies. 684p. 1979. 87.95x (ISBN 0-470-26741-0). Halsted Pr.

Ecological Relationships. N. Gilbert et al. (Illus.). 1976. text ed. 13.95x (ISBN 0-7167-0486-2). W H Freeman.

Ecological Strategies of Xylem Evolution. Sherwin Carlquist. LC 74-76382. (Illus.). 1975. 20.00x (ISBN 0-520-02730-2). U of Cal Pr.

Ecological Systems & the Environment. Theodore C. Foin, Jr. LC 75-25010. (Illus.). 640p. 1976. text ed. 19.50 (ISBN 0-395-20666-9); inst. manual 1.00 (ISBN 0-395-20667-7). HM.

Ecological Transition. John W. Bennett. 1976. text ed. 27.00 (ISBN 0-08-017867-7); pap. text ed. 16.00 (ISBN 0-08-017868-5). Pergamon.

Ecology. Taylor R. Alexander. (Golden Guide Ser). 160p. 1973. PLB 9.15 (ISBN 0-307-64359-X, Golden Pr); pap. 1.95 o.p. (ISBN 0-307-24359-1). Western Pub.

Ecology. J. Bendick. LC 75-8904. (Science Experiences Ser). (gr. 3-5). 1975. 4.90 o.p. (ISBN 0-531-01442-8). Watts.

Ecology. Peter Farb. LC 63-22074. (Life Nature Library Ser.). (Illus.). (gr. 5 up). 1970. PLB 8.97 o.p. (ISBN 0-8094-0627-6, Pub. by Time-Life). Silver.

Ecology. rev. ed. John Hoke. (First Books Ser.). (Illus.). 96p. (gr. 4-6). 1977. PLB 6.45 (ISBN 0-531-00745-6). Watts.

Ecology. Stanley L. Weinberg & Herbert J. Stolze. (Action Biology Ser.). (gr. 9-12). 1974. pap. text ed. 3.20 (ISBN 0-205-04147-7, 6741479). Allyn.

Ecology: A Textbook. H. Remmert. (Illus.). 300p. 1980. pap. 21.30 (ISBN 0-387-10059-8). Springer-Verlag.

Ecology Alphabet. Joyce Wolf. (Illus.). (gr. 3-6). 1981. PLB price not set (ISBN 0-671-42692-3). Messner.

Ecology: An Evolutionary Approach. J. Merritt Emlen. LC 71-172805. 1973. text ed. 19.95 (ISBN 0-201-01894-2). A-W.

Ecology & Behavior of Nocturnal Primates: Prosimians of Equatorial West Africa. Pierre Charles-Dominique. Tr. by R. D. Martin. LC 77-1227. 1977. 20.00x (ISBN 0-231-04362-7). Columbia U Pr.

Ecology & Behavior of the Black Rhinoceros (Diceros Bicornis L.) A Field Study. R. Schenkel & L. Schenkel-Hulliger. (Illus.). 100p. (Orig.). 1969. pap. text ed. 16.50. Parey Sci Pubs.

Ecology & Coal Resource Development, 2 vols. International Congress for Energy & the Ecosystem, University of North Dakota, 12-16 June 1978. Ed. by Mohan K. Wali. LC 78-26238. 1980. 140.00 (ISBN 0-08-023863-7). Pergamon.

Ecology & Consciousness. 2nd ed. Ed. by Richard Grossinger. 226p. (Orig.). 1980. pap. 6.95 (ISBN 0-913028-71-1). North Atlantic.

Ecology & Conservation of Natural Resources. Ray J. Davis. 1978. lib. bdg. 6.65 (ISBN 0-931054-02-8). Clark Pub.

Ecology & Earth History. R. N. Fiennes. 250p. 1980. 40.00x (Pub. by Croom Helm England). State Mutual Bk.

Ecology & Ekistics. Constantino Doxiadis. LC 76-20459. (Illus.). 1978. lib. bdg. 17.50x (ISBN 0-89158-624-5). Westview.

Ecology & Energetics of Contrasting Social Systems in the Phainopepia. Glenn E. Walsberg. (Publications in Zoology: Vol. 108). 1977. 8.50x (ISBN 0-520-09562-6). U of Cal Pr.

Ecology & Environmental Management: A Geographical Perspective. C. C. Park. LC 79-5208. (Westview Studies in Physical Geography). 224p. 1980. lib. bdg. 24.50x (ISBN 0-89158-698-9). Westview.

Ecology & Evolution of an Andean Hummingbird (Oreotrochilus Estella) F. Lynn Carpenter. (Publications in Zoology: Vol. 106). 1976. pap. 8.95x (ISBN 0-520-09545-6). U of Cal Pr.

Ecology & Evolution of Communities. Ed. by Martin L. Cody & Jared M. Diamond. LC 74-27749. (Illus.). 838p. 1975. text ed. 29.50x (ISBN 0-674-22444-2, Belknap Pr); pap. 12.50x (ISBN 0-674-22446-9). Harvard U Pr.

Ecology & Pollution - Air. Martin J. Gutnik. (First Experiments in Science & Nature Ser.). (Illus.). 48p. (gr. 2-4). 1973. PLB 7.95 o.p. (ISBN 0-516-00522-7). Childrens.

Ecology & Religion in History. Ed. by David Spring & Eileen Spring. 1974. pap. 3.95x o.p. (ISBN 0-06-131829-9, TB1829, Torch). Har-Row.

Ecology & Reproduction of the Tasmanian Bandicoots (Perameles gunni & Isodon obesulus) G. E. Heinsohn. (U. C. Publ. in Zoology: Vol. 80). 1966. pap. 7.00x (ISBN 0-520-09337-2). U of Cal Pr.

Ecology & the Politics of Scarcity: Prologue to a Political Theory of Steady State. William Ophuls. LC 76-46436. (Illus.). 1977. pap. text ed. 9.95x (ISBN 0-7167-0481-1). W H Freeman.

Ecology & the Quality of Life. S. J. Kaplan & E. Kivy-Rosenberg. (Illus.). 308p. 1973. 23.75 (ISBN 0-398-02828-1). C C Thomas.

Ecology Control & Economic Developement in East African History: The Case of Tanganyika 1850-1950. Helge Kjekshus. 1977. 20.00x (ISBN 0-520-03384-1). U of Cal Pr.

Ecology Controversy: Opposing Viewpoints. rev. ed. Ed. by Gary E. McCuen & David L. Bender. (Opposing Viewpoints Ser.: Vol. 3). (Illus.). (gr. 9 up). 1973. lib. bdg. 8.95 (ISBN 0-912616-27-X); pap. text ed. 3.95 (ISBN 0-912616-09-1). Greenhaven.

Ecology: Cycle & Recycle. Grace H. Kolbas. LC 72-81035. (Basic Biology in Color Ser.). (Illus.). 192p. (gr. 9 up). 1972. 12.95 (ISBN 0-8069-3558-8); PLB 11.69 (ISBN 0-8069-3559-6). Sterling.

Ecology-Environment Handbook. James E. Hill & Ervin Y. Kedar. LC 78-57574. 1978. pap. text ed. 6.75 (ISBN 0-8191-0525-2). U Pr of Amer.

Ecology, Evolution, & Population Biology: Readings from Scientific American. Intro. by Edward O. Wilson. LC 73-17448. (Illus.). 1974. text ed. 19.95x (ISBN 0-7167-0888-4); pap. text ed. 9.95x (ISBN 0-7167-0887-6). W H Freeman.

Ecology Game. M. A. Tribe & D. Peacock. (Basic Biology Course Ser.). (Illus.). 1976. 44.50 (ISBN 0-521-21030-5). Cambridge U Pr.

Ecology of Arboreal Folivores. Ed. by G. Gene Montgomery. LC 78-3103. (Symposia of the National Zoological Park Ser.: No. 3). (Illus.). 574p. 1978. 35.00x (ISBN 0-87474-646-9); pap. 15.00x (ISBN 0-87474-647-7). Smithsonian.

Ecology of Faith. Joseph Sittler. LC 61-10278. 112p. 1970. pap. 0.50 (ISBN 0-8006-1882-3, 1-1882). Fortress.

Ecology of Fishes. rev ed. G. V. Nikolsky. Orig. Title: Biology of Fishes. (Illus.). 1978. pap. 4.95 (ISBN 0-87666-505-9, H-999). TFH Pubns.

Ecology of Fresh Waters. Brian Moss. 360p. 1980. pap. 29.95x (ISBN 0-470-26942-1). Halsted Pr.

Ecology of Freshwater Fish Production. Ed. by Shelby D. Gerking. LC 77-92407. 1978. 61.95 (ISBN 0-470-99362-6). Halsted Pr.

Ecology of Highlands. M. S. Mani & L. E. Giddings. (Monographiae Biologicae: No. 40). (Illus.). 236p. 1980. lib. bdg. 58.00 (ISBN 90-6193-093-6, Pub. by Dr. W. Junk). Kluwer Boston.

Ecology of Housing Destruction: Economic Effects of Public Intervention in the Housing Market. Peter D. Salins. LC 79-3845. 176p. 1980. 12.50x (ISBN 0-8147-7811-9); pap. 6.00x (ISBN 0-8147-7812-7). NYU Pr.

Ecology of Human Disease. Jacques M. May. LC 58-13432. 1958. 7.50 o.p. (ISBN 0-910922-11-X). MD Pubns.

Ecology of Language: Essays by Einar Haugen. Einar Haugen. Ed. by A. S. Dil. LC 73-183888. (Language Science & National Development Ser.). xvi, 366p. 1972. 18.50x (ISBN 0-8047-0802-9). Stanford U Pr.

Ecology of Marine Sediments. J. S. Gray. (Cambridge Studies in Modern Biology: No. 2). (Illus.). 170p. Date not set. price not set (ISBN 0-521-23553-7); pap. price not set (ISBN 0-521-28027-3). Cambridge U Pr.

Ecology of Natural Resources. Ian Simmons. LC 74-4812. 424p. 1974. pap. text ed. 14.95 (ISBN 0-470-79194-2). Halsted Pr.

Ecology of Preschool Behaviour. P. K. Smith & K. J. Connolly. LC 79-42647. (Illus.). 400p. Date not set. 49.50 (ISBN 0-521-22331-8). Cambridge U Pr.

Ecology of Resource Degradation & Renewal. M. J. Chadwick & G. T. Goodman. LC 75-5776. (British Ecological Society Symposia Ser.). 450p. 1976. 50.95 (ISBN 0-470-14295-2). Halsted Pr.

Ecology of Small Boat Marinas. (Marine Technical Report: No. 5). 1973. pap. 1.00 (ISBN 0-938412-17-5). URI MAS.

Ecology of Soil Organisms. Allison L. Brown. LC 78-313368. 1978. text ed. 16.95 o.p. (ISBN 0-435-60620-4); pap. text ed. 8.95x (ISBN 0-435-60621-2). Heinemann Ed.

Ecology of the Gwembe Tonga. Thayer Scudder. 1962. pap. text ed. 9.75x (ISBN 0-7190-1276-7). Humanities.

Ecology of the Heathlands. C. H. Gimingham. LC 73-3968. 266p. 1972. text ed. 21.95x o.p. (ISBN 0-412-14980-X, Pub. by Chapman & Hall). Methuen Inc.

Ecology of the Heathlands. C. H. Gimingham. LC 73-3968. 266p. 1972. 21.95 o.p. (ISBN 0-470-30210-0). Halsted Pr.

Ecology of the Public Schools: An Inquiry into Community Countrol. Leonard J. Fein. LC 70-128661. 1971. pap. 5.50 (ISBN 0-672-63526-7). Pegasus.

Ecology: Science of Survival. Laurence Pringle. (Illus.). (gr. 7 up). 1971. 8.95 (ISBN 0-02-775230-5). Macmillan.

Ecology: The Man-Made Planet. Don Fabun. 1971. pap. text ed. 2.50x (ISBN 0-02-475350-5, 47535). Macmillan.

Econome Politique. Joachim F. De Villeneuve. (Principal French Demographic Works of the 18th Century Ser.). (Fr.). 1976. lib. bdg. 35.00x o.p. (ISBN 0-8287-1366-9); pap. text ed. 25.00x o.p. (ISBN 0-685-71509-4). Clearwater Pub.

Econometric Analysis by Control Methods. Gregory C. Chow. (Wiley Series in Probability & Mathematical Statistics). 325p. 1981. 31.95 (ISBN 0-471-08706-8, Pub. by Wiley-Interscience). Wiley.

Econometric Analysis of International Tourism. George N. Paraskevopoulos. (Lecture Ser.: No. 31). (Illus.). 110p. (Orig.). 1977. pap. 8.50x (ISBN 0-8002-2743-3). Intl Pubns Serv.

Econometric Estimation. J. C. Rowley. Ed. by Bernard Corry & Brian Henry. LC 72-7811. (Handbooks in Economic Analysis Ser). 234p. 1973. text ed. 19.95 (ISBN 0-470-74360-3). Halsted Pr.

Econometric Estimation of Cost Functions for the Regulated Transportation Industries. Richard H. Spady. LC 78-75058. (Outstanding Dissertations in Economics Ser.). 1979. lib. bdg. 25.00 (ISBN 0-8240-4135-6). Garland Pub.

Econometric Model of the Export Sector. L. Alan Winters. (Cambridge Studies in Applied Econometrics). 192p. Date not set. price not set (ISBN 0-521-23720-3). Cambridge U Pr.

Econometric Model of the Life Insurance Sector of the U. S. Economy. Cummins. LC 73-11654. 1975. 24.95 (ISBN 0-669-89490-7). Lexington Bks.

Econometric Model Performance: Comparative Simulation Studies of the U. S. Economy. Ed. by Lawrence R. Klein & Edwin Burmeister. LC 76-20145. (Orig.). 1976. 15.00x (ISBN 0-8122-7714-7). U of Pa Pr.

Econometric Model Performance in Forecasting & Policy Assessment. W. Allen Spirey & William J. Wrobleski. 1979. pap. 4.25 (ISBN 0-8447-3327-X). Am Enterprise.

Econometric Modeling of World Commodity Policy. F. Gerard Adams & Jere R. Behrman. LC 77-18596. (Wharton Econometric Studies Ser.: No. 2). (Illus.). 1978. 21.00 (ISBN 0-669-02111-3). Lexington Bks.

Econometric Models for the Developing Economies: A Case Study of Greece. Nikos Vernadakis. LC 78-61886. (Praeger Special Studies). 1979. 21.95 (ISBN 0-03-047231-8). Praeger.

Econometric Models of the Housing Sector: A Policy-Oriented Survey. J. Eric Fredland & C. Duncan Macrae. (Institute Paper). 109p. 1978. pap. 5.00 (ISBN 0-87766-232-0, 23600). Urban Inst.

Econometric Models of U.S. Energy Demand. Robert Halvorsen. LC 77-81791. (Illus.). 1978. 18.95 (ISBN 0-669-01942-9). Lexington Bks.

Econometric Models of World Agricultural Commodity Markets: Cocoa, Coffee, Tea, Wool, Cotton, Sugar, Wheat, Rice. F. Gerard Adams & Jere R. Behrman. LC 76-3624. 128p. 1976. text ed. 20.00 o.p. (ISBN 0-88410-290-4). Ballinger Pub.

Econometric Models, Techniques & Applications. Michael D. Intriligator. (Illus.). 1978. pap. 22.95 ref. (ISBN 0-13-223255-3). P-H.

Econometric Studies in Energy Demand & Supply. G. S. Maddala et al. LC 78-2886. (Praeger Special Studies). 1978. 22.95 (ISBN 0-03-042266-3). Praeger.

Econometric Theory. Arthur S. Goldberger. LC 64-10370. (Wiley Series in Probability & Mathematical Statistics). (Illus.). 1964. 29.95 (ISBN 0-471-31101-4). Wiley.

Econometrics. 2nd ed. Ronald J. Wonnacott & Thomas H. Wonnacott. LC 78-31257. (Probability & Mathematical Statistics Ser.). 1979. text ed. 26.95 (ISBN 0-471-95981-2); solutions manual (ISBN 0-471-07837-9). Wiley.

Economic Activity. G. C. Harcourt et al. 1967. 45.00 (ISBN 0-521-05199-1); pap. 13.95x (ISBN 0-521-09427-5). Cambridge U Pr.

Economic Adjustment to an Energy-Short World. Lawrence A. Veit. (Atlantic Papers Ser.: No. 38). 78p. 1980. write for info. 0.00 (ISBN 0-916672-78-6). Allanheld.

Economic Advice & Executive Policy: Recommendations from Past Members of the Council of Economic Advisers. Ed. by Werner Sichel. LC 77-7807. (Praeger Special Studies). 1978. 20.95 (ISBN 0-03-022381-4). Praeger.

Economic Advice & Presidential Leadership. Edward S. Flash, Jr. LC 65-24587. 1965. 22.50x (ISBN 0-231-02827-X). Columbia U Pr.

Economic Advisory Council 1930-1939. S. Howson & D. Winch. LC 75-38187. (Illus.). 1977. 68.50 (ISBN 0-521-21138-7). Cambridge U Pr.

Economic Analysis. 3rd ed. C. E. Ferguson & Charles Maurice. 1978. text ed. 18.50x (ISBN 0-256-02027-2). Irwin.

Economic Analysis: An Introduction. R. J. Barnes. 412p. 1971. 12.95 (ISBN 0-408-70220-6); pap. 7.95 (ISBN 0-408-70233-8). Butterworths.

Economic Analysis of Agricultural Projects. J. Price Gittinger. (World Bank Ser). (Illus.). 240p. 1972. 15.00x (ISBN 0-8018-1386-7); pap. 5.50x (ISBN 0-8018-1403-0). Johns Hopkins.

Economic Analysis of Crime: Selected Readings. Lawrence J. Kaplan & Dennis Kessler. (Illus.). 432p. 1976. 24.50 (ISBN 0-398-03407-9); pap. 17.75 (ISBN 0-398-03408-7). C C Thomas.

Economic Analysis of Environmental Problems. Ed. by Edwin S. Mills. (Universities-National Bureau Conference Ser: No. 26). 1975. 17.50 (ISBN 0-87014-267-4). Columbia U Pr.

Economic Analysis of Fisheries Management Plans. Lee Anderson. 300p. 1981. text ed. 49.95 (ISBN 0-250-40389-7). Ann Arbor Science.

Economic Analysis of Forestry Projects. (FAO Forestry Paper: No. 17). 208p. 1980. pap. 15.00 (ISBN 92-5-100827-2, F-1907, FAO). Unipub.

Economic Analysis of Forestry Projects. (FAO Forestry Paper Ser.: No. 17, Suppl. 1). 243p. 1980. pap. 13.00 (ISBN 92-5-100830-2, F1959, FAO). Unipub.

Economic Analysis of Industrial Projects. Lynn E. Bussey. (International Ser. in Industrial & System Engineering). (Illus.). 1978. ref. 24.95 (ISBN 0-13-223388-6). P-H.

Economic Analysis of Projects. Lyn Squire & Herman G. Van der Tak. LC 75-40228. (World Bank Research Publication Ser). (Illus.). 166p. 1976. 10.00x o.p. (ISBN 0-8018-1817-6); pap. 5.00x (ISBN 0-8018-1818-4). Johns Hopkins.

Economic Analysis of Provincial Land Use Policies in Ontario. M. W. Frankena & D. T. Scheffman. (Ontario Economic Council Research Studies). 1980. pap. 7.50 (ISBN 0-8020-3364-4). U of Toronto Pr.

Economic Analysis of Solar Industrial Process Heat Systems: A Methodology to Determine Annual Required Revenue & Internal Rate of Return. W. C. Dickinson & K. C. Brown. 1980. pap. 6.95 (ISBN 0-89934-012-1). Solar Energy Info.

Economic Analysis of the Soviet-Type System. Ed. by Judith Thornton. LC 75-12468. 256p. 1976. 54.00 (ISBN 0-521-20718-5). Cambridge U Pr.

Economic & Administrative History of Early Indonesia. F. H. Naerssen & R. C. Jongh. 1977. text ed. 43.50x (ISBN 90-04-04918-5). Humanities.

Economic & Business Issues of the Nineteen Eighties. Ed. by Joseph Pluta. LC 80-68658. 235p. (Orig.). 1980. pap. 7.00 (ISBN 0-87755-242-8). U of Tex Busn Res.

Economic & Business: Issues of the 1980's. Ed. by Joseph E. Pluta. 1980. 7.00. U of Tex Busn Res.

Economic & Commercial Geography of India. 2nd rev. ed. T. C. Sharma & O. Continho. (Illus.). 400p. 1980. text ed. 22.50 (ISBN 0-7069-0546-6, Pub. by Vikas India). Advent Bk.

Economic & Financial Analysis of Capital Investments. G. T. Stevens, Jr. 1979. text ed. 26.95 (ISBN 0-471-04851-8); solutions manual avail. (ISBN 0-471-05001-6). Wiley.

Economic & Monetary Union in Europe: The Economic Implications of Monetary Integration. Geoffrey Denton. LC 74-18622. 118p. 1975. 19.95 (ISBN 0-470-20940-2). Halsted Pr.

Economic & Policy Problems in Satellite Communications. Ed. by Joseph N. Pelton & Marcellus S. Snow. LC 75-44937. 1976. text ed. 25.95 (ISBN 0-275-23730-3). Praeger.

Economic & Political Development of the Sudan. Francis Lees & Hugh C. Brooks. LC 77-5252. (Illus.). 1978. lib. bdg. 28.50x (ISBN 0-89158-816-7). Westview.

Economic & Political Peace, Vol. 2. Shirley Telford. LC 76-51755. 1977. 6.95 (ISBN 0-9600202-5-X). William & Rich.

Economic & Social Change in a Midland Town: Victorian Nottingham, 1815-1900. Roy A. Church. LC 66-5409. (Illus.). 1966. 22.50x (ISBN 0-678-05038-4). Kelley.

Economic & Social Consequences of Nuclear Attacks on the United States. Arthur M. Katz. Date not set. write for info. (ISBN 0-88410-096-0). Ballinger Pub.

Economic & Social Foundations of European Civilization. Alfons Dopsch. LC 68-9591. 1969. Repr. of 1937 ed. 16.50 o.p. (ISBN 0-86527-050-3). Fertig.

Economic & Social History of Ancient Greece: An Introduction. M. M. Austin & P. Vidal-Naquet. 1978. 27.50x (ISBN 0-520-02658-6); pap. 6.95 (ISBN 0-520-04267-0). U of Cal Pr.

Economic & Social History of New England 1620-1789, 2 Vols. William B. Weedon. 1963. Set. text ed. 25.00x (ISBN 0-391-00493-X). Humanities.

Economic & Social History of Southern Africa, Vol. 3. Ed. by Z. A. Konczacki & J. M. Konczacki. 1981. 27.50x (ISBN 0-7146-3099-3, F Cass Co). Biblio Dist.

Economic & Social Security. 4th ed. J. G. Turnbull et al. 728p. 1973. 21.95 (ISBN 0-471-06643-5). Wiley.

Economic & Social Security. 4th ed. John G. Turnbull et al. LC 68-5498. 700p. 1973. 21.95x (ISBN 0-8260-8766-3). Ronald Pr.

Economic Approach to Differential Demographic Behavior in Turkey. Samuel S. Lieberman. LC 78-75054. (Outstanding Dissertations in Economics Ser.). 1979. lib. bdg. 25.00 (ISBN 0-8240-4132-1). Garland Pub.

Economic Areas of the United States. Donald J. Bogue & Calvin L. Beale. LC 61-9161. (Illus.). 1961. 35.00 (ISBN 0-02-904400-6). Free Pr.

Economic Aspects of Education. Maureen Woodhall. (General Ser). 130p. (Orig.). 1972. pap. text ed. 8.00x (ISBN 0-85633-011-6, NFER). Humanities.

Economic Aspects of Health Services. A. J. Culyer & K. G. Wright. 190p. 1978. 35.00x (ISBN 0-85520-227-0, Pub. by Martin Robertson England). Biblio Dist.

Economic Aspects of Special Education. (Special Education Ser.). 1979. pap. 9.25 (ISBN 92-3-101514-1, U869, UNESCO). Unipub.

Economic Aspects of the Energy Crisis. Harry W. Richardson. LC 75-8360. 256p. 1975. 19.95 (ISBN 0-669-03327-8). Lexington Bks.

Economic Aspects of the War. Edwin J. Clapp. 1915. 42.50x (ISBN 0-685-69798-3). Elliots Bks.

Economic Assistance to China & Korea: 1949-50 (March, June, June, July 1949; January 1950) Ed. by Richard D. Challener. (Legislative Origins of American Foreign Policy Ser.: Vol. 7). 1979. lib. bdg. 31.00 (ISBN 0-8240-3036-2). Garland Pub.

Economic Balance & a Balanced Budget. Marriner S. Eccles. LC 72-2367. (FDR & the Era of the New Deal Ser). 328p. 1973. Repr. of 1940 ed. lib. bdg. 35.00 (ISBN 0-306-70479-X). Da Capo.

Economic Basis of Protection. Simon Patten. (Neglected American Economists Ser.). 1974. lib. bdg. 50.00 (ISBN 0-8240-1025-6). Garland Pub.

Economic Behaviour: An Introduction. Colin Harbury. (Illus., Orig.). 1980. text ed. 27.50x (ISBN 0-04-330305-6, 2532); pap. 11.50x (ISBN 0-04-330306-4, 2533). Allen Unwin.

Economic Benefits from Four Employment & Training Programs. Nicholas M. Kiefer. LC 78-75061. (Outstanding Dissertations in Economics Ser.). 1979. lib. bdg. 15.00 (ISBN 0-8240-4138-0). Garland Pub.

Economic Benefits of Preserving Old Buildings. LC 76-5086. (Illus.). 1976. pap. 7.95 (ISBN 0-89133-037-2). Preservation Pr.

Economic Calculation in the Socialist Society. Trygve J. Hoff. LC 79-51861. 1981. Repr. of 1949 ed. 21.50 (ISBN 0-88355-954-4). Hyperion Conn.

Economic Causes of Imperialism. Martin Wolfe. LC 77-38965. (Major Issues in History Ser.). 1972. pap. text ed. 6.95x o.p. (ISBN 0-471-95951-0). Wiley.

Economic Challenge of the Arabs. Gian P. Casadio. LC 75-35111. 1976. 22.95 (ISBN 0-347-01067-9, 99390-5, Pub. by Saxon Hse). Lexington Bks.

Economic Change in Pre-Colonial Africa: Senegambia in the Era of the Slave Trade, 2 vols. Philip D. Curtin. LC 74-5899. 1975. Vol. 1. 30.00 (ISBN 0-299-06640-1); Vol. 2. 30.00x (ISBN 0-299-06650-9). U of Wis Pr.

Economic Change in the Philadelphia Region, 1810-1850. Diane Lindstrom. LC 77-23582. 1978. 17.50x (ISBN 0-231-04272-8). Columbia U Pr.

Economic Co-operation in the Commonwealth. G. Arnold. 1967. 22.00 (ISBN 0-08-012449-6); pap. 10.75 (ISBN 0-08-012448-8). Pergamon.

Economic Commentaries. Sir Dennis H. Robertson. LC 79-1589. 1981. Repr. of 1956 ed. 17.00 (ISBN 0-88355-894-7). Hyperion Conn.

Economic Commission for Europe & Energy Conservation. 76p. 1980. pap. 7.00 (UN80-2E4, UN). Unipub.

Economic Concepts: A Programmed Approach. 6th ed. Robert C. Bingham. (Illus.). 384p. 1981. pap. text ed. 7.95 (ISBN 0-07-044936-8, C). McGraw.

Economic Concepts & Systems Analysis: An Introduction for Public Managers. Wright & Tate. 1973. 8.95 (ISBN 0-201-08745-6). A-W.

Economic Conditions of East & Southeast Asia: A Bibliography of English-Language Material, 1965 to 1977. Compiled by Virginia Chen. LC 78-57762. 840p. 1978. lib. bdg. 45.00 (ISBN 0-313-20565-5, CEC/). Greenwood.

Economic Consequences of the New Rice Technology. 402p. 1978. pap. 20.00 (R012, IRRI). Unipub.

Economic Consequences of World Inflation on Semi-Dependent Countries. Robert E. Looney. LC 78-65351. 1978. pap. text ed. 10.75 (ISBN 0-8191-0654-2). U Pr of Amer.

Economic Crime in Europe. L. H. Leigh. Date not set. write for info. (ISBN 0-312-22788-4). St Martin.

Economic Crises. Edward D. Jones. LC 79-51862. 1981. Repr. of 1900 ed. 21.50 (ISBN 0-88355-955-2). Hyperion Conn.

Economic Crisis & American Society. Manuel Castells. 285p. 20.00; pap. 7.50. Princeton U Pr.

Economic Crisis & Crisis Theory. Paul Mattick, Sr. LC 80-5459. Orig. Title: Krisen und Krisentheorien. 228p. 1980. 22.50 (ISBN 0-87332-179-0). M E Sharpe.

Economic Crisis, Cities & Regions: An Analysis of Current Urban & Regional Problems in Australia. Frank J. Stilwell. 192p. 1980. 14.50 (ISBN 0-08-024810-1); pap. 8.95 (ISBN 0-08-024809-8). Pergamon.

Economic Decision Analysis. 2nd ed. Walter J. Fabrycky & G. J. Thuesen. 1980. text ed. 22.95 (ISBN 0-13-223248-0). P-H.

Economic Development. rev. ed. Benjamin Higgins. (Illus.). 1968. 17.95x (ISBN 0-393-09714-5, NortonC). Norton.

Economic Development: A Scientific American Book. Scientific American Editors. LC 80-22326. (Illus.). 1980. text ed. 13.95x (ISBN 0-7167-1273-3); pap. text ed. 6.95x (ISBN 0-7167-1274-1). W H Freeman.

Economic Development & Planning: Essays in Honour of Jan Tinbergen. Ed. by Willy Sellekaerts. LC 73-92712. 288p. 1974. 22.50 o.p. (ISBN 0-87332-055-7). M E Sharpe.

Economic Development & Population Growth in Rhode Island. Kurt B. Mayer. LC 53-5994. 70p. 1953. pap. 2.00 (ISBN 0-87057-033-1, Pub. by Brown U Pr). Univ Pr of New England.

Economic Development & the Dynamics of Class: Industrialization, Power & Control in Monterrey, Mexico. Menno Vellinga. 1979. pap. text ed. 21.50x (ISBN 90-232-1636-9). Humanities.

Economic Development & the Labor Market in Japan. Koji Taira. LC 78-111459. (Studies of the East Asian Institute Ser). 1970. 17.50x (ISBN 0-231-03272-2). Columbia U Pr.

Economic Development & the Use of Energy Resources in Communist China. Yuan-li Wu. LC 63-15122. (Publications Ser.: No. 30). 275p. 1963. 10.00 (ISBN 0-8179-1301-7). Hoover Inst Pr.

Economic Development As an Adaptive Process. R. H. Day & I. Singh. LC 76-9173. (Illus.). 1977. 44.50 (ISBN 0-521-21114-X). Cambridge U Pr.

Economic Development in East Central Europe. Tr. by Ivan T. Berend & Gyorgy Ranki. LC 73-6542. (Institute on East Central Europe Ser.). 1976. pap. 10.00x (ISBN 0-231-08349-1). Columbia U Pr.

Economic Development in Southeast Asia: The Chinese Dimension. Yuan-li Wu & Chun-hsi Wu. LC 79-2455. (Publication Ser.: No. 209). 232p. 1980. pap. text ed. 8.95 (ISBN 0-8179-7092-4). Hoover Inst Pr.

Economic Development in the Soviet Union. Stanley H. Cohn. 1970. pap. text ed. 3.95x o.p. (ISBN 0-669-52688-6). Heath.

Economic Development in the Third World. Michael P. Todaro. LC 76-49626. (Illus.). 1977. text ed. 17.95x (ISBN 0-582-44628-7). Longman.

Economic Development in the Third World. 2nd ed. Michael P. Todaro. (Illus.). 544p. 1981. text ed. 17.95 (ISBN 0-582-29532-7). Longman.

Economic Development of a Small Planet. Benjamin Higgins & Jean D. Higgins. (Illus.). 1979. 14.95 (ISBN 0-393-05697-X); pap. text ed. 8.95x (ISBN 0-393-09084-1). Norton.

Economic Development of Bangladesh Within a Socialist Framework: Proceedings of a Conference Held by the International Economic Association at Daca. Ed. by E. A. Robinson & Keith Griffin. LC 74-8438. (International Economic Assoc. Ser.). 1974. 44.95 (ISBN 0-470-72803-5). Halsted Pr.

Economic Development of Continental Europe 1780-1870. 2nd ed. Alan S. Milward & S. B. Saul. (Illus.). 1973. text ed. 39.95x (ISBN 0-04-330229-7); pap. text ed. 15.95x (ISBN 0-04-330299-8). Allen Unwin.

Economic Development of France & Germany 1815-1914. 4th ed. John H. Clapham. 1935. 50.50 (ISBN 0-521-04664-5); pap. 15.95 (ISBN 0-521-09150-0, 150). Cambridge U Pr.

Economic Development of Japan: Growth & Structural Change, 1868-1938. rev. ed. William W. Lockwood. 23.50 (ISBN 0-691-03014-6); pap. 7.50 o.p. (ISBN 0-691-00001-8). Princeton U Pr.

Economic Development of Latin America. 2nd ed. C. Furtado. LC 74-121365. (Latin American Studies: No.8). (Illus.). 280p. 1977. 37.50 (ISBN 0-521-21197-2); pap. 9.95x (ISBN 0-521-29070-8). Cambridge U Pr.

Economic Development of Panama: The Impact of World Inflation on an Open Economy. Robert E. Looney. LC 74-33038. (Illus.). 1976. text ed. 31.95 (ISBN 0-275-05390-3). Praeger.

Economic Development of Revolutionary Cuba: Strategy & Performance. Archibald R. Ritter. LC 73-3670. (Special Studies). (Illus.). 350p. 1974. text ed. 34.95 (ISBN 0-275-28727-0). Praeger.

Economic Development of Russia, 1905-1914. 2nd ed. Margaret S. Miller. LC 67-3033. Repr. of 1926 ed. 24.00x (ISBN 0-678-05074-0). Kelley.

Economic Development of Socialist Vietnam 1955-80. G. Nguyen Hung. LC 77-11149. (Praeger Special Studies). 1977. 23.95 (ISBN 0-275-24080-0). Praeger.

Economic Development of South Korea: The Political Economy of Success. L. L. Wade & B. S. Kim. LC 78-2665. (Praeger Special Studies). 1978. 25.95 (ISBN 0-03-043591-9). Praeger.

Economic Development of the British Coal Industry. Neil Buxton. 1979. 56.00 (ISBN 0-7134-1994-6, Pub. by Batsford England). David & Charles.

Economic Development of the Middle East: An Outline of Planned Reconstruction After the War. Alfred Bonne. LC 79-51856. 1981. Repr. of 1945 ed. 17.50 (ISBN 0-88355-949-8). Hyperion Conn.

Economic Development of the North Atlantic Community: Historical Introduction to Modern Economics. Dudley Dillard. 1967. text ed. 21.95 (ISBN 0-13-223305-3). P-H.

Economic Development of the Third World Since 1900. Paul Bairoch. Tr. by Cynthia Postan. LC 74-16706. (Illus.). 1975. pap. 7.50x (ISBN 0-520-03554-2). U of Cal Pr.

Economic Development of the United States. rev. ed. Ralph Gray & John M. Peterson. 1974. text ed. 15.95x o.p. (ISBN 0-256-01549-X). Irwin.

Economic Development of Western Europe, 4 vols. Warren C. Scoville & J. Clayburn Laforce. Incl. Vol. 1. Middle Ages & the Renaissance. pap. text ed. 2.95x o.p. (ISBN 0-669-26906-9); Vol. 2. The Sixteenth & Seventeenth Centuries. pap. text ed. o.p. (ISBN 0-669-26914-X); Vol. 3. The Eighteenth & Early Nineteenth Centuries. pap. text ed. o.p. (ISBN 0-669-26922-0); Vol. 4. The Late Nineteenth & Early Twentieth Centuries. pap. text ed. 2.95x o.p. (ISBN 0-669-26930-1). 1969. Heath.

Economic Development, Peace, & International Law. Wil D. Verwey. 1972. text ed. 36.50x (ISBN 90-232-0992-3). Humanities.

Economic Development, Poverty & Income Distribution. Wm. Loehr & J. Powelson. LC 77-23270. 1977. lib. bdg. 27.50x (ISBN 0-89158-248-7). Westview.

Economic Diplomacy & the Origins of the Second World War: Germany, Britain, France, & Eastern Europe, 1930-1939. David E. Kaiser. LC 80-7536. 352p. 1980. 25.00 (ISBN 0-691-05312-X); pap. 12.50 (ISBN 0-691-10101-9). Princeton U Pr.

Economic Disparity. W. L. Henderson & L. C. Ledebur. LC 79-96833. 1970. 10.95 (ISBN 0-02-914440-X); pap. text ed. 10.95 (ISBN 0-02-914400-0). Free Pr.

Economic Doctrines of Knut Wicksell. Carl G. Uhr. (Institute of Business & Economic Research UC Berkeley). 1960. 27.50x (ISBN 0-520-01290-9). U of Cal Pr.

Economic Education: A Guide to Information Sources. Ed. by Catherine A. Hughes. LC 73-17576. (Economics Information Guide Ser.: Vol. 6). 1977. 30.00 (ISBN 0-8103-1290-5). Gale.

Economic Effects of Annexation: A Second Case Study in Richmond, Virginia. Thomas Muller & Grace Dawson. (Institute Paper). 91p. 1976. pap. 2.50 (ISBN 0-87766-165-0, 14400). Urban Inst.

Economic Effects of Exchange-Rate Changes. new ed. Klaus-Walter Riechel. LC 78-58926. 1978. 17.95 (ISBN 0-669-02376-0). Lexington Bks.

Economic Effects of the Public Works Expenditures, 1933-1938. United States National Resources Planning Board, Public Works Committee. Ed. by J. K. Galbraith & G. G. Johnson. (FDR & the Era of the New Deal Ser). vii, 131p. 1975. Repr. of 1940 ed. lib. bdg. 20.00 (ISBN 0-306-70713-6). Da Capo.

Economic Efficiency of Financial Markets. Jan Mossin. 1977. 18.95 (ISBN 0-669-01004-9). Lexington Bks.

Economic Environment of International Business. 2nd ed. R. Vernon & L. T. Wells. 272p. 1976. pap. text ed. 12.95x (ISBN 0-13-224311-3). P-H.

Economic Environment of International Business. 3rd ed. Louis T. Wells, Jr. & Raymond Vernon. (Illus.). 272p. 1981. text ed. 13.95 (ISBN 0-13-224329-6). P-H.

Economic-Environmental-Energy Interactions. Ed. by T. R. Lakshmanan. P. Nijkamp. (Studies in Applied Regional Science: Vol. 16). 224p. 1980. lib. bdg. 18.95 (ISBN 0-89838-023-5, Martinus Nijhoff Pubs). Kluwer Boston.

Economic Essays on Developing Countries. U Tun Wai. LC 80-83264. 512p. 1980. 70.00 (ISBN 90-286-0150-3). Sijthoff & Noordhoff.

Economic Evaluation & Investment Decision Methods. 3rd ed. Franklin J. Stermole. 1980. text ed. 22.50 (ISBN 0-9603282-0-3); solutions manual 6.50 (ISBN 0-9603282-3-8). Invest Eval.

Economic Evaluation of Soviet Socialism. Alan Aboucher. (Pergamon Policy Studies). 1979. text ed. 19.25 (ISBN 0-08-023870-X). Pergamon.

Economic Evaluation of Urban Renewal. Jerome Rothenberg. (Studies of Government Finance). 1967. 12.95 (ISBN 0-8157-7592-X); pap. 4.95 (ISBN 0-8157-7591-1). Brookings.

Economic Exchange & Social Interaction in Southeast Asia: Perspectives from Prehistory, History, & Ethnography. Ed. by Karl L. Hutterer. LC 77-95147. (Michigan Papers on South & Southeast Asia: No. 13). (Illus.). 300p. 1977. pap. 7.50x (ISBN 0-89148-013-7). Ctr S&SE Asian.

Economic Factors in Population Growth: Proceedings. Ed. by Ansley J. Coale. LC 74-17375. 600p. 1976. 54.95 (ISBN 0-470-16147-7). Halsted Pr.

Economic Facts, 4 vols. Agricutural Economics Dept., U. of Nanking, Chengtu. LC 78-74325. (Modern Chinese Economy Ser.: Vol. 11). 1980. Set. lib. bdg. 165.00 (ISBN 0-8240-4260-3). Garland Pub.

Economic Forecasting-Models or Markets? James B. Ramsey. LC 80-21911. (Cato Papers Ser.: No. 15). 112p. 1980. pap. 5.00 (ISBN 0-932790-28-3). Cato Inst.

Economic Foreign Policies of Industrial States. Ed. by Wilfred L. Kohl. LC 76-43584. 1977. 21.50 (ISBN 0-669-00958-X). Lexington Bks.

Economic Foreign Policy of the United States. Benjamin H. Williams. 1967. Repr. 19.00 (ISBN 0-86527-051-1). Fertig.

Economic Foundations of British Overseas Expansion 1815-1914. Peter J. Cain. (Studies in Economic & Social History). 1980. pap. text ed. 5.25x (ISBN 0-333-23284-4). Humanities.

Economic Foundations of Political Power. Randall Bartlett. LC 73-3899. 1973. 12.95 (ISBN 0-02-901870-6). Free Pr.

Economic Freedom, Stability & Growth. Gardner Ackley et al. 1972. 8.40 (ISBN 0-932826-05-9); pap. 3.95 (ISBN 0-685-85517-1). New Issues MI.

Economic Future of the United States. Irving Leveson. (Hudson Institute Studies on the Prospects for Mankind). 300p. 1981. lib. bdg. 27.50x (ISBN 0-86531-097-1). Westview.

Economic Geography. John W. Alexander. 1963. text ed. 16.95 o.p. (ISBN 0-13-225144-2). P-H.

Economic Geography. 2nd ed. John W. Alexander & L. Gibson. 1979. 20.95 (ISBN 0-13-225151-5). P-H.

Economic Geography. Joseph H. Butler. LC 80-14542. 402p. 1980. 23.95 (ISBN 0-471-12681-0). Wiley.

Economic Geography. James O. Wheeler & Peter O. Muller. LC 80-21536. 450p. 1981. text ed. 20.95 (ISBN 0-471-93760-6). Wiley.

Economic Geography of East Africa. A. M. O'Connor. (Advanced Economic Geography Ser.). 1971. lib. bdg. 24.00x (ISBN 0-7135-1626-7). Westview.

Economic Geography of Romania. David Turnock. (Advanced Economic Geography Ser.). 1974. lib. bdg. 28.50x (ISBN 0-7135-1628-3). Westview.

Economic Geography of the World. Ed. by V. Maksakovsky. (Illus.). 1978. 10.00 (ISBN 0-8285-0002-9). Progress Pubs.

Economic Geography of West Africa. H. P. White & M. B. Gleave. (Advanced Economic Geography Ser.). 1971. pap. text ed. 16.50x (ISBN 0-7135-1721-2). Westview.

Economic Geography of Western Europe. P. R. Odell & Bert Van Der Knapp. 1980. write for info. (ISBN 0-06-318087-1, IntlDept). Har-Row.

Economic Growth: Analysis & Policy. W. A. Eltis. (Orig.). 1966. text ed. 5.50x (ISBN 0-09-079462-1, Hutchinson U Lib); pap. text ed. 2.75x (ISBN 0-09-079463-X, Hutchinson U Lib). Humanities.

Economic Growth & Development in Jordan. Michael P. Mazur. (Special Studies on the Middle East). 1979. lib. bdg. 29.50x (ISBN 0-89158-455-2). Westview.

Economic Growth & Disparities: A World View. S. Jumper et al. 1980. 20.95 (ISBN 0-13-225680-0). P-H.

Economic Growth & Distribution in China. N. Lardy. (Illus.). 1978. 29.95 (ISBN 0-521-21904-3). Cambridge U Pr.

Economic Growth & Resources: Natural Resources, Vol III. Christopher Bliss. LC 79-4430. 1979. 37.50x (ISBN 0-312-23316-7). St Martin.

Economic Growth & Stability. Gottfried Haberler. LC 73-92965. (Principles of Freedom Ser.). 1976. Repr. of 1974 ed. 10.00x o.p. (ISBN 0-8402-1337-9, Caroline Hse Inc). Green Hill.

Economic Growth & Stability: An Analysis of Economic Change & Policies. Gottfried Haberler. LC 73-92965. (Principles of Freedom Ser.). 291p. 1974. 10.00x o.p. (ISBN 0-8402-1337-9). Nash Pub.

Economic Growth & Stability: An Analysis of Economic Change & Policies. Gottfried Haberler. (Principles of Freedom Ser.). 319p. 1980. text ed. 10.00x (ISBN 0-8402-1337-9). Humanities.

Economic Growth & the Generation of Waterborne Wastes. (Marine Technical Report: No. 12). 1973. pap. 1.00 o.p. (ISBN 0-686-23174-0). URI MAS.

Economic Growth Controversy. Ed. by Andrew Weintraub et al. LC 73-75076. 200p. 1973. 12.00 o.p. (ISBN 0-87332-038-7). M E Sharpe.

Economic Growth Debate: Are There Limits to Growth? Laurence Pringles. (Impact Ser). (gr. 9 up). 1978. lib. bdg. 6.90 s&l (ISBN 0-531-01322-7). Watts.

Economic Growth in a Free Market. George H. Borts & Jerome L. Stein. LC 64-13735. 1964. 20.00x (ISBN 0-231-02666-8). Columbia U Pr.

Economic Growth in Britain & France 1780-1914: Two Paths to the Twentieth Century. Patrick O'Brien & Caglar Keyder. 1978. text ed. 27.50x (ISBN 0-04-330288-2). Allen Unwin.

Economic Growth in Twentieth Century Britain. Derek Aldcroft & Peter Fearon. 1970. 8.75x (ISBN 0-333-10041-7); pap. text ed. 4.75x (ISBN 0-333-10595-8). Humanities.

Economic Growth or Stagnation. Ed. by Jules Backman. LC 78-10874. (ITT Key Issue Lecture Ser.). 168p. text ed. 9.95 (ISBN 0-672-97323-5); pap. text ed. 4.95 (ISBN 0-672-97322-7). Bobbs.

Economic Growth Versus the Environment. Richard Lecomber. LC 75-5605. 1975. pap. 6.50x (ISBN 0-470-52100-7). Halsted Pr.

Economic Healing. rev. ed. A.R.E. New York Members. 29p. 1974. pap. 1.25 (ISBN 0-87604-074-1). ARE Pr.

Economic History of Argentina. Laura Randall. LC 77-24388. 1977. 20.00x (ISBN 0-231-03358-3). Columbia U Pr.

Economic History of Britain Since Seventeen Hundred: Volume 2: 1860 to the 1970s. Ed. by R. Floud & D. McCloskey. LC 79-41645. (Illus.). 504p. Date not set. price not set (ISBN 0-521-23167-1); pap. text ed. price not set (ISBN 0-521-29843-1). Cambridge U Pr.

Economic History of Canada: A Guide to Information Sources. Trevor J. Dick. LC 73-17571. (Economics Information Guide Ser.: Vol. 9). 1978. 30.00 (ISBN 0-8103-1292-1). Gale.

Economic History of Colonialism. Sadananda Choudhury. 1979. text ed. 13.50x (ISBN 0-391-01852-3). Humanities.

Economic History of England. D. J. Chappell. 320p. 1980. pap. 12.95x (ISBN 0-7121-0587-5). Intl Ideas.

Economic History of Europe. Shepard B. Clough et al. LC 68-27379. (Documentary History of Western Civilization Ser). 1968. 15.00x o.s.i. (ISBN 0-8027-2005-6). Walker & Co.

Economic History of Medieval Europe. N. J. Pounds. LC 73-93716. (Illus.). 544p. 1974. text ed. 21.00x (ISBN 0-582-48266-6); pap. 10.95x, 1977 (ISBN 0-582-48680-7). Longman.

Economic History of Milk Marketing, Vol. III. Leland Spencer & Charles J. Blanford. LC 77-90779. 1977. text ed. 30.00 o.p. (ISBN 0-88244-078-0). Grid Pub.

Economic History of Modern France. Francois Caron. Tr. by Barbara Bray from Fr. (Columbia Economic History of the Modern World). 1979. 18.50x (ISBN 0-231-03860-7). Columbia U Pr.

Economic History of the United States Prior to 1860: An Annotated Bibliography. new ed. Thomas Orsagh et al. LC 75-1162. 100p. 1975. text ed. 4.50 (ISBN 0-87436-205-9). ABC-Clio.

Economic History of the United States. M. L. Primack & J. F. Willis. 1980. 16.95. A-W.

Economic History of the United States. Martin L. Primack & James F. Willis. 1979. 18.95 (ISBN 0-8053-8010-8). Benjamin-Cummings.

Economic History of Transport in Britain. 3rd ed. Christopher I. Savage. 1974. text ed. 16.50x (ISBN 0-09-121470-X, Hutchinson U Lib). Humanities.

Economic History of Turkey, Eighteen Hundred to Nineteen Fourteen. Charles Issawi. LC 80-444. (Publications of the Center for Middle Eastern Studies: No. 13). 1981. lib. bdg. 20.00x (ISBN 0-226-38603-1). U of Chicago Pr.

Economic History of West Africa. A. G. Hopkins. 450p. 1973. 22.50x (ISBN 0-231-03739-2). Columbia U Pr.

Economic History of World Population. 7th ed. Ed. by Carlo M. Cipolla. (Illus.). 1978. text ed. 16.00x (ISBN 0-06-491138-1). B&N.

Economic Impact of Arts & Cultural Institutions: A Model for Assessment & a Case Study in Baltimore, Report No. 6. (National Endowment for the Arts Research Division Reports). 96p. 1977. pap. 3.50x (ISBN 0-89062-094-6, Pub. by Ctr Cult Res). Pub Ctr Cultures.

Economic Impact of the Patent System: A Study of the British Experiment. C. T. Taylor & Z. A. Silberston. LC 73-77173. (Department of Applied Economics Monographs, No. 23). (Illus.). 400p. 1973. 54.00 (ISBN 0-521-20255-8). Cambridge U Pr.

Economic Impact of TVA. Ed. by John R. Moore. LC 67-12217. 1967. 10.50x (ISBN 0-87049-072-9). U of Tenn Pr.

Economic Impacts of Land Development: Employment, Housing & Property Values. Thomas Muller. (Land Development Impact Ser.). 148p. 1976. pap. 3.95 (ISBN 0-87766-173-1, 15800). Urban Inst.

Economic Imperialism. Leonard Woolf. LC 68-9627. 1970. Repr. of 1920 ed. 12.25 (ISBN 0-86527-053-8). Fertig.

Economic Importance of Exports of the United States. (Significant Issues Ser.: Vol. II, No. 5). 119p. 1980. pap. 10.00 (ISBN 0-89206-019-0, CSIS013, CSIS). Unipub.

Economic Importance of Exports to the United States, Vol. Ii. Jack Carlson & Hugh Graham. LC 80-66694. (Significant Issues Ser.: No. 6). 128p. 1980. 5.95 (ISBN 0-89206-019-0). CSI Studies.

Economic Indicators & the GPID: An Attempt to Bring Economics Back into the Church Without Losing the Faith. 27p. 1980. pap. 5.00 (ISBN 92-808-0134-1, TUNU 068, UNU). Unipub.

Economic Influences Upon Educational Progress in the United States 1820-1850. Frank T. Carlton. LC 66-11657. (Orig.). 1966. text ed. 8.75 (ISBN 0-8077-1143-8); pap. text ed. 4.00x (ISBN 0-8077-1140-3). Tchrs Coll.

Economic Information, Decision, & Prediction, 3 vols. Jacob Marschak. (Theory & Decision Library: No. 7). 1980. Vol. I, 389 Pp. pap. 14.95 (ISBN 90-277-1195-X, Pub. by D. Reidel); Vol. II, 362 Pp. pap. 14.95 (ISBN 90-277-1196-8); Vol. III, 399 Pp. pap. 14.95 (ISBN 90-277-1197-6). Kluwer Boston.

Economic Inquiries & Studies, 2 vols. Robert Giffen. (Development of Industrial Society Ser.). 916p. 1981. Repr. 65.00x (ISBN 0-7165-1758-2, Pub. by Irish Academic Pr). Biblio Dist.

Economic Institutions Compared. Peter Wiles. LC 76-6175. 608p. 1977. 34.95 (ISBN 0-470-15083-1). Halsted Pr.

Economic Integration & the Law of Gatt. Pierre Lortie. LC 75-3626. (Special Studies). (Illus.). 202p. 1975. text ed. 25.95 (ISBN 0-275-05230-3). Praeger.

Economic Integration: Concepts, Theories & Problems. Ed. by Mihaly Simai & Katalin Garam. LC 78-308400. 423p. 1977. 30.00x (ISBN 963-05-1188-6). Intl Pubns Serv.

Economic Integration in Africa. Peter Robson. LC 68-25582. 1969. 14.95x o.s.i. (ISBN 0-8101-0033-9). Northwestern U Pr.

Economic Integration in Central America. Ed. by William R. Cline & Enrique Delgado. LC 78-60708. 1978. 21.95 (ISBN 0-8157-1470-X). Brookings.

Economic Integration of Nuclear Power Stations in Electric Power Systems. (Illus., Orig.). 1971. pap. 52.50 (ISBN 92-0-050071-4, ISP266, IAEA). Unipub.

Economic Integration: Worldwide, Regional, Sectoral: Proceedings. Congress of the International Economic Association, 4th, Budapest, Hungary. Ed. by Fritz Machlup. LC 76-10281. 1977. 39.95 (ISBN 0-470-01381-8). Halsted Pr.

Economic Interdependence in Southeast Asia. Ed. by Theodore Morgan & Nyle Spoelstra. LC 68-9021. 1969. 27.50x (ISBN 0-299-05150-1). U of Wis Pr.

Economic Interest, Militarism, & Foreign Policy: Essays on German History. Eckart Kehr. Ed. by Gordon A. Craig. Tr. by Grete Heinz from Ger. 1977. 18.50x (ISBN 0-520-02880-5). U of Cal Pr.

Economic Issues & Policies: Readings in Introductory Economics. 3rd ed. John E. Elliott & Arthur Grey. 1975. pap. text ed. 10.50 (ISBN 0-395-19824-0). HM.

Economic Issues for Consumers. 2nd ed. Roger L. Miller. (Illus.). 1978. text ed. 17.50 (ISBN 0-8299-0151-5); pap. text ed. 6.50 study guide (ISBN 0-8299-0217-1); instrs.' manual avail. (ISBN 0-8299-0560-X). West Pub.

Economic Issues for Consumers. 3rd ed. Roger L. Miller. (Illus.). 600p. 1980. text ed. 19.95 (ISBN 0-8299-0396-8). West Pub.

Economic Landscape: A Theoretical Introduction. Foust. (Geography Ser.). 1978. text ed. 18.95 (ISBN 0-675-08432-6). Merrill.

Economic Liberalism. Hermann Levy. LC 79-51864. 1981. Repr. of 1913 ed. 14.50 (ISBN 0-88355-956-0). Hyperion Conn.

Economic Liberties & the Constitution. Bernard H. Siegan. LC 80-15756. 1981. 19.50x (ISBN 0-226-75663-7). U of Chicago Pr.

Economic Library of Jacob H. Hollander. Jacob H. Hollander. Ed. by Elsie A. Marsh. LC 67-14032. 1966. Repr. of 1937 ed. 18.00 (ISBN 0-8103-3103-9). Gale.

Economic Life in the Bombay Gujerat: 1818-1939. R. D. Choksey. 14.00x o.p. (ISBN 0-210-22648-X). Asia.

Economic Man in Relation to His Natural Environment, 2 Vols. Charles R. Noyes. LC 48-7550. 1948. 27.50x (ISBN 0-231-01646-8). Columbia U Pr.

Economic Man in Sha Tin: Vegetable Gardeners in a Hong Kong Valley. Goran Aijmer. (Scandanavian Institute of Asian Studies Monograph: No. 43). (Orig.). 1980. pap. text ed. 9.25x (ISBN 0-7007-0135-4). Humanities.

Economic Man: The Anthropolgy of Economics. Harold K. Schneider. LC 73-8493. (Illus.). 1974. 12.95 (ISBN 0-02-927940-2). Free Pr.

Economic Mineral Deposits. 3rd rev. ed. M. L. Jensen & A. M. Bateman. 608p. 1981. text ed. 24.95 (ISBN 0-471-09043-3). Wiley.

Economic Mineral Deposits. 3rd ed. M. L. Jensen & A. M. Bateman. LC 78-9852. 1979. text ed. 25.95 (ISBN 0-471-01769-8). Wiley.

Economic Models: An Exposition. E. F. Beach. 227p. 1957. text ed. 11.25 (ISBN 0-471-06072-0, Pub. by Wiley). Krieger.

Economic Models, Estimation & Risk Programming: Essays in Honor of Gerhard Tintner. Ed. by K. A. Fox et al. LC 72-98260. (Lecture Notes in Operations Research & Mathematical Economics: Vol. 15). 1969. pap. 21.90 o.p. (ISBN 0-387-04638-0). Springer-Verlag.

Economic Modernization of France, 1730-1880. Roger Price. LC 75-14447. 1975. 24.95 (ISBN 0-470-69722-9). Halsted Pr.

Economic Opportunity & Crime. Marvin Ross. 1977. pap. text ed. 12.20x o.p. (ISBN 0-685-87412-5). Renouf.

Economic Perspective on the Evolution of Graduate Education: A Technical Report Presented to the National Board on Graduate Education. Stephen P. Dresch. 88p. 1974. pap. text ed. 2.00 (ISBN 0-309-02221-5). Natl Acad Pr.

Economic Perspectives. Sir John Hicks. 1977. text ed. 19.50x (ISBN 0-19-828407-1). Oxford U Pr.

Economic Perspectives: An Annual Survey of Economics, Vol. 1. Ed. by M. B. Ballbon. 280p. 1979. 35.00 (ISBN 3-7186-0001-3). Harwood Academic.

Economic Perspectives: An Annual Survey of Economics, Vol. 2. Ed. by M. B. Ballabon. 300p. 1980. lib. bdg. 45.00 (ISBN 0-470-26662-7). Harwood Academic.

Economic Philosophy of History. 1975. 59.50 (ISBN 0-89266-094-5). Inst Econ Finan.

Economic Philosophy of History & Basic Patterns in the Growth & Decline of Nations. Carlo M. Flumiani. (Illus.). 117p. 1981. 59.85 (ISBN 0-930008-77-4). Inst Econ Finan.

Economic Planning. 2nd rev. ed. A. N. Agrawal & Kundan Lal. 400p. 1980. text ed. 18.95 (ISBN 0-7069-1256-X, Pub. by Vikas India). Advent Bk.

Economic Planning. Zoltan Kenessey. 1977. 22.50x (ISBN 0-231-03571-3). Columbia U Pr.

Economic Planning in Soviet Russia. Boris Brutzkus. Tr. by Gilbert Gardner from Ger. LC 79-51857. 1981. Repr. of 1935 ed. 19.75 (ISBN 0-88355-950-1). Hyperion Conn.

Economic Planning Studies. Ed. by Frank Long. (International Studies in Economics & Econometrics: No. 8). 198p. 1980. pap. 11.95 (ISBN 90-277-1194-1, Pub. by D. Reidel). Kluwer Boston.

Economic Point of View: An Essay in the History of Economic Thought. 2nd ed. Israel M. Kirzner. LC 75-42449. (Studies in Economic Theory). 228p. 1976. 12.00; pap. 4.95. NYU Pr.

Economic Policies & Price Stability in China. Tong-Eng Wang. LC 80-620008. (China Research Monographs: No. 16). (Illus.). 1980. pap. write for info. (ISBN 0-912966-24-6). IEAS Ctr Chinese Stud.

Economic Policy & Income Distribution in Columbia. Ed. by R. Albert Berry. Ronald Soligo. (Westview Replica Edition Ser.). 1979. lib. bdg. 25.50x (ISBN 0-89158-558-3). Westview.

Economic Policy & Projects: The Development of a Consumer Society in Early Modern England. Joan Thirsk. 1978. 24.95x (ISBN 0-19-828274-5). Oxford U Pr.

Economic Policy in Postwar Japan: Growth Versus Economic Democracy. Kozo Yamamura. (Center for Japanese & Korean Studies, UC Berkeley). 1967. 21.50x (ISBN 0-520-01369-7). U of Cal Pr.

Economic Policy in Socialist Yugoslavia. R. Bicanic. LC 72-80588. (Soviet & East European Studies). (Illus.). 270p. 1973. 38.50 (ISBN 0-521-08631-0). Cambridge U Pr.

Economic Policy Reform in Mexico: A Case Study for Developing Countries. Leopoldo Solis. LC 80-26937. (Pergamon Press Series on International Development). 225p. 1981. 25.00 (ISBN 0-08-026330-5). Pergamon.

Economic Prerequisite to Democracy. Dan Usher. 224p. 1981. 17.50x (ISBN 0-231-05280-4). Columbia U Pr.

Economic Principles Applied. Ed. by C. V. Brown. 192p. 1980. pap. text ed. cancelled (ISBN 0-85520-001-4, Pub. by Martin Robertson England). Biblio Dist.

Economic Principles in Action. Robert L. Moore. (Illus.). 1979. pap. text ed. 8.95 (ISBN 0-13-226845-0). P-H.

Economic Problem. Ralph G. Hawtrey. LC 79-1581. 1981. Repr. of 1926 ed. 27.50 (ISBN 0-88355-886-6). Hyperion Conn.

Economic Problem. 5th rev. ed. Robert L. Heilbroner & Lester C. Thurow. (Illus.). 1978. ref. ed. 19.95 (ISBN 0-13-233338-4); student companion 8.95 (ISBN 0-13-233353-8). P-H.

Economic Problem of the Danubian States: A Study in Economic Nationalism. Frederick Hertz. LC 68-9662. 1970. 13.50 (ISBN 0-86527-054-6). Fertig.

Economic Problems of Latin America. John M. Hunter & James W. Foley. 1975. text ed. 20.95 (ISBN 0-395-18941-1). HM.

Economic Problems of Socialism in the U.S.S.R. Joseph Stalin. pap. 1.25 (ISBN 0-8351-0068-5). China Bks.

Economic Prospects & Policies in the Industrial Countries. Tripartite report by Saxteen economists from the European Community, Japan & North America. 1977. pap. 2.00 (ISBN 0-8157-2089-0). Brookings.

Economic Querist. G. L. Shackle. LC 72-96679. 120p. 1973. 17.95 (ISBN 0-521-20188-8). Cambridge U Pr.

Economic Realities & Female Crime: Program Choices & Economic Rehabilitation. Jane R. Chapman. LC 79-3785. 240p. 1980. 21.95x (ISBN 0-669-03515-7). Lexington Bks.

Economic Reform in Rumanian Industry. Iancu Spigler. (Economic Reforms in East European Industry Ser.). (Illus.). 194p. 1973. 15.95x o.p. (ISBN 0-19-215339-0). Oxford U Pr.

Economic Reforms in Eastern Europe & Prospects for the 1980s. NATO. (NATO Colloquim, 16-18 April 1980, Brussels, Belgium). (Illus.). 325p. 1980. 60.00 (ISBN 0-08-026801-3). Pergamon.

Economic Regulation & Consumer Welfare: The Federal Trade Commission Since 1970. Ed. by Kenneth Clarkson et al. (Illus.). 448p. Date not set. price not set (ISBN 0-521-23378-X). Cambridge U Pr.

Economic Regulatory Policies. Ed. by James E. Anderson. LC 76-44023. 232p. 1977. pap. 6.95 (ISBN 0-8093-0818-5). S Ill U Pr.

Economic Relations Between East & West: Prospects & Problems. Tripartite report by fifteen experts from the European Community, Japan, & North America. 1978. pap. 2.00 (ISBN 0-8157-2091-2). Brookings.

Economic Relations Between Socialist Countries & the Third World. Ed. by Deepak Nayyar. LC 77-84409. 294p. 1978. text ed. 25.50x (ISBN 0-86598-000-4). Allanheld.

Economic Rise of Early America. G. M. Walton & J. F. Shepherd. LC 78-13438. (Illus.). 1979. 26.95 (ISBN 0-521-22282-6); pap. 6.50x (ISBN 0-521-29433-9). Cambridge U Pr.

Economic Rivalries in China. Grover Clark. 1932. 37.50x (ISBN 0-685-69799-1). Elliots Bks.

Economic Scenes: Theory in Today's World. 2nd ed. Stanley L. Brue & Donald R. Wentworth. (Illus.). 1980. text ed. 11.95 (ISBN 0-13-233510-7). P-H.

Economic Soverignty & Regional Policy. Ed. by John Vaizey. LC 74-22003. 1975. 32.95 (ISBN 0-470-89777-5). Halsted Pr.

Economic Special-Opportunity Conduct & Crime. Pawel Horoszowski. LC 78-24829. 222p. 1980. 24.95x (ISBN 0-669-02849-5). Lexington Bks.

Economic Stabilization in Developing Countries. William R. Cline & Sidney Weintraub. LC 80-70079. 514p. 1981. 26.95 (ISBN 0-8157-1466-1); pap. 11.95 (ISBN 0-8157-1465-3). Brookings.

Economic Stabilization in Latin America: Political Dimensions. Ed. by Alejandro Foxley & Laurence Whitehead. 120p. 1980. pap. 16.50 (ISBN 0-08-026788-2). Pergamon.

Economic Status of Australian Aborigines. J. C. Altman & J. P. Nieuwenhuysen. LC 78-14917. 1979. 34.50 (ISBN 0-521-22421-7). Cambridge U Pr.

Economic Structure. Peter Musgrave. (Aspects of Modern Sociology Ser). 1969. text ed. 4.00x (ISBN 0-582-48804-4); pap. text ed. 2.50x (ISBN 0-582-48805-2). Humanities.

Economic Studies: Contributions to the Critique of Economic Theory. David P. Levine. 1977. 28.00x (ISBN 0-7100-8573-7). Routledge & Kegan.

Economic Studies on Hungary's Agriculture. Benet. 1977. 14.00 (ISBN 0-9960000-4-6, Pub. by Kaido Hungary). Heyden.

Economic Study of Chinese Agriculture. Chi-Yu Tang. LC 78-74306. (Modern Chinese Economy Ser.: Vol. 14). 514p. 1980. lib. bdg. 55.00 (ISBN 0-8240-4262-X). Garland Pub.

Economic Superpowers & the Environment: The U.S., the Soviet Union, & Japan. Donald R. Kelley et al. LC 76-1003. 1976. text ed. 22.95x (ISBN 0-7167-0720-9); pap. text ed. 10.95x (ISBN 0-7167-0721-7). W H Freeman.

Economic Survey Methods. John B. Lansing & James N. Morgan. LC 71-633672. 448p. 1971. cloth 14.00 (ISBN 0-87944-009-0); pap. 8.00 (ISBN 0-87944-008-2). U of Mich Soc Res.

Economic Survey of Europe in Nineteen Seventy-Seven: The European Economy in Nineteen Seventy-Eight, Pt.1. 166p. 1980. pap. 12.00 (UN79-2E1, UN). Unipub.

Economic Survey of Japan, 1978-1979. 28th ed. Economic Planning Agency (Govt. of Japan) LC 51-61351. (Illus.). 204p. (Orig.). 1979. pap. 35.00x (ISBN 0-8002-2757-3). Intl Pubns Serv.

Economic Survey of Latin America 1977. 536p. 1979. pap. 22.00 (ISBN 0-686-68952-6, UN79/2G1, UN). Unipub.

Economic Survey of Latin America 1977. United Nations. LC 50-3616. 536p. (Orig.). 1978. pap. 22.00x (ISBN 0-8002-1067-0). Intl Pubns Serv.

Economic Survey of Latin America 1977. United Nations. LC 50-3616. 462p. 1977. pap. 22.00x (ISBN 0-8002-1066-2). Intl Pubns Serv.

Economic Survey 1919-1939. W. Arthur Lewis. 1949. pap. text ed. 9.95x (ISBN 0-04-330051-0). Allen Unwin.

Economic System in the United Kingdom. 2nd ed. Ed. by Derek Morris. 1977. 34.95x (ISBN 0-19-877141-X). Oxford U Pr.

Economic Systems: How Resources Are Allocated. Rolf Eidem & Staffan Viotti. LC 78-19199. 1978. text ed. 18.95 (ISBN 0-470-26364-4). Halsted Pr.

Economic Theory. George B. Richardson. (Orig.). 1964. pap. text ed. 2.50x (ISBN 0-09-072653-7, Hutchinson U Lib). Humanities.

Economic Theory & Exhaustible Resources. P. S. Dasgupta & G. M. Heal. LC 79-51749. (Cambridge Economic Handbooks Ser.). 1980. 42.50 (ISBN 0-521-22991-X); pap. 16.95x (ISBN 0-521-29761-3). Cambridge U Pr.

Economic Theory & Operations Analysis. 4th ed. W. Baumol. 1977. 20.95 (ISBN 0-13-227132-X). P-H.

Economic Theory & Organization. Alfred G. McArthur & John W. Loveridge. (Illus.). 400p. 1980. pap. 16.95x. Intl Ideas.

Economic Theory & Practice in the Asian Setting, 4 vols. Committee on Economics Teaching Material for Asian Universities. Incl. Vol. 1. Macroeconomics. LC 75-20408. o.p. (ISBN 0-470-14272-3); Vol. 2. Microeconomics. LC 75-20409 (ISBN 0-470-14273-1); Vol. 3. Economics of Agriculture. LC 75-20412. o.p. (ISBN 0-470-14270-7); Vol. 4. Economics of Development. LC 75-20411 (ISBN 0-470-14271-5). (Economic Theory & Practice in the Asian Setting Ser.). 1975. Vols. 2 & 4. pap. 9.95 ea. Halsted Pr.

Economic Theory & the Antitrust Dilemma. Peter Asch. LC 78-127658. (Illus.). 1970. 24.95 (ISBN 0-471-03443-6, Pub. by Wiley-Interscience). Wiley.

Economic Theory in Retrospect. M. Blaug. LC 77-7899. 1978. 24.95x (ISBN 0-521-21733-4). Cambridge U Pr.

Economic Theory of Agricultural Land Tenure. J. M. Currie. LC 80-41114. (Illus.). Date not set. price not set (ISBN 0-521-23634-7). Cambridge U Pr.

Economic Theory of Modern Society. M. Morishima. Tr. by D. W. Anthony from Japanese. LC 75-39375. (Illus.). 332p. 1976. 49.50 (ISBN 0-521-21088-7); pap. 15.95x (ISBN 0-521-29168-2). Cambridge U Pr.

Economic Theory of Pollution Control. Paul Burrows. 240p. 1980. text ed. 25.00x (ISBN 0-262-02150-1); pap. text ed. 8.95 (ISBN 0-262-52056-7). MIT Pr.

Economic Theory of Price Indices: Two Essays on the Effects of Taste, Quality & Technological Change. Franklin M. Fisher & Karl Shell. (Economic Theory & Mathematical Economics Ser). 1972. 15.00 (ISBN 0-12-257750-7). Acad Pr.

Economic Theory of Social Institutions. Andrew Schotter. (Illus.). 240p. Date not set. 29.50 (ISBN 0-521-23044-6). Cambridge U Pr.

Economic Theory: The Elementary Relations of Economic Life. David P. Levine. 1978. 28.00 (ISBN 0-7100-8837-X). Routledge & Kegan.

Economic Thought & Ideology in Seventeenth-Century England. Joyce O. Appleby. LC 77-85527. 304p. 1980. pap. 4.95 (ISBN 0-691-00779-9). Princeton U Pr.

Economic Thought in Kievan Rus. Bohdan S. Wynar. 128p. (Ukrainian.). 1975. pap. 7.50x (ISBN 0-87287-162-2). Ukrainian Acad.

Economic Thought of the Twentieth Century. Claudio Napoleoni. Tr. by Alessandro Cigno. 174p. 1981. pap. 12.50x (ISBN 0-85520-009-X, Pub. by Martin Robertson England). Biblio Dist.

Economic Transformation of Spain & Portugal. Eric N. Baklanoff. LC 76-12842. (Praeger Special Studies). 1978. 24.95 (ISBN 0-275-23380-4). Praeger.

Economic Trends & Problems in the Early Republican Period: 1931. Institute of Pacific Relations. LC 78-74312. (Modern Chinese Economy Ser.: Vol. 25). 537p. 1980. lib. bdg. 55.00 (ISBN 0-8240-4273-5). Garland Pub.

Economic Value of Agrometeorological Information & Advice. (Technical Note Ser.: No. 164). 52p. 1981. pap. 10.00 (ISBN 92-63-10526-X, W478, WMO). Unipub.

Economic Value of Education. Theodore W. Schultz. LC 63-15453. 1963. 12.00x (ISBN 0-231-02640-4). Columbia U Pr.

Economic Way of Thinking. 3rd ed. Paul Heyne. 400p. 1980. pap. text ed. 12.95 (ISBN 0-574-19295-6, 13-2295); instr's. guide avail. (ISBN 0-574-19296-4, 13-2296); study guide 3.95 (ISBN 0-574-19297-2, 13-2297). SRA.

Economic Workbooks & Data. D. I. Trotman-Dickenson. 1969. 16.50 (ISBN 0-08-012958-7); pap. 7.75 (ISBN 0-08-012957-9). Pergamon.

Economical Construction of Concrete Dams. Compiled By American Society of Civil Engineers. 568p. 1973. pap. text ed. 19.75 (ISBN 0-87262-043-3). Am Soc Civil Eng.

Economics. 2nd ed. William P. Albrecht, Jr. (Illus.). 1979. text ed. 18.95 o.p. (ISBN 0-13-227546-5); study guide & wkbk. 8.95 o.p. (ISBN 0-13-227553-8). P-H.

Economics. J. A. Allport & C. M. Stewart. LC 77-28479. 1978. 19.50 (ISBN 0-521-22013-0); pap. 15.50x. Cambridge U Pr.

Economics. 2nd ed. Daniel R. Fusfeld. 928p. 1976. 19.95x (ISBN 0-669-90571-2); instructor's manual free (ISBN 0-669-90589-5); study guide 7.95x (ISBN 0-669-90597-6); transparency masters 15.00 (ISBN 0-669-00244-5); test item file to adopters free (ISBN 0-669-00081-7). Heath.

Economics. David R. Kamerschen & George Vredeveld. (Cliffs Course Outlines Ser.). (Illus.). 186p. 1975. pap. text ed. 4.95 (ISBN 0-8220-1500-5). Cliffs.

Economics. Duncan McDougal & James Quirk. 800p. 1981. text ed. 18.95 (ISBN 0-574-19405-3, 13-2405); instr's. guide avail. (ISBN 0-574-19406-1, 13-2406); study guide 6.50 (ISBN 0-574-19407-X, 13-2407). SRA.

Economics. Edward Marcus & Mildred R. Marcus. 1978. pap. text ed. 12.95 (ISBN 0-8403-1892-8). Kendall-Hunt.

Economics. Jack Rudman. (Undergraduate Program Field Test Ser.: UPFT-6). (Cloth bdg. avail. on request). pap. 9.95 (ISBN 0-8373-6006-4). Natl Learning.

Economics. 11th ed. Paul A. Samuelson. (Illus.). 1980. text ed. 18.95 (ISBN 0-07-054595-2); instructor's manual 6.95 (ISBN 0-07-054596-0); study guide 7.95 (ISBN 0-07-053271-0); test bank 10.95 (ISBN 0-07-054597-9); transparency masters 20.00 (ISBN 0-07-054598-7); overhead transparencies 225.00 (ISBN 0-07-075000-9). McGraw.

Economics. Lewis C. Solomon. LC 79-25514. 832p. 1980. text ed. 18.95 (ISBN 0-201-07635-7); avail. student guide 8.95 (ISBN 0-201-07637-3). A-W.

Economics. S. E. Thomas. (Teach Yourself Ser.). 1975. pap. 2.95 o.p. (ISBN 0-679-10381-3). McKay.

Economics: A Critical Approach. M. A. Van Meerhaeghe. 516p. 1971. 19.50x (ISBN 0-8448-0042-2). Crane-Russak Co.

Economics: A General Introduction. 4th ed. Lloyd G. Reynolds. 1973. text ed. 18.95 (ISBN 0-256-01400-0). Irwin.

Economics: A Tool for Understanding Society. Thomas A. Riddell et al. LC 78-62552. (Economics Ser.). (Illus.). 1979. text ed. 12.95 (ISBN 0-201-06352-2); instr's manual avail. (ISBN 0-201-06353-0). A-W.

Economics: Advanced Test for the G.R.E. 3rd ed. James W. Morrison. LC 78-5776. 1980. pap. 5.95 (ISBN 0-668-04548-5, 4548). Arco.

Economics: An Anti Text. Ed. by Francis Green & Petter Nore. 1977. text ed. 20.75x (ISBN 0-333-21201-0); pap. text ed. 7.75x (ISBN 0-333-21202-9). Humanities.

Economics: An Introduction to Analysis & Policy. 10th ed. George L. Bach. (Illus.). 1980. text ed. 19.95 (ISBN 0-13-227231-8); student wkbk. 8.95 (ISBN 0-13-227199-0). P-H.

Economics: An Introduction to the World Around You. 2nd ed. Dennis J. Weidenaar & Emanuel T. Weiler. LC 78-67942. (Economics Ser.). (Illus.). 1979. text ed. 14.95 (ISBN 0-201-08517-8); instr's manual avail. (ISBN 0-201-08516-X). A-W.

Economics & Corporate Strategy. C. J. Sutton. LC 79-4198. (Illus.). 1980. 31.50 (ISBN 0-521-22669-4); pap. 8.95x (ISBN 0-521-29610-2). Cambridge U Pr.

Economics & Decision Making for Environmental Quality. Ed. by J. Richard Conner & Edna Loehman. LC 74-6056. 1974. pap. 4.95 (ISBN 0-8130-0508-6). U Presses Fla.

Economics & Demography. Ian Bowen. (Studies in Economics). 1976. text ed. 19.95x (ISBN 0-04-330268-8); pap. text ed. 8.95x (ISBN 0-04-330269-6). Allen Unwin.

Economics & Education: Principles & Applications. D. Rogers & H. Ruchlin. LC 74-143519. 1971. text ed. 14.95 (ISBN 0-02-926690-4). Free Pr.

Economics & Equality. Ed. by Aubrey Jones. 176p. 1976. 27.00x (ISBN 0-86003-010-5, Pub. by Allan Pubs England). State Mutual Bk.

Economics & Finance: Index to Periodical Articles, Nineteen Forty-Seven to Nineteen Seventy-One. Second Supplement. Joint Bank-Fund Library, Washington, D.C. (Library Catalogs-Bib. Guides). 1979. lib. bdg. 95.00 (ISBN 0-8161-0302-X). G K Hall.

Economics & Financing of Education: A Systems Approach. 3rd ed. Roe L. Johns & Edgar L. Morphet. LC 74-30213. (Illus.). 496p. 1975. ref. ed. 19.95 (ISBN 0-13-229898-8). P-H.

Economics & Foreign Policy: A Guide to Information Sources. Mark R. Amstutz. LC 74-11566. (Vol. 7). 1977. 30.00 (ISBN 0-8103-1321-9). Gale.

Economics & Politics of East-West Trade. J. Wilczynski. 10.00x o.p. (ISBN 0-8464-0351-X). Beekman Pubs.

Economics & Public Policy: Principles, Problems & Applications. Jim Golden & Bob Baldwin. 1979. pap. text ed. 8.95 (ISBN 0-89529-098-7). Avery Pub.

Economics & Public Policy: The Automobile Pollution Case. Donald N. Dewees. 208p. 1974. 21.00x (ISBN 0-262-04043-3). MIT Pr.

Economics & Social Goals: An Introduction. Harry D. Hutchinson. LC 72-93643. (Illus.). 514p. 1973. pap. text ed. 11.95 (ISBN 0-574-17975-5, 13-0975); instr's guide avail. (ISBN 0-574-17976-3, 13-0976). SRA.

Economics & Social Problems. Max E. Fletcher. LC 78-69590. (Illus.). 1979. pap. text ed. 13.25 (ISBN 0-395-26508-8); inst. manual 0.55 (ISBN 0-395-26509-6). HM.

Economics & Society. 2nd ed. Leonard Weiss. 576p. 1981. text ed. 18.95 (ISBN 0-471-03160-7). Wiley.

Economics & Society. Leonard W. Weiss. LC 74-18054. 576p. 1975. 18.95 (ISBN 0-471-92704-X, Pub. by Wiley-Hamilton). Wiley.

Economics & Technical Change. Arnold Heertje. LC 77-76757. 1979. pap. 13.95x (ISBN 0-470-26598-1). Halsted Pr.

Economics & Technology in Nineteenth Century American Thought: The Neglected American Economists. Michael Hudson. (Neglected American Economists Ser.). 1974. lib. bdg. 50.00 (ISBN 0-8240-1037-X). Garland Pub.

Economics & the Black Exodus: An Analysis of Negro Emigration from the Southern United States; 1910-70. Flora Gill. LC 78-75070. (Outstanding Dissertations in Economics Ser.). 1979. lib. bdg. 22.00 (ISBN 0-8240-4144-5). Garland Pub.

Economics & the Crisis of Ecology. 2nd ed. Narindar Singh. 1979. pap. 3.95x (ISBN 0-19-561078-4). Oxford U Pr.

Economics & the Design of Small Farmer Technology. Ed. by Alberto Valdes et al. 1978. text ed. 16.00 (ISBN 0-8138-1910-5). Iowa St U Pr.

Economics & the Idea of Mankind. Ed. by Berthold F. Hoselitz. LC 65-12109. 1965. 20.00x (ISBN 0-231-02750-8). Columbia U Pr.

Economics & the Public Purpose. John K. Galbraith. 1975. pap. 2.50 o.p. (ISBN 0-451-08428-4, E8428, Sig). NAL.

Economics & the Public Purpose. John K. Galbraith. 1980. pap. 2.95 (ISBN 0-451-61864-5, ME1864, Ment). NAL.

Economics & the Theory of Games. Michael Bacharach. LC 76-27665. 1977. lib. bdg. 23.50x (ISBN 0-89158-704-7). Westview.

Economics & World Order: From the 1970's to the 1990's. Ed. by Jagdish N. Bhagwati. LC 73-179966. 1972. 16.95 (ISBN 0-02-895600-1); pap. text ed. 5.95 (ISBN 0-02-903470-1). Free Pr.

Economics: Applications to Agriculture & Agribusiness. 3rd ed. Ewell P. Roy et al. x, 455p. 1981. 17.00 (ISBN 0-8134-2113-6, 2113); text ed. 12.75x. Interstate.

Economics: Applications to Agriculture & Agribusiness. 2nd ed. Ewell P. Roy et al. x, 455p. 1981. 18.00 o.p. (ISBN 0-8134-2113-6, 2113); text ed. 13.50x o.p. (ISBN 0-685-64698-X). Interstate.

Economics As a Coordination Problem: The Contributions of Friedrich A. Hayek. Gerald P. O'Driscoll, Jr. LC 77-23382. (Studies in Economic Theory). 171p. 1978. 15.00; pap. 4.95. NYU Pr.

Economics: Concepts, Applications, Analysis. Roy J. Sampson & Thomas W. Calmus. 425p. 1974. text ed. 18.50 (ISBN 0-395-17812-6); instructors' manual 1.25 (ISBN 0-395-17856-8); study guide 6.95 (ISBN 0-395-17804-5). HM.

Economics: Concepts, Themes & Applications. Don R. Leet & John A. Shaw. 464p. 1980. pap. text ed. 14.95x (ISBN 0-534-00793-7); 6.95xwkbk. (ISBN 0-534-00826-7). Wadsworth Pub.

Economics, Culture & Society. Robert Ghelardi. 1976. 12.95 o.s.i. (ISBN 0-440-02341-6). Delacorte.

Economics Deciphered: A Layman's Guide. Maurice Levi. LC 80-68173. 192p. 1981. 11.95 (ISBN 0-465-01794-0). Basic.

Economics, Ecology, Ethics: Essays Toward a Steady-State Economy. Ed. by Herman E. Daly. LC 79-29712. (Illus.). 1980. text ed. 17.95x (ISBN 0-7167-1178-8); pap. text ed. 8.95x (ISBN 0-7167-1179-6). W H Freeman.

Economics Education Fourteen to Sixteen. B. Holley & V. Skelton. 250p. 1981. pap. text ed. 15.25x (ISBN 0-85633-215-1, NFER). Humanities.

Economics, Environmental Policy & the Quality of Life. William J. Baumol et al. 1979. 15.95 (ISBN 0-13-231365-0); pap. 9.95 (ISBN 0-13-231357-X). P-H.

Economics: Facts, Theory & Policy. Chris C. Rhoden. LC 75-35954. 1976. text ed. 16.95 (ISBN 0-471-71802-5); instructor's manual avail. (ISBN 0-471-71801-7). Wiley.

Economics, Finance & Development: Subject Headings Used in the Main Catalog of the Joint Bank-Fund Library. Joint Bank-Fund Library (Washington, D. C.) 1979. lib. bdg. 88.00 (ISBN 0-8161-0276-7). G K Hall.

Economics for Administrators. J. N. Mongia. 600p. 1981. text ed. 40.00x (ISBN 0-7069-1293-4, Pub by Vikas India). Advent Bk.

Economics for Agriculturalists: A Beginning Text in Agricultural Economics. John Sjo. LC 75-26011. (Agricultural Economics Ser.). 1976. text ed. 17.95 o.p. (ISBN 0-88244-072-1). Grid Pub.

Economics for Consumers. 7th ed. Leland Gordon & Stewart Lee. 693p. 1977. text ed. 16.95 (ISBN 0-442-22242-4). Van Nos Reinhold.

Economics for Everybody. Gerson Antell & Walter Harris. (Orig.). (gr. 11-12). 1973. text ed. 12.50 (ISBN 0-87720-621-X); pap. text ed. 5.83 (ISBN 0-87720-610-4). AMSCO Sch.

Economics for Managers. P. C. Crowson & B. A. Richards. (Illus.). 248p. 1978. pap. 16.95x (ISBN 0-7131-3397-X). Intl Ideas.

Economics for Pleasure. 2nd ed. George L. Shackle. 1968. 38.50 (ISBN 0-521-06282-9); pap. 11.95x (ISBN 0-521-09507-7, 170). Cambridge U Pr.

Economics for Professional Studies. Henry Toch. (Illus.). 240p. 1977. pap. 12.95 (ISBN 0-7121-0568-9, Pub. by Macdonald & Evans England). Intl Ideas.

Economics for Students. 8th ed. J. L. Hanson. (Illus.). 240p. 1978. pap. text ed. 9.95x (ISBN 0-7121-0572-7, Pub. by Macdonald & Evans England). Intl Ideas.

Economics for the Smart Businessman Who knows Nothing of Economics. Hypolite La Grande. (Illus.). 50p. 1974. 37.50 (ISBN 0-913314-25-0). Am Classical Coll Pr.

Economics from the Consumer's Perspective. Lewis Mandell. LC 74-34343. (Illus.). 300p. 1975. text ed. 15.95 (ISBN 0-574-18205-5, 13-2205); instr's guide avail. (ISBN 0-574-18206-3, 13-2206). SRA.

Economics in America: Opposing Viewpoints. Ed. by David L. Bender & Gary E. McCuen. (Opposing Viewpoints Ser.: Vol. 13). (Illus.). (gr. 9-12). 1976. lib. bdg. 10.95 (ISBN 0-912616-38-5); pap. text ed. 4.95 (ISBN 0-912616-19-9). Greenhaven.

Economics in Health Care. Ed. by Lewis E. Weeks & Howard J. Berman. LC 77-10860. 1977. text ed. 25.00 (ISBN 0-89443-026-2). Aspen Systems.

Economics in Institutional Perspective: Memorial Essays in Honor of K. William Kapp. Ed. by Rolf Steppacher et al. LC 76-41116. 1977. 16.95 (ISBN 0-669-00977-6). Lexington Bks.

Economics in Managing Radioactive Wastes. (Technical Reports Ser.: No. 83). (Orig.). 1968. pap. 3.25 (ISBN 92-0-125168-8, IAEA). Unipub.

Economics in One Lesson. Henry Hazlitt. 218p. 1981. pap. 4.95 (ISBN 0-87000-517-0). Arlington Hse.

Economics in Our Time: Concepts & Issues. Dwight R. Lee & Robert F. McNown. LC 74-18924. 224p. 1975. pap. text ed. 5.95 (ISBN 0-574-18222-5, 13-2220); instr's guide avail. (ISBN 0-574-18221-7, 13-2221). SRA.

Economics in Our Time: Macro Issues. Robert F. McNown & Dwight R. Lee. LC 76-374. 224p. 1976. pap. text ed. 5.95 (ISBN 0-574-19260-3, 13-2260); instr's guide avail. (ISBN 0-574-19261-1, 13-2261). SRA.

Economics in Society Series. Helburn et al. Incl. Concepts & Institutions. text ed. 10.93 softbound (ISBN 0-201-02856-5); tchr's guide 8.32 (ISBN 0-201-02902-2); Industry Performance. text ed. softbound o.p. (ISBN 0-201-02857-3); tchrs' guide o.p. (ISBN 0-201-02903-0). (gr. 9-12). 1974 (Sch Div). A-W.

Economics in the Future: Toward a New Paradigm. Ed. by Kurt C. Dopfer. LC 76-2600. 1976. 21.00x (ISBN 0-89158-548-6). Westview.

Economics: Institutions & Analysis. Gerson Antell. (gr. 10-12). 1970. 5.83 (ISBN 0-87720-609-0). AMSCO Sch.

Economics, Mental Health, & the Law. Jeffrey Rubin. LC 78-19571. (Illus.). 1978. 17.95 (ISBN 0-669-02629-8). Lexington Bks.

Economics of Abundance. Robert Theobald. 162p. 14.95x (ISBN 0-8290-0296-0); pap. text ed. 6.95x (ISBN 0-8290-0297-9). Irvington.
Economics of African Countries. Ed. by Edith J. Whetham & Jean I. Currie. LC 69-12931. (Illus.). 1969. 30.50 (ISBN 0-521-07070-8); pap. 11.95x (ISBN 0-521-09534-4). Cambridge U Pr.
Economics of Aging. 2nd ed. James H. Schulz. 208p. 1979. pap. text ed. 8.95x (ISBN 0-534-00772-4). Wadsworth Pub.
Economics of Agricultural Development. John W. Mellor. LC 66-19491. (Illus.). 1966. 25.00x (ISBN 0-8014-0297-2); pap. 7.95 (ISBN 0-8014-9102-9, CP102). Cornell U Pr.
Economics of Agricultural Production. Edward Witkowski & Arnold Wells. LC 78-22717. 1979. text ed. 15.95 (ISBN 0-88284-072-X). Alfred Pub.
Economics of Agriculture. R. Cohen. (Cambridge Economic Handbook Ser.). 1949. 10.95x (ISBN 0-521-08754-6). Cambridge U Pr.
Economics of Airborne Emissions. Douglas R. Mackintosh. LC 72-89646. (Special Studies in U. S. Economic, Social & Political Issues). 1973. 29.50x (ISBN 0-275-28668-1); pap. text ed. 12.95x (ISBN 0-8290-0139-5). Irvington.
Economics of American Agriculture. 3rd ed. Walter W. Wilcox et al. (Illus.). 512p. 1974. ref. ed. 19.95 (ISBN 0-13-229666-7). P-H.
Economics of Bank Credit Cards. Thomas Russell. LC 73-9383. (Special Studies). 150p. 1975. text ed. 25.00 (ISBN 0-275-09390-5). Praeger.
Economics of Being a Woman. Dee Dee Ahern & Betsy Bliss. 1976. 8.95 o.s.i. (ISBN 0-02-500610-X). Macmillan.
Economics of Black Community Development: An Analysis & Program for Autonomous Growth & Development. Frank G. Davis. 1976. pap. text ed. 9.50x (ISBN 0-8191-0008-0). U Pr of Amer.
Economics of Book Publishing in Developing Countries. (Reports & Papers on Mass Communications: No. 79). (Illus.). 44p. 1977. pap. 2.50 (ISBN 92-3-101422-6, U177, UNESCO). Unipub.
Economics of Change in Less Developed Countries. David Colman & Fred Nixson. LC 78-9708. 1978. pap. 15.95 (ISBN 0-470-26436-5). Halsted Pr.
Economics of Co-Determination. Ed. by David Heathfield. 1978. text ed. 20.75x (ISBN 0-8419-5029-6). Holmes & Meier.
Economics of Communication: A Selected Bibliography with Asbstracts. Karen P. Middleton & Meheroo Jussawalla. LC 80-50505. (Pergamon Policy Studies on Internatioanl Development). 250p. 1981. 25.00 (ISBN 0-08-026325-9). Pergamon.
Economics of Communication: A Selected Bibliography with Abstracts Published in Cooperation with the Eeast-West Center, Hawaii. Karen P. Middleton & Meheroo Jussawalla. LC 80-20505. (Pergamon Policy Studies on International Development). 1981. 25.000 (ISBN 0-08-026325-9). Pergamon.
Economics of Computers. William F. Sharpe. LC 71-89567. 1969. 22.50x (ISBN 0-231-03266-8); pap. 10.00x (ISBN 0-231-08310-6). Columbia U Pr.
Economics of Contract Law. Anthony T. Kronman & Richard A. Posner. 1979. pap. text ed. 6.95 (ISBN 0-316-50471-8). Little.
Economics of Corporation & Securities Regulation. Richard A. Posner & Kenneth E. Scott. (Orig.). 1981. text ed. write for info (ISBN 0-316-71435-6). Little.
Economics of Crime: An Anthology of Recent Work. Ed. by Ralph Andreano & John J. Siegfried. 1980. 16.25x (ISBN 0-470-26836-0); pap. text ed. 10.50 (ISBN 0-470-26837-9). Halsted Pr.
Economics of Crime & Law Enforcement. Lee R. McPheters & William B. Stronge. (Illus.). 520p. 1976. 26.75 (ISBN 0-398-03415-X). C C Thomas.
Economics of Decision: A Practical Decision System for Business & Management. Herbert E. Kierulff. 1976. 13.50 (ISBN 0-8046-7107-9). Kennikat.
Economics of Defence. Gavin Kennedy. 1975. 17.95 o.p. (ISBN 0-571-10740-0, Pub. by Faber & Faber). Merrimack Bk Serv.
Economics of Developement. 3rd ed. Everett E. Hagen. 1980. 18.95x (ISBN 0-256-02318-2). Irwin.
Economics of Development. rev. ed. Everett E. Hagen. 1975. text ed. 17.50x o.p. (ISBN 0-256-01735-2). Irwin.
Economics of Disability: International Perspectives. Ed. by Susan Hammerman & Stephen Maikowski. (Illus.). 200p. (Orig.). 1981. pap. write for info. (ISBN 0-9605554-0-4). Rehab Intl.
Economics of Dry Farming in Tamil Nadu. R. K. Sampath & Jayalakshmi Ganesan. 128p. 1974. 4.50 (ISBN 0-88253-431-9). Ind-US Inc.
Economics of Empire: Britain, Africa & the New Imperialism, 1870-1895. William G. Hynes. (Illus.). 1979. text ed. 22.00 (ISBN 0-582-64234-5). Longman.
Economics of Energy. M. G. Webb & Martin J. Ricketts. LC 79-18708. 1980. 25.95x (ISBN 0-470-26841-7). Halsted Pr.
Economics of Environmental & Natural Resources Policy. Ed. by J. A. Butlin. 200p. 1981. lib. bdg. 27.50x (ISBN 0-86531-190-0); pap. text ed. 14.00x (ISBN 0-86531-196-X). Westview.
Economics of Environmental Quality. Edwin S. Mills. (Illus.). 1978. 12.95 (ISBN 0-393-09043-4). Norton.
Economics of European Imperialism. Alan Hodgart. (Foundations of Modern History Ser.). 1978. 7.95 (ISBN 0-393-05667-8); pap. 4.95x (ISBN 0-393-09061-2). Norton.
Economics of Exchange Rates. Jacob A. Frenkel & Harry G. Johnson. (Economics Ser.). 1978. text ed. 14.95 (ISBN 0-201-02374-1); pap. text ed. 9.50 (ISBN 0-201-02376-8). A-W.
Economics of Fibre Markets: Interdependence Between Man-Made Fibres, Wool, & Cotton. C. A. Tisdell & P. W. McDonald. 1979. text ed. 45.00 (ISBN 0-08-022468-7). Pergamon.
Economics of Food Grain Distribution: The Asian Scene. 1977. pap. 7.75 (ISBN 92-833-1401-8, APO19, APO). Unipub.
Economics of Food Processing. W. Smith Greig. (Illus.). 1971. text ed. 28.50 o.p. (ISBN 0-87055-096-9). AVI.
Economics of Future Trading. B. Goss & B. S. Yamey. LC 75-6266. 1976. 27.95 (ISBN 0-470-97115-0). Halsted Pr.
Economics of Growth. 2nd ed. Jamshed K. Mehta. 1970. pap. 6.50x (ISBN 0-210-31183-5). Asia.
Economics of Health. Herbert E. Klarman. LC 65-14323. 1965. 17.50x (ISBN 0-231-02797-4). Columbia U Pr.
Economics of Health & Medical Care: Proceedings. International Economic Association Conference, Tokyo. Ed. by Mark Perlman. LC 73-20107. 1974. 39.95 (ISBN 0-470-68051-2). Halsted Pr.
Economics of Health Care - Finance & Delivery. Seymour E. Harris. LC 73-17612. 1974. 25.00x (ISBN 0-8211-0725-9); text ed. 22.50x (ISBN 0-685-72313-5). McCutchan.
Economics of Health Resources. Richard A. Ward. LC 74-12804. 160p. 1975. text ed. 11.95 (ISBN 0-201-08522-4). A-W.
Economics of Health Resources. Richard A. Ward. 150p. 1975. 10.25 (ISBN 0-686-68580-6, 14914). Hospital Finan.
Economics of High-Rise Apartment Buildings of Alternate Design Configuration. Compiled By American Society of Civil Engineers & Richard D. Steyert. 192p. 1972. pap. text ed. 6.00 (ISBN 0-87262-038-7). Am Soc Civil Eng.
Economics of Hire Purchase Credit. S. K. Basu. 1971. 10.00x (ISBN 0-210-98135-0). Asia.
Economics of Individual & Population Aging. R. L. Clark & J. J. Spengler. LC 79-19495. (Cambridge Surveys of Economic Literature Ser.). (Illus.). 1980. 24.95 (ISBN 0-521-22883-2); pap. 8.95 (ISBN 0-521-29702-8). Cambridge U Pr.
Economics of Industrial Organization. William G. Shepherd. LC 78-6285. 1979. 19.95 (ISBN 0-13-231464-9). P-H.
Economics of Inequality. A. B. Atkinson. (Illus.). 308p. 1975. 16.50x (ISBN 0-19-877024-3); pap. 9.95x (ISBN 0-19-877076-6). Oxford U Pr.
Economics of Inflation. J. A. Trevithick & C. Mulvey. LC 75-256. 184p. 1975. 24.95 (ISBN 0-470-88775-3); pap. 12.95x (ISBN 0-470-26894-8). Halsted Pr.
Economics of Innovation. 2nd ed. John E. Parker. (Illus.). 1978. text ed. 38.00x (ISBN 0-582-44612-0). Longman.
Economics of Integration: A Book of Readings. Ed. by Melvyn B. Krauss. 1973. pap. text ed. 14.95x (ISBN 0-04-330222-X). Allen Unwin.
Economics of Interdependence. Richard N. Cooper. (Council on Foreign Relations Ser.). 1980. pap. 6.50x (ISBN 0-231-05071-2, Pub. by Morningside). Columbia U Pr.
Economics of International Business. R. H. Mason et al. 464p. 1981. Repr. of 1975 ed. text ed. 23.50 (ISBN 0-89874-248-X). Krieger.
Economics of International Business. R. Hal Mason et al. LC 74-18476. (Management & Administration Ser). 464p. 1975. text ed. 20.50 o.p. (ISBN 0-471-57528-3); instructor's manual avail. o.p. (ISBN 0-471-57529-1). Wiley.
Economics of International Tax Avoidance: Political Power Versus Economic Law. Barry Bracewell-Milnes. (International Taxation Ser.: No. 2). 120p. 1980. lib. bdg. 29.00 (ISBN 90-2000-633-9, Pub. by Kluwer Law & Taxation Publishers). Kluwer Boston.
Economics of Invention & Innovation: With a Case Study of the Development of the Hovercraft. P. S. Johnson. 329p. 1975. 36.00x (ISBN 0-85520-078-2, Pub by Martin Robertson England). Biblio Dist.
Economics of Irrigation Rates - a Study of Punjab & Uttar Phadesh. N. Ansari. 1968. 9.00x o.p. (ISBN 0-210-22536-X). Asia.
Economics of Justice. Richard A. Posner. LC 80-25075. (Illus.). 448p. 1981. text ed. 25.00 (ISBN 0-674-23525-8). Harvard U Pr.
Economics of Kentucky Coal. Curtis E. Harvey. LC 76-51160. (Illus.). 192p. 1977. 13.00x (ISBN 0-8131-1358-X). U Pr of Ky.
Economics of Labor Relations. 8th ed. Gordon F. Bloom & Herbert R. Northrup. 1977. text ed. 19.50x (ISBN 0-256-01910-X). Irwin.
Economics of Leisure & Recreation. R. W. Vickerman. (Studies in Planning & Control). 1975. text ed. 25.00x o.p. (ISBN 0-333-18300-2). Verry.
Economics of Ludwig Von Mises: Toward a Critical Reappraisal. Laurence S. Moss. LC 75-41380. (Studies in Economic Theory). 129p. 1976. 12.00; pap. 3.95. NYU Pr.
Economics of Medical Care. M. M. Hauser. (University of York Studies in Economics). 1972. text ed. 27.50x o.p. (ISBN 0-04-330213-0). Allen Unwin.
Economics of Mineral Extraction. Ed. by Gerhard Anders et al. W. Phillip Gramm. LC 79-22949. 334p. 1980. 29.95 (ISBN 0-03-053171-3). Praeger.
Economics of Minorities: A Guide to Information Sources. Kenneth Gagala. LC 73-17573. (Economics Information Guide Ser: Vol. 2). 339p. 1976. 30.00 (ISBN 0-8103-1294-8). Gale.
Economics of Modern Britain: An Introduction to Macroeconomics. John Black. 272p. 1979. 24.50x (ISBN 0-85520-274-2, Pub by Martin Robertson England); pap. 9.95x (ISBN 0-85520-273-4). Biblio Dist.
Economics of Modern Britain: An Introduction to Macroeconomics. 2nd ed. John Black. 256p. 1981. 24.50x (ISBN 0-686-28828-9, Pub. by Martin Robertson England); pap. 9.95x (ISBN 0-686-28829-7). Biblio Dist.
Economics of Natural Disaster Relief in Australia. J. R. Bulter & D. P. Doessel. LC 79-50570. (Centre for Research on Federal Financial Relations - Research Monograph: No. 27). 147p. (Orig.). 1980. pap. text ed. 14.95 (ISBN 0-7081-1073-8, 0565). Bks Australia.
Economics of Natural Resources. Richard Lecomber. LC 78-23595. 247p. 1979. 24.95 (ISBN 0-470-26546-9). Halsted Pr.
Economics of New Educational Media. (Educational Methods & Techniques Ser: No. 1). (Illus.). 1977. pap. 13.50 (ISBN 92-3-101423-4, U180, UNESCO). Unipub.
Economics of New Food Product Development. Norman W. Desrosier & John N. Desrosier. (Illus.). 1971. 28.50 (ISBN 0-87055-102-7). AVI.
Economics of Nuclear & Coal Power. Saunders Miller. LC 76-24361. (Illus.). 1976. text ed. 24.95 (ISBN 0-275-23710-9). Praeger.
Economics of Nuclear Fuels. (Illus., Orig.). 1968. pap. 30.00 (ISBN 92-0-050668-2, IAEA). Unipub.
Economics of Offshore Oil & Gas Supplies. Frederick W. Mansvelt-Beck & Karl M. Wiig. LC 76-54558. (Illus.). 1977. 17.95 (ISBN 0-669-01306-4). Lexington Bks.
Economics of Personal Injury. Debapriya Ghosh et al. LC 75-28611. (Illus.). 1975. 17.00 o.p. (ISBN 0-347-01111-X, 00312-3, Pub. by Saxon Hse). Lexington Bks.
Economics of Pollution. Kenneth E. Boulding & Elvis J. Stahr. LC 70-179973. (Charles C. Moskowitz Lectures). 158p. 1971. 10.00x (ISBN 0-8147-0967-2). NYU Pr.
Economics of Pollution Control in the Non-Ferrous Metals Industry. M. H. Atkins & J. F. Lowe. (Illus.). 1979. 35.00 (ISBN 0-08-022458-X). Pergamon.
Economics of Poverty & Discrimination. 2nd ed. B. R. Schiller. (Illus.). 224p. 1976. pap. 9.95 o.p. (ISBN 0-13-232009-6). P-H.
Economics of Production & Innovation: An Industrial Perspective. Gerhard Rosegger. (Illus.). 1980. 41.00 (ISBN 0-08-024047-X); pap. 17.50 (ISBN 0-08-024046-1). Pergamon.
Economics of Property Rights. Eirik G. Furubotn & Svetozar Pejovich. LC 73-14644. 1975. 25.00 (ISBN 0-88410-251-3); pap. 12.50 (ISBN 0-88410-278-5). Ballinger Pub.
Economics of Public Choice. Ed. by Robert D. Leiter & Gerald Sirkin. (Illus.). 202p. 1976. text ed. 18.00x (ISBN 0-8290-0397-5). Irvington.
Economics of Public Education. 3rd ed. Charles S. Benson. LC 77-77670. (Illus.). 1978. text ed. 20.50 (ISBN 0-395-18619-6). HM.
Economics of Public Finance. Alan S. Blinder & Robert M. Solow. (Studies of Government Finance). 14.95 (ISBN 0-8157-0998-6); pap. 6.95 (ISBN 0-8157-0997-8). Brookings.
Economics of Public Finance. C. T. Sandford. 1969. pap. 7.70 o.p. (ISBN 0-08-013468-8); pap. 7.00 o.p. (ISBN 0-08-013467-X). Pergamon.
Economics of Public Finance. 2nd ed. C. T. Sandford. LC 77-6680. 1977. text ed. 27.00 (ISBN 0-08-021843-1); pap. text ed. 14.00 (ISBN 0-08-021842-3). Pergamon.
Economics of Public Policy: The Micro View. John C. Goodman & Edwin G. Dolan. (Illus.). 1979. pap. text ed. 8.50 (ISBN 0-8299-0238-4); instrs.' manual avail. (ISBN 0-8299-0481-6). West Pub.
Economics of Public Services: Proceedings. LC 75-37750. 1977. 49.95 (ISBN 0-470-01374-5). Halsted Pr.
Economics of Research & Technology. Keith Norris & John Valzey. (Studies in Economics Ser.). 1973. text ed. 18.95 o.p. (ISBN 0-04-330227-0); pap. text ed. 10.95x (ISBN 0-04-330228-9). Allen Unwin.
Economics of Resources. Ed. by Robert D. Leiter & Stanley L. Friedlander. (Illus.). 250p. 1976. text ed. 18.00x (ISBN 0-8290-0396-7). Irvington.
Economics of Small Firms: Return from the Wilderness. Graham Bannock. 120p. 1981. 14.50x (ISBN 0-631-11391-6, Pub. by Basil Blackwell). Biblio Dist.
Economics of Social Issues. 4th ed. Richard H. Leftwich & Ansel M. Sharp. 1980. pap. text ed. 9.95x (ISBN 0-256-02310-7); write for info. wkbk. & student guide (ISBN 0-256-02355-7). Business Pubns.
Economics of Solar & Non-Renewable Energy Technologies. Michael D. Yokell. 1981. write for info (ISBN 0-88410-619-5). Ballinger Pub.
Economics of Solar Energy & Conservation Systems, 3 vols. Frank Kreith & R. E. West. 1980. 69.95 ea. Vol. 1, 320p (ISBN 0-8493-5229-0). Vol. 2, 32 O.p (ISBN 0-8493-5230-4). Vol. 3, 288p (ISBN 0-8493-5231-2). CRC Pr.
Economics of Soviet Planning. Abram Bergson. LC 80-13737. (Studies in Comparative Economics: No. 5). (Illus.). xxii, 394p. 1980. Repr. of 1964 ed. lib. bdg. 30.00x (ISBN 0-313-22413-7, BEES). Greenwood.
Economics of Stock Market Action. Ken W. Jordon. (New Stock Market Library). (Illus.). 1979. deluxe ed. 39.85 (ISBN 0-918968-33-X). Inst Econ Finan.
Economics of Taxation. Simon James & Christopher Nobes. 320p. 1978. 33.00x (ISBN 0-86003-507-7, Pub. by Allan Pubs England); pap. 16.50x (ISBN 0-86003-607-3). State Mutual Bk.
Economics of Teacher Supply. A. Zabalza et al. LC 78-967. (Illus.). 1979. 49.50 (ISBN 0-521-22078-5). Cambridge U Pr.
Economics of the Arts. Ed. by Mark Blaug. LC 76-5889. 1976. 27.50 o.p. (ISBN 0-89158-613-X). Westview.
Economics of the Black Market. S. K. Ray. (Replica Edition Ser.). 250p. 1981. lib. bdg. 20.00x (ISBN 0-86531-149-8). Westview.
Economics of the Canadian Financial System. R. Shearer & D. Bond. 1972. 21.95 (ISBN 0-13-229781-7). P-H.
Economics of the Central Chin Tribes. H. N. Stevenson. (Illus.). 1969. Repr. of 1943 ed. text ed. 15.50x (ISBN 0-576-59276-5). Humanities.
Economics of the Davis-Bacon Act: An Analysis of Prevailing Wage Laws. John Gould & George Bittlingmayer. 1980. pap. 4.25 (ISBN 0-8447-3381-4). Am Enterprise.
Economics of the Developing Countries. rev. 4th ed. H. Myint. Ed. by Michael Parkin. 160p. 1973. pap. text ed. 9.25x (ISBN 0-09-118261-1, Hutchinson U Lib). Humanities.
Economics of the Environment. Horst Siebert. LC 80-7442. 1981. price not set (ISBN 0-669-03693-5). Lexington Bks.
Economics of the European Community. A. M. El-Agraa. 1980. 37.50 (ISBN 0-312-23285-3). St Martin.
Economics of the Firm: Theory & Practice. 2nd ed. Arthur A. Thompson, Jr. (Illus.). 1977. 19.95 (ISBN 0-13-231407-X); pap. 8.95 study guide & wkbk. (ISBN 0-13-227553-8). P-H.
Economics of the Green Revolution in Pakistan. Mahmood H. Khan. LC 75-19796. (Special Studies), (Illus.). 320p. 1975. text ed. 26.95 (ISBN 0-275-55680-8). Praeger.
Economics of the Imagination. Kurt Heinzelman. LC 79-4019. 1980. lib. bdg. 18.50x (ISBN 0-87023-274-6). U of Mass Pr.
Economics of the Pharmaceutical Industry. W. Duncan Reekie. 145p. 1975. text ed. 26.00x (ISBN 0-8419-5009-1). Holmes & Meier.
Economics of the Property Tax. Dick Netzer. (Studies of Government Finance). 326p. 1966. pap. 5.95 (ISBN 0-8157-6039-6). Brookings.
Economics of the Public Sector. 2nd ed. Robert H. Haveman. LC 76-186. (Introduction to Economics Ser). 224p. 1976. text ed. 9.50x (ISBN 0-471-36182-8, Pub. by Wiley-Hamilton). Wiley.

Economics of the Recovery Program. Douglas V. Brown et al. LC 70-163644. (FDR & the Era of the New Deal Ser). 1971. Repr. of 1934 ed. lib. bdg. 22.50 (ISBN 0-306-70197-9). Da Capo.

Economics of Tramp Shipping. B. N. Metaxas. (Illus.). 304p. 1971. text ed. 27.50x (ISBN 0-485-11127-6, Athlone Pr). Humanities.

Economics of Transport. M. R. Bonavia. (Cambridge Economic Handbook Ser). 1954. 10.95x (ISBN 0-521-08752-X). Cambridge U Pr.

Economics of Transport Appraisal. A. J. Harrison. LC 74-10625. 250p. 1974. 21.95 o.p. (ISBN 0-470-35577-8). Halsted Pr.

Economics of Transportation. 7th ed. D. Philip Locklin. 1972. text ed. 19.25x (ISBN 0-256-00301-7). Irwin.

Economics of Transportation & Logistics. Marvin L. Fair & Ernest W. Williams, Jr. 1975. 17.50x (ISBN 0-256-01628-3). Business Pubns.

Economics of Unemployment in Britain. Creedy. 1981. text ed. price not set (ISBN 0-408-10703-0). Butterworth.

Economics of University Behavior. David Garvin. 1980. 17.50 (ISBN 0-12-276550-8). Acad Pr.

Economics of Urban Problems. 2nd ed. Arthur C. Schreiber et al. LC 75-31004. (Illus.). 480p. 1976. text ed. 18.50 (ISBN 0-395-20619-7). HM.

Economics of Urban Transport. Kenneth Button. (Illus.). 1977. 21.95 (ISBN 0-566-00148-9, 00720-X, Pub. by Saxon Hse). Lexington Bks.

Economics of VAT: Preserving Efficiency, Capitalism & Social Progress. Richard W. Lindholm. LC 80-8428. 1980. 19.95 (ISBN 0-669-04111-4). Lexington Bks.

Economics of Welfare Policies. Margaret S. Gordon. LC 63-14113. 1964. 15.00x (ISBN 0-231-02639-0). Columbia U Pr.

Economics of Welfare, Rural Development, & Natural Resources in Agriculture, 1940s - 1970s. Ed. by Lee R. Martin. (Survey of Agricultural Economics Literature: Vol. 3). 720p. 1981. 35.00x (ISBN 0-8166-0819-9). U of Minn Pr.

Economics of Women & Work. Ed. by Alice H. Amsden. LC 80-15970. 1980. write for info. (ISBN 0-312-23670-0). St Martin.

Economics of Work & Pay. 2nd ed. Albert Rees. (Illus.). 1979. text ed. 14.95 scp (ISBN 0-06-045354-0, HarpC). Har-Row.

Economics of World Grain Trade. Thomas Grennes et al. LC 77-13715. (Praeger Special Studies). 1978. 22.95 (ISBN 0-03-022836-0). Praeger.

Economics, Peace & Laughter. John K. Galbraith. 288p. 1972. pap. 1.75 (ISBN 0-451-04954-3, E4954, Sig). NAL.

Economics: Principles & Applications. David Rassmussen & Charles Haworth. LC 78-2245. 672p. 1979. text ed. 17.95 (ISBN 0-574-19280-8, 13-2280); instr's guide avail. (ISBN 0-574-19281-6, 13-2281); study guide 6.50 (ISBN 0-574-19282-4, 13-2282); lecture resource supplement 3.75 (ISBN 0-574-19284-0, 13-2284). SRA.

Economics: Principles & Policies in an Open Economy. Ian Drummond. 1976. text ed. 17.50 (ISBN 0-256-01776-X); wkbk 4.50 (ISBN 0-256-01870-7). Irwin.

Economics: Principles & Policy from a Christian Perspective. Tom Rose. LC 76-41727. 1977. 12.95 (ISBN 0-915134-22-5); pap. instr's man. 3.95 (ISBN 0-915134-23-3). American Ent Texas.

Economics: Principles in Action. 2nd ed. Philip C. Starr. 1978. pap. 14.95x (ISBN 0-534-00588-8); wkbk. 7.95x (ISBN 0-534-00589-6). Wadsworth Pub.

Economics: Principles, Problems & Policies. 8th, rev. ed. Campbell R. McConnell. (Illus.). 992p. 1980. text ed. 19.95x (ISBN 0-07-044930-9, C); instructor's manual 15.00 (ISBN 0-07-044931-7); study guide 7.95x (ISBN 0-07-044932-5); economics concepts 9.95x (ISBN 0-07-044936-8); transparency masters avail. (ISBN 0-07-044934-1). McGraw.

Economics: Private & Public Choice. James D. Gwartney & Richard Stroup. 1980. 19.95 (ISBN 0-12-311040-8); instrs'. manual & test bank 3.00 (ISBN 0-12-311055-6). Test Bank (ISBN 0-12-311043-2). Acad Pr.

Economics Problem Solver. Research & Education Association Staff. LC 80-53175. (Illus.). 1088p. (Orig.). pap. text ed. 16.85x (ISBN 0-87891-524-9). Res & Educ.

Economics: Problems, Principles, Priorities. Frederick L. Golladay. LC 76-19511. 1978. 19.95 (ISBN 0-8053-3302-9); instr's man. 3.95 (ISBN 0-8053-3304-5); study guide 8.95 (ISBN 0-8053-3303-7). Benjamin-Cummings.

Economics: Public & Private Choice. James D. Gwartney. 1976. 15.95 o.p. (ISBN 0-12-311050-5); coursebook 5.95 o.p. (ISBN 0-12-311051-3). Acad Pr.

Economics: The Essential Knowledge Which Everybody, but Absolutely Everybody Ought to Possess of Economics & Economic Forecasting. C. M. Flumiani. (Essential Knowledge Ser.). (Illus.). 1978. plastic spiral bdg. 21.45 (ISBN 0-89266-115-1). Am Classical Coll.

Economie Rurale Namuroise au Bas Moyen Age (1199-1429, 2 vols. Leopold Genicot. LC 80-2028. 1981. Repr. of 1943 ed. Set. 79.50 (ISBN 0-404-18565-7). Vol. 1 (ISBN 0-404-18566-5). Vol. 2 (ISBN 0-404-18567-3). AMS Pr.

Economies & the Environment. Matthew Edel. (Foundations of Modern Economics Ser). (Illus.). 160p. 1973. pap. 6.95 ref. ed. o.p. (ISBN 0-13-231308-1). P-H.

Economies with Exhaustible Resourses. Hung-po Chao. LC 78-74998. (Outstanding Dissertations on Energy Ser.). 1979. lib. bdg. 15.50 (ISBN 0-8240-3980-7). Garland Pub.

Economist Looks at Society. G. Schachter & E. Dale. 1973. pap. 11.95x o.p. (ISBN 0-471-00951-2). Wiley.

Economist's Handbook: A Manual of Statistical Sources. Gerlof Verwey. LC 74-157492. 1971. Repr. of 1934 ed. 32.00 (ISBN 0-8103-3728-2). Gale.

Economizing Abundance: A Noninflationary Future. Robert Theobald. LC 79-125096. 151p. 1970. pap. 3.95x (ISBN 0-8040-0611-3). Swallow.

Economy & Class Structure of German Fascism. Alfred Sohn-Rethel. 1978. text ed. 15.50x (ISBN 0-906336-00-7, Trans. by M. Sohn-Rethel); pap. text ed. 7.75x (ISBN 0-906336-01-5). Humanities.

Economy & Ecological Equilibrium. P Muller. 100p. 1975. pap. text ed. 24.00 (ISBN 0-08-019681-0). Pergamon.

Economy & Society: A Study in the Integration of Economic & Social Theory. Talcott Parsons & Neil J. Smelser. 1965. pap. 2.95 o.s.i. (ISBN 0-02-923950-8). Free Pr.

Economy & Society in Baroque Portugal, 1668-1703. Carl A. Hanson. LC 80-17588. (Illus.). 320p. 1981. 22.50x (ISBN 0-8166-0969-1). U of Minn Pr.

Economy & Society in Pre-Industrial South Africa. Ed. by Shula Marks & Anthony Atmore. (Illus.). 385p. (Orig.). 1980. pap. 25.00; pap. text ed. 9.95 (ISBN 0-582-64656-1). Longman.

Economy Cars, 1981. rev. ed. Ed. by Michael L. Green. (Buyer's Guide Ser.). 96p. (Orig.). Date not set. pap. 2.50 (ISBN 0-89552-073-7). DMR Pubns.

Economy Cook Book. Mary Griffiths. LC 77-91748. 1978. 8.95 (ISBN 0-7153-7542-3). David & Charles.

Economy Cookbook: Lower Cost Foods & How to Prepare Them. June Roth. (Berkley-Dorison House Bks.). (Illus.). (YA) 1978. 7.95 o.p. (ISBN 0-685-85769-7, Dist. by Putnam). Berkley Pub.

Economy of Brazil. Ed. by Howard S. Ellis. 1969. 21.50x (ISBN 0-520-01520-7). U of Cal Pr.

Economy of Cities. Jane Jacobs. LC 69-16413. 1969. 5.95 o.p. (ISBN 0-394-42296-1). Random.

Economy of Early Renaissance Europe. H. A. Miskimin. LC 75-16607. (Illus.). 204p. 1975. 21.50 (ISBN 0-521-21017-8); pap. 7.95x (ISBN 0-521-29021-X). Cambridge U Pr.

Economy of Energy Conservation in Educational Facilities. 82p. (Orig.). 1973. pap. text ed. 4.00. Interbk Inc.

Economy of Europe in an Age of Crisis: 1600 to 1750. J. De Vries. LC 75-30438. (Illus.). 240p. 1976. 29.50 (ISBN 0-521-21123-9); pap. 7.95x (ISBN 0-521-29050-3). Cambridge U Pr.

Economy of High Wages. Jacob Schoenhof. (Neglected American Economists Ser.). 1974. lib. bdg. 50.00 (ISBN 0-8240-1030-2). Garland Pub.

Economy of Nature & the Evolution of Sex. Michael T. Ghiselin. 1974. 21.50x (ISBN 0-520-02474-5). U of Cal Pr.

Economy of Saudi Arabia. Donald M. Moliver & Paul J. Abbondante. 200p. 1980. 21.95 (ISBN 0-03-057004-2). Praeger.

Economy of Socialist Cuba: A Two-Decade Appraisal. Carmelo Mesa-Lago. 296p. 1981. price not set (ISBN 0-8263-0578-4); pap. price not set (ISBN 0-8263-0585-7). U of NM Pr.

Economy of the Later Renaissance Europe: 1460-1600. A. Miskimin. LC 75-17120. (Illus.). 1977. pap. 26.95 (ISBN 0-521-21608-7); pap. 7.95x (ISBN 0-521-29208-5). Cambridge U Pr.

Economy of the Roman Empire Quantitative Studies. R. Duncan-Jones. LC 72-93146. (Illus.). 320p. 1974. 51.00 (ISBN 0-521-20165-9). Cambridge U Pr.

Economy of the USSR During World War II. N. A. Voznesensky. 8.00 (ISBN 0-8183-0233-X). Pub Aff Pr.

Economy-Wide Models & Development Planning. Ed. by Charles Blitzer et al. (World Research Bank Publications Ser). (Illus.). 1975. pap. 7.95x (ISBN 0-19-920074-2). Oxford U Pr.

Ecophysics: The Application of Physics to Ecology. James P. Wesley. (Illus.). 368p. 1974. 26.75 (ISBN 0-398-02959-8); pap. 18.50 (ISBN 0-398-03077-4). C C Thomas.

Ecoscience: Population, Resources, Environment. Paul R. Ehrlich et al. LC 77-6824. (Illus.). 1977. text ed. 47.95x (ISBN 0-7167-0567-2); pap. text ed. 23.95x (ISBN 0-7167-0029-8). W H Freeman.

Ecosystem of the "Sick" Child: Implications for Classification & Intervention for Disturbed & Mentally Retarded Children. Ed. by Suzanne Salzinger et al. 1980. 25.00 (ISBN 0-12-617250-1). Acad Pr.

Ecosystems Modeling in Theory & Practice: An Introduction with Case Histories. Ed. by Charles A. Hall & John W. Day, Jr. LC 76-57204. 1977. 40.00 (ISBN 0-471-34165-7, Pub. by Wiley-Interscience). Wiley.

Ecotopia. Ernest Callenbach. LC 74-84366. 168p. (Orig.). 1975. 10.00 (ISBN 0-9604320-0-0); pap. 3.45 (ISBN 0-9604320-1-9). Banyan Tree.

Ecstasy & "the Praise of Folly". M. A. Screech. 267p. 1980. 49.50x (ISBN 0-7156-1361-8, Pub. by Duckworth England). Biblio Dist.

Ecstasy's Captive. Nelle McFather. 1979. pap. 2.50 (ISBN 0-505-51380-3). Tower Bks.

Ecuador: Conflicting Political Culture & the Quest for Progress. Martz. 4.95x o.p. (ISBN 0-205-03569-8, 7635699). Allyn.

Ecumenical Creed? Ed. by Hans Kung & Jurgen Moltmann. (Concilium Ser.: Vol. 118). (Orig.). 1978. pap. 4.95 (ISBN 0-8164-2198-6). Crossroad NY.

Ecumenical Documents of the Faith: The Creed of Nicea; Three Epistles of Cyril; the Tome of Leo; the Chalcedonian Definition. 4th ed. Ed. by T. Herbert Bindley. LC 79-8708. viii, 246p. 1980. Repr. of 1950 ed. lib. bdg. 22.25x (ISBN 0-313-22197-9, BIOD). Greenwood.

Ecumenical Perspective & the Modernization of Jewish Religion: A Study in the Relationship Between Theology & Myth. S. Daniel Breslauer. 1978. pap. 7.50 (ISBN 0-89130-236-0, 140005). Scholars Pr Ca.

Eczema: Its Nature, Cure & Prevention. Arthur Bobroff. (Illus.). 264p. 1962. pap. 22.75 photocopy ed. spiral (ISBN 0-398-00184-7). C C Thomas.

Ed Cartier: The Known & the Unknown. Ed. by Dean Cartier. 1977. 15.00 (ISBN 0-938192-01-9). De La Ree.

Ed Emberley's Big Green Drawing Book. Ed Emberley. LC 79-16247. (Illus.). (gr. k up). 1979. 6.95 (ISBN 0-316-23595-4); pap. 4.95 (ISBN 0-316-23596-2). Little.

Ed Emberley's Crazy Mixed-up Face Game. Ed Emberley. (Illus.). 32p. (gr. 1 up). 1981. 8.95 (ISBN 0-316-23420-6); pap. 4.95 (ISBN 0-316-23421-4). Little.

Ed Emberly's Big Orange Drawing Book. Ed Emberly. (Illus.). 96p. 1980. 8.95 (ISBN 0-316-23418-4); pap. 4.95 (ISBN 0-316-23419-2). Little.

Ed Heinemann: Combat Aercraft Designer. Edward H. Heinemann & Rosario Rausa. LC 79-87869. (Illus.). 296p. 1980. 18.95 (ISBN 0-87021-264-8). Naval Inst Pr.

Ed King Kommemorative Kalender Nineteen Eighty-One. Mark Rowland. 1980. pap. 4.95. World Food.

Edades: Kites & Visions. Lydia R. Ingle. (Illus.). 103p. 1980. pap. 7.50x (ISBN 0-686-28646-4). Cellar.

Eddie & Gardenia. Carolyn Haywood. (Illus.). (gr. 3-7). 1951. PLB 7.92 (ISBN 0-688-31255-1). Morrow.

Eddie & Louella. Carolyn Haywood. (Illus.). (gr. 3-7). 1959. PLB 7.92 (ISBN 0-688-31254-3). Morrow.

Eddie & the Fire Engine. Carolyn Haywood. (Illus.). (gr. 1-5). 1949. PLB 7.92 (ISBN 0-688-31252-7). Morrow.

Eddie Couldn't Find the Elephants. Edith Battles. LC 74-13997. (Self Starter Bks.). (Illus.). 32p. (gr. k-2). 1974. 6.50g (ISBN 0-8075-1877-8). A Whitman.

Eddie Gold's White Sox & Cubs Trivia Book. Eddie Gold. 144p. 1981. pap. 3.95 (ISBN 0-695-81574-1). Follett.

Eddie Macon's Run. James McLendon. 1980. pap. 2.95 (ISBN 0-451-09518-9, E9518, Sig). NAL.

Eddie Makes Music. Carolyn Haywood. (Illus.). (gr. 3-7). 1957. PLB 8.40 (ISBN 0-688-31256-X). Morrow.

Eddie the Dog Holder. Carolyn Haywood. (Illus.). (gr. 3-7). 1966. PLB 7.92 (ISBN 0-688-31253-5). Morrow.

Eddie the Dog Holder. Carolyn Haywood. (gr. 3-5). 1980. pap. 1.75 (ISBN 0-671-56050-6). Archway.

Eddie's Green Thumb. Carolyn Haywood. (Illus.). (gr. 3-7). 1964. PLB 7.92 (ISBN 0-688-31257-8). Morrow.

Eddie's Green Thumb. Carolyn Haywood. (Illus.). (gr. 3-5). 1980. pap. 1.75 (ISBN 0-671-56051-4). PB.

Eddie's Happenings. Carolyn Haywood. (Illus.). (gr. 3-7). 1971. PLB 7.92 (ISBN 0-688-31258-6). Morrow.

Eddie's Menagerie. Carolyn Haywood. (Illus.). (gr. 4-6). 1978. 8.95 (ISBN 0-688-22158-0); PLB 8.59 (ISBN 0-688-32158-5). Morrow.

Eddie's Menagerie. Carolyn Haywood. (Illus.). (gr. 3-5). 1980. pap. 1.75 (ISBN 0-671-56049-2). PB.

Eddie's Pay Dirt. Carolyn Haywood. (Illus.). (gr. 3-7). 1953. PLB 7.92 (ISBN 0-688-31259-4). Morrow.

Eddie's Valuable Property. Carolyn Haywood. LC 74-17499. (Illus.). 192p. (gr. 3-7). 1975. 8.25 (ISBN 0-688-22014-2); PLB 7.92 (ISBN 0-688-32014-7). Morrow.

Eden Hotel. Gary Gryst. 1980. 1.50 (ISBN 0-917554-08-6). Maelstrom.

Eden Passion. Marilyn Harris. 1980. pap. 2.50 (ISBN 0-345-28537-9). Ballantine.

Eden Phillpots on Dartmoor. Kenneth F. Day. (Illus.). 248p. 1981. 19.95 (ISBN 0-7153-8118-0). David & Charles.

Eden Seekers. Malcolm Clark, Jr. 320p. 1981. 15.00 (ISBN 0-686-69047-8). HM.

Eden's Horizon. George Madison. 1977. pap. 1.50 o.p. (ISBN 0-445-04004-1). Popular Lib.

Edgar Allan. John Neufeld. LC 68-31175. (Illus.). (gr. 5-8). 1968. 9.95 (ISBN 0-87599-149-1). S G Phillips.

Edgar Allan Poe. 2nd ed. Vincent Buranelli. (U.S. Authors Ser.: No. 4). 1977. lib. bdg. 9.95 (ISBN 0-8057-7189-1). Twayne.

Edgar Allan Poe. Ed. by Vincent Buranelli. LC 77-7265. (Twaynes's U. S. Authors Ser.). 166p. 1977. pap. text ed. 4.95 (ISBN 0-672-61502-9). Bobbs.

Edgar Allan Poe. Hanns H. Ewers. 55p. 1980. Repr. of 1917 ed. lib. bdg. 10.00 (ISBN 0-8495-1347-2). Arden Lib.

Edgar Allan Poe. George E. Woodberry. LC 80-19049. (American Men & Women of Letters Ser.). 360p. 1980. pap. 5.95 (ISBN 0-87754-152-3). Chelsea Hse.

Edgar Allan Poe Companion. J. A. Hammond. (Companion Ser.). (Illus.). 1981. 27.50x (ISBN 0-389-20172-3). B&N.

Edgar Allan Poe: His Works & Influence. Charles Haines. LC 74-3352. (Biography Ser). 160p. (gr. 7 up). 1974. PLB 5.90 o.p. (ISBN 0-531-02737-6). Watts.

Edgar Allan Poe, Stories & Poems. Edgar A. Poe. (Classics Ser). (gr. 9 up). pap. 1.50 (ISBN 0-8049-0008-6, CL-8). Airmont.

Edgar Allan Poe: The Unknown Poe. Ed. by Raymond Foye. LC 80-2431. 1980. pap. 5.95 (ISBN 0-87286-110-4). City Lights.

Edgar Cayce Handbook for Health Through Drugless Therapy. Harold J. Reilly & Ruth H. Brod. (Illus.). 356p. 1975. 10.95 o.s.i. (ISBN 0-02-601960-4). Macmillan.

Edgar Cayce Handbook for Health Through Drugless Therapy. Harold J. Reilly & Ruth H. Brod. 1977. pap. 3.50 (ISBN 0-515-05825-4). Jove Pubns.

Edgar Cayce on Atlantis. Edgar E. Cayce. Ed. by Hugh L. Cayce. 176p. 1968. pap. 2.25 (ISBN 0-446-89918-6, 9918-6). Warner Bks.

Edgar Cayce on Diet & Health. Margaret Gammon & Carol I. Read. 192p. (Orig.). 1969. pap. 2.25 (ISBN 0-446-92690-6). Warner Bks.

Edgar Cayce on Dreams. Harmon H. Bro. 224p. 1968. pap. 2.25 (ISBN 0-446-92687-6). Warner Bks.

Edgar Cayce on Healing. Mary E. Carter & William A. McGarey. 208p. 1972. pap. 2.25 (ISBN 0-446-92692-2). Warner Bks.

Edgar Cayce on Prophecy. Mary E. Carter. 208p. 1968. pap. 2.25 (ISBN 0-446-92694-9). Warner Bks.

Edgar Cayce on Religion & Psychic Experience. Harmon H. Bro. Ed. by Hugh L. Cayce. (Orig.). 1970. pap. 2.25 (ISBN 0-446-92696-5). Warner Bks.

Edgar Cayce Reader. Ed. by Hugh L. Cayce. 192p. 1969. pap. 2.25 (ISBN 0-446-92698-1). Warner Bks.

Edgar Cayce's Story of Jesus. Ed. by Jeffrey Furst. 1970. pap. 1.95 o.p. (ISBN 0-425-03225-6, Medallion). Berkley Pub.

Edgar Fawcett. Stanley R. Harrison. (U. S. Authors Ser.: No. 201). lib. bdg. 10.95 (ISBN 0-8057-0248-2). Twayne.

Edgar Lee Masters: The Spoon River Poet & His Critics. John T. Flanagan. LC 74-20530. 1974. 10.00 (ISBN 0-8108-0741-6). Scarecrow.

Edgar Poe & His Critics. Sarah H. Whitman. 81p. 1967. pap. 2.50 (ISBN 0-910120-03-X). Americanist.

Edgar Poe & His Critics. Sarah H. P. Whitman. LC 80-26202. 105p. Repr. of 1949 ed. 9.00x (ISBN 0-686-69559-3). Gordian.

Edgar Rice Burroughs: The Man Who Created Tarzan, 2 vols. Irwin Porges. 640p. 1976. Set. pap. 10.00 o.p. (ISBN 0-345-25131-8); Vol. 1. (ISBN 0-345-25947-5); Vol. 2. (ISBN 0-685-66521-6). Ballantine.

Edgar Wallace. Margaret Lane. 423p. 1980. Repr. lib. bdg. 30.00 (ISBN 0-8495-3259-0). Arden Lib.

Edgar Watson Howe. S. J. Sackett. (U. S. Authors Ser.: No. 195). lib. bdg. 10.95 (ISBN 0-8057-0383-7). Twayne.

Edge No. Thirty: Towering Nightmare. George C. Gilman. 1979. pap. 1.75 (ISBN 0-523-41312-2). Pinnacle Bks.

Edge, Number Thirty-Six: Town on Trial. George G. Gilman. 160p. 1981. pap. 1.75 (ISBN 0-523-40867-6). Pinnacle Bks.

Edge of a Kingdom. Elizabeth G. Waddell. LC 79-66934. 1981. 5.95 (ISBN 0-533-04419-7). Vantage.

Edge of an Era. Hannah R. Lurie. 1974. 3.00 o.p. (ISBN 0-685-76701-9). Know Inc.

Edge of Fear. Joyce Morton. (YA) 1978. 5.95 (ISBN 0-685-84747-0, Avalon). Bouregy.

Edge of Fear. LaVada Weir. LC 74-859. (Laurie Newman Adventures Ser). 32p. (gr. 3-9). 1974. 5.95 (ISBN 0-87191-338-0). Creative Ed.

Edge of Glass. Cathering Gaskin. 240p. 1981. pap. 2.50 (ISBN 0-553-14362-X). Bantam.

Edge of Impossibility: Tragic Forms in Literature. Joyce Carol Oates. LC 77-188692. 1972. 10.95 (ISBN 0-8149-0675-3). Vanguard.

Edge of Madness: Prisons & Prison Reform in America. Robert A. Liston. LC 79-186756. 128p. (gr. 7 up). 1972. PLB 5.88 o.p. (ISBN 0-531-02025-8). Watts.

Edge of Paradise: A Collection of Color Woodcuts. Evelyn A. Domjan. Ed. by Jane Emig. LC 78-73442. (Illus.). 1979. 20.00x (ISBN 0-933652-14-3). Domjan Studio.

Edge of Reality: A Progress Report on Unidentified Flying Objects. J. Allen Hynek & Jacques Vallee. LC 75-13226. (Illus.). 288p. 1976. 14.95 o.p. (ISBN 0-8092-8209-7); pap. 5.95 o.p. (ISBN 0-8092-8150-3). Contemp Bks.

Edge of Spring. Helen Bianchin. (Harlequin Presents Ser.). 192p. 1981. pap. 1.50 (ISBN 0-373-10415-4, Pub. by Harlequin). PB.

Edge of Temptation. Anne Mather. (Harlequin Presents Ser.). 192p. (Orig.). 1981. pap. 1.50 (ISBN 0-373-10405-7, Pub. by Harlequin). PB.

Edge of the Alphabet. Janet Frame. LC 62-16268. 1962. 4.95 o.p. (ISBN 0-8076-0194-2). Braziller.

Edge of the Forest. Agnes Smith. (Illus.). 202p. (gr. 7 up). 1974. 9.00 (ISBN 0-686-28761-4). Westwind Pr.

Edge of the Ocean. William White, Jr. LC 78-80953. (Living Nature Ser.). (Illus.). (gr. 6 up). 1977. 7.95 (ISBN 0-8069-3582-0); PLB 7.49 (ISBN 0-8069-3583-9). Sterling.

Edge of the Sea. Rachel Carson. 1971. pap. 0.95 o.p. (ISBN 0-451-04368-5, Q4368, Sig). NAL.

Edge of Twilight. Paula Christian. LC 78-54182. 1978. pap. 6.50x (ISBN 0-931328-00-4). Timely Bks.

Edgecombe Country: A Brief History. Alan D. Watson. (Illus.). 1979. pap. 2.00 (ISBN 0-86526-127-X). NC Archives.

Edges. Ed. by Ursula K. Le Guin & Virginia Kidd. 1980. pap. write for info. (ISBN 0-671-83532-7). PB.

Edges of Love. Frances C. Kerns. (Orig.). 1980. pap. 2.50 (ISBN 0-446-91093-7). Warner Bks.

Edible & Useful Wild Plants of the United States & Canada. Saunders. LC 75-46193. (Illus.). 320p. 1976. pap. 4.00 (ISBN 0-486-23310-3). Dover.

Edible & Useful Wildplants. Alan MacPherson & Sue MacPherson. (Illus.). 1979. pap. 7.95 (ISBN 0-87108-533-X). Pruett.

Edible City Resource Manual. Richard Britz et al. (Illus.). 320p. (Orig.). 1981. pap. 11.50 (ISBN 0-913232-97-1). W Kaufmann.

Edible Garden Weeds of Canada. Adam F. Szczawinski & Nancy J. Turner. (Illus.). 1978. pap. 9.95 (ISBN 0-660-00026-1, 56327-8, Pub. by Natl Mus Canada). U of Chicago Pr.

Edible Indoor Garden. Peggy Hardigree. 320p. 1981. 16.95 (ISBN 0-312-23689-1); pap. 7.95 (ISBN 0-312-23690-5). St Martin.

Edible Mushrooms. 2nd, rev. ed. Clyde M. Christensen. (Illus.). 136p. 1981. 12.95 (ISBN 0-8166-1049-5); pap. 6.95 (ISBN 0-8166-1050-9). U of Minn Pr.

Edible Ornamental Garden. John Bryan & Coralie Castle. LC 73-91941. (Illus.). 192p. (Orig.). 1974. pap. 4.95 (ISBN 0-912238-47-X) (ISBN 0-912238-46-1). One Hund One Prods.

Edible Wild Fruits & Nuts of Canada. Nancy J. Turner & Adam F. Szczawinski. (Illus.). 1979. pap. 9.95 spiral bdg. (ISBN 0-660-00128-4, 56328-6, Pub. by Natl Mus Canada). U of Chicago Pr.

Edible Wild Plants: Of Eastern North America. rev. ed. Merritt L. Fernald et al. LC 58-7977. (Illus.). 1958. 15.00 o.p. (ISBN 0-06-070810-7, HarpT). Har-Row.

Edible Wild Plants of Martha's Vineyard: And Other Coastal Parts of New England. Linsey Lee. LC 75-24889. (Illus., Orig.). 1979. pap. 4.95 (ISBN 0-932384-03-X). Tashmoo.

Edible Woman. Margaret Atwood. 1976. pap. 2.25 (ISBN 0-445-08466-9). Popular Lib.

Edificare My Iglesia. Tr. by Melvin Hodges. (Spanish Bks.). 1979. 1.50 (ISBN 0-8297-0544-9); wkbk. 0.80 (ISBN 0-8297-0545-7). Life Pubs Intl.

Edifice of Taharqa by the Sacred Lake of Karnak. Richard A. Parker et al. LC 77-76345. (Brown Egyptological Studies: No. 8). 154p. 1979. 60.00x (ISBN 0-87057-151-6, Pub. by Brown U Pr). Univ Pr of New England.

Edinburgh. David Daiche. 1979. 22.50 (ISBN 0-241-89878-1, Pub. by Hamish Hamilton England). David & Charles.

Edinburgh & South-East Scotland: Regional Archaeology. Graham Ritchie & Anne Ritchie. 1972. 5.50x o.p. (ISBN 0-435-32971-5). Heinemann Ed.

Edinburgh & the Medical Revolution. R. D. Lobban. LC 78-51669. (Cambridge Introduction to the History of Mankind Ser.). (Illus.). (YA) 1980. pap. 3.95 (ISBN 0-521-22028-9). Cambridge U Pr.

Edinburgh Conference, 1979: International Workshop on Human Gene Mapping, 5th, July 1979. Ed. by H. J. Evans et al. (Human Gene Mapping Ser.: No. 5). (Illus.). vi, 236p. 1980. pap. 39.00 (ISBN 3-8055-0649-X). S Karger.

Edinburgh Course in Applied Linguistics, Vol. 2. Ed. by J. P. Allen & S. Pit Corder. (Language & Language Learning Ser). 388p. 1975. 24.00 o.p. (ISBN 0-19-437123-9); pap. text ed. 17.00x (ISBN 0-19-437058-5). Oxford U Pr.

Edinburgh Course in Applied Linguistics: Readings for Applied Linguistics, Vol. 1. Ed. by J. P. Allen & S. Pit Corder. (Language & Language Learning Ser.). 284p. 1973. 15.25 o.p. (ISBN 0-19-437122-0); pap. 9.00x (ISBN 0-19-437057-7). Oxford U Pr.

Edinburgh Course in Applied Linguistics: Techniques in Applied Linguistics, Vol. 3. Ed. by J. P. Allen & S. Pit Corder. (Language & Language Learning Ser). 386p. 1974. 24.00 o.p. (ISBN 0-19-437124-7); pap. text ed. 13.95x (ISBN 0-19-437059-3). Oxford U Pr.

Edinburgh in Colour. John Hutchinson. (Illus.). 96p. 1980. 17.95 (ISBN 0-7134-1998-9, Pub. by Batsford England). David & Charles.

Edinburgh in the Age of Sir Walter Scott. Douglas Young. (Centers of Civilization Ser.: No. 17). 1965. 5.95 o.p. (ISBN 0-8061-0661-1). U of Okla Pr.

Edinburgh Reel. Iona MacGregor. (gr. 5 up). 1968. 5.95 o.p. (ISBN 0-571-08362-5, Pub. by Faber & Faber). Merrimack Bk Serv.

Edinburgh Review & Poetic Truth. A. H. Qureshi. (Costerus New Ser.: No. 16). 1978. pap. text ed. 8.75x (ISBN 90-6203-752-6). Humanities.

Edinburgh Seventy-Seven: History-Production-Memory. Ed. by Claire Johnston. (EIFF Ser.). 1978. pap. 6.00 (ISBN 0-918432-17-0). NY Zoetrope.

Edinburgh Seventy-Six: Psychoanalysis, Cinema, Avante-Garde. Ed. by Claire Johnston. (EIFF Ser.). 1978. pap. 5.00 (ISBN 0-918432-16-2). NY Zoetrope.

Edison. (MacDonald Educational Ser.). (Illus., Arabic.). 3.50 (ISBN 0-686-53089-6). Intl Bk Ctr.

Edison Blue Amberol Recordings: 1912-1914. Ed. by Ronald Dethlefson. (American Popular Series Live Recordings). (Illus.). 1980. 19.95 (ISBN 0-937612-00-6). A P M Pr.

Edith & the Duckling. Dare Wright. LC 80-1664. (Illus.). 48p. (ps-3). 1981. 8.95a (ISBN 0-385-17100-5); PLB (ISBN 0-385-17101-3). Doubleday.

Edith & Woodrow. Tom Shachtman. 288p. 1981. 12.95 (ISBN 0-399-12446-2). Putnam.

Edith Sitwell: A Biography. Geoffrey Elborn. LC 80-1985. 312p. 1981. 14.95 (ISBN 0-385-13467-3). Doubleday.

Edith Sitwell: A Unicorn Among Lions. Victoria Glendinning. LC 80-2721. (Illus.). 384p. 1981. 17.95 (ISBN 0-394-50439-9). Knopf.

Edith Sitwell: Selected Letters 1919-1964. Edith Sitwell. LC 72-134662. 1970. 12.50 (ISBN 0-8149-0678-8). Vanguard.

Edith Wharton. Richard H. Lawson. LC 77-40. (Modern Literature Ser.). 1977. 10.95 (ISBN 0-8044-2496-9). Ungar.

Edith Wharton. Margaret B. McDowell. LC 75-44094. (U. S. Authors Ser.: No. 265). 1976. lib. bdg. 10.95 (ISBN 0-8057-7164-6). Twayne.

Edith Wharton. Margaret B. McDowell. LC 75-44094. (Twayne's U. S. Authors Ser.). 158p. 1976. pap. text ed. 4.95 (ISBN 0-672-61509-6). Bobbs.

Edith Wharton: A Study of Her Fiction. Blake Nevius. (California Library Reprint Ser). 1976. 18.50x (ISBN 0-520-03180-6). U of Cal Pr.

Edith Wharton & Henry James: The Story of Their Friendship. Millicent Bell. LC 65-10196. 1965. 6.50 o.p. (ISBN 0-8076-0295-7). Braziller.

Edith Wharton Omnibus. Edith Wharton. (Encore Edition). 1978. 4.95 (ISBN 0-684-16933-9, ScribT). Scribner.

Edith Wharton's Argument with America. Elizabeth Ammons. LC 79-48000. 232p. 1980. 15.00x (ISBN 0-8203-0513-8). U of Ga Pr.

Editing British & American Literature: 1880-1920. Ed. by Eric Domville. LC 76-7323. (Conference on Editorial Problems Ser.). 1976. lib. bdg. 16.50 (ISBN 0-8240-2409-5). Garland Pub.

Editing Canadian Texts. Ed. by Francess G. Halpenny. (Conference on Editorial Problems Ser.). 1976. lib. bdg. 16.50 (ISBN 0-8240-2407-9). Garland Pub.

Editing Eighteenth Century Novels. Ed. by G. E. Bently, Jr. (Conference on Editorial Problems Ser.). 1976. lib. bdg. 16.50 (ISBN 0-8240-2408-7). Garland Pub.

Editing Eighteenth-Century Texts. Ed. by D. I. Smith. (Conference on Editorial Problems Ser.). 1976. lib. bdg. 16.50 (ISBN 0-8240-2402-8). Garland Pub.

Editing Medieval Texts. Ed. by George Rigg. LC 76-52722. (Conference on Editorial Problems Ser.: Vol. 12). 1977. lib. bdg. 16.50 (ISBN 0-8240-2426-5). Garland Pub.

Editing Nineteenth-Century Fiction, Vol. 13. Ed. by Jane Millgate. LC 78-3393. (Conference on Editorial Problems Ser.). 1978. lib. bdg. 16.50 (ISBN 0-8240-2428-1). Garland Pub.

Editing Nineteenth Century Texts. Ed. by John M. Robson. (Conference on Editorial Problems Ser.). 1976. lib. bdg. 16.50 (ISBN 0-8240-2401-X). Garland Pub.

Editing of Renaissance Dramatic Texts: English, Italian, & Spanish. Ed. by Anne Lancashire. LC 76-7324. (Conference on Editorial Problems Ser.: No. 11). 1976. lib. bdg. 16.50 (ISBN 0-8240-2410-9). Garland Pub.

Editing Seventeenth Century Prose. Ed. by D. I. Smith. (Conference on Editorial Problems Ser.). 1976. lib. bdg. 16.50 (ISBN 0-8240-2405-2). Garland Pub.

Editing Sixteenth Century Texts. Ed. by R. J. Schoeck. (Conference on Editorial Problems Ser). 1976. lib. bdg. 16.50 (ISBN 0-8240-2400-1). Garland Pub.

Editing Super Eight. Tim Copestake. (Illus.). 1980. cancelled o.p. (ISBN 0-8038-2387-8). Hastings.

Editing Super Eight. Timothy Copestake. (Illus.). 288p. 1980. 19.95 (ISBN 0-240-50997-8). Focal Pr.

Editing Texts of the Romantic Period. Ed. by John D. Baird. (Conference on Editorial Problems Ser.). 1976. lib. bdg. 16.50 (ISBN 0-8240-2406-0). Garland Pub.

Editing the Small Magazine. 2nd ed. Rowena Ferguson. 208p. 1976. 15.00x (ISBN 0-231-03866-6); pap. 6.00x (ISBN 0-231-03970-0). Columbia U Pr.

Editing Twentieth Century Texts. Ed. by Francess G. Halpenny. (Conference on Editorial Problems Ser.). 1976. lib. bdg. 16.50 (ISBN 0-8240-2404-4). Garland Pub.

Editing Your Own Newsletter. Mark Beach. 76p. 1980. pap. 6.95x (ISBN 0-9602664-2-9, Pub. by Coast to Coast Bks). Intl Schol Bk Serv.

Editor at Large. Leavitt F. Morris. 160p. 1981. 12.50 (ISBN 0-682-49705-3). Exposition.

Editor, Author, & Publisher. Ed. by William J. Howard. (Conference on Editorial Problems Ser.). 1976. lib. bdg. 16.50 (ISBN 0-8240-2403-6). Garland Pub.

Editor to Author: The Letters of Maxwell E. Perkins. Maxwell E. Perkins. (Illus.). 1979. 12.50 o.p. (ISBN 0-684-16173-7, ScribT). Scribner.

Editorial & Political Cartooning. Syd Hoff. LC 75-45314. (Illus.). 1976. 14.95 (ISBN 0-87396-078-5). Stravon.

Editorial Page. Washington Post Writers Group. 1977. pap. text ed. 8.75 (ISBN 0-395-24015-8). HM.

Editorial Writing, Ethics, Policy Practice. M. Lyle Spencer. 362p. 1980. Repr. of 1924 ed. lib. bdg. 30.00 (ISBN 0-89984-419-7). Century Bookbindery.

Editorially Speaking. O. W. Polen. 1975. pap. 1.25 (ISBN 0-87148-300-9). Pathway Pr.

Editor's Choice: Literature & Graphics from the U. S. Small Press, 1965-1977. Ed. by Morty Sklar & Jim Mulac. LC 79-64861. (Contemporary Anthology Ser.: No. 2). (Illus.). 501p. 1980. 14.50 (ISBN 0-930370-05-8); pap. 9.50 (ISBN 0-930370-04-X); signed, numbered ed. 25.00 (ISBN 0-930370-06-6). Spirit That Moves.

Editor's Essays of Two Decades. Alan Swallow. LC 72-94406. 401p. 1962. 7.95 (ISBN 0-8040-0073-5). Swallow.

Editor's Manual. Ed. by Julien Elfenbein. (Illus.). 1970. 15.00 o.p. (ISBN 0-686-08528-0, SP1). Am Journal Nurse.

Edmond Rostand. Alba Amoia. (World Authors Ser.: No. 420). 1978. lib. bdg. 12.50 (ISBN 0-8057-6260-4). Twayne.

Edmund Burke: A Philosophical Enquiry into the Origin of Our Ideas of the Sublime & Beautiful. James T. Boulton. 1967. 11.50x (ISBN 0-7100-1140-7). Humanities.

Edmund Burke & His Literary Friends. Donald C. Bryant. 323p. 1980. Repr. of 1939 ed. lib. bdg. 35.00 (ISBN 0-8482-0133-7). Norwood Edns.

Edmund Burke & the American Revolution. Charles R. Ritcheson. (Sir George Watson Lectures). 1976. pap. text ed. 1.25x (ISBN 0-7185-1154-9, Leicester). Humanities.

Edmund Burke & the Critique of Political Radicalism. Michael Freeman. LC 80-16266. 264p. 1980. lib. bdg. 21.00 (ISBN 0-226-26175-1). U of Chicago Pr.

Edmund Clarence Stedman. Robert J. Sholnick. (United States Authors Ser.: No. 286). 1977. lib. bdg. 12.50 (ISBN 0-8057-7188-3). Twayne.

Edmund Dulac. Colin White. (Encore Edition). (Illus.). 1975. 10.95 o.p. (ISBN 0-684-15470-6, ScribT). Scribner.

Edmund Husserl & His Critics: An International Bibliography (1894-1979) Francois Lapointe. (Bibliographies of Famous Philosophers: Vol. 4). 352p. 1980. 27.50 (ISBN 0-912632-42-9). Philos Document.

Edmund Spenser: The Faerie Queene. Ed. by Thomas P. Roche, Jr. & C. P. O'Donnell. 1247p. 1981. text ed. 40.00x (ISBN 0-300-02705-2); pap. 12.95x (ISBN 0-300-02706-0). Yale U Pr.

Edmund Waller. Jack G. Gilbert. (English Authors Ser.: No. 266). 1979. lib. bdg. 13.50 (ISBN 0-8057-6763-0). Twayne.

Edmund Wilson: Our Neighbor from Talcottville. Richard H. Costa. (York State Bks.). (Illus.). 192p. 1980. 11.95 (ISBN 0-8156-0163-8). Syracuse U Pr.

Edmund's Auto Pedia. (Orig.). 1980. pap. 2.50 (ISBN 0-440-02954-6). Dell.

Edmund's Nineteen Eighty-One Foreign Car Prices. Ed. by William R. Badnow. (Edmund's Car Price Guides Ser.). (Orig.). 1981. pap. 2.50 (ISBN 0-440-02207-X, Pub. by Edmund). Dell.

Edmund's Nineteen Eighty-One New Car Prices. Ed. by William R. Badnow. (Orig.). 1981. pap. 2.50 (ISBN 0-440-02236-3, Pub. by Edmund). Dell.

Edmund's Nineteen Eighty One New Car Prices. (Orig.). 1980. pap. 2.50 o.p. (ISBN 0-440-02953-8). Dell.

Edmund's Nineteen Eighty-One Used Car Prices. Ed. by William R. Badnow. (Edmund's Car Price Guides Ser.). (Orig.). 1981. pap. 2.50 (ISBN 0-440-02209-6, Pub. by Edmund). Dell.

Edmund's United States Coin Prices. Ed. by William R. Badnow. (Orig.). 1981. pap. 2.50 (ISBN 0-440-01794-7, Pub. by Edmund). Dell.

Edmund's United States Coin Prices. (Orig.). 1980. pap. 2.50 o.p. (ISBN 0-440-08995-6). Dell.

Edmund's Used Car Prices. Ed. by William R. Badnow. (Orig.). Date not set. pap. price not set (ISBN 0-440-02952-X, Pub by Edmund). Dell.

Edmund's Used Car Prices. (Orig.). 1980. pap. 2.50 o.p. (ISBN 0-440-02952-X). Dell.

Edna St. Vincent Millay. Norman A. Brittin. (U. S. Authors Ser.: No. 116). 1967. lib. bdg. 9.95 (ISBN 0-8057-0496-5). Twayne.

Edouard Boubat: Great Contemporary Photographer. Bernard George. LC 73-7351. (Men & Movements Ser.: Vol. 3). (Illus.). 96p. 1974. 10.95 o.s.i. (ISBN 0-02-542980-9). Macmillan.

Edouard Boubat: Great Contemporary Photographer. Bernard George. (Photography, Men & Movements Ser.: Vol. 3). (Illus.). 96p. 1974. pap. 5.95 o.s.i. (ISBN 0-02-000350-1, Collier). Macmillan.

Edouard Seguin: A Study of an Educational Approach to the Treatment of Mentally Defective Children. Mabel E. Talbot. LC 64-23753. 1964. pap. text ed. 3.50x (ISBN 0-8077-2242-1). Tchrs Coll.

EDP Auditing: A Primer. Joseph Sardinas & John G. Burch. 200p. 1981. pap. text ed. 10.95 (ISBN 0-471-12305-6). Wiley.

EDP Institute, August 22-25, 1976: Proceedings. Ed. by Janice H. Welke. 1977. pap. 8.75 (ISBN 0-89154-054-7). Intl Found Employ.

EDP Institute, Los Angeles, Nov. 4-7, 1979: Proceedings. Ed. by Mary E. Brennan. 95p. 1980. pap. 10.00 (ISBN 0-89154-127-6). Intl Found Employ.

EDP Systems for Credit Management. Conon D. Whiteside. LC 74-156330. 1971. 23.95 (ISBN 0-471-94080-1, Pub. by Wiley-Interscience). Wiley.

Edsel Affair. C. Gayle Warnock. LC 80-81129. (Illus.). 278p. 1980. 16.95 (ISBN 0-686-28039-3). Pro West.

Eduardo Mallea. H. Ernest Lewald. (World Authors Ser.: No. 433). 1977. lib. bdg. 12.50 (ISBN 0-8057-6273-6). Twayne.

Eduardo Mallea: Todo verdor perecera. Ed. by D. L. Shaw. 1968. 8.30 (ISBN 0-08-012868-8); pap. 5.75 (ISBN 0-08-012867-X). Pergamon.

Eduardo Marquina. Manual De La Nuez. LC 76-5796. (World Authors Ser.: Spain: No. 396). 1976. lib. bdg. 12.50 (ISBN 0-8057-6238-8). Twayne.

Eduardo Paolozzi. Frank Whitford. (Tate Gallery Art Ser.). (Illus.). 1977. 3.95 o.p. (ISBN 0-8120-5144-0). Barron.

Educability & Group Differences. Arthur R. Jensen. LC 72-9126. (Illus.). 416p. 1973. 10.95 o.s.i. (ISBN 0-06-012194-7, HarpT). Har-Row.

Educable Mentally Retarded Child: Guidance & Curriculum. Kathleen B. Waite. (Illus.). 592p. 1971. text ed. 54.75 (ISBN 0-398-02002-7). C C Thomas.

Educated American Women: Life-Styles & Self-Portraits. Eli Ginzberg & Alice M. Yohalem. LC 66-28964. 1966. 14.50x (ISBN 0-231-03027-4); pap. 5.00x (ISBN 0-231-03604-3). Columbia U Pr.

Educated Woman in America: Selected Writings of Catharine Beecher, Margaret Fuller & M. Carey Thomas. Ed. by Barbara M. Cross. LC 65-23578. (Illus.). 1965. text ed. 8.75 (ISBN 0-8077-1221-3); pap. text ed. 4.00x (ISBN 0-8077-1218-3). Tchrs Coll.

Educating Act: A Phenomenological View. J. Gordon Chamberlin. LC 80-6076. 202p. 1981. lib. bdg. 17.75 (ISBN 0-8191-1449-9); pap. text ed. 8.75 (ISBN 0-8191-1450-2). U Pr of Amer.

Educating Adolescent Girls. E. M. Chandler. (Unwin Education Books Ser.). 240p. (Orig.). 1980. text ed. 27.50x (ISBN 0-04-370096-9); pap. text ed. 10.50x (ISBN 0-04-370097-7). Allen Unwin.

Educating Adolescents with Behavior Disorders. Gwen Brown et al. (Special Education Ser.). 448p. Date not set. text ed. 18.95 (ISBN 0-675-08056-8). Merrill.

Educating an Urban People: The New York Experience. Ed. by Diane Ravitch & Ronald Goodenow. 1981. text ed. 22.50 (ISBN 0-8077-2600-1). Tchrs Coll.

Educating Children with Learning & Behavior Problems. M. Kozloff. LC 74-11304. 1974. 29.95 (ISBN 0-471-50630-3, Pub. by Wiley-Interscience). Wiley.

Educating Children with Severe Maladaptive Behaviors. William Stainback & Susan Stainback. 1980. 24.50 (ISBN 0-8089-1269-0). Grune.

Educating Diabetic Patients. George Steiner & Patricia A. Lawrence. 1981. text ed. price not set (ISBN 0-8261-2760-6); pap. text ed. price not set (ISBN 0-8261-2761-4). Springer Pub.

Educating Disturbed Adolescents: Theory & Practice. Payton Towns. (Current Issues in Behavioral Psychology Ser.). 1981. 19.50 (ISBN 0-8089-1312-3). Grune.

Educating Emotionally Disturbed Children. Norris G. Haring & E. L. Phillips. (Psychology & Human Development in Education Ser.). 1962. text ed. 17.95 o.p. (ISBN 0-07-026420-1, C). McGraw.

Educating Exceptional Children. 3rd ed. Samuel A. Kirk & James J. Gallagher. LC 78-69609. (Illus.). 1979. text ed. 17.95 (ISBN 0-395-26526-6); inst. manual 0.80 (ISBN 0-395-26529-0); test item supplement 0.75 (ISBN 0-395-28699-9). HM.

Educating Exceptional Children in a Changing Society. Harold D. Love. (Illus.). 264p. 1974. 13.75 (ISBN 0-398-02905-9). C C Thomas.

Educating Exceptional Pupils: An Introduction to Contemporary Practices. Kathryn Blake. LC 80-15222. (Illus.). 528p. 1981. text ed. 15.95 (ISBN 0-201-00083-0). A-W.

Educating for Christian Missions. Arthur L. Walker, Jr. (Orig.). 1981. pap. 5.95 (ISBN 0-8054-6934-6). Broadman.

Educating for Leisure-Centered Living. 2nd ed. Charles K. Brightbill & Tony A. Mobley. LC 76-47010. 1977. pap. text ed. 10.50 (ISBN 0-471-94914-0). Wiley.

Educating for Responsible Action. Nicholas Wolterstorff. 152p. (Orig.). 1980. pap. 6.95 (ISBN 0-8028-1857-9). Eerdmans.

Educating for the World View. Change Magazine Editors. LC 80-68195. 80p. 1980. pap. 3.00 (ISBN 0-915390-26-4). Change Mag.

Educating Gifted & Talented Learners. Don Sellin & Jack Birch. LC 80-19565. 372p. 1980. text ed. 24.50 (ISBN 0-89443-295-8). Aspen Systems.

Educating Our Masters. Reeder. 1980. text ed. 30.00x (ISBN 0-7185-5036-6, Leicester). Humanities.

Educating the Ablest. 2nd ed. John C. Gowan et al. LC 78-61876. 1979. pap. text ed. 12.50 (ISBN 0-87581-235-X). Peacock Pubs.

Educating the Child Who Is Different. Maria Egg. LC 68-11293. (John Day Bk.). 1968. 6.95 o.s.i. (ISBN 0-381-98095-2, A22260, TYC-T). T Y Crowell.

Educating the Deaf: Psychology, Principles & Practices. Donald F. Moores. LC 77-72896. (Illus.). 1977. text ed. 18.50 (ISBN 0-395-24486-2). HM.

Educating the Forgotten Half: Structured Activities for Learning. James L. Lee & Charles J. Pulvino. 1978. pap. text ed. 7.95 (ISBN 0-8403-1873-1). Kendall-Hunt.

Educating the Gifted: Acceleration & Enrichment. Ed. by William C. George et al. LC 79-7559. (Hyman Blumberg Symposium on Research in Early Childhood Education). 1980. text ed. 16.00x o.p. (ISBN 0-8018-2260-2); pap. text ed. 4.95x (ISBN 0-8018-2266-1). Johns Hopkins.

Educating the Handicapped: Where We've Been, Where We're Going. Mitchell Lazarus. 1980. pap. 11.95 (ISBN 0-87545-019-9). Natl Sch PR.

Educating the User. Ed. by I. Malley. 1979. pap. 11.50x (ISBN 0-85365-761-0, Pub. by Lib Assn England). Oryx Pr.

Educating the Worker-Citizen. Joel Spring. (Educational Policy, Planning & Theory). 1980. pap. text ed. 9.95 (ISBN 0-582-28075-3). Longman.

Educating Young Handicapped Children: A Developmental Approach. S. Gray Garwood. LC 79-13200. 1979. text ed. 24.75 (ISBN 0-89443-099-8). Aspen Systems.

Education, 6 pts. Incl. Pt. 1. General, 46 vols. Set. 3645.00x (ISBN 0-686-01168-6); Pt. 2. British Museum, 4 vols. Set. 342.00x (ISBN 0-686-01169-4); Pt. 3. Fine Arts, 6 vols. Set. 495.00x (ISBN 0-686-01170-8); Pt. 4. Poorer Classes, 9 vols. Set. 621.00x (ISBN 0-686-01171-6); Pt. 5. Public Libraries, 2 vols. Set. 153.00x (ISBN 0-686-01172-4); Pt. 6. Scientific & Technical, 8 vols. Set. 684.00x (ISBN 0-686-01173-2). (British Parliamentary Papers Ser.). 1971 (Pub. by Irish Academic Pr Ireland). Biblio Dist.

Education. 2nd ed. Ronald King. LC 77-1388. (Aspects of Modern Sociology: Social Structure of Modern Britain). 1977. pap. text ed. 10.50x (ISBN 0-582-48550-9). Longman.

Education. Edmund O'Connor. Ed. by Malcolm Yapp & Edmund O'Connor. (World History Ser.). (Illus.). 32p. (gr. 10). 1980. Repr. of 1977 ed. lib. bdg. 5.95 (ISBN 0-89908-147-9); pap. text ed. 1.95 (ISBN 0-89908-122-3). Greenhaven.

Education. Jack Rudman. (Undergraduate Program Field Test Ser.: UPFT-7). (Cloth bdg. avail. on request). pap. 9.95 (ISBN 0-8373-6007-2). Natl Learning.

Education. Ellen G. White. 324p. 1952. 6.50 (ISBN 0-8163-0042-9, 05151-6); pap. 4.50 o.p. (ISBN 0-8163-0043-7, 05152-4). Pacific Pr Pub Assn.

Education: A Beginning. 2nd ed. William Van Til. 624p. 1974. text ed. 18.50 (ISBN 0-395-17576-3); instructors' manual 1.50 (ISBN 0-395-17850-9). HM.

Education: A Way Ahead. Mary Warnock. 1979. 20.00x (ISBN 0-631-11281-2, Pub. by Basil Blackwell England); pap. 8.50x (ISBN 0-631-12902-2). Biblio Dist.

Education Act, Nineteen Eighteen. Lawrence Andrews. (Students Library of Education Ser.). 1976. 9.95x (ISBN 0-7100-8409-9). Routledge & Kegan.

Education After School. Tyrrell Burgess. 1977. 18.95x (ISBN 0-575-02237-X). Intl Ideas.

Education & Advancement of Women. Jacqueline Chabaud. (Orig.). 1971. pap. 6.00 (ISBN 92-3-100842-0, U182, UNESCO). Unipub.

Education & Collective Bargaining. Ed. by Anthony M. Cresswell & Michael J. Murphy. LC 76-46121. xviii, 513p. 1976. 14.00 (ISBN 0-8211-0227-3, Co-Pub. & Co-Distrib. by McCutchan); pap. 13.00 (ISBN 0-87367-769-2, Co-Pub. & Co-Distrib. by McCutchen). Phi Delta Kappa.

Education & Collective Bargaining: Readings in Policy & Research. Ed. by Anthony M. Cresswell & Michael J. Murphy. LC 76-46121. 1977. 20.50 (ISBN 0-685-78476-2); text ed. 18.50x 10 or more copies (ISBN 0-8211-0227-3). McCutchan.

Education & Colonialism. Ed. by Philip G. Altbach & Gail P. Kelly. LC 77-22777. (Educational Policy, Planning, & Theory Ser.). 1978. pap. text ed. 10.95x (ISBN 0-582-28003-6). Longman.

Education & Community: A Radical Critique of Innovative Schooling. Donald W. Oliver. LC 76-2114. 1977. 19.75 (ISBN 0-8211-1406-9); text ed. 17.75x in copies of ten (ISBN 0-685-80407-0). McCutchan.

Education & Day Care for Young Children in Need: The American Experience. Tessa Blackstone. 72p. 1973. pap. text ed. 1.90x (ISBN 0-7199-0875-2, Pub. by Bedford England). Renouf.

Education & Desegregation in Eight Schools. Center for Equal Education & John Egerton. LC 77-80528. 1977. pap. 3.60 (ISBN 0-912008-14-8). Integrated Ed Assoc.

Education & Development in the Third World. Richard D'Aeth. 138p. 1976. 18.95 (ISBN 0-347-01003-8, 99846-X, Pub. by Saxon Hse). Lexington Bks.

Education & Development in Western Europe, the United States, & the U.S.S.R. A Comparative Study. Raymond Poignant. LC 72-77012. (Illus.). 1969. text ed. 12.75x (ISBN 0-8077-2009-7). Tchrs Coll.

Education & Economic Growth in India. S. C. Goel. LC 75-904970. 1975. 9.50x o.p. (ISBN 0-333-90101-0). South Asia Bks.

Education & Education-Related Serials: A Directory. Wayne J. Krepel & Charles R. Duvall. LC 76-47040. 1977. lib. bdg. 15.00x o.p. (ISBN 0-87287-131-2). Libs Unl.

Education & Employment: A Critical Appraisal. Martin Carnoy. (Fundamentals of Educational Planning Ser: No. 26). 1978. pap. 4.75 (ISBN 92-803-1078-X, U779, UNESCO). Unipub.

Education & Employment in India: The Policy Nexus. T. N. Dhar et al. LC 76-52202. 1976. 12.50x o.p. (ISBN 0-88386-802-4). South Asia Bks.

Education & Evangelism: A Profile of the Protestant Colleges. Carnegie Commission on Higher Education. Ed. by C. Robert Pace. LC 70-39711. (Illus.). 129p. 1972. 6.95 o.p. (ISBN 0-07-010045-4, P&RB). McGraw.

Education & First Principles: A Historical Perspective. Earl T. Willis. LC 80-16408. ix, 132p. 1980. 12.74 (ISBN 0-8130-0646-5). U Presses Fla.

Education & Health of the Partially Seeing Child. 4th ed. Winifred Hathaway. LC 59-65156. 1959. 18.00x (ISBN 0-231-02356-1). Columbia U Pr.

Education & Income Distribution in Asia. P. Richards & M. Leonor. 208p. 1981. 35.50x (ISBN 0-7099-2201-9, Pub. by Croom Helm Ltd England). Biblio Dist.

Education & Industry in the Nineteenth Century: The English Disease? G. W. Roderick & M. D. Stephens. (Illus.). 196p. 1978. pap. text ed. 10.95 (ISBN 0-582-48719-6). Longman.

Education & Inequality. Caroline H. Persell. LC 76-46707. 1977. 12.95 o.s.i. (ISBN 0-02-925140-0). Free Pr.

Education & Inquiry. John Anderson. Ed. by D. Z. Phillips. 228p. 1980. 27.00x (ISBN 0-389-20075-1). B&N.

Education & Jobs. S. Parmaji. 1979. text ed. 9.25x (ISBN 0-391-01828-0). Humanities.

Education & Modernization in Asia. Don Adams. LC 75-100852. 1970. pap. 6.95 (ISBN 0-201-00028-8). A-W.

Education & Nuclear Energy. (Orig.). 1960. pap. 2.75 (ISBN 92-0-171060-7, IAEA). Unipub.

Education & Philosophy: A Practical Approach. Keith Thompson. 1977. pap. 8.50x (ISBN 0-631-94440-0, Pub. by Basil Blackwell England). Biblio Dist.

Education & Politics. Robert E. Jennings. 1978. 14.50x o.s.i. (ISBN 0-7134-0474-4). Hippocrene Bks.

Education & Politics. Robert E. Jennings. 1976. 32.00 (ISBN 0-7134-0474-4, Pub. by Batsford England); pap. 15.95 (ISBN 0-7134-0475-2). David & Charles.

Education & Politics at Harvard. Carnegie Commission on Higher Education. Ed. by S. M. Lipset & D. Riesman. LC 75-34137. 448p. 1975. 18.50 o.p. (ISBN 0-07-010114-0, P&RB). McGraw.

Education & Politics in Tropical Africa. 301p. 1979. pap. 25.00 (ISBN 0-914970-33-X, CM 004, Conch Mag). Unipub.

Education & Poverty. Thomas I. Ribich. LC 67-30600. (Studies in Social Economics). 1968. 10.95 (ISBN 0-8157-7430-3). Brookings.

Education & Psychology: The State of the Union. Ed. by Frank Farley & Neal J. Gordon. LC 80-82902. 300p. 1981. write for info (ISBN 0-8211-0506-X); text ed. write for info. McCutchan.

Education & Public Policy. Seymour E. Harris. 1965. 8.75x o.p. (ISBN 0-685-92818-7); text ed. 7.00x o.p. (ISBN 0-8211-0712-7). McCutchan.

Education & Regional Development, Vol. II. OECD Staff. 460p. (Orig., Bi-lingual-English & French). 1980. pap. 20.00 (ISBN 92-64-01996-0). OECD.

Education & Rehabilitation Techniques. James S. Payne et al. LC 74-6176. 322p. 1974. text ed. 24.95 (ISBN 0-87705-163-1); pap. text ed. 9.95 (ISBN 0-87705-225-5). Human Sci Pr.

Education & Social Change. E. J. King. 1966. text ed. 15.00 (ISBN 0-08-012059-8); pap. text ed. 7.75 (ISBN 0-08-012058-X). Pergamon.

Education & Social Change: A Photographic Study of Peru. Deborah Barndt. 1980. pap. text ed. 19.95 (ISBN 0-8403-2283-6). Kendall-Hunt.

Education & Social Change in Nineteenth Century Massachusetts. C. F. Kaestle & M. A. Vinovskis. LC 78-32130. (Illus.). 1980. 27.50 (ISBN 0-521-22191-9). Cambridge U Pr.

Education & Social Change: Themes from Ontario's Past. Ed. by Michael B. Katz & Paul H. Mattingly. LC 74-21635. 324p. 1975. 15.00x (ISBN 0-8147-5372-8); pap. 6.00x (ISBN 0-8147-5422-8). NYU Pr.

Education & Social Control. Rachel Sharp & Anthony Green. 1975. 19.50x (ISBN 0-7100-8160-X); pap. 10.00 (ISBN 0-7100-8161-8). Routledge & Kegan.

Education & Social Integration. William O. Stanley. 1953. text ed. 8.75x (ISBN 0-8077-2197-2). Tchrs Coll.

Education & Social Justice. Denis Lawton. LC 74-31568. (Sage Studies in Social & Educational Change: Vol 7). 1977. 18.00x (ISBN 0-8039-9946-1); pap. 9.95x (ISBN 0-8039-9867-8). Sage.

Education & Social Mobility in the Soviet Union: 1921-1934. Sheila Fitzpatrick. LC 78-58788. (Soviet & East European Studies). 1979. 39.95 (ISBN 0-521-22325-3). Cambridge U Pr.

Education & Social Problems. C. Weinberg. LC 72-129289. 1971. pap. text ed. 4.50 o.s.i. (ISBN 0-02-934950-8). Free Pr.

Education & Society in England, 1780-1870. Johnson. (Studies in Economic & Social History). 1980. pap. text ed. 11.50x (ISBN 0-391-01131-6). Humanities.

Education & Society in Nineteenth Century Nottingham. David Wardle. LC 71-154512. (Texts & Studies in the History of Education). (Illus.). 1971. 24.50 (ISBN 0-521-08206-4). Cambridge U Pr.

Education & Society in Tudor England. Joan Simon. LC 79-50915. 1979. 47.50 (ISBN 0-521-22854-9); pap. 14.95x (ISBN 0-521-29679-X). Cambridge U Pr.

Education & Sociology. Emile Durkheim. LC 55-11002. 1956. 10.95 (ISBN 0-02-907920-9). Free Pr.

Education & State Politics: The Developing Relationship Between Elementary, Secondary & Higher Education. Michael D. Usdan et al. LC 69-17673. (Orig.). 1969. text ed. 9.25x (ISBN 0-8077-2291-X). Tchrs Coll.

Education & the American Indian: The Road to Self-Determination Since 1928. 2nd ed. Margaret C. Szasz. LC 77-11742. (Illus.). 252p. 1979. pap. 5.95x (ISBN 0-8263-0468-0). U of NM Pr.

Education & the Community. Eric Midwinter. LC 75-20256. 163p. 1976. 12.95 (ISBN 0-470-60239-2). Halsted Pr.

Education & the Democratic Ideal. Steven M. Cahn. LC 78-27155. 1979. 14.95 (ISBN 0-88229-589-6); pap. 8.95 (ISBN 0-88229-661-2). Nelson-Hall.

Education & the Development of Reason. Ed. by R. F. Dearden et al. (International Library of the Philosophy of Education). 1972. 38.00x (ISBN 0-7100-7201-5). Routledge & Kegan.

Education & the Economics of Human Capital. R. A. Wykstra. LC 75-153078. 1971. 15.95 (ISBN 0-02-935610-5). Free Pr.

Education & the Education of Teachers. R. S. Peters. (International Library of the Philosophy of Education). 1977. 18.00x (ISBN 0-7100-8469-2). Routledge & Kegan.

Education & the Endangered Individual: A Critique of Ten Modern Thinkers. Brian V. Hill. LC 73-82283. 322p. 1974. pap. text ed. 7.00x (ISBN 0-8077-2432-7). Tchrs Coll.

Education & the French Revolution. H. C. Barnard. (Cambridge Texts & Studies in the History of Education: No. 5). 1969. 32.50 (ISBN 0-521-07256-5). Cambridge U Pr.

Education & the Law: Cases & Materials on Public Schools. 2nd ed. William R. Hazard. LC 78-50788. 1978. text ed. 17.95 (ISBN 0-02-914230-X). Free Pr.

Education & the Many Faces of the Disadvantaged: Cultural & Historical Perspectives. Ed. by William W. Brickman & Stanley Lehrer. LC 74-37166. 380p. 1972. pap. text ed. 11.95x o.p. (ISBN 0-471-10355-1). Wiley.

Education & the Mass Media in the Soviet Union & Eastern Europe. Ed. by Bohdan Harasymiw. LC 75-19789. (Special Studies). 1976. text ed. 24.95 (ISBN 0-275-56170-4). Praeger.

Education & the Modern Mind. W. R. Niblett. (Orig.). 1967. pap. 4.50 (ISBN 0-686-24604-7, Pub. by Faber & Faber). Merrimack Bk Serv.

Education & the Philosophy of Experimentalism. John L. Childs. 264p. 1980. Repr. of 1931 ed. lib. bdg. 25.00 (ISBN 0-89760-115-7). Telegraph Bks.

Education & the Political Order. Ted Tapper & Brian Salter. 1978. text ed. 26.00x (ISBN 0-333-22691-7); pap. text ed. 11.75x (ISBN 0-333-22692-5). Humanities.

Education & the Presidency. Chester E. Finn, Jr. LC 75-32871. (Politics of Education Ser.). 1977. 18.95 (ISBN 0-669-00365-4). Lexington Bks.

Education & the Social Order. Bertrand Russell. (Unwin Paperbacks). 1980. pap. 4.50 (ISBN 0-04-370080-2). Allen Unwin.

Education & the University. F. R. Leavis. 1979. 23.95 (ISBN 0-521-22610-4); pap. 6.50 (ISBN 0-521-29573-4). Cambridge U Pr.

Education & the Working Class. Brian Jackson & Dennis Marsden. (Reports of the Institute of Community Studies). 1968. Repr. of 1962 ed. 19.50x (ISBN 0-7100-3916-6). Routledge & Kegan.

Education & Training for Full Employment. Seymour Wolfbein. LC 67-23754. 1967. 20.00x (ISBN 0-231-02946-2). Columbia U Pr.

Education & Western Civilization-the Long View: An Attempt to Gain Perspective. Mowat G. Fraser. LC 73-91097. 1974. 9.00 o.p. (ISBN 0-682-47867-9, University); pap. 3.50 o.p. (ISBN 0-682-47868-7). Exposition.

Education As a Social Problem. Rudolf Steiner. LC 70-83525. 1969. 5.95 o.p. (ISBN 0-910142-08-4). Anthroposophic.

Education As an Art. Rudolf Steiner. (Spiritual Science Library). 128p. 1980. 10.00x (ISBN 0-8334-0707-4); pap. 4.50 (ISBN 0-8334-1707-X). Steinerbks.

Education As Cultural Imperialism. Martin Carnoy. LC 73-93964. (Educational Policy, Planning, & Theory Ser.). 1978. 10.95 (ISBN 0-582-28021-4); pap. 9.95x (ISBN 0-582-28018-4). Longman.

Education As Existential Possibility. Gari Lesnoff-Caravaglia. LC 76-171469. 112p. 1972. 7.50 o.p. (ISBN 0-8022-2068-1). Philos Lib.

Education at Berkeley: Report of the Select Committee on Education. rev. ed. Charles C. Muscatine. 1968. 15.00x o.p. (ISBN 0-520-00909-6); pap. 1.95 o.p. (ISBN 0-520-00912-6, CAL149). U of Cal Pr.

Education Before Five. Betty Boegehold. 1978. pap. 7.50x (ISBN 0-8077-2557-9). Tchrs Coll.

Education by Choice: The Case for Family Control. John E. Coons & Stephen D. Sugarman. LC 77-20318. 1978. 12.95 (ISBN 0-520-03613-1); pap. 4.95 (ISBN 0-520-03837-1). U of Cal Pr.

Education Careers. Don Lawson. (Career Concise Guides Ser.). (Illus.). (gr. 7-12). 1977. lib. bdg. 6.45 s&l (ISBN 0-531-01281-6). Watts.

Education, Class Language & Ideology. Noelle Bisseret. 1979. 16.00x (ISBN 0-7100-0118-5). Routledge & Kegan.

Education, Culture & Politics in Modern France. 2nd ed. W. D. Halls. text ed. 21.00 (ISBN 0-08-018962-8); pap. text ed. 10.50 (ISBN 0-08-018961-X). Pergamon.

Education, Culture & Politics in West Germany. Arthur Hearnden. Ed. by Edmanuel J. King. 153p. 1976. text ed. 21.00 (ISBN 0-08-019916-X); pap. text ed. 10.50 (ISBN 0-08-019915-1). Pergamon.

Education Curriculum for the Moderately, Severely & Profoundly Mentally Handicapped Pupil. Jane L. Adams. 96p. 1980. pap. 11.75 (ISBN 0-398-03264-5). C C Thomas.

Education Democracy & Discussion. David Bridges. (General Ser.). 1979. pap. text ed. 18.75 (ISBN 0-85633-176-7, NFER). Humanities.

Education Dilemma. John Simmons. (Illus.). 1980. 35.00 (ISBN 0-08-024304-5); pap. 17.25 (ISBN 0-08-024303-7). Pergamon.

Education, Economy, & Society: A Reader in the Sociology of Education. Ed. by A. H. Halsey et al. LC 61-9167. 1965. pap. text ed. 10.95 (ISBN 0-02-913700-4). Free Pr.

Education, Employment & Leisure. M. P. Carter. 1963. pap. 4.40 o.p. (ISBN 0-08-010321-9). Pergamon.

Education, Employment & Migration. P. Ritterband. LC 76-62584. (ASA Rose Monographs). (Illus.). 1978. 19.95 (ISBN 0-521-21586-2); pap. 6.95x (ISBN 0-521-29192-5). Cambridge U Pr.

Education et Societe En Russie Dans le Second Tiers Du XIXe Siecle. Alain Besancon. (Civilisations et Societes: No. 40). 1974. pap. 18.80x (ISBN 90-2797-545-0). Mouton.

Education for a Changing Civilization: Three Lectures Delivered on the Luther Laflin Kellogg Foundation at Rutgers University 1926. William H. Kilpatrick. 143p. 1980. Repr. of 1926 ed. lib. bdg. 15.00 (ISBN 0-89760-426-1). Telegraph Bks.

Education for a Global Century: Issues & Some Solutions. Council on Learning's National Task Force. LC 80-69769. 112p. (Orig.). Date not set. pap. 7.95 (ISBN 0-915390-29-9). Change Mag.

Education for All People: A Grassroots Primer. Ronald Walker & Institute for Responsive Action Staff. 155p. (Orig.). 1979. pap. text ed. 6.00 (ISBN 0-917754-09-3). Inst Responsive.

Education for Childbirth & Parenthood. Elizabeth R. Perkins. 180p. 1980. bds. 27.50x (ISBN 0-7099-0273-5, Pub. by Croom Helm Ltd England). Biblio Dist.

Education for Citizen Action: Challenge for the Secondary Curriculum. Fred M. Newmann. LC 74-30963. 250p. 1975. 15.00 (ISBN 0-8211-1305-4); text ed. 14.00 (ISBN 0-685-52139-7). McCutchan.

Education for Clinical Social Work: A Special Issue of Clinical Social Work Journal. Ed. by Mary Gottesfeld. LC 77-81412. 1977. text ed. 12.95 (ISBN 0-87705-323-5). Human Sci Pr.

Education for Communism: School & State in the People's Republic of Albania. John I. Thomas. LC 69-17329. (Studies: No. 22). 131p. 1969. 6.50 (ISBN 0-8179-3221-6); pap. 4.00 (ISBN 0-8179-3222-4). Hoover Inst Pr.

Education for Community Psychiatry, Vol. 6. GAP Committee on Med. Education. LC 62-2872. (Report No. 64). 1967. pap. 2.00 (ISBN 0-87318-089-5). Adv Psychiatry.

Education for Crime Prevention & Control. R. J. McLean. (Criminal Law Education & Research Center Ser.). (Illus.). 168p. 1975. 13.75 (ISBN 0-398-03226-2). C C Thomas.

Education for Family Life: Some New Policies for Child Care. Richard C. Whitfield. 161p. 1980. pap. text ed. 10.00 (ISBN 0-340-25524-2). Verry.

Education for Fullness. Himangshir B. Mukerjee. 20.00x (ISBN 0-210-33845-8). Asia.

Education for Justice (Participant Handbook) Ed. by Thomas Fenton. LC 74-83519. 120p. 1975. pap. 3.95x o.p. (ISBN 0-88344-120-9). Orbis Bks.

Education for Leisure. H. Dan Corbin & William J. Tait. (Illus.). 160p. 1973. ref. ed. 9.50 o.p. (ISBN 0-13-240531-8). P-H.

Education for Modern Man: A New Perspective. Sidney Hook. 235p. 1973. Repr. of 1963 ed. text ed. 15.00x (ISBN 0-391-00317-8). Humanities.

Education for National Efficiency: The Contribution of Sidney & Beatrice Webb. Ed. by E. J. Brennan. 218p. 1975. text ed. 20.75x (ISBN 0-485-11151-9, Athlone Pr). Humanities.

Education for Negroes in Mississippi Since Nineteen Hundred & Ten. Charles H. Wilson, Sr. 1974. 20.00 (ISBN 0-89020-011-4). Brown Bk.

Education for Personal Autonomy. H. J. Blackham. 211p. 1978. pap. text ed. 7.40x (ISBN 0-7199-0936-8, Pub. by Bedford England). Renouf.

Education for Positive Mental Health: A Review of Existing Research & Recommendations for Future Studies. James A. Davis. LC 64-15607. (Monographs in Social Research: No. 5). 1965. 7.95x (ISBN 0-202-09009-4). NORC.

Education for Safe Living. 4th ed. Herbert Stack & J. D. Elkow. (Illus.). 1966. text ed. 15.95 (ISBN 0-13-239194-5). P-H.

Education for Sale. Eric Midwinter. (Classroom Close-Ups Ser.). 1977. text ed. 12.50x o.p. (ISBN 0-04-371049-2); pap. text ed. 4.95x o.p. (ISBN 0-04-371050-6). Allen Unwin.

Education for Severely Handicapped Hearing Impaired Students. Doris Naiman. 84p. 1981. pap. text ed. 6.95x (ISBN 0-913072-34-6). Natl Assn Deaf.

Education for the Disabled in War & Industry: Army Hospital Schools. Arthur G. Crane. (Columbia University. Teachers College. Contributions to Education: No. 110). Repr. of 1921 ed. 17.50 (ISBN 0-404-55110-6). AMS Pr.

Education for the Future: The Case for Radical Change. P. A. Coggin. 170p. 1979. 29.00 (ISBN 0-08-023729-0). Pergamon.

Education for the Gifted. Ed. by Robert J. Havighurst. LC 52-11216. (National Society for the Study of Education Yearbooks Ser: No. 57, Pt. 2). pap. 4.50x o.s.i. (ISBN 0-226-60047-5). U of Chicago Pr.

Education for the Professions of Medicine, Law, Theology, & Social Welfare. Carnegie Commission on Higher Education. LC 73-6591. 304p. 1973. 12.95 o.p. (ISBN 0-07-010065-9, P&RB). McGraw.

Education for Traditional Food Procurement in the Orinoco Delta. Kenneth Ruddle & Ray Chesterfield. (University of California Publications in Ibero-Americana Ser.: Vol. 53). 1977. pap. 14.50x (ISBN 0-520-09551-0). U of Cal Pr.

Education for Tragedy: Essays in Disenchanted Hope for Modern Man. Kenneth D. Benne. LC 67-17847. 216p. 1967. pap. 3.75x (ISBN 0-8131-0124-7). U Pr of Ky.

Education for Uncertainty. Ed. by Edmund J. King. LC 78-63118. (Sage Annual Review of Social & Educational Change: Vol. 2). 1978. 18.50x (ISBN 0-8039-9896-1); pap. 9.95x (ISBN 0-8039-9897-X). Sage.

Education for Values. Ed. by David C. McClelland. 1981. text ed. 18.50x (ISBN 0-8290-0090-9). Irvington.

Education for What? British Policy Versus Local Initiative. Charles H. Lyons et al. (Foreign & Comparative Studies-Eastern African Ser.: No. 13). 100p. 1973. pap. 4.50x (ISBN 0-915984-10-5). Syracuse U Foreign Comp.

Education for World Understanding. J. L. Henderson. 1969. 12.25 (ISBN 0-08-013217-0); pap. 5.75 (ISBN 0-08-013216-2). Pergamon.

Education Futurism 1985: Challenges for Schools & Their Administrators. Walter G. Hack et al. LC 72-158486. 1971. 16.00x (ISBN 0-8211-0720-8); text ed. 14.50x (ISBN 0-685-02004-5). McCutchan.

Education Handbook for Black Families. Delores L. Friedman. LC 79-6537. (Illus.). 456p. 1980. 14.95 (ISBN 0-385-14881-X). Doubleday.

Education Handbook for Parents of Handicapped Children. Stanley I. Mopsik & Judith A. Agard. LC 78-67848. 1980. 22.50 (ISBN 0-89011-511-7). Abt Assoc.

Education, Health & Behavior. Ed. by M. Rutter et al. 390p. 1981. Repr. of 1970 ed. text ed. price not set (ISBN 0-89874-268-4). Krieger.

Education, Health & Housing. 1979. text ed. 23.25x (ISBN 0-566-00298-1, Pub. by Gower Pub Co England). Renouf.

Education II Revised. rev. ed. V. M. Kerensky et al. LC 74-156846. 1975. 14.25 o.s.i. (ISBN 0-87812-127-7). Pendell Pub.

Education in a Changing Society. Ed. by Antonia Kloskowska & Guido Martinotti. LC 76-22903. (Sage Studies in International Sociology: Vol. 11). 1977. 18.00x (ISBN 0-8039-9983-6); pap. 9.95x (ISBN 0-8039-9984-4). Sage.

Education in a Dynamic Society: A Contemporary Sourcebook. Westby-Gibson. 1972. 8.95 (ISBN 0-201-08537-2). A-W.

Education in a Rural Environment. (Education & Rural Development Ser.: No. 2). 63p. 1980. pap. 7.00 (ISBN 92-3-101764-0, U1046, UNESCO). Unipub.

Education in a Small Democracy, New Zealand. Ian A. McLaren. (World Education Ser.). 1974. 16.00 (ISBN 0-7100-7798-X). Routledge & Kegan.

Education in an Industrial Society. G. H. Bantock. 1973. 8.50 (ISBN 0-571-04791-2, Pub. by Faber & Faber). Merrimack Bk Serv.

Education in Ancient Rome. Stanley F. Bonner. (Campus Ser: No. 198). (Illus.). 1977. 25.00x (ISBN 0-520-03439-2); pap. 10.95x (ISBN 0-520-03501-1). U of Cal Pr.

Education in Angola 1878-1914. Michael A. Samuels. LC 70-122747. (Illus.). 1970. pap. text ed. 9.75x (ISBN 0-8077-2087-9). Tchrs Coll.

Education in Asia & Oceania: Reviews, Reports, & Notes. (UNESCO Regional Office for Education in Asia & Oceania: Vol.17). 99p. 1980. pap. 9.00 (UB88, UNESCO Reginal Office). Unipub.

Education in British West Indies. Eric E. Williams. 1968. pap. 6.00 (ISBN 0-685-20859-1). Univ Place.

Education in Crisis: A Sociological Analysis of Schools & Universities in Transition. Ronald G. Corwin. LC 73-12844. 380p. 1974. pap. text ed. 16.95 (ISBN 0-471-17521-8). Wiley.

Education in Depressed Areas. Ed. by A. Harry Passow. LC 63-15449. 1963. pap. 7.25x (ISBN 0-8077-1887-4). Tchrs Coll.

Education in Florida Past & Present. Ed. by Victor Mamatey. (Florida State U. Studies: No. 15). 1954. pap. 2.50 o.p. (ISBN 0-8130-0463-2). U Presses Fla.

Education in France 1848-1870. R. D. Anderson. 300p. 1975. 29.95x (ISBN 0-19-827311-8). Oxford U Pr.

Education in India Today. O. P. Shah. 1980. 15.00x (ISBN 0-8364-0634-6, Pub. by Mukhopadhyay India). South Asia Bks.

Education in Kenya: An Historical Study. James R. Sheffield. LC 72-88639. (Illus.). 126p. 1973. pap. text ed. 5.25x (ISBN 0-8077-2419-X). Tchrs Coll.

Education in Latin America: A Bibliography. Ludwig Lauerhass & Vera L. De A Raujo-Haugse. (Reference Books Ser.). lib. bdg. 55.00 (ISBN 0-8161-8516-6). G K Hall.

Education in Leicestershire, 1540-1940. Ed. by Brian Simon. 1968. text ed. 11.50x (ISBN 0-7185-1076-3, Leicester). Humanities.

Education in Malaysia. 2nd ed. Francis W. Kee & Ee T. Hong. 1975. pap. text ed. 5.00 (ISBN 0-686-60350-8, 00101). Heinemann Ed.

Education in Movement Gymnastics. W. M. Cameron & Peggy Pleasance. 1974. 4.00 o.p. (ISBN 0-8238-0166-7). Plays.

Education in Nineteenth Century Britain. C. A. Fox et al. (Government & Society in Nineteenth Century Britain Ser.). 246p. 1977. 25.00x (ISBN 0-7165-2211-X, Pub. by Irish Academic Pr Ireland). Biblio Dist.

Education in Parapsychology: Proceedings, International Conference, San Francisco, 1975. Ed. by Betty Shapin & Lisette Coly. LC 76-19467. 1976. 13.50 (ISBN 0-912328-28-2). Parapsych Foun.

Education in Psychology: James McKeen Cattell's Journal & Letters from Germany & England 1880-1888. Ed. by Michael M. Sokal. 768p. 1980. text ed. 30.00x (ISBN 0-262-19185-7). MIT Pr.

Education in Rebhausen: A German Village. Richard L. Warren. Ed. by George Spindler & Louise Spindler. (Case Studies in Education & Culture). 128p. pap. text ed. 6.95x (ISBN 0-8290-0321-5). Irvington.

Education in Rural America: A Reassessment of Conventional Wisdom. Jonathon P. Sher. LC 76-57184. 1977. lib. bdg. 26.00x (ISBN 0-89158-201-0); pap. text ed. 10.50x (ISBN 0-89158-203-7). Westview.

Education in Social Change. Eugene Sullivan. 5.50x (ISBN 0-210-22206-9). Asia.

Education in Systems Science: Report & Procedings, Germany, 21-25 Feb., 1978. Ed. by B. A. Bayraktar et al. LC 79-83871. 1979. 44.95 (ISBN 0-470-26704-6). Halsted Pr.

Education in the Arab Region Viewed from the 1970 Marrakesh Conference. (Educational Studies & Documents, No. 1). (Illus.). 57p. (Orig.). 1972. pap. 2.50 (ISBN 92-3-100918-4, U185, UNESCO). Unipub.

Education in the Cities of England. Ed. by Peter C. Raggatt. LC 73-94130. (Sage Contemporary Social Science Issues: No. 11). 1974. pap. 4.95x (ISBN 0-8039-0395-2). Sage.

Education in the Eighteenth Century. Ed. by John Browning. LC 79-18182. (Eighteenth Century Ser.). 145p. 1979. lib. bdg. 27.50 (ISBN 0-8240-4006-6). Garland Pub.

Education in the History of Medicine. Ed. by John E. Blake. 1968. 14.25 o.s.i. (ISBN 0-02-841460-8). Hafner.

Education in the Technological Society: The Vocational-Liberal Studies Controversy in the Early Twentieth Century. Arthur G. Wirth. LC 81-618. 272p. 1980. lib. bdg. 18.75 (ISBN 0-8191-1222-4); pap. text ed. 10.50 (ISBN 0-8191-1223-2). U Pr of Amer.

Education in the Two Germanies. Arthur Hearnden. LC 75-46557. 1974. 23.75x (ISBN 0-89158-539-7). Westview.

Education in the United States: A Documentary History, 5 vols. Compiled by Sol Cohen. LC 73-3099. 1974. Set. lib. bdg. 200.00 (ISBN 0-313-20141-2). Greenwood.

Education in the United States: An Interpretive History. Robert L. Church. LC 75-22764. 1976. text ed. 14.95 (ISBN 0-02-905490-7). Free Pr.

Education in the U.S.S.R. Delbert Long & Roberta Long. LC 80-82681. (Fastback Ser.: No. 148). (Orig.). 1980. pap. 0.75 (ISBN 0-87367-148-1). Phi Delta Kappa.

Education in the USSR. Joseph I. Zajda. (International Studies in Education & Social Change). (Illus.). 200p. 1980. 29.00 (ISBN 0-08-025807-7); pap. 12.00 (ISBN 0-08-025806-9). Pergamon.

Education in Two Languages: A Guide for Bilingual Teachers. Judith Walker. LC 78-65847. 1979. pap. text ed. 7.00 (ISBN 0-8191-0674-7). U Pr of Amer.

Education in West Germany: A Quest for Excellence. Hans G. Lingens & Barbara Lingens. LC 79-93116. (Fastback Ser.: No. 140). (Orig.). 1980. pap. 0.75 (ISBN 0-87367-140-6). Phi Delta Kappa.

Education in Western Australia. Ed. by W. D. Neal. 324p. 1980. 22.50x (ISBN 0-85564-147-9, Pub. by U of West Australia Pr Australia). Intl Schol Bk Serv.

Education, Income & Human Behavior. Carnegie Commission on Higher Education. Ed. by T. Juster. 1974. 21.95 o.p. (ISBN 0-07-010068-3, P&RB). McGraw.

Education Index. Incl. Vols. 9-19, 1953-69; Vols. 20-29, 1969-79; Vol. 30, 1980. 60.00 ea. Wilson.

Education Index, Vols. 1-8. 1929-53. 50.00 ea. (ISBN 0-685-22246-2). Wilson.

Education, Inequality & National Policy. Ed. by Nelson F. Ashline et al. LC 75-21833. 224p. 1976. 18.95 (ISBN 0-669-00053-1). Lexington Bks.

Education: Key to Conservation. Conservation Education Association. Incl. Bk. 1. Important Characteristics of a Good Local Program. (Illus.). 8p. 1965. pap. text ed. o.p. (ISBN 0-685-22440-6, 869); Bk. 2. Planning a State Program in Conservation Education. (Illus.). 16p. 1965. pap. text ed. 0.30 (ISBN 0-8134-0870-9, 870); Bk. 3. Twenty-Five Key Guides for Preparing Conservation Education Publications & Visual Aids. (Illus.). 16p. 1965. pap. text ed. 0.30 (ISBN 0-8134-0871-7, 871); Bk. 5. Selected List of Filmstrips on the Conservation of Natural Resources. (Illus.). 48p. 1968. pap. text ed. 0.50 (ISBN 0-685-22443-0, 1040). LC 65-23951. Interstate.

Education Laws Nineteen Seventy-Eight: A Guide to New Directions in Federal Aid. David Savage. 120p. 1979. pap. 11.95 (ISBN 0-87545-015-6). Natl Sch PR.

Education, Learning & Productivity. Victor D. Norman. 1976. pap. text ed. 12.50x (ISBN 8-200-02344-3, Dist. by Columbia U Pr). Universitet.

Education Literature Nineteen Hundred & Seven to Nineteen Thirty-Two, 12 vols. Ed. by Malcolm C. Hamilton. 1979. Set. lib. bdg. 363.00 (ISBN 0-685-94396-8). Garland Pub.

Education Literature Nineteen Hundred & Seven to Nineteen Thirty-Two, Vol. 1. Ed. by Malcolm C. Hamilton. 1979. lib. bdg. 33.00 (ISBN 0-8240-3700-6). Garland Pub.

Education Literature, Nineteen Hundred & Seven to Nineteen Thirty-Two, Vol. 7. Ed. by Malcolm C. Hamilton. 1979. lib. bdg. 33.00 (ISBN 0-8240-3706-5). Garland Pub.

Education Literature, Nineteen Hundred & Seven to Nineteen Thirty-Two, Vol. 8. Ed. by Malcolm C. Hamilton. 1979. lib. bdg. 33.00 (ISBN 0-8240-3707-3). Garland Pub.

Education Literature, Nineteen Hundred & Seven to Nineteen Thirty-Two, Vol. 10. Ed. by Malcolm C. Hamilton. 1979. lib. bdg. 33.00 (ISBN 0-8240-3709-X). Garland Pub.

Education Literature, Nineteen Hundred & Seven to Nineteen Thirty-Two, Vol. 11. Ed. by Malcolm C. Hamilton. 1979. lib. bdg. 33.00 (ISBN 0-8240-3710-3). Garland Pub.

Education, Manpower, & Development in South & Southeast Asia. Muhammad S. Huq. LC 74-19336. (Special Studies). (Illus.). 240p. 1975. 18.95 (ISBN 0-275-09120-1). Praeger.

Education of a Congressman: The Newsletters of Morris K. Udall. Morris K. Udall. LC 72-79739. 1972. pap. text ed. 7.50 (ISBN 0-672-61312-3). Bobbs.

Education of a Memoir. Margaret Frances. 1981. 13.95 (ISBN 0-533-04673-4). Vantage.

Education of a True Believer. Lev Kopelev. Tr. by Gary Kern from Rus. LC 79-3397. 15.95 (ISBN 0-06-012476-8, HarpT). Har-Row.

Education of a Woman Golfer. Nancy Lopez. 192p. 1980. pap. 6.95 (ISBN 0-346-12492-1). Cornerstone.

Education of Adults: A World Perspective. 229p. 1976. pap. 11.50 (ISBN 92-3-101246-0, U186, UNESCO). Unipub.

Education of American Physicians: Historical Essays. Ed. by Ronald L. Numbers. 1980. 35.00x (ISBN 0-520-03611-5). U of Cal Pr.

Education of an American Soccer Player. Shep Messing & David Hirshey. LC 78-8099. (Illus.). 1978. 8.95 (ISBN 0-396-07568-1). Dodd.

Education of an Outdoorsman. Cecil E. Heacox. 1976. 9.95 (ISBN 0-87691-187-4). Winchester Pr.

Education of Black Philadelphia: The Social & Educational History of a Minority Community, Nineteen Hundred to Nineteen Fifty. Vincent P. Franklin. LC 79-5045. (Illus.). 1979. 19.95 (ISBN 0-8122-7769-4). U of Pa Pr.

Education of Children Through Motor Activity. James H. Humphrey. 220p. 1975. 16.75 (ISBN 0-398-03471-0). C C Thomas.

Education of Don Juan. Robin Hardy. 1981. pap. 3.50 (ISBN 0-451-09764-5, E9764, Sig). NAL.

Education of Exceptional Children & Youth. 3rd ed. William M. Cruickshank & G. Orville Johnson. (Illus.). 736p. 1975. 21.95 (ISBN 0-13-240382-X). P-H.

Education of Exceptional Learners. 2nd ed. Frank M. Hewett & Steven R. Forness. 1977. text ed. 18.50 (ISBN 0-205-05729-2); instr's manual avail. (ISBN 0-205-05783-7). Allyn.

Education of Good Men. Maurice Leonard Jacks. LC 80-19910. 192p. 1980. Repr. of 1955 ed. lib. bdg. 19.50x (ISBN 0-313-22800-0, JAEG). Greenwood.

Education of Homebound or Hospitalized Children. Frances P. Connor. LC 64-16622. (Orig.). 1964. pap. text ed. 4.25x (ISBN 0-8077-1185-3). Tchrs Coll.

Education of Hyman Kaplan. Leonard Q. Ross. LC 38-6588. (gr. 10 up). 1968. pap. 1.95 (ISBN 0-15-627811-1, HPL29, HPL). HarBraceJ.

Education of Jesus Christ. James Ramsey. LC 80-84438. (Shepherd Classics Ser.). 130p. 1979. pap. 5.95 (ISBN 0-87983-236-3). Keats.

Education of le Corbusier. Paul V. Turner. LC 76-23658. (Outstanding Dissertations in the Fine Arts - Twentieth Century). (Illus.). 1977. Repr. of 1971 ed. lib. bdg. 48.00 (ISBN 0-8240-2732-9). Garland Pub.

Education of Little Tree. Forrest Carter. 1976. 9.95 (ISBN 0-440-02319-X). Delacorte.

Education of Little Tree. Forrest Carter. (gr. 7-12). 1981. pap. 1.50 (ISBN 0-440-92200-3, LE). Dell.

Education of Orthopaedic Surgeons. Association of Bone & Joint Surgeons. Ed. by Marshall R. Urist. (Clinical Orthopaedics Ser., Vol. 75). 1971. 15.00 (ISBN 0-685-22853-3). Lippincott.

Education of Patrick Silver. Jerome Charyn. 208p. 1981. pap. 2.75 (ISBN 0-380-01698-2, 53603, Bard). Avon.

Education of Poor & Minority Children: A World Bibliography, 2 vols. Compiled by Meyer Weinberg. LC 80-29441. 1981. lib. bdg. 95.00 (ISBN 0-313-21996-6, WEC/). Greenwood.

Education of Slow Learning Children. 2nd ed. A. E. Tansley & R. Gulliford. (Orig.). 1966. text ed. 15.00x (ISBN 0-7100-2170-4); pap. text ed. 3.50x (ISBN 0-7100-4650-2). Humanities.

Education of Steven Bell. Dan Theis. LC 76-54277. (Sports Fiction Ser.). (Illus.). (gr. 5-10). 1977. PLB 7.30 (ISBN 0-8172-0806-2). Raintree Pubs.

Education of the Eighties: A Central Issue. Ed. by Brian Simon. William Taylor. 256p. 1981. 45.00 (ISBN 0-7134-3679-4, Pub. by Batsford England); pap. 14.95 (ISBN 0-7134-3680-8). David & Charles.

Education of the Gifted Child. Ed. by Anthony Pugliese. 39p. 1977. pap. 9.00 o.p. (ISBN 0-686-00905-3, D-108). Essence Pubns.

Education of the Hearing Impaired. C. Joseph Giangreco & Marianne R. Giangreco. (Illus.). 204p. 1976. pap. 15.50 (ISBN 0-398-00673-3). C C Thomas.

Education of the Infant & Young Child. Ed. by Victor H. Denenberg. LC 77-137617. 1970. 16.50 (ISBN 0-12-209150-7). Acad Pr.

Education of the Minority Child: A Comprehensive Bibliography of 10,000 Selected Entries. Ed. by Meyer Weinberg. 1970. 12.95 o.p. (ISBN 0-685-38479-9); pap. 5.95 o.p. (ISBN 0-912008-01-6). Integrated Ed Assoc.

Education of the Poor: The History of a National School 1824-1974. Pamela Silver & Harold Silver. (Routledge Library in the History of Education). 208p. 1974. 22.00x (ISBN 0-7100-7804-8). Routledge & Kegan.

Education of the Self: A Trainer's Manual. Gerald Weinstein et al. LC 76-9529. (Mandala Series in Education). 155p. 1976. pap. text ed. 9.95 (ISBN 0-916250-16-4). Irvington.

Education of the Spanish-Speaking Urban Child: A Book of Readings. Earl J. Ogletree & David Garcia. (Illus.). 504p. 1975. 34.50 (ISBN 0-398-03335-8). C C Thomas.

Education of the Trainable Mentally Retarded: Curriculum, Methods, Materials. Freddie W. Litton. LC 77-10772. (Illus.). 1978. text ed. 16.95 (ISBN 0-8016-3023-1). Mosby.

Education of Women During the Renaissance. Mary A. Cannon. LC 79-2933. 182p. 1981. Repr. of 1916 ed. 16.00 (ISBN 0-8305-0100-2). Hyperion Conn.

Education of Women in the Italian Renaissance. Melinda K. Blade. Ed. by Arthur F. Ide. LC 79-19011. (Woman in History Ser.: Vol. 21). (Illus.). 90p. (Orig.). 1981. 20.00 (ISBN 0-86663-024-4); pap. 14.95 (ISBN 0-86663-050-3). Ide Hse.

Education Officer & His World. Derek Birley. 1970. 10.50 (ISBN 0-7100-6811-5); pap. 4.95 (ISBN 0-7100-7704-1). Routledge & Kegan.

Education, Opportunity & Social Inequality: Changing Prospects in Western Society. Raymond Boudon. LC 73-14646. (Urban Research Ser.). 208p. 1974. 20.95 (ISBN 0-471-09105-7, Pub. by Wiley-Interscience). Wiley.

Education-Psychology Journals: A Scholar's Guide. Darlene B. Arnold & Kenneth O. Doyle, Jr. LC 74-23507. 1975. 10.00 (ISBN 0-8108-0779-3). Scarecrow.

Education, Religion, & the Supreme Court. Ed. by Richard C. McMillan. LC 78-74196. (Special Studies Ser.: No. 6). 1979. 4.95 (ISBN 0-932180-05-1). Assn Baptist Profs.

Education sentimentale de Flaubert: Le Monde en creux. new ed. Pierre Cogny. (Collection themes et textes). 270p. (Orig., Fr.). 1975. pap. 6.75 (ISBN 2-03-035030-3, 2685). Larousse.

Education Since Eighteen Hundred. Ivor Morrish. (Unwin Education Books). 1970. pap. text ed. 10.95x (ISBN 0-04-370030-6). Allen Unwin.

Education, Social Science, & the Judicial Process. Ray C. Rist & Ronald J. Anson. LC 77-962. 1977. pap. text ed. 7.50x (ISBN 0-8077-2532-3). Tchrs Coll.

Education, Society & Change. Reitman. 496p. 1981. pap. text ed. 13.50 (ISBN 0-205-07254-2, 2373541); free tchr's ed. (ISBN 0-205-07255-0, 237255X). Allyn.

Education, Society & Human Nature: An Introduction to the Philosophy of Education. Anthony O'Hear. 192p. 1981. price not set (ISBN 0-7100-0747-7); pap. price not set (ISBN 0-7100-0748-5). Routledge & Kegan.

Education That Is Christian. Lois E. Le Bar. 9.95 (ISBN 0-8007-0078-3). Revell.

Education: the State of Debate: Problems Facing Education in the United States, Britain, & Canada. John Vaizey. 1976. text ed. 17.95x (ISBN 0-7156-0986-6). Intl Ideas.

Education, Unemployment & Economic Growth. Sorkin. LC 73-11656. 1974. 16.95 (ISBN 0-669-85498-0). Lexington Bks.

Educational Administration. Society of Education Officers. Ed. by Kenneth Brooksbank. 300p. (Orig.). 1981. pap. text ed. 16.95 (ISBN 0-900313-65-X). Longman.

Educational Administration & Organizational Behavior. Mark E. Hanson. 1978. text ed. 18.95 (ISBN 0-205-06164-8). Allyn.

Educational Administration: The Developing Decades. Ed. by Luverne Cunningham et al. LC 76-27956. 1977. 20.00x (ISBN 0-8211-0226-5); text ed. 18.00x (ISBN 0-685-71408-X). McCutchan.

Educational Administration Today: An Introduction. Richard Saxe. LC 79-91196. 1980. 18.50 (ISBN 0-8211-1858-7); text ed. 16.50 10 or more copies (ISBN 0-686-65584-2). McCutchan.

Educational Alternatives for Colonized People: Models for Liberation. Robert L. Williams. (Illus.). 128p. 1974. 9.95 (ISBN 0-8046-7077-3). Kennikat.

Educational & Career Services for Adults. James M. Heffernan. LC 79-3279. 1981. write for info. (ISBN 0-669-03440-1). Lexington Bks.

Educational & First Principles: A Historical Perspective. Earl T. Willis. LC 80-16406. 1980. 12.75 (ISBN 0-8130-0646-5). U Presses Fla.

Educational & Psychological Measurement & Evaluation. 5th ed. Kenneth Hopkins & Julian Stanley. (Illus.). 528p. 1972. ref. ed. 19.95 (ISBN 0-13-236281-3). P-H.

Educational & Psychosocial Aspects of Deafness. Ed. by Richard E. Hardy & John G. Cull. (American Lectures in Social & Rehabilitation Psychology Ser.). (Illus.). 216p. 1979. text ed. 16.75 (ISBN 0-398-03002-2). C C Thomas.

Educational & the Development of Reason, 3 pts. R. F. Dearden et al. Incl. Pt. 1. Critique of Current Educational Aims. pap. 7.95 (ISBN 0-7100-8084-0); Pt. 2. Reason. pap. 7.95 (ISBN 0-7100-8101-4); Pt. 3. Education & Reason. pap. 6.95 (ISBN 0-7100-8102-2). 1975. Routledge & Kegan.

Educational Anthropology: An Introduction. George F. Kneller. LC 65-14252. 171p. 1965. pap. text ed. 9.50x o.p. (ISBN 0-471-49513-1). Wiley.

Educational Applications of the WISC-R: A Handbook of Interpretive Strategies & Remedial Recommendations. Charles L. Nicholson & Charles L. Alcorn. LC 79-66967. 104p. 1980. pap. text ed. 9.70x (ISBN 0-87424-160-X). Western Psych.

Educational Assessment. Karlheinz Ingenkamp. (Council of Europe European Trend Reports on Educational Research: No. 3). (Orig.). 1977. pap. text ed. 15.00x (ISBN 0-85633-130-9, NFER). Humanities.

Educational Assessment of Learning Problems: Testing for Teaching. new ed. Gerald Wallace & Stephen C. Larsen. 1978. text ed. 20.95 (ISBN 0-205-06090-0). Allyn.

Educational Assessment of Learning Problems: Testing for Teaching. Gerald Wallace & Stephen C. Larsen. 1978. pap. text ed. 12.95 (ISBN 0-205-06089-7). Allyn.

Educational Audiology for the Limited Hearing Infant. Doreen Pollack. (Illus.). 256p. 1979. text ed. 14.75 (ISBN 0-398-01501-5). C C Thomas.

Educational Change & Architectural Consequences. LC 68-57806. (Illus.). 88p. 1968. pap. 2.00 (ISBN 0-89192-050-1). Interbk Inc.

Educational Change in Sweden. Rolland G. Paulston. LC 68-29907. (Illus.). 1968. text ed. 9.25x (ISBN 0-8077-1892-0). Tchrs Coll.

Educational Choice Second Labor Markets in Japan. Mary J. Bowman. LC 80-25557. 320p. 1981. lib. bdg. 19.00x (ISBN 0-226-06923-0). U of Chicago Pr.

Educational Cooperation Between Developed & Developing Countries. H. M. Phillips. LC 75-19807. (Praeger Special Studies). (Illus.). 352p. 1976. text ed. 32.00 (ISBN 0-275-55900-9). Praeger.

Educational Development in Africa, 3 vols. 1969. pap. 12.50 ea. (U196, UNESCO); Vol. 1. pap. (ISBN 92-803-1034-8, U197); Vol. 2. pap. (ISBN 92-803-1035-6, U198); Vol. 3. pap. (ISBN 92-803-1036-4). Unipub.

Educational Documents Abstracts, 1978. Educational Resources Information Center (ERIC) LC 72-75009. 1979. 90.00 (ISBN 0-02-692870-1). Macmillan Info.

Educational Documents Index, 1978. Educational Resources Information Center (ERIC) LC 71-130348. 1979. 60.00 (ISBN 0-02-692880-9). Macmillan Info.

Educational Drama. Brian Peachment. (Illus.). 232p. 1976. pap. 13.95x (ISBN 0-7121-0552-2, Pub. by Macdonald & Evans England). Intl Ideas.

Educational Drama for Today's Schools. Ed. by R. Baird Shuman et al. LC 78-15115. 1978. 11.00 (ISBN 0-8108-1166-9). Scarecrow.

Educational Environments & Effects: Evaluation, Policy, & Productivity. Ed. by Herbert J. Walberg. LC 78-62101. (Education Ser). 1979. 17.00 (ISBN 0-8211-2259-2); text ed. 15.20 in ten or more copies (ISBN 0-685-65115-0). McCutchan.

Educational Evaluation. W. Popham. 1975. 18.95 (ISBN 0-13-240515-6). P-H.

Educational Evaluation: Analysis & Responsibility. Michael W. Apple et al. LC 73-17611. 1974. 17.90 (ISBN 0-8211-0011-4); text ed. 16.20 in ten or more copies (ISBN 0-685-42624-6). McCutchan.

Educational Film Locator: Of the Consortium of University Film Centers & R. R. Bowker. 2nd ed. 2500p. 1980. 50.00 (ISBN 0-8352-1295-5). Bowker.

Educational Finance: An ERIC Bibliography. Educational Resources Information Center. 1972. pap. 9.95 o.s.i. (ISBN 0-02-468880-0). Macmillan Info.

Educational Finance in India. Atmanand Misra. 1962. 18.50 o.p. (ISBN 0-210-34001-0). Asia.

Educational Financing & Policy Goals for Primary Schools: Australia, Canada, Germany, Vol. I. (Document Ser.). 1979. 12.50 (ISBN 92-64-11899-3). OECD.

Educational Financing & Policy Goals for Primary Schools: Netherlands, Norway, Sweden, Italy, Vol. III. (Document Ser.). 1979. 12.50 (ISBN 92-64-11901-9). OECD.

Educational Financing & Policy Goals for Primary Schools: Vol. II United Kingdom, United States, Yugoslavia. (Document Ser.). 1979. 12.50 (ISBN 92-64-11900-0). OECD.

Educational Fund Raising Manual: Major Gift Societies. Stanley R. McAnally. 1970. pap. 5.00 (ISBN 0-89964-021-4). CASE.

Educational Futures Sourcebook II: Selections from the Second Conference of the World Future Society's Education Section. Ed. by Kathleen M. Redd & Arthur M. Harkins. 1980. write for info. World Future.

Educational Futurism: In Pursuance of Survival. John P. Pulliam & Jim R. Bowman. 164p. 1975. pap. 3.95x (ISBN 0-8061-1299-9). U of Okla Pr.

Educational Governance & Administration. T. Sergrovanni et al. 1980. 18.95 (ISBN 0-13-236653-3). P-H.

Educational Ideas of Charles Fourier. David Zeldin. LC 67-31331. 1969. 22.50x (ISBN 0-678-05019-8). Kelley.

Educational Ideologies. William O'Neill. (Orig.). 1981. pap. text ed. 17.95x (ISBN 0-8302-2305-3). Goodyear.

Educational Imperatives in a Changing Culture. Ed. by William W. Brickman. LC 67-24846. 1967. 8.00 o.p. (ISBN 0-8122-7563-2). U of Pa Pr.

Educational Innovation in Indonesia. (Experiments & Innovations in Education - Asia Ser: No. 13). 50p. 1976. pap. 2.50 (ISBN 92-3-101225-8, U200, UNESCO). Unipub.

Educational Innovation in Iran. 35p. (Orig.). 1975. pap. 2.50 (ISBN 92-3-101215-0, U201, UNESCO). Unipub.

Educational Innovation in the Republic of Korea. 43p. 1975. pap. 2.50 (ISBN 92-3-101224-X, U202, UNESCO). Unipub.

Educational Innovations in Latin America. Richard L. Cummings & Donald A. Lemke. LC 73-390. 1973. 13.50 (ISBN 0-8108-0585-5). Scarecrow.

Educational Investment in an Urban Society: Costs, Benefits, & Public Policy. Ed. by Melvin R. Levin & Alan Shank. LC 70-110397. (Illus.). 1970. pap. text ed. 12.75x (ISBN 0-8077-1684-7). Tchrs Coll.

Educational Judgments. Ed. by James F. Doyle. (International Library of the Philosophy of Education). 1973. 25.00 (ISBN 0-7100-7458-1); pap. 9.50 (ISBN 0-7100-8082-4). Routledge & Kegan.

Educational Leadership & Declining Enrollments. Ed. by Lewis B. Mayhew. LC 74-12823. 1974. 15.50x (ISBN 0-8211-1214-7); text ed. 14.00x (ISBN 0-685-14293-0). McCutchan.

Educational Measurement. 2nd ed. Richard H. Lindeman & Peter F. Merenda. 1979. pap. text ed. 9.95x (ISBN 0-673-15096-8). Scott F.

Educational Media Yearbook 1980. 6th ed. Ed. by James W. Brown & Shirley N. Brown. LC 73-4891. 400p. 1980. lib. bdg. 25.00x (ISBN 0-87287-223-8). Libs Unl.

Educational Methods & Materials. Eleanor Stocks. 1977. pap. text ed. 7.50x (ISBN 0-8191-0174-5). U Pr of Amer.

Educational Opportunity & the Home. Gordon W. Miller. (Sociology of Education Ser). 1971. text ed. 3.50x (ISBN 0-582-32453-X); pap. text ed. 3.00x (ISBN 0-582-32454-8). Humanities.

Educational Organization & Administration. Ed. by Donald A. Erickson. LC 76-18037. (Readings in Educational Research Ser.). 1977. 25.00 (ISBN 0-8211-0415-2); text ed. 22.50 10 or more copies (ISBN 0-685-71413-6). McCutchan.

Educational Organization & Administration. 3rd ed. Edgar L. Morphet et al. LC 73-18138. (Illus.). 432p. 1974. ref. ed. 18.95 (ISBN 0-13-236711-4). P-H.

Educational Performance Contracting: An Evaluation of an Experiment. Edward M. Gramlich & Patrica P. Koshel. (Studies in Social Experimentation). 76p. 1975. pap. 3.95 (ISBN 0-8157-3239-2). Brookings.

Educational Philosophy for the Future. Spencer J. Maxcy. LC 77-18479. 1978. pap. text ed. 10.00x (ISBN 0-8191-0420-5). U Pr of Amer.

Educational Philosophy of National Socialism. G. E. Kneller. 1941. 42.50x (ISBN 0-685-69834-3). Elliots Bks.

Educational Planning & Decision Making: A View Through the Organizational Process. C. Kenneth Tanner & Earl J. Williams. LC 80-8631. 1981. write for info. (ISBN 0-669-04330-3). Lexington Bks.

Educational Planning for Educational Success. Arthur W. Steller. LC 80-82685. (Fastback Ser.: No. 152). (Orig.). 1980. pap. 0.75 (ISBN 0-87367-152-X). Phi Delta Kappa.

Educational Policy & International Assessment: Implications of the IEA Surveys of Achievement. Ed. by Alan C. Purves et al. LC 74-30962. (National Society for the Study of Education, Contemporary Educational Issues Ser). 250p. 1975. 15.25 (ISBN 0-8211-1515-4); pap. text ed. 13.75 (ISBN 0-685-52137-0). McCutchan.

Educational Policy & Planning: Goals for Educational Policy in Sweden. Organization Fro Economic Cooperation & Development. 185p. (Orig.). 1980. pap. text ed. 8.50x (ISBN 92-64-01999-5, 91 80 02 3). OECD.

Educational Policy & the Law. David L. Kirp & Mark G. Yudof. LC 73-17609. 1974. 32.00 (ISBN 0-8211-1015-2); text ed. 29.00x (ISBN 0-685-42636-X). McCutchan.

Educational Policy & the Mission Schools: Case Studies from the British Empire. Ed. by Brian Holmes. 1967. text ed. 16.75x (ISBN 0-7100-6002-5). Humanities.

Educational Policy-Making: A Study of Interest Groups & Parliament. Maurice Kogan. 1975. pap. text ed. 9.95x o.p. (ISBN 0-04-370064-0). Allen Unwin.

Educational Policy-Making & the State Legislature: The New York Experience. Mike M. Milstein & Robert E. Jennings. LC 78-185780. (Special Studies in U.S. Economic, Social & Political Issues). 1973. 28.00x (ISBN 0-275-28719-X). Irvington.

Educational Products for the Exceptional Child. Ed, by Market Linkage Project for Special Education. 1981. 45.00x (ISBN 0-912700-84-X). Oryx Pr.

Educational Programs in the Health Field. American Hospital Association. LC 79-24621. 48p. 1979. pap. 7.50 (ISBN 0-87258-283-3, 3502). Am Hospital.

Educational Provision 16-19. J. Dean & B. Choppin. (General Ser.). (Orig.). 1977. pap. text ed. 7.75x (ISBN 0-85633-129-5, NFER). Humanities.

Educational Psychology. Marcellus Buoncompagni. (Library of Scientific Psychology). (Illus.). 1979. 27.50 (ISBN 0-89266-179-8). Am Classical Coll Pr.

Educational Psychology. 2nd ed. Janice T. Gibson. (Illus.). 1972. text ed. 13.95 (ISBN 0-13-236968-0). P-H.

Educational Psychology. David W. Johnson. (Illus.). 1979. pap. 17.95 ref. ed. (ISBN 0-13-236760-2). P-H.

Educational Psychology. 2nd ed. Walter B. Kolesnik. 1970. text ed. 15.95 o.p. (ISBN 0-07-035303-4, C); instructor's manual 3.95 o.p. (ISBN 0-07-035305-0). McGraw.

Educational Psychology. 6th ed. Rudolf Pintner et al. (Orig.). 1970. pap. 4.95 (ISBN 0-06-460023-8, CO 23, COS). Har-Row.

Educational Psychology: A Developmental Approach. 3rd ed. Richard Sprinthall & Normal Sprinthall. LC 80-15223. (Illus.). 624p. 1981. pap. text ed. 14.95 (ISBN 0-201-06872-9). A-W.

Educational Psychology: A Developmental Approach. 2nd ed. Richard C. Sprinthall & Norman A. Sprinthall. LC 76-17721. (Illus.). 1977. text ed. 15.50 o.p. (ISBN 0-201-06821-4); instr's manual o.p. 3.50 o.p. (ISBN 0-201-06822-2). A-W.

Educational Psychology: An Introduction. 2nd ed. Owen et al. 1981. pap. text ed. 15.95 (ISBN 0-316-67729-9); tchrs'. manual free (ISBN 0-316-67730-2). Little.

Educational Psychology & Instructional Decisions. Nelson DuBois et al. 1979. pap. text ed. 16.95x (ISBN 0-256-02056-6). Dorsey.

Educational Psychology & Its Classroom Applications. 2nd ed. M. Daniel Smith. 1978. pap. text ed. 16.95 (ISBN 0-205-06025-0); instr's man avail. (ISBN 0-205-06026-9); student guide avail. (ISBN 0-205-06028-5); tests avail. (ISBN 0-205-06027-7). Allyn.

Educational Psychology for Teachers. Anita Woolfolk & Lorraine Nicolich. (Illus.). 1980. text ed. 17.95 (ISBN 0-13-240598-9); pap. 6.95 studyguide & wkbk. (ISBN 0-13-240556-3). P-H.

Educational Psychology in a Changing World. Gerda Siann & Denis Ugwuegbu. (Illus.). 256p. (Orig.). 1980. text ed. 22.50x (ISBN 0-04-370099-3, 2587); pap. text ed. 11.50x (ISBN 0-04-370100-0, 2588). Allen Unwin.

Educational Psychology: The Instructional Enedeavor. 2nd ed. C. M. Charles. LC 75-43611. 1976. pap. text ed. 12.00 (ISBN 0-8016-0952-6). Mosby.

Educational Reform for a Changing Society. new ed. Research for Better Schools, Inc. Ed. by Louis Rubin. 1978. text ed. 19.95 (ISBN 0-205-05827-2). Allyn.

Educational Reforms & Innovations in Africa. (Experiments & Innovations in Education Ser.: No. 34). 1979. pap. 4.75 (ISBN 92-3-101560-5, U 866, UNESCO). Unipub.

Educational Research. 2nd ed. L. R. Gay. (Illus.). 464p. 1981. write for info student guide (ISBN 0-675-08021-5); price not set student guide (ISBN 0-675-08020-7); instr's. manual 3.95 (ISBN 0-686-69490-2). Merrill.

Educational Research: An Introduction. 3rd ed. Walter R. Borg & Meredith D. Gall. LC 77-17723. 1978. text ed. 17.95x (ISBN 0-582-28056-7); instrs' manual free (ISBN 0-582-28120-2). Longman.

Educational Research: Competencies for Analysis & Application. L. R. Gay. (Illus.). 368p. 1976. text ed. 17.95 (ISBN 0-675-08636-1); student suppl. 7.50 (ISBN 0-675-08600-0); instructor's manual 3.95 (ISBN 0-686-67249-6). Merrill.

Educational Research Council. (gr. 2). 1974. pap. text ed. 5.60 (ISBN 0-205-03885-9, 8038856); tchrs'. guide 12.00 (ISBN 0-205-03884-0, 8038848). Allyn.

Educational Research in Classrooms & Schools. Louis Cohen. 1977. text ed. 25.10 (ISBN 0-06-318047-2, IntlDept). Har-Row.

Educational Research in Europe: Proceedings. First All-European Conference for Directors of National Research Institutions in Education, Hamburg 26-29 April 1976. Ed. by M. Dino Carelli & Peter Sachsenmeier. 142p. 1977. pap. text ed. 19.50 (ISBN 90-265-0250-8, Pub. by Swets Pub Serv Holland). Swets North Am.

Educational Research on New Developments in Primary Education. Ed. by Louis Legrand. (Council of Europe Trends Ser.). 206p. 1980. pap. text ed. 29.75x (ISBN 0-85633-190-2, NFER). Humanities.

Educational Research: Selected Readings. William Gephart & Robert Ingle. 1969. text ed. 15.95x (ISBN 0-675-09521-2). Merrill.

Educational Research: The Art & Science of Investigation. George J. Mouly. 1978. text ed. 18.50 (ISBN 0-205-05812-4); instr's manual (ISBN 0-205-05813-2). Allyn.

Educational Software Directory: Apple II Edition. Sterling Swift Publishing Co. 104p. 1981. pap. 11.95 (ISBN 0-88408-141-9); Educational 9.95. Sterling Swift.

Educational Strategies & Services for Exceptional Children. George R. Taylor & Stanley E. Jackson. (Illus.). 276p. 1976. 19.75 (ISBN 0-398-03530-X). C C Thomas.

Educational Subnormality. Sally Tomlinson. (International Library of Sociology Ser.). 300p. 1981. price not set (ISBN 0-7100-0697-7). Routledge & Kegan.

Educational Supervision: A Handbook. Lloyd W. Dull. (Illus.). 504p. 1981. text ed. 18.95 (ISBN 0-675-08060-6). Merrill.

Educational System of India. Shri Prakash. 1980. 9.50 (ISBN 0-391-02182-6). Humanities.

Educational Systems of Africa. Martena Sasnett & Inez Sepmeyer. 1966. 65.00x (ISBN 0-520-01122-8). U of Cal Pr.

Educational Technology in Curriculum Development. 2nd ed. Derek Rowntree. 1981. text ed. 18.95 (ISBN 0-06-318169-X, IntlDept); pap. text ed. 10.25 (ISBN 0-06-318170-3). Har-Row.

Educational Theories of the Sophists. Ed. by James L. Jarrett. LC 71-108882. 1969. text ed. 8.25 (ISBN 0-8077-1565-4); pap. text ed. 4.00 (ISBN 0-8077-1564-6). Tchrs Coll.

Educational Theory: An Introduction. T. W. Moore. (Students Library of Education Ser.). 1974. 11.00x (ISBN 0-7100-7918-4); pap. 6.00 (ISBN 0-7100-8463-3). Routledge & Kegan.

Educational Theory & the Preparation of Teachers. John Wilson. (General Ser.). 200p. 1975. pap. text ed. 15.25x (ISBN 0-85633-080-9, NFER). Humanities.

Educational Therapy in the Elementary School: An Educational Approach to the Learning Problems of Children. Patrick Ashlock & Alberta Stephen. 120p. 1970. pap. 14.75 photocopy ed. spiral (ISBN 0-398-00060-3). C C Thomas.

Educational Therapy Materials from the Ashlock Learning Center. Patrick Ashlock & Sister Marie Grant. (Illus.). 440p. 1976. pap. 34.50 (ISBN 0-398-02218-6). C C Thomas.

Educational Toys in America: Eighteen Hundred to the Present. Karen Hewitt & Louise Roomet. (Illus.). 151p. (Orig.). 1979. pap. 10.00 (ISBN 0-87451-988-8). U Pr of New Eng.

Educational Vouchers: Concepts & Controversies. George R. LaNoue. LC 78-187726. (Illus.). 1972. text ed. 8.95x (ISBN 0-8077-1660-X); pap. text ed. 5.75x (ISBN 0-8077-1661-8). Tchrs Coll.

Educational Writings. John Locke. Ed. by James L. Axtell. LC 68-18341. (Illus.). 1968. 42.50 (ISBN 0-521-04073-6). Cambridge U Pr.

Educations of Man. Frederich Froebel. Tr. by W. N. Hailmann from German. (Contributions to the History of Psychology B, I: Psychometrics Ser.). 1978. Repr. of 1887 ed. write for info. (ISBN 0-89093-161-5). U Pubns Amer.

Educator's Fact Book on School Organization. William C. Miller. LC 73-95011. 1973. pap. 3.60 (ISBN 0-8224-2610-2). Pitman Learning.

Educators Grade Guide to Free Teaching Aids. 26th rev. ed. Ed. by Kathleen S. Nehmer et al. LC 56-2444. 1980. looseleaf 33.25 (ISBN 0-87708-105-0). Ed Prog.

Educator's Guide to Communication. Kenneth A. Polcyn. LC 78-89216. 116p. 1973. pap. text ed. 2.50 (ISBN 0-89192-017-X, Pub. by Acad Ed Dev). Interbk Inc.

Educator's Guide to Psychological Tests: Descriptions & Classroom Implications. Constance Tarczan. (Illus.). 128p. 1975. 12.75 (ISBN 0-398-02427-8); pap. 8.75 (ISBN 0-398-02491-X). C C Thomas.

Educators, Parents & Exceptional Children. Robert Marion. (Illus.). 275p. 1980. text ed. write for info. (ISBN 0-89443-334-2). Aspen Systems.

Educator's Resource Guide to Special Education: Terms-Laws-Tests-Organizations. William F. Davis. 270p. 1980. text ed. 17.95 (ISBN 0-205-06876-6). Allyn.

Educreation: Education for Creation, Growth & Change. 2nd ed. Paul Ritter. 1978. text ed. 51.00 (ISBN 0-08-021475-4); pap. text ed. 26.00 (ISBN 0-08-021476-2). Pergamon.

Edvard Kardelj: The Historical Roots of Non-Alignment. Nikolaos A. Stavrou. LC 80-5251. 95p. 1980. pap. text ed. 6.00 (ISBN 0-8191-1066-3). U Pr of Amer.

Edvard Munch. J. P. Hodin. (World of Art Ser.). (Illus.). 1972. pap. text ed. 9.95 (ISBN 0-19-519936-7). Oxford U Pr.

Edvard Munch. N. C. Stang. Tr. by Carol J. Knudsen. (Tokens of Norway Ser). (Illus.). 305p. (Orig.). 1972. pap. 15.00x (ISBN 82-518-0010-2). Intl Pubns Serv.

Edvard Munch: Masterpieces from the Artist's Collection in the Munch Museum in Oslo. Johan H. Langaard & Reidar Revold. LC 64-20212. (Illus.). 72p. 1972. 25.00x o.p. (ISBN 0-87663-175-8). Universe.

Edward Albee. Richard E. Amacher. LC 68-24299. (U. S. Authors Ser.: No. 141). 1968. lib. bdg. 10.95 (ISBN 0-8057-0011-0). Twayne.

Edward & the Horse. Ann Rand & Olle Eksell. LC 61-6121. (Illus.). (gr. k-2). 1961. 3.25 o.p. (ISBN 0-15-225202-9, HJ). HarBraceJ.

Edward Bawden: A Book of Cuts. Intro. by Ruari McLean. (Illus.). 84p. 1979. 15.00 (ISBN 0-85967-456-8, Pub. by Scolar Pr England); pap. 7.95 (ISBN 0-85967-457-6, Pub. by Scolor Pr England). Biblio Dist.

Edward, Benjamin & Butter. Malcolm Hall. (Illus.). 48p. (gr. 6-9). 1981. PLB 6.99 (ISBN 0-698-30731-3). Coward.

Edward Carpenter: Eighteen Forty-Four to Nineteen Twenty Nine. C. Tsuzuki. LC 80-40152. 240p. 1980. 34.50 (ISBN 0-521-23371-2). Cambridge U Pr.

Edward Dowden. Kathryn R. Ludwigson. (English Authors Ser.: No. 148). lib. bdg. 10.95 (ISBN 0-8057-1164-3). Twayne.

Edward, Edward. Lolah Burford. LC 73-182446. 576p. 1973. 8.95 o.s.i. (ISBN 0-02-518200-5). Macmillan.

Edward Everett Hale. John R. Adams. (U.S. Authors Ser.: No. 284). 1977. lib. bdg. 9.95 (ISBN 0-8057-7186-7). Twayne.

Edward Fitzgerald. Iran B. Jewett. (English Authors Ser.: No. 205). 1977. lib. bdg. 9.95 (ISBN 0-8057-6675-8). Twayne.

Edward Gibbon. R. N. Parkinson. (English Authors Ser.: No. 159). 1973. lib. bdg. 10.95 (ISBN 0-8057-1218-6). Twayne.

Edward Gibbon's Library: A Catolgue. Ed. by Geoffrey Keynes. (Illus.). 288p. 1980. Repr. of 1940 ed. 30.00x (ISBN 0-906795-02-8). U Pr of Va.

Edward Gordon Craig. Denis Bablet. Tr. by D. Woodward. LC 66-23134. (Illus.). 1966. 7.75 (ISBN 0-87830-042-2). Theatre Arts.

Edward Gordon Craig & the Pretenders: A Production Revisited. Frederick J. Marker & Lise-Lone Marker. (Special Issues Ser.). (Illus.). Date not set. price not set (ISBN 0-8093-0966-1). S Ill U Pr.

Edward Granville Browne & the Baha'i Faith. H. M. Balyuzi. (Illus.). 1970. 10.95 o.s.i. (ISBN 0-85398-023-3, 7-31-14, Pub. by G Ronald England). Baha'i.

Edward H. Chamberlin. Romney Robinson. LC 74-147309. 1971. pap. 2.00 (ISBN 0-231-03005-3). Columbia U Pr.

Edward Hopper: The Art & the Artist. Gail Levin. (Illus.). 1980. 29.95 (ISBN 0-393-01374-X). Norton.

Edward I & the Throne of Scotland 1290-1296: An Edition of the Record Sources for the Great Cause, 2 vols. E. L. Stones & Grant G. Simpson. 1979. 165.00x (ISBN 0-19-713308-8). Oxford U Pr.

Edward J. Dent: Selected Essays. Ed. by H. Taylor. LC 78-62111. (Illus.). 1979. 34.50 (ISBN 0-521-22174-9). Cambridge U Pr.

Edward Jarvis & the Medical World of Nineteenth-Century America. Gerald N. Grob. LC 78-3771. 1978. 15.00x (ISBN 0-87049-239-X). U of Tenn Pr.

Edward John Carnell: Defender of the Faith. John A. Sims. LC 78-57980. 1978. pap. text ed. 9.00 (ISBN 0-8191-0658-5). U Pr of Amer.

Edward Lear & His World. John Lehmann. LC 77-73133. (Enore Edition). (Illus.). 1977. 3.95 (ISBN 0-684-16548-1, ScribT). Scribner.

Edward Lear's Nonsense. Edward Lear. (Illus.). 1977. pap. 1.75 (ISBN 0-486-22744-8). Dover.

Edward Lewis Wallant. David Galloway. (United States Authors Ser.: No. 319). 1979. lib. bdg. 13.50 (ISBN 0-8057-7250-2). Twayne.

Edward MacDowell: A Study. 2nd ed. Lawrence Gilman. LC 67-27455. (Music Ser). 1969. Repr. of 1908 ed. lib. bdg. 17.50 (ISBN 0-306-70979-1). Da Capo.

Edward Munch. Thomas M. Messer. LC 70-142783. (Library of Great Painters Ser.). (Illus.). 168p. 1973. 35.00 (ISBN 0-8109-0333-4). Abrams.

Edward Phillip's History of the Literature of England & Scotland. Daniel G. Calder & Charles Forker. (Salzburg Studies in English Literature, Poetic Drama & Poetic Theory: No. 21). 134p. (A translation from the Compendios Enumeratio Poetarum). 1973. pap. text ed. 25.00x (ISBN 0-391-01338-6). Humanities.

Edward Prince of Wales & Aquitaine: A Biography of the Black Prince. Richard Barber. (Illus.). 1978. 17.50 o.p. (ISBN 0-684-15864-7, ScribT). Scribner.

Edward R. Murrow: The War Years. R. Franklin Smith. (Orig.). 1978. pap. 5.95x (ISBN 0-932826-04-0). New Issues MI.

Edward Rose, Negro Trail Blazer. Harold W. Felton. (Illus.). (gr. 5-9). 1967. 5.95 o.p. (ISBN 0-396-05597-4). Dodd.

Edward S. Curtis: Photographer of the North American Indian. Victor Boesen & Florence C. Graybill. LC 76-53435. (gr. 7 up). 1977. 6.95 (ISBN 0-396-07430-8). Dodd.

Edward Sheriff Curtis: Visions of a Vanishing Race. Florence C. Graybill & Victor Boesen. LC 76-16579. (Illus.). 1976. 35.00 o.s.i. (ISBN 0-690-01162-8, TYC-T). T Y Crowell.

Edward Steichen. Photos by Edward Steichen. LC 77-70071. (History of Photography Ser). (Illus.). 1978. 8.95 (ISBN 0-89381-006-1). Aperture.

Edward T. & William A. Potter, American Victorian Architects. Sarah B. Landau. Ed. by Sydney J. Freedberg. LC 78-74371. (Outstanding Dissertations in the Fine Arts Ser.). (Illus.). 1979. lib. bdg. 60.50 (ISBN 0-8240-3955-6). Garland Pub.

Edward Taylor. Norman S. Grabo. (U. S. Authors Ser.: No. 8). lib. bdg. 12.95 (ISBN 0-8057-0720-4). Twayne.

Edward Taylor Vs. Solomon Stoddard: The Nature of the Lord's Supper, Vol. II. Thomas M. Davis & Virginia L. Davis. (American Literary Manuscripts Ser.). 1981. lib. bdg. 30.00 (ISBN 0-8057-9653-3). Twayne.

Edward Taylor's "Church Record" & Related Sermons. Ed. by Thomas M. Davis & Virginia L. Davis. (American Literary Manuscripts Ser.: Vol. 1). 1981. lib. bdg. 35.00 (ISBN 0-8057-9650-9). Twayne.

Edward Taylor's Minor Poetry, Vol. 3. Ed. by Thomas M. Davis & Virginia L. Davis. (American Literary Manuscripts Ser.). 1981. lib. bdg. 35.00 (ISBN 0-8057-9654-1). Twayne.

Edward the Confessor. Frank Barlow. LC 70-104107. (English Monarchs Series). (Illus.). 1970. 19.50x (ISBN 0-520-01671-8). U of Cal Pr.

Edward the Eighth. Frances Donaldson. LC 74-31274. (Illus.). 1975. 17.50 (ISBN 0-397-00765-5). Lippincott.

Edward the Fourth. Charles Ross. LC 74-79771. (English Monarchs Ser). (Illus.). 1975. 35.00x (ISBN 0-520-02781-7). U of Cal Pr.

Edward the Second: A Chronicle Play. Bertolt Brecht. Tr. & intro. by Eric Bentley. (Orig.). 1970. pap. 1.95 (ISBN 0-394-17111-X, B119, BC). Grove.

Edward Thomas in the Countryside. Ed. & intro. by Roland Gant. 1977. 14.95 (ISBN 0-571-10799-0, Pub. by Faber & Faber). Merrimack Bk Serv.

Edward Thurlow. Ed. by Donald H. Reiman. Incl. Hermilda in Palestine...with Other Poems. Repr. of 1812 ed; Sonnets of Edward, Lord Thurlow: Select Poems, 1821. Repr. of 1819 ed. LC 75-31267. (Romantic Context Ser.: Poetry 1789-1830). 1978. lib. bdg. 43.00 (ISBN 0-8240-2213-0). Garland Pub.

Edward Thurlow, Second Baron Thurlow (1781-1829) Ed. by Donald H. Reiman. LC 75-31265. (Romantic Context Ser.: Poetry 1789-1830). 1978. lib. bdg. 47.00 (ISBN 0-8240-2211-4). Garland Pub.

Edward Weston: His Life & Photographs. rev. ed. Ben Maddow. LC 79-7058. (Illus.). 1979. 375.00 (ISBN 0-89381-043-6); ltd. ed. 300.00 (ISBN 0-89381-045-2). Aperture.

Edward Weston: Nudes. Charis Wilson. LC 77-80022. (Illus.). 1977. 25.00 (ISBN 0-89381-020-7); ltd ed 350.00 (ISBN 0-89381-025-8); pap. 14.95 (ISBN 0-89381-026-6). Aperture.

Edward Wilmot Blyden: Pan-Negro Patriot, 1832-1912. Hollis R. Lynch. (West African History Ser). (Illus.). 1970. pap. 4.95 (ISBN 0-19-501268-2, GB). Oxford U Pr.

Edward Wilson of the Antarctic. G. Seaver. 14.50 (ISBN 0-685-91531-X). Transatlantic.

Edwardian Architecture: A Handbook. Alastair Service. (World of Art Ser.). (Illus.). 1978. 17.95 (ISBN 0-19-519979-0); pap. 9.95 (ISBN 0-19-519982-0). Oxford U Pr.

Edwardian Childhoods. Thea Thompson. (Illus.). 256p. 1981. 27.50 (ISBN 0-7100-0676-4). Routledge & Kegan.

Edwardian Occasions. Samuel Hynes. 250p. 1972. 14.95 (ISBN 0-19-519709-7). Oxford U Pr.

Edwardian Radicalism 1900-1914. A. J. Morris. 288p. 1974. 22.00 (ISBN 0-7100-7866-8). Routledge & Kegan.

Edwardian Season. John S. Goodall. LC 79-89479. (Illus.). 64p. 1980. 7.95 (ISBN 0-689-50155-2, McElderry Bk). Atheneum.

Edwardian Shopping. R. H. Langbridge. LC 75-24631. 1976. 25.00 (ISBN 0-7153-7068-5). David & Charles.

Edwardian Times. (Picture Panorama of British History Ser.). 1977. pap. 4.95 (ISBN 0-263-06245-7). Transatlantic.

Edwardians & Late Victorians. Ed. by Richard Ellman. LC 60-13103. 1960. 15.00x (ISBN 0-231-02418-5). Columbia U Pr.

Edwardians: The Remaking of British Society. Paul Thompson. LC 75-10897. (Illus.). 396p. 1975. 15.00x (ISBN 0-253-31941-2). Ind U Pr.

Edwin Arlington Robinson. Hoyt C. Franchere. LC 68-24295. (U. S. Authors Ser.: No. 137). 1968. lib. bdg. 9.95 (ISBN 0-8057-0632-1). Twayne.

Edwin Arlington Robinson: Centenary Essays. Ed. by Ellsworth Barnard. LC 77-111377. 192p. 1969. 12.00x (ISBN 0-8203-0252-X). U of Ga Pr.

Edwin Broun Fred: Scientist, Administrator, Gentleman. Diane Johnson. 1974. 20.00 (ISBN 0-299-06580-4). U of Wis Pr.

Edwin Muir. Elgin W. Mellown. (English Authors Ser.: No. 248). 1979. lib. bdg. 12.95 (ISBN 0-8057-6687-1). Twayne.

Edwin Muir: A Master of Modern Poetry. Michael J. Phillips. LC 78-67103. 1978. 19.50 (ISBN 0-915144-54-9). Hackett Pub.

Edwin Newman on Language: Strictly Speaking & a Civil Tongue. Edwin Newman. 1980. pap. 6.95 (ISBN 0-446-97459-5). Warner Bks.

Edwin O'Connor. Hugh Rank. (U. S. Authors Ser.: No. 242). 1974. lib. bdg. 9.95 (ISBN 0-8057-0555-4). Twayne.

EEC & Eastern Europe. A. Shlaim & G. N. Yannopoulos. LC 78-51675. 1979. 45.00 (ISBN 0-521-22072-6). Cambridge U Pr.

EEC & the Mediterranean Countries. Ed. by A. Shlaim & G. Yannopoulos. LC 75-3858. (Illus.). 356p. 1976. 54.00 (ISBN 0-521-20817-3). Cambridge U Pr.

EEC & The Third World. Ed. by K. B. Lall & H. S. Chopra. 500p. 1980. text ed. 31.00x (ISBN 0-391-02004-8). Humanities.

EEG & Clinical Neurophysiology. Ed. by H. Lechner & A. Aranibar. (International Congress Ser.: No. 506). 128p. 1979. 24.50 (ISBN 0-444-90111-6, Excerpta Medica). Elsevier.

EEG Instrumentation and Technology. E. T. Richey & Richard Namon. (Illus.). 218p. 1976. 29.75 (ISBN 0-398-03426-5). C C Thomas.

EEG Recording. 2nd ed. M. L. Hector. LC 79-40117. (Illus.). 1980. text ed. 29.95 (ISBN 0-407-00136-0). Butterworths.

EEG Technology. 3rd ed. R. Cooper & J. W. Osselton. Ed. by J. C. Shaw. (Illus.). 304p. 1980. text ed. 29.95 (ISBN 0-407-16002-7). Butterworths.

Eel Capture, Culture, Processing & Marketing. David M. Forrest. (Illus.). 206p. 20.25 (ISBN 0-85238-070-4, FN). Unipub.

Eel Culture. Atsushi Usui. (Illus.). 190p. 19.50 (FN). Unipub.

Eels Strange Journey. Judi Friedman. LC 75-20136. (Let's Read & Find Out Science Bk). (Illus.). 40p. (gr. k-3). 1976. PLB 7.89 (ISBN 0-690-01007-9, TYC-J). T Y Crowell.

Eenie-Meenie-Minie-Mo & Other Counting-Out Rhymes. Carl Withers. (Illus.). 1970. pap. 1.75 (ISBN 0-486-22414-7). Dover.

Eerdmans' Concise Bible Encyclopedia. Ed. by Pat Alexander. LC 80-19885. (Illus.). 256p. (Orig.). 1981. pap. 8.95 (ISBN 0-8028-1876-5). Eerdmans.

Eerdmans' Concise Bible Handbook. Ed. by David Alexander & Pat Alexander. LC 80-20131. (Illus.). 384p. (Orig.). 1981. pap. 9.95 (ISBN 0-8028-1875-7). Eerdmans.

Eerdmans' Handbook to the Bible. David Alexander & Patricia Alexander. 1973. 19.95 (ISBN 0-8028-3436-1). Eerdmans.

Eero Saarinen. Allan Temko. (Makers of Contemporary Architecture Ser). (Orig.). 1966. 6.95 o.s.i. (ISBN 0-8076-0199-3); pap. 3.95 o.s.i. (ISBN 0-8076-0391-0). Braziller.

Efesios y Filemon. Marilyn Kunz & Catherine Schell. Tr. by Julio Orozco from Eng. LC 77-83811. (Encuentros Biblicos Ser.). 55p. (Orig., Span.). 1977. pap. 1.25 (ISBN 0-89922-095-9). Edit Caribe.

Effect of an Unconstitutional Statute. O. P. Field. LC 74-146273. (American Constitutional & Legal History Ser). 1971. Repr. of 1935 ed. lib. bdg. 35.00 (ISBN 0-306-70118-9). Da Capo.

Effect of Constant Light on Visual Processes. Ed. by Theodore P. Williams & B. N. Baker. LC 79-26293. 465p. 1980. 45.00 (ISBN 0-306-40328-5, Plenum Pr). Plenum Pub.

Effect of Diet on Endurance. Irving Fisher. 1918. 14.50x o.p. (ISBN 0-686-51377-0). Elliots Bks.

Effect of Disease States on Drug Pharmokinetics. LC 76-43119. 1976. 21.00 (ISBN 0-917330-11-0). Am Pharm Assn.

Effect of Genetic Variance on Nutritional Requirements of Animals. National Academy of Sciences. 1975. 6.50 (ISBN 0-309-02342-4). Natl Acad Pr.

Effect of Judicial Review on Federal-State Relations in Australia, Canada, & the United States. Richard E. Johnston. LC 70-80045. 1969. 20.00x (ISBN 0-8071-0901-0). La State U Pr.

Effect of Man on the Landscape: The Lowland Zone. Ed. by Susan Limbrey & J. G. Evans. 160p. 1980. pap. 29.95x (ISBN 0-900312-60-2, Pub. by Council Brit Arch England). Intl Schol Bk Serv.

Effect of Modern Agriculture on Rural Developement. Ed. by Gyorgy Enyedi & Ivan Volgyes. LC 80-25232. (Pergamon Policy Studies on International Developement Comparative Rural Transformations Ser.). (Illus.). 280p. 1981. 32.50 (ISBN 0-08-027179-0). Pergamon.

Effect of Processing on the Nutritional Value of Feeds. Agricultural Board. National Research Council. (Illus.). 536p. 1973. pap. 14.50 (ISBN 0-309-02116-2). Natl Acad Pr.

Effect of Repeated Electroshock on Learning in Depressives. J. C. Brengelmann. (Monographien Aus Dem Gesamtgebiete der Neurologie: Vol. 84). (Illus.). 1959. 12.40 o.p. (ISBN 0-387-02447-6). Springer-Verlag.

Effect of Selective Consumption on Voluntary Intake & Digestibility of Tropical Forages. 100p. 1980. pap. 48.75 (ISBN 90-220-0729-4, PDC 206, Pudoc). Unipub.

Effect of Surface on Behavior of Metals. C. J. Bailey. 6.00 o.p. (ISBN 0-685-28357-7). Philos Lib.

Effect of the Demographics of Individual Households on Their Telephone Useage. Ed. by Belinda B. Brandon. 432p. 1980. write for info. (ISBN 0-88410-695-0). Ballinger Pub.

Effect of the New Rice Technology on Family Labor Utilization in Laguna. (IRRI Research Paper Ser.: No. 42). 17p. 1979. pap. 5.00 (R082, IRRI). Unipub.

Effect of the War in Southeastern Europe. David Mitrany. LC 75-114590. 1973. Repr. 16.50 (ISBN 0-86527-055-4). Fertig.

Effect of Vehicle Characteristics on Road Accidents. I. S. Jones. 200p. 1976. text ed. 34.00 (ISBN 0-08-018963-6). Pergamon.

Effecting Change in Large Organizations. Eli Ginzberg. LC 57-13484. 1957. 15.00x (ISBN 0-231-02249-2). Columbia U Pr.

Effective Behavior in Organizations. rev. ed. Allan R. Cohen et al. 1980. 18.95x (ISBN 0-256-02283-6). Irwin.

Effective Behavior in Organizations: Learning from the Interplay of Cases, Concepts & Student Experiences. Allan R. Cohen et al. 1976. text ed. 16.50x o.p. (ISBN 0-256-01773-5). Irwin.

Effective Business & Technical Presentations. 2nd ed. George L. Morrisey. LC 74-24920. 224p. 1975. pap. text ed. 8.95 (ISBN 0-201-04828-0). A-W.

Effective Business Communication. 2nd ed. Herta Murphy & Charles Peck. Ed. by William J. Kane. (Illus.). 1976. pap. text ed. 15.95 o.p. (ISBN 0-07-044061-1, C). ans. to test questions 4.95 o.p. (ISBN 0-07-044067-0). McGraw.

Effective Business Relocation. William N. Kinnard & Stephen D. Messnen. LC 78-113590. 1970. 16.95 (ISBN 0-669-58420-7). Lexington Bks.

Effective Classroom Management. abr. ed. Carl J. Wallen & LaDonna Wallen. 1978. pap. text ed. 10.95 (ISBN 0-205-05985-6); text ed. 18.95 (ISBN 0-205-05893-0). Allyn.

Effective Clinician: His Methods & Approach to Diagnosis & Care. Philip A. Tumulty. LC 73-77942. 379p. 1973. text ed. 15.00 (ISBN 0-7216-8915-9). Saunders.

Effective Communication. Learning Systems Ltd. 1968. pap. text ed. 4.20 (ISBN 0-08-014048-3). Pergamon.

Effective Communication for Public Safety Personnel. M. T. Barnett & J. L. Smith. LC 76-46125. 1978. pap. text ed. 9.20 (ISBN 0-8273-1658-5); instructor's guide 1.60 (ISBN 0-8273-1659-3). Delmar.

Effective Communication in Real Estate Management. Lyle York. LC 79-67426. 183p. 1979. 18.00 (ISBN 0-913652-21-0). Realtors Natl.

Effective Communication on the Job. 3rd ed. Ed. by William K. Fallon. 273p. 1981. 15.95 (ISBN 0-8144-5698-7). Am Mgmt.

Effective Computer: A Management by Objectives Approach. John Humble & John W. Humble. LC 73-79243. 160p. 1974. 14.95 (ISBN 0-8144-5334-1). AM Mgmt.

Effective Computer Audit Practices Manual ECAP- Map-11: A Manual in Installments. William E. Perry & Javier F. Kuong. 1980. 495.00 (ISBN 0-686-27136-X). Management Advisory Pubns.

Effective Data Base Design. William Inmon. (P-H Ser. in Data Processing Management). (Illus.). 240p. 1981. text ed. 24.95 (ISBN 0-13-241489-9). P-H.

Effective Decisions & Emotional Fulfillment. Rolland S Parker. LC 76-54652. 1977. 13.95 (ISBN 0-88229-303-6). Nelson-Hall.

Effective Delegation. Didactic Systems Staff. Tr. by Euro-Training & Luis Garcia De Leon. (Simulation Game Ser.). 1971. pap. 24.90 (ISBN 0-89401-145-6); pap. 21.50 two or more; pap. 24.90 french ed. (ISBN 0-89401-017-4); pap. 21.50 ea. two or more; pap. 24.90 spanish ed. (ISBN 0-89401-018-2); pap. 21.50 ea. two or more spanish eds. Didactic Syst.

Effective Educational & Behavioral Programming for Severely & Profoundly Handicapped Students. Dorothy Popovich. (Illus.). 300p. (Orig.). 1981. pap. text ed. 14.95 (ISBN 0-933716-14-1). P H Brookes.

Effective Employee Assistance: A Comprehensive Guide for the Employer. Joseph A. Muldoon & Mitchell Berdie. 1980. 49.95 (ISBN 0-89638-048-3). CompCare.

Effective Evaluation: Improving the Usefulness of Evaluation Results Through Responsive & Naturalistic Approaches. Egon G. Guba & Yvonna S. Lincoln. LC 80-8909. (Social & Behavioral Science Ser.). 1981. text ed. price not set (ISBN 0-87589-493-3). Jossey-Bass.

Effective Football Coaching. Donald E. Fuoss & Rowland Smith. 264p. 1980. text ed. 14.95 (ISBN 0-205-07125-2). Allyn.

Effective Front Office Operations. Michael L. Kasavana. 352p. text ed. 16.95 (ISBN 0-8436-2200-8). CBI Pub.

Effective Industrial Marketing. Peter M. Chisnall. LC 76-54987. (Illus.). 1977. text ed. 20.00x (ISBN 0-582-45067-5). Longman.

Effective Ingredients of Successful Psychotherapy. Jerome D. Frank & Rudolph Hoehn-Saric. LC 78-937. 1978. 17.50 (ISBN 0-87630-168-5). Brunner-Mazel.

Effective Interpersonal Communication: A Manual for Skill Development. Eugene W. Kelly, Jr. 1977. pap. text ed. 7.50x (ISBN 0-8191-0125-7). U Pr of Amer.

Effective Interviewing for Employment Selection. C. T. Goodworth. 138p. 1979. text ed. 22.00x (ISBN 0-220-67005-6, Pub. by Busn Bks England). Renouf.

Effective Library. B. Totterdell & J. Bird. Ed. by M. Redfern. 1976. 31.00x (ISBN 0-85365-248-1, Pub. by Assn England). Oryx Pr.

Effective Management. Michael A. Hitt et al. (Management Ser). (Illus.). 1979. text ed. 18.50 (ISBN 0-8299-0196-5); pap. study guide 6.95 (ISBN 0-686-67442-1); instrs.' manual avail. (ISBN 0-8299-0489-1); transparency masters avail. (ISBN 0-8299-0490-5); study guide 6.95 (ISBN 0-8299-0246-5). West Pub.

Effective Management Coaching. 2nd ed. Edwin J. Singer. (Management in Perspective Ser.). 212p. 1979. pap. 11.50x (ISBN 0-85292-248-5). Intl Pubns Serv.

Effective Management for Engineers & Scientists. Leon A. Wortman. 264p. 1981. 17.95 (ISBN 0-471-05523-9, Ronald Pr). Wiley.

Effective Management Through Work Planning. Stanley D. Duffendack. 1971. 28.95 (ISBN 0-932078-00-1). GE Tech Prom & Train.

Effective Marketing Logistics: The Analysis Planning & Control of Distribution Operations. Graham Buxton. 1975. 37.50x (ISBN 0-8419-5007-5). Holmes & Meier.

Effective Methods of EDP Quality Assurance. William E. Perry. (Illus.). 347p. (Orig.). 1978. pap. 28.50 (ISBN 0-89435-007-2). QED Info Sci.

Effective Motivation Through Performance Appraisal. V. R. Buzzotta et al. 1980. Repr. of 1977 ed. 18.50 (ISBN 0-88410-499-0). Ballinger Pub.

Effective Municipal Police Organization. G. Douglas Gourley. (Criminal Justice Ser). 1970. pap. text ed. 3.95x (ISBN 0-02-474610-X, 47461). Macmillan.

Effective Nurse: Leader & Manager. Laura M. Douglass. LC 80-10860. (Illus.). 1980. pap. text ed. 9.95 (ISBN 0-8016-1448-1). Mosby.

Effective Policy Implementation. Ed. by Daniel Mazmanian & Paul A. Sabatier. LC 79-3041. (Policy Study Organization Bks.). 1981. 23.95x (ISBN 0-669-03311-1). Lexington Bks.

Effective Prayer. Ernest Holmes. 1966. pap. 2.50 (ISBN 0-911336-02-8). Sci of Mind.

Effective Prayer. J. Oswald Sanders. pap. 3.50 (ISBN 0-8024-2322-1). Moody.

Effective Prayer Life. Chuck Smith. LC 78-27511. 96p. 1980. pap. 1.95 (ISBN 0-936728-03-5). Word for Today.

Effective Project Management Techniques. Compiled By American Society of Civil Engineers. 84p. 1973. pap. 5.00 (ISBN 0-87262-058-1). Am Soc Civil Eng.

Effective Psychotherapy. Ed. by L. B. Fierman. LC 65-2314. 1965. 15.95 (ISBN 0-02-910140-9). Free Pr.

Effective Psychotherapy: A Handbook of Research. Alan S. Gurman & Andrew M Razin. LC 76-23300. 1977. pap. 35.75 (ISBN 0-08-019508-3). Pergamon.

Effective Public Relations. 5th ed. Allen H. Center & Scott H. Cutlip. (Illus.). 1978. ref. 19.95 (ISBN 0-13-245035-6). P-H.

Effective Publications for Colleges & Universities. rev. ed. Kelvin J. Arden & William J. Whalen. 1978. pap. 16.50 (ISBN 0-89964-034-6). CASE.

Effective Reading Instruction for Slow Learners. Donald C. Cushenbery & Kenneth J. Gilreath. 178p. 1972. 14.75 (ISBN 0-398-02543-6). C C Thomas.

Effective Reference Librarian. Diana M. Thomas et al. (Library & Information Science). 1981. write for info. (ISBN 0-12-688720-9). Acad Pr.

Effective Sales Incentive Compensation. John W. Barry & Porter J. Henry. (Illus.). 192p. 1980. write for info. (ISBN 0-07-003860-0, P&RB). McGraw.

Effective Salesmanship. Richard T. Hise. 480p. 1980. text ed. 17.95 (ISBN 0-03-054676-1). Dryden Pr.

Effective Scutboy. Gary S. Firestein & Robert A. Harrell. LC 80-25057. (Illus.). 96p. 1981. pap. text ed. 6.00 (ISBN 0-668-05159-0, 5159). Arco.

Effective Security Management. Charles A. Sennewald. LC 78-6058. (Illus.). 1978. 15.95 (ISBN 0-913708-30-5). Butterworths.

Effective Speaker. Edward S. Strother & Alan W. Huckleberry. LC 68-7238. (Illus.). 1968. text ed. 15.50 (ISBN 0-395-05441-9). HM.

Effective Speaking & Presentation for the Company Executive. Clive T. Goodworth. 204p. 1980. text ed. 12.25x (Pub. by Busn Bks England). Renouf.

Effective Student Council in the Mid-Seventies. rev ed. Earl Reum & Oveta Cummings. 48p. 1973. pap. text ed. 3.00 o.p. (ISBN 0-88210-047-5). Natl Assn Principals.

Effective Supervisory Practices. Intl City Management Assn. LC 77-28712. (Municipal Management Ser.). 1978. pap. text ed. 19.50 (ISBN 0-87326-019-8). Intl City Mgt.

Effective Teaching: Basic Principles & Activities for Individualizing Instruction. rev. ed. June Crabtree. 96p. (Orig.). 1981. pap. 5.95 (ISBN 0-87239-454-9, 3653). Standard Pub.

Effective Technical Writing & Speaking. 2nd ed. Barry T. Turner. 220p. 1978. text ed. 22.00x (ISBN 0-220-66344-0, Pub. by Busn Bks England). Renouf.

Effective Therapeutic Communications. Ann Lore. (Illus.). 128p. 1981. pap. 10.95 (ISBN 0-87619-842-6). R J Brady.

Effective Time Management: A Practical Workbook. James Davidson. LC 78-6126. 1978. 9.95 (ISBN 0-87705-332-4). Human Sci Pr.

Effective University: A Management by Objectives Approach. Graeme Norris. 1978. text ed. 23.00x (ISBN 0-566-00242-6, Pub. by Gower Pub Co England). Renouf.

Effective Use of ANS COBOL Computer Programming Language: A Supplemental Text for Programmers Working with IBM's OS & DOS Systems. Laurence S. Cohn. LC 75-5584. (Business Data Processing Ser). 178p. 1975. 20.95 (ISBN 0-471-16436-4, Pub. by Wiley-Interscience). Wiley.

Effective Use of Electricity in Buildings. (IEE Conference Publication Ser.: No. 186). (Illus.). 217p. 1980. softcover 36.00 (ISBN 0-85296-215-0). Inst Elect Eng.

Effective Use of Volunteers in Hospitals, Homes & Agencies. Harold Kurtz & Margaret Burrows. 132p. 1971. pap. 12.50 photocopy ed., spiral (ISBN 0-398-01069-2). C C Thomas.

Effective Visitation. Marie Frost. (Peter Panda Ser.). 1977. pap. 1.25 (ISBN 0-87239-145-0, 42037). Standard Pub.

Effective Voluntary Board of Directors: What Is Is & How It Works. William R. Conrad, Jr. & William E. Glenn. LC 76-13425. 186p. 1976. pap. 7.95x (ISBN 0-8040-0735-7). Swallow.

Effective Warehousing. 2nd ed. J. A. Burton. LC 75-323434. (Illus.). 368p. 1973. 12.50x (ISBN 0-7121-0566-2). Intl Pubns Serv.

Effective Writer's Companion. P. Joseph Canavan. 1981. pap. text ed. 8.95x (ISBN 0-673-15449-1). Scott F.

Effective Writing for Engineers-Managers-Scientists. H. Tichy. LC 66-21062. 1966. 18.50 (ISBN 0-471-86778-0, Pub. by Wiley-Interscience). Wiley.

Effective Writing: Methods & Examples. Kenneth R. Bindseil & Imogene B. Dickey. LC 77-72907. (Illus.). 1977. pap. text ed. 10.95 (ISBN 0-395-24950-3); inst. manual & suppl. tests 0.25 (ISBN 0-395-24949-X). HM.

Effective Writing Techniques. Dean L. Overman. LC 79-1212. (Orig.). 1980. pap. 4.95 (ISBN 0-671-09168-9). Monarch Pr.

Effective Year-Round Bible Ministries. Margaret M. Self. LC 80-52962. Orig. Title: Effective Summer Bible Ministries. 160p. 1981. pap. 3.95 (ISBN 0-8307-0751-4, 5414318). Regal.

Effectiveness of a Prison & Parole System. abr ed. Daniel Glaser. LC 79-93448. 1969. pap. 7.95 (ISBN 0-672-60842-1). Bobbs.

Effectiveness of Correctional Treatment: A Survey of Treatment Evaluation Studies. Douglas Lipton et al. LC 74-14730. (Illus.). 768p. 1975. text ed. 46.50 (ISBN 0-275-05580-9). Praeger.

Effectiveness of Policing. Ed. by R. V. G. Clarke & J. M. Hough. 184p. 1980. 19.95x (ISBN 0-566-00297-3, 03295-6, Pub by Gower Pub Co England). Lexington Bks.

Effectiveness of Punishment, Especially in Relation to Traffic Offenses. Wolf Middendorff. LC 68-9171. (New York University Criminal Law Education & Research Center Pubns. Ser.: Vol. 5). 1968. 12.50x (ISBN 0-8377-0826-5). Rothman.

Effectiveness of Union-Management Safety & Health Committees. Thomas A. Kochan et al. LC 77-22038. 1977. pap. 2.75 (ISBN 0-911558-02-0). Upjohn Inst.

Effects & Functions of Television: Children & Adolescents. Ed. by Manfred Meyer & Ursula Nissen. 1979. pap. 14.80 (ISBN 0-89664-171-6, Pub. by K G Saur). Shoe String.

Effects of Agricultural Production on Nitrates in Food & Water with Particular Reference to Isotope Studies. (Illus.). 158p. (Orig.). 1974. pap. 10.75 (ISBN 92-0-111174-6, IAEA). Unipub.

Effects of Air Pollutants on Plants. Ed. by T. A. Mansfield. LC 75-32449. (Society for Experimental Biology Seminar Ser.: No. 1). (Illus.). 180p. 1976. 39.50 (ISBN 0-521-21087-9); pap. 14.95x (ISBN 0-521-29039-2). Cambridge U Pr.

Effects of Anisotrophy & Irradiation on the Creep Behavior of Zircaloy-2. Glenn E. Lucas. LC 78-75012. (Outstanding Dissertations on Energy Ser.). 1979. lib. bdg. 35.00 (ISBN 0-8240-3987-4). Garland Pub.

Effects of Drugs on Learning & Memory. Ed. by Anthony Pugliese. 1977. pap. 9.50 o.p. (ISBN 0-686-00906-1, D-109). Essence Pubns.

Effects of Environmental Regulations on Housing Costs. David E. Dowall & Jesse Mingilton. (CPL Bibliographies: No. 6). 67p. 1979. pap. 7.00 (ISBN 0-86602-006-3). CPL Biblios.

Effects of Fluorides in Animals. Committee on Animal Nutrition. LC 74-4061. (Illus.). 76p. 1974. pap. 4.25 (ISBN 0-309-02219-3). Natl Acad Pr.

Effects of Heating on Foodstuffs. Ed. by R. J. Priestly. (Illus.). 1979. 62.10x (ISBN 0-85334-797-2, Pub. by Applied Science). Burgess-Intl Ideas.

Effects of Hospitalization on Children: Models for Their Care. Ed. by Evelyn K. Oremland & Jerome D. Oremland. (Illus.). 360p. 1973. text ed. 18.50 (ISBN 0-398-02729-3). C C Thomas.

Effects of Low Doses of Radiation on Crop Plants. (Technical Reports Ser.: No. 64). (Illus.). 58p. (Orig.). 1966. pap. 3.25 (ISBN 92-0-115466-6, IAEA). Unipub.

Effects of Mass Communication. Joseph T. Klapper. LC 60-14402. 1960. text ed. 14.95 (ISBN 0-02-917380-9). Free Pr.

Effects of Metals on Cells, Subcellular Elements, & Macromolecules. Ed. by Jack Maniloff et al. (Illus.). 416p. 1970. text ed. 28.75 (ISBN 0-398-01210-5). C C Thomas.

Effects of Microelectronic Technologies on Employment Prospects. K. Green & Rod Coombs. 240p. 1980. text ed. 36.75x (ISBN 0-566-00418-6, Pub. by Gower Pub Co England). Renouf.

Effects of Noise on Hearing. Ed. by Donald Henderson et al. LC 75-14576. 1976. 43.50 (ISBN 0-89004-012-5). Raven.

Effects of Nuclear War. Office of Technology Assessment, Congress of the U.S. LC 79-8544. 160p. text ed. 9.95 (ISBN 0-916672-36-0). Allanheld.

Effects of Pollutants on Aquatic Organisms. Ed. by A. P. Lockwood. LC 75-32448. (Society for Experimental Biology Seminar Ser.: No. 2). 180p. 1976. 39.50 (ISBN 0-521-21103-4); pap. 14.95x (ISBN 0-521-29044-9). Cambridge U Pr.

Effects of Psychological Therapy. 2nd, enl. ed. S. J. Rachman & G. T. Wilson. (FEBS Ser.: Vol. 24). 400p. 1980. 53.00 (ISBN 0-08-024675-3); pap. 16.00 (ISBN 0-08-024674-5). Pergamon.

Effects of Psychotherapy. S. Rachman. 196p. 1971. 25.00 (ISBN 0-08-016805-1); pap. 12.75 (ISBN 0-08-016807-8). Pergamon.

Effects of Radiation on Cellular Proliferation & Differentiation. 1968. pap. 26.75 (ISBN 92-0-010268-9, IAEA). Unipub.

Effects of Regulations on Housing Costs: Two Case Studies. ULI Research Division. LC 77-82249. (ULI Research Report Ser.: No. 27). (Illus.). 34p. 1977. pap. 11.75 (ISBN 0-87420-327-9). Urban Land.

Effects of Social Security on Income & the Capital Stock. Michael R. Darby. 1979. pap. 4.25 (ISBN 0-8447-3329-6). Am Enterprise.

Effects of Taurine on Excitable Tissue. Ed. by James J. Kocsis et al. 1980. write for info. (ISBN 0-89335-125-3). Spectrum Pub.

Effects of Taxation on Base Metal Mining in Canada. Brian W. Mackenzie & Michel L. Bolodeau. 190p. (Orig.). 1979. pap. text ed. 9.50x (ISBN 0-88757-012-7, Pub. by Ctr Resource Stud Canada). Renouf.

Effects of the Works Program on Rural Relief. Rebecca Farnham & Irene Link. LC 73-165682. (FDR & the Era of the New Deal Ser). 1971. Repr. of 1938 ed. lib. bdg. 15.00 (ISBN 0-306-70345-9). Da Capo.

Effects of Urban Growth: A Population Impact Analysis. Richard P. Appelbaum et al. LC 75-23952. (Illus.). 1976. 32.50 (ISBN 0-275-55980-7). Praeger.

Effects of Various Diseases on the Development of Atherosclerosis. Anatolii M. Vikhert & Valentin S. Zhdanov. Ed. by James E. Muller. LC 80-13069. 220p. 1981. 9.50 (ISBN 0-08-025555-8). Pergamon.

Effects of Weapons on Ecosystems. J. P. Robinson. LC 79-41226. (Illus.). 76p. 1979. 11.50 (ISBN 0-08-025656-2). Pergamon.

Effects on Human Health of Subtherapeutic Use of Antimicrobials in Animal Feeds. Committee to the Human Health Effects of Subtherapeutic Antibiotic Use in Animal Feeds. LC 80-81486. 1980. pap. text ed. 10.25 (ISBN 0-309-03044-7). Natl Acad Pr.

Effectual Fervent Prayer. A. W. Pink. Ed. by Donald R. White. 176p. 1981. 8.95 (ISBN 0-8010-7059-7). Baker Bk.

Efficacy of Treatment Procedures in Periodontics. Diarmuid Shanley. 340p. 1980. 68.00 (ISBN 0-931386-43-8). Quint Pub Co.

Efficiency & Empire. Arnold White. Ed. by G. R. Searle. LC 70-131993. (Society & Victorians: No. 15). 315p. 1973. Repr. of 1901 ed. text ed. 17.25x (ISBN 0-901759-42-2). Humanities.

Efficiency in Government Through Systems Analysis. Roland N. McKean. LC 58-7902. 1958. 31.95 (ISBN 0-471-58773-7, Pub. by Wiley-Interscience). Wiley.

Efficiency in Liberal Education. Carnegie Commission on Higher Education. Ed. by H. R. Bowen & G. R. Douglas. 1971. 9.95 o.p. (ISBN 0-07-010034-9, P&RB). McGraw.

Efficiency in the Social Services. Alan Williams & Robert Anderson. (Aspects of Social Policy Ser.). 1975. 14.00x (ISBN 0-631-16570-3, Pub. by Basil Blackwell); pap. 12.50x (ISBN 0-631-16580-0). Biblio Dist.

Efficient Accounting & Record Keeping. Dennis M. Doyle. Ed. by David Brownstone. LC 78-2474. (Small Business Profit Program Ser.). 1978. pap. text ed. 4.95 (ISBN 0-471-05044-X). Wiley.

Efficient Accounting & Record Keeping, 5 vol. set. Dennis M. Doyle. LC 78-2474. (Wiley Small Business Ser.). 1977. 19.95 o.p. (ISBN 0-471-04295-1). Wiley.

Efficient Capital Markets & Accounting: A Critical Analysis. Thomas Dyckman et al. (Comtemporary Topics in Accounting Ser.). (Illus.). 144p. 1975. pap. 9.95 (ISBN 0-13-246967-7). P-H.

Efficient Comfort Conditioning. W. G. Berl & W. R. Powell. 1979. lib. bdg. 23.00x (ISBN 0-89158-290-8). Westview.

Efficient Electricity Use: A Reference Book on Energy Management for Engineers, Architects, Planners, & Managers. 2nd ed. Ed. by Craig B. Smith. 1978. 49.00 (ISBN 0-08-023227-2). Pergamon.

Efficient Energy Management. Harold P. Mahon et al. (Illus.). 496p. 1981. 24.95 (ISBN 0-13-791434-2). P-H.

Efficient Port. R. B. Oram & C. C. Baker. 1971. 17.25 (ISBN 0-08-016396-3). Pergamon.

Effigies. William K. Wells. (Orig.). 1980. pap. 2.95 (ISBN 0-440-12245-7). Dell.

Effluents from Livestock. Ed. by J. K. Gasser et al. (Illus.). v, 712p. 1980. 80.00x (ISBN 0-85334-895-2). Burgess-Intl Ideas.

Effortless Childbirth...No Such Thing?-a Bibliography. Compiled by Michael A. Weinberg. 57p. (Orig.). 1980. text ed. 3.50 (ISBN 0-9601014-9-7). Weinberg.

EFTS: Electronic Funds Transfer Systems - Elements & Impact. Mark Bender. 112p. 1975. 12.95 (ISBN 0-8046-9119-3, Natl U). Kennikat.

Egermeier's Bible Story Book. Elsie G. Egermeirer. 1975. pap. 1.95 (ISBN 0-89129-010-9). Jove Pubns.

Egg & I. Betty MacDonald. LC 45-336. 1963. 10.95 (ISBN 0-397-00279-3). Lippincott.

Egg Book. Illus. by Jack Kent. LC 74-13662. (Illus.). 32p. (ps-1). 1975. 5.95g o.s.i. (ISBN 0-02-750200-7). Macmillan.

Egg Cookbook. Jackie Hobbs et al. (Illus.). 136p. (Orig.). 1979. pap. 6.75 (ISBN 0-589-01220-7, Pub. by Reed Books Australia). C E Tuttle.

Egg; or, the Memoirs of Gregory Giddy, Esq., with the Lucubrations of Messrs. F. Flimsy, F. Florid, Etc., 1772. (Flowering of the Novel, 1740-1775 Ser: Vol. 99). 1974. lib. bdg. 50.00 (ISBN 0-8240-1198-8). Garland Pub.

Egg Science & Technology. 2nd ed. William J. Stadelman & Owen J. Cotterill. (Illus.). 1977. lib. bdg. 28.50 (ISBN 0-87055-261-9); pap. text ed. 19.50 (ISBN 0-87055-292-9). AVI.

Egg Tree. Katherine Milhous. (Illus.). 32p. (gr. k-3). pap. 2.95 (ISBN 0-689-70492-5, A-119, Aladdin). Atheneum.

Egghead Republic. Arno Schmidt. LC 80-670270. 164p. 1980. 12.00 (ISBN 0-7145-2591-X, Pub. by M. Boyars). Merrimack Bk Serv.

Eggless Cookbook. Helen R. Sattler. LC 77-169071. 224p. 1972. 8.95 o.p. (ISBN 0-498-01049-X). A S Barnes.

Eggs & Cheese. The Editors of Time-Life Books. (Good Cook Ser.). (Illus.). 176p. 1981. 12.95 (ISBN 0-8094-2887-3). Time-Life.

Eggs As Usual Breakfast Etc. Nidra Poller. 26p. (gr. 2 up). 1980. PLB 10.00 stiched binding (ISBN 0-686-68704-3) Lawrence Hill.

Eggs, Milk & Cheese. Peggie Benton & Ninette Lyon. 1971. 10.95 (ISBN 0-571-08302-1, Pub. by Faber & Faber). Merrimack Bk Serv.

Eggs, Milk & Cheese. Ninette Lyon & Peggie Benton. 288p. 1971. 12.50x (ISBN 0-571-08302-1). Intl Pubns Serv.

Egil's Saga. Tr. by Hermann Palsson & Paul Edwards. 1977. pap. 2.95 (ISBN 0-14-044321-5). Penguin.

Eglise Latine et le Protestantisme, Au Point De Vue De l'Eglise d'Orient. Aleksiei S. Khomiakov. LC 80-2362. 1981. Repr. of 1872 ed. 49.00 (ISBN 0-404-18908-3). AMS Pr.

Eglogs, Epytaphes, & Sonettes, (1563) Barnabe Googe. LC 68-24209. (Illus.). 1969. Repr. of 1563 ed. lib. bdg. 20.00x (ISBN 0-8201-1060-4). Schol Facsimiles.

Egmont. Johann W. Goethe. Ed. by H. M. Waidson. (German Text Ser.). 1960. pap. 9.95x (ISBN 0-631-01670-8, Pub. by Basil Blackwell). Biblio Dist.

Ego & Archetype. Edward F. Edinger. 1973. pap. 6.95 (ISBN 0-14-021728-2, Pelican). Penguin.

Ego & Milieu: Theory & Practice of Environmental Therapy. John Cumming & Elaine Cumming. LC 62-18829. 1962. pap. 7.95x (ISBN 0-202-26044-5). Aldine Pub.

Ego Functions in Schizophrenics, Neurotics, & Normals: A Systematic Study of Conceptual, Diagnostic, & Therapeutic Aspects. Leopold Bellak et al. LC 73-3199. (Personality Processes Ser.). 688p. 1973. 39.95 (ISBN 0-471-06413-0, Pub. by Wiley-Interscience). Wiley.

Ego, Hunger & Aggression: The Beginning of Gestalt Therapy. Frederick S. Perls. LC 68-28547. 1969. pap. 2.95 (ISBN 0-394-70558-0, Vin). Random.

Ego King, 2 vols. in 1. James T. Henke & John Dean. Incl. Archetype Approach to Elizabethean Political Thought & Shakespeare's Henry VII Plays; Shakespeare's Romances & Herodotus' Histories. (Salzburg Studies in English Literature: Jacobean Drama Studies: No. 74). 1977. pap. text ed. 25.00x (ISBN 0-391-01405-6). Humanities.

Ego Psychology & Communication: Theory for the Interview. Norman A. Polansky. LC 74-116533. 1971. 17.95x (ISBN 0-202-26052-6). Aldine Pub.

Ego-States & Hidden Observers & the Women in Black & the Lady in White. John G. Watkins & Helen H. Watkins. (Sound Seminars Ser.). 1980. transcript & tapes 29.50x (ISBN 0-88432-066-9, 29400-29401). J Norton Pubs.

Egon Ronay's Lucasa Guide 1981: To Hotels, Resturants, Inns in Great Britain & Ireland & Guide to 740 Furnished Apartments in London. rev. ed. Egon Ronay. LC 74-644899. (Illus.). 830p. 1981. pap. 12.95 (ISBN 0-03-058958-4). HR&W.

Egon Ronay's Nineteen Eighty-One Pub Guide. rev. ed. Egon Ronay. (Illus.). 1981. pap. price not set (ISBN 0-14-005813-3, Pub. by Auto Assn-British Tourist Authority England). Merrimack Bk Serv.

Egon Schiele: Watercolors & Drawings. Galerie St. Etienne. (Illus.). 155p. 1968. pap. 12.00 o.p. (ISBN 0-910810-01-X). Johannes.

Egon Schiele: World of Art. Frank Whitford. (Illus.). 288p. 1981. 17.95 (ISBN 0-19-520245-7); pap. 9.95 (ISBN 0-19-520246-5). Oxford U Pr.

Egotistical Sublime: A History of Wordsworth's Imagination. Henry J. Jones. LC 78-2460. ix, 212p. 1979. Repr. of 1954 ed. lib. bdg. 19.25x (ISBN 0-313-20307-5). Greenwood.

Egoyomi & Surimono: Their History & Development. Matthi Forrer. (Illus.). 1977. pap. text ed. 23.00x (ISBN 90-70265-01-X). Humanities.

Egypt. Jacques Berque. (Illus.). 1972. 37.50 o.p. (ISBN 0-686-24608-X, Pub. by Faber & Faber). Merrimack Bk Serv.

Egypt. Nina Nelson. 1978. 22.50 (ISBN 0-7134-3181-4). David & Charles.

Egypt. Helen O'Clery. LC 79-436011. (Pegasus Books: No. 17). (Illus.). 185p. 1968. 7.50x (ISBN 0-234-77155-0). Intl Pubns Serv.

Egypt. Michael Von Haag. LC 77-70186. (Countries Ser.). (Illus.). 1977. lib. bdg. 7.95 (ISBN 0-686-51151-4). Silver.

Egypt: Activities & Projects in Color. Josie Farnay & Claude Soleillant. LC 78-66309. (Illus.). 1979. 9.95 (ISBN 0-8069-4554-0); PLB 9.29 (ISBN 0-8069-4555-9). Sterling.

Egypt & East Mediterranean World 2200-1900 B.C. W. Ward. (Arab Background Ser.). 1971. 18.00x (ISBN 0-685-72041-1). Intl Bk Ctr.

Egypt & the Fertile Crescent, 1516-1922: A Political History. Peter M. Holt. LC 66-18429. 1969. pap. 6.95 (ISBN 0-8014-9079-0, CP79). Cornell U Pr.

Egypt & the Holy Land in Historic Photographs: Seventy-Seven Views. Francis Frith. Ed. by Julia Van Haaften. 112p. 1981. pap. 7.00 (ISBN 0-486-24048-7). Dover.

Egypt: Burdens of the Past, Options for the Future. John Waterbury. LC 78-3248. (Illus.). 336p. 1978. pap. 9.95x (ISBN 0-253-28092-3). Ind U Pr.

Egypt: Economic Management in a Period of Transition. Khalid Ikram. LC 80-552. (World Bank Country Economic Report). (Illus.). 464p. 1981. text ed. 32.50x (ISBN 0-8018-2418-4); pap. text ed. 10.50x (ISBN 0-8018-2419-2). Johns Hopkins.

Egypt in Modern Times. John Richmond. LC 77-1969. 1977. 17.50x (ISBN 0-231-04296-5). Columbia U Pr.

Egypt in the Arab World 1952-1970: The Elements of a Dynamic Foreign Policy. A. I. Dawisha. LC 76-7517. 1976. 32.95 (ISBN 0-470-19960-1). Halsted Pr.

Egypt-Israel Treaty & the Peace-War Prospects for the World. John S. Watterson. (Illus.). 1979. deluxe ed. 59.75 (ISBN 0-930008-40-5). Inst Econ Pol.

Egypt of the Pharaohs: An Introduction. Alan Gardiner. (Illus.). 1966. pap. 7.95 (ISBN 0-19-500267-9, 165, GB). Oxford U Pr.

Egypt: Rebirth on the Nile. Lila Perl. (gr. 5-9). 1977. 8.75 o.p. (ISBN 0-688-22106-8); lib. bdg. 8.88 (ISBN 0-688-32106-2). Morrow.

Egypt Since Cromer, 2 Vols. G. A. Lloyd. LC 68-9625. 1970. Repr. Set. 28.50 (ISBN 0-86527-056-2). Fertig.

Egyptian Army in Politics: Pattern for New Nations. Panayiotis J. Vatikiotis. LC 72-6216. 300p. 1975. Repr. of 1961 ed. lib. bdg. 25.50x (ISBN 0-8371-6473-7, VAEA). Greenwood.

Egyptian Art. Cyril Aldred. (World of Art Ser.). (Illus.). 300p. 1980. 17.95 (ISBN 0-19-520223-6); pap. 9.95 (ISBN 0-19-520224-4). Oxford U Pr.

Egyptian Boats. Geoffrey Scott. LC 80-27676. (Carolrhoda on My Own Bk). (Illus.). 48p. (gr. k-3). 1981. PLB 5.95 (ISBN 0-87614-138-6). Carolrhoda Bks.

Egyptian Book of the Dead: The Papyrus of Ani in the British Museum. E. A. Wallis Budge. 1967. pap. 5.95 (ISBN 0-486-21866-X). Dover.

Egyptian Book of the Dead: The Papyrus of Ani. E. A. Budge. 12.50 (ISBN 0-8446-1764-4). Peter Smith.

Egyptian Childhood. Taha Hussein. (Arab Writers Series). 200p. (Orig.). 1980. 10.00x (ISBN 0-89410-210-9); pap. 5.00x (ISBN 0-89410-211-7). Three Continents.

Egyptian Designs in Modern Stitchery. Pauline Fischer & Mary L. Smith. LC 78-11162. (Illus.). 1979. 14.95 o.p. (ISBN 0-87690-316-2). Dutton.

Egyptian Drawings. William Peck & John Ross. LC 78-52246. (Illus.). 1978. 24.95 o.p. (ISBN 0-525-09691-4). Dutton.

Egyptian Earth. A. R. Sharkawi. Tr. by Desmond Stewart from Arabic. 255p. 1973. pap. 3.00 (ISBN 0-88253-121-2). Ind-US Inc.

Egyptian Economy 1952-1972. Robert Mabro. (Economies of the World Ser). 368p. 1974. text ed. 24.00x (ISBN 0-19-877030-8). Oxford U Pr.

Egyptian Gods: A Handbook. A. W. Shorter. 1978. 12.00 (ISBN 0-7100-0037-5). Routledge & Kegan.

Egyptian Magic. E. Wallis Budge. (Illus.). 1979. pap. 6.95 (ISBN 0-7100-0135-5). Routledge & Kegan.

Egyptian Plays. Ed. by Denys Johnson-Davies. (Arab Writers Series). 220p. (Orig.). 1981. 10.00 (ISBN 0-89410-236-2); pap. 5.00 (ISBN 0-89410-237-0). Three Continents.

Egyptian Religion. E. Wallis Budge. (Illus.). 1979. pap. 6.95 (ISBN 0-7100-0134-7). Routledge & Kegan.

Egyptian Revival: Its Sources, Monuments, & Meaning, 1808-1858. Richard G. Carrott. (Illus.). 1978. 24.50 (ISBN 0-520-03324-8). U of Cal Pr.

Egyptian Short Stories. Tr. by Denys Johnson-Davies from Arabic. 1978. 9.00 (ISBN 0-89410-038-6); pap. 5.00 (ISBN 0-89410-039-4). Three Continents.

Egyptian Stelae, Relief & Printings from the Petrie Collection. H. M. Stewart. (Modern Egyptology Ser.). 100p. 40.00x (ISBN 0-85668-171-7, Pub. by Aris & Phillips England). Intl Schol Bk Serv.

Egyptian Way of Death: Mummies & the Cult of the Immortal. Ange-Pierre Leca. LC 78-68326. (Illus.). 312p. 1981. 12.95 (ISBN 0-385-14609-4). Doubleday.

Egyptians. Anne Millard et al. LC 77-86182. (Peoples of the Past Ser.). (Illus.). 1977. lib. bdg. 7.95 (ISBN 0-686-51156-5). Silver.

Egypt's Liberal Experiment, 1922-1936. Afaf L. Al-Sayyid-Marsot. 1977. 20.00x (ISBN 0-520-03109-1). U of Cal Pr.

Egypt's Young Rebels: "Young Egypt", 1933-1952. James P. Jankowski. LC 75-8654. (Publications Ser.: No.145). 1975. 7.00 (ISBN 0-8179-6451-7). Hoover Inst Pr.

Ehe Ist Tot: Lang Lebe Die Ehe! Craig A. Guggenbuhl. 1976. pap. 6.00 o.p. (ISBN 0-89192-086-2). Interbk Inc.

Ehrengard. Isak Dinesen. LC 74-17033. 1975. pap. 1.95 (ISBN 0-394-71431-8, Vin). Random.

Ehrerecht der Orientalischen Kirche. Joseph Zhishman. LC 80-2367. 1981. Repr. of 1864 ed. 63.50 (ISBN 0-404-18918-0). AMS Pr.

Ei, Deus. Tr. by Frank Foglio. (Portuguese Bks.). 1979. 1.25 (ISBN 0-8297-0791-3). Life Pubs Intl.

Eichmann in Jerusalem: A Report of the Banality of Evil. rev ed. Hannah Arendt. 1977. pap. 3.50 (ISBN 0-14-004450-7). Penguin.

EIFAC Fishing Gear Intercalibration Experiments. 92p. 1980. pap. 7.50 (ISBN 92-5-100864-7, F1954, FAO). Unipub.

Eiffel Tower & Other Mythologies. Roland Barthes. Tr. by Richard Howard. 152p. 1979. 9.95 (ISBN 0-8090-4115-4); pap. 4.95 (ISBN 0-8090-1391-6). Hill & Wang.

Eiger Sanction. Trevanian. 1973. pap. 2.25 (ISBN 0-380-00176-4, 42671). Avon.

Eight American Writers. Ed. by Norman Foerster et al. 1963. 19.95x (ISBN 0-393-09524-X, NortonC). Norton.

Eight Approaches to Teaching Composition. Timothy R. Donovan & Ben W. McClelland. 160p. 1980. pap. 6.50 (ISBN 0-8141-1303-6). NCTE.

Eight Boyle Lectures on Atheism. Richard Bentley. Ed. by Rene Wellek. LC 75-11196. (British Philosophers & Theologians of the 17th & 18th Centuries: Vol. 3). 1976. Repr. of 1692 ed. lib. bdg. 42.00 (ISBN 0-8240-1752-8). Garland Pub.

Eight Chinese Plays. Tr. by William Dolby. 1978. 13.00x (ISBN 0-231-04488-7). Columbia U Pr.

Eight Exciting Adventures. Mary Verdick. Ed. by Harry Rich & Richard Smolinski. (Pal Paperbacks Ser., Kit A). (Illus., Orig.). (gr. 7-12). 1976. pap. text ed. 1.25 (ISBN 0-8374-3489-0). Xerox Ed Pubns.

Eight Expressionist Plays. August Strindberg. Tr. by Arvid Paulson. LC 65-11852. 512p. 1972. 15.00x (ISBN 0-8147-6556-4); pap. 8.00 (ISBN 0-8147-6558-0). NYU Pr.

Eight Haunted Stories. Ed. by Robert Vitarelli. (Pal Paperbacks Ser., Kit B). (Illus., Orig.). (gr. 7-12). 1973. pap. text ed. 1.25 (ISBN 0-8374-3519-6). Xerox Ed Pubns.

Eight-Hundred Years of Finnish Architecture. J. M. Richards. (Illus.). 1978. 32.00 (ISBN 0-7153-7512-1). David & Charles.

Eight Immortal Flavors. rev. & expanded ed. Johnny Kan & Charles L. Leong. Ed. by Bonnie Dahan. LC 79-53192. 256p. 1980. 10.95 (ISBN 0-89395-032-7); pap. 6.95 (ISBN 0-89395-060-2). Cal Living Bks.

Eight Language Dictionary of Medical Technology. Ed. by Ronald Albert & Harry Hahnewald. LC 78-40828. 1979. 75.00 (ISBN 0-08-023763-0). Pergamon.

Eight Lithographs: Murals at Jiquilpan. J. C. Orozco. Set. 12.50 (ISBN 0-911268-06-5). Rogers Bk.

Eight Men. Richard Wright. (gr. 10 up). 1969. pap. 1.50 o.s.i. (ISBN 0-515-02034-6, V2034). Jove Pubns.

Eight Modern Writers. John I. Stewart. (Oxford History of English Literature Ser.). 1963. 37.50x (ISBN 0-19-812207-1). Oxford U Pr.

Eight Nights: A Chanukah Counting Book. Jane Bearman. Ed. by Daniel B. Syme. LC 78-60781. (Illus.). 1979. pap. 4.50 (ISBN 0-8074-0025-4, 102562). UAHC.

Eight-Place Tables of Trigonometric Functions for Every Second of Arc. Jean Peters. 1963. 35.00 (ISBN 0-8284-0174-8); thumb index ed. 39.00 (ISBN 0-8284-0185-3). Chelsea Pub.

Eight Plays for Boys. N. L. Clay. pap. text ed. 3.25x o.p. (ISBN 0-435-21002-5). Heinemann Ed.

Eight Plays from Off-Off Broadway. Ed. by Nick Orzel & Michael Smith. 1966. pap. 4.95 o.p. (ISBN 0-672-50656-4). Bobbs.

Eight Rate & Prepayment Mortgage Yield Table No. 56. Financial Publishing Co. 12.50 o.p. (ISBN 0-685-02556-X). Finan Pub.

Eight Scandanavian Novelists: Criticism & Reviews in English. Compiled by John Budd. LC 80-24895. 192p. 1981. lib. bdg. 25.00 (ISBN 0-313-22869-8, BSN/). Greenwood.

Eight Short, Short Stories & Sketches. James T. Farrell. 1981. write for info. (ISBN 0-933292-08-2); pap. price not set (ISBN 0-933292-07-4). Arts End.

Eight-Step Grapevine. Dara Wier. LC 80-65699. (Poetry Ser.). 1980. 9.95 (ISBN 0-915604-37-X); pap. 4.95 (ISBN 0-915604-38-8). Carnegie-Mellon.

Eight Stories from the Rest of the Robots. Isaac Asimov. 1978. pap. 1.50 (ISBN 0-515-04551-9). Jove Pubns.

Eight Thousand & Eighty Six Book. Russell Rector & George Alexy. 1980. pap. 16.99 (ISBN 0-931988-29-2). Osborne-McGraw.

Eight Thousand Eighty Microcomputer Experiments. Howard Boyet. 416p. 1979. pap. 16.95 (ISBN 0-918398-08-8). Dilithium Pr.

Eight Words for Thirsty. Ann Sigford. LC 79-13892. (Story of Environmental Action Ser.). (Illus.). (gr. 7 up). 1979. PLB 8.95 (ISBN 0-87518-183-X). Dillon.

Eight Years in Another World. Harding Lemay. LC 80-69363. 1981. 10.95 (ISBN 0-689-11149-5). Atheneum.

Eighteen Editions of the Dewey Decimal Classification. John P. Comaromi. LC 76-10604. 1976. 10.00x (ISBN 0-910608-17-2). Forest Pr.

Eighteen Eighty-Eight Message. Robert Wieland. LC 80-10807. (Horizon Ser.). 1980. pap. 4.50 (ISBN 0-8127-0283-2). Southern Pub.

Eighteen-Forty Census of the Republic of Texas. Ed. by Gifford White. 19.50 (ISBN 0-8363-0029-7). Jenkins.

Eighteen Forty-Three Rebecca Eighteen Forty-Seven. Abbot Cutler. (Chapbook Ser.: No. 4). 64p. (Orig.). 1981. pap. 4.95 (ISBN 0-937672-03-3). Rowan Tree.

Eighteen-Hundred Riddles, Enigmas & Conundrums. Darwin A. Hindman. (Orig.). (gr. 4 up). 1963. pap. 2.50 (ISBN 0-486-21059-6). Dover.

Eighteen Ninety-Five to Nineteen Eleven. Roy J. Wright & Richard M. Wagner. (Cincinnati Streetcars: No.5). 1971. pap. 4.75 o.s.i. (ISBN 0-914196-10-3). Trolley Talk.

Eighteen Ninety-Seven Sears Roebuck Catalogue. abr. ed. Ed. by Fred L. Israel. LC 80-69200. (Illus.). 320p. 1981. pap. 2.75 (ISBN 0-87754-138-8). Chelsea Hse.

Eighteen Ninetys' Stories, Verses & Essays. Ed. by Leon Cantrell. (Portable Australian Authors Ser.). 1978. 12.75x (ISBN 0-7022-1037-4); pap. 8.50x (ISBN 0-7022-1038-2). U of Queensland Pr.

Eighteen Silent Years. Gordon Lindsay. (Life of Christ & Parable Ser.). 0.95 o.p. (ISBN 0-89985-162-2). Christ Nations.

Eighteen Stories. Heinrich Boll. Tr. by Leila Vennewitz from Ger. 1966. 6.95 o.p. (ISBN 0-07-006403-2, GB); pap. 3.95 o.p. (ISBN 0-07-006416-4). McGraw.

Eighteen Thirty Federal Population Census Index of Ohio, 2 vols. Ohio Family Historians. 1976. Repr. of 1964 ed. 42.50 set (ISBN 0-911060-06-5). Vol. 1 (ISBN 0-911060-04-9). Vol. 2 (ISBN 0-911060-05-7). Ohio Lib Foun.

Eighteen Twenty Federal Population Census Index of Ohio. Ohio Family Historians. 1976. Repr. of 1964 ed. 29.75 (ISBN 0-685-70950-7). Ohio Lib Foun.

Eighteen Years in the Khyber, 1879-1898. Robert Warburton. (Illus.). 15.50x o.p. (ISBN 0-19-636057-9). Oxford U Pr.

Eighteenth Brumaire of Louis Bonaparte. Marx. 1978. pap. 1.95 (ISBN 0-8351-0578-4). China Bks.

Eighteenth Century. Ed. by Pat Rogers. LC 78-15568. (Context of English Literature). 1978. text ed. 28.50x (ISBN 0-8419-0421-9); pap. text ed. 14.50x (ISBN 0-8419-0422-7). Holmes & Meier.

Eighteenth Century Background: Studies on the Idea of Nature in the Thought of the Period. Basil Willey. LC 40-31307. 1941. 20.00x (ISBN 0-231-01234-9). Columbia U Pr.

Eighteenth Century Bibliographies. Francesco Cordasco. LC 70-8541. 1970. 9.50 o.p. (ISBN 0-8108-0288-0). Scarecrow.

Eighteenth-Century Constitution: Documents & Commentary. E. N. Williams. (English Constitutional History Ser). 47.95 (ISBN 0-521-06810-X); pap. 14.95x (ISBN 0-521-09123-3). Cambridge U Pr.

Eighteenth Century Creche. Hanns Swarzenski. (Illus.). 1966. 7.50 (ISBN 0-87846-046-2); pap. 2.00 (ISBN 0-87846-162-0). Mus Fine Arts Boston.

Eighteenth Century Creche. Hanns Swarzenski. LC 66-25450. (Illus.). 1966. pap. 2.00 (ISBN 0-87846-142-6, Pub. by Mus Fine Arts Boston). C E Tuttle.

Eighteenth Century Education: Selected Sources. Ed. by Victor E. Neuberg. (Social History of Education Second Ser.: No. 2). 1981. 25.00x (ISBN 0-7130-0011-2, Pub. by Woburn Pr England). Biblio Dist.

Eighteenth-Century Encounters: Essays on Literature & Society in the Age of Walpole. Pat Rogers. 220p. 1980. 21.00x (ISBN 0-389-20090-5). B&N.

Eighteenth Century England Seventeen Fourteen to Seventeen Eighty-Four. 2nd ed. Dorothy Marshall. (A History of England Ser.). (Illus.). 572p. 1975. pap. text ed. 14.50 (ISBN 0-582-48316-6). Longman.

Eighteenth-Century English Literature: Modern Essays in Criticism. Ed. by James L. Clifford. (Orig.). 1959. pap. 5.95 (ISBN 0-19-500682-8, GB). Oxford U Pr.

Eighteenth-Century English Poetry. Peter Thorpe. LC 74-17807. 14.95 (ISBN 0-88229-196-3); pap. 7.95x (ISBN 0-88229-581-0). Nelson-Hall.

Eighteenth-Century Florida: Life on the Frontier. Ed. by Samuel Proctor. LC 76-5852. (Papers on the Annual Bicentennial Symposia: No. 3). 1976. 7.00 (ISBN 0-8130-0523-X). U Presses Fla.

Eighteenth-Century Florida: The Impact of the American Revolution. Ed. by Samuel Proctor. LC 78-1870. (Papers of the Annual Bicentennail Symposia: No. 5). 1978. 9.00 (ISBN 0-8130-0589-2). U Presses Fla.

Eighteenth Century Gold Boxes of Europe. Kenneth J. Snowman. (Illus.). 1966. 70.00 o.p. (ISBN 0-571-06800-6, Pub. by Faber & Faber). Merrimack Bk Serv.

Eighteenth Century Imitative Counterpoint: Music for Analysis. Wallace Berry & Edward Chudacoff. (Orig.). 1969. pap. 20.95 (ISBN 0-13-246843-3). P-H.

Eighteenth Century in Russia. Ed. by J. G. Garrard. (Illus.). 348p. 1973. 29.95x (ISBN 0-19-815638-3). Oxford U Pr.

Eighteenth Century Novel: The Idea of the Gentleman. Homai J. Shroff. 1978. text ed. 13.50x (ISBN 0-391-01067-0). Humanities.

Eighteenth Century Philosophy. Lewis W. Beck. LC 66-10364. (Orig.). 1966. pap. text ed. 6.95 (ISBN 0-02-902100-6). Free Pr.

Eighteenth Century Poetry & Prose. 3rd ed. Ed. by L. I. Bredvold et al. 1493p. 1973. text ed. 21.95 (ISBN 0-8260-1281-7). Wiley.

Eighteenth Century Russia: A Select Bibliography of Works Published Since 1955. P. H. Clendenning & R. Bartlett. (Russian Bibliography Ser.: No. 3). (Illus.). 260p. 1981. 18.00 (ISBN 0-89250-110-3); pap. 8.95 (ISBN 0-89250-111-1). Orient Res Partners.

Eighteenth Century Spanish Literature. R. Merritt Cox. (World Authors Ser.: No. 526). 1979. lib. bdg. 10.95 (ISBN 0-8057-6367-8). Twayne.

Eighteenth-Century Studies: In Honor of Donald F. Hyde. Ed. by W. H. Bond. LC 77-123045. (Illus.). xv, 424p. 1970. 30.00x (ISBN 0-8139-0446-3, Grolier Club). U Pr of Va.

Eighteenth Century Waifs. John Ashton. LC 68-58971. 1968. Repr. of 1887 ed. 18.00 (ISBN 0-8103-3517-4). Gale.

Eighteenth Emergency. Betsy Byars. (gr. 4-6). 1974. pap. 1.75 (ISBN 0-380-00099-7, 51367, Camelot). Avon.

Eighth A-J Assembling. Ed. by Richard Kostelanetz & Henry J. Korn. (Illus.). 1978. pap. 4.95 (ISBN 0-685-49935-9). Assembling Pr.

Eighth Circle. Stanley Ellin. (Foul Play Press Ser.). 224p. 1981. pap. 4.95 (ISBN 0-914378-67-8). Countryman.

Eighth Day of the Week. 3rd ed. Bernard R. Belden. Ed. by Bamman A. Henry. (Kaleidoscope Ser.). 1978. pap. text ed. 6.08 (ISBN 0-201-40881-3, Sch Div); tchr's. ed. 6.64 (ISBN 0-201-40882-1). A-W.

Eighth Grade. Frieda Van Atta. 1.00 ea. Gr. 6 (ISBN 0-394-40976-0). Gr. 7 (ISBN 0-394-40977-9). Gr. 8 (ISBN 0-394-40978-7). Random.

Eighth International Congress on X-Ray Optics & Microanalysis. Ed. by Donald R. Beaman et al. LC 77-18656. 665p. 90.00 (ISBN 0-87812-180-3). Pendell Pub.

Eighth Sin. Stefan Kanfer. 1979. pap. 2.50 o.p. (ISBN 0-425-04263-4). Berkley Pub.

Eighth Symposium on Nucleic Acids Chemistry: Proceedings. (Nucleic Acids Symposium Ser.: No. 8). 198p. 1980. 20.00 (ISBN 0-904147-28-2). Info Retrieval.

Eighth Tower. John Keel. 1977. pap. 1.75 o.p. (ISBN 0-451-07460-2, E7460, Sig). NAL.

Eighties Odes. Mary Gribble. 1981. 4.75 (ISBN 0-8062-1662-X). Carlton.

Eighty-Eight Rue de Charonne: Adventures in Wood Finishing. George Frank. LC 80-54431. (Illus.). 128p. 1981. 9.95 (ISBN 0-918804-06-X, Dist. by Van Nostrand Reinhold). Taunton.

Eighty-Eighty - Eighty-Eighty-Five Software Design, Bk 2. Christopher A. Titus et al. LC 78-57207. 1979. pap. 10.95 (ISBN 0-672-21615-9, 21615). Sams.

Eighty-Eighty - ZEighty Assembly Language: Techniques for Improved Programming. Alan R. Miller. 224p. 1980. pap. text ed. 8.95 (ISBN 0-471-08124-8). Wiley.

Eighty-Eighty A - Eighty Eighty-Five Assembly Language Programming. Lance A. Leventhal. (Assembly Language Programming Ser.: No. 1). (Orig.). 1978. pap. text ed. 15.99 (ISBN 0-931988-10-1). Osborne-McGraw.

Eighty-Eighty A Bugbook: Microcomputer Interfacing & Programming. Peter R. Rony et al. LC 77-77399. 1977. pap. 11.95 (ISBN 0-672-21447-4). Sams.

Eighty-Eighty, Eighty-Eighty-Five, Software Design, Bk. 1. David Larson et al. LC 78-57207. 1978. pap. 10.95 (ISBN 0-672-21541-1). Sams.

Eighty-Eighty Machine Language Programming for Beginners. Ron Santore. LC 78-53003. 1978. pap. 7.95 (ISBN 0-918398-14-2). Dilithium Pr.

Eighty Eighty-Nine I-O Processor Handbook. Jerry Kane. 200p. (Orig.). 1980. pap. 6.99 (ISBN 0-931988-39-X). Osborne-McGraw.

Eighty Eighty-Six Primer: An Introduction to Its Architecture, System Design & Programming. Stephen P. Morse. 224p. 1980. pap. 9.95 (ISBN 0-8104-5165-4). Hayden.

Eighty English Folk Songs from the Southern Appalachians. Ed. by Cecil Sharp & Maud Karpeles. 1969. pap. 2.45 o.p. (ISBN 0-262-61006-X). MIT Pr.

Eighty-First Site. Tony Kenrick. 1980. 10.00 (ISBN 0-453-00379-6, H379). NAL.

Eighty-First Site. Tony Kenrick. 1981. pap. 2.75 (ISBN 0-451-09600-2, E9600, Sig). NAL.

Eighty Million Eyes. Ed McBain. 192p. (Orig.). 1975. pap. 1.25 (ISBN 0-345-29292-8). Ballantine.

Eighty-One Sheriff Street. Gertrude Ford. 272p. 1981. 10.95 (ISBN 0-8119-0343-5). Fell.

Eighty Talks for Orthodox Young People. A. M. Coniaris. 1975. pap. 3.50 (ISBN 0-937032-16-6). Light&Life Pub Co MN.

Eighty Thousand Governments: The Politics of Subnational America. George Berkley & William J. Fox. 1978. text ed. 17.95 (ISBN 0-205-06007-2). Allyn.

Eighty Woodcraft Projects. Ronald P. Oumet. 320p. 1980. 17.95 (ISBN 0-8246-0260-9). Jonathan David.

Eighty Years of Cinema. Peter Cowie. LC 75-5175. (Illus.). 1977. 17.50 o.p. (ISBN 0-498-01762-1). A S Barnes.

Eileen Gray: Designer. J. Stewart Johnson. LC 79-33188. (Illus.). 1979. pap. 7.95 (ISBN 0-87070-308-0). Museum Mod Art.

Ein Fliehendes Pferd. Martin Walser. (Suhrkamp Taschenbuecher: St 600). 176p. (Ger.). 1980. pap. text ed. 3.90 (ISBN 3-518-37100-2, Pub. by Insel Verlag Germany). Suhrkamp.

Ein Messer Fuer Den Ehrlichen Finder. Joerg Steiner. (Suhrkamp Taschenbuecher: 583). 208p. (Ger.). 1980. pap. text ed. 3.90 (ISBN 3-518-37083-9, Pub. by Insel Verlag Germany). Suhrkamp.
Einfuehrung in das Altet Estament. Werner H. Schmidt. (De Gruyter Lehrbuch Ser.). 1979. text ed. 28.25x (ISBN 3-11-002445-4). De Gruyter.
Einfuehrung in Die Aesthetik Adornos. Karl Sauerland. (De Gruyter Studienbuch). 1979. pap. text ed. 16.50x (ISBN 3-11-007167-3). De Gruyter.
Einfuehrung in die Mischna. Chanoch Albeck. (Studia Judaica, 6). 493p. 1971. 41.75x (ISBN 3-11-006429-4). De Gruyter.
Einfuhrung in Die Phanomenologie. Wilhelm Reyer. LC 78-66737. (Phenomenology Ser.: Vol. 11). 475p. 1980. lib. bdg. 44.00 (ISBN 0-8240-9559-6). Garland Pub.
Einleitung in die Allegemeine Sprachwissenschaft. August F. Pott. Bd. with Zur Literature der Sprachenkunde. (Amsterdam Classics in Linguistics, 1800-1925: No. 10). (Orig.). 1979. pap. text ed. 62.75x (ISBN 90-272-0871-9). Humanities.
Einstein: A Centenary Volume. Ed. by A. P. French. LC 78-25968. (Illus.). 1979. text ed. 20.00 (ISBN 0-674-24230-0); pap. 8.95 (ISBN 0-674-24231-9). Harvard U Pr.
Einstein Anderson Makes up for Lost Time. Seymour Simon. (Einstein Anderson, Science Sleuth Ser.). (Illus.). 96p. (gr. 3-7). 1981. 6.95 (ISBN 0-670-29067-X). Viking Pr.
Einstein As I Knew Him. Alan W. Roberts. 7.95 (ISBN 0-89523-001-1). Green Hill.
Einstein: The First Hundred Years. Ed. by Maurice Goldsmith et al. (Illus.). 188p. 1980. 19.95 (ISBN 0-08-025019-X). Pergamon.
Einstein: The Life & Times. Ronald W. Clark. (Illus.). 1972. pap. 3.95 (ISBN 0-380-01159-X, 44123). Avon.
Einstein: The Life & Times. Ronald W. Clark. LC 71-149419. 1971. 15.00 o.s.i. (ISBN 0-690-00448-6, TYC-T). T Y Crowell.
Einstein: The Man & His Achievement. Ed. by G. J. Whitrow. LC 72-98113. 94p. 1973. pap. 2.25 (ISBN 0-486-22934-3). Dover.
Einstein's Brain. Mark Olshaker. 324p. 1981. 10.95 (ISBN 0-87131-342-1). M Evans.
Einstein's Theory of Relativity. rev. ed. Max Born. 1962. pap. 4.95 (ISBN 0-486-60769-0). Dover.
EIS Cumulative: 1978. Herner & Co. Staff. LC 79-640191. 1979. text ed. 75.00 (ISBN 0-87815-025-0). Info Resources.
EIS Cumulative 1979. Herver & Co. Staff. LC 79-640191. 459p. 1979. 75.00 (ISBN 0-87815-029-3). Info Resources.
Eisenhower Administration, Nineteen Fifty-Three to Nineteen Sixty-One: A Documentary History, 2 vols. Robert L. Branyan. LC 71-164935. 1971. Set. lib. bdg. 85.00 (ISBN 0-313-20126-9). Greenwood.
Eisenhower & Berlin, Nineteen Forty Five: The Decision to Halt at the Elbe. Stephen E. Ambrose. (Essays in American History Ser). (Illus.). 1967. pap. 4.95 (ISBN 0-393-05342-3). Norton.
Eisenhower & the Cold War. Robert A. Divine. (Illus.). 160p. 1981. 14.95 (ISBN 0-19-502823-6). Oxford U Pr.
Eisenhower & the Cold War. Robert A. Divine. 160p. 1981. pap. 3.95 (ISBN 0-19-502824-4, 621, GB). Oxford U Pr.
Eisenhower & the Jews. Judah Nadich. (Return to Zion Ser.). (Illus.). 271p. 1980. Repr. of 1953 ed. lib. bdg. 20.00x (ISBN 0-87991-122-0). Porcupine Pr.
Eisenhower As President. Ed. by Dean Albertson. (Orig.). 1963. pap. 2.95 o.p. (ISBN 0-8090-0061-X, AmCen). Hill & Wang.
Eisenhower Deception. Clive Egleton. LC 80-69372. 1981. 10.95 (ISBN 0-689-11127-4). Atheneum.
Eisenhower Declassified. Virgil Pinkley & James F. Scheer. 1979. 12.95 o.p. (ISBN 0-8007-1063-0). Revell.
Eisenhower Diaries. Ed. & intro. by Robert H. Ferrell. (Illus.). 1981. 1.95 (ISBN 0-393-01432-0). Norton.
Eisenhower the President: Crucial Days, 1951-1960. William B. Ewald, Jr. LC 80-22929. 420p. 1981. 12.95 (ISBN 0-13-246868-9). P-H.
Eisenstaedt: Germany. Klaus Honnef et al. (Illus.). 112p. (Orig.). 1981. pap. 12.50 (ISBN 0-87474-530-6). Smithsonian.
Eisenstaedt's Guide to Photography. Alfred Eisenstaedt. (Illus.). 176p. 1981. pap. 11.95 (ISBN 0-14-046483-2). Penguin.
Eisenstein: Three Films: Battleship Potemkin, October, Alexander Nevsky. Ed. by Jay Leyda. LC 74-6548. (Icon Editions: Masterworks Film Ser). (Illus.). 1974. pap. 4.95 o.s.i. (ISBN 0-06-430055-2, IN-55, HarpT). Har-Row.
E.I.T Review. V. Faires & J. Richardson. 1961. 19.95 (ISBN 0-13-279604-X). P-H.
Either-Or, 2 Vols. Soren Kierkegaard. Tr. by W. Lowrie. 1971. Vol. 1. 19.50x (ISBN 0-691-07177-2); Vol. 2. pap. 4.95 (ISBN 0-691-07178-0); Vol 1. pap. 4.95 (ISBN 0-691-01976-2); Vol. 2. pap. 4.95 (ISBN 0-691-01977-0). Princeton U Pr.
Ejecutivo Bajo Stress. Alexander Hamilton Institute, Inc. Ed. by James M. Jenks. (Illus.). 72p. (Orig., Span.). 1976. pap. 44.75x (ISBN 0-86604-008-0, A783158). Hamilton Inst.
Ejercicios de espanol. J. G. Bruton. (gr. 9 up). 1968. 5.15 (ISBN 0-08-012838-6); pap. 4.30 (ISBN 0-08-012837-8). Pergamon.
Ejido Organization in Mexico Nineteen Thirty-Four to Nineteen Seventy-Six. Dana Markiewicz. LC 79-620057. (Special Studies: Vol. 1). 1980. pap. text ed. 6.50 (ISBN 0-87903-501-3). UCLA Lat Am Ctr.
Ekco Economy Cookbook. 7.95 (ISBN 0-916752-25-9). Green Hill.
Ekwall Reading Inventory. Ekwall. 1979. pap. text ed. 6.95 (ISBN 0-205-06674-7); dupl. masters avail. (ISBN 0-205-06676-3). Allyn.
El Alamein. Michael Carver. 1979. 24.00 (ISBN 0-7134-2148-7, Pub. by Batsford England). David & Charles.
El Dorado: The Gold of Ancient Columbia. The Center for Inter-American Relations & The American Federation of Arts. LC 74-175969. (Illus.). 150p. 1980. pap. 14.95 (ISBN 0-295-95736-0). U of Wash Pr.
El Gesticulador: Pieza Para Demagogos En Tres Actos. R. Visigli. Ed. by R. Ballinger. (Span.). 1963. 8.95 (ISBN 0-13-273771-X). P-H.
El Greco. Leo Bronstein. (Library of Great Painters Ser). (Illus.). 1950. 35.00 (ISBN 0-8109-0155-2). Abrams.
El Greco. Jack Lassaigne. (Illus.). 264p. 1974. 28.00 (ISBN 0-500-18142-X); pap. 11.50 (ISBN 0-500-20136-6). Transatlantic.
El Greco Puzzle. John Murphy. 288p. 1976. pap. 1.50 o.p. (ISBN 0-345-25053-2). Ballantine.
El-Hi Textbooks in Print 1980. 11th ed. LC 70-105104. 1980. 35.00 o.p. (ISBN 0-8352-1260-2). Bowker.
El-Hi Textbooks in Print 1981. 800p. 1981. 38.00 (ISBN 0-8352-1357-9). Bowker.
El Intrepido Francisco: Vida y Ministerio de un Editor Evangelico. Mary J. Stewart. 1980. pap. 1.25 (ISBN 0-311-01069-5). Casa Bautista.
El Salvador. Alistair White. (Illus.). 1973. lib. bdg. 19.75x (ISBN 0-510-39523-6). Westview.
El Salvador in Pictures. Sterling Publishing Company Editors. LC 73-93604. (Visual Geography Ser.). (Illus.). 64p. (gr. 5 up). 1974. PLB 4.99 (ISBN 0-8069-1181-6); pap. 2.95 (ISBN 0-8069-1180-8). Sterling.
El Salvador: Landscape & Society. David Browning. (Illus.). 350p. 1971. 29.95x (ISBN 0-19-823208-X). Oxford U Pr.
El Tesoro De la Sierra Madre. B. Traven. Ed. by M. Rodriguez. (Span.). 1963. 8.95 (ISBN 0-13-273771-X). P-H.
Elastic Retort: Essays in Literature & Ideas. Kenneth Rexroth. LC 73-6425. 228p. 1973. 7.95 o.p. (ISBN 0-8164-9168-2). Continuum.
Elastic Solutions for Soil & Rock Mechanics. H. G. Poulos & E. H. Davis. LC 73-17171. (Soil Engineering Ser.). 424p. 1974. text ed. 39.95 (ISBN 0-471-69565-3). Wiley.
Elastic Waves in Solids: Applications to Signal Processing. E. Dieulesaint & D. Royer. LC 80-49980. 1981. write for info. (ISBN 0-471-27836-X, Pub. by Wiley-Interscience). Wiley.
Elasticity in Engineering Mechanics. Arthur P. Boresi & Paul P. Lynn. (Civil Engineering & Engineering Mechanics Ser.). 1974. 31.95 (ISBN 0-13-247080-2). P-H.
Elasticity, Theory & Applications. Herbert Reismann & Peter S. Pawlik. LC 80-10145. 1980. 36.00 (ISBN 0-471-03165-8, Pub. by Wiley Interscience). Wiley.
Elasticity: Theory & Applications. Adel S. Saada. LC 72-86670. 1974. text ed. 41.00 (ISBN 0-08-017053-6); pap. text ed. 27.50 (ISBN 0-08-017972-X); solutions manual 0.50 (ISBN 0-686-66891-X). Pergamon.
Elastokinetik. Kurt Hohenemser. LC 50-2567. (Ger). 9.95 (ISBN 0-8284-0055-5). Chelsea Pub.
Elbow. Thomas G. Wadsworth. (Illus.). 272p. 1981. text ed. price not set (ISBN 0-443-01931-2). Churchill.
Elder & His Work. Robert Taylor, Jr. 6.95 (ISBN 0-89315-041-X); pap. 6.95 (ISBN 0-89315-042-8). Lambert Bk.
Elder Edda. Ed. by Paul B. Taylor & W. H. Auden. 1975. pap. 2.95 o.p. (ISBN 0-571-10319-7, Pub. by Faber & Faber). Merrimack Bk Serv.
Elder Olson. Thomas E. Lucas. (U. S. Authors Ser.: No. 188). lib. bdg. 10.95 (ISBN 0-8057-0568-6). Twayne.
Eldercare: A Practical Guide to Clinical Geriatrics. Ed. by Mary O'Hara-Deveraux et al. 1980. write for info. (ISBN 0-8089-1285-2). Grune.
Elderly in Modern Society. Anthea Tinker. (Social Policy in Modern Britain Ser.). (Illus.). 320p. 1981. pap. text ed. 13.95x (ISBN 0-582-29513-0). Longman.
Elderly in the Environment: Northern Europe. John McRae. (Illus.). 119p. (Orig.). 1975. pap. 7.50 (ISBN 0-8130-0687-2). U Presses Fla.
Elderly Patients & Their Doctors. Marie Haug. 1981. text ed. price not set (ISBN 0-8261-3570-6). Springer Pub.
Elders, Shades, & Women: Ceremonial Change in Lango, Uganda. Richard T. Curley. 1973. 17.50x (ISBN 0-520-02149-5). U of Cal Pr.
Eldridge Cleaver: Ice & Fire. George Otis. pap. 1.95 (ISBN 0-89728-026-1, 664956). Omega Pubns OR.
Eleanor: A Novel. Rhoda Lerman. LC 78-15140. 304p. 1980. 10.95 (ISBN 0-03-021066-6); pap. 4.95 (ISBN 0-03-057643-1). HR&W.
Eleanor Dark. A. Grove Day. LC 75-23369. (World Authors Ser.: Australia: No. 382). 1976. lib. bdg. 12.50 (ISBN 0-8057-6224-8). Twayne.
Eleanor Farjeon's Poems for Children. Eleanor Farjeon. (Illus.). (gr. 4-6). 1951. 4.95 o.p. (ISBN 0-397-30193-6). Lippincott.
Eleanor of Aquitaine: A Biography. Marion Meade. Orig. Title: Eagle in the Court of Love: the Life of Eleanor of Aquitaine. (Illus.). 1977. 13.95 o.p. (ISBN 0-8015-2231-5). Dutton.
Eleanor of Aquitaine: A Biography. Marion Meade. (Illus.). 1980. pap. 6.95 (ISBN 0-8015-2232-3). Dutton.
Eleanor Roosevelt. Jane Goodsell. LC 71-106573. (Biography Ser.). (Illus.). (gr. 2-5). 1970. PLB 7.89 (ISBN 0-690-25626-4, TYC-J). T Y Crowell.
Eleanor Roosevelt: An American Conscience. Tamara Hareven. LC 74-26539. (FDR & the Era of the New Deal Ser). (Illus.). xx, 326p. 1975. Repr. of 1968 ed. lib. bdg. 29.50 (ISBN 0-306-70705-5). Da Capo.
Eleanor Roosevelt: Reluctant First Lady. Lorena Hickok. LC 79-26769. (Illus.). 176p. 1980. 8.95 (ISBN 0-396-07835-2). Dodd.
Electing Our Own Bishops, Concilium 137. Ed. by Peter Huizing & Knut Walf. (New Concilium 1980). 128p. 1980. pap. 5.95 (ISBN 0-8245-0116-0). Crossroad NY.
Election. C. H. Spurgeon. 1978. pap. 1.25 (ISBN 0-686-00503-1). Pilgrim Pubns.
Election & Consensus in the Church. Ed. by Giuseppe Alberigo & Anton Weiler. (Concilium Ser.: Religion in the Seventies: Church History, Vol. 77). 156p. 1972. pap. 4.95 (ISBN 0-8164-2533-7). Crossroad NY.
Election Campaign Handbook. D. Gaby & M. Treusch. 1976. 35.00 o.p. (ISBN 0-13-247098-5). P-H.
Election Day. Mary K. Phelan. LC 67-15402. (Holiday Ser.). (Illus.). (gr. k-3). 1967. 8.95 (ISBN 0-690-25661-2, TYC-J); PLB 6.89 (ISBN 0-690-25662-0). T Y Crowell.
Election Index: Nineteen Eighty. Ed. by Anna L. Brownson. LC 59-13987. 1980. pap. 8.00 (87289). Congr Staff.
Election of 1980: Reports & Interpretations. Gerald M. Pomper. 224p. (Orig.). 1980. 12.95 (ISBN 0-934540-10-1); pap. text ed. 7.95 (ISBN 0-934540-09-8). Chatham Hse Pubs.
Election Process. 2nd ed. A. Reitman. 1980. 5.95. Oceana.
Electioneering in a Democracy: Campaigns for Congress. D. A. Leuthold. LC 68-22891. 1968. pap. text ed. 6.95x o.p. (ISBN 0-471-52991-5). Wiley.
Elections & Parties. Ed. by Max Kaase & Klaus Von Beyme. LC 78-63119. (German Political Studies: Vol. 3). 1979. 20.00x (ISBN 0-8039-9888-0); pap. 9.95x (ISBN 0-8039-9889-9). Sage.
Elections Without Choice. Ed. by Guy Hermet et al. LC 77-16116. 1978. 17.95 (ISBN 0-470-99292-1). Halsted Pr.
Elections '80. Congressional Quarterly. Ed. by Congressional Quarterly. 250p. 1980. pap. text ed. 6.95 (ISBN 0-87187-199-8). Congr Quarterly.
Electocardiography for Nurses: Physiological Correlates Electrical Disturbances of the Heart. Jeanette Kernicki & Kathi Weiler. 304p. 1981. 17.95 (ISBN 0-471-05752-5, Pub. by Wiley Med). Wiley.
Electoral Behavior: A Comparative Handbook. Richard Rose. LC 72-11285. (Illus.). 1974. 35.00 (ISBN 0-02-926810-9). Free Pr.
Electoral College. Lucius Wilmerding, Jr. 1958. 15.00 (ISBN 0-8135-0294-2). Rutgers U Pr.
Electoral Facts from 1832-1853, Impartially Stated. A Complete Political Gazetteer. Charles Dod. Ed. by H. J. Hanham. 388p. 1972. Repr. of 1853 ed. 25.00x (ISBN 0-8476-6051-6). Rowman.
Electoral Participation: A Comparative Analysis. Ed. by Richard Rose. LC 80-41015. (Sage Studies in Contemporary Political Sociology). 358p. 1980. 25.00 (ISBN 0-8039-9811-2). Sage.
Electoral Politics at the Local Level in the German Federal Republic. Linda L. Dolive. LC 76-26473. (U of Fla. Social Science Monographs: No. 56). (Illus.). 1976. pap. 4.00 (ISBN 0-8130-0554-X). U Presses Fla.
Electoral Politics in the Middle East: Issues, Voters & Elites. Ed. by Jacob M. Landau et al. (Publication Ser.: No. 241). 400p. 1980. 29.95 (ISBN 0-8179-7411-3). Hoover Inst Pr.
Electoral Profile of Alaska. Thomas A. Morehouse & Gordon S. Harrison. LC 73-620227. (Joint Institute of Social & Economic Research Ser.: No. 37). 104p. 1973. pap. 3.00 (ISBN 0-295-95336-5). U of Wash Pr.
Electoral Reform in War & Peace, 1906-1918. Martin Pugh. 1978. 20.00 (ISBN 0-7100-8792-6). Routledge & Kegan.
Electra. Euripides. Tr. by Moses Hadas. LC 63-23331. pap. 2.95 (ISBN 0-672-60186-9, LLA26). Bobbs.
Electra. Euripides. Tr. by Gilbert Murray. 1905. pap. text ed. 3.95x (ISBN 0-04-882030-X). Allen Unwin.
Electra. Sophocles. Tr. by Richard C. Jebb. 1950. pap. 1.80 o.p. (ISBN 0-672-60185-0, LLA25). Bobbs.
Electra & Other Plays. Sophocles. Tr. by E. F. Watling. Incl. Women of Trachis; Philoctetes. (Classics Ser.). (YA) (gr. 9 up). 1953. pap. 2.95 (ISBN 0-14-044028-3). Penguin.
Electre. Jean Giraudoux. Ed. by James S. Patty. LC 65-19222. (Fr.). 1965. pap. text ed. 4.95x (ISBN 0-89197-138-6). Irvington.
Electric & Magnetic Fields. 3rd ed. Stephen S. Attwood. (Illus.). 1966. pap. 4.50 o.p. (ISBN 0-486-61753-X). Dover.
Electric Blues Guitar. Green Note Music Publications Staff. (Contemporary Guitar Styles Ser). (Illus.). 96p. (Orig., Prog. Bk.). 1977. pap. 8.95 (ISBN 0-912910-05-4). Green Note Music.
Electric Church. Ben Armstrong. LC 78-27699. 1979. pap. 4.95 (ISBN 0-8407-5685-2). Nelson.
Electric Circuit Analysis. Margaret R. Taber & Eugene Silgalis. LC 78-69525. (Illus.). 1979. text ed. 19.50 (ISBN 0-395-26706-4); inst. manual write for info. 0.95 (ISBN 0-395-26707-2). HM.
Electric Circuit Theory. R. Yorke. LC 80-41323. (Applied Electricity & Electronics Ser.). (Illus.). 272p. 1981. 30.00 (ISBN 0-08-026133-7); pap. 15.00 (ISBN 0-08-026132-9). Pergamon.
Electric Circuits. Robert A. Bartkowiak. LC 72-14366. 478p. 1973. text ed. 21.50 scp (ISBN 0-7002-2421-1, HarpC); sol. manual scp 4.50 (ISBN 0-8102-0040-6). Har-Row.
Electric Circuits Problem Solver: A Supplement to Any Class Text. Research & Education Association Staff. LC 79-92401. (Illus.). 1056p. 1980. pap. text ed. 22.85 (ISBN 0-87891-517-6). Res & Educ.
Electric Company Joke Book. Byron Preiss. (gr. 1-5). 1973. PLB 5.38 (ISBN 0-307-64824-9, Golden Pr). Western Pub.
Electric Components, Instruments & Troubleshooting. D. Metzger. 1981. 28.95 (ISBN 0-13-250266-6). P-H.
Electric Controls for Refrigeration & Air Conditioning. Billy C. Langley. 1974. 18.95 (ISBN 0-13-247072-1); pap. 13.95 ref. ed. (ISBN 0-13-247064-0). P-H.
Electric Current & Atmospheric Motion. S. Kato & R. G. Roper. (Advances in Earth & Planetary Sciences Ser.: No. 7). 294p. 1980. 24.50x (ISBN 0-89955-314-1, Pub. by JSSP Japan). Intl Schol Bk Serv.
Electric Drilling Rig Handbook. Will McNair. 256p. 1980. 37.50 (ISBN 0-87814-120-0). Pennwell Pub.
Electric Fields of the B. Paul L. Nunez. (Illus.). 500p. 1981. text ed. 35.00x (ISBN 0-19-502796-5). Oxford U Pr.
Electric Fish. Caroline Arnold. LC 80-12479. (Illus.). 64p. (gr. 4-6). 1980. 6.95 (ISBN 0-688-22237-4); PLB 6.67 (ISBN 0-688-32237-9). Morrow.
Electric Floor Warming with Notes on Ceiling Heating. John J. Barton. 1967. 23.50x o.p. (ISBN 0-685-20576-2). Transatlantic.
Electric Foil Fencing. Istvan Lukovich. (Illus.). 1971. 16.50x (ISBN 0-392-05526-0, SpS). Soccer.
Electric Kiln Ceramics: A Potter's Guide to Clay & Glazes. Richard Zakin. LC 80-68274. (Illus.). 256p. 1981. 24.50 (ISBN 0-686-69517-8). Chilton.
Electric Load Modeling. James B. Woodward. LC 78-75001. (Outstanding Dissertations on Energy). 1980. lib. bdg. 32.00 (ISBN 0-8240-3981-5). Garland Pub.
Electric Machine Design. Balbir Singh. 464p. 1981. text ed. 27.50x (ISBN 0-7069-1111-3, Pub. by Vikas India). Advent Bk.
Electric Machines & Transformers. Leonard Anderson. (Illus.). 336p. 1980. text ed. 18.95 (ISBN 0-8359-1615-4); instr's. manual free. Reston.

Electric Man. Carol Adorjan. LC 80-27107. (Prime Time Adventures Ser.). (Illus.). 64p. (gr. 4 up). 1981. PLB 7.95 (ISBN 0-516-02104-4). Childrens.

Electric Melting Practice. A. G. Robiette. 412p. 1972. 52.95 (ISBN 0-470-72787-X). Halsted Pr.

Electric Motor Control. Walter Alerich. LC 73-13484. 236p. 1975. pap. 7.00 (ISBN 0-8273-1157-5); lab. manual 4.80 (ISBN 0-8273-1159-1); instructor's guide 1.60 (ISBN 0-8273-1158-3). Delmar.

Electric Motor Test & Repair. 2nd ed. Jack Beater. LC 66-24043. 1966. vinyl 6.95 o.p. (ISBN 0-8306-6097-6, 97). TAB Bks.

Electric Motors. 3rd ed. Rex Miller & Edwin P. Anderson. LC 77-71584. 1977. 10.95 (ISBN 0-672-23264-2). Audel.

Electric, Optic, & Acoustic Interactions in Dielectrics. Donald F. Nelson. LC 78-25964. 1979. 36.95 (ISBN 0-471-05199-3, Pub. by Wiley-Interscience). Wiley.

Electric Power & the Civil Engineer: Proceedings. Compiled by American Society of Civil Engineers. 688p. 1974. pap. text ed. 39.50 (ISBN 0-87262-070-0). Am Soc Civil Eng.

Electric Power at Low Temperatures. Michael Rechowicz. (Monographs in Electrical & Electronic Engineering). (Illus.). 150p. 1975. 36.00x (ISBN 0-19-859312-0). Oxford U Pr.

Electric Power in the United States: Models & Policy Analysis. Martin L. Baughman et al. 1979. text ed. 32.50x (ISBN 0-262-02130-7). MIT Pr.

Electric Power Systems. 2nd ed. B. M. Weedy. LC 71-37109. 453p. 1972. 20.50 o.p. (ISBN 0-471-92445-8, Pub. by Wiley-Interscience). Wiley.

Electric Power Systems. 3rd ed. B. M. Weedy. LC 79-40081. 27.50 (ISBN 0-471-27584-0, Pub. by Wiley-Interscience). Wiley.

Electric Power Today. Compiled By American Society of Civil Engineers. 80p. 1979. pap. text ed. 6.75 (ISBN 0-87262-180-4). Am Soc Civil Eng.

Electric Radish & Other Jokes. Susan Thorndike. LC 75-183615. 48p. (gr. 1-3). 1973. PLB 4.95 (ISBN 0-385-06401-2). Doubleday.

Electric Smelting Processes. A. G. Robiette. LC 73-2039. (Illus.). 276p. 1973. 42.95 (ISBN 0-470-72786-1). Halsted Pr.

Electric Vegetarian: Natural Cooking the Food Processor Way. Paula Szilard & Juliana J. Woo. 1981. 12.95. Johnson VA.

Electric Vegetarian: Natural Cooking the Food Processor Way. Paula Szilard & Juliana J. Woo. 1980. pap. 10.95 (ISBN 0-933472-50-1). Johnson Colo.

Electric Vehicle E-016R: Inevitable? 1980. 800.00 (ISBN 0-89336-189-5). BCC.

Electric Wishing Well. Joseph J. DiCerto. 1976. 14.95 (ISBN 0-02-531320-7). Macmillan.

Electrical & Mechanical Oscillations. D. S. Jones. (Library of Mathematics). 1968. pap. 5.00 (ISBN 0-7100-4346-5). Routledge & Kegan.

Electrical Assembly & Wiring. Ed. by E. Bethell et al. (Engineering Craftsmen: No. G4). (Illus.). 1969. spiral bdg. 21.00x (ISBN 0-85083-031-1). Intl Ideas.

Electrical Blueprint Reading. John Traister. LC 75-5415. (Illus.). 1975. pap. 5.95 o.p. (ISBN 0-672-21181-5, 21181). Sams.

Electrical Breakdown of Gases. J. M. Meek & J. D. Craggs. 878p. 1978. 139.50 (ISBN 0-471-99553-3). Wiley.

Electrical Circuits. 2nd ed. Charles S. Siskind. 1965. text ed. 17.95 o.p. (ISBN 0-07-057744-7, G). McGraw.

Electrical Circuits Problems & Laboratory Manual. Roger C. Conant. (Illus.). 1980. 4.50x (ISBN 0-917974-33-6). Waveland Pr.

Electrical Code Diagrams. 7th ed. B. Z. Segall. LC 61-10921. (Illus.). 1978. 55.00 (ISBN 0-930234-01-4). Peerless.

Electrical Collectibles: Relics of the Electrical Age. Don Fredgant. (Illus.). 1981. pap. 9.95 (ISBN 0-914598-04-X). Padre Prods.

Electrical Conduction in Solid Materials: Physico-Chemical Bases & Possible Applications. J. P. Suchet. 204p. 1976. text ed. 27.00 (ISBN 0-08-018052-3). Pergamon.

Electrical Construction Cost Estimating. Harry Cubit. (Illus.). 320p. 1981. 27.50 (ISBN 0-07-014885-6). McGraw.

Electrical Control for Machines. Kenneth Rexford. LC 80-70918. (Electrical Maintenance Ser.). (Illus.). 332p. 1981. pap. text ed. 9.80 (ISBN 0-8273-1983-5); write for info. instr's guide (ISBN 0-8273-1984-3). Delmar.

Electrical Coronas: Their Basic Physical Mechanisms. Leonard B. Loeb. 1965. 35.00x o.p. (ISBN 0-520-00765-4). U of Cal Pr.

Electrical Course for Apprentices & Journeymen. Roland Palmquist. LC 73-85725. 1973. 10.95 (ISBN 0-672-23209-X). Audel.

Electrical Defibrillation. W. A. Tacker & L. A. Geddes. 224p. 1980. 69.95 (ISBN 0-8493-5359-9). CRC Pr.

Electrical Double Layer. M. J. Sparnaay. 427p. 1973. text ed. 64.00 (ISBN 0-08-016852-3). Pergamon.

Electrical Energy Generation: Economics, Reliability & Rates. Joseph Vardi & Benjamin Avi-Itzhak. 192p. 1981. text ed. 24.95x (ISBN 0-262-22024-5). MIT Pr.

Electrical Energy Management. Lawrence J. Vogt & David A. Conner. LC 77-156. 1977. 14.95 (ISBN 0-669-01457-5). Lexington Bks.

Electrical Engineering & Economics & Ethics for Professional Engineering Examinations. John S. Lyons & Stanley W. Dublin. Ed. by Lawrence J. Hollander. (Professional Engineering Examinations Ser.). (Illus.). 320p. 1970. 23.95 (ISBN 0-8104-5715-6). Hayden.

Electrical Engineering: Concepts & Applications. A. Bruce Carlson & David G. Gisser. LC 80-21519. (Electrical Engineering Ser.). 640p. 1981. text ed. price not set (ISBN 0-201-03940-0). A-W.

Electrical Engineering Experiments. U. S. Bhatnagar. 5.50x o.p. (ISBN 0-210-33848-2). Asia.

Electrical Engineering Fundamentals. 2nd ed. Robert B. Angus, Jr. (Illus.). 1968. 18.95 (ISBN 0-201-00250-7). A-W.

Electrical Engineering Principles & Testing Methods. Rhys Lewis. (Illus.). 1973. 22.30x (ISBN 0-85334-564-3, Pub. by Applied Science). Burgess-Intl Ideas.

Electrical Engineering Review Manual. 2nd ed. Raymond B. Yarbrough. LC 80-81797. (Engineering Review Manual Ser.). (Illus.). 443p. 1980. pap. 24.50 (ISBN 0-936754-00-1); wkbk. 7.00 (ISBN 0-936754-03-6). Prof Engine.

Electrical Engineers Handbook: Electric Communication & Electronics. 4th ed. H. Pender & K. McIlwain. (Wiley Engineers Handbook Ser.). 1950. 39.95 (ISBN 0-471-67848-1, Pub. by Wiley-Interscience). Wiley.

Electrical Engineers Handbook: Electrical Power. 4th ed. H. Pender & W. Del Mar. (Wiley Engineers Handbook Ser.). 1949. 40.00 (ISBN 0-471-67881-3, Pub. by Wiley-Interscience). Wiley.

Electrical Equipment Testing & Maintenance Handbook. Paul Gill. 350p. 1981. text ed. 16.95 (ISBN 0-8359-1625-1). Reston.

Electrical Events Associated with Primary Photosynthetic Reactions in Chloroplast Membranes. (Agricultural Research Reports Ser.: No. 905). 86p. 1981. pap. 16.75 (ISBN 90-220-0756-1, PDC 218, Pudoc). Unipub.

Electrical Experiments. Francis G. Rayer. LC 75-368193. (Pegasus Books: No. 13). (Illus.). (gr. 9 up). 1968. 7.50x (ISBN 0-234-77997-7). Intl Pubns Serv.

Electrical Fitting, Vol. 1. Ed. by R. T. Anderson et al. (Engineering Craftsmen: No. G3). (Illus.). 1968. spiral bdg. 18.50x (ISBN 0-85083-015-X). Intl Ideas.

Electrical Fitting, Vol. 2. Ed. by J. R. Bisby et al. (Engineering Craftsmen: No. G23). (Illus.). 1969. spiral bdg. 23.50x (ISBN 0-685-90132-7). Intl Ideas.

Electrical Fundamentals, 2 pts. J. J. De France. Incl. Pt. 1. Direct Current; Pt. 2. Indirect Current. 1969. Set. text ed. 21.95 (ISBN 0-13-247197-3). P-H.

Electrical Guide to DC-AC Circuit Analysis. Ernest A. Loerg. 1979. pap. text ed. 9.95 (ISBN 0-89669-006-7). Collegium Bk Pubs.

Electrical Inspection. Ed. by R. Davey et al. (Engineering Craftsmen: No. G24). (Illus.). 1969. spiral bdg. 24.95x (ISBN 0-85083-066-4). Intl Ideas.

Electrical Inspection Guidebook. John E. Traister. (Illus.). 1979. text ed. 19.95 (ISBN 0-8359-1629-4). Reston.

Electrical Installation Calculations, Vol. 1. 3rd ed. A. J. Watkins. 100p. 1980. 13.00x (ISBN 0-7131-3422-4, Pub. by Arnold Pubs England). State Mutual Bk.

Electrical Installation Calculations: SJ Units, Vol. 2. 2nd ed. A. J. Watkins. 106p. 1980. 13.00x (Pub. by Arnold Pubs England). State Mutual Bk.

Electrical Installation Calculations: S1 Units, Vol. 3. A. J. Watkins. 154p. 1980. 13.00x (ISBN 0-7131-3224-8, Pub. by Arnold Pubs England). State Mutual Bk.

Electrical Installation Theory & Practice. 2nd ed. E. L. Donnelly. (Illus.). 1972. pap. text ed. 14.95x (ISBN 0-245-51007-9). Intl Ideas.

Electrical Installations Technology. I. C. Whitfield. 1968. 25.00 (ISBN 0-08-012704-5); pap. text ed. 11.25 (ISBN 0-08-012703-7). Pergamon.

Electrical Interference. Rocco F. Ficchi. (Illus.). 1964. 11.45 o.p. (ISBN 0-8104-5512-9). Hayden.

Electrical Load-Curve Coverage: Proceedings. Symposium on Load-Curve Coverage in Future Electrical Power Generating Systems, Rome, Oct. 1977. Ed. by United Nations Economic Commission for Europe. LC 78-40342. (Illus.). 1979. text ed. 105.00 (ISBN 0-08-022422-9). Pergamon.

Electrical Machinery, Transformers, & Control. Harold W. Gingrich. (Illus.). 1978. ref. 19.95 (ISBN 0-13-247320-8). P-H.

Electrical Machines: An Introduction to Principles & Characteristics. J. D. Edwards. 1973. text ed. 14.95x (ISBN 0-7002-0267-6). Intl Ideas.

Electrical Machines & Their Applications. J. Hindmarsh. LC 79-20595. (Illus.). 800p. (Arabic.). 1981. pap. 20.00 (ISBN 0-08-026158-2). Pergamon.

Electrical Maintenance & Installation: Part One. 2nd ed. Ed. by F. Butcher et al. (Engineering Craftsmen: No. J2). (Illus.). 1975. spiral bdg. 22.50x (ISBN 0-685-90134-3). Intl Ideas.

Electrical Maintenance & Installation: Supplementary Training Material. Ed. by J. Reagan et al. (Engineering Craftsmen: No. J22S). (Illus.). 1976. pap. text ed. 19.95x (ISBN 0-85083-329-9). Intl Ideas.

Electrical Measurement Systems for Biological & Physical Scientists. Weber & McLean. 1976. 19.95 (ISBN 0-201-04593-1). A-W.

Electrical Measuring Instruments. E. Handscombe. (Wykeham Technology Ser.: No. 2). 1970. 9.95x (ISBN 0-8448-1173-4). Crane Russak Co.

Electrical Methods of Geophysical Prospecting. 2nd ed. Keller. 400p. Date not set. text ed. price not set (ISBN 0-08-025979-0). Pergamon.

Electrical Network Science. Robert B. Kerr. (Illus.). 1977. text ed. 23.95 (ISBN 0-13-247627-4). P-H.

Electrical Phenomena in the Heart. Ed. by Walmor C. De Mello. (Clinical Engineering Ser). 1972. 47.25 (ISBN 0-12-208950-2). Acad Pr.

Electrical Power Systems, Vol. 1. 2nd ed. A. E. Guile & W. Paterson. LC 77-1789. 1977. text ed. 52.00 (ISBN 0-08-021728-1); pap. text ed. 17.00 (ISBN 0-08-021729-X). Pergamon.

Electrical Power Systems Technology. Dale R. Patrick & Stephen W. Fardo. LC 79-63821. 1979. pap. 12.95 (ISBN 0-672-21607-8). Sams.

Electrical Power Technology. Theodore Wildi. 704p. 1981. write for info. solns. manual (ISBN 0-471-07764-X); price not set solns. manual (ISBN 0-471-09239-8). Wiley.

Electrical Principles & Practices. 2nd ed. James E. Adams. 1973. text ed. 17.25 (ISBN 0-07-000281-9, G); ans. key 1.50 (ISBN 0-07-000282-7). McGraw.

Electrical Principles for Technicians. R. Hamilton. (Electrical & Telecommunications Technicians Ser.). (Illus.). 200p. 1980. 37.50 (ISBN 0-19-859360-0). Oxford U Pr.

Electrical Principles Three Checkbook. May Bird. text ed. write for info. (ISBN 0-408-00636-6); pap. text ed. write for info. (ISBN 0-408-00601-3). Butterworth.

Electrical Principles Two Checkbook. May Bird. 1981. text ed. price not set (ISBN 0-408-00635-8); pap. text ed. price not set (ISBN 0-408-00600-5). Butterworth.

Electrical Properties of Polymers. A. R. Blythe. LC 77-85690. (Solid State Science Ser.). 1979. 49.50 (ISBN 0-521-21902-7). Cambridge U Pr.

Electrical Properties of Polymers. A. R. Blythe. LC 77-85690. (Cambridge Solid State Science Ser.). (Illus.). 201p. 1980. pap. text ed. 13.95x (ISBN 0-521-29825-3). Cambridge U Pr.

Electrical Properties of Wood & Line Design. M. Darveniza. (Illus.). 197p. (Orig.). 1980. pap. text ed. 36.25x (ISBN 0-7022-1523-6). U of Queensland Pr.

Electrical Safety Engineering. W. F. Cooper & Fordham. 1977. 52.95 (ISBN 0-408-00289-1). Butterworths.

Electrical Science, Bk. 1. Norman Balabanian & Wilbur LePage. 1970. 14.95 o.p. (ISBN 0-07-003543-1, C). McGraw.

Electrical Specifications for Building Construction. John E. Traister. (Illus.). 1978. text ed. 16.95 (ISBN 0-87909-214-9). Reston.

Electrical Stimulation Research Techniques. Ed. by Michael M. Patterson & Raymond P. Kesner. (Methods in Physiological Psychology Ser.). 1981. price not set (ISBN 0-12-547440-7). Acad Pr.

Electrical Timekeeping. 2nd ed. F. Hope-Jones. (Illus.). 1976. 18.95x (ISBN 0-7198-0070-6). Intl Ideas.

Electrical Transport in Solids. K. C. Kao & W. Hwang. (International Series in the Science of the Solid State: Vol. 14). 1981. 120.00 (ISBN 0-08-023973-0). Pergamon.

Electrical Wiring - Commercial. 4th rev. ed. Ray C. Mullin & Robert L. Smith. LC 80-65467. (Electrical Trades Ser.). (Illus.). 208p. 1981. pap. text ed. 10.00 (ISBN 0-8273-1953-3); price not set instr's. guide (ISBN 0-8273-1954-1). Delmar.

Electrical Wiring & Lighting for Home & Office. Edward L. Safford, Jr. LC 73-86765. (Illus.). 204p. 1974. 7.95 o.p. (ISBN 0-8306-3671-4); pap. 4.95 (ISBN 0-8306-2671-9, 671). TAB Bks.

Electrical Wiring-Commercial. Ray C. Mullin & Robert L. Smith. LC 77-92084. 1978. pap. 10.56 (ISBN 0-8273-1412-4); instructor's guide 1.60 (ISBN 0-8273-1413-2). Delmar.

Electrical Wiring: Design & Construction. R. Johnson & R. Cox. 1981. Repr. 19.95 (ISBN 0-13-247650-9). P-H.

Electrical Wiring: Design & Construction. Robert C. Johnson. 1971. ref. ed. 19.95 (ISBN 0-13-247635-5). P-H.

Electrical Wiring-Industrial. Robert L. Smith. LC 77-92083. 1978. pap. text ed. 10.20 (ISBN 0-8273-1414-0); instr's. guide 1.60 (ISBN 0-8273-1415-9). Delmar.

Electrical Wiring-Residential. Ray C. Mullin. LC 77-90331. 1978. pap. 10.56 (ISBN 0-8273-1410-8); instructor's guide 1.60 (ISBN 0-8273-1411-6). Delmar.

Electrical Wiring Residential: Based on 1981 National Electrial Code. 7th ed. Ray C. Mullin. 288p. 1981. 14.95. Van Nos Reinhold.

Electrical Wiring: Residential, Utility Bldgs, & Service Areas. Thomas Colvin. 10.95 (ISBN 0-89606-030-6). Green Hill.

Electricidad. Harlan Wade. Tr. by Mamie M. Contreras from Eng. LC 78-26829. (Book About Ser.). (Illus., Sp.). (gr. k-3). 1979. PLB 7.30 (ISBN 0-8172-1488-7). Raintree Pubs.

Electricidad Basica Para Apparatas Caseros. Tr. by Jose Pacheko from Eng. (Illus.). 140p. (Span.). 1975. 20.00 (ISBN 0-938336-10-X). Whirlpool.

Electricite. Harlan Wade. Tr. by Claude Potvin & Rose-Ella Potvin. (Book About Ser.). (Illus., Fr.). (gr. k-3). 1979. PLB 7.30 (ISBN 0-8172-1463-1). Raintree Pubs.

Electricity. Byron J. Alpers & Mitchell L. Afrow. (Shoptalk - Vocational Reading Skills). (gr. 9-12). 1978. pap. text ed. 5.12 (ISBN 0-205-05821-3, 4958217); tchrs'. guide 5.40 (ISBN 0-205-05824-8). Allyn.

Electricity. Mark W. Bailey. LC 77-27324. (Read About Science Ser.). (Illus.). (gr. k-3). 1978. PLB 9.95 (ISBN 0-8393-0085-9). Raintree Child.

Electricity. Boy Scouts Of America. LC 19-600. (Illus.). 48p. (gr. 6-12). 1974. pap. 0.70x (ISBN 0-8395-3206-7, 3206). BSA.

Electricity. 2nd ed. C. A. Coulson & T. J. Boyd. (Longman Mathematical Texts Ser.). (Illus.). 1979. pap. text ed. 18.95 (ISBN 0-582-44281-8). Longman.

Electricity. Howard H. Gerrish. LC 77-95064. 1978. text ed. 4.80 (ISBN 0-87006-259-X). Goodheart.

Electricity. Los Angeles Unified School District. Ed. by Richard A. Vorndran. LC 77-73243. 96p. (gr. 7-9). 1978. pap. text ed. 4.40 (ISBN 0-02-820440-9). Glencoe.

Electricity. McKnight Staff Members & Wilbur R. Miller. LC 78-53389. (Basic Industrial Arts Ser.). (Illus.). 1978. 6.00 (ISBN 0-87345-794-3); softbound 4.48 (ISBN 0-87345-786-2). McKnight.

Electricity. Edward Victor. (Beginning Science Books). (Illus.). (gr. 2-4). 1967. 2.50 o.p. (ISBN 0-695-82166-0); PLB 3.39 o.p. (ISBN 0-695-42166-2). Follett.

Electricity. rev. ed. Harlan Wade. LC 78-26825. (Book About Ser.). (Illus.). (gr. k-3). 1979. PLB 7.30 (ISBN 0-8172-1537-9). Raintree Pubs.

Electricity & Atomic Physics. Philip Parker. 1971. text ed. 6.95x o.p. (ISBN 0-435-68650-X). Heinemann Ed.

Electricity & Basic Electronics. Stephen R. Matt. LC 79-6346. (Illus.). 1980. text ed. 11.96 (ISBN 0-87006-285-9). Goodheart.

Electricity & Electronics. Howard H. Gerrish & William E. Dugger, Jr. LC 79-6345. (Illus.). 1980. text ed. 11.96 (ISBN 0-87006-310-3); lab manual 4.96 (ISBN 0-87006-263-8). Goodheart.

Electricity & Electronics Laboratory Manual. William Dugger & Dale R. Patrick. (Illus.). 1980. 4.96 (ISBN 0-87006-310-3). Goodheart.

Electricity & Electronics Laboratory Manual. rev. ed. Dale Patrick & William E. Dugger, Jr. (Illus.). 372p. (gr. 7 up). 1980. 4.96. Goodheart.

Electricity & Magnetism. 3rd ed. B. I. Bleaney & B. Bleaney. (Illus.). 1976. pap. 32.50x (ISBN 0-19-851141-8). Oxford U Pr.

Electricity & Magnetism, 2 Vols. James C. Maxwell. (Illus.). 1891. pap. text ed. 6.50 ea.; Vol. 1. pap. text ed. (ISBN 0-486-60636-8); Vol. 2. pap. text ed. (ISBN 0-486-60637-6). Dover.

Electricity & Magnetism. Francis W. Sears. (Illus.). 1951. 17.95 (ISBN 0-201-06900-8). A-W.

Electricity & Modern Physics. 2nd ed. G. A. Bennet. 1974. pap. text ed. 17.95x (ISBN 0-7131-2459-8). Intl Ideas.

Electricity, Electronics & Electromagnetics: Principles & Applications. Robert L. Boylestad & L. Nashelsky. (Illus.). 1977. text ed. 20.95 (ISBN 0-13-248310-6). P-H.

Electricity-Electronics: Principles & Applications. Joseph M. DeGuilmo. LC 79-54909. (Electronics Technology Ser.). (Illus.). 672p. (Orig.). 1981. pap. 19.60 (ISBN 0-8273-1686-0); price not set instr's. guide (ISBN 0-8273-1687-9). Delmar.

Electricity Experiments for Children. Gabriel Reuben. (gr. 5-9). pap. 2.25 (ISBN 0-486-22030-3). Dover.

Electricity for Technicians. 2nd ed. Charles M. Thomson & Abraham Marcus. (Illus.). 512p. 1975. ref. ed. 18.95 (ISBN 0-13-248658-X). P-H.

Electricity Four: AC Motors & Generators, Controls, Alternators. Walter N. Alerich. LC 79-93325. (Electrical Trades Ser.). 224p. 1981. pap. 6.60 (ISBN 0-8273-1363-2); instructor's guide 1.10 (ISBN 0-8273-1364-0). Delmar.

Electricity-Four: Motors, Generators, Controls. W. N. Alerich. 224p. 1975. pap. 6.20 o.p. (ISBN 0-8273-1155-9); instructor's guide 1.45 o.p. (ISBN 0-8273-1156-7). Delmar.

Electricity from MHD-1966, 3 vols. (Illus., Orig.). 1966. Vol. 1. pap. 38.75 (ISBN 92-0-030366-8, IAEA); Vol. 2. pap. 63.75 (ISBN 92-0-030466-4); Vol. 3. pap. 57.25 (ISBN 92-0-030566-0). Unipub.

Electricity from MHD 1968, 6 Vols. (Illus., Orig.). 1969. pap. 24.75 ea. (IAEA); Vol. 1. pap. (ISBN 92-0-030468-0); Vol. 2. pap. (ISBN 92-0-030568-7); Vol. 3. pap. (ISBN 92-0-030668-3); Vol. 4. pap. (ISBN 92-0-030768-X); Vol. 5. pap. (ISBN 92-0-030868-6); Vol. 6. pap. (ISBN 92-0-030968-2). Unipub.

Electricity from the Sun: Photovoltaic Energy. Richard Livingstone. (Energy Systems Bks.). (Illus.). 160p. 1981. pap. 7.95 (ISBN 0-07-038150-X). McGraw.

Electricity Fundamentals. Glenn E. Baker & Leonard R. Crow. LC 73-131131. 1971. 13.95 (ISBN 0-672-20795-8). Bobbs.

Electricity in the Seventeenth & Eighteenth Centuries: A Study of Early Modern Physics. J. L. Heilbron. 1979. 46.75x (ISBN 0-520-03478-3). U of Cal Pr.

Electricity Made Simple. Henry Jacobowitz. pap. 3.50 (ISBN 0-385-00436-2, Made). Doubleday.

Electricity One. rev., 2nd ed. Ed. by Harry Mileaf. (Illus.). (gr. 10-12). 1976. pap. 6.60 (ISBN 0-8104-5945-0). Hayden.

Electricity One: Devices, Circuits, Materials. Thomas S. Kubala. LC 79-93322. (Electrical Trades Ser.). 98p. 1981. pap. text ed. 4.80 (ISBN 0-8273-1357-8); instr's manual 1.00 (ISBN 0-8273-1358-6). Delmar.

Electricity One-Four. rev., 2nd, combined ed. Ed. by Harry Mileaf. (Illus.). (gr. 10-12). 1976. 16.60x (ISBN 0-8104-5919-1). Hayden.

Electricity One-Seven. Ed. by Harry Mileaf. Incl. Electricity Two. rev., 2nd ed. pap. (ISBN 0-8104-5946-9); Electricity Four. 2nd ed. pap. (ISBN 0-8104-5948-5); Electricity Five. pap. (ISBN 0-8104-5949-3); Electricity Six. rev., 2nd ed. pap. (ISBN 0-8104-5950-7); Electricity Seven. pap. o.p. (ISBN 0-8104-5550-1). (Illus.). (gr. 10-12). 1978. pap. 6.60 ea.; ea 2.15, transparencies; exam sets, vols. 1-7 0.50 ea.; transparency set 1252.00 (ISBN 0-685-46436-9). Hayden.

Electricity One-Seven. combined, rev., 2nd ed. Ed. by Harry Mileaf. (Illus.). (gr. 10-12). 1976. 25.95x (ISBN 0-8104-5952-3). Hayden.

Electricity One-Seven, 7 vols. rev., 2nd ed. Ed. by Harry Mileaf. (Illus.). (gr. 10-12). 1976. pap. 46.20 set (ISBN 0-8104-5944-2). Hayden.

Electricity Planning & the Environment: Toward a New Role for Government in the Decision Process. Dennis Dusik. Date not set. price not set (ISBN 0-88410-638-1). Ballinger Pub.

Electricity Seven. rev., 2nd ed. Harry Mileaf. (gr. 10 up). 1978. pap. 6.60 (ISBN 0-8104-5951-5). Hayden.

Electricity Three. Walter N. Alerich. LC 79-93324. (Electrical Trades Ser.). 232p. 1981. pap. 6.60 (ISBN 0-8273-1361-6); instructor's guide 1.50 (ISBN 0-8273-1362-4). Delmar.

Electricity Three. rev., 2nd ed. Harry Mileaf. (gr. 10 up). 1977. pap. 6.60 (ISBN 0-8104-5947-7). Hayden.

Electricity-Three: Motors, Generators, Controls. W. N. Alerich. 256p. 1974. pap. 6.00 o.p. (ISBN 0-8273-1153-2); instructor's guide 1.45 o.p. (ISBN 0-8273-1154-0). Delmar.

Electricity: Today's Technologies, Tomorrow's Alternatives. Electric Power Research Institute. (Illus.). 128p. (Orig.). 1981. pap. 7.95 (ISBN 0-86576-003-9). Pub Serv Ctr.

Electricity Two: Devices, Circuits, Materials. Thomas S. Kubala. LC 79-93323. (Electrical Trades Ser.). 104p. 1981. pap. text ed. 4.40 (ISBN 0-8273-1151-6); instr's guide 1.45 (ISBN 0-8273-1152-4). Delmar.

Electro Buyers' Guide 1980. 1980. pap. 27.50x (ISBN 3-9208-1913-6). Intl Pubns Serv.

Electrobiology of Nerve, Synapse & Muscle. Ed. by John P. Reuben et al. LC 75-14587. 1976. 34.50 (ISBN 0-89004-030-3). Raven.

Electrocardiogram: A Self-Study Course in Clinical Electrocardiography (a Tape Presentation) Emanuel Stein. LC 75-8186. (Illus.). 1976. pap. text ed. 16.50 (ISBN 0-7216-8585-4); tapes 85.00 (ISBN 0-7216-9893-X). Saunders.

Electrocardiography: Practical Applications with Vectorial Principles. 2nd ed. Edward K. Chung. (Illus.). 693p. 1980. text ed. 42.50 (ISBN 0-06-140642-2, Harper Medical). Harrow.

Electrochemical Data, Vol. A: Organic, Organometallic, & Biochemical Substances, Pt. 1, L. Meites & P. Zuman. LC 74-14958. 727p. 1974. 60.00 (ISBN 0-471-59200-5, Pub. by Wiley-Interscience). Wiley.

Electrochemical Methods: Fundamentals & Applications. Allen J. Bard & Larry R. Faulkner. LC 79-24712. 718p. 1980. text ed. 29.95 (ISBN 0-471-05542-5); tchrs' manual avail. (ISBN 0-471-07788-7). Wiley.

Electrochemical Stripping Analysis. F. Vydra et al. Tr. by J. Tyson. LC 76-10946. (Series on Analytical Chemistry). 1977. 60.95 (ISBN 0-470-15131-5). Halsted Pr.

Electrochemistry. Ed. by H. R. Thirsk. 1977. text ed. 27.50 (ISBN 0-08-021676-5). Pergamon.

Electrochemistry: A Reformaulation of the Basic Principles. H. G. Hertz. (Lecture Notes in Chemistry: Vol. 17). (Illus.). 254p. 1980. pap. 24.80 (ISBN 0-387-10008-3). Springer-Verlag.

Electroconvulsive Therapy. American Psychiatric Association. LC 78-69521. (Task Force Report: No. 14). 200p. 1978. pap. 10.00 (ISBN 0-685-94003-9, P228-0). Am Psychiatric.

Electroconvulsive Therapy: An Appraisal. Ed. by Robert L. Palmer. (Illus.). 320p. 1981. text ed. 59.50x (ISBN 0-19-261266-2). Oxford U Pr.

Electrode Kinetics. John Albery. (Oxford Chemistry Ser). (Illus.). 196p. 1975. 24.95x (ISBN 0-19-855433-8). Oxford U Pr.

Electrode Placement for EMG Biofeedback. John V. Basmajian & R. Blumenstein. (Illus.). 96p. 1980. softcover 8.95 (ISBN 0-683-00376-3). Williams & Wilkins.

Electrodeposition of Chromium from Chromic Acid Solutions. George Dubpernell. LC 77-549. 1977. text ed. 16.00 (ISBN 0-08-021925-X). Pergamon.

Electrodynamics & Classical Theory of Fields & Particles. A. O. Barut. (Illus.). 256p. 1980. pap. text ed. 4.50 (ISBN 0-486-64038-8). Dover.

Electroencephalography (EEG) of Human Sleep: Clinical Applications. Robert L. Williams et al. LC 73-20032. 192p. 1974. 34.50 (ISBN 0-471-94686-9, Pub. by Wiley Medical). Wiley.

Electroforming. 2nd rev. ed. Peter Spiro. 1971. 40.00x (ISBN 0-901994-34-0). Intl Pubns Serv.

Electroless & Other Nonelectrolytic Plating Techniques: Recent Developments. Ed. by J. I. Duffy. LC 80-19494. (Chemical Tech. Rev. 171). (Illus.). 366p. 1981. 45.00 (ISBN 0-8155-0818-2). Noyes.

Electrolysis, Key to a Beautiful Body. Julius Shapiro. LC 80-24691. (Illus.). 246p. 1981. 8.95 (ISBN 0-396-07903-2). Dodd.

Electrolytes. Ed. by B. Pesce. 1962. 37.00 (ISBN 0-08-009597-6); pap. 22.00 (ISBN 0-08-013778-4). Pergamon.

Electrolytes & Neuropsychiatric Disorders. Ed. by P. E. Alexander. (Illus.). 351p. 1981. text ed. 45.00 (ISBN 0-89335-122-9). Spectrum Pub.

Electrolytic Production of Magnesium. K. L. Strelets. 1977. 56.95 (ISBN 0-470-99320-0). Halsted Pr.

Electromagnetic Concepts & Applications. J. Skitok & R. Marshall. 1981. 28.00 (ISBN 0-13-248963-5). P-H.

Electromagnetic Fields. Ronald K. Wangsness. LC 78-15027. 1979. text ed. 25.95 (ISBN 0-471-04103-3); solutions manual avail. (ISBN 0-471-05936-6). Wiley.

Electromagnetic Fields & Relativistic Particles. Emil Konopinski. (International Series in Pure & Applied Physics). (Illus.). 640p. 1981. text ed. 25.95x (ISBN 0-07-035264-X, C). McGraw.

Electromagnetic Fields & Waves. 2nd ed. Paul Lorrain & Dale R. Corson. LC 72-94872. (Illus.). 1970. text ed. 25.95x (ISBN 0-7167-0331-9); solutions to problems avail. W H Freeman.

Electromagnetic Fields & Waves. Vladimir Rojansky. LC 79-52648. 1980. pap. text ed. 7.95 (ISBN 0-486-63834-0). Dover.

Electromagnetic Fields, Energy, & Waves. Leonard M. Magid. 808p. 1981. Repr. of 1972 ed. text ed. write for info. (ISBN 0-89874-221-8). Krieger.

Electromagnetic Fields: Sources & Media. Alan M. Portis. LC 78-7585. 1978. text ed. 29.95 (ISBN 0-471-01906-2); solutions manual o.p. (ISBN 0-471-03717-6). Wiley.

Electromagnetic Horn Antennas. Ed. by A. W. Love. LC 75-44649. 1976. 28.95 (ISBN 0-87942-075-8). Inst Electrical.

Electromagnetic Interactions in Elastic Solids. Ed. by H. Parkus. (CISM Courses & Lectures: Vol. 257). (Illus.). 425p. 1980. pap. 38.10 (ISBN 0-387-81509-0). Springer-Verlag.

Electromagnetic Lifetimes & Properties of Nuclear States. 1962. 5.00 (ISBN 0-309-00974-X). Natl Acad Pr.

Electromagnetic Radiation. F. H. Read. LC 79-41484. (Manchester Physics Ser.). 352p. 1980. 58.50 (ISBN 0-471-27718-5); pap. 23.00 (ISBN 0-471-27714-2). Wiley.

Electromagnetic Theory of Gratings. R. Petit. (Topics in Current Physics Ser.: Vol. 22). (Illus.). 284p. 1981. 38.35 (ISBN 0-387-10193-4). Springer-Verlag.

Electromagnetic Wave Propagation: Proceedings. Ed. by M. Desirant & J. L. Michiels. 1960. 94.50 (ISBN 0-12-211550-3). Acad Pr.

Electromagnetic Waves & Radiating Systems. 2nd ed. Edward C. Jordan & K. G. Balmain. 1968. ref. ed. 27.95 (ISBN 0-13-249995-9). P-H.

Electromagnetics & the Environment: Remote Sensing & Telecommunications. Warren L. Flock. (Illus.). 1979. ref. 28.00 (ISBN 0-13-248997-X). P-H.

Electromagnetics Induction in the Earth & Moon. Ed. by U. Schmucker. (Advances in Earth & Planetary Sciences Ser.: No. 9). 200p. 1980. lib. bdg. 26.50 (ISBN 90-277-1131-3, Pub. by D. Reidel). Kluwer Boston.

Electromagnetism. I. S. Grant & W. R. Phillips. LC 73-17668. (Manchester Physics Ser). 1975. 45.25 (ISBN 0-471-32245-8); pap. 19.25 (ISBN 0-471-32246-6, Pub. by Wiley-Interscience). Wiley.

Electromagnetism. D. F. Lawden. (Problem Solvers Ser.). (Illus.). 1973. pap. text ed. 6.50x o.p. (ISBN 0-04-538002-3). Allen Unwin.

Electromagnetism. John C. Slater & Nathaniel H. Frank. LC 69-17476. (Illus.). 1969. pap. text ed. 3.50 (ISBN 0-486-62263-0). Dover.

Electromagnetism & Quantum Theory. D. M. Grimes. (Electrical Science Ser). 1969. 25.00 o.p. (ISBN 0-12-303150-8). Acad Pr.

Electromagnetism for Engineers: In SI-Metric Units. 2nd ed. P. Hammond. 1978. text ed. 30.00 (ISBN 0-08-022103-3); pap. text ed. 10.75 (ISBN 0-08-022104-1). Pergamon.

Electromagnetism: Principles & Applications. Paul Lorrain & Dale R. Corson. LC 78-1911. (Illus.). 1979. pap. text ed. 14.95x (ISBN 0-7167-0064-6); sol. manual 3.95x (ISBN 0-7167-1105-2). W H Freeman.

Electromechanical Devices for Energy Conversion & Control Systems. V. Del Toro. 1968. ref. ed. 26.95 (ISBN 0-13-250068-X). P-H.

Electromedical Instrumentation: A Guide for Medical Personnel. P. Eergveld. LC 77-85711. (Techniques of Measurement in Medicine Ser.: No. 2). (Illus.). 1980. 29.50 (ISBN 0-521-21892-6); pap. 9.95 (ISBN 0-521-29305-7). Cambridge U Pr.

Electron & Pion Interactions with Nuclei at Intermediate Energies. Ed. by W. Bertozzi et al. (Studies in High Energy Physics: Vol. 2). 716p. 1981. 55.00 (ISBN 3-7186-0015-3). Harwood Academic.

Electron Beam X-Ray Microanalysis. Kurt F. Heinrich. 608p. 1980. text ed. 42.50 (ISBN 0-442-23286-1). Van Nos Reinhold.

Electron Beams, Lenses & Optics, Vols. 1 & 2. A. B. El-Kareh & J. C. El-Kareh. 1970. Vol. 1. 48.50 (ISBN 0-12-238001-0); Vol. 2. 48.00 (ISBN 0-12-238002-9). Acad Pr.

Electron-Ion Exchangers: A New Group of Redoxites. A. V. Kozhevnikov. Ed. by A. Pick. Tr. by R. Kondor from Rus. LC 74-32247. 129p. 1975. 27.95 (ISBN 0-470-50626-1). Halsted Pr.

Electron Micrographic Atlas of Viruses. Robley C. Williams & Harold W. Fisher. (Illus.). 152p. 1974. 22.75 (ISBN 0-398-03153-3). C C Thomas.

Electron Microprobe Analysis. Reed. LC 74-94356. (Monographs on Physics). (Illus.). 350p. 1975. 59.95 (ISBN 0-521-20466-6). Cambridge U Pr.

Electron Microscopy & Analysis. P. J. Goodhew & L. E. Cartwright. LC 74-32449. (Wykeham Science Ser.: No. 33). 1975. 9.95x (ISBN 0-8448-1160-2). Crane Russak Co.

Electron Microscopy & Cell Structure. M. A. Tribe et al. LC 75-6284. (Basic Biology Course Ser.: No. 2). (Illus.). 120p. 1975. 24.95 (ISBN 0-521-20657-X) pap. 11.95x (ISBN 0-521-20557-3); film 15.95x (ISBN 0-521-20907-2); tape commentary for film 15.95x (ISBN 0-521-20965-X). Cambridge U Pr.

Electron Microscopy & Microanalysis of Crystalline Materials. Ed. by J. A. Belk. (Illus.). 1979. 36.30x (ISBN 0-85334-816-2, Pub. by Applied Science). Burgess-Intl Ideas.

Electron Microscopy & Structure of Materials: Proceedings of the Fifth Annual Symposium on the Structure & Properties of Materials, Berkeley, September, 1971. Ed. by Gareth Thomas et al. 1972. 50.00x (ISBN 0-520-02114-2). U of Cal Pr.

Electron Microscopy & X-Ray Applications, Vol.2. Ed. by P. Russell. 200p. 1981. text ed. write for info. (ISBN 0-250-40379-X). Ann Arbor Science.

Electron Microscopy at Molecular Dimensions. Ed. by W. Daumeister. (Proceedings in Life Sciences). (Illus.). 300p. 1980. 57.90 (ISBN 0-387-10131-4). Springer-Verlag.

Electron Microscopy in Biology, Vol.1. Jack D. Griffith. (Electron Microscopy in Biology Ser.). 325p. 1981. 32.50 (ISBN 0-471-05525-5, Pub. by Wiley-Interscience). Wiley.

Electron Microscopy in Human Medicine, Vol. 7: Digestive System. (Electron Microscopy in Human Medicine Ser.). 250p. 1980. 58.00 (ISBN 0-07-032507-3, HP). McGraw.

Electron Microscopy in Human Medicine: Vol. 9, Urogenital System & Breast. Jans V. Johannessen. (Illus.). 396p. 1980. text ed. 74.00 (ISBN 0-07-032508-1, HP). McGraw.

Electron Microscopy of Cells & Tissues. Fritiof S. Sjostrand. Vol. 1, 1967. 50.50, by subscription 41.00 (ISBN 0-12-647550-4). Acad Pr.

Electron Microscopy of Plant Viruses: Bibliography 1939-1965. Compiled by Juergen Brandes. 91p. (Orig.). 1967. pap. 16.00x (ISBN 3-489-12200-3). Intl Pubns Serv.

Electron Microscopy: Principles & Practices. Richard E. Crang & Jack A. Ward. 80p. (Incl. sound filmstrip). 1975. pap. text ed. 150.00 o.p. (ISBN 0-7216-9880-8). Saunders.

Electron Molecule Scattering. Sanborn C. Brown. LC 79-12705. (Wiley Series in Plasma Physics). 1980. 24.95 (ISBN 0-471-05205-1, Pub. by Wiley-Interscience). Wiley.

Electron Optics, 2 pts. 2nd ed. P. Grivet. Incl. Pt. 1. Optics. pap. 14.50 (ISBN 0-08-016226-6); Pt. 2. Instruments. pap. 16.00 (ISBN 0-08-016228-2). 1972. Set. 67.00 (ISBN 0-08-016086-7). Pergamon.

Electron Optics. 3rd ed. O. E. Klemperer & M. E. Barnett. LC 74-118065. (Cambridge Physics Monographs). (Illus.). 1970. 68.50 (ISBN 0-521-07928-4). Cambridge U Pr.

Electron Paramagnetic Resonance in Compounds of Transition Elements. 2nd ed. S. A. Al'tshuler & B. M. Kozyrev. Tr. by A. Barouch from Rus. LC 74-8208. 589p. 1975. 82.95 (ISBN 0-470-02523-9). Halsted Pr.

Electron Paramagnetic Resonance of Transition Ions. A. Abragam & B. Bleaney. (International Series of Monographs on Physics). 1970. 84.00x (ISBN 0-19-851250-3). Oxford U Pr.

Electron-Photon Shower Distribution Function: Tables for Lead, Copper & Air Absorbers. H. Messel & D. F. Crawford. LC 69-16049. 1970. 180.00 (ISBN 0-08-013374-6). Pergamon.

Electron Physics: The Physics of the Free Electron. 2nd ed. O. Klemperer. 280p. 1972. 14.50x (ISBN 0-408-70223-0); pap. 10.95x (ISBN 0-408-70229-X). Butterworths.

Electron Scattering from Complex Nuclei Pts. A & B. Herbert Uberall. (Pure & Applied Physics Ser: Vol. 25). 1971. Pt. A. 51.00 (ISBN 0-12-705701-3); Pt. B. 48.50 (ISBN 0-12-705702-1); Set. 81.00 (ISBN 0-685-02415-6). Acad Pr.

Electron Spin Double Resonance Spectroscopy. Larry Kevan & Lowell D. Kispert. LC 75-44418. 380p. 1976. 37.50 (ISBN 0-471-47340-5, Pub. by Wiley-Interscience). Wiley.

Electron Spin Resonance. N. M. Atherton. LC 73-14031. (Illus.). 435p. 1973. 66.95 (ISBN 0-470-03600-1). Halsted Pr.

Electron Spin Resonance: A Comprehensive Treatise on Experimental Technique. C. P. Poole. 922p. 1967. 50.00 (ISBN 0-470-69386-X). Wiley.

Electron States & Optical Transitions in Solids. F. Bassani & Pastori Parravicini. 312p. 1976. text ed. 44.00 (ISBN 0-08-016846-9). Pergamon.

Electron Transfer Reactions. R. D. Cannon. LC 79-41278. 1980. text ed. 84.95 (ISBN 0-408-10646-8). Butterworths.

Electron Tubes. Yujiro Koike. (Eng.). 1972. 37.50x (ISBN 0-8002-1389-0). Intl Pubns Serv.

Electronic Amplifiers: Theory, Design, & Use. Charles H. Evans. LC 76-3950. 1979. pap. text ed. 13.20 (ISBN 0-8273-1626-7); instr's manual 2.25 (ISBN 0-8273-1627-5). Delmar.

Electronic & Ionic Impact Phenomena: Slow Position & Muon Collisions - & Notes on Recent Advances, Vol. 5. Harrie Massey et al. (International Ser. of Monographs on Physics). (Illus.). 596p. 1974. 69.00x (ISBN 0-19-851283-X). Oxford U Pr.

Electronic & Newer Ceramics. Ed. by J. J. Svec et al. 1959. 14.95 (ISBN 0-8436-0604-5). CBI Pub.

Electronic & Structural Properties of Amorphous Semiconductors. Ed. by P. G. LeComber & P. G. LeComber. 1973. 87.50 (ISBN 0-12-440550-9). Acad Pr.

Electronic & Switching Circuits. S. M. Bozic et al. (Illus.). 1975. pap. 17.95x (ISBN 0-7131-3339-2). Intl Ideas.

Electronic Assembly. Clyde Herrick & Gerry Howery. 176p. 1980. text ed. 14.95 o.p. (ISBN 0-8359-1639-1); pap. text ed. 10.95 o.p. (ISBN 0-8359-1638-3). Reston.

Electronic Briefcase: The Office of the Future. Robert A. Russel. 52p. 1978. pap. text ed. 3.00x (ISBN 0-920380-05-0, Pub. by Inst Res Pub Canada). Renouf.

Electronic Calculator Handbook for Pilots. Martin Winger. (Illus.). Date not set. spiral bdg. 3.95 (ISBN 0-911721-77-0, Pub. by Winger). Aviation.

Electronic Calculators for Business Use. Flora M. Locke. LC 78-1852. 1978. pap. text ed. 15.95 (ISBN 0-471-03579-3); tchrs. manual avail. (ISBN 0-471-03766-4). Wiley.

Electronic Circuit Analysis & Design. William H. Hayt & Gerold W. Nevdeck. LC 75-31032. (Illus.). 384p. 1976. text ed. 24.95 (ISBN 0-395-21919-1); ans. to selected problems incl. (ISBN 0-685-63236-9); solutions manual 1.00 (ISBN 0-395-21923-X). HM.

Electronic Circuit Devices. Frank Harris. (Avionics Technician Training Course Ser.). (Orig.). 1981. pap. write for info. (ISBN 0-89100-192-1). Aviation Maintenance.

Electronic Circuits & Systems. R. A. King. LC 74-31175. 1975. 19.95 (ISBN 0-470-47779-2); solutions to problems manual 3.50 (ISBN 0-470-01399-0). Halsted Pr.

Electronic Circuits: Digital & Analog. Charles A. Holt. LC 77-11654. 1978. 26.95x (ISBN 0-471-02313-2); tchr's manual avail. (ISBN 0-471-03044-9). Wiley.

Electronic Circuits for Technicians. Lloyd Temes. (Illus.). 1970. text ed. 15.50 o.p. (ISBN 0-07-063485-8, G); answers 1.50 o.p. (ISBN 0-07-063486-6). McGraw.

Electronic Circuits for the Behavioral & Biomedical Sciences: A Reference Book of Useful Solid-State Circuits. Mitchell H. Zucker. LC 76-81921. (Illus.). 1969. text ed. 22.95x (ISBN 0-7167-0918-X). W H Freeman.

Electronic Circuits Notebook: Proven Designs for Systems Applications. Ed. by Samuel Weber. LC 80-29479. (Electronic Magazine Bks.). (Illus.). 344p. (Orig.). 1981. professional 14.95 (ISBN 0-07-606720-3, R-026). McGraw.

Electronic Communications. 2nd ed. Roddy & Coolen. (Illus.). 640p. 1980. text ed. 19.95 (ISBN 0-8359-1631-6); instr's. manual free. Reston.

Electronic Components & Measurements. Bruce D. Wedlock & James K. Roberge. 1969. ref. ed. 22.95 (ISBN 0-13-250464-2). P-H.

Electronic Computer Memory Technology. W. B. Riley. 1971. 27.50 o.p. (ISBN 0-07-052915-9, P&RB). McGraw.

Electronic Computers Made Simple. Henry Jacobowitz. LC 62-7648. 1963. pap. 3.95 (ISBN 0-385-03225-0, Made). Doubleday.

Electronic Data Processing & Computers for Commercial Students. E. A. Bird. (Illus.). 1972. text ed. 19.95x (ISBN 0-434-90140-7); pap. text ed. 11.95x (ISBN 0-434-90141-5). Intl Ideas.

Electronic Data Processing in Libraries. 1975. text ed. 19.50 (ISBN 3-7940-5214-5). K G Saur.

Electronic Democracy: Television's Impact on the American Political Process. Anne Saldich. LC 79-18592. (Praeger Special Studies). 142p. 1979. 21.95 (ISBN 0-03-052146-7). Praeger.

Electronic Design with Integrated Circuits. David J. Comer. LC 80-23365. (Electrical Engineering Ser.). (Illus.). 416p. 1981. text ed. 24.95 (ISBN 0-201-03931-1). A-W.

Electronic Design's Gold Book, 4 vols. 3072p. (Multi-vol.). 1980-81. Set. 35.00 (ISBN 0-685-50904-4). Hayden.

Electronic Devices & Circuit Theory. 2nd ed. R. Boylestad & L. Nashelsky. 1978. 21.95 (ISBN 0-13-250340-9). P-H.

Electronic Devices & Circuits, Vols. 1-3. G. J. Pridham. LC 67-26692. Vol. 1. 1968. 22.00 (ISBN 0-08-012549-2); Vol. 2. 1969. o.p. (ISBN 0-08-013461-0); Vol. 3. 1972. 21.00 (ISBN 0-08-016626-1); Vol. 1. pap. 9.25 (ISBN 0-08-012548-4); Vol. 3. pap. 7.75 (ISBN 0-08-016755-1). Pergamon.

Electronic Drafting & Design. 3rd ed. Nicholas M. Raskhodoff. (Illus.). 1977. text ed. 19.95 (ISBN 0-13-250613-0). P-H.

Electronic Drafting Techniques & Excercises. George Shiers. (Illus.). 1963. pap. text ed. 12.95 (ISBN 0-13-250605-X). P-H.

Electronic Drawing & Technology. Ulises M. Lopez & George E. Warrin. LC 77-16452. (Electronic Technology Ser.). 1978. text ed. 19.95 (ISBN 0-471-02377-9); solutions manual avail. (ISBN 0-471-03715-X). Wiley.

Electronic Engineering Applications of Two Port Systems. H. B. Gatland. 1976. text ed. 32.00 (ISBN 0-08-018069-8); pap. 16.00 (ISBN 0-08-019866-X). Pergamon.

Electronic Engineers Master, 2 vols. LC 58-9813. 1980. 50.00 (ISBN 0-89047-046-4). Herman Pub.

Electronic Engineer's Reference Book. 4th ed. L. W. Turner. 1976. text ed. 79.95x (ISBN 0-408-00168-2). Butterworths.

Electronic Equipment Wiring & Assembling: Part One. Ed. by D. Adams et al. (Engineering Craftsmen: No. G5). 1968. spiral bdg. 15.50x (ISBN 0-85083-014-1). Intl Ideas.

Electronic Equipment Wiring & Assembling: Part Two. Ed. by N. F. Clark et al. (Engineering Craftsmen: No. G25). (Illus.). 1969. spiral bdg. 24.95x (ISBN 0-685-90137-8). Intl Ideas.

Electronic Experimentation in Semiconductor & Vacuous Media. Ernest A. Joerg & Nat A. Polito. 1979. pap. text ed. 9.50 (ISBN 0-89669-038-5). Collegium Bk Pubs.

Electronic Experimenter's Manual. David A. Findlay. (Illus.). 1959. 7.95 o.p. (ISBN 0-498-09369-7). A S Barnes.

Electronic Experiments. F. G. Rayer. (Pegasus Books). 1971. 10.50x (ISBN 0-234-77485-1). Intl Pubns Serv.

Electronic Feto-Maternal Monitoring: Antepartum-Intrapartum. Luis A. Cibils. (Illus.). 600p. 1981. text ed. 56.00 (ISBN 0-88416-192-7). PSG Pub.

Electronic Flash. Jim Cornfield. LC 76-1544. (Petersen's How-to Photographic Library). (Illus.). 80p. 1976. pap. 4.50 o.p. (ISBN 0-8227-0126-X). Petersen Pub.

Electronic Flash Photography: A Complete Guide to the Best Equipment & Creative Techniques. Ron Carraher & Colleen Chartier. 136p. 1980. 24.95 (ISBN 0-442-21463-4); pap. 14.95 (ISBN 0-442-21335-0). Van Nos Reinhold.

Electronic Fundamentals & Applications: Integrated & Discrete Systems. 5th ed. John D. Ryder. (Illus.). 640p. 1975. 25.95 (ISBN 0-13-251371-4). P-H.

Electronic Funds Transfers: Regulation E Compliance 1980. (Commercial Law & Practice Course Handbook Series 1979-80: Vol. 230). 1980. pap. 25.00 (ISBN 0-685-90320-6, A4-3073). PLI.

Electronic Ignition Systems. Marvin Tepper. (gr. 10 up). 1977. pap. 5.95 (ISBN 0-8104-5746-6). Hayden.

Electronic Industries Information Sources. Ed. by Gretchen R. Randle. LC 67-31262. (Management Information Guide Ser.: No. 13). 1968. 30.00 (ISBN 0-8103-0813-4). Gale.

Electronic Inspection & Test, 2 vols. Ed. by D. Adams et al. (Engineering Craftsmen: No. G26). (Illus.). 1969. Set. sprial bdg. 36.50x (ISBN 0-85083-035-4). Intl Ideas.

Electronic Instrumentation. 2nd ed. Sol D. Prensky. 1971. ref. ed. 21.95 (ISBN 0-13-251645-4). P-H.

Electronic Instrumentation & Measurement Techniques. 2nd ed. William D. Cooper. LC 77-24528. (Illus.). 1978. ref. ed. 20.95 (ISBN 0-13-251710-8). P-H.

Electronic Integrated Systems Design. Hans R. Camenzind. LC 78-12195. (Illus.). 342p. 1980. Repr. of 1972 ed. lib. bdg. 18.50 (ISBN 0-88275-763-6). Krieger.

Electronic Interpretation of Organic Chemistry: A Problems-Oriented Text. F. M. Menger & L. Mandell. 215p. 1980. text ed. 27.50 (ISBN 0-306-40379-X, Plenum Pr); pap. text ed. 12.50 (ISBN 0-306-40391-9, Plenum Pr). Plenum Pub.

Electronic Invasion. rev. 2nd ed. Robert M. Brown. (Illus.). 192p. 1975. pap. 7.15 (ISBN 0-8104-0825-2). Hayden.

Electronic Inventions & Discoveries. 2nd rev. & exp. ed. Geoffrey W. Dummer. 1978. text ed. 45.00 (ISBN 0-08-022730-9); pap. text ed. 16.50 (ISBN 0-08-023223-X). Pergamon.

Electronic Journalism. William A. Wood. LC 67-25305. 1967. 15.00x (ISBN 0-231-02875-X). Columbia U Pr.

Electronic Maintenance, Vol. 1. Ed. by S. D. Coates et al. (Engineering Craftsmen: No. J4). (Illus.). 1969. spiral bdg. 24.95x (ISBN 0-85083-027-3). Intl Ideas.

Electronic Maintenance, Vol. 2. Ed. by I. Davidson et al. (Engineering Craftsmen: No. J24). (Illus.). 1970. spiral bdg. 18.95x (ISBN 0-685-90140-8). Intl Ideas.

Electronic Materials & Devices. David H. Navon. 1975. text ed. 23.95 (ISBN 0-395-18917-9); solutions manual 5.20 (ISBN 0-395-19374-5). HM.

Electronic Measurements for Scientists, 4 modules. H. V. Malmstadt et al. Incl. Module 1. Electronic Analog Measurements & Transducers. pap. text ed. 8.95 with experiments (ISBN 0-8053-6903-1); with lab summaries 7.95 (ISBN 0-8053-6908-2); Module 2. Control of Electrical Quantities in Instrumentation. pap. text ed. 8.95 with experiments (ISBN 0-8053-6904-X); with lab summeries 7.95 (ISBN 0-8053-6909-0); Module 3. Digital & Analog Data Conversions. pap. text ed. 8.95 with experiments (ISBN 0-8053-6905-8); with lab summaries 7.95 (ISBN 0-8053-6910-4); Module 4. Optimization & Electronic Measurements. pap. text ed. 8.95 with experiments (ISBN 0-8053-6906-6); pap. text ed. 5.95 with summaries (ISBN 0-8053-6911-2). 1974. Benjamin-Cummings.

Electronic Microsurgery of Skin. Ed. by J. W. Mali (Current Problems in Dermatology: Vol. 9). (Illus.). 1981. soft cover 48.00 (ISBN 3-8055-3080-3). S Karger.

Electronic Music for Young People. Willman. write for info. (ISBN 0-87628-210-9). Ctr Appl Res.

Electronic Music Production. Alan Douglas. LC 74-75216. (Illus.). 156p. 1974. 7.95 o.p. (ISBN 0-8306-4718-X); pap. 3.95 (ISBN 0-8306-3718-4, 718). TAB Bks.

Electronic Music Synthesizers. Delton T. Horn. (Illus.). 168p. 1980. 10.95 (ISBN 0-8306-9722-5); pap. 5.95 (ISBN 0-8306-1167-3, 1167). TAB Bks.

Electronic Music: Systems, Techniques & Controls. 2nd ed. Allen Strange. 1981. pap. text ed. 7.95x (ISBN 0-697-03602-2). Wm C Brown.

Electronic News Financial Fact Book & Directory: 1980. Book Research Staff. (Illus.). 640p. 1980. pap. text ed. 90.00 (ISBN 0-87005-360-4). Fairchild.

Electronic News Financial Fact Book & Directory: 1979. Book Research Staff. (Illus.). 616p. 1979. pap. text ed. 80.00 (ISBN 0-87005-308-6). Fairchild.

Electronic Nightmare: The New Communications & Freedom. John Wicklein. LC 80-54199. 320p. 1981. 15.95 (ISBN 0-670-50658-3). Viking Pr.

Electronic Principles: Physics, Models & Circuits. Paul E. Gray & Campbell L. Searle. LC 78-107884. 1969. text ed. 34.95x (ISBN 0-471-32398-5). Wiley.

Electronic Projects for Musicians. Craig Anderton. LC 75-27789. 136p. (Orig.). 1975. pap. 7.95 (ISBN 0-8256-9502-3). Guitar Player.

Electronic Projects in Hobbies. F. G. Rayer. 1979. pap. 7.95 o.p. (ISBN 0-686-60308-7, NB 98). Hayden.

Electronic Reliability. Geoffrey W. Dummer. Ed. by N. B. Griffin. 1966. 16.00 (ISBN 0-08-011448-2); pap. 7.75 (ISBN 0-08-011447-4). Pergamon.

Electronic States of Molecules & Atom Clusters. G. Del Re et al. (Lecture Notes in Chemistry: Vol. 13). (Illus.). 180p. 1980. pap. 17.50 (ISBN 0-387-09738-4). Springer-Verlag.

Electronic Structure & the Properties of Solids: The Physics of the Chemical Bond. Walter A. Harrison. LC 79-17364. (Illus.). 1980. text ed. 29.95x (ISBN 0-7167-1000-5); instr's guide avail. (ISBN 0-7167-1220-2). W H Freeman.

Electronic Structure of Atoms & Molecules: A Survey of Rigorous Quantum Mechanical Results. Henry F. Schaefer. 1972. text ed. 12.95 (ISBN 0-201-06726-9). A-W.

Electronic Structure of Molecules: Theory & Application to Inorganic Molecules. G. Doggett. 1972. 49.00 (ISBN 0-08-016588-5). Pergamon.

Electronic Surveying & Navigation. Simo H. Laurila. LC 75-41461. 512p. 1976. 37.50 (ISBN 0-471-51865-4, Pub. by Wiley-Interscience). Wiley.

Electronic Systems, Bk. 8. W. Bolton. LC 80-41394. (Study Topics in Physics Ser.). 96p. 1980. pap. text ed. write for info. (ISBN 0-408-10659-X). Butterworths.

Electronic Systems-Theory & Applications. Henry Zanger. LC 76-18714. (Illus.). 1977. text ed. 20.95 (ISBN 0-13-252155-5). P-H.

Electronic Techniques in Anesthesia & Surgery. 2nd ed. D. W. Hill. (Illus.). 448p. 1973. 39.95 (ISBN 0-407-16401-4). Butterworths.

Electronic Techniques: Shop Practices & Construction. 2nd ed. R. Villanucci et al. 1981. 21.00 (ISBN 0-13-252486-4). P-H.

Electronic Techniques: Shop Practices & Construction. Robert S. Villanucci et al. (Illus.). 1974. ref. ed. 20.95 (ISBN 0-13-252494-5). P-H.

Electronic Transitions & the High Pressure Chemistry & Physics of Solids. H. G. Drickamer & C. W. Frank. LC 72-12341. (Studies in Chemical Physics). 220p. 1973. text ed. 29.50x o.p. (ISBN 0-412-11650-2, Pub. by Chapman & Hall). Methuen Inc.

Electronic Transitions & the High Pressure Chemistry & Physics of Solids. H. G. Drickamer & C. W. Frank. LC 72-12341. (Studies in Chemical Physics). 330p. 1973. 29.50 o.p. (ISBN 0-470-22180-1). Halsted Pr.

Electronics. Byron J. Alpers & Mitchell L. Afrow. (Shoptalk - Vocational Reading Skills). (gr. 9-12). 1978. pap. text ed. 5.12 (ISBN 0-205-05822-1, 4958225); tchrs'. guide 5.40 (ISBN 0-205-05824-8). Allyn.

Electronics. Boy Scouts Of America. LC 19-600. (Illus.). 72p. (gr. 6-12). 1977. pap. 0.70x (ISBN 0-8395-3279-2, 3279). BSA.

Electronics. J. Dilson. (Quick & Easy Series). 1966. pap. 2.95 o.s.i. (ISBN 0-02-079800-8, Collier). Macmillan.

Electronics: A Contemporary Approach. W. Gothmann. 1980. 18.95 (ISBN 0-13-252254-3). P-H.

Electronics: An Elementary Introduction for Beginners. 2nd ed. L. W. Owers. (Illus.). (gr. 10-12). 1978. pap. text ed. 11.95x (ISBN 0-291-39659-3). Intl Ideas.

Electronics & Nuclear Physics. Thomas Duncan. (gr. 9-12). text ed. 14.95 (ISBN 0-7195-2003-7). Transatlantic.

Electronics & Radio: An Introduction. M. Nelkon & H. I. Humphreys. 1975. pap. text ed. 11.95x (ISBN 0-435-68335-7). Heinemann Ed.

Electronics Buyer's Guide, 1980. Date not set. pap. 30.00 (ISBN 0-07-054596-0). McGraw.

Electronics: Circuits & Devices. R. J. Smith. LC 72-12833. 1973. 23.95x o.p. (ISBN 0-471-80181-X). Wiley.

Electronics Construction & Assembly. George Ritchie. (Illus.). 1980. lib. bdg. 16.95 (ISBN 0-13-250472-3). P-H.

Electronics: Devices, Discrete & Integrated Circuits. Arthur H. Seidman & Jack L. Waintraub. (Electronics Technology Ser.). 1977. text ed. 22.95 (ISBN 0-675-08494-6); instr's manual 3.95 (ISBN 0-685-75491-X). Merrill.

Electronics Engineer's Handbook. 2nd ed. Donald G. Fink & Donald Christiansen. 2496p. Date not set. 46.50 (ISBN 0-07-020981-2). McGraw.

Electronics Explained: A Handbook for the Layman. Peter Laurie. (Illus.). 144p. 1980. 31.95 (ISBN 0-571-11514-4, Pub. by Faber & Faber); pap. 16.95 (ISBN 0-571-11593-4, Pub. by Faber & Faber). Merrimack Bk Serv.

Electronics Five. rev., 2nd ed. Harry Mileaf. 1978. pap. 6.60 (ISBN 0-8104-5958-2). Hayden.

Electronics for Appliances. John Brittan. Ed. by A. Ross Sabin. (Illus.). 172p. (gr. 11). 1979. 20.00 (ISBN 0-938336-09-6). Whirlpool.

Electronics for Engineers. H. Ahmed & P. J. Spreadbury. LC 72-93138. (Illus.). 280p. (Orig.). 1973. 34.95 (ISBN 0-521-20114-4); pap. 12.50x (ISBN 0-521-09789-4). Cambridge U Pr.

Electronics for Modern Communication. George J. Augerbauer. (Illus.). 672p. 1974. ref. ed. 21.95 (ISBN 0-13-252338-8). P-H.

Electronics for Scientists & Engineers. 2nd ed. R. Ralph Benedict. (Illus.). 1975. 25.95x (ISBN 0-13-252353-1). P-H.

Electronics for Technicians. P. W. Crane. 1971. pap. 9.00 o.p. (ISBN 0-08-016101-4). Pergamon.

Electronics for Technicians. Abraham Marcus. LC 69-10789. 1969. ref. ed. 18.95x (ISBN 0-13-252387-6). P-H.

Electronics for Technicians Three. S. A. Knight. (Newnes-Butterworth Technical Ser.). (Illus.). 192p. 1980. pap. text ed. 15.95 (ISBN 0-408-00458-4). Butterworths.

Electronics for Technicians Two. Stephen A. Knight. (TEC Technicians Ser.). (Illus.). 1978. pap. 9.95 (ISBN 0-408-00324-3). Butterworths.

Electronics Four. 2nd rev. ed. Harry Mileaf. (gr. 10 up). 1977. pap. 7.25 (ISBN 0-8104-5957-4). Hayden.

Electronics: From Theory into Practice, 2 vols. 2nd ed. Jack Fisher & Bruce Gatland. 538p. 1975. Combined Ed. 34.00 (ISBN 0-08-019857-0); Vol. 1. pap. text ed. 15.50 (ISBN 0-08-019855-4); Vol. 2. pap. text ed. 15.50 (ISBN 0-08-019856-2). Pergamon.

Electronics in Action, Bk. 1. new ed. George Delpit & Stephen Johnson. (gr. 10-12). 1975. text ed. 10.60 (ISBN 0-87002-022-6); wkbk & ans. sheet 2.60 (ISBN 0-87002-039-0). Bennett IL.

Electronics in Action, Bk. 2. George H. Delpit. (gr. 9-12). 1972. text ed. 11.44 (ISBN 0-87002-115-X); wkbk & ans. sheet 2.52 (ISBN 0-87002-143-5); tchr's guide avail. (ISBN 0-685-24134-3). Bennett IL.

Electronics in Our World: A Survey. Gregory J. Nunz. LC 70-146682. (Illus.). 1972. ref. ed. 19.95 (ISBN 0-13-252288-8). P-H.

Electronics in the Life Sciences. S. Young. LC 73-8083. 198p. 1973. 17.95 (ISBN 0-470-97943-7). Halsted Pr.

Electronics: Level II. Peter Beards. (Illus.). 192p. 1980. pap. text ed. 12.95x (ISBN 0-7121-0581-6). Intl Ideas.

Electronics Made Simple. rev. ed. Henry Jacobowitz. LC 64-20579. pap. 3.50 (ISBN 0-385-01227-6, Made). Doubleday.

Electronics Math. W. Deem. 1980. 19.95 (ISBN 0-13-252304-3). P-H.

Electronics One. rev., 2nd ed. Ed. by Harry Mileaf. (Illus.). (gr. 10-12). 1976. pap. 6.60 (ISBN 0-8104-5954-X). Hayden.

Electronics One-Seven, 7 vols. rev. 2nd ed. Ed. by Harry Mileaf. (Illus.). (gr. 10-12). 1976. Set. pap. 46.85 (ISBN 0-8104-5953-1). Hayden.

Electronics One-Seven. rev. 2nd ed. Ed. by Henry Mileaf. (Illus.). (gr. 10-12). 1976. 27.50x (ISBN 0-8104-5961-2); exam sets, vols. 1-7 0.50 ea.; transparencies 1270.45 (ISBN 0-685-70978-7). Hayden.

Electronics Seven. rev., 2nd ed. Harry Mileaf. (gr. 10 up). 1978. pap. 6.60 (ISBN 0-8104-5960-4). Hayden.

Electronics Six. rev., 2nd ed. Ed. by Harry Mileaf. (Illus.). (gr. 10-12). 1976. pap. 6.60 (ISBN 0-8104-5959-0). Hayden.

Electronics Three. rev., 2nd ed. Ed. by Harry Mileaf. (Illus.). (gr. 10-12). 1976. pap. 6.60 (ISBN 0-8104-5956-6). Hayden.

Electronics Two. rev., 2nd ed. Ed. by Harry Mileaf. (Illus.). (gr. 10-12). 1976. pap. 6.60 (ISBN 0-8104-5955-8). Hayden.

Electronics Unraveled: A New Commonsense Approach. James Kyle. LC 74-79583. (Illus.). 228p. 1974. pap. 5.95 o.p. (ISBN 0-8306-3691-9, 691). TAB Bks.

Electrons & Gods. rev. ed. Alan Isaacs. Date not set. cancelled (ISBN 0-89793-007-X). Hunter Hse.

Electrons & Phonons. J. M. Ziman. (International Series of Monographs on Physics). 1960. 67.00x (ISBN 0-19-851235-X). Oxford U Pr.

Electrons at the Fermi Surface. Ed. by Michael Springford. LC 79-50509. (Illus.). 496p. 1980. 85.00 (ISBN 0-521-22337-7). Cambridge U Pr.

Electrons in Crystalline Solids: Trieste Lectures, 1972. (Illus.). 753p. (Orig.). 1974. pap. 44.00 (ISBN 92-0-130073-5, IAEA). Unipub.

Electrons in Liquid Ammonia. J. C. Thompson. (Monographs on the Physics & Chemistry of Materials). (Illus.). 1976. 55.00x (ISBN 0-19-851343-7). Oxford U Pr.

Electrons in Metals. C. M. Hurd. LC 80-11429. 344p. 1980. Repr. of 1975 ed. lib. bdg. write for info. (ISBN 0-89874-157-2). Krieger.

Electronystagmography: Technical Aspects & Atlas. Joseph U. Toglia. (Illus.). 168p. 1976. 18.50 (ISBN 0-398-03537-7). C C Thomas.

Electronystagmography: What Is ENG? Wallace Rubin & Charles Norris. 116p. 1974. pap. 16.25 spiral (ISBN 0-398-03098-7). C C Thomas.

Electrophoresis & Immunochemical Reactions in Gels: Techniques & Interpretation. Leo P. Cawley et al. LC 77-93631. (Illus.). 1978. pap. text ed. 20.00 (ISBN 0-89189-038-6, 45-2-035-00). Am Soc Clinical.

Electrophoresis & Isoelectric Focusing in Polyacrylamide Gel: Advances of Methods & Theories, Biochemical & Clinical Applications. Ed. by Robert Allen & H. Rainer Maurer. LC 73-94225. (Illus.). 1974. 61.75x (ISBN 3-11-004344-0). De Gruyter.

Electrophoresis in the Separation of Biological Macromolecules. O. Gaal et al. LC 77-28502. 1980. 72.75 (ISBN 0-471-99602-5, Pub. by Wiley-Interscience). Wiley.

Electrophoresis Nineteen Seventy-Nine: Methods & Theories, Biochemical & Clinical Applications. Ed. by B. J. Radola. 700p. 1980. 116.00x (ISBN 3-11-008154-7). De Gruyter.

Electrophotography. rev, 2nd ed. R. M. Schaffert. LC 75-20099. 989p. 1975. 94.95 (ISBN 0-470-75696-9). Halsted Pr.

Electrophysiology & Layout of the Auditory Nervous System. J. Donald Harris. LC 73-18092. (Studies in Communicative Disorders Ser). 1974. pap. text ed. 3.95 (ISBN 0-672-61286-0). Bobbs.

Electroslag Remelting & Plasma Arc Melting. National Materials Advisory Board, National Research Council. LC 76-13351. (Illus.). 1976. pap. 7.25 (ISBN 0-309-02505-2). Natl Acad Pr.

Electrostatics in Reprography. W. A. Cook. (Reprographic Lib.). Date not set. 8.95 (ISBN 0-8038-1899-8). Hastings.

Electrosurgery in Dentistry. 2nd ed. Maurice J. Oringer. LC 70-186952. (Illus.). 1150p. 1975. text ed. 65.00 (ISBN 0-7216-7001-6). Saunders.

Electrosurgery in Dentistry: Theory & Application in Clinical Practice. William F. Malone. (American Lectures in Dentistry Ser.). (Illus.). 248p. 1974. pap. 24.75 photocopy ed. (ISBN 0-398-02917-2). C C Thomas.

Electrosurgical Apparatus & Their Application in Dermatology. Kenneth H. Burdick. (American Lecture in Dermatology Ser.). (Illus.). 74p. 1966. 11.75 (ISBN 0-398-00259-2). C C Thomas.

Elegant & Learned Discourse on the Light of Nature, 1652: Nathanael Colverwel (1618-1651) Nathanael Culverwel. Ed. by Rene Wellek. LC 75-11215. (British Philosophers & Theologians of the 17th & 18th Centuries Ser.). 1978. lib. bdg. 42.00 (ISBN 0-8240-1769-2). Garland Pub.

Elegant Auctioneers. Wesley Towner. (Illus.). 632p. 1970. 10.00 (ISBN 0-8090-4171-5). Hill & Wang.

Elegant Beast. Leonard Lubin. LC 80-52645. (Illus.). 48p. 1981. pap. 10.95 (ISBN 0-670-29097-1, Studio). Viking Pr.

Elegant Homes of America One Hundred Years Ago, 2 vols. Skip Whitson. (Sun Historical Ser.). (Illus.). 1977. Vol. 1. pap. 3.50 (ISBN 0-89540-046-4, SB-046); Vol. 2. pap. 3.50 (ISBN 0-89540-047-2, SB-047). Sun Pub.

Elegant Hors d'Oeuvre. Margon Edney & Ede Grimm. Ed. by Elizabeth Rand & Diane Polster. LC 77-86167. (Illus.). 1977. plastic comb 5.95 (ISBN 0-914488-13-9). Rand-Tofua.

Elegant Meals with Inexpensive Meats. Ortho Books Editorial Staff. LC 78-57890. (Illus.). 1979. pap. 4.95 (ISBN 0-917102-75-4). Ortho.

Elegant Nightmares: The English Ghost Story from le Fanu to Blackwood. Jack Sullivan. LC 77-92258. 155p. 1980. pap. 4.95 (ISBN 0-8214-0569-1, 0569E). Ohio U Pr.

Elegies, 3 bks. Propertius. Ed. by W. A. Camps. 1961-67. Bk. 1. text ed. 22.50 (ISBN 0-521-06000-1); pap. 8.50x (ISBN 0-521-29210-7); Bk. 2. text ed. 22.50 (ISBN 0-521-06001-X); Bk. 3. text ed. 16.95 (ISBN 0-521-06002-8). Cambridge U Pr.

Elegies for Sir Philip Sidney. LC 80-14236. 1980. 45.00x (ISBN 0-8201-1345-X). Schol Facsimiles.

Elegy to the Memory of the Late Duke of Bedford; Written on the Evening of His Interment, Repr. Of 1820. Amelia Opie. Bd. with Mary Tighe (Nee Blackford) (1772-1810) Psyche: with Other Poems. 3rd ed. Repr. of 1811 ed. LC 75-31245. (Romantic Context Ser.: Poetry 1789-1830: Vol. 94). 1978. lib. bdg. 47.00 (ISBN 0-8240-2193-2). Garland Pub.

Elemental Analysis of Biological Materials. (Technical Reports Ser.: No. 197). 371p. 1980. pap. 45.50 (ISBN 0-686-62997-3, IDC-197, IAEA). Unipub.

Elementare Zahlentheorie. Edmund Landau. LC 49-235. (Ger). 9.95 (ISBN 0-8284-0026-1). Chelsea Pub.

Elementary Accounting. rev. 4th ed. Royal D. Bauer & Paul H. Darby. (Orig.). 1973. pap. 3.95 (ISBN 0-06-460150-1, CO 50, COS). Har-Row.

Elementary Accounting. Reynolds et al. 1978. 18.95 (ISBN 0-03-018021-X). Dryden Pr.

Elementary Accounting. 2nd ed. Issac N. Reynolds et al. LC 80-65808. 1040p. 1981. pap. text ed. 19.95 (ISBN 0-03-058144-3). Dryden Pr.

Elementary Accounting: A Logical Approach. F. D. Litzinger et al. LC 77-86162. (Accounting Ser.). 1978. pap. text ed. 18.95 o.p. (ISBN 0-88244-160-4). Grid Pub.

Elementary Algebra. Daniel L. Auvil & Charles Poluga. LC 77-76194. (Illus.). 1978. text ed. 14.95 (ISBN 0-201-00137-3); student supplement 3.25 (ISBN 0-201-00138-1). A-W.

Elementary Algebra. Cohen & Cameron. 480p. 1981. pap. text ed. 16.95 (ISBN 0-205-07308-5, 5671728); free tchr's ed. (ISBN 0-205-07309-3). Allyn.

Elementary Algebra. D. Cohen & R. Cameron. LC 75-27504. 1976. 16.95 o.p. (ISBN 0-8465-0950-4); instr's guide 2.95 o.p. (ISBN 0-8465-0951-2). Benjamin-Cummings.

Elementary Algebra. Roy Dubisch & Vernon Hood. LC 76-3846. 1977. text ed. 18.95 (ISBN 0-8053-2338-4); instr's guide 3.95 (ISBN 0-8053-2339-2). Benjamin-Cummings.

Elementary Algebra. Harold R. Jacobs. LC 78-10744. (Illus.). 1979. text ed. 12.95x (ISBN 0-7167-1047-1); tchrs. guide 7.95x (ISBN 0-7167-1075-7); test masters 7.95x (ISBN 0-7167-1077-3); transparency masters 50.00x (ISBN 0-7167-1076-5). W H Freeman.

Elementary Algebra. Richard E. Johnson. 1980. 16.95 (ISBN 0-8053-5052-7). Benjamin-Cummings.

Elementary Algebra. 3rd ed. Robert A. Moon & Robert D. Davis. (Mathematics Ser.). 528p. 1980. pap. text ed. 14.95 (ISBN 0-675-08158-0); instructor's manual 3.95 (ISBN 0-686-63339-3). Merrill.

Elementary Algebra. 4th ed. Donald S. Russell & Collins. 1971. text ed. 13.95x o.p. (ISBN 0-205-03282-6, 563282X); study guide 5.95x o.p. (ISBN 0-205-03283-4, 5632838). Allyn.

Elementary Algebra. Gene Sellers. LC 80-23171. 475p. (Orig.). 1981. pap. text ed. 17.95 (ISBN 0-8185-0434-X). Brooks-Cole.

Elementary Algebra. William Zlot et al. (Sourcebook of Fundamental Mathematics Ser.). 156p. 1973. pap. 6.50 (ISBN 0-685-91066-0, Pub. by W & W). Krieger.

Elementary Algebra: A Guided Inquiry. Sherman Stein & Calvin Crabill. LC 78-179131. 96p. (Orig.). 1972. text ed. 17.50 (ISBN 0-395-12669-X); instr. ed. 18.95 (ISBN 0-395-12670-3); solution key. pap. 2.15 (ISBN 0-395-13756-X). HM.

Elementary Algebra: A Programmed Approach. Anthony J. Pettofrezzo & Lee H. Armstrong. 1980. pap. text ed. 14.95x (ISBN 0-673-15293-6). Scott F.

Elementary Algebra: A Self-Study Course. Frances S. Mangan. 1979. pap. text ed. 16.95 (ISBN 0-8403-1978-9, 40197800). Kendall-Hunt.

Elementary Algebra by Example. William Brett & Michael Sentlowitz. LC 76-11979. (Illus.). 1977. pap. text ed. 14.95 (ISBN 0-395-24425-0); inst. manual 1.75 (ISBN 0-395-24426-9). HM.

Elementary Algebra for College Students: A Revision of a First Course in Algebra. June Wood & David Outcalt. (Mathematics Ser.). 1977. text ed. 15.95 (ISBN 0-675-08510-1); instructor's manual 3.95 (ISBN 0-685-74280-6). Merrill.

Elementary Algebra for College Students. H. S. Bear & N. G. Mouck. 1968. text ed. 12.95 o.p. (ISBN 0-201-00432-1, 00433). A-W.

Elementary Algebra for College Students. Mary P. Dolciani & Robert H. Sorgenfrey. LC 78-146720. 1971. text ed. 14.95 o.p. (ISBN 0-395-12069-1); tchrs. guide. pap. 4.00 o.p. (ISBN 0-395-12071-3); answers to even-numbered problems 1.65 o.p. (ISBN 0-395-12070-5). HM.

Elementary Algebra for College Students. 5th ed. Irving Drooyan & William Wooton. LC 78-31666. 1980. text ed. 18.50 (ISBN 0-471-03607-2); solutions manual 7.95 (ISBN 0-471-05868-8); test (ISBN 0-471-05911-0). Wiley.

Elementary Algebra for College Students. D. Franklin Wright & Kenneth E. Lindgren. 1971. text ed. 14.95x o.p. (ISBN 0-669-52134-5); instructor's guide free o.p. (ISBN 0-669-52142-6). Heath.

Elementary Algebra: Lecture-Lab. 2nd ed. Arthur Heywood. 1977. pap. text ed. 14.95x o.p. (ISBN 0-8221-0190-4). Dickenson.

Elementary Algebra Skills for College. Harry Lewis. (Orig.). 1980. pap. text ed. 14.95 (ISBN 0-442-20396-9). D Van Nostrand.

Elementary Algebra: Structure & Skills. 4th ed. Irving Drooyan et al. LC 76-15018. 390p. 1977. text ed. 18.50 (ISBN 0-471-22249-6); 5.95x (ISBN 0-471-01825-2). Wiley.

Elementary Algebra with Geometry. Irving Drooyan & William Wooton. LC 75-35736. 334p. 1976. text ed. 18.50 (ISBN 0-471-22245-3). Wiley.

Elementary Algebra Without Trumpets or Drums. Martin M. Zuckerman. 448p. 1976. text ed. 17.80x (ISBN 0-205-04895-1); instructor's manual free (ISBN 0-685-57481-4); student wkbk 6.95 (ISBN 0-205-05824-8). Allyn.

Elementary ALGOL. Alan Brundritt. (Illus.). 80p. 1976. pap. text ed. 9.95 (ISBN 0-7121-0549-2, Pub. by Macdonald & Evans Engalnd). Intl Ideas.

Elementary Analysis, Vol. 2. K. S. Snell & J. B. Morgan. 1966. 22.00 (ISBN 0-08-011777-5); pap. 10.75 (ISBN 0-08-011776-7). Pergamon.

Elementary Analysis of Variance for the Behavioral Sciences. R. Meddis. LC 72-12493. (Illus.). 129p. 1973. pap. text ed. 10.50x (ISBN 0-470-59007-6). Halsted Pr.

Elementary & Middle School Social Studies Curriculum Program, Activities, Materials. James L. Barth. LC 78-71367. 1979. pap. text ed. 11.00 (ISBN 0-8191-0667-4). U Pr of Amer.

Elementary Anecdotes in American English. L. A. Hill. (Anecdotes in American English Ser.). (Illus.). 72p. 1980. 2.50x (ISBN 0-19-502601-2). Oxford U Pr.

Elementary Applied Calculus: A Short Course. 2nd ed. Raymond F. Coughlin. 1978. text ed. 19.90 (ISBN 0-205-05965-1); instr's man. avail. (ISBN 0-205-05966-X). Allyn.

Elementary Applied Statistics: For Students in Behavioral Science. Linton C. Freeman. LC 65-14256. 1965. text ed. 18.95x (ISBN 0-471-27780-0). Wiley.

Elementary Applied Symbolic Logic. Bangs L Tapscott. (Illus.). 512p. 1976. text ed. 16.95 (ISBN 0-13-252940-8). P-H.

Elementary Biochemistry: An Introduction to the Chemistry of Living Cells. Julian Davies & Barbara S. Littlewood. (P-H Biology Ser.). (Illus.). 1979. ref. 18.95 (ISBN 0-13-252809-6). P-H.

Elementary Blueprint Reading: For Beginners in Machine Shop Practice. 115p. 1970. pap. 3.60 o.p. (ISBN 0-8273-0083-2); instructor's guide 1.45 o.p. (ISBN 0-8273-0084-0). Delmar.

Elementary Blueprint Reading for Machinists. David Taylor. LC 80-65572. (Blueprint Reading Ser.). 160p. 1981. pap. text ed. 4.60 (ISBN 0-8273-1895-2); instr's. guide 1.50 (ISBN 0-8273-1892-8). Delmar.

Elementary Business Statistics: The Modern Approach. 3rd ed. John E. Freund & F. J. Williams. (Illus.). 1977. 19.95 (ISBN 0-13-253062-7). P-H.

Elementary Calculus. George Hadley. LC 68-11022. 1968. 17.95x (ISBN 0-8162-3524-4). Holden-Day.

Elementary Calculus for Business, Economics & Social Sciences. Chaney Anderson & R. C. Pierce, Jr. 1975. text ed. 17.50 (ISBN 0-395-18960-8); instructors manual 1.90 (ISBN 0-395-18959-4). HM.

Elementary Calculus from an Advanced Viewpoint. George B. Thomas et al. 1967. 17.95 (ISBN 0-201-07558-X). A-W.

Elementary Chemical Calculations. 3rd rev. ed. Amba Prasad & G. P. Kashyap. 1967. pap. 2.50x o.p. (ISBN 0-210-27017-9). Asia.

Elementary Chemical Theory & Problems. N. M. Shah. pap. 2.50x o.p. (ISBN 0-210-22665-X). Asia.

Elementary Chemical Thermodynamics. D. C. Firth. 1969. pap. 4.50x o.p. (ISBN 0-19-914001-4). Oxford U Pr.

Elementary Chinese Readers, 4 vols. Incl. Vol. 1 (ISBN 0-8351-0778-7); Vol. 2 (ISBN 0-8351-0779-5); Vol. 3 (ISBN 0-8351-0780-9); Vol. 4 (ISBN 0-8351-0781-7). 1980. pap. 4.95 ea. China Bks.

Elementary Classical Analysis. Jerrold E. Marsden. LC 74-5764. (Illus.). 1974. text ed. 24.95x (ISBN 0-7167-0452-8). W H Freeman.

Elementary Classical Hydrodynamics. B. Chirgwin & C. A. Plumpton. 1968. 19.50 (ISBN 0-08-012406-2); pap. 9.75 (ISBN 0-08-012405-4). Pergamon.

Elementary Classical Physics, 2 vols. 2nd ed. Richard T. Weidner et al. 1973. text ed. 22.95x combined edition o.p. (ISBN 0-685-27996-0, 737574); Vol. 1. text ed. 20.95x o.p. (ISBN 0-205-03597-3, 7335970); Vol. 2. text ed. 20.95x o.p. (ISBN 0-205-03598-1, 7335989). Vol. 2. sol. man. 4.95 o.p. (ISBN 0-205-04010-1, 7340109). Allyn.

Elementary Complex Variables. W. Smith. LC 43-87526. 352p. 1974. text ed. 16.95x (ISBN 0-675-08870-4). Merrill.

Elementary Contemporary Mathematics. 2nd ed. Merlin M. Ohmer et al. LC 70-186167. 1972. pap. text ed. 19.50x o.p. (ISBN 0-471-00401-4). Wiley.

Elementary Decision Theory. Herman Chernoff & L. E. Moses. LC 59-9337. (Illus.). 1959. 24.95 (ISBN 0-471-15213-7). Wiley.

Elementary Differential Equations. 3rd ed. William E. Boyce & Richard C. Di Prima. LC 75-35565. 1977. text ed. 20.95x (ISBN 0-471-09339-4). Wiley.

Elementary Differential Equations. 3rd ed. William T. Martin et al. 1981. text ed. 22.95 (ISBN 0-8162-5435-4). Holden-Day. Postponed.

Elementary Differential Equations & Boundary Value Problems. 3rd ed. William E. Boyce & Richard C. DiPrima. LC 75-45093. 1977. 20.95x (ISBN 0-471-09334-3). Wiley.

Elementary Differential Equations with Applications. William R. Derrick & Stanley I. Grossman. LC 75-12094. 1976. text ed. 18.95 o.p. (ISBN 0-201-01470-X). A-W.

Elementary Differential Equations with Applications. 2nd ed. William R. Derrick & Stanley I. Grossman. (Mathematics Ser.). (Illus.). 576p. 1981. text ed. price not set (ISBN 0-201-03162-0). A-W.

Elementary Differential Equations with Applications: A Short Course. William R. Derrick & Stanley I. Grossman. (Illus.). 448p. 1976. text ed. 16.95 o.p. (ISBN 0-201-01472-6); ans. bk. avail. o.p. (ISBN 0-201-01471-8). A-W.

Elementary Differential Equations with Applications: A Short Course. 2nd ed. William R. Derrick & Stanley I. Grossman. (Mathematics Ser.). (Illus.). 384p. 1981. text ed. 18.95 (ISBN 0-201-03164-7). A-W.

Elementary Differential Equations with Linear Algebra. 2nd ed. Ross L. Finney & Donald E. Ostberg. LC 75-12096. (Mathematics Ser.). 704p. 1976. text ed. 20.95 (ISBN 0-201-05515-5). A-W.

Elementary Differential Geometry. Barrett O'Neill. 1966. text ed. 20.95 (ISBN 0-12-526750-9); answer bklt. 3.00 (ISBN 0-12-526756-8). Acad Pr.

Elementary Discriptive Statistics: For Those Who Think They Can't. Arthur P. Coladarci & Theodore Coladarci. 144p. 1979. pap. text ed. 6.95x (ISBN 0-534-00782-1). Wadsworth Pub.

Elementary Dynamic Programming. John W. Norman. LC 75-13746. (Illus.). 110p. 1975. pap. 11.50x (ISBN 0-8448-0719-2). Crane-Russak Co.

Elementary Economics from the Higher Standpoints. R. M. Goodwin. LC 72-116842. 1970. 35.50 (ISBN 0-521-07923-3). Cambridge U Pr.

Elementary Education in India: The Unfinished Business. J. P. Naik. 1966. 6.50x (ISBN 0-210-22509-2). Asia.

Elementary Electrochemistry. 3rd ed. Burgess. 1981. text ed. price not set (ISBN 0-408-70931-6). Butterworth.

Elementary Electrochemistry. 2nd ed. A. R. Denaro. 246p. 1971. pap. 9.95 (ISBN 0-408-70071-8). Butterworths.

Elementary Engineering Fracture Mechanics. rev. ed. D. Broek. 450p. 1978. 60.00x (ISBN 90-286-0208-9); pap. 20.00x (ISBN 90-286-0218-6). Sijthoff & Noordhoff.

Elementary Finite Element Method. C. S. Desai. (Civil Engineering & Engineering Mechanics Ser.). (Illus.). 1979. ref. ed. 26.95 (ISBN 0-13-256636-2). P-H.

Elementary Fluid Mechanics. 5th ed. John K. Vennard & Robert L. Street. LC 74-31232. 740p. 1975. text ed. 26.95 (ISBN 0-471-90587-9). Wiley.

Elementary Fluid Mechanics. Frank M. White. (Illus.). 1979. text ed. 21.95 (ISBN 0-07-069667-5, C); write for info solution manual (ISBN 0-07-069668-3). McGraw.

Elementary Fluid Mechanics: SI Edition. 5th ed. John K. Vennard & Robert L. Street. LC 76-4885. 1976. 26.95 (ISBN 0-471-90589-5) (ISBN 0-685-68753-8). Wiley.

Elementary Food Science. 2nd ed. John T. Nickerson & Louis J. Ronsivall. 1980. pap. text ed. 19.00 (ISBN 0-87055-318-6). AVI.

Elementary Forestry. Bobby Collins & Fred White. 1981. text ed. 15.95 (ISBN 0-8359-1647-2); instr's. manual free (ISBN 0-8359-1646-4). Reston.

Elementary Forms of the Religious Life. Emile Durkheim. Tr. by Joseph W. Swain. 1965. 12.95 (ISBN 0-02-908000-2); pap. text ed. 7.95 (ISBN 0-02-908010-X). Free Pr.

Elementary FORTRAN. T. M. Petersen. (Illus.). 176p. 1976. pap. text ed. 10.95x (ISBN 0-7121-0548-4, Pub. by Macdonald & Evans England). Intl Ideas.

Elementary Functions. new ed. Margaret Hutchinson. LC 73-89294. (Mathematics Ser). 352p. 1974. text ed. 14.95x o.p. (ISBN 0-675-08855-0); instructor's manual 3.95 o.p. (ISBN 0-686-66942-8). Merrill.

Elementary Functions. Adil Yaqub. 368p. 1975. text ed. 17.50 (ISBN 0-395-17093-1); instructors manual pap. 2.25 (ISBN 0-395-17871-1). HM.

Elementary Functions: Algebra & Analytic Geometry. Gus Klentos & Joseph Newmyer, Jr. 448p. 1975. pap. text ed. 15.95 (ISBN 0-675-08827-5); media: audiocassettes 160.00, 2-6 sets, 100.00 ea., 7 or more sets, 75.00 ea. (ISBN 0-675-08774-0); instructor's manual 3.95 (ISBN 0-686-67047-7). Merrill.

Elementary Functions & Analytic Geometry. H. Flanders & Justin J. Price. 1973. text ed. 18.95 (ISBN 0-12-259655-2); instr's manual 3.00 (ISBN 0-12-259656-0). Acad Pr.

Elementary Functions: Pre-Calculus Mathematics. D. Franklin Wright & Kenneth E. Lindgren. 1973. text ed. 15.95x o.p. (ISBN 0-669-84285-0); instructor's guide free o.p. (ISBN 0-669-84798-4). Heath.

Elementary Functions: Trigonometry. Gus Klentos & Joseph Newmyer, Jr. LC 73-87838. 1974. text ed. 15.95 (ISBN 0-675-08864-X); media: audiocassettes 140.00, 2-6 sets, 95.00 ea., 7 or more sets, 70.00 ea. (ISBN 0-675-08865-8). Merrill.

Elementary General Relativity. C. Clarke. 131p. 1980. pap. 19.95x (ISBN 0-470-26930-8). Halsted Pr.

Elementary General Thermodynamics. M. V. Sussman. LC 74-133896. 1972. text ed. 22.95 (ISBN 0-201-07358-7). A-W.

Elementary Geometry. Vincent H. Haag et al. 1970. text ed. 14.95 (ISBN 0-201-02658-9); instructor's manual 2.00 (ISBN 0-201-02659-7). A-W.

Elementary Geometry from an Advanced Standpoint. 2nd ed. Edwin E. Moise. LC 73-2347. 1974. text ed. 17.95 (ISBN 0-201-04793-4). A-W.

Elementary Guide to Reliability. 2nd ed. Geoffrey W. Dummer & R. C. Winton. LC 73-16199. 66p. 1974. pap. text ed. 7.00 (ISBN 0-08-017821-9). Pergamon.

Elementary Harmony. 3rd ed. William J. Mitchell. 1965. 17.50x (ISBN 0-13-257279-6). P-H.

Elementary Harmony: Theory & Practice. 2nd ed. Robert W. Ottman. LC 70-105451. 1970. text ed. 16.95 (ISBN 0-13-257451-9); wkbk 10.95 (ISBN 0-13-257469-1). P-H.

Elementary Human Physiology. Terence A. Rogers. (Illus.). 1961. text ed. 18.95x (ISBN 0-471-73062-9). Wiley.

Elementary Introduction into the Elliott's Wave Theory. Ralph N. Elliott. (New Stock Market Reference Library). (Illus.). 91p. 1981. 27.55 (ISBN 0-918968-92-5). Inst Econ Fina.

Elementary Introduction to Number Theory. 2nd ed. Calvin T. Long. 208p. 1972. text ed. 13.95x o.p. (ISBN 0-669-62703-8). Heath.

Elementary Introduction to the Theory of Probability. 5th ed. Boris V. Gnedenko & Alexander Y. Khinchin. Tr. by Leon F. Boron. 1961. pap. text ed. 3.00 (ISBN 0-486-60155-2). Dover.

Elementary Kinetics of Membrane Carrier Transport. K. D. Neame & T. G. Richards. LC 72-2047. (Illus.). 120p. 1972. pap. 14.95 (ISBN 0-470-63078-7). Halsted Pr.

Elementary Knowledge: A Story of the Creation of the Hebrew Alaphabet. Peter Haden. (Illus.). 68p. 1981. 22.50 (ISBN 0-87663-357-2). Universe.

Elementary Linear Alebra. 3rd ed. Howard Anton. 384p. 1981. text ed. 19.95 (ISBN 0-471-05338-4). Wiley.

Elementary Linear Algebra. Stanley Grossman. 400p. 1980. text ed. 19.95x (ISBN 0-534-00746-5). Wadsworth Pub.

Elementary Linear Algebra. 3rd rev. ed. Paul C. Shields. (Illus.). 1980. text ed. 17.95x (ISBN 0-87901-121-1). Worth.

Elementary Linear Algebra with Applications. Francis G. Florey. LC 78-9412. (Illus.). 1979. ref. ed. 18.95 (ISBN 0-13-258251-1). P-H.

Elementary Linear Algebra with Applications. Adil Yaqub & Hal G. Moore. LC 79-18743. (Mathematics Ser.). 1980. text ed. 17.50 (ISBN 0-201-08825-8). A-W.

Elementary Linear Programming with Applications. Bernard Kolman & Robert Beck. (Computer Science & Applied Mathematics Ser.). 1980. text ed. 19.95 (ISBN 0-12-417860-X). Acad Pr.

Elementary Logic. Nancy D. Simco & Gene G. James. 1976. text ed. 15.95x (ISBN 0-8221-0156-4). Dickenson.

Elementary Luo Grammar, with Vocabularies. Roy L. Stafford. 1967. pap. 2.00x o.p. (ISBN 0-19-639396-5). Oxford U Pr.

Elementary Mathematical Analysis. Anthony E. Labarre. 1961. 15.95 (ISBN 0-201-04110-3). A-W.

Elementary Mathematical Ecology. John Vandermeer. LC 80-15664. 320p. 1981. 25.00 (ISBN 0-471-08131-0, Pub. by Wiley-Interscience). Wiley.

Elementary Mathematical Methods. Donald D. Paige et al. LC 77-2683. 1978. 19.95 (ISBN 0-471-65756-5); tchrs. manual avail. (ISBN 0-471-04057-6). Wiley.

Elementary Mathematics. Donald F. Devine & Jerome E. Kaufmann. LC 76-24805. 1977. text ed. 20.95 (ISBN 0-471-20970-8); instructor's manual avail. (ISBN 0-471-02394-9). Wiley.

Elementary Mathematics. Qazi Zameeruddin et al. 1975. 10.50 (ISBN 0-7069-0388-9, Pub. by Vikas India). Advent Bk.

Elementary Mathematics: A Fundamentals & Techniques Approach. Samuel R. Filippone & Michael Z. Williams. LC 75-19539. (Illus.). 448p. 1976. text ed. 17.50 (ISBN 0-395-20028-8); inst. manual 3.25 (ISBN 0-395-20029-6). HM.

Elementary Mathematics Diagnosis & Correction Kit. Francis M. Fennel. 1980. pap. 17.95x comb-bound (ISBN 0-87628-295-8). Ctr Appl Res.

Elementary Mathematics for Basic Chemistry & Physics. S. M. Gabbay. 128p. (Orig.). 1980. pap. 9.95 (ISBN 0-960-722-0-7). Basic Science Prep Ctr.

Elementary Mathematics for Teachers. John L. Kelley & Donald Richert. LC 70-11612. 1970. text ed. 18.95x (ISBN 0-8162-4654-8); sol. man 2.50x (ISBN 0-8162-4664-5). Holden-Day.

Elementary Mathematics: Its Structure & Concepts. 2nd ed. M. F. Willerding. LC 71-100328. 1970. text ed. 21.95 o.p. (ISBN 0-471-94665-6). Wiley.

Elementary Mathematics Laboratory Experiences. Joseph Hooten & Michael Mahaffey. 1973. pap. text ed. 7.95 (ISBN 0-675-09038-5). Merrill.

Elementary Mathematics Method. Max E. Jerman & Edward C. Beardslee. (Illus.). 1978. text ed. 16.50 (ISBN 0-07-032531-6, C); 3.95 (ISBN 0-07-032532-4). McGraw.

Elementary Mathematics of Price Theory. Clark L. Allen. 1966. pap. 9.95x (ISBN 0-534-00655-8). Wadsworth Pub.

Elementary Matrix Algebra for Psychologists & Social Scientists. A. G. Hammer. LC 72-117464. 212p. 1971. 12.75 (ISBN 0-08-017502-3). Pergamon.

Elementary Matrix Theory. Howard Eves. 1980. pap. 5.50 (ISBN 0-486-63946-0). Dover.

Elementary Mechanics of Solids. P. P. Benham. (Illus.). 1965. 19.50 (ISBN 0-08-011216-1); pap. text ed. 8.25 o.p. (ISBN 0-08-011215-3). Pergamon.

Elementary Metallurgy & Metallography. 2nd ed. Arthur M. Shrager. (Illus.). 1961. pap. text ed. 5.00 (ISBN 0-486-60138-2). Dover.

Elementary Microstudies of Human Tissues. James V. Bradley. (Illus.). 376p. 1972. pap. 36.50 (ISBN 0-398-02240-2). C C Thomas.

Elementary Modern Physics. new ed. Atam P. Arya. LC 73-1466. 1974. text ed. 18.95 (ISBN 0-201-00304-X). A-W.

Elementary Number Theory. rev. ed. Burton. 390p. 1980. text ed. 20.95 (ISBN 0-205-06965-7, 5669650). Allyn.

Elementary Number Theory. David M. Burton. 368p. 1976. text ed. 18.95x o.s.i. (ISBN 0-205-04814-5). Allyn.

Elementary Number Theory. 2nd ed. Underwood Dudley. LC 78-5661. (Mathematical Sciences Ser.). (Illus.). 1978. text ed. 17.95x (ISBN 0-7167-0076-X); ans. book avail. W H Freeman.

Elementary Number Theory. 2nd ed. Edmund Landau. LC 57-8494. 12.00 (ISBN 0-8284-0125-X). Chelsea Pub.

Elementary Partial Differential Equations for Engineers & Scientists. J. C. Wilhoit, Jr. LC 78-62181. 1978. pap. text ed. 11.00 (ISBN 0-8191-0501-5). U Pr of Amer.

Elementary Particle Theory: Relativistic Groups & Analyticity. N. Svartholm. (Nobel Symposium Ser.). 1969. 43.95 (ISBN 0-470-83842-6). Halsted Pr.

Elementary Particles & Their Currents. Jeremy Bernstein. LC 68-21404. (Physics Ser.). (Illus.). 1968. text ed. 26.95x (ISBN 0-7167-0324-6). W H Freeman.

Elementary Persian Grammar. Lawrence P. Elwell-Sutton. pap. 19.95 (ISBN 0-521-09206-X). Cambridge U Pr.

Elementary Physical Education: A Developmental Approach. 2nd ed. Daniel B. Arnheim & Robert A. Pestolesi. LC 77-26214. 1978. text ed. 15.95 (ISBN 0-8016-0326-9). Mosby.

Elementary Physics. A. F. Abbott & M. Nelkon. Ed. by Michael Sayer. 1971. pap. 5.50x ea. o.p.; Pt. 1. pap. (ISBN 0-435-67654-7); Pt. 2. pap. (ISBN 0-435-67655-5); pap. text ed. 9.50x combined ed. o.p. (ISBN 0-435-67656-3). Heinemann Ed.

Elementary Physics. 2nd ed. Frederick W. Van Name & David Flory. (Illus.). 352p. 1974. ref. ed. 16.95 (ISBN 0-13-259515-X); pap. 4.95 study guide & wkbk. (ISBN 0-13-259523-0). P-H.

Elementary Physics: Classical & Modern. Richard T. Weidner & Robert L. Sells. 1975. text ed. 26.95x (ISBN 0-205-04647-9, 7346476); instr's. man. free (ISBN 0-205-04648-7). Allyn.

Elementary Physics of Sound for Speech Pathology & Audiology. Gordon F. Holloway & Gordon Berkey. LC 73-571. (Illus.). 244p. 1981. 14.50 (ISBN 0-87527-190-1). Green. Postponed.

Elementary Plane Geometry. R. David Gustafson & Peter D. Frisk. LC 72-5840. 320p. 1973. text ed. 17.95x (ISBN 0-471-33700-5); tchrs'. manual avail. (ISBN 0-471-33701-3). Wiley.

Elementary Plane Rigid Dynamics. H. W. Harkness. (Orig.). 1964. 20.00 (ISBN 0-12-325350-0); pap. 8.50 (ISBN 0-12-325356-X). Acad Pr.

Elementary Plane Surveying. 4th ed. Raymond E. Davis & J. W. Kelly. (Illus.). 1967. text ed. 20.50 (ISBN 0-07-015771-5, C); solutions 1.50 (ISBN 0-07-015772-3). McGraw.

Elementary Platen Presswork. rev. ed. Ralph W. Polk. (gr. 11-12). 1971. 7.96 (ISBN 0-87002-109-5). Bennett IL.

Elementary Practical Organic Chemistry: Pt. 2, Qualitative Organic Analysis. 2nd ed. A. I. Vogel. 1966. 16.95 (ISBN 0-471-90963-7). Halsted Pr.

Elementary Price Theory. 2nd ed. Peter C. Dooley. (Illus., Orig.). 1973. pap. text ed. 9.95x (ISBN 0-13-259531-1). P-H.

Elementary Price Theory. Benjamin Ward. LC 67-15673. (Orig.). 1967. pap. text ed. 3.00 o.s.i. (ISBN 0-02-933950-2). Free Pr.

Elementary Principal's Handbook: A Guide to Effective Action. abr. ed. Larry W. Hughes & Gerald C. Ubben. 1978. text ed. 17.95 (ISBN 0-205-06080-3). Allyn.

Elementary Principles of Behavior. Donald L. Whaley & Richard Malott. (Orig.). 1971. pap. text ed. 15.95 (ISBN 0-13-259499-4). P-H.

Elementary Probability & Statistical Reasoning. Howard E. Reinhardt & Don O. Loftsgaarden. 1976. text ed. 16.95x (ISBN 0-669-00300-3); instructor's manual free (ISBN 0-669-00241-0). Heath.

Elementary Psychiatry for Medical Undergraduates. Roshen S. Master. 1968. 10.00x (ISBN 0-210-22708-7). Asia.

Elementary Quantitative Chemistry. Esmarch S. Gilreath. (Illus.). 1969. pap. 10.95x (ISBN 0-7167-0146-4). W H Freeman.

Elementary Quantum Mechanics. Nevill Mott & M. Berry. LC 76-189453. (Wykeham Science Ser.: No. 22). 1972. 9.95x (ISBN 0-8448-1124-6). Crane Russak Co.

Elementary Quantum Mechanics. David S. Saxon. LC 68-16996. (Illus.). 1968. text ed. 24.95x (ISBN 0-8162-7562-9). Holden-Day.

Elementary Radiation Physics. G. S. Hurst & J. E. Turner. LC 70-949221. 166p. 1970. 15.95 o.p. (ISBN 0-471-42472-2, Pub. by Wiley). Krieger.

Elementary Radiation Physics. G. S. Hurst & J. E. Turner. 180p. 1981. Repr. of 1970 ed. text ed. 15.50 (ISBN 0-89874-249-8). Krieger.

Elementary Reader in English. rev. ed. Robert J. Dixson. (Illus., Orig.). (gr. 9-12). 1971. pap. text ed. 2.75 (ISBN 0-88345-044-5, 17977); cassettes 40.00 (ISBN 0-685-19790-5); tapes o.p. 40.00 (ISBN 0-685-19791-3). Regents Pub.

Elementary School Career Education: A Humanistic Model. Frank R. Cross. LC 73-92002. (Occupational Education Ser.). 160p. 1974. pap. text ed. 7.95x (ISBN 0-675-08824-0). Merrill.

Elementary School Health Education: Ecological Perspectives. 2nd ed. Donald B. Stone et al. 1980. pap. text ed. 12.95x (ISBN 0-697-07385-8); instructor's manual avail. (ISBN 0-697-07386-6). Wm C Brown.

Elementary School Kid's Book of Lists. Kid's Stuff People. 240p. (gr. 1-8). 1981. pap. text ed. 7.95 (ISBN 0-86530-047-X, IP 47X). Incentive Pubns.

Elementary School Libraries. 2nd ed. Jean E. Lowrie. LC 71-9962. 1970. 10.00 (ISBN 0-8108-0305-4). Scarecrow.

Elementary School of the Future: A Guide for Parents. Carl H. Delacato. 108p. 1969. pap. 11.50 photocopy ed. spiral (ISBN 0-398-00419-6). C C Thomas.

Elementary School Organization & Administration. 4th ed. Henry J. Otto & David C. Sanders. LC 64-11518. (Illus.). 1960. text ed. 24.50x (ISBN 0-89197-529-2); pap. text ed. 12.95x (ISBN 0-89197-743-0). Irvington.

Elementary School Physical Education: Toward Inclusion. Don Morris. (Brighton Ser. in Health & Physical Education). (Illus.). 1980. text ed. 15.95 (ISBN 0-89832-012-7). Brighton Pub Co.

Elementary School Science: Why & How. Kenneth D. George et al. 1973. pap. text ed. 7.95x (ISBN 0-669-83162-X). Heath.

Elementary School Teacher. Dorothy G. Petersen. LC 64-11899. (Illus.). 1964. 25.00x (ISBN 0-89197-139-4); pap. text ed. 14.95x (ISBN 0-89197-744-9). Irvington.

Elementary Science of Metals. J. W. Martin & R. A. Hull. LC 73-75479. (Wykeham Science Ser.: No. 1). 1969. 9.95x (ISBN 0-8448-1103-3). Crane Russak Co.

Elementary Seismology. Charles F. Richter. LC 58-5970. (Geology Ser.). (Illus.). 1958. 31.95x (ISBN 0-7167-0211-8). W H Freeman.

Elementary Semiconductor Physics. H. C. Wright. 21.95 (ISBN 0-442-30198-7). Litton Educ Pub.

Elementary Social Studies: A Skills Emphasis. Richad W. Servey. 600p. 1981. text ed. 17.95 (ISBN 0-205-07213-5, 2372134). Allyn.

Elementary Social Studies: An Inter-Disciplinary Approach. Marjorie A. Crutchfield. (Elementary Education Ser.). 1978. text ed. 13.95 (ISBN 0-675-08365-6); instructor's manual 3.95 (ISBN 0-685-86835-4). Merrill.

Elementary Solid State Physics: Principles & Applications. M. Ali Omar. LC 73-10593. 1974. text ed. 25.95 (ISBN 0-201-05482-5). A-W.

Elementary Spanish: A Conversational Approach. Francisco Ugarte. LC 66-30529. 1967. 11.95 (ISBN 0-672-63163-6). Odyssey Pr.

Elementary Stability & Bifurcation Theory. G. Iooss & D. Joseph. (Undergraduate Texts in Mathematics Ser.). (Illus.). 286p. 1981. 22.00 (ISBN 0-387-90526-X). Springer-Verlag.

Elementary Statistical Mechanics. G. A. Wyllie. 1970. pap. text ed. 3.00x (ISBN 0-09-101321-6, Hutchinson U Lib). Humanities.

Elementary Statistical Methods in Psychology & Education. 2nd ed. Paul J. Blommers & Robert A. Forsyth. LC 76-11983. (Illus.). 608p. 1976. text ed. 18.95 (ISBN 0-395-24340-8); study manual 8.50 (ISBN 0-395-24339-4); solutions manual 1.35 (ISBN 0-395-24341-6). HM.

Elementary Statistics. George Hadley. LC 69-11850. (Illus.). 1969. 17.95x (ISBN 0-8162-3544-9). Holden-Day.

Elementary Statistics. 4th ed. Paul G. Hoel. LC 75-33400. (Probability & Mathematical Statistics Ser). 400p. (Arabic Translation available). 1976. text ed. 19.95 (ISBN 0-471-40302-4); instr's manual avail. (ISBN 0-471-40269-9); wkbk. 7.95 (ISBN 0-471-01613-6). Wiley.

Elementary Statistics. 3rd ed. Robert Johnson. LC 79-17146. 1980. text ed. 16.95 (ISBN 0-87872-232-7). Duxbury Pr.

Elementary Statistics. 3rd ed. J. T. Spence et al. (Illus.). 288p. 1976. ref. ed. 14.95 (ISBN 0-13-260109-5); wkbk. 6.95 (ISBN 0-13-260091-9). P-H.

Elementary Statistics. M. F. Triola. 1980. 16.95 (ISBN 0-8053-9305-6); instrs manual 3.95 (ISBN 0-8053-9307-2). A-W.

Elementary Statistics. Mario F. Triola. 16.95 (ISBN 0-8053-9305-6); pap. text ed. 3.95 (ISBN 0-8053-9307-2). Benjamin-Cummings.

Elementary Statistics: A Problem Solving Approach. Andrew L. Comrey. 1975. text ed. 17.95x (ISBN 0-256-01675-5). Dorsey.

Elementary Statistics: A Workbook. K. Hope. 1966. 13.75 (ISBN 0-08-012132-2); pap. 7.00 (ISBN 0-08-012131-4). Pergamon.

Elementary Statistics: An Applied Approach. Neil R. Ullman. LC 77-10828. 1978. text ed. 18.95 (ISBN 0-471-02105-9); tchrs'. manual avail.; wkbk & study guide 6.95x (ISBN 0-471-03209-3). Wiley.

Elementary Statistics for Business. Siskin Johnson. LC 78-13691. (Illus.). 1979. text ed. 17.95 (ISBN 0-87872-188-6); study guide 7.95 (ISBN 0-686-65910-4). Duxbury Pr.

Elementary Statistics for Business. Terrell. 1979. 17.95 (ISBN 0-7216-8797-0). Dryden Pr.

Elementary Steam Power Engineering. 3rd ed. Edgar MacNaughton. 1948. text ed. 32.95x (ISBN 0-471-56034-0). Wiley.

Elementary Steel Structures. Yuan-Yu Hsieh. (Civil Engineering & Engineering Mechanics Ser). (Illus.). 192p. 1973. ref. ed. 24.95 (ISBN 0-13-260158-3). P-H.

Elementary Stories for Reproduction. Leslie A. Hill. 64p. 1965. pap. 2.50x (ISBN 0-19-432541-5). Oxford U Pr.

Elementary Structural Mechanics. Tung Au. 1963. text ed. 26.95 (ISBN 0-13-260455-8). P-H.

Elementary Structures Reconsidered: Levi-Strauss on Kinship. Francis Korn. 1973. 17.50x (ISBN 0-520-02476-1). U of Cal Pr.

Elementary Survey Analysis. James A. Davis. (Methods of Social Science Ser). (Illus.). 1971. pap. text ed. 10.95 (ISBN 0-13-260547-3). P-H.

Elementary Teachers Guide to Free Curriculum Materials. 37th rev. ed. Ed. by Kathleen S. Nehmer. LC 44-52255. 1980. pap. 15.00 (ISBN 0-87708-104-2). Ed Prog.

Elementary Technical Mathematics. 3rd ed. Frank L. Juszli & Charles A. Rodgers. (Illus.). 1980. text ed. 17.95 (ISBN 0-13-260869-3). P-H.

Elementary Technical Mathematics. 2nd ed. Frank L. Juszli & Charles A. Rodgers, Jr. 1969. text ed. 16.95 o.p. (ISBN 0-13-260786-7). P-H.

Elementary Technical Mathematics with Calculus. Frank L. Juszli & Charles A. Rodgers. LC 72-75381. (Illus.). 1971. text ed. 19.95x (ISBN 0-13-272724-2). P-H.

Elementary Textbook of Psychoanalysis. rev. ed. Brenner, Charles, M.D. 280p. 1974. pap. 3.50 (ISBN 0-385-09884-7, Anch). Doubleday.

Elementary Theory of Analytic Functions of One or Several Complex Variables. rev. ed. Henri Cartan. 1963. 23.50 (ISBN 0-201-00901-3, Adv Bk Prog). A-W.

Elementary Theory of Elastic Plates. L. G. Jaeger. 1964. 16.50 (ISBN 0-08-010342-1); pap. 7.75 (ISBN 0-08-010341-3). Pergamon.

Elementary Theory of Microeconomic Behavior. 2nd ed. Josef Hadar. LC 70-171435. 1974. text ed. 18.95 (ISBN 0-201-02672-4). A-W.

Elementary Theory of Structures. Hsieh Yuan-Yu. (Civil Engineering Ser). 1970. ref. ed. 25.95 (ISBN 0-13-261552-5). P-H.

Elementary Theory of Structures. Wang Chu-Kia & Eckel. (Civil Engineering Ser.). (Illus.). 1957. text ed. 23.50 o.p. (ISBN 0-07-068134-1, C). McGraw.

Elementary Thermodynamics for Geologists. B. J. Wood & D. G. Fraser. (Illus.). 1976. pap. text ed. 14.95x (ISBN 0-19-859927-7). Oxford U Pr.

Elementary Topology. 2nd ed. Michael C. Gemignani. LC 73-168763. (Mathematics Ser). 1972. text ed. 17.95 (ISBN 0-201-02340-7). A-W.

Elementary Treatise on Human Physiology. Francois Magendie. Tr. by John Revere from Fr. Bd. with Mind & the Brain. Alfred Binet; An Essay. T. H. Huxley. (Contributions to the History of Psychology, Vol. IV, Pt. E: Physiological Psychology). 1978. Repr. of 1844 ed. 30.00 (ISBN 0-89093-177-1). U Pubns Amer.

Elementary Vectors: SI Units. 3rd ed. E. E. Wolstenholme. LC 77-30311. 1978. text ed. 7.50 (ISBN 0-08-021679-X); pap. text ed. 4.20 (ISBN 0-08-021654-4); tchr's. ed. 2.55 (ISBN 0-08-021655-2). Pergamon.

Elementary Wave Mechanics: With Applications to Quantum Chemistry. 2nd ed. Walter Heitler. 1956. 8.00x o.p. (ISBN 0-19-851103-5); pap. 8.50x (ISBN 0-19-851115-9). Oxford U Pr.

Elementary Wave Optics. Robert H. Webb. 1969. text ed. 22.95 (ISBN 0-12-739550-4). Acad Pr.

Elements. Gail Kay Haines. LC 74-180164. (First Bks). (Illus.). 96p. (gr. 4 up). 1972. PLB 4.90 o.p. (ISBN 0-531-00746-4). Watts.

Elements. Sharon Wright & Rick Fontes. (Orig.). 1979. pap. 5.00 o.p. (ISBN 0-930138-07-4). Harold Hse.

Elements of Abstract Linear Algebra. Hiram Paley & Paul M. Weichsel. LC 76-160668. 1972. text ed. 29.50x (ISBN 0-03-081311-5). Irvington.

Elements of Accident Investigation. Ted S. Ferry. 72p. 1978. pap. 10.75 spiral (ISBN 0-398-03752-3). C C Thomas.

Elements of Acoustics. Samuel Temkin. 544p. 1981. text ed. 23.95 (ISBN 0-471-05990-0). Wiley.

Elements of Advanced Quantum Theory. John M. Ziman. LC 69-16290. (Illus.). 1969. 32.95 (ISBN 0-521-07458-4); pap. 14.95 (ISBN 0-521-09949-8). Cambridge U Pr.

Elements of Algebra. 3rd ed. Francis J. Meuller. (Illus.). 496p. 1981. text ed. 16.95 (ISBN 0-13-262469-9). P-H.

Elements of Algebra & Algebraic Computing. John D. Lipson. 420p. 1980. text ed. 34.50 (ISBN 0-201-04115-4). A-W.

Elements of Analytical Dynamics. Rudolf Kurth. 200p. 1976. text ed. 28.00 (ISBN 0-08-019848-1). Pergamon.

Elements of Applied Stochastic Processes. U. Narayan Bhat. LC 70-178140. (Probability & Mathematical Statistics Ser.). 368p. 1972. 35.95 (ISBN 0-471-07199-4, Pub. by Wiley-Interscience). Wiley.

Elements of Applied Thermodynamics. 4th ed. W. A. Brockett et al. LC 77-73341. 1978. text ed. 23.95x (ISBN 0-87021-169-2). Naval Inst Pr.

Elements of Arithmetic, Algebra, & Geometry. William Forman & Lester L. Gavurin. LC 78-159159. 1972. text ed. 18.95 (ISBN 0-471-00654-8); solns. manual & tchr's guide 6.95 (ISBN 0-471-00731-5). Wiley.

Elements of Bayesian Statistics. Hans W. Gottinger. (De Gruyter Lehrbuch). 288p. 1979. pap. text ed. 28.25x (ISBN 3-11-007169-X). De Gruyter.

Elements of Biological Science. 2nd ed. William T. Keeton. 1973. text ed. 17.95x (ISBN 0-393-09346-8). Norton.

Elements of Brahmanism in the Transcendentalism of Emerson. Leyla Goren. LC 80-2534. 1981. Repr. of 1959 ed. 18.50 (ISBN 0-404-19260-2). AMS Pr.

Elements of Buddhist Iconography. Amanda K. Coomaraswamy. (Illus.). 130p. 1972. Repr. of 1935 ed. 22.50x (ISBN 0-8002-1390-4). Intl Pubns Serv.

Elements of Business & Economic Statistics: Learning by Objectives. Harry E. McAllister. LC 74-23909. 576p. 1975. text ed. 23.95 (ISBN 0-471-58120-8); tchrs. manual avail. (ISBN 0-471-02113-X). Wiley.

Elements of Business Statistics. Gulezian. 1979. 18.95 (ISBN 0-7216-4351-5). Dryden Pr.

Elements of Calculus & Analytic Geometry. 4th ed. George Thomas. Date not set. text ed. 20.80 (ISBN 0-201-07664-0, Sch Div); price not set tchrs. commentary (ISBN 0-201-07665-9); price not set solutions manual (ISBN 0-201-07666-7); price not set self study manual (ISBN 0-201-07667-5). A-W.

Elements of Cartography. 4th ed. Arthur Robinson et al. LC 78-1670. 1978. 24.95 (ISBN 0-471-01781-7). Wiley.

Elements of Ceramics. 2nd ed. Frederick H. Norton. LC 72-9316. 1974. text ed. 19.95 (ISBN 0-201-05306-3). A-W.

Elements of Chemical Kinetics & Reactor Calculations: A Self-Paced Approach. H. Scott Fogler. (Illus.). 512p. 1974. pap. 24.95 ref. ed. (ISBN 0-13-263442-2). P-H.

Elements of Chemical Thermodynamics. 2nd ed. Leonard K. Nash. LC 79-87040. 1970. pap. text ed. 6.95 (ISBN 0-201-05236-9). A-W.

Elements of Classical Physics. M. C. Martin & C. A. Hewett. LC 73-3450. 1975. text ed. 26.00 (ISBN 0-08-017098-6). Pergamon.

Elements of Classical Thermodynamics. A. B. Pippard. 1966. pap. text ed. 9.95x (ISBN 0-521-09101-2). Cambridge U Pr.

Elements of Cobol Programming. Wilson T. Price & Jack L. Olson. LC 77-187112. 1977. pap. text ed. 14.50 (ISBN 0-03-018371-5). Dryden Pr.

Elements of Combinatory Logic. Frederic B. Fitch. LC 73-86892. 176p. 1974. 10.50x o.p. (ISBN 0-300-01523-2). Yale U Pr.

Elements of Computer Programming (Fortran) Marxer & Hartford. LC 75-153725. (Illus.). 224p. 1973. 8.00 (ISBN 0-8273-0413-7); tchr's manual 2.00 (ISBN 0-8273-0414-5). Delmar.

Elements of Conducting. 2nd ed. Emil Kahn. LC 75-4317. (Illus.). 1975. pap. text ed. 12.95 (ISBN 0-02-871050-9). Schirmer Bks.

Elements of Continuum Mechanics. C. A. Truesdell. 1966. pap. 14.70 o.p. (ISBN 0-387-03683-0). Springer-Verlag.

Elements of Control Systems Analysis: Classical & Modern Approaches. Chen Chih-Fan & J. Haas. 1967. ref. ed. 25.95 (ISBN 0-13-263509-7). P-H.

Elements of Cost-Benefit Analysis. E. J. Mishan. 1976. pap. text ed. 7.50x (ISBN 0-04-300066-5). Allen Unwin.

Elements of Criminal Due Process. Phillip E. Johnson. (Criminal Justice Ser.). 1975. pap. text ed. 11.95 (ISBN 0-685-99579-8); pap. text ed. write for info (ISBN 0-8299-0620-7). West Pub.

Elements of Critical Philosophy. Anthony F. Willich. Ed. by Rene Wellek. LC 75-11266. (British Philosophers & Theologians of the 17th & 18th Centuries: Vol. 65). 1977. Repr. of 1798 ed. lib. bdg. 42.00 (ISBN 0-8240-1815-X). Garland Pub.

Elements of Data Processing. Marxer. LC 75-153725. 215p. 1974. pap. 8.80 (ISBN 0-8273-0410-2); tchr's manual 2.00 (ISBN 0-8273-0411-0). Delmar.

Elements of Debate. Donald Klopf & James McCroskey. LC 69-17545. (Orig.). 1969. lib. bdg. 6.50 o. p. (ISBN 0-668-01899-2); pap. 5.00 (ISBN 0-668-01901-8). Arco.

Elements of Diatomic Molecular Spectra. Brian Dunford. LC 68-13548. (Chemistry Ser). (Illus., Orig.). 1968. pap. 10.95 (ISBN 0-201-01615-X). A-W.

Elements of Differential Equations. Wilfred Kaplan. 1964. 16.95 (ISBN 0-201-03632-0). A-W.

Elements of Discourse Understanding. Aravind Joshi et al. LC 80-29393. (Illus.). 352p. Date not set. price not set (ISBN 0-521-23327-5). Cambridge U Pr.

Elements of Drama. J. L. Styan. 1960. 36.00 (ISBN 0-521-06574-7); pap. text ed. 9.95x (ISBN 0-521-09201-9). Cambridge U Pr.

Elements of Dynamic Symmetry. Jay Hambidge. (Illus.,). pap. text ed. 3.00 (ISBN 0-486-21776-0). Dover.

Elements of Ecology & Field Biology. Robert L. Smith. 1977. text ed. 19.50 scp (ISBN 0-06-046329-5, HarpC); instructor's manual avail. (ISBN 0-685-74055-2). Har-Row.

Elements of Economics. Wallace C. Peterson. 500p. 1973. text ed. 15.95x (ISBN 0-393-09417-0). Norton.

Elements of Elasticity. D. S. Dugdale. 1968. 23.00 (ISBN 0-08-012634-0); pap. 11.25 (ISBN 0-08-012633-2). Pergamon.

Elements of Electricity. 4th ed. William H. Timbie & A. C. Kusko. LC 53-6444. 1953. text ed. 22.95x (ISBN 0-471-86955-4). Wiley.

Elements of Electronic Instrumentation & Measurement. Joseph Carr. (Illus.). 1979. text ed. 18.95 (ISBN 0-8359-1650-2); students manual avail. (ISBN 0-8359-1651-0). Reston.

Elements of Engineering Electromagnetics. N. Narayana Rao. (Illus.). 1977. 25.95 (ISBN 0-13-264150-X). P-H.

Elements of Engineering Mechanics. Peter Likins. (Illus.). 550p. 1973. text ed. 24.50 o.p. (ISBN 0-07-037852-5, C); solutions manual 4.50 o.p. (ISBN 0-07-037853-3). McGraw.

Elements of English: An Introduction to the Principles of the Study of Language. William Branford. 1967. text ed. 7.25x (ISBN 0-7100-1106-7). Humanities.

Elements of English Architecture. Hugh Braun. (Illus.). 212p. 1980. Repr. 22.50 (ISBN 0-7153-5775-1). David & Charles.

Elements of Environmental Analysis. George Tolley et al. (Environmental Policy Ser.: Vol. I). 1981. write for info. (ISBN 0-88410-625-X). Ballinger Pub.

Elements of Environmental Health. David F. Newton. LC 93-91307. (Public Service Technology Ser.). 362p. 1974. text ed. 16.95 (ISBN 0-675-08832-1). Merrill.

Elements of Estimating. David S. Hall. 1972. 21.50 o.p. (ISBN 0-7134-0526-0, Pub. by Batsford England). David & Charles.

Elements of Fiction: An Anthology. Ed. by Robert Scholes. 984p. 1981. pap. text ed. 9.95x (ISBN 0-19-502881-3). Oxford U Pr.

Elements of Finance for Managers. B. K. Watts. (Illus.). 256p. 1976. pap. 12.95x (ISBN 0-7121-0551-4, Pub. by Macdonald & Evans England). Intl Ideas.

Elements of Folk Psychology: Outlines of Psychological History of the Development of Mankind. Wilhelm M. Wundt. Tr. by E. L. Schaub from German. (Contributions to the History of Psychology Ser.). 1980. Repr. of 1916 ed. 30.00 (ISBN 0-89093-317-0). U Pubns Amer.

Elements of Food Engineering. John C. Harper. (Illus.). 1976. lib. bdg. 28.50 o.p. (ISBN 0-87055-218-X); pap. text ed. 17.00 (ISBN 0-87055-299-6). AVI.

Elements of Food Production & Baking. 2nd ed. Joseph F. Vastano. LC 77-26070. 1978. text ed. 14.95 (ISBN 0-672-97096-1); tchr's manual 6.67 (ISBN 0-672-97095-3); wkbk. 6.50 (ISBN 0-672-97094-5). Bobbs.

Elements of Food Technology. Ed. by Norman W. Desrosier. (Illus.). 1977. pap. 19.50 (ISBN 0-87055-284-8). AVI.

Elements of Functional Analysis. I. J. Maddox. LC 71-85726. 1970. text ed. 29.95 (ISBN 0-521-07617-X); pap. 12.50x (ISBN 0-521-29266-2). Cambridge U Pr.

Elements of General Phonetics. D. Abercrombie. 1967. 6.50x (ISBN 0-85224-028-7, Pub. by Edinburgh U Pr Scotland). Columbia U Pr.

Elements of Geographical Hydrology. B. J. Knapp. (Illus.). 1978. pap. text ed. 6.95x (ISBN 0-04-551030-X). Allen Unwin.

Elements of Graphics: How to Prepare Charts & Graphs for Effective Reports. Robert Lefferts. LC 80-8209. (Illus.). 192p. 1981. 12.95 (ISBN 0-06-012578-0, HarpT). Har-Row.

Elements of Group Therapy for Physicists. 2nd ed. A. W. Joshi. LC 76-51385. 1977. 12.95 (ISBN 0-470-99062-7). Halsted Pr.

Elements of Growth & Decline of Urban Development & Policy. Leo Van Den Berg et al. Date not set. 48.01 (ISBN 0-08-023156-X). Pergamon.

Elements of Hamiltonian Mechanics. 2nd ed. D. Ter Haar. 1971. 15.00 (ISBN 0-08-016726-8). Pergamon.

Elements of Hearing Science: A Programmed Text. Arnold M. Small. LC 77-20110. (Communications Disorders Ser.). 1978. 11.95 (ISBN 0-471-01732-9). Wiley.

Elements of Heat Transfer. 3rd ed. Max Jakob & G. A. Hawkins. LC 57-12230. 1957. text ed. 25.95x (ISBN 0-471-43725-5). Wiley.

Elements of Human Anatomy & Physiology. Richard A. Boolootian. LC 76-3681. 550p. 1976. text ed. 17.95 (ISBN 0-8299-0086-1); instrs.' manual avail. (ISBN 0-8299-0460-3). West Pub.

Elements of Human & Social Geography (Some Anthropological Perspectives) Eric Sunderland. LC 73-10060. 120p. 1974. text ed. 15.00 (ISBN 0-08-017689-5); pap. text ed. 7.00 (ISBN 0-08-017690-9). Pergamon.

Elements of Human Genetics. 2nd ed. L. L. Cavalli-Sforza. LC 76-58969. 1977. pap. text ed. 8.95 (ISBN 0-8053-1874-7). Benjamin-Cummings.

Elements of Injection Moulding of Thermoplastics. Ed. by Learning Systems Ltd. (Illus., Orig.,). (gr. 10 up). 1969. pap. text ed. 5.95 (ISBN 0-85334-043-9). Transatlantic.

Elements of Integrated Control of Sorghum Pests. (FAO Plant Production & Protection Ser.: No. 19). 167p. 1980. pap. 9.00 (ISBN 92-5-100884-1, F1943, FAO). Unipub.

Elements of International Law. Henry Wheaton. LC 78-157426. (American Constitutional & Legal History Ser). 360p. 1972. Repr. of 1836 ed. lib. bdg. 39.50 (ISBN 0-306-70206-1). Da Capo.

Elements of Intuitionism. Michael Dummett & Robert Minio. (Oxford Logic Guides Ser.). 1977. text ed. 37.50x (ISBN 0-19-853158-3). Oxford U Pr.

Elements of Japanese Law: Studies in Japanese Law & Government. Joseph E. De Becker. 1979. Repr. of 1916 ed. 34.00 (ISBN 0-89093-210-7). U Pubns Amer.

Elements of Life: Approach to Chemistry for the Health Sciences. Alan Sherman & Sharon J. Sherman. (Illus.). 1980. text ed. 19.95 (ISBN 0-13-266130-6); lab. man. 8.95 (ISBN 0-13-266148-9). P-H.

Elements of Linear Circuits. Ronald E. Scott. 1965. 20.95 (ISBN 0-201-06842-7). A-W.

Elements of Literature: Essay, Fiction, Poetry, Drama, Film. Ed. by Robert Scholes et al. (Illus.). 1978. pap. text ed. 10.95x (ISBN 0-19-502265-3). Oxford U Pr.

Elements of Loadbearing Brickwork. D. Lenczner. 125p. 1972. text ed. 19.50 (ISBN 0-08-016814-0). Pergamon.

Elements of Logic. 2nd ed. Stephen Barker. (Illus.). 336p. 1974. text ed. 12.95 o.p. (ISBN 0-07-003718-3, C); instructor's manual 3.95 o.p. (ISBN 0-07-003719-1); study guide by A, Levinson 6.95 o.p. (ISBN 0-07-037382-5). McGraw.

Elements of Marine Ecology. 3rd ed. R. V. Tait. (Illus.). 304p. 1981. pap. write for info. (ISBN 0-408-71054-3). Butterworth.

Elements of Mathematical Biology. Alfred J. Lotka. Orig. Title: Elements of Physical Biology. 1957. pap. text ed. 6.00 (ISBN 0-486-60346-6). Dover.

Elements of Mathematical Logic. 2nd ed. J. Lukasiewicz. (International Series in Pure & Applied Mathematics: Vol. 31). 1964. 12.10 o.p. (ISBN 0-08-010393-6); pap. 5.00 o.p. (ISBN 0-08-013695-8). Pergamon.

Elements of Mathematical Logic & Set Theory. J. Slupecki & L. Borkowski. 1967. 32.00 o.p. (ISBN 0-08-011096-7). Pergamon.

Elements of Mathematical Statistics. C. V. Charlier & J. A. Greenwood. 1947. pap. 5.25 o.s.i. (ISBN 0-02-842770-X). Hafner.

Elements of Mathematics: Commutative Algebra. N. Bourbaki. 1972. 57.50 (ISBN 0-201-00644-8, Adv Bk Prog). A-W.

Elements of Mathematics: Lie Groups & Lie Algebras, Part 1. Nocolas Bourbaki. 1975. pap. 57.50 (ISBN 0-201-00643-X, Adv Bk Prog). A-W.
Elements of Mechanics of Materials. 4th ed. G. Olsen. 1981. 23.95 (ISBN 0-13-267013-5). P-H.
Elements of Mechanics of Materials. 3rd ed. Gerner A. Olsen. (Illus.). 704p. 1974. ref. ed. 23.95 (ISBN 0-13-266999-4). P-H.
Elements of Meteorology. Richmond W. Longley. LC 71-110172. 1970. text ed. 19.50 o.p. (ISBN 0-471-54445-0). Wiley.
Elements of Meteorology. 3rd ed. Albert Miller & Jack Thompson. 1979. text ed. 18.95 (ISBN 0-675-08293-5); instructor's manual 3.95 (ISBN 0-686-67289-5). Merrill.
Elements of Micro-Programming. J. Raymond. (Span.). 1981. 24.50 (ISBN 0-13-273797-3). P-H.
Elements of Microbiology. 1st ed. Michael Pelczar, Jr. & E. C. S. Chan. (Illus.). 704p. (Orig.). text ed. 19.95 (ISBN 0-07-049240-9, C); 10.95 (ISBN 0-07-049241-7); instrs'. 5.50 (ISBN 0-07-049230-1). McGraw.
Elements of Microprogramming. Dilip Banerji & Jacque Raymond. (Illus.). 416p. 1981. text ed. 24.50 (ISBN 0-13-267146-8). P-H.
Elements of Mineralogy. Brian Mason & L. G. Berry. LC 68-13311. (Geology Ser.). (Illus.). 1968. 25.95x (ISBN 0-7167-0235-5). W H Freeman.
Elements of Mining. 3rd ed. Robert S. Lewis & G. B. Clark. LC 64-14990. 1964. 49.95 (ISBN 0-471-53331-9). Wiley.
Elements of Modern Physics. 2nd ed. Alfred T. Goble & D. K. Baker. (Illus.). 1971. 19.95 (ISBN 0-8260-3425-X). Wiley.
Elements of Modern Pure Geometry. M. S. Anjaneyulu. 6.50x (ISBN 0-210-26948-0). Asia.
Elements of Moral Science, 2 vols. James Beattie. Ed. by Rene Wellek. LC 75-11195. (British Philosophers & Theologians of the 17th & 18th Centuries: Vol. 2). 1976. Repr. of 1793 ed. Set. lib. bdg. 84.00 (ISBN 0-8240-1751-X); lib. bdg. 42.00 ea. Garland Pub.
Elements of Moral Science. James Beattie. LC 75-45348. 1168p. 1976. Repr. of 1790 ed. lib. bdg. 85.00 (ISBN 0-8201-1167-8). Schol Facsimilies.
Elements of New Testament Greek. John W. Wenham. 1966. text ed. 7.50x (ISBN 0-521-09842-4); key 2.50x (ISBN 0-521-06769-3). Cambridge U Pr.
Elements of Non-Linear Functional Analysis. Richard A. Graff. LC 78-14727. (Memoirs: No. 206). 1980. Repr. of 1978 ed. 8.40 (ISBN 0-8218-2206-3). Am Math.
Elements of Nuclear Power. D. J. Bennet. LC 72-13693. 207p. 1972. pap. 17.95x (ISBN 0-470-01354-0). Halsted Pr.
Elements of Numerical Analysis. Peter K. Henrici. LC 64-23840. 1964. 23.95 (ISBN 0-471-37241-2). Wiley.
Elements of Numerical Analysis. James Singer. (Illus.). 1964. text ed. 21.95 (ISBN 0-12-646450-2). Acad Pr.
Elements of Nursing. Nancy Roper et al. (Illus.). 1980. text ed. 44.00 (ISBN 0-443-02198-8); pap. text ed. 27.50x (ISBN 0-443-01577-5). Churchill.
Elements of Orchestration. Gordon Jacob. LC 76-15191. 1976. Repr. of 1962 ed. lib. bdg. 22.25x (ISBN 0-8371-8955-1, JAEO). Greenwood.
Elements of Outdoor Recreation Planning. B. L. Driver. 316p. 1974. pap. text ed. 5.95x (ISBN 0-472-08284-1). U of Mich Pr.
Elements of Palaeontology. Claude Babin. LC 79-13223. 446p. 1980. 57.00 (ISBN 0-471-27577-8, Pub. by Wiley-Interscience); pap. 22.50 (ISBN 0-471-27576-X). Wiley.
Elements of Palaeontology. Rhona M. Black. (Illus.). 1970. 54.50 (ISBN 0-521-07445-2); pap. 16.95x (ISBN 0-521-09615-4). Cambridge U Pr.
Elements of Pediatric Anesthesia. 2nd ed. C. R. Stephen et al. (American Lecture Anesthesiology Ser). (Illus.). 216p. 1970. 17.75 (ISBN 0-398-01855-3). C C Thomas.
Elements of Physical Chemistry. Moncrief & Jones. 1976. 20.95 (ISBN 0-201-04897-3). A-W.
Elements of Physical Geography. 2nd ed. Arthur N. Strahler & Alan H. Strahler. LC 78-23776. 1979. text ed. 21.95x (ISBN 0-471-04459-8); tchrs. manual avail. (ISBN 0-471-05004-0); study guide 7.95x (ISBN 0-471-05005-9). Wiley.
Elements of Physical Geology. James H. Zumberge & Clemens A. Nelson. LC 75-26843. 432p. 1976. text ed. 20.50x (ISBN 0-471-98674-7). Wiley.
Elements of Physical Metallurgy. 3rd ed. Albert G. Guy & John J. Hren. LC 72-9315. 1974. text ed. 25.95 (ISBN 0-201-02633-3). A-W.
Elements of Physical Oceanography. H. J. McLellan. 1966. 18.00 (ISBN 0-08-011320-6). Pergamon.
Elements of Physics, 2 vols. 5th ed. George Shortley & Dudley Williams. (Illus.). 1971. Combined. text ed. 27.95 (ISBN 0-13-268383-0); Vol. 1. text ed. 17.95 (ISBN 0-13-268367-9); Vol. 2. text ed. 17.95 (ISBN 0-13-268375-X). P-H.
Elements of Poetry. Robert Scholes. (Orig.). 1969. pap. text ed. 2.95x (ISBN 0-19-501047-7). Oxford U Pr.
Elements of Police Supervision. William Melnicoe & Jan Mennig. (Criminal Justice Ser). (Illus.). 1969. text ed. 10.95x (ISBN 0-02-476400-0, 47640). Macmillan.
Elements of Police Supervision. 2nd ed. William B. Melnicoe & Jan Mennig. 1978. text ed. 11.95 (ISBN 0-02-476000-5). Macmillan.
Elements of Political Economy, with Special Reference to the Industrial History of Nations. Robert E. Thompson. (Neglected American Economists Ser.). 1974. lib. bdg. 50.00 (ISBN 0-8240-1020-5). Garland Pub.
Elements of Probability Theory. L. Z. Rumshiskii. 1965. 26.00 (ISBN 0-08-010534-3); pap. 12.75 (ISBN 0-08-013609-5). Pergamon.
Elements of Production-Operations Management. Elwood S. Buffa. 256p. 1981. pap. text ed. 10.95 (ISBN 0-471-08532-4). Wiley.
Elements of Public Speaking. Joseph DeVito. (Illus.). 480p. 1980. pap. text ed. 14.50 scp (ISBN 0-06-041653-X, HarpC); avail. Har-Row.
Elements of Quantum Theory. rev. enl. 2nd ed. Frank J. Bockhoff. LC 76-41769. 1976. text ed. 24.50 (ISBN 0-201-00799-1, Adv Bk Prog). A-W.
Elements of Quaternions, 2 Vols. 3rd ed. William R. Hamilton. Ed. by Charles J. Joly. LC 68-54711. 1969. Repr. of 1901 ed. Set. 49.50 (ISBN 0-8284-0219-1). Chelsea Pub.
Elements of Radiation Protection. Ronald V. Scheele & Jack Wakley. (Illus.). 112p. 1980. pap. 10.25 (ISBN 0-398-03267-X). C C Thomas.
Elements of Real Analysis. 2nd ed. Robert G. Bartle. LC 75-15979. 480p. 1975. text ed. 24.95 (ISBN 0-471-05464-X); arabic translation avail. Wiley.
Elements of Rehabilitation in Nursing: An Introduction. Rose M. Boroch. LC 76-4590. (Illus.). 1976. pap. text ed. 13.95 (ISBN 0-8016-1425-2). Mosby.
Elements of Research: A Guide for Writers. Carol T. Williams & Gary K. Wolfe. LC 78-12170. (Illus.). 1979. pap. text ed. 5.95 (ISBN 0-88284-070-3). Alfred Pub.
Elements of Research in Nursing. 2nd ed. Eleanor W. Treece & James W. Treece, Jr. LC 76-7521. (Illus.). 1977. pap. text ed. 12.95 (ISBN 0-8016-5104-2). Mosby.
Elements of Rhetoric. Richard Whately. Ed. by Douglas Ehninger. LC 63-14292. (Landmarks in Rhetoric & Public Address Ser). 509p. 1963. Repr. of 1846 ed. 12.95x (ISBN 0-8093-0101-6). S Ill U Pr.
Elements of Sampling Theory. Vic Barnett. 1975. pap. text ed. 12.50x (ISBN 0-8448-0614-5). Crane-Russak Co.
Elements of Social Organization. 3rd ed. Raymond W. Firth. LC 80-24763. (Josiah Mason Lectures Ser., 1947). (Illus.). xi, 260p. 1981. Repr. of 1961 ed. lib. bdg. 28.50x (ISBN 0-313-22745-4, FIES). Greenwood.
Elements of Social Scientific Thinking. 2nd ed. Kenneth R. Hoover. 1981. text ed. 12.95 (ISBN 0-686-63365-2); pap. text ed. 4.95x (ISBN 0-312-24187-9). St Martin.
Elements of Soil Mechanics for Civil & Mining Engineers. 4th ed. Geoffrey N. Smith. (Illus.). 370p. 1978. text ed. 15.00x (ISBN 0-8464-0367-6); pap. 12.00x (ISBN 0-8464-0368-4). Beekman Pubs.
Elements of Solid State Physics. M. N. Rudden & J. Wilson. LC 79-41730. 208p. 1980. 40.00 (ISBN 0-471-27750-9, Pub. by Wiley-Interscience); pap. 17.00 (ISBN 0-471-27749-5). Wiley.
Elements of Solition Theory. George L. Lamb. LC 80-13373. (Pure & Applied Mathematics: Texts & Monographs). 1980. 29.95 (ISBN 0-471-04559-4, Pub. by Wiley-Interscience). Wiley.
Elements of Spatial Structure. A. D. Cliff et al. LC 74-12973. (Geographical Studies: No. 6). (Illus.). 206p. 1974. 37.50 (ISBN 0-521-20689-8). Cambridge U Pr.
Elements of Speech Communication: Achieving Competency. David M. Jabusch & Stephen Littlejohn. LC 80-82760. (Illus.). 464p. 1981. pap. text ed. 11.50 (ISBN 0-395-29730-3); instrs' manual 0.75 (ISBN 0-395-29731-1). HM.
Elements of Stagecraft. James W. Baker. LC 77-25899. 1978. pap. text ed. 11.50x (ISBN 0-88284-053-3). Alfred Pub.
Elements of Statistical Inference. 5th ed. Huntsberger & Billingsley. 416p. 1981. text ed. 15.95 (ISBN 0-205-07305-0, 5673054); free tchr's ed. (ISBN 0-205-07306-9); free student's guide (ISBN 0-205-07307-7). Allyn.
Elements of Statistical Inference. 4th ed. David V. Huntsberger & Patrick Billingsley. 1977. text ed. 18.95x (ISBN 0-205-05734-9); instructors manual avail. (ISBN 0-205-05735-7); student supplement 6.95 (ISBN 0-205-05736-5). Allyn.
Elements of Statistical Inference for Education & Psychology. D. Lynch & David V. Huntsberger. 512p. 1976. text ed. 17.95x o.p. (ISBN 0-205-05014-X); man. of test items avail. o.p. (ISBN 0-205-05016-6); solutions manual avail. o.p (ISBN 0-205-05017-4). Allyn.
Elements of Statistical Thermodynamics. 2nd ed. Leonard K. Nash. 1974. 6.95 (ISBN 0-201-05229-6). A-W.
Elements of Steelmaking Practice. J. D. Sharp. 1966. 14.50 (ISBN 0-08-011437-7); pap. 5.00 o.p. (ISBN 0-08-011436-9). Pergamon.
Elements of Stereochemistry: With a Section on Coordination Compounds. E. L. Eliel & F. Basolo. 1969. 6.95 (ISBN 0-471-23745-0). Wiley.
Elements of Stochastic Processes with Applications to the Natural Sciences. Norman T. Bailey. LC 63-23220. (Probability & Mathematical Statistics Ser.: Applied Probability & Statistics Section). 1964. 29.50 (ISBN 0-471-04165-3, Pub by Wiley-Interscience). Wiley.
Elements of Supervision. 2nd ed. W. R. Spriegel et al. LC 57-5934. 1957. 21.95 (ISBN 0-471-81774-0). Wiley.
Elements of Surgical Treatment in the Delivery of Periodontal Therapy. Richard Chaikin. (Illus.). 177p. 1978. 54.00 (ISBN 3-87652-661-2). Quint Pub Co.
Elements of Symbolic Logic. Hans Reichenbach. 444p. 1980. pap. 7.00 (ISBN 0-486-24004-5). Dover.
Elements of System-Dynamic Simulation: A Textbook with Exercises. T. J. Ferrari. LC 78-10505. 1978. pap. text ed. 16.95 (ISBN 0-470-26548-5). Halsted Pr.
Elements of Technical Writing. M. Y. Barnett. LC 73-13487. 1974. 10.00 (ISBN 0-8273-0356-4); instructor's guide 1.60 (ISBN 0-8273-0357-2). Delmar.
Elements of the Art of Packing As Applied to Special Juries Particularly in Cases of Libel Law. Jeremy Bentham. Ed. by David Berkowitz & Samuel Thorne. LC 77-86672. (Classics of English Legal History in the Modern Era Ser.: Vol. 116). 1979. Repr. of 1821 ed. lib. bdg. 55.00 (ISBN 0-8240-3153-9). Garland Pub.
Elements of the Behavioral Code. F. DeFeudis & P. DeFeudis. 1978. 52.50 (ISBN 0-12-208760-7). Acad Pr.
Elements of the Common Lawes of England. Francis Bacon. LC 77-26477. (English Experience Ser.: No. 164). 104p. 1969. Repr. of 1630 ed. 25.00 (ISBN 90-221-0164-9). Walter J Johnson.
Elements of the Common Lawes of England, 2 pts, Repr. Of 1630. Sir Francis Bacon. Bd. with John Cowell: The Institutes of the Lawes of England, Digested into the Method of the Civill or Imperiall Institutions. Repr. of 1651 ed. LC 77-86558. (Classics of English Legal History in the Modern Era: Vol. 67). 1978. lib. bdg. 55.00 (ISBN 0-8240-3054-0). Garland Pub.
Elements of the Differential & Integral Calculus. new & rev. ed. W. A. Granville et al. 1962. text ed. 25.50 (ISBN 0-471-00206-2). Wiley.
Elements of the Theory of Computation. Harry R. Lewis & Christos H. Papadimitriou. (Software Ser.). (Illus.). 496p. 1981. text ed. 22.50 (ISBN 0-13-273417-6). P-H.
Elements of the Theory of Functions. Konrad Knopp. Tr. by Frederick Bagemihl. 1952. pap. text ed. 2.75 (ISBN 0-486-60154-4). Dover.
Elements of the Theory of Markov Processes & Their Applications. Albert T. Bharucha-Reid. (Probability & Statistics Ser). 1960. 38.00 o.p. (ISBN 0-07-005156-9, P&RB). McGraw.
Elements of Theology. 2nd ed. Proclus. Tr. by E. R. Dodds. 1963. 23.50x o.p. (ISBN 0-19-814160-2). Oxford U Pr.
Elements of Thermal Technology. Seely. Date not set. price not set (ISBN 0-8247-1174-2). Dekker.
Elements of Trigonometry. Adelbert F. Hackert & Charles L. Duff. LC 73-140782. text ed. 15.95x o.p. (ISBN 0-669-61598-6); manual free o.p. (ISBN 0-669-61606-0). Heath.
Elements of Tropical Ecology. J. Yanney Ewusie. (Orig.). 1980. pap. text ed. 16.50 (ISBN 0-435-93700-6). Heinemann Ed.
Elements of Water Supply & Waste Water Disposal. 2nd ed. Gordon M. Fair et al. LC 72-151032. (Illus.). 1971. 35.95 (ISBN 0-471-25115-1). Wiley.
Elements of Weaving. Azalea S. Thorpe & J. L. Larson. Ed. by Mary Lyon. LC 67-11164. (Illus.). 10.95 o.p. (ISBN 0-385-03473-3). Doubleday.
Elements of X-Ray Crystallography. A. J. Wilson. 1970. 20.95 (ISBN 0-201-08698-0). A-W.
Elements of X-Ray Diffraction. 2nd ed. B. D. Cullity. LC 77-73950. (Illus.). 1978. text ed. 26.95 (ISBN 0-201-01174-3). A-W.
Elements of Zoology. Paul B. Weisz. 1968. text ed. 16.00 o.p. (ISBN 0-07-069103-7, C); instructor's manual 2.00 o.p. (ISBN 0-07-069104-5); study guide by Brenner 7.50 o.p. (ISBN 0-07-007639-1). McGraw.
Elena. Marilyn Granbeck. (Orig.). pap. 2.25 (ISBN 0-515-04420-2). Jove Pubns.
Elena: A Love Story of the Russian Revolution. Judith Egan. LC 80-39613. 320p. 1981. 11.95 (ISBN 0-89919-028-6). Ticknor & Fields.
Elena Quiroga. Phyllis L. Boring. (World Authors Ser.: No.459). 1977. lib. bdg. 12.50 (ISBN 0-8057-6296-5). Twayne.
Elena's Secrets of Mexican Cooking. Elena Zelayeta. 1968. pap. 4.95 (ISBN 0-385-00197-5, Dolp). Doubleday.
Elephant. Byron Barton. LC 74-154301. (Illus.). (ps-2). 1971. 4.95 (ISBN 0-395-28764-2, Clarion). HM.
Elephant & the Lotus Essays in Philosophy & Culture. V. S. Naravane. 1964. 15.00x (ISBN 0-210-26853-0). Asia.
Elephant Book. Charles Nicholas. (Illus.). 24p. (gr. k-1). 1976. PLB 5.38 (ISBN 0-307-68980-8, Golden Pr). Western Pub.
Elephant Boy. William Kotzwinkle. (ps-3). 1970. 3.95 o.p. (ISBN 0-374-32013-6). FS&G.
Elephant Eater. Allysia J. Arreola. Ed. by Marlene Kamei. 12p. (Orig.). 1977. pap. 2.00 (ISBN 0-935684-00-X). Plumbers Ink.
Elephant Girl. Ivor Cutler. (Illus.). 32p. (ps-1). 1976. 6.25 (ISBN 0-688-22065-7); PLB 6.00 (ISBN 0-688-32065-1). Morrow.
Elephant Have Right of Way. Betty Leslie-Melville & Jock Leslie-Melville. LC 72-84927. 264p. 1973. 6.95 o.p. (ISBN 0-385-07943-5). Doubleday.
Elephant Is Soft & Mushy. S. Gross. LC 79-28642. (Illus.). 128p. 1980. pap. 6.95 (ISBN 0-396-07823-0). Dodd.
Elephant Island: An Antarctic Expedition. Chris Furse. (Illus.). 1979. 27.50 (ISBN 0-904614-02-6, Pub. by Anthony Nelson Ltd, England). Buteo.
Elephant-Lore of the Hindus: The Elephant-Sport (Matanga-Lila) of Nilakantha. Nilakantha. Ed. by Franklin Edgerton. 1931. 32.50x (ISBN 0-686-50042-3). Elliots Bks.
Elephant Man. Bernard Pomerance. LC 79-7792. 1979. 8.95 (ISBN 0-394-50642-1). Grove.
Elephant on Wheels. Alida Thatcher. (Eager Readers Ser). (gr. k-3). 1975. PLB 5.00 (ISBN 0-307-60807-7, Golden Pr). Western Pub.
Elephant Seals. Louise C. Brown. LC 78-25623. (Skylight Bks.). (Illus.). (gr. 2-5). 1979. 4.95 (ISBN 0-396-07665-3). Dodd.
Elephant Set, 10 bks. Bob Reese et al. Ed. by Alton Jordon. (Illus.). (gr. k-6). 1977. Set. PLB 35.00 (ISBN 0-89868-011-5); Set. pap. 17.50 (ISBN 0-89868-044-1). ARO Pub.
Elephants. Cynthia Overbeck. (Lerner Natural Science Bks.). (Illus.). (gr. 4-9). 1981. PLB 7.95 (ISBN 0-8225-1452-4). Lerner Pubns.
Elephants. Edmund Rogers. LC 77-13964. (Animals of the World Ser.). (Illus.). (gr. 4-8). 1977. PLB 10.65 (ISBN 0-8172-1076-8). Raintree Pubs.
Elephants. Wildlife Education, Ltd. (Zoobooks). (Illus.). 20p. (Orig.). 1980. pap. 1.00 (ISBN 0-937934-00-3). Wildlife Educ.
Elephants. Herbert S. Zim. (Illus.). (gr. 3-7). 1946. PLB 6.48 (ISBN 0-688-31262-4). Morrow.
Elephants & Other Land Giants. (Wild, Wild World of Animals Ser.). (Illus.). 1976. 10.95 (ISBN 0-913948-05-5). Time-Life.
Elephants & Other Land Giants. LC 76-1868. (Wild, Wild World of Animals). (Illus.). (gr. 5 up). 1976. PLB 11.97 (ISBN 0-685-73292-4, Pub. by Time-Life Television). Silver.
Elephant's Ballet. Robert C. Kemper. LC 77-22165. 1977. 6.95 (ISBN 0-8164-0373-2). Crossroad NY.
Elephant's Child. Rudyard Kipling. LC 73-104661. (gr. k-3). 1970. 7.95 (ISBN 0-8027-6020-1); PLB 7.85 o.s.i. (ISBN 0-8027-6021-X). Walker & Co.
Elephants in the Living Room, Bears in the Canoe. Earl Hammond et al. LC 77-802. (gr. 5-7). 1977. 8.95 o.s.i. (ISBN 0-440-02251-7). Delacorte.
Elephants on the Beach. Irene Brady. (Illus.). 32p. (gr. 2-5). 1979. 7.95 (ISBN 0-684-16115-X). Scribner.
Elephants: The Vanishing Giants. Dan Freeman. (Illus.). 192p. 1981. 20.00 (ISBN 0-399-12567-1). Putnam.
Eleusis & the Eleusinian Mysteries. George E. Mylonas. 1961. 22.50x (ISBN 0-691-03513-X); pap. 8.95 (ISBN 0-691-00205-3). Princeton U Pr.
Elevation Sea Level. Barb Sisson. LC 79-67521. 1981. 5.95 (ISBN 0-533-04473-1). Vantage.

Eleven Area Health Education Centers: The View from the Grass Roots. Charles E. Odegaard. LC 80-50250. (Carnegie Council on Policy Studies in Higher Education). (Illus.). 808p. (Orig.). 1980. pap. 20.00 (ISBN 0-295-95748-4, Pub. by Carnegie Coun Policy). U of Wash Pr.
Eleven Commandments. Lehman Strauss. 1946. pap. 3.50 (ISBN 0-87213-814-3). Loizeaux.
Eleven Great Cantatas in Full Vocal & Instrumental Score. Johann S. Bach. 352p. 1976. pap. 8.50 (ISBN 0-486-23268-9). Dover.
Eleven Harrow House. Gerald Browne. 1979. pap. 2.25 o.s.i. (ISBN 0-440-12315-1). Dell.
Eleven Hungry Cats. Noburo Baba. Tr. by Alvin Tresselt. LC 79-93858. Orig. Title: Eleven Pikino Neko. (Illus.). (gr. k-3). 1970. 5.95 o.s.i. (ISBN 0-8193-0384-4, Four Winds); PLB 5.41 o.s.i. (ISBN 0-8193-0385-2). Schol Bk Serv.
Eleven Kinds of Loneliness: Short Stories. Richard Yates. LC 72-603. 230p. 1962. Repr. lib. bdg. 19.75x (ISBN 0-8371-5727-7, YALO). Greenwood.
Eleven Out of Twelve: A Bibliography. Julia Atkinson. 95p. (Orig.). 1980. pap. 4.00x (ISBN 0-931040-03-5). Independence Unltd.
Eleventh Annual Estate Planning Institute. (Estate Planning & Administration Course Handbook Ser. 1979-80: Vol. 113). 1980. 25.00 (ISBN 0-685-63715-8, D4-5131). PLI.
Eleventh Annual Institute on International Taxatio. (Tax Law & Estate Planning Course Handbook Ser. 1980-81: Vol. 147). 1980. 25.00 (ISBN 0-685-63717-4, J4-3479). PLI.
Eleventh Annual Institute on Securities Regulation. Ed. by Arthur Fleischer, Jr. et al. LC 70-125178. 593p. 1980. text ed. 50.00 (ISBN 0-686-69167-9, B2-1275). PLI.
Eleventh Commandment. Lester Del Rey. 1976. pap. 1.50 (ISBN 0-345-29641-9). Ballantine.
Eleventh Here's How. Eastman Kodak Company. LC 79-55802. (Here's How Ser.). (Illus.). 1979. pap. 4.25 (ISBN 0-87985-230-5). Eastman Kodak.
Eli. Bill Peet. LC 77-17500. (gr. k-3). 1978. reinforced bdg. 8.95 (ISBN 0-395-26454-5). HM.
Eli Terry & the Connecticut Shelf Clock. Kenneth D. Roberts. LC 72-97556. 1973. 27.00 (ISBN 0-913602-06-X). K Roberts.
Eli Whitney & the Whitney Armory. Cooper et al. (Illus.). 95p. 8.95 (ISBN 0-9603662-0-2); pap. 4.95 (ISBN 0-686-63873-5). Arma Pr.
Elie Wiesel. Ted L. Estess. LC 80-5337. (Modern Literature Ser.). 160p. 1980. 10.95 (ISBN 0-8044-2184-6). Ungar.
Elie Wiesel: A Bibliography. Molly Abramowitz. LC 74-17166. (Author Bibliographies Ser.: No. 22). 1974. 10.00 (ISBN 0-8108-0731-9). Scarecrow.
Elihu the Elephant. Gale Brennan. (Illus.). 1980. 5.95g (ISBN 0-516-09102-6). Childrens.
Elijah Jeremiah Phillips' Great Journey. Paul Ricchiuti. (Hello World Ser.). 1975. pap. 1.65 (ISBN 0-8163-0185-9, 05303-3). Pacific Pr Pub Assn.
Elijah P. Lovejoy, Abolitionist Editor. Merton L. Dillon. LC 80-11000. ix, 190p. 1980. Repr. of 1961 ed. lib. bdg. 18.75x (ISBN 0-313-22352-1, DIEJ). Greenwood.
Elijah, the Man Who Did Not Die. Gordon Lindsay. (Old Testament Ser.). 1.25 (ISBN 0-89985-149-5). Christ Nations.
Elijah, The Whirlwind Prophet. Gordon Lindsay. (Old Testament Ser.). 1.25 (ISBN 0-89985-148-7). Christ Nations.
Elimination Play in Bridge. Terence Reese & Roger Trezel. LC 76-55902. 1977. pap. 3.95 (ISBN 0-8119-0361-3). Fell.
Elio Vittorini. Joy H. Potter. (World Authors Ser.: No. 518). 1979. lib. bdg. 14.95 (ISBN 0-8057-6359-7). Twayne.
Eliot Porter Calendar 1981. Eliot Porter. 1981. 6.95 (ISBN 0-525-03004-2). Dutton.
Eliphalet Nott. Codman Hislop. LC 71-161696. (Illus.). 1971. 27.50x (ISBN 0-8195-4037-4, Pub. by Wesleyan U Pr). Columbia U Pr.
Elisa. Edmond De Goncourt. Tr. by M. Crosland from Fr. 190p. 1975. Repr. of 1959 ed. 16.50 (ISBN 0-86527-242-5). Fertig.
Elisabeth & the Marsh Mystery. Felice Holman. (Illus.). (gr. k-3). 1966. 4.95g o.s.i. (ISBN 0-02-744090-7). Macmillan.
Elisabeth Stevens Nineteen Eighty-One Guide to Baltimore's Inner Harbor. Elisabeth Stevens. (Illus.). 64p. 1981. pap. 2.50 (ISBN 0-916144-86-0). Stemmer Hse.
Elisabeth the Bird Watcher. Felice Holman. (Illus.). (gr. k-3). 1963. 5.95 (ISBN 0-02-744250-0). Macmillan.
Elisabeth the Treasure Hunter. Felice Holman. (gr. k-3). 1964. 4.95g o.s.i. (ISBN 0-02-744300-0). Macmillan.
Elise. Sara Reavin. (Orig.). 1980. pap. 2.95 (ISBN 0-451-09483-2, SG). NAL.
Elite & Development. Sachchidananda & Lal. 286p. 1980. text ed. 15.75x (ISBN 0-391-02129-X). Humanities.
Elite Images of Dutch Politics: Accommodation & Conflict. Samuel J. Eldersvels et al. 296p. 1981. text ed. 15.00x (ISBN 0-472-10009-2). U of Mich Pr.
Elite Schools: A Profile of Prestigious Independent College Preparatory Schools. Leonard Baird. LC 76-48376. 1977. 17.95 (ISBN 0-669-01146-0). Lexington Bks.
Elite Structure & Ideology: A Theory with Applications to Norway. John Higley et al. 377p. 1976. 20.00x (ISBN 0-231-04068-7). Columbia U Pr.
Elites & Change in the Kentucky Mountains. H. Dudley Plunkett & Mary J. Bowman. LC 76-160049. (Illus.). 216p. 1973. 13.50x (ISBN 0-8131-1275-3). U Pr of Ky.
Elites & Economic Development: Comparative Studies on the Political Economy of Latin American Cities. John Walton. LC 75-620108. (Latin American Monographs: No. 41). 272p. 1977. 14.95x (ISBN 0-292-72017-3); pap. 6.95 (ISBN 0-292-72018-1). U of Tex Pr.
Elites & Masses: An Introduction to Political Sociology. Martin Marger. 1980. text ed. 15.95 (ISBN 0-442-25410-5); instr's. manual 2.00 (ISBN 0-442-24628-5). D Van Nostrand.
Elites & Power in British Society. Ed. by P. Stanworth & A. Giddens. LC 73-92788. (Studies in Sociology: No. 8). (Illus.). 280p. 1974. 29.95 (ISBN 0-521-20441-0); pap. 9.95x (ISBN 0-521-09853-X). Cambridge U Pr.
Elites & Their Education. David Boyd. (General Ser). 160p. 1973. pap. text ed. 12.00x (ISBN 0-85633-025-6, NFER). Humanities.
Elites in American History: The Civil War to the New Deal. Philip H. Burch. 300p. text ed. 20.00x (ISBN 0-8419-0595-9). Holmes & Meier.
Elites in American History: The Federalist Years to the Civil War, Vol. 1. Philip H. Burch, Jr. 320p. 1981. text ed. 20.00x (ISBN 0-8419-0594-0). Holmes & Meier.
Elites in American History: The New Deal to the Carter Administration, Vol. 3. Philip H. Burch, Jr. 1980. text ed. 19.50x (ISBN 0-8419-0565-7); pap. text ed. 14.50x (ISBN 0-8419-0566-5). Holmes & Meier.
Elites in the Middle East. Ed. by I. William Zartman. 270p. 1980. 24.95 (ISBN 0-03-055961-8). Praeger.
Elites of Barotseland, 1878-1969: A Political History of Zambia's Western Province. Gerald L. Caplan. 1970. 22.50x (ISBN 0-520-01758-7). U of Cal Pr.
Elixir of Hate. George A. England. 1976. lib. bdg. 12.95x (ISBN 0-89968-176-X). Lighthouse Pr NY.
Eliza. Jean A. Bartlett. (Torment of Aaron Burr Ser.: No. 3). 1977. pap. 1.75 o.p. (ISBN 0-445-04012-2). Popular Lib.
Eliza Ou le Voyage Aux Glaciers Du Mont S. Bernard. Maria L. Cherubini. Ed. by Philip Gossett & Charles Rosen. LC 76-49216. (Early Romantic Opera Ser.). 1979. lib. bdg. 82.00 (ISBN 0-8240-2933-X). Garland Pub.
Eliza Stanhope. Joanna Trollope. 1980. pap. 2.25 o.s.i. (ISBN 0-440-12356-9). Dell.
Elizabeth. Jessica Hamilton. 1977. pap. 1.75 o.p. (ISBN 0-445-04013-0). Popular Lib.
Elizabeth: A Puerto Rican-American Child Tells Her Story. Joe Molnar. LC 74-10713. (Illus.). (gr. 4-6). 1975. PLB 5.90 (ISBN 0-531-02795-3). Watts.
Elizabeth & the English Reformation. William P. Haugaard. LC 68-23179. 1968. 49.50 (ISBN 0-521-07245-X). Cambridge U Pr.
Elizabeth Appleton. John O'Hara. 312p. 1974. pap. 1.50 o.p. (ISBN 0-445-03039-9). Popular Lib.
Elizabeth Barrett Browning. Virginia L. Radley. (English Authors Ser.: No. 136). lib. bdg. 9.95 (ISBN 0-8057-1064-7). Twayne.
Elizabeth Barrett Browning Concordance, 4 vols. Ed. by Gladys W. Hudson. LC 73-5735. 1973. Set. 125.00 (ISBN 0-8103-1003-1). Gale.
Elizabeth Bayley Seton. Annabelle M. Melville. 1976. lib. rep. ed. 20.00x (ISBN 0-684-14735-1, ScribT). Scribner.
Elizabeth Bayley Seton. Annabelle M. Melville. 1976. pap. 2.25 (ISBN 0-89129-218-7). Jove Pubns.
Elizabeth Bishop: A Bibliography, 1927-1979. Candace W. MacMahon. LC 79-13063. 1980. 20.00x (ISBN 0-8139-0783-7). U Pr of Va.
Elizabeth Blackwell. Matthew G. Grant. LC 73-15858. 1974. PLB 5.95 (ISBN 0-87191-307-0). Creative Ed.
Elizabeth Cady Stanton: A Radical for Women's Rights. Lois W. Banner. (Library of American Biography). 189p. 1980. pap. text ed. 4.95 (ISBN 0-316-08030-6). Little.
Elizabeth Cady Stanton-Susan B. Anthony: Correspondence, Writings, Speeches. Ed. by Ellen Dubois. LC 80-6190. (Studies in the Life of Women Ser.). 1981. 17.95x (ISBN 0-8052-3759-3); pap. 6.95 (ISBN 0-8052-0672-8). Schocken.
Elizabeth Catches a Fish. Jane R. Thomas. LC 76-28318. (Illus.). (gr. 1-4). 1977. 6.95 (ISBN 0-395-28827-4, Clarion). HM.
Elizabeth David Classics: Mediterranean Food, French Country Cooking, Summer Cooking. Elizabeth David. LC 80-7648. (Illus.). 672p. 1980. 15.95 (ISBN 0-394-49153-X). Knopf.
Elizabeth, Elizabeth. Eileen Dunlop. LC 76-46758. (gr. 5 up). 1977. 6.95 o.p. (ISBN 0-03-019311-7). HR&W.
Elizabeth First. Neville Williams. LC 74-187567. 224p. 1972. 4.95 o.p. (ISBN 0-385-01104-0). Doubleday.
Elizabeth Gail & the Strange Birthday Party. Hilda Stahl. (gr. 4-6). 1980. 1.95 (ISBN 0-8423-0724-9). Tyndale.
Elizabeth Gail & the Terrifying News. Hilda Stahl. (gr. 4-8). 1980. 1.95 (ISBN 0-8423-0725-7). Tyndale.
Elizabeth Gaskell. Angus Easson. 1979. 22.00x (ISBN 0-7100-0099-5). Routledge & Kegan.
Elizabeth Gaskell. Winifred Gerin. (Ser. K). (Illus.). 352p. 1980. pap. 9.95 (ISBN 0-19-281296-3). Oxford U Pr.
Elizabeth Grotesque. Neil Rhodes. 208p. 1980. 35.00 (ISBN 0-7100-0599-7). Routledge & Kegan.
Elizabeth I. Lacey B. Smith. LC 79-54031. (Problems in Civilization Ser.). (Orig.). 1980. pap. text ed. 3.95x (ISBN 0-88273-407-5). Forum Pr MO.
Elizabeth Macarthur & Her World. Hazel King. 240p. 1980. 27.50x (ISBN 0-424-00080-6, Pub. by Sydney U Pr Australia). Intl Schol Bk Serv.
Elizabeth of York: the Mother of Henry Eighth: The Mother of Henry 8. Nancy L. Harvey. (Illus.). 324p. 1973. 6.95 o.s.i. (ISBN 0-02-548590-3). Macmillan.
Elizabethan & Jacobean Tragedy: An Anthology. Robert Ornstein & Hazelton Spencer. 1964. pap. text ed. 7.95x o.p. (ISBN 0-669-21477-9). Heath.
Elizabethan Domestic Drama: A Survey of the Origins, Antecedents,& Nature of the Domestic Play in England, 1500-1640, 2 vols. Andrew Clark. (Salzburg Studies in English Literature, Jacobean Drama Studies: Vol. 49). 455p. (Orig.). 1975. Set. pap. text ed. 50.25x (ISBN 0-391-01345-9). Humanities.
Elizabethan Erotic Narratives: Irony & Pathos in the Ovidian Poetry of Shakespeare, Marlowe, & Their Contemporaries. William Keach. 1977. 19.50 (ISBN 0-8135-0830-4). Rutgers U Pr.
Elizabethan Journal. Ed. by G. B. Harrison. 1974. 25.50x (ISBN 0-7100-7881-1). Routledge & Kegan.
Elizabethan Military Science: The Books & the Practice. Henry J. Webb. (Illus.). 1965. 25.00x (ISBN 0-299-03810-6). U of Wis Pr.
Elizabethan Minor Epics. Ed. by Elizabeth S. Donno. LC 63-20343. 1963. 22.50x o.p. (ISBN 0-231-02530-0). Columbia U Pr.
Elizabethan Miscellany No. Two. Ed. by James Hogg. (Salzburg Studies in English Literature, Elizabethan & Renaissance Studies: No. 71). 1978. pap. text ed. 25.00x (ISBN 0-391-01420-X). Humanities.
Elizabethan Music & Musical Criticism. Morrison C. Boyd. LC 73-1837. 392p. 1974. pap. 4.95x o.p. (ISBN 0-8122-1071-9). U of Pa Pr.
Elizabethan Prisons & Prison Scenes, 2 vols. E. D. Pendry. (Salzburg Studies in English Literature, Elizabethan & Renaissance Studies: No. 17). (Illus.). 385p. 1974. Set. pap. text ed. 50.25 (ISBN 0-391-01496-X). Humanities.
Elizabethan Privateering Fifteen Eighty-Three - Sixteen Three. Kenneth R. Andrews. 1964. 35.50 (ISBN 0-521-04032-9). Cambridge U Pr.
Elizabethan Privy Council in the Fifteen Seventies. Michael B. Pulman. LC 73-115497. 1971. 22.75x (ISBN 0-520-01716-1). U of Cal Pr.
Elizabethan Prodigals. Richard Helgerson. 1977. 14.50x (ISBN 0-520-03264-0). U of Cal Pr.
Elizabethan Renaissance: The Life of the Society. A. L. Rowse. (Illus.). 320p. 1972. lib. rep. ed. 20.00x (ISBN 0-684-15656-3, ScribT). Scribner.
Elizabethan Song Book. W. H. Auden & Chester Kallman. Ed. by Noah Greenberg. 1968. pap. 6.50 (ISBN 0-686-16377-X, Pub. by Faber & Faber). Merrimack Bk Serv.
Elizabethan Stage Doctor As a Dramatic Convention. Philip C. Kolin. (Salzburg Studies in English Literature, Elizabethan & Renaissance Studies Ser.: No. 41). 212p. (Orig.). 1975. pap. text ed. 25.00x (ISBN 0-391-01450-1). Humanities.
Elizabethan Theatre Seven. Ed. by G. R. Hibbard. 220p. 1980. 18.50 (ISBN 0-208-01815-8, Archon). Shoe String.
Elizabethan Theatre Six. Ed. by G. R. Hibbard. (Elizabethan Theatre Ser.). 1978. 15.00 (ISBN 0-208-01636-8, Archon). Shoe String.
Elizabethan Verse Romances. Ed. by M. M. Reese. (Routledge English Texts). 1971. 7.95 (ISBN 0-7100-4517-4); pap. 2.95 (ISBN 0-7100-4518-2). Routledge & Kegan.
Elizabethan Village. Anthony Fletcher. (Then & There Ser.). (Illus.). 1972. pap. text ed. 2.65x (ISBN 0-582-20409-7). Longman.
Elizabethan Virginal Book. E. W. Naylor. LC 70-87638. (Music Ser). 1970. Repr. of 1905 ed. lib. bdg. 25.00 (ISBN 0-306-71792-1). Da Capo.
Elizabethan Zoo. Pliny. Ed. by M. St. Clare Byrne. Tr. by Philemon Holland & Edward Topsell. LC 79-88477. (Illus.). 192p. 1979. 15.00 (ISBN 0-87923-300-1, Nonpareil Bks.); pap. 7.95 (ISBN 0-87923-299-4). Godine.
Elizabethans at Home. Lu E. Pearson. (Illus.). 1957. 32.50x (ISBN 0-8047-0494-5); pap. 6.95 o.p. (ISBN 0-8047-0495-3, SP46). Stanford U Pr.
Elizabethans Errant. D. W. Davis. LC 67-16462. 1967. 9.50 (ISBN 0-8014-0098-8). Brown Bk.
Elizabeth's First Day at School. Patricia Relf. (Golden Storytime Bk.). (Illus.). 24p. 1981. 1.95 (ISBN 0-307-11957-2, Golden Pr). Western Pub.
Elizabeth's Tower. A. C. Stewart. LC 72-4063. 220p. (gr. 6-9). 1972. 9.95 (ISBN 0-87599-193-9). S G Phillips.
Elk of North America. Olaus J. Murie. LC 79-83649. (Illus.). 376p. (gr. 7-12). 1979. 13.50 (ISBN 0-933160-02-X); pap. 9.95 (ISBN 0-933160-03-8). Teton Bkshop.
Elkhorn Tavern. large print ed. Douglas C. Jones. 1981. Repr. of 1980 ed. 12.95 (ISBN 0-89621-273-4). Thorndike Pr.
Ella Fannie Elephant Riddle Book. Ann Bishop. LC 74-14931. (Riddle Bk.). (Illus.). 40p. (gr. 1-3). 1974. 5.75g (ISBN 0-8075-1966-9). A Whitman.
Ella's Dream. Elizabeth Gunn. 1979. 14.95 (ISBN 0-241-89847-1, Pub. by Hamish Hamilton England). David & Charles.
Ellen. Paul Ricchiuti. LC 76-44051. (Destiny Ser). 1976. pap. 4.50 o.p. (ISBN 0-8163-0255-3, 05312-4). Pacific Pr Pub Assn.
Ellen & the Gang. Frieda Friedman. (Illus.). (gr. 3-7). 1963. PLB 7.44 o.p. (ISBN 0-688-31263-2). Morrow.
Ellen & the Queen. Gillian Avery. LC 74-10287. (Illus.). 128p. (gr. 3-5). 1975. 5.95 o.p. (ISBN 0-525-66415-7). Elsevier-Nelson.
Ellen C. Sabin: Proponent of Higher Education for Women. Estelle Pau On Lau. 1978. pap. text ed. 7.50x (ISBN 0-8191-0469-8). U Pr of Amer.
Ellen Knauff Story. Ellen R. Knauff. LC 73-21679. (Civil Liberties in American History Ser.). 242p. 1974. Repr. of 1952 ed. lib. bdg. 29.50 (ISBN 0-306-70238-X). Da Capo.
Ellen Middleton, a Tale, 1844. Georgiana Fullerton. Ed. by Robert L. Wolff. LC 75-471. (Victorian Fiction Ser). 1975. lib. bdg. 66.00 (ISBN 0-8240-1549-5). Garland Pub.
Ellen Tebbits. Beverly Cleary. (Illus.). (gr. 3-7). 1951. 7.75 (ISBN 0-688-21264-6); PLB 7.44 (ISBN 0-688-31264-0). Morrow.
Ellen Terry & Bernard Shaw: A Correspondence. Ed. by Christopher St. John. LC 78-76887. 3.25 (ISBN 0-87830-043-0). Theatre Arts.
Ellen's Blue Jays. Dorothy Sterling. LC 61-7823. (ps-5). pap. 1.49 (ISBN 0-385-08056-5). Doubleday.
Ellery Channing. Robert N. Hudspeth. (U. S. Authors Ser.: No. 223). 1973. lib. bdg. 10.95 (ISBN 0-8057-0131-1). Twayne.
Ellery Queen Presents. Erle S. Gardner. Bd. with Erle Stanley Gardner; Amazing Adventures of Lester Leith. 192p. 1981. 9.95. Davis Pubns.
Ellery Queen Presents: Erle Stanley Gardner's The Amazing Adventures of Lester Leith. Ed. by Ellery Queen. 192p. 1981. 9.95 (ISBN 0-8037-1653-2). Davis Pubns.
Ellery Queen's Circumstantial Evidence. Ed. by Ellery Queen. 287p. 1980. 9.95 (ISBN 0-8037-2213-3). Davis Pubns.
Ellery Queen's Cops & Capers. Ed. by Ellery Queen. LC 77-81935. 1977. pap. 1.50 o.p. (ISBN 0-89559-001-8). Davis Pubns.
Ellery Queen's Crime Cruise Round the World. Ed. by Ellery Queen. 288p. 1981. 9.95 (ISBN 0-8037-2189-7). Davis Pubns.
Ellery Queen's Crimes & Consequences. Ed. by Ellery Queen. LC 77-82626. 1977. pap. 1.50 o.p. (ISBN 0-89559-002-6). Davis Pubns.
Ellery Queen's Doors to Mystery. Ed. by Ellery Queen. 288p. 1981. 9.95 (ISBN 0-8037-2194-3). Davis Pubns.
Ellery Queen's Giants of Mystery. 1976. 8.95 (ISBN 0-8037-4362-9). Davis Pubns.
Ellery Queen's X Marks the Plot. Ed. by Ellery Queen. LC 77-81937. pap. 1.95 o.p. (ISBN 0-89559-004-2). Davis Pubns.
Ellicott's Four Volume Bible Commentary (Unabridged) Charles J. Ellicott. 4580p. 1981. Repr. 119.95 (ISBN 0-310-43878-0). Zondervan.
Ellie. Herbert Kastle. 1973. 7.95 o.p. (ISBN 0-440-02312-2). Delacorte.

Ellinor, or the World As It Is, 4 vols. Mary Ann Hanway. LC 73-22145. (Feminist Controversy in England, 1788-1810 Ser.). 1974. Set. lib. bdg. 80.00 (ISBN 0-8240-0867-7); lib. bdg. 50.00 ea. Garland Pub.
Elliott Coues: Naturalist & Frontier Historian. Paul R. Cutright & Michael J. Brodhead. LC 80-12424. (Illus.). 510p. 1981. 28.95 (ISBN 0-252-00802-2). U of Ill Pr.
Ellipse. Mannis Charosh. LC 73-132293. (Young Math Ser). (Illus.). (gr. 1-4). 1971. 7.95 (ISBN 0-690-25856-9, TYC-J). T Y Crowell.
Elliptic Functions: A Primer. Eric H. Neville. Ed. by W. J. Langford. 211p. 1972. text ed. 25.00 (ISBN 0-08-016369-6). Pergamon.
Elliptic Functions & Elliptic Curves. P. Du Val. (Condon Mathematical Society Lecture Notes Ser.: No. 9). (Illus.). 200p. 1972. 26.50 (ISBN 0-521-20036-9). Cambridge U Pr.
Ellsworth & the Cats from Mars. Patience Brewster. (Illus.). 32p. (gr. 1-5). 1981. 9.95 (ISBN 0-395-29612-9, Clarion). HM.
Ellsworth on Ellsworth. Ralph E. Ellsworth. LC 80-12656. 171p. 1980. 10.00 (ISBN 0-8108-1311-4). Scarecrow.
Elmdon, Continuity & Change in a Northwest Essex Village. Jean Robin. LC 79-12964. (Illus.). 1980. 41.50 (ISBN 0-521-22820-4). Cambridge U Pr.
Elmer & the Dragon. Ruth Gannett. (Orig.). (gr. k-6). 1980. pap. 1.25 (ISBN 0-440-41761-9, Pub. by YB). Dell.
Elmer & the Dragon. Ruth S. Gannett. (Illus.). (gr. 4-6). 1950. PLB 5.99 o.s.i. (ISBN 0-394-91120-2). Random.
Elmer Gantry. Sinclair Lewis. LC 79-15937. 1979. Repr. of 1927 ed. lib. bdg. 12.50x (ISBN 0-8376-0441-9). Bentley.
Elmer Rice: A Playwright's Vision of America. Anthony F. Palmieri. LC 78-75182. 248p. 1980. 19.50 (ISBN 0-8386-2333-6). Fairleigh Dickinson.
Elmer Rice: Three Plays. Elmer Rice. Incl. The Adding Machine; Street Scene; Dream Girl. 239p. 1965. 4.25 (ISBN 0-8090-0735-5, Mermaid). Hill & Wang.
Elohist & North Israelite Traditions. Alan W. Jenks. LC 76-40189. (Society of Biblical Literature. Monograph). 1977. 9.00 (ISBN 0-89130-088-0, 060022); pap. 7.50 (ISBN 0-89130-145-3). Scholars Pr Ca.
Eloise Wilkin Four Baby's First Golden Books, 4 bks. Illus. by Eloise Wilkin. (Illus.). (ps). Date not set. boxed set 4.95 (ISBN 0-307-13650-7, Golden Pr). Western Pub.
Elope to Death. John Creasey. LC 76-43493. 1977. 6.95 o.p. (ISBN 0-03-020621-9). HR&W.
Eloquent Animals. Flora Davis. 1979. pap. 2.25 o.p. (ISBN 0-425-04039-9). Berkley Pub.
Eloquent Light. Nancy Newhall. (Illus.). 200p. 1980. 47.50, after june 30, 1981 60.00 (ISBN 0-89381-066-5); after June 31, 1981 60.00 (ISBN 0-686-65238-X). Aperture.
Eloquent Light: The Cinematography of James Wong Howe. Todd Rainsberger. LC 80-26542. (Illus.). 218p. 1981. 17.50 (ISBN 0-498-02405-9). A S Barnes.
Els Quatre Gats: Art in Barcelona Around Nineteen Hundred. Marylyn McCully. LC 77-72143. 1978. 27.50 o.p. (ISBN 0-691-03928-3). Princeton U Pr.
Elsa. rev. ed. Joy Adamson. (Illus.). (gr. 1 up). 1963. PLB 4.99 o.s.i. (ISBN 0-394-91117-2). Pantheon.
Else Lasker-Schuler, the Broken World. H. W. Cohn. LC 73-80481. (Anglica Germanica Ser.: No. 2). 172p. 1974. 42.50 (ISBN 0-521-20292-2). Cambridge U Pr.
Elsevier's Dictionary of Financial Terms. F. J. Thomson. LC 79-11810. 496p. (Eng., Ger., Span., Fr., Ital., Dutch.). 1979. 122.00 (ISBN 0-686-62653-2). Elsevier.
Elsie Dinsmore. Martha Finley. Ed. by Alison Lurie & Justin G. Schiller. LC 75-32168. (Classics of Children's Literature Ser.: 1621-1932). PLB 38.00 (ISBN 0-8240-2281-5). Garland Pub.
Elson's Music Dictionary. Louis C. Elson. LC 70-173097. xii, 306p. 1972. Repr. of 1905 ed. 20.00 (ISBN 0-8103-3268-X). Gale.
Elton John. Paula Taylor. (Rock 'n Pop Stars Ser.). (Illus.). (gr. 4-12). 1975. PLB 5.95 (ISBN 0-87191-457-3); pap. 2.95 (ISBN 0-685-82738-0). Creative Ed.
Elura: Art & Culture. T. V. Pathy. (Illus.). 190p. 1980. text ed. 31.00x (ISBN 0-391-01758-6). Humanities.
Elusive Daniel Defoe. Laura Curtis. 200p. 1981. 19.50x (ISBN 0-389-20063-8). B&N.
Elusive Harmony. Mary Burchell. (Alpha Books). 80p. (Orig.). 1978. pap. text ed. 2.25x (ISBN 0-19-424163-7). Oxford U Pr.
Elusive Isabel. Jacques Futrelle. 1976. lib. bdg. 14.95x (ISBN 0-89968-164-6). Lighthouse Pr NY.
Elusive Memory. Gertrude Mace. (YA) 1978. 5.95 (ISBN 0-685-85777-8, Avalon). Bouregy.
Elusive Mind. H. D. Lewis. (Muirhead Library of Philosophy). 1969. text ed. 26.00x (ISBN 0-00-430013-0). Humanities.
Elusive Peace: The Middle East, Oil & the Economic & Political Future of the World. Jonathan H. Mobley. (The Major Currents in Contemprary World History Lib.). (Illus.). 122p. 1981. 46.55 (ISBN 0-930008-79-0). Inst Econ Pol.
Elusive Pimpernel. Emmuska Orczy. 1976. lib. bdg. 15.75x (ISBN 0-89968-073-9). Lightyear.
Elusive Presence: The Discovery of John H. Finley & His America. Marvin E. Gettleman. LC 79-10547. (Illus.). 1979. 15.95 (ISBN 0-88229-312-5); pap. 8.95 (ISBN 0-88229-695-7). Nelson-Hall.
Elusive Reform: The New French Universities, 1968-1978. Habiba S. Cohen. (Westview Replica Edition). 1978. lib. bdg. 23.75x (ISBN 0-89158-195-2). Westview.
Elusive Republic: Political Economy in Jeffersonian America. Drew R. McCoy. LC 79-20952. (Institute for Early American History & Culture Ser.). x, 268p. 1980. 21.50x (ISBN 0-8078-1416-4). U of NC Pr.
Elusive Science: Origins of Experimental Psychical Research. Seymour H. Mauskopf & Michael R. McVaugh. LC 80-7991. (Illus.). 400p. 1981. text ed. 24.50x (ISBN 0-8018-2331-5). Johns Hopkins.
Elusive Self: Psyche & Spirit in Virginia Woolf's Novels. Louise A. Poresky. LC 79-64503. 288p. 1981. 22.50 (ISBN 0-87413-170-7, 170). U Delaware Pr.
Elusive Treasure. Brian Fagan. LC 77-8478. (Encore Edition). (Illus.). 1977. 7.95 o.p. (ISBN 0-684-16212-1, ScribT). Scribner.
Elves & the Shoemaker. (Illus.). Arabic 2.50x (ISBN 0-685-82822-0). Intl Bk Ctr.
Elves & the Shoemaker. Ed. by Alma Gilleo. LC 65-2642. (Holiday Tales). (Illus.). (ps). 1977. pap. 21.00 10 bks. & 1 casette (ISBN 0-89290-013-X). Soc for Visual.
Elves & the Shoemaker. Freya Littledale. LC 75-12500. (Illus.). 32p. (gr. k-3). 1975. 4.95 (ISBN 0-590-07426-1, Four Winds). Schol Bk Serv.
Elves & the Shoemaker. Freya Littledale. (Illus.). (gr. k-3). 1977. pap. 1.95 (ISBN 0-590-01441-2, Schol Pap); pap. 3.50 bk. & record (ISBN 0-590-20615-X). Schol Bk Serv.
Elves & the Shoemaker. Illus. by Jim Robison. (Tell-a-Tale Readers). (Illus.). (gr. k-3). 1975. PLB 4.77 (ISBN 0-307-68496-2, Whitman). Western Pub.
Elves, Fairies & Gnomes. Lee B. Hopkins. LC 79-19753. (Illus.). (ps-2). Date not set. 5.95 (ISBN 0-394-84351-7); PLB 5.99 (ISBN 0-394-94351-1). Knopf.
Elves, Gnomes & Other Little People: A Coloring Book. John O'Brien. (Illus.). 48p. 1980. pap. 2.00 (ISBN 0-486-24049-5). Dover.
Elvis. Jerry Hopkins. (Illus.). 480p. 1972. pap. 2.50 o.s.i. (ISBN 0-446-81665-5). Warner Bks.
Elvis. Richard Mann. 1977. pap. cancelled o.s.i. (ISBN 0-89728-027-X, 688974). Omega Pubns OR.
Elvis & His Friends. Maria Gripe. LC 75-8002. (Illus.). 224p. 1976. 6.95 o.s.i. (ISBN 0-440-02272-X, Sey Lawr); PLB 6.46 o.s.i. (ISBN 0-440-02273-8). Delacorte.
Elvis: Images & Fancies. Ed. by Jac L. Tharpe. LC 79-26044. 1980. 12.50 (ISBN 0-87805-113-9); pap. 6.00 (ISBN 0-87805-114-7). U Pr of Miss.
Elvis: Portrait of a Friend. Marty Lacker et al. 384p. 1980. pap. 2.95 (ISBN 0-553-13824-3). Bantam.
Elvis Presley. Mick Farren & Pearce Marchbank. 1978. pap. 4.95 (ISBN 0-8256-3921-2, Omnibus). Music Sales.
Elvis Presley. Bernard Kling & Heinz Plehn. 1980. pap. 12.95 (ISBN 0-8256-3945-X). Music Sales.
Elvis Presley. Paula Taylor. LC 74-14546. (Rock'n Pop Stars Ser.). (Illus.). 32p. (gr. 3-6). 1974. PLB 5.95 (ISBN 0-87191-394-1); pap. 2.95 (ISBN 0-89812-103-5). Creative Ed.
Elvis Presley Scrapbook. James R. Parish. 160p. (Orig.). 1975. pap. 7.95 o.p. (ISBN 0-345-27594-2). Ballantine.
Elvis, We Love You Tender. Dee Presley et al. 1981. pap. 3.50 o.s.i. (ISBN 0-440-12323-2). Dell.
Ely: Too Black, Too White. abr. ed. Ely Green. Ed. by Arthur Chitty & Elizabeth Chitty. (RL 10). 1971. pap. 1.95 o.p. (ISBN 0-451-61075-X, MJ1075, Ment). NAL.
Emancipation & Equal Rights: Politics & Constitutionalism in the Civil War Era. Herman Belz. 1978. 10.95 (ISBN 0-393-05692-9); pap. 4.95x (ISBN 0-393-09016-7). Norton.
Emancipation of Joe Tepper. Pat E. Dexter. LC 76-26594. (gr. 4-12). 1976. 6.50 o.p. (ISBN 0-525-66519-6). Elsevier-Nelson.
Emancipation of Robert Sadler. Robert Sadler & Marie Chapian. LC 75-14063. (Illus.). 256p. 1975. 7.95 (ISBN 0-87123-132-8, 230132). Bethany Fell.
Emanicipation of Robert Sadler. Robert Sadler & Marie Chapian. LC 75-14063. 1976. pap. 3.95 (ISBN 0-87123-133-6, 210133). Bethany Fell.
Embattled Witness: Memories of a Time of War. Bernard Haring. 1976. 6.95 (ISBN 0-8164-0312-0). Crossroad NY.
Emblematum Libellus Cum Commentariis. Andrea Alciati. LC 75-27869. (Renaissance & the Gods Ser.: Vol. 25). (Illus.). 1977. Repr. of 1621 ed. lib. bdg. 73.00 (ISBN 0-8240-2074-X). Garland Pub.
Emblems of Reality: Discovering Experience in Language. Melvin B. Ralston & Don R. Cox. LC 72-81654. 256p. 1973. pap. text ed. 5.95x (ISBN 0-02-476750-6). Macmillan.
Embrace My Scarlet Heart. Anne-Mariel Shepherd & Don Shepherd. 1977. pap. 1.75 o.s.i. (ISBN 0-515-04268-4). Jove Pubns.
Embrace the Fury. Jessica March. 1978. pap. 1.95 o.p. (ISBN 0-449-13973-5, GM). Fawcett.
Embraces. Sharon Wagner. (Orig.). 1980. pap. 2.50 (ISBN 0-89083-666-3, Kable News Co). Zebra.
Embriologia. Maurice Fitzgerald. (Span.). 1980. pap. text ed. 16.50 (ISBN 0-06-313120-X, Pub. by HarLA Mexico). Har-Row.
Embroidered Boxes. Jane Lemon. (Illus.). 208p. 1980. 30.00 (ISBN 0-571-11606-X, Pub. by Faber & Faber). Merrimack Bk Serv.
Embroiderer's Portfolio of Flower Designs. Eszter Haraszty. (Illus.). 1981. 22.95 (ISBN 0-87140-643-8). Liveright.
Embroidering Our Heritage: The Dinner Party Needlework. Judy Chicago & Susan Hill. (Illus.). 1980. pap. 15.95 (ISBN 0-385-14569-1, Anch). Doubleday.
Embroidering Our Heritage: The Dinner Party Needlework. Judy Chicago & Susan Hill. LC 79-6645. (Illus.). 288p. 1980. 34.95 (ISBN 0-385-14568-3, Anchor Pr). Doubleday.
Embroidery. Cecile Dreesman. (Illus.). 1969. 9.95 (ISBN 0-02-533470-0). Macmillan.
Embroidery. Nora Hana. (Illus.). 1977. 6.95 (ISBN 0-8467-0239-8, Pub. by Two Continents). Hippocrene Bks.
Embroidery & Nature. Jan Messent. (Illus.). 168p. 1980. 22.75 (ISBN 0-8231-4258-2). Branford.
Embroidery Design. Enid Mason. (Illus.). 128p. 1969. 8.50 (ISBN 0-8231-4010-5). Branford.
Embroidery Designs. Ondori Publishing Company Staff. (Ondori Embroidery Ser: Vol. 3). (Illus.). 65p. 1975. pap. 4.50 (ISBN 0-87040-358-3). Japan Pubns.
Embroidery for Beginners. Ondori Staff. (Ondori Needlework Ser.). (Orig.). (gr. 6 up). 1978. pap. 5.50 (ISBN 0-87040-429-6). Japan Pubns.
Embroidery for Children's Clothing. Ondori Publishing Co. (Ondori Needlecraft Ser.). (Illus., Orig.). 1977. pap. 6.50 (ISBN 0-87040-414-8). Japan Pubns.
Embroidery for Fun. Ondori Publishing Company Staff. (Ondori Embroidery Ser: Vol. 4). (Illus.). 137p. 1975. pap. 5.95 (ISBN 0-87040-359-1). Japan Pubns.
Embroidery for Schools. Joan Nicholson. 1977. 16.95 (ISBN 0-7134-0241-5, Pub. by Batsford England). David & Charles.
Embroidery from Traditional English Patterns. Ruby Evans. (Illus.). 1971. 8.25 o.p. (ISBN 0-8231-4026-1). Branford.
Embroidery Magic on Patterned Fabrics. Betty Parker & Edith Martin. LC 76-14976. (Encore Edition). (Illus.). 160p. 1976. 5.95 o.p. (ISBN 0-684-15704-7, ScribT). Scribner.
Embroidery Motifs from Dutch Samplers. Albarta Meulenbelt-Nieuwburg. 1975. 24.00 (ISBN 0-7134-2875-9, Pub. by Batsford England). David & Charles.
Embroidery of All Russia. Mary Gostelow. (Encore Edition). (Illus.). 1978. 3.95 (ISBN 0-684-16542-2, ScribT). Scribner.
Embroidery Schiffli Multi Head. Coleman Schneider. (Illus.). 1978. Repr. of 1968 ed. 35.00 (ISBN 0-9601662-1-1). C Schneider.
Embroidery South Africa. Mary Gostelow. (Illus.). 1977. 20.00 (ISBN 0-263-06232-5). Transatlantic.
Embroidery: Step-by-Step. Macmillan. LC 76-8262. (Step-by-Step Craft Ser.). (Illus.). 1976. pap. 5.95 o.s.i. (ISBN 0-02-011820-1, 01182, Collier). Macmillan.
Embroidery Stitches. Barbara Snook. 1975. pap. 13.50 (ISBN 0-7134-2611-X, Pub. by Batsford England). David & Charles.
Embryology & Phylogeny in Annelids & Arthropods. D. L. Anderson. LC 73-1019. 492p. 1974. 50.00 (ISBN 0-08-017069-2). Pergamon.
Embryology for Surgeons. Stephen W. Gray & John E. Skandalakis. LC 72-126453. (Illus.). 1972. 44.00 (ISBN 0-7216-4220-9). Saunders.
Embryology of Angiosperms. S. S. Bhojwani & S. P. Bhatnagar. 1978. 14.00 (ISBN 0-7069-0335-8, Pub. by Vikas India). Advent Bk.
Embryology Review. William K. Matcalf. (Basic Science Review Bks.). 1974. spiral binding 8.50 (ISBN 0-87488-207-9). Med Exam.
Embryos & How They Develop. Marie M. Jenkins. LC 74-23547. (Illus.). 192p. (gr. 7 up). 1975. 7.95 (ISBN 0-8234-0254-1). Holiday.
Emendation of R. G. Collingwood's Doctrine of Absolute Presuppositions. Kenneth L. Ketner. (Graduate Studies: No. 4). 41p. (Orig.). 1973. pap. 2.00 (ISBN 0-89672-011-X). Tex Tech Pr.
Emerald. Suzan Jarvis. (Orig.). 1980. pap. 1.95 (ISBN 0-532-23120-1). Manor Bks.
Emerald Chicks. L. V. Roper. (Renegade Roe Ser.: No. 2). 176p. 1976. pap. 1.25 o.p. (ISBN 0-445-00332-4). Popular Lib.
Emerald Necklace. Diana Brown. 1981. pap. 1.95 (ISBN 0-451-09727-0, J9727, Sig). NAL.
Emerald Station. Daoma Winston. 1974. pap. 1.95 (ISBN 0-380-00738-X, 38281). Avon.
Emeralds (Poetry) facsimile ed. Michael A. Weinberg. (Illus.). 25p. 1971. write for info. (ISBN 0-9601014-0-3). Weinberg.
Emergence. Julia Atkinson. 360p. 1974. pap. 9.00 ltd. ed. (ISBN 0-931040-02-7). Independence Unltd.
Emergence. Cynthia MacAdams. 1979. pap. 9.95 o.p. (ISBN 0-525-47522-2). Dutton.
Emergence & Growth of an Urban Region: The Developing Urban Detroit Area Vol. 3-A Concept for Future Development. Constantinos A. Doxiadis. LC 66-29622. 1969. 20.00x (ISBN 0-8143-1506-2). Wayne St U Pr.
Emergence & Growth of an Urban Region: The Developing Urban Detroit Area, Vol. 2, Future Alternatives. Constantinos A. Doxiadis. LC 66-29622. 1969. 20.00x (ISBN 0-8143-1505-4). Wayne St U Pr.
Emergence of Andhra Pradesh. K. V. Narayana Rao. 350p. 1974. lib. bdg. 12.50 (ISBN 0-88253-472-6). Ind-US Inc.
Emergence of Being: Through Indian & Greek Thought. Richard A. Gyory. LC 78-70692. 1978. pap. text ed. 9.50 (ISBN 0-8191-0646-1). U Pr of Amer.
Emergence of Classes in Algeria: Colonialism & Socio-Political Change. Marnia Lazreg. LC 76-7955. (Westview Special Studies on Social Political, & Economic Development Ser). 250p. 1976. 30.00x (ISBN 0-89158-107-3). Westview.
Emergence of Contemporary Judaism, 4 vols. Incl. Vol. 2. A Survey of Judaism from the 7th to the 17th Centuries. Phillip Sigal. LC 77-831. (Pittsburgh Theological Monographs: No. 12). 1977. Set. pap. text ed. 10.95 (ISBN 0-915138-14-X). Pickwick.
Emergence of Contemporary Judaism: The Foundation of Judaism from Biblical Origins to the Sixth Century A. D, Vol. 1, Pts. 1 & 2. Phillip Sigal. Incl. Pt. 1. From the Origins to the Separation of Christianity. (Pittsburgh Theological Monographs: No. 29). pap. text ed. 17.50 (ISBN 0-686-64852-8); Pt. 2. Rabbinic Judaism. (Pittsburgh Theological Monographs: No. 29a). pap. text ed. 15.75 (ISBN 0-915138-46-8). 1980. pap. text ed. 31.25 set (ISBN 0-915138-46-8). Pickwick.
Emergence of Contemporary Judaism: Vol. 1, the Foundations of Judaism from Biblical Origins to the Sixth Century A.D. Pt. 1 from the Origins to the Separation of Christianity. Phillip Sigal. (Pittsburgh Theological Monographs: No. 29). 1980. pap. text ed. 17.50 (ISBN 0-915138-30-1). Pickwick.
Emergence of Indian Nationalism. Anil Seal. (Political Change in Modern Asia: No. 1). (Illus.). 1968. 39.95 (ISBN 0-521-06274-8); pap. 11.50x (ISBN 0-521-09652-9). Cambridge U Pr.
Emergence of Man. enl. & rev. ed. John E. Pfeiffer. LC 72-79686. (Illus.). 576p. (YA) 1972. 17.95 o.p. (ISBN 0-06-013329-5, HarpT). Har-Row.
Emergence of Maoism: Mao-Tse-Tung, Ch'en Po-Ta, & the Search for Chinese Theory, 1935-1945. Raymond F. Wylie. LC 79-64221. 368p. 1980. 25.00x (ISBN 0-8047-1051-1). Stanford U Pr.
Emergence of Metropolitan America, 1915-1966. Blake McKelvey. LC 68-18695. (Illus.). 1968. 21.00 (ISBN 0-8135-0571-2). Rutgers U Pr.
Emergence of Modern India. Arthur Lall. LC 80-25028. 288p. 1981. 17.95 (ISBN 0-231-03430-X). Columbia U Pr.
Emergence of Pakistan. Chaudhri M. Ali. LC 79-163081. 1967. 22.50x (ISBN 0-231-02933-0). Columbia U Pr.
Emergence of Probability. I. Hacking. LC 74-82224. 216p. 1975. 29.95 (ISBN 0-521-20460-7). Cambridge U Pr.
Emergence of Social Work. 2nd ed. Neil Gilbert & Harry Specht. LC 80-83097. 484p. 1981. pap. text ed. 12.95 (ISBN 0-87581-266-X). Peacock Pubs.
Emergence of Spanish America: Vicente Rocafuerte & Spanish Americanism, 1808-1832. O. Jaime Rodriguez. LC 74-22972. 392p. 1976. 26.50x (ISBN 0-520-02875-9). U of Cal Pr.
Emergence of the Eastern World. G. L. Seidler. 1968. 28.00 (ISBN 0-08-012637-5). Pergamon.

Emergence of the Nation, 1783-1815. John C. Miller. 190p. 1972. pap. 7.95x (ISBN 0-673-05764-X). Scott F.
Emergence of the Romanian Nation State. Gerald S. Bobango. (East European Monographs: No. 58). 1979. 17.00x (ISBN 0-914710-51-6, Dist. by Columbia U Pr). East Eur Quarterly.
Emergence of the Welfare State in Britain & Germany. Ed. by Wolfgang J. Mommsen. 350p. 1981. 31.00x (ISBN 0-7099-1710-4, Pub. by Croom Helm LTD England). Biblio Dist.
Emergence of Victorian Consciousness. Ed. by George L. Levine. LC 66-24458. 1967. pap. text ed. 6.95 (ISBN 0-02-918890-3). Free Pr.
Emergence of Youth Societies. David Gottlieb et al. LC 66-13598. 1966. 10.50 o.s.i. (ISBN 0-02-912600-2). Free Pr.
Emergencies in Child Psychiatry: Emotional Crises of Children, Youth and Their Families. G. C. Morrison. 516p. 1975. 32.75 (ISBN 0-398-03229-7). C C Thomas.
Emergencies in Obstetrics & Gynecology. Arnold W. Cohen. (Clinics in Emergency Medicine Ser.). (Illus.). 224p. 1981. lib. bdg. 20.00 (ISBN 0-443-08130-1). Churchill.
Emergency! Rona Beame. LC 76-5778. (Illus.). 64p. (gr. 3-5). 1977. PLB 6.97 (ISBN 0-671-32824-7). Messner.
Emergency & Disaster Nursing Continuing Education Review. Karl D. Davis et al. 1976. spiral bdg. 8.00 o.p. (ISBN 0-87488-371-7). Med Exam.
Emergency & Law, with Special Reference to India. Nirmal C. Chatterjee & P. Parameswara Rao. 1966. 7.50x (ISBN 0-210-22741-9). Asia.
Emergency Cardiac Care. 2nd ed. Robert S. Huszar. (Illus.). 350p. 1981. pap. text ed. 14.95 (ISBN 0-87619-863-9). R J Brady.
Emergency Care. 2nd ed. H. Grant & R. Murray, Jr. LC 78-17756. (Illus.). 1978. 12.50 (ISBN 0-87618-886-2). R J Brady.
Emergency Care: Assessment & Intervention. 2nd ed. Ed. by Carmen G. Warner et al. LC 77-18285. (Illus.). 1978. 19.95 (ISBN 0-8016-4744-4). Mosby.
Emergency Care Manual: A Systems Approach. 2nd. ed. Burton A. Waisbren. 1980. pap. 9.50 (ISBN 0-87488-984-7). Med Exam.
Emergency Childbirth Handbook. Barbara Anderson & Pamela Shapiro. 1979. pap. 7.40 (ISBN 0-8273-1761-1). Delmar.
Emergency Department Organization & Management. 2nd ed. American College of Emergency Physicians. Ed. by A. L. Jenkins & John H. Van De Leuv. LC 78-13594. (Illus.). 1978. text ed. 27.50 (ISBN 0-8016-0122-3). Mosby.
Emergency Disputes: A National Labor Policy Problem. 41p. 1961. pap. 1.50 (ISBN 0-87330-002-5). Indus Rel.
Emergency Encounters: A Study of an Urban Ambulance Service. James M. Mannon. (National University Publications, Sociology of Medicine Ser.). 1981. 15.00 (ISBN 0-8046-9281-5). Kennikat.
Emergency Intervention. Ed. by Jane A. Piliavin et al. 1981. price not set (ISBN 0-12-556450-3). Acad Pr.
Emergency Management of the Critical Patient. Ed. by J. Clifford Findeiss. LC 74-81651. (Emergency Medical Care Ser.: Vol. 2). (Illus.). 288p. 1975. text ed. 22.95 (ISBN 0-8151-3223-9, Pub. by Symposia Special). Year Bk Med.
Emergency Medical Care. Ed. by William M. Portnoy et al. LC 77-70083. (Illus.). 1977. 19.95 (ISBN 0-669-01364-1). Lexington Bks.
Emergency Medical Technician Examination Review Book, Vol. 1. Warner F. Bowers & David C. Dimendberg. 1969. spiral bdg. 9.50 (ISBN 0-87488-465-9). Med Exam.
Emergency Medical Technician Examination Review, Vol. 2. Warner F Bowers & David C. Dimendberg. 1972. spiral bdg. 9.50 (ISBN 0-87488-466-7). Med Exam.
Emergency Medicine Case Studies. James T. McRae. LC 79-88721. 1979. pap. 15.50 (ISBN 0-87488-002-5). Med Exam.
Emergency Nursing. C. Luise Riehl. (YA) (gr. 9 up). 1970. 10.64 (ISBN 0-87002-009-9). Bennett IL.
Emergency Nursing: Principles & Practice. Susan A. Budassi & Janet Barber. LC 80-21629. (Illus.). 775p. 1980. pap. text ed. 24.95 (ISBN 0-8016-0451-6). Mosby.
Emergency Patient Care for the EMT: A Guide for the EMT. Janet Barber & Peter Dillman. 1981. 15.95 (ISBN 0-8359-1671-5). Reston.
Emergency Powers: The Executive Order. Tom Peasner. pap. 1.75 (ISBN 0-918700-07-8). Duverus Pub.
Emergency Preparedness Education: An Overview. R. Stoffer & Rick Lavalla. 74p. pap. 3.00 (ISBN 0-913724-23-8). Survival Ed Assoc.
Emergency Preparedness. Boy Scouts of America. LC 19-600. (Illus.). 64p. (gr. 6-12). 1974. pap. 0.70x (ISBN 0-8395-3366-7, 3366). BSA.
Emergency Psychiatric Care. H. Resnik & H. Ruben. LC 74-11791. (Illus.). 1975. pap. 12.95 (ISBN 0-913486-15-9). Charles.
Emergency Psychiatric Treatment: A Handbook of Secondary Prevention. L. D. Hankoff. 100p. 1969. 8.75 (ISBN 0-398-00771-3). C C Thomas.
Emergency Psychiatry. Beverly J. Fauman & Michael Fauman. (Illus.). 150p. 1981. write for info. softcover (3046-9). Williams & Wilkins.
Emergency Reading Teacher's Manual. Edward B. Fry. 107p. (Orig.). 1979. pap. text ed. 6.00x (ISBN 0-89061-207-2, 752S). Jamestown Pubs.
Emergency Response to Crisis. Jeffrey Mitchell & H. L. Resnik. (Illus.). 256p. 1981. text ed. 15.95 (ISBN 0-87619-856-6); pap. 12.95 (ISBN 0-87619-828-0). R J Brady.
Emergency-Room Care. 4th ed. Charles Eckert. 1981. text ed. price not set; pap. text ed. price not set. Little.
Emergency-Room Care. 3rd ed. Ed. by Charles Eckert. 1976. 22.50 (ISBN 0-316-20873-6); pap. 15.95 (ISBN 0-316-20874-4). Little.
Emergency Room Journal Articles. 2nd ed. Abraham Gelperin & Eve A. Gelperin. 244p. 1977. spiral bdg. 14.00 o.p. (ISBN 0-87488-795-X). Med Exam.
Emergency Squads. Taylor. (gr. 5 up). 1980. PLB 7.90 (ISBN 0-531-04117-4, A48). Watts.
Emergency Survival. Charles A. Lehman. Ed. by Diane M. Fessler. (Illus.). 160p. 1979. pap. 6.95 (ISBN 0-935810-03-X). Primer Pubs.
Emergency: Ten Thirty-Three. Hilary Milton. (gr. 5 up). 1977. PLB 7.90 s&l (ISBN 0-531-02905-0). Watts.
Emergency Transfer of the High Risk Neonate: A Working Manual for Medical, Nursing & Administrative Personnel. Angelo Ferrara & Anantham Harin. LC 79-17689. (Illus.). 1979. pap. text ed. 25.00 (ISBN 0-8016-1565-8). Mosby.
Emergency Treatment of Acute Respiratory Disease. 3rd ed. Llewellyn W. Springer. (Illus.). 180p. 1981. pap. text ed. 11.95 (ISBN 0-87619-862-0). R J Brady.
Emergency Treatment of Acute Respiratory Diseases: A Manual for Ambulance & Emergency Room Personnel. rev. ed. Llewellyn W. Stringer. LC 73-4419. (Illus.). 101p. 1972. pap. 8.95 (ISBN 0-87618-073-X). R J Brady.
Emergent Church: The Future of Christianity in a Post-Bourgeois World. Johann B. Metz. 160p. (Ger.). 1981. 10.95 (ISBN 0-8245-0036-9). Crossroad NY.
Emerging Arts: Management, Survival, & Growth. Joan Jeffri. LC 80-18784. 301p. 1980. 22.59 (ISBN 0-03-056707-6). Praeger.
Emerging Careers. Warren D. Gribbons & Paul R. Lohnes. LC 68-20557. 1968. text ed. 11.00x (ISBN 0-8077-1474-7). Tchrs Coll.
Emerging China. Ed. by Thomas Draper. (Reference Shelf Ser.). 1980. 6.25 (ISBN 0-8242-0644-4). Wilson.
Emerging Church. Ronald J. Wilkinks. (To Live Is Christ Ser.). 1981. pap. 4.10 (ISBN 0-697-01760-5). Wm C Brown.
Emerging City. Scott A. Greer. LC 62-11851. 1965. pap. text ed. 5.95 (ISBN 0-02-912960-5). Free Pr.
Emerging Conceptual Frameworks in Family Analyses. Ed. by F. Ivan Nye & Felix M. Berardo. (Special Studies on the Family). 356p. 1981. 13.95 (ISBN 0-03-057043-3). Praeger.
Emerging Entertainment: The Drama of the American People to 1828. Walter J. Meserve. LC 77-74444. 352p. 1977. 17.50x (ISBN 0-253-37007-8). Ind U Pr.
Emerging Form in Architecture: Conversations with Lev Zetlin. Forrest Wilson. LC 75-8912. (Illus.). 224p. 1975. 21.50 (ISBN 0-8436-0150-7). CBI Pub.
Emerging from the Chrysalis: Studies in Rituals of Women's Initiation. Bruce Lincoln. LC 80-24189. (Illus.). 208p. 1981. text ed. 18.50 (ISBN 0-674-24840-6). Harvard U Pr.
Emerging Indonesia. Donald Wilhelm. (Illus.). 192p. 1980. 25.00x (ISBN 0-389-20105-7). B&N.
Emerging Issues in Black Economic Development. Benjamin F. Bobo & Alford E. Osborne, Jr. LC 76-10500. (Illus.). 1976. 12.95 (ISBN 0-669-00718-8). Lexington Bks.
Emerging Lay Ministries. Dennis Geaney. 1979. 9.95 o.p. (ISBN 0-8362-3305-0). Andrews & McMeel.
Emerging Methods in Environmental Design & Planning. Ed. by Gary T. Moore. 1970. 20.50x o.p. (ISBN 0-262-13057-2); pap. 6.95 (ISBN 0-262-63048-6). MIT Pr.
Emerging Network Marketplace. Herbert S. Dordick et al. (Communication & Information Science Ser.). 288p. 1980. 24.95 (ISBN 0-89391-036-8). Ablex Pub.
Emerging Patterns of Administrative Accountability. Lesley Browder, Jr. LC 73-146309. 1971. 21.00x (ISBN 0-8211-0117-X); text ed. 19.00x (ISBN 0-685-04197-2). McCutchan.
Emerging Rights of Children in Treatment for Mental & Catastrophic Illnesses. Frank H. Marsh. LC 79-66481. 1979. text ed. 13.75 (ISBN 0-8191-0829-4); pap. text ed. 7.50 (ISBN 0-8191-0830-8). U Pr of Amer.
Emerging Strategic Environment: Implications for Ballistic Missile Defense. 75p. 1980. pap. 6.50 (ISBN 0-89549-008-0, IFPA 10, IFPA). Unipub.
Emerging Strategic Environment: Implications for Ballistic Missile Defense. Leon Goure et al. LC 79-53108. 75p. 1979. 6.50. Inst Foreign Policy Anal.
Emerging Technologies in Aerospace Structures, Design, Structural Dynamics & Materials. Ed. by J. R. Vinson. 326p. 1980. 40.00 (H00157). ASME.
Emerging Technology: Instructional Uses of the Computer in Higher Education. Carnegie Commission on Higher Education. Ed. by Roger Levien. LC 72-2. (Illus.). 480p. 1972. 18.95 o.p. (ISBN 0-07-010041-1, P&RB). McGraw.
Emerging Theoretical Models in Social & Political History. Ed. by Allan G. Bogue. LC 73-87857. (Sage Contemporary Social Science Issues: No. 9). 4.95x (ISBN 0-8039-0321-9). Sage.
Emerging Universe: Essays on Contemporary Astronomy. Ed. by William C. Saslaw & Kenneth C. Jacobs. LC 72-188526. 120p. 1972. 9.95x (ISBN 0-8139-0397-1). U Pr of Va.
Emerging Woman: Career Analysis & Outlooks. Ed. by Samuel H. Osipow. (Career Programs Ser). 176p. 1975. pap. text ed. 11.95x (ISBN 0-675-08733-3). Merrill.
Emerson: A Study of the Poet As Seer. Robert M. Gay. LC 80-2533. 1981. Repr. of 1928 ed. 32.75 (ISBN 0-404-19259-9). AMS Pr.
Emerson & Goethe. Frederick B. Wahr. 197p. 1980. Repr. of 1915 ed. lib. bdg. 25.00 (ISBN 0-8492-2979-0). R West.
Emerson & Social Reform. Adapa R. Rao. 132p. 1981. text ed. 10.25 (ISBN 0-391-02199-0). Humanities.
Emerson & the Orphic Poet in America. R. A. Yoder. LC 76-24599. 1978. 17.50x (ISBN 0-520-03317-5). U of Cal Pr.
Emerson & Thoreau: Transcendentalists in Conflict. Joel Porte. LC 80-2512. 1981. Repr. of 1966 ed. 29.50 (ISBN 0-404-19060-X). AMS Pr.
Emerson Bibliographies. Ed. by J. R. Bryer & R. A. Rees. LC 80-2526. (AMS Anthology Ser.). 1981. 34.50 (ISBN 0-404-19255-6). AMS Pr.
Emerson Centenary. LC 80-2531. (AMS Anthology Ser.). 1981. 49.50 (ISBN 0-404-19256-4). AMS Pr.
Emerson, Haber & Dorsen's Political & Civil Rights in the United States, Vol. I. 4th ed. Norman Dorsen et al. 1976. lawyers ed. 48.00 (ISBN 0-316-23624-1); students ed 28.00 (ISBN 0-316-19046-2); pap. 8.95 1980 suppl (ISBN 0-316-19105-1); Little.
Emerson, His Muse & Message. Ramakrishna. 312p. 1980. lib. bdg. 35.00 (ISBN 0-8482-5869-X). Norwood Edns.
Emerson in Concord. Edward W. Emerson. LC 79-78149. (Library of Lives & Letters). (Illus.). 1970. Repr. of 1889 ed. 18.00 (ISBN 0-8103-3601-4). Gale.
Emerson on Education: Selections. Ed. by Howard M. Jones. LC 66-11655. (Orig.). text ed. 9.50 (ISBN 0-8077-1587-5); pap. text ed. 4.00x (ISBN 0-8077-1584-0). Tchrs Coll.
Emerson on Race & History: An Examination of English Traits. Philip L. Nicoloff. LC 80-2540. 1981. Repr. of 1961 ed. 33.50 (ISBN 0-404-19266-1). AMS Pr.
Emerson on the Soul. Jonathan Bishop. LC 80-2527. 1981. Repr. of 1964 ed. 29.50 (ISBN 0-404-19251-3). AMS Pr.
Emerson the Essayist: An Outline of His Philosophical Development Through 1836, 2 vols. Kenneth W. Cameron. LC 80-2529. 1981. Repr. of 1945 ed. Set. 92.00 (ISBN 0-404-19280-7). Vol. 1 (ISBN 0-404-19281-5). Vol. 2 (ISBN 0-404-19282-3). AMS Pr.
Emerson: The Nineteenth Century. LC 80-2541. (AMS Anthology Ser.). 1981. 57.50 (ISBN 0-404-19257-2). AMS Pr.
Emerson: The Twentieth Century. LC 80-2547. 1981. 57.50 (ISBN 0-404-19273-4). AMS Pr.
Emerson, the Wisest American. Phillips Russell. LC 80-2544. 1981. Repr. of 1929 ed. 37.00 (ISBN 0-404-19269-6). AMS Pr.
Emerson's Angle of Vision: Man & Nature in American Experience. Sherman Paul. LC 80-2542. 1981. Repr. of 1952 ed. 33.50 (ISBN 0-404-19267-X). AMS Pr.
Emerson's Essays: First & Second Series Complete. Ralph W. Emerson. (Apollo Eds.). (YA) (gr. 9-12). pap. 4.95 (ISBN 0-8152-0001-3, A1, TYC-T). T Y Crowell.
Emerson's Library. Walter R. Harding. LC 80-2535. 1981. Repr. of 1967 ed. 37.50 (ISBN 0-404-19261-0). AMS Pr.
Emerson's "Nature" Origin, Growth, Meaning. 2nd, enl. ed. Ed. by Merton M. Sealts, Jr. & Alfred R. Ferguson. LC 78-13945. (Illus.). 236p. 1979. 12.95x o.p. (ISBN 0-8093-0891-6); pap. 6.95 (ISBN 0-8093-0900-9). S Ill U Pr.
Emerson's Plutarch. Edmund G. Berry. LC 80-2525. 1981. Repr. of 1961 ed. 37.00 (ISBN 0-404-19250-5). AMS Pr.
Emerson's Use of the Bible. Harriet R. Zink. 75p. 1980. Repr. of 1935 ed. lib. bdg. 15.00 (ISBN 0-8495-6206-6). Arden Lib.
Emigrant Indians of Kansas: A Critical Bibliography. William E. Unrau. LC 79-2169. (Newberry Library Center for the History of the American Indian Bibliographical Ser.). 96p. (Orig.). 1980. pap. 3.95x (ISBN 0-253-36816-2). Ind U Pr.
Emigrants. Johan Bojer. Tr. by A. G. Jayne from Norwegian. LC 78-9813. 1978. pap. 4.95 (ISBN 0-8032-6051-2, BB 673, Bison). U of Nebr Pr.
Emigrants. Vilhelm Moberg. (Emigrants Saga: No. 1). 1971. pap. 2.75 (ISBN 0-445-08561-4). Popular Lib.
Emigrants' Guide to California. Joseph E. Ware. LC 79-87627. (American Scene Ser). (Illus.). 64p. 1972. Repr. of 1932 ed. lib. bdg. 12.50 (ISBN 0-306-71806-5). Da Capo.
Emigrants of Ahadarra: A Tale of Irish Life. William Carleton. Ed. by Robert L. Wolff. (Ireland Nineteenth Century Fiction Ser. Two: Vol. 42). 320p. 1979. lib. bdg. 32.00 (ISBN 0-8240-3491-0). Garland Pub.
Emigration, 28 vols. (British Parliamentary Papers Ser.). 1971. Set. 2196.00x (ISBN 0-7165-1494-X, Pub. by Irish Academic Pr Ireland). Biblio Dist.
Emigration & the Chinese Lineage: The 'Mans' in Hong Kong & London. James L. Watson. 1975. 17.50x (ISBN 0-520-02647-0). U of Cal Pr.
Emigration from Europe 1815-1914: Select Documents. Ed. by Charlotte Erickson. (Documents in Economic History). 1976. text ed. 17.00x (ISBN 0-7136-1616-4). Humanities.
Emil & the Piggy Beast. Astrid Lindgren. Tr. by Michael Heron. LC 72-91228. 128p. (gr. 2-6). 1973. 5.95 o.p. (ISBN 0-695-80356-5, T0356). Follett.
Emil Brunner. P. Jewett. LC 61-10788. pap. 0.95 o.p. (ISBN 0-87784-425-9). Inter-Varsity.
Emil in the Soup Tureen. Astrid Lindgren. LC 79-93795. (Illus.). (gr. 2-6). 1970. 5.95 o.p. (ISBN 0-695-82210-1). Follett.
Emil und die Detektive. Erich Kastner. (Easy Readers, B). 1979. pap. 3.75 (ISBN 0-88436-297-3). EMC.
Emile Durkheim: Contributions to L'Annee Sociologique. Ed. by Yash Nandan. LC 79-54670. 1980. 27.50 (ISBN 0-02-907980-2). Free Pr.
Emile, Julie & Other Writings. abr. ed. Jean-Jacques Rousseau. Tr. & intro. by R. L. Archer. LC 52-18638. 1964. pap. 3.50 (ISBN 0-8120-0062-5). Barron.
Emile Lessore, 1805-1876: His Life & Work. Richard L. Smith. Bd. with Sydney Cove Medallion. (Monographs in Wedgwood Studies: Nos. 3 & 4). 1979. 9.00 (ISBN 0-912014-52-0). Buten Mus.
Emile of Jean Jacques Rousseau. William Boyd. (No. 11). 1962. text ed. 8.50 (ISBN 0-8077-1110-1); pap. text ed. 3.95x (ISBN 0-8077-1107-1). Tchrs Coll.
Emile: Or, Education. Jean-Jacques Rousseau. 1955. 10.50x (ISBN 0-460-00518-9, Evman); pap. 3.95 (ISBN 0-460-01518-4). Dutton.
Emile Zola. Bede. (Columbia Essays on Modern Writers Ser.: No. 69). 1974. pap. 2.00 (ISBN 0-231-02977-2). Columbia U Pr.
Emile Zola. Elliott M. Grant. (World Authors Ser.: France: No. 10). 1966. lib. bdg. 9.95 (ISBN 0-8057-2996-8). Twayne.
Emile Zola. Bettina L. Knapp. LC 79-48079. (Modern Literature Ser.). 160p. 1980. 10.95 (ISBN 0-8044-2482-9). Ungar.
Emilia Galotti. Gotthold Lessing. Ed. by E. L. Stahl. (Blackwell's German Text Ser.). 1973. pap. 9.95x (ISBN 0-631-01390-3, Pub. by Basil Blackwell). Biblio Dist.
Emilio Rabasa: Life & Works. Lorum H. Stratton. (Graduate Studies: No. 8). (Orig.). 1974. pap. 5.00 (ISBN 0-89672-015-2). Tex Tech Pr.
Emil's Pranks. Astrid Lindgren. (gr. 1-3). PLB 5.97 o.p. (ISBN 0-695-40158-0). Follett.
Emily Dickinson. Paul J. Ferlazzo. (U.S. Authors Ser.: No. 280). 1976. lib. bdg. 12.50 (ISBN 0-8057-7180-8). Twayne.
Emily Dickinson. Ed. by Paul J. Ferlazzo. (Twayne's U. S. Authors Ser.). 168p. 1976. pap. text ed. 4.95 (ISBN 0-672-61511-8). Bobbs.
Emily Dickinson: Her Letter to the World. Polly Longsworth. LC 65-14902. (gr. 7 up). 1965. 8.95 (ISBN 0-690-25945-X, TYC-J). T Y Crowell.

Emily Post Book of Etiquette for Young People. Ed. by Elizabeth L. Post. LC 67-25416. (Funk & W Bk.). (gr. 7 up). 1967. 9.95 o.s.i. (ISBN 0-308-50002-4, TYC-T). T Y Crowell.

Emily Post Institute Book of Home Entertaining. Emily Post. 1981. 12.95 (ISBN 0-690-01970-X). Lippincott & Crowell.

Emily Post's Wedding Etiquette: Wonderful World of Weddings. Ed. by Elizabeth L. Post. (Funk & W Bk.). (Illus.). 1970. 14.95 (ISBN 0-308-50005-9, TYC-T). T Y Crowell.

Emily the Traveling Guinea Pig. Emma Smith. (gr. 1-5). 1960. 6.95 (ISBN 0-8392-3007-9). Astor-Honor.

Emily Upham's Revenge. Avi. LC 77-13739. (gr. 5-8). 1978. 6.95 (ISBN 0-394-83506-9); PLB 6.99 (ISBN 0-394-93506-3). Pantheon.

Emily's Bunch. Laura J. Numeroff & Alice N. Richter. LC 78-2637. (Illus.). (gr. k-3). 1978. 8.95 (ISBN 0-02-768430-X, 76843). Macmillan.

Emily's Runaway Imagination. Beverly Cleary. (Illus.). (gr. 3-7). 1961. 8.25 (ISBN 0-688-21267-0); PLB 7.92 (ISBN 0-688-31267-5). Morrow.

Eminent Victorians. Lytton Strachey. 1969. pap. 3.50 (ISBN 0-15-628697-1, HPL40, HPL). HarBraceJ.

Emirate of Aleppo. Suhail Zakkar. (Arab Background Ser.). 1971. 20.00x (ISBN 0-685-77108-3). Intl Bk Ctr.

Emission, Absorption & Transfer of Radiation in Heated Atmospheres. B. H. Armstrong & R. W. Nicholls. 319p. 1972. text ed. 50.00 (ISBN 0-08-016774-8). Pergamon.

Emission Control Technology for Industrial Boilers. Ed. by A. E. Martin. LC 80-26046. (Pollution Tech. Rev. 74 Ser.: Energy Tech. Rev. 62). (Illus.). 405p. 1981. 48.00 (ISBN 0-8155-0833-6). Noyes.

Emission Electronics. L. N. Dobretsov & M. V. Gomoyunova. 44.95 (ISBN 0-470-21680-8). Halsted Pr.

Emission Spectroscopy. Ed. by Ramon M. Barnes. LC 75-30672. 1976. 49.00 (ISBN 0-12-786137-8). Acad Pr.

Emma. Jane Austen. 1964. pap. 1.75 (ISBN 0-451-51357-6, CE1357, Sig Classics). NAL.

Emma. Jane Austen. Ed. by Ronald Blythe. (English Library Ser). 1966. pap. 2.50 (ISBN 0-14-043010-5). Penguin.

Emma. new ed. Jane Austen. Ed. by Stephen Parrish. (Norton Critical Editions). 430p. 1972. pap. 4.95x (ISBN 0-393-09667-X). Norton.

Emma. Jane Austen. lib. bdg. 15.95x (ISBN 0-89966-242-0). Buccaneer Bks.

Emma. Jane Austen. pap. 1.75. Bantam.

Emma. Wendy Kesselman. LC 77-15161. (Illus.). 32p. (gr. k-3). 1980. 7.95a (ISBN 0-385-13461-4); PLB (ISBN 0-385-13462-2). Doubleday.

Emma Lazarus: Poet of Liberty. Irving Gerber. 1979. of 10 6.75 set (ISBN 0-87594-183-4). Book Lab.

Emmanuel Mounier & the New Catholic Left, 1930 to 1950. John Hellman. 276p. 1981. 35.00x (ISBN 0-8020-2399-1). U of Toronto Pr.

Emmanuelle One. Emmanuelle Arsan. Tr. by Lowell Bair. LC 78-139255. 1980. pap. 2.95 (ISBN 0-394-17657-X, B439, BC). Grove.

Emmanuelle Two. Emmanuelle Arsan. Tr. by Anselm Hollo from Fr. LC 74-24995. 1974. 3.25 (ISBN 0-394-17891-2, B453, BC). Grove.

Emmeline. Judith Rossner. 1980. 12.95 (ISBN 0-671-22938-9). S&S.

Emmeline: The Orphan of the Castle. Charlotte Smith. Ed. by Anne H. Ehrenpreis. (Oxford English Novels Ser). 1971. 16.95x (ISBN 0-19-255322-4). Oxford U Pr.

Emmet Otter's Jug-Band Christmas. Russell Hoban. LC 76-117560. (Illus.). 48p. (ps-3). 1978. Repr. of 1971 ed. 4.95 (ISBN 0-590-17707-9, Four Winds); lib. bdg. 4.95 (ISBN 0-590-07707-4). Schol Bk Serv.

Emmett's Clinical Urography, 3 vols. 4rd ed. David M. Witten et al. LC 76-19614. (Illus.). 1977. Set. 110.00 (ISBN 0-685-04797-0); Vol. 1. (ISBN 0-7216-9472-1); Vol. 2. (ISBN 0-7216-9473-X); Vol. 3. (ISBN 0-7216-9474-8). Saunders.

Emmie. Jeanette Seymour. 1980. pap. write for info. (ISBN 0-671-83129-1). PB.

Emmotionally Disturbed Child in the Classroom. 2nd ed. Hewett & Taylor. 416p. 1980. text ed. 17.95 (ISBN 0-205-06725-5, 2467259). Allyn.

Emmy, Beware! Harriette S. Abels. (Prime Time Adventures Ser.). (Illus.). 64p. (gr. 4 up). 1981. PLB 7.95 (ISBN 0-516-02105-2). Childrens.

Emmy Noether: 1882-1935. A. Dick. (Supplement Ser.: No. 13). 72p. (Ger.). 1970. pap. 12.00 (ISBN 3-7643-0519-3). Birkhauser.

Emotion. W Lyons. LC 79-2521. (Cambridge Studies in Philosophy). 240p. 1980. 35.50 (ISBN 0-521-22904-9). Cambridge U Pr.

Emotion & Object. J. R. Wilson. LC 76-179160. 240p. 1972. 23.95 (ISBN 0-521-08450-4). Cambridge U Pr.

Emotion & the Educative Process: A Report of the Committee on the Relation of Emotion to the Educative Process. Daniel A. Prescott. 323p. 1980. Repr. of 1938 ed. lib. bdg. 25.00 (ISBN 0-89760-707-4). Telegraph Bks.

Emotion, Thought,& Therapy: A Study of Hume & Spinoza & the Relationship of Philosophical Theories of the Emotions to Psychological Theories of Therapy. Jerome Neu. LC 76-20010. 1977. 18.50x (ISBN 0-520-03288-8). U. of Cal Pr.

Emotional Adjustment to Illness. K. Noonan. LC 73-13485. 168p. 1975. pap. 6.60 (ISBN 0-8273-0347-5); instructor's guide 1.60 (ISBN 0-8273-0348-3). Delmar.

Emotional Care of Hospitalized Children: An Environmental Approach. 2nd ed. Madeline Petrillo & Sirgay Sanger. LC 79-27462. 450p. 1980. pap. text ed. 10.95 (ISBN 0-397-54343-3). Lippincott.

Emotional Common Sense: How to Avoid Self-Destructiveness. Rolland S. Parker. LC 72-9758. 238p. 1973. 9.95 o.p. (ISBN 0-06-013278-7, HarpT). Har-Row.

Emotional Disorders: Diagnosis & Pharmacological Treatment. 3rd ed. A. DiMascio & H. Goldberg. 1980. 15.95 (ISBN 0-87489-255-4). Med Economics.

Emotional Disorders in Children & Adolescents: Medical & Psychological Approaches to Treatment. new ed. Ed. by Pirooz Sholevar et al. LC 79-17849. 1980. text ed. 60.00 (ISBN 0-89335-084-2). Spectrum Pub.

Emotional Flooding, Vol. I: An Official Publication of the National Institute for the Psychotherapies. Ed. by Paul T. Olsen. LC 74-12620. (New Directions in Psychotherapy Ser.). 1976. 22.95 (ISBN 0-87705-239-5). Human Sci Pr.

Emotional Health: In the World of Work. Harry Levinson. LC 63-20323. 1964. 12.95x o.p. (ISBN 0-06-033540-8, HarpT). Har-Row.

Emotional Problems & the Gospel. Vernon Grounds. 160p. 1976. pap. text ed. 2.95 o.p. (ISBN 0-310-25311-X). Zondervan.

Emotional Rehabilitation of the Geriatric Patient. Kurt Wolff. 248p. 1970. 16.75 (ISBN 0-398-02111-2). C C Thomas.

Emotional Well-Being Through Rational Behavior Training. 3rd rev. ed. David S. Goodman. (Illus.). 256p. 1978. pap. 12.50 (ISBN 0-398-03750-7). C C Thomas.

Emotionally Disturbed & Deviant Children: New Views & Approaches. William Rhodes & James L. Paul. LC 77-17630. 1978. ref. ed. 16.95 (ISBN 0-13-274662-X). P-H.

Emotionally Disturbed Child. J. Louis Despert. LC 79-97700. 1970. pap. 2.95 (ISBN 0-385-07035-7, A720, Anch). Doubleday.

Emotionally Disturbed Child: A Book of Readings. Larry A. Faas. (Illus.). 400p. 1975. 22.75 (ISBN 0-398-00539-7). C C Thomas.

Emotionally Disturbed Child in the Classroom. 2nd ed. Frank M. Hewett. text ed. 16.95x o.s.i. (ISBN 0-205-06725-5). Allyn.

Emotionally Troubled Adolescent & the Family Physician. Ed. by Michael G. Kalogerakis. 144p. 1973. 11.50 (ISBN 0-398-02844-3). C C Thomas.

Emotionally Troubled Child. Robert L. Mason, Jr. et al. 196p. 1976. 18.50 (ISBN 0-398-03557-1). C C Thomas.

Emotions & Adult Learning. William S. More. 1974. 19.95 (ISBN 0-347-01050-4, 93633-2, Pub. by Saxon Hse England). Lexington Bks.

Emotions & the Will. Alexander Bain. (Contributions to the History of Psychology Ser.: No. 5, Pt. a: Orientations). 1978. Repr. of 1859 ed. 30.00 (ISBN 0-89093-154-2). U Pubns Amer.

Emotions Can Heal, Emotions Can Harm. rev. 2nd ed. John Barton & Margaret Barton. Orig. Title: Loving Affirmations. (Illus.). 157p. 1978. pap. 5.00 (ISBN 0-937216-02-X). J&M Barton.

Emotions: Can You Trust Them? James Dobson. LC 79-91703. 144p. 1980. text ed. 6.95 (ISBN 0-8307-0730-1, 5109108). Regal.

Emotions: Their Parameters & Measurement. Ed. by Lennart Levi. LC 74-80539. 1975. 46.50 (ISBN 0-89004-019-2). Raven.

EMP Radiation & Protective Techniques. L. W. Ricketts et al. LC 76-19091. 1976. 37.95 o.p. (ISBN 0-471-01403-6, Pub. by Wiley-Interscience). Wiley.

Empedocles - the Extant Fragments. Ed. by M. R. Wright. LC 80-17923. 416p. 1981. text ed. 45.00 (ISBN 0-300-02475-4). Yale U Pr. Postponed.

Emperor & the Nightingale. Hans C. Andersen. LC 78-18065. (Illus.). (gr. 1-4). 1979. PLB 5.21 (ISBN 0-89375-134-0); pap. 1.50 (ISBN 0-89375-112-X). Troll Assocs.

Emperor Frederick Second of Hohenstaufen, Immutator Mundi. Thomas C. Van Cleve. (Illus.). 618p. 1972. 45.00x (ISBN 0-19-822513-X). Oxford U Pr.

Emperor Horikawa Diary: Sanuki no Suke Nikki. Fujiwara no Nagako. Tr. by Jennifer Brewster from Japanese. LC 77-89194. 1978. text ed. 14.00x (ISBN 0-8248-0605-0). U Pr of Hawaii.

Emperor Jones. 2nd ed. Eugene O'Neill. Ed. by Max J. Herzberg. (Orig.). 1960. pap. 6.50x (ISBN 0-13-274902-5). P-H.

Emperor Julian. Robert Browning. LC 75-13159. 1976. 15.00 o.p. (ISBN 0-520-03034-6); pap. 4.95 o.p. (ISBN 0-520-03731-6). U of Cal Pr.

Emperor Julian. Constance Head. LC 75-15724. (World Leaders Ser.: No. 53). 1976. lib. bdg. 12.50 (ISBN 0-8057-7650-8). Twayne.

Emperor of the Earth: Modes of Eccentric Vision. Czeslaw Milosz. LC 76-20005. 1977. 14.95 (ISBN 0-520-03302-7). U of Cal Pr.

Emperor of the Last Days. Ron Goulart. (Orig.). 1977. pap. 1.50 o.p. (ISBN 0-445-03201-4). Popular Lib.

Emperor Penguins. Kazue Mizumura. LC 69-10486. (Let's Read & Find Out Science Bk). (Illus.). (gr. k-3). 1969. PLB 7.89 (ISBN 0-690-26088-1, TYC-J). T Y Crowell.

Emperors & Biography: Studies in the Historia Augusta. Ronald Syme. 1971. 24.95x o.p. (ISBN 0-19-814357-5). Oxford U Pr.

Emperor's Candlesticks. Emmuska Orczy. 1976. lib. bdg. 13.75x (ISBN 0-89968-075-5). Lightyear.

Emperor's New Clothes. Hans C. Andersen. Ed. by Jack Delano & Irene Delano. (Illus.). 1971. 4.95 o.p. (ISBN 0-394-82105-X, BYR); PLB 5.99 (ISBN 0-394-92105-4). Random.

Emperor's New Clothes. (Children's Library of Picture Bks.). (Illus.). 10p. (ps). 1979. 1.95 (ISBN 0-89346-170-9, TA48, Pub. by Froebel-Kan Japan). Heian Intl.

Emperor's Virgin. Sylvia Fraser. LC 80-1064. 408p. 1980. 12.95 (ISBN 0-385-17237-0). Doubleday.

Emperor's Virgin. Sylvia Fraser. 320p. 1981. pap. 2.95 (ISBN 0-686-68903-8). Bantam.

Emphasis: Natural History. Thomas Scandone. 1979. coil binging 12.95 (ISBN 0-88252-098-9). Paladin Hse.

Empire. Samuel R. Delaney & Howard Chayken. LC 78-19575. 1978. 19.95 o.p. (ISBN 0-399-12245-1). Berkley Pub.

Empire. Samuel R. Delaney & Howard Chayken. 1978. pap. 9.95 o.p. (ISBN 0-425-03900-5, Medallion). Berkley Pub.

Empire & Commerce in Africa. Leonard Woolf. LC 67-24602. 1968. 20.00 (ISBN 0-86527-058-9). Fertig.

Empire & Liberty: American Resistance to British Authority, 1755-1763. Alan Rogers. 1975. 17.50x (ISBN 0-520-02275-0). U of Cal Pr.

Empire & the Papacy, Nine Eighteen to Twelve Seventy-Three. 8th ed. Thomas F. Tout. LC 80-18865. (Periods of European History: Period II). (Illus.). vii, 526p. 1980. Repr. of 1965 ed. lib. bdg. 35.00x (ISBN 0-313-22372-6, TOEP). Greenwood.

Empire Blues. Taylor Branch. 1981. 14.95 (ISBN 0-671-23096-4). S&S.

Empire Builder Extraordinary Sir George Goldie: His Philosophy of Government & Empire. D. J. Muffett. (Illus.). 1978. text ed. 22.50x (ISBN 0-904980-18-9). Humanities.

Empire Builders. James Hicks. (Emergence of Man Ser.). (Illus.). 1974. 9.95 (ISBN 0-8094-1320-5); lib. bdg. avail. (ISBN 0-685-48126-3). Time-Life.

Empire Builders. Jim Hicks. LC 74-75832. (Emergence of Man Ser). 160p. (gr. 6 up). 1974. lib. bdg. 9.63 o.p. (ISBN 0-8094-1321-3, Pub. by Time-Life). Silver.

Empire for Liberty: The Genesis & Growth of the United States of America, 1865-1960, 2 vols. Dumas Malone et al. LC 60-5002. (Illus., Vol. 1 to 1865, vol. 2 since 1865). 1960. Boxed Set. 82.00x (ISBN 0-89197-532-2). Irvington.

Empire Furniture 1800 to 1825. Serge Grandjean. 1966. 26.00 o.p. (ISBN 0-571-06666-6, Pub. by Faber & Faber). Merrimack Bk Serv.

Empire of the Amorites. Albert T. Clay. (Yale Oriental Researches Ser.: No. VI). 1919. 29.50x (ISBN 0-685-69801-7). Elliots Bks.

Empire of the Ants & Other Stories. Wells. (gr. 7-12). pap. 1.25 (ISBN 0-590-11845-5, Schol Pap). Schol Bk Serv.

Empire of the Steppes. Rene Grousset. LC 77-108759. 1970. 37.50 (ISBN 0-8135-0627-1). Rutgers U Pr.

Empire State Building Book. Steven Heller et al. (Illus.). 96p. 1980. 14.95 (ISBN 0-312-24456-8); pap. 7.95 (ISBN 0-686-65894-9). St Martin.

Empire Strikes Back. Donald F. Glut. 1980. pap. 2.25 (ISBN 0-345-28392-9, Del Rey). Ballantine.

Empire to Welfare State: English History Nineteen Six to Nineteen Seventy-Six. 2nd ed. T. O. Lloyd. (Short Oxford History of the Modern World Ser.). (Illus.). 1979. 37.50x (ISBN 0-19-913132-5); pap. 12.95x (ISBN 0-19-913243-7). Oxford U Pr.

Empire Unpossess'd: An Essay on Gibbon's "Decline & Fall of the Roman Empire". Lionel Gossman. LC 80-24008. (Illus.). 176p. Date not set. price not set (ISBN 0-521-23453-0). Cambridge U Pr.

Empire Without End: Three Historians of Rome. Lidia S. Mazzolani. Tr. by Joan McConnell & Mario Pel. LC 76-20672. (Helen & Kurt Wolff Bk). 1976. Repr. of 1972 ed. 10.95 (ISBN 0-15-128780-5). HarBraceJ.

Empirical Basis for Change in Education. Wesley Becker. LC 73-156886. (Illus.). 1971. pap. text ed. 10.95 (ISBN 0-574-18426-0, 13-1426); instr's guide avail. (ISBN 0-574-18427-9, 13-1427). SRA.

Empirical Studies of Indiana Politics. Ed. by James B. Kessler. LC 79-85089. (Illus.). 320p. 1970. 13.95x (ISBN 0-253-31950-1). Ind U Pr.

Empirical Study of Education in Twenty-One Countries: A Technical Report. Gilbert F. Peaker. LC 75-30533. (International Studies in Evaluation Ser: No. 8). 232p. 1976. 12.95 o.p. (ISBN 0-470-67456-3). Halsted Pr.

Empiricism & Ethics. David H. Monro. 1967. pap. 32.95 (ISBN 0-521-05752-3). Cambridge U Pr.

Employee Absenteeism in Both the Public & Private Sectors: An Annotated Bibliography to 1979. John J. Miletich. (Public Administration Ser.: Bibliographies: P-639). 53p. 1981. pap. 8.25. Vance Biblios.

Employee Assistance Program. James T. Wrich. 1974. pap. 2.95 (ISBN 0-89486-097-6). Hazelden.

Employee Assistance Program. rev. ed. James T. Wrich. 1980. 7.95. Hazelden.

Employee Benefit Plans & the Economy: Learning Guide, CEBS Course IX. 2nd ed. 1980. spiral 13.00 (ISBN 0-89154-132-2). Intl Found Employ.

Employee Benefits: A Guide for Hospitals. Alex Steinforth. LC 80-12159. 124p. 1980. 22.50 (ISBN 0-89443-290-7). Aspen Systems.

Employee Benefits & Plans & the Economy: Answers to the Questions on the Subject Matter for the Learning Guide, CEBS Course IX. 2nd ed. 62p. spiral bdg. 13.00 (ISBN 0-89154-132-2); pap. text ed. 10.00 (ISBN 0-89154-133-0). Intl Found Employ.

Employee Benefits Institutes & Seminars for Company Sponsored Plans, 1978: Proceedings. Ed. by Jack Pearson. (Orig.). 1979. pap. 7.50 (ISBN 0-89154-095-4). Intl Found Employ.

Employee Benefits Management. Ed by H. Wayne Snider. 240p. Date not set. price not set (ISBN 0-937802-00-X). Risk & Ins.

Employee Contributions & Delinqukidncies Under ERISA Institute, las Vegas, Nov. 12-15, 1978. Ed. by Mary Brennen. (Orig.). 1979. pap. 7.50 (ISBN 0-89154-097-0). Intl Found Employ.

Employee Counseling in Industry & Government: A Guide to Information Sources. Ed. by Theodore P. Peck. LC 79-16028. (Management Information Guide Ser.: No. 37). 1979. 30.00 (ISBN 0-8103-0837-1). Gale.

Employee Drug Abuse: A Manager's Guide for Action. Carl D. Chambers & Richard D. Heckman. LC 73-183372. 1972. 15.95 (ISBN 0-8436-0718-1). CBI Pub.

Employee Health Benefits: HMOs & Mandatory Dual Choice. Jeffrey A. Prussin. LC 76-24131. 1976. 49.50 (ISBN 0-912862-27-0). Aspen Systems.

Employee Relations Initiatives in Canadian Mining. 85p. (Orig.). 1979. pap. text ed. 5.00x (ISBN 0-88757-014-3, Pub. by Ctr Resource Stud Canada). Renouf.

Employee Remuneration & Profit Sharing. Richard Greenhill. 224p. 1980. 45.00x (ISBN 0-85941-123-0, Pub. by Woodhead-Faulkner England). State Mutual Bk.

Employee Reports: How to Communicate Financial Information to Employees. Anthony Hilton. (Illus.). 200p. 1980. 29.95 (ISBN 0-85941-057-9). Herman Pub.

Employees in Nursing Homes: National Nursing Home Survey, 1977. Al Sirrocco. Ed. by Klaudia Cox. (Ser. Fourteen: No. 25). 50p. 1981. pap. text ed. 1.50 (ISBN 0-8406-0213-8). Natl Ctr Health Stats.

Employer-Employee Committees & Worker Participaton. (Key Issues Ser.: No. 20). 1976. pap. 3.00 (ISBN 0-87546-221-9). NY Sch Indus Rel.

Employer Pension Plan Membership & Household Wealth. William R. Waters. LC 79-92473. (S. S. Huebner Foundation Monograph: No. 10). (Illus.). 1981. pap. price not set (ISBN 0-918930-10-3). Huebner Foun Insur.

Employer's Guide to Interviewing, Strategies & Tactics for Picking a Winner. Robert L. Genua. (Illus.). 1979. 12.95 (ISBN 0-13-274696-4, Spec); pap. 5.95 (ISBN 0-13-274688-3, Spec). P-H.

Employer's Guide to the Law on Health, Safety & Welfare at Work. 2nd ed. Ewan Mitchell. 471p. 1977. text ed. 36.75x (ISBN 0-220-66341-6, Pub. by Busn Bks England). Renouf.

Employing Civilians for Police Work. Alfred I. Schwartz et al. 1975. pap. 3.50 o.p. (ISBN 0-87766-139-1, 11700). Urban Inst.

Employing the Handicapped: A Practical Compliance Manual. A. B. Zimmer. 530p. 1981. 19.95 (ISBN 0-8144-5525-5). Am Mgmt.

Employment After CETA: Outcomes of Recent Research. 1980. 4.00. Comm Coun Great NY.

Employment & Basic Needs in Portugal. International Labour Office, Geneva. (Illus.). 228p. 1979. 22.80 (ISBN 9-22-102202-1); pap. 17.10 (ISBN 9-22-102072-X). Intl Labour Office.

Employment & Economic Growth in Urban China, 1949-57. Christopher Howe. LC 76-152641. (Contemporary China Institute Publications). (Illus.). 1971. 34.95 (ISBN 0-521-08172-6). Cambridge U Pr.

Employment & Technology Choice in Asian Agriculture. William H. Bartsch. LC 76-58540. (Special Studies). 1977. text ed. 20.95 (ISBN 0-275-24280-3). Praeger.

Employment Conditions in Europe. (Illus.). 206p. 1972. 18.00 o.p. (ISBN 0-7161-0166-1, Gower). Unipub.

Employment Conditions in Europe. Margaret Stewart. (Illus.). 249p. 1976. 25.00 o.p. (ISBN 0-7161-0307-9, Gower). Unipub.

Employment Discrimination Litigation 1979. (Litigation & Administrative Practice Course Handbook Ser.: Vol. 136). 1979. pap. 20.00 (ISBN 0-685-90322-2, H4-4801). PLI.

Employment Discrimination: The Impact of Legal & Administrative Remedies. Ray Marshall et al. LC 78-17333. 1978. 22.95 (ISBN 0-03-045356-9). Praeger.

Employment Dismissal Without Fear. Dennis D. Hunt. LC 78-6692. 1979. 14.95 (ISBN 0-7153-7700-0). David & Charles.

Employment Effects of Multinational Enterprises: The Case of the United States. D. Kujawa. Ed. by International Labour Office. (Research on Employment Effects of Multinational Enterprises. Working Papers Ser.: No. 12). 53p. (Orig.). 1980. pap. 8.55. Intl Labour Office.

Employment Effects on the Clothing Industry of Changes in International Trade: Second Tripartite Technical Meeting for the Clothing Industry, Geneve, 1980, Report III. International Labour Office. ii, 49p. (Orig.). 1980. pap. 7.15 (ISBN 92-2-102433-4). Intl Labour Office.

Employment Grievances & Disputes Procedures in Great Britain. K. W. Wedderburn & P. L. Davies. LC 71-84788. 1969. 25.00x (ISBN 0-520-01408-1). U of Cal Pr.

Employment, Growth & Basic Needs: A One-World Problem. Ed. by ILO International Labour Office. LC 77-70278. 256p. 1977. pap. 3.95 (ISBN 0-686-28705-3). Overseas Dev Council.

Employment, Growth, & Basic Needs: A One-World Problem. International Labour Office. LC 77-70278. (Special Studies). 1977. text ed. 18.95 o.p. (ISBN 0-03-021601-X); pap. 3.95 o.p. (ISBN 0-03-021606-0). Praeger.

Employment in Developing Nations. Ed. by Edward O. Edwards. LC 74-16724. 1974. 22.50x (ISBN 0-231-03873-9); pap. 11.00x (ISBN 0-231-03874-7). Columbia U Pr.

Employment in Latin America. Regional Employment Programme for Latin America & the Caribbean. (Praeger Special Studies). 1978. 22.95 (ISBN 0-03-042131-4). Praeger.

Employment in South Asia: Problems, Prospects & Prescriptions. Ronald Ridker. (Occasional Papers: No. 1). 74p. 1971. 1.00 (ISBN 0-686-28697-9). Overseas Dev Council.

Employment, Income, & Welfare in the Rural South. Brian Rungeling et al. LC 77-10612. (Praeger Special Studies). 1977. 33.95 (ISBN 0-03-023041-1). Praeger.

Employment Interviewing. 5th ed. John M. Fraser. (Illus.). 224p. 1978. pap. 13.95 (ISBN 0-7121-0570-0, Pub. by Macdonald & Evans England). Intl Ideas.

Employment of Merchant Seamen. Jonathan S. Kitchen. 658p. 1980. 150.00x (ISBN 0-85664-527-3, Pub. by Croom Helm Ltd England). Biblio Dist.

Employment of Nurses: Nursing Labour Turnover in the NHS. G. Mercer. 185p. 1979. 37.00x (ISBN 0-7099-0015-5, Pub. by Croom Helm Ltd England). Biblio Dist.

Employment of Teachers. Donald Gerwin. LC 73-20854. 1974. 20.00x (ISBN 0-8211-0610-4); text ed. 18.00x (ISBN 0-685-42632-7). McCutchan.

Employment of the Middle-Aged: Papers from Industrial Gerontology Seminars. Ed. by Gloria M. Shatto. (Illus.). 232p. 1972. 15.75 (ISBN 0-398-02408-1). C C Thomas.

Employment: Outlook & Insights. A Collection of Essays on Industrialised Market-Economy Countries. International Labour Office, Geneva. Ed. by David H. Freedman. (Illus.). 148p. (Orig.). 1979. 17.10 (ISBN 9-22-102155-6); pap. 11.40 (ISBN 0-686-65773-X). Intl Labour Office.

Employment Policies in Developing Countries. J. Mouly & E. Costa. 1975. text ed. 35.00x (ISBN 0-04-330245-9). Allen Unwin.

Employment Problem in Less Developed Countries. Organization for Economic Cooperation & Development. (Employment Ser.: No. 1). 156p. 1971. 7.50 o.p. (ISBN 0-686-14735-9). OECD.

Employment Security in the Public Sector: A Symposium. Ed. by Joseph Adler & Robert E. Doherty. 1974. pap. 2.00 (ISBN 0-87546-204-9). NY Sch Indus Rel.

Employment, Technology & Development. Amartya Sen. (Economic Development Ser.). 204p. 1975. text ed. 22.50x (ISBN 0-19-877052-9); pap. text ed. 3.50x (ISBN 0-19-877053-7). Oxford U Pr.

Employment Testing & Minority Groups. Doris B. Rosen. (Key Issues Ser.: No. 6). 1970. pap. 2.00 (ISBN 0-87546-239-1). NY Sch Indus Rel.

Emplumada. Lorna D. Cervantes. LC 80-54063. (Pitt Poetry Ser.). 1981. 9.95 (ISBN 0-8229-3436-1); pap. 4.50 (ISBN 0-8229-5327-7). U of Pittsburgh Pr.

Empowered to Care. Pastoral Care Office. 1980. pap. 8.25 (ISBN 0-8309-0291-0). Herald Hse.

Empowerment. Ed. by Chogyam Trungpa. LC 76-17439. 1978. pap. 3.95 o.p. (ISBN 0-87773-705-1, Prajna). Great Eastern.

Empresa y la Funcion De Personal. Antonio De La Luz. 7.50 (ISBN 0-8477-2620-7); pap. 6.25 (ISBN 0-8477-2609-6). U of PR Pr.

Empress. Sylvia Wallaca. 336p. 1981. pap. 2.95 (ISBN 0-553-14589-4). Bantam.

Empty Box Haiku. John Espey. 24p. (Orig.). 1980. s & l wrappers 30.00 (ISBN 0-936576-02-2). Symposium Pr.

Empty Distance Carries... Munda & Oraon Folk - Songs. Sitakant Mahapatra. 1976. lib. bdg. 14.00 (ISBN 0-89253-096-0); flexible bdg. 4.80 (ISBN 0-89253-146-0). Ind-US Inc.

Empty Fortress: Infantile Autism & the Birth of the Self. Bruno Bettelheim. LC 67-10886. 1967. 16.95 (ISBN 0-02-903130-3); pap. text ed. 8.95 (ISBN 0-02-903140-0). Free Pr.

Empty House. Michael Gilbert. (Penguin Crime Monthly Ser.). 1980. pap. 2.50 (ISBN 0-14-005142-2). Penguin.

Empty Place to Stay & Other Selected Poems. Roger Kopland. Tr. by Ria Leigh-Loohuizen from Dutch. 74p. 1980. pap. text ed. 4.00 (ISBN 0-918786-22-3). Lost Roads.

Empty Polling Booth. Arthur T. Hadley. 1978. 8.95 o.p. (ISBN 0-13-274928-9). P-H.

Empty Seat. Phyllis Green. LC 79-21813. (gr. 4 up). 1980. 7.50 o.p. (ISBN 0-525-66660-5). Elsevier-Nelson.

Empty Squirrel. Carol Carrick. LC 80-16475. (Read-Alone Bk.). (Illus.). 64p. (gr. 1-3). 1981. 5.95 (ISBN 0-688-80293-1); PLB 5.71 (ISBN 0-688-84293-3). Greenwillow.

Empty Words. John Cage. LC 78-27212. 1979. 17.50 (ISBN 0-8195-5032-9, Pub. by Wesleyan U Pr). Columbia U Pr.

Empty World. John Christopher. (gr. 7-9). 1978. PLB 10.95 (ISBN 0-525-29250-0). Dutton.

Emulation & Invention. Brooke Hindle. (Anson G. Phelps Lectureship Ser. on Early American History). (Illus.). 224p. 1981. text ed. 19.50x (ISBN 0-8147-3409-X). NYU Pr.

Emyr Humphreys. I. Williams. (Writers of Wales). 1980. pap. 9.00 (ISBN 0-7083-0750-7). Verry.

En Camino! A Cultural Approach to Beginning Spanish. 2nd ed. Eduardo Neale-Silva & Robert L. Nicholas. 1980. text ed. 15.95x (ISBN 0-673-15411-4); pap. text ed. 5.95x wkbk. (ISBN 0-673-15441-6). Scott F.

En Contacto: A First Course in Spanish. Pablo Valencia & Franca Merlonghi. 1980. pap. text ed. 16.75 (ISBN 0-395-27846-5); tchrs' ed. 18.70 (ISBN 0-395-27847-3); wkbk. 5.50 (ISBN 0-395-27848-1); recordings 154.36 (ISBN 0-395-27849-X). HM.

En Francais: Practical Conversational French. 2nd ed. Dana Carton & Anthony Caprio. 1980. text ed. write for info. (ISBN 0-442-21215-1); write for info. instr's. manual (ISBN 0-442-21218-6); write for info. tape (ISBN 0-442-21219-4); write for info. cassette (ISBN 0-442-21220-8). D Van Nostrand.

En la Casa De Mi Padre. Tr. by Corrie Ten Boom. (Spanish Bks.). (Span.). 1978. 1.90 (ISBN 0-8297-0547-3). Life Pubs Intl.

En las Huellas de los Heroes: 14 Lecciones, Tomo 4. Bernice C. Jordan. (Pasos De Fe Ser.). (Span.). pap. text ed. 2.25 (ISBN 0-86508-407-6); figuras 7.95 (ISBN 0-86508-408-4). BCM Inc.

En Onda. new ed. Ed. by Constantine C. Stathatos & Richard V. Teschner. 250p. 1975. pap. text ed. 6.95x (ISBN 0-393-09284-4). Norton.

En Route. Joris K. Huysmans. Tr. by C. Kegan Paul from Fr. LC 76-15215. xi, 313p. 1976. Repr. of 1918 ed. 17.50 (ISBN 0-86527-243-3). Fertig.

En Su Fuerza. Tr. by Gwen Wilkerson. (Spanish Bks.). (Span.). 1979. 1.50 (ISBN 0-8297-0910-X). Life Pubs Intl.

En Sus Pasos. Charles M. Sheldon. Tr. by Ruth Reuben from Eng. Orig. Title: In His Steps. 92p. (Span.). 1980. pap. 1.50 (ISBN 0-311-37011-X). Casa Bautista.

En Torno a los Origenes del Feudalismo, 3 vols. Claudio Sanchez-Albornoz y Menduina. LC 80-2004. 1981. Repr. of 1942 ed. Set. 110.00 (ISBN 0-404-18590-8). Vol. 1 (ISBN 0-404-18591-6). Vol. 2 (ISBN 0-404-18592-4). Vol. 3 (ISBN 0-404-18593-2). AMS Pr.

Enabling Acts: Selected Essays in Criticism. Louis Coxe. LC 76-4485. 1976. 11.00x (ISBN 0-8262-0200-4). U of Mo Pr.

Enactment: Greek Tragedy. Albert Cook. LC 78-153076. 175p. 1971. 13.95 (ISBN 0-8040-0539-7). Swallow.

Enameling, Step by Step. William Harper. (Step by Step Craft Ser). (Illus.). 80p. 1973. PLB 9.15 o.p. (ISBN 0-307-62006-9, Golden Pr); pap. 2.95 o.p. (ISBN 0-307-42010-8). Western Pub.

Enantiomers, Racemates & Resolutions. Sam Wilen & J. Jacques. Ed. by Andre Collet. 350p. 1981. 35.00 (ISBN 0-471-08058-6, Pub. by Wiley-Interscience). Wiley.

Enchained in Film. Vladimir Mayakovsky & Lily Brik. Tr. by Helen Segall. (Illus.). 1981. 15.00x (ISBN 0-931556-01-5); pap. 6.50 (ISBN 0-931556-03-1). Translation Pr.

Enchanted Doll, Repr. Of 1849 Ed. Mark Lemon. Bd. with Tinykin's Transformations. Repr. of 1869 ed. LC 75-32163. (Classics of Children's Literature, 1621-1932: Vol. 27). (Illus.). 1977. PLB 38.00 (ISBN 0-8240-2276-9). Garland Pub.

Enchanted Ground: Americans in Italy, 1760-1980. Erik Amfitheatrof. 256p. 1980. 14.95 (ISBN 0-316-03700-1). Little.

Enchanted Land. Jude Deveraux. 1980. pap. 2.50 (ISBN 0-686-69270-5, 76422). Avon.

Enchanted Pilgrimage. Clifford D. Simak. LC 74-16617. 224p. 1975. 6.95 o.p. (ISBN 0-399-11477-7, Dist. by Putnam). Berkley Pub.

Enchanted Places. Christopher Milne. (Illus.). (gr. 9 up). 1975. 8.25 o.p. (ISBN 0-525-29293-4). Dutton.

Enchanted Quill. Autumn Stanley. 1978. pap. 1.00 o.p. (ISBN 0-931832-10-1). No Dead Lines.

Enchanted Twilight. Kristin Michaels. Bd. with Song of the Heart. 1980. pap. 2.25 (ISBN 0-451-09536-7, 9536, Sig). NAL.

Enchanted Voyager: The Life of J. B. Rhine, an Authorized Biography. Denis Brian. 1981. 15.00 (ISBN 0-13-275107-0). P-H.

Enchanted Wanderer: The Life of Carl Maria Von Weber. Lucy Stebbins & Richard P. Stebbins. LC 80-2301. 1981. Repr. of 1940 ed. 39.50 (ISBN 0-404-18870-2). AMS Pr.

Enchanting Evil: No. 5. Barbara Cartland. 1978. pap. 1.50 o.s.i. (ISBN 0-515-04812-7). Jove Pubns.

Enchanting Experience: Naples - Marco Island. Frank F. Tenney, Jr. Ed. by Doug Woolfolk. (Illus.). 112p. 1981. 10.00 (ISBN 0-86518-016-4). Moran Pub Corp.

Enchanting Jenny. Zabrina Faire. (Orig.). 1979. pap. 1.75 (ISBN 0-446-94103-4). Warner Bks.

Enchantment of Chile. Allan Carpenter. LC 79-8561. (Enchantment of South America Ser). (Illus.). (gr. 5 up). 1969. PLB 10.00 o.p. (ISBN 0-516-04505-9). Childrens.

Enchantment of Costa Rica. Allan Carpenter. LC 71-157829. (Enchantment of Central America Ser). (Illus.). (gr. 5 up). 1971. PLB 10.00 o.p. (ISBN 0-516-04515-6). Childrens.

Enchantment of Venezuela. Allan Carpenter & Enno R. Haan. LC 70-85964. (Enchantment of South America Ser). (Illus.). (gr. 5 up). 1970. PLB 10.00 o.p. (ISBN 0-516-04511-3). Childrens.

Enchantress from the Stars. Sylvia L. Engdahl. LC 74-98609. 1970. sparton bdg. 8.69 (ISBN 0-689-20508-2). Atheneum.

Enchiridion. Epictetus. Tr. by T. W. Higginson. 1955. pap. 2.50 (ISBN 0-672-60170-2, LLA8). Bobbs.

Enchiridion Legum: A Discourse. Bd. with John Brydall: Speculum Juris Anglicani: or, a View of the Laws of England, As They Are Divided into Statute, Common-Law & Customs. John Brydall. LC 77-86567. (Classics of English Legal History in the Modern Era: Vol. 69). 1978. Repr. of 1673 ed. lib. bdg. 55.00 (ISBN 0-8240-3056-7). Garland Pub.

Enciclopedia Alfabetica Garzanti, 5 vols. (It.). 1970. 315.00 (ISBN 0-8277-3058-6). Maxwell Sci Intl.

Enciclopedia Barsa, 16 vols. (Illus.). 1980. Set. 479.00 (ISBN 0-85229-308-9). Ency Brit Ed.

Enciclopedia Brasileira Globo, 12 vols. (Portugese.). 1977. Set. inc. atlas 435.00. Pergamon.

Enciclopedia Hoepli, 14 vols. (Ital.). 1976. Set. 550.00. Pergamon.

Enciclopedia Italiana Di Scienze, Lettere ed Arti, (Treccani, 41 vols. (It). 1928-1961. Set. 3100.00 (ISBN 0-8277-3018-7). Maxwell Sci Intl.

Enciclopedia Labor, 11 vols. 5th ed. (Span.). 1975-1977. 595.00 (ISBN 0-8277-3020-9). Maxwell Sci Intl.

Enciclopedia Powszechna, 4 vols. (Pol.). 1973-1976. Set. 180.00. Pergamon.

Enciclopedia Universal Illustrada Europeo-Americana (Espasa) Supplement 1969/1970. 1976. 50.00 o.p. (ISBN 0-685-73310-6). Maxwell Sci Intl.

Enciclopedia Universal Ilustrada Europeo-Americana, (Espasa, 100 vols. & 18 supplements. (Span.). 1907. Set. 3685.00 (ISBN 0-8277-3021-7). Maxwell Sci Intl.

Enciclopedia Universal Sopena, 10 vols. (Span.). 1980. Set. 425.00. Pergamon.

Enciclopedia Universale Rizzoli-Larousse, 15 vols. (It.). 1966-1971. 1085.00 (ISBN 0-8277-3022-5). Maxwell Sci Intl.

Enciklopedija Leksikografskog Zavoda, 6 vols. (Serbo-Croatian.). 1966-1969. 295.00 (ISBN 0-8277-3068-3). Maxwell Sci Intl.

Encircled Kingdom: Legends & Folktales of Laos. Jewell R. Coburn. LC 79-53838. (Illus.). 100p. 1979. 8.95 (ISBN 0-918060-03-6). Burn-Hart.

Enclosure of Ocean Resources: Economics & the Law of the Sea. Ross D. Eckert. LC 78-70388. (Publications Ser.: No. 210). (Illus.). 1979. 16.95 (ISBN 0-8179-7101-7). Hoover Inst Pr.

Encomion of Lady Pecunia: Or, the Praise of Money. Richard Barnfield. LC 74-80162. (English Experience Ser.: No. 642). 24p. 1974. Repr. of 1598 ed. 3.50 (ISBN 90-221-0642-X). Walter J Johnson.

Encore. John G. Boucher & Andre O. Hurtgen. (Allyn & Bacon French Program Ser.). (gr. 9-12). 1976. text ed. 15.12 (ISBN 0-205-04903-6, 3649032); tchrs'. guide 5.12 (ISBN 0-205-04904-4, 3649040). Allyn.

Encore! Encore! A New Ziggy Treasury. Tom Wilson. (Illus.). (gr. 4 up). 1979. 12.95 (ISBN 0-8362-1150-2); pap. 8.95 (ISBN 0-8362-1151-0). Andrews & McMeel.

Encore for Eleanor. Bill Peet. (gr. k-3). 1981. 9.95 (ISBN 0-395-29860-1). HM.

Encore for Reform: The Old Progressives & the New Deal. Otis L. Graham, Jr. (Orig.). 1967. pap. 4.95 (ISBN 0-19-500745-X, GB). Oxford U Pr.

Encounter at Shimoda: Search for a New Pacific Partnership. Ed. by Herbert Passin & Akira Iriye. (Special Studies on China & East Asia). 1979. lib. bdg. 24.50x (ISBN 0-89158-467-6). Westview.

Encounter Groups & Psychiatry. (Task Force Report: No. 1). 27p. 1970. pap. 5.00 (ISBN 0-685-24863-1, P246-0). Am Psychiatric.

Encounter on Burrows Hill & Other Poems. Conrad Hilberry. LC 69-10511. 1968. 4.50 o.p. (ISBN 0-8214-0041-X). Ohio U Pr.

Encounter on the Narrow Ridge: Martin Buber's Life & Thought, 2 vols. 1981. boxed set 75.00 (ISBN 0-686-65888-4). Dutton. Postponed.

Encounter: Readings for Thinking, Talking, Writing. 2nd ed. Joan G. Roloff. LC 73-7356. (Illus.). 416p. 1974. pap. text ed. 6.95x (ISBN 0-02-477150-3). Macmillan.

Encounter: Theory & Practice of Encounter Groups. Ed. by Arthur Burton. LC 73-92889. (Social & Behavioral Science Ser.). 1969. 12.95x o.p. (ISBN 0-87589-044-X). Jossey-Bass.

Encounter with a New World: A Reading-Writing Text for Speakers of English As a Second Language. D. Fassler & N. Lay. 1979. pap. 7.95 (ISBN 0-13-274910-6). P-H.

Encounter with an Angry God. Carobeth Laird. 1977. pap. 2.25 (ISBN 0-345-28464-X). Ballantine.

Encounter with Darkness. John A. MacMillan. 116p. pap. 1.95 (ISBN 0-87509-287-X). Chr Pubns.

Encounter with Erikson: Historical Interpretation & Religious Biography. Donald Capps et al. LC 76-44434. (American Academy of Religion, Formative Contemporary Thinkers Ser.: No. 2). 1977. pap. 9.00 (ISBN 0-685-85749-2, 010402). Scholars Pr Ca.

Encounter with God: A Theology of Christian Experience. Morton Kelsey. 288p. 1972. pap. 5.95 (ISBN 0-87123-123-9, 210123); study guide 1.25 (ISBN 0-87123-506-4, 210506). Bethany Fell.

Encounter with Israel: A Challenge to Conscience. Alice Eckardt & Roy Eckardt. 1970. 7.95 o.p. (ISBN 0-8096-1783-8, Assn Pr). Follett.

Encounter with Sociology: The Term Paper. 2nd ed. Leonard Becker, Jr. & Clair Gustafson. 1976. pap. 4.95x (ISBN 0-87835-056-X). Boyd & Fraser.

Encounter with Terminal Illness. Ruth Kopp & Stephen Sorenson. 256p. 1980. 9.95 (ISBN 0-310-41600-0). Zondervan.

Encounter with the Divine in Mesopotamia & Israel. H. W. Saggs. (Jordan Lectures in Comparative Religion, 12th Ser). 1978. text ed. 31.25x (ISBN 0-485-17412-X, Athlone Pr). Humanities.

Encounter with Zen: Writings on Poetry & Zen. Lucien Stryk. 1981. 16.95 (ISBN 0-8040-0405-6); pap. 8.95 (ISBN 0-8040-0406-4). Swallow.

Encountering Aborigines, a Case Study: Anthropology & the Australian Aboriginal. Kenelm O. Burridge. LC 72-1191. 272p. 1974. 23.00 (ISBN 0-08-017071-4); pap. 12.00 (ISBN 0-08-017646-1). Pergamon.

Encountering Evil: Live Options in Theodicy. Ed. by Stephen T. Davis. LC 80-84647. 1981. pap. 7.95 (ISBN 0-686-69554-2). John Knox.

Encountering Myself: Contemporary Christian Meditations. Harry J. Cargas. LC 76-56519. 1977. 6.95 (ISBN 0-8164-0372-4). Crossroad NY.

Encountering New Testament Manuscripts. Jack Finegan. pap. 7.95 (ISBN 0-8028-1836-6). Eerdmans.

Encountering Society: Introductory Readings in Sociology. Janet K. Mancini & Franklyn A. Robbins. LC 80-8253. 219p. 1980. pap. text ed. 10.50 (ISBN 0-8191-1181-3). U Pr of Amer.

Encounters. J. Garton-Springer et al. (Orig.). 1980. pap. text ed. 8.95x (ISBN 0-435-28477-0); tchrs. bk. 17.95 (ISBN 0-435-28476-2); tapes 144.00 (ISBN 0-435-28474-6); cassettes 128.00 (ISBN 0-435-28473-8). Heinemann Ed.

Encounters in Organizational Behavior: Problem Situations. R. D. Joyce. 1972. text ed. 18.50 (ISBN 0-08-017013-7); pap. text ed. 9.25 (ISBN 0-08-017116-8). Pergamon.

Encounters: India's Westerly Trade in the Bronze Age. Shereen Ratnagar. 240p. 1981. 17.95 (ISBN 0-19-561253-1). Oxford U Pr.

Encounters of the Fourth Kind. R. L. Hymers. Orig. Title: UFO's & Bible Prophecy. pap. 1.95 (ISBN 0-89728-028-8, 698609). Omega Pubns OR.

Encounters: Two Studies in the Sociology of Interaction. Erving Goffman. LC 61-16844. (Orig.). 1961. pap. 4.95 (ISBN 0-672-60818-9). Bobbs.

Encounters with Arithmetic. Thomas Carnevale & Robert Shloming. 449p. 1979. pap. text ed. 14.95 (ISBN 0-15-522596-0, HC); instructor's manual avail. (ISBN 0-15-522597-9). HarBraceJ.

Encounters with Lenin. Nikolay Valentinov. Tr. by Paul Rosta & Brian Pearce. 1980. cancelled (ISBN 0-915042-04-5). Lib Soc Sci.

Encounters with the Invisible World: Being Ten Tales of Ghosts, Witches, & the Devil Himself in New England. Marilynne K. Roach. LC 76-22186. (Illus.). (gr. 5-9). 1977. 7.95 (ISBN 0-690-01277-2, TYC-J). T Y Crowell.

Encouragement to Colonies. William Alexander. LC 68-54607. (English Experience Ser.: No. 63). (Illus.). 47p. 1968. Repr. of 1624 ed. 11.50 (ISBN 90-221-0063-4). Walter J Johnson.

Encouraging Girls in Mathematics. Lorelei R. Brush. LC 79-55774. (Illus.). 1980. text ed. 16.00 (ISBN 0-89011-542-7). Abt Assoc.

Encouraging One Another. Gene A. Getz. 1981. pap. 3.95 (ISBN 0-88207-256-0). Victor Bks.

Encuentro Con Jesus. Robert E. Adams. (Illus.). Date not set. pap. 1.20 (ISBN 0-311-04657-6). Casa Bautista.

Enculturation in Latin America: An Anthology. new ed. Ed. by Johannes Wilbert. LC 76-620078. (Latin American Studies: Vol. 37). (Orig.). 1976. pap. 13.95 (ISBN 0-87903-028-3). UCLA Lat Am Ctr.

Encyclopaedia Britannica, 30 vols. Ed. by Warren E. Preece. 1980. write for info. (ISBN 0-85229-387-9). Ency Brit Ed.

Encyclopaedia of Religions. Maurice A. Canney. LC 75-123370. 1970. Repr. of 1921 ed. 28.00 (ISBN 0-8103-3856-4). Gale.

Encyclopaedia of Sport, 2 vols. Ed. by Hedley Peek & F. G. Aflalo. LC 75-23210. (Illus.). 1976. Repr. of 1897 ed. Set. 135.00 (ISBN 0-8103-4207-3). Gale.

Encyclopaedia of the Labour Movement, 3 vols. 7th ed. Ed. by Hastings B. Lees-Smith. LC 73-167033. xxv, 1132p. 1972. Repr. of 1928 ed. Set. 115.00 (ISBN 0-8103-3028-8). Gale.

Encyclopaedia Sherlockiana. Jack Tracy. 1979. pap. 7.95 (ISBN 0-380-46490-X, 46490). Avon.

Encyclopaedias: Their History Throughout the Ages. 2nd ed. Robert L. Collison. (Illus.). 1966. 18.00 o.s.i. (ISBN 0-02-843100-6). Hafner.

Encyclopaedic Dictionary of Physics, 9 vols., 5 suppls. Ed. by J. Thewlis. Incl. Vol. 1. Abbe Refractometer to Compensated Bars. 1961. 37.00 (ISBN 0-08-006540-6); Vol. 2. Compensator to Epecadmium Neutrons. 1961. 37.00 (ISBN 0-08-006541-4); Vol. 3. Epitaxy to Intermediate Image. 1961. 37.00 (ISBN 0-08-006542-2); Vol. 4. Intermediate Stage to Neutron Resonance Level. 1962. 37.00 (ISBN 0-08-006543-0); Vol. 5. Neutron Scattering to Radiation Constants. 1962. 37.00 (ISBN 0-08-006544-9); Vol. 6. Radiation, Continuous, to Stellar Luminosity. 1962. 37.00 (ISBN 0-08-006545-7); Vol. 7. Stellar Magnitude to Zwitter Ion. 1963. 37.00 (ISBN 0-08-006546-5); Vol. 8. Subject & Author Indexes. 1963. 37.00 (ISBN 0-08-006749-2); Vol. 9. Multilingual Glossary. 1964. 77.50 (ISBN 0-08-009928-9); Supplementary Volumes, 5 vols. 1966. Vol 1, 1966. 25.00 (ISBN 0-08-011835-6); Vol 2, 1967. 31.00 (ISBN 0-08-011889-5); Vol. 3, 1969. 31.00 (ISBN 0-08-012447-X); Vol. 4, 1971. 42.50 (ISBN 0-08-006359-4); Vol. 5, 1975. 50.00 (ISBN 0-08-017056-0); Vol. 6, Date Not Set. price not set (ISBN 0-08-020642-5). 635.00 set (ISBN 0-08-018296-8). Pergamon.

Encyclopaedic Dictionary of Science & War. Charles M. Beadnell. LC 74-164093. 1971. Repr. of 1943 ed. 20.00 (ISBN 0-8103-3753-3). Gale.

Encyclopedia Americana, 30 vols. Ed. by Bernard S. Cayne. LC 80-84517. (Illus.). 1981. write for info. (ISBN 0-7172-0112-0). Grolier Ed Corp.

Encyclopedia Americana, 30 vols. Ed. by Bernard S. Cayne. LC 79-55176. (Illus.). 1980. write for info o.p. (ISBN 0-7172-0111-2). Grolier Ed Corp.

Encyclopedia Brown Activity Book. Jim Razzi. (gr. 2-5). 1980. pap. 1.25 (ISBN 0-686-57990-9). Bantam.

Encyclopedia Brown & the Case of the Midnight Visitor, No. 13. Donald J. Sobol. (Encyclopedia Brown Ser.). 96p. 1980. pap. 1.50 (ISBN 0-553-15076-6). Bantam.

Encyclopedia Brown Carries on. Donald J. Sobol. LC 79-6340. (Illus.). 80p. (gr. 3-7). 1980. 6.95 (ISBN 0-590-07562-4, Four Winds). Schol Bk Serv.

Encyclopedia Brown Finds the Clues. Donald J. Sobol. LC 66-10230. (Encyclopedia Brown Ser.: No. 3). (Illus.). (gr. 2-6). 1966. 5.95 o.p. (ISBN 0-525-67204-4); pap. 2.98 (ISBN 0-525-67802-6). Elsevier-Nelson.

Encyclopedia Brown Puzzle & Game Books. Jim Razzi. (gr. 4-8). 1980. pap. 1.25 (ISBN 0-686-57991-7). Bantam.

Encyclopedia Brown Shows the Way, No. 9. Donald J. Sobol. 96p. (gr. 3-6). 1981. pap. 1.50 (ISBN 0-553-15107-X). Bantam.

Encyclopedia Brown Takes the Case. Sobol. (gr. 3-6). pap. 1.50 o.p. (ISBN 0-671-56016-6, 56016). Archway.

Encyclopedia Brown Tracks Them Down, No. 8. Donald J. Sobol. 96p. (gr. 3-6). 1981. pap. 1.50 (ISBN 0-553-15093-6). Bantam.

Encyclopedia Brown's Fourth Book of Games & Puzzles. Jim Razzi. 64p. (gr. 4-6). 1981. pap. 1.50 (ISBN 0-553-15110-X). Bantam.

Encyclopedia Brown's Record Book of Weird & Wonderful Facts. Donald J. Sobol. (gr. k-6). 1981. pap. price not set (ISBN 0-440-42361-9, YB). Dell.

Encyclopedia Brown's Third Book of Games & Puzzles. Jim Razzi. 64p. (Orig.). (gr. 4-6). 1981. pap. 1.50 (ISBN 0-553-15077-4). Bantam.

Encyclopedia Buyers' Guide. Ed. by Roger Sween. vi, 74p. 1981. pap. 4.50 (ISBN 0-914054-51-1). Index Co.

Encyclopedia Buying Guide. 3rd ed. Kenneth F. Kister. LC 76-645701. 388p. 1981. 22.50 (ISBN 0-8352-1353-6). Bowker.

Encyclopedia Hebraica, 32 vols. Incl. Supplement. (Heb.). 1949. 1250.00. Maxwell Sci Intl.

Encyclopedia International, 20 vols. Ed. by Edward Humphrey. LC 80-84815. (Illus.). 1981. write for info. (ISBN 0-7172-0712-9). Grolier Ed Corp.

Encyclopedia International, 20 vols. Ed. by Edward Humphrey. LC 79-67180. (Illus.). 1980. write for info o.p. (ISBN 0-7172-0711-0). Grolier Ed Corp.

Encyclopedia of Air Warfare. (Illus.). 256p. 1975. 17.95 o.s.i. (ISBN 0-690-00606-3, TYC-T). T Y Crowell.

Encyclopedia of Amazing but True Facts. Doug Storer. LC 79-91385. (Illus.). 448p. 1980. 9.95 (ISBN 0-8069-0184-5); lib. bdg. 9.89 (ISBN 0-8069-0185-3). Sterling.

Encyclopedia of American Architecture. Hunt. 100p. Date not set. 35.00 (ISBN 0-07-031299-0). McGraw.

Encyclopedia of American Art. Chanticleer Press. Ed. by Cy Nelson. 670p. 1981. 39.95 (ISBN 0-525-93164-3). Dutton.

Encyclopedia of American History. bicentennial, 5th ed. Ed. by Richard B. Morris & Jeffrey B. Morris. LC 74-15840. (Illus.). 1260p. (YA) 1976. 29.95 o.s.i. (ISBN 0-06-013081-4, HarpT); lib. bdg. 26.79 (ISBN 0-06-013083-0). Har-Row.

Encyclopedia of Ancient Civilizations. Ed. by Arthur Cotterell. Colin Renfrew. 320p. 1980. 29.95 (ISBN 0-8317-2790-X). Mayflower Bks.

Encyclopedia of Animated Cartoon Series: Nineteen Hundred & Nine to Nineteen Seventy-Nine. Jeff Lenburg. (Illus.). 1981. 24.95 (ISBN 0-87000-441-7). Arlington Hse.

Encyclopedia of Antiques. Harold Lewis Bond. LC 74-31297. (Illus.). 389p. 1975. Repr. of 1945 ed. 30.00 (ISBN 0-8103-4206-5). Gale.

Encyclopedia of Asian Cooking. Jeni Wright. (Illus.). 224p. 1980. 20.00 (ISBN 0-7064-0990-6); pap. 9.95 (ISBN 0-7064-1354-7). Mayflower Bks.

Encyclopedia of Atmospheric Sciences & Astrogeology. Ed. by R. Fairbridge. (Encyclopedia of Earth Sciences Ser: Vol. II). 1967. 58.00 (ISBN 0-12-786458-X). Acad Pr.

Encyclopedia of Aviation. Reference International. LC 77-72699. (Encore Edition). (Illus.). 1977. 5.95 (ISBN 0-684-16921-5, ScribT). Scribner.

Encyclopedia of Aviculture, 3 vols. Ed. by A. Rutgers & K. A. Norris. Incl. Vol. 1. 1970 (ISBN 0-7137-0800-X); Vol. 2. 1973 (ISBN 0-7137-0801-8); Vol. 3. 1977 (ISBN 0-7137-0802-6). (Illus.). 37.50 ea. (Pub. by Blandford Pr England). Sterling.

Encyclopedia of Batik Designs. Leo O. Donahue. LC 80-67121. 520p. 1981. 60.00 (ISBN 0-87982-035-7). Art Alliance.

Encyclopedia of Biblical Theology: The Concise Sacramentum Verbi. J. B. Bauer. 1172p. 1981. 29.50 (ISBN 0-8245-0042-3). Crossroad NY.

Encyclopedia of Bioethics, 4 vols. Ed. by Warren T. Reich. LC 78-8821. 1978. Set. 230.00 (ISBN 0-02-926060-4). Free Pr.

Encyclopedia of Business Information Sources. 4th, rev. ed. Ed. by Paul Wasserman et al. LC 79-24771. 1980. 85.00 (ISBN 0-8103-0368-X). Gale.

Encyclopedia of Business Letters in Four Languages, 3 vols. Ulrich Bar. LC 72-3331. 1972. Set. 59.00 o.p. (ISBN 0-668-02670-7). Arco.

Encyclopedia of Cage & Aviary Birds. Cyril H. Rogers. 15.95 (ISBN 0-7207-0802-8, Pub. by Michael Joseph). Merrimack Bk Serv.

Encyclopedia of Canvas Embroidery Stitch Patterns. rev. ed. Katharine Ireys. LC 72-78267. (Illus.). 160p. 1977. 10.95 o.s.i. (ISBN 0-690-01665-4, TYC-T); pap. 6.95 (ISBN 0-690-01666-2, TYC-T). T Y Crowell.

Encyclopedia of Chemical Technology, 12 vols. 3rd ed. Kirk & Othmer. Incl. Vol. 1. A-Alkanolamines. 967p (ISBN 0-471-02037-0); Vol. 2. Alkoxides, Metals & Antibiotics (Peptides) 1036p (ISBN 0-471-02038-9); Vol. 3. Antibiotics (Phenazines) 958p (ISBN 0-471-02039-7); Vol. 4. Blood, Coagulants & Anticoagulants to Cardiovascular Agents. 930p (ISBN 0-471-02040-0); Vol. 5. Castor Oil to Chlorosulfuric Acid. 880p (ISBN 0-471-02041-9); Vol. 6. Chocolate & Cocoa to Copper. 869p (ISBN 0-471-02042-7); Vol. 7. Copper Alloys to Distillations (ISBN 0-471-02043-5); Vol. 8. Diuretics to Emulsions (ISBN 0-471-02044-3); Vol. 9. Enamels: Porcelain or Vitreous to Ferrites. 902p (ISBN 0-471-02062-1); Vol. 10. Ferroelectrics to Fluorine Compounds. 962p (ISBN 0-471-02063-X); Vol. 11. Fluorine Compounds to Gold & Gold Compounds (ISBN 0-471-02064-8); Vol. 12. Gravity Concentration to Hidroxy Carboxylic Acids (ISBN 0-471-02065-6). 1978-80. 145.00 ea. (Pub. by Wiley-Interscience). Wiley.

Encyclopedia of Chemical Technology, Vol. 1. 3rd ed. Ed. by R. E. Kirk & D. F. Othmer. LC 64-22188. 1978. 145.00 o.p. (ISBN 0-471-02037-0, Pub. by Wiley-Interscience). Wiley.

Encyclopedia of Chemical Technology, Vol. 2. 3rd ed. Ed. by R. E. Kirk & D. F. Othmer. LC 77-15820. 1978. 145.00 o.p. (ISBN 0-471-02038-9, Pub. by Wiley-Interscience). Wiley.

Encyclopedia of Chemical Trademarks & Synonyms, Vol. 1 A-E. H. Bennett. 1981. 55.00 (ISBN 0-8206-0286-8). Chem Pub.

Encyclopedia of China Today. F. M. Kaplan & J. M. Sobin. 352p. 1979. 37.50x (ISBN 90-286-0439-1). Sijthoff & Noordhoff.

Encyclopedia of Cockatoos. Steve Kates. (Illus.). 221p. 1980. 20.00 (ISBN 0-87666-896-1, H-1023). TFH Pubns.

Encyclopedia of Comic Book Heroes: Batman, Vol. 1. Michael L. Fleisher. LC 75-19237. (Illus.). 320p. 1976. pap. 8.95 o.s.i. (ISBN 0-02-080090-8, Collier). Macmillan.

Encyclopedia of Dowsing. Deek Gladson. 4.00 o.s.i. (ISBN 0-89316-606-5). Exanimo Pr.

Encyclopedia of Embroidery Stitches, Including Crewel. Marion Nichols. LC 72-97816. (Illus.). 224p. (Orig.). 1974. pap. 5.95 (ISBN 0-486-22929-7). Dover.

Encyclopedia of Estate Planning. Robert S. Holzman. LC 80-19441. 312p. 1980. 50.00 (ISBN 0-932648-15-0). Boardroom.

Encyclopedia of Fairies: Hobgoblins, Brownies, Bogies, & Other Supernatural Creatures. Katharine M. Briggs. LC 76-12939. (Illus.). (gr. 4 up). 1978. pap. 4.95 (ISBN 0-394-73467-X). Pantheon.

Encyclopedia of Financial & Personal Survival: Six Hundred Fifty Coping Strategies. Kaiman Lee & Rita Yang. LC 80-130472. 1980. 210.00 (ISBN 0-915250-34-9). Environ Design.

Encyclopedia of Food Engineering. Carl W. Hall et al. (Illus.). 1971. lib. bdg. 75.00 (ISBN 0-87055-086-1). AVI.

Encyclopedia of Food Science. Martin S. Peterson & Arnold H. Johnson. (Illus.). 1978. lib. bdg. 79.50 (ISBN 0-87055-227-9). AVI.

Encyclopedia of Food Technology. Ed. by Arnold Johnson & Martin Peterson. (Technologic Food Encyclopedia). (Illus.). 1974. 75.00 (ISBN 0-87055-157-4). AVI.

Encyclopedia of Football. 14th ed. Roger Treat. Ed. by Pete Palmer. LC 75-38433. (Illus.). 1976. 14.95 o.p. (ISBN 0-498-01906-3). A S Barnes.

Encyclopedia of Furniture. Joseph Aaronson. 1970. 53.00 (ISBN 0-7134-0802-2, Pub. by Batsford England). David & Charles.

Encyclopedia of Furniture Making. Ernest Joyce. LC 76-49087. (Illus.). 1979. 17.50 (ISBN 0-8069-8302-7); PLB 14.99 (ISBN 0-8069-8303-5). Sterling.

Encyclopedia of Geographic Information Sources. 3rd ed. Ed. by Paul Wasserman et al. LC 78-55032. 1978. 45.00 (ISBN 0-8103-0374-4). Gale.

Encyclopedia of Geomorphology. Ed. by R. Fairbridge. LC 68-58342. (Encyclopedia of Earth Sciences Ser: Vol. III). 1968. 78.00x (ISBN 0-12-786459-8). Acad Pr.

Encyclopedia of Gerbils. David Robinson. 224p. 1980. 9.95 (ISBN 0-87666-915-1, H-974). TFH Pubns.

Encyclopedia of Governmental Advisory Organizations. 3rd ed. Ed. by Linda Sullivan. 800p. 1981. 175.00 (ISBN 0-8103-0253-5). Gale.

Encyclopedia of Governmental Advisory Organizations: A Reference Guide to Presidential Advisory Committees, Public Advisory Committees, Interagency Committees & Other Government-Related Boards, Panels, Task Forces, Commissions, Conferences, & Other Similar Bodies Serving in a Consultative, Coordinating, Advisory, Research, or Investigative Capacity. 2nd ed. Linda E. Sullivan & Anthony T. Kruzas. LC 75-15619. 400p. 1975. 110.00 o.p. (ISBN 0-8103-0251-9); New Governmental Advisory Organizations: Periodical Supplement (inter-ed sub.) 95.00 o.p. (ISBN 0-8103-0252-7). Gale.

Encyclopedia of Guinea Pigs. Margaret Elward & Catherine E. Whiteway. (Illus.). 224p. 1980. 9.95 (ISBN 0-87666-916-X, H-975). TFH Pubns.

Encyclopedia of Hardware. Tom Philbin. LC 78-52965. 1978. 12.00 o.p. (ISBN 0-8015-2335-4, Hawthorn); pap. 6.95 (ISBN 0-8015-2336-2, Hawthorn). Dutton.

Encyclopedia of Health & Beauty. Simona Morini. 1977. pap. 2.50 o.p. (ISBN 0-445-04095-5). Popular Lib.

Encyclopedia of Health & Nutrition. Max Warmbrand. 1974. pap. 1.95 o.s.i. (ISBN 0-515-03413-4, Y3413). Jove Pubns.

Encyclopedia of Health & the Human Body. Compiled by Gerry Newman. (Illus.). (gr. 7 up). 1977. PLB 16.90 s&l (ISBN 0-531-01331-6). Watts.

Encyclopedia of Homonyms-Sound Alikes: Condensed & Abridged Edition. Dora Newhouse. LC 76-50944. (gr. 4-12). 1978. text ed. 9.95 (ISBN 0-918050-02-2); pap. 6.95 (ISBN 0-918050-00-6). Newhouse Pr.

Encyclopedia of How It Works. Ed. by Donald Clarke. LC 76-56962. (Illus.). 1977. 16.95 (ISBN 0-89479-002-1). A & W Pubs.

Encyclopedia of How It's Made. Donald Clarke. LC 78-58391. (Illus.). 1978. 16.95 (ISBN 0-89479-035-8). A & W Pubs.

Encyclopedia of Indian Philosophies: Bibliography of Indian Philosophies. Ed. by Karl H. Potter. 844p. 1970. Vol. 1, 1973. 25.00x (ISBN 0-7189-2126-7); Vol. 2, 1977. 32.50x (ISBN 0-691-07183-7). Intl Pubns Serv.

Encyclopedia of Indians of the Americas, Vols. 1-9. LC 75-170347. 1974-1981. 59.00 ea. (ISBN 0-403-03586-4). Scholarly.

Encyclopedia of Indians of the Americas, Vols. 1-8. Ed. by Harry Waldman. LC 74-5088. 1974-81. lib. bdg. 59.00 ea. Scholarly.

Encyclopedia of Infantry Weapons of World War II. Ian Hogg. LC 76-51525. Orig. Title: Infantry Weapons of World War II by Sidney Mayer. (Illus.). 1977. 15.95 o.p. (ISBN 0-690-01447-3, TYC-T). T Y Crowell.

Encyclopedia of Information Systems & Services. 3rd ed. Ed. by Anthony T. Kruzas. LC 78-14575. 1030p. 1978. 135.00 o.p. (ISBN 0-8103-0940-8). Gale.

Encyclopedia of Information Systems & Services. 4th ed. Ed. by John Schmittroth, Jr. & Anthony T. Kruzas. 1500p. 1980. 175.00 (ISBN 0-8103-0942-4). Gale.

Encyclopedia of Instrumentation & Control. Douglas M. Considine. 814p. 1981. Repr. text ed. write for info. (ISBN 0-89874-281-1). Krieger.

Encyclopedia of Islam, 5 vols. Ed. by B. Lewis et al. Incl. Vol. 1. A-B: Fasc. 1-22. Ed. by H. A. Gibb et al. 1960. text ed. 182.25x (ISBN 90-040-0530-7); Vol. 2. C-G: Fasc. 23-40. Ed. by B. Lewis et al. 1965. 178.75x (ISBN 90-040-0531-5); Vol. 3. H-Iram: Fasc. 41-60. 1969. text ed. 217.75x (ISBN 90-040-3275-4); Vols. 4 & 5. I-Ram &K-Ha: Fasc. 61-78. 1978. text ed. 275.00 (ISBN 0-685-23323-5). Humanities.

Encyclopedia of Knives. Norman Strung. LC 76-10288. (Illus.). 1976. 12.50 o.s.i. (ISBN 0-397-01164-4). Lippincott.

Encyclopedia of Knots & Fancy Rope Work. 4th ed. Raoul Graumont & John Hensel. (Illus.). 1953. 22.50 (ISBN 0-87033-021-7). Cornell Maritime.

Encyclopedia of Linguistics, Information & Control. A. R. Meetham. 1969. 115.00 (ISBN 0-08-012337-6). Pergamon.

Encyclopedia of Live Foods. Charles O. Masters. (Illus.). 336p. 1975. 9.95 (ISBN 0-87666-093-6, PS-730). TFH Pubns.

Encyclopedia of Mental Health. Ed. by Albert Deutsch. LC 63-7150. 1970. Repr. of 1963 ed. 45.00 (ISBN 0-8108-0357-7). Scarecrow.

Encyclopedia of Missions: Descriptive, Historical, Biographical, Statistical. 2nd ed. Ed. by Henry Otis Dwight et al. LC 74-31438. 851p. 1975. Repr. of 1904 ed. 44.00 (ISBN 0-8103-3325-2). Gale.

Encyclopedia of Motorcycling. George Bishop. (Illus.). 1980. 16.95 (ISBN 0-686-68350-1). Putnam.

Encyclopedia of Music in Canada. Ed. by Helmut Kallmann et al. 1504p. 1981. 45.00 (ISBN 0-8020-5509-5). U of Toronto Pr.

Encyclopedia of Mysticism: & the Mystery Religions. John Ferguson. (Illus.). 14.95 (ISBN 0-8164-9310-3). Crossroad NY.

Encyclopedia of Nautical Knowledge. W. A. McEwen & A. H. Lewis. LC 53-9685. 1953. 15.00 (ISBN 0-87033-010-1). Cornell Maritime.

Encyclopedia of Occult Sciences. LC 75-78148. 1975. Repr. of 1939 ed. 22.00 (ISBN 0-8103-3120-9). Gale.

Encyclopedia of Occultism & Parapsychology: A Compedium of Information on the Occult Sciences, Magic, Demonology, Superstitions, Spiritism, Mysticism, Metaphysics, Psychical Science & Parapsycholgy. 2nd ed. Leslie Shepard. (Illus.). 400p. 1981. 125.00 (ISBN 0-8103-0196-2). Gale.

Encyclopedia of Occultism & Parapsychology: A Compendium of Information on the Occult Sciences, Magic, Demonology, Superstition, Spiritism, Mysticism, Metaphysics, Psychical Science & Parapsychology, 2 vols. Ed. by Leslie Shepard. LC 77-92. (Illus., Supplemented by Occultism update). 1978. Set. 90.00 (ISBN 0-8103-0185-7); pap. 45.00 occultism update: a periodical supplement (4 issues subscription) (ISBN 0-685-79636-1). Gale.

Encyclopedia of Occultism & Parapsychlogy: Vols. 1 & 2. Leslie A. Shepard. 1980. pap. 19.90 boxed set (ISBN 0-380-50112-0). Vol. 1 (ISBN 0-380-48835-3, 48835). Vol. 2 (ISBN 0-380-48975-9, 48975). Avon.

Encyclopedia of Oceanography. Ed. by R Fairbridge. LC 66-26059. (Encyclopedia of Earth Sciences Ser: Vol. I). 1966. 90.00 (ISBN 0-12-786457-1). Acad Pr.

Encyclopedia of One-Liner Comedy. Robert Orben. LC 73-150910. 1971. 8.95 (ISBN 0-385-06698-8). Doubleday.

Encyclopedia of Organic Gardening. Ed. by Organic Gardening & Farming Magazine. LC 77-25915. 1978. 21.95 (ISBN 0-87857-225-2). Rodale Pr Inc.

Encyclopedia of Pet Mice. Tony Jones. (Illus.). 224p. 1979. 9.95 (ISBN 0-87666-910-0, H-973). TFH Pubns.

Encyclopedia of Philosophy, 4 vols. Ed. by Paul Edwards. LC 67-10059. 1973. Set. 150.00 (ISBN 0-02-894950-1). Free Pr.

Encyclopedia of Physical Education, Fitness & Sports: Philosophy, History, Programs Administration, & Related Organizations, Vol. I. James S. Bosco. Ed. by Mary A. Turner & Thomas K. Cureton, Jr. (Illus.). 850p. Date not set. 38.00 (ISBN 0-89832-018-6). Brighton Pub Co. Postponed.

Encyclopedia of Physics. Ed. by Rita G. Lerner & George L. Trigg. 1980. text ed. 99.50 (ISBN 0-201-04313-0). A-W.

Encyclopedia of Polymer Science & Technology, 16 vols. H. F. Mark et al. Incl. Vol. 1. 1964 (ISBN 0-470-56970-0); Vol. 2. 1965 (ISBN 0-470-56973-5); Vol. 3. 1965 (ISBN 0-470-56975-1); Vol. 4. 1966 (ISBN 0-470-56977-8); Vol. 5. 1966 (ISBN 0-470-56979-4); Vol. 6. 1967 (ISBN 0-470-56980-8); Vol. 7. 1967 (ISBN 0-470-56981-6); Vol. 8. 1968 (ISBN 0-470-56982-4); Vol. 9. 1968 (ISBN 0-470-56983-2); Vol. 10. 1969 (ISBN 0-471-56984-4); Vol. 11. 1969 (ISBN 0-471-56969-0); Vol. 12. 1970 (ISBN 0-471-56992-5); Vol. 13. 1970 (ISBN 0-471-56993-3); Vol. 14. 1971 (ISBN 0-471-56994-1); Vol. 15. 1971 (ISBN 0-471-56995-X); Vol. 16. Index. 1972 (ISBN 0-471-56996-8). LC 64-22188. 85.00 ea.; Set. write for info. (ISBN 0-471-04184-X); supplements for vols. 1-2 avail. Supplement, Vol. 1 (ISBN 0-471-56997-6). Supplement, Vol. 2 (ISBN 0-471-56998-4). Wiley.

Encyclopedia of Practical Photography, 14 vols. American Photographic Book Publishing Co. & Eastman Kodak Co. 1978. Set. lib. bdg. 223.30 (ISBN 0-8174-3200-0); Set. 159.95 (ISBN 0-8174-3050-4). Amphoto.

Encyclopedia of Pre-Historic Life. Rodney Steel & Anthony Harvey. (Illus.). 1979. 24.95 (ISBN 0-07-060920-9). McGraw.

Encyclopedia of Psychoanalysis. Ed. by Ludwig Eidelberg. LC 67-28974. 1968. 35.00 (ISBN 0-02-909340-6). Free Pr.

Encyclopedia of Quotations About Music. Ed. by Nat Shapiro. (Da Capo Quality Paperbacks Ser.). 1981. pap. 7.95 (ISBN 0-306-80138-8). Da Capo.

Encyclopedia of Rawhide & Leather Braiding. Bruce Grant. LC 72-10407. (Illus.). 1972. 22.50 (ISBN 0-87033-161-2). Cornell Maritime.

Encyclopedia of Religion. Vergilius Ferm. LC 75-36508. 844p. 1976. Repr. of 1945 ed. lib. bdg. 55.00x (ISBN 0-8371-8638-2, FEEOR). Greenwood.

Encyclopedia of Religious Quotations. Frank S. Mead. 1976. pap. 2.25 (ISBN 0-89129-194-6). Jove Pubns.

Encyclopedia of Rhythms: Instrumental Forms of Harmony. Joseph Schillinger. LC 76-10326. (Music Rerint Ser.). 1976. Repr. of 1966 ed. lib. bdg. 35.00 (ISBN 0-306-70782-9). Da Capo.

Encyclopedia of Seven Thousand, Seven Hundred Illustrations. Paul L. Tan. (Illus.). 2400p. 1979. 34.95 (ISBN 0-88469-096-2). BMH Bks.

Encyclopedia of Ships & Seafaring. Ed. by Eugene Koleshnik et al. (Illus.). 256p. 1980. 14.95 (ISBN 0-517-53738-9, Michelman Bks). Crown.

Encyclopedia of Slot Machines. Robert N. Geddes & Daniel R. Mead. (Illus.). 300p. 1980. write for info. (ISBN 0-934422-17-6). Mead Co.

Encyclopedia of Social Work, 2 vols. 1977 ed. Ed. by John Turner. LC 30-30948. 40.00x (ISBN 0-87101-074-7, CHO-075-C). Natl Assn Soc Wkrs.

Encyclopedia of Softbilled Birds. Matthew M. Vriends. (Illus.). 221p. 1980. 12.95 (ISBN 0-87666-891-0, H-1026). TFH Pubns.

Encyclopedia of Sports. Frank G. Menke. 1977. pap. 8.95 (ISBN 0-385-12262-4, Dolp). Doubleday.

Encyclopedia of Statistical Sciences, 2 vols. Samuel Ketz & Norman L. Johnson. 500p. 1981. Vol. 1. 82.50 (ISBN 0-471-05546-8, Pub. by Wiley-Interscience); Vol. 2. 82.50 (ISBN 0-471-05547-6). Wiley.

Encyclopedia of Superstitions, Folklore & the Occult Sciences of the World, 3 Vols. Ed. by Cora L. Daniels & C. M. Stevans. LC 70-141151. 1971. Repr. of 1903 ed. 72.00 (ISBN 0-8103-3286-8). Gale.

Encyclopedia of Surfactants, Vol. 2. M. Ash & I. Ash. 1981. 75.00 (ISBN 0-8206-0287-6). Chem Pub.

Encyclopedia of Textiles. American Fabrics Magazine. 55.00 (ISBN 0-87245-507-6). Textile Bk.

Encyclopedia of Textiles. 3rd ed. Ed. by American Fabrics Magazine. (Illus.). 1980. 49.95 (ISBN 0-13-276576-4, Busn). P-H.

Encyclopedia of the Alkaloids, Vol. 1, (a-h), Vol. 2, (i-z) Ed. by J. S. Glasby. LC 75-17753. 1423p. 1975. Set. 95.00 (ISBN 0-306-30845-2, Plenum Pr). Plenum Pub.

Encyclopedia of the American Theatre. Edwin Bronner. LC 45-2439. (Illus.). 1980. 30.00 (ISBN 0-498-01219-0). A S Barnes.

Encyclopedia of the Arts, 2 vols. Ed. by Dagobert Runes & Harry G. Schrickey. Date not set. Repr. of 1946 ed. Set. 42.00 (ISBN 0-8103-4162-X). Gale.

Encyclopedia of the Biological Sciences. Peter Gray. LC 80-28590. 1056p. 1981. Repr. lib. bdg. price not set (ISBN 0-89874-326-5). Krieger.

Encyclopedia of the Musical Theatre. Stanley Green. LC 76-21069. 1976. 17.50 (ISBN 0-396-07221-6). Dodd.

Encyclopedia of the Violin. Alberto Bachmann. Ed. by Albert E. Weir. Tr. by Frederick H. Martens from Ger. LC 65-23406. (Music Ser). 1966. Repr. of 1925 ed. lib. bdg. 29.50 (ISBN 0-306-70912-0). Da Capo.

Encyclopedia of the Water-Lily. Charles O. Masters. (Illus.). 512p. 1974. text ed. 14.95 (ISBN 0-87666-168-1, H-944). TFH Pubns.

Encyclopedia of Theology: The Concise Sacramentum Mundi. rev., abr. ed. Ed. by Karl Rahner. 1536p. 1975. 39.50 (ISBN 0-8164-1182-4). Crossroad NY.

Encyclopedia of U. S. Government Benefits. new ed. Ed. by Roy A. Grisham, Jr. & Paul D. McConaughy. LC 66-22903. (Illus.). 1977. 11.95 o.s.i. (ISBN 0-308-10335-1, TYC-T). T Y Crowell.

Encyclopedia of United States Silver & Gold Commemorative Coins: 1892-1954. Anthony Swiatek & Walter Breen. LC 80-14074. (Illus.). 224p. 1980. 16.95 (ISBN 0-668-04765-8, 4765-8). Arco.

Encyclopedia of Wood. U. S. Dept. of Forestry. LC 77-7728. (Illus.). 384p. 1980. pap. 12.95 (ISBN 0-8069-8890-8). Sterling.

Encyclopedia of World Air Power. Christopher J. Freeman. (Illus.). 1980. 17.95 (ISBN 0-517-53754-0). Crown.

Encyclopedia of World Costume. Doreen Yarwood. (Illus.). 1978. 27.50 (ISBN 0-684-15805-1, ScribT). Scribner.

Encyclopedia of World Literature in the Twentieth Century. 2nd rev. ed. Ed. by Leonard S. Klein. (Illus.). Date not set. 75.00 (ISBN 0-8044-3135-3). Ungar.

Encyclopedia of World Rivers. LC 79-87898. 1980. 24.95 (ISBN 0-528-81048-0). Rand.

Encyclopedia of World Soccer. Richard Henshaw. LC 78-26570. (Illus.). 1979. 25.00 o.p. (ISBN 0-915220-34-2). New Republic.

Encyclopedia on How to Cut Overhead. Carl Heyel & Arnold Naidich. 1980. 89.95. Busn Res Pubns.

Encyclopedia Science Supplement, 1980. Grolier Incorporated. Ed. by Herbert Kondo. LC 64-7603. (Illus.). 1979. write for info. o.p. (ISBN 0-7172-1510-5). Grolier Ed Corp.

Encyclopedia Science Supplement, 1981. Grolier Incorporated. Ed. by Herbert Kondo. LC 64-7603. (Illus.). 1980. write for info. (ISBN 0-7172-1511-3). Grolier Ed Corp.

Encyclopedia: Selections. Denis Diderot. Tr. by Thomas Cassirer & Nelly S. Hoyt. LC 65-26535. 1965. pap. 8.80 o.p. (ISBN 0-672-60479-5). Bobbs.

Encyclopedia Yiddishanica. Endel Markowitz. LC 79-89973. (Illus.). 450p. 1980. 24.95 (ISBN 0-933910-03-7); pap. write for info. (ISBN 0-933910-04-5). Haymark.

Encyclopedic Dictionary of Mathematics, 2 vols. Ed. by Shokichi Iyanaga & Yukiyosi Kawada. 1977. Set. text ed. 150.00 (ISBN 0-262-09016-3); pap. text ed. 40.00x (ISBN 0-262-59010-7). MIT Pr.

Encyclopedic Dictionary of Roman Law. Adolf Berger. LC 53-7641. (Transactions Ser.: Vol. 43, Pt. 2). 1980. Repr. of 1953 ed. 10.00 (ISBN 0-87169-435-2). Am Philos.

Encyclopedic Directory of Ethnic Newspapers & Periodicals in the United States. 2nd rev. ed. Lubomyr R. Wynar & Anna T. Wynar. LC 76-23317. 248p. 1976. PLB 20.00x (ISBN 0-87287-154-1). Libs Unl.

Encyclopedic Directory of Ethnic Organizations in the United States. Lubomyr R. Wynar. LC 75-28150. 440p. 1975. lib. bdg. 25.00x (ISBN 0-87287-120-7). Libs Unl.

Encyclopedic Handbook of Medical Psychology. S. Krauss et al. LC 75-33106. 1976. 19.95 (ISBN 0-407-00044-5). Butterworths.

Encyclopedie, 18 vols. Ed. by Diderot & D'Alembert. (Fr., 12 vols. of plates & 6 texts). 1971-1979. 190.00 ea. (ISBN 0-8277-3025-X). Maxwell Sci Intl.

Encyclopedie de l'electricite, 2 vols. Pierre De Jussieu-Pontcarral. (Illus.). 1970. 82.50x ea. Larousse.

Encyclopedie Des Arts Decoratifs et Industriels Modernes Au XXeme Siecle, 12 vols. Ed. by Wolfgang M. Freitag. Incl. Vol. 1. Preface (ISBN 0-8240-2488-5); Vol. 2. Architecture (ISBN 0-8240-2489-3); Vol. 3. Architectural Ornamentation & Sculpture (ISBN 0-8240-2490-7); Vol. 4. Furniture (ISBN 0-8240-2491-5); Vol. 5. Furniture Hardware & Accessories (ISBN 0-8240-2492-3); Vol. 6. Textiles & Paper Products (ISBN 0-8240-2493-1); Vol. 7. Art of the Book (ISBN 0-8240-2494-X); Vol. 8. Toys, Scientific & Musical Instruments, Vehicles of Transportation (ISBN 0-8240-2495-8); Vol. 9. Costume & Fashion Design (ISBN 0-8240-2496-6); Vol. 10. Stage Design, Photography & Film (ISBN 0-8240-2497-4); Vol. 11. Environment - Street & Garden (ISBN 0-8240-2498-2); Vol. 12. Teaching of the Decorative Arts (ISBN 0-8240-2499-0). LC 76-29204. (Illus.). Set. lib. bdg. 660.00 (ISBN 0-685-76428-1); lib. bdg. 55.00 ea. Garland Pub.

Encyclopedie Francaise, 22 Vols. (Fr.). 1935-1969. 1300.00 (ISBN 0-8277-3024-1). Maxwell Sci Intl.

Encyclopedie of Diderot & D'Alembert. John Lough. 42.00 (ISBN 0-521-07604-8). Cambridge U Pr.

Encyclopedie; Ou, Dictionnaire Raisonne Des Sciences, Des Arts et Des Metiers, 35 Vols. Ed. by Diderot & D'Alembert. 1751. Repr. 4750.00 (ISBN 0-8277-3054-3). Maxwell Sci Intl.

End. Herbert Douglass. LC 79-88435. (Dimension Ser.). 1979. 7.95 (ISBN 0-8163-0341-X); pap. 5.95 (ISBN 0-8163-0328-2, 20251-5). Pacific Pr Pub Assn.

End & the Beginning. Raymond Etteldorf. 1979. pap. text ed. 5.25x (ISBN 0-86140-012-7). Humanities.

End & the Beginning. James Hanley. 1978. pap. 1.95 o.p. (ISBN 0-445-04173-0). Popular Lib.

End & the Beginning: The Nicaraguan Revolution. John A. Booth. (Special Studies on Latin America & the Caribbean). (Illus.). 225p. (Orig.). 1981. lib. bdg. 20.00x (ISBN 0-89158-939-2); pap. text ed. 10.00x (ISBN 0-86531-148-X). Westview.

End & the Myth. Paul O'Neill. (Old West Ser.). (Illus.). 1979. lib. bdg. 12.96 (ISBN 0-686-51083-6). Silver.

End As a Man. Calder Willingham. LC 47-1581. 8.95 (ISBN 0-8149-0238-3). Vanguard.

End Essentials. Richard Kostelanetz. Bd. with End Appendix. LC 79-313. LC 79-51582. 1979. 5.95 (ISBN 0-686-59587-4). Assembling Pr.

End-Essentials. Richard Kostelanetz. Bd. with End - Appendix "Intelligent Writing" Reconsidered. LC 79-51580 (ISBN 0-8108-1246-0). LC 79-57582. 1979. 12.50 (ISBN 0-8108-1247-9). Scarecrow.

End of Affluence: A Blueprint for Your Future. Paul R. Ehrlich & Anne H. Ehrlich. 320p. 1974. pap. 2.50 (ISBN 0-345-29049-6). Ballantine.

End of Innocence. Jacqueline Cummins. 1961. 8.95 (ISBN 0-8392-1028-0). Astor-Honor.

End of Innocence. Jonathan Daniels. LC 73-37285. (FDR & the Era of the New Deal Ser.). 351p. 1972. Repr. of 1954 ed. 35.00 (ISBN 0-306-70423-4). Da Capo.

End of It. Mitchell Goodman. LC 79-66117. 286p. 1980. 15.95 (ISBN 0-933256-10-8); pap. 7.95 (ISBN 0-933256-11-6). Second Chance.

End of Me Old Cigar & Jack & Jill. John Osborne. 1975. 8.95 o.p. (ISBN 0-571-10856-3, Pub. by Faber & Faber); pap. 3.95 (ISBN 0-571-10857-1). Merrimack Bk Serv.

End of Medicine. Rick J. Carlson. LC 75-6856. (Health, Medicine & Society Ser). 1975. pap. 22.95 (ISBN 0-471-13494-5, Pub. by Wiley-Interscience). Wiley.

End of Order: Versailles, Nineteen Nineteen. Charles L. Mee, Jr. 410p. 1980. 15.95 (ISBN 0-525-09810-0). Dutton.

End of Reparations. Hjalmar Schacht. Tr. by Lewis Gannett. LC 79-1590. 1981. Repr. of 1931 ed. 19.75 (ISBN 0-88355-895-5). Hyperion Conn.

End of Tether. Edith H. Gividen. 1981. 6.95 (ISBN 0-8062-1609-3). Carlton.

End of the Byzantine Empire. D. M. Nicol. 109p. 1980. text ed. 17.50x (ISBN 0-8419-5826-2). Holmes & Meier.

End of the Cattle Trail. J. L. Hill. LC 73-94430. (Illus.). 1969. 8.95 (ISBN 0-8363-0030-0). Jenkins.

End of the Chapter. John Galsworthy. (Encore Edition). 1970. 5.95 o.p. (ISBN 0-684-15944-9, ScribT). Scribner.

End of the Days. Arthur E. Bloomfield. LC 51-9505. 1961. 5.95 (ISBN 0-87123-122-0, 210122). Bethany Fell.

End of the Game: And Other Stories. Julio Cortazar. 1978. pap. 5.95 (ISBN 0-06-090637-5, CN 637, CN). Har-Row.

End of the Keynesian Era: Essays on the Disintegration of the Keynesian Political Economy. Ed. by Robert Skidelsky. LC 77-8878. 1977. text ed. 21.00x (ISBN 0-8419-0329-8); pap. text ed. cancelled (ISBN 0-8419-0340-9). Holmes & Meier.

End of the Notables. Daniel Halevy. Ed. by Alain Silvera. Tr. by June Guicharnaud from Fr. LC 73-6009. 192p. 1974. 17.50x (ISBN 0-8195-4066-8, Pub. by Wesleyan U Pr); pap. 9.00x (ISBN 0-8195-6030-8). Columbia U Pr.

End of the Post-War Era: Documents on Great Power Relations, 1968-1975. Ed. by J. Mayall & C. Navari. LC 79-50512. 1980. 59.50 (ISBN 0-521-22698-8). Cambridge U Pr.

End of the Rainbow. Mary A. Crenshaw. 224p. 1981. 12.95 (ISBN 0-02-528810-5). Macmillan.

End of the Rainbow. Diane E. Finley. 192p. (YA) 1975. 5.95 (ISBN 0-685-50845-5, Avalon). Bouregy.

End of the Road. John Margolies. Ed. by C. Ray Smith. 96p. 1981. pap. 12.95 (ISBN 0-14-005840-0). Penguin.

End of the Road. John Margolies. Ed. by C. Ray Smith. (Illus.). 96p. 1981. 22.95 (ISBN 0-670-29482-9, Studio). Viking Pr.

End of the Search. Marchette Chute. 1960. 6.95 o.p. (ISBN 0-525-09812-7). Dutton.

End of the Summer. Rosamunde Pilcher. 160p. 1976. pap. 1.25 o.p. (ISBN 0-345-24858-9). Ballantine.

End of the Tito Era: Yugoslavia's Dilemmas. Slobodan Stankovic. (Publication Ser.: No. 236). 168p. 1981. 9.95 (ISBN 0-8179-7362-1). Hoover Inst Pr.

End of the World: An Introduction to Contemporary Drama. Maurice Valency. 1980. 19.95x (ISBN 0-19-502639-X). Oxford U Pr.

End of Track. James H. Kyner & Hawthorne Daniel. LC 60-12942. (Illus.). 1960. pap. 2.75 (ISBN 0-8032-5115-7, BB 101, Bison). U of Nebr Pr.

End of Tradition: Cultural Change & Development in the Municipio of Cunha, Sao Paulo, Brazil. Robert W. Shirley. LC 76-129535. (Institute of Latin America Studies). 1971. 20.00x (ISBN 0-231-03193-9). Columbia U Pr.

End Product: The First Taboo. Dan Sabbath & Mandel Hall. 1977. pap. 4.95 (ISBN 0-916354-76-8). Urizen Bks.

End Times New Testament. David Wilkerson. pap. 3.95 o.p. (ISBN 0-912376-11-2). Chosen Bks Pub.

End to Innocence. Sheldon B. Kopp. 1978. 9.95 (ISBN 0-02-566470-0). Macmillan.

End to Innocence: Facing Life Without Illusions. Sheldon Kopp. 208p. 1981. pap. 2.95 (ISBN 0-553-13327-6). Bantam.

End to Torment: A Memoir of Ezra Pound. H. D., pseud. Ed. by Norman H. Pearson & Michael King. LC 78-27149. 1979. pap. 3.95 (ISBN 0-8112-0720-X, NDP476). New Directions.

End User's Guide to Data Base. J. Martin. 1981. 21.50 (ISBN 0-13-277129-2). P-H.

Endangered & Threatened Plants & Animals of North Carolina: Proceedings of a Symposium on Endangered & Threatened Biota of N. C., Biological Concerns. John E. Cooper et al. LC 76-18670. (Illus.). 1977. pap. text ed. 8.00 o.p. (ISBN 0-917134-01-X). NC Natl Hist.

Endangered & Threatened Plants of the United States. Edward S. Ayensu & Robert A. DeFilipps. LC 77-25138. (Illus.). 403p. 1978. 25.00x (ISBN 0-87474-222-6). Smithsonian.

Endangered Animals. Dean Morris. LC 77-8365. (Read About Animals Ser.). (Illus.). (gr. k-3). 1977. PLB 9.95 (ISBN 0-8393-0011-5). Raintree Child.

Endangered Birds of the World: The ICPB Bird Red Data Book. Warren B. King. 624p. 1981. text ed. 19.95x (ISBN 0-87474-584-5); pap. text ed. 8.95 (ISBN 0-87474-583-7). Smithsonian.

Endangered Harvest: The Future of Bay Area Farmland. John Hart & Larry Orman. (Orig.). 1980. pap. 3.00 (ISBN 0-9605262-0-X). PFOS.

Endangered Hope: Experiences in Psychiatric Aftercare Facilities. David K. Reynolds & Norman L. Farberow. 1978. 12.95 (ISBN 0-520-03457-0). U of Cal Pr.

Endangered Plants. Dorothy C. Hogner. LC 77-2310. (Illus.). (gr. 3-7). 1977. 8.95 (ISBN 0-690-01362-0, TYC-J). T Y Crowell.

Endangered Predators. John Harris & Aleta Pahl. LC 75-34051. 96p. (gr. 4-7). 1976. PLB 6.95 (ISBN 0-385-08012-3). Doubleday.

Endangered Sector. Waldemar A. Nielsen. LC 79-15772. 1979. 15.00x (ISBN 0-231-04688-X). Columbia U Pr.

Endangered Species. Sandra Hochman. 1978. pap. 2.25 (ISBN 0-380-42366-9, 42366). Avon.

Endangered Species & Other Fables with a Twist. Fritz Eichenberg. LC 79-15247. (Illus.). 1979. 27.50 (ISBN 0-916144-42-9); pap. 14.95 (ISBN 0-916144-43-7). Stemmer Hse.

Endeavors in Psychology: Selections from the Personology of Henry A. Murray. Henry A. Murray. Ed. by Edwin S. Shneidman. LC 80-7598. 656p. 1981. 30.00 (ISBN 0-06-014039-9, HarpT). Har-Row.

Endeavors of Art: A Study of Form in Elizabethan Drama. Madeleine Doran. (Illus.). 1954. pap. text ed. 8.50x (ISBN 0-299-01084-8). U of Wis Pr.

Endemic Goitre & Thyroid Function in Central Africa. F. Delange. Ed. by F. Falkner et al. (Monographs in Pediatrics: Vol. 2). (Illus.). xvi, 160p. 1974. 44.50 (ISBN 3-8055-1687-8). S Karger.

Endgame. Samuel Beckett. Tr. by Samuel Beckett from Fr. 1958. pap. 2.45 (ISBN 0-394-17208-6, E96, Ever). Grove.

Endgame: The Inside Story of Salt II. Strobe Talbott. 288p. 1980. pap. 4.95 (ISBN 0-06-090809-2, CN 809, CN). Har-Row.

Endings & Beginnings: A Harvesting. Sandra H. Albertson. 1980. 8.95 (ISBN 0-394-50627-8). Random.

Endings: In Modern Theory & Practice. P. C. Griffiths. LC 76-46161. (Encore Edition). (Illus.). 1977. 3.95 o.p. (ISBN 0-684-16194-X, ScribT). Scribner.

Endless Dark: Stories of Underground Adventure. Compiled by Phyllis R. Fenner. LC 77-5494. (Illus.). (gr. 7 up). 1977. 8.25 (ISBN 0-688-22122-X); PLB 7.92 (ISBN 0-688-32122-4). Morrow.

Endless Life: The Selected Poems. Lawrence Ferlinghetti. 224p. 1981. 14.95 (ISBN 0-8112-0796-X, NDP516); pap. 4.95 (ISBN 0-8112-0797-8). New Directions.

Endless Love. Scott Spencer. 1980. pap. 2.75 (ISBN 0-686-69252-7, 50823). Avon.

Endless Party. Etienne Delessert. Tr. by Jeffrey Tabberner from Fr. Orig. Title: San Fin la Fete. (Illus.). 32p. (ps-3). 1981. 9.95 (ISBN 0-19-279753-0). Oxford U Pr.

Endlichen und Unendlichen Graphen. Denes Koenig. LC 51-3002. (Ger). 12.95 (ISBN 0-8284-0072-5). Chelsea Pub.

Endocardial Cushion Defects: Embryology, Anatomy & Angiography. Richard B. Towbin. 280p. 1981. 32.50 (ISBN 0-87527-252-5). Green.

Endocrine & Genetic Diseases of Childhood & Adolescence. Ed. by Lytt I. Gardner. LC 74-4561. (Illus.). 1404p. 1975. text ed. 75.00 o.p. (ISBN 0-7216-3991-7). Saunders.

Endocrine Aspects of Malnutrition: Marasmus, Kwashiorkor & Psychosocial Deprivation. Ed. by L. I. Gardner & P. Amacher. LC 73-88110. 1973. 27.00 (ISBN 0-685-48386-X). Raven.

Endocrine Control in Neoplasia. Ed. by Rameshwar K. Sharma & Wayne E. Criss. LC 77-72623. (Progress in Cancer Research & Therapy Ser.: Vol. 9). 1978. 41.00 (ISBN 0-89004-244-6). Raven.

Endocrine Control of Sexual Behavior. Ed. by Carlos Beyer. LC 78-24620. (Comprehensive Endocrinology Ser.). 1979. text ed. 39.00 (ISBN 0-89004-207-1). Raven.

Endocrine Emergencies. Robert S. Mecklenburg. LC 79-26132. 60p. (Orig.). 1978. pap. 5.00x (ISBN 0-9601944-2-8). MARC.

Endocrine Functions of the Brain. Ed. by Marcella Motta. (Comprehensive Endocrinology Ser.). 493p. 1980. text ed. 42.50 (ISBN 0-89004-343-4). Raven.

Endocrine Pathology. William H. Hartmann et al. LC 78-11793. (Anatomic Pathology Slide Seminar Proceedings Ser.). (Illus.). 1979. pap. text ed. 15.00 o.p. (ISBN 0-89189-054-8, 50-1-043-00); slides 84.00 o.p. (ISBN 0-686-67346-8, 01-0-077-01). Am Soc Clinical.

Endocrine Pathology: General & Surgical. 2nd ed. J. M. Bloodworth, Jr. (Illus.). 950p. 1981. write for info. (0854-4). Williams & Wilkins.

Endocrine Pharmacology: Physiological Basis & Theraputic Applications. P. J. Bentley. LC 79-19487. (Illus.). 700p. 1981. 75.00 (ISBN 0-521-22673-2). Cambridge U Pr.

Endocrine Rhythms: Comprehensive Endocrinology. Ed. by Dorothy T. Krieger. LC 77-75655. 1979. 34.50 (ISBN 0-89004-234-9). Raven.

Endocrine System: Disease, Diagnosis, Treatment. L. Wartofsky. (Clinical Monographs Ser.). (Illus.). 1973. pap. 7.95 (ISBN 0-87618-060-8). R J Brady.

Endocrinological Imaging. James H. Thrall. 280p. 1981. 25.00 (ISBN 0-87527-235-5). Green.

Endocrinology. Graham J. Goldworthy. LC 80-18704. 184p. 1981. 34.95 (ISBN 0-470-27034-9). Halsted Pr.

Endocrinology. David A. Ontjes & Louis E. Underwood. (Medical Examination Review Books: Vol. 33). 1975. spiral bdg. 16.50 (ISBN 0-87488-131-5). Med Exam.

Endocrinology: A Review of Clinical Endocrinology. Ed. by Ernest L. Mazzaferri. LC 79-91978. (Medical Outline Ser). 1980. pap. 18.50 (ISBN 0-87488-614-7). Med Exam.

Endocrinology Case Studies. 2nd ed. Ernest L. Mazzaferri & Thomas G. Skillman. 1975. spiral bdg. 14.00 (ISBN 0-87488-008-4). Med Exam.

Endocrinology in Anaesthesia & Surgery. H. Stoeckel & T. Omaya. (Anaesthesiology & Intensive Care Medicine Ser.: Vol. 132). (Illus.). 205p. 1981. pap. 55.60 (ISBN 0-387-10211-6). Springer-Verlag.

Endocrinology, Neuroendocrinology, Neuropeptides- Part 1: Proceedings of the 28th International Congress of Physiological Sciences, Budapest, 1980. Ed. by E. Stark et al. LC 80-42047. (Advances in Physiological Sciences: Vol. 13). (Illus.). 350p. 1981. 40.00 (ISBN 0-08-026827-7). Pergamon.

Endocrinology, Neuroendocrinology, Neuropeptides-Part II: Proceedings of the 28th International Congress of Physiological Sciences, Budapest, 1980. Ed. by E. Stark et al. LC 80-42046. (Advances in Physiological Sciences Ser.: Vol. 14). (Illus.). 350p. 1981. 40.00 (ISBN 0-08-026871-4). Pergamon.

Endocrinology of Calcium Metabolism. Ed. by John A. Parsons. (Comprehensive Endocrinology Ser.). 375p. 1981. 36.00 (ISBN 0-89004-344-2). Raven.

Endocrinology of Cancer, 2 vols. David P. Rose. 1979. Vol. 1, 160p. 49.95 (ISBN 0-8493-5337-8); Vol. 2, 160p. 49.95 (ISBN 0-8493-5338-6). CRC Pr.

Endocytosis & Exocytosis in Host Defence, Vol. 17. Ed. by L. Edebo. (Monographs in Allergy). (Illus.). 240p. 1981. pap. 78.00 (ISBN 3-8055-1865-X). S Karger.

Endodontic Therapy. 2nd ed. Franklin S. Weine. LC 75-38723. (Illus.). 1976. 37.50 (ISBN 0-8016-5382-7). Mosby.

Endogenous & Exogenous Opiate Agonists & Antagonists: Proceedings of the International Narcotic Club Conference, 11-15 June 1979, North Falmouth, Massachusetts, USA. Ed. by E. Leong Way. (Book Supplement to Pergamon Journal Life Sciences). (Illus.). 600p. 1980. 66.00 (ISBN 0-08-025488-8). Pergamon.

Endogenous Intellectual Creativity: Reflections on Some ETIC & EMIC Paradigms. 22p. 1980. pap. 5.00 (ISBN 92-808-0118-X, TUNU098, UNU). Unipub.

Endogenous Peptides & Centrally Acting Drugs. Ed. by A. Levy et al. (Progress in Biochemical Pharmacology Ser.: Vol. 16). (Illus.). 200p. 1980. 49.25 (ISBN 3-8055-0831-X). S Karger.

Endometrial Carcinoma & Its Treatment: The Role of Irradiation, Extent of Surgery & Approach to Chemotherapy. Laman A. Gray, Sr. (Illus.). 240p. 1977. 29.75 (ISBN 0-398-03608-X). C C Thomas.

Endometrium. W. B. Robertson. (Postgraduate Pathology Ser.). 1981. text ed. 52.95 (ISBN 0-407-00171-9). Butterworth.

Endorphins. Ed. by E. Costa & Marco Trabucchi. LC 77-18301. (Advances in Biochemical Psychopharmacology Ser.: Vol. 18). 1978. 35.00 (ISBN 0-89004-226-8). Raven.

Endoscopic Retrograde Cholangiopancreatography. Tadayoshi Takemoto. LC 78-78228. (Illus.). 1979. 69.75 (ISBN 0-89640-032-8). Igaku-Shoin.

Endoscopy. Berci. (Illus.). 1976. 84.50 o.p. (ISBN 0-8385-2216-5). ACC.

Endosseous Dental Implants. Taylor. (Illus.). 1970. 19.25 (ISBN 0-407-16770-6). Butterworths.

Endosymbiosis & Cell Research. Ed. by W. Schwemmler & H. Schenk. 900p. 1980. text ed. 107.00x (ISBN 3-11-008299-3). De Gruyter.

Ends of the Circle. Paul O. Williams. 208p. (Orig.). 1981. pap. 2.25 (ISBN 0-345-29551-X, Del Rey). Ballantine.

Ends of the Earth. Roy C. Andrews. LC 78-164078. (Towers Bks). (Illus.). x, 355p. 1972. Repr. of 1929 ed. 18.00 (ISBN 0-8103-3923-4). Gale.

Endurance Cars. Sylvia Wilkinson. (World of Racing Ser.). (Illus.). 48p. (gr. 4 up). 1981. PLB 9.25 (ISBN 0-516-04712-4). Childrens.

Endurance of Life. Macfarlane Burnet. 1976. LC 78-54323. (Illus.). 1978. 27.50 (ISBN 0-521-22114-5). Cambridge U Pr.

Endurance of Life. Macfarlane Burnet. (Illus.). 1980. pap. 8.95 (ISBN 0-521-29783-4). Cambridge U Pr.

Enduring Asylum: Cycles of Institutional Reform at Worcester State Hospital. Ed. by Joseph P. Morrissey et al. 1980. 31.50 (ISBN 0-8089-1291-7). Grune.

Enduring Ghetto: Sources & Readings. Ed. by David R. Goldfield & James B. Lane. 1973. pap. text ed. 3.95 o.p. (ISBN 0-397-47285-4). Lippincott.

Enduring Visions: One Thousand Years of Southwestern Indian Art. Ed. by Donnelley Erdman & Philip M. Holstein. LC 79-52784. (Illus.). 1979. pap. 12.95 (ISBN 0-934324-00-X, Pub. by Aspen Ctr Visual Arts). Pub Ctr Cult Res.

Eneas: A Twelfth-Century French Romance. Tr. by John A. Yunck from Fr. (Record of Civilization, Sources & Studies: No. 93). 272p. 1974. 12.50x (ISBN 0-231-03823-2). Columbia U Pr.

Enemies: A Love Story. Isaac B. Singer. 1977. pap. 2.95 (ISBN 0-449-24065-7, Crest). Fawcett.

Enemies of the System. Brian Aldiss. 112p. 1981. pap. 1.95 (ISBN 0-380-53793-1, 53793). Avon.

Enemies of the System: A Tale of Homo Uniformis. Brian Aldiss. LC 77-11541. 1978. 7.95 o.s.i. (ISBN 0-06-010054-0, HarpT). Har-Row.

Enemies Within. Michael Z. Lewin. 1979. pap. 1.75 o.p. (ISBN 0-425-04029-1). Berkley Pub.

Enemy. Desmond Bagley. LC 76-42058. 1978. 7.95 o.p. (ISBN 0-385-04873-4). Doubleday.

Enemy Coast Ahead. Guy Gibson. 1976. 9.95 o.p. (ISBN 0-7181-1519-8, Pub. by Michael Joseph). Merrimack Bk Serv.

Enemy in Camp. Jane T Dailey. (Harlequin Presents Ser.). 192p. 1980. pap. 1.50 (ISBN 0-373-10373-5, Pub. by Harlequin). PB.

Enemy in Sight. Bill Bragg. (Orig.). 1980. pap. 1.75 (ISBN 0-505-51530-X). Tower Bks.

Enemy in Sight. Alexander Kent. pap. 1.95 (ISBN 0-515-05375-9). Jove Pubns.

Enemy of the People. Stan Barstow. 1980. pap. 3.95 (ISBN 0-7145-3651-2). Riverrun NY.

Enemy Within. John Creasey. 1977. pap. 1.25 o.p. (ISBN 0-445-00454-1). Popular Lib.

Energi. Paul Williams. 1978. pap. 2.50 (ISBN 0-446-91955-1). Warner Bks.

Energi. Paul Williams. 1976. pap. 3.95 o.p. (ISBN 0-446-87250-4). Warner Bks.

Energie: Economie et Prospective. A. Gardel. LC 79-40986. (Illus.). 1979. 82.00 (ISBN 0-08-024782-2). Pergamon.

Energize with Isometric Quickies. Naomi Watson. LC 77-76947. (Illus., Orig.). 1977. 8.95 o.p. (ISBN 0-918766-06-0); pap. 4.95 (ISBN 0-918766-02-8). Butterfly Pr.

Energizing Your Investments. Venita VanCaspel. 1980. pap. 1.50 (ISBN 0-8359-1678-2). Reston.

Energy. Irving Adler. LC 71-10143. (Reason Why Ser). (Illus.). (gr. 3-6). 1970. PLB 7.89 (ISBN 0-381-99609-3, A23400, JD-J). John Day.

Energy. LC 19-600. 64p. 1978. pap. 0.70x (ISBN 0-8395-3335-7). BSA.

Energy, 3 vols. Incl. Vol. I. Demands Resources, Impact, Technology, & Policy. rev. ed. S. S. Penner & L. Icerman. 1974. 28.50 (ISBN 0-201-05572-4); pap. 16.50 (ISBN 0-201-05573-2); Vol. II. Non-Nuclear Energy Technologies. S. S. Penner & L. Icerman. 1975. 26.50 (ISBN 0-201-05568-6); pap. 16.50 (ISBN 0-201-05569-4); Vol. III. Nuclear Energy & Energy Policies. 1976. 29.50 (ISBN 0-201-05564-3); pap. 19.50 (ISBN 0-201-05565-1). (Illus., Adv Bk Prog). A-W.

Energy. Michael Kahan. 1981. 16.95 (ISBN 0-936278-00-5). Green Hill.

Energy. Eric Oatman. 1980. 5.75 o.p. (ISBN 0-8242-0646-0). Wilson.

Energy. rev. ed. Mitchell Wilson. LC 63-21614. (Life Science Library). (Illus.). (gr. 5 up). 1969. PLB 8.97 o.p. (ISBN 0-8094-0460-5, Pub. by Time-Life). Silver.

Energy--a Global Outlook: The Case for Effective International Co-operation. Hassan T. Abdulhadi. LC 80-41616. (Illus.). 300p. 1980. 40.00 (ISBN 0-08-027292-4); pap. 15.00 (ISBN 0-08-027293-2). Pergamon.

Energy- War: Breaking the Nuclear Links. Amory B. Lovins & L. H. Lovins. LC 80-8713. 228p. 1981. pap. 4.95 (ISBN 0-06-090852-1, CN 852, CN). Har-Row.

Energy: A Multimedia Guide for Children & Young Adults. Judith H. Higgins. LC 78-15611. (Selection Guide Ser.: No. 2). 195p. 1979. text ed. 16.50 (ISBN 0-87436-266-0, Co-Pub. by Neal-Schuman). ABC-Clio.

Energy: A National Issue. Francis X. Murray. LC 76-52878. (Illus.). 1976. pap. text ed. 3.95 (ISBN 0-89206-001-8). CSI Studies.

Energy: An Introduction to Physics. Robert H. Romer. LC 75-35591. (Illus.). 1976. 21.95x (ISBN 0-7167-0357-2); tchr's guide avail. W H Freeman.

Energy Analysis: A New Public Policy Tool. Ed. by Martha W. Gilliland. LC 77-15895. (AAAS Selected Symposium Ser.: No. 9). (Illus.). 1978. lib. bdg. 17.00x (ISBN 0-89158-437-4). Westview.

Energy Analysis & Agriculture: An Application to U.S. Corn Production. Vaclav Smil & Paul Nachman. (Special Studies in Agricultural Science & Policy). 175p. 1981. lib. bdg. 22.00x (ISBN 0-86531-167-6). Westview.

Energy & Agriculture. 302p. 1981. pap. 18.00 (ISBN 0-643-02654-1, CSIRO 56, CSIRO). Unipub.

Energy & Architecture: The Solar & Conservation Potential. Christopher Flavin. LC 80-54002. (Worldwatch Papers). 1980. pap. 2.00 (ISBN 0-916468-39-9). Worldwatch Inst.

Energy & Combustion Science: Selected Papers from Progress in Energy & Combustion Science. Ed. by N. A. Chigier. LC 79-40860. (Illus.). 1979. 41.00 (ISBN 0-08-024781-4); pap. 15.75 (ISBN 0-08-024780-6). Pergamon.

Energy & Economic Development in India. R. K. Pachauri. LC 77-12718. (Praeger Special Studies). 1977. 23.95 (ISBN 0-03-022371-7). Praeger.

Energy & Economic Growth in the United States. Edward L. Allen. 1979. text ed. 22.50x (ISBN 0-262-01062-3). MIT Pr.

Energy & Employment. Willis J. Nordlund & R. Thayne Robson. LC 79-22133. 1980. 20.95 (ISBN 0-03-055291-5). Praeger.

Energy & Environment: Readings from Scientific American. Commentary by Raymond Siever. LC 79-21980. (Illus.). 1980. text ed. 19.95x (ISBN 0-7167-1052-8); pap. text ed. 9.95x (ISBN 0-7167-1053-6). W H Freeman.

Energy & Environment: The Four Energy Crises. G. Tyler Miller, Jr. 1975. pap. text ed. 5.95x o.p. (ISBN 0-534-00407-5). Wadsworth Pub.

Energy & Environment: The Four Energy Crises. 2nd ed. G. Tyler Miller, Jr. 208p. 1980. pap. text ed. 7.95x (ISBN 0-534-00836-4). Wadsworth Pub.

Energy & Environmental Balance. Earl F. Murphy. (Pergamon Policy Studies). 1980. 36.00 (ISBN 0-08-025082-3). Pergamon.
Energy & Environmental Issues: The Making & Implementation of Public Policy Issues. Michael Steinman. LC 78-13871. 224p. 1979. 19.95 (ISBN 0-669-02699-9). Lexington Bks.
Energy & How We Lost It. Johnny Mitchell. LC 78-62621. 128p. 1979. 9.95 (ISBN 0-88415-431-9). Pacesetter Pr.
Energy & Materials in Three Sectors of the Economy: A Dynamic Model with Technological Change As an Endogenous Variable. Alfred L. Levinson. LC 78-75010. (Outstanding Dissertations on Energy Ser.). 1979. lib. bdg. 15.50 (ISBN 0-8240-3983-1). Garland Pub.
Energy & Order in the Poetry of Swift. A. B. England. LC 78-75200. 1980. 12.00 (ISBN 0-8387-2367-5). Bucknell U Pr.
Energy & People. Mark Diesendorf. LC 80-670075. 1980. pap. 11.95x (ISBN 0-909509-12-3, Pub. by Soc Res Sci). Intl Schol Bk Serv.
Energy & Power: A Scientific American Book. Scientific American Editors. LC 75-180254. (Illus.). 1971. pap. text ed. 7.95x (ISBN 0-7167-0938-4). W H Freeman.
Energy & Power in Your Community: How to Analyze Where It Comes from, How Much It Costs, & Who Controls It. Elizabeth Schaefer & Jim Benson. (Illus.). 140p. (Orig.). 1980. pap. text ed. 6.00 (ISBN 0-937786-03-9). Inst Ecological.
Energy & Resource Development of Continental Margins. Ed. by Teh Fu Yen & Don Walsh. LC 80-14813. (Illus.). 238p. 1980. 33.00 (ISBN 0-08-025127-7). Pergamon.
Energy & Security. David Deese & Joseph Nye. 1980. 14.50 (ISBN 0-88410-640-3). Ballinger Pub.
Energy & Security. Ed. by Gregory Treverton. LC 80-67838. (Adelphi Library: Vol. 1). 172p. 1980. text ed. 29.50 (ISBN 0-916672-71-9). Allanheld.
Energy & Society. Timothy J. Healy. (Illus.). 400p. 1976. pap. text ed. 10.95x (ISBN 0-87835-049-7). Boyd & Fraser.
Energy & Society: The Solar Nuclear Alternative. Secretariat for Futures Studies, Stockholm. 1980. 40.00 (ISBN 0-08-024758-X); pap. 18.00 (ISBN 0-08-024759-8). Pergamon.
Energy & the Atmosphere: A Physical-Chemical Approach. Ian M. Campbell. LC 76-57689. 1977. 50.75 (ISBN 0-471-99482-0); pap. 20.95 (ISBN 0-471-99481-2, Pub. by Wiley-Interscience). Wiley.
Energy & the Developing Nations. Ed. by Peter Auer. (Pergamon Policy Studies on Energy). (Illus.). 400p. 1981. 50.00 (ISBN 0-08-027527-3). Pergamon.
Energy & the Environment: Interactions, Vol. I, Pts. A & B. Louis Theodore et al. 1980. Pt. A, 208p. 57.95 (ISBN 0-8493-5562-1); Pt. B, 192p. 54.95 (ISBN 0-8493-5563-X). CRC Pr.
Energy & the Future. Milton Rothman. LC 74-11447. (Illus.). 128p. (gr. 7 up). 1975. PLB 5.90 o.p. (ISBN 0-531-02796-1). Watts.
Energy & the Imagination: A Study of the Development of Blake's Thought. Morton D. Paley. 1970. 27.00x (ISBN 0-19-811682-9). Oxford U Pr.
Energy & the Mitochondrion. David E. Green & Harold Baum. 1970. 12.95 (ISBN 0-12-297950-8). Acad Pr.
Energy & the National Defense. Howard Bucknell. Ed. by Vincent Davis. LC 79-57566. (Essays for the Third Century). 256p. 1981. 19.50 (ISBN 0-8131-0402-5). U Pr of Ky.
Energy & the Oceans. Andre Brin. 1981. pap. text ed. write for info. (ISBN 0-86103-024-9, Westbury Hse). Butterworth.
Energy & the Urban Environment. Ed. by Regina S. Axelrod. LC 79-3523. (Conflict & Resolution). (Illus.). 1981. write for info. (ISBN 0-669-03460-6). Lexington Bks.
Energy & the Way We Live. Ed. by Melvin Kranzberg et al. LC 79-25054. (Illus.). 520p. 1980. lib. bdg. 16.00x (ISBN 0-87835-092-6); pap. text ed. 7.95x (ISBN 0-87835-084-5); study guide 2.95x (ISBN 0-87835-089-6); pap. text bd. with study guide 9.95 (ISBN 0-87835-090-X). Boyd & Fraser.
Energy & War: Breaking the Nuclear Link. Amory B. Lovins & L. Hunter Lovins. 180p. 1980. 10.00 (ISBN 0-913890-44-8). Friends Earth.
Energy & Water Use Forecasting. American Water Works Association. (AWWA Handbooks-General Ser.). (Illus.). 104p. 1980. pap. text ed. 10.00 (ISBN 0-89867-236-8). Am Water Wks Assn.
Energy & World Politics. Mason Willrich. LC 75-12058. 1978. pap. text ed. 7.95 (ISBN 0-02-935800-0). Free Pr.
Energy Aspects of the Forest Industries: Proceedings of a Seminar Organized by the Timber Committee of the United Nations Economic Commission for Europe, Udine, Italy 13-17 Nov. 1978. Ed. by United Nations Economic Commission for Europe, Geneva, Switzerland. LC 79-42869. (Illus.). 428p. 1979. 63.00 (ISBN 0-08-025661-9). Pergamon.
Energy at the Surface of the Earth. David H. Miller. 1981. 49.50 (ISBN 0-12-497150-4). Acad Pr.
Energy Auditing & Conservation: Methods, Measurement, Management, & Case Studies. Ed. by Yacov Y. Haimes. LC 79-23048. 261p. 1980. pap. text ed. 22.95 (ISBN 0-89116-175-9). Hemisphere Pub.
Energy Balances in the Production & End-Use of Alcohols Derived from Biomass. TRW - Energy Systems Planning Division. 125p. 1981. pap. 15.00 (ISBN 0-89934-116-0). Solar Energy Info.
Energy Balances of OECD Countries, 1974 to 1978. Organization for Economic Cooperation & Development & IEA. 166p. (Orig., Eng. & Fr.). 1980. pap. 9.00x (ISBN 92-64-02056-X, 6180013). OECD.
Energy Band Theory. Joseph Callaway. (Pure and Applied Physics: Vol. 16). 1964. 44.00 o.s.i. (ISBN 0-12-155250-0). Acad Pr.
Energy Basis for Man & Nature. 2nd ed. Howard T. Odum & Elisabeth C. Odum. (Illus.). 352p. 1981. text ed. 19.50 (ISBN 0-07-047511-3, C); pap. text ed. 12.95 (ISBN 0-07-047510-5, C); instrs'. manual avail. McGraw.
Energy Bibliography & Index, Vol. 3. Texas A & M University Library. 1400p. 1980. 295.00 (ISBN 0-87201-975-6). Gulf Pub.
Energy Bibliography & Index, Vol. 4. Texas A & M University Library. 1400p. 1981. 295.00 (ISBN 0-87201-284-0). Gulf Pub.
Energy Changes in Biochemical Reactions. Irving M. Klotz. (Orig.). 1967. pap. text ed. 7.95 (ISBN 0-12-416260-6). Acad Pr.
Energy Choices in a Democratic Society. Consumption, Location, & Occupational Patterns Resource Group Synthesis Panel of the Committee on Nuclear & Alternative Energy Systems. LC 80-81335. (Study of Nuclear & Alternative Energy Systems Ser.). xvii, 136p. 1980. pap. text ed. 6.50 (ISBN 0-309-03045-5). Natl Acad Pr.
Energy Cogeneration Handbook: Criteria for Central Plant Design. George Polimeros. 264p. 1981. 39.50 (ISBN 0-8311-1130-5). Indus Pr.
Energy Conservation & Economic Growth. Ed. by Charles J. Hitch. (AAAS Selected Symposium: No. 22). (Illus.). 1978. lib. bdg. 20.00x (ISBN 0-89158-354-8). Westview.
Energy Conservation & Energy Management in Buildings. Ed. by A. F. Sherratt. (Illus.). 1976. text ed. 74.50x (ISBN 0-85334-684-4, Pub. by Applied Science). Burgess-Intl Ideas.
Energy Conservation & Home Improvement, E-024. Business Communications Staff. 1977. 525.00 o.p. (ISBN 0-89336-021-X). BCC.
Energy Conservation & Home Improvements, E-024. Ed. by Business Communications. 1980. cancelled (ISBN 0-89336-214-X, E-024). BCC.
Energy Conservation & Use of Renewable Energies in the Bio-Industries: Proceedings of the International Seminar on Energy Conservation & the Use of Solar & Other Renewable Energies in Agriculture, Horticulture & Fishculture, 15-19 September, 1980, Polytechnic of Central London. Ed. by Frederick Vogt. LC 80-49739. (Illus.). 580p. 1981. 100.00 (ISBN 0-08-026866-8). Pergamon.
Energy Conservation & Use of Solar & Other Renewable Energy: Proceedings. Ed. by Frederick Vogt. (Illus.). 580p. 1981. 100.00 (ISBN 0-08-026866-8). Pergamon.
Energy Conservation Idea Handbook. 171p. (Orig.). 1980. pap. 12.00 (ISBN 0-89492-047-2). Acad Educ Dev.
Energy Conservation in Building Heating & Air Conditioning Systems. Ed. by R. Gopal. 1978. 18.00 (ISBN 0-685-66798-7, H00116). ASME.
Energy Conservation in the Built Environment. Ed. by R. G. Courtney. 1978. text ed. 60.00x (ISBN 0-904406-28-8). Longman.
Energy Conservation in Transportation. (Energy Reference Library Ser.: No. 2). (Illus.). Date not set. Repr. of 1979 ed. 18.00 (ISBN 0-8103-1023-6). Gale.
Energy Conservation: Proceedings of the Energy Research & Development Administration Conference Held at the University of Miami, Dec. 1975. Ed. by T. Nejat Veziroglu. 1977. pap. text ed. 110.00 (ISBN 0-08-022134-3). Pergamon.
Energy Conservation: Psychological Perspectives. Ed. by Andrew Baum & Jerome E. Singer. (Advances in Environmental Psychology Ser.: Vol. 3). 224p. 1981. text ed. 19.95 (ISBN 0-89859-063-9). L Erlbaum Assocs.
Energy Conservation Through Waste Utilization: Proceedings of the ASME National Waste Conference, 1978. 1978. 90.00 o.p. (ISBN 0-685-37578-1). ASME.
Energy Consumption & Conservation. Gary Hammerstrom. (Learning Packages in Policy Issues: No. 2). (Illus.). 58p. (Orig.). 1977. pap. text ed. 3.00 (ISBN 0-936826-11-8). Pol Stud Assocs.
Energy Consumption in Manufacturing. John G. Myers et al. LC 74-8111. (Ford Foundation Energy Policy Project Ser.). 736p. 1974. text ed. 40.00 (ISBN 0-88410-307-2); pap. text ed. 25.00 o.s.i. (ISBN 0-88410-323-4). Ballinger Pub.
Energy: Conversion & Utilization. Jerrold H. Krenz. 448p. 1976. text ed. 23.95x (ISBN 0-205-05421-8). Allyn.
Energy Conversion: Electromechanical, Direct, Nuclear. Edward M. Walsh. (Illus.). 1967. 21.95 (ISBN 0-8260-9125-3). Wiley.
Energy Conversion Engineering. Richard C. Bailie. LC 78-11969. (Ser. of Graduate Textbooks, Monographs & Research Papers). (Illus.). 1978. text ed. 21.50 (ISBN 0-201-00840-8). A-W.
Energy Couple. D. Q. Corey & J. P. Maas. (Illus.). 160p. 1980. 9.95 (ISBN 0-398-03964-X). C C Thomas.
Energy Crisis. Tad Szulc. LC 74-17335. 160p. 1974. PLB 7.45 (ISBN 0-531-02752-X). Watts.
Energy Crisis, Vol. 4. Ed. by Lester A. Sobel. 1980. lib. bdg. 17.50 (ISBN 0-87196-284-5). Facts on File.
Energy Crisis & the Environment: An International Perspective. Ed. by Donald R. Kelley. LC 76-24355. (Praeger Special Studies). 1977. text ed. 29.95 (ISBN 0-275-23850-4). Praeger.
Energy Crisis & U. S. Foreign Policy. Ed. by Joseph S. Szyliowicz & Bard E. O'Neill. LC 74-3140. (Special Studies). (Illus.). 280p. 1975. text ed. 31.50 (ISBN 0-275-09040-X); pap. text ed. 11.95 (ISBN 0-275-88840-1). Praeger.
Energy Crisis: Nineteen Seventy-Seven to Nineteen Seventy-Nine, Vol. 4. Ed. by Lester A. Sobel. 1980. lib. bdg. 17.50 (ISBN 0-87196-284-5). Facts on File.
Energy Demand Vs. Supply. Ed. by Diana Reische. (Reference Shelf Ser: Vol. 47, No. 5). 1975. 6.25 (ISBN 0-8242-0573-1). Wilson.
Energy Development in the Southwest: Problems of Water, Fish & Wildlife in the Upper Colorado River Basin. Ed. by Walter O. Spofford, Jr. et al. LC 80-8020. (Resources for the Future Research Ser.: Paper R-18). 1980. Set Of 2 Vols. pap. text ed. 25.00x (ISBN 0-8018-2495-8). Johns Hopkins.
Energy Development in the Western United States: Impact on Rural Areas. Steven H. Murdock & F. Larry Leistritz. LC 79-18478. 384p. 1979. 32.95 (ISBN 0-03-051351-0). Praeger.
Energy Devices & Processes: Proceedings of a Workshop on the Second Law of Thermodynamics, Held at the George Washington University, Wash. D. C., 14-16 Aug. 1979. Ed. by A. B. Cambel. 300p. 1980. pap. 60.00 (ISBN 0-08-026704-1). Pergamon.
Energy, Ecology & the Environment. Richard Wilson & William Jones. 353p. 1974. 10.95 (ISBN 0-12-757550-2). Acad Pr.
Energy, Economic Growth, & Equity in the U. S. Narisimhan P. Kannan. LC 78-31204. (Praeger Special Studies). 1979. 23.95 (ISBN 0-03-046616-4). Praeger.
Energy Economics. Samuel M. Dix. Date not set. 25.00 (ISBN 0-918998-05-0). Energy Educ. Postponed.
Energy Economics & Policy. James M. Griffin & Henry B. Steele. 1980. text ed. 18.95 (ISBN 0-12-303950-9). Acad Pr.
Energy Economics: Growth, Resources & Policies. R. J. Eden et al. (Illus.). 445p. Date not set. 34.95 (ISBN 0-521-23685-1). Cambridge U Pr.
Energy: Economy & Prospective: A Handbook for Engineers & Economists. A. Gardel. (Illus.). 480p. 1981. 82.00 (ISBN 0-08-025427-6). Pergamon.
Energy Economy in Design. Ranjit Banerji. LC 77-13289. 1979. lib. bdg. 16.00 (ISBN 0-88275-621-4). Krieger.
Energy Education: Goals & Practices. Rodney F. Allen. LC 79-93115. (Fastback Ser.: No. 139). (Orig.). 1980. pap. 0.75 (ISBN 0-87367-139-2). Phi Delta Kappa.
Energy Efficiency in Industry. Norman L. Dean. 1980. 30.00 (ISBN 0-88410-056-1). Ballinger Pub.
Energy Efficient Building Handbook. 1981. 45.00 (ISBN 0-89336-283-2). BCC.
Energy-Efficient Buildings. Architectural Record Magazine. Ed. by Walter F. Wagner, Jr. & Architectural Record. (Architectural Record Book). (Illus.). 256p. 1980. 22.95 (ISBN 0-07-002344-1). McGraw.
Energy Efficient Purchasing: A Guide for Local Governments. Richard M. Gecoma et al. 75p. 1980. pap. 7.50 (ISBN 0-89854-064-X). U of GA Inst Govt.
Energy, Environment & Building. P. Steadman. LC 74-21715. (Urban & Architectural Studies: No. 3). (Illus.). 294p. 1975. 36.00 (ISBN 0-521-20694-4); pap. 11.95x (ISBN 0-521-09926-9). Cambridge U Pr.
Energy, Environment, Population & Food: Our Four Interdependent Crises. George L. Tuve. LC 76-40351. 1976. 29.95 (ISBN 0-471-02091-5, Pub. by Wiley-Interscience); pap. 13.50 (ISBN 0-471-02090-7). Wiley.
Energy-Environment Source Book. rev. ed. John M. Fowler. 1978. pap. 5.00 o.p. (ISBN 0-686-53816-1, 471-14692). Natl Sci Tchrs.
Energy Ethics: A Christian Response. Ed. by Dieter T. Hessel. (Orig.). 1979. pap. 4.25 (ISBN 0-377-00094-9). Friend Pr.
Energy Fact Book, 1976. Ed. by Theodore F. Watts. LC 75-45508. (Illus.). 200p. 1976. 8.95 (ISBN 0-916646-00-9); pap. 4.95 (ISBN 0-916646-01-7). Tetra Tech.
Energy Factbook 1980-1981. Richard C. Dorf. 1980. 16.95 (ISBN 0-07-017623-X); pap. 7.95 (ISBN 0-07-017629-9). McGraw.
Energy Flow & Power Factor in Nonsinusoidal Circuits. W. Shepherd & P. Zand. LC 78-51684. (Illus.). 1979. 59.50 (ISBN 0-521-21990-6). Cambridge U Pr.
Energy for Developed & Developing Countries: Proceedings. Center for Theoretical Studies. Ed. by Behram Kursunogl & Arnold Perlmutter. 1981. price not set (ISBN 0-88410-634-9). Ballinger Pub.
Energy for Industry. Ed. by P. W. O'Callaghan. LC 78-41102. (Illus.). 1979. text ed. 75.00 (ISBN 0-08-022704-X). Pergamon.
Energy for Life: Photosynthesis & Respiration. Betty D. Allamong & Thomas R. Mertens. LC 76-10181. (Self-Teaching Guides Ser.). 1976. pap. text ed. 4.95 o.p. (ISBN 0-471-02263-2). Wiley.
Energy for Man. Hans Thirring. 1976. pap. 7.50x (ISBN 0-06-131861-2, TB 1861, Torch). Har-Row.
Energy for Survival. Ed. by Harry Messel. (Illus.). 368p. 1979. 38.00 (ISBN 0-08-024794-6); pap. 15.00 (ISBN 0-08-024791-1). Pergamon.
Energy for Survival: The Alternative to Extinction. Wilson Clark. LC 72-89297. (Illus.). 672p. 1974. 12.50 o.p. (ISBN 0-385-03501-2, Anchor Pr). Doubleday.
Energy for Survival: The Alternative to Extinction. Wilson Clark. LC 72-89297. 672p. 1975. pap. 5.95 (ISBN 0-385-03564-0). Doubleday.
Energy from Biological Processes. Office of Technology Assessment. 205p. 1981. lib. bdg. 34.50 (ISBN 0-89934-090-3); pap. 22.50 (ISBN 0-89934-107-1). Solar Energy Info.
Energy from Biological Processes. Office of Technology Assessment, U.S. Congress. 200p. 1981. lib. bdg. 20.00x (ISBN 0-86531-171-4). Westview.
Energy from Biological Processes, Vol. 2. Office of Technology Assessment. Date not set. lib. bdg. price not set (ISBN 0-89934-119-5); pap. price not set (ISBN 0-89934-120-9). Solar Energy Info.
Energy from Biomass in Europe. Ed. by W. Palz & P. Chartier. (Illus.). xii, 248p. 1981. 35.00x (ISBN 0-85334-934-7). Intl Ideas.
Energy from Heaven & Earth. Edward Teller. LC 79-4049. (Illus.). 1979. text ed. 17.95x (ISBN 0-7167-1063-3); pap. text ed. 9.95x (ISBN 0-7167-1064-1). W H Freeman.
Energy: From Opulence to Sufficiency. Jerrold H. Krenz. LC 79-15059. 24.95 (ISBN 0-03-057001-8). Praeger.
Energy: From Surplus to Scarcity? Ed. by K. A. Inglis. LC 73-22112. (Illus.). 242p. 1974. 29.95 (ISBN 0-470-42731-0). Halsted Pr.
Energy from the Sun. Melvin Berger. LC 75-33310. (Let's-Read-&-Find-Out Bk). (Illus.). 40p. (gr. k-3). 1976. PLB 7.89 (ISBN 0-690-01056-7, TYC-J). T Y Crowell.
Energy from the Waves. D. Ross. (Illus.). 1979. text ed. 23.00 (ISBN 0-08-023271-X); pap. text ed. 8.25 (ISBN 0-686-67668-8). Pergamon.
Energy from the Waves. 2nd rev. ed. D. Ross. LC 80-41076. (Illus.). 160p. 1981. 21.00 (ISBN 0-08-026715-7); pap. 9.00 (ISBN 0-686-68875-9). Pergamon.
Energy from the West: A Technology Assessment of Western Energy Resource Development. University of Oklahoma Science & Public Policy Program. LC 80-5936. (Illus.). 500p. 1981. 25.00 (ISBN 0-8061-1750-8); pap. 9.95 (ISBN 0-8061-1751-6). U of Okla Pr.
Energy Future: The Report of the Energy Project at the Harvard Business School. Ed. by Robert Stobaugh & Daniel Yergin. 1980. pap. 2.95 (ISBN 0-345-29349-5). Ballantine.
Energy Futures of Developing Countries: The Neglected Victims of the Energy Crisis. Ed. by Harlan Cleveland. 1980. 19.95 (ISBN 0-03-058669-0). Praeger.

Energy, Heating & Thermal Comfort. Building Research Establishment. (Building Research Ser.: Vol. 4). 1979. 38.00 (ISBN 0-904406-99-7). Longman.

Energy: Hydrocarbon Fuels & Chemical Resources. Don K. Rider. 600p. 1981. 40.00 (ISBN 0-471-05915-3, Pub. by Wiley-Interscience). Wiley.

Energy in a Finite World: Vol. I: Paths to a Sustainable Future. Ed. by Wolf Hafele. 296p. 1981. 16.50 (ISBN 0-88410-641-1). Ballinger Pub.

Energy in a Finite World: Vol. II: Global Systems Analysis. Ed. by Wolf Hafele. 826p. 1981. reference 45.00 (ISBN 0-88410-642-X). Ballinger Pub.

Energy in America: Fifteen Views. Ed. by Center for the Study of the American Experience. 300p. 1981. 22.50 (ISBN 0-88474-103-6). Transaction Bks.

Energy in Australia. Hugh Saddler. 215p. 1981. text ed. 19.95x (ISBN 0-86861-298-7, 2646). Allen Unwin.

Energy in Evolution: Teilhard's Physics of the Future. John O'Manique. (Teilhard Study Library). 1969. text ed. 4.00x (ISBN 0-900391-23-5). Humanities.

Energy in Perspective. Jerry B. Marion. 1974. 9.95 (ISBN 0-12-472275-X). Acad Pr.

Energy in the Balance. Ed. by British Association for the Advancement of Science. 260p. 1980. pap. text ed. 23.40 (ISBN 0-86103-031-1). Butterworths.

Energy in the City Environment. Ed. by N. Y. Board of Trade & Robert Rickles. LC 72-96106. 200p. 1973. 12.50 o.p. (ISBN 0-8155-5019-7, NP). Noyes.

Energy in the Developing World: The Real Energy Crisis. Ed. by V. Smil & W. E. Knowland. 394p. 1980. 74.00x (ISBN 0-19-854425-1); pap. 34.95x (ISBN 0-19-854421-9). Oxford U Pr.

Energy in Transition: A Report on Energy Policy & Future Options. Mans Lonnroth & Peter Steen. 1980. 10.95 (ISBN 0-520-03881-9). U of Cal Pr.

Energy in Transition, Nineteen Eighty-Five to Two Thousand Ten. Committee on Nuclear & Alternative Energy Systems, National Research Council & National Academy of Sciences. LC 79-27389. (Illus.). 1980. text ed. 25.95x (ISBN 0-7167-1227-X); pap. 12.95x (ISBN 0-7167-1228-8). W H Freeman.

Energy Index Nineteen Eighty. Ed. by Monica Pronin. LC 73-89098. 600p. 1981. 135.00 (ISBN 0-89947-010-6). Environ Info.

Energy, Inflation & International Economic Relations: Atlantic Institute Studies - Two. Curt Gasteyger et al. LC 75-19764. (Special Studies). (Illus.). 256p. 1975. text ed. 24.95 (ISBN 0-275-01250-6). Praeger.

Energy: International Cooperation or Crisis. Aktoine Ayoub. 272p. 1980. pap. 20.00x (ISBN 0-686-63152-8, Pub. by Laval). Intl Schol Bk Serv.

Energy Issues & Alliance Relationships: The United States, Western Europe and Japan. Robert L. Pfaltzgraff, Jr. LC 80-81711. (Special Reports). 72p. 1980. 6.50 (ISBN 0-89549-019-6). Inst Foreign Policy Anal.

Energy Losses & Ion Ranges in Solids. M. Kumakhov. 1981. cancelled (ISBN 3-7186-0059-5). Harwood Academic.

Energy Losses & Ion Ranges in Solids. M. Kumakhov & F. Komarov. 400p. 1981. price not set (ISBN 0-677-21220-8). Gordon.

Energy Management. Henry & Symonds. 352p. 1980. 23.50. Dekker.

Energy Managers' Handbook. 2nd ed. Gordon Payne. 1980. text ed. 25.00 (ISBN 0-86103-032-X); pap. text ed. 19.50 (ISBN 0-86103-033-8). Butterworths.

Energy Metabolism. Laurence E. Mount. LC 80-40265. (Studies in the Agricultural & Food Sciences). (Illus.). 416p. 1980. text ed. 79.95 (ISBN 0-408-10641-7). Butterworths.

Energy Methods in Applied Mechanics. Henry L. Langhaar. LC 62-10925. 1962. 28.95 (ISBN 0-471-51711-9, Pub. by Wiley-Interscience). Wiley.

Energy Methods in Stress Analysis. T. H. Richards. LC 79-29647. (Engineering Science Ser.). 410p. 1980. pap. 26.95 (ISBN 0-470-27068-3). Halsted Pr.

Energy Methods in Stress Analysis: With an Introduction to Finite Element Techniques. T. H. Richards. (Ellis Horwood Series in Engineering Science). 1977. 58.95 (ISBN 0-470-98960-2). Halsted Pr.

Energy Momentum Tensors. Robert Hermann. (Interdisciplinary Mathematics Ser: No. 4). 153p. 1973. 11.00 (ISBN 0-915692-03-1). Math Sci Pr.

Energy of Slaves. Leonard Cohen. LC 72-75749. 192p. 1973. pap. 2.95 o.s.i. (ISBN 0-670-00376-X). Penguin.

Energy Options: Real Economics & the Solar-Hydrogen System. John O. Bockris. 441p. 1980. 32.95x (ISBN 0-470-26915-4). Halsted Pr.

Energy Philosophy: A System of Self-Mastery & Increased Personal Energy. Roy Jorgensen. LC 80-83506. (Illus.). 260p. (Orig.). 1980. pap. 7.95 (ISBN 0-938226-01-0). Pacific Edns.

Energy Picture: Problems & Prospects. Ed. by Joseph E. Pluta. LC 80-68659. 185p. 1980. pap. 6.00. U of Tex Busn Res.

Energy Plant Sites: Community Planning for Large Projects. David Myhra. Ed. by McKinley Conway & L. L. Liston. LC 79-54253. (Illus.). 1980. pap. 35.00x (ISBN 0-910436-13-4). Conway Pubns.

Energy Policy & Forecasting: Economic, Financial, & Technological Dimensions. Glenn R. DeSouza. LC 79-9671. (Arthur D. Little Bk.). 1980. write for info. (ISBN 0-669-03614-5). Lexington Bks.

Energy Policy for India. Ed. by Rajendra K. Pachauri. 1980. 22.50x (ISBN 0-8364-0620-6, Pub by Macmillan India). South Asia Bks.

Energy Policy for the Manufacturing Sector. 155p. 1980. pap. 13.25 (ISBN 92-833-1459-X, APO 90, APO). Unipub.

Energy Policy in Iran: Domestic Choices & International Implications. Bijan Mossavar-Rahmane. LC 80-27995. (PPS on Science & Technnology Ser.). (Illus.). 160p. 1981. 15.00 (ISBN 0-08-026293-7). Pergamon.

Energy Policy in Perspective: Today's Problems, Yesterday's Solution. Ed. by Craufurd D. Goodwin. LC 80-22859. 600p. 1980. 29.95 (ISBN 0-8157-3202-3); pap. 14.95 (ISBN 0-8157-3201-5). Brookings.

Energy Policy in the United States: Social & Behavioral Dimensions. Seymour Warkov. LC 78-8454. (Praeger Special Studies). 1978. 26.50 (ISBN 0-03-043486-6). Praeger.

Energy Policy: Strategies for Uncertainty. P. Lesley Cook & A. John Surrey. 240p. 1977. 36.00x (ISBN 0-85520-213-0, Pub. by Martin Robertson England). Biblio Dist.

Energy Policy: The Global Challenge. Peter N. Nemetz. 1979. pap. text ed. 20.50x (ISBN 0-920380-30-1, Pub. by Inst Res Pub Canada). Renouf.

Energy Potential: Toward a New Electromagnetic Field Theory. Carol White. Tr. by James Cleary. 1978. pap. 7.95 (ISBN 0-918388-04-X, QC665.E4W45, Univ Edns). New Benjamin.

Energy: Power for People. Laurence Pringle. (Science for Survival Ser.). (Illus.). 128p. (gr. 7 up). 1975. 9.95 (ISBN 0-02-775330-1). Macmillan.

Energy Prices, Inflation, & Economic Activity. Ed. by Knut A. Mork. 1980. reference 22.50 (ISBN 0-88410-691-8). Ballinger Pub.

Energy Principles in Structural Mechanics. Theodore R. Tauchert. 394p. 1981. Repr. of 1974 ed. lib. bdg. price not set (ISBN 0-89874-309-5). Krieger.

Energy: Proceedings. Gas Dynamics Symposium - 7th Biennial - 1968. Ed. by Lawrence B. Holmes. 1968. 12.75x o.s.i. (ISBN 0-8101-0123-8). Northwestern U Pr.

Energy R & D Decision Making for Canada. Karen Hartley. 108p. 1979. pap. text ed. 3.00x (ISBN 0-920380-40-9, Pub. by Inst Res Pub Canada). Renouf.

Energy: Readings from Scientific American. Intro. by S. Fred Singer. LC 78-31979. (Illus.). 1979. text ed. 17.95x (ISBN 0-7167-1082-X); pap. text ed. 8.95x (ISBN 0-7167-1083-8). W H Freeman.

Energy Reference Handbook. 3rd ed. Ed. by Thomas F. Sullivan & Martin L. Heavner. LC 80-84728. 400p. 1981. 28.50 (ISBN 0-86587-082-9). Gov Insts.

Energy Regulation by the Federal Power Commission. Stephen G. Breyer & Paul W. MacAvoy. LC 74-273. (Studies in the Regulation of Economic Activity). 163p. 1974. 10.95 (ISBN 0-8157-1076-3). Brookings.

Energy Research & Development Programme, 2 vols. in one. Commission of the European Communities, Brussels, Belgium. 1979. lib. bdg. 121.05 (ISBN 90-247-2220-9, Martinus Nijhoff Pubs). Kluwer Boston.

Energy Research, Development, & Demonstration in the IEA Countries: 1979 Review of National Programmes. OECD-IEA. (Illus.). 153p. (Orig.). 1980. pap. text ed. 12.00x (ISBN 92-64-12067-X, 61-80-03-1). OECD.

Energy Research Guide. Newell B. Mack et al. 1981. write for info (ISBN 0-88410-097-9). Ballinger Pub.

Energy Research Programs. Ed. by Jaques Cattell Press. 450p. 1981. 75.00 (ISBN 0-8352-1352-8). Bowker.

Energy Research Programs Directory. Ed. by Jaques Cattell Press. 944p. 1980. 75.00 (ISBN 0-8352-1242-4). Bowker.

Energy Reserves & Supplies in the ECE Region. 74p. 1980. pap. 7.00 (ISBN 0-686-68953-4, UN79/2E24, UN). Unipub.

Energy Resources. J. R. McMullan et al. (Resource & Environmental Science Ser.). 1978. pap. text ed. 9.95 (ISBN 0-470-99377-4). Halsted Pr.

Energy Resources. Andrew L. Simon. LC 74-28320. 176p. 1975. text ed. 23.00 (ISBN 0-08-018750-1); pap. text ed. 13.25 (ISBN 0-08-018751-X). Pergamon.

Energy Resources & Conservation Related to Built Environment: Proceedings of the International Conference, Dec. 7-12, 1980, Miami Beach, Florida, 2 vols. Ed. by Oktay Ural. (Pergamon Policy Studies on International Development). 1290p. 1981. Set. 150.00 (ISBN 0-08-027170-7). Pergamon.

Energy, Resources & Policy. Richard C. Dorf. LC 76-45151. 1978. text ed. 18.95 (ISBN 0-201-01673-7); instr's guide 2.50 (ISBN 0-201-01674-5). A-W.

Energy Resources Recovery in Arid Lands. Ed. by Klaus D. Timmerhaus. (Illus.). 200p. 1981. price not set (ISBN 0-8263-0582-2); pap. price not set (ISBN 0-8263-0583-0). U of NM Pr.

Energy Saver's Cookbook. Marina Polvay. (Creative Cooking Ser.). (Illus.). 320p. 1980. 19.95 (ISBN 0-13-277616-2, Spec); pap. 9.95 (ISBN 0-13-277608-1). P-H.

Energy Saving Decorating. new ed. Judy Lindahl. (Illus.). 128p. (Orig.). 1981. pap. 4.95 (ISBN 0-9603032-3-5). Lindahl.

Energy Saving Devices for Residential & Commercial E-037. 1980. 775.00 (ISBN 0-89336-252-2). BCC.

Energy Saving Guide: Tables for Assessing the Profitability of Energy Saving Measures with Explanatory Notes and Worked Examples. Published for the Commission of the European Communities. G. Helcke. LC 80-41528. 230p. 1981. 45.00 (ISBN 0-08-026738-6); pap. 15.50 (ISBN 0-08-026739-4). Pergamon.

Energy Saving Ideas for Mobile Equipment Designers. Society of Automotive Engineers. 1980. 12.00 (ISBN 0-89883-240-3). Soc Auto Engineers.

Energy-Saving Projects. Sunset Editors. LC 80-53485. (Illus.). 96p. (Orig.). 1981. pap. 3.95 (ISBN 0-376-01230-7, Sunset Bks.). Sunset-Lane.

Energy-Saving Projects for the Home. William A. Henkin. Ed. by Ortho Books Editorial Staff. LC 80-66348. (Illus.). 112p. (Orig.). 1981. pap. 5.95 (ISBN 0-917102-86-X, Ortho Bks). Chevron Chem.

Energy Savings Devices for Residential & Commercial E-037. 1979. 600.00 o.p. (ISBN 0-89336-193-3). BCC.

Energy Shock: After the Oil Runs Out. Lawrence Solomon. LC 80-1072. 224p. 1981. 17.95 (ISBN 0-385-17160-9); pap. 9.95 (ISBN 0-385-17161-7). Doubleday.

Energy: Sources of Power. Anthony E. Schwaller. LC 79-57017. (Technology Series). (Illus.). 446p. 1980. text ed. 15.95 (ISBN 0-87192-122-7, 000-4). Davis Pubns.

Energy: Sources of Print & Nonprint Materials. Ed. by Maureen Crowley. LC 79-26574. (Neal-Schuman Sourcebook Ser.). 341p. 1980. 19.95x (ISBN 0-918212-16-2). Neal-Schuman.

Energy Statistics: A Guide to Information Sources. Ed. by Sarojini Balachandran. LC 80-13338. (Natural World Information Guide Ser.: Vol. 1). 272p. 1980. 30.00 (ISBN 0-8103-1419-3). Gale.

Energy Storage. Johannes Jensen. (Illus.). 1979. text ed. 19.95 (ISBN 0-408-00390-1). Butterworths.

Energy Storage: Transactions of the First International Assembly on Energy Storage, Held in Dubrovnik, Yugoslavia, 1979. Ed. by J. Silverman. LC 80-40771. (Illus.). 512p. 1980. 100.00 (ISBN 0-08-025471-3). Pergamon.

Energy Syndrome: Comparing National Responses to the Energy Crisis. Leon N. Lindberg. LC 76-6772. (Illus.). 1977. 17.95 (ISBN 0-669-00662-9). Lexington Bks.

Energy Systems in the United States. Amr et al. Date not set. price not set (ISBN 0-8247-1275-7). Dekker.

Energy Systems of Extended Endurance in the 1-100 Kilowatt Range for Undersea Applications. National Academy Of Sciences. 1968. 5.75 (ISBN 0-309-01702-5). Natl Acad Pr.

Energy Systems: Solar, Wind, Water, Geothermal. James R. Critser, Jr. (Ser. 11-78). 1979. 125.00 (ISBN 0-914428-58-6). Lexington Data.

Energy Systems: Solar, Wind, Water, Geothermal. James R. Critser, Jr. (Ser. 11-77). 1978. 125.00 (ISBN 0-914428-47-0). Lexington Data.

Energy Systems: Solar, Wind, Water, Geothermal. James R. Critser, Jr. (Ser. 11-79). 1981. 125.00 (ISBN 0-914428-70-5). Lexington Data.

Energy Technology & Global Policy: A Selection of Contributing Papers to the Conference on Energy Policies & the International System. Ed. by Stephen Arthur Saltzman. LC 76-49648. 276p. 1977. text ed. 21.15 (ISBN 0-87436-243-1). ABC-Clio.

Energy Technology: Expanding Energy Supplies, Vol. VII. Ed. by Richard F. Hill. LC 80-66431. (Illus.). 1400p. 1980. pap. text ed. 45.00 (ISBN 0-86587-006-3). Gov Insts.

Energy Technology Series, 6 vols. Incl. Vol. 2. International. Ed. by Thomas F Sullivan. LC 75-13612. (Illus.). 344p. 1975. pap. text ed. 25.00 (ISBN 0-86587-001-2); Vol. 3. Commercialization. Ed. by Dr. Richard F. Hill. LC 76-12198. (Illus.). 335p. 1976. pap. text ed. 25.00 (ISBN 0-86587-002-0); Vol. 4. Confronting Reality. Ed. by Dr. Richard F. Hill. LC 77-76832. (Illus.). 1977. pap. text ed. 30.00 (ISBN 0-86587-003-9); Vol. 5. Challenges to Technology. Ed. by Dr. Richard F. Hill. LC 78-55582. (Illus.). 1044p. 1978. pap. text ed. 38.00 (ISBN 0-86587-004-7); Vol. 6. Achievements in Perspective. Ed. by Dr. Richard F. Hill. LC 78-55582. (Illus.). 1168p. 1979. pap. text ed. 38.00 (ISBN 0-86587-005-5). Set. pap. text ed. 169.00 (ISBN 0-86587-007-1); microfiche 10.00 (ISBN 0-86587-000-4). Gov Insts.

Energy, the Biomass Options. Henry R. Bungay. LC 80-19645. 448p. 1981. 22.50 (ISBN 0-471-04386-9, Pub. by Wiley-Interscience). Wiley.

Energy: The Countdown: A Report to the Club of Rome. Thierry De Montbrial. LC 78-41103. (Illus.). 1979. 45.00 (ISBN 0-08-024225-1); pap. 14.00 (ISBN 0-08-024224-3). Pergamon.

Energy: The Created Crisis. Anthony C. Sutton. LC 78-73737. (Illus.). 1979. 12.95 (ISBN 0-916728-04-8). Bks in Focus.

Energy: The New Look. Margaret O. Hyde. 128p. (gr. 7-9). 1981. 7.95 (ISBN 0-07-031552-3). McGraw.

Energy: The Next Twenty Years. Ed. by Hans Landsberg. LC 79-5226. 656p. 1979. reference 27.00 (ISBN 0-88410-092-8); pap. 11.95 (ISBN 0-88410-094-4). Ballinger Pub.

Energy: The Solar Hydrogen Alternative. J. O. Bockris. LC 75-19125. 1976. 34.95 (ISBN 0-470-08429-4). Halsted Pr.

Energy: The Ultimate Resource? Earl Cook. Ed. by Salvatore J. Natoli. LC 77-87402. (Resource Papers for College Geography). (Illus.). 1978. pap. 4.00 (ISBN 0-89291-127-1). Assn Am Geographers.

Energy to Prosper. Steffen Langfeldt. 138p. (Orig.). 1980. pap. 6.95x (ISBN 0-935190-04-X). AM Books CA.

Energy, to Use or Abuse? John Davis. (Illus.). 186p. (Orig.). 1979. pap. 5.00x (ISBN 0-905381-00-9). Intl Pubns Serv.

Energy Tomorrow. Peter Harsany. (Illus.). 1980. 17.50 (ISBN 0-686-64249-X). Heinman.

Energy: Transactions in Time. Don Fabun. 1971. pap. text ed. 1.95x (ISBN 0-685-03674-X, 47536). Macmillan.

Energy Transformations in Mammals: Regulatory Mechanisms. Frederick L. Hoch. LC 74-135326. (Illus.). 1971. 10.00 o.p. (ISBN 0-7216-4700-6). Saunders.

Energy Transitions: Long-Term Perspectives. Ed. by Lewis J. Perelman et al. (AAAS Selected Symposium: No. 48). 250p. 1980. lib. bdg. 18.50x (ISBN 0-89158-862-0). Westview.

Energy Transmission & Transportation E-018. Jack T. Miskell. 1979. 675.00 o.p. (ISBN 0-89336-190-9). BCC.

Energy Use & Conservation Incentives: A Study of the Southwestern United States. William H. Cunningham & Sally C. Lopreato. LC 77-7485. (Praeger Special Studies). 1977. text ed. 22.95 (ISBN 0-03-022276-1). Praeger.

Energy Use on the Farm. James D. Ritchie. Ed. by Virginia Case. (Illus.). 400p. 1981. 32.50 (ISBN 0-89999-029-0). Structures Pub.

Energy Utilization & Enviromental Health: Methods for Prediction & Evaluation of Impact on Human Health. Richard A. Wadden. LC 78-9688. (Environmental Science & Technology.: Texts & Monographs). 200p. 1978. 31.95 (ISBN 0-471-04185-8, Pub. by Wiley-Interscience). Wiley.

Energy War: Reports from the Front. Harvey Wasserman. 270p. 1979. 12.95 (ISBN 0-88208-105-5); pap. 5.95 (ISBN 0-88208-106-3). Lawrence Hill.

Energy, Winter, & Schools: Chronology of Decision Crisis. David K. Wiles. (Politics of Education Ser.). (Illus.). 1979. 18.95 (ISBN 0-669-02544-5). Lexington Bks.

Energybook, No. 1: Natural Sources & Backyard Applications. Ed. by John Prenis. LC 74-84854. (Illus.). 117p. (Orig.). 1975. lib. bdg. 12.90 (ISBN 0-914294-22-9); pap. 5.95 (ISBN 0-914294-21-0). Running Pr.

Enfant Noir. Camara Laye. Ed. by Joyce A. Hutchinson. 1966. pap. text ed. 5.95x (ISBN 0-521-05357-9). Cambridge U Pr.

Enfants Terribles. Jean Cocteau. (Easy Readers, B). (Illus.). 1977. pap. text ed. 3.75 (ISBN 0-88436-286-8). EMC.

Enfin Malherbe: The Influence of Malherbe on French Lyric Prosody, 1605-1674. Claude K. Abraham. LC 70-160042. 368p. 1971. 18.00x (ISBN 0-8131-1254-0). U Pr of Ky.

Enfoque Arqueologico del Mundo de la Biblia. Moises Chavez. LC 76-25325. 138p. (Orig., Span.). pap. 3.25 (ISBN 0-89922-076-2). Edit Caribe.

Enforcement of Morals. Patrick Devlin. 1970. pap. 4.95 (ISBN 0-19-500305-5, GB). Oxford U Pr.

Eng. & Span. Colombia. 37p. (Eng. & Sp.). 1977. pap. text ed. 2.00 ea. o.p. OAS.

Engaged to Jarrod Stone. Carole Mortimer. (Harlequin Presents Ser.). 192p. pap. 1.50 (ISBN 0-373-10388-3, Pub. by Harlequin). PB.

Engaged to Murder. M. V. Heberden. LC 80-8412. 224p. 1981. pap. 2.25 (ISBN 0-06-080533-1, P 533, CN). Har-Row.

Engaging in Mission: A Study-Action Guide. William R. Forbes. (Orig.). 1980. pap. 2.25 (ISBN 0-377-00102-3). Friend Pr.

Engels on Capital. new ed. Frederick Engels. LC 73-94192. 132p. 1974. 6.00 o.p. (ISBN 0-7178-0408-9); pap. 1.75 (ISBN 0-7178-0409-7). Intl Pub Co.

Engelsk-Svensk Ordbok (Prisma Modern) 5th ed. Bror Danielsson. 396p. 1979. text ed. 15.00x o.p. (ISBN 91-518-0550-2, SW205); Svensk-engelsk, 3rd Ed. text ed. 17.50x o.p. (ISBN 9-1518-0942-7, SW-204). Vanous.

Engelsman's General Construction Cost File 1981. Coert Engelsman. 409p. 1980. pap. text ed. 29.95 (ISBN 0-442-12222-5). Van Nos Reinhold.

Engelsman's General Construction Cost Guide, 1980. Coert Engelsman. 1980. pap. text ed. 28.50 (ISBN 0-442-12218-7). Van Nos Reinhold.

Engine-Ear: Fifty Years of Engineering. Lewis A. Schmidt. (Illus.). 1977. 6.95 o.p. (ISBN 0-533-02937-6). Vantage.

Engine Fourteen-Fourteen. Friedrich Feld. LC 65-23882. (Illus.). (gr. 3-5). 1963. 3.95g o.p. (ISBN 0-8075-2057-8). A Whitman.

Engine Logbook. Aviation Maintenance Publishers. 77p. 1975. pap. 4.95 (ISBN 0-89100-187-5, E*A-E*F*L-1). Aviation Maintenance.

Engine Maintenance & Repair. David MacLean. (Boatowners How-to Guides). (Illus.). 1977. pap. 5.95 (ISBN 0-8306-6943-4, 943). TAB Bks.

Engine Repair: Head Assembly & Valve Gear. Bob Barkhouse. LC 74-21562. 500p. (gr. 10-12). 1974. text ed. 18.48 (ISBN 0-87345-101-5). McKnight.

Engine Service. W. Lewis. 256p. 1980. pap. 11.95 (ISBN 0-13-277236-1). P-H.

Engine Swapping. 5th, rev. ed. Ed. by Hot Rod Magazine Editors. (Hot Rod Shop Ser.). 192p. 1981. pap. 8.95 (ISBN 0-8227-6014-2). Petersen Pub.

Engineer and the City. National Academy of Engineering. 1969. 7.00 (ISBN 0-309-00125-0). Natl Acad Pr.

Engineer & the Industrial Corporation. R. Richard Ritti. LC 73-133913. 1971. 17.50x (ISBN 0-231-03373-7). Columbia U Pr.

Engineer-Chief & Assistant Engineer & Oiler: Limited to Service in the Mineral & Oil Industry. rev. ed. Ed. by Richard A. Block. (Illus.). 82p. 1975. pap. text ed. 12.00 (ISBN 0-934114-07-2). Marine Educ.

Engineer in the Community. 172p. 1980. 45.00x (Pub. by Telford England). State Mutual Bk.

Engineer-in-Training License Review. 8th ed. C. Dean Newnan. LC 76-27234. 1976. pap. 11.95 o.p. (ISBN 0-910554-22-6). Eng Pr.

Engineer-in-Training Review Manual. 5th ed. Michael R. Lindeburg. LC 80-81799. (Engineering Review Manual Ser.). (Illus.). 760p. 1980. pap. 26.50 (ISBN 0-932276-14-8); wkbk. 7.00 (ISBN 0-932276-16-4). Prof Engine.

Engineer in Transition to Management. I. Gray. LC 78-61533. (IEEE Reprint Ser.). 1979. pap. 18.95 (ISBN 0-471-05212-4); pap. 12.50 (ISBN 0-471-05213-2, Pub. by Wiley-Interscience). Wiley.

Engineered Report Writing. Melba W. Murray. LC 68-26960. 138p. 1969. 12.95 (ISBN 0-87814-006-9). Pennwell Pub.

Engineered Work Measurement. 3rd ed. Delmar W Karger & Franklin H. Bayha. LC 77-2626. (Illus.). 1977. 27.50 (ISBN 0-8311-1118-6). Indus Pr.

Engineering. Boy Scouts Of America. LC 19-600. (Illus.). 48p. (gr. 6-12). 1978. pap. 0.70x (ISBN 0-8395-3376-4, 3376). BSA.

Engineering. Jack Rudman. (Undergraduate Program Field Test Ser.: UPFT-8). (Cloth bdg. avail. on request). pap. 9.95 (ISBN 0-8373-6008-0). Natl Learning.

Engineering: A Decision Making Process. George E. Morris. LC 76-13090. (Illus.). 1977. pap. text ed. 8.95 (ISBN 0-395-24546-X). HM.

Engineering Analysis. Dennistown W. Ver Planck & B. R. Teare. LC 54-8420. 1954. 23.95x (ISBN 0-471-90618-2). Wiley.

Engineering & Construction of an Oil Production Platform. Norwegian Petroleum Society. 1980. 70.00x (ISBN 82-7270-015-8, Pub. by Norwegian Info Norway). State Mutual Bk.

Engineering & Contracting Procedure for Foundations. Compiled By American Society of Civil Engineers. (Manual & Report on Engineering Practice Ser.: No. 8). 1953. pap. text ed. 3.00 (ISBN 0-87262-204-5). Am Soc Civil Eng.

Engineering & Medicine. National Academy Of Engineering. LC 74-606277. (Illus., Orig.). 1970. pap. 7.25 (ISBN 0-309-01768-8). Natl Acad Pr.

Engineering & Technical Handbook. Donald G. McNeese & Albert L. Hoag. 1957. ref. ed. 21.95 (ISBN 0-13-277434-8). P-H.

Engineering & Technology Degrees, 1980, 3 pts. Incl. Pt. 1. By Schools. 25.00; Pt. 2. By Minorities. 75.00; Pt. 3. By Curriculum. 25.00. 1981. Set. 100.00 (201-80). AAES.

Engineering & Technology Enrollments, 1979, 2 pts. Incl. Pt. 1. Engineering Enrollments. 45.00; Pt. 2. Technology Enrollments. 45.00. 1980. Set. 75.00. AAES.

Engineering & the Liberal Arts: A Technologist's Guide to History, Literature, Philosophy, Art & Music. Samuel C. Florman. 1968. 24.50 o.p. (ISBN 0-07-021385-2, P&RB). McGraw.

Engineering Anthropometry Methods. J. A. Roebuck, Jr. et al. LC 74-34272. (Human Factors Ser). 459p. 1975. 45.95 (ISBN 0-471-72975-2, Pub. by Wiley-Interscience). Wiley.

Engineering Applications, No. 1: Installation & Maintenance of Engines in Fishing Vessels. (FAO Fisheries Technical Paper Ser.: No. 196). 136p. 1980. pap. 7.25 (ISBN 92-5-100862-0, F1948, FAO). Unipub.

Engineering Applications of Correction & Spectral Analysis. Julius S. Bendat & Allan G. Piersol. LC 79-25926. 1980. 29.95 (ISBN 0-471-05887-4, Pub. by Wiley-Interscience). Wiley.

Engineering Applications of Fracture Analysis: Proceedings of the First National Conference on Fracture Held in Johannesburg, South Africa, 7-9 November 1979. Ed. by G. G. Garrett & D. L. Marriott. LC 80-41074. (International Ser. on the Strength & Fractures of Materials & Structures). (Illus.). 440p. 1980. 60.00 (ISBN 0-08-025437-3). Pergamon.

Engineering at Cambridge University, 1783-1965. Thomas J. Hilken. 1967. 26.95 (ISBN 0-521-05256-4). Cambridge U Pr.

Engineering Calculations in Radiative Heat Transfer. W. A. Gray & R. Muller. LC 73-17321. 176p. 1974. text ed. 29.00 (ISBN 0-08-017786-7); pap. text ed. 13.25 (ISBN 0-08-017787-5). Pergamon.

Engineering Contracts & Specifications. 4th ed. R. W. Abbett. LC 63-14072. 1963. 24.95 (ISBN 0-471-00035-3, Pub by Wiley-Interscience). Wiley.

Engineering Craft Studies: Monitoring a New Syllabus. S. M. Barry. (General Ser.). (Illus.). 28p. 1974. pap. text ed. 3.75x (ISBN 0-85633-048-5, NFER). Humanities.

Engineering Descriptive Geometry. Steve M. Slaby. (Orig.). 1969. pap. 4.95 (ISBN 0-06-460101-3, CO 101, COS). Har-Row.

Engineering Design. J. Stephenson & R. A. Callander. LC 73-5277. 705p. 1974. 39.95 (ISBN 0-471-82210-8, Pub. by Wiley-Interscience). Wiley.

Engineering Design: A Synthesis of Stress Analysis & Materials Engineering. 2nd ed. J. H. Faupel & F. E. Fisher. LC 80-16727. 1980. 40.00 (ISBN 0-471-03381-2, Pub. by Wiley-Interscience). Wiley.

Engineering Design Graphics. 3rd ed. James H. Earle. LC 76-2931. 1977. text ed. 22.95 (ISBN 0-201-01774-1). A-W.

Engineering Design Graphics Problems-One. J. H. Earle. 1976. pap. text ed. 8.50 o.p. (ISBN 0-201-01719-9). A-W.

Engineering Drawing & Construction. 2nd ed. L. C. Mott. (Illus.). 1976. pap. 12.50x (ISBN 0-19-859114-4). Oxford U Pr.

Engineering Drawing & Design. C. H. Jensen. 1968. text ed. 18.95 o.p. (ISBN 0-07-094866-6, G). McGraw.

Engineering Drawing & Graphic Technology. 12th ed. Thomas E. French & Charles J. Vierck. (Illus.). 1978. lib. bdg. 19.95 (ISBN 0-07-022158-6, C); problems 10.50 (ISBN 0-07-022160-X); tchr. manual 3.95 (ISBN 0-07-022159-6). McGraw.

Engineering Drawing for Advanced Students. P. M. Dunne. 1967. pap. 4.20 (ISBN 0-08-012135-7). Pergamon.

Engineering Drawing for Technicians, Vol. 1. O. Ostrowsky. (Illus.). 94p. 1979. pap. 11.00x (ISBN 0-7131-3408-9). Intl Ideas.

Engineering Drawing from the Beginning. M. F. Cousins. 1964. Vol. 1. 1964. 28.00 (ISBN 0-08-010839-3); pap. 11.25 (ISBN 0-08-010840-7). Pergamon.

Engineering Economic Analysis. rev. ed. Donald G. Newnan. LC 79-13237. 470p. 1980. text ed. 21.95 (ISBN 0-910554-31-5). Eng Pr.

Engineering Economic Analysis & Expanded Interest Tables. 2nd ed. Michael R. Lindeburg. (Engineering Review Manual Ser.). 134p. 1980. pap. 8.50 (ISBN 0-932276-25-3). Prof Engine.

Engineering Economics. Robert L. Mitchell. 1980. 29.50 (ISBN 0-471-27640-5, Pub. by Wiley-Interscience); pap. text ed. 16.00 o.p. (ISBN 0-686-65932-5). Wiley.

Engineering Economy. 5th ed. W. J. Fabrycky & G. J. Thuesen. (Illus.). 1977. text ed. 21.95 (ISBN 0-13-277491-7). P-H.

Engineering Economy: Analysis of Capital Expenditures. 3rd ed. Ed. by Gerald W. Smith. 1979. text ed. 22.95 (ISBN 0-8138-0552-X). Iowa St U Pr.

Engineering Electromagnetics. 4th ed. William H. Hayt, Jr. (Electrical Engineering Ser.). (Illus.). 512p. 1981. text ed. 28.95 (ISBN 0-07-027395-2, C); solutions manual 4.95 (ISBN 0-07-027396-0). McGraw.

Engineering Electromagnetics. D. T. Thomas. 416p. 1972. text ed. 31.00 (ISBN 0-08-016778-0). Pergamon.

Engineering Enrollments, Nineteen Seventy-Nine by School & by Curriculum for All Students Including a Breakdown by Women, Minorities & Foreign Nationals. 45.00 (ISBN 0-686-27583-7, 207A-279). AAES.

Engineering Eponyms. 2nd rev. ed. Ed. by C. P. Auger. 1975. 15.50x (ISBN 0-85365-437-9, Pub. by Lib Assn England). Oryx Pr.

Engineering Equipment for Foundries: Proceedings. Seminar on Engineering Equipment for Foundries & Advanced Methods of Producing Such Equipment, Geneva, 1977. Ed. by United Nations Economic Commission for Europe, Geneva. (Illus.). 1979. text ed. 81.00 (ISBN 0-08-022421-0). Pergamon.

Engineering Ethics: Proceedings. Compiled By American Society of Civil Engineers. 120p. 1977. pap. text ed. 7.00 (ISBN 0-87262-173-1). Am Soc Civil Eng.

Engineering Field Theory. A. J. Baden-Fuller. 272p. 1973. text ed. 32.00 (ISBN 0-08-017033-1); pap. text ed. 16.25 (ISBN 0-08-017034-X). Pergamon.

Engineering Fluid Mechanics. John A. Roberson & Clayton T. Crowe. 1975. text ed. 20.95 o.p. (ISBN 0-395-18607-2); sol. manual 5.35 o.p. (ISBN 0-395-18782-6). HM.

Engineering Fluid Mechanics. 2nd ed. John A. Roberson & Clayton T. Crowe. LC 79-87855. (Illus.). 1980. text ed. 24.50 (ISBN 0-395-28357-4); solutions manual 2.50 (ISBN 0-395-28358-2). HM.

Engineering for Dairy & Food Products. 2nd ed. Arthur W. Farrall. LC 79-1171. (Illus.). 1980. lib. bdg. 28.50 (ISBN 0-88275-859-4). Krieger.

Engineering for Protection from Natural Disasters: Proceedings. International Conference Held in Bangkok, Jan. 7-9, 1980 & Pisidhi Karasudhi. Ed. by Worsak Kanok-Nukulchai. 1980. write for info. (ISBN 0-471-27895-5, Pub. by Wiley-Interscience). Wiley.

Engineering for Resolution of the Energy-Environment Dilemma. Committee on Power Plant Siting. LC 79-186370. (Illus.). 1972. pap. 10.75 (ISBN 0-309-01943-5). Natl Acad Pr.

Engineering Fundamentals. new ed. R. L. Shell & N. P. Jeffries. LC 74-32613. 150p. 1975. 10.50x (ISBN 0-87263-032-3). SME.

Engineering Geological Maps: A Guide to Their Preparation. (Earth Science Ser.: No. 15). (Illus.). 79p. 1976. pap. 14.50 (ISBN 0-685-66204-7, U222, UNESCO). Unipub.

Engineering Geology. Christopher C. Mathewson. (Illus.). 416p. 1981. text ed. 24.95 (ISBN 0-675-08032-0). Merrill.

Engineering Geology Case Histories: Decay & Preservation of Stone, No. 11. Erhard M. Winkler. LC 58-2632. 1978. pap. 10.00x (ISBN 0-8137-4011-8). Geol Soc.

Engineering Geology Case Histories: Geologic Mapping for Environmental Purposes, No. 10. Ed. by H. F. Ferguson. LC 73-90839. (Illus., Orig.). 1974. pap. 5.50x o.p. (ISBN 0-8137-4010-X). Geol Soc.

Engineering Graphic Modelling. Tjalve Andraeson & Schmidt. (Illus.). 1979. 11.95 (ISBN 0-408-00305-7). Butterworths.

Engineering Graphics Problem Book. C. Gordon Sanders et al. 1977. perfect bdg. 9.95 (ISBN 0-8403-8004-6). Kendall-Hunt.

Engineering Heat Transfer. Bhalchandra V. Karlekar & Robert M. Desmond. (Illus., Orig.). 1977. text ed. 24.50 (ISBN 0-8299-0054-3); solutions manual avail. (ISBN 0-8299-0497-2). West Pub.

Engineering Heat Transfer, SI Version. James R. Welty. LC 78-5179. 1978. text ed. 29.95 (ISBN 0-471-02860-6). Wiley.

Engineering Hydraulics. Ed. by Hunter Rouse. 1950. 52.50 (ISBN 0-471-74283-X, Pub. by Wiley-Interscience). Wiley.

Engineering Hydrology Today. Institute of Civil Engineers, UK. 152p. 1980. 65.00x (ISBN 0-7277-0012-X, Pub. by Telford England). State Mutual Bk.

Engineering Intelligent Systems: Concepts, Theory, & Applications. Robert M. Glorioso & Fernando C. Osorio. (Illus.). 512p. 1980. 27.00 (ISBN 0-932376-06-1). Digital Pr.

Engineering Management. David I. Cleland & Dundar F. Kocaoglu. (Industrial Engineering & Management Science Ser.). (Illus.). 528p. 1980. text ed. 21.95 (ISBN 0-07-011316-5, C). McGraw.

Engineering Materials. 2nd rev. ed. Surendra Singh. 1980. text ed. 12.50x (ISBN 0-7069-0789-2, Pub. by Vikas India). Advent Bk.

Engineering Materials: An Introduction to Their Properties & Applications. M. F. Ashby & D. R. Jones. (International Ser. on Materials Science & Technology: Vol. 34). (Illus.). 120p. 1980. 36.00 (ISBN 0-08-026139-6); pap. 11.50 (ISBN 0-08-026138-8). Pergamon.

Engineering Materials & Their Applications. Richard Flinn & Paul K. Trojan. 1975. 22.95 (ISBN 0-395-18916-0); instructor's manual 2.50 (ISBN 0-395-19378-8). HM.

Engineering Materials & Their Applications. 2nd ed. Richard A. Flinn & Paul K. Trojan. (Illus.). 753p. 1981. text ed. 22.95 (ISBN 0-395-29645-5); write for info. instr's manual (ISBN 0-395-29646-3). HM.

Engineering Materials & Their Testing, Pt. 1. D. S. Naidu. 7.50x (ISBN 0-210-27000-4). Asia.

Engineering Mechanics. W. W. Hagerty & H. J. Plass, Jr. LC 75-4730. 672p. 1975. Repr. of 1967 ed. 19.50 o.p. (ISBN 0-88275-266-9). Krieger.

Engineering Mechanics, 2 vols. J. L. Heriam. Incl. Vol. 1. Statics: SI Version. text ed. 18.95 (ISBN 0-471-05558-1); Arabic ed. (ISBN 0-471-06312-6); Vol. 2. Dynamics: SI Version. text ed. 17.95 (ISBN 0-471-05559-X); Arabic ed. (ISBN 0-471-06311-8). LC 79-11173. 1980. Wiley.

Engineering Mechanics, 2 vols. J. L. Heriam. Incl. Vol. 1. Statics. text ed. 18.95x (ISBN 0-471-59460-1); Vol. 2. Dynamics. text ed. 19.95x (ISBN 0-471-59461-X). LC 77-24716. 1978. Wiley.

Engineering Mechanics, 2 vols. 2nd ed. A. Higdon & Stiles. Incl. Vol. I. Statics (ISBN 0-13-279398-9); Vol. II. Dynamics (ISBN 0-13-279406-3). (Civil Engineering & Engineering Mechanic Ser.). (Illus.). 928p. 1976. 27.95x (ISBN 0-13-279380-6). P-H.

Engineering Mechanics. 3rd ed. A. Higdon et al. Incl. Vol. 1. Statics. 21.95 (ISBN 0-13-279273-7); Vol. 2. Dynamics. 21.95 (ISBN 0-13-279281-8). 1968. 27.95 set (ISBN 0-13-279299-0). P-H.

Engineering Mechanics, 2 vols. T. C. Huang. Incl. Vol. 1. Statics (ISBN 0-201-03005-5); Vol. 2. Dynamics (ISBN 0-201-03006-3). 1967. 16.95 ea.; 24.95 set (ISBN 0-201-03007-1). A-W.

Engineering Mechanics, 2 vols. Lawrence E. Malvern. Incl. Vol. 1. Statics. ref. ed. 19.95x (ISBN 0-13-278663-X); Vol. 2. Dynamics. ref. ed. 19.95x (ISBN 0-13-278671-0). (Illus.). 352p. 1976. P-H.

Engineering Mechanics, 2 vols. 3rd ed. I. Shames. 1980. Vol. 1, Statics. 21.95 (ISBN 0-13-279141-2); Vol. 2, Dynamics. 21.95 (ISBN 0-13-279158-7); combined ed. 27.95 (ISBN 0-13-279166-8). P-H.

Engineering Mechanics: Second Vector Edition, 2 vols. Archie Higdon et al. Incl. Vol. 1. Statics, SI Version (ISBN 0-13-279018-1); Vol. 2. Dynamics, SI Version (ISBN 0-13-279026-2). (Illus.). 1979. 18.95 ea. o.p. P-H.

Engineering Mechanics Specialty Conference, 3rd. Compiled by American Society of Civil Engineers. 952p. 1979. pap. text ed. 55.00 (ISBN 0-87262-192-8). Am Soc Civil Eng.

Engineering Mechanics: Statics, Vol. 1. Higdon & Stiles. (Civil Engineering & Engineering Mechanic Ser.). (Illus.). 400p. 1976. 17.95x o.p. (ISBN 0-13-279398-9). P-H.

Engineering Mechanics: Statics & Dynamics Combined. J. L. Meriam. LC 78-518. 1978. text ed. 28.95x (ISBN 0-471-01979-8); tchrs'. manual avail. (ISBN 0-471-02753-7). Wiley.

Engineering Mechanics: Statics & Dynamics. D. H. Pletta & D. Frederick. (Illus.). 1969. 25.95 (ISBN 0-8260-7190-2). Wiley.

Engineering Mechanics: Statics & Dynamics, 2 vols. Joseph F. Shelley. (Illus.). 1980. Set. text ed. 28.95 (ISBN 0-07-056555-4). Statics Vol. text ed. 19.95 (ISBN 0-07-056551-1); Dynamics Vol. text ed. 18.95 (ISBN 0-07-056553-8); solutions manual 11.95. Statics Vol (ISBN 0-07-056552-X). Dynamics Vol (ISBN 0-07-056554-6). McGraw.

Engineering Mechanics, 2nd Vector Ed., Vol. 2: Dynamics. A. Highdon et al. (Civil Engr. & Engr. Mechanics Ser). 1976. 21.95 (ISBN 0-13-279406-3). P-H.

Engineering: Modeling & Computation. Walter J. Gajda, Jr. & William E. Biles. LC 77-74378. (Illus.). 1977. text ed. 19.95 (ISBN 0-395-25585-6); solutions manual 0.50 (ISBN 0-395-25584-8). HM.

Engineering of Microprocessor Systems: Guidelines on System Development. C. D. Nabavi. LC 79-40952. 1979. 21.00 (ISBN 0-08-025435-7); pap. 7.25 (ISBN 0-08-025434-9). Pergamon.
Engineering of Restraint. Fred Powledge. 1.00 (ISBN 0-686-68336-6). Pub Aff Pr.
Engineering Plasticity. G. R. Calladine. 1969. 24.00 (ISBN 0-08-013970-1); pap. 13.25 (ISBN 0-08-013969-8). Pergamon.
Engineering Plasticity by Mathematical Programming: Proceedings. NATO Advanced Study Institute, University of Waterloo, Canada 2-12, August 1977. Ed. by M. Z. Cohn & G. Maier. LC 78-8474. (Illus.). 1979. 55.00 (ISBN 0-08-022735-X); pap. 34.00 (ISBN 0-08-022736-8). Pergamon.
Engineering Plasticity: Theory & Its Application to Metal Forming, Processes. R. A. Slater. LC 73-10606. 1977. text ed. 43.95 (ISBN 0-470-79647-2). Halsted Pr.
Engineering Principles for Electrical Tehcnicians, 2 vols. T. A. Lovelace. 1975. pap. text ed. 19.95x. Vol. 1 (ISBN 0-17-741108-2). Vol. 2 (ISBN 0-17-741109-0). Intl Ideas.
Engineering Properties of Soils & Rocks. F. G. Bell. (Illus.). 144p. 1981. pap. text ed. 12.50 (ISBN 0-408-00537-8). Butterworths.
Engineering Quantities & Systems of Units. Rhys Lewis. LC 72-3115. (Illus.). 176p. 1972. 13.95 o.p. (ISBN 0-470-53377-3). Halsted Pr.
Engineering Reliability: New Techniques & Applications. Chanan Singh & B. S. Dhillon. LC 80-18734. (Systems Engineering & Analysis Ser.). 425p. 1981. 36.95 (ISBN 0-471-05014-8, Pub. by Wiley-Interscience). Wiley.
Engineering Science for Technicians, Vol. 1. I. McDonagh et al. (Illus.). 1977. pap. 11.00x (ISBN 0-686-67754-4). Intl Ideas.
Engineering Science for Technicians, Vol. 2. McDonagh et al. (Illus.). 1978. pap. 11.00x (ISBN 0-7131-3398-8). Intl Ideas.
Engineering Simulation Using Small Scientific Computers. M. J. Shah. (Illus.). 336p. 1976. 23.95x (ISBN 0-13-279422-5). P-H.
Engineering Societies in the Life of a Country. 174p. 1980. 24.00x (ISBN 0-901948-02-0, Pub. by Telford England). State Mutual Bk.
Engineering Soil Mechanics. J. Tuma & M. Abdel-Hady. 1973. ref. ed. 24.95x (ISBN 0-13-279505-1). P-H.
Engineering Statistics with a Programmable Calculator. William Volk. Ed. by Robert L. Davidson. (Illus.). 320p. 1981. text ed. 17.50 (ISBN 0-07-067552-X, P&RB). McGraw.
Engineering Surveying, Vol. 1. 2nd ed. W. Schofield. (Illus.). 1978. pap. 15.95 (ISBN 0-408-00333-2). Butterworths.
Engineering Surveying: Problems & Solutions. F. A. Shepherd. (Illus.). 1977. pap. text ed. 21.00x (ISBN 0-7131-3370-8). Intl Ideas.
Engineering Technology One. Nunney. 1981. text ed. price not set (ISBN 0-408-00511-4). Butterworth.
Engineering Technology Problem Solving. Irvine. Date not set. price not set (ISBN 0-8247-1169-6). Dekker.
Engineering Thermodynamics. R. E. Balzhiser & M. R. Samuels. (Illus.). 1977. text ed. 26.95 (ISBN 0-13-279570-1). P-H.
Engineering Thermodynamics. James E. John & William L. Haberman. 1979. text ed. 23.50 (ISBN 0-205-06570-8); solutions man. avail. (ISBN 0-205-06571-6). Allyn.
Engineering Thermodynamics: An Introductory Textbook. James B. Jones & George A. Hawkins. LC 60-10316. (Illus.). 1960. text ed. 28.95x (ISBN 0-471-44946-6). Wiley.
Engineering Uses of Coherent Optics. Ed. by E. R. Robertson. LC 75-22978. 560p. 1976. 145.00 (ISBN 0-521-20879-3). Cambridge U Pr.
Engineering Wall & Partition Components for Prefabrication. Norris T. Pindar, 3rd. (Illus.). 128p. 1981. 13.50 (ISBN 0-89047-008-1). Herman Pub. Postponed.
Engineering Woodworking, Vol. 1. 2nd ed. Ed. by J. Clark et al. (Engineering Craftsmen: No. K1). (Illus.). 1975. spiral bdg. 31.50x (ISBN 0-85083-280-2). Intl Ideas.
Engineering Woodworking, Vol. 2. Ed. by M. Green et al. (Engineering Craftsmen: No. K21). (Illus.). 1977. spiral bdg. 21.00x (ISBN 0-85083-340-X). Intl Ideas.
Engineers & Engineering of the Renaissance. William B. Parsons. 1968. 18.50x o.p. (ISBN 0-262-16024-2); pap. 9.95x (ISBN 0-262-66026-1). MIT Pr.
Engineers at Work: A Casebook. Carl H. Vesper. 1975. pap. text ed. 10.50 (ISBN 0-395-18407-X). HM.
Engineers' Computer Handbook. A. Ryder & E. Malcolmson. 336p. 1980. 95.00x (ISBN 0-7277-0078-2, Pub. by Telford England). State Mutual Bk.
Engineers' Manual. 2nd ed. Ralph G. Hudson. 1939. 17.50 (ISBN 0-471-41844-7, Pub. by Wiley-Interscience). Wiley.
Engineers' Metric Manual & Buyers' Guide. D. S. Lock. 1975. text ed. 230.00 (ISBN 0-08-018220-8). Pergamon.
Engineers Salary Survey: Special Industry Report. 199p. 1980. 75.00 (ISBN 0-686-27580-2, 301-80). AAES.
Engines. Peter R. Limburg. LC 74-77243. (First Bks). (gr. 4-6). 1969. PLB 4.90 o.p. (ISBN 0-531-00705-7). Watts.
Engines, Fuels & Lubricants: Perspective on the Future. Society of Automotive Engineers. 1980. 15.00 (ISBN 0-89883-242-X). Soc Auto Engineers.
Engines of Change: United States Interests & Revolution in Latin America. George C. Lodge. (YA) 1970. 8.95 o.p. (ISBN 0-394-42344-5). Knopf.
England: An Intended Guyde, for English Travailers. John Norden. LC 79-84125. (English Experience Ser.: No. 944). 84p. 1979. Repr. of 1625 ed. lib. bdg. 14.00 (ISBN 90-221-0944-5). Walter J Johnson.
England & Germany, 1740-1914. Bernadotte E. Schmitt. 1967. Repr. 16.50 o.p. (ISBN 0-685-09545-2). Fertig.
England & Ireland Since 1800. P. J. O'Farrell. 189p. 1975. text ed. 7.75x o.p. (ISBN 0-19-215814-7); pap. text ed. 3.95x (ISBN 0-19-289045-X). Oxford U Pr.
England & Scotland, 1560-1707. Douglas Nobbs. LC 80-25749. xxi, 173p. 1981. Repr. of 1952 ed. lib. bdg. 19.75x (ISBN 0-313-22773-X, NOES). Greenwood.
England & the Continent in the Eighth Century. Wilhelm Levison. (Ford Lectures Ser). 1946. 24.95x (ISBN 0-19-821232-1). Oxford U Pr.
England & the English, 2 vols. Edward Bulwer-Lytton. 723p. 1971. Repr. of 1833 ed. 45.00x (ISBN 0-7165-1592-X, Pub. by Irish Academic Pr Ireland). Biblio Dist.
England As It Is: Political, Social & Industrial in the Middle of the Nineteenth Century, 2 vols. William Johnston. (Development of Industrial Society Ser.). 721p. 1980. 60.00x (ISBN 0-7165-1774-4, Pub. by Irish Academic Pr). Biblio Dist.
England Before the Conquest. Ed. by Peter Clemoes & Kathleen Hughes. LC 76-154508. (Illus.). 1971. 53.95 (ISBN 0-521-08191-2). Cambridge U Pr.
England in Colour. John Burke. 1972. 27.00 (ISBN 0-7134-0022-6, Pub. by Batsford England). David & Charles.
England in Colour. J. H. Peel. 1969. 14.95 (ISBN 0-7134-0017-X, Pub. by Batsford England). David & Charles.
England in Egypt. 13th ed. Alfred Milner. LC 68-9624. 1971. Repr. of 1920 ed. 17.00 (ISBN 0-86527-331-6). Fertig.
England in Eighteen Thirty Five, 3 vols. Frederick Von Raumer. 908p. 1971. Repr. of 1836 ed. 84.00x (ISBN 0-686-28334-1, Pub. by Irish Academic Pr). Biblio Dist.
England in Pictures. Sterling Publishing Company Editors. LC 65-15825. (Visual Geography Ser.). (Illus., Orig.). (gr. 6 up). PLB 4.99 (ISBN 0-8069-1055-0); pap. 2.95 (ISBN 0-8069-1054-2). Sterling.
England in the Age of Hogarth. D. Jarett. (Illus.). 256p. 1980. text ed. 13.75x (ISBN 0-246-64064-2). Humanities.
England in the Age of Hogarth. Derek Jarrett. 1979. 14.95x (ISBN 0-8464-0101-0). Beekman Pubs.
England in the Age of Thomas More. Derek Wilson. (Illus.). 1980. text ed. 15.50x (ISBN 0-246-10943-2). Humanities.
England in the Age of Thomas More. Derek Wilson. 1979. 17.95x (ISBN 0-8464-0106-1). Beekman Pubs.
England in the Days of Old. William Andrews. LC 68-21752. 1968. Repr. of 1897 ed. 18.00 (ISBN 0-8103-3545-X). Gale.
England in the Restoration & Early Eighteenth Century: Essays on Culture & Society. Ed. by H. T. Swedenberg, Jr. LC 72-149943. 272p. 1972. 20.00x (ISBN 0-520-01973-3). U of Cal Pr.
England in the Seventeenth Century. new ed. Maurice Ashley. 273p. 1980. 20.00x; pap. 9.95. B&N.
England in 1815 & 1845. A. Alison. 98p. 1971. Repr. of 1845 ed. 15.00x (ISBN 0-7165-1699-3, Pub. by Irish Academic Pr Ireland). Biblio Dist.
England, Ireland, & America. Richard Cobden. LC 77-28350. 1980. text ed. 15.95x (ISBN 0-915980-44-4). Inst Study Human.
England of Elizabeth. A. L. Rowse. LC 78-53293. 1978. 25.00 (ISBN 0-299-07720-9); pap. 8.95 (ISBN 0-299-07724-1). U of Wis Pr.
England Under the Yorkists & Tudors 1471 - 1603. P. J. Helm. (Illus.). 1968. text ed. 9.50x (ISBN 0-7135-0541-9); pap. text ed. 9.75x (ISBN 0-7135-0542-7). Humanities.
England's Baltic Trade in the Early Seventeenth Century. J. K. Fedorowicz. LC 78-67629. (Cambridge Studies in the Economic History). (Illus.). 1980. 42.50 (ISBN 0-521-22425-X). Cambridge U Pr.
England's First State Hospitals & the Metropolitan Asylums Board 1867-1930. Gwendoline M. Ayers. LC 75-126766. (Wellcome Institute of the History of Medicine). (Illus.). 1971. 30.00x (ISBN 0-520-01792-7). U of Cal Pr.
England's High Chancellor: Francis Bacon-a Romance. Richard Ince. 324p. 1980. Repr. of 1935 ed. lib. bdg. 35.00 (ISBN 0-89984-297-6). Century Bookbindery.
England's Michelangelo: A Biography of George Frederic Watts. Wilfred Blunt. (Illus.). 1978. 25.00 (ISBN 0-241-89174-4, Pub. by Hamish Hamilton England). David & Charles.
England's Parnassus: Or, the Choysest Flowers of Our Moderne Poets. Robert Allot. LC 72-167. (English Experience Ser.: No. 216). 510p. Repr. of 1600 ed. 62.00 (ISBN 90-221-0216-5). Walter J Johnson.
Engle, Ladder of Angels. (Orig.). 1979. 17.50 (ISBN 0-8164-0443-7). Crossroad NY.
Englische Schauerroman um 1880 unter Berucksichtigung der unbekannten Bucher. Jakob Brauchli. Ed. by E. F. Bleiler. LC 78-60913. (Fiction of Popular Culture Ser.: Vol. 2). 260p. 1979. lib. bdg. 26.00 (ISBN 0-8240-9666-5). Garland Pub.
English. John Colson & Greta Colson. (Illus.). 212p. tape included 17.50x o.p. (ISBN 0-686-09303-8, Dist. by Hippocrene Books Inc.). Leviathan Hse.
English: A Comprehensive Course. Harold Levine. (Orig.). (gr. 11-12). 1970. pap. text ed. 4.83 (ISBN 0-87720-303-2). AMSCO Sch.
English: A Literary Foundation Course. R. S. Fowler & A. J. Dick. 1975. text ed. 18.95x o.p. (ISBN 0-04-428032-7); pap. text ed. 9.50x o.p. (ISBN 0-04-428033-5). Allen Unwin.
English: Advance Placement Exam. Max Nadel & Arthur Sherrer. 320p. (gr. 9-12). 1980. pap. text ed. 4.95 (ISBN 0-8120-2070-7). Barron.
English Agriculture in Eighteen Fifty & Eighteen Fifty-One. James Caird. LC 67-16347. Repr. of 1852 ed. 20.00x (ISBN 0-678-05033-3). Kelley.
English Air. D. E. Stevenson. LC 75-29720. 1976. 7.95 o.p. (ISBN 0-03-016841-4). HR&W.
English Almanacs: Fifteen Hundred to Eighteen Hundred: Astrology & the Popular Press. Bernard Capp. LC 78-74212. (Illus.). 1979. 38.50x (ISBN 0-8014-1229-3). Cornell U Pr.
English America & the Restoration Monarchy of Charles II: Trans-Atlantic Politics, Commerce & Kinship. Jack M. Sosin. LC 80-16215. xii, 389p. 1981. 25.00x (ISBN 0-8032-4118-6). U of Nebr Pr.
English & American Judges As Lawmakers. Louis L. Jaffe. 1969. 16.95x (ISBN 0-19-825193-9). Oxford U Pr.
English & Japanese in Contrast. Taylor. 1979. 6.95 (ISBN 0-88345-356-8). Regents Pub.
English & Pre-Test: Placement Tests. William E. Lockhart. (Michigan Prescriptive Program Ser.). (gr. 10). 1975. wkbk. 1.50 (ISBN 0-89039-125-4). Ann Arbor Pubs.
English Antiques: The Age of Elegance 1700-1830. Donald Wintersgill. LC 75-4162. (Illus.). 272p. 1975. 18.00 o.p. (ISBN 0-688-02931-0). Morrow.
English-Arabic; Arabic-English Dictionary. E. A. Elias. pap. 12.00x. Intl Bk Ctr.
English-Arabic; Arabic-English Dictionary. John Wortabet. 1979. pap. 15.00x. Intl Bk Ctr.
English-Arabic Collegiate Dictionary. Elias. 9.50 (ISBN 0-686-27677-9). Colton Bk.
English-Arabic Dictionary. Al-Manar & Hasan Karmi. 1971. lib. bdg. 25.00x (ISBN 0-685-77120-2). Intl Bk Ctr.
English-Arabic Dictionary. Al-Mawrid & Munir Ba'Albaki. 1980. 45.00 (ISBN 0-685-82805-0). Intl Bk Ctr.
English-Arabic Dictionary. Al-Mawrid & Munir Ba'Albaki. 1978. pocket dictionary 5.50x (ISBN 0-685-85419-1). Intl Bk Ctr.
English-Arabic Dictionary. Al Manar. 1971. 25.00x. Intl Bk Ctr.
English-Arabic Dictionary: Al-Mawrid. Munir Ba'Albaki. 1981. 45.00 (ISBN 0-686-69401-5). Intl Bk Ctr.
English-Arabic Dictionary: Colloquial Arabic of Egypt. Socrates Spiro. 1974. 20.00x (ISBN 0-685-77124-5). Intl Bk Ctr.
English-Arabic Dictionary for Accounting & Finance. Adnan Abdeen. LC 79-41213. 1981. 22.95 (ISBN 0-471-27673-1, Pub. by Wiley-Interscience). Wiley.
English-Arabic Dictionary of Economics & Commerce. M. Hansen. 16.00x (ISBN 0-686-65471-4). Intl Bk Ctr.
English-Arabic Dictionary of Economics. (Libraire du Liban). pap. 6.95x (ISBN 0-686-60606-X). Intl Bk Ctr.
English-Arabic Dictionary of Petroleum Terms & the Oil Industry. A. Khatib. (Illus.). 1975. 40.00x (ISBN 0-685-72036-5). Intl Bk Ctr.
English-Arabic Dictionary of Scientific & Technical Terms. A. Khatib. (Illus.). 1974. 40.00x (ISBN 0-685-82821-2). Intl Bk Ctr.
English-Arabic Learner's Dictionary. F. Steingass. 1972. 18.00x (ISBN 0-685-77127-X). Intl Bk Ctr.
English-Arabic Lexicon. George P. Bagder. 75.00x (ISBN 0-685-72042-X). Intl Bk Ctr.
English-Arabic Pocket Dictionary. Al-Mawrid Al Quareb & Munir Ba'Alabaki. 1980. pap. 5.50x. Intl Bk Ctr.
English-Arabic Pocket Dictionary. John Wortabet. 1980. pap. 5.50x. Intl Bk Ctr.
English-Arabic Reader's Dictionary. J. John Abcarius. 1974. 16.00x (ISBN 0-685-72043-8). Intl Bk Ctr.
English-Arabic Student Dictionary. Ba'Albaki. 12.00 (ISBN 0-686-53115-9). Intl Bk Ctr.
English-Arabic Vocabulary: Students Pronouncing Dictionary. Merrill Y. Van Wagoner et al. LC 80-81198. 452p. (Orig.). 1980. pap. text ed. 10.00x (ISBN 0-87950-028-X). Spoken Lang Serv.
English Architecture. Bruce Allsopp & Ursula Clark. (Illus.). 1979. 18.00 (ISBN 0-85362-177-2, Oriel). Routledge & Kegan.
English Architecture: A Concise History. David Watkin. (World of Art Ser.). (Illus.). 1979. 17.95 (ISBN 0-19-520147-7); pap. 9.95 (ISBN 0-19-520148-5). Oxford U Pr.
English Art Thirteen Hundred Seven to Fourteen Sixty-One. Joan Evans. LC 79-91817. (Illus.). 272p. 1980. Repr. of 1949 ed. lib. bdg. 40.00 (ISBN 0-87817-261-0). Hacker.
English Art, 1100-1216. Thomas S. Boase. (Oxford History of English Art Ser.). (Illus.). 1953. 37.50x (ISBN 0-19-817202-8). Oxford U Pr.
English Art, 1216-1307. Peter Brieger. (Oxford History of English Art Ser.). 1957. 33.00x (ISBN 0-19-817203-6). Oxford U Pr.
English Art 1714-1800. Joseph Burke. (Oxford History of English Art). (Illus.). 620p. 1975. 39.95 (ISBN 0-19-817209-5). Oxford U Pr.
English Art, 871-1100. David T. Rice. (Oxford History of English Art Ser). (Illus.). 1952. 24.95x o.p. (ISBN 0-19-817201-X). Oxford U Pr.
English As a Foreign Language. 3rd ed. R. A. Close. 224p. (Orig.). 1981. pap. text ed. 10.95x (ISBN 0-04-425025-8, 2638). Allen Unwin.
English As a Second Language: A Reader. 3rd ed. Edward T. Erazmus & Harry J. Cargas. 1980. pap. text ed. 9.95 (ISBN 0-697-03958-7). Wm C Brown.
English As a Second Language: An Interdisciplinary Approach, Vol. 4. Clara Velazquez et al. 208p. 1980. pap. 9.95 (ISBN 0-8403-2279-8). Kendall-Hunt.
English As a Second Language from Theory to Practice. rev. ed. Mary Finocchiaro. 230p. 1974. text ed. 4.95 (ISBN 0-88345-222-7). Regents Pub.
English As a Second Language: Phase Four: Let's Continue. William Samelson. (Illus.). 1979. text ed. 13.95 (ISBN 0-8359-1727-4); pap. text ed. 10.95 (ISBN 0-8359-1726-6); instrs'. manual avail. (ISBN 0-8359-1728-2). Reston.
English As a Second Language Phase I: Let's Converse. William Samelson. (Illus.). 1980. text ed. 13.95 (ISBN 0-8359-1730-4); pap. text ed. 10.95 (ISBN 0-8359-1729-0); free instrs' manual. Reston.
English As a Second Language: Phase Three - Let's Write. (Illus.). 352p. 1976. 13.95 (ISBN 0-87909-263-7); pap. text ed. 8.95 (ISBN 0-87909-262-9); instrs'. manual avail. Reston.
English As a Second Language Phase Two: Let's Read. William Samuelson. (Illus.). 464p. 1975. text ed. 13.95 (ISBN 0-87909-258-0); pap. text ed. 8.95 (ISBN 0-87909-257-2); instrs'. manual avail. Reston.
English As a Second Language: Phase Zero Plus, Let's Begin. Samelson. (Illus.). 288p. 1980. text ed. 13.95 (ISBN 0-8359-1725-8); pap. text ed. 10.95 (ISBN 0-8359-1724-X). Reston.
English As We Speak It in Ireland. Patrick W. Joyce. LC 68-26579. 1971. Repr. of 1910 ed. 24.00 (ISBN 0-8103-3356-2). Gale.
English Association Handbook of Societies & Collections. Ed. by A. E. Percival. 1977. pap. 5.50x (ISBN 0-85365-449-2, Pub. by Lib Assn England). Oryx Pr.
English Associations of Working Men. Joseph M. Baernreither. Tr. by A. Taylor. LC 66-28040. 1966. Repr. of 1889 ed. 22.000 (ISBN 0-8103-3078-4). Gale.
English at School: The Wood & the Trees. Derrick Sharp. LC 79-40705. (Language Teaching Methodology Ser.). (Illus.). 128p. 1980. 13.95 (ISBN 0-08-024553-6); pap. 7.95 (ISBN 0-08-024552-8). Pergamon.
English at Your Fingertips: Teacher's Manual. Rosella Bernstein. 1979. pap. text ed. 3.95x o.p. (ISBN 0-87789-141-9). English Lang.
English Benedictines, Fifteen Forty to Sixteen Eighty-Eight: Reformation to Revolution. David Lunn. (Illus.). 282p. 1980. 24.95x. B&N.
English Bible: From KJV to NIV. Jack P. Lewis. 400p. 1981. 15.95 (ISBN 0-8010-5599-7). Baker Bk.

English Biblical Translation. A. C. Partridge. (Andre Deutsch Language Library). 1973. lib. bdg. 20.00x (ISBN 0-233-96129-1). Westview.

English Blue & White Porcelain of the Eighteenth Century. 2nd ed. Bernard Watney. 1973. 41.00 (ISBN 0-571-04796-3, Pub. by Faber & Faber). Merrimack Bk Serv.

English Book-Illustration of To-Day: Appreciations of the Work of Living English Illustrators with Lists of Their Books. Rose E. Sketchley. LC 78-179655. (Illus.). xxx, 175p. 1974. Repr. of 1903 ed. 24.00 (ISBN 0-8103-4052-6). Gale.

English Book Trade. Majorie Plant. 1974. text ed. 27.50x o.p. (ISBN 0-04-655012-7). Allen Unwin.

English Book Trade, Sixteen Sixty to Eighteen Fifty-Three. Ed. by Stephen Parks. Incl. Vol. 1 (ISBN 0-8240-0950-9); Vol. 2 (ISBN 0-8240-0951-7); Vol. 3 (ISBN 0-8240-0952-5); Vol. 4 (ISBN 0-8240-0953-3); Vol. 5 (ISBN 0-8240-0954-1); Vol. 6 (ISBN 0-8240-0955-X); Vol. 7 (ISBN 0-8240-0956-8); Vol. 8 (ISBN 0-8240-0957-6); Vol. 9 (ISBN 0-8240-0958-4); Vol. 10 (ISBN 0-8240-0959-2); Vol. 11 (ISBN 0-8240-0960-6); Vol. 12 (ISBN 0-8240-0961-4); Vol. 13 (ISBN 0-8240-0962-2); Vol. 14 (ISBN 0-8240-0963-0); Vol. 15 (ISBN 0-8240-0964-9); Vol. 16 (ISBN 0-8240-0965-7); Vol. 17 (ISBN 0-8240-0966-5); Vol. 18 (ISBN 0-8240-0967-3); Vol. 19 (ISBN 0-8240-0968-1); Vol. 20 (ISBN 0-8240-0969-X); Vol. 21 (ISBN 0-8240-0970-3); Vol. 22 (ISBN 0-8240-0971-1); Vol. 23 (ISBN 0-8240-0972-X); Vol. 24 (ISBN 0-8240-0973-8); Vol. 25 (ISBN 0-8240-0974-6); Vol. 26 (ISBN 0-8240-0975-4); Vol. 27 (ISBN 0-8240-0976-2); Vol. 28 (ISBN 0-8240-0977-0). 1974. lib. bdg. 50.00 per vol. (ISBN 0-686-57687-X). Garland Pub.

English Book Trade, Sixteen Sixty to Eighteen Fifty-Three. Ed. by Stephen Parks. Incl. Vol. 29 (ISBN 0-8240-0978-9); Vol. 30 (ISBN 0-8240-0979-7); Vol. 31 (ISBN 0-8240-0980-0); Vol. 32 (ISBN 0-8240-0981-9); Vol. 33, 2 vols (ISBN 0-8240-0982-7); Vol. 34 (ISBN 0-8240-0983-5); Vol. 35 (ISBN 0-8240-0984-3); Vol. 36 (ISBN 0-8240-0985-1); Vol. 37 (ISBN 0-8240-0986-X); Vol. 38 (ISBN 0-8240-0987-8). 1974. lib. bdg. 50.00 per vol. (ISBN 0-686-57688-8). Garland Pub.

English Books & Readers, 3 vols. Henry S. Bennett. 1970. Vol 1. 65.00 (ISBN 0-521-07609-9); Vol 2. 54.00 (ISBN 0-521-04153-8); Vol 3. 47.00 (ISBN 0-521-07701-X); 140.00 set (ISBN 0-521-08857-7). Cambridge U Pr.

English Broadsheets. Peter Abbs. (Second Ser.). 1970. pap. text ed. 4.95x o.p. (ISBN 0-435-10005-X); tchrs's ed 2.25x o.p. (ISBN 0-435-10007-6). Heinemann Ed.

English Broadsheets. Ed. by Peter Abbs. (Introductory Ser.). 1971. pap. text ed. 3.95x o.p. (ISBN 0-435-10008-4); tchr's ed. 2.95x o.p. (ISBN 0-435-10010-6). Heinemann Ed.

English Broadsheets. Ed. by Peter Abbs. (First Ser.). 1971. pap. text ed. 4.95x o.p. (ISBN 0-435-10002-5); tchrs' ed. 2.95x o.p. (ISBN 0-435-10003-3). Heinemann Ed.

English Business Letters. F. W. King & D. Ann Cree. (Illus.). 1980. pap. text ed. 4.00x (ISBN 0-582-55353-9). Longman.

English Cameo Glass. Ray Grover & Lee Grover. (Illus.). 1980. 30.00 (ISBN 0-517-53815-6). Crown.

English-Canadian Literature to 1900: A Guide to Information Sources. Ed. by R. G. Moyles. LC 73-16986. (American Literature, English Literature, & World Literatures in English Information Guide Ser.: Vol. 6). 208p. 1976. 30.00 (ISBN 0-8103-1222-0). Gale.

English Carol. Erik Routley. LC 73-9129. (Illus.). 272p. 1973. Repr. of 1959 ed. lib. bdg. 22.25x (ISBN 0-8371-6989-5, ROEC). Greenwood.

English Castles. Allen R. Brown. 1976. 33.00 (ISBN 0-7134-3119-9). David & Charles.

English Cathedral Music. 5th, rev. ed. Edmund H. Fellowes. Ed. by J. A. Westrup. LC 80-24400. (Illus.). xi, 283p. 1981. Repr. of 1973 ed. lib. bdg. 27.50x (ISBN 0-313-22643-1, FEEC). Greenwood.

English Catholic Community, 1570-1850. John Bossy. (Illus.). 1976. 29.95x (ISBN 0-19-519847-6). Oxford U Pr.

English Chamber Music. Ernst Meyer. LC 71-127181. (Music Ser). (Illus.). 1970. Repr. of 1946 ed. lib. bdg. 27.50 (ISBN 0-306-70037-9). Da Capo.

English Charlemagne Romances. Ed. by Sidney J. Herrtage. Incl. Pt. 1. Sir Ferumbras. 1879. 14.95x (ISBN 0-19-722569-1); Pt. 6. Tail of Rauf Coilyear, with the Fragments of Roland & Vernagu & Otuel. Ed. by Sidney J. Herrtage. 164p. 1882. 12.95x (ISBN 0-19-722513-6). Oxford U Pr.

English Children in the Olden Time. Jessie Bedford. 336p. 1980. Repr. of 1907 ed. lib. bdg. 30.00 (ISBN 0-8492-3777-7). R West.

English Children's Books. Percy Muir. 1979. 53.00 (ISBN 0-7134-2246-7, Pub. by Batsford England). David & Charles.

English-Chinese & Chinese-English Dictionary. 1977. 7.95 (ISBN 0-8351-0725-6). China Bks.

English Church & the Papacy, from the Conquest to the Reign of John. Zachary N. Brooke. LC 80-2228. 1981. Repr. of 1931 ed. 37.50 (ISBN 0-404-18756-0). AMS Pr.

English Church & the Papacy in the Middle Ages. Ed. by Clifford H. Lawrence. 1965. 20.00 o.p. (ISBN 0-8232-0645-9). Fordham.

English Church Architecture. Mark Child. (Illus.). 120p. 1981. 19.95 (ISBN 0-7134-2776-0, Pub. by Batsford England). David & Charles.

English Church in the Fourteenth Century. W. A. Pantin. (Medieval Academy Reprints for Teaching Ser.). 1980. pap. 5.00x (ISBN 0-8020-6411-6). U of Toronto Pr.

English Church Monuments. Brian Kemp. 240p. 1980. 53.00 (ISBN 0-7134-1735-8, Pub. by Batsford England). David & Charles.

English Church, Ten Hundred to Ten Sixty-Six. Frank Barlow. 1979. pap. text ed. 13.95 (ISBN 0-582-49049-9). Longman.

English Church Under Henry I. M Brett. (Oxford Historical Monographs). 288p. 1975. 37.50x (ISBN 0-19-821861-3). Oxford U Pr.

English Civil War & After, 1642-1658. Ed. by R. H. Parry. LC 74-111423. 1970. pap. 4.95x (ISBN 0-520-01783-8, CAMPUS 30). U of Cal Pr.

English Clergy: The Emergence & Consolidation of a Profession, 1558-1642. Rosemary O'Day. 1979. text ed. 31.25x (ISBN 0-7185-1167-0, Leicester). Humanities.

English Colloquial Arabic Dict. Raja Nasr. 1972. 18.00x (ISBN 0-685-77122-9). Intl Bk Ctr.

English Comedians at the Habsburg Court in Graz 1607-1608. Orlene Murad. (Salzburg Studies in Elizabethan & Renaissance Ser.: No. 81). 1978. pap. text ed. 25.00x (ISBN 0-391-01487-0). Humanities.

English Comedy. Allan Rodway. LC 74-25377. 1975. 20.00x (ISBN 0-520-02935-6). U of Cal Pr.

English: Commentaries by Alistair Cooke from Masterpiece Theatre. Alistair Cooke. LC 80-2701. (Illus.). 240p. 1981. cancelled (ISBN 0-394-51907-8). Knopf.

English Common Law in the Early American Colonies. Paul S. Reinsch. LC 75-110969. (American Constitutional & Legal History Ser). 1970. Repr. of 1899 ed. lib. bdg. 14.95 (ISBN 0-306-71910-X). Da Capo.

English Composition. Charles H. Vivian & Bernetta M. Jackson. (Orig.). 1961. pap. 4.50 (ISBN 0-06-460102-1, CO 102, COS). Har-Row.

English Composition. Barrett Wendell. 316p. 1980. Repr. of 1903 ed. lib. bdg. 30.00 (ISBN 0-8495-5654-6). Arden Lib.

English Composition in Eastern Colleges 1850-1940. John M. Wozniak. LC 78-59125. (Illus.). 1978. pap. text ed. 11.75 (ISBN 0-8191-0549-X). U Pr of Amer.

English Comprehensive, Three & Four Years. Gay Kelly-Crocker et al. LC 56-35602. (High School Exams & Answer Ser). (gr. 11-12). 1977. pap. 3.50 (ISBN 0-8120-0197-4). Barron.

English Connection: A Text for Speakers of Englisn As a Second Language. Gail Fingado et al. (English Ser.). 416p. 1981. text ed. 12.95 (ISBN 0-87626-236-1). Winthrop.

English Constitution. Walter Bagehot. (World's Classics Ser.). 1933. 10.95 (ISBN 0-19-250330-8). Oxford U Pr.

English Constitution. Walter Bagehot. LC 77-86594. (Classics of English Legal History in the Modern Era Ser.: Vol. 84). 1978. Repr. of 1867 ed. lib. bdg. 55.00 (ISBN 0-8240-3071-0). Garland Pub.

English Conversation Practice. Kenneth Methold. 1975. pap. text ed. 3.00x (ISBN 0-582-55221-4). Longman.

English Correspondence of Saint Boniface & His Friends in England. St. Boniface et al. Tr. by Edward Kylie. LC 66-30729. (Medieval Library). (Illus.). 209p. 1966. Repr. of 1926 ed. 19.50x (ISBN 0-8154-0028-4). Cooper Sq.

English Costume for Sports & Outdoors Recreation: From the Sixteenth to the Nineteenth Centuries. Phyllis Cunnington & Alan Mansfield. (Illus.). 1978. Repr. of 1969 ed. text ed. 23.50x (ISBN 0-7136-1017-4). Humanities.

English Costume from the Second Century BC to the Present Day. Doreen Yarwood. 1973. 30.00 (ISBN 0-7134-0853-7, Pub. by Batsford England). David & Charles.

English Costume of the Early Middle Ages. I. Brooke. (English Costume Ser.). 1977. Repr. of 1936 ed. text ed. 10.00x (ISBN 0-7136-0154-X). Humanities.

English Cotton Industry & the World Market 1815-1896. D. A. Farnie. (Illus.). 1979. 49.50x (ISBN 0-19-822478-8). Oxford U Pr.

English Country House: An Art & a Way of Life. Olive Cook. (Illus.). 1979. 19.95 (ISBN 0-500-24090-6). Thames Hudson.

English County Maps: Their Indentification, Cataloguing & Physical Care of a Collection. R. J. Lee. 1955. pap. 4.30x (ISBN 0-85365-002-0, Pub. by Lib Assn England). Oryx Pr.

English Court Odes 1660-1820. Rosamond McGuiness. (Oxford Monographs on Music). (Illus.). 250p. 1971. 22.50x o.p. (ISBN 0-19-816119-0). Oxford U Pr.

English Courts of Law. 5th ed. H. G. Hanbury & D. C. Yardley. 1979. 14.50x (ISBN 0-19-219139-X). Oxford U Pr.

English Critical Essays: Twentieth Century. Ed. by Phyllis M. Jones. (World's Classics Ser.). 7.95 (ISBN 0-19-250405-3). Oxford U Pr.

English Culture & the Decline of the Industrial Spirit, 1850-1980. Martin Wiener. (Illus.). 256p. Date not set. 15.95 (ISBN 0-521-23418-2). Cambridge U Pr.

English Cursive Book Hands, Twelve Hundred to Fifteen Hundred. M. B. Parkes. 1980. 27.50x (ISBN 0-520-04080-5). U of Cal Pr.

English Decoration in the 18th Century. John Fowler & John Cornforth. (Illus.). 1978. 29.95 o.p. (ISBN 0-214-20033-7, 8057, Dist. by Arco). Barrie & Jenkins.

English Delftware. 2nd ed. F. H. Garner & Michael Archer. 1972. 28.00 (ISBN 0-571-04756-4, Pub. by Faber & Faber). Merrimack Bk Serv.

English Dialects. G. L. Brook. (Andre Deutsch Language Library). 1972. PLB 13.50x (ISBN 0-233-95641-7). Westview.

English Dialects: An Introduction. Martyn F. Wakelin. 1972. pap. text ed. 13.00x (ISBN 0-485-12020-8, Athlone). Humanities.

English Dialogues of the Dead: A Critical History, an Anthology & a Check List. Frederick M. Keener. 300p. 1973. 18.50x (ISBN 0-231-03695-7). Columbia U Pr.

English Diaries: A Review of English Diaries from the Sixteenth to the Twentieth Century with an Introduction on Diary Writing. Arthur Ponsonby. LC 75-152247. 1971. Repr. of 1923 ed. 21.00 (ISBN 0-8103-3711-8). Gale.

English Drama. Ed. by Marie Axton & R. Williams. LC 76-57099. 1977. 32.00 (ISBN 0-521-21588-9). Cambridge U Pr.

English Drama: A Critical Introduction. Gamini Salgado. 1981. write for info. (ISBN 0-312-25429-6). St Martin.

English Drama & Theatre, 1800-1900: A Guide to Information Sources. Ed. by Leonard W. Conolly & J. P. Wearing. LC 73-16975. (American Literature, English Literature, & World Literatures in English Information Guide Ser.: Vol. 12). 1978. 30.00 (ISBN 0-8103-1225-5). Gale.

English Drama (Excluding Shakespeare) Select Bibliographical Guides. Ed. by Stanley Wells. 320p. 1975. text ed. 18.95x (ISBN 0-19-871034-8); pap. text ed. 9.50x (ISBN 0-19-871028-3). Oxford U Pr.

English Drama in Transition, 1880-1920. Ed. by Henry F. Salerno. Incl. Liars. Henry A. Jones; Second Mrs. Tanqueray. Arthur W. Pinero; Importance of Being Earnest. Oscar Wilde; Major Barbara. George B. Shaw; Admirable Crichton. James M. Barrie; Silver Box. John Galsworthy; Deirdre. William B. Yeats; Playboy of the Western World. John M. Synge; Our Betters. W. Somerset Maugham. LC 67-25504. 512p. (Orig.). 1968. pap. 9.50 (ISBN 0-685-23230-1). Pegasus.

English Drama, Nineteen Hundred-Nineteen Fifty: A Guide to Information Sources. E. H. Mikhail. LC 74-11523. (American Literature, English Literature & World Literatures in English Information Guide Ser.: Vol. 11). 1977. 30.00 (ISBN 0-8103-1216-6). Gale.

English Drama, Sixteen Sixty-Eighteen Hundred: A Guide to Information Sources. Ed. by Frederick M. Link. LC 73-16984. (American Literature English Literature & World Literatures in English Information Guide Ser.: Vol.9). 360p. 1976. 30.00 (ISBN 0-8103-1224-7). Gale.

English Drama: The Beginnings of the Modern Period, 1900-1930. Allardyce Nicoll. 115.00 (ISBN 0-521-08416-4). Cambridge U Pr.

English Drama to Sixteen Sixty (Excluding Shakespeare): A Guide to Information Sources. Ed. by F. Elaine Penninger. LC 73-16988. (American Literature, English Literature, & World Literatures in English Information Guide Ser.: Vol. 5). vi, 520p. 1976. 30.00 (ISBN 0-8103-1223-9). Gale.

English Dramatic Form, Sixteen-Sixty to Seveenteen-Sixty: An Essay in Generic History. Laura Brown. LC 80-25702. 264p. 1981. 19.50x (ISBN 0-300-02585-8). Yale U Pr.

English Eccentrics & Eccentricities. John Timbs. LC 69-18076. 1969. Repr. of 1875 ed. 20.00 (ISBN 0-8103-3556-5). Gale.

English Ecclesiastical Tenants-in-Chief & Knight Service, Especially in the Thirteenth & Fourteenth Centuries. Helena M. Chew. LC 80-2310. 1981. Repr. of 1932 ed. 32.50 (ISBN 0-404-18558-4). AMS Pr.

English Embroidery. Barbara Snook. (Illus.). 135p. 1975. 12.50 (ISBN 0-263-05579-5). Transatlantic.

English Enamel Boxes. Susan Benjamin. (Illus.). 1978. 15.95 o.p. (ISBN 0-670-29679-1, Studio). Viking Pr.

English English. 2nd ed. Ed. by Norman W. Schur. 300p. 1980. 28.00 (ISBN 0-8103-1096-1). Verbatim.

English English: A Descriptive Dictionary. Norman W. Schur. LC 77-20390. 1980. 24.95 (ISBN 0-930454-05-7). Verbatim.

English Engraved Silver. Charles Oman. (Illus.). 1979. 42.00 (ISBN 0-571-10498-3, Pub. by Faber & Faber). Merrimack Bk Serv.

English Epigrams. Ed. by William D. Adams. LC 74-77039. 1974. Repr. of 1878 ed. 20.00 (ISBN 0-8103-3700-2). Gale.

English Essays. Intro. by J. H. Lobban. 257p. 1980. Repr. lib. bdg. 30.00 (ISBN 0-89987-507-6). Century Bookbindery.

English Essays of Edward Gibbon. Edward Gibbon. Ed. by Patricia B. Craddock. 1972. 59.00 (ISBN 0-19-812496-1). Oxford U Pr.

English Essentials: With Self-Scoring Exercises. Herbert B. Nelson. (Quality Paperback: No. 52). (Orig.). 1977. pap. 3.95 (ISBN 0-8226-0052-8). Littlefield.

English Experiences. Janet Gonzalez-Mena. Incl. Program for English Experiences. (Illus.). 142p. pap. 12.95 (ISBN 0-88499-225-X); My Book. (Illus.). 48p. pap. 2.95 (ISBN 0-88499-238-1). LC 75-5307. (gr. 4 up). 1975. Set. 38.95 (ISBN 0-88499-238-1). Inst Mod Lang.

English Face of Machiavelli. Felix Raab. LC 65-1256. 1964. 15.00x o.p. (ISBN 0-8020-1300-7). U of Toronto Pr.

English Fairy & Other Folktales. Ed. by Edwin S. Hartland. LC 68-21772. 1968. Repr. of 1890 ed. 18.00 (ISBN 0-8103-3465-8). Gale.

English Farm Wagon: Origins & Structure. J. Geraint Jenkins. (Illus.). 264p. 1981. 22.50 (ISBN 0-7153-8119-9). David & Charles.

English Farmers & the Politics of Protection. Travis L. Crosby. 228p. 1977. text ed. 20.75x (ISBN 0-85527-116-7). Humanities.

English Fiction, Nineteen Hundred to Nineteen Fifty: A Guide to Information Sources. Ed. by Thomas J. Rice. LC 73-16989. (American Literature, English Literature, and World Literatures in English Information Guide Ser.: Vol. 20). 680p. 1979. 30.00 (ISBN 0-8103-1217-4). Gale.

English Fiction, Sixteen Sixty to Eighteen Hundred: A Guide to Information Sources. Ed. by Jerry Beasley. LC 74-11526. (American Literature, English Literature & World Literatures in English Information Guide Ser.: Vol. 14). 1978. 30.00 (ISBN 0-8103-1226-3). Gale.

English Field Systems. Howard L. Gray. 1981. Repr. of 1915 ed. lib. bdg. 20.00x (ISBN 0-678-08069-0). Kelley.

English Folk-Lore. Thomas F. Thiselton-Dyer. LC 75-150242. Repr. of 1878 ed. 20.00 (ISBN 0-8103-3680-4). Gale.

English Folk Poetry: Structure & Meaning. Roger Dev Renwick. LC 79-5260. (American Folklore Society Ser.). 256p. 1980. 17.00x (ISBN 0-8122-7777-5). U of Pa Pr.

English Folk-Rhymes: A Collection of Traditional Verses Relating to Places & Persons, Customs, Superstitions, Etc. G. F. Northall. LC 67-23918. 1967. Repr. of 1892 ed. 22.00 (ISBN 0-8103-3455-0). Gale.

English Folk Songs Collected, Arranged & Provided with Symphonies & Accompaniments for the Pianoforte. William A. Barrett. 95p. 1980. Repr. of 1891 ed. lib. bdg. 15.00 (ISBN 0-8492-3758-0). R West.

English for Academic & Technical Purposes: Studies in Honor of Louis Trimble. Ed. by Larry Selinker et al. (Orig.). 1981. pap. 13.95 (ISBN 0-88377-178-0). Newbury Hse.

English for Careers. Leila R. Smith. LC 76-54780. (Read & Replay Ser). 1977. pap. text ed. 15.95x (ISBN 0-471-80176-3). Wiley.

English for Careers Business Professionals & Technical. 2nd ed. Leial R. Smith. 528p. 1981. pap. text ed. 13.95 (ISBN 0-471-08991-5). Wiley.

English for Electrical Engineers. M. McAllister & G. Madama. (Illus.). 1977. pap. text ed. 10.25 (ISBN 0-582-52437-7). Longman.

English for Everybody. Ellsworth Barnard. LC 79-18238. (Orig.). 1979. pap. 5.00 (ISBN 0-686-26670-6). Dinosaur.

English for International Communication: InterCom, Bk. 1. Richard C. Yorkey et al. (Illus.). 200p. 1981. pap. text ed. price not set (ISBN 0-278-49201-0); price not set tchr's. ed. (ISBN 0-278-49216-9); price not set wkbk (ISBN 0-278-49230-4); price not set audio prog. (ISBN 0-278-49245-2). Litton Educ Pub.

English for International Conferences: A Language Course for Those Working in the Field of Science, Economics, Politics & Administration. Anthony Fitzpatrick. (MFLP Ser.). 64p. 1980. pap. 60.00 includes 4 cassettes (ISBN 0-08-027225-8). Pergamon.

English for Life, Vol. I: People & Places. V. J. Cook. (Illus.). 144p. 1980. 3.95 (ISBN 0-08-024564-1). Pergamon.

English for Maturity. 2nd ed. David Holbrook. 1967. 25.95 (ISBN 0-521-05286-6); pap. 9.95x (ISBN 0-521-09134-9, 134). Cambridge U Pr.

English for Meaning. David Holbrook. 241p. 1980. pap. text ed. 16.25x (ISBN 0-85633-184-8, NFER). Humanities.

English for Modern Business. 3rd ed. Erwin Keithley & Margaret H. Thompson. 1977. pap. text ed. 11.95 (ISBN 0-256-01852-9). Irwin.

English for Nurses. D. Austin & T. Crosfield. (Illus.). 144p. 1976. pap. text ed. 4.50x (ISBN 0-582-55019-X); tchrs' notes 2.25x (ISBN 0-582-55244-3). Longman.

English for Speakers of Mandarin Chinese. Isabella Y. Yen. (English As a Foreign Language Ser.). 356p. 1981. text & cassettes 85.00x (ISBN 0-87950-603-2); cassettes 80.00 (ISBN 0-686-69430-9). text ed. 10.00x (ISBN 0-87950-301-7). Spoken Lang Serv.

English for Speakers of Spanish: El Ingles Hablado. F. B. Agard et al. 1980. text & cassettes 65.00 (ISBN 0-87950-312-2); cassettes, 5 dual tracts 60.00 (ISBN 0-87950-311-4). Spoken Lang Serv.

English for Speakers of Vietnamese. William W. Gage. (English As a Foreign Language Ser.). 366p. 1981. text & 9 cassettes 85.00 (ISBN 0-87950-617-2); cassettes separate 80.00 (ISBN 0-87950-616-4). Spoken Lang Serv.

English for Specific Purposes. R. MacKay & A. Mountford. (Applied Linguistics & Language Study). 1978. pap. text ed. 9.00x (ISBN 0-582-55090-4). Longman.

English for the English. George Sampson. Ed. by D. Thompson. LC 70-108111. (Studies in the Tests & History of Education). 1970. 14.95 (ISBN 0-521-07848-2); pap. 5.95 (ISBN 0-521-09964-1). Cambridge U Pr.

English for the Foreign Physician. Jose M. Martins. (Illus.). 136p. 1974. photocopy ed. 12.75 (ISBN 0-398-01227-X). C C Thomas.

English for the Rejected. David Holbrook. (Orig.). 1964. pap. 9.95x (ISBN 0-521-09215-9). Cambridge U Pr.

English for You. Robert O'Neal & Alan C. Love. 1972. pap. text ed. 8.95x o.p. (ISBN 0-669-74369-0); instructor's manual free o.p. (ISBN 0-669-74385-2). Heath.

English: Franco, Slav & Flank Defence. John L. Watson. (Contemporary Chess Openings Ser.). (Illus.). 112p. 1981. 19.50 (ISBN 0-7134-2690-X, Pub. by Batsford England). David & Charles.

English-French-Arabic Dictionary of Diplomacy & International Terms. Fouk al-Ada. 30.00x (ISBN 0-685-54026-X). Intl Bk Ctr.

English-French-Arabic Dictionary of Political Idioms. Wahba. 30.00x (ISBN 0-686-65473-0). Intl Bk Ctr.

English-French-Arabic Trilingual Dictionary. Jerwan Sabek. 35.00 (ISBN 0-686-63569-8). Intl Bk Ctr.

English, French, German & Italian Techniques of Singing: A Study in National Tonal Preferences & How They Relate to Functional Efficiency. Richard Miller. LC 76-58554. (Illus.). 1977. 12.00 (ISBN 0-8108-1020-4). Scarecrow.

English-French Glossary of Educational Terminology. Robert L. Gieber. LC 80-5652. 212p. 1980. lib. bdg. 18.00 (ISBN 0-8191-1344-1); pap. text ed. 9.25 (ISBN 0-8191-1345-X). U Pr of Amer.

English Furniture: An Illustrated Handbook. Maurice Tomlin. 1972. 26.00 o.p. (ISBN 0-571-08381-1, Pub. by Faber & Faber). Merrimack Bk Serv.

English Furniture Eighteen Hundred to Eighteen Fifty-One. Edward T. Joy. (Illus.). 318p. 1977. 60.00 (ISBN 0-85667-031-6, Pub. by Sotheby Parke Bernet England). Biblio Dist.

English Furniture: From Gothic to Sheraton. Herbert Cescinsky. (Illus.). 1968. pap. 10.00 (ISBN 0-486-21929-1). Dover.

English Garden. Laurence Fleming & Alan Gore. (Illus.). 256p. 1981. 26.00 (ISBN 0-7181-1816-2). Merrimack Bk Serv.

English Garner, 12 Vols. Ed. by Edward Arber. Repr. of 1890 ed. write for info. Cooper Sq.

English Genealogy. 2nd ed. Anthony R. Wagner. (Illus.). 1972. 45.00x (ISBN 0-19-822334-X). Oxford U Pr.

English Gentleman. Douglas Sutherland. 1980. pap. 2.95 (ISBN 0-14-005597-5). Penguin.

English Gentleman: Containing Sundry Excellent Rules - How to Demeane or Accomodate Himselfe in the Manage of Publike or Private Affairs. Richard Brathwait. LC 74-28836. (English Experience Ser.: No. 717). 1975. Repr. of 1630 ed. 35.00 (ISBN 90-221-0717-5). Walter J Johnson.

English Gentleman's Child. Douglas Sutherland. (Illus.). 1981. pap. 3.50 (ISBN 0-14-005782-X). Penguin.

English Gentleman's Wife. Douglas Sutherland. 96p. 1981. pap. 2.95 (ISBN 0-14-005734-X). Penguin.

English-German Dictionary of Chemistry & Chemical Technology. 2nd ed. Ed. by Technishe Universitaet, Dresden. LC 76-455777. 1978. 47.50x (ISBN 0-8002-0401-8). Intl Pubns Serv.

English Gold Coins: Ancient to Modern Times. Emery M. Norweb. LC 68-9275. (Illus.). 96p. 1968. pap. text ed. 10.00x (ISBN 0-910386-44-7, Pub. by Cleveland Mus Art). Ind U Pr.

English Goldsmiths & Their Marks. Charles J. Jackson. 22.50 (ISBN 0-486-21206-8). Dover.

English Grammar. George O. Curme. (Orig.). 1947. pap. 3.95 (ISBN 0-06-460061-0, CO 61, COS). Har-Row.

English Grammar, 2 vols. Gordon Lish. (gr. 9-12). 1972. pap. text ed. 9.00 each incl. tchrs' manual & test (ISBN 0-8449-2700-7). Learning Line.

English Grammar for Students of French. Jacqueline Morton. LC 79-87578. 1979. pap. 4.50 (ISBN 0-934034-00-1). Olivia & Hill.

English Grammar for Students of German. Cecile Zorach. LC 80-82773. 1980. pap. 4.50 (ISBN 0-934034-02-8). Olivia & Hill.

English Grammar for Students of Spanish. Emily Spinelli. LC 79-90976. 1980. pap. 4.50 (ISBN 0-934034-01-X). Olivia & Hill.

English Grammatical Structure. L. G. Alexander et al. 255p. 1975. text ed. 27.00x (ISBN 0-582-55325-3). Longman.

English-Greek Dictionary: A Vocabulary of the Attic Language. S. C. Woodhouse. 1971. Repr. of 1910 ed. 45.00 (ISBN 0-7100-2324-3). Routledge & Kegan.

English Gypsies & Their Language. Charles G. Leland. LC 68-22035. 1969. Repr. of 1874 ed. 22.00 (ISBN 0-8103-3883-1). Gale.

English Gypsy Caravan. Ward C. Jackson & Denis E. Harvey. 1974. 16.95 (ISBN 0-7153-5680-1). David & Charles.

English Hawking & Hunting in the Boke of St. Albans. facsimile ed. Ed. by Rachel Hands. (Oxford English Monographs). (Illus.). 264p. 1975. 55.00x (ISBN 0-19-811715-9). Oxford U Pr.

English Heartland. Robert Beckinsale & Monica Beckinsale. (Illus.). 434p. 1980. 39.50x (ISBN 0-7156-1389-8, Pub. by Duckworth England). Biblio Dist.

English Heritage. J. H. Plumb et al. LC 77-92987. (Illus., Orig.). 1978. pap. text ed. 11.95x (ISBN 0-88273-350-8). Forum Pr MO.

English-Hindi Dictionary. large ed. 19.50 (ISBN 0-87557-034-8); small ed. 15.00 (ISBN 0-686-66962-2). Saphrograph.

English Hindi Dictionary. R. C. Pathak, 1979. 11.00 (ISBN 0-89744-970-3). Auromere.

English Historical Documents: 1874-1914, Vol. XII, Part 2. Ed. by W. D. Handcock. (English Historical Documents Ser.). (Illus.). 1978. 55.00x (ISBN 0-19-519994-4). Oxford U Pr.

English Historical Facts: Sixteen Hundred & Three to Sixteen Eighty-Eight. Chris Cook & John Wroughton. 231p. 1981. 32.50x (ISBN 0-8476-6295-0). Rowman.

English History: A Survey. George N. Clark. 1971. 21.95 o.p. (ISBN 0-19-822339-0). Oxford U Pr.

English History in the Making: Readings from the Sources from 1689, 2 vols. William L. Sachse. LC 67-10154. 1970. Vol. 1. pap. text ed. 13.95x (ISBN 0-471-00494-4); Vol. 2. pap. text ed. 12.95 o.p. (ISBN 0-471-00497-9). Wiley.

English History, Nineteen Nineteen to Nineteen Forty-Five. Alan J. Taylor. LC 65-27513. 1970. pap. 7.95 (ISBN 0-19-500304-7, GB311, GB). Oxford U Pr.

English History, 1919-1945. Alan J. Taylor. (Oxford History of England Ser). 1965. 33.00x (ISBN 0-19-821715-3). Oxford U Pr.

English Home. Doreen Yarwood. 1979. 30.00 (ISBN 0-7134-0805-7, Pub. by Batsford England). David & Charles.

English Hospital Statistics: Eighteen Sixty Seven to Nineteen Thirty Eight. Robert Pinker. 1966. text ed. 6.95x o.p. (ISBN 0-435-32700-3). Heinemann Ed.

English Hours. Henry James. 376p. 1980. cancelled (ISBN 0-8180-1129-7). Horizon.

English Humanists & Reformation Politics Under Henry Eighth & Edward Sixth. James K. McConica. 1965. 29.95x (ISBN 0-19-821450-2). Oxford U Pr.

English Hymnal. 1933. 18.50 (ISBN 0-19-231111-5); words only 7.95x (ISBN 0-19-231108-5). Oxford U Pr.

English Hymnal Service Book. 1962. 14.50x (ISBN 0-19-231120-4); words only 5.50x (ISBN 0-19-231121-2). Oxford U Pr.

English-Icelandic Dictionary (1976) Sigurdur O. Bogason. 1978. 75.00 (ISBN 0-685-29251-7). Heinman.

English Idioms. James M. Dixon. LC 73-163172. vi, 288p. 1975. Repr. of 1927 ed. 24.00 (ISBN 0-8103-3986-2). Gale.

English Idioms & Americanisms for Foreign Students, Professionals & Physicians. J. E. Schmidt. 544p. 1972. text ed. 26.50 (ISBN 0-398-02400-6). C C Thomas.

English Idioms: And How to Use Them. 4th ed. Jennifer Seidl & W. McMordie. 1978. pap. text ed. 5.95x (ISBN 0-19-432764-7). Oxford U Pr.

English in Agriculture. Alan Mountford. (English in Focus Ser.). (Illus.). 1978. pap. text ed. 6.95x (ISBN 0-19-437514-5); tchr's ed. 9.25x (ISBN 0-19-437506-4). Oxford U Pr.

English in Australia Now. David Holbrook. LC 76-183224. 250p. 1973. 26.50 (ISBN 0-521-08469-5); pap. text ed. 9.95x (ISBN 0-521-09706-1). Cambridge U Pr.

English in Basic Medical Science. Joan Maclean. (English in Focus Ser.). (Illus.). 1975. pap. text ed. 6.95x (ISBN 0-19-437515-3); tchr's ed. 11.00x (ISBN 0-19-437503-X). Oxford U Pr.

English in India. Vinayak K. Gokak. 1964. 7.50x (ISBN 0-210-34041-X). Asia.

English in Mechanical Engineering. Eric H. Glendinning. (English in Focus Ser). 1975. pap. text ed. 6.95x (ISBN 0-19-437512-9); tchr's ed. 11.95x (ISBN 0-19-437501-3). Oxford U Pr.

English in Physical Science. J. P. Allen & H. G. Widdowson. (English in Focus Ser). (Illus.). 1974. Student's Edition. pap. 6.95x (ISBN 0-19-437510-2); Tchr's Edition. 9.25x (ISBN 0-19-437504-8). Oxford U Pr.

English in Primary Schools. Geoffrey R. Roberts. 1972. 12.00x (ISBN 0-7100-7308-9); pap. 5.00 (ISBN 0-7100-7309-7). Routledge & Kegan.

English in Workshop Practice. Alan Mountford. (English in Focus Ser.). 1975. pap. text ed. 6.95x (ISBN 0-19-437511-0); tchrs'. ed. 9.25x (ISBN 0-19-437502-1). Oxford U Pr.

English Institute-Emerson: Prophecy, Metamorphosis, & Influence. Ed. by David Levin. (Selected Papers from the English Institute Ser). 192p. 1975. 12.50x (ISBN 0-231-04000-8). Columbia U Pr.

English Interiors: 1790-1848. John Cornforth. (Quest for Comfort Ser.). (Illus.). 1978. 29.95 o.p. (ISBN 0-686-01032-9, 8056, Dist. by Arco). Barrie & Jenkins.

English-Kikuyu Dictionary. A. R. Barlow. Tr. by T. G. Benson. 340p. 1975. 24.95x (ISBN 0-19-864407-8). Oxford U Pr.

English Lakeland: Cumbria. rev. ed. British Tourist Authority. (Illus.). 114p. 1981. pap. write for info. (ISBN 0-86143-037-9, Pub. by Auto Assn-British Tourist Authority England). Merrimack Bk Serv.

English Lands of the Abbey of Bec. Majorie Morgan. 1946. 8.00x o.p. (ISBN 0-19-822302-1). Oxford U Pr.

English Landscape Garden. H. F. Clark. (Illus.). 128p. 1980. text ed. 16.50x (ISBN 0-904387-38-0). Humanities.

English Language, 2 vols. W. F. Bolton & D. J. Crystal. Incl. Vol. 1. 1490-1839. 39.00 (ISBN 0-521-04280-1); pap. 10.50x (ISBN 0-521-09379-1); Vol. 2. 1858-1964. 1965. 49.00 (ISBN 0-521-07325-1); pap. 12.50x (ISBN 0-521-09545-X). 1966. Cambridge U Pr.

English Language. C. L. Wrenn. Date not set. Repr. of 1949 ed. lib. bdg. 22.50 (ISBN 0-89760-901-8). Telegraph Bks.

English Language: An Introduction. Nelson Francis. (gr. 12). 1965. 4.95x (ISBN 0-393-09629-7, NortonC); pap. text ed. 6.95x (ISBN 0-393-09925-3). Norton.

English Language & Literature: Teaching Area Exam for the National Teacher Examination. Arco Editorial Board. LC 65-23055. (Orig.). 1967. pap. 3.95 o.s.i. (ISBN 0-668-01319-2). Arco.

English Language & Orientation Programs in the United States. 130p. 1980. 5.00 (IIE). Unipub.

English Language Arts, Intermediate Level. Joseph Bellafiore. (Illus.). (gr. 7-9). 1969. text ed. 10.00 (ISBN 0-87720-308-3); pap. text ed. 5.83 (ISBN 0-87720-307-5); wkbk. ed. 6.83 (ISBN 0-87720-347-4). AMSCO Sch.

English Language Cookbooks, Sixteen Hundred to Nineteen Seventy-Three. Ed. by Lavonne Axford. LC 76-23533. 1976. 62.00 (ISBN 0-8103-0534-8). Gale.

English Language: Its Origin & History. Rudolph C. Bambas. LC 80-5237. (Illus.). 333p. 1980. 12.95x (ISBN 0-8061-1661-7). U of Okla Pr.

English Lantern Clocks. W. J. Hana. (Illus.). 1979. 14.95 (ISBN 0-7137-1011-X, Pub by Blandford Pr England). Sterling.

English Laws for Women in the Nineteenth Century. Caroline Norton. LC 79-2948. 188p. 1981. Repr. of 1854 ed. 17.00 (ISBN 0-8305-0111-8). Hyperion Conn.

English Legal History. 2nd ed. L. B. Curzon. 352p. 1979. pap. 12.95x (ISBN 0-7121-0578-6, Pub. by Macdonald & Evans England). Intl Ideas.

English Liberalism & the State: Individualism or Collectivism. Harold J. Schultz. LC 70-158945. (Problems in European Civilization Ser.). 1972. pap. text ed. 4.95x o.p. (ISBN 0-669-73361-X). Heath.

English Life in the Middle Ages. Louis F. Salzman. (Illus.). 1926. 24.95x (ISBN 0-19-821251-8). Oxford U Pr.

English Linguistics. James R. Smith. 1978. 2.50 (ISBN 0-8403-1436-1). Kendall-Hunt.

English Literary Criticism: Romantic & Victorian. Ed. by Daniel G. Hoffman & Samuel Hynes. 334p. 1980. Repr. of 1963 ed. text ed. 20.00x (ISBN 0-8290-0125-5); pap. text ed. 8.95x (ISBN 0-8290-0455-6). Irvington.

English Literary Journal to Nineteen Hundred: A Guide to Information Sources. Ed. by Robert B. White, Jr. LC 73-16998. (American Literature English Literature & World Literatures in English Information Guide Ser.: Vol. 8). 250p. 1977. 30.00 (ISBN 0-8103-1228-X). Gale.

English Literary Terms in Poetological Texts of the Sixteenth Century, 3 vols. Ursula Kuhn. (Salzburg Studies in English Literature, Elizabethan & Renaissance Studies: Nos. 32-34). 1071p. 1974. Set. pap. text ed. 75.25x (ISBN 0-391-01452-8). Humanities.

English Literature, 2 Vols. Bernard Grebanier. (Orig.). (gr. 9 up). text ed. 7.00 ea. Vol. 1 1959 (ISBN 0-8120-5037-1). Vol. 2 1948. Vol. 1. pap. 3.95 (ISBN 0-8120-0065-X); Vol. 2. pap. 4.50 (ISBN 0-8120-0066-8). Barron.

English Literature from Dryden to Burns. Alan D. McKillop. (Illus.). 1948. 34.00x (ISBN 0-89197-145-9). Irvington.

English Literature in Our Time & the University. F. R. Leavis. LC 78-73128. 1979. 26.50 (ISBN 0-521-22609-0); pap. 7.50 (ISBN 0-521-29574-2). Cambridge U Pr.

English Literature in the Age of Disguise. Ed. by Maximillian E. Novak. 1977. 15.00x o.p. (ISBN 0-520-03342-6). U of Cal Pr.

English Literature in the Earlier Seventeenth Century: 1600-1660. 2nd ed. Douglas Bush. (Oxford History of English Literature Ser.). 1962. 37.50x (ISBN 0-19-812202-0). Oxford U Pr.

English Literature in the Early Eighteenth Century, 1700-1740. Bonamy Dobree. (Oxford History of English Literature Ser.). 1959. 37.50x (ISBN 0-19-812205-5). Oxford U Pr.

English Literature in the Sixteenth Century Excluding Drama. Clive S. Lewis. (Oxford History of English Literature Ser.). 1954. 37.50x (ISBN 0-19-812204-7). Oxford U Pr.

English Love Poems. Ed. by John Betjeman & Geoffrey Taylor. 1964. pap. 6.95 (ISBN 0-571-07065-5, Pub. by Faber & Faber). Merrimack Bk Serv.

English Love Songs. Allen Percival. (Illus.). 256p. 1980. 27.50x (ISBN 0-389-20147-2). B&N.

English Made Easier. Joseph Bellafiore. (Orig.). (gr. 7-12). 1974. wkbk. 7.33 (ISBN 0-87720-344-X); pap. text ed. 5.92 (ISBN 0-87720-342-3). AMSCO Sch.

English Made Simple. rev. ed. Arthur Waldhorn & Arthur Zeiger. 1954. pap. 3.50 (ISBN 0-385-01208-X, Made). Doubleday.

English Made Simple Jr. Series. Jack E. Venema & John Waldman. pap. 3.50 (ISBN 0-385-00986-0, Made). Doubleday.

English Madrigal Composers. 2nd ed. Edmund H. Fellowes. 1948. pap. 9.95x (ISBN 0-19-315144-8). Oxford U Pr.

English Madrigal Verse: 1588-1632. 3rd ed. Ed. by Edmund H. Fellowes. 1967. 59.00x (ISBN 0-19-811474-5). Oxford U Pr.

English Medieval Graffiti. Violet Pritchard. 1967. 47.50 (ISBN 0-521-05998-4). Cambridge U Pr.

English Men of Letters, Walter Savage Landor. Sidney Colvin. Ed. by John Morley. 224p. 1980. Repr. of 1881 ed. lib. bdg. 15.00 (ISBN 0-89760-117-3). Telegraph Bks.

English Mind. Henry O. Taylor. 1962. pap. 0.95 o.s.i. (ISBN 0-02-067750-2, Collier). Macmillan.

English Miracle Plays, Moralities & Interludes: Specimens of the Pre-Elizabethan Drama. 8th ed. Ed. by A. W. Pollard. 1979. pap. 16.95x (ISBN 0-19-871098-4). Oxford U Pr.

English Monosyllables: A Minimal Pair Locator List for English As a Second Language. Ted Plaister. 1965. pap. 2.00x o.p. (ISBN 0-8248-0022-2, Eastwest Ctr). U Pr of Hawaii.

English Mummers & Their Plays: Traces of Ancient Mystery. Alan Brody. LC 77-92855. (Folklore & Folklife Ser). (Illus.). 1971. 12.00x (ISBN 0-8122-7611-6). U of Pa Pr.

English Mystery Plays. Ed. by Peter Happe. (English Library). 714p. 1980. pap. 4.95 (ISBN 0-14-043093-8). Penguin.

English Myths & Traditions. Henry Bett. (Illus.). 144p. 1980. Repr. of 1952 ed. lib. bdg. 17.50 (ISBN 0-8414-2921-9). Folcroft.

English Naive Painting. James Ayres. (Illus.). 168p. 1980. 29.95 (ISBN 0-500-23308-X). Thames Hudson.

English National Opera Guides: Caida, Generentola, Fidelio, Magic Flute, Vol. I. Ed. by Nicholas John. 1981. 25.00. Riverrun NY.

English Neoclassical Art. David Irwin. 1966. 19.95 o.p. (ISBN 0-571-06678-X, Pub. by Faber & Faber). Merrimack Bk Serv.

English-Norsk Dictionary: Gyldendals. new ed. B. Berulfsen. 1978. 18.50x (ISBN 8-2573-0007-1, N481); Norsk-English. 18.50x (ISBN 8-2573-0006-3, N-482). Vanous.

English Novel Explication: Supplement II, Through 1979. Christion J. Kloesel & Jeffrey R. Smitten. (Novel Explication Ser.). 312p. 1981. 27.50 (ISBN 0-208-01709-7). Shoe String.

English Novel: Form & Function. Dorothy Van Ghent. pap. 5.95x (ISBN 0-06-131050-6, TB1050, Torch). Har-Row.

English Novel: Select Bibliographical Guides. Ed. by A. E. Dyson. 384p. 1974. text ed. 19.50x (ISBN 0-19-871033-X); pap. 7.95x o.p. (ISBN 0-19-871027-5). Oxford U Pr.

English "O". Charles McCreadie & John McGonigal. 1974. pap. text ed. 3.95x o.p. (ISBN 0-435-10500-0). Heinemann Ed.

English on the Delaware: Sixteen Ten to Sixteen Eighty-Two. C. A. Weslager. 1967. 19.50 (ISBN 0-8135-0548-8). Rutgers U Pr.

English One & Two: A Contemporary Approach, 2 Bks. Robert W. Boynton et al. (gr. 7-9). 1971. Bk. 1. 6.50x o.p. (ISBN 0-8104-5611-7); Bk. 2. text ed. 7.50x o.p. (ISBN 0-8104-5613-3); tchrs.' manual, bk. 1 o.p. (ISBN 0-8104-5612-5); tchrs.' manual, bk. 2 free o.p. (ISBN 0-8104-5614-1); transparencies, bk. 1 o.p. 125.95 o.p. (ISBN 0-8104-5615-X); transparencies, bk. 2 o.p. 112.15 o.p. (ISBN 0-8104-5616-8); lp record, bk. 2 o.p. 5.95 o.p. (ISBN 0-8104-5617-6). Hayden.

English Oral Production. Elizabeth K. Anttila. 1980. pap. write for info. (ISBN 0-8477-3333-5). U of PR Pr.

English Parish Churches As Works of Art. Alec Clifton-Taylor. 1974. 24.00 (ISBN 0-7134-2776-0, Pub. by Batsford England). David & Charles.

English People in the Eighteenth Century. Dorothy Marshall. LC 80-16871. (Illus.). xvi, 288p. 1980. Repr. of 1956 ed. lib. bdg. 27.50x (ISBN 0-313-21080-2, MAENP). Greenwood.

English People on the Eve of Colonization, 1603-1630. Wallace Notestein. (New American Nation Ser). 1954. 15.00x o.s.i. (ISBN 0-06-013220-5, HarpT). Har-Row.

English Period Furniture. Charles Hayward. LC 77-155926. (Illus.). 1971. 10.00 o.p. (ISBN 0-684-12443-2, ScribT). Scribner.

English Philosophic Lyric. Louise H. Zwager. 208p. 1980. Repr. of 1931 ed. lib. bdg. 30.00 (ISBN 0-8495-6225-2). Arden Lib.

English Phonology & Phonological Theory. R. Lass. LC 76-650. (Studies in Linguistics: No. 17). 240p. 1976. 39.50 (ISBN 0-521-21039-9). Cambridge U Pr.

English Phrase Book for Vietnamese Speakers: Useful & Practical Phrases & Expressions Needed by Vietnamese. Nguyen-Dinh-Hoa. LC 75-34842. 1975. pap. 3.25 (ISBN 0-8048-1193-8). C E Tuttle.

English Place-Names. Kenneth Cameron. 1977. 22.50 (ISBN 0-7134-0841-3). David & Charles.

English Poems. John Milton. Ed. by W. W. Skeat. (World's Classics Ser). 7.95 o.p. (ISBN 0-19-250182-8). Oxford U Pr.

English Poems of C. S. Calverley. C. S. Calverley. Ed. by Hilda D. Spear. 116p. 1974. pap. text ed. 7.50x (ISBN 0-7185-1119-0, Leicester). Humanities.

English Poems of George Herbert. George Herbert. Ed. by C. A. Patrides. (Rowman & Littlefield University Library). 247p. 1974. 10.00x (ISBN 0-87471-551-2); pap. 4.50x (ISBN 0-87471-552-0). Rowman.

English Poets & the National Ideal. Ernest De Selincourt. 119p. 1980. Repr. of 1916 ed. text ed. 20.00 (ISBN 0-8492-4226-6). R West.

English-Polish Dictionary of Science & Technology. 5th ed. Ed. by Sergiusz Czerni & Maria Skrzynska. 1976. 30.00x (ISBN 0-686-23574-6). Intl Learn Syst.

English-Polish-Polish-English Chemical Dictionary. Ed. by Dobromila Kryt & Bazyli Semniuk. LC 79-393179. 912p. 1979. 32.50x (ISBN 83-204-0004-X). Intl Pubns Serv.

English Political Caricature: A Study of Opinion & Propaganda, 2 vols. M. Dorothy George. Incl. Vol. 1. To 1792. 42.00x (ISBN 0-19-817130-7); Vol. 2. 1793-1832. 42.00x (ISBN 0-19-817131-5). 1959. Oxford U Pr.

English Political Parties & Leaders in the Reign of Queen Anne, 1702-1710. Wm. T. Morgan. (Yale Historical Studies, Miscellany: No. VII). 1920. 47.50x (ISBN 0-685-69845-9). Elliots Bks.

English Popular Education: Seventeen Eighty to Nineteen Seventy. 2nd ed. D. Wardle. LC 75-41713. 208p. 1976. 22.50 (ISBN 0-521-21202-2); pap. 7.95x (ISBN 0-521-29073-2). Cambridge U Pr.

English Popular Literature: Eighteen Nineteen to Eighteen Fifty-One. Louis James. 1976. 22.50x (ISBN 0-231-04140-3). Columbia U Pr.

English Porcelain Figures of the Eighteenth Century. Arthur Lane. 1961. 23.00 (ISBN 0-571-04027-6, Pub. by Faber & Faber). Merrimack Bk Serv.

English Primary Education: A Sociological Description, 2 vols. W. A. Blyth. Incl. Vol. 1. Schools. text ed. 8.75x o.p. (ISBN 0-7100-3462-8); pap. text ed. 4.25x (ISBN 0-7100-6164-1); Vol. 2. Background. text ed. 6.00x (ISBN 0-7100-3485-7); pap. text ed. 4.25x (ISBN 0-7100-6165-X). (International Library of Sociology & Social Reconstruction). 1965. Humanities.

English Printing Fourteen Seventy-Six to Nineteen Hundred. Henry R. Plomer. 360p. 1980. Repr. of 1916 ed. lib. bdg. 35.00 (ISBN 0-8482-5576-3). Norwood Edns.

English Prints for the Collector. Stephen Calloway. LC 80-19370. (Illus.). 240p. 1981. 50.00 (ISBN 0-87951-120-6). Overlook Pr.

English Prison Officer Since Eighteen Fifty: A Study in Conflict. J. E. Thomas. (International Library of Social Policy). 1972. 22.00x (ISBN 0-7100-7280-5). Routledge & Kegan.

English Proficiency: Developing Your Reading & Writing Power, Bk. 1. Richard M. Bossone & Amy E. Ashe. 320p. (gr. 7-9). 1980. 10.32 (ISBN 0-07-006589-6, W); tchrs. manual 6.00 (ISBN 0-07-006590-X). McGraw.

English Prose & Criticism in the Nineteenth Century: A Guide to Information Sources. Ed. by Harris W. Wilson & Diane L. Hoeveler. LC 74-11527. (American Literature, English Literature, & World Literature in English Info. Guide Ser.: Vol. 18). 1979. 30.00 (ISBN 0-8103-1235-2). Gale.

English Prose, Prose Fiction, & Criticism to 1660: A Guide to Information Sources. Ed. by S. K. Heninger, Jr. LC 73-16980. (American Literature, English Literature, & World Literatures in English Information Guide Ser.: Vol. 2). 350p. 1975. 30.00 (ISBN 0-8103-1233-6). Gale.

English Proverbs & Proverbial Phrases: A Historical Dictionary. George L. Apperson. LC 70-76017. 1969. Repr. of 1929 ed. 24.00 (ISBN 0-8103-3881-5). Gale.

English Proverbs & Proverbial Phrases. William C. Hazlitt. LC 67-23914. 1969. Repr. of 1907 ed. 24.00 (ISBN 0-8103-3199-3). Gale.

English Public Revenue Sixteen Sixty to Sixteen Eighty-Eight. C. D. Chandaman. (Illus.). 400p. 1975. 55.00x (ISBN 0-19-828268-0). Oxford U Pr.

English-Reader's Dictionary. 2nd ed. Ed. by Albert S. Hornby & E. C. Parnwell. 1969. pap. 5.95x (ISBN 0-19-431116-3). Oxford U Pr.

English Reading Test. Harold V. King & Russell N. Campbell. 1956. pap. 15.00 set of 20 tests (ISBN 0-87789-029-3); pap. 0.50 eRT answer key (ISBN 0-87789-030-7). Eng Language.

English Renaissance Literature: Introductory Lectures. Frank Kermode et al. 1974. 13.00x o.p. (ISBN 0-85641-022-5, Pub. by Basil Blackwell England); pap. 5.25x o.p. (ISBN 0-85641-023-3). Biblio Dist.

English Renaissance Studies: Presented to Dame Helen Gardner in Honour of Her Seventieth Birthday. John Carey. (Illus.). 312p. 1980. 44.00x (ISBN 0-19-812093-1). Oxford U Pr.

English Review. pocket ed. 150p. (gr. 7-12). 1981. pap. text ed. 2.50 (ISBN 0-8120-2197-5). Barron. Postponed.

English Review Manual. 2nd ed. James A. Gowen. 1970. text ed. 10.95 (ISBN 0-07-023881-2, C); pap. text ed. 10.95 o.p. (ISBN 0-07-023880-4); instructor's guide & test answers 5.95 (ISBN 0-07-023883-9). McGraw.

English Revised Bible: Holy Bible As Revised, 1881-1885. 10.95 (ISBN 0-19-526831-8). Oxford U Pr.

English Revolution, Sixteen Eighty-Eight to Sixteen Eighty-Nine. George M. Trevelyan. (YA) (gr. 9 up). 1965. pap. 4.95 (ISBN 0-19-500263-6, GB). Oxford U Pr.

English Rising in Fourteen Fifty. George Kriehn. (Perspectives in European History Ser.: No. 37). vii, 131p. 1980. Repr. of 1882 ed. lib. bdg. 15.00x (ISBN 0-87991-081-X). Porcupine Pr.

English Rogue, Described in the Life of Meriton Latroon, a Witty Extravagant: Being a Complete History of the Most Eminent Cheats of Both Sexes. Richard Head & Francis Kirkman. LC 80-2483. 1981. Repr. of 1928 ed. 73.50 (ISBN 0-404-19117-7). AMS Pr.

English Roman Life. Anthony Munday. Ed. by Phillip J. Ayres. (Studies in Tudor & Stewart Literature Ser.). (Illus.). 142p. 1980. 22.00 (ISBN 0-19-812635-2). Oxford U Pr.

English Romantic Poetry & Prose. Ed. by Russell Noyes. 1956. 19.95x (ISBN 0-19-501007-8). Oxford U Pr.

English Romantic Poetry, Eighteen Hundred-Eighteen Thirty-Five: A Guide to Information Sources. Ed. by Donald Reiman. LC 74-11527. (American Literature, English Literature, & World Literatures in English Information Guide Ser.: Vol. 27). 1979. 30.00 (ISBN 0-8103-1231-X). Gale.

English Romantic Poets & Essayists: A Review of Research & Criticism. rev. ed. Ed. by Carolyn Washburn Houtchens & Lawrence Huston Houtchens. LC 66-12599. 1966. 17.50x (ISBN 0-8147-0205-8). NYU Pr.

English Romantic Poets: Modern Essays in Criticism. 2nd ed. Ed. by M. H. Abrams. 592p. 1975. pap. 7.95 (ISBN 0-19-501946-6, 35, GB). Oxford U Pr.

English-Rumanian Dictionary. Serban Andronescu. 15.00 (ISBN 0-685-20187-2, 064-X). Saphrograph.

English Rural Community: Myddle Under the Tudors & Stuarts. David G. Hey. (Illus.). 260p. 1974. text ed. 17.50x (ISBN 0-7185-1115-8, Leicester). Humanities.

English-Russian Biological Dictionary. 3rd ed. Ed. by O. I. Chibisova & L. A. Kozar. LC 78-40145. 1980. text ed. 120.00 (ISBN 0-08-023163-2). Pergamon.

English-Russian Dictionary. 6th ed. Vladimir K. Muller. 17.50 (ISBN 0-685-20186-4, 067-4). Saphrograph.

English-Russian Dictionary of Chemistry & Technology of Polymers. P. G. Babaevsky et al. Ed. by F. I. Yashinskaya & E. B. Trostyanskaya. 1978. text ed. 75.00 o.p. (ISBN 0-08-022944-1). Pergamon.

English-Russian Dictionary of Nabokov's "Lolita". A. D. Nakhimovsky & V. A. Paperno. (Rus. & Eng.). 1981. 16.50x (ISBN 0-88233-443-3); pap. 7.50x (ISBN 0-88233-444-1). Ardis Pubs.

English-Russian Dictionary of Petroleum Chemistry & Processing: Soviet Ed. 2nd rev. & enl. ed. Ed. by V. V. Kedrinsky. 1978. text ed. 100.00 o.p. (ISBN 0-08-022945-X). Pergamon.

English-Russian Dictionary of Reliability & Quality Control. Y. G. Kovalenko. LC 77-70279. 1977. text ed. 67.00 (ISBN 0-08-021933-0). Pergamon.

English-Russian Physics Dictionary. Ed. by D. M. Tolstoi. LC 78-40718. 1979. 75.00 (ISBN 0-08-023057-1). Pergamon.

English Satire. James R. Sutherland. 1958. 26.50 (ISBN 0-521-06584-4). Cambridge U Pr.

English School: Its Architecture & Organization, Vol. 2. Seaborne & Lowe. (Illus.). 1977. 50.00x (ISBN 0-7100-8408-0). Routledge & Kegan.

English Secretary. Angell Day. LC 67-10122. 1967. Repr. of 1599 ed. 35.00 (ISBN 0-8201-1012-4). Schol Facsimiles.

English Self-Taught. Eugene J. Hall. Incl. Bk. 1. 372p (ISBN 0-88345-210-3, 18140); Bk. 2. 401p (ISBN 0-88345-211-1, 18143); Bk. 3 (ISBN 0-88345-212-X, 18146); Bk. 4 (ISBN 0-88345-213-8, 18149); Bk. 5 (ISBN 0-88345-214-6, 18152); Bk. 6 (ISBN 0-88345-215-4, 18155). (gr. 7 up). 1974. wkbk. 8.25 ea.; 6-cassette album 60.00 ea. filmstrips 65.00 ea.; cassette, filmstrip & worktext sets 125.00 ea.; worktexts 1-6 & cassettes 325.00 (ISBN 0-685-48092-5). Regents Pub.

English Self-Taught, Bk. 7. Eugene J. Hall. 382p. (gr. 7 up). 1974. 8.25 (ISBN 0-88345-221-9); cassettes 60.00 (ISBN 0-685-53166-X). Regents Pub.

English Self-Taught, Bk. 8. Eugene J. Hall. (English Self-Taught Ser.). 358p. (gr. 7 up). 1975. 8.25 (ISBN 0-88345-223-5); cassettes 60.00 (ISBN 0-685-59324-X). Regents Pub.

English Self-Taught, Bk. 9. Eugene J. Hall. (English Self-Taught Ser.). 331p. (gr. 7 up). 1975. 8.25 (ISBN 0-88345-224-3); cassettes 60.00 (ISBN 0-685-59322-3). Regents Pub.

English Self-Taught, Bk. 10. Eugene J. Hall. (English Self-Taught Ser.). 318p. (gr. 7 up). 1975. 8.25 (ISBN 0-88345-225-1); cassettes 60.00 (ISBN 0-685-59326-6). Regents Pub.

English Self-Taught, Bk. 11. Eugene J. Hall. (Illus.). 315p. 1975. pap. 8.25 (ISBN 0-88345-226-X); cassettes 60.00 (ISBN 0-685-62261-4). Regents Pub.

English Self-Taught, Bk. 12. Eugene J. Hall. (Illus.). 308p. 1976. pap. 8.25 (ISBN 0-88345-227-8); cassettes 60.00 (ISBN 0-685-63972-X). Regents Pub.

English Setter. (Illus.). 1976. bds. 2.25 o.p. (ISBN 0-668-03984-1). Arco.

English Setters. Ed. by Beverly Pisano. (Illus.). 128p. 1980. 2.95 (ISBN 0-87666-716-7, KW102). TFH Pubns.

English Seventeenth-Century Verse, 2 vols. Ed. by Richard S. Sylvester. (Illus.). 720p. 1974. Vol I. pap. 6.95 (ISBN 0-393-00675-1, Norton Lib); Vol. 2. pap. 7.95 (ISBN 0-393-00676-X). Norton.

English Short Stories of the Nineteenth Century. Ed. by H. Bergner. 1969. bound 31.20 (ISBN 0-685-05222-2); pap. 12.90 (ISBN 0-685-05223-0). Adler.

English Silver 1675-1825. rev. ed. Stephen G. Ensko & Edward Wenham. (Illus.). 144p. 1980. 24.95x (ISBN 0-938186-00-0). Arcadia Pr.

English Sixth Form: A Case Study in Curriculum Research. Philip H. Taylor & W. A. Reid. (International Library of Sociology). 1974. 14.00 (ISBN 0-7100-7832-3). Routledge & Kegan.

English Sixth Form College: An Educational Concept. R. Wearing-King. 1969. pap. 5.50 o.p. (ISBN 0-08-013214-6). Pergamon.

English Skills. 2nd ed. John Langan. (Illus.). 416p. 1980. text ed. 7.95x (ISBN 0-07-036265-3, C); instructor's manual 3.95x (ISBN 0-07-036266-1). McGraw.

English Skills Handbook: Reading & Writing. Harvey S. Wiener & Charles Bazerman. LC 76-14015. (Illus.). 1976. pap. text ed. 8.25 (ISBN 0-395-20595-6); instructor's manual 0.75 (ISBN 0-395-20669-3). HM.

English Society & Government in the Fifteenth Century. Ed. by C. M. Crowder. LC 68-79460. (Selections from History Today Ser.,No. 2). (Illus.). 1967. 5.00 (ISBN 0-05-000809-9); pap. 3.95 (ISBN 0-685-09164-3). Dufour.

English Sound Changes. G. L. Brook. 175p. 6.00x (ISBN 0-7190-0111-0, Pub.by Manchester U Pr England). State Mutual Bk.

English Sounds & Spelling. L. McClelland et al. 1979. pap. 6.95 (ISBN 0-13-282954-1). P-H.

English-Spanish Guide for Medical Personnel. Ed. by Joseph Armengol et al. 1966. pap. 3.50 (ISBN 0-87488-721-6). Med Exam.

English-Spanish, Spanish-English Dictionary of Communications & Electronic Terms. Roger L. Freeman. 1972. 37.50 (ISBN 0-521-08080-0). Cambridge U Pr.

English Spelling: Roadblock to Reading. Godfrey Dewey. LC 77-141240. 1971. text ed. 15.75x (ISBN 0-8077-1242-6). Tchrs Coll.

English Springer Spaniels. Frank W. Hill. Ed. by Christina Foyle. (Foyle's Handbks). 1973. 3.95 (ISBN 0-685-55817-7). Palmetto Pub.

English Springer Spaniels. Diane McCarty & Mrs. Janet Henneberry. (Illus.). 1980. 2.95 (ISBN 0-87666-687-X, KW-081). TFH Pubns.

English Stage Ser. Attack & Defense, 1577-1730, 50 vols. Ed. by Arthur Freeman. lib. bdg. 50.00 ea.; lib. bdg. 1600.00 set (ISBN 0-685-41743-3). Garland Pub.

English Step by Step with Pictures. new ed. Boggs & Dixson. (gr. 7-12). 1980. pap. text ed. 3.75 (ISBN 0-88345-416-5, 18186). Regents Pub.

English Step by Step with Pictures. rev. ed. Robert J. Dixson & Ralph S. Boggs. (Illus., Orig.). (gr. 4 up). 1971. pap. text ed. 2.45 o.p. (ISBN 0-88345-046-1, 17978). Regents Pub.

English Stories. Arturo Vivante. LC 75-19938. (Illus.). 64p. (Orig.). 1975. pap. 4.95 o.p. (ISBN 0-914908-27-8). Street Fiction.

English Structure Exercises. Elizabeth K. Anttila. pap. 1.85 (ISBN 0-8477-3300-9). U of PR Pr.

English Study Material: High School Equivalency-GED. William E. Lockhart. (Michigan Prescriptive Program Ser.). 1975. pap. text ed. 4.50 (ISBN 0-89039-121-1). Ann Arbor Pubs.

English Subtitles. Peter Porter. 64p. 1981. pap. 11.95 (ISBN 0-19-211942-7). Oxford U Pr.

English Surnames, 2 Vols. 4th ed. Mark A. Lower. LC 68-22037. 1968. Repr. of 1875 ed. Set. 20.00 (ISBN 0-8103-3129-2). Gale.

English: Syllabus. Norman H. Crowhurst. 138p. 1974. pap. text ed. 7.45 (ISBN 0-89420-073-9, 171050); cassette recordings 130.25 (ISBN 0-89420-145-X, 171000). Natl Book.

English Synodalia of the Thirteenth Century. C. R. Cheney. 1968. Repr. of 1941 ed. 16.50x (ISBN 0-19-821396-4). Oxford U Pr.

English Syntax: An Outline for Clinicians & Teachers of Language Handicapped Children. Charles Hargis. (Illus.). 232p. 1977. 15.75 (ISBN 0-398-03558-X). C C Thomas.

English Table in History & Literature. Charles Cooper. LC 68-21760. 1968. Repr. of 1929 ed. 15.00 (ISBN 0-8103-3520-4). Gale.

English Taxation, Sixteen Forty to Seventeen Ninety-Nine. William Kennedy. Repr. of 1913 ed. 22.50x (ISBN 0-678-05060-0). Kelley.

English Teacher: Basic Traditions & Successful Innovations. Joseph Mersand. 1977. 15.00 (ISBN 0-8046-9170-3); pap. text ed. 8.95 (ISBN 0-8046-9175-4). Kennikat.

English Teacher's Companion: A Survey of the Media. Ed. by Lewis Gardner. LC 74-82110. 160p. 1975. pap. 3.95 (ISBN 0-590-09588-9, Citation). Schol Bk Serv.

English Teaching Perspectives. Donn Byrne. 1980. pap. text ed. 7.50x (ISBN 0-582-74604-3). Longman.

English Theatre & John Keats. Harry R. Beaudry. (Salzburg Studies in English Literature, Poetic Drama & Poetic Theory: No. 13). 240p. 1973. pap. 25.00x (ISBN 0-391-01321-1). Humanities.

English Theatrical Literature Fifteen Fifty-Nine to Nineteen Hundred: A Bibliography Incorporating Lowe's Bibliographical Account. James F. Arnott & J. W. Robinson. 1971. Repr. 45.00 (ISBN 0-8277-0415-1). British Bk Ctr.

English Through Drama. C. Parry. LC 72-184902. (Illus.). 250p. 1972. 24.95 (ISBN 0-521-08483-0); pap. 9.95x (ISBN 0-521-09741-X). Cambridge U Pr.

English-Tibetan Colloquial Dictionary. C. A. Bell. 1977. Repr. of 1920 ed. 18.50x (ISBN 0-8364-0401-7). South Asia Bks.

English Transition Theory, Sixteen Fifty to Eighteen Hundred. T. R. Steiner. (Approaches to Translation Studies: No. 2). 159p. (Orig.). 1976. pap. text ed. 23.00x (ISBN 90-232-1276-2). Humanities.

English Utilitarians. 2nd ed. John Plamenatz. 1958. text ed. 18.50x (ISBN 0-631-05420-0). Humanities.

English Verb. F. R. Palmer. (Linguistics Library). (Illus.). 280p. 1974. text ed. 16.95x (ISBN 0-582-52454-7); pap. text ed. 10.95x (ISBN 0-582-52458-X). Longman.

English Verb Auxiliaries. 2nd ed. W. F. Twaddell. LC 63-10462. 1978. pap. 1.50 (ISBN 0-87057-072-2, Pub. by Brown U Pr). Univ of Pr New England.

English Verse. T. R. Barnes. 1967. 49.50 (ISBN 0-521-04109-0); pap. 10.95x (ISBN 0-521-09433-X, 433). Cambridge U Pr.

English Verse, 5 vols. William Peacock. Incl. Vol. 1. Early Lyrics to Shakespeare. 6.95 (ISBN 0-19-250308-1); Vol. 2. Campion to the Ballads. 7.95 (ISBN 0-19-250309-X); Vol. 3. Dryden to Wordsworth. 7.95 (ISBN 0-19-250310-3); Vol. 4. Scott to E. B. Browning. 10.95 (ISBN 0-19-250311-1); Vol. 5. Longfellow to Rupert Brooke. 7.95 (ISBN 0-19-250312-X). (World's Classics Ser). Oxford U Pr.

English Verse Eighteen Thirty to Eighteen Ninety. Ed. by Bernard Richards. (Longman Annotated Anthologies of English Verse: Vol. 6). 543p. 1980. text ed. 33.00 (ISBN 0-582-48387-5); pap. text ed. 19.95 (ISBN 0-582-48388-3). Longman.

English Verse Satire, Fifteen Ninety to Seventeen Sixty-Five. Raman Selden. 1978. text ed. 22.50x (ISBN 0-04-827016-4). Allen Unwin.

English Verse 1300-1500. John Burrow. LC 76-7591. (Longman Annotated Anthologies of English Verse). 1977. text ed. 26.00x (ISBN 0-582-48367-0); pap. text ed. 12.95x (ISBN 0-582-48368-9). Longman.

English Verse, 1701-50. D. F. Foxon. Incl. Vol. 1. Catalogue; Vol. 2. Indexes. 1975. 540.00 (ISBN 0-521-08144-0). Cambridge U Pr.

English Versification: 1570-1980: a Reference Guide with a Global Appendix. Ed. by T. V. Brogan. LC 80-8861. 832p. 1981. text ed. 47.50x (ISBN 0-8018-2541-5). Johns Hopkins.

English Vice: Beating, Sex & Shame in Victorian England & After. Ian Gibson. (Illus.). 364p. 1978. 27.50 (ISBN 0-686-26719-2, Pub. by Duckworth England). Biblio Dist.

English-Vietnamese Phrase Book with Useful Word List: For Vietnamese Speakers. Nguyen Hy Quang. LC 75-24856. (Vietnamese Refugee Education Ser.: No. 1). 1975. pap. text ed. 4.00x (ISBN 0-87281-043-7). Ctr Appl Ling.

English Village. Richard Muir. (Illus.). 208p. 1980. 19.95 (ISBN 0-500-24106-6). Thames Hudson.

English Villages. John Burke. (Illus.). 200p. 1975. 11.50 o.s.i. (ISBN 0-7134-2932-1). Hippocrene Bks.

English-Wappo Vocabulary. J. O. Sawyer. (U. C. Publ. in Linguistics: Vol. 43). 1965. pap. 7.50x (ISBN 0-520-09238-4). U of Cal Pr.

English Without Teacher & Dictionary: English-Arabic. J. R. Mouthany. 7.95x. Intl Bk Ctr.

English Woodcuts: Fourteen Eighty to Fifteen Thirty-Five. Edward Hodnett. (Illus.). 611p. 1973. 45.00x o.p. (ISBN 0-19-721728-1). Oxford U Pr.

English Wool Trade in the Middle Ages. T. H. Lloyd. LC 76-11086. (Illus.). 1977. 53.50 (ISBN 0-521-21239-1). Cambridge U Pr.

English Word Power for Physicians & Other Professionals: A Vigorous & Cultured Vocabulary. J. E. Schmidt. 240p. 1971. 19.75 (ISBN 0-398-01666-6). C C Thomas.

English Works. R. Ascham. Ed. by W. A. Wright. 1970. Repr. of 1904 ed. 49.50 (ISBN 0-521-07768-0). Cambridge U Pr.

English Works of Giles Fletcher, the Elder. Giles Fletcher. Ed. by Lloyd E. Berry. (Illus.). 1964. 40.00 (ISBN 0-299-03370-8). U of Wis Pr.

English Writers on Education, Fourteen Eighty to Sixteen Hundred & Three. Ed. by Foster Watson. LC 67-18716. 1967. Repr. of 1906 ed. 20.00x (ISBN 0-8201-1048-5). Schol Facsimiles.

Englishman & His History. Herbert Butterfield. LC 76-121754. 1970. Repr. of 1944 ed. 9.50 o.p. (ISBN 0-208-00993-0, Archon). Shoe String.

Englishman in Kansas; or, Squatter Life & Border Warfare. T. H. Gladstone. LC 74-155700. 1971. 14.95x (ISBN 0-8032-0800-6); pap. 3.95 (ISBN 0-8032-5742-2, BB 536, Bison). U of Nebr Pr.

Englishman's Greek Concordance of the New Testament. rev. ed. George V. Vigram. 1980. pap. 23.95 (ISBN 0-8054-1388-X). Broadman.

Englishman's Greek Concordance of the New Testament: Numerically Coded to Strong's Exhaustive Concordance. rev. ed. 1980. Repr. 23.95 (ISBN 0-8010-3357-8). Baker Bk.

Englishman's Home. J. H. Peel. LC 78-52159. 1978. 14.95 (ISBN 0-7153-7637-3). David & Charles.

Englishwoman in America. Isabella L. Bird. 1966. pap. 9.50x (ISBN 0-299-03524-7). U of Wis Pr.

Englishwoman's Review of Social & Industrial Questions, Vols. 13 & 14. Ed. by Janet H. Murray & Myra Stark. 1979. lib. bdg. 44.00 ea. Garland Pub.

Engranes. Harlan Wade. Tr. by Mamie M. Contreras from Eng. LC 78-26614. (Book About Ser.). Orig. Title: Gears. (Illus., Sp.). (gr. k-3). 1979. PLB 7.30 (ISBN 0-8172-1486-0). Raintree Pubs.

Engraved Designs of William Blake. Lawrence Binyon. LC 67-25542. (Graphic Art Ser). 1967. Repr. of 1926 ed. lib. bdg. 65.00 (ISBN 0-306-70956-2). Da Capo.

Engraved Gems: The Ionides Collection. John Boardman. LC 68-17325. (Illus.). 1968. 16.95x o.s.i. (ISBN 0-8101-0048-7). Northwestern U Pr.

Engraved Glass & Other Decorated Glass. Robert T. Matthews. LC 76-48555. (Illus.). 1978. soft bound 10.95 (ISBN 0-9601150-1-3). R T Matthews.

Engrenages. Harlan Wade. Tr. by Claude Potvin & Rose-Ella Potvin. (Book About Ser.). Orig. Title: Gears. (Illus., Fr.). (gr. k-3). 1979. PLB 7.30 (ISBN 0-8172-1461-5). Raintree Pubs.

ENGUIDE: A Guide to Bibliographic Data for Users of Environmental Information. Franklin Institute. 100p. 1980. pap. text ed. 14.95. Franklin Inst Pr.

Enhanced Oil Recovery: Secondary & Tertiary Methods. Ed. by M. M. Schumacher. LC 77-15224. (Chemical Technology Review No. 103; Energy Technology Review No. 22). (Illus.). 1978. 32.00 o.p. (ISBN 0-8155-0692-9). Noyes.

Enhanced Recovery. M. Latil. 275p. 1980. 24.95 (ISBN 0-87201-775-3). Gulf Pub.

Enhanced Recovery of Residual & Heavy Oils. 2nd ed. Ed. by M. M. Schumacher. LC 80-19812. (Energy Tech. Rev. 59; Chemical Tech. Rev. 174). (Illus.). 378p. 1981. 48.00 (ISBN 0-8155-0816-6). Noyes.

Enhancement of Food Production for the United States: World Food & Nutrition Study. Board on Agriculture & Renewable Resources, National Research Council. LC 75-37121. xiii, 174p. 1975. pap. 6.00 (ISBN 0-309-02435-8). Natl Acad Pr.

Enhancing Global Human Rights. Jorge I. Dominguez et al. (Illus.). 1979. text ed. 9.95 o.p. (ISBN 0-07-017397-4, P&RB); pap. text ed. 6.95 o.p. (ISBN 0-07-017398-2). McGraw.

Enhancing Hospital Efficiency: A Guide to Expanding Beds Without Bricks. John E. Peterson et al. (Illus.). 1980. text ed. 15.00 (ISBN 0-914904-45-0). Health Admin Pr.

Enhancing Self-Concept in Early Childhood: Theory & Practice. Shirley C Samuels. LC 76-58348. 1977. text ed. 24.95 (ISBN 0-87705-316-2); pap. 11.95 (ISBN 0-87705-353-7). Human Sci Pr.

Enhancing Wellness. Carolyn C. Clark. 1981. text ed. 26.95 (ISBN 0-8261-2950-1); pap. text ed. 16.95 (ISBN 0-8261-2951-X). Springer Pub.

Enid Starkie. Joanna Richardson. LC 73-10563. (Illus.). 320p. 1974. 7.95 o.s.i. (ISBN 0-02-602910-3). Macmillan.

Enigma. Joan Ehlis. 1981. 4.95 (ISBN 0-8062-1673-5). Carlton.

Enigma of Economic Growth: A Case Study of Israel. David Horowitz. LC 77-184338. (Special Studies in International Economics & Development). 1972. 27.50x (ISBN 0-275-28272-4). Irvington.

Enigma of Evil. Alfred Schutze. 1978. pap. 7.95 (ISBN 0-903540-10-X, Pub by Floris Books). St George Bk Serv.

Enigma of Felix Frankfurter. H. N. Hirsch. LC 80-68184. 320p. 1981. 14.95 (ISBN 0-465-01979-X). Basic.

Enigma of Out-Of-Body Travel. Susy Smith. LC 65-18998. 1965. 4.95 o.p. (ISBN 0-912326-15-8). Garrett-Helix.

Enigma of Soviet Petroleum: Half Empty or Half Full? Marshall Goldman. (Illus.). 216p. (Orig.). 1980. text ed. 19.95x (ISBN 0-04-333015-0, 2509); pap. 7.95 (ISBN 0-04-333016-9, 2510). Allen Unwin.

Enigma of Stonehenge. John Fowles & Barry Brukoff. LC 80-11472. (Illus.). 128p. 1980. 19.95 (ISBN 0-671-40116-5). Summit Bks.

Enigma of the Eighties: Environment, Economic, Energy. Thomas A. Dougherty. (Science of Advanced Materials Process Engineering Ser). (Illus.). 1979. 55.00 o.p. (ISBN 0-686-15770-2). Soc Adv Material.

Enigma of the Mind. Robert Campbell. LC 75-39976. (Human Behavior). (Illus.). (gr. 5 up). 1976. lib. bdg. 9.99 o.p. (ISBN 0-8094-1946-7, Pub. by Time-Life). Silver.

Enigmas & Mysteries. LC 76-18373. (New Library of the Supernatural: Vol. 14). 1977. 8.95 o.p. (ISBN 0-385-11321-8). Doubleday.

Enigmes. Simenon. (Easy Reader, B). pap. 3.75 (ISBN 0-88436-058-X, FRA201051). EMC.

Enigmes De la Deuxienne Epitre De Paul Aux Corinthiens: Etudes Exegetique De 2 Cor. J. F. Collange. LC 71-154504. (Society for New Testament Studies Monographs: No. 18). 1972. 49.50 (ISBN 0-521-08135-1). Cambridge U Pr.

Enjoy. Alan Bennett. 80p. 1981. pap. 8.95 (ISBN 0-571-11734-1, Pub. by Faber & Faber). Merrimack Bk Serv.

Enjoy Europe by Train. William J. Dunn. LC 73-19289. 1974. pap. 5.95 o.p. (ISBN 0-684-13789-5, SL514, ScribT). Scribner.

Enjoying a Profitable Business. 2nd ed. A. C. Hazel & A. S. Reid. 251p. 1976. text ed. 18.50x (ISBN 0-220-66287-8, Pub. by Busn Bks England). Renouf.

Enjoying Archives: What They Are, Where to Find Them, How to Use Them. David Iredale. 1973. 14.95 (ISBN 0-7153-5669-0). David & Charles.

Enjoying Embroidery. Anna Wilson. LC 74-32170. (Illus.). 120p. 1975. 10.25 o.p. (ISBN 0-8231-4032-6). Branford.

Enjoying Food on a Diabetic Diet. Edith M. Meyer. LC 73-16511. 240p. 1974. pap. 4.95 (ISBN 0-385-01344-2, Dolp). Doubleday.

Enjoying Intimacy with God. J. Oswald Sanders. 218p. 1980. pap. 4.95 (ISBN 0-8024-2346-9). Moody.

Enjoying Ireland. rev. ed. William Kehoe & Constance Kehoe. 288p. 1981. pap. 5.95 (ISBN 0-8159-5406-9). Devin.

Enjoying Maine. Bill Caldwell. LC 77-78126. 1978. 9.95 (ISBN 0-930096-01-0). G Gannett.

Enjoying Nature's Marvels. Jack Aistrop. LC 61-9014. (Illus.). (gr. 5-9). 1960. 6.95 (ISBN 0-8149-0250-2). Vanguard.

Enjoying Pets. Jack Aistrop. LC 55-7891. (gr. 5-10). 6.95 (ISBN 0-8149-0251-0). Vanguard.

Enjoying Single Parenthood. Bryan M. Knight. 176p. 1981. pap. 6.95 (ISBN 0-442-29623-1). Van Nos Reinhold.

Enjoying Soccer. Jean Carlson. LC 76-9118. (Illus.). 1976. 6.95 (ISBN 0-914842-09-9); pap. 3.95 (ISBN 0-914842-10-2). Madrona Pubs.

Enjoying the Psalms, 2 vols. William MacDonald. 1981. pap. 4.95 ea. Vol. 1 (ISBN 0-937396-34-6). Vol. 2 (ISBN 0-937396-35-4). Walterick Pubs.

Enjoying the World of Art. Pierre Belves & Francois Mathey. (Illus.). (gr. 6 up). 1966. PLB 12.00 (ISBN 0-87460-100-2). Lion.

Enjoying World History. Henry Abraham & Irwin Pfeffer. (gr. 10-12). 1977. text ed. 11.58 (ISBN 0-87720-620-1); pap. text ed. 7.50 (ISBN 0-87720-618-X). AMSCO Sch.

Enjoying Your Garden. M. J. Jefferson-Brown. 1970. 4.75 o.p. (ISBN 0-8231-6034-3). Branford.

Enjoying Your Restricted Diet. Ed. by Margaret B. Salmon & Althea E. Quigley. (Illus.). 328p. 1972. 15.75 (ISBN 0-398-02396-4). C C Thomas.

Enjoyment of Amy. John Colleton. 1980. pap. write for info. (ISBN 0-671-83659-5). PB.

Enjoyment of Drama. 2nd ed. Milton Marx. LC 61-15689. (Goldentree Books in English Literature). 1961. pap. text ed. 8.95x (ISBN 0-89197-609-4). Irvington.

Enjoyment of Music. 4th ed. Joseph Machlis. LC 76-62482. (Illus.). 1977. 16.95x (ISBN 0-393-09118-X); shorter 14.95x (ISBN 0-393-09125-2); workbk 4.95x (ISBN 0-393-09122-8); instructor's guide gratis (ISBN 0-393-09129-5). Norton.

Enjoyment of Poetry. Max Eastman. 1951. lib. rep. ed. 20.00x (ISBN 0-684-15162-6, ScribT). Scribner.

Enlightened Despotism. John G. Gagliardo. LC 67-14301. (AHM Europe Since 1500 Ser.). (Orig.). 1967. pap. 5.95x (ISBN 0-88295-735-X). AHM Pub.

Enlightened England. rev. ed. Ed. by Wylie Sypher. (Illus.). 1962. 14.95x o.p. (ISBN 0-393-09425-1, NortonC). Norton.

Enlightenment. Malcolm Vapp. Ed. by Margaret Killingray et al. (Greenhaven World History Ser.). (Illus.). 32p. (gr. 10). 1980. lib. bdg. 5.95 (ISBN 0-89908-225-4); pap. text ed. 1.95 (ISBN 0-89908-200-9). Greenhaven.

Enlightenment & Despair. G. Hawthorn. LC 76-7803. 1976. 32.95 (ISBN 0-521-21308-8); pap. 9.95x (ISBN 0-521-29093-7). Cambridge U Pr.

Enlightenment in America. Ernest Cassara. LC 74-20962. (World Leaders Ser: No. 50). 1975. lib. bdg. 10.95 (ISBN 0-8057-3675-1). Twayne.

Enlightenment in America. Henry F. May. LC 75-32349. 1976. 24.95 (ISBN 0-19-502018-9). Oxford U Pr.

Enlightenment in America. Henry F. May. LC 75-32349. 1978. pap. 6.95 (ISBN 0-19-502367-6, GB529, GB). Oxford U Pr.

Enlightenment Tradition. Robert Anchor. LC 78-62855. (Cal Ser.: No. 411). 1979. 12.50x (ISBN 0-520-03805-3); pap. 3.95 (ISBN 0-520-03784-7). U of Cal Pr.

Enlisted Soldier's View of the Civil War: The Wartime Papers of Joseph R. Ward, Jr. Ed. by D. Duane Cummins & Daryl Hohweiler. (Illus., Orig.). 1981. pap. price not set (ISBN 0-9605732-0-8). Belle Pubns.

Enneagrams: A Game of Nine Letter-Words. Ian D Graves. (Oleander Games & Pastimes Ser.: Vol. 4). (Illus.). 64p. 1981. 9.95 (ISBN 0-900891-78-5); pap. 4.75 (ISBN 0-900891-79-3). Oleander Pr.

Ennui. Maria Edgeworth. Ed. by Robert L. Wolff. (Ireland Nineteenth Century Fiction Ser. Two: Vol. 3). 428p. 1979. lib. bdg. 32.00 (ISBN 0-8240-3452-X). Garland Pub.

Eno Collection of New York City Views. New York Public Library. Ed. by Frank Weitenkampf. LC 79-162522. (Illus.). 1971. Repr. of 1925 ed. 20.00 (ISBN 0-8103-3744-4). Gale.

Enoch & Noah, Patriarchs of the Deluge. Gordon Lindsay. (Old Testament Ser.). 1.25 (ISBN 0-89985-125-8). Christ Nations.

Enola Gay. Gordon Thomas & Max M. Witts. LC 76-44343. 1977. 35.00x (ISBN 0-8128-2150-5). Stein & Day.

Enola Gay. Gordon Thomas & Max M. Witts. 400p. pap. 2.75 (ISBN 0-671-42116-6). PB.

Enormous Egg. Oliver Butterworth. (gr. 4-6). 1956. 8.95 (ISBN 0-316-11904-0, Pub. by Atlantic Monthly Pr). Little.

Enormous Room. new ed. E. E. Cummings. LC 77-114387. 1950. 5.95 (ISBN 0-87140-956-9); pap. 3.25 (ISBN 0-87140-001-4, L-001). Liveright.

Enormous Turnip. (Illus.). Arabic 2.50x (ISBN 0-685-82823-9). Intl Bk Ctr.

Enough. Donald E. Westlake. 1978. pap. 1.75 o.p. (ISBN 0-449-23768-0, Crest). Fawcett.

Enough Said: Poems 1974-1979. Philip Whalen. LC 80-16530. 96p. 1980. ltd. ed. 35.00 (ISBN 0-912516-48-8); pap. 4.95 (ISBN 0-912516-49-6). Grey Fox.

Enough! The Revolt of the American Consumer. Doris Faber. LC 72-81486. 192p. (gr. 7 up). 1972. 4.95 (ISBN 0-374-32193-0). FS&G.

Enquire Within Upon Everything. 1978. 11.95 o.p. (ISBN 0-214-20424-3, 8035, Dist. by Arco). Barrie & Jenkins.

Enquiridion De Mecanografiar Fichas Catalograficas Segun las Normas De la Descripcion Bibliografica Internacionel Para Monografias Publicadadas for Separado, Manual 1. Donald J. Lehnus. (Serie Bibliotecologica). pap. 1.85 o.s.i. (ISBN 0-8477-0901-9). U of PR Pr.

Enquiries Concerning the Human Understanding. 2nd ed. David Hume. Ed. by L. A. Selby-Bigge. Bd. with Concerning the Principles of Morals. LC 80-13382. xl, 371p. 1980. Repr. of 1902 ed. 30.00x (ISBN 0-313-22462-5, HUEH). Greenwood.

Enquiry into the Doctrine Concerning Libels, Warrants, & the Seizure of Papers. Ed. by David S. Berkowitz & Samuel E. Thorne. LC 77-86678. (Classics of English Legal History in the Modern Era Ser.: Vol. 52). 99p. 1979. lib. bdg. 40.00 (ISBN 0-8240-3151-2). Garland Pub.

Enquiry into the Doctrine, Lately Propagated, Concerning Libels, Warrants, & the Seizure of Papers. facsimile ed. Father of Candor. LC 76-121100. (Civil Liberties in American History Ser.). 136p. Repr. of 1764 ed. 17.50 (ISBN 0-306-71970-3). Da Capo.

Enquiry into the Duties of the Female Sex. Thomas Gisborne. Ed. by Gina Luria. LC 74-8236. (Feminist Controversy in England, 1788-1810 Ser.). 1974. lib. bdg. 50.00 (ISBN 0-8240-0860-X). Garland Pub.

Enquiry into the Formation of Washington's Farewell Address. Horace Binney. LC 74-98692. 1969. Repr. of 1859 ed. lib. bdg. 32.50 (ISBN 0-306-71840-5). Da Capo.

Enquiry into the Ideas of Space & Time. Edmund Law. Ed. by Rene Wellek. LC 75-11230. (British Philosophers & Theologians of the 17th & 18th Century: Vol. 31). 1976. Repr. of 1734 ed. lib. bdg. 42.00 (ISBN 0-8240-1783-8). Garland Pub.

Enquiry into the Question Whether Juries Are, or Are Not, Judges of the Law. Joseph Towers & Francis Maseres. Ed. by David S. Berkowitz & Samuel E. Thorne. LC 77-86680. (Classics of English Legal History in the Modern Era Ser.: Vol. 51). 228p. 1979. lib. bdg. 40.00 (ISBN 0-8240-3150-4). Garland Pub.

Enquiry into the Validity of the British Claim to a Right of Visitation & Search of the American Vessels Suspected to Be Engaged in the African Slave-Trade. Henry Wheaton. LC 78-91668. Repr. of 1842 ed. 11.75x (ISBN 0-8371-2072-1). Negro U Pr.

Enquiry Learning in Social Studies. Graham Whitehead. (Australian Council for Educational Research Ser.: No. 101). (Illus.). 1978. pap. 25.00x (ISBN 0-85563-164-3). Verry.

Enrico Baj. (Filipacchi Art Ser.). (Illus.). 72p. 1980. 25.00 (ISBN 0-88254-536-1, Pub by Filipacchi France). Hippocrene Bks.

Enrique Jardiel Poncela. Douglas R. McKay. LC 74-6487. (World Authors Ser.: Spain: No. 333). 1974. lib. bdg. 10.95 (ISBN 0-8057-2462-1). Twayne.

Ensayo y Su Ensenanza: Dos Ejemplos Puertorriquenos. Julio Lopez Gonzalez. LC 80-17712. (Coleccion Mente y Palabra). 146p. 1980. 6.25 (ISBN 0-8477-0568-4); pap. 5.00 (ISBN 0-8477-0569-2). U of PR Pr.

Ensenando Con Exito. Tr. by Myer Pearlman. (Spanish Bks.). 1978. 1.75 (ISBN 0-8297-0548-1). Vida Pubs.

Ensenanos a Orar. Elaine Dull & Jo Anne Sekowsky. Tr. by Todd H. Fast. (Estudio Biblico De Aglow: No. E-2(S)). 64p. (Span.). 1980. pap. 1.95 (ISBN 0-930756-55-X, 4220-E2). Women's Aglow.

Ensenanza Bilingue. Ricardo Garcia. LC 76-16879. (Fastback Ser.: No. 84s). (Sp.). 1976. pap. 0.75 (ISBN 0-87367-084-1). Phi Delta Kappa.

Enslaved Brains. Eando Binder. (YA) 1971. 4.95 o.p. (ISBN 0-685-23397-9, Avalon). Bouregy.

Ensor. Robert Delevoy. (Alpine Fine Arts Collection). (Illus.). 367p. 1981. 135.00 (ISBN 0-686-64750-5, Pub by Alpine Fine Arts). Hippocrene Bks.

Entailed Hat. George A. Townsend. LC 55-14663. (Illus.). 1955. 10.00 (ISBN 0-87033-135-3, Pub. by Tidewater). Cornell Maritime.

Entanglement. Catherine Fellows. (Regency Romance Ser.). 1979. pap. 1.75 o.p. (ISBN 0-449-24079-7, Crest). Fawcett.

Entdeckung des Orgons Erster Teil die Funktion des Orgasmus. Wilhelm Reich. 390p. 1968. 35.00 (ISBN 0-374-13976-8). FS&G.

Entendamonos: Manual de Conversacion. 2nd ed. Carlos Garcia-Prada & William E. Wilson. (Span). 1959. pap. text ed. 9.15 (ISBN 0-395-04481-2). HM.

Entendamos. Walter A. Henrichsen. Tr. by David A. Cook from Eng. 112p. (Orig., Span.). 1979. pap. 2.75 (ISBN 0-89922-131-9). Edit Caribe.

Enter a Murderer. Ngaio Marsh. (Mystery Ser.). 192p. 1981. pap. 2.25 (ISBN 0-515-05943-9). Jove Pubns.

Enter a Spy: The Double Life of Christopher Marlowe. Herbert Lom. (Illus.). 112p. 1978. 9.00x (ISBN 0-8476-6258-6). Rowman.

Enter Certain Players: Edwards, Mac Liammoir & the Gate 1928-1978. Ed. by Peter Luke. (Illus.). 1978. text ed. 26.00x (ISBN 0-85105-346-7, Dolmen Pr); pap. text ed. 9.25x (ISBN 0-85105-345-9). Humanities.

Enter Dr. Nikola! Guy Boothby. LC 80-22357. (Dr. Nikola, Master of Occult Mystery: No. 1). 256p. 1980. Repr. of 1975 ed. lib. bdg. 9.95x (ISBN 0-89370-632-9). Borgo Pr.

Enter the Actress. Rosamond Gilder. (Illus.). 1959. pap. 1.95 (ISBN 0-87830-502-5, 2). Theatre Arts.

Enter the Colonies Dancing: A History of Dance in Australia Nineteen Thirty-Five to Nineteen Forty. Edward H. Pask. 188p. 1980. 32.00x (ISBN 0-19-550589-1). Oxford U Pr.

Enter the Quiet: Everyone's Way to Meditation. James Whitehill. LC 79-2996. (Illus.). 192p. (Orig.). 1980. pap. 5.95 (ISBN 0-06-069365-7, RD 312). Har-Row.

Entering BASIC. 2nd ed. John Sack & Judy M. Gabriel. 160p. 1980. pap. text ed. 7.95 (ISBN 0-574-21270-1, 13-4270). SRA.

Entering Industry: A Guide for Young Professionals. Fred W. Billmeyer & Richard N. Kelley. LC 75-22283. 281p. 1975. 25.50 (ISBN 0-471-07285-0, Pub. by Wiley-Interscience). Wiley.

Entero-Insular Axis. Ed. by W. Creutzfeldt. (Frontiers of Hormone Research: Vol. 7). (Illus.). x, 310p. 1980. 69.00 (ISBN 3-8055-0795-X). S Karger.

Enterostomal Therapy. Harriett J. May. LC 76-19894. 1977. pap. 13.00 (ISBN 0-89004-144-X). Raven.

Enterprise & Society. Vinayshil Gautam. 1979. text ed. 8.00x (ISBN 0-391-01861-2). Humanities.

Enterprise & Trade in Victorian Britain: Essays in Historical Economics. Donald N. McCloskey. (Illus.). 240p. 1981. text ed. 35.00x (ISBN 0-04-942170-0, 2617-8); pap. text ed. 14.95x (ISBN 0-04-942171-9). Allen Unwin.

Enterprise Denied: Origins of the Decline of American Railroads, 1897-1917. Albro Martin. LC 71-159673. 1971. 20.00x (ISBN 0-231-03508-X); pap. 10.00x (ISBN 0-231-08362-9). Columbia U Pr.

Enterprise in Radio: WWL & the Business of Broadcasting in America. C. Joseph Pusateri. LC 79-9598. 378p. 1980. text ed. 20.25 (ISBN 0-8191-0954-1); pap. text ed. 12.00 (ISBN 0-8191-0955-X). U Pr of Amer.

Enterprise Monopoly in the United States, 1899-1958. G. Warren Nutter & Henry Einhorn. LC 69-15570. 1969. 20.00x (ISBN 0-231-02974-8). Columbia U Pr.

Enterprise of Public Administration. C. Dwight Waldo. Ed. by Victor Jones. LC 80-13764. (Chandler & Sharp Publications in Poltical Science). 224p. (Orig.). 1980. pap. text ed. 6.95 (ISBN 0-88316-537-6). Chandler & Sharp.

Enterprise Versus Bureaucracy: The Development of Structural Air-Raid Precautions During the 2nd World War. Lord Baker of Windrush. 1978. text ed. 12.75 (ISBN 0-08-022149-1). Pergamon.

Enterprise Zones. Stuart Butler. (Illus.). 192p. 1981. text ed. 12.50 (ISBN 0-87663-350-5). Universe.

Enterprising Minx. Marian Lorraine. (Orig.). 1981. pap. 1.50 (ISBN 0-440-12270-8). Dell.

Entertainers. Clive Unger-Hamilton. (Illus.). 320p. 1980. 29.95 (ISBN 0-312-25694-9). St Martin.

Entertaining. Robert Carrier. LC 78-58768. (Illus.). 1978. 16.95 (ISBN 0-89479-034-X). A & W Pubs.

Entertaining. Karen O. Sweeney. (Concise Guides Ser.). (Illus.). (gr. 5-8). 1978. PLB 6.45 s&l (ISBN 0-531-01415-0). Watts.

Entertaining: Complete Menus for All Occasions. Ann Willan. (Illus.). 216p. 1981. 22.50 (ISBN 0-7134-3408-2, Pub. by Batsford England). David & Charles.

Entertaining with Wine. Pamela V. Price. 1976. 15.95x (ISBN 0-7198-2613-6). Intl Ideas.

Entertainment & Ritual Six Hundred to Sixteen Hundred. Peter A. Bucknell. (Illus.). 223p. 1979. 29.50x (ISBN 0-8476-6239-X). Rowman.

Entertainment Language. Jim Richey. (Survival Vocabulary Ser.). (Illus.). 48p. (gr. 7-12). 1979. pap. text ed. 2.45 (ISBN 0-915510-34-0). Janus Bks.

Entertainment, Publishing & the Arts: Agreement & the Law, 3 vols. Alexander Lindey. LC 80-10991. 1963. 60.00 ea. (ISBN 0-87632-005-1). Boardman.

Entertainments. Judith Olney. (Illus.). 196p. 1981. 19.95 (ISBN 0-8120-5410-5). Barron.

Entertainments for Elizabeth I. Jean Wilson. (Studies in Elizabethean & Renaissance Culture Ser. II). 179p. 1980. 27.50x (ISBN 0-8476-6820-7). Rowman.

Enthalpy-Entropy Diagram for Steam. D. C. Hickson & F. R. Taylor. 1964. pap. 3.95x (ISBN 0-631-97470-9, Pub. by Basil Blackwell England). Biblio Dist.

Enthusiasm: A Study of a Word & Its Relatives. Susie I. Tucker. LC 79-161296. 1972. 29.50 (ISBN 0-521-08263-3). Cambridge U Pr.

Enthusiasm Makes the Difference. Norman V. Peale. LC 67-26078. 1967. 8.95 o.p. (ISBN 0-13-283200-3). P-H.

Enthusiasts in Love. Audrey Curling. 1978. pap. 1.75 o.p. (ISBN 0-445-04260-5). Popular Lib.

Entire New Healing Approach. Pieter Los. 1981. 8.95 (ISBN 0-533-04361-1). Vantage.

Entirely Entertaining. Ed. by George D. Lamborn. 212p. (Orig.). 1979. pap. 5.95. Jr League Montclair-Newark.

Entirely for God. Elizabeth Isichei. (Cistercian Studies: No. 43). 132p. 1980. pap. 11.95 (ISBN 0-87907-943-6). Cistercian Pubns.

Entity Process: The Accumulation of a Physical Property As a Function of Mortality & Magnitude of Rank. Frank Reynolds East. 1977. 10.00 o.p. (ISBN 0-682-48630-2, University). Exposition.

Entomology. Cedric Gillot. 690p. 1980. 49.50 (ISBN 0-306-40366-8, Plenum Pr); pap. text ed. 22.50 (ISBN 0-306-40514-8, Plenum Pr). Plenum Pub.

Entomology in the U. S. A. Ed. by Gupta. 1976. 5.00 (ISBN 0-686-17552-2). Entomol Soc.

Entomology: Investigative Activities for Could-Be Bug Buffs. F. Neil Mathews & Linda H. Smith. 1978. pap. 3.95 (ISBN 0-936386-03-7). Creative Learning.

Entoptychine Pocket Gophers (Mammalia, Geomyoidea) of the Early Miocene John Day Formation, Oregon. John M. Rensberger. (U. C. Publ. in Geological Sciences: Vol. 90). 1973. pap. 11.50x (ISBN 0-520-09392-5). U of Cal Pr.

Entourage: A Tracing File for Architecture & Interior Design Drawing. Ernest Burden. (Illus.). 256p. 1981. 15.95 (ISBN 0-07-008930-2). McGraw.

Entrance. Lila Ray. (Redbird Bk.). 1976. 6.75 (ISBN 0-89253-512-1); flexible bdg. 4.00 (ISBN 0-89253-124-X). Ind-US Inc.

Entrances to Nowhere. Joan C. Hand. LC 76-770231. (Poetry Ser.). (Illus.). o. p. 8.95x (ISBN 0-89304-015-0, CCC110); signed ltd. ed. 15.00x (ISBN 0-89304-044-4); pap. 3.95x (ISBN 0-89304-014-2); pap. 4.95x signed ltd. ed. o.p. (ISBN 0-89304-043-6). Cross Cult.

Entremeses. Miguel De Cervantes. (Span). 4.50x o.s.i. (ISBN 0-686-00862-6). Colton Bk.

Entrepreneur. James D. Nisbet. Ed. by Betty Folts. (Illus.). 1976. 10.00 (ISBN 0-686-63615-5). Capital Tech.

Entrepreneur As Culture Hero: Preadaptations for Nigerian Economic Development. Bernard Belasco. LC 79-10475. (Praeger Special Studies). (Illus.). 256p. 1980. 23.95 (ISBN 0-03-052096-7). Praeger.

Entrepreneurial Function: Text & Cases on Smaller Firms. Larue T. Hosmer et al. LC 76-50928. (Illus.). 1977. text ed. 21.95 (ISBN 0-13-283093-0). P-H.

Entrepreneurial Growth & Development Programmes in Northern India: A Sociological Analysis. K. L. Sharma & Harnek Singh. 1980. 12.50x (ISBN 0-8364-0649-4, Pub. by Abhinav India). South Asia Bks.

Entrepreneurial Manager in the Small Business: Text Readings & Cases. William Naumes. LC 77-83029. (Illus.). 1978. text ed. 17.95 (ISBN 0-201-05201-6). A-W.

Entrepreneurial Woman. Sandra Winston. 240p. 1980. pap. 2.95 (ISBN 0-553-13479-5). Bantam.

Entrepreneurs. Robert L. Shook. LC 79-2735. (Illus.). 192p. 1981. pap. 3.95 (ISBN 0-06-464043-4, B*N 4043). Har-Row.

Entrepreneur's Manual: Business Start-Ups, Spin-Offs, & Innovative Management. Richard M. White. LC 76-55520. 1976. 17.50 (ISBN 0-8019-6454-7). Chilton.

Entrepreneurs of Ideology: Neoconservative Publishers in Germany, 1890-1933. Gary D. Stark. LC 80-14906. 384p. 1981. 26.50x (ISBN 0-8078-1452-0). U of NC Pr.

Entrepreneurs: Twelve Who Took Risks & Succeeded. Robert L. Shook. LC 79-2735. (Illus.). 192p. 1981. pap. 3.95 (ISBN 0-06-464043-4, BN 4043, EH). Har-Row.

Entrepreneurship & Economic Development. P. Kilby. LC 79-122279. 1971. 19.95 (ISBN 0-02-917270-5). Free Pr.

Entrepreneurship & Venture Management: Text & Readings. Clifford M. Baumback & Joseph R. Mancuso. (Illus.). 368p. 1975. pap. text ed. 12.95 (ISBN 0-13-283119-8). P-H.

Entrepreneurship in Britain, Seventeen Fifty to Nineteen Thirty-Nine. R. H. Campbell & R. G. Wilson. (Documents in Economic History). 1975. text ed. 13.00x (ISBN 0-7136-1524-9). Humanities.

Entrepreneurship in the Eighties. Gordon Baty. 1981. text ed. 17.95 (ISBN 0-8359-1745-2); pap. text ed. 12.95 (ISBN 0-8359-1744-4). Reston.

Entretiens Sur Andre Gide: Decades Du Centre Culturel International De Cerisy-la-Salle. Ed. by Marcel Arland & Jean Mouton. (Nouvelle Ser.: No. 3). 1967. pap. 20.50x (ISBN 90-2796-014-3). Mouton.

Entretiens Sur L'art et la Psychanalyse: Decades Du Centre International De Cerisy-la-Salle. Ed. by Andre Berge et al. (Nouvelle Serie: No. 6). 1968. pap. 27.05x (ISBN 90-2796-017-8). Mouton.

Entretiens Sur le Surrealisme. Ed. by Ferdinand Alquie. (Decades Du Centre Culturel International De Cerisy-la-Salle, Nouvelle Ser.: No. 8). (Illus.). 1968. pap. 45.30x (ISBN 90-279-6018-6). Mouton.

Entropy: A New World View. Jeremy Rifkin & Ted Howard. 324p. 1980. 11.95 (ISBN 0-670-29717-8). Viking Pr.

Entropy & Energy Levels. R. P. Gasser & W. G. Richards. (Oxford Chemistry Ser.). (Illus.). 150p. 1974. pap. text ed. 7.95x (ISBN 0-19-855490-7). Oxford U Pr.

Entropy & Low Temperature Physics. John S. Dugdale. (Orig.). pap. text ed. 3.50x (ISBN 0-09-078251-8, Hutchinson U Lib). Humanities.

Entropy Minimax Sourcebook. Ed. by Ronald Christiensen. (Entropy Minimax Sourcebook Ser.: Vol. IV). 1981. lib. bdg. 59.50 (ISBN 0-938876-07-4). Entropy Ltd.

Entropy Minimax Sourcebook: Applications. Ed. by R. Christensen. 800p. 1981. 59.50 (ISBN 0-686-28919-6). Entropy Ltd.

Entropy Minimax Sourcebook: Computer Implementation. R. Christensen. x, 254p. 1980. 37.50. Entropy Ltd.

Entropy Minimax Sourcebook: General Description. R. Chistensen. 700p. 1981. text ed. 29.50 (ISBN 0-686-28918-8). Entropy Ltd.

Entropy Minimax Sourcebook: Philosophical Origins. R. Christensen. x, 218p. 1980. 32.50. Entropy Ltd.

Entry of the Slavs into Christendom: An Introduction to the Medieval History of the Slav. A. P. Vlasto. LC 70-98699. 1970. 44.50 (ISBN 0-521-07459-2). Cambridge U Pr.

Entsiklopediia Russkikh Pisatelei. Il'la Nikolaevich Ignatov. LC 75-561569. (Illus., Rus.). 1972. 37.00 (ISBN 0-918884-12-8). Slavia Lib.

Altfranzosischen Liederhandschriften Ihr Verhaltniss, Ihre/Entstehung & Ihre Bestimmung. Eduard Schwan. LC 80-2169. Repr. of 1886 ed. 39.50 (ISBN 0-404-19033-2). AMS Pr.

Entstehung Des Lehnswesens. Viktor Menzel. LC 80-2015. 1981. Repr. of 1890 ed. 18.50 (ISBN 0-404-18579-7). AMS Pr.

Entstehung und Entwicklung Einer Wissenschaftlichen Tatsache: Einfuehrung in Die Lehre Vom Denkstil und Denkkollektiv. Ludwik Fleck. (Suhrkamp Taschenbuecher Wissenschaft: Stw 312). 248p. (Ger.). 1980. pap. text ed. 7.80 (ISBN 0-686-64690-8, Pub. by Insel Verlag Germany). Suhrkamp.

Entwicklung der paediatrischen Haematologie und Onkologie. Ed. by H. P. Wagner. (Paediatrische Fortbildungskurse fuer die Praxis: Vol. 50). (Illus.). 1980. soft cover 24.00 (ISBN 3-8055-0229-X). S Karger.

Enumeration of Chinese Materia Medica. Hu Shiu-Ying. 200p. 1981. 21.50 (ISBN 0-295-95744-1, Pub by Chinese Univ Hong Kong). U of Wash Pr.

Envases De Vidrio, Destinados a Preparados De Tocador. (Productos Latinoamericanos Incluidos En el Sistema Generalizado De Preferencias De los Estados Unidos Ser.). 20p. 1977. pap. text ed. 3.00 (ISBN 0-8270-3485-7). OAS.

Enviame a Mi: Aventuras de los esposos Davis, fundadores de la C. B. P. Olivia S. De Lerin. 64p. 1980. pap. 1.25 (ISBN 0-311-01062-8). Casa Bautista.

Environment. Irving Adler. LC 75-35526. (Reason Why Ser.). (Illus.). 1976. lib. bdg. 7.89 (ISBN 0-381-99617-4, JD-J). John Day.

Environment & Aging. M. Powell Lawton. LC 79-26816. (Social Gerontology Ser.). (Orig.). 1980. pap. text ed. 7.95 (ISBN 0-8185-0378-5). Brooks-Cole.

Environment & Archeology: An Ecological Approach to Prehistory. 2nd ed. Karl Butzer. LC 74-115938. (Illus.). 1971. 25.95x (ISBN 0-202-33023-0). Aldine Pub.

Environment & Behavior: A Dynamical Perspective. C. J. Holahan. LC 77-25400. (Plenum Social Ecology Ser.). (Illus.). 206p. 1977. 14.95 (ISBN 0-306-31086-4, Plenum Pr). Plenum Pub.

Environment & Behavior: Planning & Everyday Urban Life. J. Douglas Porteous. LC 76-1752. 1977. text ed. 16.95 (ISBN 0-201-05867-7). A-W.

Environment & Cognition. Ed. by William H. Ittelson. LC 72-7698. 1973. 23.00 o.p. (ISBN 0-12-785363-4). Acad Pr.

Environment & Development in Africa. United Nations Environment Programme, Nairobi & Environment Training Programme, Dakar. (UNEP Studies). (Illus.). 100p. Date not set. 15.71 (ISBN 0-08-025667-8). Pergamon.

Environment & Energy: Environmental Aspects of Energy Production & Use with Particular Reference to New Technologies. Ed. by United Nations Economic Commission for Europe, Geneva, Switzerland. LC 79-40550. 1979. 21.00 (ISBN 0-08-024468-8). Pergamon.

Environment & Equity: A Regulatory Challenge. Daniel R. Mandelker. (Regulation of American Business & Industry (RABI) Ser.). 240p. 1981. 24.95 (ISBN 0-07-039864-X, P&RB). McGraw.

Environment & Human Efficiency. E. C. Poulton. (American Lectures in Living Chemistry Ser.). (Illus.). 336p. 1972. 26.75 (ISBN 0-398-01515-5). C C Thomas.

Environment & Plant Ecology. J. R. Etherington & W. Armstrong. LC 74-3725. 347p. 1975. 31.75 o.p. (ISBN 0-471-24615-8); pap. 19.95 (ISBN 0-471-99737-4). Wiley.

Environment & Policy: The Next Fifty Years. Ed. by William R. Ewald, Jr. LC 68-27344. 476p. 1968. pap. 4.95x (ISBN 0-253-12265-1). Ind U Pr.

Environment & Pollutions: Sources, Health Effects, Monitoring & Control. Francis K. Leh & Richard K. Lak. (Illus.). 308p. 1974. 19.75 (ISBN 0-398-03030-8). C C Thomas.

Environment & Science. Ed. by Brian J. O'Brien. (Way '79 Ser.). 1979. 18.95x (ISBN 0-85564-148-7, Pub. by U of W Austral Pr). Intl Schol Bk Serv.

Environment & Services. 2nd ed. Peter Burberry. (Mitchell's Building Construction Ser.). 1978. pap. 13.95 (ISBN 0-470-26352-0). Halsted Pr.

Environment & Society: A Book of Readings on Environmental Policy, Attitudes & Values. Robert Roelofs et al. 448p. 1974. pap. text ed. 12.95 (ISBN 0-13-283374-3). P-H.

Environment & the American Experience: A Historian Looks at the Ecological Crisis. Donald W. Whisenhunt. LC 74-80068. (National University Publications). 1974. 12.95 (ISBN 0-8046-9071-5). Kennikat.

Environment & Trade: The Relation of International Trade & Environmental Policy. Ed. by Seymour J. Rubin & Thomas R. Graham. 380p. 1981. text ed. 28.50 (ISBN 0-86598-032-2). Allanheld.

Environment As Hazard. Ian Burton & Robert W. Kates. (Illus.). 1978. text ed. 12.95x (ISBN 0-19-502221-1); pap. text ed. 7.95x (ISBN 0-19-502222-X). Oxford U Pr.

Environment: Costs, Conflicts, Action. Ed. by John Cairns, Jr. & K. Dickson. 180p. 1974. 22.50 o.p. (ISBN 0-8247-6121-9). Dekker.

Environment, Ideology & Policy. Francis Sandbach. LC 80-65192. 254p. 1980. text ed. 26.50 (ISBN 0-916672-53-0). Allanheld.

Environment in Engineering Education. (Studies in Engineering Education: No. 9). 110p. 1980. pap. 9.25 (ISBN 92-3-101793-4, U1028, UNESCO). Unipub.

Environment Index Nineteen Eighty. Ed. by Monica Pronin. LC 73-189498. 800p. 1981. 135.00 (ISBN 0-89947-011-4). Environ Info.

Environment Law Review: Annual. Ed. by H. Floyd Sherrod. Incl. 1970 (ISBN 0-87632-042-6); 1971 (ISBN 0-87632-048-5); 1972 (ISBN 0-87632-082-5); 1973 (ISBN 0-87632-090-6); 1974 (ISBN 0-87632-115-5). 39.50 ea. o.p. Boardman.

Environment, Man & Economic Change: Essays Presented to S.H. Beaver. Ed. by A. D. Phillips & B. J. Turton. (Illus.). 500p. 1975. text ed. 42.00x (ISBN 0-582-50114-8). Longman.

Environment: North & South an Economic Interpretation. Charles Pearson & Anthony Pryor. LC 77-11143. 37.95 (ISBN 0-471-02741-3, Pub. by Wiley-Interscience). Wiley.

Environment of Change. Ed. by Aaron W. Warner. LC 79-79572. (Seminar on Technology & Social Change Ser). 1969. 20.00x (ISBN 0-231-03151-3). Columbia U Pr.

Environment of Early Man in the British Isles. John C. Evans. LC 74-29803. 256p. 1975. 20.00x (ISBN 0-520-02973-9). U of Cal Pr.

Environment of Human Settlements: Human Well-Being in Cities, Vol. 2. World Environment & Resources Council (WERC) Brussels, Apr. 1976. Ed. by Pierre Laconte et al. LC 76-5192. 1977. text ed. 75.00 (ISBN 0-685-74703-4). Pergamon.

Environment of Industrial Marketing. Donald E. Vinson & Donald Sciglimpaglia. LC 74-20124. (Marketing Ser.). 1975. pap. text ed. 12.95 (ISBN 0-88244-074-8). Grid Pub.

Environment of the First Line Supervisors. R. Trojanowicz. 1980. 13.95 (ISBN 0-13-282848-0). P-H.

Environment Policies for the 1980's. Organization for Economic Cooperation & Development. 110p. (Orig.). 1980. pap. text ed. 9.00x (ISBN 92-64-12049-1, 9780021). OECD.

Environment, Society & Rural Change in Latin America: The Past, Present & Future in the Country. David A. Preston. LC 79-41481. 1980. write for info. (ISBN 0-471-27713-4, Pub. by Wiley-Interscience). Wiley.

Environment, The Human Impact. Compiled by Rosemary E. Amidei. 1973. pap. 5.00 (ISBN 0-87355-001-3). Natl Sci Tchrs.

Environmental Aerodynamics. R. S. Scorer. LC 77-23909. (Mathematics & Its Applications Ser.). 1978. 69.95 (ISBN 0-470-99270-0). Halsted Pr.

Environmental Analysis for Management. James P. Baughman et al. 1974. text ed. 19.50x (ISBN 0-256-01561-9). Irwin.

Environmental & Land Controls Legislation. Daniel R. Mandelker. 1976. 30.00 (ISBN 0-672-82486-8, Bobbs-Merrill Law); 1980 suppl. 10.00 (ISBN 0-672-84303-X). Michie.

Environmental Applications of General Physics. John I. Shonle. 1974. text ed. 7.95 (ISBN 0-201-07058-8). A-W.

Environmental Aspects of Irrigation & Drainage: Proceedings. ASCE Irrigation & Drainage Division, July 1976. Compiled By American Society of Civil Engineers. 752p. 1976. pap. text ed. 37.50 (ISBN 0-87262-171-5). Am Soc Civil Eng.

Environmental Aspects of Nuclear Power Stations. (Illus., Orig.). 1971. pap. 63.75 (ISBN 92-0-020071-0, ISP261, IAEA). Unipub.

Environmental Assessment of the Hospital Industry. 1979. 15.00 o.p. (ISBN 0-87258-289-2, 1220). Am Hospital.

Environmental Behaviour of Radionuclides Released in the Nuclear Industry. (Illus.). 749p. (Orig., Eng., Fr. & Rus.). 1974. pap. 59.00 (ISBN 92-0-020473-2, ISP345, IAEA). Unipub.

Environmental Benefits & Costs of Solar Energy. Michael D. Yokell. LC 79-3688. 1980. 16.95 (ISBN 0-669-03468-1). Lexington Bks.

Environmental Biology. E. J. Barrington. LC 80-12090. (Resource & Environmental Science). 244p. 1980. pap. 17.95x (ISBN 0-470-26967-7). Halsted Pr.

Environmental Carcinogenesis. Occurrence Risk Evaluation & Mechanisms: Proceedings. International Conference on Environmental Carcinogenesis, Amsterdam, May 1979. Ed. by P. Emmelot & E. Kriek. 402p. 1979. 58.75 (ISBN 0-444-80158-8, North Holland). Elsevier.

Environmental Careers. James Hahn & Lynn Hahn. (Career Concise Guides Ser). (Illus.). 72p. (gr. 7 up). 1976. PLB 4.90 o.p. (ISBN 0-531-01132-1). Watts.

Environmental Change. Andrew Goudie. (Contemporary Problems in Geography Ser.). (Illus.). 1977. 29.95x (ISBN 0-19-874073-5); pap. 9.50x (ISBN 0-19-874074-3). Oxford U Pr.

Environmental Chemistry. P. Liss et al. LC 80-12132. (Resource & Environmental Science). 184p. 1980. pap. text ed. 14.95x (ISBN 0-470-26968-5). Halsted Pr.

Environmental Chemistry. John W. Moore & Elizabeth A. Moore. 1976. 21.95 (ISBN 0-12-505050-X). Acad Pr.

Environmental Chemistry: Air & Water Pollution. 2nd ed. H. Stephen Stoker & Spencer L. Seager. 1976. pap. 7.95x (ISBN 0-673-07978-3). Scott F.

Environmental Communications. 1980. pap. 5.95 (ISBN 0-8478-0280-9). Rizzoli Intl.

Environmental Concerns: A Bibliography of U.S. Government Publications, 1971-1973. Janet L. Burk & Stephen Hayes. 1975. 4.00 (ISBN 0-932826-06-7). New Issues MI.

Environmental Contamination by Radioactive Materials. (Illus., Orig., Eng., Fr. & Span.). 1969. pap. 39.75 (ISBN 92-0-020169-5, IAEA). Unipub.

Environmental Context of Aging. Ed. by Thomas O. Byerts et al. LC 78-20645. 256p. 1979. lib. bdg. 24.50 (ISBN 0-8240-7115-8). Garland Pub.

Environmental Control: Priorities, Policies & the Law. Frank P. Grad et al. LC 79-155361. 1971. 17.50x (ISBN 0-231-03563-2). Columbia U Pr.

Environmental Controls: The Impact on Industries. Robert A. Leone. LC 75-32222. 304p. 1976. 16.95 (ISBN 0-669-00345-X). Lexington Bks.

Environmental Cooperation Among Industrialized Countries: The Role of Regional Organizations. Nancy K. Hetzel. LC 79-5438. 1980. pap. text ed. 12.75 (ISBN 0-8191-0886-3). U Pr of Amer.

Environmental Cooperation in the North Atlantic Area. Marshall E. Wilcher. LC 79-3423. 1980. pap. text ed. 9.00 (ISBN 0-8191-0890-1). U Pr of Amer.

Environmental Design & Human Behavior: A Psychology of the Individual in Society. Ed. by Leonard Krasner. (Pergamon General Psychology Ser.). 1980. 29.50 (ISBN 0-08-023858-0). Pergamon.

Environmental Designs for Handicapped Children. J. Singh Sandhu & Horst Hendriks-Jansen. (Illus.). 1976. 24.95 (ISBN 0-685-81670-2, 00709-9, Pub. by Saxon Hse). Lexington Bks.

Environmental Economics. David W. Pearce. LC 75-44207. (Modern Economics Ser.). 1976. text ed. 19.95x (ISBN 0-582-44622-8); pap. text ed. 10.95x (ISBN 0-582-44623-6). Longman.

Environmental Economics. 2nd ed. Joseph J. Seneca & Michael K. Taussig. (Illus.). 1979. ref. ed. 18.95 (ISBN 0-13-283291-7). P-H.

Environmental Economics: A Guide to Information Sources. Ed. by Barry C. Field & Cleve E. Willis. (Man & the Environment Information Guide Ser.: Vol. 8). 1979. 30.00 (ISBN 0-8103-1433-9). Gale.

Environmental Economics: An Introduction for Students of the Resource & Environmental Sciences. Alan Cottrell. (Resource & Environmental Science Ser.). 1978. pap. text ed. 6.95 (ISBN 0-470-99395-2). Halsted Pr.

Environmental Education - Facility Resources. LC 75-85019. (Illus.). 64p. 1971. pap. 2.00 (ISBN 0-89192-051-X). Interbk Inc.

Environmental Education - Key Issues of the Future: Proceedings of the Conference Held at the College of Technology, Farnborough, England. Ed. by Hughes-Evans. LC 77-827. 1977. pap. text ed. 12.00 (ISBN 0-08-021490-8). Pergamon.

Environmental Education: A Guide to Information Sources. Ed. by William B. Stapp & Mary D. Liston. LC 73-17542. (Man & the Environment Information Guide Ser.: Vol. 1). 350p. 1975. 30.00 (ISBN 0-8103-1337-5). Gale.

Environmental Education in Australia. Russell Linke. 300p. 1980. text ed. 17.50x (ISBN 0-86861-361-4, 2339). Allen Unwin.

Environmental Education in the Elementary School: A Selection of Articles Reprinted from "Science & Children". rev. ed. Compiled by Leonard J. Garigliano & Beth J. Knape. 1977. pap. 4.75 (ISBN 0-87355-007-2). Natl Sci Tchrs.

Environmental Education in the Light of the Tbilisi Conference. (Education on the Move Ser.: No. 3). 100p. 1980. pap. 7.00 (ISBN 92-3-101787-X, U1035, UNESCO). Unipub.

Environmental Education: Principles, Methods & Applications. Ed. by Trilochan S. Bakshi & Zev Naveh. (Environmental Science Research Ser.: Vol. 18). 300p. 1980. 32.50 (ISBN 0-306-40433-8, Plenum Pr). Plenum Pub.

Environmental Effects of Complex River Development: International Experience. Ed. by Gilbert F. White. LC 77-3943. (Westview Special Studies in Natural Resources & Energy Management). (Illus.). 1977. lib. bdg. 20.00 o.p. (ISBN 0-89158-249-5). Westview.

Environmental Effects of Cooling Systems at Nuclear Power Plants: Proceedings. (Illus.). 829p. 1975. pap. 72.25 (ISBN 92-0-020075-3, ISP378, IAEA). Unipub.

Environmental Effects of Dams & Impoundments in Canada: Experience & Precepts. (Bulletin: No. 205). 1981. pap. 4.75 (ISBN 0-660-10485-7, SSC 147, SSC). Unipub.

Environmental Evaluation: Perception & Public Policy. Ervin H. Zube. LC 80-11860. (Basic Concepts in Environment & Behavior Ser.). (Orig.). 1980. pap. text ed. 6.95 (ISBN 0-8185-0377-7). Brooks-Cole.

Environmental Factor: An Approach for Managers. D. J. Davison. LC 77-20123. 1978. 27.95 (ISBN 0-470-99351-0). Halsted Pr.

Environmental Factors in Respiratory Disease. Ed. by Douglas H. Lee. (Environmental Science Ser.). 1972. 22.00 (ISBN 0-12-440655-6). Acad Pr.

Environmental Factors in the Heating of Buildings. L. E. Anapol'Skaya & L. S. Gandin. Ed. by P. Greenberg. Tr. by H. Olaru from Rus. LC 75-6609. 238p. 1975. 32.50 (ISBN 0-470-02557-3). Halsted Pr.

Environmental Forces on Engineering Structures. Ed. by C. A. Brebbia et al. LC 79-16733. 1979. 59.95x (ISBN 0-470-26820-4). Halsted Pr.

Environmental Foundations of European History. Derwent S. Whittlesey. (Perspectives in European History Ser.: No. 38). xiii, 160p. 1980. Repr. of 1949 ed. lib. bdg. 15.00x (ISBN 0-87991-074-7). Porcupine Pr.

Environmental Geology. Donald R. Coates. LC 80-21272. 736p. 1980. text ed. 23.00 (ISBN 0-471-06379-7). Wiley.

Environmental Geology. 2nd ed. Edward Keller. 1979. text ed. 19.95 (ISBN 0-675-08296-X). Merrill.

Environmental Geomorphology & Landscape Conservation, 3 vols. Ed. by Donald R. Coates. Incl. Vol. 1. Prior to 1900. 1972. 43.50 (ISBN 0-12-786241-2); Vol. 2. Urban Areas. 464p. 1974. 39.00 (ISBN 0-12-786242-0); Vol. 3. Non-Urban Regions. 496p. 1973. 43.50 (ISBN 0-12-786243-9). LC 72-77882. (Benchmark Papers in Geology Ser.). (Illus.). Acad Pr.

Environmental Geosciences: Interaction Between Natural Systems & Man. Arthur N. Strahler & Alan H. Strahler. LC 72-10325. 1973. 24.95 (ISBN 0-471-83163-8). Wiley.

Environmental Glossary. Ed. by G. William Frick. LC 80-67274. 225p. 19.50 (ISBN 0-86587-080-2). Gov Insts.

Environmental Glossary. Ed. by G. William Frick. LC 80-67274. 1980. 19.50 (ISBN 0-86587-080-2). Gov Insts.

Environmental Hazards in the British Isles. Allen H. Perry. (Illus.). 192p. (Orig.). 1981. text ed. 27.50 (ISBN 0-04-910069-6, 2601); pap. text ed. 14.95 (ISBN 0-04-910070-X, 2602). Allen Unwin.

Environmental, Health & Control Aspects of Coal Conversion: An Information Overview, 2 vols. Braunstein & Copenhaver. 1338p. 1981. Set. text ed. 90.00 (ISBN 0-250-40445-1). Ann Arbor Science.

Environmental Health & Safety. Herman Koren. LC 72-11634. 338p. 1974. text ed. 26.00 o.p. (ISBN 0-08-017077-3); pap. text ed. 14.50 (ISBN 0-08-017623-2). Pergamon.

Environmental Health & Safety in the Hospital Laboratory. Patricia A. Flury. (Illus.). 200p. 1978. 23.75 (ISBN 0-398-03773-6). C C Thomas.

Environmental Health Chemistry: The Chemistry of Environmental Agents As Potential Human Hazards. James D. McKinney. LC 80-65510. (Illus.). 656p. 1981. 47.50 (ISBN 0-250-40352-8). Ann Arbor Science.

Environmental History of the Near & Middle East Since the Last Ice Age. Ed. by William C. Brice. 1978. 52.00 o.s.i. (ISBN 0-12-133850-9). Acad Pr.

Environmental Impact Assessment. Timothy O'Riordan & Richard D. Hey. (Illus.). 1977. 24.95 (ISBN 0-685-81671-0, 00706-4, Pub. by Saxon Hse). Lexington Bks.

Environmental Impact Assessment: a bibliography with abstracts. Brian D. Clark et al. LC 79-67626. 524p. 1980. 59.95 (ISBN 0-8352-1255-6, Co-Pub. by Mansell Info England). Bowker.

Environmental Impact Assessment: An Interdisciplinary Approach. R. Dresnack & E. Golub. (Theoretical & Applied Environmental Reviews Ser.). 200p. 1980. cancelled (ISBN 0-686-61666-9). Harwood Academic.

Environmental Impact of Mining. C. G. Down & J. Stocks. LC 77-23129. 1977. 59.95 (ISBN 0-470-99086-4). Halsted Pr.

Environmental Impact of Nonpoint Source Pollution. Ed. by Michael R. Overcash & James M. Davidson. LC 79-56118. (Illus.). 1981. 29.95 (ISBN 0-250-40339-0). Ann Arbor Science.

Environmental Impact of Nuclear Power Plants. Ed. by R. A. Karam et al. LC 75-23351. 1977. text ed. 54.00 (ISBN 0-08-019956-9). Pergamon.

Environmental Impact of Stratospheric Flight. Climatic Impact Committee. 1975. pap. 11.00 (ISBN 0-309-02346-7). Natl Acad Pr.

Environmental Impact: Proceedings. ASCE Urban Transportation Division, May 1973. Compiled By American Society of Civil Engineers. 400p. 1974. pap. text ed. 16.00 (ISBN 0-87262-063-8). Am Soc Civil Eng.

Environmental Impact Statements. Michael Greenberg et al. Ed. by Salvatore J. Natoli. LC 78-59102. (Resource Papers for College Geography Ser.). (Illus.). 1978. pap. text ed. 4.00 (ISBN 0-89291-131-X). Assn Am Geographers.

Environmental Impacts of International Civil Engineering Projects & Practices: Proceedings. Compiled By American Society of Civil Engineers. 272p. pap. text ed. 18.00 (ISBN 0-87262-129-4). Am Soc Civil Eng.

Environmental Indices. Herbert Inhaber. LC 75-34290. (Environmental Science & Technology Ser). 176p. 1976. 26.00 (ISBN 0-471-42796-9, Pub. by Wiley-Interscience). Wiley.

Environmental Isotope Data No. 1: World Survey of Isotope Concentration in Precipitation (1953-1963) (Technical Reports Ser.: No. 96). (Orig.). 1969. pap. 17.25 (ISBN 92-0-145069-9, IAEA). Unipub.

Environmental Isotope Data No. 2: World Survey of Isotope Concentration in Precipitation (1964-1965) (Technical Reports Ser.: No. 117). (Illus., Orig.). 1970. pap. 20.50 (ISBN 92-0-145070-2, IDC117, IAEA). Unipub.

Environmental Isotope Data No. 3: World Survey of Isotope Concentration in Precipitation (1966-1967) (Technical Reports Ser.: No. 129). (Illus.). 402p. (Orig.). 1972. pap. 18.75 (ISBN 92-0-145271-3, IAEA). Unipub.

Environmental Isotope Data No. 4: World Survey of Isotope Concentration in Precipitation (1968-1969) (Technical Reports Ser.: No. 147). (Illus.). 334p. (Orig.). 1973. pap. 20.00 (ISBN 92-0-145173-3, IAEA). Unipub.

Environmental Isotope Data No. 5: World Survey of Isotope Concentration in Precipitation (1970-1971) (Technical Report Ser: No. 165). 309p. 1975. pap. 16.75 (ISBN 92-0-145075-3, IAEA). Unipub.

Environmental Isotope Data No. 6: World Survey of Isotope Concentration in Precipitation (1972-1975) (Technical Reports Ser.: No. 192). 1979. pap. 17.25 (ISBN 92-0-145179-2, IDC192, IAEA). Unipub.

Environmental Issues: Family Impact. Evelyn Eldridge & Nancy Meredith. 1976. pap. text ed. 10.95 o.p. (ISBN 0-8087-0518-0). Burgess.

Environmental Law: A Guide to Information Sources. Mortimer Schwartz. LC 73-17541. (Man & the Environment Information Guide Series: Vol. 6). 1977. 30.00 (ISBN 0-8103-1339-1). Gale.

Environmental Law & Policy. 2nd ed. Richard B. Stewart & James E. Krier. (Contemporary Legal Education Ser.). 1978. 25.00 (ISBN 0-672-82859-6, Bobbs-Merrill Law). Michie.

Environmental Law & the Siting of Facilities: Issues in Land Use & Coastal Zone Management. Michael S. Baram. LC 76-2664. 200p. 1976. text ed. 17.50 o.p. (ISBN 0-88410-417-6). Ballinger Pub.

Environmental Law: Cases & Materials. Roger W. Findley & Daniel A. Farber. (American Casebook Ser.). 639p. 1981. text ed. 19.95. West Pub.

Environmental Law Handbook. 6th rev. ed. J. Gordon Arbuckle et al. LC 76-41637. 349p. 1979. 39.50 (ISBN 0-86587-076-4). Gov Insts.

Environmental Law in Japan: An International Perspective. Julian Gresser et al. (Illus.). 1980. text ed. 60.00x (ISBN 0-262-07076-6). MIT Pr.

Environmental Legislation: A Sourcebook. Ed. by Mary R. Sive. LC 75-61. 1976. text ed. 42.95 (ISBN 0-275-05470-5). Praeger.

Environmental Management Handbook for Hydrocarbon Processing Plants. Ed. by James D. Wall. (Illus.). 224p. (Orig.). 1980. pap. 16.95 (ISBN 0-87201-265-4). Gulf Pub.

Environmental Management in Local Government: A Study of Local Response to Federal Mandate. Alan H. Magazine. LC 77-12818. (Praeger Special Studies). 1977. 22.95 (ISBN 0-03-040786-9). Praeger.

Environmental Management of Mineral Wastes. Ed. by G. T. Goodman & M. H. Chadwick. 382p. 1978. 42.50x (ISBN 90-286-0728-5). Sijthoff & Noordhoff.

Environmental Mediation & Conflict Management: A Selection of Papers Presented at the 5th Annual Conference of the NAEP, Washington Dc, April 21-23 1980. Ed. by R. Rajagopal. 120p. 1981. pap. 10.00 (ISBN 0-08-026261-9). Pergamon.

Environmental Mediation: The Search for Consensus. Ed. by Laura M. Lake. (Social Impact Assessment Ser.). 1979. lib. bdg. 24.00x (ISBN 0-89158-587-7). Westview.

Environmental Misuse in the Soviet Union. Ed. by Fred Singleton. LC 75-19823. (Special Studies). (Illus.). 140p. 1976. text ed. 24.95 (ISBN 0-275-56210-7). Praeger.

Environmental Modeling & Decision Making: The United States Experience. Holcomb Research Institute. LC 76-28798. 1976. text ed. 20.95 (ISBN 0-275-24190-4). Praeger.

Environmental Monitoring. Commission on Natural Resources. 1977. pap. 7.75 (ISBN 0-309-02639-3). Natl Acad Pr.

Environmental Monitoring in Emergency Situations. (Safety Ser.: No. 18). (Illus., Orig.). 1966. pap. 7.50 (ISBN 92-0-123266-7, ISP118, IAEA). Unipub.

Environmental Noise Control. Edward B. Magrab. LC 75-20233. 299p. 1975. 27.50 (ISBN 0-471-56344-7, Pub. by Wiley-Interscience). Wiley.

Environmental Physiology. Ed. by J. G. Phillips. LC 74-22107. 198p. 1975. 12.95x (ISBN 0-470-68490-9). Halsted Pr.

Environmental Physiology of Animals. Ed. by J. Bligh. LC 76-25459. 1977. pap. text ed. 24.95 (ISBN 0-470-98925-4). Halsted Pr.

Environmental Physiology of Fishes. Ed. by M. A. Ali. (NATO Advanced Study Institutes Ser, A-Life Sciences: Vol. 35). 685p. 1981. 69.50 (ISBN 0-306-40574-1, Plenum Pr). Plenum Pub.

Environmental Physiology: Proceedings of the 28th International Congress of Physiological Sciences, Budapest, 1980 (Including the Satellite Symposium on Sports Physiology) Ed. by F. Obal & G. Benedek. LC 80-42102. (Advances in Physiological Sciences: Vol. 18). (Illus.). 375p. 1981. 40.00 (ISBN 0-08-027339-4). Pergamon.

Environmental Planning: A Guide to Information Sources. Ed. by Michael J. Meshenberg. LC 73-17538. (Man & the Environment Information Guide Ser.: Vol. 3). 480p. 1976. 30.00 (ISBN 0-8103-1340-5). Gale.

Environmental Planning: Perception & Behavior. Thomas Saarinen. LC 75-19533. (Illus.). 288p. 1976. pap. text ed. 10.50 (ISBN 0-395-20618-9). HM.

Environmental Policy. Ed. by Dean Mann. (Orig.). 1980. pap. 5.00 (ISBN 0-918592-43-7). Policy Studies.

Environmental Policy Analysis: Operational Methods & Models. Peter Nijkamp. LC 79-41778. 283p. 1980. 44.00 (ISBN 0-471-27763-0, Pub. by Wiley-Interscience). Wiley.

Environmental Policy & Administrative Change: Implementation of the National Environmental Policy Act. Richard N. Andrews. LC 76-7265. (Illus.). 1976. 21.50 (ISBN 0-669-00682-3). Lexington Bks.

Environmental Policy in Australia. Alan Gilpin. (Australian Environment Ser.: No. 8). (Illus.). 380p. 1981. text ed. 36.25x (ISBN 0-7022-1366-7); pap. text ed. 21.75x (ISBN 0-7022-1367-5). U of Queensland Pr.

Environmental Policy: Water Quality, Vol. 3. George S. Tolley et al. 1981. write for info. (ISBN 0-88410-632-2). Ballinger Pub.

Environmental Politics. Ed. by Stuart S. Nagel. LC 74-3138. (Special Studies). 250p. 1974. 34.95 (ISBN 0-275-09030-2). Praeger.

Environmental Politics & the Coal Coalition. Richard H. Vietor. LC 79-5277. (Environmental History Ser.: No. 2). 304p. 1980. 18.50 (ISBN 0-89096-094-1). Tex A&M Univ Pr.

Environmental Pollution Atmosphere, Land, Water & Noise. H. M. Dix. LC 80-40287. (Institution of Environmental Sciences Ser.). 300p. 1981. 38.50 (ISBN 0-471-27797-5, Pub. by Wiley-Interscience); pap. write for info. (ISBN 0-471-27905-6). Wiley.

Environmental Pollution by Chemicals. Colin Walker. 1980. pap. text ed. 7.75x (ISBN 0-09-123891-9, Hutchinson U Lib). Humanities.

Environmental Problems - Behavioral Solutions. John D. Cone & Steven C. Hayes. LC 80-12471. (Environment & Behavior Ser.). 280p. (Orig.). 1980. pap. text ed. 8.95 (ISBN 0-8185-0392-0). Brooks-Cole.

Environmental Problems in Medicine. Ed. by William D. McKee. (Illus.). 880p. 1975. text ed. 48.75 (ISBN 0-398-02962-8). C C Thomas.

Environmental Protection: The International Dimension. David A. Kay et al. 320p. 1981. text ed. 28.50 (ISBN 0-86598-034-9). Allanheld.

Environmental Protest & Citizen Politics in Japan. Margaret A. McKean. 300p. 1981. 28.50x (ISBN 0-520-04115-1). U of Cal Pr.

Environmental Quality. Ed. by W. R. Sewell. LC 74-78558. (Sage Contemporary Social Science Issues: Vol. 13). 1974. 4.95x (ISBN 0-8039-0438-X). Sage.

Environmental Quality & Residuals Management. Allen V. Kneese & Blair T. Bower. LC 79-2181. (Resources for the Future Ser.). 1979. 25.00x (ISBN 0-8018-2245-9); pap. 7.95x (ISBN 0-8018-2286-6). Johns Hopkins.

Environmental Quality & Social Behavior: Strategies for Research. M. H. David. 1973. pap. 6.25 (ISBN 0-309-02048-4). Natl Acad Pr.

Environmental Quality & Water Development. Ed. by Charles R. Goldman et al. LC 72-83739. (Illus.). 1973. 34.95x (ISBN 0-7167-0256-8). W H Freeman.

Environmental Quality: Global Aspects of Chemistry, Toxicology & Technology As Applied to the Environment, 5 vols. Ed. by F. Coulston & F. Korte. Vol. 1, 1972. 27.50 (ISBN 0-12-227001-0); Vol. 2, 1973. 36.00 (ISBN 0-12-227002-9); Vol. 3, 1974. 32.00 (ISBN 0-12-227003-7); Vol.4, 1975. 27.50 (ISBN 0-12-227004-5); Vol. 5, 1976. 24.00 (ISBN 0-12-227005-3). Acad Pr.

Environmental Quality: With Emphasis on Urban Problems. Ed. by J. T. Coppock & C. B. Wilson. 207p. 1974. 17.95 (ISBN 0-470-17205-3). Halsted Pr.

Environmental Regulation & the Allocation of Coal: A Regional Analysis. Alan M. Schlottmen. LC 76-56841. (Special Studies). 1977. text ed. 21.95 (ISBN 0-275-24090-8). Praeger.

Environmental Rights & Remedies, 2 vols. Victor J. Yannacone, Jr. et al. LC 79-118365. 1972. 90.00 (ISBN 0-686-14502-X). Lawyers Co-Op.

Environmental Risk Assessment: Scope 15. Ann V. Whyte & Ian Burton. LC 79-42903. (Physics in Medicine & Biology Ser.). 157p. 1980. 30.00 (ISBN 0-471-27701-0, Pub. by Wiley-Interscience). Wiley.

Environmental Science. Boy Scouts of America. LC 19-600. (Illus.). 64p. (gr. 6-12). 1972. pap. 0.70x (ISBN 0-8395-3363-2, 3363). BSA.

Environmental Science: The Way the World Works. Bernard J. Nebel. (Illus.). 1980. text ed. 18.95 (ISBN 0-13-283002-7). P-H.

Environmental Statutes - 1980. 551p. (Orig.). pap. text ed. 12.95 o.p. (ISBN 0-86587-075-6). Gov Insts.

Environmental Statutes: 1981 Edition. 663p. 1981. pap. 16.96 (ISBN 0-86587-089-6). Gov Insts.

Environmental Studies: A Field & Laboratory Approach. James W. Morrison & James Hall. LC 77-5372. 1978. lib. bdg. 11.95 o.p. (ISBN 0-668-04458-6, 4144); pap. text ed. 7.95 o.p. (ISBN 0-668-04144-7). Arco.

Environmental Studies: Issues & Choices for Society. ReVelle. 1980. text ed. 18.95 (ISBN 0-442-22069-3); instr's. manual 3.95 (ISBN 0-442-25753-8). D Van Nostrand.

Environmental Studies of a Marine Ecosystem: South Texas Outer Continental Shelf. Ed. by R. Warren Flint & Nancy N. Rabalais. (Illus.). 272p. 1981. text ed. 35.00x (ISBN 0-292-72030-0). U of Tex Pr.

Environmental Studies of Port Valdez. Ed. by D. W. Hood et al. (Occasional Pub. Ser. No. 3). 15.00 (ISBN 0-914500-01-5). U of AK Inst Marine.

Environmental Studies of Port Valdez: Data Vol. 1. (Occasional Pub. Ser. No. 3a). 10.00 (ISBN 0-914500-02-3). U of AK Inst Marine.

Environmental Studies: The Construction of an 'A' Level Syllabus. Ed. by S. M. Carson. 1973. pap. text ed. 6.25x (ISBN 0-85633-029-9, NFER). Humanities.

Environmental Study of a Nuclear Plant at Charlestown: Rhode Island. Coastal Resources Center. (Marine Technical Report Ser.: No. 33). 1974. pap. 5.00 (ISBN 0-938412-07-8). URI MAS.

Environmental Surveillance Around Nuclear Installations, 2 vols. (Illus.). 927p. (Orig.). 1974. Set. pap. 73.00 (ISBN 92-0-020074-5, ISP353, IAEA). Unipub.

Environmental Technologies in Architecture. Bertram Y. Kinzey, Jr. & H. M. Sharp. (Illus.). 1963. ref. ed. 28.95 (ISBN 0-13-283226-7). P-H.

Environmental Toxicology. John H. Duffus. (Environmental Science Ser.). 132p. 1981. 15.95 (ISBN 0-470-27051-9). Halsted Pr.

Environmental Toxicology: A Guide to Information Sources. Robert L Rudd. LC 73-17540. (Man & the Environmrnt Information Guide Ser.: Vol. 7). 1977. 30.00 (ISBN 0-8103-1342-1). Gale.

Environmental Use & the Market. Hugh Macauley, Jr. & Bruce Yandle, Jr. LC 77-91. 1977. 17.95 (ISBN 0-669-01431-1). Lexington Bks.

Environmental Values, 1860-1972: A Guide to Information Sources. Ed. by Loren C. Owings. LC 73-17539. (Man & the Environment Information Guide Ser.: Vol. 4). 593p. 1976. 30.00 (ISBN 0-8103-1343-X). Gale.

Environmental Variables & the Prevention of Mental Illness. Ed. by Paul M. Insel. LC 79-3521. 240p. 1980. 25.95x (ISBN 0-669-03457-6). Lexington Bks.

Environments & Organizations: Theoretical & Empirical Perspectives. Marshall W. Meyer et al. LC 76-50706. (Social & Behavioral Science Ser.). (Illus.). 1978. text ed. 16.95x (ISBN 0-87589-374-0). Jossey-Bass.

Environments As Therapy for Brain Dysfunction. Ed. by Roger N. Walsh & William T. Greenough. LC 76-1116. (Advances in Behavioral Biology Ser.: Vol. 17). 376p. 1976. 35.00 (ISBN 0-306-37917-1, Plenum Pr). Plenum Pub.

Envy. Yury Olesha. Tr. by Thomas Berczynski from Rus. (Orig.). 1979. pap. 4.50 (ISBN 0-88233-091-8). Ardis Pubs.

Envy: A Theory of Social Behaviour. Helmut Schoeck. Tr. by Michael Glenny & Betty Ross. LC 69-14842. (Helen & Kurt Wolff Bk). Orig. Title: Neid. 408p. 1972. pap. 3.95 o.p. (ISBN 0-15-628798-6, HB241, Harv). HarBraceJ.

Envy: A Theory of Social Behaviour. Helmut Schoeck. Tr. by Michael Glenny & Betty Ross. LC 69-14842. 1966. 28.50x (ISBN 0-15-128952-2). Irvington.

Envy & Gratitude. Melanie Klein. 1975. 17.50 o.p. (ISBN 0-440-05014-6, Sey Lawr). Delacorte.

Envy & Other Works. Yuri Olesha. Tr. by Andrew R. MacAndrew. 320p. 1981. pap. 4.95 (ISBN 0-393-00042-7). Norton.

Enzymatic Basis of Detoxication, Vol. 1. Ed. by William B. Jakoby. (Biochemical Pharmacology & Toxicology Ser.). 1980. 43.00 (ISBN 0-12-380001-3). Acad Pr.

Enzymatic Basis of Detoxication, Vol. 2. William B. Jakoby. LC 80-17350. (Biochemical Pharmacology & Toxicology Ser.). 1980. lib ed 38.50 (ISBN 0-12-380002-1). Acad Pr.

Enzymatic Methods of Analysis. G. G. Guilbault. 1970. 45.00 (ISBN 0-08-006989-4). Pergamon.

Enzymatic Reaction Mechanisms. Christopher Walsh. LC 78-18266. (Illus.). 1979. text ed. 34.95x (ISBN 0-7167-0070-0). W H Freeman.

Enzymatic Release of Vasoactive Peptides: Workshop Conferences HOECHST. Ed. by Franz Gross et al. (Illus.). 430p. 1980. text ed. 41.00 (ISBN 0-89004-458-9). Raven.

Enzyme Defects & Immune Dysfunction. Ciba Foundation. (Ciba Foundation Symposium Ser.: No. 68). 1979. 35.20 (ISBN 0-444-90088-8, Excerpta Medica). Elsevier.

Enzyme Engineering: Future Directions. Ed. by Lemual B. Wingard et al. 535p. 1980. 59.50 (ISBN 0-306-40442-7, Plenum Pr). Plenum Pub.

Enzyme Handbook, 2 Vols. T. E. Barman. LC 69-19293. 1969. Set. 51.70 (ISBN 0-387-04423-X). Springer-Verlag.

Enzyme Histochemistry & Its Application in the Study of Neoplasms. M. S. Burstone. 1963. 62.00 o.s.i. (ISBN 0-12-146950-6). Acad Pr.

Enzyme Immunoassay. Edward T. Maggio. 304p. 1980. lib. bdg. 69.95 (ISBN 0-8493-5617-2). CRC Pr.

Enzyme Inhibitors. V. Brodbeck. 270p. (Orig.). Date not set. pap. price not set. Verlag Chemie.

Enzyme Kinetics. Ed by D. V. Roberts. LC 76-11091. (Cambridge Chemistry Texts Ser.). (Illus.). 1977. 57.50 (ISBN 0-521-21274-X); pap. 16.95x (ISBN 0-521-29080-5). Cambridge U Pr.

Enzyme Molecule. W. Ferdinand. LC 76-7530. 1976. 17.25 (ISBN 0-471-01822-8, Pub by Wiley-Interscience); pap. 14.95 (ISBN 0-471-01821-X). Wiley.

Enzyme Regulation & Metabolic Diseases. F. Belfiore. (Illus.). xxiv, 880p. 1980. 149.25 (ISBN 3-8055-0005-X). S Karger.

Enzyme Structure & Mechanism. Alan Fersht. LC 77-6441. (Illus.). 1977. pap. text ed. 14.95x (ISBN 0-7167-0188-X). W H Freeman.

Enzyme Therapy in Genetic Diseases: Part 2. Ed. by Robert J. Desnick. LC 79-48026. (Alan R. Liss Ser.: Vol. 16, No. 1). 1980. 64.00. March of Dimes.

Enzyme Therapy in Genetic Diseases: Proceedings, No. 2. 2nd ed. Ed. by Robert J. Desnick. LC 79-48026. (Birth Defects: Original Article Ser.: Vol. XVI, No. 1). 568p. 1980. 26.00 (ISBN 0-8451-1035-7). A R Liss.

Enzymes. Ed. by Paul D. Boyer. Incl. Vol. 1. Enzyme Structure, Control. 3rd. ed. 1970. 51.00 (ISBN 0-12-122701-4); Vol. 2. Kinetics, Mechanisms. 3rd. ed. 1970. 51.00 (ISBN 0-12-122702-2); Vol. 3. Peptide Bond Hydrolysis. 3rd ed. 1971. 62.50 (ISBN 0-12-122703-0); Vol. 4. 1971. 62.50 (ISBN 0-12-122704-9); Vol. 5. 1971. 62.50 (ISBN 0-12-122705-7); Vol. 6. 1972. 62.50 (ISBN 0-12-122706-5); Vol. 7. 1972. 62.50 (ISBN 0-12-122707-3); Vol. 8. 1973. 55.00 (ISBN 0-12-122708-1); Vol. 9. 1973. 55.00 (ISBN 0-12-122709-X); Vol. 10. 1974. 62.50 (ISBN 0-12-122710-3); Vol. 11. 1975. 62.50 (ISBN 0-12-122711-1); Vol. 12. 1975. 59.00 (ISBN 0-12-122712-X); Vol. 13. 1976. 62.50 (ISBN 0-12-122713-8). 629.00 set (ISBN 0-685-23119-4); student ed. 1973 22.50 (ISBN 0-12-122750-2). Acad Pr.

Enzymes. Jolin B. Haldane. 1965. 12.95x o.p. (ISBN 0-262-08021-4). MIT Pr.

Enzymes. M. A. Tribe et al. LC 75-14642. (Cambridge Biology Course Ser.: Bk. 7). (Illus.). 128p. 1975. 35.50 (ISBN 0-521-20870-X); limp bdg. 10.95x (ISBN 0-521-20960-9). Cambridge U Pr.

Enzymes & Isoenzymes: Structure, Properties & Function. Ed. by D. Shugar & D. Shugar. 1970. 50.00 (ISBN 0-12-640860-2). Acad Pr.

Enzymes & Neurotransmitters in Mental Disease: Based on a Symposium Held at the Technion Faculty of Medicine, Haifa, Israel August 28-30 1979. Earl Usdin et al. LC 80-40130. 640p. 1980. 98.00 (ISBN 0-471-27791-6, Pub. by Wiley-Interscience). Wiley.

Enzymes As Drugs. John C. Holcenberg & Joseph Roberts. LC 80-20641. 450p. 1981. 55.00 (ISBN 0-471-05061-X, Pub. by Wiley-Interscience). Wiley.

Enzymological Aspects of Food Irradiation. (Illus., Orig.). 1969. pap. 6.50 (ISBN 92-0-111169-X, IAEA). Unipub.

Enzymology of the Cell Surface. A. Rothstein. Bd. with Tension at the Cell Surface. E. N. Harvey. (Protoplasmatologia: Vol. 2e, Pts. 4-5). (Illus.). iv, 116p. 1954. 24.80 o.p. (ISBN 0-387-80345-9). Springer-Verlag.

Eocene & Oligocene Foraminifera from the Santa Cruz Mountains, California. W. W. Fairchild et al. (U. C. Publ. in Geological Sciences: Vol. 81). 1969. pap. 7.50x (ISBN 0-520-09184-1). U of Cal Pr.

Eocene Copper Basin Flora of Northeastern Nevada. Daniel Axelrod. (U. C. Publ. in Geological Sciences: Vol. 59). 1966. pap. 7.50x (ISBN 0-520-09160-4). U of Cal Pr.

Eoin Macneill: Scholar & Man of Action, 1867 - 1945. Michael Tierney. Ed. by F. X. Martin. (Illus.). 492p. 1981. 67.50x (ISBN 0-19-822440-0). Oxford U Pr.

Eosinophil in Health & Disease. Ed. by Adel A. Mahmoud & K. Frank Austen. 1980. 39.50 (ISBN 0-8089-1274-7). Grune.

Eothen. A. W. Kinglake. LC 71-93107. 1970. pap. 4.50x (ISBN 0-8032-5711-2, BB 509, Bison). U of Nebr Pr.

Ephemerides of Phialo. Stephen Gosson. LC 73-170404. (English Stage Ser.: Vol. 3). lib. bdg. 50.00 (ISBN 0-8240-0586-4). Garland Pub.

Ephemerides 1890-1950. A. LeRoi Simmons. 407p. 1970. text ed. 17.00 (ISBN 0-9605126-0-8). Aquarian Bk Pubs.

Ephemeris Nineteen Fifty to Nineteen Seventy-Five. A. LeRoi Simmons. (Illus.). 375p. 1977. 14.00 (ISBN 0-9605126-1-6). Aquarian Bk Pubs.

Ephesians. Irving L. Jensen. (Bible Self-Study Ser). 1973. pap. 2.25 (ISBN 0-8024-1049-9). Moody.

Ephesians. Lionel Swain. (New Testament Message Ser.). 9.95 (ISBN 0-89453-136-0); pap. 4.95 (ISBN 0-89453-201-4). M Glazier.

Ephesians. Geoffrey Wilson. 1978. pap. 2.95 (ISBN 0-85151-263-1). Banner of Truth.

Ephesians: An Exposition. W. A. Criswell. 288p. 1974. 11.95 (ISBN 0-310-22780-1). Zondervan.

Ephesians: An Exposition. W. A. Criswell. 308p. 1981. pap. 6.95 (ISBN 0-310-22781-X). Zondervan.

Ephesians & Colossians. T. K. Abbott. LC 40-15742. (International Critical Commentary Ser.). 392p. Repr. of 1979 ed. 21.00x (ISBN 0-567-05030-0). Attic Pr.

Ephesians: Living in God's Household. Robert Baylis. LC 76-43523. (Fisherman Bible Study Guide). 45p. 1976. pap. 1.95 (ISBN 0-87788-223-1). Shaw Pubs.

Ephesians, the Epistle of Christian Maturity. Keith L. Brooks. (Teach Yourself the Bible Ser). 1944. pap. 1.75 (ISBN 0-8024-2333-7). Moody.

Epic Hero & the Decline of Heroic Poetry. Peter Hagin. 182p. 1980. Repr. of 1964 ed. lib. bdg. 25.00 (ISBN 0-89987-361-8). Darby Bks.

Epic in Africa. Isidore Okpewho. 1979. 17.50 (ISBN 0-231-04400-3). Columbia U Pr.

Epic Mythology. rev. ed. E. Washburn Hopkins. LC 76-75358. 1968. Repr. of 1915 ed. 16.00x (ISBN 0-8196-0228-0). Biblo.

Epic of Latin America. John A. Crow. 1000p. 1980. 29.95 (ISBN 0-520-04107-0); pap. 14.95 (ISBN 0-520-03776-6, CAL. NO. 458). U of Cal Pr.
Epic of Modern Man: A Collection of Readings. 2nd ed. Leften Stavrianos. LC 77-138472. 1971. pap. text ed. 13.95 (ISBN 0-13-283333-6). P-H.
Epic of Survival: The Story of Anti-Semitism. Samuel Glassman. LC 80-69018. 400p. 20.00 (ISBN 0-8197-0481-4). Bloch.
Epic of the Cid. Tr. by J. Gerald Markley. LC 61-14564. 1961. pap. 3.95 (ISBN 0-672-60259-8, LLA77). Bobbs.
Epic of the Kings: Shah- nama. Ferdowsi. (Persian Heritage Ser). 1973. 27.00 (ISBN 0-7100-1367-1). Routledge & Kegan.
Epic of the New World. (Eng. & Span.). 1971. pap. 1.00 Eng. ed. (ISBN 0-8270-4555-7); pap. 1.00 Span. ed. (ISBN 0-8270-4560-3). OAS.
Epic of Women. Arthur O'Shaughnessy. Ed. by Ian Fletcher & John Stokes. LC 76-20148. (Decadent Consciousness Ser.). 1978. lib. bdg. 38.00 (ISBN 0-8240-2780-9). Garland Pub.
Epic Poem on the Life of William Clarke Quantrill: An Epic on the Life of William Clarke Quantrill. Charles Boer. LC 74-189194. 148p. 1972. 8.00 (ISBN 0-8040-0572-9); pap. 4.50 (ISBN 0-8040-0573-7). Swallow.
Epicoene; or, the Silent Woman. Ben Jonson. Ed. by L. Beaurline. LC 65-23327. (Regents Renaissance Drama Ser). 1966. 9.95x (ISBN 0-8032-0266-0); pap. 2.95x (ISBN 0-8032-5266-8, BB 216, Bison). U of Nebr Pr.
Epicurean Pursuit of Pleasure. William Hyde. (Illus.). 1980. Repr. of 1904 ed. deluxe ed. 47.95 (ISBN 0-89901-009-1). Found Class Reprints.
Epicurean Recipes of California Winemakers. Wine Advisory Board. Ed. by Donna Bottrell. (Illus.). 1978. 5.95 (ISBN 0-932664-00-8). Wine Appreciation.
Epicurus: An Introduction. J. M. Rist. LC 70-177939. 200p. 1972. 34.00 (ISBN 0-521-08426-1); pap. 7.95 (ISBN 0-521-29200-X). Cambridge U Pr.
Epidemic! Larry R. Leichter. 368p. (Orig.). 1980. pap. 2.50 (ISBN 0-89083-644-2). Zebra.
Epidemic Disease in Fifteenth Century England: The Medical Response & the Demographic Consequences. Robert S. Gottfried. (Illus.). 1978. 19.50 (ISBN 0-8135-0861-4). Rutgers U Pr.
Epidemics. Geoffrey Marks & William K. Beatty. LC 76-2584. 1978. pap. 4.95 o.p. (ISBN 0-684-15893-0, ScribT). Scribner.
Epidemiologic Reviews: 1980, Vol. 2. Ed. by Philip E. Sartwell & Neal Nathanson. LC 79-7564. (Epidemiologic Reviews Ser.). (Illus.). 240p. 1980. text ed. 13.50x (ISBN 0-8018-2404-4). Johns Hopkins.
Epidemiological Psychiatry. Brian Cooper & H. G. Morgan. (American Lectures Living Chemistry). (Illus.). 232p. 1973. 17.75 (ISBN 0-398-02581-9). C C Thomas.
Epidemiology. International Cancer Congress, 12th, Buenos Aires, 5-11 October. Ed. by Jillian Birch. LC 79-40693. (Advances in Medical Oncology, Research & Education Ser.: Vol. III). (Illus.). 1979. 68.00 (ISBN 0-08-024386-X). Pergamon.
Epidemiology & Community Health in Warm Climate Countries. R. Cruickshank et al. LC 75-5573. (Illus.). 512p. 1976. text ed. 32.00 (ISBN 0-443-01303-9); pap. text ed. 26.50x (ISBN 0-443-01145-1). Churchill.
Epidemiology & Control of Gastrointestinal Parasites of Sheep in Australia. 153p. pap. 11.00 (ISBN 0-643-00301-0, CO21, CSIRO). Unipub.
Epidemiology & Plant Disease Management. Jan C. Zadoks & Richard D. Schein. (Illus.). 1979. text ed. 22.95x (ISBN 0-19-502451-6); pap. text ed. 9.95x (ISBN 0-19-502452-4). Oxford U Pr.
Epidemiology for the Health Sciences: A Primer on Epidemiologic Concepts & Their Uses. Donald F. Austin & S. Benson Werner. (Illus.). 88p. 1979. pap. 5.25 (ISBN 0-398-02949-0). C C Thomas.
Epidemiology for the Infection Control Nurse. Ed. by Elizabeth Barrett-Connor et al. LC 77-13128. (Illus.). 1978. text ed. 18.95 (ISBN 0-8016-0744-2). Mosby.
Epidemiology of Anencephalus & Spina Bifida. J. Mark Elwood & J. Harold Elwood. (Illus.). 424p. 1980. text ed. 69.50x (ISBN 0-19-261220-4). Oxford U Pr.
Epidemiology of Cancer in Texas: Incidence Analyzed by Type, Ethnic Group, & Geographic Location. Eleanor J. Macdonald & Evelyn B. Heinze. LC 77-85516. 1978. 56.00 (ISBN 0-89004-203-9). Raven.
Epidemiology of Cancer of Selected Sites. Jerzy Staszewski. LC 74-1096. 300p. 1975. 25.00 o.p. (ISBN 0-88410-114-2). Ballinger Pub.
Epidemiology of Dementia. Ed. by James A. Mortimer & Leonard M. Schuman. (Illus.). 200p. 1981. text ed. 18.95x (ISBN 0-19-502906-2). Oxford U Pr.
Epidemiology of Hospital Associated Infections. Peter C. Fuchs. LC 79-17036. 1980. text ed. 25.00 (ISBN 0-89189-072-6, 45-7-011-00). Am Soc Clinical.
Epidemiology of Human Mycotic Diseases. Yousef Al-Doory. (Illus.). 364p. 1976. 36.50 (ISBN 0-398-03380-3). C C Thomas.
Epidemiology of Mental Retardation. Rick Heber. (Illus.). 136p. 1970. 11.75 (ISBN 0-398-00817-5). C C Thomas.
Epidemology & Public Health. 2nd ed. Ed. by Ronald Gold & Bonnie C. Yankaskas. LC 79-83719. (Clinical Sciences PreTest Self-Assessment & Review Ser.). (Illus.). 1980. 9.95 (ISBN 0-07-050967-0). McGraw-Pretest.
Epidemiology of Diabetes in Developing Countries. M. M. Ahuja. 124p. 1980. pap. 5.95x (ISBN 0-89955-316-8, Pub. by Interprint India). Intl Schol Bk Serv.
Epidermal Keratinocyte Differentiation & Fibrillogenesis. Ed. by M. Prunieras. (Frontiers of Matrix Biology Ser.: Vol. 9). (Illus.). 240p. 1980. 72.00 (ISBN 3-8055-0893-X). S Karger.
Epididymis & Fertility: Biology & Pathology. Ed. by C. G. Bollack & A. Clavert. (Progress in Reproductive Biology Ser.: Vol. 8). (Illus.). viii, 192p. 1981. 58.75 (ISBN 3-8055-2157-X). S Karger.
Epigrammata Graeca: From the Beginning to the Garland of Phillip. Ed. by Denys Page. (Oxford Classical Texts Ser). 350p. 1975. 24.95x (ISBN 0-19-814581-0). Oxford U Pr.
Epigrams to Live & Die by. Roberta Mendel. (Sketchbook Ser.). (Illus., Orig.). 1981. pap. 4.00 (ISBN 0-936424-08-7, 008). Pin Prick.
Epilepsies. 3rd ed. John M. Sutherland & Mervyn Eadie. (Illus.). 176p. 1980. pap. text ed. 10.00x (ISBN 0-443-02184-8). Churchill.
Epilepsies of Childhood. Niall F. O'Donohue. Ed. by J. Apley. LC 79-40722. (Postgraduate Pediatric Ser.). 1979. text ed. 46.95 (ISBN 0-407-00138-7). Butterworths.
Epilepsy. J. Majkowski. (Monographs in Neural Sciences: Vol. 5). (Illus.). 1980. pap. 56.50 (ISBN 3-8055-0635-X). S Karger.
Epilepsy. Alvin Silverstein & Virginia B. Silverstein. LC 74-31382. (gr. 4-7). 1975. 5.95 (ISBN 0-397-31615-1); pap. 1.95 o.p. (ISBN 0-397-31624-0). Lippincott.
Epilepsy: A Study of the Idiopathic Disease. William A. Turner. LC 73-82850. 289p. 1973. Repr. of 1907 ed. 11.00 (ISBN 0-911216-62-6). Raven.
Epilepsy: A Window to Brain Mechanisms. Ed. by Joan S. Lockard & Arthur A. Ward, Jr. 296p. 1980. text ed. 29.50 (ISBN 0-89004-499-6). Raven.
Epilepsy & Behavior Nineteen Seventy-Nine: Proceedings. Workshop Held in the Leeuwenhorst Congress Centre Noordwijkerhout, Nov. 23-25, 1979. Ed. by B. M. Kulig. 1980. text ed. 21.00 (ISBN 90-265-0332-6, Pub by Swets Pub Serv Holland). Swets North Am.
Epilepsy & the Oral Manifestations of Phenytoin Therapy. T. M. Hassell. (Monographs in Oral Science: Vol. 9). (Illus.). 200p. 1980. pap. 89.25 (ISBN 3-8055-1008-X). S Karger.
Epilepsy Explained. Mary V. Laidlaw. (Patient Handbook Ser.). 1980. pap. text ed. 3.50 (ISBN 0-443-01962-2). Churchill.
Epilepsy Fact Book. Harry Sands & Frances C. Minters. (Illus.). 1979. pap. 8.95 (ISBN 0-684-16823-5, ScribT). Scribner.
Epilepsy Handbook. 2nd ed. Louis D. Boshes & Frederic A. Gibbs. (Illus.). 206p. 1972. 17.50 (ISBN 0-398-02194-5). C C Thomas.
Epilepsy, Pregnancy, & Child. Ed. by D. Janz et al. 1981. text ed. price not set (ISBN 0-89004-654-9). Raven.
Epilepsy: The Eighth International Symposium. Ed. by J. Kiffin Penry. LC 76-58059. 1977. 19.00 (ISBN 0-89004-190-3). Raven.
Epileptic Seizures: Clinical & Electrographic Features, Diagnosis & Treatment. Henri Gastaut & Roger Broughton. 304p. 1972. pap. 32.50 photocopy ed. spiral (ISBN 0-398-02290-9). C C Thomas.
Epilogue. Mark W. Magnan, Jr. 1979. 9.95 (ISBN 0-533-04507-X). Vantage.
Epiphany. Merrill R. Abbey & O. C. Edwards. LC 74-76935. (Proclamation 1: Aids for Interpreting the Lessons of the Church Year, Ser. A: Ser. A). 64p. (Orig.). 1974. pap. 1.95 (ISBN 0-8006-4062-4, 1-4062). Fortress.
Epiphany. Paul J. Achtemeier & Elizabeth R. Achtemeier. LC 73-79349. (Proclamation 1: Aids for Interpreting the Lessons of the Church Year, Ser. C). 64p. 1973. pap. 2.50 (ISBN 0-8006-4052-7, 1-4052). Fortress.
Epiphany. C. Fitzsimons Allison & Werner H. Kelber. LC 74-24900. (Proclamation 1: Aids for Interpreting the Lessons of the Church Year). 64p. 1974. pap. 1.95 (ISBN 0-8006-4072-1, 1-4072). Fortress.
Epiphany. Joseph A. Burgess & Albert C. Winn. Ed. by Elizabeth Achtemeier et al. LC 79-7377. (Proclamation 2: Aids for Interpreting the Lessons of the Church Year, Ser. A). 64p. (Orig.). 1980. pap. 2.50 (ISBN 0-8006-4092-6, 1-4092). Fortress.
Epiphany. Richard I. Pervo & William J. Carl, III. Ed. by Elizabeth Achtemeier et al. LC 79-7377. (Proclamation 2: Aids for Interpreting the Lessons of the Church Year, Ser. C). 64p. 1979. pap. 2.50 (ISBN 0-8006-4085-3, 1-4085). Fortress.
Episcopal Church & Its Work. rev. ed. Powel M. Dawley. (Orig.). 1955. 3.50, case o.p. (ISBN 0-8164-0125-X); pap. 2.95 (ISBN 0-8164-2017-3, SP6). Crossroad NY.
Episcopal Church Welcomes You: An Introduction to Its History, Worship & Mission. William B. Gray & Betty Gray. LC 73-17898. 168p. 1974. 6.95 o.p. (ISBN 0-8164-0253-1); pap. 2.95 (ISBN 0-8164-2087-4). Crossroad NY.
Episcopal Colleagues of Archbishop Thomas Becket. David Knowles. 1971. Repr. 14.95 (ISBN 0-521-05493-1). Cambridge U Pr.
Episcopalian's Dictionary. Howard Harper. 1975. 8.95 (ISBN 0-8164-1166-2); pap. 4.50 (ISBN 0-8164-2100-5). Crossroad NY.
Episcopate in the Kingdom of Leon in the Twelfth Century. R. A. Fletcher. (Historical Monographs). (Illus.). 1978. 36.00x (ISBN 0-19-821869-9). Oxford U Pr.
Episodes at the Olive Press. Don Pate. LC 79-24125. (Horizon Ser.). 1980. pap. 4.50 (ISBN 0-8127-0269-7). Southern Pub.
Episodes of Violence in U.S. History, 3 vols. Ed. by Leon Friedman. Incl. Vol. 1. Dynamite. Louis Adamic. LC 80-21964; Vol. 2. The Dorr War. Arthur M. Mowry. LC 80-21969; Vol. 3. The Molly Maguires. Wayne G. Broehl, Jr. LC 80-21794. (Illus.). 750p. 1981. Repr. of 1970 ed. Set. 50.00 (ISBN 0-87754-133-7). Chelsea Hse.
Epistemics & Economics: A Critique of Economic Doctrine. George L. Shackle. LC 72-76091. (Illus.). 400p. 1973. 54.00 (ISBN 0-521-08626-4). Cambridge U Pr.
Epistemological Problems of Economics. Ludwig Von Mises. (Institue for Humane Studies Ser. in Economic Theory). 264p. 1981. 20.00x (ISBN 0-8147-8757-6); pap. 7.00x (ISBN 0-8147-8758-4). NYU Pr.
Epistle of James. Sophie Laws. LC 80-8349. (Harper's New Testament Commentaries Ser.). 288p. 1981. 14.95 (ISBN 0-06-064918-6, HarpR). Har-Row.
Epistle of Paul to the Galatians. Alan Cole. (Tyndale Bible Commentaries). 1964. pap. 2.95 (ISBN 0-8028-1408-5). Eerdmans.
Epistle of Paul to the Galatians. J. Koehler. Tr. by E. E. Sauer. 1957. 2.95 (ISBN 0-8100-0038-5). Northwest Pub.
Epistle of Saint James. Joseph B. Mayor. 1977. 19.25 (ISBN 0-686-12971-7). Klock & Klock.
Epistle of St. Jude & the Second Epistle of Peter. Joseph B. Mayor. 1978. 15.25 (ISBN 0-686-12945-8). Klock & Klock.
Epistle to Professor David McCutchion. S. Mokashi-Punekar. (Writers Workshop Redbird Book Ser.). 19p. 1975. 4.80 (ISBN 0-88253-534-X); pap. text ed. 4.00 (ISBN 0-88253-533-1). Ind-US Inc.
Epistle to the Ephesians. Frederick F. Bruce. 1962. 7.95 (ISBN 0-8007-0083-X). Revell.
Epistle to the Hebrews: Its Meaning & Message. James T. Hudson. 78p. Repr. of 1937 ed. 3.50 (ISBN 0-567-02144-0). Attic Pr.
Epistle to the Romans. 6th ed. Karl Barth. Tr. by Edwyn C. Hoskyns. 1968. pap. 8.95 (ISBN 0-19-500294-6, GB). Oxford U Pr.
Epistle to the Romans. Ed. by K. E. Kirk. (Clarendon Bible Ser.). (Illus.). 1937. pap. 5.95x (ISBN 0-19-826116-0). Oxford U Pr.
Epistle to the Son of the Wolf. rev. ed. Baha'u'llah. Tr. by Shoghi Effendi. LC 53-18798. 1976. 10.00 (ISBN 0-87743-048-9, 7-03-01). Baha'i.
Epistles from Bath, or, Q's Letters to His Yorkshire Relations, Repr. Of 1817. Thomas H. Bayly. Bd. with Rough Sketches of Bath, Imitations of Horace & Other Poems. Repr. of 1817 ed; Parliamentary Letters, & Other Poems. Repr. of 1818 ed; Dandies of the Present & the Macaronies of the Past: A Rough Sketch. Repr. of 1819 ed; Tribute of a Friend. Repr. of 1819 ed; Mournful Recollections. Repr. of 1820 ed; Small Talk. Repr. of 1820 ed; Erin, & Other Poems. Repr. of 1822 ed; Outlines of Edinburgh, & Other Poems. Repr. of 1822 ed. LC 75-31154. (Romantic Context Ser.: Poetry 1789-1830: Vol. 10). 1979. lib. bdg. 47.00 (ISBN 0-8240-2109-6). Garland Pub.
Epistles of David-Kaka to Plalm'n. David McCutchion. (Writers Workshop Greybird Book Ser.). 94p. 1975. 12.00 (ISBN 0-88253-536-6); pap. text ed. 4.80 (ISBN 0-88253-535-8). Ind-US Inc.
Epistles of George Fox. Ed. by Samuel Tuke. LC 78-24657. 1979. pap. 2.95 (ISBN 0-913408-46-8). Friends United.
Epistles of John & Jude. Irving L. Jenson. (Bible Self-Study Ser). 128p. (Orig.). 1971. pap. 2.25 (ISBN 0-8024-1062-6). Moody.
Epistles of Paul: Hebrews. (Banner of Truth Geneva Series Commentaries). 1978. 21.95. Banner of Truth.
Epistles of Paul the Apostle to the Thessalonians. C. F. Hogg & W. E. Vine. 5.95 (ISBN 0-89315-040-1). Lambert Bk.
Epistles of Paul to the Corinthians. Arthur P. Stanley. Date not set. 20.95 (ISBN 0-86524-051-5). Klock & Klock.
Epistles of Paul to the Philippians & Philemon. Jacobus J. Muller. (New International Commentary on the New Testament). 1955. 10.95 (ISBN 0-8028-2188-X). Eerdmans.
Epistles of Peter. Edgar C. James. (Teach Yourself the Bible Ser.). 1964. pap. 1.75 (ISBN 0-8024-2355-8). Moody.
Epistles of St. Peter. J. H. Jowett. LC 78-94111. 1970. 6.95 o.p. (ISBN 0-8254-2950-1). Kregel.
Epistles to the Ephesians & Colossians. E. K. Simpson & Frederick F. Bruce. (New International Commentary on the New Testament). 1958. 12.95 (ISBN 0-8028-2193-6). Eerdmans.
Epistolario, a Cura Di Luisa Cambi. Vincenzo Bellini. LC 80-2262. (Illus.). 1981. Repr. of 1943 ed. 56.00 (ISBN 0-404-18815-X). AMS Pr.
Epistolario De Juan Ignacio Molina. Ronan & Hanisch. (Sp.). 1980. 11.60 (ISBN 0-8294-0360-4). Loyola.
Epistolarity: Approaches to a Form. Janet Altman. 1981. write for info. (ISBN 0-8142-0313-2). Ohio St U Pr.
Epistres Morales et Familieres Du Traverseur (Poitiers, 1545) Jean Bouchet. (Classiques De la Renaissance En France: No. 4). 1970. 35.90x (ISBN 90-2796-345-2). Mouton.
Epistularum Libri Decem. Pliny. Ed. by Roger A. Mynors. (Oxford Classical Texts). 1963. 18.95x (ISBN 0-19-814643-4). Oxford U Pr.
Epitaph for Vocational Guidance: Myths, Actualities, Implications. Ruth Barry & Beverly Wolf. LC 62-13478. 1962. text ed. 10.25x (ISBN 0-8077-1047-4). Tchrs Coll.
Epitaph of a Small Winner. Machado De Assis. 1977. pap. 2.25 (ISBN 0-380-01712-1, 33878, Bard). Avon.
Epitaphs: Graveyard Humour & Eulogy. William H. Beable. LC 79-154494. 246p. Repr. of 1925 ed. 15.000 (ISBN 0-8103-3374-0). Gale.
Epitaxial Growth, Pts. A & B. Ed. by J. W. Matthews. (Materials Science & Technology Ser). 1975. Pt. A. 52.75 (ISBN 0-12-480901-4); Pt. B. deluxe ed. 49.00 (ISBN 0-12-480902-2). Acad Pr.
Epithelial Ion & Water Transport. Ed. by Anthony D. Macknight & John P. Leader. 380p. 1981. 35.00 (ISBN 0-89004-537-2). Raven.
Epithelial Transport in the Lower Vertebrates. Ed. by B. Lahlou. LC 79-50884. (Illus.). 1980. 55.00 (ISBN 0-521-22748-8). Cambridge U Pr.
Epitome of Certaine Late Aspersions Cast at Civilians. William Clerk. LC 79-84095. (English Experience Ser.: No.915). 56p. 1979. Repr. of 1631 ed. lib. bdg. 7.00 (ISBN 90-221-0915-1). Walter J Johnson.
Epitome of the Laws of Nova Scotia, 4 vols. Beamish Murdoch. LC 73-26626. 1034p. Repr. of 1833 ed. Set. 90.00x (ISBN 0-912004-04-5). W W Gaunt.
Epoch. Ed. by Robert Silverberg & Roger Elwood. (YA) 1975. 10.95 o.p. (ISBN 0-399-11460-2, Dist. by Putnam). Berkley Pub.
Epoch & Artist. David Jones. 1973. pap. 6.95 (ISBN 0-571-10152-6, Pub. by Faber & Faber). Merrimack Bk Serv.
Epochs in the Life of Jesus. A. T. Robertson. (A. T. Robertson Library Ser). 1974. pap. 2.95 o.p. (ISBN 0-8010-7624-2). Baker Bk.
Epochs in the Life of Simon Peter. A. T. Robertson. (A. T. Robertson Library Ser). 1974. pap. 3.95 o.p. (ISBN 0-8010-7626-9). Baker Bk.
Epochs of Greek & Roman Biography. Duane R. Stuart. LC 67-19532. 1928. 12.00x (ISBN 0-8196-0193-4). Biblo.
Eponyms Dictionaries Index: A Compilation of Terms Based on Names of Actual or Legendary Persons. Ed. by James Ruffner et al. LC 76-20341. 1977. 68.00 (ISBN 0-8103-0688-3). Gale.
Epyllion from Theocritus to Ovid. Mary M. Crump. Ed. by Steele Commager. LC 77-70761. (Latin Poetry Ser.). 1978. lib. bdg. 32.00 (ISBN 0-8240-2966-6). Garland Pub.
Equal Coverage for the Mentally Ill. 1972. 1.00 o.p. (ISBN 0-685-77442-2, 164). Am Psychiatric.
Equal Justice: The Supreme Court in the Warren Era. Arthur J. Goldberg. LC 72-167921. (Julius Rosenthal Memorial Lecture Ser.: 1971). 100p. 1971. 7.95x o.s.i. (ISBN 0-8101-0363-X). Northwestern U Pr.

Equal Opportunities & Equal Treatment for Men & Women Workers: Workers with Family Responsibilities, Report V (1) Ed. by International Labour Office. 84p. (Orig.). 1980. pap. 10.00 (ISBN 92-2-102405-9). Intl Labour Office.

Equal Opportunity Handbook for Hotels, Restaurants & Institutions. Arch Stokes. LC 79-859. 1979. 14.95 (ISBN 0-8436-2148-6). CBI Pub.

Equal Rights Amendment: A Bibliographic Study. Compiled by Equal Rights Amendment Project. Ed. by Anita Miller & Hazel Greenberg. LC 76-24999. 400p. 1976. lib. bdg. 22.50 (ISBN 0-8371-9058-4, ERA/). Greenwood.

Equal Rights for Children. Howard Cohen. 172p. 1981. 13.50x (ISBN 0-8476-6772-3). Rowman.

Equal Under Law. rev. ed. Jacobus TenBroek. Orig. Title: Anti Slavery Origins of the 14th Amendment. 1965. pap. 1.95 o.s.i. (ISBN 0-02-037810-6, Collier). Macmillan.

Equalities & Inequalities in Education: Proceedings. Eugenics Society Annual Symposium, 11th, London, 1973. Ed. by Peter R. Cox et al. 1976. 19.50 (ISBN 0-12-194240-6). Acad Pr.

Equality. William Ryan. 1981. 15.95 (ISBN 0-394-50493-3). Pantheon.

Equality & Efficiency: The Big Tradeoff. Arthur M. Okun. 124p. 1975. 10.95 (ISBN 0-8157-6476-6); pap. 4.95 (ISBN 0-8157-6475-8). Brookings.

Equality & Freedom, Vols. 1-3. International Association for Philosophy of Law & Social Philosophy. 1977. Set. 35.00 (ISBN 0-379-00657-X). Oceana.

Equality & Social Policy. Albert Weale. (International Library of Welfare & Philosophy). 1978. 16.00 (ISBN 0-7100-8770-5); pap. 7.95 (ISBN 0-7100-8771-3). Routledge & Kegan.

Equality in Public School Finance. Russell S. Harrison. LC 76-15879. (Illus.). 1976. 19.95 (ISBN 0-669-00785-4). Lexington Bks.

Equality, Liberty & Perfectionism. Vinit Haksar. (Clarendon Library of Logic & Philosophy Ser.). 310p. 1979. text ed. 24.95x (ISBN 0-19-824418-5). Oxford U Pr.

Equality, Moral Incentives, & the Market. Joseph H. Carens. LC 80-36774. (Illus.). 1981. lib. bdg. 19.00x (ISBN 0-226-09269-0). U of Chicago Pr.

Equality of Distribution of Police Services: A Case Study of Washington, D.C. Peter B. Bloch. 27p. 1974. pap. 1.50 o.p. (ISBN 0-87766-113-8, 65000). Urban Inst.

Equality of Distribution of Recreation Services: A Case Study of Washington, D.C. Donald M. Fisk & Cynthia A. Lancer. 46p. 1974. pap. 3.00 o.p. (ISBN 0-87766-129-4, 88000). Urban Inst.

Equality of Opportunity Reconsidered: Values in Education for Tomorrow, Proceedings. Third Colloquy for Directors of National Research Institutions in Education, Hamburg, 12-14 September 1978, Educational Research in Europe. Ed. by M. Dino Carelli & John G. Morris. 234p. 1979. pap. text ed. 19.50 (ISBN 90-265-0296-6, Pub. by Swets Pub Serv Holland). Swets North Am.

Equality of Opportunity Within & Among Nations. Ed. by Khadija Haq. LC 77-14405. (Praeger Special Studies). 1977. 27.95 (ISBN 0-03-040856-3). Praeger.

Equations. James Blount. 1981. 5.75 (ISBN 0-8062-1653-0). Carlton.

Equestrianism. Dorian Williams. (Illus.). 237p. 1980. 19.95 (ISBN 0-8069-9228-X, Pub by Guinness Superlatives England). Sterling.

Equilibrium. John C. Kiley. LC 79-54813. 1980. pap. 6.95 (ISBN 0-89615-047-X). Guild of Tutors.

Equilibrium & Disequilibrium: A Quantitative Analysis of Economic Interaction. Michael G. Allingham. LC 73-9639. 192p. 1973. text ed. 22.50 o.p. (ISBN 0-88410-252-1). Ballinger Pub.

Equilibrium Configurations of Degenerate Gaseous Masses. G. S. Saakyan. Tr. by C. F. Hall from Rus. LC 74-13583. 294p. 1974. 52.95 (ISBN 0-470-74805-2). Halsted Pr.

Equilibrium Constants of Liquid-Liquid Distribution Reactions, Pt. 3: Compound Forming Extractants, Solvating Solvents & Inert Solvents. Ed. by Y. Marcus et al. 1977. pap. text ed. 12.25 (ISBN 0-08-022032-0). Pergamon.

Equilibrium Credit Rationing. William R. Keeton. LC 78-75066. (Outstanding Dissertations in Economics). 1980. lib. bdg. 30.00 (ISBN 0-8240-4142-9). Garland Pub.

Equilibrium of Shell Structures. Jacques Heyman. (Oxford Engineering Science Ser.). (Illus.). 1977. text ed. 24.95x (ISBN 0-19-856139-3). Oxford U Pr.

Equilibrium Properties of Aqueous Solutions of Single Strong Electrolytes. E. A. Guggenheim & R. H. Stokes. LC 79-20329. 1970. 28.00 (ISBN 0-08-013445-9). Pergamon.

Equilibrium, Stability, & Growth: A Multi-Sectoral Analysis. Michio Morishima. 1964. 27.00x (ISBN 0-19-828145-5). Oxford U Pr.

Equilibrium-Stage Separation Operations in Chemical Engineering. Ernest J. Henley & J. D. Seader. LC 80-13293. 816p. 1981. text ed. 27.95 (ISBN 0-471-37108-4, Pub by Wiley-Interscience). Wiley.

Equilibrium Statistical Mechanics. 2nd ed. Frank C. Andrews. LC 74-17197. 288p. 1975. 20.95 (ISBN 0-471-03123-2, Pub by Wiley-Interscience). Wiley.

Equilibrium Thermodynamics in Petrology: An Introduction. Roger Powell. 1978. text ed. 21.60 (ISBN 0-06-318061-8, IntlDept); pap. text ed. 15.70 (ISBN 0-06-318073-1, IntlDept). Har-Row.

Equine Nutrition. A. C. Hardman. (Illus.). 128p. 1981. 17.95 (ISBN 0-7207-1244-0). Merrimack Bk Serv.

Equinox: A Gathering of T'ang Poets. Tr. by David Gordon from Chinese. LC 73-181682. xx, 88p. 1975. 9.95 (ISBN 0-8214-0162-9); pap. 3.50 o.s.i. (ISBN 0-8214-0173-4). Ohio U Pr.

Equinox Vol. V, No. 2. Aleister Crowley & Marcelo R. Motta. LC 78-68846. 1979. 31.00 (ISBN 0-933454-00-7); deluxe ed. 93.00 limited (ISBN 0-933454-01-5). Troll Pub.

Equipment Design Handbook for Refineries & Chemical Plants, Vol. 2. 2nd ed. Frank L. Evans. (Illus.). 400p. 1980. 32.95 (ISBN 0-87201-255-7). Gulf Pub.

Equipment Leasing. Ed. by Bruce E. Fritch & Albert F. Reisman. LC 80-83480. 1980. 75.00 (ISBN 0-685-85340-3, A1-1273). PLI.

Equipment Leasing, 1980. (Commercial Law & Practice Course Handbook Ser., 1979-80: Vol. 236). 1980. 25.00 (ISBN 0-686-50962-5, A4-3084). PLI.

Equipped for Good Work: A/Guide for Pastorso. Joe H. Cohen. 1981. 14.95 (ISBN 0-88289-271-1). Pelican.

Equitation. Henry Wynmalen. (Illus.). 21.85 (ISBN 0-85131-138-5, Dist. by Sporting Book Center). J A Allen.

Equity & Efficiency in Public Policy. Robert Buchele & Howard Cohen. (Learning Packages in the Policy Sciences: No. 15). (Illus.). 30p. (Orig.). 1978. pap. text ed. 2.00 (ISBN 0-936826-04-5). Pol Stud Assocs.

Equity Funding Papers: The Anatomy of a Fraud. Lee J. Seidler et al. LC 77-9921. (Accounting & Information Systems Ser.). 1977. text ed. 24.95x (ISBN 0-471-02273-X). Wiley.

Equity in the City. Ed. by P. N. Troy. 192p. 1981. text ed. 22.50x (ISBN 0-86861-250-2, 2647). Allen Unwin.

Equity, Income, & Policy: Comparative Studies in Three Worlds of Development. Ed. by Irving L. Horowitz. LC 76-2904. (Special Studies). 1977. text ed. 32.95 (ISBN 0-275-56570-X). Praeger.

Equity Laws of U.S. 1981 ed. 120p. 1981. 5.00 (ISBN 0-87526-206-6). Gould.

Equity Side of the Exchequer. W. H. Bryson. LC 73-93394. (Cambridge Studies in English Legal History). 280p. 1975. 36.00 (ISBN 0-521-20406-2). Cambridge U Pr.

Equity: Theory & Research. Walster et al. 1978. pap. text ed. 11.95 (ISBN 0-205-05929-5). Allyn.

Equity Valuation: Models, Analysis & Implications. David F. Hawkins & Walter J. Campbell. LC 78-67167. 1978. 3.50 (ISBN 0-910586-26-8). Finan Exec.

Equivocal Predication: George Herbert's Way to God. A. Heather Asals. 152p. 1981. 25.00x (ISBN 0-8020-5536-2). U of Toronto Pr.

Era de las Tinieblas. Justo L. Gonzalez. (Y Hasta Lo Ultimo De la Tierra: una Historia Ilustrada Del Christianismo Ser.: Tomo III). (Illus.). 199p. (Orig., Span.). 1978. pap. 4.50 (ISBN 0-89922-128-9). Edit Caribe.

Era de los Altos Ideales. Justo L. Gonzalez. (Y Hasta Lo Ultimo De la Tierra: una Historia Ilustrada Del Christianismo Ser.: Tomo IV). (Illus.). 197p. (Orig., Span.). 1979. pap. 4.50 (ISBN 0-89922-135-1). Edit Caribe.

Era De los Conquistadores. Justo L. Gonzalez. (Y Hasta Lo Ultimo de la Tierra: una Historia Ilustrada del Cristianismo: Tomo VII). (Illus.). 218p. (Span.). 1981. pap. 4.50 (ISBN 0-89922-162-9). Edit Caribe.

Era de los Gigantes. Justo L. Gonzalez. (Y Hasta Lo Ultimo De la Tierra: una Historia Ilustrada Del Christianismo Ser.: Tomo II). (Illus.). 184p. (Orig., Span.). 1978. pap. 4.50 (ISBN 0-89922-117-3). Edit Caribe.

Era de los Martires. Justo L. Gonzalez. (Y Hasta Lo Ultimo De la Tierra: una Historia Ilustrada Del Christianismo Ser.: Tomo I). (Illus.). 189p. (Orig., Span.). 1978. pap. 4.50 (ISBN 0-89922-109-2). Edit Caribe.

Era de los Reformadores. Justo L. Gonzalez. (Y Hasta Lo Ultimo De la Tierra: una Historia Ilustrada Del Christianismo Ser.: Tomo VI). (Illus.). 219p. (Orig., Span.). 1980. pap. 4.50 (ISBN 0-89922-154-8). Edit Caribe.

Era de los Suenos Frustrados. Justo L. Gonzalez. (Y Hasta Lo Ultimo De la Tierra: una Historia Ilustrada Del Christianismo Ser.: Tomo V). (Illus.). 182p. (Orig., Span.). 1979. pap. 4.50 (ISBN 0-89922-139-4). Edit Caribe.

ERA: Equality in Bondage. Eugenie Shelley. pap. 1.75 (ISBN 0-918700-08-6). Duverus Pub.

Era of Expansion: 1800-1848. Don E. Fehrenbacher. LC 68-8713. (American Republic Ser.). 1969. pap. text ed. 8.95x (ISBN 0-471-25691-9). Wiley.

Era of German Expressionism. Paul Raabe. 1980. 25.00 (ISBN 0-7145-0698-2); pap. 8.95 (ISBN 0-7145-0699-0). Riverrun NY.

Era of Good Feelings. George Dangerfield. LC 51-14815. 1963. pap. 5.50 (ISBN 0-15-629000-6, H034, Hbgr). HarBraceJ.

Era of Good Feelings & the Age of Jackson, 1816-1841. Compiled by Robert V. Remini & Edwin A. Miles. LC 79-84211. (Goldentree Bibliographies in American History). 1979. text ed. 18.95x (ISBN 0-88295-578-0); pap. text ed. 13.95x (ISBN 0-88295-579-9). AHM Pub.

Era of Theodore Roosevelt: 1900-1912. George E. Mowry. (New American Nation Ser). 1958. 15.00x o.s.i. (ISBN 0-06-013095-4, HarpT). Har-Row.

Eranos Yearbooks, Papers from, 6 vols. Ed. by Joseph Campbell. Tr. by R. Manheim & R. F. Hull. Incl. Vol. 1. Spirit & Nature. (Illus.). 1954. 18.50 o.p. (ISBN 0-691-09736-4); Vol. 2. The Mysteries. 1955. 20.00 (ISBN 0-691-09734-8); pap. 5.95 (ISBN 0-691-01823-5); Vol. 3. Man & Time. (Illus.). 1957. 17.50 (ISBN 0-691-09732-1); Vol. 4. Spirtual Disciplines. (Illus.). 1960. 25.00 (ISBN 0-691-09737-2); Vol. 5. Man & Transformation. (Illus.). 1964. 20.00 (ISBN 0-691-09733-X); pap. 5.95 (ISBN 0-691-01834-0); Vol. 6. Mystic Vision. 1969. 25.00 (ISBN 0-691-09735-6). (Bollingen Ser.: No. 30). Set. Princeton U Pr.

Erase Words. Keith Abbott. LC 76-58861. (Illus.). 1977. pap. 2.95 (ISBN 0-912652-35-7, Dynamite Books); pap. 8.95 signed ed. (ISBN 0-912652-36-5). Blue Wind.

Erasmus Darwin. Donald M. Hassler. (English Authors Ser.: No. 160). 1974. 10.95 (ISBN 0-8057-1138-4). Twayne.

Erdoel-Lexikon (Crude Oil Dictionary) 5th rev. ed. K. Kramer. LC 72-313250. 1972. 20.00x (ISBN 3-7785-0233-6). Intl Pubns Serv.

Ergodic & Information Theory. Ed. by Robert M. Gray & Lee D. Davisson. (Benchmark Papers in Electrical Engineering & Computer Science: Vol. 19). 1977. 40.50 (ISBN 0-12-786590-X). Acad Pr.

Ergometry: Basics of Medical Exercise Testing. Harald Mellerowicz. Ed. by Vojin N. Smodlaka. Tr. by Allan L. Rice from Ger. 1981. text ed. write for info. (ISBN 0-8067-1241-4). Urban & S.

Ergonomic Principles in the Design of Hand Tools. T. M. Fraser. Ed. by International Labour Office. (Occupational Safety & Health Ser.: No. 44). (Illus.). vii, 93p. (Orig.). 1980. pap. 8.55 (ISBN 0-686-69012-5). Intl Labour Office.

Ergonomics of the Home. E. Grandjean. LC 73-13221. 344p. 1973. 34.95 (ISBN 0-470-32180-6). Halsted Pr.

Ergot Compounds & Brain Function: Neuroendocrine & Neuropsychiatric Aspects. Menek Goldstein et al. 1980. text ed. 44.50 (ISBN 0-89004-450-3). Raven.

Eric. Doris Lund. LC 74-7061. 1974. 11.95 (ISBN 0-397-01046-X). Lippincott.

Eric Brighteyes. H. Rider Haggard. Ed. by R. Reginald & Douglas Menville. LC 80-24107. (Newcastle Forgotten Fantasy Library: Vol. 2). 319p. 1980. Repr. of 1974 ed. lib. bdg. 10.95x (ISBN 0-89370-501-2). Borgo Pr.

Eric Dolphy: A Musical Biography & Discography. Vladimir Simosko & Barry Tepperman. LC 73-16248. (Illus.). 164p. 1974. 12.50 o.p. (ISBN 0-87474-142-4). Smithsonian.

ERIC Educational Documents Index, 1966-1971: Institutions. new ed. Macmillan Information Division. 1973. 20.00 o.s.i. (ISBN 0-02-468840-1). Macmillan Info.

Eric Gill - Autobiography. Eric Gill. LC 68-54231. (Illus.). 1969. Repr. of 1941 ed. 12.00x (ISBN 0-8196-0220-5). Biblo.

Eric Gill: Twentieth Century Book Designer. rev. ed. Elizabeth Brady. LC 73-18453. 150p. 1974. lib. bdg. 10.00 (ISBN 0-8108-0640-1). Scarecrow.

Eric Gurney's Pop-up Book of Cats. Eric Gurney. LC 74-19317. (Pop-up Bks). (Illus.). (ps-2). 1974. 4.95 (ISBN 0-394-82825-9, BYR). Random.

Eric Heiden: Winner in Gold. Nathan Aaseng. LC 80-16982. (Achievers Ser.). (Illus.). (gr. 4-9). 1980. PLB 5.95g (ISBN 0-8225-0481-2). Lerner Pubns.

Eric Hoffer, an American Odyssey. Calvin Tomkins. LC 68-28887. (Illus.). 1968. 5.50 o.p. (ISBN 0-525-09948-4). Dutton.

Eric Louis Kohler: Accounting's Man of Principles. W. W. Cooper & Yuji Ijiri. (Illus.). 1978. 14.95 (ISBN 0-8359-1773-8). Reston.

Eric, or Little by Little. Frederick W. Farrar. LC 75-32199. (Classics of Children's Literature, 1621-1932: Vol. 60). (Illus.). 1976. Repr. of 1892 ed. PLB 38.00 (ISBN 0-8240-2309-9). Garland Pub.

Eric Partridge in His Own Words. Ed. by David Crystal. 224p. 1981. 12.95 (ISBN 0-02-528960-8). Macmillan.

Eric Sloane's Double Barrel. Eric Sloane. Incl. Cracker Barrel; Second Barrel. (Funk & W Bk.). 1969. boxed set 17.95 o.s.i. (ISBN 0-308-70111-9, 711100, TYC-T). T Y Crowell.

Eric Sloane's Sketchbook Calender for 1979. Eric Sloane. (Funk & W Bk.). (Illus.). 1978. 3.95 o.s.i. (ISBN 0-308-10348-3, TYC-T). T Y Crowell.

Erica Wilson's Embroidery Book. Erica Wilson. LC 78-123841. (Illus.). 224p. 1973. 17.50 o.p. (ISBN 0-684-13018-1, ScribT). Scribner.

Erich Salomon, No. 10. Illus. by Erich Salomon. LC 77-80021. (Aperture History of Photography Ser.). (Illus.). 1978. paper over boards 8.95 (ISBN 0-89381-023-1). Aperture.

Erich's Sunrise. Alexandre Ely. 176p. 1981. 7.50 (ISBN 0-682-49709-6). Exposition.

Erie Canal. Peter Spier. LC 70-157625. (gr. 1-3). 1970. pap. 1.95 (ISBN 0-385-05234-0, Zephyr). Doubleday.

Erie Canal. Ed. by Barbara K. Walker & Warren S. Walker. (Selected Source Materials for College Research Papers). 1963. pap. text ed. 2.95x o.p. (ISBN 0-669-21600-3). Heath.

Erin & Britannia: The Historical Backround to a Modern Tragedy. Michael L. Landon. LC 79-27005. (Illus.). 288p. 1981. text ed. 18.95 (ISBN 0-88229-643-4); pap. text ed. 8.95 (ISBN 0-88229-766-X). Nelson-Hall.

Erin-Go-Bragh or Irish Life Pictures. William H. Maxwell. Ed. by Robert L. Wolff. (Ireland Nineteenth Century Fiction Ser. Two: Vol. 52). 742p. 1979. lib. bdg. 32.00 (ISBN 0-8240-3501-1). Garland Pub.

Erin's Ecstasy. Sylvie F. Sommerfield. 320p. (Orig.). 1980. pap. 2.50 (ISBN 0-89083-656-6). Zebra.

Erkenntnis Fuer Freie Menschen. rev. ed. Paul Feyerabend. (Edition Suhrkamp. Neue Folge: es.NF 11). 270p. (Ger.). 1980. pap. text ed. 6.50 (ISBN 3-518-11011-X, Pub. by Insel Verlag Germany). Suhrkamp.

Ermine Tales: More Memoirs of the Earl of Carnarvon. Porchey. (Illus.). 158p. 1980. 14.50x (ISBN 0-297-77763-7, Pub. by Weidenfeld & Nicolson England). Biblio Dist.

Ermintrude. Nancy Moore & Edward Leight. LC 60-9730. (Illus.). (ps). 1960. 4.95 (ISBN 0-8149-0370-3). Vanguard.

Ernest Berke: Paintings & Sculptures of the Old West. Walt Wiggins. (Pintores Press Art Book Series: No. 2). (Illus.). 144p. 1980. 50.00 (ISBN 0-934116-03-2). Pintores Pr.

Ernest Dowson. 3rd ed. Mark Longaker. LC 68-1016. 1967. 9.00x o.p. (ISBN 0-8122-7560-8). U of Pa Pr.

Ernest Hemingway. Earl H. Rovit. (U. S. Authors Ser.: No. 41). 1963. lib. bdg. 9.95 (ISBN 0-8057-0364-0). Twayne.

Ernest Hemingway. Samuel Shaw. LC 78-134827. (Modern Literature Ser.). 10.95 (ISBN 0-8044-2823-9). Ungar.

Ernest Hemingway: A Life Story. Carlos Baker. 1980. pap. 4.95 (ISBN 0-380-50039-6, 50039, Discus). Avon.

Ernest Hemingway & His World. Anthony Burgess. LC 77-93899. (Illus.). 1978. 12.50 (ISBN 0-684-15661-X, ScribT). Scribner.

Ernest Hemingway: Selected Letters. Ed. by Carlos Baker. 960p. 1981. 25.00 (ISBN 0-684-16765-4, ScribT). Scribner.

Ernest Holmes: The Man. Reginald Armor. 1977. pap. 4.95 (ISBN 0-911336-66-4). Sci of Mind.

Ernesto 'Che' Guevara: Modern Revolutionary, Guerilla Theorist. Jay Mallin. Ed. by D. Steve Rahmas. (Outstanding Personalities Ser.: No. 53). 32p. (Orig.). (gr. 7-12). 1973. lib. bdg. 2.75 incl. catalog cards (ISBN 0-87157-556-6); pap. 1.50 vinyl laminated covers (ISBN 0-87157-056-4). SamHar Pr.

Ernie & Bert Book. Norman Stiles. (Sesame Street Shape Bks.). (Illus.). (ps-1). 1977. PLB 5.38 (ISBN 0-307-68879-8, Golden Pr). Western Pub.

Ernie & Bert Present Finish the Story. (Wipe off Bks.). 9p. (ps). 2.39 (ISBN 0-307-01844-X, Golden Pr). Western Pub.

Ernie Takes a Bath: A Counting Book (Sesame Street) (Play & Learn Ser.). (Illus.). (ps-k). 1977. 2.95 (ISBN 0-307-10737-X, Golden Pr). Western Pub.

Ernie's Telephone Call. Ray Sipherd. (Tell-a-Tale Readers). (Illus.). (gr. k-2). 1978. PLB 4.77 (ISBN 0-307-68652-3, Whitman). Western Pub.

Ernie's Work of Art. Valjean McLenigham. (Young Reader Ser.). (Illus.). (gr. k-3). 1979. PLB 5.00 (ISBN 0-307-60109-9, Golden Pr). Western Pub.

Ernst Cassirer. Seymour W. Itzkoff. (World Leaders Ser.: No. 60). 1977. lib. bdg. 12.50 (ISBN 0-8057-7712-1). Twayne.
Ernst Fuchs. Ernst Fuchs. (Contemporary Art Ser.). (Illus.). 1979. 65.00 (ISBN 0-8109-0903-0). Abrams.
Ernst Junger. Gerhard Loose. (World Authors Ser.: Germany: No. 323). 1974. lib. bdg. 10.95 (ISBN 0-8057-2479-6). Twayne.
Ernst Koch's Prinz Rosa-Stramin: Ein Beitrag Zur Hessischen Literaturgeschichte. Herman Froeb. pap. 7.00 (ISBN 0-384-17029-3). Johnson Repr.
Ernst Troeltsch & the Future of Theology. Ed. by J. P. Clayton. LC 75-44576. 1976. 32.50 (ISBN 0-521-21074-7). Cambridge U Pr.
Eroica. Mara Rostov. 1978. pap. 1.95 (ISBN 0-515-04469-5). Jove Pubns.
Eroica: A Novel About Beethoven. Carl Pidoll. LC 57-7677. 7.95 (ISBN 0-8149-0184-0). Vanguard.
Eros & Civilization. Herbert Marcuse. LC 66-3219. 320p. 1974. pap. 6.95 (ISBN 0-8070-1555-5, BP496). Beacon Pr.
Eros in Art. Ed. by Jack Bacon. (Illus.). 1969. 10.00 (ISBN 0-910550-03-4). Elysium.
Eros on Crutches. Adolf Guggenbuhl-Craig. Tr. by Gary V. Hartman from Ger. 126p. (Orig.). 1980. pap. text ed. 7.00 (ISBN 0-88214-315-8). Spring Pubns.
Erosion & Environment. M. Holy. (Environmental Sciences & Applications: Vol. 9). (Illus.). 266p. 1980. 58.00 (ISBN 0-08-024466-1). Pergamon.
Erotic Massage. (Illus.). pap. 5.00 (ISBN 0-910550-33-6). Centurion Pr.
Erotic Tales of Old Russia. Aleksandr N. Afanasev. Tr. by Yury Perkov. (Orig., Eng. & Rus.). 1980. pap. 5.95 (ISBN 0-933884-07-9). Berkeley Slavic.
Erotic World of Faery. Maureen Duffy. 1980. pap. 3.50 (ISBN 0-686-69241-1, 48108, Discus). Avon.
Eroticism in Western Art. Edward Lucie-Smith. (World of Art Ser.). (Illus.). 1972. pap. 9.95 (ISBN 0-19-519946-4). Oxford U Pr.
Errand into the Wilderness. Perry G. Miller. LC 56-11285. 1956. 10.00x (ISBN 0-674-26151-8, Belknap Pr); pap. 4.95 (ISBN 0-674-26155-0). Harvard U Pr.
Errol Flynn: The Untold Story. Charles Higham. 1981. pap. 3.50 (ISBN 0-440-12307-0). Dell.
Error Analysis: Perspectives on Second Language Acquisition. Jack Richards. (Applied Linguistics & Language Study Ser.). 1974. pap. text ed. 9.00x (ISBN 0-582-55044-0). Longman.
Error & Deception in Science: Essays on Biological Aspects of Life. Jean Rostand. 1960. text ed. 3.50x (ISBN 0-391-01976-7). Humanities.
Error-Free Computation: Why It Is Needed & Methods for Doing It. Robert T. Gregory. LC 80-23923. 148p. (Orig.). 1980. 6.50 (ISBN 0-89874-240-4). Krieger.
Error of Judgement. Henry Denker. 1980. pap. write for info. (ISBN 0-671-81959-3). PB.
Error Patterns in Computation. 2nd ed. Robert B. Ashlock. (Elementary Education Ser.). 128p. 1976. pap. text ed. 7.95x (ISBN 0-675-08654-X). Merrill.
Errors in English & Ways to Correct Them. 2nd ed. Harry Shaw. (gr. 7-12). 1970. pap. 3.95 (ISBN 0-06-463240-7, EH 240, EH). Har-Row.
Erste Jahr. 4th ed. Margaret K. Bluske & Elizabeth K. Walther. (Illus.). 1980. text ed. 16.50 scp (ISBN 0-06-040788-3, HarpC); Programmed Assisant Bk. scp 8.50 (ISBN 0-06-040795-6); instructor's manual free; scp tapes 260.00 (ISBN 0-686-65944-9). Har-Row.
Erte. Charles Spencer. (Illus.). 192p. 1980. 25.00 (ISBN 0-517-54391-5); pap. 10.95 (543915). Potter.
Erte's Costumes & Sets for "Der Rosenkavalier" in Full Color. Erte. (Illus.). 48p. 1980. pap. 6.95 (ISBN 0-486-23998-5). Dover.
Erwin Piscator's Political Theatre: The Development of Modern German Drama. C. D. Innes. LC 72-183223. (Illus.). 256p. 1972. 42.50 (ISBN 0-521-08456-3); pap. 10.50x (ISBN 0-521-29196-8). Cambridge U Pr.
Eryri: The Mountains of Longing. Amory Lovins & Philip H. Evans. Ed. & pref. by David R. Brower. (Earth's Wild Places Ser). (Illus.). 177p. 1971. 19.95 o.s.i. (ISBN 0-8415-0129-7). Friends Earth.
Erythrocyte Pathobiology: Proceedings. Instrumentation Laboratory Spring Symposium, Boston, Ma, April 1980. Ed. by Donald F. Wallach. (Progress in Clinical & Biological Research Ser.: No. 54). 250p. 1981. price not set (ISBN 0-8451-0054-8). A R Liss.
Erythrocyte Structure & Function: Proceedings. International Conference on Red Cell Metabolism & Function, 3rd, Ann Arbor, Michigan, Oct., 1974. Ed. by George Brewer. LC 75-999. (Progress in Clinical & Biological Research: Vol. 1). 812p. 1975. 55.00x (ISBN 0-8451-0001-7). A R Liss.
Erzaehlungen. Boell. (Easy Reader, D). pap. 3.75 (ISBN 0-88436-108-X, GEA301052). EMC.
Es Will Abend Werden. William Lauterbach. Ed. by Mentor Kujath. 1978. pap. 1.95 (ISBN 0-8100-0101-2, 26-0511). Northwest Pub.
ES 1 Skillbooklet. Barbara Crane. (Crane Reading System - English Ser.). (Illus.). (gr. k-2). 1977. pap. text ed. 12.20 per 10 (ISBN 0-89075-037-8). Crane Pub Co.
Esa Soy Yo. Gladys Hunt. Tr. by Grace S. Roberts from Eng. LC 77-83671. 172p. (Orig., Span.). 1977. pap. 2.25 (ISBN 0-89922-094-0). Edit Caribe.
Esau & Jacob. Joaquim M. Machado de Assis. Tr. by Helen Caldwell. 1965. 12.95 (ISBN 0-520-00788-3). U of Cal Pr.
Escalating Corporate Telephone Bill: Remedies & Opportunities. Harry Newton. 1980. 25.00 (ISBN 0-686-12129-5). Telecom Lib.
Escalera De la Predicacion. Tr. by Floyd Woodworth. (Spanish Bks.). 1978. 1.80 (ISBN 0-686-28804-1). Life Pubs Intl.
Escapade. Joan Smith. 1977. pap. 1.50 o.p. (ISBN 0-449-23232-8, Crest). Fawcett.
Escape & Evasion: Seventeen Stories of Downed Pilots Who Made It Back. James W. Kilbourne. Ed. by Carrol V. Glines. (Air Force Academy Ser.). (Illus.). 192p. 1973. 9.95 (ISBN 0-02-563000-8). Macmillan.
Escape from Bondage. W. C. Chalk. pap. text ed. 2.75x o.p. (ISBN 0-435-11228-7). Heinemann Ed.
Escape from Childhood: The Needs & Rights of Children. John Holt. LC 73-18060. 1974. 7.95 o.p. (ISBN 0-525-09955-7). Dutton.
Escape from Eden: A Novel. Catherine L. Clay. LC 77-77112. 232p. 1980. 9.95 (ISBN 0-86533-005-0). Amber Crest.
Escape from Evil. Ernest Becker. LC 75-12059. 1976. pap. 3.95 (ISBN 0-02-902340-8). Free Pr.
Escape from Freedom. Erich Fromm. 1971. pap. 3.50 (ISBN 0-380-01167-0, 54296, Discus). Avon.
Escape from Islam. Jaryl Strong. 1981. pap. 3.95 (ISBN 0-8423-0712-5). Tyndale.
Escape from New York. Mike McQuay. 192p. (Orig.). 1981. pap. 2.50 (ISBN 0-553-14914-8). Bantam.
Escape from Nowhere. Jeannette Eyerly. LC 69-11995. (gr. 7 up). 1969. 9.95 (ISBN 0-397-31070-6). Lippincott.
Escape from Predicament: Neo-Confucianism and China's Evolving Political Culture. Thomas A. Metzger. LC 76-25445. 208p. 1977. 17.50x (ISBN 0-231-03979-4). Columbia U Pr.
Escape from Scepticism: Liberal Education As If Truth Mattered. Christopher Derrick. 2.45 (ISBN 0-89385-002-0). Green Hill.
Escape from Singapore. Ian Skidmore. LC 73-13242. 198p. 1974. 7.95 o.p. (ISBN 0-684-13638-4, ScribT). Scribner.
Escape from Splatterbang. Nicholas Fisk. LC 79-11494. (Illus.). (gr. 5-9). 1979. 8.95 (ISBN 0-02-735260-9, 73526). Macmillan.
Escape from Stress. Kenneth Lamott. 1975. pap. 1.95 o.p. (ISBN 0-425-03212-4). Berkley Pub.
Escape from Terror. Bill Basansky & David Manuel. Orig. Title: Babunia. 1977. pap. 1.95 pocketsize o.p. (ISBN 0-88270-254-8). Logos.
Escape from the Coming Tribulation. Guy Duty. LC 75-17979. 160p. (Orig.). 1975. pap. 2.95 (ISBN 0-87123-131-X, 210131). Bethany Fell.
Escape from the Crater: More Adventures of the Hydronauts. Carl L. Biemiller. LC 74-2714. 216p. (gr. 6-9). 1974. 4.95 o.p. (ISBN 0-385-07133-7). Doubleday.
Escape from the Self: A Study in Contemporary Poetry & Poetics. Karl Malkoff. LC 77-22880. 1977. 15.00x (ISBN 0-231-03720-1). Columbia U Pr.
Escape from Tomorrow. Sereta Lanning. LC 78-16559. (Pacesetters Ser.). (Illus.). (gr. 4 up). 1978. PLB 7.95 (ISBN 0-516-02169-9). Childrens.
Escape from Utopia: My Ten Years in Synanon. William Olin. 300p. 1981. 12.95 (ISBN 0-913300-53-5); pap. 6.95 (ISBN 0-913300-54-3). Unity Pr.
Escape from Velos. Marion M. Markham. (Prime Time Adventures Ser.). (Illus.). 64p. (gr. 4 up). 1981. PLB 7.95 (ISBN 0-516-02106-0). Childrens.
Escape into Daylight. Geoffrey Household. (gr. 5-7). 1977. pap. 1.25 o.s.i. (ISBN 0-671-29845-3). Archway.
Escape of Alexander M'Connel of Lexington, Ky. from Captivity by the Indians: In: Hunt's Family Almanac, Repr. Of 1855 Ed. Bd. with Western Review & Miscellaneous Magazine, a Monthly Publication Devoted to Literature & Science: Vol. 177-179; Vol. 1, 353-358; Tale of Other Times... the History of the Captivity of Jonas Groves with the Indians: In: Western Herald & Steubenville Gazette, v. 13, no. 33-34, Aug. 12, 19, 1820; Little Osage Captive, an Authentic Narrative. Elias Cornelius. Repr. of 1822 ed; Interesting Narrative. Anne Jamison. Repr. of 1824 ed; Brief Narrative of the Sufferings of Lt. Nathan'l Segar Who Was Taken Prisoner by the Indians & Carried to Canada During the Revolutionary War. Repr. of 1825 ed; Narrative of William Biggs While He Was a Prisoner with the Kickapoo Indians. Repr. of 1825 ed. LC 75-7059. (Indian Captivities Ser.: Vol. 37). 1977. lib. bdg. 44.00 (ISBN 0-8240-1661-0). Garland Pub.
Escape! Strange Places Where You Can Live Free: Antarctica, Blimps, Treehouses, Etc. Jon Fisher. 1979. pap. cancelled o.p. (ISBN 0-686-23958-X). Loompanics.
Escape the Drug Scene. LaDean Griffin. pap. 3.95 (ISBN 0-89036-141-X). Hawkes Pub Inc.
Escape the River. Roy Brown. LC 76-179440. 160p. (gr. 6 up). 1972. 5.95 (ISBN 0-395-28893-2, Clarion). HM.
Escape to Athena. Patrica Blane. 1979. pap. 1.95 o.p. (ISBN 0-425-04066-6). Berkley Pub.
Escape to King Alfred. Geoffrey Trease. LC 58-9224. (gr. 6 up). 1958. 6.95 (ISBN 0-8149-0428-9). Vanguard.
Escape to Witch Mountain. Alexander Key. (gr. 5-7). 1975. pap. 1.95 (ISBN 0-671-42453-X). Archway.
Escaped Cock. D. H. Lawrence. Ed. by Gerald M. Lacy. 175p. 1976. pap. 4.00 (ISBN 0-87685-170-7). Black Sparrow.
Escola Dominical. (Portugese Bks.). (Port.). 1979. 1.45 (ISBN 0-8297-0799-9). Life Pubs Intl.
Esconderiho. Tr. by Corrie T. Boom. (Portuguese Bks.). 1979. 1.00 (ISBN 0-8297-0779-4). Life Pubs Intl.
Escritos Desconocidos De Jose Marti. Carlos Ripoll. 1971. 10.50 (ISBN 0-88303-001-2). E Torres & Sons.
Escuela Biblica 002a: A Growing Church School. Kenneth D. Blazier. Tr. by Evelyn R. De Olivieri from Eng. 64p. (Span.). 1981. pap. 3.25 (ISBN 0-8170-0928-0). Judson.
Escuela Dominical, Corazon De la Iglesia. Tr. by Ralph Williams. (Spanish Bks.). 1979. 1.30 (ISBN 0-8297-0550-3). Life Pubs Intl.
Escuela Dominical En Accion. C. H. Benson. Tr. by Fernando P. Villalobos from Eng. (Curso Para Maestros Cristianos: No. 6). Orig. Title: Sunday School Success. 122p. (Span.). 1972. pap. 2.50 (ISBN 0-89922-018-5); instructor's manual 1.50 (ISBN 0-89922-019-3). Edit Caribe.
Escuela Puertorriquena. Gomez Tejera & Cruz Lopez. 1970. 16.95 (ISBN 0-87751-004-0, Pub by Troutman Press). E Torres & Sons.
Esenin: A Biography in Memoirs, Letters, & Documents. Ed. by J. Davies. 400p. 1981. 22.50 (ISBN 0-88233-491-3). Ardis Pubs. Postponed.
Esforca-Te Para Ganhar Almas. Tr. by Orlando Boyer. (Portugese Bks.). (Port.). 1979. 1.60 (ISBN 0-8297-0662-3). Life Pubs Intl.
Eskimo: Arctic Hunters & Trappers. Sonia Bleeker. (Illus.). (gr. 3-6). 1959. PLB 6.67 (ISBN 0-688-31275-6). Morrow.
Eskimo Birthday. Tom Robinson. LC 74-23750. (Illus.). (gr. 2-5). 1975. 5.25 (ISBN 0-396-07065-5). Dodd.
Eskimo Boy Today. Byron Fish et al. LC 79-174339. (Illus.). (gr. 7 up). 1971. 6.95 o.p. (ISBN 0-88240-005-3). Alaska Northwest.
Eskimo Boyhood: An Autobiography in Psychosocial Perspective. Charles C. Hughes. LC 73-80465. (Illus.). 440p. 1974. 17.50x (ISBN 0-8131-1301-6). U Pr of Ky.
Eskimo Crafts & Their Cultural Backgrounds. Jeremy Comins. LC 75-9573. (Illus.). 128p. (gr. 5 up). 1975. PLB 6.96 o.p. (ISBN 0-688-51705-6). Lothrop.
Eskimo School on the Andreafsky: A Study of Effective Bicultural Education. Judith S. Kleinfeld. LC 79-4520. 22.95 (ISBN 0-03-048366-2). Praeger.
Eskimos. Mary Bringle. LC 72-10431. (Illus.). 96p. (gr. 4-7). 1973. PLB 3.90 o.p. (ISBN 0-531-00785-5). Watts.
Eskimos. Jill Hughes. (Civilization Library). (Illus.). (gr. 5-8). 1978. PLB 6.90 s&l (ISBN 0-531-01427-4). Watts.
Eskimos. Herbert Wally. (International Library Ser.). (Illus.). 128p. (gr. 7 up). 1976. PLB 6.90 o.p. (ISBN 0-531-02124-6). Watts.
Eskimos & Explorers. Wendell H. Oswalt. LC 78-10723. (Illus.). 368p. 1979. 15.00 (ISBN 0-88316-532-5). Chandler & Sharp.
ESL Operations: Techniques for Learning While Doing. Gayle L. Nelson & Thomas A. Winters. (Orig.). 1980. pap. text ed. 4.95 (ISBN 0-88377-149-7). Newbury Hse.
ESOP for the Eighties. Robert A. Frisch. 1981. 14.95 (ISBN 0-87863-003-1). Farnswth Pub.
Esophagus: Reflex & Primary Motor Disorders. 2nd ed. Robert D. Henderson. (Illus.). 312p. 1980. lib. bdg. 39.00 (ISBN 0-683-03948-2). Williams & Wilkins.
Esoteric Astrology. Alan Leo. 1978. pap. 6.95 (ISBN 0-685-62085-9). Weiser.
Esoteric Astrology. Alan Leo. (Astrologer's Library). 1978. pap. 6.95 (ISBN 0-89281-181-1). Inner Tradit.
Esoteric Encyclopedia of Eternal Knowledge. Vernon Howard. LC 80-6203. 256p. 1981. 9.95 (ISBN 0-8128-2797-X); pap. 6.95 (ISBN 0-8128-6117-5). Stein & Day.
Esoteric Mind Power. Vernon Howard. 196p. 1980. pap. 5.50 (ISBN 0-87516-401-3). De Vorss.
Esoteric Philosophy of Love & Marriage. Dion Fortune. pap. 4.95 (ISBN 0-685-01081-3). Weiser.
Esoteric Writings of H. P. Blavatsky. Helena P. Blavatsky. LC 79-6547. (Illus.). 500p. (Orig.). 1980. pap. 8.75 (ISBN 0-8356-0535-3, Quest). Theos Pub Hse.
Esotericism of the Popol Vuh. Raphael Girard. LC 78-74712. 1979. softcover 7.50 (ISBN 0-911500-14-6). Theos U Pr.
Esoterism & Symbol. R. A. Schwaller de Lubicz. (Illus.). 1981. 5.95 (ISBN 0-89281-014-9). Inner Tradit.
ESP. Tom Aylesworth. LC 74-26797. (Impact Bks.). (Illus.). 72p. (gr. 4-8). 1975. PLB 6.90 (ISBN 0-531-00826-6). Watts.
ESP (English for Specific Purposes) The Present Position. Pauline C. Robinson. (Pergamon Institute of English). 1980. pap. 8.95 (ISBN 0-08-024585-4). Pergamon.
ESP & Parapsychology: A Critical Re-Evaluation. C. E. Hansel. LC 79-56361. (Impact Ser.). 325p. (Orig.). 1980. 16.95 (ISBN 0-87975-119-3); pap. 8.95 (ISBN 0-87975-120-7). Prometheus Bks.
E.S.P. & Psychology. Cyril Burt. LC 75-16165. 179p. 1975. 19.95 (ISBN 0-470-12531-4). Halsted Pr.
ESP: Beyond Time & Distance. T. C. Lethbridge. 1965. 10.00 (ISBN 0-7100-1740-5). Routledge & Kegan.
ESP Experiments with LSD Twenty-Five & Psilocybin. Roberto Cavanna & Emilio Servadio. LC 64-24271. (Parapsychological Monograph No. 5). 1964. pap. 3.00 (ISBN 0-912328-08-8). Parapsych Foun.
ESP, Extrasensory Perception. Simeon Edmonds. pap. 2.00 o.p. (ISBN 0-87980-207-3). Wilshire.
ESP in Relation to Rorschach Test Evaluation. Gertrude Schmeidler. LC 60-2760. (Parapsychological Monograph No. 2). 1960. pap. 2.00 (ISBN 0-912328-04-5). Parapsych Foun.
ESP Research Today: A Study of Developments in Parapsychology Since 1960. J. Gaither Pratt. LC 73-3098. 1973. 10.00 (ISBN 0-8108-0609-6). Scarecrow.
ESP, Seers & Physics. Milbourne Christopher. LC 78-127607. (Illus.). 1970. 10.95 o.s.i. (ISBN 0-690-26815-7, TYC-T); pap. 5.95 o.s.i. (ISBN 0-690-01674-3, TYC-T). T Y Crowell.
ESP: Your Psychic Powers & How to Test Them. William R. Akins. (gr. 4 up). 1980. PLB 6.45 (ISBN 0-531-02947-6). Watts.
Espagne. Ed. by Daniel Moreau. (Collection monde et voyages). (Illus.). 159p. (Fr.). 1973. 21.00x (ISBN 2-03-053101-4). Larousse.
Espana: Sintesis De Su Civilizacion. rev. & enl. 2nd ed. Jeronimo Mallo. Ed. by Juan Rodriguez-Castellano. (Illus.). 1970. text ed. 10.95x o.p. (ISBN 0-684-41351-5, ScribC). Scribner.
Espana y Su Civilizacion. 2nd ed. Francisco Ugarte. LC 64-23908. 1965. 9.95 (ISBN 0-672-63165-2). Odyssey Pr.
Espanol a lo vivo: Level 1. 4th ed. Terrence L. Hansen & Ernest J. Wilkins. LC 77-27041. 1978. text ed. 17.50x (ISBN 0-471-01807-4); wkbk 6.95 (ISBN 0-471-03453-3); tapes 16.95 (ISBN 0-471-01782-5); tchr's manual avail. (ISBN 0-471-04151-3). Wiley.
Espanol, Comencemos: Pupil's Edition. 3rd ed. Conrad J. Schmitt. Ed. by Teresa Chimienti. LC 80-13033. (Illus.). 280p. (Span.). (gr. 7). 1980. text ed. 10.60 (ISBN 0-07-055573-7, W); tchr's ed. 11.96 (ISBN 0-07-055574-5); wkbk. 3.80 (ISBN 0-07-055575-3); tests 66.00 (ISBN 0-07-055576-1); filmstrips 93.32 (ISBN 0-07-098991-5); test replacements 39.60 (ISBN 0-07-055577-X). McGraw.
Espanol Comercial. Nelly E. Santos. (Illus.). 410p. 1981. text ed. 17.50 scp (ISBN 0-06-045725-2, HarpC). Har-Row.
Espanol De America. Rosario. 1970. 12.95 (ISBN 0-685-73205-3, Pub by Troutman Press). E Torres & Sons.

Espanol Rapido. P. M. Quinlan & W. V. Compton. Ed. by P. H. Hargreaves. 1971. 6.50 (ISBN 0-249-44089-X). Transatlantic.

Espanol: Sigamos, Pupil's Edition. 3rd ed. Conrad J. Schmitt. Ed. by Teresa Chimienti. LC 80-13032. (Illus.). 282p. (Span.). (gr. 8). 1980. text ed. 11.64 (ISBN 0-07-055578-8, W); tchrs. ed. 13.16 (ISBN 0-07-055579-6); wkbk. avail. (ISBN 0-07-055575-3); filmstrips 93.92 (ISBN 0-07-098994-X). McGraw.

Especiall Observations in the Last Time of the Pestilence. LC 72-171780. (English Experience Ser.: No. 405). 28p. 1971. Repr. of 1625 ed. 7.00 (ISBN 90-221-0405-2). Walter J Johnson.

Especially for Husbands. Michael Campion & Wilmer Zehr. (When Was the Last Time Ser.). (Illus.). 1978. pap. 4.95 (ISBN 0-87123-136-0, 210136). Bethany Fell.

Especially for Parents. Michael Campion & Wilmer Zehr. (When Was the Last Time Ser.). (Illus.). 1978. pap. 4.95 (ISBN 0-87123-137-9, 210137). Bethany Fell.

Especially for Wives. Michael A. Campion. (When Was the Last Time Ser.). 1979. pap. 4.95 (ISBN 0-87123-138-7, 210138). Bethany Fell.

ESPecially Irene: A Guide to Psychic Awareness. Irene F. Hughes. LC 70-189997. 160p. 1972. pap. 1.95 (ISBN 0-8334-1730-4). Steinerbks.

E.S.P.Ionage. William S. Doxey. 1979. pap. 1.95 (ISBN 0-505-51363-3). Tower Bks.

Espiritismo. S. D. Fernandez. (Coleccion Doctrinas Modernas: No. 1). 1980. pap. 0.55 (ISBN 0-311-05025-5, Edit Mundo). Casa Bautista.

Espiritu Mismo. Tr. by Ralph Higgs. (Spanish Bks.). 1979. 1.90 (ISBN 0-8297-0551-1). Life Pubs Intl.

Espiritu Santo. Billy Graham. Tr. by A. Edwin Sipowicz from Eng. Orig. Title: Holy Spirit. 252p. (Span.). 1980. pap. 3.95 (ISBN 0-311-09096-6). Casa Bautista.

Espiritu Santo en la Experiencia del Cristiano. J. D. Crane. Tr. by Olivia De Lerin. 1979. 3.50 (ISBN 0-311-09093-1). Casa Bautista.

Espiritu Santo y Tu. Tr. by Dennis Bennett & Rita Bennett. (Spanish Bks.). (Span.). 1978. 1.95 (ISBN 0-8297-0439-6). Life Pubs Intl.

Espiritu Siempre Eterno Del Mexico Americano. Guadalupe C. Quintanilla & James B. Silman. 1977. pap. text ed. 8.25 (ISBN 0-8191-0121-4). U Pr of Amer.

Espuela Land & Cattle Company: The Study of a Foreign-Owned Ranch in Texas. William C. Holden. LC 70-84084. (Illus.). 1970. 9.00 (ISBN 0-87611-023-5). Tex St Hist Assn.

ESQ. a Lawyers Desk Treasure, Release No. 1. rev ed. LC 76-8795. 1979. 27.50 (ISBN 0-915362-14-7). M K Heller.

Esquire's Jazz Books, 3 vols. Paul E. Miller. Incl. 1944 Jazz Book (ISBN 0-306-79525-6); 1945 Jazz Book (ISBN 0-306-79526-4); 1946 Jazz Book (ISBN 0-306-79527-2). (Roots of Jazz Ser.). (Repr. of 1944-46 ed.). 1979. Set. 50.00 (ISBN 0-306-79528-0); 19.50 ea. Da Capo.

Essai de Statistique. Jacques-Antoine Mourgue. (Principal French Demographic Works of the 18th Century Ser.). (Fr.). 1977. lib. bdg. 25.00x o.p. (ISBN 0-8287-0647-6); pap. text ed. 15.00x o.p. (ISBN 0-685-75746-3). Clearwater Pub.

Essai Sur la Conception Juridique De la Propriete Fonciere Dans le Tres Anciendroit Normand: Premiere Partie, la Conception Feodale. Henri Lagoulle. LC 80-2020. 1981. Repr. of 1902 ed. 47.50 (ISBN 0-404-18574-6). AMS Pr.

Essai Sur la Justice Primitive, Pour Servir de Principe Generateur au Seul Ordre Social Qui Peut Assurer a l'Homme Tous Ses Droits et Tous Sesmoyens de Bonheur. Abbe Pierre D'Olivier. (Fr.). 1977. lib. bdg. 15.00x o.p. (ISBN 0-8287-0245-4); pap. text ed. 5.00x o.p. (ISBN 0-685-75748-X). Clearwater Pub.

Essai Sur la Statistique De la Population Francaise: Consideree Sous Quelque-Uns De Ses Rapports Physiques et Moraux. A. d'Angeville. (Reeditions: No. 6). 1970. 65.30 (ISBN 0-686-20911-7). Mouton.

Essai sur Laforgue et les Derniers Vers suivi de Laforgue et Baudelaire. J. A. Hiddleston. LC 80-66331. (French Forum Monographs: No. 23). 132p. (Orig., Fr.). 1980. pap. 9.50 (ISBN 0-917058-22-4). French Forum.

Essai sur l'Application de l'Analyse aux Probabilites des Decisions Rendues a la Pluralite des Voix. Marie J. Condorcet. LC 75-113124. 495p. (Fr.). 1973. Repr. of 1785 ed. 27.50 (ISBN 0-8284-0252-3). Chelsea Pub.

Essai Sur les Origines et la Fondation Du Duche De Normandie. Henri Prentout. LC 80-2214. 1981. Repr. of 1911 ed. 39.00 (ISBN 0-404-18776-5). AMS Pr.

Essai Sur les Probabilites De la Duree De la Vie Humaine. Antoine Deparcieux. (Principal French Demographic Works of the 18th Century Ser.). (Fr.). 1976. lib. bdg. 60.00x o.p. (ISBN 0-8287-0261-6). pap. text ed. 50.00x o.p. (ISBN 0-685-71513-2). Clearwater Pub.

Essai Sur Thomas Gray. Roger Martin. 458p. 1980. Repr. of 1934 ed. lib. bdg. 100.00 (ISBN 0-89984-335-2). Century Bookbindery.

Essais de semiotique poetique: Avec des etudes sur Apollinaire, Bataille, Hugo, Jarry, Mallarme, Michaux, Nerval, Rimbaud, Roubaud. A. Greimas. (Collection L). 240p. (Orig., Fr.). 1972. pap. 13.95 (ISBN 2-03-036002-3, 2666). Larousse.

Essay Concerning Aspect: Some Considerations of a General Character Arising from the Abbe Darrigol's Analysis of the Basque Verb. John Anderson. (Janua Linguarum Ser. Minor: No. 167). 1973. pap. text ed. 20.00x (ISBN 90-2792-408-2). Mouton.

Essay Concerning Human Understanding. John Locke. 1979. pap. 11.50x (ISBN 0-460-00984-2, Evman). Dutton.

Essay for the Recording of Illustrious Providences. Increase Mather. LC 77-17526. 1977. Repr. of 1684 ed. lib. bdg. 40.00 (ISBN 0-8201-1299-2). Schol Facsimiles.

Essay of Dramatic Poesy, A Defence of Dramatic Poesy, & Preface to the Fables. John Dryden. Ed. by John L. Mahoney. LC 65-26522. 1965. pap. text ed. 4.95x (ISBN 0-672-60298-9). Irvington.

Essay on Anaxagoras. M. Schofield. LC 79-10348. (Cambridge Classical Studies). 1980. 24.50 (ISBN 0-521-22722-4). Cambridge U Pr.

Essay on Atomism: From Democritus to 1960. Lancelot L. Whyte. LC 61-14236. 1961. 12.50x (ISBN 0-8195-3019-0, Pub. by Wesleyan U Pr). Columbia U Pr.

Essay on Christian Philosophy. Jacques Maritain. Tr. by Edward H. Flannery. 1955. 20.00x (ISBN 0-89197-150-5). Irvington.

Essay on Drapery, 1635. William Scott. (Kress Library of Business & Economics: No. 9). 1953. pap. 5.00x (ISBN 0-678-09904-9, Baker Lib). Kelley.

Essay on Epic Poetry. William Hayley. LC 68-17013. 1968. Repr. of 1782 ed. 31.00x (ISBN 0-8201-1026-4). Schol Facsimiles.

Essay on Government. James Mill. Ed. by Currin V. Shields. (gr. 9 up). 1955. pap. 2.95 (ISBN 0-672-60215-6, LLA47). Bobbs.

Essay on Hardy. J. Bayley. LC 77-80826. 1978. 23.95 (ISBN 0-521-21814-4). Cambridge U Pr.

Essay on Irish Bulls. Maria Edgeworth. Ed. by Robert L. Wolff. (Ireland Nineteenth Century Fiction, Ser. Two: Vol. 2). 1979. lib. bdg. 46.00 (ISBN 0-8240-3451-1). Garland Pub.

Essay on Judicial Power & Unconstitutional Legislation. Brinton Coxe. LC 79-99476. 1970. Repr. of 1893 ed. 39.50 (ISBN 0-306-71853-7). Da Capo.

Essay on King Lear. S. L. Goldberg. LC 73-84318. 212p. 1974. 33.50 (ISBN 0-521-20200-0); pap. 10.50x (ISBN 0-521-09831-9). Cambridge U Pr.

Essay on Language. George Grace. 1981. write for info.; pap. price not set. Hornbeam Pr.

Essay on Man. Alexander Pope. Ed. by Frank Brady. 1965. pap. 2.50 (ISBN 0-672-61159-7, LLA103). Bobbs.

Essay on Man: An Introduction to a Philosophy of Human Culture. Ernst Cassirer. 1962. pap. 5.45 (ISBN 0-300-00034-0, Y52). Yale U Pr.

Essay on Metaphysics. Robin G. Collingwood. 364p. 1940. 24.95x (ISBN 0-19-824121-6). Oxford U Pr.

Essay on Pope. Frederick M. Keener. LC 74-1260. 192p. 1974. 20.00x (ISBN 0-231-03827-5). Columbia U Pr.

Essay on Sculpture, in a Series of Epistles to John Flaxman...with Notes...(Plates Engraved by Blake) William Hayley. Ed. by Donald H. Reiman. LC 75-31210. (Romantic Context Ser.: Poetry 1789-1830: Vol. 61). 1979. Repr. of 1800 ed. lib. bdg. 47.00 (ISBN 0-8240-2160-6). Garland Pub.

Essay on the Constitutional Prohibitions Against Legislation Impairing the Obligation of Contracts, & Against Retroactive & Ex Post Facto Laws. Henry C. Black. xxvi, 355p. 1980. Repr. of 1887 ed. lib. bdg. 32.50x (ISBN 0-8377-0312-3). Rothman.

Essay on the Foundations of Our Knowledge. Antoine A. Cournot. Tr. by M. H. Moore. 1956. pap. 3.95 (ISBN 0-672-60400-0). Bobbs.

Essay on the Freedom of the Will. Arthur Schopenhauer. Tr. by Konstantin Kolenda. LC 59-11675. 1960. pap. 3.95 (ISBN 0-672-60248-2, LLA70). Bobbs.

Essay on the Language & Versification of Chaucer. Thomas Tyrwhitt. 76p. 1980. Repr. of 1775 ed. text ed. 15.00 (ISBN 0-8492-8409-0). R West.

Essay on the Law of Bailments. Sir William Jones. Ed. by David S. Berkowitz. Samuel E. Thorne. LC 77-86562. (Classics of English Legal History in the Modern Era Ser.: Vol. 14). 132p. 1979. lib. bdg. 40.00 (ISBN 0-8240-3063-X). Garland Pub.

Essay on the Learning of Contingent Remainders & Executory Devises, 2 vols. 10th ed. Charles Fearne. Ed. by Charles Butler & Josiah W. Smith. 1980. Repr. of 1844 ed. Set. PLB 95.00x (ISBN 0-8377-0539-8). Rothman.

Essay on the Life of the Honorable Major-General Israel Putnam, Repr. Of 1788 Ed. David Humphreys. Bd. with Genuine & Correct Account of the Captivity, Sufferings & Deliverance of Mrs. Jemima Howe. Jemima Howe. Repr. of 1792 ed; Affecting History of Mrs. Howe. Repr. of 1815 ed. LC 75-7040. (Indian Captivities Ser.: Vol. 19). 1977. lib. bdg. 44.00 (ISBN 0-8240-1643-2). Garland Pub.

Essay on the Nature & Conduct of the Passions & Affections, 1742. 3rd ed. Francis Hutcheson. LC 76-81361. (History of Psychology Ser). 1969. Repr. of 1742 ed. 38.00x (ISBN 0-8201-1058-2). Schol Facsimiles.

Essay on the Nature, the End, and the Means of Imitation in the Fine Arts. A. C. Quatremere de Quincy. Ed. by Sydney J. Freedberg. LC 77-25763. (Connoisseurship, Criticism, & Art History: Vol. 18). 468p. 1979. lib. bdg. 48.00 (ISBN 0-8240-3276-4). Garland Pub.

Essay on the Origin of Human Knowledge. Etienne Bonnot de Condillac. Tr. by Thomas Nugent from Fr. LC 76-161929. (Hist. of Psych. Ser.). 1971. Repr. of 1756 ed. 42.00x (ISBN 0-8201-1090-6). Schol Facsimiles.

Essay on the Origin of Thought. Jurij Moskvitin. LC 72-85540. 297p. 1974. 15.00x (ISBN 0-8214-0156-4). Ohio U Pr.

Essay on the Principles of Education, Physiologically Considered. Charles Collier. Bd. with Art of Instructing the Infant Deaf & Dumb. (Contributions to the History of Psychology, Vol. V, Pt. B: Psychometrics & Educational Psychology). 1980. Repr. of 1856 ed. 30.00 (ISBN 0-89093-319-7). U Pubns Amer.

Essay on the Principles of Human Action, 1805. William Hazlitt. LC 70-75943. (Hist. of Psych. Ser.). 1969. 28.00x (ISBN 0-8201-1053-1). Schol Facsimiles.

Essay on the Trial by Jury. Lysander Spooner. LC 70-166097. (Civil Liberties in American History Ser). 1971. Repr. of 1852 ed. lib. bdg. 25.50 (ISBN 0-306-70320-3). Da Capo.

Essay on the True Art of Playing Keyboard Instruments. Carl P. Bach. Ed. by William J. Mitchell. (Illus.). 1948. 16.95x (ISBN 0-393-09716-1, NortonC). Norton.

Essay on Theological Method. Gordon D. Kaufman. LC 75-31656. (American Academy of Religion. Studies in Religion: No. 11). 1975. pap. 6.00 (ISBN 0-89130-307-3, 010011). Scholars Pr Ca.

Essay on West African Therapeutics. Johnson. (Traditional Healing Ser.: No. 7). 1981. 15.00 (ISBN 0-932426-09-3, Trado-Medic Bks); pap. 7.50 (ISBN 0-932426-10-7, Trado-Medic Bks). Conch Mag.

Essay on West African Therapeutics. O. Johnson. Ed. by Philip Singer & Elizabeth A. Titus. 1981. 17.50 (ISBN 0-932426-09-3). Trado-Medic.

Essay on Yugoslav Society. Branko Horvat. Tr. by Henry F. Mins from Yug. LC 79-77456. 1969. 15.00 o.p. (ISBN 0-87332-009-3). M E Sharpe.

Essay: Structure & Purpose. Richard Cherry et al. 1975. pap. text ed. 9.95 (ISBN 0-395-18610-2). HM.

Essay: Subjects & Stances. Ed. by Edward P. Corbett. (English Literature Ser). (277). 1974. pap. text ed. 8.50 (ISBN 0-13-283515-0). P-H.

Essay Towards an Indian Bibliography. Thomas W. Field. LC 67-14026. 1967. Repr. of 1873 ed. 18.00 (ISBN 0-8103-3327-9). Gale.

Essay Towards the Theory of the Ideal or Intelligible World, 2 Vols., 1701 & 1704. John Norris. Ed. by Rene Wellek. LC 75-11243. (British Philosophers & Theologians of the 17th & 18th Centuries Ser.). 1978. Set. lib. bdg. 42.00 (ISBN 0-8240-1795-1). Garland Pub.

Essay Upon Reason & the Nature of Spirits. Richard Burthogge. LC 75-11204. (British Philosophers & Theologians of the 17th & 18th Centuries: Vol. 10). 1976. Repr. of 1694 ed. lib. bdg. 42.00 (ISBN 0-8240-1759-5). Garland Pub.

Essayes or Counsels, Civill & Morall. Francis Bacon. 1974. text ed. 16.95x o.p. (ISBN 0-8277-2150-1); pap. text ed. 12.00x o.p. (ISBN 0-8277-3730-0). British Bk Ctr.

Essays. Kathryn A. Blake & Mary L. McBee. 1978. pap. text ed. 7.95 (ISBN 0-02-472160-3). Macmillan.

Essays. Winthrop M. Daniels. 1943. 17.50x (ISBN 0-685-89750-8). Elliots Bks.

Essays. William Godwin. 293p. 1980. Repr. of 1873 ed. lib. bdg. 35.00 (ISBN 0-8492-4974-0). R West.

Essays & Data on American Ethnic Groups. Ed. by Thomas Sowell. 420p. 1978. 15.00 (ISBN 0-87766-211-8, 20800). Urban Inst.

Essays & Lectures. Oscar Wilde. Ed. by Peter Stansky & Rodney Shewan. LC 76-17753. (Aesthetic Movement & the Arts & Crafts Movement Ser.). 1978. Repr. of 1908 ed. lib. bdg. 44.00x (ISBN 0-8240-2455-9). Garland Pub.

Essays & Miscellany. Hubert H. Bancroft. LC 67-29422. (Works of Hubert Howe Bancroft Ser.). 1967. Repr. of 1888 ed. 25.00x (ISBN 0-914888-42-0). Bancroft Pr.

Essays & Poems of Arnold. Intro. by Frederick W. Roe. 497p. 1980. Repr. of 1928 ed. lib. bdg. 30.00 (ISBN 0-8492-7717-5). R West.

Essays & Studies, Vol. 32, 1979. Dieter Mehl. (New Series of Essays & Studies). 1979. text ed. 18.00x (ISBN 0-391-01035-2). Humanities.

Essays & Studies in English. Members of English Dept. of University of Michigan. 231p. 1980. Repr. of 1932 ed. lib. bdg. 40.00 (ISBN 0-686-65606-7). Century Bookbindery.

Essays & Studies Nineteen Eighty, Vol.33. Inga-Stina Ewbank. (Essays & Studies). 158p. 1980. pap. text ed. 22.00x (ISBN 0-391-01766-7). Humanities.

Essays & Studies 1978, No. 31. 1978. text ed. 18.00x (ISBN 0-391-00838-2). Humanities.

Essays by Divers Hands: Being the Transactions of the Royal Society of Literature. Ed. by Brian Fothergwill. (New Series: Vol. XLI). 147p. 1980. 22.50x (ISBN 0-8476-3530-9). Rowman.

Essays by Divers Hands L: Innovation in Contemporary Literature. Ed. by Vincent Cronin. (Being the Transactions of a Royal Society of Literature, New Ser.: Vol. XL). 162p. 1979. 21.50x (ISBN 0-8476-3043-9). Rowman.

Essays Designed to Elucidate the Science of Political Economy, While Serving to Explain & Defend the Policy of Protection to Home Industry, As a System of National Cooperation for the Elevation of Labor. Horace Greeley. (Neglected American Economists Ser.). 1974. lib. bdg. 50.00 (ISBN 0-8240-1006-X). Garland Pub.

Essays for Ralph Shaw. Ed. by Norman D. Stevens. LC 75-6664. 219p. 1975. 10.00 (ISBN 0-8108-0815-3). Scarecrow.

Essays from the New England Academic Librarians' Writing Seminar. Ed. by Norman D. Stevens. LC 80-21502. 230p. 1980. 12.50 (ISBN 0-8108-1365-3). Scarecrow.

Essays from "The Quarterly Review". James Hannay. 390p. 1980. Repr. of 1861 ed. lib. bdg. 45.00 (ISBN 0-89984-282-8). Century Bookbindery.

Essays from the World of Music. Ernest Newman. LC 77-17326. (Music Reprint Ser.: 1978). (Illus.). 1978. Repr. of 1956 ed. lib. bdg. 22.50 (ISBN 0-306-77519-0). Da Capo.

Essays, Humor, & Poems of Nathaniel Ames. Sam Briggs. LC 77-75945. (Illus.). 1969. Repr. of 1891 ed. 21.00 (ISBN 0-8103-3826-2). Gale.

Essays in American Zionism Nineteen-Seventeen to Nineteen Forty-Eight. Ed. by Melvin Urofsky. 1979. 12.50 (ISBN 0-930832-56-6). Herzl Pr.

Essays in Ancient & Modern Historiography. Arnaldo Momigliano. LC 76-41484. 1977. lib. bdg. 22.50x (ISBN 0-8195-5010-8, Pub. by Wesleyan U Pr). Columbia U Pr.

Essays in Antiquity. Peter Green. 1960. 12.95 (ISBN 0-7195-0558-5). Dufour.

Essays in Applied Economics. Arthur C. Pigou. Repr. of 1930 ed. 21.00x (ISBN 0-678-05077-5). Kelley.

Essays in Binocular Vision. J. R. Charnwood. 1970. Repr. of 1950 ed. 8.75 o.s.i. (ISBN 0-02-842790-4). Hafner.

Essays in Biochemistry, Vols. 1-5 & 8-15. Ed. by Paul N. Campbell & G. D. Greville. Incl. Vol. 1. 1965 (ISBN 0-12-158101-2); Vol. 2. 1966 (ISBN 0-12-158102-0); Vol. 3. 1967 (ISBN 0-12-158103-9); Vol. 4. 1968 (ISBN 0-12-158104-7); Vol. 5. 1970 (ISBN 0-12-158105-5); Vol. 8. 1972 (ISBN 0-12-158108-X); Vol. 9. 1974 (ISBN 0-12-158109-8); Vol. 10. 1974 (ISBN 0-12-158110-1); Vol. 11. 1976 (ISBN 0-12-158111-X); Vol. 12. 1977 (ISBN 0-12-158112-8); Vol. 13. 1978 (ISBN 0-12-158113-6); Vol. 14. 1978 (ISBN 0-12-158114-4); Vol. 15. 1979 (ISBN 0-12-158115-2). (Illus.). pap. 13.00 ea. Acad Pr.

Essays in British Business History. Ed. by Barry Supple. 1977. 29.95x (ISBN 0-19-877087-1); pap. 16.50x (ISBN 0-19-877088-X). Oxford U Pr.

Essays in Chinese Poetry. Ed. by James W. Miller. 1981. text ed. 18.00 (ISBN 0-89581-452-8, Asian Humanities). Lancaster-Miller.

Essays in Creativity. Stanley Rosner & Lawrence Abt. LC 74-11096. 214p. 1974. 15.00x (ISBN 0-88427-012-2); pap. 6.95 o.p. (ISBN 0-88427-013-0, Dist. by Caroline Hse). North River.

Essays in Criminal Science. Gerhard O. Mueller. (New York University Criminal Law Education & Research Center Pubns: Vol. 1). 1960. 17.50x (ISBN 0-8377-0828-1). Rothman.

Essays in Czech History. R. R. Betts. 1969. text ed. 25.75x (ISBN 0-485-11095-4, Athlone Pr). Humanities.

Essays in Development Policy. Bimal Jalan. LC 75-904389. 1975. 9.00x o.p. (ISBN 0-88386-622-6). South Asia Bks.

Essays in Economic Analysis. Ed. by M. J. Artis. A. R. Nobay. LC 75-46207. (Illus.). 422p. 1976. 49.50 (ISBN 0-521-21154-9). Cambridge U Pr.

Essays in Economic Development. V. K. Rao. 1966. pap. 5.50x o.p. (ISBN 0-210-98182-2). Asia.

Essays in Economic Theory. Simon Patten. Ed. by Rexford G. Tugwell. (Neglected American Economists Ser.). 1974. lib. bdg. 50.00 (ISBN 0-8240-1029-9). Garland Pub.

Essays in Economic Transition. S. J. Patel. 10.00x (ISBN 0-210-22659-5). Asia.

Essays in Eighteenth-Century English Literature. Louis A. Landa. LC 80-7541. (Princeton Ser. of Collected Essays). 270p. 1980. 20.00 (ISBN 0-691-06449-0); pap. 7.95 (ISBN 0-691-01375-6). Princeton U Pr.

Essays in English History: World History in Six Dimensions. Paul Harrison Silfen. LC 74-80691. 1975. 4.00 o.p. (ISBN 0-682-48047-9, University). Exposition.

Essays in European Economic History 1500-1800. Ed. by Peter Earle. 282p. 1974. 22.50x (ISBN 0-19-877054-5). Oxford U Pr.

Essays in Feminism. Vivian Gornick. LC 77-6884. 1978. 12.95 o.s.i. (ISBN 0-06-011627-7, HarpT). Har-Row.

Essays in Freedom & Rebellion. Henry W. Nevinson. 1921. 13.50x (ISBN 0-686-51378-9). Elliots Bks.

Essays in Freethinking, Vol. 1. Chapman Cohen. 1980. pap. 4.00. Am Atheist.

Essays in French & German History: World History in Six Dimensions. Paul Harrison Silfen. 1976. 6.50 o.p. (ISBN 0-682-48375-3, University). Exposition.

Essays in General Relativity. Ed. by Frank J. Tipler. LC 80-517. 1980. 30.00 (ISBN 0-12-691380-3). Acad Pr.

Essays in Gothic Fiction: From Horace Walpole to Mary Shelley. Stephen R. Van Luchene. Ed. by Devendra P. Varma. LC 79-8488. (Gothic Studies & Dissertations Ser.). 1980. lib. bdg. 25.00x (ISBN 0-405-12649-2). Arno.

Essays in Greek & Roman History: World History in Six Dimensions. Paul Harrison Silfen. 1975. 4.50 o.p. (ISBN 0-682-48279-X, University). Exposition.

Essays in Hellenistic Poetry. Heather White. (London Studies in Classical Philology: Vol. 5). 81p. 1981. pap. text ed. 17.25x (ISBN 90-70265-52-4, Pub. by Gieben Holland). Humanities.

Essays in Honour of Professor Erwin Sturzl on His 60th Birthday, 2 vols. Ed. by James Hogg. (Salzburger Studien: No. 10). 1980. pap. text ed. 34.75x ea. Vol. 1 (ISBN 0-391-01923-6). Vol. 2 (ISBN 0-391-01924-4). Humanities.

Essays in Honour of Professor Tyrus Hillway. Ed. by Erwin A. Sturzl. (Salzburg Studies in English Literature, Romantic Reassessment Ser.: No. 65). (Illus.). 1977. pap. text ed. 25.00x (ISBN 0-391-01539-7). Humanities.

Essays in Humanistic Anthropology: Festschrift in Honor of Davis Bidney. Bruce T. Grindal & Dennis M. Warren. LC 78-66121. (Orig.). 1979. pap. text ed. 13.75 (ISBN 0-8191-0682-8). U Pr of Amer.

Essays in Indian Protohistory. Ed. by D. Agrawal & D. Chakravarti. 1980. text ed. 42.00x (ISBN 0-391-01866-3). Humanities.

Essays in International Economics. Peter B. Kenan. (Princeton Series of Collected Essays). 432p. 1980. 22.50 (ISBN 0-691-04225-X); pap. 5.95 (ISBN 0-691-00364-5). Princeton U Pr.

Essays in Interpersonal Dynamics. Warren Bennis et al. 1979. pap. text ed. 7.95x (ISBN 0-256-02231-3). Dorsey.

Essays in Jewish Intellectual History. Alexander Altman. LC 80-54471. 336p. 1981. text ed. 20.00 (ISBN 0-87451-192-5). U Pr of New Eng.

Essays in Labor Market Analysis. Ed. by Orley C. Ashenfelter & Wallace Oates. LC 77-9421. 1978. 41.95 (ISBN 0-470-99222-0). Halsted Pr.

Essays in Law & Politics. Francis D. Wormuth. Ed. by Dalmas H. Nelson & Richard L. Sklar. (National University Pubns. Multi-Disciplinary Studies in the Law). 1978. 16.50 (ISBN 0-8046-9211-4). Kennikat.

Essays in Law & Society. Ed. by Geoff Mungham & Zenon Bankowski. 216p. (Orig.). 1980. pap. 18.00 (ISBN 0-7100-0489-3). Routledge & Kegan.

Essays in Legal Ethics. Geo W. Warvelle. xiii, 234p. 1980. Repr. of 1902 ed. lib. bdg. 22.50x (ISBN 0-8377-1305-6). Rothman.

Essays in Legal History in Honor of Felix Frankfurter. Morris D. Forkosch. 1966. 17.50 (ISBN 0-672-80026-8, Bobbs-Merrill Law). Michie.

Essays in Legal Philosophy. Ed. by Robert S. Summers. (Library Reprint Ser.). 1976. 18.50x (ISBN 0-520-03213-6). U of Cal Pr.

Essays in Medical Sociology: Journeys into the Field. Renee C. Fox. LC 79-10413. (Health, Medicine & Society: a Wiley Interscience Ser.). 1979. 22.95 (ISBN 0-471-27040-7, Pub. by Wiley-Interscience). Wiley.

Essays in Medieval Life & Thought. John H. Mundy et al. LC 65-25472. 1955. 12.00x (ISBN 0-8196-0159-4). Biblo.

Essays in Morality & Ethics. Ed. by James Gaffney. LC 80-80578. 224p. (Orig.). 1980. pap. 8.95 (ISBN 0-8091-2248-0). Paulist Pr.

Essays in Musicology: In Honor of Dragan Plamenac on His 70th Birthday. Ed. by Gustave Reese & Robert J. Snow. LC 77-8220. (Music Reprint, 1978 Ser.). (Illus.). 1977. Repr. of 1969 ed. lib. bdg. 32.50 (ISBN 0-306-77408-9). Da Capo.

Essays in Neurochemistry & Neuropharmacology, 4 vols. Ed. by M. B. Youdim et al. LC 76-21043. 1977-80. Vol. 1. 37.95 (ISBN 0-471-99424-3, Pub. by Wiley-Interscience); Vol. 2. 30.75 (ISBN 0-471-99516-9); Vol. 3. 33.50 (ISBN 0-471-99613-0, Pub. by Wiley-Interscience); Vool. 4. 67.50 (ISBN 0-471-27645-6). Wiley.

Essays in Neurochemistry & Neuropharmacology, Vol. 5. Ed. by M. B. Youdim & W. Lovenberg. Tr. by D. F. Sharman & J. R. Lagnado. 152p. 1981. 47.00 (ISBN 0-471-27879-3, Pub. by Wiley-Interscience). Wiley.

Essays in Nineteenth Century Economic History: The Old Northwest. Ed. by David Klingaman & Richard Vedder. LC 74-80811. xiv, 356p. 1975. 16.00x (ISBN 0-8214-0170-X). Ohio U Pr.

Essays in Persuasion: On Seventeenth-Century English Literature. Frank L. Huntley. LC 80-14477. 1981. 14.00x (ISBN 0-226-36088-1). U of Chicago Pr.

Essays in Politics & International Relations. A. Appadorai. 15.00x (ISBN 0-210-98160-1). Asia.

Essays in Population History, 3 vols. Sherburne F. Cook & Woodrow Borah. Incl. Vols. 1 & 2. Mexico & the Caribbean. 1971. 27.50x ea. Vol. 1 (ISBN 0-520-01764-1). Vol. 2 (ISBN 0-520-02272-6); Vol. 3. Mexico & California. 1979. 25.00x (ISBN 0-520-03560-7). U of Cal Pr.

Essays in Public Economics. Ed. by Agnar Sandmo. LC 77-7. 1978. 31.95 (ISBN 0-669-01424-9). Lexington Bks.

Essays in Radical Empiricism & Pluralistic Universe: Radical Empiricism. William James. 1971. pap. 2.25 o.p. (ISBN 0-525-47256-8). Dutton.

Essays in Rebellion. Henry W. Nevinson. 241p. 1980. Repr. of 1913 ed. lib. bdg. 30.00 (ISBN 0-8495-4018-6). Arden Lib.

Essays in Russian & Soviet History, in Honor of Geroid Tanquary Robinson. Ed. by John S. Curtiss. LC 62-9706. 1963. 22.00x (ISBN 0-231-02521-1). Columbia U Pr.

Essays in Russian History: World History in Six Dimensions. Paul Harrison Silfen. LC 74-80692. 1975. 4.00 o.p. (ISBN 0-682-48048-7, University). Exposition.

Essays in Social History. Ed. by M. W. Flinn & T. C. Smout. (Illus.). 304p. 1974. pap. 14.95x (ISBN 0-19-877017-0). Oxford U Pr.

Essays in Social Theory. Steven Lukes. LC 77-8505. 1977. text ed. 17.50x (ISBN 0-231-04450-X). Columbia U Pr.

Essays in Socioeconomic Evolution. Morris A. Copeland. 1981. 10.00 (ISBN 0-533-04328-X). Vantage.

Essays in Sociological Theory. rev. ed. Talcott Parsons. 1964. pap. text ed. 9.95 o.s.i. (ISBN 0-02-924030-1). Free Pr.

Essays in the History of Materialism. G. V. Plekhanov. 1968. 16.50 (ISBN 0-86527-061-9). Fertig.

Essays in the History of New York City: A Memorial to Sidney Pomerantz. Ed. by Irwin Yellowitz. (National University Pubns. Interdisciplinary Urban Ser.). 1978. 13.95 (ISBN 0-8046-9208-4). Kennikat.

Essays in the Philosophy of Mathematics. R. L. Goodstein. 1965. text ed. 12.50x (ISBN 0-7185-1044-5, Leicester). Humanities.

Essays in the Philosophy of Religion: Based on the Sarum Lectures, 1971. H. H. Price. 130p. 1972. 11.95x (ISBN 0-19-824376-6). Oxford U Pr.

Essays in the Theory & Measurement of Consumer Behavior. Angus Deaton. 300p. Date not set. price not set (ISBN 0-521-22565-5). Cambridge U Pr.

Essays in the Theory of Employment. Joan Robinson. LC 78-14138. (Illus.). 1981. Repr. of 1950 ed. 18.50 (ISBN 0-88355-812-2). Hyperion Conn.

Essays in Toxicology, Vols. 1-7. Ed. by F. R. Blood. Incl. Vol. 1. 1969. o. p. 22.50 (ISBN 0-12-107601-6); pap. 11.50 (ISBN 0-12-107651-2); Vol. 2. 1970. 31.50 (ISBN 0-12-107602-4); pap. 11.50 (ISBN 0-12-107652-0); Vol. 3. Wayland J. Hayes, Jr. 1972. 19.00 (ISBN 0-12-107603-2); pap. 11.50 (ISBN 0-12-107653-9); Vol. 4. 1973. 31.50 (ISBN 0-12-107604-0); pap. write for info. o. p.; Vol. 5. 1974. 31.00 (ISBN 0-12-107605-9); Vol. 6. 1975. 31.50 (ISBN 0-12-107606-7); lib ed. 46.00 (ISBN 0-12-107674-1); microfiche 23.00 (ISBN 0-12-107675-X); Vol. 7. 1976. 36.00 (ISBN 0-12-107607-5); lib ed. 44.00 (ISBN 0-12-107676-8); microfiche 27.00 (ISBN 0-12-107677-6). Acad Pr.

Essays in Translation from French. Robert L. Ritchie & C. J. Simons. text ed. 27.50x (ISBN 0-521-06092-3); pap. 10.95x (ISBN 0-521-09205-1). Cambridge U Pr.

Essays in World History from Antiquity to the Present. Paul Harrison Silfen. 1976. 17.50 o.p. (ISBN 0-682-48482-2, University). Exposition.

Essays Lovecraftian. Darrell Schweitzer. LC 80-19213. 120p. 1980. Repr. lib. bdg. 9.95x (ISBN 0-89370-096-7). Borgo Pr.

Essays, Moral & Divine. Sir William Anstruther. LC 74-170474. (English Stage Ser.: Vol. 40). lib. bdg. 50.00 (ISBN 0-8240-0623-2). Garland Pub.

Essays, Moral & Political, 2 vols. Robert Southey. 865p. 1971. Repr. of 1832 ed. 70.00x (ISBN 0-686-28336-8, Pub. by Irish Academic Pr). Biblio Dist.

Essays of a Biologist. Julian Huxley. 304p. 1980. Repr. of 1929 ed. lib. bdg. 25.00 (ISBN 0-8495-2274-9). Arden Lib.

Essays of a String Teacher: Come Let Us Rosin Together. Clifford A. Cook. LC 73-77584. 1973. 7.50 o.p. (ISBN 0-682-47690-0). Exposition.

Essays of an Atheist Activist. Jon G. Murray. 1980. pap. 3.29. Am Atheist.

Essays of an Information Scientist, 3 vols. Eugene Garfield. LC 77-602. Vols. 1 & 2 (1962-1976) 25.00 (ISBN 0-89495-001-0); Vol. 3 (1977-1978) 15.00 (ISBN 0-89495-000-2, EOIS2W). Vol. 3 (ISBN 0-89495-000-2). ISI Pr.

Essays of Elia. Charles Lamb. Incl. Last Essays of Elia. 1954. 11.50x (ISBN 0-460-00014-4, Evman); pap. 4.50 (ISBN 0-460-01014-X, Evman). Dutton.

Essays of Emerson. Ralph W. Emerson. Ed. by Robert E. Spiller. pap. 2.50 (ISBN 0-671-44900-1). WSP.

Essays of George Eliot. Ed. by Thomas Pinney. LC 74-18488. 1963. 20.00x (ISBN 0-231-02619-6). Columbia U Pr.

Essays of Mark Van Doren: Nineteen Twenty-Four to Nineteen Seventy-Two. Mark Van Doren. Ed. by William Claire. LC 79-8411. (Contributions in American Studies: No. 47). (Illus.). xxv, 270p. 1980. lib. bdg. 25.00 (ISBN 0-313-22098-0, CEV/). Greenwood.

Essays of To-Day. F. H. Pritchard. 258p. 1980. Repr. lib. bdg. 20.00 (ISBN 0-89984-378-6). Century Bookbindery.

Essays of U. S. Adhesive Postage Stamps. Clarence Brazer. LC 75-40503. 1977. 35.00x (ISBN 0-88000-081-3). Quarterman.

Essays on a Science of Mythology: The Myths of the Divine Child & the Mysteries of Eleusis. rev. ed. Carl G. Jung & Carl Kerenyi. (Bollingen Ser.: Vol. 22). 1969. 12.50 (ISBN 0-691-09851-4); pap. 3.95 (ISBN 0-691-01756-5). Princeton U Pr.

Essays on Actions & Events. Donald Davidson. 320p. 1980. 29.50x (ISBN 0-19-824529-7); pap. 9.95x (ISBN 0-19-824637-4). Oxford U Pr.

Essays on Adam Smith. Ed. by Andrew S. Skinner & Thomas Wilson. 1976. 59.00x (ISBN 0-19-828191-9). Oxford U Pr.

Essays on American Foreign Policy. Ed. by Margaret F. Morris & Sandra L. Myres. LC 73-19500. (Walter Prescott Webb Memorial Lectures Ser.: No. 8). 120p. 1974. 8.95x (ISBN 0-292-72009-2). U of Tex Pr.

Essays on an America in Transition. David Rodnick. LC 75-126861. (Orig.). 1972. 10.00x (ISBN 0-912570-03-2). Caprock Pr.

Essays on Analytical Chemistry: In Memory of Professor Anders Ringbom. Ed. by Erkki Wanninen. LC 77-4103. 1977. text ed. 82.00 (ISBN 0-08-021596-3). Pergamon.

Essays on & in the Chicago Tradition. Don Patinkin. LC 79-55770. (Illus.). xii, 315p. 1981. 29.75 (ISBN 0-8223-0439-2). Duke.

Essays on Aristotle's Ethics. Ed. by Amelie O. Rorty. (Major Thinkers Ser.). 1981. 20.00x (ISBN 0-520-03773-1, CAMPUS 245); pap. 4.95x (ISBN 0-520-04041-4). U of Cal Pr.

Essays on Art & Ontology. Leone Vivante. Tr. by Arturo Vivante from It. 1980. 15.00x (ISBN 0-87480-100-1). U of Utah Pr.

Essays on Behavioral Economics. George Katona. LC 80-15510. (Illus.). 108p. 1980. 10.50 (ISBN 0-87944-257-3). U of Mich Soc Res.

Essays on Biblical Interpretation. Paul Ricoeur. Ed. by Lewis S. Mudge. LC 80-8052. 192p. (Orig.). 1980. pap. 7.95 (ISBN 0-8006-1407-0, 1-1407). Fortress.

Essays on Bibliography. Vito J. Brenni. LC 75-14082. 1975. 18.00 (ISBN 0-8108-0826-9). Scarecrow.

Essays on Binding & Fusion. Michael Brame. (Linguistics Research Monograph: Vol. 4). 1981. text ed. 32.00 (ISBN 0-932998-04-6). Noit Amrofer.

Essays on Bonhoeffer. Ed. by A. J. Klassen. 1981. pap. 5.95 (ISBN 0-8028-1744-0). Eerdmans.

Essays on Borneo Societies. Ed. by Victor T. King. (Hull Monographs on South-East Asia: No. 7). (Illus.). 1979. pap. 24.95x (ISBN 0-19-713434-3). Oxford U Pr.

Essays on Business Finance. 4th ed. Marvin Waterman et al. LC 57-1744. 1952. 10.00 (ISBN 0-685-73275-4). Masterco Pr.

Essays on Chinese Civilization. Derk Bodde. Ed. by Charles Le Blanc & Dorothy Borei. LC 80-8586. (Princeton Ser. of Collected Essays). 504p. 1981. 25.00x (ISBN 0-691-03129-0); pap. 8.95x (ISBN 0-691-00024-7). Princeton U Pr.

Essays on Constitutional Laws & Equity. Henry Schofield. LC 79-38814. (American Constitutional & Legal History Ser). (Illus.). 1972. Repr. lib. bdg. 75.00 (ISBN 0-306-70450-1). Da Capo.

Essays on Deviance & Marginality. Jerry S. Meneker. LC 79-66577. 1979. pap. text ed. 7.75 (ISBN 0-8191-0844-8). U Pr of Amer.

Essays on Econometrics & Planning. C. R. Rao. 1965. 37.00 (ISBN 0-08-011025-8). Pergamon.

Essays on Economic Policy. J. Marcus Fleming. LC 77-15991. 1978. 25.00x (ISBN 0-231-04366-X). Columbia U Pr.

Essays on Economic Policy I: Collected Essays, Vol. 3. Nicholas Kaldor. LC 80-18155. 293p. 1980. text ed. 39.50x (ISBN 0-8419-0453-7). Holmes & Meier.

Essays on Economic Policy II: Collected Economic Essays, Vol. 4. Nicholas Kaldor. LC 80-18155. 320p. 1980. 39.50x (ISBN 0-8419-0454-5). Holmes & Meier.

Essays on Economic Stability & Growth: Collected Economic Essays, Vol. 2. Nicholas Kaldor. LC 80-18145. 302p. 1980. text ed. 39.50x (ISBN 0-8419-0452-9). Holmes & Meier.

Essays on Educational Reformers. Robert H. Quick. 568p. 1980. Repr. of 1902 ed. lib. bdg. 35.00 (ISBN 0-8495-4428-9). Arden Lib.

Essays on Educators. R. S. Peters. (Unwin Education Bks). 160p. 1981. text ed. 19.95x (ISBN 0-04-370103-5, 2626-7); pap. text ed. 7.95x (ISBN 0-04-370104-3). Allen Unwin.

Essays on Financial Institutions in Mississippi. 1976. pap. 3.00 (ISBN 0-938004-03-4). U MS Bus Econ.

Essays on Freedom of Action. Ed. by Ted Honderich. 1978. pap. 7.95 (ISBN 0-7100-8883-3). Routledge & Kegan.

Essays on Function & Evolution in Behaviour. Ed. by Gerard Baerends et al. (Illus.). 350p. 1975. 55.00x (ISBN 0-19-857382-0). Oxford U Pr.

Essays on Imperialism. Michael B. Brown. (Illus.). 1972. pap. text ed. 5.25x (ISBN 0-85124-110-7). Humanities.

Essays on Jewish Life & Thought. Ed. by Joseph L. Blau et al. LC 57-11757. 1959. 22.50x (ISBN 0-231-02171-2). Columbia U Pr.

Essays on John Maynard Keynes. Ed. by M. Keynes. LC 74-12975. (Illus.). 304p. 1975. 38.50 (ISBN 0-521-20534-4). Cambridge U Pr.

Essays on John Maynard Keynes. Ed. by Milo Keynes. LC 74-12975. (Illus.). 1980. pap. 11.95 (ISBN 0-521-29696-X). Cambridge U Pr.

Essays on Karamzin: Russian Man of Letters, Political Thinker, Historian, 1766-1826. Ed. by J. L. Black. (Slavistic Printings & Reprints: No.309). 232p. 1975. pap. text ed. 43.50x (ISBN 90-2793-251-4). Mouton.

Essays on la Mujer. Ed. by Rosaura Sanchez & Rosa M. Cruz. (Anthology Ser.: No. 1). 200p. (Orig.). 1977. pap. 6.35 (ISBN 0-89551-020-0). Ucla Chicano Stud.

Essays on Linguistic Themes. Yakov Malkiel. LC 68-15588. 1968. 19.50x (ISBN 0-520-00798-0). U of Cal Pr.

Essays on Literary Art: Tennyson, Wordsworth, Jane Austen, Thoreau. Hiram M. Stanley. 164p. 1980. Repr. of 1897 ed. lib. bdg. 25.00 (ISBN 0-8414-8035-4). Folcroft.

Essays on Machine Intelligence & Other Topics. Donald Michie. 250p. 1981. write for info. (ISBN 0-677-05560-9). Gordon.

Essays on Machine Intelligence & Other Topics. Donald Michie. 250p. 1981. price not set (ISBN 0-677-05560-9). Gordon.

Essays on Medieval Agriculture & General Problems of the Medieval Economy. M. M. Postan. (Illus.). 300p. 1973. 38.50 (ISBN 0-521-08744-9). Cambridge U Pr.
Essays on Medieval Civilization. Ed. by Bede K. Lackner & Kenneth R. Philp. LC 77-17068. (Walter Prescott Webb Memorial Lecture Ser: No. 12). 1978. 10.95 (ISBN 0-292-72023-8). U of Tex Pr.
Essays on Modern Politics & History. Ed. by Han Kyo Kim. LC 75-91958. xiv, 255p. 1969. 13.95x (ISBN 0-8214-0079-7). Ohio U Pr.
Essays on Opera & English Music: In Honor of Sir Jack Westrup. Ed. by F. W. Sternfeld et al. (Illus.). 1975. 30.50x (ISBN 0-631-15890-1, Pub. by Basil Blackwell). Biblio Dist.
Essays on Penal Desert. Ed. by Andrew Von Hirsch. 1980. cancelled (ISBN 0-88410-796-5). Ballinger Pub.
Essays on Philosophical Method. R. M. Hare. (New Studies in Practical Philosophy). 1972. 11.95x (ISBN 0-520-02178-9). U of Cal Pr.
Essays on Politics & Culture. John S. Mill. Ed. by Gertrude Himmelfarb. 8.00 (ISBN 0-8446-0801-7). Peter Smith.
Essays on Realism. Georg Lukacs. 1980. text ed. 26.00x (ISBN 0-391-02179-6). Humanities.
Essays on Schubert. Maurice J. Brown. LC 77-22216. (Music Reprint Ser.). (Illus.). 1977. Repr. of 1966 ed. lib. bdg. 25.00 (ISBN 0-306-77439-9). Da Capo.
Essays on Sean O'Casey's Autobiographies: Reflections Upon the Mirror. Robert G. Lowery. 1981. text ed. 22.50x (ISBN 0-06-494392-5). B&N.
Essays on Social Organization & Values. Raymond Firth. (Social Anthropology Monographs: No. 28). 1969. pap. text ed. 9.50x (ISBN 0-485-19628-X, Athlone Pr). Humanities.
Essays on Some of the First Principles of Metaphysicks, Ethicks, & Theology. Asa Burton. LC 73-4839. (History of Psychology Ser). 440p. 1973. Repr. of 1824 ed. lib. bdg. 43.00x (ISBN 0-8201-1114-7). Schol Facsimiles.
Essays on Some Unsettled Questions of Political Economy. 2nd ed. John S. Mill. LC 68-25642. Repr. of 1874 ed. 15.00x (ISBN 0-678-00390-4). Kelley.
Essays on the Active Powers of Man. Thomas Reid. Ed. by Rene Wellek. LC 75-11251. (British Philosophers & Theologians of the 17th & 18th Centuries: Vol. 50). 1977. Repr. of 1788 ed. lib. bdg. 42.00 (ISBN 0-8240-1802-8). Garland Pub.
Essays on the American Revolution. Ed. by Stephen G. Kurtz & James H. Hutson. 350p. 1973. pap. text ed. 5.95x (ISBN 0-393-09419-7). Norton.
Essays on the Constitution: Aspects of Canadian Law & Politics. Frank R. Scott. 1977. 27.50x (ISBN 0-8020-2238-3); pap. 8.50 (ISBN 0-8020-6297-0). U of Toronto Pr.
Essays on the Constitution of the United States. Ed. by M. Judd Harmon. (National University Pubns. Multi-Disciplinary Studies in the Law). 1978. 15.00 (ISBN 0-8046-9210-6). Kennikat.
Essays on the Constitutional History of the United States in the Formative Period, 1775-1789. J. Franklin Jameson. LC 78-99473. (American Constitutional & Legal History Ser.). 1970. Repr. of 1889 ed. lib. bdg. 32.50 (ISBN 0-306-71856-1). Da Capo.
Essays on the Development of the International Legal Order: In Memory of Haro F. van Panhuys. Ed. by Frits Kalshoven et al. 240p. 1980. 50.00x (ISBN 90-286-0360-3). Sijthoff & Noordhoff.
Essays on the Gilded Age. Ed. by Margaret F. Morris. LC 72-8266. (Walter Prescott Webb Memorial Lectures Ser: No. 7). 110p. 1973. 8.95 (ISBN 0-292-72004-1). U of Tex Pr.
Essays on the Gita. Sri Aurobindo. 1979. 7.50 (ISBN 0-89744-907-X); lib. bdg. 14.00 (ISBN 0-89744-906-1); pap. 6.00 (ISBN 0-89744-908-8). Auromere.
Essays on the Heidelberg Catechism. Bard Thompson et al. LC 63-21522. 1963. pap. 5.95 (ISBN 0-8298-0325-4). Pilgrim NY.
Essays on the Law & Economics of Local Governments. Ed. by Daniel Rubinfeld. (Papers on Public Econmics Ser.: Vol. 3). 253p. (Orig.). 1980. pap. text ed. 7.50 (ISBN 0-87766-262-2, 27200). Urban Inst.
Essays on the Lord's Supper. Oscar Cullmann & Franz J. Leenhardt. LC 58-8979. 1958. pap. 3.95 (ISBN 0-8042-3748-4). John Knox.
Essays on the Making of the Constitution. Ed. by Leonard W. Levy. (Orig.). 1969. pap. 5.95x (ISBN 0-19-500954-1). Oxford U Pr.
Essays on the Manchurian Problem. Shu-Hsi Hsu. (Studies in Chinese History & Civilization). 349p. 1977. 22.00 (ISBN 0-89093-093-7). U Pubns Amer.
Essays on the Metaphysical Foundation of Personal Identity. John A. Reuscher. LC 80-6067. 111p. 1981. lib. bdg. 16.50 (ISBN 0-8191-1471-5); pap. text ed. 7.25 (ISBN 0-8191-1472-3). U Pr of Amer.
Essays on the Metaphysics of Descartes. Marthinus Versfeld. LC 68-26210. 1968. Repr. of 1940 ed. 10.00 (ISBN 0-8046-0481-9). Kennikat.
Essays on the Moral Concepts. R. M. Hare. LC 70-187322. (New Studies in Practical Philosophy). 150p. 1972. 11.95x (ISBN 0-520-02231-9). U of Cal Pr.
Essays on the New Working Class. Serge Mallet. Ed. by Dick Howard & Dean Savage. Tr. by Dick Howard from Fr. LC 75-34904. 240p. (Orig.). 1975. 12.90 (ISBN 0-914386-13-1); pap. 4.50 (ISBN 0-914386-14-X). Telos Pr.
Essays on the Philippine Novel in English. Ed. by Joseph A. Galdon. 168p. 1980. 17.50x (ISBN 0-686-28638-3); pap. 8.50x (ISBN 0-686-28639-1). Cellar.
Essays on the Principles of Morality & Natural Religion. Henry H. Kames. Ed. by Rene Wellek. LC 75-11227. (British Philosophers & Theologians of the 17th & 18th Centuries: Vol. 29). 1976. Repr. of 1751 ed. lib. bdg. 42.00 (ISBN 0-8240-1781-1). Garland Pub.
Essays on the Sabbath in Early Christianity. Kenneth A. Strand. 1979. pap. text ed. 4.80 (ISBN 0-89039-140-8). Ann Arbor FL.
Essays on the Semitic Background of the New Testament. Joseph A. Fitzmyer. LC 74-83874. (Society of Biblical Literature. Sources for Biblical Study). 1974. pap. 10.50 (ISBN 0-89130-309-X, 060305). Scholars Pr Ca.
Essays on the Sociology of Culture. Ed. by Karl Mannheim. (International Library of Sociology). 1969. 17.50x o.s.i. (ISBN 0-7100-3349-4). Routledge & Kegan.
Essays on the Sound Pattern of English. Ed. by Didier Goyvaerts & Geoffrey Pullum. (Illus.). 1975. text ed. 82.25x (ISBN 0-685-95917-1). Humanities.
Essays on the Theory & Practice of Imperialism. Wadada D. Nabudere. 192p. 1980. text ed. 22.25x (ISBN 0-906383-02-1); pap. text ed. 9.25x (ISBN 0-906383-03-X). Humanities.
Essays on the Viennese Classical Style: Gluck, Haydn, Mozart, Beethoven. H. C. Landon. LC 74-119133. 1970. 6.95 o.s.i. (ISBN 0-02-567890-6). Macmillan.
Essays on Thomas Mann. Georg Lukacs. Tr. by Stanley Mitchell from Ger. 1979. Repr. of 1965 ed. 16.50 (ISBN 0-86527-245-X). Fertig.
Essays on Troilus & Criseyde. Ed. by Mary Salu. (Chaucer Studies: No. III). 143p. 1979. 23.75x (ISBN 0-8476-6236-5). Rowman.
Essays on Urban America. Ed. by Margaret F. Morris & Elliott West. LC 74-31058. (Walter Prescott Webb Memorial Lectures: No. 9). 128p. 1975. 8.95x (ISBN 0-292-72011-4). U of Tex Pr.
Essays on Value & Distribution. Nicholas Kaldor. 1960. 12.95 (ISBN 0-02-916980-1). Free Pr.
Essays on Walter Prescott Webb. Ed. by Kenneth R. Philp & Elliott West. (Walter Prescott Webb Memorial Lectures: No. 10). 160p. 1976. 8.95 (ISBN 0-292-72016-5). U of Tex Pr.
Essays on Zionism & the Contemporary Jewish Condition. Ed. by Nathan Rotenstreich. 1981. price not set. Herzl Pr.
Essays: Religious Meditations; Places of Perswasion & Disswasion. Francis Bacon. LC 68-54612. (English Experience Ser.: No. 17). Repr. of 1597 ed. 9.50 (ISBN 90-221-0017-0). Walter J Johnson.
Essays Toward Realistic Syntax. new ed. Michael K. Brame. LC 79-67347. (Linguistics Research Monograph: Vol. 2). 1979. text ed. 32.00x (ISBN 0-932998-01-1). Noit Amrofer.
Essays Upon the Law of Contracts & Agreements, 2 vols. in 1. John J. Powell. Ed. by David Berkowitz & Samuel Thorne. LC 77-86628. (Classics of English Legal History in the Modern Era Ser.: Vol. 86). 1979. Repr. of 1970 ed. lib. bdg. 55.00 (ISBN 0-8240-3073-7). Garland Pub.
Essays: Vol. 2, English & Other Critical Miscellanies. Thomas Carlyle. 1964. 5.00x (ISBN 0-460-00704-1, Evman); pap. 2.95 (ISBN 0-460-01704-7, Evman). Dutton.
Essence & the Vocation of Man. Eric S. Mortensen. (Illus.). 1980. deluxe ed. 37.55 (ISBN 0-89266-231-X). Am Classical Coll Pr.
Essence of Organic Chemistry. Jane M. Cram & Donald J. Cram. LC 77-73957. (Chemistry Ser.). 1978. text ed. 18.95 (ISBN 0-201-01031-3); study guide 5.50 (ISBN 0-201-01032-1). A-W.
Essence of Self-Defense. Hidy Ochiai. 1979. 14.95 o.p. (ISBN 0-8092-7378-0); pap. 7.95 (ISBN 0-8092-7377-2). Contemp Bks.
Essence of Social Research: A Copernican Revolution. Charles W. Lachenmeyer. LC 72-87692. 1973. 14.95 (ISBN 0-02-917720-0). Free Pr.
Essence of the Vedas & Allied Scriptures. Basdeo Bissoondayal. 1966. pap. 1.80 (ISBN 0-88253-126-3). Ind-US Inc.
Essene Plan. Leo F. Motylewski. LC 76-14499. 1976. 8.75 (ISBN 0-8022-2183-1). Philos Lib.
Essential Algebra. 2nd ed. Carol L. Johnston & Alden T. Willis. 1978. pap. text ed. 16.95x (ISBN 0-534-00579-9). Wadsworth Pub.
Essential Algebra & Trigonometry. Doris S. Stockton. LC 77-76337. (Illus.). 1978. text ed. 18.75 (ISBN 0-395-25413-2); inst. manual 0.70 (ISBN 0-395-25414-0). HM.
Essential Anatomy. 3rd, rev. ed. J. P. Lumley et al. (Illus.). 1981. pap. text ed. write for info. (ISBN 0-443-02003-5). Churchill.
Essential Arithmetic. 2nd ed. Carol L. Johnston & Alden T. Willis. 1977. 15.95x (ISBN 0-534-00513-6). Wadsworth Pub.
Essential Calculus: With Applications in Business, Biology, & Behavioral Sciences. Margaret L. Lial & Charles D. Miller. 346p. 1975. 16.95x o.p. (ISBN 0-673-07959-7). Scott F.
Essential Christianity. rev. ed. Walter Martin. 128p. 1980. pap. 3.95 (ISBN 0-88449-043-2). Vision Hse.
Essential Cinema: Essays on Films in The Collection of Anthology Film Archives. Ed. by P. Adams Sitney. LC 74-10371. (Anthology Film Archives Series). 380p. 1975. 20.00x (ISBN 0-8147-7767-8); pap. 9.00x (ISBN 0-8147-7768-6). NYU Pr.
Essential College Algebra. Doris S. Stockton. LC 78-69526. (Illus.). 1979. text ed. 16.95 (ISBN 0-395-26544-4); inst. manual 0.90 (ISBN 0-395-26538-X). HM.
Essential College Survival Handbook: An Insider's Guide to Making College Work for You. Ralph Carnes & Valerie Carnes. 224p. 1981. 12.95 (ISBN 0-87223-684-6); pap. 6.95 (ISBN 0-87223-694-3). Playboy.
Essential Community: Local Government in the Year 2000. Laurence Rutter. Ed. by Barbara Moore. LC 80-16901. (Municipal Management Ser.). (Illus.). 170p. (Orig.). 1980. pap. 15.00 (ISBN 0-87326-994-2). Intl City Mgt.
Essential Computer Dictionary & Speller for Secretaries, Managers, & Office Personnel. JoAnne C. Mayer & Charles J. Sippl. (Illus.). 256p. 1980. text ed. 14.95 (ISBN 0-13-284364-1, Spec); pap. 6.95 (ISBN 0-13-284356-0). P-H.
Essential Concepts in Immunology. Irving Weissman et al. LC 78-57262. 1978. 10.95 (ISBN 0-8053-4406-3). Benjamin-Cummings.
Essential Delsarte. John W. Zorn. LC 68-12619. 1968. 10.00 (ISBN 0-8108-0044-6). Scarecrow.
Essential Edinburgh. Alan Hamilton. (Illus.). 1978. pap. 7.95 (ISBN 0-233-96984-5). Transatlantic.
Essential English. Lewis & Lyman. 1981. pap. text ed. write for info. Goodyear.
Essential Erasmus. Desiderius Erasmus. Tr. by John P. Dolan. (Orig.). 1964. pap. 2.50 (ISBN 0-451-61877-7, ME1877, Ment). NAL.
Essential Factors of Social Evolution. Thomas N. Carver. 1935. 17.50 (ISBN 0-89020-007-6). Brown Bk.
Essential Frankfurt School Reader. Andrew Arato et al. 1978. 17.50 (ISBN 0-916354-30-X); pap. 7.95 (ISBN 0-916354-31-8). Urizen Bks.
Essential Gandhi. Mohandas K. Gandhi. 1963. text ed. 6.50x o.p. (ISBN 0-04-320009-5). Allen Unwin.
Essential Hepatology. T. S. Chen & P. S. Chen. 1977. 29.95 (ISBN 0-409-95005-X). Butterworths.
Essential Human Anatomy & Physiology. 2nd ed. Barbara R. Landau. 1980. text ed. 20.95x (ISBN 0-673-15249-9). Scott F.
Essential Invertebrate Zoology. 2nd ed. Ed. by M. S. Laverack & J. Dando. LC 78-25963. 1979. pap. text ed. 14.95 (ISBN 0-470-26605-8). Halsted Pr.
Essential Lenny Bruce. Ed. by John Cohen. 1974. pap. 1.75 o.p. (ISBN 0-345-24386-2). Ballantine.
Essential Math, Science, & Computer Terms for College Freshmen. William F. Shanahan. LC 79-3323. (Illus.). 1981. pap. 5.95 (ISBN 0-671-18435-0). Monarch Pr.
Essential Math Skills. Leo Gafney & John C. Beers. Ed. by Peter Devine. 224p. 1980. pap. text ed. 5.20 (ISBN 0-07-010260-0, W); tchr's ed. 6.08 (ISBN 0-07-010261-9); Webstermasters tests 4.52 (ISBN 0-07-010262-7). McGraw.
Essential Mathematics. 3rd ed. Mervin L. Keedy & Marvin L. Bittinger. 1980. pap. text ed. 16.95 (ISBN 0-201-03837-4). A-W.
Essential Mathematics: A Modern Approach. 2nd ed. Mervin L. Keedy & Marvin L. Bittinger. LC 76-9337. (Illus.). 1977. pap. text ed. 14.95 o.p. (ISBN 0-201-03728-9); instr's manual 3.00 o.p. (ISBN 0-201-03742-4). A-W.
Essential Mathematics for College Freshmen. Central State University Dept. of Mathematics. 1978. pap. text ed. 10.95 (ISBN 0-8403-1518-X). Kendall-Hunt.
Essential Mathematics for College Students. 3rd ed. Francis J. Mueller. (Illus.). 320p. 1976. pap. 13.95 (ISBN 0-13-286518-1). P-H.
Essential Mathematics for Economists. 2nd ed. J. Black & J. F. Bradley. LC 79-40826. 1980. 48.50 (ISBN 0-471-27659-6, Pub. by Wiley-Interscience); pap. cancelled (ISBN 0-471-27660-X). Wiley.
Essential Mathematics for General Chemistry. Robert L. Osburn. LC 74-32574. 128p. 1975. text ed. 5.95 o.p. (ISBN 0-471-65704-2). Wiley.
Essential Methods in Business Statistics. Edward N. Dubois. 1964. text ed. 16.95 (ISBN 0-07-017875-5, C); solutions manual 4.95 (ISBN 0-07-017874-7). McGraw.
Essential Middle School. Jon W. Wiles & Joseph Bondi, Jr. (Illus.). 432p. Date not set. text ed. 16.95 (ISBN 0-675-08086-X). Merrill.
Essential Neurology. William Pryse-Phillips & T. J. Murray. LC 77-91653. 1978. 25.00 (ISBN 0-87488-740-2). Med Exam.
Essential of International Trade. David H. Wyatt. LC 79-88237. (ALA ESP Ser.). (Illus.). v, 205p. (Orig.). 1979. pap. text ed. 10.00 (ISBN 0-934270-07-4). Am Lang Acad.
Essential of Palynology. P. Krishnan Nair. 1966. 5.00x (ISBN 0-210-26918-9). Asia.
Essential Oils: Individual Essential Oils of the Plant Families, 6 vols. Ernest Guenther. Vol. 1, 444p. 25.20 (ISBN 0-88275-073-9); Vol. 2, 866p. 46.50 (ISBN 0-88275-338-X); Vol. 3, 794p. 39.75 (ISBN 0-88275-163-8); Vol. 4, 766p. 36.50 (ISBN 0-88275-074-7); Vol. 5, 526p. 25.50 (ISBN 0-88275-354-1); Vol. 6, 498p. 28.50 (ISBN 0-88275-092-5); 180.00 set (ISBN 0-88275-953-1). Krieger.
Essential Organic Chemistry for Students of the Life Sciences. A. P. Ryles et al. LC 78-31504. 1980. 40.95 (ISBN 0-471-27582-4, Pub. by Wiley-Interscience); pap. 14.00 (ISBN 0-471-27581-6, Pub. by Wiley-Interscience). Wiley.
Essential Otolaryngology: A Board Preparation & Concise Reference. 2nd ed. Ed. by Keat-Jin Lee. 1977. spiral bdg. 19.50 (ISBN 0-87488-313-X). Med Exam.
Essential Paul Elmer More: A Selection of His Writings. Ed. by Byron C. Lambert. 1972. 12.95 o.s.i. (ISBN 0-87000-162-0). Arlington Hse.
Essential Portuguese Grammar. Alexander da R. Prista. LC 66-20416. 1966. lib. bdg. 9.50x (ISBN 0-88307-579-2). Gannon.
Essential Precalculus. Raymond McGivney et al. 464p. 1980. text ed. 18.95x (ISBN 0-534-00766-X); solutions manual 3.95 (ISBN 0-534-00842-9). Wadsworth Pub.
Essential Precalculus. Doris S. Stockton. LC 77-75647. (Illus.). 1978. text ed. 18.75 (ISBN 0-395-25417-5); inst. manual 1.70 (ISBN 0-395-25418-3). HM.
Essential Principles of Psychiatry. S. Crown. LC 72-128608. 1970. text ed. 13.50 (ISBN 0-911216-16-2). Raven.
Essential Prose. Ed. by Dorothy Van Ghent & Willard Maas. LC 10-527. 1965. pap. 10.55 o.p. (ISBN 0-672-61329-8). Bobbs.
Essential Readings in Logical Positivism. Ed. by Oswald Hanfling. 320p. 1981. pap. 14.95x (ISBN 0-631-12566-3, Dist. by Basil Blackwell). Biblio Dist.
Essential Relativity. rev. ed. W. Rindler. (Texts & Monographs in Physics). (Illus.). 284p. 1980. pap. 19.80 (ISBN 0-387-10090-3). Springer-Verlag.
Essential Secretarial Studies. Sheila T. Stanwell & Josephine Shaw. 1974. pap. 17.50x (ISBN 0-7131-1788-5). Intl Ideas.
Essential Self. Eugene Raudsepp. (Best Thoughts Ser.). (Illus.). 80p. (Orig.). 1981. pap. 2.50 (ISBN 0-8431-0388-4). Price Stern.
Essential Skills Series, 20 bks. Walter Pauk. Incl. Bk. 1 (ISBN 0-89061-100-9, ESS1); Bk. 2 (ISBN 0-89061-101-7, ESS2); Bk. 3 (ISBN 0-89061-102-5, ESS3); Bk. 4 (ISBN 0-89061-103-3, ESS4); Bk. 5 (ISBN 0-89061-104-1, ESS5); Bk. 6 (ISBN 0-89061-105-X, ESS6); Bk. 7 (ISBN 0-89061-106-8, ESS7); Bk. 8 (ISBN 0-89061-107-6, ESS8); Bk. 9 (ISBN 0-89061-108-4, ESS9); Bk. 10 (ISBN 0-89061-109-2, ESS10); Bk. 11 (ISBN 0-89061-110-6, ESS11); Bk. 12 (ISBN 0-89061-111-4, ESS12); Bk. 13 (ISBN 0-89061-112-2, ESS13); Bk. 14 (ISBN 0-89061-113-0, ESS14); Bk. 15 (ISBN 0-89061-114-9, ESS15); Bk. 16 (ISBN 0-89061-115-7, ESS16); Bk. 17 (ISBN 0-89061-116-5, ESS17); Bk. 18 (ISBN 0-89061-117-3, ESS18); Bk. 19 (ISBN 0-89061-118-1, ESS19); Bk. 20 (ISBN 0-89061-119-X, ESS20). (gr. 6-12). 1976. pap. text ed. 2.40x ea; 20 bk. set (ISBN 0-89061-098-3). Jamestown Pubs.
Essential Spanish Grammar. Seymour Resnick. (Orig.). 1963. pap. 2.00 (ISBN 0-486-20780-3). Dover.
Essential Spanish Grammar. Seymour Resnick. LC 63-4093. 1959. lib. bdg. 9.50x (ISBN 0-88307-577-6). Gannon.
Essential Surgery for Nurses. M. A. Henderson. (Illus.). 240p. 1980. pap. text ed. 12.00 (ISBN 0-443-01737-9). Churchill.

Essential Trigonometry. Doris S. Stockton. LC 78-69543. (Illus.). 1979. text ed. 15.95 (ISBN 0-395-26539-8); inst. manual 0.90 (ISBN 0-395-26545-2). HM.

Essential Writings of Karl Marx. Ed. by David Caute. 1970. pap. 2.95 o.s.i. (ISBN 0-02-072620-1, Collier). Macmillan.

Essentials for the Scientific & Technical Writer. Hardy Hoover. 224p. 1981. pap. 4.00 (ISBN 0-486-24060-6). Dover.

Essentials in Pressure Monitoring: Blood & Other Body Fluids. Jozef Cywinski. (Tardieu Ser.: No. 3). (Illus.). 120p. 1980. pap. 20.00 (ISBN 90-247-2385-X). Kluwer Boston.

Essentials of Accounting. 2nd ed. R. N. Anthony. LC 76-10413. 1977. pap. 10.95 (ISBN 0-201-00252-3); instr's guide 0.50 (ISBN 0-201-00258-2). A-W.

Essentials of Accounting. John W. Buckley & Kevin M. Lightner. 1975. pap. 17.95x (ISBN 0-685-70779-2). Dickenson.

Essentials of American Government. rev. ed. Ernst B. Schultz. LC 75-2476. (gr. 9 up). 1975. pap. text ed. 5.95 (ISBN 0-8120-0642-9). Barron.

Essentials of Anorectal Surgery. Stanley M. Goldberg et al. (Illus.). 416p. 1980. text ed. 37.50 (ISBN 0-397-50417-9). Lippincott.

Essentials of Astrological Analysis. Marc E. Jones. LC 60-15588. 1974. 16.50 o.p. (ISBN 0-87878-011-4, Sabian). Great Eastern.

Essentials of Astronomy. 2nd ed. Lloyd Motz & Anneta Duveen. LC 76-19068. 1977. 20.00x (ISBN 0-231-04009-1). Columbia U Pr.

Essentials of Aviation Technology: Aviation Mechanics. Noel W. Schutz, Jr. & Bruce L. Derwing. LC 80-51692. (ALA ESP Ser.). (Illus.). xii, 180p. (Orig.). 1980. pap. text ed. 10.00 (ISBN 0-934270-10-4). Am Lang Acad.

Essentials of Basic Life Support. Jack L. Winkelman. (Orig.). 1981. pap. text ed. write for info. (ISBN 0-8087-2385-5). Burgess.

Essentials of Basic Mathematics. 2nd ed. Allyn J. Washington et al. LC 72-92390. (gr. 9-12). 1973. text ed. 14.95 o.p. (ISBN 0-8465-8544-8). Benjamin-Cummings.

Essentials of Biblical Hebrew. rev. ed. Kyle M. Yates. Ed. by J. J. Owens. 1955. 8.00x (ISBN 0-06-069710-5, HarpR). Har-Row.

Essentials of Biology: A Basic Text of Current Biological Thought. C. Leland Rodgers. LC 74-8166. (gr. 10-12). 1974. pap. 5.95 (ISBN 0-8120-0236-9). Barron.

Essentials of Brass Playing. Fred Fox. LC 77-85127. 1978. pap. 6.00 (ISBN 0-913650-03-X). Volkwein Bros.

Essentials of Brownian Motion & Diffusion. Ed. by Frank B. Knight. (Mathematical Surveys: Vol. 18). Date not set. cancelled (ISBN 0-8218-1518-0). Am Math.

Essentials of Buddhist Philosophy. 3rd ed. J. Takakusu. 1975. Repr. 7.50 (ISBN 0-8426-0826-5). Orient Bk Dist.

Essentials of Business Law. William T. Schantz & Leonard F. Robertson. 1977. text ed. 11.28 (ISBN 0-02-478190-8). Macmillan.

Essentials of Canine & Feline Electrocardiography. Lawrence P. Tilley. LC 79-14374. (Illus.). 1979. 32.50 (ISBN 0-8016-4963-3). Mosby.

Essentials of Cell Biology. 2nd ed. Robert D. Dyson. 1978. text ed. 18.95 (ISBN 0-205-06117-6). Allyn.

Essentials of Child Development & Personality. Paul H. Mussen et al. 480p. 1980. text ed. 19.50 scp (ISBN 0-06-044693-5, HarpC); study guide by ray v. peters 6.50 (ISBN 0-06-045141-6). Har-Row.

Essentials of Chiropody for Students. 6th ed. J. Michael Dalton & Katharina Kuipers. 1969. 7.95 o.p. (ISBN 0-571-04623-1, Pub. by Faber & Faber). Merrimack Bk Serv.

Essentials of Clinical Cardiology. Won R. Lee. (Illus.). 443p. (Orig.). 1980. pap. text ed. 24.95 (ISBN 0-89303-008-2). Charles.

Essentials of Clinical Dental Assisting. 2nd. ed. Joseph E. Chasteen. LC 80-372. (Illus.). 1980. 18.95 (ISBN 0-8016-0976-3). Mosby.

Essentials of College Geography. C. Langdon White et al. LC 58-6374. (Illus.). 1958. text ed. 18.95x (ISBN 0-89197-553-5); pap. text ed. 8.95x (ISBN 0-89197-752-X). Irvington.

Essentials of Communicable Disease. Ed. by Mary E. McInnes. LC 74-28353. 402p. 1975. 14.95 (ISBN 0-8016-2545-9). Mosby.

Essentials of Comparative Government. rev. ed. Samuel A. Johnson. LC 63-16873. (gr. 9-12). 1973. pap. text ed. 3.50 (ISBN 0-8120-0052-8). Barron.

Essentials of Conducting. Lazare Saminsky. (Student's Music Library). 1957. 6.95 (ISBN 0-234-77403-7). Dufour.

Essentials of Cons. Behavior. Block & Roering. 1979. 19.95 (ISBN 0-03-041961-1). Dryden Pr.

Essentials of Cost Accounting. John Dearden. (Orig.). 1969. pap. text ed. 10.95 (ISBN 0-201-01484-X); instructor's guide 0.50 (ISBN 0-201-01496-3). A-W.

Essentials of Creative Advertising. Don E. Schultz. LC 80-70203. 1981. pap. text ed. 9.95 (ISBN 0-87251-045-X). Crain Bks.

Essentials of Dental Radiography for Dental Assistants & Hygienists. 2nd ed. Wolf F. DeLyre. (Illus.). 1980. text ed. 16.95 (ISBN 0-13-285676-X). P-H.

Essentials of Discipleship. Francis M. Cosgrove. LC 79-93015. 1980. pap. 4.95 (ISBN 0-89109-442-3). NavPress.

Essentials of Drug Product Quality: Concepts & Methodology. Mahmoud M. Abdel-Monem & James G. Henkel. LC 77-27069. (Illus.). 1978. text ed. 19.95 (ISBN 0-8016-0031-6). Mosby.

Essentials of Echocardiography. B. Termini & Y. Lee. (Illus.). 1976. 18.50 (ISBN 0-87489-094-2). Med Economics.

Essentials of Economic Analysis: Vol. 1, Microeconomics. Siegfried B. Ayatey. LC 79-66234. 1979. pap. text ed. 10.50 (ISBN 0-8191-0803-0). U Pr of Amer.

Essentials of Economic Analysis: Vol. 2, Macroeconomics. Siegfried B. Ayatey. LC 79-66234. 1979. pap. text ed. 9.00 (ISBN 0-8191-0804-9). U Pr of Amer.

Essentials of Educational Measurement. 3rd ed. Robert L. Ebel. LC 78-13392. 1979. ref. ed. 18.95 (ISBN 0-13-286013-9). P-H.

Essentials of Educational Research: Methodology & Design. 2nd ed. Carter V. Good. (Orig.). 1972. pap. text ed. 18.95 (ISBN 0-13-285841-X). P-H.

Essentials of Electricity. 3rd ed. William H. Timbie & Arthur L. Pike. LC 63-8053. 1963. text ed. 19.55x (ISBN 0-471-87036-6). Wiley.

Essentials of Electricity-Electronics. 3rd ed. Morris Slurzberg & William Osterheld. 1965. text ed. 17.95 (ISBN 0-07-058260-2, G); answers 1.50 (ISBN 0-07-058261-0). McGraw.

Essentials of Electronics. F. H. Mitchell & F. H. Mitchell, Jr. (Physics Ser). 1970. text ed. 17.95 (ISBN 0-201-04761-6). A-W.

Essentials of Elementary School Mathematics. Max D. Larsen & James L. Fejfar. 1974. text ed. 18.95 (ISBN 0-12-438640-7); solution manual 3.00 (ISBN 0-12-438642-3). Acad Pr.

Essentials of English. Joseph Bellafiore. (gr. 7-9). 1970. pap. text ed. 4.42 (ISBN 0-87720-341-5); wkbk. 5.67 (ISBN 0-87720-349-0). AMSCO Sch.

Essentials of English. rev. ed. Vincent F. Hopper et al. LC 67-20430. 224p. (gr. 9 up). 1973. text ed. 5.95 (ISBN 0-8120-5031-2); pap. 3.95 (ISBN 0-8120-0059-5). Barron.

Essentials of Exercise Physiology. Larry G. Shaver. (Orig.). 1980. pap. 14.95 (ISBN 0-8087-4200-0). Burgess.

Essentials of Finance. Ray G. Jones & Dean Dudley. (Illus.). 1978. 19.95 (ISBN 0-13-286088-0). P-H.

Essentials of Financial Management: Text & Cases. George C. Philippatos. LC 73-86413. 1974. text ed. 17.95x (ISBN 0-8162-6716-2); wkbk. 4.95 (ISBN 0-8162-6696-4). Holden-Day.

Essentials of Financial Statement Analysis. Robert T. Sprouse & Robert J. Swieringa. (Economics Ser). 480p. (Prog. Bk.). 1972. 12.95 (ISBN 0-201-07170-3). A-W.

Essentials of Fire Fighting, IFSTA 200. IFSTA Committee. Ed. by John D. Peige et al. LC 77-75408. (Illus.). 1977. pap. text ed. 15.00 (ISBN 0-87939-000-X). Intl Fire Serv.

Essentials of Forensic Medicine. 3rd rev. ed. C. J. Polson & D. J. Gee. LC 72-87949. 732p. 1973. 75.00 (ISBN 0-08-017023-4). Pergamon.

Essentials of Forestry Practice. 3rd ed. Charles H. Stoddard. LC 78-6652. 1978. text ed. 17.95 (ISBN 0-471-07262-1). Wiley.

Essentials of Geriatric Medicine. George Adams. 1978. pap. text ed. 7.95x (ISBN 0-19-261216-6). Oxford U Pr.

Essentials of Higher Physics. Mary Webster. 1978. pap. text ed. 9.50x o.p. (ISBN 0-435-68836-7). Heinemann Ed.

Essentials of Histology. 8th ed. Gerrit Bevelander & Judith A. Ramaley. LC 78-4847. 1979. text ed. 19.95 (ISBN 0-8016-0669-1). Mosby.

Essentials of Homoeopathic Prescribing. D. Shepherd. 78p. 1970. pap. 3.00x (ISBN 0-8464-1008-7). Beekman Pubs.

Essentials of Hospital Finance. William O. Cleverley. LC 78-7447. (Illus.). 1978. text ed. 21.95 (ISBN 0-89443-035-1). Aspen Systems.

Essentials of Industrial & Organizational Psychology. William C. Howell. 1976. pap. 9.95x (ISBN 0-256-01806-5). Dorsey.

Essentials of Investing. Keith V. Smith & David K. Eiteman. 1974. text ed. 18.95 (ISBN 0-256-01554-6). Irwin.

Essentials of Investments. C. Ronald Sprecher. LC 77-74380. (Illus.). 1977. text ed. 19.25 (ISBN 0-395-25454-X); inst. manual 0.70 (ISBN 0-395-25455-8). HM.

Essentials of Japanese Constitutional Law. Shinichi Fujii. (Studies in Japanese Law & Government). 459p. 1979. Repr. of 1940 ed. 32.50 (ISBN 0-89093-214-X). U Pubns Amer.

Essentials of Life & Health. 3rd ed. 425p. 1981. pap. text ed. 12.95 (ISBN 0-394-32570-2). Random.

Essentials of Management. W. Jack Duncan. LC 77-81236. 1978. text ed. 19.95 (ISBN 0-03-039826-6). Dryden Pr.

Essentials of Management. 3rd ed. Joseph L. Massie. (Essentials of Management Ser.). (Illus.). 1979. ref. 15.95 (ISBN 0-13-286351-0); pap. 9.95 ref. (ISBN 0-13-286344-8). P-H.

Essentials of Management. Sheldon Wise. LC 79-88238. (ALA ESP Ser.). (Illus.). v, 110p. (Orig.). 1979. pap. text ed. 6.25 (ISBN 0-934270-06-6). Am Lang Acad.

Essentials of Management: A Behavioral Approach. Justin G. Longenecker. 1977. text ed. 14.95 (ISBN 0-675-08552-7); instructor's manual 3.95 (ISBN 0-686-67520-7). Merrill.

Essentials of Management for First-Line Supervision. Robert W. Eckles et al. LC 73-17037. 642p. 1974. text ed. 23.95 (ISBN 0-471-23000-6, Pub. by Wiley Hamilton). Wiley.

Essentials of Management Science: Applications to Decision Making. David Anderson et al. (Illus.). 1978. text ed. 19.95 (ISBN 0-8299-0147-7); study guide 7.95 (ISBN 0-8299-0202-3); test bank avail. (ISBN 0-8299-0455-7); instrs.' manual avail. (ISBN 0-8299-0453-0); transparency masters avail. (ISBN 0-8299-0454-9). West Pub.

Essentials of Management Science-Operations Research. Elwood S. Buffa & James S. Dyer. LC 77-23799. (Manangement & Administration Ser.). 1978. text ed. 22.95 (ISBN 0-471-02003-6); tchrs. manual avail. (ISBN 0-471-02004-4). Wiley.

Essentials of Managerial Finance: Principles & Practice. Steven E. Bolten & Robert L. Conn. LC 80-80961. (Illus.). 800p. 1981. text ed. 17.95 (ISBN 0-395-20462-3); write for info. instr's manual (ISBN 0-395-20461-5). HM.

Essentials of Marketing. E. Jerome McCarthy. 1979. 18.50 (ISBN 0-256-02142-2); pap. 5.95x student aid (ISBN 0-256-02242-9). Irwin.

Essentials of Marketing. 2nd ed. Richard R. Still & Edward W. Cundiff. LC 79-170644. 1972. ref. ed. 10.95 (ISBN 0-13-286468-1). P-H.

Essentials of Mathematics. 4th ed. Russell V. Person. LC 79-10708. 1980. text ed. 19.95 (ISBN 0-471-05184-5); study guide avail. (ISBN 0-471-06288-X); solutions manual avail. (ISBN 0-471-07752-6). Wiley.

Essentials of Mathematics: Precalculus- a Programmed Text, 3 bks. Vernon E. Howes. LC 75-9733. 1975. Bk. 1: Algebra I. text ed. 18.95x (ISBN 0-471-41736-X); Bk. 2: Algebra II. text ed. o.p. (ISBN 0-471-41737-8); Bk. 3: Trigonometric Functions & Applications. text ed. 18.95x (ISBN 0-471-41738-6); instr's manual avail. (ISBN 0-471-41739-4). Wiley.

Essentials of Mechanics. Donald F. Young et al. (Illus.). 576p. 1974. text ed. 9.25 (ISBN 0-8138-1110-4). Iowa St U Pr.

Essentials of Medical Ultrasound. Ed. by M. H. Repacholi & D. A. Bewell. (Medical Methods Ser.). (Illus.). 1981. 24.50 (ISBN 0-89603-028-8). Humana.

Essentials of Merchandise Information: Nontextiles. Leon Levy et al. LC 66-10398. 1968. pap. text ed. 9.20 o.p. (ISBN 0-8224-0273-4); wkbk 3.16 o.p. (ISBN 0-8224-0250-5); tchrs'. manual & key 2.80 o.p. (ISBN 0-8224-0613-6). Pitman Learning.

Essentials of Meteorology. D. H. McIntosh et al. (Wykeham Science Ser.: No. 3). 1973. pap. 11.75x (ISBN 0-8448-1354-0). Crane-Russak Co.

Essentials of Modern Chemistry. Philip Perlman. LC 78-2344. (gr. 9-12). 1979. pap. 6.95 (ISBN 0-8120-0646-1). Barron.

Essentials of Modern Chemistry. rev. ed. Philip Perlman. 472p. (gr. 9-12). 1981. pap. text ed. 6.95 (ISBN 0-8120-2278-5). Barron. Postponed.

Essentials of Modern Physics Applied to the Study of the Infrared. A. Hadni. 1967. 64.00 (ISBN 0-08-011902-6). Pergamon.

Essentials of Music for New Musicians. Dennis K. Kiely. (Illus.). 192p. 1975. pap. text ed. 10.95 (ISBN 0-13-286492-4). P-H.

Essentials of Nematodology: Camallanata of Animals & Man & Diseases Caused by Them, Vol. 22. V. M. Ivashkin. 1977. 64.95 (ISBN 0-470-99321-9). Halsted Pr.

Essentials of Nematodology: Vol. 13, Oxyurata of Animals & Man. K. I. Skrjabin et al. 1976. 69.95 (ISBN 0-470-98978-5). Halsted Pr.

Essentials of Neuropathology. Sydney S. Schochet, Jr. & William F. McCormick. (Illus.). 1979. pap. 13.95 (ISBN 0-8385-2269-6). ACC.

Essentials of Nutrition & Diet Therapy. 2nd ed. Sue R. Williams. LC 77-18733. (Illus.). 1978. pap. text ed. 13.95 (ISBN 0-8016-5571-4). Mosby.

Essentials of Oral Biology. David Adams. (Dental Ser.). (Illus.). 152p. 1981. text ed. 12.50 (ISBN 0-443-02095-7). Churchill.

Essentials of Paleobotany. Ashok C. Shukla & Shital P. Misra. 1975. 15.00 (ISBN 0-7069-0381-1, Pub. by Vikas India). Advent Bk.

Essentials of Parenting in the First Years of Life. Barbara Gross & Bernard Shuman. LC 79-23739. (Orig.). 1980. pap. text ed. 3.95 (ISBN 0-87868-184-1). Child Welfare.

Essentials of Patient Representative Programs in Hospitals. Society of Paitent Representatives of the American Hospital Association. LC 78-26889. 1978. pap. 8.75 (ISBN 0-87258-255-8, 1251). Am Hospital.

Essentials of Periodontics. 2nd ed. Elizabeth A. Pawlak & Hoag. LC 80-13361. (Illus.). 1980. pap. text ed. 13.95 (ISBN 0-8016-3764-3). Mosby.

Essentials of Personnel Management. Mitchell S. Novit. (Essentials of Management Ser.). (Illus.). 1979. ref. 14.95 (ISBN 0-13-286617-X); pap. 6.95 ref. (ISBN 0-13-286609-9). P-H.

Essentials of Petroleum: A Key to Oil Economics. 2nd, rev. ed. Paul H. Frankel. 188p. 1969. 24.00x (ISBN 0-7146-1220-0, F Cass Co). Biblio Dist.

Essentials of Physics. rev. ed. Herman Gewirtz. LC 67-30941. (gr. 9-12). 1974. 12.95 (ISBN 0-8120-6062-8); pap. text ed. 6.95 (ISBN 0-8120-0278-4). Barron.

Essentials of Political Science. Samuel A. Johnson. LC 65-25692. (Orig.). (gr. 10 up). 1971. pap. text ed. 3.95 (ISBN 0-8120-0146-X). Barron.

Essentials of Prayer. E. M. Bounds. (E. M. Bounds Ser. on Prayer). 144p. 1980. pap. 1.95 (ISBN 0-8024-6723-7). Moody.

Essentials of Precalculus Mathematics. M. D. Larsen & R. J. Shumway. (Mathematics Ser.). 1971. 12.95 (ISBN 0-201-04123-5); instructor's manual 4.00 (ISBN 0-201-04124-3). A-W.

Essentials of Psychiatric Nursing. 10th ed. Dorothy A. Mereness & Cecelia M. Taylor. LC 77-10817. (Illus.). 1978. text ed. 17.95 (ISBN 0-8016-3399-0). Mosby.

Essentials of Psychological Testing. 3rd ed. Lee J. Cronbach. (Murphy-Holtzman Ser). 1970. text ed. 24.50 scp (ISBN 0-06-041421-9, HarpC); test items avail. (ISBN 0-06-361421-9). Har-Row.

Essentials of Psychology. Walter Mischel & Harriet N. Mischel. 1977. text ed. 14.95 o.p. (ISBN 0-394-31860-9). Random.

Essentials of Psychology. R. Silverman. 1979. pap. 14.95 (ISBN 0-13-286658-7); study guide & wkbk. 6.95 (ISBN 0-13-286666-8). P-H.

Essentials of Psychology & Life. 10th ed. Philip G. Zimbardo. 1979. text ed. 17.95x (ISBN 0-673-15184-0). Scott F.

Essentials of Psychology: Exploration & Application. Dennis L. Coon. (Illus.). 1979. pap. text ed. 14.50 (ISBN 0-8299-0241-4); study guide 6.50 (ISBN 0-8299-0244-9); instrs.' manual avail. (ISBN 0-8299-0468-9); study guide 6.50. West Pub.

Essentials of Public Communicaton. James R. Andrews. LC 78-18182. 1979. text ed. 11.95 (ISBN 0-471-02357-4); tchrs. manual avail. (ISBN 0-471-04278-1). Wiley.

Essentials of Qualitative Analysis. A. Holderness & J. Lambert. 1974. pap. text ed. 3.95x (ISBN 0-435-65535-3). Heinemann Ed.

Essentials of Real Estate. David Sirota. (Illus.). 304p. 1980. ref. ed. 19.95; pap. 16.95 (ISBN 0-8359-1776-2). Reston.

Essentials of Real Estate Economics. 2nd ed. Dennis J. McKenzie & Richard M. Betts. (California Real Estate Ser.). 304p. 1980. text ed. 18.95 (ISBN 0-471-08334-8). Wiley.

Essentials of Real Estate Finance. 2nd ed. David Sirota. 424p. 1979. pap. 22.95 (ISBN 0-88462-265-7). Real Estate Ed Co.

Essentials of Renal Pathophysiology. Saulo Klahr. 1981. 10.95 (ISBN 0-8036-5377-8). Davis Co.

Essentials of Respiratory Disease. R. B. Cole. LC 75-35316. (Illus.). 278p. 1976. 16.00 o.p. (ISBN 0-397-58187-4, Pub. by Blackwell Medical). Mosby.

Essentials of Retailing. Ruth Keyes & Ronald Cushman. LC 76-55081. (Illus.). 1977. text ed. 13.95 (ISBN 0-87005-183-0). Fairchild.

Essentials of Russian. 4th ed. Andre Von Gronicka & Helen Bates-Yakobson. 1964. text ed. 16.95 (ISBN 0-13-287706-6). P-H.

Essentials of Sociology, Second Edition: From "Sociology: A Text with Adapted Readings". 6th ed. Leonard Broom & Philip Selznick. 324p. 1979. pap. text ed. 14.95 scp (ISBN 0-06-040976-2, HarpC); instructor's manual free (ISBN 0-06-361496-0); doing essentials of sociology: chapter guides, projects, tool kits scp 7.50 (ISBN 0-06-040979-7). Har-Row.

Essentials of Speech Communication. R. Ross. 1979. pap. 10.95 (ISBN 0-13-289314-2). P-H.

Essentials of Stage Lighting. Hunton D. Sellman. LC 75-187988. (Illus.). 1972. 16.95 (ISBN 0-13-289207-3). P-H.

Essentials of Stage Scenery. Samuel Selden, Jr. & Thomas Rezzuto. LC 70-182307. (Illus.). 1972. 16.95 (ISBN 0-13-289215-4). P-H.

Essentials of Statistics. R. Mason. 1976. pap. text ed. 13.95 (ISBN 0-13-289561-7). P-H.

Essentials of Statistics in Marketing. C. S. Greensted et al. 1974. 17.95 (ISBN 0-470-32630-1). Halsted Pr.

Essentials of Successful Preaching. Amar B. Rambisoon. 1981. 6.50 (ISBN 0-8062-1706-5). Carlton.

Essentials of Supervisory Management. Lester R. Bittel. LC 80-13784. (Illus.). 288p. 1980. softcover 12.95 (ISBN 0-07-005571-8, G); instrs'. manual & key 4.50 (ISBN 0-07-005572-6). McGraw.

Essentials of Teaching Elementary School Music. Robert E. Nye & Vernice T. Nye. (Illus.). 288p. 1974. 15.95 (ISBN 0-13-289280-4); pap. 11.95 (ISBN 0-13-289272-3). P-H.

Essentials of Testing. John C. Marshall & Loyde W. Hales. LC 74-158875. (Education Ser.). 1972. pap. text ed. 6.95 (ISBN 0-201-04508-7). A-W.

Essentials of Theism. Denis J. Hawkins. LC 72-9373. 151p. 1973. Repr. of 1949 ed. lib. bdg. 16.75x (ISBN 0-8371-6579-2, HAET). Greenwood.

Essentials of Trigonometry. 2nd rev. ed. Joseph B. Rosenbach et al. 1974. text ed. 18.95x (ISBN 0-471-01104-5). Wiley.

Essentials of Wesleyan Theology: A Contemporary Affirmation. Paul Mickey. 160p. 1980. pap. 4.95 (ISBN 0-310-39151-2). Zondervan.

Essex. Norman Scarfe. (Shell Guide Ser.). (Illus.). 1968. 13.95 (ISBN 0-571-08868-6, Pub. by Faber & Faber). Merrimack Bk Serv.

EST: Making Life Work. Robert Hargove. 1976. 7.95 o.p. (ISBN 0-440-02405-6). Delacorte.

EST: Playing the Game the New Way. Carl Frederick. 1976. 7.95 o.p. (ISBN 0-440-02364-5). Delacorte.

Established in Eden. Carole C. Carlson. 1978. 6.95 o.p. (ISBN 0-8007-0943-8). Revell.

Establishing Austin's Colony: The First Book Printed in Texas, with the Laws, Orders, & Contracts of Colonization. Stephen F. Austin. Ed. by David B. Gracy, 2nd. (Illus.). 9.50 (ISBN 0-8363-0031-9). Jenkins.

Establishing Controls & Auditing the Computerized Accounting System. Elise G. Jancura & Robert V. Boos. 224p. 1980. text ed. 19.95 (ISBN 0-442-80507-1). Van Nos Reinhold.

Establishing Instructional Goals. James Popham & Eva Baker. 1970. pap. text ed. 8.95 (ISBN 0-13-289256-1). P-H.

Establishment. Howard Fast. 1980. pap. 3.25 o.s.i. (ISBN 0-440-12296-1). Dell.

Establishment of Innocence. Harvey Aronson & Mike McGrady. 1977. pap. 1.95 o.p. (ISBN 0-425-03288-4). Berkley Pub.

Establishment of the European Hegemony: 1415-1715: Trade & Exploration in the Age of the Renaissance. Ed. by John H. Parry. pap. 3.95x (ISBN 0-06-131045-X, TB1045, Torch). Har-Row.

Estadistica Aplicada. 3rd ed. Taro Yamane. (Span.). 1974. 12.50 o.p. (ISBN 0-06-319775-8, IntlDept). Har-Row.

Estadistica Con Problemas. Taro Yamane. (Span.). 1979. pap. text ed. 13.00 (ISBN 0-06-319777-4, Pub. by HarLA Mexico). Har-Row.

Estadistica en Investigacion. Jack Levin. (Span.). 1979. pap. text ed. 7.80 (ISBN 0-06-315012-3, Pub. by HarLA Mexico). Har-Row.

Estados Unidos en su Bicentenario: Homenaje de la OEA. (Span.). 1977. 3.00 (ISBN 0-685-80048-2). OAS.

Estampas del Valle. new ed. Rolando Hinojosa. 1978. 7.50 (ISBN 0-915808-26-9); pap. 4.50 (ISBN 0-685-87637-3). Editorial Justa.

Estampas Espanolas. J. A. Barquero. (Span.). 7.50 (ISBN 84-241-5632-3). E Torres & Sons.

Estanflacion. Howard Sherman. (Span.). 1980. pap. text ed. 7.60 (ISBN 0-06-317152-X, Pub. by HarLA Mexico). Har-Row.

Estate & Financial Planning for the Closely Held Corporation 1980 Course Handbook. (Tax Law & Estate Planning Course Handbook Ser., 1979-80: Vol. 107). 1980. pap. 25.00 (ISBN 0-686-50961-7, D4-5124). PLI.

Estate Planning, Vols. 1-6. A. James Casner. 1980. text ed. 250.00 (ISBN 0-316-13148-2). Vol. 1. Vol. 2 (ISBN 0-316-13149-0). Vol. 3 (ISBN 0-316-13150-4). Vol. 4 (ISBN 0-316-13151-2). Vol. 5 (ISBN 0-316-13152-0). Vol. 6 (ISBN 0-316-13153-9). Little.

Estate Planning for Everyone. rev. ed. Patrick F. Flaherty & Richard S. Ziegler. LC 78-4761. (Funk & W Bk.). 1979. 14.95 o.s.i. (ISBN 0-308-10346-7, TYC-T). T Y Crowell.

Estate Planning for Everyone. rev. ed. Patrick F. Flaherty & Richard Ziegler. LC 80-8314. (Illus.). 1981. 14.95 (ISBN 0-690-01943-2, HarpT). Har-Row.

Estate Planning for the Small Business Owner. John C. Howell. 176p. 1980. pap. 5.95 (Spec). P-H.

Estate Planning: What Anyone Who Owns Anything Must Know. Peter E. Lippett. (Illus.). 1979. 16.95 (ISBN 0-8359-1778-9). Reston.

Estates. Gould Staff Editors. (Supplemented annually). 1980. looseleaf 7.50 (ISBN 0-87526-140-X). Gould.

Estates & Revolutions: Essays in Early Modern European History. H. G. Koenigsberger. LC 71-132141. (Illus.). 1971. 18.50x o.p. (ISBN 0-8014-0605-6). Cornell U Pr.

Estates & Trusts. 5th ed. Gilbert T. Stephenson & Norman A. Wiggins. (Risk & Insurance Ser.). 480p. 1973. text ed. 18.95 (ISBN 0-13-289546-3). P-H.

Estates, Gifts & Fiducuaries: Planning & Taxation. 3rd ed. George M. Schain. Ed. by Jeffrey S. Gold. 444p. 1980. 29.95 (ISBN 0-07-055120-0, P&RB); wkbk. & 10 cassettes 195.00 (ISBN 0-07-079056-6). McGraw.

Estates of the Higher Nobility in Fourteenth-Century England. George A. Holmes. LC 80-2024. 1981. Repr. of 1957 ed. 25.00 (ISBN 0-404-18570-3). AMS Pr.

Estebanico. Helen R. Parish. 128p. (gr. 7 up). 1974. 5.95 o.p. (ISBN 0-670-29814-X). Viking Pr.

Esteeming. Churches Alive Inc. (Love One Another Bible Study). 1979. wkbk. 1.50 (ISBN 0-934396-03-5). Churches Alive.

Estetica Gregoriana. Paolo A. Ferretti. LC 77-5498. (Music Reprint Ser.). 1977. Repr. of 1934 ed. lib. bdg. 35.00 (ISBN 0-306-77414-3). Da Capo.

Estevan. (gr. 1). 1974. pap. text ed. 2.80 (ISBN 0-205-03879-4, 8038791); tchrs'. guide 12.00 (ISBN 0-205-03866-2, 803866X). Allyn.

Esther. Henry Adams. Ed. by Robert Spiller. LC 38-18393. 1976. Repr. lib. bdg. 34.00x (ISBN 0-8201-1187-2). Schol Facsimiles.

Esther. George Lawson. LC 80-8072. (Kregal Timeless Classics Ser.). 1981. 9.95 (ISBN 0-8254-3124-7). Kregel.

Esther. L. B. Paton. LC 8-30156. (International Critical Commentary Ser.). 360p. Repr. of 1908 ed. text ed. 20.00x (ISBN 0-567-05009-2). Attic Pr.

Esther: Courage in Crisis. Margaret Hess. 1980. pap. 2.50 (ISBN 0-88207-216-1). Victor Bks.

Esther: The Star & the Sceptre. Gini Andrews. 272p. 1980. 9.95 (ISBN 0-310-20180-2). Zondervan.

Esther Waters. George Moore. (World's Classics). 1968. 14.95 (ISBN 0-19-250594-7). Oxford U Pr.

Esther's Town. Deemer Lee. 190p. 1980. 12.95 (ISBN 0-8138-0460-4). Iowa St U Pr.

Esthetic Basis of Greek Art. Rhys Carpenter. LC 59-13530. (Midland Bks.: No. 19). (Illus.). 1959. pap. 2.50x o.p. (ISBN 0-253-20019-9). Ind U Pr.

Esthetic of Jean Cocteau. Lydia Crowson. LC 77-95326. 206p. 1978. text ed. 12.50x (ISBN 0-87451-149-6). U Pr of New Eng.

Esthetics of Negligence: La Fontaine's Contes. John C. Lapp. LC 72-142130. 1971. 42.00 (ISBN 0-521-08067-3). Cambridge U Pr.

Esthetics: The Keystone Guide to Skin Care. Christine Valmy. 1979. pap. 16.00 (ISBN 0-912126-36-1, 1257-00). Keystone Pubns.

Estienne Jodelle, Le Recueil de Inscriptions, 1558: A Literary & Iconographical Exegesis. Victor E. Graham & W. McAllister Johnson. LC 79-163818. (Illus.). 1972. 20.00x (ISBN 0-8020-1752-5). U of Toronto Pr.

Estimated World Requirements of Narcotic Drugs in 1980. 60p. 1980. pap. 6.00 (ISBN 0-686-68954-2, UN80/11/1, UN). Unipub.

Estimates of Some Englishmen & Scotchmen. Walter Bagehot. 453p. 1980. Repr. of 1858 ed. lib. bdg. 40.00 (ISBN 0-89987-060-0). Darby Bks.

Estimating & Project Management for Small Construction Firms. Seymour Berger & Jules B. Godel. 1977. pap. text ed. 8.80 o.p. (ISBN 0-8273-1763-8). Delmar.

Estimating for Builders & Surveyors. 2nd ed. Hugh Enterkin & Gerald Reynolds. 1978. pap. 18.50x (ISBN 0-434-90542-9). Intl Ideas.

Estimating for Building & Civil Engineering Works. 7th ed. Crystal-Smith. 1981. text ed. write for info. (ISBN 0-408-00515-7). Butterworth.

Estimating for Heating & Ventilating. 3rd ed. John J. Barton. (Illus.). 29.50x (ISBN 0-408-00072-4). Transatlantic.

Estimating for Residential Construction. H. A. Van Orman. LC 76-14083. 1978. pap. text ed. 12.00 (ISBN 0-8273-1605-4); instructor's guide 1.60 (ISBN 0-8273-1606-2). Delmar.

Estimating Home Building Costs. W. P. Jackson. 288p. (Orig.). 1981. pap. 14.00 (ISBN 0-910460-80-9). Craftsman.

Estimating in Building Construction. 2nd ed. Frank R. Dagostino. (Illus.). 1978. ref. ed. 19.95 (ISBN 0-87909-275-0); text ed. 15.95 (ISBN 0-87909-275-0); solutions manual free (ISBN 0-8359-2749-0). Reston.

Estimating Manufacturing Costs. Richard Clugston. LC 78-185563. (Illus.). 214p. 1971. 14.95 (ISBN 0-8436-0811-0). CBI Pub.

Estimating Residential Construction. Alonzo Wass. (Illus.). 1980. text ed. 21.95 (ISBN 0-13-289942-6). P-H.

Estimating the Size of Animal Populations. 1st ed. J. G. Blower et al. 96p. (Orig.). 1981. text ed. 22.50x (ISBN 0-04-591017-0); pap. text ed. 9.95x (ISBN 0-04-591018-9). Allen Unwin.

Estimation. Charles F. Linn. LC 75-106574. (Young Math Ser.). (Illus.). (gr. 1-4). 1970. PLB 6.89 o.p. (ISBN 0-690-27028-3, TYC-J); filmstrip with record 12.85 o.p. (ISBN 0-690-27029-1); filmstrip with cassette 15.85 o.p. (ISBN 0-690-27031-3). T Y Crowell.

Estimation. Charles F. Linn. LC 75-106574. (Crocodile Paperbacks Ser.). (Illus.). 40p. (gr. 1-4). 1972. pap. 1.45 o.p. (ISBN 0-690-27033-X, TYC-J). T Y Crowell.

Estimation of Animal Abundance. 2nd ed. George A. Seber. 1981. 55.00 (ISBN 0-02-852010-6). Macmillan.

Estimation of Recent Trends in Fertility & Mortality in the Republic of Korea. 1980. 3.75 (ISBN 0-309-02890-6). Natl Acad Pr.

Estimation of Resources & Reserves. M. A. Adelman & G. M. Kaufman. 1981. price not set (ISBN 0-88410-644-6). Ballinger Pub.

Estimation of Soviet Defense Expenditures, 1955-75: An Unconventional Approach. William T. Lee. LC 76-24357. (Special Studies). 1977. text ed. 36.50 (ISBN 0-275-56900-4). Praeger.

Esto Creemos los Bautistas. James E. Giles. Date not set. pap. 1.90 (ISBN 0-311-09091-5). Casa Bautista.

Estrangement, Alienation, & Exploitation: A Sociological Approach to Historical Materialism. John Torrance. LC 77-8246. 1977. 25.00x (ISBN 0-231-04448-8). Columbia U Pr.

Estrangement: Marx's Conception of Human Nature & the Division of Labor. Isidor Wallimann. LC 80-929. (Contributions in Philosophy: No. 16). 240p. 1981. lib. bdg. 29.95 (ISBN 0-313-22096-4, WAE/). Greenwood.

Estrangement of Great Britain & Japan, 1917-1935. Malcolm D. Kennedy. LC 71-77517. (Illus.). 1969. 20.00x (ISBN 0-520-01431-6). U of Cal Pr.

Estrogen Receptors in Human Breast Cancer. Ed. by W. L. McGuire et al. LC 74-14484. 1975. 27.00 (ISBN 0-89004-015-X). Raven.

Estrogens & Brain Function: Neural Analysis of a Hormone-Controlled Mammalian Reproductive Behavior. D. W. Pfaff. (Illus.). 272p. 1980. 24.90 (ISBN 0-387-90487-5). Springer-Verlag.

Estrogens & Cancer. Steven G. Silverberg & Francis J. Major. LC 78-17275. 1978. 32.95 (ISBN 0-471-04172-6, Pub. by Wiley Medical). Wiley.

Estructura Electronica De los Solidos. (Serie De Fisica: No. 3). (Span.). 1974. pap. 1.00 (ISBN 0-8270-1044-3). OAS.

Estructuras Algebraicas II (Algebra Lineal) (Serie De Matematica: No. 12). 160p. (Span.). 1971. pap. 1.00 (ISBN 0-8270-6285-0). OAS.

Estructuras Algebraicas III (Grupos Finitos) (Serie De Matematicas: No. 14). (Span.). 1973. pap. 1.25 o.p. (ISBN 0-685-34528-9). OAS.

Estuaries, Geophysics, & the Environment. Geophysics Study Committee. LC 77-82812. (Studies in Geophysics). (Illus.). 1977. pap. text ed. 8.50 (ISBN 0-309-02629-6). Natl Acad Pr.

Estuarine & Coastal Land Reclamation & Water Storage. J. Phillips & B. Knights. (Illus.). 256p. 1979. 28.95 (ISBN 0-566-00252-3, Pub. by Teakfield Ltd England). Lexington Bks.

Estuarine Ecosystem. Donald S. McLusky. (Tertiary Level Biology Ser.). 176p. 1981. 34.95 (ISBN 0-470-27127-2). Halsted Pr.

Estuarine Environment. Ed. by R. S. Barnes. J. Green. (Illus.). 1972. 26.00x (ISBN 0-85334-539-2, Pub. by Applied Science). Burgess-Intl Ideas.

Estuarine Hydrography & Sedimentation. Ed. by K. R. Dyer. LC 78-67308. (Illus.). 1980. 47.50 (ISBN 0-521-22435-7); pap. 15.95 (ISBN 0-521-29496-7). Cambridge U Pr.

Estuarine Processes, 2 vols. Ed. by M. Wiley. Vol. 1. 1976. 35.00 (ISBN 0-12-751801-0); Vol. 2. 1977. 31.50 (ISBN 0-12-751802-9). Acad Pr.

Estudio Comparativo De las Legislaciones Latino Americanas Sobre Regulacion y Control de la Inversin Privada Extranjera. (Span.). 1975. 10.00 (ISBN 0-8270-5235-9). OAS.

Estudio de la Biblia. John Tickle. Tr. by Olimpia Diaz, Sr. from Eng. 96p. 1980. pap. 1.95 (ISBN 0-89243-131-8). Liguori Pubns.

Estudio De Planificacion Nucleoelectrica Para Venezuela. 1979. pap. 32.25 (ISBN 92-0-359078-1, ISP486, IAEA). Unipub.

Estudio Sectorial Sobre Empresas Transacionales En America Latina: La Industria Automotriz. 71p. (Span.). 1977. Repr. of 1974 ed. 5.00 (ISBN 0-8270-3300-1). OAS.

Estudios de Ingles: Intermedio-Avanzado. Eugene J. Hall. (gr. 9 up). 1965. pap. text ed. 2.95 (ISBN 0-88345-049-6, 17388); Set. records 40.00 (ISBN 0-685-48111-5); Set. cassettes 40.00 (ISBN 0-685-48112-3). ans. key 1.00 (ISBN 0-686-67014-0). Regents Pub.

Estudios En el Nuevo Testamento. A. T. Robertson. Tr. by Sara A. Hale from Eng. Orig. Title: Studies in the New Testament. 224p. (Span.). Date not set. pap. price not set (ISBN 0-311-03629-5). Casa Bautista.

Estudios Sobre el Nuevo Testamento. A. T. Robertson. 1978. Repr. of 1973 ed. 2.85 o.p. (ISBN 0-311-03629-5). Casa Bautista.

Eta Feudale, 2 vols. Carlo G. Mor. LC 80-2016. 1981. Repr. of 1952 ed. Set. 110.00 (ISBN 0-404-18609-2). AMS Pr.

Etats Unis. Ed. by Daniel Moreau. (Collection monde et voyages). (Illus.). 159p. (Fr.). 1973. 21.00x (ISBN 2-03-053106-5, 3895). Larousse.

Etching of Glass & Sandblasting. Nord. (Illus.). 80p. 1980. 6.95 (ISBN 0-935656-01-4, 101 B). Chrome Yellow.

Etching Techniques. Peter Coker. 1976. 22.50 (ISBN 0-7134-3063-X, Pub. by Batsford England). David & Charles.

Etchings of Jacques Bellange. Amy N. Worthen & Sue W. Reed. (Illus.). 1976. pap. 6.00 (ISBN 0-87846-094-2, Pub. by Desmoines Art Center). Mus Fine Arts Boston.

Etctera: Graphic Devices. Typony. 176p. 1980. pap. 12.95 (ISBN 0-442-24456-8). Van Nos Reinhold.

Eternal Champion: A Fantastic Romance. Michael Moorcock. LC 77-3797. 1978. Repr. 10.95 o.s.i. (ISBN 0-06-013014-8, HarpT). Har-Row.

Eternal Desire. Clarissa Ross. 1979. pap. 2.50 (ISBN 0-515-04818-6). Jove Pubns.

Eternal Feminine: Selected Poems of Goethe. Johann W. Goethe. Ed. by Frederick Ungar. LC 76-15651. 192p. 1980. 14.50 (ISBN 0-8044-2256-7). Ungar.

Eternal Fire. Calder Willingham. LC 63-7498. 1962. 8.95 (ISBN 0-8149-0237-5). Vanguard.

Eternal Flame: Aspects of Ghalib's Life & Works. K. N. Sud. 1969. 5.50x o.p. (ISBN 0-8426-1558-X). Verry.

Eternal India. Indira Gandhi. LC 80-51191. Orig. Title: Inde. (Illus.). 260p. 1980. 50.00 (ISBN 0-86565-003-9). Vendome.

Eternal Judgment. Derek Prince. (Foundation Ser.: Bk. VII). 1965-66. pap. 1.50 (ISBN 0-934920-06-0, B-16). Derek Prince.

Eternal Now. Paul Tillich. LC 63-17938. 1963. pap. 3.95 (ISBN 0-684-71907-X, SL114, ScribT). Scribner.

Eternal Poetry of Romantic Love. James W. Riley. (Illus.). 1979. deluxe ed. 31.45 (ISBN 0-930582-47-0). Gloucester Art.

Eternal Principles of Managerial Excellence for the Benefit of Businessmen: Corporate Executives, Junior Clerks, Housewives, Students, Politicians, Statesmen & Anyone Genuinely Interested in Improving His Station in Life. Carlo M. De Flumiani. (Illus.). 1977. 34.75 (ISBN 0-89266-061-9). Am Classical Coll Pr.

Eternal Promise. Thomas Kelly. LC 77-71637. 1977. pap. 2.45 (ISBN 0-913408-30-1). Friends United.

Eternal Savage. Edgar R. Burroughs. 192p. 1977. pap. 1.95 (ISBN 0-441-21805-9). Ace Bks.

Eternal Wool. Evelyn A. Domjan. Ed. by Peggy Brogan. (Illus.). 160p. 1980. 25.00 (ISBN 0-933652-15-1). Domjan Studio.

Eternity in Their Hearts. Don Richardson. LC 80-50542. 1981. text ed. 8.95 (ISBN 0-8307-0739-5, 5108608). Regal. Postponed.

Ethan Frome. lib. rep. ed. Edith Wharton. 1911. 12.50x (ISBN 0-684-15326-2, ScribT); pap. 2.45 (ISBN 0-684-71927-4, SL8, ScribT); text ed. 4.40 (ISBN 0-684-51564-4, ScribC); pap. text ed. 2.92 (ISBN 0-684-51565-2, ScribC). Scribner.

Ethanol: Farm & Fuel Issues. Schnittker Assocs. 160p. 1981. pap. 19.50 (ISBN 0-89934-096-2). Solar Energy Info.

Ethanol, Methanol, & Gasohol. J. R. Williams et al. (Illus.). 200p. 1981. 18.75 (ISBN 0-250-40382-X). Ann Arbor Science.

Ethical & Legal Issues of Social Experimentation. Ed. by Alice M. Rivlin & P. Michael Timpane. (Studies in Social Experimentation). 180p. 1975. 10.95 (ISBN 0-8157-7482-6); pap. 4.95 (ISBN 0-8157-7481-8). Brookings.

Ethical Argument Against Government. John T. Sanders. LC 80-488. 271p. 1980. text ed. 18.25 (ISBN 0-8191-1015-9); pap. text ed. 9.25 (ISBN 0-8191-1016-7). U Pr of Amer.

Ethical Choice. R. N. Beck & J. B. Orr. LC 70-122282. 1970. pap. text ed. 7.95 (ISBN 0-02-902060-3). Free Pr.

Ethical Conflicts in Computer Science & Technology. Donn B. Parker. vi, 201p. 1979. 20.00 (ISBN 0-88283-009-0); wkbk 15.00 (ISBN 0-88283-010-4). AFIPS Pr.

Ethical Constraints & Imperatives in Medical Research. Maurice B. Visscher. (American Lectures in Behavioral Science & Law Ser.). 128p. 1975. 12.50 (ISBN 0-398-03404-4). C C Thomas.

Ethical Decisions in Medicine. 2nd ed. Howard Brody. 1981. pap. text ed. write for info (ISBN 0-316-10899-5). Little.

Ethical Decisions in Physical Education & Sport. Edward J. Shea. (Illus.). 232p. 1978. 19.75 (ISBN 0-398-03787-6). C C Thomas.

Ethical Dilemmas & the Education of Policymakers. Joel L. Fleishman & Bruce L. Payne. LC 80-10230. (Teaching of Ethics Ser.). 76p. 1980. pap. 4.00 (ISBN 0-916558-05-3). Hastings Ctr Inst Soc.

Ethical Dimensions in the Health Professions. Ruth B. Purtilo & Christine K. Cassel. 200p. 1981. text ed. price not set (ISBN 0-7216-7411-9). Saunders.

Ethical Foundations of Marxism. rev. ed. Eugene Kamenka. 1972. 22.00x (ISBN 0-7100-7360-7). Routledge & Kegan.

Ethical Issues in Business: A Philosophical Approach. T. Donaldson & P. Werhare. 1979. pap. 11.50 (ISBN 0-13-290064-5). P-H.

Ethical Issues in Death & Dying. Thom Beauchamp & Seymour Perlin. 1978. pap. 11.50 (ISBN 0-13-290114-5). P-H.

Ethical Issues in Health Care. Margot J. Fromer. LC 80-25058. 350p. 1981. pap. text ed. 14.95 (ISBN 0-8016-1728-6). Mosby.

Ethical Issues in Sex Therapy & Research, Vol. 2. Ed. by William H. Masters et al. 456p. 1980. text ed. 22.50 (ISBN 0-316-54989-4). Little.

Ethical Issues of Imformed Consent in Dentistry. Richard Warner & Herman Segal. 112p. 1980. pap. 12.00 (ISBN 0-931386-33-0). Quint Pub Co.

Ethical Issues of Population Aid. Ed. by Daniel Callahan. 1980. text ed. 22.50x o.p. (ISBN 0-8290-0120-4). Irvington.

Ethical Issues of Population Aid: Culture, Economics & International Assistance. Ed. by Daniel Callahan & Phillip G. Clark. 1981. text ed. 24.50x (ISBN 0-8290-0364-9). Irvington.

Ethical Judgment: The Use of Science in Ethics. Abraham Edel. LC 55-7339. 1964. pap. text ed. 3.00 o.s.i. (ISBN 0-02-908090-X). Free Pr.

Ethical Patterns in Early Christian Thought. E. Osborn. LC 75-10040. 288p. 1976. 34.00 (ISBN 0-521-20835-1). Cambridge U Pr.

Ethical Perspectives on Business & Society. Yerachmiel Kugel & Gladys W. Gruenberg. LC 77-3106. 1977. 16.95 (ISBN 0-669-01482-6). Lexington Bks.

Ethical Principles in the Conduct of Research with Human Participants. American Psychological Association. 1973. pap. 4.50 (ISBN 0-685-56746-X). Am Psychol.

Ethical Studies: Selected Essays. Francis H. Bradley. 1951. pap. 4.95 (ISBN 0-672-60189-3, LLA28). Bobbs.

Ethical Theories: A Book of Readings with Revisions. 2nd ed. A. I. Melden. 1967. text ed. 18.95 (ISBN 0-13-290122-6). P-H.

Ethical Theory & Business. Ed. by Tom L. Beauchamp & Norman E. Bowie. (Illus.). 1979. text ed. 17.50 (ISBN 0-13-290460-8). P-H.

Ethical Theory from Hobbes to Kant. W. C. Swabey. LC 60-53161. 1961. 4.75 (ISBN 0-8022-1680-3). Philos Lib.

Ethical Theory of Clarence Irving Lewis. J. Roger Saydah. LC 68-20935. 1969. 10.00 o.p. (ISBN 0-8214-0050-9). Ohio U Pr.

Ethical Wisdom East &-or West. Ed. by George F. McLean. LC 78-106891. (Proceedings of the American Catholic Philosophical Association: Vol. 51). 1977. pap. 8.00 (ISBN 0-918090-11-3). Am Cath Philo.

Ethics. Aristotle. Tr. by John Warrington. 1963. 12.95x (ISBN 0-460-00547-2, Evman). Dutton.

Ethics. Alfred C. Ewing. 1965. pap. text ed. 6.95 (ISBN 0-02-910030-5). Free Pr.

Ethics. H. Nowell-Smith. 1958. 7.50 o.p. (ISBN 0-8022-1232-8). Philos Lib.

Ethics: A Bibliography. Richard H. Lineback. LC 76-24747. (Reference Library of the Humanities Ser.: Vol. 65). 1976. lib. bdg. 25.00 o.p. (ISBN 0-8240-9933-8). Garland Pub.

Ethics: Accounting Student Perceptions. James H. Sellers & Edward E. Milam. 50p. (Orig.). 1980. pap. 4.50 (ISBN 0-938004-00-X). U MS Bus Econ.

Ethics: An Introduction to Theories & Problems. William S. Sahakian. 272p. (Orig.). 1974. pap. 3.95 (ISBN 0-06-460139-0, CO 139, COS). Har-Row.

Ethics & Belief. Peter Baelz. LC 76-15425. 1977. pap. 3.95 (ISBN 0-8164-1229-4). Crossroad NY.

Ethics & Educational Policy. Ed. by Kenneth A. Strike & Kieran Egan. (International Library of the Philosophy of Education). 1978. 18.50x (ISBN 0-7100-8423-4); pap. 7.95 (ISBN 0-7100-0483-4). Routledge & Kegan.

Ethics & Engineering Curricula. Robert J. Baum. LC 80-10099. (Teaching of Ethics Ser.). 79p. 1980. pap. 4.00 (ISBN 0-916558-12-6). Hastings Ctr Inst Soc.

Ethics & Foreign Policy. Donald F. McHenry. LC 80-68410. (Distinguished Cria Lecture on Morality & Foreign Policy Ser.). 1980. pap. 4.00 (ISBN 0-87641-220-7). Coun Rel & Intl.

Ethics & Society: A Marxist Interpretation of Value. Milton Fisk. LC 79-3513. 1980. 28.00x (ISBN 0-8147-2564-3). NYU Pr.

Ethics & Society in England: The Revolution in the Social Sciences, 1870-1914. Reba N. Soffer. 1978. 22.75x (ISBN 0-520-03521-6). U of Cal Pr.

Ethics & the Search for Values. Ed. by Luis E. Navia & Eugene Kelly. LC 80-82123. 1980. pap. text ed. 12.95 (ISBN 0-87975-139-8). Prometheus Bks.

Ethics & Theology from the Other Side: Sounds of Moral Struggle. Enoch H. Oglesby. LC 79-62897. 1979. pap. text ed. 9.00 (ISBN 0-8191-0706-9). U Pr of Amer.

Ethics for Science Policy: Proceedings. Ed. by T. Segerstedt. (Illus.). 35.00 (ISBN 0-08-024464-5); pap. 13.75 (ISBN 0-08-024463-7). Pergamon.

Ethics for Scientific Researchers. 2nd ed. Charles E. Reagan. 184p. 1971. 11.75 (ISBN 0-398-01558-9). C C Thomas.

Ethics for the Affluent. Peter L. Danner. LC 80-5528. 424p. 1980. lib. bdg. 22.50 (ISBN 0-8191-1163-5); pap. text ed. 14.25 (ISBN 0-8191-1164-3). U Pr of Amer.

Ethics in a Permissive Society. William Barclay. LC 70-175157. 1972. 9.95 (ISBN 0-06-060415-8, Harpr). Har-Row.

Ethics in an Age of Pervasive Technology. Ed. by Melvin Kranzberg. 220p. 1980. lib. bdg. 25.00x (ISBN 0-89158-686-5). Westview.

Ethics in Business. Thomas R. Masterson & J. Carlton Nunan. 240p. 1969. text ed. 18.50x (ISBN 0-8290-0288-X). Irvington.

Ethics in Business Conduct: A Guide to Information Sources. Ed. by Portia Christian & Richard Hicks. LC 77-127411. (Management Information Guides Ser.: No. 21). 1970. 30.00 (ISBN 0-8103-0821-5). Gale.

Ethics in Human Communication. Richard L. Johannesen. LC 74-24780. 176p. pap. text ed. 5.95x (ISBN 0-917974-58-1). Waveland Pr.

Ethics in Nursing. Martin Benjamin & Joy Curtis. 250p. 1981. text ed. 13.95x (ISBN 0-19-502836-8); pap. text ed. 7.95x (ISBN 0-19-502837-6). Oxford U Pr.

Ethics in Social Research: Protecting the Interests of Human Subjects. Robert T. Bower & Priscilla De Gasparis. LC 78-19452. 1978. 24.95 (ISBN 0-03-046406-4). Praeger.

Ethics in the Education of Business Managers. Charles W. Powers & David Vogel. LC 80-10147. (Teaching of Ethics Ser.). 81p. 1980. pap. 5.00 (ISBN 0-916558-10-X). Hastings Ctr Inst Soc.

Ethics in the New Testament: Change & Development. Jack T. Sanders. LC 74-26342. 160p. 1975. 8.95 (ISBN 0-8006-0404-0, 1-404). Fortress.

Ethics in the Soviet Union Today. Howard L. Parsons. 1967. pap. 1.00 (ISBN 0-89977-016-9). Am Inst Marxist.

Ethics in the Undergraduate Curriculum. Bernard Rosen & Arthur L. Caplan. LC 80-12351. (Teaching of Ethics Ser.). 67p. 1980. pap. 4.00 (ISBN 0-916558-13-4). Hastings Ctr Inst Soc.

Ethics: Inventing Right & Wrong. J. L. Mackie. 1977. pap. 2.50 (ISBN 0-14-021957-9, Pelican). Penguin.

Ethics of Aristotle: The Nicomachean Ethics. rev ed. Ed. by Hugh Tredennick. Tr. by J. A. Thomson. 1977. pap. 3.95 (ISBN 0-14-044055-0). Penguin.

Ethics of Belief. James Livingston. LC 74-18616. (American Academy of Religion. Studies in Religion). 1974. pap. 7.50 (ISBN 0-88420-121-X, 010009). Scholars Pr Ca.

Ethics of Buddhism. S. Tachibana. 1975. text ed. 11.75x (ISBN 0-7007-0077-3). Humanities.

Ethics of Buddhism. Pref. by Shundo Tachibana. LC 74-20477. 288p. 1975. Repr. of 1926 ed. text ed. 18.50x (ISBN 0-06-496720-4). B&N.

Ethics of Competition. Frank H. Knight. (Midway Reprint Ser.). 1935. pap. 15.00x (ISBN 0-226-44687-5). U of Chicago Pr.

Ethics of Corporate Conduct. Ed. by Clarence Walton. (American Assembly Ser.). (Illus.). 1977. pap. 4.95 (ISBN 0-13-290536-1, Spec). P-H.

Ethics of Deliberate Death. Eike-Henner W. Kluge. (National University Publications, Multidisciplinary Studies in the Law). 1981. 17.50 (ISBN 0-8046-9264-5). Kennikat.

Ethics of Fetal Research. Paul Ramsey. LC 74-27633. 96p. 1975. 8.95x (ISBN 0-300-01879-7); pap. 2.95x (ISBN 0-300-01880-0). Yale U Pr.

Ethics of G.E. Moore: A New Interpretation. John Hill. 156p. 1976. Repr. text ed. 16.75x o.p. (ISBN 0-685-66836-3). Humanities.

Ethics of Health Care. Institute of Medicine. Ed. by Laurence Tancredi. LC 74-28130. xi, 313p. 1974. pap. 8.25 (ISBN 0-309-02249-5). Natl Acad Pr.

Ethics of Intensity in American Fiction. Anthony C. Hilfer. 264p. 1981. text ed. 19.95x (ISBN 0-292-72029-7). U of Tex Pr.

Ethics of International Economics: An Innovative Approach to World Affairs. Sidney H. Scheuer. 192p. 1980. 8.50 (ISBN 0-682-49653-7). Exposition.

Ethics of Manipulation: Issues in Medicine, Behavior Control & Genetics. Bernard Haring. 200p. 1976. 8.95 (ISBN 0-8164-0289-2). Crossroad NY.

Ethics of Martin Luther King, Jr. Ervin Smith. (Studies in American Religion: Vol. 2). 1981. soft cover 24.95x (ISBN 0-88946-974-1). E Mellen.

Ethics of Resource Allocations. Ed. by K. Boyd. 128p. 1980. text ed. 12.00x (ISBN 0-85224-368-5, Pub. by Edinburgh U Pr Scotland). Columbia U Pr.

Ethics of Speech Communication. 2nd ed. Thomas R. Nilsen. LC 72-86834. 1974. pap. 3.50 (ISBN 0-672-61300-X, SC10). Bobbs.

Ethics of the Business System. Marshall Missner. LC 79-22806. 1980. pap. 8.95 (ISBN 0-88284-100-9). Alfred Pub.

Ethics of the Fathers. Philip Blackman. 166p. 1980. pap. 3.95 (ISBN 0-910818-15-0). Judaica Pr.

Ethics of World Religions. Arnold D. Hunt & Robert B. Grotty. (Illus.). (gr. 9-12). 1978. lib. bdg. 8.95 (ISBN 0-912616-74-1); pap. 3.95 (ISBN 0-912616-73-3). Greenhaven.

Ethics on a Catholic University Campus: Symposium. Ed. by James Barry. 1980. pap. 5.95 (ISBN 0-8294-0369-8). Loyola.

Ethics, Politics & Epistemology: A Study in the Unity of Hume's Thought. Aryeh Botwinick. LC 80-5809. 197p. 1980. lib. bdg. 17.50 (ISBN 0-8191-1288-7); pap. text ed. 9.00 (ISBN 0-8191-1289-5). U Pr of Amer.

Ethics, Professionalism, & Maintaining Competence: Proceedings. ASCE Professional Activities Committee Conference, March 1977. Compiled By American Society of Civil Engineers. 360p. 1977. pap. text ed. 18.50 (ISBN 0-87262-076-X). Am Soc Civil Eng.

Ethics Teaching in Higher Education. Ed. by Daniel Callahan & Sissela Bok. (Hastings Center Monograph Ser.). 275p. 1980. 19.50 (ISBN 0-306-40522-9). Plenum Pub.

Ethics: Theory and Practice. Jacques P. Thiroux. 1977. pap. text ed. 5.95 (ISBN 0-02-479230-6). Macmillan.

Ethics, Value, & Reality: Selected Papers of Aurel Kolnai. Aurel Kolnai. LC 77-83145. 1978. 25.00 (ISBN 0-915144-39-5); pap. text ed. 12.50 (ISBN 0-915144-40-9). Hackett Pub.

Ethiopia. Barbara Nolen. LC 70-131149. (First Bks). (Illus.). (gr. 4-6). 1971. PLB 4.90 o.p. (ISBN 0-531-00733-2). Watts.

Ethiopia & the Red Sea: The Rise & Decline of the Solomonic Dynasty & Muslim-European Rivalry in the Region. Mordechai Abir. 272p. 1980. 25.00x (ISBN 0-7146-3164-7, F Cass Co). Biblio Dist.

Ethiopia, the Horn of Africa, & U. S. Policy. John H. Spencer. LC 77-87562. (Foreign Policy Reports Ser.). 1977. 5.00 (ISBN 0-89549-005-6). Inst Foreign Policy Anal.

Ethiopia: The Modernization of Autocracy. Robert L. Hess. Ed. by Gwendolen M. Carter. LC 79-120290. (Africa in the Modern World Ser). (Illus.). 294p. 1971. pap. 6.95x (ISBN 0-8014-9107-X, CP107). Cornell U Pr.

Ethiopian Journeys: Travels in Ethiopia 1969-72. Paul B. Henze. (Illus.). 1978. lib. bdg. 39.50 o.p. (ISBN 0-510-44220-X). Westview.

Ethiopian Perspectives: A Bibliographical Guide to the History of Ethiopia. Compiled by Clifton F. Brown. LC 77-89111. (African Bibliographic Center, Special Bibliographic Series, New Series: No. 5). lib. bdg. 22.50 (ISBN 0-8371-9850-X, BET/). Greenwood.

Ethiopians Speak: Studies in Cultural Background. Wolf Leslau. Incl. No. I. Harari. (U. C. Publ. in Near Eastern Studies: Vol. 7). 1965. pap. 11.50x (ISBN 0-520-09300-3); No. II. Chaha. (U. C. Publ. in Near Eastern Studies: Vol. 9). 1966. pap. 10.50x (ISBN 0-520-09303-8). U of Cal Pr.

Ethiopic Book of Enoch, 2 vols. Ed. by M. A. Knibb. 1979. 89.00x set (ISBN 0-19-826163-2). Oxford U Pr.

Ethnic Almanac. Stephanie Bernardo. LC 78-14694. (Illus.). 576p. 1981. 19.95 (ISBN 0-385-14143-2). Doubleday.

Ethnic Almanac. Stephanie Bernardo. LC 80-14694. (Illus.). 576p. 1981. pap. 10.95 (ISBN 0-385-14144-0, Dolp). Doubleday.

Ethnic America. Ed. by Marjorie P. Weiser. (Reference Shelf Ser.: Vol. 50, No. 2). 1978. 6.25 (ISBN 0-8242-0623-1). Wilson.

Ethnic America: A History. Thomas Sowell. (Illus.). 336p. 1981. 16.95 (ISBN 0-465-02074-7). Basic.

Ethnic & Political Nations in Europe. Jaroslav Krejci & V. Velimsky. 1980. write for info. St Martin.

Ethnic & Racial Segregation Patterns in the New York City Metropolis: Residential Patterns Among White Ethnic Groups, Blacks & Puerto Ricans. Nathan Kantrowitz. LC 72-86840. (Special Studies in U.S. Economic, Social & Political Issues). 1973. 29.50x (ISBN 0-275-06550-2). Irvington.

Ethnic Autonomy: Comparative Dynamics - the Americas, Europe & the Developing World. Ed. by Raymond L. Hall. (Pergamon Policy Studies). 1979. 47.00 (ISBN 0-08-023683-9); pap. 10.95 (ISBN 0-08-023682-0). Pergamon.

Ethnic Change. Ed. by Charles F. Keyes. LC 80-54426. (Publications on Ethnicity & Nationality of the School of International Studies: No. 2). 306p. 1981. 20.00 (ISBN 0-295-95812-X). U of Wash Pr.

Ethnic Chicago. Ed. by Peter D. Jones & Melvin G. Holli. 336p. (Orig.). 1981. pap. 12.95 (ISBN 0-8028-1821-8). Eerdmans.

Ethnic Chronologies Series, 31 vols. 1979. Set. 275.00 (ISBN 0-379-00494-1). Oceana.

Ethnic Conflict in International Relations. Astri Suhrke & Lela G. Noble. LC 77-83444. (Praeger Special Studies). 1978. 24.95 (ISBN 0-03-040681-1). Praeger.

Ethnic Dilemma in Social Services. Shirley Jenkins. LC 80-2155. (Illus.). 1981. 14.95 (ISBN 0-02-916400-1). Free Pr.

Ethnic Diversity & Conflict in Eastern Europe. Ed. by Peter F. Sugar. 500p. 1980. 22.50 (ISBN 0-87436-297-0). ABC-Clio.

Ethnic Drinking Subcultures. Andrew Greeley & William C. McCready. LC 79-13904. 144p. 1980. 18.95 (ISBN 0-03-052731-7). Praeger.

Ethnic Enterprise in America: Business & Welfare Among Chinese, Japanese, & Blacks. Ivan H. Light. 1972. 15.75x (ISBN 0-520-01738-2); pap. 5.75x (ISBN 0-520-02485-0). U of Cal Pr.

Ethnic Film & Filmstrip Guide for Libraries & Media Centers: A Selective Filmography. Lubomyr R. Wynar & Lois Buttlar. LC 80-18056. 277p. 1980. lib. bdg. 25.00x (ISBN 0-87287-233-5). Libs Unl.

Ethnic Groups & Social Change in a Chinese Market Town. C. Fred Blake. (Asian Studies at Hawaii: No. 27). 192p. (Orig.). 1981. pap. 10.50x (ISBN 0-8248-0720-0). U Pr of Hawaii.

Ethnic Groups of America; Their Morbidity, Mortality & Behavior Disorders, Vol. 2: The Blacks. Ed. by Ailon Shiloh & Ida C. Selavan. (Illus.). 312p. 1974. 24.50 (ISBN 0-398-03022-7); pap. 17.50 (ISBN 0-398-03023-5). C C Thomas.

Ethnic Groups of America: Their Morbidity, Mortality & Behavior Disorders, Vol. 1. The Jews. Ed. by Ailon Shiloh & Ida C. Selevan. (Illus.). 446p. 1973. text ed. 24.50 (ISBN 0-398-02610-6); pap. text ed. 17.50 (ISBN 0-398-02619-X). C C Thomas.

Ethnic Heritage Studies Program Catalog: 1974-1979. Regina McCormick. (Illus.). 152p. (Orig.). 1980. pap. 9.95 (ISBN 0-89994-247-4). Soc Sci Ed.

Ethnic Identities in a Transnational World. Ed. by John F. Stack, Jr. LC 80-1199. (Contributions in Political Science Ser.: No. 52). 264p. 1981. lib. bdg. 27.50 (ISBN 0-313-21088-8, SEI/). Greenwood.

Ethnic Information Sources of the United States: A Guide to Organizations, Agencies, Foundations, Institutions, Media, Commercial & Trade Bodies, Government Programs, Research Institutes, Libraries & Museums, Etc. Ed. by Paul Wasserman & Jean Morgan. LC 76-4642. 350p. 1976. 70.00 (ISBN 0-8103-0373-6). Gale.

Ethnic Jewelry: Design & Inspiration for Craftsmen & Collectors. Dona Z. Meilach. Ed. by Brandt Aymar. (Illus.). 192p. 1981. pap. 19.95 (ISBN 0-517-52974-2, Harmony). Crown.

Ethnic Jewelry: Design & Inspiration for Craftsmen & Collectors. Dona Z. Meilach. Ed. by Brant Aymar. 1981. price not set. Crown.

Ethnic Myth: Race, Ethnicity & Class in America. Stephen Steinberg. LC 80-69377. 1981. 12.95 (ISBN 0-689-11151-7). Atheneum.

Ethnic Patterns in American Cities. Stanley Lieberson. LC 63-7551. 1962. 15.95 (ISBN 0-02-918980-2). Free Pr.

Ethnic Politics in Malaysia. Raj K. Vasil. (Illus.). 234p. 1980. text ed. 16.00x (ISBN 0-391-01770-5). Humanities.

Ethnic Resurgence in Modern Democratic States: A Multidisciplinary Approach to Human Resources & Conflict. Ed. by Uri Ra'Anan. (Pergamon Policy Studies). 1980. 32.50 (ISBN 0-08-024647-8). Pergamon.

Ethnic Russia in the U. S. S. R. The Dilemma of Dominance. Ed. by Edward Allworth. LC 79-22959. (Pergamon Policy Studies Ser.). 270p. 37.50 (ISBN 0-08-023700-2). Pergamon.

Ethnic Serials: At Selected University of California Libaries. 1977. pap. 5.50x o.p. (ISBN 0-686-16210-2). Asian Am Stud.

Ethnic Soldiers: State Security in a Divided Society. Cynthia Enloe. LC 79-5418. 269p. 1980. 19.00x (ISBN 0-8203-0507-3). U of Ga Pr.

Ethnic Studies Sampler: The Best of the Title IX Project Materials. Ed. by Frances Haley. (Orig.). 1981. pap. write for info. (ISBN 0-89994-251-2). Soc Sci Ed.

Ethnic Voters & the Election of Lincoln. Ed. by Frederick C. Luebke. LC 72-139370. xxxii, 226p. 1971. 13.95x (ISBN 0-8032-0796-4); pap. 3.25x (ISBN 0-8032-5738-4, BB 567, Bison). U of Nebr Pr.

Ethnicity. A. M. Greeley. (Concilium Ser.: Vol. 101). 1977. pap. 4.95 (ISBN 0-8164-2145-5). Crossroad NY.

Ethnicity & Mental Health: Research & Recommendations. Joseph Giordano. 1980. pap. 2.00 (ISBN 0-87495-006-6). Am Jewish Comm.

Ethnicity & Political Integration: Ashanti, Ghana. Minion K. Morrison. (Foreign & Comparative Studies Program African Ser.: No. XXXVI). 1981. pap. text ed. price not set (ISBN 0-915984-59-8). Syracuse U Foreign Comp.

Ethnicity & U. S. Foreign Policy. Ed. by Abdul A. Said. LC 77-7812. (Praeger Special Studies). 1978. 22.95 (ISBN 0-03-021806-3). Praeger.

Ethnicity at Work. Ed. by Sandra Wallman. 1979. text ed. 26.75 o.p. (ISBN 0-8419-5056-3); pap. text ed. 14.50x (ISBN 0-8419-5057-1). Holmes & Meier.

Ethnicity in Contemporary Africa. Robert H. Bates. LC 73-86994. (Foreign & Comparative Studies-Eastern African Ser.: No. 14). 59p. 1973. pap. 3.50x (ISBN 0-915984-11-3). Syracuse U Foreign Comp.

Ethnicity in Modern Africa. Ed. by Brian M. Du Toit. LC 78-58295. (Special Studies on Africa Ser.). 1978. lib. bdg. 27.50x (ISBN 0-89158-314-9). Westview.

Ethnicity in the United States: A Preliminary Reconnaissance. Andrew M. Greeley. LC 74-11483. (Urban Research Ser). 384p. 1974. 23.95 (ISBN 0-471-32465-5, Pub. by Wiley-Interscience). Wiley.

Ethnicity on the Great Plains. Ed. by Frederick C. Luebke. LC 79-17743. (Illus.). xxxiv, 237p. 1980. 15.95x (ISBN 0-8032-2855-4). U of Nebr Pr.

Ethnics in a Borderland: An Inquiry into the Nature of Ethnicity & Reduction of Ethnic Tensions in a One-Time Genocide Area. Feliks Gross. LC 77-94741. (Contributions in Sociology: No. 32). 1978. lib. bdg. 19.95 (ISBN 0-313-20310-5, GET/). Greenwood.

Ethnics in American Politics: American Indians. Frances Svensson. LC 72-88751. (Critical Issues in Political Science Ser.). 1973. pap. 2.95 o.p. (ISBN 0-8087-1972-6). Burgess.

Ethnics, Machines, & the American Urban Future. Ed. by Scott Greer. 1981. pap. text ed. 14.25x (ISBN 0-87073-227-7); pap. text ed. 7.95x (ISBN 0-87073-228-5). Schenkman.

Ethnoarchaeology. Ed. by Carol Kramer. 1979. 25.00x (ISBN 0-231-04182-9). Columbia U Pr.

Ethnoarchaeology. Ed. by Carol Kramer. 1980. pap. 10.00x (ISBN 0-231-04182-9). Columbia U Pr.

Ethnographic Atlas of Ifugao. Harold C. Conklin. LC 79-689774. (Illus.). 124p. 1980. text ed. 75.00x (ISBN 0-300-02529-7). Yale U Pr.

Ethnographic Bibliography of North America, 5 vols. 4th ed. George P. Murdock & Timothy O'Leary. Incl. Vol. 1. 492p (ISBN 0-87536-205-2); Vol. 2. 294p (ISBN 0-87536-207-9); Vol. 3. 304p (ISBN 0-87536-209-5); Vol. 4. 292p (ISBN 0-87536-211-7); Vol. 5. 444p (ISBN 0-87536-213-3). LC 75-17091. (Behavior Science Bibliographies Ser.). 1975. text ed. 35.00 ea. HRAFP.

Ethnographic Film. Karl G. Heider. LC 76-10454. (Illus.). 1976. text ed. 6.95x (ISBN 0-292-72020-3); pap. text ed. 5.95x (ISBN 0-292-72025-4). U of Tex Pr.

Ethnographica Carpatho-Balcanica. Bela Gunda. (Illus.). 427p. (Eng, Fr. & Ger.). 1979. 45.00x (ISBN 963-05-1747-7). Intl Pubns Serv.

Ethnography & Language in Educational Settings, Vol. 5. Ed. by Judith Green & Cynthia Wallat. (Advances in Discourse Processes Ser.). 368p. 1980. text ed. 29.50 (ISBN 0-89391-035-X). Ablex Pub.

Ethnography of a Chiropractic Clinic: Definitions of a Deviant Situation. James B. Cowie & Julian B. Roebuck. LC 75-2811. (Illus.). 1975. 14.95 (ISBN 0-02-906730-8). Free Pr.

Ethnography of Malinowski: The Trobriand Islands, 1915-18. Bronislaw Malinowski. Ed. by Michael W. Young. (Illus.). 1979. 24.00x (ISBN 0-7100-0013-8); pap. 12.95 (ISBN 0-7100-0100-2). Routledge & Kegan.

Ethnography of Santa Clara Pueblo. W. W. Hill. Ed. by Charles H. Lange. (Illus.). 550p. 1981. 35.00x (ISBN 0-8263-0555-5). U of NM Pr.

Ethnography of Southwestern Angola: The Hero People, Vol. 3. Carlos Esterman. LC 75-8794. (Illus.). 1981. text ed. 39.50x (ISBN 0-8419-0206-2, Africana). Holmes & Meier.

Ethnography of Variation: Selected Writings on Pidgins & Creoles. Hugo Schuchardt. Ed. & tr. by T. L. Markey. (Linguistica Extranea: Studia 3). 174p. 1979. lib. bdg. 7.50 (ISBN 0-89720-003-9); pap. 5.50 (ISBN 0-89720-004-7). Karoma.

Ethnological Notebooks of Karl Marx: Studies of Morgan, Phear, Maine, Lubbock. Karl Marx. Ed. by Lawrence Krader. 448p. 1972. text ed. 52.00x (ISBN 90-0232-0924-9). Humanities.

Ethnology in Folklore. George L. Gomme. LC 79-75802. 1969. Repr. of 1892 ed. 15.00 (ISBN 0-8103-3832-7). Gale.

Ethnology of Law. 2nd ed. Leopold J. Pospisil. LC 77-75811. 1978. pap. text ed. 6.95 (ISBN 0-8465-5825-4). Benjamin-Cummings.

Ethnopharmacologic Search for Psychoactive Drugs: Proceedings. Ed. by Daniel Efron et al. LC 79-3955. 1979. Repr. of 1967 ed. text ed. 26.00 softcover (ISBN 0-89004-047-8). Raven.

Ethnopsychoanalysis: Psychoanalysis & Anthropology As Complementary Frames of Reference. George Devereux. LC 74-16708. 1978. 27.50x (ISBN 0-520-02864-3). U of Cal Pr.

Ethocratie Ou le Gouvernement Fonde Sur la Morale. Paul-Henri Thiry Holbach. (Fr.). 1977. lib. bdg. 33.00x o.p. (ISBN 0-8287-0441-4); pap. text ed. 23.00x o.p. (ISBN 0-685-77009-5). Clearwater Pub.

Ethology & Ethics of Farm Animal Production. Ed. by D. W. Folsch. (Animal Management Ser.: No. 6). 144p. (Ger. & Eng.). 1978. pap. 19.50 (ISBN 3-7643-1004-9). Birkhauser.

Ethology & Nonverbal Communication in Mental Health: An Interdisciplinary Biopsychosocial Exploration. S. A. Corson & E. O'Leary Corson. LC 79-41689. (International Ser. in Biopsychosocial Sciences). (Illus.). 290p. 1980. 48.00 (ISBN 0-08-023728-2). Pergamon.

Ethology & Society: Towards an Anthropological View. Hilary Callan. 1970. 22.50x (ISBN 0-19-823161-X). Oxford U Pr.

Ethos of Restoration Comedy. Ben R. Schneider, Jr. LC 70-140670. 1971. 10.00 (ISBN 0-252-00151-6). U of Ill Pr.

Ethyl Alcohol Production & Use As a Motor Fuel. Ed. by J. K. Paul. LC 79-22900. (Energy Tech Review, Chemical Tech Review No. 51: No. 144). (Illus.). 1980. 48.00 (ISBN 0-8155-0780-1). Noyes.

Ethylene Oxide Control in Hospitals. William J. Daley et al. LC 79-22184. 48p. (Orig.). 1979. pap. 6.25 (ISBN 0-87258-291-4, 1400). Am Hospital.

Ethylenethiourea. Ed. by P. C. Kearney. 14p. 1977. pap. text ed. 10.00 (ISBN 0-08-022026-6). Pergamon.

Ethylenimine & Other Aziridines: Chemistry - Applications. O. C. Dermer & G. E. Ham. 1969. 67.00 (ISBN 0-12-209650-9). Acad Pr.

Etica Christiana del Amor. Norman Geisler. Tr. by Arnoldo Canclini from Eng. LC 77-15813. 126p. (Orig., Span.). 1977. pap. 2.50 (ISBN 0-89922-103-3). Edit Caribe.

Etica Para la Era Atomica. facsimile ed. Ana M. O'Neill. 6.25 (ISBN 0-8477-2815-3); pap. 5.00 o.s.i. (ISBN 0-8477-2807-2). U of PR Pr.

Etidorhpa. John U. Lloyd. 386p. 1981. pap. 15.00 (ISBN 0-89540-004-9). Sun Pub.

Etienne Pasquier. L. Clark Keating. (World Authors Ser.: France: No. 241). lib. bdg. 10.95 (ISBN 0-8057-2674-8). Twayne.

Etiology of Cleft Lip & Cleft Palate. Ed. by Michael Melnick & David Bixler. (Progress in Clinical & Biological Research: Vol. 46). 566p. 1980. 40.00 (ISBN 0-8451-0046-7). A R Liss.

Etiquette for Today. Sheila Ostrander. (Illus., Orig.). (gr. 9-12). 1967. pap. 3.50 (ISBN 0-06-463272-5, EH 272, EH). Har-Row.

Etiquette, Your Ticket to Good Times. Helen Hoke. LC 70-93223. (First Bks). (Illus.). (gr. 4-6). 1970. PLB 4.90 o.p. (ISBN 0-531-00686-7). Watts.

Etiudy Po Psikhologii Tvorchestva. I. D. Ermakov. (Rus.). 1981. 15.00 (ISBN 0-88233-500-6); pap. 5.00 (ISBN 0-88233-501-4). Ardis Pubs.

Etoile du Nord. Giacomo Meyerbeer. LC 76-49198. (Early Romantic Opera Ser.: Vol. 22). 1980. lib. bdg. 82.00 (ISBN 0-8240-2921-6). Garland Pub.

Etranger. A. Camus. Ed. by G. Brae & C. Lynes. 1955. pap. 7.95 o.p. (ISBN 0-13-530790-2). P-H.

Etranger de Camus: Un Texte, ses lecteurs, leurs lectures. new ed. B. Fitch. (Collection L). 176p. (Orig., Fr.). 1972. pap. 13.95 (ISBN 2-03-036005-8). Larousse.

Etruscan Art. Otto J. Brendel. 1979. pap. 15.00 (ISBN 0-14-056143-9, Pelican). Penguin.

Etruscan Red-Figured Vase-Painting at Caere. Mario A. Del Chiaro. 1975. 35.00x (ISBN 0-520-02578-4). U of Cal Pr.

Etruscans. D. Hamblin. LC 74-25453. (Emergence of Man Ser.). (Illus.). 160p. (gr. 6 up). 1975. lib. bdg. 9.63 o.p. (ISBN 0-8094-1292-6). Silver.

Etruscans. Dora J. Hamblin. (Emergence of Man Ser.). (Illus.). 1975. 9.95 (ISBN 0-8094-1291-8); lib. bdg. avail. (ISBN 0-685-72432-8). Time-Life.

Etruscans. rev. ed. Massimo Pallottino. Ed. by David Ridgway. Tr. by J. Cremona from It. LC 74-6082. (Illus.). 320p. 1975. 12.50x (ISBN 0-253-32080-1). Ind U Pr.

Etruscans: Their Art & Civilization. Emeline Richardson. LC 64-15817. (Illus.). 1976. pap. 9.50 (ISBN 0-226-71235-4, P670, Phoen). U of Chicago Pr.

Etude de l'expression francaise: Cours elementaire I - le francais. (Illus., Fr.). 1969. 7.25 (ISBN 0-685-13911-5, 4019). Larousse.

Etude Sur le Mouvement Communaliste a Paris En 1871. Gustave Lefrancais. (Commune De Paris en 1871). (Fr.). 1977. lib. bdg. 28.75x o.p. (ISBN 0-8287-0520-8); pap. text ed. 18.75x o.p. (ISBN 0-685-77002-8). Clearwater Pub.

Etude Sur Le Mouvement D'art Decoratif En Allemagne. Charles E. Jeanneret, pseud. LC 68-26652. (Architecture & Decorative Art Ser). (Fr). 1968. Repr. of 1912 ed. lib. bdg. 22.50 (ISBN 0-306-71147-8). Da Capo.

Etude Sur les Ministeriales En Flandre et En Lotharingie. Francois L. Ganshof. LC 80-2029. 1981. Repr. of 1926 ed. 44.50 (ISBN 0-404-18563-0). AMS Pr.

Etude sur l'Histoire des Alleux en France avec une Carte des Pays Allodiaux. Emile Chenon. LC 80-2036. 1981. Repr. of 1888 ed. 33.00 (ISBN 0-404-18557-6). AMS Pr.

Etudes. Maurits I. Boas. LC 80-70949. 160p. 1981. 9.95 (ISBN 0-8119-0344-3). Fell.

Etudes De Theologie Positive Sur la Sainte Trinite: Theories Grecques Des Processions Divines. Theodore De Regnon. LC 80-2363. (Troisieme Ser., II). 1981. Repr. of 1893 ed. 67.00 (ISBN 0-404-18915-6). AMS Pr.

Etudes Franques, I: Aux Origines De la Noblesse. Joseph Balon. LC 80-2202. 1981. Repr. of 1963 ed. 16.50 (ISBN 0-404-18551-7). AMS Pr.

Etudes Litteraires Slavo-Romanes. Riccardo Picchio. (Studia Historica et Philologica Ser.: Vol. VI). (Fr.). 1978. write for info. o.p. (ISBN 8-7774-0005-4, Pub. by Licosa Editrice Italy). Schoenhof.

Etudes Rurales, Vol. 14, Nos. 53-56. Agriculture et Societes En Asie Du Sudest. (Illus.). 1974. pap. 50.50x (ISBN 0-686-20910-9). Mouton.

Etudes Sur la Naissance Des Principautes Territoriales En France, IXe-IXe Siecle. Jan Dhondt. LC 80-2033. 1981. Repr. of 1948 ed. 38.50 (ISBN 0-404-18560-6). AMS Pr.

Etudes sur la Poesie Latine: Nature et Mission du Poete. Jean Cousin. Ed. by Steele Commager. LC 77-70760. (Latin Poetry Ser.). 1979. Repr. of 1945 ed. lib. bdg. 28.00 (ISBN 0-8240-2965-8). Garland Pub.

Etymological Dictionary of Family & Christian Names. William Arthur. LC 68-17911. 1969. Repr. of 1857 ed. 24.00 (ISBN 0-8103-3107-1). Gale.

Etymological Dictionary of Harari. Wolf Leslau. (U. C. Publ. in Near Eastern Studies: Vol. 1). 1963. pap. 9.00x (ISBN 0-520-09293-7). U of Cal Pr.

Etymological Dictionary of Modern English, 2 Vols. Ernest Weekley. 1967. pap. text ed. 6.00 ea.; Vol. 1. pap. text ed. (ISBN 0-486-21873-2); Vol. 2. pap. text ed. (ISBN 0-486-21874-0). Dover.

Etymological Dictionary of Pre-Thirteenth Century Turkish. Gerard Clauson. 1040p. 1972. 125.00x (ISBN 0-19-864112-5). Oxford U Pr.

Etymological Dictionary of the English Language. rev. & enl. ed. Ed. by Walter W. Skeat. 1910. 58.00x (ISBN 0-19-863104-9). Oxford U Pr.

Etymological Dictionary of the Russian Language. Alexander G. Preobrazhensky. LC 52-3699. (Columbia Slavic Studies). 50.00 (ISBN 0-231-01889-4). Columbia U Pr.

Etymology & Usage of Peirar in Early Greek Poetry. Ann L. Bergren. (American Philological Association, American Classical Studies). 1975. pap. 6.00 (ISBN 0-89130-242-5, 400402). Scholars Pr Ca.

Eucalypts for Wood Production. W. E. Hillis & A. G. Brown. 1980. 50.00x (ISBN 0-643-02245-7, Pub. by CSJRO Australia). State Mutual Bk.

Eucalyptus Seed. D. J. Boland et al. (Illus.). 191p. 1980. 25.00x (ISBN 0-643-02586-3, Pub. by Timber Pr.). Intl Schol Bk Serv.

Eucharist & Our Everyday Life. Bernard Haring. (Orig.). 1979. pap. 3.95 (ISBN 0-8164-0037-7). Crossroad NY.

Eucharistic Theology. Joseph M. Powers. 1972. pap. 3.95 (ISBN 0-8164-2545-0). Crossroad NY.

Eucharistic Theology of Theodore Beza: Development of the Reformed Doctrine. Jill Raitt. LC 74-188907. (American Academy of Religion. Studies in Religion). 1972. pap. 7.50 (ISBN 0-89130-156-9, 010004). Scholars Pr Ca.

Eucharius Rosslin in the Younger: On Minerals & Mineral Products. Ed. by Johanna Schwind-Belkin & Earle R. Caley. (Arts Medica, Abeilung IV: Landessprachliche und Mittelalterliche Medizin I). 415p. 1978. text ed. 150.00x (ISBN 3-11006-907-5). De Gruyter.

Euclidean & Non-Euclidean Geometries: Development & History. 2nd ed. Marvin J. Greenberg. LC 79-19348. (Illus.). 1980. text ed. 19.95x (ISBN 0-7167-1103-6); instrs. manual & answer book avail. W H Freeman.

Euclides Vindicatus. 2nd ed. Girolamo Saccheri. Tr. by George B. Halstead from Lat. 1980. text ed. 12.95 (ISBN 0-8284-0289-2). Chelsea Pub.

Eudora Welty. Elizabeth Evans. LC 80-53702. (Modern Literature Ser.). 180p. 1981. 9.95 (ISBN 0-8044-2187-0). Ungar.

Eudora Welty. Ruth M. Vande Kieft. (U. S. Authors Ser.: No. 15). 1962. lib. bdg. 9.95 (ISBN 0-8057-0776-X). Twayne.

Eugene C. Barker: Historian. William C. Pool. LC 76-627820. (Illus.). 1971. 10.50 (ISBN 0-87611-025-1). Tex St Hist Assn.

Eugene Carson Blake: Prophet with Portfolio. R. Douglas Brackenridge. LC 77-25281. (Illus.). 1978. 12.95 (ISBN 0-8164-0383-X). Crossroad NY.

Eugene Delacroix: His Life & Works. Charles Baudelaire. Ed. by Sydney J. Freedberg. LC 77-18676. (Connoisseurship Criticism & Art History Ser.: Vol. 2). (Illus.). 1979. lib. bdg. 24.00 (ISBN 0-8240-3258-6). Garland Pub.

Eugene Ionesco. Richard N. Coe. 1968. pap. 1.50 (ISBN 0-394-17161-6, B 235, BC). Grove.

Eugene Ionesco. Leonard C. Pronko. LC 65-16380. (Columbia Essays on Modern Writers Ser.: No. 7). (Orig.). 1965. pap. 2.00 (ISBN 0-231-02681-1, MW7). Columbia U Pr.

Eugene Onegin: A Novel in Verse, 2 vols. Aleksandr Pushkin. Tr. by Vladimir Nabokov from Russ. LC 80-8730. (Bollingen Ser.: Vol. LXXII). 1460p. 1981. 80.00x (ISBN 0-691-09744-5); pap. 18.00 (ISBN 0-691-01837-5). Princeton U Pr.

Eugene Onegin: Revised & Enlarged Edition. rev. enlarged ed. Alexander Pushkin. Tr. by Walter Arndt. 304p. 1981. pap. 5.95 (ISBN 0-525-47591-5). Dutton.

Eugene O'neill. rev. ed. Frederic I. Carpenter. (United States Authors Ser.: No. 66). 1979. lib. bdg. 9.95 (ISBN 0-8057-7267-7). Twayne.

Eugene O'Neill. Horst Frenz. Tr. by Helen Sebba. LC 79-143188. (Modern Literature Ser.). 1971. 10.95 (ISBN 0-8044-2211-7); pap. 3.45 (ISBN 0-8044-6159-7). Ungar.

Eugene O'neill's Tragic Vision. C. P. Sinha. 1981. text ed. 16.00 (ISBN 0-391-02203-2). Humanities.

Eugene, Oregon--a Guide: America's Most Livable City. Mike Helm. LC 79-63656. (Illus.). 1979. 5.95 (ISBN 0-931742-01-3). Rainy Day Oreg.

Eugene V. Debs. Harold W. Currie. LC 76-3780. (U. S. Authors Ser.: No. 267). 1976. lib. bdg. 12.50 (ISBN 0-8057-7167-0). Twayne.

Eugenia. Clare Darcy. 1977. 8.95 o.s.i. (ISBN 0-8027-0556-1). Walker & Co.

Eugenics: Galton & After. Charles P. Blacker. LC 78-20452. 1981. Repr. of 1952 ed. 25.00 (ISBN 0-88355-832-7). Hyperion Conn.

Eugenics: Hereditarian Attitudes in American Thought. Mark H. Haller. 1963. 15.50x o.p. (ISBN 0-8135-0429-5). Rutgers U Pr.

Eugenics: Then & Now. Ed. by Carl J. Bajema. LC 75-43761. (Benchmark Papers in Genetics Ser: Vol. 5). 400p. 1976. 40.50 (ISBN 0-12-786110-6). Acad Pr.

Eugenie & Napoleon III. David Duff. LC 78-57058. (Illus.). 1978. 12.95 o.p. (ISBN 0-688-03338-5). Morrow.

Eugenie Grandet. Honore De Balzac. Tr. by Ellen Marriage. 1955. 7.95x (ISBN 0-460-00169-8, Evman); pap. 1.95 o.p. (ISBN 0-460-01169-3, EP1169). Dutton.

Eugenie Grandet. Honore De Balzac. (Literature Ser). (gr. 10-12). 1970. pap. text ed. 3.42 (ISBN 0-87720-746-1). AMSCO Sch.

Eugenie, That Spanish Woman. F. W. Kenyon. 1978. pap. 1.95 (ISBN 0-505-51301-3). Tower Bks.

Euglena: An Experimental Organism for Biochemical & Biophysical Studies. Jerome J. Wolken. LC 67-13378. 204p. 1967. 19.50 (ISBN 0-306-50086-8, Plenum Pr). Plenum Pub.

Eukaryotic Gene Regulation, 2 vols. Gerald M. Kolodny. 1980. Vol. 1, 224p. 55.95 (ISBN 0-8493-5225-8); Vol. 2, 256p. 59.95 (ISBN 0-8493-5226-6). CRC Pr.

Eulogies of Howard, a Vision, Repr. Of 1791. William Hayley. Ed. by Donald H. Reiman. Bd. with Ballads, Founded on Anecdotes Relating to Animals, with Prints...by William Blake. Repr. of 1805 ed; Poems on Serious & Sacred Subjects, Printed Only As Private Tokens of Regard, for the Particular Friends of the Author. Repr. of 1818 ed. LC 75-31209. (Romantic Context Ser.: Poetry 1789-1830: Vol. 60). 1979. lib. bdg. 47.00 (ISBN 0-8240-2159-2). Garland Pub.

Eumenides. Aeschylus. Tr. by Gilbert Murray. 1925. pap. text ed. 3.95x (ISBN 0-04-882007-5). Allen Unwin.

Euphausiacea Bibliography: A World Literature Survey. M. A. McWhinnie et al. 1981. 50.01 (ISBN 0-08-024649-4). Pergamon.

Euphonia & the Flood. Mary Calhoun. LC 75-19274. (ps-4). 1976. 5.95 o.s.i. (ISBN 0-8193-0836-6, Four Winds); PLB 5.41 o.s.i. (ISBN 0-8193-0837-4); pap. 1.95 o.s.i. (ISBN 0-8193-0907-9, Pippin). Schol Bk Serv.

Euphrates & Tigris: Mesopotamian Ecology & Destiny. Ed. by J. Rzoska. (Monographiae Biologicae: No. 38). (Illus.). 122p. 1980. lib. bdg. 31.50 (ISBN 90-6193-090-1). Kluwer Boston.

Euphrates Exile. Alan D. MacDonald. LC 80-1920. 1981. Repr. of 1936 ed. 34.00 (ISBN 0-404-18979-2). AMS Pr.

Euphrosine et Coradin Ou le Tyran Corrige. Etienne N. Mehul. Ed. by Phillip Gossett & Charles Rosen. LC 76-49224. (Early Romantic Opera Ser.: No. 38). 1980. lib. bdg. 82.00 (ISBN 0-8240-2937-2). Garland Pub.

Eupsychian Management. Abraham H. Maslow. 1965. pap. text ed. 10.50 (ISBN 0-256-00353-X). Irwin.

Eura & Zephrya...with Poetical Pieces, Repr. Of 1816. David Booth. Bd. with Elizabeth Hitchener (1783?-1822) The Fire-Side Bagatelle, Containing Enigmas on the Chief Towns of England & Wales. Elizabeth Hitchener. Repr. of 1818 ed; Weald of Sussex, a Poem. Repr. of 1822 ed. LC 75-31163. (Romantic Context Ser.: Poetry 1789-1830: Vol. 18). 1978. lib. bdg. 47.00 (ISBN 0-8240-2117-7). Garland Pub.

Eurail Guide: How to Travel Europe & All the World by Train 1981. 11th ed. Marvin L. Saltzman & Kathryn S. Muileman. LC 72-83072. 816p. 1981. pap. 9.95 (ISBN 0-912442-11-5). Eurail Guide.

Eureka. Dale Seymour & Richard Gidley. 1967. pap. 5.95 wkbk. o.p. (ISBN 0-88488-048-6). Creative Pubns.

Eurekas. Albert Goldbarth. 24p. 1981. pap. 3.95 (ISBN 0-918518-21-0). St Luke TN.

Euripides. Ed. by James Diggle. Bd. with Phaeton. LC 73-96084. (Classical Texts & Commentaries: No. 12). (Illus.). 1970. 42.50 (ISBN 0-521-07700-1). Cambridge U Pr.

Euripides' Electra. Euripides. Ed. by J. D. Denniston. 1979. pap. 14.95x (ISBN 0-19-872094-7). Oxford U Pr.

Euripides Five: Three Tragedies. Euripides. Ed. by David Grene & Richard Lattimore. Incl. Electra. Tr. by Emily T. Vermeule; The Phoenician Women. Tr. by Elizabeth Wyckoff; The Bacchae. Tr. by William Arrowsmith. LC 55-5787. 228p. 1959. pap. 3.95 (ISBN 0-226-30784-0, P312, Phoen). U of Chicago Pr.

Euripides: Heracles: With Introduction & Commentary. Ed. by Godfrey W. Bond. 448p. 1981. 45.00 (ISBN 0-19-814012-6). Oxford U Pr.

Euro-American System: Economic & Political Relations Between North America & Western Europe. Ed. by Ernst-Otto Czempiel & Dankwart A. Rustow. LC 76-4557. 1976. 31.00x (ISBN 0-89158-601-6). Westview.

Euro-Bank: Its Origins, Management & Outlook. 2nd ed. Steven I. Davis. LC 80-13337. 154p. 1980. 24.95x (ISBN 0-470-26955-3). Halsted Pr.

Euro-Bank: It's Origins, Managements & Outlook. Steven I. Davis. LC 76-15912. 1976. 19.95 (ISBN 0-470-15060-2). Halsted Pr.

Euro-barometer Three: European Men & Women, May 1975. Jacques-Rene Rabier & Ronald Inglehart. LC 79-83750. 1979. codebook 8.00 (ISBN 0-89138-989-X). ICPSR.

Euro-Dollar Market & the International Finance System. Geoffrey Bell. 112p. 1973. 18.95 o.p. (ISBN 0-470-06405-6). Halsted Pr.

Eurocommunism: A New Kind of Communism? Annie Kriegel. Tr. by Peter S. Stern. LC 77-92081. (Publications 194). 145p. 1978. 12.00 (ISBN 0-8179-6941-1). Hoover Inst Pr.

Eurocommunism & Detente. Ed. by Rudolph L. Tokes. LC 77-92750. 1978. cobee 25.00x (ISBN 0-8147-8161-6); pap. 11.00x cobee (ISBN 0-8147-8162-4). NYU Pr.

Eurocommunism & Eurosocialism: The Left Confronts Modernity. Ed. by Bernard E. Brown. 400p. text ed. 22.50x (ISBN 0-8290-0394-0); pap. text ed. 12.95x (ISBN 0-8290-0395-9). Irvington.

Eurocommunism & the Atlantic Alliance. James E. Dougherty & Diane K. Pfaltzgraff. LC 76-53142. (Special Reports Ser.). 1977. 3.00 (ISBN 0-89549-003-X). Inst Foreign Policy Anal.

Eurocommunism between East & West. Ed. by Vernon V. Aspaturian et al. LC 80-7489. 384p. 1980. 32.50x (ISBN 0-253-32346-0); pap. 9.95x (ISBN 0-253-20248-5). Ind U Pr.

Eurocommunism: The Ideological & Political-Theoretical Foundations. Ed. by George Schwab. LC 80-26864. (Contributions in Political Science: No. 60). 352p. 1981. lib. bdg. 25.00 (ISBN 0-313-22908-2). Greenwood.

Eurocommunism: The Ideological & Political-Theoretical Foundations. Ed. by George Schwab. (Contributions in Political Science: No. 60). (Illus.). 352p. 1981. lib. bdg. 25.00 (ISBN 0-313-22908-2, SEU/). Greenwood.

Eurocommunism: Theoretical, Political & Ideological Foundations. Ed. by George Schwab. 300p. 1980. cancelled (ISBN 0-935764-03-8). Ark Hse NY.

Eurocomp Seventy-Eight: Proceedings. European Computing Congress. Ed. by Online Conferences Ltd. 1978. text ed. 108.00x (ISBN 0-903796-23-6, Pub. by Online Conferences England). Renouf.

Euromarkets & International Financial Policies. D. F. Lomax & P. T. Gutmann. 275p. 1980. 29.95x (ISBN 0-470-26923-5). Halsted Pr.

Europa Administration: Directory of Administration & Justice for the European Community. Ed. by Walter Duic. 1161p. 1976. text ed. 110.00 (ISBN 3-7940-3017-6, Pub. by K G Saur). Gale.

Europa Yearbook Nineteen Eighty-One, 2 vols. 22nd ed. (Illus.). 3600p. 1981. 150.00. Gale.

Europa Yearbook 1980: A World Survey, 1980, 2 v0ls. 21st ed. LC 59-2942. iii, 607p. 1980. Set. 150.00 (ISBN 0-686-65097-2). Vol. 1 (ISBN 0-905118-46-4). Vol. 2 (ISBN 0-905118-47-2). Intl Pubns Serv.

Europe - Through the Back Door. 2nd ed. Rick Steves. 112p. 1981. pap. 5.95 (ISBN 0-686-28770-3). Steves Wide World.

Europe: A Geographical Survey of the Continent. Roy Mellor & E. Alistair Smith. LC 78-10171. 1979. 15.00x (ISBN 0-231-04708-8). Columbia U Pr.

Europe After the Rain. Alan Burns. 1980. pap. cancelled (ISBN 0-7145-0222-7). Riverrun NY.

Europe & Africa. Carol Cosgrove-Twitchett. 212p. 1978. text ed. 25.50x (ISBN 0-566-00182-9, Pub. by Gower Pub Co England). Renouf.

Europe & America. Burgess. 8.50 o.s.i. (ISBN 0-8027-0324-0). Walker & Co.

Europe & the British Health Service. Lord Wade. 94p. 1974. pap. text ed. 2.50x (ISBN 0-7199-0890-6, Pub. by Bedford England). Renouf.

Europe & the Middle East. Albert Hourani. 1980. 20.00x (ISBN 0-520-03742-1). U of Cal Pr.

Europe & the Superpower Balance. A. W. DePorte. LC 79-92257. (Headline Ser.: No. 247). (Illus.). 80p. (gr. 11-12). 1979. pap. 2.00 (ISBN 0-87124-058-0). Foreign Policy.

Europe & the United States: The Future of the Relationship. Karl Kaiser. LC 73-75612. 146p. 1973. 3.95 o.p. (ISBN 0-910416-18-4, F70037); pap. 2.50 o.p. (ISBN 0-685-31761-7, F70038). Columbia Bks.

Europe & World Energy. H. Maull. LC 80-40488. (Illus.). 1980. text ed. 43.95 (ISBN 0-408-10629-8). Butterworths.

Europe Between Revolutions, Eighteen Fifteen to Eighteen Forty-Eight. Jacques Droz. LC 80-66909. (History of Europe Ser.; Cornell Paperbacks Ser.). 228p. 1980. pap. 4.95 (ISBN 0-8014-9206-8). Cornell U Pr.

Europe Business Travel Guide. Paddington Press. 480p. 1981. 19.95 (ISBN 0-87196-338-8); pap. 11.95 (ISBN 0-87196-344-2). Facts on File.

Europe Centric Historiography of Russia: An Analysis of the Contribution by Russian Emigre Historians in the USA, 1925-55, Concerning 19th Century Russian History. Elizabeth Beyerly. LC 72-94444. (Studies in European History: No. 11). 385p. 1973. text ed. 88.25x (ISBN 90-2792-515-1). Mouton.

Europe Dimensions: A Study-Activity Guide. Carol B. Francis. (Orig.). 1981. pap. 3.95 (ISBN 0-377-00108-2). Friend Pr.

Europe: Discovery Trips. 3rd ed. Sunset Editors. LC 80-80855. (Illus.). 144p. 1980. pap. 5.95 (ISBN 0-376-06173-1, Sunset Bks). Sunset-Lane.

Europe, Eighteen Eighty to Nineteen Forty-Five. J. M. Roberts. (General History of Europe Ser.). 1972. pap. text ed. 11.95x (ISBN 0-582-48310-7). Longman.

Europe Emerges: Transition Toward an Industrial World-Wide Society, 600-1750. Robert L. Reynolds. (Illus.). 1961. pap. 8.95x (ISBN 0-299-02294-3). U of Wis Pr.

Europe from the Renaissance to Waterloo. 3rd ed. Robert Ergang. 1967. text ed. 19.95x (ISBN 0-669-22814-1). Heath.

Europe in Crisis Fifteen Ninety-Eight to Sixteen Forty-Eight. Geoffrey Parker. LC 80-66912. (History of Europe Ser.; Cornell Paperbacks Ser.). 384p. 1980. pap. 5.95 (ISBN 0-8014-9209-2). Cornell U Pr.

Europe in Retrospect: A Brief History of the Past Two Hundred Years. Raymond F. Betts. (Orig.). 1979. pap. 6.95 (ISBN 0-669-01366-8). Heath.

Europe in the Age of Negotiation. Pierre Hassner. LC 73-83410. (Washington Papers: No. 8). 1973. 3.50x (ISBN 0-8039-0281-6). Sage.

Europe in the Central Middle Ages 962-1154. 2nd ed. C. Brooke. LC 75-308112. (General History of Europe Ser.). 404p. 1975. pap. text ed. 11.95 (ISBN 0-582-48476-6). Longman.

Europe in the Eighteenth Century 1713-1783. 2nd ed. M. S. Anderson. (General History of Europe Ser.). 1977. text ed. 24.00x (ISBN 0-582-48671-8); pap. text ed. 11.50x (ISBN 0-582-48672-6). Longman.

Europe in the Fourteenth & Fifteenth Centuries. Denys Hay. (General History of Europe Ser.). 1970. pap. text ed. 9.95x (ISBN 0-582-48343-3). Longman.

Europe in the Late Middle Ages. Ed. by Beryl S. Highfield & John Hale. (Illus., Orig.). 1970. pap. 7.95 (ISBN 0-571-09413-9, Pub. by Faber & Faber). Merrimack Bk Serv.

Europe in the Nineteenth Century 1830-1880. H. Hearder. (General History of Europe Ser.). (Illus.). 1966. text ed. 16.00x (ISBN 0-582-48212-7); pap. text ed. 10.95x (ISBN 0-582-48344-1). Longman.

Europe in the Reformation. Peter J. Klassen. (Illus.). 1979. pap. text ed. 13.95 (ISBN 0-13-292136-7). P-H.

Europe in the Russian Mirror. Alexander Gerschenkron. LC 76-96090. 1970. 23.95 (ISBN 0-521-07721-4). Cambridge U Pr.

Europe in the Sixteenth Century. H. G. Koenigsberger & George L. Mosse. (General History of Europe Ser.). (Illus.). 1971. pap. text ed. 9.95x (ISBN 0-582-48345-X). Longman.

Europe in the Twentieth Century. Peter Lane. (Twentieth Century World History Ser.). 1978. 16.95 (ISBN 0-7134-0984-3). David & Charles.

Europe of the Dictators Nineteen Nineteen to Nineteen Forty-Five. Elizabeth Wiskemann. LC 80-66913. (History of Europe Ser.; Cornell Paperbacks Ser.). 287p. 1980. pap. 5.95 (ISBN 0-8014-9210-6). Cornell U Pr.

Europe on Twenty Dollars a Day: 1980-81 Edition. 1981. pap. 7.95 (ISBN 0-671-41420-8). Frommer-Pasmantier.

Europe: Privilege & Protest Seventeen Thirty to Seventeen Eighty-Nine. Olwen H. Hufton. LC 80-66911. (History of Europe Ser.; Cornell Paperbacks Ser.). 398p. 1980. pap. 5.95 (ISBN 0-8014-9208-4). Cornell U Pr.

Europe Reshaped Eighteen Forty-Eight to Eighteen Seventy-Eight. J. A. Grenville. LC 80-66910. (History of Europe Ser.; Cornell Paperbacks Ser.). 412p. 1980. pap. 5.95 (ISBN 0-8014-9207-6). Cornell U Pr.

Europe Rules the World. Trevor Cairnes. LC 79-41598. (Cambridge Introduction to the History of Mankind: Bk. 9). (Illus.). 96p. (Orig.). Date not set. pap. price not set (ISBN 0-521-22710-0). Cambridge U Pr.

Europe Seventeen Eighty to Eighteen Thirty. Franklin L. Ford. (General History of Europe Ser.). 1971. pap. text ed. 10.50x (ISBN 0-582-48346-8). Longman.

Europe Since Seveteen Fifteen: A Modern History. Eugen Weber. (Illus.). 790p. 1972. pap. text ed. 12.95x (ISBN 0-393-09404-9). Norton.

Europe Since the Second World War. J. R. Thackrah. 288p. 1979. pap. 9.95x (Pub. by Macdonald & Evans England). Intl Ideas.

Europe Since Waterloo. 3rd ed. Robert Ergang & Donald G. Rohr. 1967. text ed. 19.95x (ISBN 0-669-22830-3). Heath.

Europe Since World War Two: The Big Chance. rev. enlarged ed. Norman Luxenburg. LC 78-26092. 330p. 1979. 18.95x (ISBN 0-8093-0911-4). S Ill U Pr.

Europe: The World of the Middle Ages. Edward M. Peters. (Illus.). 1977. text ed. 24.95 (ISBN 0-13-291898-6). P-H.

Europe Two Thousand. Ed. by Peter Hall. LC 77-9479. 1977. 16.00x (ISBN 0-231-04462-3). Columbia U Pr.

Europe Without Defense? 48 Hours That Could Change the Face of the World. Robert Close. LC 79-4693. (Pergamon Policy Studies). (Illus.). 22.00 (ISBN 0-08-023108-X). Pergamon.

European Americana: A Chronological Guide to Writings on the Americas Published in Europe 1493-1600, Vol. I. John Alden. 467p. 1980. 50.00 (ISBN 0-918414-03-2). Readex Bks.

European & African Stereotypes in Twentieth-Century African Fiction. Sarah L. Milbury-Steen. (Gotham Library). 208p. 1981. 24.50x (ISBN 0-8147-5378-7); pap. 12.00 (ISBN 0-8147-5379-5). NYU Pr.

European Chemical Industries Review, 1974-75. (Illus.). 488p. 1975. 60.00 o.p. (ISBN 0-7161-0238-2, Gower). Unipub.

European Cities & Society. 2nd ed. James S. Curl. (Illus.). 1972. pap. 14.95x (ISBN 0-249-44109-8). Intl Ideas.

European Communities: A Guide to Information Sources. Ed. by J. Bryan Collester. LC 73-17506. (International Relations Information Guide Ser.: Vol. 3). 1979. 30.00 (ISBN 0-8103-1322-7). Gale.

European Communities-The Social Policy of the First Phase: The European Coal & Steel Community 1951-1970, Vol. 1. Doreen Collins. 1975. 48.50x (ISBN 0-85520-083-9, Pub by Martin Robertson England). Biblio Dist.

European Community: A New Path to Peaceful Union. Walter Hallstein. 1964. 6.25x (ISBN 0-210-31238-6). Asia.

European Community in the Nineteen Seventies. Ed. by Steven J. Warnecke. LC 79-170277. (Special Studies in International Politics & Government). 1972. 29.50x (ISBN 0-275-28224-4); pap. text ed. 16.50x (ISBN 0-89197-753-8). Irvington.

European Community in World Affairs: Political Influence & Economic Reality. Werner Feld. LC 75-44209. (Illus.). 250p. 1976. 12.50 (ISBN 0-88284-040-1); pap. text ed. 7.95x (ISBN 0-88284-037-1). Alfred Pub.

European Community Law & National Law. John Usher. (Studies on Contemporary Europe: No. 3). 96p. (Orig.). 1981. text ed. 15.95x (ISBN 0-04-341017-0, 2593); pap. text ed. 6.95x (ISBN 0-04-341018-9, 2594). Allen Unwin.

European Computer Survey Nineteen Sixty-Nine to Seventy. 6th ed. Computer Consultants Ltd. LC 74-102635. 1970. 675.00 (ISBN 0-08-016026-3). Pergamon.

European Computer Users Handbook, 1969-70. Computer Consultants Ltd. LC 63-25287. 1970. 46.00 (ISBN 0-08-016027-1). Pergamon.

European Costume. Doreen Yarwood. 1975. 53.00 (ISBN 0-7134-3020-6, Pub. by Batsford England). David & Charles.

European Demographic System: 1500 to 1820. Michael W. Flinn. LC 80-19574. (Studies in Comparative History: No. 11). 220p. 1981. text ed. 15.00 (ISBN 0-8018-2426-5). Johns Hopkins.

European Detours: A Trave Guide to Unsual Sights. Nino Lo Bello. (Illus.). 176p. 1981. 8.95 (ISBN 0-8437-3375-6). Hammond Inc.

European Diplomatic History 1815-1914: Documents & Interpretations. Herman N. Weill. LC 74-171719. 1972. 15.00 o.p. (ISBN 0-682-47375-8, University); pap. 5.00 o.p. (ISBN 0-682-47327-8). Exposition.

European Direct Investment in the U.S.A. Before World War I. Peter J. Buckley & Brian R. Roberts. 1981. 25.00 (ISBN 0-312-26940-4). St Martin.

European Direct Mail Databook: 1976. Ed. by Peter Found. 1976. pap. 27.00 o.p. (ISBN 0-7161-0284-6, Gower). Unipub.

European Directory of Economic Planning & Corporate Planning, 1973-74. 442p. 1975. 32.00 o.p. (ISBN 0-7161-0172-6, Gower). Unipub.

European Directory of Economics & Corporate Planning. rev. ed. 317p. 1976. 32.00 o.p. (ISBN 0-7161-0287-0, 2870, Gower). Unipub.

European Directory of Market Research Surveys. 1443p. 1976. 42.50 o.p. (ISBN 0-7161-0282-X, Gower). Unipub.

European Drawings, 1375-1825. Cara D. Denison & Helen B. Mules. (Fine Art Ser.). (Illus.). 316p. (Orig.). 1981. pap. price not set. Dover.

European Economic Community & United Kingdom Engineering Companies. The British Mechanical Engineering Confederation in Association with 'Engineering' 57p. 1980. 78.75x (ISBN 0-89771-002-9). State Mutual Bk.

European Economic History: The Ancient World. William I. Davisson & James E. Harper. LC 75-172518. (Illus.). 1972. 24.00x (ISBN 0-89197-153-X); pap. text ed. 10.95x (ISBN 0-89197-154-8). Irvington.

European Economic Integration & the United States. Lawrence B. Krause. 1968. 11.95 (ISBN 0-8157-5034-X). Brookings.

European Economic Issues: Agriculture, Economic Security, Industrial Democracy, the OECD. John S. Marsh. LC 76-30359. (Special Studies). 1977. text ed. 28.95 (ISBN 0-275-24410-5). Praeger.

European Elections & British Politics. David Butler & David Marquand. 208p. 1981. text ed. 25.00 (ISBN 0-582-29528-9); pap. text ed. 11.95 (ISBN 0-582-29529-7). Longman.

European Empire Building. William Cohen. LC 79-57459. (Problems in Civilization Ser.). (Orig.). 1980. pap. text ed. 3.95x (ISBN 0-88273-410-5). Forum Pr MO.

European Energy Outlook to Nineteen Eighty-Five. George Ray & Colin Robinson. LC 80-455974. 123p. 1978. pap. text ed. 135.00x (ISBN 0-8002-1405-6). Intl Pubns Serv.

European Environmental Policy East & West. Fullenbach. 1981. text ed. price not set (ISBN 0-408-10689-1). Butterworth.

European Eocene Equidae (Perissodactyla) D. E. Savage et al. (U. C. Publ. in Geological Sciences: Vol. 56). 1965. pap. 7.00x (ISBN 0-520-09157-4). U of Cal Pr.

European Historical Fiction & Biography for Children & Young People. 2nd ed. Jeanette K. Hotchkiss. LC 72-1599. 1972. 10.00 (ISBN 0-8108-0515-4). Scarecrow.

European History, Nineteen Four to Nineteen Sixty-Eight. Elizabeth Eccleshare & Valerie St. Johnston. 1975. pap. text ed. 3.95x o.p. (ISBN 0-435-31171-9). Heinemann Ed.

European History Seventeen Eighty-Nine to Nineteen Fourteen. C. A. Leeds. 448p. 1979. pap. 13.95x (ISBN 0-7121-0575-1, Pub. by Macdonald & Evans England). Intl Ideas.

European Ideologies Since Seventeen Eighty-Nine: Rebels, Radicals & Political Ferment. Thomas E. Hachey & Ralph E. Weber. 200p. (Orig.). 1981. pap. text ed. 5.50 (ISBN 0-89874-082-7). Krieger.

European Ideologies Since Seventeen Eighty-Nine: Rebels, Radicals & Political Ferment. Thomas E. Hachey & Ralph E. Weber. LC 80-12562. 1980. pap. 6.50 (ISBN 0-89874-082-7). Krieger.

European Industrial Organization. Alex Jacquemin & Henry W. De Jong. LC 76-58378. (Problems of Economic Integration Ser.). 1977. 22.95 (ISBN 0-470-99079-1). Halsted Pr.

European Industrial Relations. Ed. by Industrial Democracy in Europe (IDE) International Research Group. (Illus.). 256p. 1981. 45.00 (ISBN 0-19-827254-5). Oxford U Pr.

European Integration: Select International Bibliography of Theses & Disserations 1957-1977. Ed. by J. P. Siemers. 240p. 1979. 47.50x (ISBN 90-286-0166-X). Sijthoff & Noordhoff.

European Intellectual History Since Seventeen Eighty-Nine. 3nd ed. R. Stromberg. 1981. pap. 4.95 (ISBN 0-13-291955-9). P-H.

European Intellectual History Since 1789. 2nd ed. Roland N. Stromberg. LC 74-23541. 384p. 1975. pap. text ed. 14.95x (ISBN 0-13-292003-4). P-H.

European Labor & Multinationals. Paul J. Weinberg. LC 78-9449. (Praeger Special Studies). 1978. 21.95 (ISBN 0-03-044256-7). Praeger.

European Left: Italy, France, & Spain. Ed. by William E. Griffith. LC 79-7711. 272p. 1979. 25.95 (ISBN 0-669-03199-2). Lexington Bks.

European Literature & the Latin Middle Ages. E. R. Curtius. Tr. by Willard R. Trask. LC 52-10619. (Bollingen Ser., Vol. 36). 682p. 1953. 30.00 (ISBN 0-691-09739-9); pap. 7.50 (ISBN 0-691-01793-X). Princeton U Pr.

European Marine Biology Symposium, Fourth. Ed. by D. J. Crisp. (Illus.). 1971. 97.50 (ISBN 0-521-08101-7). Cambridge U Pr.

European Marketing Data & Statistics 1979-80. 16th ed. 1979. 107.50x (ISBN 0-686-60656-6, Euromonitor). Nichols Pub.

European Miracle: Environments, Economies & Geopolitics in the History of Europe & Asia. E. L. Jones. 274p. Date not set. text ed. price not set (ISBN 0-521-23588-X); pap. text ed. price not set (ISBN 0-521-28055-9). Cambridge U Pr.

European Monetary System: Its Promise & Prospects. Ed. by Philip H. Trezise. LC 79-55581. 96p. 1979. pap. 4.50 (ISBN 0-8157-8531-3). Brookings.

European Monetary Unification. G. Magnifico. LC 73-303. 1973. 21.95 (ISBN 0-470-56525-X). Halsted Pr.

European Monetary Unification & Its Meaning for the United States. Ed. by Lawrence B. Krause & Walter S. Salant. LC 73-1084. 1973. 12.95 (ISBN 0-8157-5032-3). Brookings.

European National Oil Companies. L. E. Grayson. 256p. 1981. price not set (ISBN 0-471-27861-0, Wiley-Interscience). Wiley.

European Organ, 1450-1850. Peter Williams. LC 78-57080. (Illus.). 336p. 1978. Repr. of 1966 ed. 27.50x (ISBN 0-253-32083-6). Ind U Pr.

European Origins of the Brethren. Donald F. Durnbaugh. 463p. 1958. 8.95 (ISBN 0-87178-256-1). Brethren.

European Paint Manufacturers, Nineteen Seventy-Seven to Nineteen Seventy-Nine. 3rd ed. 186p. (Orig.). 1977. pap. 55.00x (ISBN 90-6156-514-6). Intl Pubns Serv.

European Paraliament: What It Is - What It Does - How It Works. Michael Palmer. 128p. 1981. 14.50 (ISBN 0-08-024536-6); pap. 7.20 (ISBN 0-08-024535-8). Pergamon.

European Parliament. John Fitzmaurice. LC 78-67229. (Praeger Special Studies). 1979. 20.95 (ISBN 0-03-046221-5). Praeger.

European Parliament & the National Parliaments. V. Herman & M. P. Van Schendelen. 1978. text ed. 26.50x (ISBN 0-566-00251-5, Pub. by Gower Pub Co England). Renouf.

European Parliamentary Procedure: A Comparative Handbook. Gilbert F. Campion. LC 78-59009. (Illus.). 1981. Repr. of 1953 ed. 22.50 (ISBN 0-88355-684-7). Hyperion Conn.

European Petroleum Related Industries. Norwegian Petroleum Society. 109p. 1980. 75.00x (ISBN 82-7270-016-6, Pub. by Norwegian Info Norway). State Mutual Bk.

European Pharmacopoeia, Vol. 1. 1st ed. Pharmaceutical Society of Great Britain. 400p. 1969. 45.00 o.p. (ISBN 0-85369-066-9, Pub. by Pharmaceutical). Rittenhouse.

European Pharmacopoeia, Vol. 2. 1st ed. Pharmaceutical Society of Great Britain. 568p. 1971. 45.00 o.p. (ISBN 0-85369-079-0, Pub. by Pharmaceutical). Rittenhouse.

European Pharmacopoeia, Vol. 3. 488p. 1976. 65.00 o.p. (ISBN 0-685-69632-4, Pub. by Pharmaceutical). Rittenhouse.

European Pharmacopoeia, Nineteen Eighty to Eighty-Two, Part 1. 2nd ed. 237p. 1980. 175.00 (ISBN 2-7160-0079-4, Pub. by Maisonneuve France). Rittenhouse.

European Plastics Nineteen Seventy-Eight to Nineteen Eighty. 5th ed. 339p. (Orig.). 1978. pap. 55.00x (ISBN 90-6156-516-2). Intl Pubns Serv.

European Political Parties. Ed. by S. Henig & J. Pinder. (Political & Economic Planning Ser.). 1970. text ed. 32.50x o.p. (ISBN 0-04-327030-1). Allen Unwin.

European Portraits Sixteen Hundred to Nineteen Hundred in The Art Institute of Chicago. Susan Wise & David Piper. LC 78-57638. (Illus.). 183p. (Orig.). 1978. pap. 10.00x (ISBN 0-86559-029-X). Art Inst Chi.

European Publishers' Catalog Annual: 1980. 80000p. 1980. catalog collection 410.00 (ISBN 0-930466-32-2). Meckler Bks.

European Reminiscences Musical & Otherwise. Louis C. Elson. LC 72-125046. (Music Ser). (Illus.). 301p. 1972. Repr. of 1896 ed. lib. bdg. 29.50 (ISBN 0-306-70011-5). Da Capo.

European Retail Trades, Nineteen Seventy-Five to Seventy-Six. (Illus.). 378p. 1976. pap. 60.00 o.p. (ISBN 0-7161-0286-2, Gower). Unipub.

European Right: A Historical Profile. Ed. by Hans Rogger & Eugen Weber. 1965. pap. 7.95x (ISBN 0-520-01080-9, CAL124). U of Cal Pr.

European Scientific Co-Operation: Priorities & Perspectives. (Science Policy Studies & Documents Ser.). 52p. 1973. pap. 2.50 (ISBN 92-3-101012-3, U227, UNESCO). Unipub.

European Security & the Atlantic System. Ed. by William T. Fox & Warner R Schilling. LC 72-4248. (Institute for War & Peace Studies). 276p. 1973. 17.00x (ISBN 0-231-03640-X). Columbia U Pr.

European Security: Prospects for the 1980's. Ed. by Leebaert. (Illus.). 1979. 15.95 (ISBN 0-669-02518-6). Lexington Bks.

European Social Policy, Today & Tomorrow. Michael Shanks. 1977. text ed. 19.50 (ISBN 0-08-021444-4); pap. text ed. 7.75 (ISBN 0-08-021443-6). Pergamon.

European Solders Fifteen Fifty to Sixteen Fifty. Angela Parker & Geoffrey Parker. (Cambridge Introduction to the History of Mankind Ser.). (gr. 4-5). 1977. pap. text ed. 3.95 (ISBN 0-521-21020-8). Cambridge U Pr.

European Technology for Obtaining Energy from Solid Waste. Ed. by D. J. De Renzo. LC 78-61896. (Energy Technology Review No. 74: Pollution Technology Review No. 54). (Illus.). 1978. 39.00 (ISBN 0-8155-0730-5). Noyes.

European Transport Aircraft Since 1910. John Stroud. LC 66-28846. 1966. 15.95 o.p. (ISBN 0-370-00095-1). Aero.

European Unification in the Sixties. Miriam Camps. (Council on Foreign Relations Ser). 1966. 8.95 o.p. (ISBN 0-07-009697-X, P&RB). McGraw.

European Universities, Nineteen Seventy-Five to Eighty-Five: Proceedings of the 5th General Assembly of the Standing Conference of Rectors & Vice-Chancellors of the European Universities, Bologna, 1974. Ed. by Alain Nicollier. LC 75-4331. 1975. pap. text ed. 28.00 (ISBN 0-08-019710-8); French Ed. pap. text ed. 34.00 (ISBN 0-08-019711-6). Pergamon.

European War Crimes Trials: A Bibliography. Inge S. Neumann. Ed. by Robert A. Rosebaum. LC 77-18934. (Additional material furnished by the Wiener Library, London). 1978. Repr. of 1951 ed. lib. bdg. 17.50x (ISBN 0-313-20210-9, NEEW). Greenwood.

European Weapons & Armour. Ewart Oakeshott. (Illus.). 277p. 1980. 29.95 (ISBN 0-686-68855-4). Beinfeld Pub.

European Witch Craze in the Sixteenth & Seventeenth Centuries & Other Essays. Hugh R. Trevor-Roper. 1969. pap. 3.95x (ISBN 0-06-131416-1, TB1416, Torch). Har-Row.

European Witch Trials: Their Foundations in Popular Learned Culture, 1300-1500. Richard Kieckhefer. 1976. 21.50x (ISBN 0-520-02967-4). U of Cal Pr.

European Witchcraft. Ed. by E. William Monter. LC 76-89682. 1969. pap. text ed. 10.95x (ISBN 0-471-61402-5). Wiley.

European Yearbook-Annuaire Europeen, Vol. XXVI. Ed. by A. H. Robertson. 696p. (Fr., Eng.). 1980. lib. bdg. 110.00 (ISBN 90-247-2298-5, Pub. by Marinus Nijhoff). Kluwer Boston.

Europeans. Henry James. 176p. 1976. Repr. of 1878 ed. lib. bdg. 12.95x (ISBN 0-89244-018-X). Queens Hse.

Europeans in the Sudan Eighteen Thirty Four to Eighteen Seventy Eight. Ed. by Paul Santi & Richard Hill. (Illus.). 352p. 1980. 45.00 (ISBN 0-19-822718-3). Oxford U Pr.

Europe's Crucial Years: The Diplomatic Background of World War I, 1902-1914. Dwight E. Lee. LC 73-91315. (Illus.). 500p. 1974. text ed. 27.50x (ISBN 0-87451-094-5). U Pr of New Eng.

Europe's Free Trade Area Experiment. H. Corbet & D. Robertson. 1971. pap. 11.30 o.p. (ISBN 0-08-016233-9). Pergamon.

Europe's Futures Europe's Choices: Models of Western Europe in the 1970's. Alastair Buchan. LC 77-83385. 1969. 20.00x (ISBN 0-231-03305-2). Columbia U Pr.

Europe's Hidden Flea Markets & Budget Antique Shops. John H. Byrns. (Illus., Orig.). 1968. pap. 2.95 o.p. (ISBN 0-8038-1888-2). Hastings.

Europe's Middle Ages: Five Sixty-Five to Fifteen Hundred. Karl F. Morrison. 1970. pap. 7.95x (ISBN 0-673-05792-5). Scott F.

Europe's Steppe Frontier, Fifteen Hundred to Eighteen Hundred: A Study of the Eastward Movement in Europe. William H. McNeill. LC 64-22248. (Midway Reprint Ser.). 252p. 1964. 10.50x o.s.i. (ISBN 0-226-56151-8); pap. 9.50x (ISBN 0-226-56152-6). U of Chicago Pr.

Europe's Wonderful Little Hotels & Inns. Hilary Rubenstein. (Illus.). 512p. 1981. 12.95 (ISBN 0-312-92188-8); pap. 8.95 (ISBN 0-312-92189-6). St Martin.

Europe's Wonderful Little Hotels & Inns. 3rd rev. ed. Ed. by Hilary Rubinstein. (Illus.). 512p. 1981. 14.95 (ISBN 0-86553-038-6); pap. 8.95 (ISBN 0-312-92189-6). Congdon & Lattes.

Europe's Wonderful Little Hotels & Inns: 1979-1980. Ed. by Hilary Rubinstein. (Illus.). 1979. 10.95 o.p.; pap. 5.95 (ISBN 0-525-03383-1). Dutton.

Europump Terminology -- Glossary of Pump Applications in English, German, French, Italian, & Spanish. (Illus.). 1979. 135.00x (ISBN 0-85461-071-5). Intl Ideas.

Eurydice: Or, the Nature of Opera. Dyneley Hussey. LC 80-2283. 1981. Repr. of 1929 ed. 17.50 (ISBN 0-404-18849-4). AMS Pr.

Eurythmy. Marjorie Spock. (Illus.). 148p. (Orig.). 1980. pap. 9.95 (ISBN 0-910142-88-2). Anthroposophic.

Eusebius As Church Historian. Robert M. Grant. 192p. 1980. 29.95 (ISBN 0-19-826441-0). Oxford U Pr.

Eusebius of Caesarea & the Arian Crisis. Colm Luibheid. 128p. 1981. 18.50x (ISBN 0-7165-2277-2, Pub. by Irish Academic Pr Ireland). Biblio Dist.

Eustace Diamonds. Anthony Trollope. 1976. lib. bdg. 14.95x (ISBN 0-89968-140-9). Lightyear.

Euterpeiad or Musical Intelligencer, 3 Vols. Ed. by John R. Parker. LC 65-23389. (Music Ser). 1977. Repr. of 1820 ed. Set. lib. bdg. 75.00 (ISBN 0-306-70920-1). Da Capo.

Euthanasia & the Right to Death: The Case for Voluntary Euthanasia. Ed. by A. B. Downing. (Contemporary Issues Ser.: No. 2). 1970. text ed. 17.25x (ISBN 0-391-00022-5). Humanities.

Euthryphro. Plato. Ed. by John Burnet. Bd. with Apology of Socrates; Crito. 1924. 11.95x (ISBN 0-19-814015-0). Oxford U Pr.

Euthyphro, Apology Crito: With the Death Scene from Phaedo. Plato. Tr. by F. J. Church & R. D. Cummings. Bd. with Apology; Crito. (gr. 9up). 1956. pap. 2.50 (ISBN 0-672-60166-4, LLA4). Bobbs.

Eutrophication: Causes, Consequences, Correctives. Division Of Biology And Agriculture. LC 68-62704. 1969. text ed. 14.75 (ISBN 0-309-01700-9). Natl Acad Pr.

Eutrophication of Deep Lakes: Proceedings of Seminar Held in Oslo, Norway June 1978. Ed. by S. H. Jenkins. (Progress in Water Technology Ser.: Vol. 12, No. 2). (Illus.). 208p. 1980. pap. 47.00 (ISBN 0-08-026024-1). Pergamon.

Eva Hesse. Lucy R. Lippard. LC 76-17380. (Illus.). 1976. 25.00x (ISBN 0-8147-4971-2); pap. 10.95 (ISBN 0-8147-4972-0). NYU Pr.

Eva Peron. Nicholas Fraser & Marysa Navarro. (Illus.). 1981. 14.95 (ISBN 0-393-01457-6). Norton.

Eva Peron & Other Plays. Copi. 1980. pap. 4.95 (ISBN 0-7145-3563-X). Riverrun NY.

Eva Peron: The Myths of a Woman. Julie Taylor. LC 79-19547. x, 176p. 1981. pap. write for info. (ISBN 0-226-79144-0). U of Chicago Pr.

Eva Peron: The Myths of a Woman. Julie Taylor. LC 79-19547. (Illus.). 1980. 15.00 (ISBN 0-226-79143-2); pap. 5.95 (ISBN 0-226-79144-0). U of Chicago Pr.

Evacuation of Americans from Beirut. Crawford. (Arab Background Ser.). 1972. pap. 3.95x (ISBN 0-685-77093-1). Intl Bk Ctr.

Evalore. Eva Jones. 1979. pap. 1.95 o.p. (ISBN 0-449-23912-8, Crest). Fawcett.

Evaluated Kinetic Data for High Temperature Reactions, Vol. 3. D. L. Baulch et al. 1977. 99.95 (ISBN 0-408-70787-9). Butterworths.

Evaluating a Community Psychiatric Service: The Camberwell Register 1964-1971. Ed. by J. K. Wing & Anthea M. Hailey. (Nuffield Publications). (Illus.). 468p. 1972. 24.95x o.p. (ISBN 0-19-721372-3). Oxford U Pr.

Evaluating a Second Language Program. Gilbert A. Jarvis & Shirley J. Adams. (Language in Education Ser.: No. 19). 1979. pap. 2.95 (ISBN 0-87281-105-0). Ctr Appl Ling.

Evaluating Action Programs: Readings in Social Action & Education. Carol H. Weiss. 1972. pap. text ed. 14.95x (ISBN 0-205-03247-8, 813247X). Allyn.

Evaluating Alcohol & Drug Abuse Treatment Effectiveness. Ed. by Linda C. Sobell. 1979. 22.00 (ISBN 0-08-022997-2). Pergamon.

Evaluating Alternative Law-Enforcement Policies. Ed. by Ralph Baker & Fred Meyer. LC 79-1541. (Policy Studies Organization Bk.). (Illus.). 240p. 1979. 19.95 (ISBN 0-669-02898-3). Lexington Bks.

Evaluating & Optimizing Public Policy. Ed. by Dennis Palumbo. 1980. pap. 5.00 (ISBN 0-686-62286-3). Policy Studies.

Evaluating & Optimizing Public Policy. Ed. by Dennis J. Palumbo et al. LC 80-8598. (Policy). 1981. price not set (ISBN 0-669-04306-0). Lexington Bks.

Evaluating & Supervising Teachers: Research & Methods. Eliot G. Spack. 1978. pap. 10.00 o.p. (ISBN 0-686-00907-X, D-116). Essence Pubns.

Evaluating Classroom Instruction: A Source-Book of Instruments. Gary D. Borich & Susan K. Madden. LC 76-2953. 1977. text ed. 18.95 (ISBN 0-201-00842-4). A-W.

Evaluating Clinical Competence in the Health Profession. Margaret K. Morgan & David M. Irby. LC 77-26935. (Illus.). 1978. text ed. 18.95 (ISBN 0-8016-3493-8). Mosby.

Evaluating Correctional & Community Settings. Rudolf H. Moos. LC 73-17450. 400p. 1975. 23.95 (ISBN 0-471-61502-1, Pub. by Wiley-Interscience). Wiley.

Evaluating Educational Environments. Robert M. Smith et al. 1978. pap. text ed. 7.95 (ISBN 0-675-08388-5); instructor's manual 3.95 (ISBN 0-686-67978-4). Merrill.

Evaluating Educational Performance. Herbert J. Walberg. LC 73-17613. 1974. 19.50x (ISBN 0-685-42644-0); text ed. 17.50x (ISBN 0-685-42645-9). McCutchan.

Evaluating Evaluation. Andrew D. Cohen et al. LC 79-56013. (Bilingual Ed. Ser.: No. 6). 71p. 1979. pap. text ed. 5.75x (ISBN 0-87281-109-3). Ctr Appl Ling.

Evaluating Executive & Other Salaried Positions: Specific Programs & Approaches. 1974. 9.00 o.p. (ISBN 0-8144-6202-2). Am Mgmt.

Evaluating Federal Support for Poverty Research. Committee on Evaluation of Poverty Research. 1979. pap. 6.50 (ISBN 0-309-02894-9). Natl Acad Pr.

Evaluating Hospital-Based Ambulatory Care: A Case Study. William C. Stratmann & Ralph Ullman. LC 77-11403. 1980. 24.95 (ISBN 0-669-02096-6). Lexington Bks.

Evaluating in-Service Training for Teachers. Ed. by Colin McCabe. 129p. 1981. pap. text ed. 22.00x (ISBN 0-85633-205-4, NFER). Humanities.

Evaluating Information: A Guide for Users of Social Science Research. Jeffrey Katzer et al. LC 77-88057. (Sociology). (Illus.). 1978. pap. text ed. 7.95 (ISBN 0-201-00948-X). A-W.

Evaluating Instructional Programs. new ed. Bruce W. Tuckman. 1979. text ed. 18.95 (ISBN 0-205-06172-9). Allyn.

Evaluating Instructional Technology. Christopher K. Knapper. (New Pattern in Learning Ser.). 163p. 1980. 26.95x (ISBN 0-470-26994-4). Halsted Pr.

Evaluating Internal Control: Concepts, Guidelines, Procedures, Documentation. Kenneth P. Johnson & Henry R. Jaenicke. LC 79-23172. 1980. 39.95 (ISBN 0-471-05620-0, Ronald). Wiley.

Evaluating Occupational Education & Training Programs. Tim L. Wentling & Tom E. Lawson. 356p. 1975. text ed. 17.95x o.p. (ISBN 0-205-05048-4, 2250489L). Allyn.

Evaluating Our Performance: An Advisory for Boards of Trustees & School Heads. Nais School Administration & Trustee Committees. 1978. pap. 6.50 (ISBN 0-934338-30-2). NAIS.

Evaluating Performance in Physical Education. B. Don Franks & Helga Deutsch. 1973. text ed. 14.95 (ISBN 0-12-266050-1). Acad Pr.

Evaluating Pupil Growth: Principles of Tests & Measurements. 5th ed. J. Stanley Ahmann & Marvin D. Glock. 492p. 1975. text ed. 17.95x o.p. (ISBN 0-205-04497-2, 2244969); tests free o.p. (ISBN 0-685-50740-8); workbook 3.95 o.p. (ISBN 0-685-50741-6). Allyn.

Evaluating Quality of Care: Analytic Procedures, Monitoring Techniques. M. Clinton Miller & Rebecca G. Knapp. LC 79-4482. 1979. 30.95 (ISBN 0-89443-091-2). Aspen Systems.

Evaluating Social Action Projects. 161p. 1981. pap. 9.25 (ISBN 92-3-101807-8, U1052, UNESCO). Unipub.

Evaluating Social Programs: Theory, Practice, & Politics. Ed. by Peter H. Rossi & Walter Williams. LC 75-183473. (Quantitative Studies in Social Relations). 320p. 1972. text ed. 23.00 (ISBN 0-12-785739-7). Acad Pr.

Evaluating Social Projects in Developing Countries. Howard E. Freeman et al. 239p. (Orig.). 1980. pap. text ed. 9.00x (ISBN 92-64-12040-8). OECD.

Evaluating Student Progress in Learning the Practice of Nursing. Alice R. Rines. LC 63-19048. (Orig.). 1963. pap. 4.75x (ISBN 0-8077-2036-4). Tchrs Coll.

Evaluating Student Progress: Principles of Tests & Measurements. 6th ed. Ahmann & Glock. 540p. 1980. text ed. 17.95 (ISBN 0-205-06561-9, 246561-2); test manual (ISBN 0-205-06562-7, 246562-0). Allyn.

Evaluating Tax Shelter Offerings: 1980 Course Handbook. Alan S. Rosenberg. LC 80-80759. 512p. 1980. pap. text ed. 25.00 (ISBN 0-686-68823-6, J4-3477). PLI.

Evaluating Teachers & Administrators: A Performance Objective Approach. George B. Redfern. (Westview Special Studies in Education). 186p. 1980. lib. bdg. 18.50x (ISBN 0-89158-760-8); pap. text ed. 9.50x (ISBN 0-89158-890-6). Westview.

Evaluating Teaching: A Handbook of Positive Approaches. Robert C. Hawley. LC 75-35053. (Orig.). 1976. pap. 9.50 (ISBN 0-913636-07-X). Educ Res MA.

Evaluating the Impact of Nutrition & Health Programs. Ed. by Robert E. Klein et al. LC 79-11321. 476p. 1979. 29.50 (ISBN 0-306-40164-9, Plenum Pr). Plenum Pub.

Evaluating Transnational Programs in Government & Business. Ed. by Kenneth W. Grundy et al. 1980. 29.50 (ISBN 0-08-025101-3). Pergamon.

Evaluating Treatment Environments: A Social Ecological Approach. Rudolf H. Moos. LC 73-17450. (Wiley-Interscience Ser. Health, Medicine, & Society). 304p. 1974. 27.50 (ISBN 0-471-61503-X, Pub. by Wiley-Interscience). Wiley.

Evaluating with Validity. Ernest R. House. LC 80-14695. (Illus.). 295p. 1980. 20.00 (ISBN 0-8039-1438-5); pap. 9.95 (ISBN 0-8039-1439-3). Sage.

Evaluation & Care of Severely Disturbed Children & Their Families. Leon Hoffman. 1981. text ed. write for info. (ISBN 0-89335-129-6). Spectrum Pub.

Evaluation & Improvement of Teaching (in Secondary Schools) Charles W. Knudsen. 538p. 1980. Repr. of 1932 ed. lib. bdg. 30.00 (ISBN 0-89984-302-6). Century Bookbindery.

Evaluation & Management of the Violent Patient: Guidelines in the Hospital & Institution. John R. Lion. 88p. 1972. 8.75 (ISBN 0-398-02542-8). C C Thomas.

Evaluation & Measurement Techniques for Digital Computer Systems. Mansford E. Drummond, Jr. (Illus.). 352p. 1973. ref. ed. 24.00x (ISBN 0-13-292102-2). P-H.

Evaluation & Prediction of Subsidence: Proceedings. Engineering Foundation Conference, Jan. 1978. Compiled By American Society of Civil Engineers. 600p. 1978. pap. text ed. 36.00 (ISBN 0-87262-137-5). Am Soc Civil Eng.

Evaluation & Regulation of Body Build & Composition. Albert R. Behnke, Jr. & Jack H. Wilmore. (International Research Monograph Series in Physical Education). (Illus.). 224p. 1974. ref. ed. 11.95 (ISBN 0-13-292284-3). P-H.

Evaluation Concepts & Methods: Shaping Policy for the Health Administrator. Paul C. Nutt. (Health Care Administration: Vol. 14). (Illus.). 364p. 1981. text ed. 29.95 (ISBN 0-89335-094-X). Spectrum Pub.

Evaluation, Diagnosis, & Treatment of Occlusal Problems. Peter E. Dawson. LC 74-12409. 1974. 49.50 (ISBN 0-8016-1216-0). Mosby.

Evaluation in Education. new ed. W. James Popham. LC 74-12822. 601p. 1974. 21.00 (ISBN 0-8211-1512-X); text ed. 19.00 (ISBN 0-685-57220-X). McCutchan.

Evaluation in Education, Vol. 3. Ed. by B. H. Choppin & T. N. Postlethwaite. (Reviews in Educational Evaluation Ser.). 250p. 1980. 56.00 (ISBN 0-08-026066-7). Pergamon.

Evaluation in Education: Foundations of Competency Assessment & Program Review. Richard M. Wolf. LC 78-25743. 1979. 19.95 (ISBN 0-03-049116-9). Praeger.

Evaluation in Education: International Progress, Vol. 1. Ed. by B. Choppin & N. Postlethwaite. 1979. text ed. 56.00 (ISBN 0-08-023352-X). Pergamon.

Evaluation in Physical Education. 2nd ed. Margaret J. Safrit. (Illus.). 1980. text ed. 15.95 (ISBN 0-13-292250-9). P-H.

Evaluation in Physical Education: Assessing Motor Behavior. Margaret J. Safrit. LC 72-5427. (Illus.). 336p. 1973. text ed. 15.95x (ISBN 0-13-292227-4). P-H.

Evaluation in the Management of Human Services. Ed. by C. Clifford Atkinsson, Jr. et al. 1978. 33.00 (ISBN 0-12-066350-3). Acad Pr.

Evaluation in the Planning Process. N. Lichfield et al. 336p. 1976. text ed. 36.00 (ISBN 0-08-017843-X); pap. text ed. 19.50 (ISBN 0-08-018243-7). Pergamon.

Evaluation of Ambient Air Quality by Personnel Monitoring, Vols. 1 & 2. 2nd ed. Adrian L. Linch. (Vol. 1-336pp., vol. 2-304pp.). 1981. Vol. 1. 69.95 (ISBN 0-8493-5293-2); Vol. 2. 69.95 (ISBN 0-8493-5294-0). CRC Pr.

Evaluation of an Intervention Programme for Disadvantaged Children. Thomas Kellagham. (General Ser.). (Illus., Orig.). 1977. pap. text ed. 16.50x (ISBN 0-85633-124-4, NFER). Humanities.

Evaluation of Behavior Therapy: Issues, Evidence & Research Strategies. Alan E. Kazdin & G. Terence Wilson. LC 80-10311. xx, 230p. 1980. pap. 4.50x (ISBN 0-8032-7752-0, BB 745, Bison). U of Nebr Pr.

Evaluation of Biomaterials. George D. Winter. LC 79-42730. (Advances in Biomaterials Ser.). 1980. 135.00 (ISBN 0-471-27658-8, Pub. by Wiley-Interscience). Wiley.

Evaluation of Components for Underground Heat Distribution Systems. Federal Construction Council - Building Research Advisory Board. 1964. pap. 2.75 (ISBN 0-309-01196-5). Natl Acad Pr.

Evaluation of Composition Instruction. Barbara Davis et al. LC 80-68774. 160p. (Orig.). 1981. pap. 6.95x (ISBN 0-918528-11-9). Edgepress.

Evaluation of Continuing Education for Professionals: A Systems View. Ed. by Preston P. Le Breton. LC 79-4923. 340p. (Orig.). 1979. pap. 11.50 (ISBN 0-295-95693-3, Pub. by Div Acad Prof Progs). U of Wash Pr.

Evaluation of Dam Safety: Proceedings. Engineering Foundation Conference, Nov. 1976. Compiled By American Society of Civil Engineers. 532p. 1977. pap. text ed. 16.00 (ISBN 0-87262-088-3). Am Soc Civil Eng.

Evaluation of Driver Education: A Study of History, Philosophy, Research Methodology, & Effectiveness in the Field of Driver Education. Frederick L. McGuire & Ronald C. Kersh. (California Library Reprint Series: No. 24). 1971. 15.75x (ISBN 0-520-01931-8). U of Cal Pr.

Evaluation of Drug Activities: Pharmacometrics, 2 Vols. Ed. by D. R. Laurence & A. L. Bacharach. 1965. Vol. 1. 59.00 (ISBN 0-12-438301-7); Vol. 2. 59.00 (ISBN 0-12-438302-5). Acad Pr.

Evaluation of Econometric Models. Ed. by Jan Kmenta & James B. Ramsey. 1980. 39.50 (ISBN 0-12-416550-8). Acad Pr.

Evaluation of Graduates of Associate Degree Nursing Programs. Mildred L. Montag. LC 72-84012. 1972. pap. text ed. 4.50x (ISBN 0-8077-1828-9). Tchrs Coll.

Evaluation of Industrial Disability. 2nd ed. Packard Thurber. Ed. by California Medical Association & Industrial Accident Commission. 1960. pap. 4.50x (ISBN 0-19-501143-0). Oxford U Pr.

Evaluation of Information Services & Products. Donald W. King & Edward C. Bryant. LC 76-141595. (Illus.). 306p. 1971. text ed. 21.95 (ISBN 0-87815-003-X). Info Resources.

Evaluation of New Science: Worksheets for Scottish Integrated Science. S. H. Kellington & A. C. Mitchell. 1978. pap. text ed. 9.50x o.p. (ISBN 0-435-57500-7). Heinemann Ed.

Evaluation of Operation Neighborhood. Peter B. Bloch & David I. Specht. 1973. pap. 7.00 o.p. (ISBN 0-87766-089-1, 26000). Urban Inst.

Evaluation of Plant & Soil Fertility. D. Davidescu & V. Davidescu. 1980. write for info. (ISBN 0-85626-123-8, Pub. by Abacus Pr). Intl Schol Bk Serv.

Evaluation of Policy-Related Rehabilitation Research. Monroe Berkowitz et al. LC 75-23957. (Illus.). 244p. 1975. text ed. 23.95 (ISBN 0-275-01260-3). Praeger.

Evaluation of Postal Service Wage Rates. Douglas K. Adie. 1977. pap. 3.75 (ISBN 0-8447-3265-6). Am Enterprise.

Evaluation of Proteins for Humans. C. E. Bodwell. (Illus.). 1977. lib. bdg. 37.50 (ISBN 0-87055-215-5). AVI.

Evaluation of Public Health Hazards from Microbiological Contamination of Foods. Committee On Food Protection. 1964. pap. 3.75 (ISBN 0-309-01195-7). Natl Acad Pr.

Evaluation of Quality of Care in Psychiatry: Proceedings of a Symposium Held at the Queen St. Mental Health Centre, Toronto, Canada, June 22, 1979. A. G. Awad et al. LC 80-94280. 140p. 1980. 21.00 (ISBN 0-08-025364-4). Pergamon.

Evaluation of Radiation Emergencies & Accidents: Selected Criteria & Data. Edward J. Vallario. (Technical Reports Ser.: No. 152). (Illus.). 135p. (Orig.). 1974. pap. 12.50 (ISBN 92-0-125074-6, IAEA). Unipub.

Evaluation of Recreation & Park Programs. William F. Theobald. LC 78-24227. 1979. 19.95x (ISBN 0-471-01797-3). Wiley.

Evaluation of Risk in Business Investment. J. C. Hull. LC 80-40136. (Illus.). 192p. 1980. 27.00 (ISBN 0-08-024075-5); pap. 15.00 (ISBN 0-08-024074-7). Pergamon.

Evaluation of Seed Protein Alterations by Mutation Breeding: Proceedings. (Illus.). 1976. pap. 18.25 (ISBN 92-0-111076-6, IAEA). Unipub.

Evaluation of Sensibility & Reeducation of Sensation of the Hand. A. Lee Dellon. (Illus.). 140p. 1981. write for info. (2427-2). Williams & Wilkins.

Evaluation of Social Programs. Ed. by Clark C. Abt. LC 76-40712. (Illus.). 503p. 1977. 29.95 (ISBN 0-8039-0735-4). Sage.

Evaluation of Social Programs. Ed. by Clark C. Abt. (Illus.). 503p. 1979. pap. 12.95 (ISBN 0-8039-1412-1). Sage.

Evaluation of Teaching in Medical Schools. Robert M. Rippey. LC 80-19891. (Medical Education Ser.). 1980. text ed. 19.95 (ISBN 0-8261-3440-8). Springer Pub.

Evaluation of the CDS-CDTE Heterojuction Solar Cell. Paul B. Parks. LC 78-74996. (Outstanding Dissertations on Energy Ser.). 1979. lib. bdg. 14.00 (ISBN 0-8240-3991-2). Garland Pub.

Evaluation of the Concept of Storing Radioactive Wastes in Bedrock Below the Savannah River Plant Site. Committee on Radioactive Waste Management. (Illus.). 88p. 1972. pap. 3.50 (ISBN 0-309-02035-2). Natl Acad Pr.

Evaluation of the Salmonella Problem. Committee On Salmonella - Division Of Biology And Agriculture. LC 76-600461. (Illus., Orig.). 1969. pap. 7.00 (ISBN 0-309-01683-5). Natl Acad Pr.

Evaluation of Toxicological Data for the Protection of Public Health: Proceedings of an International Colloquium, Luxemburg, 1976. Ed. by W. J. Hunter & G. P. Smeets. 1977. pap. text ed. 57.00 (ISBN 0-08-021998-5). Pergamon.

Evaluation of Trawl Performance by Statistical Inference of the Catch. G. A. Motte & Y. Iitaka. (Marine Technical Report Ser.: No. 36). 1975. pap. 2.00 (ISBN 0-938412-08-6). URI MAS.

Evaluation of Uranium Resources. 1979. pap. 39.75 (ISBN 92-0-141079-4, ISP507, IAEA). Unipub.

Evaluation of Urban Public Transport Alternatives. Terry Thomas. Date not set. cancelled (ISBN 0-08-023734-7). Pergamon.

Evaluation Planning at the National Institute of Mental Health: A Case History. Pamela Horst et al. 166p. 1974. pap. 5.00 o.p. (ISBN 0-87766-097-2, 27000). Urban Inst.

Evaluation: Practical Guidelines. George W. Renwick. LC 79-92378. (Intercultural Handbks.). (Illus.). 1980. pap. text ed. 4.50 (ISBN 0-933662-08-4). Intercult Pr.

Evaluation Primer Workbook: Practical Exercises for Educators. Arlene Fink & Jacqueline Kosecoff. LC 77-88462. (Illus.). 57p. 1980. pap. 7.95 (ISBN 0-8039-1481-4). Sage.

Evaluation Primer Workbook: Practical Exercises for Health Professionals. Arlene Fink & Jacqueline Kosecoff. LC 77-88463. (Illus.). 89p. 1980. pap. 8.95 (ISBN 0-8039-1482-2). Sage.

Evaluation: Promise & Performance. Joseph S. Wholey. (Institute Paper). 226p. 1979. pap. 7.50 (ISBN 0-87766-250-9, 25100). Urban Inst.

Evaluation Research in Education. W. W. Cooley & P. R. Lohnes. LC 75-37696. 352p. 1976. 16.50 (ISBN 0-470-01398-2). Halsted Pr.

Evaluation Research Methods: A Basic Guide. Ed. by Leonard Rutman. LC 77-17264. (Sage Focus Editions: Vol. 3). 1977. 18.95x (ISBN 0-8039-0907-1); pap. 9.95x (ISBN 0-8039-0908-X). Sage.

Evaluation Research: Methods of Assessing Program Effectiveness. Carol H. Weiss. (Methods of Social Science Ser). (Illus.). 176p. 1972. pap. text ed. 10.95 (ISBN 0-13-292193-6). P-H.

Evaluation Roles. Arieh Lewy & David Nevo. 500p. 1981. price not set (ISBN 0-677-16290-1). Gordon.

Evaluation Strategies in Criminal Justice. William Davidson et al. (Pergamon General Psychology Ser.). Date not set. 27.51 (ISBN 0-08-024664-8). Pergamon.

Evaluation Studies Review Annual, Vol. 4. rev. ed. Ed. by Lee Sechrest et al. LC 76-15865. (Illus.). 766p. 1979. 35.00 (ISBN 0-8039-1329-X). Sage.

Evaluation Thesaurus. 2nd ed. Michael Scriven. LC 80-68775. 149p. 1980. pap. text ed. 6.95x (ISBN 0-918528-08-9). Edgepress.

Evaluation to Improve Learning. Benjamin S. Bloom & George F. Madaus. (Illus.). 352p. (Orig.). 1981. pap. text ed. 13.95 (ISBN 0-07-006109-2). McGraw.

Evaluations of Drug Interactions: 1976. 2nd ed. LC 76-14501. 30.00 (ISBN 0-917330-10-2); 1978 supplement 9.00 (ISBN 0-917330-20-X). Am Pharm Assn.

Evaluative Methods in Psychiatric Education. H. L. Muslin et al. 220p. 1974. pap. 10.00 (ISBN 0-685-65574-1, P182-0). Am Psychiatric.

Evaluator & Management. Ed. by Herbert C. Schulberg & Jeanette M. Jerrell. LC 79-19458. (Sage Research Progress Ser. in Evaluation: Vol. 4). (Illus.). 1979. 12.95x (ISBN 0-8039-1304-4); pap. 6.50x (ISBN 0-8039-1305-2). Sage.

Evalution Guidebook-a Set of Practical Guidelines for the Educational Evaluator. W. James Popham. 1972. pap. 5.95 o.p. (ISBN 0-932166-01-6). Instruct Object.

Evalution of Staff Development in Technical & Further Education: A Proposed Methodology. Adrian Fordham & John Ainley. (Australian Council for Educational Research Monograph: No. 7). 266p. 1980. pap. text ed. 22.50 (ISBN 0-85563-207-0). Verry.

Evan Fry's Illustrations from Radio Sermons. Ed. by Norman D. Ruoff. LC 74-84763. 1975. 6.50 o.p. (ISBN 0-8309-0131-0). Herald Hse.

Evangel Reader. Charles W. Conn. 1958. 3.25 (ISBN 0-87148-275-4). Pathway Pr.

Evangel Sermons. Wade H. Horton. LC 76-57860. 1977. pap. 2.95 (ISBN 0-87148-287-8). Pathway Pr.

Evangelical Awakenings in Africa. J. Edwin Orr. LC 74-32018. (Awakening Ser). 272p. 1975. pap. 4.95 (ISBN 0-87123-128-X, 210138). Bethany Fell.

Evangelical Awakenings in Eastern Asia. J. Edwin Orr. LC 74-30353. (Awakening Ser). 192p. (Orig.). 1975. pap. 4.95 (ISBN 0-87123-126-3, 210126). Bethany Fell.

Evangelical Awakenings in Latin America. J. Edwin Orr. LC 77-16148. (Awakening Ser). 1978. pap. 4.95 (ISBN 0-87123-130-1, 210130). Bethany Fell.

Evangelical Awakenings in Southern Asia. J. Edwin Orr. LC 74-32019. (Awakening Ser). 256p. (Orig.). 1975. pap. 4.95 (ISBN 0-87123-127-1, 210127). Bethany Fell.

Evangelical Awakenings in the South Seas. J. Edwin Orr. LC 76-26966. (Awakening Ser). 1977. pap. 4.95 (ISBN 0-87123-129-8, 210129). Bethany Fell.

Evangelical Mind & the New School Presbyterian Experience: A Case Study of Thought & Theology in Nineteenth-Century America. George M. Marsden. LC 75-118731. (Publications in American Studies: No. 20). 1970. 18.50x o.p. (ISBN 0-300-01343-4). Yale U Pr.

Evangelical Missions Quarterly, Vols. 7-9. Ed. by James W. Reapsome et al. LC 71-186301. 1973. Set. 13.95x (ISBN 0-87808-707-9). William Carey Lib.

Evangelical Missions Quarterly, Vols. 10-12. Ed. by James Reapsome et al. LC 71-186301. (Illus.). 1978. Set. 16.95x (ISBN 0-87808-708-7). William Carey Lib.

Evangelical Missions Quarterly, Vols. 13-15. Ed. by James Reapsome et al. LC 71-186301. 803p. 1980. Repr. 19.95 (ISBN 0-87808-709-5). William Carey Lib.

Evangelical Precepts of the Revelation. Clyde C. Cox. 1972. 4.95 (ISBN 0-87148-278-9). Pathway Pr.

Evangelical Roots: A Tribute to Wilbur Smith. Kenneth Kantzer. LC 77-17963. 1977. 8.95 o.p. (ISBN 0-8407-5120-6). Nelson.

Evangelical Succession. D. N. Samuel. 144p. pap. 7.95 (ISBN 0-227-67834-6). Attic Pr.

Evangelical Sunday School Lesson Commentary 1978-79. James E. Humbertson. 1979. 5.50 o.p. (ISBN 0-87148-290-8). Pathway Pr.

Evangelical Sunday School Lesson Commentary, 1979-80. Ed. by James E. Humbertson. 448p. 1979. 5.95 (ISBN 0-87148-291-6). Pathway Pr.

Evangelical Theology. A. A. Hodge. 1976. pap. 5.45 (ISBN 0-85151-236-4). Banner of Truth.

Evangelical Theology, Eighteen Thirty-Three to Eighteen Fifty-Six: A Response to Tractarianism. Ed. by Peter Toon & Peter Martin. LC 79-16701. (New Foundations Theological Library Ser.). 254p. 18.50 (ISBN 0-8042-3703-4). John Knox.

Evangelical-Unification Dialogue. Ed. by Richard Quebedeaux & Rodney Sawatsky. LC 79-89421. (Conference Ser.: No. 3). (Orig.). 1979. pap. text ed. 7.95 (ISBN 0-932894-02-X). Unif Theol Seminary.

Evangelicos, los Catolicos y la Virgen Maria. Stephen Benko. Tr. by Alfonso Olmedo from Eng. Orig. Title: Protestants, Catholics & Mary. Date not set. pap. price not set (ISBN 0-311-05041-7). Casa Bautista.

Evangeline & Other Poems. Henry W. Longfellow. (Classics Ser.). (gr. 7 up). pap. 1.50 (ISBN 0-8049-0094-9, CL-94). Airmont.

Evangelio Segun San Lucas. Marilyn Kunz & Catherine Schell. Tr. by Grace S. Roberts from Eng. LC 75-42950. (Encuentros Biblicos). 64p. (Orig., Span.). pap. 1.25 (ISBN 0-89922-063-0). Edit Caribe.

Evangelio y Epistolas De Juan: Texto Programado. Weldon E. Viertel. 304p. (Span.). 1981. pap. write for info. (ISBN 0-311-04347-X). Casa Bautista.

Evangelios-Para que vino Jesus? 14 Lecciones, Tomo 2. Bernice C. Jordan. (Pasos De Fe Ser.). (Span.). pap. text ed. 2.25 (ISBN 0-86508-411-4); figuras 7.95 (ISBN 0-86508-412-2). BCM Inc.

Evangelios-Quien es Jesus? 14 Lecciones, Tomo 1. Bernice C. Jordan. (Pasos De Fe Ser.). (Span.). pap. text ed. 2.25 (ISBN 0-86508-409-2); figuras 7.95 (ISBN 0-86508-410-6). BCM Inc.

Evangelism & Your Church. C. J. Miller. 1980. pap. 2.95 (ISBN 0-87552-290-4). Presby & Reformed.

Evangelism As a Lifestyle. Jim Petersen. LC 80-83874. 1980. pap. 3.95 (ISBN 0-89109-475-X). NavPress.

Evangelism in the Early Church. Michael Green. 1970. pap. 5.95 (ISBN 0-8028-1612-6). Eerdmans.

Evangelism: The Church on Fire! Robert L. Sumner. 220p. 1960. 4.75 (ISBN 0-87398-211-8, Pub. by Bibl Evang Pr). Sword of Lord.

Evangelism: The Ministry of the Church. Ed. by Richard Hughes & Joseph A. Serig. 1981. pap. 12.00 (ISBN 0-8309-0304-6). Herald Hse.

Evangelismo En Accion. Leroy Watkins. 1979. 4.95 (ISBN 0-311-13831-4). Casa Bautista.

Evangelismo Personal. Tr. by Myer Pearlman. (Spanish Bks.). 1978. 1.25 (ISBN 0-8297-0552-X). Life Pubs Intl.

Evangelist: Eighteen Thirty-Two to Eighteen Forty-Two, 10 vols. Walter Scott. 1980. Repr. text ed. 99.95 (ISBN 0-89900-226-9). College Pr Pub.

Evangelization in the World Today. Ed. by Norbert Greinacher. (Concilium Ser.: Vol. 114). 1979. pap. 4.95 (ISBN 0-8164-2610-4). Crossroad NY.

Evans of the Army. Steve Gelman. LC 64-11699. 3.95 o.p. (ISBN 0-385-03986-7). Doubleday.

Evapotranspiration from Rice Fields. (IRRI Research Paper Ser.: No. 34). 15p. 1979. pap. 5.00 (R074, IRRI). Unipub.

Evasive Peace. John Davis. 1970. pap. 2.95 (ISBN 0-911026-01-0). New World Press NY.

Evatt the Enigma: Controverial Australian. Allan Dalziel. 9.95x (ISBN 0-392-07809-0, SpS). Soccer.

Eve & Henry James: Portraits of Women & Girls in His Fiction. Edward Wagenknecht. LC 77-18613. 1978. 12.50 o.p. (ISBN 0-8061-1422-3). U of Okla Pr.

Eve & the Others. Edith Thomas. Tr. by Estelle Eirinberg from Fr. LC 75-36694. Orig. Title: Eve et les Autres. 125p. 1976. case bound 6.95 (ISBN 0-916868-01-X); pap. 3.50 (ISBN 0-685-65847-3). Continent Edns.

Eve of Saint Venus. Anthony Burgess. 128p. 1979. pap. 1.95 (ISBN 0-393-00915-7). Norton.

Eveil de l'Europe. B. Guillemain. (Histoire universelle Larousse de poche). (Fr). pap. 3.50 (ISBN 0-685-13913-1). Larousse.

Evel Knievel. Larry Batson. LC 74-18302. (Sports Superstars Ser). (Illus.). 32p. (gr. 3-6). 1974. PLB 5.95 (ISBN 0-87191-385-2); pap. 2.75 o. p. (ISBN 0-89812-191-4). Creative Ed.

Evel Knievel: Motorcycle Daredevil. Dorothy C. Schmitz. LC 77-70889. (Pros Ser.). (Illus.). (gr. 2). 1977. PLB 6.45 (ISBN 0-913940-61-5). Crestwood Hse.

Evelina. Fanny Burney. 1958. 5.00x o.p. (ISBN 0-460-00352-6, Evman). Dutton.

Evelina: Or, the History of a Young Lady's Entrance into the World. Frances Burney. Ed. by Edward A. Bloom. (Oxford English Novels Ser & Oxford Paperbacks Ser). 1968. pap. 4.95x (ISBN 0-19-281075-8). Oxford U Pr.

Eveline: The Amorous Adventures of a Victorian Lady. LC 80-8915. 352p. 1981. pap. 3.25 (ISBN 0-394-17892-0, BC). Grove.

Evelyn Innes, Repr. Of 1898 Ed. George Moore. Ed. by Robert L. Wolff. Bd. with Sister Teresa. Repr. of 1901 ed. LC 75-464. (Victorian Fiction Ser). 1975. lib. bdg. 66.00 (ISBN 0-8240-1542-8). Garland Pub.

Evelyn Sharp Collection. Louise A. Svendsen. LC 78-51870. (Illus.). 1978. soft cover 7.50 (ISBN 0-89207-012-9). S R Guggenheim.

Evelyn Underhill. Christopher Armstrong. LC 75-33401. 1976. 8.95 o.p. (ISBN 0-8028-3474-4). Eerdmans.

Evelyn Waugh. Calvin W. Lane. (English Authors Ser.: No. 301). 1981. lib. bdg. 9.95 (ISBN 0-8057-6793-2). Twayne.

Evelyn Waugh. David Lodge. LC 78-136497. (Columbia Essays on Modern Writers Ser.: No. 58). 48p. 1971. pap. 2.00 (ISBN 0-231-03258-7, MW58). Columbia U Pr.

Evelyn Waugh, Writer: The Making of a Man of Letters. Robert M. Davis. 270p. 1980. 21.95x (ISBN 0-937664-00-6). Pilgrim Bks OK.

Evelyn Waugh's Officers, Gentlemen & Rogues: The Fact Behind His Fiction. Gene D. Phillips. LC 75-26546. 195p. 1975. 11.95 (ISBN 0-88229-172-6); pap. 7.95 (ISBN 0-88229-495-4). Nelson Hall.

Even Big Guys Cry. Alex Karas & Herb Gluck. LC 77-71376. 1977. 8.95 o.p. (ISBN 0-03-017371-X). HR&W.

Even More Challenging Baseball Quiz Book. David Nemec. 1978. pap. 1.95 o.s.i. (ISBN 0-02-023200-4, Collier). Macmillan.

Even Revolutionaries Like Chocolate Chip Cookies: Selected Cartoons from "Still a Few Bugs in the System". Gary B. Trudeau. (Doonesbury Ser.). (Illus.). 128p. 1974. pap. 1.75 (ISBN 0-445-00622-6). Popular Lib.

Even the Dog Won't Eat My Meat Loaf. Carl Larsen. LC 79-19887. 1980. pap. 5.95 (ISBN 0-89645-011-2). Media Ventures.

Evening Before the Diesel: A History of the Grand Trunk Western Railroad. Charles R. Foss. (Illus.). 1980. 44.95 (ISBN 0-87108-552-6). Pruett.

Evening Edged in Gold. Arno Schmidt. LC 79-3373. (Helen & Kurt Wolff Bk.). 224p. 1980. 74.95 (ISBN 0-15-129376-7). HarBraceJ.

Evening Gray, Morning Red: A Handbook of American Weather Wisdom. Barbara Wolff. LC 76-15640. (Ready to Read Ser.). (Illus.). (gr. 1-4). 1976. 8.95 (ISBN 0-02-793320-2, 79332). Macmillan.

Evening Light Songs. 512p. 4.50. Faith Pub Hse.

Evening Star. Martin Evans. (Illus.). 224p. (Orig.). 1980. pap. 16.50x (ISBN 0-85242-634-8). Intl Pubns Serv.

Evening Sun Turned Crimson. Herbert E. Huncke. LC 79-2555. 1980. 15.00x o.p. (ISBN 0-916156-45-1); pap. 5.00x (ISBN 0-916156-43-5); signed & numbered ed. 25.00x (ISBN 0-916156-44-3). Cherry Valley.

Event Horse. Sheila Willcox. LC 73-5923. (Illus.). 160p. 1973. 9.95 (ISBN 0-397-01000-1). Lippincott.

Event of the Qur'an. Kenneth Cragg. 1971. text ed. 17.95x o.p. (ISBN 0-04-297024-5). Allen Unwin.

Eventing. Caroline Silver. LC 76-28058. 1977. 15.95 (ISBN 0-312-27090-9). St Martin.

Events & Their Afterlife. A. C. Charity. 1966. 39.95 (ISBN 0-521-04622-X). Cambridge U Pr.

Events & Wisdoms. Donald Davie. LC 65-21077. (Wesleyan Poetry Program: Vol. 27). (Orig.). 1965. 10.00x (ISBN 0-8195-2027-6, Pub. by Wesleyan U Pr); pap. 4.95x (ISBN 0-8195-1027-0). Columbia U Pr.

Events That Changed My Life. Hal Lindsey. 1977. pap. 0.98 o.s.i. (ISBN 0-88449-026-2). Vision Hse.

Events That Shook the World. Shirley Algieri. Ed. by Thomas J. Mooney. (Pal Paperbacks Ser., Kit B). (Illus., Orig.). (gr. 7-12). 1974. pap. text ed. 1.25 (ISBN 0-8374-3513-7). Xerox Ed Pubns.

Ever After. 10.00 (ISBN 0-8015-2419-9, Hawthorn). Dutton.

Ever After. Elswyth Thane. (Williamsburg Ser.: No. 3). 1981. lib. bdg. 17.95 (ISBN 0-8161-3165-1, Large Print Bks). G K Hall.

Ever Been Irritated? Dan Day. (Uplook Ser.). 31p. 1972. pap. 0.75 (ISBN 0-8163-0070-4, 05630-9). Pacific Pr Pub Assn.

Ever Get Depressed. Katie Tom. (Uplook Ser.). 1977. pap. 0.75 (ISBN 0-8163-0280-4). Pacific Pr Pub Assn.

Ever-Ready Eddie. Carolyn Haywood. LC 68-27687. (Illus.). (gr. 3-7). 1968. 7.25 o.p. (ISBN 0-688-21277-8); PLB 6.96 o.p. (ISBN 0-688-31277-2). Morrow.

Ever Since Sinai. 3rd ed. Jakob J. Petuchowski. LC 79-64324. 1979. pap. text ed. 4.95 (ISBN 0-930038-11-8). Arbit.

Ever-Victorious Army: A History of the Chinese Campaign Under Lt. Col. C. G. Gordon & of the Suppression of the T'ai P'ing Rebellion. Andrew Wilson. (Studies in Chinese History & Civilization). 395p. 1977. 24.75 (ISBN 0-89093-078-3). U Pubns Amer.

Everest: Expedition to the Ultimate. Reinhold Messner. (Illus.). 1979. 18.95 (ISBN 0-19-520135-3). Oxford U Pr.

Everest: Goddess of the Wind. Ronald Faux. (Illus.). 1978. 13.95 (ISBN 0-550-20361-3, Pub. by Two Continents); pap. 7.95 (ISBN 0-550-20351-6). Hippocrene Bks.

Everest: The West Ridge. Thomas F. Hornbein. LC 80-16088. (Illus.). 224p. 1980. Repr. of 1965 ed. 17.50 (ISBN 0-916890-90-2). Mountaineers.

Everett Massacre. Walker C. Smith. LC 72-151619. (Civil Liberties in American History Ser.). 1971. Repr. of 1920 ed. lib. bdg. 32.50 (ISBN 0-306-70150-2). Da Capo.

Everett Spruce: A Portfolio of Eight Paintings. Everett Spruce. (Blaffer Ser. of Southwestern Art: No. 1). 1958. 40.00 (ISBN 0-292-73387-9). U of Tex Pr.

Everflowing Streams. Michael Bausch & Ruth Duck. 96p. (Orig.). 1981. pap. 3.95 (ISBN 0-8298-0428-5). Pilgrim NY.

Everglades. Archie Carr. (American Wilderness Ser). (Illus.). 1973. 12.95 (ISBN 0-8094-1172-5). Time-Life.

Everglades. Archie Carr. LC 72-96548. (American Wilderness Ser). (Illus.). 1973. lib. bdg. 11.97 (ISBN 0-8094-1173-3, Pub. by Time-Life). Silver.

Everglades: The Story Behind the Scenery. Jack De Golia. Ed. by Gweneth R. DenDooven. LC 78-71200. (Illus.). 1978. 7.95 (ISBN 0-916122-56-5); pap. 3.50 (ISBN 0-916122-55-7). K C Pubns.

Evergreen: A Guide to Basic Writing. Susan C. Fawcett & Alvin Sandberg. LC 79-89001. 1980. pap. text ed. 9.95 (ISBN 0-395-28694-8); instrs' manual 0.35 (ISBN 0-395-28695-6). HM.

Evergreen Garden Trees & Shrubs: A Macmillan Color Indentification Guide. Anthony Huxley. LC 73-8709. (Illus.). 192p. 1973. 7.95 o.s.i. (ISBN 0-02-557960-6). Macmillan.

Evergreens. James U. Crockett. (Encyclopedia of Gardening Ser). (Illus.). 1971. 11.95 (ISBN 0-8094-1105-9); lib. bdg. avail. (ISBN 0-685-02974-3). Time-Life.

Evergreens. James U. Crockett. LC 78-140420. (Time-Life Encyclopedia of Gardening). (Illus.). (gr. 6 up). 1971. lib. bdg. 11.97 (ISBN 0-8094-1106-7, Pub. by Time-Life). Silver.

Evergreens. H. Peter Loewer. (Illus.). 144p. Date not set. 11.95 (ISBN 0-8027-0662-2). Walker & Co.

Everlasting Exiles. Wallace West. (YA) 5.95 (ISBN 0-685-07431-5, Avalon). Bouregy.

Everlasting Flowers. Macmillan. (Illus.). 72p. 1976. 9.95 (ISBN 0-02-578300-9). Macmillan.

Everlasting Life in Biblical Thought. Philip B. Harner. 1981. 6.95 (ISBN 0-8062-1611-5). Carlton.

Everlasting Man. G. K. Chesterton. 280p. 1974. pap. 2.95 (ISBN 0-385-07198-1, Im). Doubleday.

Everlasting Sky: New Voices from the People Named the Chippewa. Gerald Vizenor. LC 70-189729. (Illus.). (gr. 7 up). 1972. 7.95 (ISBN 0-02-792250-2, CCPr). Macmillan.

Evermore. Barbara Steward & Dwight Steward. 1978. 7.95 o.p. (ISBN 0-688-03278-8). Morrow.

Eversonian Plateau. Henry M. Barton. 1981. 4.95 (ISBN 0-8062-1567-4). Carlton.

Everson's Best Farm Manual & Helpful Hints. Ralph Everson & Mary Everson. LC 80-68664. (Illus.). 300p. (Orig.). 1980. pap. 9.95 (ISBN 0-89708-027-0). And Bks.

Everwidening Circle: A Workable Plan for Women's Bible Studies. Naomi Wright. LC 77-18361. 1978. pap. 3.95 (ISBN 0-930014-17-0). Multnomah.

Every Believer a Minister. Rex Edwards. LC 78-59308. (Dimension Ser.). 1979. pap. 5.95 (ISBN 0-8163-0234-0). Pacific Pr Pub Assn.

Every Body Is Beautiful. Ron Fletcher & Alan Ebert. (Illus.). 1978. 14.95 o.p. (ISBN 0-397-01312-4). Lippincott.

Every Boy's Judo. Anthony P. Harrington. (Illus.). (YA) (RL 7). 1971. pap. 0.95 o.p. (ISBN 0-451-06407-0, Q6407, Sig). NAL.

Every Child a Winner: Individualized Instruction. Gertrude Noar. 150p. 1981. pap. price not set (ISBN 0-89874-340-0). Krieger.

Every Child Can Learn. Staff of NCCE. 1980. pap. 0.50 (ISBN 0-934460-11-6). NCCE.

Every-Day Book, 2 Vols. William Hone. LC 67-12945. 1967. Repr. of 1827 ed. Set. 76.00 (ISBN 0-8103-3005-9). Gale.

Every Day in the Year: A Political Epitome of the World's History. Ed. by James L. Ford & Mary K. Ford. LC 68-17941. 1969. Repr. of 1902 ed. 18.00 (ISBN 0-8103-3105-5). Gale.

Every Employee a Manager. M. Scott Myers. Ed. by William R. Newton. (Illus.). 1981. 16.50 (ISBN 0-07-044269-X, P&RB). McGraw.

Every First Monday: A History of Canton, Texas. David N. Wren. 7.95 (ISBN 0-685-48793-8). Nortex Pr.

Every Four Years: The American Presidency. Ed. by Robert C. Post. 1980. 21.95 (ISBN 0-89599-005-9). Smithsonian Expo Bks.

Every Four Years: The American Presidency. Smithsonian Institution. (Smithsonian Exposition Bk.). (Illus.). 1980. 21.95 (ISBN 0-89577-005-9). Norton.

Every Kid Can Win. Terry Orlick & Cal Botterill. LC 74-19385. 190p. 1975. 13.95 (ISBN 0-88229-194-7); pap. 8.95 (ISBN 0-88229-471-7). Nelson-Hall.

Every Man Heart Lay Down. Lorenz Graham. LC 75-109899. (Illus.). (gr. 2-5). 1970. 8.95 (ISBN 0-690-27134-4, TYC-J). T Y Crowell.

Every Man Is Innocent Until Proven Broke. Brant Parker & Johnny Hart. (Wizard of Id Ser.). (Illus.). 1978. pap. 1.50 (ISBN 0-449-13650-7, GM). Fawcett.

Every Member Evangelism for Today. rev. ed. Roy J. Fish. LC 75-12289. 128p. 1976. pap. 4.95 (ISBN 0-06-061551-6, RD125, HarpR). Har-Row.

Every Person's Guide to Good Self-Esteem. Margaret Holmes. (Illus.). 1980. pap. 12.95 o.p. (ISBN 0-930490-17-7). Future Shop.

Every Pilot's Guide to Aviation Fuel Economy. Orson Kellogg. (Illus.). 64p. (Orig.). 1980. pap. 4.95 (ISBN 0-935802-00-2). Taxlogs.

Every Second Child. Archie Kalokerinos. LC 80-84435. 138p. 1981. pap. 2.95 (ISBN 0-87983-250-9). Keats.

Every Second Year: Congressional Behavior & the Two-Year Term. Charles O. Jones. 1967. 9.95 (ISBN 0-8157-4712-8); pap. 3.95 (ISBN 0-8157-4711-X). Brookings.

Every Wall a Door. Anne Dooley. 1974. pap. 2.95 o.p. (ISBN 0-525-47380-7). Dutton.

Every Whit Whole. Michael Drury. LC 78-18389. 1978. 5.95 (ISBN 0-396-07578-9). Dodd.

Every Woman in Her Humor: A Critical Edition. Archie M. Tyson. Ed. by Stephen Orgel. LC 79-54327. 300p. 1980. lib. bdg. 33.00 (ISBN 0-8240-4479-7). Garland Pub.

Every Woman's Guide to Getting Ready for the Career You Want. Donna Goldfein. LC 80-83692. 128p. (Orig.). 1981. pap. 5.95 (ISBN 0-89087-935-4). Celestial Arts.

Every Woman's Guide to Hysterectomy: Taking Charge of Your Own Body. Dee Dee Jameson & Bobbie Schwalb. LC 77-14339. (Illus.). 1978. 8.95 o.p. (ISBN 0-13-292821-3, Spec); pap. 3.95 o.p. (ISBN 0-13-292813-2, Spec). P-H.

Everybody Counts: A T. A. Self-Help Book for Math Aversion. Peter Blum. 54p. (Orig.). 1981. pap. 6.95 (ISBN 0-9605756-0-X). Math Counsel Inst.

Everybody Needs Somebody Sometime. Gerald Dahl. 190p. 1980. 3.95 (ISBN 0-8407-5751-4). Nelson.

Everybody Takes Turns. Dorothy Corey. Ed. by Fay Ann. LC 79-18652. (Self-Starter Ser.). (Illus.). (ps-1). 1980. 6.50g (ISBN 0-8075-2166-3). A Whitman.

Everybody's Book of Bicycle Riding. Thom Lieb. Ed. by Chuck McCullagh. (Illus.). 336p. 1981. 12.95 (ISBN 0-87857-322-4); pap. 9.95 (ISBN 0-87857-323-2). Rodale Pr Inc.

Everybody's Business: An Almanac. Ed. by Milton Moskowitz et al. Michael Katz. LC 80-7736. (Illus.). 008p. 1980. 21.00 (ISBN 0-06-250620-X, HarpR); pap. 9.95 (ISBN 0-06-250621-8). Har-Row.

Everybody's Virgin Islands. James E. Moore. 1979. pap. 8.95 (ISBN 0-397-01324-8). Lippincott.

Everybody's Weaving Book. Alfred A. Lewis. Ed. by Julienne Krasnoff. LC 75-31512. (Illus.). 192p. 1976. 14.95 o.s.i. (ISBN 0-02-571270-5, 57127). Macmillan.

Everyday Art. Lewis F. Day. LC 76-17763. (Aesthetic Movement Ser.: Vol. 19). 1977. Repr. of 1882 ed. lib. bdg. 44.00 (ISBN 0-8240-2468-0). Garland Pub.

Everyday Birds. Tony Soper. LC 76-20134. 1976. 10.50 (ISBN 0-7153-7277-7). David & Charles.

Everyday Costume in Britain. Audrey Barfoot. 1972. 14.95 (ISBN 0-7134-1901-6, Pub. by Batsford England). David & Charles.

Everyday Credit Checking. new ed. Sol Barzman. 256p. Date not set. (ISBN 0-690-01875-4). Lippincott & Crowell. Postponed.

Everyday Credit Checking: A Practical Guide. Sol Barzman. 256p. 1973. 9.95 (ISBN 0-690-27107-7, TYC-T). T Y Crowell.

Everyday Credit Checking: A Practical Guide. rev. ed. Sol Barzman. LC 80-82080. 289p. 1980. 13.95 (ISBN 0-934914-36-2). NACM.

Everyday Herbs for Cooking & Healing. Catherine J. Frompovich & Joanne M. Hays. 1980. 100 frame filmstrips, cassette, text 15.00 (ISBN 0-935322-11-6). C J Frompovich.

Everyday Heroes. Frank Hughes. 1981. pap. 2.50 (ISBN 0-8439-0885-8, Leisure Bks). Nordon Pubns.

Everyday History of Somewhere. Ray Raphael. (Illus.). 192p. pap. 10.00 (ISBN 0-933280-11-4). Island Pr.

Everyday Home Repairs. Michael Smith. pap. 2.95 (ISBN 0-7153-7553-9). David & Charles.

Everyday Is Easter in Alabama. Robert H. Couch. LC 76-21358. (Illus.). 1976. 10.00 (ISBN 0-916624-02-1). TSU Pr.

Everyday Japanese. Eldora Thorlin & Noah Brannen. LC 69-19854. 180p. 1969. 3.95 (ISBN 0-8348-0037-3). Weatherhill.

Everyday Korean. Eldora Thorlin & Taesoon Henthorn. LC 71-183519. 180p. 1972. 3.95 (ISBN 0-8348-0069-1). Weatherhill.

Everyday Law Made Simple. Jack Last et al. LC 77-15164. 1978. softbound 3.50 (ISBN 0-385-12921-1, Made). Doubleday.

Everyday Life in Prehistoric Times. Marjorie Quennell & C. H. Quennell. 1959. 19.95 (ISBN 0-7134-1673-4, Pub. by Batsford England). David & Charles.

Everyday Life in Roman & Anglo-Saxon Times. C. H. Quennell. 1969. 19.95 (ISBN 0-7134-1675-0, Pub. by Batsford England). David & Charles.

Everyday Life of the Incas. Anne Kendall. 1978. pap. 14.95 (ISBN 0-7134-1072-8, Pub. by Batsford England). David & Charles.

Everyday Life of the Maya. Ralph Whitlock. 1976. 19.95 (ISBN 0-7134-3232-2, Pub. by Batsford England). David & Charles.

Everyday Life of the North American Indian. John Manchip-White. 1979. 22.50 (ISBN 0-7134-0043-9, Pub. by Batsford England). David & Charles.

Everyday Math: Tables, Graphs, & Scale. Marjorie Fineberg. LC 79-730692. (Illus.). 1979. pap. text ed. 99.00 (ISBN 0-89290-129-2, A514-SATC). Soc for Visual.

Everyday Medical Handbook. George Thosteson. 304p. 1977. pap. 1.75 o.p. (ISBN 0-449-13761-9, 0-449-13761-9, GM). Fawcett.

Everyday Poems for the Jewish Child. Sora Malka & Solomon Silverstein. (Illus.). 44p. (Orig.). (ps-6). 1980. pap. 2.50 (ISBN 0-89655-050-8). BRuach HaTorah.

Everyday Prayers. William Barclay. LC 60-5326. (Harper Jubilee Bk.). 1976. pap. 1.95 o.p. (ISBN 0-06-060394-1, HJ-27, HarpR). Har-Row.

Everyday Production of Baked Goods. 2nd ed. A. B. Barrows. (Illus.). 1975. text ed. 17.95 (ISBN 0-8436-2062-5). CBI Pub.

Everyday Reasoning. Evelyn M. Barker. (Illus.). 304p. 1981. pap. text ed. 8.95 (ISBN 0-13-293407-8). P-H.

Everyday Sayings: Their Meanings Explained, Their Origins Given. Charles N. Lurie. LC 68-28334. 1968. Repr. of 1928 ed. 24.00 (ISBN 0-8103-0158-X). Gale.

Everyday Speech: How to Say What You Mean. Bess Sondel. 1950. pap. 3.50 (ISBN 0-06-463239-3, EH 239, EH). Har-Row.

Everygirls Companion. Ed. by Abraham L. Furman. LC 68-11184. (Everygirls Library). (gr. 5-9). 1968. 4.25 o.p. (ISBN 0-8313-0051-5); PLB 6.19 (ISBN 0-685-13773-2). Lantern.

Everygirls Mystery Stories. Ed. by Abraham L. Furman. (Illus.). (gr. 6-10). PLB 6.19 o.p. (ISBN 0-8313-0061-2). Lantern.

Everyhow Remarkable. Victoria Lincoln. (gr. 2-4). 1967. 3.50 o.s.i. (ISBN 0-02-759130-1, CCPr). Macmillan.

Everyman in Europe: Essays in Social History, Vol. 1. Istvan Deak. 224p. 1981. pap. text ed. 9.95 (ISBN 0-13-293621-6). P-H.

Everyman Medieval Miracle Plays. Ed. by A. C. Cawley. pap. 3.25 (ISBN 0-525-47036-0, Evman). Dutton.

Everyman's Book of British Ballads. Ed. by Roy Palmer. (Illus.). 256p. 1981. 22.50x (ISBN 0-460-04452-4, Pub. by J. M. Dent England). Biblio Dist.

Everyman's Book of English Love Poems. Ed. by John Hadfield. 234p. 1980. cancelled (ISBN 0-460-04445-1, Pub. by J M Dent). Biblio Dist.

Everyman's Dictionary of Abbreviations. rev. ed. Ed. by John Paxton. 408p. 1981. 20.00x (ISBN 0-8476-6973-4). Rowman.

Everyman's Dictionary of Economics. 2nd ed. Arthur Seldon & F. G. Pennance. LC 65-5820. 516p. 1976. 16.50x (ISBN 0-460-03023-0). Intl Pubns Serv.

Everyman's Guide to Auto Maintenance. George Zwick. LC 73-78200. (Illus.). 192p. 1973. pap. 4.95 (ISBN 0-8306-2648-4); pap. 4.95 (ISBN 0-8306-2648-4, 648). TAB Bks.

Everyman's Guide to Tax Havens. Adam Starchild. 112p. (Orig.). 1980. pap. 6.00 (ISBN 0-87364-203-1). Paladin Ent.

Everyone Goes As a Pumpkin. Judith Vigna. Ed. by Caroline Rubin. LC 77-14254. (Self-Starter Books Ser.). (Illus.). 32p. (ps-1). 1977. 6.50g (ISBN 0-8075-2186-8). A Whitman.

Everyone Is Going Somewhere. Suzanne Rosenblatt. LC 75-35920. (Illus.). 32p. (gr. k-2). 1976. 4.95 o.s.i. (ISBN 0-02-777700-6, 77770). Macmillan.

Everyone Knows What a Dragon Looks Like. Jay Williams. LC 74-13121. (Illus.). 32p. (gr. k-3). 1976. 9.95 (ISBN 0-590-07284-6, Four Winds); pap. 5.95 (ISBN 0-590-07751-1). Schol Bk Serv.

Everyone: The Timeless Myth of Everyman Reborn. Frederick Franck. LC 77-25590. 1978. 12.50 o.p. (ISBN 0-385-14357-5); pap. 6.95 o.p. (ISBN 0-385-13329-4). Doubleday.

Everyone's Guide to Food Self-Sufficiency. Walter Gullett & Jane Fellows Gullett. 1980. 7.95 (ISBN 0-87961-096-4); pap. 3.95 (ISBN 0-87961-095-6). Naturegraph.

Everyone's Guide to Four-Wheel Drive. William Hampton. (Illus.). 1980. cancelled (ISBN 0-8092-7113-3); pap. cancelled (ISBN 0-8092-7112-5). Contemp Bks.

Everyone's Guide to Opening Doors by Telephone. 2nd ed. Sam Aronson. (Illus.). 338p. 1981. 17.95 (ISBN 0-686-27230-7). S Aronson.

Everyone's Guide to Saving Gas. Rene Hollander & Bernard Percy. (Illus., Orig.). 1979. pap. 2.95 (ISBN 0-9603194-0-9). Old Oaktree.

Everyone's Guide to Theosophy. Harry Benjamin. 1969. 10.95 (ISBN 0-7229-0130-5). Theos Pub Hse.

Everyone's Income Tax Guide. rev. ed. S. Jay Lasser. 192p. 1980. write for info. (ISBN 0-937782-00-9). Hilltop Pubns.

Everyone's Money Book. Jane B. Quinn. 1980. pap. 9.95 (ISBN 0-440-55725-9, Dell Trade Pbks). Dell.

Everyone's United Nations. 477p. 1979. pap. 7.95 (ISBN 0-686-68955-0, UN79.1/5, UN). Unipub.

Everything All at Once. Adam LeFevre. LC 77-14847. (Wesleyan Poetry Program: Vol. 89). 1978. pap. 10.00x (ISBN 0-8195-2089-6, Pub. by Wesleyan U Pr); pap. 4.95 (ISBN 0-8195-1089-0). Columbia U Pr.

Everything: An Alphabet, Number, Reading, Counting & Color Identification Bk. Richard Hefter & Martin S. Moskof. LC 72-153656. (Illus.). (gr. k-2). 1971. 5.95 o.s.i. (ISBN 0-8193-0488-3, Four Winds); PLB 5.41 o.s.i. (ISBN 0-8193-0489-1). Schol Bk Serv.

Everything Book of Floors, Walls, & Ceilings. Greener. (Illus.). 250p. 1980. 14.95 (ISBN 0-8359-1803-3); pap. 7.95 (ISBN 0-8359-1802-5). Reston.

Everything Happened to Susan. Barry Malzberg. 1978. pap. 1.50 (ISBN 0-505-51221-1). Tower Bks.

Everything in the Window. Shirley Faessler. 1980. 10.95 (ISBN 0-316-25986-1, Pub. by Atlantic-Little Brown). Little.

Everything Moves. Seymour Simon. LC 75-21069. (Illus.). 48p. (gr. 1-4). 1976. 5.95 o.s.i. (ISBN 0-8027-6239-5); PLB 5.85 o.s.i. (ISBN 0-8027-6238-7). Walker & Co.

Everything That Has Been Shall Be Again. John Gilgun. (Illus.). 1981. 100.00 (ISBN 0-931460-11-5); pap. 7.50 (ISBN 0-931460-13-1). Bieler.

Everything That Linguists Have Always Wanted to Know About Logic: but Were Ashamed to Ask. James D. McCawley. LC 80-345. (Illus.). 528p. 1981. lib. bdg. 35.00x (ISBN 0-226-55617-4); pap. text ed. 12.50x (ISBN 0-226-55618-2). U of Chicago Pr.

Everything That Rises Must Converge. Flannery O'Connor. 269p. 1965. 10.00 (ISBN 0-374-15012-5); pap. 4.95 (ISBN 0-374-50464-4, N287). FS&G.

Everything to Gain: A Guide to Self-Fulfillment Through Logoanalysis. James C. Crumbaugh. LC 72-80164. 1973. 10.95 (ISBN 0-911012-14-1). Nelson-Hall.

Everything You Always Wanted to Know About Drinking Problems & Then a Few Things You Didn't Want to Know. Daniel Fairchild et al. 7.50 (ISBN 0-932194-04-4). Green Hill.

Everything You Always Wanted to Know About Mergers, Acquisitions & Divestitures but Didn't Know Whom to Ask. Roger Kuppinger. LC 78-71201. 1978. 12.95 (ISBN 0-686-24646-2). R Kuppinger.

Everything You Always Wanted to Know About Solar Energy: But Didn't Know Who to Ask. Barry J. Farrands. Ed. by Dale Sinclair. LC 80-81372. (Illus.). 425p. (Orig.). 1980. pap. 39.95x (ISBN 0-936982-00-4). Promise Corp.

Everything You Need to Grow a Messianic Synagogue. Phillip E. Goble. LC 74-28017. (Orig.). 1974. pap. 3.95 (ISBN 0-87808-421-5). William Carey Lib.

Everything You Need to Know About Monsters & Still Be Able to Get to Sleep. Daniel Cohen. LC 79-6589. (Illus.). 128p. (gr. 4 up). 1981. 7.95a (ISBN 0-385-15803-3); PLB (ISBN 0-385-15804-1). Doubleday.

Everything You Need to Know for a Cassette Ministry. Viggo B. Sogaard. LC 74-20915. 224p. 1975. pap. 3.95 (ISBN 0-87123-125-5, 210125). Bethany Fell.

Everything You Need to Know to Have Great Looking Hair. Louis Gignac & Jacqueline Warsaw. LC 80-51999. (Illus.). 144p. 1981. 14.95 (ISBN 0-670-30040-3). Viking Pr.

Everything You Never Wanted to Know About Yourself or the Cancer Syndrome. Terrence Gouedy. (Illus.). 64p. 1980. 12.50 (ISBN 0-682-49640-5). Exposition.

Everything You Should Know About Chiropractic. Chester A. Wilk. LC 80-53014. 1980. write for info. Wilk Pub.

Everything You Want to Know About Astrology, Numerology, How to Win. Zolar. LC 72-3135. (Zolar's Everything You Want to Know Ser.). 224p. 1972. pap. 1.50 (ISBN 0-668-02656-1). Arc Bks.

Everything You Want to Know About Dreams, Lucky Numbers, Omens, Oils & Incense. Zolar. LC 70-188859. (Zolar's Everything You Want to Know Ser.). 226p. 1972. pap. 1.95 (ISBN 0-668-02600-6). Arc Bks.

Everything You Wanted to Know About Ageing. Dr. Vernon Coleman. 1976. 9.95 o.p. (ISBN 0-86033-036-2). Gordon-Cremonesi.

Everything Your Heirs Need to Know About You. David S. Magee. Ed. by J. Magee Dugan. 160p. 1980. write for info. Jama Bks.

Everything's Great in Seventy-Eight. Ray Collins. (Illus.). 1978. pap. 3.95 (ISBN 0-914842-30-7). Madrona Pubs.

Everywoman: A Gynaecological Guide for Life. Derek Llewellyn-Jones. (Illus.). 1978. 11.95 (ISBN 0-571-04961-3, Pub. by Faber & Faber); pap. 4.95 (ISBN 0-571-04960-5). Merrimack Bk Serv.

Everywoman's Book. Paavo Airola. 1979. cloth 17.95 (ISBN 0-932090-00-1). Health Plus.

Everywoman's Book. Paavo Airola. (Illus.). 640p. 1981. pap. 12.95 (ISBN 0-932090-10-9). Health Plus.

Everywoman's Guide to a New Image. Peggy Granger. LC 75-37070. 1976. pap. 3.95 o.p. (ISBN 0-89087-916-8). Les Femmes Pub.

Everywoman's Guide to College. Eileen Gray. LC 75-10576. 1975. pap. 3.95 o.p. (ISBN 0-89087-903-6). Les Femmes Pub.

Everywoman's Guide to Financial Independence. Mavis A. Groza. LC 76-11371. 128p. 1976. pap. 3.95 o.p. (ISBN 0-89087-918-4). Les Femmes Pub.

Everywoman's Guide to Political Awareness. Phyllis Butler & Dorothy Gray. LC 75-37073. 1976. pap. 3.95 o.p. (ISBN 0-89087-914-1). Les Femmes Pub.

Everywoman's Health: The Complete Guide to Body & Mind. Ed. by D. S. Thompson. LC 79-6095. (Illus.). 792p. 1980. 19.95 (ISBN 0-385-15567-0). Doubleday.

Eve's Orphans: Mothers & Daughters in Medieval English Literature. Nikki Stiller. LC 79-8954. (Contributions in Women's Studies: No. 16). (Illus.). xii, 152p. 1980. lib. bdg. 19.95 (ISBN 0-313-22067-0, SEO/). Greenwood.

Eve's Ransom. George Gissing. 125p. 1980. pap. 3.00 (ISBN 0-486-24016-9). Dover.

Eve's Rib. Mariette Nowak. 272p. 1981. pap. 5.95 (ISBN 0-312-27240-5). St Martin.

Evidence. William J. Edgar. LC 80-67262. 471p. 1980. lib. bdg. 22.75 (ISBN 0-8191-1292-5); pap. text ed. 13.75 (ISBN 0-8191-1293-3). U Pr of Amer.

Evidence. John Weisman. Date not set. pap. 2.25 (ISBN 0-686-69452-X, E9724, Sig). NAL. Postponed.

Evidence & Assurance. N. M. Nathan. LC 79-50505. (Cambridge Studies in Philosophy). 1980. 29.50 (ISBN 0-521-22517-5). Cambridge U Pr.

Evidence & Explanation in Social Science. Gerald Studdert-Kennedy. 1975. 24.00x (ISBN 0-7100-8157-X). Routledge & Kegan.

Evidence & Procedures for Boundary Location. Curtis M. Brown & Winfield H. Eldridge. LC 62-18988. (Illus.). 1962. 32.50 (ISBN 0-471-10663-1, Pub. by Wiley-Interscience). Wiley.

Evidence Code-Federal. Gould Editorial Staff. (Supplemented annually). 1981. looseleaf 8.50 (ISBN 0-87526-207-4). Gould.

Evidence for the Origin of the Mactridae (Bivalvia) in the Cretaceous. LouElla R. Saul. (U. C. Publ. in Geological Sciences: Vol. 97). 1973. pap. 9.00x (ISBN 0-520-09426-3). U of Cal Pr.

Evidence for the Patrolman. Floyd N. Heffron. (Police Science Ser). (Illus.). 192p. 1972. 12.75 (ISBN 0-398-00820-5). C C Thomas.

Evidence for the Resurrection of Jesus Christ. Richard Riss. LC 76-50978. 1977. pap. 1.95 (ISBN 0-87123-134-4, 200134). Bethany Fell.

Evidence in a Nutshell, State & Federal Rules. 2nd ed. Paul F. Rothstein. (Nutshell Ser.). 401p. 1981. pap. text ed. 6.95 (ISBN 0-8299-2131-1). West Pub.

Evidence Law of New York Quizzer 1981. Gould Editorial Staff. 1981. text ed. 7.50x (ISBN 0-87526-220-1). Gould.

Evidence of Chemical Heterogeneity in the Earth's Mantle. Mineralogical Society Geochemistry Group, November 1 & 2, 1978. Ed. by D. K. Bailey et al. (Illus.). 357p. 1980. text ed. 100.00x (ISBN 0-85403-144-8, Pub. by Royal Soc London). Scholium Intl.

Evidence of Conflation in Mark? A Study in the Synoptic Problem. Thomas R. Longstaff. LC 76-40001. (Society of Biblical Literature. Dissertation Ser.: No. 28). (Illus.). 1977. pap. 7.50 (ISBN 0-89130-086-4, 060128). Scholars Pr Ca.

Evidence of Evolution. Nicholas Hotton. LC 68-24491. (Illus.). 160p. 1968. 4.95 (ISBN 0-8281-0341-0, JO42-0, Co-Pub. by Smithsonian). Am Heritage.

Evidence of Love. Shirley A. Grau. 1978. pap. 1.95 o.p. (ISBN 0-449-23766-4, Crest). Fawcett.

Evidence of the Imagination: Studies of Interactions Between Life & Art in English Romantic Literature. Ed. by Donald H. Reiman et al. LC 77-14673. 1978. 17.50x (ISBN 0-8147-7372-9); pap. 5.00x (ISBN 0-8147-7373-7). NYU Pr.

Evidence Technician. Jack Rudman. (Career Examination Ser.: C-2748). (Cloth bdg. avail. on request). 1980. pap. 10.00 (ISBN 0-8373-2748-2). Natl Learning.

Evidence That Demands a Verdict. rev. ed. Josh McDowell. LC 78-75041. 1979. 10.95 (ISBN 0-918956-57-9); pap. 6.95 (ISBN 0-918956-46-3). Campus Crusade.

Evidencia que Condeno a Aida Skripnikova. Michael Bordeaux. Tr. by Pedro Vega from Eng. 123p. (Orig., Span.). 1975. pap. 1.50 (ISBN 0-89922-060-6). Edit Caribe.

Evidencias Cristianas. Tr. by Alice A. Luce. (Spanish Bks.). (Span.). 1978. 1.25 (ISBN 0-8297-0554-6). Life Pubs Intl.

Evidential Documents. James V. Conway. (Police Science Ser). (Illus.). 288p. 1978. 19.75 (ISBN 0-398-00342-4). C C Thomas.

Evil & Danger of Stage Plays. Arthur Bedford. LC 72-170479. (English Stage Ser.: Vol. 43). lib. bdg. 50.00 (ISBN 0-8240-0626-7). Garland Pub.

Evil Eye. Ed. by Clarence Maloney. LC 76-16861. (Illus.). 1976. 17.50x (ISBN 0-231-04006-7). Columbia U Pr.

Evil Eye: The Origins & Practices of Superstition. Frederick Elworthy. (188 Ils). 1970. pap. 2.95 o.s.i. (ISBN 0-02-075980-0, Collier). Macmillan.

Evil Image: Two Centuries of Gothic Short Fiction & Poetry. Patricia L. Skarda & Nora C. Jaffe. (Illus.). 1981. pap. 7.95 (ISBN 0-452-00549-3, F549, Meridan Bks). NAL.

Evil in the Morning of the World: Phenomenological Approaches to a Balinese Community. John S. Lansing. LC 74-620023. (Michigan Papers on South & South East Asia No. 6). (Illus.). 104p. 1974. pap. 4.50x (ISBN 0-89148-006-4). Ctr S&SE Asian.

Evil of the Day. Thomas Sterling. LC 80-8414. 224p. 1981. pap. 2.25 (ISBN 0-06-080529-3, P529, PL). Har-Row.

Evil Spirit. Alexandre Shirvanzade. Tr. by Nishan Parlakian from Armenian. LC 78-65962. Orig. Title: Char Voki. (Illus.). xxxvi, 146p. 1980. 6.95 (ISBN 0-934728-00-3); pap. 4.95 (ISBN 0-934728-01-1). St Vartan.

Evil That Men Do: The Story of the Nazis. Arnold P. Rubin. LC 77-22722. (gr. 7 up). 1977. PLB 8.29 o.p. (ISBN 0-671-32852-2). Messner.

Evil: The Shadow Side of Reality. John A. Sanford. 176p. 1981. 10.95 (ISBN 0-8245-0037-7). Crossroad NY.

Evils of the Factory System Demonstrated by Parliamentary Evidence. Compiled by Charles Wing. LC 67-19730. Repr. of 1837 ed. 27.50x (ISBN 0-678-05096-1). Kelley.

Evinrude One & Two Cylinder Outboard Tune-up & Repair Manual. Clarence Coles & Howard Young. 1980. pap. 11.95 (ISBN 0-89330-008-X). Caroline Hse.

Evinrude Outboards, Forty to One Hundred & Forty HP: 1965-1977. (Illus.). 248p. 8.00 o.p. (ISBN 0-89287-218-7, B647). Western Marine Ent.

Evinrude Outboards, One and One Half to Thirty-Five HP: 1965-1978. (Illus.). 192p. 8.00 o.p. (ISBN 0-89287-229-2, B644). Western Marine Ent.

Evita--First Lady: A Biography of Eva Peron. John Barnes. LC 78-3185. 1979. pap. 2.95 (ISBN 0-394-17087-3, B425, BC). Grove.

Evita: The Lgend of Eva Peron, 1919-1952. Andrew Weber & Tim Rice. 1979. pap. 5.95 (ISBN 0-380-46433-0, 46433). Avon.

Evita: The Woman with the Whip. Mary Main. LC 79-27288. 286p. 1980. 8.95 (ISBN 0-396-07834-6). Dodd.

Evolution. Theodosius Dobzhansky et al. LC 77-23284. (Illus.). 1977. text ed. 25.95x (ISBN 0-7167-0572-9). W H Freeman.

Evolution. rev. ed. Ruth Moore. LC 62-20276. (Life Nature Library). (gr. 5 up). 1969. PLB 8.97 o.p. (ISBN 0-8094-0620-9, Pub. by Time-Life). Silver.

Evolution. Ruth Moore. (Young Readers Library). (Illus.). 1977. lib. bdg. 7.95 (ISBN 0-686-51089-5). Silver.

Evolution. Frank H. Rhodes. (Golden Guide Ser). (Illus.). 1974. PLB 9.15 (ISBN 0-307-64360-3, Golden Pr); pap. 1.95 o.p. (ISBN 0-307-24360-5). Western Pub.

Evolution: A Scientific American Book. Scientific American Editors. LC 78-10747. (Illus.). 1978. text ed. 15.95x (ISBN 0-7167-1065-X); pap. text ed. 7.95x (ISBN 0-7167-1066-8). W H Freeman.

Evolution Above the Species Level. Bernard Rensch. Tr. by Altevogt. LC 58-13505. (Columbia Biological Ser.: No. 19). 1960. 30.00x (ISBN 0-231-02296-4). Columbia U Pr.

Evolution & Classification of Flowering Plants. Arthur Cronquist. pap. 5.00 o.p. (ISBN 0-89327-212-4). NY Botanical.

Evolution & Consciousness: Human Systems in Transition. Ed. by Erich Jantsch & Conrad H. Waddington. (Illus.). 1976. 26.50 (ISBN 0-201-03438-7, Adv Bk Prog); pap. 14.50 (ISBN 0-201-03439-5). A-W.

Evolution & Education. Michael J. Grady. 1977. pap. text ed. 10.75x (ISBN 0-8191-0135-4). U Pr of Amer.

Evolution & Human Origins: An Introduction to Physical Anthropology. 2nd ed. B. J. Williams. (Illus.). 1979. text ed. 12.95 scp (ISBN 0-06-047121-2, HarpC). Har-Row.

Evolution & Morphology of the Trilobita, Trilobitoidea, & Merostomata. Anders Martinsson. 1975. pap. 70.00x (ISBN 82-00-04963-9, Dist. by Columbia U Pr). Universitet.

Evolution & Society. J. W. Burrow. 1966. 29.95 (ISBN 0-521-04393-X); pap. 9.95x (ISBN 0-521-09600-6). Cambridge U Pr.

Evolution & Speciation: Essays in Honor of M.J.D. White. W. R. Atchley & David S. Woodruff. (Illus.). 496p. Date not set. price not set (ISBN 0-521-23823-4). Cambridge U Pr.

Evolution & the Bible. Cora Reno. 1979. pap. 1.25 (ISBN 0-8024-0131-7). Moody.

Evolution & the Ecology of the Dinosaurs. L. B. Halstead. (Illus.). 1978. 12.95 o.p. (ISBN 0-8467-0559-1, Pub. by Two Continents). Hippocrene Bks.

Evolution & the Fossil Record: Readings from Scientific American. Intro. by Leo F. Laporte. LC 77-26073. (Illus.). 1978. text ed. 19.95x (ISBN 0-7167-0291-6); pap. text ed. 9.95x (ISBN 0-7167-0290-8). W H Freeman.

Evolution & the Founders of Pragmatism. Philip Wiener. 304p. 1972. pap. 5.95x (ISBN 0-8122-1043-3, Pa Paperbks). U of Pa Pr.

Evolution & Variation of Multigene Families. T. Ohta. (Lecture Notes in Biomathematics: Vol. 37). 131p. 1980. pap. 9.80 (ISBN 0-387-09998-0). Springer-Verlag.

Evolution, Brain & Behavior in Vertebrates, 2 vols. Ed. by R. B. Masterton et al. Incl. Vol. 1. Modern Concepts. 29.95 (ISBN 0-470-15045-9); Vol. 2. Persistent Problems. 14.95 (ISBN 0-470-15046-7). LC 76-6499. 1976. Halsted Pr.

Evolution: Concepts & Consequences. 2nd ed. Lawrence S. Dillon. LC 77-9033. (Illus.). 1978. pap. text ed. 17.50 (ISBN 0-8016-1299-3). Mosby.

Evolution et Structure De la Langue Francaise. Walter Von Wartburg. 22.50 (ISBN 3-7720-0013-4). Adler.

Evolution for Everyone. Paul R. Gastonguay. LC 73-5809. (BSCS Ser.). 320p. 1974. pap. 5.95 (ISBN 0-672-63642-5). Pegasus.

Evolution in Age-Structured Populations. B. Charlesworth. LC 79-8909. (Cambridge Studies in Mathematical Biology: No. 1). 250p. 1980. 44.50 (ISBN 0-521-23045-4); pap. 13.50 (ISBN 0-521-29786-9). Cambridge U Pr.

Evolution in Changing Environments: Some Theoretical Explorations. Richard Levins. LC 68-20871. (Monographs in Population Biology: No. 2). (Illus.). 1968. 12.50x (ISBN 0-691-07959-5); pap. 5.50x (ISBN 0-691-08062-3). Princeton U Pr.

Evolution in Plant Design. D. L. Duddington. (Illus.). 1969. 7.95 o.p. (ISBN 0-571-09065-6, Pub. by Faber & Faber). Merrimack Bk Serv.

Evolution in Science & Religion. Robert A. Millikan. 1935. 42.50x (ISBN 0-686-51381-9). Elliots Bks.

Evolution in the Microbial World: Proceedings. Ed. by M. J. Carlile & J. J. Skehel. (Illus.). 450p. 1974. 49.50 (ISBN 0-521-20416-X). Cambridge U Pr.

Evolution, Marxism & Christianity. Claude Cuenot et al. (Teilhard Study Library). 1967. text ed. 3.50x (ISBN 0-900391-06-5). Humanities.

Evolution of Air Breathing in Vertebrates. D. J. Randall et al. LC 80-462. (Illus.). 176p. Date not set. 27.50 (ISBN 0-521-22259-1). Cambridge U Pr.

Evolution of American Society, 1700-1815. James A. Henretta. (Civilization & Society Ser). 1973. pap. text ed. 6.95x (ISBN 0-669-84608-2). Heath.

Evolution of American Urban Society. 2nd ed. Howard P. Chudacoff. (Illus.). 256p. 1981. pap. text ed. 10.95 (ISBN 0-13-293605-4). P-H.

Evolution of Australian Foreign Policy (1938-1965) Alan Watt. 44.00 (ISBN 0-521-06747-2); pap. 12.95x (ISBN 0-521-09552-2). Cambridge U Pr.

Evolution of Balzac's Comedie Humaine. E. Preston Dargan & Bernard Weinberg. LC 72-91802. 441p. 1973. Repr. of 1942 ed. lib. bdg. 16.50x (ISBN 0-8154-0452-2). Cooper Sq.

Evolution of Behavior. Jerram Brown. 900p. 1975. text ed. 19.95x (ISBN 0-393-09295-X). Norton.

Evolution of Bioenergetic Processes. E. Broda. LC 75-6847. 220p. 1975. text ed. 30.00 o.p. (ISBN 0-08-018275-5); pap. text ed. 18.00 (ISBN 0-08-022651-5). Pergamon.

Evolution of British Town Planning. G. E. Cherry. LC 74-470. (Illus.). 275p. 1974. 24.95 (ISBN 0-470-15350-4). Halsted Pr.

Evolution of Chinese Tz'u Poetry: From Late T'ang to Northern Sung. Kang-I Sun Chang. LC 79-3195. (Illus.). 1980. 17.50x (ISBN 0-691-06425-3). Princeton U Pr.

Evolution of Coinage. George MacDonald. viii, 148p. 1980. 20.00 (ISBN 0-916710-73-4). Obol Intl.

Evolution of Consciousness: Studies in Polarity. Ed. by Shirley Sugerman et al. LC 75-27592. (Illus.). 1976. lib. bdg. 17.50x (ISBN 0-8195-4094-3, Pub. by Wesleyan U Pr). Columbia U Pr.

Evolution of Cost Accounting. S. Paul Garner. LC 76-41238. (Accounting History Classics Ser.: Vol. 1). (Illus.). 432p. 1976. pap. 11.95 (ISBN 0-8173-8900-8). U of Ala Pr.

Evolution of Crop Plants. Ed. by N. W. Simmonds. LC 78-40509. (Illus.). 1979. pap. text ed. 18.95 (ISBN 0-582-44496-9). Longman.

Evolution of Desert Biota. Ed. by David Goodall. (Illus.). 1976. 12.95x (ISBN 0-292-72015-7). U of Tex Pr.

Evolution of Designs. P. Steadman. LC 78-18255. (Cambridge Urban & Architectural Studies: No. 5). 32.50 (ISBN 0-521-22302-4). Cambridge U Pr.

Evolution of Dutch Catholicism, 1958-1974. John A. Coleman. LC 74-22958. 1979. 25.00x (ISBN 0-520-02885-6). U of Cal Pr.

Evolution of Early Man. Bernard Wood. (Illus.). 1978. 12.95 o.p. (ISBN 0-8467-0560-5, Pub. by Two Continents). Hippocrene Bks.

Evolution of Educational Thought: Lectures on the Formation & Development of Secondary Education in France. Emile Durkheim. Tr. by Peter Collins from Fr. 1977. 25.00x (ISBN 0-7100-8446-3). Routledge & Kegan.

Evolution of Electric Batteries in Response to Industrial Needs. Samuel Ruben. (Illus.). 100p. 1978. 7.95 (ISBN 0-8059-2455-8). Dorrance.

Evolution of Electronic Music. David Ernst. LC 76-41624. (Illus.). 1977. pap. text ed. 10.95 (ISBN 0-02-870880-6). Schirmer Bks.

Evolution of Ethics. Ed. by E. Hershey Sneath. 1927. 42.50x (ISBN 0-685-69867-X). Elliots Bks.

Evolution of Executive Departments of the Continental Congress, 1774-1789. Jennings B. Sanders. 6.00 (ISBN 0-8446-0888-2). Peter Smith.

Evolution of Fashion: Pattern & Cut from 1066-1930. Hamilton Hill & Bucknell. 25.00x (ISBN 0-7134-0851-0). Drama Bk.

Evolution of Giant Firms in Britain. S. J. Prais. LC 76-18410. (NIEST Economic & Social Studies Ser.: No. 30). (Illus.). 1977. 41.50 (ISBN 0-521-21356-8). Cambridge U Pr.

Evolution of Hitler's Germany. Horst Von Maltitz. 480p. 1973. 12.95 o.p. (ISBN 0-07-067608-9, P&RB). McGraw.

Evolution of Human Consciousness. John H. Crook. (Illus.). 462p. 1980. 39.00x (ISBN 0-19-857174-7). Oxford U Pr.

Evolution of Human Sexuality. Donald Symons. 368p. 1981. pap. 6.95 (ISBN 0-19-502907-0, GB 638, OPB). Oxford U Pr.

Evolution of IBP, Vol. 1. Ed. by E. B. Worthington. LC 75-2722. (International Biological Programme Ser.). (Illus.). 276p. 1975. 49.50 (ISBN 0-521-20736-3). Cambridge U Pr.

Evolution of Igneous Rocks. Norman L. Bowen. 1928. pap. 5.00 (ISBN 0-486-60311-3). Dover.

Evolution of Industry in STPI Countries. (Science & Technology for Development: STPI Module 2). 67p. 1981. pap. 5.00 (ISBN 0-88936-257-2, IDRC TS19, IDRC). Unipub.

Evolution of Love. Sydney L. Mellen. LC 80-18028. 1981. text ed. 15.95x (ISBN 0-7167-1271-7); pap. text ed. 8.95x (ISBN 0-7167-1272-5). W H Freeman.

Evolution of Mammals. L. B. Halstead. (Illus.). 1981. 12.95 o.p. (ISBN 0-8467-0561-3, Pub. by Two Continents). Hippocrene Bks.

Evolution of Management Thought. 2nd ed. Daniel A. Wren. LC 78-10959. (Management & Administration Ser.). 1979. text ed. 22.95 (ISBN 0-471-04695-7). Wiley.

Evolution of Man's Capacity for Culture. Ed. by James N. Spuhler. LC 59-10223. (Waynebooks Ser: No. 17). 1959. pap. text ed. 3.95x (ISBN 0-8143-1114-8). Wayne St U Pr.

Evolution of Mechanics. Pierre M. Duhem. Ed. by G. A. Oravas. (Genesis & Method Ser.: No. 1). Orig. Title: L'evolution De la Mecanique. 234p. 1980. Repr. 47.50x (ISBN 90-286-0688-2). Sijthoff & Noordhoff.

Evolution of Melanism: The Study of a Recurring Necessity, with Special Reference to Industrial Melanism in the Lepidoptera. Bernard Kettlewell. (Illus.). 448p. 1973. 49.00x (ISBN 0-19-857370-7). Oxford U Pr.

Evolution of Michael Krayton's Idea. Louise Westling. (Salzburg Studies in Literature, Elizabethan & Renaissance Studies: No. 37). 187p. 1974. pap. text ed. 25.00x (ISBN 0-391-01564-8). Humanities.

Evolution of OPEC Strategy. Fariborz Ghadar. LC 76-48377. 1977. 20.50 (ISBN 0-669-01147-9). Lexington Bks.

Evolution of Physical Oceanography: Essays in Honor of Henry Stommel. Ed. by Bruce A. Warren & Carol Wunsch. 768p. 1980. 37.50x (ISBN 0-262-23104-2). MIT Pr.

Evolution of Political Society: An Evolutionary View. Morton Fried. (Orig.). 1968. pap. text ed. 4.95x (ISBN 0-394-30787-9, RanC). Random.

Evolution of Population Theory: A Documentary Sourcebook. Ed. by Johannes Overbeek. LC 76-43138. (Contributions in Sociology: No. 23). 1977. lib. bdg. 16.95 (ISBN 0-8371-9313-3, OVP/). Greenwood.

Evolution of Protein Structure & Function: A Symposium in Honor of Prof. Emil L. Smith. Ed. by David S. Sigman & Mary Brazier. LC 80-18140. (UCLA Forum in Medical Science Ser.: Vol. 21). 1980. 25.00 (ISBN 0-12-643150-7). Acad Pr.

Evolution of Psychological Theory: 1650 to the Present. Richard Lowry. LC 70-116540. 1971. 14.95x (ISBN 0-202-25061-X). Aldine Pub.

Evolution of Science & Technology in STPI Countries. (Science & Technology for Development Ser.: STPI Module 3). 43p. 1981. pap. 5.00 (ISBN 0-88936-255-6, IDRC TS20, IDRC). Unipub.

Evolution of Sedimentary Rocks. Robert M. Garrels & Fred T. Mackenzie. (Illus.). 1971. text ed. 14.95x (ISBN 0-393-09959-8, NortonC). Norton.

Evolution of Sex. J. Maynard Smith. LC 77-85689. (Illus.). 1978. 35.50 (ISBN 0-521-21887-X); pap. 9.95x (ISBN 0-521-29302-2). Cambridge U Pr.

Evolution of Singlehanders. D. H. Clarke. 1976. 9.95 o.p. (ISBN 0-679-50706-X). McKay.

Evolution of Social Behavior: Hypotheses & Empirical Tests. Ed. by H. Markl & M. Feldman. (Dahlem Workshop Reports,Life Sciences Research Report Ser.: No. 18). (Illus.). 261p. (Orig.). 1980. pap. text ed. 22.50 (ISBN 0-89573-033-2). Verlag Chemie.

Evolution of Syntactic Theory in Sanskrit Grammar: Syntax of the Sanskrit Infinitive Ser. Madhav Deshpande. (Linguista Extranea: Studia: No. 10). 164p. 1980. 10.50 (ISBN 0-89720-029-2); pap. 7.50 (ISBN 0-89720-030-6). Karoma.

Evolution of the Borhyaenidae, Extinct South American Predaceous Marsupials. Larry G. Marshall. (Publications in Geological Sciences: Vol. 117). 1978. pap. 11.00x (ISBN 0-520-09571-5). U of Cal Pr.

Evolution of the Comprehensive School 1926-1966. David Rubinstein & Brian Simon. (Students Library of Education). 1970. text ed. 5.25x (ISBN 0-7100-6357-1). Humanities.

Evolution of the Earth. 3rd ed. Robert H. Dott & Roger L. Batten. (Illus.). 576p. 1980. text ed. 22.95 (ISBN 0-07-017625-6, C); write for info. McGraw.

Evolution of the Egyptian National Image: From Its Origins to Ahmad Lufti al-Sayyid. Charles Wendell. 1973. 30.00x (ISBN 0-520-02111-8). U of Cal Pr.

Evolution of the Gas Industry. Malcolm W. Peebles. 256p. 1981. 25.00x (ISBN 0-8147-6580-7). NYU Pr.

Evolution of the Human Mind. Norman L. Munn. LC 75-146722. (Illus., Orig.). 1971. pap. text ed. 8.95 (ISBN 0-395-11149-8, 3-39665). HM.

Evolution of the International Monetary System 1945-1977. Brian Tew. 1979. pap. 10.95 (ISBN 0-470-26705-4). Halsted Pr.

Evolution of the Machine. Ritchie Calder. LC 68-17249. (Illus.). 160p. 1968. 4.95 (ISBN 0-8281-0342-9, J040-0, Co-Pub. by Smithsonian). Am Heritage.

Evolution of the Nervous System. 2nd ed. Harvey B. Sarnat & Martin G. Netsky. (Illus.). 425p. 1981. text ed. 19.50x (ISBN 0-19-502775-2); pap. text ed. 13.95x (ISBN 0-19-502776-0). Oxford U Pr.

Evolution of the Nigerian State: The Southern Phase, 1898-1914. T. N. Tamuno. (Ibadan History Ser.). (Illus.). 250p. 1972. text ed. 14.00x (ISBN 0-391-00232-5). Humanities.

Evolution of the Six-Four Chord: A Chapter in the History of Dissonant Treatment. Glen Haydon. LC 75-125052. (Music Ser). 1971. Repr. of 1933 ed. lib. bdg. 19.50 (ISBN 0-306-70017-4). Da Capo.

Evolution of the Theories & Techniques of Standard Costs. Ellis Sowell. LC 73-2027. 548p. 1973. 15.00 (ISBN 0-8173-8901-6). U of Ala Pr.

Evolution of the Unit Train, 1960-1969. John T. Starr, Jr. LC 73-92655. (Research Papers Ser.: No. 158). (Illus.). 233p. 1976. pap. 8.00 o.p. (ISBN 0-89065-065-9). U Chicago Dept Geog.

Evolution of the Vertebrates: A History of the Backboned Animals Through Time. 2nd ed. Edwin H. Colbert. LC 67-84960. 1969. 21.50 o.p. (ISBN 0-471-16466-6, Pub. by Wiley-Interscience). Wiley.

Evolution of the Vertebrates: A History of the Backboned Animals Through Time. 3rd ed. Edwin H. Colbert. LC 79-27621. 544p. 1980. 25.00 (ISBN 0-471-04966-2, Pub. by Wiley Interscience). Wiley.

Evolution of Urban Society: Early Mesopotamia & Prehispanic Mexico. Robert McC. Adams. LC 66-15195. (Lewis Henry Morgan Lectures Ser.). 1966. 13.95x (ISBN 0-202-33016-8). Aldine Pub.

Evolution of Vertebrate Endocrine Systems. P. K. Pang & A. Epple. (Texas Tech Univ. Graduate Studies: No. 21). 404p. (Orig.). 1980. 35.00 (ISBN 0-89672-077-2); pap. 25.00 (ISBN 0-89672-076-4). Tex Tech Pr.

Evolution of Veterinary Pathology in Russia, Eighteen Sixty to Nineteen Thirty. Leon Z. Saunders. LC 79-52502. (Illus.). 1980. 25.00x o.p. (ISBN 0-8014-1191-2). Cornell U Pr.

Evolution of War: A Study of Its Role in Early Societies. Maurice R. Davie. 1929. 12.50x (ISBN 0-686-51382-7). Elliots Bks.

Evolution of Weapons & Warfare. T. N. Dupuy. LC 80-781. 350p. 1980. 14.95 (ISBN 0-672-52050-8). Bobbs.

Evolution of Womens' Rights, 16 vols. Tennie C. Claflin et al. 1973. lib. bdg. 2500.00 o.p. (ISBN 0-686-66806-5). Gordon Pr.

Evolution, Welfare & Time in Economics. Anthony M. Tang et al. (Illus.). 1976. 17.95 (ISBN 0-669-00736-6). Lexington Bks.

Evolutionary & Genetic Biology of Primates, 2 Vols. Ed. by John Buettner-Janusch. Set. 73.00 ea. o.p.; Vol. 1. 44.50 o.p. (ISBN 0-12-140201-0); Vol. 2. 44.50 o.p. (ISBN 0-12-140202-9). Acad Pr.

Evolutionary Biology. Douglas J. Futuyma. LC 78-27902. (Illus.). 1979. text ed. 19.50x (ISBN 0-87893-199-6). Sinauer Assoc.

Evolutionary Biology, Vol. 7. Ed. by Max K. Hecht et al. LC 67-11961. (Illus.). 314p. 1974. 27.95 (ISBN 0-306-35407-1, Plenum Pr). Plenum Pub.

Evolutionary Biology, Vol. 9. Ed. by Max K. Hecht et al. (Illus.). 458p. 1976. 35.00 (ISBN 0-306-35409-8, Plenum Pr). Plenum Pub.

Evolutionary Biology, Vols. 12 & 13. Ed. by M. K. Hecht et al. (Illus.). 1980. 32.50 ea. (Plenum Pr). Vol. 12, 388p (ISBN 0-306-40267-X). Vol. 13, 335p (ISBN 0-306-40510-5). Plenum Pub.

Evolutionary Biology of the New World Monkeys & Continental Drift. Ed. by Russell L. Ciochon & A. B. Chiarelli. (Advances in Primatology Ser.). 500p. 1981. 49.50 (ISBN 0-306-40487-7, Plenum Pr). Plenum Pub.

Evolutionary Changes to the Primate Skull & Dentition. C. L. Lavelle et al. (Illus.). 308p. 1977. 43.75 (ISBN 0-398-03618-7). C C Thomas.

Evolutionary Ecology of Animal Migration. R. Robin Baker. LC 78-34. (Illus.). 1978. text ed. 117.50x (ISBN 0-8419-0368-9). Holmes & Meier.

Evolutionary Explanation in the Social Sciences: An Emerging Paradigm. Philippe Van Parijs. (Philosophy & Society Ser.). 1981. 25.00x (ISBN 0-8476-6288-8). Rowman.

Evolutionary Metaphysics: The Development of Peirce's Theory of Catagories. Joseph L. Esposito. LC 80-15736. (Illus.). x, 152p. 1980. 15.00x (ISBN 0-8214-0551-9). Ohio U Pr.

Evolutionary Operation; A Statistical Method for Process Improvement. George E. Box & Norman R. Draper. LC 68-56159. (Applied Probability & Mathematical Statistics Ser). 1969. 27.50 (ISBN 0-471-09305-X, Pub. by Wiley-Interscience). Wiley.

Evolutionary Paleoecology of the Marine Biosphere. James W. Valentine. (Illus.). 512p. 1973. ref. ed. 26.95 (ISBN 0-13-293720-4). P-H.

Evolutionary Vision: Toward a Unifying Paradigm of Physical, Biological, & Sociocultural Evolution. Ed. by Erich Jantsch. (AAAS Selected Symposium: No. 6). 200p. 1981. lib. bdg. 17.50x (ISBN 0-86531-140-4). Westview.

Evolving Culture: A Cross-Cultural Study of Surinam, West Africa & the Caribbean. Charles J. Wooding. LC 80-5612. 343p. 1981. lib. bdg. 21.75 (ISBN 0-8191-1377-8); pap. text ed. 12.00 (ISBN 0-8191-1378-6). U Pr of Amer.

Evolving Techniques in Japanese Woodblock Prints. Gaston Petit & Amadio Arboleda. LC 77-75974. (Illus.). 1978. 18.50 (ISBN 0-87011-309-7). Kodansha.

Evolving: The Theory & Processes of Organic Evolution. Francisco J. Ayala & James W. Valentine. 1979. text ed. 18.95 (ISBN 0-8053-0310-3). Benjamin-Cummings.

Evolving Universe. Donald Goldsmith. 1981. 18.95 (ISBN 0-8053-3327-4). Benjamin-Cummings.

Evoning Female: Woman in Psychosocial Context. Carole L. Heckerman. LC 79-4240. 1979. text ed. 24.95 (ISBN 0-87705-392-8); pap. text ed. 9.95 (ISBN 0-87705-411-8). Human Sci Pr.

Evonne Goolagong. Charles Morse & Ann Morse. LC 74-796. (Creative's Superstars Ser). 32p. 1974. 5.50 o.p. (ISBN 0-87191-339-9). Creative Ed.

Ewbank's Indiana Criminal Law, 2 vols. Ed. by Symmes. 1956. with 1980 suppl. 75.00 (ISBN 0-672-84086-3, Bobbs-Merrill Law); 1980 suppl. 37.50 (ISBN 0-672-84282-3). Michie.

Ewings. John O'Hara. 352p. 1972. pap. 1.25 o.p. (ISBN 0-445-00136-4). Popular Lib.

Ewings of Dallas. 384p. (Orig.). 1980. pap. 2.75 (ISBN 0-553-14439-1). Bantam.

Ex Officio. Timothy Culver. LC 70-106590. 512p. 1970. 6.95 (ISBN 0-87131-006-6). M Evans.

Exact Methods in Linguistic Research. O. S. Akhmanova et al. Tr. by David G. Haynes & Dolores V. Mohr. 1963. 20.00x (ISBN 0-520-00542-2). U of Cal Pr.

Exact Sciences in Antiquity. 2nd ed. O. Neugebauer. LC 57-12342. (Illus.). 240p. 1970. Repr. of 1957 ed. 10.00 (ISBN 0-87057-044-7, Pub. by Brown U Pr). Univ Pr of New England.

Exam Secret. Dennis B. Jackson. pap. 3.00 (ISBN 0-87980-033-X). Wilshire.

Examen Chronologique des Monnais Frappes par la Communaute des Macedoniens Avant, Pendant et Apes la Conquete Romaine. H. F. Bompois. (Illus.). 102p. (Fr.). 20.00 (ISBN 0-916710-77-7). Obol Intl.

Examen De Ingenios, the Examination of Mens Wits. Juan de Dios Huarte Navarro. Tr. by R. Carew. LC 75-26368. (English Experience Ser.: No. 126). 1969. Repr. of 1594 ed. 28.50 (ISBN 90-221-0126-6). Walter J Johnson.

Examinacions of Thorpe & Oldcastell. William Thorpe. LC 74-28889. (English Experience Ser.: No. 766). 1975. Repr. of 1530 ed. 7.00 (ISBN 90-221-0766-3). Walter J Johnson.

Examination & Analysis of Starch & Starch Products. Ed. by J. A. Radley. (Illus.). 1976. 63.30x (ISBN 0-85334-692-5, Pub. by Applied Science). Burgess-Intl Ideas.

Examination & Valuation of Mineral Property. 4th ed. Roland D. Parks. (Illus.). 1957. 27.50 (ISBN 0-201-05730-1, Adv Bk Prog). A-W.

Examination of Dr. Reid's Inquiry into the Human Mind. Joseph Priestley. Ed. by Rene Wellek. LC 75-11249. (British Philosophers & Theologians of the 17th & 18th Centuries Ser.). 1978. Repr. of 1774 ed. lib. bdg. 42.00 (ISBN 0-8240-1800-1). Garland Pub.

Examination of Plato's Doctrines, 2 vols. I. M. Crombie. **Incl. Vol. 1. Plato on Man & Society. 1962. text ed. 24.75x (ISBN 0-7100-3608-6); Vol. 2. Plato on Knowledge & Reality. 1963. text ed. 40.50x (ISBN 0-391-01053-0). (International Library of Philosophy & Scientific Method). Set. text ed. 40.50x (ISBN 0-686-66629-1). Humanities.**

Examination of Questionable Payments & Practices. Tom Kennedy & Charles E. Simon. LC 78-14195. (Praeger Special Studies). 1978. 34.50 (ISBN 0-03-046321-1). Praeger.

Examination of the Child with Minor Neurological Dysfunction. 2nd ed. Bert C. Touwen. (Clinics in Developmental Medicine Ser.: No. 71). 150p. 1979. 25.00 (ISBN 0-685-24730-9). Lippincott.

Examination of the Hand. George L. Lucas. (Illus.). 248p. 1972. text ed. 19.75 (ISBN 0-398-02347-6). C C Thomas.

Examination of Water for Pollution Control: Handbook for Management & Analysts. M. J. Suess. (Illus.). 1700p. 1981. 300.00 (ISBN 0-08-025255-9). Pergamon.

Examination Reforms in Sri-Lanka. (International Bureau of Education Ser: Experiments & Innovations in Education, No. 24). 1977. pap. 2.50 (ISBN 92-3-101348-3, U231, UNESCO). Unipub.

Examination Review for Dental Assistants. Betty Jo Lorenzen. LC 79-53191. (Dental Assisting Ser.). 1981. 6.60 (ISBN 0-8273-1672-0). Delmar.

Examining Controversies in Adult Education. Burton W. Kreitlow. LC 80-27058. (Higher Education Ser.). 1981. text ed. price not set (ISBN 0-87589-488-7). Jossey-Bass.

Examining Deviance Experimentally: Selected Readings. Darrell J. Steffensmeier & Robert M. Terry. LC 74-32334. 311p. 1975. pap. text ed. 8.50x (ISBN 0-88284-021-5). Alfred Pub.

Examining the Gospels. Al Cooper. 1981. 4.75 (ISBN 0-8062-1601-8). Carlton.

Examining the Metric Issues. Ed. by Priscilla Adams. 85p. 1976. pap. 4.00 (ISBN 0-916148-08-4). Am Natl.

Example of Jesus Christ: Imago Christi. James Stalker. LC 80-82322. (Orig.). 1980. pap. 5.95 (ISBN 0-87983-231-2). Keats.

Example of Melville. Warner Berthoff. 1972. pap. 2.25 o.p. (ISBN 0-393-00595-X, Norton Lib). Norton.

Example of Science: An Anthology for College Composition. Robert E. Lynch & Thomas B. Swanzey. 320p. 1981. pap. text ed. 9.95 (ISBN 0-686-69275-6). P-H.

Examples Illustrating AACR2. Eric J. Hunter & Nicholas J. Fox. 192p. 1980. pap. 12.50 (ISBN 0-8389-3249-5). ALA.

Examples of a Treatise on Universal Justice or the Fountains of Equity, by Aphorisms. Francis Bacon & Richard Francis. Ed. by David S. Berkowitz & Samuel E. Thorne. LC 77-86639. (Classics of English Legal History in the Modern Era Ser.: Vol. 33). 125p. 1979. lib. bdg. 40.00 (ISBN 0-8240-3082-6). Garland Pub.

Examples of Gregorian Chant & Other Sacred Music of the 16th Century. Compiled by G. F. Soderlund & Samuel H. Scott. LC 70-129090. (Orig.). 1971. 15.95 (ISBN 0-13-293753-0). P-H.

Excalibur. John Jakes. (Orig.). 1980. pap. 2.50 o.s.i. (ISBN 0-440-12291-0). Dell.

Excalibur. Sanders A. Laubenthal. 1977. pap. 1.95 o.p. (ISBN 0-345-25635-2). Ballantine.

Excalibur Briefing: Understanding Paranormal Phenomena. Thomas E. Bearden. LC 78-12936. (Walnut Hill Bk.). (Illus., Orig.). 1980. pap. 8.95 (ISBN 0-89407-015-0). Strawberry Hill.

Excalibur III: Story of a P-51 Mustang. Robert C. Mikesh. LC 78-606028. (Famous Aircraft of the National Air & Space Museum Ser.: No. 1). (Illus.). 76p. 1978. pap. 5.95 (ISBN 0-87474-635-3). Smithsonian.

Excavation Handbook. Horace K. Church. 1980. 49.50 (ISBN 0-07-010840-4). McGraw.

Excavation of Abri Pataud, Les Eyzies (Dordoane) Stratigraphy. Hallam L. Movius, Jr. LC 76-52630. (American School of Prehistoric Bulletins Ser.: No. 31). (Illus.). 1977. pap. 30.00 (ISBN 0-87365-534-6). Peabody Harvard.

Excavation of an Iron Age Settlement, Bronze Age Ring-Ditches & Roman Features at Ashville Trading Estate, Abingdon (Oxfordshire) Michael Parrington. 166p. 1980. pap. 24.00x (ISBN 0-900312-50-5, Pub. by Coun Brit Arch England). Intl Schol Bk Serv.

Excavation of the Abri Pataud, Les Eyzies (Dordogne) Ed. by Hallam L. Movius, Jr. LC 74-77559. (American School of Prehistoric Research Bullentins Ser.: No. 30). (Illus.). 1975. pap. 30.00 (ISBN 0-87365-533-8). Peabody Harvard.

Excavations at Altar De Sacrificios: Architecture, Settlement, Burials & Caches. A. Ledyard Smith. LC 72-126638. (Peabody Museum Papers: Vol. 62, No. 2). 1972. pap. 25.00 (ISBN 0-87365-178-2). Peabody Harvard.

Excavations at Little Waltham. P. A. Rahtz. 74p. 1980. pap. 48.00 (ISBN 0-900312-64-5, Pub. by Coun Brit Arch England). Intl Schol Bk Serv.

Excavations at Nippur: Twelfth Season. McGuire Gibson et al. LC 78-59117. (Oriental Institute Communications Ser.: No. 23). (Illus.). 1978. pap. 22.00x (ISBN 0-918986-22-2). Oriental Inst.

Excavations at St. Mary's Church, Deerhurst. P. A. Rahtz. 74p. 1980. pap. 11.95x (ISBN 0-900312-35-1, Pub. by Coun Brit Arch England). Intl Schol Bk Serv.

Excavations at Seibal. Ed. by Gordon Willey. LC 74-77554. (Peabody Museum Memoirs Ser.: No. 13-1&2). (Illus.). 1975. pap. 40.00 (ISBN 0-87365-685-7). Peabody Harvard.

Excavations at Seibal: Department of Peten, Guatemala, 3 vols. Incl. Vol. 14, No. 1. Artifacts. Gordon R. Willey; Vol. 14, No. 2. Reconnaissance of Cancuen. Gair Tourtellot, 3rd et al; Vol. 14, No. 3. Brief Reconnaissance of Itzan. Gair Tourtellot et al. LC 76-53126. (Memoirs of the Peabody Museum of Archaeology & Ethnology Harvard University: Vol. 14). 1978. Set. 35.00 (ISBN 0-87365-686-5). Peabody Harvard.

Excavations at Seibal: Major Architecture & Caches & Analysis of Fine Paste Ceramics. Ledyard Smith. Ed. by Jeremy A. Subloff. (Peabody Museum Memoirs Ser.: Vol. 15, No. 1 & 2). 1981. pap. price not set (ISBN 0-87365-687-3). Peabody Harvard.

Excavations at Star Carr: An Early Mesolithic Site at Seamer Near Scarborough, Yorkshire. J. Desmond Clark. LC 75-172830. (Illus.). 226p. 1971. 65.00 (ISBN 0-521-08394-X). Cambridge U Pr.

Excavations at Tepe Yahya, Iran, 1967-1969: Progress Report No. 1. C. C. Lamberg-Karlovsky. LC 74-143902. (ASPR Bulletin: No. 27). 1970. pap. text ed. 12.00 (ISBN 0-87365-528-1). Peabody Harvard.

Excavations in Medievel Southampton 1953-1969. Colin Platt et al. Incl. Vol. 1. The Excavation; Vol. 2. The Finds. (Illus.). 1975. Set. text ed. 75.00x (ISBN 0-7185-1123-9, Leicester). Humanities.

Excavations in Southeastern Guatemala: 1976-1978. Ed. by Lawrence H. Feldman & Gary H. Walters. (Miscellaneous Publications in Anthropology Ser.: No. 9, Reports 1 & 2). (Illus.). 1980. pap. 5.00x (ISBN 0-913134-80-5). Mus Anthro Mo.

Excellence & Leadership in a Democracy. Ed. by Stephen R. Graubard & Gerald Holton. LC 62-20743. 1962. text ed. 20.00x (ISBN 0-231-02567-X). Columbia U Pr.

Excellence of Exposition: Practical Procedure in Expository Preaching. Douglas M. White. 1977. 4.25 (ISBN 0-87213-938-7). Loizeaux.

Excellency & Praehemînence of the Law of England. Thomas Williams & John Somers. Ed. by David S. Berkowitz & Samuel E. Thorne. LC 77-86674. (Classics of English Legal History in the Modern Era Ser.: Vol. 50). 357p. 1979. lib. bdg. 40.00 (ISBN 0-8240-3099-0). Garland Pub.

Excellent & Material Discourse, Proving What Great Danger Will Hand Over Our Heads. LC 72-5694. (English Experience Ser.: No. 497). 32p. 1973. Repr. of 1626 ed. 6.00 (ISBN 90-221-0497-4). Walter J Johnson.

Exceptional Child. 2nd ed. Lita Schwartz. 1979. pap. text ed. 8.95x (ISBN 0-534-00633-7). Wadsworth Pub.

Exceptional Child Grows Up: Guidelines for Understanding & Helping the Brain Injured Adolescent & Young Adult. Ernest Siegel. 1978. 8.95 (ISBN 0-87690-112-7); pap. 4.95 (ISBN 0-87690-155-0). Dutton.

Exceptional Child Through Literature. Elliot Landau et al. (Illus.). 1978. ref. ed. 10.95 (ISBN 0-13-293860-X). P-H.

Exceptional Children: A Developmental View. Marvin D. Wyne & Peter D. O'Connor. 1979. pap. text ed. 16.95x (ISBN 0-669-95786-0). Heath.

Exceptional Children: An Introductory Survey to Special Education. William L. Heward & Michael D. Orlansky. (Special Education Ser.). 480p. 1980. text ed. 17.95 (ISBN 0-675-08179-3); instructor's manual 3.95 (ISBN 0-686-63187-0). Merrill.

Exceptional Children: Educational Resources & Perspectives. Samuel A. Kirk & Francis E. Lord. 464p. 1974. pap. text ed. 11.95 (ISBN 0-395-18027-9). HM.

Exceptional Children: Introduction to Special Education. Daniel P. Hallahan & James M. Kauffman. (Special Education Ser.). 1978. ref. ed. 18.95 (ISBN 0-13-293944-4). P-H.

Exceptional Individual. 3rd ed. Charles W. Telford & James Sawrey. LC 76-44470. (Illus.). 1977. ref. ed. 18.95x (ISBN 0-13-293837-5). P-H.

Exceptional Infant: Psychosocial Risks in Infant-Environment Transactions, Vol. 4. Ed. by Douglas B. Sawin et al. LC 80-14270. (Exceptional Infant Ser.). 1980. 32.50 (ISBN 0-87630-222-3). Brunner-Mazel.

Exceptional Previews: A Self-Evaluation Handbook for Special Education Students. Carol Cartwright & Sara J. Forsberg. 1979. pap. text ed. 8.95x (ISBN 0-534-00629-9). Wadsworth Pub.

Exceptional Teaching: Individually Planned Educations. 2nd ed. Owen R. White & Norris G. Haring. (Special Education Ser.). 368p. 1980. text ed. 17.95 (ISBN 0-675-08156-4); instructor's manual 3.95 (ISBN 0-686-63188-9). Merrill.

Excerpts from the Curry County Echoes, Vol. II. Edith W. Jones. (Illus.). 110p. (Orig.). 1981. pap. 47.00 (ISBN 0-932368-08-5). Curry County.

Excersise Manual in Immunology. Lazar M. Schwartz & Paula Schwartz. LC 75-14774. 324p. 1975. 15.00 (ISBN 0-686-65368-8). Krieger.

Excess & Surplus Lines Manual. Bernard J. Daenzer. 1981. 186.00 (ISBN 0-930868-01-3). Merritt Co.

Excessive Liability - Duties & Responsibilities of the Insurer. Pat Magarick. LC 75-44308. 1976. with 1978 suppl. 30.00 (ISBN 0-87632-157-0). Boardman.

Exchange & Power in Social Life. Peter M. Blau. LC 64-23827. 1964. 23.95 (ISBN 0-471-08030-6). Wiley.

Exchange & Production: Theory in Use. 2nd ed. Armen A. Alchian & William R. Allen. 1977. pap. 14.95x (ISBN 0-534-00493-8). Wadsworth Pub.

Exchange & Trade Controls-Principles & Procedures of Regulating International Economic Transaction. Jozef Swidrowski. 480p. 1975. 50.00 (ISBN 0-7161-0223-4). Herman Pub.

Exchange Media of Colonial Mexico. Wilbur T. Meek. (Perspectives in Latin American History Ser.: No. 5). vi, 114p. 1980. Repr. of 1948 ed. lib. bdg. 13.50x (ISBN 0-87991-070-4). Porcupine Pr.

Exchange of Christendom: The International Entrepot at Dover, 1622-1651. J. S. Kepler. 200p. 1976. text ed. 17.25x (ISBN 0-7185-1144-1, Leicester). Humanities.

Exchange of Clowns. Theodore Wilden. 228p. 1981. 11.95 (ISBN 0-316-94051-8). Little.

Exchange of Expertise: The Counterpart System in the New International Order. Ed. by Irving R. Spitzberg, Jr. (Westview Replica Edition). 1978. lib. bdg. 20.25 o.p. (ISBN 0-89158-280-0). Westview.

Exchange of Gifts. Marilyn M. Brown. (Illus.). (gr. 10-12). 1980. pap. 6.95 (ISBN 0-938536-00-1). Wilton.

Exchange Reactions. (Illus., Orig., Eng. & Fr.). 1965. pap. 18.75 (ISBN 92-0-040265-8, IAEA). Unipub.

Exchange Risk & Corporate International Finance. Robert Z. Aliber. LC 78-4645. 1978. 24.95 (ISBN 0-470-26307-5). Halsted Pr.

Exchange Risk & Exposure: Current Developments in International Financial Management. Ed. by Richard M. Levich & Clas G. Wihlborg. LC 79-5181. (Illus.). 224p. 1980. 22.95 (ISBN 0-669-03246-8). Lexington Bks.

Exchange Show: A Documentation. Ed. by Nancy Vachon. LC 79-124425. (Illus.). 79p. (Orig.). 1979. pap. 5.95 (ISBN 0-87870-084-6). Memphis St Univ.

Excise Crisis: Society & Politics in the Age of Walpole. Paul Langford. 194p. 1975. 23.00x (ISBN 0-19-822437-0). Oxford U Pr.

Excitation & Propagation of Elastic Waves. J. A. Hudson. LC 79-4505. (Monographs on Mechanics & Applied Mathematics Ser.). (Illus.). 1980. 38.50 (ISBN 0-521-22777-1). Cambridge U Pr.

Excited State in Chemical Physics, Vol. Two. J. William McGowan. (Advances in Chemical Physics: Vol. 45). 616p. 1981. 45.95 (ISBN 0-471-05119-5, Pub. by Wiley-Interscience). Wiley.

Excited States, Vols. 1 & 2. Ed. by Edward C. Lim. Vol. 1, 1974. 46.00 (ISBN 0-12-227201-3); Vol. 2, 1975. 52.50 (ISBN 0-12-227202-1); Vol. 3, 1978. 40.00 (ISBN 0-12-227203-X). Acad Pr.

Excited States of Matter. Ed. by Charles W. Shoppee. (Graduate Studies: No. 2). (Illus., Orig.). 1973. pap. 8.00 (ISBN 0-89672-009-8). Tex Tech Pr.

Excitement of Change: A Book of Personal Growth. Benjamin V. White & Helen White. 190p. 1975. 7.95 (ISBN 0-8164-1206-5). Crossroad NY.

Exciting Electric Machine Inventions. Laithwaite. pap. 3.95 (ISBN 0-08-017249-0). Pergamon.

Exciting River Running in the U.S. Elizabeth Medes. 1979. 9.95 o.p. (ISBN 0-8092-7508-2); pap. 5.95 o.p. (ISBN 0-8092-7507-4). Contemp Bks.

Exciting Western Stories. Compiled by Harriet Ross. (Illus.). 160p. (gr. 4-7). 1981. PLB 7.21 (ISBN 0-87460-312-9). Lion.

Excitons: Their Properties & Uses. Donald C. Reynolds & Thomas C. Collins. 1981. 36.00 (ISBN 0-12-586580-5). Acad Pr.

Exclusion of Women from the Priesthood: Divine Law or Sex Discrimination? Ida Raming. Tr. by Norman R. Adams. LC 76-23322. 280p. 1976. 13.50 (ISBN 0-8108-0957-5). Scarecrow.

Exclusions of a Rhyme: Poems & Epigrams. J. V. Cunningham. LC 60-8072. 120p. (Orig.). 1960. 7.00x (ISBN 0-8040-0763-2); pap. 4.50 (ISBN 0-8040-0102-2). Swallow.

Exclusive Economic Zone. W. C. Extavour. 384p. 1979. 30.00x o.p. (ISBN 90-286-0838-9). Sijthoff & Noordhoff.

Excursion Flora of the British Isles. 3rd ed. A. R. Clapham et al. LC 79-51679. 600p. Date not set. 29.95 (ISBN 0-521-23290-2). Cambridge U Pr.

Excursion Flora of the British Isles. 2nd ed. Arthur R. Clapham et al. LC 68-20329. 1968. 28.95 (ISBN 0-521-04656-4). Cambridge U Pr.

Excursion into Creative Sociology. Monica B. Morris. LC 76-19023. 1977. 15.00x (ISBN 0-231-03987-5); pap. 7.00x (ISBN 0-686-67485-5). Columbia U Pr.

Excursions in Southeastern Geology: Field Trip Guidebooks, 2 vols. Ed. by Robert W. Frey. Incl. Vol. I. Field Trips-1-13. pap. 25.00 (ISBN 0-913312-48-7); Vol. II. Field Trips-14-23. pap. 25.00 (ISBN 0-913312-49-5). (Illus., Orig.). 1980. Set. pap. 40.00 (ISBN 0-913312-50-9). Am Geol.

Excursions in Victorian Bibliography. Michael Sadleir. 240p. 1980. Repr. of 1922 ed. lib. bdg. 35.00 (ISBN 0-8492-8205-5). R West.

Excursions into Mathematics. Anatole Beck et al. LC 68-57963. (Illus.). 1969. text ed. 16.95x (ISBN 0-87901-004-5). Worth.

Excursions: Selected Literary Essays. Robert Boyers. (Literary Criticism Ser). 1976. 15.00 (ISBN 0-8046-9148-7, Natl U). Kennikat.

Excuse Me! Certainly! Louis Slobodkin. LC 59-15200. (Illus.). (gr. 1-3). 1959. 5.95 (ISBN 0-8149-0403-3). Vanguard.

Excuses: How to Spot Them, Deal with Them, & Stop Using Them. Sven Wahlroos. (Illus.). 1981. 11.95 (ISBN 0-02-623300-2). Macmillan.

Executive Under Stress. Alexander Institute, Inc. Ed. by Jamess M. Jenks. (Illus.). 71p. (Orig.). 1976. pap. 49.25x (ISBN 0-86604-007-2, A783157). Hamilton Inst.

Execution. Robert Mayer. 1979. 8.95 o.p. (ISBN 0-670-30050-0). Viking Pr.

Execution of Charles Horman. Thomas Hauser. 272p. 1979. pap. 2.75 (ISBN 0-380-49098-6, 49098, Discus). Avon.

Execution of Isaac Hayne. new ed. David K. Bowden. LC 76-20850. (Illus.). 1977. 9.95 (ISBN 0-87844-037-2); ltd signed ed 12.95 (ISBN 0-87844-014-3). Sandlapper Store.

Execution of Maximilian: A Hapsburg Emperor Meets Disaster in the New World. Robin McKown. LC 73-3427. (World Focus Bks). (Illus.). (gr. 7 up). 1973. PLB 6.45 (ISBN 0-531-02165-3). Watts.

Execution of Mayor Yin & Other Stories from the Great Proletarian Cultural Revolution. Johsi Chen. Tr. by Nancy Ing & Howard Goldblatt. LC 78-1956. 248p. 1978. 10.95 (ISBN 0-253-12475-1); pap. 4.95 (ISBN 0-253-20231-0). Ind U Pr.

Executioner. Pierre Boulle. LC 61-15474. 1961. 8.95 (ISBN 0-8149-0065-8). Vanguard.

Executioner: Miami Massacre. Don Pendleton. (Executioner Ser, No. 4). 1970. pap. 1.95 (ISBN 0-523-41068-9). Pinnacle Bks.

Executioner: Nightmare in New York. Don Pendleton. (Executioner Ser, No. 7). (Orig.). 1971. pap. 1.95 (ISBN 0-523-41071-9). Pinnacle Bks.

Executioner: Vegas Vendetta. Don Pendleton. (Executioner Ser. No. 9). (Orig.). 1971. pap. 1.95 (ISBN 0-523-41073-5). Pinnacle Bks.

Executioners. John D. MacDonald. 1978. pap. 1.75 o.p. (ISBN 0-449-14059-8, GM). Fawcett.

Executioner's Song. Norman Mailer. 1980. 3.95 (ISBN 0-686-68993-3). Warner Bks.

Executive Air Fleet. Joseph Kleinpeter. (Illus.). 1979. pap. 4.95 (ISBN 0-911721-52-5, Pub. by J Kleinpeter). Aviation.

Executive & Management Development for Business & Government: A Guide to Information Sources. Ed. by Agnes O. Hanson. LC 76-8337. (Management Information Guide Ser.: No. 31). 490p. 1976. 30.00 (ISBN 0-8103-0831-2). Gale.

Executive Compensation. David R. Roberts. LC 58-12851. 1959. 8.50 o.s.i. (ISBN 0-02-926590-8). Free Pr.

Executive Compensation Survey of the Retailing Industry. 120p. 1981. 60.00 (P53680). Natl Ret Merch.

Executive Computing. J. M. Nevison. 1981. pap. text ed. 8.95 (ISBN 0-201-05248-2). A-W.

Executive, Congress, & Foreign Policy: Studies of the Nixon Administration. John Lehman. LC 76-13835. (Special Studies). 1976. text ed. 23.95 (ISBN 0-275-56490-8). Praeger.

Executive Decision Making Through Simulation. 2nd ed. Paul Cone. LC 79-165985. pap. text ed. 9.95x (ISBN 0-675-09762-2). Merrill.

Executive Decisions & Operations Research. 2nd ed. David W. Miller & Martin K. Starr. 1969. ref. ed. 21.00 (ISBN 0-13-294538-X). P-H.

Executive Ease & Dis-Ease. H. Beric Wright. LC 75-1072. 1975. 19.95 (ISBN 0-470-96450-2). Halsted Pr.

Executive Game. 3rd ed. Richard C. Henshaw & James R. Jackson. 1978. pap. text ed. 9.95 (ISBN 0-256-02034-5). Irwin.

Executive Handbook to Minicomputers. Robert A. Bonelli. (Illus.). text ed. 14.00 (ISBN 0-89433-090-X). Petrocelli.

Executive Health. A. Melhuish. 190p. 1978. text ed. 24.50x (ISBN 0-220-66351-3, Pub. by Busn Bks England). Renouf.

Executive Housekeeping. Auren Uris. 1976. 7.95 o.p. (ISBN 0-688-03000-9). Morrow.

Executive Leadership. Nathan Axelrod. 1969. pap. text ed. 9.10 (ISBN 0-672-96054-0); tchr's manual 5.00 (ISBN 0-672-96055-9). Bobbs.

Executive Leadership: How to Get It - & Make It Work. Mary E. Tramel & Helen Reynolds. (Illus.). 272p. 1981. 13.95 (ISBN 0-13-294132-5, Spec); pap. 6.95 (ISBN 0-686-69280-2). P-H.

Executive Look. Mortimer Levitt. LC 80-66011. (Illus.). 1981. 14.95 (ISBN 0-689-11078-2). Atheneum.

Executive Nothing Book. 1977. pap. 3.95 o.s.i. (ISBN 0-446-87540-6). Warner Bks.

Executive Orders Relating to Indian Reservations: 1855-1922, 2 vols. in 1. LC 75-13936. 1975. Repr. of 1922 ed. lib. bdg. 40.00 (ISBN 0-8420-2065-9). Scholarly Res Inc.

Executive Power in the United States: A Study of Constitutional Law. Adolphe De Chambruh. LC 74-75460. 303p. 1974. Repr. 32.00x (ISBN 0-912004-13-4). W W Gaunt.

Executive Privilege Vs. Democratic Accountability: The Special Assistant to the President for National Security Affairs, 1961-1969. P. M. Kamath. 485p. 1980. text ed. 33.75x (ISBN 0-391-02173-7). Humanities.

Executive Protection Manual. Jan Reber & Paul Shaw. 1976. 39.95 (ISBN 0-916070-02-6); soft cover 29.95. MTI Tele.

Executive Role in Health Service Delivery Organizations. Ingrid K. Kuhl. 1977. 5.00. Assn Univ Progs Hlth.

Executive Sales Control Atlas. rev. ed. American Map Company. 1979. 77.90 (ISBN 0-8416-9557-1). Am Map.

Executive Secretarial Procedures. 5th ed. Irene Place & Edward E. Byers. LC 79-9097. (Illus.). 1980. text ed. 15.80 (ISBN 0-07-050255-2); instrs'. manual & key 5.50 (ISBN 0-07-050257-9). McGraw.

Executive Security: A Corporate Guide to Effective Response to Abduction & Terrorism. Richard B. Cole. LC 80-14662. 336p. 1980. 24.95 (ISBN 0-471-07736-4, Pub. by Wiley Interscience). Wiley.

Executive Success: Stresses, Problems, & Adjustment. Eugene E. Jennings. LC 67-27560. 1967. 18.95x (ISBN 0-89197-156-4); pap. text ed. 6.95x (ISBN 0-89197-157-2). Irvington.

Executive Suite. Cameron Hawley. 1977. pap. 1.95 o.p. (ISBN 0-445-08578-9). Popular Lib.

Executive Survival Manual. Thomas V. Bomoma & Dennis P. Slevin. LC 78-16130. 1978. pap. 11.95 (ISBN 0-8436-2137-0). CBI Pub.

Executive Tune-Up: Personal Effectiveness Skills for Business & Professional People. Karl Albrecht. (Illus.). 224p. 1981. text ed. 13.95 (ISBN 0-13-294215-1, Spec); pap. text ed. 6.95 (ISBN 0-13-294207-0, Spec). P-H.

Executive Typewriting. 2nd ed. Charles E. Reigel & Edward A. Perkins. (Illus.). 256p. (gr. 12 up). 1980. practice set in envelope container 13.75 (ISBN 0-07-051826-2); instrs'. guide & visual key 4.95 (ISBN 0-07-051827-0). McGraw.

Executive's Guide to Coping with Stress, Tension & Anxiety-Producing Situations: (or, How to Take Control of Your Life) Mary VanMeer. 200p. (Orig.). 1981. write for info. o.s.i. (ISBN 0-937826-01-4). VanMeer Pubns.

Executive's Guide to Finding a Superior Job. William A. Cohen. LC 78-7370. (Illus.). 1978. 13.95 (ISBN 0-8144-5475-5). Am Mgmt.

Executive's Guide to Forecasting. John C. Chambers et al. LC 74-2433. (Managers Guide Ser.). 320p. 1974. 27.50 (ISBN 0-471-14335-9, Pub. by Wiley-Interscience). Wiley.

Executive's Handbook of Balanced Physical Fitness: A Guide to a Personalized Exercise Program. Thomas DeCarlo. (Illus.). 1975. pap. 4.95 o.p. (ISBN 0-8096-1900-8, Assn Pr). Follett.

Executive's Illustrated Primer of Long-Range Planning. Richard Levin. (Illus.). 240p. 1981. text ed. 11.95 (ISBN 0-13-294140-6). P-H.

Executives Under Pressure. Judi Marshall & Cary L. Cooper. LC 78-72594. (Praeger Special Studies Ser.). 1979. 20.95 (ISBN 0-03-049496-6). Praeger.

Executive's Wife. N. H. Burger. 1968. 5.95 o.s.i. (ISBN 0-02-518160-2). Macmillan.

Executivo Sob Tensao. Alexander Hamilton Institute, Inc. Ed. by James M. Jenks. (Illus.). 71p. (Orig., Portuguese.). 1978. pap. 50.75x (ISBN 0-86604-009-9). Hamilton Inst.

Exegetical Method of the Greek Translator of the Book of Job. Donald H. Gard. (Society of Biblical Literature Monographs: No. 8). 1952. pap. 7.50 (ISBN 0-89130-178-X, 060008). Scholars Pr Ca.

Exemplars for the New Social Studies: Instruction in the Elementary Schools. Frank L. Ryan. LC 70-137484. (Illus.). 1971. pap. text ed. 9.95x (ISBN 0-13-294686-6). P-H.

Exemplary History of the Novel: The Quixotic Versus the Picaresque. Walter L. Reed. LC 80-17908. 1981. lib. bdg. 22.00x (ISBN 0-226-70683-4). U of Chicago Pr.

Exenterative Surgery of the Pelvis. John S. Spratt, Jr. et al. LC 72-90729. (Major Problems in Clinical Surgery Ser.: No. 12). (Illus.). 177p. 1973. text ed. 9.95 (ISBN 0-7216-8523-4). Saunders.

Exer-Sex. Bonnie Prudden. (Illus.). 1980. pap. 3.95 (ISBN 0-553-10698-8). Aquarian Pr.

Exercices de Verbes. M. Fourel. Incl. No. 1. 60p. 1969 (ISBN 0-87774-031-3); No. 2. 86p. 1969; No. 3. 102p. 1969 (ISBN 0-87774-033-X); No. 4. 75p. 1967 (ISBN 0-87774-034-8). (Fr.). pap. text ed. 3.50 ea. Schoenhof.

Exercise & Aging: The Scientific Basis. Papers Presented Before the College of Sports Medicine & Robert Serfass. (Illus.). 224p. 1981. text ed. 12.95 (ISBN 0-89490-042-0). Enslow Pubs.

Exercise & Health: The Evidence & the Implications. Gregory S. Thomas et al. LC 80-23376. 128p. 1981. lib. bdg. 17.50 (ISBN 0-89946-048-8). Oelgeschlager.

Exercise & Tape Manual for Movement Is Life. Eva D. Garnet. (Illus.). 200p. 1981. spiral bdg. 15.00 (ISBN 0-916622-20-7). Princeton Bk Co.

Exercise & the Heart: Guidelines for Exercise Programs. Ed. by Robert L. Morse. (Illus.). 292p. 1974. 28.75 (ISBN 0-398-02365-4). C C Thomas.

Exercise & the Lung. Ed. by Jerry A. Dempsey & Charles E. Reed. 1977. 35.00x (ISBN 0-299-07220-7). U of Wis Pr.

Exercise Book. Leslie Michener & Gerald Donaldson. LC 78-7096. (Illus.). 1978. 15.00 o.p. (ISBN 0-03-045521-9); pap. 8.95 o.p. (ISBN 0-685-27620-1). HR&W.

Exercise in Health & Disease. Francis Nagle & Henry Montoye. (Illus.). 440p. 1981. write for info. (ISBN 0-398-04120-2). C C Thomas.

Exercise in the Office: Easy Ways to Better Health & Firmer Figures. Robert R. Spackman, Jr. LC 68-25554. (Arcturus Books Paperbacks). 112p. pap. 3.95 (ISBN 0-8093-0317-5). S Ill U Pr.

Exercise of Arms. Jacob De Gheyn. LC 77-146168. (Illus.). 1976. Repr. of 1607 ed. 65.00 o.p. (ISBN 0-07-016237-9); Edition Of 10 Copies, Hand Colored & Illuminated In Gold & Silver. 1000.00 o.p. (ISBN 0-686-15687-0). Arma Pr.

Exercise Physiology: Energy, Nutrition & Human Performance. William D. McArdle et al. LC 80-20156. (Illus.). 508p. 1981. text ed. 17.50 (ISBN 0-8121-0682-2). Lea & Febiger.

Exercise Plus Pregnancy Program: Exercises for Before, During & After Pregnancy. Cedeno et al. LC 80-14278. (Illus.). 192p. 1980. 10.95 (ISBN 0-688-03697-X, Quill); pap. 4.95 (ISBN 0-686-68533-4, Quill). Morrow.

Exercises for the Autonomic Nervous System: You Need Them! I. S. Pickering. (Illus.). 112p. 1981. price not set (ISBN 0-398-04454-6); pap. price not set (ISBN 0-398-04466-X). C C Thomas.

Exercises for the Mature Adult. Lois Ellfeldt & Charles L. Lowman. (Illus.). 120p. 1973. pap. 9.75 spiral (ISBN 0-398-02750-1). C C Thomas.

Exercises in Elementary Algebra. J. Richard Lux & Richard S. Pieters. (gr. 8-9). 1977. pap. text ed. 4.75x (ISBN 0-88334-087-9) (ISBN 0-685-39242-2). Ind Sch Pr.

Exercises in English Patterns & Usage. 2nd ed. Ronald Mackin & Jennifer Seidl. 1979. pap. text ed. 6.95x (ISBN 0-19-432717-5). Oxford U Pr.

Exercises in French Phonics. Francis W. Nachtmann. 1970. spiral bdg. 5.95x (ISBN 0-673-05988-X). Scott F.

Exercises in Introductory Physics. Robert B. Leighton & Rochus E. Vogt. (Physics Ser). (Orig.). 1969. pap. text ed. 4.95 (ISBN 0-201-04215-0). A-W.

Exercises in Modern Mathematics. D. T. Marjoram. 1965. text ed. 6.95 (ISBN 0-08-011004-5); pap. 5.40 (ISBN 0-08-011003-7). Pergamon.

Exercises in Physical Geography. 2nd ed. Arthur N. Strahler. 328p. 1975. pap. text ed. 10.95x (ISBN 0-471-83177-8); instructor's ed. avail. (ISBN 0-471-83157-3). Wiley.

Exercises in Plane Geometry. James D. Bristol & David A. Penner. (Illus., Orig.). (gr. 9-10). 1976. pap. text ed. 4.75x (ISBN 0-88334-086-0). Ind Sch Pr.

Exercises in Pre-Algebra. Paul F. Butler. (gr. 6-8). 1977. pap. text ed. 4.75x (ISBN 0-88334-041-0) (ISBN 0-685-39243-0). Ind Sch Pr.

Exercises in Probability & Statistics for Mathematics Undergraduates. N. A. Rahman. 1967. 10.95 o.s.i. (ISBN 0-02-850770-3). Hafner.

Exercises in Probability & Statistics. 2nd ed. N. A. Rahman. 1981. 35.00 (ISBN 0-02-850760-6). Macmillan Info.

Exercises in Reading & Writing. Alexandra Davis & O. B. Davis. (gr. 10-11). 1978. pap. text ed. 5.60x (ISBN 0-8104-5935-3). Hayden.

Exercises in Spanish. Susanne Vasi & Joseph Tomasino. 229p. 1981. pap. text ed. 3.25 (ISBN 0-88345-421-1, 18638). Regents Pub.

Exercises in Spanish. new ed. Susanne Vasi & Joseph Tomasino. 200p. 1980. pap. 3.25 (ISBN 0-88345-446-7, 18638); cassettes 25.00. Regents Pub.

Exercises in Spoken Hindi. R. S. McGregor. (Illus.). 1970. 32.50 (ISBN 0-521-07487-8); tape 49.50 (ISBN 0-521-07488-6). Cambridge U Pr.

Exercises in Style. Edmund Miller. 68p. 1980. pap. 4.00x (ISBN 0-9600486-3-4). Edmund Miller.

Exercises in Style. 2nd ed. Raymond Queneau. Tr. by Barbara Wright from Fr. LC 80-26102. Orig. Title: Exercises De Style. (Illus.). 208p. 1981. 12.95 (ISBN 0-8112-0803-6); pap. 4.95 (ISBN 0-8112-0789-7, ND513). New Directions.

Exercising for Fitness. C. P. Gilmore. Ed. by Time-Life Books. (Health Ser.). (Illus.). 176p. 1981. 12.95 (ISBN 0-8094-3754-6). Time Life.

Exergy Method of Energy Systems Analysis. John E. Ahern. LC 79-24500. 1980. 27.50 (ISBN 0-471-05494-1, Pub. by Wiley-Interscience). Wiley.

Exeter Blitz. David Rees. (gr. 6 up). 1980. 7.95 (ISBN 0-525-66683-4). Elsevier-Nelson.

Exeter Book. Ed. by George P. Krapp & Elliott V. Dobie. LC 36-30684. 1936. 20.00x (ISBN 0-231-08767-5). Columbia U Pr.

Exeter Impressions. new ed. Robert Gambee. (Illus.). 206p. 1980. 14.95 (ISBN 0-8038-1961-7). Hastings.

Exhaustive Parallel Intervals. Richard Kostelanetz. LC 79-51581. 1980. 15.00; signed & lettered, A-Z 50.00; pap. 5.95 (ISBN 0-918406-09-9). Future Pr.

Exhibit. Leslie Hollander. 384p. (Orig.). 1981. pap. 2.75 (ISBN 0-523-41479-X). Pinnacle Bks.

Exhibit Medium: Theory & Practice of Trade Show Participation. David Maxwell. (Illus.). 144p. 1978. 24.95 (ISBN 0-89047-030-8). Herman Pub.

Exhibition Catalogue Manual in Use in the Library of the Metropolitan Museum of Art. Ed. by Lucy C. Ho. (Illus.). 40p. 1974. 2.50 (ISBN 0-87099-099-3). Metro Mus Art.

Exhibition Catalogue, 1883 & Gazette, 1888-1889. Rational Dress Association. Ed. by Peter Stansky & Rodney Shewan. LC 76-18323. (Aesthetic Movement & the Arts & Crafts Movement Ser.). 1978. lib. bdg. 44.00x (ISBN 0-8240-2456-7). Garland Pub.

Exhibition Catalogues from the Fogg Art Museum, 10 vols. facsimile ed. Incl. Tiepolo: A Bicentenary Exhibition, 1770-1970. George Knox. lib. bdg. 55.00 (ISBN 0-685-76417-6); Degas Monotypes: Essay, Catalogue & Checklist. Eugenia P. Janis. lib. bdg. 60.50 (ISBN 0-685-76418-4); Ingres' Sculptural Sytle: A Group of Unknown Drawings. Phyllis Hattis. Repr. of 1973 ed. lib. bdg. 23.00 (ISBN 0-685-76419-2); Three American Painters: Kenneth Noland, Jules Olitski, Frank Stella. Michael Fried. Repr. of 1965 ed. lib. bdg. 16.50 (ISBN 0-685-76420-6); Gods & Heroes: Baroque Images of Antiquity. Eunice Williams. Repr. of 1968 ed. lib. bdg. 40.00 (ISBN 0-685-76421-4); Frederick M. Watkins Collection. Repr. of 1973 ed. lib. bdg. 38.00 (ISBN 0-685-76422-2); Eucharistic Vessels of the Middle Ages. Heidi R. Kaufmann et al. Repr. of 1975 ed. lib. bdg. 23.00 (ISBN 0-685-76423-0); Works of Art from the Collection of Paul J. Sachs. Agnes Mongan. Repr. of 1966 ed. lib. bdg. 38.00 (ISBN 0-685-76424-9); Harvard Honors Lafayette. Agnes Mongan et al. Repr. of 1976 ed. lib. bdg. 23.00 (ISBN 0-685-76425-7); Benjamin Franklin: A Perspective. Louise T. Ambler. Repr. of 1975 ed. lib. bdg. 23.00 (ISBN 0-685-76426-5). (Illus.). 1977. Garland Pub.

Exhibition in Memory of Agnes Rindge Claflin. LC 78-55009. (Illus.). 1978. pap. 3.00 (ISBN 0-89192-273-3, Pub. by Vassar Art Gallery). Interbk Inc.

Exhibition of Character & Genre Pictures. Ed. by Theodore Reff. (Modern Art in Paris 1855 to 1900 Ser.). 112p. 1981. lib. bdg. 44.00 (ISBN 0-8240-4727-3). Garland Pub.

Exhibition: Scenes from the Life of John Merrick. Thomas Gibbons. 1980. pap. 1.25 (ISBN 0-686-68848-1). Dramatists Play.

Exhibitionism Description, Assessment, & Treatment. Ed. by Daniel J. Cox & Reid J. Daitzman. 1980. lib. bdg. 32.50 (ISBN 0-8240-7033-X). Garland Pub.

Exhibitions of Art Nouveau. Ed. by Theodore Reff. (Modern Art in Paris Ser.). 486p. 1981. lib. bdg. 44.00 (ISBN 0-8240-4732-X). Garland Pub.
Exhibitions of Barbizon & Landscape Art. Ed. by Theodore Reff. (Modern Art in Paris 1855 to 1900 Ser.). 449p. 1981. lib. bdg. 44.00 (ISBN 0-8240-4737-0). Garland Pub.
Exhibitions of Classicizing Art. Ed. by Theodore Reff. (Modern Art in Paris 1855 to 1900 Ser.). 395p. 1981. lib. bdg. 44.00 (ISBN 0-8240-4735-4). Garland Pub.
Exhibitions of Draftsmen & Illustrations. Ed. by Theodore Reff. (Modern Art in Paris, 1855 to 1900, Ser.). 241p. 1981. lib. bdg. 44.00 (ISBN 0-8240-4744-3). Garland Pub.
Exhibitions of Impressionist Art, Bk. I. Ed. by Theodore Reff. (Modern Art in Paris 1855 to 1900 Ser.). 356p. 1981. lib. bdg. 44.00 (ISBN 0-8240-4741-9). Garland Pub.
Exhibitions of Impressionist Art, Bk. II. Ed. by Theodore Reff. (Modern Art in Paris 1855 to 1900 Ser.). 259p. 1981. lib. bdg. 44.00 (ISBN 0-8240-4742-7). Garland Pub.
Exhibitions of Later Realist Art. Ed. by Theodore Reff. (Modern Art in Paris 1855 to 1900 Ser.). 320p. 1981. lib. bdg. 44.00 (ISBN 0-8240-4740-0). Garland Pub.
Exhibitions of Modern Drawings. Ed. by Theodore Reff. (Modern Art in Paris 1855 to 1900 Ser.). 251p. 1981. lib. bdg. 44.00 (ISBN 0-8240-4724-9). Garland Pub.
Exhibitions of Modern European Art. Ed. by Theodore Reff. (Modern Art in Paris 1855 to 1900 Ser.). 500p. 1981. lib. bdg. 44.00 (ISBN 0-8240-4725-7). Garland Pub.
Exhibitions of Modern Prints. Ed. by Theodore Reff. (Modern Art in Paris 1855 to 1900 Ser.). 339p. 1981. lib. bdg. 44.00 (ISBN 0-8240-4726-5). Garland Pub.
Exhibitions of Realist Art, Bk. I. Ed. by Theodore Reff. (Modern Art in Paris 1855 to 1900 Ser.). 518p. 1981. lib. bdg. 44.00 (ISBN 0-8240-4738-9). Garland Pub.
Exhibitions of Realist Art, Bk. II. Ed. by Theodore Reff. (Modern Art in Paris 1855 to 1900 Ser.). 345p. 1981. lib. bdg. 44.00 (ISBN 0-8240-4739-7). Garland Pub.
Exhibitions of Romantic Art. Ed. by Theodore Reff. (Modern Art in Paris 1855 to 1900 Ser.). 340p. 1981. lib. bdg. 44.00 (ISBN 0-8240-4736-2). Garland Pub.
Exhibitions of Sculpture. Ed. by Theodore Reff. (Modern Art in Paris 1855 to 1900 Ser.). 394p. 1981. lib. bdg. 44.00 (ISBN 0-8240-4745-1). Garland Pub.
Exhibitions of Symbolists & Nabi. Ed. by Theodore Reff. (Modern Art in Paris 1855 to 1900 Ser.). 254p. 1981. lib. bdg. 44.00 (ISBN 0-8240-4743-5). Garland Pub.
Exhibitions of the Rosicrucian Salon. Ed. by Theodore Reff. (Modern Art in Paris 1855 to 1900 Ser.). 354p. 1981. lib. bdg. 44.00 (ISBN 0-8240-4730-3). Garland Pub.
Exhibitions of the Salon Des Cent, 1894 to 1895. Ed. by Theodore Reff. (Modern Art in Paris 1855 to 1900 Ser.). 175p. 1981. lib. bdg. 44.00 (ISBN 0-8240-4731-1). Garland Pub.
Exhibitions of the Society of Printmakers. Ed. by Theodore Reff. (Modern Art in Paris 1855 to 1900 Ser.). 262p. 1981. lib. bdg. 44.00 (ISBN 0-8240-4729-X). Garland Pub.
Exhibitions: Universal Marketing Tools. Alfred Alles. LC 73-1796. 260p. 1973. 21.95 (ISBN 0-470-02332-5). Halsted Pr.
Exhibits Directory: 1981. Ed. by Stanley E. Hicks. 92p. (Orig.). 1981. pap. 20.00 (ISBN 0-933636-01-6). AAP.
Exhibits Schedule-Annual Directory of Trade & Industrial Shows. Sales Meeting Magazine Research Staff. 300p. (Annual). 65.00x (ISBN 0-89047-047-2). Herman Pub.
Exhortation & Controls: The Search for a Wage - Price Policy, 1945-1971. Craufurd D. Goodwin. (Studies in Wage-Price Policy). 1975. 16.95 (ISBN 0-8157-3208-2); pap. 7.95 (ISBN 0-8157-3207-4). Brookings.
Exigent Subjects. Association of Bone & Joint Surgeons. Ed. by Marshall R. Urist. (Clinical Orthopaedics Ser., Vol. 68). 1970. 12.00 o.p. (ISBN 0-685-22848-7). Lippincott.
Exil. Saint-John Perse. Ed. by Roger Little. (Athlone French Poets Ser.). 1973. text ed. 19.50x (ISBN 0-685-45862-8, Athlone Pr); pap. text ed. 10.50x (ISBN 0-485-12706-7). Humanities.
Exile & Return: The Struggle for a Jewish Homeland. Martin Gilbert. LC 78-9780. (Illus.). 1978. 12.95 o.s.i. (ISBN 0-397-01249-7). Lippincott.
Exile Governments. Alicja Iwanska. LC 76-40139. 192p. 1981. text ed. 13.25x (ISBN 0-87073-555-1); pap. text ed. 7.95x (ISBN 0-87073-553-5). Schenkman.
Exile in the Wilderness: The Life of Chief Factor Archibald McDonald, 1790-1853. Jean M. Cole. LC 79-5361. (Illus.). 288p. 1980. 15.95 (ISBN 0-295-95704-2). U of Wash Pr.
Exile of the World: From the Silence of the Bible to the Silence of Auschwitz. Andre Neher. 224p. 1980. 16.95 (ISBN 0-8276-0176-X, 465). Jewish Pubn.
Exiled from Earth. Ben Bova. LC 74-133120. (gr. 5-12). 1971. PLB 9.95 (ISBN 0-525-29425-2); pap. 0.95 o.p. (ISBN 0-525-45016-5). Dutton.
Exiles. Michael J. Arlen. 160p. 1976. pap. 1.75 o.p. (ISBN 0-345-25196-2). Ballantine.
Exiles. William S. Long. 1980. pap. 2.75 o.s.i. (ISBN 0-440-12369-0). Dell.
Exiles - Passage to Ararat. Michael J. Arlen. 1978. pap. 5.95 (ISBN 0-374-51460-7). FS&G.
Exiles: A Facsimile of Notes, Manuscripts & Galley Proofs. James Joyce. Ed. by Michael Groden. LC 77-18397. (James Joyce Archive Ser.). 1978. lib. bdg. 104.00 (ISBN 0-8240-2810-4). Garland Pub.
Exiles & Citizens: Spanish Republicans in Mexico. Patricia W. Fagen. LC 72-3781. (Latin American Monographs: No. 29). 272p. 1973. 12.95x (ISBN 0-292-72002-5). U of Tex Pr.
Exile's Odyssey: The Memoirs of an American Deserter. Parker F. Smith. LC 78-75338. (Illus.). 1979. 12.00 o.p. (ISBN 0-498-02387-7). A S Barnes.
Exiles of Florida. Joshua R. Giddings. Intro. by Arthur W. Thompson. LC 64-19159. (Floridiana Facsimile & Reprint Ser). (Illus.). 1964. Repr. of 1858 ed. 10.75 (ISBN 0-8130-0085-8). U Presses Fla.
Exilius; or The Banish'd Roman. Jane Barker. LC 70-170536. (Foundations of the Novel Ser.: Vol. 25). lib. bdg. 50.00 (ISBN 0-8240-0537-6). Garland Pub.
Existence & Imagination: The Theatre of Henry De Montherlant. John Batchelor. 1967. text ed. 11.50x (ISBN 0-391-00421-2). Humanities.
Existence & Love: A New Approach in Existential Phenomenology. William A. Sadler, Jr. LC 68-17052. 1970. pap. 3.95 o.p. (ISBN 0-684-71883-9, SL235, ScribT). Scribner.
Existence & Presence: The Dialectics of Divinity. Laurence L. Cassidy. LC 80-5881. 246p. 1981. lib. bdg. 16.50 (ISBN 0-8191-1486-3); pap. text ed. 7.50 (ISBN 0-8191-1487-1). U Pr of Amer.
Existence & Utopia: The Social & Political Thought of Martin Buber. Bernard Susser. LC 78-75188. 260p. 1981. 15.00 (ISBN 0-8386-2292-5). Fairleigh Dickinson.
Existence of God. John H. Hick. 1964. pap. 3.95 (ISBN 0-02-085450-1). Macmillan.
Existence of God. Richard Swinburne. 1979. 39.00x (ISBN 0-19-824611-0). Oxford U Pr.
Existence, Relatedness & Growth: Human Needs in Organizational Settings. Clayton P. Alderfer. LC 78-156839. 1972. 15.95 (ISBN 0-02-900390-3). Free Pr.
Existential Anxiety: Angst. James Park. (Existential Freedom Ser.: No. 5). 1974. pap. 2.00x (ISBN 0-89231-005-7). Existential Bks.
Existential Battles: The Growth of Norman Mailer. Laura Adams. LC 74-27710. 192p. 1976. 12.00x (ISBN 0-8214-0182-3); pap. 4.75 (ISBN 0-8214-0401-6). Ohio U Pr.
Existential Errands. Norman Mailer. 320p. 1973. pap. 1.75 (ISBN 0-451-05422-9, E5422, Sig). NAL.
Existential Freedom, No. 3. James Park. 1973. pap. 2.00x (ISBN 0-89231-003-0). Existential Bks.
Existential Imagination. Ed. by Frederick Karl & Leo Hamalian. pap. 1.95 o.p. (ISBN 0-449-30779-4, C779, Prem). Fawcett.
Existential Man: The Challenge of Psychotherapy. R. E. Johnson. 1971. 9.50 (ISBN 0-08-016325-4). Pergamon.
Existential Marxism in Postwar France: From Sartre to Althusser. M. Poster. 1975. 23.50x (ISBN 0-691-07212-4); pap. 5.95 (ISBN 0-691-01994-0). Princeton U Pr.
Existential Metapsychiatry. Thomas Hora. 12.95 (ISBN 0-8164-0337-6). Crossroad NY.
Existential Neurosis. E. K. Lederman. (Illus.). 150p. 1972. 10.60 (ISBN 0-407-17040-5). Butterworths.
Existential Psychotherapy. Irvin D. Yalom. LC 80-50553. 524p. 1980. 18.50 (ISBN 0-465-02147-6). Basic.
Existential Sentences & Negation in Russian. Leonard H. Babby. (Linguistica Extranea: Studia: No. 8). 199p. 1980. 12.50 (ISBN 0-89720-013-6); pap. 7.50 (ISBN 0-89720-014-4). Karoma.
Existential Sentences in English. Gary L. Milsark. Ed. by Jorge Hankamer. LC 78-66570. (Outstanding Dissertations in Linguistics Ser.). 1979. lib. bdg. 30.00 (ISBN 0-8240-9678-9). Garland Pub.
Existential Sociology. Ed. by J. D. Douglas & J. M. Johnson. LC 76-47198. 1977. 34.50 (ISBN 0-521-21515-3); pap. 10.95x (ISBN 0-521-29225-5). Cambridge U Pr.
Existential Sociology of Jean-Paul Sartre. Gila J. Hayim. LC 80-10131. 176p. 1980. lib. bdg. 13.50x (ISBN 0-87023-298-3). U of Mass Pr.
Existential Structures: An Analytic Enquiry. Roger A. Kenyon. LC 76-4222. 1976. 6.00 (ISBN 0-8022-2181-5). Philos Lib.
Existential Structures: An Analytic Inquiry. Roger A. Kenyon. LC 76-4222. 1976. 6.00 o.p. (ISBN 0-8022-2181-5). Philos Lib.
Existential Thinking. Bernard J. Boelen. LC 68-5783. 1971. pap. 6.95 (ISBN 0-8164-2546-9). Crossroad NY.
Existential Understanding of Death: A Phenomenology of Ontological Anxiety. James Park. (Existential Freedom Ser.: No. 6). 72p. 1975. pap. 2.00x (ISBN 0-89231-006-5). Existential Bks.
Existentialism. Wesley Barnes. LC 67-28536. (Orig.). (gr. 10 up). 1968. pap. text ed. 3.25 (ISBN 0-8120-0275-X). Barron.
Existentialism. John Macquarrie. 1973. pap. 2.95 (ISBN 0-14-021569-7, Pelican). Penguin.
Existentialism. Patricia F. Sanborn. LC 68-27983. (Traditions of Philosophy Ser). (Orig.). 1968. pap. 4.95 (ISBN 0-672-63535-6). Pegasus.
Existentialism & Thomism. Joseph C. Mihalich. (Quality Paperback: No. 170). 1969. pap. 2.50 (ISBN 0-8226-0170-2). Littlefield.
Existentialism: for & Against. Paul Roubiczek. (Orig.). 32.95x (ISBN 0-521-06140-7); pap. 8.95 (ISBN 0-521-09243-4). Cambridge U Pr.
Existentialism from Dostoevsky to Sartre. Ed. by Walter A. Kaufmann. 1958. 8.50 (ISBN 0-8446-2355-5). Peter Smith.
Existentialism in Sociology. I. Craib. LC 75-44579. 280p. 1976. 32.50 (ISBN 0-521-21047-X). Cambridge U Pr.
Existentialist Thinkers & Thoughts. Frederick Patka. LC 62-9770. 1962. 4.75 o.p. (ISBN 0-8022-1285-9). Philos Lib.
Existentialist Tradition. Ed. by Nino Langiulli. LC 78-150930. 1971. pap. 2.95 o.p. (ISBN 0-385-04567-0, Anch). Doubleday.
Exit Laughing. Irvin S. Cobb. LC 73-19798. 1974. Repr. of 1941 ed. 28.00 (ISBN 0-8103-3687-1). Gale.
Exit Sherlock Holmes: The Great Detective's Final Days. Robert L. Hall. LC 76-56152. 1977. 7.95 o.p. (ISBN 0-684-14849-8, ScribT). Scribner.
Exit Thirteen. Monte Piliawsky. LC 78-59599. 1979. 10.00 o.p. (ISBN 0-89430-026-1). Morgan-Pacific.
Exit Thirty Six: A Fictional Chronicle. Robert F. Capon. 250p. 1975. 7.95 (ISBN 0-8164-0262-0). Crossroad NY.
Exit, Voice, & Loyalty: Responses to Decline in Firms, Organizations, & States. Albert O. Hirschman. LC 77-99517. 1970. 8.95x (ISBN 0-674-27650-7); pap. 2.50 (ISBN 0-674-27660-4). Harvard U Pr.
Exito. Luis Palau. Tr. by Edwin Sipowicz from Eng. LC 78-57804. 144p. (Orig., Span.). 1978. pap. 3.50 (ISBN 0-89922-115-7). Edit Caribe.
Exits: Dying Words & Last Moments. Scott Slater & Alec Solomita. 1980. 7.95 (ISBN 0-525-93070-1). Dutton.
Exits off a Toll Road. Steven Lewis. LC 75-6211. 53p. 1975. pap. 5.00 (ISBN 0-915316-11-0); pap. 2.50 limited signed ed. (ISBN 0-685-56251-4). Pentagram.
Exitus. Radomir Konstantinovic. 1980. 10.95 (ISBN 0-7145-0223-5). Riverrun NY.
Exodus. Irving L. Jensen. (Bible Self-Study Ser). 1970. pap. 2.95 (ISBN 0-8024-1002-2). Moody.
Exodus. Leon Uris. LC 62-16691. 1958. 14.95 (ISBN 0-385-05082-8). Doubleday.
Exodus. Leon Uris. 608p. 1981. pap. 3.50 (ISBN 0-553-14867-2). Bantam.
Exodus--Exodus: The Cabalistic Bible. Albert L. Schutz. Ed. by Anne N. Lowenkopf. (Orig.). Date not set. 15.50 (ISBN 0-686-69116-4); pap. 8.95 (ISBN 0-936596-04-X). Quantal.
Exodus: A Hermeneutics of Freedom. J. Severino Croatto. 112p. (Orig.). 1981. pap. 4.95 (ISBN 0-88344-111-X). Orbis Bks.
Exodus: A Study Guide Commentary. F. B. Huey, Jr. 1977. pap. 3.50 (ISBN 0-310-36053-6). Zondervan.
Exodus of Corporate Headquarters from New York City. Wolfgang Quante. LC 75-19809. (Special Studies). (Illus.). 234p. 1976. text ed. 27.95 (ISBN 0-275-55770-7). Praeger.
Exorcism. Olga Hoyt. (Illus.). (gr. 7 up). 1978. 7.45 (ISBN 0-531-01480-0). Watts.
Exorcism: Fact Not Fiction. Ed. by Martin Ebon. pap. 1.25 (ISBN 0-451-05701-5, Y5701, Sig). NAL.
Exorcism of Anneliese Michel. Felicitas D. Goodman. LC 80-910. 312p. 1981. 12.95 (ISBN 0-385-15789-4). Doubleday.
Exoterica: Poems & Drawings. V. P. Tollerton, Jr. (Illus.). 48p. 1980. 3.95 (ISBN 0-915102-01-3). Eastham Edns.
Exotic Alphabets & Ornaments. William Rowe. (Illus.). 80p. (Orig.). 1974. pap. 3.50 (ISBN 0-486-22989-0). Dover.
Exotic Atoms Nineteen Seventy-Nine: Fundamental Interactions & Structure of Matter. Kenneth Crowe et al. (Ettore Majorana International Science Ser., Physical Science: Vol. 4). 410p. 1980. 45.00 (ISBN 0-306-40322-6, Plenum Pr). Plenum Pub.
Exotic Food Guide. Marty Olmstead & Jan Weimer. Ed. by Jan Leonard. LC 80-66583. (Savvy San Francisco Ser.). (Illus.). 64p. (Orig.). 1980. pap. text ed. 2.50 (ISBN 0-89395-050-5). Cal Living Bks.
Exotic Japan: The Traveler's Wonderland. Boye De Mente. LC 72-21365. (Illus.). 160p. 1976. pap. 3.95 (ISBN 0-914778-12-9). Phoenix Bks.
Exotic Marine Fishes. Herbert R. Axelrod et al. (Illus.). 608p. 1973. 15.00 (ISBN 0-87666-102-9, H938); looseleaf bdg. o.p. 20.00 (ISBN 0-87666-103-7). Tfh Pubns.
Exotic Nudes. Andre De Dienes. (Illus.). 4.95 (ISBN 0-910550-04-2). Elysium.
Exotic Tropical Fishes. rev. ed. H. Axelrod et al. (Illus.). 1302p. 1980. 25.00 (ISBN 0-87666-543-1, H-1028); looseleaf 30.00. TFH Pubns.
Exotic Tropical Fishes. Herbert R. Axelrod et al. 9.95 (ISBN 0-87666-051-0, H-907); looseleaf 20.00 (ISBN 0-87666-052-9, H-907L). TFH Pubns.
Exotic Vegetables: How to Grow & Cook Them. Ken Kraft & Pat Kraft. (Illus.). 1977. 8.95 o.s.i. (ISBN 0-8027-0560-X); pap. 3.95 o.s.i. (ISBN 0-8027-7109-2). Walker & Co.
Exotica Series Three: Pictorial Cyclopedia of Exotic Plants. 10th, rev. ed. Alfred B. Graf. LC 72-90669. (Illus.). 1980. 78.00 (ISBN 0-911266-15-1). Roehrs.
Expanded Bond Values Tables. Financial Publishing Co. No. 63. pocket ed. 27.50 (ISBN 0-685-02541-1); No. 83. desk ed. 36.00 (ISBN 0-685-02542-X). Finan Pub.
Expanded Campus: Current Issues in Higher Education 1972. Ed. by Dyckman W. Vermilye. LC 72-6043. (Higher Education Ser.). 1972. 12.95x o.p. (ISBN 0-87589-143-8). Jossey-Bass.
Expanded Panorama Bible Study Course. Alfred T. Eade. (Illus.). 8.95 (ISBN 0-8007-0086-4). Revell.
Expanded Role of the Nurse. (Contemporary Nursing Ser.). 325p. 1973. 6.50 (ISBN 0-937126-10-1, C10). Am Journal Nurse.
Expanded Universe. Robert A. Heinlein. Ed. by Jim Baen. 1980. pap. 8.95 (ISBN 0-441-21883-0). Ace Bks.
Expanded Voice: The Art of Thomas Traherne. Stanley Stewart. LC 71-111800. 1970. 10.00 (ISBN 0-87328-045-8). Huntington Lib.
Expanding Circle: Ethics and Sociobiology. Peter Singer. 1981. 10.95 (ISBN 0-374-15112-1). FS&G.
Expanding Cooperative Horizons. Ed. by Beryle Stanton. (Illus.). 500p. 1980. 12.00; pap. 9.50. Am Inst Cooperation.
Expanding Earth. Pascual Jordan. Ed. by Arthur Beer. 224p. 1971. 34.00 (ISBN 0-08-015827-7). Pergamon.
Expanding Family: Childbearing. Carole L. Blair & Elizabeth M. Salerno. LC 75-30278. 1976. pap. text ed. 11.95 (ISBN 0-316-09915-5). Little.
Expanding Laser Industry GB-050. 1980. 850.00 (ISBN 0-89336-253-0). BCC.
Expanding School Environment. Commission on Educational Issues. 1978. pap. 6.50 (ISBN 0-934338-38-8). NAIS.
Expanding Society: Britain 1830-1900. G. Kitson Clark. 1967. 23.95 (ISBN 0-521-05897-X). Cambridge U Pr.
Expanding the Environmental Responsibility of Local Government: Claremont's Environmental Task Force & Its Recommendations. Ed. by Eleanor Cohen. LC 72-83451. (Environmental Studies Ser: No. 3). 1972. pap. 10.00x (ISBN 0-912102-07-1). Cal Inst Public.
Expanding Your Teaching Potential: A Role Clarification Guide for Educators & Human Service Workers. Susan Campbell. LC 76-58637. 1980. pap. 9.95 (ISBN 0-8290-0349-5). Irvington.
Expanding Your Vocabulary. Barbara Gregorich. LC 78-730053. (Illus.). 1978. pap. text ed. 99.00 (ISBN 0-89290-126-8, 327-SATC). Soc for Visual.
Expans'd Hieroglyphicks: A Study of Sir John Denham's Coopers Hill, with a Critical Edition of the Poem. Brendan O Hehir. LC 68-27163. 1968. 20.00x (ISBN 0-520-01496-0). U of Cal Pr.
Expansion, Conflict, & Reconstruction 1825-1880. The Educational Research Council. (American Adventure Concepts & Inquiry Ser). (Orig.). (gr. 8). 1975. pap. text ed. 8.96 (ISBN 0-205-04629-0, 8046298). Allyn.
Expansion Joints in Buildings. Building Research Advisory Board. LC 74-9845. 1974. pap. 3.75 (ISBN 0-309-02233-9). Natl Acad Pr.
Expansion of Europe. John Hargreaves. (History Today Ser). 1968. 5.00 (ISBN 0-05-001655-5); pap. 3.95 (ISBN 0-685-00928-9). Dufour.

Expansion of Europe: The First Phase. Ed. by James Muldoon. LC 77-81455. (Middle Ages Ser). 1977. 16.00x (ISBN 0-8122-7729-5); pap. 7.95x (ISBN 0-8122-1091-3). U of Pa Pr.

Expansion of the Federal Union Eighteen Hundred & One to Eighteen Forty-Eight. Wayne A. Frederick & Thomas T. Lyons. (Illus.). 296p. (Orig.). (gr. 10-12). 1978. pap. text ed. 4.50x (ISBN 0-88334-116-6). Ind Sch Pr.

Expansive Cement Concretes. 1973. pap. 22.25 (ISBN 0-685-85116-8, SP-38). ACI.

Expansive Elite: District Politics & State Policy-Making in India. Donald B. Rosenthal. 1977. 22.75x (ISBN 0-520-03160-1). U of Cal Pr.

Expansive Soils, 2 vols. Donald Snethen. LC 66-140. 900p. 1981. pap. text ed. 46.00 (ISBN 0-87262-245-2). Am Soc Civil Eng.

Expectant Fathers. Sam Bittman & Sue Zalk. LC 78-54666. 1979. 12.95 (ISBN 0-8015-2444-X, Hawthorn). Dutton.

Expectant Mother. Redbook Editors. pap. 2.50 (ISBN 0-671-42413-0). PB.

Expectation of the Poor. B. N. Vaughan. 192p. 1972. pap. 3.50 o.p. (ISBN 0-8170-0571-4). Judson.

Expectations: A Completely Unexpected Guide to Planned & Unplanned Parenthood. Andre Sala & Margot Duxler. (Illus.). 100p. 1981. pap. 2.95 (ISBN 0-399-50516-4, Perigee). Putnam.

Expectations & Actions: Expectancy-Value Models in Psychology. Ed. by Norman T. Feather. 400p. 1981. professional reference text 24.95 (ISBN 0-89859-080-9). L Erlbaum Assocs.

Expectations & Possiblities. Joseph D. Batten. LC 80-17102. 368p. 1981. text ed. write for info. (ISBN 0-201-00093-8). A-W.

Expectations, Forecasting & Control--a Provisional Textbook of Macroeconomics: Volume II, Prices, Market & Turning Points. William Frazer. LC 80-1361. 439p. 1980. lib. bdg. 25.50 (ISBN 0-8191-1290-9); pap. text ed. 16.25 (ISBN 0-8191-1291-7). U Pr of Amer.

Expedition to Earth. Arthur C. Clarke. 1975. pap. 1.95 (ISBN 0-345-28467-4). Ballantine.

Expedition Two Thousand Sixty-One. Duncan Sidwell. LC 73-145608. (Illus.). 1971. text ed. 2.95x (ISBN 0-521-08087-8). Cambridge U Pr.

Expeditions of John Charles Fremont, Supplement: Proceedings of the Court Martial. Ed. by Mary L. Spence & Donald Jackson. 1973. 17.50 (ISBN 0-252-00403-5). U of Ill Pr.

Expense Analysis: Condominiums, Cooperatives, & Planned Unit Developments. Ed. by Kenneth Anderson. 1980. lib. bdg. 30.00 (ISBN 0-912104-41-4). Inst Real Estate.

Expensive People. Joyce C. Oates. LC 68-8084. 1968. 10.95 (ISBN 0-8149-0170-0). Vanguard.

Expensive Place to Die. Len Deighton. 1980. pap. 2.25 o.p. (ISBN 0-425-04470-X). Berkley Pub.

Experiemntal Approach to Organizational Developement. 2nd ed. D. Harvey & H. Brown. 1981. pap. 10.95 (ISBN 0-13-295360-9). P-H.

Experience Analysis in Industrial Planning. Jean-Paul Sallenave. LC 76-7164. (Illus.). 1976. 17.95 (ISBN 0-669-00658-0). Lexington Bks.

Experience & Conduct. S. Korner. LC 75-44578. 1976. 38.50 (ISBN 0-521-21075-5). Cambridge U Pr.

Experience & Conduct: A Philosophical Enquiry into Practical Thinking. S. Korner. LC 75-44578. 270p. 1980. pap. 13.50 (ISBN 0-521-29943-8). Cambridge U Pr.

Experience & Environment: Major Influences on the Development of the Young Child, Vol. II. Bruce L. White et al. LC 72-10354. (Early Childhood Education Ser.). (Illus.). 1978. ref. ed. 25.95x (ISBN 0-13-294819-2). P-H.

Experience & God. John E. Smith. 1968. 9.95x (ISBN 0-19-501207-0). Oxford U Pr.

Experience & Its Modes. M. Oakeshott. LC 77-85696. 1978. 38.50 (ISBN 0-521-05852-X). Cambridge U Pr.

Experience & Reflection. Edgar A. Singer. Ed. by C. West Churchman. LC 57-11956. 1959. 15.00 o.p. (ISBN 0-8122-7039-8). U of Pa Pr.

Experience & the Growth of Understanding. D. W. Hamlyn. (International Library of the Philosophy of Education Ser.). 1978. 17.50x (ISBN 0-7100-8735-7). Routledge & Kegan.

Experience & Theory. Stephan Korner. 1966. text ed. 19.25x (ISBN 0-7100-3628-0). Humanities.

Experience & Trends in Nuclear Law. (Legal Ser.: No. 8). 169p. (Orig.). 1973. pap. 10.75 (ISBN 92-0-176072-8, IAEA). Unipub.

Experience from Operating & Fuelling Nuclear Power Plants. (Illus.). 721p. (Orig., Eng., Fr. & Span.). 1974. pap. 45.00 (ISBN 92-0-050274-1, IAEA). Unipub.

Experience in Action: A Psychomotor Psychology. Albert Pesso. LC 72-96481. 263p. 1973. 13.00x (ISBN 0-8147-6559-9). NYU Pr.

Experience of Breastfeeding. Sheila Kitzinger. 255p. (Orig.). 1980. pap. 3.50 (ISBN 0-14-005591-6). Penguin.

Experience of Dying. Alois Muller. (Concilium Ser.: Religion in the Seventies: Vol. 94). pap. 4.95 (ISBN 0-8164-2578-7). Crossroad NY.

Experience of Dying. E. Mansell Pattison. 1977. text ed. 13.95 (ISBN 0-13-294629-7, Spec); pap. text ed. 4.95 (ISBN 0-13-294611-4). P-H.

Experience of God. Charles Magsam. LC 73-89314. 256p. 1975. 7.95x o.p. (ISBN 0-88344-123-3); pap. 4.95x o.p. (ISBN 0-88344-124-1). Orbis Bks.

Experience of Labour in Eighteenth Century Industry. John Rule. 1980. 25.00 (ISBN 0-312-27664-8). St Martin.

Experience of Literature. 2nd ed. Gene Montague et al. 1970. pap. text ed. 12.95x (ISBN 0-13-294728-5). P-H.

Experience of Love: Understanding Natural Family Planning. Ingrid Trobisch & Elisabeth Roetzer. Date not set. 6.95 (ISBN 0-8007-1184-X). Revell. Postponed.

Experience of Music. Bennett Reimer & Edward Evans. (Illus.). 384p. 1973. text ed. 18.95 (ISBN 0-13-294553-3); wkbk. 9.95 (ISBN 0-13-294876-1); records 18.95 (ISBN 0-13-294900-8); library of records 110.50 (ISBN 0-13-294892-3); demonstration record 129.95. P-H.

Experience of Nothingness. Michael Novak. 1971. pap. 3.95x (ISBN 0-06-131938-4, TB 1938, Torch). Har-Row.

Experience of Teaching & Learning: A Phenomenology of Education. William A. Adams. LC 80-81902. 175p. (Orig.). 1980. pap. 6.95 (ISBN 0-937668-00-1). Psych Pr WA.

Experience of the Inner Worlds. Gareth Knight. 1975. 12.50 (ISBN 0-685-67326-X). Weiser.

Experience of the Spirit. Ed. by Peter Huizing & William Bassett. (Concilium Ser.: Religion in the Seventies: Vol. 99). 1976. pap. 4.95 (ISBN 0-8164-2096-3). Crossroad NY.

Experience, Reason & God, Vol. 8. Ed. by Eugene T. Long. (Studies in Philosophy & the History of Philosophy: Vol. 8). 1980. write for info. (ISBN 0-8132-0553-0, Dist. by Isbs). Intl Schol Bk Serv.

Experience with Abortion. Ed. by G. W. Horobin. LC 73-77171. (Illus.). 280p. 1973. 69.50 (ISBN 0-521-20240-X). Cambridge U Pr.

Experience Worketh Hope. A. J. Gossip. (Scholar As Preacher Ser.). 206p. 1945. text ed. 7.75 (ISBN 0-567-04423-8). Attic Pr.

Experiences in Groups. W. R. Bion. LG 61-7884. 1981. text ed. 12.95x (ISBN 0-465-02174-3). Basic.

Experiences in Interpersonal Communication. Theodore S. Grove. (Illus.). 224p. 1976. pap. 11.95 (ISBN 0-13-294975-X). P-H.

Experiences in Language: Tools & Techniques for Language Arts Methods. 2nd ed. Walter T. Petty et al. 544p. 1976. text ed. 14.95x o.p. (ISBN 0-205-05474-9). Allyn.

Experiences in Math for Young Children. R. Charlesworth & D. J. Radeloff. LC 77-80039. 1978. pap. text ed. 7.20 (ISBN 0-8273-1660-7); instructor's guide 1.60 (ISBN 0-8273-1661-5). Delmar.

Experiences in Music for Young Children. M. C. Pugmire. LC 76-4304. (gr. 10-12). 1977. pap. text ed. 10.00 (ISBN 0-8273-0567-2); instructor's guide 2.00 (ISBN 0-8273-0568-0); tape cassette 5.75 (ISBN 0-8273-0566-4). Delmar.

Experiences in Public Administration. Briscoe & Leonardson. 1980. pap. text ed. 7.95 (ISBN 0-87872-248-3). Duxbury Pr.

Experiences in Science for Young Children. Donald B. Neuman. LC 76-53185. 1978. pap. text ed. 8.80 (ISBN 0-8273-1642-9); instructor's guide 1.75 (ISBN 0-8273-1643-7). Delmar.

Experiences in Visual Thinking. 2nd ed. Robert H. McKim. LC 80-437. (Orig.). 1980. pap. text ed. 12.95 (ISBN 0-8185-0411-0). Brooks-Cole.

Experiences in Zero Base Budgeting. Ed. by Joseph L. Hebert. LC 77-23884. 1977. text ed. 15.00 (ISBN 0-89433-033-0). Petrocelli.

Experiences of a Special Indian Agent. rev. ed. E. E. White. (Western Frontier Library: No. 29). (Illus.). 1966. 5.95 o.p. (ISBN 0-8061-0680-8). U of Okla Pr.

Experiences of God. Jurgen Moltmann. Tr. by Margaret Kohl from Ger. LC 80-8046. 96p. 1980. pap. 3.95 (ISBN 0-8006-1406-2, 1-1406). Fortress.

Experiences of Recent High School Graduates. new ed. Ed. by George J. Nolfi. LC 78-2075. 1978. 19.95 (ISBN 0-669-02264-0). Lexington Bks.

Experiences of the Unwed Mother As a Parent: A Longitudinal Study of Unmarried Mothers Who Keep Their First Born. Mignon Sauber & Elaine Rubinstein. 1965. pap. 3.50 (ISBN 0-86671-001-9). Comm Coun Great NY.

Experiences with My Cockatiels. rev. ed. E. L. Moon. 1976. 4.95 (ISBN 0-87666-759-0, AP-1280). TFH Pubns.

Experiences with Three Tillage Systems on a Marine Loam Soil I: 1972-1975. (Agricultural Research Reports Ser.: No. 899). 100p. 1981. pap. 18.50 (ISBN 90-220-0741-3, PDC 219, Pudoc). Unipub.

Experiencias En Espanol. Frank Gonzalez-Mena & Janet Gonzalez-Mena. Ed. by A. Medrano. Tr. by Frank Gonzalez-Mena & Janet Gonzalez-Mena. (Illus.). 192p. (Orig., Span.). (gr. k-3). 1976. pap. text ed. 12.95 tchrs ed. (ISBN 0-88499-232-2); wkbk. 2.95 (ISBN 0-88499-234-9); program package 38.95 (ISBN 0-88499-233-0). Inst Mod Lang.

Experiencing Biography. Robert Beck. (Literature Ser.). (gr. 10 up). 1978. pap. text ed. 6.20x (ISBN 0-8104-6034-3); 1.75 (6125). Hayden.

Experiencing Hypnosis: Theraputic Aproaches to Altered States. Milton H. Erickson & Ernest L. Rossi. 300p. 1979. text ed. 34.50x incl. audio cassette (ISBN 0-8290-0246-4). Irvington.

Experiencing Life Through Mathematics, Vol. 1. rev. ed. Michael A. Usher & Robert Bormuth. (Illus.). 128p. (Orig.). (gr. 8-12). 1978. pap. text ed. 4.92x (ISBN 0-913688-66-5); tchrs. ed. 6.00x (ISBN 0-913688-67-3). Pawnee Pub.

Experiencing Life Through Mathematics, Vol. 2. Michael Usher & Robert Bormuth. (Illus.). (gr. 9-12). 1980. pap. text ed. 4.92 (ISBN 0-913688-68-1); tchr's ed. 6.00x (ISBN 0-913688-69-X). Pawnee Pub.

Experiencing Music. Wingell. 1981. 15.95 (ISBN 0-88284-116-5); instr's. manual free (ISBN 0-88284-131-9); wkbk. 4.95 (ISBN 0-88284-117-3); record set 30.00 (ISBN 0-88284-132-7). Alfred Pub.

Experiencing Science: Profiles in Discovery. Jeremy Bernstein. 1980. pap. 5.95 (ISBN 0-525-47636-9). Dutton.

Experiencing Social Psychology. Ayala M. Pines & Christina Maslach. 1978. pap. text ed. 8.95x (ISBN 0-394-31281-3). Random.

Experiencing Social Research. John F. Runcie. 1980. pap. text ed. 7.95 o.p. (ISBN 0-256-02304-2). Dorsey.

Experiencing Social Research. rev. ed. John F. Runcie. 1980. pap. 8.95x (ISBN 0-256-02304-2). Dorsey.

Experiencing the Holy Spirit. Jim McNair. LC 77-9262. 1977. pap. 3.50 (ISBN 0-87123-135-2, 210135). Bethany Fell.

Experiential Approach to Organization Development. D. Harvey & Donald R. Brown. (Illus.). 336p. 1976. pap. text ed. 12.95 (ISBN 0-13-294983-0). P-H.

Experiential Exercises & Cases in Management. Fremont Kast & James Rosenzweig. (Illus.). 1976. text ed. 11.95 (ISBN 0-07-033343-2); instructor's manual 4.95 (ISBN 0-07-033344-0). McGraw.

Experiential Psychotherapy Within Families. Walter Kempler. 320p. 1981. 20.00 (ISBN 0-87630-267-3). Brunner-Mazel.

Experiential Taxonomy: A New Approach to Teaching & Learning. Norman Steinaker & M. Robert Bell. LC 79-1141. (Educational Psychology Ser.). 1979. 15.00 o.s.i. (ISBN 0-12-665550-2). Acad Pr.

Experiment As a Social Occassion. Paul Wuebben et al. 330p. 1974. 12.00x o.p. (ISBN 0-87709-720-8); pap. 5.95x o.p. (ISBN 0-87709-220-6). Boyd & Fraser.

Experiment in Criticism. Clive S. Lewis. 1961. 23.95 (ISBN 0-521-05553-9); pap. 6.50 (ISBN 0-521-09350-3). Cambridge U Pr.

Experiment in Education. Sybil Marshall. (Illus.). 28.95 (ISBN 0-521-05680-2); pap. 9.95x (ISBN 0-521-09372-4). Cambridge U Pr.

Experiment in Empathy. S. Natale. (General Ser). 99p. (Orig.). 1972. pap. text ed. 10.00x (ISBN 0-901225-86-X, NFER). Humanities.

Experiment in Liberty. Ronald E. Osborn. 1978. 2.95 (ISBN 0-8272-0804-9). Bethany Pr.

Experiment in Management: Personnel Decentralization in the Tennessee Valley Authority. Robert S. Avery. LC 54-11202. 1954. 12.50x (ISBN 0-87049-010-9). U of Tenn Pr.

Experiment in Nursery Education. Ed. by Martin Woodhead. (Orig.). 1976. pap. text ed. 13.75x (ISBN 0-85633-122-8, NFER). Humanities.

Experiment in the Ruralization of Education: IPAR & the Cameroonian Reform. 113p. (Orig.). 1975. pap. 4.75 (ISBN 92-3-101172-3, U229, UNESCO). Unipub.

Experiment Perilous. Renee C. Fox. LC 59-6816. 264p. 1974. pap. 6.50x (ISBN 0-8122-1040-9). U of Pa Pr.

Experiment That Works. Bernard Lipnick. 1976. 12.50x (ISBN 0-914536-02-8). Bloch.

Experiment with Death. E. X. Ferrars. LC 80-2739. (Crime Club Ser.). 192p. 1981. 9.95 (ISBN 0-385-17523-X). Doubleday.

Experiment with Truth. Asif Currimbhoy. (Writers Workshop Bluebird Book Ser.). 62p. 1975. 10.00 (ISBN 0-88253-538-2); pap. text ed. 4.80 (ISBN 0-88253-537-4). Ind-US Inc.

Experiment with Untruth: India Under Emergency. Michael D. Henderson. 1978. 12.50x (ISBN 0-8364-0128-X). South Asia Bks.

Experimental & Clinical Neurotoxicology. Peter S. Spencer & Herbert Schaumburg. (Illus.). 952p. 1980. lib. bdg. 110.00 (ISBN 0-683-07854-2). Williams & Wilkins.

Experimental Animal Behavior: A Selection of Laboratory Exercises. Michael H. Hansell & John J. Aitken. (Illus.). 1977. 29.95x (ISBN 0-216-90325-4). Intl Ideas.

Experimental Animal Physiology: A Contemporary Systems Approach. 3rd ed. Kenneth Ottis et al. (Orig.). 1980. pap. text ed. 11.95 (ISBN 0-8403-2151-1). Kendall-Hunt.

Experimental Approach to Biology. 2nd ed. Peter Abramoff & Robert G. Thomson. (Illus.). 1976. lab manual 10.95x (ISBN 0-7167-0578-8); individual experiments 0.50 (ISBN 0-685-55248-9); instr's hndbk. avail. (ISBN 0-685-55249-7). W H Freeman.

Experimental Approach to Electro-Chemistry. N. J. Selley. LC 77-7914. 1977. 24.95 (ISBN 0-470-99204-2). Halsted Pr.

Experimental Archeology. Ed. by Daniel Ingersoll et al. LC 77-4250. 1977. 27.50x (ISBN 0-231-03658-2). Columbia U Pr.

Experimental Basis of Modern Biology. James A. Ramsay. LC 64-21564. (Illus.). 1969. text ed. 49.50x (ISBN 0-521-06027-3); pap. 12.50x (ISBN 0-521-09575-1). Cambridge U Pr.

Experimental Behavior: A Basis for the Study of Mental Disturbance. Ed. by J. Cullen. (Illus.). 440p. 1974. 25.00x (ISBN 0-7165-2231-4, Pub by Irish Academic Pr). Biblio Dist.

Experimental Biochemistry. 2nd ed. John M. Clark, Jr. & Robert L. Switzer. (Illus.). 1977. lab. manual 12.95x (ISBN 0-7167-0179-0). W H Freeman.

Experimental Biology. 2nd ed. Richard W. Van Norman. LC 74-105444. 1970. ref. ed. 19.95 (ISBN 0-13-294710-2). P-H.

Experimental Biology with Micro-Organisms. J. W. Garbutt & A. J. Bartlett. 1972. pap. text ed. 4.95 (ISBN 0-408-70228-1); teachers' guide 12.95 (ISBN 0-408-70240-0). Butterworths.

Experimental Certificate of Extended Education: Summer 1974. D. Duckworth. (General Ser.). 99p. 1975. pap. text ed. 12.50x (ISBN 0-85633-082-5, NFER). Humanities.

Experimental Chemistry. 5th ed. Russell A. Geanangel & Wesley W. Wendlandt. 1979. pap. text ed. 8.95 (ISBN 0-8403-2355-7). Kendall-Hunt.

Experimental Chemistry. 2nd ed. Saul Geffner & Paul Lauren. (gr. 10-12). 1968. pap. text ed. 6.17 (ISBN 0-87720-113-7); wkbk ed. 7.00 (ISBN 0-87720-115-3). AMSCO Sch.

Experimental Chemistry: An Introduction. Robert J. Artz. (Illus.). 311p. 1980. instructor's manual free (ISBN 0-316-05279-5); lab manual 7.95 (ISBN 0-316-05278-7). Little.

Experimental Chemistry: Laboratory Manual for Chemistry 14. Charles G. Haas & Pennsylvania State Univ. Chemistry Dept. 1978. pap. text ed. 4.50 (ISBN 0-8403-1913-4). Kendall-Hunt.

Experimental Chemotherapy, 5 vols. Ed. by Robert J. Schnitzer & F. Hawking. 1963-68. Vol. 1. 91.00 (ISBN 0-12-628401-6); Vol. 2. 65.00 (ISBN 0-12-628402-4); Vol. 3. 65.00 (ISBN 0-12-628403-2); Vol. 4. 65.00 (ISBN 0-12-628404-0); Vol. 5. 65.00 (ISBN 0-12-628405-9); Set. 271.00 (ISBN 0-685-23205-0). Acad Pr.

Experimental Community Psychology: A Psychology for the 21th Century. George W. Fairweather & William S. Davidson. Date not set. write for info. (ISBN 0-88410-363-3). Ballinger Pub. Postponed.

Experimental Design & Analysis. Wayne Lee. LC 74-12241. (Psychology Ser.). (Illus.). 1975. text ed. 23.95x (ISBN 0-7167-0772-1); wkbk. 5.95x (ISBN 0-7167-0763-2). W H Freeman.

Experimental Design & Interpretation. Ed. by Raymond O. Collier, Jr. & Thomas J. Hummel. LC 76-18039. (Readings in Educational Research Ser.). 1977. 25.00 (ISBN 0-8211-0225-7); text ed. 22.50 10 or more copies (ISBN 0-685-71415-2). McCutchan.

Experimental Designs. 2nd ed. W. G. Cochran & G. M. Cox. LC 57-5908. 1957. 28.95 (ISBN 0-471-16203-5). Wiley.

Experimental Didactics of Ernst Otto. E. E. Cochran. 1950. pap. 19.70x (ISBN 3-11-003210-4). De Gruyter.

Experimental Ecology & the Feeding of Fishes. V. S. Ivlev. 1961. 32.50x (ISBN 0-685-89751-6). Elliots Bks.

Experimental Education for Pupils Aged Ten to Fourteen. European Research in Curriculum & Evaluation, a Report of the European Contact Workshop Held in Austria in December 1976 by the Committee for the Educational Research of the Council of Europe Council for Cultural Cooperation. Ed. by John Eggleston. 218p. 1977. pap. text ed. 22.50 (ISBN 0-686-27810-0, Pub. by Swets Pub Serv Holland). Swets North Am.
Experimental Electronics for Students. K. J. Close & Y. Yarwood. 227p. cancelled (ISBN 0-470-26767-4). Halsted Pr.
Experimental Embryology of Echinoderms. Sven Horstadius. (Illus.). 201p. 1973. 29.95x (ISBN 0-19-857373-1). Oxford U Pr.
Experimental Food Chemistry. Nell I. Mondy. (Illus.). 1980. pap. text ed. 15.50 (ISBN 0-87055-343-7). AVI.
Experimental Foods Laboratory Manual. Margaret McWilliams. (Illus.). 1977. spiral bdg. 11.95x (ISBN 0-916434-22-2). Plycon Pr.
Experimental Foundations of Modern Immunology. William R. Clark. LC 80-13565. 372p. 1980. text ed. 18.95 (ISBN 0-471-04088-6). Wiley.
Experimental Fun with the Yo-Yo. Al G. Renner. LC 78-23569. (Illus.). (gr. 5 up). 1979. 5.95 (ISBN 0-396-07657-2). Dodd.
Experimental Geneticist: An Introductory Laboratory Manual. Patricia St. Lawrence et al. (Illus.). 1974. pap. 7.95x (ISBN 0-7167-0588-5); lab separates 0.50 ea. (ISBN 0-685-39560-X); instr's guide avail. W H Freeman.
Experimental Hematology Today: 1980. Ed. by S. J. Baum et al. (Illus.). xii, 290p. 1980. 84.50 (ISBN 3-8055-1705-X). S Karger.
Experimental Hematology Today 1981. Ed. by S. J. Baum et al. (Illus.). xiv, 240p. 1981. 84.50 (ISBN 3-8055-2255-X). S Karger.
Experimental High-Resolution Electron Microscopy. J. C. Spence. (Monographs on the Physics & Chemistry of Materials). (Illus.). 384p. 1981. 74.00 (ISBN 0-19-851365-8). Oxford U Pr.
Experimental Induction of Some Collagen Diseases. Kitasu Suzue. (Illus.). 1974. pap. 7.50 o.p. (ISBN 0-89640-015-8). Igaku-Shoin.
Experimental Jurisprudence & the Scienstate. Frederick K. Beutel. (Illus.). 404p. (Orig.). 1975. text ed. 55.00x o.p. (ISBN 3-7694-0400-9); pap. text ed. 34.00 o.p. (ISBN 3-7694-0404-1). Rothman.
Experimental Linguistics: Integration of Theories & Applications. G. Prideaux. (Story-Scientia Linguistics Ser.: No. 3). 1980. text ed. 57.75x (ISBN 90-6439-164-5). Humanities.
Experimental Liturgy Book. Robert F. Hoey. 1969. pap. 4.95 (ISBN 0-8164-1029-1). Crossroad NY.
Experimental Mechanics, Vol. 1: Proceedings, International Congress on Experimental Mechanics - 1st. Ed. by B. E. Rossi. 1963. 60.00 (ISBN 0-08-013346-0). Pergamon.
Experimental Meson Spectroscopy. Ed. by Charles Baltay & Arthur H. Rosenfeld. LC 78-137009. (Illus.). 1970. 32.50x (ISBN 0-231-03477-6). Columbia U Pr.
Experimental Method: A Guide to the Art of Experiment for Students of Science & Engineering. D. G. Martin & W. G. Wood. (Illus.). 106p. (Orig.). 1974. pap. text ed. 4.75x (ISBN 0-485-12022-4, Athlone Pr). Humanities.
Experimental Methodology. 2nd ed. Christensen. 432p. 1980. text ed. 17.95 (ISBN 0-205-06960-6, 7969600). Allyn.
Experimental Methodology. Larry Christensen. 1977. text ed. 15.95x o.p. (ISBN 0-205-05721-7); instr's manual avail. o.p. (ISBN 0-205-05722-5). Allyn.
Experimental Models of Epilepsy: A Manual for the Laboratory Worker. Ed. by D. P. Purpura et al. LC 72-181308. (Illus.). 615p. 1972. 39.00 (ISBN 0-911216-26-X). Raven.
Experimental Neutron Thermalization. P. A. Egelstaff & M. J. Poole. LC 79-86201. 1970. 60.00 (ISBN 0-08-006533-3). Pergamon.
Experimental Organic Chemistry. Michael P. Doyle & William S. Mungall. LC 79-18392. 1980. text ed. 18.95 (ISBN 0-471-03383-9); tchrs' manual 2.50 (ISBN 0-471-08053-5). Wiley.
Experimental Organic Chemistry. 4th ed. Charles A. MacKenzie. LC 70-138824. (Illus.). 1971. pap. text ed. 17.95 (ISBN 0-13-294785-4). P-H.
Experimental Petrology: Basic Principles & Techniques. Alan D. Edgar. 221p. 1973. 34.95x (ISBN 0-19-854402-2). Oxford U Pr.
Experimental Physics for Students. R. Whittle & J. Yarwood. LC 73-15219. 400p. 1974. text ed. 18.95x o.p. (ISBN 0-470-94131-6). Halsted Pr.
Experimental Physiology. V. V. Kulshrestha. 1977. 8.95 (ISBN 0-7069-0551-2, Pub. by Vikas India). Advent Bk.
Experimental Psychobiology: A Laboratory Manual. Ed. by Benjamin L. Hart. (Illus.). 1976. 10.95x (ISBN 0-7167-0731-4). W H Freeman.
Experimental Psycholinguistics. S. Glucksberg & J. H. Danks. LC 75-2408. 250p. 1975. 10.00 o.p. (ISBN 0-470-30840-0). Halsted Pr.
Experimental Psychology. 2nd ed. Burton G. Andreas. LC 78-171910. 1972. text ed. 23.95x (ISBN 0-471-02905-X). Wiley.
Experimental Psychology. 2nd ed. Benton J. Underwood. (Illus.). 1966. 19.95 (ISBN 0-13-295113-4); wkbk. - problems in experimental design & influence 6.95 (ISBN 0-13-295147-9). P-H.
Experimental Psychology: A Methodological Approach. 3rd ed. Frank J. McGuigan. LC 77-25206. (Illus.). 1978. ref. ed. 19.95 (ISBN 0-13-295162-2). P-H.
Experimental Psychology: Research Tactics & Their Applications. D. Chris Anderson & John G. Borkowski. 1978. 16.95x (ISBN 0-673-07866-3). Scott F.
Experimental Psychology: Tactics of Behavioral Research. John G. Borkowski & D. Chris Anderson. 1977. pap. 11.95x (ISBN 0-673-15085-2). Scott F.
Experimental Psychology: Theory & Practice. Philip J. Dunham. LC 77-5688. (Harper's Experimental Psychology Ser.). (Illus.). 1977. text ed. 19.50 scp (ISBN 0-06-041805-2, HarpC); tchr's manual free (ISBN 0-06-361783-8). Har-Row.
Experimental Radiological Health Physics. Daniel A. Gollnick. LC 77-7638. (Illus.). 260p. 1978. 25.00 (ISBN 0-08-023201-9); pap. 11.25 (ISBN 0-08-020524-0). Pergamon.
Experimental Reactor Physics. A. Edward Profio. LC 75-35735. 832p. 1976. 42.50 (ISBN 0-471-70095-9, Pub. by Wiley-Interscience). Wiley.
Experimental Stress Analysis. 2d ed. James W. Dally & William F. Riley. LC 77-393. (Illus.). 1977. text ed. 27.50x (ISBN 0-07-015204-7, C); solutions manual 9.95 (ISBN 0-07-015205-5). McGraw.
Experimental Stress Analysis. G. S. Holister. (Cambridge Engineering Pubns.). 1967. 47.95 (ISBN 0-521-05312-9). Cambridge U Pr.
Experimental Studies for General Chemistry. 2nd ed. Malcom Nicol et al. 1974. lab manual 9.95x (ISBN 0-8162-6441-4). Holden-Day.
Experimental Studies of the Differential Effect in Life Setting. P. Sailaja & K. R. Rao. LC 72-84013. (Parapsychological Monograph No. 13). 1973. pap. 3.50 (ISBN 0-912328-20-7). Parapsych Foun.
Experimental Study of Food. 2nd ed. Ada M. Campbell & Marjorie Penfield. LC 78-69535. (Illus.). 1979. text ed. 19.95 (ISBN 0-395-26666-1). HM.
Experimental Surgery in Farm Animals. R. W. Dougherty. (Illus.). 1981. write for info. (ISBN 0-8138-1540-1). Iowa St U Pr.
Experimental Techniques in Physical Metallurgy. Valentin T. Cherepin & A. K. Mallick. 1967. 20.00x (ISBN 0-210-22503-3). Asia.
Experimental Techniques in Quantitative Chemical Analysis. Vinay Kumar. LC 80-69043. 183p. (Orig.). 1981. pap. text ed. 10.00 (ISBN 0-8191-1509-6). U Pr of Amer.
Experimental Testing of Public Policy: Proceedings, 1974. Social Science Research Council Conference on Social Experiments. Ed. by Robert F. Boruch & Henry W. Riecken. LC 75-30613. 180p. 1976. 20.25x (ISBN 0-89158-004-2). Westview.
Experimental World Literacy Programme: A Critical Assessment. 198p. 1976. pap. 9.25 (ISBN 92-3-101314-9, U232, UNESCO). Unipub.
Experimentation in American Religion: The New Mysticisms & Their Implications for the Churches. Robert Wuthnow. 1978. 18.95 (ISBN 0-520-03446-5). U of Cal Pr.
Experimentation in Biology: An Introduction to Design & Analysis. W. J. Ridgman. (Tertiary Level Biology Ser.). 234p. 1976. pap. text ed. 14.95 (ISBN 0-470-15216-8). Halsted Pr.
Experimentation with Microprocessor Applications. Thomas Davis. (Orig.). 1980. pap. text ed. 9.95 (ISBN 0-8359-1812-2). Reston.
Experimentele Untersuchungen Zur Schwermetallresistenz Von Sumersen Makrophyten. H. Schuster. (Dissertationes Botanica 50 Ser.). (Illus., Ger.). 1980. pap. text ed. 20.00x (ISBN 3-7682-1229-7). Lubrecht & Cramer.
Experimentelle Untersuchungen Uber Die Psychologischen Grundlagen der Sprachlichen Analogiebildung. Albert Thumb & Karl Marbe. (Classics in Psycho-Linguistics). 108p. 1980. text ed. 28.50x (ISBN 0-686-61364-3). Humanities.
Experimenting in Psychology. Robert Gottsdanker. (P-H Ser. in Experimental Psychology). (Illus.). 1978. ref. ed. 17.95x (ISBN 0-13-295501-6). P-H.
Experimenting in the Hearing & Speech Sciences: 1978. Barry Voroba. LC 78-63106. (Illus.). 204p. 1978. 21.95 (ISBN 0-9601970-2-8); pap. 14.95 (ISBN 0-9601970-1-X); ring binder 29.95 (ISBN 0-9601970-0-1). Starkey Labs.
Experimenting with Truth: The Fusion of Religion with Technology Needed for Humanity's Survival. Rustrum Roy. (Hibbert Lectures: 1979). (Illus.). 228p. 1981. 29.00 (ISBN 0-08-025820-4); pap. 14.50 (ISBN 0-08-025819-0). Pergamon.
Experiments & Research with Humans: Values in Conflicts. Academy Forum, National Academy of Science. LC 75-13985. (Illus.). 224p. 1975. pap. 7.00 (ISBN 0-309-02347-5). Natl Acad Pr.
Experiments for Chemistry: 1046L. Michael Guttman. 1976. coil bdg. 3.75 (ISBN 0-88252-047-4). Paladin Hse.
Experiments for College Chemistry. Harold Goldwhite & Cornelius T. Moynihan. 1971. pap. text ed. 10.95 scp (ISBN 0-06-042388-9, HarpC). Har-Row.
Experiments for Electricity & Electronics. 2nd ed. Nelson Fuller & Rex Miller. LC 78-7708. 1978. pap. 3.33 (ISBN 0-672-97260-3); tchr's guide 7.50 (ISBN 0-685-91575-1). Bobbs.
Experiments in a Search for God: The Edgar Cayce Path of Application. Mark A. Thurston. 1976. pap. 3.95 (ISBN 0-87604-090-3). ARE Pr.
Experiments in Atomic Physics. Friedrich et al. (gr. 12). text ed. 6.95 (ISBN 0-7195-0467-8). Transatlantic.
Experiments in Cell Physiology. Lester Packer. 1967. text ed. 14.50 (ISBN 0-12-543450-2). Acad Pr.
Experiments in Digital Principles. 2nd ed. Donald P. Leach. (Illus.). 176p. 1980. 14.95x (ISBN 0-07-036916-X, G). McGraw.
Experiments in Environmental Chemistry: A Laboratory Manual. P. D. Vowles & D. W. Connell. LC 80-40270. (Pergamon Ser. on Environmental Science: Vol. 4). (Illus.). 108p. 1980. 23.00 (ISBN 0-686-61744-4); pap. 9.95 (ISBN 0-08-024009-7). Pergamon.
Experiments in General & Biomedical Instrumentation. Morris Tischler. Ed. by Mark Haas. (Illus.). 176p. 1980. pap. text ed. 8.95x (ISBN 0-07-064781-X, G). McGraw.
Experiments in General Chemistry. 4th ed. Russell S. Drago & Theodore L. Brown. 1977. text ed. 12.95 (ISBN 0-205-05702-0); instr's manual avail. (ISBN 0-205-05703-9). Allyn.
Experiments in Genetic Engineering: Advanced Bacterial Genetics Manual. Ed. by R. Davis et al. 150p. (Orig.). 1980. cancelled lab manual (ISBN 0-87969-130-1). Cold Spring Harbor.
Experiments in Genetics with Drosophila. M. W. Strickberger. LC 62-16158. 1962. pap. 12.95x (ISBN 0-471-83373-8). Wiley.
Experiments in Hearing. Georg Von Bekesy. LC 77-4715. 756p. 1980. Repr. of 1960 ed. lib. bdg. 32.50 (ISBN 0-88275-552-8). Krieger.
Experiments in Light, Electricity, & Modern Physics, Laboratory Manual. Dennis C. Henry & Edward B. Nelson. 1978. pap. text ed. 7.50 (ISBN 0-8403-1889-8). Kendall-Hunt.
Experiments in Mechanics, Wave Motion, & Heat, Laboratory Manual. Christopher Goertz et al. 1977. pap. text ed. 5.50 o.p. (ISBN 0-8403-1750-6). Kendall-Hunt.
Experiments in Meteorology: Investigations for the Amateur Scientist. L. W. Trowbridge. LC 70-171324. 312p. 1973. 7.95 o.p. (ISBN 0-385-08238-X). Doubleday.
Experiments in Metropolitan Government. James F. Horan & G. Thomas Taylor, Jr. LC 77-7816. (Praeger Special Studies). 1978. 27.95 (ISBN 0-03-022336-9). Praeger.
Experiments in Microprocessors & Digital Systems. Douglas V. Hall & Marybelle B. Hall. (Illus.). 176p. 1981. 7.95x (ISBN 0-07-025576-8, G). McGraw.
Experiments in Modern Physics. Adrian Melissinos. 1966. text ed. 23.95 (ISBN 0-12-489850-5). Acad Pr.
Experiments in Molecular Genetics. Jeffrey H. Miller. LC 72-78914. (Illus.). 466p. 1972. 32.00 (ISBN 0-87969-106-9). Cold Spring Harbor.
Experiments in Operant Behavior. Ellen P. Reese. LC 64-18142. (Century Psychology Ser.). (Illus.). 1981. pap. text ed. 12.95x (ISBN 0-89197-159-9). Irvington.
Experiments in Optical Illusion. Nelson F. Beeler & Franklyn M. Branley. LC 51-5642. (Illus.). (gr. 5-9). 1951. 7.95 (ISBN 0-690-27507-2, TYC-J). T Y Crowell.
Experiments in Organic Chemistry. Solomon Marmor. 1981. text ed. write for info. (ISBN 0-8087-3966-2). Burgess.
Experiments in Personality, 2 vols. Ed. by Hans J. Eysenck. Incl. Vol. 1. Psychogenetics & Psychopharmacology (ISBN 0-7100-1356-6); Vol. 2. Psychodynamics & Psychodiagnostics (ISBN 0-7100-1357-4). 1960. pap. text ed. 19.00x (ISBN 0-685-23320-0). Humanities.
Experiments in Physical Chemistry. 3rd ed. J. M. Wilson & R. J. Newcombe. Date not set. 48.01 (ISBN 0-08-023808-4); pap. 18.01 (ISBN 0-08-023807-6). Pergamon.
Experiments in Physical Chemistry. 2nd rev. ed. J. R. Wilson et al. 1968. 41.00 (ISBN 0-08-012541-7). Pergamon.
Experiments in Physical Chemistry. 2nd rev. ed. Ed. by J. R. Wilson et al. R. J. Newcombe & A. R. Denaro. LC 68-18536. 1978. 16.25 (ISBN 0-08-023798-3). Pergamon.
Experiments in Physics. Peter J. Nolan & Raymond E. Bigliani. 1981. pap. text ed. price not set (ISBN 0-8087-1446-5). Burgess.
Experiments in Polymer Science. Edward A. Collins et al. LC 73-650. 530p. 1973. pap. text ed. 18.95 (ISBN 0-471-16585-9, Pub. by Wiley-Interscience). Wiley.
Experiments in Practical Spirituality: Keyed to a Search for God, Book II. Mark A. Thurston. (Illus.). 147p. (Orig.). 1980. pap. 4.95 (ISBN 0-87604-122-5). ARE Pr.
Experiments in Prose. Ed. by Eugene Wildman. LC 70-77128. (Illus.). 351p. 1969. 13.95x (ISBN 0-8040-0103-0); pap. 5.95x (ISBN 0-8040-0104-9). Swallow.
Experiments in Space Science. rev. ed. Peter Greenleaf. LC 79-13299. (Illus.). 176p. 1980. lib. bdg. 8.95 (ISBN 0-668-05104-3, 4812-3); pap. 4.95 (ISBN 0-668-04812-3). Arco.
Experiments in Strengths of Materials. Bela I. Sandor. (Illus.). 1980. pap. text ed. 9.95 (ISBN 0-13-295329-3). P-H.
Experiments in Telecommunications. Morris Tischler. Ed. by Mark Haas. (Linear Integrated Circuit Applications Ser.). (Illus.). 176p. (gr. 12 up). 1980. pap. text ed. 7.95x (ISBN 0-07-064782-8). McGraw.
Experiments with a Microscope. Nelson F. Beeler & Franklyn M. Branley. LC 56-9796. (Illus.). (gr. 5-11). 1957. 7.95 (ISBN 0-690-28004-1, TYC-J). T Y Crowell.
Experiments with Everyday Objects: Science Activities for Children, Parents & Teachers. Kevin Goldstein-Jackson et al. LC 77-13232. (Illus.). 1978. 13.95 (ISBN 0-13-295287-4, Spec); pap. 3.95 (ISBN 0-13-295279-3, Spec). P-H.
Experiments with Light. Nelson F. Beeler & Franklyn M. Branley. LC 58-5591. (Illus.). (gr. 5-11). 1957. 7.95 (ISBN 0-690-28217-6, TYC-J). T Y Crowell.
Experiments with Mixtures: Designs, Models & the Analysis of Mixtures Data. John A. Cornell. LC 80-22153. 275p. 1981. 21.95 (ISBN 0-471-07916-2, Pub. by Wiley-Interscience). Wiley.
Experiments with Normal & Transformed Cells. Ed. by R. Crow et al. 175p. 1979. lab manual 18.00x (ISBN 0-87969-123-9). Cold Spring Harbor.
Expert Consumer: A Complete Handbook. K. Eisenberger. 1977. 13.95 (ISBN 0-13-295402-8, Spec); pap. 5.95 (ISBN 0-13-295394-3). P-H.
Expert Gardener: A Treatise Containing Certaine Necessary, Secret, & Ordinary Knowledges in Grafting. LC 74-80178. (English Experience Ser.: No. 659). (Illus.). 54p. 1974. Repr. of 1640 ed. 6.00 (ISBN 90-221-0659-4). Walter J Johnson.
Expert-Generated Data: Applications in International Affairs. Gerald W. Hopple & James A. Kuhlman. (Westview Replica Edition Ser.). 225p. 1981. lib. bdg. 22.50x (ISBN 0-89158-870-1). Westview.
Expert Obedience Class Training for Dogs: The Instructors Manual. Winifred G. Strickland. LC 70-138028. (Illus.). 1971. 10.95 o.s.i. (ISBN 0-02-615040-9). Macmillan.
Expert Systems in a Microelectronic Age. Donald Michie. 200p. 1980. 22.50x (ISBN 0-85224-381-2, Pub by Edinburgh U Pr Scotland). Columbia U Pr.
Experts Crossword Puzzle Dictionary. Herbert M. Baus. LC 72-84960. pap. 4.50 (ISBN 0-385-04788-6, Dolp). Doubleday.
Expetations in Economics. George L. Shackle. LC 78-14143. (Illus.). 1979. Repr. of 1952 ed. 16.00 (ISBN 0-88355-816-5). Hyperion Conn.
Explaining America: The Federalist. Garry Wills. LC 79-6542. 336p. 1981. 14.95 (ISBN 0-385-14689-2). Doubleday.
Explaining Emotions. Ed. by Amelie O. Rorty. 1980. 30.00x (ISBN 0-520-03775-8); pap. 7.95x (ISBN 0-520-03921-1, CAMPUS NO. 232). U of Cal Pr.
Explaining the Brain. W. Ritchie Russell & A. J. Dewar. (Illus.). 180p. 1975. 11.50x (ISBN 0-19-217650-1); pap. text ed. 5.95x (ISBN 0-19-289079-4). Oxford U Pr.
Explanation & Meaning: An Introduction to Philosophy. Daniel M. Taylor. LC 73-116837. (Illus.). 1970. 23.95 (ISBN 0-521-07910-1); pap. 6.95x (ISBN 0-521-09617-0). Cambridge U Pr.
Explanation in Archeology: An Explicit Scientific Approach. Patty J. Watson et al. LC 73-158340. (Illus.). 1971. 15.00x (ISBN 0-231-03544-6). Columbia U Pr.

Explanation in the Behavioural Sciences. Ed. by R. Borger & F. Cioffi. LC 71-105497. 1970. 57.50 (ISBN 0-521-07820-2); pap. 16.95x (ISBN 0-521-09905-6). Cambridge U Pr.

Explanation of Behaviour. Charles Taylor. 1964. text ed. 17.00x (ISBN 0-391-00099-3); pap. text ed. 9.75x (ISBN 0-7100-0491-5). Humanities.

Explanation of Social Behaviour. R. Harre & Paul F. Secord. (Quality Paperback: No. 269). 327p. 1979. pap. 5.95 (ISBN 0-8226-0269-5). Littlefield.

Explanatory & Pronouncing Dictionary of the Noted Names of Fictions. William A. Wheeler. LC 66-25811. 1966. Repr. of 1889 ed. 18.00 (ISBN 0-8103-0165-2). Gale.

Explanatory Notes to Accompany Wunder-Form No. 11: Health & Developmental Questionnaire. new ed. Ray C. Wunderlich, Jr. 1974. pap. 1.55 (ISBN 0-910812-16-0). Johnny Reads.

Explication Du Tableau Economique. Nicolas Baudeau. (Fr.). 1977. lib. bdg. 24.00x o.p. (ISBN 0-8287-0063-X); pap. text ed. 14.00x o.p. (ISBN 0-685-74925-8). Clearwater Pub.

Exploded Form: The Modernist Novel in America. James M. Mellard. LC 79-25993. 224p. 1980. 15.00 (ISBN 0-252-00801-4). U of Ill Pr.

Exploding Mystery of Prayer. Helen S. Shoemaker. (Orig.). 1978. pap. 3.95 (ISBN 0-8164-2183-8). Crossroad NY.

Exploitation of East Africa, 1856-1890: The Slave Trade & the Scramble. Reginald Coupland. LC 67-31335. 1968. 16.75x o.s.i. (ISBN 0-8101-0068-1). Northwestern U Pr.

Exploitation of Illness in Capitalist Society. Howard Waitzkin & Barbara Waterman. LC 73-19706. (Studies in Sociology Ser). 1974. pap. text ed. 3.95 (ISBN 0-672-61327-1). Bobbs.

Exploits of Brigadier Gerard. Arthur Conan Doyle. 15.95 (ISBN 0-7195-3227-2). Transatlantic.

Exploits of Moominpappa. Tove Jansson. 1978. pap. 1.50 (ISBN 0-380-41665-4, 41665, Camelot). Avon.

Exploraciones Chicano-Riquenas. Ruth V. Sasscer et al. 224p. 1981. pap. text ed. 7.95 (ISBN 0-394-32651-2). Random.

Explorando: Affective Learning Activities for Intermediate Practice in Spanish. C. Christensen. 1977. pap. text ed. 9.50 (ISBN 0-13-295980-1). P-H.

Exploration & Language. Alice Yardley. LC 72-95335. 152p. 1973. 3.25 o.p. (ISBN 0-590-07330-3, Citation). Schol Bk Serv.

Exploration Diaries of H. M. Stanley. Richard Stanley & Alan Neame. LC 62-11208. (Illus.). 1962. 10.00 (ISBN 0-8149-0212-X). Vanguard.

Exploration for Uranium Ore Depostis. (STI-PUB-434). (Illus.). 1977. pap. 77.75 (ISBN 92-0-040076-0, ISP434, IAEA). Unipub.

Exploration of the Colorado River & Its Canyons. John W. Powell. Orig. Title: Canyons of the Colorado. (Illus.). 1895. pap. 5.00 (ISBN 0-486-20094-9). Dover.

Exploration of the Inner World: A Study of Mental Disorder and Religious Experience. Anton T. Boisen. 1971. pap. 6.50x (ISBN 0-8122-1020-4, Pa Paperbks). U of Pa Pr.

Explorations in African Systems of Thought. Ed. by Ivan Karp & Charles S. Bird. LC 80-7492. 352p. 1980. 22.50x (ISBN 0-253-19523-3). Ind U Pr.

Explorations in Chemistry. Charles Gray. (Illus.). (gr. 5 up). 1965. PLB 8.95 o.p. (ISBN 0-525-29433-3). Dutton.

Explorations in Cognition. Donald A. Norman & David E. Rumelhart. LC 74-32244. (Psychology Ser.). (Illus.). 1975. text ed. 27.95x (ISBN 0-7167-0736-5). W H Freeman.

Explorations in Convention Decision Making: The Democratic Party in the 1970s. Denis Sullivan et al. LC 76-4527. (Illus.). 1976. text ed. 14.95x (ISBN 0-7167-0488-9); pap. text ed. 7.95x (ISBN 0-7167-0487-0). W H Freeman.

Explorations in Cross-Cultural Psychology. Douglass R. Price-Williams. LC 74-28740. (Publications in Anthropology Ser.). 144p. 1975. 7.50x (ISBN 0-88316-515-5). Chandler & Sharp.

Explorations in Early Southeast Asian History: The Origins of Southeast Asian Statecraft. Ed. by Kenneth R. Hall & John K. Whitmore. LC 76-6836. (Michigan Papers on South & Southeast Asia: No. 11). (Illus.). 350p. 1976. pap. 7.50x (ISBN 0-89148-011-0). Ctr S&SE Asian.

Explorations in Economics. James F. Willis & Martin L. Primack. LC 76-13973. (Illus.). 1977. text ed. 19.95 (ISBN 0-395-24524-9); inst. manual 3.00 (ISBN 0-395-24525-7); wkbk. 6.95 (ISBN 0-395-24757-8); test bank 4.50 (ISBN 0-395-24526-5). HM.

Explorations in General Theory in Social Science: Essays in Honor of Talcott Parsons, Vol. 1 & 2. Ed. by Jan J. Loubser et al. LC 75-8427. (Illus.). 1976. Vol. 1. 40.00 (ISBN 0-02-919370-2); Vol. 2. 40.00 (ISBN 0-02-919380-X); 75.00 set (ISBN 0-02-919360-5). Free Pr.

Explorations in Government: Collected Papers 1951-1968. W. J. M. Mackenzie. LC 74-6722. 1975. 24.95 (ISBN 0-470-56285-4). Halsted Pr.

Explorations in Group Work: Essays in Theory & Practice. Ed. by Saul Bernstein. LC 76-50518. 1976. text ed. 12.00x (ISBN 0-89182-000-0); pap. text ed. 6.75x (ISBN 0-89182-001-9). Charles River Bks.

Explorations in Language & Meaning: Towards a Semantic Anthropology. Malcolm Crick. LC 76-17290. 1977. text ed. 27.95 (ISBN 0-470-15144-7). Halsted Pr.

Explorations in Managing. Allen A. Zoll, III. (Illus.). 356p. 1974. text ed. 14.95 o.p. (ISBN 0-201-08812-6); pap. text ed. 9.95 (ISBN 0-201-08814-2). A-W.

Explorations in Musical Materials: A Working Approach to Making Music. James Yannatos. (Illus.). 1978. pap. text ed. 14.50 (ISBN 0-13-295956-9). P-H.

Explorations in National Cinema. Glasser et al. Ed. by Ben Lawton & Janet Staiger. (Film Studies Annual, 1977: Pt. 1). (Illus.). 1977. pap. 6.00 (ISBN 0-913178-52-7). Redgrave Pub Co.

Explorations in Nursing Research. Henry Wechsler. Ed. by Anne Kibrick. LC 79-719. 1979. text ed. 24.95 (ISBN 0-87705-379-0); pap. text ed. 12.95 (ISBN 0-87705-399-5). Human Sci Pr.

Explorations in Personal Health. Michael S. Haro et al. LC 76-10900. (Illus.). 1977. text ed. 15.75 (ISBN 0-395-24478-1); inst. manual 1.25 (ISBN 0-395-24479-X). HM.

Explorations in Psychological Experimentation. James H. Shaffer. LC 79-65010. 1979. pap. text ed. 8.75 (ISBN 0-8191-0778-6). U Pr of Amer.

Explorations in Quantitative African History. Bruce Fetter et al. Ed. by Joseph P. Smaldone. LC 77-17537. (Foreign & Comparative Studies-African Ser.: No. 27). 1978. pap. 7.00x (ISBN 0-915984-24-5). Syracuse U Foreign Comp.

Explorations in Shakespeare's Language: Some Problems of Word Meaning in the Dramatic Text. Hilda M. Hulme. LC 77-4361. 1977. pap. text ed. 10.95x (ISBN 0-582-48726-9). Longman.

Explorations in Social Geography. Herbert G. Kariel & Patricia E. Kariel. LC 71-173959. 1972. text ed. 15.95 (ISBN 0-201-03634-7). A-W.

Explorations in the Biology of Language. Noam Chomsky et al. Ed. by Edward Walker. LC 78-18352. (Higher Mental Processes Ser.). (Illus.). 256p. 1978. text ed. 22.50 (ISBN 0-89706-000-8). Bradford Bks.

Explorations in Transpersonal Psychotherapy. Ed. by Seymour Boorstein & Kathleen Speeth. LC 80-51704. 1980. 19.95 (ISBN 0-8314-0060-9). Sci & Behavior.

Explorations of Kamchatka: North Pacific Scimitar. Stepan P. Krasheninnikov. Tr. by E. A. Crownhart-Vaughan. LC 72-79116. (North Pacific Studies Ser.: No. 1). (Illus.). 1972. 14.95 (ISBN 0-87595-033-7). Oreg Hist Soc.

Explorations of Pere Marquette. Jim A. Kjelgaard. (Landmark Ser.: No. 17). (Illus.). (gr. 4-6). 1951. PLB 5.99 (ISBN 0-394-90317-X). Random.

Explorations: The English Language Course of the British European Centre. British European Centre, Paris. (Pergamon Institute of English Courses Ser.). 160p. 1981. pap. 5.95 (ISBN 0-08-025358-X). Pergamon.

Exploratory Business: Selling, Office Occupation, Shorthand. 4th ed. F. J. Dame et al. 1965. 5.68 o.p. (ISBN 0-07-015235-7, G). McGraw.

Exploratory Data Analysis. Frederick Hartwig & Brian E. Dearing. LC 79-67621. (Quantitative Applications in the Social Sciences: No. 16). (Illus.). 1979. pap. 3.50x (ISBN 0-8039-1370-2). Sage.

Exploratory Electricity. Ed. by Joseph Arnold & Kenneth Schank. (gr. 9-12). 1960. text ed. 5.00 (ISBN 0-87345-276-3). McKnight.

Exploratory Study on Responsibility, Liability & Accountability for Risks in Construction. Building Research Advisory Board. 1978. pap. 6.75 (ISBN 0-309-02791-8). Natl Acad Pr.

Explore the Book, 6 vols. in 1. J. Sidlow Baxter. 24.85 (ISBN 0-310-20620-0). Zondervan.

Explorers. new ed. R. Humble. (Seafarers Ser.). (Illus.). 1978. 13.95 (ISBN 0-8094-2658-7). Time-Life.

Explorers. Richard Humble. LC 78-1292. (Seafarers Ser.). (Illus.). 1978. lib. bdg. 11.97 (ISBN 0-686-50984-6). Silver.

Explorers from Britain. Christopher McCarthy. 1978. 16.95 (ISBN 0-7134-0988-6, Pub. by Batsford England). David & Charles.

Explorers into Africa. Josephine Kamm. LC 72-116440. (Illus.). (gr. 7-10). 1970. 8.95 (ISBN 0-02-749380-6, CCPr). Macmillan.

Explorers Ltd. Source Book. rev. & enl. ed. Compiled by Explorers Ltd. LC 76-26224. (Illus.). 1977. 15.00 o.s.i. (ISBN 0-06-011259-X, HarpT); pap. 7.95 (ISBN 0-06-011252-2, TD-257, HarpT). Har-Row.

Explorers of Man. H. R. Hays. Ed. by Ann Reit. LC 70-135645. (Surveyor Ser). (Illus.). (gr. 9 up). 1971. 5.95 o.s.i. (ISBN 0-02-743460-5, CCPr). Macmillan.

Explorers of Space: Eight Stories of Science Fiction. Ed. by Robert Silverberg. LC 74-30399. (Science Fiction Ser.). 224p. 1975. 7.95 o.p. (ISBN 0-525-66439-4). Elsevier-Nelson.

Explorers of the Arctic & Antarctic. Edward F. Dolan, Jr. (World in the Making Series). (Illus.). (gr. 7 up). 1968. 3.95g o.s.i. (ISBN 0-02-732630-6, CCPr). Macmillan.

Exploring a Career in Home Economics. James Hahn & Lynn Hahn. (Careers in Depth Ser.). 140p. (gr. 7-12). 1981. lib. bdg. 5.97 (ISBN 0-8239-0530-6). Rosen Pr.

Exploring a Coral Reef. Robert F. Burgess. (Illus.). (gr. 3-5). 1972. 4.95g o.s.i. (ISBN 0-02-716130-7). Macmillan.

Exploring Advertising. Ed. by Otto Kleppner & Irving Settel. (Illus.). 1969. pap. text ed. 10.95 (ISBN 0-13-296020-6). P-H.

Exploring Agribusiness. 3rd ed. Ewell P Roy. (Illus.). (gr. 9-12). 1980. 15.35 (ISBN 0-8134-2098-9, 2098); text ed. 11.50x (ISBN 0-685-64700-5). Interstate.

Exploring Animal Homes. Theodore Rowland-Entwistle. (Explorer Bks). (Illus.). (gr. 3-5). 1978. 2.95 (ISBN 0-531-09093-0); PLB 6.45 s&l (ISBN 0-531-09106-6). Watts.

Exploring Animal Journeys. Theodore Rowland-Entwistle. (Explorer Bks.). (Illus.). (gr. 3-5). 1978. 2.95 (ISBN 0-531-09094-9); PLB 6.45 s&l (ISBN 0-531-09100-7). Watts.

Exploring Behavior & Experience: Readings in General Psychology. Ed. by Robert M. Stutz et al. LC 75-135022. (Illus.). 1971. pap. text ed. 10.95 (ISBN 0-13-296368-X). P-H.

Exploring Books with Children. Iris M. Tiedt. LC 78-69530. (Illus.). 1978. text ed. 16.75 (ISBN 0-395-25498-1). HM.

Exploring Books with Gifted Children. Nancy Polette & Marjorie Hamlin. LC 80-23721. 1980. lib. bdg. 17.50x (ISBN 0-87287-216-5). Libs Unl.

Exploring Brazilian Bureaucracy: Performance & Pathology. Robert T. Daland. LC 80-67246. 455p. 1981. lib. bdg. 24.24 (ISBN 0-8191-1468-5); pap. text ed. 15.75 (ISBN 0-8191-1469-3). U Pr of Amer.

Exploring Careers for the Gifted. Fenton Keyes. (Careers in Depth Ser.). (Illus.). 160p. (gr. 7-12). 1981. lib. bdg. 5.97 (ISBN 0-8239-0533-0). Rosen Pr.

Exploring Careers in Animal Care. Charlotte Lobb. (Careers in Depth Ser.). (Illus.). 140p. (gr. 7-12). 1980. lib. bdg. 5.97 (ISBN 0-8239-0536-5). Rosen Pr.

Exploring Careers in Child Care. McKnight Staff. LC 74-82448. (gr. 8-12). 1974. text ed. 14.64 (ISBN 0-87345-573-8); teacher's guide 30.00 (ISBN 0-87345-576-2); activity manual 5.00 (ISBN 0-87345-574-6). McKnight.

Exploring Careers in Hospitality & Food Service. McKnight Staff. LC 75-18678. (gr. 8-12). 1975. text ed. 16.64 (ISBN 0-87345-605-X); teacher's guide 30.00 (ISBN 0-87345-606-8). McKnight.

Exploring Careers in Industry. Miller et al. LC 74-14422. (gr. 7-9). 1975. text ed. 14.64 (ISBN 0-87345-108-2). McKnight.

Exploring Careers in Science. Stanley J. Shapiro. (Careers in Depth Ser.). (Illus.). 140p. 1981. lib. bdg. 5.97 (ISBN 0-8239-0535-7). Rosen Pr.

Exploring Careers in Special Education. Marilyn Jones. (Careers in Depth Ser.). (Illus.). 128p. 1981. lib. bdg. 5.97 (ISBN 0-8239-0539-X). Rosen Pr.

Exploring Coastal New England: Gloucester to Kennebunkport. Barbara Clayton & Kathleen Whitley. LC 79-624. (Illus.). 1979. 10.95 (ISBN 0-396-07572-X); pap. 6.95 (ISBN 0-396-07698-X). Dodd.

Exploring Competency Based Education. Robert W. Houston. LC 74-76532. 1974. 17.00x (ISBN 0-8211-0752-6); text ed. 15.25x (ISBN 0-685-42635-1). McCutchan.

Exploring Costume History. Valerie Cumming. (Illus.). 72p. 1981. 17.95 (ISBN 0-7134-1829-X, Pub. by Batsford England). Doubleday.

Exploring Crater Lake Country. Ruth Kirk. LC 75-9506. (Illus.). 96p. 1975. pap. 4.95 o.p. (ISBN 0-295-95397-7). U of Wash Pr.

Exploring Cuzco. Peter Frost. (Illus.). 139p. 1981. pap. 7.95 (ISBN 0-933982-05-4). Bradt Ent.

Exploring Data Analysis: The Computer Revolution in Statistics. W. J. Dixon & W. L. Nicholson. 1974. 20.00x (ISBN 0-520-02470-2). U of Cal Pr.

Exploring Dialects. Walt Wolfram & Donna Christian. (Dialects & Educational Equity Ser.: No. 2). 1979. pap. 2.50 (ISBN 0-87281-121-2). Ctr Appl Ling.

Exploring Drafting. John R. Walker. LC 78-15883. (Illus.). 320p. 1978. text ed. 10.96 (ISBN 0-87006-262-X); wkbk. 4.40 (ISBN 0-87006-295-6); metric wkbk 4.40 (ISBN 0-87006-242-5). Goodheart.

Exploring Earth Science. Robert E. Kilburn & Peter S. Howell. (Junior High Science Program Ser.). (gr. 7-9). 1981. text ed. 15.52 (ISBN 0-205-06733-6, 6967337); tchrs'. guide & tests 9.96 (ISBN 0-205-06734-4); 7.20 (ISBN 0-205-06735-2, 6967353). Allyn.

Exploring Earth Science. Walter A. Thurber et al. (gr. 7-12). 1976. text ed. 15.52 (ISBN 0-205-04734-3, 6947344); tchrs'. guide 4.40 (ISBN 0-205-04737-8, 6947379); tests 44.00 (ISBN 0-205-04740-8, 6947409); tchrs'. guide 7.20 (ISBN 0-205-04739-4, 6947395); record bk. 7.20 (ISBN 0-205-04738-6, 6947387). Allyn.

Exploring Electricity & Electronics: Basic Fundamentals. rev. ed. H. Gerrish & W. Dugger, Jr. LC 80-20830. (Illus.). 208p. 1981. text ed. 9.96 (ISBN 0-87006-308-1). Goodheart.

Exploring Electricity-Electronics with the Electrical Team. Kraus & Rollain. LC 76-3947. (Illus.). 1979. pap. 10.80 (ISBN 0-8273-1166-4); research manual 3.40 (ISBN 0-8273-1167-2); instructor's guide 2.00 (ISBN 0-8273-1168-0). Delmar.

Exploring Elementary Mathematics: A Small-Group Approach for Teaching. Julian Weissglass. LC 79-14931. (Mathematical Sciences Ser.). (Illus.). 1979. text ed. 15.95x (ISBN 0-7167-1027-7); instr's manual 3.95x (ISBN 0-7167-1223-7). W H Freeman.

Exploring Emergency Service. Boy Scouts Of America. (Illus.). 64p. 1971. pap. 3.00x (ISBN 0-8395-6609-3, 6609). BSA.

Exploring English: Anthology of Irish Short Stories. Ed. by Augustine Martin. 367p. 1967. pap. 4.95 (ISBN 0-7171-0056-1). Irish Bk Ctr.

Exploring English Character. Geoffrey Gorer. LC 55-11159. 14.95 (ISBN 0-87599-040-1). S G Phillips.

Exploring Fabric Printing. Stuart Robinson & Patricia Robinson. (Illus.). (gr. 7 up). 1972. 12.00 (ISBN 0-8231-7021-7). Branford.

Exploring Fabrics. McKnight Staff. LC 76-53072. (gr. 7-12). 1977. text ed. 14.64 (ISBN 0-87345-613-0); tchr's ed. 34.67 (ISBN 0-87345-615-7). McKnight.

Exploring from the Chesapeake Bay to the Poconos. rev. ed. Annette Carter. LC 75-14092. (Illus.). 272p. 1975. 8.95 o.p. (ISBN 0-397-01099-0); pap. 4.95 o.p. (ISBN 0-397-01108-3). Lippincott.

Exploring Funcions. Ed. by H. G. Widdowson. (Reading & Thinking in English Ser.). 136p. 1979. pap. text ed. 5.95x (ISBN 0-19-451353-X); tchr's. ed. 8.95x (ISBN 0-19-451354-8). Oxford U Pr.

Exploring Genesis. John Phillips. 582p. 1980. 10.95 (ISBN 0-8024-2408-2). Moody.

Exploring Heat. Alexander Efron. (Modern Physics Ser.). (Illus.). 1969. pap. 3.15 o.p. (ISBN 0-8104-5656-7). Hayden.

Exploring Hebrews. John Phillips. 1977. 10.95 (ISBN 0-8024-2406-6). Moody.

Exploring How the Bible Came to Be. Paul B. Maves & Mary C. Maves. (Getting to Know Your Bible Ser). 128p. (Orig.). (gr. 4 up). 1973. pap. 1.75 (ISBN 0-687-12428-X). Abingdon.

Exploring Human Sexuality. Louis Janda & Karen Klenke-Hamel. (Orig.). 1980. pap. 9.95 (ISBN 0-442-25869-0); instr's. manual 2.50 (ISBN 0-442-25732-5). D Van Nostrand.

Exploring Human Values: Psychological & Philosophical Considerations. Richard A. Kalish & Kenneth W. Collier. LC 80-21875. 1980. pap. text ed. 9.95 (ISBN 0-8185-0331-9). Brooks-Cole.

Exploring Iowa's Past: A Guide to Prehistoric Archaeology. Lynn M. Alex. LC 80-21391. (Illus.). 180p. 1980. pap. 7.95 (ISBN 0-87745-108-7). U of Iowa Pr.

Exploring Journalism Careers. Thomas Pawlick. (Career in Depth Ser.). (Illus.). 1981. lib. bdg. 5.97 (ISBN 0-8239-0515-2). Rosen Pr.

Exploring Kittens. Nobuo Honda. (Illus., Orig.). 1980. pap. 5.95 (ISBN 0-89346-142-3). Heian Intl.

Exploring Life Science. Robert E. Kilburn & Peter S. Howell. (Junior High Science Program Ser.). (gr. 7-9). 1981. text ed. 15.52 (ISBN 0-205-06728-X, 6967280); tchrs'. ed. with tests 9.96 (ISBN 0-205-06729-8, 696739-0); record bk. 7.20 (6967302). Allyn.

Exploring Life Science. Walter A. Thurber & Robert E. Kilburn. (gr. 7-9). 1975. text ed. 15.52 (ISBN 0-205-04555-3, 6945554); tchrs'. guide 4.40 (ISBN 0-205-04556-1, 6945562); record bk. 7.20 (ISBN 0-205-04562-6, 6945627); tchrs'. ed. 7.20 (ISBN 0-205-04563-4, 6945635); tests & dup. masters 44.00 (ISBN 0-205-04557-X, 6945570). Allyn.

Exploring Living Environments. McKnight Staff. LC 77-82245. (gr. 7-12). 1977. text ed. 14.64 (ISBN 0-87345-619-X); tchr's ed. 34.67 (ISBN 0-87345-620-3). McKnight.

Exploring Man's Environment. J. Y. Wang et al. 1973. pap. text ed. 10.95 (ISBN 0-8465-3051-1). Benjamin-Cummings.

Exploring Marriage & the Family. David Knox. 1979. text ed. 16.95x (ISBN 0-673-15046-1). Scott F.

Exploring Materials with Young Children. Roy Sparkes. 1975. pap. 13.50 (ISBN 0-7134-2926-7, Pub. by Batsford England). David & Charles.

Exploring Mathematics on Your Own. Donovan A. Johnson & William H. Glenn. Incl. No. 1. **Invitation to Mathematics. pap. o.p. (ISBN 0-685-30036-6); No. 2. The World of Measurement. pap. o.p. (ISBN 0-7195-1659-5); No. 3. Number Patterns (ISBN 0-7195-1661-7); No. 4. The Theorem of Pythagoras. pap. o.p. (ISBN 0-7195-1663-3); No. 5. The World of Statistics. pap. o.p. (ISBN 0-7195-1665-X); No. 6. Sets, Sentences & Operations (ISBN 0-7195-1667-6); No. 7. Fun with Mathematics. pap. o.p. (ISBN 0-7195-1669-2); No. 8. Understanding Numeration Systems (ISBN 0-7195-1671-4); No. 9. Short Cuts in Calculating. pap. o.p. (ISBN 0-7195-1673-0); No. 10. Graphs. pap. o.p. (ISBN 0-7195-1675-7); No. 11. Calculating Devices. pap. o.p. (ISBN 0-685-30037-4); No. 12. Topology (ISBN 0-7195-1679-X); No. 13. Logic & Reasoning in Mathematics. pap. o.p. (ISBN 0-685-30038-2); No. 14. Curves. pap. o.p. (ISBN 0-7195-1683-8); No. 15. Probability & Chance. pap. o.p. (ISBN 0-7195-1685-4); No. 16. Basic Concepts of Vectors. pap. o.p. (ISBN 0-7195-1687-0); No. 17. Finite Mathematical Systems. o.p. (ISBN 0-7195-1689-7); No. 18. Computer Programming (ISBN 0-7195-1881-4); No. 19. Matrices (ISBN 0-7195-2013-4); No. 20. Infinite Numbers (ISBN 0-7195-3097-0); No. 21. Permutations & Groups (ISBN 0-7195-2909-3); No. 22. Numbers: Their Personalities & Properties. (gr. 10-12). 1973. Nos. 1-18. pap. 5.95 ea. (ISBN 0-685-30033-1); No. 19. pap. 5.95x (ISBN 0-685-30034-X); Nos.20-22. pap. 5.95 (ISBN 0-685-30035-8). Transatlantic.**

Exploring Matter & Nuclear Energy. Alexander Efron. (Modern Physics Ser.). (Illus.). 1969. pap. 3.75 o.p. (ISBN 0-8104-5658-3). Hayden.

Exploring Mental Health Parameters, Vol. III. Ed. by Fred R. Crawford. LC 80-67929. (Orig.). 1980. pap. 8.00 (ISBN 0-89937-030-6). Ctr Res Soc Chg.

Exploring Metalworking. John R. Walker. LC 75-31808. 1976. text ed. 9.98 (ISBN 0-87006-199-2); wkbk. 3.20 (ISBN 0-87006-169-0). Goodheart.

Exploring Metric Drafting. John R. Walker. LC 79-24019. (Illus.). 320p. 1980. text ed. 10.96 (ISBN 0-87006-289-1). Good Heart.

Exploring Mime. Mark Stolzenberg. LC 79-65068. (Illus.). 1979. 10.95 (ISBN 0-8069-7028-6); lib. bdg. 9.89 (ISBN 0-8069-7029-4). Sterling.

Exploring Music. 3rd ed. Robert Hickok. LC 78-62545. (Illus.). 1979. text ed. 15.95 (ISBN 0-201-02929-4); instructor's manual 3.00 (ISBN 0-201-02932-4); student's wkbk. 4.95 (ISBN 0-201-02933-2); record 21.95 (ISBN 0-201-02934-0). A-W.

Exploring Music. Ernst Krenek. 1980. pap. 4.95 (ISBN 0-7145-0226-X). Riverrun NY.

Exploring Mysticism: A Methodological. Frits Staal. LC 74-76391. 1975. 22.75x (ISBN 0-520-02726-4); pap. 4.95 (ISBN 0-520-03119-9, CAL 313). U of Cal Pr.

Exploring Nova Scotia. Lance Feild. LC 79-4903. (Illus.). 192p. 1978. lib. bdg. 10.25 o.p. (ISBN 0-914788-16-7). East Woods.

Exploring Other Worlds. Ed. by Sam Moskowitz. (Orig.). 1963. pap. 0.95 o.s.i. (ISBN 0-02-023110-5, Collier). Macmillan.

Exploring Participation. Ian Mangham & Paul Bate. 320p. 1981. 38.50 (ISBN 0-471-27921-8, Pub. by Wiley-Interscience). Wiley.

Exploring Patchwork. Doris Marston. 1972. 5.75 o.p. (ISBN 0-8231-5040-2). Branford.

Exploring Photography. rev. ed. Fern Kennedy. (Illus.). 448p. 1980. 22.50 (ISBN 0-8174-2529-2); pap. 12.95 (ISBN 0-8174-2194-7). Amphoto.

Exploring Physical Science. Robert E. Kilburn & Peter S. Howell. (Junior High Science Program Ser.). (gr. 7-9). 1981. text ed. 15.52 (ISBN 0-205-06738-7, 6967388); tchrs'. guide & tests 3.60 (ISBN 0-205-06739-5, 696739-6); record bk. 7.20 (ISBN 0-205-06740-9, 696740-X). Allyn.

Exploring Power Mechanics. Harold T. Glenn. (Illus.). (gr. 7-12). 1973. 11.96 (ISBN 0-87002-119-2); prog. wkbk. 3.32 (ISBN 0-87002-150-8). Bennett IL.

Exploring Power Technology. John R. Walker. LC 76-2567. (Illus.). 1976. text ed. 9.96 (ISBN 0-87006-207-7); wkbk. 3.20 (ISBN 0-87006-216-6). Goodheart.

Exploring Prehistoric England. P. J. Helm. (Illus.). 8.50 (ISBN 0-912728-13-2). Newbury Bks Inc.

Exploring Professional Cooking. rev. ed. Ray & Lewis. (gr. 9-12). 1980. text ed. 14.60 (ISBN 0-87002-315-2); student guide 6.08 (ISBN 0-87002-163-X); tchr's guide 10.00 (ISBN 0-87002-302-0); visual masters 10.60 (ISBN 0-87002-172-9). Bennett IL.

Exploring Professional Cooking. Mary Ray & Evelyn Lewis. (gr. 10-12). 1976. text ed. 12.80 o.p. (ISBN 0-87002-161-3); tchr guide 10.00 o.p. (ISBN 0-87002-167-2); wkbk 6.08 o.p. (ISBN 0-87002-163-X). Bennett IL.

Exploring Psi in the Ganzfeld. Carl L. Sargent. LC 80-82752. (Parapsychological Monograph Ser.: No. 17). (Illus.). 1980. pap. text ed. 6.00 (ISBN 0-912328-33-9). Parapsych Foun.

Exploring Religion. Schmidt. 1980. text ed. 12.95 (ISBN 0-87872-244-0). Duxbury Pr.

Exploring Religious Meaning. 2nd ed. Robert Monk et al. (Illus.). 1980. text ed. 13.95 (ISBN 0-13-297515-7). P-H.

Exploring Revelation. John Phillips. 288p. 1974. 10.95 (ISBN 0-8024-2407-4). Moody.

Exploring Rocks, Minerals, Fossils in Colorado. Richard M. Pearl. LC 64-25339. (Illus.). 215p. 1969. 12.95 (ISBN 0-8040-0105-7, SB). Swallow.

Exploring Romans. John Phillips. 250p. 1971. 10.95 (ISBN 0-8024-2405-8). Moody.

Exploring Science in the Elementary Schools. Donald P. Kauchak & Paul Eggen. 384p. 1980. pap. text ed. 11.50x (ISBN 0-528-61270-0); instr. manual free (ISBN 0-528-61271-9). Rand.

Exploring Shorthand. M. Zelter. 96p. 1980. text ed. 4.60 (ISBN 0-7715-0735-6). Forkner.

Exploring Social Problems. Cary S. Kart. LC 77-26096. 1978. pap. text ed. 8.50 (ISBN 0-88284-060-6). Alfred Pub.

Exploring Social Psychology. Robert A. Baron & Donn Byrne. 1978. text ed. 13.95x (ISBN 0-205-06529-5); instr's man. avail. (ISBN 0-205-06546-5). Allyn.

Exploring Social Space: Participant's Manual. Michel P. Richard & John Mann. LC 72-88813. 1973. pap. text ed. 7.95 (ISBN 0-02-926410-3). Free Pr.

Exploring Speech Communication: An Introduction. Mary Forrest & Margot Olson. 320p. 1981. pap. text ed. 9.56 (ISBN 0-8299-0381-X). West Pub.

Exploring Spirit: America & the World, Then & Now. Daniel Boorstin. LC 77-4454. 1977. pap. 2.45 (ISBN 0-394-72423-2, V-423, Vin). Random.

Exploring Teaching in Early Childhood Education. Helen F. Robison. 1977. text ed. 16.95 (ISBN 0-205-05550-8). Allyn.

Exploring Techniques: Exploring for the Handicapped. Boy Scouts of America, Exploring Division. (Exploring Techniques Ser.). (gr. 9-12). pap. text ed. 0.60x o.s.i. (ISBN 0-8395-6675-1). BSA.

Exploring Technology. E. Allen Bame & Paul Cummings. (Technology Series). (Illus.). 288p. 1980. text ed. 12.95 (ISBN 0-87192-112-X, 000-3); tchr's. guide 13.25 (ISBN 0-87192-114-6); activity manual 6.95 (ISBN 0-87192-113-8). Davis Pubns.

Exploring the Age of Dinosaurs. David Lambert. (Explorer Bks). (Illus.). (gr. 3-5). 1978. 2.95 o.p. (ISBN 0-531-09095-7); PLB 4.90 s&l o.p. (ISBN 0-531-09101-5). Watts.

Exploring the Bible. Owen Rachleff. LC 78-15262. (Illus.). 360p. 1981. 39.95 (ISBN 0-89659-008-9). Abbeville Pr.

Exploring the Deep. Andrei Aksyonov & Alexander Chernov. (gr. 7 up). 1980. PLB 6.90 (ISBN 0-531-02126-2, BO3). Watts.

Exploring the Galaxies. Simon Mitton. LC 76-42913. (Encore Edition). (Illus.). 1978. pap. 1.95 (ISBN 0-684-16912-6, ScribT). Scribner.

Exploring the Ganzfeld. Carl L. Sargent. LC 80-82752. (Parapsychological Monograph: No. 17). 1980. pap. 6.00 (ISBN 0-912328-33-9). Parapsych Foun.

Exploring the Great Basin. Gloria G. Cline. LC 63-8988. (American Exploration & Travel Ser.: Vol. 39). (Illus.). 254p. 1963. pap. 6.95 (ISBN 0-8061-1014-7). U of Okla Pr.

Exploring the Great Ice Age. Christopher Maynard. (Explorer Bks.). (Illus.). (gr. 3-5). 1979. 2.95 (ISBN 0-531-09128-7); PLB 6.45 s&l (ISBN 0-531-09113-9). Watts.

Exploring the Industries. Chris H. Groneman & Gary E. Grannis. LC 79-55313. 1980. pap. text ed. 14.40 (ISBN 0-8273-1757-3); instr's manual 1.55 (ISBN 0-8273-1758-1). Delmar.

Exploring the Latin American Mind. Seymour B. Liebman. LC 76-6847. 225p. 1976. 14.95 (ISBN 0-88229-134-3). Nelson-Hall.

Exploring the Metropolitan Community. Ed. by John C. Bollens. 1961. 21.50x (ISBN 0-520-00141-9). U of Cal Pr.

Exploring the New Testament. Rachel Henderlite. (Orig.). (gr. 6 up). 1946. pap. 4.95 (ISBN 0-8042-0240-0). John Knox.

Exploring the Old Testament. Rachel Henderlite. (Orig.). (gr. 6 up). 1945. pap. 4.95 (ISBN 0-8042-0120-X). John Knox.

Exploring the Oregon Coast by Car. Marje Blood. LC 80-25484. (Illus.). 224p. (Orig.). 1980. pap. 6.95 (ISBN 0-916076-41-5). Writing.

Exploring the Past. Valerie Lynch. LC 69-18749. (Finding Out About Science Ser). (Illus.). (gr. 3-6). 1970. PLB 5.79 o.p. (ISBN 0-381-99759-6, A24560, JD-J). John Day.

Exploring the Planets. Roy A. Gallant. LC 67-17267. (gr. 7-9). 1967. 7.95a (ISBN 0-385-07430-1); PLB (ISBN 0-385-07432-8). Doubleday.

Exploring the Planets. Jonathan Rutland. (Explorer Bks). (Illus.). (gr. 3-5). 1978. 2.95 o.p. (ISBN 0-531-09092-2); PLB 4.90 s&l o.p. (ISBN 0-531-09103-1). Watts.

Exploring the Relationship Between Child Abuse & Deliquency. Ed. by Robert J. Hunner. LC 79-5178. 320p. 1981. text ed. 19.50 (ISBN 0-916672-31-X). Allanheld.

Exploring the Santa Barbara Backcountry. Dennis R. Gagnon. LC 73-77044. (Illus.). 150p. (Orig.). 1981. pap. 5.95 (ISBN 0-934136-13-0). Western Tanager.

Exploring the Scriptures. John Phillips. 1965. Repr. 10.95 (ISBN 0-8024-2410-4). Moody.

Exploring the Spectrum. Philip S. Allahan. (Illus.). Date not set. 8.95 (ISBN 0-8159-5405-0). Devin. Postponed.

Exploring the Sun. William Jaber. LC 80-10985. (Illus.). 96p. (gr. 4 up). 1980. PLB 7.29 (ISBN 0-671-32997-9). Messner.

Exploring the Universe. W. Protheroe et al. (Science Ser.). 1979. text ed. 19.95 (ISBN 0-675-08313-3); instructor's manual 3.95 (ISBN 0-686-67277-1). Merrill.

Exploring the Universe. 2nd ed. William M. Protheroe et al. (Illus.). 480p. 1981. text ed. 19.95 (ISBN 0-675-08154-8); instr's. manual 3.95 (ISBN 0-686-69491-0). Merrill.

Exploring the Universe. 2nd ed. Ed. by Louise B. Young. (Illus.). 1971. 12.95x (ISBN 0-19-501381-6); pap. 10.95 o.p. (ISBN 0-19-501380-8). Oxford U Pr.

Exploring the Unknown: Great Mysteries Reexamined. Charles J. Cazeau & Stuart D. Scott, Jr. (Da Capo Quality Paperbacks Ser.). (Illus.). 1981. pap. 8.95 (ISBN 0-306-80139-6). Da Capo.

Exploring the Violent Earth. Jonathan Rutland. (gr. 3-5). 1980. 2.95 (ISBN 0-531-09177-5); PLB 6.45 (ISBN 0-531-09167-8). Watts.

Exploring the World of Data Processing. Claude J. DeRossi. LC 74-28054. (Illus.). 272p. 1975. 14.95 (ISBN 0-87909-259-9); instr's. manual free. Reston.

Exploring the World of Leaves. Raymond A. Wohlrabe. LC 75-15865. (Illus.). 160p. (gr. 7 up). 1976. 10.95 (ISBN 0-690-00511-3, TYC-J). T Y Crowell.

Exploring the World of Plastics. Gerald L. Steele. LC 75-42964. (gr. 8-12). 1977. text ed. 15.72 (ISBN 0-87345-411-1). McKnight.

Exploring the World of Robots. Jonathan Rutland. (Explorer Books). (Illus.). (gr. 3-5). 1979. 2.95 (ISBN 0-531-09130-9); PLB 6.45 s&l (ISBN 0-531-09115-5). Watts.

Exploring the World of Social Insects. Hilda Simon. LC 74-178823. (Illus.). (gr. 6 up). 1962. 6.95 (ISBN 0-8149-0390-8). Vanguard.

Exploring the World of Speed. Jonathan Rutland. (Explorer Books). (Illus.). (gr. 3-5). 1979. 2.95 (ISBN 0-531-09129-5); PLB 6.45 s&l (ISBN 0-531-09114-7). Watts.

Exploring Transportation Occupations. Charles S. Winn & L. A. Walsh. (Careers in Focus Ser.). 1976. text ed. 5.32 (ISBN 0-07-071023-6, G); tchr's. manual & key 3.30 (ISBN 0-07-071024-4); wksheet booklet 13.28 (ISBN 0-07-071054-6). McGraw.

Exploring Triangles: Paper-Folding Geometry. Jo Phillips. LC 74-14862. (Young Math Ser.). (Illus.). 40p. (gr. k-3). 1975. 6.95 o.p. (ISBN 0-690-00644-6, TYC-J); PLB 7.89 (ISBN 0-690-00645-4). T Y Crowell.

Exploring UFOs. Jonathan Rutland. (gr. 3-5). 1980. 2.95 (ISBN 0-531-09176-7); PLB 6.45 (ISBN 0-531-09166-X). Watts.

Exploring Under the Sea. Brian Williams. (Explorer Books). (Illus.). (gr. 3-5). 1979. 2.95 (ISBN 0-531-09133-3); PLB 6.45 s&l (ISBN 0-531-09118-X). Watts.

Exploring Unification Theology. 2nd ed. Ed. by M. Darrol Bryant & Susan Hodges. LC 78-63274. (Conference Ser.: No. 1). 1978. pap. text ed. 7.95x (ISBN 0-932894-00-3). Unif Theol Seminary.

Exploring University Mathematics, 3 Vols. N. J. Hardiman. Vol. 1. 1967. text ed. 15.00 (ISBN 0-08-011990-5); Vol. 2. 1966. text ed. 16.50 (ISBN 0-08-012567-0); Vol. 3. 1969. text ed. 15.00 (ISBN 0-08-012903-X); Vol. 1. pap. 7.00 (ISBN 0-08-011991-3); Vol. 2 1968. pap. 7.75 (ISBN 0-08-012566-2); Vol. 3 1969. pap. 7.00 (ISBN 0-08-012902-1). Pergamon.

Exploring, Visualizing, Communicating: A Composition Text. William R. West & Stephen H. Stremnel. (Ser. in English Composition). 1979. pap. text ed. 7.95 (ISBN 0-13-297556-4). P-H.

Exploring War & Weapons. Brian Williams. (Explorer Books). (Illus.). (gr. 3-5). 1979. 2.95 (ISBN 0-531-09132-5); PLB 6.45 s&l (ISBN 0-531-09117-1). Watts.

Exploring Weather. Patrick Moore & Henry Brinton. (gr. 4 up). 4.50 (ISBN 0-685-20579-7). Transatlantic.

Exploring with Computers. Gary Bitter. (Illus.). (gr. 4-7). 1981. PLB price not set (ISBN 0-671-34034-4). Messner.

Exploring Woodworking. Fred W. Zimmerman. LC 79-12354. (Illus.). 1979. text ed. 9.96 (ISBN 0-87006-276-X); wkbk. 3.20 (ISBN 0-87006-281-6). Goodheart.

Exploring Word. David Holbrook. (Orig.). 1967. 26.50 (ISBN 0-521-05288-2); pap. 9.95x (ISBN 0-521-09425-9). Cambridge U Pr.

Explosion at Donner Pass. Gary McCarthy. (Orig.). 1981. pap. 1.95 (ISBN 0-553-14745-5). Bantam.

Explosion Investigation. H. J. Yallop. 280p. 1980. 15.00x (ISBN 0-7073-0272-2, Pub. by Scottish Academic Pr Scotland). Columbia U Pr.

Explosion: The Day Texas City Died. Walter Brough & Michael Sutton. 1980. pap. 2.75 (ISBN 0-686-69244-6, 75838). Avon.

Explosions: Course, Prevention, Protection. W. Bartknecht. Tr. by H. Burg & T. Almond. (Illus.). 251p. 1981. 74.40 (ISBN 0-387-10216-7). Springer-Verlag.

Explosive & Toxic Hazardous Materials. 2nd ed. J. H. Meidl. Date not set. cancelled (ISBN 0-685-48939-6, 47658). Macmillan.

Explosive & Toxic Hazardous Materials. James Meidl. Ed. by Harvey Gruber. (Glencoe Press Fire Science Ser). 1970. text ed. 14.95x (ISBN 0-02-476380-2, 47638). Macmillan.

Explosive Muscular Power for Championship Football. John Jesse. LC 68-58253. pap. 4.95 (ISBN 0-87095-032-0). Athletic.

Explosive Welding, Forming, Plugging, & Compaction. Ed. by I. Berman & J. W. Schroeder. (PVP: No. 44). 119p. 1980. 20.00 (H00171). ASME.

Explosives. Gail K. Haines. LC 75-26707. (Illus.). 32p. 1976. 6.25 (ISBN 0-688-22058-4); lib. bdg. 6.00 (ISBN 0-688-32058-9). Morrow.

Explosives & Bomb Disposal Guide. Robert R. Lenz. (Illus.). 320p. 1976. 15.75 (ISBN 0-398-01097-8). C C Thomas.

Explosives & Homemade Bombs. 2nd ed. Joseph Stoffel. (Illus.). 324p. 1977. 24.75 (ISBN 0-398-02424-3). C C Thomas.

Exponential & Critical Experiments, 3 vols. (Illus., Eng., Fr., Rus. & Span.). 1964. Vol. 1. 24.25 (ISBN 92-0-050064-1, ISP79-1, IAEA); Vol. 2. 23.75 (ISBN 92-0-050164-8, ISP79-2); Vol. 3. 20.00 (ISBN 92-0-050264-4, ISP79-3). Unipub.

Export Directory of German Industries, 1980. 27th ed. Intro. by H. Reihlen. LC 57-16210. 1332p. (Orig.). 1980. pap. 55.00x (ISBN 0-8002-2695-X). Intl Pubns Serv.

Export Grafics USA 1980-81. Graphic Arts Trade Journal Intl Inc. Ed. by G. A. Humphrey & Lydia Miura. (Illus.). 94p. (Orig.). 1980. pap. 10.00 (ISBN 0-910762-06-6). Graph Arts Trade.

Export-Import Financing: A Practical Guide. G. W. Schneider. 1974. 29.95 (ISBN 0-8260-7915-6). Ronald Pr.

Export-Import Traffic Management & Forwarding. 6th ed. Alfred Murr. LC 79-18987. 1979. 22.50x (ISBN 0-87033-261-9). Cornell Maritime.

Export Inspection: Systems in Asia. 1977. pap. 4.50 (ISBN 92-833-2002-6, APO20, APO). Unipub.

Export Marketing French. A. Nuss. 1979. pap. text ed. 7.95 (ISBN 0-582-35157-X); casettes 30.00 (ISBN 0-582-37361-1). Longman.

Export Marketing German. R. Heidemann. 1978. pap. text ed. 7.95 (ISBN 0-582-35158-8); cassettes 30.00x (ISBN 0-582-37374-3). Longman.

Export Marketing of Capital Goods to the Socialist Countries of Eastern Europe. M. R. Hill. 200p. 1978. text ed. 45.75x (ISBN 0-566-03004-7, Pub. by Gower Pub Co England). Renouf.

Export Potential for Photovoltaic Systems. Pacific Northwest Laboratory. 210p. 1980. pap. 19.95 (ISBN 0-89934-014-8). Solar Energy Info.

Export: Processing Zones in Asia; Some Dimensions. (Illus.). 1977. 10.00 (ISBN 92-833-1039-X, APO21, APO); pap. 10.00 (ISBN 92-833-1040-3). Unipub.

Export Promotion: The Case of Brazil. Jose A. Savasini. LC 78-16883. (Praeger Special Studies). 1978. 21.95 (ISBN 0-03-041616-7). Praeger.

Exporting for Small & Medium Sized Firms. Daniel Enet. 150p. 1977. text ed. 22.00x (ISBN 0-220-66329-7, Pub. by Busn Bks England). Renouf.

Exporting: Practical Handbook for Entrepreneurs & Managers. rev. ed. Allan J. Siposs. (Illus.). 103p. (Orig.). 1978. pap. 25.00x (ISBN 0-935402-01-2). Intl Comm Serv.

Exporting Technical Education. 97p. 1968. 4.50 (ISBN 0-686-68834-1, IIE24, IIE). Unipub.

Exporting to China & Japan. D. O. Davis. cancelled (ISBN 0-932812-04-X). Bradley CPA.

Exporting Workers. Suzanne Paine. LC 74-19528. (Department of Applied Economics, Occasional Papers Ser.: No. 41). 224p. 1974. 34.95 (ISBN 0-521-20631-6); pap. 15.95x (ISBN 0-521-09879-3). Cambridge U Pr.

Exports & Economic Growth of Developing Countries. Alfred Maizels. LC 68-26987. (Publications of the National Institute of Economic & Social Research: No. 25). 1969. 42.50 (ISBN 0-521-06959-9). Cambridge U Pr.

Exposition & the English Language: Introductory Studies. 2nd ed. Ed. by James L. Sanderson & Walter K. Gordon. (Orig.). 1969. pap. text ed. 15.50 (ISBN 0-13-298026-6). P-H.

Exposition of Galatians. W. A. Criswell. 160p. 1980. pap. 5.95 (ISBN 0-310-22791-7). Zondervan.

Exposition of Genesis, 2 Vols. Herbert C. Leupold. Vol. 1. 12.95 (ISBN 0-8010-5549-0); Vol. 2. 12.95 (ISBN 0-8010-5522-9). Baker Bk.

Exposition of Proverbs, 2 vols. in 1. George Lawson. LC 80-8070. (Kregal Timeless Classics Ser.). 796p. 1981. Repr. of 1810 ed. 14.95 (ISBN 0-8254-3123-9). Kregel.

Exposition of St. Paul's Epistles. Richard Sibbes. 1978. Repr. 14.95 (ISBN 0-85151-246-1). Banner of Truth.

Exposition of the Epistle of Jude. Thomas Manton. 1978. 12.00 (ISBN 0-686-12957-1). Klock & Klock.

Exposition of the Gospel of John, 4 Vols. in 1. Arthur W. Pink. 1945. 22.95 (ISBN 0-310-31180-2). Zondervan.

Exposition of the Revelation of Jesus Christ. Walter Scott. LC 79-88736. 1979. Repr. 14.50 (ISBN 0-8254-3731-8). Kregel.

Expositions & Developments. Igor Stravinsky & Robert Craft. (Orig.). 1981. pap. 4.95 (ISBN 0-520-04403-7, CAL 503). U of Cal Pr.

Expository Dictionary of New Testament Words. W. E. Vine. 1978. 13.95 (ISBN 0-8407-5138-9). Nelson.

Expository Outlines from Paul's Epistles. Archie L. Edwards, Sr. (Sermon Outline Ser.). 1978. pap. 1.95 (ISBN 0-8010-3333-0). Baker Bk.

Expository Outlines from Romans. Croft M. Pentz. (Sermon Outline Ser.). 48p. (Orig.). 1980. pap. 1.95 (ISBN 0-8010-7045-7). Baker Bk.

Expository Sermons on the Book of Daniel. W. A. Criswell. 14.95 (ISBN 0-310-22800-X). Zondervan.

Expository Sermons on the Epistles of Peter. W. A. Criswell. 216p. (Orig.). 1980. pap. 4.95 (ISBN 0-310-22811-5). Zondervan.

Expository Writing: From Thought to Action. Holly Hickler & C. Lowell May. 1979. pap. text ed. 5.32 (ISBN 0-205-06190-7, 4961900); wkbk. 5.36 (ISBN 0-205-06191-5, 4961919); tchrs.' guide 3.20 (4961927). Allyn.

Expostion of the Four Gospels. Herschel H. Hobbs. 1977. pap. 19.95 (ISBN 0-8054-1370-7); Matthew, John, Mark, & Luke. Broadman.

Exposure. Art Gallery of Ontario. 1976. 29.95 o.p. (ISBN 0-688-03052-1). Morrow.

Exposure Control in Enlarging. George L. Wakefield. 1972. 9.95 o.p. (ISBN 0-85242-005-6, Pub. by Fountain). Morgan.

Exposure Manual. 3rd ed. J. F. Dunn & G. L. Wakefield. 1978. 21.95 o.p. (ISBN 0-85242-361-6, Pub. by Fountain). Morgan.

Express Yourself. R. W. Jepson. (Teach Yourself Ser.). 1974. pap. 2.95 o.p. (ISBN 0-679-10427-5). McKay.

Expressing Your Feelings: The Key to an Intimate Relationship. Theresa Crenshaw & Roger Crenshaw. 240p. (Orig.). (gr. 11-12). 1981. pap. text ed. 9.95x (ISBN 0-8290-0252-9). Irvington.

Expression & Meaning. J. R. Searle. LC 79-12271. 1979. 19.95 (ISBN 0-521-22901-4). Cambridge U Pr.

Expression of Results in Quantum Chemistry. new ed. Ed. by D. H. Whiffen. 1978. pap. text ed. 6.60 o.p. (ISBN 0-08-022367-2). Pergamon.

Expressionism. Wolf-Dieter Dube. (World of Art Ser.). (Illus.). 1977. pap. 9.95 (ISBN 0-19-519933-2). Oxford U Pr.

Expressionism--German Institution, 1905-1920. Paul Vogt et al. Tr. by Joachim Neugroschel. LC 80-67038. (Illus.). 336p. (Orig., Eng. & Ger.). 1980. pap. 17.95 (ISBN 0-89207-024-2). S R Guggenheim.

Expressionism: German Painting 1905-1920. Paul Vogt. Tr. by Antony Vivis & Robert E. Wolf. (Illus.). 1980. 35.00 (ISBN 0-8109-0852-2). Abrams.

Expressionists. Carl Zigrosser. 1957. 12.50 o.p. (ISBN 0-8076-0040-7). Braziller.

Expressive Therapy: A Creative Arts Approach to Depth-Oriented Therapy. Arthur Robbins. LC 80-13005. 300p. 1980. text ed. 19.95x (ISBN 0-87705-101-1). Human Sci Pr.

Expressman. David Nevin. (Old West Ser.). (Illus.). 1974. 12.95 (ISBN 0-8094-1484-8). Time-Life.

Expressmen. David Nevin. LC 74-12941. (Old West). (Illus.). (gr. 5 up). 1974. kivar 12.96 (ISBN 0-8094-1486-4, Pub. by Time-Life). Silver.

Expropriation in International Law. rev. ed. Samy Friedman. Tr. by Ivor C. Jackson from Fr. LC 80-26295. (Library of World Affairs: No. 20). 236p. 1981. Repr. of 1953 ed. lib. bdg. 29.75x (ISBN 0-313-20840-9, FREI). Greenwood.

Expropriation of Foreign Investments in Latin America. Harald Knudsen. 356p. 1975. pap. 19.50x (ISBN 8-200-01385-5, Dist. by Columbia U Pr). Universitet.

Expulsion of a Minority: Essays on Ugandan Asians. Michael Twaddle. (Commonwealth Papers Ser: No. 18). 96p. 1975. pap. text ed. 21.25x (ISBN 0-485-17618-1, Athlone Pr). Humanities.

Extant Collections of Early Black Newspapers: A Research Guide to the Black Press, 1880-1915, with an Index to the Boston Guardian, 1902-1904. Georgetta M. Campbell. LC 80-51418. 433p. 1981. 28.50x (ISBN 0-87875-197-1). Whitston Pub.

Extant Music of Rodrigo De Ceballos & Its Sources. Robert J. Snow. LC 78-70024. (Detroit Studies in Music Bibliography Ser.: No. 44). 1980. 17.50 (ISBN 0-89990-001-1). Info Coord.

Extended (Experiential) Awareness, Purposeful Relaxation, & Multiple (Differentiated Psychophysiological) Feeling States, Set-CA. Russell E. Mason. 1975. pap. 50.00x (ISBN 0-89533-013-X); Notes, Feeling Training, Substitution & Goal Achievement Training incl.; tape-1a; t-2. t-3; t-4; t-5A (ISBN 0-89533-034-2); t-7. F I Comm.

Extending Canadian Health Insurance: Options for Pharmacare & Denticare. R. G. Evans & M. F. Williamson. (Ontario Economic Council Research Studies). 1978. pap. 12.00 (ISBN 0-8020-3353-9). U of Toronto Pr.

Extending Economics Within the Curriculum. Ed. by Keith Robinson & Robert Wilson. (Direct Editions Ser). (Orig.). 1978. pap. 16.00 (ISBN 0-7100-8629-6). Routledge & Kegan.

Extending the Limits of Reliability Theory. Harold Goldberg. 300p. 1981. 30.00 (ISBN 0-471-07799-2, Pub. by Wiley Interscience). Wiley.

Extension Education & Rural Development, Vol. 1: International Experience in Communication & Innovation. Bruce R. Crouch & Shankarish Chamala. LC 79-41221. 1981. price not set (ISBN 0-471-27829-7, Pub. by Wiley-Interscience). Wiley.

Extension Education & Rural Development, Vol. 2: International Experience in Strategies for Planned Change. Bruce L. Crouch & Shankarish Chamala. LC 79-41221. 1981. price not set (ISBN 0-471-27675-8, Pub. by Wiley-Interscience). Wiley.

Extensions of Minimal Transformation Groups. I. U. Bronstein. 327p. 1979. 47.50x (ISBN 90-286-0368-9). Sijthoff & Noordhoff.

Exterior & Interior Trim. John E. Ball. LC 75-6060. 264p. 1975. pap. 8.60 (ISBN 0-8273-1120-6); instructor's guide 1.60 (ISBN 0-8273-1121-4). Delmar.

Exterior Lighting for Industry & Security. S. L. Lyons. (Illus.). xiv, 320p. 1980. 50.00x (ISBN 0-85334-879-0, Pub. by Applied Science). Burgess-Intl Ideas.

Exterior Water-Based Trade Paint Formulations. Ernest W. Flick. LC 80-19212. 349p. 1981. 36.00 (ISBN 0-8155-0820-4). Noyes.

External & Internal Characters, Horizontal & Vertical Distribution, Luminescence, & Food of the Dwarf Pelagic Shark, Euproomicrus bispinatus. D. L. Hubbs et al. (Bulletin of the Scripps Institution of Oceanography: Vol. 10). 1967. pap. 6.50x (ISBN 0-520-09314-3). U of Cal Pr.

External Assistance & Indian Economic Growth. S. Stanley Katz. 5.00x (ISBN 0-210-98137-7). Asia.

External Ear Malformations: Epidemiology, Genetics & Natural History. LC 79-2501. (Alan R. Liss Ser.: Vol. 15, No. 9). 1979. 18.00 (ISBN 0-8451-1034-9). March of Dimes.

External Galaxies & Quasi-Stellar Objects: Proceedings. International Astronomical Union Symposium, 44th, Uppsala, Sweden, 1970. Ed. by D. S. Evans. LC 77-154736. (Illus.). 549p. 1972. 40.50 (ISBN 0-387-91092-1). Springer-Verlag.

External Public Debt Prospects of the Non-Oil-Exporting Developing Countries. Gordon W. Smith. LC 77-90866. (Monographs: No. 10). 64p. 1977. 4.00 (ISBN 0-686-28685-5). Overseas Dev Council.

External Role of the European Community. Gunnar Sjostedt. 1977. 24.95 (ISBN 0-566-00172-1, 01455-9, Pub. by Saxon Hse England). Lexington Bks.

External Skeletal Fixation. Dana C. Mears. (Illus.). 584p. 1981. write for info. (5900-9). Williams & Wilkins.

Externalities & Welfare. David K. Whitcomb. LC 71-172174. (Columbia Studies in Economics: No. 6). 144p. 1972. 20.00x (ISBN 0-231-03586-1). Columbia U Pr.

Extinct & Vanishing Birds of the World. 2nd ed. James C. Greenway, Jr. (Illus.). 11.00 (ISBN 0-8446-2164-1). Peter Smith.

Extinction & Survival in Human Populations. Ed. by Charles D. Laughlin, Jr. & Ivan A. Brady. LC 76-17596. 1978. 22.50x (ISBN 0-231-04418-6); pap. 10.00x (ISBN 0-231-04419-4). Columbia U Pr.

Extra Class Radio Amateur License Guide. Martin Schwartz. LC 79-54856. 1980. pap. 1.50 (ISBN 0-912146-11-7). AMECO.

Extra Drills & Practices. Willard D. Sheeler. 1978. 4.25 (ISBN 0-89285-039-6). English Lang.

Extra Success Potential: The Art of Out-Thinking & Out-Sensing Others in Business & Everyday Life. Harold Sherman & Al Pollard. 200p. 1981. pap. 5.95 (ISBN 0-13-298109-2). P-H.

Extract from the Klamath Indians of SW Oregon. Albert Gatschet. Repr. of 1890 ed. pap. 4.50 (ISBN 0-8466-0118-4, SJS118). Shorey.

Extraction Metallurgy. 2nd ed. J. D. Gilchrist. 1978. 50.00 (ISBN 0-08-021711-7); pap. 17.00 (ISBN 0-08-021712-5). Pergamon.

Extraction with Supercritical Gases. Ed. by G. M. Schneider et al. 1980. 48.80 (ISBN 3-527-25854-X). Verlag Chemie.

Extraordinary Black Book. 2nd ed. John Wade. (Development of Industrial Society Ser.). 576p. 1980. Repr. 35.00x (ISBN 0-7165-1588-1, Pub. by Irish Academic Pr). Biblio Dist.

Extraordinary Envoy: General Hiroshi Oshima & Diplomacy in the Third Reich 1934-1939. Carl Boyd. LC 79-9600. 246p. 1980. text ed. 18.50 (ISBN 0-8191-0957-6); pap. text ed. 9.75 (ISBN 0-8191-0958-4). U Pr of Amer.

Extrapolate. Richard Kostelanetz. 50p. 1975. pap. 2.00 (ISBN 0-685-61221-X); signed 50.00 (ISBN 0-685-61222-8). Assembling Pr.

Extrapyramidal System & Its Disorders. International Conference on Parkinson's Disease, No. 6. Ed. by Louis J. Poirier et al. LC 78-57817. (Advances in Neurology Ser.: Vol. 24). 1979. text ed. 53.00 (ISBN 0-89004-369-8). Raven.

Extrasensory Ecology: Parapsychology & Anthropology. Ed. by Joseph K. Long. LC 77-6367. 1977. 19.50 (ISBN 0-8108-1036-0). Scarecrow.

Extraterritorial Antitrust: The Sherman Act vs. the Market Entry Strategy of Selected Multinational Corporations. James B. Townsend, Jr. LC 79-18802. (Special Studies in International Economics & Business). 1980. lib. bdg. 28.50x (ISBN 0-89158-483-8). Westview.

Extraterritoriality in China: The Case Against Abolition. H. G. Woodhead et al. LC 78-74343. 189p. (The growth & decline of rural industrial enterprise in North China. Extent & effects of industrialization in China the modern Chinese economy). 1980. lib. bdg. 22.00 (ISBN 0-8240-4280-8). Garland Pub.

Extraterritoriality in Japan & the Diplomatic Relations Resulting in Its Abolition, Eighteen Fifty-Three to Eighteen Ninety-Nine. F. C. Jones. 1931. 18.50x (ISBN 0-686-51384-3). Elliots Bks.

Extravagant Things: A Catalog of Indulgences. Phillip S. Schulz. (Illus.). 450p. (Orig.). 1980. pap. cancelled (ISBN 0-8092-7044-7). Contemp Bks.

Extremal Methods & Systems Analysis. Ed. by A. V. Fiacco et al. (Lecture Notes in Economics & Mathematical Systems Ser.: Vol. 174). 545p. 1980. pap. 39.30 (ISBN 3-540-09730-9). Springer-Verlag.

Extremum & Variational Principles in Mechanics. CISM (International Center for Mechanical Sciences), Dept. for General Mechanics, Technical Univ. of Brunswick, 1970. Ed. by H. Lippmann. (CISM Pubns. Ser.: No. 54). (Illus.). ii, 239p. 1972. pap. 29.00 (ISBN 0-387-81115-X). Springer-Verlag.

Extrusion of Foods. Judson M. Harper. 1981. Vol. 1. 59.95 (ISBN 0-8493-5203-7); Vol. 2. 46.95 (ISBN 0-8493-5204-5). CRC Pr.

Extrusion of Plastics. 3rd ed. E. G. Fisher. LC 75-4359. 1976. 28.95 (ISBN 0-470-15012-2). Halsted Pr.

Exuberant Years: A Guide for Junior High Leaders. Ginny W. Holderness. LC 75-13458. 128p. 1976. pap. 6.50 (ISBN 0-8042-1225-2). John Knox.

Exurbs: Urban Residential Developments in the Countryside. Dinker I. Patel. LC 79-48040. 151p. 1980. text ed. 15.50 (ISBN 0-8191-1001-9); pap. text ed. 8.00 (ISBN 0-8191-1002-7). U Pr of Amer.

Eydie Mae: How I Conquered Cancer Naturally. Chris Loeffler. pap. 2.95 (ISBN 0-686-10146-4). Prod Hse.

Eye. Davson. 1974. Vol. 5. 61.00, by subscription 49.50 (ISBN 0-12-206755-X); Vol. 6. 57.00, by subscription 41.25 (ISBN 0-12-206756-8). Acad Pr.

Eye. Kathleen Elgin. LC 67-10136. (Human Body Ser). (Illus.). (gr. 4-6). 1967. PLB 4.90 o.p. (ISBN 0-531-01172-0). Watts.

Eye. Gordon K. Klintworth & Maurice B. Landers. LC 75-19061. 236p. 1976. 18.50 (ISBN 0-683-04628-4). Krieger.

Eye, Vol. 2. R. C. Augusteyn & H. B. Collin. Ed. by David F. Horrobin. (Annual Research Reviews). 344p. 1980. 36.00 (ISBN 0-88831-083-8). Eden Med Res.

Eye & Ear Fun, 3 bks. Clarence R. Stone. 1946. 2.64 ea. o.p. Bk. 1 (ISBN 0-07-061701-5). Bk. 2 (ISBN 0-07-061702-3). Bk. 4 (ISBN 0-07-061703-1). McGraw.

Eye & Inborn Errors of Metabolism: Proceedings. Symposium Held at the Radcliffe Infirmary, Oxford, England, April, 1975 Sponsod by the National Foundation - March of Dimes. Ed. by Daniel Bergsma et al. LC 76-12112. (Birth Defects-Original Article Ser: Vol. 12, No. 3). 620p. 1976. 69.00x (ISBN 0-8451-1003-9). A R Liss.

Eye-Body Connection. Jessica Maxwell. (Illus., Orig.). 1980. pap. 6.95 (ISBN 0-446-87950-9). Warner Bks.

Eye Color, Sex, & Children's Behavior. A. L. Gary & John A. Glover. LC 76-3642. 208p. 1976. 14.95 (ISBN 0-88229-213-7). Nelson-Hall.

Eye: Disease, Diagnosis, Treatment. T. Meredith. (Illus.). 1975. pap. 7.95 (ISBN 0-87618-068-3). R J Brady.

Eye for an Eye. Anthony Trollope. Ed. by Robert L. Wolff. (Ireland Nineteenth Century Fiction - Ser. Two: Vol. 56). 440p. 1979. lib. bdg. 32.00 (ISBN 0-8240-3505-4). Garland Pub.

Eye in the Pyramid. Robert J. Shea & Robert A. Wilson. 304p. 1975. pap. 1.95 o.s.i. (ISBN 0-440-14688-7). Dell.

Eye in the Text: Essays on Perception, Mannerist to Modern. Mary A. Caws. LC 80-8540. (Princeton Essays on the Arts Ser.: No. 11). (Illus.). 334p. 1981. 17.50x (ISBN 0-691-06453-9); pap. 6.95x (ISBN 0-691-01377-2). Princeton U Pr.

Eye Injuries. Edward Zagora. (Illus.). 618p. 1970. text ed. 59.75 (ISBN 0-398-02139-2). C C Thomas.

Eye Movement Disorders. Andrew J. Gay et al. LC 74-10747. 1974. 23.00 o.p. (ISBN 0-8016-1763-4). Mosby.

Eye Movements & Information Processing in Mentally Retarded Children. Frederic J. Boersma & Walter Muir. (Modern Approaches to the Diagnosis & Instruction of Multi-Handicapped Children Ser.: Vol. 14). 100p. 1975. text ed. 21.50 (ISBN 90-237-4125-0, Pub. by Swets Pub Serv Holland). Swets North Am.

Eye-Movements & Visual Perception. R. W. Ditchburn. (Illus.). 420p. 1973. 49.00x (ISBN 0-19-857371-5). Oxford U Pr.

Eye Movements: ARVO Symposium, 1976. Ed. by B. A. Brooks & F. J. Bajandas. 223p. 1977. 22.50 (ISBN 0-306-31082-1, Plenum Pr). Plenum Pub.

Eye Movements: Cognition & Visual Perception. Ed. by Dennis F. Fisher et al. (Eye Movements Ser.). 368p. 1981. ref. 19.95 (ISBN 0-89859-084-1). L Erlbaum Assocs.

Eye Movements, Surprise Reactions & Cognitive Development. Keri M. Wilton & Frederic J. Boersma. (Modern Approaches to the Diagnosis & Instruction of Multi-Handicapped Children: Vol. 13). 78p. 1973. text ed. 17.75 (ISBN 90-237-4117-X, Pub. by Swets Pub Serv Holland). Swets North Am.

Eye of Shiva: Eastern Mysticism & Science. Amaury De Riencourt. LC 80-22032. 221p. 1981. 8.95 (ISBN 0-688-00038-X); pap. 4.95 (ISBN 0-686-63396-2). Morrow.

Eye of the Hurricane: Switzerland in World War Two. Urs Schwarz. 150p. 1980. lib. bdg. 18.00 (ISBN 0-89158-766-7). Westview.

Eye of the Lens. Langdon Jones. (Illus.). 173p. 1973. pap. 1.25 o.s.i. (ISBN 0-02-021800-1, Collier). Macmillan.

Eye of the Mind. Lynn Biederstadt. 256p. 1981. 12.95 (ISBN 0-399-90108-6). Marek.

Eye of the Needle. Ken Follett. (Illus.). 1981. pap. 3.50 (ISBN 0-451-09913-3, E9913, Sig). NAL.

Eye of the Peacock. Dodge & Safonov. (YA) 5.95 (ISBN 0-685-07432-3, Avalon). Bouregy.

Eye of the Scarecrow. Wilson Harris. (Orig.). 1974. pap. 3.95 (ISBN 0-571-10557-2, Pub. by Faber & Faber). Merrimack Bk Serv.

Eye of the Storm. Joseph Bishop. 1976. pap. 4.95 (ISBN 0-912376-16-3). Chosen Bks Pub.

Eye of the Tiger. Wilbur Smith. LC 75-14841. 312p. 1976. 7.95 o.p. (ISBN 0-385-11264-5). Doubleday.

Eye Spy: A Collection of Tricky, Sneaky, Puzzling Pictures to Test Your Eyes & Memory. Doug Anderson. LC 80-52329. (Illus.). 128p. (gr. 4 up). 1980. 6.95 (ISBN 0-8069-4628-8); PLB 6.69 (ISBN 0-8069-4629-6). Sterling.

Eye: Structure & Function in Disease. Gordon K. Klintworth. 200p. 1976. 19.50 o.p. (ISBN 0-683-04628-4). Williams & Wilkins.

Eye Winker, Tom Tinker, Chin Chopper. Tom Glazer. (Illus.). 1978. pap. 1.95 o.p. (ISBN 0-385-13344-8). Doubleday.

Eye-Witness Identification. Nathan R. Sobel. LC 72-85036. 1972. 25.00 (ISBN 0-87632-083-3); 1979 supplement incl. (ISBN 0-685-99205-5). Boardman.

Eye-Witness Identification in Criminal Cases. Patrick M. Wall. 248p. 1975. 14.75 (ISBN 0-398-02009-4). C C Thomas.

Eyes. (MacDonald Educational Ser.). (Illus., Arabic.). 3.50 (ISBN 0-686-53074-8). Intl Bk Ctr.

Eyes. 3rd ed. S. J. Miller. (Operative Surgery Ser.). 1976. 49.95 (ISBN 0-407-00609-5). Butterworths.

Eyes. Felice Picano. 1977. pap. 1.95 o.s.i. (ISBN 0-440-12427-1). Dell.

Eyes & Seeing. Joan E. Rahn. LC 80-23988. (Illus.). 128p. (gr. 5-9). 1981. PLB 8.95 (ISBN 0-689-30828-0). Atheneum.

Eyes Don't Always Want to Stay Open: Poems. Phillip Lopate. LC 74-34536. 1976. pap. 4.00 (ISBN 0-915342-12-X). SUN.

Eyes, Ears, Nose & Throat: Operative Surgery Ser. Vol. 10. Stewart Duke-Elder & Maxwell Ellis. (Illus.). 350p. 1970. 26.00 o.p. (ISBN 0-397-58032-0). Lippincott.

Eyes in the Rock: Selected Poems. David Rokeah. (Poetry in Europe Ser.). 78p. 1968. 5.95 (ISBN 0-8040-0106-5). Swallow.

Eyes of Autumn: An Experiment in Poetry. Deb K. Das. 13p. 1975. 6.00 (ISBN 0-88253-706-7). Ind-US Inc.

Eyes of Sarsis. Andrew J. Offut & Richard K. Lyon. (Orig.). 1980. pap. write for info. (ISBN 0-671-82679-4). PB.

Eyes of the Interred. Miguel A. Asturius. 1973. 15.00 o.p. (ISBN 0-440-02378-5, Sey Lawr). Delacorte.

Eyes of the Mind. Jose C. Rodriguez. 1981. 12.50 (ISBN 0-533-04591-6). Vantage.

Eyes of the Woods. Joseph Altsheler. 1976. lib. bdg. 12.95x (ISBN 0-89968-145-X). Lightyear.

Eyes on the Land. Gary Elder. 32p. 1980. pap. 3.00 (ISBN 0-88235-043-9). San Marcos.

Eyes on the Wilderness. Helmut Hirnschall. 175p. 1975. text ed. 5.95 (ISBN 0-919654-39-8). Hancock Hse.

Eyes to Behold. Michael Gaydos. 1980. pap. 2.50 o.p. (ISBN 0-89221-069-9). New Leaf.

Eyewitness. Jean-Michel Folon. 64p. 1980. 55.00 (ISBN 0-8109-0906-5). Abrams.

Eyewitness. John Minahan. 176p. (Orig.). 1981. pap. 2.25 (ISBN 0-380-77388-0, 77388). Avon.

Eyewitness: A Journalist Covers the Twentieth Century. Edmund Demaitre. (Illus.). 450p. 1981. 17.50 (ISBN 0-8044-1218-9). Ungar.

Eyewitness Auschwitz. Filip Mueller. LC 78-66257. (Illus.). 192p. 1981. pap. 6.95 (ISBN 0-8128-6084-5). Stein & Day.

Eyewitness: The Growth of Photography. Elizabeth McCausland. Ed. by Susan D. Peters. (Illus.). 250p. 1981. 22.50 (ISBN 0-8180-1421-0). Horizon.

Eyewitnesses to American Jewish History: East European Immigration 1881-1920, Pt. 3. Ed. by Azriel Eisenberg et al. (Illus.). 1978. pap. 5.00 (ISBN 0-8074-0017-3, 144061); tchrs'. guide 5.00 (ISBN 0-8074-0021-1, 204063). UAHC.

Eyewitnesses to American Jewish History: The German Immigration 1800-1875, Pt. 2. Ed. by Azriel Eisenberg et al. (Illus.). 1977. pap. 5.00 (ISBN 0-8074-0016-5, 144059); tchrs'. guide 5.00 (ISBN 0-8074-0020-3, 204062). UAHC.

Eyewitnesses to American Jewish History: 1492 - 1793, Pt. 1. Ed. by Azriel Eisenberg et al. 1976. pap. 5.00 (144060); tchrs'. guide 5.00 (ISBN 0-8074-0019-X, 204061). UAHC.

Eyewitnesses to Jewish History: From Five Eighty-Six B. C. E. to Nineteen Sixty-Seven. Ed. by Azriel Eisenberg et al. (gr. 9-12). 1972. text ed. 12.50 (ISBN 0-8074-0076-9, 144066); tchrs'. guide 5.00 (ISBN 0-8074-0057-2, 204067). UAHC.

Eyvind Johnson. Gavin Orton. (World Authors Ser.: Sweden: No. 150). lib. bdg. 10.95 (ISBN 0-8057-2468-0). Twayne.

Ezechiel und Deuterojesaja: Beruehrungen in der Heilserwartung der beiden grossen Exilspropheten. Dieter Baltzer. (Beiheft 121 Zur Zeitschrift fuer die alttestamentliche Wissenschaft Ser.). 1971. 34.00x (ISBN 3-11-001756-3). De Gruyter.

Ezekial Daniel. Irving L. Jensen. 1970. pap. 2.25 (ISBN 0-8024-1026-X). Moody.

Ezekiel. G. A. Cooke. LC 38-12281. (International Critical Commentary Ser.). 608p. Repr. of 1936 ed. text ed. 23.00x (ISBN 0-567-05016-5). Attic Pr.

Ezekiel. Arno C. Gaebelein. LC 72-88419. 1918. 5.50 (ISBN 0-87213-217-X). Loizeaux.

Ezekiel Mphahlele. Ursula A. Barnett. LC 76-18881. (World Authors Ser.: No. 417). 1976. lib. bdg. 12.50 (ISBN 0-8057-6257-4). Twayne.

Ezekiel: Notes. H. A. Ironside. Date not set. 6.50 (ISBN 0-87213-359-1). Loizeaux.

Ezekiel One. Walther Zimmerli. Ed. by Frank M. Cross, Jr. & Klaus Baltzer. LC 75-21540. (Hermenia: a Critical & Historical Commentary on the Bible). 558p. 1979. 32.95 (ISBN 0-8006-6008-0, 20-6008). Fortress.

Ezra - Esther. Irving L. Jensen. (Bible Self-Study Ser). 1970. pap. 2.25 (ISBN 0-8024-1015-4). Moody.

Ezra & Nehemiah. L. W. Batten. LC 13-12806. (International Critical Commentary Ser.). 400p. Repr. of 1913 ed. 20.00x (ISBN 0-567-05008-4). Attic Pr.

Ezra & Nehemiah & the Return from Babylon. Gordon Lindsay. (Old Testament Ser.). 1.25 (ISBN 0-89985-154-1). Christ Nations.

Ezra-Nehemiah-Esther. Ruben M. Ratzlaff & Paul T. Butler. (Bible Study Textbook Ser.). 1979. 13.00 (ISBN 0-89900-014-2). College Pr Pub.

Ezra Pound. G. Fraser. 1979. cancelled (ISBN 0-685-99623-9). Chips.

Ezra Pound. James F. Knapp. (United States Author Ser.: No. 348). 1979. 9.95 (ISBN 0-8057-7286-3). Twayne.

Ezra Pound. Jeannette Lander. LC 71-134828. (Modern Literature Ser.). 1971. 10.95 (ISBN 0-8044-2486-1); pap. 3.45 (ISBN 0-8044-6380-8). Ungar.

Ezra Pound: An Introduction to the Poetry. Bernetta Quinn. LC 72-6830. (Introductions to Modern American Poetry Ser.). 225p. 1973. 15.00x (ISBN 0-231-03282-X). Columbia U Pr.

Ezra Pound & the Visual Arts. Ezra Pound. Ed. by Harriet Zinnes. LC 80-36720. 352p. 1980. 25.95 (ISBN 0-8112-0772-2). New Directions.

Ezra Pound: The Last Rower. C. David Heymann. (Seaver-Grove Bk.). 1980. pap. 6.95 o.p. (ISBN 0-394-17748-7). Grove.

Ezra Pound: The Last Rower. a Political Profile. C. David Heymann. LC 80-52073. 320p. 1980. pap. 6.95 (ISBN 0-394-17748-7). Seaver Bks.

F

F Book of Readings for Teaching Reading in Elementary School. Sterl Artley. 1974. pap. text ed. 6.95x (ISBN 0-87543-114-3). Lucas.

F. D. R. & the Supreme Court Fight, Nineteen Thirty-Seven: A President Tries to Reorganize the Federal Judiciary. Frank B. Latham. LC 71-180166. (Focus Books). (Illus.). 72p. (gr. 7 up). 1971. PLB 4.90 o.p. (ISBN 0-531-02451-2). Watts.

F D R: The Other Side of the Coin. Hamilton Fish. 255p. 1976. pap. 8.00 (ISBN 0-911038-64-7, Inst Hist Rev). Noontide.

F D R's New Deal. Don Lawson. LC 78-4775. (Illus.). (gr. 7 up). 1979. 8.95 (ISBN 0-690-03953-0, TYC-J). T Y Crowell.

F-Eighteen Hornet, Vol. 29. J. Stevenson. (Aero Ser.). 104p. 1981. 7.95 (ISBN 0-8168-0608-X). Aero.

F-F-Frank Polk: An Uncommonly Frank Autobiography. Frank Polk. LC 78-51848. 136p. pap. 9.50 (ISBN 0-87358-276-4). Northland.

F-Four Phantom. Bill Gunston. (Illus.). 1977. 9.95 o.p. (ISBN 0-684-15298-3, ScribT). Scribner.

F-Four Phantom. G. G. O'Rourke. (Famous Aircraft Ser.). (Illus., Orig.). 1969. pap. 4.95 o.p. (ISBN 0-668-02221-3). Arco.

F-Four Phantom Two. G. G. O'Rourke. LC 78-79407. (Illus.). 1979. pap. 4.95 (ISBN 0-8168-5645-1). Aero.

F-Four-U Corsair in Action. pap. 4.95 (ISBN 0-89747-028-1). Squad Sig Pubns.

F-Fourteen Tomcat. Arthur Reed. (Illus.). 1978. 12.50 (ISBN 0-684-15881-7, ScribT). Scribner.

F. M. Dostoevsky: His Image of Man. Miriam Sajkovic. LC 62-20690. 1962. 8.00x o.p. (ISBN 0-8122-7368-0). U of Pa Pr.

F M from Antenna to Audio. Leonard Feldman. LC 73-82884. (Illus., Orig.). 1969. pap. 4.95 o.p. (ISBN 0-672-20723-0, 20723). Sams.

F. Marion Crawford Companion. John C. Moran. LC 80-1707. (Illus.). 608p. 1981. lib. bdg. 45.00 (ISBN 0-313-20926-X, MCC/). Greenwood.

F. Max Muller & the Rg-Veda. Ronald Neufeldt. 1980. 16.00x (ISBN 0-8364-0040-2). South Asia Bks.

F. Scott Fitzgerald. rev ed. Kenneth Eble. (U.S. Authors Ser.: No. 36). 1977. lib. bdg. 9.95 (ISBN 0-8057-7183-2). Twayne.

F. Scott Fitzgerald. Kenneth Eble. LC 77-429. (Twayne's U. S. Authors Ser.). 187p. 1977. pap. text ed. 4.95 (ISBN 0-672-61503-7). Bobbs.

F. Scott Fitzgerald. Rose A. Gallo. LC 76-15650. (Modern Literature Ser.). 1978. 10.95 (ISBN 0-8044-2225-7). Ungar.

F. Scott Fitzgerald & the American Dream. William A. Fahey. LC 73-4523. (Twentieth-Century American Writers Ser). (gr. 6 up). 1973. 8.95 (ISBN 0-690-00078-2, TYC-J). T Y Crowell.

F. Scott Fitzgerald & the Craft of Fiction. Richard D. Lehan. LC 66-5059. (Crosscurrents-Modern Critiques Ser.). 221p. 1966. 13.95 (ISBN 0-8093-0216-0). S Ill U Pr.

F. Scott Fitzgerald: His Art & His Technique. James E. Miller, Jr. LC 64-16900. (Gotham Library). 1964. pap. 5.00 (ISBN 0-8147-0309-7). NYU Pr.

F. Scott Fitzgerald in Minnesota: His Homes & Haunts. John J. Koblas. LC 78-21979. (No. 18). 1978. pap. 3.75 (ISBN 0-87351-134-4). Minn Hist.

FAA Flight Test Guides. rev. ed. Ernest J. Gentle et al. LC 74-77533. 112p. 1976. pap. 2.95 (ISBN 0-8168-5702-4). Aero.

Fab Fifties. Norman Jacobs. LC 79-63383. 1979. pap. 1.95 (ISBN 0-931064-09-0). Starlog.

Fab Fifties. Norman Jacobs. 1980. pap. 2.25. O'Quinn Studio.

Fabelhafte Getraume Von Taifun Willi. Higgins. pap. write for info. (ISBN 0-914162-57-8). Knowles.

Faber Book of Animal Stories. Ed. by Johnny Morris. 1978. 9.95 (ISBN 0-571-11221-8, Pub. by Faber & Faber). Merrimack Bk Serv.

Faber Book of Ballads. Ed. by Matthew Hodgart. 1965. 11.95 o.p. (ISBN 0-571-06236-9, Pub. by Faber & Faber). Merrimack Bk Serv.

Faber Book of Children's Verse. Ed. by Janet A. Smith. 1962. 8.95 (ISBN 0-571-05273-8, Pub. by Faber & Faber). Merrimack Bk Serv.

Faber Book of Comic Verse. Ed. by Michael Roberts. 1978. 15.00 (ISBN 0-571-04833-1, Pub. by Faber & Faber); pap. 8.95 (ISBN 0-571-11263-3). Merrimack Bk Serv.

Faber Book of Greek Legends. Ed. by Kathleen Lines. 1973. 9.95 (ISBN 0-571-09830-4, Pub. by Faber & Faber). Merrimack Bk Serv.

Faber Book of Northern Folk-Tales. Ed. by Kevin Crossley-Holland. (Illus.). 157p. (gr. 3-12). 1981. 11.95 (ISBN 0-571-11519-5, Pub. by Faber & Faber). Merrimack Bk Serv.

Faber Book of Nursery Stories. Ed. by Barbara Ireson. (gr. k-3). 1967. 8.95 (ISBN 0-571-06623-2). Transatlantic.

Faber Book of Nursery Verse. Barbara Ireson. (gr. 4 up). 8.95 (ISBN 0-571-06335-7). Transatlantic.

Faber Book of Poems & Places. Intro. by Geoffrey Grigson. 408p. 1980. 19.95 (ISBN 0-571-11647-7, Pub. by Faber & Faber). Merrimack Bk Serv.

Faber Book of Twentieth Century Verse. 3rd ed. Ed. by John Heath-Stubbs & David Wright. 1975. 16.95 (ISBN 0-571-04884-6, Pub. by Faber & Faber); pap. 8.95 (ISBN 0-571-04887-0). Merrimack Bk Serv.

Faber Pocket Medical Dictionary. rev. ed. P. A. Riley & P. J. Cunningham. (Illus.). 1974. 4.95 o.p. (ISBN 0-571-04844-7, Pub. by Faber & Faber). Merrimack Bk Serv.

Faber Storybook. Kathleen Lines. (Illus.). (ps-5). 1972. pap. 3.95 o.p. (ISBN 0-571-10176-3, Pub. by Faber & Faber). Merrimack Bk Serv.

Faberge & His Contemporaries: The India Early Minshall Collection of the Cleveland Museum of Art. Henry Hawley. LC 67-28951. (Illus.). 148p. 1967. 10.00x (ISBN 0-910386-10-2, Pub. by Cleveland Mus Art). Ind U Pr.

Faberge Imperial Eggs & Other Fantasies. Hermoine Waterfield & Christopher Forbes. (Illus.). 1978. 19.95 o.p. (ISBN 0-684-15966-X, ScribT). Scribner.

Faber's Anatomical Atlas for Nurses & Students. A. K. Maxwell et al. 1962. pap. text ed. 5.95 (ISBN 0-571-06461-2, Pub. by Faber & Faber). Merrimack Bk Serv.

Faberware Convection Turbo-Oven Cookbook. Margaret D. Murphy. Ed. by Marilyn Kostick. LC 80-68017. (Illus.). 144p. 1980. 8.95 (ISBN 0-916752-44-5). Dorison Hse.

Fabian Essays in Socialism. Ed. by George B. Shaw. 1967. 7.00 (ISBN 0-8446-1403-3). Peter Smith.

Fabian Socialism. George D. Cole. LC 68-21432. Repr. of 1943 ed. 21.00x (ISBN 0-678-05020-1). Kelley.

Fabian Socialism & English Politics, Eighteen Eighty-Four - Nineteen Eighteen. A. M. McBriar. 1962. pap. 14.95x (ISBN 0-521-09351-1). Cambridge U Pr.

Fabiola; or, the Church of the Catacombs, 1854. Nicholas P. Wiseman. Ed. by Robert L. Wolff. LC 75-454. (Victorian Fiction Ser). 1975. lib. bdg. 66.00 (ISBN 0-8240-1533-9). Garland Pub.

Fable-Books Printed in the Low Countries: A Concise Bibliography Until 1800. John Landwehr. 1963. text ed. 16.00x (ISBN 90-6004-096-1). Humanities.

Fable of the Good Lion. Ernest Hemingway. 28p. 1981. 4.95 (ISBN 0-8120-5276-5). Barron.

Fable of the Lion & the Scorpion. Diane Wakoski. 1975. pap. 2.50x (ISBN 0-915316-19-6). Pentagram.

Fabled Doctor Jim Jordan. F. Roy Johnson. 1968. 4.95 (ISBN 0-930230-08-6). Johnson NC.

Fables. facsimile ed. John Gay. 1969. 20.00x (ISBN 0-85417-056-1, Pub. by Scolar Pr England). Biblio Dist.

Fables. Arnold Lobel. LC 79-2004. (Illus.). 48p. (gr. 1-4). 1980. 8.95 (ISBN 0-06-023973-5, HarpJ); PLB 8.79 (ISBN 0-06-023974-3). Har-Row.

Fables, Ancient & Modern: Adapted for the Use of Children, 2 vols. in 1. William Godwin. LC 75-32153. (Classics of Children's Literature, 1621-1932: Vol. 19). 1976. Repr. of 1805 ed. PLB 38.00 (ISBN 0-8240-2267-X). Garland Pub.

Fables & Fabulists, Ancient & Modern. Thomas Newbigging. LC 70-78212. 1971. Repr. of 1895 ed. 18.00 (ISBN 0-8103-3770-3). Gale.

Fables & Vaudevilles & Plays: Theatre More-or-Less at Random. Norman D. Dietz. LC 68-16685. 176p. (Orig.). 1968. pap. 4.25 (ISBN 0-936520-00-0). Norman & Sandra.

Fables of Aesop. Aesop. Ed. by Joseph Jacobs. (New Children's Classics). (gr. 3 up). 1964. 4.95g o.s.i. (ISBN 0-02-700160-1). Macmillan.

Fables of Aggression: Wyndham Lewis, the Modernist As Fascist. Fredric Jameson. 1979. 12.95x (ISBN 0-520-03792-8). U of Cal Pr.

Fables of Aggression: Wyndham Lewis, the Modernist As Facist. Fredric Jameson. 1981. pap. 5.95 (ISBN 0-520-04398-7, CAL 496). U of Cal Pr.

Fables of Fact: The New Journalism As New Fiction. John Hellmann. LC 80-23881. 175p. 1981. 11.95 (ISBN 0-252-00847-2). U of Ill Pr.

Fables of the Jewish Aesop Translated from the Fox Fables of Berechiah Ha-Nakdan. Tr. by Moses Hadas. LC 66-27477. (Illus.). 1966. 15.00x (ISBN 0-231-02967-5). Columbia U Pr.

Fabre: Poet of Science. G. V. Legros. LC 73-152059. 1971. 7.50 o.p. (ISBN 0-8180-0218-2). Horizon.

Fabric Crafts. Jennyfer Crommelin. LC 79-20121. (Pegasus Books: No. 26). 1970. 7.50x (ISBN 0-234-77275-1). Intl Pubns Serv.

Fabric Decoration Book. Patricia E. Gaines. LC 75-4543. (Illus.). 240p. 1975. 14.95 o.p. (ISBN 0-688-02903-5). Morrow.

Fabric Furnishings. Margaret Butler & Beryl Greves. 1972. 27.00 (ISBN 0-7134-2754-X, Pub. by Batsford). David & Charles.

Fabric of Existentialism: The Philisophical & Literary Sources. Richard Gill & Ernest Sherman. 1973. text ed. 20.95 (ISBN 0-13-298216-1). P-H.

Fabric of the Universe. Denis Postle. (Illus.). 208p. 1976. 5.95 (ISBN 0-517-52623-9). Crown.

Fabric Painting & Dyeing for the Theatre. Deborah Dryden. 1981. 27.50x (ISBN 0-89676-056-1). Drama Bk.

Fabric Printing & Dyeing. David Green. (Illus.). (gr. 7 up). 1972. 12.00 (ISBN 0-8231-7025-X). Branford.

Fabric Printing & Dyeing at Home. Georgina Alexander. (Illus.). 80p. 1976. 20.00 (ISBN 0-7135-1893-6). Transatlantic.

Fabric Science. 4th ed. Joseph Pizzuto. Rev. By Arthur Price & Alan Cohen. (Illus.). 1980. ring-binder, wkbk. 14.50 (ISBN 0-87005-265-9). Fairchild.

Fabricated Foods. Ed. by George E. Inglett. (Illus.). 395p. 1975. lib. bdg. 25.00 (ISBN 0-87055-179-5). AVI.

Fabricated Man: The Ethics of Genetic Control. Paul Ramsey. LC 78-123395. 1970. 12.00x (ISBN 0-300-01373-6); pap. 3.45x (ISBN 0-300-01374-4, YF6). Yale U Pr.

Fabrication of Water Reactor Fuel Elements. 1978. pap. 70.75 (ISBN 9-2005-0079-X, ISP499, IAEA). Unipub.

Fabriche E I Disegni Di Palladio. Ottavio B. Sgamozzi. Date not set. 22.95 (ISBN 0-8038-0079-7). Hastings.

Fabricopedia. J. Hayward. (Illus.). 1974. 1.45 o.p. (ISBN 0-684-14048-9, SL563, ScribT). Scribner.

Fabrics & Threads for Schools. Anne Coleman. 1977. 17.95 (ISBN 0-7134-0187-7, Pub. by Batsford England). David & Charles.

Fabrics for Clothing. Eleanor J. Gawne. (gr. 10-12). 1973. pap. text ed. 4.60 (ISBN 0-87002-149-4). Bennett IL.

Fabrics for Historic Buildings. 2nd ed. Jane C. Nylander. LC 80-18918. (Illus.). 68p. 1980. pap. 6.95 (ISBN 0-89133-081-X). Preservation Pr.

Fabrics of Culture: The Anthology of Clothing & Adornment. Ed. by Justine Cordwell & Ronald A. Schwartz. (World Anthropology Ser.). 1979. text ed. 63.50x (ISBN 90-279-7910-3). Mouton.

Fabulacion De Enea-the Keeper of the Flame. Gladys Zaldivar. Tr. by Elias L. Rivers from Eng. & Span. (Coleccion Vortex). 67p. pap. 14.95 (ISBN 0-89729-200-6). Ediciones.

Fabularum Liber. Hyginus et al. LC 75-27848. (Renaissance & the Gods Ser.: Vol. 6). 1976. Repr. of 1535 ed. lib. bdg. 73.00 (ISBN 0-8240-2055-3). Garland Pub.

Fabulas De Iriarte. (Span.). 8.95 (ISBN 84-241-5418-5). E Torres & Sons.

Fabulas de Samaniego. (Span.). 8.95 (ISBN 84-241-5621-8). E Torres & Sons.

Fabulas Ilustradas. (Span.). 8.95 (ISBN 84-241-5414-2). E Torres & Sons.

Fabulous Cars of the 1920s & 1930s. Richard L. Knudson. LC 80-343. (Superwheels & Thrill Sports Bks.). (Illus.). (gr. 4 up). 1981. PLB 6.95 (ISBN 0-8225-0504-5). Lerner Pubns.

Fabulous Creature. Zilpha K. Snyder. LC 80-18977. 252p. (gr. 5-9). 1981. PLB 9.95 (ISBN 0-689-30829-9). Atheneum.

Fabulous Fireball. D. S. Halacy, Jr. (Illus.). (gr. 7 up). 1957. 4.95g o.s.i. (ISBN 0-02-741340-3). Macmillan.

Fabulous Fondue Cookbook. Carmel B. Reingold & William I. Kaufman. (Orig.). 1970. pap. 1.50 o.s.i. (ISBN 0-515-02311-6, V2311). Jove Pubns.

Fabulous Food Processor. Judith Gethers. 384p. (Orig.). 1981. pap. 7.95 (ISBN 0-345-29586-2). Ballantine.

Fabulous Fox: An Anthology of Fact & Fiction. Johanna Johnston. LC 78-21031. (Illus.). (gr. 5 up). 1979. 5.95 (ISBN 0-396-07652-1). Dodd.

Fabulous Histories, Designed for the Instruction of Children, Respecting Their Treatment of Animals, Repr. Of 1786 Ed. Sarah Trimmer. Bd. with Dairyman's Daughter. Legh Richmond. Repr. of 1810 ed. LC 75-32147. (Classics of Children's Literature, 1621-1932: Vol. 13). 1976. PLB 38.00 (ISBN 0-8240-2261-0). Garland Pub.

Fabulous Investment Potential of Singles. 4th, rev. ed. Don Bale, Jr. 1980. pap. 5.00. Bale Bks.

Fabulous Investment Potential of Liberty Walking Half Dollars. rev. 3rd ed. Don Bale, Jr. 1975. pap. 5.00 o.p. (ISBN 0-912070-05-6). Bale Bks.

Fabulous Investment Potential of Liberty Walking Half Dollars. 4th, rev. ed. Ed. by Don Bale, Jr. 1980. pap. 5.00. Bale Bks.

Fabulous Investment Potential of Singles. rev. 3rd ed. Don Bale, Jr. 1975. pap. 5.00 o.p. (ISBN 0-912070-13-7). Bale Bks.

Fabulous Investment Potential of Uncirculated Singles. rev. 3rd ed. Don Bale, Jr. 1975. pap. 5.00 o.p. (ISBN 0-912070-11-0). Bale Bks.

Fabulous Investment Potential of Uncirculated Singles. 4th, rev. ed. Don Bale, Jr. 1980. pap. 5.00. Bale Bks.

Fabulous Manticora. Josephine Lee. LC 75-25784. 1976. 6.95 o.p. (ISBN 0-381-99619-0, JD-J). John Day.

Fabulous Riverboat. Philip J. Farmer. 256p. 1973. pap. 2.25 (ISBN 0-425-04817-9, Medallion). Berkley Pub.

Fabulous Voyage of the Pegasus. Hugh Popham. LC 59-6591. (Illus.). (gr. 4-8). 1959. 7.95 (ISBN 0-87599-092-4). S G Phillips.

Face at the Brillstone Window. Florence P. Heide & Roxanne Heide. Ed. by Kathy Pucini. LC 78-15060. (Pilot Bks). (Illus.). (gr. 4-9). 1979. 6.95g (ISBN 0-8075-2216-3). A Whitman.

Face at the Window. Annie Mueser. (Pal Paperbacks, - Pal Skills II Ser.). (Illus.). (gr. 5-12). 1980. pap. text ed. 1.25 (ISBN 0-8374-6808-6). Xerox Ed Pubns.

Face in the Portrait. Rosemary Carter. (Harlequin Presents Ser.). 192p. (Orig.). 1981. pap. 1.50 (ISBN 0-373-10410-3, Pub. by Harlequin). PB.

Face Language. Robert Whiteside. LC 74-4418. 1974. 9.95 (ISBN 0-8119-0231-5). Fell.

Face Lifting by Exercise. 9th ed. Senta M. Runge. LC 56-6321. (Illus.). 1977. Repr. of 1961 ed. 16.00 (ISBN 0-9601042-1-6). Allegro Pub.

Face Lifts for All Seasons. Anne Marx. 1980. 7.00 (ISBN 0-8233-0322-5). Golden Quill.

Face of a Hero. Pierre Boulle. LC 56-12030. 1956. 8.95 (ISBN 0-8149-0070-4). Vanguard.

Face of Black Music. Valerie Wilmer. LC 76-18115. (Photography Ser.). 1976. lib. bdg. 18.50 (ISBN 0-306-70756-X); pap. 7.95 (ISBN 0-306-80039-X). Da Capo.

Face of Chalk. Melissa Davies. 1977. pap. 1.50 o.p. (ISBN 0-445-04008-4). Popular Lib.

Face of China: As Seen by Photographers & Travelers, 1860 to 1912. Commentary by Nigel Cameron. (Illus.). 1980. pap. 14.95 o.p. (ISBN 0-89381-031-2). Aperture.

Face of China As Seen by Photographers or Travelers: 1860-1930. Nigel Cameron. LC 78-53932. (Illus.). 1978. 25.00 (ISBN 0-89381-029-0); pap. 14.95 (ISBN 0-89381-031-2). Aperture.

Face of Emotion. Carroll E. Izard. (Century Psychology Ser.). (Illus.). 1981. Repr. of 1971 ed. text ed. 24.50x (ISBN 0-8290-0059-3). Irvington.

Face of Fear. Brian Coffey. 1978. pap. 1.95 o.p. (ISBN 0-345-27117-3). Ballantine.

Face of Man: Expressions of Uniersal Emotion in a New Guinea Village. Paul Ekman. LC 79-12934. 154p. 1980. lib. bdg. 25.00 (ISBN 0-8240-7130-1). Garland Pub.

Face of North America: The Natural History of a Continent. Peter Farb. (YA) 1963. 12.50 o.s.i. (ISBN 0-06-070746-1, HarpT). Har-Row.

Face of Rock & Roll. Bruce Pollock & John Wagman. LC 78-2402. (Illus.). 1978. pap. 12.95 o.p. (ISBN 0-03-042871-8). HR&W.

Face of the Ancient Orient. Sabatino Moscati. pap. 2.95 (ISBN 0-385-01397-3, A289, Anch). Doubleday.

Face of the Deep. Bruce C. Heezen & Charles D. Hollister. 1971. pap. 13.95x (ISBN 0-19-501277-1). Oxford U Pr.

Face of the Earth: Frontality in Two-Dimensional Mesoamerican Art. Cecilia F. Klein. LC 75-23799. (Outstanding Dissertations in the Fine Arts - Native American Art). (Illus.). 1976. lib. bdg. 41.00 (ISBN 0-8240-1994-6). Garland Pub.

Face on the Cutting Room Floor: The Story of Music & Television Censorship. Murray Schumach. LC 73-19776. (Civil Liberties in American History Ser.). (Illus.). 306p. 1974. Repr. of 1956 ed. lib. bdg. 19.50 (ISBN 0-306-70603-2). Da Capo.

Face Out Front. R. R. Irvine. (Orig.). 1977. pap. 1.25 o.p. (ISBN 0-445-00449-5). Popular Lib.

Face the Nation: The Collected Transcripts from the CBS Radio & Television Broadcasts, 1954-1978, 21 vols. Incl. Vol. 1, 1954-1955. 465p (ISBN 0-03-941431-0); Vol. 2, 1956. 418p (ISBN 0-03-091432-9); Vol. 3, 1957. 443p (ISBN 0-03-091433-7); Vol. 4, 1958. 409p (ISBN 0-03-091434-5); Vol. 5, 1959. 420p (ISBN 0-03-091435-3); Vol. 6, 1960-1961. 499p (ISBN 0-03-091436-1); Vol. 7, 1963-1964. 435p (ISBN 0-03-091437-X); Vol. 8, 1965. 316p (ISBN 0-03-091438-8); Vol. 9, 1966. 344p (ISBN 0-03-091439-6); Vol. 10, 1967. 390p (ISBN 0-03-091440-X); Vol. 11, 1968. 384p (ISBN 0-03-091441-8); Vol. 12, 1969. 353p (ISBN 0-03-091442-6); Vol. 13, 1970. 393p (ISBN 0-03-091443-4); Vol. 14, 1971. 416p (ISBN 0-03-091445-0); Vol. 15, 1972. 418p (ISBN 0-8108-0822-6); Vol. 16, 1973. 398p (ISBN 0-8108-0823-4); Vol. 17, 1974. 375p (ISBN 0-8108-0824-2); Vol. 18, 1975. 382p (ISBN 0-8108-0916-8); Vol. 19, 1976. 382p (ISBN 0-8108-1021-2); Vol. 20, 1977. 371p (ISBN 0-8108-1021-2); Vol. 21, 1978. 365p (ISBN 0-8108-1021-2). 29.50 ea. Microfilming Corp.

Face to Face. Frank M. Cortina. LC 76-184745. 250p. 1972. 20.00x (ISBN 0-231-03635-3). Columbia U Pr.

Face to Face. Ved Mehta. LC 57-9323. 1978. pap. 4.95 (ISBN 0-19-520014-4, GB537, GB). Oxford U Pr.

Face to Face Classroom Sets, Nos. 1-2. 1969-70. 40.00 ea. o.p. (ISBN 0-02-734460-6, CCPr); No. 1. (ISBN 0-685-27123-4, 73446); No. 2. (ISBN 0-02-734550-5, 73455). Macmillan.

Face-to-Face Interaction: Research, Methods, & Theory. S. Duncan & D. W. Fiske. LC 77-1841. 1977. 18.50 o.p. (ISBN 0-470-99113-5). Halsted Pr.

Face to Face to Face: An Experiment in Intimacy. Gordon Clanton & Chris Downing. 256p. 1976. pap. 1.95 o.p. (ISBN 0-345-25116-4). Ballantine.

Face: What It Means. Margaret W. Buck. LC 78-56844. 1980. 7.95 (ISBN 0-87212-138-0); pap. 4.95 (ISBN 0-87212-106-2). Libra.

Faced with Love. Adrianne Marcus. (Illus., Orig.). 1978. pap. 4.50 (ISBN 0-914278-13-4). Copper Beech.

Facelift Without Surgery: A Four Point Program to Maintain a Youthful Face. Ruth Jody & Vicki Lindner. LC 78-21474. 1979. 9.95 (ISBN 0-397-01313-2). Lippincott.

Faces About the Cross. Clovis G. Chappell. (Glovis Chappell Library). pap. 3.95 (ISBN 0-8010-2364-5). Baker Bk.

Faces in My Time. Anthony Powell. LC 80-14843. (No. 3). (Illus.). 256p. 1981. 14.95 (ISBN 0-03-021001-1). HR&W.

Faces in the City. James Kavanaugh. 1972. 6.95 (ISBN 0-87690-164-X). Dutton.

Faces in the Water. Janet Frame. 1961. 4.95 o.s.i. (ISBN 0-8076-0149-7). Braziller.

Faces in the Water. Phyllis Naylor. LC 80-24057. 180p. (gr. 6 up). 1981. PLB 9.95 (ISBN 0-689-30823-X). Atheneum.

Faces of Findhorn: Images of a Planetary Family. Ed. by Findhorn Community. LC 78-20160. (Illus.). 192p. 1980. 12.95 (ISBN 0-06-011268-9, HarpT). Har-Row.

Faces of Germany: An Introduction to the German People. Margaret Wightman. (Illus.). 1971. 14.95x (ISBN 0-245-50399-4). Intl Ideas.

Faces of Hollywood. Clarence S. Bull. LC 68-27205. (Illus.). 1968. 4.98 o.p. (ISBN 0-498-06844-7, Encore). A S Barnes.

Faces of Nature: Fashioned by God. Florence H. Roddy. 96p. 1980. 3.95 (ISBN 0-8059-2759-X). Dorrance.

Faces of Power: Constancy & Change in U.S. Foreign Policy from Truman to Johnson. Seyom Brown. 1968. 20.00x (ISBN 0-231-03089-4); pap. 7.50x (ISBN 0-231-08597-4). Columbia U Pr.

Facets. Dorothy Sinha. 8.00 (ISBN 0-89253-739-6); flexible cloth 4.80 (ISBN 0-89253-740-X). Ind-US Inc.

Facets of Genetics: Readings from Scientific American. Intro. by Adrian Srb et al. LC 78-99047. 1970. pap. text ed. 9.95x (ISBN 0-7167-0949-X). W H Freeman.

Facets of Hellenic Life. John Scarborough. LC 75-29704. (Illus.). 320p. 1976. pap. text ed. 14.25 (ISBN 0-395-20368-6). HM.

Facets of Plato's Philosophy. Ed. by W. H. Werkmeister. 1976. pap. text ed. 21.75x (ISBN 90-232-1362-9). Humanities.

Facets of Prayer. F. Bakker. Tr. by Cornelis Pronk & Fredericka Pronk. (Summit Bks.). 96p. 1981. pap. 2.45 (ISBN 0-8010-0796-8). Baker Bk.

Facets of Taoism: Essays in Chinese Religion. Ed. by Welch et al. LC 77-28034. 307p. 1981. pap. 7.95x (ISBN 0-300-02673-0). Yale U Pr.

Facets of Taoism: Essays in Chinese Religion. Ed. by Holmes Welch & Anna Seidel. LC 77-28034. 1979. 27.50x (ISBN 0-300-01695-6). Yale U Pr.

Facets of the Enlightenment: Studies in English Literature & Its Contexts. Bertrand H. Bronson. 1968. 19.50x (ISBN 0-520-00176-1). U of Cal Pr.

Facets of U.S. Interventionism. M. S. Venkatarmani. 300p. 1980. 18.50x (ISBN 0-391-01958-9). Humanities.

Facial Features in Neurologic Syndromes. Paul D. Dyken & Max D. Miller. LC 79-17012. (Illus.). 1979. text ed. 56.50 (ISBN 0-8016-1485-6). Mosby.

Facial Palsies. J. Moldaver & J. Conley. (Illus.). 272p. 1980. 35.75 (ISBN 0-398-03988-7). C C Thomas.

Facial Trauma & Concomitant Problems - Evaluation & Treatment. Ed. by William B. Irby. LC 74-524. 1974. text ed. 34.50 o.p. (ISBN 0-8016-2348-0). Mosby.

Facial Trauma & Concomitant Problems: Evaluation & Treatment. 2nd ed. William B. Irby. LC 79-15473. 1979. text ed. 39.50 (ISBN 0-8016-2349-9). Mosby.

Facilitating Children's Development: A Systematic Guide to Open Learning, 2 vols. Meier. Incl. Vol. I. Infant & Toddler Learning Episodes. 22.95 (ISBN 0-8391-1261-0); Vol. II. Learning Episodes for Older Preschoolers. 24.50 (ISBN 0-8391-1339-0). 1979. Univ Park.

Facilitating Community Change: A Basic Guide. Donald R. Fessler. LC 76-12768. 146p. 1976. pap. 11.50 (ISBN 0-88390-121-8). Univ Assocs.

Facilities in Ports for the Reception of Oil Residues: Results of an Enquiry Made in 1972. 145p. 1973. 16.50 (IMCO). Unipub.

Facilities in Ports for the Reception of Oil Residues: Results of an Enquiry Made in 1972, Supplement 1976. 27p. 1976. 7.00 (I MCO). Unipub.

Facilities in Ports for the Reception of Oily Wastes. 202p. 1980. pap. 24.75 (ISBN 92-801-1097-7, IMCO60, IMCO). Unipub.

Facilities in Sports & Physical Education. Eugene Ezersky & Richard Theibert. LC 75-46556. (Illus.). 1976. text ed. 11.95 (ISBN 0-8016-1534-8). Mosby.

Facing Death. Robert E. Kavanaugh. 1974. pap. 3.50 (ISBN 0-14-003812-4). Penguin.

Facing Death & Grief. George Marshall. 250p. 1981. 15.95 (ISBN 0-87975-140-1). Prometheus Bks.

Facing Financial Exigency. Ed. by Frank R. Kemerer & Ronald P. Satryb. LC 76-45606. (Illus.). 1977. 16.95 (ISBN 0-669-01114-2). Lexington Bks.

Facing Four. Monika Varma. (Greybird Book). 47p. 1975. 8.00 (ISBN 0-88253-758-X); pap. 4.80 (ISBN 0-88253-849-7). Ind-US Inc.

Facing Labor Issues in China. Chuan-Hua Lowe. (Studies in Chinese History & Civilization). 1977. Repr. of 1938 ed. 17.50 (ISBN 0-89093-082-1). U Pubns Amer.

Facing off, Checking, & Goaltending--Perhaps. Gary Paulsen. LC 78-21079. (Sports on the Light Side Ser.). (Illus.). (gr. 4-6). 1979. PLB 9.65 (ISBN 0-8172-0183-1). Raintree Pubs.

Facing Reality. C. L. James et al. (Illus.). 174p. 1974. pap. 3.00 (ISBN 0-935590-05-6). Bewick Edns.

Facing Terminal Illness. Mark Peachey. 72p. 1981. pap. 2.25 (ISBN 0-8361-1948-7). Herald Pr.

Facing the Chair: Story of the Americanization of Two Foreign-Born Workmen. John Dos Passos. LC 72-104066. (Civil Liberties in American History Ser). 1970. Repr. of 1927 ed. 14.95 (ISBN 0-306-71871-5). Da Capo.

Facing the Future: Church & Family Together. Ed. by Gary R. Collins. 1976. pap. 3.95 o.p. (ISBN 0-87680-845-3, 98086). Word Bks.

Facing the Gods. Hillman et al. Ed. by James Hillman. 171p. (Orig.). 1980. pap. text ed. 8.50 (ISBN 0-88214-312-3). Spring Pubns.

Facing the International Energy Problem, 1900 to 2000. Amos Jordan et al. 20.95 (ISBN 0-03-056162-0). Praeger.

Facing the Music. Harold C. Schonberg. 1981. 14.95 (ISBN 0-671-25406-5). Summit Bks.

Facing the Scalpel: What to Expect, What to Beware of When You Have an Operation. John A. MacDonald. (Illus.). 144p. 1981. 10.95 (ISBN 0-13-299198-5); pap. 4.95 (ISBN 0-13-299180-2). P-H.

Facsimile Atlas to the Early History of Cartography: Reproductions of the Most Important Maps Printed in the Fifteenth & Sixteenth Centuries. Adolf E. Nordenskiold. (Illus.). 256p. 1973. pap. text ed. 12.95 (ISBN 0-486-22964-5). Dover.

Facsimile of British Museum Ms. Harley 2253. Ed. by Neil R. Ker. (Early English Text Society Ser.). 1965. 29.50x o.p. (ISBN 0-19-722255-2). Oxford U Pr.

Facsimiles of Two Papers by Bayes, 2 vols. in 1. Thomas Bayes. Ed. by W. Edwards Deming. 1963. 7.50 o.s.i. (ISBN 0-02-841120-X). Hafner.

Fact & Comment. Malcolm S. Forbes. 1974. 7.95 o.p. (ISBN 0-394-49187-4). Knopf.

Fact & Fancy in International Economic Relations: An Essay on International Monetary Reform. Thomas Balogh. LC 73-7993. 132p. 1973. text ed. 19.50 (ISBN 0-08-017740-9). Pergamon.

Fact & Fiction in B. F. Skinner's & Utopia. R. Puligandla. LC 73-21001. 114p. 1974. 10.00 (ISBN 0-87527-130-8). Green.

Fact & Relevance: Essays on Historical Method. M. M. Postan. 1971. 26.95 (ISBN 0-521-07841-5). Cambridge U Pr.

Fact & Symbol: Essays in the Sociology of Art & Literature. Cesar Grana. 1971. 12.95 (ISBN 0-19-501285-2). Oxford U Pr.

Fact Book for Academic Administrators 1980. Ed. by Charles J. Anderson. 1980. 25.00 (ISBN 0-8268-1197-3). ACE.

Fact Book on Higher Education in the South: Nineteen Seventy-Nine & Nineteen Eighty. rev. ed. Steven S. Smartt. 1980. pap. 3.50. S Regional Ed.

Fact Book on Higher Education in the South: 1977 & 1978. rev. ed. James R. Mingle. 1978. pap. 3.00 o.p. (ISBN 0-686-23906-7). S Regional Ed.

Fact-Book on Hypertension, High Blood Pressure & Your Diet. Carlson Wade. LC 74-31668. (Pivot Original Health Book Ser). (Illus.). 128p. (Orig.). 1975. pap. 1.95 (ISBN 0-87983-095-6). Keats.

Fact-Book on Vitamins & Other Food Supplements. Carlson Wade. LC 72-86040. (Pivot Original Health Book). 128p. 1972. pap. 1.50 (ISBN 0-87983-028-X). Keats.

Fact, Fancy & Fable. Henry Reddall. LC 68-25519. 1968. Repr. of 1889 ed. 18.00 (ISBN 0-8103-3093-8). Gale.

Fact, Fantasy, Folklore. Greta Lipson. (gr. 3-12). 1977. 9.95 (ISBN 0-916456-11-0, GA71). Good Apple.

Fact into Fiction: English Literature & the Industrial Scene 1750-1850. Ivanka Kovacevic. 416p. 1975. text ed. 16.00x (ISBN 0-7185-1130-1, Leicester). Humanities.

Fact of Literature: Three Essays on Public Material. Frederic Will. 215p. (Orig.). 1973. pap. text ed. 20.00x (ISBN 9-0620-3377-6). Humanities.

Faction & Parliament: Essays in Early Stuart History. Ed. by Kevin Sharpe. LC 77-30635. 1978. 33.00x (ISBN 0-19-822468-0). Oxford U Pr.

Factional Politics in an Indian State: The Congress Party in Uttar Pradesh. Paul R. Brass. 1965. 20.00x (ISBN 0-520-00167-2). U of Cal Pr.

Factious People: Politics & Society in Colonial New York. Patricia U. Bonomi. LC 74-156803. 1971. 20.00x (ISBN 0-231-03509-8); pap. 7.50x (ISBN 0-231-08329-7). Columbia U Pr.

Factor Analysis & Measurement in Sociological Research: A Multi-Dimensional Perspective. Ed. by David J. Jackson & Edgar F. Borgatta. (Sage Studies in International Sociology: Vol. 21). 320p. 1981. 20.00 (ISBN 0-8039-9814-7) (ISBN 0-8039-9815-5). Sage.

Factor Analytic Studies: 1941-1975, 5 vols. Sukit Hinman & Brian Bolton. Set. 32.50 (ISBN 0-686-64136-1). Whitston Pub.

Factorial Design. B. L. Raktoe et al. (Wiley Series in Probability & Mathematical Statistics). 250p. 1981. 23.95 (ISBN 0-471-09040-9, Pub. by Wiley-Interscience). Wiley.

Factors Affecting Calf Crop. Ed. by Tony J. Cunha et al. LC 66-22000. (Illus.). 1967. 16.00 (ISBN 0-8130-0053-X). U Presses Fla.

Factors Affecting Medical Services Utilization: A Behavioral Approach. Terence F. Kelly & George J. Schieber. 1972. pap. 3.50 o.p. (ISBN 0-87766-036-0, 21000). Urban Inst.

Factors Affecting the Action of Narcotics. Ed. by M. W. Adler et al. LC 78-2999. (Monographs of the Mario Negri Institute for Pharmacological Research). 1978. 49.00 (ISBN 0-89004-272-1). Raven.

Factors Affecting the Use & Non-Use of Contraception Findings from a Comparative Analysis of Selected KAP Surveys. (Population Studies: No. 69). 109p. 1979. pap. 9.00 (ISBN 0-686-68956-9, UN79/13/6, UN). Unipub.

Factors in Depression. Ed. by Nathan S. Kline. LC 74-77571. 1974. 24.50 (ISBN 0-911216-79-0). Raven.

Factors in the Location of Florida Industry. M. L. Greenhut & Marshall R. Colberg. LC 62-63440. (FSU Studies: No. 36). (Illus.). 108p. 1962. 5.25 (ISBN 0-8130-0649-X). U Presses Fla.

Factors in the Selection of Marine Machinery & Plant with Particular Reference to Reliability, Maintenance & Cost. Institute of Marine Engineers. (Illus.). 104p. 1972. limp bdg. 15.00x (ISBN 0-900976-91-8, Pub. by Inst Marine Eng). Intl Schol Bk Serv.

Factors Influencing the Economical Application of Food Irradiation. (Illus.). 137p. (Orig.). 1973. pap. 9.25 (ISBN 92-0-111373-0, IAEA). Unipub.

Factors of Growth & Investment Policies: An International Approach. United Nations Economic Commission for Europe. 1978. pap. 23.00 (ISBN 0-08-021992-6). Pergamon.

Factors Related to the Professional Development of Librarians. Elizabeth W. Stone. LC 75-7741. (Illus.). 1969. 10.00 (ISBN 0-8108-0274-0). Scarecrow.

Factors Relevant to the Decommissioning of Land-Based Nuclear Reactor Plants. (Safety Ser.: No. 52). 28p. 1981. pap. 4.75 (ISBN 0-686-69440-6, ISP 541, IAEA). Unipub.

Factors Used to Increase the Susceptibility of Individuals to Forceful Indoctrination; Observations & Experiments, Vol. 3. Group for the Advancement of Psychiatry. (Symposium: No. 3). 1956. pap. 2.00 (ISBN 0-87318-043-7). Adv Psychiatry.

Factory. Antler. LC 80-25727. (Pocket Poets Ser.: No. 38). (Orig.). 1980. 8.50 (ISBN 0-87286-123-6); pap. 3.00 (ISBN 0-87286-122-8). City Lights.

Factory Management. K. G. Lockyer. 24.50x (ISBN 0-392-07793-0, SpS). Soccer.

Factory Organization & Management. N. F. Saunders. 24.50x (ISBN 0-392-07812-0, SpS). Soccer.

Factory Outlet Shopping Guide for New Jersey & Rockland County-1980. Jean D. Bird. 1979. pap. 2.95 o.p. (ISBN 0-913464-43-0). FOSG Pubns.

Factory Outlet Shopping Guide for New York City-Westchester-Long Island-1980. Jean D. Bird. 1979. pap. text ed. 2.95 o.p. (ISBN 0-913464-44-9). FOSG Pubns.

Factory Outlet Shopping Guide for North & South Carolina-1980. Jean D. Bird. 1979. pap. 2.95 o.p. (ISBN 0-913464-46-5). FOSG Pubns.

Factory Outlet Shopping Guide for Pennsylvania, 1980. 1979. pap. 2.95 o.p. (ISBN 0-913464-48-1). FOSG Pubns.

Factory Outlet Shopping Guide for Washington D. C.-Maryland-Virginia-Delaware-1980. Jean D. Bird. 1979. pap. 2.95 o.p. (ISBN 0-913464-45-7). FOSG Pubns.

Factory System Illustrated. William Dodd. LC 67-28260. (Illus.). Repr. of 1842 ed. 24.00x (ISBN 0-678-05043-0). Kelley.

Factotum. Charles Bukowski. 200p. 1980. 14.00 (ISBN 0-87685-264-9); pap. 6.00 (ISBN 0-87685-263-0). Black Sparrow.

Facts About Aging. Daniel S. Liang. 120p. 1973. pap. 6.75 (ISBN 0-398-02727-7). C C Thomas.

Facts About "Drug Abuse". The Drug Abuse Council. LC 79-54668. (Illus.). 1980. 14.95 (ISBN 0-02-907720-6). Free Pr.

Facts About Finland. A. Benz. 1976. pap. 4.50x (ISBN 9-5110-4105-3, F525). Vanous.

Facts About Furs. rev. ed. Great Nilsson et al. Tr. by Animal Welfare Institute. LC 80-65265. (Illus.). 257p. 1980. pap. text ed. 3.00 (ISBN 0-938414-02-X). Animal Welfare.

Facts About Israel. 2nd ed. Ed. by Hanan Sher. LC 55-19995. (Illus.). 232p. (Orig.). 1978. pap. 5.00x (ISBN 0-8002-2247-4). Intl Pubns Serv.

Facts About Lutherans. Albert P. Stauderman. 1959. pap. 0.65 (ISBN 0-8006-1832-7, 1-1832). Fortress.

Facts About Syphilis & Gonorrhea, 2 bks. (gr. 10-12). 1972. pap. text ed. 6.00 each (ISBN 0-8449-1228-X). Learning Line.

Facts About the Fifty States. rev. ed. Sue R. Brandt. (First Bks.). (Illus.). (gr. 4 up). 1979. PLB 6.45 s&l (ISBN 0-531-02899-2). Watts.

Facts About the Human Body. Marianne Tully & Mary A. Tully. (First Bks.). (Illus.). (gr. 4-6). 1977. PLB 6.45 s&l (ISBN 0-531-00395-7). Watts.

Facts About the Presidents. 4th ed. Joseph M. Kane. 1981. write for info. (ISBN 0-8242-0013-6). Wilson.

Facts About the Presidents. 3rd ed. Joseph N. Kane. 1974. 15.00 o.p. (ISBN 0-8242-0538-3). Wilson.

Facts & Artifacts of Ancient Middle America: A Glossary of Terms & Words Used in the Archaeology & Art History of Pre-Columbian Mexico & Central America. Compiled by Curt Muser. 1978. 16.95 o.p. (ISBN 0-525-10215-9); pap. 9.95 o.p. (ISBN 0-525-47489-7). Dutton.

Facts & Fancies for the Curious from the Harvest-Fields of Literature. Ed. by Charles C. Bombaugh. LC 68-23464. 1968. Repr. of 1905 ed. 15.00 (ISBN 0-8103-3085-7). Gale.

Facts & Fantasies About Alcohol. Shirley Schwarzrock & C. Gilbert Wrenn. (Coping with Ser.). (Illus.). (gr. 7-12). 1971. pap. text ed. 1.30 (ISBN 0-913476-13-7). Am Guidance.

Facts & Fantasies About Drugs. Shirley Schwarzrock & C. Gilbert Wrenn. (Coping with Ser.). (Illus.). (gr. 6-9). 1970. pap. text ed. 1.30 (ISBN 0-913476-12-9). Am Guidance.

Facts & Fantasies About Smoking. Shirley Schwarzrock & C. Gilbert Wrenn. (Coping with Ser.). (Illus.). 40p. (gr. 7-12). 1971. pap. text ed. 1.30 (ISBN 0-913476-14-5). Am Guidance.

Facts & Feelings in the Classroom. Louis J. Rubin. LC 77-186190. 224p. 1973. 8.95 (ISBN 0-8027-0382-8); pap. 4.50 o.s.i. (ISBN 0-8027-7087-8). Walker & Co.

Facts & Figures: A Layman's Guide to Conducting Surveys. Bill Burges. 125p. (Orig.). 1976. pap. text ed. 4.25 (ISBN 0-917754-02-6). Inst Responsive.

Facts & Observations Relative to the Influence on Manufactures Upon Health & Life. David Noble. 81p. 1971. Repr. of 1843 ed. 13.00x (ISBN 0-686-28333-3, Pub. by Irish Academic Pr). Biblio Dist.

Facts for a Change: Citizen Action Research for a Better Schools. Bill Burges. 125p. (Orig.). 1976. pap. text ed. 5.00 (ISBN 0-917754-03-4). Inst Responsive.

Facts, Frauds, & Phantasms: A Survey of the Spiritualist Movement. McHargue, Georgess (Compiler) LC 73-180090. 312p. (gr. 6-9). 1972. PLB 4.95 o.p. (ISBN 0-385-05305-3). Doubleday.

Facts of Baccarat. rev. ed. Walter I. Nolan. 1976. pap. 1.50 (ISBN 0-89650-018-7). Gamblers.

Facts of Blackjack. rev. ed. Walter I. Nolan. 1976. pap. 1.50 (ISBN 0-89650-019-5). Gamblers.

Facts of Craps. rev. ed. Walter I. Nolan. 1976. pap. 1.50 (ISBN 0-89650-020-9). Gamblers.

Facts of Roulette. Walter I. Nolan. 1970. pap. 1.50 (ISBN 0-89650-022-5). Gamblers.

Facts of Slots. Walter I. Nolan. 1970. pap. 1.50 (ISBN 0-89650-023-3). Gamblers.

Facts on File: Dictionary of Astronomy. John Daintith. (Illus.). 1979. 17.50 (ISBN 0-87196-326-4). Facts on File.

Facts on File Dictionary of Biology. Ed. by John Daintith. 288p. 1981. 14.95 (ISBN 0-87196-510-0). Facts on File.

Facts on File Dictionary of Chemistry. Ed. by John Daintith. 224p. 1981. 14.95 (ISBN 0-87196-513-5). Facts on File.

Facts on File Dictionary of Mathematics. Ed. by John Daintith. 224p. 1981. prepub. 14.95 (ISBN 0-87196-512-7). Facts on File.

Facts on File Dictionary of Physics. Ed. by John Daintith. 248p. 1981. 14.95 (ISBN 0-87196-511-9). Facts on File.

Facts, Values & Ethics. James H. Olthius. 1968. pap. text ed. 18.00x (ISBN 9-0232-0487-5). Humanities.

Facts, Words & Beliefs. L. S. Sprigge. (International Library of Philosophy & Scientific Method). 1970. text ed. 15.00x (ISBN 0-391-00069-1). Humanities.

Faculty & Teacher Bargaining: The Impact of Unions on Education. Ed. by George W. Angell. LC 80-8769. 1981. write for info. (ISBN 0-669-04360-5). Lexington Bks.

Faculty Bargaining: Change & Conflict. Carnegie Commission on Higher Education. 1975. 14.50 o.p. (ISBN 0-07-010111-6, P&RB). McGraw.

Faculty Development Through Workshops. Carole J. Bland. 232p. 1980. text ed. 15.50 (ISBN 0-398-03940-2); pap. 11.50 (ISBN 0-398-04002-8). C C Thomas.

Faculty Involvement in Library Instruction. Ed. by H. Rader. LC 76-21914. (Library Orientation Ser.: No. 6). 1976. 10.00 (ISBN 0-87650-070-X). Pierian.

Fading Partnership, America & Europe After Thirty Years. Simon Serfaty. LC 78-19755. 128p. 1979. 19.95 (ISBN 0-03-041816-X). Praeger.

Fads: America's Crazes, Fevers & Fancies from the 1890s to the 1970s. Peter L. Skolnik et al. LC 77-886. (Illus.). 1978. 9.95 o.p. (ISBN 0-690-01215-2, TYC-T); pap. 5.95 o.p. (ISBN 0-690-01216-0, TYC-T). T Y Crowell.

Fads & Fancies. Deny Sutton. LC 79-64887. (Illus.). 240p. 1980. 25.00 (ISBN 0-8390-0263-7). Allanheld & Schram.

Fads & Foibles in Modern Sociology & Related Sciences. Pitirim Sorokin. LC 76-154. 357p. 1976. Repr. of 1956 ed. lib. bdg. 26.75x (ISBN 0-8371-8733-8, SOFF). Greenwood.

Faerie Queene, 2 Vols. Edmund Spenser. Ed. by J. C. Smith. (Oxford English Texts Ser.). 1909. 89.00x (ISBN 0-19-811824-4). Oxford U Pr.

Faerie Queene: The Mutability Cantos & Selections from the Minor Poems, Bks. 1 & 2. Edmund Spenser. Ed. by Robert L. Kellogg & Oliver L. Steele. LC 65-22702. (Orig.). 1965. pap. 9.95 (ISBN 0-672-63034-6). Odyssey Pr.

Fagothey's Right & Reason: Ethics in Theory & Practice. 7th ed. Milton Gonsalves. 630p. 1981. text ed. 19.95 (ISBN 0-8016-1541-0). Mosby.

Fail Safe Investing: How to Make Money with Less Than Ten Thousand Dollars...Without Losing Sleep. Peter Nagan. 192p. 1981. 9.95 (ISBN 0-399-12616-3). Putnam.

Failed Promise of Nuclear Power: The Story of Light Water. Irvin C. Bupp & Jean-Claude Derian. LC 77-20419. (Illus.). 241p. 1981. pap. 5.95 (ISBN 0-465-02273-1). Basic.

Failure Diagnoses & Performance Monitoring. Pau. Date not set. price not set (ISBN 0-8247-1018-5). Dekker.

Failure in Polymers: Molecular Phenomenological Aspects. (Advances in Polymer Science Ser.: Vol. 27). (Illus.). 1978. 37.80 (ISBN 0-387-08829-6). Springer-Verlag.

Failure of a Revolution. Sebastian Haffner. LC 72-373. 221p. 1973. 10.95 o.p. (ISBN 0-912050-23-3, Library Pr). Open Court.

Failure of Democracy in South Korea. Sungjoo Han. 1974. 18.50x (ISBN 0-520-02437-0). U of Cal Pr.

Failure of Liberalism in Japan: Shedehara Kijuro's Encounter with Anti-Liberals. Toru Takemoto. LC 78-68695. 1979. pap. text ed. 10.50 (ISBN 0-8191-0698-4). U Pr of Amer.

Failure of Materials in Mechanical Design: Analysis, Prediction, Prevention. J. A. Collins. 700p. 1981. 25.00 (ISBN 0-471-05024-5, Pub. by Wiley-Interscience). Wiley.

Failure of Modern Art As an Aesthetic Instrument for the Emotional & Moral Uplifting of Mankind. Virgil De Leon. (Illus.). 1978. deluxe bdg. 37.50 (ISBN 0-930582-00-4). Gloucester Art.

Failure of the American Democracy: Degenerative Forces in Contemporary United States Society. enl ed. Spencer Fleming. LC 72-88744. (Illus.). 65p. 1973. 37.50 (ISBN 0-913314-13-7). Am Classical Coll Pr.

Failure of the Franklin National Bank. Joan E. Spero. LC 79-18851. 1980. 17.50 (ISBN 0-231-04788-6). Columbia U Pr.

Failure of the Greatest 20th Century Conspiracy for the Economic & Political Restructuring of the World: The Unexpected, Incredible Developments Resulting from Such a Failure. Elliot Wilcox. (Illus.). 207p. 1976. 55.00 (ISBN 0-89266-003-1). Am Classical Coll Pr.

Failure of the NRA. Bernard Bellush. (Norton Essays in American History Ser). 197p. 1976. 8.95x (ISBN 0-393-05548-5); pap. 4.95x (ISBN 0-393-09223-2). Norton.

Failure of the Prussian Reform Movement, 1807-1819. Walter M. Simon. LC 73-80591. 1971. Repr. 17.00 (ISBN 0-86527-062-7). Fertig.

Failure of the Sexual Revolution. George Frankl. 190p. 1974. text ed. 6.75x o.p. (ISBN 0-900707-35-6). Humanities.

Failure of U.S. Energy Policy. Richard Mancke. 1974. 15.00x (ISBN 0-231-03787-2); pap. 6.00x (ISBN 0-231-03853-4). Columbia U Pr.

Failure of World Monetary Reform, 1971-74. John Williamson. LC 77-71278. 221p. 1977. 15.00x (ISBN 0-8147-9173-5); pap. 6.00x (ISBN 0-8147-9174-3). NYU Pr.

Failure: The Back Door to Success-Leader's Guide. Joe Ragont. pap. 3.95 (ISBN 0-8024-2517-8). Moody.

Failures in Organization Development & Change: Cases & Essays for Learning. Philip H. Mirvis & David N. Berg. LC 77-21625. 1977. 29.95 (ISBN 0-471-02405-8). Ronald Pr.

Failures of Criticism. rev. ed. Henri Peyre. Orig. Title: Writers & Their Critics. 363p. (Orig.). 1944. 15.00x (ISBN 0-8014-0335-9); pap. 4.95 (ISBN 0-8014-9055-3, CP55). Cornell U Pr.

Faint-Hearted Felon. Pauline Pryor. (Candlelight Romance Ser.). (Orig.). Date not set. pap. 1.50 (ISBN 0-440-12506-5). Dell.

Faint Spirits. George Feldman. (Illus.). 1981. pap. 6.95 (ISBN 0-89407-036-3). Strawberry Hill.

Faint Trails: An Introduction to the Fundamentals of Adult Adoptee/Birth Parent Reunification Searches. Hal Aigner. 104p. (Orig.). 1980. pap. 4.95 (ISBN 0-937572-00-4). Paradigm Pr.

Fair American. Elizabeth Coatsworth. (Illus.). (gr. 3-7). 1968. 3.95g o.s.i. (ISBN 0-02-720270-4). Macmillan.

Fair Annie of Old Mule Hollow. Beverly C. Crook. (YA) (gr. 7 up). 1979. pap. 1.95 (ISBN 0-380-49007-2, 49007). Avon.

Fair Blows the Wind. Louis L'Amour. 1978. 7.95 o.p. (ISBN 0-525-10260-4). Dutton.

Fair Competition: The Law & Economics of Antitrust Policy. Joel B. Dirlam. LC 73-100157. Repr. of 1954 ed. lib. bdg. 18.75x (ISBN 0-8371-2971-0, DIFC). Greenwood.

Fair Day & Another Step Begun. Katie L. Lyle. LC 73-17014. 160p. (gr. 7 up). 1974. 8.95 (ISBN 0-397-31500-7). Lippincott.

Fair Employment Interviewing. Jean L. Rogers & Walter L. Fortson. LC 76-1747. 128p. 1976. text ed. 8.95 (ISBN 0-201-06469-3). A-W.

Fair Game. George Bartram, pseud. LC 73-7356. 250p. 1973. 6.95 o.s.i. (ISBN 0-02-507580-2). Macmillan.

Fair Game: A History of Hunting, Shooting & Animal Conservation. Erich Hobusch. Tr. by Ruth Michaelis-Jena & Patrick Murray. LC 80-19008. (Illus.). 280p. 1981. 29.95 (ISBN 0-668-05101-9, 5101). Arco.

Fair Game? Inequality & Affirmative Action. John C. Livingston. LC 79-13422. 1979. text ed. 14.95x (ISBN 0-7167-1131-1); pap. text ed. 7.95x (ISBN 0-7167-1132-X). W H Freeman.

Fair Haven: A Work in Defence of the Miraculous Element in Our Lord's Ministry Upon Earth. Samuel Butler. Ed. by Robert L. Wolff. LC 75-1503. (Victorian Fiction Ser). 1975. Repr. of 1873 ed. lib. bdg. 66.00 (ISBN 0-8240-1578-9). Garland Pub.

Fair Housing & Exclusionary Land Use. National Committee Against Discrimination in Housing. LC 74-13552. (Research Report Ser.: No. 23). 1974. pap. text ed. free o.p. (ISBN 0-87420-323-6). Urban Land.

Fair Is My Love. Frances S. Moore. (YA) 1971. 5.95 (ISBN 0-685-23395-2, Avalon). Bouregy.

Fair Maid of the West, Parts I & II. Thomas Heywood. Ed. by Robert K. Turner, Jr. LC 67-15069. (Regents Renaissance Drama Ser). 1967. pap. 3.25x (ISBN 0-8032-5263-3, BB 226, Bison). U of Nebr Pr.

Fair Maid of the West: Pt.I, a Critical Edition. Thomas Heywood. Ed. by Brownell Salomon. (Salzburg Studies in English Literature, Jacobean Drama Studies Ser.: No. 36). 209p. 1976. pap. text ed. 25.00x (ISBN 0-391-01408-0). Humanities.

Fair Moralist; or, Love & Virtue, 1745. Charlotte McCarthy. Ed. by Michael F. Shugrue. Bd. with Case of John Nelson, Written by Himself, 1745. John Nelson. (Flowering of the Novel, 1740-1775 Ser: Vol. 16). 1974. lib. bdg. 50.00 (ISBN 0-8240-1115-5). Garland Pub.

Fair Penitent. Nicholas Rowe. Ed. by Malcolm Goldstein. LC 69-10354. (Regents Restoration Drama Ser). 1969. 5.95x (ISBN 0-8032-0367-5); pap. 1.65x (ISBN 0-8032-5367-2, BB 270, Bison). U of Nebr Pr.

Fair Penitent & Jane Shore. Nicholas Rowe. 254p. 1980. Repr. of 1907 ed. lib. bdg. 30.00 (ISBN 0-89987-714-1). Darby Bks.

Fair Play: Ethics in Sport & Education. P. C. McIntosh. 1979. text ed. 27.50 o.p. (ISBN 0-435-80579-7); pap. text ed. 14.95x. Heinemann Ed.

Fair Play Settlers of the West Branch Valley, 1769 to 1784: A Study of Frontier Ethnography. George D. Wolf. (Illus., Orig.). 1969. 5.00 (ISBN 0-911124-31-4); pap. 3.00 (ISBN 0-911124-30-6). Pa Hist & Mus.

Fair Rosalind: The American Career of Helena Modjeska, 1877-1907. Marion M. Coleman. LC 69-10370. (Illus.). 1969. 20.00 (ISBN 0-910366-07-1). Alliance Coll.

Fair Shine the Day. Sylvia Thorpe. 1977. pap. 1.75 o.p. (ISBN 0-449-23229-8, Crest). Fawcett.

Fair Slaughter. Howard Barker. 1980. pap. 3.95 (ISBN 0-7145-3654-7). Riverrun NY.

Fair Syrian, 2 vols. Robert Bage. LC 78-60845. (Novel 1720-1805 Ser.: Vol. 10). 1980. Set. lib. bdg. 62.00 (ISBN 0-8240-3659-X). Garland Pub.

Fair Warning. Mignon G. Eberhart. 176p. 1975. pap. 0.95 o.p. (ISBN 0-445-00648-X). Popular Lib.

Fair-Weather Flying. Richard L. Taylor. LC 73-20989. (Illus.). 224p. 1974. 12.95 (ISBN 0-02-616700-X). Macmillan.

Fair Wind to Virginia. Cornelia Meigs. (Illus.). (gr. 4-6). 1964. 7.95g (ISBN 0-02-765700-0). Macmillan.

Fairbanks: A Pictorial History. Claus M. Naske & Ludwig J. Rowinski. Ed. by Donna R. Friedman. (Illus.). 208p. 1981. pap. price not set (ISBN 0-89865-108-5). Donning Co.

Fairchild's Designer: Stylist Handbook, 2 vols. Debbie A. Gioello. (Illus.). 1979. Vol. 1. (ISBN 0-87005-332-9); Vol. 2. (ISBN 0-87005-333-7); Set. 35.00; tracing pad 7.95 (ISBN 0-87005-334-5). Fairchild.

Fairchild's Financial Manual of Retail Stores: 1979. Book Division Staff. (Illus.). 1979. pap. text ed. 40.00 o.p. (ISBN 0-87005-310-8). Fairchild.

Fairchild's Textile & Apparel Financial Directory: 1980. Book Division Research Staff. 260p. 1980. text ed. 45.00 (ISBN 0-87005-361-2). Fairchild.

Fairchild's Textile & Apparel Financial Directory: 1979. Book Division Research Staff. (Illus.). 230p. 1979. pap. text ed. 40.00 (ISBN 0-87005-309-4). Fairchild.

Faire & Easie Way to Heaven: Covenant Theology & Antinomianism in Early Massachusetts. William K. Stoever. LC 77-14851. 1978. 20.00x (ISBN 0-8195-5024-8, Pub. by Wesleyan U Pr). Columbia U Pr.

Fairer Slice of the Cake: The Task Ahead. Lynda K. Taylor. 228p. 1976. text ed. 21.00x (ISBN 0-220-66284-3, Pub. by Busn Bks England). Renouf.

Fairest Hunting. H. P. Hewett. (Illus.). 3.25 o.p. (ISBN 0-85131-065-6, Dist. by Sporting Book Center). J A Allen.

Fairies. E. L. Gardner. 11.95 (ISBN 0-8356-5090-1). Theos Pub Hse.

Fairies. Avril Rodway. (Leprechaun Library). (Illus.). 64p. 1981. 3.95 (ISBN 0-399-12610-4). Putnam.

Fairies at Work & Play. G. Hodson. pap. 5.95 (ISBN 0-7229-5232-5). Theos Pub Hse.

Fairness Doctrine & the Media. Steven J. Simmons. LC 77-85740. 1978. 15.95 (ISBN 0-520-03585-2). U of Cal Pr.

Fairness in Selecting Employees. Richard D. Arvey. LC 78-74678. 1979. pap. text ed. 6.95 (ISBN 0-201-00070-9). A-W.

Fairs & Circuses. Paul White. (Junior Reference Ser.). (Illus.). 64p. (gr. 7 up). 1972. 7.95 (ISBN 0-7136-1323-8). Dufour.

Fairy & Folk Tales of the Irish Peasantry. Ed. by William B. Yeats. 416p. 1973. 12.95 (ISBN 0-02-632640-X). Macmillan.

Fairy Mythology. Keightley. LC 74-16410. 1975. Repr. of 1870 ed. 30.00 (ISBN 0-8103-3466-6). Gale.

Fairy Mythology of Shakespeare. Alfred T. Nutt. 49p. 1980. Repr. of 1900 ed. lib. bdg. 10.00 (ISBN 0-8495-4019-4). Arden Lib.

Fairy Rings & Other Mushrooms. Gladys Conklin. LC 73-76799. (Illus.). (gr. k-3). 1973. PLB 4.95 (ISBN 0-8234-0223-1). Holiday.

Fairy Tale. S. Steinberg. 1981. pap. 2.50 (ISBN 0-440-10181-6). Dell.

Fairy Tale of New York. J. P. Donleavy. 352p. 1973. 7.95 o.s.i. (ISBN 0-440-02624-5, Sey Lawr). Delacorte.

Fairy Tale of the Green Snake & the Beautiful Lily. Johann W. Von Goethe. 80p. 1980. pap. 3.50 (ISBN 0-8334-1769-X). Steinerbks.

Fairy Tales & Legends from Romania. Ed. by Ioana Sturdza et al. (Illus.). 1972. 21.00x (ISBN 0-8057-5655-8). Irvington.

Fairy Tales & the Female Imagination. Jennifer Waelti-Walters. 225p. 1981. price not set (ISBN 0-920792-07-3). Eden Women.

Fairy Tales for Me. Wilma D. Pepper. 184p. (gr. 1). 1967. 2.50x o.p. (ISBN 0-89039-053-3). Ann Arbor Pubs.

Fairy Tales from East & West. Annabel William-Ellis. (Illus., Orig.). 1978. pap. 2.95 (ISBN 0-8467-0535-4, Pub. by Two Continents). Hippocrene Bks.

Fairy Tales from Everywhere. Annabel Williams-Ellis. (Illus., Orig.). 1978. pap. 2.95 (ISBN 0-8467-0533-8, Pub. by Two Continents). Hippocrene Bks.

Fairy Tales from Here & There. Annabel Williams-Ellis. (Illus., Orig.). 1978. pap. 2.95 (ISBN 0-8467-0536-2, Pub. by Two Continents). Hippocrene Bks.

Fairy Tales from Many Lands. Illus. by Arthur Rackham. (Large Format Ser.). (Illus.). 1978. pap. 5.95 o.p. (ISBN 0-14-004914-2). Penguin.

Fairy Tales from Near & Far. Annabel Williams-Ellis. (Illus., Orig.). 1978. pap. 2.95 (ISBN 0-8467-0534-6, Pub. by Two Continents). Hippocrene Bks.

Fairy Tales from the Barbary Coast. P. Lux. (gr. 1-4). 1971. 7.95 (ISBN 0-584-62366-6). Transatlantic.

Fairy Tales of Birds & Beasts, Vol. 1. Compiled by Beth Brown. (Illus.). 128p. (gr. 3-7). 1981. PLB 8.95 (ISBN 0-87460-375-7). Lion.

Fairy Tales of Puerto Rico. David Garcia. (Children's Bks: No. 166). (Illus.). 50p. (gr. 1-5). 1981. 6.95 (ISBN 0-934642-02-8). Puerto Rico Almanacs.

Fairy Tales of Ronald M. Nottingham Sr. Ronald M. Nottingham. 1979. 4.95 (ISBN 0-533-03888-X). Vantage.

Fairy Worlds & Workers: A Natural History of the Middle Kingdom. Marjorie Spock. 1980. pap. 5.95 (ISBN 0-916786-46-3). St George Bk Serv.

Fairyland. Gyo Fujikawa. (Gyo Fujikawa Tiny Board Books). (Illus.). 14p. (ps-k). 1981. 1.95 (ISBN 0-448-15139-1). G&D.

Fairy's Gift. Cicely M. Barker. (Cicely Mary Barker Storybks). (Illus.). (gr. k-4). 1977. 3.95 (ISBN 0-685-78524-6, Pub. by Two Continents). Hippocrene Bks.

Faith. Louis Bauman. pap. 2.50 (ISBN 0-88469-026-1). BMH Bks.

Faith. Hans-Jurgen Hermission & Eduard Lohse. Tr. by Douglas Stott. LC 80-22542. (Biblical Encounter Ser.). 176p. 1981. pap. 6.95 (ISBN 0-687-12520-0). Abingdon.

Faith According to St. John of the Cross. Pope John Paul, II. Tr. by Jordan Aumann. LC 80-82265. Orig. Title: Doctrina de Fide apud S. Joannem a Cruce. 376p. (Orig.). 1981. price not set (ISBN 0-89870-010-8); pap. price not set (ISBN 0-89870-005-1). Ignatius Pr.

Faith & History: A Comparison of Christian & Modern Views of History. Reinhold Niebuhr. (Lib. Rep. Ed.). 1949. 17.50x (ISBN 0-684-15318-1, ScribT). Scribner.

Faith & Its Counterfeits. Donald G. Bloesch. 108p. (Orig.). 1981. pap. 3.95 (ISBN 0-87784-822-X). Inter Varsity.

Faith & Justice. Margaret Betz. LC 80-50259. 176p. (gr. 11-12). 1980. pap. text ed. 4.20x (ISBN 0-88489-114-3); tchr's guide 5.00x (ISBN 0-88489-121-6). St Mary's.

Faith & Life. B. B. Warfield. 1974. pap. 5.45 (ISBN 0-85151-188-0). Banner of Truth.

Faith & Politics. Reinhold Niebuhr. Ed. & intro. by Ronald H. Stone. LC 68-29097. 1968. 6.50 o.p. (ISBN 0-8076-0459-3). Braziller.

Faith & Practice. Frank E. Wilson. (Orig.). 1941. pap. 4.95 o.p. (ISBN 0-8192-1082-X). Morehouse.

Faith & Practice of the Quakers. Rufus M. Jones. 181p. 1980. pap. 3.95 (ISBN 0-913408-57-3). Friends United.

Faith & Prayer. H. M. Richards, Jr. (Uplook Ser.). 32p. 1971. pap. 0.75 (ISBN 0-8163-0071-2, 06010-3). Pacific Pr Pub Assn.

Faith & Reason in Kierkegaard. F. Russell Sullivan. LC 78-60695. 1978. pap. text ed. 7.50 (ISBN 0-8191-0559-7). U Pr of Amer.

Faith & Science in an Unjust World, Vol. 2: Reports & Recommendations. Ed. by Paul Abrecht. LC 80-81141. 224p. 1980. pap. 6.95 (ISBN 0-8006-1391-0, 1-1391). Fortress.

Faith & Science: Mutual Responsibility for a Human Future. William S. Lea. 1979. 1.50 (ISBN 0-686-28776-2). Forward Movement.

Faith & the Adolescent. Pierre Babin. 1967. 3.95 (ISBN 0-8164-1030-5). Crossroad NY.

Faith & the Prospects of Economic Collapse. Robert Lee. LC 80-82187. 144p. 1981. pap. 6.95 (ISBN 0-8042-0814-X). John Knox.

Faith at an Early Age. Marjorie Gilbert. (Illus.). 1973. pap. 1.50 (ISBN 0-89570-078-6). Claretian Pubns.

Faith at the Top. Wesley Pippert. LC 73-88676. 192p. 1973. pap. 1.50 o.p. (ISBN 0-912692-28-6). Cook.

Faith Despite the KGB. Hermann Hartfeld. Tr. by Henry Wagner. LC 80-66491. 224p. 1980. pap. 4.95 (ISBN 0-915684-74-8). Christian Herald.

Faith Experience: Communal Spirituality for Justice. Paul S. Roy. 240p. (Orig.). 1981. pap. 8.95 (ISBN 0-8091-2380-0). Paulist Pr.

Faith for Moderns. 2nd rev. ed. Robert Gordis. LC 76-136424. 1971. pap. 6.95x (ISBN 0-8197-0001-0, 10001). Bloch.

Faith for the Times, Pt. 3: The Fruit of Deliverance. Alan Redpath. 1976. 3.95 o.p. (ISBN 0-8007-0779-6). Revell.

Faith for Today. E. Flesseman-Van Leer. Tr. by John E. Steely. LC 79-56514. (Special Studies Ser.: No. 7). 1980. 6.95 (ISBN 0-932180-06-X). Assn Baptist Profs.

Faith, Hope, & Charity: Mother's Poems. Edith Barrows. 4.00 o.p. (ISBN 0-8062-1183-0). Carlton.

Faith, Hope & Clarity. Gordon Kainer. LC 77-72499. (Redwood Ser.). 1977. pap. 3.95 (ISBN 0-8163-0314-2, 06022-8). Pacific Pr Pub Assn.

Faith in History & Society: Toward a Practical Fundamental Theology. Johann B. Metz. 1979. 12.95 (ISBN 0-8164-0426-7). Crossroad NY.

Faith Is for People. Paul Little. (Orig.). 1977. pap. 3.95 (ISBN 0-88449-057-2). Vision Hse.

Faith Is Still There. David H. Read. LC 80-21395. (Orig.). 1981. pap. 4.95 (ISBN 0-687-12650-9). Abingdon.

Faith It or Fake It? Fritz Ridenour. LC 73-120783. 1978. pap. 1.95 (ISBN 0-8307-0441-8, S114-1-86). Regal.

Faith, Keyes, & Clark's Industrial Chemicals. 4th ed. Frederick A. Lowenheim & Marguerite K. Moran. LC 75-17951. 904p. 1975. 74.95 (ISBN 0-471-54964-9, Pub. by Wiley-Interscience). Wiley.

Faith of America. Fred Bauer. (Illus.). 1980. 19.95 (ISBN 0-8499-0280-0). Word Bks.

Faith of an Educationist. Khwaja G. Saiyidain. 1966. 10.25x o.p. (ISBN 0-210-26986-3). Asia.

Faith of Billy Graham. T. S. Settel. 1970. pap. 1.25 o.p. (ISBN 0-451-07104-2, Y7104, Sig). NAL.

Faith of Catholics: An Introduction. rev. ed. Richard Chilson. LC 72-81229. 192p. 1976. pap. 3.45 (ISBN 0-8091-1873-4, Deus). Paulist Pr.

Faith of John Dryden: Change & Continuity. G. Douglas Atkins. LC 80-12890. 208p. 1980. 14.00x (ISBN 0-8131-1401-2). U Pr of Ky.

Faith of Our Fathers. Cardinal Gibbons. LC 80-51331. 1980. write for info. o.p. (ISBN 0-89555-158-6). Tan Bks Pubs.

Faith of Our Fathers. Lawrence H. Waddy. 1975. pap. 3.95x (ISBN 0-8192-4063-X). Morehouse.

Faith of Our Feminists. Josephine L. Jessup. LC 65-23482. 1950. 9.00x (ISBN 0-8196-0158-6). Biblo.

Faith of the Christian Church. rev. ed. Gustaf Aulen. Tr. by Eric H. Wahlstrom from Swedish. LC 61-5302. 416p. 1973. pap. 5.75 (ISBN 0-8006-1655-3, 1-1655). Fortress.

Faith of the Church. James A. Pike & W. Norman Pittenger. (Orig.). 1951. pap. 3.95 (ISBN 0-8164-2019-X, SP3). Crossroad NY.

Faith, Psychology & Christian Maturity. Millard Sall. 1977. pap. 4.95 (ISBN 0-310-32431-9). Zondervan.

Faith, Reason, & the Plague in Seventeenth-Century Tuscany. Carlo M. Cipolla. 128p. 1981. pap. 3.95 (ISBN 0-393-00045-1). Norton.

Faith That Persuades. J. Edwin Orr. LC 76-62924. (Harper Jubilee Book). 1977. pap. 1.95 o.p. (ISBN 0-06-066939-X, HJ 30, HarpR). Har-Row.

Faith That Works: Eleven Studies in James. Andrew T. LePeau & Phyllis J. LePeau. 72p. (Orig.). 1980. pap. 2.25 (ISBN 0-87784-365-1). Inter Varsity.

Faith to Live by. Kenneth D. Barney. LC 76-27929. (Radiant Life). 128p. 1977. pap. 1.95 (ISBN 0-88243-899-9, 02-0899); teacher's ed. 2.50 (ISBN 0-88243-171-4, 32-0171). Gospel Pub.

Faith to Live by. Derek Prince. 1977. pap. 3.50 (ISBN 0-686-12768-4, B-29). Derek Prince.

Faith to Live By. Derek Prince. 1977. pap. 3.50 (ISBN 0-89283-042-5). Servant.

Faith Under Fire: Biblical Interpretations of Suffering. Danile J. Simundson. LC 79-54119. 158p. 1980. pap. 4.95 (ISBN 0-8066-1756-X, 10-2195). Augsburg.

Faith Without Fantasy. Robert M. McMillan. LC 80-66541. 1981. 2.95 (ISBN 0-8054-5285-0). Broadman.

Faithful & Fair: Transcending Sexist Language in Worship. Keith Watkins. LC 80-39698. 128p. 1981. pap. 4.95 (ISBN 0-687-12707-6). Abingdon.

Faithful Friendship. Dorothy Devers. 1980. 2.00 (ISBN 0-686-28777-0). Forward Movement.

Faithful Magistrates & Republican Lawyers: Creators of Virginia Legal Culture, 1680-1810. A. G. Roeber. LC 80-19524. (Studies in Legal History). 352p. 1981. 24.00x (ISBN 0-8078-1461-X). U of NC Pr.

Faithless Lollybird. Joan Aiken. LC 77-72999. (gr. 6-9). 1978. PLB 6.95 (ISBN 0-385-13074-0). Doubleday.

Faith's Checkbook. Charles H. Spurgeon. pap. 2.50 (ISBN 0-8024-0014-0, 35-14). Moody.

Fake Giants & Other Great Hoaxes. Timothy Bay. LC 80-21132. (gr. 4-10). 1980. pap. 1.95 (ISBN 0-88436-766-5). EMC.

Fakehat Al Bustan: Concise All Arabic Dictionary. Addullah Bustani. 1970. 40.00x (ISBN 0-685-72029-2). Intl Bk Ctr.

Fakers. Danny Korem & Paul Meier. 1980. cancelled o.p. (ISBN 0-8007-1130-0). Revell.

Fakers: Exploding the Myths of the Supernatural. Danny Korem & Paul Meier. (Illus.). 1981. 8.95 (ISBN 0-8010-5431-1). Baker Bk.

Falcon & the Snowman: A True Story of Friendship & Espionage. Robert Lindsey. 1980. pap. 2.95 (ISBN 0-671-41160-8). PB.

Falcon Claw: The Motion Picture. Sid Campbell. Ed. by Mahi Morales. 115p. 1980. pap. 7.50 (ISBN 0-937610-01-1). Dimond Pubs.

Falcon Comet Fairlane Handbook of Maintenance & Repair: 1960-1965 Models. Ed. by Clymer Publications. (Illus.). 1965. pap. 7.95 (ISBN 0-89287-249-7, A160). Clymer Pubns.

Falcon for a Queen. Catherine Gaskin. 320p. 1977. pap. 1.75 o.p. (ISBN 0-449-23074-0, Crest). Fawcett.

Falcon for a Queen. Catherine Gaskin. 336p. 1981. pap. 2.50 (ISBN 0-553-14543-6). Bantam.

Falcon for a Witch. Catherine Darby. (Falcon Ser.: No. 1). 1975. pap. 1.25 o.p. (ISBN 0-445-00313-8). Popular Lib.

Falcon Rising. Catherine Darby. (Falcon Ser.: No. 8). 1976. pap. 1.25 o.p. (ISBN 0-445-00405-3). Popular Lib.

Falcon to the Lure. Catherine Darby. (Falcon Ser: No. 12). 1978. pap. 1.75 o.p. (ISBN 0-445-04322-9). Popular Lib.

Falconer. John Cheever. 1978. pap. 2.75 (ISBN 0-345-28589-1). Ballantine.

Falconer's Island. Katherine Kent. (Orig.). 1981. pap. write for info. (ISBN 0-671-41783-5). PB.

Falconer's Lure. Antonia Forest. (Illus.). (gr. 5 up). 1957. 6.50 (ISBN 0-571-06548-1, Pub. by Faber & Faber). Merrimack Bk Serv.

Falconhurst Fancy. Kyle Onstott. 1978. lib. bdg. 14.30x (ISBN 0-89966-248-X). Buccaneer Bks.

Falconry & Hawking. Glasier. 53.00 (ISBN 0-7134-0232-6). David & Charles.

Falconry in Arabia. Mark Allen. (Illus.). 143p. Date not set. 40.00 (ISBN 0-89182-034-5). Charles River Bks.

Falcons Return: Restoring an Endangered Species. John Kaufmann & Heinz Meng. (Illus.). 128p. (gr. 7 up). 1975. PLB 7.92 (ISBN 0-688-32027-9). Morrow.

Falcon's Shadow. Anne Maybury. 1977. pap. 2.25 (ISBN 0-441-22583-7). Ace Bks.

Falkland Road: Prostitutes of Bombay. Mary E. Mark. LC 80-11778. (Illus.). 96p. 1981. 25.00 (ISBN 0-394-50987-0); pap. 12.95 (ISBN 0-394-74000-9). Knopf.

Falk's Graphical Solutions. Hansson-Falk. 8.00 o.p. (ISBN 0-686-00160-5). Columbia Graphs.

Fall from Grace. Victor Canning. LC 80-83325. 224p. 1981. 9.95 (ISBN 0-688-00195-5). Morrow.

Fall Guy. Jay Cronley. 1979. pap. 1.95 o.p. (ISBN 0-451-08890-5, J8890, Sig). NAL.

Fall in & Cheer. John R. Coyne, Jr. LC 78-7751. 1979. 8.95 o.p. (ISBN 0-385-11119-3). Doubleday.

Fall Is Here! Jane B. Moncure. LC 75-14019. (Illus.). (ps-2). 1975. 5.50 (ISBN 0-913778-13-3). Childs World.

Fall Line. Nancy Mack & Peter Sanders. LC 75-22010. (Venture Ser, a Reading Incentive Program). (Illus.). 76p. (gr. 7-12,RL 4.5-6.5). 1975. text ed. 23.25 ea. pack of 5 (ISBN 0-8172-0245-5). Follett.

Fall of America: Poems of These States, 1965-1971. Allen Ginsberg. LC 72-84228. (Pocket Poets Ser.: No. 30). 190p. 1972. pap. 4.00 (ISBN 0-87286-063-9). City Lights.

Fall of Cambria, a Poem, 2 vols. in 1. Joseph Cottle. LC 75-31186. (Romantic Context Ser.: Poetry 1789-1830: Vol. 38). 1978. Repr. of 1808 ed. lib. bdg. 47.00 (ISBN 0-8240-2137-1). Garland Pub.

Fall of Constantinople, Fourteen Fifty-Three. Steven Runciman. LC 65-10383. (Illus.). 1969. 32.50 (ISBN 0-521-06165-2); pap. 9.95x (ISBN 0-521-09573-5). Cambridge U Pr.

Fall of Imperial China. Frederic Wakeman, Jr. LC 74-27854. (Transformation of Modern China Ser.). 1975. 10.95 (ISBN 0-02-933690-2); pap. text ed. 7.95 (ISBN 0-02-933680-5). Free Pr.

Fall of Jerusalem. Abdullah Schleifer. LC 79-178713. (Illus.). 256p. 1972. 7.50 o.p. (ISBN 0-85345-204-0, CL2040); pap. 3.45 (ISBN 0-85345-249-0, PB2490). Monthly Rev.

Fall of Jerusalem, A Dramatic Poem, Repr. Of 1820 Ed. Henry H. Milman. Bd. with Belshazzar: A Dramatic Poem. Repr. of 1822 ed. LC 75-31233. (Romantic Context: Poetry 1789-1830 Ser.: Vol. 84). 1977. lib. bdg. 47.00 (ISBN 0-8240-2183-5). Garland Pub.

Fall of Paris: The Siege & the Commune 1870-71. Alistair Horne. 464p. 1981. pap. 2.95 (ISBN 0-14-005210-0). Penguin.

Fall of Princes, 4 pts. John Lydgate. Ed. by Henry Bergen. Incl. Pt. 1. Books 1-2. o.p. (ISBN 0-19-722572-1); Pt. 2. Books 3-5. 19.95x o.p. (ISBN 0-19-722573-X); Pt. 3. Books 6-9. o.p. (ISBN 0-19-722574-8); Pt. 4. Biographical Introduction, Notes & Glossary. o.p. (ISBN 0-19-722575-6). (Early English Text Society Ser.). 1924. Oxford U Pr.

Fall of the Incas. Shirley Glubok. (gr. 4 up). 1967. 5.95 o.s.i. (ISBN 0-02-736000-8). Macmillan.

Fall of the President. Washington Post Staff. 232p. 1974. 8.95 o.p. (ISBN 0-440-04550-9). Delacorte.

Fall of the Wild, the Rise of the Zoo. Robert Bendiner. (Illus.). 256p. 1981. 13.95 (ISBN 0-525-10270-1). Dutton.

Fall of Worlds. Francine Mezo. 320p. (Orig.). 1980. pap. 2.50 (ISBN 0-380-75564-5, 75564). Avon.

Fall River Tragedy: With an Essay on the True Borden Murderer by Edouard Libris. rev. ed. Ed. by Edwin Porter & Edouard Libris. 350p. 1981. lib. bdg. 15.00; pap. 10.00. Forty Whacks.

Fallacies in Mathematics. Edwin A. Maxwell. 1959. 12.95 (ISBN 0-521-05700-0). Cambridge U Pr.

Fallacy of Social Science Research: A Critical Examination & New Qualitative Model. Pablo G. Casanova. (PPS on Social Policy Ser.). 75p. 1981. 15.00 (ISBN 0-08-027549-4). Pergamon.

Fallax opus: Poet & Reader in the Elegies of Propertius. John Warden. (Phoenix Supplementary Volumes Ser.). 1980. 15.00x (ISBN 0-8020-5470-6). U of Toronto Pr.

Fallen Angel. Sally Mitchell. 1981. write for info. (ISBN 0-87972-155-3); pap. write for info. (ISBN 0-87972-156-1). Bowling Green Univ.

Fallen Angels: Endless Race. Ursula Holden. 192p. 1981. pap. 1.95 (ISBN 0-523-41273-8). Pinnacle Bks.

Fallen Crown: Three French Mary Stuart Plays of the Seventeenth Century. Michael G. Paulson. LC 79-6812. 207p. 1980. text ed. 17.00 (ISBN 0-8191-0959-2); pap. text ed. 9.25 (ISBN 0-8191-0960-6). U Pr of Amer.

Fallible Fiend. L. Sprague De Camp. 160p. 1981. pap. 1.95 (ISBN 0-345-29367-3, Del Rey). Ballantine.

Falling. Susan F. Schaeffer. 288p. 1973. 6.95 o.s.i. (ISBN 0-686-66747-6). Macmillan.

Falling in Love Again. Pamela Wallace. 288p. (Orig.). 1981. pap. 2.75 (ISBN 0-523-41055-7). Pinnacle Bks.

Falling in Place. Ann Beattie. 352p. 1981. pap. 2.95 (ISBN 0-445-04650-3). Popular Lib.

Falling off the Roof. Karen Lindsey. LC 75-21788. 72p. 1975. pap. 4.95 (ISBN 0-914086-08-1). Alicejamesbooks.

Falling Rolls in Secondary Schools, Pt. 1. Eric Briault & Frances Smith. 1980. pap. text ed. 16.00x (ISBN 0-85633-207-0, NFER). Humanities.

Falling Rolls in Secondary Schools, Pt. 2. Eric Briault & Frances Smith. 403p. 1980. pap. text ed. 27.50x (ISBN 0-85633-208-9, NFER). Humanities.

Falling Star. Lisa Eisenberg. LC 79-52653. (Laura Brewster Mysteries Ser.). (Illus.). 64p. (gr. 4 up). 1980. PLB 7.95 (ISBN 0-516-02205-9). Childrens.

Falling Torch. Algis Budrys. 1978. pap. 1.50 o.s.i. (ISBN 0-515-04649-3). Jove Pubns.

Fallon. L'Amour. 160p. (Orig.). 1981. pap. 2.25 (ISBN 0-553-14534-7). Bantam.

Falls the Shadow. Regina Ross. 248p. 1974. 6.95 o.p. (ISBN 0-440-02642-3). Delacorte.

Falsche Agentin: Reader 4. Rita M. Walbruck. LC 80-22162. (Auf Heisser Spur Ser.). (gr. 9-12). 1981. pap. 1.95 (ISBN 0-88436-853-X). EMC.

Falschungen Erzbischof Lanfranks Von Canterbury. Heinrich Boehmer. LC 80-2233. 1981. Repr. of 1902 ed. 29.50 (ISBN 0-404-18754-4). AMS Pr.

False Clues. Ron Schreiber. LC 77-88109. (Illus.). 1978. pap. 3.50 (ISBN 0-930762-01-0). Calamus Bks.

False Colours. Georgette Heyer. 1977. pap. 1.50 o.p. (ISBN 0-449-23169-0, Crest). Fawcett.

False Fleeting Perjur'd Clarence. Michael Hicks. (Illus.). 272p. 1980. text ed. 22.00x (ISBN 0-904387-44-5). Humanities.

False Presence of the Kingdom. Jacques Ellul. 4.95 (ISBN 0-8164-0235-3). Crossroad NY.

False Promise of Codetermination. Alfred L. Thimm. LC 80-8422. 288p. 1980. 27.95x (ISBN 0-669-04108-4). Lexington Bks.

False Scent. Ngaio Marsh. 1978. pap. 1.75 o.p. (ISBN 0-425-03999-4, Dist. by Putnam). Berkley Pub.

False Spring. Pat Jordan. LC 74-31082. 288p. 1975. 7.95 (ISBN 0-396-07078-7). Dodd.

Falsehood & Truth. Charlotte E. Tonna. Ed. by Robert L. Wolff. Bd. with Conformity. LC 75-488. (Victorian Fiction Novels of Faith & Doubt Ser.). 1975. Repr. of 1841 ed. lib. bdg. 66.00 (ISBN 0-8240-1564-9). Garland Pub.

Falsification & Belief. Alastair McKinnon. 1979. lib. bdg. 21.00 (ISBN 0-917930-33-9); pap. text ed. 5.50x (ISBN 0-917930-13-4). Ridgeview.

Falstaff. Giuseppe Verdi. 480p. 1980. pap. 10.95 (ISBN 0-486-24017-7). Dover.

Falter Tom & the Water Boy. Maurice Duggan. LC 59-12200. (Illus.). (gr. 3-6). 1959. 6.95 (ISBN 0-87599-027-4). S G Phillips.

Fame & Love in New York. Ed Sanders. (New World Writing Ser.: No. 17). (Illus.). 320p. 1980. 17.95 (ISBN 0-913666-31-9); pap. 7.95 (ISBN 0-913666-32-7). Turtle Isl Foun.

Fame & Obscurity. Gay Talese. 1981. pap. 3.25 (ISBN 0-440-12620-7). Dell.

Fame Game. Rona Jaffe. 1976. Repr. of 1969 ed. lib. bdg. 12.25x (ISBN 0-89966-131-9). Buccaneer Bks.

Familia Caesaris: A Social Study of the Emperor's Freedmen & Slaves. P. R. Weaver. LC 76-171686. (Illus.). 1972. 42.95 (ISBN 0-521-08340-0). Cambridge U Pr.

Familia De Pascula Duarte. Ed. by C. Cela et al. 1961. pap. 7.95 o.p. (ISBN 0-13-528307-8). P-H.

Familial Hyperbilirubinemia: Proceedings of the Workshop on Familial Disorders of Hepatic Bilirubin Metabolism Held in Venice, Italy 23rd-24th May 1980. L. Okolicsanyi. 250p. 1981. 42.00 (ISBN 0-686-69369-8, Pub. by Wiley-Interscience). Wiley.

Familial Organization. Robert F. Winch et al. LC 77-2434. (Illus.). 1978. 17.95 (ISBN 0-02-935340-8). Free Pr.

Familiar Allusions: A Hand-Book of Miscellaneous Information. William A. Wheeler. LC 66-24371. 1966. Repr. of 1882 ed. 26.00 (ISBN 0-8103-0166-0). Gale.

Familiar Animals & How to Draw Them. Amy Hogeboom. (gr. 1-4). 3.95 o.s.i. (ISBN 0-8149-0323-1). Vanguard.

Familiar Quotations. Ed. by John Bartlett. 1958. 4.75 o.p. (ISBN 0-8022-0077-X). Philos Lib.

Familiar Quotations from French & Italian Authors. Craufurd T. Ramage. LC 68-22042. Orig. Title: Beautiful Thoughts from French & Italian Authors Ser. 1968. Repr. of 1904 ed. 18.00 (ISBN 0-8103-3191-8). Gale.

Familiar Quotations from German & Spanish Authors. Craufurd T. Ramage. LC 68-2043. (With English translations). Repr. of 1904 ed. 18.00 (ISBN 0-8103-3192-6). Gale.

Familiar Quotations from Greek Authors. Craufurd T. Ramage. LC 68-22044. Orig. Title: Beautiful Thoughts from Greek Authors. 1968. Repr. of 1895 ed. 18.00 (ISBN 0-8103-3193-4). Gale.

Familiar Reptiles & Amphibians of America. Will Barker. LC 62-14599. (Familiar Nature Ser.). (Illus.). 1964. PLB 9.87 o.p. (ISBN 0-06-070421-7, HarpT). Har-Row.

Familiar Short Sayings of Great Men. Ed. by Samuel A. Bent. LC 68-30643. 1968. Repr. of 1887 ed. 22.00 (ISBN 0-8103-3182-9). Gale.

Familiar Subjects: Polaroid SX-70 Impressions. Norman Locks. LC 78-4754. (Illus.). 1978. 12.95 o.p. (ISBN 0-685-29945-7, HarpR); pap. 6.95 o.p. (ISBN 0-06-250530-0, RD 282, HarpR). Har-Row.

Familiar Territory: Observations on American Life. Joseph Epstein. 1979. 13.95 (ISBN 0-19-502604-7). Oxford U Pr.

Familiar to All. Derek Parker. (Illus.). 1978. 8.95 o.p. (ISBN 0-224-01112-X, Pub. by Chatto Bodley Jonathan). Merrimack Bk Serv.

Familias De Arrabal: Un Estudio Sobre Desarrollo y Desigualdad. Helen I. Safa. LC 80-19853. ix, 191p. Date not set. pap. price not set (ISBN 0-8477-2455-7). U of PR Pr.

Families. Jane Howard. 1980. pap. 2.75 (ISBN 0-425-04486-6). Berkley Pub.

Families. Rhodri Jones. 1971. pap. text ed. 2.50x o.p. (ISBN 0-435-14500-2). Heinemann Ed.

Families. Meredith Tax. (Illus.). 32p. (ps-3). 1981. 7.95 (ISBN 0-316-83240-5, Pub. by Atlantic). Little.

Families, Alcoholism & Therapy. Charles P. Barnard. (Illus.). 184p. 1981. text ed. 16.50 (ISBN 0-398-04157-1); pap. text ed. 12.75 (ISBN 0-398-04173-3). C C Thomas.

Families & Communities: A New View of American History. David J. Russo. LC 74-11389. 1974. 7.00x (ISBN 0-910050-29-5). AASLH.

Families & Communities As Educators. Hope Leichter. LC 79-63. 1979. text ed. 11.95 o.p. (ISBN 0-8077-2560-9); pap. text ed. 10.95 (ISBN 0-8077-2559-5). Tchrs Coll.

Families & Survivors. Alice Adams. 192p. 1976. pap. 1.50 o.s.i. (ISBN 0-446-78974-7). Warner Bks.

Families & Their Learning Environments. Kevin Marjoribanks. 1979. 22.00x (ISBN 0-7100-0167-3). Routledge & Kegan.

Families Are God's Idea. Roy Lessin. (God's Idea Books Ser.). (Illus.). 32p. (ps-4). 1981. pap. 1.25 (ISBN 0-87123-177-8, 210177). Bethany Fell.

Families Are Like That. Child Study Association of America. LC 73-21647. (Illus.). 192p. (gr. 1-5). 1975. PLB 7.49 o.p. (ISBN 0-690-00433-8, TYC-J). T Y Crowell.

Families Divided: The Impact of Migrant Labour in Lesotho. Colin Murray. (African Studies: No. 29). (Illus.). 236p. Date not set. price not set (ISBN 0-521-23501-4). Cambridge U Pr.

Families Headed by Women in New York City: An Analysis of the 1970 Census Facts. 1975. pap. 2.00 (ISBN 0-86671-069-8). Comm Coun Great NY.

Families in an Urban Mold: Policy Implications of an Australian-U.S. Comparison. Ludwig L. Geismar & Shirley Geismar. (Pergamon Policy Studies). 1979. 27.00 (ISBN 0-08-023379-1). Pergamon.

Families in Former Times. J. L. Flandrin. LC 78-18095. (Themes in the Social Sciences Ser.). (Illus.). 1979. 39.50 (ISBN 0-521-22323-7); pap. 9.95x (ISBN 0-521-29449-5). Cambridge U Pr.

Families in the Military System. Ed. by Hamilton J. McCubbin et al. LC 75-44398. (Sage Ser. on Armed Forces & Society: Vol. 9). 1976. 24.00x (ISBN 0-8039-0667-6). Sage.

Families, Individuals, & Marriage. 2nd ed. Michael Sporakowski & Mary W. Hicks. 1976. pap. text ed. 8.95 o.p. (ISBN 0-8403-0789-6). Kendall-Hunt.

Families of Black Prisoners: Survival & Progress. L. Alex Swan. (University Book Ser.). 1981. 188.95 (ISBN 0-8161-8412-7). G K Hall.

Families of Hearing-Impaired Children. Albert T. Murphy. 1979. pap. 4.50 (ISBN 0-88200-128-0). Bell Assn Deaf.

Families of Ireland. Edward MacLysaght. 450p. 1980. 40.00x (ISBN 0-686-26446-0, Pub. by Irish Academic Pr). Biblio Dist.

Families Sharing God. Barbara O. Webb. 48p. 1981. pap. 3.50 (ISBN 0-8170-0900-0). Judson.

Families Today: A Research Sampler on Families & Children, 2 vols. Bette Runck et al. LC 79-66976. (Science Monographs: No. 1). (Illus., Orig.). 1980. Vol. 1. pap. 8.50 (ISBN 0-686-27076-2); Vol. 2. pap. 8.00 (ISBN 0-686-27077-0). Gov Printing Office.

Families Under Stress. William D. Brown. 154p. 1977. pap. text ed. 7.95 (ISBN 0-87619-844-2). R J Brady.

Families Under Stress: A Psychological Interpretation. Tony Manocchio & William Petitt. 1975. 18.00 (ISBN 0-7100-8176-6). Routledge & Kegan.

Familles Normales. Paul Montel. LC 73-14649. xiii, 301p. 1974. text ed. 12.00 (ISBN 0-8284-0271-X). Chelsea Pub.

Family. Robert O. Blood, Jr. LC 71-161235. 1972. text ed. 15.95 (ISBN 0-02-904150-3). Free Pr.

Family. Helen Oxenbury. (Baby Board Bks.). (Illus.). 12p. (ps-k). Date not set. boards 3.50 (ISBN 0-671-42110-7, Little Simon). S&S.

Family. Pa Chin. 7.95 (ISBN 0-8351-0589-X). China Bks.

Family. Seymour Rossel. (gr. 4 up). 1980. PLB 6.45 (ISBN 0-531-04102-6). Watts.

Family. Ed. by Alice S. Rossi et al. 1978. 10.95 (ISBN 0-393-01167-4); pap. 6.95x (ISBN 0-393-09064-7). Norton.

Family. Ed Sanders. 1972. pap. 1.95 (ISBN 0-380-00771-1, 24802). Avon.

Family! Sylvia R. Tester. LC 80-12373. (Picture Word Bks.). (Illus.). 32p. (ps-1). 1980. PLB 5.50 (ISBN 0-89565-156-4). Childs World.

Family. Robert Wernick. (Human Behavior Ser.). 1974. 9.95 (ISBN 0-8094-1908-4); lib. bdg. avail. (ISBN 0-685-50862-5). Time-Life.

Family. Robert Wernick. LC 74-17706. (Human Behavior Ser.). (Illus.). 1974. lib. bdg. 9.99 o.p. (ISBN 0-686-51075-5). Silver.

Family. Elizabeth Wrangham et al. Ed. by Malcolm Yapp et al. (World History Ser.). (Illus.). 32p. (gr. 10). 1980. lib. bdg. 5.95 (ISBN 0-89908-148-7); pap. text ed. 1.95 (ISBN 0-89908-123-1). Greenhaven.

Family - in Crisis or in Transition. Ed. by Andrew M. Greeley. (Concilium: Vol. 121). (Orig.). 1979. pap. 4.95 (ISBN 0-8164-2201-X). Crossroad NY.

Family: A Church Challenge for the 80's. Dolores Curran. (Orig.). 1980. pap. 3.50 (ISBN 0-03-057549-4). Winston Pr.

Family ADVENTures. Bruce Clanton. LC 80-51060. (ps-6). 1980. pap. 3.95 (ISBN 0-89390-018-4). Resource Pubns.

Family Advice Services. Aryeh Leissner. 1967. pap. text ed. 3.00x (ISBN 0-582-32408-4). Humanities.

Family Affairs. Catherine Gaskin. LC 79-8832. 528p. 1980. 12.95 (ISBN 0-385-13468-1). Doubleday.

Family Album. David Galloway. 1980. 12.95 (ISBN 0-7145-3682-2); pap. 6.95 (ISBN 0-7145-3785-3). Riverrun NY.

Family Album: A Novel. David Galloway. LC 77-84387. 1978. 8.95 o.p. (ISBN 0-15-130153-0). HarBraceJ.

Family: An Historical & Social Study. Charles F. Thwing & Carrie F. Thwing. 258p. 1980. Repr. of 1913 ed. lib. bdg. 40.00 (ISBN 0-8495-5157-9). Arden Lib.

Family: An Introduction. 2nd ed. J. Ross Eshleman. 1978. text ed. 18.95 (ISBN 0-205-05949-X); instr's man. avail. (ISBN 0-205-05950-3). Allyn.

Family: An Introduction. 3rd ed. J. Ross Eshleman. 640p. 1981. text ed. 19.90 (ISBN 0-205-07241-0, 817241-2); tchrs'. ed. free (ISBN 0-205-07242-9). Allyn.

Family Ancestral Record: Adult Genealogy Starter Kit. Duane S. Crowther. LC 78-52113. 1978. 4.50 (ISBN 0-88290-088-9). Horizon Utah.

Family & Alternate Life-Styles. Nick Stinnett & Craig W. Birdsong. LC 77-16593. 1978. text ed. 15.95 (ISBN 0-88229-208-0). Nelson-Hall.

Family & Colour in Jamaica. 2nd ed. Fernando Henriques. 1968. text ed. 9.00x (ISBN 0-261-62000-2). Humanities.

Family & Community Functioning: A Manual of Measurement for Social Work Practice & Policy. Ludwig L. Geismar. LC 77-163429. 1971. 8.00 o.p. (ISBN 0-8108-0415-8). Scarecrow.

Family & Community Functioning: A Manual of Measurement for Social-Work Practice & Policy. 2nd, rev. ed. Ludwig L. Geismar. LC 80-17785. 317p. 1980. 15.00 (ISBN 0-8108-1332-7); pap. 9.75 (ISBN 0-8108-1341-6). Scarecrow.

Family & Fortune: Studies in Aristocratic Finance in the Sixteenth & Seventeenth Centuries. Lawrence Stone. (Illus.). 1973. 29.95x (ISBN 0-19-822401-X). Oxford U Pr.

Family & Inheritance. Ed. by J. Goody et al. LC 76-10402. (Past & Present Publications Ser.). (Illus.). 1976. 45.00 (ISBN 0-521-21246-4); pap. 13.95x (ISBN 0-521-29354-5). Cambridge U Pr.

Family & Kinship in Modern Britain. Christopher Turner. (Students Library of Sociology). 1969. text ed. 3.75x (ISBN 0-7100-6535-3); pap. text ed. 1.50x (ISBN 0-7100-6347-4). Humanities.

Family & Marriage. Ed. by John Mogey. (International Studies in Sociological & Social Anthropology). 1963. pap. text ed. 12.50x (ISBN 90-040-1046-7). Humanities.

Family & Other Business Groups in Economic Development: The Case of Nicaragua. Harry W. Strachan. LC 75-25025. (Special Studies). (Illus.). 160p. 1976. text ed. 21.95 (ISBN 0-275-56050-3). Praeger.

Family & Public Policy: The Issue of the 1980s. John J. Dempsey. (Illus.). 120p. 1981. text ed. price not set (ISBN 0-933716-15-X). P H Brookes.

Family & Social Change: Comparative Perspectives. Mark Hutter. 500p. 1981. text ed. 16.95 (ISBN 0-471-08394-1). Wiley.

Family & the State: Considerations for Social Policy. R. M. Moroney. LC 75-45230. (Illus.). 1976. pap. text ed. 8.50x (ISBN 0-582-48493-6). Longman.

Family As Educator. Ed. by Hope J. Leichter. LC 75-16252. 1975. 8.75x (ISBN 0-8077-2497-1); pap. 6.00x (ISBN 0-8077-2496-3). Tchrs Coll.

Family Bible Encyclopedia, 2 vols. Alvera Mickelsen & Berkley Mickelsen. Incl. Volume I (A-K (ISBN 0-89191-100-6); Volume II (L-Z (ISBN 0-89191-127-8). LC 78-55384. (Illus.). 1978. 9.95 ea.; Set. 16.95 (ISBN 0-89191-201-0). Cook.

Family Bike Rides. Milton Grossberg. (Illus.). 128p. (Orig.). 1981. pap. 5.95 (ISBN 0-87701-148-6). Chronicle Bks.

Family Book About Sexuality. Mary S. Calderone & Eric W. Johnson. LC 79-2592. (Illus.). 320p. 1981. 14.95 (ISBN 0-690-01910-6, HarpT). Har-Row.

Family Book of Best Loved Poems. George, David L. (Compiler) 1952. 9.95 (ISBN 0-385-01421-X). Doubleday.

Family Book of Camping Lists. Charles Farmer & Kathleen Farmer. (Illus.). 224p. (Orig.). 1981. pap. 6.95 (ISBN 0-8117-2136-1). Stackpole.

Family Book of Crafts. Sterling Publishing Company Editors. LC 72-95199. (Illus.). 576p. (gr. 6 up). 1973. 20.00 (ISBN 0-8069-5250-4); PLB 17.59 (ISBN 0-8069-5251-2). Sterling.

Family Book of Praise: Or Would You Rather Be a Hippopotamus? Mary J. Tully. (Illus.). 128p. (Orig.). 1980. 7.95 (ISBN 0-8215-6543-5); pap. 5.95 (ISBN 0-8215-6542-7). Sadlier.

Family Book of Sexuality. Mary S. Calderone & Eric W. Johnson. 1981. 14.95 (ISBN 0-690-01910-6, H&R). Lippincott.

Family Breakdown in Late Eighteenth Century France: Divorces in Rouen 1792-1803. Roderick Phillips. (Illus.). 288p. 1980. 55.00 (ISBN 0-19-822572-5). Oxford U Pr.

Family Budget Standard. rev ed. 1971. pap. 4.00 (ISBN 0-86671-008-6). Comm Coun Great NY.

Family, Bureaucracy, & the Elderly. Ed. by Ethel Shanas & Marvin B. Sussman. LC 76-44090. 1977. 12.75 (ISBN 0-8223-0381-7). Duke.

Family-Centered Care of Children & Adolescents: Nursing Concepts in Child Health. Jo J. Tackett & Mabel Hunsberger. 800p. 1981. text ed. price not set (ISBN 0-7216-8740-7). Saunders.

Family Centered Community Nursing: A Sociocultural Framework. Ed. by Adina M. Reinhardt & Mildred D. Quinn. LC 73-8681. 1973. pap. text ed. 12.50 (ISBN 0-8016-4102-0). Mosby.

Family Christmas Tree Book. Tomie De Paola. LC 80-12081. (Illus.). 32p. (ps-3). 1980. PLB 8.95 (ISBN 0-8234-0416-1). Holiday.

Family Circle Creative Low-Calorie Cooking. 1978. pap. 1.95 o.p. (ISBN 0-345-25940-8). Ballantine.

Family Circle Creative Needlecrafts. Ed. by Family Circle. LC 77-9240. (Illus.). 1979. 14.95 o.p. (ISBN 0-13-301853-9). P-H.

Family Circle Guide to Self-Help. Glen Evans. 1979. pap. 2.25 o.p. (ISBN 0-345-27394-X). Ballantine.

Family Communication. Sven Wahlroos. LC 73-11831. 300p. 1974. 8.95 o.s.i. (ISBN 0-02-622400-3). Macmillan.

Family Communication: Keeping Connected in Changing Times. Maureen Miller. LC 80-80226. 1980. pap. 7.95 (ISBN 0-8091-2220-0). Paulist Pr.

Family Conspiracy. Joan Phipson. LC 64-11494. (Illus.). (gr. 4-6). 1964. 5.95 o.p. (ISBN 0-15-227110-4, HJ). HarBraceJ.

Family Crises. Robert Neuhaus & Ruby Neuhaus. LC 73-85104. 1974. pap. 12.95 (ISBN 0-675-08890-9). Merrill.

Family Crucible. Augustus Y. Napier & Carl A. Whitaker. 320p. 1980. pap. 3.95 (ISBN 0-553-13576-7). Bantam.

Family Decision-Making: Sex Roles & Change Over the Life Cycle. John Scanzoni & Maximiliane Szinovacz. LC 80-18243. (Sage Library of Social Research: Vol. 111). (Illus.). 312p. 1980. 18.00 (ISBN 0-8039-1533-0); pap. 8.95 (ISBN 0-8039-1534-9). Sage.

Family Designed Learning. Thorwald Esbensen & Philip Richards. LC 74-83216. 1976. pap. 4.95 (ISBN 0-8224-2825-3). Pitman Learning.

Family Doctors & Public Policy: A Study of Manpower Distribution. John Butler. (International Library of Social Policy). 1973. 19.00 (ISBN 0-7100-7640-1). Routledge & Kegan.

Family Dog. rev. ed. Richard A. Wolters. 1975. 8.95 (ISBN 0-87690-173-9). Dutton.

Family Dolls' Houses. Vivien Greene. 176p. 1974. 23.00 (ISBN 0-8231-3030-4). Branford.

Family Economic Behavior. Eleanor B. Sheldon. LC 73-10458. 400p. 1973. 15.00 o.p. (ISBN 0-397-59058-X). Lippincott.

Family Estate Planning Guide, 2 vols. 2nd ed. Homer I. Harris. LC 71-114348. 1971. 95.00 (ISBN 0-686-14504-6). Lawyers Co-Op.

Family Factbook. 2nd ed. 670p. 1981. price not set (ISBN 0-8379-4602-6). Marquis.

Family Failing. Honor Arundel. LC 72-3231. 160p. (gr. 6 up). 1972. 7.95 o.p. (ISBN 0-525-66256-1). Elsevier-Nelson.

Family Faith. J. C. Wenger. (No. 10). 72p. 1981. pap. 0.95 (ISBN 0-686-69151-2). Herald Pr.

Family Farming in a Developing Economy. R. K. Lahiri. 1979. pap. text ed. 8.00x (ISBN 0-391-01851-5). Humanities.

Family Financial Survival. Linda Ginsberg. LC 80-70436. (Illus.). 192p. (Orig.). 1981. pap. 8.95 (ISBN 0-89087-315-1). Celestial Arts.

Family Formation in an Age of Nascent Capitalism. Ed. by D. Levine. 1977. 20.00 (ISBN 0-12-445050-4). Acad Pr.

Family Fortune. Mignon G. Eberhart. 1978. pap. 1.75 o.p. (ISBN 0-445-04203-6). Popular Lib.

Family Foundations. Paul Meier & Richard Meier. 96p. (Orig.). 1981. 8.95 (ISBN 0-8010-6117-2); pap. 4.95 (ISBN 0-8010-6122-9). Baker Bk.

Family, Friends, & Poetry. Marlan Beilke. 12p. 1980. pap. 5.00 (ISBN 0-918466-09-1). Quintessence.

Family Fun & Togetherness. Wayne Rickerson. 1979. pap. 3.95 (ISBN 0-88207-641-8). Victor Bks.

Family: Functions, Conflicts & Symbols. Peter J. Stein et al. (Sociology Ser.). 1977. pap. text ed. 12.95 (ISBN 0-201-07362-5). A-W.

Family Game: A Situational Approach to Effective Parenting. Paul Hersey & Ken Blanchard. LC 77-92163. 1978. 9.95 o.p. (ISBN 0-201-03068-3); pap. 5.95 o.p. (ISBN 0-201-03069-1). A-W.

Family Gathering. T. Alan Broughton. 1977. 7.95 o.p. (ISBN 0-525-10310-4). Dutton.

Family Guareschi: Chronicles of the Past & Present. Giovanni Guareschi. Tr. by L. K. Conrad from It. 1970. 6.50 o.p. (ISBN 0-374-15233-0). FS&G.

Family Guide to Amusement Centers: From Disneyland to Jungle Habitat. Susan Hunter. (Illus.). 1975. 9.95 o.s.i. (ISBN 0-8027-0451-4); pap. 5.95 (ISBN 0-8027-7092-4). Walker & Co.

Family Handyman Handbook of Carpentry Plans Projects. Ed. by Family Handyman Editors. 1980. 15.95 (ISBN 0-8306-9728-4); pap. 9.95 (ISBN 0-8306-1110-X, 1110). TAB Bks.

Family Handyman Handbook of Home Improvement & Remodeling. Family Handyman Magazine Editors. (Illus.). 1979. 14.95 o.p. (ISBN 0-8306-9863-9); pap. 9.95 (ISBN 0-8306-1084-7, 1084). TAB Bks.

Family Handyman Home Improvement Book. Family Handyman Magazine Editors. (Encore Edition). (Illus.). 1979. pap. 4.95 (ISBN 0-684-16319-5, ScribT). Scribner.

Family Health & Medical Guide. Good Housekeeping Editors. LC 78-51129. (Illus.). 928p. 1979. 19.95 (ISBN 0-87851-023-0). Hearst Bks.

Family Health Encyclopedia: An International Reference in the Health Sciences, Vols. 1 & 2. 1970. Set. 25.00 o.p. (ISBN 0-397-55952-6). Lippincott.

Family Historian's Handbook. Yaffa Draznin. 1978. pap. 2.50 o.s.i. (ISBN 0-515-04516-0). Jove Pubns.

Family Horse. George A. Martin. 12.50 (ISBN 0-88427-020-3). Green Hill.

Family Howl. Betty Dinneen. LC 80-25385. (Illus.). 96p. (gr. 4-6). 1981. PLB 8.95 (ISBN 0-02-732150-9). Macmillan.

Family in Australia: Social, Demographic & Psychological Aspects. Jerzy Krupinski & Alan Stoller. 273p. 1974. text ed. 18.70 o.p. (ISBN 0-08-017374-8). Pergamon.

Family in Australia: Social, Demographic & Psychological Aspects. 2nd ed. Jerzy Krupinski & Alan Stoller. 1978. text ed. 31.00 (ISBN 0-08-022260-9); pap. text ed. 13.25 (ISBN 0-08-022259-5). Pergamon.

Family in Child Health Care. Pat Azarnoff & Carol Hardgrove. 240p. 1981. pap. 14.95 (ISBN 0-471-08663-0, Pub. by Wiley-Med). Wiley.

Family in Classical China. Hiran P. Wilkinson. (Studies in Chinese History & Civilization). 239p. 1977. Repr. of 1926 ed. 19.50 (ISBN 0-89093-035-6). U Pubns Amer.

Family in History. Ed. by Charles E. Rosenberg. LC 75-14962. (Haney Foundation Ser.). 1975. 12.95 (ISBN 0-8122-7702-3); pap. 5.95 (ISBN 0-8122-1100-6). U of Pa Pr.

Family in Rural Society. Ed. by Raymond T. Coward & William M. Smith. (Special Studies in Contemporary Social Issues). 280p. 1981. lib. bdg. 25.00x (ISBN 0-86531-121-8). Westview.

Family in Search of a Future: Alternate Models for Moderns. Ed. by Herbert A. Otto. LC 75-111879. 1970. pap. text ed. 9.95 (ISBN 0-13-302869-0). P-H.

Family in Social Context. 4th ed. Gerald R. Leslie. (Illus.). 1979. text ed. 15.95x (ISBN 0-19-502423-0). Oxford U Pr.

Family in the American Economy. Hazel Kyrk. LC 53-12266. (Midway Reprint). (Illus.). 1976. pap. text ed. 18.00x (ISBN 0-226-46621-3). U of Chicago Pr.

Family in Transition: Rethinking Marriage, Sexuality, Child Rearing & Family Organization. 3rd ed. 579p. 1980. pap. text ed. 9.95 (ISBN 0-316-79722-7); free test bank by Harrentsian (ISBN 0-316-79704-9). Little.

Family Interaction. Ralph H. Turner. LC 71-118627. (Illus.). 505p. 1970. 21.95 (ISBN 0-471-89300-5). Wiley.

Family Is... Brinkley. (gr. 9-12). 1981. text ed. 7.92 (ISBN 0-87002-320-9). Bennett IL.

Family Is the Patient: An Approach to Behavioral Pediatrics for the Clinician. Bayard W. Allmond et al. LC 79-16622. 1979. pap. text ed. 19.95 (ISBN 0-8016-0131-2). Mosby.

Family Issues of Employed Women in Europe & America. Ed. by Andree Michel. (International Studies in Sociology & Social Anthropology: Vol. 11). (Illus.). 166p. 1971. text ed. 24.00x (ISBN 90-040-2633-9). Humanities.

Family Law & Child Welfare: Selected Current Trends in Legal Social Work Practice. Ed. by John Lemmon. (Law & Social Work Quarterly Ser.: Vol. 1, No. 1). 112p. 1981. text ed. 12.95 (ISBN 0-917724-64-X). Haworth Pr.

Family Legend, Repr. Of 1810 Ed. Joanna Baillie. Bd. with Metrical Legends of Exalted Characters. Repr. of 1821 ed. LC 75-31147. (Romantic Context: Poetry 1789-1830 Ser.: Vol. 4). 1977. lib. bdg. 47.00 (ISBN 0-8240-2103-7). Garland Pub.

Family Library Series, 3 bks. Ed. by Jean Watson. Incl. Pilgrim's Progress: In Modern English. John Bunyan. 6.95 (ISBN 0-310-38810-4); Princess & Curdie. George MacDonald; Princess & the Goblin. George MacDonald. (gr. 3 up). 1980. Set. slipcased 19.85 (ISBN 0-310-42718-5). Zondervan.

Family Life & Child Development: Selective Bibliography Cumulative Through 1979. Book Review Committee. (Jewish Board of Family & Children Services). 1979. pap. 3.00 (ISBN 0-87183-187-2). Jewish Bd Family.

Family Life & Illicit Love in Earlier Generations. Peter Laslett. 1977. 47.50 (ISBN 0-521-21408-4); pap. 12.95x (ISBN 0-521-29221-2). Cambridge U Pr.

Family Life & Morality: Studies in Black & White. William Gibson. LC 79-57076. 116p. 1980. pap. text ed. 7.50 (ISBN 0-8191-0969-X). U Pr of Amer.

Family Life Education: Focus on Student Involvement. K Green. LC 75-4098. 1975. pap. 4.00 (ISBN 0-686-14989-0, 261-08420). Home Econ Educ.

Family Life in a Northern Thai Village: A Study of the Structural Significance of Women. Sulamith H. Potter. 1978. 12.00x (ISBN 0-520-03430-9); pap. 4.95x (ISBN 0-520-04044-9). U of Cal Pr.

Family Life in America. Mel Albin & Dominick Cavallo. (Illus.). 350p. 1980. 8.95 (ISBN 0-686-64847-1). Revisionary.

Family Life in the U.S.A. Gladys Alesi & Dora Pantell. (gr. 9-12). 1962. pap. text ed. 2.75 (ISBN 0-88345-055-0). Regents Pub.

Family Life of Sick Children: A Study of Families Coping with Chronic Childhood Disease. Lindy Burton. 1975. 22.50x (ISBN 0-7100-8171-5); pap. 7.50 (ISBN 0-7100-8172-3). Routledge & Kegan.

Family Lifeline. Agnes C. Ducey. LC 80-820. (Ducey Bks.). (Illus.). 160p. 1981. 9.95x (ISBN 0-9605110-0-8); pap. 7.50x (ISBN 0-9605110-1-6). World Issues.

Family, Lineage & Civil Society: A Study of Society, Politics & Mentality in the Durham Region, 1500-1640. M. E. James. 240p. 1973. 33.00x (ISBN 0-19-822408-7). Oxford U Pr.

Family Living. University of Missouri - Home Economics Resource Unit. text ed. 2.00x spiral bdg. (ISBN 0-87543-023-6). Lucas.

Family Living in the Bible. Edith Deen. (Family Lib Ser.). 1969. pap. 1.25 (ISBN 0-89129-107-5). Jove Pubns.

Family Living Skill Book. Boy Scouts of America. (Illus.). 32p. (gr. 3-4). 1974. pap. 0.50x (ISBN 0-8395-6587-9, 6587); tchr's guide 0.30 (ISBN 0-685-41688-7, 18-327). BSA.

Family Mark Twain, 2 vols. Mark Twain. 1975. boxed set 20.00 o.s.i. (ISBN 0-06-010128-8, HarpT). Har-Row.

Family Marriage & Social Change. 2nd ed. Richard R. Clayton. 1979. text ed. 16.95x (ISBN 0-669-01957-7); inst. manual free (ISBN 0-669-01956-9). Heath.

Family Matters. Kitty Burns Florey. 1981. pap. 2.25 (ISBN 0-451-09667-3, 9667, Sig). NAL.

Family Mediation Workbook. Cook et al. Ed. by Donice Polk. 90p. (Orig.). 1980. pap. 10.00. D Polk.

Family Medical Handbook. 2nd ed. Ed. by David K. Carding. 226p. 1981. 14.95 (ISBN 0-571-18027-2). Merrimack Bk Serv.

Family Mental Health: Theory & Practice. Rae Sedgwick. LC 80-20160. (Illus.). 296p. 1980. pap. text ed. 9.95 (ISBN 0-8016-4447-X). Mosby.

Family Ministry: Family Life Through the Church. Charles M. Sell. 272p. 11.95 (ISBN 0-310-42580-8). Zondervan.

Family Minus. Fernando Krahn. LC 76-18093. (Illus.). 40p. (ps-3). 1977. 5.95 o.s.i. (ISBN 0-8193-0860-9, Four Winds); PLB 5.41 o.s.i. (ISBN 0-8193-0861-7). Schol Bk Serv.

Family Names & Their Story. Sabine Baring-Gould. LC 68-23136. 1969. Repr. of 1910 ed. 15.00 (ISBN 0-8103-0151-2). Gale.

Family, No. Three: Commitments. Leila Andrews. LC 76-56770. 1977. pap. 1.50 o.p. (ISBN 0-345-25706-5). Ballantine.

Family, No. Two: Transitions. Leila Andrews. 1977. pap. 1.50 o.p. (ISBN 0-345-25705-7). Ballantine.

Family Nursing. C. Luise Riehl. (Illus.). 384p. 1974. text ed. 15.00 (ISBN 0-87002-154-0). Bennett IL.

Family Nursing: A Study Guide. 2nd ed. Evelyn G. Sobol & Paulette Robischon. (Illus.). 182p. 1975. pap. 7.95 o.p. (ISBN 0-8016-4727-4). Mosby.

Family Nursing: Theory & Assessment. Marilyn M. Friedman. 337p. 1981. pap. 16.50 (ISBN 0-8385-2532-6). ACC.

Family of God: The Meaning of Church Membership. LeRoy Lawson. LC 80-53497. 64p. (Orig.). 1981. pap. 1.50 (ISBN 0-87239-432-8, 39970). Standard Pub.

Family of Outcasts. Seymour Rubenfeld. LC 65-20000. 1965. 12.95 (ISBN 0-02-927580-6). Free Pr.

Family Papers: A Return to Purgatory. Burton Blatt et al. (Illus., Orig.). 1980. pap. 8.95 (ISBN 0-582-28154-7). Longman.

Family Passover. Anne Rosen et al. LC 79-89298. 64p. (gr. 2 up). 1980. 6.95 (ISBN 0-8276-0169-7, 452). Jewish Pubn.

Family Photographs: Content, Meaning & Effect. Julia Hirsch. LC 80-25591. (Illus.). 160p. 1981. 12.95 (ISBN 0-19-502889-9). Oxford U Pr.

Family Planning & Preventive Psychiatry. S. Okpaku. 1981. 20.00 (ISBN 0-89388-003-5). Okpaku Communications.

Family Planning Communication: A Critique of the Indian Programme. Sumanta Banerjee. (Illus.). 218p. 1980. text ed. 10.50x (ISBN 0-391-02169-9). Humanities.

Family Planning the Natural Way. Josef Roetzer. Date not set. pap. 6.95 (ISBN 0-8007-1185-8). Revell. Postponed.

Family Planning Under the Emergency: Policy Implications of Incentives & Disincentives. V. A. Panandiker et al. (Illus.). 1979. text ed. 8.50x (ISBN 0-391-01011-5). Humanities.

Family Policy. Ed. by Sheila B. Kamerman & Alfred J. Kahn. 1978. 27.50x (ISBN 0-231-04464-X); pap. 12.50x (ISBN 0-231-04465-8). Columbia U Pr.

Family Portrait. Dobos et al. 1977. pap. text ed. 6.95x o.p. (ISBN 0-534-00560-8). Wadsworth Pub.

Family Portrait. alternate ed. Dobos et al. 1978. pap. text ed. 6.95x o.p. (ISBN 0-534-00691-4). Wadsworth Pub.

Family Portrait: A Study of Contemporary Life Styles. 2nd alt. ed. David E. Dobos et al. 192p. 1980. pap. text ed. 6.95x (ISBN 0-534-00876-3). Wadsworth Pub.

Family Portrait: A Study of Contemporary Life Styles. 2nd ed. David E. Dobos et al. 264p. 1980. pap. text ed. 6.95x (ISBN 0-534-00874-7). Wadsworth Pub.

Family Portrait, from a Mother's Diary. Anne M. Zanzucchi. Tr. by Lenny Szczesniak from It. LC 81-80031. Orig. Title: Giorno per Giorno. 100p. 1981. pap. 2.95 (ISBN 0-911782-19-2). New City.

Family Practice: Foundation of Changing Health Care. Geyman. LC 79-18290. 1979. 28.50 (ISBN 0-8385-2537-7). ACC.

Family Practice in the Medical School. Geyman. 1977. 8.00 o.p. (ISBN 0-686-51335-5). ACC.

Family Practice Review. Robert E. Pieroni & F. Scutchfield. 1978. spiral bdg. 16.50 (ISBN 0-87488-134-X). Med Exam.

Family Practice Review, Vol. 2. Robert E. Pieroni. LC 79-91973. 1980. pap. 14.50 (ISBN 0-87488-181-1). Med Exam.

Family Practice Specialty Board Recertification Review. 3rd ed. John E. Verby. 1978. spiral bdg. 16.50 (ISBN 0-87488-309-1). Med Exam.

Family Property Settlements Future Interest. 2nd ed. Browder et al. (Contemporary Legal Education Ser.). 1973. 19.00 o.p. (ISBN 0-672-81869-8, Bobbs-Merrill Law). Michie.

Family Quiz Book. Christina Calveley. 1981. pap. 2.95 (ISBN 0-14-005507-X). Penguin.

Family Record Book. 7.95 o.p. (ISBN 0-685-26807-1). Warman.

Family Research: A Source Book, Analysis & Guide to Federal Funding, 2 vols. Wakefield Washington Associates, Inc. LC 79-7732. (Illus.). 1979. Set. lib. bdg. 95.00 (ISBN 0-313-21139-6, WFR/). Greenwood.

Family Resource Management: Principles & Applications. Ruth E. Deacon & Francille M. Firebaugh. 280p. 1980. text ed. 16.95 (ISBN 0-205-06994-0, 4569946); tchr's. manual free (ISBN 0-205-07000-0). Allyn.

Family River Rafting Guide: 1979. Alvin Fixler. LC 79-83686. (Illus.). 1979. pap. write for info. o.p. (ISBN 0-89803-006-4). Caroline Hse.

Family Romance. Richard Wollheim. 256p. 1969. 5.95 o.p. (ISBN 0-374-15292-6). FS&G.

Family Roots of School Learning & Behavior Disorders. Ed. by Robert Friedman. 360p. 1973. 19.75 (ISBN 0-398-02469-3); pap. 11.50 (ISBN 0-398-02472-3). C C Thomas.

Family Secrets: Recipes from Grandma Fowler's Kitchen. Ed. by Mary L. Rothenbuehler. (Illus., Orig.). 1981. pap. 2.25 (ISBN 0-939010-00-3). Zephyr.

Family, Sex & Marriage in England, Fifteen Hundred to Eighteen Hundred. abr. ed. Lawrence Stone. LC 79-2028. (Illus.). 1980. pap. 8.95 (ISBN 0-06-090735-5, CN 735, CN). Har-Row.

Family Shadow: Sources of Suicide & Schizophrenia. David K. Reynolds & Norman L. Farberow. 188p. 1981. 14.95 (ISBN 0-520-04213-1). U of Cal Pr.

Family Social Welfare: Helping Troubled Families. Frances L. Feldman & Frances H. Scherz. LC 67-18276. 1967. 18.95x (ISBN 0-202-36001-6). Aldine Pub.

Family, Society, & the Individual. 4th ed. William M. Kephart. LC 76-13094. (Illus.). 1977. text ed. 16.95 (ISBN 0-395-24247-9); inst. manual 1.00 (ISBN 0-395-24246-0). HM.

Family, Society, & the Individual. 5th ed. William M. Kephart. LC 80-81847. (Illus.). 624p. 1981. text ed. 16.95 (ISBN 0-395-29760-5); instr's. manual 0.75 (ISBN 0-395-29761-3). HM.

Family Strengths: Positive Models for Family Life. Ed. by Nick Stinnett et al. LC 80-50917. x, 518p. 1980. 21.50x (ISBN 0-8032-4125-9); pap. 9.95x (ISBN 0-8032-9122-1). U of Nebr Pr.

Family Structure & Effective Health Behavior: The Energized Family. Lois Pratt. LC 75-29817. (Illus.). 256p. 1976. pap. text ed. 10.50 (ISBN 0-395-18702-8). HM.

Family Structure in Nineteenth Century Lancashire. Michael Anderson. LC 79-164448. (Cambridge Studies in Sociology: No. 5). (Illus.). 1971. 29.50 (ISBN 0-521-08237-4). Cambridge U Pr.

Family Tapestry: Five Generations of the Curwens of Walnut Hill & Their Various Relatives. Patricia T. Davis. LC 72-14325. (Illus.). 224p. 1972. lib. bdg. 10.00 (ISBN 0-915010-15-1). Sutter House.

Family That Changed. Francine S. Spilke. (Divorced Family Ser.). (Illus.). 32p. (ps). 1979. 6.95 (ISBN 0-517-53785-0, Michelman Bks). Crown.

Family That Listens. Norman Wright. 1978. pap. 3.95 (ISBN 0-88207-633-7). Victor Bks.
Family Therapy. rev. ed. Zuk. 1981. 19.95x (ISBN 0-87705-430-4); pap. 12.95x (ISBN 0-87705-955-1). Human Sci Pr.
Family Therapy: A Comparison of Approaches. new ed. Susan L. Jones. LC 80-10161. (Illus.). 1980. text ed. 14.95 (ISBN 0-87619-625-3). R J Brady.
Family Therapy: A Handbook. George Thorman. LC 65-28619. 1965. pap. 6.50x o.p. (ISBN 0-87424-047-6). Western Psych.
Family Therapy: An Introduction to Theory & Technique. 2nd ed. Gerald D. Erickson & Terrence P. Hogan. 448p. (Orig.). 1980. pap. text ed. 12.95 (ISBN 0-8185-0437-4). Brooks-Cole.
Family Therapy & Evaluation Through Art. Hanna Y. Kwiatkowska. (Illus.). 304p. 1978. 26.75 (ISBN 0-398-03729-9). C C Thomas.
Family Therapy & Social Change. Neil Solomon. 1981. text ed. 22.50x (ISBN 0-8290-0088-7); audio cassette incl. Irvington.
Family Therapy: Full Length Case Studies. Ed. by Peggy Papp. LC 77-16641. 1977. 14.95 o.p. (ISBN 0-470-99355-3). Halsted Pr.
Family Therapy: The Major Approaches. Ed. by Robert J. Green & James L. Framo. 620p. 1981. text ed. 30.00 (ISBN 0-8236-1885-4). Intl Univs Pr.
Family Therapy: The Treatment of Natural Systems. Sue Walrond-Skinner. (Library of Social Work). 1976. 19.00 (ISBN 0-7100-8325-4); pap. 8.95 (ISBN 0-7100-8326-2). Routledge & Kegan.
Family Therapy: Theory & Practice. Philip J. Guerin, Jr. 516p. 1976. lib. bdg. 24.50 o.p. (ISBN 0-470-15089-0). Halsted Pr.
Family Therapy Workbook. Irene Goldenberg & Herbert Goldenberg. 1980. pap. text ed. 4.95 (ISBN 0-8185-0412-9). Brooks-Cole.
Family Ties. Deborah A. Holmes. LC 77-82171. 1979. pap. 2.25 o.p. (ISBN 0-87216-426-8). Playboy Pbks.
Family to Family. Betty F. Griffin. 78p. 1980. pap. text ed. 5.75 (ISBN 0-88200-140-X, 16008). Alexander Graham.
Family Treatment in Social Work Practice. Ed. by Oliver Harris & Curtis Janzen. LC 79-91098. 300p. 1980. pap. text ed. 7.95 (ISBN 0-87581-254-6). Peacock Pubs.
Family Tree. Margaret Storey. LC 73-10040. (Illus.). 196p. (gr. 4-7). 1973. 5.95 o.p. (ISBN 0-525-66330-4). Elsevier-Nelson.
Family Tree. Dorothy Yates. 1967. 4.50 o.p. (ISBN 0-374-15320-5). FS&G.
Family Tree Ancestral Tablets. William H. Whitmore. 1955. pap. 7.75 (ISBN 0-8048-0684-5). C E Tuttle.
Family Violence. Richard J. Gelles. LC 79-14813. (Sage Library of Social Research: Vol. 84). (Illus.). 1979. 18.00x (ISBN 0-8039-1234-X); pap. 8.95x (ISBN 0-8039-1235-8). Sage.
Family Violence. George Thorman. 196p. 1980. text ed. 16.50 (ISBN 0-398-03953-4). C C Thomas.
Family Wilderness Handbook. Mary S. Welch. (Orig.). 1973. pap. 1.65 o.p. (ISBN 0-345-23253-4). Ballantine.
Family, Women, & Socialization in the Kibbutz. Menachem Gerson. LC 78-57188. (Illus.). 1978. 17.95 (ISBN 0-669-02371-X). Lexington Bks.
Family Word Finder. Readers Digest Editors. 832p. 1975. 16.95 (ISBN 0-89577-023-7, Pub by Reader's Digest). Norton.
Family World Atlas. Ed. by Paul Tiddens. LC 73-3377. (Illus.). 1978. 14.95 (ISBN 0-528-83092-9); deluxe ed. 16.95 (ISBN 0-528-83115-1). Rand.
Family Worship. Paul Henshaw & H. Weemshall. 84p. 1981. pap. 2.25x (ISBN 0-8358-0421-6). Upper Room.
Family Years: A Guide to Positive Parenting. Michael C. Macpherson. 146p. (Orig.). 1981. pap. 5.95 (ISBN 0-03-059131-7). Winston Pr.
Family: Yesterday, Today, Tomorrow. Walter Goodman & Elaine Goodman. LC 74-32069. 128p. (gr. 7 up). 1975. 7.95 (ISBN 0-374-32260-0). FS&G.
Famine. Rhoda Blumberg. LC 78-6837. (Impact Bks.). (Illus.). (gr. 9 up). 1978. PLB 6.90 s&l (ISBN 0-531-02201-3). Watts.
Famine in Russia, 1891-1892. Richard G. Robbins, Jr. LC 74-8528. (Studies of the Russian Institute of Columbia University). 1975. 17.50x (ISBN 0-231-03836-4). Columbia U Pr.
Famine: Ireland, 8 vols. (British Parliamentary Papers Ser.). 1971. Set. 702.00x (ISBN 0-7165-1495-8, Pub. by Irish Academic Pr Ireland). Biblio Dist.
Famine: Its Causes Effects & Management. J. R. Robson. (Food & Nutrition in History & Anthropology Ser.). 109p. 1980. write for info. (ISBN 0-677-16180-8). Gordon.
Famines in India, 1850-1965. 2nd ed. B. M. Bhatia. 10.50x (ISBN 0-210-33854-7). Asia.
Famous American Statesmen. William O. Stevens. (Illus.). (gr. 7-9). 1953. 5.95 o.p. (ISBN 0-396-03449-7). Dodd.
Famous Americans, 2 bks. Joel Legunn. (Janus Stamp & Story Ser.). (Illus.). 64p. (gr. 6-12). 1980. 2.85 ea. Bk. 1 Before 1860 (ISBN 0-915510-44-8). Bk. 2 After 1860 (ISBN 0-915510-45-6). Janus Bks.
Famous Architectural Illustrations from Distant Lands. James A. Salvadori. (Illus.). 137p. 1981. 59.45 (ISBN 0-930582-96-9). Gloucester Art.
Famous Authors: Women. Edward F. Harkins. LC 73-173098. Date not set. Repr. of 1906 ed. 18.00 (ISBN 0-8103-4306-1). Gale.
Famous Brand Names, Emblems and Trademarks. Marjorie Stiling. LC 80-69353. (Illus.). 64p. 1981. 8.95 (ISBN 0-7153-8098-2). David & Charles.
Famous British Women Novelists. Norah Smaridge. LC 67-22722. (Illus.). (gr. 7-9). 1967. 5.95 (ISBN 0-396-05612-1). Dodd.
Famous Cases of Circumstantial Evidence, 2 vols. in 1. Intro. by S. M. Phillipps. 1980. Repr. of 1878 ed. lib. bdg. 42.50x (ISBN 0-8377-1002-2). Rothman.
Famous Curses. Daniel Cohen. (gr. 3-6). pap. 1.75 (ISBN 0-671-41867-X). Archway.
Famous Custom & Show Cars. George Barris & Jack Scagnetti. (Illus.). 160p. (YA) 1973. PLB 12.95 (ISBN 0-525-29610-7). Dutton.
Famous Dishes of the World. Wina Born. Tr. by Marian Powell. (Illus.). 1973. pap. 3.95 o.s.i. (ISBN 0-02-009240-7, Collier). Macmillan.
Famous Duels & Assassinations. Lewis Melville & Reginald Hargreaves. LC 72-178619. (Illus.). 288p. 1974. Repr. of 1929 ed. 18.00 (ISBN 0-8103-3973-0). Gale.
Famous Fantastic Classics, No. 2. LC 74-20652. 160p. 1980. Repr. of 1974 ed. lib. bdg. 10.95x (ISBN 0-89370-025-8). Borgo Pr.
Famous First Facts. 4th ed. Ed. by Joseph N. Kane. 1981. write for info. Wilson.
Famous Firsts for Teachers. Charles A. Weiner et al. 1976. pap. text ed. 1.75x (ISBN 0-8134-1844-5, 1844). Interstate.
Famous Flaws. Alice Loomer. LC 76-8411. 320p. 1976. 9.95 o.s.i. (ISBN 0-02-575101-8, 57510). Macmillan.
Famous French Painters. Roland J. McKinney. LC 60-9152. (Illus.). (gr. 7-9). 1960. 5.95 (ISBN 0-396-04360-7). Dodd.
Famous Frontiersmen. John W. Moyer. LC 76-13740. (Illus.). (gr. 4-8). 1972. 6.95 o.p. (ISBN 0-528-82807-X). Rand.
Famous Game of Chesse-Play. Arthur Saul. LC 74-80216. (English Experience Ser.: No. 691). 1974. Repr. of 1614 ed. 5.00 (ISBN 90-221-0691-8). Walter J Johnson.
Famous Generals. Duncan Townson. LC 78-70608. (Illus.). (gr. 4-6). 1979. PLB 6.90 s&l (ISBN 0-531-09120-1). Watts.
Famous Guns from the Smithsonian Collection. Hank W. Bowman. LC 67-16180. (Illus.). 1966. lib. bdg. 3.50 o.p. (ISBN 0-668-01606-X). Arco.
Famous Guns That Won the West. James Wycoff. LC 68-16740. (Illus.). 1975. pap. 2.00 o.p. (ISBN 0-668-03829-2). Arco.
Famous Indian Chiefs. John W. Moyer. LC 76-13741. (Illus.). (gr. 4-8). 1957. 6.95 o.p. (ISBN 0-528-82808-8). Rand.
Famous Literary Teams for Young People. Norah Smaridge. LC 76-53636. (Famous Biographies Ser). (gr. 7 up). 1977. 5.95 (ISBN 0-396-07407-3). Dodd.
Famous Long Ago. Raymond Mungo. 1970. 3.95 (ISBN 0-8070-6182-4, Pub. by Montana Bks); pap. 1.95 (ISBN 0-8070-6183-2). Madrona Pubs.
Famous Miss Burney: The Diaries & Letters of Fanny Burney. Ed. by Barbara Schrank & David J. Supino. LC 75-25622. (John Day Bk.). 1976. 9.95 o.s.i. (ISBN 0-381-98285-8, TYC-T). T Y Crowell.
Famous Modern Negro Musicians. Penman Lovinggood. LC 77-22215. (Music Reprint Ser.). (Illus.). 1977. Repr. lib. bdg. 15.00 (ISBN 0-306-77523-9). Da Capo.
Famous Monster Funbooks. William Johnson. (Illus.). 48p. (Orig.). 1981. pap. 2.50 (ISBN 0-89844-030-0). Troubador Pr.
Famous Movie Detectives. Michael R. Pitts. LC 79-17474. 367p. 1979. 18.50 (ISBN 0-8108-1236-3). Scarecrow.
Famous Mysteries of Modern Times. Leonard Gribble. 1977. 9.50 (ISBN 0-584-10240-2). Transatlantic.
Famous Names in Engineering. Carvill. 1981. text ed. price not set (ISBN 0-408-00536-X). Butterworth.
Famous Old Cars. Hank W. Bowman. LC 57-14442. (Illus.). 1957. lib. bdg. 6.95 o.p. (ISBN 0-668-00597-1). Arco.
Famous Old Cars. Hank W. Bowman. LC 57-14442. (Illus.). 1978. pap. 2.95 o.p. (ISBN 0-668-04311-3, 4311). Arco.
Famous People on Film. Carol A. Emmens. LC 77-3449. 1977. 16.50 (ISBN 0-8108-1051-4). Scarecrow.
Famous Personalities of Flight Cookbook. Mary Henderson. LC 80-20331. (Illus.). 136p. 1981. pap. 4.95 (ISBN 0-87474-515-2). Smithsonian.
Famous Political Trials. Andrew David. LC 79-16923. (On Trial Ser.). (Illus.). (YA) (gr. 5 up). 1980. PLB 6.95g (ISBN 0-8225-1429-X). Lerner Pubns.
Famous Pulp Classics, No. 1. LC 74-20653. 1975. 5.00 (ISBN 0-913960-12-8). Fax Collect.
Famous Pulp Classics, No. 1. LC 80-23995. 100p. 1980. Repr. of 1974 ed. lib. bdg. 10.95x (ISBN 0-89370-026-6). Borgo Pr.
Famous Pulp Classics, No. 2. LC 74-20652. 1975. 5.00 (ISBN 0-913960-11-X). Fax Collect.
Famous Sayings & Their Authors: A Collection of Historical Sayings in English, French, German, Greek, Italian, & Latin. Edward Latham. LC 68-26582. 1970. Repr. of 1904 ed. 18.00 (ISBN 0-8103-3141-1). Gale.
Famous Secret Societies. John H. Lepper. LC 73-143638. 1971. Repr. of 1932 ed. 20.00 (ISBN 0-8103-3648-0). Gale.
Famous Tragedy of the Rich Jew of Malta. Christopher Marlowe. 1974. text ed. 12.00 (ISBN 0-8277-3901-X); pap. text ed. 5.95 (ISBN 0-8277-2388-1). British Bk Ctr.
Famous Women Tennis Players. Trent Frayne. LC 78-22428. (Famous Biographies Ser.). (Illus.). 1979. 6.95 (ISBN 0-396-07681-5). Dodd.
Fan. Bob Randall. 288p. 1978. pap. 2.50 (ISBN 0-446-91887-3). Warner Bks.
Fan-Qui in China in 1836-7, 3 vols. C. T. Downing. (Illus.). 980p. 1972. Repr. of 1838 ed. 84.00x (ISBN 0-7165-2026-5, Pub. by Irish Academic Pr Ireland). Biblio Dist.
Fan the Deck. rev. ed. Robert B. Cahill & Herbert J. Herbic. 1980. pap. text ed. 4.55 (ISBN 0-933282-02-8). Stack the Deck.
Fanatics. Peter Hill. LC 78-53482. 1978. 7.95 o.p. (ISBN 0-684-15821-3, ScribT). Scribner.
Fancy Dress for Children. Barbara Snook. 1975. 2.95 o.s.i. (ISBN 0-7134-2635-7). Hippocrene Bks.
Fancy Dress from Nursery Tales. Jean Greenhowe. (Illus.). 88p. 1976. 10.50 o.s.i. (ISBN 0-7134-2918-6). Hippocrene Bks.
Fancy for Pigeons. Jack Kligerman. LC 77-92316. (Illus.). 1978. 12.00 o.p. (ISBN 0-8015-4043-7). Dutton.
Fancy Pants: Creative Patterns for Making Baby's First Wardrobe. Pieke Stuvel. (Illus.). 1979. pap. 4.95 (ISBN 0-8015-0484-8, Hawthorn). Dutton.
Fandora's Story. Betty H. Hyatt. LC 81-80089. (House of Lancien Ser.). 192p. (Orig.). 1981. pap. 1.95 (ISBN 0-87216-790-9). Playboy Pbks.
Fane Fragment of the 1461 Lord's Journal. Wm. H. Dunham. (Yale Historical Pubs., Manuscripts & Edited Texts: No. XIV). 1935. 34.50x (ISBN 0-685-69813-0). Elliots Bks.
Fanfare: A Celebration of Belief. Nancy Spiegelberg & Dorothy Purdy. LC 80-25519. (Illus., Orig.). 1981. pap. 5.95 (ISBN 0-930014-56-1). Multnomah.
Fanfare for the Stalwart. Thomas G. Wheeler. LC 67-22813. (gr. 8 up). 1967. 9.95 (ISBN 0-87599-139-4). S G Phillips.
Fangs. William Dobson. (Orig.). 1980. pap. 1.95 (ISBN 0-451-09346-1, J9346, Sig). NAL.
Fannie Lou Hamer. June Jordan. LC 70-184982. (Biography Ser.). (Illus.). (gr. 1-5). 1972. 6.95 o.p. (ISBN 0-690-28893-X, TYC-J); PLB 7.89 (ISBN 0-690-28894-8). T Y Crowell.
Fannie Mae Guide to Buying, Financing & Selling Your Home. rev. ed. Ed. by Curt Tuck. LC 78-1017. 1978. pap. 5.95 (ISBN 0-385-14382-6, Dolp). Doubleday.
Fanny. Erica Jong. 1981. pap. 6.95 (ISBN 0-452-25273-3, Z5273, Plume). NAL.
Fanny Burney. Sarah Kilpatrick. LC 80-5891. (Illus.). 256p. 1981. 14.95 (ISBN 0-8128-2761-9). Stein & Day.
Fanny Burney & Her Friends: Select Passages from Her Diary & Other Writings. Frances B. Arblay. LC 75-76135. 1969. Repr. of 1890 ed. 15.00 (ISBN 0-8103-3896-3). Gale.
Fanny Crosby's Story. S. Trevena Jackson. (Christian Biography Ser.). 198p. 1981. pap. 2.95 (ISBN 0-8010-5127-4). Baker Bk.
Fanny Elssler. Ivor Guest. LC 74-105507. (Illus.). 1970. 20.00x (ISBN 0-8195-4022-6, Pub. by Wesleyan U Pr). Columbia U Pr.
Fanny Farmer Junior Cookbook. rev. ed. Wilma L. Perkins. (Illus.). (gr. 5 up). 1957. 6.95 (ISBN 0-316-69932-2). Little.
Fanny Keats. Marie Adami. 1938. 34.50x (ISBN 0-686-51385-1). Elliots Bks.
Fanny Kemble. Dorothy Marshall. LC 77-3854. (Illus.). 1978. 8.95 o.p. (ISBN 0-312-28162-5). St Martin.
Fanny Kemble's America. John A. Scott. LC 72-7557. (Women of America Ser). (Illus.). 168p. (gr. 5-9). 1973. 8.95 (ISBN 0-690-28911-1, TYC-J). T Y Crowell.
Fanny Runs in Honolulu. Martha T. Amos. (Illus.). 64p. 1981. 5.00 (ISBN 0-682-49718-5). Exposition.
Fanny, the American Kemble: Her Journals & Unpublished Letters. Fanny K Wister. LC 72-80474. 227p. 1972. 10.00x (ISBN 0-932068-00-6). South Pass Pr.
Fans. W. C. Osborne. 1977. text ed. 26.00 (ISBN 0-08-021725-7); pap. text ed. 14.00 (ISBN 0-08-021726-5). Pergamon.
Fans: Design & Operation of Centrifugal, Axial Flow & Cross Flow Fans. B. Eck. LC 72-137613. 612p. 1974. 105.00 (ISBN 0-08-015872-2). Pergamon.
Fans from the East. Carol Dorington-Ward. (Illus.). 1979. 18.95 o.p. (ISBN 0-670-30705-X, Debrett's Peerage, Ltd.). Viking Pr.
Fans: How We Go Crazy Over Sports. Michael Roberts. LC 76-26880. 1978. 8.95 o.s.i. (ISBN 0-915220-20-2); pap. 3.95 o.p. (ISBN 0-915220-46-6). New Republic.
Fanshen the Magic Bear. (gr. 1-5). 1.50. New Seed.
Fantanimals. Keith Havens. (Illus.). 48p. (Orig.). (ps-3). 1980. pap. 2.95 (ISBN 0-89542-938-1). Ideals.
Fantasex. Rolf Milonas. 1977. pap. 1.50 o.p. (ISBN 0-345-25657-3). Ballantine.
Fantasies of Sex. (Illus.). 4.95 (ISBN 0-910550-34-4). Centurion Pr.
Fantastic Art. Ed. by David Larkin. (Illus., Orig.). 1975. pap. 5.95 o.p. (ISBN 0-345-25038-9). Ballantine.
Fantastic Cornell Woolrich. Ed. by Charles G. Waugh & Martin H. Greenberg. (Alternatives Ser.). 416p. Date not set. price not set (ISBN 0-8093-1008-2). S Ill U Pr.
Fantastic Fables. Ambrose Bierce. 160p. 1976. Repr. of 1911 ed. lib. bdg. 8.75 (ISBN 0-89190-184-1). Am Repr-Rivercity Pr.
Fantastic Feats of Doctor Boox. Andrew Davies. (gr. 4-6). 1977. pap. 1.25 (ISBN 0-590-10335-0, Schol Pap). Schol Bk Serv.
Fantastic Homemade Book. Steven Lindblom. (gr. 1-12). 1979. 8.95 (ISBN 0-395-28481-3); pap. 3.95 (ISBN 0-395-28482-1). HM.
Fantastic Imagination. Ed. by Robert M. Z Boyer & Kenneth J. Zahorski. 1976. pap. 2.25 (ISBN 0-380-00956-0, 32326). Avon.
Fantastic Lives: Autobiographical Essays by Notable Science Fiction Writers. Ed. by Martin H. Greenberg. (Alternatives Ser.). 216p. 1981. 15.00 (ISBN 0-8093-0987-4). S Ill U Pr.
Fantastic Tales of Fitz-James O'Brien. 1980. 9.95 (ISBN 0-7145-3617-2). Riverrun NY.
Fantastic Toys. Monika Beisner. LC 74-79249. (Picture Bk). (Illus.). 24p. (gr. k-2). 1974. 5.95 o.s.i. (ISBN 0-695-80504-5); PLB 6.99 o.s.i. (ISBN 0-695-40504-7). Follett.
Fantastic Worlds. S. Holton. 1978. pap. 7.95 (ISBN 0-931064-03-1). Starlog Pr.
Fantastic Worlds. Robert Skotak & Scot Holton. Ed. by Howard Zimmerman & Robin Snelson. (Illus.). (gr. 3 up). 1978. pap. 7.95 (ISBN 0-931064-03-1). Starlog.
Fantastic Worlds: Myths, Tales, & Stories. Ed. by Eric S. Rabkin. 1979. 17.95 (ISBN 0-19-502542-3, GB 572); pap. 6.95 (ISBN 0-19-502541-5). Oxford U Pr.
Fantasy & Commonsense in Education. John Wilson. LC 79-10938. 134p. 1979. 18.95x (ISBN 0-470-26707-0). Halsted Pr.
Fantasy & Feeling in Education. Richard M. Jones. LC 68-29430. 1968. 15.00x (ISBN 0-8147-0220-1). NYU Pr.
Fantasy & Imagination in the Mexican Narrative. Ross Larson. LC 77-3019. 1977. pap. 8.50x (ISBN 0-87918-032-3). ASU Lat Am St.
Fantasy & Science Fiction, April Nineteen Sixty-Five. Ed. by Edward L. Ferman & Martin H. Greenberg. (Alternatives Ser.). 160p. Date not set. price not set (ISBN 0-8093-1007-4). S Ill U Pr.
Fantasy Annual III. Terry Carr. (Orig.). 1981. pap. 2.95 (ISBN 0-671-41272-8). PB.
Fantasy Art. Wieland Schmeid. (Alpine Fine Arts Collection). (Illus.). 475p. 1981. 65.00 (ISBN 0-686-64751-3, Pub by Alpine Fine Arts). Hippocrene Bks.
Fantasy of Reason: The Life & Thought of William Godwin. Don Locke. (Illus.). 1980. 28.00 (ISBN 0-7100-0387-0). Routledge & Kegan.
Fantasy Readers Guide, No. 1: The John Spencer Fantasy Publications. Michael Ashley. 54p. 1980. Repr. of 1979 ed. lib. bdg. 8.95 cancelled (ISBN 0-89370-099-1). Borgo Pr.
Fantasy Readers Guide to Ramsey Campbell. Michael Ashley. 64p. 1980. Repr. lib. bdg. 8.95x (ISBN 0-89370-098-3). Borgo Pr.
Fantasy Stories of George Macdonald, 4 vols. Ed. by Glenn Sadler. 1980. pap. 12.95 set (ISBN 0-8028-1858-7); pap. 2.95 ea. (ISBN 0-686-68801-5). Eerdmans.
Fantasy: The Golden Age of Fantastic Illustration. Brigid Peppin. (Signet Art Books). (Illus.). 1976. pap. 6.95 o.p. (ISBN 0-451-79971-2, G9971, Sig). NAL.

Fantasy Tradition in American Literature: From Irving to le Guin. Brian Attebery. LC 80-7670. 256p. 1980. 17.50x (ISBN 0-253-35665-2). Ind U Pr.

Fantasy Voices, No. 1: Interviews with Fantasy Authors. Jeffrey M. Elliot. LC 80-22575. (Milford Series: Popular Writers of Today: Vol. 31). 64p. (Orig.). 1981. lib. bdg. 8.95x (ISBN 0-89370-146-7); pap. text ed. 2.95x (ISBN 0-89370-246-3). Borgo Pr.

Fantasy Voyages: Great Science Fiction from the Saturday Evening Post. LC 79-55717. 1979. 7.95 (ISBN 0-89387-036-6). Sat Eve Post.

Fantazius Mallare: A Mysterious Oath. Ben Hecht. LC 78-6637. (Illus.). 1978. pap. 3.95 o.p. (ISBN 0-15-630160-1, Harv). HarBraceJ.

FAO Catalogue of Small Scale Fishing Gear. Ed. by C. Nedelec. (Illus.). 192p. 24.25 (ISBN 0-85238-077-1, FN). Unipub.

FAO Evaluation of Malthion Residues in Food. 28p. 1980. pap. 6.00 (F1977, FAO). Unipub.

FAO Fertilizer Yearbook, 1978. (FAO Statistical Ser.: No. 23). 115p. 1979. 18.50 (ISBN 9-2500-0783-3, F1634, FAO). Unipub.

FAO Production Yearbook, Vol. 33. 309p. 1980. pap. 25.25 (ISBN 92-5-000936-4, F2050, FAO). Unipub.

FAO Species Catalogue, Vol. 1: Shrimps & Prawns of the World; an Annotated Catalogue of Species of Interest to Fisheries. (FAO Fisheries Synopsis Ser.: No. 125, Vol. 1). 287p. 1980. pap. 15.50 (ISBN 92-5-100896-5, F1939, FAO). Unipub.

FAO Trade Yearbook 1978. (Statistical Ser.: No. 24). 361p. 1980. 21.75 (ISBN 92-5-000795-7, F1860, FAO). Unipub.

FAO Trade Yearbook, 1979, Vol. 33. 357p. 1981. 30.25 (ISBN 92-5-000965-8, F2106, FAO). Unipub.

FAO-UNEP Workshop on the Aquatic Sciences & Fisheries Information System (ASFIS) (FAO Fisheries Report Ser.: No. 243). 49p. 1981. pap. 6.00 (ISBN 92-5-000991-7, F2109, FAO). Unipub.

FAO-WHO Evaluation of Chlordane Residues in Food. 68p. 1973. pap. 6.00 (F1974, FAO). Unipub.

FAO-WHO Evaluation of Diazinon Residues in Food. 61p. 1973. pap. 6.00 (F1975, FAO). Unipub.

FAO-WHO Evaluation of Dichlorvos Residues in Food. 82p. 1973. pap. 6.00 (F1979, FAO). Unipub.

FAO-WHO Evaluation of Dieldrin Residues in Food. 99p. 1973. pap. 6.00 (F1978, FAO). Unipub.

FAO-WHO Evaluation of Endosulfan Residues in Food. 33p. 1973. pap. 6.00 (F1982, FAO). Unipub.

FAO-WHO Evaluation of Ethion Residues in Food. 42p. 1973. pap. 6.00 (F1973, FAO). Unipub.

FAO-WHO Evaluation of Parathion Residues in Food. 20p. 1973. pap. 6.00 (F1976, FAO). Unipub.

FAO-WHO Evaluation of Phosphamidon Residues in Food. 25p. 1973. pap. 6.00 (F1981, FAO). Unipub.

FAO-WHO Evaluation of Residues of Fentin Compounds in Food. 51p. 1973. pap. 6.00 (F1980, FAO). Unipub.

Far Away & Long Ago. W. H. Hudson. 350p. 1981. 14.95 (ISBN 0-8180-0251-4). Horizon.

Far Beyond Distance. Everett A. Gillis. 64p. 1981. 8.00 (ISBN 0-938328-01-8). Pisces Pr TX.

Far Call. Gordon R. Dickson. 1978. pap. 2.25 o.s.i. (ISBN 0-440-12284-8). Dell.

Far Distant Oxus. abr. ed. Katharine Hull & Pamela Whitlock. LC 69-11300. (gr. 5-8). 1969. 4.95g o.s.i. (ISBN 0-02-745760-5). Macmillan.

Far East: A Concise History. F. C. Jones. 1966. 11.25 (ISBN 0-08-011642-6); pap. 5.75 (ISBN 0-08-011641-8). Pergamon.

Far East: A History of Western Impacts & Eastern Responses (1830 - 1975) 6th ed. Paul H. Clyde & Burton F. Beers. (Illus.). 576p. 1976. 19.95 (ISBN 0-13-302968-9). P-H.

Far East & Australasia 1980-1981. 12th ed. LC 74-417170. 1500p. 1980. 100.00x (ISBN 0-905118-51-0). Intl Pubns Serv.

Far Eastern Crisis. Henry L. Stimson. 1975. Repr. of 1936 ed. 16.50 (ISBN 0-86527-327-8). Fertig.

Far Eastern Politics in the Postwar Period. Harold M. Vinacke. LC 55-10400. 1956. 20.00x (ISBN 0-89197-548-9); pap. text ed. 8.95x (ISBN 0-89197-756-2). Irvington.

Far Eastern Republic of Siberia. Henry K. Norton. LC 79-2917. (Illus.). 1981. Repr. of 1923 ed. 25.00 (ISBN 0-8305-0086-3). Hyperion Conn.

Far Eastern Trade Eighteen-Sixty to Nineteen-Fourteen. Francis E. Hyde. (Merchant Adventurers Ser.). 1979. text ed. 9.75x (ISBN 0-7136-1345-9). Humanities.

Far Field. Theodore Roethke. LC 64-12105. 1971. pap. 2.95 (ISBN 0-385-04692-8, Anch). Doubleday.

Far from Home. Ouida Sebestyen. 192p. (gr. 7 up). 1980. 8.95g (ISBN 0-316-77932-6, Pub. by Atlantic-Little Brown). Little.

Far from Home. Walter Tevis. LC 80-1073. (Double D Science Fiction Ser.). 192p. 1981. 9.95 (ISBN 0-385-17036-X). Doubleday.

Far from the Reservation: The Transracial Adoption of American Indian Children. David Fanshel. LC 70-181701. 1972. 12.50 o.p. (ISBN 0-8108-0454-9). Scarecrow.

Far Horizons. Michael Wagman. 1980. 12.95 (ISBN 0-440-02815-9). Delacorte.

Far North: Two Thousand Years of American Eskimo & Indian Art. Henry B. Collins et al. LC 77-3132. (Illus.). 320p. 1977. 22.50x (ISBN 0-253-32120-4); pap. 17.50x (ISBN 0-253-28105-9). Ind U Pr.

Far off Rhapsony. Anne-Marie Sheridan. LC 76-54898. 1977. 8.95 (ISBN 0-671-22601-0). S&S.

Far Out Facts About the Bible. William Coleman. (gr. 4-9). 1980. pap. 2.50 (ISBN 0-89191-336-X). Cook.

Far Side of Despair: A Personal Account of Depression. Russell K. Hampton. LC 74-33177. 224p. 1975. 11.95 (ISBN 0-88229-106-8). Nelson-Hall.

Far Side of Despair: Eighteen Thirty to Eighteen Sixty. Ray A. Billington. (New American Nation Ser.). (Illus.). pap. 4.95x (ISBN 0-06-133012-4, TB 3012, Torch). Har-Row.

Far Traveller. A. Bertram Chandler. (Science Fiction Ser). (Orig.). 1979. pap. 1.50 o.p. (ISBN 0-87997-444-3, UW1444). DAW Bks.

Faraway Friends. Gyo Fujikawa. (Gyo Fujikawa Tiny Board Books). (Illus.). 14p. (ps-k). 1981. 1.95 (ISBN 0-448-15103-0). G&D.

Faraway Lurs. Harry Behn. (Children's Literature Ser.). 1981. PLB 8.95 (ISBN 0-8398-2722-9). Gregg.

Faraway Lurs. Henry Behn. (YA) (gr. 7 up). 1975. pap. 1.25 (ISBN 0-380-00696-0, 22053). Avon.

Farbenvolle Untergang: Osterreichisches Lesebuck. Ed. by H. Zohn. 1971. pap. 9.50 (ISBN 0-13-199000-4). P-H.

Farberware Convection Turbo Oven Cookbook. Margaret D. Murphy. 1981. 8.95 (ISBN 0-916752-44-5). Green Hill.

Farce: Amorous Intrigue & Deception 1. Ed. by Walter H. Rubsamen. (Ballad Opera Ser.). 1974. lib. bdg. 50.00 (ISBN 0-8240-0911-8). Garland Pub.

Farce: Amorous Intrigue & Deception 2. Ed. by Walter H. Rubsamen. (Ballad Opera Ser.). 1974. lib. bdg. 50.00 (ISBN 0-8240-0912-6). Garland Pub.

Farce, Broad or Satirical. Ed. by Walter H. Rubsamen. (Ballad Opera Ser.). 1974. lib. bdg. 50.00 (ISBN 0-8240-0910-X). Garland Pub.

Farce: Magical Transformation & Necromancy. Ed. by Walter H. Rubsamen. (Ballad Opera Ser.). 1974. lib. bdg. 50.00 (ISBN 0-8240-0909-6). Garland Pub.

Farce of the Drunk Monk. P. Lal. Tr. by P. Lal from Sanskrit. 30p. 1973. pap. text ed. 4.00 (ISBN 0-88253-301-0). Ind-US Inc.

Fardorougha, the Miser; or, the Convicts of Lisnamona. William Carleton. Ed. by Robert L. Wolff. (Ireland Nineteenth Century Fiction - Ser. Two: Vol. 37). 481p. 1979. lib. bdg. 32.00 (ISBN 0-8240-3486-4). Garland Pub.

Farewell Discourse & the Final Prayer of Jesus: An Exposition of John 14-17. D. A. Carson. 196p. 1981. 9.95 (ISBN 0-8010-2460-9). Baker Bk.

Farewell Fatigue. Natalie Rogers. LC 78-17132. (Illus.). 1978. pap. 2.95 o.p. (ISBN 0-668-04664-3, 4664). Arco.

Farewell Manchester. Caroline Ramsden. (Illus.). 6.50 o.p. (ISBN 0-85131-066-4, Dist. by Sporting Book Center). J A Allen.

Farewell to Alexandria: Solutions to Space, Growth & Performance Problems of Libraries. Ed. by Daniel Gore. LC 75-35345. 224p. 1976. lib. bdg. 15.00 (ISBN 0-8371-8587-4, GGP/). Greenwood.

Farewell to Arms. Ernest Hemingway. LC 67-13157. 1929. lib. rep. ed. 17.50x (ISBN 0-684-15562-1, ScribT); pap. 3.95 (ISBN 0-684-71797-2, SL61, ScribT). Scribner.

Farewell to Babylon. Bode Sowande. 179p. (Orig.). 1979. 9.00 (ISBN 0-89410-107-2); pap. 5.00 (ISBN 0-89410-106-4). Three Continents.

Farewell to Europe. Walter Laqueur. 336p. 1981. 12.95 (ISBN 0-316-51475-6). Little.

Farewell to Shady Glade. Bill Peet. (gr. k-3). 1981. pap. 3.95x (ISBN 0-395-31128-4). HM.

Farewell to the Westerns. G. M. Kichenside. LC 75-2915. 1975. 13.50 (ISBN 0-7153-7069-3). David & Charles.

Farewell to Thee. Marian Forrester. 1978. pap. 2.25 (ISBN 0-505-51309-9). Tower Bks.

Farfeluches a la campagne. Alain Gree & Luis Camps. (Illus.). 1973. 8.95 (ISBN 0-88332-234-X, 2914). Larousse.

Farfeluches a la maison. Alain Gree & Luis Camps. (Illus.). 1973. 8.95 (ISBN 0-88332-235-8, 2915). Larousse.

Farfeluches a l'ecole. Alain Gree & Luis Camps. (Illus.). 1973. 8.95 (ISBN 0-88332-236-6, 2907). Larousse.

Farfeluches aiment les Animaux-Love the Animals. Alain Gree. (Illus., Fr.). 1980. 8.95 (ISBN 2-203-12313-3). Larousse.

Farfeluches au bord de la mer. Alain Gree & Luis Camps. (Illus.). 1973. 8.95 (ISBN 0-88332-237-4, 2913). Larousse.

Farfeluches au cirque. Alain Gree & Luis Camps. (Illus.). 1973. 8.95 (ISBN 0-88332-238-2, 2916). Larousse.

Farfeluches au marche. Alain Gree & Luis Camps. (Illus.). 1973. 8.95 (ISBN 0-88332-239-0, 2909). Larousse.

Farfeluches au zoo. (Farfeluches Ser.). (Illus.). (gr. 1). 1976. 8.95 (ISBN 0-88332-240-4, 2905). Larousse.

Farfeluches choisissent un metier: The Farfeluches Choose a Career. (Illus.). (gr. 8). 1978. 8.95 (ISBN 0-88332-101-7, 2906). Larousse.

Farfeluches en pleine action. (Farfeluches Ser.). (Illus.). (gr. 1). 1976. 6.95 o.p. (ISBN 0-88332-241-2, 2911). Larousse.

Farfeluches font des achats. Alain Gree. (Illus., Fr.). (gr. k-3). 1979. 8.95 (ISBN 0-88332-114-9). Larousse.

Farfeluches prennent le train. Alain Gree & Luis Camps. (Illus.). 1973. 8.95 (ISBN 0-88332-242-0, 2918). Larousse.

Farfeluches sur la route. Alain Gree & Luis Camps. (Illus.). 1973. 8.95 (ISBN 0-88332-243-9, 2917). Larousse.

Fargher's English Manx Dictionary. Douglas C. Fargher. 1979. text ed. 6.75x (ISBN 0-904980-23-5). Humanities.

Fargo, No. 1. John Benteen. 1980. pap. 1.75 (ISBN 0-505-51481-8). Tower Bks.

Fargo: A Pictorial History. Nancy E. Hanson. (Illus.). 205p. 1981. pap. price not set. Donning Co.

Fargo & the Texas Rangers. John Benteen. 1977. pap. 1.25 (ISBN 0-505-51126-6, BT51126). Tower Bks.

Fargo No. 3: Alaska Steel. John Benteen. (Orig.). 1980. pap. 1.50 (ISBN 0-505-51502-4). Tower Bks.

Fargo No. 4: Massacre River. John Benteen. (Orig.). 1980. pap. 1.50 (ISBN 0-505-51521-0). Tower Bks.

Fargo North Decoder, His Coat & Hat. Tom Dunsmuir. (Electric Company Ser). (gr. 1-5). 1973. PLB 5.38 (ISBN 0-307-64820-6, Golden Pr). Western Pub.

Fargo: Panama Gold, No. 2. John Benteen. 1980. pap. 1.75 (ISBN 0-505-51482-6). Tower Bks.

Farley Goes to the Doctor. Emily P. Kingsley. (Sesame Street Early Bird Bks). (Illus.). 32p. (ps). 1981. 3.50 (ISBN 0-307-11605-0, Golden Pr). Western Pub.

Farm. Louis Bromfield. 1979. pap. 2.50 (ISBN 0-380-41715-4, 41715). Avon.

Farm. (Golden Photo Board Bks.). (Illus.). 12p. (ps). 1980. 1.50 (ISBN 0-307-06074-8, Golden Pr). Western Pub.

Farm. Henry Humphrey. LC 76-23768. (gr. 1-3). 1978. 6.95a (ISBN 0-385-01388-4); PLB (ISBN 0-385-03447-4). Doubleday.

Farm. David Kherdian. LC 79-64355. 1979. 6.95 (ISBN 0-89756-026-4). Two Rivers.

Farm Amalgamation in Western Europe. A. H. Maunder & G. P. Hirsch. 132p. 1979. text ed. 21.00x (ISBN 0-566-00253-1, Pub. by Gower Pub Co England). Renouf.

Farm & Cooperative Alcohol Plant Study: Technical & Economic Assessment As a Commercial Venture. Raphael Katzen Associates International, Inc. 230p. 1981. pap. 20.00 (ISBN 0-89934-117-9). Solar Energy Info.

Farm & Factory: The Mill Experience & Women's Lives in New England, Eighteen Thirty to Eighteen Sixty. Thomas Dublin. LC 80-28084. 220p. 1981. 15.00x (ISBN 0-231-05118-2). Columbia U Pr.

Farm & Food Policy: Issues of the 1980s. Don Paarlberg. LC 79-17496. x, 338p. 1980. 16.50x (ISBN 0-8032-3656-5). U of Nebr Pr.

Farm & Nation in Japan: Agrarian Nationalism, 1870-1940. Thomas R. Havens. LC 73-16744. 352p. 1974. 22.00x (ISBN 0-691-03101-0). Princeton U Pr.

Farm & Personal Finance. Ed. by J. R. Brake. LC 68-13437. (gr. 9-12). 1968. pap. 3.50 (ISBN 0-8134-0115-1, 115). Interstate.

Farm & Ranch Management. Boy Scouts of America. (Illus.). 32p. (gr. 6-12). 1980. pap. 0.70x (3348). BSA.

Farm & Ranch Management. Ronald D. Kay. Ed. by James E. Vastyan. (Agricultural Sciences Publications). (Illus.). 384p. Date not set. text ed. 15.95 (ISBN 0-07-033462-5, C). McGraw.

Farm & Ranch Real Estate Law. John M. Cartwright. LC 70-189071. 1972. 45.00 (ISBN 0-686-14537-2). Lawyers Co-Op.

Farm & Rural Energy Planning Manual. Louise Gorenflo et al. (Illus.). 80p. (Orig.). 1981. pap. 5.00 (ISBN 0-937786-04-7). Inst Ecological.

Farm & the Village. George E. Evans. (Illus.). (gr. 5 up). 1969. 8.95 (ISBN 0-571-08804-X, Pub. by Faber & Faber); pap. 4.95 (ISBN 0-571-10551-3). Merrimack Bk Serv.

Farm & Village Boyhood. Fred Lape. LC 80-17303. (Illus.). 200p. 9.95 (ISBN 0-8156-0162-X, York State Bks). Syracuse U Pr.

Farm Animal Behaviour. 2nd ed. Andrew F. Fraser. (Illus.). 291p. 1980. pap. 14.75 (ISBN 0-8121-0739-X). Lea & Febiger.

Farm Animal Management. N. S. Sastry & C. K. Thomas. 1976. text ed. 17.50 (ISBN 0-7069-0454-0, Pub. by Vikas India). Advent Bk.

Farm Animals. Illus. by Lisa Bonforte. LC 80-53106. (Board Bks.). (Illus.). 14p. (ps). 1981. boards 2.95 (ISBN 0-394-84767-9). Random.

Farm Animals. Hans Helweg. LC 79-27483. (Picturebacks Ser.). (Illus.). 32p. (ps-3). 1980. PLB 3.99 (ISBN 0-394-93733-3); pap. 1.25 (ISBN 0-394-83733-9). Random.

Farm Animals in Color. H. Clausen & E. Tipsen. (Illus.). 1970. 9.95 (ISBN 0-7137-0539-6, Pub by Blandford Pr England). Sterling.

Farm Book. Jan Pfloog. (ps-1). 1964. PLB 5.38 (ISBN 0-307-68905-0, Golden Pr). Western Pub.

Farm Equipment of the Roman World. K. D. White. LC 73-82450. (Illus.). 248p. 1975. 58.00 (ISBN 0-521-20333-3). Cambridge U Pr.

Farm Fever: Finding & Buying Country Land. Jerry Baker & Dan Kibbie. LC 76-30861. (Funk & W Bk.). 1977. 11.95 o.s.i. (ISBN 0-308-10299-1, TYC-T). T Y Crowell.

Farm Gas Engines & Tractors. 4th ed. Fred R. Jones. 1963. text ed. 18.50 o.p. (ISBN 0-07-032780-7, C). McGraw.

Farm in Calabria & Other Poems. David Ray. Ed. by Morty Sklar. LC 80-123410. (Outstanding Author Ser.: No. 3). (Illus.). 32p. (Orig.). 1980. pap. 2.00 (ISBN 0-930370-08-2). Spirit That Moves.

Farm Journal's Best-Ever Cookies. Patricia A. Ward. LC 80-948. (Illus.). 1980. 12.95 (ISBN 0-385-17146-3). Doubleday.

Farm Journal's Complete Pie Cookbook. Editors Of Farm Journal & Nell B. Nichols. LC 65-16174. 6.95 o.p. (ISBN 0-385-01843-6). Doubleday.

Farm Journal's Country Cookbook. rev. & enl. ed. Editors Of Farm Journal & Nell B. Nichols. LC 73-175372. 480p. 1972. 10.95 (ISBN 0-385-03036-3). Doubleday.

Farm Journal's Country-Style Microwave Cookbook. Farm Journal Food Editors. 128p. (Orig.). 1980. pap. 3.50x. Farm Journal.

Farm Journal's Everyday Favorite Recipes. Farm Journal Food Editors. 128p. (Orig.). 1980. pap. 3.50x (ISBN 0-89795-011-9). Farm Journal.

Farm Journal's Freezing & Canning Cookbook. rev. ed. Editors Of Farm Journal et al. LC 77-81787. 1978. 10.95 (ISBN 0-385-13444-4). Doubleday.

Farm Journal's Speedy Skillet Meals. Patricia A. Ward. (Illus.). 232p. 1980. 8.95 (ISBN 0-89795-009-7). Farm Journal.

Farm Labor in the United States. Charles E. Bishop. LC 66-28037. 1967. 27.50x (ISBN 0-231-02985-3). Columbia U Pr.

Farm Labour in South Africa. Ed. by Francis Wilson. Alide Kooy. pap. 21.00 o.p. (ISBN 0-949968-91-9). Verry.

Farm-Level Constraints to High Yields in Asia: Nineteen Seventy-Four to Nineteen Seventy-Seven. 411p. 1979. pap. 24.50 (R013, IRRI). Unipub.

Farm Level Water Management in Selected Asian Countries. 159p. 1980. pap. 13.25 (ISBN 92-833-1461-1, APO 88, APO). Unipub.

Farm Machines. Nicholas Wykeham. LC 78-20396. (Machine World Ser.). (Illus.). (gr. 2-4). 1979. PLB 9.95 (ISBN 0-8172-1328-7). Raintree Pubs.

Farm Management in Africa: The Principles of Production & Planning. Martin Upton. 1973. 37.50x (ISBN 0-19-215646-2). Oxford U Pr.

Farm Mechanics. Boy Scouts Of America. LC 19-600. (Illus.). 64p. (gr. 6-12). 1958. pap. 0.70x (ISBN 0-8395-3346-2, 3346). BSA.

Farm Mechanization, Employment, & Income in Nepal: Traditional & Mechanized Farming in Bara District. (IRRI Research Paper Ser.: No. 38). 9p. 1979. pap. 5.00 (R078, IRRI). Unipub.

Farm Plan. Elizabeth H. Bente. 64p. 1981. 6.00 (ISBN 0-682-49671-5). Exposition.

Farm Planning & Control. 2nd ed. C. S. Barnard & J. S. Nix. LC 79-10572. 1980. 72.50 (ISBN 0-521-22658-9); pap. 23.95x (ISBN 0-521-29604-8). Cambridge U Pr.

Farm Planning & Control. C. S. Barnard & J. S. Nix. LC 72-85436. (Illus.). 522p. 1973. 52.50 (ISBN 0-521-08738-4); pap. 19.95x (ISBN 0-521-29079-1). Cambridge U Pr.

Farm Planning in the Early Stages of Development. (Agricultural Services Bulletin: No. 1). 106p. 1968. pap. 6.00 (F1971, FAO). Unipub.

Farm, Ranch & Country Vacations. Pat Dickerman. LC 60-2113. (Illus.). 1979. pap. 5.95 o.p. (ISBN 0-913214-02-7). Berkshire Traveller.

Farm, Ranch, & Country Vacations. Pat Dickerman. (Illus.). 1981. pap. 7.95 (ISBN 0-913214-03-5). Farm & Ranch.

Farm, Ranch, Countryside Guide. Patricia Dickerman. LC 60-2113. 256p. 1981. 7.95 (ISBN 0-913214-03-5). Berkshire Traveller.

Farm Sales & Pick Your Own. 91p. 1980. pap. 9.95 (ISBN 0-901361-28-3, Pub. by Grower Bks England). Intl Schol Bk Serv.

Farm Tractor Maintenance. Arlen D. Brown & Ivan G. Morrison. LC 62-13066. 256p. 1962. 5.50 o.p. (ISBN 0-8134-0032-5); text ed. 4.25x o.p. (ISBN 0-685-57258-7). Interstate.

Farm Tractors in Color. Michael Williams. LC 74-20544. (Macmillan Color Ser.). (Illus.). 208p. 1975. 8.95 (ISBN 0-02-629300-5, 62930). Macmillan.

Farm Waggons & Carts. James Arnold. LC 76-57081. 1977. 22.50 (ISBN 0-7153-7330-7). David & Charles.

Farm Water Management for Rice Cultivation. 1977. pap. 11.00 (ISBN 92-833-1404-2, APO 65, APO). Unipub.

Farm Workshop & Maintenance. Ed. by Farmers Weekly. (Illus.). 192p. 1972. text ed. 15.95x (ISBN 0-8464-0404-4). Beekman Pubs.

Farmer & His Cows. Louise L. Floethe. (Illus.). (gr. 1-5). 1957. reinforced bdg. 5.95 (ISBN 0-684-12396-7, ScribJ). Scribner.

Farmer Grover. Norman Stiles. (Illus.). 24p. (ps-4). 1977. PLB 5.38 (ISBN 0-307-68878-X, Golden Pr). Western Pub.

Farmer Hoo & the Baboons. Ida Chittum. LC 77-132357. (Illus.). (ps-3). 1971. 4.95 o.s.i. (ISBN 0-440-02582-6); PLB 4.58 o.s.i. (ISBN 0-440-02584-2). Delacorte.

Farmer in the Second World War. Walter W. Wilcox. LC 72-2389. (FDR & the Era of the New Deal Ser). 426p. 1973. Repr. of 1947 ed. lib. bdg. 39.50 (ISBN 0-306-70474-9). Da Capo.

Farmer in the Sky. Robert A. Heinlein. 224p. 1975. pap. 1.75 (ISBN 0-345-27596-9). Ballantine.

Farmer Takes a Hand: The Electric Power Revolution in Rural America. Marquis Childs. LC 73-19736. (Fdr & the Era of the New Deal Ser.). (Illus.). 256p. 1974. Repr. of 1952 ed. lib. bdg. 29.50 (ISBN 0-306-70478-1). Da Capo.

Farmer, the Rooks & the Cherry Tree. John Cunliffe. LC 80-65671. (Illus.). 32p. (ps-2). 1980. 8.95 (ISBN 0-233-96571-8). Andre Deutsch.

Farmer's Alphabet. Mary Azarian. (gr. 1-4). 1981. 10.95 (ISBN 0-87923-394-X); pap. 6.95 (ISBN 0-87923-397-4). Godine.

Farmer's & Rancher's Medical Guide. Nicholas C. Leone & Elisabeth C. Phillips. 1980. 12.95 (ISBN 0-679-51025-7). McKay.

Farmers & Towns, Rural-Urban Relations in Highland Bolivia. David A. Preston. 197p. 1980. 14.95x (ISBN 0-86094-009-8, Pub. by GEO Abstracts England); pap. 11.40x (ISBN 0-86094-008-X, Pub. by GEO Abstracts England). State Mutual Bk.

Farmers, Bureaucrats, & Middlemen: Historical Perspectives on American Agriculture. Ed. by Trudy H. Peterson. LC 80-14609. (Illus.). 514p. 1981. 19.95 (ISBN 0-88258-083-3). Howard U Pr.

Farmers' Cookbook: A Collection of Favorite Recipes, Economical Meal Planning Methods & Other Tips & Pointers for America's Farm Kitchens. Mitzi Ayala. (Illus.). 240p. 1981. 12.50 (ISBN 0-686-69457-0). Harbor Pub CA.

Farmers Hotel. John O'Hara. 128p. 1973. pap. 1.25 o.p. (ISBN 0-445-00161-5). Popular Lib.

Farmers in Revolt: The Revolutions of 1893 in the Province of Santa Fe, Argentina. Ezequiel Gallo. (Institute of Latin American Studies Monograph: No. 7). (Illus.). 108p. 1976. text ed. 21.00x (ISBN 0-485-17707-2, Athlone Pr). Humanities.

Farmers on Relief & Rehabilitation. Berta Asch & A. R. Mangus. LC 78-165678. (FDR & the Era of the New Deal Ser.). 1971. Repr. of 1937 ed. lib. bdg. 22.50 (ISBN 0-306-70340-8). Da Capo.

Farmers Primer on Growing Rice. 221p. 1979. pap. 14.50 (R024, IRRI). Unipub.

Farmer's Tax Guide. Charles F. Lein, Jr. LC 77-99077. (Illus.). 1978. pap. 3.95 o.p. (ISBN 0-8015-2558-6). Dutton.

Farmers Without Farms: Agricultural Tenancy in Nineteenth-Century Iowa. Donald L. Winters. LC 78-4021. (Contributions in American History Ser.: No. 79). (Illus.). 1978. lib. bdg. 17.50 (ISBN 0-313-20408-X, WFL/). Greenwood.

Farming for Profit in a Hungry World: Capital & the Crisis in Agriculture. Michael Perelman. LC 76-43229. 256p. 1978. text ed. 16.00 (ISBN 0-916672-88-3); pap. text ed. 7.50 (ISBN 0-916672-55-7). Allanheld.

Farming Hazards in the Drought Area. R. S. Kifer & H. L. Stewart. LC 78-165600. (FDR & the Era of the New Deal Ser). 1971. Repr. of 1938 ed. lib. bdg. 25.00 (ISBN 0-306-70348-3). Da Capo.

Farming in Great Britain. Frank Huggett. (Junior Reference Ser.). (Illus.). 64p. (gr. 7 up). 1970. 7.95 (ISBN 0-7136-1527-3). Dufour.

Farming Systems in the Tropics. 3rd ed. Hans Ruthenberg. 400p. 1980. 89.00 (ISBN 0-19-859481-X). Oxford U Pr.

Farming the Edge of the Sea. 2nd ed. Edwin S. Iversen. (Illus.). 440p. 37.50 (ISBN 0-85238-079-8, FN). Unipub.

Farming the Waters. Peter R. Limburg. LC 80-23362. (Illus.). 256p. 1981. 10.95 (ISBN 0-8253-0009-6). Beaufort Bks NY.

Farming with Animal Power. (Better Farming Ser.: No. 14). 1979. pap. 2.25 (ISBN 92-5-100157-X, F71, FAO). Unipub.

Farmland, USA. Harold Hamil. LC 75-18756. (Illus.). 112p. 1975. 25.00 (ISBN 0-913504-24-6); deluxe ed. 100.00 (ISBN 0-913504-61-0). Lowell Pr.

Farmstead Book One. Ed. by Paul Harmond. (Illus.). 1978. lib. bdg. 16.50 (ISBN 0-88930-020-8, Pub. by Cloudburst Canada); pap. 8.95 (ISBN 0-88930-019-4). Madrona Pubs.

Farnham's Freehold. Robert A. Heinlein. pap. 2.25 (ISBN 0-425-04856-X, Dist. by Putnam). Berkley Pub.

Farnsworth Score. Rex Burns. 1978. pap. 1.75 o.p. (ISBN 0-425-03749-5, Medallion). Berkley Pub.

Faroese Knitting Patterns. Foroysk Bindingarmynstur. 60p. 1980. pap. 10.95 (ISBN 0-906191-17-3, Pub. by Thule Pr England). Intl Schol Bk Serv.

Farrah: An Unauthorized Biography of Farrah Fawcett-Majors. Pat Burstein. (Illus.). (RL 7). 1977. pap. 1.50 o.p. (ISBN 0-451-07723-7, W7723, Sig). NAL.

Farriery. J. Hickman. (Illus.). 1976. 29.75 (ISBN 0-85131-228-4, Dist. by Sporting Book Center). J A Allen.

Farthest-Away Mountain. Lynne Reid Banks. LC 77-72412. (gr. 4-7). 1977. 5.95 (ISBN 0-385-12876-2). Doubleday.

Fascinante Mundo De la Biblia. Nelson B. Keyes. Orig. Title: Story of the Bible World. (Illus.). 216p. (Span.). 1980. 15.95 (ISBN 0-311-03664-3, Edit Mundo); pap. 11.95 (ISBN 0-311-03665-1, Edit Mundo). Casa Bautista.

Fascinating Womanhood. Helen Andelin. 320p. 1980. pap. 2.75 (ISBN 0-553-13988-6). Bantam.

Fascinating World of the Japanese Artist: A Collection of Essays on Japanese Art. Ed. by H. M. Kaempfer & Jhr. W. Sickinghe. 1979. text ed. 20.00x (ISBN 0-87093-156-3). Humanities.

Fascism. Alan Cassels. LC 73-13716. (Illus.). 1975. pap. 9.95x (ISBN 0-88295-718-X). AHM Pub.

Fascism: An Anthology. Ed. by Nathanael Greene. LC 67-30582. (Orig.). 1968. pap. 8.95x (ISBN 0-88295-736-8). AHM Pub.

Fascism & the Industrial Leadership in Italy, 1919-1940: A Study in the Expansion of Private Power Under Fascism. Roland Sarti. LC 79-138636. 1971. 21.50x (ISBN 0-520-01855-9). U of Cal Pr.

Fascism in Britain: An Annotated Bibliography. Philip Rees. 1978. text ed. 27.50x (ISBN 0-391-00908-7). Humanities.

Fascism in Ferrara Nineteen Fifteen to Nineteen Twenty-Five. Paul Corner. (Oxford Historical Monographs). 312p. 1975. 36.00x (ISBN 0-19-821857-5). Oxford U Pr.

Fascism in the Contemporary World: Ideology, Evolution, Resurgence. Anthony J. Joes. LC 77-14141. (Westview Special Study Ser.). 1978. pap. text ed. 9.50x (ISBN 0-89158-159-6). Westview.

Fascism in Western Europe Nineteen Hundred to Nineteen Forty-Five. H. R. Kedward. LC 78-135658. 1971. 12.00x (ISBN 0-8147-4551-2). NYU Pr.

Fascism: The Meaning & Experience of Reactionary Revolution. J. D. Formann. LC 73-11480. (gr. 7 up). 1974. 6.90 o.p. (ISBN 0-685-47544-1); pap. 3.95. Watts.

Fascist Dictatorship in Italy. Gaetano Salvemini. 1967. 18.50 (ISBN 0-86527-063-5). Fertig.

Fascist Dictatorships. C. A. Hills. 1979. 16.95 (ISBN 0-7134-0979-7, Pub. by Batsford England). David & Charles.

Fascist Ego: A Political Biography of Robert Brasillach. William R. Tucker. 1975. 30.00x (ISBN 0-520-02710-8). U of Cal Pr.

Fascist Intellectual: Drieu la Rochelle. Robert Soucy. 1979. 27.50x (ISBN 0-520-03463-5). U of Cal Pr.

Fascist Italy. Alan Cassels. LC 68-9740. (AHM Europe Since 1500 Ser.). (Illus.). 1968. pap. 5.95x (ISBN 0-88295-719-8). AHM Pub.

Fascist Movements in Austria: From Schonerer to Hitler. Francis L. Carsten. LC 76-22935. (Sage Studies in Twentieth Century History: Vol. 7). 1977. 20.00x (ISBN 0-8039-9992-5); pap. 9.95x (ISBN 0-8039-9857-0). Sage.

Fascist Persuasion in Radical Politics. A. James Gregor. LC 73-2463. 424p. 1974. 21.50 (ISBN 0-691-07556-5). Princeton U Pr.

Fascisti Exposed: A Year of Fascist Domination. Giacomo Matteotti. LC 68-9637. 1969. Repr. of 1924 ed. 10.50 (ISBN 0-86527-064-3). Fertig.

Fashion Accessories. Fairchild Market Research Division. (Fact File Ser). (Orig.). 1979. pap. 10.00 (ISBN 0-87005-319-1). Fairchild.

Fashion Accessories. 2nd ed. Leslie R. Peltz. 1980. pap. 8.95 (ISBN 0-672-97275-1); tchrs. manual 3.33 (ISBN 0-672-97276-X). Bobbs.

Fashion & Costume in Color: Fashion & Costume in Color: Seventeen Sixty to Nineteen Twenty. Jack Casson-Scott. (Illus.). 1972. 10.95 (ISBN 0-02-522500-6). Macmillan.

Fashion & Fetishism: A Social History of the Corset, Tight-Lacing & Other Forms of Body-Sculpture in the West. David Kunzle. (Illus.). 300p. 1981. 27.50x (ISBN 0-8476-6276-4). Rowman.

Fashion Bags. Eunice Wilson & Joanne Gile. 1979. 14.95 (ISBN 0-7134-1073-6). David & Charles.

Fashion Bead Embroidery. Natalie Giltsoff. 88p. 1971. 8.75 (ISBN 0-8231-4025-3). Branford.

Fashion Business: It's All Yours. Estelle Hamburger. 1976. scp 11.95 (ISBN 0-06-453503-7, HarpC); pap. text ed. 11.50 scp (ISBN 0-06-453502-9). Har-Row.

Fashion Buying. 1968. pap. 7.60 (ISBN 0-672-96044-3). Bobbs.

Fashion Buying & Merchandising. Packard et al. LC 76-13571. (Illus.). 384p. 1976. 13.95 (ISBN 0-87005-142-3). Fairchild.

Fashion, Color, Line, & Design. 2nd ed. Leslie R. Peltz. 1980. 9.90 (ISBN 0-672-97278-6); pap. 3.33 (ISBN 0-672-97277-8). Bobbs.

Fashion Crochet. Jean Kinmond. (Illus.). 1972. 7.25 o.p. (ISBN 0-8231-5035-6). Branford.

Fashion Design Drawing. Patrick J. Ireland. LC 73-134681. 1972. pap. 10.95 (ISBN 0-470-42837-6). Halsted Pr.

Fashion Design for Moderns. 2nd ed. Rosalie K. Salomon. LC 76-14535. 144p. 1976. 10.00 (ISBN 0-87005-162-8). Fairchild.

Fashion Dictionary: Fabric, Sewing, & Apparel As Expressed in the Language of Fashion. enl. ed. Ed. by Mary B. Picken. LC 72-83771. (Funk & W Bk.). (Illus.). 448p. 1972. 12.95 o.s.i. (ISBN 0-308-10052-2, F64, TYC-T). T Y Crowell.

Fashion Direction & Coordination. Susan Goschie. 1980. 9.90 (ISBN 0-672-97267-0); pap. 3.33 (ISBN 0-672-97266-2). Bobbs.

Fashion Director: What She Does & How to Be One. Elaine Jabenis. LC 72-768. 300p. 1972. text ed. 14.50x (ISBN 0-471-43125-7); pap. text ed. 9.75 (ISBN 0-471-43126-5). Wiley.

Fashion in the Age of the Black Prince: A Study of the Years 1340-1365. Stella M. Newton. (Illus.). 151p. 1980. 37.50x (ISBN 0-8476-6939-4). Rowman.

Fashion in the Thirties. Julian Robinson. (Oresko Art Bks). (Illus.). 1978. 15.95 (ISBN 0-8467-0426-9, Pub. by Two Continents); pap. 9.95 (ISBN 0-8467-0427-7). Hippocrene Bks.

Fashion Industry Careers. Doris Cassiday & Bruce Cassiday. (Career Concise Guides Ser.). (gr. 7 up). 6.45 (ISBN 0-531-01303-0). Watts.

Fashion Merchandising. 3rd ed. Mary D. Troxell & Elaine Stone. LC 80-25077. (McGraw-Hill Marketing Ser.). (Illus.). 480p. 16.50 (ISBN 0-07-065280-5). McGraw.

Fashion Merchandising Internship. 1968. wkbk. 15.50 (ISBN 0-672-96060-5). Bobbs.

Fashion Sales Promotion Handbook. 3rd ed. Arthur A. Winters & Stanley Goodman. 1967. pap. text ed. 8.95 (ISBN 0-672-96040-0); tchr's manual 5.00 (ISBN 0-672-96041-9). Bobbs.

Fashion Textiles & Laboratory Workbook. 2nd ed. Lillian Kushel. 1971. pap. 15.15 (ISBN 0-672-96046-X); wkbk & kit 28.75 (ISBN 0-672-96049-4); textile kit 15.50 (ISBN 0-686-68511-3). Bobbs.

Fashion Vocabulary & Dictation. 1969. pap. 8.50 (ISBN 0-672-96058-3). Bobbs.

Fashion with Leather. Kate Leather. 1978. 17.95 (ISBN 0-7134-1015-9, Pub. by Batsford England). David & Charles.

Fashion Writing. Polly Guerin. 1972. text ed. 15.00 (ISBN 0-672-96033-8); tchr's manual 5.00 (ISBN 0-672-96034-6). Bobbs.

Fashioning Miniatures - One More Time. Susan B. Sirkis. (Wish Booklets: Vol. 23). (Illus.). 52p. 1980. pap. 5.50x (ISBN 0-913786-23-3). Wish Bklets.

Fashions in Eyeglasses: From the 14th Century to the Present Day. rev. ed. Richard Corson. (Illus.). 1980. Repr. of 1967 ed. text ed. 70.00x (ISBN 0-7206-3282-X). Humanities.

Fashions in Hair: The First Five Thousand Years. 3rd rev. ed. Richard Corson. (Illus.). 1971. text ed. 75.00x (ISBN 0-391-00167-1). Humanities.

Fashions in Makeup. Corson. 1980. text ed. 78.00. Humanities.

Fast & Easy Needlepoint. Mary Anne Hodgson & Josephine Ruth Paine. LC 76-56302. (gr. 3-7). 1978. PLB 5.95 (ISBN 0-385-12432-5). Doubleday.

Fast As White Lightning: The Story of Stock Car Racing. Kim Chapin. (Illus.). 1981. 11.95. Dial.

Fast Break. Paul B. Ross. 1979. pap. 1.75 o.p. (ISBN 0-345-28128-4). Ballantine.

Fast Breeder Reactors. Waltar & Reynolds. 550p. Date not set. text ed. 35.00 (ISBN 0-08-025983-9); pap. text ed. 20.00 (ISBN 0-08-025982-0). Pergamon.

Fast Financing of Your Real Estate Fortune Success Kit. 2nd ed. Tyler G. Hicks. 523p. 1981. pap. 99.50 (ISBN 0-914306-46-4). Intl Wealth.

Fast Food Diet. Judith Stern & R. V. Denenberg. 160p. 1980. 9.95 (ISBN 0-13-307736-5); pap. 4.95 (ISBN 0-13-307728-4). P-H.

Fast Food Gets an "A" in School Lunch. Len Fredrick. LC 76-54649. 1977. 17.95 (ISBN 0-685-74393-4). CBI Pub.

Fast-Food King. Lisa Eisenberg. LC 79-52564. (Laura Brewster Mysteries Ser.). (Illus.). 64p. (gr. 4 up). 1980. PLB 7.95 (ISBN 0-516-02206-7). Childrens.

Fast Fourier Transform & Convolution Algorithms. H. Nussbaumer. (Springer Series in Information Sciences: Vol. 2). (Illus.). 330p. 1981. 36.60 (ISBN 0-387-10159-4). Springer-Verlag.

Fast Freeze or Slow Squeeze. Robert Sipes. LC 80-51885. 1980. 8.95 (ISBN 0-533-04731-5). Vantage.

Fast Friends. Joy Darlington. 1980. pap. 2.50 (ISBN 0-425-04742-3). Berkley Pub.

Fast Gun. Walt Coburn. 1978. pap. 1.25 (ISBN 0-505-51227-0). Tower Bks.

Fast Gun. J. T. Edson. (Orig.). 1981. pap. 1.95 (ISBN 0-425-04802-0). Berkley Pub.

Fast Life. Cynthia Wilkerson. 1979. pap. 2.25 (ISBN 0-505-51350-1). Tower Bks.

Fast Money Shoots from the Hip. Joseph M. Glazner. (Orig.). 1980. pap. 1.95 (ISBN 0-446-90164-4). Warner Bks.

Fast Neutron Activation Analysis: Elemental Data Base. John W. McKlveen. 306p. 1981. text ed. 39.95 (ISBN 0-250-40406-0). Ann Arbor Science.

Fast One. Robert Daley. 1979. pap. 2.25 o.p. (ISBN 0-345-28147-0). Ballantine.

Fast Pulsed & Burst Reactors: A Comprehensive Account of the Physics of Both Single Burst & Repetitively Pulsed Reactors. E. P. Shabalin. (Illus.). 1979. 68.00 (ISBN 0-08-022708-2). Pergamon.

Fast Reactions. J. N. Bradley. (Oxford Chemistry Ser). (Illus.). 128p. 1975. 16.95x (ISBN 0-19-855456-7). Oxford U Pr.

Fast Reactor Physics, 2 vols. (Illus., Orig., Eng., Fr. & Rus.). 1968. Vol. 1. pap. 28.00 (ISBN 0-685-12710-9, IAEA); Vol. 2. pap. 28.00 (ISBN 92-0-050568-6). Unipub.

Fast Reactor Physics Nineteen Seventy-Nine, Vol. 1. 2nd ed. 611p. 1980. pap. 71.00 (ISBN 92-0-050180-X, ISP529-1, IAEA). Unipub.

Fast Reactor Safety. John Graham. (Nuclear Science & Technology Ser.: Vol. 8). 1971. 48.00 (ISBN 0-12-294950-1). Acad Pr.

Fast Sailing Ships. David R. Macgregor. 316p. 1980. 57.00x (ISBN 0-245-51964-5, Pub. by Nautical England). State Mutual Bk.

Fast Sam, Cool Clyde, & Stuff. Myers. (YA) (gr. 7 up). 1978. pap. 1.50 (ISBN 0-380-01943-4, 45294). Avon.

Fast-Slow High-Low: A Book of Opposites. Peter Spier. LC 72-76207. (Illus.). 48p. (gr. k-3). 1972. 8.95a (ISBN 0-385-06781-X); PLB (ISBN 0-385-02876-8). Doubleday.

Fast Track: Texans & Other Strivers. Nicholas Lemann. 1981. 12.95 (ISBN 0-393-01436-3). Norton.

Fast Transforms: Algorithms, Analyses, Applications. Douglas F. Elliott & K. Ramamohan Rao. LC 79-8852. (Computer Science & Applied Mathematical Ser.). 1981. write for info. (ISBN 0-12-237080-5). Acad Pr.

Faster Reading Self-Taught. rev. ed. Harry Shefter. 1981. pap. write for info. (ISBN 0-671-83230-1). PB.

Faster Than a Speeding Bullet. Stuart Silver & Isidore Haiblum. LC 80-82221. 240p. (Orig.). 1980. pap. 2.25 (ISBN 0-87216-760-7). Playboy Pbks.

Faster Than Sound. Harvey Shapiro. LC 73-22610. (Illus.). 224p. 1975. 15.00 o.p. (ISBN 0-498-01507-6). A S Barnes.

Fastest, Cheapest, Best Way to Clean Everything. Consumer Guide. 1980. 10.95 (ISBN 0-686-62878-0, 25500). S&S.

Fastest Game in Town: Commodities. Mark R. Yarry. 192p. 1981. 9.95 (ISBN 0-13-307884-1). P-H.

Fastest Way to Get Rich: Trading in Financial Futures. Harvey Koch. LC 80-6155. 224p. 1981. 12.95 (ISBN 0-8128-2782-1). Stein & Day.

Fasti Ecclesiae Anglicanae: Series 1541-1857. John Le Neve. Incl. Vol. 1. St. Paul's, London. 1969. text ed. o.p. (ISBN 0-685-37486-6); Vol. 2. Chichester Diocese. 1971. text ed. o.p. (ISBN 0-685-37487-4); Vol. 3. Canterbury, Rochester & Winchester Dioceses. 1974. text ed. 12.00x (ISBN 0-685-37488-2). Athlone Pr). Humanities.

Fasting. Judith H. Dobrzynski. LC 78-26063. 1979. 7.95 (ISBN 0-671-18408-3); pap. 3.95 (ISBN 0-671-18355-9). Sovereign Bks.

Fasting. Jerry Falwell. 1981. pap. 2.25 (ISBN 0-8423-0849-0). Tyndale.

Fasting Rediscovered: A Guide to Health & Wholeness for Your Body-Spirit. Thomas Ryan. LC 80-81581. 176p. (Orig.). 1981. pap. 5.95 (ISBN 0-8091-2323-1). Paulist Pr.

Fasting Safely. Paul Perry. LC 78-68564. 128p. (Orig.). 1981. pap. 4.95 (ISBN 0-89037-217-9). Anderson World.

Fat Albert & the Cosby Kids: Getting It Together. Laura French. (Tell-a-Tale Readers). (Illus.). (gr. k-3). 1975. PLB 4.77 (ISBN 0-307-68598-5, Whitman). Western Pub.

Fat & Skinny. Philip Balstrino. LC 74-12306. (Let's-Read-&-Find-Out Science Bk). (Illus.). (gr. k-3). 1975. 7.95 (ISBN 0-690-00454-0, TYC-J); PLB 7.89 (ISBN 0-690-00665-9). T Y Crowell.

Fat Content & Composition of Animal Products. Agricultural & Renewable Resources Board & Food & Nutrition Board, Natural Research Council. LC 76-6496. 1976. pap. 9.75 (ISBN 0-309-02440-4). Natl Acad Pr.

Fat Ernest. Lisl Weil. LC 72-8095. (Illus.). 48p. (gr. k-3). 1973. 5.95 o.s.i. (ISBN 0-8193-0656-8, Four Winds); PLB 5.41 o.s.i. (ISBN 0-8193-0657-6). Schol Bk Serv.

Fat Free: Common Sense for Young Weight Worriers. Sara Gilbert. 112p. (gr. 6 up). 1975. 7.95 (ISBN 0-02-736410-0). Macmillan.

Fat-Free Recipes. Nevada Lampen. 1977. pap. 4.95 (ISBN 0-571-11026-6, Pub. by Faber & Faber). Merrimack Bk Serv.

Fat Is a Feminist Issue: The Anti-Diet Guide to Permanent Weight Loss. Susie Orbach. 203p. 1979. pap. 2.50 (ISBN 0-425-04380-0). Berkley Pub.

Fat Jack. Barbara Cohen. LC 80-12510. 192p. (gr. 6 up). 1980. 8.95 (ISBN 0-689-30772-1). Atheneum.

Fat Magic. Kroll. (ps-3). 1980. pap. 1.50 (ISBN 0-590-38332-9, Schol Pap). Schol Bk Serv.

Fat Men from Space. D. Manus Pinkwater. (Illus.). (gr. 4-6). 1980. pap. 0.95 (ISBN 0-440-44542-6, YB). Dell.

Fat Men from Space. Daniel M. Pinkwater. LC 77-6091. (gr. 4up). 1977. 5.50 (ISBN 0-396-07461-8). Dodd.

Fat of the Land. John Seymour. (Illus., Orig.). 1974. pap. 5.95 (ISBN 0-571-10532-7, Pub. by Faber & Faber). Merrimack Bk Serv.

Fat Polka-Dot Cat & Other Haiku. Betsy Maestro. (Illus.). 32p. (ps-1). 1976. PLB 6.95 o.p. (ISBN 0-525-29625-5). Dutton.

Fat-Soluble Vitamins. Ed. by H. F. DeLuca & J. W. Suttie. 1970. 37.50x (ISBN 0-299-05600-7). U of Wis Pr.

Fat Woman. Leon Rooke. LC 80-21893. 192p. 1981. 9.95 (ISBN 0-394-51642-7). Knopf.

Fata Morgana. William Kotzwinkle. 208p. 1980. pap. 2.95 (ISBN 0-553-11736-X). Bantam.

Fatal Curiosity. George Lillo. Ed. by William H. McBurney. LC 66-15130. (Regents Restoration Drama Ser). 1967. 5.95x (ISBN 0-8032-0364-0); pap. 1.65x (ISBN 0-8032-5364-8, BB 258, Bison). U of Nebr Pr.

Fatal Destinies: The Edgar Poe Essays. Charles Baudelaire. Tr. by Joan F. Mele from Fr. 1981. 10.95 (ISBN 0-916696-16-2); pap. 4.95 (ISBN 0-916696-17-0). Cross Country.

Fatal Flourishes. S. S. Rafferty. (gr. 7 up). 1978. pap. 1.95 (ISBN 0-380-41772-3, 41772). Avon.

Fatal Friendship: A Novel; by a Lady, 1771, 2 vols. in 1. Ed. by Michael F. Shugrue. (Flowering of the Novel, 1740-1775 Ser: Vol. 95). 1974. lib. bdg. 50.00 (ISBN 0-8240-1194-5). Garland Pub.

Fatal Glimpse. Robert K. Wilcox. 1981. pap. 2.25 (ISBN 0-8439-0899-8, Leisure Bks). Nordon Pubns.

Fatal Lozenge. Edward Gorey. (Illus.). 1960. pap. 3.50 (ISBN 0-8392-1031-0). Astor-Honor.

Fatal Mirror: Themes & Techniques in the Poetry of Fulke Greville. Richard Waswo. LC 75-188603. 1972. 10.95x (ISBN 0-8139-0392-0). U Pr of Va.

Fatal Necessity: British Intervention in New Zealand 1830-1847. Peter Adams. 1978. 23.00x (ISBN 0-19-647950-9). Oxford U Pr.

Fate & Effects of Petroleum Hydrocarbons in Marine Organisms & Ecosystems. Ed. by Douglas A. Wolfe. LC 77-76464. 1977. text ed. 67.00 (ISBN 0-08-021613-7). Pergamon.

Fate, Logic & Time. Steven M. Cahn. 1967. 10.50x o.p. (ISBN 0-300-00341-2). Yale U Pr.

Fate of a Cockroach. Tewfik A. Hakim. (African Writers Ser.). 1973. pap. text ed. 3.95 (ISBN 0-435-90117-6). Heinemann Ed.

Fate of a Cockroach & Other Plays. Tewfik Al-Hakim. Tr. by Denys Johnson-Davies from Arabic. 184p. 1980. 9.00 (ISBN 0-89410-196-X); pap. 5.00 (ISBN 0-89410-197-8). Three Continents.

Fate of Drugs in the Organism: A Bibliographic Survey, Vol. 4. Jean L. Hirtz. 1979. 82.50 (ISBN 0-8247-6587-7). Dekker.

Fate of Facts in a World of Men: Foreign Policy & Intelligence Making. Thomas L. Hughes. (Headline Ser.: 233). 1976. pap. 2.00 (ISBN 0-87124-038-6, 76-45580). Foreign Policy.

Fate of French-E in English: The Plural of Nouns Ending in-th, Vol. 7. C. T. Onions et al. Ed. by Steele Commager. Incl. Basic; Problems of Spelling Reform; Pure English of the Soil; Inflected English; Critique of Pure English; Retrospect. (Society of Pure English Ser.). 1979. lib. bdg. 42.00 (ISBN 0-8240-3671-9). Garland Pub.

Fate of Innocence. Gerald J. Goldberg. 1965. pap. text ed. 7.50x (ISBN 0-13-308189-3). P-H.

Fate of Mary Rose. Caroline Blackwood. 256p. 1981. 11.95 (ISBN 0-671-42321-5). Summit Bks.

Fate of Pollutants in the Air & Water Environments, 2 pts. I. H. Suffet. LC 76-58408. (Advances in Environmental Science & Technology). 1977. Pt. 1. 37.50 (ISBN 0-471-83539-0, Pub. by Wiley-Interscience); Pt. 2. 37.50 (ISBN 0-471-01803-1). Wiley.

Fate of Small Business in Nazi Germany. A. R. Gurland et al. LC 74-12275. 160p. 1975. Repr. of 1943 ed. 14.25 (ISBN 0-86527-065-1). Fertig.

Fate of the Dollar. Martin Mayer. 1981. Repr. pap. 3.50 (ISBN 0-451-09612-6, E9612, Sig). NAL.

Fate of the Revolution. Walter Laquer. 1967. 5.95 o.s.i. (ISBN 0-02-568330-6). Macmillan.

Fate Stepped in. D. L. Stasio. 256p. 1981. 10.50 (ISBN 0-682-49726-6). Exposition.

Fateful Years: Memoirs of a French Ambassador in Berlin, 1931-1938. Andre Francois-Poncet. LC 76-80549. 295p. 1973. Repr. of 1949 ed. 18.00 (ISBN 0-86527-066-X). Fertig.

Fates of Nations: A Biological Theory of History. Paul Colinvaux. 1980. 12.95 (ISBN 0-671-25204-6). S&S.

Fates of the Princes of Dyfed. Kenneth Morris. Ed. by R. Reginald & Douglas Menville. LC 80-19430. (Newcastle Forgotten Fantasy Library: Vol. 15). 362p. 1980. Repr. of 1978 ed. lib. bdg. 10.95x (ISBN 0-89370-514-4). Borgo Pr.

Father. August Strindberg. Ed. & tr. by Valborg Anderson. Bd. with Dream Play. LC 64-20118. (Crofts Classics Ser.). 1964. pap. text ed. 2.95x (ISBN 0-88295-096-7). AHM Pub.

Father Alberione's Prayerbook. James Alberione. 1974. plastic bdg. 4.00 o.s.i. (ISBN 0-8198-0291-3). Dghtrs St Paul.

Father & Son. Edmund Gosse. 1963. pap. 4.95 (ISBN 0-393-00195-4, Norton Lib). Norton.

Father Book: Pregnancy & Beyond. Alliance of Perinatal Research & Services, Inc. 1981. 17.50 (ISBN 0-87491-618-6); pap. 8.95 (ISBN 0-87491-422-1). Acropolis.

Father Butler, the Lough Dearg Pilgrim. William Carleton. Ed. by Robert L. Wolff. (Ireland Nineteenth Century Fiction - Ser. Two: Vol. 33). 306p. 1979. lib. bdg. 32.00 (ISBN 0-8240-3482-1). Garland Pub.

Father, Child & Sex Role: Paternal Determinants in Personality Development. Henry B. Biller. 1971. pap. 9.95 (ISBN 0-669-02517-8). Lexington Bks.

Father Clement, 1823. Grace Kennedy. Ed. by Robert L. Wolff. Bd. with Father Oswald 1842. LC 75-445. (Victorian Fiction Ser). 1975. lib. bdg. 66.00 (ISBN 0-8240-1525-8). Garland Pub.

Father Daughter. Jasper Evian. 256p. 1980. 10.95 (ISBN 0-02-536700-5). Macmillan.

Father Divine. Sara Harris. 1971. pap. 1.95 o.s.i. (ISBN 0-02-033070-7, Collier). Macmillan.

Father Eustace: A Tale of the Jesuits. Frances M. Trollope. Ed. by Robert L. Wolff. LC 75-448. (Victorian Fiction Ser.). 1975. Repr. of 1847 ed. lib. bdg. 66.00 (ISBN 0-8240-1528-2). Garland Pub.

Father Fox's Pennyrhymes. Clyde Watson. LC 71-146291. (Illus.). (gr. k-3). 1971. 8.95 (ISBN 0-690-29213-9, TYC-J); PLB 8.79 (ISBN 0-690-29214-7). T Y Crowell.

Father Has Come. Fernando L. Dasbach. 113p. 1981. 10.00. Regenbogen-Verlag.

Father Henson's Story of His Own Life. Josiah Henson. 1962. pap. 1.50 o.s.i. (ISBN 0-87091-017-5, AE). Corinth Bks.

Father: His Role in Child Development. David B. Lynn. LC 74-77547. 1974. text ed. 12.95 (ISBN 0-8185-0302-5); pap. text ed. 10.95 (ISBN 0-686-66953-3). Brooks-Cole.

Father in a Fix. Neil Boyd. LC 80-15258. 256p. 1980. 9.95 (ISBN 0-688-03643-0). Morrow.

Father-Infant Relationship: Observational Studies in Family Settings. Ed. by Frank A. Pedersen. LC 79-20514. (Praeger Special Studies Ser.). 196p. 1980. 22.95 (ISBN 0-03-049506-7). Praeger.

Father of Comfort. Basilea Schlink. 1971. pap. 2.95 (ISBN 0-87123-156-5, 200156). Bethany Fell.

Father of Fires. Kenneth M. Cameron. (ARMS Saga Ser.: Bk. 1). 320p. 1981. pap. 2.95 (ISBN 0-445-04640-6). Popular Lib.

Father Power. Biller, Henry, Ph.D. & Dennis Meredith. 400p. 1975. pap. 3.50 (ISBN 0-385-11125-8, Anch). Doubleday.

Father...a Son...& a Three-Mile Run. Keith Leenhouts. 1977. pap. 2.25 (ISBN 0-310-27512-1). Zondervan.

Fathering: Participation in Labor & Birth. Celeste R. Phillips & Joseph T. Anzalone. LC 77-13224. (Illus.). 1978. pap. 9.50 (ISBN 0-8016-3919-0). Mosby.

Fatherlove: Learning to Give the Best You've Got. D. Bruce Lockerbie. LC 80-711. 240p. 1981. 10.95 (ISBN 0-385-15865-3, Galilee). Doubleday.

Fathers. Allen Tate. LC 60-3394. 306p. 1960. pap. 5.95x (ISBN 0-8040-0108-1, 12). Swallow.

Fathers & Mothers. A. Vitale et al. 140p. 1973. pap. 7.00 (ISBN 0-88214-306-9). Spring Pubns.

Fathers & Sons. Thomas Babe. pap. 2.50 (ISBN 0-686-69574-7). Dramatists Play.

Fathers & Sons. Ivan Turgenev. Ed. by Ralph E. Matlaw. (Critical Editions). (Annotated). (gr. 9-12). 1966. pap. text ed. 5.95x (ISBN 0-393-09652-1, 9652, NortonC). Norton.

Fathers & Sons. Ivan Turgenev. (Literature Ser). (gr. 10-12). 1970. pap. text ed. 3.42 (ISBN 0-87720-724-0). AMSCO Sch.

Fathers & Sons. Ivan Turgenev. Tr. by Rosemary Edmonds. (Classics Ser). 1965. pap. 2.95 (ISBN 0-14-044147-6). Penguin.

Fathers Are People Too. D. L. Stewart. (Illus.). 128p. (Orig.). 1980. pap. 4.95 (ISBN 0-938492-01-2). Journal Herald.

Fathers: Daughters, Sons, Fathers Reveal Their Deepest Feelings. Robert Meister. 224p. 1981. 12.95 (ISBN 0-399-90107-8). Marek.

Father's Day. Jerry Klein. 176p. 1981. pap. 4.95 (ISBN 0-933180-24-1). Kickapoo.

Father's Day: A Novel of Power, Passion & Conscience. Eugene Kennedy. LC 80-2566. 528p. 1981. 13.95 (ISBN 0-385-15415-1). Doubleday.

Father's Days. Katherine Brady. 1981. pap. 2.95 (ISBN 0-440-12475-1). Dell.

Fathers, Fathers, Fathers. Eleanor R. Young. (Early Childhood Bk.). (Illus.). (ps-2). PLB 4.95 o.p. (ISBN 0-513-01108-0). Denison.

Father's Influence on Children. Marshall L. Hamilton. LC 76-41799. 1977. 13.95 (ISBN 0-88229-142-4); pap. 7.95 (ISBN 0-88229-503-9). Nelson-Hall.

Father's Legacy to His Daughters. John Gregory. Ed. by Gina Luria. LC 73-22031. (Feminist Controversy in England, 1788-1810 Ser.). 1974. lib. bdg. 50.00 (ISBN 0-8240-0863-4). Garland Pub.

Fathers to Daughters: The Legal Foundations of Female Emancipation. Peggy A. Rabkin. LC 79-6830. (Contributions in Legal Studies: No. 11). ix, 214p. 1980. lib. bdg. 25.00 (ISBN 0-313-20670-8, RFD/). Greenwood.

Fathers Without Partners: A Study of Fathers & the Family After Marital Separation. Kristine M. Rosenthal & Harry F. Keshet. 1981. 15.95x (ISBN 0-8476-6281-0). Rowman.

Fathers Without Theology. Marjorie Strachey. LC 58-6625. 1958. 4.00 o.p. (ISBN 0-8076-0056-3). Braziller.

Fathom. Marc Hammond. (Orig.). 1979. pap. 2.25 o.s.i. (ISBN 0-515-05121-7). Jove Pubns.

Fathom Five. Robert Westall. LC 80-11223. 256p. (gr. 7 up). 1980. 8.95 (ISBN 0-688-80286-9); PLB 8.59 (ISBN 0-688-84286-0). Greenwillow.

Fatigue & Microstructure. 1979. 64.00 (ISBN 0-87170-075-1). ASM.

Fatigue Design. 2nd ed. Carl C. Osgood. (International Series on the Strenth & Fracture of Materials & Structures). 500p. 1981. 65.00 (ISBN 0-08-026167-1); pap. 33.00 (ISBN 0-08-026166-3). Pergamon.

Fatigue Design of Machine Components. L. Sors. 224p. 1971. text ed. 42.00 (ISBN 0-08-016138-3). Pergamon.

Fatigue Eighty-One. 1981. text ed. price not set (ISBN 0-86103-042-7, Westbury Hse). Butterworth.

Fatigue Life of Prestressed Concrete Beams: Reinforced Concrete Research Council, No. 19. Compiled By American Society of Civil Engineers. 96p. 1977. pap. text ed. 7.00 (ISBN 0-87262-094-8). Am Soc Civil Eng.

Fatigue of Concrete. 1974. pap. 16.25 o.p. (ISBN 0-685-85118-4, SP-41); pap. 11.95 members o.p. (ISBN 0-685-85119-2). ACI.

Fatigue of Welded Structures. 2nd ed. T. R. Gurney. LC 78-21885. (British Welding Research Association Ser.). (Illus.). 1980. 66.00 (ISBN 0-521-22558-2). Cambridge U Pr.

Fatigue Resistance: Testing & Forecasting. Society of Automotive Engineers. 1979. 13.50 (ISBN 0-89883-219-5). Soc Auto Engineers.

Fatigue: What Causes It, What It Does to You, What You Can Do About It. new ed. Ray C. Wunderlich, Jr. (Illus.). 59p. 1976. pap. 2.10 (ISBN 0-910812-18-7). Johnny Reads.

Fatima. Francis Johnston. (The Great Sign). 1980. Repr. of 1979 ed. write for info. Tan Bks Pubs.

Fatima: The Great Sign. Francis Johnston. 1980. 3.50 (ISBN 0-911988-37-8, Co-Pub by Augustine Pr England). AMI Pr.

Fats Waller: His Life & Times. Joel Vance. 1979. pap. 2.25 o.p. (ISBN 0-425-04065-8). Berkley Pub.

Faulkner: A Biography, 2 vols. Joseph Blotner. (Illus.). 1974. Boxed Set. 30.00 (ISBN 0-394-47452-X). Random.

Faulkner & Black-White Relations: A Psychoanalytic Approach. Lee C. Jenkins. LC 80-21937. 288p. 1981. 20.00x (ISBN 0-231-04744-4). Columbia U Pr.

Faulkner & Dostoevsky: Influence & Confluence. Jean Weisgerber. Tr. by Dean McWilliams from Fr. LC 72-85537. xxii, 383p. 1974. 16.00 (ISBN 0-8214-0149-1). Ohio U Pr.

Faulkner & the French New Novelist. Tran Qui-Phiet. LC 80-66067. (Scholarly Monographs). 85p. 1980. pap. 7.50 (ISBN 0-8408-0503-9). Carrollton Pr.

Faulkner in the University: Class Conferences at the University of Virginia, 1957-1958. Ed. by Frederick L. Gwynn & Joseph L. Blotner. LC 59-13713. (Illus.). 1977. Repr. of 1959 ed. 13.95x (ISBN 0-8139-0843-4). U Pr of Va.

Faulkner: the Unappeased Imagination: A Collection of Critical Essays. Glenn O. Carey. 290p. 1980. 18.50x (ISBN 0-87875-181-5). Whitston Pub.

Faulkner's Intruder in the Dust: A Critical Study of the Typescripts. Patrick H. Samway. LC 79-57439. 408p. 1980. 28.50x (ISBN 0-87875-186-6). Whitston Pub.

Faulkner's Intruder in the Dust: Novel into Film. Regina K. Fadiman. LC 77-8417. (Illus.). 1978. 14.50x (ISBN 0-87049-214-4). U of Tenn Pr.

Faulkner's Yoknapatawpha Comedy. Lyall H. Powers. 296p. 1980. 18.50x (ISBN 0-472-08727-4). U of Mich Pr.

Fault & Joint Development in Brittle & Semi-Brittle Rock. N. J. Price. 1966. 23.00 (ISBN 0-08-011275-7); pap. 10.75 (ISBN 0-08-011274-9). Pergamon.

Fault Lines. James Carroll. 288p. 1980. 11.95 (ISBN 0-686-62569-2). Little.

Fauna & Flora of the Bible. 2nd ed. 1972. pap. 2.00 (ISBN 0-8267-0021-7, 08513). United Bible.

Faunal Provinces in Space & the Time: Geological Journal Special Issue, No. 4. F. A. Middlemiss et al. (Liverpool Geological Society & the Manchester Geological Association). 1980. 32.50 (ISBN 0-471-27751-7, Pub. by Wiley-Interscience). Wiley.

Faune Ichthyologique Du London Clay: Text & Atlas. Edgar Casier. (Illus.). xiv, 496p. 1966. 87.50x (ISBN 0-565-00654-1, Pub. by British Mus Nat Hist England). Sabbot-Natural Hist Bks.

Faust. new ed. Johann W. Von Goethe. Ed. by Cyrus Hamlin. Tr. by Walter Arndt from Ger. (Critical Edition Ser). 24p. 1976. pap. text ed. 5.45x (ISBN 0-393-09208-9). Norton.

Faust. Robert Nye. 290p. 1981. 12.95 (ISBN 0-399-12606-6). Putnam.

Faust, Pts. 1 & 2. abr. ed. Johann W. Von Goethe. Tr. by Louis MacNiece. 1960. pap. 4.95 (ISBN 0-19-500410-8). Oxford U Pr.

Faust Legend in Music. James W. Kelly. LC 74-75893. (Detroit Reprints in Music). 1976. 10.00 (ISBN 0-911772-81-2). Info Coord.

Faust, Parts 1 & 2. Johann W. Von Goethe. Tr. by Charles E. Passage. (Orig.). 1965. pap. 8.95 (ISBN 0-672-60414-0). Bobbs.

Faust-the Tragedy: Part One. Johann W. Von Goethe. Tr. by John Prudhoe from Ger. 157p. 1974. pap. 7.00x (ISBN 0-06-492465-3). B&N.

Faustin. Edmond De Goncourt. Tr. by G. Monkshood from Fr. 1976. Repr. of 1906 ed. 16.00 (ISBN 0-86527-267-0). Fertig.

Fauvism & Expressionism. B. Denvir. LC 77-80181. (Modern Movements in Art Ser.). 1978. pap. 1.95 (ISBN 0-8120-0878-2). Barron.

Fauvism Reexamined. Ellen C. Oppler. LC 75-23805. (Outstanding Dissertations in the Fine Arts - 20th Century). (Illus.). 1976. lib. bdg. 45.00 (ISBN 0-8240-1999-7). Garland Pub.

Favor. Nicholas Guild. 320p. 1981. 12.95 (ISBN 0-312-28512-4). St Martin.

Favorite Andrew Dang Fairy Tale Books in Many Colors: Red, Green & Blue Fairy Tale Books. Andrew Lang. (Illus.). 1979. pap. 14.95 boxed set (ISBN 0-486-23407-X). Dover.
Favorite Children's Stories from China & Tibet. Lotta C. Hume. LC 61-6219. (Illus.). (gr. 1-4). 1962. bds. 13.50 (ISBN 0-8048-0179-7). C E Tuttle.
Favorite Fairy Tales Told in Scotland. Virginia Haviland. (Illus.). (gr. 3 up). 1963. 6.95 (ISBN 0-316-35043-5); PLB o.p. (ISBN 0-316-35061-3). Little.
Favorite Movies: Critics' Choice. Ed. by Philip Nobile. 320p. 1973. 8.95 o.s.i. (ISBN 0-02-589800-0). Macmillan.
Favorite New England Recipes. Sara B. Stamm. (Illus.). 304p. 1972. pap. 9.75 (ISBN 0-911658-87-4). Yankee Bks.
Favorite New Orleans Recipes. Suzanne Ormond et al. LC 78-18841. 1979. English Ed. spiral bdg. 4.95 (ISBN 0-88289-198-7); French Ed. spiral bdg. 5.95 (ISBN 0-88289-199-5); Spanish Ed. spiral bdg. 5.95 (ISBN 0-88289-200-2); Combined Ed. spiral bdg. 10.95 (ISBN 0-88289-197-9). Pelican.
Favorite Nursery Tales. Walt Disney. (Illus.). (ps-3). 1977. PLB 5.00 (ISBN 0-307-12068-6, Golden Pr). Western Pub.
Favorite Paintings from the Cincinnati Art Museum. Millard F. Rogers, Jr. LC 80-66965. (Illus.). 104p. (Orig.). 1980. pap. 14.95 (ISBN 0-89659-159-X). Abbeville Pr.
Favorite Poems. Ed. by Al Bryant. 96p. 1972. pap. 2.50 (ISBN 0-310-22072-6). Zondervan.
Favorite Poems for Children Coloring Book. Susan Gaber. (Illus.). 48p. (Orig.). (ps-3). 1980. pap. 2.00 (ISBN 0-486-23923-3). Dover.
Favorite Poems in Large Print. Virginia S. Reiser. 1981. lib. bdg. 17.95 (ISBN 0-8161-3160-0, Large Print Bks). G K Hall.
Favorite Poems Old & New. Ed. by Helen Ferris. (gr. 3-7). 1957. 11.95a (ISBN 0-385-07696-7); PLB (ISBN 0-385-06249-4). Doubleday.
Favorite Recipes from the Microwave Times. (Illus.). 1980. 6.95 (ISBN 0-918620-20-1). Recipes Unltd.
Favorite Recipes of California Winemakers. Wine Advisory Board. Ed. by Lee Hecker. (Illus.). 1963. 5.95 (ISBN 0-932664-03-2). Wine Appreciation.
Favorite Stories & Illustrations. Zeno C. Tharp. 144p. 1956. 2.95 (ISBN 0-87148-327-0); pap. 2.25 (ISBN 0-87148-328-9). Pathway Pr.
Favorite Stories for Boys & Girls. Domenick Bava. 160p. (gr. k-6). 1980. PLB 6.95 (ISBN 0-89962-023-X). Todd & Honeywell.
Favorite Tales of Monsters & Trolls. George Jonsen. LC 76-24182. (Pictureback Library Editions). (ps-2). 1978. PLB 4.99 (ISBN 0-394-93477-6, BYR). Random.
Favorite Uncle Remus. Joel C. Harris. Ed. by George Van Santvoord & Archibald C. Coolidge. (gr. 4-8). 12.95 (ISBN 0-395-06800-2). HM.
Favorite Wisconsin Fish & Game Recipes. 1976. 1.95 o.p. (ISBN 0-932558-04-6). Wisconsin Sptm.
Favour of Your Company: Invitations to London Social Events, 1750 to 1850. Victoria Moger. (Illus.). 48p. 1980. pap. 14.00 (ISBN 0-913720-09-7). Sandstone.
Favourite Stories from Asia. Tr. by Leon Comber. (Favourite Stories Ser.). 1971. pap. text ed. 1.25 (ISBN 0-686-65609-1). Heinemann Ed.
Fawn. John Marston. Ed. by Gerald A. Smith. LC 65-11518. (Regents Renaissance Drama Ser). 1965. 7.95x (ISBN 0-8032-0276-8); pap. 1.65x (ISBN 0-8032-5275-7, BB 209, Bison). U of Nebr Pr.
Fawn of Spring-Vale, the Clarionet, & Other Tales, 3 vols. William Carleton. Ed. by Robert L. Wolff. (Ireland Nineteenth Century Fiction - Ser. Two: Vol. 38). 1068p. 1979. Set. lib. bdg. 96.00 (ISBN 0-8240-3487-2). Garland Pub.
FBI. Melvin Berger. LC 77-1395. (First Books Ser.). (gr. 4-6). 1977. PLB 6.45 (ISBN 0-531-01285-9). Watts.
Fe Incommovible. Jesse Winley. Ed. by Esteban Marosi & Angela Whidden. Tr. by Susana B. Lacy. 218p. (Span.). 1980. pap. 1.60 (ISBN 0-8297-0979-7). Vida Pubs.
Fear--Typewriter in the Sky. L. Ron Hubbard. 1977. pap. 1.50 o.p. (ISBN 0-445-04006-8). Popular Lib.
Fear & Courage. Stanley J. Rachman. LC 78-464. (Psychology Ser.). (Illus.). 1978. text ed. 17.95x (ISBN 0-7167-0089-1); pap. text ed. 8.95x (ISBN 0-7167-0087-5). W H Freeman.
Fear & Force Versus Education. Charles Wieder. LC 77-11235. 1978. pap. 4.95 (ISBN 0-8283-1706-2). Branden.
Fear at Brillstone. Florence P. Heide et al. LC 78-1307. (Pilot Bks.). (gr. 4-9). 1978. 6.95g (ISBN 0-8075-2304-6). A Whitman.
Fear Brokers: Peddling the Hate Politics of the New Right. Thomas J. McIntyre & John C. Obert. LC 80-70413. 384p. 1981. pap. 7.95 (ISBN 0-8070-3247-6, BP 620). Beacon Pr.
Fear in a Handful of Dust. John Ives. 1979. pap. 1.95 o.s.i. (ISBN 0-685-92516-1). Jove Pubns.
Fear into Anger: A Manual of Self-Defense for Women. Py Bateman. LC 77-19122. (Illus.). 1978. 15.95 (ISBN 0-88229-441-5); pap. 8.95 (ISBN 0-88229-603-5). Nelson-Hall.
Fear, Love, & Worship. C. FitzSimons Allison. pap. 3.95 (ISBN 0-8164-2020-3, SP17). Crossroad NY.
Fear of Crime: In Public Housing. Gene Fisher. 1981. 8.50 (ISBN 0-8062-1573-9). Carlton.
Fear of Freedom. Francis Biddle. LC 76-138496. (Civil Liberties in American History Ser). 1971. Repr. of 1951 ed. lib. bdg. 37.50 (ISBN 0-306-70073-5). Da Capo.
Fear of Looking; or Scopophilic-Exhibitionistic Conflicts. David W. Allen. LC 73-80875. 250p. 1974. 9.95x (ISBN 0-8139-0448-X). U Pr of Va.
Fear of Love. Carole Mortimer. (Harlequin Presents Ser.). 192p. 1980. pap. 1.50 (ISBN 0-373-10377-8, Pub. by Harlequin). PB.
Fear of Power: An Analysis of Anti-Statism in Three French Writers. Preston King. 1967. text ed. 6.25x (ISBN 0-391-01977-5). Humanities.
Fear of the Word: Censorship & Sex. Eli Oboler. LC 74-6492. 1974. 12.00 (ISBN 0-8108-0724-6). Scarecrow.
Fear on Ice. Earle Rice, Jr. (Storytellers Ser.). (Illus.). 64p. (gr. 5 up). 1981. PLB 7.95 (ISBN 0-516-02262-8). Childrens.
Fear Round About. George Bellairs. 1981. 9.95 (ISBN 0-8027-5441-4). Walker & Co.
Fear Without Childbirth. Irene Kampen. LC 77-19272. 1978. 8.95 o.p. (ISBN 0-397-01277-2). Lippincott.
Fearful Void. Geoffrey Moorhouse. LC 73-19977. (Illus.). 1974. 10.00 o.p. (ISBN 0-397-01019-2). Lippincott.
Fearfully & Wonderfully Made. Paul Brand & Phillip Yancey. 224p. 8.95 (ISBN 0-310-35450-1). Zondervan.
Fearless Cooking for One. Michele Evans. 1980. 13.95 (ISBN 0-671-24416-7). S&S.
Fearless Flying: The Complete Program for Relaxed Air Travel. Albert G. Forgione & Frederic M. Bauer. 1980. 11.95 (ISBN 0-395-29123-2); pap. 6.95. HM.
Fearless Leroy. Osmond Molarsky. (Illus.). (gr. 4-7). 1977. 6.95 o.p. (ISBN 0-8098-0008-X). Walck.
Fears & Phobias. Neil Olshan & Julie Dreyer. (gr. 7 up). 1980. PLB 7.90 (ISBN 0-531-02865-8, B08). Watts.
Fearsome Brat. George Mendoza. LC 73-133625. (Illus.). (gr. k-3). 1971. 6.75 (ISBN 0-688-41306-4); PLB 6.48 o.p. (ISBN 0-688-51306-9). Lothrop.
Feasibility of a Global Observation & Analysis Experiment. National Academy Of Sciences. 1966. pap. 5.00 (ISBN 0-309-01290-2). Natl Acad Pr.
Feasibility of Fertility Planning: Micro Perspectives. Ed. by T. Scarlett Epstein & Darrell Jackson. 1977. text ed. 37.00 (ISBN 0-08-021452-5); pap. text ed. 12.25 (ISBN 0-08-021837-7). Pergamon.
Feasibility of Health Maintenance Organizations in Texas. LBJ School of Public Affairs. LC 75-620099. (Policy Research Project Report Ser.: No. 11). 1975. 3.00 (ISBN 0-89940-607-6). LBJ Sch Public Affairs.
Feasibility Study of the SAT Performance of High-Ability Students from 1960 to 1974(Valedictorian Study) T. A. Donlon & G. Echternacht. 1977. 3.00 (ISBN 0-87447-044-7, 251712). College Bd.
Feasible Planning for Social Change. Robert Morris & Robert H. Binstock. LC 66-15763. 1966. 15.00x (ISBN 0-231-02746-X). Columbia U Pr.
Feast for Spiders. Kenneth L. Evans. 1980. pap. 1.95 (ISBN 0-451-09484-0, J9484, Sig). NAL.
Feast of All Saints. Anne Rice. 640p. 1981. pap. 2.95 (ISBN 0-449-24378-8, Crest). Fawcett.
Feast of Ashes. Sally Rosenbluth. LC 80-13195. 1980. 12.95 (ISBN 0-689-11071-5). Atheneum.
Feast of Joy: Ministering the Lord's Supper in the Free Tradition. Keith Watkins. 1977. pap. 2.50 (ISBN 0-8272-1006-X). Bethany Pr.
Feast or Famine? The Energy Future. Franklyn M. Branley. LC 79-7817. (Illus.). 128p. (gr. 5 up). 1980. 7.95 (ISBN 0-690-04040-7, TYC-J); PLB 7.89 (ISBN 0-690-04041-5). T Y Crowell.
Feasting Free on Wild Edibles. Bradford Angier. LC 72-6088. (Illus.). 320p. 1972. pap. 6.95 (ISBN 0-8117-2006-3). Stackpole.
Feasting Naturally: From Your Own Recipes. Mary A. Pickard. LC 80-68229. 1980. spiral bdg. 7.95 (ISBN 0-934474-18-4). Cookbook Pubs.
Feasting on Raw Foods. Ed. by Charles Gerras. (Illus.). 1980. 14.95 (ISBN 0-87857-271-6); pap. 9.95 o.p. (ISBN 0-87857-271-6). Rodale Pr Inc.
Feasting with Mine Enemy: Rank & Exchange Among Northwest Coast Societies. Abraham Rosman & Paula G. Rubel. LC 74-133033. 1971. 17.50x (ISBN 0-231-03483-0). Columbia U Pr.
Feasting...Naturally. Mary A. Pickard. LC 79-64450. 1979. softbound with spiral plastic bdg. 6.95 (ISBN 0-934474-05-2). Cookbook Pubs.
Feasts for Two. Paul Rubinstein. 256p. 1975. pap. 1.50 o.p. (ISBN 0-445-03099-2). Popular Lib.
Feasts for Two: A Cookbook of Menus & Recipes for Fifty Fabulous Meals. Paul Rubinstein. LC 72-92453. 256p. 1973. 9.95 (ISBN 0-02-605830-8). Macmillan.
Feasts of the Lord. Robert Thompson. pap. 5.95 (ISBN 0-89728-029-6, 645571). Omega Pubns OR.
Feather Arts: Beauty, Wealth, & Spirit from Five Continents. Phyllis Rabineau. Ed. by Patricia Williams. LC 78-774595. (Illus.). 88p. (Orig.). 1979. pap. 7.95 (ISBN 0-914868-08-X). Field Mus.
Feather Fashions & Bird Preservation. Robin W. Doughty. LC 72-619678. 1975. 16.50x (ISBN 0-520-02588-1). U of Cal Pr.
Feather for Daedalus: Explorations in Science & Myth. Kim Malville. LC 79-1955. (Physics Ser.). 152p. 1975. pap. text ed. 6.95 o.p. (ISBN 0-8465-4335-4, 54335). Benjamin-Cummings.
Feather Star. Patricia Wrightson. LC 63-7901. (Illus.). (gr. 7 up). 1963. 4.95 o.p. (ISBN 0-15-227501-0, HJ). HarBraceJ.
Featherbedding & Technological Change. Ed. by Paul A. Weinstein. (Studies in Economics). 1965. pap. text ed. 2.95 o.p. (ISBN 0-669-25924-1). Heath.
Feathered Serpent: The Rise & Fall of the Aztecs. Ruth Karen. LC 78-22129. (Illus.). 192p. 1979. 9.95 (ISBN 0-590-07413-X, Four Winds). Schol Bk Serv.
Feathers in the Fire. Catherine Cookson. 288p. 1981. pap. 2.25 (ISBN 0-553-13936-3). Bantam.
Feathers in the Wind, Bk. 1. Wilma R. Westphal. (Orion Ser.). 160p. 1981. pap. write for info. (ISBN 0-8127-0309-X). Southern Pub.
Feathers in the Wind, Bk. 2. Wilma Westphal & Chester Westphal. (Orion Ser.). 160p. 1981. pap. price not set (ISBN 0-8127-0322-7). Southern Pub.
Feature Films As History. Ed. by Kenneth Short. LC 80-28715. 192p. 1981. price not set (ISBN 0-87049-314-0). U of Tenn Pr.
Feature Writing for Newspapers. Daniel R. Williamson. 1975. 12.50 (ISBN 0-8038-2312-6); pap. text ed. 6.95x (ISBN 0-8038-2313-4). Hastings.
Features of Person & Society in Swat-Collected Essays on Pathans: Selected Essays of Frederik Barth, Vol. II. Fredrik Barth. (International Library of Anthropology Ser.). 208p. 1981. 32.00 (ISBN 0-7100-0620-9). Routledge & Kegan.
Featuring the Saint. Leslie Charteris. 1980. pap. 1.95 (ISBN 0-441-23155-1). Charter Bks.
Febold Feboldson: Tall Tales from the Great Plains. Compiled by Paul R. Beath. LC 62-8725. (Illus.). 1962. pap. 4.95 (ISBN 0-8032-5012-6, BB 161, Bison). U of Nebr Pr.
Febold Feboldson, the Fix It Farmer. new ed. Carol B. York. LC 79-66321. (Illus.). 48p. (gr. 4-6). 1980. lib. bdg. 4.89 (ISBN 0-89375-312-2); pap. 1.50 (ISBN 0-89375-311-4). Troll Assocs.
February Revolution: Petrograd, 1917. Tsuyoshi Hasegawa. LC 80-50870. (Publications on Russia of the School of International Studies: No. 9). (Illus.). 675p. 1981. 25.00 (ISBN 0-295-95765-4). U of Wash Pr.
Fed: A History of the South Wales Miners in the Twentieth Century. Hywel Francis & David Smith. (Illus.). 530p. 1980. text ed. 33.75x (ISBN 0-85315-489-9). Humanities.
Federal Administrative Proceedings. Walter Gellhorn. LC 70-138237. 150p. 1972. Repr. of 1941 ed. lib. bdg. 13.50x (ISBN 0-8371-5594-0, GEFA). Greenwood.
Federal Affairs Handbook Nineteen Seventy-Nine to Nineteen Eighty. rev. ed. Ed. by Eric Wentworth. 1979. pap. 27.50 (ISBN 0-89964-044-3). CASE.
Federal Agency Practices on Use of Piping. Building Research Advisory Board. 1967. pap. 6.25 (ISBN 0-309-01572-3). Natl Acad Pr.
Federal & State Court Systems: A Guide. Ed. by Fannie J. Klein. LC 76-47480. 1977. 18.50 (ISBN 0-88410-219-X); pap. 9.95 (ISBN 0-88410-795-7). Ballinger Pub.
Federal & State Impact on Citizen Participation in the Schools. Don Davies et al. 147p. (Orig.). 1978. pap. text ed. 5.00 (ISBN 0-917754-04-2). Inst Responsive.
Federal Aviation Regulations for Aviation Mechanics. 6th ed. Federal Aviation Administration. (Aviation Maintenance Training Course Ser.). 442p. 1980. pap. 10.00 (ISBN 0-89100-177-8, E*A-F*A*R-1E). Aviation Maintenance.
Federal Aviation Regulations for Pilots, Nineteen Eighty. Federal Aviation Administration. Ed. by Aviation Book Company. 128p. 1980. pap. 3.50 (ISBN 0-911721-66-5). Aviation.
Federal Aviation Regulations for Pilots. Aero Staff. LC 60-10472. 112p. 1981. pap. write for info. (ISBN 0-8168-5737-7). Aero.
Federal Aviation Regulations for Pilots: 1981 Edition. Ed. by Pan American Navigation Service Staff. LC 73-644468. 1981. soft bdg. 3.50 (ISBN 0-87219-014-5). Pan Am Nav.
Federal Aviation Regulations Handbook for Pilots. 2nd ed. Federal Aviation Administration. (Pilot Training Ser.). (Illus.). 448p. 1980. pap. 6.95 (ISBN 0-89100-185-9, E*A-R*P-1A). Aviation Maintenance.
Federal Budget Policy. 3rd ed. David J. Ott & Attiat F. Ott. (Studies of Government Finance). 1977. 12.95 (ISBN 0-8157-6710-2); pap. 4.95 (ISBN 0-8157-6709-9). Brookings.
Federal Career Guide. R. B. Uleck Associates. (Illus., Orig.). 1979. pap. 5.95 (ISBN 0-937562-03-3). Uleck Assoc.
Federal Challenge: S.1236. Peter F. Rousmaniere. (Government Auditing Ser.). 52p. 1979. pap. 6.00 (ISBN 0-916450-30-9). Coun on Municipal.
Federal Constitution of Switzerland. Switzerland. Constitution. Tr. by Christopher Hughes. Repr. of 1954 ed. lib. bdg. 15.00x (ISBN 0-8371-4036-6, SWFC). Greenwood.
Federal Control of Business-Antitrust Laws. Austin T. Stickells. LC 72-84857. (Commercial Law Library). 930p. 1972. 55.00 (ISBN 0-686-02629-2). Lawyers Co-Op.
Federal Convention & the Formation of the Union of the American States. Ed. by Winton U. Solberg. LC 58-9959. (YA) (gr. 9 up). 1958. pap. 10.95 (ISBN 0-672-60024-2, AHS19). Bobbs.
Federal Courtroom Evidence. Joseph W. Cotchett & Arnold B. Elkind. LC 75-26155. 1980. incl. 1979 suppl. 29.50 (ISBN 0-911110-20-8). Parker & Son.
Federal Courts: Jurisdiction & Practice. Theodore Schussler. 152p. 1980. 5.50 (ISBN 0-87526-036-5). Gould.
Federal Equal Employment Opportunity: Politics & Public Personnel Administration. David H. Rosenbloom. LC 77-954. (Special Studies). 1976. text ed. 24.95 (ISBN 0-275-24420-2). Praeger.
Federal Evidence, Vol. 5. David W. Louisell & Christopher B. Mueller. LC 76-46689. 1978. 275.00 (ISBN 0-686-22901-0). Lawyers Co-Op.
Federal Executive: The President & the Bureaucracy. Thomas A. Timberg. LC 77-17490. (Orig.). 1978. pap. text ed. 7.95x (ISBN 0-89197-641-8). Irvington.
Federal Fast Finder. 1981. pap. 5.00 (ISBN 0-686-26066-X). Wash Res.
Federal Financial System. Daniel Selko. LC 75-8891. (FDR & the Era of the New Deal Ser.). xii, 606p. 1975. Repr. of 1940 ed. lib. bdg. 59.50 (ISBN 0-306-70708-X). Da Capo.
Federal Fiscal Policy in the Postwar Recessions. Wilfred Lewis, Jr. (Studies of Government Finance). 311p. 1962. 9.95 (ISBN 0-8157-5242-3). Brookings.
Federal Funding of Civilian Research & Development: A Report to the Experimental Technology Incentives Program, U. S. Dept. of Commerce. new ed. A.D. Little, Inc. Ed. by Michael Michaelis. LC 76-43308. 1977. 35.50x (ISBN 0-89158-205-3). Westview.
Federal Government & Educational R&D. Richard A. Dershimer. LC 74-293. (Politics of Educations Ser.). (Illus.). 1976. 18.95 (ISBN 0-669-92700-7). Lexington Bks.
Federal Government & Urban Problems: HUD: Successes, Failures, & the Fate of Our Cities. M. Carter McFarland. LC 77-26301. 1978. lib. bdg. 28.00x (ISBN 0-89158-085-9). Westview.
Federal Government Is Run by Idiots: Political Commentary. James E. Joyce. (Illus.). 1980. 3.50 (ISBN 0-932212-19-0). Avery Color.
Federal Grants-in-Aid: Maximizing Benefits to the States. Anita S. Harbert. LC 76-12854. 1976. text ed. 24.95 (ISBN 0-275-23370-7). Praeger.
Federal Health Programs: Improving the Health-Care System? Ed. by Stuart Altman & Harvey M. Sapolsky. LC 79-48059. (University Health Policy Consortium Ser.). 1981. 24.95x (ISBN 0-669-03690-0). Lexington Bks.
Federal Hill: A Baltimore National Historic District. Norman G. Rukert. Ed. by Max Robinson. LC 80-65865. (Illus.). 128p. (Orig.). 1980. 12.95 (ISBN 0-910254-14-1); pap. 6.95 (ISBN 0-910254-15-X). Bodine.
Federal Income Tax: Its Sources & Applications. C. McCarthy et al. 1980. 20.95 o.p. (ISBN 0-13-308965-7). P-H.
Federal Income Tax: Nineteen Eighty Edition. Ed. by Charles B. Edelson et al. (Illus.). 1980. pap. text ed. 10.95 o.p. (ISBN 0-8359-1871-8); free instrs' manual o.p. Reston.

Federal Income Tax: Nineteen Eighty-One Edition. Edelson et al. 250p. (Orig.). 1981. pap. text ed. 10.95 (ISBN 0-8359-1873-4); instrs. manual avail. (ISBN 0-8359-1874-2). Reston.

Federal Income Tax, 1981 Edition: Its Sources & Applications. Clarence McCartney et al. (Illus.). 912p. 1980. text ed. 21.95 (ISBN 0-13-309005-1). P-H.

Federal Income Taxation of Business Enterprise. Bernard Wolfman. 1095p. 1971. 24.50 (ISBN 0-316-95113-7); pap. 1979 suppl. o.p. (ISBN 0-316-95114-5). Little.

Federal Income Taxation of Corporations & Stockholders in a Nutshell. 2nd ed. Jonathan Sobeloff & Peter P. Weidenbruch. (Nutshell Ser.). 351p. 1981. pap. 6.95 (ISBN 0-8299-2122-2). West Pub.

Federal Income Taxation of Domestic & Foreign Business Transactions. Samuel C. Thompson, Jr. (Contemporary Legal Education Ser.). 1200p. 1980. 40.00 (ISBN 0-672-84075-8); text ed. 25.00 (ISBN 0-686-68532-6). Bobbs.

Federal Income Taxation of Estates & Beneficiaries. M. Carr Ferguson et al. 749p. (Orig.). 1970. text ed. 40.00 (ISBN 0-316-27889-0); text ed. 12.50 1979 supplement (ISBN 0-316-27899-8). 1980 supplement (ISBN 0-316-27900-5). Little.

Federal Income Taxation of Insurance Companies. 3rd ed. Gerald Lenrow et al. LC 78-26091. 1979. 46.50 (ISBN 0-471-05193-4, Pub. by Ronald). Wiley.

Federal Income Taxation, 1981. Dale Bandy & Randy Swad. 250p. 1981. pap. text ed. 12.95 (ISBN 0-13-308502-3). P-H.

Federal Investment in Knowledge of Social Problems. Study Project on Social Research & Development, National Research Council. LC 78-7928. 1978. pap. text ed. 7.00 (ISBN 0-309-02747-0). Natl Acad Pr.

Federal Jurisdiction: A General View. Henry J. Friendly. 199p. 1973. 15.00x (ISBN 0-231-03741-4). Columbia U Pr.

Federal Jurisdiction: Tensions in the Allocation of Judicial Power. Martin H. Redish. 370p. 1980. 25.00 (ISBN 0-672-84196-7). Michie.

Federal Justice. Homer Cummings & Carl McFarland. LC 76-109552. (American Constitutional & Legal History Ser). 1970. Repr. of 1937 ed. lib. bdg. 49.50 (ISBN 0-306-71906-1). Da Capo.

Federal Lands: Their Use & Management. Marion Clawson & Burnell Held. LC 57-12121. (Illus.). 1965. pap. 5.95x (ISBN 0-8032-5034-7, BB 318, Bison). U of Nebr Pr.

Federal Law of Employment Discrimination in a Nutshell. rev. ed. Mack A. Player. LC 80-22475. (Nutshell Ser.). 357p. 1980. pap. text ed. 6.95 (ISBN 0-8299-2111-7). West Pub.

Federal-Metropolitan Politics & the Commuter Crisis. Michael N. Danielson. LC 65-16197. (Illus.). 1965. 16.00x (ISBN 0-231-02782-6). Columbia U Pr.

Federal Mine Electrical Certification: Surface & Underground. National School of Mines. LC 79-87486. 1979. text ed. 35.00 (ISBN 0-930206-02-9). M-A Pr.

Federal Mineral Policies, Nineteen Forty-Five to Seventy-Five: A Survey of Federal Activities That Affected the Canadian Mineral Industry. Margot J. Wojciechowski. 87p. (Orig.). 1979. pap. 3.50x (ISBN 0-686-63135-8, Pub. by Ctr Resource Stud Canada). Renouf.

Federal Personnel Procedures Reference Manual. rev. ed. Byrd W Walker, Jr. 1246p. 1976. pap. text ed. 20.00 (ISBN 0-87771-009-0). Grad School.

Federal Policy & American Indian Health Needs. Everett R. Rhoades. LC 74-10495. 32p. 1974. pap. 1.00 o.p. (ISBN 0-913456-38-1). Interbk Inc.

Federal Polity. B. M. Sharma & L. P. Choudhry. 15.00x (ISBN 0-210-26930-8). Asia.

Federal Principle: A Journey Through Time in Quest of Meaning. S. Rufus Davis. 1978. 16.50x (ISBN 0-520-03146-6). U of Cal Pr.

Federal Programs & City Politics: The Dynamics of the Aid Process in Oakland. Jeffrey L. Pressman. (Oakland Project Ser). 1975. 18.50x (ISBN 0-520-02749-3); pap. 4.95x (ISBN 0-520-03508-9). U of Cal Pr.

Federal-Provincial Collaboration: The Canada-New Brunswick General Development Agreement. Donald J. Savoie. (Institute of Public Administration of Canada (IPAC) Ser.). 220p. 1981. 25.00x (ISBN 0-7735-0373-0); pap. 11.95x (ISBN 0-7735-0374-9). McGill-Queens U Pr.

Federal Public Land & Resources Law. George C. Coggins & Charles F. Wilkinson. (University Casebook Ser.). 1018p. 1981. text ed. write for info. (ISBN 0-88277-022-5). Foundation Pr.

Federal Rathole. Donald Lambro. 1975. 7.95 o.p. (ISBN 0-87000-294-5). Arlington Hse.

Federal Regulation: Hospital Attorney's Desk Reference. American Society of Hospital Attorneys. 244p. (Orig.). 1980. pap. 35.00 (ISBN 0-87258-321-X, 1430). Am Hospital.

Federal Regulation of Mine Safety, Health & Reclamation, Vol. 179. (Commercial Law & Practice Course Handbook Ser 1977-78). 1978. soft cover 20.00 o.p. (ISBN 0-685-47623-5, A4-3006). PLI.

Federal Regulation of New Industrial Plants Course Handbook. (Real Estate Law & Practice Course Handbook Ser., 1977-78: Vol. 149). 1978. pap. 20.00 o.p. (ISBN 0-685-59709-1, N4-4314). PLI.

Federal Regulations: Ethical Issues & Social Research. Ed. by Murray L. Wax & Joan Cassell. (AAAS Selected Symposium: No. 36). 1979. lib. bdg. 22.50x (ISBN 0-89158-487-0). Westview.

Federal Regulatory Directory Nineteen Eighty to Eighty One. Congressional Quarterly Inc. Ed. by Congressional Quarterly Inc. 931p. 1980. pap. text ed. 25.00 (ISBN 0-87187-153-X). Congr Quarterly.

Federal Reorganization. Ed. by Peter Szanton. 1981. pap. 12.95x (ISBN 0-934540-11-X). Chatham Hse Pubs.

Federal Reorganization: What Have We Learned? Ed. by Peter Szanton. (Chatham House Series on Change in American Politics). 184p. 1981. pap. text ed. 12.95x (ISBN 0-934540-11-X). Chatham Hse Pubs.

Federal Republic, Europe & the World: Perspectives in West Germany Foreign Policy. Martin Saeter. 120p. 1980. text ed. 15.00x (ISBN 82-00-05315-6). Universitet.

Federal Republic in Spain: Pi y Margall & the Federal Republican Movement, 1868-74. Charles A. Hennessy. LC 80-13187. xiv, 299p. 1980. Repr. of 1962 ed. lib. bdg. 26.75x (ISBN 0-313-22458-7, HEFP). Greenwood.

Federal Reserve Conspiracy & the Rockefellers: Their Gold Corner. Emanuel Josephson. LC 68-29455. (Blacked-Out History Ser.). 374p. 1968. 12.50 (Pub. by Chedney); pap. 8.00. Alpine Ent.

Federal Reserve Policy Reappraised, 1951-1959. Daniel S. Ahearn. LC 63-10522. 1963. 18.00x (ISBN 0-231-02575-0). Columbia U Pr.

Federal Reserve System. Benjamin H. Beckhardt. LC 70-184746. 1971. 25.00x o.p. (ISBN 0-231-03536-5). Columbia U Pr.

Federal Rules of Criminal Procedure. 2nd ed. Ed. by Michele G. Hermann. LC 80-10646. 1980. looseleaf with 1978 rev. pages 35.00 (ISBN 0-87632-106-6). Boardman.

Federal Rules of Evidence. 2nd ed. LC 78-92961. 1979. looseleaf 35.00 (ISBN 0-87632-088-4). Boardman.

Federal Rules of Evidence Manual. 2nd ed. Stephen A. Saltzburg & Kenneth R. Redden. 1977. with 1979 suppl 50.00 (ISBN 0-87215-200-6); 1980 suppl. 22.50 (ISBN 0-87215-338-X). Michie.

Federal Staff Directory, 1981. Ed. by Charles B. Brownson & Anna L. Brownson. 960p. 1981. casebound 25.00 (ISBN 0-686-69484-8). Congr Staff.

Federal-State Health Policies & Impacts: The Politics of Implementation. Christa Altenstetter & James W. Bjorkman. LC 78-62173. (Illus.). 1978. pap. text ed. 7.75 (ISBN 0-8191-0503-1). U Pr of Amer.

Federal Statutory Law of Employment Discrimination. Charles A. Sullivan et al. 1000p. 1980. text ed. 45.00 (ISBN 0-672-83697-1). Bobbs.

Federal System in Constitutional Law. G. Herman Pritchett. (Illus.). 1978. pap. 11.95 ref. ed. (ISBN 0-13-308460-4). P-H.

Federal Tax Policy. rev. ed. Joseph A. Pechman. (Brookings Institute Studies of Government Finance). 1971. pap. text ed. 5.95x (ISBN 0-393-09987-3). Norton.

Federal Tax Policy. 3rd ed. Joseph A. A. Pechman. LC 76-54901. (Studies of Government Finance). 1977. 14.95 (ISBN 0-8157-6978-4); pap. 6.95 (ISBN 0-8157-6977-6). Brookings.

Federal Tax Return Manual: 1981. Commerce Clearing House. 1980. ring binder 57.00 (ISBN 0-686-64882-X). Commerce.

Federal Tax System of the United States: A Survey of Law & Administration. Joseph P. Crockett. LC 72-100154. Repr. of 1955 ed. lib. bdg. 17.50x (ISBN 0-8371-3681-4, CRTS). Greenwood.

Federal Tax Treatment of the Family. Harold M. Groves. LC 76-55946. (Brookings Institution, Studies of Government Finance Ser). 1977. Repr. of 1963 ed. lib. bdg. 15.00x (ISBN 0-8371-9425-3, GRFT). Greenwood.

Federal Taxation As an Instrument of Social & Economic Policy: A Symposium. Ed. by I. J. Goffman. LC 72-5017. 104p. 1972. Repr. of 1968 ed. lib. bdg. 15.00 (ISBN 0-306-70501-X). Da Capo.

Federal Taxation: Corporations, Partnerships, Estates & Trusts. Hoffman. 420p. 1979. write for info. (ISBN 0-8299-0491-3); solutions manual avail. West Pub.

Federal Taxation of Estates, Gifts, & Trusts. Ted D. Engelbrecht et al. (Illus.). 528p. 1981. 32.95. P-H.

Federal Taxation of Estates, Gifts, & Trusts. 3rd ed. 645p. 1980. 55.00 (ISBN 0-686-28716-9, T118C). ALI-ABA.

Federal Taxation of Gifts, Trusts & Estates. Douglas A. Kahn & Lawrence W. Waggoner. 1980. 1980 suppl. 6.95 (ISBN 0-316-48201-3). Little.

Federal Taxes & Management Decisions. rev. ed. Ray M. Sommerfeld. 1978. pap. text ed. 12.95 (ISBN 0-256-02069-8). Irwin.

Federal Trade Commission: A Fiftieth Anniversary Symposium. M. Handler et al. LC 78-152229. (Symposia on Law & Society Ser). 1971. Repr. of 1964 ed. lib. bdg. 22.50 (ISBN 0-306-70119-7). Da Capo.

Federal Trial Handbook. Robert S. Hunter. LC 74-15928. 1974. 50.00 (ISBN 0-686-14509-7). Lawyers Co-Op.

Federal Usurpation. Franklin Pierce. xx, 437p. 1980. Repr. of 1908 ed. lib. bdg. 35.00x (ISBN 0-8377-1007-3). Rothman.

Federal Work, Security, & Relief Programs. Arthur Burns & Edward Williams. LC 71-166956. (FDR & the Era of the New Deal Ser). 1971. Repr. of 1941 ed. lib. bdg. 15.00 (ISBN 0-306-70356-4). Da Capo.

Federalism & Clean Waters: The 1972 Water Pollution Control Act. Harvey Lieber. LC 74-33980. (Illus.). 288p. 1975. 22.50 (ISBN 0-669-99150-3). Lexington Bks.

Federalism & Constitutional Change. William S. Livingston. LC 74-9226. 380p. 1974. Repr. of 1956 ed. lib. bdg. 29.00x (ISBN 0-8371-7623-9, LIFC). Greenwood.

Federalism & Regional Development: Case Studies on the Experience in the United States & the Federal Republic of Germany. Ed. by George W. Hoffman. (Illus.). 784p. 1981. text ed. 40.00x (ISBN 0-292-73825-0). U of Tex Pr.

Federalism & the Regulatory Process. Richard J. Schultz. 91p. 1979. pap. text ed. 1.50x (ISBN 0-686-68857-0, Pub. by Inst Res Pub Canada). Renouf.

Federalism, Bureaucracy, & Public Policy: The Politics of Highway Transport Regulation. Richard J. Schultz. (IPAC Ser.). 237p. 1980. 20.95x (ISBN 0-7735-0360-9); pap. 10.95x (ISBN 0-7735-0362-5). McGill-Queens U Pr.

Federalism: History & Current Significance of a Form of Government. Ed. by J. C. Boogman & G. N. Van Der Plaat. (Illus.). 307p. 1980. pap. 16.90 (ISBN 90-247-9003-4, Pub by Martinus Nijhoff). Kluwer Boston.

Federalist. Ed. by Jacob E. Cooke. LC 61-6971. 1961. 35.00x (ISBN 0-8195-3016-6, Pub. by Wesleyan U Pr). Columbia U Pr.

Federalist Era, Seventeen Eighty Nine to Eighteen-One. John C. Miller. (New American Nation Ser.). (Illus.). pap. 6.95x (ISBN 0-06-133027-2, TB 3027, Torch). Harrow.

Federalist Papers. Ed. by Lester Dekoxher. LC 75-42310. pap. 2.95 o.p. (ISBN 0-8028-1620-7). Eerdmans.

Federalist Papers. 2nd ed. Ed. by Roy P. Fairfield. LC 80-8862. 368p. 1981. pap. text ed. 5.95x (ISBN 0-8018-2607-1). Johns Hopkins.

Federalist Papers: Essays by Hamilton, Madison & Jay. 2nd ed. Ed. by Roy P. Fairfield. LC 66-24210. pap. 2.95 o.p. (ISBN 0-385-07146-9, A239, Anch). Doubleday.

Federalist: Selections. Madison Hamilton. Ed. by Henry S. Commager. LC 49-11364. (Crofts Classics Ser.). 1949. pap. text ed. 2.75x (ISBN 0-88295-041-X). AHM Pub.

Federalist Years: The Years in Review Seventeen Eighty-Nine to Eighteen Hundred. Eric Rothschild. 109p. (gr. 9-12). 1980. pap. text ed. 25.00 (ISBN 0-667-00576-5). Microfilming Corp.

Federalization of Presidential Primaries. Austin Ranney. 1978. pap. 3.25 (ISBN 0-8447-3297-4). Am Enterprise.

Federally Assisted New Communities: New Dimensions in Urban Development. Hugh Mields, Jr. LC 73-78874. (Special Report Ser.). (Illus.). 1973. pap. 4.75 (ISBN 0-87420-557-3). Urban Land.

Federation of the West Indies. John Mordecai. LC 67-24014. 1968. 16.75x o.s.i. (ISBN 0-8101-0172-6). Northwestern U Pr.

Federico Fellini: An Annotated International Bibliography. Barbara A. Price & Theodore Price. LC 77-26310. 1978. 13.50 (ISBN 0-8108-1104-9). Scarecrow.

Federico Garcia Lorca. Carl W. Cobb. (World Authors Ser.: Spain: No. 23). 1968. lib. bdg. 9.95 (ISBN 0-8057-2544-X). Twayne.

Federico Garcia Lorca & Sean O'Casey: Powerful Voices in the Wilderness. Katie B. Davis. (Salzburg Studies in English Literature: Poetic Drama & Poetic Theory: No. 43). 1978. text ed. 25.00x (ISBN 0-391-01357-2). Humanities.

Federico Garcia Lorca y Su Mundo: Ensayo De una Bibliografia General. Joseph L. Laurenti & Joseph Siracusa. LC 74-2252. (Author Bibliographies Ser.: No. 15). 1974. 11.00 (ISBN 0-8108-0713-0). Scarecrow.

Fee-Based Information Services: The Commercial Sector. Richard W. Boss & Lorig Maranjian. 199p. 1980. 24.95 (ISBN 0-8352-1287-4). Bowker.

Feed Formulations. 2nd ed. T. W Perry. LC 74-83600. 1975. 12.35 o.p. (ISBN 0-8134-1670-1); text ed. 9.25x o.p. (ISBN 0-685-64706-4, 1670). Interstate.

Feed Formulations. 3rd ed. Ed. by T. W. Perry. 1981. 12.35 (ISBN 0-8134-2174-8); text ed. 9.25x. Interstate.

Feed from Animal Wastes: State of Knowledge. (FAO Animal Production & Health Paper Ser.: No. 18). 201p. 1981. pap. 10.75 (ISBN 92-5-100946-5, F2100, FAO). Unipub.

Feed Me, I'm Yours. Vicki Lansky. 176p. 1981. pap. 2.25 (ISBN 0-553-12640-7). Bantam.

Feed Your Kids Right. Lendon Smith. 1980. pap. 4.95 (ISBN 0-440-52704-X, Dell Trade Pbks). Dell.

Feedback & Control Systems. A. C. McDonald & H. Lowe. 1981. text ed. 19.95 (ISBN 0-8359-1898-X). Reston.

Feedback & Organization Development: Using Data-Based Methods. David A. Nadler. (Illus.). 1977. pap. text ed. 7.50 (ISBN 0-201-05006-4). A-W.

Feedback Systems: Input-Output Properties. C. A. Desoer & M. Vidyasagar. (Electrical Science Ser.). 1975. 43.50 (ISBN 0-12-212050-7). Acad Pr.

Feeding Ponies. William C. Miller. (Illus.). pap. 4.35 (ISBN 0-85131-211-X, Dist. by Sporting Book Center). J A Allen.

Feeding the Flame. T. Lobsang Rampa. pap. 2.50 (ISBN 0-685-01079-1). Weiser.

Feeding the Horse. Date not set. lib. bdg. 10.75 (ISBN 0-936032-04-9). Thoroughbred Own & Breed.

Feeding the Russian Fur Trade: Provisionment of the Okhotsk Seaboard & the Kamchatka Peninsula, 1639-1856. James R. Gibson. LC 79-81319. (Illus.). 1969. 27.50x (ISBN 0-299-05230-3). U of Wis Pr.

Feeding Your Horse. Diane R. Tuke. (Illus.). 104p. (Orig.). 1980. pap. 13.10 (ISBN 0-85131-334-5). J A Allen.

Feel Fit-Come Alive. Roger Pontefract. (Illus.). 144p. 1979. text ed. 19.50x (ISBN 0-19-217583-1). Oxford U Pr.

Feel of Feel. D. N. Moorty. (Redbird Bk.). 1976. lib. bdg. 8.00 (ISBN 0-89253-097-9); flexible bdg. 4.80 (ISBN 0-89253-133-9). Ind-US Inc.

Feel of the Work Place: Understanding & Improving Organization Climate. Fritz Steele & Stephen Jenks. LC 76-12802. (Illus.). 1977. pap. text ed. 8.95 (ISBN 0-201-07213-0). A-W.

Feel Younger, Live Longer. LC 76-56979. (Illus.). 1977. 12.50 o.s.i. (ISBN 0-528-81798-1); pap. 7.95 (ISBN 0-528-88195-7). Rand.

Feeling Alive. B. Milbauer & K. K. Jacobson. (Getting in Touch Ser: Bk. 2). (gr. 5-8). 0.95 o.p. (ISBN 0-531-02093-2, Q26). Watts.

Feeling Alive After 65: The Complete Medical Guide for Senior Citizens & Their Families. Robert B. Taylor. (Illus.). 224p. 1973. 8.95 o.p. (ISBN 0-87000-226-0). Arlington Hse.

Feeling Fine: Enhancing Your Well-Being. Jeanne S. Segal. (Orig.). 1980. pap. 7.95 (ISBN 0-913300-51-9). Unity Pr.

Feeling Good. David D. Burns. 1981. pap. 3.95 (ISBN 0-451-09804-8, E9804, Signet Bks). NAL.

Feeling Good: A Book About You & Your Body. Sara Gilbert. LC 78-5306. 192p. (gr. 7 up). 1979. 7.95 (ISBN 0-590-07510-1, Four Winds). Schol Bk Serv.

Feeling Good: The New Mood Therapy. David Burns. LC 80-12694. (Illus.). 388p. 1980. 12.95 (ISBN 0-688-03633-3). Morrow.

Feelings. Judy Dunn. LC 70-125915. (Illus.). (gr. k-3). 1970. PLB 6.75 (ISBN 0-87191-045-4). Creative Ed.

Feelings. Esther L. Jones. 1981. 4.95 (ISBN 0-8062-1651-4). Carlton.

Feelings: A Collection of Poems & Potpourri. Candy Fink. 1981. 4.95 (ISBN 0-533-04838-9). Vantage.

Feelings Are There. Brenda S. Pittman. 1981. 4.50 (ISBN 0-8062-1553-4). Carlton.

Feelings Between Brothers & Sisters. Marcia Conta & Maureen Reardon. LC 75-20172. (Identity I Ser.). (Illus.). 32p. (gr. k-3). 1975. Repr. of 1974 ed. PLB 7.95 o.p. (ISBN 0-8172-0039-8). Raintree Pubs.

Feelings Between Friends. Marcia Conta & Maureen Reardon. LC 75-19348. (Moods & Emotions Ser.). (Illus.). 32p. (gr. k-3). 1975. Repr. of 1974 ed. PLB 8.95 (ISBN 0-8172-0041-X). Raintree Pubs.

Feelings Between Kids & Grownups. Marcia Conta & Maureen Reardon. LC 75-19383. (Moods & Emotions Ser.). (Illus.). 32p. (gr. k-3). 1975. Repr. of 1974 ed. PLB 8.95 (ISBN 0-8172-0043-6). Raintree Pubs.

Feelings Between Kids & Parents. Marcia Conta & Maureen Reardon. LC 75-19398. (Identity I Ser.). (Illus.). 32p. (gr. k-3). 1975. Repr. of 1974 ed. PLB 7.95 o.p. (ISBN 0-8172-0045-2). Raintree Pubs.

Feelings from A to Z. Pat Visser. (Young Reader Ser.). (Illus.). (gr. k-3). PLB 5.00 (ISBN 0-307-60200-1, Golden Pr). Western Pub.

Feet First: The Complete Guide to Foot Care. Ruth Winter. (Orig.). 1981. pap. 6.95 (ISBN 0-87701-204-0). Chronicle Bks.

Féininger's Chicago: 1941. Andreas Feininger. (Illus.). 80p. 1980. 12.50 (ISBN 0-486-24007-X); pap. 5.00 (ISBN 0-486-23991-8). Dover.

Feldman Method. rev. ed. Andrew H. Thomson. LC 70-92025. 1977. 9.95 (ISBN 0-910580-01-4); pap. 5.95 (ISBN 0-910580-95-2). Farnswth Pub.

Feldspars. Ed. by W. S. Mackenzie. LC 73-87831. 700p. 1974. 59.50x (ISBN 0-8448-0251-4). Crane-Russak Co.

Felicia. Leonora Blythe. (Regency Romance Ser.). 1978. pap. 1.75 o.p. (ISBN 0-449-23754-0, Crest). Fawcett.

Felicia, the Critic. Ellen Conford. (gr. 4-6). 1978. pap. 1.75 (ISBN 0-671-42061-5). Archway.

Felicia the Critic. Ellen Conford. (Illus.). (gr. 4-6). 1978. pap. 1.25 (ISBN 0-671-29883-6). PB.

Felicia to Charlotte, Seventeen Forty-Four to Seventeen Forty-Nine, 2 vols. in 1. Mary Collyer. (Flowering of the Novel, 1740-1775 Ser: Vol. 13). 1974. lib. bdg. 50.00 (ISBN 0-8240-1112-0). Garland Pub.

Felicidad Del Nino. Tr. by James Dobson. (Spanish Bks.). (Span.). 1978. 1.90 (ISBN 0-8297-0893-6). Life Pubs Intl.

Felipe the Bullfighter. Robert Vavra. LC 68-10006. (Illus.). (gr. 4-6). 4.95 o.p. (ISBN 0-15-227510-X, HJ); PLB 3.99 o.p. (ISBN 0-15-227511-8). HarBraceJ.

Felisa & the Magic Tikling Bird. Jodi P. Belknap. LC 73-79571. (gr. 1-7). 1973. 5.95g (ISBN 0-89610-014-6). Island Her.

Felix Adler. Robert S. Guttchen. LC 73-15952. (World Leaders Ser.: No. 32). 1974. lib. bdg. 10.95 (ISBN 0-8057-3650-6). Twayne.

Felix Adler & Ethical Culture. Horace L. Friess. (Illus.). 320p. 1981. 20.00x (ISBN 0-231-05184-0). Columbia U Pr.

Felix Bloch & Twentieth Century Physics. H. Gutfreund et al. Ed. by M. Chodorow et al. (Rice University Studies: Vol. 66, No. 3). 247p. 1980. pap. 5.50x (ISBN 0-89263-246-1). Rice Univ.

Felix Diaz, the Porfirians, & the Mexican Revolution. Peter V. Henderson. LC 80-13934. xiv, 239p. 1981. 18.50x (ISBN 0-8032-2312-9). U of Nebr Pr.

Felix Feneon & the Language of Art Criticism. Joan U. Halperin. Ed. by Donald B. Kuspit. (Studies in Fine Arts: Criticism). 277p. 1980. 27.95 (ISBN 0-8357-1091-2, Pub. by UMI Res Pr). Univ Microfilms.

Felix Holt, the Radical. George Eliot. 1964. 17.95x (ISBN 0-460-00353-4, Evman); pap. 8.95 (ISBN 0-460-01353-X, Evman). Dutton.

Fellah & Townsman in the Middle East: Studies in Social History. Gabriel Baer. 1981. 30.00x (ISBN 0-7146-3126-4, F Cass Co). Biblio Dist.

Fellaheen. Henry H. Ayrout. Tr. by Hilary Wayment. LC 79-2849. 179p. 1981. Repr. of 1945 ed. 17.00 (ISBN 0-8305-0025-1). Hyperion Conn.

Fellcraft. J. A. Ingram. 12.50x (ISBN 0-392-07812-0, SpS). Soccer.

Fellini on Fellini. Frederico Fellini. 1976. 7.95 o.p. (ISBN 0-440-02528-1, Sey Lawr). Delacorte.

Fellini the Artist. Edward Murray. LC 75-25423. (Illus.). 1976. 12.00 (ISBN 0-8044-2648-1). Ungar.

Fellow-Crafts Ritual. Winston McCoy. 1981. 4.95 (ISBN 0-8062-1608-5). Carlton.

Fellow of Infinite Jest: Recollections & Anecdotes of William Lyon Phelps. Florence H. Barber. 1949. 19.50x (ISBN 0-685-89752-4). Elliots Bks.

Fellowship of Song: Popualr Singing Traditions in East Suffolk. Ginette Dunn. (Illus.). 254p. 1980. 30.00x (ISBN 0-7099-0044-9, Pub. by Croom Helm Ltd England). Biblio Dist.

Fellowship of the Craft: Conrad on Ships & Seamen & the Sea. Chester F. Burgess. (Literary Criticism Ser.). 1976. 12.00 (ISBN 0-8046-9116-9, Natl U). Kennikat.

Fellowship of the Talisman. Clifford D. Simak. 1979. pap. 2.25 (ISBN 0-345-27592-6, Del Rey Bks). Ballantine.

Fellowship: Three Letters from John. John G. Mitchell. LC 77-18501. (Orig.). 1974. pap. text ed. 3.95 (ISBN 0-930014-06-5). Multnomah.

Fell's Beginner's Guide to Bridge for All Ages. Lucille Place. LC 75-13971. 1975. pap. 4.95 (ISBN 0-8119-0362-1). Fell.

Fell's Beginner's Guide to Flower Arrangement. Betty Byrne. LC 75-583. 1976. pap. 4.95 (ISBN 0-8119-0363-X). Fell.

Fell's Beginner's Guide to Magic. Walter B. Gibson. LC 76-17125. 160p. 1976. 7.95 (ISBN 0-8119-0271-4); pap. 4.95 (ISBN 0-8119-0364-8). Fell.

Fell's Beginner's Guide to Motorcycling. Bill Kaysing. LC 76-17052. 1976. pap. 4.95 (ISBN 0-8119-0365-6). Fell.

Fell's Beginner's Guide to Tropical Fish & Fish Tanks. Reginald Dutta. LC 75-4357. 1975. 7.95 (ISBN 0-8119-0254-4). Fell.

Fell's Guide to Buying, Building & Financing a Home. M. Robert Beasley. LC 63-21657. 1963. 9.95 (ISBN 0-8119-0039-8). Fell.

Fell's Guide to Coins & Money Tokens of the World. Ian Angus. LC 74-75383. Orig. Title: Coins & Money Tokens. (Illus.). 128p. 1974. 8.95 (ISBN 0-8119-0237-4). Fell.

Fell's Guide to Commercial Art. Roy P. Nelson & Byron Ferris. LC 66-14801. (gr. 10 up). 8.95 (ISBN 0-8119-0041-X). Fell.

Fell's Guide to Doubling the Performance of Your Car. William Hampton. 192p. 1977. 8.95 o.s.i. (ISBN 0-8119-0267-6); pap. 4.95 o.p. (ISBN 0-88391-053-5). Fell.

Fell's Guide to Operating Shortwave Radio. Charles J. Vlahos. (gr. 9 up). 1969. 8.95 o.s.i. (ISBN 0-8119-0047-9). Fell.

Fell's Guide to Plant Training, Pruning & Tree Surgery. K. R. Hammett. LC 75-583. (Illus.). 1975. 8.95 (ISBN 0-8119-0260-9). Fell.

Fell's Guide to Small Boat Navigation. rev. ed. Charles Farrell. LC 61-17228. (Illus.). 1974. 8.95 (ISBN 0-8119-0049-5). Fell.

Fell's Guide to the Art of Cartooning. Roy P. Nelson. pap. 4.95 o.s.i. (ISBN 0-88391-022-5, Aim-High). Fell.

Fell's Guide to Winning Backgammon. Walter Gibson. LC 74-75381. 1974. pap. 4.95 (ISBN 0-8119-0365-6). Fell.

Fell's International Coin Book. 6th rev. ed. Charles Andrews. LC 53-11213. 320p. 1976. 7.95 (ISBN 0-8119-0367-2); pap. 4.95 (ISBN 0-88391-052-7). Fell.

Fell's Official Guide to Diving. Harry Froboess. pap. 4.95 (ISBN 0-8119-0368-0). Fell.

Fell's Official Guide to Diving: Plain, High, Fancy, Platform, Comedy & Acrobatic. Harry Froboess. LC 65-15502. (gr. 7 up). 1965. 8.95 (ISBN 0-8119-0052-5). Fell.

Fell's Official Guide to Knots & How to Tie Them. Walter Gibson. LC 61-9266. 1961. pap. 4.95 (ISBN 0-8119-0369-9). Fell.

Fell's Teen Age Guide to Skin & Scuba Diving. George Sullivan. LC 65-18211. 1975. 8.95 (ISBN 0-8119-0261-7); pap. 4.95 (ISBN 0-8119-0370-2). Fell.

Fell's United States Coin Book. 9th rev. ed. Charles J. Andrews. LC 73-11213. (Illus.). 156p. 1981. 9.95 (ISBN 0-8119-0349-4); pap. 5.95 (ISBN 0-8119-0421-0). Fell.

Fell's U.S Coin Book. 8th rev. ed. Charles Andrews. LC 73-11213. (Illus.). 1975. pap. 4.95 (ISBN 0-8119-0371-0). Fell.

Felony Arrests: Their Prosecution & Disposition in New York City's Courts. (Vera Studies in Criminal Justice (Professional Studies)). (Illus.). 192p. (Orig.). 1981. 17.50 (ISBN 0-582-28195-4); pap. 6.95 (ISBN 0-582-28187-3). Longman.

Felton & Fowler's Best, Worst & Most Unusual. Bruce Felton & Mark Fowler. LC 75-9895. 288p. (YA) 1975. 10.95 (ISBN 0-690-00569-5, TYC-T). T Y Crowell.

Female: A Novel of Another Time. Paul I. Wellman. 3.95 o.p. (ISBN 0-686-67650-5). Doubleday.

Female Adolescent Development. Ed. by Max Sugar. LC 78-31743. 1979. 22.50 (ISBN 0-87630-192-8). Brunner-Mazel.

Female Aegis, or the Duties of Women from Childhood to Old Age. Ed. by Gina Luria. LC 74-8248. (Feminist Controversy in England, 1788-1810 Ser.). 1974. lib. bdg. 50.00 (ISBN 0-8240-0858-8). Garland Pub.

Female American; or, the Adventures of Unca Eliza Winkfield, 1767, 2 vols. in 1. Ed. by Michael F. Shugrue. (Flowering of the Novel, 1740-1775 Ser: Vol. 79). 1974. lib. bdg. 50.00 (ISBN 0-8240-1178-3). Garland Pub.

Female Athlete: A Coach's Guide to Conditioning & Training. 2nd ed. Carl E. Klafs & M. Joan Lyon. LC 77-27418. (Illus.). 1978. pap. text ed. 11.95 (ISBN 0-8016-2681-1). Mosby.

Female Breast. (Illus.). pap. 5.00 (ISBN 0-910550-35-2). Centurion Pr.

Female Complaints: Lydia Pinkham & the Business of Women's Medicine. Sarah Stage. (Illus.). 304p. 1981. pap. 4.95 (ISBN 0-393-00033-8). Norton.

Female Consumer. Rosemary Scott. LC 75-31648. 300p. 1976. 32.95 (ISBN 0-470-76789-8). Halsted Pr.

Female Critick: Letters in Drollery from Ladies to Their Humble Servants. Bd. with Iter-Lunare: A Voyage to the Moon. David Russen. LC 71-17054. (Foundations of the Novel Ser.: Vol. 4). lib. bdg. 50.00 (ISBN 0-685-41747-6). Garland Pub.

Female Eunuch. Germaine Greer. (McGraw-Hill Paperback Ser.). 360p. 1980. pap. 5.95 (ISBN 0-07-024375-1). McGraw.

Female Experience: An American Documentary AHS-90. Ed. by Gerda Lerner. 1977. 13.95 (ISBN 0-672-51555-5); pap. text ed. 9.95 (ISBN 0-672-61248-8). Bobbs.

Female Hero in Folklore & Legend. Tristam P. Coffin. LC 75-14412. (Illus.). 192p. 1975. 10.95 o.p. (ISBN 0-8164-9263-8). Continuum.

Female Hierarchies. Ed. by Lionel Tiger. Heather T. Fowler. 1978. lib. bdg. 12.50 o.p. (ISBN 0-202-01161-5). Beresford Bk Serv.

Female-Male: Living Together. Bobby R. Patton & Bonnie R. Patton. (Interpersonal Communication Ser.). (Illus.). 1976. pap. text ed. 5.95 (ISBN 0-675-08643-4); instructor's manual 3.95 (ISBN 0-686-67248-8). Merrill.

Female Marine: Adventures of Miss Lucy Brewer. 2nd ed. Lucy Brewer. LC 65-23390. 1966. Repr. of 1817 ed. 14.95 (ISBN 0-306-70913-9). Da Capo.

Female of the Species. M. Kay Martin & Barbara Voorhies. 448p. 1974. 22.50x (ISBN 0-231-03875-5); pap. 10.00x (ISBN 0-231-03876-3). Columbia U Pr.

Female of the Species. Alexandra Roudybush. LC 77-12872. 1978. 7.95 o.p. (ISBN 0-385-13652-8). Doubleday.

Female Offender. Ed. by Annette M. Brodsky. LC 75-27014. (Sage Contemporary Social Science Issues: Vol. 19). 1975. 4.95x (ISBN 0-8039-0568-8). Sage.

Female Offender: A Total Look at Women in the Criminal Justice System. Ed. by Laura Crites. 1977. 21.50 (ISBN 0-669-00635-1). Lexington Bks.

Female Poets of America: With Portraits, Biographical Notices, & Specimens of Their Writings. Thomas Read. LC 76-9777. (Illus.). 1978. Repr. of 1857 ed. 50.00 (ISBN 0-8103-4290-1). Gale.

Female Poets of Great Britain. Ed. by Frederic Rowton. (Illus.). 600p. 1981. 18.95 (ISBN 0-8143-1664-6). Wayne St U Pr.

Female Power & Male Dominance: On the Origins of Sexual Inequality. Peggy R. Sanday. LC 80-18461. (Illus.). 256p. Date not set. text ed. price not set (ISBN 0-521-23618-5); pap. text ed. price not set (ISBN 0-521-28075-3). Cambridge U Pr.

Female Primate. Linda M. Fedigan. (Illus.). 1981. write for info. (ISBN 0-920792-03-0); pap. write for info. EPWP.

Female Quixote: or the Adventures of Arabella, 1752, 2 vols. in 1. Charlotte Lennox. Ed. by Michael F. Shugrue. (Flowering of the Novel, 1740-1775 Ser: Vol. 36). 1974. lib. bdg. 50.00 (ISBN 0-8240-1135-X). Garland Pub.

Female Reader. Ed. by Mary Wollstonecraft. LC 79-27565. 1980. 47.00x (ISBN 0-8201-1347-6). Schol Facsimiles.

Female Reproductive System: Dynamics of Scanning & Transmission Electron Microscopy. Alex Ferenczy & Ralph M. Richart. LC 73-17486. 401p. 1974. 64.95 (ISBN 0-471-25730-3, Pub. by Wiley-Medical). Wiley.

Female Roles: A Facilitator's Guide. Ed. by Clarke G. Carney & Sarah Lynne McMahon. LC 76-58237. 286p. 1977. pap. 15.50 (ISBN 0-88390-135-8). Univ Assocs.

Female Scholars: A Tradition of Learned Women Before 1800. Ed. by Jeanie R. Brink. (Illus.). 1980. 17.95 (ISBN 0-920792-02-2). EPWP.

Female Sexual Slavery. Kathleen Barry. 336p. 1981. pap. 3.95 (ISBN 0-380-54213-7, 54213, Discus). Avon.

Female Sexuality: New Psychoanalytic Views. J. Chasseguet-Smirgel et al. LC 79-107974. Orig. Title: Recherches Psychanalytiques Nouvelles Sur La Sexualite Feminine. 1970. 8.95 o.p. (ISBN 0-472-21900-6). U of Mich Pr.

Female Spectator: English Women Writers Before 1800. Ed. by Mary R. Mahl & Helene Koon. LC 76-26430. (Midland Bks.: No. 224). 320p. 1977. 15.00x (ISBN 0-253-32166-2); pap. 5.95x (ISBN 0-253-20224-8). Ind U Pr.

Female Sterilization by Vaginal Tubal Ligation. Herbert P. Brown & Stephan N. Schanzer. 200p. 1981. text ed. 15.00 (ISBN 0-88416-356-3). PSG Pub.

Female Studies, Two. Ed. by Florence Howe. 165p. 1970. pap. 5.00x o.p. (ISBN 0-912786-02-7). Know Inc.

Female World. Jessie Bernard. LC 80-69880. (Illus.). 1981. 17.95 (ISBN 0-02-903000-5). Free Pr.

Feminine Forever. Robert A. Wilson. LC 66-11166. (Illus.). 224p. 1966. 8.95 (ISBN 0-87131-049-X). M Evans.

Feminine Gymnastics. 3rd rev. ed. Phyllis Cooper. 1980. pap. 11.95 spiral bdg. (ISBN 0-8087-2962-4). Burgess.

Feminine Image in Literature. Barbara Warren. (Humanities Ser). 280p. (gr. 9-12). 1974. pap. text ed. 7.10x (ISBN 0-8104-5068-2). Hayden.

Feminine Mystique. Betty Friedan. 1977. pap. 2.50 (ISBN 0-440-12498-0). Dell.

Feminine Personality & Conflict. Judith M. Bardwick et al. LC 80-24191. (Contemporary Psychology Ser.). vii, 102p. 1981. Repr. of 1970 ed. lib. bdg. 19.75 (ISBN 0-313-22504-4, BAFP). Greenwood.

Feminine Plural: Stories by Women About Growing up. Ed. by Stephanie Spinner. LC 76-187798. (gr. 7 up). 1972. 8.95 (ISBN 0-02-786040-X). Macmillan.

Feminine Principle. Judith Miles. LC 75-5828. 160p. 1975. kivar 3.50 (ISBN 0-87123-159-X, 210159). Bethany Fell.

Feminine Principle. Judith Miles. LC 75-5828. 160p. 1976. pap. 2.50 (ISBN 0-87123-160-3, 200160). Bethany Fell.

Feminine: Readings in Sexual Mythology & the Liberation of Women. Ed. by Betty Roszak & Theodore Roszak. (Orig.). 1970. pap. 4.95x (ISBN 0-06-131952-X, TB 1952, Torch). Har-Row.

Feminism & Materialism. Ed. by Annette Kuhn & Annmarie Wolpe. 1978. 22.50x (ISBN 0-7100-0072-3); pap. 9.00 (ISBN 0-7100-0074-X). Routledge & Kegan.

Feminism & Process Thought: The Harvard Divinity School-Claremont Center for Process Studies Symposium Papers. Sheila G. Davaney. (Symposium Ser.: Vol. 5). 1980. soft cover 9.95x (ISBN 0-88946-903-2). E Mellen.

Feminism & Socialism in China. Elisabeth J. Croll. 1978. 27.50 (ISBN 0-7100-8816-7). Routledge & Kegan.

Feminism & Suffrage: The Emergence of an Independent Women's Movement in America, 1848-1869. Ellen C. DuBois. LC 77-90902. 1978. 17.50x o.p. (ISBN 0-8014-1043-6). Cornell U Pr.

Feminism & Suffrage: The Emergence of an Independent Women's Movement in America Eighteen Forty-Eight to Eighteen Sixty-Nine. Ellen C. DuBois. 1978. 17.50 (ISBN 0-8014-1043-6); pap. 4.95 1980 ed. (ISBN 0-8014-9182-7). Cornell U Pr.

Feminism in American Politics: A Study of Ideological Influence. Claire K. Fulenwider. LC 79-25131. 182p. 1980. 20.95 (ISBN 0-03-053461-5). Praeger.

Feminist Collage: Educating Women in the Visual Arts. Ed. by Judy Loeb. LC 79-15468. 1979. 14.95x (ISBN 0-8077-2561-7). Tchrs Coll.

Feminist Criticism: Essays on Theory, Poetry & Prose. Ed. by Cheryl L. Brown & Karen Olson. LC 78-8473. 1978. 18.00 (ISBN 0-8108-1143-X). Scarecrow.

Feminist Drama: Definition & Critical Analysis. Janet Brown. LC 79-22382. 167p. 1979. 10.00 (ISBN 0-8108-1267-3). Scarecrow.

Feminist Erotica. Ed. by Celeste West. (Illus., Orig.). 1981. 20.00 (ISBN 0-685-96697-6). Booklegger Pr.

Feminist Issues in Behavior Therapy. Ed. by Elaine A. Blechman. (Women: Counseling, Therapy & Mental Health Services Ser.: Vol. 1, No. 1). 112p. 1980. text ed. cancelled (ISBN 0-917724-24-0). Haworth Pr.

Feminist Literary Criticism: Explorations in Theory. Ed. by Josephine Donovan. LC 75-12081. 96p. 1975. pap. 4.50x (ISBN 0-8131-1334-2). U Pr of Ky.

Feminist Movement in Germany 1894-1933. Richard T. Evans. LC 75-31571. (Sage Studies in Twentieth Century History: Vol. 6). (Illus.). 1976. 17.50x (ISBN 0-8039-9951-8); pap. 8.95x (ISBN 0-8039-9996-8). Sage.

Feminist Papers: From Adams to De Beauvoir. Ed. by Alice S. Rossi. 600p. 1973. 22.50x (ISBN 0-231-03795-3). Columbia U Pr.

Feminist Tarot: A Guide to Intrapersonal Communication. 4th ed. Sally Gearhart & Susan Rennie. (Illus.). 1981. pap. write for info. (ISBN 0-930436-01-6). Persephone.

Feminist Theatre Groups. Dinah L. Leavitt. LC 80-10602. 159p. 1980. lib. bdg. 10.95x (ISBN 0-89950-005-6). McFarland & Co.

Feminists: Women's Emancipation Movements in Europe, America & Australasia 1840-1920. Richard J. Evans. LC 77-77490. 1977. text ed. 20.00x (ISBN 0-06-492037-2); pap. text ed. 8.50x (ISBN 0-06-492044-5). B&N.

Feminization of American Culture. Ann Douglas. 1978. pap. 3.95 (ISBN 0-380-01968-X, 51870, Discus). Avon.

Femme Dirigee Par l'Esprit. Beverly LaHaye. Ed. by Annie Cosson. Tr. by Michele Schneider from Eng. 175p. (Fr. & English.). 1979. pap. 1.85 (ISBN 0-8297-0972-X). Vida Pubs.

Femmes Fatales. Claude Mauriac. Tr. by Henry Wolff. 1980. pap. 4.95 (ISBN 0-7145-0232-4). Riverrun NY.

Femoral Neck Fractures & Hip Joint Injuries. D. S. Muckle. LC 77-82681. 1977. 29.50 o.p. (ISBN 0-471-03799-0, Pub. by Wiley Medical). Wiley.

Fen Tiger. Catherine Marchant. 1981. pap. 2.75 (ISBN 0-440-12502-2). Dell.

Fenaroli's Handbook of Flavor Ingredients, 2 vols. 2nd ed. Ed. & tr. by Thomas E. Furia. LC 72-152143. (Handbk. Ser). 1975. Vol. 1, 560p. 59.95 (ISBN 0-87819-534-3); Vol. 2, 944p. 69.95 (ISBN 0-87819-532-7). CRC Pr.

Fence. Bruce McGinnis. LC 79-64395. 1979. 10.00 (ISBN 0-8149-0821-7). Vanguard.

Fence: A New Look at the World of Property Theft. Marilyn E. Walsh. LC 76-5266. (Contributions in Sociology Ser.: No. 21). (Illus., Orig.). 1976. lib. bdg. 15.00 (ISBN 0-8371-8910-1, WTF/). Greenwood.

Fences & Gates. 3rd ed. Sunset Editors. LC 70-140162. (Illus.). 96p. 1971. pap. 2.95 (ISBN 0-376-01104-1, Sunset Bks). Sunset-Lane.

Fences, Hedges & Walls. Jack Kramer. LC 74-11055. (Illus.). 128p. 1975. 8.95 o.p. (ISBN 0-684-13891-3, ScribT). Scribner.

Fencing. I. Vass. (Illus.). 1977. 13.00 (ISBN 0-912728-95-7). Newbury Bks Inc.

Fenelon. James H. Davis, Jr. (World Authors Series: No. 542). 1979. lib. bdg. 14.95 (ISBN 0-8057-6384-8). Twayne.

Fenelon on Education. H. C. Barnard. (Cambridge Texts & Studies in the History of Education: No. 1). 1966. 24.50 (ISBN 0-521-04107-4). Cambridge U Pr.

Fenetres Sur la France. new ed. Yvone Lenard. (Verbal-Active French Ser.). (Illus.). (gr. 11-12). 1976. text ed. 15.68 (ISBN 0-06-582101-7, SchDept); tchr's ed. 22.36 (ISBN 0-06-582205-6); wkbk. 4.00 (ISBN 0-06-582303-6); tests 3.56 (ISBN 0-06-582603-5); tchrs. test ed. 4.00 (ISBN 0-06-582701-5); tapes 216.04 (ISBN 0-06-582802-X). Har-Row.

Feng Chin. Dominic Cheung. (World Authors Ser.: No. 515). 1979. lib. bdg. 13.95 (ISBN 0-8057-6356-2). Twayne.

Fenimore Cooper: The Critical Heritage. Ed. by George Dekker & John P. McWilliams. (Critical Heritage Ser). 318p. 1973. 27.00x (ISBN 0-7100-7635-5). Routledge & Kegan.

Fenland. A. K. Parker & D. Pye. LC 76-29114. (British Topographical Ser.). (Illus.). 1977. 14.95 (ISBN 0-7153-7296-3). David & Charles.

Fenland Chronicle. Ed. by Sybil Marshall. LC 66-21652. 1981. pap. 10.95 (ISBN 0-521-28043-5). Cambridge U Pr.

Fenland: Its Ancient Past & Uncertain Future. H. Godwin. LC 77-8824. (Illus.). 1978. 32.50 (ISBN 0-521-21768-7). Cambridge U Pr.

Feodalite En France Du X. Au XII. Siecle. Edouard Perroy. LC 80-2012. 1981. Repr. of 1956 ed. 24.50 (ISBN 0-404-18584-3). AMS Pr.

Feodor Dostoevsky. Ernest J. Simmons. LC 77-76254. (Columbia Ser.: No. 40). (Orig., Pap). 1969. pap. 2.00 (ISBN 0-231-03205-6, MW40). Columbia U Pr.

Fer-De-Lance. Rex Stout. 1979. pap. 1.75 o.s.i. (ISBN 0-515-05115-2). Jove Pubns.

Feral Livestock in Anglo-America. Tom McKnight. (Publications in Geography Ser.: Vol. 16). 1964. pap. 6.50x (ISBN 0-520-09146-9). U of Cal Pr.

Ferber: A Biography of Edna Ferber. Julie Goldsmith Gilbert. LC 76-57512. 1978. 10.50 o.p. (ISBN 0-385-03960-3). Doubleday.

Ferdinand & Isabella. Melveena McKendrick & J. H. Elliott. LC 68-14974. (Horizon Caravel Bks). (Illus.). 153p. (gr. 6 up). 1968. 9.95 (ISBN 0-8281-0395-X, J03501-03); PLB 12.89 (ISBN 0-06-024165-9, Dist. by Har-Row). Am Heritage.

Ferdinand De Saussure. Jonathan Culler. (Modern Masters Ser.). 1977. pap. 3.95 (ISBN 0-14-004369-1). Penguin.

Ferenc Deak. Bela Kiraly. Ed. by Arthur W. Brown et al. (World Leaders Ser.: No. 39). 1975. lib. bdg. 10.95 (ISBN 0-8057-3030-3). Twayne.

Ferenc Molnar. Clara Gyorgyey. (World Author Ser.--Hungary: No. 574). 1980. lib. bdg. 13.95 (ISBN 0-8057-6416-X). Twayne.

Ferguson's Trail. Charles A. Seltzer. 1979. pap. 1.25 (ISBN 0-505-51357-9). Tower Bks.

Ferme Du Pere Mathieu. Lucette Lafitte. 1958. text ed. 2.95x (ISBN 0-521-05508-3). Cambridge U Pr.

Ferment in Eastern Europe. Ed. by Irwin Isenberg. (Reference Shelf Ser: Vol. 37, No. 1). 1965. 6.25 (ISBN 0-8242-0084-5). Wilson.

Ferment in Labor. Jerome Wolf. Ed. by Fred Krinsky & Joseph Boskin. (Insight Series: Studies in Contemporary Issues). (Illus.). 128p. 1968. pap. text ed. 4.95x (ISBN 0-02-479150-4, 47915). Macmillan.

Ferment of Knowledge: Studies in the Historiography of Eighteenth-Century Science. Ed. by G. S. Rousseau & R. Porter. LC 80-40001. 550p. 1980. 39.50 (ISBN 0-521-22599-X). Cambridge U Pr.

Fermentation Products & Processes, C-018: Developments. Ed. by BCC Staff. 1978. 750.00 o.p. (ISBN 0-89336-145-3). BCC.

Fermentation Products: Processes & New Developments, C-018. Ed. by Business Communications. 1980. 800.00 (ISBN 0-89336-222-0). BCC.

Fermentation: 1977: Annual Reports. Perlman. 1977. 29.50 (ISBN 0-12-040301-3). Acad Pr.

Fermi Surface: Its Concept, Determination & Use in the Physics of Metals. A. P. Cracknell & K. C. Wong. (Monographs on the Physics & Chemistry of Materials). (Illus.). 558p. 1973. 65.00x (ISBN 0-19-851330-5). Oxford U Pr.

Fernan Caballero. Lawrence H. Klibbe. (World Authors Ser.: Spain: No. 259). 1971. lib. bdg. 10.95 (ISBN 0-8057-2187-8). Twayne.

Fernan Gonzalez, First Count of Castile: The Man & the Legend. Manuel Marquez-Sterling. LC 80-15095. (Romance Monographs: No. 40). (Illus.). 160p. 1980. write for info. Romance.

Fernand Cortez Ou la Conquete Du Mexique, 2 vols. Gasparo Spontini. Ed. by Phillip Gossett & Charles Rosen. LC 76-49226. (Early Romantic Opera Ser.: No. 43). 1980. lib. bdg. 82.00 (ISBN 0-8240-2942-9). Garland Pub.

Fernand Crommelynck. Bettina L. Knapp. (World Authors Ser.: No. 444). 1978. lib. bdg. 12.50 (ISBN 0-8057-6286-8). Twayne.

Fernando Arrabal. Peter L. Podol. (World Authors Ser.: No. 499 (Spain)). 1978. 13.50 (ISBN 0-8057-6340-6). Twayne.

Fernando Botero. Carter Ratcliff. LC 80-66283. (Illus.). 272p. 1980. 75.00 (ISBN 0-89659-146-8). Abbeville Pr.

Fernhill Series, 8 bks. Incl. Daring Rabbit (ISBN 0-310-40362-6, 11473); Foolish Rabbit (ISBN 0-310-40342-1, 11471); Otter Helps Out (ISBN 0-310-40372-3, 11474); Rabbit in Danger (ISBN 0-310-40352-9, 11472); Rabbit Runs Away (ISBN 0-310-40382-0, 11475); Rabbits in Trouble (ISBN 0-310-40402-9, 11477); Rabbits to the Rescue (ISBN 0-310-40332-4, 11470); Three Rabbits with a Secret (ISBN 0-310-40392-8, 11476). (Illus.). (gr. k-2). 1980. pap. 0.95 ea. Zondervan.

Ferns. P. Perl. (Encyclopedia of Gardening Ser.). (gr. 6 up). 1977. PLB 11.97 (ISBN 0-8094-2559-9). Silver.

Ferns. Philip Perl. (Encyclopedia of Gardening). 1977. 11.95 (ISBN 0-8094-2558-0). Time-Life.

Ferns & Palms. (Countryside Houseplant Bks). 1977. pap. 0.98 o.p. (ISBN 0-307-11905-X, Golden Pr). Western Pub.

Ferns & Palms for Interior Decoration: Garden Library. Jack Kramer. LC 73-326. (Illus.). 128p. 1972. pap. 4.95 o.p. (ISBN 0-684-12931-0, SL365, ScribT); encore edition 2.95 o.p. (ISBN 0-684-15255-X, ScribT). Scribner.

Ferns, Fern Allies & Conifers of Australia. H. T. Clifford & J. Constantine. (Illus.). 150p. 1980. text ed. 24.25x (ISBN 0-7022-1447-7). U of Queensland Pr.

Ferns for Modern Living. Elaine Davenport. Ed. by Helen V. Wilson. (Modern Living Ser.). (Illus.). 80p. (Orig.). 1977. pap. 2.95 (ISBN 0-89484-004-5, 10105). Merchants Pub Co.

Ferns of Hongkong. Harry H. Edie. (Illus.). 285p. (Orig.). 1977. pap. 14.00x o.p. (ISBN 962-209-002-8, Pub. by Hong Kong U Pr). Paragon.

Fernwaerme Schweiz. 1978. pap. 7.50 o.p. (ISBN 0-89192-197-4). Interbk Inc.

Fernwood. Marcella Thum. 1978. pap. 1.75 o.p. (ISBN 0-449-23443-6, Crest). Fawcett.

Ferrari. Ed. by Stan Grayson. (Automobile Quarterly Lib.). (Illus.). 300p. 1975. 27.50 o.p. (ISBN 0-525-10445-3). Dutton.

Ferrari Berlinetta Boxer. Mel Nichols. (Autohistory Ser.). (Illus.). 1979. 12.95 (ISBN 0-85045-326-7, Pub. by Osprey Pubns. England). Motorbooks Intl.

Ferrari Cars Nineteen Sixty-Nine to Nineteen Seventy-Three. Ed. by R. M. Clarke. (Brooklands Bks.). (Illus., Orig.). 1980. pap. 11.95. Motorbooks Intl.

Ferrari Cars: 1962-1966. R. M. Clarke. (Brooklands Bks.). (Illus.). 100p. 1979. pap. 11.95 (ISBN 0-906589-57-6, Pub. by Enthusias England). Motorbooks Intl.

Ferrari Dino 206GT, 246GT & GTS. Jan Webb. (AutoHistory Ser.). (Illus.). 128p. 1980. 12.95 (ISBN 0-85045-365-8, Pub. by Osprey England). Motorbooks Intl.

Ferrari: The Early Berlinettas & Competition Coupes. (Illus.). 80p. (Orig.). 1974. pap. 10.95 (ISBN 0-914792-00-8, Pub. by DB Pubns). Motorbooks Intl.

Ferrari: The Early Spyders & Competition Roadsters. (Illus.). 128p. (Orig.). 1975. pap. 10.95 (ISBN 0-914792-01-6, Pub. by DB Pubns). Motorbooks Intl.

Ferrari: The Gran Turismo & Competition Berlinettas. (Illus.). 94p. (Orig.). 1977. pap. 10.95 (ISBN 0-914792-02-4, Pub. by DB Pubns). Motorbooks Intl.

Ferraris for the Road. Henry Rasmussen. (Illus.). 1980. 39.95 (ISBN 0-87938-117-5). Motorbooks Intl.

Ferrets & Ferreting. Iain Brodie. (Illus.). 1979. 9.95 (ISBN 0-7137-0903-0, Pub. by Blandford Pr England). Sterling.

Ferri Metallographia: Recent Examination Methods in Metallography & the Metallography of Welds, Vol. 4. Lambert. 1980. write for info. (ISBN 0-85501-165-3). Heyden.

Ferrocement Materials & Applications. 1979. 23.25 (SP-61); 17.75. ACI.

Ferroelectrics to Fluorine Compounds, Organic, Vol. 10. 962p. 1980. 145.00 (ISBN 0-471-02063-X). Wiley.

Ferromagnetic Resonance. Ed. by S. V. Vonsovskii. 1966. 34.00 (ISBN 0-08-011027-4); pap. 21.00 (ISBN 0-08-013670-2). Pergamon.

Ferromagnetodynamics: The Dynamics of Magnetic Bubbles Domains & Domain Walls. T. H. Odel. 232p. 1981. 54.95 (ISBN 0-470-27084-5). Halsted Pr.

Ferry Story. Terry Lawhead. LC 78-16743. (Illus.). (gr. k-6). 1978. pap. 4.95 o.p. (ISBN 0-914718-33-9). Pacific Search.

Fertile Fields: Recollections & Reflections of a Busy Life. Abraham Dobin. LC 74-290. (Illus.). 480p. 1975. 8.95 o.p. (ISBN 0-498-01545-9). A S Barnes.

Fertile Image. Paul Nash. 1975. 6.95 (ISBN 0-571-10636-6, Pub. by Faber & Faber). Merrimack Bk Serv.

Fertile Stars. Brian O'Leary. (Illus.). 1981. 12.95. Everest Hse.

Fertility & Deprivation. Janet Askham. LC 75-2718. (Papers in Sociology Ser.: No. 5). (Illus.). 192p. 1975. 24.95 (ISBN 0-521-20795-9). Cambridge U Pr.

Fertility & Family Life in an Indian Village. Thomas Poffenberger. LC 75-9025. (Michigan Papers on South & Southeast Asia: No. 10). (Illus.). 114p. 1975. pap. 4.50x (ISBN 0-89148-010-2). Ctr S&SE Asian.

Fertility & Mortality Changes in Thailand, 1950-1975. 1980. 3.50 (ISBN 0-309-02943-0). Natl Acad Pr.

Fertility Control: Biologic & Behavioral Aspects. Ed. by Rochelle Shain & Carl J. Pauerstein. (Illus.). 500p. 1980. 35.00 (ISBN 0-06-142376-9, Harper Medical). Har-Row.

Fertility Control in India. M. E. Khan & C. V. Prasad. 1980. 14.00x (ISBN 0-8364-0628-1, Pub. by Manohar India). South Asia Bks.

Fertility Fallacy: Sexuality in the Post-Pill Age. Lynn S. Baker. LC 80-50715. 224p. 1981. 11.95 (ISBN 0-7216-1492-2). Saunders.

Fertility Fallacy: Sexuality in the Post Pill Age. Lynn S. Baker. LC 80-50715. 224p. 1981. 11.95 (ISBN 0-03-057656-3). HR&W.

Fertility Handbook. Judith A. Fenton & Aaron S. Lifchez. (Orig.). 1980. 12.95 (ISBN 0-517-53991-8); pap. 5.95 (ISBN 0-517-54125-4). Potter.

Fertility of Working Women: A Synthesis of International Research. Ed. by Stanley Kupinsky. LC 76-12861. (Praeger Special Studies). 1977. text ed. 37.50 (ISBN 0-275-23100-3). Praeger.

Fertilization: Comparative Morphology, Biochemistry & Immunology, 2 vols. Ed. by Charles B. Metz & Alberto Monroy. Incl. Vol. 1. 1967. 55.50 (ISBN 0-12-492650-9); Vol. 2. 1969. 63.50 (ISBN 0-12-492651-7). Set. 96.50 (ISBN 0-685-23219-0). Acad Pr.

Fertilizer Distribution & Credit Schemes for Small-Sclae Farmers. (FAO Fertilizer Bulletin Ser.: No. 1). 47p. 1980. pap. 7.50 (ISBN 92-5-100837-X, F 1900, FAO). Unipub.

Fertilizer Distribution in Selected Asian Countries. 1979. pap. 13.25 (ISBN 92-833-1453-0, APO75, APO). Unipub.

Fertilizer Management Practices for Maize: Results of Experiments with Isotopes. (Technical Reports Ser.: No. 121). (Orig.). 1971. pap. 5.50 (ISBN 92-0-115770-3, IAEA). Unipub.

Fertilizers & Soil Amendments. R. Rollett et al. 1981. 24.00 (ISBN 0-13-314336-8). P-H.

Fertilizers & Soil Fertility. Ulysses S. Jones. (Illus.). 1979. text ed. 16.95 (ISBN 0-8359-1960-9); instrs'. manual avail. (ISBN 0-8359-1961-7). Reston.

Festiniog Adventure: The Festiniog Railway's Deviation Project. Brian Hollingsworth. LC 80-68683. (Illus.). 160p. 1981. 16.95 (ISBN 0-7153-7956-9). David & Charles.

Festival. Charles Morris. LC 66-12904. 1966. 4.00 o.s.i. (ISBN 0-8076-0346-5). Braziller.

Festival. Schutz, Prior of Taize. LC 73-17913. (Orig.). 1974. pap. 2.95 (ISBN 0-8164-2583-3). Crossroad NY.

Festivals & Celebrations. Roland Auguet. (International Library). 128p. (gr. 7 up). 1975. PLB 6.90 o.p. (ISBN 0-531-02117-3). Watts.

Festivals & Dances of Panama. Lila R. Cheville & Richard A. Cheville. (Illus.). 187p. (Orig.). 1981. pap. 8.50 (ISBN 0-913714-53-4). Legacy Bks.

Festivals in Asia. Compiled by Asian Cultural Centre for Unesco. LC 75-30415. (Illus.). 68p. (gr. 9-12). 1975. 7.95 (ISBN 0-87011-265-1). Kodansha.

Festivals Sourcebook: A Reference Guide to Fairs, Festivals, & Celebrations. 1st ed. Ed. by Paul Wasserman & Esther Herman. LC 76-48852. 1977. 68.00 (ISBN 0-8103-0311-6). Gale.

Festive Cakes of Christmas. Norma J. Voth. 80p. 1981. pap. 2.95 (ISBN 0-8361-1956-8). Herald Pr.

Festschrift for Jacob Ornstein: Studies in General Linguistics & Sociolinguistics. Edward L. Blansitt, Jr. & Richard V. Teschner. (Orig.). 1980. pap. text ed. 16.95 (ISBN 0-88377-172-1). Newbury Hse.

Festschrift for Maurice Goldhaber. new ed. Ed. by Gerald Reinberg et al. LC 80-20599. (Transaction Ser.: Vol. 40). 293p. 1980. 25.00 (ISBN 0-89766-086-2). NY Acad Sci.

Fetal & Maternal Medicine. Ed. by E. J. Quilligan & Norman Kretchmer. LC 79-4345. 1979. 44.50 (ISBN 0-471-50737-7, Pub. by Wiley Medical). Wiley.

Fetal Heart Monitoring. J. T. Curran. 1975. 21.95 (ISBN 0-407-00014-3). Butterworths.

Fetal Monitoring. Roger Freeman & Thomas Garite. (Illus.). 187p. 1980. lib. bdg. 27.00 (ISBN 0-683-03378-6). Williams & Wilkins.

Fetal Monitoring & Fetal Assesment in High Risk Pregnancy. Susan M. Tucker & Sandra Bryant. 1978. pap. text ed. 11.95 (ISBN 0-8016-5121-2). Mosby.

Fetal Physiology & Medicine. R. W. Beard & P. W. Nathanielsz. LC 76-20126. (Illus.). 1976. text ed. 32.00 (ISBN 0-7216-1600-3). Saunders.

Fetal Pig. Hazel E. Field. (Illus.). 1939. pap. 0.75x o.p. (ISBN 0-8047-0359-0). Stanford U Pr.

Fetch Felix. Derrick Patrick. (Illus.). 192p. 1981. 22.50 (ISBN 0-241-10371-1, Pub. by Hamish Hamilton England). David & Charles.

Fetishes. (Illus.). pap. 5.00 (ISBN 0-910550-36-0). Centurion Pr.

Feud at Mendoza. Marshall Grover. 1977. pap. 1.25 (ISBN 0-505-51187-8). Tower Bks.

Feud at Spanish Ford. Frank Bonham. 1978. pap. 1.50 o.p. (ISBN 0-425-03771-1). Berkley Pub.

Feud at Spanish Ford. Frank Bonham. 1981. pap. 1.95 (ISBN 0-425-04837-3). Berkley Pub.

Feudal Germany. James W. Thompson. LC 80-2001. 1981. Repr. of 1928 ed. 67.50 (ISBN 0-404-18601-7). AMS Pr.

Feudal Kingdom of England: 1042-1216. Frank Barlow. (Illus.). 1972. pap. text ed. 10.95 (ISBN 0-582-48237-2). Longman.

Feudal Military Service in England: A Study of the Constitutional & Military Powers of the Barones in Medieval England. Ivor J. Sanders. LC 80-23778. (Oxford Historical Ser., British Ser.). xv, 173p. 1980. Repr. of 1956 ed. lib. bdg. 19.25x (ISBN 0-313-22725-X, SAFM). Greenwood.

Feudal Monarchy in France & England from the Tenth to the Thirteenth Century. Charles E. Petit-Dutaillis. LC 80-2011. 1981. Repr. of 1936 ed. 44.50 (ISBN 0-404-18585-1). AMS Pr.

Feuerbach. Marx W. Wartofsky. LC 76-9180. 1977. 47.50 (ISBN 0-521-21257-X). Cambridge U Pr.

Feuilles D'Automne. Victor Hugo. Ed. by L. Bisson. (French Texts Ser.). 1964. pap. text ed. 4.50x o.p. (ISBN 0-631-00420-3, Pub. by Basil Blackwell). Biblio Dist.

Fever. Ed. by James M. Lipton. 1980. text ed. 34.50 (ISBN 0-89004-451-1). Raven.

Fever Moon. Susannah Howe. (Orig.). 1978. pap. 1.95 (ISBN 0-515-04550-0). Jove Pubns.

Few Chapters in Workshop Reconstruction & Citizenship, Repr. Of 1894. C. R. Ashbee. Ed. by Peter Stansky & Rodney Shewan. Bd. with Endeavor Towards the Teaching of John Ruskin & William Morris (1901. LC 76-18324. (Aesthetic Movement & the Arts & Crafts Movement Ser.: Vol. 27). 1978. lib. bdg. 44.00 (ISBN 0-8240-2476-1). Garland Pub.

Few Days in Weasel Creek. Joanna Brent. LC 80-84368. 224p. 1981. pap. 2.50 (ISBN 0-87216-818-2). Playboy Pbks.

Few Fair Days. Jane Gardam. LC 71-187794. (Illus.). (gr. 5 up). 1972. 4.95g o.s.i. (ISBN 0-02-735790-2). Macmillan.

Few Pieces of Australia, 1979. Louis A. Denger. 1981. 8.95 (ISBN 0-533-04458-8). Vantage.

Few Reasons for Doubting the Inspiration of the Bible. Robert G. Ingersoll. 1976. pap. 3.00. Am Atheist.

Fewer Pupils - Surplus Space. LC 74-79145. 56p. 1974. pap. 4.00 (ISBN 0-89192-052-8). Interbk Inc.

Feynman Lectures on Physics, 3 Vols. R. P. Feynman et al. Vol. 1. text ed. 18.95 (ISBN 0-201-02010-6); Vol. 2. text ed. 18.95 (ISBN 0-201-02011-4); Vol. 3. text ed. 18.95 (ISBN 0-201-02014-9); Set. pap. 29.95 (ISBN 0-201-02115-3); exercises for vols 2 & 3 2.95 (ISBN 0-685-03072-5). Vol. 2 Excercises (ISBN 0-201-02017-3). Vol. 3 Excercises (ISBN 0-201-02019-X). exercises for vol. 1 2.50 (ISBN 0-686-66303-9). A-W.

Fez in the Age of the Marinides. Roger Le Tourneau. Tr. by Besse A. Clement. LC 61-6496. (Centers of Civilization Ser: No. 4). 1961. 5.95 (ISBN 0-8061-0482-1); pap. 3.95 (ISBN 0-8061-1198-4). U of Okla Pr.

Fflokes' Cartoon Companion to Classic Mythology. Michael Fflokes. LC 78-15270. (Illus.). 1978. 10.50 (ISBN 0-7153-7585-7). David & Charles.

Ffolks. Jack Davies. 320p. (Orig.). 1980. pap. 2.50 (ISBN 0-515-05430-5). Jove Pubns.

Fi Khota Ali: Christian & Islamic Teaching. Salhab. (Arabic.). 12.00x (ISBN 0-686-63563-9). Intl Bk Ctr.

FIA Yearbook of Automobile Sport. Ed. by P. Stephens. (Illus.). 800p. 1981. pap. 43.95 (ISBN 0-85059-497-9). Aztex.

Fianza Satisfecha: Attributed to Lope De Vega. Ed. by W. M. Whitby & R. R. Anderson. 1971. 42.00 (ISBN 0-521-07912-8). Cambridge U Pr.

Fiat Nineteen Sixty-Nine to Eighty-One. LC 80-70348. (Illus.). 262p. 1980. pap. 8.95. Chilton.

Fiat Service--Repair Handbook: 124 Series, 1967-1980. Mike Bishop. Ed. by Jeff Robinson. (Illus.). 1978. pap. 10.95 (ISBN 0-89287-156-3, A156). Clymer Pubns.

Fiat Service-Repair Handbook: 131 Series, 1975-1977. Jim Combs. Ed. by Eric Jorgensen. (Illus.). 1978. pap. 10.95 (ISBN 0-89287-197-0, A158). Clymer Pubns.

Fiat: 128 & X1-9, 1971-1979--Service, Repair Handbook. 3rd ed. Mike Bishop. Ed. by Eric Jorgensen. (Illus.). 1978. pap. 10.95 (ISBN 0-89287-282-9, A157). Clymer Pubns.

Fiber: A Bibliography (Knotting, Stitchery & Surface Design) 1979. 5.70 (ISBN 0-88321-039-8). Am Craft.

Fiber Diffraction Methods. Ed. by Alfred D. French & Kenncorwin H. Gardner. LC 80-21566. (ACS Symposium Ser.: No. 141). 1980. 34.50 (ISBN 0-8412-0589-2). Am Chemical.

Fiber Optics & Lightwave Communications Standard Dictionary. Martin H. Weik. 320p. 1980. text ed. 18.50 (ISBN 0-442-25658-2). Van Nos Reinhold.

Fiber Reinforced Concrete. 1974. pap. 23.25 (ISBN 0-685-85120-6, SP-44) (ISBN 0-685-85121-4). ACI.

Fiberarts Design Book. Ed. by Fiberarts Magazine. (Illus.). 176p. 1980. 24.95 (ISBN 0-8038-2394-0, Visual Communications); pap. 15.95 (ISBN 0-8038-2395-9). Hastings.

Fiberglass Boat Design & Construction. Robert J. Scott. LC 72-83719. 1973. 12.50 (ISBN 0-8286-0059-7). De Graff.

Fiberglass Boats. Boughton Cobb, Jr. (Illus.). 1978. 9.95 (ISBN 0-87165-015-0, Yachting-Zd). Ziff-Davis Pub.

Fiberglass Repairs. Paul J. Petrick. LC 76-17811. (Illus.). 1976. 6.00 (ISBN 0-87033-222-8). Cornell Maritime.

Fiberglass Rod Making. Dale P. Clemens. 1974. 14.95 (ISBN 0-87691-136-X). Winchester Pr.

Fiberoscopy of Gastric Diseases. Kenji Tsuneoka & Tadayushi Takemoto. (Illus.). 250p. 1973. 95.50 (ISBN 0-89640-043-3). Igaku-Shoin.

Fibonacci Method of Trading in Stocks & Commodities, 2 vols. in 1. Ed. by Alphonse De Rockville. (Illus.). 1979. deluxe ed. 64.75 (ISBN 0-918968-39-9). Inst Econ Finan.

Fibonacci Rhythm Theory As It Applies to Life, History, & the Future of the Stock Market. Leonardo Fibonacci & Carlo M. Flumiani. (Illus.). 1976. 77.50 (ISBN 0-89266-041-4). Am Classical Coll Pr.

Fibonacci's Secret Discoveries into the Occult Power of Numbers. Ed. by Ludwig Steiner. (Illus.). 1979. 57.50 (ISBN 0-89266-150-X). Am Classical Coll Pr.

Fibre Optics. D. A. Hill. 176p. 1977. text ed. 29.50x (ISBN 0-220-66333-5, Pub. by Busn Bks England). Renouf.

Fibres & Fabrics. John Bird & Ed Catherall. LC 77-82983. (Teaching Primary Science Ser.). (Illus.). 1977. pap. text ed. 6.95 (ISBN 0-356-05076-9). Raintree Child.

Fibrinolysis. Daniel L. Kline & K. N. Reddy. 256p. 1980. 64.95 (ISBN 0-8493-5425-0). CRC Pr.

Fibrous Composites in Structural Design. Ed. by Edward M. Lenoe et al. 900p. 1980. 85.00 (ISBN 0-306-40354-4). Plenum Pub.

Ficciones. Jorge L. Borges. Ed. & intro. by Anthony Kerrigan. 1962. pap. 3.45 (ISBN 0-394-17244-2, E368, Ever). Grove.

Fichte, Marx, & the German Philosophical Tradition. Tom Rockmore. LC 80-13194. 232p. 1980. 16.50x (ISBN 0-8093-0955-6). S Ill U Pr.

Fichte's Critique of All Revelation. J. G. Fichte. Tr. by G. D. Green. LC 77-77756. 1978. 26.95 (ISBN 0-521-21707-5). Cambridge U Pr.

Fiction & Drama in Eastern & Southeastern Europe: Evolution & Experiment in the Postwar Period. Henrik Birnbaum & Thomas Eekman. (UCLA Slavic Studies: Vol. 1). ix, 463p. 1980. 24.95 (ISBN 0-89357-064-8). Slavica.

Fiction & the Camera Eye: Visual Consciousness in Film & the Modern Novel. Alan Spiegel. LC 75-22353. 1976. 12.95x (ISBN 0-8139-0598-2). U Pr of Va.

Fiction & the Fiction Industry. J. A. Sutherland. 1978. text ed. 20.75x (ISBN 0-485-11177-2, Athlone Pr). Humanities.

Fiction for Youth: A Recommended Guide to Books. Ed. by Lillian Shapiro. 300p. 1981. 19.95 (ISBN 0-918212-34-0). Neal-Schuman.

Fiction in the Middle School. C. Field & D. C. Hamley. 1975. 14.95 o.p. (ISBN 0-686-63991-X, Pub. by Batsford England). David & Charles.

Fiction of Paul Bowles: The Soul Is the Weariest Part of the Body. Hans Bertens. (Costerus Ser.: No. XXI). (Orig.). 1979. pap. text ed. 28.50x (ISBN 90-6203-992-8). Humanities.

Fiction of Ruth Prawer Jhabvala. Haydn M. Williams. (Writers Workshop Greybird Book Ser.). 60p. 1975. 12.00 (ISBN 0-88253-540-4); pap. text ed. 4.80 (ISBN 0-88253-539-0). Ind-US Inc.

Fiction of Samuel Beckett: Form & Affect. H. Porter Abbott. LC 79-186102. (Perspectives in Criticism Ser.: No. 22). 1973. 19.50x (ISBN 0-520-02202-5). U of Cal Pr.

Fiction of the Absurd: Pratfalls in the Void. Dick Penner. (Orig.). 1980. pap. 3.50 (ISBN 0-451-61904-8, ME1904, Ment). NAL.

Fiction Writer's Handbook. Hallie Burnett & Whit Burnett. LC 74-1797. 1979. pap. 3.95 (ISBN 0-06-463492-2, EH 492, EH). Har-Row.

Fictional Father: Lacanian Readings of the Text. Ed. by Robert C. Davis. LC 80-26222. 240p. 1981. lib. bdg. 15.00x (ISBN 0-87023-111-1). U of Mass Pr.

Fictional Lives. Hugh Fleetwood. 166p. 1981. 13.95 (ISBN 0-241-10434-3, Pub. by Hamish Hamilton England). David & Charles.

Fictions of Resolution in Three Victorian Novels. Deirdre David. LC 80-16262. 304p. 1981. text ed. 20.00x (ISBN 0-231-04980-3). Columbia U Pr.

Fictions of the Self: 1550-1800. Arnold Weinstein. LC 80-7558. 344p. 1981. 20.00 (ISBN 0-691-06448-2); pap. 9.95 ltd. ed. (ISBN 0-691-10107-8). Princeton U Pr.

Fictitious & Symbolic Creatures in Art with Special Reference to Their Use in British Heraldry. John Vinycomb. LC 76-89300. (Illus.). 1969. Repr. of 1906 ed. 18.00 (ISBN 0-8103-3147-0). Gale.

Fictive Discourse & the Structures of Literature: A Phenomenological Approach. rev. exp. ed. Felix Martinez-Bonati. Tr. by Philip W. Silver from Span. (Illus.). 200p. 1981. 15.00x (ISBN 0-8014-1308-7). Cornell U Pr.

Fidalgos & Philanthropists: The Santa Casa de Misericordia of Bahia, 1550-1755. A. J. Russell-Wood. 1968. 27.50x (ISBN 0-520-01108-2). U of Cal Pr.

Fiddledust. Ross Edwards. LC 65-25807. 102p. 1965. 4.95 (ISBN 0-8040-0109-X). Swallow.

Fiddlefoot Jones of the North Woods. Philip D. Jordan. LC 57-7687. (Illus.). (gr. 4-7). 6.95 (ISBN 0-8149-0340-1). Vanguard.

Fiddlers in Fiction. Ed. by Murray J. Levith. (Illus.). 220p. 1979. 9.95 (ISBN 0-87666-616-0, Z-27). Paganiniana Pubns.

Fiddlin' Around. Peggy J. Schoenhofer. 1977. 4.50 o.p. (ISBN 0-682-48724-4). Exposition.

Fidel Castro on Internationalism, Nineteen Seventy-Five to Nineteen Eighty. 1981. 30.00 (ISBN 0-87348-610-2); pap. 7.95 (ISBN 0-87348-610-2). Path Pr NY.

Fidelio: Beethoven. Forbes Deane et al. Tr. by Tom Hammond & Rodney Blumer. 1981. pap. 4.95 (ISBN 0-7145-3823-X). Riverrun NY.

Fiedler: The Colorful Mr. Pops. Robin Moore. (Music Reprint Ser.). (Illus.). 1980. Repr. of 1968 ed. lib. bdg. 27.50 (ISBN 0-306-76008-8). Da Capo.

Field. Dola DeJong. Ed. by Maxwell Perkins. Tr. by A. V. Van Duyn from Dutch. LC 79-84437. 1979. 15.95 (ISBN 0-933256-02-7); pap. 7.95 (ISBN 0-933256-05-1). Second Chance.

Field & Equipment Record Book. new ed. Ed. by Tom Corey. 1979. pap. 9.45 (ISBN 0-932250-07-6); ringed binder 15.95. Doane Agricultural.

Field & Meadow. Etta S. Ress. LC 60-6114. (Community of Living Things Ser). (Illus.). (gr. 4-8). 1967. PLB 7.45 (ISBN 0-87191-016-0). Creative Ed.

Field Approach to Biology. R. W. Wilson & D. F. Wright. 1972. pack 6.50x o.p. (ISBN 0-435-59940-2). Heinemann Ed.

Field Archery. Don Stamp. (Illus.). 1980. 15.95 (ISBN 0-7136-1981-3). Transatlantic.

Field Artillery Battalions of the U. S. Army, 2 vols. 1979. Set. 49.90 (ISBN 0-9602404-2-X); Vol. 1. 24.95 (ISBN 0-9602404-0-3); Vol. 2. 24.95 (ISBN 0-9602404-2-X). Centaur Dumfries.

Field Athletics. Carl Johnson. (Ep Sport Ser). (Illus.). 113p. 1978. 12.95 (ISBN 0-8069-9114-3, Pub by EP Publishing England). Sterling.

Field Book of Mountaineering & Rock Climbing. Tom Lyman & Bill Riviere. (Illus.). 256p. 1975. 9.95 (ISBN 0-87691-162-9). Winchester Pr.

Field Book of Mountaineering & Rock Climbing. Tom Lyman & Bill Riviere. LC 78-50762. (Illus.). 1978. pap. 5.95 o.p. (ISBN 0-684-15584-2, ScribT). Scribner.

Field Book Wind River Range. rev. ed. Orrin H. Bonney & Lorraine G. Bonney. (Illus.). 1968. pap. 5.95 with 1975 supp. (ISBN 0-685-07191-X). Bonney.

Field Crop Disease Handbook. Robert F. Nyvall. (Illus.). 1979. lib. bdg. 45.00 (ISBN 0-87055-336-4); pap. text ed. 25.00 (ISBN 0-87055-344-5). AVI.

Field-Effect & Bipolar Power Transistor Physics. Adolph Blicher. 1981. write for info. (ISBN 0-12-105850-6). Acad Pr.

Field Engineering for Agricultural Development. Norman Hudson. (Oxford Tropical Handbooks). (Illus.). 160p. 1975. 29.95x (ISBN 0-19-859442-9). Oxford U Pr.

Field Engineer's Manual. Robert O. Parmley. 608p. 1981. 19.50 (ISBN 0-07-048513-5, P&RB). McGraw.

Field Excursion, Central Texas: Tertiary Bentonites of Central Texas. R. L. Folk et al. 53p. 1973. Repr. of 1961 ed. 1.25 (GB 3). Bur Econ Geology.

Field Excursions, East Texas: Clay, Glauconite, Ironstone Deposits. T. E. Brown et al. (Illus.). 48p. 1969. 1.00 (GB 9). Bur Econ Geology.

Field Geology in Britain. J. G. C. Anderson & T. R. Owen. Date not set. 36.01 (ISBN 0-08-022054-1); pap. 12.01 (ISBN 0-08-022055-X). Pergamon.

Field Guide to Astronomy Without a Telescope. W. A. Dexter. (Earth Science Curriculum Project Pamphlet Ser.). (gr. 11-12). 1971. pap. text ed. 3.20 (ISBN 0-395-02623-7). HM.

Field Guide to Australian Shells. Barry R. Wilson & Keith Gillett. (Illus.). 288p. 1979. 25.75 (ISBN 0-589-50120-8, Pub. by Reed Books Australia). C E Tuttle.

Field Guide to Beaches. J. H. Hoyt. (Earth Science Curriculum Project Pamphlet Ser). 1971. pap. 3.20 (ISBN 0-395-02621-0, 2-14607). HM.

Field Guide to Birds of Prey of Australia. Frank T. Morris. 124p. 29.95 (ISBN 0-686-62178-6). Eastview.

Field Guide to Edible Wild Plants. Bradford Angier. LC 73-23042. (Illus.). 256p. 1974. write for info. (ISBN 0-8117-0616-8); pap. 8.95 (ISBN 0-8117-2018-7). Stackpole.

Field Guide to Fossils. J. R. Beerbower. (Earth Science Curriculum Project Pamphlet Ser). 1971. pap. 3.20 (ISBN 0-395-02618-0, 2-14604). HM.

Field Guide to Lakes. J. Verduin. (Earth Science Curriculum Project Pamphlet Ser). 288p. 1971. pap. 3.20 (ISBN 0-395-02622-9, 2-14608). HM.

Field Guide to Layered Rocks. T. Freeman. (Earth Science Curriculum Project Pamphlet Ser). 1971. pap. 3.20 (ISBN 0-395-02617-2). HM.

Field Guide to Marine Invertebrates. Idaz Greenberg. (Illus.). 1980. plastic card 3.95 (ISBN 0-913008-11-7). Seahawk Pr.

Field Guide to Medicinal Wild Plants. Bradford Angier. LC 78-19112. (Illus.). 320p. 1978. pap. 9.95 (ISBN 0-8117-2076-4). Stackpole.

Field Guide to Medicinal Wild Plants. Bradford Angier. LC 78-19112. (Illus.). 320p. 1978. 14.95 (ISBN 0-8117-0552-8). Stackpole.

Field Guide to New Mexico Birds. Lawrence Murphy & Bernadette Murphy. Ed. by Ronald P. Ratkevich. (Illus.). 1979. pap. 3.95 (ISBN 0-932680-02-X). Dinograph SW.

Field Guide to Outdoor Photography. C. Boyd Pfeiffer. LC 76-55380. (Illus.). 224p. 1977. pap. 3.95 (ISBN 0-8117-2261-9). Stackpole.

Field Guide to Plutonic & Metamorphic Rocks. W. D. Romey. (Earth Science Curriculum Project Pamphlet Ser). 1971. pap. 3.20 (ISBN 0-395-02619-9). HM.

Field Guide to Rock Weathering. R. E. Boyer. (Earth Science Curriculum Project Pamphlet Ser). 1971. pap. 3.20 (ISBN 0-395-02615-6, 2-14601). HM.

Field Guide to Snow Crystals. Edward R. LaChapelle. LC 70-85215. (Illus.). 108p. 1969. pap. 7.95 (ISBN 0-295-95040-4). U of Wash Pr.

Field Guide to Soils. H. Foth & H. S. Jacobs. (Earth Science Curriculum Project Pamphlet Ser). 1971. pap. 3.20 (ISBN 0-395-02616-4). HM.

Field Guide to the Atmosphere. Vincent J. Schaefer & John A. Day. (Illus.). 384p. 1981. 13.95 (ISBN 0-395-24080-8). HM.

Field Guide to the Birds. 4th ed. Roger T. Peterson. 1980. 15.00 (ISBN 0-395-26621-1); limited ed. 75.00 (ISBN 0-395-29930-6); pap. 9.95 (ISBN 0-395-26619-X). HM.

Field Guide to the Birds: A Completely New Guide to All the Birds of Eastern and Central North America. 4th ed. Roger T. Peterson. 1980. 15.00 (ISBN 0-395-26621-1); ltd. ed. 50.00 (ISBN 0-686-65213-4); pap. 9.95 (ISBN 0-395-26619-X). HM.

Field Guide to the Birds of Mexico. Ernest P. Edwards. LC 78-185930. (Illus., With 1978 appendix bound in plastic ring binding). 1972. pap. 12.00 set (ISBN 0-911882-03-0). E P Edwards.

Field Guide to the Butterflies of the Pacific Northwest. James R. Christensen. LC 80-52967. (GEM Bks. - Natural History). (Illus.). 200p. (Orig.). 1981. pap. 12.95 (ISBN 0-89301-074-X). U Pr of Idaho.

Field Guide to the Common Sea & Estuary Fishes of Ono-Tropical Australia. J. M. Thomson. 144p. 1980. 17.95x (ISBN 0-00-219271-3, Pub. by W Collins Ausftralia). Intl Schol Bk Serv.

Field Guide to the Study of American Literature. Harold H. Kolb, Jr. LC 75-22033. 1976. 10.00x (ISBN 0-8139-0626-1); pap. 4.95x (ISBN 0-8139-0664-4). U Pr of Va.

Field Guide to Wilderness Living. Catherine Gearing. LC 72-97849. 224p. 1973. pap. 3.95 (ISBN 0-8127-0057-0). Southern Pub.

Field Hockey: The Coach & the Player. 2nd ed. Mildred J. Barnes & Richard G. Kentwell. 1978. text ed. 18.95 (ISBN 0-205-06512-0). Allyn.

Field Inspection of Building Construction. Thomas H. McKaig. 1958. 24.95 o.p. (ISBN 0-07-045108-7, P&RB). McGraw.

Field Instrumentation in Geotechnical Engineering. British Geotechnical Society. LC 73-9535. 720p. 1974. 49.95 (ISBN 0-470-10475-9). Halsted Pr.

Field Interrogation. 2nd ed. Allen P. Bristow. (Illus.). 168p. 1980. 9.75 (ISBN 0-398-00226-6). C C Thomas.

Field Investigation of Underground Heat Distribution Systems. Building Research Advisory Board - Federal Construction Council. 1963. pap. 5.75 o.p. (ISBN 0-309-01144-2). Natl Acad Pr.

Field Ionization & Field Desorption Mass Spectroscopy. H. D. Beckey. 1978. text ed. 46.00 (ISBN 0-08-020612-3). Pergamon.

Field Ionization Mass Spectrometry. H. D. Beckey. LC 79-146601. 1971. 52.00 (ISBN 0-08-017557-0). Pergamon.

Field Key to the Flowering Plants of Iceland. Pat Wolseley. 60p. 1980. pap. 8.95x (ISBN 0-906191-42-4, Pub. by Thule Pr England). Intl Schol Bk Serv.

Field Manual for Museums. (Museums & Monuments Ser., No. 12). (Illus., Orig.). 1970. pap. 11.50 (ISBN 92-3-100839-0, U237, UNESCO). Unipub.

Field Manual of Procedures for Postmortem Examination of Alaskan Marine Mammals. Ed. by F. H. Fay et al. write for info. (ISBN 0-914500-09-0). U of AK Inst Marine.

Field Notes: & Butterflies Beget Butterflies. C. Margaret Hall. LC 77-74865. 1978. 5.00 (ISBN 0-87212-084-8). Libra.

Field of Death. Stephen Overholser. LC 77-75875. 1977. 6.95 o.p. (ISBN 0-385-13204-2). Doubleday.

Field of Life & Death. Hsiao Hung. Tr. by Howard Goldblatt & Ellen Yeung. Bd. with Tales of Hulan River. LC 78-19549. (Chinese Literature in Translation Ser.). 320p. 1979. 14.95x (ISBN 0-253-15821-4). Ind U Pr.

Field of Stones: A Study of the Art of Shen Chou (1427-1509) Richard Edwards. (Illus.). 131p. 1962. 15.00x (ISBN 0-87474-398-2). Smithsonian.

Field of Vision. Wright Morris. LC 56-8525. 251p. 1974. 11.50x (ISBN 0-8032-3060-5); pap. 3.50 (ISBN 0-8032-5789-9, BB 577, Bison). U of Nebr Pr.

Field Photography: Beginning & Advanced Techniques. Alfred A. Blaker. LC 75-33382. (Illus.). 1976. text ed. 26.95x (ISBN 0-7167-0518-4); field supplement incl. W H Freeman.

Field Poems. Barbara Drake. (Illus.). 1975. 1.00 o.p. (ISBN 0-686-23606-8). Stone Pr MI.

Field Problems of Tropical Rice. 95p. 1974. pap. 5.00 (R006, IRRI). Unipub.

Field Research: A Manual for Logistics & Management of Scientific Studies in Natural Settings. Judith Fiedler. LC 78-62562. (Social & Behavioral Science Ser.). (Illus.). 1978. text ed. 13.95x (ISBN 0-87589-381-3). Jossey-Bass.

Field Research: Strategies for a Natural Society. Leonard Schatzman & Anselm L. Strauss. (Methods of Social Science Ser.). 176p. 1973. pap. text ed. 9.95 (ISBN 0-13-314351-1). P-H.

Field Sales Manager's Problem Solver. LC 78-52315. 1978. 9.95 o.p. (Hawthorn); pap. 4.95 (ISBN 0-8015-2606-X, Hawthorn). Dutton.

Field Sales Performance Appraisal. Clark Lambert. LC 79-18567. (Marketing Management Ser.). 1979. 24.95 (ISBN 0-471-04781-3, Pub by Ronald Pr). Wiley.

Field Test Sections Save Cost in Tunnel Support. Compiled By American Society of Civil Engineers. 64p. 1975. pap. 9.75 o.p. (ISBN 0-87262-161-8). Am Soc Civil Eng.

Field Theoretical Methods in Many-Body Systems. D. A. Kirzhnits. Tr. by A. J. Meadows. 1967. 60.00 (ISBN 0-08-011779-1). Pergamon.

Field Theoretical Methods in Particle Physics. Ed. by Werner Ruhl. (NATO Advanced Study Institutes Ser., Ser. B: Physics: Vol. 55). 608p. 1980. 69.50 (ISBN 0-306-40444-3, Plenum Pr). Plenum Pub.
Field Theory & Particle Analysis. T. D. Lee. (Contemporary Concepts in Physics Ser.). 1981. 35.00 (ISBN 0-686-69595-X); pap. 14.00 (ISBN 0-686-69596-8). Harwood Academic.
Field Theory & Particle Physics. Ed. by T. D. Lee. (Concepts in Contemporary Physics Ser.: Vol. 1). 575p. 1981. 35.00 (ISBN 0-686-65734-9); pap. 14.00 (ISBN 0-686-65735-7). Harwood Academic.
Field Theory & Strong Interactions: Proceedings. Ed. by P. Urban. (Acta Physica Austriaca Supplementum Ser.: No. 22). (Illus.). 815p. 1981. 98.00 (ISBN 0-387-81615-1). Springer-Verlag.
Field Work. Seamus Heaney. 1981. pap. 4.95 (ISBN 0-374-51620-0). FS&G.
Field Work of a Museum Naturalist: Alaska Southeast, 1919-1921; Alaska Far North, 1921-1922. Alfred M. Bailey. (Museum Pictorial: No. 22). 1971. pap. 2.25 o.p. (ISBN 0-916278-49-2). Denver Mus Natl Hist.
Field-Work Projects in Biology. Marjorie Hingley. (Illus.). 176p. 1980. 11.95 o.p. (ISBN 0-7137-0964-2, Pub by Blandford Pr England). Sterling.
Fieldbook. Boy Scouts Of America. LC 67-14537. (Illus.). 576p. (gr. 6-12). 1967. flexible bdg. 3.95x (ISBN 0-8395-3201-6, 3201). BSA.
Fielder's Choice: An Anthology of Baseball Fiction. Jerry Holtzman. 1979. 12.95 o.p. (ISBN 0-15-130681-8). HarBraceJ.
Fieldguide to the Birds of the Eastern Himalayas. Salim Ali. (Illus.). 1978. 15.95x (ISBN 0-19-560595-0). Oxford U Pr.
Fielding's Art of Fiction. Maurice O. Johnson. LC 61-5547. 1961. 7.50x o.p. (ISBN 0-8122-7260-9). U of Pa Pr.
Fielding's Caribbean, 1981. rev. ed. Margaret Zellers. LC 79-64015. 1981. Fieldingflex 10.95 (ISBN 0-688-03713-5). Fielding.
Fielding's Europe, 1981. 34th, rev. ed. Temple Fielding. 1030p. 1980. Fieldingflex bdg. 10.95 (ISBN 0-688-03776-3). Morrow.
Fielding's Favorites: Hotels & Inns, Europe 1980. 9th ed. Dodge Fielding. LC 79-642516. 1981. Fieldingflex 5.95 (ISBN 0-688-00293-5). Fielding.
Fielding's Low-Cost Europe 1981. 15th ed. Nancy Fielding & Temple Fielding. LC 75-640820. (Illus.). 1981. pap. 5.95 (ISBN 0-688-61215-6). Fielding.
Fielding's Low-Cost Europe, 1981. 15th, rev. ed. Temple Fielding & Nancy Fielding. (Illus.). 872p. 1980. Fieldingflex bdg. 5.95 (ISBN 0-688-03777-1). Morrow.
Fielding's Selective Shopping Guide to Europe 1981. 25th ed. Nancy Fielding & Temple Fielding. LC 57-9112. 1981. pap. 4.95 spiral bdg. (ISBN 0-688-61213-X). Fielding.
Fielding's Worldwide Guide to Cruises. 320p. 1981. Fieldingflex 11.95 (ISBN 0-688-00422-9). Morrow.
Fieldmouse Goes to War. Edward Kennard. (Wild & Woolly West Ser.: No. 41). (Illus., Eng. & Hopi.). 1977. pap. 2.50 (ISBN 0-910584-47-8). Filter.
Fields, Bk. 5. W. Bolton. LC 80-41166. (Study Topics in Physics Ser.). 96p. 1980. pap. text ed. write for info. (ISBN 0-408-10656-5). Butterworths.
Fields Above the Sea. William Lavendar. (Orig.). pap. 2.75 (ISBN 0-515-05390-2). Jove Pubns.
Fields & Fences. new ed. William D. Sheldon et al. (gr. 2). 1973. text ed. 7.96 (ISBN 0-205-03532-9, 5235324); tchrs'. guide 7.96 (ISBN 0-205-03533-7, 5235332); activity bk. 3.92 (ISBN 0-205-03534-5, 5235340); tchr's activity bk. 3.92 (ISBN 0-205-03535-3, 5235359); activities masters 28.00 (ISBN 0-205-03536-1, 5235367). Allyn.
Fields, Factories & Workshops Tomorrow. Peter Kropotkin. Ed. by Colin Ward. 1975. pap. 3.45x o.p. (ISBN 0-06-131858-2, TB1858, Torch). Har-Row.
Fields of Change Among the Iteso of Kenya. Ivan Karp. (International Library of Anthropology). 1978. 21.00x (ISBN 0-7100-8863-9). Routledge & Kegan.
Fields of Experience. J. H. Walsh & F. Tomlinson. 1968. pap. text ed. 2.50x o.p. (ISBN 0-435-10921-9). Heinemann Ed.
Fields of Force: The Development of a World View from Faraday to Einstein. William Berkson. 1974. 30.00 (ISBN 0-7100-7626-6). Routledge & Kegan.
Fields of Light: An Experiment in Critical Reading. Reuben A. Brower. LC 80-19289. xii, 218p. 1980. Repr. of 1951 ed. lib. bdg. 23.50x (ISBN 0-313-22653-9, BRFI). Greenwood.
Fields of Praise: The Official History of the Welsh Rugby Union, 1881-1981. David Smith & Gareth Williams. (Illus.). 505p. 1981. text ed. 47.50 (ISBN 0-7083-0766-3). Verry.
Fields of Transformation. Bika Reed. (Illus.). 1981. 8.95 (ISBN 0-89281-016-5). Inner Tradit.
Fieldwork in Geography. J. E. Archer & T. H. Dalton. 1970. 25.00 (ISBN 0-7134-2101-0, Pub. by Batsford England). David & Charles.
Fieldwork in Geology. I. M. Simpson. (Introducing Geology Ser.). (Illus.). 1977. pap. text ed. 5.50x (ISBN 0-04-550025-8). Allen Unwin.
Fieldwork in Medieval Archaeology. Christopher Taylor. 1975. 30.00 (ISBN 0-7134-2850-3, Pub. by Batsford England); pap. 14.50 (ISBN 0-7134-2872-4). David & Charles.
Fieldworker & the Field: Problems & Challenges in Sociological Investigation. M. N. Srinivas et al. 300p. 1979. text ed. 13.95x (ISBN 0-19-561118-7). Oxford U Pr.
Fiends & Creatures. Ed. by Marvin Kaye. 192p. 1975. pap. 1.25 o.p. (ISBN 0-445-00289-1). Popular Lib.
Fierce the Lion. Illus. by Evaline Ness. LC 80-10172. (Illus.). 32p. (ps-3). 1980. PLB 8.95 (ISBN 0-8234-0412-9). Holiday.
Fiery Hunt & Other Plays. Charles F. Olson. Ed. by George F. Butterick. LC 76-48311. (Writing Ser: No. 36). 150p. 1977. pap. 4.00 (ISBN 0-87704-033-8). Four Seasons Foun.
Fiery World I. rev. ed. (Agni Yoga Ser.). 1969. 9.00x (ISBN 0-933574-09-6). Agni Yoga Soc.
Fiery World II. 2nd ed. 1978. Repr. of 1947 ed. softbd. 9.00 (ISBN 0-933574-10-X). Agni Yoga Soc.
Fiery World III. (Agni Yoga Ser.). 1948. flexible cover 9.00x (ISBN 0-933574-11-8). Agni Yoga Soc.
Fiesta System and Economic Change. Waldemar R. Smith. LC 77-390. 1977. 16.00x (ISBN 0-231-04180-2). Columbia U Pr.
Fifteen. Eve Bunting. (Young Romance Ser.). (Illus.). (gr. 3-9). 1978. PLB 5.95 (ISBN 0-87191-632-0); pap. 2.95 (ISBN 0-89812-064-0). Creative Ed.
Fifteen. Beverly Cleary. (Illus.). (gr. 6-9). 1956. 8.75 (ISBN 0-688-21285-9); PLB 8.40 (ISBN 0-688-31285-3). Morrow.
Fifteen. Beverly Cleary. (gr. 7-12). 1980. pap. 1.75 (ISBN 0-440-92559-2, LFL). Dell.
Fifteen American Authors Before 1900: Bibliographic Essays on Research & Criticism. Ed. by Robert A. Rees & Earl N. Harbert. LC 77-157395. 1971. 30.00x (ISBN 0-299-05910-3); pap. 8.95x (ISBN 0-299-05913-8). U of Wis Pr.
Fifteen Centuries of Children's Literature: An Annotated Chronology of British & American Works in Historical Context. Ed. by Jane Bingham & Grayce Scholt. LC 79-8584. (Illus.). l, 540p. 1980. lib. bdg. 35.00 (ISBN 0-313-22164-2, BCL/). Greenwood.
Fifteen Cities in China. 1980. pap. 4.95 (ISBN 0-8351-0736-1). China Bks.
Fifteen-Eighty-Seven, a Year of No Significance: The Mingdynasty in Decline. Ray Huang. LC 80-5392. (Illus.). 396p. 1981. 19.95x (ISBN 0-300-02518-1). Yale U Pr.
Fifteen False Propositions About God. Jack Spicer. 1974. pap. 2.50 (ISBN 0-686-28709-6). Man-Root.
Fifteen Famous Latin Americans. Helen M. Bailey & Maria C. Grijalva. (gr. 1-6). 1971. text ed. 6.64 o.p. (ISBN 0-13-314609-X). P-H.
Fifteen Longer Poems of Rabindranath Tagore. Rabindranath Tagore. Tr. by Rabindra N. Choudhury from Bengali. 248p. 1975. lib. bdg. 15.00 (ISBN 0-88253-735-0). Ind-US Inc.
Fifteen Minute-a-Day Natural Face Lift. M. J. Saffon. 112p. 1981. pap. 3.95 (ISBN 0-446-97788-8). Warner Bks.
Fifteen Over Seventy: Counsel from My Elders. James Maas. (Illus.). 1980. pap. 3.95 (ISBN 0-915288-42-7). Shameless Hussy.
Fifteen Poems from a Classical Tamil Anthology. Tr. by A. K. Ramanujan. (Translated from Tamil). 8.00 (ISBN 0-89253-774-4); flexible cloth 4.00 (ISBN 0-89253-775-2). Ind-US Inc.
Fifteen Prose Poems. Lokenath Bhattacharya. Tr. by Nikhiles Guha from Bengali. (Saffronbird Book Ser). 25p. 1975. flexible cloth 4.80 (ISBN 0-88253-709-1). Ind-US Inc.
Fifteen Tips on Handling Job Interviews. Charles R. Grice, Jr. Ed. by S. Michele McFadden. 1981. pap. text ed. 0.65 (ISBN 0-89262-043-9). Career Pub.
Fifteen Years in Hawken Lode. John D. Baird. 15.00 (ISBN 0-88227-011-7). Gun Room.
Fifteenth Antiques & Their Prices. (Illus.). 1980. 10.95 (ISBN 0-911594-01-9). Warman.
Fifteenth Century Art & Architecture. LC 76-14068. (Garland Library of the History of Art). 1976. lib. bdg. 50.00 (ISBN 0-8240-2416-8). Garland Pub.
Fifteenth Century Basse Dances. James L. Jackman. LC 79-7767. (Dance Ser.). (Illus.). 1980. Repr. of 1964 ed. lib. bdg. 14.00x (ISBN 0-8369-9295-4). Arno.
Fifteenth Century Florentine Studies: The Palazzo Medici & a Ledger for the Church of San Lorenzo. Isabelle Hyman. LC 76-23631. (Outstanding Dissertations in the Fine Arts - Fifteenth Century). (Illus.). 1977. Repr. of 1968 ed. lib. bdg. 70.00 (ISBN 0-8240-2700-0). Garland Pub.
Fifteenth Century, Thirteen Ninety-Nine to Fourteen Eighty-Five. Ernest F. Jacob. (Oxford History of England Ser.). 1961. 33.00x (ISBN 0-19-821714-5). Oxford U Pr.
Fifth Army at War. George Forty. (Illus.). 144p. 1980. 17.50 (ISBN 0-684-16615-1, ScribT). Scribner.
Fifth Assembling. new ed. Ed. by Richard Kostelanetz & Henry J. Korn. (Illus.). 300p. (Orig.). 1974. pap. 4.95 (ISBN 0-685-49921-9). Assembling Pr.
Fifth Book of Virgil Finlay. Ed. by Gerry De La Ree. (Illus.). 1979. 15.75 (ISBN 0-938192-02-7). De La Ree.
Fifth Brazilian Symposium on Theoretical Physics. E. Ferreira. 1975. pap. 35.00 (ISBN 0-470-98956-4). Halsted Pr.
Fifth Column & Four Stories of the Spanish Civil War. Ernest Hemingway. LC 70-182369. 1969. pap. 3.45 (ISBN 0-684-12723-7, SL329, ScribT); Hudson River Edition. 12.50x (ISBN 0-684-15815-9). Scribner.
Fifth Conference on Automated Deduction, les Arcs Proceedings. Ed. by W. Bibel & R. Kowalski. (Lecture Notes in Computer Science: Vol. 87). (Illus.). 385p. 1980. pap. 22.00 (ISBN 0-387-10009-1). Springer-Verlag.
Fifth Day. Mary Q. Steele. (Illus.). (gr. 6-9). 1978. 8.25 (ISBN 0-688-80146-3); PLB 7.92 (ISBN 0-688-84146-5). Greenwillow.
Fifth Direction. Theodore Enslin. (Orig.). 1980. limited signed ed. 20.00x (ISBN 0-915316-81-1); pap. 5.00x (ISBN 0-915316-80-3). Pentagram.
Fifth Down. Alex B. Allen. LC 73-7317. (Springboard Sports Ser.). (Illus.). 64p. (gr. 3-5). 1974. 5.75g (ISBN 0-8075-2432-8). A Whitman.
Fifth Energy Resource Conference: Proceedings. Ed. by R. William De Vore et al. (Illus.). 1978. pap. text ed. 7.50 (ISBN 0-89779-006-5); microfiche 2.50 (ISBN 0-89779-007-3). OES Pubns.
Fifth Gospel: The Experience of Black Christian Values. Joseph G. Healey. LC 80-25033. (Illus.). 320p. (Orig.). 1981. pap. 7.95 (ISBN 0-88344-013-X). Orbis Bks.
Fifth Horseman. Larry Collins & Dominique Lapierre. 1980. 13.95 (ISBN 0-671-24316-0). S&S.
Fifth Horseman Is Riding. Larry Van Goetham. LC 73-10786. 160p. 1974. 4.95 o.s.i. (ISBN 0-02-621600-0). Macmillan.
Fifth Infantry Division in Thee ETO. (Divisional Ser.: No. 18). (Illus.). 254p. 1980. Repr. of 1945 ed. 27.50. Battery Pr.
Fifth Institute on Coal Mine Health & Safety: Proceedings. Ed. by R. T. Reeder. (Fifth Proceedings Ser.). (Illus.). 380p. (Orig.). 1980. pap. text ed. 12.00 (ISBN 0-918062-41-1). Colo Sch Mines.
Fifth International Symposium on Biotelemetry, Sapporo, June 1980 & Kyoto, June 1980. Ed. by H. P. Kimmich. (Biotelemetry & Patient Monitoring Journal: Vol. 7, No. 1). 52p. 1980. 19.75 (ISBN 3-8055-1073-X). S Karger.
Fifth International Symposium on Jet Cutting Technology: Proceedings. (International Symposiums on Jet Cutting Technology Ser.). 1980. 99.00 (ISBN 0-906085-41-1, Dist. by Air Science Co.). BHRA Fluid.
Fifth Mad Report on Spy Vs. Spy. Antonio Prohias. (Mad Ser.). (Illus., Orig.). 1978. pap. 1.75 (ISBN 0-446-94422-X). Warner Bks.
Fifth Profession: Becoming a Psychotherapist. William E. Henry et al. LC 71-148655. (Social & Behavioral Science Ser.). 1971. 14.95x o.p. (ISBN 0-87589-088-1). Jossey-Bass.
Fifth Queen. Ford Madox Ford. LC 63-13786. (Consists of: Fifth Queen, Privy Seal, & Fifth Queen Crowned). 1963. 15.00 (ISBN 0-8149-0099-2). Vanguard.
Fifth Season. Michael Sheridan. LC 78-7507. 52p. 1978. 7.50 (ISBN 0-8214-0405-9); pap. 4.00 (ISBN 0-8214-0407-5). Ohio U Pr.
Fifth Symposium on the Structure of Low-Medium Mass Nuclei. Ed. by J. P. Davidson & Bernard D. Kern. LC 73-77254. (Illus.). 312p. 1973. 17.00x (ISBN 0-8131-1293-1). U Pr of Ky.
Fifty Best of Baltimore & Ohio Railroad, Bk. 1. Howard N. Barr. (Illus.). 1977. 12.00 (ISBN 0-934118-16-7). Barnard Robert.
Fifty Best of Baltimore & Ohio Railroad, Bk. 3. John C. Kelly. (Illus.). 1977. 12.00 (ISBN 0-934118-02-7). Barnard Robert.
Fifty Best of Baltimore & Ohio Railroad, Bk. 5. Bob Loranz. (Illus.). 1979. 12.00 (ISBN 0-934118-04-3). Barnard Robert.
Fifty Best of New York Central Railroad, Bk. 1. Herbert H. Harwood, Jr. (Illus.). 1977. 12.00 (ISBN 0-934118-09-4). Barnard Robert.
Fifty Best of Pennsylvania Railroad, Bk. 4. Bob Lorenz. (Illus.). 1979. 12.00 (ISBN 0-934118-08-6). Barnard Robert.
Fifty Best WIM Reviews. Ed. by S. Diane Bogus. (Illus.). Date not set. pap. cancelled (ISBN 0-934172-04-8). WIM Pubns.
Fifty Billion Dollars: My Thirteen Years with the RFC (1932-1945) Jesse H. Jones. LC 74-31415. (FDR & the Era of the New Deal Ser.). (Illus.). xvi, 631p. 1975. Repr. of 1951 ed. lib. bdg. 55.00 (ISBN 0-306-70715-2). Da Capo.
Fifty Chess Masterpieces: 1941-1944. Reuben Fine. Orig. Title: Chess Marches on. 1977. pap. 3.50 o.p. (ISBN 0-486-23450-9). Dover.
Fifty Common Birds of Oklahoma & the Southern Great Plains. George M. Sutton. LC 77-24336. (Illus.). 113p. 1981. pap. 6.95 (ISBN 0-8061-1704-4). U of Okla Pr.
Fifty Contemporary Poets: The Creative Process. Ed. by Alberta Turner. LC 76-56750. 1977. text ed. 15.95x (ISBN 0-582-28024-9, Pub by McKay); pap. 9.95x (ISBN 0-582-28025-7). Longman.
Fifty Craft Ideas with Patterns. Loretta Reese. LC 80-53363. (Illus.). 64p. (Orig.). pap. 3.50 (ISBN 0-87239-427-1, 2144). Standard Pub.
Fifty Craft Projects with Bible Verses & Patterns. Maureen Biddle. LC 80-53872. (Illus.). 64p. (Orig.). 1981. pap. 3.50 (ISBN 0-87239-428-X, 2148). Standard Pub.
Fifty Dollar Gift. Evalyne S. Grand. 178p. 1979. 11.95 (ISBN 0-86629-017-6). Sunrise MO.
Fifty Dutch & Flemish Novelists. Ed. by Joost De Wit & Stanley H. Barkan. 220p. 25.00 (ISBN 0-89304-031-2); pap. 15.00 (ISBN 0-89304-032-0). Cross Cult.
Fifty Epic Paintings of American History. Henry S. Commager. LC 79-88368. (Illus.). 104p. (Orig.). pap. 9.95 (ISBN 0-89659-064-X). Abbeville Pr.
Fifty Famous Faces in Transition. Burt Berliner. 1980. pap. write for info. (ISBN 0-671-41127-6, Fireside). S&S.
Fifty Favorite Rhymes of Mother Goose. Illus. by Florence S. Winship. (Illus.). 24p. (gr. k-1). 1976. PLB 7.15 o.p. (ISBN 0-307-69053-9, Golden Pr). Western Pub.
Fifty Favourite Bible Stories. Ed. by Ernest H. Hayes. 1947. pap. 4.55 (ISBN 0-08-006196-6, Religious Educ Pr). Pergamon.
Fifty-Fifth Annual of Advertising, Editorial & Television Art & Design. Art Directors Club of New York. (Illus., Orig.). 1976. 29.95 o.p. (ISBN 0-8230-1908-X, Pub. by Art Directors Club). Watson-Guptill.
Fifty-Fifty Consultation: A Guide to Getting Your Expertise Used. Peter Block. (Illus.). 200p. 1981. text ed. price not set (ISBN 0-89384-052-1). Learning Concepts.
Fifty Fighting Years: The Communist Party of South Africa, 1921-1971. A. Lerumo. (Illus.). 1971. 4.00 o.p. (ISBN 0-8285-9101-6). Inkululeko.
Fifty Five Days: The Fall of South Vietnam. Alan Dawson. LC 77-22768. 1978. 12.50 o.p. (ISBN 0-13-314476-3). P-H.
Fifty-Four-Forty or Fight. Marjorie W. Campbell. (Canadian Jackdaw Ser: No. C28). 1974. 5.95 o.s.i. (ISBN 0-670-31223-1, Grossman). Viking Pr.
Fifty-Four-Forty or Fight. Emerson Hough. 1976. lib. bdg. 17.75x (ISBN 0-89968-043-7). Lightyear.
Fifty Golden Years of Oscar: The Official History of the Academy of Motion Picture Arts & Sciences. Robert Osborne. (Illus.). 1979. 24.95 (ISBN 0-912076-30-5); pap. 12.97 o.s.i. (ISBN 0-912076-29-1). ESE Calif.
Fifty Great Horror Stories. Canning. Date not set. 4.98 (ISBN 0-517-13671-6). Bonanza.
Fifty Great Mini-Trips for Illinois. Jack Osler. (Illus.). 1978. pap. 2.95 o.s.i. (ISBN 0-89645-006-6). Media Ventures.
Fifty Great Mini-Trips for Washington D. C. - Virginia. Jack Osler & Tricia Burgin. (Jack Osler's Mini-Trip Ser.). Date not set. pap. price not set (ISBN 0-89645-009-0). Media Ventures. Postponed.
Fifty Great Mini-Trips in Florida. rev ed. Jack Osler & George Griffin. (Jack Osler's Mini Trips Ser.). (Illus.). Date not set. pap. cancelled (ISBN 0-89645-012-0). Media Ventures.
Fifty Great Sea Stories. Joseph Conrad et al. 768p. 1980. Repr. lib. bdg. 30.00 (ISBN 0-686-68073-1). Arden Lib.
Fifty Hikes in Eastern Pennsylvania. Carolyn Hoffman. (Illus., Orig.). 1981. pap. price not set (ISBN 0-89725-018-4). NH Pub Co.
Fifty Hikes in the Adirondacks. Barbara McMartin. LC 79-92569. (Fifty Hikes Ser.). (Illus., Orig.). 1980. pap. 8.95 (ISBN 0-89725-015-X). NH Pub Co.
Fifty Hikes in Vermont. rev. ed. Ruth Sadlier & Paul Sadlier. LC 79-92572. (Fifty Hike Ser.). (Illus.). 1981. pap. 7.95 (ISBN 0-89725-013-3). NH Pub Co.

Fifty IC Projects You Can Build. Ronald M. Benrey. (Illus.). 1970. pap. 7.15 (ISBN 0-8104-0723-X). Hayden.
Fifty Major Film-Makers. Ed. by Peter Cowie. LC 73-107. (Illus.). 384p. 1976. 20.00 o.p. (ISBN 0-498-01255-7). A S Barnes.
Fifty More Hikes in Maine. Cloe Catlett. LC 79-92571. (Fifty Hikes Ser.). (Illus., Orig.). 1980. pap. 8.95 (ISBN 0-89725-017-6). NH Pub Co.
Fifty Needlepoint Stitches. J. & P. Coats Ltd. (Illus.). 1977. pap. 2.95 (ISBN 0-684-14786-6, ScribT). Scribner.
Fifty New Creative Poodle Grooming Styles. Faye Meadows. LC 79-25786. (Illus.). 1980. spiral 9.95 (ISBN 0-668-04857-3). Arco.
Fifty-Ninth Art Directors Annual. Art Directors Club of New York. Ed. by Miriam L. Solomon. (Illus.). 672p. 1980. 34.95 (ISBN 0-937414-00-X). ADC NY.
Fifty One Colt Navies. Nathan L. Swayze. LC 67-19544. (Illus., Indexed). 1967. 15.00 (ISBN 0-9600228-0-5). Gun Hill.
Fifty-One Paper Craft Projects. Pat Karch. LC 79-91249. (Illus.). 64p. (Orig.). 1979. pap. 3.50 (ISBN 0-87239-391-7, 2139). Standard Pub.
Fifty-One Sycamore Lane. Marjorie W. Sharmat. LC 73-129754. (Illus.). (gr. 3-7). 1971. 7.95 (ISBN 0-02-782340-7). Macmillan.
Fifty-One Top Quarter Horses: A Pedigree Study. Paul R. Mattson. 1980. pap. 9.95 (ISBN 0-686-28067-9). PRESCOB.
Fifty Plays for Holidays. Ed. by Sylvia E. Kamerman. (gr. 3-6). 1975. Repr. 9.95 (ISBN 0-8238-0033-4). Plays.
Fifty Poems. Boris Pasternak. (Unwin Books). 1963. 6.50 o.p. (ISBN 0-04-891022-8); pap. 2.95 (ISBN 0-04-891023-6). Allen Unwin.
Fifty Poems by E. E. Cummings. 1973. pap. 2.50 (ISBN 0-8015-2616-7, Hawthorn). Dutton.
Fifty Poems for Men & Mice. Tony Woloszyn. 1981. 4.95 (ISBN 0-8062-1594-1). Carlton.
Fifty Poems (with Translation) Hafiz. Ed. by A. J. Arberry. 1947. 44.50 (ISBN 0-521-04039-6). Cambridge U Pr.
Fifty Psalms: A New Translation. Huub Oosterhuis. 1974. pap. 3.50 (ISBN 0-8164-2581-7). Crossroad NY.
Fifty-Second Annual of Advertising, Editorial & Television Art & Design with the 13th Annual Copy Awards. The Art Directors Club of N. Y. & The Copy Club of N. Y. (Illus.). 576p. 1973. slipcased 29.95 o.p. (ISBN 0-8230-1905-5, Pub. by Art Directors Club). Watson-Guptill.
Fifty-Second Annual Yearbook. Ed. by American Bureau of Metal Statistics Editorial Staff. 1973. 25.00 (ISBN 0-685-39802-1). Am Bur Metal.
Fifty-Seven How-To-Do-It Charts. Harry L. Hiett. 1980. pap. 5.00 (ISBN 0-911380-48-5). Signs of Times.
Fifty Short Science Fiction Tales. Ed. by Isaac Asimov & Groff Conklin. 1963. pap. 2.95 (ISBN 0-02-016390-8, Collier). Macmillan.
Fifty Strategies for Experiential Learning: Book One. Ed. by Louis Thayer. LC 75-27735. Orig. Title: Affective Education. 230p. 1976. pap. 13.50 (ISBN 0-88390-108-0). Univ Assocs.
Fifty Strategies for Experimental Learning: Book Two. Ed. by Louis Thayer. 260p. (Orig.). 1981. pap. write for info. (ISBN 0-88390-164-1). Univ Assocs.
Fifty-Two Artists: Photographs by Hans Namuth. Intro. by Hans Namuth. (Illus., Exhibit portfolio). 12.00 (ISBN 0-89062-012-1, Pub. by Comm Visual). Pub Ctr Cult Res.
Fifty-Two Hundred Holley Carburetor Handbook. (Orig.). 1981. pap. 3.95 (ISBN 0-89586-050-3). H P Bks.
Fifty Two Special Day Invitation Illustrations. Billy Apostolon. (Preaching Helps Ser.). pap. 1.95 o.p. (ISBN 0-8010-0082-3). Baker Bk.
Fifty-Two Story Telling Programs. Carl G. Johnson. (Paperback Prog. Ser.). (Orig.). 1964. pap. 2.50 o.p. (ISBN 0-8010-5004-9). Baker Bk.
Fifty Villas of Our Time. R. Aloi. (Illus.). 1970. 40.00 (ISBN 0-685-47307-4). Heinman.
Fifty Ways for Antique Dealers to Beat Inflation. Edwin G. Warman. (Illus.). 1975. 5.95 o.p. (ISBN 0-685-55900-9). Warman.
Fifty Ways to Have Fun with Old Newspapers. Bill Severn. (Illus.). (gr. 3-7). 1977. 7.95 o.p. (ISBN 0-679-20402-4); pap. 3.50 o.p. (ISBN 0-679-20630-2). McKay.
Fifty Years Below Zero. Charles D. Brower. LC 42-22432. (Illus.). 1942. 8.95 (ISBN 0-396-02379-7). Dodd.
Fifty Years of Aviation Knowledge. Frederic H. Breise. 108p. 1981. 9.75 (ISBN 0-938576-00-3). F H Breise.
Fifty Years of English Song, 2 vols. Ed. by Henry F. Randolph. (Illus.). 290p. 1981. Repr. of 1888 ed. lib. bdg. 150.00 (ISBN 0-8495-4574-9). Arden Lib.
Fifty Years of Modern Art 1916-1966. Edward B. Henning. LC 66-21228. (Illus.). 220p. 1966. 17.50x (ISBN 0-910386-06-4, Pub. by Cleveland Mus Art). Ind U Pr.
Fifty Years of Music in Boston. Honor McCusker. 3.00. Boston Public Lib.
Fifty Years of National Progress, 1837-1887. M. G. Mulhall. 126p. 1971. Repr. of 1887 ed. 17.00x (ISBN 0-7165-1584-9, Pub. by Irish Academic Pr Ireland). Biblio Dist.
Fifty Years of Public Service: Personal Recollections of Shelby M. Cullom. Shelby Cullom. LC 75-87504. (American Public Figures Ser). Repr. of 1911 ed. lib. bdg. 45.00 (ISBN 0-306-71410-8). Da Capo.
Fifty Years of Sathers: The Sather Professorship of Classical Literature in the University of California, Berkeley, 1913-14-1963-64. Sterling Dow. 1965. 14.50x (ISBN 0-520-00353-5). U of Cal Pr.
Fifty Years of the Herbalist Almanac: An Anthology. Clarence Meyer. Ed. by David C. Meyer. (Illus.). 1977. pap. 6.95 (ISBN 0-916638-02-2). Meyerbooks.
Fifty Years of Victorian London. Stella Margetson. Date not set. 5.95 o.p. (ISBN 0-8038-7737-4). Hastings.
Fifty Years on the Old Frontier As Cowboy, Hunter, Guide, Scout, & Ranchman. James H. Cook. LC 57-5951. 310p. 1957. 14.95 (ISBN 0-8061-0364-7). U of Okla Pr.
Fifty Years on the Owl Hoot Trail: Jim Herron, the First Sheriff of No Man's Land, Oklahoma Territory. Harrys E. Chrisman & Jim Herron. LC 73-75735. (Illus.). 356p. 1969. 12.00 o.p. (ISBN 0-8040-0114-6, SB); pap. 7.95 (ISBN 0-8040-0614-8, Sb). Swallow.
Fifty Years-The New York Daily News in Pictures. Ed. by Worth Gatewood. LC 78-24843. (Illus.). 1979. 17.95 o.p. (ISBN 0-385-15025-3); pap. 8.95 o.p. (ISBN 0-385-15024-5, Dolp). Doubleday.
Fifty Years with Science. J. G. Crowther. (Illus.). 1970. text ed. 12.50x (ISBN 0-248-65220-6). Humanities.
Figaro. Gerda Scowen. 1981. 4.95 (ISBN 0-8062-1604-2). Carlton.
Figgie Hobbin. Charles Causley. 1974. 4.95 (ISBN 0-8027-6131-3); PLB 4.85 o.s.i. (ISBN 0-8027-6132-1). Walker & Co.
Fight Back: A Woman's Guide to Self-Defense. Emil Farkas & Margaret Leeds. LC 78-2536. (Illus.). 1978. 10.95 o.p. (ISBN 0-03-021051-8); pap. 6.95 o.p. (ISBN 0-03-021056-9). HR&W.
Fight Back: & Don't Get Ripped off. David Horowitz. LC 78-19498. 304p. 1981. pap. 2.95 (ISBN 0-06-250392-8, P 5001, PL). Har-Row.
Fight for Conservation. Gifford Pinchot. LC 10-19948. (Americana Library Ser.: No. 5). 180p. 1967. Repr. of 1910 ed. 10.50 (ISBN 0-295-97861-9, AL5). U of Wash Pr.
Fight for Family Planning. Audrey Leathard. 1980. text ed. 37.50x (ISBN 0-8419-5068-7). Holmes & Meier.
Fight for Freedom. William Lefkowitz. Ed. by Thomas J. Mooney. (Pal Paperbacks Ser., Kit A). (Illus., Orig.). (gr. 7-12). 1976. pap. text ed. 1.25 (ISBN 0-8374-3503-X). Xerox Ed Pubns.
Fight for Peace, 2 vols. Devere Allen. LC 74-147439. (Library of War & Peace; Histories of the Organized Peace Movement). Set. lib. bdg. 76.00 (ISBN 0-8240-0228-8); lib. bdg. 38.00 ea. Garland Pub.
Fight for the Valley. Lee Deighton. 160p. 1981. pap. 1.75 (ISBN 0-345-29076-3). Ballantine.
Fight in the Mountains. Christian Bernhardsen. Tr. by Franey Sinding. LC 68-28800. (gr. 7 up). 1968. 4.50 o.p. (ISBN 0-15-227523-1, HJ). HarBraceJ.
Fight It Out, Work It Out, Love It Out. Claire Pomery. LC 76-56499. 1977. 8.95 o.p. (ISBN 0-385-00468-0). Doubleday.
Fight of the Few. Richard Hough. Date not set. pap. 2.50 (ISBN 0-440-12771-8). Dell.
Fight or Die. Todhunter Ballard. Orig. Title: Westward the Monitors Roar. 1977. pap. 1.50 (ISBN 0-505-51184-3). Tower Bks.
Fightback: For the Sake of the People, for the Sake of the Land. Simon J. Ortiz. LC 80-51953. (Literature Ser.: No. 1). (Orig.). 1980. pap. 6.95 (ISBN 0-934090-03-3). U of NM Nat Am Stud.
Fighter Aces of the U. S. A. Raymond Toliver & Trevor Constable. LC 79-53300. (Illus.). 1979. 24.95 (ISBN 0-8168-5792-X). Aero.
Fighter & Prophet: The Vladimir Jabotinsky Story-the Later Years. Joseph B. Schechtman. (Return to Zion Ser.). (Illus.). 643p. 1981. Repr. of 1961 ed. lib. bdg. 35.00x (ISBN 0-87991-142-5). Porcupine Pr.
Fighter Command: A Study of Air Defence 1914-1960. Peter Wykeham. Ed. by James Gilbert. LC 79-7303. (Flight: Its First Seventy-Five Years Ser.). (Illus.). 1979. Repr. of 1960 ed. lib. bdg. 24.00x (ISBN 0-405-12209-8). Arno.
Fighter Over Finland: The Memorirs of a Fighter Pilot. Eino Luukkanen. Ed. by James Gilbert & William Green. Tr. by Mauno A. Salo. LC 79-7282. (Flight: Its First Seventy-Five Years Ser.). (Illus.). 1979. Repr. of 1963 ed. lib. bdg. 20.00x (ISBN 0-405-12191-1). Arno.
Fighter Pilots of World War II. Robert Jackson. 1977. pap. 1.50 (ISBN 0-505-51192-4). Tower Bks.
Fighter Tactics & Strategy Nineteen Fourteen to Nineteen Seventy. 2nd ed. Edward H. Sims. LC 80-68106. (Illus.). 266p. 1980. 12.95 (ISBN 0-8168-8795-0). Aero.
Fighters. George Bennett & Pete Hamill. LC 77-12839. (Illus.). 1978. pap. 7.95 o.p. (ISBN 0-385-13524-6, Dolp). Doubleday.
Fighters & Lovers: Theme in the Novels of John Updike. Joyce B. Markle. LC 72-96469. 1973. 12.00x (ISBN 0-8147-5362-0). NYU Pr.
Fighters: Attack & Training Aircraft, 1914-1919. Kenneth Munson. (Illus.). 1968. 8.95 (ISBN 0-02-588070-5). Macmillan.
Fighters Defending the Reich. Bryan Philpott. (World War Two Photo Album: No. 4). (Illus.). 96p. 1981. pap. 5.95 (ISBN 0-89404-044-8). Aztex.
Fighters in Service: Attack & Training Aircraft Since 1960. rev. ed. Kenneth Munson. LC 75-12742. (Illus.). 168p. 1975. 8.95 (ISBN 0-02-587960-X, 58796). Macmillan.
Fighters, Nineteen Thirty-Nine to Nineteen Forty-Five: World War Two. Kenneth Munson. (Illus.). 1969. 8.95 (ISBN 0-02-588010-1). Macmillan.
Fighters of World War Two. Charles W. Cain. (Illus.). 128p. 1979. 16.50x (ISBN 0-85383-414-8). Intl Pubns Serv.
Fighters Over the Mediterranean. Bryan Philpott. (World War Two Photo Album: No. 6). (Illus.). 96p. 1981. pap. 6.95 (ISBN 0-89404-048-0). Aztex.
Fighting Back. Rocky Bleier & Terry O'Neil. (Illus.). 288p. 1976. pap. 2.75 (ISBN 0-446-95704-6). Warner Bks.
Fighting Back. rev. ed. Rocky Bleier & Terry O'Neil. LC 75-12865. (Illus.). 240p. 1980. 12.95 (ISBN 0-8128-2767-8). Stein & Day.
Fighting Back. Ronni Sandroff. 1979. pap. 1.95 o.s.i. (ISBN 0-515-05120-9). Jove Pubns.
Fighting Back: A Manual for Survival with Cancer. Margaret C. Keatinge. LC 79-67759. 146p. 1980. 8.95 (ISBN 0-533-04480-4). Vantage.
Fighting Back: How to Cope with the Medical, Emotional, Legal Consequences of Rape. Janet Bode. 1978. 12.95 (ISBN 0-02-512050-6). Macmillan.
Fighting Depression. Harvey Ross. 221p. (Orig.). 1975. pap. 1.95. Larchmont Bks.
Fighting Editor; or, Warren & the Appeal. George D. Brewer. (American Newspapermen 1790-1933 Ser.). 211p. 1974. Repr. of 1910 ed. 14.50x o.s.i. (ISBN 0-8464-0030-8). Beekman Pubs.
Fighting Fisherman: The Life of Yvon Durelle. Raymond Fraser. LC 80-703. (Illus.). 288p. 1981. 11.95 (ISBN 0-385-15863-7). Doubleday.
Fighting for Life: Contest, Sexuality, & Consciousness. Walter J. Ong. LC 80-66968. (Illus.). 240p. 1981. 14.95 (ISBN 0-8014-1342-7). Cornell U Pr.
Fighting Giants: Joshua-Solomon 14 Lessons, Vol. 3. Bernice C. Jordan. (Footsteps of Faith Ser.). (gr. 3-9). 1957. pap. text ed. 1.95 (ISBN 0-86508-031-3); figures 7.95 (ISBN 0-86508-032-1). BCM Inc.
Fighting Indians of the West. Dee Brown & Martin F. Schmitt. 256p. 1975. pap. 1.95 o.p. (ISBN 0-345-24538-5). Ballantine.
Fighting Jane: Mayor Jane Byrne & the Chicago Machine. Bill Granger & Lori Granger. 1980. 12.95 (ISBN 0-8037-2470-5). Dial.
Fighting Knives. Frederick J. Stephens. LC 80-10699. (Illus.). 144p. 1980. 14.95 (ISBN 0-668-04955-3, 4955-3). Arco.
Fighting Mad. Mad Magazine Editors. (Mad Ser.). (Illus.). 192p. 1974. pap. 1.75 (ISBN 0-446-88872-9). Warner Bks.
Fighting Man of Mars. Edgar R. Burroughs. 1976. pap. 1.95 (ISBN 0-345-27840-2). Ballantine.
Fighting Men. Willard Manus. 200p. 1981. 12.95 (ISBN 0-915572-55-9); pap. 6.95 (ISBN 0-915572-54-0). Panjandrum.
Fighting One O Nine: A Pictorial History of the Messerschmitt BF 109 in Action. Uwe Feist et al. LC 77-76232. 1978. 10.50 o.p. (ISBN 0-385-05679-6). Doubleday.
Fighting Racism in World War Ii. George Breitman. 1980. 20.00 (ISBN 0-913460-81-8); pap. 5.95 (ISBN 0-913460-82-6). Monad Pr.
Fighting Ramrod. Charles N. Heckelmann. 1977. pap. 1.25 o.p. (ISBN 0-445-04058-0). Popular Lib.
Fighting Redtails: America's First Black Airmen. Warren Halliburton. LC 78-13173. (Famous Firsts Ser.). (Illus.). 1978. lib. bdg. 7.35 (ISBN 0-686-51098-4). Silver.
Fighting Sail. new ed. A. B. Whipple. Ed. by Time-Life Books. (Seafarers Ser.). (Illus.). 1978. 13.95 (ISBN 0-8094-2654-4). Time-Life.
Fighting Sail. Cal Whipple. LC 78-52043. (Seafarers Ser.). (Illus.). 1978. lib. bdg. 11.97 (ISBN 0-686-50985-4). Silver.
Fighting Ships Nineteen Eighty to Nineteen Eighty-One. Moore. 1980. 135.00 (ISBN 0-531-03937-4). Watts.
Fighting Ships Nineteen Seventy-Nine to Nineteen Eighty. Moore. 1980. 99.50 (ISBN 0-531-03913-7). Watts.
Fighting Submarine. Edwyn Gray. 192p. Date not set. pap. 2.25 (ISBN 0-523-41399-8). Pinnacle Bks.
Fighting Terms. Thom Gunn. 39p. 1970. pap. 1.95 o.p. (ISBN 0-571-09390-6, Pub. by Faber & Faber). Merrimack Bk Serv.
Fighting the Plague in Seventeenth-Century Italy. Carlo M. Cipolla. (Curti Lecture Ser.). 168p. 1981. 13.50 (ISBN 0-299-08340-3); pap. 4.95 (ISBN 0-299-08344-6). U of Wis Pr.
Fighting Whales As Whalers Knew Them. John R. Spears. (American Culture Library Bk). (Illus.). 137p. 1981. 27.45 (ISBN 0-89266-289-1). Am Classical Coll Pr.
Figurae of Joachim of Fiore. Marjorie Reeves & Beatrice Hirsch-Reich. (Oxford-Warburg Studies). (Illus.). 380p. 1972. text ed. 36.00x (ISBN 0-19-920038-6). Oxford U Pr.
Figuras De Plata. Compiled by Pablo Deiros. 1978. pap. 3.15 (ISBN 0-311-42053-2, Edit Mundo). Casa Bautista.
Figurative Tradition & the Whitney Museum of American Art: Paintings & Sculpture from the Permanent Collection. Patricia Hills & Roberta K. Tarbell. LC 80-12650. 192p. 1980. 25.00 (ISBN 0-87413-184-7). U Delaware Pr.
Figure Drawing: Structure, Anatomy & Expressive Design of Human Form. N. Goldstein. 1976. 18.95 (ISBN 0-13-314765-7). P-H.
Figure Drawing: The Structure, Anatomy, & Expressive Design of Human Form. Nathan Goldstein. (Illus.). 330p. 1981. text ed. 20.95 (ISBN 0-13-314518-2); pap. text ed. 17.95 (ISBN 0-13-314435-6). P-H.
Figure It Out. D. P. Barnard. 1976. pap. 1.25 o.p. (ISBN 0-449-13532-2, P3532, GM). Fawcett.
Figure Skating. Noyes. 1979. pap. 3.95 (ISBN 0-8015-2626-4, Hawthorn). Dutton.
Figure Skating. Marion B. Proctor. (Physical Education Activities Ser). 1969. pap. text ed. 3.25x (ISBN 0-697-07011-5); teacher's manual avail. Wm C Brown.
Figure Skating. Carlo Wolter. (First Books). (Illus.). (gr. 4 up). 1977. s&l 6.45 (ISBN 0-531-00396-5). Watts.
Figures of Cricket. S. Vaidya. 4.00x o.p. (ISBN 0-210-33858-X). Asia.
Figures of Reality: A Perspective on the Poetic Imagination. Roger Cardinal. (Illus.). 245p. 1980. 23.50x (ISBN 0-389-20064-6). B&N.
Figurinen der Comedia Dell'arte. Intro. by Karl Riha. (Insel Buecherei: 1007). 100p. pap. 9.10 (ISBN 3-458-19007-4, Pub. by Insel Verlag Germany). Suhrkamp.
Figuring. Sahkuntala Devi. 160p. 1981. pap. 3.95 (ISBN 0-06-463530-9, EH). Har-Row.
Filamentary A-Fifteen Superconductors. Ed. by Masaki Suenaga & Alan F. Clark. (Cryogenic Materials Ser.). 385p. 1980. 45.00 (ISBN 0-306-40622-5). Plenum Pub.
Filamentous Fungi. Ed. by John E. Smith & David Berry. Incl. Vol. 1. Industrial Mycology. LC 75-2101. 340p. 59.00 (ISBN 0-470-80187-5); Vol. 2. Biosynthesis & Metabolism. LC 75-41613. 79.50 (ISBN 0-470-15005-X); Vol. 3. Developmental Mycology. LC 75-2101. 54.95 (ISBN 0-470-99352-9). (Filamentous Fungi Ser.: Vols. 1-3). 1975-78. Halsted Pr.
Filaree. Marguerite Noble. 272p. 1980. pap. 2.50 (ISBN 0-345-28709-6). Ballantine.
Filarete's Treatise on Architecture: Being the Treatise by Antonio Di Piero Averlino, Known As Filarete, 2 Vols. Filarete. Tr. by John R. Spencer. (Publications in the History of Art Ser.: No. 16). (Illus.). 1965. Set. 70.00x o.p. (ISBN 0-300-00970-4). Yale U Pr.
File Management & Information Retrieval Systems: A Manual for Managers & Technicians. Suzanne L. Gill. LC 80-22785. (Illus.). 300p. 1981. lib. bdg. 16.50 (ISBN 0-87287-229-7). Libs Unl.
File on the Tsar. Anthony Summers & Tom Mangold. 1978. pap. 2.50 (ISBN 0-515-04508-X). Jove Pubns.
File Processing with Cobol. Donald Beil. (Illus.). 1981. text ed. 19.95 (ISBN 0-8359-1985-4); pap. text ed. 13.95 (ISBN 0-8359-1984-6). Reston.
Files of the Massachusetts Superior Court, 1859-1959: An Analysis & a Plan for Action. Michael S. Hindus et al. (Reference Publications Ser.). 1980. lib. bdg. 50.00 (ISBN 0-8161-9037-2). G K Hall.
Filet Crochet. F. W. Kettelle. 1978. pap. 1.50 (ISBN 0-486-23745-1). Dover.
Filial Deprivation & Foster Care. Shirley Jenkins & Elaine Norman. LC 72-3564. 320p. 1972. 16.00x (ISBN 0-231-03575-6). Columbia U Pr.
Filigree Architecture: Metal & Glass Construction. (Illus.). 216p. (Eng. Fr. & Ger.). 1980. text ed. 19.00 (ISBN 0-89192-298-9). Interbk Inc.

Filing & Records Management. Irene M. Place & E. L. Popham. 1966. text ed. 12.95x (ISBN 0-13-314625-1). P-H.

Filing Practice Workbook. 3rd ed. Donald Connor. (gr. 9-12). 1975. pap. 2.00 (ISBN 0-8224-2002-3); key 0.96 (ISBN 0-8224-2006-6). Pitman Learning.

Filing: Syllabus. 2nd ed. Joanne Piper. 1979. pap. text ed. 6.95 (ISBN 0-89420-037-2, 327007); cassette recordings 104.25 (ISBN 0-89420-146-8, 106000). Natl Book.

Filing Systems & Records Management. 3rd ed. Jeffrey R. Stewart, Jr. et al. LC 80-21605. (Illus.). 240p. 1981. text ed. 10.95 (ISBN 0-07-061471-7, G); instructor's manual & key avail. (ISBN 0-07-061473-3); practice materials avail. (ISBN 0-07-061472-5). McGraw.

Filipino Immigrant. Dorian Sikat. Date not set. 7.50 (ISBN 0-682-49405-4). Exposition. Postponed.

Filippino Lippi's Strozzi Chapel in Santa Maria Novella. J. Russell Sale. Ed. by Sydney J. Freedberg. LC 78-74376. (Outstanding Dissertations in the Fine Arts Ser.). (Illus.). 1979. lib. bdg. 47.00 (ISBN 0-8240-3963-7). Garland Pub.

Filippo Brunelleschi: The Cupola of Santa Maria Del Fiore. Howard Saalman. (Studies in Architecture). (Illus.). 391p. 1980. 140.00 (ISBN 0-8390-0268-8). Allanheld & Schram.

Filippo Strozzi & the Medici: Favour & Finance in Sixteenth-Century Florence & Rome. Melissa M. Bullard. LC 79-51822. (Cambridge Studies in Early Modern History). 216p. 1980. 24.50 (ISBN 0-521-22301-6). Cambridge U Pr.

Fill the Heavens with Commerce: Chicago Aviation 1855 to 1926. Neal Callahan & David Young. (Illus.). 250p. 1981. 15.00 (ISBN 0-914090-99-2). Chicago Review.

Filled with the Spirit. Robert C. Cunningham. LC 73-190446. 1972. pap. 0.75 (ISBN 0-88243-712-7, 02-0712). Gospel Pub.

Fillers & Extenders for Plastics P-031R. 1977. 525.00 o.p. (ISBN 0-89336-199-2). BCC.

Filling Gaps: An Interpersonal Skills Approach. Anthony Russo. 1978. pap. 6.95 (ISBN 0-89529-044-8). Avery Pub.

Filling the Bill. Aileen Fisher. (Nature Ser). (gr. k-6). 1973. PLB 6.96 (ISBN 0-8372-0864-5); filmstrip & record 18.00 (ISBN 0-8372-0209-4); cassette & filmstrip avail. (ISBN 0-8372-0875-0). Bowmar-Noble.

Filly for Joan. Clarence W. Anderson. (Illus.). (gr. 3-7). 1962. 4.95g o.s.i. (ISBN 0-02-703620-0). Macmillan.

Film: A Reference Guide. Robert A. Armour. LC 79-6566. (American Popular Culture). xxiv, 251p. 1980. lib. bdg. 29.95 (ISBN 0-313-22241-X, AFR/). Greenwood.

Film Actors Guide: Western Europe. James R. Parish. LC 77-22485. 1977. 28.50 (ISBN 0-8108-1044-1). Scarecrow.

Film: An Introduction. John L. Fell. LC 73-18865. (Illus.). 274p. 1975. pap. 10.95 (ISBN 0-02-758911-0). Praeger.

Film and-as Literature. John Harrington. (Illus.). 1977. pap. text ed. 11.95 (ISBN 0-13-315945-0). P-H.

Film & Dreams. Ed. by Vlada Petric. 1981. pap. 8.50 (ISBN 0-913178-61-6). Redgrave Pub Co.

Film & Literature. Morris Beja. 1979. pap. text ed. 10.95 (ISBN 0-582-28094-X). Longman.

Film & TV Graphics, 2. Ed. by Walter Herdeg. (Visual Communication Bks.). (Illus.). 1976. 39.50 (ISBN 0-8038-2322-3). Hastings.

Film Animation As a Hobby. Andrew Hobson & Mark Hobson. LC 75-14523. 60p. 1975. 6.95 o.p. (ISBN 0-8069-5330-6); PLB 6.69 o.p. (ISBN 0-8069-5331-4). Sterling.

Film As Film. V. T. Perkins. (Orig.). 1972. pap. 2.25 o.p. (ISBN 0-14-021477-1, Pelican). Penguin.

Film As Film: Understanding & Judging Movies. V. F. Perkins. lib. bdg. 9.50x o.p. (ISBN 0-88307-423-0). Gannon.

Film Book Bibliography: 1940-1975. Jack Ellis et al. LC 78-4055. 1979. 31.00 (ISBN 0-8108-1127-8). Scarecrow.

Film Career of Alain Robbe-Grillet. William Van Wert. Ed. by Ronald Gottesman. (Three Directors Set). 1979. pap. 7.80 (ISBN 0-913178-58-6). Redgrave Pub Co.

Film Career of Alain Robbe-Grillet. William F. Van Wert. (Orig.). 1979. pap. 7.80 (ISBN 0-913178-59-4, Pub. by Two Continents). Hippocrene Bks.

Film Career of Billy Wilder. Steve Seidman. Ed. by Ronald Gottesman. (Three Director Set). 1978. pap. 7.80 (ISBN 0-913178-58-6). Redgrave Pub Co.

Film Career of Buster Keaton. George Wead & George Lellis. Ed. by Ronald Gottesman. (Three Director Set). 1978. pap. 7.80 (ISBN 0-913178-57-8). Redgrave Pub Co.

Film-Cinema-Movie: A Theory of Experience. Gerald Mast. LC 75-34679. (Illus.). 256p. 1977. 17.50 o.p. (ISBN 0-06-012822-4, HarpT). Har-Row.

Film Composers in America: A Checklist of Their Work. Clifford McCarty. LC 72-4448. (Music Ser.). 196p. 1972. Repr. of 1953 ed. lib. bdg. 19.50 (ISBN 0-306-70495-1). Da Capo.

Film Criticism: An Index to Critics' Anthologies. Richard Heinzkill. LC 75-20159. 1975. 10.00 (ISBN 0-8108-0840-4). Scarecrow.

Film Directors: A Guide to Their American Films. James R. Parish & Michael R. Pitts. LC 74-17398. (Illus.). 1974. 18.50 (ISBN 0-8108-0752-1). Scarecrow.

Film Directors Guide: Western Europe. James R. Parish et al. LC 76-1891. (Illus.). 1976. 13.50 (ISBN 0-8108-0908-7). Scarecrow.

Film Experience. Roy Huss & Norman Silverstein. LC 67-28833. (Illus.). 1968. 8.95 o.p. (ISBN 0-06-032967-X, HarpT). Har-Row.

Film Facts. Cobbett Steinberg. 350p. 1980. 17.95 (ISBN 0-87196-313-2). Facts on File.

Film Form. Sergei Eisenstein. LC 49-8349. 1969. pap. 3.95 (ISBN 0-15-630920-3, HB153, Harv). HarBraceJ.

Film: Form & Function. George Wead & Geore Lellis. LC 80-82804. (Illus.). 512p. 1981. pap. text ed. 12.95 (ISBN 0-395-29740-0). HM.

Film Genre: Theory & Criticism. Ed. by Barry K. Grant. LC 77-8908. 1977. 12.00 (ISBN 0-8108-1059-X). Scarecrow.

Film: Historical-Theoretical Speculations. Buscombe et al. Ed. by Ben Lawton & Janet Staiger. (Film Studies Annual, 1977: Pt. 2). (Orig.). 1977. pap. 6.00 (ISBN 0-913178-53-5). Redgrave Pub Co.

Film in History: Restaging the Past. Pierre Sorlin. (Illus.). 226p. 1980. 21.50x (ISBN 0-389-20130-8). B&N.

Film in the Third Reich: A Study of the German Cinema, 1933-1945. David S. Hull. 1969. 17.50 (ISBN 0-520-01489-8). U of Cal Pr.

Film Library Techniques: Principles of Administration. Helen P. Harrison. (Studies in Media Management). Date not set. 17.50 (ISBN 0-8038-2294-4). Hastings.

Film Makers on Film Making. Ed. by Harry M. Geduld. LC 67-25134. (Midland Bks.: No. 104). 1967. Repr. 10.00x o.p. (ISBN 0-253-12600-2). Ind U Pr.

Film Music: From Violins to Video. James L. Limbacher. LC 73-16153. 1974. 25.00 (ISBN 0-8108-0651-7). Scarecrow.

Film on the Left: American Documentary Film from 1931 to 1942. William Alexander. LC 80-8534. (Illus.). 364p. 1981. 27.50x (ISBN 0-691-04678-6); pap. 12.50x (ISBN 0-691-10111-6). Princeton U Pr.

Film Programmer's Guide to 16mm Rentals. 3rd ed. Ed. by Kathleen Weaver. 1980. pap. 21.25 (ISBN 0-934456-02-X). Reel Res.

Film: Readings in the Mass Media. Allen Kirschner. LC 70-158977. 1971. pap. 7.50 (ISBN 0-672-73221-1). Odyssey Pr.

Film: Real to Reel. rev. ed. David Coynik. (Illus., Orig.). 1976. pap. text ed. 10.95 scp (ISBN 0-06-382530-9, HarpC). Har-Row.

Film Review Annual, 1979. Ed. by Jerome S. Ozer. 1980. lib. bdg. 60.00x (ISBN 0-89198-124-1). Ozer.

Film Review, Nineteen Seventy-Seven to Seventy-Eight. Ed. by F. Maurice Speed. (Illus.). 1978. 15.00 (ISBN 0-491-02211-5). Transatlantic.

Film Review: 1979-1980. F. Maurice Speed. (Illus.). 1980. 8.95 (ISBN 0-8015-2632-9, Hawthorn). Dutton.

Film Scripts Four: A Hard Day's Night, The Best Man, Darling. Ed. by George P. Garrett et al. LC 71-135273. (Orig.). 1972. Set. 18.95x (ISBN 0-89197-162-9); pap. text ed. 8.95x ea.; instruc. manual free avail. Irvington.

Film Scripts Three: The Apartment, The Misfits, Charade. Ed. by George P. Garrett et al. LC 71-135273. (Orig.). 1972. pap. 18.95x set (ISBN 0-89197-165-3); pap. text ed. 8.95x ea.; instructor's manual free avail. (ISBN 0-685-26613-3). Irvington.

Film Scripts Two: High Noon, Twelve Angry Men, The Defiant Ones. Ed. by George P. Garrett et al. LC 71-135273. (Orig.). 1971. pap. 16.50x set (ISBN 0-89197-165-3); pap. text ed. 6.95x ea.; instructor's manual free avail. (ISBN 0-8290-0137-9). Irvington.

Film Sense. Sergei Eisenstein. LC 47-6064. 1969. pap. 4.95 (ISBN 0-15-630935-1, HB154, Harv). HarBraceJ.

Film Service Profiles. Compiled by Kay Salz. LC 80-10394. 56p. (Orig.). 1980. pap. 5.00 (ISBN 0-935654-00-3, Pub. by Ctr for Arts Info). Pub Ctr Cult Res.

Film Seventy-Two to Seventy-Three: An Anthology by the National Association of Film Critics. Ed. by David Denby. LC 73-1746. 304p. 1973. 7.95 o.p. (ISBN 0-685-32270-X); pap. 3.95 o.p. (ISBN 0-672-51871-6). Bobbs.

Film-Star Portraits of the Fifties: 163 Glamor Photos. John Kobal. (Illus.). 164p. (Orig.). 1980. pap. 6.95 (ISBN 0-486-24008-8). Dover.

Film Theory & Criticism: Introductory Readings. 2nd ed. Ed. by Gerald Mast & Marshall Cohen. (Illus.). 1979. 26.95x (ISBN 0-19-502503-2); pap. text ed. 9.95x (ISBN 0-19-502498-2). Oxford U Pr.

Filmarama: The Flaming Years, 1920-1929, Vol. 2. Compiled by John Stewart. LC 75-2440. 1977. 30.00 (ISBN 0-8108-1008-5). Scarecrow.

Filmarama: The Formidable Years, 1893-1919, Vol. 1. Compiled by John Stewart. LC 75-2440. 401p. 1975. 18.00 (ISBN 0-8108-0802-1). Scarecrow.

Filmgoer's Companion. Leslie Halliwell. 1978. pap. 9.95 (ISBN 0-380-00430-5, 50419). Avon.

Filmguide to Henry V. Harry M. Geduld. LC 73-75788. (Filmguide Ser: No. 7). 96p. 1973. 5.00x (ISBN 0-253-39313-2); pap. 1.75x (ISBN 0-253-29314-6). Ind U Pr.

Filmguide to la Passion de Jeanne d'arc. David Bordwell. LC 72-88634. (Filmguide Ser: No. 1). 96p. 1973. 5.00x (ISBN 0-253-39301-9); pap. 1.75 (ISBN 0-253-39302-7). Ind U Pr.

Filmguide to The General. E. Rubinstein. LC 72-88637. (Filmguide Ser: No. 5). 96p. 1973. 5.00x (ISBN 0-253-39309-4); pap. 1.75x (ISBN 0-253-39310-8). Ind U Pr.

Filmguide to Two Thousand One: A Space Odyssey. Carolyn Geduld. LC 72-88635. (Filmguide Ser.: No. 3). 96p. 1973. 5.00x (ISBN 0-253-39305-1); pap. 1.75x (ISBN 0-253-39306-X). Ind U Pr.

Filming for Television. A. Arthur Englander & Paul Petzold. (Library of Film & Television Practice). Date not set. 21.50 (ISBN 0-8038-2320-7). Hastings.

Filming Sports: The How-to Book for Coaches, Sports Information Directors, Motion Picture - Still Sports Photographers (S-65) Ed. by Eastman Kodak Company. (Illus.). 288p. (Orig.). 1981. pap. 19.95 (ISBN 0-87985-268-2). Eastman Kodak.

Filmography of the Third World: An Annotated List of 16mm Films. Helen W. Cyr. LC 76-22584. 1976. 13.50 (ISBN 0-8108-0940-0). Scarecrow.

FilmRow Executive BlackBook. Ralph Zucker. 400p. 1981. pap. write for info. (ISBN 0-686-27694-9). Filmrow Pubns.

Filmrow: The Executive BlackBook of the Theatrical Motion Picture Marketing Business. Ralph Zucker. 400p. (Orig.). 1981. write for info. Filmrow Pubns.

Films & Coatings for High Technology Applications. Rointan F. Bunshah. (Engineering Ser.). (Illus.). 600p. 1981. text ed. 60.00 o.p. (ISBN 0-686-69160-1). Lifetime Learn.

Films Ex Libris: Literature in Sixteen mm & Video. Salvatore J. Parlato. LC 80-10181. (Illus.). 283p. 1980. lib. bdg. 15.95x (ISBN 0-89950-006-4). McFarland & Co.

Films in the Classroom: A Practical Guide. Hannah E. Miller. LC 78-21941. 1979. lib. bdg. 13.50 (ISBN 0-8108-1184-7). Scarecrow.

Films of Alan Ladd. Marilyn Henry & Ron DeSourdis. (Illus.). 256p. 1981. 16.95 (ISBN 0-8065-0736-5). Citadel Pr.

Films of Alfred Hitchcock. Michael S. Lasky & Robert A. Harris. (Illus.). pap. 7.95 (ISBN 0-8065-0619-9). Citadel Pr.

Films of Anthony Quinn. Alvin H. Marill. 1977. pap. 6.95 (ISBN 0-8065-0570-2). Citadel Pr.

Films of Barbara Streisand. David Castell. (Films of...Ser.). (Illus.). (gr. 7-12). 1978. Repr. of 1974 ed. PLB 5.95 (ISBN 0-912616-78-4). Greenhaven.

Films of Bela Lugosi. Richard Bojarski. 1980. 16.95 (ISBN 0-8065-5071-6). Lyle Stuart.

Films of Carl-Theodor Dreyer. David Bordwell. 1981. 23.50 (ISBN 0-520-03987-4). U of Cal Pr.

Films of Charlton Heston. Jeff Rovin. (Films of...Ser.). (Illus.). 256p. 1980. pap. 7.95 (ISBN 0-8065-0741-1). Citadel Pr.

Films of Charlton Heston. John Williams. Ed. by David Castell. (Films of...Ser.). (Illus.). (gr. 7-12). 1978. Repr. of 1974 ed. PLB 5.95 (ISBN 0-912616-80-6). Greenhaven.

Films of Clint Eastwood. Mark Whitman. Ed. by David Castell. (Films of...Ser.). (Illus.). (gr. 7-12). 1978. Repr. of 1973 ed. PLB 5.95 (ISBN 0-912616-75-X). Greenhaven.

Films of Elizabeth Taylor. Susan D'Arcy. Ed. by David Castell. (Films of...Ser.). (Illus.). (gr. 7-12). 1978. Repr. of 1974 ed. PLB 5.95 (ISBN 0-912616-83-0). Greenhaven.

Films of Ingrid Bergman. Lawrence J. Quirk. (Illus.). 226p. 1975. pap. 6.95 (ISBN 0-8065-0480-3). Citadel Pr.

Films of Jack Nicholson. Bruce Braithwaite. Ed. by David Castell. (Films of...Ser.). (Illus.). (gr. 7-12). 1978. Repr. PLB 5.95 (ISBN 0-912616-76-8). Greenhaven.

Films of Jacques Tati. Brent Maddock. LC 77-11084. 1977. 10.00 (ISBN 0-8108-1065-4). Scarecrow.

Films of James Dean. Mark Whitman. Ed. by David Castell. (Films of...Ser.). (Illus.). (gr. 7-12). 1978. Repr. of 1974 ed. PLB 5.95 (ISBN 0-912616-88-1). Greenhaven.

Films of Jane Fonda. George Haddad-Garcia. (Illus.). 256p. 1981. 16.95 (ISBN 0-8065-0752-7). Citadel Pr.

Films of John Garfield. Howard Gelman. 1977. pap. 6.95 (ISBN 0-8065-0620-2). Citadel Pr.

Films of Judy Garland. Brian Baxter. Ed. by David Castell. (Films of...Ser.). (Illus.). (gr. 7-12). 1978. Repr. of 1974 ed. PLB 5.95 (ISBN 0-912616-81-4). Greenhaven.

Films of Leni Riefenstahl. David B. Hinton. LC 78-7036. 1978. 10.00 (ISBN 0-8108-1141-3). Scarecrow.

Films of Liza Minelli. Susan D'Arcy. Ed. by David Castell. (Films of...Ser.). (Illus.). (gr. 7-12). 1978. Repr. of 1973 ed. PLB 5.95 (ISBN 0-912616-82-2). Greenhaven.

Films of Marlon Brando. Bruce Braithwaite. Ed. by David Castell. (Films of...Ser.). (Illus.). (gr. 7-12). 1978. Repr. of 1974 ed. PLB 5.95 (ISBN 0-912616-86-5). Greenhaven.

Films of Michael Caine. Emma Andrews. Ed. by David Castell. (Films of...Ser.). (Illus.). (gr. 7-12). 1978. Repr. of 1974 ed. PLB 5.95 (ISBN 0-912616-90-3). Greenhaven.

Films of Myrna Loy. Lawrence J. Quirk. 1980. 16.95 (ISBN 0-8065-0735-7). Lyle Stuart.

Films of Norma Shearer. Jack Jacobs & Myron Braum. LC 74-9286. (Illus.). 320p. 1976. 17.50 o.p. (ISBN 0-498-01552-1). A S Barnes.

Films of Paul Newman. Kenneth Thompson. Ed. by David Castell. (Films of...Ser.). (Illus.). (gr. 7-12). 1978. Repr. of 1974 ed. PLB 5.95 (ISBN 0-912616-87-3). Greenhaven.

Films of Rita Hayworth. Gene Ringgold. 1977. pap. 6.95 (ISBN 0-8065-0574-5). Citadel Pr.

Films of Robert Redford. David Castell. (Films of... Ser.). (Illus.). (gr. 7-12). 1978. Repr. of 1973 ed. PLB 5.95 (ISBN 0-912616-77-6). Greenhaven.

Films of Robert Taylor. Lawrence J. Quirk. (Illus.). 1979. pap. 6.95 (ISBN 0-8065-0667-9). Citadel Pr.

Films of Roger Moore. John Williams. Ed. by David Castell. (Films of...Ser.). (Illus.). (gr. 7-12). 1979. Repr. of 1974 ed. PLB 5.95 (ISBN 0-912616-89-X). Greenhaven.

Films of Ronald Colman. Lawrence J. Quirk. (Illus.). 1979. pap. 6.95 (ISBN 0-8065-0668-7). Citadel Pr.

Films of Sean Connery. Emma Andrews. Ed. by David Castell. (Films of...Ser.). (Illus.). (gr. 7-12). 1978. Repr. of 1974 ed. PLB 5.95 (ISBN 0-912616-85-7). Greenhaven.

Films of Sherlock Holmes. Chris Steinbrunner & Norman Michaels. 1980. pap. 9.95 (ISBN 0-8065-0739-X). Lyle Stuart.

Films of Shirley MacLaine. Patricia Erens. LC 76-50188. (Illus.). 1978. 17.50 (ISBN 0-498-01993-4); pap. 7.95 o.p. (ISBN 0-498-02302-8). A S Barnes.

Films of Sophia Loren. Tony Crawley. (Illus.). pap. 6.95 (ISBN 0-8065-0700-4). Citadel Pr.

Films of Steve McQueen. Joanna Campbell. Ed. by David Castell. (Films of... Ser.). (Illus.). (gr. 7-12). 1978. Repr. of 1973 ed. PLB 5.95 (ISBN 0-912616-84-9). Greenhaven.

Films of Tennessee Williams. Gene D. Phillips. LC 76-50204. (Illus.). 256p. 1980. 20.00 o.p. (ISBN 0-87982-025-X). Art Alliance.

Films of the Fifties. Andrew Dowdy. LC 75-2132. 242p. 1975. 6.95 o.p. (ISBN 0-688-00198-X); pap. 3.50 o.p. (ISBN 0-688-05198-7). Morrow.

Films of the Forties. Tony Thomas. 1977. pap. 6.95 (ISBN 0-8065-0571-0). Citadel Pr.

Films of Vincent Price. Iain F. McAsh. Ed. by David Castell. (Films of...Ser.). (Illus.). (gr. 7-12). 1978. Repr. of 1973 ed. PLB 5.95 (ISBN 0-912616-79-2). Greenhaven.

Films of William Holden. Lawrence J. Quirk. 256p. 1973. 12.00 (ISBN 0-8065-0375-0); pap. 6.95 (ISBN 0-8065-0517-6). Citadel Pr.

Films on Film History. Anthony Slide. LC 79-17662. 242p. 1979. 13.00 (ISBN 0-8108-1238-X). Scarecrow.

Films on Solid Surfaces. J. G. Dash. 1975. 42.50 (ISBN 0-12-203350-7). Acad Pr.

Filmstrips. LaMond F. Beatty. Ed. by James E. Duane. LC 80-21338. (Instructional Media Library: Vol. 4). (Illus.). 104p. 1981. 13.95 (ISBN 0-87778-164-8). Educ Tech Pubns.

Fils Du Fauconnier. Ed. by Louise C. Seibert & Lester G. Crocker. (Fr.). 1963. pap. text ed. 6.95x (ISBN 0-684-41431-7, ScribC). Scribner.

Filters & Filtration. R. H. Warring. (Illus.). 1969. 35.00x (ISBN 0-85461-025-1). Intl Ideas.

Fin M'Coul: The Giant of Knockmany Hill. Illus. & retold by Tomie De Paola. LC 80-2254. (Illus.). 32p. (ps-3). 1981. PLB 10.95 (ISBN 0-8234-0384-X); pap. 4.95 (ISBN 0-8234-0385-8). Holiday.

Final Act. Inter-American Statistical Conference - 6th - Santiago, Chile - 1972. (Eng, Fr, Port, & Span.). pap. 1.00 ea. o.p. OAS.

Final Act: Meeting of Consultation. Ministers of Foreign Affairs of the American Republics-5th-Santiago-Chile 1959. (Port. & Fr.). pap. 1.00 ea. o.p. OAS.

Final Act: Meeting of Consultation. Ministers of Foreign Affairs of the American Republics-6th-San Jose-Costa Rica-1960. (Sp.). pap. 1.00 (ISBN 0-8270-1675-1). OAS.

Final Act: Meeting of Consultation. Ministers of Foreign Affairs of the American Republics-7th-San Jose-Costa Rica-1960. (Sp.). pap. 1.00 (ISBN 0-8270-1700-6). OAS.

Final Act: Meeting of Consultation. Ministers of Foreign Affairs of the American Republic-8th-Punta Del Este-Uruguay-1962. (Eng., Span. & Port.). pap. 1.00 ea. o.p. OAS.

Final Act: Meeting of Consultation. Ministers of Foreign Affairs of the American Republics-12th-Washington D. C.-1968. (Span. & Eng.). pap. 1.00 Eng. ed. (ISBN 0-8270-1735-9); pap. 1.00 Span ed. (ISBN 0-8270-1740-5). OAS.

Final Act: Meeting of Consultation. Ministers of Foreign Affairs of the American Republics-15th Quito, Ecuador. (Eng., Span., Fr.). 1974. pap. 1.00 Eng. ed. (ISBN 0-8270-1745-6); pap. 1.00 Span. ed. (ISBN 0-8270-1750-2); pap. 1.00 French ed. (ISBN 0-8270-1755-3). OAS.

Final Conflict: Omen III. Gordon McGill. (Orig.). 1980. pap. 2.50 (ISBN 0-451-09584-7, E9584, Sig). NAL.

Final Contributions to the Problems & Methods of Psycho-Analysis. Sandor Ferenczi. Ed. by Michael Balint. Tr. by Eric Mosbacher from Ger. LC 80-19817. (Brunner-Mazel Classics in Psychoanalysis Ser.: No. 8). 450p. 1980. Repr. of 1955 ed. 20.00 (ISBN 0-87630-256-8). Brunner-Mazel.

Final Countdown. Martin Caidin. 240p. (Orig.). 1980. pap. 2.25 (ISBN 0-553-12155-3). Bantam.

Final Countdown. R. H. Pierson & G. S. Stevenson. LC 66-23433. (Stories That Win Ser.). 1966. pap. 0.95 o.p. (ISBN 0-8163-0118-2, 06100-2). Pacific Pr Pub Assn.

Final Curtain. Ngaio Marsh. 288p. 1980. pap. 1.95 (ISBN 0-515-05554-9). Jove Pubns.

Final Days. Woodward & Carl Bernstein. 1976. pap. 2.50 (ISBN 0-380-00844-0, 31104). Avon.

Final Death, No. 29. Warren Murphy. (Destroyer Ser.). 1977. pap. 1.75 (ISBN 0-523-40885-4). Pinnacle Bks.

Final Deduction. Rex Stout. 144p. 1981. pap. 1.95 (ISBN 0-553-12205-3). Bantam.

Final Edition. Arthur Miller. 384p. (Orig.). 1981. pap. 2.75 (ISBN 0-523-41170-7). Pinnacle Bks.

Final Events on Planet Earth. Norman R. Gulley. LC 77-24206. (Horizon Ser.). 1977. pap. 4.50 (ISBN 0-8127-0144-5). Southern Pub.

Final Fortress: The Campaign for Vicksburg, 1862-1863. Samuel Carter, III. (Illus.). 384p. 1980. 19.95 (ISBN 0-312-28943-X). St Martin.

Final Hour. Taylor Caldwell. 608p. 1978. pap. 2.95 (ISBN 0-449-24221-8, Crest). Fawcett.

Final Larval Instars of the Ichneumonidae. John Short. (Memoir Ser.: No. 25). (Illus.). 508p. 1978. 35.00 (ISBN 0-686-26663-3). Am Entom Inst.

Final Notice. Jonathan Valin. LC 80-16654. 256p. 1980. 8.95 (ISBN 0-396-07898-2). Dodd.

Final Payments. Mary Gordon. 320p. 1981. pap. 2.75 (ISBN 0-345-29554-4). Ballantine.

Final Proof. Marie Reno. 1977. pap. 1.25 o.p. (ISBN 0-445-04059-9). Popular Lib.

Final Report. Lagos Conference, 1964. 1964. pap. 2.50 (ISBN 92-3-100565-0, U243, UNESCO). Unipub.

Final Solution. rev. ed. Gerald Reitlinger. 1961. pap. 4.95 o.p. (ISBN 0-498-04021-6, Prpta). A S Barnes.

Final Statistical Report of the Federal Emergency Relief Administration. U. S. Federal Works Agency. LC 76-179755. (FDR & the Era of the New Deal Ser). 406p. 1972. Repr. of 1942 ed. lib. bdg. 42.50 (ISBN 0-306-70455-2). Da Capo.

Final Take. Paul Peterson. 1980. pap. write for info. (ISBN 0-671-81678-0). PB.

Final Testimonies. Karl Barth. LC 77-8088. 1977. 3.95 o.p. (ISBN 0-8028-3497-3). Eerdmans.

Final Verdict. Adela R. St. Johns. pap. 2.50 (ISBN 0-451-07994-9, E7994, Sig). NAL.

Finality & Intelligence. Leszek Figurski. LC 78-62252. 1978. pap. text ed. 9.00 (ISBN 0-8191-0565-1). U Pr of Amer.

Finality of Faith. James D. Bales. pap. 2.50 (ISBN 0-89315-051-7). Lambert Bk.

Finality Testament: Book of Life. Kevin Templin. 1981. 5.75 (ISBN 0-8062-1679-4). Carlton.

Finally Home. Juliann DeKorte. (Illus.). 1977. 5.95 o.p. (ISBN 0-8007-0934-9). Revell.

Finally It's Friday: School & Work in Mid-America, 1921-1933. Loren Reid. 288p. 1981. 19.95 (ISBN 0-8262-0330-2). U of Mo Pr.

Finance & Enterprise in Early America: A Study of Stephen Girard's Bank, 1812-1831. Donald R. Adams, Jr. LC 77-20301. 1978. 15.00x (ISBN 0-8122-7736-8). U of Pa Pr.

Finance & Industrialization in the Austro-Hungarian Empire, 1873-1914. R. L. Rudolph. LC 75-2736. (Illus.). 350p. 1976. 47.50 (ISBN 0-521-20878-5). Cambridge U Pr.

Finance & Protection of Investments in Developing Countries. Ingrid Delupis. LC 73-12149. 183p. 1973. 27.95 (ISBN 0-470-20637-3). Halsted Pr.

Finance & Trade. Fred Sanderson & Harold Cleveland. LC 74-78422. (Policy Papers Ser.: The Washington Papers, No. 14). 1974. 3.50x (ISBN 0-8039-0443-6). Sage.

Finance As a Dynamic Process. Edwain J. Elton & Martin J. Gruber. (Foundations of Finance Ser.). (Illus.). 176p. 1975. ref. ed. 14.95 (ISBN 0-13-314690-1); pap. text ed. 10.95 (ISBN 0-13-314682-0). P-H.

Finance Capital: A Study of the Latest Phase of Capitalist Development. Rudolf Hilferding. Tr. by Tom Bottomore from Ger. 500p. 1981. 60.00 (ISBN 0-7100-0618-7). Routledge & Kegan.

Finance Dictionary, German-English, English-German. Friedrich K. Feldbausch. 205p. 1972. 18.75x o.p. (ISBN 0-900537-02-7, Dist. by Hippocrene Books Inc.). Leviathan Hse.

Finance for Managers. Walter S. Goff. 296p. 1980. pap. text ed. 14.95x (ISBN 0-7121-0636-7). Intl Ideas.

Finance for the Non-Accountant. 3rd ed. L. E. Rockley. 337p. 1979. pap. 12.25x (ISBN 0-220-67022-6, Pub. by Busn Bks England). Renouf.

Finance for the Nonfinancial Manager. Herbert T. Spiro. LC 76-56371. 1977. 19.95 (ISBN 0-471-01788-4, Pub. by Wiley-Interscience). Wiley.

Finance for the Nonfinancial Manager, Student Edition. Herbert T. Spiro. LC 76-56371. 1978. 19.95x (ISBN 0-471-04803-8, Pub. by Wiley-Interscience); tchr's manual avail. (ISBN 0-471-05952-8). Wiley.

Finance for the Purchasing Executive. L. E. Rockley. 191p. 1978. text ed. 24.50x (ISBN 0-220-66362-9, Pub. by Busn Bks England). Renouf.

Finance in China. Srinvas Wagel. LC 78-74334. (Modern Chinese Economy Ser.). 447p. 1980. lib. bdg. 55.00 (ISBN 0-8240-4268-9). Garland Pub.

Finance of International Trade. Brian Kettell. LC 80-28878. (Illus.). xviii, 175p. 1981. lib. bdg. 40.00 (ISBN 0-89930-011-1, KFI/, Quorum Bks). Greenwood.

Finance of Local Government. 6th rev. ed. N. P. Hepworth. (New Local Government Ser.: No. 6). 328p. 1981. pap. text ed. 15.95x (ISBN 0-04-352087-1, 2405). Allen Unwin.

Finances of Europe. Daniel Strasser. LC 77-24408. (Praeger Special Studies). 1977. text ed. 31.95 (ISBN 0-03-022386-5). Praeger.

Financial Accounting. 3rd ed. James J. Benjamin et al. LC 80-67311. (Illus.). 737p. 1980. pap. text ed. 18.95 (ISBN 0-931920-21-3); practice problems 4.95x; study guide 5.95x; work papers 6.95x. Dame Pubns.

Financial Accounting. 3rd ed. Bierman. 1978. 20.95 (ISBN 0-7216-1704-2). Dryden Pr.

Financial Accounting. R. M. Copeland et al. LC 79-18276. 1980. 19.95 (ISBN 0-471-17173-5); working papers & study guide avail. Wiley.

Financial Accounting. William W. Pyle & Kermit D. Larson. 1980. 19.50x (ISBN 0-256-02259-3). Irwin.

Financial Accounting. K. Fred Skousen et al. 1981. text ed. write for info. (ISBN 0-87901-156-4); write or info. study guide (ISBN 0-87901-157-2); write for info. practice set, vol. 2 (ISBN 0-87901-159-9); price not set practice set, vol. 2 (ISBN 0-87901-160-2); write for info. working papers (ISBN 0-87901-158-0). Worth.

Financial Accounting: A Basic Approach. Albert Slavin et al. 756p. 1980. text ed. 19.95 (ISBN 0-03-048906-7). Dryden Pr.

Financial Accounting: A Distillation of Experience. George O. May. 1972. Repr. of 1943 ed. text ed. 13.00 (ISBN 0-914348-05-1). Scholars Bk.

Financial Accounting: A Programmed Text. 4th ed. James D. Edwards et al. 1978. Vol. 1. text ed. 17.95x (ISBN 0-256-02010-8); Vol. 2. text ed. 14.50x (ISBN 0-256-02008-6); work papers 6.50x (ISBN 0-256-02013-2); Vol. 2. work papers 6.50x (ISBN 0-256-02015-9); Vol. 1. study guide & review manual 5.50x (ISBN 0-256-02011-6); Vol. 2. study guide & review manual 5.50x (ISBN 0-256-02009-4); mini-practice set 4.00x (ISBN 0-256-02014-0). Irwin.

Financial Accounting: An Events Approach. William J. Schrader et al. 520p. 1981. text ed. 18.95x (ISBN 0-931920-29-9). Dame Pubns.

Financial Accounting: An Introductory Study. J. L. Livingstone & Harry D. Kerrigan. LC 76-5615. (Accounting Ser.). 1977. text ed. 19.95 o.p. (ISBN 0-88244-100-0). Grid Pub.

Financial Accounting: Basic Concepts. 3rd. ed. Earl A. Spiller, Jr. 1977. text ed. 19.50 (ISBN 0-256-01906-1). Irwin.

Financial Accounting Concepts. 2nd ed. James H. Rossell & William Frasure. (Business Ser.). 1974. 19.95 (ISBN 0-675-08860-7); instructor's manual 3.95 (ISBN 0-686-67215-1). Merrill.

Financial Accounting: Concepts & Principles. David F. Fetyko. 768p. 1980. text ed. 17.95x (ISBN 0-534-00753-8, Kent Pub.); guide 6.95xstudy (ISBN 0-534-00851-8); papers 6.95xworking (ISBN 0-534-00846-1). Kent Pub Co.

Financial Accounting: Concepts & Uses. 2nd ed. Rudolph W. Schattke & Howard G. Jensen. 1978. text ed. 19.95 (ISBN 0-205-05901-5); transparencies avail. (ISBN 0-205-05902-3); checklist avail. (ISBN 0-205-05903-1); practice set 5.95 (ISBN 0-205-05904-X); sol. man. avail. (ISBN 0-205-05905-8); study guide 6.95 (ISBN 0-205-05906-6); working papers 6.95 (ISBN 0-205-05907-4); tests avail. (ISBN 0-205-05908-2); sample pkg. avail. (ISBN 0-205-05909-0). Allyn.

Financial Accounting Estimates Through Statistical Sampling by Computer. Maurice S. Newman. LC 76-23400. (Systems & Controls for Financial Management Ser.). 27.95 (ISBN 0-471-01567-9). Ronald Pr.

Financial Accounting Information: An Introduction to Its Preparation & Use. A. T. Montgomery. LC 77-83023. 1978. text ed. 17.95 (ISBN 0-201-04924-4); instr's man. avail. (ISBN 0-201-04923-6). A-W.

Financial Accounting: Principles & Issues. 2nd ed. Michael H. Granof. (Illus.). 1980. text ed. 19.95 (ISBN 0-13-314153-5). P-H.

Financial Administration of the Church. Ed. by William Bassett & Peter Huizing. (Concilium Ser.: Vol. 117). (Orig.). 1978. pap. 4.95 (ISBN 0-8164-2197-8). Crossroad NY.

Financial Administration Under the T'ang Dynasty. D. C. Twitchett. 54.00 (ISBN 0-521-07823-7). Cambridge U Pr.

Financial Advice for Physicians. John N. Sheagren. 132p. 1972. text ed. 11.75 (ISBN 0-398-02409-X). C C Thomas.

Financial Aid Through Social Work. Michael P. Jackson & B. Michael Valencia. (Library of Social Work Ser.). 1979. 17.00x (ISBN 0-7100-0176-2). Routledge & Kegan.

Financial Analysis & Business Decisions on the Pocket Calculator. Jon M. Smith. LC 75-39752. (Systems & Controls for Financial Management Ser.). 320p. 1976. 21.50 (ISBN 0-471-80184-4, Pub. by Wiley-Interscience). Wiley.

Financial Analysis & the New Community Development Process. Richard L. Heroux & William A. Wallace. LC 72-92458. (Special Studies in U.S. Economic, Social, & Political Issues). 1973. 28.50x (ISBN 0-275-28646-0). Irvington.

Financial Analysis: Principles & Procedures. Jerry Viscione. LC 76-13794. (Illus.). 1977. pap. text ed. 9.50 (ISBN 0-395-24455-2); inst. manual with solutions 1.50 (ISBN 0-395-24454-4). HM.

Financial Analyst's Handbook. Ed. by Summer N. Levine. Incl. Vol. 1. Portfolio Management. 1540p. 37.50 (ISBN 0-87094-082-1); Vol. 2. Analysis by Industry. 1032p. o.p. (ISBN 0-87094-083-X). LC 74-81386. 1975. Dow Jones-Irwin.

Financial & Accounting Guide for Nonprofit Organizations. 3rd ed. Malvern J. Gross, Jr. & William Warshauer, Jr. 1979. 32.50 (ISBN 0-471-04974-3). Ronald Pr.

Financial & Accounting Handbook for the Service Industries. Jerome Solomon. 560p. 1981. 29.95 (ISBN 0-8436-0854-4). CBI Pub.

Financial & Cost Accounting for Management. 7th ed. A. H. Taylor & H. Shearing. (Illus.). 384p. 1979. pap. text ed. 15.95x (ISBN 0-7121-0633-2, Pub. by Macdonald & Evans England). Intl Ideas.

Financial & Economic History of the African Tropical Territories. Alan Pim. 1970. Repr. of 1940 ed. 15.00 (ISBN 0-87266-046-X). Argosy.

Financial & Managerial Accounting in Health Care Facilities. Robert Broyles. 600p. Date not set. text ed. price not set (ISBN 0-89443-340-7). Aspen Systems.

Financial & Managerial Control: A Health Care Perspective. Edward J. Lusk & Janice G. Lusk. LC 78-10606. 1979. text ed. 38.50 (ISBN 0-89443-036-X). Aspen Systems.

Financial & Operating Results of Department & Speciality Stores. 75p. 1980. pap. text ed. 45.00 (ISBN 0-686-60190-4, C134). Natl Ret Merch.

Financial Aspects of Industrial Leasing Decisions: Implications for Marketing. Paul F. Anderson. LC 77-75139. (MSU Business Studies Ser.). 1977. pap. 6.50 (ISBN 0-87744-145-6). Mich St U Busn.

Financial Broker-Finder-Business Broker-Consultant Success Kit. 2nd ed. Tyler G. Hicks. 485p. 1981. pap. 99.50 (ISBN 0-686-69033-8). Intl Wealth.

Financial Capitalization Rate Tables No. 73. Financial Publications. 25.00 o.p. (ISBN 0-685-47819-X). Finan Pub.

Financial Compound Interest & Annuity Tables No. 376. 6th ed. Financial Publishing Co. 40.00 (ISBN 0-685-02543-8). Finan Pub.

Financial Deepening in Economic Development. Edward S. Shaw. (Economic Development Ser.). 225p. 1973. text ed. 10.95x (ISBN 0-19-501633-5); pap. text ed. 4.95x (ISBN 0-19-501632-7). Oxford U Pr.

Financial Deepening in the Asian Countries. George J. Viksnins. 96p. (Orig.). 1980. pap. 6.50x (ISBN 0-8248-0745-6). U Pr of Hawaii.

Financial Dimensions of Marketing Management. Frank H. Mossman et al. LC 77-14990. (Wiley Series on Marketing Management). 1978. 22.95 (ISBN 0-471-03376-6). Wiley.

Financial Education of Children & Teenagers. C. M. Flumiani. (Idea Books Ser.). (Illus.). 1978. 24.50 (ISBN 0-89266-127-5). Am Classical Coll Pr.

Financial Handbook. 4th ed. J. I. Bogen & S. S. Shipman. 1208p. 1968. 40.95 (ISBN 0-471-06556-0). Wiley.

Financial Handbook. rev. 4th ed. Ed. by Jules I. Bogen et al. (Illus.). 1250p. 1968. 40.95 (ISBN 0-8260-1160-8). Ronald Pr.

Financial Help in Social Work: A Study of Preventive Work with Families Under the Children & Young Persons Act, 1963. J. S. Heywood & B. K. Allen. 102p. 1971. 21.00x (ISBN 0-7190-0487-X, Pub. by Manchester U Pr England). State Mutual Bk.

Financial History of the New Japan. T. F. M. Adams & Iwao Hoshii. LC 75-185642. (Illus.). 547p. 1972. 22.50x (ISBN 0-87011-157-4). Kodansha.

Financial History of the United States. Margaret G. Myers. LC 70-104900. 1970. 22.50x (ISBN 0-231-02442-8); pap. 7.50x (ISBN 0-231-08309-2). Columbia U Pr.

Financial Information, Accounting & the Law: Cases & Materials. James Cox. 1980. text ed. 20.00 (ISBN 0-316-15861-5). Little.

Financial Institution Management. Neil Seitz & Frederick Yeager. 450p. 1982. text ed. 18.95 (ISBN 0-8359-2022-4); instr's. manual free (ISBN 0-8359-2023-2). Reston.

Financial Institutions. 5th ed. Donald P. Jacobs et al. 1972. text ed. 17.50x o.p. (ISBN 0-256-00262-2). Irwin.

Financial Institutions. Peter S. Rose & Donald R. Fraser. 1980. 18.95x (ISBN 0-256-02205-4). Business Pubns.

Financial Institutions & Industrialization in the Rhineland, 1815-1870. Richard Tilly. (Illus.). 1966. 20.00x (ISBN 0-299-03920-X). U of Wis Pr.

Financial Institutions & Markets. David S. Kidwell & Richard L. Peterson. LC 80-65804. 640p. 1981. text ed. 18.95 (ISBN 0-03-046066-2). Dryden Pr.

Financial Institutions & Markets. Murray E. Polakoff et al. 1970. text ed. 21.95 (ISBN 0-395-05062-6). HM.

Financial Institutions & Markets in a Changing World. Ed. by Donald R. Fraser & Peter S. Rose. 1980. pap. 12.95x (ISBN 0-256-02201-1). Business Pubns.

Financial Integration in Western Europe. Etienne S. Kirschen et al. LC 68-58869. 1969. 20.00x (ISBN 0-231-03200-5). Columbia U Pr.

Financial Interdependence & Variability in Exchange Rates. Ralph C. Bryant. 1980. pap. 2.50 (ISBN 0-8157-1127-1). Brookings.

Financial Intermediaries: An Introduction. 2nd ed. Benton E. Gup. LC 79-87858. 1979. text ed. 19.50 (ISBN 0-395-28138-5); instrs' manual 1.50 (ISBN 0-395-28157-1). HM.

Financial Intermediaries: An Introduction. Benton E. Gup. LC 75-31005. (Illus.). 416p. 1976. text ed. 18.50 o.p. (ISBN 0-395-19828-3); inst. manual 2.25 o.p. (ISBN 0-395-19827-5). HM.

Financial Management. 2nd ed. Eugene F. Brigham. LC 78-56209. 1979. text ed. 22.95 (ISBN 0-03-045401-8). Dryden Pr.

Financial Management. Robert Frame & Dudley Curry. LC 73-89292. (Business Ser.). 576p. 1974. text ed. 17.95 (ISBN 0-675-08852-6); media: audiocassettes & filmstrips 450.00, 2-7 sets, 380.00 ea., 8-15 sets, 340.00 ea., 16 or more sets, 275.00 ea. (ISBN 0-675-08807-0); instructor's manual 3.95 (ISBN 0-686-66911-8). Merrill.

Financial Management. 4th ed. Robert W. Johnson. 1971. text ed. 20.95x (ISBN 0-205-03231-1, 1032313); tchrs. manual o.p. 2.00 (ISBN 0-685-00328-0). Allyn.

Financial Management: A Capital Market Approach. John J. Clark et al. 1976. text ed. 19.95 (ISBN 0-205-05445-5, 105445-7); instructor's manual free (ISBN 0-205-05447-1, 105447-3). Allyn.

Financial Management: An Introduction. S. H. Archer et al. 724p. 1979. 23.50 (ISBN 0-471-02987-4); study guide 9.50 (ISBN 0-471-02988-2). Wiley.

Financial Management & Policy. 5th ed. James C. Van Horne. (Illus.). 1980. text ed. 21.00 (ISBN 0-13-315820-9). P-H.
Financial Management: Cases. Larry Gitman & Edward A. Moses. 1978. text ed. 19.50 (ISBN 0-8299-0167-1); instrs.' manual avail. (ISBN 0-8299-0480-8). West Pub.
Financial Management: Cases & Readings. rev. ed. Victor L. Andrews & Pearson Hunt. 1976. text ed. 19.95x (ISBN 0-256-01746-8). Irwin.
Financial Management Decision Game (Fingame) Leroy D. Brooks. 1975. pap. text ed. 9.50x (ISBN 0-256-01668-2). Irwin.
Financial Management Education in Health Administration Programs. 1979. 6.00. Assn Univ Progs Hlth.
Financial Management for Contractors. Fails Management Institute. Ed. by I. J. Jackson & Marita Kennihan. (Illus.). 224p. 1981. 22.50 (ISBN 0-07-019887-X). McGraw.
Financial Management for the Arts: A Guidebook for Arts Organizations. Charles A. Nelson & Frederick J. Turk. LC 75-43360. (Illus.). 52p. (Orig.). 1975. pap. text ed. 5.95 (ISBN 0-915400-01-4). Am Council Arts.
Financial Management for the Hospitality Industry. Michael M. Coltman. LC 79-378. 1979. text ed. 16.95 (ISBN 0-8436-2141-9). CBI Pub.
Financial Management in Agriculture. 2nd. ed. John A. Hopkin et al. (Illus.). 1979. 18.35 (ISBN 0-8134-2037-7); text ed. 13.75x (ISBN 0-685-34803-2). Interstate.
Financial Management in the Shipping Industry. Phillip C. Cheng. LC 79-15869. 1979. 27.50x (ISBN 0-87033-249-X, 249X). Cornell Maritime.
Financial Management of Condominium & Homeowner's Associations. Community Management Corporation. LC 76-21960. (Special Report Ser.). 1976. 14.50 (ISBN 0-87420-569-7). Urban Land.
Financial Management of Health Care Facilities. William O. Cleverley. LC 76-4034. 1976. 26.00 (ISBN 0-912862-20-3). Aspen Systems.
Financial Management of Health Care Facilities. William O. Cleverley. 394p. 1976. 18.75 (ISBN 0-686-68581-4, 14915). Hospital Finan.
Financial Management of Health Care Organizations: A Referenced Outline & Annotated Bibliography. AUPHA Task Force on Financial Management. 237p. 1978. 8.00 (ISBN 0-686-68588-1, 14921). Hospital Finan.
Financial Management of Health Care Organizations: A Referenced Outline & Annotated Bibliography. LC 78-62119. 8.00 o.p. (ISBN 0-686-24301-3). Assn Univ Progs Hlth.
Financial Management of Health Institutions. John B. Silvers & C. K. Prahalad. 339p. 1974. 17.95 (ISBN 0-686-68576-8, 14910). Hospital Finan.
Financial Management of Hospitals. 4th ed. Howard J. Berman & Lewis E. Weeks. LC 79-16947. (Illus.). 1979. text ed. 29.50 (ISBN 0-914904-33-7). Health Admin Pr.
Financial Management of Hospitals. 3rd ed. Howard W. Berman & Lewis E. Weeks. (Illus.). 585p. 1976. 17.50 (ISBN 0-686-68573-3, 1496). Hospital Finan.
Financial Management of the Small Firm. Ernest W. Walker & J. William Petty, II. LC 78-873. (Illus.). 1978. ref. 18.95 (ISBN 0-13-316091-2). P-H.
Financial Management: Self-Correcting Problems. Jerome S. Osteryoung. (Finance & Real Estate Ser.). 1976. pap. text ed. 7.95 o.p. (ISBN 0-88244-105-1). Grid Pub.
Financial Management: Theory & Applications. Robert C. Higgins. LC 76-25053. 600p. 1977. text ed. 19.50 (ISBN 0-574-19240-9, 13-2240); instr's guide avail. (ISBN 0-574-19241-7, 13-2241). SRA.
Financial Market Rates & Flows. James C. Van Horne. (Illus.). 1978. pap. text ed. 10.95 (ISBN 0-13-316190-0). P-H.
Financial Marketing. LC 80-67814. (Marketing Ser.). 1980. pap. 4.95 (ISBN 0-87251-051-4). Crain Bks.
Financial Markets & the Economy. 2nd ed. Charles Henning et al. (Illus.). 1978. ref. 19.95 (ISBN 0-13-316083-1). P-H.
Financial Markets in the Capitalist Process. Douglas Vickers. LC 77-20308. (Illus.). 1978. 16.00x (ISBN 0-8122-7739-2). U of Pa Pr.
Financial Markets: The Accumulation & Allocation of Wealth. Roland I. Robinson & Dwayne Wrightsman. Orig. Title: Money & Capital Markets. (Illus.). 512p. 1974. text ed. 18.95 o.p. (ISBN 0-07-053273-7, C). McGraw.
Financial Measurement for Managers. G. L. Jones. 1976. pap. text ed. 13.95x (ISBN 0-7131-3367-8). Intl Ideas.
Financial Monthly Mortgage Handbook: 6 per Cent to 15 per Cent No. 158. 3rd ed. Financial Publications. 17.50 (ISBN 0-685-47820-3). Finan Pub.
Financial Monthly Refun Table, 78's Method No. 227. Financial Publishing Co. 20.00 (ISBN 0-685-02545-4). Finan Pub.
Financial Mortgage Guide No. 149. 2nd ed. Financial Publishing Co. 5.00 o.p. (ISBN 0-685-02546-2). Finan Pub.
Financial Motivation for Executives. Graef S. Crystal. LC 77-116716. 1970. 12.95 o.p. (ISBN 0-8144-5230-2). Am Mgmt.
Financial Pass-Through Yield & Value Tables for GNMA Mortgage-Backed Securities No. 715. rev. 5th ed. Ed. by Financial Pub Editors. 25.00 (ISBN 0-685-47818-1). Finan Pub.
Financial Phenomenon: An Investigation of the Rise & Fall of the Slater Walker Empire. Charles Raw. LC 77-17675. 1978. 12.95 o.p. (ISBN 0-06-013506-9, HarpT). Har-Row.
Financial Planning for Study in the United States: A Guide for Students from Other Countries. rev. ed. LC 67-31259. 1980. per copy 2.00 o.p. (ISBN 0-87447-045-5, 235880); 100 or more copies 0.40 o.p. (ISBN 0-685-71518-3). College Bd.
Financial Planning for the Executive. Paul A. Randle & Philip R. Swensen. (Finance Ser.). (Illus.). 300p. 1981. text ed. 15.95. Lifetime Learn.
Financial Planning for the Independent Professional. Herbert T. Spiro. LC 78-18179. 1978. 26.95 (ISBN 0-471-03111-9, Pub. by Wiley-Interscience). Wiley.
Financial Planning for Your Family. J. K. Lasser Tax Institute. 1979. 10.95 (ISBN 0-671-96099-7); pap. 2.95 (ISBN 0-346-12410-7). Cornerstone.
Financial Planning Guide for Your Money Matters. Malcolm MacGregor. LC 78-55443. (Illus.). 1978. spiral wkbk 5.95 (ISBN 0-87123-154-9, 210154). Bethany Fell.
Financial Policy & Economic Growth. Samir A. Makdisi. LC 78-31561. (Modern Middle East Ser.). 1979. 20.00x (ISBN 0-231-04614-6). Columbia U Pr.
Financial Real Estate Handbook No. 512. 256p. 1980. pap. 6.50 (ISBN 0-686-64811-0). Finan Pub.
Financial Report Surveys, 18 vols. Set. pap. 150.50 o.p. (ISBN 0-685-58508-5). Am Inst CPA.
Financial Reporting: An Accounting Revolution. William H. Beaver. (Contemporary Topics in Accounting Ser.). (Illus.). 240p. 1981. text ed. 12.95 (ISBN 0-13-316141-2); pap. text ed. 9.95 (ISBN 0-13-316133-1). P-H.
Financial Reporting in Japan. R. J. Ballon et al. LC 75-30179. (Illus.). 305p. 1976. 15.00x (ISBN 0-87011-269-4). Kodansha.
Financial Reporting Techniques in Twenty Industrial Companies Since 1861. Richard Vangermeersch. LC 79-1238. (U of Fla. Accounting Ser.: No. 9). write for info. (ISBN 0-8130-0624-4). U Presses Fla.
Financial Resources for Disabled Individuals. Institute for Information Studies et al. Ed. by Carolyn Vash & Marjorie Boyer Crane. LC 80-84166. 70p. 1980. pap. write for info. (ISBN 0-935294-06-6). Inst Info Stud.
Financial Self-Assessment: A Workbook for Colleges. Nathan Dickmeyer & K. Scott Hughes. 72p. 1980. pap. text ed. 15.00 (ISBN 0-915164-11-6). Natl Assn Coll.
Financial Solidarity for Development: Efforts & Institutions of the Members of OPEC 1973-1976 Review, Vol. 1. 117p. 1979. pap. 15.00 (ISBN 0-686-68957-7, 79/2D9, UN). Unipub.
Financial Solidarity for Development: Statistical Annex, Vol. 2. 83p. 1979. pap. 15.00 (ISBN 0-686-68958-5, UN79/2D9, UN). Unipub.
Financial Statement Analysis: A New Approach. Baruch Lev. (Contemporary Topics in Accounting Ser: Foundations of Finance). (Illus.). 288p. 1974. pap. text ed. 8.95 (ISBN 0-13-316364-4). P-H.
Financial Statement Analysis: Theory, Application & Interpretation. rev. ed. Leopold A. Bernstein. 1978. 20.95x (ISBN 0-256-02004-3). Irwin.
Financial Statements. 7th ed. Stewart Y. McMullen. 1979. 20.95 (ISBN 0-256-02165-1). Irwin.
Financial Statements: How to Read & Interpret Them for Success in the Stock Market. Henry R. Hoffmaster. (Illus.). 1980. deluxe ed. 49.45 (ISBN 0-918968-62-3). Inst Econ Finan.
Financial Strategy. William E. Fruhan, Jr. 1979. 17.95 (ISBN 0-256-02228-3). Irwin.
Financial Support to the Fishing Industry. OECD. (Illus.). 161p. (Orig.). 1980. pap. 6.50x (ISBN 92-64-12087-4, 53-80-01-1). OECD.
Financial System. J. O. Light & William L. White. 1979. 19.95x (ISBN 0-256-02120-1). Irwin.
Financial Systems for Community Health Organizations: A Manager's Guide. Charles L. Harper et al. 1981. text ed. 24.95 (ISBN 0-534-97976-9). Lifetime Learn.
Financial Tactics & Terms for the Sophisticated International Investor. Harry D. Schultz. LC 72-9152. (Illus.). 184p. 1974. 10.00 o.p. (ISBN 0-06-013808-4, HarpT). Har-Row.
Financial Theory & Corporate Policy. Thomas E. Copeland & J. Fred Weston. LC 78-73366. 1979. text ed. 21.95 (ISBN 0-201-00971-4); solution manual 5.95 (ISBN 0-201-00972-2). A-W.
Financing & Charges for Wastewater Systems. Compiled By American Society of Civil Engineers. 72p. 1973. pap. text ed. 4.00 (ISBN 0-87262-057-3). Am Soc Civil Eng.
Financing & Managing State & Local Government. Richard W. Lindholm & Hortojo Wignjowijoto. LC 78-19227. (Illus.). 1979. 29.95 (ISBN 0-669-02434-1). Lexington Bks.
Financing & Risk in Developing Countries. Ed. by Stephen H. Goodman. LC 78-63013. (Praeger Special Studies). 1978. 22.50 (ISBN 0-03-042281-7). Praeger.
Financing Black Economic Development. Timothy Bates & William Bradford. (Institute for Research on Poverty Policy Analysis Ser.). 1979. 17.50 (ISBN 0-12-081650-4); pap. 8.50 (ISBN 0-12-081652-0). Acad Pr.
Financing Business Firms. 6th ed. James E. Wert & Glenn V. Henderson. 1979. text ed. 18.95 (ISBN 0-256-02182-1). Irwin.
Financing Capital Formation for Local Governments. Ann R. McWatters. LC 79-10333. (Research Report: No. 79-3). 1979. pap. 3.00x (ISBN 0-87772-266-8). Inst Gov Stud Berk.
Financing Community Colleges. Walter I. Garms. LC 76-54165. 1977. text ed. 9.25x (ISBN 0-8077-2510-2). Tchrs Coll.
Financing Education in a Climate of Change. 2nd ed. Burrup. 19.95x (ISBN 0-205-05696-2, 2256967). Allyn.
Financing Equal Educational Opportunity: Alternatives for State Finance. Joel S. Berke et al. LC 79-190059. 300p. 1972. 16.60x (ISBN 0-8211-0120-X); text ed. 15.00x (ISBN 0-685-24959-X). McCutchan.
Financing Foreign Trade in Eastern Europe: Problems of Bilateralism & Currency Inconvertibility. John S. Garland. LC 76-24351. 1977. text ed. 23.95 (ISBN 0-275-23800-8). Praeger.
Financing Goods. LC 57-7094. 609p. 1957. text ed. 20.00 (ISBN 0-9605500-0-3). A G Sweetser.
Financing Government in a Federal System. George F. Break. (Studies of Government Finance). 1980. 17.95 (ISBN 0-8157-1068-2); pap. 6.95 (ISBN 0-8157-1067-4). Brookings.
Financing Health Care for the Elderly: Medicare, Medicaid & Private Health Insurance. Judith Feder & John Holahan. (Health Policy & the Elderly Ser.). 106p. 1979. pap. 5.50 (ISBN 0-87766-244-4, 24900). Urban Inst.
Financing Health Care for the Poor. John Holahan. LC 74-25273. (Illus.). 1975. 17.95 (ISBN 0-669-97634-2). Lexington Bks.
Financing Industrial Investment. John C. Carrington & George T. Edwards. LC 78-65708. 1979. 29.95 (ISBN 0-03-049761-2). Praeger.
Financing Mining Projects in Developing Countries. Marian Radetzki & Stephen Zorn. 1980. 35.00x (Pub. by Mining Journal England). State Mutual Bk.
Financing of Economic Development. W. Newlyn. (Illus.). 1978. 37.50x (ISBN 0-19-828402-0). Oxford U Pr.
Financing of Health Care - An Inquiry Anthology. Lewis E. Weeks et al. LC 79-13436. (Illus.). 1979. pap. text ed. 14.00 (ISBN 0-914904-34-5); pap. text ed. 17.00 (ISBN 0-914904-35-3). Health Admin Pr.
Financing of Indian Education. Atmanand Misra. 1968. 7.50x o.p. (ISBN 0-210-31188-6). Asia.
Financing of Planned Development in India. S. Prakash. 1968. 7.50 (ISBN 0-8426-1682-9). Verry.
Financing Part-Time Students: The New Majority in Postsecondary Education. 1974. 4.75 o.p. (ISBN 0-685-48013-5). ACE.
Financing Politics: Recent Wisconsin Elections. David Adamany. LC 79-84948. 1969. 24.50 (ISBN 0-299-05430-6). U of Wis Pr.
Financing Presidential Campaigns. Delmer D. Dunn. (Studies in Presidential Selection). 1972. pap. 4.95 (ISBN 0-8157-1961-2). Brookings.
Financing Procedures of British Foreign Trade. Stephen Carse et al. LC 79-18146. 160p. 1980. 24.95 (ISBN 0-521-22534-5). Cambridge U Pr.
Financing Real Estate. James H. Boykin. LC 77-205. (Special Ser. in Real Estate & Urban Land Economics). (Illus.). 1979. 28.95 (ISBN 0-669-01449-4); price not set instrs' manual (ISBN 0-669-03998-5). Lexington Bks.
Financing Real Estate in California. Homer C. Davey & Albert Sharum. 1976. text ed. 20.50 scp (ISBN 0-06-453607-6, HarpC). Har-Row.
Financing Social Securtiy. Ed. by Colin D. Campbell. 1979. 15.25 (ISBN 0-8447-2140-9); pap. 8.25 (ISBN 0-8447-2140-9). Am Enterprise.
Financing Soviet Schools. Harold J. Noah. LC 66-29416. (Orig.). 1967. text ed. 9.25x (ISBN 0-8077-1857-2); pap. text ed. 7.00x (ISBN 0-8077-1854-8). Tchrs Coll.
Financing State & Local Governments. 3rd ed. James A. Maxwell & J. Richard Aronson. LC 76-54871. (Studies of Government Finance). 1977. 14.95 (ISBN 0-8157-5512-0); pap. 5.95 (ISBN 0-8157-5511-2). Brookings.
Financing Survival Manual for Small Business. Laurie H. Hutzler. (Illus.). 1981. pap. 15.00 (ISBN 0-937542-05-9). Legal Mgmt Serv.
Financing the Capital Requirements of the U. S. Airline Industry in the 1980's. Robert W. Mandell. LC 79-7747. 192p. 1979. 21.95 (ISBN 0-669-03215-8). Lexington Bks.
Financing the Civil Service Retirement System. Dan M. McGill. 1979. 11.00x (ISBN 0-256-02250-X). Irwin.
Financing the Growth of Electric Utilities. David L. Scott. LC 75-25024. (Illus.). 1976. text ed. 22.95 (ISBN 0-275-56460-6). Praeger.
Financing the Metropolis. Ed. by Kent Mathewson & William B. Neenan. 352p. 1980. 29.95 (ISBN 0-03-056886-2). Praeger.
Financing the Solar Home. David Barrett et al. LC 77-3858. 1977. 22.95 (ISBN 0-669-01684-5). Lexington Bks.
Financing University Education. A. R. Prest. (Institute of Economic Affairs, Occasional Papers Ser.: No. 12). pap. 2.50 (ISBN 0-255-69603-5). Transatlantic.
Financing Urban & Rural Development Through Betterment Levies: The Latin American Experience. Jorge Macon & Jose Merino Manon. LC 76-24359. (Special Studies). 1977. text ed. 24.50 (ISBN 0-275-23970-5). Praeger.
Finansim: A Financial Management Simulation. 2nd ed. Paul S. Greenlaw et al. 1979. pap. text ed. 11.50 (ISBN 0-8299-0248-1); instrs.' maual avail. (ISBN 0-8299-0613-4). West Pub.
Finches & Other Seed-Eating Birds. Robin L. Restall. (Illus.). 1975. 19.95 (ISBN 0-571-10353-7, Pub. by Faber & Faber). Merrimack Bk Serv.
Finches of Australia: A Folio. Frank T. Morris. (Illus.). 124p. 65.00 (ISBN 0-7018-1000-9). Eastview.
Finch's Fortune. Mazo De La Roche. 1976. pap. 1.50 o.p. (ISBN 0-449-23053-8, Crest). Fawcett.
Finchy: A Memoir of Peter Finch by His Former Wife. Yolande Finch. (Illus.). 1981. 12.95 (ISBN 0-671-61008-2, Wyndham Bks). S&S.
Find a Stranger, Say Goodbye. Lois Lowry. (gr. 7-9). 1979. pap. 1.95 (ISBN 0-671-42062-3). Archway.
Find a Stranger, Say Goodbye. Lois Lowry. (YA) (gr. 7-9). 1979. pap. 1.75 (ISBN 0-671-29999-9). PB.
Find-a-Word Puzzles for Vo-Ag Students: Set 1. Alvin Halcombe. 1981. pap. 9.95 (ISBN 0-8134-2164-0, 2164). Interstate.
Find and Use Your Spiritual Gifts. John E. Packo. 117p. (Orig.). 1980. pap. 2.95 (ISBN 0-87509-293-4); avail. leaders guide 1.25 (ISBN 0-87509-294-2). Chr Pubns.
Find Debbie! Roy Brown. LC 75-25511. (gr. 7-12). 1976. 7.95 (ISBN 0-395-28894-0, Clarion). HM.
Find, Fix & Strike! The Fleet Air Arm at War 1939-45. John Winton. (Illus.). 192p. 1981. 28.50 (ISBN 0-7134-3488-0, Pub. by Batsford England). David & Charles.
FIND: Frye's Index to Nonverbal Data. Jerry K. Frye. LC 80-51053. 344p. 1980. 39.95 (ISBN 0-936992-01-8); pap. 29.95 (ISBN 0-936992-02-6). U of Minn Comp Ctr.
Find of a Lifetime: Sir Arthur Evans & the Discovery of Knossos. Sylvia Horowitz. LC 80-36851. (Illus.). 288p. 1981. 14.95 (ISBN 0-670-13575-5). Viking Pr.
Find Out by Touching. Paul Showers. LC 60-13242. (Let's-Read-&-Find-Out Science Bk). (Illus.). (gr. k-3). 1961. PLB 7.89 (ISBN 0-690-29782-3, TYC-J). T Y Crowell.
Find the Changeling. Gregory Benford & Gordon Eklund. 1980. pap. 2.50 (ISBN 0-440-12604-5). Dell.
Find the Magician! Hank Whittemore. LC 80-5510. 276p. 1980. 11.95 (ISBN 0-670-31738-1). Viking Pr.
Finder. John Chambers. LC 80-23928. 168p. (gr. 4-6). 1981. PLB 8.95 (ISBN 0-689-30803-5). Atheneum.
Finders, Keepers. Annabel Johnson & Edgar Johnson. LC 80-69994. 192p. (gr. 7 up). 1981. 7.95 (ISBN 0-590-07790-2, Four Winds). Schol Bk Serv.
Finders Weepers. Miriam Chaikin. LC 79-9608. (Illus.). 128p. (gr. 3-6). 1980. 8.95 (ISBN 0-06-021176-8, HarpJ); PLB 8.79 (ISBN 0-06-021177-6). Har-Row.
Findex: The Dictionary of Market Research Reports, Studies & Surveys. Ed. by Thomas E. Miller & Lisa Sher. 1981. 125.00 (ISBN 0-931634-07-5). Info Clearing House.
Finding a Girl in America. Andre Dubus. 1981. pap. 6.95 (ISBN 0-87923-393-1). Godine.

Finding a Job: A Resource Guide for the Middle Aged & Retired. Norman Sprague & Hilary F. Knatz. 1978. pap. 9.25 o.p. (ISBN 0-685-62973-2). Adelphi Univ.

Finding & Exploiting Your Opponents Weaknesses. Rex Lardner. LC 74-12730. 1978. 4.95 o.p. (ISBN 0-385-09103-6). Doubleday.

Finding & Fixing the Older Home. Joseph F. Schram. LC 76-25112. (Illus.). 1976. 13.95 (ISBN 0-912336-32-3); pap. 6.95 (ISBN 0-912336-33-1). Structures Pub.

Finding & Preparing Precious & Semiprecious Stones. James A. Peterson. (Illus.). 96p. 1974. pap. 6.95 o.p. (ISBN 0-8096-1826-5, Assn Pr). Follett.

Finding Birds Around the World. Peter Alden & John Gooders. (Illus.). 704p. 1980. 16.95 (ISBN 0-395-29114-3). HM.

Finding Birds in Mexico. 2nd ed. Ernest P. Edwards. LC 68-58738. (Illus., Incl. 1976 Supplement to Finding Birds in Mexico). 1968. pap. 12.00 set (ISBN 0-911882-05-7). E P Edwards.

Finding Birds in Panama. 2nd ed. Ernest P. Edwards & Horace Loftin. LC 73-21847. (Illus.). 1971. softcover 5.00 (ISBN 0-911882-02-2). E P Edwards.

Finding Career Alternatives for Teachers: A Step-by-Step Guide. Anne Miller. 84p. (Orig.). 1979. pap. 9.95 (ISBN 0-9604134-0-5). Apple Pub Co.

Finding Facts: Interviewing, Observing, Using Reference Sources. W. Rivers. 1975. pap. 8.95 (ISBN 0-13-316364-4). P-H.

Finding Families: An Ecological Approach to Family Assessment in Adoption. Ann Hartman. LC 78-26537. (Sage Human Services Guides: Vol. 7). 1979. pap. 6.50x (ISBN 0-8039-1216-1). Sage.

Finding Freedom. Billy Graham. pap. 1.25 o.p. (ISBN 0-310-25062-5). Zondervan.

Finding God in Everyday Life. Kevin Coughlin. 80p. (Orig.). 1981. pap. 3.95 (ISBN 0-8091-2351-7). Paulist Pr.

Finding Home. David Kherdian. LC 80-22805. 256p. (gr. 7 up). 1981. 8.95 (ISBN 0-688-00400-8); PLB 8.59 (ISBN 0-688-00401-6). Greenwillow.

Finding Money: A Businessman's Guide to Sources of Financing. James G. Hellmuth. 227p. 1980. 50.00 (ISBN 0-932648-12-6). Boardroom.

Finding My Way. Riker. (gr. 9-12). 1979. pap. 7.52 (ISBN 0-87002-304-7); student guide 2.52 (ISBN 0-87002-309-8); tchr's guide 2.64 (ISBN 0-87002-311-X). Bennett IL.

Finding of the Third Eye. Vera S. Alder. 1980. pap. 3.95 (ISBN 0-87728-056-8). Weiser.

Finding One to Ten. George Adamson. (Illus.). (ps-5). 1968. 5.95 (ISBN 0-571-08330-7, Pub. by Faber & Faber). Merrimack Bk Serv.

Finding Out About Bible Times. Deborah Manley. 1980. write for info. (ISBN 0-89191-339-4). Cook.

Finding Out About the Past. Mae B. Freeman. (Gateway Ser.: No. 44). (Illus.). (gr. 4-8). 1967. 2.95 o.p. (ISBN 0-394-80144-X, BYR); PLB 5.99 (ISBN 0-394-90144-4). Random.

Finding Out About Trucks. Art Timms. LC 80-14559. (Finding-Out Books). (Illus.). 64p. (gr. 4-9). 1980. PLB 6.95 (ISBN 0-89490-037-4). Enslow Pubs.

Finding, Reading & Interpreting Nursing Research. Patricia Trussell et al. LC 80-84150. 225p. 1981. text ed. price not set (ISBN 0-913654-70-1). Nursing Res.

Finding Roman Britain. Jenniger Laing. 1977. 11.50 o.p. (ISBN 0-7153-7406-0). David & Charles.

Finding Solutions: Learning How to Deal with Life's Problems & Decisions. Ed. by James D. Cisek & Anthea George. (Illus.). (gr. 6-10). 1980. wkbk 3.95 (ISBN 0-9604510-0-5); lab manual 4.95 (ISBN 0-9604510-1-3). Life Skills.

Finding the Way. Dale E. Rogers. Orig. Title: God Has the Answers. 64p. 1973. 3.95 o.p. (ISBN 0-8007-0604-8). Revell.

Finding the Way. new ed. William D. Sheldon et al. (gr. 5). 1973. text ed. 10.80 (ISBN 0-205-03557-4, 523557X); tchrs'. guide 10.30 (ISBN 0-205-03558-2, 5235588); activity bk. 3.96 (ISBN 0-205-03559-0, 5235596); tchrs' activity bk 3.96 (ISBN 0-205-03560-4, 523560X); activities masters 28.00 (ISBN 0-205-03561-2, 5235618). Allyn.

Finding Your Way in the Outdoors. Robert L. Mooers, Jr. (Illus.). 1972. 6.95 o.p. (ISBN 0-525-10505-0). Dutton.

Fine & Handsome Captain. Frances Lynch. 1977. pap. 1.50 o.p. (ISBN 0-449-23269-7, Crest). Fawcett.

Fine & Private Place. Peter S. Beagle. 256p. 1976. pap. 2.25 (ISBN 0-345-29001-1). Ballantine.

Fine Art of Baseball: A Complete Guide to Strategy, Skills, & Systems. 2nd ed. L. Watts, III. (Illus.). 1973. 15.95 (ISBN 0-13-316968-5). P-H.

Fine Art of Being Clever...for Fun & Profit. Linda Arden. LC 78-55993. (Illus.). 1978. softcover 12.95 o.p. (ISBN 0-930490-11-8). Future Shop.

Fine Art of Mixing Drinks. rev. ed. David A. Embury. LC 58-5572. 1948. pap. 3.50 (ISBN 0-385-09683-6, C177, Dolp). Doubleday.

Fine Art of Needlepoint. Muriel B. Crowell. (Illus.). 128p. 1973. 10.95 (ISBN 0-690-29799-8, TYC-T). T Y Crowell.

Fine Art of Tennis Hustling. Rex Lardner. 128p. (Orig.). 1975. pap. 3.50 (ISBN 0-8015-2638-8, Hawthorn). Dutton.

Fine Art of Understanding Patients. R. C. Bates. 1968. pap. 5.95 (ISBN 0-87489-019-5). Med Economics.

Fine Art Reproductions. (Illus.). 1978. 32.50 o.p. (ISBN 0-8212-1119-6). NYGS CT.

Fine-Art Weaving. Irene Waller. (Illus.). 144p. 1980. 24.00 (ISBN 0-7134-0412-4, Pub. by Batsford England). David & Charles.

Fine Arts: A Bibliographic Guide to Basic Reference Works, Histories & Handbooks. 2nd ed. Donald L. Ehresmann. LC 79-9051. 1979. lib. bdg. 25.00x (ISBN 0-87287-201-7). Libs Unl.

Fine Arts Cookbook. Ed. by Mrs. Robert L. Ahern. (Illus.). 1970. spiral bdg. 7.95 (ISBN 0-87846-163-9). Mus Fine Arts Boston.

Fine Arts Cookbook, Two. Compiled by Carl F. Zahn. (Illus.). 195p. 1981. 14.95 (ISBN 0-8436-2211-3). CBI Pub.

Fine Arts in America. Joshua C. Taylor. LC 78-23643. (History of American Civilization Ser.: No. 27). xvi, 264p. 1981. pap. 7.95 (ISBN 0-226-79151-3). U of Chicago Pr.

Fine Companion. Shakerly Marmion. Ed. by Richard Sonnershein & Stephen Orgel. LC 78-66827. (Renaissance Drama Ser.). 1979. lib. bdg. 33.00 (ISBN 0-8240-9731-9). Garland Pub.

Fine English Cookery. Michael Smith. 1977. pap. 5.95 o.p. (ISBN 0-571-11128-9, Pub. by Faber & Faber). Merrimack Bk Serv.

Fine Furniture. A. W. Marlow. LC 55-13928. 1977. pap. 8.95 (ISBN 0-8128-2250-1). Stein & Day.

Fine Mechanisms & Precision Instruments, Principles of Design. W. Trylinski. 1971. 75.00 (ISBN 0-08-006361-6). Pergamon.

Fine Needle Aspiration Biopsy of the Rat Liver - Cytological, Cytochemical & Biochemical Methods: Proceedings of a Workshop on Technique & Application of Fine Needle Aspiration Biology in Experimental Toxicology, Zurich, 1979. Ed. by G. Zbinden. (Illus.). 70p. 1980. 29.00 (ISBN 0-08-025508-6). Pergamon.

Fine Particles Processing, 2 vols. Ed. by P. Somasundaran. LC 79-57344. (Illus.). 1865p. 1980. text ed. 45.00x (ISBN 0-89520-275-1). Soc Mining Eng.

Fine Particulate Pollution. United Nations Economic Commission for Europe. 1978. text ed. 30.00 (ISBN 0-08-023399-6). Pergamon.

Fine Points of Tennis. Paul Metzler. LC 77-93309. (Illus.). 1978. 8.95 (ISBN 0-8069-4118-9); lib. bdg. 8.29 (ISBN 0-8069-4119-7). Sterling.

Fine Prints: Collecting, Buying & Selling. Cecile Shapiro & Lauris Mason. LC 76-9200. (Illus.). 1976. 10.95 o.p. (ISBN 0-06-013853-X, HarpT). Har-Row.

Fine-Tuning: An NCCB Report on Noncommercial Radio. Judith Becker et al. 1980. pap. 3.00 (ISBN 0-9603466-4-3). NCCB.

Fine Woodworking Biennial Design Book. Fine Woodworking Magazine. (Illus.). 1978. pap. 7.95 o.p. (ISBN 0-918804-00-0, ScribT). Scribner.

Fine Woodworking Biennial Design Book. Fine Woodworking magazine Editors. LC 77-79327. (Illus.). 1977. pap. 9.95 (ISBN 0-918804-00-0, Dist. by Van Nostrand Nostrand Reinhold). Taunton.

Fine Woodworking Techniques, No. 1. Fine Woodworking Magazine Editors. LC 78-58221. (Illus.). 1978. 14.95 (ISBN 0-918804-02-7, Dist. by Nostrand Reinhold). Taunton.

Fine Woodworking Techniques, No. 2. Fine Woodworking Magazine Editors. LC 80-52056. (Illus.). 208p. 1980. 14.95 (ISBN 0-918804-09-4, Dist. by Van Nostrand Reinhold). Taunton.

Fine Woodworking Techniques One. Fine Woodworking Magazine. (Illus.). 1978. 9.95 o.p. (ISBN 0-918804-02-7, ScribT). Scribner.

Finer Points of Riding. rev. ed. A. K. Frederiksen. (Illus.). pap. 8.75 (ISBN 0-85131-323-X, Dist. by Sporting Book Center). J A Allen.

Finest Kind O'day: Lobstering in Maine. Bruce A. McMillan. LC 77-3049. (gr. 2 up). 1977. 8.95 (ISBN 0-397-31763-8). Lippincott.

Finest of Fulness. Ed. by Ras Robinson. 192p. 1979. pap. 3.95 (ISBN 0-937778-00-1). Fulness Hse.

Finger Acupressure. Pedro Chan. 1976. pap. 1.95 (ISBN 0-345-27868-2). Ballantine.

Finger Frolics: Fingerplays for Young Children. 2nd ed. Liz Cromwell & Dixie Hibner. 1976. pap. 7.95 (ISBN 0-933212-09-7, Dist. by Gryphon House). Partner Pr.

Finger Game Miracle. Nancy Kelton. LC 76-46408. (When They Were Young Ser.). (Illus.). (gr. k-3). 1977. PLB 7.95 (ISBN 0-8172-0452-0). Raintree Pubs.

Finger Paint & Pudding Prints. Ann S. Wiseman. LC 80-14353. (Illus.). 32p. (gr. k-3). 1980. PLB 5.95 (ISBN 0-201-08346-9, 8346, A-W Childrens). A-W.

Finger Plays for Nursery & Kindergarten. Emilie Poulsson. LC 74-165397. (Illus.). (ps-k). 1971. pap. 2.00 (ISBN 0-486-22588-7). Dover.

Finger Puppets: Easy to Make, Fun to Use. Laura Ross. LC 78-155752. (Illus.). (gr. k-3). 1971. PLB 6.96 o.p. (ISBN 0-688-51613-0). Lothrop.

Finger Rhymes. Marc Brown. LC 80-10173. (Illus.). 32p. (ps-3). 1980. PLB 8.95 (ISBN 0-525-29732-4, Unicorn). Dutton.

Finger-Ring Lore. William Jones. LC 67-24357. 1968. Repr. of 1890 ed. 25.00 (ISBN 0-8103-3449-6). Gale.

Finger Spelling Fun. David A. Adler. (gr. 1-3). 1980. PLB 7.90 (ISBN 0-531-04140-9). Watts.

Finger Weaving: Indian Braiding. Alta R. Turner. (Little Craft Book Ser.). (Illus.). 48p. (gr. 3 up). 1973. 4.95 o.p. (ISBN 0-8069-5264-4); PLB 5.89 o.p. (ISBN 0-8069-5265-2). Sterling.

Fingermath, Bk. 1. Peter K. Gurau & E. A. Lieberthal. (Fingermath Ser.). 1979. pap. 4.00 pupil's ed. (ISBN 0-07-025221-1, W); tchr's. ed. 8.00 (ISBN 0-07-025231-9). McGraw.

Fingermath Book. Peter K. Gurau & Edwin M. Lieberthal. Ed. by Leo Gafney. (Fingermath Ser.: Bk. 3). 192p. (gr. 3-8). 1980. pap. text ed. 4.40 (ISBN 0-07-025223-8, W); tchrs. ed. 8.80 (ISBN 0-07-025233-5). McGraw.

Fingerprint. Patricia Wentworth. 240p. 1980. pap. 1.95 (ISBN 0-553-13948-7). Bantam.

Fingerprint Detective. Robert H. Millimaki. (gr. 4-7). 1973. 10.95 (ISBN 0-397-31484-1). Lippincott.

Fingerprint Handbook. Annita T. Field. (Police Science Ser). (Illus.). 196p. 1976. 14.75 (ISBN 0-398-00562-1). C C Thomas.

Fingerprint Owls & Other Fantasies. Marjorie P Katz. Ed. by Herbert M. Katz. LC 72-85648. (Illus.). 54p. 1981. pap. 3.95 (ISBN 0-87131-341-3). M Evans.

Fingerprint Owls & Other Fantasies. Marjorie P. Katz. LC 72-85648. 64p. 1981. pap. cancelled (ISBN 0-87131-341-3). M Evans.

Fingerprinting. Boy Scouts Of America. LC 19-600. (Illus.). 36p. (gr. 6-12). 1964. pap. 0.70x (ISBN 0-8395-3287-3, 3287). BSA.

Fingerprints: History, Law & Romance. George W. Wilton. LC 70-164057. 1971. Repr. of 1938 ed. 20.00 (ISBN 0-8103-3755-X). Gale.

Fingertip Devotions. Amy Bolding. 1970. 2.95 (ISBN 0-8010-0798-4). Baker Bk.

Fingertip Reference for Dental Materials. Sandra P. Hall & Felice L. Hirsch. LC 79-54689. (Dental Assisting Ser.). 121p. 1981. pap. text ed. 8.00 (ISBN 0-8273-1863-4). Delmar.

Finish Me off. Hillary Waugh. 1978. pap. 1.75 (ISBN 0-505-51324-2). Tower Bks.

Finish with Engines. Mike Peyton. 96p. 1980. 9.00x (ISBN 0-245-53409-1, Pub. by Nautical England). State Mutual Bk.

Finished. M. David Sisler, Jr. 1978. pap. 2.50 (ISBN 0-87148-333-5). Pathway Pr.

Finished Rake: or Gallantry in Perfection. Bd. with Secret History of Mama Oella, Princess Royal of Peru; Masterpiece of Imposture. Elizabeth Harding; Temple Rakes: or Innocence Preserved. LC 73-170585. (Foundations of the Novel Ser.: Vol. 57). lib. bdg. 50.00 (ISBN 0-8240-0569-4). Garland Pub.

Finishing off. Patrick J. Galvin. LC 77-24521. (Successful Book). (Illus.). 1977. 13.95 (ISBN 0-912336-50-1); pap. 6.95 (ISBN 0-912336-51-X). Structures Pub.

Finishing Processes in Printing. A. G. Martin. (Library of Printing Technology). Date not set. 22.00 (ISBN 0-8038-2289-8). Hastings.

Finishing Technology. rev. ed. George A. Soderberg. (gr. 10-12). 1969. text ed. 15.96 (ISBN 0-87345-016-7). McKnight.

Finishing Touch. Bruce Bliven, Jr. LC 78-1356. (Illus.). 1978. 8.95 (ISBN 0-396-07534-7). Dodd.

Finite & Infinite Dimensional Linear Spaces. Jarvinen. 185p. 1981. price not set. Dekker. Postponed.

Finite Element Analysis: Fundamentals. Richard H. Gallagher. (Civil Engr. & Engr. Mechanics Ser.). (Illus.). 416p. 1975. 26.95 (ISBN 0-13-317248-1). P-H.

Finite Element Method. 3rd ed. O. C. Zienkiewicz. (Illus.). 1978. text ed. 34.95 (ISBN 0-07-084072-5, C). McGraw.

Finite Element Method: A Basic Introduction for Engineers. K. C. Rockey et al. LC 74-6671. 239p. 1975. 25.95 o.p. (ISBN 0-470-72927-9). Halsted Pr.

Finite Element Method: A Basic Introduction. K. C. Rockey et al. 239p. 1980. pap. text ed. 19.95x (ISBN 0-470-26979-0). Halsted Pr.

Finite Element Method: A First Approach. Alan J. Davies. (Oxford Applied Mathematics & Computing Science Ser.). (Illus.). 300p. 1980. 49.50x (ISBN 0-19-859630-8); pap. 27.50x (ISBN 0-19-859631-6). Oxford U Pr.

Finite Element Method for Engineers. Kenneth H. Huebner. LC 74-17452. 448p. 1975. 35.00 (ISBN 0-471-41950-8, Pub. by Wiley-Interscience). Wiley.

Finite Element Method in Engineering. Ed. by S. S. Rao. LC 80-40817. 400p. 1981. 51.00 (ISBN 0-08-025467-5); pap. 18.00 (ISBN 0-08-025466-7). Pergamon.

Finite Element Methods for Engineers. Roger T. Fenner. (Illus.). 1976. 23.50 o.p. (ISBN 0-333-18340-1); pap. text ed. 16.95x (ISBN 0-333-18656-7). Scholium Intl.

Finite Elements: An Introduction, Vol. I. Eric B. Becker et al. (Illus.). 256p. 1981. 24.95 (ISBN 0-13-317057-8). P-H.

Finite Elements in Fluids, 3 vols. Ed. by R. H. Gallagher et al. Incl. Vol. 1. Viscous Flow & Hydrodynamics. 290p. 1975. 55.75 (ISBN 0-471-29045-9); Vol. 2. Mathematical Foundations, Aerodynamics, & Lubrication. 287p. 1975. 55.75 (ISBN 0-471-29046-7); Vol. 3. 1978. 55.75 (ISBN 0-471-99630-0). LC 74-13573 (Pub. by Wiley-Interscience). Wiley.

Finite Free Resolutions. D. G. Northcott. LC 75-31397. (Tracts in Mathematics Ser.: No. 71). 250p. 1976. 49.50 (ISBN 0-521-21155-7). Cambridge U Pr.

Finite Groups. 2nd ed. Daniel Gorenstein. xvii, 517p. 1980. 22.50 (ISBN 0-8284-0301-5). Chelsea Pub.

Finite Groups & Finite Geometrics. T. Tsuzuku. (Cambridge Tracts in Mathematics Ser.: No. 78). (Illus.). 250p. Date not set. price not set (ISBN 0-521-22242-7). Cambridge U Pr.

Finite Markov Processes & Applications. Marius Iosifescu. LC 79-42726. 250p. 1980. 32.50 (ISBN 0-471-27677-4). Wiley.

Finite Mathematics. Steven C. Althoen & Robert J. Bumcrot. (Illus.). 1978. text ed. 16.95x (ISBN 0-393-09046-9). Norton.

Finite Mathematics. Martin Eisen & Carole Eisen. 1978. text ed. 15.95x (ISBN 0-02-472450-5). Macmillan.

Finite Mathematics. 2nd ed. James W. Thomas & Ann M. Thomas. 1978. text ed. 17.80 (ISBN 0-205-05996-1); instr's man. avail. (ISBN 0-205-05997-X). Allyn.

Finite Mathematics. N. A. Weiss & M. L. Yoselof. LC 74-20001. (Illus.). ix, 628p. 1975. text ed. 17.95x (ISBN 0-87901-039-8). Worth.

Finite Mathematics: A Modeling Approach. Marvin L. Bittinger & J. Conrad Crown. LC 76-14656. (Illus.). 1977. text ed. 16.95 o.p. (ISBN 0-201-00832-7); instr's manual 2.50 o.p. (ISBN 0-201-00833-5). A-W.

Finite Mathematics: A Modeling Approach. 2nd ed. J. Conrad Crown & Marvin L. Bittinger. LC 80-19472. (Mathematics Ser.). (Illus.). 480p. 1981. text ed. 15.95 (ISBN 0-201-03145-0). A-W.

Finite Mathematics: An Introduction to Mathematical Models. Ruric E. Wheeler & W. D. Peeples. LC 73-89593. (Contemporary Undergrad Math Ser). 1974. text ed. 18.95 (ISBN 0-8185-0117-0); instr's. manual o.p. (ISBN 0-685-46781-3). Brooks-Cole.

Finite Mathematics & Calculus with Applications to Business. Paul G. Hoel. LC 73-19505. 464p. 1974. text ed. 18.50x (ISBN 0-471-40430-6); tchr's manual avail. (ISBN 0-471-40432-2). Wiley.

Finite Mathematics & Its Applications. Robert E. Rector & Earl J. Zwick. LC 78-69547. (Illus.). 1979. text ed. 17.50 (ISBN 0-395-27206-8); inst. manual 0.75 (ISBN 0-395-27207-6). HM.

Finite Mathematics: From Sets to Game Theory. Adelbert Hackert. 1974. text ed. 15.95x o.p. (ISBN 0-669-81125-4); instructor's manual free o.p. (ISBN 0-669-90258-6). Heath.

Finite Mathematics with Applications for Business & Social Sciences. 3rd ed. Abe Mizrahi & Michael Sullivan. LC 78-12522. 1979. text ed. 19.95 (ISBN 0-471-03336-7); tchrs. manual avail. (ISBN 0-471-05507-7); study guide avail. (ISBN 0-471-05499-2). Wiley.

Finite Mathematics: With Applications in Business, Biology, & Behavioral Sciences. Margaret L. Lial & Charles D. Miller. 1977. 17.95x (ISBN 0-673-15044-5). Scott F.

Finite Mathematics: With Applications to Business & the Social Sciences. Ruric E. Wheeler & W. D. Peeples, Jr. LC 80-13916. 550p. 1980. text ed. 19.95 (ISBN 0-8185-0418-8). Brooks-Cole.

Finite Mathematics with Business Applications. 2nd ed. John G. Kemeny et al. (Quantitative Analysis for Business Ser). 1972. ref. ed. 19.95 (ISBN 0-13-317321-6). P-H.

Finite Mathematics with Calculus for the Management, Life & Social Sciences. William R. Derrick & Judith L. Derrick. LC 78-18639. (Illus.). 1979. text ed. 18.95 (ISBN 0-201-01400-9). A-W.

Finite Mathematics with Models. Gareth Williams. 1976. text ed. 17.80x (ISBN 0-205-04913-3); instr's manual free (ISBN 0-205-04914-1). Allyn.

Finite Simple Groups & Their Classifications. Michael Aschbacher. LC 79-20927. (Yale Mathematical Monograph: No. 7). (Orig.). 1980. pap. text ed. 6.95 (ISBN 0-300-02449-5). Yale U Pr.

Finite State Markovian Decision Processes. Cyrus Derman. (Mathematics in Science & Engineering Ser.: Vol. 67). 1970. 25.50 (ISBN 0-12-209250-3). Acad Pr.

Finite-Strip Method in Bridge Engineering. Yew C. Loo & Anthony R. Cusens. (Viewpoint Publication Ser.). (Illus.). 1979. pap. text ed. 22.50 (ISBN 0-7210-1041-5). Scholium Intl.

Finite Strip Method in Structural Analysis. Y. K. Cheung. Ed. by B. G. Neal. 130p. 1976. text ed. 32.00 (ISBN 0-08-018308-5). Pergamon.

Finland & Europe: The Period of Autonomy & the International Crises, 1808-1914. Juhani Paasivirt. Ed. by D. G. Kirby. Tr. by Anthony F. Upton from Finnish. (Nordic Ser.: Vol. 7). 300p. 1981. 29.50x (ISBN 0-8166-1046-0). U of Minn Pr.

Finland, Germany & the Soviet Union, 1940-1941: The Petsamo Dispute. H. Peter Krosby. (Illus.). 1968. 22.50x (ISBN 0-299-05140-4). U of Wis Pr.

Finley Peter Dunne. Grace Eckley. (United States Authors Ser.: No. 402). 1981. lib. bdg. 11.95 (ISBN 0-8057-7295-2). Twayne.

Finley Peter Dunne & Mr. Dooley: The Chicago Years. Charles Fanning. LC 77-75483. (Illus.). 304p. 1978. 16.00x (ISBN 0-8131-1365-2). U Pr of Ky.

Finn Family Moomintroll. Tove Jansson. 1975. pap. 1.95 (ISBN 0-380-00350-3, 51771, Camelot). Avon.

Finnegans Wake: A Facsimile of Buffalo Notebooks VI.B.1 - VI.B.4. James Joyce. Ed. by Michael Groden. LC 77-11978. (James Joyce Archive Ser.). 1978. lib. bdg. 104.00 (ISBN 0-8240-2828-7). Garland Pub.

Finnegans Wake: A Facsimile of Buffalo Notebooks VI.B.5 - VI.B.8. James Joyce. Ed. by Michael Groden. LC 77-12610. (James Joyce Archive Ser.). 1978. lib. bdg. 104.00 (ISBN 0-8240-2829-5). Garland Pub.

Finnegans Wake: A Facsimile of Buffalo Notebooks VI.B.9 - VI.B.12. James Joyce. Ed. by Michael Groden. LC 77-14619. (James Joyce Archive Ser.). 1978. lib. bdg. 104.00 (ISBN 0-8240-2830-9). Garland Pub.

Finnegans Wake: A Facsimile of Buffalo Notebooks VI.B.33 - VI.B.36. James Joyce. Ed. by Michael Groden. LC 78-1112. (James Joyce Archive Ser.). 1978. lib. bdg. 104.00 (ISBN 0-8240-2836-8). Garland Pub.

Finnegans Wake: A Facsimile of Buffalo Notebooks VI.B.37 - VI.B.40. James Joyce. Ed. by Michael Groden. LC 78-1109. (James Joyce Archive Ser.). 1978. lib. bdg. 104.00 (ISBN 0-8240-2837-6). Garland Pub.

Finnegans Wake: A Facsimile of Buffalo Notebook VI. A. James Joyce. Ed. by Michael Groden. LC 78-1113. (James Joyce Archive Ser.). 1978. lib. bdg. 104.00 (ISBN 0-8240-2827-9). Garland Pub.

Finnegans Wake: A Facsimile of Buffalo Notebooks VI. B. 17-20. James Joyce. Ed. by Michael Groden. LC 78-17967. (James Joyce Archive Ser.: Vol. 33). lib. bdg. 104.00 (ISBN 0-8240-2832-5). Garland Pub.

Finnegans Wake: A Facsimile of Buffalo Notebooks VI. B. 13-16. James Joyce. Ed. by Michael Groden. LC 78-9769. (James Joyce Archive Ser.). 1978. lib. bdg. 104.00 (ISBN 0-8240-2831-7). Garland Pub.

Finnegans Wake: A Facsimile of Buffalo Notebooks VI. B. 29-32. James Joyce. Ed. by Michael Groden. LC 78-4178. (James Joyce Archive Ser.: Vol. 36). lib. bdg. 104.00 (ISBN 0-8240-2835-X). Garland Pub.

Finnegans Wake: A Facsimile of Buffalo Notebooks VI. B. 25-28. James Joyce. Ed. by Michael Groden. LC 78-4135. (James Joyce Archive Ser.). 1978. lib. bdg. 104.00 (ISBN 0-8240-2834-1). Garland Pub.

Finnegans Wake: A Facsimile of Buffalo Notebooks VI. B. 21-24. James Joyce. Ed. by Michael Groden. LC 78-17966. (James Joyce Archive Ser.: Vol. 34). 1978. lib. bdg. 104.00 (ISBN 0-8240-2833-3). Garland Pub.

Finnegans Wake: A Facsimile of Buffalo Notebooks VI. C. 1,2,3,4,5,7. James Joyce. Ed. by Michael Groden. LC 78-1114. (James Joyce Archive Ser.). 1978. lib. bdg. 104.00 (ISBN 0-8240-2840-6). Garland Pub.

Finnegans Wake: A Facsimile of Buffalo Notebooks VI. C. 12,13,14,17,11,18. James Joyce. Ed. by Michael Groden. LC 78-51001. (James Joyce Archive Ser.). 1978. lib. bdg. 104.00 (ISBN 0-8240-2842-2). Garland Pub.

Finnegans Wake: A Facsimile of Buffalo Notebooks VI. C. 6,8,9,10,15,16. James Joyce. Ed. by Michael Groden. LC 78-51002. (James Joyce Archive Ser.). 1978. lib. bdg. 104.00 (ISBN 0-8240-2841-4). Garland Pub.

Finnegans Wake: A Facsimile of Buffalo Notebooks VI.B. 41-44. James Joyce. LC 78-4174. (James Joyce Archive Ser.). 1978. lib. bdg. 104.00 (ISBN 0-8240-2838-4). Garland Pub.

Finnegans Wake: Book I: A Facsimile of the Galley Proofs Volume II. James Joyce. Ed. by Michael Groden. LC 77-23060. (James Joyce Archive Ser.). 1978. lib. bdg. 104.00 (ISBN 0-8240-2846-5). Garland Pub.

Finnegans Wake: Book I: A Facsimile of the Galley Proofs Volume I. James Joyce. Ed. by Michael Groden. LC 77-23060. (James Joyce Archive Ser.). 1978. lib. bdg. 104.00 (ISBN 0-8240-2845-7). Garland Pub.

Finnegans Wake: Book I, Chapter I: A Facsimile of Drafts, Typescripts & Proofs. James Joyce. Ed. by James Groden. LC 78-896. (James Joyce Archive Ser.). 1978. lib. bdg. 104.00 (ISBN 0-8240-2843-0). Garland Pub.

Finnegans Wake: Book I, Chapter 8: a Facsimile of Drafts, Typescripts, & Proofs. James Joyce. Ed. by Michael Groden. LC 78-4039. (James Joyce Archive Ser.). 1978. lib. bdg. 104.00 (ISBN 0-8240-2862-7). Garland Pub.

Finnegans Wake: Book I, Chapters 2-3: a Facsimile of Drafts, Typescripts, & Proofs. James Joyce. Ed. by Michael Groden. LC 78-4140. (James Joyce Archive Ser.). 1978. lib. bdg. 104.00 (ISBN 0-8240-2844-9). Garland Pub.

Finnegans Wake: Book I, Chapters 4-5: a Facsimile of Drafts, Typescripts, & Proofs. James Joyce. Ed. by Michael Groden. LC 78-4138. (James Joyce Archive Ser.). 1978. lib. bdg. 104.00 (ISBN 0-8240-2860-0). Garland Pub.

Finnegans Wake: Book I, Chapters 6-7: a Facsimile of Drafts, Typescripts, & Proofs. James Joyce. Ed. by Michael Groden. LC 78-8959. (James Joyce Archive Ser.: Vol. 62). 1978. lib. bdg. 104.00 (ISBN 0-8240-2861-9). Garland Pub.

Finnegans Wake: Book II, Chapter I: A Facsimile of Drafts, Typescripts, & Proofs. James Joyce. Ed. by Michael Groden. LC 77-11681. (James Joyce Archive Ser.). 1978. lib. bdg. 104.00 (ISBN 0-8240-2849-X). Garland Pub.

Finnegans Wake: Book II, Chapter 2: A Facsimile of Drafts, Typescripts, & Proofs, Vol. 1. James Joyce. Ed. by Michael Groden. LC 77-18399. (James Joyce Archive Ser.). 1978. lib. bdg. 104.00 (ISBN 0-8240-2853-8). Garland Pub.

Finnegans Wake: Book II, Chapter 2: A Facsimile of Drafts, Typescripts, & Proofs, Vol. II. James Joyce. Ed. by Michael Groden. LC 77-18399. (James Joyce Archive Ser.). 1978. lib. bdg. 104.00 (ISBN 0-8240-2854-6). Garland Pub.

Finnegans Wake: Book II, Chapter 3: a Facsimile of Drafts, Typescripts, & Proofs, Vol. 1. James Joyce. Ed. by Michael Groden. LC 77-10573. (James Joyce Archive Ser.). 1978. lib. bdg. 104.00 (ISBN 0-8240-2850-3). Garland Pub.

Finnegans Wake: Book II, Chapter 3: A Facsimile of Drafts, Typescripts, & Proofs, Vol. II. James Joyce. Ed. by Michael Groden. LC 77-10573. (James Joyce Archive Ser.). 1978. lib. bdg. 104.00 (ISBN 0-8240-2851-1). Garland Pub.

Finnegans Wake: Book II, Chapter 4: A Facsimile of Drafts, Typescripts, & Proofs. James Joyce. Ed. by Michael Groden. LC 77-84971. (James Joyce Archive Ser.). 1978. lib. bdg. 104.00 (ISBN 0-8240-2852-X). Garland Pub.

Finnegans Wake: Book III: A Facsimile of the Galley Proofs. James Joyce. Ed. by Michael Groden. LC 77-22951. (James Joyce Archive Ser.). 1978. lib. bdg. 104.00 (ISBN 0-8240-2847-3). Garland Pub.

Finnegans Wake: Book III, Chapter 3: A Facsimile of Drafts, Typescripts, & Proofs, Vol. 1. James Joyce. Ed. by Michael Groden. LC 78-899. (James Joyce Archive Ser.). 1978. lib. bdg. 104.00 (ISBN 0-8240-2856-2). Garland Pub.

Finnegans Wake: Book III, Chapter 3: A Facsimile of Drafts, Typescripts, & Proofs, Vol. II. James Joyce. Ed. by Michael Groden. LC 78-899. (James Joyce Archive Ser.). 1978. lib. bdg. 104.00 (ISBN 0-8240-2857-0). Garland Pub.

Finnegans Wake: Book III, Chapter 4: A Facsimile of Drafts, Typescripts, & Proofs. James Joyce. Ed. by Michael Groden. LC 78-4465. (James Joyce Archive Ser.). 1978. lib. bdg. 104.00 (ISBN 0-8240-2858-9). Garland Pub.

Finnegans Wake: Book III, Chapters 1 & 2: A Facsimile of Drafts, Typescripts, & Proofs. James Joyce. Ed. by Michael Groden. LC 78-898. (James Joyce Archive Ser.). 1978. lib. bdg. 104.00 (ISBN 0-8240-2855-4). Garland Pub.

Finnegans Wake: Book III, Chapters 1-4: a Facsimile of Transition Pages. James Joyce. Ed. by Michael Groden. LC 78-17968. (James Joyce Archive Ser.). 1978. lib. bdg. 104.00 (ISBN 0-8240-2859-7). Garland Pub.

Finnegans Wake: Book IV: A Facsimile of Drafts, Typescripts, & Proofs. James Joyce. Ed. by Michael Groden. LC 77-22867. (James Joyce Archive Ser.). 1978. lib. bdg. 104.00 (ISBN 0-8240-2848-1). Garland Pub.

Finnegans Wake Gazetteer. Louis O. Mink. LC 77-74443. 600p. 1978. 25.00x (ISBN 0-253-32210-3). Ind U Pr.

Finney & Miller's Principles of Accounting, Introductory. 8th ed. G. Johnson & J. Gentry. 1980. 19.95 (ISBN 0-13-317370-4); Pt. 1. working papers 5.95 (ISBN 0-13-317594-4); Part 2. working papers 5.95 (ISBN 0-13-317602-9); practice set 7.95 (ISBN 0-13-317636-3); student guide 6.95 (ISBN 0-13-317628-2). P-H.

Finney Lives On. V. Raymond Edman. 1970. pap. 3.95 (ISBN 0-87123-150-6, 210150). Bethany Fell.

Finney on Revival. Charles G. Finney. Ed. by E. E. Shelhamer. 128p. 1974. pap. 1.95 (ISBN 0-87123-151-4, 200151). Bethany Fell.

Finney's Systematic Theology. Charles G. Finney. LC 76-3500. Orig. Title: Finney's Lectures on Systematic Theology. 1976. pap. 5.95 (ISBN 0-87123-153-0, 210153). Bethany Fell.

Finnish Deluxe Dictionary: English-Finnish. 2nd ed. R. Hurme & M. Pesonen. 1978. 85.00x (ISBN 9-5100-5699-5, F-565). Vanous.

Finnish Dictionary. 10th ed. E. Riikon & A. Tuomikowski. 1979. text ed. 45.00x (ISBN 9-5110-0343-7, F560). Vanous.

Finnish-English, English-Finnish Dictionary, 2 Vols. 11th ed. A. Wuolle. 1978-79. Set. 35.00 (ISBN 951-0-09469-2). Finnish-Eng (ISBN 9-5100-8500-6). Eng.-Finnish (ISBN 951-0-08500-6). Heinman.

Finnish-English-Finnish Pocket Dictionary. Ed. by A. Wuolle. 1978. pap. text ed. 9.50x (ISBN 9-5100-7468-3, F559). Vanous.

Finnish for Foreigners, 3 vols. M. Aaltio. Set. pap. 30.00 (ISBN 0-686-66991-6). Vol. 1 (ISBN 9-5110-0397-6). Vol. 2 (ISBN 9-5110-1483-8) (ISBN 9-5110-1919-8). Heinman.

Finnish for Foreigners, Pt. 3. M. H. Paitio. 1975. 13.50x (ISBN 9-5110-1919-8, F-566). Vanous.

Finnish for Foreigners, Pt. 1: Lessons 1-25. 9th ed. M. J. Aaltio. (Illus.). 254p. 1976. pap. text ed. 13.50x (ISBN 951-1-00397-6, F561); cassette a, 35.00x cassettes b-e, 100.00x open reel, 4.50x exercises 40.00x (ISBN 0-686-66923-1). Vanous.

Finnish for Foreigners: Pt 2, Lessons 27 to 40. 8th rev. ed. M-H Aaltio. (Illus.). 192p. 1976. pap. text ed. 13.50x (ISBN 951-1-01483-8, F 562). Vanous.

Finnish Pocket Dictionary, Finnish-English - English-Finnish. new ed. 391p. (Engl. & Finnish.). 1978. pap. text ed. 9.50x (ISBN 9-5100-7468-3, F559). Vanous.

Finnish Revolution. Anthony F. Upton. (Nordic Ser.: Vol. 3). 600p. 1981. 39.50x (ISBN 0-8166-0905-5). U of Minn Pr.

Finnish Small Dictionary: Finnish-English, Vol. 2. 11th ed. Aino Wuolle. 1976. text ed. 20.00x (ISBN 9-5100-0074-4, F558). Vanous.

Finns & the Lapps: How They Live & Work. John L. Irwin. 171p. 1973. text ed. 8.95 (ISBN 0-03-030206-4, HoltC). HR&W.

Finta Cameriera. Gaetano Latilla. Ed. by Howard M. Brown. LC 76-21007. (Italian Opera 1640-1770 Ser.: Vol. 37). 1978. lib. bdg. 75.00 (ISBN 0-8240-2636-5). Garland Pub.

Finton the Fish: Visual Discriminations for Children. Marjorie E. Olson. (Illus.). 29p. (gr. k-1). 1974. pap. text ed. 2.00x (ISBN 0-89039-100-9). Ann Arbor FL.

Fiona. Catherine Gaskin. 288p. 1977. pap. 1.75 o.p. (ISBN 0-449-23238-7, Crest). Fawcett.

Fiona's Flea. Beverly Keller. (Illus.). 64p. (gr. 7-10). 1981. PLB 6.99 (ISBN 0-698-30719-4). Coward.

Fire. Edward E. Daub. LC 77-26664. (Read About Ser.). (Illus.). (gr. k-3). 1978. PLB 9.95 (ISBN 0-8393-0080-8). Raintree Child.

Fire. Gail K. Haines. LC 74-13396. (Illus.). 32p. (gr. 1-5). 1975. PLB 6.48 (ISBN 0-688-32009-0). Morrow.

Fire. Leonard Rule. LC 73-161698. (New Citizen Books). (Illus.). 80p. 1973. 10.50x (ISBN 0-85340-229-9). Intl Pubns Serv.

Fire & Ice. Andrew Tobias. (Illus.). 1977. pap. 2.25 o.s.i. (ISBN 0-446-82409-7). Warner Bks.

Fire & Ice: The Arkansas Diamonds. Kent Biffle. (Illus.). 220p. Date not set. pap. 5.95 (ISBN 0-87870-108-7). Memphis St Univ.

Fire & Ice: The Cascade Volcanoes. 2nd ed. Stephen Harris. LC 75-36435. (Illus.). 1980. pap. 7.95 (ISBN 0-89886-009-1). Mountaineers.

Fire & Ice: The Cascade Volcanoes. rev. ed. Stephen L. Harris. LC 75-36435. (Illus.). 320p. (YA) 1980. pap. 7.95 (ISBN 0-89886-009-1, Copublished with The Mountaineers). Pacific Search.

Fire & Ice: The Charles Revson-Revlon Story. Andrew Tobias. LC 76-6124. 1976. 10.00 o.p. (ISBN 0-688-03023-8). Morrow.

Fire & Smoke Retardant Chemicals, C-004. 1976. 450.00 o.p. (ISBN 0-89336-067-8). BCC.

Fire & Smoke Retardant Chemicals Outlook C-004R. 1980. 825.00 (ISBN 0-89336-205-0). BCC.

Fire & the Gold. Phyllis Whitney. (YA) (RL 7). 1974. pap. 1.50 (ISBN 0-451-07320-7, W7320, Sig). NAL.

Fire & the Rose Are One. Sebastian Moore. 176p. 1980. 9.95 (ISBN 0-8164-0468-2). Seabury.

Fire & Theft Security Systems. 2nd ed. Byron Wels. (Illus.). 1976. 8.95 o.p. (ISBN 0-8306-6956-6, 956); pap. 5.95 (ISBN 0-8306-5956-0). TAB Bks.

Fire Apparatus Practices. 6th ed. IFSTA Committee. Ed. by Gene Carlson & Charles Orton. LC 80-82822. (IFSTA Ser.: No. 106). 1980. pap. text ed. 7.00 (ISBN 0-87939-040-9). Intl Fire Serv.

Fire Apparatus Practices: 106. IFSTA Committee. Ed. by Everett Hudiburg. (Illus.). 1970. pap. text ed. 6.00 o.p. (ISBN 0-87939-006-9). Intl Fire Serv.

Fire at Sea. Gordon Carlson. Ed. by Mary Verdick. (Beginning Pal Paperbacks Ser.). (Illus., Orig.). (gr. 7-12). 1977. pap. text ed. 1.25 (ISBN 0-8374-3461-0). Xerox Ed Pubns.

Fire Below Zero. Barnaby Conrad. (Orig.). 1981. pap. 2.75 (ISBN 0-440-12524-3). Dell.

Fire Brand. J. Larcombe Rees. (Pathfinder Ser.). 128p. (gr. 2-6). 1980. pap. 2.50 (ISBN 0-310-37911-3, 0017P). Zondervan.

Fire Bride. Julia Wherlock. (Orig.). 1980. pap. write for info. (ISBN 0-671-41295-7). PB.

Fire Canto. Deb K. Das. 8.00 (ISBN 0-89253-487-7); flexible cloth 4.00 (ISBN 0-89253-488-5). Ind-US Inc.

Fire Cloud. Kenneth McKenney. 1980. pap. 2.50 (ISBN 0-380-50054-X, 50054). Avon.

Fire Company Apparatus & Procedure. 2nd ed. Lawrence W. Erven. (Fire Science Ser). (Illus.). 360p. 1974. text ed. 14.95x (ISBN 0-02-474150-7, 47415). Macmillan.

Fire Control, Vol. 8. Building Research Establishment. 1978. 38.00x (ISBN 0-86095-805-1). Longman.

Fire Department Cartoons. 48p. 1.00 (ISBN 0-913452-07-6). Jesuit Bks.

Fire Department Company Officer. IFSTA Committee. Ed. by Gene Carlson & Charles Orton. LC 80-85349. (Orig.). 1981. pap. text ed. 7.00 (ISBN 0-87939-043-3). Intl Fire Serv.

Fire Department Management: Scope & Method. David B. Gratz. (Fire Science Ser). 1972. text ed. 13.95x (ISBN 0-02-474620-7, 47462). Macmillan.

Fire Department Officer: 301. IFSTA Committee. Ed. by Everett Hudiburg. (Illus.). 1967. pap. text ed. 3.50 o.p. (ISBN 0-87939-018-2). Intl Fire Serv.

Fire Department Safety Program: Safety Two. National Fire Protection Association. LC 79-720641. (Illus.). 1979. pap. text ed. 60.00 (ISBN 0-87765-164-7, SL-54). Natl Fire Prot.

Fire Detection for Life Safety. Committee on Fire Research, National Research Council. LC 76-53105. 1977. pap. 7.75 (ISBN 0-309-02600-8). Natl Acad Pr.

Fire Drill. Bob Reese et al. Ed. by Dan Wasserman. (Ten Word Bks.). (Illus.). (gr. k-1). 1979. PLB 4.50 (ISBN 0-89868-071-9); pap. 1.95 (ISBN 0-89868-082-4). ARO Pub.

Fire Engine Book. (Golden Play & Learn Bk.). 14p. (ps). Date not set. pap. 2.95 (ISBN 0-307-10739-6, Golden Pr). Western Pub.

Fire Engines. (Golden Sturdy Shape Bks.). (Illus.). 14p. (ps). 1981. 2.95 (ISBN 0-307-12263-8, Golden Pr). Western Pub.

Fire Engines in Color. Arthur Ingram & Denis Bishop. (Illus.). 235p. 1980. 9.95 (ISBN 0-7137-0627-9, Pub. by Blandford Fr England). Sterling.

Fire-Fiend & the Raven. Charles D. Gardette & Edgar A. Poe. 1973. 7.50 (ISBN 0-938192-03-5). De La Ree.

Fire Fighters. rev. ed. Rhoda Blumberg. (First Bks. Ser). (Illus.). 72p. (gr. 4). 1976. PLB 6.45 (ISBN 0-531-00850-9). Watts.

Fire Flood & Other Stories. Vonda McIntyre. 1981. pap. 2.50 (ISBN 0-671-83631-5). PB.

Fire Gardens of Maylandia. Rhea Sanders. 1980. 10.00 (ISBN 0-937684-10-4). Tradd St Pr.

Fire in My Bones. A. Elisabeth McFadden & R. W. Spalding. LC 78-71387. (Destiny Ser.). 1979. pap. 4.95 (ISBN 0-8163-0319-3, 06217-4). Pacific Pr Pub Assn.

Fire in My Bones. D. Stacey. 1976. pap. 4.30 (ISBN 0-08-018054-X). Pergamon.

Fire in My Bones. 2nd ed. Fred M. Wood. 1981. pap. 3.50 (ISBN 0-8054-1219-0). Broadman.

Fire in the Barley. Frank Parrish. LC 78-27819. (Dan Mallet Novel of Suspense Ser.). 1979. 7.95 (ISBN 0-396-07684-X). Dodd.

Fire in the Brand: An Introduction to the Creative Work & Theology of John Wesley. Howard A. Slaatte. 1963. 4.00 o.p. (ISBN 0-682-41125-6). Exposition.

Fire in the Islands! The Acts of the Holy Spirit in the Solomon Islands. Alison Griffiths. LC 77-71627. (Illus.). 1977. pap. 3.95 (ISBN 0-87788-264-9). Shaw Pubs.

Fire in the Minds of Men. James H. Billington. LC 79-2750. 677p. 1980. 25.00 (ISBN 0-465-02405-X). Basic.

Fire in the Streets. Milton Viorst. 1981. 8.95 (ISBN 0-671-42814-4, Touchstone). S&S.

Fire in the Wind. Alan Riefe. 1976. pap. 1.25 o.p. (ISBN 0-445-00423-1). Popular Lib.

Fire in Your Life. Irving Adler. LC 55-9930. (Illus.). (YA) (gr. 5-9). 1955. PLB 7.89 (ISBN 0-381-99991-2, A27060, JD-J). John Day.

Fire Investigation: A Practical Guide for Fire Students & Officers, Insurance Investigators, Loss Adjustors, & Police Officers. M. F. Dennett. (Illus.). 80p. 1980. 17.25 (ISBN 0-08-024741-5); pap. 9.75 (ISBN 0-08-024742-3). Pergamon.

Fire Island. Burt Hirschfeld. (Orig.). 1970. pap. 2.50 (ISBN 0-380-00232-9, 50427). Avon.

Fire Island Pines. William Delligan. 1977. pap. 1.95 o.p. (ISBN 0-445-04020-3). Popular Lib.

Fire: Its Many Faces & Moods. James J. O'Donnell. LC 80-10123. 192p. (gr. 7 up). 1980. PLB 7.79 (ISBN 0-671-33021-7). Messner.

Fire Mate. Olga Cossi. LC 77-1334. (Illus.). 1977. 5.50 o.p. (ISBN 0-8309-0163-9). Independence Pr.

Fire Mountain. Janet Cullen-Tanaka. 288p. (Orig.). 1980. pap. 2.50 (ISBN 0-89083-646-9). Zebra.

Fire of Genius: Inventors of the Past Century. Ernest V. Heyn et al. LC 75-21227. 12.95 o.p. (ISBN 0-385-03776-7). Doubleday.

Fire of Life: The Smithsonian Book of the Sun. Smithsonian. (Illus.). 1981. 24.95 (ISBN 0-89599-006-7). Smithsonian Expo.

Fire on the Earth. Ralph Martin. 1975. pap. 1.95 (ISBN 0-89283-021-2). Servant.

Fire on the Mountain Top. Gloria Faizi. 1973. pap. 1.25 (ISBN 0-685-55705-7, 7-31-68). Baha'i.

Fire Out of the Stone. 2nd ed. Dane Rudhyar. LC 79-89943. Date not set. cancelled (ISBN 0-89793-020-7). Hunter Hse.

Fire Protection Administration for Small Communities & Fire Protection Districts. Commerce & Community Affairs Dept. LC 79-93086. (Illus.). 1980. pap. text ed. 15.00 (ISBN 0-87939-037-9). Intl Fire Serv.

Fire Protection Directory 1979. (Benn Directories Ser.). 1979. 52.50 (ISBN 0-686-52399-7, Pub by Benn Pubns). Nichols Pub.

Fire Protection for the Design Professional. Ed. by Rolf Jensen. LC 75-9508. 198p. 1975. 29.95 (ISBN 0-8436-0152-3). CBI Pub.

Fire Protection in Nuclear Power Plants. (Safety Ser.: No. 50-SG-D2). 1979. pap. 6.50 (ISBN 92-0-123779-0, ISP 536, IAEA). Unipub.

Fire Protection Manual for Hydrocarbon Processing Plants, Vol. 2. Ed. by Charles H. Vervalin. (Illus.). 300p. 1981. text ed. 49.95 (ISBN 0-87201-288-3). Gulf Pub.

Fire Related Codes, Laws & Ordinances. Vince Clet. 1978. text ed. 12.95x (ISBN 0-02-471760-6). Macmillan.

Fire Resistance of Non-Loadbearing Exterior Walls. Building Research Advisory Board. 1951. pap. 3.50 o.p. (ISBN 0-309-00076-9). Natl Acad Pr.

Fire Retardants: Proceeding of the First European Conference on Flammability & Fire Retardants. Ed. by ViJay M. Bhatnagar. LC 78-66105. 1979. pap. 35.00 (ISBN 0-87762-264-7). Technomic.

Fire Safety Training in Health Care Institutions. American Hospital Association. LC 75-20295. (Illus.). 60p. 1975. pap. 10.00 (ISBN 0-87258-163-2, 1595). Am Hospital.

Fire Sale. Robert Klane. 1977. pap. 1.75 o.p. (ISBN 0-449-23350-2, Crest). Fawcett.

Fire Sciences Dictionary. Ed. by B. W. Kuvshinoff et al. LC 77-3489. 1977. 20.50 (ISBN 0-471-51113-7, Pub. by Wiley-Interscience). Wiley.

Fire Screen. James Merrill. LC 71-86549. 1969. pap. 6.95 (ISBN 0-689-10185-6). Atheneum.

Fire Service First Aid Practices, IFSTA Committee: 109. Ed. by John Peige et al. LC 77-75409. 1977. pap. text ed. 7.00 (ISBN 0-87939-009-3). Intl Fire Serv.

Fire Service Instructor Training. 4th ed. ISTA Committee. Ed. by Gene Carlson. (Illus.). 1981. pap. text ed. 7.00 (ISBN 0-87939-045-X, IFSTA 302). Intl Fire Serv.

Fire Service Instructor Training: 303. Ifsta Committee. Ed. by Everett Hudiburg. (Illus.). 1970. pap. text ed. 6.00 o.p. (ISBN 0-87939-020-4). Intl Fire Serv.

Fire Service Pumps & Hydraulics. Warren E. Isman. LC 76-3943. 1977. pap. 8.40 (ISBN 0-8273-0591-5). Delmar.

Fire Service Reference Guide Addendum: 502a. Connie Williams. 1978. pap. text ed. 1.50 (ISBN 0-87939-026-3). Intl Fire Serv.

Fire Service Reference Guide: 502. Ed. by John D. Peige & Jerry Laughlin. LC 77-80386. 1977. pap. text ed. 6.00 (ISBN 0-87939-031-X). Intl Fire Serv.

Fire Service Rescue Practices. 5th ed. IFSTA Committee. Ed. by Gene Carlson. (IFSTA Ser.: No. 108). 1981. pap. 7.00 (ISBN 0-87939-044-1). Intl Fire Serv.

Fire Station Book. Nancy Bundt. LC 80-16617. (Illus.). 32p. (ps-3). 1981. PLB 5.95g (ISBN 0-87614-126-2). Carolrhoda Bks.

Fire Storm. Robb White. (gr. 5-9). 1979. 7.95a (ISBN 0-385-14630-2); PLB (ISBN 0-385-14631-0). Doubleday.

Fire Stream Practices. 6th ed. IFSTA Committee. Ed. by Gene Carlson & Charles Orton. LC 80-80447. (IFSTA: No. 105). (Illus.). 206p. 1980. pap. text ed. 7.00 (ISBN 0-87939-041-7). Intl Fire Serv.

Fire Suppression & Detection Systems. John L. Bryan. LC 73-7367. (Fire Science Ser). (Illus.). 320p. 1974. text ed. 14.95 (ISBN 0-02-473920-0, 47392). Macmillan.

Fire That Consumes. Henry De Montherlant. Tr. by Vivian Cox from Fr. LC 80-51842. Orig. Title: Ville Dont le Prince Est un Enfant. 88p. 1980. 24.00 (ISBN 0-9604392-1-8). G F Ritchie.

Fire Time. Poul Anderson. 256p. 1975. pap. 2.25 (ISBN 0-345-28692-8). Ballantine.

Fire Ventilation Practices. 6th ed. IFSTA Committee. Ed. by Gene Carlson & Charles Orton. LC 80-84149. (IFSTA Ser.: No. 107). 1981. pap. text ed. 70.00 (ISBN 0-87939-039-5). Intl Fire Serv.

Fire Ventilation Practices: 107. IFSTA Committee. Ed. by Everett Hudiburg & Carl McCoy. (Illus.). 1970. pap. text ed. 6.00 o.p. (ISBN 0-87939-007-7). Intl Fire Serv.

Fire Watch. Alan D. Burke. 1980. 12.95 (ISBN 0-316-11683-1, Pub. by Atlantic-Little Brown). Little.

Firearms Blueing & Browning. R. H. Angier. 160p. 1936. 9.95 (ISBN 0-685-20387-5). Stackpole.

Firearms Control: A Study of Armed Crime & Firearms Control in England & Wales. Colin Greenwood. (Illus.). 272p. 1972. 25.00 (ISBN 0-7100-7435-2). Routledge & Kegan.

Firearms Curiosa. Lewis Winant. LC 54-7114. (Illus.). 1961. 9.95 o.p. (ISBN 0-686-15793-1). Ray Riling.

Firearms Encyclopedia. George Nonte. (Outdoor Life Bk.). 1973. 19.95 o.s.i. (ISBN 0-06-013213-2, HarpT). Har-Row.

Firearms in American History. Michael Berger. LC 78-11652. (First Bks.). (Illus.). (gr. 5 up). 1979. PLB 6.45 (ISBN 0-531-02255-2). Watts.

Firearms in Colonial America: The Impact of History & Technology 1492-1792. M. L. Brown. LC 80-27221. (Illus.). 450p. 1980. 45.00 (ISBN 0-87474-290-0). Smithsonian.

Firearms Investigation, Identification & Evidence. Hatcher et al. (Illus.). 548p. 1977. Repr. 24.50 (ISBN 0-8117-0612-5). Stackpole.

Fireball. John Christopher. LC 80-22094. (gr. 5-7). 1981. PLB 9.95 (ISBN 0-525-29738-3). Dutton.

Fireball Mystery. Mary Adrian. (Illus.). (gr. 2-6). 1977. 6.95 (ISBN 0-8038-2325-8). Hastings.

Firebirds. W. C. Chalk. 1971. pap. text ed. 2.50x o.p. (ISBN 0-435-11198-1). Heinemann Ed.

Firebrand. Ann F. Barron. 1977. pap. 1.95 o.p. (ISBN 0-449-13863-1, GM). Fawcett.

Firebrands. Sahle Sellassie. (Orig.). 9.00 (ISBN 0-89410-103-X); pap. 5.00 (ISBN 0-89410-102-1). Three Continents.

Firebrands. George Smith. LC 80-82222. 384p. (Orig.). 1980. pap. 2.95 (ISBN 0-87216-765-8). Playboy Pbks.

Firebrand's Woman. Vanessa Royall. (Orig.). 1980. pap. 2.95 o.s.i. (ISBN 0-440-12597-9). Dell.

Firebug. Neild Oldham. Ed. by Tom Mooney. (Pal Paperbacks Ser.). (Illus., Orig.). (gr. 7-12). 1976. pap. text ed. 1.25 (ISBN 0-8374-3488-2). Xerox Ed Pubns.

Firecrest Round the World. Alain Gerbault. 1981. 12.50 (ISBN 0-679-51026-5). McKay.

Fired. Khamal S. Opoku. 64p. 1980. pap. 5.00 (ISBN 0-682-49636-7). Exposition.

Firefacts: The Consumer's Guide to Wood Heat. Jerry Kipp. 256p. 1980. 14.95 (ISBN 0-914378-61-9); pap. 9.95 (ISBN 0-914378-58-9). Countryman.

Firefighter, F. D. 7th ed. Robert E. McGannon. LC 80-25047. 256p. (Orig.). 1981. pap. 8.00 (ISBN 0-668-05170-1, 5170). Arco.

Firefighter Study Guide: FSTA, 500. 1st ed. Ed. by Jerry Laughlin et al. LC 79-84380. 1979. pap. 5.00 (ISBN 0-87939-033-6). Intl Fire Serv.

Firefighters Occupational Safety: 209. 1st ed. IFSTA Committee. Ed. by Jerry Laughlin & Connie Osterhout. LC 79-83647. 1979. pap. text ed. 7.00 (ISBN 0-87939-028-X). Intl Fire Serv.

Fireflies. Rabindranath Tagore. (Illus.). 1928. 11.95 (ISBN 0-02-615980-5). Macmillan.

Firehouse. Dennis Smith & Jill Freedman. (Illus.). 1978. pap. 7.95 o.p. (ISBN 0-385-12577-1, Dolp). Doubleday.

Firelands Art Review 1977. Joel Rudinger. (Anthology of the Arts Ser.: No. 2). 1977. pap. 3.00x o.p. (ISBN 0-918342-04-X). Cambric.

Fireless Cookery. Heidi Kirschner. 144p. 1981. pap. 5.95 (ISBN 0-914842-58-7). Madrona Pubs.

Firelord. Parke Godwin. LC 80-497. (Science Fiction Ser.). 416p. 1980. 12.95 (ISBN 0-385-17070-X). Doubleday.

Fireman: A Personal Account. Neil Wallington. LC 78-65762. 1979. 17.95 (ISBN 0-7153-7723-X). David & Charles.

Firemanship. Boy Scouts Of America. LC 19-600. (Illus.). 64p. (gr. 6-12). 1968. pap. 0.70x (ISBN 0-8395-3317-9, 3317). BSA.

Firemen at War: The Work of London's Firefighters in the Second World War. Neil Wallington. LC 80-68692. (Illus.). 160p. 1981. 19.95 (ISBN 0-7153-7964-X). David & Charles.

Fireplace in the Home. Trudy West. LC 74-81060. (Illus.). 160p. 1976. 16.95 (ISBN 0-7153-6751-X). David & Charles.

Fireplace Stoves, Hearths, & Inserts. Geri Harrington. LC 80-7587. (Illus.). 192p. 1980. 20.00 (ISBN 0-06-011821-0, HarpT). Har-Row.

Fireplace Stoves, Hearths, & Inserts: A Guide & Catalog. Geri Harrington. LC 80-7587. (Illus.). 192p. 1980. pap. 8.95 (ISBN 0-06-090804-1, CN 804, CN). Har-Row.

Fireplaces. Robert E. Jones & Monte Burch. Ed. by Shirley M. Horowitz. LC 80-67153. (Illus.). 144p. (Orig.). 1980. 12.95 (ISBN 0-932944-25-6); pap. 5.95 (ISBN 0-932944-26-4). Creative Homeowner.

Fireplaces & Wood Stoves. M. E. Daniels. LC 76-26948. (Illus.). 1977. 13.95 (ISBN 0-672-52175-X). Bobbs.

Fireplaces & Wood Stoves. M. E. Daniels. LC 76-26948. (Illus.). 1978. pap. 7.95 (ISBN 0-672-52402-3). Bobbs.

Fireplaces: How to Build. rev ed. Sunset Editors. LC 79-90337. (Illus.). 96p. 1980. pap. 3.95 o.p. (ISBN 0-376-01155-6, Sunset Bks). Sunset-Lane.

Fireplay. William Wingate. 1978. pap. 1.95 o.s.i. (ISBN 0-515-04782-1). Jove Pubns.

Firepower. S. W. Karl. (Orig.). 1979. pap. 2.25 (ISBN 0-532-23182-1). Manor Bks.

Fireproofing: Chemistry, Technology, & Applications. P. Thiery & J. H. Goundry. (Illus.). 1970. 22.30x (ISBN 0-444-20062-2, Pub. by Applied Science). Burgess-Intl Ideas.

Fires & Human Behaviour. David Canter. LC 79-41489. 338p. 1980. 30.00 (ISBN 0-471-27709-6, Pub. by Wiley-Interscience). Wiley.

Fires in the Sky: The Birth & Death of Stars. Roy A. Gallant. LC 78-4339. (Illus.). 176p. (gr. 5-9). 1978. 8.95 (ISBN 0-590-07475-X, Four Winds). Schol Bk Serv.

Fires on the Plain. Shohei Ooka. Tr. by Ivan Morris from Japanese. 254p. 1957. pap. 5.95 (ISBN 0-8048-1379-5). C E Tuttle.

Fireship. Joan D. Vinge. 1978. pap. 1.75 o.s.i. (ISBN 0-440-15794-3). Dell.

Fireweed & Other Poems. William H. Matchett. LC 80-52963. (Illus.). 64p. (Orig.). 1980. 15.00 (ISBN 0-930954-14-9); pap. 9.00 (ISBN 0-930954-15-7). Tidal Pr.

Fireweeds: Poems. Theodore Weiss. 1976. 9.95 o.s.i. (ISBN 0-02-625750-5). Macmillan.

Fireweeds: Poems. Theodore Weiss. 1976. pap. 5.95 o.s.i. (ISBN 0-02-071000-3, Collier). Macmillan.

Firewind. Hank Searls. LC 80-648. 384p. 1981. 12.95 (ISBN 0-385-17084-X). Doubleday.

Fireworks: A Gunsite Anthology. Jeff Cooper. LC 80-83992. 1981. 19.95 (ISBN 0-916172-07-4). Janus Pr.

Fireworks: Nine Stories in Various Disguises. Angela Carter. LC 80-8706. 144p. 1981. 8.95 (ISBN 0-06-014852-7, HarpT). Har-Row.

Firm of Girdlestone. A. Conan Doyle. LC 80-65205. (Conan Doyle Centennial Ser.). (Illus.). 364p. 1981. 16.95 (ISBN 0-934468-42-7). Gaslight.

Firm up Your Thighs in Fifteen Minutes a Day. Anita Columbo & Franco Columbu. (Anita & Franco Columbu's Shape up in Minutes-a-Day Program). (Illus., Orig.). 1980. pap. 1.95 (ISBN 0-8092-7078-1); prepack 93.60 (ISBN 0-8092-7022-6). Contemp Bks.

Firmament of Time. rev. ed. Loren Eiseley. LC 60-11032. 1960. pap. 4.95 (ISBN 0-689-70068-7, 95). Atheneum.

First Across! The U. S. Navy's Transatlantic Flight of 1919. Richard K. Smith. LC 72-85396. 1973. 11.00 (ISBN 0-87021-184-6). Naval Inst Pr.

First Act in China: The Story of the Sian Mutiny. James M. Bertram. LC 74-31223. (China in the 20th Century Ser). Orig. Title: Crisis in China. (Illus.). xxii, 284p. 1975. Repr. of 1938 ed. lib. bdg. 27.50 (ISBN 0-306-70687-3). Da Capo.

First Adventure. Elizabeth Coatsworth. (Illus.). (gr. 4-6). 1950. 3.50 o.s.i. (ISBN 0-02-720380-8). Macmillan.

First Afghan War: 1838-42. James A. Norris. LC 67-21962. 1967. 65.00 (ISBN 0-521-05838-4). Cambridge U Pr.

First Aid. Boy Scouts of America. LC 19-600. (Illus.). 64p. (gr. 6-12). 1972. pap. 0.55x o.p. (ISBN 0-8395-3276-8, 3276). BSA.

First Aid. Boy Scouts of America. (Illus.). 56p. (gr. 6-12). 1981. pap. 0.70x. BSA.

First Aid & Care of Small Animals. rev. ed. Ed. by Ernest P. Walker & Animal Welfare Institute. (Illus.). 54p. 1980. pap. text ed. 2.00 (ISBN 0-938414-04-6). Animal Welfare.

First Aid & Care of Wild Birds. J. E. Cooper & J. T. Eley. 1979. 28.00 (ISBN 0-7153-7664-0). David & Charles.

First Aid & Emergency Care Workbook. 2nd new ed. Brent Hafen & Keith Karren. (Illus.). 1980. 10.00x (ISBN 0-89582-024-2). Morton Pub.

First Aid & Emergency Medical Care. James H. Rogers et al. 128p. 1980. pap. text ed. 6.95 (ISBN 0-8403-2242-9). Kendall-Hunt.

First Aid & Emergency Rescue. Lawrence Erven. Ed. by Harvey Gruber. LC 71-110984. (Fire Science Ser). (Illus.). 215p. 1970. pap. text ed. 9.95x (ISBN 0-02-474370-4, 47437). Macmillan.

First Aid at Your Fingertips. D. Lawson-Wood & J. Lawson-Wood. 56p. 1976. pap. 4.00x (ISBN 0-8464-1009-5). Beekman Pubs.

First Aid: Contemporary Practices & Principles. Ed. by Brent Q. Hafen et al. LC 72-82623. 1972. spiral bdg. 6.95 o.p. (ISBN 0-8087-0837-6). Burgess.

First Aid for Boaters & Divers. Sea Grant. 128p. 1980. pap. 4.95 (ISBN 0-695-81425-7). Follett.

First Aid for Emergency Crews: A Manual on Emergency First Aid Procedures for Ambulance Crews, Law Enforcement Officers, Fire Service Personnel, Wrecker Drivers, Hospital Staffs, Industry, Nurses. Carl B. Young, Jr. (Illus.). 192p. 1970. 10.75 (ISBN 0-398-02134-1). C C Thomas.

First Aid for Hill Walkers & Climbers. Jane Renouf & Stewart Hulse. (Illus.). 169p. 1978. pap. 5.95 (ISBN 0-14-046293-7). Bradt Ent.

First Aid for Pets: The Pet Owner's Complete Guide to Emergency Care of Dogs, Cats & Other Small Animals. Robert W. Kirk. 1978. 10.95 o.p.; pap. 7.95 (ISBN 0-87690-275-1). Dutton.

First Aid for Your Car. Robert Scharff. 1980. pap. 2.50 (ISBN 0-451-09416-6, E9416, Sig). NAL.

First Aid for Your Dog. Margaret R. Shelton et al. Ed. by Christina Foyle. 1972. 3.95 (ISBN 0-685-55804-5). Palmetto Pub.

First Aid in Mental Health. Joy Melville. 192p. 1981. text ed. cancelled o.s.i. (ISBN 0-04-362033-7, 2563); pap. 11.50 o.s.i. (ISBN 0-04-362034-5, 2564). Allen Unwin.

First Aid Principles & Procedures. Pamela B. Do Carmo & Angelo T. Patterson. (Illus.). 256p. 1976. pap. text ed. 8.95 (ISBN 0-13-317933-8). P-H.

First Aid Skill Book. Boy Scouts of America. (Illus.). 32p. (gr. 3-4). 1974. pap. 0.50x (ISBN 0-8395-6588-7, 18-328); tchr's guide 0.30 (ISBN 0-685-41687-9). BSA.

First Aid Step by Step. T. McCarthy. (Illus.). 1977. pap. 11.00x (ISBN 0-433-20451-6). Intl Ideas.

First Aid without Panic. Joel Hartley. 1977. pap. 2.50 o.p. (ISBN 0-445-08603-3). Popular Lib.

First Amendment in a Free Society. Ed. by Jonathan Bartlett. (Reference Shelf Ser.: Vol. 50, No. 6). 1979. 6.25 (ISBN 0-8242-0627-4). Wilson.

First American: A Story of North American Archaeology. C. W. Ceram. 1972. pap. 2.95 (ISBN 0-451-61862-9, ME1862, Ment). NAL.

First American Circus Ever. Irving L. Burnside. LC 78-15552. (Famous Firsts Ser.). (Illus.). 1978. lib. bdg. 7.95 (ISBN 0-686-51099-2). Silver.

First American Constitutions: Republican Ideology & the Making of State Constitutions in the Revolutionary Era. Willi P. Adams. Tr. by Rita Kimber & Robert Kimber. LC 79-10887. xviii, 351p. 1980. 23.50x (ISBN 0-8078-1388-5). U of NC Pr.

First American Cook Book. Amelia Simmons. 1966. pap. 3.50 (ISBN 0-917420-00-4). Buck Hill.

First Americans. Robert Claiborne. (Emergence of Man Ser). (Illus.). 170p. 1973. 9.95 (ISBN 0-8094-1267-5); lib. bdg. avail. (ISBN 0-685-31460-X). Time-Life.
First Americans. Robert Claiborne. LC 73-75294. (Emergence of Man Ser). (Illus.). (gr. 6 up). 1973. lib. bdg. 9.63 o.p. (ISBN 0-8094-1268-3, Pub. by Time-Life). Silver.
First Americans: Tribes of North America. Jane W. Watson. (I Am Reading Bk.). (Illus.). (gr. 1-4). 1980. 4.95 (ISBN 0-394-84194-8); PLB 5.99 (ISBN 0-394-94194-2). Pantheon.
First Among Equals: Great Britain & Venezuela, 1810-1910. George E. Carl. Ed. by David J. Robinson. LC 80-17481. (Dellplain Latin American Studies: No. 5). (Illus.). 188p. (Orig.). 1980. pap. 17.75 (ISBN 0-8357-0574-9, SS-00142, Pub. by Syracuse U Dept Geog). Univ Microfilms.
First & Last Freedom. Jiddu Krishnamurti. LC 74-25687. 228p. 1975. pap. 4.95 (ISBN 0-06-064831-7, RD 91, HarpR). Har-Row.
First & Last Journeys of Thoreau, 2 vols. in 1. Henry D. Thoreau. Ed. by Franklin B. Sanborn. LC 80-2520. 1981. Repr. of 1905 ed. 45.00 (ISBN 0-404-19068-5). AMS Pr.
First & Second Corinthians. Ed. by John Hayes. write for info (ISBN 0-8042-3239-3). John Knox.
First & Second Kings. James E. Smith. LC 78-300507. (Bible Study Textbook Ser.). (Illus.). 1975. 16.50 (ISBN 0-89900-012-6). College Pr Pub.
First & Second Messengers: New Vistas. Ed. by E. Costa et al. LC 75-14583. (Advances in Biochemical Psychopharmacology Ser: Vol. 15). 1976. 41.50 (ISBN 0-89004-084-2). Raven.
First & Second Peter. Gordon H. Clark. 1980. pap. 4.95. Presby & Reformed.
First & Second Peter. Irving L. Jensen. (Bible Self-Study Ser). 1971. pap. 2.25 (ISBN 0-8024-1060-X). Moody.
First & Second Peter. Donald Senior. (New Testament Message Ser.). 9.95 (ISBN 0-89453-143-3); pap. 4.95 (ISBN 0-89453-208-1). M Glazier.
First & Second Samuel. Irving L. Jensen. (Bible Self-Study Ser.). 1970. pap. 2.25 (ISBN 0-8024-1009-X). Moody.
First & Second Samuel. H. P. Smith. LC 99-1607. (International Critical Commentary Ser.). 462p. 1899. text ed. 20.00x (ISBN 0-567-05005-X). Attic Pr.
First & Second Thessalonians. Keith L. Brooks. (Teach Yourself the Bible Ser). 1961. pap. 1.75 (ISBN 0-8024-2645-X). Moody.
First & Second Thessalonians. Irving L. Jensen. (Bible Self-Study Ser.). 112p. 1974. pap. 2.25 (ISBN 0-8024-1053-7). Moody.
First & Second Thessalonians. James M. Reese. Ed. by Wilfrid Harrington & Donald Senior. (New Testament Message Ser.: Vol. 16). 130p. 1980. 9.95 (ISBN 0-89453-139-5); pap. 4.95 (ISBN 0-89453-204-9). M Glazier.
First & Second Thessalonians. Geoffrey Wilson. 1975. pap. 2.45 (ISBN 0-85151-227-5). Banner of Truth.
First & Second Timothy & Titus. Irving L. Jensen. (Bible Self-Study Ser.). 1973. pap. 2.25 (ISBN 0-8024-1054-5). Moody.
First & Second Timothy & Titus: Letters to Two Young Men. Calvin W. Becker. (Teach Yourself the Bible Ser). 1961. pap. 1.75 (ISBN 0-8024-2646-8). Moody.
First & the Fifth. O. John Rogge. LC 71-140377. (Civil Liberties in American History Ser). 1971. Repr. of 1960 ed. lib. bdg. 35.00 (ISBN 0-306-70087-5). Da Capo.
First Approach to Economics. E. V. Morgan. pap. 26.00x (ISBN 0-392-07843-0, SpS). Soccer.
First Asian Symposium on Intellectual Creativity in Endogenous Culture. 74p. 1980. pap. 6.75 (ISBN 92-808-0189-9, TUNU081, UNU). Unipub.
First Aviators. Curt Prendergast. (The Epic of Flight). (Illus.). 176p. (Orig.). 1981. 12.95 (ISBN 0-8094-3262-5). Time-Life.
First Baby in Camp. William P. Bennett. 68p. pap. 3.50 (ISBN 0-8466-0161-3, SJS161). Shorey.
First Bible Lessons. Jean Baxendale. (Illus., Orig.). (ps). 1955. pap. 6.95 (ISBN 0-87239-328-3, 2861). Standard Pub.
First Birth: A Family Turning Point. Doris B. Entwisle & Susan G. Doering. LC 80-22741. (Illus.). 304p. 1981. text ed. 25.00x (ISBN 0-8018-2408-7). Johns Hopkins.
First Blood. David Morrell. 256p. 1976. pap. 1.75 o.p. (ISBN 0-449-22976-9, Crest). Fawcett.
First Blue Jeans. Ricki Dru. LC 78-14398. (Famous Firsts Ser.). (Illus.). 1978. lib. bdg. 7.35 (ISBN 0-686-51100-X). Silver.
First Blues: Rags, Ballads & Harmonium Songs Nineteen Seventy-One to Nineteen Seventy-Four. LC 75-23082. 1975. 14.95 (ISBN 0-916190-04-8); pap. 6.00 (ISBN 0-916190-05-6). Full Court NY.
First Book Atlas. 2nd ed. C. S. Hammond & Co. (First Bks). (gr. 4 up). 1973. PLB 4.90 o.p. (ISBN 0-531-00473-2). Watts.
First Book of Africa. rev ed. Langston Hughes. (First Bks). (Illus.). (gr. 4-6). 1965. PLB 4.90 o.p. (ISBN 0-531-00452-X). Watts.
First Book of Air. David C. Knight. (First Bks). (Illus.). (gr. 4-6). 1961. PLB 4.90 o.p. (ISBN 0-531-00453-8). Watts.
First Book of Airplanes. rev. ed. Jeanne Bendick. LC 75-31880. (First Bks. Ser). (Illus.). 72p. (gr. 4). 1976. PLB 6.45 (ISBN 0-531-00455-4). Watts.
First Book of American History. Henry S. Commager. (First Bks.). (Illus.). (gr. 4-6). 1957. PLB 4.90 (ISBN 0-531-00458-9); pap. 1.95 o.p. (ISBN 0-531-02305-2). Watts.
First Book of American Negroes. Margaret B. Young. (First Bks). (Illus.). (gr. 4-6). 1967. PLB 6.45 (ISBN 0-531-00592-5); pap. 1.25 (ISBN 0-531-02306-0). Watts.
First Book of Ancient China. Richard L. Walker. LC 72-83645. (First Bks). (Illus.). (gr. 7 up). 1969. PLB 4.90 o.p. (ISBN 0-531-00699-9). Watts.
First Book of Ancient Egypt. Charles A. Robinson, Jr. (First Bks). (Illus.). (gr. 4-6). 1960. PLB 6.45 (ISBN 0-531-00462-7). Watts.
First Book of Ancient Greece. Charles A. Robinson, Jr. (First Bks). (Illus.). (gr. 4-6). 1960. PLB 6.90 (ISBN 0-531-00463-5). Watts.
First Book of Ancient Rome. rev. ed. Charles A. Robinson, Jr. (First Bks). (Illus.). (gr. 4-6). 1964. PLB 6.90 (ISBN 0-531-00466-X). Watts.
First Book of Ants. Helen Hoke. LC 74-98668. (First Bks). (Illus.). (gr. k-3). 1970. PLB 4.90 o.p. (ISBN 0-531-00700-6). Watts.
First Book of Archaeology. Nora B. Kubie. (First Bks). (Illus.). (gr. 4-6). 1957. PLB 6.90 (ISBN 0-531-00470-8). Watts.
First Book of Arctic Exploration. Douglas Liversidge. LC 75-114925. (First Bks). (Illus.). (gr. 4-6). 1970. PLB 4.90 o.p. (ISBN 0-531-00711-1). Watts.
First Book of Automobiles. 2nd rev. ed. Jeanne Bendick. LC 66-10586. (First Bks). (Illus.). (gr. 4-6). 1971. PLB 6.45 (ISBN 0-531-00475-9). Watts.
First Book of Baseball. rev. ed. Benjamin Brewster. (First Bks). (Illus.). (gr. 4-6). 1963. PLB 6.45 (ISBN 0-531-00479-1). Watts.
First Book of Basketball. rev ed. Don Schiffer. LC 77-3219. (First Bks.). (Illus.). (gr. 4-6). 1977. lib. bdg. 6.45 s&l (ISBN 0-531-01289-1). Watts.
First Book of Bears. Robert Whitehead & James Teason. LC 66-10585. (First Bks). (Illus.). (gr. 4-6). 1966. PLB 4.90 o.p. (ISBN 0-531-00481-3). Watts.
First Book of Bird Watching. Aubrey Burns. LC 68-11140. (First Bks). (Illus.). (gr. 4-6). 1968. PLB 4.90 o.p. (ISBN 0-531-00485-6). Watts.
First Book of Birds. Margaret Williamson. (First Bks). (Illus.). (gr. 4-6). 1951. PLB 4.90 o.p. (ISBN 0-531-00484-8). Watts.
First Book of Black Africa on the Move. Leslie Lacy. LC 77-75874. (First Bks). (Illus.). (gr. 7 up). 1969. PLB 4.90 o.p. (ISBN 0-531-00702-2). Watts.
First Book of Bolivia. William E. Carter. (First Bks). (Illus.). (gr. 4-6). 1963. PLB 4.90 o.p. (ISBN 0-531-00486-4). Watts.
First Book of Bowling. Karl Schuon. LC 66-1218. (First Bks). (Illus.). (gr. 4-6). 1966. PLB 4.90 o.p. (ISBN 0-531-00487-2). Watts.
First Book of Brazil. rev. ed. Sally Sheppard. (First Bks). (Illus.). 72p. (gr. 4-7). 1972. PLB 4.90 o.p. (ISBN 0-531-00488-0). Watts.
First Book of Bridge. Alfred Sheinwold. 1962. pap. 2.95 (ISBN 0-06-463242-3, EH 242, EH). Har-Row.
First Book of Bridge. Alfred Sheinwold. (Illus., Orig.). 1966. pap. 3.95 o.p. (ISBN 0-571-06717-4, Pub. by Faber & Faber). Merrimack Bk Serv.
First Book of Camping. rev. ed. E. C. Janes. (First Bks.). (Illus.). 72p. (gr. 3-6). 1977. PLB 6.45 (ISBN 0-531-00494-5). Watts.
First Book of Canada. rev. ed. Charles Linneaweaver. LC 67-17788. (First Bks). (Illus.). (gr. 4-6). 1967. PLB 4.90 o.p. (ISBN 0-531-00495-3). Watts.
First Book of Caves. Elizabeth Hamilton. (First Bks). (Illus.). (gr. 4-6). 1956. PLB 4.90 o.p. (ISBN 0-531-00496-1). Watts.
First Book of Cells, the Basic Structure of Life. Vicki Cobb. LC 79-101745. (First Bks). (Illus.). (gr. 7 up). 1970. PLB 4.90 o.p. (ISBN 0-531-00703-0). Watts.
First Book of Chess. I. A. Horowitz & Fred Reinfeld. 1953. pap. 2.95 (ISBN 0-06-463241-5, EH 241, EH). Har-Row.
First Book of Chess. I. A. Horowitz & Fred Reinfeld. (Illus.). 1966. pap. 3.50 o.p. (ISBN 0-571-06731-X, Pub. by Faber & Faber). Merrimack Bk Serv.
First Book of Chess. rev. ed. Joseph Leeming. Ed. by Robert S. Fenton. (First Bks.). (Illus.). (gr. 4-6). 1977. lib. bdg. 4.90 s&l o.p. (ISBN 0-531-01290-5). Watts.
First Book of Chess Strategy. G. M. Lisitsyn & B. Cafferty. 1978. pap. 9.95 (ISBN 0-7134-1423-5, Pub. by Batsford England). David & Charles.
First Book of Codes & Ciphers. Sam Epstein & Beryl Epstein. (First Bks). (Illus.). (gr. 4-6). 1956. PLB 5.90 (ISBN 0-531-00502-X). Watts.
First Book of Communist China. rev. ed. William Kinmond. (First Bks). (Illus.). 96p. (gr. 7 up). 1972. PLB 4.90 o.p. (ISBN 0-531-00506-2). Watts.
First Book of Conservation. rev. ed. Frances C. Smith. (First Bks). (Illus.). 72p. (gr. 4-6). 1972. PLB 4.90 o.p. (ISBN 0-531-00510-0). Watts.
First Book of Deserts. David C. Knight. (First Bks). (Illus.). (gr. 4-6). 1964. PLB 4.90 o.p. (ISBN 0-531-00515-1). Watts.
First Book of Drawing. Louis Slobodkin. (First Bks). (Illus.). (gr. 4-6). 1958. PLB 6.45 (ISBN 0-531-00516-X). Watts.
First Book of Eagles. Robert Whitehead. LC 68-24609. (First Bks). (Illus.). (gr. 4-6). 1968. PLB 4.90 o.p. (ISBN 0-531-00517-8). Watts.
First Book of Electrons. rev. ed. Edmund Lindop. LC 68-10435. (First Bks). (Illus.). 72p. (gr. 4-6). 1972. PLB 4.90 o.p. (ISBN 0-531-00521-6). Watts.
First Book of Electricity. Sam Epstein & Beryl Epstein. (First Bks.). (Illus.). 72p. (gr. 4-6). 1977. PLB 6.45 (ISBN 0-531-00522-4). Watts.
First Book of Energy. George R. Harrison. LC 64-17790. (First Bks). (Illus.). (gr. 4-6). 1965. PLB 4.90 o.p. (ISBN 0-531-00523-2). Watts.
First Book of England. Noel Streatfeild. (First Bks). (Illus.). (gr. 4-6). 1958. PLB 4.90 o.p. (ISBN 0-531-00524-0). Watts.
First Book of Eppe. Roderick Macleish. 384p. 1981. pap. 2.95 (ISBN 0-449-24405-9, Crest). Fawcett.
First Book of Ethics. Algernon D. Black. LC 65-13677. (First Bks). (Illus.). (gr. 4-6). 1965. PLB 4.90 o.p. (ISBN 0-531-00526-7). Watts.
First Book of Facts & How to Find Them. David C. Whitney. LC 66-12152. (First Bks). (Illus.). (gr. 4-6). 1966. PLB 4.90 o.p. (ISBN 0-531-00527-5). Watts.
First Book of Food. rev. ed. Ida Scheib & Carole E. Welker. LC 73-12477. (First Bks). (Illus.). 72p. (gr. 4-6). 1974. PLB 4.90 o.p. (ISBN 0-531-00534-8). Watts.
First Book of Gases. Vicki Cobb. LC 74-114922. (First Bks). (gr. 4-6). 1970. PLB 4.90 o.p. (ISBN 0-531-00713-8). Watts.
First Book of Glaciers. Rebecca Markus. (First Bks). (Illus.). (gr. 4-6). 1962. PLB 4.90 o.p. (ISBN 0-531-00541-0). Watts.
First Book of Graphs. rev. ed. Dyno Lowenstein. (First Bks). (Illus.). 72p. (gr. 5 up). 1976. PLB 6.45 (ISBN 0-531-00679-4). Watts.
First Book of Grasses: The Structure of Grasses Explained for Beginners. 3rd ed. Agnes Chase. LC 76-48919. (Illus.). 127p. 1977. text ed. 8.95x (ISBN 0-87474-307-9). Smithsonian.
First Book of Grasslands Around the World. Corinne J. Naden. LC 72-117184. (First Bks). (Illus.). (gr. 7 up). 1970. PLB 6.90 (ISBN 0-531-00714-6). Watts.
First Book of Hiking. C. William Harrison. LC 65-21648. (First Bks). (Illus.). (gr. 4-6). 1965. PLB 4.90 o.p. (ISBN 0-531-00547-X). Watts.
First Book of Holidays. rev. ed. Bernice Burnett. LC 74-3075. (First Bks. Ser.). (Illus.). 72p. (gr. 4-7). 1974. PLB 6.90 (ISBN 0-531-00548-8). Watts.
First Book of Hospitals. Harold Coy. LC 74-3075. (First Bks). (Illus.). (gr. 4-6). 1964. PLB 4.90 o.p. (ISBN 0-531-00550-X). Watts.
First Book of How to Make a Speech. David G. Powers. (First Bks). (Illus.). (gr. 4-6). 1963. PLB 4.90 o.p. (ISBN 0-531-00552-6); pap. 1.25 o.p. (ISBN 0-531-02301-X). Watts.
First Book of How to Run a Meeting. David G. Powers. LC 67-17556. (First Bks). (Illus.). (gr. 4-6). 1967. PLB 4.90 o.p. (ISBN 0-531-00553-4); pap. 1.25 o.p. (ISBN 0-531-02302-8). Watts.
First Book of How to Write a Report. Sue R. Brandt. LC 68-17702. (First Bks). (Illus.). (gr. 4-6). 1968. PLB 6.45 (ISBN 0-531-00554-2); pap. 0.95 o.p. (ISBN 0-685-21862-7). Watts.
First Book of Hymns. Irene Dark. (Ladybird Ser). 1968. bds. 1.49 (ISBN 0-87508-838-4). Chr Lit.
First Book of Ice Hockey. Eric Whitehead. LC 69-12390. (First Bks). (Illus.). (gr. 4-6). 1969. PLB 4.90 o.p. (ISBN 0-531-00557-7). Watts.
First Book of India. rev. ed. Jean Bothwell. LC 66-10129. (First Bks). (Illus.). (gr. 4-6). 1971. PLB 6.45 (ISBN 0-531-00559-3). Watts.
First Book of Indonesia. Frederick K. Poole. LC 70-134368. (First Bks). (Illus.). (gr. 4-6). 1971. PLB 4.90 o.p. (ISBN 0-531-00735-9). Watts.
First Book of Israel. rev. ed. Nora B. Kubie. LC 74-31166. (First Bks). (Illus.). (gr. 4-6). 1968. PLB 6.45 (ISBN 0-531-00563-1). Watts.
First Book of Italy. rev. ed. Sam Epstein & Beryl Epstein. LC 72-257. (First Bks). (Illus.). 72p. (gr. 4-6). 1972. PLB 4.90 o.p. (ISBN 0-531-00562-3). Watts.
First Book of Jazz. rev. ed. Langston Hughes. (First Bks. Ser.). (Illus.). 72p. (gr. 7-9). 1976. PLB 4.90 o.p. (ISBN 0-531-00565-8). Watts.
First Book of Kenya. F. Blanche Foster. LC 77-87928. (First Bks). (Illus.). (gr. 7 up). 1969. PLB 4.90 o.p. (ISBN 0-531-00706-5). Watts.
First Book of KIM. Jim Butterfield et al. 1978. pap. 10.75 (ISBN 0-8104-5119-0); computer program tapes 9.95 ea.; no. 00700 tape 1; no. 00800 tape 2; no. 00900 tape 3. Hayden.
First Book of Kings. F. W. Farrar. Date not set. 16.75 (ISBN 0-86524-035-3). Klock & Klock.
First Book of Letter Writing. Helen Jacobson & Florence Mischel. (First Bks). (Illus.). (gr. 4-6). 1957. PLB 4.90 o.p. (ISBN 0-531-00569-0); pap. 1.25 (ISBN 0-685-21863-5). Watts.
First Book of Local Government. rev. ed. James A. Eichner. (First Bks.). (Illus.). 72p. (gr. 6-9). 1976. PLB 6.45 (ISBN 0-531-00571-2). Watts.
First Book of Machines. Walter Buehr. (First Bks). (Illus.). (gr. 4-6). 1962. PLB 4.90 o.p. (ISBN 0-531-00574-7). Watts.
First Book of Magic. Edward Stoddard. (First Bks.). (Illus.). 72p. (gr. 4-6). 1977. PLB 6.45 (ISBN 0-531-00575-5). Watts.
First Book of Magic. Edward Stoddard. 1980. pap. 1.75 (ISBN 0-380-49221-0, 49221, Camelot). Avon.
First Book of Maps & Globes. Sam Epstein & Beryl Epstein. (First Bks). (Illus.). (gr. 4-6). 1959. PLB 4.90 o.p. (ISBN 0-531-00577-1). Watts.
First Book of Mars. rev ed. David C. Knight. LC 72-8123. (First Bks). (Illus.). 96p. (gr. 4-6). 1973. 6.45 (ISBN 0-531-00797-9). Watts.
First Book of Metal-Work. 2nd ed. Bernard Cuzner. (Illus.). 162p. 1979. pap. 7.50x (ISBN 0-905418-54-9). Intl Pubns Serv.
First Book of Meteors & Meteorites. David C. Knight. LC 69-11190. (First Bks). (Illus.). (gr. 4-6). 1969. PLB 4.90 o.p. (ISBN 0-531-00582-8). Watts.
First Book of Mexico. Sam Epstein & Beryl Epstein. LC 67-10078. (First Bks). (Illus.). (gr. 4-6). 1967. PLB 4.90 o.p. (ISBN 0-531-00583-6). Watts.
First Book of Microbes. Lucia Lewis. LC 72-254. (First Bks). (Illus.). 96p. (gr. 4 up). 1972. PLB 4.90 o.p. (ISBN 0-531-00677-8). Watts.
First Book of Microcomputers: The Home Computer Owner's Best Friend. Robert Moody. 1978. pap. 5.95 (ISBN 0-8104-5121-2). Hayden.
First Book of Mining. Patricia M. Markun. (First Bks). (Illus.). (gr. 4-6). 1959. PLB 4.90 o.p. (ISBN 0-531-00584-4). Watts.
First Book of Modern Greece. Ruth Warren. LC 66-10130. (First Bks). (Illus.). 88p. (gr. 4-6). 1972. PLB 6.45 (ISBN 0-531-00544-5). Watts.
First Book of Mythology. Kathleen Elgin. (First Bks). (Illus.). (gr. 4-6). 1955. PLB 4.90 o.p. (ISBN 0-531-00589-5). Watts.
First Book of New World Explorers. Louise D. Rich. (First Bks). (Illus.). (gr. 4-6). 1960. PLB 4.90 o.p. (ISBN 0-531-00595-X); pap. 1.25 o.p. (ISBN 0-531-02315-X). Watts.
First Book of Pearls. Eleanor R. Young. LC 72-104031. (First Bks). (Illus.). (gr. 4-6). 1970. PLB 4.90 o.p. (ISBN 0-531-00691-3). Watts.
First Book of Physical Fitness. John Walsh. (First Bks). (Illus.). (gr. 4-6). 1961. PLB 4.90 o.p. (ISBN 0-531-00610-7). Watts.
First Book of Pioneers. Walter Havighurst. (First Bks). (Illus.). (gr. 4-6). 1959. PLB 4.90 o.p. (ISBN 0-531-00611-5). Watts.
First Book of Politics. Patricia M. Markun. LC 72-93221. (First Bks). (Illus.). (gr. 4-6). 1970. PLB 4.90 o.p. (ISBN 0-531-00692-1). Watts.
First Book of Prehistoric Animals. Alice Dickinson. (First Bks). (Illus.). (gr. 4-6). 1954. PLB 4.90 o.p. (ISBN 0-531-00613-1). Watts.
First Book of Prehistoric Cave Paintings. Rebecca B. Markus. LC 68-25724. (First Bks). (Illus.). (gr. 7 up). 1968. PLB 4.90 o.p. (ISBN 0-531-00614-X). Watts.
First Book of Presidents. rev. ed. Harold Coy. LC 66-10157. (First Bks). (Illus.). (gr. 4-6). 1973. PLB 6.45 (ISBN 0-531-00615-8); pap. 1.25 (ISBN 0-531-02316-8). Watts.
First Book of Printing. Sam Epstein & Beryl Epstein. LC 72-2294. (First Bks.). (Illus.). (gr. 4-7). 1974. PLB 6.45 (ISBN 0-531-00616-6). Watts.
First Book of Puerto Rico. 2nd ed. Antonio J. Colorado. (First Bks.). (Illus.). (gr. 3-5). 1978. PLB 6.45 s&l (ISBN 0-531-01292-1). Watts.
First Book of Puzzles & Brain Twisters. Fred Walls. LC 70-100096. (First Bks). (gr. 4-6). 1970. PLB 4.90 o.p. (ISBN 0-531-00693-X). Watts.
First Book of Reconstruction. Dorothy Levenson. LC 78-117941. (First Bks). (Illus.). (gr. 4-6). 1970. PLB 4.90 o.p. (ISBN 0-531-00715-4). Watts.
First Book of Safety. Polly Bolian & Shirley Hinds. LC 76-93222. (First Bks). (Illus.). (gr. 4-6). 1970. PLB 4.90 o.p. (ISBN 0-531-00694-8). Watts.
First Book of Samuel. William G. Blaikie. 1978. 13.50 (ISBN 0-686-12946-6). Klock & Klock.

First Book of Science Experiments. Rose Wyler. LC 76-132066. (First Bks). (Illus.). (gr. 4-6). 1971. PLB 4.90 o.p. (ISBN 0-531-00623-9). Watts.

First Book of Skyscrapers. Creighton Peet. LC 64-17781. (First Bks). (Illus.). (gr. 4-6). 1964. PLB 4.90 o.p. (ISBN 0-531-00629-8). Watts.

First Book of Slavery in the United States. Leonard W. Ingraham. LC 68-27402. (First Bks). (Illus.). (gr. 4-6). 1968. PLB 6.45 (ISBN 0-531-00630-1). Watts.

First Book of Snakes. rev. ed. John Hoke. (First Bks). (Illus.). (gr. 4-6). 1956. PLB 4.90 o.p. (ISBN 0-531-00631-X). Watts.

First Book of Soccer. Clive Toye. LC 68-25725. (First Bks). (Illus.). (gr. 4-6). 1968. PLB 6.45 (ISBN 0-531-00633-6). Watts.

First Book of Soils. William H. Matthews, 3rd. LC 70-121921. (First Bks). (Illus.). (gr. 4-6). 1970. PLB 4.90 o.p. (ISBN 0-531-00716-2). Watts.

First Book of Solar Energy. John Hoke. LC 68-10336. (First Bks). (Illus.). (gr. 4-6). 1968. PLB 4.90 o.p. (ISBN 0-531-00634-4). Watts.

First Book of South America. rev. ed. William E. Carter. LC 72-249. (First Bks). (Illus.). 96p. (gr. 4-6). 1972. PLB 4.90 o.p. (ISBN 0-531-00636-0). Watts.

First Book of Space Travel. rev. ed. Jeanne Bendick. (First Bks). (Illus.). (gr. 4-6). 1969. PLB 4.90 o.p. (ISBN 0-531-00639-5). Watts.

First Book of Stones. Maribelle B. Cormack. (First Bks). (Illus.). (gr. 3-5). 1950. PLB 4.90 o.p. (ISBN 0-531-00644-1). Watts.

First Book of Swamps & Marshes. Frances C. Smith. LC 69-10887. (First Bks). (Illus.). (gr. 4-6). 1969. PLB 4.90 o.p. (ISBN 0-531-00649-2). Watts.

First Book of Switzerland. Sam Epstein & Beryl Epstein. LC 64-11911. (First Bks). (Illus.). (gr. 4-6). 1964. PLB 4.90 o.p. (ISBN 0-531-00651-4). Watts.

First Book of the American Revolution. Richard B. Morris. (First Bks). (Illus.). (gr. 4-6). 1956. PLB 4.90 o.p. (ISBN 0-531-00459-7); pap. 1.25 o.p. (ISBN 0-531-02307-9). Watts.

First Book of the Ancient Maya. Barbara Beck. LC 65-11746. (First Bks). (Illus.). (gr. 4-6). 1965. PLB 6.45 (ISBN 0-531-00464-3). Watts.

First Book of the Antarctic. Joseph B. Icenhower. (First Bks). (Illus.). (gr. 4-6). 1971. PLB 4.90 o.p. (ISBN 0-531-00468-6). Watts.

First Book of the Arab World. Ruth Warren. (First Bks). (Illus.). (gr. 4-6). 1963. PLB 4.90 o.p. (ISBN 0-531-00469-4). Watts.

First Book of the Arctic. Douglas Liversidge. LC 67-10058. (First Bks). (Illus.). (gr. 4-6). 1967. PLB 4.90 o.p. (ISBN 0-531-00472-4). Watts.

First Book of the Aztecs. Barbara Beck. LC 66-18671. (First Bks). (Illus.). (gr. 4-6). 1966. PLB 6.45 (ISBN 0-531-00476-7). Watts.

First Book of the Cabinet of the President of the U. S. James Eichner. LC 69-11536. (First Bks). (gr. 4-6). PLB 6.45 (ISBN 0-531-00491-0). Watts.

First Book of the Civil War. rev. ed. Dorothy Levenson. (First Bks.). (Illus.). (gr. 4-7). lib. bdg. 6.45 s&l (ISBN 0-531-01291-3). Watts.

First Book of the Cliff Dwellers. Rebecca Markus. LC 68-11138. (First Bks). (Illus.). (gr. 4-6). 1968. PLB 4.90 o.p. (ISBN 0-531-00501-1). Watts.

First Book of the Constitution. Richard B. Morris. (First Bks). (Illus.). (gr. 4-6). 1958. PLB 4.90 o.p. (ISBN 0-531-00511-9); pap. 1.25 o.p. (ISBN 0-531-02310-9). Watts.

First Book of the Early Settlers. Louise D. Rich. (First Bks). (Illus.). (gr. 4-6). 1960. PLB 4.90 o.p. (ISBN 0-531-00518-6); pap. 1.25 o.p. (ISBN 0-531-02312-5). Watts.

First Book of the Earth. O. Irene Sevrey. LC 67-26379. (First Bks). (Illus.). (gr. 4-6). 1958. PLB 4.90 o.p. (ISBN 0-531-00519-4). Watts.

First Book of the Emergency Room. Eleanor Kay. LC 72-11774. (First Bks). (Illus.). (gr. 4-6). 1970. PLB 4.90 o.p. (ISBN 0-531-00712-X). Watts.

First Book of the Founding of the Republic. Richard B. Morris. LC 68-10728. (First Bks). (Illus.). (gr. 4-6). 1968. PLB 4.90 o.p. (ISBN 0-531-02313-3); pap. 1.25 o.p. (ISBN 0-685-21864-3). Watts.

First Book of the Fur Trade. Louise D. Rich. LC 65-10451. (First Bks). (Illus.). (gr. 4-6). 1965. PLB 4.90 o.p. (ISBN 0-531-00539-9). Watts.

First Book of the Human Senses. Gene Liberty. (First Bks). (Illus.). (gr. 4-6). 1961. PLB 4.90 o.p. (ISBN 0-531-00555-0). Watts.

First Book of the Incas. Barbara Beck. LC 66-16579. (First Bks). (Illus.). (gr. 4-6). 1966. PLB 4.90 o.p. (ISBN 0-531-00558-5). Watts.

First Book of the Indian Wars. Richard B. Morris. (First Bks). (Illus.). (gr. 4-6). 1959. PLB 4.90 o.p. (ISBN 0-531-00560-7). Watts.

First Book of the Moon. rev. ed. Herbert Kondo. LC 72-139484. (First Bks). (Illus.). (gr. 7 up). 1971. PLB 4.90 o.p. (ISBN 0-531-00740-5). Watts.

First Book of the Neo-Narrative. Stanley Berne & Arlene Zekowski. 1954. 75.00 (ISBN 0-913844-09-8). Am Canadian.

First Book of the Netherlands. rev. ed. Angelo Cohn. (First Bks). (Illus.). (gr. 4-6). 1971. PLB 4.90 o.p. (ISBN 0-531-00593-3). Watts.

First Book of the Olympic Games. rev. ed. John Walsh. LC 63-10379. (First Bks). (Illus.). (gr. 4-6). 1971. PLB 4.90 o.p. (ISBN 0-531-00601-8). Watts.

First Book of the Opera. Noel Streatfeild. LC 65-10097. (First Bks). (Illus.). (gr. 4-6). 1967. PLB 4.90 o.p. (ISBN 0-531-00602-6). Watts.

First Book of the Red Cross. Carol Rothkopf. LC 70-134498. (First Bks). (Illus.). (gr. 4-6). 1971. PLB 4.90 o.p. (ISBN 0-531-00736-7). Watts.

First Book of the Renaissance. Neil Grant. LC 72-134366. (First Bks). (Illus.). (gr. 7 up). 1971. PLB 4.90 o.p. (ISBN 0-531-00737-5). Watts.

First Book of the Soviet Union. rev. ed. Louis L. Snyder. (First Bks). (Illus.). 96p. (gr. 7 up). 1972. PLB 6.45 (ISBN 0-531-00638-7). Watts.

First Book of the Supreme Court. Harold Coy. (First Bks). (Illus.). (gr. 7 up). 1958. PLB 4.90 o.p. (ISBN 0-531-00648-4). Watts.

First Book of the Vatican. John Deedy. LC 70-102275. (First Bks). (Illus.). (gr. 7 up). 1970. PLB 4.90 o.p. (ISBN 0-531-00697-2). Watts.

First Book of the Vikings. Louise D. Rich. (First Bks). (Illus.). (gr. 4-6). 1962. PLB 4.90 o.p. (ISBN 0-531-00660-3). Watts.

First Book of the War of 1812. Richard B. Morris. (First Bks). (Illus.). (gr. 4-6). 1961. PLB 4.90 o.p. (ISBN 0-531-00662-X). Watts.

First Book of the War with Mexico. Henry Castor. (First Bks). (Illus.). (gr. 4-6). 1964. PLB 4.90 o.p. (ISBN 0-531-00663-8). Watts.

First Book of Turkey. Emil Lengyel. LC 77-94770. (First Bks). (Illus.). (gr. 4-6). 1970. PLB 4.90 o.p. (ISBN 0-531-00695-6). Watts.

First Book of Turtles & Their Care. John Hoke. LC 78-98669. (First Bks). (Illus.). (gr. 7 up). 1970. PLB 4.90 o.p. (ISBN 0-531-00696-4). Watts.

First Book of Vegetables. Barbara L. Beck. (First Bks). (gr. 4-6). 1970. PLB 4.90 o.p. (ISBN 0-531-00717-0). Watts.

First Book of Volcanoes & Earthquakes. rev ed. Rebecca B. Markus. LC 72-2301. (First Bks). (Illus.). (gr. 4-6). 1972. PLB 4.90 o.p. (ISBN 0-531-00799-5). Watts.

First Book of Whimsy: Bits of Almost-Haiku & Other Things. Roberta Mendel. (Books for Browsers Ser.). (Illus.). 24p. (Orig.). 1978. pap. 3.00x o.p. (ISBN 0-936424-00-1, 001). Pin Prick.

First Book of Wild Bird World. C. B. Colby. (First Bks). (Illus.). (gr. 4-6). 1970. PLB 4.90 o.p. (ISBN 0-531-00698-0). Watts.

First Book of Words. Samuel Epstein & Beryl Epstein. (First Bks). (Illus.). (gr. 4-6). 1954. PLB 4.90 o.p. (ISBN 0-531-00673-5). Watts.

First Book of World War One. Louis Snyder. (First Bks). (Illus.). (gr. 7 up). 1958. PLB 6.45 (ISBN 0-531-00675-1). Watts.

First Book of World War Two. Louis Snyder. (First Bks). (Illus.). (gr. 7 up). 1958. PLB 6.45 (ISBN 0-531-00676-X); pap. 1.25 (ISBN 0-531-02319-2). Watts.

First Book on Male Liberation & Sex Equality. Frank Bertels. (Illus.). 352p. 1981. lib. bdg. 25.00 (ISBN 0-932574-05-X); pap. 15.00 (ISBN 0-932574-06-8). Brun Pr.

First-Born of Egypt. Demouzon. LC 78-54648. 1979. 8.95 o.p. (ISBN 0-85690-077-X). Peebles Pr.

First Came the Wings. Charles A. McClain. LC 79-63893. 1979. pap. 3.95x (ISBN 0-8358-0387-2). Upper Room.

First-Century Cynicism in the Epistles of Heraclitus. Harold W. Attridge. LC 76-20736. (Harvard Theological Review. Harvard Theological Studies: No. 29). 1976. pap. 6.00 (ISBN 0-89130-111-9, 020029). Scholars Pr Ca.

First-Century Judaism in Crisis: Yohanan Ben Zakkai & the Renaissance of Torah. Jacob Neusner. LC 74-14799. 208p. 1975. pap. 4.50 o.p. (ISBN 0-687-13120-0). Abingdon.

First-Century Slavery & the Interpretation of I Corinthians 7: 21. S. Scott Bartchy. LC 73-83723. (Society of Biblical Literature. Dissertation Ser.). 1973. pap. 9.00 (ISBN 0-89130-220-4, 060111). Scholars Pr Ca.

First Chinese Embassy to the West: The Journals of Kuo Sung-Tao, Liu Hsi-Hung & Chang Te-Yi. Tr. by J. D. Frodsham. (Illus.). 266p. 1974. 24.00x (ISBN 0-19-821555-X). Oxford U Pr.

First Christians: An Illustrated History of the Church. Ed. by Florence Flugaur & Mark Brokering. Tr. by John Drury from Ital. (Illus.). 124p. (gr. 4-9). 1980. 16.95 (ISBN 0-03-056823-4). Winston Pr.

First Church of Christ, Scientist, & Miscellany. Mary B. Eddy. German Ed. pap. 7.00 (ISBN 0-686-00513-9). First Church.

First Circle. Alexandr I. Solzhenitsyn. Tr. by Thomas P. Whitney from Rus. LC 68-54547. 1968. 20.00 o.p. (ISBN 0-06-013949-8, HarpT). Har-Row.

First Cities. Dora J. Hamblin. (Emergence of Man Ser.). (Illus.). 160p. 1973. 9.95 (ISBN 0-8094-1300-0); lib. bdg. avail. (ISBN 0-685-32374-9). Time-Life.

First Cities. Dora J. Hamblin. LC 73-83187. (Emergence of Man Ser.). (Illus.). 1973. lib. bdg. 9.63 o.p. (ISBN 0-686-51071-2). Silver.

First Civilizations: The Archaeology of Their Origins. Glyn Daniel. LC 68-26868. (Apollo Eds.). (Illus.). 1970. pap. 4.95 o.s.i. (ISBN 0-8152-0262-8, A262G, TYC-T). T Y Crowell.

First-Class Radiotelephone License Handbook. 4th ed. Edward M. Noll. LC 74-15459. (Illus.). 416p. 1974. pap. 8.50 o.p. (ISBN 0-672-21144-0). Sams.

First Class Radiotelephone License Handbook. 5th ed. Edward M. Noll. LC 80-52936. 1980. pap. 11.95 (ISBN 0-672-21757-0). Sams.

First Collected Edition of the Works of Oscar Wilde, 15 Vols. Oscar Wilde. Ed. by Robert Ross. 1969. Repr. of 1922 ed. Set. 225.00x o.p. (ISBN 0-06-497659-9). B&N.

First Contributions to Psycho-Analysis. Sandor Ferenczi. Tr. by Ernest Jones from Ger. LC 80-19815. (Brunner-Mazel Classics in Psycholoanalysis Ser.: No. 6). Orig. Title: Sex in Psychoanalysis. 340p. 1980. Repr. 20.00 (ISBN 0-87630-254-1). Brunner-Mazel.

First Convention. Thomas McCarthy. 1978. pap. text ed. 6.25x (ISBN 0-85105-340-8, Dolmen Pr). Humanities.

First Corinthians. Keith L. Brooks. (Teach Yourself the Bible Ser). 1964. pap. 1.75 (ISBN 0-8024-2649-2). Moody.

First Corinthians. Jerome Murphy-O'Connor. (New Testament Message Ser.: Vol. 10). 172p. 1980. 9.95 (ISBN 0-89453-133-6); pap. 4.95 (ISBN 0-89453-198-0). M Glazier.

First Corinthians. Geoffrey Wilson. 1978. pap. 3.95. Banner of Truth.

First Corinthians (Adult Workbook) Darrell Conley. pap. 1.95 (ISBN 0-89315-052-5). Lambert Bk.

First Course in Abstract Algebra. 2nd ed. John B. Fraleigh. LC 75-9010. 1976. 19.95 (ISBN 0-201-01984-1). A-W.

First Course in Algebra. Linsley Wyant & James Stakkestad. (Page-Ficklin Math Ser). 1976. pap. 12.95 (ISBN 0-8087-3710-4). Burgess.

First Course in Algebra & Number Theory. Edwin Weiss. 1971. text ed. 21.95 (ISBN 0-12-743150-0). Acad Pr.

First Course in Algebraic Topology. C. Kosniowski. LC 79-41682. 280p. 1980. 44.50 (ISBN 0-521-23195-7); pap. 15.95 (ISBN 0-521-29864-4). Cambridge U Pr.

First Course in Calculus. 4th ed. Serge Lang. LC 77-76193. (Mathematics Ser.). (Illus.). 1978. text ed. 20.95 (ISBN 0-201-04149-9). A-W.

First Course in Calculus with Analytic Geometry. Harley Flanders et al. 1973. 19.95 (ISBN 0-12-259657-9); instrs' manual 3.00 (ISBN 0-12-259658-7). Acad Pr.

First Course in Continuum Mechanics. 2nd ed. Yuan-Cheng Fung. (International Series in Dynamics). (Illus.). 1977. 26.95 (ISBN 0-13-318311-4). P-H.

First Course in Data Processing. J. D. Couger & F. McFadden. 1977. 21.95 (ISBN 0-471-17738-5). Wiley.

First Course in Data Processing with BASIC. Dan Couger & Fred McFadden. LC 80-22130. 450p. 1981. pap. text ed. 17.95 (ISBN 0-471-08046-2). Wiley.

First Course in Data Processing with BASIC, COBOL, FORTRAN, RPG II. 2nd ed. Dan Couger & Fred McFadden. LC 80-22129. 550p. 1981. pap. text ed. 17.50 (ISBN 0-471-05581-6). Wiley.

First Course in Differential Equations. F. G. Hagin. (Illus.). 384p. 1975. text ed. 18.95 (ISBN 0-13-318394-7). P-H.

First Course in Differential Geometry. Chuan-Chih Hsiung. LC 80-22112. (Pure & Applied Mathematics Ser.). 375p. 1981. 24.00 (ISBN 0-471-07953-7, Pub. by Wiley-Interscience). Wiley.

First Course in Fundamentals of Mathematics. Edwin I. Stein. (gr. 7-12). 1978. text ed. 13.96 (ISBN 0-205-05540-0, 5655404); tchr's guide 2.00 (ISBN 0-205-05541-9, 5655412). Allyn.

First Course in Linear Algebra. Raymond A. Beauregard & John B. Fraleigh. LC 72-5648. 1973. text ed. 20.50 (ISBN 0-395-14017-X, 3-03230); solutions manual. pap. 2.15 (ISBN 0-395-14018-8, 3-03231). HM.

First Course in Linear Algebra. 2nd ed. Daniel Zelinsky. 1973. text ed. 18.95 (ISBN 0-12-779060-8). Acad Pr.

First Course in Mathematical Analysis. John C. Burkill. 1962. 23.95x (ISBN 0-521-04381-6); pap. 13.95x (ISBN 0-521-29468-1). Cambridge U Pr.

First Course in Mathematical Statistics. George G. Roussas. LC 71-183673. 1973. text ed. 24.95 (ISBN 0-201-06522-3). A-W.

First Course in Modern Mathematics, Vol. 1. Marie Anderson. 1973. text ed. 5.95x o.p. (ISBN 0-435-50018-X); pap. text ed. 5.95x with answers o.p. (ISBN 0-435-50019-8). Heinemann Ed.

First Course in Modern Mathematics, Vol. 2. Marie Anderson. 1972. text ed. 3.95x o.p. (ISBN 0-435-50020-1); pap. text ed. 5.95x with answers o.p. (ISBN 0-435-50021-X). Heinemann Ed.

First Course in Modern Mathematics, Vol. 3. Marie Anderson. 1973. text ed. 3.95x o.p. (ISBN 0-435-50022-8); pap. text ed. 5.95x with answers o.p. (ISBN 0-435-50023-6). Heinemann Ed.

First Course in Modern Mathematics, Vol. 4. Marie Anderson. 1971. text ed. 3.95x o.p. (ISBN 0-435-50016-3); pap. text ed. 5.95x with answers o.p. (ISBN 0-435-50017-1). Heinemann Ed.

First Course in Ordinary Differential Equations. 4th ed. Walter Leighton. 1976. text ed. 21.95x (ISBN 0-534-00435-0). Wadsworth Pub.

First Course in Ordinary Differential Equations. 5th ed. Walter Leighton. 304p. 1980. text ed. 21.95x (ISBN 0-534-00837-2). Wadsworth Pub.

First Course in Partial Differential Equations: With Complex Variables & Transform Methods. Hans F. Weinberger. 1965. 28.95 (ISBN 0-471-00623-8). Wiley.

First Course in Probability & Statistics. Henrick J. Malik & Kenneth Mullen. LC 72-1941. 1973. text ed. 16.95 (ISBN 0-201-04413-7). A-W.

First Course in Quantitative Analysis. Ray U. Brumblay. LC 77-93982. (Chemistry Ser). 1970. text ed. cancelled (ISBN 0-201-00726-6). A-W.

First Course in Rational Continuum Mechanics: General Concepts, Vol. 1. Clifford A. Truesdell. (Pure & Applied Math Ser.). Vol. 1, 1977. 32.00 (ISBN 0-12-701301-6); Vol. 2, 1981. write for info. (ISBN 0-12-701302-4). Acad Pr.

First Course in Rings, Fields & Vector Spaces. P. B. Bhattacharya & S. K. Jain. 1977. 10.95 (ISBN 0-470-99047-3, 76-55303). Halsted Pr.

First Course in Statistics. R. Loveday. text ed. 6.95x (ISBN 0-521-05601-2). Cambridge U Pr.

First Course in Stochastic Processes. 2nd ed. Samuel Karlin. 1975. text ed. 22.95 (ISBN 0-12-398552-8). Acad Pr.

First Course in Technical English, Bk. 2. Lynette Beardwood et al. (Illus.). 1979. pap. text ed. 5.95x (ISBN 0-435-28758-3); tchr's ed. 7.50x (ISBN 0-435-28759-1); 24.00tape (ISBN 0-435-28760-5); cassette 22.00 (ISBN 0-435-28031-7). Heinemann Ed.

First Course of Homological Algebra. D. G. Northcott. LC 72-97873. 250p. 1973. 29.95 (ISBN 0-521-20196-9). Cambridge U Pr.

First Course of Homological Algebra. D. G. Northcott. LC 72-87873. 217p. 1980. pap. 12.50x (ISBN 0-521-29976-4). Cambridge U Pr.

First Crop. Gertrude Bell. LC 72-89608. (Illus.). (gr. 5-8). 1973. 6.50 o.p. (ISBN 0-8309-0082-9). Independence Pr.

First Crossword Puzzle Book. Leslie Hill & P. R. Popkin. 64p. 1968. pap. text ed. 2.95x (ISBN 0-19-432551-2). Oxford U Pr.

First Crusade. Steven Runciman. LC 80-40228. (Illus.). 224p. 1980. 19.95 (ISBN 0-521-23255-4). Cambridge U Pr.

First Crusade: The Chronicle of Fulcher of Chartres & Other Source Materials. Ed. by Edward Peters. LC 74-163384. (Middle Ages Ser). 1971. 9.50x (ISBN 0-8122-7643-4); pap. text ed. 5.95x (ISBN 0-8122-1017-4, Pa Paperbks). U of Pa Pr.

First Day of Spring & Other Prose: Stories & Other Prose. Raymond Knister. Ed. by Peter Stevens. LC 76-10475. (Literature of Canada Ser: No. 17). 376p. 1975. pap. 7.95 (ISBN 0-8020-6198-2). U of Toronto Pr.

First Deadly Sin. Lawrence Sanders. 1980. pap. 2.95 (ISBN 0-425-04692-3). Berkley Pub.

First Dictionary of Linguistics & Phonetics. David Crystal. (Language Library Ser.). 404p. 1980. lib. bdg. 32.50x (ISBN 0-86531-051-3, Pub. by Andre Deutsch); pap. text ed. 12.00 (ISBN 0-86531-050-5). Westview.

First Do No Harm. Natalee Greenfield. 176p. 1981. pap. 1.95 (ISBN 0-448-17227-5, Tempo). G&D.

First Do No Harm... A Dying Woman's Battle Against the Physicians & Drug Companies Who Misled Her About the Hazards of the Pill. Natalee S. Greenfield. 1976. 7.95 (ISBN 0-8467-0198-7, Pub. by Two Continents). Hippocrene Bks.

First Edition? Statements of Selected North American, British Commonwealth, & Irish Publishers on Their Methods of Designating First Editions. Ed. by Edward N. Zempel & Linda A. Verkler. LC 77-89503. 1977. 12.50 (ISBN 0-930358-00-7); pap. 7.95 (ISBN 0-930358-01-5). Spoon River.

First Epistle of St. Peter. 2nd ed. Edward G. Selwyn. (Thornapple Commentaries Ser.). 517p. 1981. pap. 10.95 (ISBN 0-8010-8199-8). Baker Bk.
First Epistle to Timothy. Henry P. Liddon. 1978. 6.00 (ISBN 0-686-12944-X). Klock & Klock.
First European Elections: A Handbook & Guide. Chris Cook. 1979. text ed. 20.75x (ISBN 0-391-00989-3); pap. text ed. 10.00x (ISBN 0-391-00990-7). Humanities.
First Explorers. John Vernon. 1978. 14.95 (ISBN 0-7134-0986-X, Pub. by Batsford England). David & Charles.
First Farmers. Jonathan N. Leonard. LC 73-85264. (Emergence of Man Ser). (Illus.). (gr. 6 up). 1973. lib. bdg. 9.63 o.p. (ISBN 0-8094-1305-1, Pub. by Time-Life). Silver.
First Farmers. Jonathan N. Leonard. (Emergence of Man Ser.). (Illus.). 1973. 9.95 (ISBN 0-8094-1304-3); lib. bdg. avail. (ISBN 0-685-41616-X). Time-Life.
First Fast Draw. Louis L'Amour. 160p. (Orig.). 1980. pap. 2.25 (ISBN 0-553-14538-X). Bantam.
First Ferro Boat Book. Pete Greenfield. Ed. by Denny Desoutter. (Practical Handbooks for the Yachtsman Ser.). (Illus.). 1979. 15.00 (ISBN 0-370-30066-1); pap. 10.50 (ISBN 0-370-30090-4). Transatlantic.
First Fifty Years. David Filbeck. LC 80-65966. 400p. 1980. pap. 5.95 (ISBN 0-89900-060-6). College Pr Pub.
First Fifty Years: The Cleveland Museum of Art 1916-1966. Carl Wittke. LC 66-21227. (Illus.). 176p. 1966. 10.00x (ISBN 0-910386-09-9, Pub. by Cleveland Mus Art). Ind U Pr.
First Fire. Francesca Greer. (Orig.). 1979. pap. 2.50 o.s.i. (ISBN 0-446-81915-8). Warner Bks.
First Fire: Central & South American Indian Poetry. Hugh Fox. LC 77-11528. 1978. pap. 5.95 o.p. (ISBN 0-385-03815-1, Anchor Pr). Doubleday.
First Flowers of Our Wilderness: American Painting, the Colonial Period. James T. Flexner. (History of American Painting Ser.: Vol. 1). (Illus.). 390p. 1980. pap. 5.00 (ISBN 0-486-22180-6). Dover.
First Foods. rev. ed. Marion Cronan & June Atwood. (gr. 7-9). 1976. text ed. 11.88 (ISBN 0-87002-168-0); tchr's guide avail. Bennett IL.
First Four Years Are the Hardest: A Handbook for Campus Christians. Michael Pountney. LC 80-19792. (Illus.). 110p. (Orig.). 1980. pap. 3.95 (ISBN 0-87784-451-8). Inter-Varsity.
First Freedom. M. L. Ernst. LC 73-166324. (Civil Liberties in American History Ser.). 316p. 1971. Repr. of 1946 ed. lib. bdg. 29.50 (ISBN 0-306-70242-8). Da Capo.
First Freedom. Bryce W. Rucker. LC 68-11651. (Arcturus Books Paperbacks). 340p. 1971. pap. 9.95 (ISBN 0-8093-0498-8). S Ill U Pr.
First French Republic, 1792-1804. M. J. Sydenham. 1974. 23.75x (ISBN 0-520-02577-6). U of Cal Pr.
First Gentlemen of Virginia: Intellectual Qualities of the Early Colonial Ruling Class. Louis B. Wright. LC 40-247. pap. 3.95 (ISBN 0-8139-0247-9). U Pr of Va.
First Geography of Jamaica. 2nd ed. F. C. Evans. (Illus.). 48p. (gr. 5-8). 1973. 4.75x (ISBN 0-521-20252-3). Cambridge U Pr.
First Geography of the Eastern Caribbean. F. C. Evans. (Illus.). 48p. (gr. 5 up). 1972. text ed. 4.75x (ISBN 0-521-08312-5). Cambridge U Pr.
First Geography of the West Indies. F. C. Evans. (gr. 5 up). 1974. 5.95x (ISBN 0-521-20112-8). Cambridge U Pr.
First Geography of Trinidad & Tobago. 2nd ed. F. C. Evans. LC 67-21957. (Illus.). text ed. 4.75x (ISBN 0-521-20180-2). Cambridge U Pr.
First Glance at Adrienne Von Speyr. Hans Urs Von Balthasar. Tr. by Antje Lawry & Sr. Sergia Englund. LC 79-91933. Orig. Title: Erster Blick Auf Adrienne Von Speyr. 220p. (Orig.). 1981. pap. 6.95 (ISBN 0-89870-003-5). Ignatius Pr.
First Grade Takes a Test. Miriam Cohen. LC 80-10316. (Illus.). 32p. (ps-3). 1980. 7.95 (ISBN 0-688-80265-6); PLB 7.63 (ISBN 0-688-84265-8). Greenwillow.
First Grammatical Treatise: The Earliest Germanic Phonology. 2nd, rev. ed. Ed. by Einar Haugen. (Classics of Linguistics Ser). (Illus.). 112p. 1973. text ed. 15.00x (ISBN 0-582-52491-1). Longman.
First Group Therapy Book. Edward L. Pinney, Jr. 224p. 1970. text ed. 11.50 (ISBN 0-398-01490-6). C C Thomas.
First Hebrew Primer for Adults. Ethelyn Simon et al. (Orig.). 1981. pap. text ed. 12.95 (ISBN 0-939144-01-8). EKS Pub Co.
First Horsemen. Frank Trippet. (Emergence of Man Ser.). (Illus.). 1974. 9.95 (ISBN 0-8094-1278-0); lib. bdg. avail. (ISBN 0-685-50286-4). Time-Life.
First Horsemen. Frank Trippett. (gr. 6 up). 1974. PLB 11.56 o.p. (ISBN 0-8094-1279-9, Pub. by Time-Life). Silver.
First I Say the Shema. Molly Cone. (Shema Primary Ser: No. 1). (Illus., Orig.). (gr. 1). 1971. pap. text ed. 5.00 (ISBN 0-8074-0134-X, 101081). UAHC.
First Images of America: The Impact of the New World. Ed. by Fredi Chiappelli. LC 75-7191. 1976. 130.00x (ISBN 0-520-03010-9). U of Cal Pr.
First Immortals. E. L. Arch. (YA) 5.95 (ISBN 0-685-07433-1, Avalon). Bouregy.
First International Conference on Uranium Mine Waste Disposal. Ed. by Charles O. Brawner. LC 80-69552. (Illus.). 626p. 1980. 22.00x (ISBN 0-89520-279-4). Soc Mining Eng.
First International Symposium on Groundwater Ecology. Proceedings, Schlitz, September 1975. Ed. by Siegfried Husmann. 232p. 1976. pap. text ed. 29.95 (ISBN 90-265-0240-0, Pub. by Swets Pub Serv Holland). Swets North Am.
First into the Air: The First Airplanes. David McMullen & Susan McMullen. LC 78-15141. (Famous Firsts Ser.). (Illus.). 1978. lib. bdg. 7.35 (ISBN 0-686-51101-8). Silver.
First John: A Commentary. Gordon H. Clark. 1980. pap. 4.75 (ISBN 0-87552-166-5). Presby & Reformed.
First Kings & Chronicles. rev.ed ed. Ed. by Irving L. Jensen. (Bible Self-Study Ser). (Illus.). 1968. pap. 2.25 (ISBN 0-8024-1011-1). Moody.
First LACUS Forum: Proceedings. Linguistic Association of Canada & the U.S. Ed. by Adam Makkai & Valerie Makki. pap. text ed. 10.95 (ISBN 0-685-69725-8). Hornbeam Pr.
First Ladies. Rhoda Blumberg. LC 77-2617. (First Bks.). (gr. 4-6). 1977. PLB 6.45 (ISBN 0-531-01286-7). Watts.
First Ladies. Kathleen Prindiville. (gr. 4-6). 1964. 4.95 o.s.i. (ISBN 0-02-775150-3). Macmillan.
First Ladies of the White House: Washington Thru Nixon. Lee Brooks. LC 76-86857. (Illus.). 156p. 1981. 12.50 (ISBN 0-87319-022-X). C Hallberg.
First Lady of Versailles: Marie Adelaide of Savory, Dauphine of France. Lucy Norton. (Illus.). 1978. 15.00 o.s.i. (ISBN 0-397-01051-6). Lippincott.
First Lensman. E. E. Smith. 1973. pap. 1.75 (ISBN 0-515-05332-5). Jove Pubns.
First Lessons in Grammar. Samuel S. Greene. Repr. of 1848 ed. write for info. (ISBN 0-8201-1349-2). Schol Facsimil.
First Level Nursing-Study Modules. Venner M. Farley. (Nursing-Registered Ser.). 1981. pap. 10.00 (ISBN 0-8273-1873-1); write for info. instrs'. guide (ISBN 0-8273-1875-8). Delmar.
First Line Defense: The U. S. Navy Since 1945. Paul B. Ryan. (Publication Ser.: No. 237). 336p. 1981. 14.95 (ISBN 0-8179-7371-0). Hoover Inst Pr.
First-Line Management: Approaching Supervision Effectively. rev. ed. Lawrence L. Steinmetz & H. Ralph Todd, Jr. 1979. pap. 10.50x (ISBN 0-256-02213-5). Business Pubns.
First-Line Patient Care Management. Barbara J. Stevens. LC 76-499. 192p. 1976. 13.25 o.s.i. (ISBN 0-913654-25-6); pap. 8.95 o.s.i. (ISBN 0-913654-26-4). Nursing Res.
First-Line Supervisor's Manual. Glen D. King. (Police Science Ser.). 160p. 1976. 10.75 (ISBN 0-398-01017-X). C C Thomas.
First Lines for the Practice of Physic. William Cullen. Bd. with Physiology. E. Peart. (Contributions to the History of Psychology Ser., Vol. XII, Pt. A: Orientations). 1980. Repr. of 1822 ed. 30.00 (ISBN 0-89093-314-6). U Pubns Amer.
First Living Things. Julian May. LC 79-119799. (Illus.). (gr. k-3). 1970. reinforced bdg. 4.50 o.p. (ISBN 0-8234-0177-4). Holiday.
First Look at Cats. Millicent E. Selsam & Joyce Hunt. LC 80-7673. (First Look at Ser.). (Illus.). 32p. (gr. 1-4). 1981. 7.95 (ISBN 0-8027-6398-7); PLB 8.85 (ISBN 0-8027-6399-5). Walker & Co.
First Look at Dogs. Millicent Selsam & Joyce Hunt. Tr. by Harriett Springer. (First Look at Ser.). 32p. (gr. 1-4). 1981. 7.95 (ISBN 0-8027-6409-6); lib. bdg. 8.85 (ISBN 0-8027-6421-5). Walker & Co.
First Look at Fish. Millicent Selsam & Joyce Hunt. LC 72-81377. (First Look at Ser). 32p. (gr. 2-4). 1972. 4.50 o.s.i. (ISBN 0-8027-6119-4); PLB 5.39 (ISBN 0-8027-6120-8). Walker & Co.
First Look at Flowers. Millicent E. Selsam & Joyce Hunt. LC 76-57063. (First Look at Ser.). (Illus.). (gr. k-3). 1977. 5.95 o.s.i. (ISBN 0-8027-6281-6); PLB 6.85 (ISBN 0-8027-6282-4). Walker & Co.
First Look at Frogs, Toads & Salamanders. Millicent E. Selsam & Joyce Hunt. (First Look at Ser.). (Illus.). 32p. (gr. 2-4). 1976. 5.50 o.s.i. (ISBN 0-8027-6243-3); PLB 6.85 (ISBN 0-8027-6244-1). Walker & Co.
First Look at Insects. Millicent E. Selsam & Joyce Hunt. LC 73-92451. (First Look at Ser). (Illus.). 32p. (gr. 2-4). 1974. 5.50 o.s.i. (ISBN 0-8027-6181-X); PLB 5.39 (ISBN 0-8027-6182-8). Walker & Co.
First Look at Leaves. Millicent E. Selsam. Ed. by Millicent E. Selsam & Joyce Hunt. LC 72-81376. (First Look at Ser). (Illus.). 32p. (gr. 2-4). 1972. 5.39 o.s.i. (ISBN 0-8027-6117-8); PLB 5.39 (ISBN 0-8027-6118-6). Walker & Co.
First Look at Sharks. Millicent Selsam et al. (First Look at Ser.). (Illus.). (gr. k-3). 1979. 7.95 o.s.i. (ISBN 0-8027-6372-3); PLB 7.85 (ISBN 0-8027-6373-1). Walker & Co.
First Look at Snakes, Lizards & Other Reptiles. Millicent E. Selsam & Joyce Hunt. LC 74-26315. (Illus.). 32p. (gr. 1-4). 1975. 5.50 o.s.i. (ISBN 0-8027-6212-3); PLB 5.39 (ISBN 0-8027-6211-5). Walker & Co.
First Look at Whales. Millicent E. Selsam & Joyce Hunt. (First Look at Ser.). (gr. k-3). 1980. 7.95 o.s.i. (ISBN 0-8027-6387-1); PLB 8.85 (ISBN 0-8027-6388-X). Walker & Co.
First Love. Bethany Strong. 1978. pap. 1.95 o.s.i. (ISBN 0-515-04504-7). Jove Pubns.
First Love & Other Tales. Ivan Turgenev. Tr. by David Magarshack. Orig. Title: Selected Tales of Ivan Turgenev. 1968. pap. 4.95 (ISBN 0-393-00444-9, Norton Lib). Norton.
First Marriage. Fanny Howe. 1977. pap. 1.75 (ISBN 0-380-01850-0, 36475). Avon.
First Medical College in Vermont, Castleton, 1818-1862. Frederick C. Waite. (Illus.). 280p. 1949. 2.00x o.p. (ISBN 0-934720-14-2). VT Hist Soc.
First Men. Edmund White. (Emergence of Man Ser.). (Illus.). 1973. 9.95 (ISBN 0-8094-1259-4); lib. bdg. avail. (ISBN 0-685-28794-7). Time-Life.
First Men. Edmund White. LC 73-93968. (Emergence of Man Ser.). (Illus.). 1973. lib. bdg. 9.63 o.p. (ISBN 0-686-51072-0). Silver.
First Month of Life. G. Stoutt. 1977. pap. 6.95 (ISBN 0-87489-067-5). Med Economics.
First Month of Life: A Parent's Guide to Care of the Newborn. Glen R. Stoutt, Jr. 1981. pap. 1.95 (ISBN 0-451-09613-4, J9613, Sig). NAL.
First Ms. Reader. Ms. Magazine Editors. 228p. (Orig.). 1973. pap. 1.95 o.s.i. (ISBN 0-446-89027-8). Warner Bks.
First New Deal. Raymond Moley. LC 66-22282. (Illus.). 1966. 12.50 o.p. (ISBN 0-15-131290-7). HarBraceJ.
First New York-Philadelphia Stage Road. James Cawley & Margaret Cawley. LC 78-75175. (Illus.). 120p. 1980. 14.50 (ISBN 0-8386-2331-X). Fairleigh Dickenson.
First Nine Months of Life. Geraldine L. Flanagan. (Illus.). 95p. 1978. Repr. of 1962 ed. 12.95x (ISBN 0-433-10600-X). Intl Ideas.
First Notebook of Head Injury. 2nd ed. K. G. Jamieson. (Illus.). 1971. 14.95 (ISBN 0-407-17350-1). Butterworths.
First Number Book. Shari Robinson. LC 80-83587. (Illus.). 96p. (gr. k-4). 1981. PLB 11.85 (ISBN 0-448-13922-7); pap. 3.95 (ISBN 0-448-47335-6). Platt.
First of Midnight. Marjorie Darke. LC 77-13435. (gr. 6 up). 1978. 6.95 (ISBN 0-395-28854-1, Clarion). HM.
First of the Penguins. Mary Q. Steele. LC 73-1964. (Illus.). 160p. (gr. 5-9). 1973. 4.95g o.s.i. (ISBN 0-02-786880-X). Macmillan.
First of the Tudors: A Study of Henry VII & His Reign. Michael Van Cleave Alexander. 280p. 1980. 22.50x (ISBN 0-8476-6259-4). Rowman.
First Offensive, 1942: Roosevelt, Marshall, & the Making of American Strategy. Richard W. Steele. LC 73-75792. 256p. 1973. 15.00x (ISBN 0-253-32215-4). Ind U Pr.
First Official NFL Trivia Book. Ted Brock & Jim Campbell. 1980. pap. 1.95 (ISBN 0-451-09541-3, J9541, Sig). NAL.
First Olympic Games. Barbara Christesen. LC 78-15976. (Famous Firsts Ser.). (Illus.). 1978. lib. bdg. 7.35 (ISBN 0-686-51102-6). Silver.
First on Mars, No. 18. Rex Gordon. (Science Fiction Rediscovery Ser.). 1976. pap. 2.25 o.p. (ISBN 0-380-00572-7, 28084). Avon.
First on the Antarctic Continent. C. E. Borchgrevink. (Illus.). 333p. 1980. Repr. of 1901 ed. 49.00x (ISBN 0-7735-0515-6). McGill-Queens U Pr.
First Over Germany: A Story of the 306th Bombardment Group. Arthur Bove. LC 80-69557. (Aviation Ser.: No. 4). (Illus.). 138p. Repr. 20.00 (ISBN 0-89839-038-9). Battery Pr.
First Over the Oceans. Melinda Blau. LC 78-12960. (Famous Firsts Ser.). (Illus.). 1978. lib. bdg. 7.35 (ISBN 0-686-51103-4). Silver.
First Part of Hieronimo. Thomas Kyd. Ed. by Andrew S. Cairncross. Bd. with Spanish Tragedy. LC 66-20826. (Regent Renaissance Drama Ser). 1967. 10.95x (ISBN 0-8032-0267-9); pap. 2.65x (ISBN 0-8032-5267-6, BB 221, Bison). U of Nebr Pr.
First Part of the Life & Raigne of King Henrie the IIII. Sir John Hayward. LC 74-28862. (English Experience Ser.: No. 742). 1975. Repr. of 1599 ed. 11.50 (ISBN 90-221-0742-6). Walter J Johnson.
First Penthouse Dwellers of America. Ruth Underhill. LC 75-23849. (Illus.). 1976. 15.00 (ISBN 0-88307-525-3); pap. 4.95 (ISBN 0-88307-526-1). Gannon.
First Person, Vol. 1. Ed. by M. D. Elevitch. 1978. pap. 7.50 (ISBN 0-916452-03-4). First Person.
First-Person America. Ann Banks. LC 80-7660. (Illus.). 320p. 1980. 13.95 (ISBN 0-394-41397-0). Knopf.
First Person: An Essay on Reference & Intentionality. Roderick Chisholm. LC 80-24910. 192p. 1981. 22.50x (ISBN 0-8166-1045-2). U of Minn Pr.
First Person, Singular. Compiled by Jerry Jones. 175p. 1981. pap. 4.95 (14018P). Impact Tenn.
First Person Singular: Living the Good Life Alone. Stephen M. Johnson. LC 76-51353. 1977. 10.00 o.p. (ISBN 0-397-01162-8). Lippincott.
First Peter, 2 vols. John Brown. 1980. 29.95 (ISBN 0-85151-204-6); Vol. 1, 577 Pp. (ISBN 0-85151-205-4); Vol. 2, 640 Pp. (ISBN 0-85151-206-2). Banner of Truth.
First Philosophers. 2nd ed. George Thomson. (Studies in Ancient Society). (Illus.). 1961-1977. pap. text ed. 6.50x (ISBN 0-85315-406-6). Humanities.
First Philosophy: An Introduction to Philosophical Issues. Max Hocutt. 272p. 1980. pap. text ed. 9.95x (ISBN 0-534-00790-2). Wadsworth Pub.
First Photographs. Gail Buckland. (Illus.). 192p. 1980. 29.95 (ISBN 0-02-518070-3). Macmillan.
First Photographs of Jerusalem: The Old City. Ed. by Ely Schiller. (Illus.). 252p. (Eng. & Heb.). 1978. 30.00x (ISBN 0-8002-2455-8). Intl Pubns Serv.
First Piatigorsky Cup. Ed. by Isaac Kashdan. (Illus.). 224p. 1980. pap. 3.50 (ISBN 0-486-24066-5). Dover.
First Picture Dictionary - English-Arabic. (Illus.). 2.50x (ISBN 0-686-53072-1). Intl Bk Ctr.
First Pink Light. Eloise Greenfield. LC 75-45478. (Illus.). 40p. (gr. k-3). 1976. PLB 7.89 (ISBN 0-690-01087-7, TYC-J). T Y Crowell.
First Planning Meeting for TOPEX. (Topex Report Ser.: No. 1). 83p. 1981. pap. 10.00 (ISBN 92-63-10565-0, W479, WMO). Unipub.
First Polish Americans: Silesian Settlements in Texas. T. Lindsay Baker. LC 78-6373. 1979. 14.95 (ISBN 0-89096-060-7). Tex A&M Univ Pr.
First Prayers for Young Catholics. Maureen Curley. (Children of the Kingdom Activities Ser.). (gr. 1-4). 1978. 7.95 (ISBN 0-686-13686-1). Pflaum Pr.
First Principles of Composition, 4 vols. Eugene H. Soules. Incl. Vol. 1-Using a Dictionary to Avoid Spelling Errors (ISBN 0-86589-001-3); Vol. 2 Editing & Revising for Correct Entence Structure (ISBN 0-86589-002-1); Vol. 3-Using Modifiers for Clarity & Effectiveness (ISBN 0-86589-003-X); Vol. 4-Analyzing Sentences for Consistency (ISBN 0-86589-004-8). 1975. Set. 11.00 (ISBN 0-86589-000-5). Individual Learn.
First Principles of the Science of Mining & Salt Mining. Franz L. Cancrinus. Tr. by Kenneth V. Bordeau & Elvi L. Bordeau. LC 80-65488. (Microform Publication: No. 10). 1980. 4.00 (ISBN 0-8137-6010-0). Geol Soc.
First Principles of Verse. Robert Hillyer. 1950. text ed. 8.95 (ISBN 0-87116-032-3). Writer.
First Principles: Topical Studies for New Converts. Gary Underwood & Marylyn Underwood. 1978. 3.45 (ISBN 0-89137-709-3). Quality Pubns.
First Printings of American Authors, 4 vols. Ed. by Matthew J. Bruccoli & C. E. Clark, Jr. LC 74-11756. (Illus.). 1978. Set. 220.00 (ISBN 0-8103-0933-5). Gale.
First Printings of American Authors: Supplement, Vol. 5. Ed. by Matthew J. Bruccoli & C. E. Clark, Jr. (Illus.). 1980. 55.00 (ISBN 0-8103-0934-3, Bruccoli Clark Bk). Gale.
First Rapprochement: England & the United States, 1795-1805. Bradford Perkins. 1967. Repr. 20.00x (ISBN 0-520-00998-3). U of Cal Pr.
First Reader in Biblical Theology: The Design of the Scriptures. Robert C. Dentan. 1965. pap. 3.95 (ISBN 0-8164-2022-X, SP20). Crossroad NY.

First Reference Library, 50 bks, Bks. 1-25. Sylvia Van Sickle. Incl. Rivers & River Life (ISBN 0-356-03790-8); Snakes & Lizards. o.p. (ISBN 0-356-03791-6); Roads & Highways (ISBN 0-356-03792-4); Ports & Harbors (ISBN 0-356-04027-5); Bridges & Tunnels (ISBN 0-356-04028-3); Towns & Cities (ISBN 0-356-04029-1); Horses & Ponies (ISBN 0-356-04030-5); Airplanes & Balloons (ISBN 0-356-04031-3); The Story of Cars. o.p. (ISBN 0-356-04032-1); Mountains (ISBN 0-356-04099-2); Electricity (ISBN 0-356-04100-X); Television (ISBN 0-356-04101-8); Photography (ISBN 0-356-04102-6); The Jungle (ISBN 0-356-04275-8); The Dog Family (ISBN 0-356-04276-6); Gypsies & Nomads. o.p. (ISBN 0-356-04277-4); Ballet & Dance (ISBN 0-356-04278-2); Paper & Printing. o.p. (ISBN 0-356-04279-0); Food & Drink (ISBN 0-356-04280-4); Cloth & Weaving (ISBN 0-356-04281-2); Lakes & Dams (ISBN 0-356-04282-0); Building (ISBN 0-356-04283-9); Butterflies & Moths (ISBN 0-356-04284-7); Vanishing Animals (ISBN 0-356-04614-1); Animals That Burrow (ISBN 0-356-04615-X). (Illus., Minimum order: 20 books). (gr. 1-4). 1976. PLB 7.30 ea. Raintree Child.

First Reference Library, Bks. 26-50. Sylvia Van Sickle. Incl. Spiders (ISBN 0-356-03669-3); Pirates & Buccaneers (ISBN 0-356-03670-7); Size (ISBN 0-356-03671-5); Fire (ISBN 0-356-03672-3); Weather (ISBN 0-356-03673-1); Deserts (ISBN 0-356-03674-X); Skyscrapers (ISBN 0-356-03675-8); Monkeys & Apes (ISBN 0-356-03676-6); Trains & Railroads (ISBN 0-356-03677-4); Trees & Woods (ISBN 0-356-03678-2); Cowboys (ISBN 0-356-03783-5); Time & Clocks (ISBN 0-356-03784-3); Light & Color (ISBN 0-356-03785-1); Birds & Migration (ISBN 0-356-03786-X); The Universe (ISBN 0-356-03787-8); Farms & Farmers. o.p. (ISBN 0-356-03788-6); Rocks & Mining. o.p. (ISBN 0-356-03789-4); Fuel & Energy (ISBN 0-356-04616-8); Animals with Shells (ISBN 0-356-04617-6); The Theater (ISBN 0-356-04618-4); Health & Disease (ISBN 0-356-04619-2); Pollution (ISBN 0-356-04620-6); The Movies. o.p.; Signals & Messages (ISBN 0-356-04622-2); Fishing. o.p. (ISBN 0-356-04623-0). (Illus., Minimum order: 20 bks.). (gr. 1-4). 1976. PLB 7.30 ea. Raintree Child.

First Report of the Central Board of His Majesty's Commissioners Appointed to Collect Information in the Manufacturing Districts: As to the Employment of Children in Factories. Great Britain, Factories Inquiry Commission. LC 71-367641. 1981. Repr. of 1833 ed. lib. bdg. 75.00x (ISBN 0-678-05226-3). Kelley.

First Rotarian. James P. Walsh. (Illus.). 351p. 1980. 14.95 (ISBN 0-906360-02-1). Scan Pub.

First Rotarian: The Life & Times of Percy Paul Harris, Founder of Rotary. James P. Walsh. Ed. by Harry Treadwell. (Illus.). 351p. 1979. 40.00 (ISBN 0-906360-02-1). Heinman.

First Scalp for Custer: The Skirmish at Warbonnet Creek, Nebraska, July 17, 1876. Paul L. Hedren. LC 80-68844. (Hidden Springs of Custeriana Ser.: No. V). (Illus.). 106p. 1981. 38.00 (ISBN 0-87062-137-8). A H Clark.

First Science Dictionary: English with Arabic Glossary. Lucas. 9.95x (ISBN 0-686-65474-9). Intl Bk Ctr.

First Seeing Eye Dogs. Burnham Holmes. LC 78-14804. (Famous Firsts Ser.). (Illus.). 1978. lib. bdg. 7.35 (ISBN 0-686-51104-2). Silver.

First Sentimental Education. Gustave Flaubert. Tr. by Douglas Garman. LC 77-149947. 275p. 1972. 16.50x (ISBN 0-520-01967-9). U of Cal Pr.

First Seven Thousand Years: A Study in Bible Chronology. Charles G. Ozanne. LC 73-114063. (Illus.). 1970. 5.00 o.p. (ISBN 0-682-47084-8, Testament). Exposition.

First Ships Round the World. W. Brownlee. LC 73-91815. (Cambridge Introduction to the History of Mankind Ser.). (Illus.). 48p. 1974. 3.95 (ISBN 0-521-20438-0). Cambridge U Pr.

First Sign of Winter. Mary B. Christian. LC 73-1066. (Illus.). 48p. (gr. k-3). 1973. 5.95 o.s.i. (ISBN 0-8193-0671-1, Four Winds); PLB 5.41 o.s.i. (ISBN 0-8193-0672-X). Schol Bk Serv.

First Songs: The Young Child Sings. Mary V. Jones. LC 76-45936. 1977. pap. 4.95 (ISBN 0-8091-2000-3); record 6.98 (ISBN 0-8091-7625-4). Paulist Pr.

First Stargazers. James Cornell. (Illus.). 288p. 1981. 17.95 (ISBN 0-684-16799-9, ScribT). Scribner.

First Step. Anne Snyder. LC 75-4867. 128p. (gr. 5-10). 1975. 5.95 o.p. (ISBN 0-03-014651-8). HR&W.

First Steps. 1966. pap. 0.95 (ISBN 0-570-03536-8, 14-1520, 14-1521). tchr's manual 1.25 (ISBN 0-570-03536-8). Concordia.

First Steps Beyond Ometrics. 1976. 3.95 (ISBN 0-89190-964-8). Am Repr-Rivercity Pr.

First Steps: Bible Stories for Children. Charles Foster. (Illus.). (gr. 5-8). 1960. pap. 2.50 (ISBN 0-8024-0023-X). Moody.

First Steps in Ballet: Home Practice in Basic Exercises. Thalia Mara & Lee Wyndham. LC 55-6550. 1955. 6.95 (ISBN 0-385-02432-0). Doubleday.

First Steps in Chess. J. N. Walker. (Chess Bks). (Illus.). 1979. 9.95 (ISBN 0-19-217580-7); pap. 6.95 (ISBN 0-19-217580-7). Oxford U Pr.

First Steps in Horsemastership. Linton M. Real. LC 72-92314. (Illus.). 7.50 o.p. (ISBN 0-668-02761-4). Arco.

First Steps in Librarianship. K. C. Harrison. (Grafton Books on Library & Information Science). 188p. 1980. lib. bdg. 26.00x (ISBN 0-233-96427-4, Pub. by Andre Deutsch). Westview.

First Steps in Reading & Writing: Books One & Two. (Gateway to English Program Ser.). (Illus., Orig.). (gr. 7-12). 1981. pap. text ed. 4.50 ea. Vol. 1 (ISBN 0-88377-186-1). Vol. 2 (ISBN 0-88377-195-0). Newbury Hse.

First Steps in Spanish. Margarita Madrigal. 111p. (gr. 3-6). 1961. pap. text ed. 2.75 (ISBN 0-88345-177-8, 17448). Regents Pub.

First Steps in Teaching Creative Dancing. Mary Joyce. LC 72-97841. (Illus.). 192p. 1973. text ed. 9.95 o.p. (ISBN 0-87484-268-9). Mayfield Pub.

First Steps in Teaching Creative Dance to Children. 2nd ed. Mary Joyce. LC 79-91834. (Illus.). 226p. 1980. pap. text ed. 7.95 (ISBN 0-87484-510-6). Mayfield Pub.

First Steps in the Kitchen. Maureen O'Connor. (Illus.). 1971. 3.95 o.p. (ISBN 0-571-09338-8, Pub. by Faber & Faber). Merrimack Bk Serv.

First Steps on Stairs. 1980. pap. 5.75 (ISBN 92-0-178580-1, IN/17/R1, IAEA). Unipub.

First Steps to Musicianship. Richard Billingham & Marie Goodkin. 256p. 1980. pap. text ed. 9.95x (ISBN 0-917974-38-7). Waveland Pr.

First Strike. Douglas Terman. 1980. pap. 2.95 (ISBN 0-671-83466-5). PB.

First Student Movement: Student Activism in the United States During the Nineteen Thirties. Ralph S. Brax. (National University Publications, Political Science Ser.). 1981. 17.50 (ISBN 0-8046-9266-1). Kennikat.

First Stunt Stars of Hollywood. Lionel Wilson. LC 78-14465. (Famous Firsts Ser.). (Illus.). 1978. lib. bdg. 7.35 (ISBN 0-686-50002-4). Silver.

First Supplement to Manuscripts, Edinburgh University Library. Edinburgh University Library. (Library Catalogs-Supplements). lib. bdg. 115.00 (ISBN 0-8161-0319-4). G K Hall.

First Teeline Workbook. I. C. Hill. 1977. pap. text ed. 4.00x (ISBN 0-435-45341-6). Heinemann Ed.

First Ten: A Penmaen Press Bibliography. Michael McCurdy & Michael Peich. LC 78-52650. (Illus.). 1978. 12.50 (ISBN 0-915778-20-3); deluxe ed. 50.00 o.p. (ISBN 0-915778-19-X). Penmaen Pr.

First Ten Years: A Diplomatic History of Israel. Walter Eytan. (Return to Zion Ser.). (Illus.). x, 239p. 1980. Repr. of 1958 ed. lib. bdg. 17.50x (ISBN 0-87991-140-9). Porcupine Pr.

First Texas Cook Book. Repr. of 1883 ed. 12.95 (ISBN 0-8363-0032-7). Jenkins.

First Thanksgiving. Lou Rogers. (Beginning-to-Read Ser.). (Illus.). (gr. 2-4). 1962. 2.50 o.p. (ISBN 0-695-82884-3); lib. ed. 2.97 o.p. (ISBN 0-695-42884-5). Follett.

First Things. Natalie Provenzano. (Illus.). (ps-1). 1980. 2.95 (ISBN 0-525-69408-0, Gingerbread). Dutton.

First Things First. Frederick Catherwood. 128p. 1981. pap. 5.95 (ISBN 0-87784-472-0). Inter Varsity.

First Things First. Joseph I. Chapman. LC 74-22523. 96p. (Orig.). 1975. pap. 2.50 o.p. (ISBN 0-8170-0649-4). Judson.

First Things First: Quality Education & the Way to Achieve It. 3.50 (ISBN 0-686-28653-7). Quality Educ.

First Things Last. David Malouf. 58p. 1981. text ed. 13.25 (ISBN 0-7022-1564-3); pap. text ed. 7.25 (ISBN 0-7022-1565-1). U of Queensland Pr.

First Things to Touch. Illus. by Mary McClain. (Floppies Ser.). (Illus.). 6p. (ps-k). Date not set. 3.95 (ISBN 0-671-42533-1, Little Simon). S&S.

First Three Tales. 3rd ed. Hans C. Andersen. pap. 5.00x (ISBN 87-14-27297-0, D715). Vanous.

First Three Years of Life. Burton L. White. 1978. pap. 4.95 (ISBN 0-380-01893-4, 37234). Avon.

First Time. Karl Fleming & Anne T. Fleming. pap. 1.95 o.p. (ISBN 0-425-03152-7). Berkley Pub.

First Time in London. Jack Meiland. LC 78-21547. 1979. pap. 5.95 (ISBN 0-684-16505-8, ScribT). Scribner.

First Time Out: Skills for Living Away from Home. Reva Camiel & Hila Michaelsen. LC 79-92821. (Illus., Orig.). (gr. 11-12). 1980. pap. 5.95 (ISBN 0-915190-26-5). Jalmar Pr.

First to Know. Anne Bernays. 1975. pap. 1.25 o.p. (ISBN 0-445-00247-6). Popular Lib.

First to Sail the World Alone: Joshua Slocum. Jan Fortman. LC 78-13720. (Famous Firsts Ser.). (Illus.). 1978. lib. bdg. 7.35 (ISBN 0-686-51105-0). Silver.

First to the Moon. Jim Collins. LC 78-13611. (Famous Firsts Ser.). (Illus.). 1978. lib. bdg. 7.35 (ISBN 0-686-51106-9). Silver.

First to the Top of the World: Admiral Peary at the North Pole. Tom Lisker. LC 78-14924. (Famous Firsts Ser.). (Illus.). 1978. lib. bdg. 7.35 (ISBN 0-686-51107-7). Silver.

First Travel Guide to the Moon: What to Pack, How to Go, & What to See When You Get There. Rhoda Blumberg. LC 80-66244. (Illus.). 80p. (gr. 5 up). 1980. 7.95 (ISBN 0-590-07663-9, Four Winds). Schol Bk Serv.

First Twenty-Five Years: A Review of the NFER 1946-71. Yates. 1971. pap. text ed. 3.00x (ISBN 0-901225-82-7, NFER). Humanities.

First Twenty Years: A Segment of Film History. 2nd ed. LC 68-58700. (Illus.). 1979. 10.00 (ISBN 0-913986-01-1). Locare.

First Two Lives of Lukas-Kasha. Lloyd Alexander. LC 77-26699. (gr. 4-7). 1978. PLB 11.95 (ISBN 0-525-29748-0). Dutton.

First Two Partes of the Acts or Unchaste Examples of the Englyshe Votaryes. John Bale. LC 79-84086. (English Experience Ser.: No. 906). 540p. 1979. Repr. of 1560 ed. lib. bdg. 40.00 (ISBN 90-221-0906-2). Walter J Johnson.

First Two Thousand Years. W. Cleon Skousen. 1953. 7.50 (ISBN 0-685-48240-5). Bookcraft Inc.

First Wild West Rodeo. Teri Crawford. LC 78-14549. (Famous Firsts Ser.). (Illus.). 1978. lib. bdg. 7.35 (ISBN 0-686-51109-3). Silver.

First Witch. Joseph Coleman. (Pal Paperbacks, - Pal Skills II Ser.). (Illus.). (gr. 5-12). 1980. pap. text ed. 1.25 (ISBN 0-8374-6812-4). Xerox Ed Pubns.

First Woman in Congress: Jeanette Rankin. Judy R. Block. LC 78-14490. (Famous Firsts Ser.). (Illus.). 1978. lib. bdg. 7.35 (ISBN 0-686-51110-7). Silver.

First Woman of Medicine: The Story of Elizabeth Blackwell. Scott Matthew. LC 78-16305. (Famous Firsts Ser.). (Illus.). 1978. lib. bdg. 7.35 (ISBN 0-686-51111-5). Silver.

First Women of the Skies. Kitty A. Crowley. LC 78-21907. (Famous Firsts Ser.). (Illus.). 1978. lib. bdg. 7.35 (ISBN 0-686-51112-3). Silver.

First Wondrous Year: You & Your Baby. Johnson & Johnson Baby Products Company. (Illus.). 1979. 16.95 (ISBN 0-02-559530-X); pap. 10.95 (ISBN 0-02-077100-2). Macmillan.

First Words Language Programme. Bill Gillham. (Illus.). 1979. text ed. 15.95x (ISBN 0-04-371059-X). Allen Unwin.

First Words Language Programme. Bill Gillham. 96p. 1980. 20.00x (Pub. by Beaconsfield England). State Mutual Bk.

First Workbook of Spanish. Ivor A. Richards et al. pap. 0.75 o.s.i. (ISBN 0-671-46896-0). WSP.

First Workshop on Grand Unification. Ed. by P. Frampton et al. (Lie Groups; History, Frontiers & Applications: Vol. XI). 250p. 1980. text ed. 30.00x (ISBN 0-915692-31-7). Math Sci Pr.

First World Disarmament: And Why It Failed. Lord Noel-Baker. 1979. 19.00 (ISBN 0-08-023365-1). Pergamon.

First World War. Ed. by Jere C. King. LC 72-80545. (Documentary History of Western Civilization Ser). 350p. 1973. 15.00x o.s.i. (ISBN 0-8027-2047-1). Walker & Co.

First World War in German Narrative Prose. Ed. by Charles N. Genno & Heinz Wetzel. LC 79-26625. 1980. 17.50x (ISBN 0-8020-5490-0). U of Toronto Pr.

First World War, Nineteen Fourteen to Nineteen Eighteen. Gerd Hardach. (History of the World Economy in the Twentieth Century Ser.: Vol. 2). 1981. pap. 6.95 (ISBN 0-520-04397-9, CAL 495). U of Cal Pr.

First World War, 1914-1918. Gerd Hardach. (History of the World Economy in the Twentieth Century Ser: Vol. 2). 1977. 20.00x (ISBN 0-520-03060-5). U of Cal Pr.

First Writers Workshop Literary Reader: An Anthology. Ed. by P. Lal. (Writers Workshop Greybird Book Ser.). 107p. 1975. 15.00 (ISBN 0-88253-542-0); pap. text ed. 6.75 (ISBN 0-88253-541-2). Ind-US Inc.

First Writers Workshop Story Anthology. P. Lal. 9.00 (ISBN 0-89253-762-0); flexible cloth 5.00 (ISBN 0-89253-763-9). Ind-US Inc.

First Year. Enid L. Meadowcroft. LC 46-22591. (Illus.). (gr. 5 up). 1946. 8.95 (ISBN 0-690-30349-1, TYC-J). T Y Crowell.

First Year Calculus. Ethan D. Bolker & Joseph W. Kitchen. LC 73-14350. 1974. pap. text ed. 13.95 (ISBN 0-201-00645-6). A-W.

First Year College Chemistry. 9th ed. John R. Lewis. (Illus., Orig.). 1971. pap. 3.95 (ISBN 0-06-460005-X, CO 5, COS). Har-Row.

First-Year Harmony Workbook. P. Friedheim. 1966. pap. text ed. 5.95 (ISBN 0-02-910710-5). Free Pr.

First Year Latin. Charles Jenney & Rogers Scudder. (New Jenney Latin Series). (gr. 10). 1975. text ed. 14.40 (ISBN 0-205-04595-2, 3945952); tchr's. guide 3.60 (ISBN 0-205-04596-0, 3945960); wkbk 5.40 (ISBN 0-205-02482-3, 3924823); tchrs'. guide to wkbk. 3.60 (ISBN 0-205-02483-1, 3924831); tests 4.12 (ISBN 0-205-02484-X, 392484X); tchrs'. ed. 4.12 (ISBN 0-205-02485-8, 3924858). Allyn.

First Year Latin. rev. ed. Charles Jenney, Jr. & Rogers V. Scudder. 1979. text ed. 14.40 (ISBN 0-205-06177-X, 396177X); wkbk. 5.40 (ISBN 0-205-06178-8, 3961796); tchrs.' guide 3.60 (3961788). Allyn.

First Year of Bereavement. Ira O. Glick et al. LC 74-12499. 536p. 1974. 20.95 (ISBN 0-471-30421-2, Pub. by Wiley-Interscience). Wiley.

First Year of Life. G. Curtis Jenkins & R. Newton. (Library of General Practice). (Illus.). 260p. 1981. pap. text ed. 18.00 (ISBN 0-443-01717-4). Churchill.

First Year of Life: Psychological & Medical Implications of Early Experience. David Shaffer & Judy Dunn. LC 78-11237. (Studies in Psychiatry). 1980. 37.95 (ISBN 0-471-99734-X, Pub. by Wiley-Interscience). Wiley.

First Year Training for Craftsmen & Technicians: An Introduction to General & Special Skills, 16 vols. Ed. by Engineering Industry Training Board. (Illus.). 1975-1976. Set. spiral bdg. 77.00x (ISBN 0-685-90143-2). Intl Ideas.

First, You Cry. Betty Rollin. LC 76-16047. 1976. 7.95 o.p. (ISBN 0-397-01167-9). Lippincott.

First You Like Me. Micky K. Marks. LC 69-13125. (Illus.). (gr. 3-7). 1969. 5.95 o.s.i. (ISBN 0-8193-0255-4, Four Winds); PLB 5.41 o.s.i. (ISBN 0-8193-0256-2). Schol Bk Serv.

First Zen Reader. Trevor P. Leggett. LC 60-12739. (Illus.). 1960. pap. 5.50 (ISBN 0-8048-0180-0). C E Tuttle.

Firstborn. Roland Cutler. 1978. pap. 1.75 o.p. (ISBN 0-449-14002-4, GM). Fawcett.

Firstfruits: A Harvest of 25 Years of Israeli Writing. Ed. & intro. by James A. Michener. 432p. 1974. pap. 1.75 o.p. (ISBN 0-449-30641-0, X641, Prem). Fawcett.

Firsts Under the Wire: The World's Fastest Horses (1900-1950) Theodus Carroll. LC 78-11476. (Famous Firsts Ser.). (Illus.). 1978. lib. bdg. 7.35 (ISBN 0-686-51108-5). Silver.

Fiscal Congress: Legislative Control of the Budget. Lance T. LeLoup. LC 79-6823. (Contributions in Political Science: No. 47). (Illus.). xii, 227p. 1980. lib. bdg. 25.00 (ISBN 0-313-22009-3, LFC/). Greenwood.

Fiscal Crisis of American Cities: Essays on the Political Economy of Urban America with Special Reference to New York. David Mermelstein & Roger Alcaly. 1977. pap. 5.95 (ISBN 0-394-72193-4, V-193, Vin). Random.

Fiscal Federalism & Grants-in-Aid. Ed. by Peter Mieszlowski & William Oakland. (Papers on Public Economics Ser.: Vol.1). 166p. (Orig.). 1979. pap. text ed. 5.50 (26300). Urban Inst.

Fiscal Harmonization in Common Markets, 2 Vols. Vol. 1. Theory, Vol. 2. Practice. Ed. by Carl S. Shoup. LC 66-14789. 1966. Set. 50.00x (ISBN 0-231-08964-3). Columbia U Pr.

Fiscal Impact of Residential & Commercial Development: A Case Study. Thomas Muller & Grace Dawson. 140p. 1972. pap. 3.00 o.p. (ISBN 0-87766-074-3, 22000). Urban Inst.

Fiscal Management & Planning in Local Government. James C Snyder. LC 76-43218. 1977. 18.95 (ISBN 0-669-01055-3). Lexington Bks.

Fiscal Reform in Bolivia: Final Report of the Bolivian Mission on Tax Reform. Richard A. Musgrave. LC 80-14943. (Illus.). 1981. pap. text ed. 15.00 (ISBN 0-915506-22-X). Harvard Law Intl Tax.

Fiscal Zoning & Land Use Controls. Edwin S. Mills & Wallace E. Oates. LC 74-21877. 224p. 1975. 19.95 (ISBN 0-669-96685-1). Lexington Bks.

Fiscal Zoning in Suburban Communities. Duane Windsor. LC 78-20632. (Illus.). 208p. 1979. 21.00 (ISBN 0-669-02751-0). Lexington Bks.

Fish. (Good Cook Ser.). (Illus.). 1979. lib. bdg. 9.30 (ISBN 0-8094-2863-6); kivar bdg. 11.97 (ISBN 0-8094-2864-4). Silver.

Fish, Amphibian & Reptile Remains from Archaeological Sites, Part I: Southeastern & Southwestern United States. Stanley J. Olsen. LC 68-56643. (Peabody Museum Papers: Vol. 56, No. 2). 1968. pap. text ed. 15.00 (ISBN 0-87365-192-8). Peabody Harvard.

Fish and Fish Dishes of Laos. Alan Davidson. LC 75-29794. (Illus.). 1975. pap. 4.75 o.p. (ISBN 0-8048-1170-9). C E Tuttle.

Fish & Game Cooking. Joan Cone. 1981. 10.95 o.p. (ISBN 0-914440-46-2); pap. 7.95 (ISBN 0-914440-45-4). EPM Pubns.

Fish & How They Reproduce. Dorothy H. Patent. LC 76-10349. (Illus.). (gr. 3-7). 1976. 8.95 (ISBN 0-8234-0285-1). Holiday.

Fish & Moose News. Bill Woodman. LC 79-27794. (Illus.). 128p. 1980. pap. 6.95 (ISBN 0-396-07825-7). Dodd.
Fish & Seafood Dishes for Foodservice Menu Planning. Eulilia C. Blair. LC 75-25636. (Foodservice Menu Planning Ser.). 240p. 1975. 16.50 (ISBN 0-8436-2086-2). CBI Pub.
Fish & Shell Fish. new ed. (Illus.). 520p. 1973. 65.00 (ISBN 0-685-41622-4). Radio City.
Fish and Shellfish. rev. ed. Ed. by A. E. Simms. (Illus.). 1973. 54.95 (ISBN 0-685-90327-3, Northwood Pub.). CBI Pub.
Fish & Shellfish Farming in Coastal Waters. P. H. Milne. (Illus.). 208p. 24.75 (ISBN 0-85238-022-4, FN). Unipub.
Fish & the Sea. Spike Noel. (Junior Reference Ser.). (Illus.). 64p. (gr. 7 up). 1972. 7.95 (ISBN 0-7136-1239-8). Dufour.
Fish & Wildlife Management. Boy Scouts of America. LC 19-600. (Illus.). 64p. (gr. 6-12). 1972. pap. 0.70x (ISBN 0-8395-3307-1, 3307). BSA.
Fish Behavior: Why Fish Do What They Do. Helmut E. Adler. (Illus.). 271p. 1975. 20.00 (ISBN 0-87666-162-2, PS-734). TFH Pubns.
Fish Book. Dick Martin. (Illus.). 24p. (gr. k-1). 1976. PLB 5.38 (ISBN 0-307-68982-4, Golden Pr). Western Pub.
Fish Book: How to Buy, Clean, Catch, Cook & Preserve Them. Jeffrey Fisher. (Illus.). 128p. 1981. 8.95 (ISBN 0-87523-196-9). Emerson.
Fish Breeding Recipes. Wolfgang Ostermoeller. (Illus.). 1973. pap. 5.95 (ISBN 0-87666-071-5, PS-693). TFH Pubns.
Fish Catching Methods of the World. 2nd ed. Andres von Brandt. (Illus.). 256p. 19.50 (ISBN 0-85238-026-7, FN). Unipub.
Fish Chromosome Methodology. T. E. Denton. (Illus.). 176p. 1973. 17.50 (ISBN 0-398-02831-1). C C Thomas.
Fish Communities in Tropical Freshwaters. Rosemary Lowe-McConnell. LC 74-75103. (Tropical Ecology Ser). Orig. Title: Ecology of Tropical Fish. (Illus.). 200p. (Orig.). 1975. 28.00x o.p. (ISBN 0-582-44348-2). Longman.
Fish Cookery. Michael Wood. (Illus.). 5.95x o.p. (ISBN 0-8464-0417-6). Beekman Pubs.
Fish Dinner in Memison. E. R. Eddison. (Del Rey Bk.). 1978. pap. 2.25 o.p. (ISBN 0-345-27222-6). Ballantine.
Fish Diseases. Mark Dulin. 1979. 2.95 (ISBN 0-87666-524-5, KW-066). TFH Pubns.
Fish Diseases: Third COPRAQ-Session. Ed. by W. Ahne. (Proceedings in Life Sciences Ser.). (Illus.). 252p. 1981. 49.80 (ISBN 0-387-10406-2). Springer-Verlag.
Fish Farming Handbook. E. Evan Brown & J. B. Gratzek. (Illus.). 1980. 19.50 (ISBN 0-87055-341-0). AVI.
Fish Feed Technology: Lectures Presented at the FAO - UNDP Training Course in Fish Feed Technology. (Agriculture Development Coordination Programme Ser.). 400p. 1980. pap. 21.50 (ISBN 92-5-100901-5, F1944, FAO). Unipub.
Fish Hatches. Joanna Cole. (Illus.). (gr. k-3). 1978. 7.95 (ISBN 0-688-22153-X); PLB 7.63 (ISBN 0-688-32153-4). Morrow.
Fish Hawk. John Kaufmann. (gr. 3-7). 1967. 6.75 (ISBN 0-688-21298-0); PLB 6.48 (ISBN 0-688-31298-5). Morrow.
Fish in Research. Ed. by O. W. Neuhaus & J. E. Halver. LC 74-107020. 1969. 32.50 (ISBN 0-12-515850-5). Acad Pr.
Fish in the Sea Is Not Thirsty. Kabir. (Translated from Hindi). 8.00 (ISBN 0-89253-602-0); flexible cloth 4.00 (ISBN 0-89253-603-9). Ind-US Inc.
Fish Is Red: The Story of the Secret War Against Castro. Warren Hinckle & William Turner. 288p. 1981. 12.95 (ISBN 0-8129-0908-9). Times Bks.
Fish-Lovers Cookbook. Mel London & Sheryl London. (Illus.). 1980. 16.95 (ISBN 0-87857-299-6). Rodale Pr Inc.
Fish of the Ocean & Shore. J. M. Thompson. 208p. 1980. 13.95x (ISBN 0-686-68861-9, Pub. by W Collins Australia). Intl Schol Bk Serv.
Fish Out of Water in English & Spanish. Tr. by Carlos Rivera & Helen Palmer. (Spanish Beginner Bks: No. 2). (gr. 2-4). 1967. 2.95 (ISBN 0-394-81598-X); PLB 5.99 (ISBN 0-394-91598-4). Random.
Fish Population Dynamics. Ed. by John A. Gulland. LC 75-45094. 1977. 50.75 (ISBN 0-471-01575-X, Pub by Wiley-Interscience). Wiley.
Fish Versus Oil. S. E. Haugan Consulting. 1980. 50.00x (Pub. by Norwegian Info Norway). State Mutual Bk.
Fishbein's Illustrated Medical & Health Encyclopedia: Family Health Guide Edition. Ed. by Morris Fishbein & Justin Fishbein. LC 78-53643. 1978. 24.95 (ISBN 0-87475-250-7). Stuttman.
Fishbowl Management: A Participative Approach to Systematic Management. Howard Sargent. LC 77-27924. 1978. 19.95 (ISBN 0-471-03574-2, Pub. by Wiley-Interscience). Wiley.
Fisher Hall, Miami University, Oxford, Ohio: Its Preservation Potential. Visnapuu & Gaede, Inc. (Consultant Service Grant Report). (Illus.). 25p. 1973. pap. 3.00 (ISBN 0-89133-012-7). Preservation Pr.
Fisher of Kilverstone. Ruddock F. Mackay. (Illus.). 559p. 1974. 19.95x (ISBN 0-19-822409-5). Oxford U Pr.
Fisheries & Aquaculture in the People's Republic of China. 32p. 1980. pap. 5.00 (ISBN 0-88936-189-4, IDRC 115, IDRC). Unipub.
Fisheries & Energy Production. Ed. by Saul B. Saila. LC 74-32513. 1975. 18.95 (ISBN 0-669-98467-1). Lexington Bks.
Fisheries Conflict in the North Atlantic: Problems of Management & Jurisdiction. Ed. by Giulio Pontecorvo. LC 74-9665. (Law of the Sea Institute Ser). 1974. text ed. 17.50 o.p. (ISBN 0-88410-020-0). Ballinger Pub.
Fisheries Ecology. Paul Hart & Tony Pitcher. 224p. 1980. 35.00x (ISBN 0-85664-894-9, Pub. by Croom Helm England). State Mutual Bk.
Fisheries Ecology of Floodplain Rivers. Robin L. Welcomme. (Illus.). 1979. text ed. 50.00 (ISBN 0-582-46310-6). Longman.
Fisheries Economics. Rognvaldur Hannesson. 1979. pap. 23.00x (ISBN 82-00-05217-6, Dist. by Columbia U Pr.). Universitet.
Fisheries Management. Robert T. Lackey. LC 80-20028. 422p. 1980. 34.95 (ISBN 0-470-27056-X). Halsted Pr.
Fisheries Oceanography. Ilmo Hela & Taivo Laevastu. (Illus.). 254p. 22.00 (ISBN 0-85238-009-7, FN). Unipub.
Fisheries of Australia. Peter Pownall. (Illus.). 160p. 1979. 20.50 (ISBN 0-85238-101-8, FN). Unipub.
Fisheries of Europe. James R. Coull. (Advanced Economic Geography Ser.). 1972. lib. bdg. 22.00x (ISBN 0-7135-1612-7). Westview.
Fisheries of the North Pacific: History, Species, Gear & Processes. rev. ed. Robert J. Browning. (Illus.). 432p. 1980. pap. 24.95 (ISBN 0-88240-128-9). Alaska Northwest.
Fisherman. Ed. by Daniel Jacobson. LC 74-34264. (Indians of North America Ser). 96p. (gr. 4-7). 1975. PLB 4.90 o.p. (ISBN 0-531-02830-5). Watts.
Fisherman & His Wife. Brothers Grimm. Tr. by Elizabeth Shub from Ger. LC 78-8133. (Illus.). (gr. k-3). 1979. 9.50 (ISBN 0-688-86003-6). Greenwillow.
Fisherman's Almanac. Dan Morris & Norman Strung. LC 70-93179. (Illus.). 1970. 5.95 o.s.i. (ISBN 0-02-587120-X). Macmillan.
Fisherman's Catalog. Vlad Evanoff. LC 76-23806. 1977. 6.95 o.p. (ISBN 0-385-12196-2). Doubleday.
Fisherman's Handbook. George Bannon. 12.50x (ISBN 0-392-06420-0, SpS). Soccer.
Fisherman's Handbook. (Illus.). 319p. 1980. 37.00 (ISBN 0-85238-106-9, FN85, FN). Unipub.
Fisherman's Handbook. John Power & Jeremy Brown. LC 70-38529. 1972. pap. 2.95 o.p. (ISBN 0-684-13752-6, SL512, ScribT). Scribner.
Fisherman's Paradise. O. S. Hintz. LC 75-322904. 1979. 9.95 (ISBN 0-370-10486-2, Pub. by Chatto Bodley Jonathan). Merrimack Bk Serv.
Fisherman's Son. Mirra Ginsburg. LC 78-31852. (Illus.). (gr. k-3). 1979. 7.95 (ISBN 0-688-80216-8); PLB 7.63 (ISBN 0-688-84216-X). Greenwillow.
Fisherman's Whore. Dave Smith. LC 73-85445. 74p. 1974. 6.50 (ISBN 0-8214-0137-8). Ohio U Pr.
Fishermen. Sally Festing. 1977. 11.95 (ISBN 0-7153-7448-6). David & Charles.
Fishermen of Galilee: The Human Ecology of a New England Coastal Community. John J. Poggie & Carl Gersuny. LC 73-93703. (Marine Bulletin: No. 17). 1974. pap. 3.00 (ISBN 0-938412-09-4). URI MAS.
Fishermen's Handbook. W. H. Perry. 1980. 60.00x (ISBN 0-686-64736-X, Pub. by Fishing News England). State Mutual Bk.
Fishermen's Handbook. Ed. by W. H. Perry. 344p. 1980. cloth 29.95x (ISBN 0-85238-106-9, Pub. by Fishing News England). State Mutual Bk.
Fishers of Men. Anita Bryant & Bob Green. (Illus.). 1973. 5.95 o.p. (ISBN 0-8007-0612-9). Revell.
Fishers of Men: The Way of the Apostles. Gordon Converse et al. LC 80-23760. 1980. 14.95 (ISBN 0-13-319673-9). P-H.
Fishes. Url N. Lanham. LC 62-9366. (Illus.). 1967. pap. 5.00 (ISBN 0-231-08581-8, 81). Columbia U Pr.
Fishes. F. Ommanney. (Young Readers Library). (Illus.). 1977. lib. bdg. 7.95 (ISBN 0-686-51090-9). Silver.
Fishes. F. D. Ommanney. LC 63-10758. (Life Nature Library). (Illus.). (gr. 5 up). 1970. PLB 8.97 o.p. (ISBN 0-8094-0622-5, Pub. by Time-Life). Silver.
Fishes. Loren Woods. (Beginning Science Bks). (gr. 2-4). 2.50 o.p. (ISBN 0-695-82890-8). Follett.
Fishes & the Forest: Explorations in Amazonian Natural History. Michael Goulding. LC 80-41201. (Illus.). 250p. 1981. 20.00x (ISBN 0-520-04131-3). U of Cal Pr.
Fishes: Guidelines for the Breeding, Care, & Management of Laboratory Animals. Institute of Laboratory Animal Resources. LC 74-3462. (Illus.). 88p. 1974. pap. 5.00 o.p. (ISBN 0-309-02213-4). Natl Acad Pr.
Fishes in North American Deserts. Robert J. Naiman & David L. Solt. 360p. 1981. 35.00 (ISBN 0-471-08523-5, Pub. by Wiley-Interscience). Wiley.
Fishes of Canada's National Capital Region. D. E. McAllister & Brian W. Coad. (Illus.). 1974. pap. text ed. 5.00x (ISBN 0-660-02014-9, 56345-6, Pub. by Natl Gallery Canada). U of Chicago Pr.
Fishes of Lakes, Rivers, & Oceans. LC 78-51971. (Wild, Wild World of Animals Ser.). (Illus.). 1978. lib. bdg. 11.97 (ISBN 0-686-51169-7). Silver.
Fishes of Lakes, Rivers & Oceans. new ed. Time-Life Television Editors. (Wild, Wild World of Animals Ser). (Illus.). 1978. 10.95 (ISBN 0-913948-20-9). Time-Life.
Fishes of the Chesapeake Bay. Samuel F. Hildebrand & William C. Schroeder. LC 72-5565. (Illus.). 388p. 1972. Repr. of 1928 ed. 8.00x. Smithsonian.
Fishes of the Nile. G. A. Boulenger. 1964. Repr. of 1907 ed. 185.00 (ISBN 3-7682-0241-0). Lubrecht & Cramer.
Fishes of the Red River Drainage, Eastern Kentucky. Branley A. Branson & Donald L. Batch. LC 73-80459. (Illus.). 76p. 1974. pap. 4.50x (ISBN 0-8131-1295-8). U Pr of Ky.
Fishes of the World: A Key to Families & a Checklist. G. U. Lindberg. LC 73-16382. (Illus.). 545p. 1974. 59.95 (ISBN 0-470-53565-2). Halsted Pr.
Fishes of the World: Illustrated Dictionary. Alwynne Wheeler. Ed. by Thomas B. Fraser. LC 75-6972. (Illus.). 400p. 1975. 12.98 o.s.i. (ISBN 0-02-626180-4, 62618). Macmillan.
Fishing. Boy Scouts Of America. LC 19-600. (Illus.). 64p. (gr. 6-12). 1974. pap. 0.70x (ISBN 0-8395-3295-4, 3295). BSA.
Fishing. Paul Neimark. (Wilderness World Ser.). (Illus.). 64p. (gr. 3 up). 1981. PLB 9.25 (ISBN 0-516-02452-3). Childrens.
Fishing. Jerolyn Nentl & Howard Schroeder. LC 80-10490. (Back to Nature Ser.). (Illus.). (gr. 3-5). 1980. lib. bdg. 5.95 (ISBN 0-89686-070-1). Crestwood Hse.
Fishing. John F. Waters. (First Bks.). (Illus.). (gr. 4-6). 1978. PLB 6.45 s&l (ISBN 0-531-01407-X). Watts.
Fishing: An Encyclopedic Guide to Tackle & Tactics for Fresh & Salt Water. Joseph D. Bates, Jr. 1974. 16.95 (ISBN 0-87690-110-0). Dutton.
Fishing Around the World. Louise L. Floethe. LC 72-498. (Illus.). 40p. (gr. 1-3). 1972. write for info. (ISBN 0-684-12948-5, ScribJ). Scribner.
Fishing Boats & Their Equipment. 182p. 1980. pap. 15.75 (ISBN 0-85238-090-9, FN 81, FN). Unipub.
Fishing Cadet's Handbook. Alfred Hodson. (Illus.). 108p. 7.50 (ISBN 0-85238-011-9, FN). Unipub.
Fishing Canals. Ken Cope. LC 79-55994. (Illus.). 1980. 17.95 (ISBN 0-7153-7887-2). David & Charles.
Fishing Days. Geoffrey Bucknell. 8.50x (ISBN 0-392-06580-0, SpS). Soccer.
Fishing for Bass: Modern Tactics & Tackle. A. D. Livingston. LC 74-8026. 1974. 8.95 o.s.i. (ISBN 0-397-01017-6). Lippincott.
Fishing for Beginners. John Fabian. 1980. pap. 2.95 (ISBN 0-689-70468-2, Aladdin). Atheneum.
Fishing for Food. Trevor Housby. pap. 2.95 (ISBN 0-7153-7546-6, Pub. by Batsford England). David & Charles.
Fishing for Fun. Byron Dalrymple. (Illus.). 192p. 1975. 8.95 o.p. (ISBN 0-87691-164-5). Winchester Pr.
Fishing Industries of Scotland 1790-1914: A Study in Regional Adaptation. Malcom Gray. LC 78-40244. 1978. 26.00x (ISBN 0-19-714105-6). Oxford U Pr.
Fishing Is for Me. Art Thomas. LC 80-13442. (Sports for Me Books Ser.). (Illus.). 48p. (gr. 2-5). 1980. PLB 5.95g (ISBN 0-8225-1096-0). Lerner Pubns.
Fishing Made Easy. Arthur L. Cone, Jr. (Illus.). 1968. 6.95 o.s.i. (ISBN 0-02-526270-X). Macmillan.
Fishing Rigs for Fresh & Salt Water. Vlad Evanoff. LC 76-26221. (Illus.). 1977. 9.95 o.p. (ISBN 0-06-011257-3, HarpT). Har-Row.
Fishing the Dry Fly As a Living Insect: An Unorthodox Method. Leonard M. Wright. (Illus.). 1972. 6.95 o.p. (ISBN 0-525-21740-1). Dutton.
Fishing the Nymph. James Quick. (Illus.). 1960. 12.95 (ISBN 0-8260-7265-8). Ronald Pr.
Fishing with Small Fry: A Parent's Guide to Teaching Children How to Fish. Jim Freeman. LC 73-77333. (Illus.). 128p. 1973. pap. 2.95 o.p. (ISBN 0-87701-035-8). Chronicle Bks.
Fishwatcher's Field Guide. Idaz Greenberg. (Illus.). 1979. plastic card 3.95 (ISBN 0-913008-10-9). Seahawk Pr.
Fishwatchers' Guide to the Inshore Fishes of the Pacific Coast. Daniel W. Gotshall. LC 77-73915. (Illus.). 1977. pap. 8.95 o.p. (ISBN 0-930118-01-4). Sea Chall.
Fishy Story. A. Piccini. (Illus.). (ps-3). 0.75 o.s.i. (ISBN 0-8198-0197-6). Dghtrs St Paul.
Fisica, Vol. I. 2nd ed. Alvaro Pinzon. (Span.). 1978. pap. text ed. 6.00 (ISBN 0-06-316668-2, Pub. by HarLA Mexico). Har-Row.
Fisica, Vol. II. 2nd ed. Alvaro Pinzon. (Span.). 1978. pap. text ed. 6.00 (ISBN 0-06-316669-0, Pub. by HarLA Mexico). Har-Row.
Fisica Cuantica. rev. ed. OAS General Secretariat Dept. of Scientific Affairs. (Monografias Cientificas (Scientific Monographs)). 62p. (Orig.). 1980. Repr. of 1971 ed. 2.00 (ISBN 0-8270-1100-8). OAS.
Fisica General, Vol. I. Beatriz Alvarenga. (Span.). 1980. pap. text ed. 5.00 (ISBN 0-06-310011-8, Pub. by HarLA Mexico). Har-Row.
Fisica Moderna. Virgilio Acosta et al. (Span.). 1975. pap. text ed. 10.50 (ISBN 0-06-310010-X, IntlDept). Har-Row.
Fisica Paraciencias E Ingenieria, Vol. II. John P. McKelvey & Howard Grotch. (Span.). 1981. pap. text ed. 14.50 (ISBN 0-06-315476-5, Pub. by HarLA Mexico). Har-Row.
Fission, Fusion & the Energy Crisis. 2nd ed. S. E. Hunt. (Illus.). 180p. 1980. 23.00 (ISBN 0-08-024734-2); pap. 11.00 (ISBN 0-08-024733-4). Pergamon.
Fission, Fusion, & the Energy Crisis. S. E. Hunt. LC 74-9926. 1974. text ed. 19.50 o.p. (ISBN 0-08-018102-3); pap. text ed. 10.50 o.p. (ISBN 0-08-018079-5). Pergamon.
Fission Gas Behaviour in Nuclear Fuels: Proceedings. Joint Research Centre, Workshop, Karlsruhe Establishment (European Inst. for Transuranium Elements), Germany, October 1978. Ed. by C. Ronchi et al. (European Applied Research Reports Special Topics Ser.). 350p. 1979. pap. text ed. 82.00 (ISBN 3-7186-0010-2). Harwood Academic.
Fist & the Letter: Revolutionary Poems of Latin America. Tr. by Roger Prentice & John M. Kirk. (Illus.). 1978. pap. 3.50 o.p. (ISBN 0-8467-0558-3, Pub. by Two Continents). Hippocrene Bks.
Fit Athlete. Roy J. Shephard. (Illus.). 1978. 16.50x (ISBN 0-19-217549-1). Oxford U Pr.
Fit for Freedom. H. Philip Constans, Jr. LC 79-6405. 141p. 1980. pap. text ed. 7.50 (ISBN 0-8191-0945-2). U Pr of Amer.
Fit to Be Styled a Typographer. James Moran. (Illus.). 66p. 1980. 32.00 (ISBN 0-913720-10-0); pap. 18.50 (ISBN 0-913720-11-9). Sandstone.
Fitness Fact Book: A Guide to Diet, Exercise & Sport. Theodore Berland. 1981. pap. 1.95 (ISBN 0-686-69109-1, J9730, Sig). NAL.
Fitness Factor: Practical Body Building for Health. Michael B. Kelly. LC 80-20432. (Illus.). 256p. 1981. 11.95 (ISBN 0-668-05115-9, 5115). Arco.
Fitness First-a-Fourteen-Day Diet & Exercise Program. Jeanne Jones & Kharma Kientzler. LC 80-11320. (Illus.). 154p. (Orig.). 1980. 9.95 o.p. (ISBN 0-89286-168-1); pap. 6.95 (ISBN 0-89286-162-2). One Hund One Prods.
Fitness for Every Body. Linda Garrison & Ann K. Read. LC 79-91831. (Illus.). 138p. 1980. pap. text ed. 3.95 (ISBN 0-87484-444-4). Mayfield Pub.
Fitness for the Working Woman. Marie F. Griffing. 1979. 9.95 o.p. (ISBN 0-8092-7425-6); pap. 5.95 (ISBN 0-8092-7424-8). Contemp Bks.
Fitness from Six to Twelve. Bonnie Prudden. LC 67-13726. (Illus.). 1972. 9.95 o.s.i. (ISBN 0-06-013436-4, HarpT). Har-Row.
Fitness of Man's Environment. Robert M. Adams et al. LC 68-20988. (Smithsonian Annual, No. 2). 250p. 1968. 15.00x (ISBN 0-87474-058-4). Smithsonian.
Fitness of the Environment: An Inquiry into the Biological Significance of the Properties of Matter. Lawrence J. Henderson. 8.00 (ISBN 0-8446-0691-X). Peter Smith.
Fitness the Footballer's Way. Barry Walsh & Peter Douglas. (Illus., Orig.). 1978. pap. 2.95 (ISBN 0-8467-0428-5, Pub. by Two Continents). Hippocrene Bks.
Fitting Death for Billy the Kid. Ramon F. Adams. LC 60-5112. (Illus.). 310p. 1981. 14.95 (ISBN 0-8061-0458-9). U of Okla Pr.

Fitting Equations to Data: Computer Analysis of Multifactor Data for Scientists & Engineers. Cuthbert Daniel. LC 79-130429. (Wiley Series in Probability & Mathematical Statistics). 1980. 21.95 o.p. (ISBN 0-471-05370-8, Pub. by Wiley-Interscience). Wiley.

Fitting Out a Moulded Hull. Fox Geen. (Illus.). 176p. 1976. pap. 10.95 (ISBN 0-685-69131-4). Transatlantic.

Fitting the Task to the Man: An Ergonomic Approach. 3rd ed. Etienne Grandjean. LC 77-447838. 379p. 1980. 35.00 (ISBN 0-85066-192-7); pap. 22.50 (ISBN 0-8002-2225-3). Intl Pubns Serv.

Fitxharbets Booke of Husbandrie: Newlie Corrected. John Fitzherbert. LC 79-84107. (English Experience Ser.: No. 926). 220p. 1979. Repr. of 1598 ed. lib. bdg. 21.00 (ISBN 90-221-0926-7). Walter J Johnson.

Fitzgerald-Hemingway Annual. Ed. by Matthew Bruccoli & C. Frazer Clark, Jr. Incl. 1969. 18.00 (ISBN 0-685-60247-8); 1970. 18.00 (ISBN 0-910972-03-6); 1971. 22.00 (ISBN 0-910972-12-5); 1972. 22.00 (ISBN 0-910972-34-6); 1973. 22.00 (ISBN 0-910972-38-9); 1974. o.s.i. (ISBN 0-910972-49-4); 1975. o.s.i. (ISBN 0-910972-54-0); 1976. 24.00 (ISBN 0-910972-62-1). LC 75-83781. IHS-PDS.

Fitzgerald-Hemingway Annual, 3 vols. Ed. by Matthew J. Bruccoli & Richard Layman. Incl. 1977 Annual. 1978 (ISBN 0-8103-0909-2); 1978 Annual. 1979 (ISBN 0-8103-0910-6); 1979 Annual. 1980 (ISBN 0-8103-0911-4). LC 75-83781. (Illus.). 44.00 ea. (Bruccoli Clark). Gale.

Fitzgerald: La Vocation de l'echec. J. Bessiere. (Collection themes et textes). 256p. (Orig., Fr.). 1972. pap. 6.75 (ISBN 2-03-035002-8, 2682). Larousse.

Fitzgerald Reader. Ed. by Artur Mizener. LC 62-9632. 1963. pap. text ed. 7.95 (ISBN 0-684-15871-X, ScribC). Scribner.

Fitzgerald's Salaman & Absal. Arthur J. Arberry. (Cambridge Oriental Ser.: No. 2). 1956. 36.00 (ISBN 0-521-05011-1). Cambridge U Pr.

Fitzgerald's the Great Gatsby: The Novel, the Critics, the Background. Ed. by Henry D. Piper. (Research Anthologies Ser). (Illus., Orig.). 1970. pap. text ed. 7.95x (ISBN 0-684-41402-3, ScribC). Scribner.

Five. Kurt Vonnegut, Jr. pap. 8.40 boxed set o.s.i. (ISBN 0-685-45986-1). Dell.

Five Ages of the Cinema. Charles H. Tarbox. (Illus.). 128p. 1980. 20.00 (ISBN 0-682-49618-9). Exposition.

Five Arches with 'philoctetes' & Other Poems. T. R. Henn. 1980. pap. text ed. 24.75x (ISBN 0-901072-92-3). Humanities.

Five Arches with Philoctetes & Other Poems. T. R. Henn. 1980. text ed. 24.75x (ISBN 0-391-02105-2). Humanities.

Five Black Lives: The Autobiographies of Venture Smith, James Mars, William Grimes, the Rev. G. W. Offley, & James L. Smith. Ed. by Arna Bontemps et al. LC 74-108647. 1971. 17.50x (ISBN 0-8195-4036-6, Pub. by Wesleyan U Pr). Columbia U Pr.

Five Books of Moses. Oswald T. Allis. 1977. Repr. of 1947 ed. pap. 4.95 (ISBN 0-8010-0108-0). Baker Bk.

Five Boys in a Cave. Richard Church. LC 51-10431. (gr. 7-9). 1951. 7.95 (ISBN 0-381-99854-1, A27660, JD-J). John Day.

Five-Branch Government: The Full Measure of Constitutional Checks & Balances. Henry J. Merry. LC 79-22499. 290p. 1980. 17.50 (ISBN 0-252-00797-1). U of Ill Pr.

Five Bushel Farm. Elizabeth Coatsworth. (Illus.). (gr. 4-6). 1939. 4.95g o.s.i. (ISBN 0-02-720480-4). Macmillan.

Five Centuries of English Bookbinding. Howard M. Nixon. (Illus.). 244p. 1978. 35.00 (ISBN 0-85967-411-8, Pub. by Scolar Pr England). Biblio Dist.

Five Civilized Tribes. Grant Foreman. (Civilization of the American Indian Ser.: No. 8). (Illus.). 1971. 14.95 o.p. (ISBN 0-8061-0033-8); pap. 7.95 (ISBN 0-8061-0923-8). U of Okla Pr.

Five Clocks. Martin Joos. LC 62-62715. 1967. pap. 3.50 (ISBN 0-15-631380-4, H058, Hbgr). HarBraceJ.

Five Constitutions. Ed. by S. E. Finer. 1980. text ed. 30.00x (ISBN 0-391-00967-2). Humanities.

Five Contemporary Turkish Poets. Ed. by Stanley H. Barkan. Tr. by Talat Sait. (Cross-Cultural Review No. 6). 48p. (Turkish & Eng.). 1980. 10.00 (ISBN 0-89304-610-8); pap. 4.00 (ISBN 0-89304-611-6). Cross Cult.

Five Cries of Youth. Merton P. Strommen. LC 73-18690. 192p. 1974. 4.95 (ISBN 0-06-067748-1, RD224, HarpR). Har-Row.

Five Deadly Guns. Ralph Hayes. (Orig.). 1980. pap. write for info. (ISBN 0-505-51522-9). Tower Bks.

Five Elements of Acupuncture & Chinese Massage. D. Lawson-Wood & J. Lawson-Wood. 96p. 1976. 8.95x (ISBN 0-8464-1010-9). Beekman Pubs.

Five Eleventh Century Hungarian Kings: Their Policies & Their Relations with Rome. Z. J. Kosztolnyik. (East European Monographs: No. 79). 288p. 1981. text ed. 20.00x (ISBN 0-914710-73-7). East Eur Quarterly.

Five Fields of Social Service. Ed. by Henry S. Maas. 208p. 1966. pap. 8.00 (ISBN 0-87101-611-7, CBO-611-C). Natl Assn Soc Wkrs.

Five Fings of Distance. Peter Lovesey. (Illus.). 197p. 1981. 10.95 (ISBN 0-312-29484-0). St Martin.

Five for Freedom: Lucretia Mott, Elizabeth Cady Stanton, Lucy Stone, Susan B. Anthony, Carrie Chapman Catt. Constance B. Burnett. LC 68-8734. (Illus.). 1968. Repr. of 1953 ed. lib. bdg. 17.50x (ISBN 0-8371-0034-8, BUFF). Greenwood.

Five for Sorrow, Ten for Joy. Rumer Godden. 256p. 1981. pap. 2.75 (ISBN 0-449-24372-9, Crest). Fawcett.

Five for Sorrow Ten for Joy: A Consideration of the Rosary. Ed. by J. Neville Ward. LC 72-96263. 200p. 1974. pap. 1.45 o.p. (ISBN 0-385-09544-9, Im). Doubleday.

Five from Me, Five from You. Shelagh Macdonald. LC 80-2695. 192p. (gr. 6 up). 1981. 8.95 (ISBN 0-233-96554-8). Andre Deutsch.

Five Generations of Obesity: A Compilation of Family Recipes Making Getting Fat Look Easy. Ed. by Mildred Tyrack & Jeannine Van Eperen. (Illus.). 116p. (Orig.). 1981. pap. 4.95 (ISBN 0-937268-03-8). Alpha Printing.

Five Go to Demon's Rock. Enid Blyton. 1980. pap. 1.95 (ISBN 0-689-70478-X, Aladdin). Atheneum.

Five Graphic Music Analyses. Heinrich Schenker. LC 69-15902. Orig. Title: Five Analyses in Sketch Form. 1969. pap. 3.50 (ISBN 0-486-22294-2). Dover.

Five Graves for Lassiter. Jack Slade. 1979. pap. 1.50 (ISBN 0-505-51409-5). Tower Bks.

Five Graves to Boot Hill. Gordon D. Shirreffs. 1977. pap. 1.25 (ISBN 0-505-51157-6). Tower Bks.

Five Great Religions. Edward Rice. LC 72-87074. (Illus.). 192p. (gr. 7 up). 1973. 9.95 (ISBN 0-590-07175-0, Four Winds). Schol Bk Serv.

Five Historic Ships from Plan to Model. George S. Parker. LC 81-22137. (Illus.). 1980. 17.50 (ISBN 0-87033-258-9). Cornell Maritime.

Five Houses: Gwathmy Siegel Architects. Ed. by Kenneth Frampton. (IAUS Catalogues Ser.). 96p. (Orig.). 1980. pap. 12.00 (ISBN 0-932628-05-2). IAUS.

Five Hundred & Eight Answers to Bible Questions. Martin R. DeHaan. 1979. pap. 5.95 (ISBN 0-310-23341-0). Zondervan.

Five Hundred & Fifty-Five Timer Applications Sourcebook. Howard M. Berlin. LC 78-56584. 1976. pap. 6.95 (ISBN 0-672-21538-1). Sams.

Five Hundred & Five Rock & Roll Questions Your Friends Can't Answer. Nicholas Schaffner & Elizabeth Schaffner. LC 80-54484. 160p. 1981. 9.95 (ISBN 0-8027-0674-6); pap. 5.95 (ISBN 0-8027-7171-8). Walker & Co.

Five Hundred Bible Study Outlines. F. E. Marsh. LC 79-2549. 382p. 1980. Repr. of 1897 ed. 8.95 (ISBN 0-8254-3229-4). Kregel.

Five Hundred Dollar Way to Start a U.S. Stamp Investment Program. Stephen L. Suffet. LC 80-230. 1980. 3.50 (ISBN 0-87576-089-9). Pilot Bks.

Five Hundred Fishing Experts & How They Catch Fish. Vlad Evanoff. LC 77-80884. (Illus.). 1978. 10.95 o.p. (ISBN 0-385-07940-0). Doubleday.

Five Hundred Five Football Questions Your Friends Can't Answer. Harold Rosenthal. 192p. 9.95 (ISBN 0-8027-0661-4); pap. 5.95 (ISBN 0-8027-7163-7). Walker & Co.

Five Hundred Five Hockey Questions Your Friends Can't Answer. Frank Polnaszek. 192p. 1980. 9.95 (ISBN 0-8027-0669-X); pap. 5.95 (ISBN 0-8027-7167-X). Walker & Co.

Five Hundred Hats of Bartholomew Cubbins. Dr. Seuss. LC 38-30610. (Illus.). (gr. k-3). 5.95 (ISBN 0-8149-0338-6). Vanguard.

Five Hundred Mail Order Ideas. A. Stern. 1978. 14.50 o.p. (ISBN 0-685-04997-3, 0-911156-27-5). Porter.

Five Hundred More Things to Make for Farm & Home. Glenn C. Cook. (Illus.). (gr. 9-12). 1944. 16.65 (ISBN 0-8134-0038-4); text ed. 13.75x (ISBN 0-685-03891-2). Interstate.

Five Hundred One German Verbs: Written in Japanese. Strutz. Date not set. pap. 4.25 (ISBN 0-8120-2182-7). Barron. Postponed.

Five Hundred Things to Do in Florida for Free. Jim Hargrove & Harry Cooper. 140p. Date not set. pap. 3.95 (ISBN 0-695-81564-4). Follett. Postponed.

Five Hundred Things to Do in Houston for Free. Jim Hargrove et al. 140p. Date not set. pap. 3.95 (ISBN 0-695-81563-6). Follett. Postponed.

Five Hundred Things to Do in Los Angeles for Free. Carol MacConaugha. 140p. 1981. pap. 3.95 (ISBN 0-695-81562-8). Follett.

Five Hundred Word Theme. 3rd ed. Lee J. Martin & Harry P. Kroitor. (Illus.). 1979. pap. text ed. 8.50 (ISBN 0-13-321588-1). P-H.

Five Hundred Word Theme Workbook. Harry Kroitor. (Illus.). 224p. 1981. pap. 6.95 (ISBN 0-13-321612-8). P-H.

Five in a Tent. Victoria Furman. LC 66-1334. (gr. 3-7). 1966. 5.95 o.s.i. (ISBN 0-8193-0133-7, Four Winds); PLB 5.41 o.s.i. (ISBN 0-8193-0134-5). Schol Bk Serv.

Five in the Forest. Jan Wahl. (Picture Bk). (Illus.). 48p. (gr. k-3). 1974. 4.95 o.p. (ISBN 0-695-80446-4); lib. ed. 4.98 o.p. (ISBN 0-695-40446-6). Follett.

Five Indian Tribes of the Upper Missouri: Sioux, Arickaras, Assiniboines, Crees & Crows. Edwin T. Denig. Ed. by John C. Ewers. (Civilization of the American Indian Ser.: No. 59). (Illus.). 1961. 12.95 (ISBN 0-8061-0493-7); pap. 6.95 (ISBN 0-8061-1308-1). U of Okla Pr.

Five Language Dictionary of Surface Coatings, Platings, Product Finishing, Plastics & Rubber. R. W. Santholzer. 1969. 60.00 (ISBN 0-08-012336-8). Pergamon.

Five Late Romantic Poets. Ed. by James Reeves. (Poetry Bookshelf). 1974. pap. text ed. 3.95 (ISBN 0-435-15074-X). Heinemann Ed.

Five Little Angels. Patricia T. Sullivan. (Illus.). 50p. 1980. pap. 1.95 (ISBN 0-933402-16-3). Charisma Pr.

Five Little Gifts. Paul Ricchiuti. (Hello World Ser.). 1975. pap. 1.65 (ISBN 0-8163-0186-7, 06265-3). Pacific Pr Pub Assn.

Five Little Peppers. (Illustrated Junior Library). (Illus.). 288p. 1981. pap. 4.95 (ISBN 0-448-11008-3). G&D.

Five Little Peppers & How They Grew. Harriet M. Lothrop. LC 75-32184. (Classics of Children's Literature, 1621-1932: Vol. 47). (Illus.). 1976. Repr. of 1880 ed. PLB 38.00 (ISBN 0-8240-2296-3). Garland Pub.

Five Little Sermons. K. D. Katrak & Usha Katrak. 9.00 (ISBN 0-89253-626-8); flexible cloth 4.80 (ISBN 0-89253-627-6). Ind-US Inc.

Five Men Under One Umbrella: And Other Ready-to-Read Riddles. Joseph Low. (Ready-to-Read Ser.). (Illus.). 64p. (gr. 1-3). 1975. 7.95 (ISBN 0-02-761460-3). Macmillan.

Five Metaphysical Poets: Donne, Herbert, Vaughan, Crashaw, Marvell. Joan Bennett. 1964. 27.50 (ISBN 0-521-04156-2); pap. 8.95x (ISBN 0-521-09238-8). Cambridge U Pr.

Five Metropolitan Governments. Melvin B Mogulof. 1972. pap. 3.50 o.p. (ISBN 0-87766-033-6, 12000). Urban Inst.

Five-Minute Feasts. Karl Wurzer. Ed. by L. Leedham. (Illus.). 176p. 1980. 12.95 (ISBN 0-88421-157-6). Butterick Pub.

Five Minutes to Midnight. Sabi Shabtai. 1981. pap. 2.95 (ISBN 0-440-12534-0). Dell.

Five Modern No Plays. Yukio Mishima. Tr. by Donald Keene from Japanese. (Illus.). 206p. 1957. pap. 6.50 (ISBN 0-8048-1380-9). C E Tuttle.

Five Modern No Plays. Yukio Mishima. Tr. by Donald Keene. 198p. Date not set. pap. 1.95 (ISBN 0-394-71883-6, Vin). Random.

Five Monographs on Business Income. Sidney S. Alexander et al. LC 73-84377. 1973. Repr. of 1950 ed. text ed. 13.00 (ISBN 0-914348-00-0). Scholars Bk.

Five More. Ner Littner. LC 80-80866. 56p. (Orig.). 1980. pap. text ed. 3.95 (ISBN 0-87868-189-2). Child Welfare.

Five Mountains: The Rinzai Zen Monastic Institution in Medieval Japan. Martin Collcutt. (Harvard East Asian Monograph: Vol. 85). (Illus.). 450p. 1981. 20.00 (ISBN 0-674-30497-7). Harvard U Pr.

Five Novels. Ronald Firbank. Incl. Valmouth; Artificial Princess; Flower Beneath the Foot; Prancing Nigger; Cardinal Pirelli. LC 49-48966. 1969. 8.50 o.p. (ISBN 0-8112-0276-3). New Directions.

Five Novels. Ronald Firbank. Incl. Valmouth: Valmouth; Artifical Princess; Flower Beneath the Foot; Prancing Nigger; Cardinal Pirelli. 1981. pap. 7.95 (ISBN 0-8112-0799-4, NDP518). New Directions.

Five Novels. Ronald Firbank. 384p. 1981. pap. 7.95 (ISBN 0-8112-0799-4, NDP518). New Directions.

Five O'Clock Charlie. Marguerite Henry. LC 62-11987. (Illus.). (gr. 2-4). 1962. 4.95 (ISBN 0-528-82618-2); pap. 2.95 (ISBN 0-528-87006-8). Rand.

Five on a Secret Trail. Enid Blyton. 1980. pap. 1.95 (ISBN 0-689-70477-1, Aladdin). Atheneum.

Five on the Black Hand Side: A Play. Charles Russell. LC 73-82643. 1973. pap. 6.95 (ISBN 0-89388-092-2). Okpaku Communications.

Five on the Western Edge. Ed. & intro. by Stephen Vincent. (Illus.). 1977. o.p. (ISBN 0-917672-01-1); pap. 4.95x (ISBN 0-917672-00-3). Momos.

Five Orders of Classic Architecture. Howard M. Hamlin. (Illus.). 148p. 1981. 69.75 (ISBN 0-930582-95-0). Gloucester Art.

Five Passengers from Lisbon. Mignon E. Eberhart. 160p. 1976. pap. 1.25 o.p. (ISBN 0-685-68756-2). Popular Lib.

Five Pennies Make a Nickel: A Piggybank Book. Rhoda Bellak & Dick Voehl. (Piggybank Bks.). 12p. (gr. k-2). 1981. text ed. 4.95 (ISBN 0-671-42562-5). Wanderer Bks.

Five per Cent Philanthropy: An Account of Housing in Urban Areas, 1840-1914. J. N. Tarn. LC 77-186253. (Illus.). 300p. 1973. 41.95 (ISBN 0-521-08506-3). Cambridge U Pr.

Five Philosophers. Ed. by Philip Wheelwright & Peter Fuss. LC 63-14019. 1963. pap. 7.50 (ISBN 0-672-63035-4). Odyssey Pr.

Five Plays. George Hitchcock. 330p. (Orig.). 1981. pap. 7.95 (ISBN 0-937310-10-7). Jazz Pr.

Five Points of Calvinism. H. Hanko et al. LC 76-47146. 1976. pap. 2.95 (ISBN 0-8254-2854-8). Kregel.

Five Points of Calvinism. Jack Seaton. 1979. pap. 0.95. Banner of Truth.

Five Points of Calvinism: A Study Guide. Edwin H. Palmer. 1972. pap. 3.95 (ISBN 0-8010-6926-2). Baker Bk.

Five Ports to Danger. Vivian Connolly. (Orig.). 1980. pap. 1.75 (ISBN 0-505-51518-0). Tower Bks.

Five Power Nuclei Which Control the Life & Destinies of the United States. Spencer Fleming. (Illus.). 200p. 1976. 31.50 (ISBN 0-913314-71-4); lib. bdg. 37.50 (ISBN 0-685-59176-X). Am Classical Coll Pr.

Five Public Philosophies of Walter Lippmann. Benjamin F. Wright. LC 73-6696. 168p. 1973. 12.95x o.p. (ISBN 0-292-72407-1). U of Tex Pr.

Five Red Herrings. Dorothy L. Sayers. 1968. pap. 2.25 (ISBN 0-380-01187-5, 51219). Avon.

Five Red Herrings. Dorothy L. Sayers. (Large Print Bks.). 1980. lib. bdg. 15.95 (ISBN 0-8161-3044-2). G K Hall.

Five Senses. Rhodri Jones. 1971. pap. text ed. 2.50x o.p. (ISBN 0-435-14506-1). Heinemann Ed.

Five Senses for One Death: Special Issue 18. Adi. pap. 1.00 o.p. (ISBN 0-685-78397-9). The Smith.

Five Sermons: Preached at the Rolls Chapel & A Dissertation Upon the Nature of Virtue. Joseph Butler. LC 50-4922. 1950. pap. 2.95 (ISBN 0-672-60182-6, LLA21). Bobbs.

Five Ships West: The Story of Magellan. Charles E. Israel. (gr. 4-6). 1966. 5.95g o.s.i. (ISBN 0-02-747410-0). Macmillan.

Five Simple Keys to Effective Evangelism: You Too Can Do It. Charles L. McKay. 1978. pap. text ed. 11.00x (ISBN 0-8191-0397-7). U Pr of Amer.

Five Smooth Stones for Pastoral Work. Eugene H. Peterson. LC 79-87751. 1980. pap. 8.95 (ISBN 0-8042-1103-5). John Knox.

Five Steps Toward a Better Marriage. David A. Thompson. 96p. (Orig.). 1980. pap. 3.95 (ISBN 0-87123-164-6, 210164). Bethany Fell.

Five Temperaments: Elizabeth Bishop, Robert Lowell, James Merrill, Adrienne Rich, John Ashbery. David Kalstone. LC 76-42655. 1977. 13.95 (ISBN 0-19-502260-2). Oxford U Pr.

Five-Thousand Years of Art: An Exhibition from the Collections of the Metropolitan Museum of Art. Thomas Schlotterback. LC 76-50228. (Whatcom Museum Ser.). (Illus.). 1976. pap. 10.00 (ISBN 0-295-95575-9). U of Wash Pr.

Five to Seven. Diana Noel. (Illus.). 144p. 1980. pap. 2.95 (ISBN 0-86072-032-2, Pub. by Quartet England). Horizon.

Five Towns. Leslie Tonner. LC 80-52418. 416p. 1981. 12.95 (ISBN 0-87223-652-8). Seaview Bks.

Five Tracts of Hasan Al-Banna: A Selection from the Majmu'at Rasa'il Al-'imam Al-Shahid Hasan Al-Banna. Hasan Wendell & Hasan Al-Banna. LC 77-83119. (Publications in Near Eastern Studies: Vol. 20). 1978. pap. 11.50x (ISBN 0-520-09584-7). U of Cal Pr.

Five Types of Ethical Theory. 8th ed. C. D. Broad. (International Library of Philosophy & Scientific Method). 1930. text ed. 25.00x (ISBN 0-7100-3080-0). Humanities.

Five Ways of Parenting: One That Works! Verne Faust. LC 79-65211. 1980. 13.95 (ISBN 0-934162-01-8). Thomas Paine Pr.

Five Were Missing ("Ransom") Lois Duncan. (RL 7). 1972. pap. 1.50 (ISBN 0-451-08678-3, W8678, Sig). NAL.

Five Who Found the Kingdom: New Testament Stories. Sandol Stoddard. LC 80-1663. (Illus.). 128p. (gr. 7). 1981. 8.95a (ISBN 0-385-17169-2); PLB (ISBN 0-385-17170-6). Doubleday.

Five Women. Denise Adler. 1980. pap. 1.95 (ISBN 0-8423-0874-1). Tyndale.

Five Words Long. 3rd ed. Mildred A. Dawson et al. Ed. by Henry A. Bamman. (Kaleidoscope Ser.). 1978. pap. text ed. 6.08 (ISBN 0-201-40875-9, Sch Div); tchr's. ed. 6.64 (ISBN 0-201-40876-7). A-W.

Five Years a Captive Among the Black-feet Indians. Sylvester Crakes. LC 75-7099. (Indian Captivities Ser.: Vol. 74). 1976. Repr. of 1858 ed. lib. bdg. 44.00 (ISBN 0-8240-1698-X). Garland Pub.

Five Years a Dragoon ('49 to '54) And Other Adventures on the Great Plains. Percival G. Lowe. 1965. pap. 7.95 o.p. (ISBN 0-8061-1089-9). U of Okla Pr.

Five Years of Military Government in Chile (1973-1978; Bernardo Elgueta et al. 300p. 1981. text ed. 25.00 (ISBN 0-930576-40-3). E M Coleman Ent.

Fix It. Robert Brightman. 7.95 (ISBN 0-916752-18-6). Green Hill.

Fix-It Duro-Loctite Guide to Home & Auto Care & Repair. Robert Brightman. LC 77-89550. (Illus.). 1978. 7.95 (ISBN 0-916752-18-6). Dorison Hse.

Fix It Guide for Women. Dorothy Carbo. LC 76-21255. 1976. pap. 2.50 o.p. (ISBN 0-668-04016-5). Arco.

Fix Your Axe: Easy Guitar Repairs You Can Do at Home. Ed. by Guitar Player Magazine & Eric Kriss. LC 75-27790. (Illus.). 72p. (Orig.). 1976. pap. 5.95 (ISBN 0-8256-9503-1). Guitar Player.

Fix Your Bicycle: All Speeds, All Major Makes, Simplified, Step by Step. 2nd ed. Eric Jorgensen. Ed. by Jeff Robinson. (Illus.). 192p. 1975. pap. text ed. 7.00 (ISBN 0-89287-035-4, X901). Clymer Pubns.

Fix Your Chevrolet. Bill Toboldt. (Illus.). 1978. 6.00 (ISBN 0-87006-255-7). Goodheart.

Fix Your Ford. Bill Toboldt. (Illus.). 1978. 6.00 (ISBN 0-87006-254-9). Goodheart.

Fix Your Volkswagen. Larry Johnson. 1980. 6.00 (ISBN 0-87006-297-2). Goodheart.

Fixed Base Operators - Management Handbook. David Cohen. Ed. by David Jones & M. Dale Hurst. (Aviation Management Ser.). 1980. pap. text ed. write for info. (ISBN 0-89100-148-4). Aviation Maintenance.

Fixed Point Theorems. D. R. Smart. LC 73-79314. (Tracts in Mathematics Ser.: No. 66). (Illus.). 160p. 1974. 23.95 (ISBN 0-521-20289-2). Cambridge U Pr.

Fixed Point Theorems. D. R. Smart. (Cambridge Tracts in Mathematics: No. 66). (Illus.). 100p. 1980. pap. 13.95x (ISBN 0-521-29833-4). Cambridge U Pr.

Fixed Rings of Finite Automorphism Groups of Associative Rings. S. Montgomery. (Lectures Notes in Mathematics Ser.: Vol. 818). 126p. 1981. pap. 9.80 (ISBN 0-387-10232-9). Springer-Verlag.

Fixed Stars & Constellations in Astrology. Vivian E. Robson. LC 73-16447. (Illus.). 1980. pap. 5.95 (ISBN 0-87728-033-9). Weiser.

Fixer. Bernard Malamud. 352p. 1966. 17.50 (ISBN 0-374-15572-0). FS&G.

Fjord Oceanography. Ed. by Howard J. Freeland et al. (NATO Conference Ser., Ser. IV: Marine Science: Vol. 4). 713p. 1980. 69.50 (ISBN 0-306-40439-7, Plenum Pr). Plenum Pub.

Flag Captain. Alexander Kent. 1979. pap. 1.95 o.p. (ISBN 0-425-04180-8). Berkley Pub.

Flag Captain. Alexander Kent. pap. 1.95 (ISBN 0-515-05349-X). Jove Pubns.

Flags of the U.S.A. enl. ed. David Eggenberger. 1964. 9.95 (ISBN 0-690-30491-9, TYC-T). T Y Crowell.

Flags of the World. rev. ed. E. M. Barraclough. LC 68-22445. (Illus.). (gr. 7 up). 1979. 30.00 (ISBN 0-7232-2015-8). Warne.

Flair: A Handbook of Classroom Ideas to Motivate the Teaching of Creative Writing. (Spice Ser). 1972. 6.50 (ISBN 0-89273-112-5). Educ Serv.

Flair Duplicating Master: Elementary Creative Writing. (Spice Ser.). (gr. k-8). 1975. 5.95 (ISBN 0-89273-516-3). Educ Serv.

Flair in the Kitchen. 1980. pap. 4.95 (ISBN 0-930756-58-4, 4230-FK). Women's Aglow.

Flambards. K. M. Peyton. pap. 3.95 (ISBN 0-14-005461-8). Penguin.

Flamboyant Mr. Colt & His Deadly Six-Shooter. Bern Keating. LC 78-8214. 1978. 9.95 o.p. (ISBN 0-385-12371-X). Doubleday.

Flame. William Sears & Robert Quigley. 1972. 3.95 (ISBN 0-85398-031-4, 7-31-81, Pub. by G Ronald England); pap. 1.95 (ISBN 0-85398-030-6, 7-31-82, Pub. by G Ronald England). Baha'i.

Flame & the Fire. Elizabeth Hanley. 1978. pap. 1.95 (ISBN 0-505-51251-3). Tower Bks.

Flame & the Flower. Kathleen E. Woodiwiss. 1976. pap. 2.50 (ISBN 0-380-00525-5, 46276). Avon.

Flame in the Night. (Encounter Ser.). (gr. 3-7). 2.25 o.s.i. (ISBN 0-8198-0234-4). Dghtrs St Paul.

Flame of Chandrapore. Aaron Fletcher. 1979. pap. 2.25 (ISBN 0-505-51342-0). Tower Bks.

Flame of Desire. Carole Mortimer. (Harlequin Presents Ser.). 192p. 1981. pap. 1.50 (ISBN 0-373-10418-9, Pub. by Harlequin). PB.

Flame of New Orleans. Frances P. Statham. 416p. 1978. pap. 1.95 o.p. (ISBN 0-449-13720-1, GM). Fawcett.

Flame of Savannah. Maggie Lyons. (Orig.). 1980. pap. 2.25 (ISBN 0-515-04745-7). Jove Pubns.

Flame of Sunset. L. P. Holmes. 1979. pap. 1.75 o.p. (ISBN 0-445-04161-7). Popular Lib.

Flame of White. Bd. with Rose of Life. 1981. write for info. (ISBN 0-935490-02-7). Euclid Pub.

Flame Retardants for Plastics, Rubber & Textiles: Including Indexes & Abstracts 1967 to 1971. James R. Critser, Jr. Incl. 285.00 (ISBN 0-914428-03-9). (Ser. 2-6771b). 1971. Lexington Data.

Flame Retardants for Plastics, Rubber, Textiles & Paper: Series No. 2-7980, July 1979 - June 1980. James R. Critser, Jr. 136p. 1981. refer. - ring bdg. 110.00 (ISBN 0-914428-73-X). Lexington Data.

Flamenco Nights. Susanna Collins. (Second Chance at Love, Contemporary Ser.: No. 1). 192p. (Orig.). 1981. pap. 1.75 (ISBN 0-515-05703-7). Jove Pubns.

Flameout. Colin Peel. LC 77-15918. 1978. 7.95 o.p. (ISBN 0-312-29546-4). St Martin.

Flameout. Colin D. Peel. LC 80-83595. 192p. 1981. pap. 2.25 (ISBN 0-87216-792-5). Playboy Pbks.

Flames of Desire. Vanessa Royall. 1978. pap. 2.25 o.s.i. (ISBN 0-440-14637-2). Dell.

Flames of Rome. Paul Maier. LC 80-2561. (Illus.). 384p. 1981. 12.95 (ISBN 0-385-17091-2, Galilee). Doubleday.

Flaming Star. Millard. (gr. 3-5). pap. 1.50 (ISBN 0-590-11923-0, Schol Pap). Schol Bk Serv.

Flamingo Park. Margaret Way. (Harlequin Romances). 192p. 1981. pap. 1.25 (ISBN 0-373-02400-2, Pub. by Harlequin). PB.

Flammable Hazardous Materials. 2nd ed. James H. Meidl. 1978. text ed. 14.95x (ISBN 0-02-476570-8). Macmillan.

Flanders Road. Claude Simon. 1961. 4.00 o.p. (ISBN 0-8076-0146-2). Braziller.

Flandre et Artois touristiques. (Illus.). 1978. text ed. 14.25x (ISBN 2-03-013927-0, 3158). Larousse.

Flannery O'Connor. Preston M. Browning, Jr. LC 74-8849. (Crosscurrents-Modern Critiques Ser.). 160p. 1974. 7.95 (ISBN 0-8093-0672-7). S Ill U Pr.

Flannery O'Connor. Dorothy T. McFarland. LC 74-78443. (Modern Literature Ser.). 140p. 1976. 10.95 (ISBN 0-8044-2609-0). Ungar.

Flannery O'Connor. Dorothy Walters. (U. S. Authors Ser.: No. 216). 1971. lib. bdg. 9.95 (ISBN 0-8057-0556-2). Twayne.

Flannery O'Connor: Her Life, Library & Book Reviews. Lorine M. Getz. (Studies in Women & Religion: Vol. 5). 1980. soft cover 24.95x (ISBN 0-88946-997-0). E Mellen.

Flannery O'Connor's Georgia. Barbara McKenzie. LC 80-10936. (Illus.). 132p. 1980. 24.95 (ISBN 0-8203-0517-0); pap. 12.50 (ISBN 0-8203-0518-9). U of Ga Pr.

Flash. Mel Juffe. LC 73-2336. 256p. 1974. 7.95 o.p. (ISBN 0-670-31743-8). Viking Pr.

Flash & the Swan. Ann Brophy. LC 80-14513. (Illus.). (gr. 5 up). 1981. 8.95g (ISBN 0-7232-6190-3). Warne.

Flash, Crash, Rumble, & Roll. Franklyn M. Branley. LC 64-18161. (Let's-Read-&-Find-Out Science Bk). (Illus.). (gr. k-3). 1964. PLB 7.89 (ISBN 0-690-30563-X, TYC-J). T Y Crowell.

Flash Gordon. Arthur B. Cover. (Orig.). pap. 2.50 (ISBN 0-515-05848-3). Jove Pubns.

Flash Gordon, No. 5. David Hagberg. 192p. (Orig.). 1981. pap. 2.25 (ISBN 0-448-17234-8, Tempo). G&D.

Flash Gordon Book. Adapted by Lynn Haney. (Illus.). 64p. 1980. 5.95 (ISBN 0-399-20782-1). Putnam.

Flash Gordon Novel, 3 vols. David Hegberg. Incl. No. 1 (ISBN 0-448-12963-9); No. 2 (ISBN 0-448-17215-1); No. 3 (ISBN 0-448-17231-3). (Flash Gordon Novel Ser.). 208p. 1980. pap. 2.25 (ISBN 0-686-64851-X, Tempo). G&D.

Flash of Green. John D. MacDonald. 1979. pap. 2.25 (ISBN 0-449-14186-1, GM). Fawcett.

Flashback!-I Didn't Know That. Alice Wilson et al. (Orig.). 1980. playscript 2.50 (ISBN 0-87602-236-0). Anchorage.

Flashpoint. George La Fountaine. 1978. pap. 1.75 o.p. (ISBN 0-449-23644-7, Crest). Fawcett.

Flask of Fields. Ed. by Richard J. Anobile. 1975. pap. 3.95 (ISBN 0-380-01189-1, 17533). Avon.

Flat & Corrugated Diaphragm Design Handbook. DiGiovanni. Date not set. price not set. Dekker.

Flat on My Face. Julia First. (gr. 4-6). 1975. pap. 1.25 (ISBN 0-380-00204-3, 52324, Camelot). Avon.

Flatland: A Romance of Many Dimensions. 5th rev ed. Edwin A. Abbott. 1963. pap. 2.95 (ISBN 0-06-463210-5, E*H 210, EH). Har-Row.

Flats, Families & the Under-Fives. Elizabeth Gittus. (International Library of Social Policy). 1976. 20.00 (ISBN 0-7100-8284-3). Routledge & Kegan.

Flatten Your Stomach in Fifteen Minutes a Day. - Anita Columbo & Franco Columbu. (Anita & Franco Columbu's Shape up in Minutes-a-Day Program). (Illus., Orig.). 1980. pap. 1.95 (ISBN 0-8092-7076-5); 93.60 (ISBN 0-8092-7022-6). Contemp Bks.

Flaubert. Benjamin F. Bart. LC 67-27410. (Illus.). 1967. 16.00 o.p. (ISBN 0-8156-0057-7); pap. 6.95 (ISBN 0-8156-0087-9). Syracuse U Pr.

Flaubert: The Problem of Aesthetic Discontinuity. Marie J. Diamond. 1975. 12.50 (ISBN 0-8046-9075-8, Natl U). Kennikat.

Flavii Cresconii Corippi Iohannidos Libri 8. Ed. by J. Diggle & F. R. Goodyear. LC 78-85717. 1970. 39.00 (ISBN 0-521-07626-9). Cambridge U Pr.

Flavius Cresconius Corippus: In Laudem Lustini Augusti Minoris. Ed. by Averil Cameron. (Illus.). 235p. 1976. text ed. 52.00x (ISBN 0-485-11157-8, Athlone Pr). Humanities.

Flavonoids. Ed. by J. Harborne & Helga Mabry. 1975. 77.00 set (ISBN 0-685-72438-7); Pt. 1. 47.50 (ISBN 0-12-324601-6); Pt. 2. 47.50 (ISBN 0-12-324602-4). Acad Pr.

Flavor: It's Chemical, Behavioral & Commercial Aspects. Charles Apt. LC 77-13274. 1978. lib. bdg. 36.50x (ISBN 0-89158-233-9). Westview.

Flavor Microbiology. Pinhas Margalith. (Illus.). 336p. 1980. 31.50 (ISBN 0-398-04083-4). C C Thomas.

Flavor of North Beach: The Insider's Guide to San Francisco's Historic Italian District. Brian St. Pierre & Mary E. Moose. 160p. (Orig.). 1981. pap. 5.95 (ISBN 0-87701-157-5). Chronicle Bks.

Flavor of Spain. Myra Waldo. 1970. pap. 1.50 o.s.i. (ISBN 0-02-010400-6, Collier). Macmillan.

Flavor of Texas. J. F. Dobie. 176p. (YA) 1975. 12.50 (ISBN 0-8363-0130-7). Jenkins.

Flavor of Wisconsin: An Informal History of Food & Eating in the Badger State. Harva Hachten. LC 80-26172. (Illus.). 300p. 1981. 12.95 (ISBN 0-87020-204-9). State Hist Soc Wis.

Flavor Technology: Profiles, Products, Applications. Henry Heath. (Illus.). 1978. lib. bdg. 39.50 (ISBN 0-87055-258-9). AVI.

Flavors of Northern Italy. Violeta Autumn. LC 80-83215. (Illus.). 168p. (Orig.). 1980. pap. 5.95 (ISBN 0-89286-164-9). One Hund One Prods.

Flavors of the Caribbean & Latin America: A Personal Collection of Recipes. Alex D. Hawkes. 1978. 14.95 o.p. (ISBN 0-670-31755-1). Viking Pr.

Flavour of Montreal. Kenneth Mitchell. (Illus.). 1977. 8.95 o.s.i. (ISBN 0-7715-9338-4). Vanguard.

Flawed Liberation: Socialism & Feminism. Ed. by Sally M. Miller. LC 80-1050. (Contributions to Women's Studies Ser.: No. 19). 240p. 1981. lib. bdg. 27.50 (ISBN 0-313-21401-8, MFL/). Greenwood.

Flawed Victory: A New Perspective on the Civil War. William L. Barney. LC 80-68972. 225p. 1980. lib. bdg. 19.00 (ISBN 0-8191-1273-9); pap. text ed. 8.75 (ISBN 0-8191-1274-7). U Pr of Amer.

Flea Market & Garage Sale Handbook. Irene Copeland. 1977. pap. 1.75 o.p. (ISBN 0-445-08624-6). Popular Lib.

Flea Market Mystery. Virginia Evansen. LC 77-16863. (gr. 5 up). 1978. 5.95 (ISBN 0-396-07521-5). Dodd.

Flea Market Price Guide. 2nd ed. Robert W. Miller. (Illus.). 6.95 o.p. (ISBN 0-87069-268-2). Wallace-Homestead.

Flea Story: I Want to Stay Here! I Want to Go There! Leo Lionni. LC 77-4322. (Illus.). (ps-2). 1977. 5.95 (ISBN 0-394-83498-4); PLB 6.99 (ISBN 0-394-93498-9). Pantheon.

Fleas. Johanna Cole. (Illus.). 64p. (gr. 3-7). 1973. PLB 6.48 (ISBN 0-688-31844-4). Morrow.

Fleas. H. Hoke & V. Pitt. LC 73-12147. (First Bks). 4.47 o.p. (ISBN 0-531-00815-0). Watts.

Flechtengattung Psora Sensu Zahlbruckner. Gotthard Schneider. (Bibliotheca Lichenologica: 13). (Illus.). 308p. (Ger.). 1980. lib. bdg. 40.00x (ISBN 3-7682-1257-2). Lubrecht & Cramer.

Fledgling. Jane Langton. LC 79-2008. 192p. (gr. 3-7). 1981. pap. 2.95 (ISBN 0-06-440121-9, Trophy). Har-Row.

Fleet Admiral King. Ernest King & Walter Whitehill. LC 78-11889. (Politics and Strategy of World War II Ser.). 1976. Repr. of 1952 ed. lib. bdg. 49.50 (ISBN 0-306-70772-1). Da Capo.

Fleet Footed Florence. Marilyn Sachs. LC 76-56330. (Illus.). 48p. (gr. 2). 1981. 8.95a (ISBN 0-385-12745-6); PLB (ISBN 0-385-12746-4). Doubleday.

Fleet: Its River, Prison, & Marriages. John Ashton. LC 68-21753. 1969. Repr. of 1888 ed. 20.00 (ISBN 0-8103-3414-3). Gale.

Fleet Street Disaster. Graham Cleverley. LC 76-25733. (Communication & Society: Vol. 7). 1976. 17.50x (ISBN 0-8039-9989-5, Co-Pub with Constable). Sage.

Fleetwood: or, The New Man of Feeling, 3 vols. William Godwin. Ed. by Ronald Paulson. LC 78-60852. (Novel 1720-1805 Ser.: Vol. 14). 1979. Set. lib. bdg. 93.00 (ISBN 0-8240-3663-8). Garland Pub.

Flemish & Dutch Paintings Fourteen Hundred to Nineteen Hundred: From the John & Mable Ringling Museum of Art. Franklin W. Robinson & William H. Wilson. LC 80-50842. (Illus.). 310p. (Orig.). 1980. pap. 25.00 (ISBN 0-916758-02-8). Ringling Mus Art.

Flesh. Michael Brodsky. Date not set. Vol. I & Ii. 10.00 ea. (ISBN 0-89396-027-6). Urizen Bks. Postponed.

Flesh. Philip J. Farmer. Bd. with Lord Tyger. 1981. pap. 2.50 (ISBN 0-451-09787-4, E9787, Sig). NAL.

Flesh & Spirit. Elizabeth Christman. 1980. pap. 2.25 (ISBN 0-686-69260-8, 52142). Avon.

Flesh & the Devil. Teresa Denys. 488p. 1981. 12.95 (ISBN 0-312-29583-9). St Martin.

Flesh Eaters. L. A. Morse. 1979. pap. 2.25 (ISBN 0-446-82633-2). Warner Bks.

Flesh Is Heir. Lincoln Kirstein. (Lost American Fiction Ser.). 1977. pap. 1.75 o.p. (ISBN 0-445-08548-7). Popular Lib.

Flesh Is Weak: An Intimate History of the Church of England. Andrew Barrow. (Illus.). 254p. 1981. 29.95 (ISBN 0-241-10234-0, Pub. by Hamish Hamilton England). David & Charles.

Fleshwound. F. W. Belland. 224p. (Orig.). 1981. pap. 2.25 (ISBN 0-515-05652-9). Jove Pubns.

Fletcher & Zenobia. Edward Gorey & Victoria Chess. LC 67-14746. (Illus.). 1967. 4.95 o.p. (ISBN 0-8015-2670-1). Dutton.

Fletcher Martin. H. Lester Cooke, Jr. LC 75-2472. (Contemporary Artists Ser.). (Illus.). 1977. 65.00 o.p. (ISBN 0-8109-0319-9). Abrams.

Fletcher Without Beaumont: A Study of the Independent Plays of John Fletcher. Mary Cone. (Salzburg Studies in English Literature, Jacobean Drama Studies: No. 60). 1976. pap. 25.00x (ISBN 0-391-01348-3). Humanities.

Fletch's Fortune. Gregory McDonald. 1978. pap. 2.25 (ISBN 0-380-37978-3, 76323). Avon.

Fleur. Sarah Nichols. (Wyndham Saga: No. 3). 1977. pap. 1.50 o.p. (ISBN 0-445-03216-2). Popular Lib.

Fleurs du Mal. Charles Baudelaire. Ed. by Enid Starkie. (French Texts Ser.). 1970. pap. text ed. 10.50x (ISBN 0-631-00410-6, Pub. by Basil Blackwell). Biblio Dist.

FLEX Review. Robert Abrams et al. LC 80-83395. 1980. pap. 21.50 (ISBN 0-87488-158-7). Med Exam.

Flexibility & Health Through Yoga. Helen M. Esser. (Illus.). 1978. pap. text ed. 8.95 (ISBN 0-8403-2236-4). Kendall-Hunt.

Flexible Life Scheduling: Breaking the Education-Work-Retirement Lockstep. Fred Best. 1979. 23.95 (ISBN 0-03-050586-0); pap. 8.95 (ISBN 0-03-050591-7). Praeger.

Flexible Rotor-Bearing System Dynamics, 3 vols, Pts. I, II, & III. Incl. Pt. I. Critical Speeds & Response of Flexible Rotor Systems. R. L. Eshleman. 1972. pap. 5.00 o.p. (ISBN 0-685-30772-7, H00042); Pt. II. Bearing Influence & Representation in Rotor Dynamics Analysis. W. Shapiro & J. H. Rumbarger. 1972. pap. text ed. 3.50 o.p. (ISBN 0-685-30773-5, H00046); Pt. III. Unbalance Response & Balancing of Flexible Rotor in Bearing. N. F. Reiger. 1973. pap. text ed. 4.00 o.p. (ISBN 0-685-30774-3, H00048). 1972. ASME.

Flexible Work Schedule: An Innovation in the Quality of Work Life. Simcha Ronen. (Illus.). 352p. 1980. 18.95 (ISBN 0-07-053607-4). McGraw.

Flick & I. Ralph J. Batschelet. 176p. 1981. 9.00 (ISBN 0-682-49717-7). Exposition.

Flicka, Ricka, Dicka & a Little Dog. Maj Lindman. LC 48-3307. (Illus.). (gr. k-2). 1946. 5.75g (ISBN 0-8075-2486-7). A Whitman.

Flicka, Ricka, Dicka & the Big Red Hen. Maj Lindman. LC 60-13634. (Illus.). (gr. k-2). 1960. 5.75g (ISBN 0-8075-2481-6). A Whitman.

Flicka, Ricka, Dicka & the Girl Next Door. Maj Lindman. (Illus.). (gr. k-2). 5.75g (ISBN 0-8075-2483-2). A Whitman.

Flicka, Ricka, Dicka & the New Dotted Dresses. Maj Lindman. (Illus.). (gr. k-2). 5.75g (ISBN 0-8075-2482-4). A Whitman.

Flicka, Ricka, Dicka & the Strawberries. Maj Lindman. (Illus.). (gr. k-2). 1944. 5.75g (ISBN 0-8075-2489-1). A Whitman.

Flicka, Ricka, Dicka & the Three Kittens. Maj Lindman. LC 41-17581. (Illus.). (gr. k-2). 1941. 5.75g (ISBN 0-8075-2490-5). A Whitman.

Flicka, Ricka, Dicka & Their New Friend. Maj Lindman. (Illus.). (gr. k-2). 1942. 5.75g (ISBN 0-8075-2487-5). A Whitman.

Flicka, Ricka, Dicka & Their New Skates. Maj Lindman. (Illus.). (gr. k-2). 1950. 5.75g (ISBN 0-8075-2488-3). A Whitman.

Flicka, Ricka, Dicka Bake a Cake. Maj Lindman. LC 55-7571. (Illus.). (gr. k-2). 1955. 5.75g (ISBN 0-8075-2480-8). A Whitman.

Flicka, Ricka, Dicka Go to Market. Maj Lindman. LC 58-9950. (Illus.). (gr. k-2). 1958. 5.75g (ISBN 0-8075-2485-9). A Whitman.

Flies of Western North America. Frank R. Cole & Evert L. Schlinger. LC 68-10687. (Illus.). 1969. 58.50x (ISBN 0-520-01516-9). U of Cal Pr.

Flight. H. Guyford Stever & James J. Haggerty. LC 65-24362. (Life Science Library). (Illus.). (gr. 5 up). 1969. PLB 8.97 o.p. (ISBN 0-8094-0469-9, Pub. by Time-Life). Silver.

Flight & Rebellion: Slave Resistence in Eighteenth Century Virginia. Gerald W. Mullin. 224p. 1972. 15.95 (ISBN 0-19-501514-2). Oxford U Pr.

Flight Before Flying. David Wragg. LC 73-93897. (Illus.). 1974. 9.95 (ISBN 0-8119-0233-1). Fell.

Flight Deck Uses for HP-25: Vol. 1, Professional Assortment. Melvin N. Peterson. 66p. 1979. spiral bdg. 10.00x (ISBN 0-938880-00-4). MNP Star.

Flight Deck Uses for the HP-41c: Vol. 1, Manual Run Mode Edition. Melvin N. Peterson. 59p. 1981. spiral bdg. 12.00x (ISBN 0-938880-01-2). MNP Star.

Flight Engineers Manual. 10th rev. ed. LC 67-30737. 1979. pap. 17.95 (ISBN 0-87219-005-6). Pan Am Nav.

Flight from Dhahran: The/True Experiences of an American Businessman Held Hostage in Saudi Arabia. John McDonald & Clyde Burleson. 256p. 1981. 10.95 (ISBN 0-13-322453-8). P-H.

Flight from Reality. Clarence B. Carson. 568p. 1969. 8.00 o.p. (ISBN 0-910614-33-4); pap. 4.00 (ISBN 0-910614-18-0). Foun Econ Ed.

Flight from the Hunter. Siegfried Stander. LC 77-76653. 1977. 7.95 o.p. (ISBN 0-312-29598-7). St Martin.

Flight from Women in the Fiction of Saul Bellow. Joseph F. McCadden. LC 80-5641. 299p. 1980. lib. bdg. 18.75 (ISBN 0-8191-1308-5); pap. text ed. 10.50 (ISBN 0-8191-1309-3). U Pr of Amer.

Flight from Work. Goran Palm. Tr. by P. Smith. LC 77-76077. 1977. 16.95 (ISBN 0-521-21668-0). Cambridge U Pr.

Flight Guide Airport & Frequency Manual, Vol. 1: Western States. Airguide Publications. Ed. by Monte Navarre. 1980. small binder 16.00 (ISBN 0-911721-14-2, Pub. by Airguide). Aviation.

Flight Guide Airport & Frequency Manual, Vol. 2: Eastern & Central States. Airguide Publications. Ed. by Monte Navarre. 1980. small binder 22.00 (ISBN 0-911721-15-0, Pub. by Airguide). Aviation.

Flight Identification of European Raptors. 2nd ed. R. F. Porter et al. (Illus.). 1976. 26.00 (ISBN 0-85661-012-7, Pub by T & A D Poyser). Buteo.

Flight Instructor, Airplane, Answer Book. Ed. by Wallace E. Manning. (Aviation Test Prep Ser.). 1979. pap. 8.95 o.p. (ISBN 0-911721-16-9, Pub. by AvTest). Aviation.

Flight Instructor Airplane Written Test Guide: Ac 61-72b. Federal Aviation Administration. 1980. pap. 6.00 (ISBN 0-685-55081-8, Pub. by Flightshop). Aviation.

Flight Instructor Manual. 2nd ed. (Pilot Training Ser.). (Illus.). 240p. 1981. pap. text ed. 11.95 (ISBN 0-88487-066-9, JS314126). Jeppesen Sanderson.

Flight Instructor Written Test Answers & Explanations. Martha King & John King. (Pilot Training Ser.). 1980. pap. 8.95 (ISBN 0-89100-191-3, E*A-61-72B*G). Aviation Mainenance.

Flight Instructor Written Test Guide. 3rd ed. Federal Aviation Administration. (Pilot Training Ser.). (Illus.). 138p. 1979. pap. 6.00 (ISBN 0-89100-137-9, E*A-A*C61-72B). Aviation Maintenance.

Flight Instructor's Manual. 2nd ed. William K. Kershner. (Illus.). 380p. 1980. pap. 15.95 (ISBN 0-8138-0635-6). Iowa St U Pr.

Flight Instructor's Written Test Questions, Answers & Explanations. combined ed. John King & Martha King. (Pilot Training Ser.). 1980. pap. 13.95 (ISBN 0-89100-200-6, E*A-A*C61-72B-1). Aviation Maintenance.

Flight into Egypt. Amos Elon. LC 79-6165. (Illus.). 264p. 1980. 10.95 (ISBN 0-385-15796-7). Doubleday.

Flight of a Dragon. Lee R. Bobker. LC 80-22670. 256p. 1981. 9.95 (ISBN 0-688-03759-3). Morrow.

Flight of Icarus. Raymond Queneau. Tr. by Barbara Wright from Fr. LC 73-76900. Orig. Title: Vol D'Icare. 192p. 1973. pap. 4.95 (ISBN 0-8112-0483-9, NDP358). New Directions.

Flight of Lies. Gavin Scott. 224p. 1981. 9.95 (ISBN 0-312-29614-2). St Martin.

Flight of Sparrows. Roy Brown. LC 72-92432. 160p. (gr. 5-8). 1973. 7.95 (ISBN 0-02-714860-2). Macmillan.

Flight of the Animals. Claudine. LC 70-153788. (Illus.). (gr. k-3). 1971. 5.95 o.s.i. (ISBN 0-8193-0492-1, Four Winds); PLB 5.41 o.s.i. (ISBN 0-8193-0493-X). Schol Bk Serv.

Flight of the Doves. Walter Macken. LC 68-12083. (gr. 4-6). 1968. 5.95g o.s.i. (ISBN 0-02-762060-3). Macmillan.

Flight of the Henny. Jan De Hartog. LC 80-8228. 265p. Date not set. 10.95 (ISBN 0-06-010983-1, HarpT). Har-Row. Postponed.

Flight of the Horse. Larry Niven. 1976. pap. 1.95 (ISBN 0-345-27549-7). Ballantine.

Flight of the Kestrel. Margaret Abbey. 1978. pap. 1.75 o.p. (ISBN 0-345-25424-4). Ballantine.

Flight of the Lone Eagle: Charles Lindbergh Flies Nonstop from New York to Paris. John T. Foster. LC 74-898. (Focus Bks). (Illus.). 72p. 1974. PLB 6.45 (ISBN 0-531-02723-6). Watts.

Flight of the Sparrow. Julia Cunningham. LC 80-12788. 144p. (gr. 5-9). 1980. 6.95 (ISBN 0-394-84501-3); PLB 6.99 (ISBN 0-394-94501-8). Pantheon.

Flight of the Vin Fin: The Wondrous Adventures of C.P. Rodgers & His Aero Machine in the Grand Coast-to-Coast 50,000 Dollar Race. Richard Stein. LC 79-51432. (Illus.). 1979. 10.95 o.p. (ISBN 0-8129-0839-2, Dist. by Har-Row). Times Bks.

Flight of the Vin Fiz. E. P. Stein. 1980. cancelled (ISBN 0-8129-0839-2). Times Bks.

Flight Seaward. Andrew Jones. LC 78-6735. 1978. 8.95 o.p. (ISBN 0-688-03359-8). Morrow.

Flight to Arras. Antoine De Saint-Exupery. Tr. by Lewis Galantiere. LC 43-12440. 1969. pap. 3.50 (ISBN 0-15-631880-6, HPL45, HPL). HarBraceJ.

Flight to Falconhurst. Kyle Onstott & Lance Horner. (Falconhurst Plantation Ser.). 1978. pap. 2.50 (ISBN 0-449-14257-4, GM). Fawcett.

Flight to Lucifer: A Gnostic Fantasy. Harold Bloom. LC 79-22095. 1980. pap. 3.95 (ISBN 0-394-74323-7, V-323, Vin). Random.

Flight to Mercury. Bruce C. Murray & Eric Burgess. LC 76-25017. (Illus.). 1976. 17.50 (ISBN 0-231-03996-4). Columbia U Pr.

Flight Toward Home. Wolfgang Ecke. Tr. by Anthony Knight. LC 78-89582. (gr. 5 up). 1970. 4.50 o.s.i. (ISBN 0-02-733260-8). Macmillan.

Flight Training Handbook. Federal Aviation Administration. LC 80-70552. (Illus.). 352p. 1981. 12.95 (ISBN 0-385-17599-X). Doubleday.

Flight Training Handbook. 2nd ed. Federal Aviation Administration. (Pilot Training Ser.). (Illus.). 325p. 1980. pap. 7.40 (ISBN 0-89100-165-4, EA-AC61-21A). Aviation Maintenance.

Flights into Time. Juba Amon-Ra. LC 80-81579. (Illus.). 52p. (Orig.). 1980. 7.50 (ISBN 0-936874-01-5, JNP-01); pap. 4.50 (ISBN 0-936874-00-7, JNP-00); special ed. 15.00 (ISBN 0-936874-02-3, JNP-02). Joyful Noise.

Flim-Flam. James Randi. (Illus.). 1980. 12.95 (ISBN 0-690-01877-0). Lippincott.

Flintlock: Its Origin & Development. Torsten Lenk. 45.00 (ISBN 0-87556-149-7). Saifer.

Flint's Emergency Treatment & Management. 6th ed. Harvey D. Cain. 1980. 19.95 (ISBN 0-7216-2312-3). Saunders.

Flip Line. Jim Moore. 300p (Orig.). 1981. pap. 2.95. Tuppence.

Flirt. Rajendra Yadav. Tr. by Jai Ratan from Hindi. Orig. Title: Kulta. 100p. 1975. pap. 1.50 (ISBN 0-88253-769-5). Ind-US Inc.

Flitters, Tatters, & the Counsellor & Other Sketches. May L. Hartley. (Nineteenth Century Fiction Ser.: Ireland: Vol. 67). 1979. lib. bdg. 46.00 (ISBN 0-8240-3516-X). Garland Pub.

FLN in Algeria: Party Development in a Revolutionary Society. Henry F. Jackson. LC 76-47889. (Contributions in Afro-American & African Studies: No. 30). (Illus.). 1977. lib. bdg. 19.95 (ISBN 0-8371-9401-6, JFA/). Greenwood.

Floater. Calvin Trillin. LC 80-17337. 1980. 9.95 (ISBN 0-89919-017-0). Ticknor & Fields.

Floating and Sinking. Franklyn M. Branley. LC 67-15396. (Let's-Read-&-Find-Out Science Bk). (Illus.). (gr. k-3). 1967. bds. 6.95 o.p. (ISBN 0-690-30917-1, TYC-J); PLB 7.89 (ISBN 0-690-30918-X). T Y Crowell.

Floating Breakwater Conference Papers, 1974. Ed. by T. Kowalski. (Marine Technical Report Ser.: No. 24). 1974. pap. 5.00 (ISBN 0-938412-10-8). URI MAS.

Floating Drilling: Equipment & Its Use. J. Riley Sheffield, Jr. (Illus.). 260p. 1980. 21.95 (ISBN 0-87201-289-1). Gulf Pub.

Floating Pound & the Sterling Area, 1931-1939. Ian Drummond. LC 80-14539. 352p. Date not set. 37.50 (ISBN 0-521-23165-5). Cambridge U Pr.

Floating Republic. George E. Manwaring & Bonamy Dobree. LC 67-72366. (Illus.). Repr. of 1935 ed. 23.00x (ISBN 0-678-05185-2). Kelley.

Floating World in Japanese Fiction. Howard Hibbett. LC 75-28976. (Illus.). 1974. pap. 5.95 (ISBN 0-8048-1154-7). C E Tuttle.

Floating Worlds. Cecelia Holland. 1976. 10.95 o.p. (ISBN 0-394-49330-3). Knopf.

Floating Zone Silicon. Keller & Mulbauer. 256p. 1981. 39.75 (ISBN 0-8247-1167-X). Dekker.

Flock. Mary Austin. LC 73-83228. (Illus.). 266p. 1973. Repr. of 1906 ed. 15.00 (ISBN 0-88307-509-1). Gannon.

Flood Control Politics: The Connecticut River Valley Problem, 1927-1950. William E. Leuchtenburg. LC 73-38834. (FDR & the Era of the New Deal Ser.). (Illus.). 1972. Repr. of 1953 ed. lib. bdg. 32.50 (ISBN 0-306-70446-3). Da Capo.

Flood of Thessaly: Proctor Bryan Waller. Ed. by Donald H. Reiman. LC 75-31248. (Romantic Context Ser.: Poetry 1789-1830). 1978. Repr. of 1823 ed. lib. bdg. 47.00 (ISBN 0-8240-2196-7). Garland Pub.

Flood Studies Conference. Institute of Civil Engineers, UK. 106p. 1980. 75.00x (ISBN 0-7277-0014-6, Pub. by Telford England). State Mutual Bk.

Floods: A Geographical Perspective. Roy C. Ward. (Focal Problems in Geography Ser.). 1978. 24.95 o.p. (ISBN 0-470-99383-9). Halsted Pr.

Floods: A Geographical Perspective Paper. Roy C. Ward. (Focal Problems in Geography Ser.). 244p. 1980. pap. text ed. 12.95x (ISBN 0-470-26965-0). Halsted Pr.

Floods & Reservoir Safety: An Engineering Guide. Institute of Civil Engineers, UK. 1980. pap. 25.00x (ISBN 0-7277-0033-2, By Telford England). State Mutual Bk.

Floodtide. Kay Thorpe. (Harlequin Presents Ser.). 192p. 1981. pap. 1.50 (ISBN 0-373-10425-1, Pub. by Harlequin). PB.

Floor Coverings. Fairchild Market Research Division. (Fact File Ser). 1978. pap. 10.00 (ISBN 0-87005-255-1). Fairchild.

Floors & Floors Maintenance. Walter L. Salter. LC 74-11222. (Illus.). 360p. 1974. 29.95 (ISBN 0-470-74992-X). Halsted Pr.

Floors & Stairways. LC 77-89982. (Home Repair & Improvement Ser.). (Illus.). 1978. lib. bdg. 11.97 (ISBN 0-686-51037-2). Silver.

Floors & Stairways. Time Life Books Editors. (Home Repair Ser.). (Illus.). 1978. 10.95 (ISBN 0-8094-2394-4). Time-Life.

Floppy Infant. 2nd ed. Ed. by Victor Dubowitz. (Clinics in Developmental Medicine Ser.: No. 76). 109p. 1980. 25.00 (ISBN 0-685-24726-0). Lippincott.

Floppy Rabbit: An Easter Musical. Myra J. Jordan & Roy E. Grant. (Illus.). 30p. (Orig.). (ps-1). 1980. pap. 4.50. Merriam-Eddy.

Flora & Fauna Design Fantasies. William Rowe. (Pictorial Archive Ser.). (Illus.). 80p. (Orig.). 1976. 4.00 (ISBN 0-486-23289-1). Dover.

Flora Balearica Etude Phytogeographique Sur les Iles Baleares, 4vols. H. Knoche. (Illus.). 240.00 (ISBN 3-87429-061-1). Lubrecht & Cramer.

Flora de Cuba, 2 vols. H. Leon & Hermano Alain. (Illus.). 2317p. (Span., Lat.). 1979. Repr. of 1946 ed. lib. bdg. 280.80 five parts bound in 2 vols. (ISBN 3-87429-077-8). Lubrecht & Cramer.

Flora Europaea. T. G. Tutin et al. Incl. Vol. 1. Lycopodiaceae to Plantanaceae. 1964. 90.00 (ISBN 0-521-06661-1); Vol. 2. Rosaceae to Umbelliferae. 1968. 90.00 (ISBN 0-521-06662-X); Vol. 3. Diapseniaceae to Myoporaceae. 90.00 (ISBN 0-521-08489-X); Vol. 4. Plantaginaceae to Compositae (& Rubiaceae) 1976. 90.00 (ISBN 0-521-08717-1). LC 64-24315. Cambridge U Pr.

Flora Europaea: Alismataceae to Orchidaceae, Vol. 5. T. G. Tutin et al. LC 64-24315. (Illus.). 1980. 105.00 (ISBN 0-521-20108-X). Cambridge U Pr.

Flora of California, Vols. 1,2 & Vol. 3, Pts. 1 & 2. W. L. Jepson. (Illus.). 1722p. 1979. Set. pap. 40.00x (ISBN 0-935628-00-2). Jepson Herbarium.

Flora of Central Texas. Robert G. Reeves. Orig. Title: Flora of South Central Texas. 1977. pap. text ed. 8.00x (ISBN 0-934786-00-3). G Davis.

Flora of Costa Rica, 4 vols. Paul C. Standley. 1980. Set. lib. bdg. 595.00 (ISBN 0-8490-3181-8). Gordon Pr.

Flora of New Mexico, 2 vols. W. C. Martin & C. R. Hutchins. (Illus.). 3000p. 1980. lib. bdg. 160.00x (ISBN 3-7682-1263-7, Pub. by Cramer Germany). Lubrecht & Cramer.

Flora of New Mexico, 2 vols. W. C. Martin & R. Hutchins. (Illus.). 3000p. 1980. Set. lib. bdg. 160.00x (ISBN 3-7682-1263-7, Pub. by Cramer Germany); Vol. 1. lib. bdg. 80.00x (ISBN 3-7682-1283-1); Vol. 2. lib. bdg. 8.00x (ISBN 3-7682-1284-X). Lubrecht & Cramer.

Flora of North America, 2 Vols. John Torrey & Asa Gray. (Classica Botanica Americana Ser.: Vol. 4). 1968. Repr. Set. 71.50 o.s.i. (ISBN 0-02-853640-1). Hafner.

Flora of Southern Illinois. John W. Voigt & Robert H. Mohlenbrock. LC 59-5094. (Illus.). 399p. 1959. 8.95x (ISBN 0-8093-0026-5). S Ill U Pr.

Flora of Southern Illinois. John W. Voigt & Robert H. Mohlenbrock. LC 73-12984. (Arcturus Books Paperbacks). 399p. 1974. pap. 3.95 (ISBN 0-8093-0662-X). S Ill U Pr.

Flora of the British Isles. 2nd ed. Arthur R. Clapham et al. 1962. 68.50 (ISBN 0-521-04657-2); illustrations, 4 pts. 28.50 ea. Cambridge U Pr.

Flora of the Chuckanut Formation of Northwestern Washington, the Equisetales, Filicales, & Coniferales. M. B. Pabst. (U. C. Publ. in Geological Sciences: Vol. 76). 1968. pap. 7.00x (ISBN 0-520-09179-5). U of Cal Pr.

Flora of the Marshes of California. Herbert L. Mason. LC 57-7960. (Illus.). 1957. 30.00x (ISBN 0-520-01433-2). U of Cal Pr.

Flora of the Prairies & Plains of Central North America. Per A. Rydberg. LC 79-166434. (Illus.). 1971. pap. 5.00 ea.; Vol. 1. pap. o.p. (ISBN 0-486-22584-4); Vol. II. pap. (ISBN 0-486-22585-2). Dover.

Flora of the Rocky Mountains & Adjacent Plains. 2nd ed. Per A. Rydberg. 1954. Repr. of 1922 ed. 24.00 o.s.i. (ISBN 0-02-851250-2). Hafner.

Flora of the Santa Barbara Region, California. Clifton F. Smth. LC 76-9164. 331p. 1976. pap. text ed. 12.50 (ISBN 0-936494-00-X). Santa Barbara Mus Nat Hist.

Flora of the Trinity Alps. William J. Ferlatte. (Illus.). 1974. 16.50x (ISBN 0-520-02089-8). U of Cal Pr.

Flora Sweet. Jeanne Sakol. 1977. pap. 1.95 o.p. (ISBN 0-345-25055-9). Ballantine.

Flora Sylvatica for Southern India, 3 vols. R. H. Beddome. 800p. 1980. 240.00 (ISBN 0-89955-313-3, Intl Bk). Intl Schol Bk Serv.

Flora Tristan: Feminist, Socialist & Free Spirit. Joyce A. Schneider. LC 80-20067. 256p. (gr. 7-9). 1980. 8.95 (ISBN 0-688-22250-1); PLB 8.59 (ISBN 0-688-32250-6). Morrow.

Flora Virgiliana. Pietro Bubani. 134p. 1974. Repr. of 1869 ed. lib. bdg. 26.00x (ISBN 3-87429-075-1). Lubrecht & Cramer.

Floral Art Book of Reference. Helen Cox. LC 70-91462. 1970. text ed. 16.50 (ISBN 0-08-007100-7). Pergamon.

Floral Biology. M. Percival. 1965. 10.50 (ISBN 0-08-010610-2); pap. 7.00 (ISBN 0-08-010609-9). Pergamon.

Floral Design & Arrangement. G. McDaniel. 250p. 1981. text ed. 16.95 (ISBN 0-8359-2072-0); instr's. manual free (ISBN 0-8359-2073-9). Reston.

Floral Doilies for Crocheting. Rita Weiss. (Illus.). 1979. pap. 1.75 (ISBN 0-486-23789-3). Dover.

Floral Embroidery. Ondori Publishing Co. Staff. (Ondori Handicrafts Ser). (Illus.). 64p. 1976. pap. 5.50 (ISBN 0-87040-365-6). Japan Pubns.

Floral Iron-on Transfer Patterns. Ed. by Rita Weiss. LC 75-21351. (Needlework Ser.). 48p. (Orig.). 1976. pap. 1.75 (ISBN 0-486-23248-4). Dover.

Florence: City of the Renaissance. Charles Haines. LC 79-182564. (Illus.). 96p. (gr. 5-9). 1972. PLB 3.90 o.p. (ISBN 0-531-00756-1). Watts.

Florence in the Age of Dante. Paul G. Ruggiers. (Centers of Civilization Ser.: No. 15). 1968. Repr. of 1964 ed. 5.95x o.p. (ISBN 0-8061-0617-4). U of Okla Pr.

Florence Lin's Chinese One-Dish Meals: The Fastest Way of Cooking Delicious, Economical, Well Balanced Meals. Florence Lin. 192p. 1981. pap. 5.95 (ISBN 0-8015-2672-8, Hawthorn). Dutton.

Florence Lin's Chinese Regional Cookbook. Florence Lin. 288p. 1975. 15.95 (ISBN 0-8015-2674-4, Hawthorn); text ed. 8.95 (ISBN 0-8015-2673-6, Hawthorn). Dutton.

Florence Lin's Chinese Vegetarian Cookbook. Florence Lin. LC 75-28686. 1977. pap. 4.95 (ISBN 0-8015-2677-9, Hawthorn). Dutton.

Florence MacCartby: An Irish Tale. Lady Morgan Sydney Owenson. Ed. by Robert L. Wolff. (Ireland Nineteenth Century Fiction, Ser. Two: Vol. 8). 1979. lib. bdg. 46.00 ea. Garland Pub.

Florence Nightingale. Anne Colver. (Illus.). (gr. 1-7). 1966. pap. 1.25 (ISBN 0-440-42620-0, YB). Dell.

Florence Nightingale in Rome: Letters Written 1847 to 1848. Ed. by Mary Keele. 1981. 12.00 (ISBN 0-87169-143-4). Am Philos.

Florence Nightingale: Saint, Reformer, or Rebel? Raymond G. Hebert. 120p. 1980. 6.50 (ISBN 0-89874-127-0). Krieger.
Florence Rena Sabin. Sybil Downing & Jane V. Barker. (Illus.). 80p. (Orig.). (gr. 5-6). 1981. pap. 5.50 (ISBN 0-87108-237-3). Pruett.
Florentine Busts: Sculpted Portraiture in the Fifteenth Century. Jane Schuyler. LC 75-23814. (Outstanding Dissertations in the Fine Arts - 15th Century). (Illus.). 1976. lib. bdg. 41.00 (ISBN 0-8240-2007-3). Garland Pub.
Florentine Codex, General History of the Things of New Spain, 12 bks. Bernardino De Sahagun. Tr. by Arthur J. Anderson & Charles E. Dibble. Incl. Bk. 1. Gods. 15.00x (ISBN 0-87480-000-5); Bk. 2. Ceremonies. 20.00 o.p. (ISBN 0-87480-001-3); Bk. 3. Origin of the Gods. 15.00x (ISBN 0-87480-002-1); Bks. 4 & 5. Soothsayers, the Omens. 20.00x (ISBN 0-87480-003-X); Bk. 6. Rhetoric & Moral Philosophy. 20.00x (ISBN 0-87480-010-2); Bk. 7. Sun, Moon & Stars, & the Binding of the Years. 15.00x (ISBN 0-87480-004-8); Bk. 8. Kings & Lords. 20.00x (ISBN 0-87480-005-6); Bk. 9. Merchants. 15.00x (ISBN 0-87480-006-4); Bk. 10. People. 20.00x (ISBN 0-87480-007-2); Bk. 11. Earthly Things. 25.00x (ISBN 0-87480-008-0); Bk. 12. Conquest of Mexico. 20.00x (ISBN 0-87480-096-X). U of Utah Pr.
Florentine Painting & Its Social Background. Frederick Antal. (Icon Editions). (Illus.). 576p. 1975. pap. 8.95x o.s.i. (ISBN 0-06-430067-6, IN-67, HarpT). Har-Row.
Florentine Renaissance Sculpture. Charles Avery. LC 78-148429. (Icon Editions). (Illus.). 282p. 1971. pap. 5.95x o.s.i. (ISBN 0-06-430038-2, IN-38, HarpT). Har-Row.
Florentine Studies. Nicolai Rubinstein. (Illus.). 1969. 15.95 o.p. (ISBN 0-571-08477-X, Pub. by Faber & Faber). Merrimack Bk Serv.
Florian: The Lippizaner. Felix Salten. Date not set. 8.75 (ISBN 0-85131-127-X, Dist. by Sporting Book Center). J A Allen.
Florid Victorian Ornament. Karl Klimsch. LC 76-58573. (Pictorial Archive Ser.). (Illus.). 1977. pap. 4.00 (ISBN 0-486-23490-8). Dover.
Florida. 28.00 (ISBN 0-89770-085-6). Curriculum Info Ctr.
Florida. Gloria L. Hahoda. (States & the Nation Ser.). (Illus.). 1976. 12.95x (ISBN 0-393-05585-X, Co-Pub by AASLH). Norton.
Florida Bird Songs. Donald Borror & Maurice L. Glitz. 1980. pap. 4.50 record & booklet (ISBN 0-486-23956-X). Dover.
Florida Educators. James Preu. LC 56-63392. (Florida State Univ. Studies). 1959. 4.50 (ISBN 0-8130-0494-2). U Presses Fla.
Florida Enchantments. Anthony Weston Dimock & Julian A. Dimock. LC 74-13789. (Illus.). 318p. 1975. Repr. of 1908 ed. 20.00 (ISBN 0-8103-4061-5). Gale.
Florida Food Fare: & Food for Thought. Lois J. Blackburn. (Illus.). 120p. (Orig.). 1980. pap. 5.00 (ISBN 0-938910-00-0). Pecalhen.
Florida for Tourists, Invalids & Settlers. George M. Barbour. Ed. by Emmett B. Peter, Jr. LC 64-19152. (Floridiana Facsimile & Reprint Ser). (Illus.). 1964. Repr. of 1882 ed. 10.75 (ISBN 0-8130-0012-2). U Presses Fla.
Florida Gardening Month by Month. Nixon Smiley. LC 78-125661. (Illus.). 1980. pap. 7.95 (ISBN 0-87024-302-0). U of Miami Pr.
Florida: In Words & Pictures. Dennis Fradin. LC 80-16681. (Young People's Stories of Our States Ser.). (Illus.). 48p. (gr. 2-5). 1980. PLB 8.65 (ISBN 0-516-03909-1). Childrens.
Florida Indians I. Howard F. Cline. Ed. by David A. Horr. (American Indian Ethnohistory Ser.). 1978. lib. bdg. 42.00 (ISBN 0-8240-0766-2). Garland Pub.
Florida Indians II. Howard F. Cline. Ed. by David A. Horr. (American Indian Ethnohistory Ser.). 1978. lib. bdg. 42.00 (ISBN 0-8240-0767-0). Garland Pub.
Florida Indians III. Charles H. Fairbanks. Ed. by David A. Horr. (American Indian Ethnohistory Ser.). 1978. lib. bdg. 42.00 (ISBN 0-8240-0759-X). Garland Pub.
Florida Literacy Test: Statewide Assessment Program of Basic Skills & Functional Literacy. Date not set. pap. 4.95 (ISBN 0-8120-2060-X). Barron. Postponed.
Florida Literacy Test: Statewide Assessment Program of Basic Skills & Functional Literacy. James W. Morrison. LC 78-6863. 1978. pap. 4.95 o.p. (ISBN 0-668-04669-4). Arco.
Florida Old & New. Frederick W. Dau. LC 74-13957. 1975. Repr. of 1934 ed. 22.00 (ISBN 0-8103-4060-7). Gale.
Florida One Hundred Years Ago. King & Treat. (Sun Historical Ser.). (Illus.). pap. 3.50 (ISBN 0-89540-055-3). Sun Pub.
Florida Ramble. Alex Shoumatoff. LC 72-9154. (Illus.). 196p. (YA) 1974. 7.95 o.p. (ISBN 0-06-013858-0, HarpT). Har-Row.
Florida Real Estate. Harwood Thompson. (Illus.). 672p. 1980. ref. ed. 19.95; text ed. 16.95 (ISBN 0-8359-2067-4). Reston.
Florida Real Estate Resource Book. Harwood Thompson & Ellis. 1978. pap. 7.95 ref. ed. (ISBN 0-87909-739-6). Reston.
Florida State Industrial Directory 1980. State Industrial Directories Corp. 1980. pap. 65.00 (ISBN 0-89910-039-2). State Indus Dir.
Florida Statistical Abstract, Nineteen Eighty. Ed. by Ralph B. Thompson. LC 67-7393. 1980. 20.00x (ISBN 0-8130-0677-5); pap. 11.50 (ISBN 0-8130-0678-3). U Presses Fla.
Florida Statistical Abstract, 1980. Ed. by Ralph B. Thompson. (Illus.). 695p. 1980. 20.00x (ISBN 0-8130-0677-5); pap. 11.50 (ISBN 0-8130-0678-3). U Presses Fla.
Florida Wild Flowers. Mary F. Baker. 1977. Repr. 5.95 (ISBN 0-9600046-1-0). Horticultural.
Florida's Aviation History. Warren J. Brown. 1980. pap. 6.95 (ISBN 0-912522-70-4). Aero-Medical.
Florida's Enchanting Islands: Sanibel & Captiva. 3rd ed. Linda Firestone & Whit Morse. LC 80-67778. (Illus., Orig.). 1980. pap. 4.95 (ISBN 0-917374-08-8). Good Life VA.
Floridas Fascinating Everglades. Rolfe F. Schell. LC 63-8861. (Illus.). 1974. 4.50 (ISBN 0-87208-004-8); pap. 2.00 (ISBN 0-87208-032-3). Island Pr.
Florida's Gubernatorial Politics in the Twentieth Century. David R. Colburn & Richard K. Sher. LC 80-10277. 19.95 (ISBN 0-8130-0644-9). U Presses Fla.
Florida's Older Population Revisited. T. Stanton Dietrich. (Illus.). vi, 78p. (Orig.). 1978. pap. 6.00 (ISBN 0-8130-0686-4). U Presses Fla.
Florida's Politics & Government. Ed. by Manning J. Dauer. LC 80-20723. (Orig.). 1980. pap. 10.00x (ISBN 0-8130-0671-6). U Presses Fla.
Floss & Stan's "Why Are My Leaves Turning Yellow & Falling Off" Answer Book. Floss Dworkin & Stan Dworkin. 1978. 9.95 o.p. (ISBN 0-87690-267-0). Dutton.
Flotation Agents & Processes: Technology & Applications. Ed. by M. W. Ranney. LC 80-19191. (Chemical Tech. Rev. 172). (Illus.). 372p. 1981. 48.00 (ISBN 0-8155-0821-2). Noyes.
Flour Power: The Art of Cooking with Flour. Christine Brady. 1979. 16.95 (ISBN 0-241-10168-9, Pub. by Hamish Hamilton). David & Charles.
Floure & the Leafe" & "the Assembly of Ladies". Ed. by D. A. Pearsall. (Old & Middle English Texts). 191p. 1980. pap. 13.00x (ISBN 0-389-20026-3). B&N.
Floury Fingers. Cecilia H. Hinde. (Illus.). 1962. 5.95 (ISBN 0-571-04522-7, Pub. by Faber & Faber); pap. 1.95 o.p. (ISBN 0-571-09075-3). Merrimack Bk Serv.
Flow Blue China: An Aid to Identification. Petra Williams. LC 77-171985. (Illus.). 225p. 1971. 12.95x o.p. (ISBN 0-914736-01-9). Fountain Hse East.
Flow Blue China, an Aid to Identification. rev. ed. Petra Williams. LC 80-70461. (Illus.). 234p. 1981. 12.95x (ISBN 0-914736-07-8). Fountain Hse East.
Flow Blue China & Mulberry Ware Similarity & Value Guide. rev. ed. Petra Williams. LC 80-68848. (Illus.). 220p. 1980. 12.95x (ISBN 0-914736-06-X). Fountain Hse East.
Flow Cytometry, Four. Ed. by O. D. Laerum. 550p. 1981. 64.00x (ISBN 8-20005-399-7). Universitet.
Flow-Induced Vibration of Power Plant Components. Ed. by M. K. Au-Yang. (PVP: No. 41). 176p. 1980. 24.00 (H00168). ASME.
Flow Injection Analysis. Jaromir Ruzicka & Elo H. Hansen. 250p. 1981. 32.50 (ISBN 0-471-08192-2, Pub. by Wiley-Interscience). Wiley.
Flow Lines to Health. 4th ed. John Barton & Margaret Barton. (Illus.). 158p. 1980. pap. 8.00 (ISBN 0-937216-04-6). J&M Barton.
Flow, Mixing & Heat Transfer in Furnaces. Ed. by Khalil. 1978. 45.00 (ISBN 0-08-022695-7). Pergamon.
Flow of Art. Henry McBride. LC 75-13774. 1975. 12.50 (ISBN 0-689-10692-0). Atheneum.
Flow of Art. Daniel Rich. LC 75-13774. 1975. 12.50 (ISBN 0-689-10692-0). Atheneum.
Flow of High Polymers: Continuum & Molecular Rheology. Stanley Middleman. LC 67-29460. 1968. 27.95 (ISBN 0-470-60235-X, Pub. by Wiley-Interscience). Wiley.
Flow of Religious Instruction. James M. Lee. 4.95 o.p. (ISBN 0-686-13703-5). Pflaum Pr.
Flow-Schemes in Organic Chemistry. Colin T. McCarty. 1976. 3.95x o.p. (ISBN 0-435-65575-2). Heinemann Ed.
Flow Visualization: Proceedings. new ed. International Symposium on Flow Visualization, Tokyo, Oct. 12-14, 1977. Ed. by Tsuyoshi Asanuma. LC 79-12407. (Thermal & Fluids Engineering Ser.). (Illus.). 413p. 1979. text ed. 89.50 (ISBN 0-89116-155-4, Co-Pub. with McGraw Intl). Hemisphere Pub.
Flowcharting: Programming, Software Design & Computer Problem Solving. Bernard B. Bycer. LC 75-16175. 326p. 1975. pap. text ed. 16.95 (ISBN 0-471-12882-1). Wiley.
Flower Adornment (Avatamsaka) Sutra: Chapter Fifteen, The Ten Dwellings. Commentary by Ch'An Master Hua. Tr. by Bhikshuni Heng Hsien et al from Chinese. (Orig.). 1981. pap. write for info. (ISBN 0-917512-30-8). Buddhist Text.
Flower Adornment (Avatamsaka) Sutra: Chapter 26, The Ten Grounds. Ch'An Master Hua. Tr. by Bhikshuni Heng Hsien from Chinese. (Illus.). 1980. pap. 7.00 (ISBN 0-917512-29-4). Buddhist Text.
Flower & Plant Production in the Greenhouse. 3rd ed. Kennard S. Nelson. LC 77-79741. (Illus.). (gr. 9-12). 1978. 15.35 (ISBN 0-8134-1965-4); text ed. 11.50x (ISBN 0-685-03893-9). Interstate.
Flower & Vegetable Plant Breeding. Leslie Watts. (Orig.). 1980. pap. 22.50 (ISBN 0-901361-35-6, Pub. by Grower Bks England). Intl Schol Bk Serv.
Flower Arrangement. (Illus.). 60p. 1980. pap. 4.50 (ISBN 0-89955-103-3, Pub. by Shufunotomo Japan). Intl Schol Bk Serv.
Flower Arrangement. E. M. Lyall. 4.50x o.p. (ISBN 0-392-03016-0, LTB). Soccer.
Flower Arrangement with a Marine Theme. Rendell. 1972. 3.95 o.p. (ISBN 0-7153-4109-X). David & Charles.
Flower Arrangements for Special Occasions. Winifrede Morrison. (Illus.). 88p. 1976. 8.95 o.s.i. (ISBN 0-7134-3088-5). Hippocrene Bks.
Flower Arranging: A Manual. 1972. 5.50 (ISBN 0-87543-106-2). Lucas.
Flower Arranging for All Occasions. rev. ed. Katherine Cutler. LC 80-2850. (Illus.). 256p. 1981. 12.95 (ISBN 0-385-18508-1). Doubleday.
Flower Arranging in House & Garden. George Smith. 15.95 (ISBN 0-7207-0958-X, Pub. by Michael Joseph). Merrimack Bk Serv.
Flower Book. Gladys Hutcheson. 95p. 1980. 19.75x (ISBN 0-7050-0071-0, Pub. by Skilton & Shaw England). State Mutual Bk.
Flower Does Not Talk: Zen Essays. Zenkei Shibayama. LC 79-109494. (Illus.). 1970. pap. 6.75 (ISBN 0-8048-0884-8). C E Tuttle.
Flower Fairies Alphabet Book. Cicely M. Barker. (Illus.). 1978. 3.95 (ISBN 0-8467-0512-5, Pub. by Two Continents). Hippocrene Bks.
Flower Fairies Birthday Book. Illus. by Cicely M. Barker. (Illus.). 157p. 1980. 5.95 (ISBN 0-216-90814-0, Pub. by Blackie England). Hippocrene Bks.
Flower Fairies of Autumn. Cicely M. Barker. (Flower Fairies Ser.). (Illus.). (gr. 2-5). 1976. 3.95 (ISBN 0-8467-0191-X, Pub. by Two Continents). Hippocrene Bks.
Flower Fairies of Spring. Cicely M. Barker. (Flower Fairies Ser.). (Illus.). (gr. 2-5). 1976. 3.95 (ISBN 0-8467-0193-6, Pub. by Two Continents). Hippocrene Bks.
Flower Fairies of Summer. Cicely M. Barker. (Flower Fairies Ser.). (Illus.). (gr. 2-5). 1976. 3.95 (ISBN 0-8467-0194-4, Pub. by Two Continents). Hippocrene Bks.
Flower Fairies of the Garden. Cicely M. Barker. (Flower Fairies Ser.). (Illus.). (gr. 2-5). 1976. 3.95 (ISBN 0-8467-0192-8, Pub. by Two Continents). Hippocrene Bks.
Flower Fairies of the Trees. Cicely M. Barker. (Flower Fairies Ser.). (Illus.). (gr. 2-5). 1976. 3.95 (ISBN 0-8467-0195-2, Pub. by Two Continents). Hippocrene Bks.
Flower Fairies of the Wayside. Cicely M. Barker. (Flower Fairies Ser.). (Illus.). (gr. 2-5). 1976. 3.95 (ISBN 0-8467-0196-0, Pub. by Two Continents). Hippocrene Bks.
Flower Fairy - a Little Book of Old Rhymes. Cicely M. Barker. (Cicely Mary Barker Storybks.). (Illus.). (gr. k-4). 1977. 3.95 (ISBN 0-8467-0257-6, Pub. by Two Continents). Hippocrene Bks.
Flower for Every Day. Margery Fish. 208p. 1981. pap. 9.95 (ISBN 0-571-11738-4, Pub. by Faber & Faber). Merrimack Bk Serv.
Flower Garden in England. Richard Gorer. (Illus.). 1975. 11.50 o.s.i. (ISBN 0-7134-2858-9). Hippocrene Bks.
Flower Lore: The Teachings of Flowers Historical, Legendary, Poetical & Symbolic. LC 79-179690. 1972. Repr. of 1879 ed. 25.00 (ISBN 0-8103-3865-3). Gale.
Flower Mother. Mary Calhoun. LC 70-168469. (Illus.). 32p. (gr. k-3). 1972. PLB 6.96 o.p. (ISBN 0-688-31303-5). Morrow.
Flower of Love. Rachel North. (Orig.). 1980. pap. 2.50 (ISBN 0-505-51525-3). Tower Bks.
Flower of the Dusk. Myrtle Reed 1976. lib. bdg. 15.75x (ISBN 0-89968-109-3). Lightyear.
Flower Painting in Watercolor. rev. ed. Mario Cooper. 144p. 1980. pap. 9.95 (ISBN 0-442-23137-7). Van Nos Reinhold.
Flower Pollination in the Phlox Family. Karen A. Grant & Verne Grant. LC 65-19809. 1965. 17.50x (ISBN 0-231-02843-1). Columbia U Pr.
Flower Pressing. Peter Bauzen & Susanne Bauzen. Tr. by Paul Kuttner from Ger. LC 77-167661. (Little Craft Book Ser.). (gr. 7 up). 1971. 5.95 (ISBN 0-8069-5186-9); PLB 6.69 (ISBN 0-8069-5187-7). Sterling.
Flowercraft. Eunice Svinicki. (Step-by-Step Crafts Ser.). (Illus.). 1977. PLB 9.15 o.p. (ISBN 0-307-62020-4, Golden Pr); pap. 1.95 (ISBN 0-307-42020-5). Western Pub.
Flowered Box: A Novel of Suspense. Thomas J. Green. LC 80-22442. 192p. 1980. 9.95 (ISBN 0-8253-0010-X). Beaufort Bks NY.
Flowering House Plants. James U. Crockett. (Encyclopedia of Gardening Ser). (Illus.). 1971. 11.95 (ISBN 0-8094-1097-4); lib. bdg. avail. (ISBN 0-685-00195-4). Time-Life.
Flowering House Plants. James U. Crockett. LC 78-140420. (Time-Life Encyclopedia of Gardening). (Illus.). 1971. lib. bdg. 11.97 (ISBN 0-8094-1098-2, Pub. by Time-Life). Silver.
Flowering House Plants Month by Month. Jack Kramer. 126p. 1973. pap. 1.95 o.s.i. (ISBN 0-346-12085-3). Cornerstone.
Flowering of American Folk Art, 1776-1876. Jean Lipman & Alice Winchester. LC 73-3081. (Illus.). 288p. 1974. 25.00 o.s.i. (ISBN 0-670-32120-6, Studio). Viking Pr.
Flowering of Ireland: Saints, Scholars & Kings. Katharine Scherman. (Illus.). 320p. 1981. 15.95 (ISBN 0-316-77284-4). Little.
Flowering of the Italian Renaissance. Andre Chastel. LC 65-27309. (Arts of Mankind Ser). 30.00 o.s.i. (ISBN 0-8076-0503-4). Braziller.
Flowering Plant Index of Illustration & Information. Garden Center of Greater Cleveland. 1979. lib. bdg. 200.00 (ISBN 0-8161-0301-1). G K Hall.
Flowering Plants: Flowering Rush to Rushes. Robert H. Mohlenbrock. LC 69-16117. (Illustrated Flora of Illinois Ser.). (Illus.). 286p. 1970. 22.95x (ISBN 0-8093-0407-4). S Ill U Pr.
Flowering Plants from Cuban Gardens. Women's Club of Havana. (Illus.). 1958. 12.95 (ISBN 0-87599-131-9). S G Phillips.
Flowering Plants: Lilies to Orchids. Robert H. Mohlenbrock. LC 69-16118. (Illustrated Flora of Illinois Ser.). (Illus.). 304p. 1970. 22.95x (ISBN 0-8093-0408-2). S Ill U Pr.
Flowering Plants: Magnolias to Pitcher Plants. Robert H. Mohlenbrock. LC 80-18529. (Illustrated Flora of Illinois Ser.). (Illus.). 256p. 1981. 18.95x (ISBN 0-8093-0920-3). S Ill U Pr.
Flowering Plants of Africa: An Analytical Key to the Genera of African Phanerogams. F. Thonner. 1962. Repr. of 1916 ed. 90.00 (ISBN 3-7682-0118-X). Lubrecht & Cramer.
Flowering Plants: Willows to Mustards. Robert H. Mohlenbrock. LC 79-10981. (Illustrated Flora of Illinois Ser.). (Illus.). 302p. 1980. 22.95x (ISBN 0-8093-0922-X). S Ill U Pr.
Flowering Response of the Rice Plant to Photoperiod: A Review of the Literature. 75p. 1976. pap. 5.00 (R023, IRRI). Unipub.
Flowering Shrubs. James U. Crockett. (Encyclopedia of Gardening Ser). (Illus.). 1972. 11.95 (ISBN 0-8094-1113-X); lib. bdg. avail. (ISBN 0-685-24678-7). Dist. by Little. Time-Life.
Flowering Shrubs. James U. Crockett. LC 78-140420. (Time-Life Encyclopedia of Gardening). (Illus.). (gr. 6 up). 1972. lib. bdg. 11.97 (ISBN 0-8094-1114-8, Pub. by Time-Life). Silver.
Flowers. H. Angel. 1975. pap. 5.00 o.p. (ISBN 0-85242-424-8, Pub. by Fountain). Morgan.
Flowers. Ruth Heller. (Creative Coloring Activity Pandabacks). (Illus.). 32p. 1981. pap. 1.25 (ISBN 0-448-49623-2). G&D.
Flowers. David Hughes. (Illus.). (ps). 1979. 1.25 (ISBN 0-370-10728-4, Pub. by Chatto Bodley Jonathan). Merrimack Bk Serv.
Flowers. Bob Reese et al. Ed. by Dan Wasserman. (Ten Word Bks.). (Illus.). (gr. k-1). 1979. PLB 4.50 (ISBN 0-89868-076-X); pap. 1.95 (ISBN 0-89868-087-5). ARO Pub.
Flowers: A Guide for Your Garden, 2 vols. Ippolito Pizzetti & Henry Cocker. LC 73-7526. (Illus.). 1300p. 1975. 60.00 o.p. (ISBN 0-8109-0127-7). Abrams.
Flowers & Flowering Plants. Arthur Aldrich. (Easy-Read Fact Book Ser.). (Illus.). 48p. (gr. 2-4). 1976. PLB 3.90 o.p. (ISBN 0-531-01214-X). Watts.
Flowers & Plants of Western Australia. rev. ed. Rica Erickson et al. 232p. 1979. 39.95 (ISBN 0-589-50116-X, Pub. by Reed Books Australia). C E Tuttle.
Flowers & Shadows. Benjamin Okri. (Drum Beat Ser.). 274p. 1980. pap. 5.00 (ISBN 0-582-64301-5). Three Continents.
Flowers & Their Story. Hilderic Friend. LC 78-175751. (Illus.). 300p. 1972. Repr. of 1907 ed. 18.00 (ISBN 0-8103-3868-8). Gale.
Flowers Are Fabulous: For Decorating. Diane Love. (Illus.). 144p. 1975. 17.50 (ISBN 0-02-575560-9). Macmillan.
Flowers Are for Keeping: How to Dry Flowers & Make Gifts & Decorations. Joella Cramblit & JoAnn Loebel. LC 79-12892. (Illus.). 128p. (gr. 5 up). 1979. PLB 8.29 (ISBN 0-671-33007-1). Messner.

Flowers Arrangers Guide to Showing. Howard Franklin. 1979. 14.95 (ISBN 0-7134-3321-3). David & Charles.

Flowers: East Coast Edition. Ed. by Little, Brown Editors. (Explorer's Notebooks). (Illus.). 32p. (Orig.). (gr. 5 up). 1981. pap. 1.95 (ISBN 0-316-52773-4). Little.

Flowers for Algernon. Daniel Keyes. LC 66-12366. 1966. 12.95 (ISBN 0-15-131510-8). HarBraceJ.

Flowers for Algernon. Daniel Keyes. (Amsco Literature Ser.). 1969. pap. text ed. 3.92 (ISBN 0-87720-751-8). AMSCO Sch.

Flowers: Free Form-Interpretive Design. Morris Benz. LC 59-15356. (Illus.). 1960. 15.00 (ISBN 0-89096-103-4). San Jacinto.

Flowers: Geometric Form. Morris Benz. LC 66-25443. (Illus.). 1973. 35.00 o.p. (ISBN 0-911982-07-8). San Jacinto.

Flowers: Geometric Form. rev., 5th ed. Morris Benz. LC 80-50568. (Illus.). 336p. 1980. 42.50 (ISBN 0-911982-12-4). San Jacinto.

Flowers in Books & Drawings, Nine Forty to Eighteen Forty. Pref. by Charles Ryskamp. LC 80-83208. (Illus.). 84p. 1980. pap. 6.95 (ISBN 0-87598-072-4). Pierpont Morgan.

Flowers in Praise: Church Flower Arrangements & Festivals. Julia Clements. LC 79-57312. (Illus.). 96p. 1980. 24.00 (ISBN 0-7134-3328-0, Pub. by Batsford England). David & Charles.

Flowers in the Attic. V. C. Andrews. pap. 2.95 (ISBN 0-686-68323-4). PB.

Flowers in the Mirror. Li, Ju-chen. Ed. & tr. by Tai-yi Lin. 1965. 20.00x (ISBN 0-520-00747-6). U of Cal Pr.

Flowers of Emptiness: Reflections on an Ashram. Sally Belfrage. 256p. 1981. 10.95 (ISBN 0-8037-2523-X). Dial.

Flowers of Greece & the Aegean. Anthony Huxley & William Taylor. (Illus.). 1977. 24.00 (ISBN 0-7011-2190-4). Transatlantic.

Flowers of Greece & the Balkans: A Field Guide. Oleg Polunin. 474p. 1980. 125.00x (ISBN 0-19-217626-9). Oxford U Pr.

Flowers of Mountain & Plain. 3rd ed. Edith S. Clements. (Illus.). 1955. Repr. of 1926 ed. 9.75 o.s.i. (ISBN 0-02-842950-8). Hafner.

Flowers of Passion. George Moore. Ed. by Ian Fletcher & John Stokes. Bd. with Pagan Poems. LC 76-20138. (Decadent Consciousness Ser.). 1978. lib. bdg. 38.00 (ISBN 0-8240-2778-7). Garland Pub.

Flowers of South-West Europe. Oleg Polunin & B. E. Smythies. (Illus.). 1973. 45.00x (ISBN 0-19-217625-0). Oxford U Pr.

Flowers of Svalbard. Olaf Ronning & Olav Bjaerevoll. (Illus.). 56p. 1981. pap. 14.00x (ISBN 82-00-05398-9). Universitet.

Flowers of the Forest. Ruth D. MacDougall. LC 80-22415. 1981. 11.95 (ISBN 0-689-11124-X). Atheneum.

Flowers of the Mediterranean. Oleg Polunin & Anthony Huxley. LC 79-670242. (Illus.). 1979. 15.95 (ISBN 0-7011-1029-5, Pub. by Chatto Bodley Jonathan); pap. 9.95 (ISBN 0-7011-2284-6). Merrimack Bk Serv.

Flowers: West Coast Edition. Ed. by Little, Brown Editors. (Explorer's Notebooks). (Illus.). 32p. (Orig.). (gr. 5 up). 1981. pap. 1.95 (ISBN 0-316-52774-2). Little.

Flowers When You Want Them: A Grower's Guide to Out-of-Season Bloom. John James. LC 77-70139. (Illus.). 1977. 10.95 o.p. (ISBN 0-8015-2679-5); pap. 5.95 o.p. (ISBN 0-8015-2680-9). Dutton.

Flowmeters: A Basic Guide & Source-Book for Users. Alan T. Hayward. LC 79-15530. 197p. 1979. 27.95x (ISBN 0-470-26732-1). Halsted Pr.

FLs & the 'new' Student. Ed. by Joseph A. Tursi. 1970. pap. 7.95x (ISBN 0-915432-70-6). NE Conf Teach.

Fluctuant Representation in Synthetic Cubism: Picasso, Braque, Gris, 1910-1920. Winthrop Judkins. LC 75-23796. (Outstanding Dissertations in the Fine Arts - 20th Century). (Illus.). 1976. lib. bdg. 53.00 (ISBN 0-8240-1991-1). Garland Pub.

Fluctuation Theory of Phase Transitions. A. Z. Patashinskii et al. Ed. by P. J. Shepherd. (International Series in Natural Philosophy: Vol. 98). (Illus.). 1979. text ed. 60.00 (ISBN 0-08-021664-1). Pergamon.

Fluctuations & Non-Linear Wave Interactions in Plasmas. A. G. Sitenko. Tr. by O. D. Kocherga. (International Series in Natural Philosophy: Vol. 107). (Illus.). 250p. 1981. 42.00 (ISBN 0-08-025051-3). Pergamon.

Fluency & Language Teaching. Richard Leeson. (Applied Linguistics & Language Study). 1976. pap. text ed. 9.00x (ISBN 0-582-55078-5). Longman.

Fluffy: The Story of a Cat. Jurg Obrist. LC 79-10446. (Illus.). 32p. (ps-3). 1981. PLB 11.95 (ISBN 0-689-30722-5). Atheneum.

Fluger. Doris Perschia. (Science Fiction Ser.). 1980. pap. 1.95 (ISBN 0-87997-577-6, UJ1577). DAW Bks.

Fluid & Blood Component Therapy in the Critically Ill. Suellyn Ellerbe. (Contemporary Issues in Critical Care Nursing). (Illus.). 224p. 1981. lib. bdg. 20.00 (ISBN 0-443-08129-8). Churchill.

Fluid & Electrolyte Metabolism in Infants & Children: A Unified Approach. William B. Weil, Jr. 1978. 32.00 (ISBN 0-8089-1028-0). Grune.

Fluid Behaviour in Biological Sciences. Leonard Leyton. (Illus.). 250p. 1975. 39.95x (ISBN 0-19-854126-0). Oxford U Pr.

Fluid, Blood, and Blood Component Administration. Burnell R. Brown, Jr. (Contemporary Anesthesia Practice Ser.: Vol. 5). 1981. write for info. (ISBN 0-8036-1271-0). Davis Co.

Fluid Clutches & Torque Converters. Walter B. Larew. LC 68-8908. (Illus.). 1968. 9.95 o.p. (ISBN 0-8019-5383-9). Chilton.

Fluid Film Lubrication. William Gross & Lee A. Matsch. Ed. by John H. Vohr & Manfred Wildman. LC 80-36889. 773p. 1980. 35.00 (ISBN 0-471-08357-7, Pub. by Wiley-Interscience). Wiley.

Fluid Flow Measurement Bibliography. Ed. by R. Rosemary Dowden. 1972. microfiche 25.00 (ISBN 0-900983-21-3, Dist. by Air Science Co.). BHRA Fluid.

Fluid Inclusion Research: Proceedings of COFFI, Vol. 10, 1977. Ed. by Edwin Roedder & Andrezj Kozlowski. 270p. 1980. pap. 10.00x (ISBN 0-472-02010-2). U of Mich Pr.

Fluid Mechanics. 5th ed. Raymond C. Binder. (Illus.). 448p. 1973. ref. ed. 25.95x (ISBN 0-13-322594-1). P-H.

Fluid Mechanics. William Bober & Richard A. Kenyon. LC 79-12977. 1980. 26.95 (ISBN 0-471-04886-0); solutions manual avail. (ISBN 0-471-04999-9). Wiley.

Fluid Mechanics. Noel DeNevers. LC 78-91144. (Engineering Ser). 1970. text ed. 24.95 (ISBN 0-201-01497-1). A-W.

Fluid Mechanics. M. Manohar & P. Krishnamachar. 500p. 1981. text ed. 25.00x (ISBN 0-7069-1188-1, Pub. by Vikas India). Advent Bk.

Fluid Mechanics. M. C. Potter & J. F. Foss. 1975. 26.95 (ISBN 0-8260-7207-0); tchrs. manual avail. (ISBN 0-471-07509-4). Wiley.

Fluid Mechanics. Ruth H. Rogers. 1978. 28.00 (ISBN 0-7100-8681-4). Routledge & Kegan.

Fluid Mechanics: A Laboratory Course. M. A. Plint & L. Boswirth. 186p. 1978. 30.00x (ISBN 0-85264-245-8, Pub. by Griffin England). State Mutual Bk.

Fluid Mechanics & Its Applications. James Murdock. LC 75-31024. (Illus.). 384p. 1976. text ed. 23.95 (ISBN 0-395-20626-X); solutions manual 2.50 (ISBN 0-395-24216-9). HM.

Fluid Mechanics for Engineers. Maurice L. Albertson et al. 1960. text ed. 25.95 (ISBN 0-13-322578-X). P-H.

Fluid Mechanics for Technicians. Thomas B. Hardison. (Illus.). 272p. 1977. ref. ed. 18.95 (ISBN 0-87909-297-1); students manual avail. Reston.

Fluid Mechanics of Large Blood Vessels. T. J. Pedley. LC 78-73814. (Cambridge Monographs on Mechanics & Applied Mathematics). (Illus.). 1980. 89.50 (ISBN 0-521-22626-0). Cambridge U Pr.

Fluid Mechanics, Thermodynamics of Turbomachinery. 2nd ed. S. L. Dixon. 1974. text ed. 19.25 o.p. (ISBN 0-08-018072-8); pap. text ed. 11.00 o.p. (ISBN 0-08-018071-X). Pergamon.

Fluid Milk Industry. 3rd ed. J. Lloyd Henderson. LC 75-137709. Orig. Title: Market Milk Industry. (Illus.). 1971. 39.50 (ISBN 0-87055-090-X). AVI.

Fluid Movers: Pumps, Compressors, Fans & Blowers. Chemical Engineering Magazine. (Chemical Engineering Bks.). (Illus.). 384p. 1980. 24.95 (ISBN 0-07-010769-6, P&RB). McGraw.

Fluid Power. 3rd ed. Harry L. Stewart & John M. Storer. LC 73-82160. 1980. 19.95 (ISBN 0-672-97224-7); instructor's manual 3.33 (ISBN 0-672-97226-3); student manual 8.95 (ISBN 0-672-97225-5). Bobbs.

Fluid Power for Aircraft: Modern Hydraulic Technology. 3rd ed. Samuel W. Merrill. 1974. pap. 10.00 (ISBN 0-914680-01-3). Intermtn Air.

Fluid Power for Industrial Use: Hydraulics, Vol. 2. Olaf A. Johnson. 224p. 1981. lib. bdg. 12.50 (ISBN 0-89874-048-7). Krieger.

Fluid Power Logic Circuit Design: Analysis, Design Methods & Worked Examples. Peter Rohner. LC 79-14178. 226p. 1979. 32.95x (ISBN 0-470-26779-8). Halsted Pr.

Fluid Power: Theory & Applications. James Sullivan. (Illus.). 480p. 1975. 18.95 (ISBN 0-87909-272-6); instrs'. manual avail. Reston.

Fluid Therapy & Disorders of Electrolyte Balance. 2nd ed. W. H. Taylor. (Illus.). 200p. 1970. 9.50 (ISBN 0-632-07430-2, Blackwell). Mosby.

Fluid Transients in Hydro-Electric Engineering Practice. Charles Jaeger. (Illus.). 1977. 62.50x (ISBN 0-216-90225-8). Intl Ideas.

Fluidic Components & Equipment, 1968-69. Ed. by Geoffrey W. Dummer & J. M. Robertson. 1969. 105.00 (ISBN 0-08-013446-7). Pergamon.

Fluidic Systems Design. C. A. Belsterling. LC 80-12189. 248p. 1981. Repr. of 1971 ed. lib. bdg. write for info. (ISBN 0-89874-169-6). Krieger.

Fluidics Applications Bibliography. Ed. by T. E. Brock. 1968. text ed. 24.00 (ISBN 0-900983-00-0, Dist. by Air Science Co.). BHRA Fluid.

Fluidics Quarterly, Vol. 11. (Illus.). 1979. 115.00 (ISBN 0-88232-052-1). Delbridge Pub Co.

Fluidics Quarterly: The Journal of Fluid Control, Vol. 13. (Illus.). 1981. 124.00 (ISBN 0-88232-062-9). Delbridge Pub Co.

Fluidised Particles. John F. Davidson & David Harrison. 1963. 27.50 (ISBN 0-521-04789-7). Cambridge U Pr.

Fluidization. Ed. by J. F. Davidson. D. L. Keairns. LC 77-82495. (Illus.). 1978. 52.50 (ISBN 0-521-21943-4). Cambridge U Pr.

Fluidization Technology: Proceedings, 2 vols. International Fluidization Conference, 1975. Ed. by Dale L. Keairns. LC 75-40106. (Thermal & Fluids Engineering Ser.). (Illus.). 1000p. 1976. Set. 119.50 (ISBN 0-89116-162-7, Co-Pub. by McGraw Intl). Hemisphere Pub.

Fluidized Bed Reactors. J. G. Yates. 1981. text ed. price not set. Butterworth.

Fluids & Blood Component Therapy in the Critically Ill. 1981. text ed. price not set (ISBN 0-443-08129-8). Churchill.

Fluids & Electrolytes. E. Kinsey Smith. Ed. by Elizabeth Brain. (Illus.). 112p. 1980. pap. text ed. 9.00 (ISBN 0-443-08101-8). Churchill.

Fluids & Electrolytes in the Surgical Patient. Carlos Pestana. 1977. pap. 10.95 o.p. (ISBN 0-683-06859-8). Williams & Wilkins.

Fluids & Electrolytes in the Surgical Patient. 2nd ed. Carlos Pestana. (Illus.). 192p. 1981. softcover 14.95 (ISBN 0-683-06860-1). Williams & Wilkins.

Fluids, Electrolytes, & Metabolism. Robert F. Wilson. 148p. 1975. pap. 11.50 (ISBN 0-398-02643-2). C C Thomas.

Fluids for Anesthesia & Surgery in the Newborn & Infant. E. J. Bennett. (Illus.). 248p. 1975. 25.50 (ISBN 0-398-03279-3). C C Thomas.

Fluids for Power Sysytems. R. H. Warring. (Illus.). 1970. 39.95x (ISBN 0-85461-040-5). Intl Ideas.

Fluorescence Assay in Biology & Medicine, 2 Vols. Sidney Udenfriend. (Molecular Biology: Vol. 3). (Illus.). Vol. 1, 1962. 46.00 (ISBN 0-12-705850-8); Vol. 2. 47.50 (ISBN 0-12-705802-8). Acad Pr.

Fluoridation-For Your Community & Your State. rev. ed. Donald R. McNeil. pap. cancelled o.s.i. (ISBN 0-685-05573-6). Am Dental.

Fluorides. Committee On Biological Effects Of Atmospheric Pollutants. LC 70-169178. (Biological Effects of Atmospheric Pollutants Ser). 1971. pap. text ed. 7.75 (ISBN 0-309-01922-2). Natl Acad Pr.

Fluorides & Dental Caries. 2nd ed. Ed. by Ernest Newbrun. (Illus.). 208p. 1978. 15.75 (ISBN 0-398-03448-6). C C Thomas.

Fluorides for Better Bones & Teeth. Association of Bone & Joint Surgeons. Ed. by Marshall R. Urist. (Clinical Orthopaedics Ser, Vol. 55). 1967. 15.00 (ISBN 0-685-14231-0). Lippincott.

Fluorine in Organic Chemistry. Richard D. Chambers. 410p. 1981. Repr. of 1973 ed. lib. bdg. price not set (ISBN 0-89874-345-1). Krieger.

Fluorocarbons: Alternatives, Markets, Problems. BCC Staff. (Illus.). 1976. 500.00 o.p. (ISBN 0-89336-092-9). BCC.

Fluorometric Techniques in Clinical Chemistry. Franklin R. Elevitch. LC 73-155034. (Illus.). 300p. 1973. 16.50 o.p. (ISBN 0-316-23250-5). Little.

Flush Times of Alabama & Mississippi. Joseph Baldwin. 1959. 7.50 (ISBN 0-8446-1589-7). Peter Smith.

Flussbpiraten Des Mississippi. Friedrich Gerstacker. (Insel Taschenbuecher: It 435). (Illus.). 551p. (Ger.). 1980. pap. text ed. 7.80 (ISBN 3-458-32135-7, Pub. by Insel Verlag Germany). Suhrkamp.

Flute. rev. ed. Philip Bate. (Instruments of the Orchestra Ser.). 1980. 17.95 (ISBN 0-393-01292-1). Norton.

Flute Technique. 4th ed. F. B. Chapman. 1973. pap. 7.75 (ISBN 0-19-318609-8). Oxford U Pr.

Flutterby. Stephen Cosgrove. (Serendipity Bks). (Illus.). (gr. k-4). 1978. PLB 6.95 (ISBN 0-87191-664-9). Creative Ed.

Fluvial Processes in Geomorphology. Luna B. Leopold et al. LC 64-10919. (Geology Ser.). (Illus.). 1964. 27.95x (ISBN 0-7167-0221-5). W H Freeman.

Fly Away Free. Joan Hewett. LC 80-50449. (Illus.). 32p. (gr. 2-5). 1981. 8.95 (ISBN 0-8027-6402-9); PLB 9.85 (ISBN 0-8027-6403-7). Walker & Co.

Fly Away Home. Christine Nostlinger. Tr. by Anthea Bell. 144p. (gr. 7 up). 1975. 5.88 o.p. (ISBN 0-531-01096-1). Watts.

Fly Casting with Lefty Kreh. Lefty Kreh & Hermann Kessler. LC 73-16374. (Illus.). 1974. 8.95 o.s.i. (ISBN 0-397-00999-2). Lippincott.

Fly-Dressing. David J. Collyer. LC 74-20454. (Illus.). 280p. 1975. 25.00 (ISBN 0-7153-6719-6). David & Charles.

Fly Dressing Materials. John Veniard. 1978. 13.95 (ISBN 0-87691-267-6). Winchester Pr.

Fly Fisherman's Complete Guide to Fishing with the Fly Rod. Ed. by Fly Fisherman Magazine. (Illus.). 1978. 14.95 (ISBN 0-87165-013-4); pap. 7.95 (ISBN 0-87165-094-0). Ziff-Davis Pub.

Fly Fishing for Panfish: A Beginner's Guide. John Malo. LC 80-26788. (Illus.). 150p. 1981. 8.95 (ISBN 0-87518-208-9). Dillon.

Fly Fishing for Trout: A Guide for Adult Beginners. Richard W. Talleur. 1974. 11.95 (ISBN 0-87691-133-5). Winchester Pr.

Fly-Fishing Heresies. Leonard M. Wright, Jr. (Illus.). 1975. 8.95 o.p. (ISBN 0-87691-203-X). Winchester Pr.

Fly-Fishing the Rockies. William C. Black. (Illus.). 160p. 1976. 9.95 o.p. (ISBN 0-87108-507-0). Pruett.

Fly Has Lots of Eyes. Beverly Amstutz. (Illus.). 1981. pap. 2.50 (ISBN 0-937836-04-4). Precious Res.

Fly High, Run Free. Jane Ratcliffe. (Illus.). 168p. 1981. 10.95 (ISBN 0-7011-2365-6, Pub. by Chatto-Bodley-Jonathan). Merrimack Bk Serv.

Fly on Instruments. George C. Larson. LC 79-7602. (Illus.). 240p. 1980. 12.95 (ISBN 0-385-14619-1). Doubleday.

Fly-Rodding for Bass. A. D. Livingston. LC 75-38710. 1976. 8.95 o.p. (ISBN 0-397-01112-1). Lippincott.

Fly Tackle: A Guide to the Tools of the Trade. Harmon Henkin. LC 75-18644. (Illus.). 1976. 9.95 o.p. (ISBN 0-397-01072-9). Lippincott.

Fly Through the Baha'i Year. Terry Ostovar. (Illus.). 48p. (Orig.). (gr. 2-6). 1980. pap. 4.95 (ISBN 0-933770-13-8). Kalimat.

Fly-Tying. William B. Sturgis. (Illus.). 1940. 8.95 o.p. (ISBN 0-684-10584-5, ScribT). Scribner.

Fly Tying & Fly Fishing for Bass & Panfish. 2nd rev. ed. Tom Nixon. LC 75-20613. 14.50 (ISBN 0-498-01826-1). A S Barnes.

Fly Tying Illustrated: For Nymphs & Lures. Freddie Rice & Freddie Rice. LC 76-2150. (Illus.). 112p. 1976. 11.95 (ISBN 0-7153-6952-0). David & Charles.

Fly Tying, Rod & Tackle Making. Ed. by Kenneth Mansfield. (Angler's Library). 1978. 4.50 o.p. (ISBN 0-214-65306-4, 8002, Dist. by Arco). Barrie & Jenkins.

Fly with the Wind, Flow with the Water. Ann Atwood. (Illus.). 32p. (gr. 1-5). 1979. 9.95 (ISBN 0-684-16103-6). Scribner.

Flyaway Kite. Gyo Fujikawa. LC 80-3353. (Gyo Fujikawa Ser.). (Illus.). 32p. (gr. k-3). 1981. 3.95 (ISBN 0-448-11747-9); PLB 9.30 (ISBN 0-448-13652-X). G&D.

Flying & Ballooning from Old Photographs. John Fabb. LC 79-56467. (Illus.). 120p. 1980. 19.95 (ISBN 0-7134-2015-4, Pub. by Batsford England). David & Charles.

Flying Birds. David Urry & Katie Urry. LC 74-110974. 1969. 7.95 (ISBN 0-910294-20-8). Brown Bk.

Flying Buccaneers: The Illustrated Story of Kenney's Fifth Air Force. Steve Birdsall. LC 77-74293. 1977. 15.00 o.p. (ISBN 0-385-03218-8). Doubleday.

Flying Circus of Physics. Jearl Walker. LC 75-5670. 224p. 1975. 11.95 (ISBN 0-471-91808-3). Wiley.

Flying Creatures. Ernest Prescott. (Easy-Read Wildlife Bk.). (Illus.). 48p. (gr. 2-4). 1976. PLB 4.90 o.p. (ISBN 0-531-00035-8). Watts.

Flying Dutchman: The Complete Text in German & English. Richard Wagner. Ed. by Brian Large & Peter Butler. (Illus.). 1975. text ed. 13.95x (ISBN 0-7156-0938-6). Intl Ideas.

Flying Fortress. Edward Jablonski. LC 65-19886. 1965. 16.95 (ISBN 0-385-03855-0). Doubleday.

Flying Free. Dick Cate. LC 76-57722. (Illus.). (gr. 4-7). 1977. 6.95 o.p. (ISBN 0-525-66535-8). Elsevier-Nelson.

Flying Fur, Fin & Scale: Strange Animals That Swoop and Soar. Mary Leister. LC 77-7620. (Illus.). (gr. 4 up). 1977. 9.95 (ISBN 0-916144-07-0). Stemmer Hse.

Flying Hand-Launched Gliders. John Kaufmann. LC 73-17236. (Illus.). 96p. (gr. 7 up). 1974. PLB 6.96 (ISBN 0-688-30108-8); pap. 2.50 o.p. (ISBN 0-688-25108-0). Morrow.

Flying High. Nancy Mack & Peter Sanders. LC 74-34425. (Venture Ser, a Reading Incentive Program). (Illus.). 80p. (gr. 7-12,RL 4.5-6.5). 1975. In Packs Of 5. text ed. 23.25 ea. pack (ISBN 0-8172-0216-1). Follett.

Flying High. Bill Powers. (Target Bks.). (Illus.). (gr. 3 up). 1978. PLB 6.45 s&l (ISBN 0-531-01461-4). Watts.

Flying Horse. (MacDonald Educational Ser.). (Illus., Arabic.). 3.50 (ISBN 0-686-53085-3). Intl Bk Ctr.

Flying Know-How. Robert N. Buck. 1975. 10.95 (ISBN 0-440-04931-8). Delacorte.

Flying Legion. George A. England. 1976. lib. bdg. 12.95 (ISBN 0-89968-177-8). Lightyear.

Flying Light Aircraft. 2nd ed. David Ogilvy. (Illus.). 224p. 1979. 20.00 (ISBN 0-7136-1854-X). Transatlantic.

Flying Model Airplanes & Helicopters by Radio Control. Edward L. Safford. (Illus.). 1977. pap. 5.95 (ISBN 0-8306-6825-X, 825). TAB Bks.

Flying Mystique. Harry Bauer. (Illus.). 1980. 9.95 (ISBN 0-440-02722-5, E Friede). Delacorte.

Flying Origami. Eiji Nakamura. LC 70-188761. (Illus.). 64p. 1972. pap. 6.50 (ISBN 0-87040-023-1). Japan Pubns.

Flying Precision Maneuvers in Light Airplanes. Ron Fowler. (Illus.). 224p. 1980. 10.95 (ISBN 0-440-02598-2). Delacorte.

Flying Reptiles, in the Age of Dinosaurs. John Kaufmann. LC 76-1919. (Illus.). 40p. (gr. 1-5). 1976. 5.75 o.p. (ISBN 0-688-22073-8); PLB 6.00 (ISBN 0-688-32073-2). Morrow.

Flying Safely. rev. ed. Richard Collins. 1981. 10.95 (ISBN 0-440-02652-0, E Friede). Delacorte.

Flying Saucer Revelations. Michael X. 1969. pap. 5.95 (ISBN 0-685-20196-1). Saucerian.

Flying Saucers. Gordon Lindsay. pap. 0.95 (ISBN 0-89985-199-1). Christ Nations.

Flying Saucers - an Analysis of the Air Force Project Blue Book Special Report No. 14: Including the C. I. A. & the Saucers. 4th ed. Leon Davidson. (Illus.). 1977. pap. 12.95 o.p. (ISBN 0-685-80881-5). Saucerian.

Flying Saucers & the Straight-Line Mystery. Aime Michel. LC 58-8787. (Illus.). 1958. 12.95 (ISBN 0-87599-077-0). S G Phillips.

Flying Saucers Are Watching Us. Otto O. Binder. 1978. pap. 1.50 (ISBN 0-505-51304-8). Tower Bks.

Flying Saucers: Magic in the Skies. Otto Billig. 256p. 1981. text ed. 14.95x (ISBN 0-87073-833-X). Schenkman.

Flying Ship. Rosemary Harris. (Illus.). (ps-5). 1975. 6.95 (ISBN 0-571-10504-1, Pub. by Faber & Faber). Merrimack Bk Serv.

Flying Shoes. Cynthia Jameson. LC 72-8126. (Illus.). 48p. (gr. k-3). 1973. 5.95 o.s.i. (ISBN 0-8193-0642-8, Four Winds); PLB 5.41 o.s.i. (ISBN 0-8193-0643-6). Schol Bk Serv.

Flying Solo: The New Art of Living Single. Kenneth Wydro. LC 77-27287. 1978. 8.95 o.p. (ISBN 0-399-12151-X, Pub. by Berkley Pub). Berkley Pub.

Flying Sorcerers. David Gerrold & Larry Niven. (A Del Rey Bk.). 1977. pap. 1.95 (ISBN 0-345-28039-3). Ballantine.

Flying Tigers. John Toland. (YA) 1979. pap. 1.50 (ISBN 0-440-92621-1, LFL). Dell.

Flying Tigers. John Toland. (Landmark Ser: No. 105). (Illus.). (gr. 7-8). 1963. PLB 5.99 (ISBN 0-394-90405-2). Random.

Flying with Broken Wings. Virginia R. Thomas. Date not set. 6.95 (ISBN 0-533-04791-9). Vantage.

Flytying Techniques. Jacqueline Wakeford. LC 80-1274. (Illus.). 176p. 1980. 29.95 (ISBN 0-385-17306-7, NLB). Doubleday.

Fo-Kuang Ssu: Literary Evidences & Buddhist Images. Marylin M. Rhie. LC 76-23690. (Outstanding Dissertations in the Fine Arts - Far Eastern). (Illus.). 1977. Repr. of 1970 ed. lib. bdg. 45.00 (ISBN 0-8240-2721-3). Garland Pub.

Fo-Sho-Hing-Tsan-King, Vol. 19. Ed. by F. Max Mueller. Tr. by Beal. (Sacred Books of the East Ser.). 15.00x (ISBN 0-8426-1398-6). Verry.

Foal to Five Years. Ann Hyland. LC 80-11310. 128p. 1980. 12.95 (ISBN 0-668-04952-9, 4952-9). Arco.

Foam Control Agents. H. T. Kerner. LC 76-17942. (Chemical Technology Review: No. 75). (Illus.). 1977. 39.00 (ISBN 0-8155-0634-1). Noyes.

Foam Sandwich Boatbuilding. Peter Wynn. LC 72-87223. (Illus.). 128p. 1972. 9.95 o.p. (ISBN 0-87742-027-0). Intl Marine.

Focal Aspects of the Industrial Revolution: 1825-42, Five Pamphlets. 198p. 1971. Repr. of 1842 ed. 25.00x (ISBN 0-7165-1562-8, Pub. by Irish Academic Pr England). Biblio Dist.

Focal Encyclopedia of Photography. Gaunt & Petzold. 1980. desk ed. 24.95 (ISBN 0-240-50680-4). Focal Pr.

Focal Guide to Movie Tilting. Philip Jenkins. (Focal Guide Ser.). (Illus.). 160p. 1981. pap. 7.95 (ISBN 0-240-51011-9). Focal Pr.

Focal Points. Georg Borgstrom. (Illus.). 288p. 1973. pap. 8.95 o.s.i. (ISBN 0-02-513650-X). Macmillan.

Focalguide to Better Pictures. David Lynch. LC 80-41302. (Focalguide Ser.). 1981. pap. 7.95 (ISBN 0-240-51053-4). Focal Pr.

Focalguide to Camera Accessories. Leonard Gaunt. (Focalguide Ser.). (Illus.). 216p. 1980. pap. 7.95 (ISBN 0-240-51043-7). Focal Pr.

Focalguide to Movie Titling. Philip Jenkins. (Focalguide Ser.). (Illus.). 1980. pap. 7.95 o.p. (ISBN 0-240-51011-9). Focal Pr.

Focalguide to Travel Photography. Peter McKenzie. LC 80-41482. (Focalguide Ser.). (Illus.). 136p. 1981. pap. 7.95 (ISBN 0-240-51072-0). Focal Pr.

Focke Wulf 190, a Famous German Fighter. Heinz J. Nowarra. LC 65-15546. (Harleyford Ser). (Illus.). 1965. 18.95 (ISBN 0-8168-6365-2). Aero.

Focke-Wulf 190 at War. encore ed. Alfred Price. LC 77-78704. (Illus.). 1978. 4.95 o.p. (ISBN 0-684-16364-0, ScribT). Scribner.

Foclair Gaeilge Bearla (Irish-English Dictionary) O'Donaill. 30.00x (ISBN 0-686-28280-9). Colton Bk.

Focus: A College English Handbook. Kim Flachmann. (Illus.). 448p. 1981. pap. text ed. 6.95 (ISBN 0-395-29728-1); instrs' manual 0.75. HM.

Focus: A Handbook of Classroom Ideas to Motivate the Teaching of Intermediate Social Studies. (Spice Ser.). 1977. 6.50 (ISBN 0-89273-125-7). Educ Serv.

Focus Changes of August Pervico. Dale Worsley. LC 80-19515. 192p. 1980. 10.00 (ISBN 0-8149-0841-1). Vanguard.

Focus Forecasting: Computer Techniques for Inventory Control. Bernard T. Smith. LC 78-6120. 1978. 19.95 (ISBN 0-8436-0761-0). CBI Pub.

Focus on America. Philip J. McFarland et al. LC 76-53136. (Focus on Literature Ser.). (Illus.). (gr. 11). 1977. text ed. 15.32 (ISBN 0-395-24962-7); tchr's guide 5.76 (ISBN 0-395-24961-9). HM.

Focus on American Catechetics: A Commentary on the General Catechetical Directory. 101p. 1972. 2.95. Natl Cath Educ.

Focus on Believing. Mary Jo Tully & Sandra J. Hirstein. (Light of Faith Ser.). (Orig.). (gr. 3 up). 1981. pap. text ed. 3.00 (ISBN 0-697-01767-2); tchr's ed. 7.60 (ISBN 0-697-01768-0). Wm C Brown.

Focus on Belonging. Mary Jo Tully & Sandra J. Hirstein. (Light of Faith Ser.). (Orig.). (gr. 2 up). 1981. pap. text ed. 2.65 (ISBN 0-697-01765-6); tchrs' ed. 7.60 (ISBN 0-697-01766-4). Wm C Brown.

Focus on Calculator Math. Charles Lund & Margaret Smart. (Illus.). (gr. 4-12). 1979. pap. text ed. 4.95 (ISBN 0-918932-66-1). Activity Resources.

Focus on Celebrating. Mary Jo Tully & Sandra J. Hirstein. (Light of Faith Ser.). (Orig.). (gr. 5 up). 1981. pap. text ed. 3.00 (ISBN 0-697-01771-0); tchrs' ed. 7.60. Wm C Brown.

Focus on Classroom Behavior: Readings & Research. W. Scott MacDonald et al. (Illus.). 170p. 1973. 11.75 (ISBN 0-398-02460-X). C C Thomas.

Focus on Composition. Ann Raimes. (Illus.). 1978. pap. 6.95x (ISBN 0-19-502238-6). Oxford U Pr.

Focus on Deafness: Selected Readings on Deafness for Paraprofessionals. Edgar D. Lawrence. 1978. pap. text ed. 10.50x (ISBN 0-8191-0389-6). U Pr of Amer.

Focus on Faith in Jesus. Ronald J. Wilkins. (To Live in Christ Ser.). 1980. pap. 3.75 (ISBN 0-697-01719-2); parish ed. 3.00 (ISBN 0-697-01720-6). Wm C Brown.

Focus on Film & Theatre. J. Hurt. 1974. pap. 2.95 (ISBN 0-13-314658-8, Spec). P-H.

Focus on Forms. Philip J. McFarland et al. LC 76-53136. (Focus on Literature Ser.). (Illus., Gr. 10). 1977. text ed. 14.80 (ISBN 0-395-24970-8); teachers guide 5.24 (ISBN 0-395-24963-5). HM.

Focus on Group Psychotherapy. Saul Scheidlinger. 1981. write for info. (ISBN 0-8236-1990-7). Intl Univs Pr.

Focus on Growth in the Church: School Ed. Joel R. Gorun. (To Live Is Christ Ser.). 1980. teacher's manual 3.85 (ISBN 0-697-01722-2). Wm C Brown.

Focus on Health: Issues & Events of 1979. Ed. by Helen Zelon. LC 80-1719. (News in Print Ser.). (Illus.). 1980. lib. bdg. 24.95x (ISBN 0-405-12879-7). Arno.

Focus on Ideas. Philip J. McFarland et al. LC 76-53136. (Focus on Literature Ser.). (Illus., Gr. 12). 1977. text ed. 15.32 (ISBN 0-395-24960-0); teachers guide 5.76 (ISBN 0-395-24959-7). HM.

Focus on Life Student Project Book. rev ed. Thomas J. Zimmerman. (To Live Is Christ Ser.). 40p. 1976. wkbk. 1.65 (ISBN 0-697-01655-2). Wm C Brown.

Focus on Living. Mary Jo Tully & Sandra J. Hirstein. (Light of Faith Ser.). (Orig.). (gr. 4 up). 1981. pap. text ed. 3.00 (ISBN 0-697-01769-9); tchrs' ed. 7.60 (ISBN 0-697-01770-2). Wm C Brown.

Focus on Loving. Mary Jo Tully & Sandra J. Hirstein. (Light of Faith Ser.). (Orig.). (gr. 1). 1981. pap. text ed. 2.65 (ISBN 0-697-01763-X); tchrs' ed. 7.60 (ISBN 0-697-01763-X). Wm C Brown.

Focus on Nurse Credentialing. Jo Hohman. LC 80-17049. 96p. (Orig.). 1980. 10.00 (ISBN 0-87258-303-1, 1460). Am Hospital.

Focus on Photography. Ronald E. Jones. Ed. by Ronald Kirchem. (Illus.). 256p. (gr. 9-12). 1980. text ed. 13.28 (ISBN 0-07-033020-4, W). McGraw.

Focus on Physical Handicap. J. Panckhurst. 158p. 1981. pap. text ed. 16.00x (ISBN 0-85633-217-8, NFER). Humanities.

Focus on Police: The Police in American Society. Ed. by C. P. Potholm & R. E. Morgan. 1976. pap. text ed. 6.95 o.p. (ISBN 0-470-15075-0); pap. text ed. 6.95 (ISBN 0-470-15077-7). Halsted Pr.

Focus on Reading. Nell McCutchan. (English As a Second Language Ser.). (Illus.). 1980. pap. text ed. 9.95 (ISBN 0-13-322776-6). P-H.

Focus on Relating. Mary Jo Tully & Sandra J. Hirstein. (Light of Faith Ser.). (Orig.). (gr. 6). 1981. pap. text ed. 3.00 (ISBN 0-697-01773-7); tchrs' ed. 7.60 (ISBN 0-697-01774-5). Wm C Brown.

Focus on Society: An Introduction to Sociology. 2nd ed. Norman W. Storer. LC 79-26376. (Sociology Ser.). (Illus.). 1980. text ed. 13.95 (ISBN 0-201-07337-4). A-W.

Focus on Teachers' Centers. Christopher Redknap. (General Ser.). 1977. pap. text ed. 13.25x (ISBN 0-85633-126-0, NFER). Humanities.

Focus on the Engineer: Today & Tomorrow. 106p. 1977. 12.50 o.p. (ISBN 0-686-27578-0, 124-78). AAES.

Focus on the Retarded Adult: Programs & Services. Schulman. LC 79-17181. 1979. pap. 18.95 (ISBN 0-8016-4367-8). Mosby.

Focus on the Science Fiction Film. W. Johnson. 1972. 5.95 o.p. (ISBN 0-13-795161-2); pap. 2.95 o.p. (ISBN 0-13-795179-5). P-H.

Focus on Viewpoints. Philip J. McFarland et al. LC 76-53136. (Focus on Literature Ser.). (Illus., Gr. 9). 1977. text ed. 14.80 (ISBN 0-395-24968-6); tcr's guide 5.24 (ISBN 0-395-24969-4). HM.

Focus on Your Language. James W. Parkinson. LC 75-17952. 279p. 1976. pap. 7.95 (ISBN 0-672-61358-1); tchrs.' manual 5.00 (ISBN 0-685-50625-8). Bobbs.

Focus Uppslagsbok, 6 vols. 3rd ed. (Swedish.). 1970-1971. 395.00 (ISBN 0-8277-3026-8). Maxwell Sci Intl.

Focusing. Eugene Gendlin. 192p. (Orig.). 1981. pap. 3.50 (ISBN 0-553-14526-6). Bantam.

Focusing Artifice: The Poetry of Robert Browning. Roma A. King, Jr. LC 68-20934. 1968. 10.00 o.p. (ISBN 0-8214-0042-8). Ohio U Pr.

Focusing Industrial Arts on Career Education. H. Bert DiPaul. LC 79-53500. (Illus.). 143p. (Orig.). (gr. 9-12). 1979. pap. 3.95 (ISBN 0-9605418-0-2). DiPaul.

Focusing of Charged Particles, 2 Vols. Ed. by A. Septier. 1967. Vol. 1. 55.25 (ISBN 0-12-636901-1); Vol. 2. 52.25 (ISBN 0-12-636902-X); Set. 87.25 (ISBN 0-685-05127-7). Acad Pr.

Focusing on Gebruder Heubach Dolls. J. Foulke. 1980. pap. 6.95 (ISBN 0-87588-148-3). Hobby Hse.

Focusing on the Strengths of Children. Linda B. Gambrell & Robert M. Wilson. LC 73-80404. 1973. pap. 4.50 (ISBN 0-8224-2900-4). Pitman Learning.

Fodor's Alaska 1980. (Fodor's Modern Travel Guides Ser.). 1980. 9.95 (ISBN 0-679-00566-8); pap. 4.95 (ISBN 0-679-00567-6). McKay.

Fodor's Australia, New Zealand & the South Pacific 1980. Ed. by Robert Fisher. (Fodor Travel Guide Ser.). (Illus.). 1980. 13.95 o.p. (ISBN 0-679-00562-5); pap. 10.95 o.p. (ISBN 0-679-00563-3). McKay.

Fodor's Austria 1980. Ed. by Robert Fisher. (Fodor Travel Guide Ser.). (Illus.). 1980. 12.95 o.p. (ISBN 0-679-00500-5). McKay.

Fodor's Austria, 1981. 1980. pap. 11.95 (ISBN 0-679-00668-0). McKay.

Fodor's Belgium & Luxembourg 1980. (Fodor's Modern Travel Guides Ser.). 1980. 12.95 o.p. (ISBN 0-679-00505-6). McKay.

Fodor's Bermuda 1980. (Fodor's Travel Guide Ser.). (Illus.). 1980. 8.95 o.p. (ISBN 0-679-00552-8); pap. 5.95 o.p. (ISBN 0-679-00553-6). McKay.

Fodor's Brazil. Ed. by Eugene Fodor. (Fodor Travel Guides). (Illus.). 1979. 8.95 o.p. (ISBN 0-679-00550-1); pap. 5.95 o.p. (ISBN 0-679-00551-X). McKay.

Fodor's Budget America, 1981. 1980. 12.50 (ISBN 0-679-00661-3); pap. 8.95 (ISBN 0-679-00662-1). McKay.

Fodor's Budget Europe, 1980. Fodor. 1979. 10.95 o.p. (ISBN 0-679-00487-4); pap. 7.95 o.p. (ISBN 0-679-00488-2). McKay.

Fodor's Budget Europe, 1981. 1980. 10.95 (ISBN 0-679-00657-5); pap. 7.95 (ISBN 0-679-00658-3). McKay.

Fodor's Budget France, 1980. Fodor. 1980. pap. 4.95 o.p. (ISBN 0-679-00484-X). McKay.

Fodor's Budget Travel in America 1980. (Fodor's Travel Guide Ser.). (Illus.). 1979. 12.50 o.p. (ISBN 0-679-00477-7); pap. 8.95 o.p. (ISBN 0-679-00478-5). McKay.

Fodor's Budget Travel in America, 1981. (Fodor Travel Guides Ser.). 640p. 1980. cancelled (ISBN 0-679-00661-3); pap. cancelled (ISBN 0-679-00662-1). McKay.

Fodor's California in Japanese. (Fodor's Travel Guide Ser.). (Illus., Japanese.). 1980. 12.95 (ISBN 0-679-00434-3); pap. 9.95 (ISBN 0-679-00435-1). McKay.

Fodor's California 1980. (Fodor's Modern Travel Guides Ser.). 1980. 9.95 o.p. (ISBN 0-679-00470-X); pap. 5.95 o.p. (ISBN 0-679-00471-8). McKay.

Fodor's Canada 1980. Ed. by Robert Fisher. (Fodor Travel Guides Ser.). (Illus.). 1977. 13.95 o.p. (ISBN 0-679-00501-3); pap. 10.95 o.p. (ISBN 0-679-00502-1). McKay.

Fodor's Caribbean & Bahamas 1980. (Fodor's Travel Guide Ser.). (Illus.). 1979. 13.95 o.p. (ISBN 0-679-00503-X); pap. 10.95 o.p. (ISBN 0-679-00504-8). McKay.

Fodor's Disney's Adventure Guide to California. (Fodor Travel Guides Ser.). 64p. (gr. 1-6). 1980. pap. 3.95 (ISBN 0-679-00577-3). McKay.

Fodor's Disney's Adventure Guide to Florida. (Fodor Travel Guides Ser.). 64p. (gr. 1-6). 1980. pap. 3.95 (ISBN 0-679-00575-7). McKay.

Fodor's Egypt 1980. (Fodor's Modern Travel Guides Ser.). 1980. 10.95 o.p. (ISBN 0-679-00564-1). McKay.

Fodor's Europe 1980. Ed. by Robert Fisher. (Fodor Travel Guides Ser.). 1979. 13.95 o.p. (ISBN 0-679-00506-4); pap. 10.95 o.p. (ISBN 0-679-00507-2). McKay.

Fodor's Farwest, 1980. Fodor. 1979. 10.95 o.p. (ISBN 0-679-00451-3); pap. 7.95 o.p. (ISBN 0-679-00452-1). McKay.

Fodor's Florida 1980. (Fodor's Modern Travel Guides Ser.). 1980. 9.95 o.p. (ISBN 0-679-00472-6); pap. 6.95 o.p. (ISBN 0-679-00473-4). McKay.

Fodor's France 1980. (Fodor's Modern Travel Guides Ser.). 1980. 13.95 o.p. (ISBN 0-679-00558-7); pap. 10.95 o.p. (ISBN 0-679-00559-5). McKay.

Fodor's Germany 1980. Ed. by Robert Fisher. (Fodor Travel Guide Ser.). 1980. 12.95 o.p. (ISBN 0-679-00508-0); pap. 9.95 o.p. (ISBN 0-679-00509-9). McKay.

Fodor's Great Britain: 1980. Eugene Fodor. (Fodor's Travel Guide Ser.). (Illus.). 1980. 12.95 o.p. (ISBN 0-679-00510-2); pap. 9.95 o.p. (ISBN 0-679-00511-0). McKay.

Fodor's Greece: 1980. Eugene Fodor. (Fodor's Travel Guide Ser.). (Illus.). 1980. 12.95 o.p. (ISBN 0-679-00560-9); pap. 9.95 o.p. (ISBN 0-679-00561-7). McKay.

Fodor's Hawaii 1980. Ed. by Robert Fisher. (Fodor Travel Guides Ser.). (Illus.). 1979. 12.95 o.p. (ISBN 0-679-00450-5); pap. 9.95 o.p. (ISBN 0-679-00469-6). McKay.

Fodor's Holland 1980. (Fodor's Modern Travel Guides Ser.). 1980. 11.95 o.p. (ISBN 0-679-00517-X). McKay.

Fodor's India & Nepal 1980. (Fodor's Travel Guide Ser.). (Illus.). 1979. 14.95 o.p. (ISBN 0-679-00514-5). McKay.

Fodor's Iran, 1979. Fodor. 1979. 12.95 o.p. (ISBN 0-679-00368-1). McKay.

Fodor's Ireland 1980. Ed. by Robert Fisher. (Fodor Travel Guide Ser.). (Illus.). 1980. 12.95 o.p. (ISBN 0-679-00515-3); pap. 9.95 o.p. (ISBN 0-679-00516-1). McKay.

Fodor's Israel: 1980. Eugene Fodor. (Fodor's Travel Guide Ser.). (Illus.). 1980. 12.95 o.p. (ISBN 0-679-00520-X); pap. 9.95 o.p. (ISBN 0-679-00521-8). McKay.

Fodor's Italy: 1980. Eugene Fodor. (Fodor's Travel Guide Ser.). (Illus.). 1980. 12.95 o.p. (ISBN 0-679-00512-9); pap. 9.95 o.p. (ISBN 0-679-00513-7). McKay.

Fodor's Japan & Korea, 1981. 1981. 13.95 (ISBN 0-679-00703-2); pap. 10.95 (ISBN 0-679-00704-0). McKay.

Fodor's Japan & South Korea 1980. (Fodor's Travel Guide Ser.). (Illus.). 1980. 13.95 o.p. (ISBN 0-679-00518-8); pap. 10.95 o.p. (ISBN 0-679-00519-6). McKay.

Fodor's Mexico 1980. Ed. by Robert Fisher. (Fodor Travel Guides Ser.). (Illus.). 1979. 13.95 o.p. (ISBN 0-679-00525-0); pap. 10.95 o.p. (ISBN 0-679-00526-9). McKay.

Fodor's New England 1980. Ed. by Robert Fisher. (Fodor Travel Guides Ser.). (Illus.). 1980. 10.95 o.p. (ISBN 0-679-00457-2); pap. 7.95 o.p. (ISBN 0-679-00458-0). McKay.

Fodor's New York 1980. (Fodor's Travel Guide Ser.). (Illus.). 1980. 9.95 o.p. (ISBN 0-679-00458-0); pap. 6.95 o.p. (ISBN 0-679-00460-2). McKay.

Fodor's People's Republic of China. Fodor. 1979. 14.95 o.p. (ISBN 0-679-00397-5); pap. 10.95 o.p. (ISBN 0-679-00398-3). McKay.

Fodor's Portugal: 1980. Eugene Fodor. (Fodor's Travel Guide Ser.). (Illus.). 1980. 11.95 o.p. (ISBN 0-679-00527-7). McKay.

Fodor's Portugal, 1981. 1980. pap. 10.95 (ISBN 0-679-00709-1). McKay.

Fodor's Scandinavia 1980. Ed. by Robert Fisher. (Fodor Travel Guide Ser.). 1979. 13.95 o.p. (ISBN 0-679-00530-7); pap. 10.95 o.p. (ISBN 0-679-00531-5). McKay.

Fodor's South America 1980. Ed. by Robert Fisher. (Fodor Travel Guides Ser.). (Illus.). 1979. 13.95 o.p. (ISBN 0-679-00532-3); pap. 10.95 o.p. (ISBN 0-679-00533-1). McKay.

Fodor's South 1980. Eugene Fodor. (Fodor's Travel Guide Ser.). 1979. 11.95 o.p. (ISBN 0-679-00463-7); pap. 7.95 o.p. (ISBN 0-679-00464-5). McKay.

Fodor's Southeast Asia 1980. Ed. by Robert Fisher. (Fodor Travel Guide Ser.). (Illus.). 1979. 13.95 o.p. (ISBN 0-679-00534-X); pap. 10.95 o.p. (ISBN 0-679-00535-8). McKay.

Fodor's Southwest 1980. Eugene Fodor. (Fodor's Travel Guide Ser.). 1979. 10.95 o.p. (ISBN 0-679-00465-3); pap. 7.95 o.p. (ISBN 0-679-00466-1). McKay.

Fodor's Soviet Union 1980. Ed. by Robert Fisher. (Fodor Travel Guide Ser.). (Illus.). 1979. 13.95 o.p. (ISBN 0-679-00536-6). McKay.

Fodor's Spain 1980. Eugene Fodor. (Fodor's Travel Guide Ser.). 1979. 12.95 o.p. (ISBN 0-679-00537-4); pap. 9.95 o.p. (ISBN 0-679-00538-2). McKay.

Fodor's Switzerland 1980. (Fodor's Modern Travel Guide Ser.). 1980. 11.95 o.p. (ISBN 0-679-00565-X). McKay.

Fodor's U. S. A. 1980. Ed. by Robert Fisher. (Fodor Travel Guide Ser.). (Illus.). 1979. 14.95 o.p. (ISBN 0-679-00467-X); pap. 10.95 o.p. (ISBN 0-679-00468-8). McKay.

Fodor's Yugoslavia 1980. (Fodor's Modern Travel Guides Ser.). 1980. 11.95 o.p. (ISBN 0-679-00540-4). McKay.

Foetal & Neonatal Physiology: Proceedings. Ed. by K. W. Cross et al. LC 72-93673. (Illus.). 600p. 1973. 95.00 (ISBN 0-521-20178-0). Cambridge U Pr.

FOF Yearbook, 1980. Facts on File Staff. 1200p. 1981. lib. bdg. 65.00 (ISBN 0-87196-039-7). Facts on File.

Fog. Mildred Lee. LC 72-81259. 250p. (gr. 7 up). 1972. 9.95 (ISBN 0-395-28911-4; Clarion). HM.

Fog & Sun, Sea & Stone: The Monterey Coast. LC 80-66365. (Illus.). 160p. (Photos & text by Steve Crouch). 1980. 23.50 (ISBN 0-912856-61-0). Graphic Arts Ctr.

Fog Burns off by Eleven O'clock. Diana Gregory. LC 80-26790. 134p. (gr. 4-8). 1981. PLB 7.95 (ISBN 0-201-04139-1, 4139, A-W Childrens). A-W.

Fog Comes on Little Pig Feet. Rosemary Wells. (gr. 7 up). 1973. pap. 1.50 o.p. (ISBN 0-380-01192-1, 48249). Avon.

Fog Island. Marilyn Ross. 1977. pap. 1.50 o.p. (ISBN 0-445-04105-6). Popular Lib.

Fog Magic. Julia Sauer. (Illus.). (gr. 3-6). 1977. pap. 1.25 (ISBN 0-671-29817-8). PB.

Foggy Rescue. Consuelo Joerns. LC 80-11375. (Illus.). 40p. (gr. k-3). 1980. 7.95 (ISBN 0-590-07744-9, Four Winds). Schol Bk Serv.

Foil. Charles A. Selberg. LC 74-30701. 224p. 1975. text ed. 9.95 (ISBN 0-201-06943-1). A-W.

Foil Fencing. 4th ed. Muriel Bower. (Physical Education Ser.). 112p. 1980. pap. text ed. write for info. (ISBN 0-697-07097-2). Wm C Brown.

Foil Fencing: Skills, Safety, Operations, & Responsibilities for the 1980s. Maxwell R. Garret & Mary H. Poulson. LC 80-18426. (Illus.). 160p. 1981. text ed. 9.75x (ISBN 0-271-00273-5). Pa St U Pr.

Fois Pour Toutes: Revision Des Structures Essentielles De la Langue Francais. Hale Sturges et al. (Illus.). 1976. pap. text ed. 6.50x (ISBN 0-88334-079-8). Ind Sch Pr.

Fold a Banana: & 146 Other Things to Do When You're Bored. Jim Erskine. (Illus.). 1978. pap. 5.95 (ISBN 0-517-53503-3, Dist. by Crown). Potter.

Fold-And-Paste Origami Storybook. Florence Sakade & Kazuhiko Sono. LC 64-22899. (gr. 1-4). 1964. bds. 4.95 o.p. (ISBN 0-8048-0189-4). C E Tuttle.

Folded Leaf. William Maxwell. LC 80-67031. 288p. 1980. pap. 7.50 (ISBN 0-87923-351-6, Nonpareil Bks). Godine.

Folding Schooner: And Other Adventures in Boat Design. Philip C. Bolger. LC 76-8779. (Illus.). 1976. 17.50 (ISBN 0-87742-083-1). Intl Marine.

Folding Screen Chinese Lyrics. Tr. by Alan Ayling et al. (Writing in Asia Ser.). 1976. pap. text ed. 5.95 (ISBN 0-686-60433-4, 00204). Heinemann Ed.

Folding Table Napkins. Marianne Von Bornstedt & Ulla Prytz. LC 72-81040. (Little Craft Book Ser.). (Illus.). 48p. (gr. 6 up). 1972. 5.95 (ISBN 0-8069-5218-0); PLB 6.69 (ISBN 0-8069-5219-9). Sterling.

Folding Table Napkins. Marianne Von Bornstedt & Ulla Prytz. LC 72-81040. (Illus.). 48p. 1981. pap. 4.95 (ISBN 0-8069-8974-2). Sterling.

Folgen der Verfolgung: Das Ueberlebenden-Syndrom. William G. Niederland. (Edition Suhrkamp. Neue Folge: esNF 15). 280p. (Orig., Ger.). 1980. pap. text ed. 7.80 (ISBN 3-518-11015-2, Pub. by Insel Verlag Germany). Suhrkamp.

Foliage House Plants. James U. Crockett. (Encyclopedia of Gardening Ser). (Illus.). 1972. 11.95 (ISBN 0-8094-1121-0); lib. bdg. avail. (ISBN 0-685-25145-4). Time-Life.

Foliage House Plants. James V. Crockett. LC 78-140420. (Time-Life Encyclopedia of Gardening). (Illus.). (gr. 6 up). 1972. lib. bdg. 11.97 (ISBN 0-8094-1123-7, Pub. by Time-Life). Silver.

Foliage Plant Production. Jasper N. Joiner. (Illus.). 608p. 1981. text ed. 24.95 (ISBN 0-13-322867-3). P-H.

Folic Acid: Biochemistry & Physiology in Relation to the Human Nutrition Requirement. Food & Nutrition Board. LC 77-8182. 1977. pap. text ed. 13.50 (ISBN 0-309-02605-9). Natl Acad Pr.

Folic Acid in Neurology, Psychiatry, & Internal Medicine. Ed. by M. I. Botez & E. H. Reynolds. LC 78-57243. 1979. text ed. 49.50 (ISBN 0-89004-338-8). Raven.

Folk & Festival Costume of the World. lib. rep. ed. R. Turner Wilcox. LC 65-23986. (Illus.). 1965. 25.00x (ISBN 0-684-15379-3, ScribT). Scribner.

Folk & Forign Costume Dolls. Linda J. Frame. (Illus.). 1980. pap. 9.95 (ISBN 0-89145-143-9). Collector Bks.

Folk & Traditional Music of the Western Continents. 2nd ed. Bruno Nettl. (Illus.). 272p. 1973. pap. 10.95 (ISBN 0-13-322933-5). P-H.

Folk Art Designs to Color or Cut. Ramona Jablonski. LC 78-13765. (International Design Library). (Illus.). 1978. pap. 2.95 (ISBN 0-916144-33-X). Stemmer Hse.

Folk Art Painting: A Bit of the Past & Present. Betty A. Vaughan. (Illus.). 52p. (Orig.). 1981. pap. 7.95 (ISBN 0-9605172-0-0). BETOM Pubns.

Folk Art to Horse-Drawn Carriages. Time-Life Books Editors. (Encyclopedia of Collectibles Ser.). (Illus.). 1979. lib. bdg. 10.98 (ISBN 0-686-50978-1). Silver.

Folk Arts of Hungary. Ed. by Walter W. Kolar. LC 80-54019. (Illus.). 190p. (Orig.). 1980. pap. 10.00 (ISBN 0-936922-01-X). Tamburitza.

Folk Arts of Norway. 2nd enl. ed. Janice S. Stewart. (Illus.). 12.50 (ISBN 0-8446-4610-5). Peter Smith.

Folk Arts of the Americas: 1981 Datebook, Organization of the American States. (Illus.). 1980. 6.95 (ISBN 0-87491-294-6). Acropolis.

Folk Classification: A Topically Arranged Bibliography of Contemporary & Background References Through 1971. Harold C. Conklin. LC 72-9400. 501p. 1972. pap. 4.00 o.p. (ISBN 0-913516-01-5). Yale U Anthro.

Folk Costumes of the World. Robert Harrold & Phyllida Legg. (Illus.). 1979. 10.95 (ISBN 0-7137-0868-9, Pub. by Blandford Pr England). Sterling.

Folk Crafts for World Friendship. Florence Temko. LC 76-4215. (gr. 3-5). 1976. 9.95 (ISBN 0-385-11115-0). Doubleday.

Folk Culture on St. Helena Island, South Carolina. Guy B. Johnson. LC 68-5945. xxiv, 183p. Repr. of 1930 ed. 15.00 (ISBN 0-8103-5015-7). Gale.

Folk Dances Around the World, Vol. 1. Janet J. Pholeric. LC 79-63544. 188p. 1980. 12.00 (ISBN 0-498-02259-5). A S Barnes.

Folk Designs from the Caucasus for Weaving & Needlework. Lyatif Kerimov. (Illus.). 6.75 (ISBN 0-8446-5054-4). Peter Smith.

Folk Embroidery of the USSR. Nina T. Klimova. 152p. 1981. 19.95 (ISBN 0-442-24464-9). Van Nos Reinhold.

Folk Festivals & the Foreign Community. Dorothy G. Spicer. LC 70-167201. 1976. Repr. of 1923 ed. 18.00 (ISBN 0-8103-4301-0). Gale.

Folk Guitar As a Profession. Happy Traum. Ed. by Dominic Milano. LC 76-57470. (Illus.). 70p. 1977. pap. 5.95 (ISBN 0-8256-9507-4). Guitar Player.

Folk Housing in Middle Virginia: A Structural Analysis of Historic Artifacts. Henry Glassie. LC 75-11653. (Illus.). 1975. 16.50x (ISBN 0-87049-173-3); pap. 9.50x (ISBN 0-87049-268-3). U of Tenn Pr.

Folk Laughter on the American Frontier. M. C. Boatright. 7.50 (ISBN 0-8446-0035-0). Peter Smith.

Folk Literature of the British Isles: Readings for Librarians, Teachers, & Those Who Work with Children & Young Adults. Eloise S. Norton. LC 78-10324. 1978. lib. bdg. 14.00 (ISBN 0-8108-1177-4). Scarecrow.

Folk-Literature of the Sephardic Jews, Vol. 1. The Judeo-Spanish Ballad Chapbooks of Yacob Abraham Yona. Samuel G. Armistead & Joseph H. Silverman. LC 71-78565. 1971. 38.50x (ISBN 0-520-01648-3). U of Cal Pr.

Folk Literature of the Yamana Indians: Martin Gusinde's Collection of Yamana Narratives. Ed. by Johannes Wilbert. LC 76-20026. 1977. 20.00x (ISBN 0-520-03299-3). U of Cal Pr.

Folk-Lore of China, & Its Affinities with That of the Aryan & Semitic Races. Nicholas B. Dennys. LC 79-89262. (Illus.). iv, 163p. 1972. Repr. of 1876 ed. 20.00 (ISBN 0-8103-3932-3). Gale.

Folk-Lore of East Yorkshire. John Nicholson. 168p. 1980. Repr. of 1972 ed. lib. bdg. 20.00 (ISBN 0-8492-1981-1). R West.

Folk-Lore of Plants. Thomas F. Thiselton-Dyer. LC 68-22054. 1968. Repr. of 1889 ed. 18.00 (ISBN 0-8103-3551-9). Gale.

Folk-Lore of Women As Illustrated by Legendary & Traditionary Tales, Folk-Rhymes, Proverbial Sayings, Superstitions Etc. Thomas F. Thiselton-Dyer. LC 68-24475. 1968. Repr. of 1906 ed. 15.00 (ISBN 0-8103-3555-7). Gale.

Folk Lore, Old Customs & Superstitions in Shakespeare Land. J. Harvey Bloom. LC 73-2830. viii, 167p. 1973. Repr. of 1930 ed. 10.00 (ISBN 0-8103-3269-8). Gale.

Folk Medicine. D. C. Jarvis. 1978. pap. 2.50 (ISBN 0-449-2416 -0, Crest). Fawcett.

Folk Medicine & Herbal Healing. George G. Meyer et al. write for info. (ISBN 0-398-04470-8). C C Thomas.

Folk Medicine of the Delaware & Related Algonkian Indians. Gladys Tantaquidgeon. LC 73-620801. (Pennsylvania Historical & Museum Commission Anthropological Ser.: No. 3). (Illus.). 145p. 1972. 7.00 (ISBN 0-911124-70-5); pap. 4.00 (ISBN 0-911124-69-1). Pa Hist & Mus.

Folk Music & Mass Media. Shyam Parmar. 1978. 7.50x o.p. (ISBN 0-8364-0137-9). South Asia Bks.

Folk Music in School. Ed. by R. Leach & R. Palmer. LC 77-71416. (Resources of Music Ser.). 1978. 17.50 (ISBN 0-521-21595-1); pap. 6.95 (ISBN 0-521-29206-9). Cambridge U Pr.

Folk Music: More Than a Song. Kristin Baggelaar & Donald Milton. LC 76-3547. (Illus.). 1976. 14.95 o.p. (ISBN 0-690-01159-8, TYC-T). T Y Crowell.

Folk of Christendom. Arthur Garrett. LC 79-92433. 1981. 49.95 (ISBN 0-8022-2363-X). Philos Lib.

Folk Origins of Indian Art. Curt Maury. LC 75-94909. (Illus.). 1969. 22.50x (ISBN 0-231-03198-X). Columbia U Pr.

Folk Poetry of Modern Greece. Roderick Beaton. LC 79-7644. (Illus.). 272p. 1980. 29.50 (ISBN 0-521-22853-0). Cambridge U Pr.

Folk Revival: The Rediscovery of a National Music. Fred Woods. (Illus.). 1979. 9.95 (ISBN 0-7137-0970-7, Pub by Blandford Pr England); pap. 4.95 (ISBN 0-7137-0993-6). Sterling.

Folk Song in England. A. L. Lloyd. 1968. pap. 3.65 o.p. (ISBN 0-7178-0278-7). Intl Pub Co.

Folk Songs & Dances of the Americas, 2 Bks. 1969. Bk. 1. pap. 1.00 (ISBN 0-8270-4450-X); Bk. 2. pap. 1.00 (ISBN 0-8270-4455-0). OAS.

Folk-Songs Mainly from West Virginia. John Harrington Cox. Ed. by George Herzog & Herbert Halpert. LC 76-58548. (Music Reprint Series). 1977. Repr. of 1939 ed. lib. bdg. 22.50 (ISBN 0-306-70786-1). Da Capo.

Folk Songs of North America. Alan Lomax. LC 60-1043. (Illus.). 1960. 14.95 o.p. (ISBN 0-385-04844-0). Doubleday.

Folk Songs of North America. Alan Lomax. (Illus.). 656p. 1975. pap. 8.95 (ISBN 0-385-03772-4, Dolp). Doubleday.

Folk Spirit of Albany. Tammis K. Groft. (Illus.). 1978. pap. 6.00 (ISBN 0-939072-00-9). Albany Hist & Art.

Folk Stories of the South. M. A. Jagendorf. LC 70-134672. (Illus.). (gr. 3 up). 1969. 8.95 (ISBN 0-8149-0000-3). Vanguard.

Folk Tale, Fiction & Saga in the Homeric Epics. Rhys Carpenter. (Sather Classical Lectures Ser.: No. 20). 1974. 17.00x (ISBN 0-520-02808-2). U of Cal Pr.

Folk Tales from Kashmir. S. L. Sadhu. 4.75x o.p. (ISBN 0-210-33861-X). Asia.

Folk Tales from Korea. Ed. & tr. by Zong In-Sob. LC 53-12953. 1979. 6.95 (ISBN 0-394-17096-2, E738, Ever). Grove.

Folk Tales from Korea. Compiled by & tr. by In Sob Zong. 176p. 1979. write for info. (ISBN 0-930878-15-9). Hollym Intl.

Folk Tales from Rajasthan. L. N. Birla. 1964. 4.75x o.p. (ISBN 0-210-34031-2). Asia.

Folk Tales of Himachal Pradesh. K. A. Seethalakshami. (Folk Tales of India Ser.: No. 8). 120p. 1972. 3.75x (ISBN 0-8002-0633-9). Intl Pubns Serv.

Folk Toys Around the World & How to Make Them. Joan Joseph. LC 72-1127. (Illus.). 96p. (gr. 5 up). 1972. 5.95 o.s.i. (ISBN 0-686-66677-1, Four Winds); PLB 5.41 o.s.i. (ISBN 0-8193-0599-5). Schol Bk Serv.

Folk Toys Around the World & How to Make Them. Joan Joseph. LC 72-1127. (Illus.). (gr. 3 up). 1972. 3.50 (ISBN 0-935738-01-0, 5016). US Comm UNICEF.

Folk Wines, Cordials & Brandies: How to Make Them, Along with the Pleasures of Their Lore. Moritz Jagendorf. LC 63-21854. (Illus.). 1963. 12.50 (ISBN 0-8149-0125-5). Vanguard.

Folklore & the Sea. 1st ed. Horace Beck. LC 73-6011. (American Maritime Library: Vol. 6). (Illus.). 1973. pap. 9.95 (ISBN 0-8195-6052-9). Columbia U Pr.

Folklore Bibliography for Nineteen Seventy-Six. Ed. by Merle E. Simmons. (Indiana University Folklore Institute Monograph Ser.: Vol. 33). 256p. 1981. text ed. 17.50 (ISBN 0-89727-023-1). Inst Study Hum.

Folklore Calendar. George Long. LC 76-78191. 1970. Repr. of 1930 ed. 19.00 (ISBN 0-8103-3367-8). Gale.

Folklore in America. Ed. by Tristram P. Coffin & Hennig Cohen. LC 79-97699. 1970. pap. 2.50 (ISBN 0-385-05071-2, A15, Anch). Doubleday.

Folklore International: Essays in Traditional Literature, Belief, & Custom in Honor of Wayland Debs Hand. Ed. by D. K. Wilgus & Carol Sommer. LC 67-16249. (Illus.). xiv, 259p. Repr. of 1967 ed. 20.00 (ISBN 0-8103-5023-8). Gale.

Folklore Nationalism & Politics. Ed. by Felix J. Oinas. 1977. pap. 9.95 (ISBN 0-89357-043-5). Slavica.

Folklore of American Weather. Eric Sloan. 1976. pap. 3.50 (ISBN 0-8015-2719-8, Hawthorn). Dutton.

Folklore of Buxar. Amir Hasan. 1978. 17.00x o.p. (ISBN 0-8364-0301-0). South Asia Bks.

Folklore of Capitalism. Thurman W. Arnold. 1937. 29.50x o.p. (ISBN 0-686-51386-X). Elliots Bks.

Folklore of Fairy-Tale. Macleod Yearsley. LC 68-31517. 1968. Repr. of 1924 ed. 18.00 (ISBN 0-8103-3457-7). Gale.

Folklore of Ireland. Sean O'Sullivan. 1974. 19.95 (ISBN 0-7134-2803-1, Pub. by Batsford England). David & Charles.

Folklore of Nepal. M. M. Sharma. 1979. 11.50x o.p. (ISBN 0-8364-0317-7). South Asia Bks.

Folklore of Other Lands: Folk Tales, Proverbs, Songs, Rhymes & Games of Italy, France, the Hispanic World & Germany. A. M. Selvi et al. 1956. 9.75 o.p. (ISBN 0-913298-24-7). S F Vanni.

Folklore of Prehistoric Sites in Britain. Leslie V. Grinsell. LC 76-8624. (Illus.). 304p. 1976. 24.00 (ISBN 0-7153-7241-6). David & Charles.

Folklore of the Cotswolds. Katherine M. Briggs. 1974. 19.95 (ISBN 0-7134-2831-7, Pub. by Batsford England). David & Charles.

Folklore of the Holy Land. James E. Hanauer. 280p. 1980. Repr. of 1935 ed. lib. bdg. 30.00 (ISBN 0-8492-5272-5). R West.

Folklore of the Jews. Angelo S. Rappoport. LC 71-167125. Repr. of 1937 ed. 18.00 (ISBN 0-8103-3864-5). Gale.

Folklore of the Oil Industry. Mody C. Boatright. LC 63-21186. 228p. 1980. Repr. of 1963 ed. 6.95 (ISBN 0-87074-007-5). SMU Press.

Folklore of the Scottish Highlands. Anne Ross. (Folklore of the British Isles Ser.). (Illus.). 174p. 1976. 11.50x (ISBN 0-87471-836-8). Rowman.

Folklore of the Sea. Margret Baker. (Illus.). 1979. 14.50 (ISBN 0-7153-7568-7). David & Charles.

Folklore: Performance & Communication. Ed. by D. Ben-Amos & K. Goldstein. LC 74-80122. (Approaches to Semiotics Ser.: No. 40). (Illus.). 308p. 1975. pap. text ed. 70.50x (ISBN 90-2793-143-7). Mouton.

Folklore Studies, Ancient & Modern. W. R. Halliday. LC 76-78175. 1971. Repr. of 1924 ed. 15.00 (ISBN 0-8103-3676-6). Gale.

Folklore Studies in the Twentieth Century: Proceedings of the Centenary Conference of the Folklore Society. Ed. by Venetia J. Newall. 1981. 85.00x (ISBN 0-8476-3638-0). Rowman.

Folklorist of the Coal Fields: George Korson's Life & Work. Angus K. Gillespie. LC 79-25839. (Illus.). 1980. 16.95 (ISBN 0-271-00255-7). Pa St U Pr.

Folksong-Plainsong: A Study in Origins & Musical Relationships. 2nd ed. G. B. Chambers. 1972. Repr. of 1956 ed. text ed. 9.50x (ISBN 0-85036-178-8). Humanities.

Folksongs of the Upper Thames. Alfred Williams. LC 68-31150. 1968. Repr. of 1923 ed. 18.00 (ISBN 0-8103-3421-6). Gale.

Folksongs of Virginia: A Checklist of the WPA Holdings at Alderman Library, University of Virginia. Bruce A. Rosenberg. LC 75-88185. 145p. 1969. 5.95 (ISBN 0-8139-0279-7). U Pr of Va.

Folkstories of Children. Brian Sutton-Smith. LC 80-5010. (American Folklore Society Ser.). 1980. 19.95x (ISBN 0-686-61087-3). U of Pa Pr.

Folktale. Stith Thompson. 1977. 20.00x (ISBN 0-520-03359-0); pap. 8.95x (ISBN 0-520-03537-2). U of Cal Pr.

Folktales from Kammu Two: A Story-Teller's Tales. Kristina Lindell et al. (Scandanavian Institute of Asian Studies Monograph: No. 40). (Orig.). 1980. pap. text ed. 10.50x (ISBN 0-7007-0131-1). Humanities.

Folktales of America, Vol 1. Catherine H. Ainsworth. LC 80-66300. (Folktales & Legends Ser.). 206p. 1980. pap. 10.00 (ISBN 0-933190-08-5). Clyde Pr.

Follain Initiation. Frank Graziano & Jean Follain. Tr. by Mary Feeney. 1979. pap. 24.00x (ISBN 0-931460-07-7). Bieler.

Follett Instant French Conversation Guide. 2.50 (ISBN 0-695-84196-3). Follett.

Follett Instent German Conversation Guide. Gerda Joseph. (Illus., Orig.). 1966. 2.50 (ISBN 0-695-84197-1). Follett.

Follett Instant Spanish Conversation Guide. Jack Joseph. (Illus., Orig.). 2.50 (ISBN 0-695-84199-8). Follett.

Follett-Velazquez Spanish & English Dictionary. rev. ed. 1977. 14.95 (ISBN 0-685-86169-4). Follett.

Follett Vest-Pocket Dictionaries: German. 344p. 1975. pap. 2.95 (ISBN 0-695-80608-4). Follett.

Follett Vest-Pocket Dictionaries: Webster Dictionary. rev. ed. 304p. 1975. pap. 2.95 (ISBN 0-695-80611-4). Follett.

Follies. Daniel M. Epstein. 1979. pap. 5.95 (ISBN 0-87951-075-7). Overlook Pr.

Follies. Daniel M. Epstein. LC 76-8059. 60p. 1977. 10.00 (ISBN 0-87951-048-X). Overlook Pr.

Follow a Fisher. Laurence Pringle. LC 72-83784. (Illus.). (gr. 2-5). 1973. 7.89 o.p. (ISBN 0-690-31237-7, TYC-J). T Y Crowell.

Follow Me. 1976. 5.95 o.p. (ISBN 0-88270-200-9); pap. 3.95 o.p. (ISBN 0-88270-201-7). Logos.

Follow Me! Charles Hunter. 1975. pap. 1.95 (ISBN 0-917726-35-9). Hunter Bks.

Follow My Black Plume. Geoffrey Trease. LC 63-13784. (gr. 6-10). 6.95 (ISBN 0-8149-0426-2). Vanguard.

Follow That Bus! Pat Hutchins. LC 76-21822. (Illus.). (gr. 2-5). 1977. PLB 7.92 (ISBN 0-688-84068-X). Greenwillow.

Follow That Ghost! Dale Fife. LC 79-11370. (Illus.). (gr. 1-5). 1979. PLB 7.95 (ISBN 0-525-30010-4, Unicorn Bk.). Dutton.

Follow the Leader. Linda DuBreuil. 1979. pap. 1.95 (ISBN 0-505-51433-8). Tower Bks.

Follow the Leader Series, 4 bks. Incl. Frightened Fisherman: Matthew 8: 23-27 (ISBN 0-310-41112-2, 11575); Greedy Tax Man: Matthew 9: 9-12 (ISBN 0-310-41122-X, 11576); Hungry Crowd: Matthew 14: 13-21 (ISBN 0-310-41142-4, 11578); Kind Soldier: Matthew 8: 5-13 (ISBN 0-310-41132-7, 11577). (Illus.). (gr. k-2). 1980. pap. 0.95 ea. Zondervan.

Follow the River. Lydia Dabcovich. LC 80-10173. (Illus.). 32p. (ps-2). 1980. PLB 8.95 (ISBN 0-525-30015-5). Dutton.

Follow the Shadows. Jocelyn Carew. 480p. (Orig.). 1980. pap. 2.75 (ISBN 0-380-41921-1, 44776). Avon.

Follow Through to Love. Elsie W. Strother. (YA) 1977. 4.95 o.p. (ISBN 0-685-73816-7, Avalon). Bouregy.

Follow Your Heart. Natalie Shipman. (YA) 1971. 5.95 (ISBN 0-685-03336-8, Avalon). Bouregy.

Follow Your Nose. Paul Showers. LC 63-15097. (Let's-Read-&-Find-Out Science Bk). (Illus.). (gr. k-3). 1963. PLB 7.89 (ISBN 0-690-31273-3, TYC-J); filmstrip with record 11.95 (ISBN 0-690-31274-1); film with cassette 14.95 (ISBN 0-690-31276-8). T Y Crowell.

Follow Your Star. Lucy Walker. 1976. pap. 1.75 (ISBN 0-345-29279-0). Ballantine.

Followers. Eve Bunting. (Science Fiction Ser.). (Illus.). (gr. 3-9). 1978. PLB 5.95 (ISBN 0-87191-627-4); pap. 2.95 (ISBN 0-89812-055-1). Creative Ed.

Followers of Christ: Perspectives on the Religious Life. Johannes B. Metz. LC 78-70817. 1979. pap. 3.95 (ISBN 0-8091-2138-7). Paulist Pr.

Following Christ. Ronald Klug. 1981. pap. 3.50 (ISBN 0-570-03826-X, 12-2791). Concordia.

Following God's Trailblazers: Kings & Prophets 14 Lessons, Vol. 4. (Footsteps of Faith Ser.). (gr. 3-9). 1958. pap. text ed. 1.95 (ISBN 0-86508-033-X); figures 7.95 (ISBN 0-86508-034-8). BCM Inc.

Following Gravity. James Applewwhite. LC 80-21578. 1981. 7.95x (ISBN 0-8139-0885-X). U Pr of Va.

Following Jesus. Segundo Galilea. Tr. by Helen Phillips. 128p. (Orig.). 1981. pap. 4.95 (ISBN 0-88344-136-5). Orbis Bks.

Following Joey Home. Meg Woodson. 160p. 1980. pap. 3.95 (ISBN 0-310-34861-7). Zondervan.

Following the Frontier: American Transportation in the Nineteenth Century. Leonard F. James. LC 68-13811. (Curriculum Related Bks). (Illus.). (gr. 5-8). 1968. 4.95 o.p. (ISBN 0-15-228827-9, HJ). HarBraceJ.

Following the Way: The Setting of John's Gospel. Bruce E. Schein. LC 79-54121. 224p. 1980. 12.50 (ISBN 0-8066-1758-6, 10-2348). Augsburg.

Folly River. Wendy Salinger. 1980. 7.95 (ISBN 0-525-10760-6). Dutton.

Folon: The Eyewitness. Jean-Michel Folon. (Illus.). 64p. 1980. 55.00 (ISBN 0-686-62699-0, 0906-5); limited edition aquatint with signed book 500.00 (ISBN 0-686-62700-8, 84909-1). Abrams.

Fond Farewell to Dying. Syd Logsdon. (Orig.). 1981. pap. text ed. 2.25 (ISBN 0-671-41099-7). PB.

Fondue: The Fine Art of Fondue, Chinese Wok & Chafing Dish Cooking. Carol D. Brent. LC 77-95289. 4.95 o.p. (ISBN 0-385-00606-3). Doubleday.

Fondues. Exner. 1981. 8.95 (ISBN 0-8120-5404-0). Barron.

Fonteyn: The Making of a Legend. Keith Money. LC 74-3578. (Illus.). 320p. 1974. 25.00 o.p. (ISBN 0-688-61163-X). Morrow.

Food. Irving Adler. LC 76-54783. (Reason Why Ser.). (Illus.). (gr. 2-5). 1977. PLB 6.89 (ISBN 0-381-90051-7, JD-J). John Day.

Food. Stanley L. Weinberg & Herbert J. Stoltze. (Action Biology Ser.). (gr. 9-12). 1974. pap. text ed. 3.20 (ISBN 0-205-04144-2, 6741444). Allyn.

Food Additives. R. J. Taylor. LC 79-42729. (Institution of Environmental Sciences Ser.). 126p. 1980. 30.00 (ISBN 0-471-27684-7, Pub. by Wiley Interscience); pap. 13.75 (ISBN 0-471-27683-9). Wiley.

Food Additives for Hyperactive Children. C. Keith Connors. 180p. 1980. 18.50 (ISBN 0-306-40400-1, Plenum Pr). Plenum Pub.

Food Additives, Student Syllabus. Ronald B. Froehlich. pap. text ed. 4.85 (ISBN 0-89420-076-3, 168008); cassette recordings 39.00 (ISBN 0-89420-205-7, 16800O). Natl Book.

Food Aid & Policy for Economic Development: An Annotated Bibliography & Directory. Melissa L. Cadet. (Illus.). 187p. (Orig.). 1981. 24.95 (ISBN 0-938398-00-8); pap. 16.95. Trans Tech Mgmt.

Food Allergy. J. W. Gerrard. (Illus.). 312p. 1980. 28.50 (ISBN 0-398-04038-9); pap. 19.75 (ISBN 0-398-04041-9). C C Thomas.

Food Allergy & the Allergic Patient: A Simple Review of Problems Encountered by the Recently Diagnosed Patient. rev. ed. E. Louis Taube. 96p. 1978. pap. 6.50 (ISBN 0-398-02733-1). C C Thomas.

Food Allergy, Its Manifestations & Control, & the Elimination Diets - a Compendium: With Important Consideration of Inhalant, Drug, & Infectant Allergy. Albert H. Rowe & Albert Rowe, Jr. (Illus.). 696p. 1972. text ed. 27.75 (ISBN 0-398-02395-6). C C Thomas.

Food Allergy: Provocative Testing & Injection Therapy. Joseph B. Miller. 160p. 1972. pap. 15.25 spiral (ISBN 0-398-02601-7). C C Thomas.

Food: An Energy Exchange System. Don Fabun. 1971. pap. text ed. 2.50x (ISBN 0-02-475370-X, 47537). Macmillan.

Food: An Informal Dictionary. Waverley Root. (Illus.). 1980. 29.95 (ISBN 0-671-22589-8). S&S.

Food Analysis Laboratory Experiments. 2nd ed. Clifton Meloan & Y. Pomeranz. (Illus.). 1980. pap. 10.50 (ISBN 0-87055-351-8). AVI.

Food Analysis Laboratory Experiments. Clifton E. Meloan & Y. Pomeranz. (Illus.). 143p. 1973. pap. text ed. 10.50 o.p. (ISBN 0-87055-149-3). AVI.

Food Analysis: Theory & Practice. rev. ed. Y. Pomeranz & Clifton E. Meloan. 1978. 23.50 (ISBN 0-87055-238-4). AVI.

Food & Agriculture: A Scientific American Book. Scientific American Editors. (Illus.). 1976. 16.95x (ISBN 0-7167-0382-3); pap. 8.95x (ISBN 0-7167-0381-5). W H Freeman.

Food & Agriculture in Global Perspective: Discussions in the Committee of the Whole of the United States. Toivo Miljan et al. (Illus.). 260p. 28.00 (ISBN 0-08-025550-7). Pergamon.

Food & Arthritis. Gaynor Maddox. (Illus.). 224p. 1973. pap. 1.25 o.p. (ISBN 0-445-00151-8). Popular Lib.

Food & Beverage Cost Controls. Bruno Maizel. LC 77-142501. 1971. text ed. 13.95 (ISBN 0-672-96077-X); tchr's manual 6.67 (ISBN 0-672-96079-6); wkbk. 6.50 (ISBN 0-672-96078-8). Bobbs.

Food & Beverage Industries: A Bibliography & Guidebook. Albert C. Vara. LC 70-102058. (Management Information Guide Ser.: No. 16). 1970. 30.00 (ISBN 0-8103-0816-9). Gale.

Food & Beverage Management. David A. Fearn. 320p. 1973. 29.95 (ISBN 0-408-70158-7). Transatlantic.

Food & Beverage Mycology. L. R. Beuchat. (Illus.). 1978. lib bdg. 35.50 o.p. (ISBN 0-87055-247-3); pap. text ed. 22.50 (ISBN 0-87055-293-7). AVI.

Food & Beverage Purchasing. Bruno Maizel. LC 77-142502. 1971. text ed. 14.95 (ISBN 0-672-96071-0); tchr's manual 5.90 (ISBN 0-672-96073-7); wkbk. 6.50 (ISBN 0-672-96072-9). Bobbs.

Food & Beverage Service. D. H. Lillicrap. (Illus.). 218p. 1971. pap. 13.95x (ISBN 0-7131-1664-1). Intl Ideas.

Food & Clothing. H. K. Idleman & E. N. Stanton. (Contemporary Consumer Ser.). 1976. text ed. 4.24 (ISBN 0-07-031689-9, G); tchr's manual & key 4.95 (ISBN 0-07-031690-2). McGraw.

Food & Cooking. Margaret Baker. (Junior Reference Ser.). (Illus.). 64p. (gr. 7 up). 7.95 (ISBN 0-7136-1465-X). Dufour.

Food & Development in the Semi-Arid Zone of East Africa. Philip W. Porter. LC 79-20312. (Foreign & Comparative Studies-African Ser.: No. XXXII). 110p. 1979. pap. text ed. 7.00x (ISBN 0-915984-54-7). Syracuse U Foreign Comp.

Food & Drug Law, Cases & Materials. Richard A. Merrill & Peter B. Hutt. LC 80-23167. (University Casebook Ser.). 959p. 1980. text ed. write for info. (ISBN 0-88277-016-0). Foundation Pr.

Food & Economics. Lois A. Hungate & Ralph W. Sherman. (Illus.). 1979. pap. text ed. 13.50 (ISBN 0-87055-229-5). AVI.

Food & Health of Western Man. James L. Mount. LC 75-11989. 270p. 1975. 19.95x (ISBN 0-470-61957-0). Halsted Pr.

Food & Heat Producing Solar Greenhouse. rev. ed. Bill Yanda & Rick Fisher. LC 79-91276. (Illus.). 208p. (Orig.). 1980. pap. 8.00 (ISBN 0-912528-20-6). John Muir.

Food & Menu Dictionary. C. Dahl. LC 77-123002. 1972. 10.95 (ISBN 0-8436-0556-1). CBI Pub.

Food & Nutrition. James J. Haggerty & William H. Sebrell, Jr. (Life Science Library). (Illus.). (gr. 5 up). 1967. PLB 10.20 o.p. (ISBN 0-8094-0481-8, Pub. by Time-Life). Silver.

Food & Nutrition Bibliography. 9th ed. 1980. pap. text ed. 12.50x (ISBN 0-912700-77-7). Oryx Pr.

Food & Nutrition Bibliography. 10th ed. 1981. pap. text ed. 12.50x (ISBN 0-912700-78-5). Oryx Pr.

Food & Population in the Middle East. Ed. by Elias H. Tuma. LC 76-57917. 83p. 1976. pap. 5.00 (ISBN 0-934484-08-2). Inst Mid East & North Africa.

Food & Population: Priorities in Decision Making. Ed. by T. Dams et al. 208p. 1979. text ed. 21.00x (ISBN 0-566-00250-7, Pub. by Gower Pub Co England). Renouf.

Food & the Consumer. Amihud Kramer. (Illus.). 1973. pap. text ed. 8.50 o.p. (ISBN 0-87055-148-5). AVI.

Food & the Consumer. rev. ed. Amihud Kramer. (Illus.). 1980. pap. text ed. 12.50 (ISBN 0-87055-339-9). AVI.

Food & Wine of Southwest France. Michael Brown. (Illus.). 216p. 1981. 35.00 (ISBN 0-7134-1847-8, Pub. by Batsford England). David & Charles.

Food & Your Well-Being. Theodore P. Labuza. (Illus.). 1977. pap. text ed. 11.95 (ISBN 0-8299-0129-9); instrs.' manual & study guide 4.95 (ISBN 0-8299-0162-0). West Pub.

Food As a Crutch. Shirley Schwarzrock & C. Gilbert Wrenn. (Coping with Ser.). (Illus.). (gr. 7-12). 1971. pap. text ed. 1.30 (ISBN 0-913476-18-8). Am Guidance.

Food-Borne Infections & Intoxications. H. Riemann. (Food Science & Technology Ser. of Monographs). 1969. 67.50 o.p. (ISBN 0-12-588350-1). Acad Pr.

Food by Appointment: Royal Recipes 1066. Michele Brown. (Illus.). 1978. 17.95 (ISBN 0-241-89635-5, Pub. by Hamish Hamilton England). David & Charles.

Food Care & Food Storage. Ser-Vol-Tel Institute. (Foodservice Career Education Ser.). 1974. pap. 4.95 (ISBN 0-8436-2014-5). CBI Pub.

Food Chains & Ecosystems: Ecology for Young Experimenters. George I. Schwartz & Bernice S. Schwartz. LC 73-15171. (gr. 5-7). 1974. 4.95 o.p. (ISBN 0-385-08000-X). Doubleday.

Food Chemicals Codex. 2nd ed. Food Protection Committee. (Illus.). 1088p. 1972. 28.00 (ISBN 0-309-01949-4). Natl Acad Pr.

Food Chemistry. Leonard W. Aurand & A. E. Woods. (Illus.). 1973. text ed. 19.50 o.p. (ISBN 0-87055-142-6). AVI.

Food Chemistry. 3rd, rev. ed. Lillian Hoagland Meyer. (Illus.). 1978. Repr. soft cover 13.50 (ISBN 0-87055-171-X). AVI.

Food Colloids. H. D. Graham. (Illus.). 1977. lib. bdg. 39.50 (ISBN 0-87055-201-5). AVI.

Food Colorimetry: Theory & Applications. F. G. Francis & F. M. Clydesdale. (Illus.). 1975. text ed. 39.50 (ISBN 0-87055-183-3). AVI.

Food Colors. Food Protection Committee & Food And Nutrition Board. LC 70-176233. 1971. pap. 3.25 o.p. (ISBN 0-309-01930-3). Natl Acad Pr.

Food Combining Handbook. Gary Null et al. 1973. pap. 1.75 (ISBN 0-515-05779-7, V3202). Jove Pubns.

Food Composition: Tables for Use in the Middle East. P. L. Pellet & Sossy Shadarevian. 1970. pap. 10.00x (ISBN 0-8156-6032-4, Am U Beirut). Syracuse U Pr.

Food Consciousness for Spiritual Development. Jacques De Langre. LC 80-84993. (Illus., Orig.). 1980. pap. 6.00 (ISBN 0-916508-05-6). Happiness Pr.

Food Conspiracy Cookbook & Member's Manual. Lois Wickstrom. (Illus.). 215p. 1973. 3.50 (ISBN 0-916176-01-0). Sproing.

Food Consumption & Planning. Ed. by K. K. Rao. 1976. 94.00 (ISBN 0-08-016459-5). Pergamon.

Food Control in Action. Ed. by P. O. Dennis et al. (Illus.). xii, 280p. 1980. 45.00x (ISBN 0-85334-894-4). Burgess-Intl Ideas.

Food Costs-Farm Prices: A Compilation or Information Relating to Agriculture. U. S. Congress, House Committee on Agriculture. (Illus.). x, 114p. 1973. Repr. of 1970 ed. 15.00 (ISBN 0-8103-3278-7). Gale.

Food Crisis in Prehistory: Over Population & Origins of Agriculture. Mark N. Cohen. LC 76-41858. 1979. 20.00x (ISBN 0-300-02016-3); pap. 7.95x (ISBN 0-300-02351-0). Yale U Pr.

Food Crops of the Lowland Tropics. Ed. by C. L. Leakey & J. B. Wills. 1977. 45.00x (ISBN 0-19-854517-7). Oxford U Pr.

Food Dehydration, 2 vols. 2nd ed. Wallace B. Van Arsdel et al. Incl. Vol. 1. Drying Methods & Phenomena. 34.50 (ISBN 0-87055-137-X); Vol. 2. Practices & Applications. 42.50 (ISBN 0-87055-138-8). (Illus.). 1973. AVI.

Food Dryer Handbook. Pamela G. Wubben. 55p. 1980. pap. 3.50 (ISBN 0-935442-02-2). One Percent.

Food, Energy & Future of Society. David Pimentel. 1980. pap. 3.00x (ISBN 0-87081-089-8). Colo Assoc.

Food, Energy & Society. David Pimentel & Marcia Pimentel. LC 79-9484. 1979. pap. 14.95x (ISBN 0-470-26840-9). Halsted Pr.

Food Engineering System, Vol. 2: Utilities. Arthur W. Farrall. (Illus.). 1979. pap. text ed. 23.50 (ISBN 0-87055-283-X). AVI.

Food Engineering Systems: Operations, Vol. No. 1. A. W. Farrall. (Illus.). 1976. lib. bdg. 37.50 (ISBN 0-87055-190-6); pap. text ed. 23.50 (ISBN 0-87055-297-X). AVI.

Food Equipment Facts. new ed. Carl Scriven & James Stevens. LC 80-67617. (First Ser.). 429p. (Orig.). 1980. pap. 9.95 (ISBN 0-9604902-0-5). Concept Design.

Food Facts & Fallacies. Allan G. Cameron. (Illus., Orig.). 1973. pap. 4.95 (ISBN 0-571-10290-5, Pub. by Faber & Faber). Merrimack Bk Serv.

Food First. Frances M. Lappe & Joseph Collins. 1979. pap. 2.95 (ISBN 0-345-29045-3). Ballantine.

Food Fit for Humans. Frank A. Wilson. 1980. 15.00x (ISBN 0-85207-132-9, Pub. by Daniel Co England). State Mutual Bk.

Food Fit for Humans. Frank A. Wilson. 1975. 7.25x (ISBN 0-8464-1011-7). Beekman Pubs.

Food Flavorings: Composition, Manufacture & Use. 2nd, rev. ed. Joseph Merory. 1968. 37.50 o.p. (ISBN 0-87055-024-1). AVI.

Food for Beauty. rev. ed. Helena Rubinstein. 256p. 1977. pap. 1.95 (ISBN 0-915962-19-5). Larchmont Bks.

Food for Fifty. 6th ed. B. B. West et al. LC 78-21921. 1979. text ed. 21.95 (ISBN 0-471-02688-3). Wiley.

Food for God's Children. Raphael Gasson. 1977. pap. 3.95 o.p. (ISBN 0-88270-255-6). Logos.

Food for Lambs. C. E. Orr. 168p. pap. 1.50. Faith Pub Hse.

Food for Modern Living. rev. ed. Irene E. McDermott et al. 1973. text ed. 12.60 o.p. (ISBN 0-397-40201-5); 14.52 o.p. (ISBN 0-397-40202-3). Lippincott.

Food for Plants. (Discovering Soils Ser.: No. 6). 33p. 1978. pap. 5.00 (ISBN 0-643-02170-1, CO13, CSIRO). Unipub.

Food for Thought. 2nd ed. T. P. Labuza & A. Elizabeth Sloan. (Illus.). 1977. pap. text ed. 8.50 (ISBN 0-87055-244-9). AVI.

Food for Today. Helen Kowtaluk & Alice Kopan. 1977. 15.00 (ISBN 0-87002-181-8); pap. 16.80 tchr. resource guide (ISBN 0-87002-187-7); student activity guide 2.60 (ISBN 0-87002-197-4). Bennett IL.

Food for War - Food for Peace: U. S. Food Aid in a Global Context. Mitchell B. Wallerstein. 378p. 1980. text ed. 30.00x (ISBN 0-262-23106-9). MIT Pr.

Food, Foreign Policy & Raw Materials Cartels. William Schneider. LC 76-492. (Strategy Papers Ser.: No. 28). 1975. 6.50x (ISBN 0-8448-0921-7); pap. 2.95x (ISBN 0-8448-0922-5). Crane-Russak Co.

Food from the Arab World. Marie Khayat. pap. 5.00x (ISBN 0-686-63568-X). Intl Bk Ctr.

Food from the Far West. or, American Agriculture. James MacDonald. 1980. lib. bdg. 69.95 (ISBN 0-8490-3187-7). Gordon Pr.

Food from the Sea: The Economics & Politics of Ocean Fisheries. Frederick W. Bell. LC 77-28756. (Special Studies in Natural Resources & Energy Management Ser.). (Illus.). 1978. lib. bdg. 30.00x (ISBN 0-89158-403-X); pap. text ed. 12.50x (ISBN 0-89158-353-X). Westview.

Food from the Seashore. Kendall McDonald. (Illus.). 128p. 1980. 11.95 (ISBN 0-7207-1183-5, Pub. by Michael Joseph); pap. 6.50 (ISBN 0-7207-1235-1). Merrimack Bk Serv.

Food from the Wild. Judy Urquhart. LC 77-85026. (Penny Pinchers Ser.). 1978. 2.95 (ISBN 0-7153-7545-8). David & Charles.

Food from Waste. Ed. by G. G. Birch et al. (Illus.). 1976. 67.20x (ISBN 0-85334-659-3, Pub. by Applied Science). Burgess-Intl Ideas.

Food, Fuel, & Shelter: A Watershed Analysis of Land-Use Trade-Offs in a Semi-Arid Region. Timothy D. Tregarthen. LC 77-19355. (Westview Special Studies in Natural Resources & Energy Management Ser.). 1978. lib. bdg. 20.00x (ISBN 0-89158-070-0). Westview.

Food Fundamentals. 3rd ed. Margaret McWilliams. LC 78-65888. 1979. 20.95x (ISBN 0-471-02691-3). Wiley.

Food Grain Distribution in Selected Asian Countries. 1979. pap. 13.25 (ISBN 92-833-1452-2, APO77, APO). Unipub.

Food Hygiene & Food Hazards. 2nd ed. A. B. Christie & Mary C. Christie. (Illus.). 1977. 12.95 o.p. (ISBN 0-571-04949-4, Pub. by Faber & Faber); pap. 5.95 (ISBN 0-571-10902-0). Merrimack Bk Serv.

Food in Civilization: How History Has Been Affected by Human Tastes. Carson I. Ritchie. 192p. 1981. 8.95 (ISBN 0-8253-0037-1). Beaufort Bks NY.

Food in History. Reay Tannahill. LC 75-160342. (Illus.). 448p. 1974. pap. 8.95 (ISBN 0-8128-1752-4). Stein & Day.

Food in Perspective: Third International Conference of Ethnological Food Research. Alexander Fenton & Trefor Owen. 1980. text ed. 34.50x (ISBN 0-85976-044-8). Humanities.

Food in Theory & Practice. Eva Medved. LC 77-76340. (Illus.). 1978. text ed. 15.95x (ISBN 0-916434-24-9). Plycon Pr.

Food in Vogue. Maxime De La Falaise. LC 79-8920. (Illus.). 336p. 1980. 15.95 (ISBN 0-385-09220-2). Doubleday.

Food Inflation Fighters Handbook. Judith L. Klinger. (Illus.). 1980. pap. 5.95 (ISBN 0-449-90030-4, Columbine). Fawcett.

Food Irradiation. (Illus., Orig., Eng., Fr., Rus. & Span.). 1966. pap. 44.00 (ISBN 92-0-010166-6, IAEA). Unipub.

Food Is Your Best Medicine. Henry G. Bieler. 256p. 1973. pap. 2.45 (ISBN 0-394-71837-2, V-837, Vin). Random.

Food Law Handbook. Harold W. Schultz. (Illus.). 1981. lib. bdg. 79.50 (ISBN 0-87055-372-0). AVI.

Food-Lover's Garden. Angelo M. Pellegrini. LC 76-106621. (Illus.). 1970. pap. 4.95 (ISBN 0-914842-06-4). Madrona Pubs.

Food Marketing. rev. ed. L. B. Darrah. 1971. 25.95 (ISBN 0-8260-2345-2). Wiley.

Food Merchandising: Principles & Practices. Theodore W. Leed & Gene A. German. LC 73-88739. (Illus.). 1973. 14.95 (ISBN 0-686-01267-4). Lebhar Friedman.

Food Microbiology. A. N. Sharpe. (Illus.). 238p. 1980. 24.75 (ISBN 0-398-04017-6). C C Thomas.

Food Microbiology: Public Health & Spoilage Aspects. M. P. De Figueiredo & D. F. Splittstoesser. (Illus.). 1976. lib. bdg. 39.50 (ISBN 0-87055-209-0). AVI.

Food: Multilingual Thesaurus. Ed. by Commission of European Communities, Directorate-Center for Research-Science & Education. 1979. 4 vols. & index 180.00 (ISBN 0-89664-036-1, Pub. by K G Saur). Gale.

Food, Nutrition, & the Young Child. Jeannette Endres & Robert E. Rockwell. LC 80-10848. (Illus.). 1980. pap. text ed. 10.95 (ISBN 0-8016-4139-X). Mosby.

Food, Nutrition & You. Fergus S. Clydesdale & F. J. Francis. (Illus.). 1977. lib. bdg. 12.95 (ISBN 0-13-323048-1); pap. text ed. 8.95 (ISBN 0-13-323030-9). P-H.

Food of Death: Fifty-One Tales. Lord Edward Dunsany. Ed. by R. Reginald & Douglas Menville. LC 80-19151. (Newcastle Forgotten Fantasy Library: Vol. 3). Orig. Title: Fifty-One Tales. 138p. 1980. Repr. of 1974 ed. lib. bdg. 9.95x (ISBN 0-89370-502-0). Borgo Pr.

Food of Love: Princess Edmond De Polignac (1865-1943) & Her Salon. Michael De Cossart. (Illus.). 1978. 21.95 o.p. (ISBN 0-241-89785-8, Pub. by Hamish Hamilton England). David & Charles.

Food Oils & Their Uses. Theodore J. Weiss. (Illus.). 1970. lib. bdg. 27.50 (ISBN 0-87055-093-4). AVI.

Food on the Frontier: Minnesota Cooking from 1850 to 1900, with Selected Recipes. Marjorie Kreidberg. LC 75-34214. (Illus.). 313p. 1975. 10.50 (ISBN 0-87351-096-8); pap. 6.50 (ISBN 0-87351-097-6). Minn Hist.

Food or Fuel: New Competition for World's Cropland. 43p. 1980. pap. 2.95 (ISBN 0-686-63000-9, WW-35, WW). Unipub.

Food Packaging. Stanley Sacharow & Roger C. Griffin, Jr. (Illus.). 1970. 25.50 o.p. (ISBN 0-87055-070-5). AVI.

Food, People & Nutrition. Eleanor F. Eckstein. (Illus.). 1980. pap. text ed. 19.50 (ISBN 0-87055-355-0). AVI.

Food Pharmacology. N. Sapeika. 200p. 1969. pap. 12.00 spiral (ISBN 0-398-01648-8). C C Thomas.

Food Plants of the North American Indians. Elias Yanovsky. 1980. lib. bdg. 49.95 (ISBN 0-8490-3108-7). Gordon Pr.

Food Policies. John R. Tarrant. LC 79-40740. (Wiley Series on Studies in Environmental Management & Resources Development). 338p. 1980. 44.50 (ISBN 0-471-27656-1, Pub. by Wiley-Interscience). Wiley.

Food Policies: The Regional Conflict. Ed. by David N. Balaam & Michael J. Carey. LC 79-48097. 280p. 1981. text ed. 24.50 (ISBN 0-916672-52-2). Allanheld.

Food Policy: The Responsibility of the United States in the Life & Death Choices. Ed. by Peter G. Brown & Henry Shue. LC 76-57803. (Illus.). 1979. pap. text ed. 8.95 (ISBN 0-02-905170-3). Free Pr.

Food Power. George Schwartz. 204p. 1981. pap. 4.95 (ISBN 0-07-055674-1). McGraw.

Food Power: A Doctor's Guide to Commonsense Nutrition. E. Earle Arnow. LC 75-185419. (Illus.). 320p. 1972. 14.95 (ISBN 0-911012-37-0). Nelson-Hall.

Food Preparation Recipes. Kathryn B. Niles. 1955. text ed. 19.50x (ISBN 0-471-63888-9). Wiley.

Food Preservation by Irradiation, Vol. I. (Illus.). 1978. pap. 51.50 (ISBN 92-0-010278-6, ISP 470-1, IAEA). Unipub.

Food Preservation by Irradiation, Vol. 2. (Illus.). 1978. pap. 37.50 (ISBN 92-0-010378-2, ISP470-2, IAEA). Unipub.

Food Price Policies & Nutrition in Latin America. (Food & Nutrition Bulletin Ser.: Suppl. 3). 170p. 1980. pap. 15.00 (ISBN 92-808-0128-7, TUNU087, UNU). Unipub.

Food Process Engineering. D. R. Heldman. (Illus.). 1975. text ed. 32.00 o.p. (ISBN 0-87055-174-4); pap. text ed. 20.00 o.p. (ISBN 0-87055-298-8). AVI.

Food Process Engineering. D. R. Heldman & R. P. Singh. (Illus.). 1981. pap. text ed. 24.00 (ISBN 0-686-69097-4). AVI.

Food Process Engineering: Vol. 1 Food Processing Systems. Ed. by P. Linko et al. (Illus.). xii, 981p. 1980. 210.00x (ISBN 0-85334-896-0). Burgess-Intl Ideas.

Food Process Engineering: Volume 2--Enzyme Engineering in Food Processing. Ed. by P. Linko et al. (Illus.). vii, 328p. 1980. 75.00x (ISBN 0-85334-897-9). Burgess-Intl Ideas.

Food Processing Operations, 3 Vols. Maynard A. Joslyn & J. L. Heid. 1963-64. 25.50 ea. o.p. Vol. 1 (ISBN 0-87055-015-2). Vol. 2 (ISBN 0-87055-016-0). Vol. 3 (ISBN 0-87055-017-9). AVI.

Food Processing Plant. Melvin Berger. (Industry at Work Ser.). (gr. 4-6). 1977. 5.90 (ISBN 0-531-01336-7). Watts.

Food Processing Waste Management. John H. Green & Amihud Kramer. (Illus.). 1979. text ed. 39.00 (ISBN 0-87055-331-3). AVI.

Food Processor Bread Cookbook. Consumer Guide. (Illus.). 1980. 14.95 (ISBN 0-671-25201-1, 25201); pap. 7.95 (ISBN 0-671-25138-4, 25138). S&S.

Food Processor Cookbook. Linda Carter & Culinary Arts Institute Staff. Ed. by Edward G. Finnegan. LC 78-54620. (Adventures in Cooking Ser). (Illus.) 1980. cancelled (ISBN 0-8326-0608-1, 1517); pap. 3.95 (ISBN 0-8326-0607-3, 2517). Delair.

Food Processor Cookbook. Fayal Greene. 1977. pap. 1.50 o.p. (ISBN 0-445-08598-3). Popular Lib.

Food Processor Recipes for Conventional & Microwave Cooking. Sharon Dlugosch & Joyce Battcher. LC 78-74899. 1979. pap. 3.50 (ISBN 0-918420-03-2); pap. 12.00 tchrs' manual (ISBN 0-918420-04-0). Brighton Pubns.

Food Production & Its Consequences. new ed. Phillip E. Smith. LC 75-28640. (Cummings Modular Program in Anthropology). 1975. text ed. 7.50 o.p. (ISBN 0-8465-6718-0); pap. text ed. 5.50 o.p. (ISBN 0-8465-6719-9). Benjamin-Cummings.

Food Products Formulary: Meats, Poultry, Fish & Shellfish. Stephan Komarik et al. (Illus.). 1974. text ed. 49.50 (ISBN 0-87055-152-3). AVI.

Food Products Formulary, Vol. 2: Cereals, Baked Goods, Dairy & Egg Products. Donald K. Tressler & William J. Sultan. (Illus.). 1975. lib. bdg. 49.50 (ISBN 0-87055-170-1). AVI.

Food Products Formulary, Vol. 3: Fruit, Vegetables & Nut Products. Donald K. Tressler & Jasper G. Woodroof. (Illus.). 1976. lib. bdg. 49.50 (ISBN 0-87055-202-3). AVI.

Food Protein Sources. Ed. by N. W. Pirie. LC 74-12962. (International Biological Programme Ser.: No. 4). (Illus.). 288p. 1975. 47.50 (ISBN 0-521-20588-3). Cambridge U Pr.

Food Proteins. Ed. by John R. Whitaker & Steven R. Tannenbaum. (Illus.). 1977. lib. bdg. 39.00 (ISBN 0-87055-230-9). AVI.

Food Quality & Nutrition: Research Priorities for Thermal Processing. Ed. by W. K. Downey. (Illus.). 1978. text ed. 71.30x (ISBN 0-85334-803-0, Pub. by Applied Science). Burgess-Intl Ideas.

Food Quality Assurance. Wilbur A Gould. (Illus.). 1977. text ed. 29.50 (ISBN 0-87055-219-8); pap. text ed. 18.50 (ISBN 0-87055-294-5). AVI.

Food: Readings from Scientific American. Intro. by Johan E. Hoff & Jules Janick. LC 73-3138. (Illus.). 1973. text ed. 17.95x (ISBN 0-7167-0876-0); pap. text ed. 9.95x (ISBN 0-7167-0875-2). W H Freeman.

Food Retailing Industry: Market Structure, Profits, & Prices. Bruce W. Marion et al. LC 78-19751. 1979. 22.95 (ISBN 0-03-046106-5). Praeger.

Food Safety. Howard R. Roberts. 448p. 1981. 39.50 (ISBN 0-471-06458-0, Pub. by Wiley-Interscience). Wiley.

Food Sanitation. Rufus K. Guthrie. 1972. text ed. 21.50 o.p. (ISBN 0-87055-122-1). AVI.

Food Sanitation. 2nd ed. Rufus K. Guthrie. (Illus.). 1980. lib. bdg. 21.50 (ISBN 0-87055-361-5). AVI.

Food Science. Helen Charley. LC 80-17047. 530p. 1970. 19.50 (ISBN 0-8260-1925-0). Wiley.

Food Science. 3rd ed. Norman N. Potter. 1978. text ed. 22.00 (ISBN 0-87055-275-9). AVI.

Food Science: A Chemical Approach. 3rd ed. Brian A. Fox & Allan G. Cameron. 1977. 10.50x (ISBN 0-8448-0938-1). Crane-Russak Co.

Food Science & Nutrition: Current Issues & Answers. Fergus Clydesdale. (Illus.). 1979. ref. 16.95 (ISBN 0-13-323162-3). P-H.

Food Security for Developing Countries. Ed. by Alberto Valdes. 350p. 1981. lib. bdg. 25.00x (ISBN 0-86531-071-8). Westview.

Food Security Issues in the Arab Near East: A Report of the United Nations Economic Commission for Western Asia. A A. El-Sherbini. LC 79-40254. (Illus.). 1979. 39.50 (ISBN 0-08-023447-X). Pergamon.

Food Service Careers. Cornelius. 1979. text ed. 14.60 (ISBN 0-87002-206-7); avail. tchr's guide; student's guide 2.96 (ISBN 0-87002-165-6). Bennett IL.

Food Service Equipment. 2nd ed. Anna K. Jernigan & Lynne N. Ross. (Illus.). 122p. 1980. pap. text ed. 6.75 (ISBN 0-8138-0550-3). Iowa St U Pr.

Food Service Facilities Planning. E. A. Kazarian. (Illus.). 1975. text ed. 25.50 (ISBN 0-87055-168-X). AVI.

Food Service Lodging English. Peter Klain. (Illus., Prog. Bk.). 1971. pap. 7.95 (ISBN 0-8436-0531-6). CBI Pub.

Food Service Management. 3rd ed. Charles E. Eshbach. LC 79-20378. 1979. pap. text ed. 11.95 (ISBN 0-8436-2176-1). CBI Pub.

Food Service Management: Study Course. Anna K. Jernigan et al. 1977. pap. text ed. 6.95 (ISBN 0-8138-0790-5). Iowa St U Pr.

Food Service Science. Laura L. Smith & Lewis J. Minor. (Illus.). 1974. pap. text ed. 19.00 (ISBN 0-87055-382-8). AVI.

Food Service Supervisor, School Lunch Manager. Arco Editorial Board. LC 65-27819. (Orig.). 1968. lib. bdg. 8.50 o.p. (ISBN 0-668-02022-9). Arco.

Food Service Systems: Analysis, Design & Implementation. Ed. by G. E. Livingston & Charlotte M. Chang. 1980. 30.50 (ISBN 0-12-453150-4). Acad Pr.

Food Service Trends. Ed. by Charles E. Eshbach. LC 74-220. 330p. 1974. 15.95 (ISBN 0-8436-0581-2). CBI Pub.

Food Study Manual. 2nd ed. Helen Charley. LC 79-75636. (Illus.). 275p. (Orig.). 1971. 14.50 (ISBN 0-8260-1940-4, 14195). Wiley.

Food Systems. Boy Scouts of America. LC 19-600. (Merit Badge Ser.). (Illus.). 48p. (gr. 6-12). 1978. pap. 0.70x (ISBN 0-8395-3399-3). BSA.

Food to Improve Your Health. Linda Pelstring & Jo A. Hauck. 256p. 1975. pap. 1.50 o.p. (ISBN 0-523-00637-3). Pinnacle Bks.

Food Values & Calorie Charts. Jules G. Szanton. (gr. 9 up). 1965. 5.95 o.s.i. (ISBN 0-8119-0059-2). Fell.

Food Values of Portions Commonly Used. 12th ed. Charles F. Church & Helen N. Church. 195p. 1975. pap. text ed. 7.95 o.p. (ISBN 0-397-54172-4). Lippincott.

Food Values of Portions Commonly Used. 13th ed. Jean Pennington & Helen N. Church. LC 80-7594. 200p. 1980. pap. 5.95 (ISBN 0-06-090819-X, CN819, CN). Har-Row.

Foodborne & Waterborne Diseases: Their Epidemiological Character. I. Jackson Tartakow & John H. Vorperian. (Illus.). 1981. pap. 19.00 (ISBN 0-87055-368-2). AVI.

Foods. 7th ed. Gladys E. Vail et al. LC 77-74376. (Illus.). 1978. text ed. 18.50 (ISBN 0-395-25521-X); inst. guide 0.90 (ISBN 0-395-25522-8); lab. manual 8.25 (ISBN 0-395-25523-6). HM.

Foods, Diet & Nutrition. 2nd ed. Ed. by Kenneth L. Jones et al. 141p. 1975. pap. text ed. 6.50 scp (ISBN 0-06-384341-2, HarpC). Har-Row.

Foods for One or Two--or More. Amy G. Ireson & Shirley F. Lipscomb. LC 77-75158. (Illus.). 1978. spiral bdg. o.p. 7.25 (ISBN 0-395-25823-5); text ed. 18.50 (ISBN 0-395-25820-0). HM.

Foods from Harvest Festivals & Folk Fairs. Anita Borghese. LC 77-968. (Illus.). 1977. 9.95 o.s.i. (ISBN 0-690-01655-7, TYC-T). T Y Crowell.

Foods in Homemaking. rev. ed. Marion L. Cronan & June Atwood. (Illus.). (gr. 9-12). 1972. text ed. 18.00 (ISBN 0-87002-121-4); tchr's guide avail. (ISBN 0-685-06847-1). Bennett IL.

Foods of the World. Time-Life Editors. 1980. 14.95 (ISBN 0-686-68054-5). Time-Life.

Foods to Improve Your Health: A Complete Guide to Over Three Hundred Foods for One Hundred One Common Ailments. Linda Pelstring & JoAnn Mauck. LC 73-83298. 224p. 1974. 3.95 (ISBN 0-8027-7147-5). Walker & Co.

Foods Under Glass, GA-046. Ed. by Business Communications Co. 1980. 675.00 (ISBN 0-89336-229-8). BCC.

Foodservice for the Extended Care Facility. Lendal H. Kotschevar. LC 72-75295. 1973. text ed. 21.95 (ISBN 0-8436-0548-0). CBI Pub.

Foodservice Operations Manual. John C. Birchfield. LC 79-15622. 1979. spiral bd. 39.95 (ISBN 0-8436-2145-1). CBI Pub.

Foodservice Purchasing. Raymond B. Peddersen. 460p. 1981. text ed. 19.95 (ISBN 0-8436-2192-3). CBI Pub.

Foodservice Refrigeration. Sandra J. Ley. (Illus.). 1980. 21.50 (ISBN 0-8436-2146-X). CBI Pub.

Foodservice Safety. Ser-Vol-Tel Institute. (Foodservice Career Education Ser.). 1974. pap. 4.95 (ISBN 0-8436-2008-0). CBI Pub.

Foodservice Vocabulary. Ser-Vol-Tel Institute. (Foodservice Career Education Ser.). 1975. pap. 4.95 (ISBN 0-8436-2007-2). CBI Pub.

Fool in Christ, Emanuel Quint. Gerhart Hauptmann. Tr. by T. Seltzer from Ger. LC 76-28694. 1977. Repr. of 1911 ed. 19.50 (ISBN 0-86527-251-4). Fertig.

Fool of Quality, 5 vols. Henry Brooke. Ed. by Ronald Paulson. LC 78-60842. (Novel 1720-1805 Ser.: Vol. 6). 1979. Set. lib. bdg. 155.00 (ISBN 0-8240-3655-7). Garland Pub.

Foolish Filly. E. Radlauer & R. S. Radlauer. LC 73-17048. (gr. 3 up). 1974. PLB 5.90 o.p. (ISBN 0-531-02680-9). Watts.

Foolish Frog. Pete Seeger & Charles Seeger. LC 73-2121. (Illus.). 40p. (gr. k-3). 1973. 7.95 (ISBN 0-02-781480-7). Macmillan.

Foolish Giant. Bruce Coville & Katherine Coville. LC 77-18522. (I-Like-to-Read Bks). (Illus.). (gr. k-2). 1978. 6.89 (ISBN 0-397-31800-6). Lippincott.

Foolish Virgin. Margaret Penn. 256p. Date not set. pap. 8.95 (ISBN 0-521-28297-7). Cambridge U Pr.

Fools & Heroes: The Changing Role of Communist Intellectuals in Czechoslovakia. Peter Hruby. 1980. 35.00 (ISBN 0-08-024276-6). Pergamon.

Fool's Crow. Thomas E. Mails. 1980. pap. 3.50 (ISBN 0-686-69256-X, 52175, Discus). Avon.

Fool's Errand. Steele MacKaye & Albion W. Tourgee. Ed. by Dean H. Keller. LC 79-6587. 1969. 8.00 o.p. (ISBN 0-8108-0279-1). Scarecrow.

Fool's Errand. Marc Norman. 1979. pap. 2.25 o.p. (ISBN 0-345-28060-1). Ballantine.

Fool's Errand. Marc Norman. 1978. 8.95 o.p. (ISBN 0-03-019301-X). HR&W.

Fools in Town Are on Our Side. Ross Thomas. 1975. pap. 1.75 (ISBN 0-380-00687-1, 28290). Avon.

Fools of Time: Studies in Shakespearean Tragedy. Northrop Frye. LC 67-5748. 1967. pap. 3.95 (ISBN 0-8020-6215-6). U of Toronto Pr.
Fool's Paradise. Ann Cooper. (Harlequin Romances Ser.). 192p. (Orig.). 1981. pap. 1.25 (ISBN 0-686-68820-1, Pub. by Harlequin). PB.
Fool's Proof. Alberta S. Carter. 256p. 1975. pap. 1.25 o.p. (ISBN 0-445-00261-1). Popular Lib.
Foot & Ankle. Bateman & Trott. 1980. 32.00. Thieme Stratton.
Foot & Shoeing. British Horse Society & Pony Club. LC 76-55015. 1976. pap. 1.95 (ISBN 0-8120-0758-1). Barron.
Foot Treadle Loom Weaving. rev ed. Edward Worst. (Illus.). 1975. pap. 4.95 (ISBN 0-88930-011-9, Pub. by Cloudburst Canada). Madrona Pubs.
Football. Ben Hodge. LC 75-6822. (Target Bks.). (Illus.). (gr. 4-6). 1977. PLB 6.45 s&l (ISBN 0-531-00768-5). Watts.
Football. George Sullivan. LC 72-2790. (All Star Sports Ser). (Illus.). 128p. (gr. 4 up). 1972. 5.95 o.p. (ISBN 0-695-80035-3); PLB 5.97 o.p. (ISBN 0-695-40035-5). Follett.
Football Book. Lawrence T. Lorimer & John Devaney. LC 77-74461. (Illus.). (gr. 5 up). 1977. PLB 5.99 (ISBN 0-394-93574-8, BYR); pap. 3.95 (ISBN 0-394-83574-3). Random.
Football Coaching. John H. McKay. (Illus.). 1966. 14.95 (ISBN 0-8260-5885-X). Wiley.
Football Fury. Steve Gelman. LC 62-8954. (gr. 6-9). 5.95 o.p. (ISBN 0-385-01428-7). Doubleday.
Football Greats. R. Broeg & Weeb Ewbank. (Illus.). 1977. pap. 4.95 (ISBN 0-8272-1007-8). Bethany Pr.
Football on Television. Ed. by Edward Buscombe. (BFI Television Monograph: No. 4). (Illus., Orig.). 1977. pap. 3.25 o.p. (ISBN 0-85170-046-2). NY Zoetrope.
Football: Picking Winners Against the Spread. A. J. Friedman. 64p. (Orig.). 1980. pap. 2.95 (ISBN 0-89650-703-3). Gamblers.
Football Playbook. Sam DeLuca. LC 74-188241. (Illus.). 1972. 8.95 o.p. (ISBN 0-8246-0143-2). Jonathan David.
Football Register: 1980 Edition. 1980. pap. 8.95 (ISBN 0-452-25249-0, Z5249, Plume). NAL.
Football Schedules Book. 4.00 (ISBN 0-686-22332-2). NAIA Pubns.
Football Scouting Workbook. Dienhart. write for info. (ISBN 0-392-07843-0). Soccer.
Football Talk. Howard Liss. 1980. pap. 1.50 (ISBN 0-671-56037-9). Archway.
Football Techniques Illustrated. rev. ed. Jim Moore & T. Micoleau. (Illus.). 1962. 11.50 (ISBN 0-8260-6215-6). Ronald Pr.
Footballers & Businessmen: The Origin of Professional Soccer in England. Steven Tischler. 180p. 1981. text ed. 24.00x (ISBN 0-8419-0658-0). Holmes & Meier.
Football's Breakaway Backs. Nathan Aaseng. LC 80-16691. (Sports Heroes Library). (Illus.). 72p. (gr. 4 up). 1980. PLB 5.95g (ISBN 0-8225-1063-4). Lerner Pubns.
Football's Cunning Coaches. Nathan Aaseng. LC 80-29252. (Sports Heroes Library). (Illus.). (gr. 4 up). 1981. PLB 5.95 (ISBN 0-8225-1065-0). Lerner Pubns.
Football's Great Quarterback: Joe Namath. Patricia M. Eldred. (Allstars Ser.). (Illus.). (gr. 2-6). 1977. PLB 5.95 o.p. (ISBN 0-87191-580-4). Creative Ed.
Football's Greatest Coach, Vince Lombardi. Gene Schoor. (Illus.). 240p. (gr. 6-7). 1974. 4.95 o.p. (ISBN 0-385-08513-3). Doubleday.
Football's Powerful Runner: Franco Harris. Thomas Braun. (Allstars Ser.). (Illus.). (gr. 2-6). 1977. PLB 5.95 o.p. (ISBN 0-87191-585-5). Creative Ed.
Football's Steadiest Kickers. Nathan Aaseng. LC 80-28868. (Sports Heroes Library). (Illus.). (gr. 4 up). 1981. PLB 5.95 (ISBN 0-8225-1069-3). Lerner Pubns.
Football's Sure-Handed Receivers. Nathan Aaseng. LC 80-17762. (Sports Heroes Library). (Illus.). 72p. (gr. 4 up). 1980. PLB 5.95g (ISBN 0-8225-1064-2). Lerner Pubns.
Football's Toughest Tight Ends. Nathan Aaseng. LC 80-27803. (Sports Heroes Ser.). (Illus.). (gr. 4 up). 1981. PLB 5.95 (ISBN 0-8225-1070-7). Lerner Pubns.
Football's Winning Quarterbacks. Nathan Aaseng. LC 80-12074. (Sports Heroes Library). (Illus.). (gr. 4 up). 1980. PLB 5.95g (ISBN 0-8225-1062-6). Lerner Pubns.
Footfalls of Indian History. Sr. Nivedita. (Illus.). pap. 2.95 o.p. (ISBN 0-87481-127-9). Vedanta Pr.
Foothpath. Ed. by Patricia C. Groth & Kitty Druck. LC 78-71325. (Illus.). 72p. (Orig.). 1978. pap. 5.00 (ISBN 0-937158-00-3). Del Valley.
Footloose in the Swiss Alps. William E. Reifsnyder. LC 74-76313. (Totebook). (Illus.). 444p. 1974. pap. 7.95 (ISBN 0-87156-102-6). Sierra.
Footloose in Vermont. Margaret Hard. (Illus., orig). 1969. 3.95 o.s.i. (ISBN 0-911570-06-3); pap. 2.00 o.s.i. (ISBN 0-911570-07-1). Vermont Bks.
Footloose with a Fishing Rod. W. E. Davies. 6.50x (ISBN 0-392-06479-0, LTB). Soccer.
Footnotes. Donald Lev. Ed. by Stanley H. Barkan. (Cross-Cultural Review Chapbook 11). 16p. 1980. pap. 2.00 (ISBN 0-89304-810-0). Cross Cult.
Footnotes & Headlines. C. Kent. (Orig.). 1970. pap. 3.45 (ISBN 0-8164-2548-5). Crossroad NY.
Footnotes & Headlines: A Play-Pray Book. M. Corita Kent. LC 67-27568. (Illus., Orig.). 1969. Repr. of 1967 ed. 6.00 (ISBN 0-8164-1032-1). Crossroad NY.
Footnotes of the Buckhorn: Centennial Edition 1881-1981. Fritz Toepperwein & Emilia Toepperwein. pap. 3.50 (ISBN 0-910722-14-5). Highland Pr.
Footnotes to American History: A Bibliographic Source Book. Harold S. Sharp. LC 76-49967. 1977. 27.50 (ISBN 0-8108-0994-X). Scarecrow.
Footnotes to Medicine. David J. Gerrick. 172p. 1980. 10.95 (ISBN 0-686-68569-5). Dayton Labs.
Footnotes to World History: A Bibliographic Source Book. Harold S. Sharp. LC 78-23417. 1979. 32.50 (ISBN 0-8108-1185-5). Scarecrow.
Footprints of Faith. David Paulson. LC 78-69673. (Redwood Ser.). 1978. pap. 3.95 (ISBN 0-8163-0196-4, 06390-9). Pacific Pr Pub Assn.
Footprints of Providence. Jeannie McReynolds. LC 77-25504. (Crown Ser.). 1978. pap. 4.50 (ISBN 0-8127-0172-0). Southern Pub.
Footprints of Robert Burns. Jessie Patrick Findlay. 174p. 1980. Repr. of 1923 ed. lib. bdg. 22.50 (ISBN 0-8492-4725-X). R West.
Footprints of the Buddha. Mary Baskett. LC 80-80133. (Illus.). 125p. (Orig.). 1980. pap. 8.95 (ISBN 0-87633-034-0). Phila Mus Art.
Footprints: Walking Through the Passages of Life. Howard Hendricks & Jeanne Hendricks. LC 80-25868. (Illus.). 96p. 1981. pap. 8.95 (ISBN 0-930014-55-3). Multnomah.
Footsteps in the Dark. Georgette Heyer. 1976. Repr. of 1932 ed. lib. bdg. 14.75x (ISBN 0-89966-122-X). Buccaneer Bks.
Footsteps into the Future. Rajni Kothari. LC 74-31357. (Preferred Worlds for the 1990's Ser.). 1975. 8.95 (ISBN 0-02-917570-4); pap. text ed. 7.95 (ISBN 0-02-917580-1). Free Pr.
Footsteps of Jesus. Jack Arvin. (Ser. Outlines). 4.95 (ISBN 0-89315-053-3). Lambert Bk.
Footwear. Iris Brooke. LC 79-109116. (Illus.). 1971. 5.95 (ISBN 0-87830-047-3). Theatre Arts.
Footwear Evidence: The Examination, Identification, & Comparison of Footwear Impressions. John R. Abbott. 100p. 1964. pap. 12.70 photocopy ed. spiral (ISBN 0-398-00003-4). C C Thomas.
Footwear: Leathercraft. Churchill Proper. LC 78-185669. (Handicraft Ser.: No. 1). (Illus.). 32p. (Orig.). (gr. 7-12). 1971. lib. bdg. 2.45 incl. catalog cards (ISBN 0-87157-901-4); pap. 1.45 vinyl laminated covers (ISBN 0-87157-401-2). SamHar Pr.
Footwear, Raw Hides & Skins & Leather Industry in OECD Countries, 1976-1977. 1979. 5.00 (ISBN 92-64-01874-3). OECD.
For a Critique of the Political Economy of the Sign. Jean Baudrillard. Tr. by Charles Levin from Fr. lib. bdg. 14.00 (ISBN 0-914386-23-9); pap. 4.50 (ISBN 0-914386-24-7). Telos Pr.
For a Living. Frances Phillips. 1981. pap. 4.00 (ISBN 0-914610-26-0). Hanging Loose.
For a New Liberty: The Libertarian Manifesto. Murray Rothbard. 1978. pap. 6.95 (ISBN 0-02-074690-3, Collier). Macmillan.
For a New Policy of International Development. Angelos T. Angelopoulos. LC 77-24420. (Praeger Special Studies). 1977. text ed. 17.95 o.p. (ISBN 0-03-022816-6); pap. 7.95 o.p. (ISBN 0-03-022821-2). Praeger.
For a Time Such As This. Jim Halsey. 1976. pap. 2.95 o.p. (ISBN 0-87552-309-9). Presby & Reformed.
For a World Like Ours. James L. Boyer. (New Testament Studies Ser.). pap. 2.95 o.p. (ISBN 0-8010-0553-1). Baker Bk.
For a World Like Ours: Studies in I Corinthians. James L. Boyer. pap. 3.95 (ISBN 0-88469-057-1). BMH Bks.
For All God's People: Ecumenical Prayer Cycle. 240p. (Orig.). 1981. pap. cancelled (ISBN 0-88344-012-1). Orbis Bks.
For Always. Eve Bunting. (Young Romance Ser.). (Illus.). (gr. 3-9). 1978. PLB 5.95 (ISBN 0-87191-636-3); pap. 2.95 (ISBN 0-89812-068-3). Creative Ed.
For & Against. L. G. Alexander. 1975. pap. text ed. 3.00x (ISBN 0-582-52306-0). Longman.
For Believers Only. J. Oswald Sanders. LC 76-15347. Orig. Title: Real Discipleship. 1977. pap. 1.95 (ISBN 0-87123-161-1, 200161). Bethany Fell.
For Better! for Worse! Caryl Rivers & Alan Lupo. 256p. 1981. 12.95 (ISBN 0-671-25446-4). Summit Bks.
For Better, for Worse: A Feminist Handbook on Marriage & Other Options. Jennifer B. Fleming & Carolyn K. Washburne. LC 77-8017. (Illus.). 1977. 14.95 o.p. (ISBN 0-684-14919-2, ScribT); pap. 7.95 o.p. (ISBN 0-684-14920-6, ScribT). Scribner.
For Better or Worse: The American Influence in the World. Ed. by Allan F. Davis. LC 80-1048. (Contributions in American Studies Ser.: No. 51). 240p. 1981. lib. bdg. 29.95 (ISBN 0-313-22342-4, DBO/). Greenwood.
For Children Mainly: Story Talks for Use in Church. A. Jason Shirah. (Orig.). 1980. pap. 3.95 (ISBN 0-8272-1010-8). Bethany Pr.
For Colored Girls Who Have Considered Suicide When the Rainbow Is Enuf: A Choreopoem. Ntozake Shange. 1977. 8.95 (ISBN 0-02-609840-7). Macmillan.
For God's Sake Run with Joy. C. Seerveld. LC 72-81234. 1973. pap. 4.95x (ISBN 0-686-00489-2). Wedge Pub.
For Gourmets with Ulcers. Toni M. Bruyere & Sidney J. Robey. 224p. 1974. pap. 1.95 o.p. (ISBN 0-06-463395-0, 395, EH). Har-Row.
For Gourmets with Ulcers. Toni M. Bruyere & Sidney J. Robey. 224p. 1981. pap. 4.95 (ISBN 0-393-00984-X). Norton. Postponed.
For Grandparents: Wonders & Worries. Myron C. Madden & Mary B. Madden. LC 80-12778. (Christian Care Bk.). 1980. pap. 5.95 (ISBN 0-664-24325-8). Westminster.
For Harmony & Strength: Japanese White-Collar Organization in Anthropological Perspective. Thomas P. Rohlen. LC 73-91668. 1974. 21.50x (ISBN 0-520-02674-8); pap. 6.95x (ISBN 0-520-03849-5). U of Cal Pr.
For-Hhundred Ideas for Ddesign, Vol.4. Morris Grossman. 376p. 1980. 13.95 (ISBN 0-8104-0950-X). Hayden.
For Jerusalem's Sake I Will Not Rest. Basilea Schlink. 1.45 (ISBN 0-551-00741-9). Evang Sisterhood Mary.
For Kicks. Dick Francis. 1980. pap. write for info. (ISBN 0-671-83499-1). PB.
For Kids Only. Intro. by Charles F. Reasoner. LC 76-28183. (Illus.). (gr. 1 up). 1977. 8.95 o.s.i. (ISBN 0-440-02738-1); pap. 4.95 (ISBN 0-440-02690-3). Delacorte.
For Love of a Pirate. Anthony Esler. LC 78-17287. 1978. 9.95 o.p. (ISBN 0-688-03375-X). Morrow.
For Love of a Rose. Antonia Ridge. 1965. 8.95 (ISBN 0-571-06469-8, Pub. by Faber & Faber); pap. 4.95 (ISBN 0-571-10118-6). Merrimack Bk Serv.
For Love or Money. Vivian Donald. pap. 1.25 (ISBN 0-451-07756-3, Y7756, Sig). NAL.
For Love: Poems Nineteen Fifty to Nineteen Sixty. Robert Creeley. LC 62-8903. (Orig.). pap. 2.95 o.p. (ISBN 0-684-71738-7, SL178, ScribT). Scribner.
For Money or Love: Boy Prostitution in America. Robin Lloyd. LC 75-40691. 1976. 8.95 (ISBN 0-8149-0773-3). Vanguard.
For Money or Love: Boy Prostitution in America. Robin Lloyd. 1977. pap. 1.95 (ISBN 0-345-27577-2). Ballantine.
For My Country. Jules-Paul Tardivel. Tr. by Sheila Fischman. LC 75-6862. (Social History of Canada Ser.). Orig. Title: Pour la Patrie. 1975. pap. 5.50 (ISBN 0-8020-6267-9). U of Toronto Pr.
For One Another: Jewish Organizations That Help Us All. Raymond A. Zwerin. (Illus.). (gr. 6). 1975. text ed. 6.00 (ISBN 0-8074-0136-6, 141420); tchr's. guide o.p. 5.00 (ISBN 0-685-48915-9, 201421). UAHC.
For One Moment. Christmas C. Kauffman. 1964. pap. 3.50 (ISBN 0-8024-3808-3). Moody.
For Ourselves, Our Families, & Our Future: The Struggle for Childbearing Rights. The Childbearing Rights Information Project. Ed. by Marian McDonald. LC 80-52554. (Illus.). 165p. (Orig.). 1980. pap. 5.00 (ISBN 0-932728-03-0). Red Sun Pr.
For Pacifists. Mohandas K. Gandhi. Ed. by Bharatan Kumarappa. 130p. (Orig.). 1981. pap. 1.50 (ISBN 0-934676-28-3). Greenlf Bks.
For Parents of a Child Whose Speech Is Delayed. 2nd ed. R. Corbin Pennington & Elizabeth James. 1980. pap. 0.50 (ISBN 0-8134-2137-3, 2137). Interstate.
For Peace & Justice: Pacifism in America, 1914-1941. Charles Chatfield. LC 70-142143. (Illus.). 1971. 16.50x (ISBN 0-87049-126-1). U of Tenn Pr.
For Rain As Well As Rainbow. Carol Amen. (Uplook Ser.). 1975. pap. 0.65 o.p. (ISBN 0-8163-0173-5, 06433-7). Pacific Pr Pub Assn.
For Seekers of God: Spiritual Talks of Mahapurush Swami Shivananda. Swami Shivananda. Tr. by Swami Vividishananda & Swami Gambhirananda. 186p. 1972. 5.79 (ISBN 0-87481-169-4); pap. 5.95 (ISBN 0-87481-130-9). Vedanta Pr.
For Socialism. Gustav Landauer. Tr. by David J. Parent from Ger. LC 78-51081. 1978. 12.00 (ISBN 0-914386-10-7); pap. 3.95 (ISBN 0-914386-11-5). Telos Pr.
For Students About Studying: A Study Skills Handbook. Rita Phipps. 1981. write for info. U of Wash Pr.
For Teenagers Only, Change Your Habits to Change Your Shape. Joanne Ikeda. LC 78-12697. 1978. pap. 5.95 (ISBN 0-915950-23-5). Bull Pub.
For Texas & Zed. Zach Hughes. 256p. (Orig.). 1976. pap. 1.25 o.p. (ISBN 0-445-00370-7). Popular Lib.
For the Birds. John Cage. 220p. 1981. 20.00 (ISBN 0-7145-2690-8, Pub. by M. Boyars). Merrimack Bk Serv.
For the Children's Hour. Carolyn S. Bailey & Clara M. Lewis. LC 73-20186. (Illus.). 336p. 1974. Repr. of 1920 ed. 30.00 (ISBN 0-8103-3958-7). Gale.
For the Common Defense. Andrew J. Goodpaster. LC 77-4562. 1977. 18.95 (ISBN 0-669-01620-9). Lexington Bks.
For the Going. Joel Bernstein. LC 74-24492. (Illus.). 1974. 3.95 (ISBN 0-915298-00-7). Sagarin Pr.
For the Greater Glory: A Church Needlepoint Handbook. Mary P. Olsen. (Illus.). 192p. 1980. 15.95 (ISBN 0-8164-0476-3). Seabury.
For the Health of Body & Soul. Stanley S. Harakas. 48p. (Orig.). 1980. pap. 1.95 (ISBN 0-916586-42-1). Hellenic Coll Pr.
For the Long Term Investor. David Coleman. 12.95 (ISBN 0-930726-05-7). Green Hill.
For the Parents of a Child Whose Speech Is Delayed. R. Corbin Pennington & Elizabeth James. LC 64-25221. 1965. pap. 0.50 o.p. (ISBN 0-8134-0015-5, 15); pap. 0.40 ea. 2-24 copies o.p.; pap. 0.32 ea. 25 or more copies o.p. Interstate.
For the People: A Consumer Action Handbook. Joanne Anderson. LC 77-73065. 1977. pap. 5.95 o.p. (ISBN 0-201-00200-0). A-W.
For the Record: Selected Statements, 1977 to 1980. Henry Kissinger. 288p. 1981. 12.95 (ISBN 0-316-49663-4). Little.
For the Sake of a Single Verse. Rainer M. Rilke. (Illus.). 40p. 1974. pap. 12.95 (ISBN 0-517-51205-X); pap. 6.95 (ISBN 0-517-51206-8). Potter.
For the Sake of Argument: Writing Editorials & Position Papers. Eileen N. Wagner. LC 79-64515. 1979. pap. text ed. 9.25 (ISBN 0-8191-0763-8). U Pr of Amer.
For the Sake of the Song. Townes Van Zandt. LC 77-20732. (Illus.). 1977. 7.50 (ISBN 0-930324-04-8); pap. 5.00 (ISBN 0-930324-05-6). Wings Pr.
For the Sake of the Song. Townes Van Zandt. 7.50 (ISBN 0-930324-04-8). Green Hill.
For the Sake of the Trust: Sherlock Holmes & the Musgrave Ritual. Edward A. Merrill. LC 80-67700. (Sherlock Holmes Monograph). (Illus.). 112p. 1981. 10.95 (ISBN 0-934468-05-2). Gaslight.
For the Shape of Your Life. Felicia Scherer. 1976. pap. text ed. 2.50 (ISBN 0-918734-14-2). Reymont.
For the Sleepwalker. Edward Hirsch. LC 80-2726. (Knopf Poetry Ser.: No. 6). 1981. 10.95 (ISBN 0-394-51474-2); pap. 5.95 (ISBN 0-394-74908-1). Knopf.
For the Story Teller, Story Telling & Stories to Tell. Carolyn S. Bailey. LC 74-23576. 1975. Repr. of 1913 ed. 24.00 (ISBN 0-8103-3802-5). Gale.
For They Are My Friends. Tom Marotta. LC 76-43510. 1977. o.p. (ISBN 0-917806-00-X); pap. 8.95 (ISBN 0-917806-01-8). Morgan.
For This I Went to College? Bil Keane. (Family Circus Ser.). (Illus.). 1978. pap. 1.50 (ISBN 0-449-14069-5, GM). Fawcett.
For Those I Loved. Martin Gray & May Gallo. (RL 10). 1974. pap. 1.95 (ISBN 0-451-06942-0, J6942, Sig). NAL.
For Those Who Live & Breathe: A Manual for Patients with Emphysema & Chronic Bronchitis. 2nd ed. Thomas L. Petty & Louise M. Nett. (Illus.). 128p. 1975. 9.75 (ISBN 0-398-02380-8). C C Thomas.
For Want of a Nail: If Burgoyne Had Won at Saratoga. Robert Sobel. (Illus.). 384p. 1973. 12.95 o.s.i. (ISBN 0-02-612250-2). Macmillan.
For We Are: Toward Understanding Your Personal Potential. Mark King. LC 74-10354. 1975. text ed. 6.00 (ISBN 0-201-03747-5). A-W.
For Weber: Essays in the Sociology of Fate. Bryan S. Turner. 360p. 1981. price not set (ISBN 0-7100-0780-9). Routledge & Kegan.
For Whom the Bell Tolls. Ernest Hemingway. 1940. 17.50x (ISBN 0-684-15316-5, ScribT); pap. 5.95 (ISBN 0-684-71798-0, SL4, ScribT). Scribner.
For Whom the Trumphets Sound. Don K. O'Shay. 1981. 13.95 (ISBN 0-533-04840-0). Vantage.
For Women Only. Anna Keefer. 112p. 1980. pap. 5.95 (ISBN 0-89305-037-7). Anna Pub.

For You. Carolyn Bartmess. 1981. 4.95 (ISBN 0-8062-1701-4). Carlton.

For Your Delight. Ed. by Ethel L. Fowler. (gr. 4-6). 1924. 5.95 o.p. (ISBN 0-571-06514-7, Pub. by Faber & Faber). Merrimack Bk Serv.

For Your Eyes Only. Ian Fleming. (James Bond Ser.). 1981. pap. 2.25 (ISBN 0-515-06074-7). Jove Pubns.

For Your Information: A Guide to Writing Reports. Richard Swanson. (Illus.). 160p. 1974. pap. text ed. 6.50 (ISBN 0-13-324905-0). P-H.

For Yourself - the Fulfillment of Female Sexuality. Lonnie Garfield Barbach. LC 74-4873. 240p. 1975. 7.95 o.p. (ISBN 0-385-05825-X); pap. 3.95 (ISBN 0-385-11245-9). Doubleday.

For Zion's Sake: A Biography of Judah L. Magnes. Norman Bentwich. (Return to Zion Ser.). (Illus.). 329p. 1980. Repr. of 1954 ed. lib. bdg. 25.00x (ISBN 0-87991-144-1). Porcupine Pr.

Foraging for Edible Wild Mushrooms. rev. ed. Karen Haard & Richard Haard. (Illus.). 1978. lib. bdg. 11.95 (ISBN 0-88930-015-1, Pub. by Cloudburst Canada); pap. 5.95 (ISBN 0-88930-017-8). Madrona Pubs.

Foraminiferal Studies in the Lower & Middle Tertiary of Soquel Creek, Santa Cruz County, California. Roberta K. Smith. (U. C. Publ. in Geological Sciences: Vol. 91). 1971. pap. 7.50x (ISBN 0-520-09389-5). U of Cal Pr.

Forbid Them Not. Louis Cassels. LC 73-75885. 1973. 2.00 o.p. (ISBN 0-8309-0097-7). Independence Pr.

Forbidden City. Anthony Esler. 1979. pap. 1.95 o.p. (ISBN 0-449-23836-9, Crest). Fawcett.

Forbidden City. Anthony Esler. LC 77-6743. 1977. 9.95 o.p. (ISBN 0-688-03219-2). Morrow.

Forbidden Disappointments. James Carroll. LC 74-80349. 1975. 6.95 (ISBN 0-8091-0195-5); pap. 3.95 (ISBN 0-8091-1842-4). Paulist Pr.

Forbidden Experiment: The Story of the Wild Boy of Aveyron. Roger Shattuck. 220p. 1980. 12.95 (ISBN 0-374-15755-3). FS&G.

Forbidden Fantasies. Mike Phillips et al. (Illus.). 128p. 1980. pap. 14.95 (ISBN 0-02-006300-8, Collier). Macmillan.

Forbidden Fires: Janice Young Brooks. LC 80-80983. (Historical Romance Ser.). 304p. (Orig.). 1980. pap. 2.50 (ISBN 0-87216-687-2). Playboy Pbks.

Forbidden Flowers: More Women's Sexual Fantasies. Nancy Friday. pap. 3.50 (ISBN 0-671-81166-5). PB.

Forbidden Game: A Social History of Drugs. Brian Inglis. LC 75-12382. 1975. 8.95 o.p. (ISBN 0-684-14428-X, ScribT). Scribner.

Forbidden Love. Caroline Courtney. 224p. 1980. pap. 1.75 (ISBN 0-446-94297-9). Warner Bks.

Forbidden River. Al Cody. (YA) 1973. 5.95 (ISBN 0-685-29160-X, Avalon). Bouregy.

Forbidden World. Ted White & Dave Bischoff. 1978. pap. 1.50 o.p. (ISBN 0-445-04328-8). Popular Lib.

Force. Harlan Wade. Tr. by Claude Potvin & Rose-Ella Potvin. (Book About Ser.). Orig. Title: Strength. (Illus., Fr.). (gr. k-3). 1979. PLB 7.30 (ISBN 0-8172-1453-4). Raintree Pubs.

Force & Energy: Physics, Bk. 1. L. J. Campbell & R. J. Carlton. (Secondary Science Ser). (Illus., Orig.). (gr. 8-11). 1974. pap. text ed. 6.95 (ISBN 0-7100-7739-4). Routledge & Kegan.

Force of Habit, a Comedy. Thomas Bernhard. Tr. by Neville Plaice & Stephen Plaice. (National Theatre Plays Ser.). 1976. pap. text ed. 4.25x (ISBN 0-435-23120-0). Heinemann Ed.

Force of Knowledge. J. M. Ziman. LC 75-23529. (Illus.). 368p. 1976. 41.50 (ISBN 0-521-20649-9); pap. 14.95x (ISBN 0-521-09917-X). Cambridge U Pr.

Force of Star Wars. Frank Allnutt. 1977. pap. 1.95 (ISBN 0-89728-030-X, 689135). Omega Pubns OR.

Force Reductions in Europe: Starting Over. Jeffrey Record. LC 80-83753. (Special Report Ser.). 92p. 1980. 6.50 (ISBN 0-89549-027-7). Inst Foreign Policy Anal.

Force Ten from Navarone. Alistair MacLean. 1979. pap. 2.50 (ISBN 0-449-23934-9, Crest). Fawcett.

Force Without War: U. S. Armed Forces As a Political Instrument. Barry M. C. Blechman & Stephen S. Kaplan. 1978. 21.95 (ISBN 0-8157-0986-2); pap. 11.95 (ISBN 0-8157-0985-4). Brookings.

Forced Labor: Maternity Care in the United States. Nancy S. Shaw. 1974. 18.50 (ISBN 0-08-017835-9); pap. text ed. 9.75 (ISBN 0-08-017834-0). Pergamon.

Forces & Fields. Mary B. Hesse. 320p. 1962. 10.00 (ISBN 0-8022-0712-X). Philos Lib.

Forces for Change in Latin America: U. S. Policy Implications. Colin I. Bradford, Jr. LC 70-181831. (Monographs: No. 5). 80p. 1971. 2.00 (ISBN 0-686-28690-1). Overseas Dev Council.

Forces of Change in Western Europe. Chamberline. (Illus.). 352p. 1980. text ed. 24.50 (ISBN 0-07-084107-1). McGraw.

Forces of Freedom in Spain 1974-1979, P-245. Samuel D. Eaton. LC 80-8383. (Illus.). 216p. 1981. pap. 11.95 (ISBN 0-8179-7452-0). Hoover Inst Pr.

Forces of Nature. P. C. Davies. LC 78-72084. (Illus.). 1979. 32.50 (ISBN 0-521-22523-X); pap. 9.95 (ISBN 0-521-29535-1). Cambridge U Pr.

Forces of Order: Police Behavior in Japan & the United States. David H. Bayley. LC 75-17304. 1976. 16.50x (ISBN 0-520-03069-9); pap. 3.95 (ISBN 0-520-03641-7). U of Cal Pr.

Forces on Leadership. Michael C. Giammatteo et al. 80p. 1981. pap. 4.00 (ISBN 0-88210-116-1). Natl Assn Principals.

Forcible Entry, Rope & Portable Extinguisher Practices, No. 101. IFSTA Committee. Ed. by John Peige et al. LC 77-94425. (Illus.). 1978. pap. text ed. 7.00 (ISBN 0-87939-032-8). Intl Fire Serv.

Forcible Rape. The Crime, the Victim, & the Criminal. Duncan Chappell et al. LC 77-3377. 1977. 22.50x (ISBN 0-231-03839-9); pap. 10.00x (ISBN 0-231-04641-3). Columbia U Pr.

Ford Bronco 1966-1980. Chilton's Automotive Editorial Dept. (Illus.). 1980. pap. 8.95 (ISBN 0-8019-6961-1). Chilton.

Ford Courier 1972-1980. Chilton's Automotive Editorial Dept. (Illus.). 1980. pap. 8.95 (ISBN 0-8019-6983-2). Chilton.

Ford Fairmont, 1978-1979: Shop Manual. Clymer Publications. Ed. by Eric Jorgensen. (Illus.). 328p. (Orig.). 1980. 10.95 (ISBN 0-89287-307-8, A174). Clymer Pubns.

Ford Fiesta, 1978 to 1980. Chilton's Automotive Editorial Dept. LC 78-20258. (Chilton's Repair & Tune-up Guides). (Illus.). 1979. pap. 8.95 (ISBN 0-8019-6846-1, 6846). Chilton.

Ford Fiesta 1978-1979 Shop Manual. Jim Combs. Ed. by Eric Jorgensen. (Illus.). 272p. 1979. pap. text ed. 10.95 (ISBN 0-89287-299-3, A173). Clymer Pubns.

Ford: Five Plays. John Ford. Ed. by Havelock Ellis. Incl. The Lover's Melancholy; 'Tis Pity She's a Whore; The Broken Heart; Love's Sacrifice; Perkin Warbeck. (Orig.). 1957. pap. 2.95 o.p. (ISBN 0-8090-0704-5, Mermaid). Hill & Wang.

Ford Madox Brown & the Pre-Raphaelite History-Picture. Lucy F. Rabin. LC 77-94725. (Outstanding Dissertations in the Fine Arts Ser.). 1979. lib. bdg. 31.00 (ISBN 0-8240-3246-2). Garland Pub.

Ford Madox Ford. Charles G. Hoffmann. (English Authors Ser.: No. 55). lib. bdg. 10.95 (ISBN 0-8057-1200-3). Twayne.

Ford Madox Ford. Sondra J. Stang. LC 77-41. (Modern Literature Ser.). 1977. 10.95 (ISBN 0-8044-2832-8). Ungar.

Ford Madox Ford: The Essence of His Art. R. W. Lid. 1964. 15.75x (ISBN 0-520-00748-4). U of Cal Pr.

Ford Model A Service Manual & Handbook of Repair & Maintenance. Victor W. Page. Ed. by Clymer Publications. 1961. pap. 9.00 o.p. (ISBN 0-89287-265-9, H525). Clymer Pubns.

Ford Model T Manual: 1922. Ed. by Ford Motor Company. (Illus.). 1949. pap. 4.00 o.p. (ISBN 0-89287-255-1, H505). Clymer Pubns.

Ford Nineteen Sixty-Eight to Seventy-Nine. (Illus.). 304p. (Spanish.). 1980. pap. 8.95. Chilton.

Ford Owner's Handbook: Models T & a Nineteen Hundred & Eight to Nineteen Twenty-Eight. Victor W. Page. Ed. by Clymer Publications. (Illus.). 1958. pap. 9.00 o.p. (ISBN 0-89287-258-6, H509). Clymer Pubns.

Ford Pick-Ups: Nineteen Sixty Five to Eighty Repair Tune-up Guide. (New Automotive Bks.). 256p. 1980. 8.95 (ISBN 0-8019-6913-1). Chilton.

Ford Pickups: 1969-1979 Shop Manual. Ray Hoy. Ed. by Eric Jorgensen. (Illus.). 368p. (Orig.). 1979. pap. text ed. 10.95 (ISBN 0-89287-303-5, A248). Clymer Pubns.

Ford Road. Lorin Sorensen. (Illus.). 1978. 19.95 (ISBN 0-87938-078-0, Pub. by Silverado Pubns Co). Motorbooks Intl.

Ford Road. Lorin Sorensen. (Illus.). 191p. 1978. 16.95 (ISBN 0-87938-078-0). Silverado.

Ford Service-Repair Handbook: Courier Pickups, 1972-1979. (Illus.). pap. 10.95 (ISBN 0-89287-198-9, A172). Clymer Pubns.

Ford Tune-up & Maintenance: Vans & Pickups, 1969-1978. Mike Bishop. Ed. by Eric Jorgensen. (Illus.). 1978. pap. 7.00 o.p. (ISBN 0-89287-231-4, A242). Clymer Pubns.

Ford Tune-Up & Repair. Ed. by Spence Murray. LC 78-65687. (Tune-up & Repair Ser.). (gr. 9-12). 1979. pap. 4.95 (ISBN 0-8227-5041-4). Petersen Pub.

Ford Tune-up Maintenance: All Models/1969-1979. Ray Hoy. Ed. by Jeff Robinson. 1977. pap. 7.95 (ISBN 0-89287-135-0, A-170). Clymer Pubns.

Ford Vans: 1969-1979 Shop Manual. Ray Hoy. Ed. by Eric Jorgensen. (Illus.). 360p. (Orig.). 1979. pap. text ed. 10.95 (ISBN 0-89287-302-7, A249). Clymer Pubns.

Ford, 1968 to 1979. Chilton's Automotive Editorial Dept. LC 78-20254. (Chilton' Repair & Tune-up Guides). (Illus.). 1979. pap. 8.95 (ISBN 0-8019-6842-9). Chilton.

Ford 4-Wheel Drive Maintenance Bronco: F-100, F-150, F-250 1969-1979. (Illus.). 1977. pap. 7.95 (ISBN 0-89287-173-3, A232). Clymer Pubns.

Ford's Freighter Travel Guide: Published Semi-Annually, March & September. 57th ed. Merrian E. Clark. Ed. by Juliann D'Ascenzo & Bonnie Wilson. LC 54-3845. (Illus.). 140p. pap. 4.95 (ISBN 0-916486-57-5). Fords Travel.

Ford's International Cruise Guide. 26th ed. Merrian E. Clark. Ed. by Bonnie Wilson & Juliann D'Ascenzo. LC 75-29725. (Illus.). 160p. 1980. pap. 5.95 o.p. (ISBN 0-916486-53-2). M Clark.

Ford's International Cruise Guide. 28th ed. Merrian E. Clark. Ed. by Bonnie Wilson & Juliann D'Ascenzo. LC 75-29725. (Illus.). 160p. 1981. pap. 5.95 (ISBN 0-916486-56-7). M Clark.

Ford's International Cruise Guide: Summer 1981. 29th ed. Merrian E. Clark. Ed. by Bonnie Wilson & Juliann D'Ascenzo. LC 75-29725. (Illus.). 160p. 1981. pap. 5.95 (ISBN 0-916486-59-1). M Clark.

Fore-Edge Painting: A Historical Survey of a Curious Art in Book Decoration. Carl J. Weber. LC 66-26931. (Illus.). 1966. 25.00 o.p. (ISBN 0-8178-3811-2). Harvey.

Forecast. Malcolm Hill. 1980. pap. 1.25 (ISBN 0-440-42607-3, YB). Dell.

Forecast of Fulfillment: A Review of Research on Predictive Assessment of the Adult Retarded for Social & Vocational Adjustment. Henry V. Cobb. LC 72-3084. (Illus.). 176p. 1972. 5.00x (ISBN 0-8077-1168-3). Tchrs Coll.

Forecasting & Policy Simulation Model of the Health Care Sector: The HRRC Prototype Microeconomic Model. Donald Yett et al. LC 74-15534. (Human Resources Research Center Monographs). (Illus.). 1979. 21.50 (ISBN 0-669-94250-2). Lexington Bks.

Forecasting College Achievement: A Survey of Aptitude Tests for Higher Education, Part I., General Considerations in the Measurement of Academic Progress. Albert B. Crawford & Paul S. Burnham. 1946. 37.50x (ISBN 0-686-51387-8). Elliots Bks.

Forecasting Crime Data. James A. Fox. LC 77-8720. (Illus.). 1978. 16.95 (ISBN 0-669-01639-X). Lexington Bks.

Forecasting in Business & Economics. C. W. Granger. LC 79-91742. (Economic Theory, Econometrics, & Mathematical Econometrics Ser.). 1979. text ed. 18.95 (ISBN 0-12-295180-8). Acad Pr.

Forecasting in International Relations: Theory, Methods, Problems, Prospects. Ed. by Nazli Choucri & Thomas W. Robinson. LC 78-19169. (Illus.). 1978. text ed. 36.95x (ISBN 0-7167-0059-X). W H Freeman.

Forecasting: Methods & Applications. Spyros Makridakis & Steven C. Wheelwright. LC 77-18806. (Management & Administration Ser.). 1978. 31.95 (ISBN 0-471-93770-3); tchrs'. manual avail. (ISBN 0-471-03726-5). Wiley.

Forecasting Methods for Management. 2nd ed. Steven C. Wheelwright & Spyros Makridakis. LC 76-42294. (Systems & Controls for Financial Management Ser). 1977. 27.95 o.p. (ISBN 0-471-02225-X, Pub. by Wiley-Interscience). Wiley.

Forecasting Methods for Management. 3rd ed. Steven C. Wheelwright & Spyros Makridakis. LC 79-23476. (Systems & Controls for Financial Management Ser.). 300p. 1980. 28.95 (ISBN 0-471-05630-8, Pub by Ronald Pr). Wiley.

Forecasting Process for the Beginning Forecaster. Hans Levenbach & James P. Cleary. (Illus.). 350p. 1981. text ed. 29.95 (ISBN 0-534-97975-0). Lifetime Learn.

Forecasting the Impact of Technological Change on Manpower Utilization & Displacement: An Analytic Summary. Alan Fechter. 1975. pap. 2.50 o.p. (ISBN 0-87766-138-3, 99000). Urban Inst.

Forecasts for Nineteen-Eighty Two. Peter Popoff & Don Tanner. LC 80-69975. (Illus.). 50p. 1980. pap. 1.00 (ISBN 0-938544-00-4). Faith Messenger.

Foreground of 'Leaves of Grass' Floyd Stovall. LC 73-87861. 288p. 1974. 17.50x (ISBN 0-8139-0523-0). U Pr of Va.

Forehanding & Backhanding - If You're Lucky. Gary Paulsen. LC 77-27046. (Sports on the Light Side Ser.). (Illus.). (gr. 3-6). 1978. PLB 9.65 (ISBN 0-8172-1158-6). Raintree Pubs.

Foreign Aid As a Moral Obligation? Theodore A. Sumberg. LC 73-86711. (Washington Papers: No. 10). 1973. 3.50x (ISBN 0-8039-0283-2). Sage.

Foreign Banking & Investment in the United States: Issues & Alternatives. Francis A. Lees. LC 76-4782. 1976. 22.95 (ISBN 0-470-15212-5). Halsted Pr.

Foreign Birds. Cyril H. Rogers. Ed. by Christina Foyle. (Foyle's Handbks). 1973. 3.95 (ISBN 0-685-55809-6). Palmetto Pub.

Foreign Body. Roderick Mann. 1975. 6.95 o.s.i. (ISBN 0-02-579420-5). Macmillan.

Foreign Devils. Irvin Fause. 288p. 1976. pap. 1.75 o.p. (ISBN 0-445-08422-7). Popular Lib.

Foreign Devils on the Silk Road: The Search for the Lost Cities & Treasures of Chinese Central Asia. Peter Hopkirk. (Illus.). 264p. 1981. lib. bdg. 27.50x (ISBN 0-87023-234-7). U of Mass Pr.

Foreign Dialects. Marguerite S. Herman & Lewis Herman. LC 58-10332. 1943. 12.95 (ISBN 0-87830-048-1). Theatre Arts.

Foreign Disinvestment by U. S. Multinational Corporations: With Eight Case Studies. Roger L. Torneden. LC 75-1136. (Special Studies). (Illus.). 174p. 1975. text ed. 24.95 (ISBN 0-275-05830-1). Praeger.

Foreign Exchange Dealer's Manual. Raymond G. Coninx. 168p. 1980. 30.00x (ISBN 0-85941-152-4, Pub. by Woodhead-Faulkner England). State Mutual Bk.

Foreign Exchange Management. R. McRae & D. Walker. 1981. 36.00 (ISBN 0-13-325357-0). P-H.

Foreign Exchange Management & the Multinational Corporation: A Manager's Guide. Abraham M. George. LC 78-19738. 1978. 28.95 (ISBN 0-03-046641-5). Praeger.

Foreign Exchange Management in Multinational Firms. Vinh Quang Tran. Ed. by Gunter Dufey. (Research for Business Decisions). 246p. 1980. 27.95 (ISBN 0-8357-1133-1, Pub. by UMI Res Pr). Univ Microfilms.

Foreign Exchange Today. Raymond G. Coninx. LC 77-11932. 1978. 19.95 (ISBN 0-470-99315-4). Halsted Pr.

Foreign Exchange Today. rev. ed. Raymond G. Coninx. 167p. 1980. 19.95 (ISBN 0-470-27025-X, Pub. by Halsted Pr). Wiley.

Foreign Exchange Yearbook, 1979: A Listing of Daily Foreign Exchange & Euro-Currency Deposit Rates for Leading World Currencies. Ed. by Trevor Underwood. 1979. 31.95 (ISBN 0-470-26694-5). Halsted Pr.

Foreign Exchange Yearbook 1981. Ed. by Trevor Underwood. 264p. 1980. 60.00x (Pub. by Woodhead-Faulkner England). State Mutual Bk.

Foreign Fictions: An Anthology of Contemporary International Short Fiction. Ed. by John Biguenet. 1978. pap. 4.95 (ISBN 0-394-72493-3, V-493, Vin). Random.

Foreign Government Offices in California: A Directory. LC 76-1641. 100p. (Orig.). 1978. pap. 7.50x o.p. (ISBN 0-912102-28-4). Cal Inst Public.

Foreign Immigrants in Early Bourbon Mexico: Seventeen Hundred to Seventeen Sixty. C. F. Nunn. LC 78-1159. (Cambridge Latin American Studies: No. 31). 1979. 35.50 (ISBN 0-521-22051-3). Cambridge U Pr.

Foreign Investment & Development in Egypt. David Carr. LC 79-1250. 1979. 20.95 (ISBN 0-03-048351-4). Praeger.

Foreign Investment & Development in the Southwest Pacific: With Special Reference to Austrailia & Indonesia. David W. Carr. LC 78-8598. (Praeger Special Studies). 1978. 24.95 (ISBN 0-03-042271-X). Praeger.

Foreign Investment & Economic Development in Asia. Ed. by Nihar Sarkar. LC 76-901639. 1976. 17.50x o.p. (ISBN 0-88386-819-9, Orient Longman). South Asia Bks.

Foreign Investment & Industrialisation in Singapore. Ed. by Helen Hughes & You-Poh Seng. LC 69-14301. 1969. 21.50 (ISBN 0-299-05420-9). U of Wis Pr.

Foreign Investment & Japan. Ed. by Robert J. Ballon & Eugene H. Lee. LC 72-85427. 340p. 1972. 12.50x (ISBN 0-87011-186-8). Kodansha.

Foreign Investment & Regional Development: The Theory & Practice of Investment Incentives, with a Case Study of Belgium. G. Richard Thoman. LC 72-85978. (Special Studies in International Economics & Development). 1973. 28.50x (ISBN 0-275-28681-9). Irvington.

Foreign Investment Codes & Location of Direct Investment. Robert E. Grosse. LC 80-15194. (Praeger Special Studies). 174p. 1980. 20.95 (ISBN 0-03-057024-7). Praeger.

Foreign Investment in Latin America: Cases & Attitudes. Marvin D. Bernstein. (Borzoi Books on Latin America Ser). 1966. pap. 3.50 o.p. (ISBN 0-394-30054-8). Knopf.

Foreign Investment in the Third World: A Comparative Study of Selected Developing Country Investment Promotion Programs. Richard D. Robinson et al. 1980. 10.00 (6005). Chamber Comm US.

Foreign Investment in the U. S. Costs & Benefits. Elliot Zupnick. LC 80-66684. (Headline Ser.: No. 249). (Illus.). 80p. (Orig.). 1980. pap. 2.00 (ISBN 0-87124-061-0). Foreign Policy.
Foreign Investment in the U. S. Fishing Industry. Jeremiah J. Sullivan & Per O. Heggelund. LC 79-2074. (Pacific Rim Research Ser.: No. 3). 208p. 1979. 21.95 (ISBN 0-669-03066-X). Lexington Bks.
Foreign Investment in the United States. Bruce Zagaris. LC 79-20638. (Praeger Special Studies Ser.). (Illus.). 334p. 1980. 26.95 (ISBN 0-03-052401-6). Praeger.
Foreign Investment in the United States: 1980 Course Handbook. Stuart R. Singer & Stanley Weiss. LC 79-92658. 617p. 1980. pap. text ed. 25.00 (ISBN 0-686-68824-4, B4-6531). PLI.
Foreign Investment: The Management of Political Risk. Dan Haendel. (Westview Special Studies in International Economics). 1978. lib. bdg. 23.50x (ISBN 0-89158-253-3). Westview.
Foreign Language Learner: A Guide for Teachers. Mary Finacchiaro & Michael Bonomo. 1973. text ed. 8.95 (ISBN 0-88345-087-9, 18071); pap. text ed. 5.95 (ISBN 0-88345-088-7, 18072). Regents Pub.
Foreign Language Learning: Research & Development. Ed. by Thomas E. Bird. Incl. Classroom Revisited. Seymour O. Simches; Innovative Foreign Language Programs. Oliver Andrews, Jr; Liberated Expression. F. Mills Edgerton. 118p. 1968. pap. 7.95x (ISBN 0-915432-68-4). NE Conf Teach Foreign.
Foreign Language Learning, Today & Tomorrow: Essays in Honor of Emma M. Birkmaier. Ed. by Jermaine D. Arendt et al. 1979. 19.25 (ISBN 0-08-024628-1). Pergamon.
Foreign Language Teacher in Today's Classroom Environment. Ed. by Warren C. Born. 1979. pap. 7.95x (ISBN 0-915432-79-X). NE Conf Teach.
Foreign Language Teachers & Tests. Ed. by Hunter Kellenberger. Incl. Foreign Language Instruction in Elementary Schools. Arthur S. Selvi; Linguistic Aids. Richard H. Walker; Qualifications of Foreign Language Teachers. Stephen A. Freeman; Role of Foreign Languages in American Life. Theodore Andersson; Teaching of Literature. Norman L. Torrey; Tests: Listening Comprehension, Other Skills. 56p. 1954. pap. 7.95x (ISBN 0-915432-54-4). NE Conf Teach Foreign.
Foreign Language Teaching: Challenges to the Profession. Ed. by G. Reginald Bishop, Jr. Incl. Case for Latin. William R. Parker; Challenge of Bilingualism. A. Bruce Gaarder; From School to College: The Problem of Continuity. Micheline Dufau; Study Abroad. Stephen A. Freeman. 158p. 1965. pap. 7.95x (ISBN 0-915432-65-X). NE Conf Teach Foreign.
Foreign Language Teaching: Ideals & Practices. Ed. by George F. Jones. Incl. Foreign Languages in Colleges & Universities. Roger L. Hadlich; Foreign Languages in Elementary School. Conrad J. Schmitt; Foreign Languages in the Secondary School. Milton R. Hahn. 62p. 1964. pap. 7.95x (ISBN 0-915432-64-1). NE Conf Teach Foreign.
Foreign Language Teaching: Meeting Individual Needs. PIE Seminar,Papers, Oxford, April 1979. Ed. by Howard B. Altman. 128p. pap. 7.95 (ISBN 0-08-024604-4). Pergamon.
Foreign Language Testing: A Practical Approach. Mary Finocchiaro & Sydney Sako. 1981. pap. text ed. 9.95 (ISBN 0-88345-362-2). Regents Pub.
Foreign Language Tests & Techniques. Ed. by Margaret Gilman. 136p. 1956. pap. 7.95x (ISBN 0-915432-56-0). NE Conf Teach Foreign.
Foreign Languages & International Studies 1981: Toward Cooperation & Integration. Ed. by Thomas H. Geno. LC 55-34379. 200p. 1981. pap. 7.95 (ISBN 0-915432-81-1). NE Conf Teach Foreign.
Foreign Languages, English As a Second & Foreign Language, & the U. S. Multinational Corporation. Marianne Inman. (Language in Education Ser.: No. 16). (Orig.). 1979. pap. text ed. 4.95x (ISBN 0-87281-102-6). Ctr Appl Ling.
Foreign Languages: Reading, Literature, Requirements. Ed. by Thomas E. Bird. Incl. Teaching of Reading. William G. Moulton; Times & Places for Literature. F. Andre Paquette; Trends in Foreign Language Requirements & Placement. John F. Gummere. 124p. 1967. pap. 7.95x (ISBN 0-915432-67-6). NE Conf Teach Foreign.
Foreign Licensing Policy in Multinational Enterprises. Piero Telesio. (Praeger Special Studies). 21.95 (ISBN 0-03-047476-0). Praeger.
Foreign Medical Graduates in America. Patricio R. Mamot. 196p. 1974. 12.75 (ISBN 0-398-02751-X). C C Thomas.
Foreign Medical Graduates in Psychiatry: Issues & Problems. Ronald Chen. LC 79-17189. 448p. 1980. 22.95x (ISBN 0-87705-485-1). Human Sci Pr.
Foreign Medical Graduates: The Case of the United States. Alfonso Mejia et al. LC 80-7576. 1980. 18.95 (ISBN 0-669-03760-5). Lexington Bks.
Foreign Ministers of Alexander First: Political Attitudes & the Conduct of Russian Diplomacy, 1801-1825. Patricia K. Grimsted. LC 69-11615. (Illus.). 1969. 20.50x (ISBN 0-520-01387-5). U of Cal Pr.
Foreign Mud. Maurice Collis. (Illus., Orig.). 1964. pap. 4.95 (ISBN 0-571-05797-7, Pub. by Faber & Faber). Merrimack Bk Serv.
Foreign Office & Foreign Policy 1898-1914. Zara S. Steiner. LC 70-85739. (Illus.). 1970. 37.50 (ISBN 0-521-07654-4). Cambridge U Pr.
Foreign Origins. David L. Kent. LC 80-85008. 100p. 1981. softcover 10.00 (ISBN 0-9604886-3-4). C M Kent.
Foreign Policies & Foreign Trade of the German Democratic Republic & the Korean Democratic People's Republic. Ed. by Kie-Taek Kim & Andis Kaulins. (German Korea Studies Group Ser.). 144p. 1980. pap. 15.00 (ISBN 0-8188-0117-4, Pub. by German Korea Stud Germany). Paragon.
Foreign Policies of Herbert Hoover, 1929-1933. William S. Myers. Ed. by Frank Freidel. LC 78-66558. (History of the United States Ser.: Vol. 14). 272p. 1979. lib. bdg. 20.00 (ISBN 0-8240-9699-1). Garland Pub.
Foreign Policies of the French Left. Ed. by Simon Serfaty. LC 79-53137. (Westview Special Studies in West European Politics & Society). 1979. lib. bdg. 16.50x (ISBN 0-89158-652-0). Westview.
Foreign Policies of the Powers. 2nd ed. F. S. Northedge. 1974. 14.95 o.p. (ISBN 0-571-04837-4, Pub. by Faber & Faber). Merrimack Bk Serv.
Foreign Policies of the Powers. Ed. by F. S. Northedge. LC 75-3762. 1975. 17.95 (ISBN 0-02-923170-1); pap. text ed. 8.95 (ISBN 0-02-923180-9). Free Pr.
Foreign Policies of West European Socialist Parties. Ed. by Werner J. Feld. LC 77-83485. (Praeger Special Studies). 1978. 20.95 (ISBN 0-03-039381-7). Praeger.
Foreign Policy Analysis. Ed. by Richard L. Merritt. LC 75-27808. (Policy Studies Organization Study). 176p. 1975. 17.95 (ISBN 0-669-00251-8). Lexington Bks.
Foreign Policy & Interdependence in Gaullist France. Edward L. Morse. LC 72-5391. (Center of International Studies). 388p. 1973. 21.50x (ISBN 0-691-05209-3). Princeton U Pr.
Foreign Policy & Its Planning. K. P. Misra. 1971. 5.50x (ISBN 0-210-22333-2). Asia.
Foreign Policy & National Intergration: The Case of Indonesia. Jon M. Reinhardt. (Monograph: No. 17). (Illus.). vi, 230p. 1971. 6.50 o.p. (ISBN 0-686-63725-9). Yale U Pr.
Foreign Policy & the Developing Nation. Richard Butwell. LC 68-55041. 244p. 1969. 13.00x (ISBN 0-8131-1185-4). U Pr of Ky.
Foreign Policy & U. S. National Security: Major Postelection Issues. William W. Whitson. LC 76-2070. (Praeger Special Studies Ser.). 384p. 1976. text ed. 32.50 (ISBN 0-275-56540-8); pap. text ed. 11.95 (ISBN 0-275-85700-X). Praeger.
Foreign Policy Behavior: The Interstate Behavior Analysis Model. Jonathan Wilkenfeld et al. LC 80-13161. (Illus.). 288p. 1980. 22.50 (ISBN 0-8039-1476-8). Sage.
Foreign Policy for a New Age. Robert G. Wesson. LC 76-13999. (Illus.). 1976. pap. text ed. 17.95 (ISBN 0-395-24652-0). HM.
Foreign Policy Making in Communist Countries. Ed. by Hannes Adomeit. LC 78-70493. (Praeger Special Studies). 172p. 1979. 22.95 (ISBN 0-03-046201-0). Praeger.
Foreign Policy Making in Developing States. Christopher Clapham. LC 77-71401. (Praeger Special Studies). 1979. 23.95 (ISBN 0-03-046691-1). Praeger.
Foreign Policy Making in the Middle East: Domestic Influences on Policy in Egypt, Iraq, Israel, & Syria. R. D. McLaurin et al. LC 76-24360. (Special Studies). 1977. text ed. 29.95 (ISBN 0-275-23870-9); pap. 9.95 (ISBN 0-275-65010-3). Praeger.
Foreign Policy Making in Western Europe: A Comparative Approach. Ed. by William Wallace & W. E. Paterson. LC 78-58844. 1978. 23.95 (ISBN 0-03-046271-1). Praeger.
Foreign Policy of American Labor. Carl Gershman. LC 75-33469. (Washington Papers: No. 29). 1975. 3.50x (ISBN 0-8039-0572-6). Sage.
Foreign Policy of Eastern Europe: New Approaches. Ed. by Ronald Linden. (Praeger Special Studies). 290p. 1980. 27.95 (ISBN 0-03-056136-1). Praeger.
Foreign Policy of France. J. Nere. (Foreign Policies of the Great Powers). 1975. 26.00x (ISBN 0-7100-7968-0). Routledge & Kegan.
Foreign Policy of Hitler's Germany: Starting World War II, 1937-1939. Gerhard L. Weinberg. LC 79-26406. 1980. 44.00x (ISBN 0-226-88511-9). U of Chicago Pr.
Foreign Policy of Iran, 1500-1941: A Developing Nation in World Affairs. Rouhollah K. Ramazani. LC 66-12469. 1966. 12.95x (ISBN 0-8139-0200-2). U Pr of Va.
Foreign Policy of Modern Japan. Robert A. Scalapino. (Campus Ser.: No. 196). 1977. 21.50 (ISBN 0-520-03196-2); pap. 6.95x (ISBN 0-520-03499-6). U of Cal Pr.
Foreign Policy of Senegal. W. A. Skurnik. xx, 308p. 1972. 13.00x o.s.i. (ISBN 0-8101-0373-7). Northwestern U Pr.
Foreign Policy of Soviet Russia: 1929-1941, 2 vols. Max Beloff. Incl. Vol. 1. 1929-1936. 1947. (ISBN 0-19-214505-3); Vol. 2. 1936-1941. 1949 (ISBN 0-19-214506-1). (Royal Institute of International Affairs Ser.). 14.95x ea. o.p. Oxford U Pr.
Foreign Policy of Thailand, 1954-1971. Ganganath Jha. 1979. text ed. 14.50x (ISBN 0-391-01012-3). Humanities.
Foreign Policy of the Soviet Union. 3rd ed. Alvin Z. Rubenstein. 448p. 1972. pap. text ed. 9.95 (ISBN 0-394-31699-1). Random.
Foreign Policy of the Third Reich. Klaus Hildebrand. 1974. 15.75x (ISBN 0-520-01965-2); pap. 5.50x (ISBN 0-520-02528-8). U of Cal Pr.
Foreign Policy of the USSR: Domestic Factors. Morton Schwartz. 1975. pap. 7.95x (ISBN 0-8221-0145-9). Dickenson.
Foreign Policy of West Germany: Formation & Contents. Ed. by Ekkehart Krippendorff & Volker Rittberger. LC 80-40149. (German Political Studies: Vol. 4). (Illus.). 372p. 1980. 20.00 (ISBN 0-8039-9818-X); pap. 9.95 (ISBN 0-8039-9819-8). Sage.
Foreign Policy Priorities 1970-1971. Foreign Policy Association. 1970. pap. 0.95 o.s.i. (ISBN 0-02-073500-6, Collier). Macmillan.
Foreign Protestants & the Settlement of Nova Scotia: The History of a Piece of Arrested British Policy in the Eighteenth Century. Winthrop P. Bell. LC 61-4799. xiv, 673p. 1961. 45.00x o.p. (ISBN 0-8020-7000-0). U of Toronto Pr.
Foreign Relations of the New States. Michael Leifer. (Studies in Contemporary Southeast Asia). 128p. 1974. text ed. 8.50x (ISBN 0-582-71042-1); pap. text ed. 5.50x (ISBN 0-582-71043-X). Longman.
Foreign Student's Guide to Dangerous English. Elizabeth Claire. (Illus.). 92p. (Orig.). 1980. pap. 4.95 (ISBN 0-937630-00-4). Eardley Pubns.
Foreign Students in the United States of America: Coping Behavior Within the Educational Environment. W. Frank Hull, IV. LC 78-19741. 1978. 23.95 (ISBN 0-03-046151-0). Praeger.
Foreign Substances & Nutrition. Ed. by J. C. Somogyi. R. Tarjan. (Bibliotheca Nutritio et Dieta: No. 29). (Illus.). 1980. pap. 49.75 (ISBN 3-8055-0621-X). S Karger.
Foreign Trade & Commerce in Ancient India. Prakash C. Prasad. 1977. 20.00x o.p. (ISBN 0-88386-981-0). South Asia Bks.
Foreign Trade & Domestic Aid. Charles R. Frank, Jr. LC 76-51821. 1977. 10.95 (ISBN 0-8157-2914-6). Brookings.
Foreign Trade & International Development. Anindya K. Bhattacharya. LC 75-27807. (Illus.). 1976. 15.95 (ISBN 0-669-00252-6). Lexington Bks.
Foreign Trade & U. S. Policy: The Case for Free International Trade. Leland B. Yeager & David G. Tuerck. LC 75-19832. (Praeger Special Studies Ser.). 275p. 1976. text ed. 29.95 (ISBN 0-275-56270-0); pap. text ed. 11.95 (ISBN 0-275-89510-6). Praeger.
Foreign Trade Criteria in Socialist Economies. Andrea Boltho. LC 78-121366. (Soviet & East European Studies). 1970. 25.50 (ISBN 0-521-07883-0). Cambridge U Pr.
Foreign Trade in a Planned Economy. Ed. by Imre Vajda & M. Simai. LC 74-149433. 1971. 38.50 (ISBN 0-521-08153-X). Cambridge U Pr.
Foreign Trade Marketplace. Ed. by George J. Schultz. LC 76-20342. 1977. 70.00 (ISBN 0-8103-0981-5). Gale.
Foreign Trade of China: Policy, Law, & Practice. Gene T. Hsiao. LC 76-7768. 1977. 27.50x (ISBN 0-520-03257-8). U of Cal Pr.
Foreign Trade Prices in the Council for Mutual Economic Assistance. E. A. Hewett. LC 73-86045. (Soviet & East European Studies). (Illus.). 212p. 1974. 35.50 (ISBN 0-521-20377-5). Cambridge U Pr.
Foreign Trade Turnover of Latin America Until 1970 & Its Prospective Development up to 1980. Arpad Orosz. LC 77-369256. (Studies on Developing Countries). 130p. (Orig.). 1976. pap. 8.50x (ISBN 0-8002-0494-8). Intl Pubns Serv.
Foreign Travel & Immunization Guide. 10th ed. Hans Neumann. 1981. pap. 5.50 (ISBN 0-87489-254-6). Med Economics.
Foreign Workers & Immigration Policy: The Case of France. Organization for Economic Cooperation & Development & C. Kennedy-Brenner. (Development Center Studies). (Illus.). 106p. (Orig.). 1980. pap. text ed. 6.00x (ISBN 92-64-11964-7, 41 79 04 1). OECD.
Foreigner. Arun Joshi. (Orient Paperback Ser). 244p. 1972. pap. 3.25 (ISBN 0-88253-106-9). Ind-US Inc.
Foreigner: A Novel. Arun Joshi. 1969. 6.00x (ISBN 0-210-98113-X). Asia.
Foreigners in Their Native Land: Historical Roots of the Mexican Americans. Ed. by David J. Weber. LC 73-77858. 1979. pap. 7.50x (ISBN 0-8263-0279-3). U of NM Pr.
Forensic Anthropology: The Structure, Morphology, & Variation of Human Bone & Dentition. Mahmoud Y. El-Najjar & K. Richard McWilliams. (Illus.). 208p. 1978. 17.50 (ISBN 0-398-03648-9). C C Thomas.
Forensic Biology for the Law Enforcement Officer. Charles G. Wilber. (Illus.). 392p. 1974. 25.75 (ISBN 0-398-03174-6). C C Thomas.
Forensic Dentistry. Irvin M. Sopher. (American Lectures in Forensic Pathology Ser.). (Illus.). 176p. 1976. 19.75 (ISBN 0-398-03474-5). C C Thomas.
Forensic Examination of Paints & Pigments. David A. Crown. (August Vollmer Criminalistics Ser). 276p. 1968. 24.75 (ISBN 0-398-00372-6). C C Thomas.
Forensic Hypnosis: The Practical Application of Hypnosis in Criminal Investigations. Whitney Hibbard & Raymond Worring. (Illus.). 400p. 1980. text ed. 34.75 (ISBN 0-398-04098-2). C C Thomas.
Forensic Medicine, 3 vols. Ed. by Cesare G. Tedeschi et al. LC 74-4593. (Illus.). 1680p. 1977. Vol. 1. 50.00 (ISBN 0-7216-8772-5); Vol. 2. 35.00 (ISBN 0-7216-8773-3); Vol. 3. 40.00 (ISBN 0-7216-8774-1); 125.00 set (ISBN 0-7216-8771-7). Saunders.
Forensic Paper Examination & Analysis. Louise Louden. LC 79-55266. (Bibliographic Ser.: No. 286). 1979. pap. 10.00 (ISBN 0-87010-057-2). Inst Paper Chem.
Forensic Psychiatry. Ed. by G. V. Morozov & Ia. M. Kalashnik. LC 76-77458. 1970. 22.50 o.p. (ISBN 0-87332-024-7). M E Sharpe.
Forensic Psychiatry: A Practical Guide for Lawyers & Psychiatrists. Robert L. Sadoff. (American Lectures in Behavioral Science & Law Ser.). 272p. 1975. 19.75 (ISBN 0-398-03412-5). C C Thomas.
Forensic Psychology. Robert Gordon. 1977. 7.95 (ISBN 0-88229-477-6). Nelson-Hall.
Forensic Psychology. Lionel Haward. 280p. 1981. 45.00 (ISBN 0-7134-2475-3, Pub. by Batsford England). David & Charles.
Forensic Psychology & Psychiatry. Ed. by Fred Wright et al. LC 80-17982. (N.Y. Academy of Sciences Annals: Vol. 347). 364p. 1980. 58.00 (ISBN 0-89766-084-6). NY Acad Sci.
Forensic Toxicology. Ed. by John S. Oliver. 320p. 1980. 50.00x (Pub. by Croom Helm England). State Mutual Bk.
Forerunner. Andre Norton. 288p. (Orig.). 1981. pap. 2.50 (ISBN 0-523-41481-1). Pinnacle Bks.
Forerunner Foray. Andre Norton. 1975. pap. 2.25 (ISBN 0-441-24621-4). Ace Bks.
Forerunners. Reed M. Holmes. 1981. pap. price not set (ISBN 0-8309-0315-1). Herald Hse.
Foreseeing the Future. Basil I. Rakoczi. 128p. 1973. pap. 1.25 o.p. (ISBN 0-06-087039-7, HW). Har-Row.
Forest. rev. ed. Ed. by Peter Farb. LC 61-17488. (Life Nature Library). (Illus.). (gr. 5 up). 1969. PLB 8.97 o.p. (ISBN 0-8094-0614-4, Pub. by Time-Life). Silver.
Forest & Forestry. 2nd ed. David Anderson & William A. Smith. LC 75-23932. (gr. 10-12). 1976. 15.35 o.p. (ISBN 0-8134-1764-3); text ed. 11.50x o.p. (ISBN 0-685-71178-1, 1764). Interstate.
Forest & Forestry. 3rd ed. Ed. by David Anderson & A. Smith William. (gr. 10-12). 1981. 14.00 (ISBN 0-8134-2169-1); text ed. 10.50x. Interstate.
Forest & Garden. William White, Jr. LC 76-19799. (Living Nature Ser.). (Illus.). (gr. 7 up). 1976. 7.95 (ISBN 0-8069-3578-2); PLB 7.49 (ISBN 0-8069-3579-0). Sterling.
Forest & Range Policy. 2nd ed. Samuel T. Dana & Sally K. Fairfax. (Illus.). 496p. 1980. text ed. 19.95 (ISBN 0-07-015288-8, P&RB). McGraw.
Forest & Range Policy: Its Development in the U. S. Samuel T. Dana. (American Forestry Ser). 1956. text ed. 18.00 o.p. (ISBN 0-07-015285-3, C). McGraw.
Forest & Shade Tree Entomology. Roger F. Anderson. LC 60-11714. 1960. 25.50 (ISBN 0-471-02739-1). Wiley.
Forest & the Sea. Marston Bates. 1965. pap. 2.45 (ISBN 0-394-70292-1, V-292, Vin). Random.

Forest & Woodland. Stephen Collins. LC 60-6114. (Community of Living Things Ser). (Illus.). (gr. 4-8). 1967. PLB 7.45 (ISBN 0-87191-015-2). Creative Ed.

Forest Biometrics. M. Prodan. 1968. 55.00 o.p. (ISBN 0-08-012441-0). Pergamon.

Forest Echo. G. A. Skrebitski. LC 66-21974. (gr. 2-4). PLB 4.35 o.s.i. (ISBN 0-8076-0414-3). Braziller.

Forest Ecology. 3rd ed. Stephen H. Spurr & Burton V. Barnes. LC 79-10007. 1980. text ed. 24.95 (ISBN 0-471-04732-5). Wiley.

Forest Energy & Economic Development. D. E. Earl. (Illus.). 140p. 1975. 22.50x (ISBN 0-19-854521-5). Oxford U Pr.

Forest Environments in Tropical Life Zones: A Pilot Study. L. R. Holdridge et al. LC 75-129847. 1971. 165.00 (ISBN 0-08-016340-8). Pergamon.

Forest Fertilization Research. 1965. 0.65 o.p. (ISBN 0-686-20729-7). SUNY Environ.

Forest Folklore, Mythology & Romance. Alexander Porteous. LC 68-26597. 1968. Repr. of 1928 ed. 18.00 (ISBN 0-8103-3456-9). Gale.

Forest Hills: An Illustrated History. Robert Minton. LC 75-14461. (Illus.). 268p. 1975. 17.95 o.p. (ISBN 0-397-01094-X). Lippincott.

Forest Home. Elizabeth M. Rourke. 1980. 5.50 (ISBN 0-8233-0314-4). Golden Quill.

Forest Hotel. Barbara S. Davis. (Illus.). 24p. (gr. k-1). 1976. PLB 5.00 (ISBN 0-307-60350-4, Golden Pr). Western Pub.

Forest Influences. (FAO-Forestry Ser.: No. 9). 307p. 1980. pap. 16.25 (ISBN 92-5-100722-5, F 1880, FAO). Unipub.

Forest Mensuration. 2nd ed. Bertram Husch et al. (Illus.). 1972. 21.95 (ISBN 0-8260-4595-2). Wiley.

Forest Microclimatology. Richard Lee. LC 77-21961. (Illus.). 1978. 20.00x (ISBN 0-231-04156-X). Columbia U Pr.

Forest of Enchantment. John Cook & Maria Cook. (Illus.). 48p. (gr. 4-6). 1979. 3.95 (ISBN 0-8059-2670-4). Dorrance.

Forest Pest Control: An Assessment of Present & Alternative Technologies, 5 vols, Vol Iv. (Pest Control Ser.). 1975. pap. 7.00 (ISBN 0-309-02413-7). Natl Acad Pr.

Forest Plants of the Monangahela National Forest. Roy B. Clarkson et al. 1980. pap. 8.95 (ISBN 0-910286-82-5). Boxwood.

Forest-Products Community: Crosset, Arkansas. (gr. 2). 1974. pap. text ed. 4.12 (ISBN 0-205-03888-3, 8038880); tchr's. guide 12.00 (ISBN 0-205-03884-0, 8038848). Allyn.

Forest Products Prices 1960-1978. (FAO Forestry Paper Ser.: No. 18). 79p. 1980. pap. 7.50 (ISBN 92-5-000881-3, F1955, FAO). Unipub.

Forest Recreation. 2nd ed. Robert W. Douglass. 1975. text ed. 19.50 (ISBN 0-08-018008-6). Pergamon.

Forest Resource Economics. G. Robinson Gregory. 512p. 1972. 22.95 (ISBN 0-8260-3605-8, 40503). Wiley.

Forest Runners. Joseph Altsheler. 1976. lib. bdg. 16.30x (ISBN 0-89968-002-X). Lightyear.

Forest Tree Planting in Arid Zones. 2nd ed. A. Y. Goor & C. W. Barney. LC 76-22314. (Illus.). 1976. 27.50 (ISBN 0-8260-3441-1, 39153, Pub. by Wiley-Interscience). Wiley.

Forest Trees of the Pacific Slope. George B. Sudworth. (Illus.). 11.00 (ISBN 0-8446-3031-4). Peter Smith.

Forest Trees of the Pacific Slope. George B. Sudworth. (Illus.). 1967. pap. 6.95 (ISBN 0-486-21752-3). Dover.

Forest Trees of the United States & Canada, & How to Identify Them. Elbert L. Little. LC 79-52527. (Illus.). 1980. pap. text ed. 2.00 (ISBN 0-486-23902-0). Dover.

Forest World. Eric Duffey. LC 79-91274. (Illus.). 224p. 1980. 18.95 (ISBN 0-89479-060-9). A & W Pubs.

Foresters, an American Tale, 1792. Jeremy Belknap. LC 71-100127. 1969. Repr. of 1792 ed. 23.00x (ISBN 0-8201-1071-X). Schol Facsimiles.

Forester's Companion. 2nd ed. N. D. James. 1966. 12.50x (ISBN 0-631-09620-5, Pub. by Basil Blackwell); pap. 8.95x (ISBN 0-631-10811-4). Biblio Dist.

Forestry. Boy Scouts Of America. LC 19-600. (Illus.). 64p. (gr. 6-12). 1971. pap. 0.70x (ISBN 0-8395-3302-0, 3302). BSA.

Forestry in National Developments: Production Systems, Conservation, Foreign Trade & Aid. Ed. by K. R. Shepherd & H. V. Richter. (Development Studies Centre - Monograph: No. 17). (Orig.). 1980. pap. 13.95 (ISBN 0-7081-1822-4, 0414, Pub. by ANUP Australia). Bks Australia.

Forests: Fresh Perspectives from Ecosystems Analysis. Proceedings. Oregon State University Biology Colloquium, 40th. Ed. by Richard H. Waring. LC 80-14883. (Illus.). 210p. 1980. pap. 12.00 (ISBN 0-87071-179-2). Oreg St U Pr.

Forests of the Sea: Life & Death on the Continental Shelf. John L. Culliney. LC 78-8208. 1979. pap. 5.95 (ISBN 0-385-14417-2, Anch). Doubleday.

Forever. Judy Blume. LC 74-22850. 1975. 8.95 (ISBN 0-87888-079-8). Bradbury Pr.

Forever After. Kate Lazlo. 288p. 1981. 10.95 (ISBN 0-686-69084-2). Dial.

Forever After. Doric Wilson. LC 80-82802. 80p. (Orig.). 1980. pap. 3.95 (ISBN 0-935672-01-X). JH Pr.

Forever Ambridge. Norman Painting. 1980. 9.95 o.p. (ISBN 0-7181-1422-1, Pub. by Michael Joseph). Merrimack Bk Serv.

Forever & Ever. Wayne Cruseturner. 240p. (Orig.). 1981. pap. 2.50 (ISBN 0-515-05529-8). Jove Pubns.

Forever Fuel: The Story of Hydrogen. Peter Hoffman. 250p. 1981. 16.00x (ISBN 0-89158-581-8). Westview.

Forever in Debt. Raymond W. Gibson. (Orig.). 1980. pap. text ed. 5.00 (ISBN 0-89536-461-1). CSS Pub.

Forever in Eden. Lorraine N. Finley. 1971. 5.00 o.p. (ISBN 0-685-02641-8). Golden Quill.

Forever Is a Hell of a Long Time. Ted Stauffer. LC 75-32995. 320p. 1976. 9.95 o.p. (ISBN 0-8092-8089-2). Contemp Bks.

Forever Panting. Peter De Vries. 1974. pap. 1.25 o.p. (ISBN 0-445-00191-7). Popular Lib.

Forever Tomorrow. Anne Duffield. 1974. pap. 1.25 o.p. (ISBN 0-425-02672-8, Medallion). Berkley Pub.

Forever Triumphant. F. J. Huegel. 96p. 1967. pap. 1.50 (ISBN 0-87123-155-7, 200155). Bethany Fell.

Forever Young. Jonathan Cott. (Illus.). 1978. 10.00 o.p. (ISBN 0-685-85032-3); pap. 5.95 (ISBN 0-394-73398-3). Random.

Forget All the Rules You Ever Learned About Graphic Design: Including the Ones in This Book. Bob Gill. 168p. 1981. 22.50. Watson-Guptill.

Forget Harry. Carrie Smith. 1981. 11.95 (ISBN 0-671-42265-0). S&S.

Forget-Me-Not Lane. Peter Nichols. 1971. 8.95 (ISBN 0-571-09855-X, Pub. by Faber & Faber); pap. 5.50 (ISBN 0-571-09857-6). Merrimack Bk Serv.

Forget the Gas Pumps-Make Your Own Fuel. Jim Wortham & Barbara Whitener. LC 79-90459. (Illus., Orig.). 1979. lib. bdg. 12.95 (ISBN 0-915216-72-8); pap. 4.95 (ISBN 0-915216-43-4). Love Street.

Forgetful Fred. Jay Williams. LC 73-12965. (Illus.). 40p. (ps-3). 1974. 5.95 o.s.i. (ISBN 0-8193-0719-X, Four Winds); PLB 5.41 o.s.i. (ISBN 0-8193-0720-3). Schol Bk Serv.

Forgetting Elena. Edmund White. 192p. 1976. pap. 1.50 o.p. (ISBN 0-445-03145-X). Popular Lib.

Forgetting's No Excuse. Mary Scott. 1973. 6.95 o.p. (ISBN 0-571-09875-4, Pub. by Faber & Faber). Merrimack Bk Serv.

Forging a Language. J. Chothia. LC 78-73239. (Illus.). 1980. 29.50 (ISBN 0-521-22569-8). Cambridge U Pr.

Forging a More Perfect Union: The Years in Review 1784-1788. Eric Rothschild & Livia Brilliant. 160p. (gr. 9-12). 1980. pap. text ed. 25.00 (ISBN 0-667-00575-7). Microfilming Corp.

Forging & Welding. rev. ed. Robert E. Smith. (Illus.). (gr. 7 up). 1956. text ed. 14.00 (ISBN 0-87345-120-1). McKnight.

Forging of an Aristocracy. Ronald Story. 1980. 16.00x (ISBN 0-8195-5044-2, Pub by Wesleyan U Pr England). Columbia U Pr.

Forging of Our Continent. Charlton Ogburn, Jr. LC 68-22959. (Illus.). 160p. 1968. 4.95 (ISBN 0-8281-0343-7, JO411-0, Co-Pub. by Smithsonian). Am Heritage.

Forging of the Cosmic Race: A Reinterpretation of Colonial Mexico. Colin M. MacLachlan & Jaime E. Rodriguez. (Illus.). 408p. 1980. 25.00 (ISBN 0-520-03890-8). U of Cal Pr.

Forging of the "Ring". C. Von Westernhagen. Tr. by Arnold Whittall & Mary Whittall. LC 76-7140. (Illus.). 1976. 27.50 (ISBN 0-521-21293-6). Cambridge U Pr.

Forging the American Republic, 1760-1815. Norman K. Risjord. LC 72-4239. 1973. pap. text ed. 8.50 (ISBN 0-201-06301-8). A-W.

Forgive & Remember: Managing Medical Failure. Charles L. Bosk. LC 78-16596. 1979. 15.00x (ISBN 0-226-06679-7). U of Chicago Pr.

Forgive & Remember: Managing Medical Failure. Charles L. Bosk. LC 78-16596. 248p. 1981. pap. 5.95 (ISBN 0-226-06680-0). U of Chicago Pr.

Forgive, Forget & Be Free. Jeanette Lockerbie. LC 80-69304. 148p. 1981. 7.95 (ISBN 0-915684-76-4). Christian Herald.

Forgive the Father: A Memoir of Changing Generations. Howard Wolf. LC 78-14396. 1978. 8.95 o.p. (ISBN 0-915220-44-X). New Republic.

Forgive Us Our Prayers. John A. Huffman, Jr. 1980. pap. 1.95 (ISBN 0-88207-519-5). Victor Bks.

Forgiveness Is a Two-Way Street. Charles W. Keysor. 132p. 1981. pap. 3.95 (ISBN 0-88207-338-9). Victor Bks.

Forgiving. Churches Alive Inc. (Love One Another Bible Study). 1979. wkbk. 1.50 (ISBN 0-934396-01-9). Churches Alive.

Forgotten Airplanes: Interesting History of Aviation Firsts. Deborah L. Platt & Keith Wiesley. 176p. 1981. 10.50 (ISBN 0-934506-04-3). Westminster Comm Pubns.

Forgotten Ambassador: The Reports of John Leighton Stuart, 1946-1949. Ed. by Kenneth W. Rea & John C. Brewer. (Replica Edition Ser.). 350p. 1981. lib. bdg. 25.00x (ISBN 0-86531-157-9). Westview.

Forgotten Arts, Book Four. (Illus.). 64p. 1979. 3.95 (ISBN 0-911658-02-5). Yankee Bks.

Forgotten Bear. pap. 3.50 incl. record (ISBN 0-590-20607-9, Schol Pap). Schol Bk Serv.

Forgotten Bear. Consuelo Joerns. LC 78-1546. (Illus.). (gr. k-3). 1978. 5.95 (ISBN 0-590-07560-8, Four Winds). Schol Bk Serv.

Forgotten Books of the American Nursery. Rosalie V. Halsey. LC 68-31084. 1969. Repr. of 1911 ed. 15.00 (ISBN 0-8103-3483-6). Gale.

Forgotten Bride. Gwen Westwood. (Harlequin Romances Ser.). 192p. 1980. pap. 1.25 o.p. (ISBN 0-373-02363-4, Pub. by Harlequin). PB.

Forgotten Empire-Vijayanagar: A Contribution to the History of India. Robert T. Sewell. (Illus.). 427p. 1972. Repr. of 1900 ed. 31.00x (ISBN 0-686-28323-6, Pub. by Irish Academic Pr). Biblio Dist.

Forgotten Father. Thomas A. Smail. 1981. pap. 5.95 (ISBN 0-8028-1879-X). Eerdmans.

Forgotten Folk-Tales of the English Counties. Ruth L. Tongue. 1970. 17.50 (ISBN 0-7100-6833-6). Routledge & Kegan.

Forgotten Glory. James Burke. (Illus.). 1979. 11.95 (ISBN 0-87244-049-4). Texian.

Forgotten Heritage: Original Folk Tales of Lowland Scotland. Ed. by Hannah Aitken. (Illus.). 168p. 1973. 11.00x (ISBN 0-87471-430-3). Rowman.

Forgotten Impulses. Todd Walton. 1981. pap. 2.50 (ISBN 0-451-09802-1, E9802, Signet Bks). NAL.

Forgotten Neighborhood: Site of an Early Skirmish in the War on Poverty. Ludwig Geismar & Jane Krisberg. LC 67-12067. 1967. 11.00 o.p. (ISBN 0-8108-0048-9). Scarecrow.

Forgotten Ones: A Sociological Study of Anglo & Chicano Retardates. Anne-Marie Henshel. 338p. 1973. 15.00x (ISBN 0-292-72403-9). U of Tex Pr.

Forgotten People: Cane River's Creoles of Color. Gary B. Mills. LC 77-452. (Illus.). 1977. 20.00x (ISBN 0-8071-0279-2); pap. 8.95 (ISBN 0-8071-0287-3). La State U Pr.

Forgotten Planet. G. Henry Smith. (YA) 5.95 (ISBN 0-685-07434-X, Avalon). Bouregy.

Forgotten Railways: Chilterns & Cotswolds. R. Davies & M. D. Grant. LC 74-83307. (Forgotten Railways Ser). (Illus.). 240p. 1975. 14.95 (ISBN 0-7153-6701-3). David & Charles.

Forgotten Railways: East Anglia. R. S. Joby. LC 76-48824. (Forgotten Railways Ser.). (Illus.). 1977. 14.95 (ISBN 0-7153-7312-9). David & Charles.

Forgotten Railways: North & Mid Wales. Rex Christiansen. LC 75-31317. (Forgotten Railways Ser.). (Illus.). 144p. 1976. 14.95 (ISBN 0-7153-7059-6). David & Charles.

Forgotten Railways: North East England. K. Hoole. (Forgotten Railways Ser.). (Illus.). 1973. 14.95 (ISBN 0-7153-5894-4). David & Charles.

Forgotten Railways: North-West England. John Marshall. LC 80-68899. (Illus.). 176p. 1981. 16.95 (ISBN 0-7153-8003-6). David & Charles.

Forgotten Railways of South East England. H. P. White. (Forgotten Railways Ser.). 1976. 14.95 (ISBN 0-7153-7286-6). David & Charles.

Forgotten Railways: Scotland. John Thomas. (Forgotten Railways Ser.). (Illus.). 144p. 1976. 14.95 (ISBN 0-7153-6961-X). David & Charles.

Forgotten Railways: South Wales. James Page. LC 79-51099. (Illus.). 1979. 19.95 (ISBN 0-7153-7734-5). David & Charles.

Forgotten Railways: The East Midlands. P. Howard Anderson. (Forgotten Railways Ser.). (Illus.). 208p. 1973. 17.95 (ISBN 0-7153-6094-9). David & Charles.

Forgotten Season. Kathleen Conlon. 177p. 1981. 9.95 (ISBN 0-312-29899-4). St Martin.

Forgotten Sector: The Training of Ancillary Staff in Hospitals. D. N. Smith. 1969. text ed. 22.00 (ISBN 0-08-013379-7); pap. text ed. 10.75 (ISBN 0-08-013378-9). Pergamon.

Forgotten Sioux: An Ethnohistory of the Lower Brule Reservation. Ernest L. Schusky. LC 75-503. (Illus.). 272p. 1975. 16.95 (ISBN 0-88229-138-6); pap. 8.95 (ISBN 0-88229-501-2). Nelson-Hall.

Forgotten Third Skill: Reading a Foreign Language. Marcelle Kellerman. LC 80-41029. (Language Teaching Methodology Ser.). 96p. 1981. 11.95 (ISBN 0-08-024599-4); pap. 7.95 (ISBN 0-08-024598-6). Pergamon.

Forgotten Truth: The Primordial Tradition. Huston Smith. LC 74-15850. (Illus.). 192p. 1976. 8.95 o.s.i. (ISBN 0-06-013902-1, HarpT). Har-Row.

Forgotten Truth: The Primordial Tradition. Huston Smith. 1977. pap. 3.95 (ISBN 0-06-090576-X, CN 576, CN). Har-Row.

Forgotten Truths. Robert Anderson. LC 80-17526. (Sir Robert Anderson Library). 1980. pap. 3.50 (ISBN 0-8254-2130-6). Kregel.

Forgotton Spurgeon. Iain H. Murray. 1978. pap. 3.95 (ISBN 0-85151-156-2). Banner of Truth.

Foriegn Cultural Policy: A Survey from a German Point of View. Hans Arnold. 1979. pap. 18.50 (ISBN 0-85496-210-7). Dufour.

Fork River Space Project. Wright Morris. LC 77-3798. 1977. 8.95 o.s.i. (ISBN 0-06-013106-3, HarpT). Har-Row.

Fork, Spoon & Finger Food. Peter French-Hodges & Catherine Althaus. (Illus.). 1975. 6.95 o.p. (ISBN 0-571-10613-7, Pub. by Faber & Faber). Merrimack Bk Serv.

Fork-Tailed Devil: P-38. Martin Caidin. (Illus.). 1976. pap. 2.25 (ISBN 0-345-28301-5). Ballantine.

Forked Tongue. Giles Lutz. 160p. 1981. pap. 1.75 (ISBN 0-345-29220-0). Ballantine.

Forkner Shorthand. 4th ed. Hamden L. Forkner, et al. 11.20x (ISBN 0-912036-10-9); pap. 9.20x (ISBN 0-912036-11-7). Forkner.

Forkner Shorthand Outlines for the Business Vocabulary. Geraldine M. Farmer & Mary S. Lore. 123p. 1972. pap. 6.60x (ISBN 0-912036-23-0). Forkner.

Form-Analysis & Exegesis: A Fresh Approach to the Interpretation of Mishnah. Jacob Neusner. 224p. 1981. 22.50x (ISBN 0-8166-0984-5); pap. 9.95x (ISBN 0-8166-0985-3). U of Minn Pr.

Form & Convention in the Poetry of Edmund Spenser. Ed. by William Nelson. LC 61-16780. (Papers of the English Institute Ser.). 1961. 15.00x (ISBN 0-231-02502-5). Columbia U Pr.

Form & Expression in Calligraphy. Donald Jackson. LC 78-20704. (Illus.). Date not set. pap. 3.95 (ISBN 0-8008-2683-3, Pentalic). Taplinger. Postponed.

Form & Function: Japanese Teapots. Masao Usui. LC 78-71255. (Form & Function Ser.: Vol. 4). (Illus.). 1981. pap. 8.95 (ISBN 0-87011-392-5). Kodansha.

Form & Function of the Body of the Greek Letter in the Non-Literary Papyri & in Paul the Apostle. John L. White. LC 75-33088. (Society of Biblical Literature. Dissertation Ser.). (Illus.). 1975. pap. 7.50 (ISBN 0-89130-048-1, 060102). Scholars Pr Ca.

Form & Function: Remarks on Art, Design & Architecture. Horatio Greenough. Ed. by Harold A. Small. 1947. pap. 3.95x (ISBN 0-520-00514-7, CAMPUS26). U of Cal Pr.

Form & Meaning: Writings on the Renaissance & Modern Art. Robert Klein. Tr. by Madeline Jay & Leon Wieseltier. LC 80-8772. 276p. 1981. pap. 7.95 (ISBN 0-691-00328-9). Princeton U Pr.

Form & Purpose in Boswell's Biographical Works. William R. Siebenschuh. 1972. 14.50x (ISBN 0-520-02246-7). U of Cal Pr.

Form & Structure of the Familiar Greek Letter of Recommendation. Chan-Hie Kim. LC 72-87887. (Society of Biblical Literature. Dissertation Ser.: No. 4). 1972. pap. 9.00 (ISBN 0-89130-160-7, 060104). Scholars Pr Ca.

Form & Structure of the Official Petition: A Study in Greek Epistolography. John L. White. LC 72-87889. (Society of Biblical Literature. Dissertations Ser.: No. 5). (Illus.). 1972. pap. 9.00 (ISBN 0-89130-161-5, 060105). Scholars Pr Ca.

Form & Style: Theses, Reports, Term Papers. 5th ed. William G. Campbell & Stephen V. Ballou. LC 77-75137. (Illus.). 1977. pap. text ed. 7.25 (ISBN 0-395-25442-6). HM.

Form & Substance: An Advance Rhetoric. Richard Coe. 400p. 1981. text ed. 10.95 (ISBN 0-471-04585-3). Wiley.

Form & Thought in Prose. 4th ed. Ed. by Wilfred Stone & Robert Hoopes. LC 77-73100. 1977. 11.95x (ISBN 0-8260-8556-3). Wiley.

Form in Modern Verse Drama, 2 vols. Douglas B. Kurdys. (Salzburg Studies in English Literature Poetic Drama & Poetic Theory Ser.: No. 17). 1972. Set. pap. 50.25x (ISBN 0-391-01454-4). Humanities.

Form in Music: An Examination of Traditional Techniques of Musical Structure & Their Application in Historical & Contemporary Styles. Wallace Berry. 1966. text ed. 20.95 (ISBN 0-13-329201-0). P-H.

Form of Housing. Sam Davis. 320p. 1981. pap. text ed. 14.95 (ISBN 0-442-27218-9). Van Nos Reinhold.

Form of Sociology: Paradigms & Crises. S. N. Eisenstadt & M. Curelaru. LC 76-7602. 386p. 1976. 25.95 (ISBN 0-471-23472-9, Pub. by Wiley-Interscience). Wiley.

Form, Space & Vision. 3rd ed. Graham Collier. LC 75-167911. 1972. pap. text ed. 18.95 (ISBN 0-13-329458-7). P-H.

Form Your Own Corporation. John C. Howell. 128p. 1980. pap. 5.95 (Spec). P-H.

Formal Approach to Discourse Anaphora. Bonnie L. Webber. Ed. by Jorge Hankamer. LC 78-67737. (Outstanding Dissertations in Linguistics Ser.). 1979. lib. bdg. 24.00 (ISBN 0-8240-9670-3). Garland Pub.

Formal Background to Mathematics: Pt. II, A & B. R. Edwards. (Universitext). 1170p. 1980. pap. 39.80 (ISBN 0-387-90513-8). Springer-Verlag.

Formal Language Theory: Perspectives & Open Problems. Ed. by Ronald V. Book. 1980. 25.00 (ISBN 0-12-115350-9). Acad Pr.

Formal Logic. 2nd ed. Arthur N. Prior. 1962. 35.00x (ISBN 0-19-824156-9). Oxford U Pr.

Formal Logic: Its Scope & Limits. 2nd ed. Richard C. Jeffrey. (Illus.). 256p. 1981. text ed. 17.95 (ISBN 0-07-032321-6, C); instr's manual 5.95 (ISBN 0-07-032322-4). McGraw.

Formal Semantics of Natural Language. Ed. by E. L. Keenan. LC 74-25657. 456p. 1975. 59.50 (ISBN 0-521-20697-9). Cambridge U Pr.

Formal Theory of Exceptions in Generative Phonology. Wim Zonneveld. (Illus.). 1978. pap. text ed. 23.00x (ISBN 0-685-92395-9). Humanities.

Formalized Planning for Institutions of Higher Learning. Jerry W. Johnson & W. Randy Boxx. 1978. 4.00 (ISBN 0-938004-04-2). U MS Bus Econ.

Format & Coding for Computer Output Microfilm: ANSI-NMA MS2-1978. National Micrographics Assn. 1978. 6.00 (ISBN 0-89258-054-2). Natl Micrograph.

Formation & Fate of Cell Organelles. International Society for Cell Biology. Ed. by Katherine B. Warren. (Proceedings: Vol. 6). 1968. 49.00 (ISBN 0-12-611906-6). Acad Pr.

Formation & Role of Excited States in Radiolysis: Special Issue of International Journal for Radiation Physics & Chemistry, Vol. 8, Nos. 1 & 2. Ajit Singh. pap. text ed. 42.00 (ISBN 0-08-019986-0). Pergamon.

Formation du vocabulaire de l'aviation. L. Guilbert. (Fr). pap. 23.75x o.p. (ISBN 0-685-13923-9). Larousse.

Formation of a Legend: van Gogh Criticism, Eighteen Ninety to Nineteen Twenty. Carol M. Zemel. Ed. by Donald B. Kuspit. (Studies in Fine Arts: Criticism). 280p. 1981. 27.95 (ISBN 0-8357-1094-7, Pub. by UMI Res Pr). Univ Microfilms.

Formation of a Modern Labor Force: Upper Silesia 1865-1914. Lawrence Schofer. LC 73-90658. 1975. 19.50x (ISBN 0-520-02651-9). U of Cal Pr.

Formation of Christian Europe: An Illustrated History of the Church. Ed. by Florence Flugaur. Tr. by John Drury. (gr. 5-9). 1980. text ed. 16.95 (ISBN 0-03-056827-7). Winston Pr.

Formation of Christian Understanding: An Essay in Theological Hermeneutics. Charles M. Wood. (Orig.). 1981. pap. price not set (ISBN 0-664-24373-8). Westminster.

Formation of Soil Material. T. R. Paton. (Illus.). 1978. text ed. 20.00x (ISBN 0-04-631009-6); pap. text ed. 9.95x (ISBN 0-04-641010-4). Allen Unwin.

Formation of the American Medical Profession: The Role of Institutions, 1780-1860. Joseph F. Kett. LC 80-14326. xi, 217p. 1980. Repr. of 1968 ed. lib. bdg. 22.00x (ISBN 0-313-22428-5, KEFO). Greenwood.

Formation of the Baltic States: A Study of the Effects of Great Power Politics Upon the Emergence of Lithuania,Latvia, & Estonia. Stanley W. Page. LC 74-80578. 1970. Repr. 14.00 (ISBN 0-86527-068-6). Fertig.

Formation of the Christian Bible. Hans Von Campenhausen. Tr. by J. A. Baker from Ger. LC 73-171495. 360p. 1977. pap. 7.50 (ISBN 0-8006-1263-9, 1-1263). Fortress.

Formation of the New Testament. Eduard Lohse. Tr. by M. Eugene Boring. LC 80-27032. 256p. (Orig.). 1981. pap. 8.95 (ISBN 0-687-13294-0). Abingdon.

Formation of the Resurrection Narratives. Reginald H. Fuller. LC 79-8885. 240p. 1980. pap. 5.95 (ISBN 0-8006-1378-3, 1-1378). Fortress.

Formation of the Workingmen's Party of the U. S. 1876. Ed. by P. Foner. (Occasional Papers: No.18). 1976. 1.25 (ISBN 0-89977-017-7). Am Inst Marxist.

Formation of Uranium Ore Deposits. (Illus.). 748p. 1975. pap. 68.00 (ISBN 92-0-040274-7, ISP374, IAEA). Unipub.

Formative Years of Social Security. Arthur J. Altmeyer. (Illus.). 1966. 22.50 (ISBN 0-299-03820-3); pap. 6.50 (ISBN 0-299-03824-6). U of Wis Pr.

Formative Years of the Israeli Labour Party: The Organization of Power, 1919-1930. Yonathan Shapiro. LC 74-22992. (Sage Studies in Twentieth Century History: Vol. 4). 1976. 17.50x (ISBN 0-8039-9936-4). Sage.

Formative Years: 1607-1763. Clarence L. Ver Steeg. (Making of America Ser). 1964. 8.95 (ISBN 0-8090-4610-5); pap. 5.95 (ISBN 0-8090-0137-3). Hill & Wang.

Formats Used in the Library Multimedia Union Catalog. LC 79-4055. 59p. 1979. 6.00 (ISBN 0-913578-19-3). Inglewood Ca.

Formerly British Honduras: A Profile of the New Nation of Belize. William D. Setzekorn. LC 74-31640. (Illus.). 300p. 1976. 7.95 (ISBN 0-9600822-1-2); pap. 3.95 (ISBN 0-685-73559-1). Ohio U Pr.

Formerly British Honduras: A Profile of the New Nation of Belize. William D. Setzekorn. (Illus.). 295p. pap. 7.95x (ISBN 0-8214-0568-3). Ohio U Pr.

Forming of the Republic (1763-1825) The Educational Research Council. (American Adventure Concept & Inquiry Ser). (gr. 8). 1975. pap. text ed. 8.96 (ISBN 0-205-04630-4, 8046301). Allyn.

Forming-Thinking-Writing: The Composing Imagination. Ann E. Berthoff. (gr. 10-12). 1978. pap. text ed. 7.50x (ISBN 0-8104-6033-5). Hayden.

Formosa Betrayed. George Kerr. LC 76-10805. (China in the 20th Century Ser.). 1976. Repr. of 1965 ed. lib. bdg. 45.00 (ISBN 0-306-70762-4). Da Capo.

Forms & Agreements for Architects, Engineers & Contractors. Albert Dib. 1976. with 1979 suppl. 110.00 (ISBN 0-87632-215-1). Boardman.

Forms & Agreements on Intellectual Property & International Licensing. 3rd ed. Leslie W. Melville. LC 78-17576. 1979. looseleaf with 1979 rev. pages 67.50 (ISBN 0-686-57648-9). Boardman.

Forms & Their Meaning in Western Art. Lincoln Rothschild. LC 74-9298. (Illus.). 320p. 1976. 15.00 o.p. (ISBN 0-498-01608-0). A S Barnes.

Forms for Safety & Security Management. Edward T. Guy & John J. Merrigan. 448p. 1980. text ed. 28.95 (ISBN 0-409-95089-0). Butterworths.

Forms Manual. SAA College & University Archives Committee. 236p. 1973. pap. 11.00 o.p. (ISBN 0-931828-04-X). Soc Am Archivists.

Forms Manual for the CPA: For Audit, Review, & Compilation of Financial Statements. Benjamin Newman. LC 80-17271. 450p. 1980. 39.95 (ISBN 0-471-05762-2, Pub. by Ronald). Wiley.

Forms of Action at Common Law. Frederic W. Maitland. 1936. text ed. 15.95x (ISBN 0-521-05657-8); pap. text ed. 7.95x (ISBN 0-521-09185-3). Cambridge U Pr.

Forms of Brief Therapy. Ed. by Simon Budman. 500p. 1981. 25.00 (ISBN 0-89862-608-0). Guilford Pr.

Forms of Discovery: Critical & Historical Essays on the Forms of the Short Poem in English. Yvor Winters. LC 66-30433. 378p. 1967. 8.95 o.p. (ISBN 0-8040-0118-9); pap. 7.95x (ISBN 0-8040-0119-7). Swallow.

Forms of Drama. Ed. by Robert W. Corrigan & Glenn M. Loney. LC 74-150136. 906p. (Orig.). 1972. pap. text ed. 9.75 (ISBN 0-395-04327-1). HM.

Forms of Evil in the Gothic Novel. Chitra P. Reddin. Ed. by Devendra P. Varma. LC 79-8472. (Gothic Studies & Dissertations Ser.). 1980. lib. bdg. 28.00x (ISBN 0-405-12669-7). Arno.

Forms of Explanation: Rethinking the Questions in Social Theory. Alan Garfinkel. LC 80-2341. 192p. 1981. 16.00x (ISBN 0-300-02136-4). Yale U Pr.

Forms of Imagination: An Anthology of Poetry, Fiction & Drama. O. B. Hardison, Jr. & Jerry L. Mills. 1972. pap. text ed. 10.95 (ISBN 0-13-329516-8). P-H.

Forms of Public Address. Robert G. King. LC 68-15020. (Speech Communication Ser). 1968. pap. 3.95 (ISBN 0-672-61077-9, SC6). Bobbs.

Forms of Silence. Herbert W. Martin. LC 79-88742. 1980. pap. 4.00 perf. bound (ISBN 0-916418-20-0). Lotus.

Forms of the Novella: 10 Short Novels. David Richter. 833p. 1981. pap. text ed. 9.95 (ISBN 0-394-32030-1). Knopf.

Forms of Verse: British & American. Sara DeFord & Clarinda H. Lott. LC 77-94257. (Illus., Orig.). 1971. 24.50x (ISBN 0-89197-169-6); pap. text ed. 12.95x (ISBN 0-89197-170-X). Irvington.

Forms of Verse, British & American. Sara DeFord & Clarinda H. Lott. LC 77-94257. 393p. Repr. 12.95 (ISBN 0-390-26000-2). New Poets.

Forms of War Government in France. Pierre Renouvin. (Economic & Social History of the World War Ser.). 1927. 47.50x (ISBN 0-685-69856-4). Elliots Bks.

Formula. 289p. 1980. pap. 12.95 (ISBN 0-8362-2702-6). Andrews & McMeel.

Formula. Steve Shagan. 352p. 1980. pap. 2.75 (ISBN 0-553-13801-4). Bantam.

Formula Book. Norman Stark. 1976. pap. 1.75 (ISBN 0-380-00840-8, 31047). Avon.

Formula for Fitness. Richard E. Hunton. 1973. pap. 1.95 o.p. (ISBN 0-8054-5218-4). Broadman.

Formula for Happiness. Spiros Zodhiates. 256p. (Orig.). 1980. pap. 8.75 (ISBN 0-89957-046-1). AMG Pubs.

Formula for Success: A Core Concept of Management. Lawrence A. Appley. LC 73-87546. 1974. 11.95 (ISBN 0-8144-5339-2). Am Mgmt.

Formula Vee: Racing, History & Chassis-Engine Prep. Andrew L. Schupack. (Orig.). 1980. 12.95 (ISBN 0-8306-9952-X); pap. 6.95 (ISBN 0-8306-2063-X, 2063). TAB Bks.

Formulacion Quimica. Erica Glyn. (Span). 1970. pap. text ed. 2.70 (ISBN 0-06-313340-7, IntlDept). Har-Row.

Formulae & Methods. G. M. Cavanaugh et al. 1964. 6.00 (ISBN 0-685-52858-8). Marine Bio.

Formulae & Theorems in Mathematics. H. E. Fernando. 1967. pap. text ed. 2.95x o.p. (ISBN 0-435-71060-5). Heinemann Ed.

Formulae for the Mariner. Richard M. Plant. LC 78-21543. (Illus.). 1978. spiral bdg. 7.00x (ISBN 0-87033-251-1). Cornell Maritime.

Formulaic & Non-Formulaic Style in the Nibelungenlied: A Computer-Based Analysis. Agnes M. Bruno. (U. C. Publications in Modern Philology, Vol. 109). 1974. pap. 9.00x (ISBN 0-520-09499-9). U of Cal Pr.

Formulary of Detergents & Other Cleaning Agents. M. Ash & I. Ash. 1980. 22.50 (ISBN 0-8206-0247-7). Chem Pub.

Formulas & Theorems in Pure Mathematics. George S. Carr. LC 78-113122. Orig. Title: Synopsis of Pure Mathematics. 1970. text ed. 35.00 (ISBN 0-8284-0239-6). Chelsea Pub.

Formulations & Computational Algorithms in Finite-Element Analysis: U. S. German Symposium. Ed. by Klaus Bathe et al. 1977. text ed. 47.50x (ISBN 0-262-02127-7). MIT Pr.

Formwork for Concrete. M. K. Hurd. 1979. 39.25 (ISBN 0-685-85098-6, SP-4) (ISBN 0-685-85099-4). ACI.

Forrest Reid. Mary C. Bryan. (English Author Ser.: No. 199). 1976. lib. bdg. 12.50 (ISBN 0-8057-6661-8). Twayne.

Forster's Women: Eternal Differences. Bonnie B. Finkelstein. LC 74-18418. 192p. 1975. 12.50x (ISBN 0-231-03893-3). Columbia U Pr.

Forsyte Saga. John Galsworthy. 1933. lib. rep. ed. 25.00x (ISBN 0-684-15368-8, ScribT). Scribner.

Forsyth Wickes Collection. Percy C. Rathbone. LC 68-27635. (Illus.). 1968. pap. 2.50 (ISBN 0-87846-036-5, Pub. by Mus Fine Arts Boston). C E Tuttle.

Forsyth Wickes Collection. Perry T. Rathbone. (Illus.). 1968. 8.50 (ISBN 0-87846-164-7). Mus Fine Arts Boston.

Forsyth's Three. Frederick Forsyth. 1152p. 1980. 15.95 (ISBN 0-670-52410-7). Viking Pr.

Fort & the Flag. Louise Grant. (N. H.-Vermont Historiettes). (Illus.). 73p. (Orig.). (gr. 3-4). 1977. pap. 2.45 (ISBN 0-915892-09-X). Regional Ctr Educ.

Fort Apache, the Bronx. Heywood Gould. 224p. (Orig.). 1981. pap. 2.50 (ISBN 0-446-91618-8). Warner Bks.

Fort at the Dry. Al Cody. (YA) 1977. 5.95 (ISBN 0-685-75640-8, Avalon). Bouregy.

Fort Bliss, a Pictorial History. Leon C. Metz & Millard G. McKinney. Ed. by Frank Mangan. Date not set. 30.00 (ISBN 0-930208-10-2). Mangan Bks. Postponed.

Fort Defiance & the Navajos. Maurice Frink. (Illus.). 150p. (Orig.). 1981. pap. 5.95 (ISBN 0-87108-585-2). Pruett.

Fort Hare Nineteen Fifteen to Nineteen Forty-Eight: The Evolution of an African College. Alexander Kerr. LC 68-22137. (Illus.). 1968. text ed. 8.50x (ISBN 0-903983-04-4). Humanities.

Fort Hays, Frontier Army Post, 1865-1889. Leo E. Oliva. LC 80-82227. (Illus.). 66p. 1980. pap. write for info. (ISBN 0-87726-020-6). Kansas St Hist.

Fort Hogan. Frank Bonham. 1980. pap. 1.75 o.p. (ISBN 0-425-04562-5). Berkley Pub.

Fort Inexpugnable De L'honneur Du Sexe Femenin. Francois De Billon. Repr. of 1555 ed. 43.00 (ISBN 0-384-04270-8). Johnson Repr.

Fort McKavett, Texas. Margaret Bierschwale. (Illus.). 1966. 15.00 (ISBN 0-685-05001-7). A Jones.

Fort Mojave, Eighteen Fifty-Nine to Eighteen Ninety: Letter of the Commanding Officers. Irene J. Brennan. 1980. pap. 26.00 (ISBN 0-89126-083-8). Military Aff Aero.

Fort Phil Kearny: An American Saga. Dee Brown. LC 62-10963. (Illus.). 1971. pap. 5.25 (ISBN 0-8032-5730-9, BB 523, Bison). U of Nebr Pr.

Fort Starvation. Frank Gruber. 160p. 1980. pap. 1.75 o.s.i. (ISBN 0-553-14180-5). Bantam.

Fort Supply: Brigham Young's Green River Experiment. Fred R. Gowans & Eugene E. Campbell. 1976. pap. 3.25 o.s.i. (ISBN 0-8425-0248-3). Brigham.

Fort Worth: The Civilized West. Caleb Pirtle. Ed. by Ellen S. Blakey & Larry P. Silvey. LC 80-66338. (American Portrait Ser.). (Illus.). 240p. 1980. 24.95 (ISBN 0-932986-11-0). Continent Herit.

Fortaleza y Ternura. Tr. by Joyce Landorf. (Spanish Bks.). (Span.). 1978. 1.90 (ISBN 0-8297-0806-5). Life Pubs Intl.

Forties. Cobell Phillips. 1974. 12.95 o.s.i. (ISBN 0-686-66970-3). Macmillan.

Forties as Reported by the New York Times. Ed. by Arleen Keylin & Jonathan Cohen. LC 80-13897. (Illus.). 1980. lib. bdg. 9.98x (ISBN 0-405-12214-4). Arno.

Fortran. Robert J. Bent & George C. Sethares. LC 80-28581. 448p. (Orig.). 1981. pap. text ed. 16.95 (ISBN 0-8185-0436-6). Brooks-Cole.

Fortran. Samuel L. Marateck. 1977. 13.95 (ISBN 0-12-470460-3); instr' manual 1978 3.00 (ISBN 0-12-470462-X). Acad Pr.

Fortran & Agol: A Programmed Course for Students of Science & Technology. A. C. Bajpai et al. LC 73-5712. (Applied Mathematics for Scientists & Technologists Ser). 276p. 1972. 20.95 o.p. (ISBN 0-471-04371-0, Pub by Wiley-Interscience). Wiley.

Fortran & Computer Mathematics for the Engineer & Scientist. R. E. Carlile & B. E. Gillett. LC 72-95446. 1974. 23.00 (ISBN 0-87814-016-6). Pennwell Pub.

FORTRAN & FAP: A Program Library, Vol. 1. Stephen M. Simpson, Jr. cancelled o.s.i. (ISBN 0-201-07022-7, Adv Bk Prog). A-W.

Fortran Autotester. Robert E. Smith & Dora E. Johnson. (Prog. Bk.). 1962. pap. 10.95 (ISBN 0-471-80337-5, Pub. by Wiley-Interscience). Wiley.

Fortran Computer Programming for Statistics: A Manual. Richard C. Fegan & Susan L. Brosche. 1979. pap. 6.95 (ISBN 0-13-329326-2). P-H.

Fortran Computer Programs. C. W. Merriam, 3rd. LC 77-14792. 1978. 24.95 (ISBN 0-669-01995-X). Lexington Bks.

Fortran for Humans. 3rd ed. Richard Didday & Rex Page. (Illus.). 450p. 1981. pap. text ed. 10.36 (ISBN 0-8299-0356-9). West Pub.

FORTRAN for IBM System-360. 1968. pap. text ed. 10.95 (ISBN 0-574-16104-X, 15-0600); guide 2.25 (ISBN 0-574-16105-8, 15-0601). SRA.

Fortran Four. 2nd ed. J. Friedmann et al. (Wiley Self Teaching Guide Ser.). 544p. 1980. pap. 10.95 (ISBN 0-471-07771-2). Wiley.

FORTRAN Four Pocket Handbook. Daniel E. Alexander & Andrew C. Messer. 96p. (Orig.). 1972. pap. 3.95 (ISBN 0-07-001015-3, SP). McGraw.

Fortran Four Primer. Richard A. Mann. LC 77-188187. 1972. pap. text ed. 11.50 scp (ISBN 0-7002-2412-2, HarpC); solutions manual avail. (ISBN 0-685-23390-1). Har-Row.

FORTRAN Four Programming & Applications. C. Joseph Sass. LC 72-93537. 328p. 1974. pap. text ed. 12.95x (ISBN 0-8162-7473-8). Holden-Day.

Fortran Four Programming for Engineers & Scientists. 2nd ed. Paul W. Murrill & Cecil L. Smith. LC 73-1689. (Illus.). 322p. 1973. pap. text ed. 14.95 scp (ISBN 0-7002-2419-X, HarpC); solution manual avail. (ISBN 0-685-28248-1). Har-Row.

Fortran Four: Standard Fortran Watfor-Watfiv. Elliot I. Organick & Loren P. Meissner. 1975. text ed. 13.95 (ISBN 0-201-05503-1). A-W.

FORTRAN Fundamentals: A Short Course. Jack Steingraber. (Computer Programming Ser.). (Illus.). 96p. 1975. pap. text ed. 5.95 (ISBN 0-8104-5860-8). Hayden.

Fortran IV. Jehosua Friedmann et al. LC 74-34044. (Self-Teaching Guides Ser). 464p. 1975. pap. text ed. 8.95 (ISBN 0-471-28082-8). Wiley.

Fortran IV. 3rd ed. Fritz A. McCameron. 1978. pap. text ed. 10.95 (ISBN 0-256-02036-1). Irwin.

Fortran IV: A Programmed Instruction Approach. 3rd ed. J. Daniel Couger & Loren E. Shannon. 1976. pap. text ed. 11.50x (ISBN 0-256-01632-1). Irwin.

Fortran IV Programming. M. G. Chopra & Ram Kumar. 248p. 1980. text ed. 22.50 (ISBN 0-7069-1040-0, Pub. by Vikas India). Advent Bk.

Fortran IV Self-Taught. Mario V. Farina. 1966. pap. 14.95 (ISBN 0-13-329722-5). P-H.

Fortran IV with Watfor & Watfiv. P. Cress et al. 1970. ref. ed. 14.95x (ISBN 0-13-329433-1). P-H.

FORTRAN Logic & Programming. Fritz A. McCameron. 1968. pap. text ed. 7.25x o.p. (ISBN 0-256-00322-X). Irwin.

FORTRAN Programming. Donald D. Spencer. 1980. pap. 8.95 (ISBN 0-686-65745-4); tchr's manual 4.95 (ISBN 0-686-65746-2); wkbk 3.95 (ISBN 0-89218-018-8). Camelot Pub.

Fortran Programming for Civil Engineers. R. McCuen. 1975. pap. 16.95 (ISBN 0-13-329417-X). P-H.

Fortran Programming with Applications to Engineering: An Introductory Fortran Manual. Jack Evett & Richard P. Pinckney. 212p. 1981. pap. 5.95 (ISBN 0-910554-32-3). Eng Pr.

FORTRAN Seventy-Seven: Featuring Structured Programming. 3rd ed. Loren P. Meissner & Elliot I. Organick. LC 78-74689. 1980. pap. text ed. 13.95 (ISBN 0-201-05499-X). A-W.

FORTRAN Seventy-Seven for Humans. Rex Page & Richard Didday. (Illus.). 1980. pap. 10.95 (ISBN 0-8299-0271-6); instrs.' manual avail. (ISBN 0-8299-0615-0). West Pub.

Fortran Techniques. A. C. Day. LC 72-78891. (Illus.). 104p. 1972. 16.95 (ISBN 0-521-08549-7); pap. 6.95x (ISBN 0-521-09719-3). Cambridge U Pr.

FORTRAN with Style. Henry F. Ledgard & Louis J. Chmura. (Computer Programming Ser.). (gr. 12 up). 1978. pap. text ed. 8.35x (ISBN 0-8104-5682-6). Hayden.

Fortress. Gabrielle Lord. 154p. 1981. 8.95 (ISBN 0-312-29978-8). St Martin.

Fortress Besieged. Chi'en Chung-shu. Tr. by Jeanne Kelly & Nathan K. Mao. LC 78-24846. (Chinese Literature in Translation Ser.). 416p. 1980. 17.50x (ISBN 0-253-16518-0). Ind U Pr.

Fortress for Well-Being: Baha'i Teachings on Marriage. (Comprehensive Deepening Program Ser). 1973. pap. text ed. 4.00 (ISBN 0-87743-070-5, 7-64-04). Baha'i.

Fortress for Well-Being: Bahai Teachings on Marriage. (Comprehensive Deepening Program Ser.: Gift Ed.). 1974. 10.00 (ISBN 0-87743-093-4, 7-64-10); pap. 5.00 (ISBN 0-87743-153-1, 7-64-11). Bahai.

Fortress Fury. Carter A. Vaughan. 1977. pap. 1.50 o.p. (ISBN 0-445-03189-1). Popular Lib.

Fortress in the Sky: B-17 Bombers. Peter M. Bowers. LC 76-17145. 256p. 1976. 18.95 (ISBN 0-913194-04-2, Pub. by Sentry). Aviation.

Forts of Tennessee. Ed. by J. Ralph Randolph. (Tennessee Ser.: Vol. 4). (Illus.). 1981. 12.95 (ISBN 0-87870-109-5). Memphis St Univ.

Forts of the Upper Missouri. Robert G. Athearn. LC 67-24466. (Illus.). xii, 340p. 1972. pap. 7.50 (ISBN 0-8032-5762-7, 555, Bison). U of Nebr Pr.

Forts of the West: Military Forts & Presidios & Posts Commonly Called Forts West of the Mississippi to 1898. Robert W. Frazer. (Illus.). 1977. 11.95 o.p. (ISBN 0-8061-0674-3); pap. 5.95 (ISBN 0-8061-1250-6). U of Okla Pr.

Fortunate Foundlings, Seventeen Forty-Four. Eliza Haywood. (Flowering of the Novel, 1740-1775 Ser: Vol. 10). 1974. lib. bdg. 50.00 (ISBN 0-8240-1109-0). Garland Pub.

Fortunate Pilgrim. Mario Puzo. 1978. pap. 2.25 (ISBN 0-449-23456-8, Crest). Fawcett.

Fortunate Strangers. Cornelius Beukenkamp, Jr. LC 80-19260. 269p. 1980. Repr. of 1971 ed. lib. bdg. 9.95x (ISBN 0-89370-600-0). Borgo Pr.

Fortunate Traveller. Derek Walcott. 1981. 10.95 (ISBN 0-374-15765-0). FS&G.

Fortunately. Remy Charlip. LC 80-36956. (Illus.). 48p. (ps-3). 1980. Repr. of 1964 ed. 8.95 (ISBN 0-590-07762-7, Four Winds). Schol Bk Serv.

Fortune & Men's Eyes. John Herbert. LC 67-31624. (Photos). 1968. pap. 4.95 (ISBN 0-394-17357-0, E457, Ever). Grove.

Fortune for a Falcon. Catherine Darby. (Falcon Ser: No. 3). 256p. (Orig.). 1975. pap. 1.25 o.p. (ISBN 0-445-00329-4). Popular Lib.

Fortune Telling for Fun. Paul Showers. LC 80-2549. 349p. 1980. Repr. of 1971 ed. lib. bdg. 10.95x (ISBN 0-89370-607-8). Borgo Pr.

Fortunes of Falstaff. John D. Wilson. 1943. 23.95 (ISBN 0-521-06830-4); pap. 6.95 (ISBN 0-521-09246-9). Cambridge U Pr.

Fortunes of Faust. E. M. Butler. 1979. 42.00 (ISBN 0-521-22562-0); pap. 10.95 (ISBN 0-521-29552-1). Cambridge U Pr.

Fortunes of Hector O'halloran & His Man, Mark Anthony O'toole. William H. Maxwell. Ed. by Robert L. Wolff. (Ireland Nineteenth Century Fiction - Ser. Two: Vol. 51). 416p. 1979. lib. bdg. 32.00 (ISBN 0-8240-3500-3). Garland Pub.

Fortunes of Love. Caroline Courtney. 1981. lib. bdg. 12.95 (ISBN 0-8161-3138-4, Large Print Bks). G K Hall.

Fortunes of Love. Caroline Courtney. 1980. pap. 1.75 (ISBN 0-446-94055-0). Warner Bks.

Fortunes of Nigel. Sir Walter Scott. Ed. by Frederick M. Link. LC 65-18715. 1965. pap. 3.25x (ISBN 0-8032-5176-9, BB 321, Bison). U of Nebr Pr.

Fortunes of the Emperors: Studies in Revolution, Exile, Abdication, Usurpation, & Deposition in Ancient Japan. Richard A Ponsonby-Fane. (Studies in Japanese History & Civilization). 1979. 28.00 (ISBN 0-89093-250-6). U Pubns Amer.

Fortunes of the Irish Language. 128p. 1954. pap. 4.50 o.p. (ISBN 0-85342-045-9). Irish Bk Ctr.

Fortune's Wheel. Rhoda Edwards. LC 78-7752. 1979. 8.95 o.p. (ISBN 0-385-11582-2). Doubleday.

Fortunoff's Child. Leslie Tonner. 1980. 10.95 (ISBN 0-8037-3354-2). Dial.

Forty Days Lost. Ben East & Jerolyn Nentl. Ed. by Howard Schroeder. LC 79-5185. (Survival Ser.). (Illus., Orig.). (gr. 3 up). 1979. PLB 5.95 (ISBN 0-89686-042-6); pap. 2.95 (ISBN 0-89686-050-7). Crestwood Hse.

Forty-Eight Preludes & Fugues of J. S. Bach. Cecil Gray. (Music Reprint Ser.). 1979. Repr. of 1938 ed. 16.00 (ISBN 0-306-79559-0). Da Capo.

Forty-Eight Signs in the Land of Israel. Gordon Lindsay. 1.25 (ISBN 0-89985-186-X). Christ Nations.

Forty Fathoms Down. Lawrence Cortesi. 1979. pap. 1.75 (ISBN 0-505-51445-1). Tower Bks.

Forty Fathoms Down (The Silent Service No. 2) Jones J. Farragut. (Orig.). 1981. pap. 2.75 (ISBN 0-440-12655-X). Dell.

Forty-First Thief. Edward A. Pollitz. 1975. 8.95 o.p. (ISBN 0-440-04837-0). Delacorte.

Forty Five - Seventy Springfield. Albert J. Frasca & Robert H. Hill. Ed. by Charles R. Suydam. LC 80-51230. (Illus.). 396p. 1980. 49.50 (ISBN 0-937500-11-9); deluxe ed. 9.50 deluxe edition (ISBN 0-937500-10-0). Springfield Pub Co.

Forty-Five Years with Labour. K. Dwarkadas. 6.95x o.p. (ISBN 0-210-33983-7). Asia.

Forty-Five Years with Philips. Frederik Philips. (Illus.). 1978. 17.95 (ISBN 0-7137-0931-6, Pub. by Blandford Pr England). Sterling.

Forty Footers. Avin H. Johnston. (Orig.). 1980. pap. 1.95 (ISBN 0-532-23215-1). Manor Bks.

Forty-Four Hours to Change Your Life: Marriage Encounter. Henry P. Durkin. (Orig.). pap. 1.25 (ISBN 0-89129-139-3). Jove Pubns.

Forty-Four Vintage. Anthony Price. LC 77-92229. 1978. 7.95 o.p. (ISBN 0-385-14028-2). Doubleday.

Forty Games for Frivolous People. Peter Wilson. (Illus.). 1979. pap. 3.95 (ISBN 0-8256-3154-8, Quick Fox). Music Sales.

Forty Innovative Programs in Early Childhood Education. Compiled by Berlie J. Fallon. LC 72-95010. (Orig.). 1973. pap. 6.75 (ISBN 0-8224-3075-4). Pitman Learning.

Forty Million Schoolbooks Can't Be Wrong. L. Ethan Ellis. LC 75-14227. (Illus.). 112p. (gr. 6 up). 1975. 8.95 (ISBN 0-02-733450-3, 73345). Macmillan.

Forty-Nine & Holding. Richard K. Smith. LC 75-11179. (Illus.). 1975. 7.95 (ISBN 0-89430-023-7). Morgan-Pacific.

Forty-Nine Percent Majority: The Male Sex Role. Deborah S. David & Robert Brannon. LC 75-18152. 352p. 1976. text ed. 9.95 (ISBN 0-201-01448-3). A-W.

Forty-Niners. W. Johnson. (Old West Ser.). (Illus.). 240p. 1974. 12.95 (ISBN 0-8094-1470-8). Time-Life.

Forty-Niners. William W. Johnson. LC 73-88997. (Old West). (Illus.). (gr. 5 up). 1974. kivar 12.96 (ISBN 0-8094-1472-4, Pub. by Time-Life). Silver.

Forty Object Sermons for Children. Joe E. Trull. (Object Lesson Ser.). 96p. 1975. pap. 2.95 (ISBN 0-8010-8831-3). Baker Bk.

Forty-One Fifty Holley Carburetor Handbook. Mike Urich. (Orig.). 1980. pap. 3.95 (ISBN 0-89586-047-3). H P Bks.

Forty-Second Street Studio. Joyce Baronio. LC 80-80678. (Illus.). 96p. 1980. 40.00 (ISBN 0-936568-00-3). Pyxidium Pr.

Forty Thousand Years of Music: Man in Search of Music. Jacques Chailley. Tr. by Rollo Myers from Fr. LC 74-31227. (Music Reprint Ser). (Illus.). xiv, 229p. 1975. Repr. of 1964 ed. lib. bdg. 25.00 (ISBN 0-306-70661-X). Da Capo.

Forty-Three Students, Thirty-Seven Chairs. Dale Hanson. LC 78-67253. 201p. 1978. 10.50 (ISBN 0-87527-193-6). Green.

Forty to Sixty- How We Waste the Middle Aged. Michael Fogarty. 250p. 1975. pap. text ed. 8.75x (ISBN 0-7199-0904-X, Pub. by Bedford England). Renouf.

Forty-Year Parallel in Presidential Election. Lawrence Cravit. 1980. 10.00 (ISBN 0-533-04611-4). Vantage.

Forty Years As a College President. Wilson H. Elkins & George H. Callcott. 130p. 1981. cancelled o.p. (ISBN 0-686-64814-5). Carrollton Pr.

Forty Years in Nuts & Bolts: The Wholesale Electrical Game. Frederick Warburton. 280p. 1980. pap. text ed. 6.95 o.p. (ISBN 0-934616-05-1). Valkyrie Pr.

Forty Years in the Mormon Church: Why I Left It. R. C. Evans. 1976. Repr. of 1920 ed. 6.50 (ISBN 0-89315-054-1). Lambert Bk.

Forty Years of Screen Credits Nineteen Twenty-Nine to Nineteen Sixty-Nine, 2 Vols. John T. Weaver. LC 76-12592. 1970. Set. 45.00 (ISBN 0-8108-0299-6). Scarecrow.

Forty Years of Spy. Leslie Ward. LC 70-81512. 1969. Repr. of 1915 ed. 22.00 (ISBN 0-8103-3575-1). Gale.

Forty Years on the Wild Frontier. Carl W. Breihan & Wayne Montgomery. (Illus.). Date not set. 15.00 (ISBN 0-8159-5518-9). Devin. Postponed.

Forum for Death Education & Counseling: Selected Proceedings from the First National Conference. Ed. by Ellen S. Zinner & Stephen F. Steele. 298p. (Orig.). 1979. pap. 11.95 (ISBN 0-536-03314-5). Ginn Custom.

Forward in Time. Ben Bova. 256p. 1974. pap. 1.25 o.p. (ISBN 0-445-08310-7). Popular Lib.

Forward: Rick Barry. Robert Geline & Priscilla Turner. LC 75-42339. (Sports Profile Ser.). (Illus.). (gr. 4-11). 1976. PLB 8.50 (ISBN 0-8172-0146-7). Raintree Pubs.

Forward to Literature. Ernest Earnest. 332p. 1980. Repr. of 1945 ed. lib. bdg. 25.00 (ISBN 0-89987-205-0). Century Bookbindery.

Forward with Nature: An Integrated Approach to World Problems of Technology, Energy & Agriculture. J. N. Mukherjee. 188p. 1979. text ed. 18.00x (ISBN 0-8426-1676-4). Verry.

Forwards. Robert Armstrong. (Stars of the NBA Ser.). (Illus.). (gr. 3-7). 1977. PLB 7.95 (ISBN 0-87191-563-4). Creative Ed.

Fossil & Living Dinoflagellates. W. A. Sarjeant. 1975. 25.00 (ISBN 0-12-619150-6). Acad Pr.

Fossil Animal Remains: Their Preparation and Conservation. A. E. Rixon. (Illus.). 296p. 1976. pap. text ed. 18.25x (ISBN 0-485-12028-3, Athlone Pr). Humanities.

Fossil Evidence: The Human Evolutionary Journey. 3rd ed. Frank E. Poirier. (Illus.). 360p. 1981. pap. text ed. 12.95 (ISBN 0-8016-3952-2). Mosby.

Fossil Hunters: In Search of Ancient Plants. Henry N. Andrews. LC 79-24101. (Illus.). 664p. 1980. 28.50 (ISBN 0-8014-1248-X). Cornell U Pr.

Fossil Macropodidae from Lake Menindee, New South Wales. R. H. Tedford. (U. C. Publ. in Geological Sciences: Vol. 64). 1967. pap. 8.50x (ISBN 0-520-09165-5). U of Cal Pr.

Fossil Mammals of Africa, No. 8: An Annotated Bibliography of the Fossil Mammals of Africa 1742-1950. A. Tindell-Hopwood & J. P. Hollyfield. 194p. 1954. pap. 16.00x (ISBN 0-565-00179-5). Sabbot-Natural Hist Bks.

Fossil Mammals of the Type Lance Formation, Wyoming, Part II, Marsupialia. W. A. Clemens, Jr. (U. C. Publ. in Geological Sciences: Vol. 62). 1966. pap. 8.00x (ISBN 0-520-09163-9). U of Cal Pr.

Fossil Mammals of the Type Lance Formation, Wyoming, Part 3: Eutheria & Summary. William A. Clemens, Jr. (U. C. Publ. in Geological Sciences: Vol. 94). 1973. pap. 9.00x (ISBN 0-520-09418-2). U of Cal Pr.

Fossil Men: Elements of Human Paleontology. Marcellin Boule. LC 78-72691. 1980. Repr. of 1923 ed. 69.50 (ISBN 0-404-18262-3). AMS Pr.

Fossil Vertebrates of Africa, 3 vols. Ed. by L. S. Leakey et al. Vol. 1, 1969. 28.60 (ISBN 0-12-440401-4); Vol. 2, 1971. 46.00 (ISBN 0-12-440402-2); Vol. 3, 1973. 29.00 (ISBN 0-12-440403-0). Acad Pr.

Fossil Vertebrates of Alabama. John T. Thurmond & Douglas E. Jones. LC 80-13075. (Illus.). 256p. 1981. 22.50x. U of Ala Pr.

Fossils. F. A. Middlemiss. (Introducing Geology Ser.). 1976. pap. text ed. 4.95x (ISBN 0-04-560005-8). Allen Unwin.

Fossils. Richard Moody. (Illus.). 128p. 1979. 8.95 (ISBN 0-600-36313-9). Transatlantic.

Fossils: An Introduction to Prehistoric Life. William H. Matthews. (Orig.). 1962. pap. 3.95 (ISBN 0-06-463280-6, EH 280, EH). Har-Row.

Fossils & Progress: Paleontology & the Idea of Progressive Evolution in the Nineteenth Century. Peter J. Bowler. LC 75-40005. 1976. lib. bdg. 14.00 o.p. (ISBN 0-88202-043-9). N Watson.

Fossils Tell of Long Ago. Aliki. LC 78-170999. (Let's-Read-&-Find-Out Science Bk). (Illus.). 40p. (gr. k-3). 1972. PLB 7.89 (ISBN 0-690-31379-9, TYC-J). T Y Crowell.

Foster & Laurie. Al Silverman. 1975. pap. 1.75 o.p. (ISBN 0-445-08403-0). Popular Lib.

Foster Care & Families: Conflicting Values & Policies. Ruth Hubbell. (Family Impact Seminar Ser.). 200p. 1981. 15.00x (ISBN 0-87722-206-1). Temple U Pr.

Foster Care of Children: Nurture & Treatment. Draza Kline & Helen-Mary F. Overstreet. LC 78-186386. (Studies of the Child Welfare League of America). 385p. 1972. 17.50x (ISBN 0-231-03601-9); pap. 8.00x (ISBN 0-231-08337-8). Columbia U Pr.

Foster Care: Theory & Practice. V. George. (International Library of Sociology & Social Reconstruction). 1970. text ed. 11.25x (ISBN 0-7100-6800-X). Humanities.

Foster Child. Marion Dane Bauer. LC 76-54291. (gr. 5 up). 1977. 6.95 (ISBN 0-395-28889-4, Clarion). HM.

Foster Parent Associations: Designs for Development. LC 73-93382. 1974. pap. 1.65 o.p. (ISBN 0-87868-110-8). Child Welfare.

Foster Parenting: An Updated Review of the Literature. Rosemarie Carbino. 49p. (Orig.). 1980. pap. text ed. 4.25 (ISBN 0-87868-178-7). Child Welfare.

Foster Parenting Young Children: Guidelines from a Foster Parent. Evelyn H. Felker. LC 73-93885. 1974. pap. 3.95 (ISBN 0-87868-119-1). Child Welfare.

Foster Sons of the Desert. Esther M. Petersen. 6.95 o.p. (ISBN 0-685-58702-9). Vantage.

Fostering Intellectual Development in Young Children. Kenneth D. Wann et al. LC 62-18037. (Orig.). 1962. pap. 6.50x (ISBN 0-8077-2305-3). Tchrs Coll.

Fotovision del Antiguo Testamento. David Alexander. Tr. by Pedro Vega from Eng. (Illus.). 157p. (Span.). 1976. 8.50 (ISBN 0-89922-062-2). Edit Caribe.

Fouche, Napoleon, & the General Police. Eric A. Arnold. LC 79-62894. 1979. pap. text ed. 9.50 (ISBN 0-8191-0716-6). U Pr of Amer.

Fougasse. Ed. by Bevis Hillier. (Illus.). 1978. 15.95 (ISBN 0-241-89462-X, Pub. by Hamish Hamilton England). David & Charles.

Foul Play. Dick O'Connor. (Sportellers Ser.). (Illus.). 64p. (gr. 5 up). 1981. PLB 7.95 (ISBN 0-516-02263-6). Childrens.

Foul: The Connie Hawkins Story. David Wolf. LC 71-117279. 1972. 7.95 o.p. (ISBN 0-03-086021-0). HR&W.

Fouling of Heat Transfer Equipment: International Conference 1979. Ed. by Euan F. Somerscales & James G. Knudsen. LC 80-28694. (Illus.). 700p. 1981. text ed. 75.00 (ISBN 0-89116-199-6). Hemisphere Pub.

Found: God's Will. John Macarthur, Jr. Orig. Title: God's Will Is Not Lost. 1977. pap. 1.75 (ISBN 0-88207-503-9). Victor Bks.

Found: Long-Term Gains from Early Intervention. Ed. by Bernard Brown. LC 78-3120. (AAAS Selected Symposium Ser.: No. 8). 1978. lib. bdg. 22.50x (ISBN 0-89158-436-6). Westview.

Foundation Analysis. Ronald F. Scott. (Civil Engineering & Engineering Mechanics Ser.). (Illus.). 496p. 1981. text ed. 27.95 (ISBN 0-13-329169-3). P-H.

Foundation & Empire. Isaac Asimov. 1976. pap. 1.95 (ISBN 0-380-00774-6, 42689). Avon.

Foundation Center National Data Book, 2 vols. 4th ed. The Foundation Center. 846p. (Orig.). 1979. pap. 45.00 (ISBN 0-87954-027-3). Foundation Ctr.

Foundation Center National Data Book, 2 vols. The Foundation Center. 840p. (Orig.). 1981. pap. 45.00 (ISBN 0-87954-039-7). Foundation Ctr.

Foundation Center Source Book Profiles. The Foundation Center. Ed. by Sherry E. Goldstein. LC 77-79015. (Ser. 3). (Orig.). 1980. pap. 200.00 (ISBN 0-87954-024-9). Foundation Ctr.

Foundation Course in French Language & Culture. rev. ed. Clifford S. Parker & Pierre Maubrey. LC 68-12139. Orig. Title: Foundation Course in French. (Illus., Fr.). 1969. text ed. 15.95x (ISBN 0-669-44149-X); tapes avail. (ISBN 0-669-44156-2); tapes. 10 reels 50.00 (ISBN 0-669-44164-3); student test bk. 1.75x (ISBN 0-669-50468-8). Heath.

Foundation Course in International Relations for African Students. Ray Ofoegbu. 224p. (Orig.). 1980. pap. text ed. 10.50x (ISBN 0-04-327058-1, AU448). Allen Unwin.

Foundation Course in Spanish. 5th ed. Laurel H. Turk & Aurelio M. Espinosa. (Illus.). 439p. 1981. text ed. 16.95 (ISBN 0-669-02637-9); wkbk. 5.95 (ISBN 0-669-02638-7); answer keys with tests avail. (ISBN 0-669-02639-5); tapescript avail. (ISBN 0-669-02640-9); reels set of 15 75.00 (ISBN 0-669-02641-7); cassettes set of 15 75.00 (ISBN 0-669-02643-3); demo tape avail. (ISBN 0-669-02644-1). Heath.

Foundation Course in Spanish. 4th ed. Laurel H. Turk et al. 1978. text ed. 16.95x o.p. (ISBN 0-669-00491-X); inst. manual free o.p. (ISBN 0-669-00492-8); wkbk. 5.95 o.p. (ISBN 0-669-00493-6); indiv. prog. 4.95x o.p. (ISBN 0-669-00993-8); reels 85.00 o.p. (ISBN 0-669-00495-2); cassettes 85.00 o.p. (ISBN 0-669-00494-4). Heath.

Foundation Design. Wayne C. Teng. (Illus.). 1962. ref. ed. 27.95x (ISBN 0-13-329805-1). P-H.

Foundation Dictionary of Russian. B. B. Anpilogova et al. Tr. by V. Korotky. Date not set. 4.50 (ISBN 0-8446-1538-2). Peter Smith.

Foundation Engineering. 2nd ed. Ralph B. Peck et al. LC 73-9877. 544p. 1974. 27.95 (ISBN 0-471-67585-7). Wiley.

Foundation Engineering in Difficult Ground. F. G. Bell. 1978. 79.95 (ISBN 0-408-00311-1). Butterworths.

Foundation Engineering: Soil Exploration & Spread Foundations. K. Szechy & L. Varga. LC 79-318873. (Illus.). 1978. 50.00x (ISBN 963-05-1489-3). Intl Pubns Serv.

Foundation for Faith. Derek Prince. (Foundation Ser.: Bk. I). 1965-66. pap. 1.75 (ISBN 0-934920-00-1, B-10). Derek Prince.

Foundation for Missions. M. Thomas Starkes. LC 80-67460. 1981. pap. 4.95 (ISBN 0-8054-6325-9). Broadman.

Foundation Fundamentals: A Guide for Grantseekers. Carol M. Kurzig. LC 80-67501. (Illus.). 148p. (Orig.). 1980. pap. 4.95 (ISBN 0-87954-026-5). Foundation Ctr.

Foundation Grants Index Nineteen Eighty. The Foundation Center. LC 72-76018. 540p. (Orig.). 1981. pap. 30.00 (ISBN 0-87954-040-0). Foundation Ctr.

Foundation Grants Index 1978. Ed. by Lee Noe. 1979. write for info. o.p. (ISBN 0-87954-020-6, Dist. by Foundation Ctr). Columbia U Pr.

Foundation Grants to Individuals. 2nd ed. Ed. by Carol Kurzig et al. LC 79-90273. 236p. 1979. pap. 15.00 (ISBN 0-87954-025-7). Foundation Ctr.

Foundation Guide for Religious Grant Seekers. Ed. by Peter S. Robinson. LC 79-19006. (Scholars Press Handbooks in Humanities Ser.: No. 1). 1979. 10.50 (ISBN 0-89130-339-1, 001501); pap. 6.00 (ISBN 0-89130-340-5). Scholars Pr Ca.

Foundation of American Education: Readings. 4th ed. James A. Johnson et al. 1979. pap. 9.85x (ISBN 0-205-06565-1). Allyn.

Foundation of Analysis in Operations Research. J. William Schmidt & Robert P. Davis. LC 80-987. (Operations Research & Industrial Engineering Ser.). 1981. 27.00 (ISBN 0-12-626850-9). Acad Pr.

Foundation of Cognitive-Development Psychology: James Mark Baldwin's Theory & Its Contemporary Meaning. Ed. by John M. Broughton & D. John Freeman-Moir. 300p. 1981. text ed. price not set (ISBN 0-89391-043-0). Ablex Pub.

Foundation of Euclidean & Non-Euclidean Geometries According to F. Klein. L. Redei. (International Series in Pure & Applied Mathematics: Vol. 97). 1968. 52.00 o.p. (ISBN 0-08-011965-4). Pergamon.

Foundation of Japanese Buddhism: The Aristocratic Age, Vol. I. Alicia Matsunaga & Daigan Matsunaga. LC 74-83654. 1974. 13.75x (ISBN 0-914910-25-6); pap. 7.75x (ISBN 0-914910-26-4). Buddhist Bks.

Foundation of Moral Goodness, 2 vols. in 1. John Blaguy. Ed. by Rene Wellek. LC 75-11194. (British Philosophers & Theologians of the 17th & 18th Centuries: Vol. 1). 1976. Repr. of 1729 ed. lib. bdg. 42.00 (ISBN 0-8240-1750-1). Garland Pub.

Foundation of Newton's Alchemy; or, "the Hunting of the Greene Lyon". Betty J. Dobbs. LC 74-31795. (Illus.). 320p. 1976. 47.50 (ISBN 0-521-20786-X). Cambridge U Pr.

Foundation of Philosophy--a Refutation of Skepticism, the True Jesus Christ, the Science of God & Man; the God of the Christians. Apostolos Makrakis. Ed. by Orthodox Christian Educational Society. Tr. by Anthony Lekatsos & Denver Cummings. 103p. 1955. 6.00x (ISBN 0-938366-07-6). Orthodox Chr.

Foundation of Political Science: Research, Methods & Scope. Ed. by Donald M. Freeman. LC 76-43130. 1978. 35.00 (ISBN 0-02-910670-2). Free Pr.

Foundation of Programming Through Basic. Peter Moulton. LC 78-21569. 1979. text ed. 14.95 (ISBN 0-471-03311-1); tchrs. manual avail. (ISBN 0-471-05414-3). Wiley.

Foundation of the Conservative Party 1830-1867. Robert Stewart. (History of the Conservative Party Ser.). (Illus.). 1978. text ed. 35.00x (ISBN 0-582-50712-X). Longman.

Foundation of the League of Arab States: Wartime Diplomacy & Inter-Arab Politics 1941-1945. Ahamad M. Gomaa. 1978. text ed. 35.00x o.p. (ISBN 0-582-78073-X). Longman.

Foundation Series, 7 bks. 1966. Set. pap. 9.95 (ISBN 0-934920-17-6). Derek Prince.

Foundation Stock. A. V. Gomez. 6.95 (ISBN 0-533-01979-6). Vantage.

Foundation Studies in Education: Justifications & New Directions: A Source Book. Margaret Gillett & John A. Laska. LC 73-7899. 1973. 13.50 (ISBN 0-8108-0671-1). Scarecrow.

Foundation Trilogy. Isaac Asimov. 1974. pap. 7.95 (ISBN 0-380-00101-2, 54403). Avon.

Foundations. Lauri F. Lee. (Gateway to English Program). (Illus.). 128p. (Orig.). 1981. tchrs' bk. 4.95 (ISBN 0-88377-176-4); student wkbk 1.95 (ISBN 0-88377-177-2). Newbury Hse.

Foundations & Principles of Health Education. Nicholas Galli. LC 77-21586. 1978. text ed. 18.95 (ISBN 0-471-29065-3). Wiley.

Foundations: Essays in Philosophy, Logic, Mathematics & Economics. Intro. by F. P. Ramsey. (International Library of Psychology, Philosophy & Scientific Method). 1978. text ed. 24.75x (ISBN 0-391-00814-5). Humanities.

Foundations for Dams: Proceedings. Engineering Foundation Conference, Mar. 1974. Compiled By American Society of Civil Engineers. 480p. 1974. pap. text ed. 27.50 (ISBN 0-87262-100-6). Am Soc Civil Eng.

Foundations for Managing the Farm Business. D. Lynn Forster & Bernard L. Erven. LC 80-20832. (Agricultural Economics Ser.). 320p. 1981. text ed. 20.95 (ISBN 0-88244-230-9). Grid Pub.

Foundations for Nursing. E. L. Brill & D. F. Kilts. 813p. 1980. text ed. 24.95 (ISBN 0-8385-2687-X). ACC.

Foundations for Reading & Writing: Workbooks 1 & 2. W. D. Sheeler et al. Ed. by A. R. Evans. (Welcome to English Ser.). (Illus.). 1977. No. 1. wkbk 2.50 ea. (ISBN 0-89285-033-7). No. 2 (ISBN 0-89285-034-5). English Lang.

Foundations for Serving Those Wth Severe & Multiple Handicaps. Jack M. Goodzeit. 300p. 1981. text ed. 24.50x (ISBN 0-8290-0268-5); pap. text ed. 12.95x (ISBN 0-8290-0269-3). Irvington.

Foundations for Teaching English As a 2nd Language: Theory & Method for Multicultural Education. Muriel Saville-Troike. 200p. 1976. pap. 8.95 (ISBN 0-13-329946-5). P-H.

Foundations in Music Theory. 2nd ed. Leon Dallin. 1967. pap. 12.95x (ISBN 0-534-00659-0). Wadsworth Pub.

Foundations in Singing: A Basic Text in the Fundamentals of Teaching & Song Interpretation - Medium-High Voice Edition. Van A. Christy. 250p. (Orig.). 1981. write for info. plastic comb bind. (ISBN 0-697-03483-6). Wm C Brown.

Foundations in Sociolinguistics: An Ethnographic Approach. Dell Hymes. LC 73-89288. (Conduct & Communication Ser.). 1974. 15.00x (ISBN 0-8122-7675-2); pap. 7.95x (ISBN 0-8122-1065-4, Pa Paperbks). U of Pa Pr.

Foundations in the Dust: The Story of Mesopotamian Exploration. rev. enl. ed. Seton Lloyd. (Illus.). 216p. 1981. 19.95 (ISBN 0-500-05038-4). Thames Hudson.

Foundations in Truth. Mary E. Fields. LC 80-67931. 275p. 1980. 10.00 (ISBN 0-87516-423-4). De Vorss.

Foundations of a Planned Economy, Vol IV Pt. 2. E. H. Carr. 1972. 19.95 (ISBN 0-02-522050-0). Macmillan.

Foundations of a Planned Economy 1926-1929. E. H. Carr. LC 76-45527. (History of Soviet Russia Ser.: Vol. 3 Pts. 1 & 2). 1977. Pt. 1. 17.50 o.p. (ISBN 0-02-522060-8, 52206); Pt. 2. 17.50 (ISBN 0-02-522070-5, 52207). Macmillan.

Foundations of Accounting Measurement. Yuji Ijiri. LC 67-15629. 1978. Repr. of 1967 ed. text ed. 13.00 (ISBN 0-914348-22-1). Scholars Bk.

Foundations of Acoustics, Basic Mathematics & Basic Acoustics. E. J. Skudrzyk. LC 76-161480. (Illus.). 1972. 130.00 (ISBN 0-387-80988-0). Springer-Verlag.

Foundations of Aerodynamics: Bases of Aerodynamic Design. 3rd ed. Arnold M. Kuethe & Chuen-Yen Chow. LC 76-20761. 1976. text ed. 29.95 (ISBN 0-471-50953-1). Wiley.

Foundations of Algebraic Topology. S. Eilenberg & N. Steenrod. (Mathematical Ser.: Vol. 15). 1952. 22.00 o.p. (ISBN 0-691-07965-X). Princeton U Pr.

Foundations of American Foreign Policy. Albert B. Hart. LC 74-109549. (Law, Politics & History Ser). 1970. Repr. of 1901 ed. lib. bdg. 32.50 (ISBN 0-306-71903-7). Da Capo.

Foundations of Analysis. 2nd ed. Edmund Landau. LC 60-15580. (gr. 9 up). 1960. text ed. 8.95 (ISBN 0-8284-0079-2). Chelsea Pub.

Foundations of Analysis: Bk. 1, a Straightforward Introduction: Logic, Sets & Numbers. K. G. Binmore. LC 79-41790. (Illus.). 200p. Date not set. 24.95 (ISBN 0-521-23322-4); pap. 12.95 (ISBN 0-521-29915-2). Cambridge U Pr.

Foundations of Analysis: Bk. 2, a Straightforward Introduction: Topological Ideas. K. G. Binmore. LC 79-41790. (Illus.). 350p. Date not set. price not set (ISBN 0-521-23350-X); pap. price not set (ISBN 0-521-29930-6). Cambridge U Pr.

Foundations of Analytic Philosophy. Ed. by Peter French et al. (Midwest Studies in Philosophy: Vol. 6). 576p. 1981. 35.00 (ISBN 0-8166-1033-9); pap. 15.00 (ISBN 0-8166-1036-3). U of Minn Pr.

Foundations of Animal Development. Arthur F. Hopper & Nathan H. Hart. (Illus.). 1979. text ed. 21.95x (ISBN 0-19-502569-5). Oxford U Pr.

Foundations of Applied Mathematics. Michael D. Greenberg. LC 77-11125. (Illus.). 1978. ref. ed. 27.95x (ISBN 0-13-329623-7). P-H.

Foundations of Archeology. Jason W. Smith. 1976. pap. 14.95x (ISBN 0-02-478680-2). Macmillan.

Foundations of Astronomy: From Big Bang to Black Holes. R. Knox. LC 79-13. 1979. 12.95 (ISBN 0-470-26638-4). Halsted Pr.

Foundations of Behavior Genetics. John L. Fuller & William R. Thompson. LC 78-4199. (Illus.). 1978. text ed. 23.95 (ISBN 0-8016-1712-X). Mosby.

Foundations of Biological Theory. E. H. Mercer. 290p. 1981. 30.00 (ISBN 0-471-08797-1, Pub. by Wiley Interscience). Wiley.

Foundations of Biophysics. A. L. Stanford, Jr. 1975. text ed. 22.75 (ISBN 0-12-663350-9). Acad Pr.

Foundations of Chemical Analysis. Omortag Budevsky. LC 79-40240. (Ellis Horwood Series in Analytical Chemistry). 372p. 1979. 59.95x (ISBN 0-470-26692-9). Halsted Pr.

Foundations of Chemical Kinetics. Sidney W. Benson. 722p. 1981. Repr. of 1960 ed. lib. bdg. write for info. (ISBN 0-89874-194-7). Krieger.

Foundations of Chemistry in the Laboratory. 4th ed. Morris Hein et al. (Orig.). 1977. pap. 10.95x (ISBN 0-8221-0206-4). Dickenson.

Foundations of Child Psychiatry. Ed. by E. Miller. 1968. 82.00 (ISBN 0-08-011826-7). Pergamon.

Foundations of Chinese Musical Art. 2nd ed. John H. Levis. (Illus.). 1963. Repr. of 1933 ed. 13.50 o.p. (ISBN 0-8188-0064-X). Paragon.

Foundations of Christian Faith. John A. Bain. 112p. Repr. of 1936 ed. 2.95 (ISBN 0-567-02015-0). Attic Pr.

Foundations of Christian Faith. Karl Rahner. 1978. 19.50 (ISBN 0-8164-0354-6). Crossroad NY.

Foundations of Classical & Quantum Statistical Mechanics. R. Jancel. 1970. 50.00 (ISBN 0-08-012823-8). Pergamon.

Foundations of Climatology. E. T. Stringer. LC 72-81920. (Illus.). 1972. text ed. 36.95x (ISBN 0-7167-0242-8). W H Freeman.

Foundations of College Chemistry. 3rd ed. Daniel B. Murphy & Viateur Rousseau. LC 79-17521. 1980. text ed. 21.95x (ISBN 0-471-04621-3); tchrs. manual avail. (ISBN 0-471-05916-1); study guide avail. (ISBN 0-471-05605-7). Wiley.

Foundations of College Chemistry: The Alternate Edition. Morris Hein. LC 80-259. 1980. text ed. 12.95 (ISBN 0-8185-0402-1). Brooks-Cole.

Foundations of Colonial America: A Documentary History, 3 vols. Ed. by W. Keith Kavenagh. LC 72-80866. 2650p. 1981. Set. pap. 55.00 (ISBN 0-87754-208-2). Chelsea Hse.

Foundations of Conditioning. Ed. by Harold B. Falls et al. 1970. text ed. 7.95 (ISBN 0-12-248055-4). Acad Pr.

Foundations of Conditioning & Learning. Ed. by Gregory A. Kimble. LC 67-10442. (Century Psychology Ser.). (Illus.). 1967. 38.50x (ISBN 0-89197-172-6); pap. text ed. 18.50x o. p. (ISBN 0-89197-762-7). Irvington.

Foundations of Contemporary Psychology. Ed. by Merle Meyer. (Illus.). 1979. text ed. 17.95x (ISBN 0-19-502327-7). Oxford U Pr.

Foundations of Continuum Thermodynamics. Ed. by J. J. Domingos et al. LC 74-23460. 337p. 1975. 42.95 (ISBN 0-470-21777-4). Halsted Pr.

Foundations of Decision Support Systems. Robert H. Bonczek et al. LC 80-1779. (Operations Research & Industrial Engineering Ser.). 1981. price not set (ISBN 0-12-113050-9). Acad Pr.

Foundations of Democracy. Ed. by F. Ernest Johnson. (Religion & Civilization Series of the Institute for Religious & Social Studies). 1964. Repr. of 1947 ed. 27.50x (ISBN 0-8154-0120-5). Cooper Sq.

Foundations of Developmental Psychology. Richard La Barba. LC 80-615. 1980. lib ed 18.95 (ISBN 0-12-432350-2); write for info. (ISBN 0-12-432355-3). Acad Pr.

Foundations of Drama. C. J. Gianakaris. 1975. pap. 9.75 (ISBN 0-395-18611-0); instr's. manual 1.75 (ISBN 0-395-18800-8). HM.

Foundations of Education. 3rd ed. Ed. by George F. Kneller. LC 78-138913. 1971. text ed. 22.95 (ISBN 0-471-49505-0). Wiley.

Foundations of Education: Dissenting Views. Ed. by James J. Shields & Colin Greer. LC 73-16438. 208p. 1974. text ed. 11.50x (ISBN 0-471-78635-7). Wiley.

Foundations of Education for Prospective Teachers. Sandford W. Reitman. 1977. text ed. 16.95x (ISBN 0-205-05677-6). Allyn.

Foundations of Education: Social Perspective. Richard D. Van Scotter et al. (Illus.). 1979. text ed. 16.95 (ISBN 0-13-329268-1). P-H.

Foundations of Educational Evaluation: Its Technology, Management, Economicas, & Futurology. Edward K. Brown. (Illus.). 200p. 1978. 10.00 (ISBN 0-8059-2519-8). Dorrance.

Foundations of Educational Research. Alfred L. Papillon. LC 78-69861. 1978. pap. text ed. 12.00 (ISBN 0-8191-0583-X). U Pr of Amer.

Foundations of Educational Research. 2nd ed. Gilbert Sax. 1979. 19.95 (ISBN 0-13-329300-9). P-H.

Foundations of Electrical Engineering. K. Simonyi. 1964. 40.00 (ISBN 0-08-010204-2); pap. 18.50 (ISBN 0-08-019001-4). Pergamon.

Foundations of Electromagnetic Theory. 3rd ed. John R. Reitz et al. LC 78-18649. (Physics Ser.). (Illus.). 1979. text ed. 23.95 (ISBN 0-201-06332-8). A-W.

Foundations of England: Or, Twelve Centuries of British History, 2 vols. James H. Ramsay. LC 80-2215. 1981. Repr. of 1898 ed. Set. 125.00 (ISBN 0-404-18780-3). Vol. 1 (ISBN 0-404-18781-1). Vol. 2 (ISBN 0-404-18782-X). AMS Pr.

Foundations of English Administrative Law: Certiorari & Mandamus in the Seventeenth Century. Edith G. Henderson. LC 63-11421. (Ames Foundation Publications Ser). 1963. 10.00x (ISBN 0-674-31351-8). Harvard U Pr.

Foundations of English Opera. 2nd ed. Edward J. Dent. LC 65-18501. (Music Ser). 1965. Repr. of 1928 ed. lib. bdg. 22.50 (ISBN 0-306-70905-8). Da Capo.

Foundations of Epidemiology. Abraham M. Lilienfeld. 275p. 1976. text ed. 12.95x o.p. (ISBN 0-19-502072-3); pap. text ed. 9.95x o.p. (ISBN 0-19-502071-5). Oxford U Pr.

Foundations of Factor Analysis. Stanley Mulaik. (McGraw-Hill Paperbacks). (Illus.). 480p. 1972. text ed. 30.00 o.p. (ISBN 0-07-043980-X, C). McGraw.

Foundations of Family Therapy. Lynn Hoffman. LC 80-68956. 416p. 1981. 25.00x (ISBN 0-465-02498-X). Basic.

Foundations of Farm Policy. Luther Tweeten. LC 71-83145. 1970. 12.50x o.p. (ISBN 0-8032-0721-2). U of Nebr Pr.

Foundations of Financial Management. Stanley B. Block & Geoffrey A. Hirt. 1978. text ed. 20.95x (ISBN 0-256-02033-7). Irwin.

Foundations of Fluid Mechanics. Shao Yuan. 1967. text ed. 26.95x (ISBN 0-13-329813-2). P-H.

Foundations of Food Science. John Hawthorn. (Illus.). 1981. text ed. price not set (ISBN 0-7167-1295-4); pap. text ed. price not set (ISBN 0-7167-1296-2). W H Freeman.

Foundations of Guidance & Counseling: Multidisciplinary Readings. Ed. by C. E. Smith & Oscar G. Mink. LC 72-75026. 1969. pap. text ed. 5.50 o.p. (ISBN 0-397-47158-0). Lippincott.

Foundations of Health. 2nd ed. Charles Bucher & Einar Olsen. (Illus.). 448p. 1976. Ref. Ed. 15.95 (ISBN 0-13-329896-5). P-H.

Foundations of Health Science. 3rd ed. Barbara O. Henkel et al. 1977. text ed. 17.95 (ISBN 0-205-05739-X). Allyn.

Foundations of Hypnosis: From Mesmer to Freud. Maurice M. Tinterow. (Illus.). 620p. 1970. 59.75 (ISBN 0-398-01928-2). C C Thomas.

Foundations of Indian Culture. Sri Aurobindo. 1979. pap. 10.00 (ISBN 0-89744-909-6). Auromere.

Foundations of Indian Federalism. K. R. Bombwall. 1967. 10.00x (ISBN 0-210-22721-4). Asia.

Foundations of Inductive Reasoning. R. Christensen. xii, 363p. 1964. 39.50 (ISBN 0-686-28748-7, 04-08-01). Entropy Ltd.

Foundations of Inference in Survey Sampling. Claes-Magnus Cassel et al. LC 77-5114. (Probability & Mathematical Statistics Ser., Probability & Statistics Section). 1977. 25.00 (ISBN 0-471-02563-1, Pub. by Wiley-Interscience). Wiley.

Foundations of Interpersonal Attraction. Ed. by Theodore Huston. 1974. 28.00 (ISBN 0-12-362950-0). Acad Pr.

Foundations of Jurisprudence. Hall. 1973. 15.00 (ISBN 0-672-81849-3, Bobbs-Merrill Law). Michie.

Foundations of Language Development a Multidisciplinary Approach, 2 vols. E. H. Lenneberg. Ed. by Elizabeth Lenneberg. 1975. Vol. 1. 35.50 (ISBN 0-12-443701-X); Vol. 2. 35.50 (ISBN 0-12-443702-8); Set. 57.00. Acad Pr.

Foundations of Law Enforcement & Criminal Justice. Robert G. Caldwell. Ed. by William Nardini. LC 76-46478. 1977. 16.95 (ISBN 0-672-61412-X). Bobbs.

Foundations of Learning & Memory. Roger M. Tarpy & Richard E. Mayer. 1978. 15.95x (ISBN 0-673-15074-7). Scott F.

Foundations of Life & Health Insurance. William T. Hold & Jerry D. Todd. (Studies in Insurance & Actuarial Science: No. 2). (Orig.). 1971. pap. 3.50 o.p. (ISBN 0-87755-068-9). U of Tex Busn Res.

Foundations of Linguistics. Franklin C. Southworth & Chander J. Daswani. LC 73-9137. (Illus.). 1974. text ed. 14.95 (ISBN 0-02-930300-1). Free Pr.

Foundations of Linguistics. D. Wunderlich. Tr. by R. Lass from Ger. LC 77-82526. (Cambridge Studies in Linguistics Monographs: No. 22). 1979. 59.95 (ISBN 0-521-22007-6); pap. 17.50x (ISBN 0-521-29334-0). Cambridge U Pr.

Foundations of Mathematical Analysis. Ed. by Johnsonbaugh & Pfaffenberger. 1981. 24.50 (ISBN 0-8247-6919-8). Dekker.

Foundations of Mathematical Genetics. A. W. Edwards. LC 76-9168. (Illus.). 1977. 23.95 (ISBN 0-521-21325-8). Cambridge U Pr.

Foundations of Mathematical Programming. William W. Claycombe & William G. Sullivan. (Illus.). 304p. 1975. 16.95 (ISBN 0-87909-282-3); students manual avail. Reston.

Foundations of Mathematics. Ian Stewart & David Tall. (Illus.). 1977. 13.50x (ISBN 0-19-853164-8); pap. 10.95x (ISBN 0-19-853165-6). Oxford U Pr.

Foundations of Maths in the Infant School. Joy Taylor. (Unwin Education Books). 1976. text ed. 17.95x o.p. (ISBN 0-04-372014-5); pap. text ed. 7.50x o.p. (ISBN 0-04-372015-3). Allen Unwin.

Foundations of Modern Art. Amedee Ozenfant. Tr. by John Rodker. (Illus.). 1952. pap. text ed. 5.00 (ISBN 0-486-20215-1). Dover.

Foundations of Modern Austrian Economics. Intro. by Edwin Dolan. LC 76-5894. (Studies in Economic Theory). 238p. 1976. 12.00; pap. 4.95. NYU Pr.

Foundations of Modern Historical Scholarship: Language, Law & History in the French Renaissance. Donald R. Kelley. LC 68-8875. 1970. 20.00x (ISBN 0-231-03141-6). Columbia U Pr.

Foundations of Modern Political Thought: The Renaissance, 2 vols. Q. Skinner. LC 78-51676. 1978. Vol. 1. 39.50 (ISBN 0-521-22023-8); Vol. 1. pap. 10.95x (ISBN 0-521-29337-5); Vol. 2. 39.50 (ISBN 0-521-22284-2); Vol. 2. pap. 10.95x (ISBN 0-521-29435-5). Cambridge U Pr.

Foundations of Molecular Pharmacology, 2 vols. J. B. Stenlake. Incl. Vol. 1. Medicinal & Pharmaceutical Chemistry. text ed. 90.00x (ISBN 0-485-11171-3); Vol. 2. The Chemical Basis of Drug Action. text ed. 46.25x (ISBN 0-485-11172-1). 1979 (Athlone Pr). Humanities.

Foundations of Morality. Henry Hazlitt. LC 72-81850. (Illus.). 398p. 1972. 12.00x o.p. (ISBN 0-8402-1297-6); pap. 4.95x o.p. (ISBN 0-686-65433-1). Nash Pub.

Foundations of Music. Wayne Barlow. LC 53-8987. (Illus.). 1953. 28.50x (ISBN 0-89197-176-9); pap. 16.50x. Irvington.

Foundations of New Testament Christology. Reginald H. Fuller. 1965. lib. rep. ed. 17.50x (ISBN 0-684-15532-X, ScribT); pap. 3.95 o.p. (ISBN 0-684-15537-0, SL772, ScribT). Scribner.

Foundations of Nigeria's Financial Infrastructure. Ed. by J. K. Onoh. 318p. 1980. 50.00x (ISBN 0-7099-0448-7, Pub. by Croom Helm Ltd England). Biblio Dist.

Foundations of Nuclear Engineering. Thomas J. Connolly. LC 77-26916. 1978. text ed. 27.95 (ISBN 0-471-16858-0); tchrs. manual 5.00 (ISBN 0-471-02971-8). Wiley.

Foundations of Ophthalmic Pathology. Ed. by Daniel M. Albert & Carmen A. Puliafito. LC 78-9871. (Illus.). 1979. 49.75 (ISBN 0-8385-2690-X). ACC.

Foundations of Optimal Control Theory. E. B. Lee & L. Markus. LC 67-22414. (SIAM Series in Applied Mathematics). 1967. 44.50 (ISBN 0-471-52263-5, Pub. by Wiley-Interscience). Wiley.

Foundations of Optimization. M. S. Bazaraa & C. M. Shetty. (Lecture Notes in Economics & Mathematical Systems Ser.: Vol. 122). 1976. pap. 9.00 (ISBN 0-387-07680-8). Springer-Verlag.

Foundations of Optimization. 2nd ed. Charles S. Beightler et al. (International Ser. in Industrial & Systems Engineering). (Illus.). 1979. text ed. 24.95 (ISBN 0-13-330332-2). P-H.

Foundations of Optimization. Douglass Wilde & C. Beightler. 1967. 22.95 o.p. (ISBN 0-13-330035-8). P-H.

Foundations of Parasitology. Gerald D. Schmidt & Larry S. Roberts. LC 76-30335. (Illus.). 1977. text ed. 23.50 o.p. (ISBN 0-8016-4339-2); pap. 19.95 o.p. (ISBN 0-8016-4345-7). Mosby.

Foundations of Parasitology. 2nd ed. Gerald D. Schmidt & Larry S. Roberts. (Illus.). 672p. 1981. pap. text ed. 24.95 (ISBN 0-8016-4344-9). Mosby.

Foundations of Paul Samuelson's Revealed Preference Theory: A Study by the Method of Rational Reconstruction. Stanley Wong. 1978. 30.00x (ISBN 0-7100-8643-1). Routledge & Kegan.

Foundations of Pediatric Nursing. 2nd ed. Violet Broadribb. (Illus., Orig.). 1973. pap. 9.50 o.p. (ISBN 0-397-54135-X). Lippincott.

Foundations of Pennsylvania Prehistory. Ed. by Barry C. Kent et al. LC 7-612349. (Pennsylvania Historical & Museum Commission Anthropological Ser.: No. 1). (Illus.). 1971. 13.00 (ISBN 0-911124-67-5). Pa Hist & Mus.

Foundations of Personnel. William F. Glueck. 1979. 18.50x (ISBN 0-256-02202-X). Business Pubns.

Foundations of Physical Education. 8th ed. Charles A. Bucher. LC 78-17035. (Illus.). 1979. 17.95 (ISBN 0-8016-0867-8). Mosby.

Foundations of Physical Education. Richard Rivenes et al. LC 77-75155. (Illus.). 1978. text ed. 14.75 (ISBN 0-395-25389-6). HM.

Foundations of Potential Theory. Oliver D. Kellogg. 1929. pap. text ed. 5.00 (ISBN 0-486-60144-7). Dover.

Foundations of Power: John Marshall, 1801-1815. George L. Haskins. (History of the Supreme Court of the United States: Vol. II). (Illus.). 900p. 1981. 60.00 (ISBN 0-02-541360-0). Macmillan.

Foundations of Practical Harmony & Counterpoint. 2nd ed. Reginald O. Morris. LC 79-10541. (Illus.). xii, 148p. 1980. Repr. of 1931 ed. lib. bdg. 15.75x (ISBN 0-313-21465-4, MOPH). Greenwood.

Foundations of Primitive Thought. Christopher R. Hallpike. (Illus.). 530p. 1979. text ed. 49.00x (ISBN 0-19-823196-2). Oxford U Pr.

Foundations of Probability. Alfred Renyi. LC 72-105221. 1970. 18.95x (ISBN 0-8162-7114-3). Holden-Day.

Foundations of Programming with Pascal. Lawrie Moore. (Series of Computers & Their Applications). 238p. 1980. 47.95 (ISBN 0-470-27022-5, Pub. by Halsted Pr). Wiley.

Foundations of Psychology. Gary S. Belkin & Ruth H. Skydell. LC 78-69566. (Illus.). 1979. text ed. 17.50 (ISBN 0-395-25363-2); annot. inst. ed. 18.95 (ISBN 0-395-25364-0); study guide 6.95 (ISBN 0-395-25365-9); test items 0.65 (ISBN 0-395-25366-7); test items manual il 0.60 (ISBN 0-395-28483-X). HM.

Foundations of Quantum Mechanics. Ed. by B. D'Espagnat. (Italian Physical Society: Course 49). 1972. 54.50 (ISBN 0-12-368849-3). Acad Pr.

Foundations of Quantum Theory. Sol Wieder. 1973. text ed. 22.95 (ISBN 0-12-749050-7). Acad Pr.

Foundations of Secure Computation. Ed. by Richard A. Demillo et al. 1978. 25.50 (ISBN 0-12-210350-5). Acad Pr.

Foundations of Solid Mechanics. Y. C. Fung. 1965. ref. ed. 26.95 (ISBN 0-13-329912-0). P-H.

Foundations of Statistical Mechanics: A Deductive Treatment. O. Penrose. LC 70-89513. (International Series in Natural Philosophy: Vol. 22). (Illus.). 1970. 23.10 o.p. (ISBN 0-08-013314-2). Pergamon.

Foundations of Stochastic Analysis. M. M. Rao. (Probability & Mathematical Statistics Ser.). 1981. price not set (ISBN 0-12-580850-X). Acad Pr.

Foundations of Structuralism: A Critique of Levi-Strauss & the Structuralist Movement. Simon Clarke. 224p. 1981. 26.50x (ISBN 0-389-20156-1). B&N.

Foundations of Syntactic Theory. Robert P. Stockwell. LC 76-8021. (Foundations of Modern Linguistics Ser.). 1977. 14.95 (ISBN 0-13-329987-2); pap. text ed. 9.95 (ISBN 0-13-329979-1); wkbk. 5.95 (ISBN 0-13-965202-7). P-H.

Foundations of Technical Mathematics. Warren Donahue. LC 75-96962. 1970. 19.95 (ISBN 0-471-21774-3). Wiley.

Foundations of the Metaphysics of Morals. Immanuel Kant. Tr. by Lewis W. Beck. Bd. with What Is Enlightenment. LC 59-11679. 1959. pap. 3.50 (ISBN 0-672-60312-8, LLA113). Bobbs.

Foundations of the Metaphysics of Morals: Text & Critical Essays. Immanuel Kant. Ed. by Robert P. Wolff. LC 68-9841. (Text & Critical Essays Ser.). 1969. pap. 6.95 (ISBN 0-672-61114-7, TC1). Bobbs.

Foundations of the Nineteenth Century, 2 vols. Houston S. Chamberlain. LC 67-29735. 1968. Repr. Set. 85.00 (ISBN 0-86527-069-4). Fertig.

Foundations of the Novel Series: Representative Early Eighteenth-Century Fiction, 71 vols. Ed. by Michael F. Shugrue. lib. bdg. 50.00 ea. Garland Pub.

Foundations of the Theory of Groupoids & Groups. Otakar Boruvka. LC 75-8625. 215p. 1976. Repr. of 1960 ed. 37.95 (ISBN 0-470-08965-2). Halsted Pr.

Foundations of the Theory of Probability. 2nd ed. Andrei N. Kolmogorov. LC 56-11512. 7.50 (ISBN 0-8284-0023-7). Chelsea Pub.

Foundations of Theoretical Phonology. James Foley. LC 76-27904. (Cambridge Studies in Linguistics Monographs: No. 2). 1977. 26.95 (ISBN 0-521-21466-1). Cambridge U Pr.

Foundations of Three Dimensional Euclidean Geometry. Vaisman. Date not set. 35.00 (ISBN 0-8247-6901-5). Dekker.

Foundations of Twentieth Century Education in England. Eric J. Eaglesham. (Students Library of Education Ser.). (Orig.). 1967. text ed. 3.00x (ISBN 0-7100-4221-3). Humanities.

Foundations of Urban Education. Ed. by William P. McLemore. 1977. pap. text ed. 9.75x (ISBN 0-8191-0172-9). U Pr of Amer.

Foundations of Vocational Education. 3rd ed. Rupert Evans & Edward Herr. Ed. by Robert E. Taylor. (Merrill Series in Career Programs). 1978. text ed. 18.95 (ISBN 0-675-08442-3). Merrill.

Foundations of Vocational Education: Social & Philosophical Concepts. J. Thompson. (Illus.). 1973. ref. ed. 17.95 (ISBN 0-13-330068-4). P-H.

Founder of Christianity. Charles H. Dodd. LC 73-90222. 1970. pap. 3.95 (ISBN 0-02-084640-1). Macmillan.

Founders & Forefathers: Who Were the People Who Made America? Martin W. Sandler et al. (People Make a Nation Ser.). (gr. 7-12). 1971. pap. text ed. 4.80 (ISBN 0-205-03437-3, 7834373). Allyn.

Founders of Neurology: One Hundred & Forty-Six Biographical Sketches by Eighty-Nine Authors. 2nd ed. Webb Haymaker & Francis Schiller. (Illus.). 640p. 1970. 24.75 (ISBN 0-398-00809-4). C C Thomas.

Founders of the Middle Ages. E. M. Rand. Date not set. 7.50 (ISBN 0-8446-2779-8). Peter Smith.

Founder's Praise. Joanne Greenberg. LC 76-3968. 1976. 8.95 o.p. (ISBN 0-03-015391-3). HR&W.

Founding Fathers of Social Science. rev. ed. Ed. by Timothy Raison. 319p. 1979. 15.95 o.p. (ISBN 0-85967-458-4, Pub. by Scolar Pr England); pap. 7.95 (ISBN 0-85967-459-2). Biblio Dist.

Founding of the Democratic Republic. Martin Diamond. LC 80-84210. 192p. 1981. pap. text ed. 5.50 (ISBN 0-87581-271-6). Peacock Pubs.

Founding of the French Socialist Party, 1893-1905. Aaron Noland. 14.25 (ISBN 0-86527-070-8). Fertig.

Founding of the Henry E. Huntington Library & Art Gallery: Four Essays. James Thorpe et al. (Illus.). 1969. 2.50 (ISBN 0-87328-105-5). Huntington Lib.

Founding of the Roman Catholic Church in Oceania 1825-1850. R. M. Wiltgen. LC 78-74665. (Illus.). 610p. 1980. text ed. 36.95 (ISBN 0-7081-0835-0, 0572). Bks Australia.

Foundling. Carol Carrick. LC 77-1587. (Illus.). (ps-4). 1977. 6.95 (ISBN 0-395-28775-8, Clarion). HM.

Foundry Engineering. F. Taylor et al. LC 59-11811. 1959. 27.95 (ISBN 0-471-84843-3). Wiley.

Foundryman's Handbook. 8th ed. Foundry Services Ltd. 1976. text ed. 13.75 (ISBN 0-08-018020-5). Pergamon.

Fountain of Discontent: The Trent Affair & Freedom of the Seas. Gordon H. Warren. LC 80-24499. (Illus.). 366p. 1981. price not set. NE U Pr.

Fountains. Sylvia Wallace. 384p. 1976. 8.95 o.p. (ISBN 0-688-03040-8). Morrow.

Fouquet. J. Melet-Sanson. (Illus.). (gr. 10-12). 1978. 10.95 (ISBN 0-8120-5280-3, Screpel). Barron.

Four African Literatures: Xhosa, Sotho, Zulu, Amharic. Albert S. Gerard. LC 74-126763. 1971. 26.50x (ISBN 0-520-01788-9). U of Cal Pr.

Four Against the Bank of England. Ann Huxley. LC 80-82216. 224p. 1980. pap. 2.50 (ISBN 0-87216-750-X). Playboy Pbks.

Four American Anthropologists. Joan T. Mark. 1980. lib. bdg. write for info. (ISBN 0-88202-190-7). N Watson.

Four & Twenty Blackbirds. Francis Brabazon. (Illus.). 52p. 1975. pap. 2.25x (ISBN 0-913078-22-0). Sheriar Pr.

Four Bears in a Box. Martha Alexander. (Illus.). 32p. (ps-3). 1981. boxed set 6.95 (ISBN 0-8037-2756-9). Dial.

Four Before Richardson: Selected English Novels, 1720-1727. Ed. by William H. McBurney. LC 63-9095. (Landmark Edition). 1978. 21.50x (ISBN 0-8032-0114-1). U of Nebr Pr.

Four Books of Architecture. Andrea Palladio. Ed. by Isaac Ware. 1738. pap. text ed. 8.95 (ISBN 0-486-21308-0). Dover.

Four Brothers in Blue. Robert G. Carter. LC 78-56909. 1978. Repr. of 1913 ed. 16.95 (ISBN 0-292-72426-8). U of Tex Pr.

Four Centuries of Cat Books: A Bibliography, 1570-1970. Claire Necker. LC 72-363. 1972. 20.50 (ISBN 0-8108-0480-8). Scarecrow.

Four Centuries of English Letters. Ed. by William B. Scoones. LC 79-142558. 1971. Repr. of 1893 ed. 22.00 (ISBN 0-8103-3638-3). Gale.

Four Centuries of Liege Gunmaking. Claude Gaier. (Illus.). 368p. 1977. 106.00x (ISBN 0-85667-028-6, Pub. by Sotheby Parke Bernet England). Biblio Dist.

Four Centuries of Modern Iraq. Stephen Longrigg. (Arab Background Ser.). 15.00x (ISBN 0-685-72044-6). Intl Bk Ctr.

Four Comedies by Pedro Calderon de la Barca. Pedro Calderon de la Barca. Tr. by Kenneth Muir. LC 80-14570. 304p. 1980. 21.50x (ISBN 0-8131-1409-8). U Pr of Ky.

Four Comedies: Lysistrata, the Congresswomen, the Acharnians, the Frogs. Aristophanes. Ed. by William Arrowsmith. (Illus.). 432p. 1969. pap. 5.95 (ISBN 0-472-06152-6, 152, AA). U of Mich Pr.

Four Contemporary Swedish Poets. Ed. by Stanley H. Barkan. Tr. by Robin Fulton & Anselm Hollo. (Cross-Cultural Review No.5). 48p. Date not set. 10.00 (ISBN 0-89304-608-6); pap. 4.00 (ISBN 0-89304-609-4). Cross Cult.

Four Critics: Croce, Valery, Lukacs, & Ingarden. Rene Wellek. LC 80-54429. (Walker-Ames Lecture Ser.). 104p. 1981. 8.95 (ISBN 0-295-95800-6). U of Wash Pr.

Four Day Week & Other Stories. Gerald Locklin. 1980. 3.00 (ISBN 0-917554-06-X). Maelstrom.

Four-Day Work Week: Blue Collar Adjustment to a Nonconventional Arrangement of Work & Leisure Time. David M. Maklan. LC 77-14308. (Prager Special Studies). 1977. 23.95 (ISBN 0-03-039916-5). Praeger.

Four Days in Philadelphia- 1776. Mary K. Phelan. LC 67-18521. (gr. 5 up). 1967. 8.95 (ISBN 0-690-31485-X, TYC-J). T Y Crowell.

Four Decades of Choral Training. Gerald F. Darrow. LC 74-31205. 1975. 10.00 (ISBN 0-8108-0791-2). Scarecrow.

Four Doctors. Benjamin Siegel. 288p. 1975. 7.95 o.p. (ISBN 0-440-04563-0). Delacorte.

Four Essays in the Theory of Uncertainty & Portfolio Choice. Jonathan Eaton. LC 78-75071. (Outstanding Dissertations in Economics). 1980. lib. bdg. 24.00 (ISBN 0-8240-4145-3). Garland Pub.

Four Essays on Gulliver's Travels. Arthur E. Case. 6.75 (ISBN 0-8446-1106-9). Peter Smith.

Four Essays on Liberty. Isaiah Berlin. 1970. 14.95 (ISBN 0-19-501242-9). Oxford U Pr.

Four Fabulous Faces: Swanson, Garbo, Crawford, Dietrich. Larry Carr. (Large Format Ser). (Illus.). 1978. pap. 12.95 o.p. (ISBN 0-14-004988-6). Penguin.

Four Families of Karimpur. Charlotte V. Wiser. LC 78-1557. (Foreign & Comparative Studies-South Asian Ser.: No. 3). (Illus.). 1978. pap. text ed. 6.50x (ISBN 0-915984-78-4). Syracuse U Foreign Comp.

Four Farces: L'obstination Des Femmes; le Cuvier: le Paste et la Tarte; Maistre Pierre Pathelin. Ed. by Barbara C. Bowen. (French Texts Ser.). 1967. pap. 10.00x (ISBN 0-631-00670-2, Pub. by Basil Blackwell). Biblio Dist.

Four Feathers. A. E. W. Mason. 1977. pap. text ed. 1.50 (ISBN 0-505-51162-2, 51162). Tower Bks.

Four, Five & Six by Tey. Josephine Tey. 1958. 8.95 o.s.i. (ISBN 0-02-617060-4). Macmillan.

Four for Tomorrow. Roger Zelazny. 192p. 1973. pap. 1.95 (ISBN 0-441-24904-3). Ace Bks.

Four French Dramatists: A Bibliography of Criticism of the Works of Eugene Brieux, Francois De Curel, Emile Fabre, Paul Hervieu. Edmund F. Santa Vicca. LC 74-7495. (Author Bibliographies Ser.: No. 17). 1974. 10.00 (ISBN 0-8108-0755-6). Scarecrow.

Four Fundamental Questions. 2nd ed. Da Free John. LC 79-92923. 1980. pap. 1.95 (ISBN 0-913922-49-8). Dawn Horse Pr.

Four Generations of Commissions: The Peale Collection of the Maryland Historical Society. LC 75-1729. (Illus.). 1975. 8.00 (ISBN 0-686-11974-6). Md. Hist.

Four Generations of Management: The Simpson-Reed Story. William G. Reed & Elwood R. Maunder. (Illus.). 1977. 16.50 o.p. (ISBN 0-89030-033-X). Forest Hist Soc.

Four Generations of Verse. Pauline M. Keith. 1981. 5.95 (ISBN 0-930142-06-3). Merlin Pr.

Four German Poets: Gunter Eich, Hilde Domin, Erich Fried, & Gunter Kunert. Gunter Eich et al. Ed. & tr. by Agnes Stein. LC 78-59474. (Contemporary Poets Ser.). 1980. 12.95 (ISBN 0-87376-034-4). Red Dust.

Four Golden Learning Bee Books. Date not set. pap. 2.95 boxed set (ISBN 0-307-13638-8, Golden Pr). Western Pub.

Four Gospels. David Brown. 15.95 (ISBN 0-85151-016-7). Banner of Truth.

Four Gospels: An Introduction, 2 Vols. Vawter, Bruce, C.M. LC 67-10408. 1969. pap. 3.50 vol. I (ISBN 0-385-01479-1, Im); Vol. 1. Volume II 3.50 (ISBN 0-385-06557-4, 255A). Vol. 2 (255B). Doubleday.

Four Gospels & Revelation. Tr. by Richmond Lattimore from Greek. 320p. 1979. 10.95 (ISBN 0-374-15801-0). FS&G.

Four Great Comedies. William Shakespeare. Incl. As You Like It; Midsummer Night's Dream; The Tempest; Twelfth Night. pap. 2.75 (ISBN 0-671-42463-7). WSP.

Four Great Makers of Modern Architecture: Gropius, le Corbusier, Mies Van der Rohe, Wright. Gropius et al. LC 78-130312. (Architecture & Decorative Art Ser.: Vol. 37). 1970. Repr. of 1963 ed. lib. bdg. 29.50 (ISBN 0-306-70065-4). Da Capo.

Four Great Railways. Michael R. Bonavia. LC 79-91498. (Illus.). 1980. 17.95 (ISBN 0-7153-7842-2). David & Charles.

Four Great Southern Cooks. Ruth Jenkins et al. LC 80-68989. (Illus.). 200p. (Orig.). 1980. pap. 7.95 (ISBN 0-938072-00-5). DuBose Pub.

Four-Handed Dentistry in Clinical Practice. Joseph E. Chasteen. LC 78-7436. 1978. text ed. 16.95 (ISBN 0-8016-0977-1). Mosby.

Four Hundred & Ninety-Five Golf Lessons by Arnold Palmer. Arnold Palmer & Earl Puckett. 1973. pap. 4.95 o.p. (ISBN 0-695-80402-2). Follett.

Four Hundred Drugs That Don't Work. Chris Coley & Sidney Wolfe. 6.95. Green Hill.

Four Hundred Ideas for Design, Vol. 3. Electronic Design. Ed. by Morris Grossman. (Illus.). 1976. 16.60 (ISBN 0-8104-5111-5). Hayden.

Four Hundred Miles from Harlem: Courts, Crime, & Correction. Max Wylie. 288p. 1972. 6.95 o.s.i. (ISBN 0-02-631900-4). Macmillan.

Four Hundred Silent Years. Gordon Lindsay. (Old Testament Ser.). 1.25 (ISBN 0-89985-158-4). Christ Nations.

Four Hundred Songs & Dances from the Stuart Masque. Ed. by Andrew J. Sabol. LC 77-6686. 661p. 1978. 100.00x (ISBN 0-87057-146-X, Pub. by Brown U Pr). Univ Pr of New England.

Four in a Wild Place. John Stallard. LC 79-152674. 1971. 6.95 o.p. (ISBN 0-393-08649-6). Norton.

Four Just Men. Edgar Wallace. 1976. lib. bdg. 14.95x (ISBN 0-89968-155-7). Lightyear.

Four Keys to Guatemala. Vera Kelsey et al. LC 77-2175. (Funk & W Bk.). (Illus.). 1978. 10.00 o.s.i. (ISBN 0-308-10293-2, TYC-T); pap. 5.95 o.s.i. (ISBN 0-308-10316-5, TYC-T). T Y Crowell.

Four-Language Technical Dictionary of Chromatography: English, German, French, Russian. H. Angele. LC 76-103000. 1971. text ed. 42.00 (ISBN 0-08-015865-X). Pergamon.

Four-Language Technical Dictionary of Heating, Ventilation & Sanitary Engineering: English, German, French, Russian. W. Lindeke. LC 79-81248. 1971. 50.00 (ISBN 0-08-006426-4). Pergamon.

Four Latin Authors. Ed. by Eberhard C. Kennedy. 1940. text ed. 7.50x (ISBN 0-521-05881-3). Cambridge U Pr.

Four Little Kittens. Kathleen Daly. (ps-1). 1957. PLB 5.00 (ISBN 0-307-60322-9, Golden Pr). Western Pub.

Four Magic Boxes. Jane B. Monroe. LC 77-12959. (Creative Dramatics Ser.). (Illus.). (ps-3). 1978. PLB 5.50 (ISBN 0-89565-007-X); pap. 2.50 (ISBN 0-89565-040-1). Childs World.

Four Major Plays. new ed. Aristophanes. Incl. The Acharnians; The Birds; The Clouds; Lysistrata. (Classics Ser). (gr. 11 up). 1968. pap. 1.50 (ISBN 0-8049-0189-9, CL-189). Airmont.

Four Major Plays of Chikamatsu. Donald Keene. LC 64-5372. 1961. 25.00x (ISBN 0-231-02490-8); pap. 6.00 (ISBN 0-231-08553-2). Columbia U Pr.

Four Marks of a Total Christian. Bruce L. Shelley. 1978. pap. 1.95 (ISBN 0-88207-512-8). Victor Bks.

Four Martyrdoms from the Pierpont Morgan Coptic Codices. Ed. by E. A. Reymond & J. W. Barns. 278p. 1974. 24.95x (ISBN 0-19-815448-8). Oxford U Pr.

Four Marys. Rinalda Roberts. 256p. (Orig.). 1976. pap. 1.25 o.p. (ISBN 0-445-00366-9). Popular Lib.

Four Minute Fun for Parent & Child. Elaine Hardt. LC 79-90463. 1978. pap. 2.95 (ISBN 0-932960-02-2). Horizons.

Four Months in a Sneak Box: A Boat Voyage of Twenty Six Hundred Miles Down the Ohio & Mississippi Rivers. Nathaniel Holmes Bishop. LC 71-142572. (Illus.). xii, 322p. 1976. Repr. of 1879 ed. 26.00 (ISBN 0-8103-4170-0). Gale.

Four of a Kind. Zeke Masters. (Orig.). 1981. pap. 1.75 (ISBN 0-671-42617-6). PB.

Four Phases of American Development: Federalism, Democracy, Imperialism, Expansion. John B. Moore. LC 72-109551. (Law, Politics & History Ser). 1970. Repr. of 1912 ed. lib. bdg. 25.00 (ISBN 0-306-71905-3). Da Capo.

Four Plays. Guenter Grass. Tr. by Ralph Manheim & A. Leslie Willson. Incl. Flood; Mister, Mister; Only Ten Minutes to Buffalo; The Wicked Cooks. LC 67-11968. 289p. 1968. pap. 3.25 o.p. (ISBN 0-15-633150-0, HB138, Harv). HarBraceJ.

Four Plays. Audrey Tolbert. 1981. 4.95 (ISBN 0-8062-1664-6). Carlton.

Four Plays, 1789-1812. William Dunlap. LC 76-46978. 300p. 1976. lib. bdg. 25.00x (ISBN 0-8201-1283-6). Schol Facsimiles.

Four Poached & Oatmeal. Robert M. Michaels. LC 80-81367. (Illus.). 50p. (Orig.). 1980. pap. 3.50 (ISBN 0-9604292-0-4). KaChunk Pr.

Four Poets on Poetry. Ed. by Don C. Allen. LC 80-20856. (Percy Graeme Turnbull Memorial Lectures on Poetry, 1958). 111p. 1980. Repr. of 1959 ed. lib. bdg. 19.50x (ISBN 0-313-22405-6, ALFP). Greenwood.

Four Political Treatises, 1533-1541. Thomas Elyot. LC 67-10273. 1967. 44.00x (ISBN 0-8201-1015-9). Schol Facsimiles.

Four Psalms: Twenty-Three, Thirty-Seven, Fifty-Two & One Hundred Twenty-One. George A. Smith. LC 80-82329. (Shepherd Classic Ser.). 1980. pap. 5.95 (ISBN 0-87983-235-5). Keats.

Four Psychologies Applied to Education: Freudian, Behavioral, Humanistic, Transpersonal. Ed. by Thomas B. Roberts. LC 74-9729. 1975. text ed. 19.50 o.p. (ISBN 0-470-72586-9); pap. text ed. 12.95x (ISBN 0-470-72588-5). Halsted Pr.

Four Puppies. Anne Heathers. (ps-2). 1960. PLB 5.00 (ISBN 0-307-61405-0, Golden Pr). Western Pub.

Four Quartets. T. S. Eliot. Ed. by Bernard Bergonzi. LC 77-127568. (Casebook Ser). 1970. pap. text ed. 2.50 o.s.i. (ISBN 0-87695-039-X). Aurora Pubs.

Four Romantic Tales from 19th Century German. Ed. by Helene Scher et al. Clemens Brentano & Achim Von Arnim. Tr. by Helene Scher from Ger. LC 75-1428. 1975. 7.50 (ISBN 0-8044-2769-0); pap. 3.95 (ISBN 0-8044-6804-4). Ungar.

Four Roses in Three Acts. Franklin Mason. LC 80-68007. 1981. 9.95 (ISBN 0-914590-64-2); pap. 4.95 (ISBN 0-914590-65-0). Fiction Coll.

Four Sacred Seasons. G. De Purucker. LC 79-63565. 1979. 4.50 (ISBN 0-911500-83-9); pap. 2.75 softcover (ISBN 0-911500-84-7). Theos U Pr.

Four Seasons. Tony Geiss. (Big Picture Bks.). (Illus.). (ps-k). 1979. 1.95 (ISBN 0-307-10820-1, Golden Pr); PLB 7.62 (ISBN 0-307-60820-4). Western Pub.

Four Seasons. Tony Geiss. (Illus.). (ps-3). 1979. PLB 5.00 (ISBN 0-307-60179-X, Golden Pr). Western Pub.

Four Seasons Cookbook. Nancy Elmont. 1981. 11.95 (ISBN 0-916752-47-X). Green Hill.

Four Seasons Cookbook. Nancy Elmont. LC 80-70101. (Illus.). 144p. 1981. 8.95 (ISBN 0-916752-47-X). Dorison Hse.

Four Seasons Cookery Book. Margaret Costa. 1979. 28.00x (ISBN 0-8464-0423-0). Beekman Pubs.

Four Seasons North: A Journal of Life in the Alaskan Wilderness. Billie Wright. LC 79-138774. (Illus.). 288p. (YA) 1973. 9.95 o.p. (ISBN 0-06-014756-3, HarpT). Har-Row.

Four Seasons of Chester County. Red Hamer. (Illus.). 96p. 1979. 24.95 (ISBN 0-9605400-0-8). Four Seas Bk.

Four Seasons of the Chesapeake Bay: Fall-Winter, Vol. II. Red Hamer. Ed. by Barbara H. Hamer. (Illus.). 128p. 1981. 27.50 (ISBN 0-9605400-2-4). Four Seas Bk.

Four Seasons of the Chesapeake Bay: Spring-Summer, Vol. 1. Red Hamer. Ed. by Barbara H. Hamer. (Illus.). 128p. 1980. 27.50 (ISBN 0-9605400-0-8). Four Seas Bk.

Four Seasons: Splendid Recipes from the World-Famous Restaurant. Tom G. Margittai & Paul Kovi. 1980. 24.95 (ISBN 0-671-25022-1). S&S.

Four Servants. Ed. by Alma Gilleo. LC 74-734828. (Fairy Tales of the Brothers Grimm Cassette Bks). (Illus.). 16p. 1976. pap. 21.00 incl. 10 bks. & one cassette (ISBN 0-89290-009-1). Soc for Visual.

Four Slaves of Cythera, a Romance in Ten Cantos. Robert Bland. Ed. by Donald H. Reiman. LC 75-31160. (Romantic Context Ser.: Poetry 1789-1830: Vol. 15). 1978. Repr. of 1809 ed. lib. bdg. 47.00 (ISBN 0-8240-2114-2). Garland Pub.

Four Springs. Edwin Honig. LC 70-189190. 60p. 1972. 6.00 (ISBN 0-8040-0580-X); pap. 2.75 o.p. (ISBN 0-8040-0581-8). Swallow.

Four Stars from the World of Sports. Clare Gault & Frank Gault. LC 75-3909. (Illus.). 112p. (gr. 3-7). 1975. 4.95 (ISBN 0-8027-6221-2); PLB 4.83 o.s.i. (ISBN 0-8027-6222-0). Walker & Co.

Four States of America. Martin J. Rodgers. 1980. 7.95 (ISBN 0-533-04562-2). Vantage.

Four Stories. Sigrid Undset. Tr. by Naomi Walford from Norwegian. LC 78-16903. 1978. Repr. of 1969 ed. lib. bdg. 19.75x (ISBN 0-313-20566-3, UNFS). Greenwood.

Four Stories for Four Seasons. Tomie de Paola. LC 76-8837. (Illus.). (ps-2). 1977. PLB 7.95 (ISBN 0-13-330175-3); pap. 3.95 (ISBN 0-13-330100-1). P-H.

Four Thousand Questions & Answers on the Bible. (YA) (gr. 7-12). pap. 1.25 o.p. (ISBN 0-685-19667-4). Jove Pubns.

Four Trojan Horses. Harry Conn. 1978. pap. cancelled o.s.i. (ISBN 0-89728-031-8, 700212). Omega Pubns OR.

Four Tudor Interludes. Ed. by J. A. Somerset. (Renaissance Library). 192p. 1974. text ed. 18.75x (ISBN 0-485-13602-3, Athlone Pr); pap. text ed. 10.00x (ISBN 0-485-12602-8, Athlone Pr). Humanities.

Four Types of Value Destruction: A Search for the Good Through an Ethical Analysis of Everyday Experience. D. D. Keyes. 1978. pap. text ed. 7.00x (ISBN 0-8191-0395-0). U Pr of Amer.

Four Ukranian Poets. Ed. by Danylo S. Struk. Tr. by Martha Bohachevska-Chomiak. 1977. write for info. o.p. (ISBN 0-685-79417-2). Cataract Pr.

Four Voyages to the New World. Christopher Columbus. Tr. by R. H. Major. 1961. pap. 1.95 o.s.i. (ISBN 0-87091-004-3, AE). Corinth Bks.

Four Way Bargello. rev. ed. Dorothy Kaestner. LC 73-14400. (Illus.). 1972. encore ed. 4.95 (ISBN 0-684-16198-2, ScribT); pap. 8.95 (ISBN 0-684-15142-1, SL 733, ScribT). Scribner.

Four Ways of Being Human. Gene Lisitzky. 1976. pap. 3.50 (ISBN 0-14-004391-8). Penguin.

Four Weekends to an Ideal Marriage. Herbert A. Glieberman & Paul Neimark. 1981. 8.95 (ISBN 0-938814-00-1). Barrington.

Four Wheel Drive Handbook. James T. Crow & Cameron A. Warren. 96p. 1976. Repr. 3.95 (ISBN 0-87880-004-2). Norton.

Four-Wheel-Drive North American Travel Guide. LC 79-63747. 1980. pap. 7.95 (ISBN 0-528-84110-6). Rand.

Four Winds Farm, Repr. Of 1887 Ed. Mary L. Molesworth. Bd. with Children of the Castle. Repr. of 1890 ed. LC 75-32192. (Classics of Children's Literature, 1621-1932: Vol. 54). (Illus.). 1976. PLB 38.00 (ISBN 0-8240-2303-X). Garland Pub.

Four Winds of Heaven. Monique R. High. 695p. 1980. 10.95 (ISBN 0-440-02573-7). Delacorte.

Four Winds of Heaven. Monique R. High. 1981. pap. 3.25 o.s.i. (ISBN 0-440-12566-9). Dell.

Four World Views. The Educational Research Council. (Human Adventure, Concepts & Inquiry Ser). (gr. 5). 1975. pap. text ed. 6.20 (ISBN 0-205-04444-1, 8044449); tchrs'. guide 4.80 (ISBN 0-205-04445-X, 8044457). Allyn.

Four Years in the Rockies: Or the Adventures of Isaac P. Rose... Giving His Experience As a Hunter & Trapper. James B. Marsh. LC 75-7120. (Indian Captivities Ser.: Vol. 94). 1976. Repr. of 1884 ed. lib. bdg. 44.00 (ISBN 0-8240-1718-8). Garland Pub.

Four Years On: A Follow-up Study at School Leaving Age of Children Formerly Attending a Traditional & Progessive Junior School. Stan Gooch & M. L. Pringle. (Studies in Child Development). (Orig.). 1966. pap. text ed. 3.50x (ISBN 0-582-32392-4). Humanities.

Four Years Voyages of Captain George Roberts. Daniel Defoe. LC 79-170566. (Foundations of the Novel Ser.: Vol. 47). lib. bdg. 50.00 (ISBN 0-8240-0559-7). Garland Pub.

Foure Bookes of Husbandry, Newely Englished & Increased by B. Googe. Conrad Heresbach. LC 72-205. (English Experience Ser.: No. 323). 1971. Repr. of 1577 ed. 49.00 (ISBN 90-221-0323-4). Walter J Johnson.

Fourier Analysis. Hans Triebel. LC 77-555434. 1977. pap. 9.50x (ISBN 0-8002-0808-0). Intl Pubns Serv.

Fourier Analysis in Several Complex Variables. Leon Ehrenpreis. (Pure & Applied Mathematics Ser.). 1970. 43.50 (ISBN 0-471-23400-1, Pub. by Wiley-Interscience). Wiley.

Fourier Analysis of Time Series: An Introduction. Peter Bloomfield. LC 75-34294. (Probability & Mathematical Statistics Ser.). 258p. 1976. 25.95 (ISBN 0-471-08256-2, Pub. by Wiley-Interscience). Wiley.

Fourier Analysis on Groups. W. Rudin. (Pure & Applied Mathematics Ser.). 1962. 30.50 (ISBN 0-470-74481-2). Wiley.

Fourier Integral & Certain of Its Applications. Norbert Wiener. 1933. pap. text ed. 3.50 (ISBN 0-486-60272-9). Dover.

Fourier Methods in Crystallography. G. N. Ramachandran & R. Srinivasan. 259p. 1970. 23.95 (ISBN 0-471-70705-8). Krieger.

Fourier Series. 2nd ed. Werner Rogosinski. LC 50-6214. 6.95 (ISBN 0-8284-0067-9). Chelsea Pub.

Fourier Series & Integrals. H. Dym & H. P. McKean. (Probability & Mathematical Statistics Ser). 1972. 39.00 (ISBN 0-12-226450-9). Acad Pr.

Fouriersche Integrale. Salomon Bochner. LC 49-22695. (Ger). 8.95 (ISBN 0-8284-0042-3). Chelsea Pub.

Fourscore Classics of Music Literature. Gustave Reese. LC 78-87616. (Music Reprint Ser). 1969. Repr. of 1957 ed. lib. bdg. 17.50 (ISBN 0-306-71620-8). Da Capo.

Foursome. E. A. Whitehead. 1972. 7.50 (ISBN 0-571-09878-9, Pub. by Faber & Faber); pap. 4.95 (ISBN 0-571-09879-7). Merrimack Bk Serv.

Fourteen Decisions for Undeclared War. John R. Howard. LC 78-62668. (Illus.). 1978. pap. text ed. 9.00 (ISBN 0-8191-0585-6). U Pr of Amer.

Fourteen Stories. Stephen Dixon. LC 80-14911. (Johns Hopkins Poetry & Fiction Program). 145p. 1980. 9.95 (ISBN 0-8018-2445-1). Johns Hopkins.

Fourteen Years in the Sandwich Islands. Charles De Varigny. Tr. by Alfons L. Korn. LC 80-26141. (Illus.). 320p. (Fr.). 1981. 24.95 (ISBN 0-8248-0709-X). U Pr of Hawaii.

Fourteeners: Colorado's Great Mountains. Perry Eberhart & Philip Schmuck. LC 72-75740. (Illus.). 128p. 1970. 12.00 (ISBN 0-8040-0122-7, SB); pap. 6.95 (ISBN 0-8040-0123-5). Swallow.

Fourteenth Air Force Story. Kenn C. Rust & Stephen Muth. (Illus.). 1977. 7.50 (ISBN 0-685-83159-0, Pub. by Hist Aviation). Aviation.

Fourteenth Amendment & the Bill of Rights: The Incorporation Theory. Charles Fairman & Stanley Morrison. LC 71-25622. (American Constitutional & Legal History Ser). 1970. Repr. of 1949 ed. lib. bdg. 29.50 (ISBN 0-306-70029-8). Da Capo.

Fourteenth Amendment & the States. Charles W. Collins. LC 74-5437. (American Constitutional & Legal History Ser.). 1974. Repr. of 1912 ed. lib. bdg. 25.00 (ISBN 0-306-70638-5). Da Capo.

Fourteenth Century English Mystics, Vol. 2. George W. Tuma. (Salzburg Studies in English Literature; Elizabethan & Renaissance Studies: No.62). 1977. pap. text ed. 25.00x (ISBN 0-391-01548-6). Humanities.

Fourteenth Century Prose & Verse. Ed. by Kenneth Sisam. (Smith, D. N., Ser). 1921. pap. 13.50x (ISBN 0-19-871093-3). Oxford U Pr.

Fourteenth Century Studies. Maude V. Clarke. Ed. by L. S. Sutherland & M. McKisack. 1937. 27.00x (ISBN 0-19-822303-X). Oxford U Pr.

Fourteenth Century, 1307-1399. May McKisack. (Oxford History of England Ser.). 1959. 34.00x (ISBN 0-19-821712-9). Oxford U Pr.

Fourteenth Day Conspiracy. Jean Gilliland. LC 80-51212. 224p. 1980. pap. 6.95 (ISBN 0-934616-09-4). Valkyrie Pr.

Fourteenth Session of the General Assembly of IUCN. Bd. with Proceedings. IUCN Technical Meeting, Fourteenth. 201p. 1980. pap. 10.00 (ISBN 2-88032-600-1, IUCN 81, IUCN). Unipub.

Fourteenth Witch. Shelley Blue & Deborah Snow. 1977. pap. 5.50 o.p. (ISBN 0-930436-00-8). Persephone.

Fourth Amendment Rights. Joseph D. Hirschel. LC 78-57161. (Illus.). 1979. 17.95 (ISBN 0-669-02361-2). Lexington Bks.

Fourth Blow. Charles Beardsley. 1980. pap. 2.50 (ISBN 0-445-04623-6). Popular Lib.

Fourth Book of Junior Authors & Illustrators. Ed. by Doris De Montreville & Elizabeth D. Crawford. 1978. 17.00 (ISBN 0-8242-0568-5). Wilson.

Fourth Book of the Chronicle of Fredegar with Its Continuations. Tr. by J. M. Wallace-Hadrill. LC 80-28086. (Medieval Classics Ser.). (Illus.). lxvii, 137p. 1981. Repr. of 1960 ed. lib. bdg. 27.50x (ISBN 0-313-22741-1, WAFRE). Greenwood.

Fourth Book of Virgil Finlay. Ed. by Gerry De La Ree. (Illus.). 1979. 15.50 o.p. (ISBN 0-686-15703-6). De La Ree.

Fourth Crossword Puzzle Book. Leslie Hill & P. R. Popkin. 62p. 1971. pap. text ed. 2.95x (ISBN 0-19-432550-4). Oxford U Pr.

Fourth Dimension. Paul Y. Cho. 1979. pap. 4.95 (ISBN 0-88270-380-3). Logos.

Fourth Dimension Simply Explained. Henry Manning. 7.50 (ISBN 0-8446-2522-1). Peter Smith.

Fourth Directory of Periodicals: Publishing Articles in English & American Literature & Language. Donna Gerstenberger & George Hendrick. LC 74-21506. 234p. 1974. 18.95x (ISBN 0-8040-0675-X); pap. 9.95x (ISBN 0-8040-0676-8). Swallow.

Fourth Floor. Hal Boswell. 1981. 8.95 (ISBN 0-533-04772-2). Vantage.

Fourth Grade Celebrity. Patricia R. Giff. (gr. k-6). 1981. pap. 1.25 (ISBN 0-440-42676-6, YB). Dell.

Fourth Institute on Coal Mine Health & Safety: Proceedings. Ed. by R. T. Reeder. 1979. 10.50 o.p. (ISBN 0-918062-07-1). Colo Sch Mines.

Fourth Inventory of Computers in Higher Education. Ed. by John W. Hamblen & Carolyn R. Landis. (EDUCOMoser. in Computing & Telecommunications in Higher Education: No. 4). 1970. lib. bdg. 30.00x (ISBN 0-89158-568-0). Westview.

Fourth Mad Declassified Papers on Spy Vs. Spy. Antonio Prohias. (Mad Ser.). (Illus.). 192p. 1974. pap. 1.75 (ISBN 0-446-94423-8). Warner Bks.

Fourth Man. Andrew Boyle. 464p. 1980. pap. 3.50 (ISBN 0-553-14245-3). Bantam.

Fourth National Congress on Child Abuse & Neglect. Ed. by Shelley Brazier. 350p. 1981. casebound 27.00 (ISBN 0-88416-313-X, 313). PSG Pub.

Fourth New Voices Annual Volume: The John W. Campbell Award Nominees. Ed. by George R. Martin. (Orig.). 1981. pap. 2.25 (ISBN 0-425-05033-5). Berkley Pub.

Fourth of July. Mary K. Phelan. LC 65-25909. (Holiday Ser.). (Illus.). (gr. k-3). 1966. PLB 7.89 (ISBN 0-690-31415-9, TYC-J). T Y Crowell.

Fourth Print Price Guide. Edwin G. Warman. Repr. of 1976 ed. 7.95 o.p. (ISBN 0-685-73594-X). Warman.

Fourth R: Research in the Classroom. Norris G. Haring et al. 1978. 15.95 (ISBN 0-675-08387-7). Merrill.

Fourth Reich. Joseph Rosenberger. (Death Merchant Ser.: No. 39). 192p. (Orig.). 1980. pap. 1.95 (ISBN 0-523-41383-1). Pinnacle Bks.

Fourth Review of Special Education. Ed. by Lester Mann & David Sabatino. 1980. 44.50 (ISBN 0-8089-1263-1). Grune.

Fourth Revolution: Instructional Technology in Higher Education. Carnegie Commission on Higher Education. LC 72-4363. (Illus.). 112p. 1972. 3.95 o.p. (ISBN 0-07-010050-0, P&RB). McGraw.

Fourth Side of the Triangle. Ellery Queen. 192p. 1975. pap. 1.75 (ISBN 0-345-28288-4). Ballantine.

Fourth Symposium on Recent & Fossil Marine Diatoms, Oslo 1976: Proceedings. Ed. by R. Simonsen. (Beiheft zur Nova Hedwigia Ser.: No. 54). (Illus.). 1977. lib. bdg. 100.00x (ISBN 3-7682-5454-2). Lubrecht & Cramer.

Fourth Thousand Years. W. Cleon Skousen. LC 66-29887. 1966. 13.95 (ISBN 0-685-48242-1). Bookcraft Inc.

Fourth Wall. Barbara Paul. 474p. 1980. Repr. of 1979 ed. large print ed. 12.95 (ISBN 0-89621-254-8). Thorndike Pr.

Fourth Way. P. D. Ouspensky. 1971. pap. 3.95 (ISBN 0-394-71672-8, Vin). Random.

Fourty-Four Pounds or Size & Piece. Virginia Jansen. (Illus.). 1978. pap. 3.50 o.p. (ISBN 0-931212-00-6, Pub. by Jansen). Caroline Hse.

Fox & Hare. Chester Anderson. LC 80-66869. (Illus.). 192p. 1980. 20.00 (ISBN 0-9601428-0-0); pap. 9.95 (ISBN 0-9601428-9-4). Entwhistle Bks.

Fox & His Vixen. Viveca Ives. 1977. pap. 1.95 o.p. (ISBN 0-345-27325-7). Ballantine.

Fox & the Grapes. Ed. by Denise W. Guynn. (Aesop's Fables Bk). (Illus.). 16p. (ps). 1980. pap. 22.00 ten bks & one cass. (ISBN 0-89290-075-X, BC14-3). Soc for Visual.

Fox at Bay: Martin Van Buren & the Presidency, 1837-1841. James C. Curtis. LC 72-111507. 248p. 1970. 13.00x (ISBN 0-8131-1214-1). U Pr of Ky.

Fox Book. Jan Pfloog. (Illus.). 24p. (gr. k-1). 1976. PLB 5.38 (ISBN 0-307-68978-6, Golden Pr). Western Pub.

Fox Book. Ed. by Richard Shaw. LC 78-161068. (Animal Art Anthology Ser). (Illus.). (gr. 2-5). 1971. PLB 4.95 o.p. (ISBN 0-7232-6082-6). Warne.

Fox Dancer. Robert J. Steelman. 1976. pap. 0.95 o.p. (ISBN 0-685-69161-6, LB370NK, Leisure Bks). Nordon Pubns.

Fox Farm. Warwick Deeping. 1976. lib. bdg. 17.75x (ISBN 0-89968-021-6). Lightyear.

Fox Finds a Friend. Walt Disney Productions. (Sturdy Shape Bks). 14p. (ps). 1981. 2.95 (ISBN 0-307-12261-1, Golden Pr). Western Pub.

Fox Friend. Elizabeth Coatsworth. (Illus.). (gr. k-2). 1966. 4.25g o.s.i. (ISBN 0-02-720510-X). Macmillan.

Fox Gold. George Moor. 1980. 12.95 (ISBN 0-7145-3615-6). Riverrun NY.

Fox Hunting. Duke Of Beaufort. LC 79-56043. (Illus.). 236p. 1980. 29.95x (ISBN 0-7153-7896-1). David & Charles.

Fox Hunting, Five Minute Lectures. (British Horse Society Ser.). 1981. pap. 2.25 (ISBN 0-8120-2097-9). Barron.

Fox in Shangri-La. Catherine J. Frompovich. (ps-2). 1978. tchr's. ed. 0.75x (ISBN 0-935322-01-9). C J Frompovich.

Fox-North Coalition. J. Cannon. LC 70-85715. 1970. 35.50 (ISBN 0-521-07606-4). Cambridge U Pr.

Fox Talbot, Photographer. Robert Lassam. (Illus.). 94p. 1981. 22.50 (ISBN 0-900193-77-8, Pub. by Compton Pr England); pap. 9.95 (ISBN 0-686-69417-1). Kent St U Pr.

Fox Trap. Robert A. Smith. 1978. pap. 1.75 o.p. (ISBN 0-449-14073-3, GM). Fawcett.

Fox Went Out on a Chilly Night. Peter Spier. LC 60-7139. (Illus.). (gr. 1-3). pap. 1.49 (ISBN 0-385-01065-6, Zephyr). Doubleday.

Foxbat. Peter Cave. (Orig.). 1979. pap. 1.95 o.s.i. (ISBN 0-515-04878-X). Jove Pubns.

Foxes. Dewey Gram. (Orig.). 1979. pap. 2.25 (ISBN 0-446-92156-4). Warner Bks.

Foxes & Physic. Geoffrey Sparrow. (Illus.). 3.75 o.p. (ISBN 0-85131-067-2, Dist. by Sporting Book Center). J A Allen.

Foxe's Book of English Martyrs. Hilda N. Schroetter. 360p. 1981. 10.95 (ISBN 0-8499-0152-9). Word Bks.

Foxe's Book of Martyrs. Foxe. Repr. 7.95 (ISBN 0-686-12388-3). Church History.

Foxe's Book of Martyrs. John Foxe. 400p. 1981. pap. 2.95 (ISBN 0-686-69320-5). Whitaker Hse.

Foxes of Kincarra. Ann R. Ritcher. 128p. 1981. 7.95 (ISBN 0-89962-209-7). Todd & Honeywell.

Foxfire Book: Hog Dressing, Log Cabin Building, Mt. Crafts, Foods Planting by the Signs, Snake Lore, Hunting Tales, Faith Healing, Moonshining & Other Affairs of Plain Living. Ed. by Eliot Wigginton. 320p. 1972. 10.95 (ISBN 0-385-07350-X, Anch); pap. 5.95 (ISBN 0-385-07353-4, Anch). Doubleday.

Foxfire Books, Bks. 1-3. Eliot Wigginton. (Illus.). 1312p. 1975. Set. pap. 20.85 (ISBN 0-385-11253-X, Anch). Doubleday.

Foxfire Five. Ed. by Eliot Wigginton. LC 78-55859. 1979. 12.95 (ISBN 0-385-14307-9, Anchor Pr); pap. 7.95 (ISBN 0-385-14308-7). Doubleday.

Foxfire Four. Ed. by Eliot Wigginton. LC 76-50803. 1977. 12.95 (ISBN 0-385-12086-9, Anchor Pr); pap. 7.95 (ISBN 0-385-12087-7, Anch). Doubleday.

Foxfire Six: Shoemaking, Gourd Banjos & Song-Bows, 100 Toys & Games, Wooden Locks, a Water-Powered Sawmill & Other Affairs of Just Plain Living. Eliot Wigginton. LC 79-6541. (Illus.). 512p. 1980. 14.95 (ISBN 0-385-15271-X, Anchor Pr); pap. 7.95 (ISBN 0-385-15272-8). Doubleday.

Foxfire Three. Ed. by Eliot Wigginton. LC 73-9183. 512p. 1975. 10.00 (ISBN 0-385-02265-4, Anchor Pr); pap. 7.95 (ISBN 0-385-02272-7, Anch). Doubleday.

Foxfire Two. Ed. by Eliot Wigginton. LC 70-163087. 12.95 (ISBN 0-385-02254-9, Anchor Pr); pap. 7.95 (ISBN 0-385-02267-0, Anch). Doubleday.

Foxglove Manor, Eighteen Eighty-Four. Robert Buchanan. Ed. by Robert Lee Wolff. LC 75-483. (Victorian Fiction Ser.). 1975. lib. bdg. 66.00 (ISBN 0-8240-1560-6). Garland Pub.

Foxman. Gary Paulsen. LC 76-57974. (gr. 6 up). 1977. 7.95 o.p. (ISBN 0-525-66543-9). Elsevier-Nelson.

Fox's Earth. Anne R. Siddons. 1981. 14.95 (ISBN 0-671-24962-2). S&S.

Foxx! Zack Tyler. (Orig.). 1981. pap. 1.95 (ISBN 0-440-12742-4). Dell.

Foxx Hunting. Zack Tyler. (Orig.). 1981. pap. 2.25 (ISBN 0-440-12451-4). Dell.

Foxx's Gold. Zack Tyler. (Orig.). 1981. pap. 1.95 (ISBN 0-440-13552-4). Dell.

Foxx's Herd. Zack Tyler. (Orig.). Date not set. pap. 1.95 (ISBN 0-440-12730-0). Dell.

Foxy Ferdinand: Tsar of Bulgaria. Stephen Constant. 352p. 1980. 17.50 (ISBN 0-531-09930-X). Watts.

Fozzie's Big Book of Sidesplitting Jokes (Please Laugh) Illus. by Tim Kirk. LC 80-23776. (Muppet Show Bks.). (Illus.). 32p. (gr. 1-5). 1981. pap. 1.95 (ISBN 0-394-84675-3). Random.

Frac's Guide to Quality School Lunch & Breakfast Programs. rev. ed. Lynn Parker et al. Ed. by Cecilia Perry. Orig. Title: Frac's Guide to the School Lunch & Breakfast Programs. 52p. 1980. pap. text ed. 1.00 (ISBN 0-934220-04-2). Food Res Action.

Fractals: Form, Chance, & Dimension. Benoit B. Mandelbrot. LC 76-57947. (Mathematics Ser.). (Illus.). 1977. text ed. 22.95x (ISBN 0-7167-0473-0). W H Freeman.

Fractional Horse-Power Electric Motors: A Guide to Types & Applications. E. K. Bottle. 209p. 1948. 10.95x (ISBN 0-85264-051-X, Pub. by Griffin England). State Mutual Bk.

Fractions. P. Driscoll et al. Ed. by K. West & D. Johnston. (Math Skills for Daily Living Ser.). (Illus.). 40p. (gr. 7-12). 1979. pap. text ed. 3.95x (ISBN 0-87453-092-X, 82092). Denoyer.

Fractions. Barbara Gregorich & Clark Odom. LC 79-730045. (Illus.). 1978. 99.00 (ISBN 0-89290-094-6, A510-SATC). Soc for Visual.

Fractions & Food: Fractions, Decimals & Electronic Communications. Learning Achievement Corporation. Ed. by Therese A. Zak. (MATCH Ser.). (Illus.). 144p. Date not set. text ed. 5.28 (ISBN 0-07-037113-X, G). McGraw.

Fractions Are Parts of Things. J. Richard Dennis. LC 73-127603. (Illus.). 40p. (gr. 2-5). 1971. 7.95 (ISBN 0-690-31520-1, TYC-J); PLB 7.89 (ISBN 0-690-31521-X); pap. 1.45 (ISBN 0-690-31522-8, TYC-J). T Y Crowell.

Fractions, Book 1: Reusable Edition. Frances F. Loose. (gr. 4). 1973. wkbk. 6.00 (ISBN 0-89039-064-9). Ann Arbor Pubs.

Fractions, Book 2: Reusable Edition. Frances F. Loose. (gr. 4-6). 1973. wkbk. 6.50 (ISBN 0-89039-066-5). Ann Arbor Pubs.

Fracture & Fatigue Control in Structures: Applications of Fracture Mechanics. Stan Rolfe & John Barson. (Illus.). 1977. text ed. 34.95 (ISBN 0-13-329953-8). P-H.

Fracture in Concrete. Ed. by W. F. Chen & E. C. Ting. LC 80-69656. 110p. 1980. pap. text ed. 12.00 (ISBN 0-87262-259-2). Am Soc Civil Eng.

Fracture Mechanics, Current Status, Future Prospects: Proceedings of a Conference Held at Cambridge University, March 16, 1979. Ed. by R. A. Smith. (Illus.). 128p. 1979. 55.00 (ISBN 0-08-024766-0). Pergamon.

Fracture Mechanics in Engineering Practice. P. Stanley. (Illus.). 1977. 86.90x (ISBN 0-85334-723-9, Pub. by Applied Science). Burgess-Intl Ideas.

Fracture of Brittle Solids. B. R. Lawn & T. R. Wilshaw. LC 74-12970. (Solid State Science Ser). (Illus.). 160p. 1975. 47.00 (ISBN 0-521-20654-5); pap. 17.50x (ISBN 0-521-09952-8). Cambridge U Pr.

Fracture of Composite Materials. G. C. Sih & V. P. Tamus. 429p. 1979. 35.00x (ISBN 90-286-0289-5). Sijthoff & Noordhoff.

Fracture of Engineering Brittle Materials. Ayal De S. Jayatilaka. (Illus.). 1979. 64.60x (ISBN 0-85334-825-1, Pub. by Applied Science). Burgess-Intl Ideas.

Fracture to the Acetabulum. E. Letournel & R. Judet. (Illus.). 420p. 1981. 162.00 (ISBN 0-387-09875-5). Springer-Verlag.

Fracture Treatment & Healing. Ed. by R. Bruce Heppenstall. LC 77-79395. (Illus.). 1087p. 1980. text ed. 75.00 (ISBN 0-7216-4638-7). Saunders.

Fractured Continent: Latin America in Close-Up. Willard L. Beaulac. LC 78-70885. (Publication Ser.: No. 225). (Illus.). 252p. 1980. 11.95 (ISBN 0-8179-7251-X). Hoover Inst Pr.

Fractures, Dislocations & Sprains. Alan E. Nourse. LC 78-6855. (First Bks). (Illus.). (gr. 4 up). 1978. PLB 6.45 s&l (ISBN 0-531-01494-0). Watts.

Fractures of the Hip, Vol. 92. Association of Bone & Joint Surgeons. Ed. by Marshall Urist. (Clinical Orthopaedics & Related Research Ser.). 1973. 15.00 (ISBN 0-685-34613-7). Lippincott.

Fraeulein Von Scuderi. E. T. Hoffmann. (Insel Taschenbuecher: It 410). (Illus.). 126p. (Ger.). 1980. pap. text ed. 3.25 (ISBN 3-458-32110-1, Pub. by Insel Verlag Germany). Suhrkamp.

Fragile Bond. Ruth Winter. 208p. 1976. 7.95 o.s.i. (ISBN 0-02-630510-0). Macmillan.

Fragile Ecosystems: Evaluation of Research & Applications in the Neotropics. Ed. by E. G. Farnworth & F. B. Golley. LC 74-8290. (Illus.). 280p. 1974. pap. 12.40 (ISBN 0-387-06695-0). Springer-Verlag.

Fragile Empires: Correspondence of Samuel Swartwout & James Morgan 1836-1856. R. R. Brunson & Feris A. Bass, Jr. 1978. 7.50 (ISBN 0-88319-032-X). Shoal Creek Pub.

Fragile Miracle of Martin Gray. David D. Duncan. LC 79-88367. (Illus.). 96p. 7.95 (ISBN 0-89659-073-9). Abbeville Pr.

Fragile Moments. Compiled by Phyllis Hobe. 1980. 14.95 (ISBN 0-8007-1176-9). Revell.

Fragment: The Autobiography of Mary Jane Mount Tanner. Ed. by Margery W. Ward. (Utah, the Mormons, & the West: No. 9). 1980. 15.00 (ISBN 0-87480-183-4, Tanner). U of Utah Pr.

Fragmenta Phytographicae Australiae, Vols.1-11 & Suppl. Ferdinand Von Mueller. 1974. 240.00 (ISBN 90-6123-311-9). Lubrecht & Cramer.

Fragmentary Class Structure. K. Roberts et al. 1977. pap. text ed. 17.95 (ISBN 0-435-82765-0); pap. text ed. 11.50 (ISBN 0-435-82766-9). Heinemann Ed.

Fragments: A Selection from the Notebooks of Paolo Soleri. LC 79-3587. (Illus.). 224p. 1981. 12.95 (ISBN 0-06-250810-5, HarpR). Har-Row.

Fragments from Greek & Roman Architecture: The Classical America Edition of Hector D'Espouy's Plates. Hector D'Espouy. (Illus.). 1981. 19.95 (ISBN 0-393-01427-4); pap. 9.95 (ISBN 0-393-00052-4). Norton.

Fragments of an Analysis with Freud. Joseph Wortis. LC 54-9792. 224p. 1975. 6.95 o.p. (ISBN 0-07-071903-9, SP); pap. 3.50 o.p. (ISBN 0-07-071904-7). McGraw.

Fragments of Empedocles. Empedocles. Tr. & intro. by William E. Leonard. LC 73-85282. 92p. 1973. 9.95 (ISBN 0-87548-300-3); pap. 3.95 (ISBN 0-87548-301-1). Open Court.

Fragonard. (Selected Artists Art Ser). (Illus.). 1977. pap. 5.95 (ISBN 0-8120-0871-5). Barron.

Fragonard. David Wakefield. (Illus.). 1977. 15.95 (ISBN 0-8467-0246-0, Pub. by Two Continents); pap. 9.95 (ISBN 0-8467-0245-2). Hippocrene Bks.

Fragrance of Beauty. Joyce Landorf. LC 74-76813. 1973. pap. 2.95 (ISBN 0-88207-231-5). Victor Bks.

Frail Vessels: Woman's Role in Women's Novels from Fanny Burney to George Eliot. Hazel Mews. 1969. text ed. 18.75x (ISBN 0-485-11105-5, Athlone Pr). Humanities.

Frame Conceptions & Text Understanding. Ed. by Dieter Metzing. (Research in Text Theory: No. 5). 167p. 1980. text ed. 42.50x (ISBN 3-11-008006-0). De Gruyter.

Frame Structure in Tudor & Stuart Drama. Steven C. Young. (Salzburg Studies in English Literature, Elizabethan & Renaissance Studies: No. 6). 189p. (Orig.). 1976. pap. text ed. 25.00x (ISBN 0-391-01577-X). Humanities.

Frames of Mind: Constraints of the Common-Sense Conception of the Mental. Adam Morton. (Illus.). 180p. 1980. text ed. 22.00x (ISBN 0-19-824607-2). Oxford U Pr.

Framework for Accountancy. 2nd ed. C. C. Magee. 336p. 1979. pap. text ed. 14.95x (ISBN 0-7121-0631-6, Pub. by Macdonald & Evans England). Intl Ideas.

Framework for Development: The EEC & the ACP. Carol C. Twitchett. 160p. 1981. text ed. 28.50x (ISBN 0-04-338094-8, 2592). Allen Unwin.

Framework for Financial Analysis. John K. Ford. 176p. 1981. pap. text ed. 9.95 (ISBN 0-13-330241-5). P-H.

Framework for the Curriculum. Penelope B. Weston. (Monographs in Curriculum Studies: No. 2). 1977. pap. text ed. 18.00x (ISBN 0-85633-137-6, NFER). Humanities.

Framework of Anglo-Saxon History to A. D. 900. K. Harrison. LC 75-13450. 176p. 1976. 31.95 (ISBN 0-521-20935-8). Cambridge U Pr.

Framework of Regional Economics in the United Kingdom. A. J. Brown. LC 72-83665. (Publications of the National Institute of Economic & Social Studies: No. 27). (Illus.). 384p. 1972. 42.50 (ISBN 0-521-08743-0). Cambridge U Pr.

Framing Guide & Steel Square Book. rev. ed. D. L. Sigmon. 312p. 1958. 9.00 (ISBN 0-914760-01-7). Cline-Sigmon.

Framing of the Constitution of the United States. Max Farrand. 1913. 20.00 (ISBN 0-300-00445-1); pap. 6.45x 1962 (ISBN 0-300-00079-0, Y53). Yale U Pr.

Framing Pictures. J. T. Burns. LC 77-83674. (Illus.). 1978. 10.95 o.p. (ISBN 0-684-15509-5, ScribT); pap. 6.95 o.p. (ISBN 0-684-15508-7, ScribT). Scribner.

Framing, Sheathing & Insulation. R. Jones. LC 73-1847. 235p. 1973. pap. 7.00 (ISBN 0-8273-0096-4); answer book 1.60 (ISBN 0-8273-0097-2). Delmar.

Framing: Step-by-Step. Eamon Toscano. (Step-by-Step Craft Ser). 1971. PLB 9.15 o.p. (ISBN 0-307-62007-7, Golden Pr); pap. 2.95 (ISBN 0-307-42007-8, Golden Pr). Western Pub.

Framingham Study: The Epidemiology of Atherosclerotic Disease. Thomas R. Dawber. LC 80-11189. (Commonwealth Fund Ser.). 1980. text ed. 17.50x (ISBN 0-674-31730-0). Harvard U Pr.

Frampton! Susan Katz. 1978. pap. 1.75 o.s.i. (ISBN 0-515-04603-5). Jove Pubns.

Fran. Fran Lance & Pat King. 132p. 1980. pap. 4.95 (ISBN 0-930756-51-7, 4230-LK1). Women's Aglow.

Fran Tarkenton. Jay H. Smith. LC 74-9863. (Creative Education Sports Superstars Ser.). (Illus.). 32p. (gr. 3-6). 1974. PLB 5.95 o. p. (ISBN 0-87191-376-3); pap. 2.75 (ISBN 0-89812-167-1). Creative Ed.

Fran Tarkenton: Master of the Gridiron. Dorothy C. Schmitz. LC 77-70890. (Pros Ser.). (Illus.). (gr. 2). 1977. PLB 6.45 (ISBN 0-913940-63-1). Crestwood Hse.

Fran Tarkenton: Scrambling Quarterback. Julian May. LC 73-80423. (Sports Close-up Ser.). (gr. 3-9). 1973. PLB 5.95 o.p. (ISBN 0-913940-03-8); pap. 2.95 o.p. (ISBN 0-913940-96-8). Crestwood Hse.

Franc-Parler. 2nd ed. Simone R. Dietiker. 1980. text ed. 16.95x (ISBN 0-669-02491-0); instrs.' guide avail. (ISBN 0-669-02494-5); wkbk. 5.95 (ISBN 0-669-02492-9); tapes-reels 45.00 (ISBN 0-669-02496-1); cassettes 45.00 (ISBN 0-669-02497-X); demo tape (ISBN 0-669-02498-8); tapescript (ISBN 0-669-02495-3). Heath.

Francais. L. Wylie & A. Begue. 1970. 14.95 o.p. (ISBN 0-13-530634-5). P-H.

Francais: Commencons. Josee Okin & Conrad J. Schmitt. 1970. text ed. 11.60 (ISBN 0-07-047500-8, W); tchr's. ed. 10.96 (ISBN 0-07-047501-6); wkbk. 3.60 (ISBN 0-07-047502-4); tapes 360.00 (ISBN 0-07-047503-2); tests 72.00 (ISBN 0-686-66095-1); Webster master replacements 36.00 (ISBN 0-07-047506-7); filmstrips 80.00 (ISBN 0-07-047504-0). McGraw.

Francais commercial, 3 vols. G. Mauger et al. Vol. 1. pap. text ed. 7.50 (ISBN 2-03-040404-7, 3760); Vol. 2. pap. text ed. 8.50 (ISBN 2-03-040405-5, 3761); Vol. 3. pap. text ed. 7.50 (ISBN 0-685-13927-1, 3762). Larousse.

Francais: Depart-Arrivee. John A. Rassias & Jacqueline De Lachapelle-Skubly. 577p. 1980. text ed. 18.95 scp (ISBN 0-06-045316-8, HarpC); instrs'. manual avail.; scp student wkbk. 6.50 (ISBN 0-06-045317-6); scp tapes 295.00 (ISBN 0-06-047493-9). Har-Row.

Francais ecrit, francais parle. A. Sauvageot. (Langue vivante). (Fr). pap. 8.25 (ISBN 0-685-13928-X, 3623). Larousse.

Francais vivant. 2nd ed. Terence L. Hansen et al. Ed. by Julian Kaplow. LC 77-27029. 1978. text ed. 17.95 (ISBN 0-471-01782-5); wkbk. 5.95 (ISBN 0-471-03539-4); tapes 1.00 (ISBN 0-471-04346-X). Wiley.

France. Joseph Barry. (Illus.). (gr. 7 up). 1965. 4.95 o.s.i. (ISBN 0-02-708460-4). Macmillan.

France. J. Beaujeu-Garnier. LC 75-28288. (World's Landscapes). (Illus.). 160p. 1976. pap. text ed. 9.50x (ISBN 0-582-48178-3). Longman.

France. Frances Chambers. (World Bibliographical Ser.: No. 13). 175p. 1980. 31.50 (ISBN 0-903450-25-9). ABC Clio.

France. rev. ed. Virginia Creed. LC 77-83911. (World Culture Ser). (Illus.). 168p. (gr. 6 up). 1978. text ed. 9.95 ea. 1-4 copies (ISBN 0-88296-188-8); text ed. 7.96 ea. 5 or more copies; tchrs'. guide 8.94 (ISBN 0-88296-369-4). Fideler.

France. Douglas Johnson. LC 75-78381. (Nations & Peoples Library). 1969. 8.50x o.s.i. (ISBN 0-8027-2105-2). Walker & Co.

France. Danielle Lifschitz. LC 75-44867. (Macdonald Countries). (Illus.). (gr. 7 up). 1976. PLB 7.95 (ISBN 0-382-06099-7, Pub. by Macdonald Ed). Silver.

France. Ronald Lloyd. (Illus.). (gr. 5-9). 1975. PLB 3.90 o.p. (ISBN 0-531-02777-5). Watts.

France - Message of Peace, Trust, Love & Faith. 1980. 5.00 (ISBN 0-8198-2601-4); pap. 3.50. Dghtrs St Paul.

France: A Modern History. rev. & enl. ed. Albert Guerard. LC 69-19782. (Illus.). 632p. 1969. 12.50x (ISBN 0-472-08390-2). U of Mich Pr.

France: A Study in Nationality. A. Siegfried. 122p. 1980. Repr. of 1930 ed. lib. bdg. 20.00 (ISBN 0-89760-826-7). Telegraph Bks.

France Actuelle. rev. ed. Camille Bauer. (Illus.). 1971. text ed. 10.50 (ISBN 0-395-04150-3, 3-03207). HM.

France & Belgium, Nineteen Thirty-Nine to Nineteen Forty. Brian Bond. Ed. by Noble Frankland & Christopher Dowling. LC 79-52237. (Politics & Strategy of the Second World War Ser.). 1979. 13.50 (ISBN 0-87413-157-X). U Delaware Pr.

France & Europe in Eighteen Forty-Eight: A Study of French Foreign Affairs in Time of Crisis. Lawrence C. Jennings. 1973. 28.50x (ISBN 0-19-822514-8). Oxford U Pr.

France & Munich. Alexander Werth. LC 68-9632. 1969. Repr. of 1939 ed. 14.25 (ISBN 0-86527-071-6). Fertig.

France & Soviet Union. rev. ed. Virginia Creed & W. A. Douglas Jackson. LC 77-83892. (World Cultures Ser.). (Illus.). 298p. (gr. 6 up). 1978. text ed. 12.43 ea. 1-4 copies (ISBN 0-88296-154-3); text ed. 9.94 ea. 5 or more copies; tchrs'. guide 8.94 (ISBN 0-88296-369-4). Fideler.

France & the Estates General of 1614. J. M. Hayden. LC 73-82456. (Studies in Early Modern History). (Illus.). 320p. 1974. 42.95 (ISBN 0-521-20325-2). Cambridge U Pr.

France & the Jacobite Rising of Seventeen Forty-Five. Francis McLynn. 256p. 1981. 26.50x (ISBN 0-85224-404-5, Pub. by Edinburgh U Pr Scotland). Columbia U Pr.

France & the United States: Their Diplomatic Relations, 1789-1914. Henry Blumenthal. 1972. pap. 2.95 o.p. (ISBN 0-393-00625-5, Norton Lib). Norton.

France, Eighteen Forty-Eight to Nineteen Forty-Five: Ambition & Love. Theodore Zeldin. 1979. pap. 8.95 (ISBN 0-19-285090-3, GB 587, GB). Oxford U Pr.

France Eighteen Forty-Eight to Nineteen Forty-Five: Politics & Anger. Theodore Zeldin. (Illus.). 1979. pap. 8.95 (ISBN 0-19-285082-2, GB578, GB). Oxford U Pr.

France Eighteen Forty-Eight to Nineteen Forty-Five: Taste & Corruption. Theodore Zeldin. 448p. 1980. pap. 8.95 (ISBN 0-19-285100-4, GB 620). Oxford U Pr.

France: Empire & Republic, 1850-1940. Ed. by David Thompson. LC 68-27380. (Documentary History of Western Civilization Ser). 1968. 15.00x o.s.i. (ISBN 0-8027-2009-9). Walker & Co.

France in Modern Times. 3rd ed. Gordon Wright. 1981. 24.95 (ISBN 0-393-01455-X). Norton.

France in Modern Times. 3rd ed. Gordon Wright. 500p. 1981. 24.95 (ISBN 0-393-95153-7); 12.95 (ISBN 0-393-95153-7). Norton.

France in Pictures. Sterling Publishing Company Editors. LC 65-24384. (Visual Geography Ser). (Illus., Orig.). (gr. 5 up). 1965. PLB 4.99 (ISBN 0-8069-1057-7); pap. 2.95 (ISBN 0-8069-1056-9). Sterling.

France in the Age Louis Thirteenth & Richelieu. Victor L. Tapie. LC 74-8919. (Illus.). 664p. 17.50 o.p. (ISBN 0-275-52530-9). Praeger.

France Motorway Atlas. 4th ed. Michelin Guides & Maps Division. pap. 3.95 (ISBN 0-686-10140-5). Michelin.

France: Ses Grandes Heures Litteraires. Andre Maman et al. (Level 4 or 5). (gr. 9-12). 1968. text ed. 15.95 (ISBN 0-07-039851-8, C); inst. manual 4.95 (ISBN 0-07-039852-6); exercises 5.95 (ISBN 0-07-039853-4); tapes 150.00 (ISBN 0-07-097885-9). McGraw.

France Since Nineteen Eighteen. Herbert Tint. 1970. 24.00 (ISBN 0-7134-1505-3, Pub. by Batsford England). David & Charles.

France Under De Gaulle. Ed. by Irwin Isenberg. (Reference Shelf Ser: Vol. 39, No. 1). 1967. 6.25 (ISBN 0-8242-0094-2). Wilson.

France Under the Directory. M. Lyons. (Illus.). 256p. 1975. 35.50 (ISBN 0-521-20785-1); pap. 10.50x (ISBN 0-521-09950-1). Cambridge U Pr.

France 1848-1945: Ambition, Love & Politics, Vol. 1. Theodore Zeldin. (Oxford History of Modern Europe Ser). (Illus.). 828p. 1973. 45.00x (ISBN 0-19-822104-5). Oxford U Pr.

France, 1848-1945: Intellect, Taste, & Anxiety, Vol. 2. Theodore Zeldin. (Oxford History of Modern Europe Ser.). 1977. text ed. 49.50x (ISBN 0-19-822125-8). Oxford U Pr.

France, 1870-1914: Politics & Society. R. D. Anderson. 1977. 22.50x (ISBN 0-7100-8575-3). Routledge & Kegan.

Frances Benjamin Johnston: Women of Class & Station. Constance W. Glenn & Leland Rice. (Illus.). 96p. (Orig.). 1979. pap. 8.00 (ISBN 0-936270-12-8). Art Mus Gall.

Frances Perkins: That Woman in FDR's Cabinet. Lillian H. Mohr. 14.95 (ISBN 0-88427-019-X). Green Hill.

France's Vietnam Policy: A Study in French-American Relations. Marianna P. Sullivan. LC 77-94749. (Contributions in Political Science: No. 12). 1978. lib. bdg. 17.50 (ISBN 0-313-20317-2, SUV/). Greenwood.

Frances Wright & the "Great Experiment". Margaret Lane. (Illus.). 50p. 1972. bds. 5.00x (ISBN 0-87471-090-1). Rowman.

Francesca. Margaret Abbey. 1976. pap. 1.25 o.p. (ISBN 0-345-25423-6). Ballantine.

Francesco Corbetta & the Baroque Guitar: With a Transcription of His Works, 2 vols. Richard T. Pinnell. Ed. by George Buelow. (Studies in Musicology). 714p. 1980. Set. 49.95 (ISBN 0-8357-1140-4, Pub. by UMI Res Pr); Vol. 1. (ISBN 0-8357-1141-2); Vol. 2. (ISBN 0-8357-1142-0). Univ Microfilms.

Francesco Guicciardini. Peter E. Bondanella. LC 75-41388. (World Authors Ser.,: Italy: No.389). 1976. lib. bdg. 10.95 (ISBN 0-8057-6231-0). Twayne.

Francesco Vettori: Florentine Citizen & Medici Servant. Rosemary D. Jones. (University of London Historical Studies: No. 34). 366p. 1972. text ed. 39.00x (ISBN 0-485-13134-X, Athlone Pr). Humanities.

Franchise Affair. Josephine Tey. LC 79-19129. 1981. Repr. of 1948 ed. lib. bdg. 10.00x (ISBN 0-8376-0446-X). Bentley.

Franchise Handbook. rev. ed. Ed. by Michael L. Green. Date not set. 12.00 (ISBN 0-89552-027-3); pap. text ed. 7.95 (ISBN 0-89552-026-5). DMR Pubns.

Franchise Riches Success Kit. 2nd ed. Tyler G. Hicks. 876p. 1981. pap. 99.50 (ISBN 0-914306-40-5). Intl Wealth.

Franchised & Independent Business: How to Evaluate, Start & Run It. Robert M. Dias. cancelled (ISBN 0-932812-05-8). Bradley CPA.

Franchising. Alfred J. Modica. (Illus.). 192p. 1981. pap. 7.95 (ISBN 0-8256-3203-X, Quick Fox). Music Sales.

Franchising. 2nd & rev. ed. Charles L. Vaughn. LC 78-24841. (Illus.). 304p. 1979. 22.95 (ISBN 0-669-02852-5). Lexington Bks.

Franciabigio. Susan R. McKillop. (California Studies in the History of Art). (Illus.). 1974. 60.00x (ISBN 0-520-01688-2). U of Cal Pr.

Francis Bacon. John Russell. (World of Art Ser.). (Illus.). 1979. 17.95 (ISBN 0-19-520113-2); pap. 9.95 (ISBN 0-19-520114-0). Oxford U Pr.

Francis Bacon - Essays. Francis Bacon. (Rowman & Littlefield University Library). 200p. 1972. 10.95x (ISBN 0-87471-666-7); pap. 4.50x (ISBN 0-87471-667-5). Rowman.

Francis Bacon: A Political Biography. Joel J. Epstein. LC 76-25617. 1977. 13.50x (ISBN 0-8214-0232-3). Ohio U Pr.

Francis Bacon: A Selection of His Works. Francis Bacon. Ed. by Sidney Warhaft. LC 65-20259. (College Classics in English Ser). 1965. pap. 8.55 (ISBN 0-672-63011-7). Odyssey Pr.

Francis Bacon & Renaissance Prose. Brian Vickers. LC 68-22664. (Illus.). 1968. 56.00 (ISBN 0-521-06709-X, X). Cambridge U Pr.

Francis Bacon & Socialized Science. Antoinette M. Paterson. (American Lectures in Philosophy). 208p. 1973. 16.75 (ISBN 0-398-02867-2). C C Thomas.

Francis Bacon: Discovery & the Art of Discourse. Lisa Jardine. (Illus.). 304p. 1975. 32.95 (ISBN 0-521-20494-1). Cambridge U Pr.

Francis Barlow: First Master of English Book Illustration. Edward Hodnett. 1978. 42.50x (ISBN 0-520-03409-0). U of Cal Pr.

Francis Book: A Celebration of the Universal Saint. Compiled By Roy Gasnick. (Illus.). 320p. 1980. 19.95 (ISBN 0-02-542760-1, Collier); pap. 12.95 (ISBN 0-02-003200-5). Macmillan.

Francis Carey Slater. John R. Doyle, Jr. (World Authors Ser.: South Africa: No. 173). lib. bdg. 10.95 (ISBN 0-8057-2834-1). Twayne.

Francis Danby: Varieties of Poetic Landscape. Eric Adams. LC 72-75185. (Studies in British Art). (Illus.). 352p. 1973. 60.00x (ISBN 0-300-01538-0). Yale U Pr.

Francis Ford Coppola. Robert K. Johnson. (Theatrical Arts Ser.). 1977. lib. bdg. 10.95 (ISBN 0-8057-9252-X). Twayne.

Francis Galton's Art of Travel. Francis Galton. LC 79-53734. (Illus.). 1979. 19.95 (ISBN 0-7153-5139-7). David & Charles.

Francis Hopkinson, the First American Poet-Composer, & James Lyon, Patriot, Preacher, Psalmodist. 2nd ed. Oscar G. Sonneck. LC 65-23393. (Music Ser). 1967. Repr. of 1905 ed. lib. bdg. 19.50 (ISBN 0-306-70918-X). Da Capo.

Francis Kafka. Ronald D. Gray. LC 72-83576. 192p. 1973. 36.00 (ISBN 0-521-20007-5); pap. 10.50x (ISBN 0-521-09747-9). Cambridge U Pr.

Francis Marion. Matthew G. Grant. LC 73-10061. 1974. PLB 5.95 (ISBN 0-87191-257-0). Creative Ed.

Francis of Assisi. Arnaldo Fortini. Tr. by Helen Moak. 900p. 1980. 29.50 (ISBN 0-8245-0116-0). Crossroad NY.

Francis Parkman. Robert L. Gale. (U. S. Authors Ser.: No. 220). 1973. lib. bdg. 10.95 (ISBN 0-8057-0582-1). Twayne.

Francis Ponge. Ian Higgins. (Athlone French Poets Ser.). 1979. text ed. 23.50x (ISBN 0-485-14612-6, Athlone Pr); pap. text ed. 10.00x (ISBN 0-485-12212-X, Anthlone Pr). Humanities.

Francis Ponge: The Power of Language. Tr. by Serge Gavronsky. 1979. 16.95x (ISBN 0-520-03441-4). U of Cal Pr.

Francis Preston Blair Family in Politics. William E. Smith. LC 70-87725. (American Scene Ser). Repr. of 1933 ed. lib. bdg. 75.00 (ISBN 0-306-71665-8). Da Capo.

Francis Thompson: A Critical Biography. Paul Van K. Thomson. LC 73-165666. 280p. 1973. Repr. of 1961 ed. text ed. 9.00 (ISBN 0-87752-155-7). Gordian.

Francis Warrington Dawson & the Politics of Restoration: South Carolina, Eighteen Seventy-Four to Eighteen Eighty-Nine. E. Culpepper Clark. LC 79-27884. (Illus.). 256p. 1980. 18.95x (ISBN 0-8173-0039-2). U of Ala Pr.

Francis William Edmonds. Maybelle Mann. LC 75-24834. (Illus.). 128p. 1975. pap. 6.00 (ISBN 0-88397-050-3). Intl Exhibit Foun.

Francis William Edmonds: Mammon & Art. Maybelle Mann. LC 76-23638. (Outstanding Dissertations in the Fine Arts - American). (Illus.). 1977. Repr. of 1972 ed. lib. bdg. 41.00 (ISBN 0-8240-2708-6). Garland Pub.

Francisco. Robert Maiorano. LC 78-4574. (Illus.). (gr. k-3). 1978. 8.95 (ISBN 0-02-762170-7, 76217). Macmillan.

Francisco Ayala. Estelle Irizarry. (World Authors Ser.: No. 450). 1977. lib. bdg. 11.95 (ISBN 0-8057-6287-6). Twayne.

Francisco Coronado. Malcolm C. Jensen. LC 73-12087. (Visual Biography Ser). (Illus.). 64p. (gr. 4-5). 1974. PLB 4.90 o.p. (ISBN 0-531-00973-4). Watts.

Francisco de Quevedo & the Neostoic Movement. Henry Ettinghausen. (Oxford Modern Languages & Literature Monographs). 190p. 1972. 29.95x (ISBN 0-19-815521-2). Oxford U Pr.

Francisco De Quevedo: La Vida del Buscon Llamado Don Pablos. Francisco De Quevedo & Barry Ife. 1977. 27.00 (ISBN 0-08-021855-5). Pergamon.

Francisco Franco: The Jewish Connection. Harry S. May. 1978. pap. text ed. 9.00x (ISBN 0-8191-0363-2). U Pr of Amer.

Francisco Javier Alagre: A Study in Mexican Literary Criticism. Allan Deck. 1976. pap. 9.00 (ISBN 0-8294-0337-X). Jesuit Hist.

Francisco Javier Clavigero, S. J., Figure of the Mexican Enlightment: His Life & Work. Charles E. Ronan. 1977. pap. 20.00x (ISBN 0-8294-0347-7). Jesuit Hist.

Francisco Lopez De Ubeda. Bruno M. Damiani. (World Authors Ser.: Spain: No. 431). 1977. lib. bdg. 12.50 (ISBN 0-8057-6271-X). Twayne.

Francisco Zuniga: Sculptor. Sheldon Reich. LC 80-18986. 1980. 35.00 (ISBN 0-8165-0665-5). U of Ariz Pr.

Francisk Skorina. 74p. 1980. pap. 4.75 (ISBN 92-3-201626-5, U 1007, UNESCO). Unipub.

Franck Taylor Bowers, Eighteen Seventy-Five-Nineteen Thirty-Two. Ed. by Richard I. Barons. LC 77-72387. 1977. pap. 5.00 (ISBN 0-937318-02-7, Pub. by Roberson Ctr.). Pub Ctr Cult Res.

Franco-British Rivalry in the Post-War Near East: The Decline of French Influence. Henry H. Cumming. LC 79-2854. (Illus.). 229p. 1981. Repr. of 1938 ed. 19.75 (ISBN 0-8305-0029-4). Hyperion Conn.

Franco-German Coalition & the Emergence of a New International Superpower: Its Effects Upon the Future Course of History. Vincenzo G. De Graziani. (Illus.). 1979. deluxe ed. 47.75 (ISBN 0-930008-31-6). Inst Econ Pol.

Franco Harris. Thomas Braun. (Creative Superstars Ser.). (Illus.). (gr. 3-9). 1975. PLB 5.95 (ISBN 0-87191-473-5); pap. 2.75 o. p. (ISBN 0-89812-169-8). Creative Ed.

Franco-Prussian War: The German Invasion of France 1870-71. Michael Howard. 1979. Repr. of 1961 ed. text ed. 26.00x (ISBN 0-246-63587-8). Humanities.

Franco Russian Alliance, 1891-1917. Georges Michon. LC 68-9610. 1969. Repr. of 1929 ed. 17.50 (ISBN 0-86527-072-4). Fertig.

Francois Hemsterhuis. Heinz Moenkemeyer. (World Authors Ser.: Netherlands: No. 277). 1975. lib. bdg. 12.50 (ISBN 0-8057-2419-2). Twayne.

Francois Truffaut. Annette Insdorf. (Theatrical Arts Ser.). 1978. lib. bdg. 9.95 (ISBN 0-8057-9253-8). Twayne.

Franconia Stories, 10 vols. in 2. Jacob Abbott. LC 75-32164. (Classics of Children's Literature, 1621-1932: Vol. 28). (Illus.). 1976. Repr. of 1853 ed. Set. PLB 60.00 (ISBN 0-8240-2277-7); PLB 38.00 ea. Garland Pub.

Frangipani Garden. Barbara Hanrahan. (Illus.). 224p. 1981. text ed. 19.25 (ISBN 0-7022-1562-7); pap. 9.75 (ISBN 0-7022-1563-5). U of Queensland Pr.

Franju. movie ed. Raymond Durgnat. LC 68-31139. 1967. 7.95 (ISBN 0-520-00366-7); pap. 1.95 (ISBN 0-520-00367-5, CAL171). U of Cal Pr.

Frank & I. Anonymous. LC 68-56363. 272p. 1980. pap. 3.50 (ISBN 0-394-17751-7, B444, BC). Grove.

Frank Aydelotte of Swarthmore. Frances Blanshard. LC 70-108646. (Illus.). 1970. 22.50x (ISBN 0-8195-4023-4, Pub. by Wesleyan U Pr). Columbia U Pr.

Frank Bear. Spencer Knight. (Orig.). 1979. pap. 1.95 (ISBN 0-532-23112-0). Manor Bks.

Frank Chamberlain Porter: Pioneer in American Biblical Interpretation. Roy A. Harrisville. LC 76-4498. (Society of Biblical Literature. Study in Biblical Scholarship). 1976. pap. 7.50 (ISBN 0-89130-104-6, 061101). Scholars Pr Ca.

Frank City (Goodbye) Joe Cottonwood. 1981. pap. price not set (ISBN 0-440-52906-9, Delta). Dell.

Frank Dalby Davison. Louise E. Rorabacher. (World Authors Ser.: No. 514). 1979. lib. bdg. 12.50 (ISBN 0-8057-6355-4). Twayne.

Frank Herbert. David M. Miller. (Starmont Reader's Guide: No. 5). 80p. 1981. Repr. lib. bdg. 9.95x (ISBN 0-89370-036-3). Borgo Pr.

Frank Herbert: Prophet of Dune. George E. Slusser. LC 78-1310. (Milford Ser: Popular Writers of Today: Vol. 14). Date not set. lib. bdg. 8.95x (ISBN 0-89370-119-X); pap. 2.95 (ISBN 0-89370-219-6). Borgo Pr. Postponed.

Frank J. North: Pawnee Scout, Commander & Pioneer. Ruby E. Wilson. (Illus.). 1981. 15.00 (ISBN 0-8040-0767-5). Swallow. Postponed.

Frank Lloyd Wright. Vincent Scully, Jr. LC 60-6075. (Masters of World Architecture Ser). (Illus.). 128p. 1960. pap. 7.95 (ISBN 0-8076-0221-3). Braziller.

Frank Lloyd Wright. M. Tanigawa. 1978. 185.00 o.p. (ISBN 0-685-05019-X, 0-911156-28-8). Porter.

Frank Lloyd Wright. Charlotte Willard. LC 71-188775. (Illus.). (gr. 7 up). 1972. 8.95 (ISBN 0-02-793070-X). Macmillan.

Frank Lloyd Wright: His Life & His Architecture. Robert C. Twombly. LC 78-9466. 1979. 22.50 (ISBN 0-471-03400-2, Pub. by Wiley-Interscience). Wiley.

Frank O'connor: An Introductory Study. Maurice Wohlgelernter. LC 76-45085. 1977. 15.00x (ISBN 0-231-04194-2). Columbia U Pr.

Frank O'Hara. Alan Feldman. (United States Authors Ser.: No. 347). 1979. 10.95 (ISBN 0-8057-7277-4). Twayne.

Frank O'Hara: Poet Among Painters. Marjorie Perloff. LC 76-16636. 1977. 12.50 o.s.i. (ISBN 0-8076-0835-1). Braziller.

Frank R. Stockton. Henry L. Golemba. (United States Authors Ser.: No. 374). 1981. lib. bdg. 11.95 (ISBN 0-8057-7288-X). Twayne.

Frank Reade Jr.'s New Electric Terror "The Thunderer"; or, the Search for the Tartar's Captive. Ed. by E. F. Bleiler. (Frank Reade Library: Vol. 2). 1980. lib. bdg. 44.00 (ISBN 0-8240-3541-0). Garland Pub.

Frank Robinson: Slugging Toward Glory. Julian May. LC 74-31949. (Sports Close-up Ser.). (gr. 3-9). 1975. PLB 5.95 o.p. (ISBN 0-913940-14-3); pap. 2.95 o.p. (ISBN 0-913940-21-6). Crestwood Hse.

Frank Sinatra. Paula Taylor. (Rock 'n Pop Stars Ser.). (Illus.). (gr. 3-6). 1975. PLB 5.95 (ISBN 0-87191-460-3); pap. 2.95 (ISBN 0-89812-109-4). Creative Ed.

Frank Sinatra: Is This Man Mafia? George Carpozi, Jr. (Orig.). 1979. pap. 2.25 (ISBN 0-532-23282-8). Manor Bks.

Frank Tashlin. Claire Johnston & Paul Willemen. (EIFF Ser.). 1978. pap. 4.00 (ISBN 0-918432-13-8). NY Zoetrope.

Frank Waters. Thomas J. Lyon. (U. S. Authors Ser.: No. 225). 1973. lib. bdg. 10.95 (ISBN 0-8057-0775-1). Twayne.

Franken, Alemannen, Bayern und Burgunder in Oberitalien, 774-962. Eduard Hlawitscka. LC 80-2025. 1981. Repr. of 1960 ed. 38.50 (ISBN 0-404-18569-X). AMS Pr.

Frankenstein. Mary Shelley. 1959. 11.50x (ISBN 0-460-00616-9, Evman); pap. 2.95 (ISBN 0-460-01616-4). Dutton.

Frankenstein. Mary Shelley. Adapted by Alice Schick & Joel Schick. LC 80-385. (Illus.). 48p. (gr. 3 up). 1980. PLB 8.44 (ISBN 0-440-02693-8); pap. 4.95 (ISBN 0-440-02692-X). Delacorte.

Frankenstein Legend: A Tribute to Mary Shelley & Boris Karloff. Donald F. Glut. LC 73-944. (Illus.). 1973. 13.50 (ISBN 0-8108-0589-8). Scarecrow.

Frankenstein Moved in on the Fourth Floor. Elizabeth Levy. LC 78-19830. (Illus.). 64p. (gr. 2-5). 1981. pap. 1.95 (ISBN 0-06-440122-7, Trophy). Har-Row.

Frankenstein: Or, the Modern Prometheus. Mary W. Shelley. Ed. by James H. Rieger. LC 72-80409. (LL Ser.). 333p. 1974. pap. text ed. 5.50 o.p. (ISBN 0-672-61020-5). Bobbs.

Frankfort: A Pictorial History. Stuart Sprague & Elizabeth Perkins. (Illus.). 1980. 16.95 (ISBN 0-89865-003-8); ltd. ed. 24.95 (ISBN 0-89865-001-1). Donning Co.

Frankfurt School Reader, Vol. II: The Post-War Years. Andrew Arato. Date not set. 17.50 (ISBN 0-89396-035-7); pap. 7.95 (ISBN 0-89396-036-5). Urizen Bks.

Frankfurt School: The Critical Theories of Max Horkheimer & Theoder W. Adorno. Zolton Tar. LC 77-2353. 1977. 23.95 (ISBN 0-471-84536-1, Pub. by Wiley-Interscience). Wiley.

Frankincense & Myrrh: A Study of the Arabian Incense Trade. N. S. Groom. (Arab Background Ser.). (Illus.). 328p. 1981. text ed. 37.00 (ISBN 0-582-76476-9). Longman.

Frankish Institutions Under Charlemagne. Francois L. Ganshof. Tr. by Bryce Lyon & Mary Lyon. LC 68-29166. 191p. 1968. 8.50x (ISBN 0-87057-108-7, Pub. by Brown U Pr). Univ Pr of New England.

Franklin, America's "Lost State". Noel B. Gerson. LC 68-19819. (Illus.). (gr. 7-10). 1968. 3.50 o.s.i. (ISBN 0-02-735920-4, CCPr). Macmillan.

Franklin D. Roosevelt. Morton J. Frisch. LC 74-16425. (World Leaders Ser.: No. 43). 1975. lib. bdg. 9.95 (ISBN 0-8057-3708-1). Twayne.

Franklin D. Roosevelt & American Foreign Policy, 1932-1945. Robert Dallek. (Galaxy Book: No. 628). 690p. 1981. pap. 9.95 (ISBN 0-19-502894-5). Oxford U Pr.

Franklin D. Roosevelt & Foreign Affairs: Second Series, Vols. 4-16. Franklin D. Roosevelt. Ed. by Donald B. Schewe. LC 68-25617. 2327p. 1979. 27.00 ea.; Set, Jan. 1937-Aug. 1939. 375.00 (ISBN 0-88354-201-3). Vol. 4, Jan.-Mar. 1973 (ISBN 0-88354-202-1). Vol. 5, Apr.-June 1937 (ISBN 0-88354-203-X). Vol. 6, July-Sept. 1937 (ISBN 0-88354-204-8). Vol. 7, Oct.-Dec. 1937 (ISBN 0-88354-205-6). Vol. 8, Jan.-Feb. 1938 (ISBN 0-88354-206-4). Clearwater Pub.

Franklin D. Roosevelt & the City Bosses. Lyle W. Dorsett. (National University Publications Interdisciplinary Urban Ser.). 1977. 12.50 (ISBN 0-8046-9186-X); pap. 4.95 o.p. (ISBN 0-8046-9203-3). Kennikat.

Franklin D. Roosevelt, Gallant President. Barbara S. Feinberg. LC 80-22307. (Illus.). 96p. (gr. 2-6). 1981. 7.50 (ISBN 0-688-00433-4); PLB 7.20 (ISBN 0-688-00434-2). Morrow.

Franklin Delano Roosevelt: A Career in Progressive Democracy. rev. ed. E. K. Lindley. LC 73-21771. (FDR & the Era of the New Deal Ser.). 366p. 1974. Repr. of 1933 ed. lib. bdg. 32.50 (ISBN 0-306-70634-2). Da Capo.

Franklin Delano Roosevelt, President for the People. Roslyn Hiebert & Ray E. Hiebert. LC 68-15570. (Biography Ser). (Illus.). (gr. 6 up). 1968. PLB 5.90 o.p. (ISBN 0-531-00920-3). Watts.

Franklin Pierce. Roy F. Nichols. LC 58-7750. 1964. 12.50x o.p. (ISBN 0-8122-7044-4). U of Pa Pr.

Franklin Watts Concise Guide to Babysitting. Rubie Saunders. LC 71-188479. (Career Concise Guides Ser.). (Illus.). 72p. (gr. 5 up). 1972. PLB 4.90 o.p. (ISBN 0-531-02563-2). Watts.

Franklin Watts Concise Guide to Good Grooming for Boys. Rubie Saunders. LC 72-1361. (Career Concise Guides Ser.). (Illus.). 72p. (gr. 5 up). 1972. PLB 5.45 o.p. (ISBN 0-531-02256-0). Watts.

Franklin's Prologue & Tale. Geoffrey Chaucer. Ed. by A. C. Spearing. (Selected Tales from Chaucer). text ed. 4.95x (ISBN 0-521-04624-6). Cambridge U Pr.

Franklin's Tale from the Canterbury Tales. Ed. by Gerald Morgan. (London Medieval & Renaissance Ser.). 144p. 1981. pap. text ed. 11.75x (ISBN 0-8419-0653-X). Holmes & Meier.

Frankly Feminine: God's Idea of Womanhood. Gloria H. Hawley. 160p. (Orig.). 1981. pap. 3.50 (ISBN 0-87239-455-7, 2969). Standard Pub.

Frankly McCarthy. Eugene McCarthy. Ed. by Carol E. Rinzler. 1.00 (ISBN 0-8183-0169-4). Pub Aff Pr.

Franks. F. J. Los. Tr. by John P. Wardle from Dutch. 112p. 1940. pap. 3.50x (ISBN 0-911038-79-5, N League). Noontide.

Frans Hals, His Life, His Paintings: A Critique of His Art. Ed. by Georg Van Der Groot. 1979. deluxe ed. 22.45 (ISBN 0-930582-27-6). Gloucester Art.

Frantz - Malm's Chemistry in the Laboratory. James B. Ifft & Julian L. Roberts, Jr. (Illus.). 1981. 8.95x (ISBN 0-7167-1238-5); tchrs. manual avail.; individual exercises 0.50 ea. W H Freeman.

Frantz Fanon: A Critical Study. Irene Gendzier. 1973. 10.00 o.p. (ISBN 0-394-46205-X). Pantheon.

Frantz Fanon: Colonialism & Alienation. Renate Zahar. Tr. by Willfried F. Feuser from Ger. LC 74-7783. (Modern Reader Paperback Ser). 144p. 1976. pap. 5.00 (ISBN 0-85345-374-8, PB-3748). Monthly Rev.

Frantz-Malm's Chemical Principles in the Laboratory. 2nd ed. Julian L. Roberts, Jr. & James B. Ifft. (Illus.). 1977. lab. manual 10.95x (ISBN 0-7167-0184-7); tchr's manual avail.; individual experiments 0.50 ea. (ISBN 0-685-99797-9). W H Freeman.

Frantz-Malm's Essentials of Chemistry in the Laboratory. 3rd ed. James B. Ifft & Julian L. Roberts. (Illus.). 1975. 9.95x (ISBN 0-7167-0175-8); individual experiments 0.50 ea.; tchr's manual avail. W H Freeman.

Franz Anton Mesmer: Physician Extraordinaire. Ann Jensen & Mary L. Watkins. LC 66-28499. 7.50 o.p. (ISBN 0-912326-19-0). Garrett-Helix.

Franz Grillparzer, a Critical Biography. Douglas Yates. 188p. 1980. Repr. of 1946 ed. lib. bdg. 22.50 (ISBN 0-8482-3111-2). Norwood Edns.

Franz Joseph I of Austria & His Empire. Anatol Murad. LC 68-17233. (Illus.). 259p. 1968. text ed. 22.50x (ISBN 0-8290-0172-7). Irvington.

Franz Kafka. Franz Baumer. Tr. by Abraham Farbstein from Ger. LC 68-3144. (Modern Literature Ser.). 1971. 10.95 (ISBN 0-8044-2024-6); pap. 3.45 (ISBN 0-8044-6014-0). Ungar.

Franz Kafka. Walter H. Sokel. LC 66-26005. (Columbia Ser.: No. 19). (Orig.). 1966. pap. 2.00 (ISBN 0-231-02751-6, MW19). Columbia U Pr.

Franz Kafka. Meno Spann. LC 75-26548. (World Authors Ser.: Austria: No. 381). 1976. lib. bdg. 9.95 (ISBN 0-8057-6182-9). Twayne.

Franz Liszt: The Man & His Music. Ed. by Alan Walker. 1978. pap. 11.95 o.p. (ISBN 0-214-20345-X, 8021, Dist. by Arco). Barrie & Jenkins.

Franz Schneider (Seventeen Thirty-Seven to Eighteen Twelve) A Thematic Catalogue of His Works. Robert N. Freeman. (Thematic Catalogues Ser.: No. 5). 1979. lib. bdg. 27.50 (ISBN 0-918728-13-4). Pendragon NY.

Fraser's Canadian Trade Directory, 1980, 3 vols. 69th ed. LC 39-5763. 1980. Set. 95.00x (ISBN 0-8002-2707-7). Intl Pubns Serv.

Frases Fundamentales Para Comunicarse. Orange County Assoc. (gr. k-12). 1975. 3.15 (ISBN 0-89075-200-1). Crane Pub Co.

Fraternal Organizations. Alvin J. Schmidt. LC 79-6187. (Greenwood Encyclopedia of American Institutions). xxxiii, 410p. 1980. lib. bdg. 35.00 (ISBN 0-313-21436-0, SFR/). Greenwood.

Fratonizing in the Office: The Book the Boss Should Never Have. Judith Heverly. 1981. 8.95 (ISBN 0-87949-177-9). Ashley Bks.

Frau Lou: Nietzsche's Wayward Disciple. Rudolph Binion. LC 68-10389. 602p. 1968. 25.00x (ISBN 0-691-06142-4, 313); pap. 7.95 o.p. (ISBN 0-691-01312-8). Princeton U Pr.

Frau Luther. Yvonne Davy. LC 78-57355. (Destiny Ser.). 1979. pap. 4.95 (ISBN 0-8163-0235-9). Pacific Pr Pub Assn.

Fraud Corruption & Holiness: The Controversy Over the Supervision of Jewish Dietary Practice in New York City. Harold P. Gastwirt. LC 74-77649. 1974. 15.00 (ISBN 0-8046-9056-1, Natl U). Kennikat.

Fraud Investigation: Fundamentals for Police. Rush G. Glick & Robert S. Newsom. (Illus.). 358p. 1974. text ed. 17.75 (ISBN 0-398-03070-7). C C Thomas.

Fraud, Politics & the Disposition of the Indians: The Iroquois Land Frontier in the Colonial Period. Georgiana C. Nammack. (Civilization of the American Indian Ser.: Vol. 97). (Illus.). 128p. 1969. 8.95x (ISBN 0-8061-0854-1). U of Okla Pr.

Frauds & Hoaxes & Swindles. Daniel Cohen. (YA) (gr. 7-12). pap. 1.25 (ISBN 0-440-92699-8, LE). Dell.

Frauen am Hofe Trajans. Hildegard Temporini. (Illus.). 1979. 66.80x (ISBN 3-11-007822-8). De Gruyter.

Fray Luis De Granada. John A. Moore. (World Authors Ser.: No. 438). 1977. lib. bdg. 12.50 (ISBN 0-8057-6276-0). Twayne.

Frazetta Four. Betty Ballantine. 96p. 1980. pap. 8.95 (ISBN 0-553-01267-3). Bantam.

Frazier Hunt's Story of General Custer. Frazier Hunt. (Monograph: No. 5). (Orig.). 1979. pap. 2.50x (ISBN 0-686-27215-3). Monroe County Lib.

Freaks: Cinema of the Bizarre. Werner Adrian. (Illus.). 104p. 1976. pap. 3.95 o.s.i. (ISBN 0-446-87101-X). Warner Bks.

Freaks of Fanaticism & Other Strange Events. Sabine Baring-Gould. LC 68-21754. 1968. Repr. of 1891 ed. 18.00 (ISBN 0-8103-3503-4). Gale.

Freaky Facts. Louis Phillips. Ed. by Meg Schneider. (Funnybones Ser.). 64p. 1981. pap. 1.50 (ISBN 0-671-42247-2). S&S.

Freaky Fillins, No. 1. Ed. by David Hartley. 48p. (Orig.). 1980. pap. 1.50 (ISBN 0-937518-00-X). Hartley Hse.

Freaky Fillins, No. 2. Ed. by Melissa Hartley. 48p. (Orig.). 1980. pap. 1.50 (ISBN 0-937518-01-8). Hartley Hse.

Freaky Fillins, No. 3. Ed. by David Hartley. 48p. (Orig.). 1980. pap. 1.50 (ISBN 0-937518-02-6). Hartley Hse.

Freaky Fillins, No. 4. Ed. by Melissa Hartley. 48p. (Orig.). 1980. pap. 1.50 (ISBN 0-937518-03-4). Hartley Hse.

Freaky Fractions. Charlie Daniel & Becky Daniel. (gr. 1-5). 1978. 4.95 (ISBN 0-916456-19-6, GA77). Good Apple.

Freaky Friday. Mary Rodgers. (gr. 7 up). 1977. pap. 1.95 (ISBN 0-06-080392-4, P392, PL). Har-Row.

Freckle Juice. Judy Blume. LC 74-161016. (Illus.). 40p. (gr. 2-5). 1971. 5.95 (ISBN 0-590-07242-0, Four Winds). Schol Bk Serv.

Freckle Juice. Judy Blume. 1978. pap. 1.25 (ISBN 0-440-42813-0, YB). Dell.

Freckles. Gene S. Porter. 1977. 9.95x (ISBN 0-89967-003-2). Harmony & Co.

Freckles. Gene S. Porter. 254p. 1980. Repr. PLB 14.95x (ISBN 0-89966-224-2). Buccaneer Bks.

Fred Bear's Field Notes. Fred Bear. LC 76-2752. 1976. 11.95 (ISBN 0-385-11690-X). Doubleday.

Fred Bear's World of Archery. Fred Bear. (Illus.). 1979. 15.95 (ISBN 0-385-11275-0). Doubleday.

Fred Boynton: Lobsterman, New Harbor Maine. Ted Van Winkle. LC 74-29368. (Illus.). 80p. 1975. 12.50 (ISBN 0-87742-050-5). Intl Marine.

Fred Flintstone's Counting Book. Leslie Max. (Play & Learn Shape Board Bks). 14p. (gr. k-3). 1981. bds. 2.95 comb bdg. (ISBN 0-89828-100-8, 6001, Pub. by Ottenheimer Pubs Inc). Tuffy Bks.

Fred Lynn. Joe Soucheray. (Sports Superstars Ser.). (Illus.). (gr. 3-9). 1977. PLB 5.95 (ISBN 0-87191-541-3); pap. 2.95 (ISBN 0-89812-175-2). Creative Ed.

Freddie Goes to Florida. Walter R. Brooks. (gr. k-6). 1980. pap. 1.75 (ISBN 0-440-42577-8, YB). Dell.

Freddus Elephantus et Horatius Porcus Saltans Cincinnatis. Edvardus C. Echols. 129p. (Orig., Latin.). (gr. 10-11). 1980. pap. text ed. 3.50x (ISBN 0-88334-139-5). Ind Sch Pr.

Freddy's Book. John Gardner. 1981. pap. 2.95 (ISBN 0-345-29544-7). Ballantine.

Freddy's Book. John Neufeld. (gr. 2-7). 1975. pap. 1.75 (ISBN 0-380-00203-5, 53298, Camelot). Avon.

Frederic Chopin: His Life & Letters. Maurycy Karasowski. Tr. by Emily Hill. Repr. of 1938 ed. lib. bdg. 32.50x (ISBN 0-8371-3968-6, KAFC). Greenwood.

Frederic Joliot-Curie. Maurice Goldsmith. 1976. text ed. 15.75x (ISBN 0-85315-342-6). Humanities.

Frederic Remington. Ernest Raboff. LC 73-75361. 36p. (gr. 3-7). 1976. 6.95 (ISBN 0-385-05033-X). Doubleday.

Frederick Denison Maurice: Rebellious Conformist, 1805-1872. Olive J. Brose. LC 74-141380. xxiii, 308p. 1971. 16.00x (ISBN 0-8214-0092-4). Ohio U Pr.

Frederick Douglass on Women's Rights. Philip S. Foner. LC 76-5326. (Contributions in Afro-American & African Studies: No. 25). (Orig.). 1976. lib. bdg. 16.95 (ISBN 0-8371-8895-4, FFD/). Greenwood.

Frederick Goddard Tuckerman. Samuel A. Golden. (U. S. Authors Ser.: No. 104). 1966. lib. bdg. 10.95 (ISBN 0-8057-0748-4). Twayne.

Frederick Jackson Turner. James D. Bennett. LC 74-32112. (U. S. Authors Ser.: No. 254). 1975. lib. bdg. 10.95 (ISBN 0-8057-7150-6). Twayne.

Frederick Law Olmsted & the American Environmental Tradition. Albert Fein. LC 72-75831. (Planning & Cities Ser). (Illus.). 160p. 1972. 10.00 (ISBN 0-8076-0650-2); pap. 7.95 (ISBN 0-8076-0649-9). Braziller.

Frederick Law Olmsted Sr: Founder of Landscape Architecture in America. Julius G. Fabos et al. LC 68-19670. (Illus.). 1968. 12.00x (ISBN 0-87023-035-2); pap. 6.00x (ISBN 0-87023-052-2). U of Mass Pr.

Frederick Manfred. Robert C. Wright. (United States Authors Ser.: No. 336). 1979. lib. bdg. 13.50 (ISBN 0-8057-7247-2). Twayne.

Frederick Pohl's Favorite Stories: Forty Years As a Science Fiction Editor. Frederick Pohl. 448p. 1981. 14.95 (ISBN 0-399-12592-2). Putnam.

Frederick the Great. Margaret Goldsmith. 218p. 1980. Repr. of 1929 ed. lib. bdg. 20.00 (ISBN 0-89760-314-1). Telegraph Bks.

Frederick the Great. Ludwig Reiners. 1960. 13.95 (ISBN 0-85496-251-4). Dufour.

Frederick the Great: A Historical Profile. Gerhard Ritter. Tr. & intro. by Peter Paret. 1968. 15.75x (ISBN 0-520-01074-4); pap. 4.95x (ISBN 0-520-02775-2). U of Cal Pr.

Frederick the Great: A Profile. Ed. by Peter Paret. (World Profiles Ser). (Orig.). 1972. 7.95 o.p. (ISBN 0-8090-4678-4); pap. 3.95 o.p. (ISBN 0-8090-1402-5). Hill & Wang.

Frederick the Great: Prussian Warrior & Statesman. Louis L. Snyder & Ida M. Brown. LC 68-24122. (Biography Ser). (Illus.). (gr. 7 up). 1968. PLB 5.90 o.p. (ISBN 0-531-00872-X). Watts.

Frederick Weisman Company Collection of California Art. 2nd ed. Ed. by Constance W. Glenn. (Illus.). 64p. 1979. pap. 8.00 (ISBN 0-936270-11-X). Art Mus Gall.

Frederick Wiseman: A Guide to References & Resources. Liz Ellsworth. (Reference Bks.). 1979. lib. bdg. 24.95 (ISBN 0-8161-8066-0). G K Hall.

Free - Lancer & the Staff Writer. 2nd ed. William L. Rivers. 1976. text ed. 14.95x (ISBN 0-534-00453-9). Wadsworth Pub.

Free, Adult, Uncensored: The Living History of the Federal Theatre Project. John O'Connor & Lorraine Brown. LC 78-9292. (Illus.). 1978. 24.95 o.p. (ISBN 0-915220-37-7); pap. 11.95 o.p. (ISBN 0-915220-38-5). New Republic.

Free Air. Sinclair Lewis. 370p. 1980. Repr. of 1919 ed. lib. bdg. 35.00 (ISBN 0-8495-3330-9). Arden Lib.

Free & Easy. 7th ed. 1980. pap. 6.75 (ISBN 0-87314-091-5). Peter Glenn.

Free & Ennobled: Source Readings in the Development of Victorian Feminism. Ed. by Carol Bauer & Lawrence Ritt. (Illus.). 1979. 46.00 (ISBN 0-08-022272-2); pap. 18.50 (ISBN 0-08-022271-4). Pergamon.

Free & Faithful in Christ: General Moral Theology for Clergy & Laity, Vol. 1. Bernard Haring. 1978. 17.50 (ISBN 0-8164-0398-8). Crossroad NY.

Free & Faithful in Christ: Light to the World, Vol. 3. Bernard Haring. 500p. 1981. 19.50 (ISBN 0-8245-0009-1). Crossroad NY.

Free & Faithful in Christ: The Truth Will Set You Free, Vol. 2. Bernard Haring. 560p. 1979. 17.50 (ISBN 0-8164-0205-1). Crossroad NY.

Free & Inexpensive Materials on World Affairs. Leonard S. Kenworthy. LC 68-56447. 1969. pap. text ed. 3.50x (ISBN 0-8077-1608-1). Tchrs Coll.

Free Association. Paul Buttenweiser. 224p. 1980. 11.95 (ISBN 0-316-11899-0). Little.

Free at Last: A Bibliography of Martin Luther King, Jr. William H. Fisher. LC 77-22202. 1977. 10.00 (ISBN 0-8108-1081-6). Scarecrow.

Free Cleveland: A Guide to Leisure Fun in the Cleveland, Ohio, Area. Phillip G. Williams. LC 80-82977. (Illus.). 1981. pap. text ed. 7.95 (ISBN 0-936284-00-5). P Gaines Co.

Free Composition-der Freie Satz, 2 vols. Heinrich Schenker. Tr. by Ernst Oster from Ger. LC 78-4420. (Music Ser.). 1979. Set. lib. bdg. 33.95x (ISBN 0-582-28073-7). Longman.

Free Discussion of the Doctrine of Materialism and Philosophical Necessity, 1778. Richard Price. Ed. by Rene Wellek. LC 75-11247. (British Philosophers & Theologians of the 17th & 18th Centuries Ser.). 1978. lib. bdg. 42.00 (ISBN 0-8240-1798-6). Garland Pub.

Free-Electron Generators of Coherent Radiation. Ed. by Stephen Jacobs et al. LC 80-11556. (Physics of Quantum Electronics: Vol. 7). 848p. 1980. text ed. cancelled (ISBN 0-201-05687-9). A-W.

Free Enquiry into the Miraculous Powers, Which Are Supposed to Have Subsisted in the Christian Church. Conyers Middleton. Ed. by Rene Wellek. LC 75-11235. (British Philosophers & Theologians of the 17th & 18th Centuries: Vol. 36). 1977. Repr. of 1749 ed. lib. bdg. 42.00 (ISBN 0-8240-1788-9). Garland Pub.

Free Enquiry into the Nature & Origin of Evil. 2nd ed. Soame Jenyns. Ed. by Rene Wellek. LC 75-11226. (British Philosophers & Theologians of the 17th & 18th Centuries: Vol. 28). 1976. Repr. of 1757 ed. lib. bdg. 42.00 (ISBN 0-8240-1780-3). Garland Pub.

Free Fall. William Golding. LC 60-5431. (YA) (gr. 9-12). 1962. pap. 2.95 (ISBN 0-15-633468-2, H010, Hbgr). HarBraceJ.

Free Fall in Crimson. John D. MacDonald. LC 80-7871. 224p. 1981. 9.95 (ISBN 0-06-014833-0, HarpT). Har-Row.

Free Fire Zone: Short Stories by Vietnam Veterans. LC 72-5875. 1973. pap. 3.50. Packrat Pr.

Free-for-All: The Reds, the Whites & the Blues. Elihu Blotnick & Barbara Robinson. (Illus.). 64p. (Orig.). 1981. pap. 6.95 (ISBN 0-915090-02-3). Calif Street.

Free-Form Bargello. Gigs Stevens. LC 77-5784. (Illus.). 1977. 14.95 o.p. (ISBN 0-684-15024-7, ScribT); pap. 7.95 o.p. (ISBN 0-684-15055-7, SL719, ScribT). Scribner.

Free Germany: The National Committee & the League of German Officers. Bodo Scheurig. Tr. by Herbert Arnold from Ger. LC 75-82540. 1969. 20.00x (ISBN 0-8195-4010-2, Pub. by Wesleyan U Pr). Columbia U Pr.

Free-Hand Sketching for Engineering & Technical Students. E. Sutton. 64p. 1980. 4.05x (ISBN 0-85950-057-8, Pub. by Thornes England). State Mutual Bk.

Free Ice Water: The Story of the Wall Drug. rev. ed. Dana C. Jennings. LC 76-92836. (Illus.). 96p. 1975. pap. 2.95 (ISBN 0-87970-139-0). North Plains.

Free-Lancer & Staff Writer: Newspaper Features & Magazine Articles. 3rd ed. William L. Rivers & Shelley Smolkin. 352p. 1980. text ed. 14.95x (ISBN 0-534-00873-9). Wadsworth Pub.

Free-Living Unarmoured Dinoflagellata. C. A. Kofoid & Olive Swezy. (Univ. of California Memoirs Ser.). (Illus.). 540p. 1974. Repr. of 1921 ed. lib. bdg. 105.00 (ISBN 3-87429-066-2). Lubrecht & Cramer.

Free Magazines for Libraries. Adeline M. Smith. LC 80-15557. 280p. 1980. lib. bdg. 16.95x (ISBN 0-89950-021-8). McFarland & Co.

Free Oscillations of the Earth. E. R. Lapwood & T. Usami. (Cambridge Monographs on Mechanics & Applied Mathematics). (Illus.). 168p. Date not set. price not set (ISBN 0-521-23536-7). Cambridge U Pr.

Free Parliaments. Roger Acherley. Ed. by David S. Berkowitz & Samuel E. Thorne. LC 77-89218. (Classics of English Legal History in the Modern Era Ser.: Vol. 65). 334p. 1979. lib. bdg. 40.00 (ISBN 0-8240-3164-4). Garland Pub.

Free Periodicals from Socialist Countries: An Annotated Bibliography. Harry G. Shaffer. 1977. 0.60 (ISBN 0-89977-018-5). Am Inst Marxist.

Free Press. Toni Delacorte et al. 240p. (Orig.). 1981. pap. 9.95 (ISBN 0-936602-15-5). Harbor Pub CA.

Free Press - Free People: The Best Cause. John Hohenberg. LC 70-133912. 1971. 20.00x o.p. (ISBN 0-231-03315-X). Columbia U Pr.

Free Press: A Do It Yourself Guide to Promote Your Interests, Organization or Business. Toni Delacorte et al. 240p. 1981. 9.95 (ISBN 0-936602-15-5). Harbor Pub CA.

Free Press, Free People: The Best Cause. John Hohenberg. LC 70-133912. 1973. pap. 3.95 o.s.i. (ISBN 0-02-914800-6). Free Pr.

Free-Radical Chemistry. D. C. Nonhebel & J. C. Walton. LC 73-97887. (Illus.). 600p. 1973. 99.00 (ISBN 0-521-20149-7). Cambridge U Pr.

Free Radicals, 2 vols. Ed. by Jay K. Kochi. LC 72-6105. (Reactive Intermediates in Organic Chemistry Ser). 713p. 1973. Vol. 1. 68.95 (ISBN 0-471-49701-0); Vol. 2. 75.00 (ISBN 0-471-49702-9, Pub by Wiley-Interscience). Wiley.

Free Rein. Robert B. Ruddell et al. (Pathfinder - Allyn & Bacon Reading Program: Level 16). (gr. 4-5). 1978. text ed. 9.12 (ISBN 0-205-05188-X, 5451884); 14.60 (ISBN 0-205-05190-1, 5451906); wkbk. 3.88. Allyn.

Free Religion: An American Faith. Stow Persons. 5.00 o.p. (ISBN 0-8446-2736-4). Peter Smith.

Free Soil, Free Labor, Free Men. Eric Foner. LC 70-97024. 1970 17.95 (ISBN 0-19-500548-1). Oxford U Pr.

Free Soil, Free Labor, Free Men: The Ideology of the Republican Party Before the Civil War. Eric Foner. 1971. pap. 5.95 (ISBN 0-19-501352-2, 342, GB). Oxford U Pr.

Free Speech in the Church. Karl Rahner. LC 79-8717. Orig. Title: Das Freie Wort in der Kirche. 112p. 1981. Repr. of 1959 ed. lib. bdg. 17.50x (ISBN 0-313-20849-2, RAFS). Greenwood.

Free Speech: Responsible Communication Under Law. 2nd ed. Robert M. O'Neil. LC 71-182877. (Orig.) 1972. pap. 3.95 (ISBN 0-672-61301-8, SC11). Bobbs.

Free Spirit: Evonne Goolagong. D. J. Herda. LC 76-16197. (Sports Profiles Ser.). (Illus.). 48p. (gr. 4-11). 1976. PLB 8.50 (ISBN 0-8172-0146-7). Raintree Pubs.

Free Spirits. Ed. by Nancy J. Peters et al. 1981. pap. price not set (ISBN 0-87286-128-7). City Lights.

Free Stuff for Home & Garden. Ed. by Free Stuff Editors. (Illus.). 120p. (Orig.). 1981. pap. 2.95 (ISBN 0-915658-27-5). Meadowbrook Pr.

Free Stuff for Travelers. Ed. by Free Stuff Editors. 120p. (Orig.). 1981. pap. 2.95 (ISBN 0-915658-29-1) Meadowbrook Pr.

Free-Style Ikebana. Stella Coe. (Modern Japanese Flower Arrangement Ser.). 1979. 11.95 o.p. (ISBN 0-214-65247-5, 8045, Dist. by Arco). Barrie & Jenkins.

Free Things for Homeowners. Yolande Flesch. 96p. (Orig.). 1981. pap. 4.95 (ISBN 0-346-12533-2). Cornerstone.

Free Thoughts on Religion, the Church, & National Happiness. Bernard Mandeville. LC 77-17171. Date not set. Repr. of 1720 ed. lib. bdg. price not set (ISBN 0-8201-1300-X). Schol Facsimiles. Postponed.

Free to Be Good or Bad. Herbert Holt. 1977. pap. 2.50 o.p. (ISBN 0-06-464005-1, BN). Har-Row.

Free to Be Thin. Marie Chapian. LC 79-15656. (Illus.). 192p. 1979. pap. 3.95 (ISBN 0-87123-560-9, 210560); study guide by Neva Coyle 64 pgs. 1.95 (ISBN 0-87123-163-8, 210163). Bethany Fell.

Free to Choose: A Guide to Effective Communication. rev. ed. H. O. Nordberg et al. LC 74-84819. 1975. 8.95 (ISBN 0-8465-4850-X, 51958). Benjamin-Cummings.

Free to Choose: A Personal Statement. Milton Friedman & Rose Friedman. 352p. 1981. pap. 2.95 (ISBN 0-380-52548-8, 52548). Avon.

Free to Read: A Guide to Effective Reading. rev. ed. H. A. Bamman et al. LC 74-84819. 1975. 9.95 (ISBN 0-8465-5835-1, 55835); 0.75 (ISBN 0-8465-5836-X, 55836). Benjamin-Cummings.

Free University: A Model for Lifelong Learning. William A. Draves. 324p. 1980. 17.95 (ISBN 0-695-81443-5, Assn Pr). Follett.

Free Verse: An Essay on Prosody. Charles O. Hartman. LC 80-10782. 225p. 1980. 14.00x (ISBN 0-691-06438-5). Princeton U Pr.

Free Verse Self. Martin J. Rosenblum. 1977. pap. text ed. 4.00 o.p. (ISBN 0-89018-005-9). Lionhead Pub.

Free Vibration Analysis of Beams & Shafts. D. J. Gorman. LC 74-20504. 448p. 1975. 35.00 (ISBN 0-471-31770-5, Pub. by Wiley-Interscience). Wiley.

Free Yourself from Pain. David Bresher & Richard Trubo. 1980. pap. write for info. (ISBN 0-671-81683-7). PB.

Freed from Witchcraft. Doreen Irvine. 192p. 1981. pap. 3.95 (ISBN 0-8407-5771-9). Nelson.

Freedom: A Guarantee for Everybody. Kenneth D. Barney. (Radiant Life Ser). 128p. 1976. pap. 1.25 (ISBN 0-88243-891-3, 02-0891, Radiant Books); teacher's ed 2.50 (ISBN 0-88243-165-X, 32-0165). Gospel Pub.

Freedom & Authority in Education. G. H. Bantick. 1970. 5.95 (ISBN 0-571-09328-0, Pub. by Faber & Faber). Merrimack Bk Serv.

Freedom & Authority in Puritan New England. Allen Guttmann. Ed. by Richard H. Brown & Van R. Halsey. (Amherst Project Units in American History). (gr. 11-12). 1970. pap. text ed. 4.52 (ISBN 0-201-02666-X, Sch Div); tchr's manual 1.92 (ISBN 0-201-02668-6). A-W.

Freedom & Constraint: A Memorial Tribute to Max Gluckman. Ed. by Myron J. Aronoff. (Illus.). 1976. pap. text ed. 22.25x (ISBN 90-232-1392-0). Humanities.

Freedom & Crisis, 2 vols. 2nd ed. Allen Weinstein & R. Jackson Wilson. 1978. Single Vol. pap. text ed. 17.95x (ISBN 0-394-31217-1); pap. 12.95 ea.; Vol. 1. (ISBN 0-394-31219-8); Vol. 2. (ISBN 0-394-31223-6); wkbks. 4.95 ea. Vol. 1 (ISBN 0-394-32294-0). Vol. 2 (ISBN 0-394-32295-9). Random.

Freedom & Crisis: An American History. Allen Weinstein. 972p. 1981. text ed. 18.95 (ISBN 0-394-32415-3). Random.

Freedom & Crisis: An American History, 2 vols. 3rd ed. Allen Weinstein. 1981. Vol. 1, 498p. pap. text ed. 12.95 (ISBN 0-394-32611-3); Vol. 2, 539p. pap. text ed. 12.95 (ISBN 0-394-32612-1). Random.

Freedom & Determinism. Ed. by Keith Lehrer. 204p. 1976. pap. text ed. 5.95x (ISBN 0-391-00537-5). Humanities.

Freedom & Development. Gabriel Almond et al. 4.75x (ISBN 0-210-22595-5). Asia.

Freedom & Development - Uhuru Na Maendeleo. Julius K. Nyerere. (Illus.). 420p. 1974. pap. 4.95x (ISBN 0-19-519772-0, GB412, GB). Oxford U Pr.

Freedom & Discipline in the Education of Young People. Leon Da Costa. (Science of Man Library Bk). (Illus.). 176p. 1976. lib. bdg. 37.50 (ISBN 0-913314-68-4). Am Classical Coll Pr.

Freedom & Domination: A Historical Critique of Civilization. Alexander Rustow. Tr. by Salvator Attanasio from Ger. LC 80-10575. 700p. 1980. 35.00x (ISBN 0-691-05304-9). Princeton U Pr.

Freedom & Education: The Beginnings of a New Philosophy. Richard L. Hopkins. LC 79-66475. 1979. text ed. 14.50 (ISBN 0-8191-0836-7); pap. text ed. 7.75 (ISBN 0-8191-0837-5). U Pr of Amer.

Freedom & Emergency Powers in the Cold War. Robert S. Rankin & Winfried R. Dallmayr. LC 63-21213. 1964. pap. text ed. 10.95x (ISBN 0-89197-531-4). Irvington.

Freedom & Fate: An Inner Life of Ralph Waldo Emerson. 2nd ed. Stephen E. Whicher. LC 74-84742. 1969. 10.00 o.p. (ISBN 0-8122-7045-2). U of Pa Pr.

Freedom & Growth in Marriage. 2nd ed. James L. McCary. LC 79-17199. 1980. text ed. 15.95 (ISBN 0-471-05341-4); tchrs' manual (ISBN 0-471-07845-X). Wiley.

Freedom & Nature: The Voluntary & the Involuntary. Paul Ricoeur. Tr. by E. V. Kohak. (Studies in Phenomenology & Existential Philosophy Ser). 1966. 22.95x (ISBN 0-8101-0208-0); pap. 9.95x (ISBN 0-8101-0534-9). Northwestern U Pr.

Freedom & Prejudice: The Legacy of Slavery in the United States & Brazil. Robert B. Toplin. LC 80-656. (Contributions in Afro-American & African Studies: No. 56). 1981. lib. bdg. 33.95 (ISBN 0-313-22008-5, TFP/). Greenwood.

Freedom & Protection: The Bill of Rights. Andrew D. Weinberger. LC 72-6217. 180p. 1972. Repr. of 1962 ed. lib. bdg. 12.75x (ISBN 0-8371-6474-5, WEFP). Greenwood.

Freedom & Reason. Richard M. Hare. (Oxford Paperbacks Ser.: No. 92). 1965. pap. text ed. 7.50x (ISBN 0-19-881092-X). Oxford U Pr.

Freedom & Rights. A. J. Milne. 1968. text ed. 10.75x (ISBN 0-04-170021-X). Humanities.

Freedom & Socialism: A Selection from Writings & Speeches 1965-1967. Julius K. Nyerere. 1970. pap. 6.95 (ISBN 0-19-501241-0, GB). Oxford U Pr.

Freedom & the Court: Civil Rights & Liberties in the United States. 3rd ed. Henry J. Abraham & Grace Doherty. 1977. 22.50 (ISBN 0-19-502135-5); pap. 6.95x (ISBN 0-19-502134-7). Oxford U Pr.

Freedom & the Critical Undertaking: Essays on Kant's Later Critiques. Mary-Barbara Zeldin. LC 80-17553. (Sponsor Ser.). 346p. (Orig.). 1980. pap. 21.75 (ISBN 0-8357-0525-0, SS-00143). Univ Microfilms.

Freedom & the Law. Bruno Leoni. LC 71-167535. 1976. 7.50x o.p. (ISBN 0-916054-18-7); pap. 4.95x o.p. (ISBN 0-8402-1215-1). Green Hill.

Freedom & the Law. Bruno Leoni. LC 71-167535. 204p. 1961. 7.50x o.p. (ISBN 0-8402-1215-1); pap. text ed. 4.95x o.p. (ISBN 0-686-65432-3). Nash Pub.

Freedom & the Welfare State. Bill Jordan. 1978. pap. 6.95 (ISBN 0-7100-8910-4). Routledge & Kegan.

Freedom at Stake. Peter Archer & Lord Reay. LC 67-15647. (Background Ser.). 1967. 6.25 (ISBN 0-8023-1118-0). Dufour.

Freedom Bound. Henrietta Buckmaster. 1967. pap. 1.25 o.s.i. (ISBN 0-02-030740-3, Collier). Macmillan.

Freedom Comes from Human Beings. Merritt Clifton. 80p. (Orig.). 1980. pap. 4.00 (ISBN 0-686-28738-X). Samisdat.

Freedom, Corruption, & Government in Elizabethan England. Joel Hurstfield. LC 73-76380. 368p. 1973. pap. text ed. 16.50x (ISBN 0-674-31925-7). Harvard U Pr.

Freedom Diet - Games Dieters Play. Leslie J. Maynard. LC 76-47654. 1977. 9.95 (ISBN 0-8119-0275-7). Fell.

Freedom Dues: Or, a Gentleman's Progress in the New World. Robert Abel. 404p. 1980. 10.95 (ISBN 0-8037-2575-2). Dial.

Freedom, Emotion & Self-Substance: The Structure of a Central Part of Spinoza's Ethics. Arne Naess. 1975. pap. text ed. 11.00x (ISBN 8-200-01459-2, Dist. by Columbia U Pr). Universitet.

Freedom Freeway. Leonard E. Read. 128p. 1979. 3.00 (ISBN 0-910614-61-X). Foun Econ Ed.

Freedom from a Self-Centered Life. William Law. Ed. by Andrew Murray. LC 77-71426. 1977. pap. 2.25 (ISBN 0-87123-104-2, 200104). Bethany Fell.

Freedom from Depression. James E. Johnson. (Orig.). 1981. pap. 2.95 (ISBN 0-88270-494-X). Logos.

Freedom from Pain Through Acupressure. Frank Z. Warren. LC 75-16632. 1976. 9.95 (ISBN 0-8119-0256-0). Fell.

Freedom from Stress. Ernest Holmes. 1964. pap. 3.50 (ISBN 0-911336-30-3). Sci of Mind.

Freedom from Stress: A Holistic Method. Phil Nuernberger. (Illus., Orig.). 1981. 10.00 (ISBN 0-89389-071-5); pap. 6.95 (ISBN 0-89389-064-2). Himalayan Intl Inst.

Freedom from the Known. Jiddu Krishnamurti. LC 69-17013. 128p. 1975. pap. 3.95 (ISBN 0-06-064808-2, RD 90, HarpR). Har-Row.

Freedom Frontiers: The Story of the American People. James I. Clark & Robert O. Remini. 1975. 13.95 (ISBN 0-02-640660-8, 64066); tchr's manual 3.48 (ISBN 0-02-640670-5, 64067). Macmillan.

Freedom in Constitutional Contract: Perspectives of a Political Economist. James M Buchanan. LC 77-89513. (Texas A&M Univ. Economics Ser.: No. 2). 328p. 1977. 22.50x (ISBN 0-89096-038-0). Tex A&M Univ Pr.

Freedom in Jeopardy: The Tyranny of Idealism. LC 68-54126. (Principles of Freedom Ser.). 1976. Repr. of 1969 ed. 9.95x o.p. (ISBN 0-916054-19-5). Green Hill.

Freedom in Jeopardy: The Tyranny of Idealism. John V. Van Sickle. LC 68-54126. (Principles of Freedom Ser.). 204p. 1969. 9.95 (ISBN 0-89617-045-4). Inst Humane.

Freedom in Meditation. Carrington, Patricia, Ph.D. LC 76-6240. 1978. pap. 3.50 (ISBN 0-385-12407-4, Anch). Doubleday.

Freedom in the World: Political Rights & Civil Liberties. Ed. by Raymond D. Gastil. 321p. (Orig.). 1981. pap. 8.95 (ISBN 0-87855-819-5). Transaction Bks.

Freedom in the World: Political Rights & Civil Liberties, 1980. Raymond D. Gastil. LC 80-66430. (Illus.). 1980. lib. bdg. 24.95 (ISBN 0-932088-02-3). Freedom Hse.

Freedom Inside the Organization: Bringing Civil Liberties to the Workplace. David Ewing. 1977. 10.00 (ISBN 0-87690-249-2). Dutton.

Freedom Is an Inside Job. Vera Channels & Mary Vestermark. LC 77-15745. 1978. 5.95 o.p. (ISBN 0-8042-2060-3). John Knox.

Freedom Is As Freedom Does. Corliss Lamont. LC 74-171384. (Civil Liberties in American History Ser.). 1972. Repr. of 1956 ed. lib. bdg. 35.00 (ISBN 0-306-70498-6). Da Capo.

Freedom Is As Freedom Does: Civil Liberties in America. Corliss Lamont. 330p. (Orig.). 1981. pap. 5.95 (ISBN 0-8180-0350-2). Horizon.

Freedom Letter. Alan Johnson. 1979. 4.95 (ISBN 0-8024-2874-6). Moody.

Freedom-Love & Playing-Love & Other Special Kinds. Paul J. Thompson. LC 78-65331. 1977. 4.95 (ISBN 0-9601288-2-4); pap. 2.95 (ISBN 0-9601288-1-6). P J Thompson.

Freedom of Access to Library Materials. John Robotham & Gerald Shields. 250p. Date not set. 16.95 (ISBN 0-918212-31-6). Neal-Schuman.

Freedom of Association, Labour Relations & Development in Asia: Asian Regional Conference, Manila, December, 1980, Ninth Session, Report II. International Labour Office. ii, 61p. (Orig.). 1980. pap. 7.15 (ISBN 92-2-102499-7). Intl Labour Office.

Freedom of Choice. Yves Simon. Ed. by Peter Wolff. LC 75-75040. xx, 167p. 1969. 10.00 o.p. (ISBN 0-8232-0840-0). Fordham.

Freedom of Choice Affirmed. Ed. by Corliss Lamont. 214p. (Orig.). 1981. pap. 4.95 (ISBN 0-8180-1329-X). Horizon.

Freedom of Choice in Housing. Social Science Panel. 80p. 1972. pap. 3.00 (ISBN 0-309-02025-5). Natl Acad Pr.

Freedom of Expression. Fred R. Berger. 224p. 1979. pap. text ed. 7.95x (ISBN 0-534-00749-X). Wadsworth Pub.

Freedom of Expression & Security: A Comparative Study of the Function of the Supreme Courts of the United States of American & India. Ajit S. Bedi. 1966. 13.95x (ISBN 0-210-31224-6). Asia.

Freedom of Forgiveness. David Angsburger. 128p. 1973. pap. 1.50 (ISBN 0-8024-2875-4). Moody.

Freedom of God's Sons: Studies in Galatians. Homer A. Kent, Jr. (New Testament Studies). (Illus.). 144p. 1976. pap. 2.95 o.p. (ISBN 0-8010-5376-5). Baker Bk.

Freedom of Sexual Love. Joseph W. Bird & Lois F. Bird. LC 67-10377. 1970. pap. 2.75 (ISBN 0-385-04341-4, Im). Doubleday.

Freedom of Simplicity. Richard J. Foster. LC 80-8351. 192p. 1981. 9.95 (ISBN 0-06-062832-4, HarpR). Har-Row.

Freedom of the News Media. Olga G. Hoyt & Edwin P. Hoyt. LC 72-93809. 192p. (gr. 6 up). 1973. 6.95 (ISBN 0-395-28910-6, Clarion). HM.

Freedom of the Press. William E. Hocking. LC 77-39587. (Civil Liberties in American History Ser). 240p. 1972. Repr. of 1947 ed. lib. bdg. 22.50 (ISBN 0-306-70231-2). Da Capo.

Freedom of the Press. G. Seldes. LC 73-146159. (Civil Liberties in American History Ser). 1971. Repr. of 1935 ed. lib. bdg. 35.00 (ISBN 0-306-70125-1). Da Capo.

Freedom of the Press & Fair Trial: Final Report with Recommendations. H. R. Medina & Association of the Bar of the City of New York. LC 67-15897. 1967. 12.50x (ISBN 0-231-03054-1). Columbia U Pr.

Freedom of the Press Vs. Public Access. Benno C. Schmidt, Jr. LC 75-19818. (Special Studies). 1976. text ed. 26.95 (ISBN 0-275-01620-X); pap. text ed. 11.95 (ISBN 0-275-89430-4). Praeger.

Freedom of the Will. Jonathan Edwards. Ed. by Arnold S. Kaufman & William K. Frankena. LC 68-22308. 1969. 24.50x (ISBN 0-672-51063-4); pap. text ed. 12.95x (ISBN 0-672-60360-8). Irvington.

Freedom or Order: Must We Choose? (Crucial Issues in American Government Ser.). (gr. 9-12). 1976. pap. text ed. 4.96 (ISBN 0-205-04905-2, 7649053). Allyn.

Freedom Road. Howard Fast. (Literature Ser). (gr. 10-12). 1970. pap. text ed. 3.92 (ISBN 0-87720-752-6). AMSCO Sch.

Freedom Seder: A New Haggadah for Passover. Arthur L. Waskow. 1970. 3.95 o.p. (ISBN 0-03-084532-7); pap. 1.50 (ISBN 0-03-084681-1). HR&W.

Freedom Through Knowledge. Epaulic. 1981. 5.50 (ISBN 0-8062-1602-6). Carlton.

Freedom to Choose. Ernest J. Gruen. 224p. 1976. pap. 2.95 (ISBN 0-88368-072-6). Whitaker Hse.

Freedom to Die: Moral & Legal Aspects of Euthanasia. rev. ed. O. Ruth Russell. LC 77-3383. 1977. 24.95 (ISBN 0-87705-311-1). Human Sci Pr.

Freedom to Learn: A View of What Education Might Become. Carl Rogers. LC 72-75629. 1969. text ed. 11.95 (ISBN 0-675-09519-0); pap. text ed. 8.95x (ISBN 0-675-09579-4). Merrill.

Freedom to Learn: An Active Learning Approach to Mathematics. E. Biggs & J. MacLean. 1969. text ed. 14.00 (ISBN 0-201-00572-7). A-W.

Freedom to Live. Ernest Holmes. 1969. pap. 3.50 (ISBN 0-911336-35-4). Sci of Mind.

Freedom Trail to Greystone. Louisa Bronte. 240p. (Orig.). 1976. pap. 1.50 o.p. (ISBN 0-345-24860-0). Ballantine.

Freedom Versus Suppression & Censorship. Charles H. Busha. LC 72-91672. (Research Studies in Library Science: No. 8). 250p. 1972. lib. bdg. 15.00x (ISBN 0-87287-057-X). Libs Unl.

Freedom's Edge: The Computer Threat to Society. Milton R. Wessel. (Illus.). 200p. 1974. pap. 8.95 (ISBN 0-201-08543-7). A-W.

Freedom's First Generation: Black Hampton, Virginia, Eighteen Sixty-One to Eighteen Ninety. Robert F. Engs. LC 79-5046. (Illus.). 1980. 15.00x (ISBN 0-8122-7768-6). U of Pa Pr.

Freefood Seafood Book. Peggy A. Hardigree. 224p. (Orig.). 1981. pap. 8.95 (ISBN 0-8117-2068-3). Stackpole.

Freehand. Lily Harmon. 1981. 13.95 (ISBN 0-671-41452-6). S&S.

Freeing the Natural Voice. Kristin Linklater & Douglas Florian. LC 75-28172. (Illus.). 1976. text ed. 12.50x (ISBN 0-910482-67-5). Drama Bk.

Freelance Business Writing Business. William R. Palmer. LC 78-78221. (Illus.). 1979. postpaid (14.95 price) 16.10 (ISBN 0-9602350-0-0); pap. 12.95 postpaid (11.95 price) (ISBN 0-9602350-1-9). Heathcote.

Freelance Photography: Advice from the Pros. Curtis W. Casewit. 1980. 10.95 (ISBN 0-02-522400-X, Collier); pap. 5.95 (ISBN 0-02-079310-3, Collier). Macmillan.

Freeman Library of Laboratory Separates in Chemistry, 1083-1122, 40 studies. Ed. by Ralph K. Birdwhistell & Rod O'Connor. 1971. loose-leaf 0.50 ea. o.p.; tchr's manual avail. o.p. W H Freeman.

Freemasonry Known by the Masonic Diploma. Apostolos Makrakis. Tr. by Denver Cummings. 135p. (Orig.). 1956. pap. 3.00x (ISBN 0-938366-42-4). Orthodox Chr.

Freer Gallery of Art, Washington D. C. John A. Pope et al. LC 80-82645. (Oriental Ceramics Ser.: Vol. 9). (Illus.). 180p. 1981. 65.00 (ISBN 0-87011-448-4). Kodansha.

Freer's Cove. Ethel Gordon. (Candlelight Romance Ser.). 1981. pap. 1.50 (ISBN 0-440-12704-1). Dell.

Freesias. Denis Smith. 90p. 1980. pap. 9.95 (ISBN 0-901361-25-9, Pub. by Grower Bks England). Intl Schol Bk Serv.

Freestyle for Michael. Hazel Krantz. LC 64-16255. (Illus.). (gr. 5-8). 3.95 (ISBN 0-8149-0345-2). Vanguard.

Freestyle Skiing. John Mohan et al. 1976. 11.95 (ISBN 0-87691-185-8). Winchester Pr.

Freestyle Skiing. John Mohan et al. 1978. pap. 8.95 (ISBN 0-87691-265-X). Winchester Pr.

Freethought in the United Kingdom & the Commonwealth: A Descriptive Bibliography. Gordon Stein. LC 80-1792. 192p. 1981. lib. bdg. 35.00 (ISBN 0-313-20869-7, SFU/). Greenwood.

Freethought in the United States: A Descriptive Bibliography. Marshall G. Brown & Gordon Stein. LC 77-91103. 1978. lib. bdg. 17.50 (ISBN 0-313-20036-X, BFT/). Greenwood.

Freeway. Peter Nichols. 1975. pap. 4.95 (ISBN 0-571-10744-3, Pub. by Faber & Faber). Merrimack Bk Serv.

Freeway Driving. Kathleen Wiegner. 1981. pap. 4.00 (ISBN 0-914610-23-6). Hanging Loose.

Freeway Under Construction. Judson Cornwall. 1978. bklt. 1.95 (ISBN 0-88270-304-8). Logos.

Freewill & Responsibility: Four Lectures. Anthony Kenny. 1978. 12.50x (ISBN 0-7100-8998-8). Routledge & Kegan.

Freeze & Please Home Freezer Cookbook. June Roth. LC 63-21654. 1968. 5.95 (ISBN 0-8119-0063-0); pap. 4.95 (ISBN 0-8119-0372-9). Fell.

Freeze Drying & Advanced Food Technology. Ed. by S. A. Goldblith et al. 1975. 98.00 (ISBN 0-12-288450-7). Acad Pr.

Freeze-Fracture: Methods, Artifacts, & Interpretations. J. E. Rash & C. S. Hudson. LC 79-109. 1979. text ed. 21.00 (ISBN 0-89004-386-8). Raven.

Freeze Frame. R. R. Irvine. 192p. 1976. pap. 1.25 o.p. (ISBN 0-445-00351-0). Popular Lib.

Freeze with Ease. Marian Burros & Lois Levine. LC 65-21466. 1968. pap. 2.95 (ISBN 0-02-009280-6, Collier). Macmillan.

Freezer Cookbook. Charlotte Erickson. (Illus.). 1981. pap. 8.95 (ISBN 0-8092-5888-9). Contemp Bks.

Freezer Cookery. Margaret D. Murphy. 7.95 (ISBN 0-916752-02-X). Green Hill.

Freezing & Irradiation of Fish. Ed. by Rudolf Kreuzer. (Illus.). 548p. 41.25 (ISBN 0-85238-008-9, FN). Unipub.

Freezing & Thawing of Concrete: Mechanisms & Control. William A. Cordon. (Monograph: No. 3). 1966. 9.00 o.p. (ISBN 0-685-85136-2, M-3); members 7.25 o.p. (ISBN 0-685-85137-0). ACI.

Freezing Preservation of Foods, 4 vols. 4th ed. Donald K. Tressler et al. Incl. Vol. 1. Principles of Refrigeration; Equipment for Freezing & Transporting Food. 32.00 (ISBN 0-87055-044-6); Vol. 2. Factors Affecting Quality in Frozen Foods. 35.00 (ISBN 0-87055-045-4); Vol. 3. Commercial Freezing Operations; Fresh Foods. 39.00 (ISBN 0-87055-046-2); Vol. 4. Freezing of Precooked & Prepared Foods. 39.00 (ISBN 0-87055-047-0). (Illus.). 1968. AVI.

Frege's Theory of Judgement. David Bell. 178p. 1979. text ed. 24.95x (ISBN 0-19-827423-8). Oxford U Pr.

Frei Otto: Form & Structure. Philip Drew. LC 76-178. (Illus.). 1976. 42.50 o.p. (ISBN 0-89158-535-4). Westview.

Freight Flows & Spatial Aspects of the British Economy. M. Chisholm & P. O'Sullivan. LC 72-83592. (Geographical Studies: No. 4). (Illus.). 140p. 1973. 27.50 (ISBN 0-521-08672-8). Cambridge U Pr.

Freight Train. Donald Crews. LC 78-2303. (Illus.). (gr. k-3). 1978. 7.95 (ISBN 0-688-80165-X); PLB 7.63 (ISBN 0-688-84165-1). Greenwillow.

Freight Trains West. Archie Lawson. (Illus.). 150p. (Orig.). 1980. 9.95 (ISBN 0-9604806-0-9); pap. 5.95 (ISBN 0-9604806-1-7). Lucas Pubs CA.

Freiheit und System Bei Hegel. Emil Angehrn. 1977. 73.00x (ISBN 3-11-006969-5). De Gruyter.

Fremde, Erzaehlung. Sinclair. (Edition Suhrkamp. Neue Folge: es. NF 7). 150p. (Orig., Ger.). 1980. pap. text ed. 4.55 (ISBN 3-518-11007-1, Pub. by Insel Verlag Germany). Suhrkamp.

Fremont Culture: A Study in Culture Dynamics on the Northern Anasazi Frontier. James H. Gunnerson. LC 79-76014. (Peabody Museum Papers: Vol. 59, No. 2). 1969. pap. text ed. 15.00 (ISBN 0-87365-172-3). Peabody Harvard.

French. Holloway Staff. (Harper Phrase Books for the Traveler Ser.). (Orig.). 1977. pap. 1.00 (ISBN 0-8467-0309-2, Pub. by Two Continents). Hippocrene Bks.

French. Jack Rudman. (Undergraduate Program Field Test Ser.: UPFT-9). (Cloth bdg. avail. on request). pap. 9.95 (ISBN 0-8373-6009-9). Natl Learning.

French Absolutism: The Crucial Phase, 1620-1629. Alexandra D. Lublinskaya. (Illus.). 1968. 44.50 (ISBN 0-521-07117-8). Cambridge U Pr.

French Against the French. Milton Dank. LC 74-10735. 1974. 12.50 o.s.i. (ISBN 0-397-01040-0). Lippincott.

French & English. Richard Faber. 1975. 13.95 (ISBN 0-571-10727-3, Pub. by Faber & Faber). Merrimack Bk Serv.

French & Indian Cruelty; Exemplified in the Life & Various Vicissitudes of Fortune, of Peter Williamson...Containing a Particular Account of the Manners, Customs, & Dress, of the Savages, Repr. Of 1757. Bd. with French & Indian Cruelty. Repr. of 1758 ed; Sufferings of... Repr. of 1796 ed; Travels & Surprising Adventures of John Thomson, Who Was Taken, & Carried to America, & Sold for a Slave There; How He Was Taken Captive by the Savages,... & His Return to Scotland. Repr. of 1761 ed; Full & Particular Account of the Sufferings of William Gatenby. Repr. of 1784 ed. (Narratives of North American Indian Captivities Ser.: Vol. 9). 1979. lib. bdg. 44.00 (ISBN 0-8240-1633-5). Garland Pub.

French & Indian War. Red Reeder. LC 76-181680. (gr. 5-9). 1972. 7.95 (ISBN 0-525-66208-1). Elsevier-Nelson.

French Arabic Dictionary, 2 vols. Cherbonneau. Set. 25.00x (ISBN 0-685-54027-8). Intl Bk Ctr.

French Architecture. Pierre Lavedan. (Illus.). 304p. 1980. 15.95 (ISBN 0-85967-366-9, Pub. by Scolar Pr England); pap. 7.95 (ISBN 0-85967-365-0). Biblio Dist.

French Are Coming. Wilma P. Hays. LC 65-22681. (Younger Reader Ser.). (Illus.). (gr. 4-7). 1965. 3.95 o.p. (ISBN 0-910412-63-4). Williamsburg.

French Art at the End of the Nineteenth Century: An Illustrated Survey. Charles G. Barrow. (Illus.). 123p. 1981. 39.45 (ISBN 0-930582-88-8). Gloucester Art.

French Atlantic Affair. Ernest Lehman. 1978. pap. 2.75 (ISBN 0-446-95258-3). Warner Bks.

French Budgetary Process. Guy Lord. LC 70-186113. 1973. 28.50x (ISBN 0-520-02196-7). U of Cal Pr.

French Cistercian Grisaille Glass. Helen J. Zakin. LC 78-74385. (Outstanding Dissertations in the Fine Arts, Fourth Ser.). 1979. lib. bdg. 44.00 (ISBN 0-8240-3971-8). Garland Pub.

French Cities in the Nineteenth Century. Ed. by John Merriman. 256p. 1981. text ed. 28.50x (ISBN 0-8419-0464-2). Holmes & Meier.

French Code of Criminal Procedure. (American Series of Foreign Penal Codes: Vol. 7). 1964. 17.50x (ISBN 0-8377-0027-2). Rothman.

French Colonial Rule & the Baule Peoples: Resistance & Collaboration, 1889-1911. Timothy C. Weiskel. (Oxford Studies in African Affairs Ser.). (Illus.). 352p. 1981. 42.50x (ISBN 0-19-822715-9). Oxford U Pr.

French Communism, 1920-1972. Ronald Tiersky. LC 74-921. 416p. 1974. 22.50x (ISBN 0-231-03754-6). Columbia U Pr.

French Communist Party in Transition: PCF-CPSU Relations & the Challenge to Soviet Authority. Annette E. Stiefbold. LC 77-83477. (Praeger Special Studies). 1978. 22.95 (ISBN 0-03-040946-2). Praeger.

French Concise Dictionary. Cassells. 1977. 8.95 (ISBN 0-02-052267-3). Macmillan.

French Consul. Lucien Bodard. 1977. 10.00 o.p. (ISBN 0-394-49321-4). Knopf.

French Conversation Through Idioms. Gerber & Storzer. Date not set. pap. 6.95 (ISBN 0-8120-2107-X). Barron. Postponed.

French Cook Book. Sunset Editors. LC 76-7666. (Illus.). 96p. 1976. pap. 3.95 (ISBN 0-376-02423-2, Sunset Bks.). Sunset-Lane.

French Cookery. Robin Howe. 4.50x (ISBN 0-392-06255-0, Ltcb). Soccer.

French Cooking Without Tears. Lyn Macdonald. (Illus.). 192p. 1980. 16.95 (ISBN 0-241-10173-5, Pub. by Hamish Hamilton England). David & Charles.

French Course for West Africa, 4 bks. Helen M. Purkis. 1962-65. Bk. 1. text ed. 5.95x (ISBN 0-521-06009-5); Bk. 2. text ed. 5.95x (ISBN 0-521-06010-9); Bk. 3. text ed. 5.95x (ISBN 0-521-06011-7); Bk. 4. text ed. 5.95x (ISBN 0-521-06012-5). Cambridge U Pr.

French Defence: Main Line Winawer. John Moles. 1975. 20.95 (ISBN 0-7134-2921-6, Pub. by Batsford England). David & Charles.

French Defence: Tarrasch Variation. Raymond Keene & Shaun Talbot. (Algebraic Chess Openings Ser.). (Illus.). 112p. 1981. pap. 11.95 (ISBN 0-7134-1898-2, Pub. by Batsford England). David & Charles.

French Deputy: Incentives & Behavior in the National Assembly. Oliver H. Woshinsky. LC 73-7960. (Illus.). 256p. 1973. 17.95 o.p. (ISBN 0-669-90159-8). Lexington Bks.

French Dialect of St. Thomas U.S. Virgin Islands: A Descriptive Grammar with Texts & Glossary. Arnold R. Highfield. 350p. 1979. pap. 10.50 (ISBN 0-89720-026-8). Karoma.

French Drawings & Sketchbooks of the Eighteenth Century. Art Institute of Chicago & Harold Joachim. LC 77-20132. 1978. write for info. (ISBN 0-226-68795-3, Chicago Visual Lib) (ISBN 0-685-84958-9). U of Chicago Pr.

French Drawings from a Private Collection: Louis XIII to Louis XVI. Ed. by Konrad Oberhuber & Beverly S. Jacoby. LC 80-65383. 182p. 1980. pap. 7.50 (ISBN 0-916724-42-5). Fogg Art.

French Drawings: Great Drawings of the Louvre. Maurice Serullaz. LC 68-23040. (Illus.). 20.00 o.s.i. (ISBN 0-8076-0472-0). Braziller.

French-English & English-French Dictionary of Commercial & Financial Terms, Phrases & Practice. 2nd ed. J. O. Kettridge. 1969. Repr. of 1968 ed. 30.00 (ISBN 0-7100-1671-9). Routledge & Kegan.

French-English & English-French Dictionary of Financial & Mercantile Terms Phrases & Practice. J. O. Kettridge. 1971. Repr. of 1934 ed. 20.00 (ISBN 0-7100-1667-0). Routledge & Kegan.

French-English & English-French Dictionary of Technical Terms & Phrases, 2 vols. J. O. Kettridge. Incl. Vol. 1. French-English. 40.00 (ISBN 0-7100-1672-7); Vol. 2. English-French. 40.00 (ISBN 0-7100-1673-5). 1970. Repr. of 1959 ed. Set. 70.00 (ISBN 0-685-25619-7). Routledge & Kegan.

French-English Dictionary for Chemists. 2nd ed. A. M. Patterson. 1954. 20.95 o.p. (ISBN 0-471-66957-1, Pub. by Wiley-Interscience). Wiley.

French-English Instant Vocabulary Francais-Anglais. Eleanor P. Cruikshank. 88p. 1980. pap. 4.00 (ISBN 0-9605284-0-7). Cruikshank.

French Enlightenment & the Jews. Arthur Hertzberg. LC 68-18996. 1968. 22.50x (ISBN 0-231-03049-5). Columbia U Pr.

French Ensor Chadwick: Scholarly Warrior. Paolo E. Coletta. LC 80-67240. 264p. 1980. lib. bdg. 18.75 (ISBN 0-8191-1153-8); pap. text ed. 10.75 (ISBN 0-8191-1154-6). U Pr of Amer.

French Explorers in the Pacific Vol. 2: The Nineteenth Century. John Dunmore. 1969. 22.00x o.p. (ISBN 0-19-821540-1). Oxford U Pr.

French Export Behavior in Third World Markets, Vol. II. Lawrence Franko & Sherry Stephenson. LC 80-66695. (Significant Issues Ser.: No. 6). 96p. 1980. 4.00. CSI Studies.

French Export Behaviour in Third World Markets. (Significant Issues Ser.: Vol. II, No. 6). 96p. 1980. pap. 7.50 (ISBN 0-89206-021-2, CSIS014, CSIS). Unipub.

French False Friends. C. W. E. Kirk-Greene. 272p. 1981. 18.95 (ISBN 0-7100-0741-8). Routledge & Kegan.

French Fiction Today: A New Direction. Leon S. Roudiez. LC 70-185392. 1972. 28.00 (ISBN 0-8135-0724-3). Rutgers U Pr.

French Finances, 1770-95: From Private Enterprise to Public Administration. J. F. Bosher. LC 73-111124. (Studies in Early Modern History). (Illus.). 1970. 46.50 (ISBN 0-521-07764-8). Cambridge U Pr.

French for Beginners. Charles Duff. 1955. pap. 3.95 (ISBN 0-06-463252-0, EH 252, EH). Har-Row.

French for Business Studies. Michelle Rover. 95p. (Fr.). 1979. pap. text ed. 4.50 (ISBN 0-582-35900-7). Longman.

French for Careers: Conversational Perspectives. Gallo & Sedwick. (Illus., Orig.). 1980. pap. text ed. 8.95 (ISBN 0-442-23883-5). D Van Nostrand.

French for English Idioms & Figurative Phrases. J. O. Kettridge. 1966. Repr. of 1940 ed. 16.00 (ISBN 0-7100-1669-7). Routledge & Kegan.

French for Reading: A Programmed Approach for Graduate Degree Requirements. Karl C. Sandberg & Eddison C. Tatham. 1972. text ed. 13.95 (ISBN 0-13-331603-3). P-H.

French Garden, Fifteen-Hundred-Eighteen-Hundred. William H. Adams. LC 78-24655. (Illus.). 1979. 19.95 (ISBN 0-8076-0918-8); pap. 9.95 (ISBN 0-8076-0919-6). Braziller.

French Grammar. 2nd ed. Francis M. Dumont. 1969. pap. 3.95 (ISBN 0-06-460035-1, CO 35, COS). Har-Row.

French Grand Opera: An Art & a Business. William L. Crosten. LC 73-171381. 132p. 1972. Repr. of 1948 ed. lib. bdg. 22.50 (ISBN 0-306-70405-6). Da Capo.

French Huguenots. Janet G. Gray. 200p. (Orig.). 1981. pap. 6.95 (ISBN 0-8010-3758-1). Baker Bk.

French Idioms & Figurative Phrases: With Many Quotations. J. O. Kettridge. 1970. Repr. of 1949 ed. 18.00 (ISBN 0-7100-1668-9). Routledge & Kegan.

French Idioms on the Way. Barbara Gerber & Gerald Storzer. (Illus.). Date not set. pap. 4.95 (ISBN 0-8120-2108-8). Barron. Postponed.

French Imperialism in the Middle East: The Failure of Policy in Syria & Lebanon, 1900-1914. William I. Shorrock. LC 75-32078. 264p. 1976. 25.00x (ISBN 0-299-07030-1). U of Wis Pr.

French Impressionists. Diane Kelder. LC 79-57411. (Abbeville Library of Art: No. 2). (Illus.). 112p. 1980. pap. 4.95 (ISBN 0-89659-093-3). Abbeville Pr.

French in Mexico & Texas, 1838-1839. Eugene Maissin. Tr. by J. L. Sheppherd. (Illus.). 1961. 35.00 (ISBN 0-685-05002-5). A Jones.

French Industrial Studies. Michael Rose. 148p. 1977. text ed. 20.50x (ISBN 0-566-00207-8, Pub. by Gower Pub Co England). Renouf.

French Influence on English Education. W. H. Armytage. (Students Library of Education). 1968. pap. text ed. 2.50x (ISBN 0-7100-4216-7). Humanities.

French Kiss. Peter Israel. 1977. pap. 1.75 (ISBN 0-380-01827-6, 36178). Avon.

French Landscape Drawings, & Sketches of the Eighteenth Century. Roseline Bacou et al. Date not set. 16.50 (ISBN 0-374-85311-8); pap. 7.50 (ISBN 0-374-86233-8). FS&G. Postponed.

French Language: History, Practice, & Stylistics. T. G. Combe & P. Rickard. 1970. 14.95x (ISBN 0-245-59995-9). Intl Ideas.

French Legation in Texas, 2 vols. Ed. by Nancy N. Barker. (Illus.). 1971-73. 12.00 ea. Vol. 1 (ISBN 0-87611-026-X). Vol. 2 (ISBN 0-87611-030-8). Tex St Hist Assn.

French Legislators 1800-1834: A Study in Quantitative History. Thomas Beck. 1975. 22.75x (ISBN 0-520-02535-0). U of Cal Pr.

French Level Three: Forty Classroom Tests. Maxim Newmark & Christopher Kendris. LC 58-47141. (High School Regents Exams & Answer Ser.). (gr. 9-12). 1977. pap. 3.50 (ISBN 0-8120-0198-2). Barron.

French Lieutenant: A Ghost Story. Richard Church. LC 71-147272. (gr. 6-8). 1972. 7.95 (ISBN 0-381-99853-3, A28920, JD-J). John Day.

French Life & Ideals. Albert Feuillerat. 1925. 34.50x (ISBN 0-685-89753-2). Elliots Bks.

French Literature: An Annotated Guide to Selected Bibliographies. Richard Kempton. LC 80-24230. (Selected Bibliographies in Language & Literature Ser.: No. 2). 56p. (Orig.). 1981. pap. 4.50x (ISBN 0-87352-951-0). Modern Lang.

French Literature: An Approach Through Close Reading. 4th ed. Wilbur M. Frohock. 1970. 5.50 (ISBN 0-87774-000-3). Schoenhof.

French Literature in the Twentieth Century. Christopher Robinson. (Comparative Literature Ser.). 288p. 1981. 15.00x (ISBN 0-389-20121-9). B&N.

French Lyric Poetry: An Anthology. Frank S. Giese & Warren F. Wilder. LC 64-7849. 1965. pap. 5.50 (ISBN 0-672-63038-9). Odyssey Pr.

French: MacCutcheon & Advance Lines. T. D. Harding. (Illus.). 130p. 1980. pap. 13.95 (ISBN 0-7134-2026-X, Pub. by Batsford England). David & Charles.

French Made Simple. Eugene Jackson & Antonio Rubio. LC 73-9033. pap. 3.50 (ISBN 0-385-08691-1, Made). Doubleday.

French Menu Cookbook. Richard Olney. LC 80-24423. (Illus.). 446p. Date not set. pap. 8.95 (ISBN 0-689-70607-3, 268). Atheneum. Postponed.

French Music Today. Claude Rostand. LC 73-4333. 146p. 1973. Repr. of 1955 ed. lib. bdg. 18.50 (ISBN 0-306-70578-8). Da Capo.

French Official Publications. Gloria Westfall. LC 80-40418. (Guides to Official Publications: Vol. 6). (Illus.). 223p. 1980. 35.00 (ISBN 0-08-021838-5). Pergamon.

French Once a Week Book, 2 bks. P. H. Hargreaves et al. 1976. pap. 5.25x ea. (Pub. by Basil Blackwell); Bk. 1, Repr. Of 1961 Ed. pap. (ISBN 0-631-97290-0); Bk. 2, Repr. Of 1962 Ed. pap. (ISBN 0-631-97300-1). Biblio Dist.

French Pacific Islands: French Polynesia & New Caledonia. Virginia Thompson & Richard Adloff. LC 71-138634. (Illus.). 1971. 32.50x (ISBN 0-520-01843-5). U of Cal Pr.

French Painting Between the Past & the Present: Artists, Critics, & Traditions from 1848 to 1870. Joseph C. Sloane. (Monographs in Art & Archaeology: No. 27). (Illus.). 300p. 1973. 27.50x (ISBN 0-691-03817-1); pap. 7.50 (ISBN 0-691-00306-8). Princeton U Pr.

French Painting from the Hermitage Museum. Anna Barskaya & Antonina Izerghina. (Illus.). 1977. 60.00 (ISBN 0-8109-0908-1). Abrams.

French Paintings of the Seventeenth & Eighteenth Centuries. rev. ed. Agnes Szigethi. Tr. by Elisabeth Hoch from Hungarian. Ed. by Bertha Gaster. (Illus.). 1977. 25.00 (ISBN 0-8283-1726-7). Branden.

French Passion. Diane Du Pont. 1977. pap. 1.95 o.p. (ISBN 0-449-13888-7, GM). Fawcett.

French Penal Code. (American Series of Foreign Penal Codes: Vol. 1). 1960. 15.00x (ISBN 0-8377-0021-3). Rothman.

French Pensions. Tony Lynes. 163p. 1967. pap. text ed. 5.00x (Pub. by Bedford England). Renouf.

French Perspectives in African Studies: A Collection of Translated Essays. Ed. by Pierre Alexandre. (International African Institute Ser.). 348p. 1973. 24.95 o.p. (ISBN 0-19-724191-3). Oxford U Pr.

French Phonetics. Eliane Burroughs. (gr. 8-12). 1972. pap. text ed. 10.00 (ISBN 0-8449-1601-3). Learning Line.

French Phonology. Foreign Service Institute. 394p. (Fr.). 1980. 60.00x (ISBN 0-88432-032-4, F250); 8 audiocassettes incl. J Norton Pubs.

French Physician, Jeannine D. Van Eperen, Eperen/jeannine D. Van. Jeannine D. Van Eperen. 128p. (Orig.). 1980. pap. 4.95 (ISBN 0-937268-00-3). Alpha Printing.

French Piano Music. Alfred Cortot. Tr. by Hilda Andrews from Fr. LC 77-4108. (Music Reprint, 1977 Ser.). 1977. Repr. of 1932 ed. 19.50 (ISBN 0-306-70896-5). Da Capo.

French Pilot, Vol.1. 224p. 1980. 30.00x (Pub. by Nautical England). State Mutual Bk.

French Pilot, Vol. 2. Malcom Robson. 256p. 1980. 33.00x (ISBN 0-245-53382-6, Pub. by Nautical England). State Mutual Bk.

French Poems in English Verse, Eighteen Fifty to Nineteen Seventy. Dorothy B. Aspinwall. LC 73-1782. 113p. 1973. lib. bdg. 10.00 (ISBN 0-8108-0599-5). Scarecrow.

French Poetry of the Renaissance. Ed. by Bernard Weinberg. LC 64-19796. (Arcturus Books Paperbacks). 260p. (Fr). 1964. pap. 6.95 (ISBN 0-8093-0135-0). S Ill U Pr.

French Political Pamphlets, Fifteen Forty-Seven to Sixteen Forty-Eight: A Catalog of Major Collections in American Libraries. Ed. by Robert O. Lindsay & John Neu. LC 78-84953. 1969. 35.00 (ISBN 0-299-04990-6). U of Wis Pr.

French Political System. Suzanne Berger. (Patterns of Government Ser.). 1974. pap. text ed. 4.95 (ISBN 0-394-31818-8). Random.

French Politicians & Elections, 1951-1968. Philip Williams. (Illus.). 1970. 41.50 (ISBN 0-521-07709-5); pap. 12.50x (ISBN 0-521-09608-1). Cambridge U Pr.

French Politics & Public Policy. Ed. by Philip Cerny & Martin Schain. 1980. write for info. (ISBN 0-312-30509-5). St Martin.

French Polity. William Safran. LC 76-58487. (Comparative Studies of Political Life Ser.). 1977. pap. 9.95x (ISBN 0-582-28102-4, Pub. by MacKay). Longman.

French Porcelain of the Eighteenth Century. 2nd ed. William B. Honey. 1972. 24.95 o.p. (ISBN 0-571-04741-6, Pub. by Faber & Faber). Merrimack Bk Serv.

French Press: Class, State, & Ideology. J. W. Freiberg. 255p 1981. 31.95 (ISBN 0-03-058309-8). Praeger.

French Pronunciation Illustrated. Lucien Guitard & Leon Marandet. text ed. 3.25x (ISBN 0-521-05156-8). Cambridge U Pr.

French Prophets: The History of a Millenarian Group in Eighteenth-Century England. Hillel Schwartz. (Illus.). 1980. 27.50x (ISBN 0-520-03815-0). U of Cal Pr.

French Prose Writers of the Fourteenth & Fifteenth Centuries. J. M. Ferrier. 1966. pap. 11.75 o.p. (ISBN 0-08-011301-X). Pergamon.

French Provincial Cookbook. Colette Black. (Orig.). 1967. pap. 0.95 o.s.i. (ISBN 0-02-009230-X, Collier). Macmillan.

French Provincial Cooking. rev. ed. Elizabeth David. LC 80-8369. (Illus.). 520p. 1981. 16.95 (ISBN 0-06-014827-6, HarpT). Har-Row.

French Provincial Police & the Fall of the Second Republic: Social Fear & Counterrevolution. Thomas R. Forstenzer. LC 80-8549. 384p. 1981. 25.00x (ISBN 0-691-05318-9). Princeton U Pr.

French Religious Wars in English Political Thought. John H. Salmon. LC 80-24621. vii, 202p. 1981. Repr. of 1959 ed. lib. bdg. 22.50x (ISBN 0-313-22221-5, SAFR). Greenwood.

French Renaissance Fountains. Naomi Miller. LC 76-23645. (Outstanding Dissertations in the Fine Arts - 16th Century). (Illus.). 1977. Repr. of 1966 ed. lib. bdg. 63.00 (ISBN 0-8240-2713-2). Garland Pub.

French Renaissance Scientific Poetry. Ed. by D. B. Wilson. (Renaissance Library). 1974. text ed. 18.75x (ISBN 0-485-13808-5, Athlone Pr); pap. text ed. 10.00x (ISBN 0-485-12808-X). Humanities.

French Review. pocket ed. 150p. (gr. 7-12). 1981. pap. text ed. 2.50 (ISBN 0-8120-2194-0). Barron. Postponed.

French Revolution. Paul H. Beik. LC 71-142852. (Documentary History of Western Civilization Ser). 1971. 15.00x o.s.i. (ISBN 0-8027-2036-6). Walker & Co.

French Revolution. Gerald P. Dartford. (gr. 9-12). 1972. pap. text ed. 3.25x (ISBN 0-88334-046-1). Ind Sch Pr.

French Revolution, 2 vols. Georges Lefebvre. Incl. From Its Origins to 1793. Tr. by Elizabeth M. Evans. Vol. 1. 20.00x (ISBN 0-231-02342-1); Vol. 1. pap. 6.00 (ISBN 0-231-08598-2); From 1793 to 1799. Tr. by John H. Stewart & James Friguglietti. Vol. 2. 20.00x (ISBN 0-231-02519-X); pap. 6.00 (ISBN 0-231-08599-0). LC 64-11939. 1962-64. Columbia U Pr.

French Revolution, 3 vols. Hippolyte A. Taine. 8.00 ea. (ISBN 0-8446-1435-1). Peter Smith.

French Revolution. Richard Tames. Ed. by Margaret Killingray et al. (Wolrd History Ser.). (Illus.). 32p. (gr. 10). 1980. Repr. lib. bdg. 5.95 (ISBN 0-89908-136-3); pap. text ed. 1.95 (ISBN 0-89908-111-8). Greenhaven.

French Revolution. 2nd ed. J. M. Thompson. (Illus.). 544p. 1980. pap. 10.95x (ISBN 0-631-11921-3, Pub. by Basil Blackwell). Biblio Dist.

French Revolution, Vol. 2. Thomas Carlyle. 1955. 6.00x o.p. (ISBN 0-460-00032-2, Evman). Dutton.

French Revolution: A Concise History. Norman Hampson. LC 74-33925. (Encore Edition). 1975. 12.50 o.p. (ISBN 0-684-14302-X, ScribT). Scribner.

French Revolution & the Psychology of Revolution. Gustave LeBon. (Social Science Classics Ser.). 337p. 1980. 19.95 (ISBN 0-87855-310-X); pap. 6.95 (ISBN 0-87855-697-4). Transaction Bks.

French Revolution of 1870-1871. Roger L. Williams. (Revolutions in the Modern World Ser.). 1969. pap. 5.95x (ISBN 0-393-09837-0, NortonC). Norton.

French Revolution Seen from the Right. p ed. Paul H. Beik. LC 70-80523. 1971. Repr. of 1956 ed. 13.75 (ISBN 0-86527-074-0). Fertig.

French Revolution: Their Gracious Pleasure, Vol. III. Claude Manceron. LC 80-36724. (Illus.). 480p. 1981. 19.95 (ISBN 0-394-50155-1). Knopf.

French Riviera Campaign of August Nineteen Forty-Four. Alan F. Wilt. LC 80-23041. 1981. price not set (ISBN 0-8093-1000-7). S Ill U Pr.

French Royalism Under the Third & Fourth Republics. Samuel Osgood. LC 79-2289. 1981. Repr. of 1961 ed. 19.00 (ISBN 0-88355-965-X). Hyperion Conn.

French Rural History: An Essay on Its Basic Characteristics. Marc Bloch. Tr. by Janet Sondheimer. (Illus.). 1966. 20.00x (ISBN 0-520-00127-3); pap. 6.95x (ISBN 0-520-01660-2, CAMPUS28). U of Cal Pr.

French Sculptors, Vol. 2. Francois Souchal. (Illus.). 464p. 1981. 200.00 (ISBN 0-85181-063-2, Pub. by Faber & Faber). Merrimack Bk Serv.

French Sculptors of the Seventeenth & Eighteenth Centuries: The Region of Louis XIV. Francois Souchal. (Reign of Louis XIV Catalogue Raisonne Ser.: Vol. 1, A-F). (Illus.). 1977. 165.00 (ISBN 0-85181-062-4, Pub. by Faber & Faber). Merrimack Bk Serv.

French Sculpture at the Beginning of the Gothic Period, 1140-1225. Marcel Aubert. LC 75-143337. (Illus.). 1972. Repr. of 1929 ed. 40.00 o.p. (ISBN 0-87817-057-X). Hacker.

French Sculpture of the Romanesque Period. Paul Deschamps. LC 78-143343. (Illus.). 1972. Repr. of 1930 ed. 40.00 o.p. (ISBN 0-87817-063-4). Hacker.

French Second Republic: A Social History. Roger Price. 1972. 32.00 (ISBN 0-7134-1117-1, Pub. by Batsford England). David & Charles.

French Six Bibliography: Critical & Biograpical References for the Study of Nineteenth Century French Literature, No. 1-7, 1954-1967. William T. Starr. (Orig.). 1945-69. Set. pap. 25.00x (ISBN 0-933444-00-1). French Inst.

French Society & the Revolution. D. Johnson. LC 76-1136. (Past and Present Publications Ser.). 300p. 1976. 26.95 (ISBN 0-521-21275-8). Cambridge U Pr.

French Sociology: Rupture & Renewal Since 1968. Ed. by Charles Lemert. 528p. 1981. 22.50x (ISBN 0-231-04698-7); pap. 10.00x (ISBN 0-231-04699-5). Columbia U Pr.

French Stage in the Nineteenth Century. Marvin Carlson. LC 72-3981. 1972. 11.50 (ISBN 0-8108-0516-2). Scarecrow.

French Symbolist Poetry: An Anthology. Tr. by John P. Houston & Mona T. Houston. LC 79-3381. 288p. 1980. 25.00x (ISBN 0-253-16725-6); pap. 10.95x (ISBN 0-253-20250-7). Ind U Pr.

French Theater Since 1930: Six Contemporary Full Length Plays. Ed. by Oreste F. Pucciani. 1954. 15.95x o.p. (ISBN 0-471-00449-9). Wiley.

French Theatre Since Eighteen Thirty. Harold Hobson. 1979. 17.95 (ISBN 0-7145-3650-4). Riverrun NY.

French: Three Thousand One Hundred Steps to Master Vocabulary. Ed. by William Jassey. LC 67-18801. (Prog. Bk.). 1969. pap. 2.95 (ISBN 0-668-01680-9). Arc Bks.

French Tragedy: The Power of Enchantment. Albert Cook. LC 80-39611. 136p. 1981. 12.00x (ISBN 0-8040-0548-6). Swallow.

French Twenty Bibliography: Critical & Bibliographical References for the Study of French Literature Since 1885, No. 32. Ed. by Douglas W. Alden. LC 77-648803. (Orig.). 1981. pap. 42.00 (ISBN 0-933444-37-0). French Inst.

French Twenty Bibliography: Provencal Upplement No. 1, Critical & Biographical References to Provencal Literature Since 1850. Ed. by J. D. Gauthier. (Orig.). 1976. pap. 12.00 (ISBN 0-933444-32-X). French Inst.

French Verse-Art. Clive Scott. LC 79-50508. 1980. 37.50 (ISBN 0-521-22689-9). Cambridge U Pr.

French Views of America in the 1930's. Donald R. Allen. Ed. by Frank Freidel. LC 78-62374. (Modern American History Ser.: Vol. 1). 1979. lib. bdg. 28.00 (ISBN 0-8240-3625-5). Garland Pub.

French Winawer: Modern & Auxiliary Lines. John Moles & Kevin Wicker. 1979. 25.50 (ISBN 0-7134-2037-5, Pub. by Batsford England). David & Charles.

French Windows. Walter Georis. 1981. 19.95 (ISBN 0-89396-029-2); pap. 9.95 (ISBN 0-89396-030-6). Urizen Bks.

French Workbook, Book 1. Eli Blume. (gr. 9 up). 1977. wkbk. 6.00 (ISBN 0-87720-993-6). AMSCO Sch.

French Workbook, Book 2. Eli Blume. (gr. 10-11). 1977. wkbk. 6.25 (ISBN 0-87720-994-4). AMSCO Sch.

French Writers of Today. Ed. by Henri Clouard & Robert Leggewie. (Illus.). 336p. (Fr.). 1965. pap. 7.95x (ISBN 0-19-500853-7). Oxford U Pr.

Frenchman's Creek. Daphne Du Maurier. LC 70-184730. 320p. 1971. Repr. lib. bdg. 12.50x (ISBN 0-8376-0412-5). Bentley.

Frenchman's Mistress. Irene Michaels. (Orig.). 1980. pap. 2.75 (ISBN 0-440-12545-6). Dell.

Frenchtown. John Rodabough. 200p. 1981. 19.95 (ISBN 0-86629-021-4). Sunrise MO.

Freneau's Published Prose: A Bibliography. Philip M. Marsh. (Author Bibliographies Ser.: No. 5). 1970. 10.00 (ISBN 0-8108-0289-9). Scarecrow.

Frenzy of Sweeney. Austin Clarke. (Dolmen Editions Ser.: No. XXIX). 1980. text ed. 26.00x (ISBN 0-85105-349-1, Dolmen Pr). Humanities.

Frequency Conversion. J. Thomson et al. (Wykeham Technology Ser.: No. 1). 1969. 9.95x (ISBN 0-8448-1172-6). Crane Russak Co.

Frequency: Response Methods in Control Systems. Ed. by A. G. MacFarlane. LC 79-90572. 1979. 39.95 (ISBN 0-87942-125-8). Inst Electrical.

Frequency Response Methods in Control Systems. Alistair G. Macfarlane. 1979. 39.95 (ISBN 0-471-06486-6, Pub. by Wiley-Interscience); pap. 25.95 (ISBN 0-471-06426-2). Wiley.

Frequency Synthesis by Phase-Lock. William F. Egan. LC 80-16917. 304p. 1980. text ed. 20.00 (ISBN 0-471-08202-3, Pub. by Wiley-Interscience). Wiley.

Frequency Synthesizers: Theory & Design. 2nd ed. Vadim Manassewitsch. LC 80-13345. 544p. 1980. 36.00 (ISBN 0-471-07917-0, Pub. by Wiley Interscience). Wiley.

Frescoes in Siena's Palazzo Pubblico, Twelve Eighty-Nine to Fifteen Thirty-Nine: Studies in Imagery & Relations to Other Communal Palaces in Tuscany. Edna C. Southard. LC 78-74381. (Fine Arts Dissertations, Fourth Ser.). (Illus.). 1980. lib. bdg. 66.00 (ISBN 0-8240-3967-X). Garland Pub.

Frescoes of the Skull: The Later Prose & Drama of Samuel Beckett. James Knowlson & John Pilling. LC 79-6153. 320p. (Orig.). 1980. pap. 4.95 postponed (ISBN 0-394-17610-3, E735, Ever). Grove.

Fresh & Salt Water. B. Bartram Cadbury. LC 60-6114. (Community of Living Things Ser). (Illus.). (gr. 4-8). 1967. PLB 7.45 (ISBN 0-87191-017-9). Creative Ed.

Fresh, Canned, & Frozen: Food from Past to Future. William Wise. LC 74-145599. (Finding-Out Books for Science & Social Studies, Grades 1-4). (Illus.). (gr. 2-4). 1971. PLB 6.95 (ISBN 0-8193-0482-4, Pub. by Parents). Enslow Pubs.

Fresh Cider & Pie. Franz Brandenberg. LC 73-585. (Illus.). 32p. (gr. k-3). 1973. 4.95g o.s.i. (ISBN 0-02-711910-6). Macmillan.

Fresh English. 3rd ed. Robert A. McQuitty & James P. Walker. 384p. 1980. pap. text ed. 17.95 (ISBN 0-8403-2244-5). Kendall-Hunt.

Fresh Fruit & Vegetable Book: A Complete Guide to Enjoying Fresh Fruits & Vegetables. Celebrity Kitchen & United Fresh Fruit & Vegetable Association. LC 80-8390. (Illus.). 320p. 1981. pap. 3.95 (ISBN 0-06-463527-9, EH 527). Har-Row.

Fresh Hope in Cancer. Maurice Finkel. 128p. 1981. pap. 6.95 (ISBN 0-914794-41-8). Wisdom Garden.

Fresh-Water Fisherman's Bible. rev. ed. Vlad Evanoff. LC 79-7684. (Outdoor Bible Ser.). (Illus.). 1980. pap. 3.95 (ISBN 0-385-14405-9). Doubleday.

Fresh Water Fishing. Zane Grey. 298p. Repr. lib. bdg. 12.75x (ISBN 0-89190-762-9). Am Repr-Rivercity Pr.

Fresh Water Fishing. Ed Moore. (Illus., Orig.). 1965. pap. 0.95 o.s.i. (ISBN 0-02-029320-8, Collier). Macmillan.

Fresh-Water Invertebrates of the United States. 2nd ed. Robert W. Pennak. LC 78-8130. 1978. 32.50 (ISBN 0-471-04249-8, Pub. by Wiley-Interscience). Wiley.

Fresh Wind of the Spirit. Kenneth C. Kinghorn. LC 74-7415. 128p. 1975. pap. 4.95 (ISBN 0-687-13495-1). Abingdon.

Freshman Calculus. 2nd ed. Robert Bonic et al. 1976. text ed. 21.95x (ISBN 0-669-96727-0); wkbk. 7.95x (ISBN 0-669-97774-8). Heath.

Freshman Chemical Engineering. Michael E. Leesley. 1979. 15.95 (ISBN 0-87201-106-2). Gulf Pub.

Freshman Seminar: A New Orientation. Robert D. Cohen & Ruth Jody. LC 77-1682. (Westview Special Studies in Higher Education Ser.). 1978. PLB 20.00x (ISBN 0-89158-098-0); pap. text ed. 9.75x (ISBN 0-89158-099-9). Westview.

Freshman Writer. Michele F. Cooper. (Illus.). 208p. (Orig.). 1972. pap. 2.95 (ISBN 0-06-460136-6, CO 136, COS). Har-Row.

Freshman Writes. Ed. by Roger M. Swanson. LC 70-179365. 1973. pap. 9.60 o.p. (ISBN 0-672-63039-7). Odyssey Pr.

Freshwater Ecology. 2nd ed. T. T. Macan. LC 73-14419. 1974. pap. 13.95 o.p. (ISBN 0-470-56149-1). Halsted Pr.

Freshwater Fish in New Zealand. R. M. McDowall. (Mobil New Zealand Nature Ser.). (Illus.). 80p. (Orig.). 1980. pap. 6.95 (ISBN 0-589-01327-0, Pub. by Reed Bks Australia). C E Tuttle.

Freshwater Fishes, Bk. 1. Herbert R. Axelrod. (Illus.). 320p. 1974. 20.00 (ISBN 0-87666-076-6, PS-713). TFH Pubns.

Freshwater Fishes of Alaska. James E. Morrow. LC 80-1116. (Illus.). 272p. (Orig.). 1980. pap. 24.95 (ISBN 0-88240-134-3). Alaska Northwest.

Freshwater Fishes of New York State: A Field Guide. Robert G. Werner. (Illus.). 270p. 1980. 20.00s (ISBN 0-8156-2233-3); pap. 11.95 (ISBN 0-8156-2222-8). Syracuse U Pr.

Freshwater Fishing. Ray Ovington. 1977. pap. 3.95 (ISBN 0-8015-2837-2, Hawthorn). Dutton.

Freshwater Life in Ireland. Cedric S. Woods. 1974. 7.00x (ISBN 0-7165-2280-2, Pub. by Irish Academic Pr Ireland); pap. 2.50x (ISBN 0-7165-2281-0). Biblio Dist.

Freshwater Molluscs of Canada. Arthur H. Clarke. (Illus.). 416p. 1981. lib. bdg. 39.95x (ISBN 0-660-00022-9, 56350-2, Pub. by Natl Mus Canada). U of Chicago Pr.

Freshwater Snails of Africa & Their Medical Importance. David S. Brown. (Illus.). 450p. 1980. 55.00 (ISBN 0-85066-145-5). Am Malacologists.

Freshwater Wetlands: A Guide to Common Indicator Plants of the Northeast. Dennis W. Magee. LC 80-26876. (Illus.). 240p. 1981. lib. bdg. 17.50x (ISBN 0-87023-316-5); pap. text ed. 7.95x (ISBN 0-87023-317-3). U of Mass Pr.

Fresno California Illustrated. Fresno City & County Historical Society. LC 80-68522. (Illus.). 192p. 1980. Repr. 13.95 (ISBN 0-914330-35-7). Pioneer Pub Co.

Fretting Corrosion. R. B. Waterhouse. 1973. text ed. 37.00 (ISBN 0-08-016902-3). Pergamon.

Freud: A Collection of Critical Essays. Perry Meisel. (Twentieth Century Views Ser.). 256p. 1981. 13.95 (ISBN 0-13-331405-7, Spec); pap. 5.95 (ISBN 0-13-331397-2). P-H.

Freud-A Man of His Century. Gunnar Brandell. Tr. by Iain White. LC 78-5347. 1979. text ed. 18.25x (ISBN 0-391-00871-4). Humanities.

Freud & Dewey on the Nature of Man. Morton Levitt. 1960. 3.75 (ISBN 0-8022-0966-1). Philos Lib.

Freud & Modern Psychology: The/Emotional Basis of Mental Illness, Vol. 1. Helen B. Lewis. (Emotions Personality & Psychotherapy Ser.). 240p. 1981. 19.50 (ISBN 0-306-40525-3, Plenum Pr). Plenum Pub.

Freud & Philosophy: An Essay on Interpretation. Paul Ricoeur. Tr. by Denis Savage. LC 70-89907. (Terry Lectures Ser). 1970. 30.00x (ISBN 0-300-01165-2); pap. 9.95 (ISBN 0-300-02189-5). Yale U Pr.

Freud & the Dilemmas of Psychology. Marie Jahoda. LC 80-17140. vi, 186p. 1981. pap. 4.50x (ISBN 0-8032-7553-6, BB 759, Bison). U of Nebr Pr.

Freud & the Kingmaker: The Visit to America - The Letters of Sigmund Freud & G. S. Hall, 1908 to 1923 & Freud's Five Lectures at Clark University. Saul Rosenzweig. LC 78-65156. 1981. 13.50 (ISBN 0-930172-03-5). Rana Hse.

Freud As Student of Religion: Perspectives on the Background & Development of His Thought. Reuben M. Rainey. LC 75-17536. (American Academy of Religion. Dissertation Ser.: No. 7). 1975. pap. 7.50 (ISBN 0-89130-012-0, 010107). Scholars Pr Ca.

Freud, Biologist of the Mind: Beyond the Psychoanalytic Legend. Frank J. Sulloway. 20.00 (ISBN 0-686-68084-7). Basic.

Freud: Dictionary of Psychoanalysis. Ed. by Frank Gaynor & Nandor Fodor. 1976. pap. 1.25 o.p. (ISBN 0-449-30725-5, P725, Prem). Fawcett.

Freud, Jews & Other Germans: Masters & Victims in Modernist Culture. Peter Gay. 1978. 15.95x (ISBN 0-19-502258-0). Oxford U Pr.

Freud, Marx & Morals. Hugh Meynell. 1981. 23.00x (ISBN 0-389-20045-X). B&N.

Freud on Broadway. W. David Sievers. LC 76-141891. 1971. Repr. of 1955 ed. lib. bdg. 17.50x (ISBN 0-8154-0366-6). Cooper Sq.

Freud on Ritual: Reconstruction & Critique. Volney P. Gay. LC 79-11385. (American Academy of Religion, Dissertation Ser.: No. 26). 1979. 12.00 (ISBN 0-89130-282-4, 010126); pap. 7.50 (ISBN 0-89130-301-4). Scholars Pr Ca.

Freud: The Psychoanalytic Adventure. Robert Ariel. LC 77-29220. 1978. pap. 10.00 o.p. (ISBN 0-03-021696-6). HR&W.

Freudian Paradigm: Psychoanalysis & Scientific Thought. Ed. by Mohammed Mujeeb-Ur Rahman. LC 73-89486. 1977. 23.95 (ISBN 0-911012-89-3); pap. 11.95 (ISBN 0-88229-461-X). Nelson-Hall.

Freudian Theory & American Religious Journals: Nineteen Hundred to Nineteen Sixty-Five. Ann E. Rosenberg. Ed. by Robert Berkhofer. (Studies in American History & Culture, III). 255p. 1980. 26.95 (ISBN 0-8357-1099-8, Pub. by UMI Res Pr). Univ Microfilms.

Freud's Incredible Conception of the Contemporary Female. Edward M. Chamberlain. (Illus.). 1979. deluxe ed. 47.45 (ISBN 0-930582-38-1). Gloucester Art.

Freud's Unfinished Journey. Louis Breger. 220p. write for info. (ISBN 0-7100-0613-6). Routledge & Kegan.

Freund & Williams' Modern Business Statistics. rev. ed. B. Perles & C. Sullivan. 1969. text ed. 17.95 (ISBN 0-13-589580-4); lab. manual & wkbk. 6.95 (ISBN 0-13-589598-7). P-H.

Freydis & Gudrid. Elizabeth Boyer. 1978. pap. 1.95 o.p. (ISBN 0-445-04278-8). Popular Lib.

Friar Bacon & Friar Bungay. Robert Greene. Ed. by Daniel Seltzer. LC 63-14697. (Regents Renaissance Drama Ser). 1963. 6.95x (ISBN 0-8032-0263-6); pap. 1.85x (ISBN 0-8032-5262-5, BB 200, Bison). U of Nebr Pr.

Friar Thomas B Aquino: His Life, Thought & Works. Weisheipl, James A., O.P. LC 73-80801. 480p. 1974. 10.00 o.p. (ISBN 0-385-01299-3). Doubleday.

Fric-Frac. Albert Spaggiari. 288p. 1981. pap. 2.50 (ISBN 0-445-04592-2). Popular Lib.

Friction. Edward Victor. (Illus.). (gr. 2-4). 1961. 2.50 o.p. (ISBN 0-695-83205-0); lib. ed. 2.97 o.p. (ISBN 0-695-43205-2). Follett.

Friction & Lubrication of Elastomers. D. F. Moore. 305p. 1972. text ed. 42.00 (ISBN 0-08-016749-7); pap. text ed. 24.00 (ISBN 0-08-019002-2). Pergamon.

Friction & Lubrication of Solids, 2 Vols. Frank P. Bowden & D. Tabor. (International Ser. of Monographs on Physics). Vol. 1. 36.00x o.p. (ISBN 0-19-851204-X). Oxford U Pr.

Friction & Wear: A Trilogy Text for Students. B. Pugh. 19.95 (ISBN 0-408-00097-X); pap. 6.95 (ISBN 0-408-00098-8). Butterworths.

Friction & Wear: Calculation Methods. I. V. Kragelsky et al. LC 80-41669. (Illus.). 450p. 1981. 75.00 (ISBN 0-08-025461-6); pap. 60.00 (ISBN 0-08-027320-3). Pergamon.

Friction & Wear in Polymer-Based Materials. V. A. Bely et al. LC 80-41825. (Illus.). 400p. 1981. 85.00 (ISBN 0-08-025444-6). Pergamon.

Friday Run. James Wood. LC 76-141319. 1969. 6.95 (ISBN 0-8149-0672-9). Vanguard.

Friday's Feast. Don Pendleton. (Executioner Ser.: No. 37). (Orig.). 1979. pap. 1.95 (ISBN 0-523-41101-4). Pinnacle Bks.

Friedberg's: Diseases of the Heart. 4th ed. Ed. by Leon Resnekov & Desmond Julian. (Illus.). 1981. write for info. (ISBN 0-443-08003-8). Churchill.

Friedrich. Hans P. Richter. Tr. by Edite Kroll. LC 78-119098. (gr. 5-8). 1970. reinforced bdg. 5.95 o.p. (ISBN 0-03-012721-1). HR&W.

Friedrich Durrenmatt. Armin Arnold. LC 78-178169. (Modern Literature Ser.). 128p. 1972. 10.95 (ISBN 0-8044-2000-9). Ungar.

Friedrich Durrenmatt. Murray B. Peppard. (World Authors Ser.: Germany: No. 87). lib. bdg. 10.95 (ISBN 0-8057-2284-X). Twayne.

Friedrich Engels: A Biography. Gustav Mayer. LC 68-9596. 1969. Repr. of 1936 ed. 22.00 (ISBN 0-86527-075-9). Fertig.

Friedrich Froebel. Robert B. Downs. (World Leaders Ser.: No. 74). 1978. lib. bdg. 10.95 (ISBN 0-8057-7668-0). Twayne.

Friedrich Gerstacker: Wild Sports in the Far West. Ed. by Edna Steeves & Harrison Steeves. LC 68-16624. 1968. 14.75 (ISBN 0-8223-0167-9). Duke.

Friedrich Meinecke & German Politics in the Twentieth Century. Robert A. Pois. LC 70-157818. 192p. 1972. 20.00x (ISBN 0-520-02045-6). U of Cal Pr.

Friedrich Nietzche & the Politics of Transfiguration. Tracy B. Strong. LC 74-81442. 380p. 1976. 23.75x (ISBN 0-520-02810-4). U of Cal Pr.

Friedrich Schiller. Charles E. Passage. LC 74-76129. (World Dramatists Ser). (Illus.). 180p. 1975. 10.95 (ISBN 0-8044-2734-8). Ungar.

Friedrich Schiller--Medicine, Psychology, & Literature: With the First English Edition of His Complete Medical & Psychological Writings. Kenneth Dewhurst & Nigel Reeves. 1978. 29.50x (ISBN 0-520-03250-0). U of Cal Pr.

Friedrich Schleiermacher. Stephen Sykes. LC 75-158145. (Makers of Contemporary Theology Ser). (Orig.). 1971. pap. 3.45 (ISBN 0-8042-0556-6). John Knox.

Friedrich Von Holstein: Politics & Diplomacy in the Era of Bismarck & Wilhelm. Norman Rich. 1965. 130.00 (ISBN 0-521-06077-X). Cambridge U Pr.

Friend. John Burningham. LC 76-16436. (Illus.). (ps-1). 1976. 2.50 (ISBN 0-690-01273-X, TYC-J); PLB 4.89 (ISBN 0-690-01274-8). T Y Crowell.

Friend & Foe: Aspects of French-American Cultural Contact in the Sixteenth & Seventeenth Centuries. Cornelius J. Jaenen. (Illus.). 1976. 15.00x (ISBN 0-231-04088-1). Columbia U Pr.

Friend & Lover: Poems. John Ditsky. LC 80-84832. (Ontario Review Press Poetry Ser.). 80p. 1981. 9.95 (ISBN 0-86538-011-2); pap. 4.95 (ISBN 0-86538-012-0). Ontario Rev NJ.

Friend at Court. 45p. 1980. pap. text ed. 2.00 (ISBN 0-938822-00-4). USTA.

Friend Can Help. Terry Berger. LC 75-19325. (Moods & Emotions Ser.). (Illus.). 32p. (gr. k-3). 1975. Repr. of 1974 ed. PLB 8.95 (ISBN 0-8172-0051-7). Raintree Pubs.

Friend Monkey. Pamela L. Travers. LC 70-161389. (gr. k-3). 1971. 6.95 o.p. (ISBN 0-15-229555-0, HJ). HarBraceJ.

Friend of China. Joyce Milton. (Books for Young Readers Ser.). (Illus.). 128p. (gr. 7 up). 1980. PLB 8.95 (ISBN 0-8038-2388-6). Hastings.

Friend of Kafka & Other Stories. Isaac B. Singer. LC 70-115752. 311p. 1970. 12.95 (ISBN 0-374-15880-0); pap. 5.95 (ISBN 0-374-51538-7). FS&G.

Friend: The Story of George Fox & the Quakers. Jane Yolen. LC 74-171865. 192p. (gr. 7 up). 1972. 6.95 (ISBN 0-395-28932-7, Clarion). HM.

Friendly Bear. Robert Bright. 1971. Repr. of 1957 ed. Softbound 1.49 o.p. (ISBN 0-385-04470-4). Doubleday.

Friendly Book. Margaret W. Brown. (ps-1). 1954. PLB 5.00 (ISBN 0-307-60592-2, Golden Pr). Western Pub.

Friendly Correspondence: Mazes to the Mind. Teresa M. Gomes. Ed. by Marlene Kamei. 35p. (Orig.). 1978. pap. 2.00 (ISBN 0-935684-01-8). Plumbers Ink.

Friendly Dolphins. Patricia Lauber. (Gateway Ser.: No. 28). (Illus.). (gr. 3-6). 1963. 3.95 (ISBN 0-394-80128-8, BYR); PLB 5.99 (ISBN 0-394-90128-2). Random.

Friendly Fairways of Michigan. Glenda Cross. LC 78-54174. (Orig.). 1978. 4.95 (ISBN 0-686-12255-0). Friendly Fairways.

Friendly Intruders: Childcare Professionals & Family Life. Carole E. Joffe. 1977. 14.95x (ISBN 0-520-02925-9); pap. 3.95 (ISBN 0-520-03934-3). U of Cal Pr.

Friendly Philosopher. Robert Crosbie. (Illus.). vii, 415p. 1934. Repr. 6.00 (ISBN 0-938998-13-7). Theosophy.

Friendly Snowman. Sharon Gordon. (Illus.). 32p. (gr. k-2). 1980. PLB 2.96 (ISBN 0-89375-377-7); pap. 0.95 (ISBN 0-89375-277-0). Troll Assocs.

Friendly Vermin: A Survey of Feral Livestock in Australia. Tom L. McKnight. (Publ. in Geography Ser.: Vol. 21). 1977. pap. 9.00x (ISBN 0-520-09558-8). U of Cal Pr.

Friendly Wolf. Paul Goble & Dorothy Goble. LC 74-77664. (Illus.). 32p. (gr. 1-3). 1975. 9.95 (ISBN 0-87888-104-2). Bradbury Pr.

Friends. Terry Berger. (Illus.). 64p. (gr. 3-5). 1981. PLB 6.97 (ISBN 0-686-69300-0). Messner.

Friends. T. Degens. 160p. (gr. 7 up). 1981. 9.95 (ISBN 0-670-33051-5). Viking Pr.

Friends. Judy Dunn. LC 77-125914. (Illus.). (gr. k-3). 1970. PLB 6.75 (ISBN 0-87191-046-2). Creative Ed.

Friends. Satomi Ichikawa. LC 76-46146. (Illus.). (ps-2). 1977. 5.95 o.s.i. (ISBN 0-8193-0870-6, Four Winds); PLB 5.41 o.s.i. (ISBN 0-8193-0871-4). Schol Bk Serv.

Friends. Elieba Levine. 288p. (Orig.). 1980. pap. 2.25 (ISBN 0-89083-645-0). Zebra.

Friends. Helen Oxenbury. (Baby Board Bks.). (Illus.). 12p. (ps). Date not set. boards 3.50 (ISBN 0-671-42111-5, Little Simon). S&S.

Friends. April Smith. (gr. 7-12). 1980. pap. 1.50 (ISBN 0-440-92666-1, LFL). Dell.

Friends. Sandy Ziegler. Ed. by Jane Buerger. 1980. 5.95 (ISBN 0-89565-174-2, 4931). Standard Pub.

Friends & Betrayers. Carl Johnes. (Orig.). Date not set. pap. 2.50 (ISBN 0-440-12570-7). Dell.

Friends & Friends of Friends. Bernard Wolff. (Illus.). 1978. pap. 8.95 o.p. (ISBN 0-525-47519-2). Dutton.

Friends at Knoll House. Joan Mellows. (A Fawcett Regency Novel Ser.). 224p. 1976. pap. 1.25 o.p. (ISBN 0-449-22530-5, P2530, Crest). Fawcett.

Friends, Followers & Factions: A Reader in Political Clientelism. Steffen W. Schmidt et al. 1977. 32.50x (ISBN 0-520-02696-9); pap. 9.95x (ISBN 0-520-03156-3). U of Cal Pr.

Friends, Guests & Colleagues: The Mufu System of the Late Ch'ing Period. Kenneth E. Folsom. 1968. 18.50x (ISBN 0-520-00425-6). U of Cal Pr.

Friends in Palestine. Christina Jones. 1981. write for info. (ISBN 0-913408-62-X). Friends United.

Friends of ABU ALI: Three More Tales of the Middle East. Dorothy O. Van Woerkom. LC 77-12624. (Ready-to-Read Ser.). (Illus.). (gr. 1-4). 1978. 8.95 (ISBN 0-02-791320-1, 79132). Macmillan.

Friends of Charlie Ant Bear. Malcolm Hall. (Break-of-Day Bk.). (Illus.). 64p. (gr. 3-5). 1980. PLB 6.59 (ISBN 0-698-30711-9). Coward.

Friends of Eddie Coyle. George V. Higgins. 176p. 1981. pap. 2.50 (ISBN 0-345-28635-9). Ballantine.

Friends of Richard Nixon. George V. Higgins. 1976. pap. 1.95 o.p. (ISBN 0-345-25226-8). Ballantine.

Friends or Acquaintances? Canada & Japan's Other Trading Partners in the Early 1980's. K. A. Hay. 52p. 1978. pap. text ed. 3.00x (ISBN 0-920380-15-8, Pub. by Inst Res Pub Canada). Renouf.

Friends till the End: A Novel. Todd Strasser. LC 80-68738. 192p. (YA) (gr. 8-12). 1981. 8.95 (ISBN 0-440-02750-0). Delacorte.

Friends to Find. Walt Disney Productions. (Winnie-the-Pooh Hunny Pot Bks.). 24p. (ps-3). 1980. PLB 5.38 (ISBN 0-307-68874-7, Golden Pr). Western Pub.

Friends with God. Catherine Marshall. (gr. 2-4). 1972. pap. 1.25 (ISBN 0-380-01199-9, 33647). Avon.

Friendship, Altruism & Morality. Lawrence Blum. (International Library of Philosophy). 256p. 1980. 20.00 (ISBN 0-7100-0582-2). Routledge & Kegan.

Friendship & Other Poems. Marguerite De Angeli. LC 79-6857. (Illus.). 48p. 1981. 5.95a (ISBN 0-385-15854-8); PLB (ISBN 0-385-15855-6). Doubleday.

Friendship & Social Relations in Children. Hugh C. Foot et al. LC 79-40637. 1980. 51.25 (ISBN 0-471-27628-6, Pub. by Wiley-Interscience). Wiley.

Friendship Game. Andrew M. Greeley. LC 79-117979. 1971. pap. 1.95 (ISBN 0-385-04230-2, Im). Doubleday.

Friendship Hedge. Gunilla B. Norris. (Illus.). 48p. (gr. 2-4). 1973. PLB 6.95 o.p. (ISBN 0-525-30210-7). Dutton.

Friendship in Death: In Twenty Letters from the Dead to the Living. Elizabeth S. Rowe. LC 70-170576. (Foundations of the Novel Ser.: Vol. 53). lib. bdg. 50.00 (ISBN 0-8240-0565-1). Garland Pub.

Friendstone. Martha Derman. 160p. (gr. 4-7). 1981. 8.95 (ISBN 0-8037-2472-1); PLB 8.44 (ISBN 0-8037-2480-2). Dial.

Frigates. M. Gruppe. (Seafarers Ser.). (Illus.). 1979. lib. bdg. 11.97 (ISBN 0-8094-2716-8); kivar bdg. 9.96 (ISBN 0-8094-2717-6). Silver.

Frightened Forest. Ann Turnbull. LC 74-19358. (gr. 3-6). 1975. 7.95 (ISBN 0-395-28884-3, Clarion). HM.

Frightened Gun, No. Thirty Two. George G. Gilman. (Edge Ser.). (Orig.). 1979. pap. 1.75 (ISBN 0-523-41314-9). Pinnacle Bks.

Frigidity: Its Cure with Hypnosis. Gilbert S. MacVaugh. LC 78-26958. 1979. 44.00 (ISBN 0-08-021748-6). Pergamon.

Fringe Benefits: A Proposal for the Future. 1979. pap. 9.50. Am Inst CPA.

Fringe of Leaves. Patrick White. 1977. pap. 1.95 (ISBN 0-380-01826-8, 36160). Avon.

Frisbee Disc Basics. D. Roddick. 1980. 8.95 (ISBN 0-13-331322-0). P-H.

Frisbee Fun. Margaret Poynter. (Illus.). (gr. 3-6). 1978. pap. 1.25 (ISBN 0-671-29885-2). PB.

Frisbee Players' Handbook. 3rd ed. Dan Poynter & Mark Danna. LC 77-79101. (Illus.). 1980. pap. text ed. 6.95 (ISBN 0-915516-20-9); pap. 9.95 with disc (ISBN 0-915516-15-2); pap. 6.95 without disc (ISBN 0-915516-19-5). Para Pub.

Frisco Epic. Gerald Locklin. 1980. 1.50 (ISBN 0-917554-07-8). Maelstrom.

Frisian. Thomas L. Markey. (Contributions to the Sociology of Language Ser.: No. 30). 1979. text ed. 40.00x (ISBN 90-279-3128-3). Mouton.

Fritz. Martin Shepard. LC 80-50243. 256p. 1981. Repr. of 1975 ed. 7.95 (ISBN 0-933256-15-9). Second Chance.

Fritz. Martin Shepard. LC 80-50243. 256p. 1980. 15.95 (ISBN 0-933256-14-0); pap. 7.95 (ISBN 0-933256-15-9). Second Chance.

Fritz & the Beautiful Horses. Jan Brett. (gr. k-3). 1981. pap. 8.95 (ISBN 0-395-30850-X). HM.

Fritz Lang. Robert Armour. (Theatrical Art Ser.). 1978. 12.50 (ISBN 0-8057-9259-7). Twayne.

Fritz Leiber. Jeff Frane. (Starmont Reader's Guide Ser.: No. 8). 64p. 1980. lib. bdg. 9.95 (ISBN 0-89370-039-8). Borgo Pr.

Fritz: The World War I Memoirs of a German Lieutenant. Fritz Nagel. Ed. by Richard A. Baumgartner. (Illus.). 160p. (Orig.). 1980. pap. 6.95 (ISBN 0-9604770-0-4). Der Angriff.

Fritzie Goes Home. Kate Pogue. (Young Reader Ser.). (Illus.). (gr. k-3). 1979. PLB 5.00 (ISBN 0-307-60301-6, Golden Pr). Western Pub.

Frog. Paula Z. Hogan. LC 78-21240. (Life Cycles Ser.). (Illus.). (gr. k-3). 1979. PLB 9.95 (ISBN 0-8172-1253-1). Raintree Pubs.

Frog. Angela Sheehan. (First Look at Nature Books). (Illus.). (gr. 2-4). 1977. 2.50 (ISBN 0-531-09080-9); pap. 6.45 s&l (ISBN 0-531-09055-8). Watts.

Frog & Toad Coloring Book. Arnold Lobel. (Illus.). 32p. (ps-3). 1981. pap. 1.95 (ISBN 0-06-023978-6, HarpJ). Har-Row.

Frog Band & Durrington. Jim Smith. (Frog Band Ser.). (Illus.). 32p. (gr. 1-3). 1980. pap. 3.95g (ISBN 0-316-80159-3). Little.

Frog Band & the Owlnapper. Jim Smith. (Illus.). 32p. (ps-3). 1981. 8.95 (ISBN 0-316-80163-1). Little.

Frog Book. Mary C. Dickerson. (Illus.). 1969. pap. 6.50 (ISBN 0-486-21973-9). Dover.

Frog Book. Ed. by Richard Shaw. LC 72-83128. (Animal Art Anthology Ser). (Illus.). 48p. (gr. 1 up). 1972. PLB 4.95 o.p. (ISBN 0-7232-6083-4). Warne.

Frog-Eating Electric Light Bug. Lester Harris. LC 78-3762. 1978. pap. 4.50 (ISBN 0-8127-0146-1). Southern Pub.

Frog Is Born. William White, Jr. LC 72-81037. (Nature Ser.). (Illus.). 96p. (gr. 5 up). 1972. 6.95 o.p. (ISBN 0-8069-3522-7); PLB 6.69 o.p. (ISBN 0-8069-3523-5). Sterling.

Frog Prints. B. L. Harwick. LC 76-13840. (Read to Myself Ser.). 48p. (gr. k-2). 1976. PLB 7.75 (ISBN 0-8172-0152-1). Raintree Pubs.

Frog Rider: Folk Tales from China. 1980. pap. 1.95 (ISBN 0-8351-0764-7). China Bks.

Frog Salad. Sally George. 256p. 1981. 9.95 (ISBN 0-684-16766-2, ScribT). Scribner.

Frogs. Aristophanes. Tr. by Gilbert Murray. 1908. pap. text ed. 3.95x (ISBN 0-04-882021-0). Allen Unwin.

Frogs. Gerald Donaldson. 127p. 1980. 14.95 (ISBN 0-442-22650-0). Van Nos Reinhold.

Frogs. Linda Sonntag. (Leprechaun Library). (Illus.). 64p. 1981. 3.95 (ISBN 0-399-12611-2). Putnam.

Frogs & Other Plays. Aristophanes. Tr. by David Barrett. Incl. Wasps; Poet & the Women. (Classics Ser.). (Orig.). 1964. pap. 2.50 (ISBN 0-14-044152-2). Penguin.

Frogs & Polliwogs. Dorothy C. Hogner. LC 56-7795. (Illus.). (gr. 2-5). 1956. 6.95 o.p. (ISBN 0-690-31769-7, TYC-J). T Y Crowell.

Frogs & Toads. Jane Dallinger. (Lerner Natural Science Bks.). (Illus.). (gr. 4-10). 1981. PLB 7.95 (ISBN 0-8225-1454-0). Lerner Pubns.

Frogs & Toads. Edward Turner & Clive Turner. Ed. by Barbara Brenner. LC 76-13653. (Young Naturalist Ser.). (Illus.). 80p. (gr. 3-7). 1976. PLB 8.25 (ISBN 0-8172-0331-1). Raintree Pubs.

Frogs & Toads. Herbert S. Zim. (Illus.). (gr. 3-7). 1950. PLB 6.48 (ISBN 0-688-31316-7). Morrow.

Frogs in the Aquarium. new ed. Werner Von Filek. Orig. Title: Frosche im Aquarium. (Illus.). 96p. (Orig.). 1973. pap. 5.95 (ISBN 0-87666-191-6, PS690). TFH Pubns.

Frogs, Toads, Salamanders & How They Reproduce. Dorothy H. Patent. LC 74-26567. (Illus.). 144p. (gr. 4-7). 1975. 8.95 (ISBN 0-8234-0255-X). Holiday.

Frogs Who Wanted a King & Other Songs from La Fontaine. Compiled by Edward Smith. LC 77-5819. (Illus.). 64p. (gr. 1 up). 1977. 11.95 (ISBN 0-590-17294-8, Four Winds). Schol Bk Serv.

From a Bare Hull. Ferenc Mate. (Illus.). 1978. 19.95 o.p. (ISBN 0-920256-00-7, ScribT). Scribner.

From a Bare Hull. Ferenc Mate. 1975. 19.95 (ISBN 0-920256-00-7). Norton.

From a Coastal Kitchen: Food & Flavor from Lull Bay. Lee Reid. (Illus.). 144p. 1981. pap. 7.95 (ISBN 0-87663-608-3). Universe.

From a Dark Lantern: A Journal. Arland Ussher. Ed. by Roger N. Parisious et al. 1978. text ed. 45.50x (ISBN 0-391-01594-X). Humanities.

From a Limestone Ledge. John Graves. LC 80-7641. (Illus.). 256p. 1980. 11.95 (ISBN 0-394-51238-3). Knopf.

From a Logical Point of View: Logico-Philosophical Essays. Willard Quine. pap. 3.95x (ISBN 0-06-130566-9, TB566, Torch). Har-Row.

From a Logical Point of View: Nine Logico-Philosophical Essays. 2nd rev. ed. Willard V. Quine. LC 61-15277. 1961. 9.00x (ISBN 0-674-32350-5); pap. 3.95x (ISBN 0-674-32351-3). Harvard U Pr.

From a Normal Beginning: The Origins of Kean College of New Jersey. Donald R. Raichle. (Illus.). 432p. 1980. 20.00 (ISBN 0-8386-4500-3). Fairleigh Dickinson.

From A to Z. Irene Coletta. (Illus.). (ps-2). 1979. 7.95g (ISBN 0-13-331678-5); pap. 2.95 (ISBN 0-13-331546-0). P-H.

From A to Z. Deborah Manley. LC 78-21027. (Ready, Set, Look Ser.). (Illus.). (gr. k-3). 1979. PLB 9.65 (ISBN 0-8172-1303-1). Raintree Pubs.

From A to Z: 200 Contemporary American Poets. Ed. by David Ray. LC 80-27328. xi, 243p. 1981. 16.95 (ISBN 0-8040-0369-6); pap. 8.95 (ISBN 0-8040-0370-X). Swallow.

From a View to a Death. Anthony Powell. 1978. pap. 2.25 o.p. (ISBN 0-445-04295-8). Popular Lib.

From a Year in Greece. Frederic Will. (Illus.). 1967. 11.50 (ISBN 0-292-73664-9). U of Tex Pr.

From Abacus to Zeus: A Handbook of Art History. J. Pierce. 1977. pap. text ed. 8.95 (ISBN 0-13-331686-6). P-H.

From Affluence to Praxis: Philosophy & Social Criticism. Mihailo Markovic. 1980. 5.95 (ISBN 0-472-64000-3). U of Mich Pr.

From Agriculture to Services: The Transformation of Industrial Employment. Joachim Singelmann. LC 78-19843. (Sage Library of Social Research: Vol. 69). 1978. 18.00x (ISBN 0-8039-1092-4); pap. 8.95x (ISBN 0-8039-1093-2). Sage.

From Alpha to Omega. Alexander Humez & Nicholas Humez. (Illus.). 256p. 1980. write for info. (ISBN 0-87923-386-9). Godine.

From Amoral to Humane Bureaucracy: The Coming Journey of Public Administration. Eugene P. Dvorin & Robert H. Simmons. (Orig.). 1972. pap. text ed. 6.50 scp (ISBN 0-06-382585-6, HarpC). Har-Row.

From an Oilfield Brat to a Child of the King. Mary M. Domstead. 1981. 5.95 (ISBN 0-533-04913-X). Vantage.

From an Understanding Heart. Evelyn Barkins. LC 76-43626. (Illus.). 34p. 1977. pap. 2.95 (ISBN 0-8119-0373-7). Fell.

From Anecdote to Experiment in Psychical Research. Robert H. Thouless. 1972. 17.50 (ISBN 0-7100-7285-6). Routledge & Kegan.

From Antiquary to Archaeologist: A Study of William Cunningham. 13.50x o.p. (ISBN 0-8464-0431-1). Beekman Pubs.

From Apes to Warlords. Solly Zuckerman. LC 77-3783. (Illus.). 1978. 22.50 o.s.i. (ISBN 0-06-014807-1, HarpT). Har-Row.

From Arithmetic to Algebra. Derek Bloomfield. (Illus.). 1976. pap. 12.95 (ISBN 0-87909-289-0); instrs'. manual avail. Reston.

From Arithmetic to Algebra. Michael St. John. 132p. (Orig.). 1980. pap. text ed. 4.50 (ISBN 0-937354-00-7, TX-334-207). Delta Systems.

From Arsenic to DDT: A History of Entomology in Western Canada. Paul W. Riegert. 400p. 1980. 30.00x (ISBN 0-8020-5499-4). U of Toronto Pr.

From Art to Science: Seventy-Two Objects Illustrating the Nature of Discovery. Cyril S. Smith. (Illus.). 1980. 25.00 (ISBN 0-262-19181-4). MIT Pr.

From Bandung to Colombo: Conference of the Non-Aligned Countries. Ed. by Sigham & Van Dihn. LC 76-162957. 1975. 7.95 (ISBN 0-89388-221-6). Okpaku Communications.

From Bed to Verse. Connie Page. Date not set. 4.75 (ISBN 0-8062-1641-7). Carlton.

From Bede to Alfred: Studies in Early Anglo-Saxon Literature & History. Dorothy Whitelock. 368p. 1980. 75.00x (ISBN 0-86078-066-X, Pub. by Variorum England). State Mutual Bk.

From Behavioral Science to Behavior Modification. Harry I. Kalish. (Illus.). 448p. 1980. 19.95 (ISBN 0-07-033245-2). McGraw.

From Being to Becoming: Time & Complexity in the Physical Sciences. Ilya Prigogine. LC 79-26774. (Illus.). 1980. text ed. 24.95x (ISBN 0-7167-1107-9); pap. text ed. 12.95x (ISBN 0-7167-1108-7). W H Freeman.

From Belasco to Brook: Great Stage Directors of the Twentieth Century. Samuel Leiter. 1981. 16.95 (ISBN 0-89676-057-X); pap. 12.95 (ISBN 0-89676-063-4). Drama Bk.

From Beowulf to Modern British Writers. 3rd ed. Ed. by John Ball. 1959. 18.95 (ISBN 0-672-63168-7). Odyssey Pr.

From Birth to Maturity. Charlotte Buhler. 1968. text ed. 11.25x (ISBN 0-7100-6244-3). Humanities.

From Birth to One Year. Marilyn Segal. LC 80-13831. (Play & Learn Ser.: Vol. 1). (Illus.). 96p. pap. 3.95 (ISBN 0-916392-50-3). Oak Tree Pubns.

From Birth to Twelve: How to Be a Successful Parent to Infants & Children. Gary D. Kannenberg. LC 80-69331. 125p. 1981. 7.95 (ISBN 0-86548-043-5). Century Twenty One.

From Blake to a Vision. Kathleen Raine. (New Yeats Papers Ser.: No. 17). 1979. pap. text ed. 11.75x (ISBN 0-85105-339-4, Dolmen Pr). Humanities.

From Bondage to Freedom. James Sprunt et al. (Orig.). 1968. pap. 4.50 (ISBN 0-8042-9020-2); tchrs' guide pap. 3.00. John Knox.

From Border to Middle Shire: Northumberland 1586-1625. S. J. Watts & S. I. Watts. (Illus.). 256p. 1975. text ed. 20.00x (ISBN 0-7185-1127-1, Leicester). Humanities.

From Borderline Adolescent to Functioning Adult: The Test of Time. James F. Masterson & Jacinta L. Costello. LC 80-14270. 300p. 1980. 19.50 (ISBN 0-87630-234-7). Brunner-Mazel.

From Brass Hat to Bowler Hat. Frances De Guinard. 1979. 19.95 (ISBN 0-241-10165-4, Pub. by Hamish Hamilton England). David & Charles.

From Brown to Bakke: The Supreme Court & School Integration, 1954-1978. Ed. by J. Harvie Wilkinson. (Galaxy Book: No. 634). 378p. 1981. pap. 6.95 (ISBN 0-19-502897-X). Oxford U Pr.

From Brown to Boston: Desegregation in Education -- 1954-1974, 2 vols. Leon Jones. LC 78-8312. 1979. Set. 72.50 (ISBN 0-8108-1147-2). Scarecrow.

From Buggy Whips to Moon Walks. Alfred G. Brown. 1978. 7.00 o.p. (ISBN 0-682-49037-7). Exposition.

From Bunchgrass to Agribusiness on the Columbia Plateau: The McGregor Land & Livestock Company, Eighteen Eighty-Two to Nineteen Seventy-Two. Alexander C. McGregor. 1980. write for info. o.p. U of Wash Pr.

From Campus to Career Success. Elwood N. Chapman. LC 78-9085. 304p. 1978. pap. text ed. 6.95 (ISBN 0-574-20580-2, 13-3580); instr's guide avail. (ISBN 0-574-20581-0, 13-3581). SRA.

From Canton to California: The Epic of Chinese Immigration. Corinne K. Hoexter. LC 76-14504. (Illus.). 320p. (gr. 7 up). 1976. 9.95 (ISBN 0-590-07344-3, Four Winds). Schol Bk Serv.

From Cape Mystery to Cape of No Return: The Saga of Men at Sea. Peter Salcher. 1978. 6.95 o.p. (ISBN 0-533-03486-8). Vantage.

From Casablanca to Berlin. Bruce Bliven, Jr. (Landmark Ser, No. 112). (gr. 5-9). 1965. 2.95 o.p. (ISBN 0-394-80412-0, BYR); PLB 5.99 (ISBN 0-394-90412-5). Random.

From Caxton to Beckett. Toppen. 1979. text ed. 42.75x (ISBN 90-6203-581-7). Humanities.

From Cell to Organism: Readings from Scientific American. Intro. by Donald Kennedy. LC 66-30156. (Illus.). 1967. text ed. 15.95x (ISBN 0-7167-0963-5); pap. text ed. 7.95x (ISBN 0-7167-0962-7). W H Freeman.

From Centennial to World War: American Society, 1876-1917. Walter T. K. Nugent. LC 76-15164. (History of American Society Ser.). 1976. pap. text ed. 7.95 (ISBN 0-672-60932-0). Bobbs.

From Chalk to Bronze: A Biography of Waldine Tauch. Alice Hutson. 1978. 6.95 (ISBN 0-88319-037-0). Shoal Creek Pub.

From Character Building to Social Treatment: The History of the Use of Groups in Social Work. Kenneth E. Reid. LC 79-6567. xviii, 249p. 1981. lib. bdg. 29.95 (ISBN 0-313-22016-6, RCB/). Greenwood.

From Charity to Social Work in England & the United States. Kathleen Woodroofe. LC 65-49593. 1962. pap. 6.50 (ISBN 0-8020-6118-4). U of Toronto Pr.

From Child to Adult: Studies in the Anthropology of Education. Ed. by John Middleton. LC 75-44039. (Texas Press Sourcebooks in Anthropolgy: No. 9). 1976. pap. 7.95x (ISBN 0-292-72416-0). U of Tex Pr.

From Childhood to Childhood: Children's Books & Their Creators. Jean Karl. (John Day Bk.). 1970. 8.95 (ISBN 0-381-98131-2, A29160, TYC-T). T Y Crowell.

From Clay to Art: A Complete Guide to the Craft of Ceramics. Ann Russell. (Illus.). 118p. 1978. 8.95 (ISBN 0-8059-2514-7). Dorrance.

From Clay to Rock: Personal Insights into Life from Simon Peter. Leslie B. Flynn. LC 80-69307. 176p. 1981. pap. 5.95 (ISBN 0-915684-79-9). Christian Herald.

From Clerk to Cleric. F. H. Cleobury. 1977. pap. 3.00 (ISBN 0-227-67825-7). Attic Pr.

From Coleridge to Gore: A Century of Religious Thought in Britain. B. M. Reardon. 1971. 15.00x o.p. (ISBN 0-582-48510-X). Longman.

From Columbus to Castro: The History of the Caribbean, 1492-1969. Eric E. Williams. LC 75-138773. (Illus.). 1971. 13.95x (ISBN 0-06-014668-0, HarpT). Har-Row.

From Columbus to Cromwell: Ireland Britain & Europe, c 1500-c.1700. James Halpin. (Illus.). 1978. pap. text ed. 5.25 large format limp bdg. o.p. (ISBN 0-7171-0808-2). Irish Bk Ctr.

From Cooper to Philip Roth: Essays on American Literature Presented to J. G. Riewald on the Occasion of His Seventieth Birthday. Ed. by Jan Bakker & D. R. Wilkinson. (Costerus New Ser.). 130p. 1980. pap. text ed. 14.25x (ISBN 90-6203-851-4). Humanities.

From Cotswolds to High Sierras. George E. Franklin. LC 66-20373. (Illus.). 167p. 1966. 4.00 (ISBN 0-87004-046-4). Caxton.

From Crested Peaks: The Story of Adams State College of Colorado. Berl McAdow. 1961. 3.95 (ISBN 0-8040-0335-1). Swallow.

From Critical Theory of Society to Theology of Communicative Praxis. Rudolf J. Siebert. LC 79-65296. 1979. pap. text ed. 9.50 (ISBN 0-8191-0783-2). U Pr of Amer.

From Cultural Rebellion to Counterrevolution: The Politics of Maurice Barres. C. Stewart Doty. LC 75-15337. 294p. 1976. 16.00 (ISBN 0-8214-0191-2). Ohio U Pr.

From Deep Within Me. Mario I. Andrade. 48p. 1978. 2.95 (ISBN 0-8059-2620-8). Dorrance.

From Democracy to Nazism: A Regional Case Study on Political Parties in Germany. Rudolf Heberle. LC 72-80556. 1970. Repr. 13.50 (ISBN 0-86527-076-7). Fertig.

From Dependence to Statehood, Vol. 1. H. H. Marshall. 1980. 50.00 (ISBN 0-379-20348-0). Oceana.

From Dependence to Statehood in Commonwealth Africa: Selected Documents, World War I to Independence. H. H. Marshall. LC 80-10407. 734p. 1980. lib. bdg. 50.00 (ISBN 0-379-20348-0). Oceana.

From Dependency to Development: Strategies to Overcome Underdevelopment & Inequality. Ed. by Heraldo Munoz. (Westview Special Studies in Social, Political, & Economic Development). 300p. 1981. lib. bdg. 26.50x (ISBN 0-89158-902-3); pap. text ed. 12.50 (ISBN 0-86531-079-3). Westview.

From Dessalines to Duvalier: Race, Colour & National Independence in Haiti. David Nicholls. LC 78-56817. (Cambridge Latin American Studies: No. 34). 1979. 39.95 (ISBN 0-521-22177-3). Cambridge U Pr.

From Destruction to Rebirth: The Holocaust & the State of Israel. Carla L. Klausner & Joseph P. Schultz. LC 78-62262. 1978. pap. text ed. 11.25 (ISBN 0-8191-0574-0). U Pr of Amer.

From Dits to Bits...a Personal History of the Electronic Computer. Herman Lukoff. LC 79-90567. 200p. 1979. 14.95 (ISBN 0-89661-002-0). Robotics Pr.

From Domesday Book to Magna Carta, 1087-1216. 2nd ed. Austin L. Poole. (Oxford History of England Ser). 1955. 33.00x (ISBN 0-19-821707-2). Oxford U Pr.

From Doon with Death. Ruth Rendell. 160p. 1976. pap. 1.95 (ISBN 0-345-29287-1). Ballantine.

From Dryden to Jane Austen: Essays on English Critics & Writers, 1660-1818. Hoyt Trowbridge. LC 76-21490. 1978. Repr. of 1977 ed. 15.00x (ISBN 0-8263-0430-3). U of NM Pr.

From Dude to Cowman. Walter Bonnheim. 180p. 1975. 5.95 (ISBN 0-914330-05-5). Western Tanager.

From Earth to Infinity: A Guide to Space Travel. Joseph J. DiCerto. LC 80-12812. (Illus.). 320p. (gr. 7 up). 1980. PLB 9.29 (ISBN 0-671-33017-9). Messner.

From Eight to Eighty (Young Adult Poetry) Helen Altvater. 100p. (Orig.). 1981. pap. 5.95 (ISBN 0-933906-17-X). Gusto Pr.

From Emperor to Citizen, Vol. I. 2nd ed. Aisin-Gioro Pu Yi. 1980. 5.95 o.p. (ISBN 0-8351-0619-5); pap. 6.95 o.p. (ISBN 0-8351-0621-7). China Bks.

From Emperor to Citizen, Vol. II. 2nd ed. Aisin-Gioro Pu Yi. 1980. 5.95 o.p. (ISBN 0-8351-0620-9); pap. 6.95 o.p. (ISBN 0-8351-0622-5). China Bks.

From Exile to Advent. 5th ed. W. Fairweather. (Handbooks for Bible Classes Ser.). 210p. pap. text ed. 3.50 (ISBN 0-567-28128-0). Attic Pr.

From Exodus to Advent. Morris Venden. LC 79-22389. (Orion Ser.). 1979. pap. 2.95 (ISBN 0-8127-0255-7). Southern Pub.

From Experience to Expression: A College Rhetoric. 2nd ed. Joseph J. Comprone. LC 80-82348. (Illus.). 528p. 1981. pap. text ed. 11.50 (ISBN 0-395-29310-3); write for info. instr's manual (ISBN 0-395-29311-1). HM.

From Fat to Fit. 2nd ed. Ann Wigmore. 96p. 1977. pap. 1.95. Hippocrates.

From Fertility Cult to Worship. Walter J. Harrelson. LC 66-14929. (Scholars Press Reprint Ser.: No. 4). pap. 9.00x (ISBN 0-89130-379-0, 00 07 04). Scholars Pr CA.

From Fire to Flood: Historic Human Destruction of Sonoran Desert Riverine Oases. Henry F. Dobyns. (Anthropological Papers Ser.: No. 20). (Illus.). 222p. (Orig.). 1981. pap. 11.95 (ISBN 0-87919-092-2). Ballena Pr.

From Flintlock to Rifle: Infantry Tactics, 1740-1866. Steven Ross. LC 77-74397. (Illus.). 1979. 15.00 (ISBN 0-8386-2051-5). Fairleigh Dickinson.

From Football to Finance: The Story of Brady Keys Jr. Eric B. Roberts. LC 70-151026. (Illus.). (gr. 7 up). 1971. 4.75 o.p. (ISBN 0-15-230265-4, HJ). HarBraceJ.

From Footpaths to Freeways: The Story of Roads. Solveig Russell. LC 78-135528. (Finding-Out Bks.). (Illus.). (gr. 1-4). 1971. PLB 6.95 (ISBN 0-8193-0442-5). Enslow Pubs.

From Freedom to Formula: The Evolution of the Eucharistic Prayer from Oral Improvisation to Written Text. Alan Bouley. (Studies in Christian Antiquity: Vol. 21). 288p. 1980. 25.00x (ISBN 0-8132-0554-9, Pub. by Cath U of America Pr). Intl Schol Bk.

From Furrows to Freeways. Raymond L. Friesen. 1981. 6.95 (ISBN 0-533-04712-9). Vantage.

From Garden to Table. Mary Norwak. (Illus.). 1978. 16.95 (ISBN 0-241-89593-6, Pub. by Hamish Hamilton England). David & Charles.

From Generation to Generation: Age Groups & Social Structure. Samuel N. Eisenstadt. LC 55-10998. 1964. pap. text ed. 6.95 (ISBN 0-02-909380-5). Free Pr.

From Germantown to Steinbach. Daniel Hertzler. 248p. 1981. pap. 7.95 (ISBN 0-8361-1949-5). Herald Pr.

From Glasgow to Saturn. Edwin Morgan. (Poetry Ser.). 1979. 6.95 o.s.i. (ISBN 0-85635-040-0, Pub. by Carcanet New Pr England). Persea Bks.

From God to Us. Norman L. Geisler & William E. Nix. 302p. (Orig.). 1974. pap. 5.50 (ISBN 0-8024-2878-9). Moody.

From Goethe to Hauptmann: Studies in a Changing Culture. Camillo Von Klenze. LC 66-23519. 1926. 10.50x (ISBN 0-8196-0178-0). Biblo.

From 'Good Order' to Glorious Revolution: Salem, Massachusetts, Sixteen Twenty-Eight to Sixteen Eighty-Nine. Christine A. Young. Ed. by Robert Berkhofer. (Studies in American History & Culture). 273p. 1980. 27.95 (ISBN 0-8357-1101-3, Pub. by UMI Res Pr). Univ Microfilms.

From Gothic to Functional Form. Alfred Boe. (Architecture & Decorative Art Ser.). 1979. Repr. of 1957 ed. 22.50 (ISBN 0-306-77544-1). Da Capo.

From Grace to Glory: Meditations of the Psalms. Murdoch Campbell. 1979. pap. 3.95 (ISBN 0-85151-028-0). Banner of Truth.

From Grammar to Paragraphs. Sarah Clark. 306p. 1981. pap. text ed. 8.95 (ISBN 0-394-32560-5). Random.

From Greek to Graffiti. Robert C. Goospeed. (Illus.). 288p. (Orig.). 1981. 15.00 (ISBN 0-682-49696-0, University); pap. 10.00 (ISBN 0-682-49706-1, University). Exposition.

From Harper Valley to the Mountain Top. Jeannie C. Riley & Jamie Buckingham. Orig. Title: Jeannie C. 180p. 1980. 8.95 (ISBN 0-912376-63-5). Chosen Bks Pub.

From Headhunters to Hallelujahs. Doris Trefren. 190p. (Orig.). 1980. pap. 3.75 (ISBN 0-89957-047-X). AMG Pubs.

From Hearth to Cookstove. Linda C. Franklin. LC 73-93247. (Collector Ser.). (Illus.). 1978. 15.00 (ISBN 0-87637-339-2, 339-02). Hse of Collectibles.

From Helgoland to Hollywood. Lawrence Telford. 160p. 1981. 8.00 (ISBN 0-682-49738-X). Exposition.

From Hell to Heaven: Memoirs from Patton's Third Army. Vernon D. McHugh. 35p. 1980. 3.95 (ISBN 0-8059-2742-5). Dorrance.

From Hell to Texas. Dwight Brickner. 1977. pap. 1.50 (ISBN 0-505-51207-6). Tower Bks.

From Heroics to Sentimentalism: A Study of Thomas Otway's Tragedies. Hazel M. Pollard. (Salzburg Studies in English Literature, Poetic Drama & Poetic Theory: No. 10). 301p. 1974. pap. text ed. 25.00x (ISBN 0-391-01500-1). Humanities.

From Holbein to Whistler: Notes on Drawing & Engraving. Alfred Brooks. (Illus.). 1920. 75.00x (ISBN 0-685-69792-4). Elliots Bks.

From Hollywood. DeWitt Bodeen. LC 73-15158. (Illus.). 512p. 1976. 15.00 o.p. (ISBN 0-498-01346-4). A S Barnes.

From Human Sentience to Drama: Principles of Critical Analysis, Tragic & Comedic. Richard Pollard & Hazel B. Pollard. LC 73-85447. ix, 310p. 1974. 14.00x (ISBN 0-8214-0135-1). Ohio U Pr.

From Hydrocarbons to Petrochemicals. Lewis F. Hatch & Sami Matar. (Illus.). 120p. 1981. 25.95x (ISBN 0-87201-374-X). Gulf Pub.

From Idea to Application: Some Selected Nuclear Techniques in Research & Development. (Illus.). 1978. pap. 25.75 (ISBN 92-0-131078-1, ISP 476, IAEA). Unipub.

From Idea to Essay. 2nd ed. JoRay McCuen & Anthony C. Winkler. 1980. pap. text ed. 8.95 (ISBN 0-574-22055-0, 13-5055); instr's guide avail. (ISBN 0-574-22056-9, 13-5056). SRA.

From Indians to Chicanos: A Sociocultural History. James D. Vigil. LC 80-18539. (Illus.). 180p. pap. text ed. 10.95 (ISBN 0-8016-5230-8). Mosby.

From Innocence Through Experience: Keats's Myth of the Poet. Priscilla W. Tate. (Salzburg Studies in English Literature, Romantic Reassessment: No. 34). 147p. 1974. pap. text ed. 25.00x (ISBN 0-391-01546-X). Humanities.

From Instinct to Identity: The Development of Personality. Louis Breger. LC 73-5766. (P-H Personality Ser). (Illus.). 400p. 1974. ref. ed. 18.95x (ISBN 0-13-331637-8). P-H.

From Isolation to Mainstream: Problems of the Colleges Founded for Negroes. Carnegie Commission On Higher Education. 1971. 1.95 o.p. (ISBN 0-07-010028-4, P&RB). McGraw.

From Jordan to Pentecost. Derek Prince. (Foundation Ser.). pap. 1.75 (ISBN 0-934920-02-8, B-12). Derek Prince.

From Karl Mannheim. Karl Mannheim. Ed. by Kurt H. Wolff. (Orig.). 1971. pap. 7.95 (ISBN 0-19-501394-8, GB). Oxford U Pr.

From Kiev to Tel Aviv: Escape from Russia. Arieh Gur. 1981. 14.00x (ISBN 0-931556-02-3). Translation Pr.

From King's College to Columbia, 1746-1800. David C. Humphrey. (Illus.). 328p. 1976. 22.50x (ISBN 0-231-03942-5). Columbia U Pr.

From Leroi Jones to Amiri Baraka: The Literary Works. Theodore R. Hudson. LC 72-97096. 256p. 1973. 12.75 (ISBN 0-8223-0296-9); pap. 6.75 (ISBN 0-8223-0454-6). Duke.

From Liquor & Loneliness to Love & Laughter. Dean Marr. 1978. 8.95 o.p. (ISBN 0-8362-6502-5); pap. 4.95 o.p. (ISBN 0-8362-6503-3). Andrews & McMeel.

From Ma Perkins to Mary Hartman: The Illustrated History of Soap Operas. Robert La Guardia. 1977. pap. 1.95 o.p. (ISBN 0-345-25562-3). Ballantine.

From Magic to Metaphor. George Worgol. LC 79-56752. (Orig.). 1980. pap. 8.95 (ISBN 0-8091-2280-4). Paulist Pr.

From Mandeville to Marx: Genesis & Triumph of Economic Ideology. Louis Dumont. LC 76-8087. 1977. lib. bdg. 16.50x o.s.i. (ISBN 0-226-16981-2). U of Chicago Pr.

From Mars Hill to Manhattan. G. Papaioannou. 1976. pap. 5.95 (ISBN 0-937032-08-5). Light & Life Pub Co MN.

From Marx to Hegel. George Lichtheim. LC 70-167871. 1971. pap. 3.95 (ISBN 0-8164-9188-7); 7.95 o.p. (ISBN 0-8164-9120-8, Continuum). Continuum.

From Mary Noble to Mary Hartman. Madeleine Edmonson & David Rounds. 1977. pap. 1.75 o.s.i. (ISBN 0-515-04423-7). Jove Pubns.

From Mathematics to Philosophy. Hao Wang. (International Library of Philosophy & Scientific Method). 420p. 1973. text ed. 29.25x (ISBN 0-391-00335-6). Humanities.

From Medicine to Miracles. Kathryn Kuhlman. LC 78-67100. 1978. pap. 1.50 (ISBN 0-87123-383-5, 200383). Bethany Fell.

From Metternich to the Beatles. Richard C. Lukas. 1973. pap. 1.95 o.p. (ISBN 0-451-61191-8, MJ1191, Ment). NAL.

From Mid-Career Through Retirement: Longitudinal Studies of the Male Work Force. Herbert S. Parnes. (Illus.). 352p. 1981. text ed. 27.50x (ISBN 0-262-16079-X). MIT Pr.

From Ming to Ch'ing: Conquest, Region, & Continuity in Seventeenth-Century China. Jonathan Spence & John E. Wills, Jr. LC 78-15560. (Illus.). 437p. 1981. pap. 8.95x (ISBN 0-300-02672-2). Yale U Pr.

From Ming to Ch'ing: Conquest, Region & Continuity in 17th Century China. Jonathan Spence & John E. Wills, Jr. LC 78-15560. (Illus.). 1979. 30.00x (ISBN 0-300-02218-2). Yale U Pr.

From Mississippi to California. Ed. by Michael D. Heaston. Date not set. 9.50 (ISBN 0-8363-0157-9). Jenkins.

From Mobilization to Revolution. Charles Tilly. LC 77-79468. (Illus.). 1978. pap. text ed. 8.95 (ISBN 0-201-07571-7). A-W.

From My Heart to Yours. Mary J. Cook. LC 77-86313. (Illus.). 1977. pap. 4.95 o.p. (ISBN 0-89769-006-0). Pine Mntn.

From My Israel Journal. Florence R. Kraut. LC 80-80528. 56p. (Orig.). 1980. pap. 2.95 (ISBN 0-686-28879-3). Preston St Pr.

From My Life. Erich Honecker. LC 80-41162. (Leaders of the World Ser.: Vol. 3). (Illus.). 500p. 1980. 24.00 (ISBN 0-08-024532-3). Pergamon.

From My Mother's Kitchen: Recipes & Reminiscences. Mimi Sheraton. LC 75-6360. (Illus.). 1979. 12.95 (ISBN 0-06-013846-7, HarpT). Har-Row.

From My Old Boat Shop: One-Lung Engines, Fantail Launches, & Other Marine Delights. Weston Farmer. LC 78-64786. (Illus.). 1979. 20.00 (ISBN 0-87742-107-2). Intl Marine.

From My Window. Andre Kertesz. 1981. 24.95 (ISBN 0-8212-1125-0). NYGS.

From Naked to Nude: Life Drawing in the Twentieth Century. Georg Eisler. LC 76-47085. (Illus.). 1977. pap. 5.95 o.p. (ISBN 0-688-08167-3). Morrow.

From Napoleon to Stalin & Other Essays. E. H. Carr. 1980. 20.00 (ISBN 0-312-30774-8). St Martin.

From Nationalism to Internationalism: US Foreign Policy Before 1917. Akira Iriye. (Foreign Policies of the Great Powers Ser.). 1977. 22.00 (ISBN 0-7100-8444-7). Routledge & Kegan.

From Near & Far. Mabel O'Donnell. (Design for Reading Ser). (Illus.). (gr. 3). 1972. text ed. 10.36 (ISBN 0-06-516006-1, SchDept); tchr's ed. 14.28 (ISBN 0-06-516204-8); wkbk. 3.20, (ISBN 0-06-516305-2)tchr's ed. 6.36 (ISBN 0-06-516405-9); phonics wkbk. & tchr's ed. 2.68 5.36 (ISBN 0-06-516314-1); dupl masters a-b with ans. key 23.20 ea.; mastery test pkg. 14.48 (ISBN 0-06-516614-0); transition papbks. 2.52 ea.; tchrs' ed. 14.20 (ISBN 0-685-02883-6); wkbk. 2.52, tchr's wkbk. for Transition Bks. 5.04 (ISBN 0-685-02884-4). Har-Row.

From Neuron to Brain: A Cellular Approach to the Function of the Nervous System. Stephen W. Kuffler & John G. Nicholls. LC 75-32228. 1976. text ed. 19.50x (ISBN 0-87893-442-1). Sinauer Assoc.

From New Deal Banking Reform to World War Two Inflation. M. Friedman & A. Schwartz. 1980. pap. 3.95 (ISBN 0-691-00363-7). Princeton U Pr.

From Night to Sunlight. Thomas Whitfield. LC 80-68874. 1980. pap. 4.95 (ISBN 0-8054-5291-5). Broadman.

From Nine to Twelve: Europe's Destiny. Ed. by J. W. Schneider. LC 80-50459. 256p. 1980. 47.50x (ISBN 90-286-0280-1). Sijthoff & Noordhoff.

From Now to Eternity (Revelation) John Heading. 1981. pap. 3.95 (ISBN 0-937396-15-X). Walterick Pubs.

From Office to Profession: The New England Ministry, 1750-1850. Donald M. Scott. LC 77-20304. 1978. 16.00x (ISBN 0-8122-7737-6). U of Pa Pr.

From One to Two Years. Don Adcock & Marilyn Segal. LC 80-13835. (Play & Learn Ser.). (Illus.). 1980. pap. 4.95 (ISBN 0-916392-51-1). Oak Tree Pubns.

From Oxford to Rome, & How It Fared with Some Who Lately Made the Journey, 1847. Elizabeth F. Harris. Ed. by Robert L. Wolff. Bd. with Rest in the Church, 1848. LC 74-449. (Victorian Fiction Ser.). 1975. lib. bdg. 66.00 (ISBN 0-8240-1529-0). Garland Pub.

From Pale to Pampa: The Jewish Immigrant Experience in Buenos Aires. Eugene Sofer. 1981. text ed. 24.00x (ISBN 0-8419-0428-6). Holmes & Meier.

From Paragraph to Essay: Readings for Progress in Writing. 3rd ed. Ed. by Woodrow Ohlsen & Frank L. Hammond. LC 76-27897. 320p. (For accelerated classes). (gr. 9-12). 1976. pap. text ed. 7.95x (ISBN 0-684-14832-3, ScribC). Scribner.

From Pariah to Patriot: The Changing Image of the German Peasant, 1770-1840. John G. Gagliardo. LC 72-80091. 352p. 1969. 15.00x (ISBN 0-8131-1187-0). U Pr of Ky.

From Particular to General Linguistics. Selected Essays 1965 to 1978. Yakov Malkiel. (Studies in Language Companion: No. 3). 1980. text ed. 68.50x (ISBN 0-391-01268-1). Humanities.

From Pauperism to Poverty. Karel Williams. 500p. 1981. 60.00 (ISBN 0-7100-0698-5). Routledge & Kegan.

From Peanuts to President. Beatrice S. Smith. LC 76-51267. (Illus.). (gr. 3-6). 1977. PLB 6.65 o.p. (ISBN 0-8172-0428-8). Raintree Pubs.

From Pearl Harbor to Okinawa. Bruce Bliven, Jr. (Landmark Ser.: No. 94). (Illus.). (gr. 5-9). 1960. PLB 5.99 (ISBN 0-394-90394-3, BYR). Random.

From Pearl Harbor to Vietnam: The Memoirs of Admiral Arthur W. Radford. Ed. by Stephen Jurika, Jr. LC 78-59466. (Publications 221 Ser.). (Illus.). 488p. 1980. 15.00 (ISBN 0-8179-7211-0). Hoover Inst Pr.

From Peasant to Farmer: A Revolutionary Strategy for Development. Raanan Weitz. LC 76-170926. (Twentieth Century Fund Study). 1971. 17.50x (ISBN 0-231-03592-6). Columbia U Pr.

From Period Three to Period Four: Chronological Studies of the Bronze Age in Southern Scandinavia & Northern Germany. Klavs Randsborg. (Archaeological Historical Ser.: No. 15). (Illus.). 1972. pap. text ed. 27.75x (ISBN 87-480-7622-8). Humanities.

From Personal to Territorial Law: Aspects of the History & Structure of the Western Legal - Constitutional Tradition. Simeon L. Guterman. 1972. 12.50 o.p. (ISBN 0-8108-0405-0). Scarecrow.

From Petals to Pinecones: A Nature Art & Craft Book. Katherine N. Cutler. LC 70-81753. (Illus.). (gr. 4 up). 1969. PLB 7.92 (ISBN 0-688-51594-0); pap. 2.95 o.p. (ISBN 0-688-45003-2). Lothrop.

From Philanthropy to Social Welfare: An American Cultural Perspective. Philip Klein. LC 68-18617. (Social & Behavioral Science Ser.). 1968. 14.95x o.p. (ISBN 0-87589-012-1). Jossey-Bass.

From Phonology to Philology: An Outline of Descriptive & Historical Spanish Linguistics. John R. Burt. LC 80-67212. 208p. 1980. lib. bdg. 17.50 (ISBN 0-8191-1310-7); pap. text ed. 9.50 (ISBN 0-8191-1311-5). U Pr of Amer.

From Physical Concept to Mathematical Structure: An Introduction to Theoretical Physics. Lynn Trainor & Mark B. Wise. LC 78-11616. (Mathematical Expositions Ser.). 1979. 25.00x (ISBN 0-8020-5432-3); pap. 10.00x (ISBN 0-8020-6432-9). U of Toronto Pr.

From Plato to Nietzsche. E. L. Allen. Orig. Title: Guide Book to Western Thought. 192p. 1977. pap. 2.25 (ISBN 0-449-30768-9, Prem). Fawcett.

From Ploughshare to Ballotbox. Derek W. Urwin. 356p. 1981. pap. 30.00x (ISBN 82-00-05394-6). Universitet.

From Policy to Administration: Essays in Honour of William A.Robson. Ed. by J. A. Griffiths. 1976. text ed. 42.50x (ISBN 0-686-67889-3). Allen Unwin.

From Pond to Prairie: The Changing World of a Pond & Its Life. Laurence Pringle. LC 70-175599. (Illus.). 40p. (gr. 4-6). 1972. 4.95g o.s.i. (ISBN 0-02-775220-8). Macmillan.

From Poor Law to Welfare State: A History of Social Welfare in America. 2nd ed. Walter I. Trattner. LC 78-58914. 1979. 14.95 (ISBN 0-02-932890-X); pap. text ed. 7.95 (ISBN 0-02-932900-0). Free Pr.

From Poverty to Power. James Allen. 184p. 1980. pap. 5.50 (ISBN 0-89540-061-8). Sun Pub.

From Prescription to Persuasion: Manipulation of Seventeenth Century Virginia Economy. John C. Rainbolt. LC 73-83268. 1974. 13.95 (ISBN 0-8046-9057-X). Kennikat.

From Primer to Pleasure in Reading. Mary F. Thwaite. LC 72-82182. (Illus.). 312p. 1972. 14.00 (ISBN 0-87675-275-X). Horn Bk.
From Problem to Program. Ed. by M. E. Wardle. (School Mathematics Project Computing Ser). (Illus.). (gr. 8-12). 1971. 16.95 (ISBN 0-521-08301-X); pap. 6.95 (ISBN 0-521-09684-7). Cambridge U Pr.
From Project to Production. A. Brichta & P. E. Sharp. LC 79-97830. 1970. 25.00 (ISBN 0-08-006638-0); pap. 13.25 (ISBN 0-08-006639-9). Pergamon.
From Prologue to Epilogue in Vietnam. Mortimer T. Cohen. LC 79-54798. (Illus.). 612p. 15.00 (ISBN 0-686-28498-4). Retriever.
From Protest to Challenge - a Documentary History of African Politics in South Africa, 1882-1964: Challenge & Violence 1953-1964, Vol. 3. Ed. by Thomas Karis et al. LC 72-152423. (Publications Ser.: No. 123). 825p. 1977. 22.50 (ISBN 0-8179-6231-X). Hoover Inst Pr.
From Puritan to Yankee: Character & the Social Order in Connecticut, 1690-1765. Richard L. Bushman. 352p. 1980. pap. 4.95 (ISBN 0-674-32551-6). Harvard U Pr.
From Quarks to Quasars. Edward Thomas. 1977. pap. text ed. 11.25x (ISBN 0-485-12024-0, Athlone Pr). Humanities.
From Quasimodo to Scarlett O'Hara: A National Board of Review Anthology. Ed. by Stanley Hochman. LC 80-53695. (Ungar Film Library). 400p. 1981. 25.00 (ISBN 0-8044-2381-4); pap. 10.95 (ISBN 0-8044-6274-7). Ungar.
From Radical Left to Extreme Right: A Bibliography of Current Periodicals of Protest, Controversy, Advocacy, or Dissent, with Dispassionate Content - Summaries to Guide Librarians & Other Educators, Vol. 3. 2nd. rev. enl. ed. Theodore J. Spahn & Janet P. Spahn. LC 76-126558. 1976. 27.50 (ISBN 0-8108-0883-8). Scarecrow.
From Rationalism to Existentialism: The Existentialist & Their Nineteenth Century Backgrounds, 1972. Robert Solomon. 1978. pap. text ed. 7.95x (ISBN 0-391-00850-1). Humanities.
From Rebellion to Revolution: Afro-American Slave Revolts in the Making of the Modern World. Eugene D. Genovese. LC 80-11386. 208p. 1981. pap. 2.95 (ISBN 0-394-74485-3, Vin). Random.
From Red to Black? The Financial Status of Private Colleges & Universities. William W. Jellema. LC 73-7155. (Higher Education Ser.). 208p. 1973. 11.95x o.p. (ISBN 0-87589-188-8). Jossey-Bass.
From Religion to Philosophy. A Study of the Origins of Western Speculation. F. M. Cornford. 1957-1979. text ed. o. p. (ISBN 0-391-01238-X); pap. text ed. 7.95x (ISBN 0-391-01239-8). Humanities.
From Rhodesia to Zimbabwe: Behind & Beyond Lancaster House. Ed. by W. H. Morris-Jones. (Studies in Commonwealth Politics & History: No. 9). (Illus.). 123p. 1980. 22.50x (ISBN 0-7146-3167-1, F Cass Co). Biblio Dist.
From Riot to Recovery: Newark After Ten Years. Ed. by Stanley B. Winters. LC 79-66424. 1979. text ed. 22.25 (ISBN 0-8191-0822-7); pap. text ed. 15.75 (ISBN 0-8191-0823-5). U Pr of Amer.
From Ritual to Record: The Nature of Modern Sports. Allen Guttmann. (Illus.). 1979. pap. 6.00x (ISBN 0-231-08369-6). Columbia U Pr.
From Ritual to Record: The Nature of Modern Sport. Allen Guttmann. LC 77-20886. (Illus.). 1978. 17.50 (ISBN 0-231-03993-X). Columbia U Pr.
From Ritual to Romance. Jessie L. Weston. Tr. by Mary M. McLaughlin. 7.50 (ISBN 0-8446-3162-0). Peter Smith.
From Ritual to Romance. Jessie L. Weston. LC 57-3633. 1957. pap. 2.95 (ISBN 0-385-09334-9, A125, Anch). Doubleday.
From Riva Ridge to Riva. Julius Keller. 4.95 o.p. (ISBN 0-685-46465-2). Vantage.
From Rock Bottom to Mountaintop. Bill Stearns. 1979. pap. 2.50 (ISBN 0-88207-580-2). Victor Bks.
From Rollo to Tom Sawyer & Other Papers. Alice M. Jordan. 160p. 1948. pap. 6.50 (ISBN 0-87675-058-7). Horn Bk.
From Romanticism to Post-Impressionism. Istvan Genthon. (Illus.). 1966. 7.50 (ISBN 0-8283-1124-2). Branden.
From Room to Room. Jane Kenyon. LC 78-60469. 68p. 1978. pap. 4.95 (ISBN 0-914086-24-3). Alicejamesbooks.
From Roosevelt to Roosevelt, 1901-1941. Ed. by Otis L. Graham, Jr. LC 70-151116. (Literature of History Ser). (Orig.). 1971. 18.95x (ISBN 0-89197-181-5); pap. text ed. 6.95x (ISBN 0-89197-182-3). Irvington.
From Russia, with Love. Ian Fleming. 256p. 1980. pap. 1.95 (ISBN 0-515-05515-8). Jove Pubns.
From Sad to Glad. Nathan S. Kline. 1981. pap. 2.95 (ISBN 0-345-29545-5). Ballantine.
From Sad to Glad: Kline on Depression. Nathan Kline. 224p. 1975. pap. 1.95 (ISBN 0-345-28502-6). Ballantine.
From Sadowa to Sarajevo: The Foreign Policy of Austria-Hungary 1866-1914. F. R. Bridge. (Foreign Policies of Great Powers Ser). (Illus.). 496p. 1972. 32.00x (ISBN 0-7100-7269-4). Routledge & Kegan.
From Sail to Steam: Recollections of Naval Life. Alfred T. Mahan. LC 68-26817. (American Scene Ser). 1968. Repr. of 1907 ed. lib. bdg. 29.50 (ISBN 0-306-71148-6). Da Capo.
From Saint Francis to Dante: Translations from the Chronicle of the Franciscan Salimbene (1221-88) Salimbene Di Adam. Ed. & tr. by G. G. Coulton. LC 68-10910. 462p. 1972. 15.00x o.p. (ISBN 0-8122-7672-8); pap. 5.95x (ISBN 0-8122-1053-0, Pa Paperbks). U of Pa Pr.
From Sartre to the New Novel. Betty T. Rahv. LC 74-77655. 176p. 1974. 12.50 (ISBN 0-8046-9076-6, Natl U). Kennikat.
From Scarface to Scarlett: American Films in the 1930s. Roger Dooley. (Illus.). 700p. 1981. 25.00 (ISBN 0-15-133789-6). HarBraceJ.
From School to Work: Effective Counselling & Guidance. Christine H. Moor. LC 74-31569. (Sage Studies in Social & Educational Change: Vol. 3). (Illus.). 1976. 18.00x (ISBN 0-8039-9947-X); pap. 9.95x (ISBN 0-8039-9856-2). Sage.
From Sea to Sea: The Growth of the United States. Harold Faber. LC 67-10351. (gr. 7 up). 1967. 5.95 o.p. (ISBN 0-374-32475-1). FS&G.
From Sea to Shining Sea. Lucille Hein. LC 75-11839. 32p. (gr. 4-8). 1975. 4.95 o.p. (ISBN 0-8170-0681-8). Judson.
From Self-Help to Health: A Guide to Self-Help Groups. David Robinson & Yvonne Robinson. 1979. 14.95 (ISBN 0-686-63745-3, Pub. by Batsford England). David & Charles.
From Selling to Managing. Ronald D. Brown. (AMACOM Executive Books). 1978. pap. 5.95 (ISBN 0-8144-7500-0). Am Mgmt.
From Serfdom to Socialism (1907) James K. Hardie. Ed. by R. E. Dowse. Bd. with Labour & the Empire (1907) James R. MacDonald; Socialist's Budget (1907) Philip Snowden. LC 74-496. 385p. 1975. 18.00 (ISBN 0-8386-1540-6). Fairleigh Dickinson.
From Seven to Seventy: Memoirs of a Painter & a Yankee. Edward Simmons. Ed. by H. Barbara Weinberg. LC 75-28891. (Art Experience in Late 19th Century America Ser.: Vol. 24). (Illus.). 1976. Repr. of 1922 ed. lib. bdg. 37.00 (ISBN 0-8240-2248-3). Garland Pub.
From Shore to Ocean Floor: How Life Survives in the Sea. Seymour Simon. LC 72-6248. (Living Things in Their Environment Ser). 72p. (gr. 4-5). 1973. PLB 5.90 (ISBN 0-531-02614-0). Watts.
From Shtetl to Suburbia: The Family in Jewish Literary Imagination. Sol Gittleman. LC 78-53646. 1979. 10.95 (ISBN 0-8070-6364-9, BP-591); pap. 4.95 (ISBN 0-8070-6365-7). Beacon Pr.
From Signs to Propositions: The Concept of Form in 18th-Century Semantic Theory. Stephen K. Land. LC 74-189426. (Linguistics Library). (Illus.). 224p. 1974. text ed. 14.95x (ISBN 0-582-55046-7). Longman.
From Single Cells to Plants. E. Thomas et al. (Wykeham Science Ser.: No. 38). 1975. 9.95x (ISBN 0-8448-1165-3). Crane Russak Co.
From Slaves to Squatters: Plantation Labor & Agriculture in Zanibar & Coastal Kenya, 1890-1925. Frederick Cooper. LC 80-5391. (Illus.). 352p. 1981. text ed. 25.00 (ISBN 0-300-02454-1). Yale U Pr.
From Smollett to James: Studies in the Novel & Other Essays Presented to Edgar Johnson. Ed. by Samuel I. Mintz et al. LC 79-25865. 1981. 27.50x (ISBN 0-8139-0663-6). U Pr of Va.
From Social Issues to Public Policy. Robert Eyestone. LC 78-13334. (Viewpoints on American Politics Ser.). 1978. pap. text ed. 8.95 (ISBN 0-471-24978-5). Wiley.
From Society to Nature: A Study of Doris Lessing's "Children of Violence". Ingrid Holmquist. (Gothenburg Studies in English: No. 46). 1980. pap. 19.75x (ISBN 91-7346-083-4). Humanities.
From Stars to Sculptures. Mabel O'Donnell et al. (Design for Reading Ser). (Subj. matter reading). (gr. 8). text ed. 12.20 (ISBN 0-06-511028-5, SchDept); tchr's manual 11.56 (ISBN 0-06-511218-0). Har-Row.
From Start to Finish. J. Hislop. (Illus.). 1978. 24.35 (ISBN 0-85131-265-9, Dist. by Sporting Book Center). J A Allen.
From State Hospital to Psychiatric Center. Murray Levine. 1980. 15.95 (ISBN 0-669-03810-5). Lexington Bks.
From Sticks & Stones: Personal Adventures in Mathematics. Paul B. Johnson. LC 74-23322. (Illus.). 552p. 1975. text ed. 16.95 (ISBN 0-574-19115-1, 13-6005); instr's guide avail. (ISBN 0-574-19116-X, 13-6006). SRA.
From Story to Stage: The Dramatic Adaptation of Prose Fiction in the Period of Shakespeare & His Contemporaries. Max Bluestone. (Studies in English Literature: No. 70). 1974. pap. 40.00x (ISBN 90-2792-697-2). Mouton.
From Strength to Strength: The First Half Century of the Formative Age of the Baha'i Faith. Eunice Braun. LC 78-9424. 1978. pap. 4.00 (ISBN 0-87743-125-6, 7-32-30). Baha'i.
From Stressors to Strains: Research into Their Interrelationships. N. Van Dijkhuizen. xii, 292p. 1980. pap. text ed. 27.75 (ISBN 90-265-0351-2). Swets North Am.
From Student to Nurse. Ida Simpson. LC 78-31933. (ASA Rose Monographs). 1979. 19.95 (ISBN 0-521-22683-X); pap. 6.95x (ISBN 0-521-29616-1). Cambridge U Pr.
From Sunset to Dawn. Leslie R. Smith. 1945. 4.95 (ISBN 0-687-13664-4). Abingdon.
From "Superman to Man". rev. ed. J. A. Rogers. 132p. 1941. 5.95 (ISBN 0-9602294-4-2). H M Rogers.
From Surrealism to the Absurd. Ed. by Wolodymyr T. Zyla. (Proceedings of the Comparative Literature Symposium: Vol. III). (Illus.). 5.00 o.s.i. (ISBN 0-89672-045-4). Tex Tech Pr.
From Surtees to Sassoon, Some Eng. Contrasts. (1938-1928) Harvey F. Darton. 222p. 1980. Repr. lib. bdg. 25.00 (ISBN 0-8492-4219-3). R West.
From Television to Home Computer: The Future of Consumer Electronics. Ed. by Angus Robertson. (Illus.). 336p. 1980. 27.50 (ISBN 0-7137-0973-1, Pub. by Blandford Pr England). Sterling.
From Tension to Tonic: The Plays of Edward Albee. Anne Paolucci. LC 75-179594. (Crosscurrents-Modern Critiques Ser.). 158p. 1972. 9.95 (ISBN 0-8093-0551-8). S Ill U Pr.
From the Abyss. Of Its Inhabitants by One of Them, London, 1903. C. F. Masterman. LC 79-56963. (English Working Class Ser.). 1980. lib. bdg. 12.00 (ISBN 0-8240-0115-X). Garland Pub.
From the Apostolic Community to Constantine. Ed. by Hubert Jedin & John P. Dolan. (History of the Church: Vol. 1). 1980. 37.50 (ISBN 0-8164-1038-0). Crossroad NY.
From the Ashes of Disgrace: A Journal from Germany, 1945-1955. Hans Speier. LC 80-21599. 336p. 1981. lib. bdg. 20.00x (ISBN 0-87023-135-9). U of Mass Pr.
From the Beginning, 5 bks. Alma Gilleo. Incl. Air Travel from the Beginning (65002-9); Communications from the Beginning (ISBN 0-89565-003-7); Dinosaurs & Other Reptiles from the Beginning (ISBN 0-89565-004-5); Land Travel from the Beginning (ISBN 0-89565-000-2); Water Travel from the Beginning (ISBN 0-89565-000-2). (Illus.). (gr. 1-4). 1977. 27.50 set (ISBN 0-685-86290-9); 5.50 ea. Childs World.
From the Beginning to Alexander the Great. Colin McEvedy & Sarah McEvedy. LC 70-135199. (Atlas of World History Ser). (Illus.). (gr. 6-10). 1971. 5.95 o.s.i. (ISBN 0-02-765530-X, CCPr). Macmillan.
From the Broken Tree. Lee Langley. 1978. 10.95 o.p. (ISBN 0-525-10988-9). Dutton.
From the Center: A Folio of Native American Art & Poetry. Ed. by Maurice Kenny. (Illus.). 30p. (Orig.). 1981. pap. 7.50 (ISBN 0-936574-03-8). Strawberry Pr NY.
From the Circle of Alcuin to the School of Auxerre. J. Marenbon. (Cambridge Studies in Medieval Life & Thought: Third Ser., Vol. 15). (Illus.). 248p. Date not set. price not set (ISBN 0-521-23428-X). Cambridge U Pr.
From the Cold War to Detente. Ed. by Peter J. Potichnyj & Jane P. Shapiro. LC 75-19808. (Praeger Special Studies Ser.). 238p. 1976. text ed. 31.95 (ISBN 0-275-56200-X). Praeger.
From the Community to the Classroom: Gathering Second Language Speech Samples. Barbara F. Freed. (Language in Education Ser.: No. 6). 1978. pap. 2.95 (ISBN 0-87281-085-2). Ctr Appl Ling.
From the Counter to the Bottom Line. Carl Warren & Merl Miller. LC 79-52263. 225p. 1979. pap. 13.95 (ISBN 0-918398-11-8). Dilithium Pr.
From the Country of Eight Islands. Tr. by Hiroaki Sato & Burton Watson. LC 80-1077. 480p. 1981. pap. 9.95 (ISBN 0-385-14030-4, Anch). Doubleday.
From the Country of Eight Islands: An Anthology of Japanese Poetry. Ed. by Hiroaki Sato & Burton Watson. 480p. 1981. 17.50 (ISBN 0-295-95798-0). U of Wash Pr.
From the Declaration of Independence to the Constitution: The Roots of American Constitutionalism. Ed. by Carl J. Friedrich & Robert G. McCloskey. 1954. pap. 4.50 (ISBN 0-672-60006-4, AHS6). Bobbs.
From the Deep Woods to Civilization: Chapters in the Autobiography of an Indian. Charles A. Eastman. LC 77-7226. (Illus.). 1977. 11.95x (ISBN 0-8032-0936-3); pap. 3.75 (ISBN 0-8032-5873-9, BB 651, Bison). U of Nebr Pr.
From the Depths: The Discovery of Poverty in the United States. Robert H. Bremner. LC 56-7622. (Illus.). 364p. 1956. 10.95x (ISBN 0-8147-0054-3); pap. 6.00x (ISBN 0-8147-0055-1). NYU Pr.
From the Diary of a Snail. Gunter Grass. Tr. by Ralph Manheim from Ger. LC 73-6680. 1973. 7.95 o.p. (ISBN 0-15-133800-0). HarBraceJ.
From the Dreadnought to Scapa Flow: The Royal Navy in the Fisher Era, 1904-1919, 5 vols. Arthur J. Marder. Incl. Vol. 1. The Road to War, 1904-1914. 1961. 28.50x (ISBN 0-19-215122-3); Vol. 3. Jutland & After. 2nd ed. 1978. 23.50x (ISBN 0-19-215841-4); Vol. 4. 1917: Year of Crisis. 1969. 24.00x (ISBN 0-19-215170-3); Vol. 5. Victory & Aftermath. 1970. 27.95x (ISBN 0-19-215187-8). Oxford U Pr.
From the Edge of the Crowd. A. J. Gossip. (Scholar As Preacher Ser.). 316p. 1924. text ed. 7.75 (ISBN 0-567-04420-3). Attic Pr.
From the Exile to Christ: Historical Introduction to Palestinian Judaism. Werner Foerster. Ed. by Gordon E. Harris. LC 64-18151. 264p. 1964. pap. 7.50 (ISBN 0-8006-0978-6, 1-978). Fortress.
From the Frontline. Ed. by Gwendolen M. Carter & E. Philip Morgan. (Special Project Ser.: No. 27). 252p. 1980. 26.95. Hoover Inst Pr.
From the Frontline: Speeches of Sir Seretse Khama. Ed. by Gwendolen Carter & E. Philip Morgan. (Special Project Ser.: 27). 252p. 1980. 26.95. Hoover Inst Pr.
From the Grass Roots. Opal Sofge. 3.95 o.p. (ISBN 0-685-48830-6). Nortex Pr.
From the Heat of the Day. Roy A. Heath. 176p. 1981. pap. 5.95 (ISBN 0-8052-8071-5, Pub. by Allison & Busby England). Schocken.
From the Heat of the Earth. Stanley H. Ward. (University of Utah Frederick William Reynolds Lecture Ser.: No. 40). 1977. pap. 1.00 (ISBN 0-87480-127-3). U of Utah Pr.
From the High Middle Ages to the Eve of the Reformation. Ed. by Hubert Jedin & John P. Dolan. (History of the Church: Vol. 4). 1980. 37.50 (ISBN 0-8164-1040-2). Crossroad NY.
From the Kudzu to the Ivy: How to Find Your College: a Southerner's Guide to Northeastern Colleges. Julie R. Brawner et al. 256p. (Orig.). (YA) (gr. 11-12). 1980. pap. 5.95. Kudzu-Ivy.
From the Land & Back. Curtis K. Stadtfield. LC 76-38946. (Illus.). 1974. pap. 2.95 o.p. (ISBN 0-684-13691-0, SL508, ScribT). Scribner.
From the Law of Moses to the Magna Carta: Essays in Ancient & Medieval History. James T. Wall. LC 79-66236. 1979. pap. text ed. 7.50 (ISBN 0-8191-0801-4). U Pr of Amer.
From the Life of the Marionettes. Ingmar Bergman. Tr. by Alan Blair. 1980. 8.95 (ISBN 0-394-51317-7); pap. 2.95 (ISBN 0-394-73970-1). Pantheon.
From the Milk River. Christine Hugh-Jones. LC 76-73126. (Cambridge Studies in Social Anthropology: No. 26). (Illus.). 1980. 24.95 (ISBN 0-521-22544-2). Cambridge U Pr.
From the Miscellania of Venantius Fortunatus. Venantius Fortunatus. Tr. by Geoffrey Cook. LC 79-17109. (Lat.). 1981. 12.00x (ISBN 0-916156-38-9); pap. 5.00x (ISBN 0-916156-40-0). Cherry Valley.
From the Missouri West. Robert Adams. (Illus.). 1980. 20.00 (ISBN 0-89381-059-2); ltd. ed., 100 copies 400.00 (ISBN 0-89381-063-0). Aperture.
From the Mixed-up Files of Mrs. Basil E. Frankweiler. E. L. Konigsburg. 1977. pap. 1.50 (ISBN 0-440-43180-8, YB). Dell.
From the Modern Repertoire: Series One. Ed. by Eric Bentley. Incl. La Parisienne. Becque; The Threepenny Opera. Brecht; Danton's Death. Buchner; The Infernal Machine. Cocteau; Fantasio. De Musset; Sweeney Agonistes. Eliot; The Love of Don Perlimplin. Lorca; Belisa in the Garden. Lorca; Round Dance. Schnitzler; The Snob. Sternheim; A Full Moon in March. Yeats. 424p. 1949. 12.50x (ISBN 0-253-12900-1). Ind U Pr.
From the Modern Repertoire: Series Two. Ed. by Eric Bentley. Incl. Galileo. Brecht; Him. Cummings; The King & The Duke. Fergusson; Electra. Giraudoux; Jest; Satire; Irony. Grabbe; The Dark Tower. MacNeice; The Epidemic. Mirabeau; Venus & Adonis. Obey; Easy Money. Ostrovsky; The Marquis of Keith. Wedekind. (Illus.). 528p. 1952. 15.00x (ISBN 0-253-12901-X). Ind U Pr.
From the Mundane to the Magnificent. Vera S. Alder. 1980. pap. 5.95 (ISBN 0-87728-504-7). Weiser.
From the Myth to Icon: Reflections of Greek Ethical Doctrine in Literature & Art. Helen North. LC 79-7619. (Cornell Studies in Classical Philology). (Illus.). 1979. 19.50x (ISBN 0-8014-1135-1). Cornell U Pr.
From the Nolichucky to Memphis: Reminiscences of a Tennessee Doctor. Samuel F. Strain. LC 79-129552. (Twentieth Century Reminiscence Ser.: No. 2). (Illus.). 1979. 13.95 (ISBN 0-87870-064-1). Memphis St Univ.

From the Orient & the Desert. Ghazi A. Algosaibi. (Illus.). 1978. pap. cancelled o.p. (ISBN 0-85362-176-4, Oriel). Routledge & Kegan.

From the Other's Point of View. J. Daniel Hess. LC 79-22405. 1980. pap. 7.95 (ISBN 0-8361-1912-6). Herald Pr.

From the Picture Press. Ed. by John Szarkowski. LC 72-82886. (Illus.). 96p. 1973. pap. 4.95 (ISBN 0-87070-334-X). Museum Mod Art.

From the Pinnacle of the Temple: Faith or Presumption. Charles Farah, Jr. 1979. 7.95 o.p. (ISBN 0-88270-361-7); pap. 4.95 (ISBN 0-88270-462-1). Logos.

From the Poetry of Sumer: Creation, Glorification, Adoration. Samuel N. Kramer. LC 78-57321. 1979. 11.95x (ISBN 0-520-03703-0). U of Cal Pr.

From the Revolution Through the Age of Jackson. J. Howe. 1973. pap. text ed. 10.95 (ISBN 0-13-331348-4). P-H.

From the Rio Grande to the Arctic: Story of the Richfield Oil Corporation. Charles S. Jones. LC 70-160504. (Illus.). 1972. 17.50 (ISBN 0-8061-0976-9); pap. 6.95 (ISBN 0-8061-1155-0). U of Okla Pr.

From the Rising of the Sun: Christians & Society in Contemporary Japan. James M. Phillips. LC 80-24609. (Illus.). 352p. (Orig.). 1981. pap. 14.95 (ISBN 0-88344-145-4). Orbis Bks.

From the School of Eloquence & Other Poems. Tony Harrison. 56p. 1978. bds. 12.50x (ISBN 0-8476-3132-X). Rowman.

From the Small Town to the Great Community: The Social Thought of Progressive Intellectuals. Jean B. Quandt. 1970. 16.00 (ISBN 0-8135-0679-4). Rutgers U Pr.

From the Stone Age to Christianity. 2nd ed. William Foxwell Albright. 1957. pap. 2.50 (ISBN 0-385-09306-3, A100, Anch). Doubleday.

From the Stone Age to the Forty-Five: Studies in Scottish Material Culture Presented to R. B. K. Stevenson, Former Keeper, National Museum of Antiquities of Scotland. Ed. by D. V. Clarke & Anne O'Connor. 1980. text ed. 34.50x (ISBN 0-85976-046-4). Humanities.

From the Terrace. John O'Hara. 1974. pap. 2.25 o.p. (ISBN 0-445-08247-X). Popular Lib.

From the Tigris to the Tiber. rev. ed. Tom B. Jones. 1978. pap. text ed. 10.50x (ISBN 0-256-01992-4). Dorsey.

From the Top. William D. Sheldon et al. (Breakthrough Ser.). (gr. 7-12). 1976. pap. text ed. 5.12 (ISBN 0-205-04110-8, 5241103); tchrs'. ed. 2.40 (ISBN 0-205-04111-6, 5241111); dup masters 22.00 (ISBN 0-205-05439-0, 5254396). Allyn.

From the Window of God to the Vanity of Man: A Study of Window Symbolism in Western Painting. Carla Gottlieb. LC 80-53355. (Illus.). 500p. 1980. 35.00 (ISBN 0-9604420-1-4); pap. 25.00 (ISBN 0-9604420-2-2). Boian Bks.

From Their Point of View: London Nineteen Eight. M. Loane. LC 79-56961. (English Working Class Ser.). 1980. lib. bdg. 27.00 (ISBN 0-8240-0113-3). Garland Pub.

From Thinking to Behaving. Louise M. Berman. LC 67-19025. (Orig.). 1967. pap. text ed. 4.00x (ISBN 0-8077-1071-7). Tchrs Coll.

From This Dark Stairway. Mignon G. Eberhart. 1976. Repr. of 1931 ed. lib. bdg. 13.20 (ISBN 0-88411-760-X). Amereon Ltd.

From This Day Forward: Staying Married When No One Else Is & Other Reckless Acts. Louise DeGrave. 228p. 1981. 10.95 (ISBN 0-316-17930-2). Little.

From This Mountain-Cerro Gordo. Robert C. Likes & Glenn R. Day. LC 75-44236. (Illus.). 86p. 1975. 7.95 (ISBN 0-912494-16-6); pap. 3.95 (ISBN 0-912494-15-8). Chalfant Pr.

From Three to Thirteen: Socialization & Achievement in School. J. A. Simms & T. H. Simms. (Longman Sociology of Education Ser.). 1969. text ed. 5.00x (ISBN 0-582-32436-X); pap. text ed. 3.00x (ISBN 0-582-32437-8). Humanities.

From Thunder Bay. Arthur Maling. LC 80-8397. 1981. 10.95 (ISBN 0-06-014832-2, HarpT). Har-Row.

From Treble Clef to Bass Clef Baritone. Reginald H. Fink. 1972. pap. 3.95 (ISBN 0-918194-05-9). Accura.

From Trinidad: An Anthology of Early West Indian Writing. Ed. by Reinhard W. Sander. LC 77-20785. 1979. text ed. 37.50x (ISBN 0-8419-0352-2, Africana). Holmes & Meier.

From Tweedledum to Tweedledee: The New Labor Government in Australia. Robert Catley. LC 74-189120. 112p. 1974. pap. 6.00x (ISBN 0-85552-022-1). Intl Pubns Serv.

From Two to Five. Kornei Chukovsky. Ed. & tr. by Miriam Morton. (YA) (gr. 7 up). 1963. pap. 3.95 (ISBN 0-520-00238-5, CAL119). U of Cal Pr.

From Two to Three Years. Don Adcock & Marilyn Segal. LC 80-13834. (Play & Learn Ser.). (Illus.). 1980. pap. 5.95 (ISBN 0-916392-52-X). Oak Tree Pubns.

From Under the Earth: America's Metals, Fuels, & Minerals. Howard E. Smith, Jr. LC 67-18546. (Curriculum Related Bks). (Illus.). (gr. 5-9). 1967. 5.25 o.p. (ISBN 0-15-230270-0, HJ). HarBraceJ.

From Under the Rubble. A. Solzhenitsyn et al. 308p. 1981. pap. 6.95 (ISBN 0-89526-890-6). Regnery-Gateway.

From Utopia to Nightmare. Chad Walsh. LC 71-38130. 190p. 1972. Repr. of 1962 ed. lib. bdg. 13.75x (ISBN 0-8371-6325-0, WAFU); pap. 4.95 (ISBN 0-8371-8959-4, WAF). Greenwood.

From Versailles to Vichy: The Third French Republic 1919-1940. Nathanael Greene. LC 75-101945. (AHM Europe Since 1500 Ser.). 1970. pap. 5.95x (ISBN 0-88295-737-6). AHM Pub.

From Versailles to Wall Street: The International Economy in the 1920's. Derek H. Aldcroft. 1977. 20.00x (ISBN 0-520-03336-1). U of Cal Pr.

From War to Cold War: 1942-48. Roy Douglas. 1980. 19.95 (ISBN 0-312-30862-0). St Martin.

From War to War: The Arab-Israeli Confrontation 1948-1967. Nadav Safran. LC 68-27991. 1969. 10.00 o.p. (ISBN 0-672-53540-8); pap. 9.95 (ISBN 0-672-63540-2). Pegasus.

From West Africa: A Social, Political & Economic Record 1917-1977, 4 vols. Ed. by Victor N. Low. 1981. Set. 130.00x (ISBN 0-7146-3055-1, F Cass Co). Biblio Dist.

From "Wiggins Wonders" Comes Psychic Phenomena. Walter Wiggins. 1981. 8.95 (ISBN 0-533-04235-6). Vantage.

From Woman to Woman: A Gynecologist Answers Questions About You & Your Body. rev. ed. Lucienne Lanson. LC 80-11226. (Illus.). 352p. 1981. 15.00 (ISBN 0-394-51293-6); pap. 8.95 (ISBN 0-394-73996-5). Knopf.

From Writers to Writing: A College Reading & Writing Workbook. L. Kirby & S. Scarry. 364p. 1978. 10.95 (ISBN 0-471-01766-3). Wiley.

From X-Rays to Quarks: Modern Physicists & Their Discoveries. Emilio Segre. LC 80-466. (Illus.). 1980. text ed. 21.95x (ISBN 0-7167-1146-X); pap. text ed. 10.95x (ISBN 0-7167-1147-8). W H Freeman.

From Youth to Constructive Adult Life: The Role of the Public School. Ed. by Ralph Tyler. LC 77-95249. (National Society for the Study of Education, Series on Contemp. Educ. Issues). 1978. 15.75 (ISBN 0-8211-1907-9); text ed. 14.25 ten copies (ISBN 0-685-04972-8). McCutchan.

Front & Center. John Houseman. 1981. pap. 6.95 (ISBN 0-671-41391-0, Touchstone Bks). S&S.

Front Office Operation. Joseph J. Haszonics. LC 77-146929. 1971. text ed. 13.50 (ISBN 0-672-96074-5); tchr's manual 5.90 (ISBN 0-672-96076-1); wkbk. 6.95 (ISBN 0-672-96075-3). Bobbs.

Front Range Restaurants: The One Hundred Best. Richard L. Fetter et al. 1980. pap. 7.95 (ISBN 0-933472-46-3). Johnson Colo.

Frontenac of New France. Ronald Syme. (Illus.). (gr. 5-9). 1969. 6.95 (ISBN 0-688-21318-9). Morrow.

Frontier & the American West. Rodman W. Paul. Ed. by Richard W. Etulain. LC 76-11622. (Goldentree Bibliographies in American History). 1977. pap. text ed. 12.95x (ISBN 0-88295-542-X). AHM Pub.

Frontier Army Sketches. James W. Steele. LC 73-99567. 1969. 7.95x (ISBN 0-8263-0159-2); pap. 2.95 o.p. (ISBN 0-8263-0233-5). U of NM Pr.

Frontier Community: Kansas City to 1870. A. Theodore Brown. LC 63-14768. 1963. 15.00x o.p. (ISBN 0-8262-0023-0). U of Mo Pr.

Frontier Development Policy in Brazil: A Study of Amazonia. Dennis J. Mahar. LC 78-19750. (Praeger Special Studies). 1979. 21.95 (ISBN 0-03-047091-9). Praeger.

Frontier Elements in a Hudson River Village. new ed. Carl Nordstrom. LC 72-91175. (National University Publications). 1973. 13.95 (ISBN 0-8046-9033-2). Kennikat.

Frontier Healers. Lee D. Willoughby. (Making of America Ser.). (Orig.). 1981. pap. 2.75 (ISBN 0-440-02608-3). Dell.

Frontier in American Development: Essays in Honor of Paul Wallace Gates. Ed. by David M. Ellis. (Illus.). 425p. 1969. 22.50x (ISBN 0-8014-0489-4). Cornell U Pr.

Frontier in American Literature. Ed. by Philip Durham & Everett Jones. LC 68-31708. 1969. pap. 8.95 (ISBN 0-672-63040-0). Odyssey Pr.

Frontier in the Formative Years, 1783-1815. Reginald Horsman. LC 76-94404. (Histories of the American Frontier Ser). (Illus.). 253p. 1979. pap. 6.50x (ISBN 0-8263-0313-7). U of NM pr.

Frontier Justice. Wayne Gard. (Illus.). 324p. 1981. 17.50 (ISBN 0-8061-0194-6); pap. 8.95 (ISBN 0-8061-1755-9). U of Okla Pr.

Frontier Lady: Recollections of the Gold Rush & Early California. Sarah Royce. Ed. by Ralph H. Gabriel. LC 76-44263. (Illus.). 1977. 10.95x (ISBN 0-8032-0909-6); pap. 2.45 (ISBN 0-8032-5856-9, BB 634, Bison). U of Nebr Pr.

Frontier Living. Edwin Tunis. LC 75-29639. (Illus.). 168p. (gr. 7 up). 1976. 12.95 (ISBN 0-690-01064-8, TYC-J). T Y Crowell.

Frontier Mission: A History of Religion West of the Southern Appalachians to 1861. Walter B. Posey. LC 66-16229. (Illus.). 448p. 1966. 14.00x (ISBN 0-8131-1119-6). U Pr of Ky.

Frontier on the Potomac. Jonathan Daniels. LC 70-37284. (FDR & the Era of the New Deal Ser). 262p. 1972. Repr. of 1946 ed. lib. bdg. 35.00 (ISBN 0-306-70425-0). Da Capo.

Frontier People of Roman Britain. Peter Salway. (Cambridge Classical Studies). 1965. 34.00 (ISBN 0-521-06187-3). Cambridge U Pr.

Frontier Spirit & Progress. Frank H. Tucker. LC 79-19372. 368p. 1981. text ed. 23.95 (ISBN 0-88229-376-1); pap. text ed. 11.95 (ISBN 0-88229-757-0). Nelson-Hall.

Frontier Trails: The Autobiography of Frank M. Canton. Frank M. Canton. Ed. by Edward E. Dale. LC 66-13415. (Western Frontier Library: Vol. 30). 258p. 1966. pap. 4.95 (ISBN 0-8061-1018-X). U of Okla Pr.

Frontier Violence. W. Eugene Hollon. 1974. 14.95 (ISBN 0-19-501750-1). Oxford U Pr.

Frontier Violence: Another Look. W. Eugene Hollon. LC 73-87617. (Illus.). 288p. 1976. pap. 4.95 (ISBN 0-19-502098-7, 475, GB). Oxford U Pr.

Frontier Wolf. Rosemary Sutcliff. LC 80-39849. (gr. 6 up). 1981. 10.95 (ISBN 0-525-30260-3). Dutton.

Frontier Woman: The Story of Mary Ronan. Ed. by H. G. Merriam. (Illus.). 1975. pap. 4.50 o.p. (ISBN 0-586-15662-5). U of MT Pubns Hist.

Frontiers in Catecholamine Research: Proceedings, International Catecholamine Symposium, 3rd, Strasbourg, France, May, 1973. Ed. by Earl Usdin & Solomon Snyder. 1974. text ed. 95.00 (ISBN 0-08-017922-3). Pergamon.

Frontiers in Liver Disease. Ed. by Paul D. Berk & Thomas C. Chalmers. (Illus.). 300p. 1981. text ed. 35.00 (ISBN 0-86577-017-4). Thieme-Stratton.

Frontiers in Neuroendocrinology, Vol. 4. Ed. by L. Martini & W. F. Ganong. LC 77-82030. 350p. 1976. 29.50 (ISBN 0-89004-033-8). Raven.

Frontiers in Neuroendocrinology, Vol. 5. Ed. by William F. Ganong & Luciano Martini. LC 77-82030. 1978. 31.00 (ISBN 0-89004-135-0). Raven.

Frontiers in Neuroendocrinology, Vol. 6. Ed. by Luciano Martini & William F. Ganong. 430p. 1979. text ed. 42.50 (ISBN 0-89004-404-X). Raven.

Frontiers in Organization & Management. William M. Evan. LC 79-20512. (Praeger Special Studies). 192p. 1980. 19.95 (ISBN 0-03-048441-3). Praeger.

Frontiers in Psychoanalysis: Between the Dream & the Pain. J. B. Pontalis. 1981. write for info. (ISBN 0-8236-2090-5). Intl Univs Pr.

Frontiers in Quantitative Criminology. Ed. by James A. Fox (Quantitative Studies in Social Relations). 1981. price not set (ISBN 0-12-263950-2). Acad Pr.

Frontiers in the Americas: A Global Perspective. Jorge Manach. Tr. by Philip H. Phenix from Span. LC 74-34325. 125p. 1975. 10.25x (ISBN 0-8077-2481-5); pap. 5.75x (ISBN 0-8077-2480-7). Tchrs Coll.

Frontiers in Therapeutic Drug Monitoring. Ed. by Gianni Tognoni et al. (Monographs of the Mario Negri Institute for Pharmacological Research). 200p. 1980. text ed. 21.50 (ISBN 0-89004-508-9). Raven.

Frontiers of Applied Geometru: Proceedings of Symposium. Les Cruces, New Mexico, January 1980. Ed. by Robin J. McLeod & Eugene L. Wachspress. 128p. 1980. pap. 23.40 (ISBN 0-08-026487-5). Pergamon.

Frontiers of Astronomy. Fred Hoyle. LC 55-6582. (Illus.). 1955. 12.50 o.s.i. (ISBN 0-06-002760-6, HarpT). Har-Row.

Frontiers of Change: Early Industrialism in America. Thomas C. Cochran. 175p. 1981. 15.00 (ISBN 0-19-502875-9). Oxford U Pr.

Frontiers of Classroom Research. Ed. by Gabriel Chanan & Sara Delamont. (General Ser.). 266p. 1975. pap. text ed. 20.75x (ISBN 0-85633-075-2, NFER). Humanities.

Frontiers of Communication: The Americas in Search of Political Culture. Karin Dovring. 176p. 1975. 6.95 (ISBN 0-8158-0328-1). Chris Mass.

Frontiers of Consciousness. Ed. by White, John Warren, 1939- 1975. pap. 2.95 (ISBN 0-380-00393-7, 48850). Avon.

Frontiers of Constitutional Liberty. P. G. Kauper. LC 70-173668. (American Constitutional & Legal History Ser.). 252p. 1972. Repr. of 1956 ed. lib. bdg. 25.00 (ISBN 0-306-70408-0). Da Capo.

Frontiers of Criminology. Ed. by H. J. Klare & D. Haxby. 1967. 21.00 (ISBN 0-08-011579-9). Pergamon.

Frontiers of Dance: The Life of Martha Graham. Walter Terry. LC 75-9871. (Women of America Ser.). (Illus.). 160p. (gr. 5-9). 1975. 10.95 (ISBN 0-690-00920-8, TYC-J). T Y Crowell.

Frontiers of Folklore. Ed. by William R. Bascom. LC 77-12784. (AAAS Selected Symposium Ser.: No. 5). (Illus.). 1978. lib. bdg. 17.00x (ISBN 0-89158-432-3). Westview.

Frontiers of Free Radical Chemistry. William A. Pryor. LC 80-19007. 1980. 27.00 (ISBN 0-12-566550-4). Acad Pr.

Frontiers of Knowledge: The Frank Nelson Doubleday Lectures at the National Museum of History & Technology at the Smithsonian Institution, Washington, D. C. Saul Bellow et al. 416p. 1975. Limited Edition. 20.00 (ISBN 0-385-04826-2). Doubleday.

Frontiers of Photography. (Life Library of Photography). (Illus.). 1972. 14.95 (ISBN 0-8094-1064-8). Time-Life.

Frontiers of Sociology. Ed. by T. R. Fyvel. 1965. text ed. 4.25x (ISBN 0-7100-1436-8); pap. text ed. 2.50x (ISBN 0-7100-6093-9). Humanities.

Frontiers of Space. rev. ed. Philip Bono & Kenneth Gatland. LC 76-2028. (Macmillan Color Ser.). 288p. 1976. 9.95 (ISBN 0-02-542810-1, 54281). Macmillan.

Frontiers of Space: Pocket Encyclopedia of Space in Color. Phillip Bono & Kenneth Gatland. (gr. 8 up). 1969. 5.95 o.s.i. (ISBN 0-02-513500-7). Macmillan.

Frontiersman from Lout to Hero: Notes on the Significance of the Comparative Method & the Stage Theory in Early American Literature & Culture. Leo J. Lemay. 1979. pap. 3.50 (ISBN 0-912296-39-9, Dist. by U Pr of Va). Am Antiquarian.

Frontiersmen. Paul O'Neil. LC 76-47101. (Old West Ser.). (Illus.). (gr. 5 up). 1977. 12.96 (ISBN 0-8094-1547-X, Pub. by Time-Life). Silver.

Frontiersmen. Paul O'Neil. (Old West Ser.). 1977. 12.95 (ISBN 0-8094-1545-3). Time-Life.

Frontiersmen in Blue: The United States Army & the Indian, 1848-1865. Robert M. Utley. LC 80-27796. (Illus.). xvi, 384p. 1981. 23.50x (ISBN 0-8032-4550-5, BB 769, Bison); pap. 9.95 (ISBN 0-8032-9550-2). U of Nebr Pr.

Frontierswomen, the Iowa Experience. Glenda Riley. (Illus.). 1981. write for info. (ISBN 0-8138-1470-7). Iowa St U Pr.

Frontiertown: The Politics of Community Building in Israel. Myron J. Aronoff. 306p. 1974. text ed. 17.00x (ISBN 0-7190-0574-4). Humanities.

Frost & Fire. Olov Isaaksson & Soren Hallgren. (Illus.). 1980. 27.50 (ISBN 0-906191-36-X, Pub. by Thule England). Intl Schol Bk Serv.

Frost, Drought & Heat Resistance. J. Levitt. (Protoplasmatologia: Vol. 8, Pt. 6). (Illus.). 1958. pap. 30.70 o.p. (ISBN 0-387-80490-0). Springer-Verlag.

Frost in May. Antonia White. (Virago Modern Classic). 221p. 1980. pap. 4.95 (ISBN 0-8037-2697-X). Dial.

Frost in the Night: A Childhood on the Eve of the Third Reich. Edith Baer. LC 79-27774. 224p. 1980. 8.95 (ISBN 0-394-84364-9); lib. bdg. 8.99 (ISBN 0-394-94364-3). Pantheon.

Frost on the Moon. Catherine Darby. (Moon Chalice Quest Ser.: No. 2). 1977. pap. 1.50 o.p. (ISBN 0-445-04010-6). Popular Lib.

Frosty: A Raccoon to Remember. Harriett E. Weaver. (gr. 5-7). 1977. pap. 1.95 (ISBN 0-671-42094-1). Archway.

Frozen & Quick-Frozen Food: New Agricultural Production & Marketing Aspects, Proceedings of a Joint Symposium, Budapest, 1977. United Nations Economic Commission for Europe & United Nations, Food & Agricultural Organization. LC 77-30194. 1977. pap. 35.00 (ISBN 0-08-022031-2). Pergamon.

Frozen Delights. Diana Collier & Nancy Goff. LC 75-42494. (Illus.). 256p. 1976. 8.95 o.s.i. (ISBN 0-690-01097-4, TYC-T). T Y Crowell.

Frozen Earth: Explaining the Ice Ages. Ronald Fodor. (Illus.). 64p. (gr. 6-12). 1981. PLB 7.95 (ISBN 0-89490-036-6). Enslow Pubs.

Frozen Fire. James Houston. (gr. 7 up). pap. 2.95 (ISBN 0-689-70489-5, A-116, Aladdin). Atheneum.

Frozen Fire. Charlotte Lamb. (Harlequin Presents Ser.). 192p. 1980. pap. 1.50 (ISBN 0-373-10380-8, Pub. by Harlequin). PB.

Frozen Hors D'oeuvre Cookbook: You've Got It Made. Jane Keyes. (Illus.). 224p. 1980. 12.95 (ISBN 0-8038-8602-0). Hastings.

Frozen Human Semen: A Royal College of Obstetricians & Gynaecologists Workshop in the Cryobiology of Human Semen & Its Role on Artificial Insemination by Donor, March 22 & 23, 1979. Ed. by David W. Richardson et al. (Developments in Obstetrics & Gynecology Ser.: No. 4). 280p. 1980. lib. bdg. 49.95 (ISBN 90-247-2370-1, Martinus Nijhoff Pubs). Kluwer Boston.
FRP Technology. R. G. Weatherhead. (Illus.). xvii, 460p. 1980. 70.00x (ISBN 0-85334-886-3). Burgess-Intl Ideas.
Fructose Cookbook. Minuha Cannon. (Illus.). 128p. (Orig.). 1979. lib. bdg. 9.25 o.p. (ISBN 0-914788-18-3); pap. 5.95 (ISBN 0-914788-18-3). East Woods.
Fruehromantische Dichtungstheorie. Armand Nivelle. (Ger). 1970. 35.90x (ISBN 3-11-002703-8). De Gruyter.
Fruit. David Hughes. (Illus.). (ps). 1979. 1.25 (ISBN 0-370-02040-5, Pub. by Chatto Bodley Jonathan). Merrimack Bk Serv.
Fruit & Vegetable Juice Processing. J. K. Paul. LC 75-532. (Food Technology Review Ser: No. 21). (Illus.). 277p. 1975. 36.00 o.p. (ISBN 0-8155-0565-5). Noyes.
Fruit & Vegetable Juice Processing Technology. 3rd ed. Philip E. Nelson & Donald K. Tressler. (Illus.). 1980. text ed. 36.00 (ISBN 0-87055-362-3). AVI.
Fruit & Vegetable Juice Processing Technology. 2nd ed. Donald K. Tressler & M. A. Joslyn. (Illus.). 1971. 36.00 o.p. (ISBN 0-87055-098-5). AVI.
Fruit Cookbook. Suzanne Topper. 1973. pap. 2.95 o.p. (ISBN 0-380-01202-2, 14803). Avon.
Fruit Flies or Tephritidae of California. Richard H. Foote & F. L. Blanc. (Bulletin of the California Insect Survey: Vol. 7). 1963. pap. 8.50x (ISBN 0-520-09032-2). U of Cal Pr.
Fruit for Tomorrow. Francena H. Arnold. pap. 2.50 (ISBN 0-310-20222-1). Zondervan.
Fruit Growing in Southern Africa. Zoe Gilbert. 1980. 25.00x (Pub. by Bailey & Swinton South Africa). State Mutual Bk.
Fruit Key & Twig Key to Trees & Shrubs. William M. Harlow. (Illus.). 6.00 (ISBN 0-8446-0678-2). Peter Smith.
Fruit of That Forbidden Tree: Restoration Poems, Songs & Jests on the Subject of Sensual Love. Ed. by John Adlard. (Fyfield Ser.). 1980. 6.95 (ISBN 0-85635-146-6, Pub. by Carcanet New Pr England); pap. 3.95 (ISBN 0-85635-147-4). Persea Bks.
Fruit of the Spirit. rev. ed. (Aglow Bible Study: Bk. 3R). 64p. 1980. pap. 1.95 (ISBN 0-930756-54-1, 4220-3R). Women's Aglow.
Fruit of the Spirit. Donald Gee. 80p. 1975. pap. 1.25 (ISBN 0-88243-501-9, 02-0501, Radiant Bks). Gospel Pub.
Fruit of the Spirit. John W. Sanderson. 144p. 1976. pap. 2.95 (ISBN 0-310-32542-0). Zondervan.
Fruit Preservation. Ed. by Duru Jagtiani. 128p. 1980. text ed. 10.50 (ISBN 0-7069-1039-7, Pub. by Vikas India). Advent Bk.
Fruitbasket Friends. JoAn Summers. LC 75-7481. (gr. 4-8). 1975. pap. 3.50 (ISBN 0-88270-121-5). Logos.
Fruited Plain: The Story of American Agriculture. Walter Ebeling. 1980. 24.50 (ISBN 0-520-03751-0). U of Cal Pr.
Fruitful & Responsible Love. Karol Wojtyla. (Orig.). 1979. pap. 2.95 (ISBN 0-8164-2237-0). Crossroad NY.
Fruitless Repentance; or, the History of Kitty le Fever, 1769, 2 vols. in 1. Ed. by Michael F. Shugrue. (Flowering of the Novel, 1740-1775 Ser: Vol. 86). 1974. lib. bdg. 50.00 (ISBN 0-8240-1185-6). Garland Pub.
Fruits & Vegetables. Erica Jong. LC 74-138876. 1971. 5.95 o.p. (ISBN 0-03-085998-0); pap. 3.95 (ISBN 0-03-085999-9). HR&W.
Fruits for Southern Florida. David Sturrock. 196p. 1980. pap. 7.95 (ISBN 0-9600046-2-9). Horticultural.
Fruits of Solitude. William Penn. pap. 3.95 (ISBN 0-913408-39-5). Friends United.
Fruto Del Espiritu. (Aglow Bible Study: Bk. 3). 64p. (Span.). 1980. pap. 1.95 (ISBN 0-930756-53-3, 4220-3(S)). Women's Aglow.
Fruto Do Espirito. Tr. by Charles R. Hembree. (Portuguese Bks.). 1979. 1.50 (ISBN 0-8297-0652-6). Life Pubs Intl.
Frutos De Mi Trasplante. Alrto Andino. LC 79-52356. (Coleccion Caniqui). 102p. (Span.). 1980. pap. 5.95 (ISBN 0-89729-230-8). Ediciones.
Fry Cooking. Ser-Vol-Tel Institute. (Foodservice Career Education Ser.). 1974. pap. 4.95 (ISBN 0-8436-2028-5). CBI Pub.
Fuchsias. Stanley Wilson. 1977. pap. 10.95 (ISBN 0-571-11047-9, Pub. by Faber & Faber). Merrimack Bk Serv.
Fuchsias in Color. Brian Proudley & Valerie Proudley. (Illus.). 206p. 1981. 12.95 (ISBN 0-7137-0754-2, Pub. by Blandford Pr England). Sterling.
Fuel Alcohol: How to Make It, How to Use It. James Ross. 160p. 1981. 9.95 (ISBN 0-312-30932-5); pap. 4.95 (ISBN 0-312-30933-3). St Martin.
Fuel Alcohol on the Farm. U.S. National Alcohols Fuels Commission. 50p. 1981. pap. 4.95 (ISBN 0-89934-097-0). Solar Energy Info.
Fuel & Energy. Herta S. Breiter. LC 77-18560. (Read About Sciences Ser.). (Illus.). (gr. k-3). 1978. PLB 9.95 (ISBN 0-8393-0083-2). Raintree Child.
Fuel & Fuel Elements for Fast Reactors, 2 vols. (Illus.). 906p. (Orig., Eng., Fr., Rus. & Span.). 1974. Vol. 1. pap. 25.75 (ISBN 92-0-050074-9, IAEA); Vol. 2. pap. 32.25 (ISBN 92-0-050174-5). Unipub.
Fuel & Lubricant Additives. BCC Staff. 1981. 800.00 (ISBN 0-89336-239-5, C-027). BCC.
Fuel & Power, 5 pts. Incl. Pt. 1. Coal Trade, 5 vols. Set. 405.00x (ISBN 0-686-01141-4); Pt. 2. Gas, 6 vols. Set. 423.00x (ISBN 0-686-01142-2); Pt. 3. Mining Accidents, 12 vols. Set. 954.00x (ISBN 0-686-01143-0); Pt. 4. Mining Districts, 2 vols. Set. 153.00x (ISBN 0-686-01144-9); Pt. 5. Mining Royalties, 3 vols. Set. 216.00x (ISBN 0-686-01145-7). (British Parliamentary Papers Ser.). 1971 (Pub. by Irish Academic Pr Ireland). Biblio Dist.
Fuel Burn-up Predictions in Thermal Reactors. (Illus., Orig., Eng. & Fr.). 1968. pap. 12.50 (ISBN 92-0-051068-X, IAEA). Unipub.
Fuel Economy of the Gasoline Engine. D. R. Blackmore & A. Thomas. LC 77-3916. 1977. 27.95 (ISBN 0-470-99132-1). Halsted Pr.
Fuel Efficiency in Industrial Practice. 288p. 1980. 11.00 (ISBN 92-833-1051-9, APO81, APO). Unipub.
Fuel from Farms. Solar Energy Research Institute. 161p. 1980. 20.95 (ISBN 0-89934-050-4, B947-PP); pap. 10.95 (ISBN 0-89934-051-2, B047-PP). Solar Energy Info.
Fuel Oil Manual. 3rd ed. Paul F. Schmidt. LC 69-10507. (Illus.). 1969. 21.00 (ISBN 0-8311-3014-8). Indus Pr.
Fuels & Fuel Technology, 2 Vols. W. Francis. 1965. Vol. 1. 27.00 (ISBN 0-08-010754-0); Vol. 2. 28.00 (ISBN 0-08-010756-7); Vol. 1. pap. 11.75 (ISBN 0-08-010753-2); Vol. 2. pap. 11.75 (ISBN 0-08-010755-9). Pergamon.
Fuels & Fuel Technology. 2nd ed. W. Francis & M. C. Peters. (Illus.). 608p. 1980. 105.00 (ISBN 0-08-025249-4); pap. 34.50 (ISBN 0-08-025250-8). Pergamon.
Fuels & Refractories. J. D. Gilchrist. 1963. 9.90 (ISBN 0-08-009780-4); pap. 4.95 (ISBN 0-08-009779-0). Pergamon.
Fuels from Biomass: Technology & Feasibility. Ed. by J. S. Robinson. LC 80-23488. (Energy Tech. Re. 61; Chem. Tech. Rev. 176). (Illus.). 377p. 1981. 48.00 (ISBN 0-8155-0824-7). Noyes.
Fuente Hispana. R. G. Marshall et al. (Level 3). (gr. 10-12). 1971. text ed. 11.95 (ISBN 0-07-040575-1, C); instructors' manual 3.95 (ISBN 0-07-040579-4); tapes 250.00 (ISBN 0-07-098975-3). test pkg. replacement 25.00 (ISBN 0-07-040578-6). McGraw.
Fuerza. Harlan Wade. Tr. by Mamie M. Contreras from Eng. LC 78-26850. (Book About Ser.). Orig. Title: Strength. (Illus., Sp.). (gr. k-3). 1979. PLB 7.30 (ISBN 0-8172-1478-X). Raintree Pubs.
Fugitive Essays: Selected Writings of Frank Chodorov. Frank Chodorov. LC 79-28720. 416p. 1980. 9.00 (ISBN 0-913966-72-X); pap. 4.00 (ISBN 0-686-63047-5). Liberty Fund.
Fugitive Facts. 2nd ed. Ed. by Robert Thorne. LC 69-19882. 1969. Repr. of 1889 ed. 20.00 (ISBN 0-8103-3750-9). Gale.
Fugue. Roger Bullivant. 1971. pap. text ed. 3.00x (ISBN 0-09-108441-5, Hutchinson U Lib). Humanities.
Fugue for an October Age. R. Martin Helick. 340p. 1980. pap. 6.95 (ISBN 0-912710-09-8). Regent Graphic Serv.
Fugue for Beginners. Eric Thiman. (YA) (gr. 9 up). 1966. 3.90 (ISBN 0-19-321770-8). Oxford U Pr.
Fulcanelli: Master Alchemist, le Mystere Des Cathedrales. 2nd ed. Fulcanelli. Tr. by Mary Sworder. (Illus.). 1977. Repr. of 1971 ed. 14.00 (ISBN 0-685-01095-3). Bro Life Bks.
Fulfillment. James M. Bryant. 1976. pap. 6.50 (ISBN 0-686-27964-6). J M Bryant.
Fulfillment. LaVyrle Spencer. 1979. pap. 2.25 (ISBN 0-380-47084-5, 47084). Avon.
Fulfillment of the Scriptures: Abraham, Moses & Piers. Ruth M. Ames. 1970. 9.95x o.s.i. (ISBN 0-8101-0301-X). Northwestern U Pr.
Fulke Greville, Lord Brooke, 1554-1628: A Critical Biography. Joan Rees. LC 79-132064. (Illus.). 1971. 17.50x (ISBN 0-520-01824-9). U of Cal Pr.
Full Account of the Wonderful Mission of Earl Lavender. John Davidson. Ed. by Ian Fletcher & John Stokes. LC 76-20049. (Decadent Consciousness Ser.: Vol. 7). 1977. Repr. of 1894 ed. lib. bdg. 38.00 (ISBN 0-8240-2756-6). Garland Pub.
Full and Particular Account of the Life and Transactions of Roger Johnson. Ed. by Michael F. Shugrue. Bd. with Life and Adventures of Gilbert Langley. Repr. of 1740 ed; True and Impartial History of the Life and Adventures of Somebody. Repr. of 1740 ed; Apology for the Life of Mrs. Shamela Andrews. Henry Fielding. Repr. of 1741 ed. (Flowering of the Novel, 1740-1775 Ser: Vol. 3). 1974. Repr. of 1740 ed. lib. bdg. 50.00 (ISBN 0-8240-1102-3). Garland Pub.
Full Assurance. Harry A. Ironside. 1937. pap. 1.50 (ISBN 0-8024-2896-7). Moody.
Full Circle. J. E. Johnson. (War Book Ser.). 288p. 1980. pap. 2.50 (ISBN 0-553-13568-6). Bantam.
Full Circle. Erich M. Remarque. LC 74-1190. 1974. 6.95 o.p. (ISBN 0-15-134100-1). HarBraceJ.
Full-Color Designs from Chinese Opera Costumes. Northeast Drama Institute. (Illus.). 1980. pap. 6.00 (ISBN 0-486-23979-9). Dover.
Full-Color Russian Folk Needlepoint Designs Charted for Easy Use. Frieda Halpern. (Needlework Ser). (Illus.). 1976. pap. 2.95 (ISBN 0-486-23451-7). Dover.
Full-Color Uniforms of the Prussian Army: Seventy-Two Plates from the Year 1830. L. Sachse & Co. (Illus.). 80p. 1981. pap. price not set (ISBN 0-486-24085-1). Dover.
Full Count. George Mason & William D. Sheldon. (Breakthrough Ser.). (RL 1). 1973. pap. text ed. 5.12 (ISBN 0-205-03336-9, 5233364); tchrs'. guide 2.40 (ISBN 0-205-03102-1, 5231027). Allyn.
Full Employment in a Free Society. Lord Beveridge. 1960. text ed. 55.00x (ISBN 0-04-331004-4). Allen Unwin.
Full Employment Program for the 1970's. Ed. by Alan Gartner et al. LC 75-36408. (Praeger Special Studies Ser.). 160p. 1976. text ed. 11.95 (ISBN 0-275-22810-X). Praeger.
Full Employment Without Inflation. John H. Pierson. LC 79-5446. 254p. 1980. text ed. 18.50 (ISBN 0-916672-39-5). Allanheld.
Full Length Animated Feature Films. Ed. by Bruno Edera. (Library of Animation Technology). Date not set. 37.50 (ISBN 0-8038-2317-7). Hastings.
Full Moon to France. Devereaux Rochester. LC 76-26250. 1977. 8.95 o.s.i. (ISBN 0-06-013586-7, HarpT). Har-Row.
Full Moons. Paul Katzeff. 1981. 12.95 (ISBN 0-8065-0737-3). Lyle Stuart.
Full of Grace & Truth, Vol. 1. Watchman Nee. Tr. by Stephen Kaung. 1980. 2.95 (ISBN 0-935008-49-7). Christian Fellow Pubs.
Full of Joy. Margaret Ragland. 1980. pap. 3.95 (ISBN 0-89137-415-9). Quality Pubns.
Full of the Moon. Chloe Fries. (Challenge Bks). (Illus.). (gr. 4-8). 1979. PLB 5.95 (ISBN 0-87191-686-X). Creative Ed.
Full-Size Stained Glass Templates: Sixteen Attractive & Easy Patterns. Ed Sibbett, Jr. (Illus.). 1979. pap. 4.00 (ISBN 0-486-23744-3). Dover.
Full Summer. Frederick Buell. LC 78-25914. (Wesleyan Poetry Program: Vol. 95). 1979. 10.00x (ISBN 0-8195-2095-0, Pub. by Wesleyan U Pr); pap. 4.95 (ISBN 0-8195-1095-5). Columbia U Pr.
Fullback in the Large Fry League. C. Paul Jackson. (Illus.). (gr. 6-9). 1965. 4.95g o.p. (ISBN 0-8038-2261-8). Hastings.
Fullness of the Spirit. Kenneth S. Wuest. 1975. pap. 2.50 (ISBN 0-8024-2897-5). Moody.
Fully Ordered Groups. A. I. Kokorin & V. M. Kopytov. Tr. by D. Louvish from Rus. LC 73-22108. 147p. 1974. 32.95 (ISBN 0-470-49887-0). Halsted Pr.
Fulness & Freedom. R. J. Lucas. Ed. by J. A. Motyer & J. R. Stott. LC 79-3635. (Bible Speaks Today Ser.). 1980. pap. 4.95 (ISBN 0-87784-602-2). Inter-Varsity.
Fulper Art Pottery: An Aesthetic Appreciation, 1909-1929. Robert Blasberg & Carol L. Bohdan. (Jordan-Volpe Gallery Ser.). (Illus.). 88p. pap. 14.95 (ISBN 0-87905-069-1). Peregrine Smith.
Fun & Fantasy Book. Buzz Featherman. LC 80-54612. (Illus.). 144p. (Orig.). 1981. pap. text ed. 6.95 (ISBN 0-932238-04-1). Word Shop.
Fun & Fantasy Book. new ed. Buzz Featherman. (Illus.). 1980. 6.95 (ISBN 0-932238-03-3). Word Shop.
Fun & Fellowship Resource Book. Helen Eisenberg & Larry Eisenberg. (Game & Party Bks.). 160p. 1981. pap. 3.95 (ISBN 0-8010-3364-0). Baker Bk.
Fun & Games. Max Brodnick. (Illus.). 1976. pap. 1.25 o.p. (ISBN 0-685-72565-0, LB394, Leisure Bks). Nordon Pubns.
Fun & Profit in Stamp Collecting. Herman Herst, Jr. (gr. 9 up). 1975. pap. 3.95 (ISBN 0-8015-2851-8, Hawthorn). Dutton.
Fun Astrology. Sondra Hill. Orig. Title: All About Astrology. (Illus.). 96p. (gr. 4-7). 1981. PLB price not set (ISBN 0-671-41629-4). Messner.
Fun at Camp. Sharon Peters. (Illus.). 32p. (gr. k-2). 1980. PLB 2.96 (ISBN 0-89375-378-5); pap. 0.95 (ISBN 0-89375-278-9). Troll Assocs.
Fun Days. Margaret Hillert. (Just Beginning-to-Read Ser.). (Illus.). (gr. 1-6). 1981. PLB 4.39 (ISBN 0-695-41546-8); pap. 1.50 (ISBN 0-695-31546-3). Follett.
Fun Encyclopedia. Elvin O. Harbin. (Illus.). (gr. 4 up). 1940. 8.95 (ISBN 0-687-13714-4). Abingdon.
Fun for All. Ed. by Steven Otfinoski. (Beginning Pal Paperbacks Ser.). (Illus., Orig.). (gr. 7-12). 1977. pap. text ed. 1.25 (ISBN 0-8374-3467-X). Xerox Ed Pubns.
Fun for Hunkydory. May Justus. (Illus.). 24p. (gr. k-3). 1976. PLB 5.00 (ISBN 0-307-60521-3, Golden Pr). Western Pub.
Fun for You. Mabel O'Donnell. (Design for Reading Ser). (Illus.). (preprimer 3). 1972. pap. 2.92 (ISBN 0-06-516002-9, SchDept). Har-Row.
Fun Ideas for Family Devotions (with Activity Pages) Ginger Jurries & Karen Mulder. (Illus.). 176p. (Orig.). 1981. pap. 5.95 (ISBN 0-87239-415-8, 2968). Standard Pub.
Fun in a Chinese Laundry: An Autobiography. Josef Von Sternberg. 352p. 1973. pap. 2.95 o.s.i. (ISBN 0-02-012870-3, Collier). Macmillan.
Fun Is Therapeutic: A Recreation Book to Help Therapeutic Recreation Leaders by People Who Are Leading Recreation. Ardis Stevens. 104p. 1972. 9.75 (ISBN 0-398-02421-9). C C Thomas.
Fun Joke Book. Bob Phillips. pap. 1.95 (ISBN 0-89081-235-7). Harvest Hse.
Fun-N-Games. Wayne Rice et al. 1977. pap. 5.95 (ISBN 0-310-35001-8). Zondervan.
Fun of Figure Skating. Maribel V. Owen. LC 60-10433. (Illus.). 1960. 11.95 o.s.i. (ISBN 0-06-071470-0, HarpT). Har-Row.
Fun of It: Random Records of My Own Flying & of Women in Aviation. Amelia Earhart. LC 71-159945. 1975. Repr. of 1932 ed. 18.00 (ISBN 0-8103-4078-X). Gale.
Fun on Wheels. Joanna Cole. (Illus.). (ps-1). 1977. 7.25 (ISBN 0-688-22102-5); PLB 6.96 (ISBN 0-688-32102-X). Morrow.
Fun Plans for Church Recreation. Ed. by Agnes D. Pylant. LC 58-8924. 1958. 4.95 (ISBN 0-8054-7501-X). Broadman.
Fun-to-Find Word Games, No. 1. 128p. 1974. pap. 0.95 o.p. (ISBN 0-445-08249-6). Popular Lib.
Fun-to-find Word Games, No. 2. (Orig.). 1974. pap. 0.95 o.p. (ISBN 0-445-00577-7). Popular Lib.
Fun-to-Find Word Games, No. 3. (Orig.). 1974. pap. 0.95 o.p. (ISBN 0-445-00587-4). Popular Lib.
Fun-to-Find Word Games, No. 4. pap. 0.95 o.p. (ISBN 0-445-00606-4). Popular Lib.
Fun-to-Make Nature Crafts. Robyn Supraner. LC 80-23399. (Illus.). 48p. (gr. 2-5). 1980. PLB 6.92 (ISBN 0-89375-440-4); pap. 1.75 (ISBN 0-89375-441-2). Troll Assocs.
Fun Ways to Holidays. Mamie G. Gamoran. (gr. 5-9). 1951. pap. 2.00 (ISBN 0-8074-0136-6, 321400). UAHC.
Fun with ABC & 1-2-3. Hal Dareff. LC 65-18659. (Illus.). (ps-2). 1965. 5.95 o.s.i. (ISBN 0-8193-0105-1, Four Winds); PLB 5.41 o.s.i. (ISBN 0-8193-0106-X). Schol Bk Serv.
Fun with Applique & Patchwork. 1970. 14.95 (ISBN 0-7134-2458-3, Pub. by Batsford England). David & Charles.
Fun with Bible Geography. Marie Chapman. LC 80-65055. (Teaching Aid Ser.). 65p. 1980. plastic spiral 3.75 (ISBN 0-89636-044-X). Accent Bks.
Fun with Brain Puzzlers. L. H. Longley-Cook. 1977. pap. 1.25 o.p. (ISBN 0-449-13755-4, GM). Fawcett.
Fun with Building Models. Roy Laming. (Learning with Fun Ser.). (Illus.). 64p. 1980. text ed. 11.50x (ISBN 0-7182-1322-X, SpS). Soccer.
Fun with Clay. Joseph Leeming. (Illus.). (gr. 7-9). 1944. 8.95 o.p. (ISBN 0-397-30095-6). Lippincott.
Fun with Collage. Jan Beaney. (Learning with Fun Ser.). (Illus.). 64p. (gr. 5 up). 1980. text ed. 11.50x (ISBN 0-7182-1320-3, LTB). Soccer.
Fun with Computers & Basic. Donald D. Spencer. LC 76-45411. 1977. pap. 6.95 (ISBN 0-89218-005-6). Camelot Pub.
Fun with Cooking. rev ed. Mae B. Freeman. (Illus.). (gr. 4-6). 1947. 3.95 (ISBN 0-394-80278-0, BYR); PLB 4.99 (ISBN 0-394-90278-5). Random.
Fun with Fabric Printing. K. Monk. 8.00 o.p. (ISBN 0-87245-231-X). Textile Bk.
Fun with Felt. Annette Feldman. 184p. 1980. 15.95 (ISBN 0-442-25774-0). Van Nos Reinhold.
Fun with Felt. Jutta Lammer. 1970. 14.95 (ISBN 0-7134-2459-1, Pub. by Batsford England). David & Charles.

Fun with Flowers. Martha Neese & Marvin Neese. LC 68-27867. (Illus.). 72p. 1980. pap. 8.95 (ISBN 0-8348-0152-3). Weatherhill.

Fun with Flowers. Marvin Neese & Martha Neese. LC 68-57453. (Illus.). 112p. 1980. pap. 8.95 (ISBN 0-8348-0153-1, Pub. by John Weatherhill Inc Japan). C E Tuttle.

Fun with Fossils. William Cartner. (Learning with Fun Ser.). (Illus.). (gr. 5 up). 1977. 11.50x (ISBN 0-7180-0713-1, LTB). Soccer.

Fun with Fruit Preservation: Leather, Drying, & Other Methods. Dora D. Flack. LC 74-78025. (Illus.). 98p. 1973. pap. 4.50 (ISBN 0-88290-023-4). Horizon Utah.

Fun with Growing Things. Joan Eckstein & Joyce Gleit. (Illus.). 1975. pap. 2.95 o.p. (ISBN 0-380-00344-9, 23861). Avon.

Fun with Magic. Alexander Van Rensselaer. LC 57-9854. (gr. 3-9). 1956. 4.95 o.p. (ISBN 0-385-02428-2). Doubleday.

Fun with Paper. Joseph Leeming. (Illus.). (gr. 4-6). 1939. 6.50 o.p. (ISBN 0-397-30061-1). Lippincott.

Fun with Paper. Robyn Supraner. LC 80-19859. (Illus.). 48p. (gr. 2-5). 1980. PLB 6.92 (ISBN 0-89375-430-7); pap. 1.75 (ISBN 0-89375-431-5). Troll Assocs.

Fun with Picture Projects. Tony Hart. LC 73-174505. (Learning with Fun Ser.). 64p. (gr. 3 up). 1973. 8.50x (ISBN 0-7182-0082-9). Intl Pubns Serv.

Fun with Scientific Experiments. Mae B. Freeman & Ira M. Freeman. (Illus.). (gr. 4-7). 1960. 3.95 o.p. (ISBN 0-394-80281-0, BYR); PLB 4.99 (ISBN 0-394-90281-5). Random.

Fun with Shells. Joseph Leeming. (Illus.). (gr. 7-9). 1958. 4.82 o.p. (ISBN 0-397-31384-5). Lippincott.

Fun with Short Wave Radio. rev. ed. Gilbert Davey. Ed. by Jack Cox. (Learning with Fun Ser.). (Illus.). 64p. 1980. text ed. 11.50x (ISBN 0-7182-1319-X, Sps). Soccer.

Fun with Stagecraft. Andrew McCallum. (Illus.). 64p. 1981. 8.95 (ISBN 0-89490-008-0). Enslow Pubs.

Fun with Weaving. Alice Gilbreath. (Illus.). 96p. (gr. 3-7). 1976. 6.25 (ISBN 0-688-22064-9); PLB 6.00 o.p. (ISBN 0-688-32063-5). Morrow.

Fun with Weaving. Eileen Hobden. (Learning with Fun Ser.). (Illus.). 64p. (gr. 5 up). text ed. 11.50x (ISBN 0-7182-1317-3, SpS). Soccer.

Fun with Words. 1977. 2.95 (ISBN 0-442-82573-0). Peter Pauper.

Funciones De Variable Compleja. Cesar Trejo. Orig. Title: Variable Compleja. (Span.). 1974. 8.30 (ISBN 0-06-319300-0, IntlDept). Har-Row.

Function & Analysis of Capital Market Rates. James C. Van Horne. LC 73-99453. 1970. pap. 10.95 ref. ed. (ISBN 0-13-331934-2). P-H.

Function & Context in Linguistics Analysis. Ed. by D. J. Allerton et al. LC 78-11603. 1979. 26.95 (ISBN 0-521-22429-2). Cambridge U Pr.

Function & Form in the Sloth. M. Goffart. 1971. 37.00 (ISBN 0-08-016090-5). Pergamon.

Function & Formation of Neural Systems, LSRR 6. Ed. by Gunther S. Stent. (Dahlem Workshop Reports Ser.). 1977. pap. 33.90 (ISBN 0-89573-090-1). Verlag Chemie.

Function & Metabolism of Phospholipids in the Central & Peripheral Nervous Systems. Ed. by Giuseppe Porcellati et al. LC 76-15617. (Advances in Experimental Medicine & Biology Ser.: Vol. 72). 412p. 1976. 45.00 (ISBN 0-306-39072-8, Plenum Pr). Plenum Pub.

Function & Molecular Aspects of Biomembrane Transport: Proceedings. International Symposium on Function & Molecular Aspects of Biomembrane Transport, Italy, April 1979. Ed. by E. Quagliariello et al. (Developments in Bioenergetics & Biomembranes Ser.: Vol. 3). 526p. 1979. 68.50 (ISBN 0-444-80149-9, North Holland). Elsevier.

Function of Criticism: Problems & Exercises. Yvor Winters. LC 57-1652. 220p. 1957. pap. 5.95x (ISBN 0-8040-0130-8, 83). Swallow.

Function of Mimesis & Its Decline. 2nd ed. John D. Boyd. LC 68-28691. 1980. pap. 8.00 (ISBN 0-8232-1046-4). Fordham.

Function of Religion: An Introduction. Louis B. Jennings. LC 79-53368. 1979. pap. text ed. 12.00 (ISBN 0-8191-0789-1). U Pr of Amer.

Function of the Lexicon in Transformational Generative Grammar. Rudolf P. Botha. (Janua Linguarum, Ser. Major: No. 38). 1968. text ed. 44.10x (ISBN 90-2790-688-2). Mouton.

Function of the Masque in Jacobean Tragedy & Tragicomedy. Marie Cornelia. (Salzburg Studies in English Literature, Jacobean Drama Studies: No. 77). 1978. pap. text ed. 25.00x (ISBN 0-391-01350-5). Humanities.

Function of the Orgasm. Wilhelm Reich. Tr. by V. Carfagno. 416p. 1973. 10.95 (ISBN 0-374-15965-3). FS&G.

Function of the Orgasm: The Discovery of the Orgone. Wilhelm Reich. Tr. by Wilhelm Reich. (Illus.). pap. 3.95 o.p. (ISBN 0-452-00337-7, FM337, Mer). NAL.

Function of the Persona in the Poetry of Byron. Jane Kirchner. (Salzburg Studies in English Literature, Romantic Reassessment: No.15). 1973. pap. text ed. 25.00x (ISBN 0-391-01446-3). Humanities.

Function Theoretic Methods in Partial Differential Equations. R. P. Gilbert. (Mathematics in Science & Engineering Ser: Vol. 54). 1969. 46.00 (ISBN 0-12-283050-4). Acad Pr.

Functional Adaptations of Marine Organisms. Ed. by F. J. Vernberg & W. B. Vernberg. (Physiological Ecology Ser.). 1981. price not set (ISBN 0-12-718280-2). Acad Pr.

Functional Administration in Physical & Health Education. Marion Johnson. LC 76-13089. (Illus.). 1977. text ed. 17.75 (ISBN 0-395-20635-9); inst. manual 1.25 (ISBN 0-395-20636-7); study guide 8.25 (ISBN 0-395-20637-5). HM.

Functional Analysis. George Bachman & Lawrence Narici. 1966. text ed. 22.95 (ISBN 0-12-070250-9). Acad Pr.

Functional Analysis. 2nd ed. L. V. Kantorovich & G. P. Akilov. 800p. 1981. 100.00 (ISBN 0-08-023036-9); pap. 35.00 (ISBN 0-08-026486-7). Pergamon.

Functional Analysis. B. V. Limaye. LC 80-84533. 400p. 1981. 17.95 (ISBN 0-470-26933-2). Halsted Pr.

Functional Analysis. 5th ed. K. Yosida. (Grundlehren der Mathematischen Wissenschaften: Vol. 123). 1978. 34.10 o.p. (ISBN 0-387-08627-7). Springer-Verlag.

Functional Analysis. 6th ed. K. Yosida. (Grundlehren der Mathematischen Wissenschaften Ser.: Vol. 123). 501p. 1980. 39.00 (ISBN 0-387-10210-8). Springer-Verlag.

Functional Analysis & Measure Theory. rev. ed. M. G. Krein et al. (Translations Ser.: No. 1, Vol. 10). 1980. 37.20 (ISBN 0-8218-1610-1, TRANS 1-10). Am Math.

Functional Analysis of Information Networks. Hal B. Becker. 296p. 1981. Repr. of 1973 ed. lib. bdg. write for info. (ISBN 0-89874-028-2). Krieger.

Functional Analysis of Information Processing. Grayce M. Booth. LC 80-11247. 288p. 1981. Repr. of 1973 ed. lib. bdg. write for info. (ISBN 0-89874-135-1). Krieger.

Functional Analysis of Politics: An Introductory Discussion. Roy E. Jones. (Orig.). 1967. text ed. 5.75x (ISBN 0-7100-5131-X); pap. text ed. 2.75x (ISBN 0-7100-5120-4). Humanities.

Functional Anatomy of Marine Mammals. R. J. Harrison. 52.00 (ISBN 0-12-328002-8). Vol. 2, 1975. Vol. 3, 1978. 59.00 (ISBN 0-12-328003-6). Acad Pr.

Functional Anatomy of the Spermatazoan. Ed. by B. Afzelius. 1975. text ed. 79.00 (ISBN 0-08-018006-X). Pergamon.

Functional & Surgical Anatomy of the Hand. 2nd ed. Emanuel B. Kaplan. 1965. 20.00 o.p. (ISBN 0-397-50137-4). Lippincott.

Functional Approach to the Interpretation of the Skull in Infancy & Childhood. K. J. Momose. LC 70-111805. (Illus.). 250p. 1981. 17.50 (ISBN 0-87527-225-8). Green.

Functional Bestiary: Laboratory Studies About Living Systems. Steven Vogel & Stephen Wainwright. (Illus., Orig.). 1969. 7.95 (ISBN 0-201-08148-2). A-W.

Functional Comprehension. Donn Byrne. 1979. pap. text ed. 2.80x o.p. (ISBN 0-582-55242-7). Longman.

Functional Design in Fishes. 3rd ed. R. McNeill Alexander. (Illus.). 1974. pap. text ed. 7.00 (ISBN 0-09-104751-X, Hutchinson U Lib). Humanities.

Functional Differential Equations & Bifurcations: Proceedings. Ed. by A. F. Ize. (Lecture Notes in Mathematics: Vol. 799). 409p. 1980. pap. 24.50 (ISBN 0-387-09986-7). Springer-Verlag.

Functional Dynamics of the Cell. Edward Bresnick & Arnold Schwartz. LC 68-14640. 1968. text ed. 20.95 (ISBN 0-12-132650-0). Acad Pr.

Functional English for Writers. 2nd ed. Kevin G. Burne et al. 1978. pap. 8.95x (ISBN 0-673-15105-0). Scott F.

Functional Histology. Myrin Borysenko et al. 1978. text ed. 17.95 (ISBN 0-316-10303-9); pap. text ed. 12.95 (ISBN 0-316-10302-0). Little.

Functional Housekeeping in Hotels & Motels. John T. Fales. LC 72-142508. 1971. text ed. 14.50 (ISBN 0-672-96080-X); tchr's manual 5.00 (ISBN 0-672-96082-6); wkbk. 6.50 (ISBN 0-672-96081-8). Bobbs.

Functional Human Anatomy: The Regional Approach. 3rd ed. Alexander Lane. 1981. pap. text ed. 15.95 (ISBN 0-8403-2340-9). Kendall-Hunt.

Functional Integration--Theory & Applications. Ed. by Jaen-Pierre Antoine & Enrique Tirapegui. 355p. 1980. 42.50 (ISBN 0-306-40573-3, Plenum Pr). Plenum Pub.

Functional Integration & Its Applications. Ed. by A. M. Arthurs & M. R. Bhagavan. 300p. 1975. 45.00x (ISBN 0-19-853346-2). Oxford U Pr.

Functional Integration & Quantum Physics. Barry Simon. (Pure & Applied Mathematics Ser.). 1979. 32.50 (ISBN 0-12-644250-9). Acad Pr.

Functional Lessons in Singing. 2nd ed. Ivan Trusler & Walter Ehret. LC 73-180598. (Illus.). 240p. 1972. pap. 14.95 ref. ed. (ISBN 0-13-331801-X). P-H.

Functional Literacy in Mali: Training for Development. Bernard Dumont. LC 73-77353. (Educational Studies & Documents, No. 10). (Illus.). 67p. (Orig.). 1973. pap. 2.50 (ISBN 92-3-101113-8, U257, UNESCO). Unipub.

Functional Mathematics for the Mentally Retarded. Daniel Peterson. LC 70-188780. text ed. 21.50x (ISBN 0-675-09097-0). Merrill.

Functional Morphology of Hepatic Vascular System. Ungvary. 1977. 17.00 (ISBN 0-9960006-7-4. Pub. by Kaido Hungary). Heyden.

Functional Morphology of the Fore-Guts of the Thalassind Crustaceans, "Callianassa californiensis" & "Upogebia pugettensis". Rex R. Powell. (U. C. Publications in Zoology: Vol. 102). 1974. pap. 6.00x (ISBN 0-520-09504-9). U of Cal Pr.

Functional Morphology of the Hip & Thigh of the Lorisiformes. J. McArdle. (Contributions to Primatology Ser.: Vol. 17). (Illus.). 148p. 1981. pap. 19.25 (ISBN 3-8055-1767-X). S Karger.

Functional Neurosurgery. Ed. by Theodore Rasmussen & Raul Marino. LC 77-85871. 1979. text ed. 34.50 (ISBN 0-89004-228-4). Raven.

Functional Organization of Descending Supraspinal Fibre Systems to the Spinal Cord: Anatomical Observations & Physiological Correlations. R. Nyberg-Hansen. (Advances in Anatomy, Embryology & Cell Biology: Vol. 39, Pt. 2). (Illus.). 1966. pap. 11.30 o.p. (ISBN 0-387-03494-3). Springer-Verlag.

Functional Programming. Peter Henderson. (Ser. in Computer Science). (Illus.). 1980. text ed. 33.95 (ISBN 0-13-331579-7). P-H.

Functional Teaching of the Mentally Retarded. 2nd ed. Max G. Frankel et al. (Illus.). 288p. 1975. 18.50 (ISBN 0-398-03361-7). C C Thomas.

Functional Toxicity of Anesthesia. David L. Bruce. LC 80-82766. (Scientific Basis of Clinical Anesthesia Ser.). 1980. 15.50 (ISBN 0-8089-1276-3). Grune.

Functional Units in Protien Biosynthesis. Ed. by R. A. Cox & A. A. Hadjiolov. 1972. 57.50 (ISBN 0-12-194550-2). Acad Pr.

Functional Writing. A. D. Van Nostrand et al. LC 77-74098 (Illus.). 1977. pap. text ed. 10.95 (ISBN 0-395-25294-6); inst. guide 0.25 (ISBN 0-395-25293-8). HM.

Functionalism. M. Abrahamson. LC 77-6828. 1978. pap. 8.95 ref. (ISBN 0-13-331900-8). P-H.

Functionalism. I. C. Jarvie. LC 72-97621. (Basic Concepts in Anthropology Ser.). 1973. pap. text ed. 2.95 o.p. (ISBN 0-8087-1018-4). Burgess.

Functionalism. Jonathan H. Turner & Alexandra Maryanski. (Series in Social Theory). 1979. pap. 6.95 (ISBN 0-8053-9338-2). Benjamin-Cummings.

Functionalism & World Politics: A Study Based on United Nations Programs Financing Economic Development. James P. Sewell. 1966. 18.50x (ISBN 0-691-07508-5). Princeton U Pr.

Functionaries. F. William Howton. 1969. 6.95; pap. 2.95 (ISBN 0-531-06454-9). Watts.

Functioning of Complex Organizations. George England et al. LC 80-21966. 352p. 1981. lib. bdg. 25.00 (ISBN 0-89946-067-4). Oelgeschlager.

Functioning of Floating Exchange Rates: Theory, Evidence & Policy Implications. Ed. by David Bigman & Teizo Taya. LC 79-21589. 1980. ref. ed. 37.50 (ISBN 0-88410-492-3). Ballinger Pub.

Functioning of Freshwater Ecosystems. Ed. by E. D. Le Cren & R. H. Lowe-McConnell. LC 79-50504. (International Biological Programme Ser.: No. 22). (Illus.). 1980. 95.00 (ISBN 0-521-22507-8). Cambridge U Pr.

Functions: An Approach to Algebra & Trigonometry. 2nd ed. Robert J. Mergener. 1978. pap. text ed. 18.50 (ISBN 0-8403-2339-5). Kendall-Hunt.

Functions of a Complex Variable, 2 vols. D. O. Tall. (Library of Mathematics). 1970. Vol. 1. pap. 2.95 (ISBN 0-7100-6567-1); Vol. 2. pap. 2.95 (ISBN 0-7100-6785-2); pap. 6.50 set (ISBN 0-685-25621-9). Routledge & Kegan.

Functions of Folk Costume in Moravian Slovakia. Petr Bogatyrev. LC 78-149915. (Approaches to Semiotics Ser: No. 5). (Illus.). 107p. 1971. text ed. 25.90x (ISBN 90-2791-756-6). Mouton.

Functions of Language in the Classroom. Ed. by Courtney B. Cazden et al. LC 78-173091. 1972. text ed. 14.25x o.p. (ISBN 0-8077-1147-0); pap. 10.95x (ISBN 0-8077-1142-X). Tchrs Coll.

Functions of Life: A Laboratory Guide for Animal Physiology. James D. Witherspoon. LC 71-100892. 1970. pap. text ed. 9.95 (ISBN 0-201-08717-0). A-W.

Functions of Mathematical Physics. Harry Hochstadt. LC 78-141199. (Pure & Applied Mathematics Ser.: Vol. 28). 1971. 32.95 (ISBN 0-471-40170-6, Pub. by Wiley-Interscience). Wiley.

Functions of One Complex Variable. J. B. Conway. Ed. by P. R. Halmos. LC 72-96938. (Lecture Notes in Mathematics: Vol. 11). (Illus.). xiv, 314p. 1973. text ed. 18.30 o.p. (ISBN 0-387-90061-6). Springer-Verlag.

Functions of Setting in the Novel: From Mrs. Radcliffe to Charles Dickens. Ann Ronald. Ed. by Devendra P. Varma. LC 79-8475. (Gothic Studies & Dissertations Ser.). 1980. lib. bdg. 25.00x (ISBN 0-405-12659-X). Arno.

Functions of Social Conflict. Lewis A. Coser. LC 56-6874. 1964. pap. text ed. 5.95 (ISBN 0-02-906810-X). Free Pr.

Functions of the Brain. David Ferrier. (Contributions to the History of Psychology E, III, Physiological Psychology Ser.). 1978. Repr. of 1886 ed. 30.00 (ISBN 0-89093-176-3). U Pubns Amer.

Fund Advisors Institute, August 1976: Proceedings. Ed. by Janice H. Welke. 1976. pap. 10.50 (ISBN 0-89154-053-9). Intl Found Employ.

Fund Advisors Institute, July 1975, Denver, Colorado: Proceedings. (Pensions). 221p. 1976. pap. 6.50 (ISBN 0-89154-039-3). Intl Found Employ.

Fund-Raising. H. Blume. (Orig.). 1977. pap. 6.95 (ISBN 0-7100-8549-4). Routledge & Kegan.

Fund-Raising & Grant-Aid: A Practical & Legal Guide for Charities & Voluntary Organisations. Ann Darnbrough & Derek Kinrade. 160p. 1980. 24.00x (ISBN 0-85941-075-7, Pub. by Woodhead-Faulkner England). State Mutual Bk.

Fund Raising by Parent-Citizen Groups. Douglas Lawson. 1976. pap. 3.50 (ISBN 0-934460-04-3). NCCE.

Fund Raising in the Black Community: History, Feasibility, & Conflict. King E. Davis. LC 75-25586. 1975. 10.00 (ISBN 0-8108-0870-6). Scarecrow.

Fund Raising in the United States. Scott M. Cutlip. LC 64-8261. 1965. 12.50 (ISBN 0-910294-21-6). Brown Bk.

Fund-Raising Projects with a World Hunger Emphasis. Paul Longacre. LC 80-83771. 72p. 1980. pap. 1.95 (ISBN 0-8361-1940-1). Herald Pr.

Fundamental Accounting Principles. 3rd canadian ed. William Pyle et al. 1980. text ed. 21.95x (ISBN 0-256-02293-3); workbook of study guides 7.95x (ISBN 0-256-02295-X); working papers 7.95x ea. Nos. 1-14 (ISBN 0-256-02295-X). Nos. 15-28 (ISBN 0-256-02296-8). practice sets 7.95x ea. No. 1 (ISBN 0-256-02297-6). No. 2 (ISBN 0-256-02298-4). Irwin.

Fundamental Accounting Principles. 8th ed. William W. Pyle et al. (Willard J. Graham Ser. in Accounting). 900p. 1978. text ed. 19.95x (ISBN 0-256-01994-0); practice sets nos. 1 & 2, wkbk. of study guides 5.95 work papers 1-14 & 15-29 5.95 ea. 5.95 ea. Irwin.

Fundamental Algebra & Trigonometry. 2nd ed. Mervin L. Keedy & Marvin L. Bittinger. (Mathematics-Remedial & Precalculus Ser.). (Illus.). 576p. 1981. text ed. 15.95 (ISBN 0-201-03839-0). A-W.

Fundamental & Clinical Bone Physiology. Ed. by Marshall R. Urist. (Illus.). 416p. 1980. text ed. 38.50 (ISBN 0-397-50470-5). Lippincott.

Fundamental ANSI Cobol Programming. James B. Maginnis. 1975. Repr. text ed. 16.95x (ISBN 0-13-339218-X). P-H.

Fundamental Aspects of Biocompatibility, 2 vols. D. F. Williams. (Biocompatibility Ser.: Vol. 1). 1981. 56.95 (ISBN 0-8493-5581-8); Vol. 2, 272p. 69.95 (ISBN 0-8493-5588-5). CRC Pr.

Fundamental Aspects of Medical Thermography. W. M. Park & B. L. Reece. 1980. 18.00x (Pub. by Brit Inst Radiology England). State Mutual Bk.

Fundamental Aspects of the Normality Rule & Their Role in Deriving Constitutive Laws of Soils. S. K. Jain. (Civil Engineering & Engineering Mechanics Ser.: No. 1). (Illus.). 178p. 1980. 23.50 (ISBN 0-9605004-0-5, 5004-0-5). Eng Pubns.

Fundamental College Algebra. 2nd ed. Mervin L. Keedy & Marvin L. Bittinger. (Mathematics-Remedial & Precalculus Ser.). 480p. 1981. text ed. 15.95 (ISBN 0-201-03847-1). A-W.

Fundamental Concepts of Elementary Mathematics. Lawrence A. Trivieri. 1977. text ed. 19.50 scp o.p. (ISBN 0-06-046675-8, HarpC); ans. to selected even numbered exercises free o.p. (ISBN 0-06-366685-5). Har-Row.
Fundamental Concepts of Estate Administration 1978. (Estate Planning & Administration Course Handbook Ser. 1980-81: Vol. 114). 1980. 25.00 (ISBN 0-685-63714-X, D4-5132). PLI.
Fundamental Concepts of Estate Planning Nineteen Seventy-Nine Course Handbook. (Tax Law & Estate Planning Course Handbook Ser., 1979-80: Vol. 112). 1980. pap. 25.00 (ISBN 0-686-50969-2, D4-5128). PLI.
Fundamental Concepts of Higher Algebra. A. Adrian Albert. LC 56-5129. 1961. pap. 1.50 o.s.i. (ISBN 0-226-01177-1, P507, Phoen). U of Chicago Pr.
Fundamental Concepts of Information Modeling. Matthew Flavin. (Yourdon Press Monograph). (Illus.). 104p. (Orig.). 1981. pap. 10.00 (ISBN 0-917072-22-7). Yourdon.
Fundamental Concepts of Mathematics. 2nd ed. R. L. Goodstein. 1978. text ed. 45.00 (ISBN 0-08-021665-X); pap. text ed. 19.25 (ISBN 0-08-021666-8). Pergamon.
Fundamental Concepts of Modern Biology. Sebastian Haskel & David Sygoda. (Orig.). (gr. 10-12). 1972. text ed. 12.41 (ISBN 0-87720-055-6); pap. text ed. 7.17 (ISBN 0-87720-054-8). AMSCO Sch.
Fundamental Concepts of Modern Chemistry. Saul L. Geffner. (Illus.). (gr. 10-12). 1968. text ed. 11.58 (ISBN 0-87720-102-1); pap. text ed. 6.58 (ISBN 0-87720-101-3). AMSCO Sch.
Fundamental Concepts of Modern Physics. Sheldon Diamond. (gr. 11-12). 1970. pap. text ed. 6.58 (ISBN 0-87720-178-1). AMSCO Sch.
Fundamental Concepts of Music. William H. Toutant. 336p. 1979. pap. text ed. 14.95x (ISBN 0-534-00743-0). Wadsworth Pub.
Fundamental Considerations in Cardiology & Diabetes. Ed. by Ralph C. Scott. (Clinical Cardiology & Diabetes Ser.: Vol. I Part I). (Illus.). 384p. 1981. 36.00 (ISBN 0-87993-135-3). Futura Pub.
Fundamental Disch. Thomas M. Disch. Ed. by Samuel R. Delany. 416p. (Orig.). 1980. pap. 2.50 (ISBN 0-553-13670-4). Bantam.
Fundamental Duties. Ed. by D. Lasok et al. 275p. 1980. 30.00 (ISBN 0-08-024048-8); pap. 12.00 (ISBN 0-08-024049-6). Pergamon.
Fundamental Electronics. James F. Turner. LC 72-169985. 480p. 1972. text ed. 19.95 (ISBN 0-675-09175-6). Merrill.
Fundamental Filing Practice. Irene Place et al. (Office Occupations Ser). (Illus.). 256p. 1973. pap. text ed. 9.95x (ISBN 0-13-332742-6). P-H.
Fundamental Formulas of Physics, 2 Vols. 2nd ed. Donald H. Menzel. (Illus.). 1960. Vol. 1. pap. text ed. 5.00 (ISBN 0-486-60595-7); Vol. 2. pap. text ed. 5.00 (ISBN 0-486-60596-5). Dover.
Fundamental Issues in Nursing. Ed. by The Journal of Nursing Administration, Staff. LC 75-14685. 96p. 1975. pap. text ed. 7.95 o.s.i. (ISBN 0-913654-12-4). Nursing Res.
Fundamental Laws of the State of Israel. Ed. by Joseph Badi. LC 61-8605. 451p. 1961. text ed. 34.00x (ISBN 0-8290-0174-3). Irvington.
Fundamental Legal Concepts of China & the West: A Comparative Study. Hyung I. Kim. (National University Publications, Multidisciplinary Studies in the Law). 1981. 17.50 (ISBN 0-8046-9275-0). Kennikat.
Fundamental Legal Documents of Communist China. Ed. by Albert P. Blaustein. 1962. 20.00x (ISBN 0-8377-0300-X). Rothman.
Fundamental Mathematics. L. J. Nachman. 657p. 1978. 20.95 (ISBN 0-471-62815-8). Wiley.
Fundamental Mathematics for the Management & Social Sciences. alt. ed. Lloyd Emerson & Laurence Paquette. 688p. 1981. text ed. 22.00 (ISBN 0-205-07166-X, 567166-3); tchrs. ed. avail. (ISBN 0-205-07169-4). Allyn.
Fundamental Mathematics for the Management & Social Sciences. 2nd ed. Lloyd Emerson & Lawrence Paquette. 1978. text ed. 22.00 (ISBN 0-205-06000-5); instr's man. avail. (ISBN 0-205-06001-3); student study guide 7.50 (ISBN 0-205-06002-1). Allyn.
Fundamental Mathematics of Life Insurance. Floyd S. Harper & Lewis C. Workman. 1970. text ed. 10.75 (ISBN 0-256-00231-2). Irwin.
Fundamental Moral Theology. Franz Bockle. Tr. by N. D. Smith from Ger. (Orig.). 1980. pap. 17.50 (ISBN 0-916134-42-3). Pueblo Pub Co.
Fundamental Physics, 2 vols. Duane Roller & Ronald Blum. Incl. Vol. 1. Mechanics, Waves & Thermodynamics; Vol. 2. Electricity, Magnetism, Light & Modern Physics. (Illus.). 1981. text ed. 22.95 ea.; text ed. 28.95 (ISBN 0-8162-7282-4); wkbk. & sol. manual avail. Holden-Day.
Fundamental Principles of Dynamic Symmetry As They Are Expressed in Nature & Art: A Mathematical & Geometrical Treatise. Jay Hambridge. (Illus.). 1979. deluxe ed. 54.75 (ISBN 0-930582-20-9). Gloucester Art.
Fundamental Principles of the Metaphysics of Morals. Immanuel Kant. Tr. by Thomas K. Abbott. 1949. pap. 2.95 (ISBN 0-672-60177-X, LLA16). Bobbs.
Fundamental Problems of Marxism. rev. ed. George V. Plekhanov. LC 69-20358. 1969. 5.95 o.p. (ISBN 0-7178-0074-1); pap. 2.25 (ISBN 0-7178-0073-3). Intl Pub Co.
Fundamental Processes in Radiation Chemistry. P. Ausloos. 753p. 1968. text ed. 32.50 (ISBN 0-470-03834-9, Pub. by Wiley). Krieger.
Fundamental Real Analysis. S. L. Gupta & Nisha Rani. 1976. 15.00 (ISBN 0-686-63607-4, Pub. by Vikas India). Advent Bk.
Fundamental Reference Sources. Frances N. Cheney. LC 73-151051. 1971. 12.00 o.p. (ISBN 0-8389-0081-X). ALA.
Fundamental Reference Sources. 2nd ed. Frances N. Cheney & Wiley J. Williams. 300p. 1980. 12.50 (ISBN 0-8389-0308-8). ALA.
Fundamental Rock Climbing. Ed. by Arthur Reidel. 1973. pap. 1.75 (ISBN 0-9601698-0-6). MIT Outing.
Fundamental Rules of Successful Investing. Richard D. Wyckoff. (Illus.). 121p. 1981. 57.85 (ISBN 0-918968-85-2). Inst Econ Finan.
Fundamental Skills & Concepts 1: Language Arts Lessons for Grades 1-3. Dorothea M. Ross & Sheila A. Ross. (Makemaster Bk.). 1980. pap. 14.95 (ISBN 0-8224-0291-2). Pitman Learning.
Fundamental Skills & Concepts 2: Arithmetic Lessons for Grades 1-3. Dorothea M. Ross & Sheila A. Ross. (Makemaster Bk.). 1980. pap. 14.95 (ISBN 0-8224-0292-0). Pitman Learning.
Fundamental Skills in Hematology. Brian H. Baker. 508p. 1980. pap. 28.50 photocopy ed. spiral (ISBN 0-398-04101-6). C C Thomas.
Fundamental Skills in Patient Care. LaVerne W. Lewis. LC 75-26993. 495p. 1976. pap. 13.75 o.p. (ISBN 0-397-54174-0). Lippincott.
Fundamental Skills in Patient Care. 2nd ed. Laverne W. Lewis. LC 79-27050. 1980. pap. text ed. 14.95 (ISBN 0-397-54283-6, 408 PGS.); 8.75 (ISBN 0-397-54335-2, 257 PGS. FOR WKBK.). Lippincott.
Fundamental Skills in Serology: Agglutination Tests, Syphilis Serology, Flourescent Staining. Leila J. Walker & Howard Taub. (Illus.). 486p. 1976. pap. 21.75 (ISBN 0-398-03510-5). C C Thomas.
Fundamental Statistical Concepts. Frederic E. Fischer. LC 72-3309. 1973. text ed. 18.50 scp (ISBN 0-06-382662-3, HarpC). Har-Row.
Fundamental Statistics for Business & Economics. Thomas R. Dyckman & L. Joseph Thomas. 1977. 19.95 (ISBN 0-13-344523-2). P-H.
Fundamental Statistics for Business & Economics. 4th abr. ed. John Neter et al. 514p. 1975. text ed. 16.95x (ISBN 0-205-04547-2); instr's manual free (ISBN 0-205-04548-0); ans. bk. 3.95 (ISBN 0-205-04567-7). Allyn.
Fundamental Statistics in Business & Economics. Byung S. Lee & Lien-Fu Huang. LC 78-68690. 1979. pap. text ed. 17.25 (ISBN 0-8191-0701-8). U Pr of Amer.
Fundamental Structures of Computer Science. William Wulf et al. LC 79-12374. 1981. text ed. 21.95 (ISBN 0-201-08725-1). A-W.
Fundamental Techniques of Direct-Screen Color Reproduction. Ed. by Eastman Kodak Company. (Illus.). 44p. 1980. pap. 5.50 (ISBN 0-87985-260-7, Q-10). Eastman Kodak.
Fundamental Techniques Veterinary Surgery. Charles D. Knecht et al. (Illus.). 250p. 1981. text ed. price not set (ISBN 0-7216-5463-0). Saunders.
Fundamental Theology. Gerald O'Collins. LC 80-82809. 288p. (Orig.). 1981. pap. 6.95 (ISBN 0-8091-2347-9). Paulist Pr.
Fundamental Theory of Servomechanisms. LeRoy A. MacColl. pap. 3.50 o.p. (ISBN 0-486-61916-8). Dover.
Fundamental Tissue Geometry. K. J. Dormer. LC 79-50235. (Illus.). 1980. 32.50 (ISBN 0-521-22326-1). Cambridge U Pr.
Fundamentalism & American Culture: The Shaping of Twentieth Century Evangelicalism, 1870-1925. George M. Marsden. (Illus.). 320p. 1980. 19.95 (ISBN 0-19-502758-2). Oxford U Pr.
Fundamentalism in Black Inner City Storefront Churches. Titus Haynes. LC 79-57584. 1980. 6.95 (ISBN 0-533-04572-X). Vantage.
Fundamentals & Applications of Digital Logic Circuits. 2nd ed. Sol Libes. 1978. pap. 9.75 (ISBN 0-8104-5661-3); exam 1.30 (ISBN 0-8104-0916-X); final exam 0.30 (ISBN 0-685-93591-4). Hayden.
Fundamentals & Modeling of Separation Processes: Absorption, Distillation, Evaporation & Extraction. C. Holland. (International Ser. in Physical & Chemical Engineering Science). (Illus.). 464p. 1975. 29.95 (ISBN 0-13-344390-6). P-H.
Fundamentals & Practice of Marketing. John Wilmshurst. 1978. pap. 14.95x (ISBN 0-434-92263-3). Intl Ideas.
Fundamentals for Maxillofacial Prosthetics. O. E. Beder. (American Lectures in Dentistry Ser.). (Illus.). 246p. 1974. 29.50 (ISBN 0-398-02916-4). C C Thomas.
Fundamentals in Nuclear Theory. (Illus., Orig.). 1967. pap. 39.75 (ISBN 92-0-130067-0, IAEA). Unipub.
Fundamentals in the First School. M. Brearley et al. (Illus.). 1974. Repr. of 1969 ed. 9.50x (ISBN 0-631-11840-3, Pub. by Basil Blackwell). Biblio Dist.
Fundamentals of Advertising Research. Alan D. Fletcher & Thomas A. Bowers. LC 78-15516. (Advertising & Journalism Ser.). 1979. 17.95 (ISBN 0-88244-178-7). Grid Pub.
Fundamentals of Aerosol Science. David T. Shaw. LC 77-19331. 1978. 36.50 (ISBN 0-471-02949-1, Pub. by Wiley-Interscience). Wiley.
Fundamentals of Air Pollution. Arthur C. Stern et al. 1973. text ed. 21.50 (ISBN 0-12-666560-5). Acad Pr.
Fundamentals of Air Pollution. Samuel J. Williamson. LC 75-186842. 1973. text ed. 23.95 (ISBN 0-201-08629-8). A-W.
Fundamentals of Alcohol Problems. James C. Kincannon. (Illus.). 300p. Date not set. pap. text ed. 10.50 (ISBN 0-8016-2695-1). Mosby. Postponed.
Fundamentals of American Government: A Programmed Approach. Neuman Pollack. 1978. pap. text ed. 13.60 (ISBN 0-205-06008-0). Allyn.
Fundamentals of Amorphous Semiconductors. National Materials Advisory Board. LC 75-188496. 128p. 1972. pap. 6.00 (ISBN 0-309-01944-3). Natl Acad Pr.
Fundamentals of Analytical Flame Spectroscopy. Cornelis T. Alkemade & Roland Herrmann. LC 79-4376. 442p. 1979. 74.95 (ISBN 0-470-26710-0). Halsted Pr.
Fundamentals of Anesthesia Care. Betty J. Smith. LC 72-86526. (Illus.). 145p. (Orig.). 1972. pap. text ed. 7.95 o.p. (ISBN 0-8016-4693-6). Mosby.
Fundamentals of Applied Kinematics. D. C. Tao. (Illus.). 1967. 17.95 (ISBN 0-201-07451-6). sol. manual o.p. 1.50 (ISBN 0-686-66351-9). A-W.
Fundamentals of Applied Physics. C. Thomas Olivo & Thomas P. Olivo. LC 77-79381. 1978. text ed. 15.00 (ISBN 0-8273-1300-4); tchr's guide 3.00 (ISBN 0-8273-1301-2). Delmar.
Fundamentals of Archaeology. Robert J. Sharer & Wendy A. Ashmore. 1979. text ed. 17.95 (ISBN 0-8053-8760-9). Benjamin-Cummings.
Fundamentals of Auditing. 2nd ed. Robert K. Mautz. LC 64-20075. 1964. text ed. 22.95x o.p. (ISBN 0-471-57785-5); solutions avail. o.p. (ISBN 0-471-57817-7). Wiley.
Fundamentals of Austrian Economics. Thomas C. Taylor. (Study in Political Economy Ser.: No. 4). 76p. (Orig.). 1980. 2.00 (ISBN 0-932790-27-5). Cato Inst.
Fundamentals of Behavior Pathology. 2nd ed. Richard M. Suinn. LC 74-30206. (Series in Psychology). 1975. text ed. 23.95x (ISBN 0-471-83547-1). Wiley.
Fundamentals of Behavioral Statistics. 4th ed. R. Runyon & A. Haber. 1980. 16.95 (ISBN 0-201-06375-1); write for info. (ISBN 0-201-06378-6); students' wkbk. 5.95 (ISBN 0-201-06376-X); test item booklet 2.50 (ISBN 0-201-06377-8); PSI study guide 6.95 (ISBN 0-201-06633-5); PSI instrs manual 2.75 (ISBN 0-201-06632-7). A-W.
Fundamentals of Biochemical Pharmacology. Ed. by Z. M. Bacq et al. LC 75-135101. 1971. text ed. 52.00 (ISBN 0-08-016453-6); pap. text ed. 24.00 (ISBN 0-08-017775-1). Pergamon.
Fundamentals of Biochemistry. Gordon Kilgour. Date not set. text ed. 21.95 (ISBN 0-442-25756-2); instr's. manual 2.00 (ISBN 0-442-25757-0). D Van Nostrand.
Fundamentals of Biometry. L. N. Balaam. 1972. 16.95 (ISBN 0-470-04571-X). Halsted Pr.
Fundamentals of Business Mathematics. Nelda W. Roueche. (Illus.). 1979. pap. 12.95 (ISBN 0-13-334441-X). P-H.
Fundamentals of Business Mathematics. Walter E. Williams & James H. Reed. 1977. text ed. 14.95x o.p. (ISBN 0-697-08015-3); wkbk 7.95x o.p. (ISBN 0-697-08019-6); instructor's manual 4.00 o.p. (ISBN 0-686-67790-0). Wm C Brown.
Fundamentals of Business Mathematics. 2nd ed. Walter E. Williams & James H. Reed. 580p. 1981. text ed. write for info. (ISBN 0-697-08049-8); wkbk avail. (ISBN 0-697-08056-0); instrs' manual avail. (ISBN 0-697-08057-9). Wm C Brown.
Fundamentals of Business Policy. Raleigh F. Steinhauer. 1978. pap. text ed. 7.50 (ISBN 0-8191-0370-5). U Pr of Amer.
Fundamentals of Business Statistics. Jerome D. Braverman. 597p. 1979. tchrs' ed. 17.95 (ISBN 0-12-128050-0); instrs'. manual 3.00 (ISBN 0-12-128052-7); solutions manual 5.50 (ISBN 0-12-128054-3). Acad Pr.
Fundamentals of Cell Pharmacology. Ed. by S. Dikstein. (Illus.). 572p. 1973. 54.75 (ISBN 0-398-02504-5). C C Thomas.
Fundamentals of Chemical Reaction Engineering. Charles D. Holland & Raymond G. Anthony. (International Ser. in the Physical & Chemical Engineering Sciences). (Illus.). 1979. text ed. 26.95 (ISBN 0-13-335596-9). P-H.
Fundamentals of Chemistry. Fred H. Redmore. (Illus.). 1979. ref. ed. 20.95 (ISBN 0-13-335158-0); lab. manual 8.95 (ISBN 0-13-335174-2); 7.95 (ISBN 0-13-335182-3); sol. manual 6.95 (ISBN 0-13-335166-1). P-H.
Fundamentals of Child Counseling. Donald B. Keat. 300p. 1974. text ed. 19.50 (ISBN 0-395-17827-4); instructor's manual 2.50 (ISBN 0-395-17859-2). HM.
Fundamentals of Circuits, Electronics, & Signal Analysis. Kendall L. Su. LC 77-74147. (Illus.). 1978. text ed. 26.95 (ISBN 0-395-25038-2); sol. manual 1.10 (ISBN 0-395-25039-0). HM.
Fundamentals of Classical Thermodynamics: SI Version. G. J. Van Wylen. (Series in Thermal & Transport Sciences). 1980. 13.95 (ISBN 0-471-04505-5). Wiley.
Fundamentals of Classical Thermodynamics: SI Version. 2nd rev. ed. Gordon J. Van Wylen & Richard E. Sonntag. LC 76-2405. 1976. text ed. 23.95 (ISBN 0-471-04188-2); solutions manual 9.00 (ISBN 0-471-04519-5); Arabic Translation avail. (ISBN 0-471-04505-5). Wiley.
Fundamentals of Clinical Hematology. Jerry L. Spivak. (Illus.). 405p. 1980. 25.00 (ISBN 0-06-142465-X, Harper Medical). Har-Row.
Fundamentals of Clinical Trials. Lawrence M. Friedman et al. 320p. 1981. 24.50 (ISBN 0-88416-296-6). PSG Pub.
Fundamentals of Co-Counseling Manual: Spanish Translation. Harvey Jackins. Tr. by Emma Ramos-Diaz & Azril Bacal. (Span.). 1981. pap. 5.00 (ISBN 0-911214-28-3). Rational Isl.
Fundamentals of College Accounting. Meral Fielding et al. LC 72-186146. 1972. text ed. 12.75 (ISBN 0-89702-027-8); wkbk. 6.20 (ISBN 0-89702-028-6); 7.40 (ISBN 0-89702-026-X). PAR Inc.
Fundamentals of College Chemistry. Denis M. Callewaert & Julien Genyea. 1980. text ed. 15.95x (ISBN 0-87901-124-6). Worth.
Fundamentals of College Geometry. 2nd ed. Edwin M. Hemmerling. (Illus.). 1970. text ed. 20.95x (ISBN 0-471-37034-7). Wiley.
Fundamentals of Complex Analysis for Mathematics, Science & Engineering. Edward B. Soff & Arthur D. Snider. (Illus.). 1976. 23.95 (ISBN 0-13-332148-7). P-H.
Fundamentals of Computer Science. Terry M. Walker. 425p. 1975. text ed. 23.95x (ISBN 0-205-04715-7). Allyn.
Fundamentals of Computers in Business: A Systems Approach. Edward A. Tomeski. LC 78-54208. 1979. text ed. 18.95x (ISBN 0-8162-8733-3); instructor's manual 4.50 (ISBN 0-8162-8734-1); wkbk. 6.00 (ISBN 0-8162-8735-X). Holden-Day.
Fundamentals of Configuration Management. Thomas T. Samaras & Frank L. Czerwinski. LC 75-127668. 1971. 35.95 (ISBN 0-471-75100-6, Pub. by Wiley-Interscience). Wiley.
Fundamentals of Construction Estimating & Cost Accounting. Keith Collier. (Illus.). 400p. 1974. 21.95 (ISBN 0-13-335604-3). P-H.
Fundamentals of Corrosion. 2nd ed. J. C. Scully. 252p. 1975. text ed. 23.00 (ISBN 0-08-018081-7); pap. text ed. 11.25 (ISBN 0-08-018080-9). Pergamon.
Fundamentals of Counseling. 2nd ed. Bruce E. Shertzer & Shelley C. Stone. 544p. 1974. text ed. 17.75 o.p. (ISBN 0-395-17580-1); instructors' manual pap. 2.00 o.p. (ISBN 0-395-17803-7). HM.
Fundamentals of Counseling. 3rd ed. Bruce E. Shertzer & Shelley C. Stone. LC 79-88448. (Illus.). 1980. text ed. 17.95 (ISBN 0-395-28580-1); instrs'. manual 1.00 (ISBN 0-395-28579-8). HM.
Fundamentals of Creative Advertising. C. Dennis Schick & Albert C. Book. 1981. write for info. (ISBN 0-87251-035-2). Crain Bks.
Fundamentals of Criminal Advocacy. F. Lee Bailey & Henry B. Rothblatt. LC 73-90861. 1974. 18.00x o.p. (ISBN 0-686-14542-9). Lawyers Co-Op.
Fundamentals of Criminal Behavior & Correctional Systems. Ed. by John G. Cull & Richard E. Hardy. (American Lectures in Social & Rehabilitation Psychology Ser.). (Illus.). 364p. 1973. 24.50 (ISBN 0-398-02637-8). C C Thomas.

Fundamentals of Criminal Investigation. 5th ed. Charles E. O'Hara & Gregory L. O'Hara. (Illus.). 928p. 1980. 26.75 (ISBN 0-398-04000-1). C C Thomas.
Fundamentals of Criminal Justice Research. Robert S. Clark. (Illus.). 1977. 18.95 (ISBN 0-669-01005-7). Lexington Bks.
Fundamentals of Cyclic Stress & Strain. Bela I. Sandor. LC 70-176415. (Illus.). 204p. 1972. text ed. 17.50x (ISBN 0-299-06100-0). U of Wis Pr.
Fundamentals of Dairy Chemistry. 2nd ed. Ed. by Byron H. Webb et al. 1974. text ed. 45.00 (ISBN 0-87055-143-4). AVI.
Fundamentals of Debate: Theory & Practice. Otto F. Bauer. 1966. pap. 6.95x o.p. (ISBN 0-673-05715-1). Scott F.
Fundamentals of Digital Systems Design. V. Thomas Rhyne. LC 72-6903. (Illus.). 560p. 1973. 27.95 (ISBN 0-13-336156-X). P-H.
Fundamentals of Dimensional Metrology. Busch & Wilkie Bros. Foundation. LC 64-12593. 428p. 1966. 10.80 (ISBN 0-8273-0193-6); instructor's guide 1.60 (ISBN 0-8273-0197-9). Delmar.
Fundamentals of Earthquake Engineering. N. M. Newmark & E. Rosenblueth. (Civil Engineering & Engineering Mechanics Ser). (Illus.). 1972. ref. ed. 33.95 (ISBN 0-13-336206-X). P-H.
Fundamentals of Economics. A. Morrice. 1972. pap. text ed. 13.95x (ISBN 0-685-83783-1). Intl Ideas.
Fundamentals of Electric Circuits. David Bell. (Illus.). 1978. ref. ed. 19.95 (ISBN 0-87909-318-8); students manual avail. Reston.
Fundamentals of Electric Circuits. 2nd ed. David Bell. 688p. 1981. text ed. 18.95 (ISBN 0-8359-2128-X); instrs. manual avail. Reston.
Fundamentals of Electric Waves. 2nd ed. H. H. Skilling. LC 74-8930. 256p. 1974. Repr. of 1948 ed. 11.75 o.p. (ISBN 0-88275-180-8). Krieger.
Fundamentals of Electricity & Automotive Electrical Systems. Thomas Weathers & Claud Hunter. (Illus.). 256p. 1981. text ed. 16.95 (ISBN 0-13-337030-5). P-H.
Fundamentals of Electricity for Agriculture. Robert J. Gustafson. (Illus.). 1980. pap. 16.50 (ISBN 0-87055-327-5). AVI.
Fundamentals of Electrocardiography. E. M. McLachlan. (Illus.). 192p. 1981. text ed. 37.50x (ISBN 0-19-261237-9); pap. text ed. 22.50x (ISBN 0-19-261199-2). Oxford U Pr.
Fundamentals of Electrochemical Analysis. Z. Galus. Tr. by G. F. Reynolds from Pol. LC 76-5838. (Series in Analytical Chemistry). 1976. 84.95 (ISBN 0-470-15080-7). Halsted Pr.
Fundamentals of Electronic Computers: Digital & Analog. Matthew Mandl. 1967. ref. ed. 17.95 (ISBN 0-13-337915-9). P-H.
Fundamentals of Electronic Devices. David A. Bell. (Illus.). 480p. 1974. 19.95 (ISBN 0-87909-276-9); students manual avail. Reston.
Fundamentals of Electronic Devices. 2nd ed. Ronald J. Tocci. Ed. by Samuel L. Oppenheimer. (Technology Ser). (Illus.). 496p. 1975. text ed. 20.95 (ISBN 0-675-08771-6); instructor's manual 3.95 (ISBN 0-686-67096-5). Merrill.
Fundamentals of Electronics. 2nd ed. E. Norman Lurch. LC 70-125273. 1971. text ed. 21.95x (ISBN 0-471-55520-7). Wiley.
Fundamentals of Electronics. 3rd ed. Norman E. Lurch. LC 79-18696. 624p. 1981. text ed. 19.95 (ISBN 0-471-03494-0); solution manual 7.00 (ISBN 0-471-03716-8). Wiley.
Fundamentals of Elementary Mathematics Geometry. Marlyn J. Behr & Dale Jungst. 326p. 1972. 17.95 (ISBN 0-12-084740-X); answer suppl. 3.00 (ISBN 0-12-084746-9). Acad Pr.
Fundamentals of Engineering Drawing. Warren J. Luzadder. 1981. 21.95 (ISBN 0-13-338350-4). P-H.
Fundamentals of Engineering Drawing for Design, Product Development & Numerical Control. 7th ed. Warren J. Luzadder. (Illus.). 1977. text ed. 17.95 (ISBN 0-13-338368-7); problems book 9.95 (ISBN 0-13-716308-8). P-H.
Fundamentals of Engineering Review. Iowa State University Research Foundation. LC 80-83440. 208p. 1980. pap. text ed. 14.95 (ISBN 0-8403-2305-0). Kendall-Hunt.
Fundamentals of Enhanced Oil Recovery. H. K. Van Poolen et al. 176p. 1980. 30.00 (ISBN 0-87814-144-8). Pennwell Pub.
Fundamentals of Entomology. Richard J. Elzinga. (Illus.). 1978. ref. ed. 21.95x (ISBN 0-13-338186-2). P-H.
Fundamentals of Entomology. 2nd ed. Richard J. Elzinga. (Illus.). 464p. 1981. text ed. 19.95 (ISBN 0-13-338194-3). P-H.
Fundamentals of Entomology & Plant Pathology. 2nd ed. Louis L. Pyenson. (Illus.). 1977. 20.50 o.p. (ISBN 0-87055-237-6). AVI.
Fundamentals of Entomology & Plant Pathology. 2nd ed. Louis L. Pyenson. (Illus.). 1980. text ed. 22.00 (ISBN 0-87055-334-8). AVI.
Fundamentals of Enzyme Kinetics. Athel Cornish-Bowden. LC 79-40116. (Illus.). 1979. text ed. 19.95 (ISBN 0-408-10617-4). Butterworths.
Fundamentals of Experimental Design. 3rd ed. Jerome L. Myers. 1979. text ed. 21.95x (ISBN 0-205-06615-1). Allyn.
Fundamentals of Experimental Psychology: A Comparative Approach. 2nd ed. Ed. by P. Robinson. 19.95 (ISBN 0-13-339135-3); pap. 5.95 wkbk (ISBN 0-13-339127-2). P-H.
Fundamentals of Experimental Psychology: A Comparative Approach. Paul W. Robinson. 400p. 1976. 19.95x (ISBN 0-13-339168-X); student guide 6.95 (ISBN 0-13-339143-4). P-H.
Fundamentals of Financial Accounting. 2nd ed. John A. Tracy. 1978. text ed. 22.95 (ISBN 0-471-88160-0); study guide 7.50 (ISBN 0-471-88161-9); tchrs. manual 14.95 (ISBN 0-471-02293-4); working papers 11.95 (ISBN 0-471-88162-7). Wiley.
Fundamentals of Financial Accounting. rev ed. Glenn A. Welsch & Robert N. Anthony. 1977. text ed. 19.00 (ISBN 0-256-01907-X); working papers 6.50 (ISBN 0-256-01958-4); practice set 5.95 (ISBN 0-256-01959-2); study guide 6.00 (ISBN 0-256-01957-6). Irwin.
Fundamentals of Financial Management. 2nd ed. Eugene F. Brigham. 627p. 1980. 20.95 (ISBN 0-03-054771-7). Dryden Pr.
Fundamentals of Financial Management. 3rd ed. J. Hanrahan & C. Dipchand. 1977. 21.95 (ISBN 0-13-339374-7). P-H.
Fundamentals of Financial Management. 4th ed. James C. Van Horne. (Illus.). 1980. text ed. 21.00 (ISBN 0-13-339408-5); study guide 8.95 (ISBN 0-13-339424-7). P-H.
Fundamentals of Finite Elements for Engineers. B. Nath. (Illus.). 256p. 1974. text ed. 25.00x (ISBN 0-485-11148-9, Athlone Pr). Humanities.
Fundamentals of Finite Mathematics. R. L. Childress. (Illus.). 1976. ref. ed. 17.95 (ISBN 0-13-339325-9). P-H.
Fundamentals of Finite Mathematics. R. W. Negus. LC 73-17469. 448p. 1974. text ed. 19.95x o.p. (ISBN 0-471-63121-3). Wiley.
Fundamentals of Finite Mathematics. Robert W. Negus. 416p. 1981. Repr. of 1974 ed. text ed. price not set (ISBN 0-89874-270-6). Krieger.
Fundamentals of Fixed Prosthodontics. 2nd ed. Herbert Schillingburg et al. (Illus.). 454p. 1981. write for info. Quint Pub Co.
Fundamentals of Fixed Prosthodontics. Herbert Shillingburg et al. (Illus.). 339p. 1978. 32.50 (ISBN 3-87652-641-8). Quint Pub Co.
Fundamentals of Fluid Mechanics. Alan L. Prasuhn. (Illus.). 1980. text ed. 24.95 (ISBN 0-13-339507-3). P-H.
Fundamentals of Fluid Mechanics. James A. Sullivan. (Illus.). 1978. ref. ed. 17.95 (ISBN 0-8359-2999-X); students manual avail. Reston.
Fundamentals of Fluid Power. William D. Wolansky et al. LC 76-13963. (Illus.). 1976. text ed. 21.50 (ISBN 0-395-18956-X); inst. manual 2.25 (ISBN 0-395-18955-1). HM.
Fundamentals of Food Canning. John M. Jackson & Byron M. Shinn. (Illus.). 1979. text ed. 29.00 (ISBN 0-87055-257-0). AVI.
Fundamentals of Food Chemistry. american ed. Werner Heimann. (Illus.). 1980. pap. text ed. 30.00 (ISBN 0-87055-356-9). AVI.
Fundamentals of Food Engineering. 3rd ed. Stanley E. Charm. 1978. pap. text ed. 22.50 (ISBN 0-87055-313-5). AVI.
Fundamentals of Food Freezing. Norman W. Desrosier & Donald K. Tressler. (Illus.). 1977. 27.50 o.p. (ISBN 0-87055-233-3); pap. text ed. 18.00 (ISBN 0-87055-290-2). AVI.
Fundamentals of Food Microbiology. Marion Fields. (Illus.). 1979. text ed. 19.00 (ISBN 0-87055-250-3). AVI.
Fundamentals of Food Process Engineering. Romeo T. Toledo. (Illus.). 1980. pap. text ed. 24.50 (ISBN 0-87055-338-0). AVI.
Fundamentals of Food Processing Operations: Ingredients, Methods & Packaging. John L. Heid & Maynard A. Joslyn. (Illus.). 1967. 25.00 (ISBN 0-87055-014-4). AVI.
Fundamentals of Forecasting. William F. Sullivan & W. Wayne Claycombe. (Illus.). 1977. ref. ed. 18.95 (ISBN 0-87909-300-5). Reston.
Fundamentals of Forestry Economics. William A. Duerr. (American Forestry Ser). 1960. text ed. 20.00 o.p. (ISBN 0-07-017978-6, C). McGraw.
Fundamentals of FORTRAN Programming: With Watfor-Watfiv. Terry M. Walker. 1975. 11.95x o.p. (ISBN 0-205-04885-4, 204885X). Allyn.
Fundamentals of Fracture Mechanics. J. F. Knott. LC 73-15844. 1974. 35.95 o.p. (ISBN 0-470-49565-0). Halsted Pr.
Fundamentals of Gastroenterology: With Self-Assessment Workbook. 3rd ed. Ed. by L. W. Powell & D. W. Piper. (Illus.). 222p. 1980. pap. text ed. 17.50 incl. wkbk. (ISBN 0-909337-26-8); wkbk. avail. ADIS Pr.
Fundamentals of General, Organic, & Biological Chemistry. John R. Holum. LC 77-10418. 1978. text ed. 23.95x (ISBN 0-471-40873-5); study guide 7.50 (ISBN 0-471-02454-6); tchr's manual avail. (ISBN 0-471-03669-2). Wiley.
Fundamentals of Genetics. 2nd ed. A. S. Islam. 520p. 1981. text ed. 27.50x (ISBN 0-7069-1238-1, Pub. by Vikas India). Advent Bk.
Fundamentals of Geomorphology. R. J. Rice. (Illus.). 1977. text ed. 32.00 (ISBN 0-582-48429-4); pap. text ed. 17.95x (ISBN 0-582-48430-8). Longman.
Fundamentals of Geotechnical Analysis. I. S. Dunn et al. LC 79-13583. 1980. text ed. 20.95 o.p. (ISBN 0-471-03698-6); solutions manual avail. o.p. (ISBN 0-471-04997-2). Wiley.
Fundamentals of Goju-Ryu Karate. Gosei Yamaguchi. Ed. by Pat Alston. LC 72-80830. (Ser.112). (Illus.). 1972. pap. text ed. 7.95 (ISBN 0-89750-007-5). Ohara Pubns.
Fundamentals of Group Child Care: A Textbook & Instructional Guide for Child Care Workers. Jack Adler. 1981. price not set reference (ISBN 0-88410-198-3). Ballinger Pub.
Fundamentals of Guidance. 4th ed. Bruce Shertzer & Shelley C. Stone. LC 80-81917. (Illus.). 576p. 1981. text ed. 18.95 (ISBN 0-395-29712-5); write for info. instr's manual (ISBN 0-395-29713-3). HM.
Fundamentals of Guidance. 3rd ed. Bruce E. Shertzer & Shelley C. Stone. LC 75-31026. (Illus.). 576p. 1976. text ed. 18.95 (ISBN 0-395-20621-9); inst. manual 2.00 (ISBN 0-395-20614-6). HM.
Fundamentals of Heat Transfer. Frank P. Incropera. Ed. by David P. DeWitt. LC 80-17209. 656p. 1981. text ed. 23.95 (ISBN 0-471-42711-X). Wiley.
Fundamentals of Heat Transfer. Lindon Thomas. (Illus.). 1980. text ed. 27.95 (ISBN 0-13-339903-6). P-H.
Fundamentals of Homeostasis. 2nd ed. Maxwell Borow. 1977. spiral bdg. 8.50 o.p. (ISBN 0-87488-758-5). Med Exam.
Fundamentals of Human Neuropsychology. Bryan Kolb & Ian Q. Whishaw. LC 80-17987. (Psychology Ser.). (Illus.). 1980. text ed. 17.95x (ISBN 0-7167-1219-9). W H Freeman.
Fundamentals of Hydraulic Systems. Ned H. Hwang. (P-H Ser. in Environmental Sciences). (Illus.). 352p. 1981. text ed. 28.95 (ISBN 0-13-340000-X). P-H.
Fundamentals of Hydro & Aeromechanics. Ludwig Prandtl & O. G. Tietjens. Tr. by L. Rosenhead. (Illus.). pap. text ed. 4.00 (ISBN 0-486-60374-1). Dover.
Fundamentals of Immunology. 4th ed. William C. Boyd. LC 66-20389. 1967. 38.95 (ISBN 0-470-09342-0, Pub. by Wiley-Interscience). Wiley.
Fundamentals of Immunology. Noel R. Rose et al. Ed. by Joan C. Zulch. (Illus.). 448p. 1973. text ed. 15.25x o.p. (ISBN 0-02-403590-4); pap. text ed. 11.50x o.p. (ISBN 0-685-30318-7). Macmillan.
Fundamentals of Individual Appraisal: Assessment Techniques for Counselors. Bruce Shertzer & James D. Linden. LC 78-69542. (Illus.). 1978. text ed. 18.95 (ISBN 0-395-26536-3); inst. manual 0.60 (ISBN 0-395-26537-1). HM.
Fundamentals of Individual Retirement Plans. Bernhart R. Snyder & Snyder. 1980. 8.95 (ISBN 0-87863-206-9). Farnswth Pub.
Fundamentals of Industrial Toxicology. Kim E. Anderson & Ronald M. Scott. (Illus.). 1981. 14.95 (ISBN 0-250-40378-1). Ann Arbor Science.
Fundamentals of Inferential Statistics for Business Analysis. 2nd ed. Howard B. Baltz. 416p. 1980. pap. text ed. 18.95 (ISBN 0-8403-2217-8). Kendall-Hunt.
Fundamentals of Instruction. John King & Martha King. (Pilot Training Ser.). 1979. pap. 2.95 (ISBN 0-89100-134-4, E*A*A*C61-90). Aviation Maintenance.
Fundamentals of Investing. Ben Branch. LC 75-26703. 1976. 21.50 (ISBN 0-471-09650-4); instructor's manual avail. (ISBN 0-471-09651-2). Wiley.
Fundamentals of Investments. Richard A. Stevenson & Edward H. Jennings. LC 75-42350. (Illus.). 580p. 1976. text ed. 16.95 (ISBN 0-8299-0077-2); instrs.' manual avail. (ISBN 0-8299-0575-8). West Pub.
Fundamentals of Investments. 2nd ed. Richard A. Stevenson & Edward H. Jennings. (Illus.). 608p. 1980. text ed. 15.95 (ISBN 0-8299-0299-6). West Pub.
Fundamentals of Juvenile Criminal Behavior & Drug Abuse. Ed. by Richard E. Hardy & John G. Cull. 276p. 1975. 18.50 (ISBN 0-398-03162-2). C C Thomas.
Fundamentals of Law Enforcement. A. F. Brandstatter & A. A. Hyman. (Criminal Justice Ser). 1972. text ed. 14.95x (ISBN 0-02-473740-2). Macmillan.
Fundamentals of Layout. F. H. Wills. LC 78-166431. 1971. lib. bdg. 11.50x (ISBN 0-88307-595-4). Gannon.
Fundamentals of Layout for Newspaper & Magazine Advertising, for Page Design of Publications & Brochures. F. H. Wills. LC 78-166431. (Illus.). 1971. pap. 3.50 (ISBN 0-486-21279-3). Dover.
Fundamentals of Leadership: A Guide for the Supervisor. Raymond J. Burby. LC 72-2644. (Illus.). 128p. (Prog. Bk.). 1972. pap. text ed. 8.95 (ISBN 0-201-00744-4). A-W.
Fundamentals of Learning. John P. Houston. 1976. text ed. 16.95 (ISBN 0-12-356850-1); instrs' manual 3.00 (ISBN 0-12-356852-8). Acad Pr.
Fundamentals of Learning & Motivation. 3rd ed. Frank A. Logan & William C. Gordon. 250p. 1981. pap. text ed. write for info. (ISBN 0-697-06634-7). Wm C Brown.
Fundamentals of Library Organisation & Administration: A Practical Guide. E. V. Corbett. 1978. 24.50x (ISBN 0-85365-540-5, Pub. by Lib Assn England); pap. text ed. 15.50x (ISBN 0-85365-840-4). Oryx Pr.
Fundamentals of Logic Design. 2nd ed. Charles H. Roth. (Electrical Engineering Ser.). (Illus.). 1979. pap. 20.95 (ISBN 0-8299-0226-0); instrs. manual avail. (ISBN 0-8299-0572-3). West Pub.
Fundamentals of Machine Design. K. D. Sharma. 1971. 12.50x (ISBN 0-210-27015-2). Asia.
Fundamentals of Management Accounting. rev. ed. Robert N. Anthony & Glenn A. Welsch. 1977. text ed. 18.95x (ISBN 0-256-01896-0); practice set 5.95x (ISBN 0-256-01957-6); study guide 6.50x (ISBN 0-256-01603-8). Irwin.
Fundamentals of Management Accounting. John A. Tracy. LC 75-26988. 565p. 1976. text ed. 21.95 (ISBN 0-471-88151-1, Pub. by Wiley-Hamilton). Wiley.
Fundamentals of Management for the Physician. Frank Moya. (Illus.). 208p. 1974. 14.75 (ISBN 0-398-02945-8). C C Thomas.
Fundamentals of Management: Functions, Behavior, Models. 3rd ed. James Donnelly et al. 1978. 18.50x (ISBN 0-256-02073-6). Business Pubns.
Fundamentals of Management Science. Efraim Turban & Jack Meredith. 1977. 19.95x (ISBN 0-256-01812-X). Business Pubns.
Fundamentals of Management: Selected Readings. 3rd ed. James Donnelly et al. 1978. pap. 9.95x (ISBN 0-256-02075-2). Business Pubns.
Fundamentals of Managerial Economics. James L. Pappas & Eugene F. Brigham. LC 79-51063. 560p. 1981. text ed. 17.95 (ISBN 0-03-040841-5). Dryden Pr.
Fundamentals of Marching. M. R. Broer & R. M. Wilson. (Illus.). 1965. 9.95 (ISBN 0-8260-1340-6). Wiley.
Fundamentals of Marketing. 6th ed. William J. Stanton. (Illus.). 704p. 1981. text ed. 19.95 (ISBN 0-07-060891-1, C); instrs. manual 10.95 (ISBN 0-07-060892-X); study guide 6.95 (ISBN 0-07-060893-8); test file 15.95 (ISBN 0-07-060894-6); transparency masters avail. (ISBN 0-07-060895-4). McGraw.
Fundamentals of Mathematical Analysis, 2 Vols. G. M. Fikhtengol'ts. 1965. Vol. 1. 25.00 (ISBN 0-08-010059-7); Vol. 2. 25.00 (ISBN 0-08-010060-0); Vol. 1. pap. 18.75 (ISBN 0-08-013473-4); Vol. 2. pap. 21.00 (ISBN 0-08-013474-2). Pergamon.
Fundamentals of Mathematics. William M. Setek, Jr. 1976. text ed. 14.95x (ISBN 0-02-478370-6). Macmillan.
Fundamentals of Mathematics. Edwin I. Stein. (gr. 7-12). 1976. text ed. 15.80 (ISBN 0-205-05003-4, 5650038); tchrs'. ed. 4.20 (ISBN 0-205-05004-2, 5650046). Allyn.
Fundamentals of Mathematics. Edwin I. Stein. (gr. 7-12). 1980. text ed. 15.80 (ISBN 0-205-06895-2, 5668956); tchrs'. guide 4.20 (ISBN 0-205-06896-0). Allyn.
Fundamentals of Mathematics for Business, Social, & Life Sciences. W. Adams. 1979. 21.95 (ISBN 0-13-341073-0). P-H.
Fundamentals of Meal Management. Margaret McWilliams. LC 78-54660. (Illus.). 1978. text ed. 16.95 (ISBN 0-916434-29-X). Plycon Pr.
Fundamentals of Meat Animal Evaluation. Minish & Lidvall. 1981. text ed. 15.95 (ISBN 0-8359-2137-9); instr's. manual free (ISBN 0-8359-2138-7). Reston.
Fundamentals of Medical Assisting, Administrative & Clinical. Mary A. Frew & David R. Frew. 1981. 16.95 (ISBN 0-8036-3858-2). Davis Co.
Fundamentals of Men's Fashion Design: A Guide to Casual Clothes. new ed. Edmund Roberts. LC 75-13691. (Illus.). 224p. 1975. 14.50x (ISBN 0-87005-104-0). Fairchild.
Fundamentals of Metal Casting. Richard A. Flinn. 1963. 20.95 (ISBN 0-201-02020-3). A-W.

Fundamentals of Metallurgical Processes. L. Coudurier & I. Wilkomirsky. 1978. text ed. 52.00 (ISBN 0-08-019612-8); pap. text ed. 17.00 (ISBN 0-08-019654-3). Pergamon.

Fundamentals of Meteorology. Louis J. Battan. 1979. 17.95 (ISBN 0-13-341131-1). P-H.

Fundamentals of Microbiology. 9th ed. Martin Frobisher et al. LC 73-88259. (Illus.). 850p. 1974. text ed. 18.95 o.p. (ISBN 0-7216-3922-4). Saunders.

Fundamentals of Modern Agriculture. C. D. Blake. 516p. 1974. 14.00 o.p. (ISBN 0-424-05290-3, Pub. by Sydney U Pr); pap. 12.75x (ISBN 0-424-06930-X, Pub. by Sydney U Pr). Intl Schol Bk Serv.

Fundamentals of Modern Marketing. 2nd ed. Edward Cundiff et al. 480p. 1976. 15.95 o.p. (ISBN 0-13-341248-2); student guide 6.95 o.p. (ISBN 0-13-341255-5). P-H.

Fundamentals of Modern Marketing. 3rd ed. Edward W. Cundiff et al. 1980. text ed. 18.95 (ISBN 0-13-341388-8). P-H.

Fundamentals of Modern Photocomposition. John W. Seybold. (Illus.). 1979. text ed. 27.50 (ISBN 0-918514-03-7); pap. text ed. 22.50 (ISBN 0-918514-02-9). Seybold.

Fundamentals of Modern Physics. Robert M. Eisberg. LC 61-6770. (Illus.). 1961. 28.50 (ISBN 0-471-23463-X). Wiley.

Fundamentals of Momentum, Heat & Mass Transfer. 2nd ed. James R. Welty et al. LC 76-16813. 897p. 1976. text ed. 31.95 (ISBN 0-471-93354-6). Wiley.

Fundamentals of Multicomponent Distillation. (Chemical Engineering Ser.). (Illus.). 624p. 1981. text ed. 39.95 (ISBN 0-07-029567-0, C). McGraw. Postponed.

Fundamentals of Municipal Bonds. Public Securities Assoc. (Illus.). 1980. cancelled (ISBN 0-89490-048-X). Enslow Pubs.

Fundamentals of Music. 3rd ed. Raymond Elliott. LC 76-139599. (Illus.). 1971. pap. text ed. 12.50 (ISBN 0-13-341305-5). P-H.

Fundamentals of Music. Richard Wink. LC 76-20867. (Illus.). 1977. pap. text ed. 14.50 (ISBN 0-395-20598-0). HM.

Fundamentals of Natural Gas. Consumers Power Company. LC 74-100858. (Supervision Ser). 1970. pap. text ed. 10.95 (ISBN 0-201-01180-8). A-W.

Fundamentals of Negotiating. new ed. Gerard I. Nierenberg. 1977. 14.95 (ISBN 0-8015-2868-2, Hawthorn); pap. 6.50 (ISBN 0-8015-2869-0, Hawthorn). Dutton.

Fundamentals of Network Analysis. Don T. Phillips & Alberto Garcia-Diaz. (Illus.). 496p. 1981. text ed. 26.95 (ISBN 0-13-341552-X). P-H.

Fundamentals of Network Analysis & Synthesis. Behrouz Peikari. (Illus.). 544p. 1974. ref. ed. 26.95 (ISBN 0-13-341321-7). P-H.

Fundamentals of Neurology. John M. Sutherland. 272p. (Orig.). 1980. pap. 23.50 (ISBN 0-909337-29-2). ADIS Pr.

Fundamentals of Neurophysiology. 2nd rev. ed. R. F. Schmidt et al. LC 74-18500. (Springer Study Ed.). (Illus.). x, 294p. 1975. pap. 12.40 o.p. (ISBN 0-387-06871-6). Springer-Verlag.

Fundamentals of Neurophysiology: Springer Study Edition. 2nd ed. Ed. by R. F. Schmidt et al. Tr. by D. Jordan & I. Jordan. 1978. pap. 15.50 (ISBN 0-387-08188-7). Springer-Verlag.

Fundamentals of Nuclear Science: With Applications in Agriculture & Biology. P. N. Tiwari. LC 74-1290. 1974. 12.95 (ISBN 0-470-87522-4). Halsted Pr.

Fundamentals of Number Significance. Marc E. Jones. LC 78-69854. 1978. 16.50 o.p. (ISBN 0-87878-015-7, Sabian). Great Eastern.

Fundamentals of Number Theory. William J. LeVeque. LC 76-55645. 1978. text ed. 19.95 (ISBN 0-201-04287-8). A-W.

Fundamentals of Numerical Analysis. Stephen G. Kellison. LC 74-78157. 1974. text ed. 17.50x (ISBN 0-256-01612-7). Irwin.

Fundamentals of Numerical Computation: International Conference. Ed. by G. Alefeld & R. D. Crigorieff. (Computing Supplementum: No. 2). (Illus.). 250p. 1980. pap. 57.90 (ISBN 0-387-81566-X). Springer-Verlag.

Fundamentals of Nursing. Margaret Magnus. (Nursing Examination Review Books: Vol. 11). 1972. pap. 6.00 (ISBN 0-87488-511-6). Med Exam.

Fundamentals of Nursing. M. Murray. 1976. text ed. 20.95x (ISBN 0-13-341354-3); student wkbk. study guide 6.95 (ISBN 0-13-341370-5). P-H.

Fundamentals of Nursing. 2nd ed. Malinda Murray. (Illus.). 1980. text ed. 20.95 (ISBN 0-13-341313-6); pap. text ed. 8.95 study guide (ISBN 0-13-341347-0). P-H.

Fundamentals of Nursing. Jack Rudman. (ACT Proficiency Examination Program: PEP-36). (Cloth bdg. avail. on request). pap. 14.95 (ISBN 0-8373-5536-2). Natl Learning.

Fundamentals of Nursing: Concepts & Procedures. Barbara B. Kozier & Glenora L. Erb. LC 78-7776. 1979. 23.95 (ISBN 0-201-03904-4, 03904, M&N Div); instr's guide 3.95 (ISBN 0-686-52327-X, 03905). A-W.

Fundamentals of Nursing Practice: Concepts, Roles & Functions. Fay L. Bower & Em O. Bevis. LC 77-26885. (Illus.). 1978. text ed. 16.95 (ISBN 0-8016-0732-9). Mosby.

Fundamentals of Nursing: The Humanities & the Sciences in Nursing. 5th ed. Elinor V. Fuerst et al. LC 74-519. 450p. 1974. text ed. 10.95 o.p. (ISBN 0-397-54152-X). Lippincott.

Fundamentals of Nutrition. 2nd ed. L. E. Lloyd et al. LC 77-16029. (Animal Science Ser.). (Illus.). 1978. text ed. 23.95x (ISBN 0-7167-0566-4). W H Freeman.

Fundamentals of Obstetrics & Gynaecology, Vol. 2: Gynaecology. Derek Llewellyn-Jones. (Illus.). 1978. 29.00 (ISBN 0-571-04929-X, Pub. by Faber & Faber); pap. 18.00 (ISBN 0-571-04958-3). Merrimack Bk Serv.

Fundamentals of Operating Room Nursing. 2nd ed. Shirley M. Brooks. LC 79-500. (Illus.). 1979. pap. 11.50 (ISBN 0-8016-0814-7). Mosby.

Fundamentals of Operations Research for Management. Shiv K. Gupta & John M. Cozzolino. LC 73-94384. (Illus.). 1975. text ed. 22.95x (ISBN 0-8162-3476-0); solutions manual 6.50x (ISBN 0-8162-3486-8). Holden-Day.

Fundamentals of Organic Chemistry. C. David Gutsche & Daniel G. Pasto. (Illus.). 1248p. 1975. 26.95 (ISBN 0-13-333443-0); solutions manual 4.95 (ISBN 0-13-333435-X). P-H.

Fundamentals of Organic Reaction Mechanisms. J. Milton Harris & Carl C. Wamser. LC 75-40275. 1976. 26.95 (ISBN 0-471-35400-7). Wiley.

Fundamentals of Organizational Behavior: An Applied Perspective. Andrew J. Du Brin. LC 72-12998. 1974. text ed. 19.25 o.p. (ISBN 0-08-017110-9); pap. text ed. 11.00 o.p. (ISBN 0-08-017111-7); 0.55 o.p. (ISBN 0-08-017112-5). Pergamon.

Fundamentals of Organizational Behavior: An Applied Perspective. 2nd ed. Andrew J. Du Brin. LC 77-12720. 1978. text ed. 44.00 (ISBN 0-08-022252-8); pap. text ed. 15.00 (ISBN 0-08-022251-X). Pergamon.

Fundamentals of Our Faith. Herschel H. Hobbs. LC 60-5200. (Orig.). 1960. pap. 4.95 (ISBN 0-8054-1702-8). Broadman.

Fundamentals of Patient-Centered Nursing. 3rd ed. Ruth V. Matheney et al. LC 72-185524. (Illus.). viii, 288p. 1972. pap. text ed. 10.50 o.p. (ISBN 0-8016-3153-X). Mosby.

Fundamentals of Personal Rapid Transit. Jack H. Irving et al. 1978. 11.95 (ISBN 0-669-02520-8). Lexington Bks.

Fundamentals of Photochemistry. K. K. Rohatgi-Mukherjee. LC 78-12088. 1979. 12.95 (ISBN 0-470-26547-7). Halsted Pr.

Fundamentals of Physical Metallurgy. John D. Verhoeven. LC 75-4600. 567p. 1975. text ed. 30.95 (ISBN 0-471-90616-6). Wiley.

Fundamentals of Physical Surveillance: A Guide for Uniformed & Plainclothes Personnel. Raymond P. Siljander. (Illus.). 288p. 1978. 24.50 (ISBN 0-398-03660-8). C C Thomas.

Fundamentals of Physics. 2nd ed. David Halliday & Robert Resnick. LC 80-17184. 1024p. 1981. text ed. write for info. (ISBN 0-471-03363-4); write for info. wkbk. (ISBN 0-471-06463-7). Wiley.

Fundamentals of Physics: Extended Version. 2nd extended ed. David Halliday & Robert Resnick. LC 80-23013. 1040p. 1981. text ed. 26.95 (ISBN 0-471-08005-5). Wiley.

Fundamentals of Physiology: The Human Body & How It Works. rev. ed. Elbert Tokay. 1970. pap. 3.95 (ISBN 0-06-463221-0, EH 221, EH). Har-Row.

Fundamentals of Pipe Drafting. Charles H. Thompson. LC 58-13471. 1958. pap. 10.00 (ISBN 0-471-85998-2, Pub. by Wiley-Interscience). Wiley.

Fundamentals of Pipe Flow. A. R. Kaplan. LC 79-23924. 1980. 39.95 (ISBN 0-471-03375-8, Pub. by Wiley-Interscience). Wiley.

Fundamentals of PL-1 Programming: A Structured Approach with PL-C. Terry M. Walker. 1977. pap. text ed. 13.95 (ISBN 0-205-04892-7). Allyn.

Fundamentals of Plant Genetics & Breeding. James R. Welsh. LC 80-14638. 450p. 1981. text ed. 23.95 (ISBN 0-471-02862-2). Wiley.

Fundamentals of Plant Pathology. Daniel A. Roberts & Carl W. Boothroyd. LC 77-169737. (Illus.). 1972. text ed. 24.95x (ISBN 0-7167-0822-1). W H Freeman.

Fundamentals of Plastic & Reconstructive Surgery. Wallace H. J. Chang. (Illus.). 424p. 1980. softcover 32.50 (ISBN 0-683-01515-X). Williams & Wilkins.

Fundamentals of Police Administration. Charles D. Hale. (Criminal Justice). 1977. text ed. 15.95 (ISBN 0-205-05688-1, 8256888); instructor's manual free (ISBN 0-205-05689-X, 825689-6). Allyn.

Fundamentals of Position Tolerance. John V. Liggett. (Manufacturing Data Ser.). (Illus.). 1970. pap. 11.75 (ISBN 0-87263-020-X). SME.

Fundamentals of Powder Coating. new ed. Ed. by Emery P. Miller & David D. Taft. (Illus.). 287p. 1974. 10.00x (ISBN 0-87263-033-1). SME.

Fundamentals of Private Pensions. 4th ed. Dan M. McGill. 1979. text ed. 17.95 (ISBN 0-256-02252-6). Irwin.

Fundamentals of Production Operations Management. Fearon et al. 171p. 1979. pap. text ed. 6.95 (ISBN 0-8299-0269-4); instrs.' manual avail. (ISBN 0-8299-0478-6). West Pub.

Fundamentals of Protective Systems: Planning, Evaluation, Selection. Albert J. Mandelbaum. (Illus.). 288p. 1973. text ed. 15.75 (ISBN 0-398-02657-2). C C Thomas.

Fundamentals of Psychological & Educational Measurement. Herman R. Tiedeman. (Illus.). 144p. 1972. 15.75 (ISBN 0-398-02429-4). C C Thomas.

Fundamentals of Psychological Medicine. R. R. Tilleard-Cole & J. Marks. LC 75-15862. 290p. 1975. 26.95 (ISBN 0-470-86791-4). Halsted Pr.

Fundamentals of Psychological Research. 3rd ed. Wood. text ed. 17.95 (ISBN 0-316-95169-2); training manual free (ISBN 0-316-95170-6). Little.

Fundamentals of Psychology. 2nd ed. Audrey Haber & Richard P. Runyon. LC 77-79460. (Psychology Ser.). (Illus.). 1978. text ed. 16.95 (ISBN 0-201-02766-6); wkbk 6.50 (ISBN 0-201-02767-4); instr's resource guide 4.50 (ISBN 0-201-02768-2). A-W.

Fundamentals of Psychology: An Introduction. Michael Gazzaniga. 1973. text ed. 18.95 (ISBN 0-12-278650-5). Acad Pr.

Fundamentals of Public Relations: Professional Guidelines, Concepts & Integrations. 2nd ed. Ed. by Lawrence W. Nolte & Dennis L. Wilcox. 1979. 16.45 (ISBN 0-08-022470-9). Pergamon.

Fundamentals of Public Speaking. 5th ed. Donald C. Bryant & Karl R. Wallace. (Illus.). 640p. 1976. pap. 14.95 (ISBN 0-13-342725-0). P-H.

Fundamentals of Pulse & Digital Circuits. 2nd ed. Ronald J. Tocci. (Electronics Technology Ser.). 1977. text ed. 20.95 (ISBN 0-675-08492-X); instructor's manual 3.95 (ISBN 0-686-67521-5). Merrill.

Fundamentals of Quantity Food Preparation: Breads, Soups & Sandwiches. Geraline B. Hardwick & Robert L. Kennedy. LC 77-20096. (Illus.). 1978. 22.95 (ISBN 0-8436-2163-X). CBI Pub.

Fundamentals of Quantity Food Preparation: Desserts & Beverages. Geraline B. Hardwick & Robert L. Kennedy. LC 74-20917. (Illus.). 364p. 1975. 22.95 (ISBN 0-8436-2051-X). CBI Pub.

Fundamentals of Queueing Theory. Donald Gross & Carl M. Harris. LC 73-20084. (Probability & Mathematical Statistics Ser.). 576p. 1974. 34.95 (ISBN 0-471-32812-X, Pub. by Wiley-Interscience). Wiley.

Fundamentals of Radiation Dosimetry. John R. Greening. (Medical Physics Handbook: No. 6). 190p. 1980. 27.00 (ISBN 0-9960020-5-7, Pub. by a Hilger England). Heyden.

Fundamentals of Radiobiology. 2nd ed. Z. M. Bacq & P. Alexander. 1971. 32.00 (ISBN 0-08-009406-6); pap. text ed. 4.15 (ISBN 0-08-012166-7). Pergamon.

Fundamentals of Radiological Science. John Hale. (Illus.). 356p. 1974. text ed. 21.50 (ISBN 0-398-02805-2). C C Thomas.

Fundamentals of Real Estate Appraisal. 2nd ed. Ventolo & Williams. 320p. (Orig.). 1979. pap. 22.95 (ISBN 0-88462-285-1). Real Estate Ed Co.

Fundamentals of Reinforced Concrete. John N. Cernica. (Illus.). 1964. 19.95 (ISBN 0-201-00945-5). A-W.

Fundamentals of Removable Prosthodontics. Dean L. Johnson & Russell J. Stratton. (Illus.). 500p. 1980. 46.00 (ISBN 0-931386-10-1). Quint Pub Co.

Fundamentals of RIA & Other Ligand Assays: A Programmed Text. Jeffrey C. Travis. (Illus.). 1977. 22.50 (ISBN 0-930914-05-8). Sci Newsletters.

Fundamentals of Risk & Insurance. 2nd ed. Emmett J. Vaughan & Curtis M. Elliot. LC 77-18769. (Wiley-Hamilton Series in Risk & Insurance). 1978. text ed. 24.50 (ISBN 0-471-90353-1); tchrs'. manual avail. (ISBN 0-471-02164-4). Wiley.

Fundamentals of Scaling & Psychophysics. John C. Baird & Elliot Noma. LC 78-6011. (Wiley Ser. in Behavior). 1978. 25.95 (ISBN 0-471-04169-6, Pub. by Wiley-Interscience). Wiley.

Fundamentals of Semiconductor Devices. Joseph Lindmayer et al. LC 76-16765. 506p. 1977. Repr. of 1965 ed. 26.50 (ISBN 0-88275-424-6). Krieger.

Fundamentals of Senior Physics. Incl. Physics of Measurement. Peter Sandery. pap. text ed. 4.95x o.p. (ISBN 0-435-68107-9, S7); Planets, Satellites, & Gravity. P. Burford et al. pap. text ed. 4.95x o.p. (ISBN 0-435-68108-7, S8); Fluid Dynamics. R. J. Booth et al. pap. text ed. 4.95x o.p. (ISBN 0-435-68109-5, S9); Sound. C. Johnson et al. pap. text ed. 4.95x o.p. (ISBN 0-435-68110-9, S10); Motion of Charged Particles in Fields. P. G. Edwards et al. pap. text ed. 4.95x o.p. (ISBN 0-435-68111-7, S11); Practical Electronics. D. B. Roberts. pap. text ed. 4.95x o.p. (ISBN 0-435-68112-5, S12); Atmospheric Electricity. W. S. Boundy. pap. text ed. o.p. (ISBN 0-435-68113-3, S13); Development of the Concept of the Atom. C. Butler et al. pap. text ed. 4.95x o.p. (ISBN 0-435-68124-9, HS5); Waves in Nature. T. M. Gibbons & C. L. Pyle. pap. text ed. 4.95x o.p. (ISBN 0-435-68125-7, HS6); Optical Systems. G. R. Fuller. pap. text ed. 4.95x o.p. (ISBN 0-435-68126-5, HS7); A.C. Circuits. B. Donnelly et al. pap. text ed. o.p. (ISBN 0-435-68127-3, HS8); Aspects of Physical Meteorology. Bruce Mason. pap. text ed. 4.95x o.p. (ISBN 0-435-68128-1, HS9); Solid State Phenomena. R. Lawrence & R. K. Maynard. pap. text ed. 4.95x o.p. (ISBN 0-435-68129-X, HS10); Special Relativity. Peter Sandery. pap. text ed. 4.95x o.p. (ISBN 0-435-68130-3, HS11). 1972. Heinemann Ed.

Fundamentals of Senior Physics Textbook, 2 bks. J. M. Mayfield & B. M. Webber. 1973. pap. text ed. 12.95x; Bk. 1. pap. text ed. 13.95 (00510); Bk. 2. pap. text ed. 13.95 (000502). Heinemann Ed.

Fundamentals of Sensation & Perception. Michael W. Levine & Jeremy M. Shefner. (Psychology Ser.). (Illus.). 480p. 1981. text ed. 19.95 (ISBN 0-201-04339-4). A-W.

Fundamentals of Sensory Physiology. Ed. by R. F. Schmidt. (Illus.). 1978. 18.50 (ISBN 0-387-08801-6). Springer-Verlag.

Fundamentals of Singing & Speaking. Teodosio Longo. 112p. 1945. 7.00x (ISBN 0-913298-54-9). S F Vanni.

Fundamentals of Social Intervention: Core Concepts & Skills for Social Work Practice. Frank M. Loewenberg. LC 76-23290. 1977. 13.50x (ISBN 0-231-03611-6). Columbia U Pr.

Fundamentals of Social Work Practice. Sanders. 1981. pap. text ed. price not set. Duxbury Pr.

Fundamentals of Soil Behavior. James K. Mitchell. LC 75-28096. (Soil Engineering Ser). 384p. 1976. text ed. 35.95 (ISBN 0-471-61168-9). Wiley.

Fundamentals of Soil Science. 6th ed. Henry D. Foth. LC 77-86509. 1978. 22.95 (ISBN 0-471-26792-9). Wiley.

Fundamentals of Solar Heating. R. Schubert & L. Ryan. 1981. 23.95 (ISBN 0-13-344457-0). P-H.

Fundamentals of Spanish Grammar. Richard Armitage et al. 1975. pap. text ed. 6.60 (ISBN 0-395-19865-8). HM.

Fundamentals of Speech Communication. 3rd ed. Bert E. Bradley. 430p. 1981. pap. text ed. write for info. (ISBN 0-697-04177-8); instr's manual avail. (ISBN 0-697-04184-0). Wm C Brown.

Fundamentals of Sports Biomechanics. Charles Simonian. (Illus.). 224p. 1981. text ed. 13.95 (ISBN 0-13-344499-6). P-H.

Fundamentals of Statistical Thermodynamcis. R. E. Sonntag & G. J. Van Wylen. LC 65-27654. 1966. text ed. 26.95x (ISBN 0-471-81360-5). Wiley.

Fundamentals of Structured Programming Using FORTRAN with SF-K & WATFIV-S. R. C. Holt & J. N. Hume. (Illus.). 1977. pap. text ed. 12.95 (ISBN 0-87909-302-1); case ed. 14.95 (ISBN 0-8359-7131-7). Reston.

Fundamentals of Systems Analysis. 2nd ed. Jerry Fitzgerald et al. LC 80-11769. 500p. 1980. text ed. 22.95 (ISBN 0-471-04968-9, Pub by Wiley College); write for info. (ISBN 0-471-08117-5). Wiley.

Fundamentals of Teaching Machine & Programmed Learning Systems, 3 vols. Leonard C. Silvern. LC 64-14098. (Illus., Prog. Bk.). 1964. Set. 50.00 (ISBN 0-685-09258-5). Ed & Training.

Fundamentals of Television: Theory & Service. new ed. Bernard Hartman. (Technology Ser). (Illus.). 272p. 1975. text ed. 18.95 (ISBN 0-675-08745-7). Merrill.

Fundamentals of Temperature, Pressure, & Flow Measurements. 2nd ed. Robert P. Benedict. LC 76-54341. 1977. 37.50 (ISBN 0-471-06561-7, Pub. by Wiley-Interscience). Wiley.

Fundamentals of Texas Government. E. Larry Dickens & Pamela S. Bertone. LC 76-2572. (Illus.). 149p. (Orig.). 1976. lib. bdg. 7.95 (ISBN 0-88408-046-3); pap. text ed. 5.95 (ISBN 0-88408-127-3). Sterling Swift.

Fundamentals of the Computing Sciences. Kurt Maly & Allen R. Hanson. (Illus.). 1978. ref. ed. 19.95 (ISBN 0-13-335240-4); supplementary vol. 11.95 (ISBN 0-13-335257-9). P-H.

Fundamentals of the Esoteric Philosophy. 2nd, rev. ed. G. De Purucker. Ed. by Grace F. Knoche. LC 78-74258. 1979. 13.50 (ISBN 0-911500-63-4); softcover 8.95 (ISBN 0-911500-64-2). Theos U Pr.

Fundamentals of the Fungi. Elizabeth Moore-Landecker. (Biological Ser). (Illus.). 1972. ref. ed. 23.95x (ISBN 0-13-339267-8). P-H.

Fundamentals of Theoretical Chemistry. R. Daudel. 1967. 26.00 (ISBN 0-08-012300-7). Pergamon.

Fundamentals of Training for Security Officers: A Comprehensive Guide to What You Should Be, Know & Do to Have a Successful Career As a Private Patrolman or Security Officer. John D. Peel. (Illus.). 344p. 1980. 17.95 (ISBN 0-398-03966-6). C C Thomas.

Fundamentals of Transmission Lines & Electromagnetic Fields. S. R. Seshadri. LC 77-128908. (Engineering Science Ser). 1971. text ed. 25.95 (ISBN 0-201-06722-6). A-W.

Fundamentals of Trial Techniques. Thomas A. Mauet. 1980. pap. text ed. 10.00 (ISBN 0-316-55082-5). Little.

Fundamentals of Vestibular Pathology. William B. Dublin. 380p. 1981. 32.50 (ISBN 0-87527-203-7). Green. Postponed.

Fundamentals of Veterinary Opthtalmology. Douglas H. Slatter. (Illus.). 400p. 1980. text ed. write for info. (ISBN 0-7216-8357-6). Saunders.

Fundamentals of Visual Science. Melvin L. Rubin & Gordon L. Walls. (Illus.). 460p. 1972. text ed. 21.50 (ISBN 0-398-01625-9). C C Thomas.

Fundamentals of Wound Management. Ed. by Thomas K. Hunt & J. Englebert. (Illus.). 612p. 1979. 29.50 (ISBN 0-8385-2837-6). ACC.

Fundamentals of Yoga: A Handbook of Theory, Practice & Application. Rammurti S. Mishra. 240p. 1974. pap. 2.50 (ISBN 0-385-00952-6, Anch). Doubleday.

Fundamentals: The Foundations of Nursing. Dorothy White et al. 324p. 1972. 16.95 (ISBN 0-13-331991-1). P-H.

Fundamentals to a Pharmacology of the Mind. Corneliu E. Giurgea. (American Lectures on Objective Psychiatry). (Illus.). 376p. 1981. text ed. 37.75 (ISBN 0-398-04130-X). C C Thomas.

Fundamentos De Administracion Financiera. Lawrence J. Gitman. Ed. by Jesus V. Herrera & Mei Mei Alicia Chu Polido. Tr. by Carlos S. Restrepo from Eng. (Span.). 1978. text ed. cancelled (ISBN 0-06-313160-9, Pub. HarLA Mexico). Har-Row.

Fundamentos De Inmunologia E Inmunoquimica. (Serie De Biologia: No. 11). (Span.). 1973. pap. 2.00 o.p. (ISBN 0-8270-6090-4). OAS.

Fundamentos De Investigacion Experimental. rev. ed. Robert Plutchik. 1975. pap. text ed. 7.00 (ISBN 0-06-316991-6, IntlDept). Har-Row.

Fundamentos Filosoficos De la Educacion. 3rd ed. Miguel A. Riestra. 5.00 o.s.i. (ISBN 0-8477-2716-5); pap. 4.35 o.s.i. (ISBN 0-8477-2717-3). U of PR Pr.

Fundammentals Learning Through Making Music. Jay Zorn & James Hanshumaker. Ed. by Sandy Feldstein. LC 79-25768. 1980. pap. 13.50 (ISBN 0-88284-105-X). Alfred Pub.

Funding Higher Education: A Six Nation Analysis. Ed. by Lyman A. Glenny. LC 79-4557. 1979. 25.95 (ISBN 0-03-049616-0). Praeger.

Funding of Social Knowledge Production & Application: A Survey of Federal Agencies. xvii, 487p. 1978. pap. 17.50 (ISBN 0-309-02780-2). Natl Acad Pr.

Fundraising: A Guide for Non-Profit Organizations. Niel Pendleton. (Illus.). 192p. 1981. 13.95 (ISBN 0-13-332163-0, Spec); pap. 6.95 (ISBN 0-13-332155-X). P-H.

Funds for the Future: Report of the Twentieth Century Fund Task Force on College & University Endowment Policy. Twentieth Century Fund, Inc. (Illus.). 1975. 7.95 o.p. (ISBN 0-07-065619-3, P&RB); pap. 4.50 o.p. (ISBN 0-07-065620-7). McGraw.

Funeral. George Abbe. 4.95 (ISBN 0-912292-03-2). The Smith.

Funeral. Andrew W. Blackwood. (Source Book for Ministers Ser.). 1972. pap. 4.95 (ISBN 0-8010-0576-0). Baker Bk.

Funeral Encyclopedia. Ed. by Charles L. Wallis. (Source Bks for Ministers Ser.). 1973. pap. 5.95 (ISBN 0-8010-9539-5). Baker Bk.

Funeral Sermons & Outlines. F. B. Meyer et al. (Ministers Handbook Ser). pap. 2.50 o.p. (ISBN 0-8010-5873-2). Baker Bk.

Funeral Service: A Bibliography of Literature on Its Past, Present, & Future, the Various Means of Disposition, & Memorialization. Barbara K. Harrah & David F. Harrah. LC 76-40340. 1976. 18.00 (ISBN 0-8108-0946-X). Scarecrow.

Funeral Urn. June Drummond. 1977. 6.95 o.s.i. (ISBN 0-8027-5363-9). Walker & Co.

Funerals Are Fatal. Agatha Christie. 1980. pap. 2.25 (ISBN 0-671-83173-9). PB.

Fungal Genetics. 4th ed. J. R. Fincham et al. (Botanical Monographs). 1979. 62.50x (ISBN 0-520-03818-5). U of Cal Pr.

Fungal Spore: Form & Function. Darrell J. Weber & W. M. Hess. LC 75-38889. 895p. 1976. 46.75 (ISBN 0-471-92332-X, Pub. by Wiley-Interscience). Wiley.

Fungal Walls & Hyphal Growth. Ed. by J. H. Burnett & A. P. Trinci. LC 78-72082. (Illus.). 1980. 68.50 (ISBN 0-521-22499-3). Cambridge U Pr.

Fungal Wilt Diseases of Plants. Ed. by M. E. Mace & A. A. Bell. 1981. price not set (ISBN 0-12-464450-3). Acad Pr.

Fungi. H. Angel. 1975. pap. 5.00 (ISBN 0-85242-425-6, Pub. by Fountain). Morgan.

Fungi: An Introduction. Lilian E. Hawker. 1966. pap. text ed. 5.75x (ISBN 0-09-078992-X, Hutchinson U Lib). Humanities.

Fungi in Agricultural Soils. K. H. Domsch & W. Gams. Tr. by P. S. Hudson from Ger. LC 72-3604. 1972. 24.50 o.p. (ISBN 0-470-21776-6). Halsted Pr.

Fungi, Man & His Environment. Roderic C. Cooke. LC 77-1460. (Illus.). 144p. 1978. text ed. 20.00x (ISBN 0-582-46034-4); pap. text ed. 6.95 (ISBN 0-582-44262-1). Longman.

Fungi of the Faeros, 2 pts. F. H. Moeller. Incl. Pt. 1. Basidiomycetes. 1945; Pt. 2. Myxomycetes, Archimycetes, Phycomycetes, Asomycetes, & Fungi Imperfecti (with Appendix to Pt. 1) 1958. (Illus.). 15.00 set (ISBN 0-934454-42-6). Lubrecht & Cramer.

Fungicides: An Advanced Treatise, Vols. 1-2. Ed. by Dewayne C. Torgeson. 1967. Vol. 1. 68.50 (ISBN 0-12-695601-4). Vol. 2. 68.50 (ISBN 0-12-695602-2). Acad Pr.

Fungous Diseases of Man. J. Walter Wilson & Orda A. Plunkett. 1965. 28.50x (ISBN 0-520-01344-1). U of Cal Pr.

Fungus Diseases of Tropical Crops. Paul Holliday. LC 79-41602. (Illus.). 500p. 1980. 125.00 (ISBN 0-521-22529-9). Cambridge U Pr.

Funhouse. Owen West. 288p. 1980. pap. 2.75 (ISBN 0-515-05726-6). Jove Pubns.

Funk & Wagnalls Crossword Puzzle Word Finder. Edmund I. Schwartz & Leon F. Landovitz. (Funk & W Bk.). 768p. 1974. 8.95 o.p. (ISBN 0-308-10126-X, TYC-T). T Y Crowell.

Funk & Wagnalls Guide to Modern World Literature. Martin Seymour-Smith. LC 73-5931. (Funk & W Bk.). 1206p. 1975. 17.50 o.p. (ISBN 0-308-10079-4, TYC-T). T Y Crowell.

Funk & Wagnalls Guide to Personal Money Management. C. Colburn Hardy. LC 75-17830. (Funk & W Bk.). (Illus.). 450p. 1976. 13.95 o.s.i. (ISBN 0-308-10213-4, TYC-T). T Y Crowell.

Funk & Wagnalls-Los Angeles Crossword Treasury, 3 vols. Margaret Farrar. (Funk & W Bk.). 1978. pap. 3.95 ea. o.s.i. (TYC-T); Vol. 1. (ISBN 0-308-10311-4); Vol. 2. (ISBN 0-308-10312-2); Vol. 3. (ISBN 0-308-10313-0). T Y Crowell.

Funk & Wagnalls Standard College Dictionary. new updated ed. Funk And Wagnalls Editors. LC 72-13007. (Funk & W Bk.). 1632p. 1977. 9.95 o.s.i. (ISBN 0-308-10309-2, TYC-T); thumb indexed 10.95 o.s.i. (ISBN 0-308-10310-6). T Y Crowell.

Funk & Wagnalls Standard Desk Dictionary. new ed. LC 76-57148. (Funk & W Bk.). 1977. 7.95 (ISBN 0-308-10280-0, TYC-T); thumb indexed 8.95 (ISBN 0-308-10272-X). T Y Crowell.

Funk & Wagnalls Standard Dictionary. 1980. pap. 2.25 (ISBN 0-451-09358-5, E9358, Sig). NAL.

Funktionen und Relationenalgebren. Lev Kaluznin & Reinhard Poschel. (Mathematische Reihe: No. 67). (Illus., Ger.). 1979. Repr. 42.00 (ISBN 3-7643-1038-3). Birkhauser.

Funktionentheorie, 2 Vols. William F. Osgood. LC 63-11319. (Ger). Vol. 1. 12.50 (ISBN 0-8284-0193-4); Vol. 2. 17.50 (ISBN 0-8284-0182-9). Chelsea Pub.

Funky. Barbara H. Herrera. LC 77-80685. (Destiny Ser.). 1978. pap. 4.95 (ISBN 0-8163-0001-1, 06829-6). Pacific Pr Pub Assn.

Funny Bones. Mike Thaler. (Illus.). 96p. (gr. 4-6). 1976. PLB 4.90 o.p. (ISBN 0-531-00349-3). Watts.

Funny Bunny. Judy Scoder. Ed. by Dan Wasserman. (Ten Word Bks.). (Illus.). (gr. k-1). 1979. PLB 4.50 (ISBN 0-89868-069-7); pap. 1.95 (ISBN 0-89868-080-8). ARO Pub.

Funny Drawing Book. Jerry Warshaw. Ed. by Caroline Rubin. LC 77-14389. (Activity Books Ser.). (Illus.). 48p. (gr. 2 up). 1978. 6.50g (ISBN 0-8075-2681-9). A Whitman.

Funny Feet. Leatie Weiss. (Easy-Read Story Books Ser.). (Illus.). (gr. k-3). 1978. PLB 6.45 s&l (ISBN 0-531-01348-0). Watts.

Funny Fizzles. Jim Molica & Bill Nellor. (Orig.). 1978. pap. 1.25 o.p. (ISBN 0-451-07973-6, Y7973, Sig). NAL.

Funny Friends in Mother Goose Land. Illus. by Pam Ford. (Tell-a-Tale Readers). (Illus.). (gr. k-3). 1979. PLB 4.77 (ISBN 0-307-68647-7, Whitman). Western Pub.

Funny, Funny World Almanac. Martin Ragaway. (Laughter Library). (Illus., Orig.). 1979. pap. 1.95 o.p. (ISBN 0-8431-0526-7). Price Stern.

Funny Magic: Easy Tricks for the Young Magician. Rose Wyler & Gerald Ames. LC 73-39866. (Illus.). 56p. (gr. k-3). 1972. 5.95 o.s.i. (ISBN 0-8193-0584-7, Four Winds); PLB 5.41 o.s.i. (ISBN 0-8193-0585-5). Schol Bk Serv.

Funny Men of the Movies. Edward Edelson. LC 75-14817. 128p. (gr. 4-7). 1976. PLB 5.95 (ISBN 0-385-09693-3). Doubleday.

Funny Mouth: Comedy Material for All Occasions. Mike Porter. 1981. spiral bdg. 12.95 (ISBN 0-914598-70-8); pap. 9.95 (ISBN 0-914598-71-6). Padre Prods.

Funny Number Tricks: Easy Magic with Arithmetic. Rose Wyler & Gerald Ames. LC 76-3439. 48p. (ps-2). 1976. 5.95 o.s.i. (ISBN 0-8193-0846-3, Four Winds); PLB 5.41 o.s.i. (ISBN 0-8193-0847-1). Schol Bk Serv.

Funny Old Bag. Lisl Weil. LC 73-13564. (Illus.). 48p. (ps-3). 1974. 5.95 o.s.i. (ISBN 0-8193-0717-3, Four Winds); PLB 5.41 o.s.i. (ISBN 0-8193-0718-1). Schol Bk Serv.

Funny Ride. Margaret Hillert. (Just Beginning-to-Read Ser.). (Illus.). 32p. (gr. 1-6). 1981. PLB 4.39 (ISBN 0-686-68656-X); pap. 1.50 (ISBN 0-695-31552-8). Follett.

Funny Side of Football. John Sullivan et al. (Illus.). 92p. (Orig.). 1980. pap. 3.95 (ISBN 0-89260-141-8). Hwong Pub.

Funnybones. Allan Ahlberg. LC 79-2472. (Illus.). 32p. (gr. k-3). 1981. 7.95 (ISBN 0-688-80238-9); PLB 7.63 (ISBN 0-688-84238-0). Greenwillow.

Fur Magic. Andre Norton. (gr. 4-6). 1978. pap. 1.75 (ISBN 0-671-41403-8). Archway.

Fur Magic. Andre Norton. (Illus.). (gr. 4-6). 1978. pap. 1.75 (ISBN 0-671-41403-8). PB.

Fur Person. May Sarton. 1973. pap. 1.50 (ISBN 0-451-08942-1, W8942, Sig). NAL.

Fur Rendezvous or Rendezvous on the Green. R. P. DeZeng. 1981. 5.95 (ISBN 0-533-04700-5). Vantage.

Fur Trade in Colonial New York, 1686-1776. Thomas E. Norton & Robert Frank. LC 73-2047. 272p. 1974. 25.00x (ISBN 0-299-06420-4). U of Wis Pr

Fur Trade Letters of Francis Ermatinger. Lois H. McDonald. LC 80-65050. (Northwest Historical Ser.: Vol. 15). (Illus.). 317p. 1980. 29.00 (ISBN 0-87062-130-0). A H Clark.

Fur Trader of the North: The Story of Pierre de la Verendrye. Ronald Syme. LC 72-13603. (Illus.). 192p. (gr. 5-9). 1973. 6.95 (ISBN 0-688-20076-1). Morrow.

Fur Trappers & Traders: The Indians, the Pilgrims, & the Beaver. Beatrice Siegel. LC 80-7671. (Illus.). 64p. (gr. 3-7). 1981. 8.50 (ISBN 0-8027-6396-0); PLB 8.85 (ISBN 0-8027-6397-9). Walker & Co.

Fur Trapping. Bill Musgrove & Gerry Blair. (Illus.). 1979. 11.95 (ISBN 0-87691-284-6). Winchester Pr.

Furies. John Jakes. (Kent Family Chronicle: No. 4). (Orig.). 1976. pap. 2.95 (ISBN 0-515-05890-4). Jove Pubns.

Furious Seasons & Other Stories. Raymond Carver. (Noel Young Bks.). 1977. cloth o.p. 10.00 (ISBN 0-88496-114-1); pap. 3.95 (ISBN 0-88496-113-3). Capra Pr.

Furnace Operations. 3rd ed. Robert D. Reed. 230p. 1981. 18.95 (ISBN 0-87201-301-4). Gulf Pub.

Furnishing Dolls' Houses. Audrey Johnson. LC 72-75079. (Illus.). 284p. 1972. 23.00 (ISBN 0-8231-3029-0). Branford.

Furniture: A Concise History. Edward Lucie-Smith. (World of Art Ser.). (Illus.). 1979. 17.95 (ISBN 0-19-520145-0); pap. 9.95 (ISBN 0-19-520146-9). Oxford U Pr.

Furniture Buyer's Handbook: How to Buy, Arrange, Maintain & Repair Furniture. Max Alth & Charlotte Alth. (Illus.). 1980. pap. 14.95 (ISBN 0-8027-0636-3); pap. 9.95 (ISBN 0-8027-7155-6). Walker & Co.

Furniture Collections of the Essex Institute. Anne Farnam et al. (E. I. Museum Booklet Ser.). (Illus.). 64p. (Orig.). 1981. 4.95 (ISBN 0-88389-102-6). Essex Inst.

Furniture Finishing. Pattou & Vaughn. LC 73-24061. (Illus.). 1973. pap. 4.95 o.p. (ISBN 0-8473-1125-2). Sterling.

Furniture: How to Make -Do, Make Over, Make Your Own. Lis King. LC 76-16409. (Illus.). 1976. pap. 4.95 (ISBN 0-8069-8356-6). Sterling.

Furniture in Twenty Four Hours. Spiros Zakas. 1976. 10.95 o.s.i. (ISBN 0-02-633390-2). Macmillan.

Furniture Maker's Handbook. Family Handyman Magazine Staff. LC 75-38972. 1977. 17.95 o.p. (ISBN 0-684-14499-9, ScribT). Scribner.

Furniture of John Henry Belter & the Rococo Revival. Marvin Schwarz et al. 1981. 24.95 (ISBN 0-525-93170-8). Dutton.

Furniture of the American Arts & Crafts Movement: Stickley & Roycroft Mission Oak. David M. Cathers. 1981. 9.95 (ISBN 0-453-00397-4, H397). NAL.

Furniture Treasury, 3 Vols. Wallace Nutting. (Illus.). Vols. 1 & 2 In 1. 29.95 (ISBN 0-02-590980-0); Vol. 3. 24.95 (ISBN 0-02-591040-X). Macmillan.

Furniture Upholstery. 2nd ed. Sunset Editors. LC 80-80858. (Illus.). 112p. 1980. pap. 4.95 (ISBN 0-376-01183-1, Sunset Bks.). Sunset-Lane.

Further Adventures of Halley's Comet. John C. Batchelor. 640p. 1981. 17.95 (ISBN 0-312-92231-0); pap. 8.95 (ISBN 0-312-92232-9). Congdon & Lattes.

Further Adventures of Puss in Boots. Nicholas S. Gray. (Illus.). (ps-5). 1971. 3.95 o.p. (ISBN 0-571-09641-7, Pub. by Faber & Faber). Merrimack Bk Serv.

Further Adventures of Robinson Crusoe. Henry Treece. LC 58-9623. (Illus.). (gr. 7-11). 1958. 9.95 (ISBN 0-87599-116-5). S G Phillips.

Further Adventures of the Family from One End Street. Eve Garnett. LC 56-12040. (Illus.). (gr. 4-7). 6.95 (ISBN 0-8149-0303-7). Vanguard.

Further Buddhist Studies: Selected Essays. Edward Conze. 1976. text ed. 13.00x o.p. (ISBN 0-85181-009-8). Verry.

Further Confessions of Zeno. Italo Svevo. Tr. by Ben Johnson & P. N. Furbank. LC 69-19076. 1969. 17.50x (ISBN 0-520-01436-7); pap. 2.45 (ISBN 0-520-01753-6, CAL226). U of Cal Pr.

Further Contributions to the Theory & Technique of Psycho-Analysis. Sandor Ferenczi. Ed. by John Rickman. Tr. by Jane I. Suttie from Ger. LC 80-19811. (Brunner-Mazel Classics in Psychoanalysis Ser.: No. 7). 480p. 1980. Repr. of 1926 ed. 20.00 (ISBN 0-87630-255-X). Brunner-Mazel.

Further Education in England & Wales. 2nd rev. ed. Leonard M. Cantor & I. F. Roberts. (Illus.). 348p. 1972. 25.00 (ISBN 0-7100-7358-5). Routledge & Kegan.

Further Engineering Dynamics. J. C. Maltbaek. 177p. 1980. pap. 21.95x (ISBN 0-470-26943-X). Halsted Pr.

Further Exercises in Modern Mathematics. D. T. Marjoram. 1966. text ed. 6.95 (ISBN 0-08-011969-7); pap. 5.40 (ISBN 0-08-011968-9). Pergamon.

Further Explorations in Group Work. Ed. by Saul Bernstein. 1976. text ed. 12.00 (ISBN 0-89182-002-7); pap. 5.75 (ISBN 0-89182-003-5). Charles River Bks.

Further Explorations in Personality. Albert I. Rabin. LC 80-19407. (Personality Processes Ser.). 240p. 1980. 19.95 (ISBN 0-471-07721-6, Pub. by Wiley-Interscience). Wiley.

Further Favourite Stories from Asia. Retold by Leon Comber. (Favourite Stories Ser.). 1978. pap. text ed. 1.25 (ISBN 0-686-60435-0, 00302). Heinemann Ed.

Further Greek Epigrams. Ed. by D. L. Page. LC 79-42646. (Illus.). 700p. Date not set. price not set (ISBN 0-521-22903-0). Cambridge U Pr.

Further Letters of Gerard Manley Hopkins, Including His Correspondence with Coventry Patmore. 2nd ed. Gerard M. Hopkins. Ed. by C. C. Abbott. 1956. 45.00x (ISBN 0-19-212116-2). Oxford U Pr.

Further Listening Comprehension Tests. J. C. Templer. 1972. pap. text ed. 2.50x (ISBN 0-435-28728-1); tchr's ed. 3.50x (ISBN 0-435-28729-X). Heinemann Ed.

Further Offshore. J. H. Illingworth. (Illus.). 1979. 30.00 o.p. (ISBN 0-229-63890-2). Scribner.

Further Pavement Reflections. Lionel Gardner. (Writers Workshop Redbird Book Ser.). 42p. 1975. 12.00 (ISBN 0-88253-544-7); pap. text ed. 4.80 (ISBN 0-88253-543-9). Ind-US Inc.

Further Recollections of a Western Ranchman: New Mexico 1883-1889, Vol. II. William French. (Illus.). 1965p. 20.00 (ISBN 0-87266-011-7). Argosy.

Further Reminiscences, 1864-1894. Sabine Baring-Gould. LC 67-23869. 1967. Repr. of 1925 ed. 15.00 (ISBN 0-8103-3050-4). Gale.

Further Studies in the Assessment of Toxic Actions: Proceedings. Ed. by P. L. Chambers & W. Klinger. (Archives of Toxicology Supplementum Ser.: No. 4). (Illus.). 507p. 1981. pap. 57.80 (ISBN 0-387-10191-8). Springer-Verlag.

Further Topics in Investigating Chemistry. L. Davies et al. 1974. text ed. 6.25x o.p. (ISBN 0-435-64162-X). Heinemann Ed.

Further Up & Further in. Welleran Poltarnees. 1981. pap. cancelled (ISBN 0-914676-03-2). Green Tiger.

Furtwangler in America. Daniel Gillis. LC 75-125028. (Illus.). 1980. Repr. of 1971 ed. 7.95 (ISBN 0-87867-079-3). Ramparts.

Fury on Ice: A Canadian-American Hockey Story. Sheldon Ilowite. LC 72-124617. 128p. (gr. 6-9). 1970. 4.95g o.s.i. (ISBN 0-8038-2284-7). Hastings.

Fury Out of Time. Lloyd Biggle, Jr. 1975. pap. 1.25 o.p. (ISBN 0-685-61045-4, LB318, Leisure Bks). Nordon Pubns.

Fury, Stallion of Broken Wheel Ranch. Miller. (gr. 3-5). 1980. pap. 1.50 (ISBN 0-590-31260-X, Schol Pap). Schol Bk Serv.

Fusion-Magnetic: Magnetic, Vol. 1. Ed. by Edward Teller. 1981. Pt.a. write for info. (ISBN 0-12-685201-4); Pt. B. write for info. (ISBN 0-12-685241-3). Acad Pr.

Fusion of Naturalism & Humanism. Bernard D. Ouden. LC 79-5348. 1979. pap. text ed. 9.00 (ISBN 0-8191-0869-3). U Pr of Amer.

Fusion Reactor Design Concepts. 1979. pap. 37.50 (ISBN 92-0-131178-8, ISP487, IAEA). Unipub.

Fusion Reactor Design Problems. (Illus.). 540p. (Orig.). 1974. pap. 26.75 (ISBN 92-0-139074-2, IAEA). Unipub.

Fusion Research, 2 vols. Thomas J. Dolan. LC 80-18383. 1000p. Set. 100.01 (ISBN 0-08-025565-5); Vol. I. pap. 25.01 (ISBN 0-08-025566-3); Vol. II. pap. 25.01 (ISBN 0-08-025567-1). Pergamon.

Fusion Technology Nineteen Seventy-Eight: Proceedings, 2 vols. Commission of the European Communities, Luxembourg. LC 79-40553. (Commission of the European Communities: Eur 6215). (Illus.). 1979. Set. pap. 235.00 (ISBN 0-08-023439-9). Pergamon.

Fusion Technology: Proceedings of the 11th Symposium, Oxford, England, Sept. 15-19, 1980, 2 vols. Commission of the European Communities, Luxembourg. (Illus.). 1000p. Date not set. Set. price not set (ISBN 0-08-025697-X). Pergamon.

Fusion Welding & Brazing of Copper & Copper Alloys. R. J. Dawson. LC 73-7969. 139p. 1973. 15.95 (ISBN 0-470-19981-4). Halsted Pr.

Fuss-Free Fit. (Illus.). 80p. 1978. pap. 1.75 (ISBN 0-918178-11-8). Simplicity.

Futility of Family Policy. Gilbert Y. Steiner. 250p. 1981. 15.95 (ISBN 0-8157-8124-5); pap. 5.95 (ISBN 0-8157-8123-7). Brookings.

Future, Vol. I. Ed. by Martin H. Greenberg et al. 384p. (Orig.). 1981. pap. 2.50 (ISBN 0-449-24366-4, Crest). Fawcett.

Future Agenda. Frwd. by Robert A. DeVries. (Education for Health Administration: Vol. 3). (Illus.). 1977. pap. text ed. 7.50 (ISBN 0-914904-23-X). Health Admin Pr.

Future & the Past: A Translation of the Gukansko, an Interpretive History of Japan Written in 1219. Ed. by Delmer M. Brown & Ichiro Lishida. LC 77-73493. 1979. 29.50x (ISBN 0-520-03460-0). U of Cal Pr.

Future As Nightmare: H. G. Wells & the Anti-Utopians. Mark R. Hillegas. LC 74-4084. (Arcturus Books Paperbacks Ser.). 212p. 1974. lib. bdg. 12.95x (ISBN 0-8093-0680-8); pap. 6.95 (ISBN 0-8093-0676-X). S Ill U Pr.

Future Business. Harriette S. Abels. Ed. by Howard Schroeder. LC 80-14859. (Our Future World Ser.). (Illus.). 48p. (gr. 6-9). 1980. PLB 5.95 (ISBN 0-89686-081-7); pap. text ed. 2.95 (ISBN 0-89686-090-6). Crestwood Hse.

Future Coal Prospects: Country & Regional Assessments, Vol. 2. Ed. by Carroll L. Wilson. 1980. 37.50 (ISBN 0-88410-098-7). Ballinger Pub.

Future Coal Supply for the World Energy Balance. Ed. by M. Grenon. (International Institute for Applied Systems Analysis. Proceedings). 1979. 125.00 (ISBN 0-08-023437-2). Pergamon.

Future Communication. Harriette S. Abels. Ed. by Howard Schroeder. LC 80-16529. (Our Future World Ser.). (Illus.). 48p. (gr. 6-9). 1980. PLB 5.95 (ISBN 0-89686-084-1); pap. text ed. 2.95 (ISBN 0-89686-093-0). Crestwood Hse.

Future Dimensions of World Food & Populations. Ed. by Richard G. Woods. (Winrock Ser.). 425p. 1981. lib. bdg. 22.50x (ISBN 0-86531-160-9). Westview.

Future Directions for Museums of American Art. Amon Carter Museum. LC 80-80501. 68p. 1980. pap. 7.95 (ISBN 0-88360-033-1). Amon Carter.

Future Economic Significance of Large Lowgrade Copper & Nickel Deposits. F. W. Prokop. Ed. by H. Borchert. (Illus.). 67p. (Orig.). 1975. pap. 32.50x (ISBN 3-443-12013-X). Intl Pubns Serv.

Future Energy Concepts. (IEE Conference Publications Ser.: No. 171). (Illus.). 1979. pap. 50.50x (ISBN 0-85296-198-7). Inst Elect Eng.

Future Explored. Timothy P. Weber. 1978. pap. 3.95 (ISBN 0-88207-763-5). Victor Bks.

Future Family. Harriette S. Abels. Ed. by Howard Schroeder. LC 80-16400. (Our Future World Ser.). (Illus.). 48p. (gr. 6-9). 1980. PLB 5.95 (ISBN 0-89686-085-X); pap. text ed. 2.95 (ISBN 0-89686-094-9). Crestwood Hse.

Future Family. Philip Campbell. LC 80-84365. 1981. pap. 4.95 (ISBN 0-933350-39-2). Morse Pr.

Future File. Paul Dickson. 1978. pap. 1.95 (ISBN 0-380-42242-5, 42242). Avon.

Future Food. Harriette S. Abels. Ed. by Howard Schroeder. LC 80-14823. (Our Future World Ser.). (Illus.). 48p. (Orig.). (gr. 6-9). 1980. PLB 5.95 (ISBN 0-89686-083-3); pap. text ed. 2.95 (ISBN 0-89686-092-2). Crestwood Hse.

Future for Coal As a Fuel & Chemical, E-004. Business Communications Co. 1980. 825.00 (ISBN 0-89336-273-5). BCC.

Future for Junior Mining in Canada. 175p. (Orig.). 1979. pap. text ed. 10.00x (ISBN 0-88757-018-6, Pub. by Ctr Resource Stud Canada). Renouf.

Future for Water-Based Resins. 1978. 725.00 (ISBN 0-89336-120-8, C-012). BCC.

Future Government. Harriette S. Abels. Ed. by Howard Schroeder. LC 80-14940. (Our Future World Ser.). (Illus.). 48p. (gr. 4 up). PLB 5.95 (ISBN 0-89686-082-5); pap. 2.95 (ISBN 0-89686-091-4). Crestwood Hse.

Future Government. Harriette S. Abels. Ed. by Howard Schroeder. LC 80-14940. (Our Future World Ser.). (Illus.). (gr. 6-9). 1980. PLB 5.95 (ISBN 0-89686-082-5); pap. 2.95 (ISBN 0-89686-091-4). Crestwood Hse.

Future Imperfect: Science Fact & Science Fiction. Ed. by Rex Malik. 219p. 1980. 25.00x (ISBN 0-903804-64-6). Nichols Pub.

Future in Our Hands. Erik Dammann. (Illus.). 1979. 25.00 (ISBN 0-08-024284-7); pap. 11.50 (ISBN 0-08-024283-9). Pergamon.

Future in the Making: Current Issues in Higher Education 1973. Ed. by Dyckman W. Vermilye. LC 73-10935. (Higher Education Ser). 224p. 1973. 11.95x o.p. (ISBN 0-87589-202-7). Jossey-Bass.

Future in the Present: Selected Writings of C. L. R. James. C. L. R. James. LC 77-73129. 228p. 1980. pap. 6.95 (ISBN 0-88208-125-X). Lawrence Hill.

Future Income Prospects for Canada's Senior Citizens. Leroy O. Stone & Michael J. MacLean. 104p. 1979. pap. text ed. 7.95x (ISBN 0-920380-13-1, Pub. by Inst Res Pub Canada). Renouf.

Future Indefinite: Decision-Making in a Transition Economy. Peter W. House & Gerard R. Ryan. LC 79-2723. 192p. 1979. 19.95 (ISBN 0-669-03231-X). Lexington Bks.

Future Interests in a Nutshell. Lawrence W. Waggoner. LC 80-20195. (Nutshell Ser.). 338p. 1980. pap. 6.95 (ISBN 0-8299-2105-2). West Pub.

Future Life. Rene Pache. 1979. pap. 6.95 (ISBN 0-8024-2900-9). Moody.

Future Maker in India: The Story of Sara Chakko. Mary L. Slater. (Orig.). 1968. pap. 0.95 o.p. (ISBN 0-377-84121-8). Friend Pr.

Future Man. Chris Morgan. (Future Studies Series). (Illus.). 208p. 1979. 16.00 (ISBN 0-8290-0144-1). Irvington.

Future Man: An Optimistic Look at What the Future Holds for Mankind. Chris Morgan. 208p. 1981. pap. 6.95 (ISBN 0-686-28897-1). Lewis Pub Co.

Future Markets for Consultancy: Professional Business Development Abroad. Reginald Bidgood. (Illus.). 160p. 1980. 21.00x (ISBN 0-7198-2830-9). Intl Ideas.

Future Medicine. Harriette S. Abels. Ed. by Howard Schroeder. LC 80-15523. (Our Future World Ser.). (Illus.). 48p. (Orig.). (gr. 6-9). 1980. PLB 5.95 (ISBN 0-89686-086-8); pap. 2.95 (ISBN 0-89686-095-7). Crestwood Hse.

Future of Academic Community Medicine in Development Countries. Willoughby Latham. LC 78-24484. 1979. 22.95 (ISBN 0-03-051116-X). Praeger.

Future of Adult Education: New Responsibilities of Colleges & Universities. Fred H. Harrington. LC 76-19499. (Higher Education Ser). 1977. 13.95x (ISBN 0-87589-301-5). Jossey-Bass.

Future of Agriculture in the Soviet Union & Eastern Europe: The 1976-1980 Five-Year Plans. Ed. by Roy Laird et al. LC 77-582. (Westview Special Studies on the Soviet Union & Eastern Europe). 1977. lib. bdg. 27.50x (ISBN 0-89158-302-5). Westview.

Future of American Government: What Will It Be? Cathryn Long & Rudie Tretten. (Crucial Issues in American Government). (gr. 9-12). 1978. pap. text ed. 4.96 (ISBN 0-205-05523-0, 7655231). Allyn.

Future of Berlin. Ed. by Martin J. Hillenbrand. LC 79-55003. (Atlantic Institute for International Affairs Research Ser.: Vol. 3). (Illus.). 313p. 1981. text ed. 27.50 (ISBN 0-916672-46-8). Allanheld.

Future of Big-City Schools: Desegregation Policies & Magnet Alternatives. Ed. by Daniel V. Levine & Robert J. Havighurst. LC 76-62900. 1977. 17.50x (ISBN 0-8211-1113-2); text ed. 15.75x 10 or more copies (ISBN 0-685-75000-0). McCutchan.

Future of Brazil. William Overholt. (Westview Special Studies on Latin America). 1978. lib. bdg. 27.50x (ISBN 0-89158-268-1). Westview.

Future of British Conurbations. Cameron. 1980. 38.00 o.p. (ISBN 0-582-44389-X). Longman.

Future of Business - Annual Review 1980-81: Practical Issues. Center for Strategic & International Studies, Georgetown University. Ed. by G. Sterling Slappey. LC 79-24081. (Pergamon Policy Studies). 110p. 1980. 16.50 (ISBN 0-08-025585-X); pap. 6.25 (ISBN 0-08-025584-1). Pergamon.

Future of Business Global Issues in the Eighties & Nineties. M. Ways et al. (Orig.). 1979. 18.25 (ISBN 0-08-022477-6); pap. 8.75 (ISBN 0-08-022476-8). Pergamon.

Future of Christian Marriage. Ed. by William W. Basset & Peter J. Huizing. (Concilium Ser.: Religion in the Seventies: Vol. 87). 1976. pap. 4.95 (ISBN 0-8164-2571-X). Crossroad NY.

Future of Cincinnati's Capital Plant. N. Humphrey et al. (America's Urban Capital Stock Ser.: Vol. 3). 66p. (Orig.). 1980. pap. 4.00 (ISBN 0-87766-264-9, 27400). Urban Inst.

Future of Cleveland's Capital Plant. N. Humphrey et al. (America's Urban Capital Stock Ser.: Vol. 2). 77p. (Orig.). 1979. pap. text ed. 4.00 (ISBN 0-87766-264-9, 26900). Urban Inst.

Future of Dollar & World Reserve System. Morrell. 1981. text ed. price not set (ISBN 0-408-10674-3); pap. text ed. price not set (ISBN 0-408-10675-1). Butterworth.

Future of Educational Telecommunications. George W. Tressel et al. LC 74-27645. 1975. 15.95x (ISBN 0-669-97691-1). Lexington Bks.

Future of Higher Education: Some Speculation & Suggestions. Carnegie Commission on Higher Education. Ed. by Alexander Mood. LC 73-6533. 192p. 1973. 10.50 o.p. (ISBN 0-07-010064-0, P&RB). McGraw.

Future of International Economic Organizations. Ed. by Don Wallace, Jr. & Helga Escobar. LC 75-44942. (Special Studies). 1977. text ed. 23.95 (ISBN 0-275-22990-4). Praeger.

Future of International Legal Order, 4 vols. Ed. by C. E. Black & Richard A. Falk. Incl. Vol. 1. Trends & Patterns. 1969. 25.00x (ISBN 0-691-09215-X); Vol. 2. Wealth & Resources. 1970. 20.00x (ISBN 0-691-09217-6); Vol. 3. Conflict Management. 416p. 1971. 22.00x (ISBN 0-691-09220-6); Vol. 4. Structure of the International Environment. 600p. 1972. 22.50x (ISBN 0-691-09221-4); pap. o.p. (ISBN 0-691-10005-5). (Center of International Studies, Princeton Univ.). Princeton U Pr.

Future of International Organization. Rudiger Jutte. 1981. 22.50 (ISBN 0-312-31476-0). St Martin.

Future of Japan & the Korean Peninsula. Ed. by Tsuneari Fukuda. Tr. by K. Jahng from Japanese. LC 78-71337. (Illus.). 1979. 12.40 (ISBN 0-930878-14-0). Hollym Intl.

Future of Marriage As an Institution. Ed. by Franz Bockle. LC 70-113057. (Concilium Ser.: Religion in the Seventies: Vol. 55). 1970. pap. 4.95 (ISBN 0-8164-2511-6). Crossroad NY.

Future of Music. E. J. Dent. 1966. pap. 5.75 (ISBN 0-08-011354-0). Pergamon.

Future of Muslim Civilization. Ziauddin Sardar. 224p. 1979. 37.00x (ISBN 0-85664-800-0, Pub. by Croom Helm Ltd England). Biblio Dist.

Future of New York City's Capital Plant. David A. Grossman. (America's Urban Capital Stock Ser.: Vol. 1). 112p. (Orig.). 1979. pap. text ed. 4.50 (ISBN 0-87766-249-5, 25700). Urban Inst.

Future of Nonfuel Minerals. John E. Tilton. 1977. 9.95 (ISBN 0-8157-8460-0). Brookings.

Future of North America: Canada, the United States, & Quebec Nationalism. Elliot J. Feldman & Neil Nevitte. 378p. 1979. pap. text ed. 9.50x (ISBN 0-87674-045-X, Pub. by Inst Res Pub Canada). Renouf.

Future of Nuclear Structure Studies. (Illus., Orig.). 1969. pap. 9.25 (ISBN 92-0-031069-9, IAEA). Unipub.

Future of Oil: A Simulation Study of the Interrelationships of Resources, Reserves, & Use 1980-2080. Peter R. Odell & Kenneth E. Rosing. 300p. 1980. 47.50x (ISBN 0-89397-097-2). Nichols Pub.

Future of Pharmaceuticals. C. Bezold. 144p. 1980. 12.00 (ISBN 0-471-08343-7, Pub. by Wiley Med). Wiley.

Future of Policing. Ed. by Alvin W. Cohn. LC 77-92833. (Sage Criminal Justice System Annuals: Vol. 9). 1978. 20.00x (ISBN 0-8039-0702-8); pap. 9.95x (ISBN 0-8039-0703-6). Sage.

Future of Political Parties. Ed. by Louis Maisel & Paul M. Sacks. LC 75-5016. (Sage Electoral Studies Yearbook: Vol. 1). 1975. 20.00x (ISBN 0-8039-0426-6); pap. 9.95x (ISBN 0-8039-0570-X). Sage.

Future of Public Broadcasting. Ed. by Douglass Cater & Michael J. Nyhan. (Special Studies). 200p. 1976. text ed. 26.95 (ISBN 0-275-56990-X); pap. text ed. 10.95 (ISBN 0-275-64590-8). Praeger.

Future of Religious Life. Ed. by Peter Huizing & Williams Basset. (Concillium Ser.: Vol. 97). pap. 4.95 (ISBN 0-8164-2094-7). Crossroad NY.

Future of Social Security. abr. ed. Peter J. Ferrara. (Cato Public Policy Research Monograph: No. 4). 100p. (Orig.). 1981. pap. 5.00 (ISBN 0-932790-26-7). Cato Inst.

Future of Social Security. Alicia H. Munnell. LC 76-51883. (Studies in Social Economics). 1977. 11.95 (ISBN 0-8157-5896-0); pap. 4.95 (ISBN 0-8157-5895-2). Brookings.

Future of Social Work Research. Ed. by David Fanshel. LC 79-92733. 246p. 1980. pap. 12.50 (ISBN 0-87101-084-4, CBQ-084-C). Natl Assn Soc Wkrs.

Future of Student Affairs: A Guide to Student Development for Tomorrow's Higher Education. Theodore K. Miller & Judith S. Prince. LC 76-19496. (Higher Education Ser.). 1976. 13.95x (ISBN 0-87589-298-1). Jossey-Bass.

Future of Synthetic Materials: The Petroleum Connection. Christopher Flavin. (Worldwatch Papers Ser.). 1980. pap. 2.00 (ISBN 0-916468-35-6). Worldwatch Inst.

Future of Teacher Education. Ed. by J. W. Tibble. 1971. 11.00 (ISBN 0-7100-7189-2). Routledge & Kegan.

Future of Technological Civilization. Victor Ferkiss. LC 73-90926. 384p. 1974. 12.50 o.s.i. (ISBN 0-8076-0738-X). Braziller.

Future of the American Past. Earl H. Brill. LC 73-17890. 1974. pap. 2.95 (ISBN 0-8164-2086-6). Crossroad NY.

Future of the American Suburbs: Survival or Extinction. Dennis P. Sobin. LC 72-154034. 1971. 11.50 (ISBN 0-8046-9014-6, Natl U). Kennikat.

Future of the British Conurbation Policies & Prescription for Change. Ed. by Gordon Cameron. 288p. 1980. lib. bdg. 38.00 (ISBN 0-582-44389-X). Longman.

Future of the Health Sciences. Stanley Lesse. 216p. 1981. text ed. 18.50x (ISBN 0-8290-0250-2). Irvington.

Future of the Inter-American System. Tom J. Farer. LC 78-31153. (Praeger Special Studies). 1979. 24.95 (ISBN 0-03-047391-8). Praeger.

Future of the Korean Peninsula. Ed. by Young C. Kim & Abraham M. Halpern. LC 77-24407. (Praeger Special Studies). 1977. text ed. 25.95 (ISBN 0-03-021846-2). Praeger.

Future of the Multinational Pharmaceutical Industries to 1990. Barrie G. James. LC 77-72268. 1977. 39.95 (ISBN 0-470-99130-5). Halsted Pr.

Future of the Printed Word. Ed. by Philip Hills. LC 80-1716. 172p. 1980. lib. bdg. 25.00 (ISBN 0-313-22693-8, HIP/). Greenwood.

Future of the Soviet Economy: 1978-1985. Ed. by Holland Hunter. (Westview Special Studies on the Soviet Union & Eastern Europe Ser.). 1978. lib. bdg. 22.50x (ISBN 0-89158-097-2). Westview.

Future of the Space Program--Large Corporations & Society: Discussions with 22 Science-Fiction Writers. Jeffrey M. Elliot. LC 80-19754. (Great Issues of the Day Ser.: Vol. 1). 64p. (Orig.). 1981. lib. bdg. 8.95x (ISBN 0-89370-140-8); pap. text ed. 2.95x (ISBN 0-89370-240-4). Borgo Pr.

Future of the Strategic Arms Race: Options for the 1970's. George W. Rathjens. 1969. pap. 0.90 (ISBN 0-87003-028-0). Carnegie Endow.

Future of the U. K. Motor Industry. Krish Bhaskar. 1979. 37.50x (ISBN 0-85038-259-9). Nichols Pub.

Future of the World Motor Industry. Krish Bhaskar. 300p. 1980. 42.50x (ISBN 0-89397-083-2). Nichols Pub.

Future of Unbelief. Gerhard Szczesny. LC 60-1665. 1961. 5.95 o.s.i. (ISBN 0-8076-0124-1); pap. 2.95 (ISBN 0-8076-0375-9). Braziller.

Future of United States Domestic Air Freight Industry. Lewis M. Schneider. 1973. text ed. 11.00 (ISBN 0-87584-106-6). Harvard U Pr.

Future Office Systems Market, 2 vols. 493p. 1980. Set. 1000.00 (ISBN 0-686-28894-7, A778). Frost & Sullivan.

Future Perfect: American Science Fiction of the Nineteenth Century. Ed. by H. Bruce Franklin. 1978. 17.50x (ISBN 0-19-502322-6). Oxford U Pr.

Future Present: The Phenomenon of Christian Worship. Marianne H. Micks. LC 75-103844. 1970. pap. 4.95 (ISBN 0-8164-2109-9). Crossroad NY.

Future Science. Harriette S. Abels. Ed. by Howard Schroeder. LC 80-19412. (Our Future World Ser.). (Illus.). 48p. (Orig.). (gr. 6-9). 1980. PLB 5.95 (ISBN 0-89686-080-9); pap. 2.95 (ISBN 0-89686-089-2). Crestwood Hse.

Future Science: Life Energies & the Physics of Paranormal Phenomena. Ed. by John White & Stanley Krippner. LC 76-23808. 600p. 1977. pap. 4.50 (ISBN 0-385-11203-3, Anch). Doubleday.
Future Sea. George S. Fichter. LC 78-57790. (Illus.). 1978. 14.95 (ISBN 0-8069-3106-X); lib. bdg. 13.29 (ISBN 0-8069-3107-8). Sterling.
Future Shape of Ministry. Urban T. Holmes. pap. 5.95 (ISBN 0-8164-2025-4). Crossroad NY.
Future Space. Harriette S. Abels. Ed. by Howard Schroeder. LC 80-16457. (Our Future World Ser.). (Illus.). 48p. (Orig.). (gr. 4 up). PLB 5.95 (ISBN 0-89686-087-6); pap. 2.95 (ISBN 0-89686-096-5). Crestwood Hse.
Future Technical Needs & Trends in the Paper Industry - II. Jack S. Barton et al. (TAPPI PRESS Reports). (Illus.). 1976. pap. 33.95 (ISBN 0-89852-364-8, 01-01-R064). TAPPI.
Future Technical Needs & Trends in the Paper Industry - III. Robert W. Hagemeyer et al. (TAPPI PRESS Reports). (Illus.). 1979. pap. 39.95 (ISBN 0-89852-378-8). TAPPI.
Future Travel. Harriette S. Abels. Ed. by Howard Schroeder. (Our Future World Ser.). (Illus.). 48p. (gr. 6-9). 1980. PLB 5.95 (ISBN 0-89686-088-4); pap. 2.95 (ISBN 0-89686-097-3). Crestwood Hse.
Future Trends in Education Policy. Jane Newitt. LC 78-19672. 1979. 16.95 (ISBN 0-669-02713-8). Lexington Bks.
Future Utility Requirements. rev. ed. BCC Staff. 1977. 650.00 (ISBN 0-89336-003-1, E-028). BCC.
Future While It Happened. Samuel Lubell. 162p. 1973. pap. 2.95x (ISBN 0-393-09321-2). Norton.
Future Without Future. Jacques Sternberg. LC 73-6427. 256p. 1973. 6.95 o.p. (ISBN 0-8164-9170-4). Continuum.
Future Worlds. Richard A. Falk. LC 75-43478. (Headline Ser.: 229). (Illus.). 1976. pap. 2.00 (ISBN 0-87124-034-3). Foreign Policy.
Future's Advocate. Edwin Carr. LC 74-82187. 1975. 10.00 o.p. (ISBN 0-8309-0121-3). Herald Hse.
Futures Conditional. Robert Theobald. LC 77-183105. 1972. pap. 7.95 (ISBN 0-672-61217-8). Bobbs.
Futures Directory. John McHale & Magda C. McHale. LC 76-51285. 1977. lib. bdg. 50.00x (ISBN 0-89158-224-X). Westview.
Futures in School Finance: Working Toward a Common Goal. Seventeenth National Conference on School Finance. Ed. by K. Forbis Jordan & Kern Alexander. LC 75-8465. 221p. 1975. 5.50 (ISBN 0-87367-757-9). Phi Delta Kappa.
Futures of Europe. W. Kennet. LC 76-9541. (Illus.). 1976. 27.50 (ISBN 0-521-21326-6). Cambridge U Pr.
Futures Research: New Directions. Ed. by Harold A. Linstone & W. H. Simmonds. 1977. text ed. 25.50 (ISBN 0-201-04096-4, Adv Bk Prog). A-W.
Futures: The Anti-Inflation Investment. Mike Geczi. 1980. pap. 2.95 (ISBN 0-686-69239-X, 75713, Discus). Avon.
Futurism. Caroline Tisdall & Angelo Bozzola. LC 77-76819. (World of Art Ser.). (Illus.). 1978. 17.95 (ISBN 0-19-519983-9); pap. 9.95 (ISBN 0-19-519980-4). Oxford U Pr.
Futurism & the International Avant-Garde. Anne D'Harnoncourt & Germano Celant. LC 80-83095. (Illus.). 144p. (Orig.). 1980. pap. 10.95 (ISBN 0-87633-037-5). Phila Mus Art.
Futurism in Education: Methodologies. Stephan P. Hencley & James R. Yates. LC 73-20853. 1974. 20.50x (ISBN 0-8211-0753-4); text ed. 18.50x (ISBN 0-685-42634-3). McCutchan.
Futurist Performance. Michael Kirby. (Illus.). 1971. pap. 3.95 o.p. (ISBN 0-525-47280-0). Dutton.
Futuristic Community Development: East Central Florida Crime Impact 1974-1984. R. Christensen et al. xxii, 390p. Date not set. pap. 15.00 (ISBN 0-686-28750-9, 04-80-04). Entropy Ltd.
Futurology: Promise, Performance, Prospects. Victor C. Ferkiss. LC 77-88625. (Policy Papers Ser.: The Washington Papers, No. 50). 1977. 3.50x (ISBN 0-8039-0977-2). Sage.
Fuzzy Duckling. Jane Werner. (ps-1). 1949. PLB 5.00 (ISBN 0-307-60557-4, Golden Pr). Western Pub.
Fuzzy Duckling. Jane Werner. (ps-1). 1949. 1.95 (ISBN 0-307-10841-4, Golden Pr); PLB 7.62 (ISBN 0-307-60841-7). Western Pub.
Fuzzy Sets & Systems: Theory & Applications. Didier Dubois & Henri Prade. LC 79-6952. (Mathematics in Science & Engineering Ser.). 1980. 65.60 (ISBN 0-12-222750-6). Acad Pr.
Fuzzy Switching & Automata: Theory & Applications. Abraham Kandel & Samuel C. Lee. LC 76-29148. (Computer Systems Engineering Ser.). 1979. 34.50x (ISBN 0-8448-1020-7). Crane-Russak Co.

G

G. B. Shaw: Creative Artist. Homer E. Woodbridge. LC 63-14294. (Arcturus Books Paperbacks). 193p. 1965. pap. 1.65 (ISBN 0-8093-0159-8). S Ill U Pr.
G. D. H. Cole. Gerald L. Houseman. (English Authors Ser.: No. 255). 1979. lib. bdg. 14.50 (ISBN 0-8057-6746-0). Twayne.
G. E. Falkland. Edward Bulwer-Lytton. Ed. by Herbert V. Thal. (First Novel Library). 1964. 5.00 (ISBN 0-304-92027-4); pap. 2.95 (ISBN 0-685-09165-1). Dufour.
G. I. Bill, the Veterans, & the Colleges. Keith W. Olson. LC 72-91667. (Illus.). 152p. 1974. 10.00x (ISBN 0-8131-1288-5). U Pr of Ky.
G I-Five Jahrestagung. Ed. by J. Muehlbacher. (Lecture Notes in Computer Science: Vol. 34). 755p. 1975. pap. 29.30 (ISBN 0-387-07410-4). Springer-Verlag.
G. K. Chesterton. Lawrence J. Clipper. (English Authors Ser.: No. 166). 1974. lib. bdg. 10.95 (ISBN 0-8057-1090-6). Twayne.
G. K. Chesterton: Radical Populist. Margaret Canovan. LC 77-73045. 1977. 10.95 o.p. (ISBN 0-15-135700-5). HarBraceJ.
G Man. Nick Carter. (Nick Carter Ser.). 224p. (Orig.). 1981. pap. 2.25 (ISBN 0-441-69656-2). Charter Bks.
G-MAP Training Manual. General Electric Company. 1970. pap. 14.95 (ISBN 0-932078-42-7). GE Tech Prom & Train.
G R P Boat Construction. Keith Figg & John Hayward. (Questions & Answers Ser.). (Illus.). 86p. (Orig.). 1979. pap. 7.50 (ISBN 0-408-00317-0). Transatlantic.
G. W. F. Hegel. Clark Butler. (World Authors Ser.: Germany: No. 461). 1977. lib. bdg. 12.50 (ISBN 0-8057-6298-1). Twayne.
G. W. Pabst. Lee Atwell. (Theatrical Arts Ser.). 1977. lib. bdg. 12.50 (ISBN 0-8057-9251-1). Twayne.
G-046 Growing Markets for Security Monitoring & Alarm Systems: G-046. BCC Staff. 1980. 750.00 (ISBN 0-89336-111-9). BCC.
GAAP for Smaller Businesses. 1976. pap. 2.25. Am Inst CPA.
GABA in Nervous System Function. Ed. by E. Roberts et al. LC 74-21983. 576p. 1976. 36.50 (ISBN 0-89004-043-5). Raven.
Gabon: Nation-Building on the Ogooue. Brian Weinstein. (Illus.). 1967. 17.00x (ISBN 0-262-23023-2). MIT Pr.
Gabriel. Jean S. Doty. LC 73-6045. (Illus.). 128p. (gr. 3-5). 1974. 4.95g o.s.i. (ISBN 0-02-732740-X). Macmillan.
Gabriel Celaya. Sharon K. Ugalda. (World Authors Ser.: No. 483 Spain). 1978. 12.50 (ISBN 0-8057-6324-4). Twayne.
Gabriel Fielding. Alfred Borrello. (English Authors Ser.: No. 162). 1974. lib. bdg. 10.95 (ISBN 0-8057-1194-5). Twayne.
Gabriel Garcia Marquez. George R. McMurray. LC 76-20409. (Modern Literature Ser.). 1977. 10.95 (ISBN 0-8044-2620-1). Ungar.
Gabriel Garcia Marquez: An Annotated Bibliography, 1947-1979. Compiled by Margaret E. Fau. LC 80-784. x, 198p. 1980. lib. bdg. 27.50 (ISBN 0-313-22224-X, FGM/). Greenwood.
Gabriel Garcia Marquez: Revolution in Wonderland. Regina Janes. 136p. 1981. text ed. 9.00x (ISBN 0-8262-0337-X). U of Mo Pr.
Gabriel Hounds. Mary Stewart. 256p. 1981. pap. 2.50 (ISBN 0-449-23946-2, Crest). Fawcett.
Gabriel Marcel. Sam Keen. LC 67-11288. (Makers of Contemporary Theology Ser). 1967. pap. 3.45 (ISBN 0-8042-0584-1). John Knox.
Gabriel Marcel on Religious Knowledge. Neil Gillman. LC 80-5061. 315p. 1980. text ed. 19.50 (ISBN 0-8191-1034-5); pap. text ed. 11.50 (ISBN 0-8191-1035-3). U Pr of Amer.
Gabriel Tellez: El Condenado por desconfiado. Ed. by D. Rogers. LC 73-7964. 172p. 1974. text ed. 22.00 (ISBN 0-08-017247-4); pap. text ed. 14.00 (ISBN 0-08-017248-2). Pergamon.
Gabriela, Clove & Cinnamon. Jorge Amado. 1974. pap. 3.95 (ISBN 0-380-01205-7, 51839, Bard). Avon.
Gabriela Mistral; Poet & Humanitarian: The Chilean Years, 1889-1922. Margaret T. Rudd & Martin C. Taylor. LC 79-2310. (Illus.). Date not set. cancelled o.p. (ISBN 0-8263-0519-9). U of NM Pr.
Gabriele D'Annunzio. Gerald Griffin. LC 77-113312. 1970. Repr. of 1935 ed. 12.50 (ISBN 0-8046-0995-0). Kennikat.
Gabriele Muunter: Between Munich & Murnau. Anne Mochon. Ed. by Peter Walsh & Paula Matthews. LC 80-21810. (Illus.). 65p. 1980. pap. 9.95 (ISBN 0-916724-19-0). Fogg Art.
Gabrielino Indians of Southern California: An Annotated Ethnohistoric Bibliography. Mary La Lone. (Occasional Papers: No. 6). 72p. 1980. pap. 4.50 (ISBN 0-917956-15-X). UCLA Arch.
Gabrielle. Theresa Conway. 1978. pap. 1.95 o.p. (ISBN 0-449-13916-6, GM). Fawcett.
Gace Bule, Trouvere Champenois. Gace Brule. LC 80-2158. (Societe Neo-Philologigue De Helsingfors Ser.: Memoires, Vol. 16). 1981. Repr. of 1951 ed. 59.50 (ISBN 0-404-19022-7). AMS Pr.
Gada: Three Approaches to the Study of African Society. Asmarom Legesse. LC 72-87783. 1973. 25.00 (ISBN 0-02-918400-2). Free Pr.
Gadabouts & Stick-at-Homes: Wild Animals & Their Habitats. Lorus Milne & Margery Milne. (Sierra Club-Scribner's Juvenile Ser.). (Illus.). 128p. (gr. 4 up). 1980. 8.95 (ISBN 0-684-16473-6). Sierra.
Gadney's Guide to One Thousand Eight Hundred International Contests, Festivals & Grants in Film & Video, Photography, TV-Radio Broadcasting, Writing, Poetry, Playwriting & Journalism: Updated Address Edition. rev. ed. Alan Gadney. LC 80-66803. 610p. 1980. 22.95 (ISBN 0-930828-03-8); pap. 15.95 (ISBN 0-930828-02-X). Festival Pubns.
Gadsen's Silent Observers: An Introduction to Natural History of Southern Arizona. Merritt S. Keasey. LC 75-103353. (Wild & Woolly West Ser.: No. 42). (Illus.). 56p. 1974. 7.00 (ISBN 0-910584-38-9); pap. 2.50 (ISBN 0-910584-68-0). Filter.
Gaelic Dictionary--Gaelic-English; English-Gaelic. Malcolm MacLennan. 632p. 1980. 45.00 (ISBN 0-08-025713-5); pap. 22.00 (ISBN 0-08-025712-7). Pergamon.
Gaelic Grammar. Calder. 352p. 12.50x (ISBN 0-686-27678-7). Colton Bk.
Gaelic Lexicon for Finnegans Wake & Glossary for Joyce's Other Works. Brendan O Hehir. 1968. 22.75x (ISBN 0-520-00952-5). U of Cal Pr.
Gaelic Without Groans. 3rd ed. John Mackechnie. 1974. pap. text ed. 4.50x (ISBN 0-05-002862-6). Longman.
Gaff Sail. Robert Simper. LC 79-90907. (Illus.). 144p. 1980. 14.95 (ISBN 0-87021-827-1). Naval Inst Pr.
Gag Galaxy Outer Space Jokes & Riddles. Gary Poole. (Illus.). 128p. (Orig.). 1981. pap. 1.25 (ISBN 0-448-17165-1, Tempo). G&D.
Gagg for the New Gospell? No: A New Gagg for an Old Goose. Richard Montagu. LC 74-28872. (English Experience Ser.: No. 751). 1975. Repr. of 1624 ed. 26.00 (ISBN 90-221-0751-5). Walter J Johnson.
Gaggle of Green Geese. V. Gilbert Beers. (Christian Home Library). (Illus.). 32p. (ps-3). 1974. 5.50 (ISBN 0-8024-2911-4). Moody.
Gaging: Practical Design & Application. Ed. by Edward S. Roth. LC 80-53424. (Manufacturing Update Ser.). (Illus.). 289p. 1981. 29.00 (ISBN 0-87263-064-1). SME.
Gaily We Parade. Sara Brewton & John E. Brewton. (Illus.). (gr. 4-6). 1967. 8.95 (ISBN 0-02-712340-5). Macmillan.
Gaining Skills in Using the Library. Eileen Corcoran. (Illus.). 1980. pap. 2.25x (ISBN 0-88323-158-1, 247). Richards Pub.
Gaining Through Losing. Evelyn Christenson. 1980. 8.95 (ISBN 0-88207-795-3). Victor Bks.
Gains & Losses. Robert L. Wolff. (Victorian Fiction Ser). Orig. Title: Faith & Doubt in Victorian England. 1975. lib. bdg. 66.00 (ISBN 0-8240-1617-3). Garland Pub.
Galactic Adventures. Fred Baker et al. LC 80-80321. (Illus.). 192p. (gr. 3-7). 1980. 7.95 (ISBN 0-528-82374-4). Rand.
Galactic Cluster. James Blish. 176p. 1972. pap. 0.95 (ISBN 0-451-05441-5, Q5441, Sig). NAL.
Galactic Empires, Vol. I. Ed. by Brian Aldiss. 1978. pap. 2.25 (ISBN 0-380-42341-3, 42341). Avon.
Galactic Patrol. E. E. Smith. 1973. pap. 1.75 (ISBN 0-515-05288-4, V3084). Jove Pubns.
Galactic Whirlpool. David Gerrold. (Star Trek Ser.). 240p. (Orig.). 1980. pap. 2.25 (ISBN 0-553-14242-9). Bantam.
Galapagos. Lester E. Harris. LC 76-23727. (Crown Ser.). 128p. (gr. 8 up). 1976. pap. 4.50 (ISBN 0-8127-0125-9). Southern Pub.
Galapagos Islands. Alfred M. Bailey. (Museum Pictorial: No. 9). 1970. pap. 1.10 o.p. (ISBN 0-916278-46-8). Denver Mus Natl Hist.
Galatians. Hans D. Betz. LC 77-78625. (Hermenia: a Critical & Historical Commentary on the Bible). 1979. 27.95 (ISBN 0-8006-6009-9, 20-6009). Fortress.
Galatians. rev. ed. Don E. Boatman & Kenny Boles. LC 70-1141. (Bible Study Textbook Ser.). (Illus.). 1976. 11.50 (ISBN 0-89900-039-8). College Pr Pub.
Galatians. E. D. Burton. LC 20-21079. (International Critical Commentary Ser.). 632p. 1920. text ed. 23.00x (ISBN 0-567-05029-7). Attic Pr.
Galatians. Irving L. Jensen. (Bible Self Study Ser). 1973. pap. 2.25 (ISBN 0-8024-1048-0). Moody.
Galatians. Carolyn Osiek. (New Testament Message Ser.). 9.95 (ISBN 0-89453-135-2); pap. 4.95 (ISBN 0-89453-200-6). M Glazier.
Galatians. Curtis Vaughan. 128p. 1972. pap. 2.50 (ISBN 0-310-33543-4). Zondervan.
Galatians. Geoffrey Wilson. 1979. pap. 3.50 (ISBN 0-85151-294-1). Banner of Truth.
Galatians & Ephesians. William Hendrikson. (New Testament Commentary). 290p. 1979. 15.95 (ISBN 0-8010-4211-9). Baker Bk.
Galatians & Romans. Frank Stagg. (Knox Pereaching Guides Ser.). 160p. (Orig.). 1980. pap. 4.50 (ISBN 0-8042-3238-5). John Knox.
Galatians & Romans. Frank Stagg. LC 79-92066. (Knox Preaching Guides Ser.). 128p. (Orig., John Hayes series editor). 1980. pap. 4.50 (ISBN 0-8042-3238-5). John Knox.
Galatians, the Epistle of Christian Liberty. Keith L. Brooks. (Teach Yourself the Bible Ser). 1963. pap. 1.75 (ISBN 0-8024-2925-4). Moody.
Galaxies. Isaac Asimov. LC 68-13034. (Beginning Science Ser). (Illus.). (gr. 2-4). 1968. 2.50 o.p. (ISBN 0-695-83315-4); PLB 2.97 o.p. (ISBN 0-695-43315-6). Follett.
Galaxies. Timothy Ferris. LC 80-13139. (Illus.). 200p. 1980. 75.00 (ISBN 0-87156-273-1). Sierra.
Galaxies & Quasars. William J. Kaufmann, 3rd. LC 79-10570. (Illus.). 1979. text ed. 17.95x (ISBN 0-7167-1133-8); pap. text ed. 8.95x (ISBN 0-7167-1134-6). W H Freeman.
Galaxies & the Universe: Lectures. Ed. by Lodewijk Woltjer. LC 68-20445. (Vetlesen Symposium, 1966). (Illus.). 1968. 15.00x (ISBN 0-231-03110-6). Columbia U Pr.
Galaxies, Islands in Space. David C. Knight. (Illus.). (gr. 4-6). 1979. 6.50 (ISBN 0-688-22180-7); PLB 6.24 (ISBN 0-688-32180-1). Morrow.
Galaxy Formation: A Personal View. John Gribbin. LC 75-31706. 1976. 24.95 (ISBN 0-470-32775-8). Halsted Pr.
Galaxy World Postage Stamp Album. Larry Grossman. (Illus.). 1980. 2.95 (ISBN 0-685-78367-7). Grossman Stamp.
Galbraith & Market Capitalism. David Reisman. LC 79-9688. 1980. 25.00x (ISBN 0-8147-7380-X); pap. 11.00x (ISBN 0-8147-7381-8). NYU Pr.
Galbraith Reader. John K. Galbraith. LC 75-19930. 1977. 15.00 (ISBN 0-87645-091-5). Gambit.
Galbraith Viewpoint in Perspective: Critical Commentary on "The Age of Uncertainty" Television Series. Ed. by Gerald L. Musgrave. LC 77-92085. (Hoover Special Project Ser). 1978. pap. 3.00 (ISBN 0-8179-4212-2). Hoover Inst Pr.
Galdos & the Art of the European Novel, Eighteen Sixty-Seven to Eighteen Eighty-Seven. Stephen Gilman. LC 80-8550. 416p. 1981. 27.50x (ISBN 0-691-06456-3). Princeton U Pr.
Galdos: The Mature Thought. Brian J. Dendle. LC 80-51013. (Studies in Romance Languages: No. 23). 216p. 1980. 16.50x (ISBN 0-8131-1407-1). U Pr of Ky.
Gale Sayers: Star Running Back. LC 73-80425. (Sports Close-up Ser.). (gr. 3-9). 1973. PLB 5.95 o.p. (ISBN 0-913940-04-6); pap. 2.50 o.p. (ISBN 0-89686-016-7). Crestwood Hse.
Galen on Language & Ambiguity "De Captionibus" (on Fallacies) An English Translation of Galen's. R. B. Edlow. (Philosophia Antiqua: No. 31). 1977. pap. text ed. 25.25x (ISBN 90-04-04869-3). Humanities.
Galilean Accent. A. J. Gossip. (Scholar As Preacher Ser.). 302p. 1926. text ed. 7.75 (ISBN 0-567-04421-1). Attic Pr.
Galilee from Alexander the Great to Hadrian, 323 B. C. E. to 135 C. E. Sean V. Freyne. 27.50 (ISBN 0-89453-099-2). M. Glazier.
Galileo. Stillman Drake. (Pastmasters Ser.). 1981. 7.95 (ISBN 0-8090-4850-7); pap. 2.95 (ISBN 0-8090-1416-5). Hill & Wang.
Galileo. (MacDonald Educational Ser.). (Illus., Arabic.). 3.50 (ISBN 0-686-53094-2). Intl Bk Ctr.
Galileo & the Art of Reasoning: Rhetorical Foundations of Logic & Scientific Method. Maurice A. Finocchiaro. (Philosophy of Science Studies: No. 61). 463p. 1980. lib. bdg. 42.00 (ISBN 90-277-1094-5, Pub. by D. Reidel); pap. 21.00 (ISBN 90-277-1095-3). Kluwer Boston.
Galileo at Work: His Scientific Biography. Stillman Drake. LC 78-5239. xxiv, 536p. 1981. pap. 9.95 (ISBN 0-226-16227-3). U of Chicago Pr.
Galileo Galilei, His Life & Work. Raymond J. Seeger. (Men of Physics Ser.). 1966. 16.50 (ISBN 0-08-012025-3); pap. 7.75 (ISBN 0-08-012024-5). Pergamon.
Galileo Galilei: Operations of the Geometric & Military Compass. Tr. by Stillman Drake from Italian. LC 78-606002. (Illus.). 95p. 1978. text ed. 5.95x (ISBN 0-87474-383-4). Smithsonian.
Galileo Galilei, Space Pioneer. Arthur S. Gregor. (gr. 2-5). 1965. 3.95 o.s.i. (ISBN 0-02-736800-9). Macmillan.

Galileo Galilei: Two New Sciences. Tr. by Stillman Drake from Lat. 456p. 1973. 25.00 (ISBN 0-299-06400-X); pap. 7.95 (ISBN 0-299-06404-2). U of Wis Pr.

Galileo Reappraised. Ed. by Carlo L. Golino. (UCLA Center for Medieval & Renaissance Studies). 1966. 14.50x (ISBN 0-520-00490-6). U of Cal Pr.

Galileo, Science & the Church. rev. ed. Jerome J. Langford. 1971. pap. 4.95 (ISBN 0-472-06173-9, 173, AA). U of Mich Pr.

Galla Monarchy: Jimma Abba Jifar, Ethiopia, 1830-1932. Herbert S. Lewis. (Illus.). 1965. 17.50x (ISBN 0-299-03690-1). U of Wis Pr.

Gallagher Plot. (Nick Carter Ser.). 1979. pap. 1.95 (ISBN 0-441-27244-4). Charter Bks.

Gallant Mrs. Stonewall. Harnett Kane. 320p. 1976. Repr. of 1957 ed. lib. bdg. 14.95x (ISBN 0-89244-075-9). Queens Hse.

Gallantry A-la-Mode. LC 79-26558. 1980. Repr. of 1674 ed. 22.00x (ISBN 0-8201-1342-5). Schol Facsimiles.

Gallathea. John Lyly. Ed. by Anne B. Lancashire. Bd. with Midas. LC 69-11445. (Regents Renaissance Drama Ser). 1970. 10.95x (ISBN 0-8032-0268-7); pap. 2.65x (ISBN 0-8032-5269-2, BB 231, Bison). U of Nebr Pr.

Gallensteine Im Roentgenbild. C. Wolpers. (Illus.). 66p. 1980. soft cover 20.50 (ISBN 3-8055-2031-X). S Karger.

Gallery of American Weathervanes & Whirligigs. Robert Bishop. (Illus.). 128p. 1981. 27.50 (ISBN 0-525-93151-1); pap. 16.95 (ISBN 0-525-47652-0). Dutton.

Gallery of Children. reissue ed. A. A. Milne. (Illus.). 1976. 4.95 o.p. (ISBN 0-679-50689-6). McKay.

Gallery of Monsters. Katy Hall & Lisa Eisenberg. (Illus.). 64p. (gr. 2-5). 1981. pap. 2.95 (ISBN 0-394-84743-1). Random.

Gallery of Presidents. Marc Pachter. LC 78-22471. (Illus.). 95p. 1979. pap. 5.95 (ISBN 0-87474-743-0). Smithsonian.

Gallery of Spiders: Poems. John R. Reed. LC 80-81894. (Ontario Review Press Poetry Ser.). 80p. 1980. 9.95 (ISBN 0-86538-005-8); pap. 4.95 (ISBN 0-86538-006-6). Ontario Rev NJ.

Galley Guide - Updated. Alex W. Moffat & C. Burnham Porter. LC 77-22546. 1977. 7.95 (ISBN 0-396-07427-8). Dodd.

Galley to Mytilene, Stories 1949-1960: Collected Stories of Paul Goodman. Paul Goodman. Ed. by Taylor Stoehr. (Vol. 4). 315p. (Orig.). 1980. 14.00 (ISBN 0-87685-360-2); deluxe ed. 25.00 (ISBN 0-87685-361-0); pap. 7.50 (ISBN 0-87685-359-9). Black Sparrow.

Galliard Book of Carols. Ed. by June Tillman et al. (Illus.). 248p. 1980. 30.00x (ISBN 0-389-20146-4). B&N.

Gallic Salt: Eighteen Fabliaux Translated from the Old French. Robert Harrison. 1974. 25.00x (ISBN 0-520-02418-4). U of Cal Pr.

Gallium-67 Imaging. Paul B. Hoffer et al. LC 77-13125. (Diagnostic & Therapeutic Radiology Ser.). 1978. 32.50 (ISBN 0-471-02601-8, Pub. by Wiley Medical). Wiley.

Gallo-Roman Muse. Dorothy Coleman. LC 79-71. 1979. 32.50 (ISBN 0-521-22254-0). Cambridge U Pr.

Galloping off in All Directions: An Anthology for Horse Lovers. LC 78-52331. (Illus.). 1978. 12.95 o.p. (ISBN 0-312-31576-7). St Martin.

Gallows Gold. James Parrette. (Orig.). 1980. pap. 1.95 (ISBN 0-89083-687-6, Kable News Co). Zebra.

Gallows Stands in Salem. Anne-Marie Bretonne. 256p. 1975. pap. 1.25 o.p. (ISBN 0-445-00276-X). Popular Lib.

Gallows Wedding. Rhona Martin. 1980. pap. 2.50 o.p. (ISBN 0-425-04299-5). Berkley Pub.

Gallstones. Joseph A. Caprini et al. (Discussions in Surgical Management Ser.). 1979. pap. 10.50 (ISBN 0-87488-953-7). Med Exam.

Gallup Poll: Public Opinion, 1980. Ed. by George H. Gallup. LC 79-56557. 320p. 1981. lib. bdg. 49.50 (ISBN 0-8420-2181-7). Scholarly Res Inc.

Galveston - Houston Electric Railway. Herb Woods. (Special Ser.: No. 22). (Illus.). 84p. 1976. pap. 6.00 o.p. (ISBN 0-916374-23-8). Interurban.

Galveston Era: The Texas Crescent on the Eve of Secession. Earl W. Fornell. (Illus.). 355p. 1976. pap. 9.95 (ISBN 0-292-72710-0). U of Tex Pr.

Gambetta & the National Defense. J. P. Bury. LC 70-80531. 1970. Repr. of 1936 ed. 17.50 (ISBN 0-86527-077-5). Fertig.

Gambit. Rex Stout. 160p. 1981. pap. 2.25 (ISBN 0-553-14646-7). Bantam.

Gambit Thirty-Three - Thirty-Four: Polish Issue. 1980. pap. 8.00. Riverrun NY.

Gambit Thirty-Two: International Theatre Review. 1978. pap. 3.00 (ISBN 0-7145-3721-7). Riverrun NY.

Gamble of the Marines. Raymond J. Toner. LC 62-19561. (Illus.). (gr. 5-7). 1963. 5.95g o.p. (ISBN 0-8075-2735-1). A Whitman.

Gambler. Max Brand. 208p. 1976. pap. 1.75 (ISBN 0-446-94328-2). Warner Bks.

Gambler. Fyodor Dostoevsky. Tr. by Andrew R. MacAndrew. 192p. 1981. pap. 4.95 (ISBN 0-393-00044-3). Norton.

Gamblers. Robert Wallace. Ed. by Time-Life Books. (Old West). (Illus.). 1979. 12.95 (ISBN 0-8094-2308-1). Time-Life.

Gamblers. Robert Wallace. LC 78-12281. (Old West Ser.). (Illus.). 1978. lib. bdg. 12.96 (ISBN 0-686-51078-X). Silver.

Gamblers & Gambling. Robert D. Herman. (Illus.). 1976. 16.95 (ISBN 0-669-00963-6). Lexington Bks.

Gambling: A Guide to Information Sources. Jack I. Gardner. LC 79-23797. (Sports, Games, & Pastimes Information Guide Ser.: Vol. 8). 1980. 30.00 (ISBN 0-8103-1229-8). Gale.

Gambling & Betting: Their Origin & Their Relation to Morality & to Religion. 3rd ed. R. H. Charles. 92p. 1928. text ed. 2.95 (ISBN 0-567-22066-4). Attic Pr.

Gambling & Society: Interdisciplinary Studies on the Subject of Gambling. William R. Eadington. (Illus.). 488p. 1976. 45.75 (ISBN 0-398-03459-1). C C Thomas.

Gambling Know-How. Irv Sutton. 64p. (Orig.). 1980. pap. 2.95 (ISBN 0-89650-716-5). Gamblers.

Gambling Nevada Style. Maurice Lemmel. LC 64-16205. pap. 2.95 (ISBN 0-385-07257-0, C476, Dolp). Doubleday.

Gambling Probabilities. Henry C. Landa. (Illus.). 1979. pap. 4.00 (ISBN 0-931974-05-4). FICOA.

Gambling Today. David Lester. 160p. 1979. text ed. 13.75 (ISBN 0-398-03952-6). C C Thomas.

Gambling: Who Really Wins? Jim Haskins. (First Bks.). (Illus.). (gr. 4 up). 1979. PLB 6.45 (ISBN 0-531-02942-5). Watts.

Gambling World. Rouge Et Noir. LC 68-22047. 1968. Repr. of 1898 ed. 20.00 (ISBN 0-8103-3551-4). Gale.

Game a Day Book. Gyles Brandreth. LC 79-91386. (Illus.). 192p. (gr. 2-12). 1980. 6.95 (ISBN 0-8069-4610-5); PLB 7.49 (ISBN 0-8069-4611-3). Sterling.

Game Bird Carving. Bruce Burk. LC 72-79365. (Illus.). 1972. 19.95 (ISBN 0-87691-080-0). Winchester Pr.

Game Bird Hunting. rev. ed. F. Phillip Rice & John I. Dahl. LC 65-14985. (Funk & W Bk.). (Illus.). 1977. 7.95 o.s.i. (ISBN 0-308-10322-X, TYC-T); pap. 4.50 (ISBN 0-308-10323-8, TYC-T). T Y Crowell.

Game Climbers Play: A Selection of One Hundred Mountaineering Articles. Ed. by Ken Wilson. (Sierra Club Paperback Library). (Illus.). 688p. 1980. pap. 9.95 o.p. (ISBN 0-87156-301-0). Sierra.

Game Cookbook. Geraldine Steindler. 1965. pap. 5.95 o.p. (ISBN 0-695-87906-5). Follett.

Game Diagram. Franklin H. Ernst, Jr. 1972. softbd 2.50x (ISBN 0-916944-19-0). Addresso'set.

Game-Generating-Games: A Trilogy of Games for Community & Classroom. Richard D. Duke & Cathy S. Greenblat. LC 79-15721. (Illus.). 1979. pap. 9.95x (ISBN 0-8039-1282-X). Sage.

Game Is Played. Amii Lorin. (Orig.). 1981. pap. 1.50 (ISBN 0-440-12835-8). Dell.

Game of Billiards. Clive Cottingham, Jr. LC 64-23471. (Illus.). 1967. 8.95 o.p. (ISBN 0-397-00322-6); pap. 5.95 (ISBN 0-397-00476-1, LP-11). Lippincott.

Game of Business. John McDonald. LC 74-5530. 1977. pap. 4.50 (ISBN 0-385-11671-3, Anch). Doubleday.

Game of Catch. Helen Cresswell. LC 76-46991. (Illus.). (gr. 3-6). 1977. 7.95 (ISBN 0-02-725440-2, 72544). Macmillan.

Game of Chess. Thomas Middleton. 1980. pap. text ed. 25.00x (ISBN 0-391-02145-1). Humanities.

Game of Chess: Marco Girolamo Vido's Scacchia Ludus. Ed. by Marion Di Cesare. (Bibliotheca, Humanistica & Reformatorica: No. 13). 1975. text ed. 27.50x (ISBN 90-6004-335-9). Humanities.

Game of Functions. Robert Froman. LC 74-2266. (Young Math Ser). (Illus.). 40p. (gr. k-3). 1974. 6.95 o.p. (ISBN 0-690-00544-X, TYC-J); PLB 6.89 (ISBN 0-690-00545-8). T Y Crowell.

Game of Go. Arthur Smith. LC 56-12653. (Illus.). 1956. pap. 5.25 (ISBN 0-8048-0202-5). C E Tuttle.

Game of Table Tennis. Dick Miles. (Illus.). 1971. 7.95 o.s.i. (ISBN 0-397-00527-X); pap. 2.95 (ISBN 0-397-00878-3, LP-59). Lippincott.

Game of Tarot. Michael Dummett. (Illus.). 600p. 1980. 95.00 (ISBN 0-7156-1014-7, Pub. by Duckworth England). Biblio Dist.

Game of the Century. J. Neal Blanton. (Illus.). 1970. 12.50 (ISBN 0-8363-0034-3). Jenkins.

Game of Truth. Edith Maxwell. (YA) (gr. 7-9). 1977. pap. 1.75 (ISBN 0-671-56004-2). PB.

Game of Words. Rgo S. Ramachandra. 1976. 8.00 (ISBN 0-89253-809-0); flexible cloth 4.80 (ISBN 0-89253-810-4). Ind-US Inc.

Game Plan II. Campus Crusade for Christ Staff. 100p. (gr. 9-12). 1980. pap. text ed. 2.25 (ISBN 0-918956-64-1). Campus Crusade.

Game Playing with BASIC. Donald D. Spencer. 1977. pap. 9.50 (ISBN 0-8104-5109-3). Hayden.

Game Playing with Computers. rev., 2nd ed. Donald D. Spencer. 320p. 1975. 19.95x (ISBN 0-8104-5103-4). Hayden.

Game, Set, & Match. William R. Cox. LC 76-13140. (gr. 5 up). 1977. 5.95 (ISBN 0-396-07400-6). Dodd.

Game Theory & Politics. Steven J. Brams. LC 74-15370. (Illus.). 1975. pap. text ed. 9.95 (ISBN 0-02-904550-9). Free Pr.

Game Theory & Related Topics. Ed. by O. Moeschlin & D. Pallaschke. LC 79-15339. 399p. 1979. 53.75 (ISBN 0-444-85342-1, North Holland). Elsevier.

Game Theory & Related Topics: Proceedings. Symposium on Game Theory & Related Topics, Hagen & Bonn, Sept. 1978. Ed. by O. Moeschlin & D. Pallaschke. 1979. 53.75 (ISBN 0-444-85342-1, North Holland). Elsevier.

Game Time. Harvey Hanson. LC 75-4776. (Illus.). 128p. (gr. 6-10). 1975. 5.90 (ISBN 0-531-02831-3). Watts.

Game with the Hole in It. Peter Dobereiner. (Illus.). 1970. 4.95 o.p. (ISBN 0-571-08923-2, Pub. by Faber & Faber); pap. 3.95 (ISBN 0-571-10421-5). Merrimack Bk Serv.

Gamebreakers of the NFL. Bill Gutman. (NFL Punt, Pass & Kick Library: No. 18). (Illus.). (gr. 5 up). 1973. 2.50 o.p. (ISBN 0-394-82501-2, BYR); PLB 3.69 (ISBN 0-394-92501-7). Random.

Gamefish of New England. Thompson. 426p. 1980. 14.95 (ISBN 0-89272-063-8). Down East.

Gamemaker. David Cohler. 1981. pap. 2.50 (ISBN 0-451-09766-1, E9766, Sig). NAL.

Gamemakers: Winning Philosophies of Eight NFL Coaches. Jack Clary. (Illus.). 256p. 1976. 10.95 o.s.i. (ISBN 0-695-80630-0). Follett.

Games. Compiled by Mary Hohenstein. 160p. (Orig.). 1980. pap. 5.95 (ISBN 0-87123-191-3, 210191). Bethany Fell.

Games. Bill Pronzini. 1978. pap. 1.75 o.p. (ISBN 0-449-23484-3, Crest). Fawcett.

Games Alcoholics Play. Claude Steiner. 1977. pap. 2.50 (ISBN 0-345-28470-4). Ballantine.

Games America Played. John Chaffee & Judi Culbertson. (Illus.). 192p. Date not set. 16.95 o.p. (ISBN 0-686-61465-8, ScribT). Scribner. Postponed.

Games & Decisions: Introduction & Critical Survey. Robert D. Luce & H. Raiffa. LC 57-12295. 1957. 27.95 (ISBN 0-471-55341-7). Wiley.

Games & Simulations in Science Education. H. I. Ellington et al. 180p. 1980. 25.00x (ISBN 0-89397-093-X). Nichols Pub.

Games & Simulations in the Foreign Language Classroom. Alice C. Omaggio. (Language in Education Ser. No. 13). (Orig.). 1979. pap. text ed. 5.95x (ISBN 0-87281-099-2). Ctr Appl Ling.

Games & Simulatons in Industrial & Labor Relations Training. Mary A. Coghill. (Key Issues Ser.: No. 7). 1971. pap. 2.00 (ISBN 0-87546-207-3). NY Sch Indus Rel.

Games & Sports the World Around. 3rd ed. Sarah E. Hunt. (Illus.). (gr. 9-12). 1964. 13.95 (ISBN 0-8260-4565-0). Ronald Pr.

Games As Models of Social Phenomena. Henry Hamburger. LC 78-23267. (Illus.). 1979. text ed. 18.95x (ISBN 0-7167-1011-0); pap. text ed. 8.95x (ISBN 0-7167-1010-2). W H Freeman.

Games at Twilight. Anita Desai. LC 79-4943. 1980. 9.95 (ISBN 0-06-011079-1, HarpT). Har-Row.

Games Book. Harriette H. Grimes & John W. Knack, Sr. (gr. 1-8). 1976. wkbk. 5.00 (ISBN 0-89039-163-7). Ann Arbor Pubs.

Games Cells Play. Max D. Lechtman et al. LC 78-57373. 1979. text ed. 7.50 (ISBN 0-8053-6094-8). Benjamin-Cummings.

Games Children Play: Instructive & Creative Play Activities for the Mentally Retarded & Developmentally Disabled Child. Manny Sternlict & Abraham Hurwitz. 128p. 1980. 12.95 (ISBN 0-442-25857-7). Van Nos Reinhold.

Games Christians Play: An Irreverent Guide to Religion Without Tears. Judi Culbertson & Patti Bard. 125p. 1973. pap. 1.25 o.p. (ISBN 0-06-087046-X, HW). Har-Row.

Games Climbers Play: A Collection of Mountaineering Writing. Ed. by Ken Wilson. LC 80-15374. (Sierra Club Paperback Library). (Illus.). 688p. 1980. pap. 9.95 (ISBN 0-87156-301-0). Sierra.

Games Doctors Play. Ed. by Claude A. Frazier. (Illus.). 424p. 1973. 29.75 (ISBN 0-398-02586-X). C C Thomas.

Game's End. Milton Dank. LC 78-12625. 1979. 8.95 (ISBN 0-397-31821-9). Lippincott.

Games for All Ages. Marjorie Wackerbarth & Lillian S. Graham. (Direction Bks). (Orig.). 1973. pap. 3.45 (ISBN 0-8010-9536-0). Baker Bk.

Games for All Occasions. Ken Anderson & Morry Carlson. pap. 2.50 (ISBN 0-310-20152-7). Zondervan.

Games for All Seasons. Alida Thacher. LC 77-19235. (Games & Activities Ser.). (Illus.). (gr. k-3). 1978. PLB 9.30 (ISBN 0-8172-1164-0). Raintree Pubs.

Games for Bible Discovery. Monte Corley & Roy Nichols. LC 79-55019. (Bible Discovery Bks.). 1979. pap. 4.25 (ISBN 0-8344-0110-X). Sweet.

Games for Cub Scouts. Boy Scouts Of America. (Illus.). 96p. 1963. pap. 1.25x (ISBN 0-8395-3844-8, 3844). BSA.

Games for Information Skills. Margaret R. Lassia. 80p. 1980. pap. text ed. 8.58x (ISBN 0-931510-06-6). Hi Willow.

Games for Language Learning. A. Wright et al. pap. 7.95 (ISBN 0-521-22170-6). Cambridge U Pr.

Games for the Science Classroom: An Annotated Bibliography. Paul B. Hounshell & Ira R. Trollinger. 1977. pap. 3.75 (ISBN 0-87355-006-4). Natl Sci Tchrs.

Games for the Super-Intelligent. James F. Fixx. 128p. 1974. pap. 1.75 (ISBN 0-445-08518-5). Popular Lib.

Games for Travel, No. 3. Richard Latta. 1981. 1.50 (ISBN 0-8431-0242-X). Price Stern.

Games for Travel, No. 3. Richard Latta. 48p. (Orig.). 1981. pap. 1.75 (ISBN 0-8431-0312-4). Price Stern.

Games for Two. Michael Ansara. (Illus.). 224p. 1981. pap. 8.95 (ISBN 0-906071-26-7). Proteus Pub NY.

Games from Many Lands. Anita Benarde. LC 71-86975. (Illus.). 64p. (gr. 3-7). 1971. PLB 7.95 (ISBN 0-87460-147-9). Lion.

Games, Games, Games, Juegos, Juegos, Juegos: Chicano Children at Play--Games & Rhymes. Ruben Sandoval & David Strick. (gr. 1 up). 1977. PLB 6.95 (ISBN 0-385-05438-6). Doubleday.

Games in Education & Development. Loyda M. Shears & Eli M. Bower. (Illus.). 392p. 1974. 27.75 (ISBN 0-398-02608-4). C C Thomas.

Games Mother Never Taught You: Corporate Gamesmanship for Women. Betty L. Harragan. 400p. 1978. pap. 2.95 (ISBN 0-446-93685-5); pap. 6.95 (ISBN 0-446-97726-8). Warner Bks.

Games of Anatoly Karpov. K. J. O'Connell & J. B. Adams. 1974. 19.95 (ISBN 0-7134-2849-X). David & Charles.

Games of Chance. Thomas Hinde. LC 66-29207. (Two complete novels). 1966. 8.95 (ISBN 0-8149-0119-0). Vanguard.

Games of Children, Their Origin & History. Henry Bett. LC 68-31218. 1968. Repr. of 1929 ed. 15.00 (ISBN 0-8103-3473-9). Gale.

Games of 'Eighty. W. H. Mefford. (Orig.). 1980. pap. 1.95 (ISBN 0-505-51494-X). Tower Bks.

Games of Robert J. Fischer. Robert Wade & K. J. O'Connell. 1973. pap. 29.95 (ISBN 0-7134-0370-5). David & Charles.

Games of the World Correspondence Chess Championships, Nos. I-VII. Ed. by T. D. Harding. (Illus.). 152p. 1980. 28.95 (ISBN 0-7134-2031-6, Pub. by Batsford England). David & Charles.

Games People Play. Eric Berne. 1978. pap. 2.75 (ISBN 0-345-29477-7). Ballantine.

Games, Sports & Exercises for the Physically Handicapped. 2nd ed. Ed. by Ronald C. Adams et al. LC 75-1079. (Illus.). 308p. 1975. pap. 14.50 o.p. (ISBN 0-8121-0514-1). Lea & Febiger.

Games They Paid Michael to Play. Elizabeth Terrell. Ed. by Sylvia Ashton. Date not set. 12.95 (ISBN 0-87949-149-3). Ashley Bks.

Games to Grow on. Stan Leonard & Donna Leonard. 1976. pap. 1.50 o.p. (ISBN 0-88207-254-4). Victor Bks.

Games to Grow On: Activities to Help Children Learn Self-Control. Lawrence E. Shapiro. (Illus.). 176p. 1981. text ed. 13.95 (ISBN 0-13-346148-3, Spec); pap. text ed. 5.95 (ISBN 0-13-346130-0, Spec). P-H.

Games to Improve Perceptual Skills of Pre-Schoolers: Ideas for Parents & Teachers. Janeen A. Johnson. 1978. pap. text ed. 0.25 (ISBN 0-8134-2049-0, 2049); for 25 copies 4.38; for 100 copies 14.75. Interstate.

Games to Learn By: One Hundred One Best Educational Games. rev. ed. Muriel Mandell. LC 58-12540. (Illus.). 128p. (gr. k-6). 1972. 5.95 o.p. (ISBN 0-8069-4520-6); PLB 5.89 o.p. (ISBN 0-8069-4521-4). Sterling.

Games to Play with the Very Young. Ed. by Polly Berrien. (Illus.). (ps-2). 1967. 1.95 o.p. (ISBN 0-394-80654-9, BYR). Random.

Games War: A Moscow Journal. Christopher Booker. 208p. 1981. 18.50 (ISBN 0-571-11755-4, Pub. by Faber & Faber); pap. 8.95 (ISBN 0-571-11763-5). Merrimack Bk Serv.

Games Without Losers. Sarah Liu & Mary L. Vittitow. LC 75-25279. (Illus.). 112p. 1975. pap. 5.95 (ISBN 0-913916-17-X). Incentive Pubns.
Games Without Words: Activities for Thinking Teachers & Thinking Children. Sydney Wolff & Caryl Wolff. (Illus.). 120p. 1977. pap. text ed. 12.50 (ISBN 0-398-03062-6). C C Thomas.
Games You Can Build Yourself. Katharina Zechlin. LC 74-82327. (Illus.). 64p. (gr. 6 up). 1975. 9.95 (ISBN 0-8069-5308-X); PLB 9.29 (ISBN 0-8069-5309-8). Sterling.
Gamesman Bridge: Play Better with Kantar. Edwin B. Kantar & Jackson Stanley. (Illus.). 1972. 5.95 o.p. (ISBN 0-87140-543-1). Liveright.
Gamesmaster Catalog. Ed. by Dana Lombardy. (Illus., Orig.). 1980. pap. 6.95 (ISBN 0-933168-02-0). Boynton & Assoc.
Gamines: How to Adopt from Latin America. Jean Nelson-Erichsen & Heino R. Erichsen. LC 79-26965. (Illus.). 1981. 12.95 (ISBN 0-87518-197-X). Dillon.
Gaming It up with Shakespeare. Patricia Ciabotti. Ed. by Linda H. Smith. 1980. pap. 3.95 (ISBN 0-936386-09-6). Creative Learning.
Gamins: How to Adopt from Latin America. Jean Nelson-Erichsen & Heino R. Erichsen. (Illus.). 1979. pap. 9.95x (ISBN 0-686-25160-1); pap. text ed. 9.95x (ISBN 0-686-25159-8). Dillon.
Gamma Image in Benign & Metabolic Bone Diseases, 2 vols. Wilfrido M. Sy. 1980. 64.95 ea. Vol. 1, 272p (ISBN 0-8493-5361-0). Vol. 2, 272p (ISBN 0-8493-5362-9). CRC Pr.
Gamma-Ray Surveys in Uranium Exploration. (Technical Reports Ser.: No. 186). 1979. pap. 12.00 (ISBN 92-0-145079-6, IDC186, IAEA). Unipub.
Gammafunktion, 2 vols. in 1. Niels Nielsen. Incl. Integrallogarithmus. LC 64-13785. (Ger.). 1965. 16.50 (ISBN 0-8284-0188-8). Chelsea Pub.
Gana. Jean Douassot. Tr. by Alexander Trocchi. 1980. 15.95 (ISBN 0-7145-0327-4). Riverrun NY.
Gandhari Dharmapada. Ed. by John Brough. (London Oriental Ser.). 1962. 34.50x o.p. (ISBN 0-19-713519-6). Oxford U Pr.
Gandhi. F. W. Rawding. LC 79-11008. (Cambridge Introduction to the History of Mankind Topic Book). (Illus.). (gr. 6). 1980. pap. 3.95 (ISBN 0-521-20715-0). Cambridge U Pr.
Gandhi. Malcolm Yapp. Ed. by Margaret Killingray & Edmund O'Connor. (World History Ser.). (Illus.). 32p. (gr. 10). 1980. Repr. of 1977 ed. lib. bdg. 5.95 (ISBN 0-89908-128-2); pap. text ed. 1.95 (ISBN 0-89908-103-7). Greenhaven.
Gandhi: A Memoir. William Shirer. 1981. 6.95 (ISBN 0-671-25080-9, Touchstone). S&S.
Gandhi Against Machiavellism: Non-Violence in Politics. Simone Panter-Brick. 1967. 7.50x (ISBN 0-210-34085-1). Asia.
Gandhi & Jinnah. Allen H. Merriam. 1980. 16.00x (ISBN 0-8364-0039-9). South Asia Bks.
Gandhi & Marx. K. G. Mashruwala. 119p. (Orig.). 1981. pap. 1.50 (ISBN 0-934676-30-5). Greenlf Bks.
Gandhi & Nehru. B. R. Nanda et al. 76p. 1979. pap. text ed. 4.50x (ISBN 0-19-561148-9). Oxford U Pr.
Gandhi on Non-Violence: Selected Texts from Gandhi's Non-Violence in Peace & War. Mohandas Gandhi. Ed. by Thomas Merton. LC 65-15672. (Orig.). 1965. pap. 2.95 (ISBN 0-8112-0097-3, NDP197). New Directions.
Gandhi Through Western Eyes. Horace Alexander. 9.00x (ISBN 0-210-22554-8). Asia.
Gandhi Today. 2nd ed. J. D. Sethi. 1979. text ed. 20.00 (ISBN 0-7069-0831-7, Pub. by Vikas India). Advent Bk.
Gandhian Way to World Peace. S. C. Gangal. 1960. 4.50x o.p. (ISBN 0-8426-1266-1). Verry.
Gang: A Study in Adolescent Behavior. Herbert Bloch & Arthur Niederhoffer. 1958. 6.00 o.p. (ISBN 0-8022-0143-1). Philos Lib.
Gang & Mrs. Higgins. George Shannon. LC 80-15957. (Read-Alone Bk.). (Illus.). 48p. (gr. 1-3). 1981. 5.95 (ISBN 0-688-80303-2); PLB 5.71 (ISBN 0-688-84303-4). Greenwillow.
Gang Girl. H. Samuel Fleischman. LC 67-17269. (gr. 7-8). 1967. 5.95 o.p. (ISBN 0-385-06290-7). Doubleday.
Ganges. Gina Douglas. LC 78-62983. (Rivers of the World Ser.). (Illus.). 1978. lib. bdg. 7.95 (ISBN 0-686-51134-4). Silver.
Ganglioside Function: Biochemical & Pharmacological Implications. Ed. by Giuseppe Porcellati et al. LC 76-7403. (Advances in Experimental Medicine & Biology Ser.: Vol. 71). 306p. 1976. 35.00 (ISBN 0-306-39071-X, Plenum Pr). Plenum Pub.
Gangster Chronicles: TV Lie-In. Michael Lasker & Richard A. Simmons. 224p. (Orig.). 1981. pap. 2.50 (ISBN 0-515-05808-4). Jove Pubns.
Gangsters on the Screen. Frank Manchel. LC 78-5953. (Illus.). (gr. 6 up). 1978. PLB 7.90 s&l (ISBN 0-531-01471-1). Watts.
Gannon Girls. Thom Racina & Joe Johnson. (Orig.). 1979. pap. 2.25 (ISBN 0-515-05384-8). Jove Pubns.
Gansebraten. Roesler. (Easy Reader, A). pap. 2.90 (ISBN 0-88436-109-8, GEA110054). EMC.
GAO: The Quest for Accountability in American Government. Frederick D. Mosher. 1979. pap. text ed. 13.25x (ISBN 0-89158-459-5). Westview.
Gaping Pig: Literature & Metamorphoses. Irving Massey. LC 74-22967. 1976. 17.50 (ISBN 0-520-02887-2). U of Cal Pr.
Garages & Carports. James E. Russell. Ed. by Shirley M. Horowitz. (Illus.). 144p. (Orig.). 1981. pap. 6.95 (ISBN 0-932944-32-9). Creative Homeowner.
Garbage Mountain: A United States Community Solves a Problem. Judith Conaway. (World of Our Own). (Illus.). 16p. (primer). 1977. 7 bks. & one cassette 15.00 (ISBN 0-89290-017-2). Soc for Visual.
Garbage World. Charles Platt. 1977. pap. 1.25 (ISBN 0-505-51164-9). Tower Bks.
Garbo. Alexander Walker. LC 80-12717. (Illus.). 192p. 1980. 19.95 (ISBN 0-02-622950-1). Macmillan.
Garcia the Centenarian & His Times. Malcolm S. Mackinley. LC 75-40206. (Music Reprint Ser.). 1975. Repr. of 1908 ed. lib. bdg. 29.50 (ISBN 0-306-70671-7). Da Capo.
Garcilaso De la Vega. Bernard Gicovate. LC 74-28304. (World Authors Ser.: Spain: No. 349). 1975. lib. bdg. 12.50 (ISBN 0-8057-2342-0). Twayne.
Garden: An Illustrated History. Julia S. Berrall. (Illus.). 1978. 22.50 o.p. (ISBN 0-670-33433-2). Viking Pr.
Garden & Patio Building Book. Sunset Editors. LC 69-13278. (Illus.). 96p. 1969. pap. 3.95 (ISBN 0-376-01213-7, Sunset Bks.). Sunset-Lane.
Garden & the Wilderness. Charles Pratt & William Maxwell. (Illus.). 159p. 1980. 50.00 (ISBN 0-8180-1420-2). Horizon.
Garden Art: The Personal Pursuit of Artistic Refinements, Inventive Concepts, Old Follies, & New Conceits for the Home Gardener. Lorraine M. Burgess. (Illus.). 192p. 1980. 25.00 (ISBN 0-8027-0665-7). Walker & Co.
Garden Book for Houston & the Gulf Coast. Ed. by River Oaks Garden Club. LC 75-5316. (Illus.). 191p. (Includes planting calendar). 1975. 8.95 (ISBN 0-88415-350-9). Pacesetter Pr.
Garden Books, Old & New. Mary Evans. LC 71-162512. 1971. Repr. of 1926 ed. 15.00 (ISBN 0-8103-3743-6). Gale.
Garden Color: Annuals & Perennials. Sunset Editors. LC 80-53479. (Illus.). 96p. 1981. pap. 3.95 (ISBN 0-376-03154-9, Sunset Bks). Sunset-Lane.
Garden Conifers in Color. Brian Proudley & Valerie Proudley. (Color Ser.). (Illus.). 1976. 9.95 (ISBN 0-7137-0807-7, Pub by Blandford Pr England). Sterling.
Garden Construction. James U. Crockett & Ogden Tanner. (Time-Life Encyclopedia of Gardening Ser.). (Illus.). 1978. lib. bdg. 11.96 (ISBN 0-686-51059-3). Silver.
Garden Construction. Ogden Tanner. Ed. by Time-Life Books. (Time-Life Encyclopdia of Gardening). (Illus.). 1978. 11.95 (ISBN 0-8094-2583-1). Time-Life.
Garden Construction Know-How. 1977. pap. 4.95 (ISBN 0-917102-69-X). Ortho.
Garden End. Peter Jones. (Illus.). 116p. 1981. 15.00 (ISBN 0-933806-09-4). Black Swan CT.
Garden Flowers in Color. Brian Proudley & Valerie Proudley. (Illus.). 1979. 12.95 (ISBN 0-7137-0911-1, Pub. by Blandford Pr England). Sterling.
Garden Flowers in Color, Vol. 1: Annuals & Bulbs. Anthony Huxley. Tr. by W. J. Spilsbury. (Pocket Encyclopedias of Flowers Ser). (Illus.). 1971. 8.95 o.s.i. (ISBN 0-02-562950-6). Macmillan.
Garden Flowers in Color, Vol. 2: Garden Perennials & Water Plants. Anthony Huxley. (Pocket Encyclopedias of Flowers Ser). 1971. 5.95 o.s.i. (ISBN 0-02-562960-3). Macmillan.
Garden Foliage for Flower Arrangement. Sybil Emberton. (Illus.). 1968. 12.95 (ISBN 0-571-08512-1, Pub. by Faber & Faber). Merrimack Bk Serv.
Garden Jungle. Densey Clyne. 184p. 1980. 27.95x (ISBN 0-00-216411-6, Pub. by W Collins Australia). Intl Schol Bk Serv.
Garden Maker's Answer Book. Lorraine M. Burgess. (Illus.). 1975 (Assn Pr). pap. 6.95 o.p. (ISBN 0-686-67236-4). Follett.
Garden of Earthly Delights. Joyce C. Oates. LC 67-19288. 1967. 10.95 (ISBN 0-8149-0171-9). Vanguard.
Garden of Earthly Delights. Joyce C. Oates. 384p. 1977. pap. 1.95 o.p. (ISBN 0-449-23194-1, Crest). Fawcett.
Garden of Eros. Dorothy Bryant. LC 78-73215. 1979. pap. 6.00 (ISBN 0-931688-03-5). Ata Bks.
Garden of Eternal Swallows. Karen E. Gordon. LC 80-50745. (Illus.). 176p. (Orig.). 1980. pap. 5.95 (ISBN 0-394-73948-5). Shambhala Pubns.
Garden of Fand. Ashok Mahajan. (Redbird Bk.). 1976. lib. bdg. 6.75 (ISBN 0-89253-122-3); flexible bdg. 4.80 (ISBN 0-89253-143-6). Ind-US Inc.
Garden of Ghosts. Marilyn Ross. 256p. (Orig.). 1974. pap. 1.25 o.p. (ISBN 0-445-00227-1). Popular Lib.
Garden of Hope: Laradon Hall. George V. Kelly & Harry Farrar. (Illus.). 240p. 1980. 12.50 (ISBN 0-87108-561-5); pap. 7.50 (ISBN 0-87108-562-3). Pruett.
Garden of Stones. M. M. Parker. LC 80-13966. 224p. 1980. 8.95 (ISBN 0-396-07858-3). Dodd.
Garden of the Golden Apples: A Bibliography of Patrick Kavanagh. Peter Kavanagh. 1972. pap. 5.00 (ISBN 0-914612-05-0). Kavanagh.
Garden of Thorns. Sally Wentworth. (Harlequin Romances Ser.). 192p. 1980. pap. 1.25 o.p. (ISBN 0-373-02361-8, Pub. by Harlequin). PB.
Garden of Unicorns. J. C. Conaway. 176p. (Orig.). 1976. pap. 1.25 o.p. (ISBN 0-345-25109-1). Ballantine.
Garden on the Moon. Pierre Boulle. LC 65-10229. 1964. 8.95 (ISBN 0-8149-0063-1). Vanguard.
Garden Pools. Leonard C. Betts. (Illus.). 1952. pap. 2.50 (ISBN 0-87666-077-4, M513). TFH Pubns.
Garden Prospect. Peter Yates. 1980. 15.00 (ISBN 0-912330-41-4); pap. 9.50 (ISBN 0-912330-42-2). Jargon Soc.
Garden Prospect: Selected Poems of Peter Yates. Peter Yates. 1980. 15.00 (ISBN 0-912330-41-4); pap. 9.50 (ISBN 0-912330-42-2). Jargon Soc.
Garden Shrubs & Trees. S. G. Harrison. 9.75x (ISBN 0-392-06725-0, LTB). Soccer.
Garden Shrubs & Trees in Color. Eigil Kiaer. (Color Ser.). (Illus.). 1959. 9.95 (ISBN 0-7137-0649-X, Pub by Blandford Pr England). Sterling.
Garden Spice & Wild Pot-Herbs: An American Herbal. Walter C. Muenscher & Myron A. Rice. LC 78-56899. (Illus.). 218p. 1978. pap. 7.95 (ISBN 0-8014-9174-6). Comstock.
Gardener--Assistant Gardener. 2nd ed. Arco Editorial Board. LC 75-27588. (Orig.). 1975. pap. 8.00 (ISBN 0-668-01340-0, 1340). Arco.
Gardener's Handbook, 3 bks. David Carr. Incl. Vol. 1. Broad-Leaved Trees. (Illus.). 144p. 24.00 (ISBN 0-7134-1306-9); pap. 14.50 o.p. (ISBN 0-7134-1306-9); Vol. 2. Conifers. (Illus.). 144p. 24.00 (ISBN 0-7134-1307-7); pap. 14.95 o.p. (ISBN 0-7134-1308-5); Vol. 3. Shrubs. (Illus.). 144p. 23.95 o.p. (ISBN 0-7134-1882-6); pap. 13.95 o.p. (ISBN 0-686-61986-2); Growing Fruit & Nuts. David Carr. (Illus.). 1980. 23.95 o.p. (ISBN 0-7134-1883-4, Pub. by Batsford England); pap. 14.50 (ISBN 0-7134-1896-6). David & Charles. (Illus.). 1980 (Pub. by Batsford England). David & Charles.
Gardener's Magic & Folklore. Margaret Baker. LC 77-73799. (Illus.). 1978. 12.50x (ISBN 0-87663-299-1). Universe.
Gardener's Trouble Shooter. Victor H. Reis. (Illus.). 1958. 8.95 o.p. (ISBN 0-911378-09-X). Sheridan.
Gardening. Boy Scouts Of America. LC 19-600. (Illus.). 48p. (gr. 6-12). 1976. pap. 0.70x (ISBN 0-8395-3240-7, 3240). BSA.
Gardening. rev. ed. Virginia Kirkus. (First Bks.). (Illus.). 72p. (gr. 4 up). 1976. PLB 4.90 o.p. (ISBN 0-531-00540-2). Watts.
Gardening & Landscaping: Lawns, Vegetables, Flowers, Trees, & Shrubs. Jules Oravetz, Sr. LC 74-28650. 1975. 9.95 (ISBN 0-672-23229-4, 23229). Audel.
Gardening by the Foot. Jacob R. Mittleider. LC 80-84564. 150p. 1981. pap. 4.95 (ISBN 0-88290-175-3, 4026). Horizon Utah.
Gardening for Beginners. Frances Hutchison. Ed. by Edwin Steffek. (Illus.). 152p. 1976. pap. 5.95 o.s.i. (ISBN 0-02-063250-9, Collier). Macmillan.
Gardening for Food. W. G. Smith. LC 71-37212. (Illus.). 192p. 1972. pap. 2.45 o.p. (ISBN 0-684-12836-5, SL427, ScribT). Scribner.
Gardening for Good Eating. Helen M. Fox. (Illus.). 278p. 1973. pap. 1.95 o.s.i. (ISBN 0-686-66736-0, Collier). Macmillan.
Gardening for Health & Nutrition. John Philbrick & Helen Philbrick. LC 79-3595. 96p. 1980. pap. 3.95 (ISBN 0-06-066535-1, RD 402). Har-Row.
Gardening for the Physically Handicapped & Elderly. Mary Chaplin. 1978. 13.50 (ISBN 0-7134-1081-7). David & Charles.
Gardening in the Upper Midwest. Leon C. Snyder. LC 77-8650. (Illus.). 1978. 12.50 (ISBN 0-8166-0833-4). U of Minn Pr.
Gardening on Chalk, Lime & Clay. Judith Berrisford. 1979. 14.95 (ISBN 0-571-10952-7, Pub. by Faber & Faber); pap. 6.95 (ISBN 0-571-11129-7). Merrimack Bk Serv.
Gardening Under Lights. James U. Crockett & Wendy B. Murphy. (Time-Life Encyclopedia of Gardening Ser.). (Illus.). 1978. lib. bdg. 11.96 (ISBN 0-686-51060-7). Silver.
Gardening Under Lights. 1.95 (ISBN 0-686-21156-1). Bklyn Botanic.
Gardening Under Lights. Ed. by Time-Life Books & Time Life Books Editors. (Encyclopedia of Gardening Ser.). (Illus.). 1978. 11.95 (ISBN 0-8094-2570-X). Time-Life.
Gardening with Color. Ed. by Staff of Ortho Books. LC 77-89690. (Illus.). 1978. pap. 4.95 (ISBN 0-917102-58-4). Ortho.
Gardening with Water, Plantings & Stone. Carroll Calkins. 156p. 1975. pap. 1.95 o.s.i. (ISBN 0-346-12176-0). Cornerstone.
Gardening with Wildflowers. Frances Tenenbaum. LC 73-1109. (Encore Editions). (Illus.). 1973. 3.95 o.p. (ISBN 0-684-15005-0, ScribT). Scribner.
Gardening Without Pests. 1979. 1.95 (ISBN 0-686-27086-X). Bklyn Botanic.
Gardening Without Soil. Sarah R. Riedman. LC 78-13088. (First Bks.). (Illus.). (gr. 4-6). 1979. PLB 6.45 s&l (ISBN 0-531-02256-0). Watts.
Gardening...Naturally. D. X. Fenten. LC 72-13790. (Illus.). 128p. (gr. 4 up). 1973. PLB 5.88 o.p. (ISBN 0-531-02625-6); pap. 2.95 (ISBN 0-531-02338-9). Watts.
Gardens Are for Eating. Stanley Schuler. (Illus.). 340p. 1975. pap. 3.95 o.s.i. (ISBN 0-02-063700-4, Collier). Macmillan.
Gardens of Adonis. Marcel Detienne. (European Philoaophy & the Human Sciences). (Illus.). 1977. text ed. 26.75x (ISBN 0-391-00611-8). Humanities.
Gardens of Britain, Five: Yorkshire & Humberside. Kenneth Lemmon. 1979. 24.00 (ISBN 0-7134-1743-9, Pub. by Batsford England). David & Charles.
Gardens of Britain, Four: Kent, Sussex & Surrey. Tom Wright. 1978. 24.00 (ISBN 0-7134-1281-X, Pub. by Batsford England). David & Charles.
Gardens of Britain, Six: Derbyshire, Leicestershire, Lincolnshire, Northamptonshire & Nottinghamshire. John Anthony. 1979. 24.00 (ISBN 0-7134-1745-5, Pub. by Batsford England). David & Charles.
Gardens of Britain, Three: Berkshire, Oxfordshire, Buckinghamshire, Bedfordshire, Hertfordshire. Richard Bisgrove. 1978. 24.00 (ISBN 0-7134-1178-3, Pub. by Batsford England). David & Charles.
Gardens of Britain, Two: Dorset, Hampshire and the Isle of Wight. Allen Patterson. 1978. 24.00 (ISBN 0-7134-0992-4, Pub. by Batsford England). David & Charles.
Gardens of Illusion: The Genius of Andre Le Nostre. F. Hamilton Hazlehurst. (Illus.). 430p. 1981. 39.95 (ISBN 0-8265-1209-7). Vanderbilt U Pr.
Gardens of Lucullus. John A. Schmidt. 1980. 10.95 (ISBN 0-533-04588-6). Vantage.
Gardens That Care for Themselves: How to Grow Neater, Healthier Plants, Cut Your Outdoor Chores in Half. Tam Mossman. LC 77-76254. 1978. 10.95 o.p. (ISBN 0-385-11171-1). Doubleday.
Gardens Without Soil. Jack Kramer. LC 75-22408. (Encore Edition). (Illus.). 1976. 3.95 o.p. (ISBN 0-684-15698-9, ScribT). Scribner.
Gardner's Kitchen. John Corry & Grace Corry. (Illus.). 128p. 1980. 9.95 (ISBN 0-87691-321-4). Winchester Pr.
Garelli Moped Owner Service-Repair: 1976-1978. Ed Scott. Ed. by Eric Jorgensen. (Illus.). 1978. pap. 6.00 (ISBN 0-89287-200-4, M435). Clymer Pubns.
Garfield at Large. Jim Davis. 1980. pap. 4.95 (ISBN 0-345-28779-7). Ballantine.
Garfield Gains Weight. Jim Davis. 128p. (Orig.). 1981. pap. 4.95 (ISBN 0-345-28844-0). Ballantine.
Gargoyles, Chimeres, & the Grotesque in French Gothic Sculpture. enl. & 2nd ed. Lester B. Bridaham. LC 68-27724. (Architecture & Decorative Art Ser.: Vol. 22). (Illus.). 1969. Repr. of 1930 ed. lib. bdg. 55.00 (ISBN 0-306-71152-4). Da Capo.
Garibaldi. Ed. by Denis M. Smith. LC 69-15335. (Great Lives Observed Ser). 1969. pap. text ed. 1.95 o.p. (ISBN 0-13-346783-X). P-H.
Garibaldi: The Revolutionary & His Men. Andrea Viotti. (Illus.). 224p. 1980. 22.50 (ISBN 0-7137-0942-1, Pub. by Blandford Pr England). Sterling.
Garland of Games & Other Diversions. Barbara Cooney. LC 69-15675. (Younger Reader Ser). (Illus., Orig.). (gr. k-3). 1969. 3.95 o.p. (ISBN 0-910412-01-4); pap. 1.95 o.p. (ISBN 0-910412-12-X). Williamsburg.
Garland of Wisdom: From the Edgar Cayce Readings. Compiled by W. H. Church. (Edgar Cayce Readings). 36p. 1975. pap. 1.25 o.p. (ISBN 0-87604-081-4). ARE Pr.
Garlanda: The Ups & Downs of an Uppity Teapot. Penny Pollock. (Illus.). 80p. (gr. 2-6). 1980. 7.95 (ISBN 0-399-20713-9). Putnam.

Garlic. Paavo Airola. 2.00 o.s.i. (ISBN 0-89557-039-4). Bi World Indus.
Garlic Kid. Thomas Starling. LC 77-91896. Orig. Title: Ringling Hall. 1978. pap. 3.95 (ISBN 0-914864-01-7). Spindrift.
Garnier's Becket: Translated from the 12th Century Vie Saint Thomas le Martyr de Cantorbire of Gannier of Pont-Sainte Maxence. Ed. by Janet Shirley. (Illus.). 191p. 1975. 20.00x (ISBN 0-87471-798-1). Rowman.
Garnishes, Relishes & Sauces for Foodservice Menu Planning. Eulalia C. Blair. LC 77-3292. (Foodservice Menu Planning Ser.). 1977. 16.50 (ISBN 0-8436-2173-7). CBI Pub.
Garrett Wade Book of Woodworking Tools. Gary Chinn. LC 79-7082. (Illus.). 1980. 17.50 (ISBN 0-690-01840-1, TYC-T). T Y Crowell.
Garrick Stage: Theatres & Audiences in the Eighteenth Century. Allardyce Nicoll. LC 79-9667. (Illus.). 192p. 1980. 25.00 (ISBN 0-8203-0510-3). U of Ga Pr.
Garrison Diversion Unit: A Case Study in Canadian-U.S. Environmental Relations. John E. Carroll & Roderick M. Logan. 56p. 1980. 5.00 (ISBN 0-88806-070-X). Natl Planning.
Garrison State in Prewar Japan & Post-War Korea: A Comparative Analysis of Military Politics. Jai-Hyup Kim. LC 77-26344. 1978. 11.25 (ISBN 0-8191-0416-7). U Pr of Amer.
Garrison's History of Neurology. Ed. by Lawrence C. McHenry, Jr. (Illus.). 568p. 1969. 22.75 (ISBN 0-398-01261-X). C C Thomas.
Garrity & Other Plays. Philip Ward. (Dramascripts Ser.). 2.50 (ISBN 0-902675-01-X). Oleander Pr.
Garry Unger & the Battling Blues. Stan Fischler. LC 76-49993. 1977. 7.95 (ISBN 0-396-07388-3). Dodd.
Garth Pig & the Ice-Cream Lady. Mary Rayner. (ps-3). pap. 2.95 (ISBN 0-689-70495-X, A-122, Aladdin). Atheneum.
Garuda Purana, Pt. 1. Ed. by J. L. Shastri. (Ancient Indian Tradition & Mythology Ser.: Vol. 12). 1979. text ed. 18.00x (ISBN 0-8426-1106-1). Verry.
Garveyism As a Religious Movement: The Institutionalization of a Black Civil Religion. Randall K. Burkett. LC 78-15728. (ATLA Monograph Ser.: No. 13). 1978. 13.50 (ISBN 0-8108-1163-4). Scarecrow.
Gary Bell Story. Gary Bell & David R. Seay. 176p. (Orig.). 1981. pap. 4.95 (ISBN 0-89081-253-5). Harvest Hse.
Gary Cooper: An Intimate Biography. Hector Arce. 272p. 1980. pap. 2.75 (ISBN 0-553-14130-9). Bantam.
Gary Player's Golf Book for Young People. Gary Player & George Sullivan. LC 79-55882. (Illus.). 112p. (gr. 7-12). 1980. 8.95 (ISBN 0-914178-35-0, 25483-9). Golf Digest.
Gary Player's Golf Clinic. Gary Player. LC 81-65104. (Illus.). 160p. 1981. pap. 6.95 (ISBN 0-910676-23-2, 6036). DBI.
Gary Snyder. Bob Steuding. LC 76-14938. (U.S. Authors Ser: No. 274). 1976. lib. bdg. 12.50 (ISBN 0-8057-7174-3). Twayne.
Gary Tong's Crazy Cut-Outs. Tong. (ps-3). pap. 1.50 (ISBN 0-590-05738-3, Schol Pap). Schol Bk Serv.
Gas & A.C. Arc Welding & Cutting. 3rd ed. Royalston F. Jennings. (gr. 7 up). 1956. pap. text ed. 5.00 (ISBN 0-87345-119-8). McKnight.
Gas Bearing Symposium. 4th ed. 1969. text ed. 29.00 (ISBN 0-686-63954-5, Dist. by Air Science Co.). BHRA Fluid.
Gas Chromatographic Applications in Microbiology & Medicine. Brij M. Mitruka. LC 74-18002. (Techniques in Pure & Applied Microbiology Ser). 496p. 1975. 55.50 (ISBN 0-471-61183-2, Pub. by Wiley Medical). Wiley.
Gas Chromatographic Detectors. D. J. David. LC 73-4773. 295p. 1974. 29.95 o.p. (ISBN 0-471-19674-6, Pub. by Wiley-Interscience). Wiley.
Gas Chromatography-Mass Spectrometry in Neurobiology. Ed. by E. Costa & B. Holmstedt. LC 73-84113. (Advances in Biochemical Psychopharmacology Ser.: Vol. 7). (Illus.). 183p. 1973. 24.50 (ISBN 0-911216-48-0). Raven.
Gas-Cooled Reactors with Emphasis on Advanced Systems, Vol. 1. 1976. pap. 34.25 (ISBN 92-0-050076-5, IAEA). Unipub.
Gas-Cooled Reactors with Emphasis on Advanced Systems Vol. 2, 1976: Proceedings. IAEA-NEA Symposium, Julich, Oct. 13-17, 1975. (Proceedings Ser.). (Illus., Orig.). 1976. pap. 44.00 (ISBN 92-0-050176-1, IAEA). Unipub.
Gas Directory & Who's Who 1979. (Benn Directories Ser.). 1979. 42.50 (ISBN 0-686-52400-4, Pub by Benn Pubns). Nichols Pub.
Gas Discharges & Their Applications. (IEE Conference Publication Ser.: No. 189). (Illus.). 560p. (Orig.). 1980. soft cover 79.00. Inst Elect Eng.
Gas Dynamics. James E. John. 1969. text ed. 25.95x (ISBN 0-205-02262-6, 3222624). Allyn.
Gas Dynamics, 2 vols. Maurice J. Zucrow & Joe D. Hoffman. LC 76-6855. 768p. Vol. 1. text ed. 44.95 (ISBN 0-471-98440-X); Vol. 2. text ed. 44.95 (ISBN 0-471-01806-6). Wiley.
Gas Engine Manual. 2nd ed. Ted Pipe. LC 76-45883. 1977. 9.95 (ISBN 0-672-23245-6). Audel.
Gas Engineers Handbook. American Gas Association. Ed. by C. George Segeler. (Illus.). 1965. 63.00 (ISBN 0-8311-3011-3). Indus Pr.
Gas-Flow & Chemical Lasers: Proceedings. new ed. International Symposium on Gas-Flow and Chemical Lasers, 2nd, Rhode-St-Genese, Belgium, Sept. 11-15, 1978. Ed. by John F. Wendt. LC 79-12779. (Illus.). 608p. 1979. text ed. 49.50 (ISBN 0-89116-147-3). Hemisphere Pub.
Gas Guzzler to Gas Sipper Manual: The Motorist's Complete Step-by-Step Do-It-Yourself Guide for Converting Your V-8 Car Engine to a V-4, Plus More Than 100 Other Ways to Save Gas & Money. George D. Russell. LC 79-92199. (Illus.). 110p. 1979. pap. 5.95 spiral bdg. (ISBN 0-935850-00-7). Rosetta Pub Co.
Gas Industry & the Environment: Proceedings. United Nations Economic Commission for Europe, Commission on Gas, Minsk, USSR, 1977. 1978. text ed. 51.00 (ISBN 0-08-022412-1). Pergamon.
Gas Lasers. C. S. Willet. 1974. text ed. 90.00 (ISBN 0-08-017803-0). Pergamon.
Gas-Phase Oxidation of Hydrocarbons. V. Y. Shtern. Ed. by B. P. Mullins. 1964. 37.50 o.p. (ISBN 0-08-010202-6). Pergamon.
Gas-Phase Reactions: Kinetics & Mechanisms. V. N. Kondratiev & E. E. Nikitin. (Illus.). 250p. 1980. 63.80 (ISBN 0-387-09956-5). Springer-Verlag.
Gas Pipe Networks: The Early History of College Radio, 1936-1946. Louis M. Bloch, Jr. (Illus.). 156p. 1981. 12.95 (ISBN 0-914276-02-6). Bloch & Co OH.
Gas Savers Guide. Consumer Guide Editors. (Orig.). 1979. pap. 1.95 (ISBN 0-449-80000-8, Columbine). Fawcett.
Gas Situation in the ECC Region Around the Year 1990. United Nations Economic Commission for Europe. (European Committee for Economic Perspectives: Vol. 18). 1979. 69.00 (ISBN 0-08-024465-3). Pergamon.
Gas-Solid Transport. George E. Klinzing. (Chemical Engineering Ser.). (Illus.). 358p. 1981. text ed. 28.50 (ISBN 0-07-035047-7, C). McGraw.
Gas Tables: Thermodynamic Properties of Air Products of Combustion & Component Gases Compressible Flow Functions Including Those of Ascher H. Shapiro & Gilbert M. Edelman. 2nd ed. Joseph H. Keenan et al. LC 79-15098. 1980. 22.50 (ISBN 0-471-02207-1, Pub. by Wiley-Interscience). Wiley.
Gas Transfer in the Lung. B. A. Hills. (Monographs in Experimental Biology: No. 19). (Illus.). 200p. 1974. 38.50 (ISBN 0-521-20167-5). Cambridge U Pr.
Gas Turbine Aero-Thermodynamics: With Special Reference to Aircraft Propulsion. Frank Whittle. LC 80-41372. 240p. 1981. 30.00 (ISBN 0-08-026719-X); pap. 17.50 (ISBN 0-08-026718-1). Pergamon.
Gas Turbine Combustor Design Problems. Ed. by Arthur H. Lefebvre. LC 79-22350. 431p. 1979. text ed. 51.75 (ISBN 0-89116-177-5). Hemisphere Pub.
Gas Turbine Engineering Applications Cycles & Characteristics. R. T. Harman. LC 80-21003. 304p. 1981. 29.95 (ISBN 0-470-27065-9). Halsted Pr.
Gas Turbine Heat Transfer: 1978. Ed. by V. L. Erickson & H. L. Julien. 1978. 18.00 (ISBN 0-685-66801-0, H00125). ASME.
Gas Turbine Theory. 2nd ed. H. Cohen et al. 1979. 19.95 o.p. (ISBN 0-470-26781-X). Halsted Pr.
Gascony: England's First Colony 1204-1453. Margaret W. Labarge. (Illus.). 276p. 1980. 24.50x (ISBN 0-389-20142-1). B&N.
Gasdynamic Lasers: An Introduction. John D. Anderson. (Quantum Electronic Ser.). 1976. 29.50 (ISBN 0-12-056950-7). Acad Pr.
Gasdynamics of Explosions & Reactive Systems: Proceedings of the Sixth International Colloquium Held in Stockholm, Sweden, 22-26 August 1977. Ed. by A. K. Openheim. (Illus.). 782p. 1980. 100.00 (ISBN 0-08-025442-X). Pergamon.
Gases, Liquids & Solids. 2nd ed. D. Tabor. LC 78-26451. (Illus.). 1980. 57.50 (ISBN 0-521-22383-0); pap. 15.95 (ISBN 0-521-29466-5). Cambridge U Pr.
Gaslights in Calcutta. K. Mahadev. 8.00 (ISBN 0-89253-677-2); flexible cloth 4.80 (ISBN 0-89253-678-0). Ind-US Inc.
Gasohol Sourcebook: (Abstracts) P. N. Cheremisinopf. 1981. text ed. 29.95 (ISBN 0-250-40425-7). Ann Arbor Science.
Gasoline Cowboy. William C. Gault. LC 73-15784. 160p. (gr. 5-7). 1974. PLB 7.95 o.p. (ISBN 0-525-30352-9). Dutton.
Gasoline: The Automotive Adventures of Charles Bates. James D. Houston. (Noel Young Bk). 128p. 1980. 8.95 (ISBN 0-88496-144-3). Capra Pr.
Gaspara Stampa, Louise Labe y Sor Juana Ines de la Cruz: Triptico Renacentista Barroco. Giovanni Guernelli. 4.65 (ISBN 0-8477-3132-4). U of PR Pr.
Gaston Goes to Mardi Gras. James Rice. LC 77-13302. (Illus.). 1977. 7.95 (ISBN 0-88289-158-8). Pelican.
Gaston Goes to Texas. James Rice. LC 78-12490. (Illus.). (ps-6). 1978. 7.95 (ISBN 0-88289-204-5). Pelican.
Gaston Lays an Offshore Pipeline. James Rice. (Illus.). 1979. 7.95 (ISBN 0-88289-177-4). Pelican.
Gaston the Green-Nosed Alligator. Illus. by James Rice. 1974. 7.95 (ISBN 0-88289-049-2). Pelican.
Gastric Secretions - Mechanism & Control. Ed. by T. K. Shnitka. 1967. 75.00 (ISBN 0-08-012412-7). Pergamon.
Gastro-Intestinal Ultrastructure: An Atlas of Scanning & Transmission Electron Micrographs. Carl J. Pfeiffer et al. 1974. 55.25 (ISBN 0-12-553750-6). Acad Pr.
Gastroenterology. 3rd ed. Ed. by Lawrence D. Wruble et al. Myron Lewis & Michael Levinson. (Medical Examination Review Book: Vol.22). 1977. spiral bdg. 16.50 (ISBN 0-87488-141-2). Med Exam.
Gastroenterology & Nutrition in Infancy, 2 vols. Ed. by Emanuel Lebenthal. 1980. Set. text ed. 115.00 (ISBN 0-89004-526-7) (ISBN 0-89004-533-X). Raven.
Gastroenterology: Foregut, Vol. 1. Ed. by J. H. Baron & F. Moody. (Butterworth International Medical Reviews). 1981. text ed. price not set (ISBN 0-407-02287-2). Butterworth.
Gastroenterology in Clinical Nursing. 3rd ed. Barbara A. Given & Sandra J. Simmons. LC 79-13048. (Illus.). 1979. pap. text ed. 17.95 (ISBN 0-8016-1855-X). Mosby.
Gastroenterology Nursing Continuing Education Review. Barbara A. Russo. 1976. spiral bdg. 8.00 o.p. (ISBN 0-87488-373-3). Med Exam.
Gastroenterology Specialty Board Review. William A. Sodeman, Jr. & Thomas A. Saladin. 1977. spiral bdg. 16.50 (ISBN 0-87488-316-4). Med Exam.
Gastrointestinal Defence Mechanisms: Proceedings of a Satellite Symposium of the 28th International Congress of Physiological Sciences, Budapest, 1980. Ed. by Gy. Mozsik et al. LC 80-41883. (Advances in Physiological Sciences: Vol. 29). (Illus.). 590p. 1981. 70.00 (ISBN 0-08-027350-5). Pergamon.
Gastrointestinal Diseases: Focus on Clinical Diagnosis. Khursheed N. Jeejeebhoy. 1979. pap. 19.50 (ISBN 0-87488-831-X). Med Exam.
Gastrointestinal Emergencies Two: Proceedings of the 2nd International Symposium on Gastrointestinal Emergencies, Rome, 7-8 June 1979. Ed. by F. R. Barany et al. (Advances in the Biosciences: Vol. 27). (Illus.). 186p. 1980. 30.00 (ISBN 0-08-024927-2). Pergamon.
Gastrointestinal Hormones. Ed. by George B. Glass. (Comprehensive Endocrinology Ser.). 1980. text ed. 92.00 (ISBN 0-89004-395-7). Raven.
Gastrointestinal Motility. Ed. by James M. Christensen. 520p. 1980. 47.50 (ISBN 0-89004-503-8, 566). Raven.
Gastrointestinal Motility. H. Duthrie. 1978. 39.50 (ISBN 0-8391-1268-8). Univ Park.
Gastrointestinal Nursing. Hazel V. Rice. (Nursing Outline Ser.). 1978. pap. 9.50 (ISBN 0-87488-392-X). Med Exam.
Gastrointestinal Pan-Endoscopy. L. H. Berry. (Illus.). 688p. 1974. 49.75- (ISBN 0-398-02912-1). C C Thomas.
Gastrointestinal Physiology. 2nd ed. Leonard R. Johnson. LC 80-23381. (Illus.). 160p. 1981. text ed. 13.95 (ISBN 0-8016-2532-7). Mosby.
Gastronomic Bibliography. Katherine G. Bitting. LC 71-168559. (Illus.). 1971. Repr. of 1939 ed. 34.00 (ISBN 0-8103-3758-4). Gale.
Gastronomical & Culinary Literature: A Survey & Analysis of Historically-Oriented Collections in the U. S. A. Barbara L. Feret. LC 78-32098. 1979. lib. bdg. 10.00 (ISBN 0-8108-1204-5). Scarecrow.
Gatehouse Mystery. (Trixie Belden Mystery Stories Ser.). (gr. 4 up). 1977. PLB 5.52 (ISBN 0-307-61526-X, Golden Pr); pap. 1.25 (ISBN 0-307-21526-1). Western Pub.
Gates' Jigs, Fixtures, Tools & Gauges. 6th ed. Ed. by G. H. Ryder. (Illus.). 1973. 17.50x (ISBN 0-291-39432-9). Intl Ideas.
Gates of Creation. Philip J. Farmer. 1977. pap. 2.25 (ISBN 0-441-27389-0). Ace Bks.
Gates of Forgiveness: Selichot. Ed. by Chaim Stern. 1980. pap. 2.00 ea. Eng. Ed (ISBN 0-916694-57-7). Hebrew Ed (ISBN 0-916694-74-7). Central Conf.
Gates of New Life. James S. Stewart. (Scholar As Preacher Ser.). 261p. Repr. of 1937 ed. pap. text ed. 10.00 (ISBN 0-567-24426-1). Attic Pr.
Gates of Prayer: The New Union Prayerbook. Ed. by Chaim Stern. 1975. English ed. 10.00 (ISBN 0-916694-01-1); Hebrew ed. 10.00 (ISBN 0-916694-00-3). Central Conf.
Gates of Repentance. Ed. by Chaim Stern. 1978. 10.00 (ISBN 0-916694-38-0); pulpit ed. 20.00 (ISBN 0-916694-40-2); Hebrew ed. 10.00 (ISBN 0-916694-39-9). Central Conf.
Gates of Sagittarius. Roland Cutler. 344p. 1980. 10.95 (ISBN 0-8037-3268-6). Dial.
Gates of the Forest. Elie Wiesel. 1969. pap. 2.75 o.s.i. (ISBN 0-380-01206-5, 51821, Bard). Avon.
Gates of the House. Chaim Stern. 1977. 6.95 (ISBN 0-916694-35-6); lib. bdg. 7.50 o.s.i. (ISBN 0-916694-42-9). Central Conf.
Gates of the Mountains. Will Henry. (Western Fiction Ser.). 1980. lib. bdg. 13.95 (ISBN 0-8398-2689-3). Gregg.
Gates of the Wind. Michael Carroll. 8.95 (ISBN 0-7195-0197-0). Transatlantic.
Gates of Understanding. Ed. by Lawrence Hoffman. LC 77-23488. 1977. text ed. 6.95 o.p. (ISBN 0-685-87866-X, 142686); pap. text ed. 4.95 (ISBN 0-8074-0009-2, 142689). UAHC.
Gates Shall Not. E. E. Cleveland. (Horizon Ser.). 96p. 1980. pap. write for info. (ISBN 0-8127-0325-1). Southern Pub.
Gateway. Frederik Pohl. (Del Rey Bk). 1978. pap. 2.50 (ISBN 0-345-29300-2). Ballantine.
Gateway to Abstract Mathematics. Edwin A. Maxwell. 11.95 (ISBN 0-521-05701-9). Cambridge U Pr.
Gateway to Heaven. Sheldon Vanauken. 336p. 1981. pap. 2.95 (ISBN 0-553-14648-3). Bantam.
Gateway to Heaven: A Novel. Sheldon Vaunauken. LC 79-3600. (Illus.). 304p. 1980. 9.95 (ISBN 0-06-068822-X). Har-Row.
Gateway to Judaism, 2 vols. Albert M. Shulman. LC 69-15777. 1971. Set. 30.00 o.p. (ISBN 0-498-06896-X, Yoseloff). A S Barnes.
Gateway to Life. Ernest Holmes. Ed. by Willis Kinnear. 96p. (Orig.). 1974. pap. 4.50 (ISBN 0-911336-59-1). Sci of Mind.
Gateway to the Heart. Debbie Camp. (Orig.). 1980. pap. 1.95 (ISBN 0-532-23208-9). Manor Bks.
Gateway to the Middle Ages: France & Britain. Eleanor S. Duckett. 1961. pap. 1.75 o.p. (ISBN 0-472-06050-3, 50, AA). U of Mich Pr.
Gateway to Wisdom: Taoist & Buddhist Contemplative & Healing Yogas Adapted for Western Students of the Way. John Blofeld. LC 79-67685. (Illus.). 1980. pap. 6.95 (ISBN 0-394-73878-0). Shambhala Pubns.
Gateways into Light. Flower A. Newhouse. LC 74-75517. 160p. 1974. pap. 6.50 (ISBN 0-910378-09-6). Christward.
Gathas of Zarathustra: A Reconstruction of the Text. M. C. Monna. 1978. pap. text ed. 34.25x (ISBN 90-6203-582-5). Humanities.
Gather, Darkness! Fritz Lieber. (Science Fiction Ser.). 1980. lib. bdg. 14.95 (ISBN 0-8398-2639-7). Gregg.
Gathered in Love. Paulist Press Team of Canadian & American Catechists. (Come to the Father Program Ser.). (Audio-vis. aids avail). (gr. 3). 1973. text ed. 2.75 child-parent bk. (ISBN 0-8091-9096-6); text ed. 2.75 spanish ed. (ISBN 0-8091-9105-9); cCD tchr. manual 7.95 (ISBN 0-8091-9098-2); parochial tchr. man. 7.95 (ISBN 0-8091-9097-4). Paulist Pr.
Gathered Sketches from the Early History of New Hampshire & Vermont: Containing Vivid & Interesting Account of a Great Variety of the Adventures of Our Forefathers, & of Other Incidents of Olden Time. Francis Chase. LC 75-7092. (Indian Captivities Ser.: Vol. 68). 1976. Repr. of 1856 ed. lib. bdg. 44.00 (ISBN 0-8240-1692-0). Garland Pub.
Gatherers. Daniel Jacobson. LC 76-9810. (Indians of North America Ser.). (Illus.). 96p. (gr. 7 up). 1977. PLB 5.90 (ISBN 0-531-00326-4). Watts.
Gathering. Virginia Hamilton. LC 80-12512. (Justice Cycle Ser.: Vol. 3). 192p. (gr. 7 up). 1980. 8.95 (ISBN 0-688-80269-9); PLB 8.59 (ISBN 0-688-84269-0). Greenwillow.
Gathering. David Manuel. LC 80-53855. 250p. (Orig.). 1980. pap. 4.95 (ISBN 0-932260-07-1). Rock Harbor.
Gathering & Writing the News: A Reporter's Complete Guide to Techniques & Ethics of News Reporting. John P. Jones. LC 75-33642. 304p. 1976. 16.95 (ISBN 0-88229-243-9); pap. 8.95x (ISBN 0-88229-583-7). Nelson-Hall.
Gathering at Greystone, No. 2. Louisa Bronte. 256p. (Orig.). 1976. pap. 1.50 o.p. (ISBN 0-345-24766-3). Ballantine.
Gathering Firewood: New Poems & Selected. David Ray. LC 74-5968. (Wesleyan Poetry Program: Vol. 75). 88p. 1974. pap. 4.95 (ISBN 0-8195-1075-0, Pub. by Wesleyan U Pr). Columbia U Pr.

Gathering of Animals: An Unconventional History of the New York Zoological Society. William Bridges. LC 74-1793. (Illus.). 480p. (YA) 1974. 12.50 o.s.i. (ISBN 0-06-010472-4, HarpT). Har-Row.

Gathering of Reason. John Sallis. LC 80-14485. (Continental Thought Ser.: Vol. 2). xii, 196p. 1981. 14.00x (ISBN 0-8214-0439-3). Ohio U Pr.

Gathering of the Ungifted: Toward a Dialogue on Christian Identity. John Meagher. 168p. 1972. 5.95 (ISBN 0-8164-1034-8). Crossroad NY.

Gathering of Wolves. Michael Hammonds. 1976. pap. 1.25 o.p. (ISBN 0-685-72564-2, LB393, Leisure Bks). Nordon Pubns.

Gathering Storm in the Churches. Jeffrey K. Hadden. LC 68-22613. 1969. 5.95 o.p. (ISBN 0-385-03326-5). Doubleday.

Gathering What the Great Nature Provided: Food Traditions of the Gitksan. People of 'Ksan. LC 79-3871. (Illus.). 128p. 1980. 17.95 (ISBN 0-295-95710-7). U of Wash Pr.

Gatitos. Jan Pfloong. Tr. by Rene Sanchez. (Illus.). 24p. (Span.). (ps-3). 1977. PLB 5.92 o.p. (ISBN 0-307-68847-X, Golden Pr). Western Pub.

Gato y Perro (Cat & Dog) (ps-3). pap. 1.50 (ISBN 0-590-05416-3, Schol Pap). Schol Bk Serv.

Gatt Activities in Nineteen Seventy-Nine & Conclusion of the Tokyo Round Multilateral Trade Negotiations. 87p. 1980. pap. 7.00 (ISBN 0-686-64630-4, G 124, GATT). Unipub.

GATT Legal System & World Trade Diplomacy. Robert E. Hudec. LC 75-23972. 416p. 1975. text ed. 28.95 o.p. (ISBN 0-275-01320-0). Praeger.

GATT Plus-A Proposal for Trade Reform: With the Text of the General Agreement. Atlantic Council of the United States. LC 76-126. (Special Studies). 208p. 1976. text ed. 24.95 (ISBN 0-275-23010-4). Praeger.

Gattungen der Pyrenomyceten, Sphaeropsideen und Melanconieen, Pt. 1. F. Petrak & H. Sydow. (Feddes Repertorium: Beiheft 27). 551p. (Ger.). 1979. Repr. of 1926 ed. lib. bdg. 97.20x (ISBN 3-87429-071-9). Lubrecht & Cramer.

Gaucho Martin Fierro. Jose Hernandez. Tr. by Frank G. Carrino et al. LC 74-12185. (Unesco Collection of Representative Works, Latin American Ser.). 192p. (Eng. & Span.). 1974. Repr. of 1872 ed. 20.00x (ISBN 0-8201-1133-3). Schol Facsimiles.

Gaudi. David Mower. (Illus.). 1977. 15.95 (ISBN 0-8467-0248-7, Pub. by Two Continents); pap. 9.95 (ISBN 0-8467-0247-9). Hippocrene Bks.

Gaudi: The Architecture in Barcelona, Antoni. Sterner. Date not set. pap. 3.50 (ISBN 0-8120-2293-9). Barron. Postponed.

Gaudy Night. Dorothy L. Sayers. 1968. pap. 2.50 (ISBN 0-380-01207-3, 42457). Avon.

Gauge Fields. N. P. Konoplyova & V. N. Popov. 300p. 1981. 60.00 (ISBN 3-7186-0045-5). Harwood Academic.

Gauge Fields, & Cartan-Enresmann Connections: Part a. Robert Hermann. LC 75-12199. (Interdisciplinary Mathematics: No. 10). 500p. 1975. 35.00 (ISBN 0-915692-09-0). Math Sci Pr.

Gauge Fields: Introduction to Quantumm Theory. L. D. Faddeev & A. A Slavnov. 1981. 28.95 (ISBN 0-8053-9016-2). A-W.

Gauge Theories of Weak Interactions. J. C. Taylor. LC 75-9092. (Cambridge Monographs on Mathematical Physics). (Illus.). 200p. 1976. 47.95 (ISBN 0-521-20896-3); pap. 12.95x (ISBN 0-521-29518-1). Cambridge U Pr.

Gauguin. Robert Goldwater. (Library of Great Painters Ser). (Illus.). 1957. 35.00 (ISBN 0-8109-0137-4). Abrams.

Gaullist Phenomenon: The Gaullist Movement in the Fifth Republic. Jean Charlot. (Studies in Political Science). 1971. text ed. 32.50x (ISBN 0-04-320069-9). Allen Unwin.

Gauntlet. Michael Butler & Dennis Shryack. 1977. pap. 1.95 o.s.i. (ISBN 0-446-89470-2). Warner Bks.

Gauvain in Old French Literature. Keith Busby. (Degre Second Ser.: No. 2). 425p. 1980. pap. text ed. 48.50x (ISBN 90-6203-831-X). Humanities.

Gavin. Bradley Biggs. (Illus.). 1980. 17.50 (ISBN 0-208-01748-8, Archon). Shoe String.

Gawain-Poet. A. C. Spearing. LC 72-112476. 1971. 42.00 (ISBN 0-521-07851-2); pap. 10.95x (ISBN 0-521-29119-4). Cambridge U Pr.

Gay American History: Lesbians & Gay Men in the U.S.A., a Documentary. Jonathan Katz. LC 76-2039. (Illus.). 1976. 19.95 o.p. (ISBN 0-690-01164-4, TY.C-T); pap. 9.95 (ISBN 0-690-01165-2, TYC-T). T Y Crowell.

Gay Astrologer. John Savage. 1981. 7.95. Ashley Bks.

Gay Cliche. Christopher Xenakis. pap. 4.95 (ISBN 0-933656-06-8). Trinity Pub Hse.

Gay Love Signs. Michael Jay. (Orig.). 1980. pap. 6.95 (ISBN 0-345-28774-6). Ballantine.

Gay Phoenix. Michael Innes. LC 79-28521. 1977. 6.95 (ISBN 0-396-07442-1). Dodd.

Gay Plays: First Collection. Ed. by William H. Hoffman. 1978. pap. 3.95 (ISBN 0-380-42788-5, 77263, Bard). Avon.

Gay Print & Coloring Book. Ray Verbsky & Don Williams. 1980. 7.95. Green Hill.

Gay Theology. Kent Philpott. 1977. pap. 2.50 o.p. (ISBN 0-88270-241-6). Logos.

Gayan, Vadan, Nirtan. Hazrat I. Khan. LC 80-52801. (The Collected Works of Hazrat Inayat Khan Ser.). 304p. 1980. 10.00 (ISBN 0-930872-21-5, 1006H); pap. 5.95 (ISBN 0-930872-16-9, 1006P). Sufi Order Pubns.

Gaylord's Badge. Richard Meade. 1976. pap. 1.25 o.p. (ISBN 0-505-50974-1, BT50974). Tower Bks.

Gays & Film. 2nd ed. Richard Dyer et al. (BFI Ser.). (Illus., Orig.). 1981. pap. 6.25 (ISBN 0-85170-106-X). NY Zoetrope.

Gays & Film. Richard Dyer et al. (BFI Ser.). 1977. pap. 5.00 o.p. (ISBN 0-85170-065-9). NY Zoetrope.

Gaywyck. Vincent Virga. 384p. 1980. 2.95 (ISBN 0-380-75820-2, 75820). Avon.

Gaza Intercept. E. Howard Hunt. LC 80-6171. 256p. 1981. 12.95 (ISBN 0-8128-2804-6). Stein & Day.

Gaze & Mutual Gaze. M. Argyle & M. Cook. LC 75-12134. (Illus.). 160p. 1976. 27.50 (ISBN 0-521-20865-3). Cambridge U Pr.

Gazelle & the Hunter. Foley. (Folk Tales Ser.). PLB 7.35 (ISBN 0-516-06480-0). Childrens.

Gazeteer of the Hyborian World of Conan. Lee Falconer. LC 80-19671. 160p. 1980. Repr. of 1977 ed. lib. bdg. 10.95x (ISBN 0-89370-031-2). Borgo Pr.

Gazetteer of the Persian Gulf, 'Oman & Central Arabia, 2 vols. John G. Lorimer. 1970. Repr. of 1914 ed. 650.00x o.p. (ISBN 0-7165-0993-8, Pub. by Irish Academic Pr Ireland). Biblio Dist.

Gazetter of Mesolithics Sites in England & Wales. John Wymer. 1980. pap. 27.60 (ISBN 0-900312-49-1, Pub. by GEO Abstracts England). State Mutual Bk.

Gbandes: A People of the Liberian Hinterland. Benjamin G. Dennis. LC 72-88580. 1973. 20.95 (ISBN 0-911012-50-8). Nelson-Hall.

G'Dee. Helen Fine. (Illus.). (gr. 4-5). 1958. text ed. 4.50 (ISBN 0-8074-0137-4, 123702). UAHC.

G'Dee's Book of Holiday Fun. Helen Fine. (Illus.). (gr. 4-6). 1961. pap. 3.00 o.p. (ISBN 0-685-20737-4, 121701). UAHC.

Gear Design Simplified. 3rd ed. Franklin D. Jones & Henry Ryffell. (Illus.). 1961. text ed. 17.00 (ISBN 0-8311-1022-8). Indus Pr.

Gear Designs & Production. Trautschold. 6.50 o.p. (ISBN 0-686-00165-6). Columbia Graphs.

Gear Metrology. C. A. Scoles & R. Kirk. 166p. 1969. 15.00x o.p. (ISBN 0-8464-0443-5). Beekman Pubs.

Gearing Down. Sam Moses & Peter Sanders. LC 74-34463. (Venture Ser, a Reading Incentive Program). (Illus.). 80p. (gr. 7-12,RL 4.5-6.5). 1975. In Packs Of 5. text ed. 23.25 ea. pack (ISBN 0-8172-0218-8). Follett.

Gears. rev. ed. Harlan Wade. LC 78-21312. (Book About Ser.). (Illus.). (gr. k-3). 1979. PLB 7.30 (ISBN 0-8172-1535-2). Raintree Pubs.

Gecekondu: Rural Migration & Urbanization in Turkey. K. H. Karpat. LC 75-12159. (Illus.). 1976. 39.95 (ISBN 0-521-20954-4). Cambridge U Pr.

GED Mathematics Test Preparation Guide: High School Equivalency Examination. Deborah Moran et al. (Cliffs Test Preparation Ser.). 182p. (gr. 10 up). 1981. pap. 3.95 (ISBN 0-8220-2016-5). Cliffs.

GED Reading Skills Test Preparation Guide: High School Equivalency Examination. William A. Covino & Margaret Coda-Messerle. (Cliffs Test Preparation Ser.). 105p. (Orig.). (gr. 10 up). 1981. pap. 2.95 (ISBN 0-8220-2014-9). Cliffs.

GED Writing Skills Test Preparation Guide: High School Equivalency Examination. Loraine J. Weber & Willam A. Covino. (Cliffs Test Preparation Ser.). 151p. (Orig.). (gr. 10 up). 1981. pap. 3.95 (ISBN 0-8220-2015-7). Cliffs.

Geek. Craig Nova. LC 74-15884. (Illus.). 208p. 1975. 8.95 o.p. (ISBN 0-06-013209-4, HarpT). Har-Row.

Geeta. Tr. by Shri P. Swami. (Orig.). 1965. pap. 4.95 (ISBN 0-571-06157-5, Pub. by Faber & Faber). Merrimack Bk Serv.

Gefieder des Huhnes: Abbild des Tieres und seiner Haltung. C. H. Burckhardt et al. (Tierhaltung: No. 9). (Illus.). 67p. (Ger.). 1979. pap. 16.00 (ISBN 3-7643-1137-1). Birkhauser.

Gegenreformation in den Furstentumern Liegnitz-Brirg-Wohlau, Ihre Vorgeschichte und Ihre Staatsrechtlichen Grundlagen. Dorothee Von Velsen. (Ger). Repr. of 1931 ed. 29.00 (ISBN 0-384-64224-1); pap. 23.00 (ISBN 0-685-02156-4). Johnson Repr.

Gegenseitige Beeinflussung und Temperatur-Wirkung bei tropischen und subtropischen Pflanzen: Bericht ueber neue experimentelle Untersuchungen an Nutzpflanzen und Arten der spontanen Vegetation. Ruediger Knapp. (Illus.). 1967. pap. 6.00 (ISBN 3-7682-0576-2). Lubrecht & Cramer.

Geheime Mission. Hans-Jost Konig. LC 75-2362. 1975. pap. 4.25 (ISBN 0-88436-181-0). EMC.

Gehenna. Conrad Aiken. 1978. 14.50 o.p. (ISBN 0-685-86329-8). Porter.

Gehoert, Geschrieben, Gelernt! M. E. Mountjoy. 1973. pap. text ed. 2.95x o.p. (ISBN 0-435-38602-6). Heinemann Ed.

Geisha Diary. Ken Noyle. (YA) 1976. 7.95 o.p. (ISBN 0-399-11795-4, Dist. by Putnam). Berkley Pub.

Geisha Story: With Doll & Flower Arrangements. Billie T. Chandler. LC 63-8717. (Illus.). 1963. brocade 5.50 o.p. (ISBN 0-8048-0205-X). C E Tuttle.

Gel Chromatography. T. Kremmer & L. Boross. LC 77-24994. 1980. 57.00 (ISBN 0-471-99548-7, Pub. by Wiley-Interscience). Wiley.

Gel Electrophoresis: A Practical Approach. 1980. write for info. Info Retrieval.

Gelignite. William Marshall. 1978. pap. 1.75 o.p. (ISBN 0-445-04289-3). Popular Lib.

Gelignite. William L. Marshall. LC 77-1402. 1977. 6.95 o.p. (ISBN 0-03-016906-2). HR&W.

Gem, a General Econometric Matrix Program. L. J. Slater. LC 76-16920. (Applied Economics, Occasional Papers Ser.: No. 46). (Illus.). 1976. pap. 11.95x (ISBN 0-521-29114-3). Cambridge U Pr.

Gem Kingdom. Paul Desautels. 1971. 25.00 (ISBN 0-394-46533-4); pap. 7.95 (ISBN 0-394-73373-8). Random.

Gem of the Wanderer. Bob Maddux. 1979. 2.95 (ISBN 0-89728-009-1). Omega Pubns OR.

Gemini. Julia Parker. (Pocket Guide to Astrology Ser.). (Orig.). 1980. pap. write for info. (ISBN 0-671-25559-2, Fireside). S&S.

Gemini. Paula Taylor. (Sun Signs Ser.). (Illus.). (gr. 4-12). 1978. PLB 5.95 (ISBN 0-685-86765-X); pap. 2.95 (ISBN 0-89812-073-X). Creative Ed.

Gemmological Instruments. P. G. Read. 1978. 29.95 (ISBN 0-408-00316-2). Butterworths.

Gemmologists' Compendium. 6th rev. ed. Robert Webster. Ed. by Allan Jobbins. 256p. 1980. 14.95 (ISBN 0-442-23885-1). Van Nos Reinhold.

Gems & Jewelry in Color. Ove Dragsted. LC 75-2391. (Illus.). 240p. 1975. 10.95 (ISBN 0-02-533500-6, 53350). Macmillan.

Gems & Jewels: Uncut Stones & Objets d'Art. Henri-Jean Schubnel. (Illus.). (gr. 8 up). 1972. PLB 8.46 o.p. (ISBN 0-307-64313-1, Golden Pr). Western Pub.

Gems & Minerals. Susan Harris. (gr. 2-4). 1980. PLB 6.45 (ISBN 0-531-03241-8). Watts.

Gems & Minerals of America: A Guide to Rock Collecting. Jay E. Ransom. LC 72-9147. (Illus.). 730p. (YA) 1975. 22.50 o.p. (ISBN 0-06-013512-3, HarpT); lib. bdg. 21.79 o.p. (ISBN 0-06-013513-1); (ISBN 0-685-50280-5). Har-Row.

Gems, Minerals, Crystals & Ores. Richard M. Pearl. 1977. pap. 4.95 o.p. (ISBN 0-307-44385-X, Golden Pr). Western Pub.

Gems of Geometry. William T. Stokes. 1978. pap. text ed. 5.95 (ISBN 0-914534-02-5). Stokes.

Gems of Truth. Myrtle S. Jessup. 64p. 1981. 5.00 (ISBN 0-682-49688-X). Exposition.

Gemstones & Minerals: A Guide for the Amateur Collector & Cutter. Paul Villiard. (Illus.). 1979. pap. 6.95 (ISBN 0-87691-282-X). Winchester Pr.

Gemstones of the Bible. 2nd ed. Percy H. Perkins, Jr. (Illus.). 150p. 1980. pap. write for info. (ISBN 0-9603090-1-2). P H Perkins.

Gemstones of the World. Walter Schumann. Ed. by Anthony T. Tennissen. LC 77-79503. (Illus.). 1977. 17.95 (ISBN 0-8069-3088-8); lib. bdg. 16.79 (ISBN 0-8069-3089-6). Sterling.

Gendai Chato Taikan: A General View of Contemporary Tea Ceremony & Ceramic Ware, 6 vols. Ed. by Tetsuzo Tanikawa & Shufunotomo Editorial Staff. (Illus., Japanese.). 1979. Set. 200.00 (ISBN 0-8048-1343-4, Pub. by Shufunotomo Co Ltd Japan). Vol. 1, 152p. Vol. 2, 164p. Vol. 3, 186p. Vol. 4, 186p. Vol. 5, 186p. Vol. 6, 200p. C E Tuttle.

Gender Advertisements. Erving Goffman. (Illus., Orig.). 1979. pap. 5.95 (ISBN 0-06-090633-2, CN 633, CN). Har-Row.

Gender, an Ethnomethodological Approach. Suzanne Kessler & Wendy McKenna. LC 77-15957. 1978. 24.95 (ISBN 0-471-58445-2, Pub. by Wiley-Interscience). Wiley.

Gender & Class Consciousness. Pauline Hunt. LC 79-22107. 1980. text ed. 36.50x (ISBN 0-8419-0580-0). Holmes & Meier.

Gender & Literary Voice. Ed. by Janet Todd. (Women & Literature: Vol. 1). 250p. 1981. text ed. 24.50x (ISBN 0-8419-0656-4); pap. text ed. 12.50x (ISBN 0-8419-0657-2). Holmes & Meier.

Gene Expression, Vol. 3: Plasmids & Phages. Benjamin Lewin. LC 73-14382. 1977. 41.95 (ISBN 0-471-53170-7, Pub. by Wiley-Interscience); pap. 18.95 (ISBN 0-471-02715-4). Wiley.

Gene Function: E. coli & Its Heritable Elements. Robert E. Glass. 450p. 1980. 60.00x (Pub. by Croom Helm England). State Mutual Bk.

Gene Function: Proceedings. FEBS Meeting, 12th, Dresden, 1978. Ed. by S. Rosenthal et al. (Federation of European Biochemical Society Ser.: Vol. 51). (Illus.). 1979. 60.00 (ISBN 0-08-023175-6). Pergamon.

Gene Interactions in Development. L. I. Korochkin. (Monographs on Theoretical & Applied Genetics: Vol. 4). (Illus.). 340p. 1980. 59.80 (ISBN 0-387-10112-8). Springer-Verlag.

Gene Structure & Expression. Ed. by D. H. Dean et al. (Ohio State University Biosciences Colloquia: No. 6). (Illus.). 369p. 1980. 22.50 (ISBN 0-8142-0321-3). Ohio St U Pr.

Gene Wolfe's Book of Days. Gene Wolfe. LC 80-1074. (Science Fiction Ser.). 192p. 1981. 9.95 (ISBN 0-385-15991-9). Doubleday.

Genealogia. Giovanni Boccaccio. LC 75-27843. (Renaissance & the Gods Ser.: Vol. 2). (Illus.). 1976. Repr. of 1494 ed. lib. bdg. 73.00 (ISBN 0-8240-2051-0). Garland Pub.

Genealogical Demography. Ed. by B. Dyke & W. T. Morrill. LC 80-17683. (Population & Social Structure: Advances in Historical Demography Ser.). 1980. 19.50 (ISBN 0-12-226380-4). Acad Pr.

Genealogical Historical Guide to Latin America. Ed. by Lyman DePlatt. LC 78-75146. (Genealogy & Local History Ser.: Vol. 4). 1978. 30.00 (ISBN 0-8103-1389-8). Gale.

Genealogical Periodical Annual Index, Nineteen Seventy Eight, Vol.17. Catherine M. Mayhew. Ed. by Laird C. Towle. xii, 167p. 1980. 12.50 (ISBN 0-917890-23-X). Heritage Bk.

Genealogical Research for Czech & Slovak Americans. Ed. by Olga K. Miller. LC 78-13086. (Genealogy & Local History Ser.: Vol. 2). (Illus.). 1978. 30.00 (ISBN 0-8103-1404-5). Gale.

Genealogical Research in Maryland: A Guide. 2nd ed. Ed. by Mary K. Meyer. LC 72-91197. 1976. 6.00 (ISBN 0-938420-05-4). Md Hist.

Genealogie. Giovanni Boccaccio. LC 75-27847. (Renaissance & the Gods Ser.: Vol. 5). (Illus., Fr.). 1976. Repr. of 1531 ed. lib. bdg. 73.00 (ISBN 0-8240-2054-5). Garland Pub.

Genealogy. Boy Scouts of America. LC 19-600. (Illus.). 32p. (gr. 6-12). 1973. pap. 0.70x (ISBN 0-8395-3383-7, 3383). BSA.

Genealogy for Children. Pamela G. Wubben. 65p. (ps-7). 1981. pap. 7.95 (ISBN 0-935442-03-0). One Percent.

Genealogy: How to Find Your Roots. Henry Gilfond. (Impact Bks.). (Illus.). (gr. 7 up). 1978. PLB 6.90 s&l (ISBN 0-531-01455-X). Watts.

Genealogy My Way. LaVonne J. Bouressa. LC 77-95808. 1977. 8.95 (ISBN 0-686-12309-3). Genealogy Res.

Genealogy Records of the First Arizona Volunteer Infantry Regiment. Lonnie E. Underhill. LC 80-24778. (Illus.). iv, 124p. 1980. pap. 18.50 (ISBN 0-933234-02-3). Roan Horse.

Genera of Flowering Plants: Angiospermae, 2 vols. J. Hutchinson. 1200p. 1980. Repr. of 1964 ed. Set. lib. bdg. 129.60x (ISBN 0-686-28721-5); Vol. I. lib. bdg. 64.80x (ISBN 3-87429-177-4); Vol. 2. lib. bdg. 64.80x (ISBN 3-87429-178-2). Lubrecht & Cramer.

Genera of Flowering Plants: Dicotyledones. John Hutchinson. 1964-67. Vol. 1. 43.50x o.p. (ISBN 0-19-854351-4); Vol. 2. 41.00x o.p. (ISBN 0-19-854361-1). Oxford U Pr.

Genera of Fungi Sporulating in Pure Culture. 2nd ed. J. A. Von Arx. (Illus.). 1974. 50.00 o.p. (ISBN 3-7682-0693-9). Lubrecht & Cramer.

Genera of Ichneumonidae, Pt. 1, Ephialtinae To Agriotypinae. Henry Townes. (Memoirs Ser: No. 11). (Illus.). 300p. 1969. 20.00 (ISBN 0-686-00418-3). Am Entom Inst.

Genera of Ichneumonidae, Pt. 2, Gelinae. Henry Townes. (Memoirs Ser: No. 12). (Illus.). 537p. 1970. 35.00 (ISBN 0-686-00419-1). Am Entom Inst.

Genera of Ichneumonidae, Pt. 3, Lycorininae To Porizontinae. Henry Townes. (Memoirs Ser: No. 13). (Illus.). 307p. 1970. 20.00 (ISBN 0-686-00420-5). Am Entom Inst.

Genera of Ichneumonidae, Pt. 4, Cremastinae To Diplazontinae. Henry Townes. (Memoirs Ser: No. 17). (Illus.). 372p. 1971. 28.00 (ISBN 0-686-01268-2). Am Entom Inst.

Genera of Soil Microfungi. O. Verona & P. Gambogi. Tr. by W. J. Byford. 320p. 1981. pap. text ed. 25.00x (ISBN 3-7682-1259-9). Lubrecht & Cramer.

Generacion de 1898 ante Espana: Antologia de literatura de temas nacionales y universales. Ed. by Sumner M. Greenfield. LC 80-80146. 400p. 1981. pap. 25.00 (ISBN 0-89295-013-7). Society Sp & Sp-Am.

General. Janet Charters. (Illus.). 1961. 7.95 (ISBN 0-7100-1173-3). Routledge & Kegan.

General Administration in the Nursing Home. 2nd, rev. ed. Wesley W. Rogers. LC 75-22325. 1976. 16.95 o.p. (ISBN 0-8436-0573-1); text ed. 11.95 o.p. (ISBN 0-685-50116-7). CBI Pub.

General Administration in the Nursing Home. 3rd ed. Wesley W. Rogers. LC 80-19106. 456p. 1980. text ed. 17.95 (ISBN 0-8436-0788-2). CBI Pub.

General Algebraic Ideas. Robert Hermann. (Interdisciplinary Mathematics Ser: No. 1). 205p. 1973. 10.00 (ISBN 0-915692-00-7). Math Sci Pr.

General & Comparative Physiology. 2nd ed. William S. Hoar. (Illus.). 896p. 1975. 24.95 (ISBN 0-13-350272-4); lab. companion 7.95 (ISBN 0-13-347724-X). P-H.

General & Inorganic Chemistry. 2nd ed. James G. Wilson & A. B. Newall. (Illus.). 1971. text ed. 19.95x (ISBN 0-521-07073-2). Cambridge U Pr.

General & Introductory View of Professor Kant's Principles. Friedrich A. Nitsch. Ed. by Rene Wellek. LC 75-11240. (British & Theologians of the 17th & 18th Centuries: Vol. 40). 1977. Repr. of 1796 ed. lib. bdg. 42.00 (ISBN 0-8240-1792-7). Garland Pub.

General & Rational Grammar: The Port-Royal Grammar. Antoine Arnauld & Claude Lancelot. Ed. by Jacques Rieux & Bernard E. Rollin. LC 74-84245. (Janua Linguarum, Series Minor: No. 208). 197p. 1975. pap. text ed. 34.10x (ISBN 90-2793-004-X). Mouton.

General & Social Systems. F. Kenneth Berrien. LC 68-29552. (Illus.). 1968. 15.00x (ISBN 0-8135-0585-2). Rutgers U Pr.

General Anesthesia, 2 vols. 4th ed. T. C. Gray & J. Nunn. Incl. Vol. 1. text ed. 94.95 (ISBN 0-407-00144-1); Vol. 2. text ed. 94.95 (ISBN 0-407-00145-X). LC 79-42889. (Illus.). 1979. Set. text ed. 189.00 (ISBN 0-407-00146-8). Butterworths.

General Anesthesia & the Central Nervous System. Leonard C. Jenkins. LC 74-81839. 554p. 1969. 22.50 o.p. (ISBN 0-88275-120-4). Krieger.

General Applied Statistics. 3rd ed. Fadil H. Zuwaylif. LC 78-67937. 1979. text ed. 15.95 (ISBN 0-201-08994-7). A-W.

General Architectural Drafting. William E. Wyatt. (gr. 10-12). 1976. text ed. 17.68 (ISBN 0-87002-072-2); student guide 3.00 (ISBN 0-87002-166-4); drafting masters 10.88 (ISBN 0-87002-189-3). Bennett IL.

General Assembly of the United Nations: A Study of Procedure & Practice. rev. ed. Sydney D. Bailey. LC 78-2810. (Carnegie Endowment for International Peace, United Nations Studies: No. 9). (Illus.). 1978. Repr. of 1964 ed. lib. bdg. 28.50x (ISBN 0-313-20336-9, BAGA). Greenwood.

General Bennet H. Young. Oscar A. Kinchen. 1981. 8.95 (ISBN 0-8158-0404-0). Chris Mass.

General Bibliographical Dictionary, 4 Vols. Friedrich A. Ebert. LC 68-19956. 1968. Repr. of 1837 ed. 130.00 (ISBN 0-8103-3304-X). Gale.

General Biology. 10th ed. George B. Noland. LC 78-27065. (Illus.). 1979. text ed. 19.95 (ISBN 0-8016-3673-6). Mosby.

General Biology Laboratory Manual. 2nd ed. Indiana University & Michael Charnego. 1978. 8.50 (ISBN 0-8403-2268-2). Kendall-Hunt.

General Botany. 5th ed. Harry J. Fuller & Donald D. Ritchie. (Illus.). 1967. pap. 4.95 (ISBN 0-06-460033-5, CO 33, COS). Har-Row.

General Botany. Wilhelm Nultsch. (Ger). 1971. text ed. 19.50 (ISBN 0-12-522850-3). Acad Pr.

General Charles G. (Chinese) Gordan's Khartoum Journal. Ed. by Lord Elton. LC 63-13658. (Illus.). 1963. 6.00 (ISBN 0-8149-0110-7). Vanguard.

General Chemistry. Ralph Becker & Wayne Wentworth. LC 72-5642. 1973. text ed. 19.50 o.p. (ISBN 0-395-16002-2, 3-03295); instructor's manual. pap. 1.50 o.p. (ISBN 0-395-16003-0, 3-03296); study guide 7.75 o.p. (ISBN 0-395-14516-3, 3-03297). HM.

General Chemistry. Ralph S. Becker & Wayne E. Wentworth. LC 79-87864. 1980. text ed. 21.95 (ISBN 0-395-25316-0); instrs'. manual 1.10 (ISBN 0-395-25317-9); study guide 8.50 (ISBN 0-395-25318-7). HM.

General Chemistry. R. A. Day, Jr. & Ronald C. Johnson. (Illus.). 592p. 1974. text ed. 20.95 (ISBN 0-13-349340-7). P-H.

General Chemistry. N. Glinka. Tr. by MIR Publishers. 710p. 1975. 18.00x o.p. (ISBN 0-8464-0446-X). Beekman Pubs.

General Chemistry. 6th ed. William H. Nebergall et al. 1980. text ed. 21.95x (ISBN 0-669-02218-7); instrs'. manual avail. (ISBN 0-669-02475-9); study guide 7.95 (ISBN 0-669-02474-0); basic lab. studies 8.95 (ISBN 0-669-02473-2); problems & solutions manual 6.95 (ISBN 0-669-02472-4). Heath.

General Chemistry. John B. Russell. (McGraw-Hill Series in Chemistry). (Illus.). 832p. 1980. text ed. 19.95 (ISBN 0-07-054310-0); instr's manual 5.95 (ISBN 0-07-054312-7); study guide 6.95 (ISBN 0-07-054313-5); study guide 5.95 (ISBN 0-07-054311-9); solutions manual 5.95 (ISBN 0-07-054314-3). McGraw.

General Chemistry. B. Richard Siebring & Mary E. Schaff. 864p. 1980. text ed. 21.95x (ISBN 0-534-00802-X); lab manual 11.95x (ISBN 0-534-00838-0); study guide 7.95x (ISBN 0-534-00839-9); solutions manual 5.95x (ISBN 0-534-00859-3). Wadsworth Pub.

General Chemistry. 2nd ed. Arthur L. Williams et al. LC 73-18784. 1974. text ed. 14.95 (ISBN 0-201-08743-X); instr. manual 2.50 (ISBN 0-201-08744-8). A-W.

General Chemistry Experiments. Jerry L. Mills & Roy E. Mitchell. (Illus.). 1979. lab manual 8.95 (ISBN 0-89582-012-9). Morton Pub.

General Chemistry Lab Text with Quantitative Analysis. Hutton. 1968. text ed. 10.95 (ISBN 0-675-09629-4). Merrill.

General Chemistry Laboratory Manual. Margaret E. Jackson et al. 1977. pap. text ed. 6.95 o.p. (ISBN 0-8403-1204-0). Kendall-Hunt.

General Chemistry: Principles & Structures. J. E. Brady & G. E. Humiston. 1975. 16.00 o.p. (ISBN 0-471-09530-3). Krieger.

General Chemistry: Principles & Structure. 2nd ed. James E. Brady & Gerard E. Humiston. LC 77-11045. 1978. text ed. 23.95 (ISBN 0-471-01910-0); write for info tchr's manual (ISBN 0-471-03666-8); wkbk. 6.50x (ISBN 0-471-03498-3). Wiley.

General Chemistry: Readings from Scientific American. Intro. by James B. Ifft & John E. Hearst. LC 73-13624. (Illus.). 1974. text ed. 19.00x o.p. (ISBN 0-7167-0886-8); pap. text ed. 8.75x o.p. (ISBN 0-7167-0885-X). W H Freeman.

General-Class Amateur Study Guide. Phil Anderson. LC 79-63865. 1979. pap. 6.50 (ISBN 0-672-21617-5). Sams.

General Climatology. 3rd ed. Howard J. Critchfield. (Illus.). 416p. 1974. ref. ed. 18.95 (ISBN 0-13-350264-3). P-H.

General Cohomology Theory & K. Theory. Peter J. Hilton. (London Mathematics Society Lecture Note Ser.: No. 1). 1970. text ed. 11.95 (ISBN 0-521-07976-4). Cambridge U Pr.

General, Comparative & Clinical Endocrinology of the Adrenal Cortex. Ed. by I. Chester-Jones & I. W. Henderson. Vol. 1, 1976. 63.50 (ISBN 0-12-171501-9); Vol. 2, 1978. 126.50 (ISBN 0-12-171502-7); Vol. 3, 1978. write for info. (ISBN 0-12-171503-5). Acad Pr.

General Demands Concerning the Late Covenent: Together with the Answers. LC 74-80156. (English Experience Ser.: No. 635). 1974. Repr. of 1638 ed. 6.00 (ISBN 90-221-0635-7). Walter J. Johnson.

General Drafting. 4th ed. Verne C. Fryklund & Frank R. Kepler. LC 78-81375. (Illus.). (gr. 9-10). 1969. text ed. 11.16 (ISBN 0-87345-095-7). McKnight.

General Ecology. 2nd ed. S. J. McNaughton & Larry L. Wolf. LC 78-23200. 702p. 1979. text ed. 17.95 (ISBN 0-03-019801-1, HoltC). HR&W.

General Economic History. Max Weber. (Social Science Classics Ser.). 1981. text ed. 19.95 (ISBN 0-87855-317-7); pap. text ed. 7.95 (ISBN 0-87855-690-7). Transaction Bks.

General Engineering Science in SI Units, 2 vols 2nd ed. G. W. Marr & R. C. Layton. 1971. Vol. 1. 11.25 (ISBN 0-08-015805-6); Vol. 2. 11.25 (ISBN 0-08-015807-2); Vol. 1. pap. 4.80 (ISBN 0-08-015804-8); Vol. 2. pap. 4.80 (ISBN 0-08-015806-4). Pergamon.

General Epistle of James. Randolph V. Tasker. (Tyndale Bible Commentaries). 1957. pap. 2.95 (ISBN 0-8028-1415-8). Eerdmans.

General Equilibrium Analysis: An Introduction to the Two Sector Model. J. C. Baldry. LC 80-82652. 256p. 1980. 29.95 (ISBN 0-470-27024-1, Pub. by Halsted Pr). Wiley.

General Equilibrium Analysis: An Introduction with Applications. David Simpson. LC 74-31814. 164p. 1975. text ed. 17.95 (ISBN 0-470-79209-4). Halsted Pr.

General Geology of the Western United States: A Laboratory Manual. rev. ed. Allen M. Bassett & Shannon O'Dunn. (Illus.). 176p. 1980. pap. text ed. 9.95x (ISBN 0-917962-67-2). Peek Pubns.

General George at Yorktown. Carole Charles. LC 75-33158. (Stories of the Revolution Ser.). (Illus.). (gr. 2-6). 1975. PLB 5.50 (ISBN 0-913778-23-0). Childs World.

General George B. McClellan, Shield of the Union. Warren W. Hassler, Jr. LC 74-9619. (Illus.). 350p. 1974. Repr. of 1957 ed. lib. bdg. 29.75x (ISBN 0-8371-7606-9, HAGG). Greenwood.

General George H. Thomas, the Indomitable Warrior. Wilbur Thomas. 1964. 25.00 o.p. (ISBN 0-682-42066-2, Lochinvar). Exposition.

General Guide to Abortion. R. Bruce Sloane & Diana F. Horvitz. LC 72-90556. 1973. 13.95 (ISBN 0-911012-30-3). Nelson-Hall.

General Guide to Paris. Raymond Denaes. 1978. pap. 9.95 (ISBN 0-933982-04-6, Pub by Editions L'indispensable). Bradt Ent.

General History of Music from the Earliest Times, 2 Vols. Thomas Busby. LC 68-21091. (Music Ser). 1968. Repr. of 1819 ed. 55.00 (ISBN 0-306-71063-3). Da Capo.

General History of the Robberies & Murders of the Most Notorious Pyrates. Charles Johnson. LC 71-170563. (Foundations of the Novel Ser.: Vol. 44). lib. bdg. 50.00 (ISBN 0-8240-0556-2). Garland Pub.

General Hospital Psychiatric Units - a National Survey. R. M. Glasscote & C. K. Kanno. pap. 1.50 o.p. (ISBN 0-685-24856-9, 154). Am Psychiatric.

General Index to Modern Musical Literature in the English Language: Including Periodicals for the Years 1915-1926. Eric Blom. LC 71-108736. (Music Ser). 1970. Repr. of 1927 ed. lib. bdg. 17.50 (ISBN 0-306-71898-7). Da Capo.

General Industrial Education. Los Angeles Unified School District. Ed. by Richard A. Vorndran. LC 77-73280. 552p. (gr. 7-9). 1978. text ed. 15.96 (ISBN 0-02-820350-X). Glencoe.

General-Industrial Machine Shop. Harold V. Johnson. 1979. text ed. 17.00 (ISBN 0-87002-293-8); student guide 2.96 (ISBN 0-87002-295-4); visual masters 13.40 (ISBN 0-87002-054-4). Bennett IL.

General Industry. John R. Lindbeck & Irving T. Lathrop. (Illus.). (gr. 7-9). 1977. 15.28 (ISBN 0-87002-185-0). student guide 4.64 (ISBN 0-87002-196-6). answer sheet free. Bennett IL.

General Insurance. 10th ed. David L. Bickelhaupt. 1979. text ed. 19.50x (ISBN 0-256-02150-3). Irwin.

General Integration & Measure. A. J. Weir. LC 73-91620. (Illus.). 344p. 1974. 35.50 (ISBN 0-521-20407-0); pap. 13.95 (ISBN 0-521-29715-X). Cambridge U Pr.

General Ledger: COM-PET Edition. Ed. by Lon Poole. 200p. 1980. pap. cancelled (ISBN 0-931988-44-6). Osborne-McGraw.

General Ledger-WANG. Lon Poole et al. 144p. (Orig.). 1979. pap. 20.00 (ISBN 0-931988-20-9). Osborne-McGraw.

General Lee. Paul B. Ricchiuti. (Uplook Ser.). 1978. pap. 0.75 (ISBN 0-8163-0198-0, 07038-3). Pacific Pr Pub Assn.

General Linguistics: An Introductory Survey. 3rd ed. R. H. Robins. (Longman Linguistics Library). (Illus.). 1980. text ed. 30.00 (ISBN 0-582-55363-6); pap. text ed. 14.95 (ISBN 0-582-55364-4). Longman.

General Math. Carolyn A. Maher et al. Ed. by Leo Gafney. 160p. 1980. pupil's ed. 4.80 (ISBN 0-07-039593-4, W); tchrs. ed. 5.20 (ISBN 0-07-039594-2). McGraw.

General Mathematics: Syllabus. 2nd ed. Al Gray & Clifford H. Matousek. 1972. pap. text ed. 5.75 (ISBN 0-89420-019-4, 350899); cassette recordings 102.55 (ISBN 0-89420-148-4, 350900). Natl Book.

General Metals. rev, 5th ed. John L. Feirer. (Industrial Education Ser.). (Illus.). 480p. (gr. 9-10). 1980. text ed. 17.32 (ISBN 0-07-020380-6, W); study guide 4.20 (ISBN 0-07-020382-2); tchrs. resource guide 3.96 (ISBN 0-07-020381-4). McGraw.

General Methodology Manual for Occupational Manuals & Projects in Marketing Series. E. L. Dorr. 1969. 6.50 o.p. (ISBN 0-07-017647-7, G); general methodology manual 3.95 o.p. (ISBN 0-07-017648-5). McGraw.

General Microbiology: The Students' Textbook. Peter Hunter. LC 76-28532. (Illus.). 500p. 1977. pap. text ed. 12.50 (ISBN 0-8016-2313-8). Mosby.

General Motors X Cars Tune-up & Repair. (Orig.). (gr. 9-12). 1981. pap. 6.95 (ISBN 0-8227-5058-9). Petersen Pub.

General Music Methods. Thomas A. Regelski. LC 80-5561. (Illus.). 448p. 1981. text ed. 12.95 (ISBN 0-02-872070-9). Schirmer Bks.

General Oceanography: An Introduction. 2nd ed. Gunther Dietrich et al. LC 80-12919. 1980. 50.00 (ISBN 0-471-02102-4, Pub. by Wiley-Interscience). Wiley.

General, Organic & Biochemistry: A Brief Introduction. H. Stephen Stoker & Michael R. Slabaugh. 1980. text ed. 18.95x (ISBN 0-673-15091-7); study guide 7.95x (ISBN 0-673-15501-3). Scott F.

General, Organic, & Biological Chemistry: Chemistry for the Living System. M. Lynn James et al. 1980. text ed. 21.95 (ISBN 0-669-01329-3); lab. guide 8.95 (ISBN 0-669-01332-3); study guide 7.95 (ISBN 0-669-01331-5); instrs'. guide free (ISBN 0-669-01330-7). Heath.

General Organizational & Administrative Concepts for University Police. Swen C. Nielsen. 96p. 1971. 9.75 (ISBN 0-398-02164-3). C C Thomas.

General Parasitology. Thomas C. Cheng. 1973. text ed. 27.00 (ISBN 0-12-170750-4). Acad Pr.

General Part of the Criminal Law of Norway. Johannes Andenaes. Tr. by T. P. Ogle. (New York University Comparative Criminal Law Project, Pubns: No. 3). 1965. 22.50x (ISBN 0-8377-0202-X). Rothman.

General Pathology. Ivan Damjanov. (Medical Outline Ser.). 1976. spiral bdg. 12.00 o.p. (ISBN 0-87488-628-7). Med Exam.

General Pathology: A Programmed Text. Thomas H. Kent. 1975. pap. 16.95 (ISBN 0-316-48920-4). Little.

General Patterns of Invertebrate Development. Gary J. Brusca. (Illus.). 134p. 1975. pap. 7.15x (ISBN 0-916422-03-8). Mad River.

General Physics. Dudley Williams & John Spangler. Date not set. text ed. price not set (ISBN 0-442-26155-1). D Van Nostrand.

General Physics Demonstration Manual. Olan E. Kruse. 1973. Repr. pap. 4.50x wkbk. (ISBN 0-934786-06-2). G Davis.

General Physics Laboratory Manual. 3rd ed. Richard L. Childers & Edwin R. Jones. 1978. pap. text ed. 4.50 o.p. (ISBN 0-8403-0034-4). Kendall-Hunt.

General Physics: Mechanics & Molecular Physics. L. D. Landau et al. 1967. 21.00 (ISBN 0-08-009106-7). Pergamon.

General Physics with Bioscience Essays. Jerry B. Marion. LC 78-4487. 1979. text ed. 23.95x (ISBN 0-471-56911-9); tchrs. manual avail. (ISBN 0-471-03672-2); study guide avail. (ISBN 0-471-03673-0). Wiley.

General Physics Workbook: Physics Problems & How to Solve Them. Foster Strong. (Illus.). 1972. wkbk. 10.95x (ISBN 0-7167-0339-4). W H Freeman.

General Physiological Processes. Irving L. Schwartz. 225p. 1973. pap. 9.50 (ISBN 0-686-65355-6). Krieger.

General Pitt-Rivers. M. W. Thompson. 1977. pap. text ed. 6.50x (ISBN 0-239-00162-1). Humanities.

General Plastics: Projects & Procedures. rev. ed. Raymond Cherry. (Illus.). (gr. 10-12). 1967. text ed. 14.64 (ISBN 0-87345-162-7). McKnight.

General Principles & Breast & Hernia. C. Rob et al. (Operative Surgery Ser.). 1977. 67.95 (ISBN 0-407-00610-9). Butterworths.

General Principles of Criminal Law. 2nd ed. Jerome Hall. 1960. 17.00 (ISBN 0-672-80035-7, Bobbs-Merrill Law). Michie.

General Principles of Quantum Mechanics. W. Pauli. 212p. 1980. pap. 17.20 (ISBN 0-387-09842-9). Springer-Verlag.

General Problem of Rolling Contact. A. L. Browne. Ed. by N. T. Tsai. (AMD: Vol. 40). 176p. 1980. 28.00 (G00173). ASME.

General Prologue to the Canterbury Tales. Geoffrey Chaucer. Ed. by J. Winny. (Selected Tales from Chaucer). 1965. text ed. 5.75x (ISBN 0-521-04629-7). Cambridge U Pr.

General Psychological Theory. Sigmund Freud. 1963. pap. 2.95 (ISBN 0-02-076350-6, Collier). Macmillan.

General Psychology. S. Sunder Das. 1964. 6.75x (ISBN 0-210-22575-0). Asia.

General Psychology. 4th ed. Douglas Fryer et al. (Orig.). 1954. pap. 3.95 (ISBN 0-06-460024-6, CO 24, COS). Har-Row.

General Psychopathology. C. Scharfetter. Tr. by Helen Marshall from Ger. LC 79-52853. (Illus.). 1980. 54.50 (ISBN 0-521-22812-3); pap. 15.95x (ISBN 0-521-29655-2). Cambridge U Pr.

General Recordkeeping, Bk. 1. 8th ed. Harry Huffman & Jeffrey R. Stewart. (Illus.). 224p. (gr. 9-11). 1980. 13.96 (ISBN 0-07-031040-8, G); tchrs. ed. 7.50 (ISBN 0-07-031043-2); activity guide & working papers 4.72 (ISBN 0-07-031041-6); tchrs. ed. for activity guide & working papers 5.25 (ISBN 0-07-031043-2). McGraw.

General Relativity. Ed. by S. W. Hawking & W. Israel. LC 78-62112. (Illus.). 900p. 1980. pap. 28.95 (ISBN 0-521-29928-4). Cambridge U Pr.

General Relativity: An Einstein Centenary Survey. Ed. by S. W. Hawking & W. Israel. LC 78-62712. (Illus.). 1979. 89.50 (ISBN 0-521-22285-0). Cambridge U Pr.

General Relativity & Gravitation: One Hundred Years After the Birth of Albert Einstein, 2 vols. Ed. by A. Held. (Illus.). 1980. Set. 99.50 (ISBN 0-686-58609-3, Plenum Pr); 57.50 ea. Vol. 1 (ISBN 0-306-40265-3). Vol. 2 (ISBN 0-306-40266-1). Plenum Pub.

General Relativity & Gravitation: Proceedings. International Conference, 7th, Tel Aviv, June 23-28, 1974. Ed. by G. Shaviv. LC 75-33824. 1976. 54.95 (ISBN 0-470-77939-X). Halsted Pr.

General Relativity from A to B. Robert Geroch. (Illus.). 238p. 1981. pap. 4.95 (ISBN 0-226-28864-1). U of Chicago Pr.

General Relativity from A to B. Robert Geroch. pap. 4.95 (ISBN 0-226-28864-1). U of Chicago Pr.

General Relativity: Papers in Honour of J. L. Synge. Ed. by L. O'Raifeartaigh. (Illus.). 287p. 1972. 29.00x o.p. (ISBN 0-19-851126-4). Oxford U Pr.

General Report: Second Tripartite Technical Meeting for the Clothing Industry, Geneva, 1980. International Labour Office. v, 154p. (Orig.). 1980. pap. 11.40 (ISBN 92-2-102431-8). Intl Labour Office.

General Rhetoric. Jacques Dubois et al. Tr. by Paul B. Burrell & Edgar M. Slotkin. LC 80-24495. (Illus.). 288p. 1981. text ed. 18.95x (ISBN 0-8018-2326-9). Johns Hopkins.

General Science. Boy Scouts of America. LC 19-600. (Illus.). 48p. (gr. 6-12). 1972. pap. 0.70x (ISBN 0-8395-3332-2, 3332). BSA.

General Science Index: June 1979-May 1980. (Sold on service basis). 1980. write for info. Wilson.

General Selection from the Works of Sigmund Freud. Sigmund Freud. LC 57-11436. 1957. pap. 2.95 (ISBN 0-385-09325-X, A115, Anch). Doubleday.

General Semantics: A Theory of Meaning Analyzed. T. C. Pollock & J. G. Spaulding. (Monographs: No. 3). 3.00x (ISBN 0-910780-03-X). Inst Gen Semantics.

General Semantics & Contemporary Thomism. Margaret Gorman. LC 62-9136. 1962. pap. 2.95x (ISBN 0-8032-5075-4, BB 146, Bison). U of Nebr Pr.

General Semantics & the Social Sciences. William J. Williams. LC 71-155970. 1972. 8.50 o.p. (ISBN 0-8022-2055-X). Philos Lib.

General Semantics Bulletin: Official Annual Journal of the Institute of General Semantics. Alfred Korzybski. Ed. by Robert Pula. 20.00 (ISBN 0-910780-00-5). Inst Gen Semantics.

General Semantics Monographs No. 4: Scientific Epistemologic Backgrounds of General Semantics. M. Swanson. 1959. 5.00x (ISBN 0-910780-04-8). Inst Gen Semantics.

General Semantics Seminar Nineteen Thirty Seven. 2nd ed. Alfred Korzybski. 1964. pap. 5.00x (ISBN 0-910780-02-1). Inst Gen Semantics.

General Shop Bench Woodworking. rev. ed. Verne C. Fryklund & Armand J. LaBerge. (Illus.). (gr. 9-10). 1955. pap. 5.80 (ISBN 0-87345-001-9). McKnight.

General Shop Metalwork. rev. ed. Alva W. Dragoo. (gr. 8-9). 1964. pap. text ed. 5.00 (ISBN 0-87345-109-0). McKnight.

General Shop Woodworking. rev. ed. Verne C. Fryklund & Armand J. LaBerge. (gr. 9-10). 1972. text ed. 12.60 (ISBN 0-87345-031-0). McKnight.

General Social Survey, 1976. National Opinion Research Center. 1977. codebk. 12.00 (ISBN 0-89138-158-9). ICPSR.

General Social Surveys, 1972-1980: Cumulative Codebook. James A. Davis & Tom W. Smith. 1980. 8.00 (ISBN 0-932132-25-1). NORC.

General Social Surveys, 1972-1980: Cumulative Codebook. James A. Davis et al. 1980. pap. 8.00 (ISBN 0-932132-25-1). NORC.

General Statistics. 3rd ed. Audrey Haber & Richard P. Runyon. LC 76-23985. 1977. text ed. 16.95 (ISBN 0-201-02729-1). A-W.

General Statutes of North Carolina, Annotated with 1979 Cum. Suppl, 17 vols. Michie Editorial Staff. Set. write for info. (ISBN 0-87215-132-8); write for info. 1979 suppl. & index (ISBN 0-87215-308-8); 1980 interim suppl. avail. (ISBN 0-87215-347-9). Michie.

General Store in Vermont: An Oral History. Jane Beck. 1980. pap. 3.50x (ISBN 0-934720-23-1). VT Hist Soc.

General Strike. R. A. Florey. 1981. 28.95 (ISBN 0-7145-3698-9). Riverrun NY.

General Strike of Eighteen Forty-Two. Mick Jenkins. (Illus.). 300p. 1980. text ed. 24.75x (ISBN 0-85315-488-0). Humanities.

General Strike 1926. Ed. by Jeffrey Skelley. 1976. text ed. 15.75x (ISBN 0-85315-337-X). Humanities.

General Studies: First Handbook for Technical Students. I. J. Finch. 1965. 15.00 (ISBN 0-08-011106-8); pap. 7.00 (ISBN 0-08-011105-X). Pergamon.

General Surgery Therapy Update Service. Ed. by Oliver H. Beahrs. (Illus.). 1979. 80.00 (ISBN 0-89289-300-1). HM Prof Med Div.

General Surgical Nursing. Jane E. DeLoach. (Nursing Outline Ser.). 1979. pap. 9.50 (ISBN 0-87488-393-8). Med Exam.

General Surgical Nursing Continuing Review. Kathryn N. Donovan. LC 80-81906. 1980. pap. 9.75 (ISBN 0-87488-318-0). Med Exam.

General System Theory: Essays on Its Foundation & Development. rev. ed. Ludwig Von Bertalanffy. LC 68-25176. 1969. 9.95 o.s.i. (ISBN 0-8076-0452-6); pap. 5.95 (ISBN 0-8076-0453-4). Braziller.

General Systematic Bacteriology: History, Nomenclature, Groups of Bacteria. Robert E. Buchanan. 1970. Repr. of 1925 ed. 21.75 o.s.i. (ISBN 0-02-842140-X). Hafner.

General Systems Philosphy for the Social & Behavioral Sciences. John W. Sutherland. Ed. by Ervin Laszlo. (International Library of Systems Theory & Philosophy Ser). 1973. 7.95 (ISBN 0-8076-0724-X); pap. 6.95 (ISBN 0-8076-0725-8). Braziller.

General Systems Theory Applied to Nursing. Arlene M. Putt. 1978. text ed. 10.95 (ISBN 0-316-72300-2). Little.

General Systems Theory: Mathematical Foundations. M. D. Mesarovic & Y. Takahara. 1975. 37.50 (ISBN 0-12-491540-X); lib ed. 48.00 (ISBN 0-12-491541-8); microfiche 27.50 (ISBN 0-12-491542-6). Acad Pr.

General Textbook of Nursing. 19th ed. Evelyn Pearce. 1975. text ed. 19.95 o.p. (ISBN 0-571-04855-2, Pub. by Faber & Faber). Merrimack Bk Serv.

General Theory of Bureaucracy. E. Jaques. LC 76-7380. 1976. 24.95 (ISBN 0-470-15097-1). Halsted Pr.

General Theory of Relativity. Paul A. Dirac. LC 75-8690. 71p. 1975. 16.95 (ISBN 0-471-21575-9, Pub. by Wiley-Interscience). Wiley.

General Topology. J. L. Kelley. (Graduate Texts in Mathematics Ser.: Vol. 27). 310p. 1975. Repr. 19.80 (ISBN 0-387-90125-6). Springer-Verlag.

General Topology. M. G. Murdeshwar. LC 80-18434. 480p. 1981. 19.95 (ISBN 0-470-26916-2). Halsted Pr.

General Topology. Stephen Willard. LC 74-100890. 1970. text ed. 19.95 (ISBN 0-201-08707-3). A-W.

General View of the Origin & Nature of the Constitution & Government of the United States. Henry Baldwin. LC 72-118027. (American Constitutional & Legal History Ser). 1970. Repr. of 1837 ed. lib. bdg. 22.50 (ISBN 0-306-71944-4). Da Capo.

General Virology. 3rd ed. S. E. Luria et al. LC 77-9498. 1978. text ed. 27.95 (ISBN 0-471-55640-8). Wiley.

General Was a Lady. Margaret Troutt. 325p. 1980. 9.95 (ISBN 0-87981-139-0); pap. 5.95 (ISBN 0-87981-141-2). Holman.

General Washington's Headquarters: Seventeen Seventy-Five to Seventeen Eighty-Three. Dorothy T. Muir. LC 76-45927. (Illus.). 1977. 19.95 (ISBN 0-916624-06-4). TSU Pr.

General Welding & Cutting. Ed. by J. Bell et al. (Engineering Craftsmen: No. F10). (Illus.). 1976. spiral bdg. 26.00x (ISBN 0-85083-330-2). Intl Ideas.

General William King. Marion J. Smith. LC 79-67417. (Illus.). 182p. 1980. 11.95 (ISBN 0-89272-072-7). Down East.

General World Atlas, No. 9550. rev. ed. American Map Co. Inc. 1979. 0.95 (ISBN 0-8416-9550-4). Am Map.

General Zoology. 5th ed. Gordon Alexander. (Illus., Orig.). 1964. pap 4.50 (ISBN 0-06-460032-7, CO 32, COS). Har-Row.

General Zoology. 5th ed. Tracy I. Storer & Robert L. Usinger. (Illus.). 864p. 1972. text ed. 17.50 o.p. (ISBN 0-07-061776-7). McGraw.

General Zoology Laboratory Guide. 3rd ed. James C. Underhill et al (Et Al). 1978. pap. 6.95 spiral bdg. (ISBN 0-8087-2108-9). Burgess.

General Zoology Laboratory Guide: Shortversion. 8th ed. Ed. by J. E. Wodsedalek. Charles F. Lytle. 237p. 1981. write for info. wire coil. Wm C Brown.

Generalised Functions. R. F. Hoskins. (Mathematics & Its Applications Ser.). 1980. pap. 43.95 (ISBN 0-470-26608-2). Halsted Pr.

Generalizations in Historical Writing. Ed. by A. V. Riasanovsky. LC 63-7860. 1964. 9.00x o.p. (ISBN 0-8122-7386-9). U of Pa Pr.

Generalized Clifford Parallelism. J. A. Tyrrell & J. G. Semple. LC 74-134625. (Tracts in Mathematics Ser.: No. 61). 1971. 23.95 (ISBN 0-521-08042-8). Cambridge U Pr.

Generalized Inverse of Matrices & Its Applications. C. R. Rao & Sujit K. Mitra. LC 74-158528. (Ser. in Probability & Statistics Section). 1971. 29.95 (ISBN 0-471-70821-6, Pub. by Wiley-Interscience). Wiley.

Generalized Networks. Richard Saeks. LC 76-162146. 1972. 34.50x (ISBN 0-03-085195-5); pap. text ed. 16.50x (ISBN 0-89197-767-8). Irvington.

Generalized Reciprocal Method of Seismic Refraction Prospecting. Derecke Palmer. Ed. by Kenneth B. Burke. (Illus.). 112p. 1980. write for info. (ISBN 0-931830-14-1). Soc Exploration.

Generalizing from the Experimental Housing Allowance Program: An Assessment of Site Characteristics. Jeanne E. Goederf. (Institute Paper). 67p. 1978. pap. 4.50 (ISBN 0-87766-224-X, 22900). Urban Inst.

Generally Speaking: How Children Learn Language. Ronald Macaulay. (Orig.). 1980. pap. text ed. 6.95 (ISBN 0-88377-162-4). Newbury Hse.

Generation Apart. J. T. Richards. (Whitmarsh Chronicles Ser.: Vol. 1). 416p. (Orig.). 1981. pap. 2.75 (ISBN 0-515-05242-6). Jove Pubns.

Generation Gap. Burl Hogins & Gerald Bryant. 1970. pap. text ed. 3.95x (ISBN 0-02-474970-2, 47497). Macmillan.

Generation in Motion: Popular Music & Culture in the 1960's. David Pichaske. LC 78-63033. (Illus.). 1979. 15.00 (ISBN 0-02-871860-7); pap. 5.95 (ISBN 0-02-871850-X). Schirmer Bks.

Generation of a Journey. Jacob Sloan. 12.00 (ISBN 0-89253-675-6); flexible cloth 4.80 (ISBN 0-89253-676-4). Ind-US Inc.

Generation of Basaltic Magma. H. S. Yoder, Jr. LC 76-29672. 1976. text ed. 8.25 o.p. (ISBN 0-685-75493-6); pap. text ed. 6.25 (ISBN 0-309-02504-4). Natl Acad Pr.

Generation of Spanish Poets, Nineteen Twenty - Nineteen Thirty-Six. C. B. Morris. LC 69-11270. (Illus.). 1969. 48.00 (ISBN 0-521-07381-2); pap. 11.50x (ISBN 0-521-29481-9). Cambridge U Pr.

Generations. Ed. by Rhodri Jones. (Themes Ser.: Bk. 4). 1969. pap. text ed. 2.95x o.p. (ISBN 0-435-14483-9); tchr's ed. 1.50x o.p. (ISBN 0-435-14487-1). Heinemann Ed.

Generations. Neela Padmanabhan. Tr. by Ka N. Subramanyam from Tamil. (Orient Paperback Ser). 192p. 1972. pap. 2.50 (ISBN 0-88253-110-7). Ind-US Inc.

Generations & Politics: A Panel Study of Young Adults & Their Parents. M. Kent Jennings & Richard G. Niemi. LC 80-8555. (Illus.). 408p. 1981. 25.00x (ISBN 0-691-07626-X); pap. 6.95x (ISBN 0-691-02201-1). Princeton U Pr.

Generations Apart: Adult Hostility to Youth. Leon Sheleff. 352p. 1981. 18.95 (ISBN 0-07-056540-6, P&RB). McGraw.

Generations in Clay: Pueblo Pottery of the American Southwest. Alfred E. Dittert, Jr. & Fred Plog. LC 80-81831. (Illus.). 168p. 1980. 27.50 (ISBN 0-87358-271-3); pap. 14.95 (ISBN 0-87358-270-5). Northland.

Generations Learning Together. Donald Griggs & Patricia Griggs. (Griggs Educational Resources Ser.). 1980. pap. 6.95 (ISBN 0-687-14050-1). Abingdon.

Generative Grammar of Afar. Loren Bliese. (SIL Publications on Linguistics Ser.). 315p. 1980. write for info. (ISBN 0-88312-083-6); price not set microfiche (ISBN 0-88312-483-1). Summer Inst Ling.

Generative Grammatical Studies in the Japanese Language. S. Y. Kuroda. Ed. by Jorge Hankamer. LC 78-66564. (Outstanding Dissertations in Linguistics Ser.). 1979. lib. bdg. 27.50 (ISBN 0-8240-9680-0). Garland Pub.

Generative Interpretation of Dialect: A Study of Modern Greek Phonology. B. Newton. LC 72-187080. (Studies in Linguistics: No. 8). (Illus.). 240p. 1973. 35.00 (ISBN 0-521-08497-0); pap. 11.95x (ISBN 0-521-29062-7). Cambridge U Pr.

Generative Phonology. F. Dell. LC 79-14139. (Illus.). 1980. 42.50 (ISBN 0-521-22484-5); pap. 9.95x (ISBN 0-521-29519-X). Cambridge U Pr.

Generative Phonology. Sanford A. Schane. (Foundations of Modern Linguistics Ser.). 176p. 1973. ref. ed. 10.95 (ISBN 0-13-350967-2); pap. text ed. 7.95 (ISBN 0-13-350959-1); wkbk. 6.50 (ISBN 0-13-350942-7). P-H.

Generative Phonology: A Case Study from French. Nigel H. Love. (Linguisticae Investigationes Supplementa: No. 4). 300p. 1980. text ed. 34.25x (ISBN 90-272-3113-3). Humanities.

Generative Rhetoric, a Teaching Guide for English Composition. Leo H. Croteau. 300p. 1980. tchrs.' ed. 25.00 (ISBN 0-9602582-0-5). Neechee Assoc.

Generators & Relations for Discrete Groups. 3rd rev. ed. H. S. Coxeter & W. O. Moser. LC 72-79063. (Ergebnisse der Mathematik und Ihrer Grenzgebiete: Vol. 14). (Illus.). 174p. 1972. 17.80 o.p. (ISBN 0-387-05837-0). Springer-Verlag.

Generic Classification of the Orsillinae of the World (Hemiptera-Heteroptera: Lygaeidae) P. D. Ashlock. (U. C. Publ. in Entomology: Vol. 48). 1967. pap. 6.00x (ISBN 0-520-09120-5). U of Cal Pr.

Generic Demands of Greek Literature. Frederic Will. 1976. pap. text ed. 14.25x (ISBN 90-6203-447-0). Humanities.

Generic Names of Moths of the World. Vol. II. Noctuoidea: Arctiidae, Ctenuchidae, Dioptidae, Lymantriidae, Notodontidae, Thaumetopoeidae & Thyretidae. A. Watson et al. Ed. by I. W. Nye. (Illus.). xiv, 228p. 1980. 58.00x (ISBN 0-565-00811-0). Sabbot-Natural Hist Bks.

Generic Revision & Skeletal Morphology of Some Cerioporid Cyclostomes, No. 291. O. B. Nye. (Bulletins of American Paleontology: Vol. 71). pap. 25.00 (ISBN 0-87710-229-5). Paleo Res.

Generous Cow. Bijou Le Tord. LC 76-14464. (Illus.). 40p. (ps-2). 1977. 5.95 o.s.i. (ISBN 0-8193-0852-8, Four Winds); PLB 5.41 o.s.i. (ISBN 0-8193-0853-6). Schol Bk Serv.

Generous Earl. Catherine Coulter. (Orig.). 1981. pap. price not set (ISBN 0-451-09899-4, Sig). NAL.

Generous Rivals or Love Triumphant. LC 72-170531. (Foundations of the Novel Ser.: Vol. 20). lib. bdg. 50.00 (ISBN 0-8240-0532-5). Garland Pub.

Generous Vine Grower. G. A. Pottebaum. (Little People's Paperbacks Ser.). 1979. pap. 0.99 (ISBN 0-8164-2252-4). Crossroad NY.

Genes & the Mind: Inheritance of Mental Illness. Ming T. Tsuang & Randall VanderMey. (Illus.). 158p. 1980. text ed. 12.95x (ISBN 0-19-261268-9). Oxford U Pr.

Genes, Cells, & Behavior: A View of Biology Fifty Years Later. Ed. by Norman H. Horowitz & Edward Hutchings, Jr. LC 80-18744. (Biology Ser.). (Illus.). 1980. text ed. 12.95x (ISBN 0-7167-1217-2). W H Freeman.

Genes, Chromosomes, & Neoplasia. M. D. Anderson Symposia on Fundamental Cancer Research, 33rd. Ed. by Frances E. Arrighi et al. 550p. 1981. 49.50 (ISBN 0-89004-532-1). Raven.

Genes, Environment & Behavior: An Interactionist Approach. Jack R. Vale. (Illus.). 470p. 1980. text ed. 21.50 scp (ISBN 0-06-046758-4, HarpC). Har-Row.

Genesee Diary: Report from a Trappist Monastery. Henri J. Nouwen. 192p. 1981. pap. 3.95 (ISBN 0-385-17446-2, Im). Doubleday.

Genesee Diary: Report from a Trappist Monastery. Henri J. M. Nouwen. LC 75-38169. 192p. 1976. 8.95 (ISBN 0-385-11368-4). Doubleday.

Genesis. John Calvin. (Geneva Commentaries Ser.). 1979. 17.95 (ISBN 0-85151-093-0). Banner of Truth.

Genesis, Vol. II. C. C. Crawford. (Bible Study Textbook Ser.). 1968. 15.00 (ISBN 0-89900-003-7). College Pr Pub.

Genesis. M. Dods. (Handbooks for Bible Classes Ser.). 224p. Repr. of 1956 ed. 3.50 (ISBN 0-567-08101-X). Attic Pr.

Genesis. Ed. by Irving L. Jensen. (Bible Self-Study Ser.). 1967. pap. 2.25 (ISBN 0-8024-1001-4). Moody.

Genesis. John Skinner. (International Critical Commentary Ser.). 640p. 1930. text ed. 23.00x (ISBN 0-567-05001-7). Attic Pr.

Genesis. John T. Willis. LC 78-52455. (Living Word Commentary Ser.: Vol. 2). 1979. 13.95 (ISBN 0-8344-0098-7). Sweet.

Genesis A. Alger N. Doane. LC 77-77437. 1978. 40.00 (ISBN 0-299-07430-7). U of Wis Pr.

Genesis: A Devotional Commentary in One Volume. Donald G. Barnhouse. 564p. 1973. 12.95 (ISBN 0-310-20470-4). Zondervan.

Genesis: A Study Guide Commentary. Leon J. Wood. 160p. 1975. pap. 3.50 (ISBN 0-310-34743-2). Zondervan.

Genesis Accounts of Creation. Claus Westermann. Ed. by Norman E. Wagner. LC 64-11858. (Facet Ser.). 1964. pap. 1.35 o.p. (ISBN 0-8006-3007-6, 1-3007). Fortress.

Genesis & Evolutionary Development of Life. A. I. Oparin. 1969. 22.75 (ISBN 0-12-527446-7). Acad Pr.

Genesis & Exodus: A Portrait of the Benson Family. David Williams. 1979. 27.00 (ISBN 0-241-10190-5, Pub. by Hamish Hamilton England). David & Charles.

Genesis & Treatment of Psychologic Disorders in the Elderly: Aging, Vol. 2. Ed. by S. Gershon & A. Raskin. LC 75-14573. 288p. 1975. 27.00 (ISBN 0-89004-004-4). Raven.

Genesis-Deuteronomy. Matthew Henry. (Commentary on the Whole Bible Ser: Vol. 1). 12.00 (ISBN 0-8007-0197-6). Revell.

Genesis-Exodus: An Access Guide. William T. Kelley. 128p. (Orig.). 1981. pap. 4.95 (ISBN 0-8215-5927-3). Sadlier.

Genesis, Exodus, Leviticus, Numbers. Foster R. McCurley. LC 78-14670. (Proclamation Commentaries: the Old Testament Witness for Preaching). 128p. 1979. pap. 3.95 (ISBN 0-8006-0593-4, 1-593). Fortress.

Genesis: Fifteen Lessons, Vol. 1. Bernice C. Jordan. (Footsteps of Faith Ser.). (gr. 3-9). 1960. pap. text ed. 1.95 (ISBN 0-86508-027-5); figures 7.95 (ISBN 0-86508-028-3). BCM Inc.

Genesis in Space & Time. Francis A. Schaeffer. LC 72-78406. 144p. 1972. pap. 3.50 (ISBN 0-87784-636-7). Inter-Varsity.

Genesis of a Music. 2nd ed. Harry Partch. LC 73-4333. (Music Reprint Ser.). 1974. lib. bdg. 29.50 (ISBN 0-306-71597-X); pap. 9.50 (ISBN 0-306-80106-X). Da Capo.

Genesis of a Painting: Picasso's Guernica. Rudolf Arnheim. (Illus.). 148p. 1981. 30.00x (ISBN 0-520-00037-4, CAL 485); pap. text ed. 10.95 (ISBN 0-520-04266-2, 485). U of Cal Pr.

Genesis of a Revolution. Ed. & tr. by Stanley Munro. (Writing in Asia Ser.). 1978. pap. text ed. 5.95x (ISBN 0-686-58245-4, 00206). Heinemann Ed.

Genesis of British Egyptology, 1549-1906. John D. Wortham. LC 78-160509. (Illus.). 1971. 9.95x o.p. (ISBN 0-8061-0981-5). U of Okla Pr.

Genesis of Hand Preference. Minnie Giesecke. LC 78-72795. Repr. of 1936 ed. 18.00 (ISBN 0-686-63637-6). AMS Pr.

Genesis of Language: The First Michigan Colloquium, 1979. Derek Bickerton et al. Ed. by Kenneth C. Hill. 159p. 1979. 15.50 (ISBN 0-89720-024-1); pap. 12.50 (ISBN 0-89720-025-X). Karoma.

Genesis of New Weapons: Decision Making for Military R&D. Ed. by Franklin A. Long & Judith Reppy. LC 80-12243. 1980. 25.00 (ISBN 0-08-025973-1). Pergamon.

Genesis of Noto: An Eighteenth-Century Sicilian City. Stephen Tobriner. 1980. 40.00x (ISBN 0-520-03526-7). U of Cal Pr.

Genesis of Structures in African Narrative: Dahomean Narratives, Vol. 2. G. M. Shreve & E. O. Arewa. (Studies in African Semiotics Ser.). 1981. 30.00 (ISBN 0-914970-01-1). Conch Mag.

Genesis of the Classical Conditioned Response. I. Martin & A. B. Levey. 164p. 1968. 25.00 (ISBN 0-08-013360-6). Pergamon.

Genesis of the Professional Officers' Corps. G. Teitler. LC 77-23307. (Sage Series on Armed Forces & Society: Vol. 11). 1977. 18.00x (ISBN 0-8039-0841-5). Sage.

Genesis One Through Eleven: Studies in Structure & Theme. Patrick D. Miller, Jr. (JSOT Supplement Ser.: No. 8). 50p. 1978. pap. text ed. 4.95x (ISBN 0-905774-07-8, Pub. by JSOT Pr England). Eisenbrauns.

Genesis: Quinze Lecciones, Tomo 1. Bernice C. Jordan. (Pasos De Fe Ser.). (Span.). pap. text ed. 2.25 (ISBN 0-86508-401-7); figuras 7.95 (ISBN 0-86508-402-5). BCM Inc.

Genesis Rock. Edwin Corley. 1981. pap. 2.75 (ISBN 0-440-12877-3). Dell.

Genesis: The Origins of Man & the Universe. John Gribbin. 1981. 13.95 (ISBN 0-440-02832-9). Delacorte.

Genesis to Deuteronomy: Notes on the Pentateuch, 6 vols. in 1. C. H. Mackintosh. LC 72-75082. 928p. 1972. 15.95 (ISBN 0-87213-617-5). Loizeaux.

Genessee Queen. Winifred Madison. LC 77-72634. (gr. 7up). 1977. 6.95 o.p. (ISBN 0-440-02809-4). Delacorte.

Genet Mission. Harry Ammon. (Essays in American History Ser.). 208p. 1973. 6.95x (ISBN 0-393-05475-6); pap. text ed. 3.95x (ISBN 0-393-09420-0). Norton.

Genetic Analysis of Traits Related to Grain Characteristics & Quality in Two Crosses of Rice. (IRRI Research Paper Ser.: No. 35). 14p. 1979. pap. 5.00 (R075, IRRI). Unipub.

Genetic & Anthropological Studies of Olympic Athletes. Ed. by Alfonso L. De Garay et al. 1974. 24.50 (ISBN 0-12-208650-3). Acad Pr.

Genetic & Environmental Hearing Loss: Syndromic & Nonsyndromic. Ed. by L. Stefan Levin & Connie Knight. (Birth Defects: Oringinal Article Ser.: Vol. XVI, No. 7). 100p. 1980. write for info. (ISBN 0-8451-1040-3). A R Liss.

Genetic & Sociological Aspects of Rice Breeding in India. (IRRI Research Paper Ser.: No. 10). 31p. 1977. pap. 5.00 (R050, IRRI). Unipub.

Genetic Aspects Anaphylactoid Reactions. Ed. by P. Dukor et al. (Par Pseudo-Allergic Reactions. Involvement of Drugs & Chemicals Ser.: Vol. 1). (Illus.). 250p. 1980. 78.00 (ISBN 3-8055-0537-X). S Karger.

Genetic Basis of Evolutionary Change. R. C. Lewontin. (Biological Ser.: Vol. 25). 336p. 1974. 20.00 (ISBN 0-231-03392-3); pap. 8.00x (ISBN 0-231-08318-1). Columbia U Pr.

Genetic Control of Natural Resistance to Infection & Malignancy. Ed. by Emil Skamene. (Perspectives in Immunology Ser.). 1980. 33.00 (ISBN 0-12-647680-2). Acad Pr.

Genetic Counseling. Ed. by Herbert Lubs & Felix de la Cruz. LC 76-52601. 1977. 37.50 (ISBN 0-89004-150-4). Raven.

Genetic Counseling: Fact, Values & Norms. Ed. by Alexander M. Capron et al. LC 79-1736. (Alan R. Liss Ser.: Vol. 15, No. 2). 1979. write for info. (ISBN 0-8451-1025-X). March of Dimes.

Genetic Counseling in Relation to Mental Retardation. J. M. Berg. 1971. pap. 6.25 (ISBN 0-08-016315-7). Pergamon.

Genetic Determinism & Children. Ed. by Ethel Tobach & Betty Rosoff. (Genes & Gender Ser.: No. 3). 176p. (Orig.). 1980. pap. text ed. 7.95 (ISBN 0-87752-221-9). Gordian.

Genetic Diseases Among Ashkenazi Jews. Ed. by Richard M. Goodman & Arno G. Motulsky. LC 77-90594. 1979. text ed. 39.00 (ISBN 0-89004-262-4). Raven.

Genetic Diseases & Developmental Disabilities: Aspects of Detection & Prevention. Ed. by Tamah L. Sadick & Siegfried M. Pueschal. (AAAS Selected Symposium: No. 33). 1979. lib. bdg. 16.00x (ISBN 0-89158-367-X). Westview.

Genetic Diseases in Pregnancy: Maternal Effects & Fetal Outcome. Ed. by Joseph D. Schulman & Joe L. Simpson. 1981. write for info. (ISBN 0-12-630940-X). Acad Pr.

Genetic Effects on Aging: Proceedings. Conference Held at Jackson Laboratory, Bar Harbor, Maine, Sept. 1976. Ed. by David E. Harrison & Daniel Bergsma. LC 77-20249. (Birth Defects Original Article Ser.: Vol. 14, No. 1). 550p. 1978. 58.00x (ISBN 0-8451-1016-0). A R Liss.

Genetic Engineering of Osmoregulation: Impact of Plant Productivity for Food, Chemicals & Energy. Ed. by Donald W. Rains et al. (Basic Life Sciences Ser.: Vol. 14). 395p. 1980. 39.50 (ISBN 0-306-40454-0, Plenum Pr). Plenum Pub.

Genetic Engineering: Principles & Methods, Vol. 1. Ed. by Jane K. Setlow & Alexander Hollaender. 277p. 1979. 29.50 (ISBN 0-306-40154-1, Plenum Pr). Plenum Pub.

Genetic Engineering: Principles & Methods, Vol. 2. Ed. by Jane K. Setlow & Alexander Hollaender. 298p. 1980. 32.50 (ISBN 0-306-40447-8, Plenum Pr). Plenum Pub.

Genetic Engineering: Threat or Promise? Laurence E. Karp. LC 76-3497. (Illus.). 320p. 1976. 17.95 (ISBN 0-88229-261-7); pap. 8.95 (ISBN 0-88229-460-1). Nelson-Hall.

Genetic Fix: New Opportunities & Dangers for You, Your Child & the Nation. Amitai Etzioni. LC 73-7350. 224p. 1973. 7.95 o.s.i. (ISBN 0-02-536410-3). Macmillan.

Genetic Improvement of Crops: Emergent Techniques. Ed. by Irwin Rubenstein et al. 232p. 1980. 22.50x (ISBN 0-8166-0966-7). U of Minn Pr.

Genetic Improvement of Seed Proteins. Board on Agriculture & Renewable Resources, National Research Council. LC 76-17097. 1976. pap. 15.25 (ISBN 0-309-02421-8). Natl Acad Pr.

Genetic Interrelationships to Improved Rice Varieties in Asia. (IRRI Research Paper Ser.: No. 23). 34p. 1979. pap. 5.00 (R063, IRRI). Unipub.

Genetic Markers in Human Blood. Eloise R Giblett. (Illus.). 1969. 22.75 (ISBN 0-632-05290-2, Blackwell). Mosby.

Genetic Mechanisms: Proceedings, Vol. 21. Cold Spring Harbor Symposia on Quantitative Biology. LC 34-8174. (Illus.). 410p. 1957. 30.00 (ISBN 0-87969-020-8). Cold Spring Harbor.

Genetic, Metabolic & Developmental Aspects of Mental Retardation. Ed. by Robert F. Murray, Jr. et al. (Illus.). 366p. 1972. 23.50 (ISBN 0-398-02531-2). C C Thomas.

Genetic Organization, Vol. 1. Ed. by E. W. Caspari & A. W. Ravin. 1969. 56.00 (ISBN 0-12-163301-2); by subscription 56.00 (ISBN 0-12-163301-2). Acad Pr.

Genetic Origins of Tumor Cells. Ed. by F. J Cleton & J. W. Simons. (Developments in Oncology Ser.: Vol. 1). xv, 125p. 1980. lib. bdg. 26.30 (ISBN 90-247-2272-1, Pub. by Martinus Nijhoff). Kluwer Boston.

Genetic Recombination: Thinking About It in Phage & Fungi. Franklin W. Stahl. LC 79-13378. (Biology Ser.). (Illus.). 1979. text ed. 28.95x (ISBN 0-7167-1037-4). W H Freeman.

Genetic Relationship of the Ainu Language. James Patrie. (Oceanic Linguistics Special Publications Ser.: No. 17). 380p. (Orig.). 1981. pap. text ed. price not set (ISBN 0-8248-0724-3). U Pr of Hawaii.

Genetic Screening: Programs, Principles & Research. Division of Medical Sciences, National Research Council. LC 75-5790. xv, 388p. 1975. pap. 10.50 (ISBN 0-309-02403-X). Natl Acad Pr.

Genetic Variability. Christopher Wills. (Illus.). 350p. 1981. text ed. 45.00x (ISBN 0-19-857570-X). Oxford U Pr.

Genetic Variation in Hormone Systems, 2 vols. John G. Shire. 1979. Vol. 1, 208p. 54.95 (ISBN 0-8493-5283-5); Vol. 2, 192p. 49.95 (ISBN 0-8493-5284-3). CRC Pr.

Genetic Variation of Viruses, Vol. 354. Ed. by Peter Palese & Bernard Roizman. LC 80-25770. 501p. 1980. write for info. (ISBN 0-89766-097-8); pap. write for info. (ISBN 0-89766-098-6). NY Acad Sci.

Genetic Vulnerability of Major Crops. National Academy of Sciences Agricultural Board. 304p. 1972. pap. 10.50 o.p. (ISBN 0-309-02030-1). Natl Acad Pr.

Genetics. D. J. Cove. LC 75-160089. (Illus.). 1972. 35.50 (ISBN 0-521-08255-2); pap. text ed. 10.95x (ISBN 0-521-09663-4). Cambridge U Pr.

Genetics. Ursula Goodenough. LC 77-26245. 840p. 1978. text ed. 19.95 (ISBN 0-03-019716-3, HoltC). HR&W.

Genetics. 2nd ed. John B. Jenkins. LC 78-69608. (Illus.). 1979. text ed. 21.95 (ISBN 0-395-26502-9); inst. manual 0.65 (ISBN 0-395-26501-0). HM.

Genetics. 2nd ed. Robert C. King. (Illus.). 1965. 12.95x (ISBN 0-19-500932-0). Oxford U Pr.

Genetics: A Basic Guide. I. J. Pedder & E. G. Wynne. 183p. 1974. pap. text ed. 5.95x (ISBN 0-393-09267-4). Norton.

Genetics: A Survey of the Principles of Heredity. 5th ed. A. M. Winchester. LC 76-14001. (Illus.). 1977. text ed. 18.95 (ISBN 0-395-24557-5); inst. manual & solutions 1.75 (ISBN 0-395-24559-1); twenty transparencies 7.75 (ISBN 0-395-24560-5). HM.

Genetics & Counseling in Cardiovascular Diseases. James J. Nora & Audrey H. Nora. (Illus.). 240p. 1978. 21.75 (ISBN 0-398-03755-8). C C Thomas.

Genetics & Education. Arthur R. Jensen. LC 72-86636. 384p. 1973. 10.95 o.s.i. (ISBN 0-06-012192-0, HarpT). Har-Row.

Genetics & Heterogeneity of Common Gastrointestinal Disorders. Ed. by Jerome I. Rotter et al. 1980. 35.00 (ISBN 0-12-598760-9). Acad Pr.

Genetics & Probability. Earl L. Green. (Illus.). 1981. text ed. 29.50x (ISBN 0-19-520159-0). Oxford U Pr.

Genetics & Social Structure: Mathematical Structuralism in Population Genetics & Social Theory. Ed. by Paul A. Ballonoff. LC 73-20412. (Benchmark Papers in Genetics Ser). 520p. 1974. 40.50 (ISBN 0-12-786125-4). Acad Pr.

Genetics & Society. Ed. by J. Bresler. LC 72-2650. 1973. pap. text ed. 7.95 (ISBN 0-201-00600-6). A-W.

Genetics & the Origin of Species. 3rd ed. Theodosius Dobzhansky. 1951. pap. 7.50x (ISBN 0-231-08551-6). Columbia U Pr.

Genetics & the Quality of Life. Ed. by C. Birch & P. Albrecht. 1976. text ed. 32.00 (ISBN 0-08-018210-0); pap. text ed. 14.30 (ISBN 0-08-019861-9). Pergamon.

Genetics As a Tool in Microbiology. Ed. by S. W. Glover & D. A. Hopwood. (Society for General Microbiology Symposium: No. 31). (Illus.). 450p. Date not set. text ed. price not set (ISBN 0-521-23748-3). Cambridge U Pr.

Genetics, Evolution, & Man. W. F. Bodmer & L. L. Cavalli-Sforza. LC 75-33990. (Illus.). 1976. 23.95x (ISBN 0-7167-0573-7). W H Freeman.

Genetics, Evolution, Race, Radiation, Biology: Essays in Social Biology, Vol. 2. Ed. by Bruce Wallace. LC 79-167789. 1972. pap. text ed. 10.95x (ISBN 0-13-351155-3). P-H.

Genetics Explosion. Alvin Silverstein & Virginia B. Silverstein. LC 79-22651. (Illus.). 160p. (gr. 7 up). 1980. 8.95 (ISBN 0-590-07517-9, Four Winds). Schol Bk Serv.

Genetics for Dog Breeders. Frederick B. Hutt. LC 79-15169. (Illus.). 1979. text ed. 17.95x (ISBN 0-7167-1069-2). W H Freeman.

Genetics in Medicine. 3rd ed. James S. Thompson & Margaret W. Thompson. LC 78-64726. (Illus.). 396p. 1980. text ed. 16.00 (ISBN 0-7216-8857-8). Saunders.

Genetics: Its Concepts & Implications. Anna C. Pai & Helen Marcue-Roberts. (Illus.). 736p. 1981. text ed. 24.95 (ISBN 0-13-351007-7). P-H.

Genetics Laboratory Investigations. 7th rev. ed. Elton J. Gardner & Thomas R. Mertens. 1980. 7.95 (ISBN 0-8087-0786-8). Burgess.

Genetics Now: Ethical Issues in Genetic Research. Ed. by John J. Buckley, Jr. LC 78-57577. 1978. pap. text ed. 9.50 (ISBN 0-8191-0528-7). U Pr of Amer.

Genetics of Algae. Ralph A. Lewin. LC 75-27297. (Botanical Monographs: Vol 12). 1976. 40.00x (ISBN 0-520-03149-0). U of Cal Pr.

Genetics of Altruism. Scott A. Boorman & Paul R. Levitt. LC 79-52792. 1980. 29.50 (ISBN 0-12-115650-8). Acad Pr.

Genetics of Bacteria & Their Viruses: Studies in Basic Genetics & Molecular Biology. 2nd ed. W. Hayes. LC 69-16199. 925p. 1976. pap. text ed. 24.95 (ISBN 0-470-36474-2). Halsted Pr.

Genetics of Epilepsy: A Review. Ed. by M. E. Newmark. J. K. Penry. 1979. 16.00 (ISBN 0-89004-394-9). Raven.

Genetics of Flowering Plants. Verne Grant. LC 74-13555. (Illus.). 1975. 27.50x (ISBN 0-231-03694-9); pap. 12.50x (ISBN 0-231-08363-7). Columbia U Pr.

Genetics of Higher Plants: Applications of Cell Culture. R. S. Chaleff. (Development & Cell Biology Monographs: No. 9). 208p. Date not set. price not set (ISBN 0-521-22731-3). Cambridge U Pr.

Genetics of Host-Parasite Interaction. Peter R. Day. LC 73-17054. (Illus.). 1974. text ed. 23.95x (ISBN 0-7167-0844-2). W H Freeman.

Genetics of Human Cancer. Ed. by John J. Mulvihill et al. LC 75-44924. (Progress in Cancer Research & Therapy: Vol. 3). 1977. 28.00 (ISBN 0-89004-110-5). Raven.

Genetics of Human Populations. L. L. Cavalli-Sforza & Walter F. Bodmer. LC 79-120302. (Biology Ser.). (Illus.). 1978. pap. text ed. 21.95x (ISBN 0-7167-1018-8). W H Freeman.

Genetics of Industrial Microorganisms. Ed. by O. K. Sebek & A. I. Laskin. (Illus.). 1979. 12.00 (ISBN 0-914826-19-0). Am Soc Microbio.

Genetics of Livestock Improvement. 3rd ed. John F. Lasley. LC 77-22807. (Illus.). 1978. ref. ed. 22.95 (ISBN 0-13-351106-5). P-H.

Genetics of Locomotor Disorders. C. O. Carter & T. J. Fairbank. (Oxford Monographs on Medical Genetics). 230p. 1974. text ed. 18.95x o.p. (ISBN 0-19-264131-X). Oxford U Pr.

Genetics of Man. 2nd ed. Paul A. Moody. (Illus.). 525p. 1975. text ed. 11.95x o.p. (ISBN 0-393-09228-3); answer bk. avail. o.p. (ISBN 0-393-09221-6). Norton.

Genetics of Microbes. Brian W. Bainbridge. (Tertiary Level Biology Ser.). 204p. 1980. pap. 30.95x (ISBN 0-470-26995-2). Halsted Pr.

Genetics of the Evolutionary Process. Theodosius Dobzhansky. LC 72-127363. 1971. 22.50x (ISBN 0-231-02837-7); pap. 10.00x (ISBN 0-231-08306-8). Columbia U Pr.

Genetics of the Horse. William E. Jones & Ralph Bogart. (Illus.). 21.00 o.p. (ISBN 0-85131-226-8, Dist. by Sporting Book Center). J A Allen.

Genetics: Readings from Scientific American. Intro. by Cedric I. Davern. LC 80-25208. (Illus.). 1981. text ed. 17.95x (ISBN 0-7167-1200-8); pap. text ed. 8.95x (ISBN 0-7167-1201-6). W H Freeman.

Genetics, Structure & Function of Blood Cells: Proceedings of the 28th International Congress of Physiological Sciences, Budapest, 1980. S. R. Hollan et al. LC 80-41876. (Advances in Physiological Sciences: Vol. 6). (Illus.). 310p. 1981. 40.00 (ISBN 0-08-026818-8). Pergamon.

Geneva Crisis. Matti Golan. 288p. 1981. 11.95 (ISBN 0-89479-073-0). A & W Pubs.

Geneva of Erstwhile. Elsie C. Wheaton. 1981. 5.95 (ISBN 0-8062-1674-3). Carlton.

Genial Idiots: The American Saga As Seen by Our Humorists. Richard Curtis. LC 68-22815. (America in the Making Ser). (Illus.). (gr. 7 up). 1968. 3.95g o.s.i. (ISBN 0-02-725530-1, CCPr). Macmillan.

Genie in the Bottle: Unravelling the Myths About Wine. Roger Morris. (Illus.). 204p. 1981. 12.95 (ISBN 0-89104-213-X); pap. 5.95 (ISBN 0-89104-198-2). A & W Pubs.

Genitourinary Problems in Women. Jack R. Robertson. (Amer. Lec. in Gynecology & Obstetrics Ser.). (Illus.). 168p. 1978. 21.75 (ISBN 0-398-03668-3). C C Thomas.

Genitourinary Radiology Case Studies. Thomas H. Johnson. 1980. pap. 16.75 (ISBN 0-87488-090-4). Med Exam.

Genius. Theodore Dreiser. 463p. 1980. Repr. of 1917 ed. lib. bdg. 17.25x (ISBN 0-89968-206-5). Lightyear.

Genius Figure in Antiquity & the Middle Ages. Jane C. Nitzsche. LC 74-17206. 1975. 15.00x (ISBN 0-231-03852-6). Columbia U Pr.

Genius of American Politics, 1958. Daniel J. Boorstin. (Walgreen Foundation Lectures). 10.50 (ISBN 0-226-06490-5, Phoen). U of Chicago Pr.

Genius of British Painting. David Piper. (Illus.). 352p. 1975. 27.50 o.p. (ISBN 0-688-00313-3). Morrow.

Genius of Christianity. Francois R. De Chateaubriand. LC 75-25532. 1975. Repr. of 1856 ed. 35.00 (ISBN 0-86527-254-9). Fertig.

Genius of George Washington. Edmund S. Morgan. 1981. 12.95 (ISBN 0-393-01440-1). Norton.

Genius of Japanese Design. Sherman E. Lee. LC 79-66246. (Illus.). 1981. 39.50 (ISBN 0-87011-395-X). Kodansha.

Genius of John Ruskin: Selections from His Writings. Ed. by John D. Rosenberg. 1979. Repr. of 1963 ed. 27.50 (ISBN 0-7100-0354-4). Routledge & Kegan.

Genius of the Early English Theater: Abraham & Isaac, Second Shepherd's Play, Everyman, Doctor Faustus, Macbeth, Volpone, Samson Agonistes. Ed. by Sylvan Barnet et al. 1962. pap. 2.50 (ISBN 0-451-61889-0, ME1889, Ment). NAL.

Genius of the West. Louis Rongier. LC 76-93466. (Principles of Freedom Ser.). 222p. 1971. 10.00 o.p. (ISBN 0-8402-5001-0). Nash Pub.

Genius of the West. Louis Rougier. LC 76-93466. (Principles of Freedom). 1976. 10.00x o.p. (ISBN 0-916054-36-5). Green Hill.

GENMIX: A General Computer Program for Two-Dimensional Parabolic Flow. Ed. by Dudley B. Spalding. LC 77-7978. 1977. text ed. 66.00 (ISBN 0-08-021708-7). Pergamon.

Genoa-Carson Valley Book, 1981-82. Ed. by Michael Miluck. (Illus.). 96p. 1981. pap. 3.00 (ISBN 0-686-28841-6). Dragon Ent.

Genocide & National Suicide. Rainer C. Baum. 1981. 25.00x (ISBN 0-8476-6970-X). Rowman.

Genome Organization & Expression in Plants. Ed. by C. J. Leaver. (NATO Advanced Study Institutes Ser., Series A, Life Sciences: Vol. 29). 600p. 1980. 59.50 (ISBN 0-306-40340-4). Plenum Pub.

Genre Painting of Eastman Johnson: The Sources & Development of His Styles & Themes. Patricia Hills. LC 76-23627. (Outstanding Dissertations in the Fine Arts - American). (Illus.). 1977. Repr. of 1973 ed. lib. bdg. 48.00 (ISBN 0-8240-2697-7). Garland Pub.

Genres of the Irish Literary Revival. Ed. by Ronald Schleifer. 190p. 1980. 16.95 (ISBN 0-937664-53-7). Pilgrim Bks OK.

Genteel Gentile: Letters of Elizabeth Cumming, 1857 - 1858. Ed. by Ray R. Canning & Beverly Beeton. (Utah, The Mormons, & The West: No. 8). 1978. 12.50 (ISBN 0-87480-163-X, Tanner). U of Utah Pr.

Gentle Annie. MacKinlay Kantor. (Western Fiction Ser.). 1980. lib. bdg. 10.95 (ISBN 0-8398-2688-5). Gregg.

Gentle Architecture. Malcolm Wells. (Illus.). 192p. 1981. 22.50 (ISBN 0-07-069245-9, P&RB). McGraw.

Gentle Art of Making Enemies. James A. Whistler. 8.50 (ISBN 0-8446-3168-X). Peter Smith.

Gentle Ben. Walt Morey. 1976. pap. 1.75 (ISBN 0-380-00743-6, 48884, Camelot). Avon.

Gentle Birth Book: A Practical Guide to Leboyer Family-Centered Delivery. Nancy Berezin. 1981. pap. 2.95 (ISBN 0-671-41990-0). PB.

Gentle Breeze of Jesus. Mel Tari & Noni Tari. LC 78-64960. 1978. pap. 2.50 (ISBN 0-89221-056-7, 056-7). New Leaf.

Gentle Brother. White Eagle. 1968. 3.95 (ISBN 0-85487-002-4). De Vorss.

Gentle Desert: Exploring an Ecosystem. Laurence Pringle. LC 77-5875. (Illus.). (gr. 3-7). 1977. 7.95 (ISBN 0-02-775380-8, 77538). Macmillan.

Gentle Desperado. Max Brand. (Max Brand Popular Classics Ser.). 160p. (Orig.). 1981. pap. 6.95 (ISBN 0-88496-157-5). Capra Pr.

Gentle Gunman. Max Brand. 1976. pap. 1.75 (ISBN 0-446-94291-X). Warner Bks.

Gentle Jungle. Toni R. Helfer. LC 80-10275. (Illus.). 336p. 1980. 9.95 (ISBN 0-8425-1790-1). Brigham.

Gentle Like a Cyclone: Stories of Horses & Their Riders. Compiled by Phyllis R. Fenner. LC 74-2499. (Illus.). 192p. (gr. 7 up). 1974. 7.25 o.p. (ISBN 0-688-21821-0); PLB 7.92 (ISBN 0-688-31821-5). Morrow.

Gentle Pirate. Jayne Castle. 1980. pap. 1.50 (ISBN 0-440-12981-8). Dell.

Gentle Spears. Arthur Dobrin. Ed. by Stanley H. Barkan. (Cross-Cultural Review Chapbook 3). 16p. 1980. pap. 2.00 (ISBN 0-89304-802-X). Cross Cult.

Gentle Vengeance. Charles LeBaron. 1981. 12.95 (ISBN 0-399-90112-4). Marek.

Gentle War: The Story of the Salvation Army. Lawrence Fellows. LC 79-14622. (Illus.). (gr. 5 up). 1979. 8.95 (ISBN 0-02-734430-4, 73443). Macmillan.

Gentleman from Philadelphia. Rebecca Baldwin. 1978. pap. 1.50 o.p. (ISBN 0-449-23559-9, Crest). Fawcett.

Gentleman George - King of Melodrama. Eric Irvin. (Illus.). 234p. 1981. text ed. 18.00x (ISBN 0-7022-1536-8). U of Queensland Pr.

Gentleman in Paradise. Harper McBride. (Orig.). 1981. pap. 1.50 (ISBN 0-440-12186-8). Dell.

Gentleman of Leisure: A Year in the Life of a Pimp. Bob Adelman. (Illus.). 224p. 1973. pap. 1.95 (ISBN 0-451-05524-1, J5524, Sig). NAL.

Gentleman Usher. George Chapman. Ed. by John H. Smith. LC 69-12399. (Regents Renaissance Drama Ser). 1970. 9.95x (ISBN 0-8032-0285-7); pap. 2.75x (ISBN 0-8032-5286-2, BB 232, Bison). U of Nebr Pr.

Gentleman's Country House & Its Plan 1835-1914. Jill Franklin. (Illus.). 272p. 1981. 40.00 (ISBN 0-7100-0622-5). Routledge & Kegan.

Gentleman's Gentleman. Julian Fane. 148p. 1981. 14.95 (ISBN 0-241-10434-3, Pub. by Hamish Hamilton England). David & Chalres.

Gentleman's Magazine Biographical & Obituary Notices, 1781-1819: An Index. Benjamin Nangle. LC 80-907. (Garland Reference Library of Humanities). 450p. 1980. 55.00 (ISBN 0-8240-9510-3). Garland Pub.

Gentleman's Magazine Library: Being a Classified Collection of the Chief Contents of the Gentleman's Magazine from 1731-1868, 13 vols. Ed. by George L. Gomme et al. Incl. Vol. 1. Manners & Customs. Repr. of 1886 ed (ISBN 0-8103-3434-8); Vol. 2. Dialect, Proverbs, & Word Lore. Repr. of 1886 ed (ISBN 0-8103-3435-6); Vol. 3. Popular Superstitions. Repr. of 1884 ed (ISBN 0-8103-3436-4); Vol. 4. English Traditional Lore. Repr. of 1885 ed (ISBN 0-8103-3437-2); Vols. 5 & 6. Archaeology. Repr. of 1886 ed (ISBN 0-8103-3438-0); Vols. 7 & 8. Romano-British Remains. Repr. of 1886 ed (ISBN 0-8103-3439-9); Vol. 9. Literary Curiosities & Notes. Ed. by Alice B. Gomme. Repr. of 1889 ed (ISBN 0-8103-3440-2); Vol. 10. Bibliographical Notes. Ed. by A. C. Bickley. Repr. of 1890 ed (ISBN 0-8103-3441-0); Vols. 11 & 12. Architectural Antiquities. Repr. of 1890 ed (ISBN 0-8103-3442-9); Vol. 13. Ecclesiology. Ed. by F. A. Milne. Repr. of 1886 ed (ISBN 0-8103-3443-7). LC 67-23900. Vols. 1-4, 9, 10, 13. 18.00 ea.; Vols. 5 & 6, 7 & 8, 11 & 12 (two Vol. Sets) 28.00 ea. (ISBN 0-8103-3355-4). Gale.

Gentlemen from Chicago. John Cashman. 288p. 1974. pap. 1.50 o.p. (ISBN 0-445-03050-X). Popular Lib.

Gentlemen in Crisis: The First Century of the Union League of Philadelphia, 1862-1962. Maxwell Whiteman. LC 75-13693. (Illus.). 372p. 1975. 12.00 (ISBN 0-915810-00-X). Union League PA.

Gentlemen Merchants. R. G. Wilson. LC 79-149804. 271p. 1971. lib. bdg. 15.00x (ISBN 0-678-06785-6). Kelley.

Gentlemen Negotiators: A Diplomatic History of World War One. Z. A. Zeman. LC 70-108149. 1971. 9.95 o.s.i. (ISBN 0-02-633450-X). Macmillan.

Gentlemen of Property and Standing: Anti-Abolition Mobs in Jacksonian America. Leonard L. Richards. 1971. pap. 4.95 (ISBN 0-19-501351-4, 347, GB). Oxford U Pr.

Gentlemen of Property & Standing: Anti-Abolition Mobs in Jacksonian America. Leonard L. Richards. LC 74-93862. 1970. 12.95 (ISBN 0-19-500082-X). Oxford U Pr.

Gentlemen of Sixteen July. Maurice & Ken Follett. 1980. 9.95 (ISBN 0-87795-298-1). Arbor Hse.

Gentlemen of Venice. James Shirley. Ed. by Wilson F. Engel. (Salzburg Studies in English Literature, Jacobean Drama Studies: No. 62). 199p. 1976. pap. text ed. 25.00x (ISBN 0-391-01521-4). Humanities.

Gentlest Art. E. V. Lucas. 422p. 1981. Repr. of 1913 ed. lib. bdg. 25.00 (ISBN 0-89987-509-2). Darby Bks.

Gently Down the Stream. Ethlyn Walkington. 1981. 5.95 (ISBN 0-8062-1606-9). Carlton.

Gently in the Highlands. Alan Hunter. LC 74-18254. 174p. 1975. 5.95 o.s.i. (ISBN 0-02-557550-3, 55755). Macmillan.

Gently Through the Woods. Alan Hunter. LC 75-15852. 191p. 1975. Repr. 5.95 o.s.i. (ISBN 0-02-557560-0, 55756). Macmillan.

Gently with the Innocents. Alan Hunter. 183p. 1974. 5.95 o.s.i. (ISBN 0-02-557530-9). Macmillan.

Gently with the Ladies. Alan Hunter. LC 74-477. 186p. 1974. 5.95 o.s.i. (ISBN 0-02-557540-6). Macmillan.

Gently with the Painters. Alan Hunter. LC 75-43639. 208p. 1976. 6.95 o.s.i. (ISBN 0-02-557570-8, 55757). Macmillan.

Gentrification & the Resegregation of American Cities. Michael Lang. 1981. price not set professional reference (ISBN 0-88410-697-7). Ballinger Pub.

Gentry & the Elizabethan State. Gareth Jones. (New History of Wales). (Illus.). 1977. text ed. 7.75x (ISBN 0-7154-0303-6). Humanities.

Gentry of Bedfordshire in the 13th & 14th Centuries. K. S. Naughton. (Occasional Papers in English Local History, Third Series: No. 2). (Illus., Orig.). 1976. pap. text ed. 8.50x (ISBN 0-7185-2032-7, Leicester). Humanities.

Gentry: The Rise & Fall of a Ruling Class. G. E. Mingay. LC 76-13576. (Themes in British Social History). (Illus.). 1976. pap. text ed. 10.95x (ISBN 0-582-48403-0). Longman.

Genuine Dying Speech of the Reverend Parson Coppock, Pretended Bishop of Carlisle: Who Was Drawn, Hanged & Quartered There, Oct. 18, 1746, for High Treason & Rebellion, Etc. Thomas Coppock. LC 80-2477. 1981. Repr. of 1746 ed. 23.50 (ISBN 0-404-19109-6). AMS Pr.

Genuine Memoirs of the Celebrated Miss Maria Brown, Exhibiting the Life of a Courtesan in the Most Fashionable Scenes of Dissipation, 1766, 2 vols. in 1. (Flowering of the Novel, 1740-1775 Ser: Vol. 75). 1974. lib. bdg. 50.00 (ISBN 0-8240-1174-0). Garland Pub.

Genus Galium (Rubiaceae) in Mexico & Central America. Lauramay T. Dempster. (Publications in Botany: No. 73). 1978. pap. 7.00x (ISBN 0-520-09578-2). U of Cal Pr.

Genus Mallophora & Related Asilid Genera in North America (Diptera: Asilidae) F. R. Cole & A. E. Pritchard. (U. C. Publ. in Entomology: Vol. 36.2). 1964. pap. 5.00x o.p. (ISBN 0-520-09108-6). U of Cal Pr.

Genus Pinus. Nicholas T. Mirov. (Illus.). 1967. 26.50 (ISBN 0-8260-6140-0, Pub. by Wiley-Interscience). Wiley.

Genus Tigridia (Iridaceae) of Mexico & Central America. Elwood Molseed. (U. C. Publ. in Botany: Vol. 54). 1970. pap. 7.50x (ISBN 0-520-09028-4). U of Cal Pr.

Geo-Bibliography of Anomalies: Primary Access to Observations of UFOs, Ghosts, & Other Mysterious Phenomena. Compiled By George M. Eberhart. LC 79-6183. xl, 1114p. 1980. lib. bdg. 59.95 (ISBN 0-313-21337-2, EBA/). Greenwood.

Geo-Metrics: The Metric Application of Geometric Tolerancing. Lowell W. Foster. (Illus.). 300p. 1974. 14.95 (ISBN 0-201-01989-2); pocket guide 9.95 (ISBN 0-201-01987-6). A-W.

Geoarchaeology: Earth Science of the Past. rev. ed. Ed. by Donald A. Davidson & Myra Shackley. LC 76-25224. 1977. lib. bdg. 45.00x (ISBN 0-89158-635-0). Westview.

Geobotanical Foundations of the Middle East. M. Zohary. 762p. 1973. text ed. 255.00 (ISBN 90-265-0157-9, Pub. by Swets Pub Serv Holland). Swets North Am.

Geochemical Transport & Kinetics. A. W. Hofmann et al. 1974. 27.00 (ISBN 0-87279-644-2, 634). Carnegie Inst.

Geochemistry. Arthur H. Brownlow. (Illus.). 1979. text ed. 23.95 (ISBN 0-13-351064-6). P-H.

Geochemistry. Victor M. Goldschmidt. Ed. by Alex Muir. (International Ser. of Monographs on Physics). 1954. 62.00x (ISBN 0-19-851210-4). Oxford U Pr.

Geochemistry & the Environment: Distribution of Trace Elements Related to the Occurrence of Certain Cancers, Cardiovascular Diseases, & Urolithiasis, Vol. III. Committee on Env. Geochem., National Research Council. (Geochemistry & the Environment Ser.). 1978. pap. text ed. 14.00x (ISBN 0-309-02795-0). Natl Acad Pr.

Geochemistry & the Environment: The Relation of Other Selected Trace Elements to Health & Disease, Vol. II. U. S. National Committee for Geochemistry. 1977. pap. 12.00 (ISBN 0-309-02548-6). Natl Acad Pr.

Geochemistry & the Environment: The Relation of Selected Trace Elements to Health & Disease, Vol. 1. National Research Council, U. S. National Committee for Geochemistry. LC 74-13309. (Illus.). ix, 113p. 1974. pap. 10.00 (ISBN 0-309-02223-1). Natl Acad Pr.

Geochemistry of Bottom Sediments Matagorda Bay System, Texas. J. H. McGowen et al. (Illus.). 64p. 1979. 1.50 (GC 79-2). Bur Econ Geology.

Geochemistry of Hydrothermal Ore Deposits. 2nd ed. Ed. by H. L. Barnes. LC 79-354. 1979. 33.00 (ISBN 0-471-05056-3, Pub by Wiley-Interscience). Wiley.

Geochemistry of Organic Substances. S. M. Manskaya & T. V. Drozdova. 1968. 60.00 (ISBN 0-08-012404-6). Pergamon.

Geochemistry of Water in Relation to Cardiovascular Disease. 1979. pap. 10.75 (ISBN 0-309-02884-1). Natl Acad Pr.

Geochronology of North America. Committee On Nuclear Sciences. 1965. pap. 7.00 (ISBN 0-309-01276-7). Natl Acad Pr.

Geodesic Math & How to Use It. Hugh Kenner. LC 74-27292. 150p. 1976. 14.95x (ISBN 0-520-02924-0); pap. 5.95 (ISBN 0-520-03054-0, CAL 323). U of Cal Pr.

Geodesy. 4th ed. G. Bomford. 840p. 1980. 139.00 (ISBN 0-19-851946-X). Oxford U Pr.

Geodynamics of the Western Pacific. Ed. by S. Uyeda et al. (Advances in Earth & Planetary Sciences Ser.: Pt. 6). 592p. 1980. 49.50x (ISBN 0-89955-315-X, Pub. by JSSP Japan). Intl Schol Bk Serv.

Geoffrey Chaucer. Nevill Coghill. Ed. by Bonamy Dobree et al. Bd. with Sir Thomas Malory. M. C. Bradbrook. LC 63-63096. (British Writers & Their Work Ser: Vol. 1). 1964. pap. 1.60x (ISBN 0-8032-5650-7, BB 450, Bison). U of Nebr Pr.

Geoffrey Chaucer. Edwin J. Howard. (English Authors Ser.: No. 1). 1964. lib. bdg. 9.95 (ISBN 0-8057-1088-4). Twayne.

Geoffrey Chaucer. John Norton-Smith. (Medieval Authors Ser.). 1974. 25.00 (ISBN 0-7100-7801-3). Routledge & Kegan.

Geoffrey Chaucer: A Selection of His Works. Geoffrey Chaucer. Ed. by Kenneth Kee. LC 66-13408. (College Classics in English Ser.). 1966. pap. 5.95 (ISBN 0-672-63017-6). Odyssey Pr.

Geoffrey Chaucer of England. Marchette Chute. 1946. 7.95 o.p. (ISBN 0-525-11257-X). Dutton.

Geoffrey of Monmouth: Historia Regum Brittaniae. Geoffrey Of Monmouth. Ed. by Jacob Hammer. 1951. 15.00 o.p. (ISBN 0-910956-31-6). Medieval Acad.

Geografia Historica Del Mundo Biblico. Tr. by Netta K. De Money. (Spanish Bks.). (Span.). 1979. 2.95 (ISBN 0-8297-0558-9). Life Pubs Intl.

Geografia Historica Do Mundo Biblico. Tr. by Netta D. De Money. (Portuguese Bks.). 1979. 2.25 (ISBN 0-8297-0723-9). Life Pubs Intl.

Geographic Perspectives on Urban Systems with Integrated Readings. Brian J. Berry & Frank E. Horton. 1970. ref. ed. 22.95 (ISBN 0-13-351312-2). P-H.

Geographical Atlas of World Weeds. Leroy Holm et al. LC 78-24280. 1979. 37.50 (ISBN 0-471-04393-1, Pub. by Wiley-Interscience). Wiley.

Geographical Basis of History. Georg W. Hegel. Ed. by George A. Rittenhouse. (Most Meaningful Classics in World Culture Ser.). (Illus.). 1979. 39.75 (ISBN 0-89266-198-4). Am Classical Coll Pr.

Geographical Change & Industrial Revolution. J. Langton. LC 78-67428. (Cambridge Geographical Studies: No. 11). (Illus.). 1980. 53.50 (ISBN 0-521-22490-X). Cambridge U Pr.

Geographical Economics. Patrick O'Sullivan. 195p. 1981. 24.95 (ISBN 0-470-27122-1). Halsted Pr.

Geographical Etymology: A Dictionary of Place-Names Giving Their Derivations. C. Blackie. LC 68-17916. 1968. Repr. of 1887 ed. 15.00 (ISBN 0-8103-3882-3). Gale.

Geographical Guide to Floras of the World. S. F. Blake. (Landmark Reprints in Plant Science). 1961. text ed. 40.00 (ISBN 0-86598-006-3). Allanheld.

Geographical Guide to Floras of the World: Pt. 1; Africa, Australia, North America, South America & Islands. Sidney F. Blake & A. C. Atwood. 1967. Repr. of 1942 ed. 13.75 o.s.i. (ISBN 0-02-841470-5). Hafner.

Geographical History of America or the Relation of Human Nature to the Human Mind. Gertrude Stein. 224p. Date not set. pap. 1.95 (ISBN 0-394-71941-7). Random.

Geographical Interpretation Through Photographs (& Interpretation of Statistics) Tan K. Hock & Ewen D. Brown. 1972. pap. text ed. 4.95x (ISBN 0-04-910048-3). Allen Unwin.

Geographical Perspectives & Urban Problems. Div. of Earth Sciences. (Illus.). 120p. 1973. pap. 8.00 (ISBN 0-309-02106-5). Natl Acad Pr.

Geographical Perspectives in Juvenile Delinquency. David J. Evans. 144p. 1980. text ed. 27.75x (ISBN 0-566-00351-1, Pub. by Gower Pub Co England). Renouf.

Geographical Regions of Nigeria. Reuben K. Udo. LC 70-94980. (Illus.). 1970. 25.00x (ISBN 0-520-01588-6). U of Cal Pr.

Geographical Survey of Africa. James M'Queen. 303p. Repr. of 1969 ed. 29.50x (ISBN 0-7146-1834-9, F Cass Co). Biblio Dist.

Geographies of the Mind: Essays in Historical Geosophy in Honor of John Kirtland Wright. Ed. by David Lowenthal & Martyn J. Bowden. (Illus.). 288p. 1976. text ed. 9.95x (ISBN 0-19-501970-9). Oxford U Pr.

Geography. 1981. text ed. 25.85 (ISBN 0-06-318186-X, Pub. by Har-Row Ltd England); pap. text ed. 13.10 (ISBN 0-06-318187-8). Har-Row.

Geography. Jack Rudman. (Undergraduate Program Field Test Ser.: UPFT-10). (Cloth bdg. avail. on request). pap. 9.95 (ISBN 0-8373-6010-2). Natl Learning.

Geography, Bk. 1. Iain Meyer & Richard Huggett. 1979. pap. text ed. 9.50 (ISBN 0-06-318096-0, IntlDept). Har-Row.

Geography & Capital. K. A. Boesler. 1976. pap. text ed. 28.00 (ISBN 0-08-019712-4). Pergamon.

Geography & Inequality. B. E. Coates et al. (Illus.). 1977. text ed. 29.95x (ISBN 0-19-874069-7); pap. text ed. 9.95x (ISBN 0-19-874070-0). Oxford U Pr.

Geography & Local Administration: A Bibliography. Keith Hoggart. (Public Administration Ser.: Bibliography P-530). 84p. 1980. pap. 9.00. Vance Biblios.

Geography & Man's Environment. Arthur N. Strahler & Alan H. Strahler. LC 76-30759. 1977. text ed. 21.95x (ISBN 0-471-01870-8). Wiley.

Geography & Mental Health. Christopher J. Smith. Ed. by Salvatore J. Natoli. LC 76-29269. (Resource Papers for College Geography Ser.). 1977. pap. text ed. 4.00 (ISBN 0-89291-119-0). Assn Am Geographers.

Geography & Planning. Thomas W. Freeman. (Repr. of 1958 ed.). 1968. pap. text ed. 2.25x (ISBN 0-09-028604-9, Hutchinson U Lib). Humanities.

Geography & Regional Administration: England & Wales: 1830-1968. 3rd ed. T. W. Freeman. 1967. text ed. 5.50x (ISBN 0-09-086610-X, Hutchinson U Lib). Humanities.

Geography & the Geography Teacher. David Hall. (Unwin Education Books: Teaching Today Ser.). 1976. text ed. 18.95x o.p. (ISBN 0-04-371043-3); pap. text ed. 11.50x (ISBN 0-04-371044-1). Allen Unwin.

Geography & the Urban Environment: Progress in Research & Applications, 3 vols. D. T. Herbert & R. J. Johnston. LC 77-13555. 1979. Vol. 1. 44.50 (ISBN 0-471-99575-4, Pub. by Wiley-Interscience); Vol. 2. 44.50 (ISBN 0-471-99725-0); Vol. 3. 51.95 (ISBN 0-471-27632-4). Wiley.

Geography As Social Science. Gordon J. Fielding. 1974. text ed. 20.50 scp (ISBN 0-06-042051-0, HarpC); inst. manual avail. (ISBN 0-06-362080-4). Har-Row.

Geography as Spatial Interaction. Edward L. Ullman. Ed. by Ronald R. Boyce. LC 79-6759. 252p. 1980. 16.50 (ISBN 0-295-95711-5). U of Wash Pr.

Geography, Ideology & Social Concern. Ed. by D. R. Stoddart. (Illus.). 1981. 26.50x (ISBN 0-389-20207-X). B&N.

Geography of Agriculture. P. A. R. Newbury. (Illus.). 336p. 1980. pap. text ed. 18.95x (ISBN 0-7121-0733-9). Intl Ideas.

Geography of American Cities. Risa Palm. (Illus.). 384p. 1981. text ed. 18.95x (ISBN 0-19-502785-X). Oxford U Pr.

Geography of American Sport: From Cabin Creek to Anaheim. John F. Rooney, Jr. 1974. text ed. 11.50 (ISBN 0-201-06491-X). A-W.

Geography of Bangladesh. Haroun Er Rashid. (Illus.). 1978. lib. bdg. 30.00x (ISBN 0-89158-356-4). Westview.

Geography of Crime & Violence: A Spatial & Ecological Perspective. Daniel E. Georges. Ed. by Salvatore Natoli. LC 78-50967. (Resource Papers for College Geography Ser.). 1978. pap. text ed. 4.00 (ISBN 0-89291-128-X). Assn Am Geographers.

Geography of Energy. Gerald Manners. 1966. pap. text ed. 3.25x (ISBN 0-09-110381-9, Hutchinson U Lib). Humanities.

Geography of Europe. 4th ed. Ed. by George W. Hoffman et al. LC 77-75128. (Illus.). 671p. 1977. 24.95 (ISBN 0-8260-4176-0). Wiley.

Geography of Europe: A Regional Analysis. Ed. by Vincent H. Malstrom. LC 72-144099. (Foundations of World Regional Geography Ser). 1971. pap. text ed. 4.95 o.p. (ISBN 0-13-351460-9). P-H.

Geography of Flowering Plants. 4th ed. Ronald Good. LC 73-85684. (Illus.). 584p. 1974. text ed. 33.00x (ISBN 0-582-46611-3). Longman.

Geography of Ghana. E. A. Boateng. 17.95 (ISBN 0-521-04272-0); pap. 8.95x (ISBN 0-521-04273-9). Cambridge U Pr.

Geography of Holiness: The Photography of Thomas Merton. Ed. by Deba Patnaik. LC 80-18604. 1980. 17.50 (ISBN 0-8298-0401-3). Pilgrim NY.

Geography of Housing. Larry S. Bourne. (Scripta Series in Geography). 290p. 1981. 27.95 (ISBN 0-470-27058-6); pap. 19.95 (ISBN 0-470-27059-4). Halsted Pr.

Geography of Industrial Society. Peter Dicken & Peter Lloyd. 1981. text ed. 25.85 (ISBN 0-06-318030-8, IntlDept); pap. text ed. 13.10 (ISBN 0-06-318048-0). Har-Row.

Geography of International Tourism. Ian M. Matley. Ed. by Salvatore J. Natoli. LC 76-18390. (Resource Papers for College Geography Ser.). (Illus.). 1976. pap. text ed. 4.00 (ISBN 0-89291-110-7). Assn Am Geographers.

Geography of Iron & Steel. 4th rev. ed. Norman J. Pounds. (Orig.). 1968. pap. text ed. 6.00x (ISBN 0-09-106261-6, Hutchinson U Lib). Humanities.

Geography of Laws & Justice: Spatial Perspectives on the Criminal Justice System. Keith D. Harries & Stanley D. Brunn. LC 77-25460. (Praeger Special Studies). 1978. 24.95 (ISBN 0-03-022331-8). Praeger.

Geography of Life. Wilfred T. Neill. LC 68-8877. (Illus.). 1969. 22.50x (ISBN 0-231-02876-8). Columbia U Pr.

Geography of Lograire. Thomas Merton. LC 78-88727. (Orig.). 1969. pap. 2.75 (ISBN 0-8112-0098-1). New Directions.

Geography of Manufacturing. Gunnar Alexandersson. 1967. pap. 6.95 ref. ed. (ISBN 0-13-351262-2). P-H.

Geography of Market Centers & Retail Distribution. Brian Berry. 1967. pap. 6.95 ref. ed. (ISBN 0-13-351304-1). P-H.

Geography of Marketing. J. Beaujeu-Garnier & A. Delobez. (Geographies for Advanced Study). (Illus.). 1979. pap. text ed. 19.95 (ISBN 0-582-48991-1). Longman.

Geography of Modern Africa. 2nd ed. William A. Hance. (Illus.). 736p. 1975. 20.50x (ISBN 0-231-03869-0). Columbia U Pr.

Geography of New York State. Ed. by John H. Thompson. LC 66-14602. (Illus.). 1977. pap. 25.00x (ISBN 0-8156-2182-5); supplement & 3 color maps o.p. 6.95x (ISBN 0-8156-2185-X); supplement only o.p. 2.95 (ISBN 0-8156-2190-6). Syracuse U Pr.

Geography of Pakistan. 4th ed. K. U. Kureshy. (Illus.). 1978. pap. text ed. 5.95x (ISBN 0-19-577222-9). Oxford U Pr.

Geography of Pollution: A Study of Greater Manchester. C. M. Wood et al. 150p. 1974. 27.00x (ISBN 0-7190-0564-7, Pub. by Manchester U Pr England). State Mutual Bk.

Geography of Population. 2nd ed. J. Beaujeu-Garnier. Tr. by S. H. Beaver from Fr. (Geographies for Advanced Study Ser). (Illus.). 1978. text ed. 25.00x (ISBN 0-582-48569-X); pap. text ed. 13.50x (ISBN 0-582-48570-3). Longman.

Geography of Post-War France: A Social & Economic Approach. Hugh D. Clout. 180p. 1972. text ed. 18.50 (ISBN 0-08-016765-9); pap. text ed. 7.75 (ISBN 0-08-016766-7). Pergamon.

Geography of Rural Development in Nigeria. Joseph T. Uyanga. LC 79-9601. 188p. 1980. pap. text ed. 9.00 (ISBN 0-8191-0956-8). U Pr of Amer.

Geography of Scotland. K. J. Lea et al. LC 77-76096. 1977. 21.95 o.p. (ISBN 0-7153-7422-2). David & Charles.

Geography of Sea Transport. A. D. Couper. 1972. text ed. 8.25x (ISBN 0-09-112850-1, Hutchinson U Lib). Humanities.

Geography of Settlement. Peter Daniel & Michael Hopkinson. (Conceptual Frameworks in Geography Ser.). (Illus.). 289p. 1979. pap. text ed. 10.95 (ISBN 0-05-003128-7). Longman.

Geography of Sierra Leone. K. C. Dalton. 1965. text ed. 5.95x (ISBN 0-521-04764-1). Cambridge U Pr.

Geography of Soils: Formation, Distribution & Management. Donal Steila. (Illus.). 256p. 1976. 8.95x (ISBN 0-13-351734-9). P-H.

Geography of State Policies. J. R. Prescott. 1968. text ed. 6.00x (ISBN 0-09-088860-X, Hutchinson U Lib). Humanities.

Geography of the Imagination. Guy Davenport. 384p. 1980. 20.00 (ISBN 0-86547-000-6); pap. 10.00 (ISBN 0-86547-001-4). N Point Pr.

Geography of the Near Past. Al Young. LC 75-21624. 1976. 6.95 o.p. (ISBN 0-03-013876-0); pap. 3.95 o.p. (ISBN 0-03-013881-7). HR&W.

Geography of the Soviet Union. 3rd ed. John C. Dewdney. LC 78-40992. (Pergamon Oxford Geography Ser.). (Illus.). 1979. text ed. 29.00 (ISBN 0-08-023739-8); pap. text ed. 13.25 (ISBN 0-08-023738-X). Pergamon.

Geography of the United States. Williams Macgraw. (gr. 8-12). 1972. pap. text ed. 9.00 each incl. 3 texts, 3 maps, tchr's manual & test (ISBN 0-8449-1000-7). Learning Line.

Geography of Tourism. H. Robinson. (Illus.). 512p. 1976. pap. 17.50x (ISBN 0-7121-0721-5, Pub. by Macdonald & Evans England). Intl Ideas.

Geography of Towns. Arthur E. Smailes. (Orig.). 1966. pap. text ed. 2.50x (ISBN 0-09-028624-3, Hutchinson U Lib). Humanities.

Geography of Transportation. Edward Taaffe & Howard L. Gauthier. (Foundations of Economic Geography Ser.). (Illus.). 224p. 1973. pap. 7.95 ref. ed. (ISBN 0-13-351387-4). P-H.

Geography of Tropical African Development: A Study of Spatial Patterns of Economic Change Since Independence. 2nd ed. Anthony M. O'Connor. LC 77-30470. 1978. text ed. 30.00 (ISBN 0-08-021847-4); pap. text ed. 11.25 (ISBN 0-08-021848-2). Pergamon.

Geography of Two Germanies. Mellor. 1978. 20.40 (ISBN 0-06-318066-9, IntlDept). Har-Row.

Geography Puzzles. Peggy Adler. (Illus.). (gr. 4-6). 1979. PLB 6.90 s&l (ISBN 0-531-02867-4). Watts.

Geography: Regions & Concepts. 2nd ed. Harm J. De Blij. LC 77-17536. 1978. text ed. 20.95x o.p. (ISBN 0-471-20051-4); tchrs. manual avail. o.p. (ISBN 0-471-04040-1); wkbk. 6.95x o.p. (ISBN 0-471-04039-8). Wiley.

Geography: Regions & Concepts. 3rd ed. Harm J. De Blij. LC 80-17961. 593p. 1981. text ed. 18.95 (ISBN 0-471-08015-2); tchr's ed. avail. (ISBN 0-471-08106-X); study guide avail. (ISBN 0-471-07882-4). Wiley.

Geography Teaching with a Little Latitude. L. J. Jay. (Classroom Close-Ups Ser.: No. 7). (Illus.). 160p. 1981. text ed. 17.95x (ISBN 0-04-371077-8, 2606); pap. text ed. 8.95x (ISBN 0-04-371078-6, AU 461). Allen Unwin.

Geography: Theory in Practice, Bk. 1, Settlements. Iain R. Meyer. 201p. (Orig.). pap. text ed. 9.50 (ISBN 0-06-318096-0, Pub. by Har-Row Ltd England). Har-Row.

Geography Theory in Practice: Book Three. Iain Meyer & Richard Huggett. 1981. pap. text ed. 13.10 (ISBN 0-06-318164-9, IntlDept). Har-Row.

Geography Theory in Practice: Book Two. Iain Meyer & Richard Huggett. 1980. pap. text ed. 13.10 (ISBN 0-06-318166-5, IntlDept). Har-Row.

Geokhimiya Translations Nineteen Sixty-Nine: A Supplement to Geochemistry International, Vol. 6. American Geological Institute. LC 74-645947. 706p. (Orig., Rus.). 1980. pap. 35.00 (ISBN 0-913312-39-8). Am Geol.

Geologic & Historic Guide to the State Parks of Texas. R. A. Maxwell. (Illus.). 197p. 1973. Repr. of 1970 ed. 3.00 (GB 10). Bur Econ Geology.

Geologic Reconnaissance of Southeastern Guatemala. Howell Williams et al. (U. C. Publ. in Geological Sciences: Vol. 50). 1964. pap. 7.50x (ISBN 0-520-09150-7). U of Cal Pr.

Geologic Story of Longhorn Cavern. W. H. Matthews. 50p. 1963. 1.00 (GB 4). Bur Econ Geology.

Geologic Story of Palo Duro Canyon. W. H. Matthews. (Illus.). 51p. 1969. 1.00 (GB 8). Bur Econ Geology.

Geologic Time. 2nd ed. Don L. Eicher. (Foundations of Earth Sciences Ser.). (Illus.). 160p. 1976. pap. 7.95 (ISBN 0-13-352484-1). P-H.

Geological Development of Svalbard During the Precambrian, Lower Palaeozoic, & Devonian. Ed. by Thore S. Winsnes. (Norsk Polarinstitutt Skrifter: Vol. 167). (Illus.). 323p. 1980. pap. text ed. 30.00x (ISBN 82-90307-03-9). Universitet.

Geological Disasters: Earthquakes & Volcanoes. Thomas G. Aylesworth. (Impact Bks.). (Illus.). 1979. PLB 6.90 s&l (ISBN 0-531-02288-9). Watts.

Geological Evolution of Australia & New Zealand. D. S. W. Brown et al. 1968. 26.00 (ISBN 0-08-012278-7); pap. 14.50 (ISBN 0-08-012277-9). Pergamon.

Geological Evolution of North America. 3rd ed. Colin W. Stearn et al. LC 78-8124. 1979. text ed. 23.95x (ISBN 0-471-07252-4). Wiley.

Geological Guide to Mammoth Cave National Park. Arthur N. Palmer. (Speleologia Ser.). (Illus.). 1981. write for info. (ISBN 0-914264-27-3, Dist. by Caroline Hse); pap. write for info. (ISBN 0-914264-28-1). Zephyrus Pr.

Geological Maps. B. Simpson. 1968. 13.75 (ISBN 0-08-012781-9); pap. 6.25 (ISBN 0-08-012780-0). Pergamon.

Geological Nomenclature. Ed. by W. A. Visser. 568p. 1980. lib. bdg. 95.00 (ISBN 90-247-2403-1). Kluwer Boston.

Geological Oceanography. Francis P. Shepard. LC 76-54533. 1977. 19.50x (ISBN 0-8448-1064-9). Crane-Russak Co.

Geological Survey of Norway. S Gjelle et al. (No. 343, Bulletin 48). pap. 16.00x (ISBN 82-00-31377-8, Dist. by Columbia U Pr.). Universitet.

Geological Survey of Norway. J Guezou & O Nilsen. (No. 340, Bulletin 47). 1979. pap. 19.00x (ISBN 82-00-31373-5, Dist. by Columbia U Pr.). Universitet.

Geological Survey of Norway, No. 354, Bulletin 52. 150p. 1980. pap. 20.00x (ISBN 8-2003-1390-5). Universitet.

Geological Survey of Norway, No. 355, Bulletin 53. 64p. 1980. pap. 14.00x (ISBN 82-00-31391-3). Universitet.

Geological Survey of Norway, No. 356, Bulletin 54. 200p. 1980. pap. 22.00x (ISBN 82-003-1392-1). Universitet.

Geological Survey of Norway, No. 358, Bulletin 55. B. A. Sturt et al. (Illus.). 60p. 1981. pap. 14.00x. Universitet.

Geological Survey of Norway, No. 359, Bulletin 56. J. B. Wielens et al. (Illus.). 60p. 1981. pap. 14.00x. Universitet.

Geological Survey of Norway, No. 360, Bulletin 57. (Illus.). 200p. 1981. pap. 24.00x (ISBN 82-00-31397-2). Universitet.

Geological Survey of Norway, No. 361, Bulletin 58. Unni H. Rowell. 1981. pap. 12.00x (ISBN 82-00-31430-8). Universitet.

Geology. Boy Scouts Of America. LC 19-600. (Illus.). 88p. (gr. 6-12). 1953. pap. 0.70x (ISBN 0-8395-3284-9, 3284). BSA.

Geology. Eugen Kolisko. 1979. pap. 3.95x (ISBN 0-906492-01-7, Pub. by Kolisko Archives). St George Bk Serv.

Geology. new ed. Lou W. Page. (Orig.). 1973. pap. text ed. 6.44 (ISBN 0-201-05653-4, Sch Div); tchr's manual 2.84 (ISBN 0-201-05654-2). A-W.

Geology. 4th rev. ed. Richard M. Pearl. 1975. pap. 4.95 (ISBN 0-06-460160-9, CO 160, Cos). Har-Row.

Geology. Jack Rudman. (Undergraduate Program Field Test Ser.: UPFT-11). (Cloth bdg. avail. on request). pap. 9.95 (ISBN 0-8373-6011-0). Natl Learning.

Geology. Walter A. Thurber et al. (Exploring Earth Science Program Ser.). (gr. 7-12). 1976. pap. text ed. 4.96 (ISBN 0-205-04741-6, 6947417). Allyn.

Geology: A Synopsis Part 2 Historical Geology. Eugene J. Tynan & J. Allen Cain. LC 79-92086. 192p. 1981. pap. text ed. 7.95 (ISBN 0-8403-2306-9). Kendall-Hunt.

Geology: A Synopsis: Pt. 1, Physical Geology. J. Allan Cain & Eugene J. Tyna. (Orig.). 1980. pap. text ed. 7.95 (ISBN 0-8403-2162-7). Kendall-Hunt.

Geology & Geohydrology of the Palo Duro Basin, Texas Panhandle: A Report on the Progress of Nuclear Waste Isolation Feasibility Studies. S. P. Dutton et al. (Illus.). 99p. 1979. 2.50 (GC 79-1). Bur Econ Geology.

Geology & Mineral Deposits of Pre-Cambrian Rocks of the Van Horn Area, Texas. P. B. King & P. T. Flawn. (Illus.). 218p. 1953. 5.75 (PUB 5301). Bur Econ Geology.

Geology & Palaeontology of Southeast Asia, Vol. XXI. T. Kobayashi et al. 381p. 1980. 52.00x (ISBN 0-86008-263-6, Pub. by U of Tokyo Pr Japan). Intl Schol Bk Serv.

Geology & Structure of Vestvagoey, Lofoten, North Norway. James F. Tull. (Geological Survey of Norway Ser: No. 333, Bulletin 42). 1978. pap. 12.00x (ISBN 82-00-31367-0, Dist. by Columbia U Pr). Universitet.

Geology & the Human Environment. David J. Leveson. (Illus.). 1980. text ed. 17.95x (ISBN 0-19-502578-4). Oxford U Pr.

Geology & Virginia. Richard V. Dietrich. LC 76-110752. (Illus.). 1971. 13.95x (ISBN 0-8139-0289-4). U Pr of Va.

Geology Explained in Dorset. John W. Parkins. LC 76-54070. (Geology Explained Ser.). (Illus.). 1977. 8.95 (ISBN 0-7153-7319-6). David & Charles.

Geology Explained in South Wales. T. R. Owen. (Geology Explained Ser.). (Illus.). 1973. 14.95 (ISBN 0-7153-5860-X). David & Charles.

Geology Explained: In the Forest of Dean & the Wye Valley. William Dreghorn. 1968. pap. 4.95 (ISBN 0-7153-4263-0). David & Charles.

Geology Explained in the Lake District. Robert Prosser. (Geology Explained Ser.). 1977. 14.95 (ISBN 0-7153-7397-8). David & Charles.

Geology Explained in the Severn Vale & Cotswolds. William Dreghorn. (Illus.). 192p. 1974. 14.95 (ISBN 0-7153-4102-2). David & Charles.

Geology Explained in the Yorkshire Dales & on the Yorkshire Coast. Derek Brumhead. LC 78-660964. 1979. 17.95 (ISBN 0-7153-7703-5). David & Charles.

Geology Field Guide: The Black Hills. Rodney M. Feldmann & Richard A. Heimlich. 208p. (Orig.). 1980. pap. 8.95 (ISBN 0-8403-2193-7). Kendall-Hunt.

Geology Field Guide: The Southern Rocky Mountains. Robert P. Larkin et al. 176p. (Orig.). 1980. pap. text ed. 9.95 (ISBN 0-8403-2207-0). Kendall-Hunt.

Geology for Civil Engineers. Adam McLean & Colin Gribble. (Illus.). 1979. text ed. 30.00x (ISBN 0-04-624002-0); pap. text ed. 14.95x (ISBN 0-685-94492-1). Allen Unwin.

Geology Illustrated. John S. Shelton. LC 66-16380. (Illus.). 1966. 24.95x (ISBN 0-7167-0229-0). W H Freeman.

Geology in Engineering. John R. Schultz & A. B. Cleaves. LC 55-7317. 1955. text ed. 28.95x (ISBN 0-471-76461-2). Wiley.

Geology Laboratory Manual: Geology from New Jersey. Robert Metz et al. LC 79-65477. (Illus.). 1979. 7.80 (ISBN 0-934434-00-X). RA Corp.

Geology Made Simple. William H. Matthews, III. LC 67-10378. 1967. pap. 2.50 o.p. (ISBN 0-385-01469-4, Made). Doubleday.

Geology of Bell County, Texas. W. S. Adkins & M. B. Arick. (Illus.). 92p. 1930. 1.00 (BULL 3016). Bur Econ Geology.

Geology of California. R. M. Norris & R. W. Webb. 379p. 1976. 21.95 (ISBN 0-471-61566-8). Wiley.

Geology of Central America, Vol. 15. 2nd ed. Richard Weyl. (Beitraege Zur Regionalen Geologie der Erde). (Illus.). 371p. 1980. lib. bdg. 88.85x (ISBN 3-443-11015-0). Lubrecht & Cramer.

Geology of Donegal. W. Pitcher & A. Berger. 435p. 1972. 55.00 o.p. (ISBN 0-471-69055-4, Pub. by Wiley). Krieger.

Geology of Edgeoya & Barentsoya: Svalbard. B. E. Lock et al. (Norsk Polarinstitutt Skrifter: Vol. 168). (Illus.). 64p. 1980. pap. text ed. 7.50x. Universitet.

Geology of Europe. Derek V. Ager. 576p. 1980. 44.95x (ISBN 0-470-26990-1). Halsted Pr.

Geology of Grayson County, Texas. F. M. Bullard. (Illus.). 72p. 1931. 0.50 (BULL 3125). Bur Econ Geology.

Geology of Hemphill County, Texas. L. C. Reed & O. M. Longnecker, Jr. (Illus.). 98p. 1932. price not set (BULL 3231). Bur Econ Geology.

Geology of Henrys Chapel Quadrangle, Northeastern Cherokee County, Texas. H. B. Stenzel. (Illus.). 119p. 1953. 3.50 (PUB 5305). Bur Econ Geology.

Geology of Hood Spring Quadrangle, Brewster County, Texas. R. W. Graces, Jr. (Illus.). 51p. 1954. 2.25 (RI 21). Bur Econ Geology.
Geology of Iowa. Wayne I. Anderson. (Illus.). 1981. write for info. (ISBN 0-8138-1505-3). Iowa St U Pr.
Geology of Ireland. Ed. by Charles H. Holland. 400p. 1980. 40.00x (ISBN 0-7073-0269-2, Pub. by Scottish Academic Pr). Columbia U Pr.
Geology of Japan. Fuyuji Takai et al. 1964. 30.00x (ISBN 0-520-01249-6). U of Cal Pr.
Geology of Mammoth Cave National Park: A Geological Guide. Arthur N. Palmer. 1980. 9.95 (ISBN 0-914264-27-3); pap. 5.95 (ISBN 0-914264-28-1). Caroline Hse.
Geology of Minnesota. Ed. by P. K. Sims & G. B. Morey. LC 73-62334. 1972. pap. 12.00 (ISBN 0-934938-00-8). Minn Geol Survey.
Geology of Oregon. 3rd ed. Ewart M. Baldwin. LC 76-4346. (Illus.). 1981. perfect bdg. 11.95 (ISBN 0-8403-2321-2). Kendall-Hunt.
Geology of Petroleum. 2nd ed. A. I. Levorsen. LC 65-25242. (Geology Ser.). (Illus.). 1967. 30.95x (ISBN 0-7167-0230-4). W H Freeman.
Geology of Potter County. L. T. Patton. (Illus.). 180p. 1923. 0.50 (BULL 2330). Bur Econ Geology.
Geology of Selected Areas in New Jersey & Eastern Pennsylvania & Guidebook of Excursions. Ed. by Seymour Subitzky & Harold E. Gill. 1969. 25.00 (ISBN 0-8135-0606-9). Rutgers U Pr.
Geology of Soils: Their Evolution, Classification, & Uses. Charles B. Hunt. LC 71-158739. (Geology Ser.). (Illus.). 1972. text ed. 28.95x (ISBN 0-7167-0253-3). W H Freeman.
Geology of Stonewall County, Texas. L. T. Patton. (Illus.). 77p. 1930. 0.50 (BULL 3027). Bur Econ Geology.
Geology of Tarrant County. W. M. Winton & W. S. Adkins. (Illus.). 122p. 1919. 0.50 (BULL 1931). Bur Econ Geology.
Geology of Texas: Vol.I, Stratigraphy. E. H. Sellards et al. (Illus.). 1007p. 1978. Repr. of 1932 ed. 8.00 (BULL 3232). Bur Econ Geology.
Geology of the Continental Margins. G. Boillot. Tr. by Alwyn Scarth from Fr. (Illus.). 160p. 1981. pap. text ed. 14.50 (ISBN 0-582-30036-3). Longman.
Geology of the East Midlands. Ed. by P. C. Sylvester-Bradley & T. D. Ford. 1968. text ed. 20.00x (ISBN 0-7185-1072-0, Leicester). Humanities.
Geology of the Glass Mountains, Texas: Part I, Descriptive Geology. P. B. King. (Illus.). 167p. 1930. 2.50 (BULL 3038). Bur Econ Geology.
Geology of the Glass Mountains, Texas: Part Ii, Faunal Summary & Correlation of the Permian Formations with Description of Brachiopoda. R. E. King. (Illus.). 146p. 1930. 2.50 (BULL 3042). Bur Econ Geology.
Geology of the Industrial Rocks & Minerals. Robert L. Bates. (Illus.). 10.00 (ISBN 0-8446-0481-X). Peter Smith.
Geology of the Late Paleozoic Horseshoe Atoll in West Texas. D. A. Myers et al. (Illus.). 113p. 1956. 2.00 (PUB 5607). Bur Econ Geology.
Geology of the Leech Lake Mountain Region, California: A Cross-Section of the North-Eastern Franciscan Belt & Its Tectonic Implications. John Suppe. (Publications in Geology, Vol. 107). 1974. pap. 11.00x (ISBN 0-520-09488-3). U of Cal Pr.
Geology of the Llano Region & Austin Area. rev. ed. V. E. Barnes et al. 154p. 1976. Repr. of 1972 ed. 1.50 (GB 13). Bur Econ Geology.
Geology of the Olduval Gorge: A Study of Sedimentation in a Semiarid Basin. Richard L. Hay. 1976. 34.50x (ISBN 0-520-02963-1). U of Cal Pr.
Geology of the Sierra Nevada. Mary Hill. LC 73-93053. (California Natural History Guides Ser.). (Illus.). 1975. 12.95x (ISBN 0-520-02801-5); pap. 5.95 (ISBN 0-520-02698-5). U of Cal Pr.
Geology of the South Atlantic Islands. Raoul C. Mitchell-Thome. (Beitraege zur regionalen Geologie der Erde: Vol. 10). (Illus.). 366p. 1970. lib. bdg. 90.05x (ISBN 3-443-11010-X, Pub by Gebrueder Borntraeger Germany). Lubrecht & Cramer.
Geology of the State of Hawaii. 2nd ed. Harold T. Stearns. (Illus.). Date not set. price not set (ISBN 0-87015-234-3). Pacific Bks.
Geology of Tom Green County. G. G. Henderson. (Illus.). 116p. 1928. 0.50 (BULL 2807). Bur Econ Geology.
Geology of Wisconsin & Upper Michigan: Including Parts of Adjacent States. Rachel K. Paull & Richard A. Paull. LC 76-27036. (Illus.). 1977. pap. text ed. 9.95 (ISBN 0-8403-1596-1). Kendall-Hunt.
Geology on the Moon. J. E. Guest & R. Greeley. LC 77-371984. (Wykeham Science Ser.: No. 43). 1977. 17.95x (ISBN 0-8448-1170-X); pap. 12.50x (ISBN 0-8448-1346-X). Crane-Russak Co.
Geology: Principles & Concepts: a Programmed Text. Dennis P. Cox & Helen R. Cox. (Illus.). 1974. pap. text ed. 12.25x o.p. (ISBN 0-7167-0262-2). W H Freeman.
Geology, Resources & Society: An Introduction to Earth Science. H. W. Menard. LC 73-17151. (Geology Ser.). (Illus.). 1974. text ed. 21.95x (ISBN 0-7167-0260-6); instructor's guide avail. W H Freeman.
Geology: The Paradox of Earth & Man. Keith Young. 416p. 1975. text ed. 20.50 (ISBN 0-395-05561-X); instructor's manual 1.25 (ISBN 0-395-18267-0). HM.
Geology: The Science of a Changing Earth. 7th, rev. ed. Ira S. Allison & Donald F. Palmer. (Illus.). 1980. text ed. 17.95x (ISBN 0-07-001123-0); pap. text ed. 15.95x (ISBN 0-07-001121-4); instr's manual 4.95x (ISBN 0-07-001122-2). McGraw.
Geology: The Science of the Earth. M. N. Stirrup. LC 78-73233. (Illus.). 1980. pap. 11.95 (ISBN 0-521-22567-1). Cambridge U Pr.
Geomagnetic Field & Life: Geomagnetobiology. A. P. Dubrov. (Illus.). 318p. 1978. 25.00 (ISBN 0-306-31072-4, Plenum Pr). Plenum Pub.
Geomathematical & Petrophysical Studies in Sedimentology, an International Symposium: Proceedings of Papers Presented at Sessions Sponsored by the International Association for Mathematical Geology at the Tenth International Congress on Sedimentology in Jerusalem, July 1979. Dan Gill & Daniel F. Merriam. (Computers & Geology Ser.: Vol. 3). (Illus.). 285p. 1979. 41.00 (ISBN 0-08-023832-7). Pergamon.
Geometric Algebra: Pure & Applied Mathematics. E. Artin. (Wiley-Interscience Ser. of Texts, Monographs & Tracts). 214p. 1957. 26.50 (ISBN 0-470-03432-7, Pub. by Wiley-Interscience). Wiley.
Geometric & Engineering Drawing. 2nd ed. K. Morling. (Illus.). 1974. pap. 15.95x (ISBN 0-7131-3319-8). Intl Ideas.
Geometric & Positional Tolerancing Reference & Work Book. 2nd ed. Aubrey Yuen. 90p. 1973. perfect bnd 7.95x (ISBN 0-912702-07-9). Global Eng.
Geometric & Positional Tolerancing Reference & Work Book. Ed. by Aubrey Yuen. 1973. 7.95x (ISBN 0-912702-07-9). Global Eng.
Geometric Approach to Homology Theory. S. Buoncristiano et al. LC 75-22980. (London Mathematical Society Lecture Note Ser.: No. 18). (Illus.). 216p. 1976. pap. text ed. 17.95x (ISBN 0-521-20940-4). Cambridge U Pr.
Geometric Approach to International Trade. Melvyn B. Krauss. LC 77-20676. 1979. text ed. 34.95 (ISBN 0-470-99353-7). Halsted Pr.
Geometric Design Standards for Highways Other Than Freeways. 1969. 1.00. AASHTO.
Geometric Introduction to Topology. C. T. Wall. LC 70-168765. 1972. text ed. 15.95 (ISBN 0-201-08432-5). A-W.
Geometric Invariant Theory. D. Mumford. (Ergebnisse der Mathematik und Ihrer Grenzgebiete: Vol. 34). (Illus.). 1965. 22.50 o.p. (ISBN 0-387-03284-3). Springer-Verlag.
Geometric Measure Theory. H. Federer. LC 69-16846. (Grundlehren der Mathematischen Wissenschaften: Vol. 153). 1969. 62.10 (ISBN 0-387-04505-8). Springer-Verlag.
Geometric Principles & Procedures for Computer Graphic Applications. Sylvan H. Chasen. LC 78-7998. (Illus.). 1978. 21.95 (ISBN 0-13-352559-7). P-H.
Geometric Quantization. Nicholas Woodhouse. (Oxford Mathematical Monographs). (Illus.). 400p. 1980. 74.00 (ISBN 0-19-853528-7). Oxford U Pr.
Geometric Structure of Systems Control Theory & Physics: Part B. Robert Hermann. LC 74-30856. (Interdisciplinary Mathematics Ser.: No. 11). 1976. 40.00 (ISBN 0-915692-14-7). Math Sci Pr.
Geometric Structure of Theory & Physics: Part A. Robert Hermann. LC 74-30856. (Interdisciplinary Mathematics Ser: No. 9). 450p. 1974. 35.00 (ISBN 0-915692-08-2). Math Sci Pr.
Geometric Symmetry. E. H. Lockwood & R. H. Macmillan. LC 77-77713. (Illus.). 1978. 28.50 (ISBN 0-521-21685-0). Cambridge U Pr.
Geometric Theory of Non-Linear Differential Equations: Backlund Transformations, & Solitons, Part B. (Interdisciplinary Mathematics: Vol. 14). 1977. pap. 33.00 (ISBN 0-915692-18-X). Math Sci Pr.
Geometric Theory of Non-Linear Differential Equations, Backlund Transformations, Solitons: Part A. Robert Hermann. LC 76-17201. (Interdisiplinary Mathematics Ser.: No. 12). 1976. 30.00 (ISBN 0-915692-16-3). Math Sci Pr.
Geometrical & Physical Optics. 2nd ed. R. S. Longhurst. LC 74-169158. (Illus.). 704p. 1974. pap. text ed. 19.95x (ISBN 0-582-44099-8). Longman.
Geometrical & Topological Methods in Gauge Theories: Proceedings. Ed. by J. P. Harnad & S. Shnider. (Lecture Notes in Physics: Vol. 129). 155p. 1980. pap. 14.00 (ISBN 0-387-10010-5). Springer-Verlag.
Geometrical Approaches to Differential Equations: Proceedings. Ed. by R. Martini. (Lecture Notes in Mathematics: Vol. 810). (Illus.). 339p. 1980. pap. 19.50 (ISBN 0-387-10018-0). Springer-Verlag.
Geometrical Design Coloring Book. Spyros Horemis. 1973. pap. 1.75 (ISBN 0-486-20180-5). Dover.
Geometrical Drawing. D. D. Agarwal et al. 1980. text ed. 10.50x (ISBN 0-7069-0802-3, Pub. by Vikas India). Advent Bk.
Geometrical Methods for Th Theory of Linear Systems: Proceedings. NATO ASI & AMS Summer Seminar in Applied Mathematics Held at Harvard University, Cambridge, Ma., June 18-29, 1979. Ed. by Christopher I. Byrnes & Clyde F. Martin. (NATO Advanced Study Institutes Series C: Mathematical & Physical Sciences, 62). 313p. 1980. lib. bdg. 39.50 (ISBN 90-277-1154-2, Pub. by D. Reidel). Kluwer Boston.
Geometrical Methods of Mathematical Physics. B. Schutz. LC 80-40211. (Illus.). 300p. 1980. 39.95 (ISBN 0-521-23271-6); pap. 16.95 (ISBN 0-521-29887-3). Cambridge U Pr.
Geometrics Two: The Application of Geometric Tolerancing Techniques. Lowell W. Foster. LC 78-67959. 1979. pap. text ed. 14.95 (ISBN 0-201-01936-1). A-W.
Geometries of Light. Eugene Warren. (Wheaton Literary Ser.). 80p. (Orig.). 1981. pap. 3.95 (ISBN 0-87788-300-9). Shaw Pubs.
Geometry. Thomas J. Cooney et al. Date not set. text ed. price not set (ISBN 0-201-00974-9, Sch Div); price not set tchr's manual (ISBN 0-201-00975-7). A-W. Postponed.
Geometry. Isidore Dressler. (Orig.). (gr. 10-12). 1973. text ed. 12.58 (ISBN 0-87720-235-4); pap. text ed. 8.33 (ISBN 0-87720-234-6). AMSCO Sch.
Geometry. Harold R. Jacobs. LC 73-20024. (Illus.). 1974. text ed. 12.95 (ISBN 0-7167-0456-0); tchr's guide 6.95x (ISBN 0-7167-0460-9); test masters 4.95x (ISBN 0-7167-0459-5); transparency masters 45.00x (ISBN 0-7167-0458-7). W H Freeman.
Geometry. new ed. Joseph Verdina. (Mathematics Ser). (Illus.). 400p. 1975. text ed. 17.95x (ISBN 0-675-08738-4); instructor's manual 3.95 (ISBN 0-685-50986-9). Merrill.
Geometry: A Guided Inquiry. Don Chakerian et al. LC 71-179132. 1972. text ed. 18.50 (ISBN 0-395-13148-0, 3-53528); tchrs. ed. 19.95 (ISBN 0-395-13149-9, 3-53529); sample test questions 1.90 (ISBN 0-395-18003-1, 3-53531); solution key pap. 4.55 (ISBN 0-685-02024-X, 3-53530). HM.
Geometry: A Modern Introduction. 2nd ed. Mervin L. Keedy & Charles W. Nelson. LC 79-178267. 1973. text ed. 13.95 (ISBN 0-201-03673-8). A-W.
Geometry: An Intuitive Approach. Margaret R. Hutchinson. LC 79-171538. 352p. 1972. 13.95x o.p. (ISBN 0-675-09427-5); instructor's manual 3.95 o.p. (ISBN 0-686-66709-3). Merrill.
Geometry: An Investigative Approach. new ed. P. O'Daffer & S. Clemens. (Grades 10-11). 1976. pap. text ed. 19.25 (ISBN 0-201-05420-5, Sch Div); tchrs. ed. 5.80 (ISBN 0-201-05421-3); wkbk. 2.75 (ISBN 0-201-05422-1). A-W.
Geometry & Design & Maintenance: Ratio, Proportion, Reading Graphs & Data. Learning Achievement Corporation. Ed. by Therese A. Zak. (MATCH Ser.). (Illus.). 128p. 1981. text ed. 5.28 (ISBN 0-07-037115-6, G). McGraw.
Geometry & Induction: Containing Geometry in the Sensible World & the Logical Problem of Induction. Jean Nicod. Tr. by J. Bell & M. Wood. LC 70-107149. 1970. 14.50x (ISBN 0-520-01689-0). U of Cal Pr.
Geometry & Measurement. Dennis Bila et al. LC 76-19445. 1976. 5.95x (ISBN 0-87901-059-2). Worth.
Geometry & Symmetry. Paul B. Yale. LC 67-28042. 1968. 17.95x (ISBN 0-8162-9964-1). Holden-Day.
Geometry & the Imagination. David Hilbert & Stephan Cohn-Vossen. LC 52-2894. (gr. 9 up). 1952. text ed. 14.95 (ISBN 0-8284-0087-3). Chelsea Pub.
Geometry & Trigonometry for the Trades: A Guided Approach. Robert A. Carman & Hale Saunders. 1981. 7.95 (ISBN 0-471-05969-2). Wiley.
Geometry by Transformations. E. A. Maxwell. LC 74-76568. (School Mathematics Project Handbook Ser). (Illus.). 200p. 1974. 42.00 (ISBN 0-521-20405-4); pap. 13.95x (ISBN 0-521-29125-9). Cambridge U Pr.
Geometry for Elementary Teachers. John E. Young & Grace A. Bush. LC 77-155559. 300p. 1971. text ed. 17.95x (ISBN 0-8162-9984-6); instr's manual 2.50 (0-8162-9994). Holden-Day.
Geometry for Teachers. C. Patrick Collier. LC 75-25017. (Illus.). 352p. 1976. text ed. 17.50 (ISBN 0-395-20661-8). solutions manual 1.90 (ISBN 0-395-24219-3). HM.
Geometry in Modules A-D, Bks. 1-4. Muriel W. Lange. (gr. 10-12). 1975. pap. text ed. 4.24 ea. (Sch Div); No. 1. pap. text ed. (ISBN 0-201-04125-1); No. 2. pap. text ed. 4.24 (ISBN 0-201-04126-X); No. 3. pap. text ed. 4.24 (ISBN 0-201-04127-8); No. 4. pap. text ed. 4.24 (ISBN 0-201-04128-6); tchr's commentary 12.44 (ISBN 0-201-04129-4). A-W.
Geometry of Complex Numbers. Hans Schwerdtfeger. LC 79-52529. 1980. pap. text ed. 4.00 (ISBN 0-486-63830-8). Dover.
Geometry of Geodesics. Herbert Busemann. (Pure and Applied Mathematics: Vol. 6). 1955. 41.00 (ISBN 0-12-148350-9). Acad Pr.
Geometry of Hunger. D. S. Halacy, Jr. (Illus.). 1972. 10.95 o.p. (ISBN 0-06-011746-X, HarpT). Har-Row.
Geometry of Loop Spaces & the Cobar Construction. Hans J. Baues. LC 80-12430. (Memoirs of the American Mathematical Society Ser.). 1980. 6.40 (ISBN 0-8218-2230-6, MEMO-230). Am Math.
Geometry of Manifolds. Richard L. Bishop & R. J. Crittenden. (Pure and Applied Mathematics Ser.: Vol. 15). 1964. text ed. 19.50 o.p. (ISBN 0-12-102450-4). Acad Pr.
Geometry of Random Fields. Robert J. Adler. 304p. 1981. 47.50 (ISBN 0-471-27844-0, Pub. by Wiley-Interscience). Wiley.
Geometry of Structural Forms. Ed. by A. Gheorghiu & V. Dragomir. (Illus.). 1978. 51.30x (ISBN 0-85334-683-6, Pub. by Applied Science). Burgess-Intl Ideas.
Geometry, Relativity & the Fourth Dimension. Rudolf V. Rucker. LC 76-22240. (Illus.). 1977. pap. text ed. 2.75 (ISBN 0-486-23400-2). Dover.
Geometry Review Guide. Isidore Dressler. (gr. 10-12). 1973. pap. text ed. 5.42 (ISBN 0-87720-215-X). AMSCO Sch.
Geomicrobiology. Erlich. Date not set. price not set (ISBN 0-8247-1183-1). Dekker.
Geomology. Cornelius S. Hurlbut, Jr. & George S. Switzer. LC 78-13262. 1979. 25.50 (ISBN 0-471-42224-X, Pub. by Wiley-Interscience). Wiley.
Geomorphological Map of Papua New Guinea. (Land Research Ser.: No. 33). (Illus.). 23p. 1979. 9.00 (ISBN 0-643-00092-5, CO17, CSIRO). Unipub.
Geomorphological Processes. E. Derbyshire et al. LC 79-5285. (Studies in Physical Geography Ser.). 312p. 1980. lib. bdg. 27.50x (ISBN 0-89158-695-4, Pub. by Dawson Pub); pap. text ed. 13.50x (ISBN 0-89158-864-7). Westview.
Geomorphological Techniques. Ed. by Andrew Goudie. (Illus.). 320p. 1981. text ed. 60.00x (ISBN 0-04-551042-3, 2632-3); pap. text ed. 29.95x (ISBN 0-04-551043-1). Allen Unwin.
Geomorphology. Robert Ruhe. 1975. text ed. 20.95 (ISBN 0-395-18553-X). HM.
Geomorphology & Climate. Ed. by Edward Derbyshire. LC 75-4523. 514p. 1976. 81.50 (ISBN 0-471-20954-6, Pub. by Wiley-Interscience). Wiley.
Geomorphology & Engineering. Ed. by Donald R. Coates. (Binghamton Symposia in Geomorphology: International Ser.: No. 7). (Illus.). 384p. 1980. text ed. 30.00x (ISBN 0-04-551040-7, 2584). Allen Unwin.
Geomorphology in Arid Regions. Ed. by Donald O. Doehring. (Binghamton Symposia in Geomorphology: International Ser.: No. 8). (Illus.). 276p. 1980. text ed. 20.00x (ISBN 0-04-551041-5, 2508). Allen Unwin.
Geomorphology in Environmental Management: An Introduction. Ronald U. Cooke & John C. Doornkamp. (Illus.). 348p. 1974. text ed. 29.50x (ISBN 0-19-874020-4); pap. text ed. 16.50x (ISBN 0-19-874021-2). Oxford U Pr.
Geomorphology Laboratory Manual with Report Forms. Marie Morisawa. LC 76-13456. 1976. pap. text ed. 13.95x (ISBN 0-471-01847-3). Wiley.
Geomorphology of Sonar Basin. Rajkumar Rai. 1980. text ed. write for info. (ISBN 0-391-01835-3). Humanities.
Geomorphology: Present Problems & Future Prospects. Ed. by Clifford Embleton et al. (Illus.). 1978. text ed. 29.95x (ISBN 0-19-874078-6). Oxford U Pr.
Geophysical Case Study of the Woodlawn Orebody, New South Wales Australia. Robert J. Whiteley. LC 79-42637. (Illus.). xviii, 592p. 1980. 80.00 (ISBN 0-08-023996-X). Pergamon.
Geophysical Predictions. Geophysics Research Board, National Research Council. LC 78-8147. (Studies in Geophysics Ser.). 1978. pap. text ed. 12.75 (ISBN 0-309-02741-1). Natl Acad Pr.
Geophysical Studies in the Norwegian-Greenland Sea. Gisle Gronlie. (Norsk Polarinstitutt Skrifter: Vol. 170). (Illus.). 117p. 1980. pap. text ed. 10.00 (ISBN 82-90307-05-5). Universitet.

Georg Brandes. Bertil Nolin. LC 76-2718. (World Authors Ser.: Denmark: No. 390). 1976. lib. bdg. 12.50 (ISBN 0-8057-6232-9). Twayne.

Georg Buchner. Ronald Hauser. (World Authors Ser.: Germany: No. 300). 1974. lib. bdg. 10.95 (ISBN 0-8057-2183-5). Twayne.

Georg Buchner. Herbert Lindenberger. LC 64-16355. (Crosscurrents-Modern Critiques Ser.). 169p. 1964. 6.95 (ISBN 0-8093-0138-5). S Ill U Pr.

Georg Forster. Thomas P. Saine. (World Authors Ser.: Germany: No. 215). lib. bdg. 10.95 (ISBN 0-8057-2316-1). Twayne.

Georg Kaiser. Ernst Schurer. (World Authors Ser.: Germany: No. 196). lib. bdg. 10.95 (ISBN 0-8057-2480-X). Twayne.

Georg Kaiser Plays, Vol. 1. Georg Kaiser. Tr. by B. J. Kenworthy. 1980. pap. 6.95 (ISBN 0-7145-0242-1). Riverrun NY.

Georg Lukacs. Ehrhard Bahr & Ruth G. Kunzer. LC 70-190350. (Modern Literature Ser.). 1972. 10.95 (ISBN 0-8044-2014-9). Ungar.

Georg Lukacs. George H. Parkinson. 1977. 16.00x (ISBN 0-7100-8678-4). Routledge & Kegan.

Georg Simmel: The Conflict in Modern Culture & Other Essays. K. Peter Etzkorn. LC 67-25064. 1968. text ed. 11.25x (ISBN 0-8077-1296-5). Tchrs Coll.

Georg Trakl. Herbert Lindenberger. (World Authors Ser.: Germany: No. 171). lib. bdg. 10.95 (ISBN 0-8057-2886-4). Twayne.

Georg Trakl: Poems. Tr. by Lucia Getsi. LC 73-79473. xi, 173p. 1973. pap. 11.00 (ISBN 0-8214-0174-2). Ohio U Pr.

George & Martha One Fine Day. James Marshall. (Illus.). (gr. k-3). 1978. reinforced bdg. 6.95 (ISBN 0-395-27154-1). HM.

George & Martha Tons of Fun. James Marshall. (gr. k-3). 1980. reinforced bdg. 6.95 (ISBN 0-395-29524-6). HM.

George & Red. Elizabeth Coatsworth. LC 69-11293. (Illus.). (gr. 4-6). 1969. 3.95g o.s.i. (ISBN 0-02-720260-7). Macmillan.

George Bancroft. Robert H. Canary. (U. S. Authors Ser.: No. 226). 1974. lib. bdg. 10.95 (ISBN 0-8057-0034-X). Twayne.

George Baxter & the Baxter Prints. Max E. Mitzman. LC 78-52165. (Illus.). 1978. 32.00 (ISBN 0-7153-7629-2). David & Charles.

George Bernard Shaw, 2 vols. Archibald Henderson. LC 79-87485. (Illus.). 1078p. 1972. Repr. of 1956 ed. Set. lib. bdg. 55.00 (ISBN 0-306-71491-4). Da Capo.

George Bernard Shaw. Eldon C. Hill. (English Authors Ser.: No. 236). 1978. lib. bdg. 9.95 (ISBN 0-8057-6709-6). Twayne.

George Bernard Shaw. John F. Matthews. LC 72-92031. (Columbia Essays on Modern Writers Ser.: No. 45). (Orig.). 1969. pap. 2.00 (ISBN 0-231-03145-9, MW45). Columbia U Pr.

George Bernard Shaw Vegetarian Cookbook. Alice Laden & R. J. Minney. 1974. pap. 1.50 o.s.i. (ISBN 0-515-03465-7, A3465). Jove Pubns.

George C. Marshall: Ordeal & Hope, 1939-1943. Forrest C. Pogue. 1966. 12.50 o.s.i. (ISBN 0-670-33686-6). Viking Pr.

George Cabot Lodge. John W. Crowley. LC 75-44429. (U. S. Authors Ser.: No. 264). 1976. lib. bdg. 10.95 (ISBN 0-8057-7165-4). Twayne.

George Canning (Seventeen Seventy to Eighteen Twenty-Seven) & William Gifford (Seventeen Fifty-Six to Eighteen Twenty-Six. Ed. by Donald H. Reiman. LC 75-31176. (Romantic Context: Poetry 1789-1830 Ser.). 1978. lib. bdg. 47.00 (ISBN 0-8240-2128-2). Garland Pub.

George Catlin: Episodes from Life Among the Indians & Last Rambles. George Catlin. Ed. by Marvin C. Ross. 354p. 1980. pap. 12.50 (ISBN 0-8061-1693-5). U of Okla Pr.

George Catlin: Episodes from "Life Among the Indians" & "Last Rambles". Ed. by Marvin C. Ross. LC 59-7959. 1979. 25.00 (ISBN 0-8061-0442-2); pap. 12.50 (ISBN 0-8061-1693-5). U of Okla Pr.

George Chapman: Action & Contemplation in His Novels. Peter Bement. (Salzburg Studies in English Literature, Jacobean Drama Studies: No. 8). 292p. 1974. pap. text ed. 25.00x (ISBN 0-391-01323-8). Humanities.

George Chapman: Aspects of Decadence in Early 17th Century Drama, 2 vols. Leonard Goldstain. (Salzburg Studies in English Literature, Jacobean Drama Studies Ser.: No. 31). 440p. 1975. Set. pap. text ed. 50.25x (ISBN 0-391-01387-4). Humanities.

George Crabbe. Terence Bareham. (Critical Studies Ser.). 245p. 1977. 19.50x (ISBN 0-06-490305-2). B&N.

George Crolx (Seventeen Eighty to Eighteen Sixty) Ed. by Donald H. Reiman. LC 75-31189. (Romantic Context Ser.: Poetry 1789-1830 Ser.). 1978. lib. bdg. 47.00 (ISBN 0-8240-2140-1). Garland Pub.

George Dance, Architect 1741-1825. Dorothy Stroud. 1971. 35.00 (ISBN 0-571-09007-9, Pub. by Faber & Faber). Merrimack Bk Serv.

George Darley (Seventeen Ninety-Five to Eighteen Forty-Six) George Darley. Ed. by Donald H. Reiman. LC 75-31193. (Romantic Context Ser.: Poetry 1789-1830). 1978. lib. bdg. 47.00 (ISBN 0-8240-2144-4). Garland Pub.

George De Forest Brush: A Joyous Painter. Nancy Bowditch. 1970. 12.50x (ISBN 0-87233-008-7). Bauhan.

George Du Maurier: The Satirist of the Victorians. T. M. Wood. 198p. 1980. Repr. of 1913 ed. lib. bdg. 35.00 (ISBN 0-89760-913-1). Telegraph Bks.

George Eliot. R. T. Jones. LC 75-114602. (British Authors Ser). 1971. 22.00 (ISBN 0-521-07832-6); pap. 6.95x (ISBN 0-521-09613-8). Cambridge U Pr.

George Eliot. Ed. by Richard Stang. (Discussions of Literature). 1960. pap. text ed. 2.95x o.p. (ISBN 0-669-21865-0). Heath.

George Eliot: A Writer's Notebook, 1854-1879, Collected Writings. Joseph Wiesenfarth. LC 80-23271. Date not set. write for info. (ISBN 0-8139-0887-6). U Pr of Va.

George Eliot & Flaubert: Pioneers of the Modern Novel. Barbara Smalley. LC 73-85446. ix, 240p. 1974. 12.00x (ISBN 0-8214-0136-X). Ohio U Pr.

George Eliot and Judaism: A Study of George Eliot's Interest & Knowledge of Judaism. William Baker. (Salzburg Studies in English Literature, Romantic Reassessment Ser.: No. 45). 272p. 1975. pap. text ed. 25.00x (ISBN 0-391-01312-2). Humanities.

George Eliot & Spinoza. Dorothy Atkins. (Salzburg Studies in English Literature: Romantic Reassessment Ser.: No. 78). 1979. pap. text ed. 25.00x (ISBN 0-391-01302-5). Humanities.

George Eliot: Centenary Essays & Unpublished Fragment. Ed. by Anne Smith. (Critical Studies Ser.). 221p. 1980. 27.50x (ISBN 0-389-20058-1). B&N.

George Eliot: Her Mind & Her Art. Joan Bennett. (Orig.). 1948. 27.50 (ISBN 0-521-04158-9); pap. 8.95x (ISBN 0-521-09174-8, 174). Cambridge U Pr.

George Eliot: Romantic Humanist--A Study of the Philosophical Structure of Her Novels. K. M. Newton. 215p. 1981. 26.50x (ISBN 0-389-20081-6). B&N.

George Eliot's Creative Conflict: The Other Side of Silence. Laura Emery. LC 75-3768. 1976. 15.75x (ISBN 0-520-02979-8). U of Cal Pr.

George Eliot's Middlemarch Notebooks: A Transcription. Ed. by John C. Pratt. Victor A. Neufeldt. LC 74-16715. 1979. 30.00x (ISBN 0-520-02867-8). U of Cal Pr.

George-Etienne Cartier: Montreal Bourgeois. Brian Young. (Illus.). 200p. 1981. 23.95x (ISBN 0-7735-0370-6); pap. 10.95x (ISBN 0-7735-0371-4). McGill-Queens U Pr.

George Fitzmaurice. Carol W. Gelderman. (English Authors Ser.: No. 252). 1979. lib. bdg. 11.95 (ISBN 0-8057-6741-X). Twayne.

George Fitzmaurice & His Enchanted Land. Howard K. Slaughter. (Irish Theatre Ser.: No. 2). (Illus., Orig.). 1972. pap. text ed. 3.25x (ISBN 0-85105-188-X, Dolmen Pr). Humanities.

George Frederic Handel. Paul H. Lang. (Illus.). 1966 22.95 (ISBN 0-393-02131-9); pap. 7.95, 1977 (ISBN 0-393-00815-0). Norton.

George Gascoigne. Ronald C. Johnson. (English Authors Ser.: No. 133). lib. bdg. 10.95 (ISBN 0-8057-1212-7). Twayne.

George Gershwin: His Journey to Greatness. David Ewen. LC 77-6821. (Illus.). 1977. Repr. of 1970 ed. lib. bdg. 25.00x (ISBN 0-8371-9663-9, EWGG). Greenwood.

George Gissing. John Goode. (Barnes & Noble Critical Study Ser). 205p. 1979. text ed. 18.50x (ISBN 0-06-492488-2). B&N.

George Gissing: Critical Essays. Ed. by Jean-Pierre Michaux. (Critical Studies). 208p. 1981. 25.00x (ISBN 0-389-20061-1). B&N.

George Gissing: The Nether World. Ed. by John Goode. LC 74-499. 432p. 1974. 20.00 o.p. (ISBN 0-8386-1543-0). Fairleigh Dickinson.

George Gordon, Lord Byron: A Comprehensive Bibliography of Secondary Materials in English, 1807-1974. Oscar J. Santucho. LC 76-41006. (Author Bibliographies Ser.: No. 30). 1977. 27.50 (ISBN 0-8108-0982-6). Scarecrow.

George Grosz. Uwe M. Schneede. (Illus.). 220p. 1981. pap. 3.75 (ISBN 0-8120-2184-3). Barron.

George Grosz: Art & Politics in the Weimar Republic. Beth I. Lewis. LC 79-143764. (Illus.). 1971. 25.00 (ISBN 0-299-05901-4). U of Wis Pr.

George H. Morris Teaches Beginners How to Ride: A Clinic for Instructors, Parents, & Students. Frwd. by Gordon Wright. LC 79-7224. (Illus.). 144p. 1981. 10.95 (ISBN 0-385-14226-9). Doubleday.

George Hamell Cook: A Life in Agriculture & Geology, 1818-1889. Jean Sidar. 1976. 13.00 (ISBN 0-8135-0827-4). Rutgers U Pr.

George Henry Durrie (1820-63), American Winter Landscapist: Renowned Through Currier & Ives. (Illus.). 240p. 1977. 34.95 (ISBN 0-686-28866-1). M Hutson.

George Henry Lewes. Edgar W. Hirshberg. (English Authors Ser.: No. 100). lib. bdg. 10.95 (ISBN 0-8057-1332-8). Twayne.

George Herbert Mead: Essays on His Social Philosophy. Ed. by John W. Petras. LC 59-11329. 1968. 9.25x (ISBN 0-8077-1902-1). Tchrs Coll.

George Joachim Goschen: The Transformation of a Victorian Liberal. T. J. Spinner, Jr. (Conference on British Studies Biographical Ser.). 268p. 1973. 39.00 (ISBN 0-521-20210-8). Cambridge U Pr.

George Kelly. Foster Hirsch. LC 75-2086. (U. S. Authors Ser.: No. 259). 1975. lib. bdg. 10.95 (ISBN 0-8057-7158-1). Twayne.

George Lewis: A Jazzman from New Orleans. Tom Bethell. 1977. 14.50 (ISBN 0-520-03212-8). U of Cal Pr.

George MacDonald: An Anthology. Ed. by C. S. Lewis. 1978. 7.95 (ISBN 0-02-570530-X). Macmillan.

George Meredith. M. Sturge Henderson. 324p. 1980. Repr. of 1907 ed. lib. bdg. 30.00. Darby Bks.

George Meredith. Hannah Lynch. 170p. 1980. Repr. of 1891 ed. lib. bdg. 10.00 (ISBN 0-8495-3335-X). Arden Lib.

George Meredith: A Reappraisal of the Novels. Mahommad Shaheen. 1980. 19.50x (ISBN 0-389-20022-0). B&N.

George Meredith: His Life & Lost Love. David Williams. 1978. 25.00 (ISBN 0-241-89630-4, Pub. by Hamish Hamilton England). David & Charles.

George Meriton. Sir Henry Spelman. Anon. Charles Fearne. Ed. by David S. Berkowitz & Samuel E. Thorne. (English Legal History Ser.: Vol. 137). 370p. 1979. lib. bdg. 55.00 (ISBN 0-8240-3174-1). Garland Pub.

George Michael's Secrets for Beautiful Hair. George Michael & Ray Lindsay. LC 79-7693. (Illus.). 256p. 1981. 19.95 (ISBN 0-385-15465-8). Doubleday.

George Mikes Introduces Switzerland. Ed. by Raffael Ganz. (Illus.). 1978. 15.95 (ISBN 0-233-96757-5). Transatlantic.

George Moore. Anthony Farrow. (English Authors Ser.: No. 244). 1978. 12.50 (ISBN 0-8057-6685-5). Twayne.

George Mueller. Faith C. Bailey. 160p. 1980. pap. 2.50 (ISBN 0-8024-0031-0). Moody.

George Mueller: Delighted in God. Roger Steer. LC 75-33488. 1979. pap. 5.95 (ISBN 0-87788-303-3). Shaw Pubs.

George Mueller: Man of Faith. Basil Miller. 160p. 1972. pap. 2.25 (ISBN 0-87123-182-4, 200182). Bethany Fell.

George Mueller: Young Rebel in Bristol. Faith Bailey. 1958. pap. 1.95 o.p. (ISBN 0-8024-0031-0). Moody.

George Muller of Bristol. Arthur T. Pierson. 1971. 9.95 (ISBN 0-8007-0106-2). Revell.

George N. Peek & the Fight for Farm Parity. Gilbert C. Fite. (Illus.). 1954. 13.95x o.p. (ISBN 0-8061-0285-3). U of Okla Pr.

George Orwell. Roberta Kalechofsky. LC 73-77054. (Modern Literature Ser.). 1973. 10.95 (ISBN 0-8044-2480-2). Ungar.

George Orwell: A Life. Bernard Crick. 1981. 19.95 (ISBN 0-316-16112-8). Little.

George Orwell & the Origins of 1984. William Steinhoff. LC 74-78989. 1975. 12.50 o.p. (ISBN 0-472-87400-4); pap. 6.50x (ISBN 0-472-08802-5). U of Mich Pr.

George Orwell: The Critical Heritage. Ed. by Jeffrey Meyers. (Critical Heritage Ser.). 432p. 1975. 30.00x (ISBN 0-7100-8255-X). Routledge & Kegan.

George Orwell: The Ethical Imagination. Sant S. Bal. 144p. 1981. text ed. 9.25 (ISBN 0-391-02202-4). Humanities.

George Rapp's Separatists: 1700-1803. Karl J. Arndt. LC 80-82896. (Illus.). 512p. (Ger. & Eng.). 1980. bilingual ed. 32.50 (ISBN 0-937640-00-X). Harmony Soc.

George Reserve Deer Herd: Population Ecology of a K-Selected Species. Dale R. McCullough. (Illus.). 1979. lib. bdg. 16.00x (ISBN 0-472-08611-1, 08611). U of Mich Pr.

George Ripley. Henry L. Golemba. (U. S. Authors Ser.: No. 281). 1977. lib. bdg. 9.95 (ISBN 0-8057-7181-6). Twayne.

George Robert Bonfield: Philadelphia Marine Painter, 1805 to 1898. Philadelphia Maritime Museum. LC 78-71198. (Illus.). 78p. (Orig.). 1978. pap. text ed. 8.00 (ISBN 0-913346-04-7). Phila Maritime Mus.

George Rogers Clark & the Revolution in Illinois, Seventeen Sixty-Three to Seventeen Eighty-Seven. Theodore C. Pease & Marguerite J. Pease. 1929. 3.00 (ISBN 0-912226-12-9). Ill St Hist So.

George Russell. Robert B. Davis. (English Authors Ser.: No. 208). 1977. lib. bdg. 10.95 (ISBN 0-8057-6677-4). Twayne.

George S. Kaufman: His Life, His Theater. Malcolm Goldstein. (Illus.). 1979. 25.00 (ISBN 0-19-502623-3). Oxford U Pr.

George Sand & the Victorian World. Paul G. Blount. LC 78-4274. 200p. 1979. 15.00x (ISBN 0-8203-0451-4). U of Ga Pr.

George Sand & the Victorians: Her Influence & Reputation in 19th Century England. Patricia Thomson. 1976. 20.00x (ISBN 0-231-04262-0). Columbia U Pr.

George Santayana. Willard E. Arnett. (World Leaders Ser). lib. bdg. 9.95 (ISBN 0-8057-3718-9). Twayne.

George Sessions Perry: His Life & Works. Maxine C. Hairston. LC 73-84416. (Illus.). 188p. 1973. 9.50 (ISBN 0-8363-0119-6). Jenkins.

George Thalben-Ball. Jonathan Rennert. (Illus.). 1979. 17.95 (ISBN 0-7153-7863-5). David & Charles.

George the Alligator. Dorothea H. Christensen. 1979. 4.50 (ISBN 0-533-04149-X). Vantage.

George the Babysitter. Shirley Hughes. LC 77-4833. Orig. Title: Helpers. (Illus.). (ps-2). 1978. PLB 8.95 (ISBN 0-13-352682-8); pap. 2.95 (ISBN 0-13-352674-7). P-H.

George the Fourth: Regent & King, 1811-1830, Vol. 2. Christopher Hibbert. LC 72-9122. (Illus.). 352p. 1974. 15.00 o.s.i. (ISBN 0-06-011886-5, HarpT). Har-Row.

George Theotokas. Thomas Doulis. (World Authors Ser.: Greece: No. 339). 1975. lib. bdg. 12.50 (ISBN 0-8057-2881-3). Twayne.

George Third & Lord Bute: The Leicester House Years. James L. McKelvey. LC 72-96682. 160p. 1973. 9.75 (ISBN 0-8223-0292-6). Duke.

George W. Littlefield, Texan. J. Evetts Haley. (Illus.). 287p. 1943. 14.95 (ISBN 0-8061-0126-1); pap. 6.95 (ISBN 0-8061-1166-6). U of Okla Pr.

George Washington. Ingri D'Aulaire & Edgar Parin D'Aulaire. (gr. 1-4). 8.95a (ISBN 0-385-07306-2); PLB (ISBN 0-385-07611-8). Doubleday.

George Washington. Robert Jones. (World Leaders Ser.: No. 80). 1979. lib. bdg. 13.50 (ISBN 0-8057-7726-1). Twayne.

George Washington. Clara I. Judson. (Beginning-to-Read Bks). (Illus.). (gr. 3). 1.50 o.p. (ISBN 0-695-33350-X). Follett.

George Washington, 5 vols. John Marshall. LC 80-25082. (American Statesmen Ser.). 2400p. 1981. Set. pap. 19.95 (ISBN 0-87754-175-2). Chelsea Hse.

George Washington: A Biography in His Own Words. George Washington. Ed. by Ralph Andrist. LC 72-76000. (Founding Father Ser). (Illus.). 416p. (YA) 1973. 15.00 o.s.i. (ISBN 0-06-010127-X, HarpT). Har-Row.

George Washington & the Making of a Nation. Marcus Cunliffe & Richard B. Morris. LC 66-2290. (American Heritage Junior Library). (Illus.). (gr. 5 up). 1966. PLB 12.89 (ISBN 0-06-021378-7, Dist. by Har-Row). Am Heritage.

George Washington & the Wolves. Ed. by Jerome Hellmuth. LC 77-20798. (Illus.). 1977. pap. 3.95 (ISBN 0-914842-23-4). Madrona Pubs.

George Washington Carver. Peter Towne. LC 74-34296. (Biography Ser.). (Illus.). 40p. (gr. 1-4). 1975. PLB 7.84 (ISBN 0-690-00777-9, TYC-J). T Y Crowell.

George Washington Carver: An American Biography. Rackham Holt. LC 62-11430. 1963. 7.95 (ISBN 0-385-03045-2). Doubleday.

George Washington, Citizen-Soldier. Charles C. Wall. LC 79-21241. 1980. 12.50x (ISBN 0-8139-0851-5); pap. 6.95 (ISBN 0-8139-0852-3). U Pr of Va.

George Washington Diamond's Account of the Great Hanging at Gainesville, 1862. Ed. by Sam Acheson & Julie O'Connell. 1963. 5.00 (ISBN 0-87611-000-6); pap. 3.50 (ISBN 0-87611-001-4). Tex St Hist Assn.

George Washington's Canal at Great Falls, Va. T. F. Hahn. 1976. 2.50 (ISBN 0-933788-55-X). Am Canal & Transport.

George Washington's Expense Account. Marvin Kitman. 1976. pap. 1.95 o.p. (ISBN 0-345-25519-4). Ballantine.

George Whitefield: The Life & Times of the Great Evangelist of the 18th Century Revival, Vol. II. Arnold Dallimore. LC 79-67152. 640p. 1980. 19.95 (ISBN 0-89107-168-7, Cornerstone Bks). Good News.

George Whitefield: The Life & Times of the Great Evangelist of the 18th Century Revival, Vol. 1. Arnold Dallimore. LC 79-67152. 598p. 1980. 19.95 (ISBN 0-89107-167-9, Cornerstone Bks). Good News.

George Whitefield's Journals. George Whitefield. 1978. 14.95 (ISBN 0-85151-147-3). Banner of Truth.

George Whitefield's Letters: 1734-1742. Goerge Whitefield. 1976. 14.95 (ISBN 0-85151-239-9). Banner of Truth.

Georges Bank: Past, Present, & Future. G. C. McLeod. (Special Studies on Natural Resources & Energy Management). 225p. 1981. lib. bdg. 22.00x (ISBN 0-86531-199-4). Westview.

Georges Braque. Raymond Cogniat. (Library of Great Painters). (Illus.). 1980. 35.00 (ISBN 0-8109-0703-8). Abrams.

Georges Duhamel. Bettina L. Knapp. (World Authors Ser.: France: No. 199). lib. bdg. 10.95 (ISBN 0-8057-2272-6). Twayne.

Georges Rouault. Pierre Courthion. (Illus.). 1977. 35.00 (ISBN 0-8109-0459-4). Abrams.

Georges Simenon. Lucille F. Becker. (World Authors Ser.: No. 456). 1977. lib. bdg. 12.50 (ISBN 0-8057-6293-0). Twayne.

Georges Simenon: A Checklist of His "Maigret" & Other Mystery Novels & Short Stories in French & in English Translations. Trudee Young. LC 76-14410. (Author Bibliographies Ser.: No. 29). 1976. 10.00 (ISBN 0-8108-0964-8). Scarecrow.

Georgetown University Papers on Languages & Linguistics. Ed. by Richard J. O'Brien. Incl. No. 1. 127p. 1970 (ISBN 0-87840-051-6); No. 2. 95p. 1971 (ISBN 0-87840-052-4); No. 4. 1972. pap. (ISBN 0-87840-054-0); No. 5. 1972. pap. (ISBN 0-87840-055-9); No. 6. 1972. pap. (ISBN 0-87840-056-7); No. 7. 1973. pap. (ISBN 0-87840-057-5); No. 9. 1975. pap. (ISBN 0-87840-059-1); No. 11. 1975. pap. (ISBN 0-87840-061-3); No. 12. 1976. pap. (ISBN 0-87840-062-1); No. 13. 1976. pap. (ISBN 0-87840-063-X); No. 14. 1978. pap. (ISBN 0-87840-064-8). pap. 2.25 ea. o.p. Georgetown U Pr.

Georgetown University Papers on Languages & Linguistics, No. 10. Douglas B. Price & Neil J. Twombly. Tr. by Mary C. Osborne et al. (Illus.). 1978. pap. 5.95 o.p. (ISBN 0-87840-065-6). Georgetown U Pr.

Georgette Heyer Compendium. Harmony Raine & Georgette Heyer. 1979. 4.95x (ISBN 0-89967-000-8). Harmony & Co.

Georgi Vins Prisoner of Conscience. Georgi Vins. Ed. by Michael Bourdeaux. Tr. by Jane Ellis from Rus. LC 75-18986. 288p. (Orig.). 1975. pap. 2.95 o.s.i. (ISBN 0-912692-84-7). Cook.

Georgia. 28.00 (ISBN 0-89770-086-4). Curriculum Info Ctr.

Georgia Colony. Ira L. Brown. LC 73-95174. (Forge of Freedom Ser). (Illus.). (gr. 5-8). 1970. 8.95 (ISBN 0-02-714900-5, CCPr). Macmillan.

Georgia Cookbook. 2nd ed. W. Gordon Ragan. LC 78-70630. (Illus.). 1980. 9.95 (ISBN 0-916620-50-6). Portals Pr.

Georgia History: A Bibliography. John E. Simpson. LC 76-15642. 1976. 18.00 (ISBN 0-8108-0960-5). Scarecrow.

Georgia History in Outline. rev. ed. Kenneth Coleman. LC 78-14087. 142p. 1978. pap. text ed. 4.00x (ISBN 0-8203-0467-0). U of Ga Pr.

Georgia: In Words & Pictures. Dennis Fradin. LC 80-26768. (Young People's Stories of Our States Ser.). (Illus.). 48p. (gr. 2-5). 1981. PLB 8.65g (ISBN 0-516-03910-5, Time Line). Childrens.

Georgia O'Keeffe: A Portrait by Alfred Stieglitz. Georgia O'Keeffe. LC 78-13467. (Illus., Co-pub. by Metropolitan Museum of Art). 1979. 45.00 (ISBN 0-670-51989-8, Studio). Viking Pr.

Georgia Property & Casualty. 1980. 14.00 (ISBN 0-930868-36-6). Merritt Co.

Georgia State Industrial Directory, 1980. State Industrial Directories Corp. 1980. pap. 50.00 (ISBN 0-89910-021-X). State Indus Dir.

Georgia Water Resources: Issues & Options. Ed. by James E. Kundell. 114p. 1980. pap. 10.00x. U of GA Inst Govt.

Georgian Dublin. Desmond Guiness. 1979. 45.00 (ISBN 0-7134-1908-3, Pub. by Batsford England). David & Charles.

Georgian England. Peter Lane. (Visual Sources Ser.). (Illus.). 96p. (gr. 7-9). 1981. 16.95 (ISBN 0-7134-3358-2, Pub. by Batsford England). David & Charles.

Georgian London. G. E. Mingay. (Illus.). 164p. 1976. 18.50 o.s.i. (ISBN 0-7134-3045-1). Hippocrene Bks.

Georgian London. G. E. Mingay. 1975. 33.00 (ISBN 0-7134-3045-1, Pub. by Batsford England). David & Charles.

Georgian People. Fred Dwyer. 1978. 16.95 (ISBN 0-7134-0045-5, Pub. by Batsford England). David & Charles.

Georgian Poetic. Myron Simon. (Library Reprint Ser.: Vol. 89). 1978. 14.50x (ISBN 0-520-03618-2); pap. 5.95x o.p. (ISBN 0-520-09495-6). U of Cal Pr.

Georgian Poetry, Nineteen Eleven to Nineteen Twenty-Two: The Critical Heritage. T. Rogers. (Critical Heritage Ser.). 1977. 29.00x (ISBN 0-7100-8278-9). Routledge & Kegan.

Georgian Satirists: Edward Young, Christopher Smart, Charles Churchill. Sherard Vines. 217p. 1980. Repr. of 1934 ed. lib. bdg. 25.00 (ISBN 0-8495-5528-0). Arden Lib.

Georgian Scene Painters & Scene Painting. Sybil Roenfeld. Date not set. price not set (ISBN 0-521-23339-9). Cambridge U Pr.

Georgian Syntax: A Study in Relational Grammar. Alice C. Harris. (Cambridge Studies in Linguistics: No. 33). (Illus.). 300p. Date not set. price not set (ISBN 0-521-23584-7). Cambridge U Pr.

Georgian Times. (Picture Panorama of British History Ser.). 1977. pap. 4.95 (ISBN 0-263-06243-0). Transatlantic.

Georgiana. Marian P. Rettke. 224p. (Orig.). 1981. pap. 2.25 (ISBN 0-515-05656-1). Jove Pubns.

Georgia's Land of the Golden Isles. Burnette Vanstory. LC 80-28565. (Illus.). 225p. 1981. 15.00 (ISBN 0-8203-0557-X); pap. 8.95 (ISBN 0-8203-0558-8). U of Ga Pr.

Georgicks of Hesoid. Hesoid. Tr. by G. Chapman. LC 74-26251. (English Experience Ser.: No. 324). 1971. Repr. of 1618 ed. 8.00 (ISBN 90-221-0324-2). Walter J Johnson.

Georgics. Virgil. Tr. by Smith P. Bovie. LC 56-11264. 1966. pap. 4.00x o.s.i. (ISBN 0-226-06778-5); pap. 4.00x (ISBN 0-226-85740-9). U of Chicago Pr.

Georgics of Virgil. L. P. Wilkinson. LC 75-79058. 1969. 55.00 (ISBN 0-521-07450-9); pap. 12.50 (ISBN 0-521-29323-5). Cambridge U Pr.

Georgie. Robert Bright. (gr. k-6). 1959. 6.95 (ISBN 0-385-07307-0); Softbound 1.95 (ISBN 0-385-08030-1). Doubleday.

Georgie Clark: Thirty Years of River Running. Georgie W. Clark & Duane Newcomb. LC 77-25448. (Illus.). 1978. 6.95 o.p. (ISBN 0-87701-105-2). Chronicle Bks.

Georgie to the Rescue. Robert Bright. LC 56-5582. (ps-1). 6.95a (ISBN 0-385-07308-9); PLB (ISBN 0-385-07613-4); Softbound 1.95 (ISBN 0-385-08067-0). Doubleday.

Georgie's Halloween. Robert Bright. LC 58-7154. (ps-3). 1971. 6.95a (ISBN 0-385-07773-4, 58-7154); softbound 1.95 (ISBN 0-385-01017-6); PLB (ISBN 0-385-07778-5). Doubleday.

Geostatistics. Pierre F. Mousset-Jones. 180p. 1980. 15.50 (ISBN 0-07-043568-5). McGraw.

Geotechnology: An Introductory Text for Students & Engineers. Albert F. Roberts. LC 76-45440. 1977. text ed. 59.00 (ISBN 0-08-019602-0); pap. text ed. 24.75 (ISBN 0-08-021594-7). Pergamon.

Geotectonic Development of California, Vol. 1. Ed. by W. G. Ernst. (Illus.). 720p. 1981. text ed. 31.95 (ISBN 0-13-353938-5). P-H.

Geotectonics. V. V. Belousov. (Illus.). 330p. 1981. 29.80 (ISBN 0-387-09173-4). Springer-Verlag.

Geothermal Energy: A Hot Prospect. Augusta Goldin. LC 80-8800. (Illus.). (gr. 7 up). 1981. 10.95 (ISBN 0-15-230662-5, HJ). HarBraceJ.

Geothermal Energy: A Novelty Becomes Resource. (Transactions: Vol. 2). (Illus.). 748p. 1980. Repr. of 1978 ed. 27.50 (ISBN 0-934412-52-9). Geothermal.

Geothermal Energy & Regional Development. Stahrl Edmunds & Adam Rose. 1979. 31.95 (ISBN 0-03-053316-3). Praeger.

Geothermal Energy & Regional Development: The Case of Imperial County, California. Ed. by Stahrl W. Edmunds & Adam Z. Rose. LC 79-19219. (Illus.). 398p. 1979. 31.95 (ISBN 0-03-053316-3). Praeger.

Geothermal: Energy for the Eighties. Ed. by Robert J. Schultz et al. (Transactions: Vol. 4). (Illus.). 835p. 1980. 28.00 (ISBN 0-934412-54-5). Geothermal.

Geothermal Energy in the Western United States: Innovation Versus Monopoly. Sheldon L. Bierman et al. LC 77-16078. (Praeger Special Studies). 1978. 34.50 (ISBN 0-03-041470-9). Praeger.

Geothermal Energy Projects: Planning & Management. Ed. by Louis J. Goodman & Ralph N. Love. (Policy Studies). 1980. 33.00 (ISBN 0-08-025095-5). Pergamon.

Geothermal Energy Utilization. Edward C. Wahl. LC 77-546. 1977. 33.00 (ISBN 0-471-02304-3, Pub. by Wiley-Interscience). Wiley.

Geothermal Resources. Robert Bowen. LC 79-41547. 243p. 1980. 59.95x (ISBN 0-470-26917-0). Halsted Pr.

Geothermal Resources & Technology in the U. S. Committee on Nuclear & Alternative Energy Systems, National Research Council. 1979. pap. text ed. 5.50 (ISBN 0-309-02874-4). Natl Acad Pr.

Geothermal Systems: Principles & Case Histories. Ed. by L. Rybach & L. J. Muffler. LC 80-40290. 328p. 1981. 70.00 (ISBN 0-471-27811-4, Pub. by Wiley-Interscience). Wiley.

Gerait's Daughter. Millie J. Ragosta. LC 80-2759. 192p. 1981. 9.95 (ISBN 0-385-17274-5). Doubleday.

Gerald Ford & the Future of the Presidency. Jerald F. TerHorst. LC 74-82727. 1974. 11.95 (ISBN 0-89388-191-0). Okpaku Communications.

Gerald Griffin: A Critical Biography 1803-1840. J. Cronin. LC 77-80831. (Illus.). 1978. 24.50 (ISBN 0-521-21800-4). Cambridge U Pr.

Gerard de Nerval. Norma Rinsler. 1973. text ed. 17.50x (ISBN 0-485-14601-0, Athlone Pr); pap. text ed. 8.75x (ISBN 0-485-12706-7, Athlone Pr). Humanities.

Gerard Manley Hopkins & the Victorian Temper. Alison G. Sulloway. 300p. 1972. 17.50x (ISBN 0-231-03645-0). Columbia U Pr.

Gerard Manley Hopkins: Selected Prose. Gerard M. Hopkins. Ed. by Gerald Roberts. (Standard Authors Ser.). 288p. 1981. 19.50x (ISBN 0-19-254173-0); pap. 8.95x (ISBN 0-19-281272-6). Oxford U Pr.

Gerardo the Unfortunate Spaniard: A Pattern for Lascivious Lovers. Cespedes Gonzalo & Meneses Gonzalo. Tr. by Leonard Digges. LC 80-2475. 1981. Repr. of 1622 ed. 142.40 (ISBN 0-404-19107-X). AMS Pr.

Gerbil for a Friend. D. Pape. (Illus.). 1979. pap. 1.50 (ISBN 0-13-353987-3). P-H.

Gerbils. Henrie. (gr. 2-5). 1980. PLB 5.90 (ISBN 0-531-04121-2, E40). Watts.

Gerbils. Paul Paradise. (Illus.). 96p. 1980. 2.95 (ISBN 0-87666-757-4, KW-037). TFH Pubns.

Gerbils. David Robinson. LC 76-9037. (Illus.). (YA) 1976. bds. 2.25 o.p. (ISBN 0-668-03987-6). Arco.

Gerbils. Alvin Silverstein & Virginia B. Silverstein. LC 75-34390. (gr. 3-6). 1976. 8.95 (ISBN 0-397-31660-7); pap. 3.95 (ISBN 0-397-31661-5). Lippincott.

Gerechte Kriege: Christentum, Islam, Marxismus. Reiner Steinweg. (Edition Suhrkamp. Neue Folge: esNF 17). 250p. (Orig., Ger.). 1980. pap. text ed. 6.50 (ISBN 3-518-11017-9, Pub. by Insel Verlag Germany). Suhrkamp.

Gerfalcon. Leslie Barringer. Ed. by R. Reginald & Douglas Menville. LC 80-19243. (Newcastle Forgotten Fantasy Library: Vol. 7). 310p. 1980. Repr. of 1976 ed. lib. bdg. 10.95x (ISBN 0-89370-506-3). Borgo Pr.

Gerhart Hauptmann. Hugh P. Garten. 1954. 22.50x o.p. (ISBN 0-686-51393-2). Elliots Bks.

Geriatric Amputee: Principles of Management. Committee On Prosthetic-Orthotic Education. LC 79-610527. (Illus., Orig.). 1971. pap. text ed. 4.25 (ISBN 0-309-01873-0). Natl Acad Pr.

Geriatric Assistant. Hazel Mummah & Marsella Smith. (Illus.). 320p. 1980. pap. text ed. 11.95 (ISBN 0-07-044015-8, HP). McGraw.

Geriatric Cardiology. R. Joe Noble & Donald A. Rothbaum. (Cardiovascular Clinics Ser.: Vol. 12, No. 1). 1981. 40.00 (ISBN 0-8036-6565-2). Davis Co.

Geriatric Contentment: A Guide to Its Achievement in Your Home. Shirley G. Desnick. 76p. 1971. text ed. 9.75 (ISBN 0-398-00440-4). C C Thomas.

Geriatric Endocrinology. Robert B. Greenblatt. LC 75-43196. (Aging Ser.: Vol. 5). 1978. 24.50 (ISBN 0-89004-112-1). Raven.

Geriatric Imperative: An Introduction to Gerontology & Clinical Geriatrics. Anne R. Somers & Dorothy R. Fabian. 320p. 1981. pap. 14.95 (ISBN 0-686-69606-9). ACC.

Geriatric Medicine for Students. John C. Brocklehurst & Thomas Hanley. LC 76-8473. (Livingstone Medical Texts Ser.). (Illus.). 1976. pap. text ed. 9.75 (ISBN 0-443-01470-1). Churchill.

Geriatric Medicine for the Primary Care Practitioner. Edward B. Elkowitz. 1981. text ed. price not set (ISBN 0-8261-3230-8); pap. text ed. price not set (ISBN 0-8261-3231-6). Springer Pub.

Geriatric Nutrition. Annette B. Natow et al. LC 80-12282. 1980. text ed. 16.95 (ISBN 0-8436-2184-2). CBI Pub.

Geriatric Procedure Manual. Joan Bretung. 192p. 1980. write for info. o.p. (ISBN 0-913292-05-2). Tiresias Pr.

Geriatrics: A Study of Maturity. 3rd ed. Esther Caldwell & Barbara Hegner. LC 79-55313. (Practical Nursing Ser.). (Illus.). 288p. 1981. pap. text ed. 8.80 (ISBN 0-8273-1935-5); instr's. guide 1.50 (ISBN 0-8273-1934-7). Delmar.

Geriatrics for Nurses & Social Workers. John Agate. (Illus.). 1972. pap. 19.95x (ISBN 0-433-00204-2). Intl Ideas.

Geriatrics in the United States: Manpower Projections & Training Considerations. Robert L. Kane et al. LC 80-8840. (Illus.). write for info. (ISBN 0-669-04386-9). Lexington Bks.

Gericault: Etude Biographique et Critique, Averc Le Catalogue Raisonne De L'Oeuvre Du Maitre. rev ed. Charles Clement. LC 73-83834. (Graphic Art Ser.). (Illus.). 550p. (Fr.). 1974. Repr. of 1879 ed. lib. bdg. 65.00 (ISBN 0-306-70643-1). Da Capo.

Germ Cells & Soma: A New Look at Old Problem. Anne McLaren. LC 80-54221. (Silliman Lectures: No. 5). (Illus.). 128p. 1981. 15.00 (ISBN 0-300-02694-3). Yale U Pr.

German. Holloway Staff. (Harper Phrase Books for the Traveler Ser.). (Orig.). 1977. pap. 1.00 (ISBN 0-8467-0310-6, Pub. by Two Continents). Hippocrene Bks.

German. Jack Rudman. (Undergraduate Program Field Test Ser.: UPFT-12). (Cloth bdg. avail. on request). pap. 9.95 (ISBN 0-8373-6012-9). Natl Learning.

German A, 5 bks. Ellert & Ellert. (gr. 8-12). 1972. pap. text ed. 7.00 each (ISBN 0-686-57754-X). Learning Line.

German: A Structural Approach. 2nd ed. Walter Lohnes & F. W. Strothman. (Illus.). 500p. 1973. text ed. 11.95x (ISBN 0-393-09345-X); tchr's ed. 3.95x (ISBN 0-393-09360-3); study guide 4.45x (ISBN 0-393-09352-2). Norton.

German: A Structural Approach. 3rd ed. Walter F. Lohnes & F. W. Strothmann. 1980. text ed. 13.95x (ISBN 0-393-95059-X); tchrs'. manual avail. (ISBN 0-393-95068-9); study guide 4.95x (ISBN 0-393-95064-6). Norton.

German Achievement Test. Vivian Greiner. (gr. 11-12). 1968. lib. bdg. 4.50 o.p. (ISBN 0-668-01697-3). Arco.

German American History & Life: A Guide to Information Sources. Ed. by Michael Keresztesi & Gary Cocozzoli. LC 79-24065. (Ethnic Studies Information Guide Ser.: Vol. 4). 1980. 30.00 (ISBN 0-8103-1459-2). Gale.

German-American Literature. Don H. Tolzmann. LC 77-21596. 1977. 17.00 (ISBN 0-8108-1069-7). Scarecrow.

German-American Relations. Ed. by W. R. Smyser. LC 79-57535. (Washington Papers: No. 74). 88p. 1980. pap. 3.50 (ISBN 0-8039-1451-2). Sage.

German Americana: A Bibliography. Don H. Tolzmann. LC 74-28085. 1975. 18.00 (ISBN 0-8108-0784-X). Scarecrow.

German-Americans. La Vern Rippley. LC 75-26917. (Immigrant Heritage of America Ser.). 1976. lib. bdg. 9.95 (ISBN 0-8057-8405-5). Twayne.

German Aviation Medicine, World War Two, 2 vols. Surgeon General, USAF. Tr. by Aero Medical Center Staff. LC 77-168949. (Illus.). 1302p. 1971. Repr. of 1950 ed. Set. lib. bdg. 75.00 (ISBN 0-87936-000-3). Scholium Intl.

German B, 3 bks. Ellert & Ellert. (gr. 8-12). 1972. pap. text ed. 7.00 each (ISBN 0-8449-1423-1). Learning Line.

German Baroque Novel. Hans Wagener. (World Authors Ser.: Germany: No. 229). lib. bdg. 10.95 (ISBN 0-8057-2356-0). Twayne.

German Bombers Over England. Bryan Philpott. (World War Two Photo Album: No. 2). (Illus.). 96p. 1981. pap. 5.95 (ISBN 0-89404-042-1). Aztex.

German Bombers Over Russia: World War Two Photo Album. Bryan Philpott. (Illus.). 96p. 1981. pap. 5.95 (ISBN 0-89404-050-2). Aztex.

German Bombers Over the Med. Bryan Philpott. (World War Two Photo Album Ser.: No. 13). (Illus.). 1980. 17.95 o.p. (ISBN 0-85059-393-X); pap. 11.95 o.p. (ISBN 0-85059-394-8). Aztex.

German Bombers Over the Med: World War Two Photo Album. Bryan Philpott. (Illus.). 96p. 1981. pap. 5.95 (ISBN 0-89404-037-5). Aztex.

German Books in Print, Nineteen Eighty to Eighty-One: Authors-Titles-Keywords, 4 vols. 10th ed. Set. 250.00 (ISBN 3-7657-0862-3, Dist by Gale Research Co.). K G Saur.

German Books in Print, Nineteen Eighty to Eighty-One: ISBN Register. 637p. 1980. 95.00 (ISBN 3-7657-0986-7, Dist. by Gale Research Co.). K G Saur.

German Books in Print, Nineteen Eighty to Eighty-One: Subject Guide, 3 vols. 3rd ed. 1980. Set. 240.00 (Dist. by Gale Research Co.). K G Saur.

German Books in Print 1979-1980, 3 vols. 9th ed. 5889p. (Ger. & Eng.). 1979. text ed. 198.00 o.p. (ISBN 0-89664-163-5). K G Saur.

German Business After the Economic Miracle. Frank Vogl. LC 73-15142. 1973. 29.95 (ISBN 0-470-90970-6). Halsted Pr.

German Capital Ships. Paul Beaver. (World War Two Photo Album Ser.: No. 14). (Illus.). 1980. 17.95 o.p. (ISBN 0-85059-395-6); pap. 11.95 o.p. (ISBN 0-85059-396-4). Aztex.

German Capital Ships: World War Two Photo Album. Paul Beaver. (Illus.). 96p. 1981. pap. 5.95 (ISBN 0-89404-038-3). Aztex.

German Churches Under Hitler: Background, Struggle & Epilogue. Ernst Helmreich. LC 78-17737. 1978. 30.00 (ISBN 0-8143-1603-4). Wayne St U Pr.

German Code of Criminal Procedure. (American Series of Foreign Penal Codes: Vol. 10). 1965. 17.50x (ISBN 0-8377-0030-2). Rothman.

German Conception of History: The National Tradition of Historical Thought from Herder to the Present. Georg G. Iggers. LC 68-17147. 1968. 20.00x (ISBN 0-8195-3088-3, Pub. by Wesleyan U Pr). Columbia U Pr.

German Concise Dictionary. Cassells. 1977. 8.95 (ISBN 0-02-052265-7). Macmillan.

German Corporation Tax Reform Law 1977. Tr. by Hugh J. Ault & Albert J. Radler. 1977. pap. text ed. 15.00x (ISBN 3-7875-5261-8). Rothman.

German Dadaist Literature. Rex W. Last. (World Authors Ser.: Germany: No. 272). 1973. lib. bdg. 10.95 (ISBN 0-8057-2361-7). Twayne.

German Delegation at the Paris Peace Conference. Alma Luckau. LC 70-80569. 1971. Repr. 25.00 (ISBN 0-86527-078-3). Fertig.

German Democratic Republic. Ed. by Lyman H. Legters. LC 77-578. 1977. lib. bdg. 24.50 o.p. (ISBN 0-89158-142-1). Westview.

German Democratic Republic: A Profile. Henry Krisch. (Nations of Contemporary Eastern Europe Ser.). 128p. 1981. lib. bdg. 16.50x (ISBN 0-89158-850-7). Westview.

German Destroyers & Escorts: World War Two Photo Album. Paul Beaver. (Illus.). 96p. 1981. pap. 5.95 (ISBN 0-89404-060-X). Aztex.

German Dictatorship: The Origins, Structure, and Effects of National Socialism. Karl D. Bracher. Tr. by Jean Steinberg from German. LC 70-95662. Orig. Title: Deutsche Diktatur: Enstehung, Struktur, & Folgen Des Nationalsozialismus. 553p. 1972. pap. text ed. 8.95x. Praeger.

German Dimension of American History. Joseph Wandel. LC 78-26050. 1979. 14.95 (ISBN 0-88229-147-5); pap. 7.95 (ISBN 0-88229-668-X). Nelson-Hall.

German Dolls II. Patricia Smith. (Illus.). 1980. pap. 9.95 (ISBN 0-89145-151-X). Collector Bks.

German Draft Penal Code E 1962. (American Series of Foreign Penal Codes: Vol. 11). 1966. 15.00x (ISBN 0-8377-0031-0). Rothman.

German Economy at War. Alan S. Milward. 1965. text ed. 14.00x (ISBN 0-485-11075-X, Athlone Pr). Humanities.

German Election Study, October 1965. DIVO Institut fuer Wirtschaftsforschung, Sozialforschung und angewandte Mathematik. 1975. codebk. 10.00 (ISBN 0-89138-109-0). ICPSR.

German-English & English-German Medical Dictionary. 6th rev. & enl. ed. D. W. Unseld. 1971. 25.00 o.p. (ISBN 3-8047-0567-7). Heinman.

German English Dictionary. John C. Traupman. 764p. (Orig.). 1981. pap. 2.50 (ISBN 0-553-14155-4). Bantam.

German-English Dictionary for Chemists. 3rd ed. A. M. Patterson. 1950. 21.95 (ISBN 0-471-66990-3, Pub. by Wiley-Interscience). Wiley.

German-English Dictionary of Technical, Scientific & General Terms. 3rd ed. A. Webel. 1969. Repr. of 1952 ed. 37.50 (ISBN 0-7100-2258-1). Routledge & Kegan.

German-English, English-German Patent Terminological Dictionary. E. B. Klaften & F. C. Allison. 1971. 50.00 (ISBN 0-685-12020-1). Heinman.

German-English Glossary of Financial & Commercial Terms. new ed. C. A. Gunston & C. M. Corner. (Ger. & Eng.). 1977. 57.50 (ISBN 3-7819-2008-9). Adler.

German Enigma: The Elitist Tradition in German Literature. Walter E. Anderson. LC 79-66491. 225p. 1981. 9.95 (ISBN 0-533-04398-0). Vantage.

German Enlightenment & the Rise of Historicism. Peter H. Reill. LC 73-87244. 318p. 1975. 27.50x (ISBN 0-520-02594-6). U of Cal Pr.

German Executive, 1890-1933. Maxwell E. Knight. LC 78-80560. (Illus.). 52p. 1973. Repr. of 1952 ed. 9.00 (ISBN 0-86527-079-1). Fertig.

German Expressionist Drama. J. M. Ritchie. Ed. by Ulrich J. Weisstein. (World Author Ser.: No. 421). 1977. lib. bdg. 9.95 (ISBN 0-8057-6261-2). Twayne.

German Expressionist Painting. Peter Selz. (Illus.). 1957. 38.50x (ISBN 0-520-01161-9); pap. 10.95 (ISBN 0-520-02515-6). U of Cal Pr.

German Expressionist Poetry. Roy F. Allen. (World Authors Ser.: No. 421). 1979. lib. bdg. 13.50 (ISBN 0-8057-6386-4). Twayne.

German Family. Ed. by Richard Evans & W. R. Lee. 224p. 1981. 27.50x (ISBN 0-389-20101-4). B&N.

German Fighters Over England. Bryan Philpott. Ed. by D. Reach. (World War 2 Photo Album: 10). (Illus.). 1979. 17.95 o.p. (ISBN 0-85059-355-7); pap. 11.75 o.p. (ISBN 0-85059-356-5). Aztex.

German Fighters Over England: World War Two Photo Album. Bryan Philpott. (Illus.). 96p. 1981. softcover 5.95 (ISBN 0-89404-056-1). Aztex.

German Fighters Over Russia. Bryan Philpott. (World War Two Photo Album: No. 16). (Illus.). 96p. 1980. pap. 5.95 (ISBN 0-89404-040-5). Aztex.

German First Year. Harry Reinert. (gr. 7-12). 1971. wkbk. 6.42 (ISBN 0-87720-583-3). AMSCO Sch.

German, Flemish, & Dutch Drawings. Roseline Bacou. (Great Drawings of the Louvre Museum Ser: Vol. 3). (Illus.). 1968. 20.00 o.s.i. (ISBN 0-8076-0474-7). Braziller.

German Folk Tales. Grimm Brothers. Tr. by Francis P. Magoun, Jr. & Alexander H. Krappe. LC 59-5095. (Arcturus Books Paperbacks). 682p. (gr. 5 up). 1969. pap. 11.95 (ISBN 0-8093-0356-6). S Ill U Pr.

German for Beginners. 2nd rev. ed. Charles Duff & Paul Stamford. 1960. pap. 3.95 (ISBN 0-06-463217-2, EH 217, EH). Har-Row.

German for Careers: Conversational Perspectives. Peter Bonnell & Frank Sedwick. (Orig.). 1980. pap. text ed. 8.95 (ISBN 0-442-20563-5). D Van Nostrand.

German for Reading: A Programmed Approach. Karl C. Sandberg & John R. Wende. 1973. pap. text ed. 14.95 (ISBN 0-13-354019-7). P-H.

German Foreign Policy, 1871-1914. Imanuel Geiss. (Orig.). 1976. pap. 18.00 (ISBN 0-7100-8303-3). Routledge & Kegan.

German Foreign Policy, 1890-1914 & Colonial Policy to 1914: A Handbook & Annotated Bibliography. Andrew R. Carlson. 1970. 10.00 (ISBN 0-8108-0296-1). Scarecrow.

German Forestry. Franz Heske. 1938. 47.50x (ISBN 0-686-51394-0). Elliots Bks.

German Graded Readers, 3 bks. Erika Meyer. Incl. Bk. 1. Auf Dem Dorfe. 2nd ed. 1964. pap. text ed. 3.90 (ISBN 0-395-04887-7, 3-37456); Bk. 2. In der Stadt. 2nd ed. 1964. pap. text ed. o.p. (ISBN 0-685-23334-0, 3-37461); Bk. 3. Genialische Jugend: Zwei Erzahlungen. 1949. pap. text ed. o.p. (ISBN 0-685-23335-9, 3-37465). LC 49-4261. HM.

German Graded Readers: Alternate Series, 3 bks. Erika Meyer. Incl. Bk. 1. Ein Briefwechsel. pap. text ed. 3.90 (ISBN 0-395-04890-7, 3-37470); Bk. 2. Akademische Freiheit. pap. text ed. o.p. (ISBN 0-685-23336-7, 3-37475); Bk. 3. Goslar. pap. text ed. o.p. (ISBN 0-685-23337-5, 3-37480). 1954. HM.

German Grammar. 3rd ed. Eric V. Greenfield. (Orig., Ger.). 1968. pap. 3.95 (ISBN 0-06-460034-3, CO 34, COS). Har-Row.

German Grammar Workbook. Robert O. Roseler & Joseph R. Reichard. 1956. pap. text ed. 2.95x (ISBN 0-89197-533-0). Irvington.

German Historians & England: A Study in Nineteenth Century Views. Charles E. McClelland. LC 79-154514. 1971. 41.00 (ISBN 0-521-08063-0). Cambridge U Pr.

German History & Civilization - 1806-1914: A Bibliography of Scholarly Periodical Literature. John C. Fout. LC 74-10803. 1974. 15.00 (ISBN 0-8108-0742-4). Scarecrow.

German in Thirty-Two Lessons. Adrienne. (Gimmick Ser.). 1979. 10.95 (ISBN 0-393-04527-7); pap. 5.95 (ISBN 0-393-04533-1). Norton.

German in Twenty Lessons. (Cortina Language Ser.). 1977. pap. 3.95 o.p. (ISBN 0-385-13009-0, Dolp). Doubleday.

German Language Press of the Americas, 3 vols. Karl J. Arndt & May Olson. 1980. Set. text ed. 321.00 (Pub. by K G Saur). Gale.

German Laws Relating to Patents, Utility Models & Trade Marks & to Inventions of Employees. J. D. Von Uexkull. 157p. 1978. pap. 23.50x (ISBN 3-452-18469-2, Pub by C Heymanns Verlag KG West Germany). Rothman.

German Legends of the Brothers Grimm, 2 vols. Ed. & tr. by Donald Ward. LC 80-24596. (Translations in Folklore Studies Ser.). (Illus.). 1981. Set. 42.00 (ISBN 0-915980-79-7). Inst Study Human.

German Lied & Its Poetry. Elaine Brody & Robert A. Fowkes. LC 76-124520. 1971. 15.00 (ISBN 0-8147-0958-3). NYU Pr.

German Literary Influence on Byron. M. Roxana Klapper. (Salzburg Studies in English Literature, Romantic Reassessment Ser.: No. 43). 1975. pap. text ed. 25.00x (ISBN 0-391-01448-X). Humanities.

German Literary Influence on Shelley. Roxana M. Klapper. (Salzburg Studies in English Literature, Romantic Reassessment: No. 42). 1974. pap. text ed. 25.00x (ISBN 0-391-01449-8). Humanities.

German Made Simple. Eugene Jackson & Adolph Geiger. LC 65-10615. pap. 3.50 (ISBN 0-385-00129-0, Made). Doubleday.

German Man of Letters: Twelve Literary Essays, Vols. 5 & 6. Ed. by Alex Natan & Brian Keith-Smith. LC 66-28772. 318p. 1973. Vol. 5. 15.95 (ISBN 0-8023-1175-X); Vol. 6. 15.95 (ISBN 0-8023-1239-X). Dufour.

German Maritime Aircraft. Bryan Philpott. (World War Two Photo Album: No. 18). (Illus.). 96p. 1981. pap. 5.95 (ISBN 0-89404-046-4). Aztex.

German Marxism & Russian Communism. John P. Plamenatz. LC 75-1135. 356p. 1975. Repr. of 1954 ed. lib. bdg. 25.25x (ISBN 0-8371-7986-6, PLGM). Greenwood.

German Medieval Literary Patronage from Charlemagne to Maximilian the First: A Critical Commentary with Special Emphasis on Imperial Promotion of Literature. William C. McDonald & Ulrich Goebel. LC 73-82154. (Amsterdamer Publikationen Zur Sprache und Literatur: No. 10). 220p. (Orig.). 1973. pap. text ed. 23.00x (ISBN 90-6203-201-X). Humanities.

German Men of Letters: Twelve Literary Essays. Ed. by Alex Natan. Vol. 1. 15.95 (ISBN 0-85496-001-5); pap. 8.95 (ISBN 0-85496-002-3); Vol. 2. pap. 15.95 (ISBN 0-85496-004-X); Vol. 3. pap. 10.95 (ISBN 0-85496-006-6). Dufour.

German Military Uniforms & Insignia, 1933-1945. We, Editors. LC 68-6985. (Illus.). 1967. 8.95 o.p. (ISBN 0-911964-00-2). Paladin Ent.

German Mind of the Nineteenth Century: A Literary & Historical Anthology. Ed. by Hermann Glaser. 416p. 1981. 19.50 (ISBN 0-8264-0041-8); pap. 8.95 (ISBN 0-8264-0044-2). Continuum.

German Mountain Troops. Bruce Quarrie. (World War Two Photo Album: No. 15). (Illus.). 96p. 1980. pap. 5.95 (ISBN 0-89404-039-1). Aztex.

German Once a Week, 2 bks. H. Eichinger et al. 1976. pap. 5.25x ea. (Pub. by Basil Blackwell). Bk. 1, 1977 (ISBN 0-631-96270-0). Bk. 2 (ISBN 0-631-96280-8). Biblio Dist.

German Paratroops in the Mediterranean: World War Two Photo Album. Bruce Quarrie. (Illus.). 96p. 1981. pap. 5.95 (ISBN 0-89404-049-9). Aztex.

German Peasant War Fifteen Twenty-Five: New Viewpoints. Bob Scribner & Gerhard Benecke. (Illus.). 1979. text ed. 22.50x (ISBN 0-04-900031-4); pap. text ed. 8.95x (ISBN 0-04-900032-2). Allen Unwin.

German Penal Code. (American Series of Foreign Penal Codes: Vol. 4). 1961. 15.00x (ISBN 0-8377-0024-8). Rothman.

German Photographic Literature, Eighteen Thirty-Nine to Nineteen Seventy-Eight: Theory, Technology, Visual. A Classified Bibliography of German-Language Photographic Publications. Ed. by Frank Heidtmann et al. 690p. 1980. 85.00 (ISBN 3-598-10026-4, Dist. by Gale Research Co.). K G Saur.

German Poetic Realism. Clifford A. Bernd. (World Authors Ser.: No. 605). 1981. lib. bdg. 12.95 (ISBN 0-8057-6447-X). Twayne.

German Poetry: A Guide to Free Appreciation. rev. ed. R. Gray. LC 75-20834. 120p. 1976. 27.50 (ISBN 0-521-20931-5); pap. 8.95x (ISBN 0-521-29000-7). Cambridge U Pr.

German Policy of Augustus: An Examination of the Archaeological Evidence. C. M. Wells. (Illus.). 340p. 1972. 28.50x (ISBN 0-19-813162-3). Oxford U Pr.

German Political Idealism. Frank Thakurdas. 368p. 1980. text ed. 22.50x (ISBN 0-391-01796-9). Humanities.

German Political Studies, Vol. 1. Ed. by Klaus Von Beyme. LC 74-82535. 1974. 20.00x (ISBN 0-8039-9927-5). Sage.

German Political System. Guido Goldman. (Patterns of Government Ser). 1974. pap. text ed. 5.95 (ISBN 0-394-31820-X). Random.

German Political Systems: Theory & Practice in the Two Germanies. Ed. by Klaus Von Beyme. LC 74-82535. (German Political Studies: Vol. 2). 1976. 20.00x (ISBN 0-8039-9963-1). Sage.

German Politics Under Soviet Occupation. Henry Krisch. LC 74-3288. 1974. 20.00x (ISBN 0-231-03835-6). Columbia U Pr.

German Polity. David P. Conradt. LC 77-17711. (Comparative Studies of Political Life Ser.). 1978. text ed. 15.95x (ISBN 0-582-28034-6); pap. text ed. 9.95x (ISBN 0-582-28033-8). Longman.

German Problem Reconsidered. David Calleo. LC 78-9683. 208p. 1980. pap. 6.95 (ISBN 0-521-29966-7). Cambridge U Pr.

German Raiders: A History of Auxiliary Cruisers of the German Navy 1895-1945. Paul Schmalenbach. LC 78-71801. (Illus.). 144p. 1980. 15.95 (ISBN 0-87021-824-7). Naval Inst Pr.

German Raiders of World War II. August K. Muggenthaler. LC 76-30612. 1977. 14.95 o.p. (ISBN 0-13-354027-8). P-H.

German Realism of the Twenties. Gregory Hedberg. (Illus.). 1980. 15.00. Minneapolis Inst Arts.

German Review. pocket ed. 150p. (gr. 7-12). 1981. pap. text ed. 2.50 (ISBN 0-8120-2195-9). Barron. Postponed.

German Review & Reference Grammar. Paul G. Krauss. (Orig.). 1962. pap. text ed. 7.95 o.p. (ISBN 0-13-354100-2). P-H.

German Review Grammar. 2nd ed. Alan J. Pfeffer. 1970. text ed. 13.95x o.p. (ISBN 0-669-52241-4); tapes. 6 reels 30.00 o.p. (ISBN 0-669-90407-4); lab drill manual o.p 1.50x o.p. (ISBN 0-669-52266-X). Heath.

German Revolution of Nineteen Eighteen. A. J. Ryder. 1967. 41.95 (ISBN 0-521-06176-8). Cambridge U Pr.

German-Romance Contact: Name-Giving in Walser Settlements. Peter N. Richardson. LC 74-79043. (Amsterdamer Publikationen Zur Sprache und Literatur: No. 15). 372p. (Orig.). 1974. pap. text ed. 34.25x (ISBN 90-6203-221-4). Humanities.

German Romantic Painting. William Vaughan. LC 80-13170. (Illus.). 288p. 1980. 45.00x (ISBN 0-300-02387-1). Yale U Pr.

German-Russians: A Bibliography. James Long. LC 78-19071. 136p. 1978. text ed. 11.95 (ISBN 0-87436-282-2). ABC-Clio.

German Seed in Texas Soil: Immigrant Farmers in Nineteenth Century Texas. Terry G. Jordan. 1966. pap. 5.95 (ISBN 0-292-72707-0). U of Tex Pr.

German Shepherd Guide. Madelaine Pickup. 6.98 o.p. (ISBN 0-385-01575-5). Doubleday.

German Shepherd Today. Winifred G. Strickland & James A. Moses. LC 73-19044. (Illus.). 512p. 1974. 17.95 (ISBN 0-02-615030-1). Macmillan.

German Shepherds. rev. ed. E. Mansfield Schalk. (Illus.). 128p. 1974. pap. 2.95 o.p. (ISBN 0-87666-297-1, HS1043). TFH Pubns.

German Short Stories, Vol. 1. 1900-1945, Vol. 2. 1945-1955, Vol. 3. 1955-1965. H. M. Waidson. Vol. 1. text ed. 4.75x (ISBN 0-521-06717-0); Vol. 2. text ed. 5.25x (ISBN 0-521-06718-9); Vol. 3. text ed. 5.75x (ISBN 0-521-07180-1). Cambridge U Pr.

German Shorthaired Pointer. L. Z. Spirer & H. F. Spirer. 1970. 9.95 (ISBN 0-87666-303-X, PS635). TFH Pubns.

German Shorthaired Pointers. Richard S. Johns. (Illus.). 128p. 1974. pap. cancelled o.p. (ISBN 0-87666-302-1, HS-1046). TFH Pubns.

German Small Arms. A. J. Cormack. (Illus.). 160p. 1979. 20.00x (ISBN 0-85383-261-7). Intl Pubns Serv.

German Social Democratic Party 1875-1933. W. L. Guttsman. (Illus.). 1981. text ed. 40.00x (ISBN 0-04-943024-6, 2613). Allen Unwin.

German Socialism & Weimar Democracy. Richard Breitman. LC 80-21412. 296p. 1981. 20.00x (ISBN 0-8078-1462-8). U of NC Pr.

German-Soviet Pact, August 23, 1939: A Nonagression Pact. Grant Neil. LC 75-8512. (World Focus Bks). (Illus.). 72p. (gr. 7 up). 1975. PLB 6.45 (ISBN 0-531-02174-2). Watts.

German Strategy Against Russia, 1939-1941. Barry Leach. (Illus.). 1973. 29.00x o.p. (ISBN 0-19-821495-2). Oxford U Pr.

German Tanks & Armoured Vehicles 1914-1945. B. T. White. LC 68-26167. (Illus.). 1966. lib. bdg. 3.50 o. p. o.p. (ISBN 0-668-01783-X); pap. 1.95 o.p. (ISBN 0-668-01784-8). Arco.

German Theater Today: A Symposium. Ed. by Leroy R. Shaw. (Dept of Germanic Languages Pubns). (Illus.). 1964. 10.00 (ISBN 0-292-73250-3). U of Tex Pr.

German Through Conversational Patterns. 3rd ed. R. M. Rogers & Arthur R. Watkins. (Illus.). 544p. 1981. text ed. 17.50 scp (ISBN 0-06-045551-9, HarpC); avail. instrs' manual; wkbk. scp 7.50 (ISBN 0-06-045554-3); tapes 229.00. Har-Row.

German Trade Unionism from Bismarck to Hitler: 1869-1933, 2 vols. John Moses. Incl. Vol. 1. Bismarck to 1918. 400p (ISBN 0-389-20072-7); Vol. 2. 1919-1933. 400p (ISBN 0-389-20073-5). 1981. 25.00x ea. B&N.

German Tradition in Literature. Ronald D. Gray. LC 65-17206. 1966. 48.00 (ISBN 0-521-05133-9); pap. 17.50 (ISBN 0-521-29278-6). Cambridge U Pr.

German Tradition of Self-Cultivation. W. H. Bruford. LC 74-79143. 336p. 1974. 47.50 (ISBN 0-521-20482-8). Cambridge U Pr.

German Wines. Heinrich Meinhard. (Illus.). 1971. 7.95 (ISBN 0-85362-107-1, Oriel). Routledge & Kegan.

German Women Writers of the Twentieth Century. Ed. by Elizabeth R. Herrmann & Edna H. Spitz. LC 78-40139. 1978. text ed. 25.00 (ISBN 0-08-021827-X); pap. text ed. 14.00 (ISBN 0-08-021828-8). Pergamon.

German Word Family Dictionary: Together with English Equivalents. Howard H. Keller. 1978. 14.95x (ISBN 0-520-03291-8). U of Cal Pr.

Germans, Poles, & Jews: The Nationality Conflict in the Prussian East, 1772-1914. William W. Hagen. LC 80-10557. (Illus.). 1980. lib. bdg. 17.50x (ISBN 0-226-31242-9). U of Chicago Pr.

Germans: The Biography of an Obsession. George Bailey. 1974. pap. 3.50 (ISBN 0-380-00140-3, 53918, Discus). Avon.

Germany. rev. ed. Gerhart H. Seger. LC 77-83909. (World Cultures Ser.). (Illus.). 188p. (gr. 6 up). 1978. text ed. 9.95 ea. 1-4 copies (ISBN 0-88296-180-2); text ed. 7.96 ea. 5 or more copies; tchrs'. guide 8.94 (ISBN 0-88296-369-4). Fideler.

Germany: A History. John E. Rodes. 719p. 1964. 19.50 o.p. (ISBN 0-03-042600-6, Pub. by HR&W). Krieger.

Germany: A Short History. Donald S. Detwiler. LC 76-4563. 288p. 1976. 14.95x (ISBN 0-8093-0491-0); pap. 7.95 (ISBN 0-8093-0768-5). S Ill U Pr.

Germany & America: Essays on Problems of International Relations & Immigration. Ed. by Hans L. Trefousse. 270p. 1981. 23.00x (ISBN 0-930888-06-5). Brooklyn Coll Pr.

Germany & Europe, 1919-1939. John Hiden. LC 77-3299. 1978. text ed. 15.00x (ISBN 0-582-48489-8); pap. text ed. 8.50x (ISBN 0-582-48490-1). Longman.

Germany & Japan: A Study in Totalitarian Diplomacy, 1933-1941. Ernst L. Presseisen. LC 68-57832. 1970. Repr. of 1958 ed. 18.50 (ISBN 0-86527-082-1). Fertig.

Germany & the Future of Europe. Ed. by Hans J. Morgenthau. (Midway Reprint Ser.). (Illus.). viii, 180p. 1975. pap. text ed. 7.00x o.s.i. (ISBN 0-226-53831-1). U of Chicago Pr.

Germany & the Two World Wars. Andreas Hillgruber. Tr. by William C. Kirby. LC 80-27036. 144p. 1981. text ed. 14.50 (ISBN 0-674-35321-8). Harvard U Pr.

Germany Confronts Modernization: German Culture & Society, 1790-1890. Robert Anchor. (Civilization & Society Ser). 224p. 1972. pap. 5.95x o.p. (ISBN 0-669-81026-6). Heath.

Germany East & West: Conflicts, Collaboration & Confrontation. Lawrence L. Whetten. LC 79-3713. 244p. 1981. 17.50x (ISBN 0-8147-9193-X). NYU Pr.

Germany, Eighteen Forty-Eight to Eighteen Seventy-Nine. John A. Moses. (History Monographs). 1973. pap. text ed. 4.50x (ISBN 0-435-31620-6). Heinemann Ed.

Germany in the Age of Bismarck. W. M. Simon. (Historical Problems: Studies & Documents). 1968. text ed. 8.95x o.p. (ISBN 0-04-943010-6). Allen Unwin.

Germany in the Age of Total War. Volker Berghahn & Martin Kitchen. 272p. 1981. 25.00x (ISBN 0-389-20186-3). B&N.

Germany in the Eighteenth Century. Walter H. Bruford. 1935. 38.50 (ISBN 0-521-04354-9); pap. 11.50x (ISBN 0-521-09259-0, 259). Cambridge U Pr.

Germany: Its Geography & Growth. K. A. Sinnhuber. 1972. 14.00 (ISBN 0-7195-1286-7). Transatlantic.

Germany, Nuclear Weapons & Alliance Relations: 1954-1966. Catherine M. Kelleher. 384p. 1975. 20.00x (ISBN 0-231-03960-3). Columbia U Pr.

Germany: People & Politics. Ed. by Robert F. Hopwood. LC 68-134435. (Selections from History Today Ser.: No. 12). (Illus.). 1969. 3.95 (ISBN 0-05-001656-3). Dufour.

Germany: Two Thousand Years, 2 Vols. rev. ed. Kurt F. Reinhardt. LC 60-53139. Vol.1. 12.00 (ISBN 0-8044-1783-0); Vol.2. 12.00 (ISBN 0-8044-1784-9); Vol.1. pap. 5.50 (ISBN 0-8044-6692-0); Vol.2. pap. 5.95 (ISBN 0-8044-6693-9). Set. pap. 10.95 (ISBN 0-8044-6691-2). Ungar.

Germany Under Direct Controls: Economic Aspects of Industrial Disarmament, 1945-1948. Nicholas Balabkins. 1964. 16.00 (ISBN 0-8135-0449-X). Rutgers U Pr.

Germany Without Bismarck. John Rohl. LC 67-26960. 1967. 22.75x (ISBN 0-520-01086-8). U of Cal Pr.

Germany's Hitler. Heinz A. Heinz. (Illus.). 1976. pap. 4.00x (ISBN 0-911038-46-9). Noontide.

Germany's Ostpolitik: Relations Between the Federal Republic & the Warsaw Pact Countries. Lawrence L. Whetten. 1971. pap. 6.50x o.p. (ISBN 0-19-285051-2). Oxford U Pr.

Germany's Third Empire. Arthur Moeller Van Den Bruck. 1972. 16.00 (ISBN 0-86527-085-6). Fertig.

Germany's Three Reichs. Edmond Vermeil. LC 68-9638. 1969. Repr. of 1944 ed. 19.00 (ISBN 0-86527-086-4). Fertig.

Germinal. Emile Zola. Tr. by Havelock Ellis. 1964. 5.00x o.p. (ISBN 0-460-00897-8, Evman); pap. op o.p. (ISBN 0-460-01897-3, EP1897). Dutton.

Germination of Seeds. 2nd ed. A. M. Mayer et al. Ed. by P. F. Wareing & A. W. Galston. 160p. 1976. text ed. 30.00 (ISBN 0-08-018966-0); pap. text ed. 18.00 (ISBN 0-08-018965-2). Pergamon.

Germplasm Bank Information Retrieval System. (IRRI Research Paper Ser.: No. 45). 24p. 1979. pap. 5.00 (R085, IRRI). Unipub.

Geronimo. Matthew G. Grant. LC 73-12203. 1974. PLB 5.95 (ISBN 0-87191-267-8). Creative Ed.

Geronimo. Ronald Syme. LC 74-16337. (Illus.). 96p. (gr. 3-7). 1975. 7.25 (ISBN 0-688-22013-4); PLB 6.96 (ISBN 0-688-32013-9). Morrow.

Geronimo: The Man, His Time, His Place. Angie Debo. LC 76-13858. (Civilization of the American Indian Ser: No.142). 1976. 14.95 (ISBN 0-8061-1333-2). U of Okla Pr.

Gerontology: A Book of Readings. Clyde B. Vedder. (Illus.). 448p. 1971. 14.75 (ISBN 0-398-01972-X). C C Thomas.

Gerontology in Higher Education. Mildred Seltzer et al. 1978. text ed. 23.95x (ISBN 0-534-00582-9). Wadsworth Pub.

Gerontology in Higher Education: Developing Institutional & Community Strength. new ed. Harvey L. Sterns et al. 1979. text ed. 23.95x (ISBN 0-534-00708-2). Wadsworth Pub.

Gershwin Years. rev. ed. Edward Jablonski & Lawrence D. Stewart. LC 73-78334. 384p. 1973. 6.95 o.p. (ISBN 0-385-02847-4). Doubleday.

Gertie & Gus. Lisl Weil. LC 77-4757. (Illus.). (gr. k-4). 1977. 5.95 o.s.i. (ISBN 0-8193-0911-7, Four Winds); PLB 5.41 o.s.i. (ISBN 0-8193-0912-5). Schol Bk Serv.

Gertrude Atherton. Charlotte S. McClure. (United States Authors Ser.: No. 324). 1979. lib. bdg. 10.95 (ISBN 0-8057-7216-2). Twayne.

Gertrude Stein. Michael J. Hoffman. (U. S. Authors Ser.: No. 268). 1976. lib. bdg. 10.95 (ISBN 0-8057-7168-9). Twayne.

Gertrude Stein in Pieces. Richard Bridgman. 1970. 18.95x (ISBN 0-19-501280-1). Oxford U Pr.

Gertrude, the Goose Who Forgot. Joanna Galdone. LC 73-19583. (Illus.). (gr. k-3). 1975. PLB 5.90 o.p. (ISBN 0-531-02735-X). Watts.

Gertrude's Follies. T. Hachtman. 80p. 1981. pap. 5.95 (ISBN 0-312-32630-0). St Martin.

Gertrudis Gomez De Avellaneda. Hugh A. Harter. (World Authors Ser.: No. 599). 1981. lib. bdg. 14.95 (ISBN 0-8057-6441-0). Twayne.

Gesammelte Abhandlungen, 3 Vols. 3rd ed. David Hilbert. LC 65-21834. (Ger). 1981. Set. 49.95 (ISBN 0-8284-0195-0). Chelsea Pub.

Gesammelte Abhandlungen, 2 Vols. in 1. Hermann Minkowski. LC 66-28570. (Ger). 35.00 (ISBN 0-8284-0208-6). Chelsea Pub.

Gesammelte Lichenologische Schriften, 2 vols. J. Mueller. Incl. Vol. 1. Lichenologische Beitraege 1-XXXV. o.p. (ISBN 0-686-22233-4). 1967. 220.00 set (ISBN 3-7682-0440-5). Lubrecht & Cramer.

Gesammelte Mathematische Abhandlungen, 2 vols. in 1. 2nd ed. Hermann A. Schwarz. LC 70-113147. (Ger). text ed. 39.50 (ISBN 0-8284-0260-4). Chelsea Pub.

Gesammelte Werke, 8 vols. 2nd ed. Karl G. Jacobi. LC 68-31427. (Illus., Ger., Includes Supplementband Vorlesugen Uber Dynamik). 1969. Vols. 1-7. 160.00 (ISBN 0-8284-0226-4); Vol. 8. 15.00 (ISBN 0-8284-0227-2). Chelsea Pub.

Geschichte der deutschen Gartenkunst, 3 vols. D. Hennebo & A. Hoffman. (Illus.). 930p. 1980. Repr. of 1962 ed. Set. lib. bdg. 187.00x (ISBN 3-87429-176-6). Lubrecht & Cramer.

Geschichte der deutschen Seeschiffart, Band I: Von der Urzeit Bis Zum Ende Des 15th Jahrhunderts. Walther Vogel. 560p. 1973. Repr. of 1915 ed. 111.75x (ISBN 3-11-002304-0). De Gruyter.

Geschichte der Serbischen Kunst von den Anfaengen bis zum Ende des Mittelalters. Svetozar Radojcic. (Illus., Ger.). 1969. 29.40x (ISBN 3-11-000267-1). De Gruyter.

Geschichte Mittelasiens im Altertum. Franz Altheim & Ruth Stiehl. (Illus., Ger.). 1970. 164.70x (ISBN 3-11-002677-5). De Gruyter.

Geschichtszahlen der Phonetik (1941) Together with Quellenatlas der Phonetik (1940) Giulio Panconcelli-Calzia. (Studies in the History of Linguistics: No. 16). 1980. text ed. 40.00x (ISBN 0-391-01649-0). Humanities.

Geschicte der Oper. Hermann Kretzschmar. LC 80-2285. 1981. Repr. of 1919 ed. 33.50 (ISBN 0-404-18853-2). AMS Pr.

Gestalt Art Experience. Janie Rhyne. LC 73-84603. 1974. text ed. 16.95 (ISBN 0-8185-0102-2). Brooks-Cole.

Gestalt Psychology: A Survey of Facts & Principles. George W. Hartmann. LC 73-16649. (Illus.). 325p. 1974. Repr. of 1935 ed. lib. bdg. 25.00x (ISBN 0-8371-7213-6, HAGE). Greenwood.

Gestalt Self Therapy. Muriel Schiffman. LC 73-75228. 240p. (Orig.). 1980. pap. 4.95 (ISBN 0-914640-02-X, Pub. by Self Therapy Pr). Wingbow Pr.

Gestalt Therapy Primer: Introductory Readings in Gestalt Therapy. F. Douglas Stephenson. (Illus.). 232p. 1975. pap. 22.75 (ISBN 0-398-03233-5). C C Thomas.

Gestalt Therapy Resources. 3rd ed. Jerry Kogan. 44p. 1980. pap. 5.00 (ISBN 0-930162-03-X). Transform Berkeley.

Gestapo. Edward Crankshaw. 1977. pap. 1.50 o.s.i. (ISBN 0-515-04236-6). Jove Pubns.

Gestational Age of the Newborn: A Clinical Manual. Lilly M. Dubowitz & Victor Dubowitz. LC 76-62906. 1977. text ed. 19.95 (ISBN 0-201-01171-9, M&N Div). A-W.

Gestational Age, Size & Maturity. Ed. by Michael Dawkins & W. G. MacGregor. (Clinics in Developmental Medicine Ser. No. 19). 115p. 1965. 9.00 (ISBN 0-685-24719-8). Lippincott.

Gesture of Balance: A Guide to Awareness, Self-Healing & Meditation. Tarthang Tulku. LC 75-5255. (Illus.). 1976. 12.95 (ISBN 0-913546-17-8); pap. 6.50 (ISBN 0-913546-16-X). Dharma Pub.

Gesture of Fleshless Sound. Gopal Honnalgere. (Writers Workshop Redbird Book Ser.). 42p. 1975. 14.00 (ISBN 0-88253-546-3); pap. text ed. 4.00 (ISBN 0-88253-545-5). Ind-US Inc.

Gestures of Despair in Medieval & Early Renaissance Art. Moshe Barasch. LC 76-4601. 1976. 28.50x (ISBN 0-8147-1006-9). NYU Pr.

Get-Away Car. Eleanor Clymer. (gr. 4-7). 1978. PLB 8.95 (ISBN 0-525-30470-3). Dutton.

Get Away Car. Eleanor Clymer. 144p. (gr. 3-6). 1981. pap. 1.75 (ISBN 0-553-15092-8). Bantam.

Get Behind Me Satan. Virgil Leach. 1977. 6.95 (ISBN 0-89137-521-X); pap. 4.95 (ISBN 0-89137-520-1). Quality Pubns.

Get Even Two. George Hayduke. (Get Even Ser.: Vol. 2). (Illus.). 170p. 1981. 9.95 (ISBN 0-87364-213-9). Paladin Ent.

Get Hired: Thirteen Ways to Get a Job. Durlynn Anema. (Illus.). 64p. (gr. 7-12). 1979. pap. text ed. 2.95 (ISBN 0-915510-35-9). Janus Bks.

Get Judge Parker! Albert Butler. (Orig.). 1980. pap. 1.75 (ISBN 0-505-51500-8). Tower Bks.

Get Me Out of Here! Gordon Carlson. Ed. by Richard Uhlich. (Bluejeans Paperbacks Ser.). (Illus., Orig.). (gr. 7-12). 1978. pap. text ed. 1.25- (ISBN 0-8374-5005-5). Xerox Ed Pubns.

Get off the Unicorn. Anne McCaffrey. LC 77-1709. 1977. pap. 2.25 (ISBN 0-345-28508-5). Ballantine.

Get on Out of Here, Philip Hall. Bette Greene. LC 79-50151. 160p. (gr. 3-6). 1981. 9.95 (ISBN 0-8037-2871-9); PLB 9.43 (ISBN 0-8037-2872-7). Dial.

Get Oppenheimer! Steven L. Newman & Mark S. Christopher. 288p. 1980. 14.95 (ISBN 0-8129-0927-5). Times Bks.

Get Out & Get Under. Max Wilk. 1981. 12.95 (ISBN 0-393-01425-8). Norton.

Get Out of Debt. Joseph P. Fortin. 160p. 1980. pap. text ed. 6.95 (ISBN 0-936256-00-1). Omega Pub Co.

Get Out There & Reap. Guin R. Tuckett. 1976. pap. 1.00 (ISBN 0-8272-1229-1). Bethany Pr.

Get Really Rich in the Coming Super Metals Boom. Gordon McLendon. 1981. pap. 4.95 (ISBN 0-671-43202-8). PB.

Get Rich in Spite of Yourself. Louis Grafe. pap. 1.50 (ISBN 0-912576-10-3). R Collier.

Get Set! Go! Shigeo Watanabe. (Illus.). 32p. (gr. 2-5). 1981. 6.95 (ISBN 0-399-20780-5); lib. bdg. 6.99 (ISBN 0-399-61175-4). Philomel.

Get Started in Dried Flower Craft. B. Amlick. 1974. pap. 2.95 o.s.i. (ISBN 0-02-011110-X, Collier). Macmillan.

Get That Nigger off the Field. Art Rust, Jr. 1976. 7.95 o.p. (ISBN 0-440-02791-8). Delacorte.

Get to Know Spain. Rosemary Hunt. 1979. pap. text ed. 7.50 (ISBN 0-435-39003-1). Heinemann Ed.

Get Well Hotel. Burstein. 113p. Date not set. lib. bdg. 4.95 (ISBN 0-07-009244-3). McGraw.

Get Well Naturally. Linda Clark. LC 65-18927. 1968. pap. 2.75 (ISBN 0-668-01762-7). Arc Bks.

Get Your Life Together. Pat Boone. pap. 3.95 (ISBN 0-89728-032-6, 578516). Omega Pubns OR.

GETAJOB. Robert R. Carkhuff et al. LC 75-1498. (Career Skills Ser.). 178p. 1975. pap. text ed. 8.95x (ISBN 0-914234-44-7). Human Res Dev Pr.

Getaway Guide II: More Short Vacations in the Pacific Northwest. Jake Rankin & Marni Rankin. 192p. 1981. pap. 8.95 (ISBN 0-914718-56-8). Pacific Search.

Getaway World, No. 4. E. E. Smith & Stephen Goldin. (Family D'alembert Ser.). (Orig.). pap. 1.75 (ISBN 0-515-04809-7). Jove Pubns.

Getting About in Towns. Paul White. (Junior Reference Ser.). (Illus.). 64p. (gr. 7 up). 7.95 (ISBN 0-7136-1691-1). Dufour.

Getting Acquainted with Accounting. 2nd ed. John L. Carey & K. Fred Skousen. LC 76-10904. (Illus.). 1977. pap. text ed. 6.25 (ISBN 0-395-24513-3). HM.

Getting Ahead in the Music Business. Ronald Zalkind. LC 79-7366. 1979. 15.00 (ISBN 0-02-872990-0); pap. 6.95 (ISBN 0-02-873000-3). Schirmer Bks.

Getting Along. Rick J. Wilks & Anne W. Millyard. LC 80-65478. 1978. pap. 4.40 (ISBN 0-8224-3377-X). Pitman Learning.

Getting Along with Your Teachers. Phyllis R. Naylor. LC 80-22319. 96p. (gr. 4-6). 1981. 7.50g (ISBN 0-687-14123-0). Abingdon.

Getting Around Cities & Towns. Winifred H. Roderman. (Survival Guide Ser.). (Illus.). 64p. (gr. 7-12). 1979. pap. text ed. 2.85 (ISBN 0-915510-30-8). Janus Bks.

Getting Away with Murder: The Law & Bishop Legrand. Hays. 1981. 14.95 (ISBN 0-690-01941-6). Lippincott & Crowell.

Getting Better: A Report on Health Care from the Salzbug Seminar. Ed. by Herbert P. Gleason. LC 80-23486. 192p. Date not set. text ed. 22.50 (ISBN 0-89946-053-4). Oelgeschlager.

Getting Better Results from the Meetings You Run. Michael Renton. LC 80-51792. (Illus.). 95p. 1980. pap. text ed. 5.95 (ISBN 0-87822-214-6, 2146). Res Press.

Getting by on One Hundred Thousand Dollars a Year & Other Sad Tales of the Seventies. Andrew Tobias. 1980. 10.95 (ISBN 0-671-25518-5). S&S.

Getting Clear. Anne K. Rush. 1973. 10.00 o.p. (ISBN 0-394-48382-0). Random.

Getting Control of Your Weight. David W. Abbott. 144p. 1980. pap. cancelled (ISBN 0-89037-187-3). Anderson World.

Getting Custody: Winning the Last Battle of a Marital War. Robert H. Woody. 1978. 10.95 (ISBN 0-02-631570-X). Macmillan.

Getting Drunk with the Birds. Richard Frost. LC 72-141385. 49p. 1971. 5.95 (ISBN 0-8214-0088-6). Ohio U Pr.

Getting Even. Woody Allen. 128p. Date not set. pap. 1.95 (ISBN 0-394-72640-5, V-640, Vin). Random.

Getting Even with Getting Old. Julia Kessler. LC 80-11045. 228p. 1980. 15.95 (ISBN 0-88229-663-9); pap. 8.95 (ISBN 0-88229-754-6). Nelson-Hall.

Getting Fit the Hard Way. Barry Walsh & Peter Douglas. (Illus.). 1981. 12.50 (ISBN 0-7137-1086-1, Pub. by Blandford Pr England). Sterling.

Getting Grants: A Creative Guide to the Grants System: How to Find Funders, Write Convincing Proposals, & Make Your Grants Work. Craig Sith & Eric Skjei. LC 78-20187. 288p. pap. 4.95 (ISBN 0-06-090834-3, CN 834, CN). Har-Row.

Getting in Shape to Ski. new ed. Hamilton. (Orig.). 1979. pap. 3.95 (ISBN 0-8015-2957-3, Hawthorn). Dutton.

Getting in the Spirit: Annual Bay Area Christmas Events. Carole T. Meyers. LC 79-19253. (Illus., Orig.). 1979. pap. write for info. (ISBN 0-917120-05-1). Carousel Pr.

Getting in Touch with Your Government. Robert A. Liston. LC 75-22333. 160p. (gr. 7 up). 1975. PLB 6.64 o.p. (ISBN 0-671-32763-1). Messner.

Getting Inside the Bible. Herbert H. Lambert. 144p. 1976. pap. 1.50 (ISBN 0-8272-1218-6). Bethany Pr.

Getting into American Medical-Veterinary Schools: A Practical "How to" Guide. Rosalie Gottfried. LC 77-93397. (gr. 8 up). 1978. pap. text ed. 5.50x (ISBN 0-931084-01-6). Argee Pub.

Getting into Business. E. N. Chapman. LC 75-20279. 1976. 17.95 (ISBN 0-471-14600-5). Wiley.

Getting into College. Frank C. Leana. 1980. 11.95 (ISBN 0-8090-4921-X); pap. 5.95 (ISBN 0-8090-1393-2). Hill & Wang.

Getting into God. D. Stuart Briscoe. 128p. 1975. pap. 2.95 (ISBN 0-310-21722-9). Zondervan.

Getting into Pro Baseball. Mike Dyer. (Getting into the Pros Ser.). (Illus.). (gr. 6 up). 1979. PLB 6.45 s&l (ISBN 0-531-01319-7). Watts.

Getting into Pro Basketball. Richard B. Lyttle. (Getting into the Pros Ser.). (Illus.). (gr. 6 up). 1979. PLB 6.45 s&l (ISBN 0-531-01451-7). Watts.

Getting into Pro Football. John D. McCallum. (Getting into the Pros Ser.). (Illus.). (gr. 6 up). 1979. PLB 6.45 s&l (ISBN 0-531-02279-X). Watts.

Getting into Pro Soccer. Stan Fischler & Richard Friedman. (Getting into the Pros Ser.). (Illus.). (gr. 6 up). 1979. PLB 6.45 s&l (ISBN 0-531-02280-3). Watts.

Getting Involoved with Business. Roy Poe et al. (Illus.). 576p. (gr. 9-10). 1980. text ed. 12.16 (ISBN 0-07-050335-4, G); learning activity kit I 4.60 (ISBN 0-07-050336-2). McGraw.

Getting It All Together: A Study in Ephesians. Roy C. Putnam. LC 76-28456. 1977. pap. 3.95 o.p. (ISBN 0-687-14114-1). Abingdon.

Getting It off the Shelf: A Methodology for Implementing Federal Research. Peter W. House & David W. Jones, Jr. LC 77-3918. (Special Studies in Public Systems Management Ser.). (Illus.). 1977. lib. bdg. 27.50x (ISBN 0-89158-347-5). Westview.

Getting It Right. Joyce Vogelman. 208p. 1981. pap. 2.25 (ISBN 0-380-77685-5). Avon.

Getting It: The Psychology of EST. Sheridan Fenwick. LC 76-20617. 1976. 7.95 o.p. (ISBN 0-397-01170-9). Lippincott.

Getting Married. Bill Duff. LC 73-331250. (New Citizen Books). (Illus.). 80p. 1973. 7.50x (ISBN 0-85340-238-8). Intl Pubns Serv.

Getting Married. Cathy Greenblat & Thomas J. Cottle. LC 80-16369. 276p. 1980. 11.95 (ISBN 0-07-024330-1). McGraw.

Getting Motivated: The Secret Behind Individual Motivations by the Man Who Was Not Afraid to Ask "Why?". Ernest Dichter. LC 78-21168. (Illus.). 1979. 14.50 (ISBN 0-08-023687-1). Pergamon.

Getting New Business Leads: A Guide for Advertising Agencies. David Lockett. LC 80-70204. 1980. 6.95 (ISBN 0-87251-062-X). Crain Bks.

Getting Organized. Stephanie Winston. 1980. pap. 5.95 (ISBN 0-446-97806-X). Warner Bks.

Getting Organized: Time & Paperwork. Stephanie Winston. 1980. pap. 2.50 (ISBN 0-446-97564-8). Warner Bks.

Getting Out. Winifred Madison. LC 75-34629. (gr. 7 up). 1976. 6.95 o.p. (ISBN 0-695-80634-3); PLB 6.99 o.p. (ISBN 0-695-40634-5). Follett.

Getting Out. Marsha Norman. 1979. pap. 2.50 (ISBN 0-380-75184-4, 75184, Bard). Avon.

Getting Out of Town. Robert Long. 16p. pap. 2.00 o.p. (ISBN 0-935252-19-3). Street Pr.

Getting Paid: Practical Credit Collection Techniques for Business & Industry. Harold B. Whalen & Robert L. Nickerson. LC 80-82730. (Illus.). 135p. (Orig.). 1980. pap. 10.00 (ISBN 0-937788-00-7). Kalum Pr.

Getting People to Read: Volunteer Programs That Work. Carl Smith & Leo Fay. LC 73-7538. 256p. 1973. 8.95 o.p. (ISBN 0-440-02836-1). Delacorte.

Getting Published. David S. Thomas & Hubert Bermont. 1974. pap. 3.95 (ISBN 0-06-090382-1, CN382, CN). Har-Row.

Getting Ready for AACR2: The Cataloger's Guide. Christa F. Hoffmann. LC 80-15168. (Professional Librarian Ser.). 225p. 1980. pap. 24.50 (ISBN 0-914236-64-4). Knowledge Indus.

Getting Ready for College: How to Settle Down & Make the Grade. George Weigand. 1981. pap. text ed. 2.25 (ISBN 0-8120-2080-4). Barron.

Getting Ready for Living Together. Richard Langsdale. LC 74-76918. (Illus.). 96p. (Orig.). 1974. pap. 1.95 o.p. (ISBN 0-8006-1302-3, 1-1302). Fortress.

Getting Ready to Cook. Ann A. Weaver. (gr. 7-12). 1974. pap. 2.80 (ISBN 0-8224-3383-4); tchrs' manual free (ISBN 0-8224-7677-0). Pitman Learning.

Getting Results from Courses, Workshops, Seminars, & Conferences: Tips for Participants. 1980. pap. 9.95 cancelled (ISBN 0-89384-059-9). Learning Concepts.

Getting Rich in Real Estate Partnerships. Ruth Baker. (Orig.). 1981. 11.95 (ISBN 0-446-51222-2). Warner Bks.

Getting Rich: The Smart Woman's Guide to Successful Money Management. Diane L. Ackerman. 288p. 1981. 11.95 (ISBN 0-89479-063-3). A & W Pubs.

Getting Started: A Preface to Writing. Harry Rougier & E. K. Stockum. (Orig.). 1970. pap. text ed. 3.95x (ISBN 0-393-09900-8, NortonC). Norton.

Getting Started: Career Education Activities for Exceptional Students. Jill S. Lamkin. 144p. 1980. pap. 5.50 (ISBN 0-86586-113-7). Coun Exc Child.

Getting Started in Alabama Real Estate. Jerry F. Bartlett. (Real Estate Ser.). 1978. pap. text ed. 12.50 (ISBN 0-8403-1879-0). Kendall-Hunt.

Getting Started in Candlemaking. Walter E. Schutz. 104p. 1972. pap. 2.95 o.s.i. (ISBN 0-02-011900-3, Collier). Macmillan.

Getting Started in Electronic Troubleshooting. William E. Long. (Illus.). 1979. ref. 17.95 (ISBN 0-8359-2487-4); instrs'. manual avail. (ISBN 0-8359-2488-2). Reston.

Getting Started in Film-Making. Lillian Schiff. LC 77-79504. (Illus.). (gr. 6 up). 1977. 7.95 (ISBN 0-8069-5382-9); PLB 7.49 (ISBN 0-8069-5383-7). Sterling.

Getting Started in General Purpose Simulation System. Kenneth A. Dunning. LC 80-28281. 117p. (Orig.). 1981. pap. 5.95x (ISBN 0-910554-34-X). Eng Pr.

Getting Started in Leathercraft. Maria Di Valentin & Louis Di Valentin. 104p. 1972. pap. 2.95 o.s.i. (ISBN 0-02-011300-5, Collier). Macmillan.

Getting Started in Plastics. Nancy M. Lang. 104p. 1972. pap. 2.95 o.s.i. (ISBN 0-02-011720-5, Collier). Macmillan.

Getting Started in Private Practice. G. Balliett. 1978. 21.50 (ISBN 0-87489-134-5). Med Economics.

Getting Started in Stamp Collecting. rev. ed. Burton Hobson. LC 62-18631. (Illus.). (gr. 4 up). 7.95 (ISBN 0-8069-6010-8); PLB 7.49 (ISBN 0-8069-6011-6). Sterling.

Getting Started in Telecommunications Management. Larry A. Arredondo. 1980. softcover 30.00 (ISBN 0-936648-04-X). Telecom Lib.

Getting Started in Tennis. Paul Metzler. LC 70-180467. (Illus.). 160p. (gr. 7 up). 1972. 7.95 o.p. (ISBN 0-8069-4050-6); PLB 7.49 o.p. (ISBN 0-8069-4051-4). Sterling.

Getting Started in Treasure Hunting. Alan Smith. (Illus.). 192p. 1981. pap. 7.95 (ISBN 0-8117-2045-4). Stackpole.

Getting Started: Urban Youth in the Labor Market. Albert Westefeld. LC 77-166952. (FDR & the Era of the New Deal Ser.). 1971. Repr. of 1943 ed. lib. bdg. 19.50 (ISBN 0-306-70358-0). Da Capo.

Getting the Author's Tone: Is He Humorous, Serious, Satirical? Walter Pauk. (Skill at a Time Ser). 64p. (gr. 9-12). 1975. pap. text ed. 2.40x (ISBN 0-89061-024-X). Jamestown Pubs.

Getting the Job You Want. Howard Dowding & Sheila Boyce. (Orig.). 1980. pap. 5.95x (ISBN 0-8464-1012-5). Beekman Pubs.

Getting the Main Point: Separating the Wheat from the Chaff. Walter Pauk. (Skill at a Time Ser). 64p. (gr. 9-12). 1975. pap. text ed. 2.40x (ISBN 0-89061-026-6). Jamestown Pubs.

Getting the Message. J. Barry DuVall et al. LC 79-57016. (Technology Ser.). 384p. 1981. text ed. 15.50 (ISBN 0-87192-123-5, 000-6); tchr's guide 18.60 (ISBN 0-87192-125-1, 00-6A); activity manual 5.95 (ISBN 0-87192-124-3, 00-6B). Davis Mass.

Getting the Most from Radio Control Systems. Fred M. Marks. Ed. by Burr Angle. LC 80-81430. (Illus.). 88p. (Orig.). 1980. pap. 8.95 (ISBN 0-89024-550-9). Kalmbach.

Getting the Most from Your Garden. Organic Gardening Editors. (Illus.). 1980. 14.95 (ISBN 0-87857-291-0). Rodale Pr Inc.

Getting the Type You Want. Tracy Sabin. (Illus.). 1980. pap. 7.95 (ISBN 0-930904-01-X). Graphic Dimens.

Getting Through: How to Make Words Work for You. Godfrey Howard. LC 80-66087. 176p. 1980. 11.95 (ISBN 0-7153-7821-X). David & Charles.

Getting to Know the Real You. Sterling G. Ellsworth & Richard G. Ellsworth. LC 80-69724. 162p. 1980. 6.95 (ISBN 0-87747-840-6). Deseret Bk.

Getting to Know Your Bible. Hans-Georg Lubkoll & Eugen Wiesnet. Tr. by David L. Scheidt from Ger. LC 75-34527. (Illus.). 64p. 1976. pap. 1.95 (ISBN 0-8006-1217-5, 1-1217). Fortress.

Getting to Know Your Faith. Paul Steeves. 1977. pap. 2.95 o.p. (ISBN 0-87784-629-4). Inter-Varsity.

Getting Well Again. Carl Simonton et al. 256p. (Orig.). 1980. pap. 2.75 (ISBN 0-553-12268-1). Bantam.

Getting Your Act Together: Goal Setting for Fun, Health & Profit. George L. Morrisey. (Wiley Self-Teaching Guide Ser.). 1980. pap. text ed. 7.95 (ISBN 0-471-08185-X). Wiley.

Getting Your Child into TV Commercials. Cindy Booth. LC 79-26106. 1980. pap. 2.95 (ISBN 0-87576-087-2). Pilot Bks.

Getting Your Executives Fit. Don T. Jacobs. LC 79-64731. (Illus.). 256p. (Orig.). 1981. pap. 12.95 (ISBN 0-89037-176-8). Anderson World.

Getting Your Horse Fit. Diana Tuke. (Illus.). pap. 5.10 (ISBN 0-85131-255-1, Dist. by Sporting Book Center). J A Allen.

Getting Your Kids to Eat Right. Barbara Richert. 192p. (Orig.). 1981. pap. 5.95 (ISBN 0-346-12519-7). Cornerstone.

Getting Your Message Across: A Practical Guide to Business Communication. Craig Aronoff et al. (Illus.). 500p. 1981. text ed. 13.95 (ISBN 0-8299-0362-3). West Pub.

Getting Your Shape in Shape: A New Weight Conditioning Program for Women. Jean Zuver. LC 80-26725. (Illus.). 128p. 1981. 7.95 (ISBN 0-498-02536-5). A S Barnes.

Getting Your Way with Parents. Tom Alquist. LC 80-68888. 128p. (Orig.). 1981. pap. 2.50 (ISBN 0-89636-065-2). Accent Bks.

Getting Your Words Across. Murray Bromberg & Milton Katz. 256p. (gr. 7-12). 1981. pap. text ed. 3.95 (ISBN 0-8120-2082-0). Barron.

Gettysburg: A Journey in Time. William Frassanito. LC 74-10597. 1976. pap. 8.95 (ISBN 0-684-14696-7, ScribT). Scribner.

Gettysburg: The Final Fury. Bruce Catton. LC 73-11896. (Illus.). 128p. 1974. slip cased 10.00 (ISBN 0-385-02060-0). Doubleday.

Geysers & Geothermal Energy. J. S. Rinehart. (Illus.). 223p. 1980. 19.80 (ISBN 0-387-90489-1). Springer-Verlag.

Gezer Two. William G. Dever. 1974. 35.00x (ISBN 0-685-56198-4). Ktav.

Ghana & Ivory Coast, Spotlight on West Africa. Lila Perl. LC 74-23106. (Illus.). 160p. (gr. 5-9). 1975. 7.92 (ISBN 0-688-31833-9). Morrow.

Ghana in the Humanities & Social Sciences, 1900-71: A Bibliography. Christian C. Aguolu. LC 73-9519. 1973. 16.50 (ISBN 0-8108-0635-5). Scarecrow.

Ghana Observed: Essays on the Politics of a West African Republic. Dennis Austin. LC 76-15398. 1976. text ed. 28.50x (ISBN 0-8419-0278-X, Africana). Holmes & Meier.

Ghana's Foreign Policy, Nineteen Fifty-Seven - Nineteen Sixty-Six: Diplomacy, Ideology, & the New State. W. Scott Thompson. LC 68-56322. 1969. 26.00x (ISBN 0-691-03076-6). Princeton U Pr.

Ghandhi: A Memoir. William L. Shirer. 1981. pap. 4.95 (ISBN 0-671-25080-9, Touchstone Bks). S&S.

Ghar Parau. David M. Judson. (Illus.). 208p. 1973. 10.00 o.s.i. (ISBN 0-02-560320-5). Macmillan.

Ghaznavids. Clifford Bosworth. (Arab Background Ser.). 1973. 15.00x (ISBN 0-685-77091-5). Intl Bk Ctr.

Ghelderode: Seven Plays, Vol. 1. Michel De Ghelderode. Incl. Chronicles of Hell; Barabbas; The Women at the Tomb; Pantagleize; The Blind Men; Three Actors & Their Drama; Lord Halewyn. 304p. (Orig.). 1960. pap. 4.95 (ISBN 0-8090-0719-3, Mermaid). Hill & Wang.

Ghenko: The Mongol Invasion of Japan. Nakaba Yamada. (Studies in Japanese History & Civilization). 1979. Repr. of 1916 ed. 25.00 (ISBN 0-89093-254-9). U Pubns Amer.

Ghent Altarpiece & the Art of Jan Van Eyck. Lotte B. Philip. LC 73-113007. (Illus.). 380p. 1980. 50.00x (ISBN 0-691-03870-8); pap. 15.00 (ISBN 0-691-00316-5). Princeton U Pr.

Ghetto Fever. Thomas V. Millea. 1968. 3.95 (ISBN 0-685-07639-3, 80530). Macmillan.

Ghetto Fighters. Tr. by Meyer Barkai. 1977. pap. text ed. 1.75 (ISBN 0-505-51159-2). Tower Bks.

Ghetto Marketplace. F. D. Sturdivant. LC 77-81932. 1969. 8.95 (ISBN 0-02-932290-1); pap. text ed. 5.95 o.p. (ISBN 0-02-932300-2). Free Pr.

Ghetto: Readings with Interpretations. Ed. by Joe T. Darden. (National University Publications, Interdisciplinary Urban Ser.). 1981. 19.50 (ISBN 0-8046-9277-7); pap. 9.95 (ISBN 0-8046-9279-3). Kennikat.

Ghetto School: Class Warfare in an Elementary School. Gerald Levy. LC 70-116067. 1970. pap. 4.95 (ISBN 0-672-63543-7). Pegasus.

Ghetto Takes Shape: Black Cleveland, 1870-1930. Kenneth L. Kusmer. (Blacks in the New World Ser.). (Illus.). 320p. 1976. 15.00 (ISBN 0-252-00289-X); pap. 4.50 (ISBN 0-252-00690-9). U of Ill Pr.

Ghost & Ghastlies. Helen Hoke. (Illus.). 192p. (gr. 4-6). 1976. PLB 7.90 (ISBN 0-531-01210-7). Watts.

Ghost & Horror Stories. Ambrose Bierce. 7.00 (ISBN 0-8446-0493-3). Peter Smith.

Ghost at the Wedding. Elna Stone. 1977. pap. 1.25 (ISBN 0-505-51145-2). Tower Bks.

Ghost Charlie. Bridwell. (Illus.). (gr. 2-3). 1980. pap. 3.50 incl. record (ISBN 0-590-24002-1, Schol Pap). Schol Bk Serv.

Ghost House Revenge. Claire McNally. 240p. (Orig.). 1981. pap. 2.50 (ISBN 0-553-14624-6). Bantam.

Ghost-Hunter & His Family. John Banim & Michael Banim. Ed. by Robert L. Wolff. (Ireland Nineteenth Century Fiction - Ser. Two: Vol. 22). 348p. 1979. lib. bdg. 32.00 (ISBN 0-8240-3471-6). Garland Pub.

Ghost Hunters. Arthur Myers. LC 80-19668. (Illus.). 160p. (gr. 7 up). 1980. PLB 9.29 (ISBN 0-671-33076-4). Messner.

Ghost Hunters: The Inside Story of Haunted Places. Harry T. Sutton. 1978. pap. 3.50 (ISBN 0-7134-1729-3, Pub. by Batsford England). David & Charles.

Ghost Lane. Jane L. Curry. LC 78-73319. 1979. 7.95 (ISBN 0-689-50129-3, Mcelderry Bk). Atheneum.

Ghost Mountain Guns. W. F. Bragg. 1981. pap. 1.75 (ISBN 0-8439-0896-3, Leisure Bks). Nordon Pubns.

Ghost Next Door. Wylly F. St. John. (Illus.). (gr. 4-7). 1980. pap. 1.75 (ISBN 0-671-56084-0). Archway.

Ghost of Bennett's Villa. Mary J. Goodwin. LC 79-88506. (Illus.). (gr. 5 up). 1981. 10.00 (ISBN 0-932632-05-X); pap. 3.95 (ISBN 0-932632-03-3). MJG Co.

Ghost of Five Owl Farm. Wilson Gage. (gr. 4-6). 1980. pap. 1.75 (ISBN 0-671-56085-9). Archway.

Ghost of Flight 401. John G. Fuller. (YA) 1978. 2.25 (ISBN 0-425-03553-0, Dist. by Putnam). Berkley Pub.

Ghost of Grannoch Moor. William MacKellar. LC 73-6028. (Illus.). (gr. 4 up). 1973. 3.95g o.p. (ISBN 0-396-06834-0). Dodd.

Ghost of Hagar. George Otis. pap. 2.50 (ISBN 0-89728-033-4, 581116). Omega Pubns OR.

Ghost of Henry James. David Plante. LC 71-118217. Date not set. cancelled (ISBN 0-87645-025-7). Gambit.

Ghost of Hidden Springs. (Meg Bks.). (gr. 3 up). 1978. pap. 1.25 (ISBN 0-307-21530-X, Golden Pr). Western Pub.

Ghost of McDow Hole. M. Clendenin. 4.75 o.p. (ISBN 0-8062-1204-7). Carlton.

Ghost of Monsieur Scarron. Janet Lewis. LC 65-16520. 378p. 1959. 10.95 (ISBN 0-8040-0076-X); pap. 6.95 (ISBN 0-8040-0133-2, 70). Swallow.

Ghost of Old Capernaum. Walter A. Dawes. (Illus.). 358p. (Orig.). 1980. pap. text ed. 24.95 (ISBN 0-686-28901-3). New Capernaum.

Ghost of Peg-Leg Peter & Other Stories of Old New York. Moritz A. Jagendorf. LC 65-17371. (Illus.). (gr. 3 up). 1965. 7.95 (ISBN 0-8149-0327-4). Vanguard.

Ghost of Staghorn. Auriel Douglas. 192p. (Orig.). 1981. pap. 1.95 (ISBN 0-523-41323-8). Pinnacle Bks.

Ghost of Stalin. Jean-Paul Sartre. LC 67-19872. 1968. 4.50 o.p. (ISBN 0-8076-0437-2). Braziller.

Ghost of the Great River Inn. Lynn Hall. 64p. 1980. PLB 5.39 (ISBN 0-695-41465-8). Follett.

Ghost of Thomas Kempe. Penelope Lively. 192p. (gr. 3-6). 1973. PLB 8.95 (ISBN 0-525-30495-9). Dutton.

Ghost of Tillie Jean Cassaway. Ellen H. Showell. LC 78-5353. (Illus.). 128p. (gr. 3-7). 1978. 6.95 (ISBN 0-590-07559-4, Four Winds). Schol Bk Serv.

Ghost of Windy Hill. Clyde R. Bulla. LC 68-11059. (gr. 3-7). 1968. 6.95 (ISBN 0-690-32763-3, TYC-J); PLB 7.89 (ISBN 0-690-32764-1). T Y Crowell.

Ghost Pirates. W. H. Hodgson. 276p. 1980. Repr. of 1909 ed. lib. bdg. 13.95x (ISBN 0-89968-209-X). Lightyear.

Ghost Plane Over Hartley Field. Larry Sutton. (Carolrhoda Mini-Mysteries). (Illus.). 32p. (gr. 1-4). 1981. PLB 4.95 (ISBN 0-87614-135-1). Carolrhoda Bks.

Ghost Ship of Fog Island. Marilyn Ross. 256p. (Orig.). 1975. pap. 1.25 o.p. (ISBN 0-445-00285-9). Popular Lib.

Ghost Stories. John Hampden. 1975. pap. 3.25 o.p. (ISBN 0-460-01952-X, Evman). Dutton.

Ghost Stories. new ed. Ed. by Barbara Walker. 128p. (gr. 7-12). 1975. PLB 6.95 o.p. (ISBN 0-07-067812-X, GB). McGraw.

Ghost Stories of Edith Wharton. Edith Wharton. LC 76-25402. 256p. 1973. lib. rep. ed. 17.50x (ISBN 0-684-14829-3, ScribT). Scribner.

Ghost Stories of Edith Wharton. Edith Wharton. 1976. pap. 1.75 o.p. (ISBN 0-445-08507-X). Popular Lib.

Ghost Sub. Roger E. Herst. 384p. 1980. pap. 2.50 (ISBN 0-89083-655-8). Zebra.

Ghost Town of Bodie. Anne Johnson & Russ Johnson. LC 67-31002. 3.45 (ISBN 0-912494-19-0); pap. 3.45 (ISBN 0-912494-02-6). Chalfant Pr.

Ghost Towns & Historical Haunts in Arizona. Thelma Heatwole. (Illus.). 144p. (Orig.). 1981. pap. 4.50 (ISBN 0-914846-10-8). Golden West Pub.

Ghost Towns & Mining Camps of New Mexico. James E. Sherman & Barbara H. Sherman. LC 72-9525. (Illus.). 270p. 1975. 13.95 (ISBN 0-8061-1066-X); pap. 6.95x (ISBN 0-8061-1106-2). U of Okla Pr.

Ghost Towns of Oklahoma. John W. Morris. (Illus.). 1978. 15.95 (ISBN 0-8061-1358-8); pap. 7.95 (ISBN 0-8061-1420-7). U of Okla Pr.

Ghost Towns of the American West. Robert Silverberg. LC 68-17081. (Illus.). (gr. 7 up). 1968. 10.95 (ISBN 0-690-32621-1, TYC-J). T Y Crowell.

Ghost Towns of the Santa Cruz Mountains. John V. Young. Ed. by Michael S. Gant. LC 79-90223. (Illus.). 156p. Date not set. pap. 4.95 (ISBN 0-934136-06-8, Paper Vision). Western Tanager. Postponed.

Ghost Towns of the Southwest: Arizona, New Mexico & Utah. Donald C. Miller. (Western Ghost Town Ser.). 1980. 14.95 (ISBN 0-87108-565-8). Pruett.

Ghost Towns of the West. 2nd ed. Sunset Editors. LC 77-72507. (Illus.). 224p. 1978. pap. 8.95 (ISBN 0-376-05313-5, Sunset Bks.). Sunset-Lane.

Ghost Trails of Wyoming. Mae Urbanek. (Illus.). 236p. 1978. 16.95; pap. 8.95. Urbanek.

Ghost Waltz: A Memoir. Ingeborg Day. LC 80-16411. 240p. 1980. 11.95 (ISBN 0-670-29485-3). Viking Pr.

Ghost Wineries of Napa Valley. Irene W. Haynes. (Illus.). 80p. (Orig.). 1980. pap. 2.40 (ISBN 0-9604904-1-8). Taylor & Friends.

Ghost with the Halloween Hiccups. Stephen Mooser. (Illus.). (gr. k-3). 1978. pap. 1.75 (ISBN 0-380-40287-4, 51953, Camelot). Avon.

Ghostly Animals. Daniel Cohen. LC 76-23751. (gr. 4-7). 1977. 6.95 o.p. (ISBN 0-385-11567-9); PLB (ISBN 0-385-11568-7). Doubleday.

Ghostly Animals of America. Patricia Clyne. LC 77-6487. (Illus.). (gr. 5 up). 1977. 5.95 (ISBN 0-396-07465-0). Dodd.

Ghostly Tales & Mysterious Happenings of Old Monterey. Randall A. Reinstedt. LC 79-110356. (Illus.). 1977. pap. 3.95 (ISBN 0-933818-04-1). Ghost Town.

Ghostly Tales of Washington Irving. Ed. by Michael Hayes. 1980. 9.95 (ISBN 0-7145-3739-X). Riverrun NY.

Ghosts. Antonia Barber. (gr. 5-7). 1975. pap. 1.95 (ISBN 0-671-42454-8). Archway.

Ghosts. Antonia Barber. (gr. 5-7). 1975. pap. 1.75 (ISBN 0-671-56001-8). PB.

Ghosts. Henrik Ibsen. 1979. 7.95x (ISBN 0-8464-0091-X). Beekman Pubs.

Ghosts. Ed McBain. (Large Print Bks.). 1980. lib. bdg. 12.95 (ISBN 0-8161-3128-7). G K Hall.

Ghosts. Ed McBain. 176p. 1981. pap. 2.25 (ISBN 0-553-14518-5). Bantam.

Ghosts Along the Cumberland: Deathlore in the Kentucky Foothills. William L. Montell. LC 74-32241. (Illus.). 283p. 1975. 13.50x (ISBN 0-87049-165-2). U of Tenn Pr.

Ghosts & Ghouls. Gwen Risedorf. LC 77-14333. (Myth, Magic & Superstition Ser.). (Illus.). (gr. 4-5). 1977. PLB 9.65 (ISBN 0-8172-1038-5). Raintree Pubs.

Ghosts & Poltergeists. Gurney Williams. (Illus.). (gr. 4-6). 1979. PLB 6.45 s&l (ISBN 0-531-02214-5). Watts.

Ghosts & Specters: Ten Supernatural Stories from the Deep South. Bruce Roberts & Nancy Roberts. LC 73-20909. 96p. (gr. 5-7). 1974. 4.95 o.p. (ISBN 0-385-00698-5). Doubleday.

Ghosts & Three Other Plays. Henrik Ibsen. LC 66-11746. 1966. pap. 2.95 (ISBN 0-385-02147-X, A215E, Anch). Doubleday.

Ghosts, Bandits & Legends of Old Monterey. Randall A. Reinstedt. LC 74-189524. (Illus.). 1974. pap. 3.50 (ISBN 0-933818-00-9). Ghost Town.

Ghosts, Ghosts, Ghosts. Ed. by Phyllis R. Fenner. (Terrific Triple Titles Ser). (Illus.). (gr. 4-6). 1952. PLB 6.90 o.p. (ISBN 0-531-01676-5). Watts.

Ghosts I Have Met, & Some Others. John K. Bangs. LC 80-19172. 191p. 1980. Repr. of 1971 ed. lib. bdg. 9.95x (ISBN 0-89370-605-1). Borgo Pr.

Ghosts in the Valley. Adi-Kent T. Jeffrey. LC 75-4658. 96p. 1971. pap. 1.50 o.p. (ISBN 0-915460-00-9). New Hope.

Ghosts, Monsters, & Wild Men: Legends of the Oregon Country. Mike Helm. (Illus.). 1981. write for info. (ISBN 0-931742-03-X). Rainy Day Oreg.

Ghosts of Hamlet. Martin Scofield. LC 79-21297. 180p. 1981. 39.50 (ISBN 0-521-22735-6). Cambridge U Pr.

Ghosts of Kampala: The Rise & Fall of Idi Amin. George I. Smith. 208p. 1980. 10.95 (ISBN 0-312-32662-9). St Martin.

Ghosts of Lee House. Frances Priddy. LC 68-27813. (gr. 7-8). 1968. 5.95 o.p. (ISBN 0-385-08952-X). Doubleday.

Ghosts of Old Miss, & Other Essays on Home. Willie Morris. 165p. 1981. 9.95. Yoknapatawpha.

Ghosts of Rowan Oak: William Faulkner's Ghost Stories for Children. Dean F. Wells. LC 80-52628. (Illus.). 64p. 1980. 9.95. Yoknapatawpha.

Ghosts of the Carolinas. Bruce Roberts & Nancy Roberts. LC 62-21045. (Orig.). 5.95 (ISBN 0-87461-952-1); pap. 4.50 (ISBN 0-87461-953-X). McNally.

Ghosts of the Gothic: Austen, Eliot, & Lawrence. Judith Wilt. LC 80-7559. 1980. 18.50 (ISBN 0-691-06439-3). Princeton U Pr.

Ghosts of the Heart. John Logan. LC 60-7239. 1960. 4.50x o.s.i. (ISBN 0-226-49110-2). U of Chicago Pr.

Ghosts of the North. Jack Hallam. LC 76-40612. (Ghosts Ser.). (Illus.). 1976. 4.50 o.p. (ISBN 0-7153-7320-X). David & Charles.

Ghosts of the Wild West. Bruce Roberts & Nancy Roberts. LC 76-2813. (YA) (gr. 6-7). 1976. 5.95 o.p. (ISBN 0-385-11299-8). Doubleday.

Ghosts: The Illustrated History. Peter Haining. LC 74-29441. (Illus.). 128p. 1975. 9.95 o.s.i. (ISBN 0-02-547410-3). Macmillan.

Ghosts' Who's Who. Jack Hallam. 1977. 7.95 (ISBN 0-7153-7452-4). David & Charles.

Ghosts, Witchcraft, & Demonology in England. Eric Maple. LC 78-53668. (Illus.). 1981. 10.95 o.p. (ISBN 0-498-02249-8). A S Barnes.

Giacometti, No. 65. (Maeght Gallery: Derriere le Miroir Ser.). (Fr.). 1977. pap. 19.95 (ISBN 0-8120-0913-4). Barron.

Giambattista & Domenico Tiepolo: A Study & Catalogue Raisonne of the Chalk Drawings. George Knox. (Illus.). 632p. 1980. 180.00 (ISBN 0-19-817313-X). Oxford U Pr.

Giant Airships. Time-Life Books Editors & Douglas Botting. (Epic of Flight). (Illus.). 176p. 1981. 12.95 (ISBN 0-8094-3270-6). Time-Life.

Giant Book of Amateur Radio Antennas. Robert J. Traister. (Illus.). 1979. pap. 8.95 (ISBN 0-8306-8802-1); pap. 8.95 (ISBN 0-8306-8802-1, 802). TAB Bks.

Giant Book of Strange but True Sports Stories. Howard Liss. LC 76-8132. (Illus.). (gr. 5-9). 1976. 3.95 (ISBN 0-394-83287-6, BYR); PLB 6.99 (ISBN 0-394-93287-0). Random.

Giant Can Do Anything. Eric Houghton. LC 80-65669. (Illus.). 32p. (ps-2). 1980. 8.95 (ISBN 0-233-96237-9). Andre Deutsch.

Giant Devil-Dingo. Dick Roughsey. LC 75-14210. (Illus.). 36p. (gr. k-3). 1975. 6.95 o.s.i. (ISBN 0-02-777840-1, 77784). Macmillan.

Giant Journey. Steven Kroll. LC 80-20512. (Illus.). 32p. (ps-3). 1981. PLB 7.95 (ISBN 0-8234-0381-5). Holiday.

Giant Killer. Vernon T. Hyman. 352p. 1981. 12.95 (ISBN 0-399-90099-3). Marek.

Giant Kippernose & Other Stories. John Cunliffe. LC 80-2694. 112p. (gr. k-5). 1981. 8.95 (ISBN 0-233-96386-3). Andre Deutsch.

Giant Molecular Clouds in the Galaxy. P. M. Solomon & M. G. Edmunds. (Illus.). 348p. 1980. 48.00 (ISBN 0-08-023068-7). Pergamon.

Giant Molecules. Herman F. Mark. LC 66-19119. (Life Science Library). (Illus.). (gr. 5 up). 1966. PLB 8.97 o.p. (ISBN 0-8094-0474-5, Pub. by Time-Life). Silver.

Giant Multipole Resonances Oak Ridge, Tennessee, October 15-17, 1979. Ed. by F. E. Bertrand. (Nuclear Science Research Conference Ser.: Vol. 1). 481p. 1980. 42.50 (ISBN 0-686-61662-6). Harwood Academic.

Giant Nursery Book of Things That Work. George Zaffo. LC 67-10020. (gr. k-1). 1967. PLB 7.95 (ISBN 0-385-06412-8). Doubleday.

Giant Panda. 1981. text ed. 29.95 (ISBN 0-442-20064-1). Van Nos Reinhold.

Giant Planets. Alan Nourse. LC 73-14515. (First Bks). (Illus.). 96p. (gr. 5 up). 1974. PLB 6.45 (ISBN 0-531-00816-9). Watts.

Giant Quiz Book. Compiled by Tom T. Wills. 256p. 1981. pap. 6.95 (ISBN 0-89104-207-5). A & W Pubs.

Giant Resonance Phenomena in Intermediate-Energy Nuclear Reactions. F. Cannata & H. Ueberall. (Springer Tracts in Modern Physics: Vol. 89). (Illus.). 112p. 1980. 29.80 (ISBN 0-387-10105-5). Springer-Verlag.

Giant Sea Creatures, Real & Fantastic. John F. Waters. LC 72-85584. (Illus.). 160p. (gr. 4-6). 1973. 4.95 o.p. (ISBN 0-695-80371-9); lib. ed. 4.98 o.p. (ISBN 0-695-40371-0). Follett.

Giant Talk: An Anthology of Third World Writings. Ed. by Quincy Troupe & Rainer Shulte. 1975. pap. 6.95 (ISBN 0-394-71443-1, V-443, Vin). Random.

Giant Trunk Mystery. Linda Boorman. 96p. (gr. 6-12). 1981. pap. 2.25 (ISBN 0-686-69419-8). Victor Bks.

Giant Who Swallowed the Wind. John Cunliffe. LC 79-64314. (Illus.). (gr. k-2). 1980. 8.95 (ISBN 0-233-96310-3). Andre Deutsch.

Giant Who Wanted Company. Lee Priestly. (Young Reader Ser.). (Illus.). (gr. k-3). 1979. PLB 5.00 (ISBN 0-307-60207-9, Golden Pr). Western Pub.

Giants. Jack Ansell. 1976. pap. 1.95 o.p. (ISBN 0-685-72627-4, T3271). Berkley Pub.

Giants. Compiled by Doug Cushman. LC 79-55012. (Deluxe Illustrated Ser.). (Illus.). 48p. (ps-3). 1980. 5.95 (ISBN 0-448-47486-7); PLB 11.85 (ISBN 0-448-13623-6). Platt.

Giants & Warriors. Retold by James Reeves. (Illus., Orig.). 1978. pap. 2.95 (ISBN 0-8467-0540-0, Pub. by Two Continents). Hippocrene Bks.

Giants Are Very Brave People. Florence P. Heide. LC 75-93857. (gr. k-3). 1970. 5.95 o.s.i. (ISBN 0-8193-0370-4, Four Winds); PLB 5.41 o.s.i. (ISBN 0-8193-0371-2). Schol Bk Serv.

Giants' Farm. Jane H. Yolen. LC 76-58317. (Illus.). (ps-3). 1977. 6.95 (ISBN 0-395-28834-7, Clarion). HM.

Giants Go Camping. Jane Yolen. LC 78-17928. (Illus.). (gr. 1-3). 1979. 6.95 (ISBN 0-395-28834-7, Clarion). HM.

Giants of Jazz. rev. ed. Studs Terkel. LC 75-20024. (Illus.). 192p. (gr. 5 up). 1975. 10.95 (ISBN 0-690-00998-4, TYC-J). T Y Crowell.

Giants' Star. James Hogan. 320p. (Orig.). 1981. pap. 2.50 (ISBN 0-345-28771-1, Del Rey). Ballantine.

Gibberellins & Plant Growth. H. N. Krishnamoorthy. LC 74-10469. 1976. 25.95 (ISBN 0-470-50797-7). Halsted Pr.

Gibbon. R. B. Mowat. 282p. 1980. Repr. of 1936 ed. lib. bdg. 30.00 (ISBN 0-8495-3827-0). Arden Lib.

Gibboniana, 17 vols. Incl. Vol. 1 (ISBN 0-8240-1338-7); Vol. 2 (ISBN 0-8240-1339-5); Vol. 3 (ISBN 0-8240-1340-9); Vol. 4 (ISBN 0-8240-1341-7); Vol. 5 (ISBN 0-8240-1342-5); Vol. 6 (ISBN 0-8240-1343-3); Vol. 7 (ISBN 0-8240-1344-1); Vol. 8 (ISBN 0-8240-1345-X); Vol. 9 (ISBN 0-8240-1346-8); Vols. 10 & 11. Set. lib. bdg. 76.00 (ISBN 0-8240-1347-6); Vol. 12 (ISBN 0-8240-1348-4); Vol. 13 (ISBN 0-8240-1349-2); Vol. 14 (ISBN 0-8240-1350-6); Vol. 15 (ISBN 0-8240-1351-4); Vol. 16 (ISBN 0-8240-1352-2); Vol. 17 (ISBN 0-8240-1353-0). (Life & Times of Seven Major British Writers Ser). 1974. lib. bdg. 47.00 ea. Garland Pub.

Gibbon's Autobiography. Edward Gibbon. Ed. by M. M. Reese. (Routledge English Texts). 1970. 7.95 (ISBN 0-7100-6923-5); pap. 4.95 (ISBN 0-7100-6925-1). Routledge & Kegan.

Gibby: The Memoirs Of a Horsey Man. Francis Gibson. 1978. pap. 8.75 (ISBN 0-85131-277-2). J A Allen.

Gibeon & Israel: The Role of Gibeon & the Gibeonites in the Political and Religious History of Early Israel. J. Blenkinsopp. LC 74-171672. (Society for Old Testament Studies Monographs). 1972. 29.50 (ISBN 0-521-08368-0). Cambridge U Pr.

Gibran in Paris. Yusaf Huwayyik. Tr. & intro. by Matti Mossa. (Gideon Detective Ser.). 192p. 1976. pap. 1.75 o.p. (ISBN 0-445-08425-1). Popular Lib.

Gibran of Lebanon. Bushrui. 15.00x (ISBN 0-685-89877-6). Intl Bk Ctr.

Gibson's Suits in Chancery, 2 vols. 5th ed. Arthur Crownover, Jr. 1100p. 1955. text ed. 50.00 (ISBN 0-87215-083-6). Michie.

Gideon. Chester Aaron. LC 80-12779. 192p. (gr. 7-11). 1981. cancelled (ISBN 0-525-30548-3). Dutton.

Gideon & the Early Judges. Gordon Lindsay. (Old Testament Ser.). 1.25 (ISBN 0-89985-135-5). Christ Nations.

Gideon Welles. John Niven. (Illus.). 500p. 1973. 27.50 (ISBN 0-19-501693-9). Oxford U Pr.

Gideon's Drive. J. J. Marric. (Gideon Detective Ser.). 1977. pap. 1.25 o.p. (ISBN 0-445-04123-4). Popular Lib.

Gideon's Fog. J. J. Marric. (Harper Novel of Suspense). 188p. 1974. 7.95 o.s.i. (ISBN 0-06-012798-8, HarpT). Har-Row.

Gideon's Fog. J. J. Marric. 1981. pap. 1.95 (ISBN 0-445-08530-4). Popular Lib.

Gideon's Men. J. J. Marric. (Gideon Detective Ser.). 1979. pap. 1.75 o.p. (ISBN 0-445-04422-5). Popular Lib.

Gideon's Night. J. J. Marric. (Gideon Detective Ser.). 1978. pap. 1.50 o.p. (ISBN 0-445-01429-6). Popular Lib.

Gideon's Power. J. J. Marric. (Gideon Detective Ser.). 1977. pap. 1.25 o.p. (ISBN 0-445-00451-7). Popular Lib.

Gideon's Press. J. J. Marric. LC 73-4154. (Harper Novel of Suspense). 192p. (YA) 1973. 7.95 o.s.i. (ISBN 0-06-012787-2, HarpT). Har-Row.

Gideon's Press. J. J. Marric. (Gideon Detective Ser.). 192p. 1981. pap. 1.95 (ISBN 0-445-00426-6). Popular Lib.

Gideon's Ride. J. J. Marric. (Gideon Detective Ser.). 1979. pap. 1.75 o.p. (ISBN 0-445-04493-4). Popular Lib.

Gideon's River. J. J. Marric. (Gideon Detective Ser.). 1977. pap. 1.25 o.p. (ISBN 0-445-04060-2). Popular Lib.

Gideon's Wrath. J. J. Marric. (Gideon Detective Ser.). 1977. pap. 1.25 o.p. (ISBN 0-445-00435-5). Popular Lib.

Gielgud: An Actor & His Time, a Memoir. John Gielgud. (Illus.). 1980. 14.95 (ISBN 0-517-54179-3). Potter.

Gifford on Courage. Frank Gifford & Charles Mangel. LC 76-21862. 320p. 1976. 9.95 (ISBN 0-87131-223-9). M Evans.

Gifford Pinchot: Forester-Politician. M. Nelson McGeary. Ed. by Frank Freidel. LC 78-66552. (History of the United States Ser.: Vol. 12). 481p. 1979. lib. bdg. 36.00 (ISBN 0-8240-9700-9). Garland Pub.

Gift. Gordon DePree & Gladis DePree. (Illus.). 128p. 1976. padded cover & boxed 10.95 (ISBN 0-310-23650-9). Zondervan.

Gift. Gordon DePree & Gladis DePree. (Illus.). 1979. pap. 7.95 (ISBN 0-310-23651-7). Zondervan.

Gift. Peter Dickinson. 192p. (gr. 7-12). 1974. 8.95 (ISBN 0-316-18427-6, Pub. by Atlantic Monthly Pr.). Little.

Gift. Edwin G. March. 1981. 6.95 (ISBN 0-8062-1635-2). Carlton.

Gift. Madeena S. Nolan. (Orig.). 1981. pap. 2.50 (ISBN 0-440-12875-7). Dell.

Gift. Cynthia Walcott. LC 76-5476. (Illus.). (gr. 1-5). 1976. 7.00 (ISBN 0-87743-105-1, 7-52-51); with cassette narration 12.00 (ISBN 0-87743-108-6, 7-52-52). Baha'i.

Gift for a Gift. Anne Rockwell. LC 73-12855. (Illus.). 48p. (gr. k-3). 1974. 5.95 o.s.i. (ISBN 0-8193-0711-4, Four Winds); PLB 5.41 o.s.i. (ISBN 0-8193-0712-2). Schol Bk Serv.

Gift for Mama. Esther Hauzig. 64p. (gr. 3-7). 1981. 8.95 (ISBN 0-670-33976-8). Viking Pr.

Gift for Tolum. Marjorie Hopkins. LC 72-272. (Illus.). 48p. (gr. k-3). 1972. 5.95 o.s.i. (ISBN 0-8193-0588-X, Four Winds); PLB 5.41 o.s.i. (ISBN 0-8193-0589-8). Schol Bk Serv.

Gift from Earth. Larry Niven. 256p. 1975. pap. 1.50 o.p. (ISBN 0-345-24509-1). Ballantine.

Gift-Giver. Joyce Hansen. 128p. (gr. 4-8). 1980. 7.95 (ISBN 0-395-29433-9, Clarion). HM.

Gift Horse. Hayes. Orig. Title: The Carousel Horse. (gr. 4-5). 1980. pap. 1.25 (ISBN 0-590-30905-6, Schol Pap). Schol Bk Serv.

Gift Horse & Other Stories. Kate C. O'Brien. 1981. 8.95 (ISBN 0-8076-0976-5). Braziller.

Gift of Adminstration. Thomas C. Campbell & Gary B. Reierson. LC 80-24594. 1981. soft cover 6.95 (ISBN 0-664-24357-6). Westminster.

Gift of Christmas. Jane B. Moncure. LC 79-10279. (Bible Story Books). (Illus.). (ps-3). 1979. PLB 5.50 (ISBN 0-89565-083-5). Childs World.

Gift of Flowers. Beverly Parkin. 64p. 1976. 4.95 o.p. (ISBN 0-8028-3479-5). Eerdmans.

Gift of Gold. Beverly Butler. LC 72-3151. (gr. 4-8). 1972. 5.95 (ISBN 0-396-06636-4). Dodd.

Gift of Gold. Beverly Butler. (YA) (gr. 7-9). 1973. pap. 1.95 (ISBN 0-671-41327-9). PB.

Gift of Grace. Arthur A. Vogel. 1980. 1.50 (ISBN 0-686-28778-9). Forward Movement.

Gift of Inner Healing. Ruth C. Stapleton. LC 75-36180. 1976. 5.95 (ISBN 0-87680-809-7, Key Word Bks.); pap. 1.75 (ISBN 0-686-67399-9, 91030). Word Bks.

Gift of Islands: Living in Figi. June Knox-Mawer. 8.75 (ISBN 0-7195-0780-4). Transatlantic.

Gift of Joy. Christian Duquoc. (Concilium Ser.: Vol. 39). pap. 6.95 (ISBN 0-8091-1578-6). Paulist Pr.

Gift of Life: A Message of Hope for the Seriously Ill. Randy Becton. (Illus.). 1978. pap. 3.95 (ISBN 0-89137-309-8). Quality Pubns.

Gift of Life: The Social & Psychological Impact of Organ Transplantation. Roberta G. Simmons et al. LC 77-2749. (Health, Medicine & Society Ser.). 1977. 29.95 (ISBN 0-471-79197-0, Pub by Wiley-Interscience). Wiley.

Gift of Love, 5 vols. Joan W. Anglund. (Illus.). 32p. 1980. Set. pap. 8.95 (ISBN 0-15-230790-7, VoyB). HarBraceJ.

Gift of Love. Romen Basu. (Greenbird Bk.). 176p. 1975. 12.00 (ISBN 0-88253-823-3); pap. 5.00 (ISBN 0-88253-824-1). Ind-US Inc.

Gift of Love. Joel S. Goldsmith. Ed. by Lorraine Sinkler. LC 75-9330. 96p. (Gift format). 1975. 4.95 (ISBN 0-06-063172-4, HarpR). Har-Row.

Gift of Magic. Lois Duncan. (Illus.). (gr. 5-7). 1972. pap. 1.75 (ISBN 0-671-56096-4). PB.

Gift of Nerve - Poems, 1966-1977. Emery E. George. 1978. 6.95 (ISBN 0-914408-06-2); pap. 3.95 (ISBN 0-685-89712-5). Kylix Pr.

Gift of Play. Maria W. Piers & Genevieve M. Landau. 123p. 1980. 9.95 (ISBN 0-8027-0657-6). Walker & Co.

Gift of Sarah Barker. Jane Yolen. LC 80-26443. 156p. (gr. 7 up). 1981. 9.95 (ISBN 0-670-64580-X). Viking Pr.

Gift of Tenderness. Compiled by Elisabeth Deane. 1979. 2.95 (ISBN 0-442-82589-7). Peter Pauper.

Gift of the Holy Spirit Today. J. Rodman Williams. (Orig.). 1980. pap. 6.95 (ISBN 0-88270-413-3). Logos.

Gift of the Magi. O. Henry. LC 78-55660. (Illus.). 1978. Repr. 7.95 (ISBN 0-672-52296-9). Bobbs.

Gift of the Magi. O. Henry. (Creative's Classics Ser.). 32p. (gr. 4-9). 1980. PLB 6.95 (ISBN 0-87191-775-0). Creative Ed.

Gift of the Magi. O. Henry. Ed. by Walter Pauk & Raymond Harris. (Jamestown Classics Ser.). (Illus.). 35p. (gr. 6-12). 1979. pap. text ed. 1.60x (ISBN 0-89061-186-6, 401); tchrs. ed. 2.50x (ISBN 0-89061-188-2, 403). Jamestown Pubs.

Gift of the Magi & Other Stories. C. G. Draper. (Hewbury House Reader Ser.: Stage 2 - Beginner). (Illus., Orig.). 1981. pap. text ed. 1.95 (ISBN 0-88377-169-1). Newbury Hse.

Gift of the Refugees: Notes of a Volunteer Family of a Refugee Camp. Hakon Torjesen et al. 1981. 9.95 (ISBN 0-9602790-3-2). The Garden.

Gift of the Sacred Dog. Paul Goble. LC 80-15843. (Illus.). 32p. (gr. k-2). 9.95 (ISBN 0-87888-165-4). Bradbury Pr.

Gift of Tongues. Larry Christenson. 1963. pap. 0.45 (ISBN 0-87123-184-0, 260184). Bethany Fell.

Gift of Wonder. Helen Lowrie Marshall. LC 67-28483. 1967. 1.95 o.p. (ISBN 0-385-09465-5). Doubleday.

Gift Outright: America to Her Poets. Ed. by Helen Plotz. LC 77-8555. (gr. 7 up). 1977. 9.25 (ISBN 0-688-80109-9); PLB 8.88 (ISBN 0-688-84109-0). Greenwillow.

Gifted & Talented. Carol Epstein. 1979. pap. 11.95 (ISBN 0-87545-017-2). Natl Sch Pr.

Gifted & the Creative: A Fifty Year Perspective. Ed. by Julian C. Stanley et al. LC 77-4790. (Hyman Blumberg Symposium Ser.: No. 6). (Illus.). 1978. text ed. 17.50x o.p. (ISBN 0-8018-1974-1); pap. 4.95 (ISBN 0-8018-1975-X). Johns Hopkins.

Gifted Child. J. B. Shields. (Exploring Education Ser.). 1968. pap. text ed. 5.00x (ISBN 0-901225-42-8, NFER). Humanities.

Gifted Child: An Annotated Bibliography. A. Start. (Bibliographic Ser.). 1971. pap. text ed. 4.25x (ISBN 0-85633-003-5, NFER). Humanities.

Gifted Child, the Family & the Community. The American Association for Gifted Children. LC 80-54030. 228p. 1981. 17.50 (ISBN 0-8027-0673-8). Walker & Co.
Gifted Children. Frank Laycock. 1979. pap. text ed. 8.95x (ISBN 0-673-15142-5). Scott F.
Gifted Disadvantaged: A Ten Year Longitudinal Study of Compensatory Education in Israel. Moshe Smilansky & David Nevo. 356p. 1980. 26.50 (ISBN 0-677-04400-3). Gordon.
Gifted in Socio-Educational Perspective. T. Ernest Newland. (Special Education Ser.). (Illus.). 448p. 1976. 18.95 (ISBN 0-13-356287-5). P-H.
Gifted Women in Politics & the Arts & Sciences. Louise M. Bachtold. LC 80-69361. 135p. 1981. perfect bdg. 10.95 (ISBN 0-86548-022-2). Century Twenty One.
Gifted Young Children. Wendy C. Roedell et al. Ed. by Abraham J. Tannenbaum. LC 80-10707. (Perspectives on Gifted & Talented Education Ser.). (Orig.). 1980. pap. text ed. 6.50x (ISBN 0-8077-2587-0). Tchrs Coll.
Giftedness, Conflict & Underachievement. Whitmore. 478p. 1980. text ed. 18.95 (ISBN 0-205-06870-7, 2468700). Allyn.
Gifts & Ministries. Arnold Bittlinger. LC 72-96403. 104p. 1973. pap. 1.95 o.p. (ISBN 0-8028-1497-2). Eerdmans.
Gifts & Other Stories. O. Henry et al. (Oxford Progressive English Readers Ser.). (Illus.). (gr. 3up). 1974. pap. text ed. 2.95x (ISBN 0-19-580574-7). Oxford U Pr.
Gifts Differing. Isabel B. Myers & Peter B. Myers. (Orig.). 1980. 21.50 (ISBN 0-89106-015-4); pap. 12.00 (ISBN 0-89106-011-1). Consulting Psychol.
Gifts from the Kitchen. Norma Myers & Joan Scobey. LC 79-8914. 320p. 1980. pap. 9.95 (ISBN 0-672-52631-X). Bobbs.
Gifts of Genius. James Thorpe. LC 80-80077. (Illus.). 200p. 1980. 10.00 (ISBN 0-87328-110-1). Huntington Lib.
Gifts of Power: The Writings of Rebecca Jackson, Black Visionary, Shaker Eldress. Ed. by Jean M. Hunez. (Illus.). 370p. 1981. lib. bdg. 20.00x (ISBN 0-87023-299-1). U of Mass Pr.
Gifts of the Child Christ, 2 vols. George MacDonald. LC 72-94606. 1972. pap. 9.95 (ISBN 0-8028-1518-9). Eerdmans.
Gifts of the Holy Spirit. C. R. Vaughan. 1975. 11.95 (ISBN 0-85151-222-4). Banner of Truth.
Gifts of Writing: Decorative Projects with Words & Art. Susan Judy & Stephen Judy. LC 80-10360. (Illus.). (gr. 5-7). 1980. 8.95 (ISBN 0-684-16522-8). Scribner.
Giftwish. Graham M. Martin. 1981. 8.95 (ISBN 0-395-30348-6). HM.
Gigantes en Canaan: 14 Lecciones, Tomo 3. Bernice C. Jordan. (Pasos de Fe Ser.). (Span.). pap. text ed. 2.25 (ISBN 0-86508-405-X); figuras 7.95 (ISBN 0-86508-406-8). BCM Inc.
Gigantic Balloon. Ruth Park. LC 76-3408. (Illus.). 40p. (gr. k-4). 1976. 5.95 o.s.i. (ISBN 0-685-66683-2, Four Winds); PLB 5.41 o.s.i. (ISBN 0-8193-0849-8); pap. 1.95 o.s.i. (ISBN 0-8193-0909-5, Pippin). Schol Bk Serv.
Gigantic Joke Book. Joseph Rosenbloom. LC 77-93310. (Illus.). (gr. 2 up). 1978. 7.95 (ISBN 0-8069-4590-7); PLB 8.29 (ISBN 0-8069-4591-5). Sterling.
Gigantick Histories of the Two Famous Giants of Guildhall. Thomas Boreman. Ed. by Alison Lurie & Justin G. Schiller. LC 75-32140. (Classics of Children's Literature Ser.: 1621-1932). PLB 38.00 (ISBN 0-8240-2256-4). Garland Pub.
Giggle Puss: Pet Jokes for Kids. Charles Keller. LC 76-44837. (Illus.). (gr. 1-4). 1977. 5.95 (ISBN 0-13-356295-6); pap. 1.95 (ISBN 0-13-356303-0). P-H.
Giggles Goggles. Elaine Laron. (Electric Company Ser.). (Illus.). (gr. 1-5). 1973. PLB 5.38 (ISBN 0-307-64825-7, Golden Pr). Western Pub.
Giggly-Wiggly, Snickety-Snick. Robyn Supraner. LC 76-14406. (Illus.). 40p. (ps-3). 1978. 7.25 (ISBN 0-590-17709-5, Four Winds); lib. bdg. 7.95 (ISBN 0-590-07709-0). Schol Bk Serv.
Gigi Bread, Gamblers & Friends. Louis H. Cappelli. LC 79-67322. 195p. 1980. 7.95 (ISBN 0-533-04449-9). Vantage.
Gila Monsters Meet You at the Airport. Marjorie W. Sharmat. LC 80-12264. (Illus.). 32p. (gr. k-3). 1980. 8.95 (ISBN 0-02-782450-0). Macmillan.
Gila: River of the Southwest. Edwin Corle. LC 51-6152. (Illus.). 1964. pap. 4.50 (ISBN 0-8032-5040-1, BB 305, Bison). U of Nebr Pr.
Gilbert & Sullivan Dictionary. Ed. by George E. Dunn. LC 72-125070. (Music Ser). 1971. Repr. of 1936 ed. lib. bdg. 14.50 (ISBN 0-306-70007-7). Da Capo.
Gilbert & Sullivan in America. Reginald Allen. LC 79-54098. (Illus.). 26p. 1979. pap. 3.00. Pierpont Morgan.
Gilbert & Sullivan: Their Lives & Times. Leslie Baily. (Large Format Ser.). (Illus.). 1979. pap. 5.95 o.p. (ISBN 0-14-005106-6). Penguin.
Gilbert Antoine de St. Maxent: The Spanish-Frenchman of New Orleans. James J. Coleman, Jr. LC 68-54600. 136p. 1980. 10.00 (ISBN 0-911116-06-0). Pelican.
Gilbert Crispin, Abbot of Westminster: A Study of the Abby Under Norman Rule. Joseph A. Robinson. LC 80-2211. 1981. Repr. of 1911 ed. 32.50 (ISBN 0-404-18785-4). AMS Pr.
Gilbert Foliot & His Letters. Adrian Morey & C. N. Brooke. (Cambridge Studies in Medieval Life & Thought). 1966. 44.95 (ISBN 0-521-05764-7). Cambridge U Pr.
Gilbert Haven: Methodist Abolitionist. William Gravely. LC 72-14179. 272p. 1973. 8.95 o.p. (ISBN 0-687-14702-6). Abingdon.
Gilbert Ryle: An Introduction to His Philosophy. William Lyons. (Harvester Studies in Philosophy: No. 21). 1980. text ed. 30.00 (ISBN 0-391-01800-0). Humanities.
Gilbert Stuart. William T. Whitley. LC 77-87680. (Library of American Art Ser). 1932. lib. bdg. 27.50 (ISBN 0-306-71712-3). Da Capo.
Gilbert Stuart & His Pupils. John H. Morgan. LC 72-96440. (Library of American Art Ser). 1969. Repr. of 1939 ed. lib. bdg. 18.50 (ISBN 0-306-71827-8). Da Capo.
Gildas: The Ruin of Britain & Other Works. Gildas. Ed. by Michael Winterbottom. 162p. 1978. 16.00x (ISBN 0-8476-6079-6). Rowman.
Gilded Age. Mark Twain & Charles D. Warner. pap. 2.75 (ISBN 0-451-51375-4, CE1375, Sig Classics). NAL.
Gilded Age: A Tale of to-Day. Mark Twain. Ed. by Bryant M. French. LC 76-183110. 1972. 8.95 (ISBN 0-672-61028-0). Bobbs.
Gilded Age City: Politics, Life, & Labor in Petersburg, Virginia, 1874-1889. William D. Henderson. LC 80-1385. (Illus.). 603p. 1980. lib. bdg. 25.50 (ISBN 0-8191-1294-1); pap. text ed. 17.50 (ISBN 0-8191-1295-X). U Pr of Amer.
Gilded Age, Eighteen Seventy-Seven to Eighteen Ninety-Six. Compiled by Vincent De Santis. LC 72-96558. (Goldentree Bibliographies in American History Ser.). 168p. (Orig.). 1973. pap. 6.95x (ISBN 0-88295-526-5). AHM Pub.
Gilded Bat. Edward Gorey. LC 66-22413. (Illus.). 1979. 5.95 (ISBN 0-396-07688-2). Dodd.
Gilded Butterflies: The Rise & Fall of the London Season. Philippa Pullar. 1979. 22.50 (ISBN 0-241-89965-6, Pub. by Hamish Hamilton England). David & Charles.
Gilded Needles. Michael McDowell. 352p. 1980. pap. 2.50 (ISBN 0-380-76398-2, 76398). Avon.
Gilded Spurs. Grace Ingram. 1979. pap. 1.95 o.p. (ISBN 0-449-23910-1, Crest). Fawcett.
Gildenford. Valerie Anand. 1979. pap. 2.50 o.p. (ISBN 0-445-04336-9). Popular Lib.
Giles & Phineas Fletcher. Frank S. Kastor. (English Authors Ser.: No. 225). 1978. lib. bdg. 12.50 (ISBN 0-8057-6696-0). Twayne.
Giles of Rome and the Medieval Theory of Conception. Anthony M. Hewson. (University of London Historical Ser: No. 38). 280p. 1975. text ed. 47.50x (ISBN 0-485-13138-2, Athlone Pr). Humanities.
Gill History of Ireland, 11 vols. Ed. by James Lydon & Margaret Maccurtin. Set. pap. 60.10 (ISBN 0-686-16761-9). Irish Bk Ctr.
Gilles de la Tourette Syndrome. Ed. by Arthur K. Shapiro et al. LC 74-21986. 1978. 32.50 (ISBN 0-89004-057-5). Raven.
Gilpin County Gold: Peter McFarlane, Mining Entrepreneur in Central City, Colorado. H. William Axford. LC 76-115034. (Illus.). xii, 210p. 1976. 12.95 (ISBN 0-8040-0550-8, SB). Swallow.
Gimme an H, Gimme an E, Gimme an L, Gimme a P. Frank Bonham. LC 80-23926. 192p. (YA) (gr. 7 up). 1980. 9.95 (ISBN 0-684-16717-4). Scribner.
Gimmicks Make Money in Retailing. 2nd ed. Betty J. Minsky. LC 71-153566. (Illus.). 200p. 1972. 8.95 (ISBN 0-87005-095-8). Fairchild.
Gimpel the Fool & Other Stories. Isaac B. Singer. Tr. by Saul Bellow et al. 1957. 9.95 (ISBN 0-374-16244-1); pap. 4.95 (ISBN 0-374-50052-5). FS&G.
Ginger Tree. Oswald Wynd. LC 77-6892. 1977. 10.95 o.p. (ISBN 0-06-014729-6, HarpT). Har-Row.
Gingerbread Boy. Retold by & illus. by Paul Galdone. LC 74-11461. 40p. (ps-3). 1975. 7.95 (ISBN 0-395-28799-5, Clarion). HM.
Gingerbread Boy. Anne McGill-Franzen. LC 79-62980. (Learn-a-Tale). (Illus.). (gr. k-2). 1979. PLB 8.25 (ISBN 0-8393-0184-7). Raintree Child.
Gingerbread Children. Ilo Orleans. (Beginning-to-Read Bks). (Illus.). 32p. (gr. 1-3). 1973. PLB 3.39 o.p. (ISBN 0-695-40433-4); pap. 1.50 o.p. (ISBN 0-695-30433-X). Follett.
Gingerbread Man. Illus. by Ed Arno. (Illus.). (gr. k-3). 1970. pap. 1.25 (ISBN 0-590-01554-0, Schol Pap); pap. 3.95 gingerbread man & three billy goats gruff (2 bks.) & 1 record (ISBN 0-590-04405-2). Schol Bk Serv.
Gingerbread Man. Illus. by Elfrieda. (Illus.). (ps-2). 1972. PLB 7.15 o.p. (ISBN 0-307-69054-7, Golden Pr). Western Pub.
Gingerbread Man. (Ladybird Ser.). (Illus., Arabic.). 2.50x (ISBN 0-686-63577-9). Intl Bk Ctr.
Gingerbread Man. Illus. by Bonnie Rutherford & Bill Rutherford. 32p. (ps-3). 1972. 1.95 (ISBN 0-307-10460-5, Golden Pr); PLB 7.62 (ISBN 0-307-60460-8). Western Pub.
Ginghams. Sy Reit. (Golden Book of Picture Postcards Ser.). (Illus.). (ps-4). 1977. pap. 0.95 o.p. (ISBN 0-307-11101-6, Golden Pr). Western Pub.
Ginghams & the Backward Picnic. Joan Bowden. (Young Reader Ser.). (Illus.). (gr. k-3). 1979. PLB 5.00 (ISBN 0-307-60148-X, Golden Pr). Western Pub.
Ginnie & the New Girl. Catherine Woolley. (Illus.). (gr. 3-7). 1954. 6.75 o.p. (ISBN 0-688-21336-7). Morrow.
Ginnie Joins In. Catherine Woolley. (Illus.). (gr. 3-7). 1951. 6.95 (ISBN 0-688-21341-3). Morrow.
Giode TP Classification in Geology. LC 80-41094. (Geology Ser.). 120p. 1981. 34.95 (ISBN 0-470-27090-X). Halsted Pr.
Giorgione's Tempesta, with Comments on Giorgione's Poetic Allegories. Edgar Wind. 1969. 19.95x o.p. (ISBN 0-19-817165-X). Oxford U Pr.
Giotto & Assisi. Millard Meiss. (Illus.). 12.95x (ISBN 0-912158-42-5). Hennessey.
Giovanni Antonio Bazze - "Il Sodoma". Andree Hayum. LC 75-23794. (Outstanding Dissertations in the Fine Arts - 16th Century). (Illus.). 1976. lib. bdg. 41.00 (ISBN 0-8240-1989-X). Garland Pub.
Giovanni Batista Sammartini Sonate a Tre Stromenti. Giovanni B. Sammartini. Ed. by Bathia D. Churgin. LC 80-12339. (Early Musical Masterworks Ser.). 80p. 1981. 20.00x (ISBN 0-8078-1446-6). U of NC Pr.
Giovanni Bellini. Giles Robertson. LC 79-93169. (Illus.). 171p. 1980. Repr. of 1968 ed. lib. bdg. 60.00 (ISBN 0-87817-273-4). Hacker.
Giovanni Segantini: A Vision of His Art & of His Letters. John L. Thompson. (Illus.). 107p. 1981. 41.85 (ISBN 0-930582-94-2). Gloucester Art.
Giovanni Verga. Giovanni Cecchetti. (World Authors Ser.: No. 489 Italy). 1978. 12.95 (ISBN 0-8057-6330-9). Twayne.
Gipsy Smith: From the Forest I Came. David Lazell. 224p. 1973. pap. 2.50 (ISBN 0-8024-2959-9). Moody.
Gipsy Wharf. Jasim Uddin. LC 70-10225. (Unesco's Pakistan Ser). (Illus.). 1970. 9.95 (ISBN 0-672-53544-0). Pegasus.
Giraffe: Its Biology, Behavior, & Ecology. Anne I Dagg & J. Bristol Foster. 210p. 1980. Repr. of 1976 ed. text ed. write for info. (ISBN 0-89874-275-7). Krieger.
Giraffe: The Silent Giant. Miriam Schlein. LC 76-7922. (Illus.). 64p. (gr. 2-5). 1976. 6.95 (ISBN 0-590-07421-0, Four Winds). Schol Bk Serv.
Giraffes at Home. Ann Cooke. LC 79-158686. (Let's-Read-&-Find-Out Science Bk.). (Illus.). (gr. k-3). 1972. 7.95 (ISBN 0-690-33082-0, TYC-J); PLB 7.89 (ISBN 0-690-33083-9). T Y Crowell.
Giraldi Cinthio on Romances. Giraldi Cinthio. Tr. by Henry L. Snuggs. LC 68-12971. 216p. 1968. 9.75x (ISBN 0-8131-1158-7). U Pr of Ky.
Giraudoux: Four Plays, Vol. 1. Jean Giraudoux. Incl. Ondine; The Enchanted; The Madwoman of Chaillot; The Apollo of Bellac. 255p. (Orig.). 1958. pap. 5.95 (ISBN 0-8090-0712-6, Mermaid). Hill & Wang.
Giraudoux: Three Plays, Vol. 2. Jean Giraudoux. Tr. by Phyllis La Farge & Peter H. Judd. Incl. Siegfried; Amphitryon 38; Electra. 247p. (Orig.). 1964. pap. 5.95 (ISBN 0-8090-0731-2, Mermaid). Hill & Wang.
Girl Alive. Margaret Thiele. LC 80-11623. (Orion Ser.). 1980. pap. 1.95 (ISBN 0-8127-0268-9). Southern Pub.
Girl at the Half-Way House. Emerson Hough. 1976. lib. bdg. 16.75x (ISBN 0-89968-044-5). Lightyear.
Girl Between. Sheila Douglas. (Harlequin Romances). 192p. 1981. pap. 1.25 (ISBN 0-373-02392-8, Pub. by Harlequin). PB.
Girl Called Al. Constance C. Greene. (Illus.). (gr. 6-8). 1969. 7.95 (ISBN 0-670-34153-3). Viking Pr.
Girl Called Rosemary. Doubtfire. (gr. 7-12). pap. 1.25 (ISBN 0-590-09243-X, Schol Pap). Schol Bk Serv.
Girl Captives of the Cheyennes: A True Story of the Capture & Rescue of 4 Pioneer Girls, 1874, Repr. Of 1927 Ed. Grace E. Meredith. Bd. with Narrative of the Captivity of Mrs. Jane Frazier: In: Thomas' History of Allegheny County, Pennsylvania. Jane Frazier. Repr. of 1930 ed; History of the Capture & Captivity of David Boyd from Cumberland County, Pennsylvania, in 1756. Ed. by Marion M. Davis. Repr. of 1931 ed; Means Massacre, Molly Finney, the Canadian Captive. Charles P. Illsley. Repr. of 1932 ed; Narrative of Titus King of Northampton, Mass., a Prisoner of the Indians in Canada, 1755-1758. Repr. of 1938 ed. LC 75-7137. (Indian Captivities Ser.: Vol. 109). 1977. lib. bdg. 44.00 (ISBN 0-8240-1733-1). Garland Pub.
Girl Cried Murder. Woolfolk. (gr. 7-12). pap. 0.95 o.p. (ISBN 0-590-05810-X, Schol Pap). Schol Bk Serv.
Girl from Pike County. Bret Harte. Ed. by Walter Pauk & Raymond Harris. (Classics Ser). (Illus.). (gr. 6-12). 1976. pap. text ed. 1.60x (ISBN 0-89061-050-9, 521); tchrs. ed. 3.00 (ISBN 0-89061-053-3, 523). Jamestown Pubs.
Girl from Samos. Menander. Tr. by E. G. Turner from Gr. 64p. 1972. pap. text ed. 5.75x (ISBN 0-485-12019-4, Athlone Pr). Humanities.
Girl from the Sea. Anne Weale. (Harlequin Presents Ser.). 192p. 1981. pap. 1.50 (ISBN 0-373-10408-1, Pub. by Harlequin). PB.
Girl in a Swing. Richard Adams. 1980. pap. 3.50 (E9662, Signet Bks). NAL.
Girl in a Swing. Richard Adams. LC 79-3480. 1980. 11.95 (ISBN 0-394-51049-6). Knopf.
Girl in Exile. Alice M. Dodge. (YA) 1969. 5.95 (ISBN 0-685-07435-8, Avalon). Bouregy.
Girl in the Golden Atom. Raymond Cummings. 1976. lib. bdg. 12.95x (ISBN 0-89968-175-1). Lightyear.
Girl in the Mirror. Zoa Sherburne. (gr. 7 up). 1966. 7.75 (ISBN 0-688-21344-8). Morrow.
Girl in the Painting. Eve Bunting. (Young Romance Ser.). (Illus.). (gr. 3-9). 1978. PLB 5.95 (ISBN 0-87191-639-8); pap. 2.95 (ISBN 0-89812-069-1). Creative Ed.
Girl in the Plain Brown Wrapper. John D. MacDonald. LC 72-8388. 1973. 8.95 (ISBN 0-397-00953-4). Lippincott.
Girl in White Armor. new ed. Albert B. Paine. (gr. 7 up). 1967. 4.50g o.s.i. (ISBN 0-02-769650-2). Macmillan.
Girl Inside. Jeannette Eyerly. 1980. pap. 1.75 (ISBN 0-425-04522-6). Berkley Pub.
Girl Like Me. Jeannette Eyerly. LC 66-10022. (gr. 7 up). 1966. 9.95 (ISBN 0-397-30869-8). Lippincott.
Girl Missing. Christine Nostlinger. Tr. by Anthea Bell from Ger. LC 76-13893. 144p. (gr. 6 up). 1976. PLB 5.90 o.p. (ISBN 0-531-00346-9). Watts.
Girl of the Woods. Grace L. Hill. 192p. 1981. pap. 1.95 (ISBN 0-553-14599-1). Bantam.
Girl Possessed. Violet Winspear. (Harlequin Presents Ser.). 192p. 1981. pap. 1.50 (ISBN 0-373-10420-0, Pub. by Harlequin). PB.
Girl Rebel: The Autobiography of Hsieh Pingying with Extracts from Her "New War Diaries". Hsieh Pingying. Tr. by Adet Lin & Anor Lin. LC 74-34583. (China in the 20th Century Ser). (Illus.). xviii, 270p. 1975. Repr. of 1940 ed. lib. bdg. 25.00 (ISBN 0-306-70691-1). Da Capo.
Girl Scout Badges & Signs: Leaders Guide. Girl Scouts of the U.S.A. Program Department. 1980. pap. text ed. 2.50 (ISBN 0-88441-327-6, 20-712). GS.
Girl Scout Cookbook. Girl Scouts of the U. S. A. Ed. by Ely List. LC 70-144349. (Illus.). 192p. 1971. 6.95 o.p. (ISBN 0-8092-9144-4); PLB avail o.p. (ISBN 0-685-28671-1). Contemp Bks.
Girl Through the Ages. Dorothy M. Stuart. LC 70-89292. (Illus.). 264p. 1969. Repr. of 1933 ed. 15.00 (ISBN 0-8103-3581-6). Gale.
Girl Watcher. James Lawson. 1977. pap. 1.95 o.s.i. (ISBN 0-446-89330-7). Warner Bks.
Girl Who Cried Flowers & Other Tales. Jane Yolen. LC 73-8903. (Illus.). 64p. (gr. 3-6). 1974. 9.95 (ISBN 0-690-00216-5, TYC-J); PLB 7.89 (ISBN 0-690-00217-3). T Y Crowell.
Girl Who Cried Flowers: And Other Tales. Jane Yolen. LC 80-26140. (Illus.). 64p. 1981. pap. 5.95 (ISBN 0-8052-0666-3). Schocken.
Girl Who Had Everything. Rae Foley. 1978. pap. 1.75 o.s.i. (ISBN 0-515-04806-2). Jove Pubns.
Girl Who Knew It All. Patricia R. Giff. (gr. k-6). 1981. pap. 1.25 (ISBN 0-440-42855-6, YB). Dell.
Girl Who Knew Tomorrow. Zoa Sherburne. (gr. 7 up). 1970. PLB 7.44 (ISBN 0-688-31347-7). Morrow.
Girl Who Lived on the Ferris Wheel. Louise Moeri. 112p. 1980. pap. 1.75 (ISBN 0-380-52506-2, 52506). Avon.
Girl Who Loved the Wind. Jane Yolen. LC 71-171012. (Illus.). (gr. k-3). 1972. 9.95 (ISBN 0-690-33100-2, TYC-J); PLB 9.89 (ISBN 0-690-33101-0). T Y Crowell.

Girl Who Loved Wild Horses. Paul Goble. LC 77-20500. (gr. k-2). 1978. 9.95 (ISBN 0-87888-121-2). Bradbury Pr.

Girl Who Married a Ghost & Other Tales from the North American Indian. Ed. by John Bierhorst. LC 77-21515. (Illus.). (gr. 5 up). 1978. 10.95 (ISBN 0-590-07505-5, Four Winds). Schol Bk Serv.

Girl Who Writes Dirty Books. Linda Dubreuil. 1975. pap. 1.50 o.p. (ISBN 0-685-51413-7, LB225KK, Leisure Bks). Nordon Pubns.

Girl with the Golden Hair. Leslie Deane. (Orig.). 1978. pap. 2.25 (ISBN 0-515-04807-0). Jove Pubns.

Girl with the Jade Green Eyes. John Boyd. 1978. 8.95 o.p. (ISBN 0-670-34164-9). Viking Pr.

Girl with the Silver Eyes. Willo D. Roberts. LC 80-12391. 192p. (gr. 4-6). 1980. 8.95 (ISBN 0-689-30786-1). Atheneum.

Girl with Wings. Doubtfire. (gr. 7-12). pap. 1.25 o.p. (ISBN 0-590-05370-1, Schol Pap). Schol Bk Serv.

Girl Without a Name. Gunnel Beckman. Tr. by Anne Parker from Swedish. LC 75-124840. (Illus.). (gr. 4-6). 1970. 5.50 o.p. (ISBN 0-15-230980-2, HJ). HarBraceJ.

Girls Are Equal Too. Dale Carlson. (Illus.). 1973. pap. 2.95 (ISBN 0-689-70433-X, Aladdin). Atheneum.

Girls Are Missing. Caroline Crane. LC 80-14784. 224p. 1980. 8.95 (ISBN 0-396-07877-X). Dodd.

Girls Can Too. Ed. by Lee B. Hopkins. LC 72-887. (Illus.). 48p. (gr. k-3). 1972. PLB 4.90 o.p. (ISBN 0-531-02587-X). Watts.

Girls' Christian Names, Their History, Meaning & Association. Helena Swan. LC 68-17935. 1968. Repr. of 1900 ed. 20.00 (ISBN 0-8103-3135-7). Gale.

Girls' Gymnastics. rev ed. Erna Wachtel & Newton C. Loken. LC 63-19163. (gr. 6 up). 1967. 6.95 (ISBN 0-8069-4310-6); PLB 7.49 (ISBN 0-8069-4311-4). Sterling.

Girls in the Velvet Frame. Adele Geras. LC 79-12352. (gr. 4-7). 1979. 8.95 (ISBN 0-689-30729-2). Atheneum.

Girls of Slender Means. Muriel Spark. 1963. 4.95 o.p. (ISBN 0-394-42637-1). Knopf.

Girodet-Trioson: An Iconographical Study. George Levitine. LC 77-94702. (Outstanding Dissertations in the Fine Arts Ser.). 1978. lib. bdg. 52.00x (ISBN 0-8240-3235-7). Garland Pub.

Girty. Richard Taylor. LC 77-82790. (New World Writing Ser.). (Illus.). 1977. pap. 4.95 o.p. (ISBN 0-913666-18-1). Turtle Isl Foun.

G.I.'s Vietnam Diary. Dominick Yezzo. LC 73-17193. 96p. (gr. 7 up). 1974. PLB 5.90 (ISBN 0-531-02684-1). Watts.

Giselle, Save the Children. Giselle Hrsch & Peggy Mann. LC 79-51194. 288p. 1980. 12.95 (ISBN 0-89696-054-4). Everest Hse.

Gissing: The Critical Heritage. Ed. by Pierre Coustillas & Colin Partridge. (Critical Heritage Ser.). 1972. 40.00 (ISBN 0-7100-7367-4). Routledge & Kegan.

Gist of the Cults. Jan K. Van Baalen. 1944. pap. 1.25 o.p. (ISBN 0-8028-1205-8). Eerdmans.

Gita Govinda. Jayadeva. Tr. by G. Keyt. 1974. 10.00 (ISBN 0-88253-488-2). Ind-US Inc.

Gita Govinda & Other Poems. Monika Varma. 4.80 (ISBN 0-89253-764-7); flexible cloth 4.00 (ISBN 0-89253-765-5). Ind-US Inc.

Gitaway Box. Hilary Milton. (gr. 4-9). 1980. pap. 2.95 (ISBN 0-89191-243-6). Cook.

Give a Magic Show! Burton Marks & Rita Marks. LC 77-5436. (gr. 2-6). 1977. 7.25 o.p. (ISBN 0-688-41819-8); PLB 6.96 (ISBN 0-688-51819-2). Lothrop.

Give a Man a Gun. Leslie Ernenwein. 1975. pap. 0.95 o.p. (ISBN 0-685-52175-3, LB239NK, Leisure Bks). Nordon Pubns.

Give All to Oregon. Cecil P. Dryden. (Illus.). 1968. 8.95 (ISBN 0-8038-2606-0). Hastings.

Give Love the Air. Faith Baldwin. 1980. pap. write for info. (ISBN 0-671-83092-9). PB.

Give Me a Child Until He's Two: Then You Take Him till He's Four! Marilyn McGinnis. LC 80-54005. 176p. pap. 4.95 (ISBN 0-8307-0785-9). Regal.

Give Me Back My Soul. Bebe Patten. 1973. pap. 1.25 o.p. (ISBN 0-8007-0645-5). Revell.

Give Me One Good Reason. Norma Klein. (YA) 1977. pap. 2.25 (ISBN 0-380-00166-7, 51292). Avon.

Give Sorrow Words: Maryse Holder's Letters from Mexico. Maryse Holder. 336p. (Orig.). 1980. pap. 2.50 (ISBN 0-380-51466-4, 51466). Avon.

Give the Lady What She Wants: The Story of Marshall Fields & Company. Lloyd Wendt & Herman Kogan. LC 52-7501. (Illus.). 1979. pap. 3.95 (ISBN 0-89708-020-3). And Bks.

Give Them Roots & Wings. Ed. by Dorothy T. Schwartz & Dorothy Aldrich. 163p. 1972. pap. 7.50, ATA members 5.00 (ISBN 0-686-13195-9). Am Theatre Assoc.

Give Up? William Cole. LC 78-6842. (Illus.). (gr. 4-6). 1978. PLB 6.45 s&l (ISBN 0-531-02249-8). Watts.

Give Us a Great Big Smile, Rosy Cole. Sheila Greenwald. (Illus.). 80p. (gr. 3 up). 1981. 7.95 (ISBN 0-316-32672-0, Pub. by Atlantic). Little.

Give Us the Tools. 1979. pap. 7.00 (ISBN 0-88936-213-0, IDRC131, IDRC). Unipub.

Give Us This Day. Carol Greene. 1980. pap. 6.50 (ISBN 0-570-03496-5, 56-1713). Concordia.

Give Us This Day. E. Howard Hunt. 240p. 1974. pap. 1.25 o.p. (ISBN 0-445-00212-3). Popular Lib.

Give Us This Day Our Daily Bread: Asking for & Sharing Life's Necessities. Colleen T. Evans. LC 78-20070. 168p. 1981. 9.95 (ISBN 0-385-14091-6, Galilee). Doubleday.

Give Your Child a Future: How to Develop a Productive Personality. John Gillmore & Eunice Gillmore. 1981. pap. 6.95 (ISBN 0-89803-038-2). Caroline Hse.

Give Your Child a Superior Mind. Seigfried Engelmann & Therese Engelmann. 320p. 1981. 5.95 (ISBN 0-346-12532-4). Cornerstone.

Give Your Child Permission to Unfold. Dorothy Bullock. LC 80-70509. 64p. (Orig.). 1981. pap. 2.95 (ISBN 0-87516-438-2). De Vorss.

Givers & Takers 2. Jane Mayhall. LC 68-55445. 78p. 1973. pap. 1.95 (ISBN 0-87130-033-8). Eakins.

Givers, Takers, & Other Kinds of Lovers. Josh McDowell. 1980. pap. 4.95 (ISBN 0-8423-1033-9). Tyndale.

Giving & Taking: Across the Foundation Desk. John M. Russell. LC 77-4865. 1977. pap. text ed. 4.95 (ISBN 0-8077-2526-9). Tchrs Coll.

Giving Birth. C. Margaret Hall. LC 79-53198. 1979. pap. 2.25 (ISBN 0-931590-03-5). Antietam Pr.

Giving Birth: Childbearing in America Today. Rita Kramer. 1979. 10.95 o.p. (ISBN 0-8092-7859-6). Contemp Bks.

Giving Cardiac Care. LC 80-27519. (Nursing Photobook). (Illus.). 160p. 1981. text ed. 12.95 (ISBN 0-916730-28-X). InterMed Comm.

Giving God What You Are. Pat Baker. 1981. pap. 3.95 (ISBN 0-8054-5333-4). Broadman.

Giving Good Weight. John McPhee. 261p. 1979. 9.95 (ISBN 0-374-16306-5); pap. 5.95 (ISBN 0-374-51600-6). FS&G.

Giving Medications Correctly & Safely. A. Bartilucci & J. Durgin. 1978. pap. 9.95 (ISBN 0-87489-216-3). Med Economics.

Giving up the Gun. Noel Perrin. LC 80-50744. 122p. 1980. pap. 4.95 (ISBN 0-394-73949-3). Random.

Giving up the Gun: Japan's Reversion to the Sword Fifteen Forty-Three to Eighteen Seventy-Nine. Noel Perrin. LC 80-50744. (Illus.). 122p. 1980. pap. 4.95 (ISBN 0-394-73949-3). Shambhala Pubns.

Giving Youth a Better Chance: Options for Education, Work, & Service. Carnegie Council on Policy Studies in Higher Education. LC 79-90851. (Carnegie Council Ser.). 1980. 14.95x (ISBN 0-87589-441-0). Jossey-Bass.

Gjon Mili: Photographs & Recollections. Gjon Mili. 1980. 40.00 (ISBN 0-8212-1116-1, 315001). NYGS.

GK One: The Publication of the General Catalogue of Printed Books in British Museum, 1881-1900. Barbara McCrimmon. 1980. write for info. (ISBN 0-208-01874-3, Linnet). Shoe String.

Gl Amanti Generosi. Francesco Mancini. Ed. by Howard M. Brown. LC 76-21035. (Italian Opera 1640-1770 Ser.). 1978. lib. bdg. 75.00 (ISBN 0-8240-2617-9). Garland Pub.

Glacial & Fluvioglacial Landforms. R. J. Price. (Geomorphology Texts: Vol. 5). (Illus.). 242p. 1973. pap. text ed. 16.95 (ISBN 0-582-48435-9). Longman.

Glacial & Periglacial Morphology, 2 vols. 2nd ed. C. Embleston & C. A. King. Incl. Vol. 1. Glacial Geomorphology. LC 75-14188. pap. 19.95 (ISBN 0-470-23893-3); Vol. 2. Periglacial Geomorphology. LC 75-14187. pap. 13.95 (ISBN 0-470-23895-X). 1975. Halsted Pr.

Glacial & Quaternary Geology. Richard F. Flint. LC 74-141198. (Illus.). 1971. 33.50 (ISBN 0-471-26435-0). Wiley.

Glacier Bay Concerto. Richard Dauenhauer. (Alaskana Book Ser.: No. 38). 120p. (Orig.). 1980. 12.95 (ISBN 0-935094-02-4); pap. 4.95 (ISBN 0-935094-04-0). Alaska Pacific.

Glacier Project: Concepts & Critiques-Selected Readings on the Glacier Theories of Organization & Management. Ed. by Jerry L. Gray. LC 75-27252. (Illus.). 350p. 1976. 27.50x (ISBN 0-8448-0716-8). Crane-Russak Co.

Glacier Tracks. Emogene Tallcott. LC 70-101479. (Illus.). (gr. 5 up). 1970. PLB 7.63 o.p. (ISBN 0-688-51118-X). Lothrop.

Glacieres or Freezing Caverns. Edwin S. Balch. Repr. of 1900 ed. 11.50 (ISBN 0-914264-32-X, Dist. by Caroline Hse). Zephyrus Pr.

Glaciers. Wendell V. Tangborn. LC 65-18702. (Let's-Read-&-Find-Out Science Bk). (Illus.). (gr. k-3). 1965. bds. 7.95 (ISBN 0-690-33118-5, TYC-J); PLB 7.89 (ISBN 0-690-33119-3). T Y Crowell.

Glaciers & Landscape: A Geomorphological Approach. D. E. Sugden & B. S. John. LC 76-11014. 1976. 19.95x (ISBN 0-470-15113-7). Halsted Pr.

Glad Rags II. Leigh Charlton & Annette Swanberg. (Illus.). 168p. (Orig.). 1981. pap. 7.95 (ISBN 0-87701-178-8). Chronicle Bks.

Glad Tidings. E. J. Waggoner. LC 72-81729. (Dimension Ser.). 1977. pap. 5.95 (ISBN 0-8163-0281-2). Pacific Pr Pub Assn.

Glad Tidings of Baha'u'llah: Being Extracts from the Sacred Writings of the Baha'is. rev. ed. Baha'U'Llah The Bab & Abdu'L-Baha. 1975. 4.95 (ISBN 0-85398-046-2, 7-15-51, Pub. by G Ronald England); pap. 2.00 (ISBN 0-85398-045-4, 7-15-52, Pub. by G Ronald England). Baha'i.

Gladiator. William Earls. (Orig.). Date not set. pap. 2.50 (ISBN 0-440-12995-8). Dell.

Gladiator: The Hill of the Dead. Andrew Quiller. 176p. (Orig.). 1975. pap. 1.25 o.p. (ISBN 0-523-22765-5). Pinnacle Bks.

Gladstone. Erich Eyck. Tr. by Bernard Miall. LC 68-56055. Repr. of 1938 ed. 25.00x (ISBN 0-678-05045-7). Kelley.

Gladstone: A Progress in Politics. Peter Stansky. 224p. 1981. pap. 4.95 (ISBN 0-393-00037-0). Norton.

Gladstone Diaries, Vols. 1 & 2# 1825-39. William E. Gladstone. Ed. by M. R. Foot. 1968. 89.00x (ISBN 0-19-821370-0). Oxford U Pr.

Gladstone Diaries: Volumes V & VI, 1844-1868. William E. Gladstone. Ed. by H. C. Matthew. (Gladstone Diaries Ser.). (Illus.). 1978. 139.00x set (ISBN 0-19-822445-1). Oxford U Pr.

Gladstone Diaries: 1840-1854, Vols. 3 & 4. William E. Gladstone. Ed. by M. R. Foot & M. R. Foot. (Illus.). 1450p. 1975. Set. 109.00x (ISBN 0-19-822425-7). Oxford U Pr.

Gladstones: A Family Biography. S. G. Checkland. LC 72-134611. 1971. 44.50 (ISBN 0-521-07966-7). Cambridge U Pr.

Gladys Aylward. Christine Hunter. 1970. pap. 1.95 (ISBN 0-8024-2986-6). Moody.

Gladys Hunt's "How to" Handbook. Gladys Hunt. LC 73-169168. 1971. pap. 1.95 (ISBN 0-87788-396-3). Shaw Pubs.

Glagol III: Al'manakh "Ardisa". Ed. by Carl R. Proffer & Ellendea Proffer. (Rus.). 1981. 15.00 (ISBN 0-88233-477-8); pap. 5.00 (ISBN 0-88233-478-6). Ardis Pubs.

Glaister's Glossary of the Book: Terms Used in Paper-Making, Printing, Bookbinding, & Publishing. Geoffrey Glaister. 1979. 75.00 (ISBN 0-520-03364-7). U of Cal Pr.

Glamorize with Lighting. A. Eugene Frazier. Ed. by Arthur F. Ide. LC 79-9441. (Good Taste Begins with You Ser.). (Illus.). iii, 50p. 1980. Repr. of 1969 ed. pap. text ed. 5.00 (ISBN 0-86663-224-7). Ide Hse.

Glance at the History of Linguistics, with Particular Regard to the Historical Study of Phonology. Holger Pedersen. Tr. by C. Henriksen & P. Henriksen. (Studies in the History of Linguistics: No. 7). (Illus.). 1980. text ed. 18.75x (ISBN 0-391-01648-2). Humanities.

Glasgow Stations. John R. Hume & Colin Johnston. 1979. 19.95 (ISBN 0-7153-7569-5). David & Charles.

Glass. Joseph Philippe. (Q Books: Where Do Things Come from?). (Illus.). 28p. 1978. 3.95 (ISBN 0-8467-0442-0, Pub. by Two Continents). Hippocrene Bks.

Glass Adonis. C. A. Trypanis. 1973. pap. 3.95 (ISBN 0-571-10170-4, Pub. by Faber & Faber). Merrimack Bk Serv.

Glass Ceramic Technology. S. Scholes. 1978. text ed. 16.70 o.p. (ISBN 0-08-019900-3). Pergamon.

Glass Dove. Sally Carrighar. 1977. pap. 1.75 (ISBN 0-380-01829-2, 36194). Avon.

Glass Engineering Handbook. 2nd ed. Errol B. Shand. 1958. 37.50 o.p. (ISBN 0-07-056395-0, P&RB). McGraw.

Glass Engraving. Barbara Norman. LC 80-18031. (Illus.). 208p. 1981. 25.00 (ISBN 0-668-05081-0, 5081). Arco.

Glass Etching-Pattern Book I: Fruit, Flowers, & Birds. Barry Nord & Elaine Nord. (Illus.). 50p. (Orig.). 1980. pap. 3.95 (ISBN 0-935656-02-2, 101C). Chrome Yellow.

Glass Etching-Pattern Book II: Wildlife, Alphabets, Geometrics. Barry Nord & Elaine Nord. (Illus.). 50p. (Orig.). 1980. pap. 3.95 (ISBN 0-935656-03-0, 101D). Chrome Yellow.

Glass Fibre for Schools. John Tiranti. (gr. 9-12). 1972. 8.95 (ISBN 0-85458-330-0); pap. 4.95 (ISBN 0-85458-340-8). Transatlantic.

Glass Fibre Yachts: Improvement & Repair. Charles Jones. 128p. 1980. 12.00x (Pub. by Nautical England). State Mutual Bk.

Glass House. Alice L. Covert. 1972. 5.95 (ISBN 0-685-25147-0, Avalon). Bouregy.

Glass House. Laura Furman. 204p. 1980. 10.95 (ISBN 0-670-34179-7). Viking Pr.

Glass in Modern Architecture of the Bauhaus Period. Arthur Korn. LC 68-11357. (Illus.). 1968. 15.00 o.s.i. (ISBN 0-8076-0440-2). Braziller.

Glass Key. Dashiell Hammett. 204p. Date not set. pap. 1.50 (ISBN 0-394-71773-2, Vin). Random.

Glass King & Other Poems. Sukanta Chaudhuri. (Writers Workshop Redbird Book Ser.). 32p. 1975. 6.00 (ISBN 0-88253-548-X); pap. text ed. 3.00 (ISBN 0-88253-547-1). Ind-US Inc.

Glass, Mosaics, & Plastic. Eric Shults. (Encore Edition). (Illus.). 1979. 3.95 (ISBN 0-684-16924-X, ScribT). Scribner.

Glass Reinforced Concrete. John L. Darlison & M. W. Fordyce. 1981. text ed. price not set. Butterworth.

Glass Ring. Mary Kennedy. LC 78-72143. (Illus.). (gr. 1-5). Date not set. price not set (ISBN 0-89799-106-0); pap. price not set (ISBN 0-89799-065-X). Dandelion Pr. Postponed.

Glass Room. Mary Towne. (Illus.). (gr. 5-7). 1972. pap. 0.75 (ISBN 0-671-29544-6). PB.

Glass-Sided Ant's Nest. Peter Dickinson. 1981. pap. 2.95 (ISBN 0-14-005864-8). Penguin.

Glass Slipper: Charles Perrault's Tales of Times Past. Tr. by John Bierhorst from Fr. LC 80-66243. (Illus.). 128p. 1981. 9.95t (ISBN 0-590-07603-5, Four Winds). Schol Bk Serv. Postponed.

Glass Teat. Harlan Ellison. 1975. pap. 1.50 o.s.i. (ISBN 0-515-03701-X, V3701). Jove Pubns.

Glass Technology: Developments Since 1978. Ed. by J. I. Duffy. LC 80-26045. (Chmical Tech. Rev. Ser.: 184). (Illus.). 323p. 1981. 48.00 (ISBN 0-8155-0838-7). Noyes.

Glassblower's Children. Maria Gripe. Tr. by Sheila La Farge from Swedish. LC 73-949. (Illus.). 160p. (gr. 3-7). 1973. PLB 6.46 o.s.i. (ISBN 0-440-03065-X, Sey Lawr). Delacorte.

Glassblowing: A Search for Form. Harvey Littleton. 136p. 1980. pap. 9.95 (ISBN 0-442-24341-3). Van Nos Reinhold.

Glassblowing: An Introduction to Artistic & Scientific Flameworking. rev. ed. Edward Carberry. LC 78-51569. (Illus.). 1980. 16.95 (ISBN 0-9601682-1-4). M G L S Pub.

Glassblowing for Laboratory Technicians. 2nd ed. R. Barbour. 1978. text ed. 45.00 (ISBN 0-08-022155-6); pap. text ed. 14.00 (ISBN 0-08-022156-4). Pergamon.

Glassmakers. Leonard E. Fisher. LC 64-16320. (Colonial Americans Ser). (Illus.). (gr. 4-6). 1964. PLB 4.90 o.p. (ISBN 0-531-01028-7). Watts.

Glastonbury: Mecca of the Westcountry. Michael Mathias & Derek Hector. LC 78-51083. (Illus.). 1979. 10.50 (ISBN 0-7153-7798-1). David & Charles.

Glastonbury Miscellany of the 15th Century: A Descriptive Index of Trinity College. A. G. Rigg. (Oxford English Monographs). 1968. 5.00x o.p. (ISBN 0-19-811713-2). Oxford U Pr.

Glaucoma & Its Medical Treatment with Cortin: Myopia Its Cause & Prevention. Emanuel Josephson. (Natural Health Ser.). 92p. (Orig.). 1937. pap. text ed. 6.95 (Pub. by Chedney). Alpine Ent.

Glaucoma: Contemporary International Concepts. Ed. by John G. Bellows. LC 79-88728. (Illus.). 448p. 1980. 54.50 (ISBN 0-89352-058-6). Masson Pub.

Glaze Projects. Richard Behrens. 3.95 (ISBN 0-934706-06-9). Prof Pubns Ohio.

Gleaning from Galatians. Gussie Lambert. (Ser. Outlines). 4.95 (ISBN 0-89315-075-4). Lambert Bk.

Gleanings. Charles L. Taylor. 1979. 2.00 (ISBN 0-686-28779-7). Forward Movement.

Gleanings: Essays in Jewish History, Letters & Art. Cecil Roth. 1967. 7.95 (ISBN 0-8197-0178-5). Bloch.

Gleanings for the Curious from the Harvest Fields of Literature: A Melange of Excerpta. Charles C. Bombaugh. LC 68-23465. 1970. Repr. of 1875 ed. 30.00 (ISBN 0-8103-3086-5). Gale.

Gleanings from Elisha. Arthur W. Pink. LC 79-181591. 288p. 1972. 10.95 (ISBN 0-8024-2962-9). Moody.

Gleanings from Paul. Arthur W. Pink. 1967. write for info. (ISBN 0-8024-2965-3). Moody.

Gleanings from the Scriptures: Man's Total Depravity. Arthur W. Pink. LC 73-80942. 1970. 10.95 (ISBN 0-8024-2966-1). Moody.

Gleanings from the Writings of Baha'u'llah. 2nd rev. ed. Baha'u 'llah. Tr. by Shoghi Effendi. LC 76-45364. 1976. 10.00 (ISBN 0-87743-111-6, 7-03-03); pap. 6.35 o.s.i. (ISBN 0-87743-112-4, 7-03-04). Baha'i.

Gleanings in Exodus. Arthur W. Pink. 1964. 10.95 (ISBN 0-8024-2975-0). Moody.

Gleanings in Genesis. Arthur W. Pink. 1922. 10.95 (ISBN 0-8024-2968-8). Moody.

Gleanings in Joshua. Arthur W. Pink. 1964. 10.95 (ISBN 0-8024-2982-3). Moody.
Gleanings in Old Garden Literature. William C. Hazlitt. LC 68-21773. 1968. Repr. of 1887 ed. 15.00 (ISBN 0-8103-3509-3). Gale.
Gleanings in the Godhead. Arthur W. Pink. 256p. 10.95 (ISBN 0-8024-2977-7). Moody.
Gleb Uspensky. Nikita I. Prutskov. (World Authors Ser.: Russia: No. 190). lib. bdg. 10.95 (ISBN 0-8057-2914-3). Twayne.
Glen Alps Retrospective: The Collagraph Idea, Nineteen Fifty Six to Nineteen Eighty. Bellevue Art Museum. LC 79-54958. (Illus.). pap. 4.95 (ISBN 0-295-95703-4). U of Wash Pr.
Glencannon: Great Stories from the Saturday Evening Post. LC 77-23723. 1977. 5.95 (ISBN 0-89387-017-X). Sat Eve Post.
Glenda. Janice M. Udry. (Illus.). (gr. 3-5). 1976. pap. 0.95 (ISBN 0-671-29784-8). PB.
Glendraco. Laura Black. LC 77-5017. 1977. 10.00 o.p. (ISBN 0-312-32917-2). St Martin.
Glenn's Datsun. Harold T. Glenn. 1975. pap. 7.95 o.p. (ISBN 0-8092-8319-0). Contemp Bks.
Glenn's Diesel & Gasoline Fuel-Injection Manual. Harold T. Glenn. (Illus.). 128p. 1973. 8.95 o.p. (ISBN 0-8092-9069-3, 1085). Contemp Bks.
Glenn's Jaguar Repair & Tune-up Guide. Harold T. Glenn. (Illus.). 1965. 8.95 (ISBN 0-8019-5083-X). Chilton.
Glenn's Triumph Repair & Tune-up Guide. Harold T. Glenn. (Illus.). 1965. 8.95 (ISBN 0-8019-1433-7). Chilton.
Glenn's Volvo Repair & Tune-up Guide. Harold T. Glenn. (Illus.). 1965. 8.95 (ISBN 0-8019-1434-5). Chilton.
Glenrose Calling. Amanda W. West. 1979. pap. 2.50 (ISBN 0-515-05081-4). Jove Pubns.
Glenway Wescott: The Paradox of Voice. Ira D. Johnson. LC 74-138301. 1971. 11.95 (ISBN 0-8046-0572-6, Natl U). Kennikat.
Gli Aeroplani Caproni: Studi-Progetti-Realizzazioni dal 1908 al 1935. Gianni Caproni. Ed. by James Gilbert. LC 79-7234. (Flight: Its First Seventy-Five Years Ser.). (Illus.). 1979. Repr. of 1936 ed. lib. bdg. 54.00x (ISBN 0-405-12150-4). Arno.
Gli Amori d'Apollo e di Dafne. Francesco Cavalli. Ed. by Howard M. Brown. LC 76-21071. (Italian Opera 1640-1770 Ser.). 1978. lib. bdg. 70.00 (ISBN 0-8240-2600-4). Garland Pub.
Gli Duoi Fratelli Rivali: The Two Rival Brothers. Giambattista Della Porta. Tr. by Louise G. Clubb from Italian. 350p. 1980. 22.50x (ISBN 0-520-03786-3). U of Cal Pr.
Gli Imbianchini Non Hanno Ricordi. Dario Fo. (Easy Readers). 1979. pap. 2.90 (ISBN 0-88436-296-5). EMC.
Glider Basics from Frist Flight to Solo. Thomas Knauff. Ed. by Allan Northcut & Debbie Northcut. LC 80-81375. (Illus.). 155p. 1980. text ed. 12.95. Knauff.
Gliding: A Handbook on Soaring Flight. 4th ed. Derek Piggott. (Illus.). 270p. 1976. 18.50x (ISBN 0-06-495570-2). B&N.
Gliding, Soaring, & Skysailing. Norman F. Smith. LC 79-27680. (Illus.). 160p. (gr. 9-12). 1980. PLB 7.79 (ISBN 0-671-32981-2). Messner.
Glimpse of Chinese Language: Peking's Language Reforms & the Teaching of Chinese in the U.S. Francis Shieh. pap. 6.50 (ISBN 0-686-09053-5, AD612722); microfiche 3.50 (ISBN 0-686-09054-3). Natl Tech Info.
Glimpse of Perfection. John F. Hornbrook. 178p. (Orig.). 1979. pap. 3.95 (ISBN 0-89841-004-5). Zoe Pubns.
Glimpses in Plant Research. Ed. by P. K. Nair. 300p. 1980. 35.00x (Pub. by Croom Helm England). State Mutual Bk.
Glimpses in Plant Research: Botanical Lectures & Essays, Vol. V. P. K. Nair. 400p. 1980. text ed. 50.00 (ISBN 0-7069-0827-9, Pub. by Vikas India). Advent Bk.
Glimpses into the Psychology of Yoga. I. K. Taimni. 1973. 10.95 (ISBN 0-8356-7290-5). Theos Pub Hse.
Glimpses of Abhidharma. Chogyam Trungpa. 1978. pap. 5.95 (ISBN 0-87773-708-8, Prajna). Great Eastern.
Glimpses of Baptist Heritage. Claude L. Howe, Jr. 1981. pap. 5.75 (ISBN 0-8054-6559-6). Broadman.
Glimpses of China from a Galloping Horse (a Woman's Journal). Norma L. Djerassi. LC 74-19098. 1975. 9.00 (ISBN 0-08-018215-1). Pergamon.
Glimpses of Colonial Society & Life at Princeton College, 1766-1773, by One of the Class of 1763. William Paterson. Ed. by W. Jay Mills. LC 72-179711. (Illus.). 182p. (Six songs). 1972. Repr. of 1903 ed. 18.00 (ISBN 0-8103-3810-6). Gale.
Glimpses of Gleams & Glooms. Cora G. Chase. 32p. 1980. 2.95 (ISBN 0-8059-2757-3). Dorrance.
Glimpses of the Beyond. Jean-Baptiste Delacour. 214p. 1974. 6.95 o.p. (ISBN 0-440-03287-3). Delacorte.
Glimpses of the Mother's Life, Vol. 2. Mira Alfassa. Ed. by Nilima Das. 335p. 1980. 11.00 (ISBN 0-89071-291-3). Matagiri.
Glinda of Oz. Frank L. Baum. 224p. 1981. pap. 2.25 (ISBN 0-345-28236-1, Del Rey). Ballantine.
Glip, Glop, Gloop: The Common School Children's Cookbook. Ed. by Sandra Graham. Isabel L. Hawley. LC 74-80786. (Illus.). 128p. (ps-6). Date not set. cancelled (ISBN 0-913636-05-3). Educ Res MA.
Glitter & Ash. Dennis Smith. 1981. pap. 2.95 (ISBN 0-451-09761-0, E9761, Sig). NAL.
Glitter-Dust. Alice Dwyer-Joyce. LC 77-25771. 1978. 7.95 o.p. (ISBN 0-312-32947-4). St Martin.
Glitter Girl. Joycelyn Day. (Second Chance at Love, Contemporary Ser.: No. 5). 192p. (Orig.). 1981. pap. 1.75 (ISBN 0-515-05878-5). Jove Pubns.
Glitter Street. Tim O'Sullivan. 1981. pap. 2.75 (ISBN 0-440-12902-8). Dell.
Glitterati. Charlotte Payne. Date not set. pap. 2.75 (ISBN 0-440-13067-0). Dell.
Glitterball. Rochelle Larkin. (Orig.). 1980. pap. 2.50 (ISBN 0-451-09525-1, E9525, Sig). NAL.
Glittering Misery. Patricia Y. Stallard. LC 77-94525. (Illus.). 1978. 10.95 o.p. (ISBN 0-88342-054-6); pap. 4.95 (ISBN 0-88342-239-5). Presidio Pr.
Global Analysis. Ed. by M. Grmela. (Lecture Notes in Mathematics: Vol. 755). 1980. pap. 20.00 (ISBN 0-387-09703-1). Springer-Verlag.
Global Analysis & Its Applications, 3 vols. (Illus.). 699p. (Orig.). 1975. Vol. 1. pap. 17.25 (ISBN 0-685-52332-2, ISP355, IAEA); Vol.2. pap. 28.00 (ISBN 0-685-52333-0); Vol. 3. pap. 24.25 (ISBN 0-685-52334-9). Unipub.
Global Development & Marketing. Robert Bartels. LC 80-11542. (Marketing Ser.). 90p. 1981. pap. text ed. 7.95 (ISBN 0-88244-223-6). Grid Pub.
Global Dialogue: The New International Economic Order. Bhashkar P. Menon. 1977. text ed. 21.00 (ISBN 0-08-021498-3); pap. text ed. 8.50 (ISBN 0-08-021499-1). Pergamon.
Global Earthquake Monitoring: Its Uses, Potentials, & Support Requirements. Ed. by Committee on Seismology. LC 77-5219. 1977. pap. text ed. 6.25 (ISBN 0-309-02608-3). Natl Acad Pr.
Global Employment Guide: Worldwide Opportunities for Profitable & Exciting Year-Round or Seasonal Jobs in Every Corner of the Globe. James N. Powell. LC 79-83725. 1979. 7.95 (ISBN 0-87863-171-2). Farnswth Pub.
Global Evangelism Rides Again: How to Protect Human Rights Without Really Trying. Ernst B. Haas. LC 78-620023. (Policy Papers in International Affairs Ser.: No. 5). 1978. pap. 2.50x (ISBN 0-87725-505-9). U of Cal Intl St.
Global Food Shortage. Lila Perl. LC 75-35860. 128p. (gr. 5-9). 1976. PLB 6.96 (ISBN 0-688-32068-6). Morrow.
Global Geology. M. A. Khan & B. Matthews. LC 75-38616. (Wykeham Science Ser.: No. 41). 1976. 8.60x (ISBN 0-8448-1168-8). Crane Russak Co.
Global History. rev. ed. Leften S. Stavrianos et al. 1979. text ed. 17.40 (ISBN 0-205-06113-3, 7861133); tchrs'. guide 4.40 (ISBN 0-205-06114-1, 7861141); tests 44.00 (ISBN 0-205-06115-X, 786115X). Allyn.
Global History of Man. Leften S. Stavrianos et al. (gr. 9-12). 1974. text ed. 17.40 (ISBN 0-205-03815-8, 7838158); tchrs'. guide 4.40 (ISBN 0-205-03816-6, 7838166); tests & dup. masters 44.00 (ISBN 0-205-02467-X, 782467X). Allyn.
Global History of Philosophy: The Patristic-Sutra Period, Vol. 3. John C. Plott. 1980. 27.00 (ISBN 0-8426-1680-2). Verry.
Global Interdependence & the Multinational Firm. Lloyd N. Cutler. LC 78-58094. (Headline Ser.: 239). 1978. pap. 2.00 (ISBN 0-87124-046-7). Foreign Policy.
Global Jigsaw Puzzle: The Story of Continental Drift. Irene Kiefer. LC 77-16188. (Illus.). (gr. 5-8). 1978. 8.95 (ISBN 0-689-30621-0). Atheneum.
Global Marine Pollution: An Overview. (Intergovernmental Oceanographic Commission Technical Ser: No. 18). 1979. pap. 4.75 (ISBN 92-3-101551-6, U863, UNESCO). Unipub.
Global Models & the International Economic Order. Sam Cole. LC 77-30175. 1977. text ed. 13.50 (ISBN 0-08-022991-3); pap. text ed. 4.45 (ISBN 0-08-022025-8). Pergamon.
Global Politics. James L. Ray. LC 78-69552. (Illus.). 1978. text ed. 15.95 (ISBN 0-395-26542-8); inst. manual 0.65 (ISBN 0-395-26540-1). HM.
Global Simulation Models: A Comparative Study. J. Clark et al. LC 74-32231. 135p. 1975. 24.95 (ISBN 0-471-15899-2, Pub. by Wiley-Interscience). Wiley.
Global Systems Dynamics. E. O. Attinger. 1970. 29.95 (ISBN 0-471-03640-4). Halsted Pr.
Global Talk. Joseph N. Pelton. LC 80-83261. 320p. 1980. write for info. (ISBN 90-286-0240-2). Sijthoff & Noordhoff.
Global Theory of Dynamical Systems: Proceedings. Ed. by Z. Nitecki & C. Robinson. (Lecture Notes in Mathematics Ser.: Vol. 819). 499p. 1981. pap. 29.50 (ISBN 0-387-10236-1). Springer-Verlag.
Global Two Thousand Report to the President of the U. S.--Entering the 21st Century: The Summary Report--Special Edition with Environment Projections & the Government's Global Model, Vol. 1. Ed. by Gerald O. Barney. (Pergamon Policy Studies Ser.). 200p. 1980. 30.00 (ISBN 0-08-024617-6); pap. 9.50 (ISBN 0-08-024616-8). Pergamon.
Globally Optimal Design. Douglass J. Wilde. LC 78-2933. 1978. 29.95 (ISBN 0-471-03898-9, Pub. by Wiley-Interscience). Wiley.
Globe. Elizabeth Spires. (Wesleyan Poetry Program Ser.: No. 101). 72p. 1981. 10.00 (ISBN 0-8195-2101-9); pap. 4.95 (ISBN 0-8195-1101-3). Wesleyan U Pr.
Globular Clusters. Ed. by D. A. Hanes & B. F. Madore. LC 79-41472. (Cambridge Astrophysics Ser.: No. 2). (Illus.). 288p. 1980. 62.50 (ISBN 0-521-22861-1). Cambridge U Pr.
Gloire D'Afrique. Roger J. Cazziol. (Illus.). 1971. text ed. 2.25x (ISBN 0-521-08181-5). Cambridge U Pr.
Glomerular Basement Membrane. Ed. by G. Lubec. (Renal Physiology: Vol. 3, No. 1-6). (Illus.). viii, 434p. 1981. pap. write for info. (ISBN 3-8055-2398-X). S Karger.
Glomerulonephritis: Morphology, Natural History, & Treatment, Pts. 1-2. Priscilla Kincaid-Smith et al. LC 73-6562. (Perspectives in Nephrology & Hypertension Ser). 1238p. 1973. Set. 77.50 (ISBN 0-471-47762-1, Pub. by Wiley-Medical). Wiley.
Gloomy Clouds Over the Danube. Margita E. Tenhonen. 169p. 1980. 7.95 (ISBN 0-533-04437-5). Vantage.
Gloomy Louie. Phyllis Green. Ed. by Ann Fay. LC 79-28533. (Illus.). (gr. 3-6). 1980. 5.75 (ISBN 0-8075-2962-1). A Whitman.
Gloria, 2 vols. in 1. Benito Perez Galdos. Tr. by C. Bell from Span. LC 73-21667. 692p. 1975. Repr. of 1882 ed. 27.50 (ISBN 0-86527-255-7). Fertig.
Gloria Dell' Arte: A Renaissance Perspective. Ed. by Katherine W. Paris. LC 79-89876. (Illus.). 88p. (Orig.). 1979. pap. 6.00 (ISBN 0-686-28885-8). Philbrook.
Glories of Mary. St. Alphonsus de Liguori. LC 79-112485. 1977. pap. 10.00 (ISBN 0-89555-021-0, 187). TAN Bks Pubs.
Glorifying God & Other Sermons. Melvin J. Wise. 4.95 (ISBN 0-89315-076-2). Lambert Bk.
Glorious Age in Africa: The Story of Three Great African Empires. Daniel Chu et al. LC 65-10280. 1965. 4.95 o.p. (ISBN 0-385-03763-5). Doubleday.
Glorious Gospel. James A. Cross. 1956. 2.95 (ISBN 0-87148-350-5). Pathway Pr.
Glorious Koran. bilingual ed. Ed. by Marmaduke Pickthall. 1696p. 1976. text ed. 50.00x (ISBN 0-04-297036-9). Allen Unwin.
Glorious Koran. Tr. by Muhammed M. Pickthall from Arabic. 1979. deluxe ed. 50.00 (ISBN 0-87773-713-4). Great Eastern.
Glorious Obsession. Abraham Unger. 1978. pap. 1.75 (ISBN 0-505-51253-X). Tower Bks.
Glorious Revolution in America. David S. Lovejoy. 1974. pap. 3.95x o.p. (ISBN 0-06-131775-6, TB1775, Torch). Har-Row.
Glorious Revolution in America: Documents on the Colonial Crisis of 1689. Ed. by Michael G. Hall et al. 1972. pap. text ed. 4.95x (ISBN 0-393-09398-0). Norton.
Glorious Scoundrel: A Biography of Captain John Smith. Noel B. Gerson. LC 78-1357. (Illus.). 1978. 7.95 (ISBN 0-396-07518-5). Dodd.
Glory. Ronald S. Joseph. 464p. (Orig.). 1980. pap. 2.75 (ISBN 0-446-85469-7). Warner Bks.
Glory: A Novel. Vladimir Nabakov. 1971. 6.95 (ISBN 0-07-045733-6, GB). McGraw.
Glory & Shame of England, 2 vols. C. Edwards Lester. (Development of Industrial Society Ser.). 905p. 1980. Repr. 36.00x (ISBN 0-7165-1789-2, Pub. by Irish Academic Pr). Biblio Dist.
Glory & the Lightning. Taylor Caldwell. 1978. pap. 2.75 (ISBN 0-449-23972-1, Crest). Fawcett.
Glory Girl. Stella G. Polk. (gr. 5-8). 1970. 6.95 o.p. (ISBN 0-8363-0036-X). Jenkins.
Glory Hand. Paul Boorstin & Sharon Boorstin. 320p. 1981. 12.95 (ISBN 0-399-90100-0). Marek.
Glory Hunter: A Life of General Custer. Frederic F. Van De Water. LC 63-20840. (Illus.). 1964. Repr. of 1934 ed. 15.00. Argosy.
Glory Land. Dorothy Dowdell. 384p. (Orig.). 1981. pap. 2.75 (ISBN 0-449-14404-6, GM). Fawcett.
Glory March. Kenneth M. Hammer. (Custeriana Monograph Ser.: No. 7). 1980. pap. 2.50. Monroe County Lib.
Glory of Christ. John Owen. 288p. 1980. pap. 6.95 (ISBN 0-8024-2988-2). Moody.
Glory of De Dienes Women. Andre De Dienes. (Illus.). 7.95 (ISBN 0-910550-05-0). Elysium.
Glory of Greece & World of Alexander. Michael Davison. LC 79-92450. (Illus.). 172p. 1980. pap. 14.95 (ISBN 0-89659-104-2). Abbeville Pr.
Glory of Nature's Form. Willis Peterson. Ed. by Robert D. Shangle. LC 79-12418. (Illus.). 160p. 1979. 27.50 (ISBN 0-89802-001-8). Beautiful Am.
Glory of the Divine Mother. S. Shankaranarayanan. 1979. 7.50 o.p. (ISBN 0-89744-957-6). Auromere.
Glory of the Jewish Holidays. 2nd ed. Hillel Seidman. LC 68-58504. (Illus.). 1980. 13.95 (ISBN 0-88400-065-6). Shengold.
Glory of the King's Daughter: Kvuda Bas Melech. Moshe Wiener. 280p. (Orig., Hebrew & Eng.). 1980. 8.95 (ISBN 0-9605406-0-1); pap. 6.95 (ISBN 0-9605406-1-X). M Wiener.
Glory Riders. Charles Heckelmann. 1977. pap. 1.25 o.p. (ISBN 0-445-04102-1). Popular Lib.
Glory Seeker. Louise MacKendrick. 1978. pap. 1.95 (ISBN 0-505-51230-0). Tower Bks.
Glosario de Technologia Educativa. OAS General Secretarliat, Dept. of Educational Affairs. (Illus.). 83p. (Span.). 1978. pap. text ed. 3.00 (ISBN 0-8270-1060-5). OAS.
Glosario De Voces Ibericas y Latinas. D. Simonet. (French-Arabic.). 1974. 18.00x (ISBN 0-685-82825-5). Intl Bk Ctr.
Glossaire Des Mots Espagnols et Portugais Derives De L'arabe. R. Dozy. 1974. 20.00x (ISBN 0-685-72045-4). Intl Bk Ctr.
Glossary of Agricultural Terms, English-Bengali. Jack A. Dabbs. LC 79-626525. 1969. 3.00 (ISBN 0-911494-05-7). Dabbs.
Glossary of Astronomy & Astrophysics. rev. ed. Ed. by Jeanne Hopkins. LC 80-5226. 224p. 1980. lib. bdg. 17.50x (ISBN 0-226-35171-8). U of Chicago Pr.
Glossary of Conference Terms. 1978. pap. 6.00 (ISBN 92-3-101566-4, U840, UNESCO). Unipub.
Glossary of Construction Industry Terms. The American Institute of Architects. pap. 1.50 (ISBN 0-913962-18-X). Am Inst Arch.
Glossary of Dialectal Place-Nomenclature. Robert C. Hope. LC 68-58761. 1968. Repr. of 1883 ed. 15.00 (ISBN 0-8103-3530-1). Gale.
Glossary of English & German Management Terms. James Coveney. 1977. pap. text ed. 6.00x (ISBN 0-582-55525-6). Longman.
Glossary of Environmental Terms (Terrestrial) U. S. Army Natick Laboratories. LC 73-2851. 149p. 1973. Repr. of 1968 ed. 18.00 (ISBN 0-8103-3277-9). Gale.
Glossary of French & English Management Terms. Ed. by James Coveney & Shelia J. Moore. 158p. 1972. pap. 6.00x (ISBN 0-582-55502-7). Longman.
Glossary of Geographical & Topographical Terms. Alexander Knox. LC 68-30592. 1968. Repr. of 1904 ed. 15.00 (ISBN 0-8103-3236-1). Gale.
Glossary of Geographical Terms. 3rd ed. Dudley Stamp & Audrey N. Clark. 1979. text ed. 35.00 (ISBN 0-582-35258-4). Longman.
Glossary of Hospital Terms. 2nd rev. ed. American Medical Record Association. 128p. 1974. 5.75 (ISBN 0-686-68577-6, 14911). Hospital Finan.
Glossary of Insurance Terms. Ed. by Robert W. Osler & John S. Bickley. 1972. 4.95 o.p. (ISBN 0-88245-004-2); pap. 3.00 o.p. (ISBN 0-88245-005-0). Merritt Co.
Glossary of Linguistic Terminology. Mario A. Pei. 1966. 20.00x (ISBN 0-231-03012-6). Columbia U Pr.
Glossary of Liturgical & Ecclesiastical Terms. Frederick G. Lee. LC 76-174069. (Tower Bks). (Illus.). xl, 452p. 1972. Repr. of 1877 ed. 21.00 (ISBN 0-8103-3949-8). Gale.
Glossary of Marine Technology Terms. Institute of Marine Engineers. 178p. 1980. pap. 15.00 (ISBN 0-434-90840-1). Sheridan.
Glossary of Modern Sailing Terms. John Rousmaniere. LC 75-31504. (Illus.). 254p. 1976. 6.95 (ISBN 0-396-07006-X). Dodd.
Glossary of Molecular Biology. Anthony Evans. LC 74-26571. 1975. 13.95 (ISBN 0-470-24740-1). Halsted Pr.
Glossary of Mongolian Technical Terms. Frederick H. Buck. LC 58-59834. (American Council of Learned Societies Publications). 79p. (Orig.). 1958. pap. 3.00x (ISBN 0-87950-257-6). Spoken Lang Serv.
Glossary of Reference on Subjects Connected with Far East. Herbert A. Giles. 328p. 1978. Repr. 17.50 (ISBN 0-89684-134-0, Pub. by Cosmo Pubns India). Orient Bk Dist.
Glossary of Sanskrit Terms & Key to Their Correct Pronunciation. Geoffrey A. Barborka. 76p. (Orig.). 1972. pap. 1.75 (ISBN 0-685-29054-9, 913004-04). Point Loma Pub.
Glossary of Spanish & English Management Terms. James Coveney & J. Amey. 1978. pap. text ed. 6.00x (ISBN 0-582-55541-8). Longman.

Glossary of Terms & Phrases. Henry P. Smith. LC 79-175746. x, 521p. 1972. Repr. of 1889 ed. 26.00 (ISBN 0-8103-3816-5). Gale.
Glossary of Terms in Sri Aurobindo's Writings. Aurobindo. 1979. 9.50 (ISBN 0-89744-980-0, Pub. by Sri Aurobindo Ashram Trust India); pap. 7.50 (ISBN 0-89744-981-9, Pub. by Sri Aurobindo Ashram Trust India). Auromere.
Glossary of Terms Used in Heraldry. Henry Gough & James Parker. (Illus.). 1966. Repr. of 1894 ed. 15.00 (ISBN 0-8103-3126-8). Gale.
Glossary of Terms Used in Heraldry. James Parker. LC 77-94021. (Illus.). (gr. 9 up). 1970. 12.50 (ISBN 0-8048-0715-9). C E Tuttle.
Glossary of the Environment. Conseil International De la Langue Francaise. LC 76-19547. (Praeger Special Studies). 1977. 21.95 (ISBN 0-275-23760-5). Praeger.
Glossary of UK Fishing Gear Terms. 1980. 39.50x (ISBN 0-686-64737-8, Pub. by Fishing News England). State Mutual Bk.
Glossary of United States Patent Practice. Louis Applebaum et al. LC 70-103702. (Eng, Fr & Ger.). 1969. 25.00 (ISBN 0-87632-037-X). Boardman.
Glossary of Words & Phrases Used in Radiology, Nuclear Medicine & Ultrasound. 2nd ed. Lewis E. Etter. 384p. 1970. pap. 32.50 photocopy ed. spiral (ISBN 0-398-00526-5). C C Thomas.
Glossary of Words, Phrases, Names & Allusions in the Works of English Authors. Robert Nares. LC 66-25635. 1966. Repr. of 1905 ed. 34.00 (ISBN 0-8103-3219-1). Gale.
Glossectomee Speech Rehabilitation. Madge Skelly. (Illus.). 180p. 1973. text ed. 14.75 (ISBN 0-398-02706-4). C C Thomas.
Gloucester Fragments. John Earle. 116p. 1980. Repr. of 1861 ed. lib. bdg. 65.00 (ISBN 0-8482-0717-3). Norwood Edns.
Gloucestershire Studies. Ed. by H. P. Finberg. 1957. text ed. 13.00x (ISBN 0-7185-1013-5, Leicester). Humanities.
Glove Compartment Road Atlas. (Illus.). 1980. 1.25 (ISBN 0-8437-2550-8). Hammond Inc.
Gloves: Their Annals & Associations. S. William Beck. LC 75-75801. 1969. Repr. of 1883 ed. 15.00 (ISBN 0-8103-3825-4). Gale.
Glow Discharge Processes: Sputtering & Plasma Etching. Brian Chapman. LC 80-17047. 432p. 1980. 31.50 (ISBN 0-471-07828-X, Pub. by Wiley-Interscience). Wiley.
Glowing Embers. Bess Gibson. 26p. 1980. 2.95 (ISBN 0-8059-2761-1). Dorrance.
Glowing Health Through Diet & Posture. D. Lawson-Wood & J. Lawson-Wood. 62p. 1973. pap. 2.50x (ISBN 0-686-68110-X). Beekman Pubs.
Glu the Emperor Penguin. Robert Hunt. LC 72-736442. (Adventures of Wild Animals Book). (Illus.). 16p. (gr. 2-5). 1978. pap. 21.00 10 bks. & one cassette (ISBN 0-89290-027-X). Soc for Visual.
Glucuronidation of Drugs & Other Compounds. G. J. Dutton. 304p. 1980. 69.95 (ISBN 0-8493-5295-9). CRC Pr.
Glue It Yourself: Woodworking Without Nails. Robert Lasson & Sidney Shupak. (Illus.). (YA) 1978. PLB 8.95 o.p. (ISBN 0-525-30722-2). Dutton.
Glutamic Acid: Advances in Biochemistry & Physiology. Ed. by L. J. Filer, Jr. et al. LC 78-56782. (Mario Negri Institute for Pharmacological Research Monographs). 1979. text ed. 38.00 (ISBN 0-89004-356-6). Raven.
Glutamine: Metabolism, Enzymology & Regulation. Ed. by Jaime Mora & Rafael Palacios. 1980. 28.00 (ISBN 0-12-506040-8). Acad Pr.
Gluttons & Libertines: Human Problems of Being Natural. Marston Bates. LC 66-11978. 1971. pap. 2.45 (ISBN 0-394-71267-6, V-267, Vin). Random.
Glycoconjugate Research: Proceedings, Vol. 1. International Symposium on Glycoconjugates, Fourth. Ed. by John D. Gregory & Roger Jeanloz. LC 79-15164. 1979. 35.00 (ISBN 0-12-301301-1). Acad Pr.
Glycogen & Its Related Enzymes of Metabolism in the Central Nervous System. M. Z. Ibrahim. (Advances in Anatomy, Embryology & Cell Biology: Vol. 52, Pt. 1). (Illus.). 90p. 1976. pap. 33.10 (ISBN 0-387-07454-6). Springer-Verlag.
Glyndebourne: A History of the Festival Opera. Spike Hughes. LC 80-70705. (Illus.). 400p. 1981. 27.50 (ISBN 0-7153-7891-0). David & Charles.
Glyph Seven: Textual Studies. 1980. 16.50x (ISBN 0-8018-2365-X); pap. 5.95 (ISBN 0-8018-2366-8). Johns Hopkins.
GM Subcompact, Nineteen Seventy One to Eighty Repair & Tune-up Guide. (New Autommotive Bks.). 256p. 1980. 8.95 (ISBN 0-8019-6935-2). Chilton.
GM X-Body Nineteen Eighty Repair & Tune-up Guide: Covers 1980 Models Only: Chevolet Citation, Oldsmobile Omega, Pontiac Phoenix, Buick Skylark. (New Automotive Bks.). 192p. 1980. 8.95 (ISBN 0-8019-6909-3). Chilton.
GMAT Graduate Management Admission Test: A Test Preparation Guide. Randolph Z. Volkell. LC 80-21793. (Wiley Self-Teaching Guide Ser.). 185p. 1980. pap. text ed. 7.95 (ISBN 0-471-05286-8). Wiley.
GMAT (Graduate Management Admissions Test) Jerry Bobrow & William A. Covino. Date not set. pap. text ed. cancelled. Cliffs.
Gnasty Gnomes. Bob Stine. (Illus.). 62p. (gr. 3-6). 1981. PLB 6.99 (ISBN 0-394-94686-3); pap. 5.95 (ISBN 0-394-84686-9). Random.
GNMA Yield & Price Equivalent Tables No. 736. 7.50 (ISBN 0-685-59987-6). Finan Pub.
Gnome, a Candle, & Me: Reflections in a Candle on a Winter's Night. George E. Sewell & Chester Delacruz. (Illus.). 60p. (Orig.). 1981. pap. 4.50 (ISBN 0-938012-00-2). Deluxe Co.
Gnome from Nome. Steve Cosgrove. (Serendipity Bks). (Illus.). (gr. k-4). 1978. PLB 6.95 (ISBN 0-87191-656-8). Creative Ed.
Gnome Named Goodwill. Irvin Martin. 59p. (gr. k-4). 1978. 3.95 (ISBN 0-8059-2619-4). Dorrance.
Gnomes & Occasions. Howard Nemerov. 1974. pap. 1.95 o.s.i. (ISBN 0-226-57255-2, PP15, Phoen). U of Chicago Pr.
Gnomes Color & Story Album. Bill Nygren. (Illus.). 32p. 1980. pap. 3.50 (ISBN 0-89844-019-X). Troubador Pr.
Gnomes Funbook. (Illus.). 48p. 1980. pap. 2.50 (ISBN 0-89844-020-3). Troubador Pr.
Gnomes Games. Larry Evans. (Illus.). 64p. 1980. pap. 4.50 (ISBN 0-89844-020-3). Troubador Pr.
Gnomes of the Night. Arthur N. Bragg. LC 64-24504. 1965. 7.00x o.p. (ISBN 0-8122-7472-5). U of Pa Pr.
Gnomids. W. C. Chalk. pap. text ed. 2.75x o.p. (ISBN 0-435-11229-5). Heinemann Ed.
Gnostic Circle. Patrizia Norelli-Bachelet. 1978. pap. 7.95 (ISBN 0-87728-411-3). Weiser.
Gnostic Dialogue. Pheme Perkins. LC 80-81441. (Theological Inquiries Ser.). 256p. 1980. pap. 6.95 (ISBN 0-8091-2320-7). Paulist Pr.
Gnostics & Their Remains. C. W. King. LC 73-76092. (Illus.). 500p. 1981. Repr. of 1887 ed. 19.50 (ISBN 0-913510-34-3). Wizards.
Gnys at Wrk: A Child Learns to Write & Read. Glenda Bissex. LC 80-14558. 1980. text ed. 17.50x (ISBN 0-674-35485-0). Harvard U Pr.
Go Ahead Series, Gr. 1. Gregory. Incl. Bk. 1. Tom's Little Feet. pap. text ed. (ISBN 0-8009-0819-8); pkg. of 10 copies 9.28 (ISBN 0-8009-0917-8); Bk. 2. Big Egg. pap. text ed. (ISBN 0-8009-0822-8); Bk. 3. Red Kite. pap. text ed. (ISBN 0-8009-0824-4); pkg. of 10 copies 9.28 (ISBN 0-8009-0921-6); Bk. 4. Grandma the Kitten. pap. text ed. (ISBN 0-8009-0826-0); pkg. of 10 copies 9.28 (ISBN 0-8009-0923-2); Bk. 5. Dog Who Wanted a Boy. pap. text ed. (ISBN 0-8009-0828-7); pap. text ed. 9.28 pkg. of 10 copies (ISBN 0-8009-0925-9). 1969. pap. text ed. 1.04 ea.; tchr's. ed. for Go Ahead Ser, Gr. 1-3 9.28 (ISBN 0-8009-0919-4). McCormick-Mathers.
Go Ahead Series, Gr. 2. Gregory. Incl. Bk. 1. Bill & I. (ISBN 0-8009-0830-9); pkg. of 10 (ISBN 0-8009-0927-5); Bk. 2. Blue Weed. pap. text ed. (ISBN 0-8009-0832-5); pkg. of 10 (ISBN 0-8009-0929-1); Bk. 3. House on Wheels. pap. text ed. (ISBN 0-8009-0834-1); pkg. of 10 (ISBN 0-8009-0931-3); Bk. 4. New Shoes. pap. text ed. (ISBN 0-8009-0836-8); pkg. of 10 (ISBN 0-8009-0934-8); Bk. 5. Balloon Book. pap. text ed. (ISBN 0-8009-0838-4); pkg. of 10 (ISBN 0-8009-0936-4); Bk. 6. An Umbrella for May. (ISBN 0-8009-0840-6); pap. text ed. kpkg. of 10 (ISBN 0-8009-0938-0); Bk. 7. Boat. pap. text ed. (ISBN 0-8009-0842-2); pkg. of 10 (ISBN 0-8009-0940-2). 1969-70. pap. text ed. 1.04 ea.; pkgs. of 10 of same title 9.28 ea.; tchr's. ed. for Go Ahead 8ser, Gr. 1-3 9.25 (ISBN 0-8009-0919-4). McCormick-Mathers.
Go Ahead Series, Gr. 3. Gregory. Incl. Bk. 2. Little Clown. pap. text ed. (ISBN 0-8009-0844-9); pkg. of 10 (ISBN 0-8009-0942-9); Bk. 2310#10#.00. Yellow Horse. pap. text ed. (ISBN 0-8009-0846-5); pkg. of 10 (ISBN 0-8009-0944-5); Bk. 3. Sue's Tree. pap. text ed. (ISBN 0-8009-0850-3); pkg. of 10 (ISBN 0-8009-0946-1); Bk. 4. Mr. Long's Long Feet. pap. text ed. (ISBN 0-8009-0853-8); pkg. of 10 (ISBN 0-8009-0948-8); Bk. 5. Nine on Team. pap. text ed. (ISBN 0-8009-0855-4); pkg. of 10 (ISBN 0-8009-0951-8); Bk. 6. Happy the Merry-Go-Round. pap. text ed. (ISBN 0-8009-0857-0); pkg. of 10 (ISBN 0-8009-0953-4). pap. text ed. 1.16 ea.; pkgs. of 10 of same title 10.60 ea.; tchr's. ed. for Go Ahead Ser, Gr. 1-3 9.28 (ISBN 0-8009-0919-4). McCormick-Mathers.
Go & Go Moku. Edward Lasker. (Illus.). 1960. pap. 3.50 (ISBN 0-486-20613-0). Dover.
Go Away Death. John Creasey. 1976. pap. 1.25 o.p. (ISBN 0-445-00427-4). Popular Lib.
Go Away, Warts! Norma Simon. Ed. by Kathleen Tucker. LC 79-28534. (Concept Bk.: Level 2). (Illus.). (gr. 3-6). 1980. 6.50g (ISBN 0-8075-2970-2). A Whitman.
Go Back to Where You Belong: Yeats's Return from Exile. George M. Harper. (New Yeats Papers Ser.: Vol. 6). 40p. 1973. pap. text ed. 3.75x (ISBN 0-85105-244-4, Dolmen Pr). Humanities.
Go-Between. L. P. Hartley. LC 54-7169. 320p. (Orig.). 1980. pap. 4.95 (ISBN 0-8128-6073-X). Stein & Day.
Go-Between God: The Holy Spirit & the Christian Mission. John V. Taylor. 1979. pap. 4.95x (ISBN 0-19-520125-6). Oxford U Pr.
Go Boy! A Lifetime Behind Bars. Roger Caron. 1978. 10.95 o.p. (ISBN 0-07-082535-1, GB). McGraw.
Go! Fight! Win! Betty L. Phillips. LC 79-53607. (Illus.). (YA) (gr. 8 up). 1981. PLB 8.89 (ISBN 0-440-02957-0); pap. 7.95 (ISBN 0-440-02956-2). Delacorte.
Go Fly a Sailplane. Linda Morrow & Ray Morrow. LC 80-65995. (Illus.). 192p. 1981. 10.95 (ISBN 0-689-11080-4). Atheneum.
Go for the Flag. Tom Weiskopf. 1969. pap. 3.50 (ISBN 0-8015-3018-0, Hawthorn). Dutton.
Go Free! The Meaning of Justification. Robert M. Horn. LC 76-4736. 128p. (Orig.). 1976. pap. 2.25 o.p. (ISBN 0-87784-644-8). Inter-Varsity.
Go Hire Yourself an Employer. rev. expanded ed. Richard K. Irish. LC 77-15159. 1978. pap. 4.95 (ISBN 0-385-13638-2, Anch). Doubleday.
Go Not Gently: Letters from a Patient with Amyotrophic Lateral Sclerosis. Frances McGill. Ed. by Lillian G. Kutscher. LC 79-48047. (Foundation of Thanatology Ser.). 1980. lib. bdg. 16.00x (ISBN 0-405-12643-3). Arno.
Go on Singing. Richard G. Champion. (Radiant Life). 128p. 1976. pap. 1.95 (ISBN 0-88243-895-6, 02-0895); teacher's ed 2.50 (ISBN 0-88243-169-2, 32-0169). Gospel Pub.
Go, Pep, & Pop: Two Hundred Fifty Tested Ideas for Lively Libraries. Virginia Baeckler & Linda Larson. LC 75-20328. 1976. pap. 4.50 (ISBN 0-916444-01-5). UNABASHED Lib.
Go Placidly Amid the Noise & Haste: Meditations on the "Desiderata". 2nd ed. Granville T. Walker. 112p. 1976. pap. 1.25 (ISBN 0-8272-1217-8). Bethany Pr.
Go Preach the Kingdom Heal the Sick. Jim Wilson. 127p. pap. text ed. 4.75 (ISBN 0-227-67659-9). Attic Pr.
Go Saddle the Sea. Joan Aiken. LC 77-76958. (gr. 6-9). 1977. PLB 7.95 (ISBN 0-385-13226-3). Doubleday.
Go See the Movie in Your Head. Joseph E. Shorr. 1977. pap. 1.95 o.p. (ISBN 0-445-04100-5). Popular Lib.
Go South Inside: Cruising the Inland Waterway. LC 77-82090. (Illus.). 1978. 17.50 (ISBN 0-87742-070-X). Intl Marine.
Go, Team, Go. John R. Tunis. (gr. 7 up). 1954. 7.75 (ISBN 0-688-21349-9). Morrow.
Go Tell It to Mrs. Golightly. Catherine Cookson. LC 80-10308. 192p. (gr. 5 up). 1980. 7.95 (ISBN 0-688-41965-8); PLB 7.63 (ISBN 0-688-51965-2). Lothrop.
Go up for Glory. Bill Russell. 1980. pap. 2.25 o.p. (ISBN 0-425-04676-1). Berkley Pub.
Go-West Guide - Los Angeles. Ernest Schworck. (Illus.). 48p. 1978. pap. 2.45 English version o.p. (ISBN 0-912076-27-5); pap. 2.45 Japanese Version o.p. (ISBN 0-912076-28-3). ESE Calif.
Go Where the Money Is: Mideast & North African Banks & Financial Institutions. 2nd ed. Tyler G. Hicks. 150p. 1981. pap. 15.00 (ISBN 0-914306-56-1). Intl Wealth.
Goa. Asif Currimbhoy. (Writers Workshop Bluebird Book Ser.). 82p. 1975. 8.00 (ISBN 0-88253-550-1); pap. text ed. 4.80 (ISBN 0-88253-549-8). Ind-US Inc.
Goa: Indian Takeover. Ed. by Avrahm Mezerik. 15.00 (ISBN 0-685-40641-5, 70). Intl Review.
Goal Ahead. Joel Reeve. LC 67-22811. (gr. 7-10). 1967. 8.95 (ISBN 0-87599-137-8). S G Phillips.
Goal Analysis. Robert F. Mager. LC 77-189630. (Illus., Orig.). 1972. pap. 4.50 (ISBN 0-8224-3476-8). Pitman Learning.
Goal of a New World Order. Shoghi Effendi. 1971. pap. 1.00 (ISBN 0-87743-100-0, 7-08-28). Baha'i.
Goal Programming & Extensions. James P. Ignizio. LC 75-12089. (Illus.). 192p. 1976. 21.95 (ISBN 0-669-00021-3). Lexington Bks.
Goal Programming Methods for Multiple Objective Integer Programs. Sang M. Lee. 1979. pap. text ed. 12.00 (ISBN 0-89806-001-X, 125). Am Inst Indus Eng.
Goal Setting. Charles L. Hughes. LC 65-26864. 1965. 12.95 (ISBN 0-8144-5116-0). Am Mgmt.
Goal to Go. Mike Neigoff. LC 70-115898. (Pilot Book Ser). (Illus.). (gr. 3-5). 1970. 6.95g (ISBN 0-8075-2974-5). A Whitman.
Goalguide: A Minicourse in Writing Goals & Behavioral Objectives for Special Education. Herbert R. Padzensky & Jane Gibson. 1975. instructors manual, (free with participant's manual & wkbk.) 1.00 (ISBN 0-8224-3487-3); wkbk. 2.50 (ISBN 0-8224-3486-5); participant's manual 3.00 (ISBN 0-8224-3485-7). Pitman Learning.
Goaling up. O. O. Bell. LC 77-91672. (Illus.). 1978. 13.95 (ISBN 0-931034-01-9). Everest Pub.
Goals & Behavior in Psychotherapy & Counseling: Readings & Questions. Jack T. Huber & Howard L. Millman. LC 73-190060. 384p. 1972. pap. text ed. 12.95 (ISBN 0-675-09092-X). Merrill.
Goals Clarification: Curriculum, Teaching, Evaluation. Ed. by Warren C. Born. 1975. pap. 7.95x. NE Conf Teach.
Goals for Engineering Profession. Date not set. 3.50 (515). AAES.
Goals in a Global Community, Vol. II. Ed. by Ervin Laszlo & Judah Bierman. 1978. text ed. 49.00 (ISBN 0-08-022973-5). Pergamon.
Goals in a Global Community: Studies on the Conceptual Foundations, Vol. I. Ed. by Ervin Laszlo. LC 77-79971. 1977. text ed. 32.00 (ISBN 0-08-022221-8). Pergamon.
Goals in Male Reproductive Research: Proceedings of Conference on Future Goals in Reproductive Medicine & Surgery, 20 September, 1979, Bethesda, Md. Ed. by Saul Boyarsky & Kenneth Polakoski. 144p. 1981. 30.00 (ISBN 0-08-025910-3). Pergamon.
Goaltending. Jacques Plante. (Illus.). 128p. 1973. pap. 2.95 o.s.i. (ISBN 0-02-081120-9, Collier). Macmillan.
Goat Husbandry. David Mackenzie. 16.75 o.p. (ISBN 0-685-20587-8). Transatlantic.
Goat Husbandry. 4th ed. David Mackenzie. Ed. by Jean Laing. (Illus.). 375p. 1981. 23.00 (ISBN 0-571-18024-8, Pub. by Faber & Faber); pap. 9.95 (ISBN 0-571-11322-2). Merrimack Bk Serv.
Goat in the Rug. Charles L. Blood & Martin Link. LC 80-17315. (Illus.). 40p. (ps-3). 1980. Repr. of 1976 ed. 8.95 (ISBN 0-590-07763-5, Four Winds). Schol Bk Serv.
Goat Owners' Scrapbook. C. E. Leach. Date not set. 7.50 (ISBN 0-686-26682-X). Dairy Goat.
Goatfoot Milktongue Twinbird. Donald Hall. LC 77-3248. (Poets on Poetry Ser.). pap. 5.95 (ISBN 0-472-40000-2). U of Mich Pr.
Goatkeeper's Guide. Jill Salmon. LC 80-69354. (Illus.). 152p. 1981. 14.95 (ISBN 0-7153-8055-9). David & Charles.
Goats, Rabbits, & Chickens. (Country Home Ser.). 96p. 2.95 (ISBN 0-88453-006-X). Berkshire Traveller.
Goats, Rabbits & Chickens. Hollis Lee. (Country Home & Small Farm Guides Ser.). (Illus.). 1978. pap. 2.95 (ISBN 0-88453-006-X). Barrington.
Goats: Their Care & Breeding. Ferial Rogers & Phyllis V. Minter. (Illus.). 100p. 1980. 3.95 (ISBN 0-686-63088-2, 4948-0, Pub. by K & R Bks England). Arco.
Goba of the Zambezi: Sex Roles, Economics & Change. Chet S. Lancaster. LC 80-24220. (Illus.). 350p. 1980. 19.95x (ISBN 0-8061-1613-7). U of Okla Pr.
Gobble-Uns'll Git You Ef You Don't Watch Out! James W. Riley. LC 74-23110. (gr. 3-5). 1975. 8.95 (ISBN 0-397-31621-6). Lippincott.
Gobierno civil y la Ley Foraker (Antecedentes historicos) Carmen I. Raffucci de Garcia. LC 79-16454. Orig. Title: Instituciones de Gobierno Civil en la Elaboracion de la Ley Foraker y Sus Antecedentes Historicos. xi, 213p. (Sp.). 1980. pap. write for info. (ISBN 0-8477-0864-0). U of PR Pr.
Gobierno y los Presidentes De los Estados Unidos De America. Joaquin Roy. (Illus.). 96p. (Orig., Span.). (gr. 8 up). 1980. pap. 7.95 (ISBN 0-89196-073-2, Domus Bks). Quality Bks IL.
Goblin, a Wild Chimpanzee. Geza Teleki & Karen Steffy. (gr. 3-6). 1977. PLB 7.95 (ISBN 0-525-30747-8). Dutton.
Goblin Market. Christina Rossetti. LC 76-115984. (gr. 1 up). 1970. PLB 7.95 o.p. (ISBN 0-525-30744-3). Dutton.
Goblin Tales. new ed. Corinne Denan. LC 79-66326. (Illus.). 48p. (gr. 2-6). 1980. lib. bdg. 4.89 (ISBN 0-89375-320-3); pap. 1.50 (ISBN 0-89375-319-X). Troll Assocs.
Goblins Giggle & Other Stories. Molly Bang. LC 72-9033. (Illus.). 57p. (gr. 4-7). 1973. reinforced bdg. 5.95 o.p. (ISBN 0-684-13226-5, ScribJ). Scribner.
Gochnour Idiom Screening Test (GIST) Elizabeth Gochnour. 1977. pap. text ed. 3.95x (ISBN 0-8134-2049-0, 1970). Interstate.
God. Phyllis God. Date not set. 7.95 (ISBN 0-533-04754-4). Vantage.
God & a Boy Named Joe. Ethel Barrett. LC 74-16957. (Venture Stories Ser.). (Illus.). 160p. (Orig.). (gr. 4-8). 1975. pap. 1.95 (ISBN 0-8307-0324-1, 57-006-04). Regal.

God & a Mouse. Angela Toigo, Sr. LC 72-84198. (Illus.). 52p. 1980. 5.00 (ISBN 0-913180-01-7). Benedict Con Adoration.

God & Caesar: Case Studies in the Relationship Between Christianity & the State. Ed. by Robert D. Linder. LC 78-187900. 140p. 1971. pap. 1.95 o.p. (ISBN 0-913446-00-9). Conf Faith & Hist.

God & Charity: Images of Eastern Orthodox Theology, Spirituality & Practice. T. Hopko et al. Ed. by Francis D. Costa. LC 79-3027. (Pan-Am Books). 103p. (Orig.). 1979. pap. text ed. 3.95 (ISBN 0-916586-34-0). Holy Cross Orthodox.

God & Evil: Reading on the Theological Problem of Evil. Nelson Pike. 1964. pap. 7.95 ref. ed (ISBN 0-13-357665-5). P-H.

God & His Church. Duane S. Crowther. LC 76-173392. (Scripture Guide Ser.). 1971. pap. 4.95 (ISBN 0-88290-006-4). Horizon Utah.

God & His Messengers. David Hofman. (Illus.). 1978. pap. 4.50 o.s.i. (ISBN 0-85398-049-7, 7-52-43, Pub. by G Ronald England). Baha'i.

God & History. J. Montgomery Boice. (Foundations of the Christian Faith: Vol 4). 292p. (Orig.). 1981. pap. 6.95 (ISBN 0-87784-746-0). Inter-Varsity.

God & History in the Old Testament. Dennis Baly. LC 76-9984. 256p. 1976. pap. 6.95x (ISBN 0-06-060369-0, RD 186, HarpR). Har-Row.

God & Man. Oscar Oppenheimer. LC 79-64099. 1979. pap. text ed. 9.00 (ISBN 0-8191-0753-0). U Pr of Amer.

God & Man: The Essential Knowledge Which Everyone, but Absolutely Everyone Ought to Possess About Human Nature & the Nature of God & How the Two Are Related. Lawrence Vinoi. (Essential Knowledge Ser. Books). (Illus.). 1978. plastic spiral bdg. 24.75 (ISBN 0-89266-118-6). Am Classical Coll Pr.

God & Me. Deborah Christensen. (Sunflower Bks. for Young Children: Bk. 3). (Illus., Orig.). (ps-2). 1980. pap. 2.00 (ISBN 0-87743-143-4, 7-53-03). Baha'i.

God & Mrs. Adam. Alma E. Blanton. (Illus.). 152p. (Orig.). 1978. pap. 4.95 (ISBN 0-938134-00-0, G-1). Loving Pubs.

God & the Astronomers. Robert Jastrow. 1980. pap. 4.95 (ISBN 0-446-97350-5). Warner Bks.

God & the "New" Psychology of Sex. Benjamin Constable. (Illus.). 265p. 1976. 43.75 (ISBN 0-89266-043-0). Am Classical Coll Pr.

God & the Problem of Evil. Sr. Concetta Belleggia. 1980. 3.75 (ISBN 0-8198-3007-0); pap. 2.50 (ISBN 0-8198-3008-9). Dghtrs St Paul.

God & the Tree & Me. Dorothy H. Brown. LC 79-66196. 1979. pap. 4.25x (ISBN 0-8358-0386-4). Upper Room.

God & Utopia. Gabriel Vahanian. LC 77-24029. 1977. 8.95 (ISBN 0-8164-0358-9). Crossroad NY.

God & Vitamins. Marjorie Holmes. LC 80-911. 360p. 1980. 10.95 (ISBN 0-385-15249-3, Galilee). Doubleday.

God & You Unlimited. Nola Stevens. (Illus.). 144p. 1980. 7.00 (ISBN 0-682-49642-1). Exposition.

God Answers Prayer. Geo. Mueller. pap. 2.95 (ISBN 0-686-27009-6). Schmul Pub Co.

God Approached: A Commentary on the Poems of William Empson. Philip Gardner & Áveril Gardner. 226p. 1978. 17.50x (ISBN 0-8476-6059-1). Rowman.

God As Dynamic Actuality: A Preliminary Study of the Process Theologies of John B. Cobb, Jr. & Schubert M. Ogden. James E. Caraway. LC 78-61388. 1978. pap. text ed. 9.75 (ISBN 0-8191-0485-X). U Pr of Amer.

God at Eventide. A. J. Russell. 1975. pap. 1.25 (ISBN 0-89129-069-9, PV069). Jove Pubns.

God Believes in Me. William V. Coleman & Patricia R. McLemore. Incl. Standard Edition-Family Bk. 24p. (gr. 4-6) (ISBN 0-87793-080-5); Simplified Edition-Classroom Bk. 32p. (gr. 2-3) (ISBN 0-87793-081-3); Standard Edition Classroom Book. 24p. (gr. 4-6) (ISBN 0-87793-079-1). (Illus., Orig.). (gr. 2-6). 1975. wkbk. 0.95 ea. o.p. Ave Maria.

God Believes in Me, Director Guide. William V. Coleman & Patricia R. McLemore. (Illus.). 24p. (Orig.). (gr. 2-6). 1975. pap. 1.25 o.p. (ISBN 0-87793-082-1); simplified family ed. gr. 2-3 0.95 o.p. (ISBN 0-87793-080-5). Ave Maria.

God Beyond Nature. R. E. Clark. LC 77-76108. (Redwood Ser.). 1978. pap. 3.95 (ISBN 0-8163-0002-X, 07345-2). Pacific Pr Pub Assn.

God Bless You, Mr. Rosewater. Kurt Vonnegut, Jr. pap. 2.50 (ISBN 0-440-12929-X). Dell.

God Calling. Ed. by A. J. Russell. (Spire Bk). 1972. pap. 2.50 (ISBN 0-8007-8096-5). Revell.

God Calling. Ed. by A. J. Russell. 1972. pap. 1.95 (ISBN 0-515-05618-9). Jove Pubns.

God Can Make It Happen. Russ Johnston. 144p. 1976. pap. 3.50 (ISBN 0-88207-741-4). Victor Bks.

God Centred Evangelism. R. B. Kuiper. 1978. pap. 3.95 (ISBN 0-85151-110-4). Banner of Truth.

God Demands Doctrinal Preaching. Ed. by Thomas B. Warren & Garland Elkins. 1978. 10.95 (ISBN 0-934916-32-2); pap. 7.95 (ISBN 0-686-23947-4). Natl Christian Pr.

God Dwells with His People. Paul M. Zehr. 216p. 1981. pap. 7.95 (ISBN 0-8361-1939-8). Herald Pr.

God Emperor of Dune. Frank Herbert. 432p. 1981. 12.95 (ISBN 0-399-12593-0). Putnam.

God Encountered, Vol. 1. David A. Clemens. LC 79-52420. (Steps to Maturity Ser.). 1973. tchrs'. manual 14.95 (ISBN 0-86508-002-X); student's manual 12.50 (ISBN 0-86508-001-1); visuals packet 4.25 (ISBN 0-86508-007-0). BCM Inc.

God for Every Day. William Maestri. 204p. 1981. 8.95 (ISBN 0-88347-123-X). Thomas More.

God Gap, 2 vols. George N. Thompson. 192p. 1980. Set. 10.00 (ISBN 0-686-28944-7). Directions Pr.

God Gave Me Miracle Hands. Lacie A. Palmer. 1981. 5.95 (ISBN 0-533-04578-9). Vantage.

God Guides Us. Sr. Mary Bothwell. (Christ Our Life Ser). (Illus.). (gr. 3). 1981. pap. text ed. 3.80 (ISBN 0-8294-0365-5); tchr's ed. 6.95 (ISBN 0-8294-0366-3). Loyola.

God Has Many Names. John Hick. 108p. 1981. text ed. 20.00x (ISBN 0-333-27747-3, Pub. by Macmillan, England); pap. text ed. 7.50 (ISBN 0-333-27758-9). Humanities.

God Has Spoken. rev. ed. J. I. Packer. LC 80-7789. (Orig.). 1980. pap. 3.95 (ISBN 0-87784-656-1). Inter-Varsity.

God, Have You Got It All Together. Ethel Barrett. LC 76-29888. (Venture Stories Ser.). 1977. pap. 1.95 (ISBN 0-8307-0434-5, S064-1-54). Regal.

God: Here & Now. Margery Wilson. 1978. pap. 4.95 (ISBN 0-87707-207-8). CSA Pr.

God, His Prophets & His Children. M. R. Bawa Muhaiyaddeen. (Illus.). 1978. pap. 4.95 (ISBN 0-914390-09-0). Fellowship Pr PA.

God, History, & Historians: An Anthology of Modern Christian Views of History. Ed. by C. T. McIntire. LC 76-47428. 1977. 22.95 (ISBN 0-19-502203-3). Oxford U Pr.

God, History & Historians: Modern Christian Views of History. Ed. by C. T. McIntire. 1977. pap. 6.95 (ISBN 0-19-502204-1, GB496, GB). Oxford U Pr.

God I Don't Understand. Kenneth Boa. 156p. 1975. pap. 3.95 (ISBN 0-88207-722-8). Victor Bks.

God-Idea of the Ancients: Or Sex in Religion. Eliza B. Gamble. LC 79-66997. 339p. 1981. Repr. of 1897 ed. 27.50 (ISBN 0-8305-0110-X). Hyperion Conn.

God, If You Exist, Prove It to Me. Thomas J. Ammerman. 1981. 6.95 (ISBN 0-8062-1595-X). Carlton.

God in Idea & Experience: The Apriori Elements of Religious Consciousness; an Epistemological Study. Rees Griffiths. 316p. Repr. of 1931 ed. text ed. 4.95 (ISBN 0-567-02128-9). Attic Pr.

God in Man Made Manifest. 1968. pap. text ed. 0.95 (ISBN 0-570-03533-3, 14-1518, 14-1519). tchr's manual 1.25 (ISBN 0-570-03534-1). Concordia.

God in the American Schools: Religious Education in a Pluralistic Society. Grant E. De Forest. (Illus.). 1979. 39.45 (ISBN 0-89266-181-X). Am Classical Coll Pr.

God in the Classroom. Marjorie E. Cook Adams. pap. 1.95 (ISBN 0-89107-116-4). Good News.

God-Inspired Orthodox Julian Calendar VS. the False Gregorian Papal Calendar. Kallistos Makris. Tr. by Jerry Vlesmas from Hellenic. 118p. (Orig.). 1971. pap. 2.00x (ISBN 0-938366-36-X). Orthodox Chr.

God Invented Sex. Charles E. Wittschiebe. LC 74-78047. (Anvil Ser.). 256p. 1974. pap. 5.95 (ISBN 0-8127-0081-3, 07366-8). Southern Pub.

God Is. Alan Hayward. 224p. 1980. pap. 4.95 (ISBN 0-8407-5746-8). Nelson.

God Is Calling His People to Forgiveness. Gene Lilly. 1977. pap. 2.25 (ISBN 0-917726-15-4). Hunter Bks.

God Is for the Emotionally Ill: A Doctor's Spiritual-Medical Approach. G. J. Guldseth. 108p. 1969. pap. 1.95 o.p. (ISBN 0-912106-72-7). Logos.

God Is Never Absent. Clark M. Williamson. 1977. pap. 2.50 (ISBN 0-8272-1230-5). Bethany Pr.

God Is No Fool. Lois A. Cheney. (Orig.). pap. 1.50 (ISBN 0-89129-251-9). Jove Pubns.

God Is Speaking to You. Harry S. Beck & James W. Gerrard. 6.95 (ISBN 0-686-05779-1). Prod Hse.

God Is with You. Swami Muktananda. (Illus., Orig.). 1978. pap. 1.25 (ISBN 0-914602-57-8). SYDA Found.

God Let Me Out of This Marriage. Denise Vicker. Ed. by John Boneck. LC 80-83459. 160p. 1981. pap. 3.50 (ISBN 0-89221-080-X). New Leaf.

God Likes Them Plain. Eric Linklater. LC 79-53455. (Short Story Index in Reprint Ser.). Date not set. Repr. of 1935 ed. 24.50x (ISBN 0-8486-5009-3). Core Collection. Postponed.

God Love You. Fulton J. Sheen. LC 80-23085. 224p. 1981. pap. 4.50 (ISBN 0-385-17486-1, Im). Doubleday.

God Loves Laughter. William Sears. 1960. 7.50 o.s.i. (ISBN 0-85398-018-7, 7-31-73); pap. 3.95 (ISBN 0-85398-019-5, 7-31-74, Pub. by G Ronald England). Baha'i.

God Loves Me. Maureen Curley. (Children of the Kingdom Ser.). (gr. 1-4). 1977. 7.95 (ISBN 0-686-13681-0). Pflaum Pr.

God Made the Animals. Mrs. James Swartzentruber. (God Is Good Ser.). 1976. 2.25 (ISBN 0-686-18185-9). Rod & Staff.

God Made the One & Only Me. Barbara Linville. LC 76-8737. (Illus.). (ps). 1976. pap. text ed. 2.25 (ISBN 0-916406-28-8). Accent Bks.

God Made the Stars. Peter Moore. (Illus.). 32p. (Orig.). (gr. k-2). 1981. pap. write for info. (ISBN 0-933770-18-9). Kalimat.

God Made the World. (Tell-a-Bible Story Ser.). (Illus.). 28p. bds. 0.69 (ISBN 0-686-68636-5, 3680). Standard Pub.

God Made the World. G. A. Pottebaum. (Little People's Paperbacks Ser.). 1979. pap. 0.99 (ISBN 0-8164-2239-7). Crossroad NY.

God Made the World (Creation) Scripture Union. (New Owl Ser.). 1978. pap. 0.49 (ISBN 0-87508-925-9). Chr Lit.

God Made Them Great. John Tallach. 1978. pap. 4.25 (ISBN 0-85151-190-2). Banner of Truth.

God Made Them Superstars. Barbara Anson. 1976. pap. 1.50 o.p. (ISBN 0-685-73454-4, LB405, Leisure Bks). Nordon Pubns.

God Makes the Difference. Joyce G. Godby. 128p. 1981. 5.00 (ISBN 0-8059-2764-6). Dorrance.

God, Man, Salt Water & the Eastern Shore. 2nd ed. William I. Tawes. LC 77-5735. (Illus.). 1977. 7.50 (ISBN 0-87033-231-7, Pub. by Tidewater). Cornell Maritime.

God Meets Man: A Theology of the Sabbath & the Second Advent. Sakae Kubo. LC 78-6616. (Anvil Ser.). 1978. pap. 7.95 (ISBN 0-8127-0171-2). Southern Pub.

God-Men: An Inquiry into Witness Lee & the Local Church. rev. ed. Neil T. Duddy & Spiritual Counterfeits Project. (Orig.). Date not set. pap. 4.95 (ISBN 0-87784-833-5). Inter-Varsity.

God, Money & You. George Otis. pap. 1.95 (ISBN 0-89728-034-2, 546638). Omega Pubns OR.

God, Money & You. George Otis. 1975. pap. 1.50 (ISBN 0-89129-004-4). Jove Pubns.

God Never Fails. Mary L. Kupferle. 1958. 2.95 o.p. (ISBN 0-87159-045-X). Unity Bks.

God of All Comfort. Hannah W. Smith. 1956. pap. 2.50 (ISBN 0-8024-0018-3). Moody.

God of Tarot. Piers Anthony. (Orig.). 1979. pap. 1.75 (ISBN 0-515-05134-9). Jove Pubns.

God of Tarot. Piers Anthony. (Orig.). 1981. pap. 2.25 (ISBN 0-425-05031-9). Berkley Pub.

God of the Oppressed. James Cone. 1978. pap. 4.95 (ISBN 0-8164-2607-4). Crossroad NY.

God of the Philosophers. Anthony Kenny. 1979. 16.50x (ISBN 0-19-824594-7). Oxford U Pr.

God of the Present Age. Eric Seldon. LC 80-26149. 1981. pap. price not set (ISBN 0-8309-0305-4). Herald Hse.

God of the Witches. Margaret Murray. (Illus.). 1970. pap. 4.95 (ISBN 0-19-501270-4, GB). Oxford U Pr.

God on Every Mountain Top. Byrd Baylor. (Illus.). 64p. (gr. 3-7). 1981. 8.95 (ISBN 0-684-16758-1). Scribner.

God Passes By. rev. ed. Shoghi Effendi. LC 44-51036. 1974. 11.00 (ISBN 0-87743-020-9, 7-08-10); pap. 6.00 (ISBN 0-87743-034-9, 7-08-11). Baha'i.

God-Players. Earl Jabay. LC 69-11637. 1970. pap. 4.95 (ISBN 0-310-26541-X). Zondervan.

God! Please Stop Drugs. Teresa Harris. Date not set. 5.95 (ISBN 0-533-04435-9). Vantage.

God Save Ireland! The Irish Conflict in the Twentieth Century. Patricia B. Stevens. LC 73-19067. 224p. (gr. 7 up). 1974. 10.95 (ISBN 0-02-788180-6). Macmillan.

God, Sex & You. M. O. Vincent. 1976. pap. 1.75 (ISBN 0-89129-191-1). Jove Pubns.

God So Loves the World. G. A. Pottebaum. (Little People's Paperbacks Ser.). 1979. pap. 0.99 (ISBN 0-8164-2244-3). Crossroad NY.

God Speaks to Women Today. Eugenia Price. pap. 2.95 (ISBN 0-310-31302-3). Zondervan.

God-Talk. John Macquarrie. (Library of Contemporary Theology). 1979. pap. 7.95 (ISBN 0-8164-2205-2). Crossroad NY.

God the Father. Russell P. Spittler. (Radiant Life). 1976. pap. 1.25 (ISBN 0-88243-898-0, 02-0898, Radiant Bks); teacher's ed 2.50 (ISBN 0-88243-170-6, 32-0170). Gospel Pub.

God the Father: Theology & Patriarchy in the Teaching of Jesus, No. 4. Robert Hamerton-Kelly. Ed. by Walter Brueggemann & John R. Donahue. LC 78-54551. (Overtures to Biblical Theology Ser). 144p. 1979. pap. 5.95 (ISBN 0-8006-1528-X, 1-1528). Fortress.

God, the Holy Spirit. George Otis & Mary Walker. pap. 1.25 (ISBN 0-685-60971-5, 532877). Omega Pubns OR.

God the Redeemer. James M. Boice. LC 77-14880. (Foundations of the Christian Faith: Vol. 2). 1978. pap. 5.95 (ISBN 0-87784-744-4). Inter-Varsity.

God They Never Knew. George Otis. 1978. pap. 3.95 (ISBN 0-89728-011-3, 678276). Omega Pubns OR.

God Thoughts. Dick Williams. 1970. pap. 1.65 (ISBN 0-8164-2026-2, SP66). Crossroad NY.

God Told Me to. C. K. Chandler. 1976. pap. 1.75 (ISBN 0-345-28580-8). Ballantine.

God Ventures. Irene B. Harrell. 1975. pap. 1.95 o.p. (ISBN 0-88270-136-3). Logos.

God vs We the People. John A. Sinclair. 1977. 7.50 o.p. (ISBN 0-682-48746-5). Exposition.

God Wants You to Be Well. Laurence H. Blackburn. 160p. 1974. pap. 3.75 (ISBN 0-8192-1189-3). Morehouse.

God Was a Stranger. Margaret Kirk. 1980. pap. 2.75 (ISBN 0-85363-130-1). OMF Bks.

God Was in Christ. D. M. Baillie. 1977. pap. 6.50 (ISBN 0-571-05685-7, Pub. by Faber & Faber). Merrimack Bk Serv.

God Wash the World & Start Again. Lorenz Graham. LC 75-109900. (Illus.). (gr. 2-5). 1971. 6.95 o.p. (ISBN 0-690-33295-5, TYC-J); PLB 6.89 o.p. (ISBN 0-690-33296-3). T Y Crowell.

God We Seek. Paul Weiss. LC 64-13476. 267p. 1964. 10.95x (ISBN 0-8093-0133-4). S Ill U Pr.

God We Seek. Paul Weiss. LC 72-11838. (Arcturus Books Paperbacks). 1973. pap. 7.95 (ISBN 0-8093-0628-X). S Ill U Pr.

God: What People Have Said About Him. Ed. by Lothar Kahn. 320p. 1980. 9.95 (ISBN 0-8246-0251-X). Jonathan David.

God, Where Are You? Meditations on the Old Testament. Carlos Mesters. Tr. by John Drury from Port. LC 76-41356. 1977. 6.95x o.p. (ISBN 0-88344-162-4). Orbis Bks.

God Who Comes. Carlo Carretto. 1976. pap. 1.50 (ISBN 0-89129-062-1). Jove Pubns.

God Who Dares to Be Man: Theology of Prayer & Suffering. Bonnell Spencer. 128p. Date not set. 12.95 (ISBN 0-8164-0478-X). Seabury.

God Who Understands Me: Studies in the Sermon on the Mount. Gladys M. Hunt. LC 75-181992. (Fisherman Bible Study Guide). 1971. pap. 1.95 (ISBN 0-87788-316-5). Shaw Pubs.

God, Why Me? Mario Martino. 1981. 4.95 (ISBN 0-8062-1703-0). Carlton.

God Within. Rene Dubos. LC 76-37224. 1972. text ed. 22.50x (ISBN 0-684-12768-7). Irvington.

God Writes Straight with Crooked Lines. Ernest A. Fitzgerald. LC 80-65997. 144p. 1981. 7.95 (ISBN 0-689-11073-1). Atheneum.

Godan. Premchand. Tr. by P. Lal. 1972. pap. 3.50 (ISBN 0-88253-069-0). Ind-US Inc.

Goddaughter. Adrian Reid. 1980. pap. 2.25 (ISBN 0-380-47571-5, 47571, 47571). Avon.

Godden's Guide to English Porcelain. Geoffrey Godden. (Illus.). 286p. 1980. text ed. 31.25x (ISBN 0-686-61566-2). Humanities.

Godden's Guide to English Porcelain. Geoffrey A. Godden. 1978. 70.00x (ISBN 0-246-11002-3, Pub. by Granada England). State Mutual Bk.

Goddess & Other Women. Joyce C. Oates. LC 74-81808. 512p. 1974. 10.95 (ISBN 0-8149-0745-8). Vanguard.

Goddess & Other Women. Joyce C. Oates. 464p. 1976. pap. 1.95 o.p. (ISBN 0-449-22774-X, C2774, Crest). Fawcett.

Goddess in the Home. Phyllis Arthur. (YA) 1971. 5.95 (ISBN 0-685-03334-1, Avalon). Bouregy.

Goddess Named Gold. Bhabani Bhattacharya. 306p. 1969. pap. 3.40 (ISBN 0-88253-016-X). Ind-US Inc.

Goddesses of Sun & Moon: Circe, Aphrodite, Medea, Niobe, & Dunquin. Karl Kerenyi. (Dunquin Ser.). 1979. pap. text ed. 7.00 (ISBN 0-88214-211-9). Spring Pubns.

Goddesses: Silkscreen Prints by Mayumi Oda. Mayumi Oda. (Lancaster-Miller Art Ser.). (Illus.). 100p. 1981. 9.95 (ISBN 0-89581-010-7). Lancaster-Miller.

Godel's Proof. Ernest Nagel & James R. Newman. LC 58-5610. 1958. 9.50 (ISBN 0-8147-0324-0); pap. 4.50x (ISBN 0-8147-0325-9). NYU Pr.

Godfather. Mario Puzo. (RL 10). 1979. pap. 2.95 (ISBN 0-451-09438-7, E9438, Sig). NAL.

Godliness & Good Learning: Four Studies on a Victorian Ideal. David Newsome. (Illus.). 1961. 10.95 (ISBN 0-7195-1015-5). Transatlantic.

Godly Rebellion: Parisian Cures & the Religious Fronde, 1652-1662. Richard Golden. LC 80-25282. 264p. 1981. 22.50x (ISBN 0-8078-1466-0). U of NC Pr.

Godmother. Hugh Fleetwood. 152p. 1980. 16.95 (ISBN 0-241-10126-3, Pub. by Hamish Hamilton England). David & Charles.

Gododdin. Desmond O'Grady. (Dolmen Editions Ser.: No. 26). (Illus.). 1977. text ed. 56.25x (ISBN 0-85105-310-6, Dolmen Pr). Humanities.

Godric. Frederick Buechner. 1980. 10.95 (ISBN 0-689-11086-3). Atheneum.

God's Adventurer. Hudson Taylor & Phyllis Thompson. (Illus.). 1978. pap. 2.25 (ISBN 0-85363-094-1). OMF Bks.

God's Altar: The World & the Flesh in Puritan Poetry. Robert Daly. LC 77-76182. 1978. 14.00x (ISBN 0-520-03480-5). U of Cal Pr.

God's Alternative: Swami Vivekenanda's Attitude to Buddhism. Lal Mani Joshi. (God Ser.: No. 841). Date not set. cancelled (ISBN 0-89007-841-6). C Stark. Postponed.

Gods & Beasts: The Nazis & the Occult. Dusty Sklar. LC 77-87197. (Illus.). 1977. 9.95 o.s.i. (ISBN 0-690-01232-2, TYC-T). T Y Crowell.

Gods, & Heroes from Viking Mythology. Brian Branston. (Illus.). 1978. 12.95 (ISBN 0-85654-029-3, Pub. by Two Continents). Hippocrene Bks.

Gods & Heroes in the Athenian Agora: Excavations of the Athenian Agora Picture Bks. John M. Camp. (No. 19). (Illus.). 1980. pap. 1.50x (ISBN 0-87661-623-6). Am Sch Athens.

Gods & Heroes of the Greeks: An Introduction to Greek Mythology. Ed. by Herbert J. Rose. 8.50 (ISBN 0-8446-5113-3). Peter Smith.

Gods & Rituals: Readings in Religious Beliefs & Practices. Ed. by John Middleton. LC 75-44032. (Texas Press Sourcebooks in Anthropology: No. 6). 1976. pap. 7.95x (ISBN 0-292-72708-9). U of Tex Pr.

Gods & Spacemen in the Ancient West. W. Raymond Drake. pap. 1.50 (ISBN 0-451-06055-5, W6055, Sig). NAL.

Gods & Symbols of Ancient Egypt: An Illustrated Dictionary. Manfred Lurker. Rev. by Peter A. Clayton. (Illus.). 144p. 1980. 16.95 (ISBN 0-500-11018-2, Quest). Thames Hudson.

Gods & the Kings: A Glance at Creative Power. Jacques Rueff. LC 72-94011. 288p. 1973. Repr. 8.95 o.s.i. (ISBN 0-02-605880-4). Macmillan.

God's Answers to Our Anxieties. James T. Jeremiah. (Direction Books Ser.). 1979. pap. 1.45 (ISBN 0-8010-5083-9). Baker Bk.

God's Bits of Wood. Ousmane Sembene. LC 75-133620. 1970. pap. 2.95 o.p. (ISBN 0-385-04430-5, Anch). Doubleday.

God's Blueprints. John McKelvie Whitworth. 1975. 25.00x (ISBN 0-7100-8002-6). Routledge & Kegan.

God's Calling: A Missionary Autobiography. Robert H. Culpepper. LC 80-68643. 1981. 4.95 (ISBN 0-8054-6323-2). Broadman.

Gods Can Die. Edwin Thumboo. (Writing in Asia Ser.). 1977. pap. text ed. 3.25 o.p. (ISBN 0-686-60436-9, 00223). Heinemann Ed.

God's Chosen People: A Theological Interpretation of the Book of Deuteronomy. Ronald E. Clements. 1968. pap. text ed. 2.50x o.p. (ISBN 0-8401-0422-7). Allenson.

God's Christ & His People. Jacob Jervell. 1977. pap. 31.00x (ISBN 82-00-01628-5, Dist. by Columbia U Pr). Universitet.

God's Church for Today. Peter Toon. LC 80-65330. (Christian Faith for Today Ser.). 144p. (Orig.). 1980. pap. 3.95 (ISBN 0-89107-183-0). Good News.

God's Country & My People. Wright Morris. LC 80-23155. (Illus.). 176p. 1981. pap. 15.95 (ISBN 0-8032-3067-2, BB 752, Bison). U of Nebr Pr.

God's Covenants & Our Time. Guy Duty. LC 73-8587. 1964. pap. 2.45 (ISBN 0-87123-180-8, 210180). Bethany Fell.

God's Daughter in Nassau. Stephen G. Burrows. 1979. 8.50 (ISBN 0-682-49497-6). Exposition.

God's Day, Today, & Everyday. Elaine B. Moore. 1980. pap. 2.95 (ISBN 0-570-03497-3, 56-1348). Concordia.

Gods Depart: The Hawaiian Kingdom, 1832-1873. new ed. Kathleen D. Mellen. (Kathleen Dickenson Mellen's Epic Saga of the Hawaiian Kingdom Ser.). 300p. 1980. pap. 7.95 o.p. (ISBN 0-8038-2708-3). Hastings.

God's Design: Focusing an Old Testament Theology. Elmer A. Martens. 368p. 1981. 12.95 (ISBN 0-8010-6115-6). Baker Bk.

God's Early Helpers. Maureen Curley. (gr. 4-7). 1974. 7.95 (ISBN 0-686-13690-X). Pflaum Pr.

God's East Wind: Sermons for the Easter Season, Ser. A. Leonard W. Mann. 64p. (Orig.). 1980. pap. text ed. 3.95 (ISBN 0-89536-449-2). CSS Pub.

God's Fool. Lawrence D. Moon. 12.95 (ISBN 0-531-09946-6). Watts.

God's Fools: Lives of Fools for Christ's Sake. Lev Puhalo. 1976. pap. 6.00 (ISBN 0-913026-79-4). St Nectarios.

God's Footprint on My Floor. Leo Van Dolson. LC 76-56996. (Horizon Ser.). 1977. pap. 4.95 (ISBN 0-8127-0132-1). Southern Pub.

God's Frontiersmen: The Yale Band in Illinois. John R. Willis. LC 79-65011. 1979. pap. text ed. 10.00 (ISBN 0-8191-0781-6). U Pr of Amer.

Gods, Ghosts & Men in Melanesia. Ed. by P. Lawrence & M. J. Meggitt. 1965. pap. 12.95x (ISBN 0-19-550147-0). Oxford U Pr.

God's Gold Mines. C. Roy Angell. LC 62-9194. 1962. 3.95 (ISBN 0-8054-5113-7). Broadman.

God's Gracious Dealings. Fred Pruitt & Lawrence Pruitt. (Illus.). 496p. 5.00. Faith Pub Hse.

God's Guidance at Dawn. Mary Light. pap. 1.00 o.p. (ISBN 0-910924-68-6). Macalester.

God's Hand in My Life. Ed. by Lawrence Geraty. LC 77-12585. (Horizon Ser.). 1977. pap. 4.95 (ISBN 0-8127-0151-8). Southern Pub.

God's Helper. Danella G. Kotrba. (Come Unto Me Ser.: Year 2, Bk. 1). 32p. (ps). 1980. pap. 1.50 (ISBN 0-8127-0211-5). Southern Pub.

God's Images: A New Vision. James Dickey. LC 78-17465. (Illus., Orig.). 1978. pap. 7.95 (ISBN 0-8164-2194-3). Crossroad NY.

God's Incomparable Word. Harold Lindsell. 1978. pap. 2.95 (ISBN 0-88207-774-0). Victor Bks.

God's Inerrant Word: An International Symposium on the Trustworthiness of Scripture. Ed. by John W. Montgomery. LC 74-4100. 288p. 1974. 7.95 (ISBN 0-87123-179-4, 230179). Bethany Fell.

God's Kingdom for Today. Peter Toon. LC 80-65331. (Christian Faith for Today Ser.). 128p. 1980. pap. 3.95 (ISBN 0-89107-188-1, Cornerstone Bks). Good News.

God's Last Metaphor: The Doctrine of the Trinity in New England Theology. Bruce M. Stephens. LC 80-11421. (American Academy of Religion Studies in Religion). 12.00x (ISBN 0-89130-385-5, 01 00 24); pap. 7.50x (ISBN 0-89130-386-3). Scholars Pr CA.

God's Marvelous Work, Bk. 1. Rosa M. Mullet. 1975. Repr. of 1980 ed. write to pub. for info. (ISBN 0-686-11149-4); tchrs. ed avail. (ISBN 0-686-11150-8). Rod & Staff.

God's Marvelous Work, Bk. 2. Rosa M. Mullet. 1979. write for info. (ISBN 0-686-25256-X); tchr's ed. avail. (ISBN 0-686-25257-8). Rod & Staff.

God's Master Key to Prosperity. Gordon Lindsay. 1.95 (ISBN 0-89985-001-4). Christ Nations.

God's Medicine of Faith. Norvel Hayes. 1978. pap. 1.95 (ISBN 0-917726-20-0). Hunter Bks.

God's Meekest Angels. Janice C. Yee. (Illus.). (gr. k-6). 1980. pap. 1.75 (ISBN 0-686-60162-9); pap. 1.05 (ISBN 0-686-66043-9). Pi Pr. Postponed.

Gods, Men & Monsters from the Greek Myths. Michael Gibson. (Illus.). 1978. 12.95 (ISBN 0-85654-027-7, Pub. by Two Continents). Hippocrene Bks.

God's Mercy Surmounting Man's Cruelty, Exemplified in the Captivity & Redemption of Elizabeth Hanson, Repr. Of 1728. Bd. with Account of the Captivity of Elizabeth Hanson. Repr. of 1760 ed; Memoirs of Odd Adventures, Strange Deliverances, & C. in the Captivity of John Gyles. Repr. of 1736 ed; Narrative of the Captivity of Nehemiah How, Who Was Taken by the Indians at the Great-Meadow Fort Above Fort Dummer. Repr. of 1748 ed; Redeemed Captive. John Norton. Repr. of 1748 ed. LC 75-7025. (Indian Captivities Ser.: Vol. 6). 1977. lib. bdg. 44.00 (ISBN 0-8240-1630-0). Garland Pub.

God's Message in Troubled Times. Frank R. Campbell. 1981. pap. 3.95 (ISBN 0-8054-2239-0). Broadman.

God's New Israel: Religious Interpretations of American Destiny. C. Cherry. 1971. pap. 11.95 (ISBN 0-13-357335-4). P-H.

God's New Society. John R. Stott. Ed. by J. A. Motyer & John R. Stott. LC 79-3636. (Bible Speaks Today Ser.). 1980. pap. text ed. 5.95 (ISBN 0-87784-587-5). Inter-Varsity.

Gods of Aquarius. Brad Steiger. 1981. pap. 2.50 (ISBN 0-425-04753-9). Berkley Pub.

Gods of Life. Neil Elliott. LC 73-8491. 192p. 1974. 7.95 o.s.i. (ISBN 0-02-535200-8). Macmillan.

Gods of Mars. Rona Randall. 1977. pap. 1.95 (ISBN 0-345-27835-6). Ballantine.

Gods of the Ancient Northmen. Georges Dumezil. Ed. & tr. by Einar Haugen. (Study of Comparative Folklore & Mythology, No. 3). 1974. 18.50x (ISBN 0-520-02044-8); CAL 371. pap. 3.95 (ISBN 0-520-03507-0). U of Cal Pr.

God's OK -- You're OK? Perspective on Christian Worship. Richard W. Baynes. LC 79-67440. 96p. (Orig.). 1981. pap. 1.95 (ISBN 0-87239-382-8, 40088). Standard Pub.

God's Other Door & the Continuity of Life. Edgar Cayce & Hugh L. Cayce. 1976. pap. 1.95 (ISBN 0-87604-007-5). ARE Pr.

God's People. William A. Kramer. LC 75-16790. 1975. lib. bdg. 7.25 (ISBN 0-8100-0010-5, 06N552). Northwest Pub.

God's People in Christ: New Testament Perspectives on the Church & Judaism, No. 7. Daniel J. Harrington. Ed. by Walter Brueggemann & John R. Donahue. LC 79-7380. (Overtures to Biblical Theology Ser.). 144p. 1980. pap. 6.50 (ISBN 0-8006-1531-X, 1-1531). Fortress.

God's People in God's World. John Gladwin. LC 80-7726. 1980. pap. 5.95 (ISBN 0-87784-607-3). Inter-Varsity.

God's People in Transition. Dan Ivins. Date not set. 5.95 (ISBN 0-8054-6932-X). Broadman. Postponed.

God's Perfect Way for You. Hazel Pickett. 1.95 o.p. (ISBN 0-910924-32-5). Macalester.

God's Perfect Will. G. Campbell Morgan. (Morgan Library). 1978. pap. 3.95 (ISBN 0-8010-6055-9). Baker Bk.

God's Plan for Us. Brian Hall & Benjamin Tonna. LC 80-81439. 128p. 1980. pap. 8.95 (ISBN 0-8091-2311-8). Paulist Pr.

God's Plot: The Paradoxes of Puritan Piety, Being the Autobiography & Journal of Thomas Shepard. Ed. by Michael McGiffert & Winfred E. Bernhard. LC 71-181364. (Commonwealth Ser.: Vol. 1). (Illus.). 250p. 1972. 15.00x (ISBN 0-87023-100-6). U of Mass Pr.

God's Presence in History: Jewish Affirmations & Philosophical Reflections. Emil L. Fackenheim. LC 79-88135. (Deems Lectureship in Philosophy Ser). 1970. 8.00x (ISBN 0-8147-0142-6). NYU Pr.

God's Priests & Warriors. Robert P. Goldman. LC 76-41255. 1977. 15.00x (ISBN 0-231-03941-7). Columbia U Pr.

God's Prison Gang. Ray Hoekstra & Walter Wagner. 1977. 6.95 o.p. (ISBN 0-8007-0840-7). Revell.

God's Promises Solve My Problems. Glenn Coon. (Harvest Ser.). 1979. pap. 3.95 (ISBN 0-8163-0334-7, 07550-7). Pacific Pr Pub Assn.

Gods Protecting Providence Man's Surest Help & Defense...Remarkable Deliverance of Divers Person, from the Devouring Waves of the Sea...& Also...the Inhumane Canibals of Florida, Repr. Of 1699 Ed. Jonathan Dickinson. Bd. with Good Fetch'd Out of Evil. Cotten Mather. Repr. of 1706 ed; Memorial of the Present Deplorable State of New England. Cotten Mather. Repr. of 1707 ed. LC 75-7023. (Indian Captivities Ser.: Vol. 4). 1977. lib. bdg. 44.00 (ISBN 0-8240-1628-9). Garland Pub.

God's Psychiatry. Charles Allen. 1963. pap. 1.75 (ISBN 0-515-05327-9). Jove Pubns.

God's Purpose & Man's Plans. Edward R. Dayton. 1976. pap. 3.75 (ISBN 0-912552-11-5). MARC.

God's Questions & Answers: Contemporary Studies in Malachi. Robert W. Bailey. LC 76-56513. 1977. pap. 3.95 (ISBN 0-8164-1228-6). Crossroad NY.

God's Reach. Glenn Clark. pap. 3.50 o.p. (ISBN 0-910924-48-1). Macalester.

God's Remedy for Depression. Vivian Clark. (Direction Bks.). (Orig.). 1980. pap. 3.50 (ISBN 0-8010-2444-7). Baker Bk.

God's Righteous Kingdom. Walter J. Chantry. 151p. (Orig.). 1980. pap. 3.50 (ISBN 0-85151-310-7). Banner of Truth.

God's Salvation for Today. Peter Toon. (Christian Faith for Today Ser.). 144p. 1981. pap. 3.95 (ISBN 0-89107-194-6, Cornerstone Bks). Good News.

God's Secret Agent. (Encounter Ser.). (gr. 3-7). 2.25 o.s.i. (ISBN 0-8198-0236-0). Dghtrs St Paul.

God's Song in My Heart: Daily Devotions. Ruth Y. Nelson. LC 56-11912. 432p. 1957. 7.50 (ISBN 0-8006-0254-4, 1-254). Fortress.

God's Soul Medicine. Solomon J. Benn, III. (Resources for Black Ministries Ser.). 64p. (Orig.). 1981. pap. 2.45 (ISBN 0-8010-0802-6). Baker Bk.

God's Sovereignty in the Lives of Twin Brothers. J. Van Zweden. pap. 1.95. Reiner.

God's Spy. 1977. 6.95 o.p. (ISBN 0-88270-213-0, H213-9); pap. 3.95 o.p. (ISBN 0-88270-214-9, P214-7). Logos.

God's Storehouse: Exodus 16 Lessons, Vol. 2. Bernice C. Jordan. (Old Testament Ser.). (gr. 3-9). 1961. pap. text ed. 1.95 (ISBN 0-86508-029-1); figures 7.95 (ISBN 0-86508-030-5). BCM Inc.

God's Trombones. James W. Johnson. (Poets Ser). 1976. pap. 3.50 (ISBN 0-14-042217-X). Penguin.

God's Trustees. new ed. Charles E. Dietze. 112p. (Orig.). 1976. pap. 1.25 (ISBN 0-8272-1216-X). Bethany Pr.

Gods Unknown. Robert Charroux. (Orig.). 1974. pap. 1.25 o.p. (ISBN 0-425-02547-0, Medallion). Berkley Pub.

God's Way of Reconciliation: Studies in Ephesians II. Martyn D. Lloyd-Jones. 1972. 10.95 (ISBN 0-8010-5519-9). Baker Bk.

God's Will for Your Life. S. Maxwell Coder. 1946. pap. 1.50 (ISBN 0-8024-3055-4). Moody.

God's Will: You Can Know It. Leslie Flynn & Bernice Flynn. 1979. pap. 2.95 (ISBN 0-88207-779-1). Victor Bks.

God's Winter Gifts. Gail Linam. 1980. pap. 2.95 (ISBN 0-8054-4158-1). Broadman.

God's Wonderful World. 1968 ed. Morris Kipper & Lenore Kipper. LC 68-56182. (Illus.). (gr. k-3). text ed. 3.50 o.p. (ISBN 0-88400-026-5); teachers' ed. 6.50 o.p. (ISBN 0-88400-028-1). Shengold.

God's Wonderful World of Fish. Illus. by Victor Mitchell. (gr. 2-6). 1978. pap. 0.79 o.p. (ISBN 0-8307-0627-5, 56-059-03). Regal.

God's Word As It Was in the Beginning. G. V. Lampkin. 1981. 6.95 (ISBN 0-533-04646-7). Vantage.

God's Word for Today. Peter Toon. (Christian Faith for Today Ser.). 144p. (Orig.). 1981. pap. 3.95 (ISBN 0-89107-193-8, Cornerstone Bks). Good News.

God's Word Made Plain. Mrs. Paul Friederichsen. (Span). 1958. pap. 2.50 (ISBN 0-8024-3041-4). Moody.

God's World: His Story. Roger L. Berry. 1981. pap. 11.45 tchrs'. guide (ISBN 0-87813-914-1). Christian Light.

Godwin & Mary: Letters of William Godwin & Mary Wollstonecraft. Ed. by Ralph M. Wardle. LC 76-13032. (Illus.). 1977. 7.95x (ISBN 0-8032-0901-0); pap. 2.65 (ISBN 0-8032-5852-6, BB 631, Bison). U of Nebr Pr.

Goergian Gentleman. Michael Brander. (Saxon House Bks.). 1974. 8.95 o.p. (ISBN 0-347-00020-7). Gordon-Cremonesi.

Goergina & the Dragon. Lee Kingman. (Illus.). (gr. 3-5). 1974. pap. 1.25 (ISBN 0-671-29892-5). PB.

Goering Testament. George Markstein. 256p. 1981. 8.95 o.p. (ISBN 0-345-28095-4); pap. text ed. 2.50 o.p. (ISBN 0-345-28047-4). Ballantine.

Goering Treasure. Gordon Davis. 288p. (Orig.). 1980. pap. 2.28 (ISBN 0-89083-692-2). Zebra.

Goethe: A Critical Introduction. Ronald D. Gray. (Orig.). 44.50 (ISBN 0-521-05134-7); pap. text ed. 14.50x (ISBN 0-521-09404-6). Cambridge U Pr.

Goethe, a Critical Introduction. Henry C. Hatfield. LC 64-24031. 1963. 12.50x (ISBN 0-674-35550-4). Harvard U Pr.

Goethe & His Age. Georg Lukacs. Tr. by Robert Anchor from Ger. 1978. Repr. of 1968 ed. 18.25 (ISBN 0-86527-256-5). Fertig.

Goethe & Inner Harmony: A Study of 'Schoene Seele' in the Apprenticeship of William Meister. D. L. Farrelly. 220p. 1973. 10.00x (ISBN 0-7165-2157-1, Pub. by Irish Academic Pr Ireland). Biblio Dist.

Goethe & Music. Frederick Sternfeld. (Music Reprint Ser.). 176p. 1979. Repr. of 1954 ed. 19.50 (ISBN 0-306-79515-9). Da Capo.

Goethe & Rousseau: Resonances of the Mind. Carl Hammer, Jr. LC 72-91665. 232p. 1973. 12.00x (ISBN 0-8131-1289-3). U Pr of Ky.

Goethe & the Novel. Eric A. Blackall. LC 75-38426. 344p. 1976. 22.50x (ISBN 0-8014-0978-0). Cornell U Pr.

Goethe & the Philosophers' Stone: Symbolical Patterns in the Parable & the Second Part of Faust. Alice Raphael. LC 64-7535. 8.50 o.p. (ISBN 0-912326-13-1). Garrett-Helix.

Goethe As Revealed in His Poetry. 2nd ed. Barker Fairley. LC 63-21991. 9.50 (ISBN 0-8044-2186-2). Ungar.

Goethes Aussere Erscheinung. Ed. by Emil Schaeffer. (Illus.). 120p. 1980. text ed. 31.20 (ISBN 3-458-04925-8, Pub. by Insel Verlag Germany). Suhrkamp.

Goethe's "Das Marchen" Translation and Analysis. Waltraud Bartscht. LC 72-132826. (Studies in Germanic Langauges & Literatures: No. 3). 112p. 1972. 9.00x (ISBN 0-8131-1237-0). U Pr of Ky.

Goethe's Die Wahlverwandtschaften. H. B. Nisbet. Ed. by Hans Reiss. (Blackwell's German Text Ser.). 1971. pap. 6.00x o.p. (ISBN 0-631-01840-9, Pub. by Basil Blackwell). Biblio Dist.

Goethe's Faust. Ed. by Roe-Merrill S. Heffner et al. Incl. Vol. I. Introduction, Pts. I & II. 584p. pap. text ed. 9.25 (ISBN 0-299-06874-9, 687); Vol. II. Vocabulary & Notes. 414p. pap. text ed. 8.25 (ISBN 0-299-06884-6, 688). LC 75-12216. 1975. U of Wis Pr.

Goethe's Faust: Its Genesis & Purport. Eudo C. Mason. 1967. 20.00x (ISBN 0-520-00821-9). U of Cal Pr.

Goethes Letzte Schweizer Reise. (Insel Taschenbuecher: No. 375). (Illus.). 438p. (Orig.). 1980. pap. text ed. 7.80 (ISBN 0-686-64714-9, Pub. by Insel Verlag Germany). Suhrkamp.

Goethe's World View: Presented in His Reflections & Maxims. Johann W. Goethe. Ed. by Frederick Ungar. Tr. by Heinz Norden. LC 63-18513. pap. 3.45 (ISBN 0-8044-6192-9). Ungar.

Goethes's Faust: The Making of Part I. John Gearey. LC 80-5826. 256p. 1981. 19.00x (ISBN 0-300-02571-8). Yale U Pr.
Goettliche Komoedie und Exegese. Manfred Bambeck. viii, 253p. 1975. pap. 47.10x (ISBN 3-11-004874-4). De Gruyter.
Goforth of China. Rosalind Goforth. 1969. pap. 3.95 (ISBN 0-87123-181-6, 200181). Bethany Fell.
Goggles. Ezra J. Keats. LC 70-78081. (Illus.). (gr. k-2). 1969. 8.95g o.p. (ISBN 0-02-749590-6). Macmillan.
Gogol. V. V. Gippius. Tr. by R. Maguire. 1981. 17.50 (ISBN 0-88233-612-6). Ardis Pubs.
Gogol. Vasily Gippius. LC 63-7522. (Slavic Reprint Ser.: No. 1). 246p. (Rus). 1971. pap. 4.75 (ISBN 0-87057-069-2, Pub. by Brown U Pr). Univ Pr of New England.
Gogol's "Overcoat" An Anthology of Critical Essays. Ed. by Elizabeth Trahan. 1981. 15.00 (ISBN 0-88233-614-2). Ardis Pubs.
Gogo's Car Breaks Down. Anne Rockwell. LC 74-2523. (ps-k). 1978. 5.95a o.p. (ISBN 0-385-00555-5); PLB (ISBN 0-385-02365-0). Doubleday.
Goin' South. Madeleine Shaner. 1978. pap. 1.95 o.s.i. (ISBN 0-515-04623-X). Jove Pubns.
Going After Cacciato. Tim O'Brien. 1979. pap. 2.25 o.s.i. (ISBN 0-440-12966-4). Dell.
Going All the Way. Dan Wakefield. 1970. 6.95 o.p. (ISBN 0-440-02955-4, Sey Lawr). Delacorte.
Going Away. Clancy Sigal. 1978. pap. 2.25 o.p. (ISBN 0-445-04210-9). Popular Lib.
Going Bananas Over Language Skills. Charlie Daniel & Becky Daniel. (gr. 2-6). 1978. 5.95 (ISBN 0-916456-22-6, GA83). Good Apple.
Going Blind. Jonathon Penner. 1978. pap. 1.75 o.s.i. (ISBN 0-515-04541-1). Jove Pubns.
Going Crazy. Otto Freidrich. 1976. pap. 1.95 (ISBN 0-380-00888-2, 31567). Avon.
Going for the Gold. Emma Lathen. 1981. 10.95 (ISBN 0-671-41407-0). S&S.
Going for the Gold. new ed. Tim Wendel. (Illus.). 228p. 1980. 10.00 (ISBN 0-88208-116-0). Lawrence Hill.
Going Hollywood. Marie Brenner. 1977. 8.95 o.s.i. (ISBN 0-440-03018-8). Delacorte.
Going Home. Peter Simpson & Ruth Levitt. (Illus.). 400p. 1981. pap. text ed. 20.00 (ISBN 0-443-01839-1). Churchill.
Going Home: A Home Care Training Program. Ernest H. Rosenbaum et al. (Illus.). 160p. 1980. 12.00 (ISBN 0-915950-49-9); three ring binder 12.00 (ISBN 0-915950-48-0). Bull Pub.
Going in Style. Robert Grossbach. (Orig.). 1979. 2.25 (ISBN 0-446-92485-7). Warner Bks.
Going International: The Experience of Smaller Companies Overseas. Gerald D. Newbould et al. LC 78-15729. 1978. 27.95 (ISBN 0-470-26493-4). Halsted Pr.
Going into Hospital. new ed. Susan Pinkus. LC 73-595891. (New Citizen Book). (Illus.). 80p. 1973. 10.50x (ISBN 0-85340-230-2). Intl Pubns Serv.
Going It Alone. George Willig & Drew Bergman. LC 78-69672. (Illus.). 160p. 1979. 12.95 (ISBN 0-385-14725-2); pap. 6.95 (ISBN 0-385-14726-0). Doubleday.
Going Metric in Catering. J. H. Croft. 1969. pap. 4.20 (ISBN 0-08-006512-0). Pergamon.
Going Metric the Fun Way. Eva-Lee Baird & Rose Wyler. LC 77-16895. (Illus.). (gr. 8-9). 1980. 7.95a (ISBN 0-385-13641-2); PLB (ISBN 0-385-13642-0). Doubleday.
Going on a Dig. Velma F. Morrison. LC 80-2776. (Illus.). 128p. (gr. 5 up). 1981. PLB 6.95 (ISBN 0-396-07915-6). Dodd.
Going Places. Aileen Fisher. (Nature Ser). (gr. k-6). 1973. PLB 6.96 (ISBN 0-8372-0865-3); filmstrip & record 18.00 (ISBN 0-8372-0210-8); filmstrip & cassette 18.00 (ISBN 0-8372-0876-9). Bowmar-Noble.
Going Places. William Stafford. 1976. pap. 2.50 (ISBN 0-915596-05-9). West Coast.
Going Places with Your Personality: A Guide to Successful Living. Charles H. Kahn et al. (Special Education Ser for slow learners). (gr. 4-12,RL 2.7). 1971. pap. 2.56 (ISBN 0-8224-3495-4); tchrs' manual free (ISBN 0-8224-3496-2). Pitman Learning.
Going Public - Securities Underwriting. Gerald J. Robinson & Klaus Eppler. LC 61-18675. (Illus.). 1971. looseleaf with 1978 rev. pages 60.00 (ISBN 0-87632-010-8). Boardman.
Going Solo: A Simple Guide to Soaring. Derek Piggott. (Illus.). 112p. 1978. pap. 8.95x. B&N.
Going Through Divorce: Facing the Problems of Adjustment. Howard M. Vollmer. 1980. 8.95 (ISBN 0-87015-198-3). Pacific Bks.
Going to Camp. Irene C. Kleeberg. (First Bks.). (Illus.). (gr. 4-6). 1978. PLB 6.45 s&l (ISBN 0-531-01488-6). Watts.
Going to Law School? Readings on a Legal Career. Thomas Ehrlich & Geoffrey C. Hazard, Jr. 252p. 1975. 8.95 (ISBN 0-316-22287-9); pap. 7.95 (ISBN 0-316-22288-7). Little.
Going to School: An Anthology of Prose About Teachers & Students. Ed. by Abraham H. Lass & Norma L. Tasman. 1981. pap. 2.95 (ISBN 0-451-61905-6, ME1905, Ment). NAL.
Going to School in 1776. John Loeper. LC 72-86940. 112p. (gr. 4-6). 1973. 8.95 (ISBN 0-689-30089-1). Atheneum.
Going to Shakespeare. John C. Trewin. 1978. text ed. 22.95x (ISBN 0-04-792010-6). Allen Unwin.
Going Too Far: The Personal Chronicle of a Feminist. Ed. by Robin Morgan. 348p. Date not set. pap. 4.95 (ISBN 0-394-72612-X, Vin). Random.
Going Very Fast in a Circle--If You Don't Run Out of Gas. Gary Paulsen. LC 78-21109. (Sports on the Light Side Ser.). (Illus.). (gr. 4-6). 1979. PLB 9.65 (ISBN 0-8172-0185-8). Raintree Pubs.
Going Wild. Jay Schleifer. Ed. by Thomas J. Mooney. (Beginning Pal Paperbacks Ser.). (Illus., Orig.). (gr. 7-12). 1977. pap. text ed. 1.25 (ISBN 0-8374-3454-8). Xerox Ed Pubns.
Going Wild: Adventures of a Zoo Vet. David Taylor. LC 80-18432. (Illus.). 242p. 1981. 12.95 (ISBN 0-8128-2756-2). Stein & Day.
Going...Teach Coordinator: Cesare Bonivento, P.I.M.E. 1980. 19.95 (ISBN 0-8198-3009-7). Dghtrs St Paul.
Gold & Silver Wyre-Drawers. Elizabeth Glover. (Illus.). 91p. 1979. 47.50x (ISBN 0-8476-3144-3). Rowman.
Gold & the Garbage in Management Theories & Prescriptions. James A. Lee. LC 80-12758. (Illus.). x, 480p. 1980. 22.95x (ISBN 0-8214-0436-9, 0436E); pap. 10.95x (ISBN 0-8214-0578-0). Ohio U Pr.
Gold at the Starbow's End. Frederick Pohl. pap. 1.25 o.p. (ISBN 0-345-22775-1). Ballantine.
Gold Bug. Edgar A. Poe. LC 76-94830. 1969. 3.00 (ISBN 0-937684-01-5). Tradd St Pr.
Gold Cities: Grass Valley & Nevada City. 2nd ed. Ed. by Jim Morely & Doris Foley. (Illus.). 96p. 1980. 9.95 (ISBN 0-8310-7136-2); pap. 3.50 (ISBN 0-8310-7135-4). Howell-North.
Gold Coin. Reidar Brodtkorb. Tr. by L. W. Kingsland. LC 66-11198. (Illus.). (gr. 5-9). 1966. 4.95 o.p. (ISBN 0-15-231155-6, HJ). HarBraceJ.
Gold Crew. Thomas N. Scortia & Frank M. Robinson. LC 79-23066. 444p. 1980. 11.95 (ISBN 0-446-51202-8); pap. 2.95 (ISBN 0-446-83522-6). Warner Bks.
Gold Crown Lane. Irmelin S. Lilius. Tr. by Marianne Helweg from Swedish. LC 79-2103. (gr. 5 up). 1980. 7.95 (ISBN 0-440-04231-3, Sey Lawr); PLB 7.45 (ISBN 0-440-04232-1). Delacorte.
Gold Dollars, & the European Currency System: The Seven Year Monetary War. Rainer Hellman. (Praeger Special Studies). 1979. 24.95 (ISBN 0-03-041611-6). Praeger.
Gold Down Under: Story of the Australian Gold Rush. Marian T Place. (Illus.). (gr. 7 up). 1969. 4.50g o.s.i. (ISBN 0-02-774440-X, CCPr). Macmillan.
Gold Dredger's Handbook. 2nd ed. Karl Von Mueller. 1980. pap. 4.00 (ISBN 0-89316-609-X); plastic bdg. 6.00 (ISBN 0-89316-610-3). Exanimo Pr.
Gold Fever. Helen Wilson. (Illus.). 1979. pap. 7.25 (ISBN 0-913814-27-X). Nevada Pubns.
Gold, Guns & Ghost Towns. W. A. Chalfant. 12.95 (ISBN 0-912494-32-8); pap. 6.95 (ISBN 0-686-63864-6). Chalfant Pr.
Gold Hunters. J. D. Borthwick. LC 70-146785. 1971. Repr. of 1917 ed. 21.00 (ISBN 0-8103-3635-9). Gale.
Gold Hunter's Field Book: How & Where to Find Gold in the United States & Canada. Jay E. Ransom. LC 74-20409. 1980. pap. 5.95 (ISBN 0-06-090775-4, CN 775, CN). Har-Row.
Gold Hunter's Field Book: How & Where to Prospect for Colors, Nuggets, & Mineral Ores of Gold by Amateur Serious Followers of Jason & the Golden Fleece. Jay E. Ransom. LC 74-20409. (Illus.). 382p. (YA) 1975. 10.95 o.p. (ISBN 0-06-013511-5, HarpT). Har-Row.
Gold Hunter's Handbook. George Sullivan. LC 80-5718. 208p. 1981. 14.95 (ISBN 0-8128-2788-0). Stein & Day.
Gold in Her Hair, No. 2. Anne Neville. (Starlight Romance Ser.). 144p. 1981. pap. 1.75 (ISBN 0-553-14364-6). Bantam.
Gold in the Black Hills. Watson Parker. (Illus.). 1966. 12.95 o.p. (ISBN 0-8061-0723-5). U of Okla Pr.
Gold in the Grass. Margaret Leatherbarrow. Ed. by Bargyla & Gylver Rateaver. LC 75-23179. (Conservation Gardening & Farming Ser: Ser. C). 1975. pap. 10.00 (ISBN 0-9600698-8-7). Rateavers.
Gold Key to Writing Your Life History. Leone N. Western. LC 80-83026. (Illus.). 124p. 1981. pap. 7.95 (ISBN 0-918146-20-8). Peninsula WA.
Gold Lovers. Robert H. Rimmer. Orig. Title: Zolotov Affair. 227p. 1980. Repr. of 1967 ed. 12.50 (ISBN 0-8290-0224-3). Irvington.
Gold Mine in Gold. rev. 3rd ed. Don Bale, Jr. 1975. pap. 5.00 o.p. (ISBN 0-912070-12-9). Bale Bks.
Gold Mine in Gold. 4th, rev. ed. Don Bale, Jr. 1980. pap. 5.00. Bale Bks.
Gold Mine in Your Pocket. rev. 3rd ed. Don Bale, Jr. 1975. pap. 5.00 o.p. (ISBN 0-912070-07-2). Bale Bks.
Gold Mine in Your Pocket. 4th, rev. ed. Don Bale, Jr. 1980. pap. 5.00. Bale Bks.
Gold Mining for Recreation. Ed. by Harvey Neese. (Illus., Orig.). 1981. pap. 4.95 (ISBN 0-87701-182-6). Chronicle Bks.
Gold Mountain. Charlotte Paul. 1977. pap. 2.25 (ISBN 0-441-29749-8). Ace Bks.
Gold of Ancient America. Allen Wardell. Orig. Title: Pre-Columbian Gold in the Museum of Fine Arts, Boston. (Illus.). 1968. 12.00 o.p. (ISBN 0-87846-153-1). Mus Fine Arts Boston.
Gold of Karinthy. Diana LaPoint. 1978. pap. 1.95 (ISBN 0-505-51261-0). Tower Bks.
Gold of the Evening. Marjorie M. Bitker. Orig. Title: Forest Path. 240p. 1975. pap. 1.25 o.p. (ISBN 0-445-00268-9). Popular Lib.
Gold of the Tigers: Selected Later Poems. Jorge L. Borges. Tr. by Alastair Reid. (Bilingual ed.). 1977. 8.95 o.p.; pap. 3.95 (ISBN 0-525-03465-X). Dutton.
Gold Panner's Handbook. Karl Van Mueller. 1981. pap. 4.00 (ISBN 0-89316-621-9); plastic bdg 6.00 (ISBN 0-686-69464-3). Exanimo Pr.
Gold Panning for Profit. Walter J. Robertson. Ed. by William R. Jones. (Illus.). 32p. 1978. pap. 2.50 (ISBN 0-89646-035-5). Outbooks.
Gold Prospecting in Ohio. David J. Gerrick. 84p. 1980. pap. 5.95 (ISBN 0-686-68570-9). Dayton Labs.
Gold Rocker Handbook. Tron Miller. 1980. pap. 4.00 (ISBN 0-89316-619-7); plastic bdg. 6.00. Exanimo Pr.
Gold Rush Country. 4th ed. Sunset Editors. LC 75-180518. (Illus.). 128p. 1972. pap. 3.95 (ISBN 0-376-06255-X, Sunset Bks). Sunset-Lane.
Gold Rush Narrow Gauge. 10.00 (ISBN 0-685-83338-0). Chatham Pub CA.
Gold Strike. Peter McCurtin. (Sundance Ser.: No. 35). 1980. pap. 1.75 (ISBN 0-8439-0819-X, Leisure Bks). Nordon Pubns.
Gold: The World Industry & Canadian Corporate Strategy. Eric Cousoneau & Peter R. Richardson. 192p. (Orig.). 1979. pap. text ed. 10.00x (ISBN 0-88757-013-5, Pub. by Ctr Resource Stud Canada). Renouf.
Gold to Remember. Mary Wibberley. (Harlequin Presents Ser.). 192p. 1981. pap. 1.50 (ISBN 0-373-10432-4, Pub. by Harlequin). PB.
Gold Tried in the Fire. Ballard. pap. 3.00 (ISBN 0-686-12401-4). Church History.
Gold Wagon. Chet Cunningham. 1980. pap. 1.50 (ISBN 0-505-51460-5). Tower Bks.
Gold Was the Mortar: The Economics of Cathedral Building. Henry Kraus. (Illus.). 1979. 35.00 (ISBN 0-7100-8728-4). Routledge & Kegan.
Gold Wings, Blue Sea: A Naval Aviator's Story. Rosario Rausa. 216p. 1981. 15.95 (ISBN 0-87021-219-2). Naval Inst Pr.
Golda Meir Story. rev. ed. Margaret Davidson. (Illus.). 240p. (gr. 3-7). 1981. 9.95 (ISBN 0-684-16877-4). Scribner.
Golda: The Life of Israel's Prime Minister. Peggy Mann. 1973. pap. 1.25 o.s.i. (ISBN 0-671-48132-0). WSP.
Goldberg's Diet Catalog. Larry Goldberg. (Illus.). 1977. 17.50 (ISBN 0-02-544480-8). Macmillan.
Golden Age. Kenneth Grahame. LC 75-32198. (Classics of Children's Literature, 1621-1932: Vol. 59). (Illus.). 1976. Repr. of 1900 ed. PLB 38.00 (ISBN 0-8240-2308-0). Garland Pub.
Golden Age, a Poetical Epistle from Erasmus D---N M.D., to Thomas Beddoes, Repr. Of 1794 Ed. Erasmus Darwin. Ed. by Donald H. Reiman. Bd. with Temple of Nature; or the Origin of Society: A Poem, with Philosophical Notes. Repr. of 1803 ed. LC 75-31195. (Romantic Context Ser.: Poetry 1789-1830: Vol. 47). 1979. lib. bdg. 47.00 (ISBN 0-8240-2146-0). Garland Pub.
Golden Age: Dutch Seventeenth Century Portraiture. William H. Wilson. LC 80-53473. (Illus.). 175p. (Orig.). 1980. pap. 8.00 (ISBN 0-916758-03-6). Ringling Mus Art.
Golden Age of American History. Ed. by Frank Freidel. LC 59-12230. (Golden Age Ser). 8.50 o.s.i. (ISBN 0-8076-0091-1). Braziller.
Golden Age of Brazil, 1695-1750: Growing Pains of a Colonial Society. C. R. Boxer. 1962. 17.50x (ISBN 0-520-00162-1); pap. 7.50x (ISBN 0-520-01550-9, CAMPUS78). U of Cal Pr.
Golden Age of Comic Books, 1937-1945. Richard O'Brien. (Orig.). 1977. pap. 6.95 o.p. (ISBN 0-345-25535-6). Ballantine.
Golden Age of Melodrama. Intro. by Michael Kilgarriff. 499p. 1975. 14.95 o.p. (ISBN 0-8238-0190-X). Plays.
Golden Age of Opera. Herman Klein. (Music Reprint Ser.). 1979. 29.50 (ISBN 0-306-70840-X). Da Capo.
Golden Age of Television. Max Wilk. 1976. 10.00 o.p. (ISBN 0-440-02950-3). Delacorte.
Golden Age of the American Poster: A Concise Edition of the American Poster Renaissance. Victor Margolin. 1976. pap. 6.95 o.p. (ISBN 0-345-25129-6). Ballantine.
Golden Age of the Luxury Car: An Anthology of Articles & Photographs from Autobody, 1927-1931. George Hildebrand. (Illus., Orig.). 1980. pap. 6.00 (ISBN 0-486-23984-5). Dover.
Golden Age of Tramways. new ed. Charles Klapper. 1974. 13.50 o.p. (ISBN 0-7153-6458-8). David & Charles.
Golden Age of Yachting. Jack Grout. Tr. by John Chamier. LC 80-51188. Orig. Title: C'etait Au Temps Des Yachtsmen. (Illus.). 240p. (Fr.). Date not set. 29.95 (ISBN 0-86565-006-3). Vendome. Postponed.
Golden Alphabet (on Psalm 119) C. H. Spurgeon. pap. 3.95 (ISBN 0-686-09094-2). Pilgrim Pubns.
Golden Anni-Verse-Ary. Sarah H. Johnston. 1981. 5.95 (ISBN 0-533-04805-2). Vantage.
Golden Aphroditis. John Grange. LC 37-5556. 1978. Repr. of 1577 ed. 22.00 (ISBN 0-8201-1177-5). Schol Facsimiles.
Golden Apple. (Sharazad Stories Ser.). (Illus., Arabic.). pap. 3.50 (ISBN 0-686-53110-8). Intl Bk Ctr.
Golden Apple: Illuminatus 2. Robert J. Shea & Robert A. Wilson. 1975. pap. 1.95 o.s.i. (ISBN 0-440-14691-7). Dell.
Golden Arithmetization. Nicholas C. Eliopoulos. 403p. (Orig.). 1980. pap. text ed. 30.00x (ISBN 0-9505396-0-3). Phystiklakis & Eliopoulos.
Golden Arrow. Bessie H. Heck. (Illus.). 160p. (gr. 5-9). 1981. 8.95 (ISBN 0-684-16882-0). Scribner.
Golden Ass. Lucius Apuleius. Ed. by Harry C. Schnur. Tr. by William Adlington. 1962. pap. 0.95 o.s.i. (ISBN 0-02-048240-X, Collier). Macmillan.
Golden Berg Who Wouldn't Dance. William Stevenson. LC 80-7943. 576p. 1980. 8.95 (ISBN 0-15-135338-7). HarBraceJ.
Golden Bible Atlas. Samuel Terrien. (Illus.). (gr. 9 up). 1957. 7.95 (ISBN 0-307-15749-0, Golden Pr); PLB 10.69 o.p. (ISBN 0-307-65749-3). Western Pub.
Golden Bird & Other Fairy Tales. Grimm Brothers. Tr. by Randall Jarrell. (Illus.). (gr. k-3). 1963. 4.50 o.s.i. (ISBN 0-02-737280-4). Macmillan.
Golden Book of Buccaneers. (gr. 3-7). Date not set. 6.95 (ISBN 0-307-16811-5, Golden Pr). Western Pub.
Golden Book of Fun & Nonsense. Ed. by Louis Untermeyer. (Illus.). (gr. 4-9). 1970. PLB 9.15 o.p. (ISBN 0-307-66507-0, Golden Pr). Western Pub.
Golden Book of Three Hundred Sixty-Five Stories. Kathryn Jackson. 1955. 6.95 (ISBN 0-307-15557-9, Golden Pr); PLB 12.23 o.p. (ISBN 0-307-65575-X). Western Pub.
Golden Booke of the Leaden Gods, Repr. Of 1577 Ed. Stephen Batman. Bd. with Third Part of the Countess of Pembroke's Yvychurch. Abraham Fraunce. Repr. of 1592 ed; Fountaine of Ancient Fiction. Richard Lynche. Repr. of 1599 ed. LC 75-27856. (Renaissance & the Gods Ser.: Vol. 13). (Illus.). 1976. lib. bdg. 73.00 (ISBN 0-8240-2062-6). Garland Pub.
Golden Bough. abr ed. James G. Frazer. 19.95 (ISBN 0-02-095560-X); pap. 8.95 (ISBN 0-685-15196-4). Macmillan.
Golden Bough, 13 vols. James G. Frazer. 5380p. 1980. Repr. of 1890 ed. Set. 375.00 (ISBN 0-312-33215-7). St Martin.
Golden Bowl. Henry James. (Illus.). 592p. 1973. pap. 1.50 o.p. (ISBN 0-445-08227-5). Popular Lib.
Golden Bowl. Frederick F. Manfred. LC 75-40838. 240p. 1976. pap. 5.95 (ISBN 0-8263-0407-9). U of NM Pr.
Golden Bowl Be Broken: Peasant Life in Four Cultures. Richard Critchfield. LC 73-77855. (Midland Bks.: No. 187). (Illus.). 320p. 1974. 12.50x (ISBN 0-253-13260-6). Ind U Pr.
Golden Bull. Nick Carter. (Nick Carter Ser.). 224p. (Orig.). 1981. pap. 2.25 (ISBN 0-441-29782-X). Charter Bks.
Golden Buttons. Ed. by Alma Gilleo. LC 74-734827. (Fairy Tales of the Brothers Grimm Cassette Bks). (Illus.). 16p. (ps). 1976. pap. 21.00 10 bks. & one cassette (ISBN 0-89290-008-3); cassette incl. (ISBN 0-685-70098-4). Soc for Visual.
Golden Century of Italian Opera: From Rossini to Puccini. William Weaver. (Illus.). 256p. 1980. 27.50 (ISBN 0-500-01240-7). Thames Hudson.
Golden Child. Penelope Fitzgerald. LC 77-93900. 1978. 7.95 o.p. (ISBN 0-684-15645-8, ScribT). Scribner.

Golden Circle: A Book of Months. Hal Borland. LC 77-23560. (Illus.). (gr. 5 up). 1977. 10.95 (ISBN 0-690-03803-8, TYC-J). T Y Crowell.
Golden Codgers: Biographical Speculations. Richard Ellmann. LC 73-86067. 208p. 1976. pap. 4.95 (ISBN 0-19-519845-X, 465, GB). Oxford U Pr.
Golden Days of Greece. Oliver Coolidge. LC 68-21599. (Illus.). (gr. 5 up). 1968. 9.95 (ISBN 0-690-33473-7, TYC-J). T Y Crowell.
Golden Days of San Simeon. Ken Murray. LC 73-130962. 1971. 14.95 (ISBN 0-385-04632-4). Doubleday.
Golden Dead. Charles R. Pike. LC 80-69219. (Jubal Cade Westerns Ser.). 128p. 1981. pap. 2.95 (ISBN 0-87754-236-8). Chelsea Hse.
Golden Door: Italian & Jewish Immigrant Mobility in New York City, 1880-1915. Thomas Kessner. 1977. text ed. 14.95 (ISBN 0-19-502116-9); pap. 4.95 (ISBN 0-19-502161-4). Oxford U Pr.
Golden Dozen. Jessyca R. Gaver. 1976. pap. 1.25 o.p. (ISBN 0-685-69151-9, LB348ZK, Leisure Bks). Nordon Pubns.
Golden Dragon: Alfred the Great & His Times. Alfred J. Mapp, Jr. LC 74-8983. 1974. 10.95 o.p. (ISBN 0-87548-293-7). Open Court.
Golden Dream: Surburbia in the 1970's. Stephen Birmingham. LC 76-57891. 1978. 10.00 o.s.i. (ISBN 0-06-010334-5, HarpT). Har-Row.
Golden Dreams. Gwen Briwtow. 224p. 1980. 11.50 (ISBN 0-686-62597-8). Lippincott.
Golden Egg Book. Margaret W. Brown. (Illus.). 32p. (ps-1). 1976. 2.95 (ISBN 0-307-12045-7, Golden Pr); PLB 7.62 (ISBN 0-307-60462-4). Western Pub.
Golden Egg Book. Margaret W. Brown. (Illus.). (ps-2). 1947. PLB 5.00 (ISBN 0-307-60456-X, Golden Pr). Western Pub.
Golden Fancy. Jennifer Blake. 1980. pap. 2.75 (ISBN 0-449-14369-4, GM). Fawcett.
Golden Fleece. Hughie Call. LC 80-38781. (Illus.). 1981. 17.95x (ISBN 0-8032-1413-8, Bison); pap. 5.25 (ISBN 0-8032-6308-2, BB 760, Bison). U of Nebr Pr.
Golden Fleece & the Heroes Who Lived Before Achilles. Padraic Colum. (Illus.). (gr. 4-6). 1962. 9.95 (ISBN 0-02-723620-X). Macmillan.
Golden Fruits. Nathalie Sarraute. Tr. by Maria Jolas from Fr. 1980. 11.95 (ISBN 0-7145-0258-8); pap. 4.95 (ISBN 0-7145-0259-6). Riverrun NY.
Golden Galatea. Florence Stevenson. (Orig.). 1979. pap. 2.25 o.s.i. (ISBN 0-515-04338-9). Jove Pubns.
Golden Gate. Alistair MacLean. 1977. pap. 2.50 (ISBN 0-449-23177-1, Crest). Fawcett.
Golden Gate Bridge! Elaine Ratner & Tim Ware. LC 80-52139. (Illus.). 1981. 18.50 (ISBN 0-916290-12-3); pap. 10.95. Squarebooks.
Golden Goddess of El Dorado. Roberta Vaughn. (Orig.). 1980. pap. write for info. (ISBN 0-671-41266-3). PB.
Golden Gondola. Barbara Cartland. (Barbara Cartland Ser.). (Orig.). pap. 1.75 (ISBN 0-515-05509-3). Jove Pubns.
Golden Hamsters. Herbert S. Zim. (Illus.). (gr. 3-7). 1951. 6.48 (ISBN 0-688-31353-1). Morrow.
Golden Happy Birthday Book. Barbara S Hazen. (Illus.). 1976. 4.95 (ISBN 0-307-16809-3, Golden Pr); PLB 10.69 o.p. (ISBN 0-307-66809-6). Western Pub.
Golden Harvest. White Eagle. 1958. 3.50 (ISBN 0-85487-017-2). De Vorss.
Golden Honeycomb. Kamala Markandaya. LC 76-27642. 1977. 10.00 o.s.i. (ISBN 0-690-01208-X, TYC-T). T Y Crowell.
Golden Horseshoe. Elizabeth Coatsworth. LC 35-18415. (Illus.). (gr. 4-6). 1968. Repr. of 1935 ed. 4.95g o.s.i. (ISBN 0-02-720590-8). Macmillan.
Golden Idol. Lisa Eisenberg. LC 79-52655. (Laura Brewster Mysteries Ser.). (Illus.). 64p. (gr. 4 up). Date not set. PLB 7.95 (ISBN 0-516-02207-5). Childrens.
Golden Key: A Study of the Fiction of George MacDonald. Robert L. Wolff. 1961. 34.50x (ISBN 0-686-51395-9). Elliots Bks.
Golden Key & Other Fantasy Stories. George MacDonald. Ed. by Glenn G. Sadler. (Fantasy Stories of George MacDonald Ser.). 176p. 1980. pap. 2.95 (ISBN 0-8028-1859-5). Eerdmans.
Golden Khersonese. Paul Wheatley. LC 73-1841. (Illus.). 388p. 1973. Repr. of 1961 ed. lib. bdg. 33.25x (ISBN 0-8371-6808-2, WHGH). Greenwood.
Golden Land. Ed. by James Reeves. (gr. 4 up). 1963. 10.95 o.p. (ISBN 0-582-15284-4). Dufour.
Golden Lasso. Fern Michaels. 192p. (Orig.). 1980. pap. 1.50 (ISBN 0-671-57032-3). S&S.
Golden Latin Artistry. L. P. Wilkinson. 1963. 42.00 (ISBN 0-521-06807-X). Cambridge U Pr.
Golden Leprechaun. Nancy J. Brooks. 124p. (gr. 3-6). 1980. 5.95 (ISBN 0-8059-2767-0). Dorrance.
Golden Locket. Juliana Davison. 1978. pap. 1.75 o.p. (ISBN 0-425-03769-X, Medallion). Berkley Pub.
Golden Lotus. Janet L. Roberts. (Orig.). 1981. pap. 2.50 (ISBN 0-446-81997-2). Warner Bks.
Golden Lotus: A Translation of the Chinese Novel, Chin P'ing Mei, 4 vols. Tr. by Clement Egerton from Chinese. 1572p. 1972. Set. 80.00 (ISBN 0-7100-7349-6); 22.00 ea. Routledge & Kegan.
Golden Mother Goose. Illus. by Alice Provensen & Martin Provensen. (Illus.). 1976. 2.95 o.p. (ISBN 0-307-13766-X, Golden Pr); PLB 7.62 o.p. (ISBN 0-307-63766-2). Western Pub.
Golden Nuggets. Estelle Y. Flota. LC 80-51806. 60p. 1981. 5.95 (ISBN 0-533-04721-8). Vantage.
Golden Nuggets, Nineteen Seventy-Two. rev. ed. (Illus.). 1977. 8.95 (ISBN 0-916700-00-3); perfect bdg. 5.95 (ISBN 0-685-93617-1). Epiphany Pr.
Golden Ones. Frank Slaughter. 1976. Repr. of 1957 ed. lib. bdg. 12.45 (ISBN 0-89190-531-6). Am Repr-Rivercity Pr.
Golden Paths. Roger Elwood. 1978. pap. 1.50 o.s.i. (ISBN 0-515-04499-7). Jove Pubns.
Golden Peaches of Samarkand: A Study of T'ang Exotics. Edward H. Schafer. 1981. 35.00x (ISBN 0-520-01144-9). U of Cal Pr.
Golden People. Roy Sparkia. 1976. pap. 1.95 o.s.i. (ISBN 0-515-03974-8). Jove Pubns.
Golden Pharaoh. Philipp Vandenberg. (Illus.). 288p. 1981. 13.95 (ISBN 0-02-621580-2). Macmillan.
Golden Picture Dictionary: A Beginning Dictionary of More Than 2500 Words. Lucille Ogle & Tina Thoburn. (Illus.). (gr. k-3). 1976. PLB 12.23 o.p. (ISBN 0-307-67861-X, Golden Pr); pap. 3.95 o.p. (ISBN 0-307-15991-4); 5.95 (ISBN 0-307-17861-7). Western Pub.
Golden Praises. Jo Petty. LC 80-944. 192p. 1981. 7.95 (ISBN 0-385-15892-0, Galilee). Doubleday.
Golden Precepts of Esotericism. 3rd, rev. ed. G. De Purucker. LC 78-74257. 1979. 5.00 (ISBN 0-911500-85-5); pap. 3.00 (ISBN 0-911500-86-3). Theos U Pr.
Golden Prize. Illus. by Cliff Schule. (Illus.). (gr. 3 up). 1979. pap. 1.25 (ISBN 0-307-21508-3, Golden Pr). Western Pub.
Golden Puma. Margaret Way. (Harlequin Romances Ser.). 192p. 1980. pap. 1.25 o.p. (ISBN 0-373-02357-X, Pub. by Harlequin). PB.
Golden Rendezvous. Alistair MacLean. 1978. pap. 2.25 (ISBN 0-449-23624-2, Crest). Fawcett.
Golden Republicanism: The Crusade for Hard Money. Clarence A. Stern. 1964. pap. 1.50 (ISBN 0-9600116-1-7). Stern.
Golden Retriever: Its Care & Training. Joan Tudor. (Illus.). 100p. 1980. 3.95 (ISBN 0-903264-33-1, 4945-6, Pub. by K & R Bks England). Arco.
Golden Retrievers. Joan Gill. Ed. by Christina Foyle. (Foyles Handbks). 1973. 3.95 (ISBN 0-685-55801-0). Palmetto Pub.
Golden Retrievers. James Walsh & Phyllis A. Walsh. (Illus.). 128p. 1980. 2.95 (ISBN 0-87666-678-0, KW 067). TFH Pubns.
Golden River to Golden Road: Society, Culture & Change in the Middle East. 3rd rev. ed. Raphael Patai. LC 70-84742. 1969. 17.00x (ISBN 0-8122-7289-7). U of Pa Pr.
Golden Road to Samarkand. Tapati Mookerji. 5.00 (ISBN 0-89253-526-1). Ind-US Inc.
Golden Serpent. Walter D. Myers. (Illus.). 40p. (gr. 1-4). 1980. 9.95 (ISBN 0-670-34445-1). Viking Pr.
Golden Slave. Poul Anderson. 256p. (Orig.). 1980. pap. 2.25 (ISBN 0-89083-651-5). Zebra.
Golden Sleepy Book. Margaret W. Brown. (Illus.). (ps-2). 1971. PLB 7.15 o.p. (ISBN 0-307-62038-7, Golden Pr). Western Pub.
Golden Slippers: An Anthology of Negro Poetry. Ed. by Arna Bontemps. (Illus.). 1941. 10.00 (ISBN 0-06-010395-7, HarpT); PLB 8.97 o.s.i. (ISBN 0-06-010404-X). Har-Row.
Golden Song Book. Katharine T. Wessells. (Illus.). (gr. 1-2). 1945. PLB 9.15 o.p. (ISBN 0-307-65708-6, Golden Pr). Western Pub.
Golden Sovereigns. Jocelyn Carew. 408p. (Orig.). 1980. pap. 2.50 (ISBN 0-380-00845-9, 47381). Avon.
Golden Spinning Wheel. Lisl Weil. LC 69-20614. (Illus.). (gr. k-3). 1969. 4.95g o.s.i. (ISBN 0-686-66482-5). Macmillan.
Golden Spy. Charles Gildon. LC 77-170519. (Foundations of the Novel Ser.: Vol. 14). lib. bdg. 50.00 (ISBN 0-8240-0526-0). Garland Pub.
Golden Stallion. Lytle Shannon. (YA) 1972. 5.95 (ISBN 0-685-02720-1, Avalon). Bouregy.
Golden State: A History of California. 2nd ed. Andrew F. Rolle & John S. Gaines. LC 79-84210. (Illus.). 1979. text ed. 12.95x (ISBN 0-88295-796-1); pap. text ed. 7.95x (ISBN 0-88295-797-X). AHM Pub.
Golden State Rails. Wesley Fox. (Illus.). 76p. 1980. pap. 8.95 (ISBN 0-9604122-0-4). W Fox.
Golden Staters. Lee D. Willoughby. 1980. pap. 2.75 (ISBN 0-440-03020-X). Dell.
Golden Stick. Gary Paulsen. LC 76-47670. (Sports Fiction Ser.). (gr. 5-10). 1977. 7.75 (ISBN 0-8172-0800-3). Raintree Pubs.
Golden Story. Daisy Aldan. 6.95 (ISBN 0-913152-49-8). Green Hill.
Golden Sword. Janet E. Morris. 384p. 1981. pap. 2.50 (ISBN 0-553-14846-X). Bantam.
Golden Tales from Long Ago, 3 vols. Ernest Nister. LC 80-7614. (Illus., 24p. ea.). (gr. 3-12). 1980. Set. 5.95 (ISBN 0-440-03015-3). Delacorte.
Golden Temple Cookbook. Yogi Bhajan. LC 78-52267. (Orig.). 1979. pap. 5.95 (ISBN 0-8015-3067-9, Hawthorn). Dutton.
Golden Thread. Philippa Burrell. 350p. 1980. 29.75x (ISBN 0-7050-0067-2, Pub. by Skilton & Shaw England). State Mutual Bk.
Golden Thread. Ken Butti & John Perlin. LC 79-25095. (Illus.). 1980. 15.95 (ISBN 0-917352-07-6); pap. 9.95 (ISBN 0-917352-08-4). Cheshire.
Golden Thread. Jean Nash. (Orig.). 1980. pap. 2.25 (ISBN 0-505-51483-4). Tower Bks.
Golden Tide. Sondra Stanford. 192p. (Orig.). 1980. pap. 1.50 (ISBN 0-671-57006-4). S&S.
Golden Trade of the Moors. 2nd ed. Edward W. Bovill & Robin Hallet. 1968. 13.50x (ISBN 0-19-215630-6); pap. 6.95x (ISBN 0-19-285045-8). Oxford U Pr.
Golden Tradition. Ed. & tr. by Ahmed Ali. (Studies in Oriental Culture). 350p. 1973. 20.00x (ISBN 0-231-03687-6); pap. 7.50x (ISBN 0-231-03688-4). Columbia U Pr.
Golden Treasury of Chinese Poetry: 121 Classical Poems. Tr. by John A. Turner. LC 75-42790. (Renditions). 352p. 1976. 12.50 (ISBN 0-295-95506-6). U of Wash Pr.
Golden Treasury of Scottish Poetry. Ed. by H. MacDiarmid. LC 77-88076. (Granger Poetry Library). 1976. Repr. of 1940 ed. 29.50x (ISBN 0-89609-027-2). Granger Bk.
Golden Treasury of Songs & Lyrics. 8th ed. Francis T. Palgrave. (gr. 9 up). 1944. 6.95 o.s.i. (ISBN 0-02-594410-X). Macmillan.
Golden Treasury of the Best Songs & Lyrical Poems in the English Language. 5th ed. Ed. by Francis T. Palgrave. (Oxford Standard Authors Ser.). (gr. 5-9). 1964. 27.00 (ISBN 0-19-254156-0). Oxford U Pr.
Golden Unicorn. Phyllis A. Whitney. 320p. 1977. pap. 2.25 (ISBN 0-449-23104-6, Crest). Fawcett.
Golden Warrior. Hope Muntz. 1978. pap. 1.95 o.p. (ISBN 0-445-04315-6). Popular Lib.
Golden Wings, & Other Stories. William Morris. Ed. by R. Reginald & Douglas Menville. LC 80-19101. (Newcastle Forgotten Fantasy Library: Vol. 8). 169p. 1980. Repr. of 1976 ed. lib. bdg. 9.95x (ISBN 0-89370-507-1). Borgo Pr.
Golden Womb of the Sun (Rig Veda) Tr. by P. Lal from Sanskrit. 40p. 1973. 6.75 (ISBN 0-89253-787-6); pap. text ed. 4.80 (ISBN 0-88253-305-3). Ind-US Inc.
Golden Years of Clyde Steamers. A. J. Paterson. LC 79-56430. (Illus.). 1979. 19.95 (ISBN 0-7153-4290-8). David & Charles.
Golden Years of the Hutterites. Leonard Gross. LC 80-10711. (Studies in Anabaptist & Mennonite History Ser.: Vol. 23). 1980. 12.95x (ISBN 0-8361-1227-X). Herald Pr.
Goldenberg Who Couldn't Dance. Everett Greenbaum. LC 79-3353. 168p. 1980. 8.95 (ISBN 0-15-136174-6). HarBraceJ.
Goldene Topf ein Marchen Aus der Neuen Zeit. E. T. Hoffmann. Ed. by W. F. Mainland. (Blackwell's German Text Ser.). 1967. pap. 9.95x (ISBN 0-631-01310-5, Pub. by Basil Blackwell). Biblio Dist.
Goldeneye. Malcolm Macdonald. LC 80-23235. (Illus.). 544p. 1981. 15.00 (ISBN 0-394-51118-2). Knopf.
Goldengrove. Darryl Ponicsan. LC 78-163586. 1971. 5.95 o.p. (ISBN 0-440-01971-0). D Ponicsan.
Goldenrod. Herbert Harker. pap. 1.95 (ISBN 0-451-08557-4, J8557, Sig). NAL.
Goldfinger. Ian Fleming. 1966. 3.95 o.s.i. (ISBN 0-02-539000-7). Macmillan.
Goldfinger. Ian Fleming. (James Bond Ser.). 272p. (Orig.). 1980. pap. 2.25 (ISBN 0-515-05839-4). Jove Pubns.
Goldfish. Anthony Evans. Ed. by Christina Foyle. (Foyle's Handbks). 1973. 3.95 (ISBN 0-685-55819-3). Palmetto Pub.
Goldfish. rev. ed. George F. Hervey & Jack Hems. (Illus.). 284p. 1981. pap. 9.50 (ISBN 0-571-11611-6, Pub. by Faber & Faber). Merrimack Bk Serv.
Goldfish. Ed. by Paul R. Paradise. (Illus.). 1979. 2.95 (ISBN 0-87666-511-3, KW-014). TFH Pubns.
Goldfish. Herbert S. Zim. (Illus.). (gr. 3-7). 1947. PLB 6.48 (ISBN 0-688-31340-X). Morrow.
Goldfish: Their Care & Breeding. Coborn. (Illus.). 96p. 1981. 3.95 (ISBN 0-903264-24-2, 5215-5, Pub. by K & R Bks England). Arco.
Goldie the Dollmaker. rev. ed. M. B. Goffstein. (Illus.). 64p. (ps-3). 1980. 6.95 (ISBN 0-374-32739-4). FS&G.
Goldilocks & the Three Bears. (Illus.). Arabic 2.50x (ISBN 0-685-82827-1). Intl Bk Ctr.
Goldilocks & the Three Bears. Ed. by Matt H. Newman. (Children's Stories Bk). (Illus.). 18p. (ps). 1980. pap. 22.00 ten bks & one cass. (ISBN 0-89290-085-7, BC13-2). Soc for Visual.
Goldilocks & the Three Bears. Illus. by Lilian Obligado. (Golden Storytime Bk. for Learning). 24p. (gr. 3-6). 1980. 1.50 (ISBN 0-307-11980-7); PLB 6.08 s&l (ISBN 0-307-61980-X). Western Pub.
Goldilocks & the Three Bears: Notated in Sutton Movement Shorthand. Valerie J. Sutton & Betty Beekman. (Illus.). 1978. pap. text ed. 3.00x (ISBN 0-914336-34-7). Move Short Soc.
Goldmaker's House. Irmelin S. Lilius. Tr. by Marianne Helweg from Swedish. LC 79-2104. (gr. 5 up). 1980. 7.95 (ISBN 0-440-04200-3, Sey Lawr); PLB 7.45 (ISBN 0-440-04201-1). Delacorte.
Goldmakers: Ten Thousand Years of Alchemy. Kurt K. Doberer. Tr. by E. W. Dickes. LC 79-8605. Repr. of 1948 ed. 29.50 (ISBN 0-404-18465-0). AMS Pr.
Goldoni: La Locandiera. Ed. by Vincent Luciani. 1980. pap. 4.95 (ISBN 0-913298-18-2). S F Vanni.
Gold's Gym Book of Strength Training for the Dedicated Athlete. Ken Sprague. LC 78-65364. (Illus.). 1979. 13.50 o.p. (ISBN 0-312-90557-2); pap. 7.95 o.p. (ISBN 0-312-90556-4). St Martin.
Goldschmiede Rheinland-Westfalens. Daten. Zeichen. Werke, 2 vols. Wolfgang Scheffler. LC 72-81568. 1200p. 1973. 267.65x (ISBN 3-11-003842-0). De Gruyter.
Goldsmiths and Silversmiths of England. Christopher Lever. LC 75-314072. (Illus.). 1975. pap. text ed. 15.75x (ISBN 0-09-121220-0). Humanities.
Goldsworthy Lowes Dickinson. E. M. Forster. Ed. by Oliver Stallybrass. (Abinger Edition of E. M. Forster Ser.). 1978. text ed. 17.75x (ISBN 0-8419-5810-6). Holmes & Meier.
Goldwyn. Arthur Marx. 1977 pap. 1.95 o.p. (ISBN 0-345-25555-0). Ballantine.
Goldyhall. Natalie Babbit. 1976. pap. 1.25 (30163, Camelot). Avon.
Golem. Alfred Bester. 1981. pap. 2.50 (ISBN 0-671-82047-8). PB.
Golem: Mystical Tales of the Ghetto. Chayim Bloch. LC 75-183055. 288p. 1972. pap. 2.95 (ISBN 0-8334-1726-6). Steinerbks.
Golem of Prague. Gershon Winkler. (Illus.). 1980. 12.95 (ISBN 0-910818-24-X); pap. 9.95 (ISBN 0-910818-25-8). Judaica Pr.
Golf. Pat Bradley. (Burns Sports Ser.). 156p. Date not set. pap. 4.95 o.p. (ISBN 0-695-81569-5). Follett.
Golf. LC 19-600. (Illus.). 72p. 1977. pap. 0.70x (ISBN 0-8395-3397-7). BSA.
Golf. John Morgan. (Sports Library). (Illus.). 1979. 12.95 (ISBN 0-8069-9116-X); pap. 6.95 (ISBN 0-8069-9118-6). Sterling.
Golf. Robert Scharff. (Quick & Easy Ser). (Orig.). 1968. pap. 2.95 o.s.i. (ISBN 0-02-081500-X, Collier). Macmillan.
Golf. Gary Wiren. (Sport Ser). (Illus.). (gr. 10 up). 1971. text ed. 4.95 ref. ed. o.p. (ISBN 0-13-358028-8); pap. 3.95 ref. ed. (ISBN 0-13-358010-5). P-H.
Golf: A Guide to Information Sources. Ed. by Joseph S. Murdoch & Janet Seagle. LC 79-23270. (Sports, Games & Pastimes Information Guide Ser.: Vol. 7). 1979. 30.00 (ISBN 0-8103-1457-6). Gale.
Golf: A Positive Approach. Carol Johnson & Ann Johnstone. LC 74-24619. 1975. pap. text ed. 6.75 (ISBN 0-201-03416-6). A-W.
Golf Book. Michael Bartlett. (Illus.). 1980. 22.95 (ISBN 0-87795-297-3) (ISBN 0-686-64654-1). Arbor Hse.
Golf Course Developments. Rees L. Jones & Guy L. Rando. LC 73-86554. (Technical Bulletin Ser.: No. 70). (Illus.). 112p. 1974. pap. 12.00 (ISBN 0-87420-070-9). Urban Land.
Golf Course Supervisor. Jack Rudman. (Career Examination Ser.: C-2774). (Cloth bdg. avail. on request). 1980. pap. 12.00 (ISBN 0-8373-2774-1). Natl Learning.
Golf Diary. James Wagenvoord. (Illus.). 160p. 1981. 6.95 (ISBN 0-312-33806-6). St Martin.
Golf Explained: How to Take Advantage of the Rules. Peter Dobereiner. LC 76-51177. 9.95 (ISBN 0-8069-4110-3); lib. bdg. 9.29 (ISBN 0-8069-4111-1); PLB write for info. Sterling.
Golf for the Connoisseur: A Golfing Anthology. Ed. by Michael Hobbs. (Illus.). 256p. 1980. 30.00 (ISBN 0-7134-1397-2, Pub. by Batsford England). David & Charles.
Golf Is Madness. Ted Barnett. LC 77-80365. (Illus.). 128p. 1977. 5.95 (ISBN 0-671-22974-5). Golf Digest.
Golf Made Easy. James Haber LC 73-20980. 1974. pap. 3.50 o.p. (ISBN 0-684-13791-7, SL517, ScribT). Scribner.

Golf Magazine's Great Golf Courses You Can Play. Golf Magazine Editors. LC 72-2208. (Illus.). 450p. 1973. 10.00 o.p. (ISBN 0-684-13431-4). Scribner.

Golf Magazine's Tips from the Teaching Pros. Golf Magazine Editors. LC 69-15310. (Illus.). 1969. 11.95 o.s.i. (ISBN 0-06-110779-4, HarpT). Har-Row.

Golf Quiz. Herbert W. Wind. LC 80-66690. (Illus.). 192p. (Orig.). 1980. pap. 8.95 (ISBN 0-914178-41-5, 41416-X). Golf Digest.

Golf Techniques: How to Improve Your Game. Parker Smith. LC 73-3048. (Concise Guide Ser). (Illus.). (gr. 5 up). 1973. PLB 4.90 o.p. (ISBN 0-531-02627-2). Watts.

Golfer's Bible. Frank Kenyon Allen et al. LC 68-11788. 1968. pap. 3.50 (ISBN 0-385-01402-3). Doubleday.

Golfing for Cats. Alan Coren. LC 75-21688. 176p. 1976. 7.95 o.p. (ISBN 0-312-33810-4). St Martin.

Golgi Centennial Symposium: Perspectives in Neurobiology. Golgi Centennial Symposium, September 1973. Ed. by Maurizo Santini. LC 74-21985. 1975. 68.50 (ISBN 0-911216-80-4). Raven.

Goliath. J. Weatherby. 288p. (Orig.). 1981. pap. 2.75 (ISBN 0-553-14593-2). Bantam.

Goliath: The Wilt Chamberlain Story. Bill Libby. LC 76-50104. 1977. 8.95 (ISBN 0-396-07392-1). Dodd.

Goliath to Gog: A Gallery of Giants from Fable, Fact, Fiction & Folklore. Sam Goldstein. (Odd Books for Odd Moments Ser.). (Illus.). 72p. (Orig.). 1980. pap. 3.95 (ISBN 0-938338-00-5). Winds World Pr.

Gollywhopper Egg. Anne Rockwell. LC 73-6042. (Ready-to-Read Ser). (Illus.). 64p. (gr. 1-4). 1974. 8.95 (ISBN 0-02-777470-8). Macmillan.

Golyi God. Boris Pil'Niak. 79p. (Orig., Rus.). 1980. 12.00 o.p. (ISBN 0-88233-452-2); pap. 5.00 (ISBN 0-88233-453-0). Ardis Pubs.

Gomez Story. W. C. Chalk. pap. text ed. 2.75x o.p. (ISBN 0-435-11224-4). Heinemann Ed.

Gompers in Canada: A Study in American Continentalism Before the First World War. Robert H. Babcock. LC 74-78507. 1974. pap. 6.50 (ISBN 0-8020-6242-3). U of Toronto Pr.

Goncourt Brothers. Richard B. Grant. (World Authors Ser.: France: No. 183). lib. bdg. 10.95 (ISBN 0-8057-2384-6). Twayne.

Gondal's Queen: A Novel in Verse. Emily J. Bronte. Ed. by Fannie E. Ratchford. LC 54-10044. (Illus.). 1977. pap. text ed. 9.95x o.p. (ISBN 0-292-72711-9). U of Tex Pr.

Gonds of Andhra Pradesh: Tradition & Change in an Indian Tribe. Christoph Von Furerhaimendorf. (Illus.). 569p. 1981. 40.00x (ISBN 0-7069-0718-3). Advent Bk.

Gone Away. Ruth Tomalin. LC 79-670253. (gr. 4 up). 1979. 10.95 (ISBN 0-571-11342-7, Pub. by Faber & Faber). Merrimack Bk Serv.

Gone Crazy & Back Again: The Rise & Fall of the Rolling Stone Generation. Robert S. Anson. LC 80-5448. 384p. 1981. 14.95 (ISBN 0-385-13114-3). Doubleday.

Gone Is Shadow's Child. J. G. Foy. 1972. pap. 1.25 (ISBN 0-89129-205-5). Jove Pubns.

Gone Is Shadow's Child. Jessie G. Foy. 1976. pap. 1.25 (ISBN 0-89129-205-5). Jove Pubns.

Gone Sailing. Helen Adam. LC 80-10659. (Illus., Orig.). 1980. 20.00 (ISBN 0-915124-30-0, Bookslinger; Small Press Distribution); pap. 5.00 (ISBN 0-915124-29-7). Toothpaste.

Gone to Earth. Mary Webb. 288p. 1979. o. p. 18.00x (ISBN 0-686-28504-2, Pub. by Duckworth); pap. 4.50x (ISBN 0-7156-1339-1). Biblio Dist.

Gone to Texas. Richard Wormser. (Illus.). (gr. 5-9). 1970. 8.25 (ISBN 0-688-21354-5). Morrow.

Gone to the Zoo. Lucy Conley. 1979. 5.10 (ISBN 0-686-25258-6). Rod & Staff.

Gone with a Wang. 1980. 8.95 (ISBN 0-440-02790-X). Delacorte.

Gone with the Wind. Margaret Mitchell. (gr. 9 up). 1936. 12.95 (ISBN 0-02-585390-2); 2 vol. lg. print ed. 13.95 (ISBN 0-02-489440-0); anniversary ed. 19.96 (ISBN 0-02-585350-3). Macmillan.

Gone with the Wind. Margaret Mitchell. 1974. pap. 3.50 (ISBN 0-380-00109-8, 49841). Avon.

Gone with the Wind. Margaret Mitchell. 1974. pap. 4.95 (ISBN 0-380-00759-2, 30445). Avon.

Gonzalo de Berceo. John E. Keller. (World Authors Ser.: Spain: No. 187). lib. bdg. 10.95 (ISBN 0-8057-2144-4). Twayne.

Goobersville Breakdown. Robert Lieberman. (Illus.). 221p. 1979. 10.95 (ISBN 0-686-60866-6); pap. 4.95 (ISBN 0-933124-00-7). Gamma Bks.

Good Americans: The Loyalists in the American Revolution. Wallace Brown. LC 69-11500. 1969. pap. 4.95 (ISBN 0-688-27754-3). Morrow.

Good & Bad Feelings. Mark Stein. LC 75-28353. (Illus.). 96p. (gr. 3-7). 1976. 6.25 o.p. (ISBN 0-688-22061-4); PLB 6.48 (ISBN 0-688-32061-9). Morrow.

Good & Evil: A New Direction. Richard Taylor. 1970. 9.95 (ISBN 0-02-616690-9); pap. 1.95 (ISBN 0-02-089680-8). Macmillan.

Good & Evil: Mythology & Folklore. Anthony S. Mercatante. LC 77-11809. (Illus.). 1978. 10.95 o.s.i. (ISBN 0-06-012968-9, HarpT). Har-Row.

Good & Evil: Two Interpretations. Martin Buber. 1953. pap. 3.95 o.p. (ISBN 0-684-71723-9, SL45, ScribT). Scribner.

Good & Inexpensive Books for Children. rev. ed. Ed. by Esther D. Hemsing. LC 72-75054. (Illus.). 1972. pap. 2.00x o.p. (ISBN 0-87173-022-7). ACEI.

Good Apple Guide to Learning Centers. Craig Borba & Michele Borba. (gr. k-6). 1978. 11.95 (ISBN 0-916456-33-1, GA86). Good Apple.

Good Apple Math Book. Gary Grimm & Don Mitchell. (gr. 3-8). 1975. 10.95 (ISBN 0-916456-00-5, GA59). Good Apple.

Good Beginnings with Dairy Goats. Jo Eberhardt. Date not set. 6.00 (ISBN 0-686-26687-0). Dairy Goat.

Good Behavior. Molly Keane. LC 80-8792. 288p. 1981. 10.95 (ISBN 0-394-51818-7). Knopf.

Good Behavior: Being a Study of Certain Types of Civility. Harold Nicolson. 7.50 (ISBN 0-8446-0822-X). Peter Smith.

Good Books Come from Devon. Ed. by David St. John Thomas. LC 80-70289. (Illus.). 108p. 1981. pap. 5.95 (ISBN 0-7153-8139-3). David & Charles.

Good Bread. Barbara J. Hansen. (Illus.). 1976. 9.95 o.s.i. (ISBN 0-02-547860-5). Macmillan.

Good Bugs & Bad Bugs in Your Garden: Backyard Ecology. Dorothy C. Hogner. LC 74-6235. (Illus.). 96p. (gr. 3-7). 1974. PLB 7.89 (ISBN 0-690-00120-7, TYC-J). T Y Crowell.

Good Buy Book -- South. Annie Moldafsky. 228p. (Orig.). 1981. pap. 4.95 (ISBN 0-528-88046-2). Rand.

Good-Bye Chicago. W. R. Burnett. 182p. 1981. 9.95 (ISBN 0-686-69110-5). St Martin.

Good-Bye, Darkness: A Memoir of the Pacific War. William Manchester. 384p. 1980. 14.95 (ISBN 0-316-54501-5). Little.

Good-Bye Kitchen. Mildred Kantrowitz. LC 76-174602. (gr. k-3). 1969. 5.95 o.s.i. (ISBN 0-8193-0542-1, Four Winds); PLB 5.41 o.s.i. (ISBN 0-8193-0543-X). Schol Bk Serv.

Good-Bye Loneliness. Jay H. Schmidt & Paul Neimark. LC 77-16766. (Illus.). 192p. 1981. pap. 6.95 (ISBN 0-8128-6095-0). Stein & Day.

Good-Bye, My Lady. James Street. (gr. 7-9). 1954. 10.95 (ISBN 0-397-00049-9). Lippincott.

Good-Bye My Lady. James Street. (gr. 7-9). 1977. pap. 1.75 (ISBN 0-671-24289-X). Archway.

Good-Bye to Earth. Leo P. Kelley. LC 78-68226. (Galaxy Five Ser.). (Illus.). 64p. (gr. 4 up). 1980. PLB 7.95 (ISBN 0-516-02252-0). Childrens.

Good-Bye to the Jungle. John R. Townsend. LC 67-10335. (gr. 7-9). 1967. PLB 5.53 o.p. (ISBN 0-397-31426-4). Lippincott.

Good Bye World. David H. Hallock. 4.95 o.p. (ISBN 0-685-58726-6). Vantage.

Good Cheer: The Romance of Food & Feasting. Frederick W. Hackwood. LC 68-9571. 1968. Repr. of 1911 ed. 18.00 (ISBN 0-8103-3508-5). Gale.

Good Communications: What Every Good Manager Should Know. J. Hargreaves. LC 76-40317. 1977. 17.95 (ISBN 0-470-98958-0). Halsted Pr.

Good Companions. Era Zistel. 1981. pap. 1.75 (ISBN 0-451-09813-7, E9813, Signet Bks). NAL.

Good Companions. large print ed. Eva Zistel. LC 80-29117. 1981. Repr. of 1980 ed. 7.95 (ISBN 0-89621-265-3). Thorndike Pr.

Good Company: Poets at Michigan. Ed. by Jeanne Rockwell & Thomas E. Noonan. LC 77-91403. 1978. 6.00 (ISBN 0-9602934-0-X). Noon Rock.

Good Cooking. Jean Stewart. 1974. pap. text ed. 7.50x o.p. (ISBN 0-435-42713-X). Heinemann Ed.

Good Crewman. Robin Brandon. 1979. 12.95x (ISBN 0-8464-0077-4). Beekman Pubs.

Good Crewman. Robin Brankon. (Illus.). 1979. 7.95 o.p. (ISBN 0-229-11502-0). Scribner.

Good Day to Die. Del Barton. 320p. 1981. pap. 2.75 (ISBN 0-445-04646-5). Popular Lib.

Good Dog Book: Loving Care. Mordecai Siegal. (Illus.). 1977. 11.95 (ISBN 0-02-610600-0). Macmillan.

Good Dog Poems. Ed. by William Cole. (Illus.). 192p. (gr. 5 up). 1980. 9.95 (ISBN 0-684-16709-3). Scribner.

Good Dog's Cook Book. Richard Graham. LC 79-92259. (Illus., Orig.). 1980. pap. 4.95 (ISBN 0-932966-06-3). Permanent Pr.

Good Earth. Pearl Buck. (Arabic.). pap. 7.95x (ISBN 0-686-63553-1). Intl Bk Ctr.

Good Earth. Pearl S. Buck. (John Day Bk.). 1931. 12.95 (ISBN 0-381-98033-2, A30860, TYC-T). T Y Crowell.

Good Earth. Pearl S. Buck. (Keith Jennison Large Type Bks). (gr. 6 up). PLB 9.95 o.p. (ISBN 0-531-00191-1). Watts.

Good Earth. Pearl S. Buck. (gr. 8-12). 1975. pap. 2.75 (ISBN 0-671-43342-3); 2.50 (ISBN 0-686-67106-6). PB.

Good Earth & Country Cooking. 2nd ed. Betty Groff & Jose Wilson. LC 73-23128. (Illus.). 256p. 1974. pap. 8.95 (ISBN 0-8117-2066-7). Stackpole.

Good Education of Youth. Ed. by Frederick C. Gruber. 1957. 12.00x o.p. (ISBN 0-8122-7049-5). U of Pa Pr.

Good English. Basil Freestone. LC 71-375014. (Pegasus Books: No. 11). (Illus.). 1968. 7.50x (ISBN 0-234-77962-4). Intl Pubns Serv.

Good Evening Everybody: From Cripple Creek to Samarkand. Lowell Thomas. (Illus.). 384p. 1976. 12.50 o.p. (ISBN 0-688-03068-8). Morrow.

Good Fight. Ruby Ratzlaff. LC 78-57356. (Redwood Ser.). pap. 3.95 (ISBN 0-8163-0232-4). Pacific Pr Pub Assn.

Good Food. Tony S. Elena, Jr. LC 80-65651. 128p. (Orig.). 1981. pap. 6.95 (ISBN 0-89087-265-1). Celestial Arts.

Good Food & Fitness. Ed. by Better Homes & Gardens Books Editors. (Illus.). 96p. 1981. 4.95 (ISBN 0-696-00635-9). Meredith Corp.

Good Food Compendium. Jo G. Brown. LC 78-22306. (Illus.). 336p. 1981. pap. 10.95 (ISBN 0-385-13523-8, Dolp). Doubleday.

Good Food for Good Health. Thelma B. Harris. LC 79-187205. (Illus.). 256p. 1971. 4.95 (ISBN 0-8127-0045-7). Southern Pub.

Good Frames & Bad: A Grammer of Frame Writing. 2nd ed. Susan M. Markle. LC 71-91153. 1969. pap. 16.50 (ISBN 0-471-57013-3); tchrs'. manual avail. (ISBN 0-471-57014-1). Wiley.

Good Friends. Scripture Union. 1978. pap. 0.49 (ISBN 0-87508-929-1). Chr Lit.

Good Friends Again: Two - Three. Vera Groomer. (Come Unto Me Ser.: Year 2, Bk. 3). 32p. (ps). 1980. pap. 1.50 (ISBN 0-8127-0272-7). Southern Pub.

Good Garb. Bill Dasheff & L. Dearborn. (Orig.). 1980. pap. 9.95 (ISBN 0-440-52588-8, Delta). Dell.

Good Goodies. Stan Dworkin & Floss Dworkin. 1979. pap. 2.50 (ISBN 0-449-23964-0, Crest). Fawcett.

Good Grief, Charlie Brown: Selected Cartoons from "Good Grief, More Peanuts", Vol. 1. Charles M. Schulz. (Peanuts Ser.). (Illus.). 1978. pap. 1.50 (ISBN 0-449-23801-6, Crest). Fawcett.

Good Grooming for Girls. Rudie Saunders. (Career Concise Guides Ser.). (Illus.). 72p. (gr. 5-9). 1976. PLB 4.90 o.p. (ISBN 0-531-02902-6). Watts.

Good Guys, the Bad Guys & the First Amendment: Free Speech Vs. Fairness in Broadcasting. Fred Friendly. 1976. 10.00 o.p. (ISBN 0-394-49725-2). Random.

Good Health Guide. Open University. 1980. text ed. 22.95 (ISBN 0-06-318150-9, IntlDept). Har-Row.

Good Health Without Drugs: Get Well & Stay Well the Natural Way. Norman D. Ford. LC 77-9226. 1978. 8.95 o.p. (ISBN 0-312-33868-6). St Martin.

Good-Hearted Youngest Brother. Emoke De Papp Severo. (Illus.). 32p. (gr. k-3). 1981. 9.95 (ISBN 0-87888-141-7). Bradbury Pr.

Good Housekeeping Exercise & Diet Program. LC 79-88981. (Illus.). 1979. 7.95 (ISBN 0-87851-025-7); pap. text ed. 3.95 (ISBN 0-87851-026-5). Hearst Bks.

Good Housekeeping Family Health & Medical Guide. LC 78-51129. (Illus.). 1979. 19.95 (ISBN 0-87851-023-0). Hearst Bks.

Good Housekeeping: Fancy Folds-Napkin Folding Step-by-Step. (Illus.). 128p. 1980. 8.95 (ISBN 0-87851-040-0). Hearst Bks.

Good Housekeeping Illustrated Cookbook. Intro. by Zoe Coulson. LC 79-92727. 512p. 1980. 19.95 (ISBN 0-87851-037-0). Hearst Bks.

Good Housekeeping Woman's Almanac. Ed. by Barbara McDowell & Hana Umlauf. 1977. pap. 3.95 o.p. (ISBN 0-685-59257-X). Newspaper Ent.

Good Humor Book. Roland Peterson. (Orig.). 1977. pap. 1.75 o.s.i. (ISBN 0-88449-060-2). Vision Hse.

Good in Existential Metaphysics. Elizabeth G. Salmon. (Aquinas Lecture). 1952. 6.95 (ISBN 0-87462-117-8). Marquette.

Good Journey. Simon J. Ortiz. LC 77-82789. (New World Writing Ser.). (Illus.). 1977. 15.00 o.p. (ISBN 0-913666-21-1); pap. 6.95 o.p. (ISBN 0-913666-20-3). Turtle Isl Foun.

Good Junk. Judith A. Enderle. (Illus.). 32p. (ps-3). 1981. 5.95 (ISBN 0-525-66720-2). Elsevier-Nelson.

Good King Wenceslas: With Illustrations & Musical Settings. Mary R. Newland. (Illus.). 32p. 1980. 7.95 (ISBN 0-8164-0474-7). Seabury.

Good Kipling. Elliot L. Gilbert. LC 73-122098. ix, 216p. 1970. 11.95x (ISBN 0-8214-0085-1). Ohio U Pr.

Good Lemonade. Frank Asche. LC 72-1361. 32p. (gr. k-3). 1976. 5.90 (ISBN 0-531-01093-7). Watts.

Good Leviathan. Pierre Boulle. LC 78-57255. 1979. 8.95 (ISBN 0-8149-0807-1). Vanguard.

Good Life. Henry Jacobsen. LC 68-11556. 96p. 1968. pap. 2.95 (ISBN 0-88207-018-5). Victor Bks.

Good Life Good Death: A Doctor's Case for Euthanasia & Suicide. Christiaan Barnard. LC 80-18839. 120p. 1980. 7.95 (ISBN 0-13-360370-9). P-H.

Good Life in Hard Times: San Francisco's '20s & '30s. Jerry Flamm. LC 76-30524. (Illus.). 1977. pap. 7.95 (ISBN 0-87701-092-7). Chronicle Bks.

Good Little Thomas Hardy. C. H. Salter. 236p. 1981. 26.50x (ISBN 0-389-20126-X). B&N.

Good Looking. David A. Sohn. LC 75-27940. 1975. 8.95 (ISBN 0-912920-47-5). North Am Pub Co.

Good Lord! Not Another Book of Snappy Answers to Stupid Questions. Al Jaffee. (Mad Ser.). (Illus., Orig.). 1980. pap. 1.75 (ISBN 0-446-94450-5). Warner Bks.

Good Memory-Good Student: A Guide to Remembering What You Learn. Harry Lorayne. LC 72-6851. 160p. (gr. 5-9). 1972. Vol. 1. 7.95 o.p. (ISBN 0-525-66322-3). Elsevier-Nelson.

Good Mornin', Vietnam. Louis Cisneros. 1981. 4.95 (ISBN 0-8062-1568-2). Carlton.

Good Morning, Chick. Mirra Ginsburg. LC 70-11352. (Illus.). 24p. (ps). 1980. 7.95 (ISBN 0-688-80284-2); PLB 7.63 (ISBN 0-688-84284-4). Greenwillow.

Good Morning: Last Poems by Mark Van Doren. Mark Van Doren. 1973. 6.95 o.p. (ISBN 0-8090-5064-1). Hill & Wang.

Good Morning, Lord: Devotions for Athletes. LeRoy Patterson. (Good Morning, Lord Ser.). 1979. 2.45 (ISBN 0-8010-7044-9). Baker Bk.

Good Morning Nutritional Breakfast Cookbook. Laurie D. Palma. LC 77-73996. 1978. 3.95 (ISBN 0-89430-005-9). Morgan-Pacific.

Good Morning Please. Teddy Sullivan. 1981. 11.95 (ISBN 0-87460-354-4); pap. 5.95. Lion.

Good Morning, Tecate. June N. Summers. (Illus.). 62p. (Orig.). 1972. pap. text ed. 4.00 (ISBN 0-686-28871-8). J N Summers.

Good Morning, Whale. Achim Broger. LC 74-9762. (Illus.). 28p. (gr. 1-3). 1975. 7.95 (ISBN 0-02-714460-7). Macmillan.

Good Morning, World. Barbara Blake. 40p. 1981. 3.50 (ISBN 0-8059-2777-8). Dorrance.

Good 'n' Mad. Mad Magazine Editors. (Mad Ser.: No. 26). (Illus.). 1976. pap. 1.75 (ISBN 0-446-94365-7). Warner Bks.

Good Neighbors & Other Strangers. Edgar Pangborn. LC 75-182023. 195p. 1973. pap. 1.50 o.s.i. (ISBN 0-02-023600-X, Collier). Macmillan.

Good News. Borghild Dahl. (gr. 7 up). 1966. PLB 5.95 o.p. (ISBN 0-525-30828-8). Dutton.

Good News About Trouble. Eddy Swieson & Howard Norton. 1978. pap. 1.95 pocketsize o.p. (ISBN 0-88270-319-6). Logos.

Good News According to Matthew. Eduard Schweizer. Tr. by David E. Green. LC 74-3717. 1975. 15.00 (ISBN 0-8042-0251-6). John Knox.

Good News, Bad News. Edwin Diamond. 1978. 14.00 (ISBN 0-262-04057-3); pap. 5.95 (ISBN 0-262-54035-5). MIT Pr.

Good News, Bad News. Edwin Diamond. 288p. (Orig.). 1980. 14.00; pap. 5.95. MIT Pr.

Good News-Bad News. Philip M. Fragasso. LC 80-15582. 176p. (gr. 4-8). 1980. PLB 7.95 (ISBN 0-201-03197-3). A-W.

Good News for Modern Man: New Testament. American Bible Society. 516p. 1980. pap. 2.95 (ISBN 0-553-14347-6). Bantam.

Good News for Today. Barbara M. Higdon. 1981. pap. write for info. (ISBN 0-8309-0298-8). Herald Hse.

Good Night! Frances H. Grimes. LC 79-87669. (Illus.). (ps-3). Date not set. price not set (ISBN 0-89799-181-8); pap. price not set (ISBN 0-89799-182-6). Dandelion Pr. Postponed.

Good-Night Owl. Pat Hutchins. LC 72-186355. (Illus.). (ps-2). 1972. 8.95 (ISBN 0-02-745900-4). Macmillan.

Good-Night, Owl! Pat Hutchins. LC 74-20794. (Illus.). 32p. (ps-2). 1976. pap. 1.95 o.s.i. (ISBN 0-02-043730-7, 04373, Collier). Macmillan.

Good Night, Sleep Tight Book. Mircea Vasiliu. (Illus.). (ps-3). 1973. PLB 7.15 o.p. (ISBN 0-307-62504-4, Golden Pr). Western Pub.

Good Night, Sweet Prince. Gene Fowler. 1978. Repr. of 1944 ed. 16.05x (ISBN 0-89966-095-9). Buccaneer Bks.

Good Night's Sleep: A Step-by-Step Program for Overcoming Insomnia & Other Sleep Problems. Jerrold S. Maxman. (Illus.). 1981. 14.95 (ISBN 0-393-01437-1). Norton.

Good Ol' Snoopy: Selected Cartoons from "Snoopy", Vol. 2. Charles M. Schulz. (Peanuts Ser.). (Illus.). 1978. pap. 1.50 (ISBN 0-449-23709-5, Crest). Fawcett.

Good Old Boy. Willie Morris. LC 80-52627. 144p. 1980. Repr. 9.95. Yoknapatawpha.

Good Old Company Towns. John W. McGrain. (Baltimore County Heritage Publication Ser.). (Illus.). 1981. pap. price not set (ISBN 0-937076-01-5). Baltimore Co Pub Lib.

Good Old Days - They Were Terrible! Otto L. Bettmann. LC 74-6050. (Illus.). 1974. 10.00 o.p. (ISBN 0-394-48689-7); pap. 4.95 (ISBN 0-394-70941-1). Random.

Good Parliament. George Holmes. 210p. 1975. 29.95x (ISBN 0-19-822446-X). Oxford U Pr.

Good People of Gomorrah. Ed. by Gordon Osing. LC 78-31841. (Illus.). 1979. pap. 6.95x (ISBN 0-918518-13-X). St Luke TN.

Good Photography Made Easy. Derek Watkins. LC 76-8616. (Leisure and Travel Ser). (Illus.). 128p. 1976. 8.95 (ISBN 0-7153-7212-2). David & Charles.

Good Pit Man. Keith Alldritt. LC 76-5367. 1976. 8.95 o.p. (ISBN 0-312-33915-1). St Martin.

Good Questions. Gerald Kaminski. (Illus.). 32p. (Orig.). (gr. k-3). 1980. pap. 3.75 (ISBN 0-931896-00-2). Cove View.

Good Rain. Alice E. Goudey. (Illus.). (gr. 1-5). 1950. PLB 5.95 o.p. (ISBN 0-525-30856-3). Dutton.

Good Reading: A Guide for Serious Readers. rev. ed. J. Sherwood Weber. 1980. pap. 3.50 (ISBN 0-451-61909-9, ME1909, Ment). NAL.

Good Samaritan. Mandevile. (Ladybird Ser.). 1979. 1.49 (ISBN 0-87508-837-6). Chr Lit.

Good Samaritan. G. A. Pottebaum. (Little People's Paperbacks Ser.). 1979. pap. 0.99 (ISBN 0-8164-2249-4). Crossroad NY.

Good Sandwiches & Picnic Dishes. Ambrose Heath. 1949. 4.00 (ISBN 0-693-11415-0). Transatlantic.

Good Seeds, the Rich Grains, the Hardy Nuts for a Healthier, Happier Life. rev. ed. Ruth Adams & Frank Murray. 303p. 1973. pap. 1.75 (ISBN 0-915962-07-1). Larchmont Bks.

Good Sex: The Healthy Man's Guide to Sexual Fulfillment. Ed. by Gary F. Kelly. 1981. pap. 2.95 (ISBN 0-451-09572-3, Sig). NAL.

Good Ships of Newport News. Alexander C. Brown. LC 76-12100. (Illus.). 1976. 12.75 (ISBN 0-87033-220-1, Pub. by Tidewater). Cornell Maritime.

Good Shooting. J. E. Ruffer. LC 79-56044. (Illus.). 208p. 1980. 22.50x (ISBN 0-7153-7917-8). David & Charles.

Good Sign Cookbook. Lisa Kaplan. LC 80-67482. (Illus.). 80p. 1980. pap. 3.50 (ISBN 0-937730-00-9). Good Sign.

Good Sleep Without Drugs. Cyril Scott. 1980. pap. 1.95 (ISBN 0-87904-012-2). Lust.

Good Soldier Svejk & His Fortunes in the War. Jaroslav Hasek. Tr. by Cecil Parrott from Czech. (Illus.). 752p. 1980. lib. bdg. 15.00x (ISBN 0-434-31375-0, Pub. by Heinemann England). Bentley.

Good Speech for the American Actor. Edith Skinner & Timothy Monich. 1980. text ed. 13.95x incl. cassette (ISBN 0-89676-039-1). Drama Bk.

Good Sport. Julia Whedon. LC 79-7670. 216p. 1981. 10.95 (ISBN 0-385-15528-X). Doubleday.

Good Stories for Anniversaries. Frances J. Olcott. LC 77-167093. (Tower Bks). (Illus.). 1971. Repr. of 1937 ed. 22.00 (ISBN 0-8103-3910-2). Gale.

Good Taste Begins with You. Alton E. Frazier. Ed. by Arthur F. Ide. LC 79-9441. (Illus., Orig.). 1980. pap. 39.00x set (ISBN 0-86663-250-6). Ide Hse.

Good, the Bad & the Rest of Us. Evelyn Slaatten. LC 80-15595. 160p. (gr. 4-6). 1980. 7.95 (ISBN 0-688-22251-X); PLB 7.63 (ISBN 0-688-32251-4). Morrow.

Good Thief. Robert Rosenblum. 1976. pap. 1.75 o.p. (ISBN 0-345-25219-5). Ballantine.

Good Times, Bad Times. James Kirkwood. 1978. pap. 2.25 (ISBN 0-449-23975-6, Crest). Fawcett.

Good Times, Bad Times. Mary Verdick. Ed. by Thomas J. Mooney. (Beginning Pal Paperbacks Ser.). (Illus., Orig.). (gr. 7-12). 1977. pap. text ed. 1.25 (ISBN 0-8374-3453-X). Xerox Ed Pubns.

Good Times for Your Family. Wayne E. Rickerson. LC 76-3934. (Orig.). 1976. pap. 3.25 o.p. (ISBN 0-8307-0427-2, 54-036-18). Regal.

Good Times with Football. (Illus.). 24p. (gr. 3-4). 1976. 4.50 (ISBN 0-912122-05-6); pap. 1.89 (ISBN 0-912122-06-4). Football Hobbies.

Good 'uns: A Memoir of H.C. "Bud Jackson. H. C. Jackson. (Illus.). 280p. 1980. 17.95 (ISBN 0-914330-38-1). Pioneer Pub Co.

Good Vibrations: The Beach Boys on Records, 1961-1980. Brad Elliott. 1981. 14.95 (ISBN 0-87650-118-8). Pierian.

Good Wives. Louisa M. Alcott. (gr. 4 up). 1979. pap. 2.25 (ISBN 0-14-031127-0, Puffin). Penguin.

Good Work, Amelia Bedelia. Peggy Parish. 1980. pap. 1.75 (49171, Camelot). Avon.

Good Writing. Judi K. Turkel & Franklynn Peterson. (New Viewpoints Vision Bks.). 320p. Date not set. 9.95 (ISBN 0-531-06376-3). Watts.

Goodbye, Arnold. P. K. Roche. LC 79-50750. (Illus.). 32p. (ps-2). 1981. pap. 2.75 (ISBN 0-8037-3033-0, Pied Piper Bk). Dial.

Goodbye Blues. Bernard Green & Ted Schwarz. 224p. 1981. 10.95 (ISBN 0-07-024337-9, GB). McGraw.

Goodbye Charlie. Evelyn Bolton. LC 74-9572. (Evelyn Bolton's Horse Stories Ser). (Illus.). 32p. (gr. 2-6). 1974. PLB 5.95 (ISBN 0-87191-369-0); pap. 2.95 (ISBN 0-89812-127-2). Creative Ed.

Goodbye, Columbus, Hello M. Michael Meyers. LC 76-15403. 1976. 8.95 o.p. (ISBN 0-688-03090-4). Morrow.

Goodbye Gutenberg: The Newspaper Revolution of the 1980's. Anthony Smith. LC 79-24263. (Illus.). 1980. 16.95 (ISBN 0-19-502709-4). Oxford U Pr.

Goodbye Mommy. Bruce K. Doman. (Gentle Revolution Ser.). (Illus.). 86p. 1977. 4.95 (ISBN 0-936676-00-0). Better Baby.

Goodbye My Lady. James Street. (YA) (gr. 7-9). 1978. pap. 1.25 (ISBN 0-671-29879-8). PB.

Goodbye Summer. Crosby Bonsall. LC 78-23245. (gr. 4-7). 1979. 7.50 (ISBN 0-688-80202-8); PLB 7.20 (ISBN 0-688-84202-X). Greenwillow.

Goodbye to a River. John Graves. LC 77-7198. (Illus.). 1977. pap. 4.95 (ISBN 0-8032-5876-3, BB 642, Bison). U of Nebr Pr.

Goodbye to Excellence: A Critical Look at Minimum Competency Testing. Mitchel Lazarus. (NAESP Studies in Education & Public Policy). 192p. (Orig.). 1981. lib. bdg. 16.00x (ISBN 0-89158-771-3); pap. text ed. 6.50x (ISBN 0-89158-897-3). Westview.

Goodbye to Good-Time Charlie. Larry Sabato. LC 78-333. (Illus.). 1978. 21.95 (ISBN 0-669-02161-X). Lexington Bks.

Goodbye to the Working Class. Roy Greenslade. LC 76-373483. 1979. 11.95 (ISBN 0-7145-2511-1, Pub. by M Boyars); pap. 6.95 (ISBN 0-7145-2523-5). Merrimack Bk Serv.

Goodenough-Harris Test Examination of Intellectual Maturity of Youths 12-17 Years: Demographic & Socioeconomic Factors. Dale B. Harris & Glenn D. Pinder. (Ser. 11: No. 159). 70p. 1976. pap. text ed. 1.50 (ISBN 0-8406-0068-2). Natl Ctr Health Stats.

Goode's World Atlas. 15th ed. Ed. by Edward B. Espenshade, Jr. Joel Morrison. LC 73-21108. 1978. text ed. 16.95 (ISBN 0-528-83061-9); pap. text ed. 10.95 (ISBN 0-528-63004-0). Rand.

Goodliest Land: North Carolina. Bruce Roberts & Nancy Roberts. LC 72-89345. (Illus.). 160p. 1973. 11.95 (ISBN 0-385-04302-3). Doubleday.

Goodman & Gilman's The Pharmacological Basis of Therapeutics. 6th ed. Ed. by Alfred G. Gilman et al. 1980. text ed. 45.00 (ISBN 0-02-344720-6). Macmillan.

Goodness! Eating Healthily. Christine Mulliss. 64p. 1977. pap. 4.00x (ISBN 0-8464-1014-1). Beekman Pubs.

Goodness Had Nothing to Do with It. Mae West. (Belvedere Bk.). 312p. 1981. pap. 6.95 (ISBN 0-87754-301-1). Chelsea Hse.

Goodnight, Dear Monster. Terry N. Morris. LC 79-26904. (Illus.). 32p. 1980. bds. 1.95 (ISBN 0-394-84221-9). Knopf.

Goodnight, Goodnight. Eve Rice. LC 79-17253. (Illus.). (gr. k-1). 1980. 6.95 (ISBN 0-688-80254-0); PLB 6.67 (ISBN 0-688-84254-2). Greenwillow.

Goodnight Ladies. Babs H. Deal. LC 77-76229. 1978. 7.95 o.p. (ISBN 0-385-00831-7). Doubleday.

Goodnight Little One. Robert Kraus. (Illus.). 32p. (ps-2). 1981. paper over board 1.95 (ISBN 0-671-41091-1, Pub. by Windmill). S&S.

Goodnight Richard Rabbit. Robert Kraus. (Illus.). 32p. (ps-2). 1981. paper over board 1.95 (ISBN 0-671-41090-3, Pub. by Windmill). S&S.

Goodwin Sands Shipwrecks. Richard Larn. (Shipwrecks Ser.). 1977. 14.95 (ISBN 0-7153-7202-5). David & Charles.

Goody Two-Shoes: A Facsimile Reproduction of the Edition of 1766. LC 68-31083. (Illus.). 1970. Repr. of 1881 ed. 15.00 (ISBN 0-8103-3516-6). Gale.

Goofy-Big Man in the Big Top. (Wipe off Bks.). 9p. (ps). Date not set. 2.39 (ISBN 0-307-01846-6, Golden Pr). Western Pub.

Goofy Goes to the Hospital. Ronnie Kraus. LC 79-91868. (Illus.). 48p. (gr. 1-3). 1981. 4.95 (ISBN 0-448-16583-X); PLB 9.30 (ISBN 0-448-13642-2). G&D.

Goofy Keeps Fit. Walt Disney Productions. (ps-1). 1979. PLB 6.08 (ISBN 0-307-61079-9, Golden Pr); pap. 1.95 o.p. (ISBN 0-307-11079-6). Western Pub.

Goofy on Cave Man Island. (Illus.). 36p. 1981. 3.95 (ISBN 0-89659-179-4). Abbeville Pr.

Goofy Presents the Olympics: A Fun & Exciting History of the Olympics from the Ancient Games to Today. Walt Disney Productions. LC 79-18177. (Illus.). 128p. (gr. 2-6). 1980. 6.95 (ISBN 0-394-84224-3, BYR); PLB 6.99 (ISBN 0-394-94224-8). Random.

Goon for Lunch. Harry Secombe. LC 75-24747. 1976. 7.95 o.p. (ISBN 0-312-34020-6). St Martin.

Goops & How to Be Them. G. Burgess. (Peter Possum Paperbacks Ser). 1967. pap. 0.95 o.p. (ISBN 0-531-05130-7). Watts.

Goose & the Golden Coins. Lorinda B. Cauley. LC 80-24591. (Illus.). 48p. (ps-3). 1981. pap. 5.95 (ISBN 0-15-232207-8, VoyB). HarBraceJ.

Goose & the Golden Coins. Retold by & illus. by Lorinda B. Cauley. LC 80-24591. (Illus.). 48p. (ps-3). 1981. 11.95 (ISBN 0-15-232206-X, HJ). HarBraceJ.

Goose Step Is Verboten. Eric Waldman. LC 64-23077. 1964. 8.50 o.s.i. (ISBN 0-02-933650-3). Free Pr.

Goosehill Gang, 4 bks. M. B. Christian. Incl. Goosehill Gang & the Chocolate Cake Caper: Illustrating 1 John 3: 18 (ISBN 0-570-03606-2, 39DD1031); Goosehill Gang & the Disappearing Dues: Illustrating Matthew 22: 39 (ISBN 0-570-03607-0, 39DD1032); Goosehill Gang & the Test Paper Thief: Illustrating Matthew 5: 39 (ISBN 0-570-03608-9, 39DD1033); Goosehill Gang & the Vanishing Sandwich: Illustrating Luke 10: 37 (ISBN 0-570-03609-7, 39DD1034). (Illus.). (gr. 1-4). 1977. pap. 3.55 set (ISBN 0-686-67954-7); pap. 0.95 ea. Concordia.

Gopher Baroque, & Other Beastly Conceits. Sandra Boynton. (Thomas Congdon Bk.). (Illus.). 1979. 13.95 o.p.; pap. 6.95 (ISBN 0-525-03469-2). Dutton.

Gor Promotion. John Norman. Incl. Tarnsman of Gor. pap. 1.75 o. p. (ISBN 0-345-27135-1); Outlaw of Gor. pap. 1.75 o. p. (ISBN 0-345-27136-X); Priest Kings of Gor. pap. 1.75 o. p. (ISBN 0-345-27199-8); Nomad of Gor. pap. 1.75 o. p. (ISBN 0-345-27346-X); Assassin of Gor. pap. 1.75 o. p. (ISBN 0-345-27347-8); Raiders of Gor. pap. 1.75 o. p. (ISBN 0-345-27200-5); Captive of Gor. pap. 2.50 (ISBN 0-345-29414-9). 1973. Ballantine.

Gorboduc, or Ferrex & Porrex. Thomas Sackville & Thomas Norton. Ed. by Irby B. Cauthen, Jr. LC 74-88095. (Regents Renaissance Drama Ser.). 1970. 6.50x (ISBN 0-8032-0288-1); pap. 1.85x (ISBN 0-8032-5289-7, BB 235, Bison). U of Nebr Pr.

Gordon Childe: Revolutions in Archaeology. Bruce G. Trigger. 224p. 1980. 22.50x (ISBN 0-231-05038-0). Columbia U Pr.

Gordon Greenidge: The Man in the Middle. Gordon Greenidge & Patrick Symes. LC 80-66424. (Illus.). 208p. 1980. 19.95 (ISBN 0-7153-8044-3). David & Charles.

Gordon of Sesame Street Storybook. Matt Robinson. (Illus.). (gr. 7-9). 1951. 4.95 (ISBN 0-394-82406-7, BYR); PLB 5.99 (ISBN 0-394-92406-1). Random.

Gordon Snidow Portrays the Cowboy Heritage Hangin'on. Bruce Berger. LC 80-83021. (Illus.). 128p. 1980. 40.00 (ISBN 0-87358-266-7); pap. 18.50 (ISBN 0-87358-265-9); ltd. ed. avail. (ISBN 0-87358-267-5). Northland.

Gordon Takes a Wife. Emily Binning. 138p. 1977. 3.75 (ISBN 0-930756-26-6, 4230-EB1). Women's Aglow.

Gordon's House. Julie Brinckloe. LC 75-33189. 48p. (ps-3). 1976. 5.95 o.p. (ISBN 0-385-06886-7); PLB write for info. o.p. (ISBN 0-385-06905-7). Doubleday.

Gordon's Medical Management of Ocular Disease. 2nd ed. Ed. by Edward A. Dunlap. (Illus.). 1976. 39.50x o.p. (ISBN 0-06-140730-5, Harper Medical). Har-Row.

Gordonstown, a New Design for America. Stuart Gordon. (Illus.). 288p. 1980. pap. 10.95 (ISBN 0-9603942-0-6). Gordonstown.

Gore Vidal. Ray L. White. (U. S. Authors Ser.: No. 135). 1968. lib. bdg. 10.95 (ISBN 0-8057-0760-3). Twayne.

Gore Vidal: A Primary & Secondary Bibliography. Robert J. Stanton. (Reference Publications). 1980. lib. bdg. 25.00 (ISBN 0-8161-8109-8). G K Hall.

Goren on Play & Defense. Charles H. Goren. LC 73-16506. 448p. 1974. 9.95 o.p. (ISBN 0-385-06753-4). Doubleday.

Goren's Bridge Complete. rev. ed. Charles H. Goren. LC 73-75161. 9.95 o.p. (ISBN 0-385-04355-4). Doubleday.

Goren's Bridge Complete. Charles H. Goren. LC 80-2247. 736p. 1981. 14.95 (ISBN 0-385-17441-1). Doubleday.

Gorey Posters. Edward Gorey. 1979. pap. 8.95 (ISBN 0-8109-2179-0). Abrams.

Gorgias. Plato. Tr. by W. C. Helmbold. LC 52-9226. 1952. pap. 3.50 (ISBN 0-672-60181-8, LLA20). Bobbs.

Gorgias. Plato. Ed. by E. R. Dodds. 1959. 34.50x (ISBN 0-19-814153-X). Oxford U Pr.

Gorgias. Plato. Tr. by Terence Irwin from Greek. (Clarendon Plato Ser.). 278p. 1979. text ed. 29.00x (ISBN 0-19-872087-4); pap. text ed. 14.95x (ISBN 0-19-872091-2). Oxford U Pr.

Gorgon's Head: A Study in Tragedy & Despair. William R. Brashear. LC 76-491558. 164p. 1977. 12.00x (ISBN 0-8203-0417-4). U of Ga Pr.

Gorilla. Colin Willock. LC 77-10372. 1978. 10.00 o.p. (ISBN 0-312-34035-4). St Martin.

Gorilla Adventure. Willard Price. (Illus.). 222p. (gr. 3-6). 1980. 8.95 (ISBN 0-224-61636-6, Pub. by Chatto Bodley Jonathan). Merrimack Bk Serv.

Gorilla Did It. Barbara S. Hazen. (Illus.). 1974. pap. 2.95 (ISBN 0-689-70438-0, Aladdin). Atheneum.

Gorillas. Kay McDearmon. LC 78-11292. (Skylight Bks.). (Illus.). (gr. 3-5). 1979. 4.95 (ISBN 0-396-07645-9). Dodd.

Gorky Rises. William Steig. LC 80-68068. (Illus.). 32p. (ps-3). 1980. 10.95 (ISBN 0-374-32752-1). FS&G.

Gormenghast. Mervyn Peake. 1976. pap. 2.50 (ISBN 0-345-27699-X). Ballantine.

Gosoku Ryu Karate: Kumite I. Takayuki Kubota. LC 80-53036. (Illus.). 160p. (Orig.). 1980. pap. 6.95 (ISBN 0-86568-010-8). Unique Pubns.

Gospel According to John. Ed. by G. Campbell Morgan. 8.95 (ISBN 0-8007-0119-4). Revell.

Gospel According to John, Pt. 1. Frank Pack. Ed. by Everett Ferguson. LC 74-7628. (Living Word Commentary Ser., Vol 5). 1975. 7.95 (ISBN 0-8344-0068-5). Sweet.

Gospel According to John, Pt. 2. Frank Pack. LC 77-8725. (Living Word Commentary Ser.: Vol. 5). 1977. 7.95 (ISBN 0-8344-0088-X). Sweet.

Gospel According to John in the Revised Standard Version. Intro. by J. C. Fenton. (New Clarendon Bible Ser). 1970. 6.95x (ISBN 0-19-836908-5). Oxford U Pr.

Gospel According to Luke, 2 parts. Anthony L. Ash. Ed. by Everett Ferguson. LC 72-77838. (The Living Word Commentary Ser., Vol. 4). 1972. 7.95 ea.; Pt 1. (ISBN 0-8344-0067-7); Pt 2. (ISBN 0-8344-0077-4). Sweet.

Gospel According to Luke. Ed. by G. Campbell Morgan. 8.95 (ISBN 0-8007-0120-8). Revell.

Gospel According to Mark. Earle McMillan. Ed. by Everett Ferguson. LC 73-8572. (Living Word Commentary Ser., Vol. 3). 1973. 7.95 (ISBN 0-8344-0066-9). Sweet.

Gospel According to Mark. Ed. by G. Campbell Morgan. 8.95 (ISBN 0-8007-0121-6). Revell.

Gospel According to Mark: An Access Guide. Daniel J. Harrington. 128p. (Orig.). 1981. pap. 4.95 (ISBN 0-8215-9835-X). Sadlier.

Gospel According to Matthew. Jack P. Lewis. Ed. by Everett Ferguson. LC 75-21256. (Living Word Commentary Ser.: Vol. 2). 1976. 7.95 (ISBN 0-8344-0065-0). Sweet.

Gospel According to Matthew. Ed. by G. Campbell Morgan. 8.95 (ISBN 0-8007-0122-4). Revell.

Gospel According to Matthew, Pt. 1. Jack Lewis. Ed. by Everett Ferguson. LC 75-21256. (The Living Word Commentary Ser.: Vol. 2). 1976. 7.95 (ISBN 0-8344-0094-4). Sweet.

Gospel According to Matthew in the Revised Standard Version. H. Benedict Green. (New Clarendon Bible Ser). 314p. 1975. 15.50x o.p. (ISBN 0-19-836918-2); pap. 7.95 (ISBN 0-19-836911-5). Oxford U Pr.

Gospel According to "Peanuts". Robert L. Short. LC 65-11632. (Illus.). 1965. pap. 2.95 (ISBN 0-8042-1968-0). John Knox.

Gospel According to St. John, 2 vols. Rudolf Schnackenburg. 1980. 29.50 ea. Vol. 1 (ISBN 0-8164-1210-3). Vol. 2 (ISBN 0-8164-0213-2). Crossroad NY.

Gospel According to St. John. Randolph V. Tasker. (Tyndale Bible Commentaries). 1960. pap. 3.95 (ISBN 0-8028-1403-4). Eerdmans.

Gospel According to St. John Vols. 1, 2, & 3, the New Testament for Spiritual Reading Vols. 7, 8, & 9. John Huckle. 1978. 6.00 ea. Crossroad NY.

Gospel According to St. Matthew. A. H. McNeile. (Thornapple Commentaries). 484p. 1980. pap. 8.95 (ISBN 0-8010-6099-0). Baker Bk.

Gospel Anchors Aweigh. Ray A. Matthews. LC 79-87732. (Destiny Ser.). 1980. pap. 4.95 (ISBN 0-8163-0382-7, 07690-1). Pacific Pr Pub.

Gospel & Islam: A Nineteen Seventy-Eight Compendium. Ed. by Don M. McCurry. 1979. pap. 9.00 (ISBN 0-912552-26-3). MARC.

Gospel & Law: Contrast or Continuum? the Hermeneautics of Dispensationalism & Covenant Theology. Daniel P. Fuller. (Orig.). 1980. pap. 10.95 (ISBN 0-8028-1808-0). Eerdmans.

Gospel & the Land: Early Christianity & Jewish Territorial Doctrine. W. D. Davies. LC 72-82228. 1974. 22.50x (ISBN 0-520-02278-5). U of Cal Pr.

Gospel Criticism & Form Criticism. W. Emery Barnes. 83p. 1936. pap. text ed. 3.50 (ISBN 0-567-02020-7). Attic Pr.

Gospel Fever. Frank G. Slaughter. LC 80-25615. 475p. 1980. Repr. of 1980 ed. large print ed. 12.95 (ISBN 0-89621-256-4). Thorndike Pr.

Gospel Fever: A Novel About America's Most Beloved TV Evangelist. Frank G. Slaughter. LC 79-6094. (Illus.). 384p. 1980. 10.95 (ISBN 0-385-15308-2). Doubleday.

Gospel Hyms, 6 vols, No. 1-6. facsimile ed. Ira D. Sankey et al. LC 70-171076. (Earlier American Music Ser.: No. 5). 512p. 1972. Repr. of 1895 ed. lib. bdg. 25.00 (ISBN 0-306-77305-8). Da Capo.

Gospel in Exodus. Henry Law. 1967. pap. 1.95 (ISBN 0-686-12516-9). Banner of Truth.

Gospel in Gotham. James B. Coffman. 3.50 (ISBN 0-89315-077-0). Lambert Bk.

Gospel in Leviticus. Joseph Seiss. LC 80-8078. 408p. 1981. 10.95 (ISBN 0-8254-3743-1). Kregel.

Gospel in Solentiname, Vol. 1. Ernesto Cardenal. Tr. by Donald Walsh from Spanish. LC 76-2681. Orig. Title: Elevangelio En Solentiname. 1976. 6.95x o.p. (ISBN 0-88344-168-3); pap. 4.95 o.p. (ISBN 0-88344-170-5). Orbis Bks.

Gospel Narrative. Louis Marin & Claude Chabrol. Tr. by Alfred M. Johnson, Jr. (Pittsburgh Theological Monographs: No. 30). 1980. pap. cancelled (ISBN 0-915138-33-6). Pickwick.

Gospel of John, 2 vols. in 1. rev. ed. W. H. Van Doren. LC 80-8080. (Kregal Bible Study Classics Ser.). 1100p. 1981. Repr. of 1878 ed. text ed. 22.95 (ISBN 0-8254-3953-1). Kregel.

Gospel of John: Addresses. H. A. Ironside. Date not set. 10.95 (ISBN 0-87213-373-7). Loizeaux.

Gospel of John: An Expositional Commentary, Vol. 4. James M. Boice. 1978. 12.95 (ISBN 0-310-21460-2). Zondervan.

Gospel of John: An Expositional Commentary, 5 vols. James M. Boice. 1979. Set. 62.75 (ISBN 0-310-21458-0). Zondervan.

Gospel of John: An Expositional Commentary, Vol. 5. James M. Boice. 1979. 12.95 (ISBN 0-310-21470-X). Zondervan.

Gospel of John: Vol. 2 (5: 1-8: 59)(Christ & Judaism) James M. Boice. 1976. 11.95 (ISBN 0-310-21430-0). Zondervan.

Gospel of John (1: 1-4: 54, Vol. 1. James M. Boice. 416p. 1975. 12.95 (ISBN 0-310-21420-3). Zondervan.

Gospel of Luke. H. A. Ironside. Date not set. 8.75 (ISBN 0-87213-376-1). Loizeaux.

Gospel of Luke. William Kelly. Date not set. 16.95 (ISBN 0-86524-046-9). Klock & Klock.

Gospel of Luke, 2 vols. in 1. W. H. Van Doren. LC 80-8079. (Kregal Bible Study Classics Ser.). 1981. Repr. of 1878 ed. 22.95 (ISBN 0-8254-3953-1). Kregel.

Gospel of Mark. H. A. Ironside. Date not set. 5.50 (ISBN 0-87213-377-X). Loizeaux.

Gospel of Matthew, Vol. I. Harold Fowler. LC 78-1064. (Bible Study Textbook Ser.). (Illus.). 1975. 13.50 (ISBN 0-89900-029-0). College Pr Pub.

Gospel of Matthew, Vol. III. Harold Fowler. (Bible Study Textbook Ser.). (Illus.). 1978. 12.95 (ISBN 0-89900-031-2). College Pr Pub.

Gospel of Matthew. H. A. Ironside. Date not set. 7.00 (ISBN 0-87213-378-8). Loizeaux.

Gospel of Matthew. David Thomas. LC 78-11502. (Kregel Bible Study Classics). Orig. Title: Genius of the Gospel. 1980. 12.95 (ISBN 0-8254-3812-8). Kregel.

Gospel of Sri Ramakrishna. Tr. by Swami Nikhilananda. LC 58-8948. (Illus.). 1106p. 15.00 (ISBN 0-911206-01-9); abridged ed., with index, 640p. 7.00 (ISBN 0-911206-02-7). Ramakrishna.

Gospel of the Comforter. Steele. pap. 5.95 (ISBN 0-686-12870-2). Schmul Pub Co.

Gospel of the Kingdom (Matthew) C. H. Spurgeon. 4.95 (ISBN 0-686-09110-8). Pilgrim Pubns.

Gospel of the Lord. Marcion Of Sinope. Tr. by James H. Hill. LC 78-63171. (Heresies II Ser.). 80p. 1980. Repr. of 1891 ed. 13.50 (ISBN 0-404-16186-3). AMS Pr.

Gospel of the Stars: A Celebration of the Mystery of the Zodiac. Peter Lemesurier. LC 78-61013. 1979. 7.95 o.p. (ISBN 0-312-34067-2). St Martin.

Gospel Poverty: Witness to the Risen Christ. Michael D. Guinan. 96p. (Orig.). 1981. pap. 3.95 (ISBN 0-8091-2377-0). Paulist Pr.

Gospel Religion of Jesus Christ. Dennis M. Battle. 52p. 1980. pap. 2.25 (ISBN 0-933464-08-8). D M Battle Pubns.

Gospel Sermons for Saint & Sinner. James B. Reesor. 107p. 1968. 2.95 (ISBN 0-87148-356-4); pap. 2.25 (ISBN 0-87148-357-2). Pathway Pr.

Gospels. Fred B. Craddock. LC 80-26270. 160p. (Orig.). 1981. pap. 6.95 (ISBN 0-687-15655-6). Abingdon.

Gospels & Contemporary Biographies in the Greco-Roman World. Clyde W. Votaw. LC 79-135748. (Facet Bks.). 72p. 1970. pap. 1.00 (ISBN 0-8006-3061-0, 1-3061). Fortress.

Gospels & the Acts. rev. ed. Chester K. Lehman. (Bible Survey Course No. 4). 1956. pap. 1.00 o.p. (ISBN 0-8361-1319-5). Herald Pr.

Gospels Then. J. Ylvisaker. 1977. Repr. 16.95 (ISBN 0-8100-0052-0). Northwest Pub.

Gospels: 14 Lessons, Vol. 1. Bernice C. Jordan. (New Testament Ser.). (gr. 3-9). 1955. pap. text ed. 1.95 (ISBN 0-86508-035-6); figures 7.95 (ISBN 0-86508-036-4). BCM Inc.

Gospels: 14 Lessons, Vol. 2. Bernice C. Jordan. (Footsteps of Faith Ser.). (gr. 3-9). 1956. pap. text ed. 1.95 (ISBN 0-86508-037-2); figures 7.95 (ISBN 0-86508-038-0). BCM Inc.

Gossamer Odyssey: The Triumph of Human-Powered Flight. Morton Grosser. (Illus.). 288p. 1981. 14.95 (ISBN 0-686-69048-6). HM.

Gossamered View with a Special Section on the Legends of Christmas. Dianne J. Morrissey. LC 80-68777. (Illus.). 92p. (Orig.). 1980. pap. 3.95 (ISBN 0-9604664-0-1). Artemis Pr.

Gossip in the First Decade of Victoria's Reign. John Ashton. LC 67-23942. 1968. Repr. of 1903 ed. 15.00 (ISBN 0-8103-3249-3). Gale.

Gossip's Story, & a Legendary Tale, 2 vols. Jane West. Ed. by Gina Luria. LC 73-22192. (Feminist Controversy in England, 1788-1810 Ser.). 1974. lib. bdg. 50.00 ea. (ISBN 0-8240-0884-7). Garland Pub.

Gotama Buddha. Hajime Nakamura. LC 77-8589. 1977. 8.95x (ISBN 0-914910-05-1); pap. 5.95x (ISBN 0-914910-06-X). Buddhist Bks.

Gotch: The Story of a Cowhorse. Luke D. Sweetman. LC 78-116053. (Illus.). 1970. pap. 4.95 (ISBN 0-8032-5726-0, BB 527, Bison). U of Nebr Pr.

Gothic Architecture. Louis Grodecki. (History of World Architecture). (Illus.). 1977. 45.00 (ISBN 0-8109-1008-X). Abrams.

Gothic Architecture in England, Western & Southern Europe with an Illustrated Glossary of Technical Words. T. Roger Smith. (Illus.). 1979. Repr. of 1880 ed. deluxe ed. 67.50 (ISBN 0-930582-19-5). Gloucester Art.

Gothic Art. Andrew Martindale. (World of Art Ser.). (Illus.). 1967. pap. 9.95 (ISBN 0-19-519924-3). Oxford U Pr.

Gothic Cathedral: Origins of Gothic Architecture & the Medieval Concept of Order. Otto Von Simson. LC 72-11946. (Illus.). 300p. 1973. pap. text ed. 5.95 (ISBN 0-691-01789-1). Princeton U Pr.

Gothic Europe Fourteen Hundred to Fifteen Hundred: The History of Dress. Margaret Scott. (The History of Dress Ser.: Vol. 1). (Illus.). 1980. text ed. 62.50 (ISBN 0-391-02148-6). Humanities.

Gothic Heroine & the Nature of the Gothic Novel. Raymond W. Mise. Ed. by Devendra P. Varma. LC 79-8465. (Gothic Studies & Dissertations Ser.). 1980. lib. bdg. 25.00x (ISBN 0-405-12675-1). Arno.

Gothic Novels of the Twentieth Century: An Annotated Bibliography. Elsa J. Radcliffe. LC 78-24357. 291p. 1979. lib. bdg. 13.00 (ISBN 0-8108-1190-1). Scarecrow.

Gothic Painted Altar Frontals from the Church of Tingelstad. Leif E. Plahter et al. (Medieval Art in Norway Ser). 107p. 1974. 32.00x (ISBN 8-200-08953-3, Dist. by Columbia U Pr). Universitet.

Gothic Revival Architecture in Ireland. Douglas Richardson. LC 76-23700. (Outstanding Dissertations in the Fine Arts Ser.). 1978. lib. bdg. 133.00x (ISBN 0-8240-2723-X). Garland Pub.

Gothic Romance: Its Appeal to Women Writers & Readers in Late Eighteenth-Century England. Bette B. Roberts. Ed. by Devendra P. Varma. LC 79-8474. (Gothic Studies & Dissertations Ser.). 1980. lib. bdg. 25.00x (ISBN 0-405-12658-1). Arno.

Gothic Strains & Bourgeois Sentiments in the Novels of Mrs. Ann Radcliffe & Her Imitations. John Garrett. Ed. by Devendra P. Varma. LC 79-8454. (Gothic Studies & Dissertations Ser.). 1980. lib. bdg. 40.00x (ISBN 0-405-12668-9). Arno.

Gothic to Fantastic: Readings in Supernatural Fiction. Sydney L. Lea. Ed. by Devendra P. Varma. LC 79-8463. (Gothic Studies & Dissertations Ser.). 1980. lib. bdg. 22.00x (ISBN 0-405-12653-0). Arno.

Gothic Tradition. Elizabeth MacAndrew. LC 79-9447. 1980. 20.00x (ISBN 0-231-04674-X). Columbia U Pr.

Gottesvergiftung. Tilmann Moser. (Suhrkamp Taschenbuecher: No. 533). 112p. 1980. pap. text ed. 3.25 (ISBN 3-518-37033-2, Pub. by Insel Verlag Germany). Suhrkamp.

Gottfried August Burger. William A. Little. (World Authors Ser.: Germany: No. 270). 1974. lib. bdg. 12.50 (ISBN 0-8057-2185-1). Twayne.

Gottfried von Strassburg. Michael S. Batts. (World Authors Ser.: Germany: No. 167). lib. bdg. 10.95 (ISBN 0-8057-2866-X). Twayne.

Gottfried Von Strassburg Tristan & Isolde. 4th ed. Ed. by Friedrich Maurer. 1977. 6.25x (ISBN 3-11-006841-9). De Gruyter.

Gourd Dancer. N. Scott Momaday. LC 75-30338. (Illus.). 96p. (YA) 1976. 9.95 o.s.i. (ISBN 0-06-012982-4, HarpT); pap. 2.95 o.s.i. (ISBN 0-06-012983-2, TD-250, HarpT). Har-Row.

Gourman Report: A Rating of Graduate & Professional Programs in American & International Universities. Jack Gourman. LC 79-91882. 119p. (Orig.). 1980. pap. 21.50 (ISBN 0-918192-03-X). Natl Ed Stand.

Gourman Report: A Rating of Undergraduate Programs in American & International Universities. 3rd ed. Jack Gourman. LC 79-918881. 124p. 1980. pap. 21.50 (ISBN 0-918192-02-1). Natl Ed Stand.

Gourmet Cookbook for Those Interested in Weight Control. Caroline Weiss et al. (Illus.). 1979. pap. 2.50 (ISBN 0-686-65552-4). Budlong.

Gourmet Cooking on a Budget. Carol Traux. 192p. (Orig.). 1976. pap. 1.95 o.p. (ISBN 0-345-25382-5). Ballantine.

Gourmet Cooking Without Salt. Eleanor P. Brenner. LC 79-6856. (Illus.). 416p. 1981. 15.95 (ISBN 0-385-14821-6). Doubleday.

Gourmet Doggie Bag Cookbook. Irvin Gans. Date not set. 6.95 (ISBN 0-533-04764-1). Vantage.

Gourmet Food on a Wheat-Free Diet. Marion N. Wood. 128p. 1979. 10.75 (ISBN 0-398-02117-1). C C Thomas.

Gourmet Gardening. Ed. by Anne Halpin. (Illus.). 256p. 1981. pap. 9.95 (ISBN 0-87857-349-6). Rodale Pr Inc.

Gourmet Minceur: A Week of Gourmet Diet Meals. Beverly Cox. LC 79-63111. (Illus., Orig.). 1977. pap. 7.95 (ISBN 0-8149-0783-0). Vanguard.

Gourmet Recipes for Diabetics: The International Diabetic Diet Book. Dorothy T. Revell. 196p. 1971. 13.75 (ISBN 0-398-02153-8). C C Thomas.

Gourmet Wine Cooking the Easy Way. 3rd ed. Wine Adsisory Bloard. Ed. by David R. Wilcox. (Illus.). 1980. 5.95 (ISBN 0-932664-01-6). Wine Appreciation.

Gourmet's Bland Diet Cookbook. Jane N. Blair. (Orig.). 1974. pap. 1.25 (ISBN 0-515-03306-5, V3306). Jove Pubns.

Gourmet's Guide to New Orleans. Natalie V. Scott & Caroline M. Jones. 112p. 1976. pap. 2.95 o.p. (ISBN 0-88289-124-3); spiral bdg. 3.95 (ISBN 0-88289-079-4). Pelican.

Gourmet's Low-Cholesterol Cookbook. Elizabeth Weiss & Rita P. Wolfson. 1974. pap. 2.25 o.p. (ISBN 0-515-05690-1, V3458). Jove Pubns.

Gousha-Chek-Chart United States Road Atlas. (Orig.). 1977. pap. 1.95 o.p. (ISBN 0-451-82049-5, XJ2049, Sig). NAL.

Gousha Chek-Chart United States Road Atlas. rev ed. (Illus.). 80p. 1980. pap. 2.25 (ISBN 0-451-82060-6, XE2060, Sig). NAL.

Gousha North American Road Atlas. rev. ed. 1981. pap. 4.50 (ISBN 0-451-82064-9, XE2064, Sig). NAL.

Gout. Association of Bone & Joint Surgeons. Ed. by Marshall R. Urist. (Clinical Orthopaedics Ser., Vol. 71). 1970. 15.00 (ISBN 0-685-22851-7). Lippincott.

Gout & Pseudogout. H. Ralph Schumacher, Jr. (Discussions in Patient Management Ser.). 1978. spiral 9.50 (ISBN 0-87488-888-3). Med Exam.

Gouverneur Morris. Theodore Roosevelt. LC 80-24746. (American Statesmen Ser.). 340p. 1981. pap. 5.95 (ISBN 0-87754-188-4). Chelsea Hse.

Gove Love the Air. Faith Baldwin. 1980. pap. write for info. (ISBN 0-671-83092-9). PB.

Goverment & Politics in India. Baljit Singh & Dhirendra Vajpeyi. 130p. (Orig.). 1981. pap. text ed. 8.95 (ISBN 0-86590-006-X). Apt Bks.

Governance of Britain. Harold Wilson. LC 76-47262. (Illus.). 1977. 10.95 o.p. (ISBN 0-06-014676-1, HarpT). Har-Row.

Governance of Federal Regulatory Agencies. David M. Welborn. LC 77-8012. 1977. 11.50x (ISBN 0-87049-216-0). U of Tenn Pr.

Governance of Higher Education: Six Priority Problems. Carnegie Commission on Higher Education. LC 73-4774. (Illus.). 272p. 1973. 8.50 o.p. (ISBN 0-07-010062-4, P&RB). McGraw.

Governance of Public Enterprise: A Case Study of Urban Mass Transit. Neil W. Hamilton & Peter R. Hamilton. LC 80-5349. 1981. 18.95. Lexington Bks.

Governance of Teacher Education. M. L. Cushman. LC 76-52063. 1977. 16.00x (ISBN 0-685-78477-0); text ed. 14.50 (ISBN 0-8211-0228-1). McCutchan.

Governance of Teacher Education. M. L. Cushman. LC 76-52063. 1977. 12.60 (ISBN 0-8211-0228-1, Co-Pub with McCutchan); pap. 7.00 (ISBN 0-87367-770-6). Phi Delta Kappa.

Governing Academic Organizations: New Problems, New Perspectives. Ed. by Gary L. Riley & Victor J. Baldridge. LC 76-56995. 1977. 20.00x (ISBN 0-8211-1715-7); text ed. 18.00x (ISBN 0-685-75001-9). McCutchan.

Governing Britain. A. Hanson & M. Walles. 1970. pap. 1.95 o.p. (ISBN 0-531-06009-8, Fontana Pap). Watts.

Governing Greater Stockholm: A Study of Policy Development & System Change. Thomas J. Anton. LC 79-94447. 1975. 20.00x (ISBN 0-520-02718-3). U of Cal Pr.

Governing Hospitals: Trustees & the New Accountabilities. Robert Cunningham, Jr. LC 75-44127. 1976. pap. 12.50 (ISBN 0-87258-182-9, 1665). Am Hospital.

Governing Metropolitan Toronto: A Social & Political Analysis 1953-1971. Albert Rose. LC 72-157821. (Institute of Governmental Studies, U. C. Berkeley & Lane Studies in Regional Government). 1973. 20.00x (ISBN 0-520-02041-3). U of Cal Pr.

Governing Nature. Earl F. Murphy. 1970. pap. 2.95 o.p. (ISBN 0-531-06464-6). Watts.

Governing New York City. Wallace S. Sayre & Herbert Kaufman. 1965. pap. 11.95x (ISBN 0-393-09657-2, NortonC). Norton.

Governing of Men. Alexander H. Leighton. 1945. 20.00x o.p. (ISBN 0-691-08607-9). Princeton U Pr.

Governing Schools: New Approaches to Old Issues. Luvern L. Cunningham. LC 70-137520. 1971. 9.95x (ISBN 0-675-09255-8); pap. text ed. 7.95 (ISBN 0-675-09256-6). Merrill.

Governing the London Region: Reorganization & Planning in the 1960's. Donald L. Foley. LC 76-157822. (Institute of Governmental Studies, UC Berkeley & Lane Studies in Regional Environment). 1972. 18.50x (ISBN 0-520-02040-5); pap. 5.75x (ISBN 0-520-02248-3, CAMPUS81). U of Cal Pr.

Governing Under Pressure: The Policy Process in a Post Parliamentary Democracy. J. J. Richardson & A. G. Jordan. 212p. 1979. 33.50x (ISBN 0-85520-237-8, Pub by Martin Robertson England); pap. 12.50x (ISBN 0-85520-314-5). Biblio Dist.

Government, 4 pts. Incl. Pt. 1. Civil Service, 12 vols. Set. 882.00x (ISBN 0-686-01119-8); Pt. 2. Diplomatic Service, 4 vols. Set. 306.00x (ISBN 0-686-01120-1); Pt. 3. Elections, 5 vols. Set. 432.00x (ISBN 0-686-01121-X); Pt. 4. Municipal Corporations, 9 vols. Set. 756.00x (ISBN 0-686-01122-8). (British Parliamentary Papers Ser.). 1971 (Pub. by Irish Academic Pr Ireland). Biblio Dist.

Government Against Poverty. Joseph A. Kershaw. (Studies in Social Economics). 174p. 1970. 10.95 (ISBN 0-8157-4902-3). Brookings.

Government & Agriculture: Growth of Federal Farm Aid. Donald C. Blaisdell. LC 72-2365. (FDR & the Era of the New Deal Ser.). 217p. 1974. Repr. of 1940 ed. lib. bdg. 27.50 (ISBN 0-306-70488-9). Da Capo.

Government & Campus: Federal Regulation of Religiously Affiliated Higher Education. Edward M. Gaffney & Philip R. Moots. LC 80-53164. 210p. 1981. text ed. 15.95 (ISBN 0-268-01003-X); pap. text ed. 8.95 (ISBN 0-268-01005-6). U of Notre Dame Pr.

Government & Common Sense: Citizens Guide to Political Thinking. William Welch. (Littlefield, Adams Quality Paperback Ser.: No. 362). 224p. (Orig.). 1981. pap. 4.95 (ISBN 0-8226-0362-4). Littlefield.

Government & Economic Choice: An Introduction to Public Finance. Thomas F. Pogue & Larry G. Sgontz. LC 77-75157. (Illus.). 1978. text ed. 18.95 (ISBN 0-395-25112-5). HM.

Government & Industry Relationships: The Lubbock Memorial Lectures, 1975. Ed. by David G. Lethbridge. 200p. 1976. text ed. 25.00 (ISBN 0-08-019733-7); pap. text ed. 17.50 (ISBN 0-08-019732-9). Pergamon.

Government & Local Power in Japan: A Study Based on the Bizen Province, 500-1700. John W. Hall. (Illus.). 1966. 22.50x (ISBN 0-691-03019-7); pap. 8.95 (ISBN 0-691-00780-2). Princeton U Pr.

Government & Local Power in Japan: A Study on Bizen Province, 500-1700. John W. Hall. LC 65-14307. (Illus.). 446p. 1980. 30.00x. Princeton U Pr.

Government & Management of Schools. George Baron & D. A. Howell. 270p. 1974. text ed. 20.75x (ISBN 0-485-11142-X, Athlone Pr). Humanities.

Government & Politics: An Introduction to Political Science. 2nd ed. Ed. by John C. Wahlke et al. 1971. 13.95 (ISBN 0-394-31031-4); tchrs. manual free (ISBN 0-394-31605-3). Random.

Government & Politics in Contemporary Israel, 1948 to Present. Alfred Katz. LC 79-5508. 1980. pap. text ed. 10.50 (ISBN 0-8191-0908-8). U Pr of Amer.

Government & Politics in India. Baljit Singh & Dhirendra Vajpeyi. 130p. 1980. text ed. 10.50 (ISBN 0-86590-008-6). Apt Bks.

Government & Politics in Zambia. Ed. by William Tordoff. LC 73-86660. (Perspectives on Southern Africa Ser). 1975. 22.75x (ISBN 0-520-02593-8). U of Cal Pr.

Government & Politics of Britain. 4th rev. ed. John P. Mackintosh. 1977. pap. text ed. 8.50x (ISBN 0-09-118481-9, Hutchinson U Lib). Humanities.

Government & Politics of Communist China. D. J. Waller. 1973. text ed. 7.75x (ISBN 0-09-102870-1, Hutchinson U Lib). Humanities.

Government & Politics of France. Vincent Wright. LC 78-9274. 1978. text ed. 24.45x (ISBN 0-8419-0409-X); pap. text ed. 9.75x (ISBN 0-8419-0410-3). Holmes & Meier.

Government & Politics of Israel. Don Peretz. 1979. lib. bdg. 23.50x (ISBN 0-89158-086-7); pap. text ed. 10.00x (ISBN 0-89158-087-5). Westview.

Government & Politics of Texas. 7th ed. 1981. text ed. 9.95 (ISBN 0-316-55422-7); tchrs'. manual free (ISBN 0-316-55423-5). Little.

Government & Politics of the Middle East & North Africa. Ed. by David E. Long & Bernard Reich. 465p. 1980. text ed. 30.00x (ISBN 0-89158-593-1); pap. text ed. 13.50x (ISBN 0-89158-871-X). Westview.

Government & Politics of West Germany. Kurt Sontheimer. 1972. text ed. 8.00x (ISBN 0-09-111130-7, Hutchinson U Lib). Humanities.

Government & Related Library & Information Services in the U. K. 3rd rev. ed. Ed. by J. Burkett. 1974. pap. 15.50 (ISBN 0-85365-127-2, Pub. by Lib Assn England). Oryx Pr.

Government & Society in Colonial Peru: The Intendant System 1784-1814. J. R. Fisher. (Univ. of London Historical Studies: No. 29). 1970. text ed. 26.25x (ISBN 0-485-13129-3, Athlone Pr). Humanities.

Government & the American Economy. 3rd ed. Merle Fainsod et al. 1959. 13.95x (ISBN 0-393-09553-3, NortonC). Norton.

Government & the Corporation. Ralph K. Winter. 1978. pap. 4.25 (ISBN 0-8447-3313-X). Am Enterprise.

Government & the Planning Process. P. H. Levin. 1976. text ed. 25.00x o.p. (ISBN 0-04-352059-6). Allen Unwin.

Government & the Sports Business. Ed. by Roger G. Noll. LC 74-279. (Studies in the Regulation of Economic Activity). 1974. 14.95 (ISBN 0-8157-6106-6); pap. 6.95 (ISBN 0-8157-6105-8). Brookings.

Government as a Source of Union Power: The Role of Public Policy in Collective Bargaining. Philip Ross. LC 65-10155. 320p. 1965. 12.50x (ISBN 0-87057-085-4, Pub. by Brown U Pr). Univ Pr of New England.

Government As Land Developer. Ed. by Neal Roberts. LC 75-41924. 1977. 21.95 (ISBN 0-669-00485-5). Lexington Bks.

Government at the Grass-Roots. 3rd ed. George S. Blair. LC 80-84554. (Illus.). 1981. 15.95 (ISBN 0-913530-25-5); pap. 10.95x (ISBN 0-913530-24-7). Palisades Pub.

Government Budgeting & PPBS: A Programmed Introduction. A. B. Turnbull. 1970. pap. 12.95 (ISBN 0-201-07615-2). A-W.

Government Budgeting with Special Reference to India. B. N. Gupta. 1967. 10.00 (ISBN 0-210-27103-5). Asia.

Government by All the People. Delos F. Wilcox. LC 72-1117. (American Constitutional & Legal History Ser.). 338p. 1972. Repr. of 1932 ed. lib. bdg. 32.50 (ISBN 0-306-70502-8). Da Capo.

Government by Pen: The Scotland of James VI & I. Maurice Lee. LC 79-16830. 224p. 1980. 16.00 (ISBN 0-252-00765-4). U of Ill Pr.

Government by the People. 10th ed. James M. Burns et al. Incl. Basic. rev. ed. LC 78-1264. text ed. 16.95 (ISBN 0-13-361162-0); study guide 3.95 (ISBN 0-13-361188-4); National. LC 78-1266. text ed. 17.95 (ISBN 0-13-361154-X); study guide 4.50 (ISBN 0-13-361220-1); National, State, Local. LC 78-1260. text ed. 19.95 (ISBN 0-13-361147-7); study guide 5.95 (ISBN 0-13-361196-5). 1978. P-H.

Government by the People, 3 pts. 11th ed. James M. Burns et al. Incl. National, State, Local. 800p. text ed. 19.95 (ISBN 0-13-361253-8); Basic. 480p. text ed. 16.95 (ISBN 0-13-361238-4); National. 640p. text ed. 17.95 (ISBN 0-13-361246-5). (Illus.). 1981. P-H.

Government Control & Multinational Strategic Management: Power Systems & Telecommunication Equipment. Yves L. Doz. LC 79-11793. (Praeger Special Studies Ser.). 298p. 1979. 24.95 (ISBN 0-03-049476-1). Praeger.

Government Controlled Enterprises: International Strategic & Policy Decisions. R. Mazzolini. LC 78-10961. 1979. 36.50 (ISBN 0-471-99727-7, Pub. by Wiley-Interscience). Wiley.

Government Department: An Organizational Perspective. D. C. Pitt & B. C. Smith. 166p. (Orig.). 1981. pap. 20.00 (ISBN 0-7100-0742-6). Routledge & Kegan.

Government Enterprise. Ed. by Wolfgang G. Friedmann & J. F. Garner. 1971. 22.50x (ISBN 0-231-03448-2). Columbia U Pr.

Government Finance: Economics of the Public Sector. 6th ed. John F. Due & Ann F. Friedlaender. 1977. text ed. 19.95x (ISBN 0-256-01399-3). Irwin.

Government Finance: National, State & Local. Wyland Gardner. LC 77-3572. 1978. 17.95 (ISBN 0-13-360743-7). P-H.

Government Guides to Health & Nutrition. Ralph L. Woods. (Orig.). 1975. pap. 1.25 o.s.i. (ISBN 0-515-03654-4, V3654). Jove Pubns.

Government Handout: A Study in the Administration of the Public Lands 1875-1891. Harold H. Dunham. LC 79-87564. (American Scene Ser). 1970. Repr. of 1941 ed. lib. bdg. 35.00 (ISBN 0-306-71433-7). Da Capo.

Government in American Society. Anthony T. Bouscaren. LC 78-62171. 1978. pap. text ed. 10.25 (ISBN 0-8191-0506-6). U Pr of Amer.

Government in France: An Introduction to the Executive Power. M. Anderson. 1970. 23.00 (ISBN 0-08-015562-6); pap. 11.25 (ISBN 0-08-015561-8). Pergamon.

Government in Metropolitan Calcutta. I. P. A. New York. 6.50x o.p. (ISBN 0-210-22663-3). Asia.

Government in Science: The U. S. Geological Survey, 1867-1894. Thomas G. Manning. LC 67-17851. (Illus.). 272p. 1967. 11.00x (ISBN 0-8131-1142-0). U Pr of Ky.

Government in Spain: The Executive at Work. Kenneth M. Medhurst. 1973. text ed. 16.50 (ISBN 0-08-016940-6). Pergamon.

Government in Sweden: The Executive at Work. N. C. Elder. 1970. 22.00 (ISBN 0-08-015534-0); pap. text ed. 10.75 (ISBN 0-08-015533-2). Pergamon.

Government in Tennessee. 3rd ed. Lee S. Greene et al. LC 75-12587. 418p. 1975. 12.50x (ISBN 0-87049-178-4); pap. 7.95 o.p. (ISBN 0-87049-180-6). U of Tenn Pr.

Government in the Classroom: Dollars & Power in the Classroom. Ed. by Mary F. Williams. LC 78-74964. 1979. 21.95 (ISBN 0-03-052751-1). Praeger.

Government in the Federal Republic of Germany: The Executive at Work. Nevil Johnson. LC 73-12759. 232p. 1974. text ed. 16.50 (ISBN 0-08-017699-2). Pergamon.

Government Information Management: A Counter-Report to the Commission on Federal Paperwork. Elliott R. Morss & Robert F. Rich. (Westview Special Studies in Information Management). 225p. 1980. lib. bdg. 26.50x (ISBN 0-89158-596-6). Westview.

Government Inspector. Nikolai V. Gogol. LC 73-187162. (Drama Editions Ser: No. 7). 1972. 2.45x (ISBN 0-8166-0640-4); pap. 1.95x (ISBN 0-8166-0642-0). U of Minn Pr.

Government Intervention in the Canadian Nuclear Industry. G. Bruce Doern. 1980. pap. text ed. 8.95x (ISBN 0-920380-46-8, Pub. by Inst Res Pub Canada). Renouf.

Government Intervention in the Developed Economy. Ed. by Peter Maunder. LC 78-72590. 1979. 25.95 (ISBN 0-03-049501-6). Praeger.

Government Management Internships & Executive Development. Thomas P. Murphy. (Illus.). 1973. 19.00 o.p. (ISBN 0-669-86363-7). Lexington Bks.

Government Nurse. Felicia Bryce. 192p. (YA) 1976. 4.95 o.p. (ISBN 0-685-66571-2, Avalon). Bouregy.

Government of British Trade Unions. Joseph Goldstein. 1953. 7.95 o.s.i. (ISBN 0-02-912250-3). Free Pr.

Government of Business. R. E. Thomas. 224p. 1976. 30.00x (ISBN 0-86003-501-8, Pub. by Allan Pubs England); pap. 15.00x (ISBN 0-86003-601-4). State Mutual Bk.

Government of Corporations. Richard Eells. LC 62-15339. 1962. 9.95 o.s.i. (ISBN 0-02-909290-6). Free Pr.

Government of Education: The Politics & Administration of Education in Britain. Keith Fenwick & Peter McBride. 256p. 1981. 20.00x (ISBN 0-85520-255-6, Pub. by Martin Robertson England); pap. 9.95x (ISBN 0-85520-254-8). Biblio Dist.

Government of Greater London. Gerald Rhodes & S. K. Ruck. (New Local Government Ser.). 1970. pap. text ed. 9.50x o.p. (ISBN 0-04-352027-8); pap. text ed. 9.50x o. p. (ISBN 0-04-352028-6). Allen Unwin.

Government of India & Reform: Polices Towards Politics & the Constitution 1916-1921, Vol. 32. Peter Robb. (London Oriental Ser). 1977. 37.50x (ISBN 0-19-713590-0). Oxford U Pr.

Government of Poland. Jean-Jacques Rousseau. Tr. by Willmoore Kendall. LC 70-167692. 1972. pap. text ed. 3.95 (ISBN 0-672-60391-8, LLA165). Bobbs.

Government of Prince Edward Island. Frank MacKinnon. LC 53-2186. 1974. 28.50x o.p. (ISBN 0-8020-7038-8). U of Toronto Pr.

Government of Queensland. Colin A. Hughes. (Governments of the Australian States & Territories Ser.). (Illus.). 322p. 1981. text ed. 36.25x (ISBN 0-7022-1515-5); pap. text ed. 19.25x (ISBN 0-7022-1516-3). U of Queensland Pr.

Government of Strangers: Executive Politics in Washington. Hugh Heclo. LC 76-51882. 1977. 15.95 (ISBN 0-8157-3536-7); pap. 6.95 (ISBN 0-8157-3535-9). Brookings.

Government of the Rhine Palatinate in the Fifteenth Century. Henry J. Cohn. 1965. 24.00x (ISBN 0-19-821454-5). Oxford U Pr.

Government of the Soviet Union: A Constitutional Approach, Vol. 1. John Yin. LC 80-82427. (Orig.). 1980. pap. 29.50 (ISBN 0-913124-41-9). Nordland Pub.

Government of the United Kingdom: Political Authority in a Changing Society. Max Beloff & Gillian Peele. (Comparitive Modern Goverment Ser.). (Orig.). 1980. 17.95x (ISBN 0-393-01344-8); pap. text ed. 6.95x (ISBN 0-393-95135-9). Norton.

Government of the United States. 3rd ed. Ernest B. Fincher. (Illus.). 384p. 1976. pap. 12.50 (ISBN 0-13-361881-1). P-H.

Government Policy & Shipbuilding. Brian Hogwood. 1979. text ed. 28.25x (ISBN 0-566-00233-7, Pub. by Gower Pub Co England). Renouf.

Government Project. Edward C. Banfield. 1951. 7.25 o.s.i. (ISBN 0-02-901440-9). Free Pr.

Government Publications. Vladimir M. Palic. 1979. text ed. 37.00 (ISBN 0-08-021457-6). Pergamon.

Government Reference Books, '70-71: A Biennial Guide to U.S. Government Publications. 2nd ed. Sally Wynkoop. LC 76-146307. 250p. 1972. 8.50 o.p. (ISBN 0-87287-062-6). Libs Unl.

Government Reference Books 76-77: A Biennial Guide to U.S. Government Publications. Ed. by Alan E. Schorr. LC 76-146307. 1978. lib. bdg. 25.00x (ISBN 0-87287-192-4). Libs Unl.

Government Reference Books 78-79: A Biennial Guide to U. S. Government Publications, 6th Biennial Volume. Walter L. Newsome. 450p. 1980. lib. bdg. 25.00x (ISBN 0-87287-192-4). Libs Unl.

Government Regulation of Accounting & Information. Ed. by A. Rashad Abdel-khalik. LC 79-26555. (University of Florida Accounting Ser.: No. 11). (Illus.). vi, 320p. (Orig.). 1980. pap. 10.00 (ISBN 0-8130-0663-5). U Presses Fla.

Government Regulation of Business Including Antitrust Information Sources. Ed. by Beatrice S. McDermott & Freada A. Coleman. LC 67-25294. (Management Information Guide Ser.: No. 11). 229p. 1967. 30.00 (ISBN 0-8103-0810-X). Gale.

Government Regulation of the Computer Industry. Bruce Gilchrist & Milton R. Wessel. LC 72-83726. ix, 247p. 1972. 12.50 (ISBN 0-88283-028-7). AFIPS Pr.

Government Regulation: Scope, Growth, Process. W. T. Stanbury. 267p. 1980. pap. text ed. 10.95x (ISBN 0-920380-48-4, Pub. by Inst Res Pub Canada). Renouf.

Government Requirements of Small Business. Roland J. Cole & Philip D. Tegeler. LC 79-3046. (Human Affairs Research Center Ser.). 192p. 1980. 18.95 (ISBN 0-669-03307-3). Lexington Bks.

Government Spending & Economic Expansion. A. E. Burns & D. S. Watson. LC 75-173452. (FDR & the Era of the New Deal Ser). 174p. 1972. Repr. of 1940 ed. lib. bdg. 20.00 (ISBN 0-306-70368-8). Da Capo.

Government Spending & Landvalues. Ed. by C. L. Harriss. LC 72-9988. 320p. 1973. 21.50x (ISBN 0-299-06320-8). U of Wis Pr.

Government Under Law. Arthur E. Sutherland. LC 68-26003. (Law, Politics & History Ser). (Illus.). 1968. Repr. of 1956 ed. lib. bdg. 45.00 (ISBN 0-306-71146-X). Da Capo.

Government Versus Trade Unionism in British Politics Since 1968. Gerald A. Dorfman. LC 78-70886. (Publication 224 Ser.). 187p. 1979. 12.95 (ISBN 0-8179-7241-2). Hoover Inst Pr.

Governmental Accounting. 5th ed. Leon E. Hay & R. M. Mikesell. 1974. text ed. 17.95x o.p. (ISBN 0-256-01543-0). Irwin.

Governmental & Intergovernmental Immunity in Australia & Canada. Colin H. McNairn. 1977. 15.00x (ISBN 0-8020-2241-3). U of Toronto Pr.

Governmental Budgeting. Jesse Burkhead. LC 56-8000. 1956. 26.95 (ISBN 0-471-12375-7). Wiley.

Governmental Controls & the Free Market: The U. S. Economy in the 1970's. Ed. by Svetozar Pejovich. LC 76-17976. 240p. 1976. 19.50x (ISBN 0-89096-020-8). Tex A&M Univ Pr.

Governmental Ethics & Conflicts of Interest in Georgia. Kipling L. McVay & Robert S. Stubbs. 227p. 1980. 15.00 (ISBN 0-87215-304-5). Michie.

Governmental Organization for the Regulation of Nuclear Power Plants. (IAEA Safety Ser.: No. 50-C-G). 43p. 1979. pap. 6.50 (ISBN 92-0-123478-3, ISP502, IAEA). Unipub.

Governmental Regulation of Business. Jesse S. Raphael. LC 66-12081. 1966. 7.95 o.s.i. (ISBN 0-02-925820-0). Free Pr.

Governmental Secrecy & National Security: The Progressive Case. A. De Volpi et al. (Pergamon Policy Studies on International Politics). (Illus.). 400p. 1980. 30.00 (ISBN 0-08-025995-2); pap. 15.00 (ISBN 0-08-027529-X). Pergamon.

Governments & Growth. F. Knox. 1976. 18.95 (ISBN 0-347-01153-5, 00787-0, Pub. by Saxon Hse). Lexington Bks.

Governments & Leaders: An Approach to Comparative Politics. Edward Feit. LC 77-77977. (Illus.). 1978. text ed. 18.75 (ISBN 0-395-25367-5). HM.

Governments & Mining Companies in Developing Countries. James Cobbe. LC 79-4851. (Special Studies in Social, Political & Economic Development). (Illus.). 1979. lib. bdg. 25.00x (ISBN 0-89158-562-1). Westview.

Governments & the Geography of Federal Spending in the U.S.A. Ronald J. Johnston. 208p. 1981. write for info. (ISBN 0-471-27865-3, Pub. by Wiley-Interscience). Wiley.

Governments Within the States. Eugene P. Dvorin & Arthur J. Misner. LC 70-136121. (Political Science Ser). 1971. pap. 5.95 (ISBN 0-201-01620-6). A-W.

Governor & the Rebel: A History of Bacon's Rebellion in Virginia. Wilcomb E. Washburn. (Illus.). 272p. 1972. pap. 5.95 (ISBN 0-393-00645-X, Norton Lib). Norton.

Governor in the Indian Constitution. V. K. Varadachari. 1980. 13.00x (ISBN 0-8364-0658-3, Pub. by Heritage India). South Asia Bks.

Governor's Land Archaeological District Excavations: The Nineteen Seventy-Six Season. Alain C. Outlaw. (Illus.). Date not set. write for info. (ISBN 0-8139-0875-2). U Pr of Va. Postponed.

Governors of Arkansas: Essays in Political Biography. Ed. by Timothy P. Donovan & Willard B. Gatewood, Jr. 1981. text ed. 24.00x (ISBN 0-938626-00-0). U of Mo Pr.

Governors of Minnesota: 1849-1971. Committee for the Inauguration of Wendell R. Anderson. (Illus.). 22p. 1971. pap. 2.00 (ISBN 0-685-47097-0). Minn Hist.

Governors of Mississippi. Cecil L. Sumners. (Governors of the State Ser.). (Illus.). 180p. 1980. 13.95 (ISBN 0-88289-237-1). Pelican.

Governors of Tennessee, Seventeen Ninety to Eighteen Thirty-Five: I. Jill S. Broer et al. Ed. by Charles W. Crawford. LC 79-129790. (Tennessee Ser.: Vol. 3). (Illus.). 1979. 12.95 (ISBN 0-87870-075-7). Memphis St Univ.

Governor's Wife on the Mining Frontier. James L. Thane, Jr. (Utah, the Mormons, & the West: No. 7). 1976. 8.50 (ISBN 0-87480-161-3, Tanner). U of Utah Pr.

Goya. J. Gudiol. (Library of Great Painters Ser). 1965. 35.00 (ISBN 0-8109-0149-8). Abrams.

Goya. Sarah Symmons. LC 77-77884. (Illus.). 1977. 15.95 (ISBN 0-8467-0354-8, Pub. by Two Continents); pap. 9.95 (ISBN 0-8467-0353-X). Hippocrene Bks.

Goya & His Critics. Nigel Glendinning. LC 76-49697. 1977. 40.00x (ISBN 0-300-02011-2). Yale U Pr.

Gozo Al Crecer, Summer/jessica De. Jessica De Summers. Date not set. pap. price not set (ISBN 0-311-38550-8, Edit Mundo). Casa Bautista.

GPSS Fortran. B. Schmidt. (Computing Ser.). 544p. 1981. write for info. (ISBN 0-471-27881-5, Pub. by Wiley-Interscience). Wiley.

Grabianski's Birds. Janusz Grabianski. LC 68-11332. (Illus.). (gr. k-3). 1968. PLB 3.95 o.p. (ISBN 0-531-01365-0). Watts.

Grabianski's Cats. Janusz Grabianski. LC 67-10577. (Illus.). (gr. k-3). 1967. PLB 4.95 o.p. (ISBN 0-531-01366-9). Watts.

Gracchi. David Stockton. 1979. 28.50x (ISBN 0-19-872104-8); pap. 12.95x (ISBN 0-19-872105-6). Oxford U Pr.

Grace. Lewis S. Chafer. pap. 6.95 (ISBN 0-310-22331-8). Zondervan.

Grace Abounding. John Bunyan. 1959. pap. 1.50 (ISBN 0-8024-3293-X). Moody.

Grace Abounding to the Chief of Sinners. John Bunyan. Ed. by Roger Sharrock. (Oxford English Texts Ser). 1962. 29.95x (ISBN 0-19-811833-3). Oxford U Pr.

Grace Abounding to the Chief of Sinners. John Bunyan. Ed. & intro. by Roger Sharrock. Bd. with Pilgrim's Progress from This World to That Which Is to Come. (Oxford Standard Authors Ser). 1966. 24.95 (ISBN 0-19-254159-5). Oxford U Pr.

Grace Alone. 1980. 3.25 (ISBN 0-8100-0110-1). Northwest Pub.

Grace & Duty of Being Spiritually Minded. John Owen. (Summit Bks). 1977. pap. 3.45 (ISBN 0-8010-6663-8). Baker Bk.

Grace & Forgiveness in Ministry. Murray S. Thompson. LC 80-23613. 176p. (Orig.). 1981. pap. 6.95 (ISBN 0-687-15680-7). Abingdon.

Grace & the Glory of God: Deliverance from Cults. Ray C. Jarman & Carmen Benson. 98p. 1968. pap. 2.95 o.p. (ISBN 0-912106-71-9). Logos.

Grace & Torah. J. M. Myers. LC 74-26343. 96p. 1975. pap. 2.95 (ISBN 0-8006-1099-7, 1-1099). Fortress.

Grace Grows Best in Winter. large print ed. Margaret Clarkson. 208p. 1975. kivar 5.95 (ISBN 0-310-22467-5). Zondervan.

Grace Livingston Hill. Jean Karr. 1976. lib. bdg. 8.20 (ISBN 0-89190-992-3). Am Repr-Rivercity Pr.

Grace Notes & Other Fragments. Joseph A. Sittler. Ed. by Robert M. Herhold & Linda M. Delloff. LC 80-8055. 128p. (Orig.). 1981. pap. 5.50 (ISBN 0-8006-1404-6, 1-1404). Fortress.

Grace of God in the Gospel. John Cheesman et al. 1976. pap. 2.45 (ISBN 0-85151-153-8). Banner of Truth.

Grace of Yielding. Derek Prince. 1977. pap. 1.50 (ISBN 0-934920-20-6, B-30). Derek Prince.

Grace of Zen: Zen Texts for Meditation. Karlfried Durckheim. 1977. pap. 3.95 (ISBN 0-8164-2151-X). Crossroad NY.

Grace Unlimited. Clark H. Pinnock. LC 75-22161. 272p. 1975. pap. 5.95 (ISBN 0-87123-185-9, 210185). Bethany Fell.

Grace Upon Grace. James Cook. 6.95. Eerdmans.

Gracie. Suzanne Roberts. LC 65-19890. (gr. 5-9). 1965. 5.95 o.p. (ISBN 0-385-05866-7). Doubleday.

Graciela: A Mexican-American Child Tells Her Story. Joe Molnar. LC 77-182297. (Illus.). 48p. (gr. 4-7). 1972. PLB 4.90 o.p. (ISBN 0-531-02023-1). Watts.

Graded Exercises & Worked Examples in Physics. 5th ed. M. Nelkon. 1977. pap. text ed. 5.95x o.p. (ISBN 0-435-68657-7). Heinemann Ed.

Graded Exercises in English. rev. ed. Robert J. Dixson. (Orig.). (gr. 8-10). 1971. pap. text ed. 2.95 (ISBN 0-88345-058-5, 18009); answer key 1.00 (ISBN 0-685-19797-2). Regents Pub.

Graded French Reader: Premiere Etape. 3rd ed. Ed. by Camille Bauer & Otto Bond. 1978. pap. text ed. 6.95x (ISBN 0-669-00876-1). Heath.

Graded German Comprehension. F. M. Christie. 1968. pap. text ed. 2.50x (ISBN 0-435-38160-1). Heinemann Ed.

Graded German Reader. 2nd ed. Hannelore Crossgrove & William C. Crossgrove. 1978. pap. text ed. 6.95x (ISBN 0-669-01533-4). Heath.

Graded Italian Reader: Prima Tappa. 2nd ed. Vincenzo Cioffari et al. 1979. pap. text ed. 6.95 (ISBN 0-669-01955-0). Heath.

Graded Problems in Chemistry to Ordinary Level. A. Holderness & J. Lambert. 1979. pap. text ed. 3.95x o.p. (ISBN 0-435-64427-0). Heinemann Ed.

Graded Readers for Students of English As a Second Language. Incl. Jack London's The Call of the Wild. Ed. by Winifred E. Jones. (3000 word level). pap. 3.25 (ISBN 0-87789-075-7); Selected Stories by American Authors. Ed. by Kenneth Croft & Edith F. Croft. (2000 word level). pap. 2.95 o.p. (ISBN 0-87789-074-9); Stephen Crane's The Red Badge of Courage. Ed. by Winifred E. Jones. (3000 word level). pap. 3.25 (ISBN 0-87789-079-X); Stories by Edgar Allan Poe. Ed. by David P. Harris. (4000 word level). pap. 3.50 (ISBN 0-87789-080-3); Stories by Edith Wharton. Ed. by Kenneth Croft & Edith F. Croft. (3000 word level). pap. 3.25 (ISBN 0-87789-078-1); Stories by Jack London. Ed. by Kenneth Croft & Edith F. Croft. (3000 word level). pap. 3.25 (ISBN 0-87789-076-5); Stories by O. Henry. Ed. by Mildred H. Larson. (3000 word level). pap. 3.25 (ISBN 0-87789-077-3); Stories by Washington Irving. Ed. by Kenneth Croft & Edith F. Croft. (2000 word level). pap. 2.95 (ISBN 0-87789-073-0); Stories of the American West. Ed. by Sara Withers. (4000 word level). pap. 3.50 (ISBN 0-87789-082-X); Two Short Novels by Henry James. Ed. by Corbin S. Carnell. (4000 word level). pap. 3.50 (ISBN 0-87789-081-1). 1973. Eng Language.

Graded Readings & Exercises in Old Icelandic. Kenneth G. Chapman. 1970. pap. 8.75x (ISBN 0-520-00221-0, CAMPUS25). U of Cal Pr.

Graded Readings in Russian History: The Formation of the Russian State. Leon Stilman. LC 60-7695. (Columbia Slavic Studies). (Illus.). (gr. 9 up). 1960. pap. 6.00x (ISBN 0-231-02390-1). Columbia U Pr.

Graded Spanish Reader. 3rd ed. Ed. by Manuel Duran. 1978. pap. text ed. 6.95x (ISBN 0-669-00880-X). Heath.

Graded Spanish Review: Grammar with Composition. 2nd ed. F. C. Tarr & Augusto Centeno. (gr. 9-12). 1973. text ed. 13.95 (ISBN 0-13-362160-X). P-H.

Grades: Research & Reporting Procedures. Donald L. Halsted & Anne M. Bober. 43p. 1978. pap. 9.00 o.p. (ISBN 0-686-00908-8, D-115). Essence Pubns.

Grades, What's So Important About Them, Anyway? Shirley Schwarzrock & C. Gilbert Wrenn. (Coping with Ser.). (Illus.). 33p. (gr. 7-12). pap. text ed. 1.30 (ISBN 0-913476-34-X). Am Guidance.

Gradient Liquid Chromatography. C. Liteanu & S. Gocan. LC 74-1008. (Ser. in Analytical Chemistry). 1974. text ed. 44.95 (ISBN 0-470-54124-5). Halsted Pr.

Gradual Awakening. Stephen Levine. LC 77-27712. 1979. pap. 4.95 (ISBN 0-385-14164-5, Anch). Doubleday.

Graduate Course in Probability. Howard G. Tucker. (Probability & Mathematical Statistics: Vol. 2). 1967. text ed. 21.95 (ISBN 0-12-702646-0). Acad Pr.

Graduate Management Admission Test. 3rd ed. Arco Editorial Board. LC 79-1214. (Arco Professional Career Examination Ser.). (Illus.). 408p. (Orig.). 1980. pap. 6.95 (ISBN 0-668-04914-6, 4914); lib. bdg. 10.00 o. p. (ISBN 0-668-04917-0). Arco.

Graduate Management Admission Test. Edward C. Gruber. 1976. pap. 6.95 (ISBN 0-671-18995-6). Monarch Pr.

Graduate Management Admission Test. 1st ed. David R. Turner. LC 77-7368. 1977. pap. 6.00 o.p. (ISBN 0-668-04360-1). Arco.

Graduate Management Admissions Test Preparation Guide. Jerry Bobrow & William A. Covino. (Cliffs Test Preparation Ser.). (Illus.). 342p. 1980. wkbk. 5.25 (ISBN 0-8220-2006-8). Cliffs.

Graduate Record Examination Aptitude Test. 5th ed. Arco Editorial Board. LC 78-15173. (Arco Professional Career Examination Ser.). (Illus.). 428p. (Orig.). 1980. pap. 6.95 (ISBN 0-668-04910-3, 4910-3); lib. bdg. 10.00 (ISBN 0-668-04915-4). Arco.

Graduate Record Examination Aptitude Test Preparation Guide. William A. Covino et al. (Cliffs Test Preparation Ser.). (Illus.). 267p. (Orig.). 1980. wkbk. 4.95 (ISBN 0-8220-2008-4). Cliffs.

Graduate Record Examination: Review for the Advanced Psychology Test. L. H. Halpert. 1980. pap. 5.95 (ISBN 0-671-18991-3). Monarch Pr.

Graduate School Adjustments to the New Depression in Higher Education. National Board on Graduate Education. 1975. pap. 6.50 (ISBN 0-309-02328-9). Natl Acad Pr.

Graduate Student Survival. W. Richard Dukelow. (Illus.). 88p. 1980. 6.75 (ISBN 0-398-04068-0). C C Thomas.

Graduate Studies: The Guide to Postgraduate Study in the UK, 1980 to 1981. 7th ed. Ed. by Careers Research & Advisory Centre. 1191p. 1980. 135.00x (ISBN 0-86021-342-0). Intl Pubns Serv.

Graduate Studies (United Kingdom), Nineteen Eighty to Eighty-One. Ed. by Careers Research & Advisory Centre. 1191p. 1980. 135.00x (ISBN 0-86021-342-0). Intl Pubns Serv.

Graduate Theses & Dissertations in ESL: 1978-79. Stephen Cooper. (Language in Education Ser.: No. 27). 1980. pap. text ed. 2.95 (ISBN 0-87281-127-1). Ctr Appl Ling.

Graduate Theses Dissertations in E S L: Nineteen Seventy-Six to Nineteen Seventy-Seven. Stephen Cooper. (Language in Education Ser.: No. 3). 1978. pap. text ed. 2.95 (ISBN 0-87281-079-8). Ctr Appl Ling.

Graduated Language Training: For Patients with Aphasia & Children with Language Deficiencies. Robert L. Keith. LC 79-91245. (Illus.). 320p. 1980. clinical test 24.95 (ISBN 0-933014-57-0). College-Hill.

Graduated Swing Method. Richard Metz. (Illus.). 128p. 1981. 12.95 (ISBN 0-684-16868-5, ScribT). Scribner.

Graduate's Guide to Success. William J. Krutza. 96p. 1976. 3.95 (ISBN 0-8010-5374-9). Baker Bk.

Graduate's Guide to the Business World. Joan L. Owens. LC 73-77700. (Illus.). 96p. 4.95x o.p. (ISBN 0-686-09301-1, Dist. by Hippocrene Books Inc.); pap. 2.50x o.p. (ISBN 0-686-09302-X). Leviathan Hse.

Graduation: A New Start. Robert Flood. 128p. 1981. pap. 5.95. Moody.

Gradwohl's Clinical Laboratory Methods & Diagnosis. 8th ed. Alex C. Sonnenwirth & Leonard Jarett. LC 79-26398. (Illus.). 1980. text ed. 115.00 (ISBN 0-8016-4741-X). Mosby.

Graff-a-Doodle Do. Lee Ames. (Illus.). 96p. 1981. pap. 3.95 (ISBN 0-686-69181-4). G&D.

Graffiti in the Big Ten. Marina N. Haan & Richard B. Hammerstrom. 164p. (Orig.). 1980. pap. 3.95 (ISBN 0-9604534-0-7). Brown Hse Gall.

Graffiti: Poems. 3rd ed. Lawrence Bantleman. (Redbird Bk.). 1976. lib. bdg. 8.00 (ISBN 0-89253-095-2); pap. text ed. 4.00 (ISBN 0-89253-132-0). Ind-US Inc.

Graft vs. Leukemia in Man & Animal Models. Ed. by James P. O'Kunewick & Ruby F. Meredith. 304p. 1981. 69.95 (ISBN 0-8493-5745-4). CRC Pr.

Graham Greene: A Descriptive Catalogue. Robert H. Miller. LC 77-92925. 88p. 1979. 12.50x (ISBN 0-8131-1383-0). U Pr of Ky.

Graham Greene: Some Critical Considerations. Ed. by Robert O. Evans. LC 63-22005. 304p. 1967. pap. 5.00x (ISBN 0-8131-0114-X). U Pr of Ky.

Graham Greene the Entertainer. Peter Wolfe. LC 72-188700. (Crosscurrents-Modern Critiques Ser.). 191p. 1972. 11.95 (ISBN 0-8093-0580-1). S Ill U Pr.

Graham Greene: The Films of His Fiction. Gene D. Phillips. LC 73-85252. 1974. pap. 7.950 (ISBN 0-8077-2376-2). Tchrs Coll.

Grail Yoga. 2nd ed. Edward Thomas. LC 74-84399. (Grail Bk). (Illus.). 128p. 1975. pap. 2.95 (ISBN 0-914896-28-8). East Ridge Pr.

Grail Yoga. Henry Thomas. 128p. 1978. pap. 3.95 (ISBN 0-8334-1715-0). Multimedia.

Grain Motor Fuel Alcohol Technical & Economic Assessment Study. Raphael Katzen Associates. 344p. 1981. pap. 39.50 (ISBN 0-89934-063-6). Solar Energy Info.

Grain of Salt. Grigory Vinokur. LC 80-17406. 208p. 1981. 9.95 (ISBN 0-8119-0330-3). Fell.

Grain Storage: Part of a System. Ed. by R. N. Sinha & William E. Muir. (Illus.). 1973. text ed. 35.50 o.p. (ISBN 0-87055-123-X). AVI.

Grain Trading As a Foundation for Total Futures Trading. Ralph M. Ainsworth. (Illus.). 197p. 1980. 79.75 (ISBN 0-918968-74-7). Inst Econ Finan.

Grains of Wheat. K. B. Kelly. (Illus.). 128p. 1981. pap. 1.95 (ISBN 0-914544-32-2). Living Flame Pr.

Gramatica Analitica. Aurelio M. Espinosa & John P. Wonder. 400p. 1975. text ed. 17.95x (ISBN 0-669-82941-2). Heath.

Gramatica Elemental Del Griego Del Nuevo Testamento. Guillermo H. Davis. Tr. by Jorge F. McKibben. 1980. Repr. of 1978 ed. 3.75 (ISBN 0-311-42008-7). Casa Bautista.

Gramatica Espanola De Repaso. 2nd ed. Francisco Ugarte. Ed. by F. L. Gordon. LC 78-81805. 1969. 8.95 (ISBN 0-672-63173-3). Odyssey Pr.

Gramatica Funcional. Clark A. Vaughan. (gr. 9-10). 1969. pap. text ed. 5.95 (ISBN 0-88334-014-3) (ISBN 0-685-39245-7). Ind Sch Pr.

Gramatica Griega Del Nuevo Testamento. H. E. Dana & J. R. Mantey. Tr. by Adolfo Robleto & Catalina De Clark. 1979. pap. 8.95 (ISBN 0-311-42010-9). Casa Bautista.

Grambling: Cradle of the Pros. Bill McIntyre. Ed. by Doug Woolfolk. (Illus.). 110p. 1980. 12.50 (ISBN 0-86518-015-6). Moran Pub Corp.

Grammaire de base. new ed. Jean Dubois. (Orig., Fr.). 1976. pap. 7.25 (ISBN 2-03-040166-8). Larousse.

Grammaire de la Langue Georgienne. Hans Vogt. (Institutt for Sammenlignende Kulturforskning Serie B.: No. 58). 278p. 1971. 27.00x (ISBN 8-200-08720-4, Dist. by Columbia U Pr). Universitet.

Grammaire Francaise: Methode Orale. Hazel J. Bullock. 1949. 22.50x (ISBN 0-89197-493-8); pap. text ed. 12.50x (ISBN 0-89197-775-9). Irvington.

Grammaire Larousse du francais contemporain. Larousse & Co. (Fr). 18.00 (ISBN 2-03-070031-2, 3746). Larousse.

Grammaire structurale du francais, 3 vols. Jean Dubois. Incl. Vol. 1. Nom et pronom. 192p (3630); Vol. 2. Verbe. 192p (3631); Vol. 3. Phrase et transformations. 180p (3632). (Fr.). pap. 14.50 ea. Larousse.

Grammaire transformationelle du francais: Syntaxe du nom. Maurice Gross. 1978. pap. text ed. 20.95 (ISBN 2-03-070343-5, 3633). Larousse.

Grammaire transformationelle du francais: Syntaxe du verbe. M. Gross. (Fr). pap. 14.50 (ISBN 0-685-13931-X). Larousse.

Grammar & Drillbook. Willard D. Sheeler. 1978. 4.25 (ISBN 0-89285-037-X). English Lang.

Grammar & L Formas: An Introduction. D. Wood. (Lecture Notes in Computer Science: Vol. 91). 314p. 1980. pap. 19.50 (ISBN 0-387-10233-7). Springer-Verlag.

Grammar Basics: A Reading-Writing Approach. Jean Malmstrom. (English Language Ser.). (gr. 10 up). 1977. pap. text ed. 6.75x (ISBN 0-8104-6025-4). Hayden.

Grammar for Reading German, Form C. rev. ed. K. Roald Bergethon & Ellis Finger. 1979. pap. text ed. 9.40 (ISBN 0-395-26085-X); instrs'. answer key 6.60 (ISBN 0-395-26084-1). HM.

Grammar of Biloxi. Paula F. Einaudi. LC 75-25114. (American Indian Linguistics Ser.). 1976. lib. bdg. 42.00 (ISBN 0-8240-1965-2). Garland Pub.

Grammar of Case: Towards a Localistic Theory. John M. Anderson. LC 71-145602. (Studies in Linguistics Ser: No. 4). (Illus.). 1971. 35.00 (ISBN 0-521-08035-5); pap. 11.95 (ISBN 0-521-29057-0). Cambridge U Pr.

Grammar of Colloquial Tibetan. Sir Charles Bell. 1977. pap. 4.00 o.p. (ISBN 0-486-23466-5). Dover.

Grammar of Conducting: A Practical Guide to Baton Technique & Orchestral Interpretation. 2nd ed. Max Rudolf. LC 79-7634. (Illus.). 1980. text ed. 17.50 (ISBN 0-02-872220-5). Schirmer Bks.

Grammar of Contemporary English. R. Quirk et al. 1976. text ed. 42.00x (ISBN 0-582-52444-X). Longman.

Grammar of Diegueno Nominals. Larry P. Gorbet. LC 75-25116. (American Indian Linguistics Ser.). 1976. lib. bdg. 42.00 (ISBN 0-8240-1967-9). Garland Pub.

Grammar of Diyari, South Australia. P. Austin. (Cambridge Studies in Linguistics Monographs: No. 32). (Illus.). 230p. Date not set. price not set (ISBN 0-521-22849-2). Cambridge U Pr.

Grammar of English Predicate Complement Constructions. Peter S. Rosenbaum. (Press Research Monographs: No. 47). 1967. 12.50x o.p. (ISBN 0-262-18023-5). MIT Pr.

Grammar of English Reflexives. Michael Helke. Ed. by Jorge Hankamer. LC 78-66542. (Outstanding Dissertations in Linguistics Ser.). 1979. lib. bdg. 22.00 (ISBN 0-8240-9684-3). Garland Pub.

Grammar of Lahu. James A. Matisoff. (U. C. Publ. in Linguistics: Vol. 75). 1973. pap. 17.75x (ISBN 0-520-09467-0). U of Cal Pr.

Grammar of Mishnaic Hebrew. M. H. Segal. 1979. pap. text ed. 12.95x (ISBN 0-19-815454-2). Oxford U Pr.

Grammar of Modern Latvian, 3 vols. T. G. Fennel & H. Gelsen. (Slavistic Printings & Reprintings: No. 303). 1980. text ed. 176.50x (ISBN 0-686-26963-2). Mouton.

Grammar of Motives. Kenneth Burke. LC 69-16741. 1969. 18.50x (ISBN 0-520-01543-6); pap. 6.95x (ISBN 0-520-01544-4). U of Cal Pr.

Grammar of Music. Thomas Busby. LC 76-20711. (Music Reprint Ser). 1976. Repr. of 1818 ed. lib. bdg. 35.00 (ISBN 0-306-70789-6). Da Capo.

Grammar of Music. Hilda Hunter. (Student's Music Library Ser). 1952. 6.95 (ISBN 0-234-77208-5). Dufour.

Grammar of New Testament Greek: Accidence & Word Formation, Vol. 2. J. H. Moulton et al. 572p. 1979. text ed. 17.50x (ISBN 0-567-01012-0). Attic Pr.

Grammar of New Testament Greek: Syntax, Vol. 3. J. H. Moulton et al. 438p. 1963. text ed. 17.50x (ISBN 0-567-01013-9). Attic Pr.

Grammar of New Testament Greek: The Prolegomena, Vol. I. 3rd ed. J. H. Moulton et al. 320p. 1978. write for info. (ISBN 0-567-01011-2). Attic Pr.

Grammar of Old Irish. R. Thurneysen. 1961. 30.00x (ISBN 0-686-00866-9). Colton Bk.

Grammar of Palestinian Jewish Aramaic. 2nd ed. William B. Stevenson. (With an Appendix on the Numerals). 1962. 13.95x (ISBN 0-19-815419-4). Oxford U Pr.

Grammar of Pawnee. Douglas R. Parks. LC 75-25121. (American Indian Linguistics Ser.). 1976. lib. bdg. 42.00 (ISBN 0-8240-1971-7). Garland Pub.

Grammar of Politics. Harold J. Laski. 1925. 47.50x o.p. (ISBN 0-686-51396-7). Elliots Bks.

Grammar of Septuagint Greek. Frederick C. Conybeare & G. Stock. 80p. 1980. pap. 5.95 (ISBN 0-310-43001-1). Zondervan.

Grammar of Southeastern Pomo. Julius Moshinsky. (Publications in Linguistics Vol. 72). 1974. pap. 11.50x (ISBN 0-520-09450-6). U of Cal Pr.

Grammar of Spoken Chinese. Yuen Ren Chao. 1968. 35.00x (ISBN 0-520-00219-9). U of Cal Pr.

Grammar of Spoken English. 3rd ed. H. E. Palmer. Ed. by R. Kingdon. LC 75-26276. 341p. 1975. 36.00 (ISBN 0-521-21097-6); pap. 10.50x (ISBN 0-521-29040-6). Cambridge U Pr.

Grammar of Tera: Transformational Syntax & Texts. Paul Newman. (U. C. Publ. in Linguistics: Vol. 57). 1970. pap. 9.50x (ISBN 0-520-09254-6). U of Cal Pr.

Grammar of the Arabic Language, 2 Vols. 3rd ed. William Wright. 1933-1967. Vol. 1. 42.00 (ISBN 0-521-06875-4); Vol. 2. pap. text ed. 27.50x (ISBN 0-521-09455-0). Cambridge U Pr.

Grammar of the Arabic Language. Wm. Wright. 1974. 25.00 (ISBN 0-685-77114-8). Intl Bk Ctr.

Grammar of the English Language. George O. Curme. 1978. 40.00 set (ISBN 0-930454-03-0). Verbatim.

Grammar of the English Language: Parts of Speech. George O. Curme. LC 77-87423. 1978. 20.00 (ISBN 0-930454-02-2). Verbatim.

Grammar of the English Language: Syntax. George O. Curme. LC 77-87422. 1978. 20.00 (ISBN 0-930454-01-4). Verbatim.

Grammar of the Gothic Language & the Gospel of St. Mark. 2nd ed. Joseph Wright. 1954. 24.95x (ISBN 0-19-811922-4). Oxford U Pr.

Grammar of the Ho Language. L. Burrows. 194p. 1980. Repr. of 1915 ed. 20.00 o.p. (ISBN 0-89684-258-4, Pub. by Cosmo Pubns India). Orient Bk Dist.

Grammar of the Icelandic or Old Norse Tonque. Rasmus K. Rask. Tr. by George W. Dasent from Danish. (Amsterdam Classics in Linguistics 1800-1925: No. 2). Orig. Title: Vejledning til det Islandskeeller gamle Nordisk Sprog. 1979. text ed. 40.00x (ISBN 90-272-0871-9). Humanities.

Grammar of the New Testament Greek: Style, Vol. 4. J. H. Moulton et al. LC 7-13420. 1976. text ed. 15.00x (ISBN 0-567-01018-X). Attic Pr.

Grammar of the Prakrit Language. 2nd rev. ed. D. C. Sircar. 6.50 (ISBN 0-89684-209-6). Orient Bk Dist.

Grammar of Tuscarora. Marianne M. Williams. LC 75-25124. (American Indian Linguistics Ser.). 1976. lib. bdg. 42.00 (ISBN 0-8240-1974-1). Garland Pub.

Grammar of Vai. William E. Welmers. (Publ. in Linguistics Ser: Vol. 84). 1977. pap. 10.75x (ISBN 0-520-09555-3). U of Cal Pr.

Grammar of Yidin. R. M. Dixon. LC 76-27912. (Cambridge Studies in Linguistics: No. 19). (Illus.). 1977. 75.00 (ISBN 0-521-21462-9). Cambridge U Pr.

Grammar, Rhetoric & Composition. Richard D. Mallery. 1967. pap. 3.95 (ISBN 0-06-463228-8, EH 228, EH). Har-Row.

Grammar School Tradition in a Comprehensive World. J. N. Hewitson. 1969. text ed. 6.50x (ISBN 0-7100-6392-X). Humanities.

Grammatica Speculativa of Thomas of Erfurt. Ed. by G. L. Bursill-Hall. (Classics of Linguistics Ser). 340p. 1972. text ed. 25.00x (ISBN 0-582-52495-4). Longman.

Grammatical Insights into the New Testament. Nigel Turner. LC 66-71386. 208p. Repr. of 1965 ed. text ed. 15.95x (ISBN 0-567-01017-1). Attic Pr.

Grammatical Structures of English & Spanish. Robert P. Stockwell et al. (Orig.). 1965. pap. 6.00x (ISBN 0-226-77504-6). U of Chicago Pr.

Grammatical Texts. Arno Poebel. (Publications of the Babylonian Section: Vol. 6). 122p. 1914. soft bound 3.00 o.p. (ISBN 0-686-11920-7). Univ Mus of U PA.

Grammatical Theory in Western Europe 1500-1700. G. A. Padley. LC 75-44573. 320p. 1976. 47.50 (ISBN 0-521-21079-8). Cambridge U Pr.

Gramophone Classical Catalogue. Ed. by Gramophone. LC 79-53740. (Illus.). 1980. 13.50 (ISBN 0-7153-7883-X). David & Charles.

Gramps & the Coon Dog. Jean Marie. Ed. by M. Karl Kulikowski. (Gusto Press Poetry Discovery Ser.). (Orig.). 1979. pap. 3.95 (ISBN 0-933906-08-0). Gusto Pr.

Gramsci & Marxist Theory. Chantal Mouffe. 1979. 26.00x (ISBN 0-7100-0357-9); pap. 14.50 (ISBN 0-7100-0358-7). Routledge & Kegan.

Gramsci & the Communist Question. Luciano Pellicani. Tr. by Mimi Watts from Ital. (Publication Ser.: No. 243). 128p. (Orig.). 1981. pap. write for info. (ISBN 0-8179-7432-6). Hoover Inst Pr.

Gramsci & the State. Christine Buci-Glucksmann. Tr. by David Fernbach from Fr. 485p. 1980. text ed. 36.50x (ISBN 0-85315-483-X). Humanities.

Gran Enciclopedia Larousse, 10 vols. & 1 supplement. (Span.). 1967. Set. 845.00 (ISBN 0-8277-3061-6). Maxwell Sci Intl.

Gran Enciclopedia Rialp, 24 vols. (Span.). 1971-1876. Set. 1425.00. Pergamon.

Gran Minoria. Leighton Ford. Tr. by Jose M. Blanch from Eng. Orig. Title: Christian Persuader. 170p. (Orig., Span.). 1969. pap. write for info. o.p. (ISBN 0-89922-005-3). Edit Caribe.

Gran Passo en Tren. Philip Mann. Tr. by Georgian Kreps from Span. (Shape Board Play Book). Orig. Title: Great Train Ride. (Illus.). 14p. (Eng.). (ps-3). 1981. bds. 3.50 plastic comb bdg. (ISBN 0-89828-201-2, 5005SP). Tuffy Bks.

Granada-Monarch: Nineteen Seventy Five to Eighty Repair & Tune-up Guide. (New Automotive Bks.). 240p. 1980. 8.95 (ISBN 0-8019-6937-9). Chilton.

Grand Atlas & Picture Book of the World. LC 77-74767. (Illus.). 1977. 35.00 o.p. (ISBN 0-528-83083-X). Rand.

Grand Beehive. Compiled by Hal Cannon. (Illus.). 88p. (Orig.). 1980. pap. 9.50 (ISBN 0-87480-190-7). U of Utah Pr.

Grand Canyon. Robert Wallace. (American Wilderness Ser). (Illus.). 1972. 12.95 (ISBN 0-8094-1144-X). Time-Life.

Grand Canyon. Robert Wallace. LC 71-179463. (American Wilderness Ser). (Illus.). (gr. 6 up). 1972. lib. bdg. 11.97 (ISBN 0-8094-1145-8, Pub. by Time-Life). Silver.

Grand Canyon: An Anthology. Bruce Babbitt. LC 78-58470. (Illus.). 1978. 15.95 (ISBN 0-87358-180-6). Northland.

Grand Canyon: An Anthology. Bruce Babbitt. LC 78-58470. (Illus.). 276p. 1980. pap. 8.95 (ISBN 0-87358-275-6). Northland.

Grand Canyon: Early Impressions. Ed. by Paul Schullery. LC 80-66185. 130p. 1981. 15.00 (ISBN 0-87081-086-3); pap. 6.95 (ISBN 0-87081-087-1). Colo Assoc.

Grand Canyon: Guide & Reference Book. Cliff McAdams. (Illus.). 100p. (Orig.). 1981. pap. 5.95 (ISBN 0-87108-577-1). Pruett.

Grand Canyon: The Story Behind the Scenery. rev. ed. Merrill D. Beal. Ed. by Gweneth R. DenDooven. LC 75-14775. (Illus.). 1978. 7.95 (ISBN 0-916122-31-X); pap. 3.00 (ISBN 0-916122-06-9). K C Pubns.

Grand Canyon Treks. rev. ed. Harvey Butchart. (Illus.). 1976. 2.95 (ISBN 0-910856-38-9). La Siesta.

Grand Canyon Treks II. Harvey Butchart. 1976. 1.95 (ISBN 0-910856-61-3). La Siesta.

Grand Canyon Wildflowers. Arthur M. Phillips, 3rd. Ed. by T. J. Priehs. LC 79-54236. (Illus.). 145p. 1979. pap. 6.50 (ISBN 0-938216-01-5). GCNHA.

Grand Central Books. Karen K. Welch et al. (Crossties Ser.). (gr. k-2). 1977. 10 copies 249.90 (ISBN 0-8332-1113-7); tchrs' manual 4.89 (ISBN 0-8332-1124-2); dupl. masters 30.99 (ISBN 0-8332-1129-3). Economy Co.

Grand Century of the Lady: 1720-1820. Arthur Calder-Marshall. (Illus.). 1976. o. p. 29.95 (ISBN 0-86033-011-7); pap. 9.95 (ISBN 0-86033-049-4). Gordon-Cremonesi.

Grand Design. Douglas Reed. 1977. pap. 2.00x (ISBN 0-911038-49-3). Noontide.

Grand Domestic Revolution: Feminism, Socialism & the American Home, 1870-1930. Dolores Hayden. (Illus.). 425p. 1981. text ed. 19.95x (ISBN 0-262-08108-3). MIT Pr.

Grand Duchess. Anne Duffield. 1973. pap. 1.25 o.p. (ISBN 0-425-02726-0, 22726, Medallion). Berkley Pub.

Grand Ecart. Jean Cocteau. Tr. by Lewis Galantiere from Fr. LC 74-22403. 153p. 1977. Repr. of 1925 ed. 14.00 (ISBN 0-86527-257-3). Fertig.

Grand Emporiums: The Illustrated History of America's Great Department Stores. Robert Hendrickson. LC 78-7555. (Illus.). 616p. 1980. pap. 9.95 (ISBN 0-8128-6092-6). Stein & Day.

Grand Enciclopedia Universale Curcio, 20 vols. (Ital.). 1976-1977. Set. 980.00. Pergamon.

Grand Experiment: The Life and Death of the TTT Program As Seen Through the Eyes of Its Evaluators. Malcolm D. Provus. LC 74-30961. 277p. 1975. 16.00 (ISBN 0-8211-1514-6); text ed. 14.50 (ISBN 0-685-52140-0). McCutchan.

Grand Huckster: Houston's Judge Roy Hofheintz, Genius of the Astrodome. Edgar Ray. (Illus.). 1980. 19.95 (ISBN 0-87870-069-2); deluxe ed. 29.95 (ISBN 0-87870-195-8). Memphis St Univ.

Grand Inquest: The Story of Congressional Investigations. Telford Taylor. LC 73-19825. 358p. 1974. Repr. of 1955 ed. lib. bdg. 35.00 (ISBN 0-306-70620-2). Da Capo.

Grand Inquisitor. Fodor Dostoyevsky. LC 56-7503. (Milestones of Thought Ser.). pap. 1.45 (ISBN 0-8044-6125-2). Ungar.

Grand Inquisitor on the Nature of Man. Fedor Dostoyevsky. Tr. by Constance Garnett. 1948. pap. 2.50 (ISBN 0-672-60237-7, LLA63). Bobbs.

Grand Island Story. Beatrice H. Castle. Ed. by James L. Carter. LC 71-11186. 1974. 4.50 (ISBN 0-938746-01-4). Marquette Cnty Hist.

Grand Jubilee. Suzette H. Elgin. 192p. 1981. 9.95 (ISBN 0-385-15877-7). Doubleday.

Grand Larousse Encyclopedique, 10 vols. 2 supplements 1975. (Fr.). Set. reg. ed. 835.00 (ISBN 0-8277-3027-6). Maxwell Sci Intl.

Grand Larousse Encyclopedique, 24 vols. (Fr.). 1973. Set. prestige ed. 1250.00 (ISBN 0-8277-3028-4). Maxwell Sci Intl.

Grand Larousse encyclopedique: Second Supplement. new ed. (Illus., Fr.). 1975. 95.00x (ISBN 2-03-000312-3, 3939). Larousse.

Grand Meaulnes. Fournier. (Easy Reader, B). pap. 3.75 (ISBN 0-88436-110-1, FRA201056). EMC.

Grand Medecin et Biologiste Cashmir - Joseph Davaine. Ed. by J. Theodorides. 1969. pap. 42.00 (ISBN 0-08-012366-X). Pergamon.

Grand National. John Welsome. 1978. pap. 1.95 o.p. (ISBN 0-449-23578-5, Crest). Fawcett.

Grand National Commentary. J. K. Pye. (Illus.). 11.35 (ISBN 0-85131-121-0, Dist. by Sporting Book Center). J A Allen.

Grand Old Duke of York. Maureen Roffey & Bernard Lodge. (Illus.). 1978. 6.95 (ISBN 0-370-10761-6, Pub. by Chatto Bodley Jonathan). Merrimack Bk Serv.

Grand Panjandrum: And 1999 Other Rare & Delightful Words & Expressions. J. N. Hook. 1980. 13.95 (ISBN 0-02-553620-6). Macmillan.

Grand Prix Champions. Mary S. Heglar. (Illus.). 1973. 7.95 (ISBN 0-87880-014-X). Norton.

Grand Prix Culinaire. Gerold Berger. 528p. Date not set. 29.95 (ISBN 0-8436-2196-6). CBI Pub.

Grand Prix World Championship. Julian May. LC 76-5460. (Sports Classics Ser.). (Illus.). (gr. 4-12). 1976. PLB 8.95 o.p. (ISBN 0-87191-506-5). Creative Ed.

Grand Sophy. Georgette Heyer. 320p. 1981. pap. 1.95 (ISBN 0-515-05928-5). Jove Pubns.

Grand Stand: An Uncommon Guide to Myrtle Beach & Its Surroundings. Nancy Rhyne. (Illus.). 160p. (Orig.). 1981. pap. 4.95 (ISBN 0-914788-36-1). East Woods.

Grand Strategy: Principles & Practices. John M. Collins. LC 73-76606. 1973. 15.00 o.s.i. (ISBN 0-87021-683-X); pap. 7.50 o.p. (ISBN 0-686-66756-5). Naval Inst Pr.

Grand Teton: The Story Behind the Scenery. Hugh Crandall. Ed. by Gweneth R. DenDooven. LC 78-57539. (Illus.). 1978. lib. bdg. 7.95 (ISBN 0-916122-47-6); pap. 3.00 (ISBN 0-916122-22-0). K C Pubns.

Grand Titration: Science & Society in East & West. Joseph Needham. LC 76-483302. 1979. pap. 7.50 (ISBN 0-8020-6359-4). U of Toronto Pr.

Granddaughter's Inglenook Cookbook. (Illus.). 322p. (Contributions of Recipes from Women of The Church of the Brethren). 1942. 7.95 (ISBN 0-87178-323-1); spiral bdg. 6.95 (ISBN 0-87178-324-X). Brethren.

Grande Enciclopedia Portuguesa E Brasileira, 40 vols. (Portuguese.). 1936-1960. Set. 1600.00 (ISBN 0-8277-3029-2). Maxwell Sci Intl.

Grande Encyclopedie, 21 vols. 77.00 ea.; index 85.00x (ISBN 0-685-36199-3). Larousse.

Grande Encyclopedie (Larousse, 21 vols. (Illus.). 13000p. (Fr.). 1972-1978. 1175.00 set (ISBN 0-8277-3030-6). Maxwell Sci Intl.

Grandes Epopeyas. (Span.). 8.95 (ISBN 84-241-5622-6). E Torres & Sons.

Grandes Heures of Jean, Duke of Berry. Ed. by Marcel Thomas. LC 75-167761. (Illus.). 192p. 1971. 70.00 (ISBN 0-8076-0613-8). Braziller.

Grandfather. Jeannie Baker. LC 78-74759. (Illus.). (gr. k-2). 1980. 8.95 (ISBN 0-233-96864-4). Andre Deutsch.

Grandfather Rock: The New Poetry & the Old. David Morse. LC 76-156048. (gr. 7 up). 1972. 6.95 o.s.i. (ISBN 0-440-03016-1). Delacorte.

Grandfather Stories of the Navajos. rev. ed. Sydney M. Callaway & Gary Witherspoon. Ed. by Broderick A. Johnson. LC 68-57898. (Illus.). 88p. 1974. 4.50 o.p. (ISBN 0-89019-006-2). Navajo Curr.

Grandfathers Are to Love. Lois Wyse. LC 67-18466. (Illus.). (gr. k-1). 1967. 2.50 o.s.i. (ISBN 0-8193-0165-5, Four Winds); boxed set with Grandmothers Are to Love 5.00 o.s.i. (ISBN 0-685-48750-4). Schol Bk Serv.

Grandfather's Land. Bob Fitch & Lynne Fitch. LC 75-190188. (gr. 5-9). 1970. PLB 6.95 (ISBN 0-87191-049-7). Creative Ed.

Grandfather's Private Zoo. Ruskin Bond. (Illus.). 95p. (gr. 3-5). 1.00 (ISBN 0-88253-345-2). Ind-US Inc.

Grandi Incisioni Su Armi D'Bagi. Mario Abbiatico. (Illus.). Repr. of 1976 ed. 30.00. Arma Pr.

Grandison Mather. Henry Harland, pseud. Ed. by Ian Fletcher & John Stokes. LC 76-24891. (Decadent Consciousness Ser.). 1977. lib. bdg. 38.00 (ISBN 0-8240-2768-X). Garland Pub.

Grandissimes. George W. Cable. 1957. pap. 5.95 o.p. (ISBN 0-8090-0025-3, AmCen). Hill & Wang.

Grandma & the Buck Deer. Joel Vance. (Illus.). 176p. 1980. 12.50 (ISBN 0-87691-322-2). Winchester Pr.

Grandma Didn't Wave Back. Rose Blue. LC 79-189568. 64p. (gr. 3-5). 1972. PLB 6.90 (ISBN 0-531-02557-8). Watts.

Grandma Haley. Aleda Renken. (Haley Adventures Ser.). 1981. pap. 2.50 (ISBN 0-570-07234-4, 39-1069). Concordia.

Grandma Is Somebody Special. Susan Goldman. Ed. by Caroline Rubin. LC 76-18980. (Self-Starter Bks.). (Illus.). 32p. (ps-1). 1976. 6.50g (ISBN 0-8075-3034-4). A Whitman.

Grandma's Tea Leaf Ironstone. Annise Heaivilin. (Illus.). 19.95 (ISBN 0-87069-323-9). Wallace-Homestead.

Grandmaster Preparation. Lyev Polugayevsky. Tr. by K. P. Neat. (Pergamon Russian Chess Ser.). (Illus.). 200p. 1981. 22.00 (ISBN 0-08-024099-2); pap. 12.00 (ISBN 0-08-024098-4). Pergamon.

Grandmasters of Chess. Harold C. Schonberg. (Illus.). 1981. 17.95 (ISBN 0-393-01403-7). Norton.

Grandmother. Jeannie Baker. (Illus.). (ps-2). 1979. PLB 8.95 (ISBN 0-233-96975-6). Andre Deutsch.

Grandmother. Georges Simenon. Tr. by Jean Stewart. LC 80-14918. (Helen & Kurt Wolff Bk.). 192p. 1980. Repr. of 1959 ed. 8.95 (ISBN 0-15-136738-8). HarBraceJ.

Grandmother Brown's Hundred Years: 1827-1927. Harriet C. Brown. Ed. by Annette K. Baxter. LC 79-8778. (Signal Lives Ser.). (Illus.). 1980. Repr. of 1929 ed. lib. bdg. 36.00x (ISBN 0-405-12827-4). Arno.

Grandmother Cat & the Hermit. Elizabeth Coatsworth. LC 70-99786. (Illus.). (gr. 3-5). 1970. 4.95g o.s.i. (ISBN 0-02-720580-0). Macmillan.

Grandmother's Amazing Housekeeping Secrets. 2nd ed. Maude D. Key. 91p. 1968. pap. 3.50 (ISBN 0-917420-01-2). Buck Hill.

Grandmothers Are to Love. Lois Wyse. LC 67-18465. (Illus.). (gr. k-1). 1967. 2.50 o.s.i. (ISBN 0-8193-0167-1, Four Winds); boxed set with Grandfathers Are to Love 5.00 o.s.i. (ISBN 0-685-48749-0). Schol Bk Serv.

Grandmother's House. J. B. Herman. (Orig.). 1980. pap. 1.75 (ISBN 0-532-23136-8). Manor Bks.

Grandmother's Pictures. Sam Cornish. 1978. pap. 0.95 (ISBN 0-380-01912-4, 30163, Camelot). Avon.

Grandpa & Me Together. Susan Goldman. Ed. by Kathleen Tucker. LC 79-18244. (Self-Starter Ser.). (Illus.). (ps-2). 1980. 6.50g (ISBN 0-8075-3036-0). A Whitman.

Grandpa Had a Windmill, Grandma Had a Churn. Louise A. Jackson. LC 77-23313. (Illus.). 40p. (gr. k-6). 1977. 6.25 o.s.i. (ISBN 0-8193-0872-2, Four Winds); PLB 5.71 o.s.i. (ISBN 0-8193-0873-0). Schol Bk Serv.

Grandpa, Me & Our House in the Tree. Barbara Kirk. LC 78-9564. (Illus.). (gr. 3-6). 1978. 8.95 (ISBN 0-02-750750-5, 75075). Macmillan.

Grandpa with a Stick: Joseph Theolin Landry - His Ancestors & Descendants. Compiled by Norma P. Evans. LC 80-67365. (Illus.). 100p. (Orig.). 1980. pap. 15.00 (ISBN 0-937418-02-1); special family ed. 15.00 (ISBN 0-937418-03-X). N P Evans.

Grandparents - Grandchildren: The Vital Connection. Arthur Kornhaber & Kenneth L. Woodward. LC 79-6083. (Illus.). 312p. 1981. 11.95 (ISBN 0-385-15577-8, Anchor Pr). Doubleday.

Grandparents Around the World. Dorka Raynor. Ed. by Caroline Rubin. LC 76-57661. (Concept Books Ser.). (Illus.). (gr. k). 1977. 6.95g (ISBN 0-8075-3037-9). A Whitman.

Grandparent's Garden of Verses. Evelyn Barkins. LC 72-96892. 1973. pap. 2.95 (ISBN 0-8119-0374-5). Fell.

Grandparents: Then God Created Grandparents & It Was Very Good. Charles W. Shedd. LC 75-42892. (Illus.). 144p. 1976. 7.95 (ISBN 0-385-11067-7); pap. 4.95 (ISBN 0-385-13115-1). Doubleday.

Grandpa's Ghost Stories. James Flora. 1980. pap. 1.95 (ISBN 0-689-70469-0, Aladdin). Atheneum.

Grange Master's America: In Defense of Freedom. Winton Weydemeyer. 272p. 1981. 12.50 (ISBN 0-682-49677-4). Exposition.

Granger Movement: A Study of Agricultural Organization & Its Political, Economic, & Social Manifestations, 1870-1880. Solon J. Buck. LC 63-9713. (Illus.). 1963. pap. 4.25x (ISBN 0-8032-5027-4, BB 166, Bison). U of Nebr Pr.

Grania: The Story of an Island. Emily Lawless. Ed. by Robert L. Wolff. (Ireland Nineteenth Century Fiction - Ser. Two: Vol. 73). 592p. 1979. lib. bdg. 32.00 (ISBN 0-8240-3522-4). Garland Pub.

Granite Lady: Poems. Susan F. Schaeffer. 150p. 1974. pap. 3.95 o.s.i. (ISBN 0-02-070750-9, Collier). Macmillan.

Granivorous Birds in Ecosystems. Ed. by J. Pinowski & S. C. Kendeigh. LC 76-47189. (International Biological Programme Ser.: No. 12). (Illus.). 1978. 79.50 (ISBN 0-521-21504-8). Cambridge U Pr.

Granny. Gertrude Wenzel. (Illus.). 272p. 1981. 12.50 (ISBN 0-682-49694-4). Exposition.

Granny & the Desperadoes. Peggy Parish. (Illus.). 40p. (gr. 1-3). 1970. 7.95g (ISBN 0-02-769890-4). Macmillan.

Granny & the Indians. Peggy Parish. LC 69-11304. (Illus.). (gr. 1-3). 1969. 7.95 (ISBN 0-02-769940-4). Macmillan.

Granny Brand, Her Story. Dorothy C. Wilson. LC 76-16721. (Illus.). 1976. 6.95 o.p. (ISBN 0-915684-11-X); pap. 3.50 o.p. (ISBN 0-915684-27-6). Christian Herald.

Granny, the Baby, & the Big Gray Thing. Peggy Parish. (Illus.). (gr. k-4). 1972. 6.95g (ISBN 0-02-769860-2). Macmillan.

Granny's Cookery Book. Frances Kitchin. LC 78-66798. (Illus.). 1978. 8.95 (ISBN 0-7153-7721-3). David & Charles.

Granny's Fish Story. Phyllis La Farge. LC 74-545. (Illus.). 36p. (ps-3). 1975. 5.95 o.s.i. (ISBN 0-8193-0760-2, Four Winds); PLB 5.41 o.s.i. (ISBN 0-8193-0761-0). Schol Bk Serv.

Granny's Special Moments Book. Alice Greenspan. (Florida Grandparents Guide Ser.). (Illus., Orig.). (ps-4). 1980. pap. 1.95 (ISBN 0-936076-01-1). Aaron Pubs.

Grant: A Biography. William S. McFeely. (Illus.). 1981. 19.95 (ISBN 0-393-01372-3). Norton.

Grant Money & How to Get It: A Handbook for Librarians. 1st ed. Richard W. Boss. 138p. 1980. 19.95 (ISBN 0-8352-1274-2). Bowker.

Grantley Manor: A Tale, 1847. Georgiana Fullerton. Ed. by Robert L. Wolff. LC 75-451. (Victorian Fiction Ser.). 1975. lib. bdg. 66.00 (ISBN 0-8240-1531-2). Garland Pub.

Grants for the Arts. Virginia White. 275p. 1980. 19.50 (ISBN 0-306-40270-X, Plenum Pr). Plenum Pub.

Grants Game: How to Win the First Time You Play. Lawrence Lee. 224p. 1981. 11.95 (ISBN 0-936602-18-X); pap. 7.95 (ISBN 0-936602-03-1). Harbor Pub CA.

Grants Game: How to Win the First Time You Play. Lawrence Lee. 224p. (Orig.). 1981. 11.95 (ISBN 0-936602-18-X); pap. 7.95 (ISBN 0-686-69117-2). Harbor Pub CA.

Grants in the Humanities: A Scholar's Guide to Funding Sources. William E. Coleman. LC 79-25697. 1980. pap. 12.95x (ISBN 0-918212-21-9). Neal-Schuman.

Grant's Method of Anatomy. 10th ed. John V. Basmajian. (Illus.). 644p. 1980. 26.95 (ISBN 0-683-00373-9). Williams & Wilkins.

Grants Register: Nineteen Eighty-One-Eighty-Three. 7th ed. Ed. by Craig Alan Lerner. 800p. 1980. 32.50x (ISBN 0-312-34407-4). St Martin.

Grantsmanship. Armand Lauffer. LC 77-10013. (Sage Human Services Guides: Vol. 1). 1977. pap. 6.00x (ISBN 0-8039-0880-6). Sage.

Grantwriting for Health Professionals. Harry Sulz. 1981. pap. price not set (ISBN 0-316-82196-9). Little.

Granulation: Monographs in Powder Science & Technology. P. J. Sherrington & R. Oliver. 1980. write for info. (ISBN 0-85501-177-7). Heyden.

Granulocyte Identification. Gerald E. Byrne, Jr. et al. LC 78-720294. (Laboratory Learning Aids Ser.). (Illus.). 1977. binder 40.00 (ISBN 0-89189-062-9, 71-5-003-00). Am Soc Clinical.

Granville Hicks. Terry L. Long. (United States Authors Ser.: No. 387). 1981. lib. bdg. 11.95 (ISBN 0-8057-7319-3). Twayne.

Granville Hicks in the 'New Masses' Granville Hicks. Ed. by Jack A. Robbins. LC 73-83265. (National University Pubns.). 1974. 22.50 (ISBN 0-8046-9042-1). Kennikat.

Grape Cure. Basil Shackleton. 1978. pap. 3.95 o.s.i. (ISBN 0-7225-0202-8). Newcastle Pub.

Grape Expeditions: Bicycle Tours of the California Wine Country, Vol. 2. Lena Emmery & Sally Taylor. (Illus.). 48p. 1980. pap. text ed. 2.40 (ISBN 0-9604904-0-X). Taylor & Friends.

Graph, Chart & Table: Interpretation for Test-Takers. David R. Turner. LC 80-14351. 224p. 1980. pap. 8.00 (ISBN 0-668-04817-4, 4817-4). Arco.

Graph Games. Frederique & Papy. LC 72-157647. (Young Math Ser). (Illus.). (gr. 1-4). 1971. PLB 7.89 (ISBN 0-690-34965-3, TYC-J). T Y Crowell.

Graph Paper From Your Copier. John Craver. (Illus.). 232p. 1980. pap. 12.95 (ISBN 0-89586-045-7). H P Bks.

Graph Theory. Frank Harary. 1969. text ed. 20.95 (ISBN 0-201-02787-9). A-W.

Graph Theory. Wataru Mayeda. LC 70-37366. 704p. 1972. 43.50 (ISBN 0-471-57950-5, Pub. by Wiley-Interscience). Wiley.

Graph Theory: Seventeen Thirty-Six to Nineteen Thirty-Six. Norman Biggs et al. (Illus.). 1976. 45.00x (ISBN 0-19-853901-0). Oxford U Pr.

Graph Theory with Applications to Engineering & Computer Science. Narsingh Deo. 1974. 25.95 (ISBN 0-13-363473-6). P-H.

Graph Theory: With Engineering Applications. David E. Johnson & Johnny R. Johnson. 350p. 1972. 32.50x (ISBN 0-8260-4775-0, Pub. by Wiley-Interscience). Wiley.

Graphemes of Tiberian Hebrew. G. M. Schramm. (U. C. Publ. in Near Eastern Studies: Vol. 2). 1964. pap. 6.00x (ISBN 0-520-09294-5). U of Cal Pr.

Graphic Artist & His Design Problems. Josef Muller-Brockmann. (Visual Communication Bks.). 1961. 29.00 o.p. (ISBN 0-8038-2618-4). Hastings.

Graphic Arts. new ed. Darvey Carlsen. (gr. 7-12). 1977. text ed. 10.48 (ISBN 0-87002-177-X); tchr's guide avail. (ISBN 0-685-57544-6). Bennett IL.

Graphic Arts. Frederick D. Kagy. LC 78-5456. (Illus.). 1978. text ed. 4.80 (ISBN 0-87006-252-2). Goodheart.

Graphic Arts. Los Angeles Unified School District. Ed. by Richard A. Vorndran. LC 77-73302. 128p. (gr. 7-9). 1978. pap. text ed. 4.40 (ISBN 0-02-820430-1). Glencoe.

Graphic Arts. McKnight Staff Members & Wilbur R. Miller. LC 78-53390. (Basic Industrial Arts Ser.). (Illus.). 1978. 6.00 (ISBN 0-87345-795-1); softbound 4.48 (ISBN 0-87345-787-0). McKnight.

Graphic Arts Encyclopedia. 2nd ed. George A. Stevenson. (Illus.). 1979. 29.95 (ISBN 0-07-061288-9). McGraw.

Graphic Arts Green Book: 1980 Midwest Edition. 1980. pap. 50.00 o.p. (ISBN 0-910880-06-9). Lewis.

Graphic Arts Green Book: 1981 Midwest Edition. 500p. 1981. pap. 50.00 (ISBN 0-910880-09-3). Lewis.

Graphic Arts Japan, Vol. 21, 1979-80. Ed. by Kaichi Sawamura. LC 64-43886. (Illus.). 190p. (Orig.). 1980. pap. 35.00x (ISBN 0-8002-2728-X). Intl Pubns Serv.

Graphic Commmunications for the Performing Arts. Ed. by David J. Skal. (Illus.). 200p. (Orig.). 1981. pap. 10.95x (ISBN 0-930452-11-9, Pub. by Theatre Comm). Pub Ctr Cult Res.

Graphic Communication. W. Bowman. LC 67-29931. (Human Communication Ser.). 1968. 22.95 (ISBN 0-471-09290-8, Pub. by Wiley-Interscience). Wiley.

Graphic Communication. John Twyford. (Illus.). 120p. (gr. 9-12). 1981. pap. 17.50 (ISBN 0-7134-3388-4, Pub. by Batsford England). David & Charles.

Graphic Communications. Richard Broekhuizen. 380p. 1979. text ed. 15.72 (ISBN 0-87345-246-1); study guide 3.96 (ISBN 0-87345-247-X); ans. key free (ISBN 0-87345-248-8). McKnight.

Graphic Design Education. Igildo Biesele. (Illus.). 190p. 1981. 67.50 (ISBN 0-8038-2712-1, Visual Communication). Hastings.

Graphic Design, San Francisco. The Institute of Graphic Designers. LC 79-23535. (Illus.). 144p. 1980. 22.50 (ISBN 0-87701-160-5). Chronicle Bks.

Graphic Graflex Photography: The Master Book for the Larger Camera. facsimile ed. Willard D. Morgan & Henry M. Lester. LC 70-167717. (Illus.). 424p. 1971. text ed. 16.00 o.p. (ISBN 0-87100-018-0). Morgan.

Graphic Guide to Industrialized Building Elements. Raymond Sluzas & Anne Ryan. LC 77-13121. (Illus.). 1977. 19.95 (ISBN 0-8436-0163-9); pap. 12.95 (ISBN 0-8436-0164-7). CBI Pub.

Graphic Layout & Design. Gerald Silver. LC 80-65062. (Graphic Arts Ser.). 216p. 1981. pap. text ed. 10.40 (ISBN 0-8273-1374-8); instructor's guide 1.60 (ISBN 0-8273-1375-6). Delmar.

Graphic Layout & Design. Gerald A. Silver. 320p. 1981. 13.95 (ISBN 0-442-26774-6). Van Nos Reinhold.

Graphic Problem Solving for Architects & Builders. Paul Lassea. LC 75-8607. 1975. 18.95 (ISBN 0-8436-0154-X); pap. 12.75 (ISBN 0-685-93090-4). CBI Pub.

Graphic Reproduction & Photography of Works of Art. John Lewis & Edwin Smith. 1969. 12.95 o.p. (ISBN 0-571-09034-6, Pub. by Faber & Faber). Merrimack Bk Serv.

Graphic Reproduction Photography. J. Burden. Date not set. 19.50 o.p. (ISBN 0-8038-5778-0). Hastings.

Graphic Reproductions. Spence. 1980. text ed. 22.64 (ISBN 0-87002-285-7); student guide 2.60 (ISBN 0-87002-319-5). Bennett IL.

Graphic Standards of Solar Energy. Spruille Braden, III. LC 77-12217. (Illus.). 1977. 19.95 o.p. (ISBN 0-8436-0165-5). CBI Pub.

Graphic Teaching Aids in Basic Anthropometry. D. R. Henning & J. R. Vincent. LC 71-635321. (Museum Brief: No. 6). (Illus.). i, 57p. 1971. pap. 2.60x (ISBN 0-913134-05-8). Mus Anthro Mo.

Graphic Work of M. C. Escher. rev. ed. M. C. Escher. 1967. 13.95 o.p. (ISBN 0-8015-3102-0). Dutton.

Graphic Work of Renoir: A Catalogue Raisonne. Joseph G. Stella. (Illus.). 112p. 1975. pap. 25.00 o.p. (ISBN 0-8390-0168-1). Allanheld & Schram.

Graphics Annual, 1980-1981: International Annual of Advertising & Editorial Graphics. Ed. by Walter Herdeg. (Visual Communications Bks.). (Illus.). 247p. 1980. 59.50 (ISBN 0-8038-2709-1). Hastings.

Graphics: Design into Production. Alec Davis. 1973. 11.95 o.p. (ISBN 0-571-08810-4, Pub. by Faber & Faber). Merrimack Bk Serv.

Graphics for Engineers: Visualizations, Communication & Design. R. P. Hoelscher et al. LC 67-29722. 1968. text ed. 28.95x (ISBN 0-471-40558-2). Wiley.

Graphics in Engineering Design. 3rd ed. Alexander Levens & William Chalk. LC 79-17291. 1980. text ed. 25.95 (ISBN 0-471-01478-8); tchrs' manual (ISBN 0-471-04998-0); wkbk. 1 a (ISBN 0-471-03133-X); wkbk. 2 a (ISBN 0-471-03214-X); wkbk. 3 a (ISBN 0-471-07749-6); solution manual 1 a; solution manual 2 a (ISBN 0-471-08104-3). Wiley.

Graphics Master, No. 2. Dean P. Lem. LC 76-41508. (Illus.). 113p. 1977. 47.50 (ISBN 0-914218-02-6). D Lem Assocs.

Graphics Posters '81: The International Annual of Poster Art. Ed. by Walter Herdeg. (Visual Communications Bks.). (Illus.). 204p. 1981. 59.50 (ISBN 0-8038-2714-8). Hastings.

Graphing Algebraic Functions. Robert M. Oman. 1979. pap. 1.95 (ISBN 0-931660-02-5). R Oman Pubns.

Graphing, Factoring Quadratic Trinomials. NAIS Task Force on Secondary Mathematics. (Occasional Papers Ser.: No. 2). (Illus.). 1978. pap. 3.25 (ISBN 0-934338-14-0). NAIS.

Grapho-Therapeutics. Paul De Sainte Colombe. 352p. 1973. pap. 1.25 o.p. (ISBN 0-445-00175-5). Popular Lib.

Grapho-Therapeutics: Pen & Pencil Therapy. Paul De Sainte Colombe. 1966. pap. 8.95 (ISBN 0-87516-297-5). De Vorss.

Graphology. Tom Aylesworth. LC 76-7048. (Career Concise Guides Ser.). (Illus.). 72p. (gr. 6 up). 1976. PLB 4.90 o.p. (ISBN 0-531-00323-X). Watts.

Graphology. Barbara Hill. (Illus.). 143p. 1981. 9.95 (ISBN 0-686-69111-3). St Martin.

Graphology Handbook. Curtis Casewit. (Illus.). 168p. (Orig.). 1980. pap. 6.95 (ISBN 0-914918-15-X). Para Res.

Graphology: The Science of Handwriting. Henry Frith. (Illus.). 128p. pap. 4.50 (ISBN 0-8334-1756-8). Steinerbks.

Graphs. rev. ed. Dino Lowenstein. (First Bks.). (Illus.). 72p. (gr. 5 up). 1976. PLB 6.45 (ISBN 0-531-00679-4). Watts.

Graphs, Codes & Designs. P. J. Cameron & J. H. Van Lint. (London Mathematical Society Lecture Notes Ser.: No. 43). 180p. 1980. 19.95x (ISBN 0-521-23141-8). Cambridge U Pr.

Grasp of Consciousness: Action & Concept in the Young Child. Jean Piaget. LC 75-43687. 352p. 1976. 16.50x (ISBN 0-674-36033-8); pap. 5.95 (ISBN 0-674-36034-6). Harvard U Pr.

Grass. Claude Simon. Tr. by Richard Howard. LC 60-6241. 1960. 4.50 o.p. (ISBN 0-8076-0100-4). Braziller.

Grass Eaters. Gary Paulsen. LC 76-10313. (Real Animals Ser.). (Illus.). 64p. (gr. 5 up). 1976. PLB 8.65 (ISBN 0-8172-0602-7). Raintree Pubs.

Grass Is Singing. Doris Lessing. 288p. 1976. pap. 1.75 o.p. (ISBN 0-445-08391-3). Popular Lib.

Grass Roots. Albert Goldman. (Orig.). 1980. pap. 2.75 (ISBN 0-446-85465-4). Warner Bks.

Grass Roots: An Anti-Nuke Sourcebook. Ed. by Fred Wilcox. LC 80-11762. (Illus.). 192p. 1980. 13.95 (ISBN 0-89594-032-9); pap. 6.95 (ISBN 0-89594-031-0). Crossing Pr.

Grass Roots in an African City: Political Behavior in Nairobi. Marc H. Ross. LC 74-34263. 192p. 1975. text ed. 22.50x (ISBN 0-262-18074-X). MIT Pr.

Grass Roots Music. Dean Tudor & Nancy Tudor. LC 78-31686. (American Popular Music on Elpee). 1979. lib. bdg. 25.00x (ISBN 0-87287-133-9). Libs Unl.

Grass Roots: Readings in State & Local Government. Erwin C. Buell & William E. Brigman. 1968. pap. 7.95x (ISBN 0-673-05904-9). Scott F.

Grass Skiing: A Complete Beginner's Book. LaVada Weir. (Illus.). 128p. (gr. 4-6). 1981. PLB 7.29 (ISBN 0-686-69301-9). Messner.

Grass War. Harley Hess. (Orig.). 1979. pap. 1.75 (ISBN 0-532-23180-5). Manor Bks.

Grasses. Jaromir Sikula. (Concise Guides Ser.). (Illus.). 1979. 7.95 (ISBN 0-600-34045-7). Transatlantic.

Grasses: Bromus to Paspalum. Robert H. Mohlenbrock. LC 71-156793. (Illustrated Flora of Illinois Ser.). (Illus.). 352p. 1972. 22.95x (ISBN 0-8093-0520-8). S Ill U Pr.

Grasses: Panicum to Danthonia. Robert H. Mohlenbrock. LC 73-6807. (Illustrated Flora of Illinois Ser). (Illus.). 398p. 1973. 22.95x (ISBN 0-8093-0521-6). S Ill U Pr.

Grasshopper King. Elizabeth B. Coker. 1981. 13.95 (ISBN 0-525-10716-9). Dutton.

Grasshopper to the Rescue. Tr. by Bonnie Carey from Rus. (Illus.). (gr. k-3). 1979. 7.50 (ISBN 0-688-22172-6); PLB 7.20 (ISBN 0-688-32172-0). Morrow.

Grasshoppers. Jane Dallinger. (Lerner Natural Science Bks.). (Illus.). (gr. 4-10). 1981. PLB 7.95 (ISBN 0-8225-1455-9). Lerner Pubns.

Grasshoppers & Crickets. Dorothy C. Hogner. LC 60-9219. (Illus.). (gr. 2-5). 1960. 7.95 (ISBN 0-690-35035-X, TYC-J); pap. 7.89 (ISBN 0-690-35036-8). T Y Crowell.

Grasshoppers & Elephants. Wilfred Burchett. 1977. pap. 4.95 (ISBN 0-916354-65-2); pap. 5.95 (ISBN 0-916354-66-0). Urizen Bks.

Grasshoppers of California (Orthoptera: Acridoidea) H. F. Strohecker et al. (Bulletin of the California Insect Survey: Vol. 10). 1968. pap. 9.00x (ISBN 0-520-09035-7). U of Cal Pr.

Grassi Block Substitution Test for Measuring Organic Brain Pathology. 2nd ed. Joseph R. Grassi. (American Lecture Psychology Ser.). (Illus.). 96p. 1970. text ed. 9.75 (ISBN 0-398-00717-9). C C Thomas.

Grassland Ecosystems of the World. Ed. by R. T. Coupland. LC 77-83990. (International Biological Programme Ser.: No. 18). 1979. 75.00 (ISBN 0-521-21867-5). Cambridge U Pr.

Grasslands of the Monsoon. R. O. Whyte. (Illus.). 1969. 7.95 o.p. (ISBN 0-571-08583-0, Pub. by Faber & Faber). Merrimack Bk Serv.

Grassroot Jungles. rev. ed. Edwin W. Teale. LC 44-5481. (Illus.). (gr. 9 up). 1937. 6.95 (ISBN 0-396-01714-2). Dodd.

Grassroots: An Illustrated History of Bluegrass & Mountain Music. Fred Hill. LC 80-67106. (Illus.). 160p. (Orig.). 1980. 15.00 (ISBN 0-914960-26-1); pap. 8.95 (ISBN 0-914960-25-3). Academy Bks.

Grassroots Philosophy for the Modern Mind. Homer T. Rosenberger. LC 75-32703. (Horizons of the Humanities: Vol. 2). 255p. 1976. lib. bdg. 9.00 (ISBN 0-917264-00-2). Rose Hill.

Grassroots Science: Guide to Activities Projects & Filmstrips, Sets 4 & 5. Judith Hardy et al. Ed. by Patricia Dambry. Incl. Set 4. Earth, Air & Water. LC 78-730899 (ISBN 0-87453-045-8); Set 5. Life-Times: The Season. LC 78-730900 (ISBN 0-87453-055-5). (Illus.). (gr. k-3). 1978. 5.00 ea.; avail. activity guide (ISBN 0-685-65927-5). Denoyer.

Grassroots: The Writer's Workbook, Form B. Susan Fawcett & Alvin Sandberg. LC 80-68139. 272p. 1981. pap. text ed. 9.75 (ISBN 0-395-29726-5); instr's. manual 0.50 (ISBN 0-395-29727-3). HM.

Grassroots: The Writer's Workbook, Form a. Susan C. Fawcett & Alvin Sandberg. LC 75-37475. 30p. 1976. pap. text ed. 9.75 (ISBN 0-395-24063-8); inst. manual 0.75 (ISBN 0-395-24274-6). HM.

Graustark. George B. McCutcheon. 1976. lib. bdg. 19.25x (ISBN 0-89968-061-5). Lightyear.

Grave Concern. Chaim Lieberman. LC 68-58650. 202p. 1968. 4.95 (ISBN 0-88400-016-8). Shengold.

Grave Mistake. Ngaio Marsh. 1980. pap. 1.95 (ISBN 0-515-05369-4). Jove Pubns.

Grave of the Right Hand. Charles Wright. LC 76-105510. (Wesleyan Poetry Program: Vol. 51). Orig. Title: Lost Displays. 1970. 10.00x (ISBN 0-8195-2051-9, Pub. by Wesleyan U Pr). Columbia U Pr.

Gravel Pit Angling. Peter Stone. LC 77-91759. (Illus.). 1978. 17.95 (ISBN 0-7153-7580-6). David & Charles.

Gravel Springs Fife & Drum: An Essay. David Evans. 1981. cancelled (ISBN 0-89267-006-1). Ctr South Folklore.

Gravel Springs Fife & Drum: Film Transcript. (Illus.). 1981. cancelled (ISBN 0-89267-007-X). Ctr South Folklore.

Grave's Company. Sarah Nichols. 256p. (Orig.). 1975. pap. 1.25 o.p. (ISBN 0-445-00252-2). Popular Lib.

Graves' Disease. Alan E. Lewis. LC 80-15624. (Discussions in Patient Management Ser.). 1980. pap. 12.00 (ISBN 0-87488-870-0). Med Exam.

Graves Papers & Other Documents Relating to the Naval Operations of the Yorktown Campaign, July to October 1781: New York Historical Society. Ed. by French E. Chadwick. LC 16-19248. (Illus.). 1916. 8.00x o.p. (ISBN 0-685-73899-X). U Pr of Va.

Gravestone Inscriptions in Northampton County Virginia. Compiled by Jean M. Mihalyka. 6.00 (ISBN 0-686-69510-0). Va State Lib.

Gravestones of Early New England: And the Men Who Made Them. Harriette M. Forbes. (Thanatology Service Ser.). 150p. 1981. Repr. of 1980 ed. 15.00 (ISBN 0-686-64831-5). Highly Specialized.

Graveyard to Let. Carter Dickson. 1978. pap. 1.50 (ISBN 0-505-51222-X). Tower Bks.

Gravitation. Charles W. Misner et al. LC 78-156043. (Physics Ser.). (Illus.). 1279p. 1973. pap. text ed. 38.95x (ISBN 0-7167-0344-0). W H Freeman.

Gravitation & Cosmology; Principles & Applications of the General Theory of Relativity. Steven Weinberg. LC 78-37175. 750p. 1972. 34.95 (ISBN 0-471-92567-5). Wiley.

Gravitation & Space Time. new ed. Hans C. Ohanian. (Illus.). 400p. 1976. text ed. 19.95x (ISBN 0-393-09198-8). Norton.

Gravitation Quanta & the Universe. A. R. Prasanna et al. LC 80-17051. 326p. 1981. 34.95 (ISBN 0-470-27007-1). Halsted Pr.

Gravitation, Quanta & the Universe: Proceedings of the Einstein Centenary Symposium Held at Ahmedabad, India 29 January to 3 February, 1979. Ed. by A. R. Prasanna et al. LC 80-17051. 326p. 1981. 34.95 (ISBN 0-470-27007-1). Halsted Pr.

Gravitational Curvature: An Introduction to Einstein's Theory. Theodore T. Frankel. LC 78-12092. (Illus.). 1979. pap. text ed. 11.95x (ISBN 0-7167-1062-5). W H Freeman.

Gravitational Physiology: Proceedings of the 28th International Congress of Physiological Sciences, Budapest, 1980. LC 80-42103. (Advances in Physiological Sciences: Vol. 19). (Illus.). 350p. 1981. 40.00 (ISBN 0-08-027340-8). Pergamon.

Gravity. George Gamow. LC 62-8840. 1962. pap. 2.50 o.p. (ISBN 0-385-01577-1, S22, Anch). Doubleday.

Gravity & Tectonics. Ed. by Kees A. De Jong & Robert Scholten. LC 73-1580. (Illus.). 502p. 1973. 47.50 (ISBN 0-471-20305-X, Pub. by Wiley-Interscience). Wiley.

Gravity & the Earth. A. H. Cook & V. T. Saunders. (Wykeham Science Ser.: No. 6). 1969. 9.95x (ISBN 0-8448-1108-4). Crane Russak Co.

Gravity Is a Mystery. Franklyn M. Branley. LC 70-101922. (Let's-Read-and-Find-Out Science Bk). (Illus.). (gr. k-3). 1970. 7.95 (ISBN 0-690-35071-6, TYC-J); PLB 7.89 (ISBN 0-690-35072-4). T Y Crowell.

Gravity Is a Push. Walter Wright. 1979. 6.95 (ISBN 0-8062-1263-2). Carlton.

Gray Boone on Antiques. Gray Boone. LC 80-84408. (Illus.). 160p. 1981. 12.95 (ISBN 0-8487-0519-X). Oxmoor Hse.

Gray Corrugated Pottery from Awatovi. James C. Gifford & S. Watson Smith. LC 78-50909. (Peabody Museum Papers: Vol. 69). 1978. pap. 20.00 (ISBN 0-87365-194-4). Peabody Harvard.

Gray Family & Allied Lines. Jo W. Linn & Gordon Gray. LC 76-42358. (Illus.). 1976. 27.50 (ISBN 0-918470-01-3). J W Linn.

Gray-Flannel Pigskin: Movers & Shakers of Pro Football. William H. Paul. LC 74-10669. 1974. 7.95 o.p. (ISBN 0-397-01025-7). Lippincott.

Gray Ghosts of Taylor Ridge. Mary F. Shura. LC 77-16861. (gr. 5 up). 1978. 5.95 (ISBN 0-396-07526-6). Dodd.

Gray Goose & Gander & Other Mother Goose Rhymes. Anne Rockwell. LC 79-6839. (Illus.). 64p. (ps-1). 1980. 8.95 (ISBN 0-690-04048-2, TYC-J); PLB 8.79 (ISBN 0-690-04049-0). T Y Crowell.

Gray Is the Color: An Exhibition of Grisaille Painting, 13th-20th Centuries. Intro. by J. Patrice Marandel. LC 73-92776. (Illus.). 1974. pap. 5.00 (ISBN 0-914412-08-6). Inst for the Arts.

Gray Itch: The Male Metapause Syndrome. Edmond C. Hallberg. 1980. pap. 2.50 (ISBN 0-446-91507-6). Warner Bks.

Gray Lensman. E. E. Smith. 1973. pap. 1.50 (ISBN 0-515-04589-6). Jove Pubns.

Gray-Scale Ultrasound: A Manual for Physician & Technical Personnel. Royal J. Bartrum, Jr. & Harte C. Crow. LC 77-72802. (Illus.). 1977. text ed. 16.50 (ISBN 0-7216-1548-1). Saunders.

Gray Wolf & Other Fantasy Stories. George MacDonald. Ed. by Glenn G. Sadler. (Fantasy Stories of George MacDonald Ser.). 200p. 1980. pap. 2.95 (ISBN 0-8028-1862-5). Eerdmans.

Graying of America: Retirement & Why You Can't Afford It. James Jorgensen. 245p. 1980. 10.95 (ISBN 0-8037-2913-8). Dial.

Graying of the Campus. Ruth Weinstock. LC 78-69846. 160p. 1978. 14.00 (ISBN 0-89192-247-4); pap. 8.00 (ISBN 0-89192-290-3). Interbk Inc.

Graying of Working America: The Coming Crisis in Retirement-Age Policy. Harold L. Sheppard & Sara E. Rix. LC 77-2528. (Illus.). 1979. pap. text ed. 6.95 (ISBN 0-02-928720-0). Free Pr.

Grays Harbor: 1885-1913. Robert A. Weinstein. (Large Format Ser.). (Illus.). 1978. pap. 7.95 o.p. (ISBN 0-14-004890-1). Penguin.

Grays Harbor: 1885-1913. Robert A. Weinstein. (Illus.). 1978. 16.95 o.p. (ISBN 0-670-34833-3, Studio). Viking Pr.

Gray's Sporting Journal. 1977. pap. 30.00 o.p. (ISBN 0-685-79971-9, T0800). Follett.

GRE (Graduate Record Examination) William A. Covino et al. Date not set. pap. text ed. cancelled. Cliffs.

Greag Engineers: From Antiquity Through the Industrial Revolution, Vol. I. Ed. by Roland Turner & Steven L. Goulden. (Illus.). 630p. 1981. 65.00x (ISBN 0-312-34574-7). St Martin.

Greased Lightning. Kenneth Vose & Lawrence DuKore. (Orig.). 1977. pap. 1.50 o.s.i. (ISBN 0-446-88399-9). Warner Bks.

Great Abnormals. Theophilus B. Hyslop. LC 79-162514. xxviii, 289p. 1971. Repr. of 1925 ed. 20.00 (ISBN 0-8103-3797-5). Gale.

Great Adventure Films. Tony Thomas. pap. 7.95 (ISBN 0-8065-0747-0). Lyle Stuart.

Great Adventure Stories. Ed. by Harriet Ross. LC 60-6579. (Illus.). 160p. (YA) 1979. PLB 6.99 (ISBN 0-87460-180-0); pap. 1.95 (ISBN 0-87460-181-9). Lion.

Great Adventures of the Old Testament. Paul Waterman. LC 22-769. (Activity Book Ser.). (ps-2). Vol. 1. pap. 0.79 (ISBN 0-87123-751-2, 220751); Vol. 2. pap. 0.79 (ISBN 0-87123-769-5). Bethany Fell.

Great Adventures of the Vikings. John Geipel. LC 77-72486. (Illus.). 48p. (gr. 5-9). 1977. 3.95 (ISBN 0-528-82204-7); PLB 3.97 o.p. (ISBN 0-528-80052-3). Rand.

Great Adventures That Changed Our World. (Illus.). 1978. 15.95 (ISBN 0-89577-048-2, Pub. by Reader's Digest). Norton.

Great Afghan Book. American School of Needlework. Ed. by Mary Thomas. (Illus.). 160p. 1981. 16.95 (ISBN 0-8069-5444-2, Columbia Hse). Sterling.

Great Ages of Man Guide & Index. (Great Ages of Man Ser.). 1967. 12.95 (ISBN 0-685-72428-X); lib. bdg. avail. (ISBN 0-685-72429-8). Time-Life.

Great Alaska Earthquake of 1964: Biology. Committee on the Alaska Earthquake. (Illus.). 320p. 1972. text ed. 21.95 (ISBN 0-309-01604-5). Natl Acad Pr.

Great Alaska Earthquake of 1964: Engineering. Committee on the Great Alaska Earthquake of 1964. (Great Alaska Earthquake of 1964 Ser.). (Illus.). 1210p. 1973. 37.50 (ISBN 0-309-01606-1). Natl Acad Pr.

Great Alaska Earthquake of 1964: Geology. Committee on the Alaska Earthquake. (Illus.). 848p. 1972. text ed. 35.00 (ISBN 0-309-01601-0). Natl Acad Pr.

Great Alaska Earthquake of 1964: Human Ecology. Committee on the Alaska Earthquake. 1970. 29.50 (ISBN 0-309-01607-X). Natl Acad Pr.

Great Alaska Earthquake of 1964: Hydrology. Committee on the Alaska Earthquake. (Great Alaskan Earthquake Ser). (Illus.). 1968. 25.00 (ISBN 0-309-01603-7). Natl Acad Pr.

Great Alaska Earthquake of 1964: Oceanography & Coastal Engineering. Committee on the Alaska Earthquake. LC 68-60037. (Illus.). 624p. 1972. 32.50 (ISBN 0-309-01605-3). Natl Acad Pr.

Great Alaska Earthquake of 1964: Seismology & Geodesy. Committee on the Alaska Earthquake. LC 68-60037. (Illus.). 592p. 1972. 25.00 (ISBN 0-309-01602-9). Natl Acad Pr.

Great Alaska Earthquake of 1964: Summary & Recommendations Including Index to Series. Committee on the Alaska Earthquake. (Illus.). 288p. 1973. 16.00 (ISBN 0-309-01608-8). Natl Acad Pr.

Great All-Time Baseball Record Book: A Unique Sourcebook of Facts, Feats & Figures. Joseph L. Reichler. (Illus.). 608p. 1981. 19.95 (ISBN 0-02-603100-0). Macmillan.

Great American Alimony Escape. David Rogers. 1979. pap. 1.95 o.p. (ISBN 0-449-14132-2, GM). Fawcett.

Great American Beer Book. James Robertson. 1980. pap. 2.95 (ISBN 0-446-93073-3). Warner Bks.

Great American Blow-up: Puffery in Advertising & Selling. Ivan L. Preston. LC 74-27313. 1975. 27.50 (ISBN 0-299-06730-0); pap. 7.95 (ISBN 0-299-06734-3). U of Wis Pr.

Great American Brands: The Success Formulas That Made Them Famous. David P. Cleary. (Illus.). 300p. 1980. text ed. 17.50 (ISBN 0-87005-338-8). Fairchild.

Great American Chewing Gum Book. Robert Hendrickson. LC 79-6055. (Illus.). 254p. 1980. 6.95 (ISBN 0-8128-6050-0). Stein & Day.

Great American Chili Book. Bill Bridges. LC 78-5384. 224p. 1981. 12.95 (ISBN 0-89256-074-6); pap. 6.95 (ISBN 0-89256-130-0). Rawson Wade.

Great American Communication Catalogue. Irving J. Rein. (Speech Communications Ser.). (Illus.). 160p. 1975. pap. 10.95 (ISBN 0-13-363580-5). P-H.

Great American Convertible: An Affectionate Guide. Robert S. Weider & George Hall. LC 77-72416. 1977. pap. 6.95 (ISBN 0-385-13123-2, Dolp). Doubleday.

Great American Desert. Donald Young. LC 80-21183. (Illus.). 64p. (gr. 4 up). 1980. PLB 7.29 (ISBN 0-671-33054-3). Messner.

Great American Desert Then & Now. W. Eugene Hollon. LC 75-5512. (Illus.). xxviii, 284p. 1975. pap. 3.95 (ISBN 0-8032-5806-2, BB 592, Bison). U of Nebr Pr.

Great American Frontier: A History of Western Pioneering. Ed. by Thomas D. Clark. LC 74-28026. (No. 87). 376p. 1975. pap. 8.95 (ISBN 0-672-60146-X, AHS-87). Bobbs.

Great American Lawyers, 8 Vols. Ed. by William D. Lewis. LC 75-157105. (Illus.). 1971. Repr. of 1909 ed. Set. text ed. 245.00x (ISBN 0-8377-2402-3). Rothman.

Great American Newspaper: The Story of the Village Voice. Kevin McAuliffe. (Encore Edition). (Illus.). 1978. 4.95 (ISBN 0-684-16588-0). Scribner.

Great American Poetry Bake-off. Robert Peters. LC 79-16090. 290p. 1979. 14.50 (ISBN 0-8108-1231-2). Scarecrow.

Great American Sculptures. William J. Clark. LC 75-28869. (Art Experience in Late 19th Century America Ser.: Vol. 5). (Illus.). 1976. Repr. of 1878 ed. lib. bdg. 44.00 (ISBN 0-8240-2229-7). Garland Pub.

Great American Sex Test: Who Are You, Sexually? Joyce D. Fleming & Leonore Tiefer. (Illus.). 1981. 10.95 (ISBN 0-02-538720-0). Macmillan. Postponed.

Great American Sports Book. George Gipe. LC 78-4707. (Illus.). 1978. 15.95 (ISBN 0-385-13091-0); pap. 7.95 o.p. (ISBN 0-385-13092-9). Doubleday.

Great American Writers: Program Guide, Vol. 1. Ed. by J. M. Heher. 100p. (gr. 9-12). 1980. pap. text ed. 7.95 (ISBN 0-667-00601-X). Microfilming Corp.

Great Ape. Fernando Krahn. (Puffin Picture Bks.). (Illus.). 1980. 1.95 (ISBN 0-14-005744-7). Penguin.

Great Apes. David A. Hamburg & Elizabeth R. McGown. 1979. text ed. 23.95 (ISBN 0-8053-3669-9). Benjamin-Cummings.

Great Apostolic Blunder Machine. John R. Fry. LC 78-3137. 1978. pap. 4.95 o.p. (ISBN 0-06-063072-8, RD 277, HarpR). Har-Row.

Great Art Madonnas Classed According to Their Significance As Types of Impressive Motherhood. Vincent J. Hurlington. (Great Art Masters Library Bk.). (Illus.). 143p. 1981. 37.45 (ISBN 0-930582-97-7). Gloucester Art.

Great Ascent. Robert L. Heilbroner. LC 62-17086. 1963. 8.95 o.s.i. (ISBN 0-06-011810-5, HarpT). Har-Row.

Great Awakening. Joseph Tracy. 1976. 11.95 (ISBN 0-85151-233-X). Banner of Truth.

Great Awakening & American Education. Douglas Sloan. LC 72-91270. 270p. 1973. pap. text ed. 5.25x (ISBN 0-8077-2381-9). Tchrs Coll.

Great Awakening: Documents Illustrating the Crisis & Its Consequences. Ed. by Alan Heimert & Perry Miller. LC 66-23537. 1967. 24.50x (ISBN 0-672-50977-6). Irvington.

Great Awakening: Documents Illustrating the Crisis & Its Consequences. Ed. by Alan E. Heimert & Perry Miller. LC 66-23537. (Orig.). 1967. pap. 9.95 (ISBN 0-672-60044-7, AHS34). Bobbs.

Great Awakening in Virginia. Gewehr. Repr. 12.00 (ISBN 0-686-12354-9). Church History.

Great Awakening, 1720-1760: Religious Revival Arouses America's Sense of Individual Liberties. Monroe Stearns. LC 73-93224. (Focus Bks). (Illus.). (gr. 7 up). 1970. PLB 4.90 o.p. (ISBN 0-531-01008-2). Watts.

Great Ball Court of Chichen Itza, Yucatan, Mexico. Marvin Cohodas. LC 77-94690. (Outstanding Dissertations in the Fine Arts Ser.). 1978. lib. bdg. 48.50 (ISBN 0-8240-3221-7). Garland Pub.

Great Ballet Paper Dolls. Nancie Swanberg. (Illus.). 32p. (Orig.). 1981. pap. 3.50 (ISBN 0-89844-027-0). Troubador Pr.

Great Balloon Escape. Jurgen Petschull. Tr. by Courtney Searls. 1981. 10.95 (ISBN 0-686-62158-1). Times Bks.

Great Barrier Reef. Craig McGregor. (World's Wild Places Ser). (Illus.). 1973. 12.95 (ISBN 0-8094-2006-6). Time-Life.

Great Barrier Reef. Craig McGregor. (World's Wild Places Ser.). (Illus.). 1977. lib. bdg. 11.97 (ISBN 0-686-51018-6). Silver.

Great Basin Kingdom: An Economic History of the Latter-Day Saints, 1830-1900. Leonard J. Arrington. LC 58-12961. (Illus.). 1966. pap. 6.95 (ISBN 0-8032-5006-1, BB362, Bison). U of Nebr Pr.

Great Bathrooms. Jeffrey Weiss. 96p. 1981. pap. 9.95 (ISBN 0-312-34486-4). St Martin.

Great Bible Stories for Children. Ed. by Lane Easterly. 5.95 o.p. (ISBN 0-8407-4988-0). Nelson.

Great Big Animal Book. Illus. by Feodor Rojankovsky. (Illus.). 1976. PLB 7.62 (ISBN 0-307-60468-3, Golden Pr). Western Pub.

Great Big Boat. Sylvia R. Tester. LC 79-12176. (Bible Story Books). (Illus.). (ps-3). 1979. PLB 5.50 (ISBN 0-89565-087-8). Childs World.

Great Big Book of Bedtime Stories. Illus. by Tibor Gergely. (Illus.). (ps-2). 1972. 7.95 (ISBN 0-307-16529-9, Golden Pr); PLB 7.62 o.p. (ISBN 0-307-66529-1). Western Pub.

Great Big Car & Truck Book. Illus. by Richard Scarry. (ps-2). 1951. 1.95 (ISBN 0-307-10473-7, Golden Pr); PLB 7.62 (ISBN 0-307-60473-X). Western Pub.

Great Big Dummy. Janet Schulman. (gr. k-6). Date not set. pap. price not set (ISBN 0-440-43072-0, YB). Dell.

Great Big Enormous Turnip. Alexei Tolstoy. LC 69-10277. (Illus.). (gr. k-3). 1969. PLB 3.90 o.p. (ISBN 0-531-01684-6). Watts.

Great Big Fire Engine Book. Illus. by Tibor Gergely. (Illus.). (gr. k-2). 1950. 1.95 (ISBN 0-307-10470-2, Golden Pr); PLB 7.62 (ISBN 0-307-60470-5). Western Pub.

Great Big Joke & Riddle Book. Ed. by Oscar Weigle. LC 79-129734. (Illus.). 224p. (gr. 1-5). 1981. 6.95 (ISBN 0-448-02584-1); PLB 10.15 (ISBN 0-448-03167-1). G&D.

Great Big Ugly Man Came up & Tied His Horse to Me: A Book of Nonsense Verse. Wallace Tripp. (Illus.). 48p. (gr. k-3). 1973. 6.95g (ISBN 0-316-85280-5); pap. 3.95 (ISBN 0-316-85281-3). Little.

Great Big Wild Animal Book. Feodor Rojankovsky. (Illus.). (ps-2). 1962. PLB 7.62 (ISBN 0-307-60452-7, Golden Pr). Western Pub.

Great Black Americans. 2nd. rev. ed. Ben Richardson & William A. Fahey. LC 75-12841. Orig. Title: Great American Negroes. (Illus.). 352p. (gr. 5 up). 1976. 10.95 (ISBN 0-690-00994-1, TYC-J). T Y Crowell.

Great Blue. Marnie R. Crowell. 1980. 9.95 (ISBN 0-8129-0905-4). Times Bks.

Great Bone Hunt. Margaret Cooper. (gr. 2-4). 1967. 2.95 o.s.i. (ISBN 0-02-724380-X). Macmillan.

Great Book of Catalogs. Steve Pinkerton & Betsy Pinkerton. 8.95 (ISBN 0-9602882-0-1). Green Hill.

Great Book of Currier & Ives' America. Walton Rawls. LC 79-89549. (Illus.). 488p. 1979. 85.00 (ISBN 0-89659-070-4). Abbeville Pr.

Great Book of French Impressionism. Diane Kelder. LC 80-66527. (Illus.). 448p. 1980. 100.00 (ISBN 0-89659-151-4). Abbeville Pr.

Great Book of French Impressionism. Horst Keller. Tr. by Alexis Brown from Ger. LC 80-13206. (Illus.). 272p. 1980. 50.00 (ISBN 0-933920-11-3). Hudson Hills.

Great Brain. John D. Fitzgerald. (Illus.). (gr. 7 up). 1971. pap. 1.50 (ISBN 0-440-40307-3, YB). Dell.

Great Brain at the Academy. John D. Fitzgerald. 176p. (gr. 3-7). 1973. pap. 1.50 (ISBN 0-440-43113-1, YB). Dell.

Great Brain Does It Again. 1976. pap. 1.50 (ISBN 0-440-42983-8, YB). Dell.

Great Brain Reforms. John D. Fitzgerald. 176p. 1975. pap. 1.50 (ISBN 0-440-44841-7, YB). Dell.

Great Bread: The Easiest Possible Way to Make Almost a Hundred Kinds. Bernice Hunt. (Illus.). 124p. 1980. pap. 5.95 (ISBN 0-14-046472-7). Penguin.

Great Bread! The Easiest Possible Way to Make Almost 100 Kinds. Bernice Hunt. (Illus.). (gr. 6 up). 1977. 8.95 o.p. (ISBN 0-670-34861-9). Viking Pr.

Great Britain. Francis Coleman. LC 75-44870. (Macdonald Countries). (Illus.). (gr. 6 up). 1976. PLB 7.95 (ISBN 0-382-06102-0, Pub. by Macdonald Ed). Silver.

Great Britain & the Commonwealth. 3rd ed. James A. Williamson. 1965. text ed. 5.50x (ISBN 0-7136-0844-7). Humanities.

Great Britain & the Congo: The Pillage of the Congo Basin. E. D. Morel. LC 68-9619. 1969. Repr. of 1909 ed. 15.50 (ISBN 0-86527-088-0). Fertig.

Great Britain & the Origins of the Pacific War: A Study of British Policy in East Asia, 1937 to 1941. Peter Lowe. (Illus.). 330p. 1977. text ed. 39.00x (ISBN 0-19-822427-3). Oxford U Pr.

Great Britain: Geographical Essays. Jean B. Mitchell. 1962. 48.00 (ISBN 0-521-05739-6); pap. 19.95x (ISBN 0-521-09986-2). Cambridge U Pr.

Great Britain, Road Atlas. Johnston & Bacon. (Illus.). 372p. 1978. pap. 11.95 (ISBN 0-7179-4239-2). Bradt Ent.

Great Britian Map. 1978. pap. 2.50 o.p. (ISBN 0-214-20167-8, 8012, Dist. by Arco). Barrie & Jenkins.

Great Bronze Age of China: An Exhibition from the People's Republic of China. Ed. by Wen Fong. (Illus.). xviii, 404p. 1980. 25.00 (ISBN 0-87099-226-0). Metro Mus Art.

Great Buffalo Hunt. Wayne Gard. LC 59-11049. (Illus.). 1968. pap. 5.95 (ISBN 0-8032-5067-3, BB 390, Bison). U of Nebr Pr.

Great Bull Market: Wall Street in the 1920's. Robert Sobel. LC 68-19795. (Essays in American History). 1968. pap. 5.95x (ISBN 0-393-09817-6, NortonC). Norton.

Great Burgerland Disaster. Betty K. Levine. LC 80-36713. 120p. (gr. 5-9). 1981. PLB 8.95 (ISBN 0-689-30815-9). Atheneum.

Great Cable Car Adventure Book. Jill Anthony & Gene Anthony. (Illus.). 192p. (Orig.). 1981. pap. 6.95 (ISBN 0-89141-120-8). Presidio Pr.

Great Camaro. Michael Lamm. (Illus.). 144p. 1978. 16.95 (ISBN 0-932128-00-9). Lamm-Morada.

Great Campaigns-- Reform & War in America Nineteen Hundred to Nineteen Twenty-Eight. Otis L. Graham, Jr. & Leon Litwack. LC 79-24302. 400p. 1980. pap. 9.95 (ISBN 0-89874-022-3). Krieger.

Great Camps of the Adirondacks. Harvey Kaiser. LC 79-90360. (Illus.). Date not set. 40.00 (ISBN 0-87923-308-7); limited edition 140.00 (ISBN 0-87923-392-3). Godine. Postponed.
Great Canadian Outback. Robert Janes. (Illus.). 1979. 19.95 (ISBN 0-295-95678-X, Pub. by Douglas & McIntyre Canada). U of Wash Pr.
Great Cars & Grand Marques: Automobile Quarterly's Great Cars & Grand Marques. Automobile Quarterly Editors. (Automobile Quarterly Marques History Ser.). 1976. 29.50 o.p. (ISBN 0-525-11612-5). Dutton.
Great Cases of Scotland Yard. Intro. by Eric Ambler. (Illus.). 1978. 12.95 (ISBN 0-89577-053-9, Pub. by Reader's Digest). Norton.
Great Cat Chase. Mercer Mayer. LC 74-13120. (Illus.). 32p. (gr. k-2). 1975. 3.95 (ISBN 0-590-07400-8, Four Winds). Schol Bk Serv.
Great Centers. Ian Thorne. (Stars of the NHL Ser.). (Illus.). (gr. 4-12). 1976. PLB 7.95 (ISBN 0-87191-492-1). Creative Ed.
Great Chess Upsets. Samuel Reshevsky. LC 74-77098. 1975. 9.95 o.p. (ISBN 0-668-03492-0); pap. 3.95 o.p. (ISBN 0-668-03493-9). Arco.
Great Chicago Melting Pot Cookbook. Agnes Feeney & John Leckel. (Illus., Orig.). 1980. pap. 6.95 (ISBN 0-89865-028-3). Donning Co.
Great Chiefs. Benjamin Capps. LC 75-744. (Old West). (Illus.). (gr. 5 up). 1975. kivar 12.96 (ISBN 0-8094-1494-5, Pub. by Time-Life). Silver.
Great Chiefs. William W. Johnson. (Old West Ser.). (Illus.). 240p. 1975. 12.95 (ISBN 0-8094-1492-9). Time-Life.
Great Christ Debate: A Quest for the Theological Reconciliation of Judaism, Christianity, & Islam. Etomar Ben Roffman. 1978. 8.50 o.p. (ISBN 0-682-49123-3). Exposition.
Great Christian Hymnal. Tillit S. Teddlie. 1965. 3.00 (ISBN 0-89137-600-3). Quality Pubns.
Great Church Fights. Leslie B. Flynn. 1976. pap. 1.95 o.p. (ISBN 0-88207-743-0). Victor Bks.
Great Church in Captivity. Steven Runciman. LC 68-29330. 1968. 42.50 (ISBN 0-521-07188-7). Cambridge U Pr.
Great Civilisations: Egypt. (Illus.). Arabic 2.50x (ISBN 0-685-82828-X). Intl Bk Ctr.
Great Composers, Bks. 1 & 2. (Illus., Arabic.). 2.50x ea. Intl Bk Ctr.
Great Composers: Reviews & Bombardments. Bernard Shaw. Ed. by Louis Crompton. LC 76-14311. (Cal. Ser.: No. 351). 1978. 28.50x (ISBN 0-520-03253-5); pap. 6.95 (ISBN 0-520-03266-7). U of Cal Pr.
Great Controversy. Ashley S. Johnson. 7.50 o.p. (ISBN 0-89225-096-8). Gospel Advocate.
Great Controversy. Ellen G. White. 1950. 5.95 (ISBN 0-8163-0035-6, 07886-5); deluxe ed. 9.50 (ISBN 0-8163-0036-4, 07882-4); pap. 0.95 (ISBN 0-8163-0037-2, 07887-3). Pacific Pr Pub Assn.
Great Cookie Thief. Emily P. Kingsley. (Sesame Street Shape Bks.). (Illus.). (ps-3). 1977. PLB 5.38 (ISBN 0-307-68877-1, Golden Pr). Western Pub.
Great Crash of Nineteen Twenty-Nine. John K. Galbraith. 1980. pap. 2.75 (ISBN 0-686-69255-1, 50799, Discus). Avon.
Great Crimes of the Century: Murderers Leave Clues, No. 8. George Carpozi, Jr. (Orig.). 1980. pap. 1.95 (ISBN 0-532-23130-9). Manor Bks.
Great Crimes of the Century: The Savage Killers, No. 7. George Carpozi, Jr. (Orig.). 1980. pap. 1.95 (ISBN 0-532-23129-5). Manor Bks.
Great Crimes of the Century: The Senseless Slayers, No. 5. George Carpozi, Jr. (Orig.). 1979. pap. 1.95 (ISBN 0-532-23165-1). Manor Bks.
Great Crimes of the Century: The Weird Murderers, No. 6. George Carpozi, Jr. (Orig.). 1979. pap. 1.95 (ISBN 0-532-23113-9). Manor Bks.
Great Crisis & Its Political Consequences. E. Varga. 14.50 (ISBN 0-86527-089-9). Fertig.
Great Dane Thor. Walter Farley. (Illus.). (gr. 5-9). 1966. 4.95 (ISBN 0-394-81582-3, BYR). Random.
Great Danes. rev. ed. Mary K. Johnston. (Illus.). 126p. 1973. pap. 2.95 o.p. (ISBN 0-87666-309-9, HS-1052). TFH Pubns.
Great Danes. Diane McCarty. (Illus.). 125p. 1980. 2.95 (ISBN 0-87666-693-4, KW-082). TFH Pubns.
Great Danes in Canada. Pat Ostova. 1980. 19.95 (ISBN 0-87714-080-4). Caroline Hse.
Great Days. Donald Barthelme. 1980. pap. write for info. (ISBN 0-671-83185-2). PB.
Great Days of the Circus. Freeman Hubbard & Leonard Farley. (American Heritage Junior Library). (Illus.). 153p. (gr. 5 up). 1962. 9.95 (ISBN 0-8281-0394-1, J010-0). Am Heritage.
Great Debate on Miracles: From Joseph Glanvill to David Hume. R. M. Burns. LC 78-75197. 300p. 1981. 20.00 (ISBN 0-8387-2378-0). Bucknell U Pr.
Great Debates, Carter Vs. Ford, 1976. Ed. by Sidney Kraus. LC 78-62422. (Midland Bks.: No. 229). (Illus.). 568p. 1979. 29.95x (ISBN 0-253-30363-X); pap. 19.50x (ISBN 0-253-20229-9). Ind U Pr.
Great Debates in American History. Marion M. Miller. 1970. Repr. of 1913 ed. 140.00 (ISBN 0-8108-0386-0). Scarecrow.
Great Debates: Kennedy vs. Nixon, 1960. Ed. by Sidney Kraus. LC 62-7487. 1977. 17.50x (ISBN 0-253-32630-3); pap. text ed. 5.95x (ISBN 0-253-32631-1). Ind U Pr.
Great Decisions Nineteen Eighty. American Foreign Policy Association. (gr. 9-12). 1980. pap. text ed. 5.20 (ISBN 0-205-06889-8, 7668899); free tchrs' guide avail. (ISBN 0-205-06890-1). Allyn.
Great Decisions Nineteen Eighty-One. Foreign Policy Association. (Illus.). 96p. (Orig.). 1981. pap. 5.00 (ISBN 0-87124-066-1). Foreign Policy.
Great Decisions 1976. Foreign Policy Association. (gr. 10-12). 1976. pap. text ed. 5.20 (ISBN 0-205-05383-1, 7653832); tchrs' guide 2.20 (ISBN 0-205-06115-X). Allyn.
Great Decisions 1978. Foreign Policy Association. (gr. 9-12). 1978. pap. 5.20 (ISBN 0-205-06076-5, 7660766); tchrs'. ed 2.20 (ISBN 0-205-06077-3, 7660774). Allyn.
Great Decisions 1979. rev. ed. Foreign Policy Association. 1979. text ed. 5.20 (ISBN 0-205-06428-0, 7664281). Allyn.
Great Defensemen. Ian Thorne. (Stars of the NHL Ser.). (Illus.). (gr. 4-12). 1976. PLB 7.95 (ISBN 0-87191-493-X). Creative Ed.
Great Depression & New Deal Monetary Policy: Two Essays. Garet Garrett & Murray N. Rothbard. LC 80-36791. (Cato Paper Ser.: No. 13). 148p. 1980. pap. 4.00 (ISBN 0-932790-19-4). Cato Inst.
Great Depression Revisited. Ed. by Karl Brunner. (Rochester Studies in Economics & Policy Issues: Vol. 2). 368p. 1980. lib. bdg. 20.00 (ISBN 0-89838-051-0, Pub by Martinus Nijhoff). Kluwer Boston.
Great Desert Race. Betty Baker. LC 80-16483. (Illus.). 144p. (gr. 5-9). 1980. PLB 8.95 (ISBN 0-02-708200-8). Macmillan.
Great Detective Stories. Ed. by Harriet Ross. LC 64-24881. (Illus.). 160p. (YA) 1981. PLB 6.99 (ISBN 0-87460-186-X); pap. 1.95 (ISBN 0-87460-187-8). Lion.
Great Dialogues of Plato. Tr. by Rouse. pap. 5.95 (ISBN 0-452-25234-2, Z5234, Plume). NAL.
Great Diamonds of the World. Edwin W. Streeter. Ed. by Joseph Hatton & A. H. Keane. LC 76-78238. 1971. Repr. of 1882 ed. 18.00 (ISBN 0-8103-3624-3). Gale.
Great Dirigibles, Their Triumphs & Disasters. John Toland. Orig. Title: Ships in the Sky: the Story of the Great Dirigibles. (Illus.). 8.50 (ISBN 0-8446-4612-1). Peter Smith.
Great Disasters. Ed. by Pat McCarthy. (Pal Paperbacks Ser., Kit A). (Illus., Orig.). (gr. 7-12). 1974. pap. text ed. 1.25 (ISBN 0-8374-3477-7). Xerox Ed Pubns.
Great Dismal Swamp: Its Science, History & Folklore. Hubert J. Davis. (Illus.). 1971. 7.50 (ISBN 0-930230-11-6). Johnson NC.
Great Divide. Bryce Walker. LC 73-81327. (American Wilderness Ser). (Illus.). (gr. 6 up). 1973. lib. bdg. 11.97 (ISBN 0-8094-1185-7, Pub. by Time-Life). Silver.
Great Divide. Bryce Walker. (American Wilderness Ser.). 1973. 12.95 (ISBN 0-8094-1184-9). Time-Life.
Great Divide: Travels in the Upper Yellowstone in the Summer of 1874. Earl Of Dunraven. LC 67-26059. (Illus.). 1967. pap. 3.95 o.p. (ISBN 0-8032-5052-5, 369, Bison). U of Nebr Pr.
Great Divorce. C. S. Lewis. 1946. 4.95 o.p. (ISBN 0-02-570550-4); pap. 1.95 (ISBN 0-02-086780-8). Macmillan.
Great Dragon Competition & Other Stories. John Cunliffe. (Illus.). (gr. k-5). 1980. 6.95 (ISBN 0-233-96472-X). Andre Deutsch.
Great Dramatists. Ed. by James Vinson & Daniel Kirkpatrick. (Great Writers of the English Language Ser.). 700p. 1979. 45.00 (ISBN 0-312-34570-4). St Martin.
Great Drawings & Illustrations from Punch Eighteen Forty-One to Nineteen Hundred-One: One Hundred Ninety-Two Works by Leech, Keene, du Maurier, May & 21 Others. Ed. by Stanley Appelbaum & Richard Kelly. (Illus.). 144p. (Orig.). 1981. pap. price not set (ISBN 0-486-24110-6). Dover.
Great Drawings of All Time, 4 vols. Ed. by Ira Moskowitz. LC 75-19869. (Illus.). 2250p. 1976. Repr. of 1962 ed. Set. 375.00 (ISBN 0-87011-294-5). Kodansha.
Great Eastern Railway. Cecil J. Allen. 14.95x (ISBN 0-392-07860-0, SpS). Soccer.
Great Eating, Great Dieting Cookbook. Arthur Darack et al. LC 77-4246. 1978. 14.95 o.s.i. (ISBN 0-690-01684-0, TYC-T). T Y Crowell.
Great Educators: Readings for Leaders in Education. Hugh C. Black et al. LC 72-88717. 1972. 19.95 (ISBN 0-911012-48-6). Nelson-Hall.
Great Endurance Horse Race. Jack Shaefer. (Illus.). 112p. (Orig.). 1981. pap. 6.95 (ISBN 0-88496-165-6). Capra Pr.
Great English Letter-Writers, 2 vols. William J. Dawson & Coningsby W. Dawson. 1980. Set. lib. bdg. 50.00 (ISBN 0-8492-4218-5). R West.
Great Escape. Paul Brickhill. 1978. pap. 2.25 (ISBN 0-449-23717-6, Crest). Fawcett.
Great Escaper. David Warren. LC 78-26629. (Raintree Great Adventures). (Illus.). (gr. 3-6). 1979. PLB 8.95 (ISBN 0-8393-0152-9). Raintree Child.
Great Estate at Work. Susanna W. Martina. LC 79-51827. (Illus.). 308p. 1980. 54.50 (ISBN 0-521-22696-1). Cambridge U Pr.
Great Events in the Life of Christ. Jerry Vines. 1979. pap. 1.95 (ISBN 0-88207-776-7). Victor Bks.
Great Events Two As Reported in the New York Times: Program Guide. Ed. by Liza Altman & Ronald R. Gonella. 107p. (gr. 7-12). 1980. pap. text ed. 7.95 (ISBN 0-667-00600-1). Microfilming Corp.
Great Exhibitions. John Allwood. 1978. 19.95 o.s.i. (ISBN 0-02-501710-1). Macmillan.
Great Expectations. Charles Dickens. Ed. by Louis Crompton. LC 62-21261. 1964. pap. 6.50 (ISBN 0-672-60967-3, LL2). Bobbs.
Great Expectations. Charles Dickens. 1979. 12.95x (ISBN 0-460-00234-1, Evman); pap. 2.95 (ISBN 0-460-01234-7). Dutton.
Great Expectations. Charles Dickens. 1962. pap. 0.95 o.s.i. (ISBN 0-02-050320-2, Collier). Macmillan.
Great Expectations. Charles Dickens. Ed. by R. D. McMaster. LC 65-2026. (College Classics in English Ser.). 1965. pap. 4.95 (ISBN 0-672-63042-7). Odyssey Pr.
Great Expectations. Charles Dickens. (World's Classics Ser.). 7.50 o.p. (ISBN 0-19-250128-3). Oxford U Pr.
Great Expectations. Charles Dickens. Ed. by Angus Calder. (English Lib.). (Orig.). (YA) (gr. 9 up). 1965. pap. 2.25 (ISBN 0-14-043003-2). Penguin.
Great Expectations. Charles Dickens. (Keith Jennison Large Type Bks). (gr. 5 up). PLB 9.95 o.p. (ISBN 0-531-00194-6). Watts.
Great Expectations. Charles Dickens. (Literature Ser). (gr. 9-12). 1970. pap. text ed. 4.17 (ISBN 0-87720-725-9). AMSCO Sch.
Great Expectations. Charles Dickens. Ed. by N. L. Clay. (Guide Novel Ser.). pap. text ed. 5.50x (ISBN 0-435-16234-9). Heinemann Ed.
Great Expectations. Charles Dickens. pap. 1.95. Bantam.
Great Expectations. Gail R. Rosensfit. (Living Literature Workbook Ser.). (Orig.). (gr. 7). Date not set. pap. 1.50 (ISBN 0-671-09249-9). Monarch Pr. Postponed.
Great Expectations for Small Schools: The Limitations of Federal Programs. William A. Firestone. 215p. 1980. 23.95 (ISBN 0-03-057397-1). Praeger.
Great Expectations for Small Schools: The Perils of Federal Programs. William A. Firestone. (Praeger Special Studies). 215p. 1980. 20.95 o.p. (ISBN 0-686-63287-7). Praeger.
Great Expectations with Reader's Guide. Charles Dickens. (gr. 10-12). 1975. pap. text ed. 7.00 (ISBN 0-87720-800-X); tchrs ed. 4.40 (ISBN 0-87720-900-6). AMSCO Sch.
Great Experiment. F. Thistlethwaite. (Illus.). 1977. pap. 11.95x (ISBN 0-521-29224-7). Cambridge U Pr.
Great Experiments in Biology. Ed. by Mordecai L. Gabriel & Seymour Fogel. 1955. pap. text ed. 14.95x (ISBN 0-13-363549-X). P-H.
Great Experiments in Psychology. 3rd ed. Henry E. Garrett. (Century Psychology Ser.). (Illus.). 1981. 29.50x (ISBN 0-89197-190-4); pap. text ed. 16.50x (ISBN 0-89197-776-7). Irvington.
Great Exploration Hoaxes. David Roberts. Ed. by Herbert Michaelman. 1981. 12.95 (ISBN 0-517-54075-4, Michaelman Books). Crown.
Great Explorers. (Horizons of Knowledge Ser.). (Illus.). 1979. lib. bdg. 17.50 (ISBN 0-87196-411-2). Facts on File.
Great Extravaganza: Portland & the Lewis & Clark Expedition. Carl Abbott. LC 80-83179. (Illus.). 104p. 1981. pap. 5.95 (ISBN 0-87595-088-4). Oreg Hist Soc.
Great Fear: Race in the Mind of America. Ed. by Gary B. Nash & Richard Weiss. LC 77-118970. 1970. 5.95 o.p. (ISBN 0-03-085270-6). HR&W.
Great Forest. Richard G. Lillard. LC 72-8129. (Illus.). 452p. 1973. Repr. of 1947 ed. lib. bdg. 39.50 (ISBN 0-306-70534-6). Da Capo.
Great Formosan Imposter. Frederic J. Foley. 126p. 1980. 7.50 (ISBN 0-89955-148-3, Pub. by Mei Ya Pub Taiwan). Intl Schol Bk Serv.
Great Founding Clans of America. Avery Kolb. 1980. 20.00 o.p. (ISBN 0-8424-0158-X). Caroline Hse.
Great Frame-Up: The Consumer's Guide to Eyeglasses. Paul D. Friend. Ed. by Debbie Hammond. 1980. 11.95 (ISBN 0-87949-181-7). Ashley Bks.
Great Frederick & Other Stories. Margaret Epp. 128p. (gr. 7 up). 1971. pap. 1.50 (ISBN 0-8024-1325-0). Moody.
Great French Writers: Madame De Sevigne. Gaston Boissier. 154p. 1980. Repr. of 1887 ed. lib. bdg. 25.00 (ISBN 0-8495-0476-7). Arden Lib.
Great Frog Swap. Ron Roy. LC 79-21966. (Illus.). 48p. (gr. 1-4). 1981. 7.95 (ISBN 0-394-84432-7); PLB 7.99 (ISBN 0-394-94432-1). Pantheon.
Great Frontier. Walter P. Webb. 1964. 14.95 (ISBN 0-292-73253-8); pap. 7.95 (ISBN 0-292-72706-2). U of Tex Pr.
Great Games by Chess Prodigies. Fred Reinfeld. (Illus.). 256p. 1972. pap. 2.95 o.s.i. (ISBN 0-02-029710-6, Collier). Macmillan.
Great Gangster Pictures. James R. Parish & Michael R. Pitts. LC 75-32402. (Illus.). 1976. 18.00 (ISBN 0-8108-0881-1). Scarecrow.
Great Garlic Cookbook. Barbara Friedlander et al. LC 75-16359. (Illus.). 160p. 1975. 12.95 o.s.i. (ISBN 0-02-541500-X, 54150). Macmillan.
Great Gates: The Story of the Rocky Mountain Passes. Marshall Sprague. LC 80-21994. (Illus.). x, 468p. 1981. 23.50x (ISBN 0-8032-4122-4); pap. 8.50 (ISBN 0-8032-9119-1, BB 742, Bison). U of Nebr Pr.
Great Gatsby. F. Scott Fitzgerald. (gr. 9-12). 1920. 6.95 o.p. (ISBN 0-684-10154-8, ScribT); text ed. 6.95 (ISBN 0-684-51515-6, ScribC); pap. 3.95 (ISBN 0-684-71760-3, SL1, ScribT); pap. text ed. 3.24 (ISBN 0-684-51516-4, SSP2, ScribC); ScribT. pap. 2.25 (ISBN 0-684-16325-X). Scribner.
Great Gatsby. F. Scott Fitzgerald. (Hudson River Edition Ser.). 1981. write for info. (ISBN 0-684-16498-1, ScribT). Scribner.
Great Georgian Houses of America, 2 Vols. Architects' Emergency Committee. (Illus.). 1970. pap. 8.95 ea. Vol. 1 (ISBN 0-486-22491-0). Vol. 2 (ISBN 0-486-22492-9). Dover.
Great Gilly Hopkins. Katherine Paterson. LC 77-27075. (gr. 5 up). 1978. 7.95 (ISBN 0-690-03837-2, TYC-J); PLB 7.89 (ISBN 0-690-03838-0). T Y Crowell.
Great Gittin up Morning: The Story of Denmark Vesey. John O. Killens. Ed. by Louis R. Rivera. (Illus.). 128p. 1980. pap. 5.50 (ISBN 0-917886-06-2). Shamal Bks.
Great Goalies. Ian Thorne. (Stars of the NHL Ser.). (Illus.). (gr. 4-12). 1976. PLB 7.95 (ISBN 0-87191-491-3). Creative Ed.
Great Goalies of Pro Hockey. Frank Orr. (Pro Hockey Library: No. 5). (Illus.). (gr. 5 up). 1973. 2.50 o.p. (ISBN 0-394-82539-X); PLB 3.69 (ISBN 0-394-92539-4). Random.
Great God Mogadon & Other Plays. Barry Oakley. 119p. 1980. pap. 10.95x (ISBN 0-7022-1437-X); pap. 6.00x (ISBN 0-7022-1437-X). U of Queensland Pr.
Great Golf Humor. Ed. by Larry Sheehan. LC 79-52547. (Illus.). 1979. 9.95x (ISBN 0-914178-31-8, 25166-X). Golf Digest.
Great-Grandfather in the Honey Tree. Sam Swayne & Zoa Swayne. (Illus.). (gr. 4-6). 1949. PLB 3.95 o.p. (ISBN 0-670-34932-1). Viking Pr.
Great-Grandmother Cat Tales. Jan Wahl. LC 76-5484. (Illus.). (gr. k-4). 1976. 3.95 o.p. (ISBN 0-394-83278-7); PLB 5.99 (ISBN 0-394-93278-1). Pantheon.
Great Grandmother Goose. Helen Cooper. LC 79-1081. (Illus.). (gr. k up). 1979. 7.95 (ISBN 0-688-80218-4); PLB 7.63 (ISBN 0-688-84218-6). Greenwillow.
Great Gray Owl: Phantom of the Nortern Forest. Robert W. Nero. LC 80-607110. (Illus.). 168p. 1980. 17.50 (ISBN 0-87474-672-8). Smithsonian.
Great Gulper. Jim Slater. LC 80-53067. (A. Mazing Monsters Ser.). (Illus.). 1981. pap. 1.25 (ISBN 0-394-84737-7). Random.
Great Gunfighters of the Kansas Cowtowns, 1867-1886. Nyle H. Miller & Joseph W. Snell. LC 63-63480. (Illus.). 1967. 16.95x (ISBN 0-8032-0123-0); pap. 4.50 (ISBN 0-8032-5137-8, BB 333, Bison). U of Nebr Pr.
Great Harry. Carolly Erickson. LC 79-21868. 1980. 14.95 (ISBN 0-671-40017-7). Summit Bks.
Great Harvest. G. A. Pottebaum. (Little People's Paperbacks Ser.). 1979. pap. 0.99 (ISBN 0-8164-2253-2). Crossroad NY.
Great Historic Places. American Heritage. 1980. pap. 4.95 (ISBN 0-686-60940-9, 24710). S&S.
Great Historic Places: An American Heritage Guide. American Heritage Editors. Ed. by Beverly Da Costa. LC 73-8836. (Illus.). 320p. 1973. 6.95 (ISBN 0-686-65705-5, 23074, Pub. by Am Heritage). S&S.
Great Historic Places: An American Heritage Guide. American Heritage Editors. Ed. by Beverley Da Costa. LC 73-8836. (Illus.). 320p. 1973. pap. 6.95 (ISBN 0-8281-0295-3, B033G). Am Heritage.

Great Historic Places of Europe: A Horizon Guide. Horizon Magazine Editors. Ed. by Beverly Hilowitz. LC 74-10941. (Illus.). 384p. 1974. 10.00 (ISBN 0-686-65706-3, 23073, Pub. by Am Heritage). S&S.
Great Historical Figures of Japan. Ed. by Hyoye Murakami & Thomas J. Harper. (Illus., Orig.). 1978. 18.50 (ISBN 0-87040-431-8). Japan Pubns.
Great Hitters of the Major Leagues. Frank Graham, Jr. (Major League Baseball Library). (Illus.). (gr. 5-9). 1969. 2.50 o.p. (ISBN 0-394-80180-6, BYR). Random.
Great Horned Owl. Jeanne F. Hill. 1980. 2.50 (ISBN 0-934834-02-4). White Pine.
Great Horror Stories. new ed. Ed. by Harriet Ross. LC 64-24882. (Illus.). 160p. (YA) 1981. PLB 6.99 (ISBN 0-87460-188-6); pap. 1.95 (ISBN 0-87460-189-4). Lion.
Great Horses of the U. S. Equestrian Team. William Steinkraus & Sam Savitt. LC 76-53434. (gr. 5 up). 1977. 6.95 (ISBN 0-396-07432-4). Dodd.
Great Humorous Stories. Ed. by Harriet Ross. LC 64-24883. (Illus.). 160p. (YA) 1979. PLB 6.99 (ISBN 0-87460-190-8); pap. 1.95 (ISBN 0-87460-191-6). Lion.
Great Hunger. Cecil Woodham-Smith. 1980. pap. 8.95 (ISBN 0-525-47643-1). Dutton.
Great I Came's of Jesus. A. M. Coniaris. 1980. pap. 5.95 (ISBN 0-686-27069-X). Light&Life Pub Co MN.
Great Ideas. Martha B. Ardiff & Eileen Seaward. (Readers Ser.: Stage 4-Intermediate). (Orig.). 1980. pap. text ed. 2.80 (ISBN 0-88377-159-4). Newbury Hse.
Great Ideas & Theories of Modern Cosmology. Jagjit Singh. 1966. pap. text ed. 4.50 (ISBN 0-486-20925-3). Dover.
Great Ideas for Banquets: Possibilities, Plans, & Patterns. Phyllis Robinson. (Paperback Program Ser.). (Orig.). 1981. pap. 7.95 (ISBN 0-8010-7706-0). Baker Bk.
Great Ideas for Teaching Economics. Burns. 846p. 1981. pap. write for info. (ISBN 0-8302-2304-5). Goodyear.
Great Ideas in Communications. A. Brown. 1968. 7.00 (ISBN 0-08-007073-6). Pergamon.
Great Ideas in Engineering. E. Larson. 6.00 o.p. (ISBN 0-08-007078-7). Pergamon.
Great Ideas in Information Theory, Language & Cybernetics. Jagjit Singh. (Orig.). 1966. pap. text ed. 4.00 (ISBN 0-486-21694-2). Dover.
Great Ideas in Music. P. Young. 6.25 (ISBN 0-08-007072-8). Pergamon.
Great Ideas in the Law-Justice: Due Process of Law. Isidore Starr. 300p. 1981. pap. text ed. 6.50 (ISBN 0-8299-1020-4). West Pub.
Great Ideas of Modern Mathematics. Jagjit Singh. (Illus.). 1959. pap. text ed. 4.00 (ISBN 0-486-20587-8). Dover.
Great Ideas of Operations Research. Jagjit Singh. (Illus., Orig.). 1968. pap. text ed. 3.50 (ISBN 0-486-21886-4). Dover.
Great Immigrants. Cecyle S. Neidle. (Immigrant Heritage of America Ser). 1972. lib. bdg. 9.95 (ISBN 0-8057-3222-5). Twayne.
Great Impeacher. Robert E. Horowitz. (Brooklyn College Studies on Society in Change Ser.). 1979. 20.00 (ISBN 0-930888-03-0). Brooklyn Coll Pr.
Great Indian Chiefs. Albert Roland. (Illus.). (gr. 6 up). 1968. 5.95g o.s.i. (ISBN 0-02-777650-6, CCPr). Macmillan.
Great Indoor Games from Trash & Other Things. Judith Conaway. LC 77-7383. (Games & Activities Ser.). (Illus.). (gr. k-4). 1977. PLB 9.30 (ISBN 0-8172-0952-2). Raintree Pubs.
Great Industries of the United States: Being an Historical Summary of the Origin, Growth, & Perfection of the Chief Industrial Arts of This Country, 2 vols. Ed. by Horace Greeley. (Neglected American Economists Ser.). 1974. Set. lib. bdg. 76.00 (ISBN 0-8240-1007-8); lib. bdg. 50.00 ea. Garland Pub.
Great Insaturation & New Atlantis. Francis Bacon. Ed. by J. Weinberger. (Croft Classics Ser.). 1980. text ed. 9.95 (ISBN 0-88295-115-7); pap. text ed. 2.95 (ISBN 0-88295-113-0). AHM Pub.
Great Instrumentalists in Historic Photographs: 275 Portraits from 1850 to 1950. James Camner. (Illus.). 1980. pap. 6.95 (ISBN 0-486-23907-1). Dover.
Great International Barbeque Book. Myra Waldo. 216p. 1981. pap. 4.95 (ISBN 0-07-067778-6). McGraw.
Great International Disaster Book. James Cornell. LC 76-20752. (Encore Editions). (Illus.). 432p. 1976. 5.95 (ISBN 0-684-16894-4, ScribT). Scribner.
Great Issues: A Forum on Important Questions Facing the American Public. Al Capp & George Wallace. 1970. 5.95. Troy State Univ.
Great Issues: A Forum on Important Questions Facing the American Public. C. Northcote Parkinson & O. K. Armstrong. 1971. 5.95. TSU Pr.
Great Issues of International Politics. 2nd ed. Ed. by Morton A. Kaplan. LC 73-84931. 576p. 1974. text ed. 24.95x (ISBN 0-202-24139-4); pap. text ed. 13.95x (ISBN 0-202-24140-8). Aldine Pub.
Great Issues of Politics. 5th ed. Leslie Lipson. (Illus.). 528p. 1976. text ed. 16.95 (ISBN 0-13-363895-2). P-H.
Great Issues 71: A Forum on Important Questions Facing the American Public. Winston S. Churchill & John Glubb. 1972. 5.95. TSU Pr.
Great Issues 72: Imortant Questions Facing the American Public. Edward Teller & Paul V. Yoder. 1973. 5.95. TSU Pr.
Great Issues 73: A Forum on Important Questions Facing the American Public, Vol. 5. Russell Kirk & John Chamberlain. 1974. 5.95. TSU Pr.
Great Issues 74: A Forum on Important Questions Facing the American Public, Vol. 6. William Tate & Thomas H. Moorer. 5.95. TSU Pr.
Great Issues 75: A Forum on Important Questions Facing the American Public, Vol. 7. Odie B. Faulk & Erik M. Von Kuehneli. LC 76-26349. (Illus.). 1976. 10.95 (ISBN 0-916624-03-X). TSU Pr.
Great Issues 76: A Forum on Important Questions Facing the American Public, Vol. 8. Ashley Montagu & David N. Rowe. LC 77-85525. 11.95 (ISBN 0-916624-11-0). Troy State Univ.
Great Issues 77: A Forum on Important Questions Facing the American Public, Vol. 9. Paul W. McCracken & Ralph Izard. LC 78-65990. 1978. 12.95 (ISBN 0-916624-26-9). TSU Pr.
Great Issues 78: A Forum on Important Questions Facing the American Public, Vol.10. Douglas E. Leach & Patrick J. Buchanan. LC 75-648855. 1979. 13.95 (ISBN 0-916624-28-5). TSU Pr.
Great Issues 79-80: A Forum on Important Questions Facing the American Public, Vol. 11. George Bush & Philip Crane. 1980. 14.95 (ISBN 0-916624-32-3). TSU Pr.
Great Jazz Artists. James L. Collier. LC 77-7212. (Illus.). 192p. (gr. 7 up). 1977. 7.95 (ISBN 0-590-07493-8, Four Winds). Schol Bk Serv.
Great Jelly of London. Paul Jennings. (Illus.). (ps-5). 1967. 6.95 (ISBN 0-571-08546-6, Pub. by Faber & Faber); pap. 2.95 (ISBN 0-571-10844-X). Merrimack Bk Serv.
Great Jewish Debates & Dilemmas: Perspectives on Moral Issues in Conflict in the 80's. Albert Vorspan. LC 80-21057. 240p. (gr. 10-12). 1980. pap. text ed. 5.95 (ISBN 0-8074-0049-1). UAHC.
Great Jewish Plays. Ed. & tr. by Joseph C. Landis. LC 66-14720. 360p. 1972. 8.95 o.s.i. (ISBN 0-8180-0504-1). Horizon.
Great Jewish Plays. Ed. by Joseph C. Landis. 1980. pap. 3.50 (ISBN 0-380-51573-3, 51573, Bard). Avon.
Great Jewish Women. Greta Fink. LC 77-99193. 1978. 8.95 (ISBN 0-8197-0458-X). Bloch.
Great Kitchens. Jeffery Weiss. 96p. 1981. pap. 9.95 (ISBN 0-312-34605-0). St Martin.
Great Kivas of Chaco Canyon & Their Relationships. Gordon Vivian & Paul Reiter. (School of American Research Monograph: No. 22). (Illus.). 112p. 1980. pap. 7.50 (ISBN 0-8263-0297-1). U of NM Pr.
Great Lakes. James P. Barry. LC 76-15641. (First Bks.). (Illus.). 72p. (gr. 4-6). 1976. PLB 4.90 o.p. (ISBN 0-531-00337-X). Watts.
Great Lakes Archaeology. Ronald J. Mason. LC 80-2340. (New World Archaeological Record Ser.). 1981. price not set (ISBN 0-12-477850-X). Acad Pr.
Great Lakes Nature Guide. rev. ed. Michigan United Conservation Clubs. 1978. pap. 1.75 (ISBN 0-933112-05-X). Mich United Conserv.
Great Lakes Triangle. Jay Gourley. 1977. pap. 1.75 o.p. (ISBN 0-449-13827-5, GM). Fawcett.
Great Legal Philosophers: Selected Readings in Jurisprudence. Ed. by Clarence Morris. LC 57-11955. 1971. pap. 8.95x (ISBN 0-8122-1008-5, Pa Paperbks). U of Pa Pr.
Great Liberation (Mahanirvana Tantra) Tr. by John Woodroffe. 7.95 o.p. (ISBN 0-89744-113-3, Pub. by Ganesh & Co. India). Auromere.
Great Linebackers of the NFL. Richard Kaplan. (NFL Punt, Pass & Kick Library: No. 12). (Illus.). (gr. 5-9). 1970. 2.50 o.p. (ISBN 0-394-80152-0, BYR); PLB 3.69 (ISBN 0-394-90152-5). Random.
Great Liners. Melvin Maddocks. (Seafarers). 1978. 13.95 (ISBN 0-8094-2662-5). Time-Life.
Great Liners. Melvin Maddocks. LC 78-1366. (Seafarers Ser.). (Illus.). 1978. lib. bdg. 11.97 (ISBN 0-686-50986-2). Silver.
Great Lion of Bechuanaland: The Life and Times of Roger Price, Missionary. Edwin W. Smith. 1957. text ed. 15.00x (ISBN 0-8401-2210-1). Allenson.
Great Lion of God. Taylor Caldwell. LC 78-97653. 1970. 12.50 o.p. (ISBN 0-385-00042-1). Doubleday.
Great Lion of God. Taylor Caldwell. 1977. pap. 2.75 (ISBN 0-449-24096-7, Crest). Fawcett.
Great Los Angeles Blizzard. Tom Racina. 1978. pap. 2.25 o.s.i. (ISBN 0-515-04718-X). Jove Pubns.
Great Los Angeles Fire. Edward Stewart. 1980. 11.95 (ISBN 0-671-25135-X). S&S.
Great Love Stories from the Saturday Evening Post. LC 76-41559. 1976. 5.95 (ISBN 0-89387-003-X). Sat Eve Post.
Great Lover. Danialle Branton. 1978. pap. 1.95 o.p. (ISBN 0-449-14039-3, GM). Fawcett.
Great Luxury Liners, 1927-1952: A Photographic Record. Willam Miller, Jr. (Illus.). 160p. Date not set. pap. 6.95 (ISBN 0-486-24056-8). Dover.
Great McGoniggle Rides Shotgun. Scott Corbett. (Illus.). (gr. 1-3). 1977. 6.95 (ISBN 0-316-15729-5, Atlantic-Little, Brown). Little.
Great McGoniggle Switches Pitches. Scott Corbett. (Illus.). 64p. (gr. 2 up). 1980. 6.95 (ISBN 0-316-15710-4, Pub. by Atlantic Monthly Pr). Little.
Great McGoniggle Rides Shotgun. Scott Corbett. (gr. k-6). 1980. pap. 0.95 (ISBN 0-440-43313-4, YB). Dell.
Great Male Dancers of the Ballet. Walter Terry. 1978. pap. 10.00 (ISBN 0-385-04197-7, Anchor Pr). Doubleday.
Great Managua Earthquake. Jay Mallin. Ed. by D. Steve Rahmas. (Events of Our Times Ser.: No. 14). 32p. (Orig.). (gr. 7-12). 1974. lib. bdg. 2.45 incl. catalog cards (ISBN 0-686-07224-3); pap. 1.25 vinyl laminated covers (ISBN 0-686-07225-1). SamHar Pr.
Great Maria. Cecelia Holland. 1974. 8.95 o.p. (ISBN 0-394-48509-2). Knopf.
Great Masks to Make. Robyn Supraner. LC 80-24077. (Illus.). 48p. (gr. 2-5). 1980. PLB 6.92 (ISBN 0-89375-436-6); pap. 1.75 (ISBN 0-89375-437-4). Troll Assocs.
Great Mathematicians. Herbert Westren Turnbull. LC 61-16934. (Illus.). 1961. usa 8.00x (ISBN 0-8147-0419-0). NYU Pr.
Great Meadow. Elizabeth M. Roberts. 224p. 1975. pap. 1.50 o.p. (ISBN 0-89176-446-1, 6446). Mockingbird Bks.
Great Meatless Meals. Frances M. Lappe & Ellen B. Ewald. (Orig.). 1976. pap. 2.25 (ISBN 0-345-29501-3). Ballantine.
Great Meatless Meals. Francis M. Lappe & Ellen B. Ewald. 160p. (Orig.). 1981. pap. 2.50. Ballantine.
Great Men of American Popular Song. rev. ed. David Ewen. LC 71-37961. 432p. 1972. 14.95 o.p. (ISBN 0-13-364182-1). P-H.
Great Menagerie: An Adaptation of the Antique Pop-up Book. Anthea Bell. LC 79-67762. (Illus.). (gr. k-3). 1980. 7.95 (ISBN 0-670-34979-8, Co-Pub. by Kestrel Books). Viking Pr.
Great Merchants. new & enl. ed. Tom Mahoney & Leonard Sloane. LC 73-14065. 384p. (YA) 1974. 12.95 o.s.i. (ISBN 0-06-012739-2, HarpT). Har-Row.
Great Migration: Emergence of the Americas, Indicated in the Readings of Edgar Cayce. Vada F. Carlson. (Orig.). 1970. pap. 1.95 (ISBN 0-87604-040-7). ARE Pr.
Great Mirror of Folly. Arthur H. Cole. (Kress Library of Business & Economics: No. 6). 1949. pap. 5.00x (ISBN 0-678-09901-4, Baker Lib). Kelley.
Great Modern European Short Stories. Ed. by Douglas Angus & Sylvia Angus. 1977. pap. 2.50 (ISBN 0-449-30781-6, Prem). Fawcett.
Great Moment. Elinor Glyn. (Barbara Cartland's Library of Love: Vol. 14). 214p. 1980. 12.95x (ISBN 0-7156-1474-6, Pub. by Duckworth England). Biblio Dist.
Great Moments in Auto Racing. Frank Orr. LC 73-18087. (Illus.). 160p. 1974. 2.50 o.p. (ISBN 0-394-82763-5); PLB 3.69 (ISBN 0-394-92763-X). Random.
Great Moments in Pro Basketball. Dave Wolf & Bill Bruns. (gr. 5-9). 1968. PLB 3.69 (ISBN 0-394-90872-4, BYR). Random.
Great Moments in Sport: Motor Cycle Racing. Peter Carrick. (Illus.). 1977. 16.95 (ISBN 0-7207-0972-5). Transatlantic.
Great Moments in Sports Car Racing. David J. Abodaher. (Illus.). 96p. (gr. 4-6). 1981. PLB 7.29 (ISBN 0-686-69302-7). Messner.
Great Money Panic: A Guide for Survival & Action. Martin D. Weiss. (Illus.). 256p. 1981. 15.95 (ISBN 0-87000-502-2). Arlington Hse.
Great Monsters of the Movies. Edward Edelson. (gr. 4-6). 1974. pap. 1.75 (ISBN 0-671-56108-1). Archway.
Great Moral Dilemmas. Ed. by R. M. MacIver. (Religion & Civilization Ser). 1964. Repr. of 1956 ed. 19.50x (ISBN 0-8154-0145-0). Cooper Sq.
Great Mother: An Analysis of the Archetype. Erich Neumann. Tr. by Ralph Manheim. (Bollingen Ser.: Vol. 47). 628p. 1972. 25.00x (ISBN 0-691-09742-9); pap. 6.95 (ISBN 0-691-01780-8). Princeton U Pr.
Great Movie Series. Ed. by James R. Parish. LC 78-146771. (Illus.). 1971. 5.98 o.p. (ISBN 0-498-07847-7, Encore). A S Barnes.
Great Movie Spectaculars. Edward Edelson. LC 76-56. 144p. (gr. 4-7). 1976. PLB 6.95 (ISBN 0-385-11180-0). Doubleday.
Great Movies Spectaculars. Edward Edelson. (Illus.). (YA) (gr. 7-9). 1977. pap. 1.50 (ISBN 0-671-29994-8). PB.
Great Muppet Caper. Ellis Weiner. 96p. 1981. pap. 8.95 (ISBN 0-553-01304-1). Bantam.
Great Mutiny: India, Eighteen Fifty-Seven. Christopher Hibbert. 472p. 1980. pap. 6.95 (ISBN 0-14-004752-2). Penguin.
Great Mysteries: An Essential Catechism. Andrew M. Greeley. (Orig.). 1976. 8.95x (ISBN 0-8164-0309-0); pap. 3.95x (ISBN 0-8164-2128-5). Crossroad NY.
Great Mystery Stories. Compiled by Eleanor M. Edwards. LC 60-6578. (Lion Classics Ser). (Illus.). 160p. (YA) 1981. lib. bdg. 6.98 (ISBN 0-87460-194-0); pap. 1.95 (ISBN 0-87460-195-9). Lion.
Great Myths of Economics. Don Paarlberg. LC 68-16213. (Principles of Freedom Ser.). 1976. Repr. of 1968 ed. 9.95x o.p. (ISBN 0-916054-20-9). Green Hill.
Great Myths of Economics. Don Paarlberg. LC 68-16213. (Principles of Freedom Ser.). (Illus.). 206p. 1968. 9.95 (ISBN 0-89617-044-6). Inst Humane.
Great Naropa Poetry Wars. Tom Clark. LC 79-55794. 1980. pap. 5.00 (ISBN 0-932274-06-4); signed ed. o.p. 20.00 (ISBN 0-932274-07-2). Cadmus Eds.
Great Negroes, Past & Present. 3rd rev. ed. Russell L. Adams. Ed. by David P. Ross, Jr. LC 72-87924. (Orig.). 1976. 12.95 (ISBN 0-910030-07-3); pap. text ed. 7.95 (ISBN 0-910030-08-1); 9 portfolios of display prints 9.95 ea. Afro-Am.
Great No Hit Games of the Major Leagues. Frank Graham, Jr. (Major League Baseball Library: No. 9). (Illus.). (gr. 1-6). 1968. 2.50 (ISBN 0-394-80189-X, BYR); PLB 3.69 (ISBN 0-394-90189-4). Random.
Great Northern Railway, Vol. III. John Wrottesley. (Illus.). 192p. 1981. 30.00 (ISBN 0-7134-3835-5, Pub. by Batsford England). David & Charles.
Great Northern Railway: Expansion & Competition, Vol. 2. John Wrottesley. 1979. 30.00 (ISBN 0-7134-1592-4, Pub. by Batsford England). David & Charles.
Great Northern Railway: Origins & Development, Vol. 1. John Wrottesley. 1979. 30.00 (ISBN 0-7134-1590-8, Pub. by Batsford England). David & Charles.
Great Northern Suburban. John Young. 1977. 19.95 (ISBN 0-7153-7477-X). David & Charles.
Great Novelists & Prose Writers. Ed. by James Vinson & Daniel Kirkpatrick. (Great Writers of the English Language Ser.). 1400p. 1979. 45.00x (ISBN 0-312-34624-7). St Martin.
Great Oak. Gerald Rose & Elizabeth Rose. (Illus.). (ps-5). 1970. 4.95 o.p. (ISBN 0-571-09251-9, Pub. by Faber & Faber). Merrimack Bk Serv.
Great Opens. Michael Hobbs. LC 76-23536. (Illus.). 1977. 8.95 o.p. (ISBN 0-498-02035-5). A S Barnes.
Great Organizers: Theory & Practice of Organizations. Ernest Dale. 1971. pap. 2.95 o.p. (ISBN 0-07-015173-3, SP). McGraw.
Great Outdoor Games from Trash & Other Things. Judith Conaway. LC 77-7785. (Games & Activities Ser.). (Illus.). (gr. k-4). 1977. PLB 9.30 (ISBN 0-8172-0950-6). Raintree Pubs.
Great Outdoors Book. Ed. by Charles R. Meck. LC 81-65103. (Illus.). 256p. (Orig.). 1981. pap. 8.95 (ISBN 0-910676-24-0, 7706). DBI.
Great Painters of China. Max Loehr. LC 79-6030. (Icon Editions). (Illus.). 336p. 1980. 29.95 (ISBN 0-06-435326-5, HarpT). Har-Row.
Great Paintings of the Old American West. Patricia J. Broder. LC 79-2401. (Illus.). 160p. 1979. 17.95 (ISBN 0-89659-068-2). Abbeville Pr.
Great Paper Airplane Factory. Charlie Daniel & Becky Daniel. (gr. 2-6). 1978. 3.95 (ISBN 0-916456-21-8, GA84). Good Apple.
Great Parties for Young Children. Cheryl C. Barron & Cathy C. Scherzer. (Illus.). 160p. 1981. 9.95 (ISBN 0-8027-0684-3); pap. 5.95 (ISBN 0-8027-7175-0). Walker & Co.
Great Pass Receivers of the NFL. Dave Anderson. (NFL Punt, Pass & Kick Library). (gr. 5-9). 1966. PLB 3.69 (ISBN 0-394-90196-7, BYR). Random.

Great Passages of the Bible. William N. McElrath. Ed. by James C. Barry. LC 63-8409. (Illus., Orig.). (gr. 6-7). 1963. pap. 3.25 tchrs' ed. (ISBN 0-8054-4907-8); pap. 1.95 students' ed. (ISBN 0-8054-4908-6). Broadman.

Great Passenger Ships: 1936-1950, Vol. 4. Arnold Kludas. (Illus.). 1977. 47.90 (ISBN 0-85059-253-4). Aztex.

Great Passenger Ships: 1951-1976, Vol. 5. Arnold Kludas. (Illus.). 1977. 47.95 (ISBN 0-85059-265-8). Aztex.

Great Peace: An Asian's Candid Report on Red China. Ed. by Raja Hutheesing. LC 74-28428. (China in the 20th Century Ser). 246p. 1975. Repr. of 1953 ed. lib. bdg. 22.50 (ISBN 0-306-70694-6). Da Capo.

Great Pendulum of Becoming. Nelvin Vos. (Orig.). 1980. pap. 8.95 (ISBN 0-8028-1828-5). Eerdmans.

Great Pennant Races of the Major Leagues. Frank Graham, Jr. (Major League Baseball Library). (Illus.). 1967. 2.50 o.p. (ISBN 0-394-80187-3, BYR). Random.

Great Perpendicular Path. Grania Davis. 1980. pap. 1.95 (ISBN 0-380-47217-1, 47217). Avon.

Great Photographers. (Life Library of Photography). (Illus.). 1971. 14.95 (ISBN 0-8094-1043-5). Time-Life.

Great Pianists Speak for Themselves. Elyse Mach. LC 79-28736. 1980. 9.95 (ISBN 0-396-07824-9). Dodd.

Great Piano Virtuosos of Our Time. Wilhelm Von Lenz. LC 72-8049. (Music Ser). 184p. 1973. Repr. of 1899 ed. lib. bdg. 12.50 (ISBN 0-306-70528-1). Da Capo.

Great Piggy Bank Robbery. Illus. by Russ Biernat. (Illus.). 32p. (Orig.). (ps). 1980. pap. 1.95 o.p. (ISBN 0-89542-934-9). Ideals.

Great Poems of the English Language, 2 vols. enl. ed. Ed. by Wallace A. Briggs & William R. Benet. LC 79-51965. (Granger Poetry Library). 1981. Repr. of 1941 ed. Set. 94.50x (ISBN 0-89609-178-3). Granger Bk.

Great Poets. Ed. by James Vinson & Daniel Kirkpatrick. (Great Writers of the English Language Ser.). 1200p. 1979. 45.00x (ISBN 0-312-34640-9). St Martin.

Great Political Theories, Vol. 1. Ed. by Michael Curtis. 1976. pap. 2.50 (ISBN 0-380-00785-1, 40626, Discus). Avon.

Great Political Theories, Vol 1. Ed. by Michael Curtis. 464p. 1981. pap. 3.95 (77222, Discus). Avon.

Great Political Theories, Vol. 2. Ed. by Michael Curtis. 1976. pap. 2.50 (ISBN 0-380-01235-9, 49858, Discus). Avon.

Great Political Theories, Vol 2. Ed. by Michael Curtis. 496p. 1981. pap. 3.95 (77230, Discus). Avon.

Great Power Competition for Overseas Bases. Robert E. Harkavy. 300p. Date not set. price not set (ISBN 0-08-025089-0). Pergamon.

Great Power Intervention in the Middle East. Ed. by Milton Leitenberg & Gabriel Sheffer. LC 79-341. (Pergamon Policy Studies). 400p. 1979. 28.00 (ISBN 0-08-023867-X). Pergamon.

Great Power Rivalry at the Turkish Straits: The Montreux Conference & Convention of 1936. Anthony R. Deluca. (East European Monographs: No. 77). 224p. 1981. text ed. 16.00x (ISBN 0-914710-71-0). East Eur Quarterly.

Great Powers & the European States System: 1815-1914. Roger Bullen & Roy Bridge. (Illus.). 224p. (Orig.). 1980. text ed. 23.00 (ISBN 0-582-49134-7); pap. text ed. 11.95 (ISBN 0-582-49135-5). Longman.

Great Powers in the Middle East Nineteen Forty-One to Nineteen Forty-Seven: The Road to the Cold War. Barry Rubin. 264p. 1980. 26.00x (ISBN 0-7146-3141-8, F Cass Co). Biblio Dist.

Great Prologue. Mark E. Petersen. LC 75-14997. 136p. 1976. pap. 1.50. Deseret Bk.

Great Prophetic Themes. Keith L. Brooks. (Teach Yourself the Bible Ser). 1962. pap. 1.50 (ISBN 0-8024-3320-0). Moody.

Great Pyramid: A Miracle in Stone. Joseph Seiss. LC 72-81590. (Illus.). 256p. 1973. pap. 2.95 (ISBN 0-8334-1735-5). Steinerbks.

Great Pyramid: A Miracle in Stone. Joseph A. Seiss. LC 80-8341. (Harper's Library of Spiritual Wisdom). 256p. 1981. pap. 5.95 (ISBN 0-06-067211-0, HarpR). Har-Row.

Great Pyramid Decoded. rev. ed. E. Raymond Capt. (Illus.). 96p. 1978. pap. 3.00 (ISBN 0-934666-01-6). Artisan Sales.

Great Pyramid: Man's Monument to Man. Tom Valentine. (Illus.). 192p. 1980. pap. 2.25 o.p. (ISBN 0-523-40453-0). Pinnacle Bks.

Great Pyramid: Signs in the Sun. John E. Gangstad. LC 76-24077. (Illus.). 200p. 1976. lib. bdg. 9.95 (ISBN 0-9603374-0-7); pap. 5.95 (ISBN 0-9603374-1-5); 1980 supplement 2.50 (ISBN 0-9603374-2-3). Di-Tri Bks.

Great Quick & Easy Cooking. Beatriz-Maria Prada. 192p. (Orig.). 1975. pap. 1.50 o.p. (ISBN 0-345-24282-3). Ballantine.

Great Rabbit Rip-off. E. W. Hildick. (McGurk Mystery Ser.: No. 4). (Illus.). (gr. 3-5). 1978. pap. 1.75 (ISBN 0-671-41106-3). PB.

Great Rabbit Rip-off: A McGurk Mystery, No. 4. E. W. Hildick. (gr. 3-5). 1978. pap. 1.75 (ISBN 0-671-41454-2). Archway.

Great Railroad War. Giles A. Lutz. LC 80-1851. (Double D Western Ser.). 192p. 1981. 9.95 (ISBN 0-385-17348-2). Doubleday.

Great Railway Bazaar. Paul Theroux. 1976. pap. 2.50 (ISBN 0-345-25191-1). Ballantine.

Great Rebellion: Mexico Nineteen Hundred & Five to Nineteen Twenty-Four. Ramon E. Ruiz. 1980. 24.95 (ISBN 0-393-01323-5). Norton.

Great Rebellion, Sixteen Forty-Two to Sixteen Sixty. Ivan Roots. pap. 17.95 (ISBN 0-7134-1399-9, Pub. by Batsford England). David & Charles.

Great Reform Act. Michael Brock. Ed. by Joel Hurstfield. (Illus.). 411p. 1974. text ed. 18.25x (ISBN 0-09-115910-5, Hutchinson U Lib); pap. text ed. 11.75x (ISBN 0-09-115911-3, Hutchinson U Lib). Humanities.

Great Religions By Which Men Live. Floyd H. Ross & Tynette Hills. Orig. Title: Questions That Matter Most Asked by the World's Religions. 1977. pap. 2.50 (ISBN 0-449-30825-1, Prem). Fawcett.

Great Republic: A History of the American People. Bernard Bailyn et al. 1977. text ed. 18.95x o.p. (ISBN 0-669-86629-6); Vol. 1. pap. text ed. 11.95x o.p. (ISBN 0-669-86637-7); Vol. 2. pap. text ed. 10.95x o.p. (ISBN 0-669-86645-8); instructor's manual free o.p. (ISBN 0-669-97881-7); study guide 5.95x o.p. (ISBN 0-669-97865-5); test item file to adopters free o.p. (ISBN 0-669-00962-8). Heath.

Great Republic: A History of the American People. 2nd ed. Bernard Bailyn et al. 1008p. 1981. text ed. 19.95 (ISBN 0-669-02753-7); pap. text ed. 12.95 vol. 1 (ISBN 0-669-02754-5); pap. text ed. 12.95 vol. 2 (ISBN 0-669-02755-3); instr's guide avail. (ISBN 0-669-02757-X); student guide 5.95 (ISBN 0-669-02756-1). Heath.

Great Revival, Seventeen Eighty-Seven to Eighteen Five: The Origins of the Southern Evangelical Mind. John B. Boles. LC 77-183349. (Illus.). 260p. 1972. 14.00x (ISBN 0-8131-1260-5). U Pr of Ky.

Great Revival: The Russian Church Under German Occupation. Wassilij Alexeev & Stavrou Theofanis. LC 76-83. text ed. 21.95 o.p. (ISBN 0-8087-0131-2). Burgess.

Great Riding Schools of the World. Dorian Williams. LC 74-14906. (Illus.). 320p. 1975. 12.98 o.s.i. (ISBN 0-02-629060-X). Macmillan.

Great Rookies of the Major Leagues. Jim Brosnan. (Major League Baseball Library: No. 3). (Illus.). (gr. 5-9). 1966. PLB 3.69 (ISBN 0-394-90186-X, BYR). Random.

Great Rope. Rosemary S. Nesbitt. 1980. Repr. lib. bdg. 5.95x (ISBN 0-686-68699-3). Mathom.

Great Round the World Maze Trip. Rick Brightfield & Glory Brightfield. (Illus.). 1977. pap. 4.95 o.p. (ISBN 0-345-25678-6). Ballantine.

Great Roxhythe. Georgette Heyer. 1976. Repr. of 1922 ed. lib. bdg. 17.55x (ISBN 0-89966-117-3). Buccaneer Bks.

Great Rulers of the African Past. Lavinia Dobler & William A. Brown. LC 65-17230. pap. 2.50 (ISBN 0-385-03845-3, 27, Zenith). Doubleday.

Great Sacrilege. James F. Wathen. LC 76-183571. 1971. 5.00 o.p. (ISBN 0-89555-016-4, 120); pap. text ed. 3.50 (ISBN 0-89555-014-8). TAN Bks Pubs.

Great San Francisco & Fire, 1906. Eric Saul & Don DeNevi. LC 80-83616. (Illus.). 176p. 25.00 (ISBN 0-89087-288-0). Celestial Arts.

Great Santini. Pat Conroy. 1979. pap. 2.50 (ISBN 0-380-00991-9, 44768). Avon.

Great Santini. Pat Conroy. 536p. Repr. of 1976 ed. 10.00 (ISBN 0-937036-00-5). Old NY Bk Shop.

Great Scenes from the World Theater, Vol. 1. Ed. by James L. Steffensen, Jr. (Orig.). 1965. pap. 2.95 (ISBN 0-380-42705-2, 42705, Bard). Avon.

Great Scenes from the World Theatre, Vol. 2. Ed. by James L. Steffensen, Jr. (Orig.). 1976. pap. 3.95 (ISBN 0-380-01220-0, 53157, Bard). Avon.

Great School Bus Controversy. Ed. by Nicolaus Mills. LC 73-16469. 356p. 1973. 15.00x (ISBN 0-8077-2430-0); pap. 8.75x (ISBN 0-8077-2431-9). Tchrs Coll.

Great Science Fiction Pictures. James R. Parish & Michael R. Pitts. LC 77-5426. 1977. 18.00 (ISBN 0-8108-1029-8). Scarecrow.

Great Science Fiction Series: Stories from the Best of the Science Fiction Series from 1944 to 1980 by 20 All-Time Favorite Writers. Ed. by Frederick Pohl et al. LC 79-1705. 416p. 1980. 16.95 (HarpT). Har-Row.

Great Sculpture of Ancient Greece. Pierre Devambez. LC 78-55511. (Reynal's World History of Great Sculpture Ser.). (Illus.). 1978. 25.00 o.p. (ISBN 0-688-61205-9). Reynal.

Great Sea Monster or a Book by You. Berthe Amoss. LC 74-30422. (Illus.). 36p. (gr. k-3). 1975. 5.95 o.s.i. (ISBN 0-685-53908-3, Four Winds); PLB 5.41 o.s.i. (ISBN 0-8193-0798-X). Schol Bk Serv.

Great Sea Stories of All Nations. Ed. by H. M. Tomlinson. 1108p. 1980. Repr. of 1930 ed. 40.00 (ISBN 0-89760-884-4). Telegraph Bks.

Great Seal of the United States. Paul F. Case. (Illus.). 1976. 2.25 (ISBN 0-938002-01-5). Builders of Adytum.

Great Shark Hunt. Hunter Thompson. 1980. pap. 3.50 (ISBN 0-445-04596-5). Popular Lib.

Great Shark Stories. Ed. by Ron Taylor & Valerie Taylor. LC 76-27279. (Illus.). 1978. 12.95 o.s.i. (ISBN 0-06-014236-7, HarpT). Har-Row.

Great Short Works of Stephen Crane: Red Badge of Courage, Monster, Maggie, Open Boat, Blue Hotel, Bride Comes to Yellow Sky & Other Works. rev. ed. Stephen Crane. Ed. by J. Colvert. pap. 2.50 (ISBN 0-06-083032-8, P3032, PL). Har-Row.

Great Short Works: The Lagoon, the Nigger of Narcissus, Youth, Heart of Darkness, Typhoon, the Secret Sharer. Joseph Conrad. 6.75 (ISBN 0-8446-0068-7). Peter Smith.

Great Showbusiness Animals. David Rothel. LC 80-16891. 1980. 19.95 (ISBN 0-498-02519-5). A S Barnes.

Great Smoky Mountains. rev. ed. Laura Thornborough. (Illus.). 1962. 7.50 (ISBN 0-87049-034-6). U of Tenn Pr.

Great Smoky Mountains Picture Book. Jim Doane. Ed. by George Castaldo. (Color Pictorial of Great Smoky Mountains Ser.: No. 1). (Illus.). 72p. (Orig.). 1981. price not set (ISBN 0-936672-13-7); pap. price not set (ISBN 0-936672-14-5). Aerial Photo.

Great Smoky Mountains: The Story Behind the Scenery. Rita Cantu. Ed. by Gweneth R. DenDooven. LC 78-78123. (Illus.). 1979. 7.95 (ISBN 0-916122-60-3); pap. 3.00 (ISBN 0-916122-59-X). K C Pubns.

Great Songwriters of Hollywood. Warren Craig. LC 79-87793. 256p. 1980. 14.95 (ISBN 0-498-02439-3). A S Barnes.

Great Souls at Prayer. Mary W. Tileston. 366p. Repr. of 1898 ed. text ed. 9.50 (ISBN 0-227-67474-X). Attic Pr.

Great South: The New Route to the Gulf. (Illus.). pap. 4.50 wrappers o.p. (ISBN 0-8363-0037-8). Jenkins.

Great Sporting Posters of the Golden Age. Sid Latham. LC 77-76772. (Illus.). 48p. 1978. pap. 11.95 (ISBN 0-8117-2115-9). Stackpole.

Great Sports Photos. Brondfield. (gr. 3-5). 1980. pap. 1.50 (ISBN 0-590-30369-4, Schol Pap). Schol Bk Serv.

Great Spy Pictures. James R. Parish & Michael R. Pitts. LC 73-19509. (Illus.). 1974. 21.00 (ISBN 0-8108-0655-X). Scarecrow.

Great Stanley Cup Playoffs. Bill Libby. (Pro Hockey Library: No. 4). (Illus.). (gr. 5 up). 1972. 2.50 o.p. (ISBN 0-394-82404-0, BYR); PLB 3.69 (ISBN 0-394-92404-5). Random.

Great State of Maine Cookbook. Ladies Aid of the Northern Maine Universalist-Unitarian Churches. 180p. 1981. 8.95 (ISBN 0-89975-002-8). World Authors.

Great Steel Strike & Its Lessons. William Z. Foster. LC 70-139202. (Civil Liberties in American History Ser). (Illus.). 1971. Repr. of 1920 ed. lib. bdg. 29.50 (ISBN 0-306-70079-4). Da Capo.

Great Stories of American Businessmen from American Heritage. Intro. by Oliver Jensen. LC 72-80701. (Illus.). 382p. 1972. 15.00 (ISBN 0-8281-0327-5, B071). Am Heritage.

Great Story Poems. rev ed. Ed. by Theodoric Jones. LC 65-24688. (Illus.). 160p. (YA) 1972. PLB 6.99 (ISBN 0-87460-204-1); pap. 2.95 (ISBN 0-87460-205-X). Lion.

Great Story Poems - Collection. Ed. by H. K. Ross. (Illus.). 160p. 1981. PLB 6.95. Lion.

Great Sundial Cutout Book. Robert Adzema & Mablen Jones. LC 78-52964. 1978. pap. 9.95 (ISBN 0-8015-3117-9, Hawthorn). Dutton.

Great Sunflower. Clifford Stone. LC 76-10020. 192p. 1976. 8.95 (ISBN 0-8149-0775-X). Vanguard.

Great Surveys of the American West. Richard A. Bartlett. LC 62-16475. (American Exploration & Travel Ser.: Vol. 38). (Illus.). 464p. 1980. pap. 9.95 (ISBN 0-8061-1653-6). U of Okla Pr.

Great Survival Resource Book. Ed. by Martha Henderson & Paladin Press. (Illus.). 188p. 1981. 19.95 (ISBN 0-87364-199-X). Paladin Ent.

Great Suspense Stories. new ed. Ed. by Harriet Ross. LC 61-5152. (Illus.). 160p. (YA) 1981. PLB 6.99 (ISBN 0-87460-206-8); pap. 1.95 (ISBN 0-87460-207-6). Lion.

Great Take-Away. Louise Mathews. LC 80-12961. (Illus.). 48p. (ps-3). 1980. PLB 7.95 (ISBN 0-396-07846-X). Dodd.

Great Texts of the Bible: Genesis-Numbers. James Hastings. 458p. Repr. of 1911 ed. text ed. 5.00x (ISBN 0-567-06701-7). Attic Pr.

Great Texts of the Bible: James-Jude. James Hastings. 439p. Repr. of 1912 ed. 5.00x (ISBN 0-567-06719-X). Attic Pr.

Great Texts of the Bible: Job-Psalm 23. James Hastings. 518p. Repr. of 1913 ed. text ed. 5.00x (ISBN 0-567-06703-3). Attic Pr.

Great Texts of the Bible: Revelation. James Hastings. 432p. Repr. of 1915 ed. 5.00x (ISBN 0-567-06720-3). Attic Pr.

Great Texts of the Bible: Romans 8-16. James Hastings. 479p. Repr. of 1911 ed. text ed. 5.00x (ISBN 0-567-06714-9). Attic Pr.

Great Texts of the Bible: Thessalonians-Hebrews. James Hastings. 495p. Repr. of 1914 ed. text ed. 5.00x (ISBN 0-567-06718-1). Attic Pr.

Great Themes. (Life Library of Photography). (Illus.). 1970. 14.95 (ISBN 0-8094-1026-5). Time-Life.

Great Toad Hunt & Other Expeditions. Howard McCord. LC 79-23842. 1980. 7.95 (ISBN 0-89594-015-9); pap. 3.95 (ISBN 0-89594-014-0). Crossing Pr.

Great Tradition: George Eliot, Henry James, Joseph Conrad. F. R. Leavis. (Gotham Library). 1963. pap. 5.00x, usa (ISBN 0-8147-0254-6). NYU Pr.

Great Transformation: The Political & Economic Origins of Our Time. Karl Polanyi. 1957. pap. 6.95 (ISBN 0-8070-5679-0, BP45). Beacon Pr.

Great United States Exploring Expedition of 1838-1842. William Stanton. LC 73-84390. (Illus.). 1975. 18.95 (ISBN 0-520-02557-1). U of Cal Pr.

Great Unsolved Cases. Arnold Madison. LC 78-6932. (Triumph Bks). (Illus.). (gr. 6 up). 1978. PLB 6.90 s&l (ISBN 0-531-01465-7). Watts.

Great Unsolved Cases. Arnold Madison. (gr. 7-12). 1980. pap. 1.25 (ISBN 0-440-93099-5, LFL). Dell.

Great Upon the Mountain: The Story of Crazy Horse, Legendary Mystic & Warrior. Vinson Brown. LC 74-13458. 1975. 9.95 (ISBN 0-02-517350-2, 51735). Macmillan.

Great Valentine's Day Balloon Race. Adrienne Adams. LC 80-19527. (Illus.). 32p. (gr. k-3). 1980. 9.95 (ISBN 0-684-16640-2). Scribner.

Great Verses from the Psalms. Charles H. Spurgeon. Ed. by Norman Hillyer. 1977. 8.95 (ISBN 0-310-32900-0). Zondervan.

Great Verses from the Psalms. Charles H. Spurgeon. 278p. 1981. pap. 6.95 (ISBN 0-310-32901-9). Zondervan.

Great Vitamin Hoax. D. Tatkon. 1967. 5.95 o.s.i. (ISBN 0-02-616300-4). Macmillan.

Great Volcano. 1965. pap. 1.50 o.p. (ISBN 0-85363-019-4). OMF Bks.

Great Voyages in Small Boats Solo Transatlantic. Ann Davison et al. 1981. 15.00 (ISBN 0-8286-0085-6). De Graff.

Great War, Nineteen Fourteen to Nineteen Eighteen. Marc Ferro. 1973. 16.00x (ISBN 0-7100-7574-X); pap. 8.95 (ISBN 0-7100-7575-8). Routledge & Kegan.

Great War on White Slavery or Fighting for the Protection of Our Girls. Clifford Roe & Charles Winick. LC 78-66466. (Prostitution Ser.: Vol. 16). 448p. 1979. lib. bdg. 40.00 (ISBN 0-8240-9712-2). Garland Pub.

Great Way West: The History & Romance of the Great Western Railway's Route from Paddington to Penzanze. David St. John Thomas. LC 75-10530. (Illus.). 1975. 14.95 (ISBN 0-7153-7063-4). David & Charles.

Great Western Album. R. C. Riley. 14.50x (ISBN 0-392-07860-0, SpS). Soccer.

Great Western Indian Fights. Potomac Corral of the Westerners. LC 60-15191. (Illus.). 1966. pap. 3.50 (ISBN 0-8032-5186-6, BB 339, Bison). U of Nebr Pr.

Great Western Pictures. James R. Parish & Michael R. Pitts. LC 76-28224. (Illus.). 1976. 20.00 (ISBN 0-8108-0980-X). Scarecrow.

Great Western Railway: A New History. Frank Booker. 1977. 14.95 (ISBN 0-7153-7455-9). David & Charles.

Great Westerns from the Saturday Evening Post. LC 76-41559. 1976. 5.95 (ISBN 0-89387-004-8). Sat Eve Post.

Great Whales. Herbert S. Zim. (Illus.). (gr. 3-7). 1951. PLB 6.48 (ISBN 0-688-31360-4). Morrow.

Great Wheel: The World, Monetary System; a Reinterpretation. Sidney E. Rolfe & James L. Burtle. LC 73-79929. (McGraw-Hill Paperbacks). 304p. 1975. pap. 4.95 (ISBN 0-07-053562-0, SP). McGraw.

Great White Wall. William R. Benet. 1916. 24.50x o.p. (ISBN 0-686-51397-5). Elliots Bks.

Great Winemakers of California. Robert Benson. (Illus.). 1977. 15.00 o.p. (ISBN 0-88496-107-9). Capra Pr.

Great Wingmen. Ian Thorne. (Stars of the NHL Ser.). (Illus.). (gr. 4-12). 1976. PLB 7.95 (ISBN 0-87191-494-8). Creative Ed.

Great Wok Cookbook. Victor S. Yung. 256p. 1974. 7.95 o.p. (ISBN 0-8402-1310-7). Nash Pub.

Great Wolf & the Good Woodsman. Helen Hoover. LC 67-18463. (Illus.). (gr. k-3). 1967. 5.95 o.s.i. (ISBN 0-8193-0169-8, Four Winds). Schol Bk Serv.

Great Women of Faith. Nancy A. Hardesty. LC 80-65440. 200p. 1980. 7.95 (ISBN 0-8010-4223-2). Baker Bk.

Great Works of Christ in America, 2 vols. Cotton Mather. 1979. Set. 37.95; Vol. 1. (ISBN 0-85151-280-1); Vol. 2. (ISBN 0-85151-280-1). Banner of Truth.

Great Zoos of the World: Their Origins & Significance. Ed. by Lord Zuckerman. (Illus.). 230p. 1980. lib. bdg. 35.00x (ISBN 0-89158-985-6). Westview.

Greater Horseshoe Bat. Roger Ransome. (Mammal Society Ser.). (Illus.). 50p. 1980. 6.95 (ISBN 0-7137-0986-3, Pub. by Blandford Pr England). Sterling.

Greater London: The Politics of Metropolitan Reform. Frank Smallwood. LC 64-25258. 1965. 28.00x (ISBN 0-672-51145-2). Irvington.

Greater Love. Beth Cary. 1922. 3.00 o.p. (ISBN 0-685-88270-5). Metaphysical.

Greater Medieval Historians: An Interpretation & a Bibliography. Indrikis Sterns. LC 80-5850. 260p. 1980. lib. bdg. 18.75 (ISBN 0-8191-1327-1); pap. text ed. 10.50 (ISBN 0-8191-1328-X). U Pr of Amer.

Greatest Book Ever Written. Fulton Oursler. 8.95 (ISBN 0-385-04175-6). Doubleday.

Greatest Book in the World & Other Papers. A. Edward Newton. LC 78-86572. (Essay & General Literature Index Reprint Ser). (Illus.). 1969. Repr. 19.50 (ISBN 0-8046-0579-3). Kennikat.

Greatest Crime. Sloan Wilson. (Adventure & Suspense Ser.). 11.50 (ISBN 0-87795-296-5). Arbor Hse.

Greatest Enemy. Douglas Reeman. pap. 2.25 (ISBN 0-515-05448-8). Jove Pubns.

Greatest Gamblers. Ruth S. Knowles. Orig. Title: Epic of American Oil Exploration. 376p. 1980. pap. 7.95 (ISBN 0-8061-1654-4). U of Okla Pr.

Greatest Gift Guide Ever. Judith King. LC 79-65184. (Illus., Orig.). 1980. pap. 4.00 (ISBN 0-9602776-0-9). Variety Pr.

Greatest Gift in the World. Og Mandino. LC 76-43508. 7.95 (ISBN 0-8119-0274-9). Fell.

Greatest Guessing Game. Robert Froman. LC 77-5463. (Young Math Book). (Illus.). (gr. 1-3). 1978. PLB 7.89 (ISBN 0-690-01376-0, TYC-J). T Y Crowell.

Greatest Indian Stories. Zane Grey. 1978. pap. 1.50 (ISBN 0-505-51303-X). Tower Bks.

Greatest Miracle in the World. Og Mandino. LC 75-12823. 1975. 7.95 (ISBN 0-8119-0255-2). Fell.

Greatest Monsters in the World. Daniel Cohen. (Illus.). (gr. 4 up). 1977. pap. 1.50 (ISBN 0-671-29990-5). PB.

Greatest of Expositions: St. Louis World's Fair, 1904. rev. ed. Ed. by Sunrise Publishing Company Editors. 1981. pap. 8.95 (ISBN 0-86629-029-X). Sunrise MO.

Greatest of These. Jane Merchant. (Orig.). pap. 1.25 (ISBN 0-89129-175-X). Jove Pubns.

Greatest Plot in History. 2nd ed. Ralph De Toledano. 1977. 8.95 o.p. (ISBN 0-87000-371-2). Arlington Hse.

Greatest Power on Earth: The International Race for Supremacy. Ronald W. Clark. LC 80-7899. (Illus.). 352p. 1981. 12.95 (ISBN 0-06-014846-2, HarpT). Har-Row.

Greatest Quiz Book Ever. Roy W. Dickson. LC 73-14252. (Illus.). 216p. (YA) 1974. 7.95 o.s.i. (ISBN 0-06-011032-5, HarpT). Har-Row.

Greatest Salesman in the World. Og Mandino. LC 68-10798. (gr. 9 up). 7.95 (ISBN 0-8119-0400-8); pap. 4.95 span. ed.. (ISBN 0-88391-020-9). Fell.

Greatest Secret in the World. Og Mandino. LC 79-175423. 200p. 1972. 7.95 (ISBN 0-8119-0212-9). Fell.

Greatest Show on Earth. Katherine Leiner & Michael Arthur. LC 80-17776. (Old Friends Ser.: Old Friends Ser.). (Illus.). 80p. 1980. 6.95 (ISBN 0-916392-62-7). Oak Tree Pubns.

Greatest Song: In Critique of Solomon. Calvin G. Seerveld. LC 69-27706. 1967. 12.95x (ISBN 0-686-27477-6). Radix Bks.

Greatest Sports Stars. Pierre Conan. Ed. by Thomas J. Mooney. (Pal Paperbacks, Pal Skills Ser.). (Illus., Orig.). (gr. 7-12). 1978. pap. text ed. 1.25 (ISBN 0-8374-6713-6). Xerox Ed Pubns.

Greatest Story Ever Told. Fulton Oursler. 1949. pap. 2.45 (ISBN 0-385-08028-X, D121, Im). Doubleday.

Greatest Thing in the World. Henry Drummond. (Inspirational Classic Ser). 1968. 4.95 (ISBN 0-8007-1078-9); pap. 1.25 (ISBN 0-8007-8018-3, Spire Bks). Revell.

Greatest Thing That Almost Happened. Don Robertson. 1977. pap. 1.95 o.s.i. (ISBN 0-446-89660-8). Warner Bks.

Greatest Work in the World. rev. ed. Willie W. White. 1975. pap. 3.95 (ISBN 0-89900-108-4). College Pr Pub.

Greatheart. Ethel M. Dell. (Barbara Cartland's Library of Love: Vol. 15). 247p. 1980. 12.95x (ISBN 0-7156-1475-4, Pub. by Duckworth England). Biblio Dist.

Greatness in Music. Alfred Einstein. LC 70-87527. 1972. Repr. of 1941 ed. lib. bdg. 25.00 (ISBN 0-306-71441-8). Da Capo.

Greatness in Music. Alfred Einstein. LC 76-6984. 1976. pap. 6.95 (ISBN 0-306-80046-2). Da Capo.

Greatness of the Kingdom. Alva J. McClain. 10.95 (ISBN 0-88469-011-3). BMH Bks.

Grebe. F. Pijlman. (Animal Environment Ser.). (Illus.). 30p. 1980. 4.95 (ISBN 0-8120-5377-X). Barron.

Grece. new ed. Ed. by Daniel Moreau. (Collection monde et voyages). 159p. (Fr.). 1973. 21.00x (ISBN 2-03-053105-7, 3897). Larousse.

Greco-Roman Tradition. Hayden V. White. (White Ser). 158p. 1973. pap. text ed. 9.50 scp (ISBN 0-06-047064-X, HarpC). Har-Row.

Greece. Jim Antoniou. LC 75-44871. (Macdonald Countries). (Illus.). (gr. 6 up). 1976. PLB 7.95 (ISBN 0-382-06104-7, Pub. by Macdonald Ed.). Silver.

Greece. Mary Jo Clogg & Richard Clogg. (World Bibliographical Ser.: No. 17). 1981. write for info. (ISBN 0-903450-30-5). ABC Clio.

Greece. Elisabeth De Stroumillo. (Thornton Cox's Traveller's Guide Ser.). (Illus.). 1974. pap. 5.95 (ISBN 0-8038-2665-6). Hastings.

Greece. John Harrison & Shirley Harrison. LC 80-50995. (Rand McNally Pocket Guide Ser.). (Illus.). 1980. pap. 3.95 (ISBN 0-528-84307-9). Rand.

Greece. Robin Mead. 1976. 24.00 (ISBN 0-7134-3080-X). David & Charles.

Greece & the Aegean. William O. Kellogg. 1975. pap. text ed. 4.95x (ISBN 0-88334-066-6). Ind Sch Pr.

Greece & the British Connection, 1935-1941. John S. Koliopoulos. 1978. 37.50x (ISBN 0-19-822523-7). Oxford U Pr.

Greece & the European Community. Hedley Bull et al. 172p. 1979. text ed. 22.25x (ISBN 0-566-00232-9, Pub. by Gower Pub Co England). Renouf.

Greece & Yugoslavia on Fifteen Dollars a Day: 1980-81 Edition. 1981. pap. 4.95 (ISBN 0-671-25176-7). Frommer-Pasmantier.

Greece in Pictures. rev. ed. Sterling Publishing Company Editors. LC 62-12596. (Visual Geography Ser). (Illus., Orig.). (gr. 6 up). PLB 4.99 (ISBN 0-8069-1023-2); pap. 2.95 (ISBN 0-8069-1022-4). Sterling.

Greece in the Bronze Age. Emily Vermeule. LC 64-23427. 406p. 1972. pap. 12.00 (ISBN 0-226-85354-3, P490, Phoen). U of Chicago Pr.

Greece in the Bronze Age. Emily T. Vermeule. LC 64-23427. (Illus.). 1964. 24.00x (ISBN 0-226-85353-5). U of Chicago Pr.

Greece: The Traveller's Guide to History & Mythology. Brian Dicks. LC 79-91497. (Illus.). 1980. 17.95 (ISBN 0-7153-7797-3). David & Charles.

Greed, Pts. 5-7. Diane Wakoski. (Orig.). 1976. pap. 10.00 (ISBN 0-87685-095-6). Black Sparrow.

Greedy Institutions. Lewis A. Coser. LC 73-10571. 1974. 12.95 (ISBN 0-02-906750-2). Free Pr.

Greedy Little Cobbler. Tony Ross. LC 79-56766. 24p. (gr. 1-6). 1980. 4.95 (ISBN 0-8120-5389-3). Barron.

Greedy Shopkeeper. Irene Mirkovic. LC 80-13034. (Illus.). 32p. (gr. k-3). 1980. pap. 2.95 (ISBN 0-15-232552-2, VoyB). HarBraceJ.

Greek. Holoway Staff. (Harper Phrase Books for the Traveler Ser.). (Orig.). 1977. pap. 1.00 (ISBN 0-8467-0311-4, Holloway). Hippocrene Bks.

Greek Americans: Struggle & Success. Charles C. Moskos, Jr. 1980. text ed. 10.95 (ISBN 0-13-365106-1); pap. text ed. 7.95 (ISBN 0-13-365098-7). P-H.

Greek & English Lexicon to the New Testament. Greenfield. 5.95 (ISBN 0-310-20350-3). Zondervan.

Greek & Latin Literary Texts from Greco-Roman Egypt. Roger A. Pack. LC 65-10786. 1967. 8.50 (ISBN 0-910294-22-4). Brown Bk.

Greek & Macedonian Art of War. Frank E. Adcock. (Sather Classical Lectures: No. 30). 1957. 12.75x (ISBN 0-520-02807-4); pap. 2.25 (ISBN 0-520-00005-6, CAL54). U of Cal Pr.

Greek & Persian Armies. Jack Cassin-Scott. (Men-at-Arms Ser.). (Illus.). 48p. 1978. pap. 7.95 (ISBN 0-85045-271-6). Hippocrene Bks.

Greek & Roman Architecture. 2nd ed. Donald S. Robertson. (Illus.). 1969. 52.00 (ISBN 0-521-06104-0); pap. 12.95x (ISBN 0-521-09452-6). Cambridge U Pr.

Greek & Roman Art. Ariane Ruskin & Michael Batterberry. (Discovering Art). (Illus.). (gr. 7 up). 1969. 9.95 o.p. (ISBN 0-07-054294-5, GB); pap. 4.95 o.p. (ISBN 0-07-054295-3). McGraw.

Greek & Roman Civilization. Educational Research Council. (Human Adventure, Concepts & Inquiry Ser). (gr. 5). 1975. pap. text ed. 6.20 (ISBN 0-205-04446-8, 8044465); tchrs.' guide 5.20 (ISBN 0-205-04447-6, 8044473). Allyn.

Greek & Roman Coins & the Study of History. J. G. Milne. (Illus.). 1977. 15.00 (ISBN 0-916710-80-7). Obol Intl.

Greek & Roman Coins & the Study of History. J. G. Milne. (Illus.). 128p. 1980. 30.00. Obol Intl.

Greek & Roman Philosophy After Aristotle. Ed. by Jason L. Saunders. LC 66-12892. (Orig.). 1966. pap. text ed. 6.95 (ISBN 0-02-927730-2). Free Pr.

Greek & Roman Pottery. R. M. Cook & R. J. Charleston. Ed. by Robert J. Charleston. LC 78-55079. (Masterpieces & Western & Near Eastern Ceramics Ser.: Vol. 2). (Illus.). 1979. 200.00 (ISBN 0-87011-343-7) (ISBN 0-686-52652-X). Kodansha.

Greek Anthology: Garland of Philip & Other Contemporary Epigrams, 2 Vols. Andrew S. Gow & D. L. Page. LC 68-10149. (Eng. & Gr.). 1968. 130.00 set (ISBN 0-521-05874-0). Cambridge U Pr.

Greek Anthology: Hellenistic Epigrams, 2 Vols. Andrew S. Gow & D. L. Page. 1965. Set. 130.00 set (ISBN 0-521-05124-X). Cambridge U Pr.

Greek Art. John Boardman. (World of Art Ser.). (Illus.). 1973. pap. 9.95 (ISBN 0-19-519917-0). Oxford U Pr.

Greek Art. R. M. Cook. (Illus.). 222p. 1976. 12.95 (ISBN 0-374-16670-6). FS&G.

Greek Art. Walter-Herwig Schuchhardt. LC 70-175860. (History of Art Ser.). (Illus.). 192p. 1972. 8.95x (ISBN 0-87663-169-3). Universe.

Greek Art & Architecture. K. McLeish. (Aspects of Greek Life). (Illus.). 1975. pap. text ed. 2.95x (ISBN 0-582-20673-1). Longman.

Greek Art & the Idea of Freedom. Denys Haynes. (Illus.). 108p. 1981. 15.95 (ISBN 0-500-23331-4). Thames Hudson.

Greek Athletics. D. Buchanan. (Aspects of Greek Life). (Illus.). 1977. pap. text ed. 2.95x (ISBN 0-582-20059-8). Longman.

Greek Basic Course, Vol. 1. Foreign Service Institute. 328p. (Gr.). 1980. 12 cassettes plus text 115.00x (ISBN 0-88432-034-0, R301, Audio-Forum). J Norton Pubs.

Greek Basic Course, Vol. 2. Foreign Service Institute. 200p. (Gr.). 12 cassettes plus text 98.00x (ISBN 0-88432-035-9, R318, Audio-Forum). J Norton Pubs.

Greek City from Alexander to Justinian. A. H. Jones. 404p. (Orig.). 1979. pap. text ed. 22.00x (ISBN 0-19-814842-9). Oxford U Pr.

Greek Coins Supplement. Frwd. by Mary B. Comstock. (Illus.). 1964. 12.50 (ISBN 0-87846-165-5); pap. 4.50 (ISBN 0-87846-166-3). Mus Fine Arts Boston.

Greek Concept of Justice: From Its Shadow in Homer to Its Substance in Plato. Eric A. Havelock. LC 78-6064. 1978. 18.50x (ISBN 0-674-36220-9). Harvard U Pr.

Greek Cookbook. Margot Phillips & Culinary Arts Institute Staff. Ed. by Edward G. Finnegan. LC 79-51590. (Adventures in Cooking Ser.). (Illus.). 1980. cancelled (ISBN 0-8326-0612-X, 1520); pap. 3.95 (ISBN 0-8326-0611-1, 2520). Delair.

Greek Cookery. 3rd ed. Nicholas Tselementes. 1956. 5.00 (ISBN 0-685-09035-3). Divry.

Greek Dances for Americans. Rozanna Mouzaki. Tr. by Athena Dallas-Damis. LC 77-25604. (Illus.). 192p. 1981. pap. 9.95 (ISBN 0-385-14041-X). Doubleday.

Greek Drama in Its Theatrical & Social Context. Peter Walcot. 1976. pap. text ed. 8.25x o.p. (ISBN 0-7083-0602-0). Verry.

Greek-English, English-Greek Pocket Dictionary. 9.00 (ISBN 0-685-58555-7). Heinman.

Greek-English Letterwriting. B. G. Revelis. 5.00 (ISBN 0-685-09036-1). Divry.

Greek-English Lexicon. 9th ed. Ed. by Henry G. Liddell & Robert Scott. 1940. 74.00x (ISBN 0-19-864214-8). Oxford U Pr.

Greek-English Lexicon: A Supplement. Henry G. Liddell & Robert Scott. Ed. by E. A. Barber et al. 1968. 22.00x (ISBN 0-19-864210-5). Oxford U Pr.

Greek-English Lexicon of the New Testament: Being Grimm's Wilke's Clavis Novi Testamenti, Transl. Revised & Enlarged. 4th ed. Ed. by J. H. Thayer. 746p. Repr. of 1901 ed. text ed. 25.00x (ISBN 0-567-01015-5). Attic Pr.

Greek-English Lexicon of the New Testament. Tr. by F. Wilbur Gingrich from Ger. Ed. by William F. Arndt et al. Tr. by F. W. Danker from Ger. LC 78-14293. (2nd rev. & augmented edition). 1979. lib. bdg. 30.00x (ISBN 0-226-03932-3). U of Chicago Pr.

Greek-English Lexicon of the New Testament. rev 2nd ed. Wilbur F. Gingrich & Frederick W. Danker. 1979. 30.00 o.p. (ISBN 0-310-20570-0). Zondervan.

Greek-English Lexicon of the New Testament. W. J. Hickie. (Direction Bks.). 1977. pap. 2.95 (ISBN 0-8010-4164-3). Baker Bk.

Greek-English Lexicon to the New Testament. William Greenfield. 216p. 1981. pap. 5.95 (ISBN 0-310-20351-1). Zondervan.

Greek Everyday Life. R. Nichols & S. Nichols. (Aspects of Greek Life Ser.). (Illus.). 1978. pap. text ed. 2.95x (ISBN 0-582-20672-3). Longman.

Greek Exploration & Seafaring. Kenneth McLeish. (Aspects of Greek Life). 1972. pap. text ed. 2.95x (ISBN 0-582-34402-6). Longman.

Greek Fathers. James Campbell. LC 63-10279. (Our Debt to Greece & Rome Ser). Repr. of 1930 ed. 16.50x (ISBN 0-8154-0046-2). Cooper Sq.

Greek Folk Religion. Martin P. Nilsson. (Illus.). 8.50 (ISBN 0-8446-0218-3). Peter Smith.

Greek Folk Religion. Martin P. Nilsson. 1972. pap. 4.95x (ISBN 0-8122-1034-4, Pa. Paperbacks). U of Pa Pr.

Greek for Beginners. L. A. Wilding. (gr. 7-12). text ed. 8.95 (ISBN 0-571-10402-9). Transatlantic.

Greek Heritage in Victorian Britain. Frank M. Turner. LC 80-24013. (Illus.). 512p. 1981. text ed. 30.00x (ISBN 0-300-02480-0). Yale U Pr.

Greek Ideals & Modern Life. Richard W. Livingstone. LC 72-82814. 1969. Repr. of 1935 ed. 10.50x (ISBN 0-8196-0245-0). Biblo.

Greek Imperialism. William S. Ferguson. LC 63-18045. 1941. 10.50x (ISBN 0-8196-0127-6). Biblo.

Greek Islands. Lawrence Durrell. (Illus.). 1978. 25.00 o.p. (ISBN 0-670-35296-9, Studio). Viking Pr.

Greek Islands. Robin Mead. LC 79-56491. (Illus.). 160p. 1980. 22.50 (ISBN 0-7134-0625-9, Pub. by Batsford England). David & Charles.

Greek Islands Cooking. Theonie Mark. 1979. 27.00 (ISBN 0-7134-1283-6, Pub. by Batsford England). David & Charles.

Greek Literature: An Anthology. Ed. by Michael Grant. (Classics Ser.). 1977. pap. 2.50 o.p. (ISBN 0-14-044323-1). Penguin.

Greek Lyrics. rev ed. Tr. by Richmond Lattimore. LC 60-51619. 1960. 5.00x o.s.i. (ISBN 0-226-46943-3). U of Chicago Pr.

Greek Made Easy. 3rd ed. George C. Divry. 1953. 5.00 (ISBN 0-685-09037-X). Divry.

Greek Monumental Bronze Sculpture of the Fifth & Fourth Centuries B.C. Caroline Houser. LC 76-23628. (Outstanding Dissertations in the Fine Arts Ser.). 1978. lib. bdg. 52.00x (ISBN 0-8240-2698-5). Garland Pub.

Greek Music, Verse & Dance. Thrasybulos Georgiades. LC 73-4336. 156p. 1973. Repr. of 1955 ed. lib. bdg. 17.50 (ISBN 0-306-70561-3). Da Capo.

Greek Myths. Olivia Coolidge. (Illus.). (gr. 7 up). 1949. 8.95 (ISBN 0-395-06721-9). HM.

Greek Myths. Robert Graves. LC 55-8278. 1959. 10.00 o.p. (ISBN 0-8076-0054-7). Braziller.

Greek Myths & Christian Mystery. Hugo Rahner. LC 79-156736. (Illus.). 1971. Repr. of 1963 ed. 17.50x (ISBN 0-8196-0270-1). Biblo.

Greek Nation, 1453-1669: The Cultural & Economic Background of Modern Greek Society. Apostolos Vacalopoulos. 472p. 1976. 32.50 (ISBN 0-8135-0810-X). Rutgers U Pr.

Greek New Testament. 3rd ed. Ed. by Kurt Aland et al. 1975. leather 16.30 (ISBN 3-438-05111-7, 56491); vinyl 7.50 (ISBN 3-438-05110-9); With Dictionary. vinyl 9.75 (ISBN 3-438-05113-3, 56492). United Bible.

Greek Oared Ships, Nine Hundred - Three Hundred Twenty-Two B.C. John S. Morrison & R. T. Williams. LC 67-19504. (Illus.). 1968. 72.00 (ISBN 0-521-05770-1). Cambridge U Pr.

Greek Oracles. Herbert W. Parke. 1967. pap. text ed. 6.25x (ISBN 0-09-084111-5, Hutchinson U Lib). Humanities.

Greek Orations: Lysias, Isocrates, Demosthenes, Aeschines, Hyperides. Ed. by W. Robert Connor. (Orig.). 1966. pap. 5.95 (ISBN 0-472-06116-X, 116, AA). U of Mich Pr.

Greek Orthodox Church: Faith, History, & Practice. Demetrios J. Constantelos. (Orig.). (YA) (gr. 9-12). 1967. pap. 1.95 (ISBN 0-8164-2029-7, SP38). Crossroad NY.

Greek Penal Code. (American Series of Foreign Penal Codes: Vol. 18). 1973. 17.50x (ISBN 0-8377-0038-8). Rothman.

Greek Philosophers: From Thales to Aristotle. W. K. Guthrie. pap. 3.95x (ISBN 0-06-131008-5, TB 1008, Torch). Har-Row.

Greek Philosophical Terms: A Historical Lexicon. F. E. Peters. LC 67-25043. 234p. 1967. 10.95x o.p. (ISBN 0-8147-0343-7); pap. 5.95 (ISBN 0-8147-6552-1). NYU Pr.

Greek Philosophy, 3 Vols. C. J. De Vogel. 1960-1964. Vol. 1. text ed. 24.00x (ISBN 90-04-02356-9); Vol. 2. text ed. 24.00x (ISBN 90-04-02357-7); Vol. 3. text ed. 42.25x (ISBN 90-040374-3-8). Humanities.

Greek Philosophy: Thales to Aristotle. Reginald E. Allen. LC 66-10363. (Orig.). 1966. pap. text ed. 6.95 (ISBN 0-02-900500-0). Free Pr.
Greek Popular Morality in the Time of Plato & Aristotle. K. J. Dover. 1975. 23.75x (ISBN 0-520-02721-3). U of Cal Pr.
Greek Position. Robert Roderick. Date not set. 14.95 (ISBN 0-671-61015-5, Wyndham). S&S.
Greek Pottery. 3rd ed. Arthur Lane. 1971. 38.00 (ISBN 0-571-04701-7, Pub. by Faber & Faber). Merrimack Bk Serv.
Greek Refinements. William H. Goodyear. (Illus.). 1912. 100.00x (ISBN 0-685-69823-8). Elliots Bks.
Greek Religion & Its Survivals. Walter W. Hyde. LC 63-10268. (Our Debt to Greece & Rome Ser). 1963. Repr. of 1930 ed. 7.50x (ISBN 0-8154-0117-5). Cooper Sq.
Greek, Roman, & Etruscan Bronzes in the MFA. 1971. 35.00 (ISBN 0-87846-060-8). Mus Fine Arts Boston.
Greek Science After Aristotle. G. E. Lloyd. LC 72-11959. (Ancient Culture & Society Ser.). (Illus.). 208p. 1973. 6.95x (ISBN 0-393-04371-1); pap. 4.95 (ISBN 0-393-00780-4). Norton.
Greek Sculpture: The Archaic Period. John Boardman. LC 77-25202. (World of Art Ser.). (Illus.). 1978. 17.95 (ISBN 0-19-520046-2); pap. 9.95 (ISBN 0-19-520047-0). Oxford U Pr.
Greek Skepticism: A Study in Epistemology. Charlotte L. Stough. LC 76-82464. 1969. 18.50x (ISBN 0-520-01604-1). U of Cal Pr.
Greek Society. 2nd ed. Frank J. Frost. 1980. pap. text ed. 7.95 (ISBN 0-669-02452-X). Heath.
Greek State at War, Pt. 1. W. Kendrick Pritchett. LC 71-633960. 1975. 18.50x (ISBN 0-520-02758-2). U of Cal Pr.
Greek State at War, Pt. 2. W. Kendrick Pritchett. LC 74-77991. 1975. 20.00x (ISBN 0-520-02565-2). U of Cal Pr.
Greek State at War, Pt. 3. W. Kendrick Pritchett. 1980. 24.50 (ISBN 0-520-03781-2). U of Cal Pr.
Greek Struggle for Independence, 1821-1833. Douglas Dakin. LC 72-89798. 1973. 22.50x (ISBN 0-520-02342-0). U of Cal Pr.
Greek Symbol Mystery. Carolyn Keene. Ed. by Wendy Barish. (Nancy Drew Ser.). (Illus.). 192p. (gr. 3-7). 1981. 7.95 (ISBN 0-671-42297-9); pap. 1.95 (ISBN 0-671-42298-7). Wanderer Bks.
Greek Text of Judges: Recensional Developments. Walter R. Bodine. LC 80-12578. (Harvard Semitic Monographs: No. 23). 15.00x (ISBN 0-89130-400-2). Scholars Pr CA.
Greek Theatre. Kenneth McLeish. (Aspects of Greek Life Ser.). (Illus.). 1972. pap. text ed. 2.95x (ISBN 0-582-34400-X). Longman.
Greek Theatre Practice. J. Michael Walton. LC 79-8580. (Contributions in Drama & Theatre Studies: No. 3). (Illus.). viii, 237p. 1980. lib. bdg. 23.95 (ISBN 0-313-22043-3, WGT/). Greenwood.
Greek Thinkers: A History of Ancient Philosophy, 4 vols. Theodor Gomperz. Incl. Vol. 1. text ed. (ISBN 0-687-01947-8); pap. text ed. (ISBN 0-7195-0498-8); Vol. 2. text ed. (ISBN 0-687-01948-6); pap. text ed. (ISBN 0-7195-0499-6); Vol. 3. text ed. (ISBN 0-7195-0500-3); pap. text ed. (ISBN 0-7195-0504-6); Vol. 4. text ed. (ISBN 0-7195-0501-1); pap. text ed. (ISBN 0-7195-0505-4). 1964. text ed. 10.00x ea.; pap. text ed. 8.25x ea. Humanities.
Greek Tragedies. Ed. by David Grene & Richmond Lattimore. Incl. Vol. 1. Agamemnon, Prometheus Bound, Oedipus the King, Antigone. 1960. pap. 4.50 (ISBN 0-226-30774-3, P41); Vol. 2. The Libation Bearers, Electra (Sophocles), Iphigenia in Tauris, Electra (Euripides), the Trojan Women. 1960. pap. text ed. 3.95 (ISBN 0-226-30775-1, P42); Vol. 3. The Eumenides, Philoctetes, Oedipus at Colonus, the Bacchae, Alcestis. 1960. pap. text ed. 3.95 (ISBN 0-226-30777-8, P43). LC 60-950. 1960 (Phoen). U of Chicago Pr.
Greek Tragedy in Action. Oliver Taplin. 1979. 20.00x (ISBN 0-520-03704-9); pap. 4.95 (ISBN 0-520-03949-1). U of Cal Pr.
Greek Tyrants. A. Andrewes. 1956. pap. 7.00x (ISBN 0-09-029564-1, Hutchinson U Lib). Humanities.
Greek Vase: Dynamic Symmetry. Jay Hambidge. (Promotion of the Arts Library Bks.). (Illus.). 131p. Date not set. Repr. of 1917 ed. 77.45 (ISBN 0-89901-030-X). Found Class Reprints.
Greek Vase-Painting in Midwestern Collections. Warren G. Moon. Ed. by Paula Prokopoff-Giannini & Susan Wegner. LC 79-56832. (Illus.). 231p. (Orig.). 1979. pap. 12.50x (ISBN 0-86559-041-9). Art Inst Chi.
Greek Vocabulary. Joint Association of Classical Teachers. 1980. pap. 5.95 (ISBN 0-521-23277-5). Cambridge U Pr.
Greek Way. Edith Hamilton. 1973. pap. 2.75 (ISBN 0-380-00816-5, 53140, Discus). Avon.
Greek Wedding. Jane A. Hodge. 320p. 1977. pap. 1.75 o.p. (ISBN 0-449-23216-6, Crest). Fawcett.
Greek Wit: A Collection of Smart Sayings & Anecdotes. Frederick A. Paley. 128p. 1980. Repr. of 1881 ed. lib. bdg. 20.00 (ISBN 0-8492-2190-0). R West.
Greek Word Building. Matthias Stehle. LC 76-14405. (Society of Biblical Literature). 1976. pap. 6.00 (ISBN 0-89130-108-9, 060310). Scholars Pr Ca.
Greek World. Eliot Porter. Ed. by Peter Levi. (Illus.). 1980. 45.00 (ISBN 0-525-11812-8). Dutton.
Greeks. Antony Andrewes. LC 66-19367. (History of Human Society Ser.). (Illus.). (YA) 1967. 7.95 o.p. (ISBN 0-394-42722-X). Knopf.
Greeks. Judith Crosher & Harry Strongman. LC 77-86190. (Peoples of the Past Ser.). (Illus.). 1977. lib. bdg. 7.95 (ISBN 0-686-51157-3). Silver.
Greeks Bearing Gifts: The Epics of Achilles & Ulysses. Bernard Evslin. LC 76-16039. (Illus.). 336p. (YA) 1976. 9.95 (ISBN 0-590-17431-2, Four Winds). Schol Bk Serv.
Greeks Had a Word for It. B. C. Taylor. 1973. pap. text ed. 2.00x (ISBN 0-8077-8018-9). Tchrs Coll.
Greeks in America. rev. ed. Jayne C. Jones. LC 68-31504. (In America Bks.). (Illus.). (gr. 5-11). 1977. PLB 5.95 (ISBN 0-8225-0215-1). Lerner Pubns.
Green Air. David Harper. 240p. 1976. pap. 1.50 o.p. (ISBN 0-445-03143-3). Popular Lib.
Green & Richmond Pediatric Diagnosis: Interpretation of Symptoms & Signs in Different Age Periods. 3rd ed. Morris Green. LC 79-65454. (Illus.). 658p. 1980. text ed. 29.00 (ISBN 0-7216-4242-X). Saunders.
Green Avenue: The Life & Writings of Forrest Reid, 1875-1947. B. Taylor. LC 79-41418. 200p. 1980. 29.50 (ISBN 0-521-22801-8). Cambridge U Pr.
Green Bay Packers. Julian May. (NFL Today Ser.). (gr. 4-8). 1980. lib. bdg. 6.45 (ISBN 0-87191-727-0); pap. 2.95 (ISBN 0-89812-230-9). Creative Ed.
Green Bay Packers. Julian May. LC 74-905. (Superbowl Champions Ser). 48p. 1974. 6.45 (ISBN 0-87191-330-5); pap. 2.95 (ISBN 0-89812-086-1). Creative Ed.
Green Blades Rising: The Anglo-Saxons. Kevin C. Crossley-Holland. LC 75-4576. (Illus.). 144p. (gr. 6-12). 1976. 8.95 (ISBN 0-395-28902-5, Clarion). HM.
Green Book: Guide for Living in Saudi Arabia. 3rd ed. Madge Pendleton et al. LC 80-82276. (Illus.). 187p. 1980. pap. 12.00x (ISBN 0-918992-03-6). Middle East Edit.
Green Brain. Frank Herbert. (Science Fiction Ser.). 1981. PLB 13.95 (ISBN 0-8398-2667-2). Gregg.
Green Broke. Carrie Young. 224p. 1981. 8.95 (ISBN 0-396-07953-9). Dodd.
Green Bronze Mirror. Lynne Ellison. LC 75-89663. Date not set. 4.95 (ISBN 0-8149-0709-1). Vanguard. Postponed.
Green Cabinet: Theocritus & the European Pastoral Lyric. Thomas G. Rosenmeyer. LC 78-82376. 1969. 18.50x (ISBN 0-520-01381-6); pap. 5.95x (ISBN 0-520-02362-5, CAMPUS90). U of Cal Pr.
Green Carnation. Robert Hichens. Ed. by Stanley Weintraub. LC 74-93105. 1970. pap. 2.45 (ISBN 0-8032-5703-1, BB 507, Bison). U of Nebr Pr.
Green Dragon: The Lives of Banastre Tarleton & Mary Robinson. Robert D. Bass. LC 57-6183. 1973. Repr. 6.95 o.p. (ISBN 0-87844-019-4). Sandlapper Store.
Green Eyes. Ben Cunningham. 1976. pap. 1.50 o.p. (ISBN 0-345-25465-1). Ballantine.
Green Fairy Book. Ed. by Andrew Lang. (gr. 4-6). 1965. pap. 4.00 (ISBN 0-486-21439-7). Dover.
Green Felt & Funny-Money: A Complete Guide to Throwing a Home Casino Party. Terri Jones & Evelyn J. Jones. Ed. by Sue Piper. (Illus.). 1980. pap. text ed. 6.95 (ISBN 0-686-28734-7). Univ Marketing.
Green Flag Over Texas: The Last Years of Spain in Texas. 2nd ed. Julia K. Garrett. LC 40-3613. (Texas Heritage Ser). (Illus.). 1969. Repr. of 1939 ed. 12.50 (ISBN 0-8363-0038-6). Jenkins.
Green Fly Swamp: Environmental Assessment. Robert Tillman. 1975. pap. 5.80 o.p. (ISBN 0-89327-228-0). NY Botanical.
Green Frontier. Wolfgang Koerner. Tr. by Patricia Crampton from Ger. (gr. 7 up). 1977. 8.25 (ISBN 0-688-22124-6); lib. bdg. 7.92 (ISBN 0-688-32124-0). Morrow.
Green Futures of Tycho. William Sleator. LC 80-23020. (gr. 5-9). 1981. PLB 9.95 (ISBN 0-525-31007-X). Dutton.
Green Goals & Greenbacks: State-Level Environmental Review Programs & Their Associated Costs. Stuart L. Hart & Gordon A. Enk. LC 79-5229. (Westview Replica Edition Ser.). (Illus.). 364p. 1979. lib. bdg. 27.50x (ISBN 0-89158-752-7). Westview.
Green Gold Harvest: A History of Logging & Its Products. Whatcom Museum of History & Art. LC 72-10060. (Whatcom Museum Ser.). (Illus.). 78p. 1969. pap. 5.00 (ISBN 0-295-95577-5). U of Wash Pr.
Green Grass Grows All Around. Hilde Hoffman. LC 68-10032. (gr. k-2). 1968. 7.95g (ISBN 0-02-744180-6). Macmillan.
Green Grass of Wyoming. Mary O'Hara. (gr. 7-9). 1946. 10.95 (ISBN 0-397-00011-1). Lippincott.
Green Guide to Health from Plants. Jean Palaiseul. 1978. 10.95 o.p. (ISBN 0-214-66891-6, 4087, Dist. by Arco). Barrie & Jenkins.
Green Hill Far Away. Peter Upton. 1978. pap. 2.25 o.p. (ISBN 0-345-27208-0). Ballantine.
Green Hills of Africa. Ernest Hemingway. 1935. Hudson River Edition. 17.50x (ISBN 0-684-16481-7); pap. 4.95 (ISBN 0-684-71799-9, SL50, ScribT). Scribner.
Green Hills of Earth. Robert A. Heinlein. 176p. (RL 7). 1973. pap. 1.75 (ISBN 0-451-09264-3, E9264, Sig). NAL.
Green Ice. Gerald A. Brown. 1978. 9.95 o.p. (ISBN 0-440-03034-X). Delacorte.
Green Knight. Vera Chapman. 1977. pap. 1.50 (ISBN 0-380-01704-0, 33795). Avon.
Green Knight & Red Mourning. Richard E. Ogden. (Orig.). 1980. pap. 1.95 (ISBN 0-532-23218-6). Manor Bks.
Green Leaf, Green Bough: Collected Poems. Robert Dunn. 25p. 1973. pap. 1.50 (ISBN 0-934676-02-X). Greenlf Bks.
Green Leaves & Gold. Monika Varma. (Writers Workshop Redbird Book Ser.). 38p. 1975. 4.80 (ISBN 0-88253-552-8); pap. text ed. 4.00 (ISBN 0-88253-551-X). Ind-US Inc.
Green Man. Kingsley Amis. LC 76-95862. 1970. 5.95 o.p. (ISBN 0-15-137040-0). HarBraceJ.
Green Mansions. William H. Hudson. (Literature Ser). (gr. 9-12). 1970. pap. text ed. 3.42 (ISBN 0-87720-726-7). AMSCO Sch.
Green Millenium. Fritz Lieber. (Science Fiction Ser.). 1980. lib. bdg. 14.95 (ISBN 0-8398-2641-9). Gregg.
Green Paradise. Heather Hill. 192p. 1981. pap. 1.50 (ISBN 0-671-57060-9). S&S.
Green Power: The Corporation & the Urban Crisis. George S. Odiorne. 208p. text ed. 22.50 (ISBN 0-8290-0290-1); pap. text ed. 12.95 (ISBN 0-8290-0291-X). Irvington.
Green Power: The Successful Way of A. G. Gaston. A. G. Gaston. (Illus.). 1977. Repr. of 1968 ed. 8.95 (ISBN 0-916624-09-9). TSU Pr.
Green Power: The Successful Way of A. G. Gaston. A. G. Gaston. (Illus.). 1978. pap. 2.95 (ISBN 0-916624-10-2). TSU Pr.
Green Revolution. B. H. Farmer. LC 76-51278. (Cambridge Commonwealth Ser.). (Illus.). 1977. lib. bdg. 32.00x (ISBN 0-89158-709-8). Westview.
Green Revolution: A Case Study of Punjab. M. S. Randhawa. LC 73-5851. 207p. 1974. 15.95 (ISBN 0-470-70795-X). Halsted Pr.
Green Revolution in India: A Perspective. Bandhudas Sen. LC 74-11066. 118p. 1974. 11.95 (ISBN 0-470-77590-4). Halsted Pr.
Green Revolution in West Pakistan: Implications of Technological Change. Leslie Nulty. LC 73-170471. (Special Studies in International Economics & Development). 1972. 26.50x (ISBN 0-89197-779-1). Irvington.
Green Ripper. John B. MacDonald. (gr. 7-12). 1980. lib. bdg. 12.95 (ISBN 0-8161-3023-X). G K Hall.
Green Russell & Gold. Elma D. Spencer. 1966. 9.95 o.p. (ISBN 0-292-73623-1). U of Tex Pr.
Green Salamander. Pamela Hill. 1978. pap. 1.95 o.p. (ISBN 0-449-23642-0, Crest). Fawcett.
Green Shaded Lamps. Cornelia Veenendaal. LC 76-55615. 64p. 1977. pap. 4.95 (ISBN 0-914086-16-2). Alicejamesbooks.
Green Shadows. Lucile V. Stevens. 192p. (YA) 1973. 5.95 (ISBN 0-685-32415-X, Avalon). Bouregy.
Green Soldiers. John Bensko. LC 80-26052. (Younger Poet Ser.: No. 76). 80p. 1981. 9.95 (ISBN 0-300-02637-4); pap. 4.95 (ISBN 0-300-02644-7). Yale U Pr.
Green Spring Valley: Its History & Heritage, 2 vols. Incl. Vol. 1. A History & Historic Houses. Dawn F. Thomas; Vol. 2. Genealogies. Robert Barnes. LC 78-53033. (Illus.). 1978. 35.00 set (ISBN 0-938420-06-2). Md Hist.
Green Thumb Book of Fruit & Vegetable Gardening. George Abraham. LC 78-85000. (Illus.). 1969. 11.95 (ISBN 0-13-365189-4). P-H.
Green Thumb Cookbook. Organic Gardening & Farming Editors. Ed. by Anne Moyer. LC 77-1745. 1977. 14.95 (ISBN 0-87857-168-X). Rodale Pr Inc.
Green Thumb Garden Handbook. rev & expanded ed. George Abraham & Katy Abraham. LC 77-22279. 1977. 14.95 (ISBN 0-13-365114-2). P-H.
Green Tiger's Caravan. Green Tiger Staff. (Illus.). 1981. pap. 8.95 (ISBN 0-914676-58-X). Green Tiger.
Green Tree & a Dry Tree. Carter Wilson. LC 79-184534. (Illus.). 320p. 1972. 7.95 o.s.i. (ISBN 0-02-630130-X). Macmillan.
Green Turtle Mysteries. John F. Waters. LC 70-158701. (Let's-Read-&-Find-Out Science Bk). (Illus.). (gr. k-3). 1972. 7.95 (ISBN 0-690-35994-2, TYC-J); PLB 7.89 (ISBN 0-690-35995-0). T Y Crowell.
Green Wisdom. Arthur Galston. LC 80-68183. 1981. 12.95 (ISBN 0-465-02712-1). Basic.
Green Wood House: How to Build & Own a Beautiful,Inexpensive House. rev. ed. Larry M. Hackenberg. LC 75-33166. 1978. 9.75x (ISBN 0-8139-0646-6); pap. 4.95 o.p. (ISBN 0-8139-0683-0). U Pr of Va.
Green Words: A Handbook. Ed. by Donald Brady. LC 79-92506. 91p. 1980. pap. text ed. 2.50 (ISBN 0-8191-0965-7). U Pr of Amer.
Greenberg's Guide to American Flyer's Gauge. Paul G. Yorkis & Jim Walsh. 160p. 1980. pap. 19.95 (ISBN 0-442-21209-7). Van Nos Reinhold.
Greenberg's Operating & Repair Manual for American Flyer Trains. Thomas Barker. Ed. by Linda Greenberg. LC 79-54103. (Illus.). 1979. pap. 6.95 (ISBN 0-89778-218-6). Greenberg Pub Co.
Greenberg's Operating & Repair Manual for Lionel Trains: 1906-1942. John Hubbard. Ed. by Bruce C. Greenberg. (Illus.). 1981. 9.95 (ISBN 0-89778-071-X). Greenberg Pub Co.
Greenberg's Price Guide to American Flyer S Gauge Trains 1945-1966. Paul Yorkis. LC 80-67942. (Illus., Orig.). 1980. 19.95 (ISBN 0-89778-225-9); pap. cancelled. Greenberg Pub Co.
Greenberg's Price Guide to Lionel Trains: 1901-1942. 2nd ed. Bruce C. Greenberg. Ed. by Linda Greenberg. (Illus.). 1979. 19.95 (ISBN 0-89778-088-4); pap. 12.95 (ISBN 0-89778-072-8). Greenberg Pub Co.
Greenberg's Price Guide to Lionel Trains: O & O-27 Trains, 1945-1977. Bruce C. Greenberg. (Illus.). 1977. pap. 12.95 o.p. (ISBN 0-89778-500-2, Pub. by Crown). Greenberg Pub Co.
Greenberg's Repair & Operating Manual for Lionel Trains. Bruce C. Greenberg. 736p. 1980. pap. 9.95 (ISBN 0-442-21363-8). Van Nos Reinhold.
Greene & Greene: Architects in the Residential Style. William R. Current & Karen Current. (Illus.). 1977. pap. 10.95 (ISBN 0-88360-036-6). Amon Carter.
Greene Forest, or a Naturall Historie. John Maplet. LC 79-84122. (English Experience Ser.: No.941). 244p. 1979. Repr. of 1567 ed. lib. bdg. 18.00 (ISBN 90-221-0941-0). Walter J Johnson.
Greenhorn on the Frontier. Ann Finlayson. LC 73-93587. (Illus.). 196p. (gr. 7-12). 1974. 5.95 o.p. (ISBN 0-7232-6104-0). Warne.
Greenhouse Effect. Harold Bernard. LC 80-8710. 256p. 1981. pap. 4.95 (ISBN 0-06-090855-6, C*N 855, CN). Har-Row.
Greenhouse Effect. Harold Bernard. 1980. 12.95 (ISBN 0-88410-633-0). Ballinger Pub.
Greenhouse Environment: The Effect of Environmental Factors on Flower Crops. John W. Mastalerz. LC 77-6793. 1977. 25.95 (ISBN 0-471-57606-9). Wiley.
Greenhouse Gardening. James V. Crockett et al. LC 76-51513. (Time-Life Encyclopedia of Gardening). (Illus.). (gr. 6 up). 1977. PLB 11.97 (ISBN 0-8094-2563-7, Pub by Time-Life). Silver.
Greenhouse Gardening. Ed. by Time-Life Books. (Encyclopedia of Gardening). (Illus.). 1977. 11.95 (ISBN 0-8094-2562-9). Time-Life.
Greenhouse Gardening for Fun. Claire Blake. (Illus.). 1967. pap. 3.95 (ISBN 0-688-06737-9). Morrow.
Greenhouse Gardening in the South. William M. Minar. LC 76-1685. (Illus.). 96p. 1976. pap. 3.95 (ISBN 0-88415-327-4). Pacesetter Pr.
Greenhouse Grower. Kennard S. Nelson. LC 76-1113. 1977. 15.35 (ISBN 0-8134-1811-9, 1811); text ed. 11.50x (ISBN 0-685-77708-1). Interstate.
Greenhouse Management: A Guide to Structures, Environmental Control, Materials Handling, Crop Programming & Business Analysis. Robert W. Langhans. (Illus.). 239p. 1980. 14.50 (ISBN 0-9604006-0-5). Halcyon Ithaca.
Greenhouse Management for Flower & Plant Production. 4th ed. Kennard S. Nelson. 1980. 15.35 (ISBN 0-8134-2070-9, 2070); text ed. 11.50x (ISBN 0-8134-2070-9). Interstate.
Greenhouse Operation & Management. P. Nelson. 1978. 18.95 (ISBN 0-87909-319-6); instrs'. manual avail. Reston.

Greenhouse Operation & Management. 2nd ed. Paul Nelson. 520p. 1981. text ed. 16.95 (ISBN 0-8359-2576-5); instr's. manual free (ISBN 0-8359-2577-3). Reston.

Greenhouse: Place of Magic. Charles H. Potter. (Illus.). 1966. 7.95 o.p. (ISBN 0-525-11818-7); Rev. Ed. 1976. pap. 4.95 o.p. (ISBN 0-87690-199-2). Dutton.

Greenhouse Tomatoes, Lettuce & Cucumbers. S. H. Wittwer & S. Honma. (Illus.). 225p. 1979. 15.00x (ISBN 0-87013-210-5). Mich St U Pr.

Greenhousing for Purple Thumbs. Fenten. LC 76-26055. (Illus.). 192p. (Orig.). 1976. 4.95 (ISBN 0-89286-105-3); pap. 4.95 (ISBN 0-89286-104-5). One Hund One Prods.

Greening of Mrs. Duckworth. Marion Duckworth. 1980. pap. 3.95 (ISBN 0-8423-1187-4). Tyndale.

Greenland Criminal Code. (American Series of Foreign Penal Codes: Vol. 16). x, 47p. 1970. 10.00x (ISBN 0-8377-0036-1). Rothman.

Greenleaf Fires. John Gould. LC 77-17824. 1978. 8.95 o.p. (ISBN 0-684-15478-1, ScribT). Scribner.

Green's Functions & Boundary Value Problems. Ivar Stakgold. LC 78-27259. (Pure & Applied Mathematics: Texts, Monographs & Tracts). 1979. 35.95 (ISBN 0-471-81967-0, Pub. by Wiley-Interscience). Wiley.

Greenwich Forum V: Europe & the Sea: the Cause for & Against a New International Regime for the North Sea and Its Approaches. Ed. by D. C. Watt. 1980. text ed. 52.00 (ISBN 0-86103-039-7). Butterworths.

Greenwich Forum VI: Britain & the Sea: the Challenges for Shipping in the 1990's. D. C. Watt. 1981. text ed. write for info. (ISBN 0-86103-049-4, Westbury Hse). Butterworths.

Greenwich Village. Fred W. McDarrah. (Orig.). 1963. pap. 1.45 o.p. (ISBN 0-87091-032-9). Corinth Bks.

Greenwich Village: A Photographic Guide. Edmund T. Delaney et al. LC 74-78593. (Illus.). 128p. (Orig.). 1976. pap. 4.00 (ISBN 0-486-23114-3). Dover.

Greenwillow. B. J. Chute. 1956. 5.95 o.p. (ISBN 0-525-11835-7). Dutton.

Greenwood's Guide to Great Lakes Shipping. rev. ed. John O. Greenwood. 700p. 1979. text ed. 30.00 (ISBN 0-685-52168-0). Freshwater.

Greenworks: Tender Loving Care for Plants. Judith Handelsman & Sara Baerwald. LC 73-1854. 1974. pap. 1.95 o.s.i. (ISBN 0-02-062890-0); pap. o.s.i. (ISBN 0-685-31477-4). Macmillan.

Greenyards. Joan Lingard. 396p. 1981. 12.95 (ISBN 0-399-12513-2). Putnam.

Greeting Card Handbook. Edward J. Hohman & Norma E. Leary. (Barnes & Noble Everyday Handbook). (Illus.). 160p. (Orig.). 1981. pap. 4.95 (ISBN 0-06-463532-5, EH532, BN). Har-Row.

Gregg Barratt's Woman. Lilian Peake. (Harlequin Presents Ser.). 192p. 1981. pap. 1.50 (ISBN 0-373-10424-3, Pub. by Harlequin). PB.

Gregg Dictation: Diamond Jubilee Series. 2nd ed. Louis A. Leslie et al. 1970. text ed. 9.96 (ISBN 0-07-037257-8, G); instructor's handbk 3.90 (ISBN 0-07-037258-6); student transcript 3.76 (ISBN 0-07-037259-4); wkbk 4.40 (ISBN 0-07-037260-8); key to wkbk 2.90 (ISBN 0-07-037261-6); tapes avail. (ISBN 0-07-086052-1) (ISBN 0-07-087482-4). McGraw.

Gregg Notehand. 2nd ed. Louis A. Leslie et al. 1968. text ed. 11.04 (ISBN 0-07-037331-0, G); instructor's guide 4.30 (ISBN 0-07-037338-8); exercises 5.18 (ISBN 0-07-037343-4); inst. key to exercises 4.30 (ISBN 0-07-037344-2). McGraw.

Gregg Shorthand. John R. Gregg et al. (Diamond Jubilee Ser). 1963. text ed. 9.80 (ISBN 0-07-024591-6, G); student transcript 3.40 (ISBN 0-07-024525-8); wkbk. 4.40 (ISBN 0-07-037308-6) (ISBN 0-686-60795-3). McGraw.

Gregg Shorthand. 2nd ed. John R. Gregg et al. (Diamond Jubilee Ser). 1972. 7.95 (ISBN 0-07-024625-4, G); text ed. 9.80 (ISBN 0-686-66105-2); instructor's handbk. 3.90 (ISBN 0-07-024626-2); students transcript 3.40 (ISBN 0-07-024627-0); wkbk 4.40 (ISBN 0-07-037250-0); key to wkbk. 2.70 (ISBN 0-07-037251-9). McGraw.

Gregg Shorthand for Colleges, Vol. 2. 2nd ed. Louis A. Leslie et al. (Diamond Jubilee Ser.). (Illus.). 448p. 1973. text ed. 14.95 (ISBN 0-07-037406-6, G); instructor's handbk. 4.35 (ISBN 0-07-037409-0); wkbk. 5.45 (ISBN 0-07-037408-2); key to wkbk. 3.10 (ISBN 0-07-037410-4); tapes avail. (ISBN 0-07-086345-8); student transcript 4.45 (ISBN 0-07-037407-4); cassettes avail. (ISBN 0-07-087615-0). McGraw.

Gregg Shorthand for Colleges, Transcription. 2nd ed. L. Et Al Leslie & C. Zoubek. LC 79-11916. (Series 90). (Illus.). 448p. 1980. text ed. 16.50 (ISBN 0-07-037760-X, G); instructor's manual 4.90 (ISBN 0-07-037764-2); wkbk. 5.95 (ISBN 0-07-037762-6); key to wkbk. 3.40 (ISBN 0-07-037763-4); student's trans. 4.45 (ISBN 0-07-037761-8); teach. dict. 12.80 (ISBN 0-686-62427-0). McGraw.

Gregg Shorthand, Functional Method. Louis A. Leslie & Charles E. Zoubek. (Diamond Jubilee Ser). 1963. text ed. 10.68 (ISBN 0-07-037310-8, G); wkbk. 4.40 (ISBN 0-07-037308-6). McGraw.

Gregg Shorthand Functional Method. 2nd ed. Louis A. Leslie & Charles E. Zoubek. (Diamond Jubilee Ser). 1971. text ed. 9.96 (ISBN 0-07-037255-1, G); inst. handbk. 3.90 (ISBN 0-07-037256-X); wkbk. 4.40 (ISBN 0-07-037250-0); key to wkbk. 2.70 (ISBN 0-07-037251-9). McGraw.

Gregg Typing for Colleges: Intensive Course. A. C. Lloyd et al. (Gregg College Typing Ser.: Series 4). 1978. pap. text ed. 9.95 (ISBN 0-07-038252-2, G); instructor's manual 12.95 (ISBN 0-07-038259-X); proofguide for lessons 2.80 (ISBN 0-07-038261-1); wk. guide for lessons 5.95 (ISBN 0-686-60821-6). McGraw.

Gregg Walker, News Photographer. Emyl Jenkins. LC 78-91739. (Illus.). (gr. 5-8). 1978. 5.95g o.p. (ISBN 0-8075-3041-7). A Whitman.

Gregor Mendel: Father of the Science of Genetics. Harry Sootin. LC 59-7933. (Illus.). (gr. 7-10). 1958. 7.95 (ISBN 0-8149-0409-2). Vanguard.

Gregorian Chant: A History of Controversy Concerning Its Rhythm. John Rayburn. LC 80-27616. xiv, 90p. 1981. Repr. of 1964 ed. lib. bdg. 19.75x (ISBN 0-313-22811-6, RAGR). Greenwood.

Gregorio & Maria Martinez Sierra. Patricia W. Oconnor. (World Authors Ser.: Spain: No. 412). 1977. lib. bdg. 12.50 (ISBN 0-8057-6252-3). Twayne.

Gregorio y Sus Puntos. Judith Vigna. Ed. by Caroline Rubin. Tr. by Alma F. Ada from Eng. LC 76-47528. (Self-Starter Books Ser.). (Illus.). 32p. (Span.). (gr. k-3). 1976. 6.50g (ISBN 0-8075-3044-1). A Whitman.

Gregory Griggs & Other Nursery Rhyme People. Arnold Lobel. LC 77-22209. (Illus.). (gr. k-3). 1978. 9.25 (ISBN 0-688-80128-5); PLB 8.88 (ISBN 0-688-84128-7). Greenwillow.

Gregory Peck. Michael Freedland. LC 80-82359. (Illus.). 320p. 1980. 10.95 (ISBN 0-688-03619-8). Morrow.

Gregory the Grub. Ethel Barrett. (ps-1). 1978. pap. 6.95 o.p. (ISBN 0-8307-0421-3, 56-028-07). Regal.

Gregory, the Terrible Eater. Mitchell Sharmat. LC 79-19172. (Illus.). 32p. (gr. k-3). 1980. 7.95 (ISBN 0-590-07586-1, Four Winds). Schol Bk Serv.

Gregory's Stitches. Judith Vigna. LC 73-22400. (Self Starter Bks.). (Illus.). 32p. (gr. k-2). 1974. 6.50g (ISBN 0-8075-3046-8). A Whitman.

Gregory's Two Hundred Home Plan Ideas. Beryl Guertner. pap. 7.50x (ISBN 0-392-05865-0, ABC). Soccer.

Gregynog: A History of the House. Ed. by G. T. Hughes. 1977. 40.00 (ISBN 0-7083-0634-9). Verry.

Grendel. John C. Gardner. 1975. pap. 2.25 (ISBN 0-345-28865-3). Ballantine.

Grenelle. Isabelle Holland. LC 80-24329. 357p. 1980. Repr. of 1976 ed. large print ed. 9.95 (ISBN 0-89621-252-1). Thorndike Pr.

Grenencourt. Iona Charles. 256p. 1975. pap. 1.25 o.p. (ISBN 0-445-00264-6). Popular Lib.

Grenz Rays: An Illustrated Guide to the Theory & Practical Applications of Soft X-Rays. Daniel Graham & John Thomson. LC 79-42745. (Illus.). 164p. 1980. 24.00 (ISBN 0-08-025525-6). Pergamon.

Gresley Pacifics: Part 1 1922-1935. O. S. Nock. (Locomotive Monographs). 1973. 14.95 (ISBN 0-7153-6336-0). David & Charles.

Gresley Pacifics, Part 2: 1935-1974. O. S. Nock. LC 74-157265. 1975. 14.95 (ISBN 0-7153-6718-8). David & Charles.

Gresley's Coaches: Coaches Built for GNR, ECJS & LNER 1905-53. Michael Harris. (Illus.). 1973. 14.95 (ISBN 0-7153-5935-5). David & Charles.

Gretchen's World. Alice Hoffer. LC 80-83354. (Illus.). 48p. (gr. k-3). 1981. 5.95 (ISBN 0-448-16560-0); PLB 11.85 (ISBN 0-448-13491-8). G&D.

Grevisse's Correct French: A Practical Guide. Maurice Grevisse. Tr. by Christopher Kendris from Fr. (gr. 11-12). 1981. pap. text ed. 8.95 (ISBN 0-8120-2169-X). Barron.

Grey Lady & the Strawberry Snatcher. Molly Bang. LC 79-21243. (Illus.). 48p. (gr. 1 up). 1980. 10.95 (ISBN 0-590-07547-0, Four Winds). Schol Bk Serv.

Greygallows. Barbara Michaels. LC 72-3149. 320p. 1972. 6.95 o.p. (ISBN 0-396-06635-6). Dodd.

Greygallows. Barbara Michaels. 1977. pap. 1.75 o.p. (ISBN 0-449-23052-X, Crest). Fawcett.

Greyhound. rev., 7th ed. H. Edwards Clarke. 222p. 1980. text ed. 24.95x (ISBN 0-09-141410-5, SpS). Soccer.

Greyhound Betting for Profit. Ross Hamilton. 64p. 1980. pap. 2.95 (ISBN 0-89650-725-4). Gamblers.

Greyhound Racing 's Precision Players. Patrick R. Cullen. (Orig.). 1980. pap. write for info. Precision Pub Co.

Greyhounds. Roy Genders. Ed. by Christina Foyle. (Foyle's Handbks). 1973. 3.95 (ISBN 0-685-55807-X). Palmetto Pub.

Greystone Heritage. Louisa Bronte. 1976. pap. 1.50 o.p. (ISBN 0-345-25161-X). Ballantine.

Greystone Tavern. Louisa Bronte. 256p. (Orig.). 1975. pap. 1.50 o.p. (ISBN 0-345-24642-X). Ballantine.

Grid Approaches for Managerial Leadership in Nursing. Robert R. Blake & Jane S. Mouton. Ed. by Mildred Tapper. LC 80-21583. (Illus.). 158p. 1980. pap. text ed. 9.95 (ISBN 0-8016-0696-9). Mosby.

Grid Approaches to Managing Stress. Robert R. Blake & Jane S. Mouton. (Illus.). 196p. 1980. 15.50 (ISBN 0-398-04093-1). C C Thomas.

Grid Metal Manual for Storage Batteries. Nels E. Hehner & Everett J. Ritchie. (Avail. in eng. & span.). 1973. 15.00 (ISBN 0-685-56652-8). IBMA Pubns.

Grid Systems in Graphic Design: A Visual Communications Manual. Josef Muller-Brockmann. (Visual Communications Bks.). (Illus.). 176p. (Eng. & Ger.). 1981. 45.00 (ISBN 0-8038-2711-3). Hastings.

Grief Counseling & Sudden Death: A Manual & Guide. Polly Doyle. (Illus.). 352p. 1980. 26.50 (ISBN 0-398-04060-5). C C Thomas.

GRIEF: Living Through It & Growing with It. Arthur Freese. 1978. pap. 3.50 (ISBN 0-06-464024-8, BN 4024, BN). Har-Row.

Grief Observed. C. S. Lewis. 1963. 4.95 (ISBN 0-8164-0137-3). Crossroad NY.

Grief Observed. C. S. Lewis. (Orig.). 1966. pap. 3.95 (ISBN 0-571-06624-0, Pub. by Faber & Faber). Merrimack Bk Serv.

Grief Response for the Critically Ill. Jean A. Werner-Beland. (Illus.). 1980. text ed. 13.95 (ISBN 0-8359-2591-9); pap. text ed. 9.95 (ISBN 0-8359-2590-0). Reston.

Griego Del Nuevo Testamento: Texto Programado, Tomo III. Irene Foulkes. 220p. (Span.). 1973. pap. text ed. 7.00 (ISBN 0-89922-054-1). Edit Caribe.

Griego Del Nuevo Testamento: Texto Programado, Tomo II. Irene Foulkes. 203p. (Span.). 1973. pap. 7.00 (ISBN 0-89922-053-3). Edit Caribe.

Griego Del Nuevo Testamento: Texto Programado, Tomo I. Irene Foulkes. 194p. (Span.). 1973. pap. 7.00 (ISBN 0-89922-052-5). Edit Caribe.

Grierson on Documentary. John Grierson. Ed. by Forsyth Hardy. 1979. pap. 6.95 (ISBN 0-571-11367-2, Pub. by Faber & Faber). Merrimack Bk Serv.

Grierson on the Movies. John Grierson. Ed. by H. Forsyth Hardy. 200p. 1981. 22.00 (ISBN 0-571-11665-5, Pub. by Faber & Faber). Merrimack Bk Serv.

Grievance Arbitration Case Studies. Arthur P. Blockhaus. LC 74-8433. 416p. 1974. 19.95 (ISBN 0-8436-0722-X). CBI Pub.

Grievance Initiation & Resolution: A Study in Steel. David A. Peach & E. Robert Livernash. 1975. text ed. 8.50 (ISBN 0-87584-112-0). Harvard U Pr.

Grievance Procedure & Arbitration: Text & Cases. James W. Robinson & Wayne L. Dernoncourt. LC 77-18573. 1978. pap. text ed. 11.00x (ISBN 0-8191-0411-6). U Pr of Amer.

Grievance-Response Mechanisms in the Ghetto. R. S. Redmount et al. LC 74-151046. (Symposia on Law & Society Ser). 1971. Repr. of 1968 ed. lib. bdg. 17.50 (ISBN 0-306-70117-0). Da Capo.

Grieve Not for Wrightsie. Nancy Brunson & Wright A. Brunson. 1978. pap. 3.95 o.p. (ISBN 0-88270-272-6). Logos.

Grievous Bodily Harm. Ted Lewis. (Orig.). pap. 2.25. Jove Pubns.

Griffin's Talon. Anne Carsley. (Orig.). 1980. pap. write for info. (ISBN 0-671-41293-0). PB.

Griffon's Nest. Betty Levin. 352p. (gr. 5-9). 1975. 10.95 (ISBN 0-02-757350-8, 75735). Macmillan.

Grigorenko Papers: Writings by General P. G. Grigorenko & Documents on His Case. Peter Grigorenko. LC 76-5912. 1976. 22.00x (ISBN 0-89158-603-2). Westview.

Grihya-Sutras, Rules of Vedic Domestic Ceremonies, Vols. 29 & 30. Ed. by F. Max Mueller. Tr. by Oldenburg & Muller. (Sacred Books of the East Ser.). 15.00x ea.; Vol. 29. (ISBN 0-8426-1399-4); Vol. 30. (ISBN 0-8426-1400-1). Verry.

Grill Cooking. Ser-Vol-Tel Institute. (Foodservice Career Education Ser.). 1974. pap. 4.95 (ISBN 0-8436-2029-3). CBI Pub.

Grilling. Zechmann. 1981. 8.95 (ISBN 0-8120-5399-0). Barron.

Grillparzer: A Critical Introduction. W. E. Yates. LC 77-158550. 1972. 47.50 (ISBN 0-521-08241-2). Cambridge U Pr.

Grim Phoenix: Reconstructing Thomas Pynchon. William M. Plater. LC 77-12833. 288p. 1978. 12.50x (ISBN 0-253-32670-2). Ind U Pr.

Grim Science: The Struggle for Power. Walter H. Slack. (National Univ. Publications, Political Science Ser.). 200p. 1981. 20.00 (ISBN 0-8046-9260-2). Kennikat.

Grime & Punnishment. Harvey C. Gordon. (Orig.). 1981. pap. 3.95 (ISBN 0-446-97026-3). Warner Bks.

Grimm's Fairy Tales. Grimm. (Illustrated Classics Ser.). (Illus.). (gr. 7-12). 1980. Repr. cancelled o.p. (ISBN 0-19-274503-4). Oxford U Pr.

Grimm's Fairy Tales. Grimm Brothers. Ed. by Rose Dobbs. (Illus.). (gr. k-3). 1955. PLB 4.39 (ISBN 0-394-80657-3, BYR); PLB 4.39 (ISBN 0-394-90657-8). Random.

Grimm's Fairy Tales. (Illustrated Junior Library). (Illus.). 384p. 1981. pap. 4.95 (ISBN 0-448-11009-1). G&D.

Grimm's Fairy Tales: Twenty Stories. Grimm Brothers. (Large Format Ser.). (Illus.). 1978. pap. 5.95 o.p. (ISBN 0-14-004908-8). Penguin.

Grimm's Grandchildren: Current Topics in German Linguistics. Herbst et al. (Longman Linguistics Library). (Illus.). 1980. text ed. 27.00 (ISBN 0-582-55487-X); pap. text ed. 15.95 (ISBN 0-582-55489-6). Longman.

Grimm's Household Tales, 2 Vols. Jakob L. Grimm. Tr. by Margaret Hunt. LC 68-31090. 1968. Repr. of 1884 ed. 40.00 (ISBN 0-8103-3463-1). Gale.

Grimm's Tales for Young & Old: The Complete Stories. Tr. by Ralph Manheim. LC 76-56318. 1977. 14.95 (ISBN 0-385-11005-7). Doubleday.

Grimm's The Musicians of Bremen. Tr. by Anne Rogers from Danish. LC 74-78599. (Illus.). 24p. (gr. 1-3). 1974. 6.95 (ISBN 0-88332-060-6, 8027). Larousse.

Grinding, Vol. 1. Ed. by J. Allen et al. (Engineering Craftsmen: No. H5). 1968. spiral bdg. 21.00x (ISBN 0-85083-013-3). Intl Ideas.

Grinding, Vol. 2. Ed. by D. W. Barlow et al. (Engineering Craftsmen: No. H.31). 1972. spiral bdg. 28.50x (ISBN 0-85083-380-9). Intl Ideas.

Grinding Technology. S. F. Krar & J. W. Oswald. LC 72-7935. 1974. pap. text ed. 11.60 (ISBN 0-8273-0208-8); instructor's guide 1.60 (ISBN 0-8273-0209-6). Delmar.

Grindle Lamfoon & the Procurnious Fleekers. Valerie H. Damon. Ed. by Dave Damon. LC 78-64526. (Illus.). (gr. 1-12). 1979. 8.95 (ISBN 0-932356-05-2); fleeker ed. 10.95 (ISBN 0-932356-06-0). Star Pubns MO.

Gringa & Barranca Abajo. Florencio Sanchez. LC 72-6355. 186p. 1973. 12.50 o.p. (ISBN 0-8386-1264-4). Fairleigh Dickinson.

Grinker's Neurology. 7th ed. Nicholas A. Vick. (Illus.). 1104p. 1976. 49.75 (ISBN 0-398-03470-2). C C Thomas.

Grinny: A Novel of Science Fiction. Nicholas Fisk. LC 74-10274. 96p. (gr. 5-8). 1974. 6.95 o.p. (ISBN 0-525-66697-4). Elsevier-Nelson.

Griot Sings: Songs from the Black World. Ed. by Edna S. Edet. LC 78-10713. Date not set. pap. 6.95 (ISBN 0-89062-064-4, Pub. by Medgar Evers Coll). Pub Ctr Cult Res.

Griot Sings: Songs from the Black World. Ed. by Edna S. Edet. 96p. (Orig.). 1978. pap. 6.95 (ISBN 0-89062-064-4, Pub. by Medgar Evers Coll). Pub Ctr Cult Res.

Griot Speaks: Stories & Folktales from the Black World. Chinwe M. Harden-Umolu. 96p. (Orig.). (gr. 3 up). 1979. pap. 8.00 (ISBN 0-89062-040-7, Pub. by Medgar Evers Coll). Pub Ctr Cult Res.

Grip, a Dog Story. Helen Griffiths. LC 78-6819. (Illus.). (gr. 5-9). 1978. 8.95 (ISBN 0-8234-0335-1). Holiday.

Grip, a Dog Story. Helen Griffiths. 1981. pap. price not set (ISBN 0-671-56034-4). Archway.

Grips or, Efforts to Revive the Host. M. D. Elevitch. LC 73-170613. 111p. 1972. 6.95 (ISBN 0-916452-02-6). First Person.

Griselda's New Year. Marjorie W. Sharmat. LC 79-11375. (Ready-to-Read). (Illus.). (gr. 1-4). 1979. 7.95 (ISBN 0-02-782420-9). Macmillan.

Grist Mills in Baltimore County, Maryland. John W. McGrain. (Baltimore County Heritage Publication). (Illus.). 40p. 1980. pap. 4.95 (ISBN 0-937076-00-7). Baltimore Co Pub Lib.

Grizzly Bear: The Narrative of a Hunter-Naturalist. William H. Wright. LC 77-1772. (Illus.). 1977. 15.50x (ISBN 0-8032-0927-4); pap. 4.95 (ISBN 0-8032-5865-8, BB 646, Bison). U of Nebr Pr.

Groans of a Lost Soul. John Bunyan. LC 68-6571. 1967. pap. 3.25 (ISBN 0-685-19830-8). Reiner.

Grocery Retailing in the Eighties. Progressive Grocer Magazine Staff. (Illus.). 1980. 12.95 (ISBN 0-911790-75-6). Prog Grocer.

Groggs Day Out. Anne Bentley. LC 80-2689. 32p. (gr. k-3). 1981. 9.95 (ISBN 0-233-97348-6). Andre Deutsch.

Groggs Have a Wonderful Summer. Anne Bentley. (Illus.). (ps-2). 1980. 8.95 (ISBN 0-233-97199-8). Andre Deutsch.

Groom Your Dog. Leon F. Whitney. (Orig.). 1962. pap. 2.00 (ISBN 0-87666-313-7, DS1023). TFH Pubns.

Groove Your Golf Swing My Way. Lee Trevino & Dick Aultman. LC 75-41853. 1976. 12.95 o.p. (ISBN 0-689-10723-4). Atheneum.

Grooves of Change: A Book of Memoirs. Herbert Samuel. (Return to Zion Ser.). (Illus.). 378p. 1980. Repr. of 1946 ed. lib. bdg. 25.00x (ISBN 0-87991-137-9). Porcupine Pr.

Grooves of Change: A Book of Memoirs. Herbert L. Samuel. LC 80-1913. 1981. Repr. of 1946 ed. 39.50 (ISBN 0-404-18985-7). AMS Pr.

Grooving the Symbol. R. W. Lid. LC 78-98886. 1970. pap. text ed. 6.95 (ISBN 0-02-918960-8). Free Pr.

Groping Giant: Russia. Wm. A. Brown, Jr. 1920. 22.50x (ISBN 0-685-69793-2). Elliots Bks.

Gross Anatomy Review. William K. Metcalf et al. (Basic Science Review Bks.). 1975. spiral bdg. 8.00 o.s.i. (ISBN 0-87488-220-6). Med Exam.

Gross Intrusion & Other Stories. Steven Berkoff. 1980. 9.95 (ISBN 0-7145-3685-7); pap. 4.95 (ISBN 0-7145-3685-7). Riverrun NY.

Gross Regional Product of Texas & Its Regions: Growth Trends & the Structure of Output. Thomas R. Plaut & Mildred C. Anderson. (Illus.). 100p. (Orig.). 1981. pap. text ed. 6.00 (ISBN 0-87755-244-4). U of Tex Busn Res.

Grosse Brockhaus, 15 vols 2 supplements 1 atlas. 16th ed. (Ger.). 1952. 270.00 o.p. (ISBN 0-8277-3032-2). Maxwell Sci Intl.

Grosse Duden-Lexikon, 8 vols. (Ger., With 2 suppl.). 1964-1969. Set. 350.00 (ISBN 0-8277-3033-0). Maxwell Sci Intl.

Grosse Pointe on Lake Sainte Claire. Theodore P. Hall & Silas Farmer. LC 73-17472. 114p. 1974. Repr. of 1886 ed. 6.00 (ISBN 0-8103-3879-3). Gale.

Grosses Vollstaendiges Universallexikon aller Wissenschaften und Kunste, 1731-1750: Suppls. 1751-54, 68 vols. (Ger.). Set. 6185.00. Pergamon.

Grossman's Guide to Wines, Beers, & Spirits. 6th rev. ed. Harold J. Grossman. (Illus.). 1977. 27.50 (ISBN 0-684-15033-6, ScribT). Scribner.

Grosvenor Estate in Mayfair: The Buildings, Pt. 2. Ed. by F. H. Sheppard. (Survey of London Ser.: Vol. 40). 429p. 1980. text ed. 143.00x (ISBN 0-485-48240-1, Athlone Pr). Humanities.

Grosz. Frank Whitford. (Oresko-Jupiter Art Bks). (Illus.). 96p. 1981. 17.95 (ISBN 0-933516-88-6, Pub. by Oresko-Jupiter England). Hippocrene Bks.

Grote Nederlandse Larousse Encyclopedie, 25 vols. (Dutch., 14 vols. avail.). 1972-1979. Set. 1845.00 (ISBN 0-8277-3052-7). Maxwell Sci Intl.

Grote Winkler Prins Encyclopedie, 20 vols. 7th ed. (Dutch.). 1975. Set. 1245.00 (ISBN 0-8277-3035-7). Maxwell Sci Intl.

Grotesque in Church Art. Thomas T. Wildridge. LC 68-30633. 1969. Repr. of 1899 ed. 15.00 (ISBN 0-8103-3077-6). Gale.

Groton Plantation: An Archaeological Study of a South Carolina Locality. James B. Stoltman. LC 74-77556. (Peabody Museum Monographs: No. 1). 1974. pap. text ed. 12.00 (ISBN 0-87365-900-7). Peabody Harvard.

Grouchy Ladybug. Eric Carle. LC 77-3170. (Illus.). (ps). 1977. 8.95 (ISBN 0-690-01391-4, TYC-J); PLB 8.79 (ISBN 0-690-01392-2). T Y Crowell.

Ground Attack Aircraft of World War II. Christopher Shores. (Illus.). 191p. 1979. 9.95 (ISBN 0-356-08338-1, Pub by Macdonald & Jane's England). Hippocrene Bks.

Ground Beef. 2nd ed. Sunset Editors. LC 73-75750. (Illus.). 80p. 1973. pap. 2.95 o.p. (ISBN 0-376-02453-4, Sunset Bks). Sunset-Lane.

Ground Cover & Other Ways to Weed-Free Gardens. Frederick A. Boddy. LC 74-78251. (Illus.). 176p. 1974. 13.50 (ISBN 0-7153-6575-4). David & Charles.

Ground Cover Fire Fighting Practices. 2nd ed. Ed. by Gene Carlson & Carles Orton. (Illus.). 1981. pap. text ed. 7.00 (ISBN 0-87939-038-7, IFSTA 207). Intl Fire Serv. Postponed.

Ground Cover Plants. Donald Wyman. (Illus.). 1956. 5.95 o.s.i. (ISBN 0-02-632030-4). Macmillan.

Ground Cover Plants. Donald Wyman. (Illus.). 192p. 1976. pap. 3.95 o.s.i. (ISBN 0-02-064020-X, Collier). Macmillan.

Ground Engineering. 132p. 1980. 75.00x (ISBN 0-901948-09-8, Pub. by Telford England). State Mutual Bk.

Ground I Walked on. George N. Shuster. 1961. 4.50 o.p. (ISBN 0-374-16692-7). FS&G.

Ground Squirrels. Colleen S. Bare. LC 80-13649. (A Skylight Bk.). (Illus.). 64p. (gr. 2-5). 1980. PLB 5.95 (ISBN 0-396-07852-4). Dodd.

Ground Studies for Pilots. 2nd ed. S. E. Taylor & H. A. Parmar. (Illus.). Date not set. 14.95 o.p. (ISBN 0-258-96983-0, ScribT). Scribner. Postponed.

Ground Studies for Pilots. S. E. Taylor & H. A. Parmar. Incl. Vol. I. Radio Aids. 3rd ed. 200p. 1979. text ed. 26.50x (ISBN 0-246-11169-0); Vol. II. Plotting & Flight Planning. 130p. 1976. text ed. 19.95x (ISBN 0-246-11176-3); Vol. III. Navigation General. 232p. 1979. text ed. 26.50x (ISBN 0-246-11177-1). Pub. by Granada England). Renouf.

Ground Subsidence. 1980. pap. 17.00x (ISBN 0-7277-0046-4, Pub. by Telford England). State Mutual Bk.

Ground Treatment by Deep Compaction. Ed. by Thomas Telford Editorial Staff, Ltd. 166p. 1980. 30.00x (ISBN 0-7277-0024-3, Pub. by Telford England). State Mutual Bk.

Ground Water Management. Compiled By American Society of Civil Engineers. (Manual & Report on Engineering Practice: No. 40). 1972. pap. text ed. 13.75 (ISBN 0-87262-216-9). Am Soc Civil Eng.

Ground Water Studies: Suppl. 3. (Studies & Reports in Hydrology: No. 7). 1978. pap. 18.00 (ISBN 92-3-101471-4, U833, UNESCO). Unipub.

Groundhog up a Tree. Glenn Shelton. 6.95 (ISBN 0-685-48817-9). Nortex Pr.

Groundhog's Day at the Doctor. Judy Delton. (Illus.). 48p. (ps-3). 1981. PLB 5.95 (ISBN 0-8193-1042-5); pap. 4.95 (ISBN 0-8193-1041-7). Parents.

Groundhog's Story. Emil E. Liers. LC 76-25629. (Crown Ser.). (primer). 1976. pap. 4.50 (ISBN 0-8127-0130-5). Southern Pub.

Grounding for the Metaphysics of Morals. Immanuel Kant. Tr. by James W. Ellington from Ger. (HPC Philosophical Classics Ser.). 125p. 1981. lib. bdg. 12.50 (ISBN 0-915145-01-4); pap. text ed. 2.75 (ISBN 0-915145-00-6). Hackett Pub.

Groundog Day. Sharon Shebar & Judy Schoder. Ed. by Alton Jordan. (Holdays Ser.). (Illus.). (gr. k-3). 1977. PLB 3.50 (ISBN 0-89868-027-1, Read Res); pap. text ed. 1.75 (ISBN 0-89868-060-3). ARO Pub.

Grounds for Comparison. Harry Levin. LC 72-75402. (Studies in Comparative Literature: No. 32). (Illus.). 448p. 1972. 18.50x (ISBN 0-674-36335-3). Harvard U Pr.

Grounds for Grammar. Gregory A. Ross. 1976. pap. text ed. 7.50x (ISBN 0-8191-0063-3). U Pr of Amer.

Grounds for Growth: Comprehensive Theory Manual. Gerry Ball. 1980. 14.95 (ISBN 0-86584-009-1). Human Dev Train.

Groundwater Monitoring. Lorne G. Everett. LC 80-82885. (Illus.). 480p. 1980. 150.00x (ISBN 0-931690-14-5). GE Tech Market.

Group. Mary McCarthy. 1980. pap. 2.75 (ISBN 0-686-69265-9, 52134). Avon.

Group & Family Therapy: 1980: An Overview. Ed. by Lewis R. Wolberg & Marvin L. Aronson. LC 72-10881. 432p. 1980. 25.00 (ISBN 0-87630-238-X). Brunner-Mazel.

Group Approach in Nursing Practice. 2nd ed. Gwen D. Marram. LC 77-14584. (Illus.). 1978. pap. text ed. 11.00 (ISBN 0-8016-3126-2). Mosby.

Group Approaches in Psychiatry. J. Stuart Whitely & John Gordon. (Social & Psychological Aspects of Medical Practice Ser.). 1979. 20.00x (ISBN 0-7100-8970-8). Routledge & Kegan.

Group Behavior: A Guide to Information Sources. Ed. by Gloria B. Gottsegen. LC 79-63744. (Psychology Information Guide Ser.: Vol. 2). 1979. 30.00 (ISBN 0-8103-1439-8). Gale.

Group Communication: Discussion Processes & Application. Alvin Goldberg & Carl Larson. LC 74-5295. (Speech Communication Ser.). (Illus.). 224p. 1975. ref. ed. 15.95x (ISBN 0-13-365221-1). P-H.

Group Communication: Essence of Synergy. John E. Baird, Jr. & Sanford B. Weinberg. 270p. 1981. pap. text ed. write for info. (ISBN 0-697-04181-6); resourse manual avail. (ISBN 0-697-04187-5). Wm C Brown.

Group Counseling: A Developmental Approach. 2nd ed. George M. Gazda. 1978. pap. text ed. 18.95 (ISBN 0-205-05958-9). Allyn.

Group Counseling & Group Psychotherapy with Rehabilitation Clients. Milton Seligman. (Illus.). 352p. 1977. 22.00 (ISBN 0-398-03585-7); pap. 17.00 (ISBN 0-398-03588-1). C C Thomas.

Group Counseling & Psychotherapy with Adolescents. Beryce W. Maclennan & Naomi Felsenfeld. LC 68-18998. 1968-70. 13.50x (ISBN 0-231-03093-2); pap. 5.00x (ISBN 0-231-08640-7). Columbia U Pr.

Group Counseling & Therapy Techniques in Special Settings. Ed. by Richard E. Hardy & John G. Cull. (American Lectures in Social & Rehabilitation Psychology Ser.). 180p. 1974. text ed. 14.50 (ISBN 0-398-03001-4). C C Thomas.

Group Counseling: Theory & Practice. 2nd ed. Don C. Dinkmeyer & James J. Muro. LC 77-83357. 1979. text ed. 14.95 (ISBN 0-87581-206-6). Peacock Pubs.

Group Crafts for Teachers & Librarians on Limited Budgets. Kristina Preslan. LC 80-13145. (Illus.). 1980. pap. 9.00x (ISBN 0-87287-218-1). Libs Unl.

Group Decision Theory. N. C. Dalkey. 1981. cancelled (ISBN 0-201-01430-0, Adv Bk Prog). A-W.

Group Development. 2nd, rev, enl. ed. Ed. by Leland P. Bradford. LC 78-51283. 234p. 1978. pap. 12.50 (ISBN 0-88390-144-7). Univ Assocs.

Group Development Through Participation Training. John McKinley. LC 78-71870. 128p. (Orig.). 1980. pap. text ed. 9.95 (ISBN 0-8091-2247-2); participant's bk. 2.50 (ISBN 0-8091-2299-5). Paulist Pr.

Group Discussion: A Practical Guide to Participation & Leadership. Gerald M. Phillips et al. LC 78-56441. (Illus.). 1978. text ed. 13.95 (ISBN 0-395-25415-9); inst. manual 0.65 (ISBN 0-395-25416-7). HM.

Group Discussion As Learning Process: Sourcebook, Student Edition. Elizabeth Flynn & John La Faso. LC 74-170013. 1972. pap. 8.95 (ISBN 0-8091-1589-1). Paulist Pr.

Group Discussion: Theory & Technique. 2nd ed. R. Victor Harnack et al. (Illus.). 1977. text ed. 16.95 (ISBN 0-13-365247-5). P-H.

Group Dynamic Law. David A. Funk. LC 80-84733. 1981. 29.50 (ISBN 0-686-68867-8). Philos Lib.

Group Dynamics. 3rd ed. Marvin Shaw. (Illus.). 560p. 1980. 21.95 (ISBN 0-07-056504-X). McGraw.

Group Dynamics & Society: A Multinational Approach. Ed. by The European Institute & Trygve Johnstad. LC 80-24932. 352p. 1980. text ed. 27.50 (ISBN 0-89946-070-4). Oelgeschlager.

Group for the Advancement of Psychiatry Publications: Bound Volumes, 9 bks, Vols. 1-9. Incl. Vols. 1-2. Reports 1-01 Through 1-34 & Symposium 2-01. 1947-56. 20.00 (ISBN 0-87318-040-2); Vol. 3. Reports 1-35 Through 1-42 & Symposiums 2-02 Through 2-05. 1956-59. 20.00 (ISBN 0-87318-055-0); Vol. 4. Reports 1-43 Through 1-53 & Symposiums 2-06 Through 2-08. 1959-62. 20.00 (ISBN 0-87318-072-0); Vol. 5. Reports 1-54 Through 1-59 & Symposiums 2-09 Through 2-11. 1962-65. 20.00 (ISBN 0-87318-084-4); Vol. 6. Reports 1-60 Through 1-69; Also Report 1-271, Originally Published in 1954. 1965-68. 20.00 (ISBN 0-87318-097-6); Vol. 7. Reports 1-70 Through 1-80, Report 1-372 & Film Guide 9-11. 1968-71. 20.00 (ISBN 0-87318-126-3); Vol. 8. Reports 1-81 Through 1-90 & Symposium 2-12. 1971-74. 30.00 (ISBN 0-87318-127-1); Index of Publications for the First Seven Volumes: Reports Nos. 1-01 Through Nos. 1-80. LC 73-76845. 1947-1971. 10.00 (ISBN 0-87318-118-2); Vol. 9. Reports 1-91 Through 1-99. 1974-77. 30.00 (ISBN 0-87318-141-7); Vol. 10. Reports 1-100 Through 1-106. 1977-1980. 40.00. Set. 186.00 (ISBN 0-87318-144-1). Adv Psychiatry.

Group Forty Seven: The Reflected Intellect. Siegfried Mandel. LC 73-8698. (Crosscurrents-Modern Critiques Ser.). 245p. 1973. 8.95 (ISBN 0-8093-0641-7). S Ill U Pr.

Group Guidance & Counseling in the Schools: Selected Readings. Ed. by James Hansen & Stanley Cramer. 1971. pap. text ed. 13.95 (ISBN 0-13-365304-8). P-H.

Group Hypnotherapy & Hypnodrama. Ed. by Ira A. Greenberg. LC 76-17012. 320p. 1977. 19.95 (ISBN 0-88229-256-0). Nelson-Hall.

Group Legal Services. Susan T. MacKenzie. (Key Issues Ser.: No. 18). 1975. pap. 3.00 (ISBN 0-87546-231-6). NY Sch Indus Rel.

Group Life: The Nature & Treatment of Its Specific Conflicts. Marshall C. Greco. 357p. 1980. Repr. of 1950 ed. lib. bdg. 35.00 (ISBN 0-89984-229-1). Century Bookbindery.

Group Meeting Sparklers. Boy Scouts of America. (Illus.). Repr. of 1962 ed. pap. text ed. 0.50x (ISBN 0-8395-3122-2). BSA.

Group Orgy. (Illus.). 4.95 (ISBN 0-910550-37-9). Centurion Pr.

Group Participation: Techniques for Leaders & Members. Harvey J. Bertcher. LC 79-175. (Sage Human Services Guides: Vol. 10). 1979. pap. 8.00x (ISBN 0-8039-1204-8). Sage.

Group Performance. James H. Davis. Ed. by Charles A. Kiesler. (Psychology-Topics in Social Psychology). 1969. pap. text ed. 6.95 (ISBN 0-201-01476-9). A-W.

Group Performance of Literature. B. Long et al. (Illus.). 1977. pap. text ed. 15.95 (ISBN 0-13-365346-3). P-H.

Group Practice Development: A Practical Handbook. John W. Field. LC 76-56948. 1976. 32.00 (ISBN 0-912862-26-2). Aspen Systems.

Group Problem Solving Process: Studies of a Valence Model. L. Richard Hoffman. LC 79-12578. 256p. 1979. 24.95 (ISBN 0-03-047636-4). Praeger.

Group Procedures: Purposes, Processes, & Outcomes. Richard C. Diedrich & H. Allan Dye. 1972. pap. text ed. 14.95 (ISBN 0-395-04364-6). HM.

Group Process As a Helping Technique. S. Thompson & J. H. Kahn. LC 79-124667. 1970. 15.00 (ISBN 0-08-016220-7); pap. 7.00 (ISBN 0-08-016219-3). Pergamon.

Group Process for Nurses. Maxine E. Loomis. LC 78-31261. (Illus.). 1979. pap. text ed. 10.50 (ISBN 0-8016-3037-1). Mosby.

Group Process for the Health Professions. 2nd ed. Edward E. Sampson & Marya Sampson. 352p. 1981. pap. 12.95 (ISBN 0-471-08279-1, Pub. by Wiley Med). Wiley.

Group Process Today: Evaluation & Perspective. Ed. by Donald S. Milman & George D. Goldman. 336p. 1974. 19.75 (ISBN 0-685-50187-6). C C Thomas.

Group Processes: An Introduction to Group Dynamics. 2nd ed. Joseph Luft. LC 76-107365. 1970. pap. 4.95 (ISBN 0-87484-146-1). Mayfield Pub.

Group Processes & Personal Change. Peter B. Smith. 1980. text ed. 18.35 (ISBN 0-06-318146-0, IntlDept); pap. text ed. 10.45 (ISBN 0-06-318151-7). Har-Row.

Group Processes & Productivity. Ivan D. Steiner. (Social Psychology Ser). 1972. 14.50 (ISBN 0-12-665350-X). Acad Pr.

Group Processes for the Health Professions. Edward E. Sampson & Marya S. Marthas. LC 77-23013. 1977. pap. 11.95 (ISBN 0-471-01987-9, Pub. by Wiley Medical). Wiley.

Group Production Organization & Technology. E. K. Ivanov. Ed. by T. J. Grayson. Tr. by E. Bishop. (Illus.). 144p. 1968. 9.95x o.p. (ISBN 0-8464-0457-5). Beekman Pubs.

Group Psychology & the Analysis of the Ego. Sigmund Freud. Ed. & tr. by James Strachey. 1975. 6.95 (ISBN 0-393-01117-8, Norton Lib); pap. 2.95 (ISBN 0-393-00770-7). Norton.

Group Psychotherapy: Practice & Development. Baroch Levine. 1979. 17.95 (ISBN 0-13-365296-3). P-H.

Group Remedy Prescriber. Eric F. Powell. 1980. 7.95 o.p. (ISBN 0-8464-1015-X). Beekman Pubs.

Group Representations in Mathematics & Physics: Battelle Seattle 1969 Rencontres. Ed. by V. Bargmann. LC 75-146233. (Lecture Notes in Physics: Vol. 6). 1971. pap. 18.30 (ISBN 0-387-05310-7). Springer-Verlag.

Group Skills in Social Work: A Four Dimensional Approach. Sue Henry. LC 80-83378. 416p. 1981. text ed. 12.50 (ISBN 0-87581-268-6). Peacock Pubs.

Group Strategy for Energy Research, Development & Demonstration. Ed. by OECD & IEA. 97p. (Orig.). 1980. pap. 8.00 (ISBN 9-2641-2124-2). OECD.

Group Theory & Chemistry. David M. Bishop. (Illus.). 310p. 1973. 39.00x (ISBN 0-19-855140-1). Oxford U Pr.

Group Theory & Quantum Mechanics. B. L. Van Der Waerden. (Grundlehren der Mathematischen Wissenschaften Ser.: Vol. 214). (Illus.). 211p. 1981. 39.00 (ISBN 0-387-06740-X). Springer-Verlag.

Group Theory for Social Workers: An Introduction. Ken Heap. 1977. text ed. 26.00 (ISBN 0-08-018956-3); pap. text ed. 11.00 (ISBN 0-08-018955-5). Pergamon.

Group Theory in Quantum Mechanics. V. Heine. 1963. 30.00 (ISBN 0-08-009242-X). Pergamon.

Group Theory Made Easy for Scientists & Engineers. N. V. Swamy & Mark A. Samuel. LC 78-11733. 1979. 18.50 (ISBN 0-471-05128-4, Pub. by Wiley-Interscience). Wiley.

Group Therapy: A Behavioral Approach. Sheldon D. Rose. (Illus.). 1977. 17.95 (ISBN 0-13-365239-4). P-H.

Group Therapy: A Source of New Meaning. Robert L. Anders & Loretta S. Bermosk. 1981. cancelled (ISBN 0-8036-0142-5). Davis Co.

Group Training Techniques: Cases, Applications & Research. Ed. by M. L. Berger & P. J. Berger. LC 72-9008. 191p. 1973. 24.95 (ISBN 0-470-06960-0). Halsted Pr.

Group Work in the Helping Profession: A Bibliography. (ASGW Publications). 1976. pap. 6.25 o.p. (ISBN 0-686-17935-8). Am Personnel.

Group Work: Learning & Practice. Nano McCaughan. (National Institute Social Service Library). 1978. text ed. 22.50x (ISBN 0-04-361029-3); pap. text ed. 8.95x (ISBN 0-04-361030-7). Allen Unwin.

Groups & Individuals. W. Doise & G. Douglas. LC 77-84800. (Illus.). 1978. 29.95 (ISBN 0-521-21953-1); pap. 8.95x (ISBN 0-521-29320-0). Cambridge U Pr.

Groups at Work: Unresolved Issues in the Study of Organizations. Alvin Zander. LC 77-82918. (Social & Behavioral Science Ser). 1977. text ed. 11.95x (ISBN 0-87589-347-3). Jossey-Bass.

Groups in Social Work: Application of Small Group Theory & Research to Social Work Practice. Margaret E. Hartford. LC 71-181782. 320p. 1972. 16.00x (ISBN 0-231-03548-9); pap. 9.00x (ISBN 0-685-23629-3). Columbia U Pr.

Groups: Theory & Experience. 2nd ed. Rodney Napier & Matti Gershenfeld. (Illus.). 448p. 1981. text ed. write for info. (ISBN 0-395-29703-6). HM.

Groups: Theory & Experience. Rodney W. Napier & Matti K. Gershenfeld. LC 72-7925. 325p. 1973. text ed. 17.95 (ISBN 0-395-12658-4, 3-40200); instructors' manual pap. 4.50 (ISBN 0-395-14048-X, 3-40201). HM.

Grouse Foolish & Other Stories. Harry Vanderweide. (Illus.). 144p. 1979. 7.95 (ISBN 0-89933-006-1). DeLorme Pub.

Grouting in Engineering Practice. Robert Bowen. LC 75-20111. 186p. 1975. 42.95 (ISBN 0-470-09221-1). Halsted Pr.

Grover Presents Finish the Picture. (Wipe-off Bks). 9p. (ps). 2.39 (ISBN 0-307-01841-5, Golden Pr). Western Pub.

Grover's Little Red Riding Hood. Norman Stiles. (Illus.). (gr. k-2). 1976. PLB 5.38 (ISBN 0-307-68934-4, Golden Pr). Western Pub.

Grover's Own Alphabet. Sol Murdocca. (Illus.). (ps-1). 1978. PLB 4.77 (ISBN 0-307-68654-X, Whitman). Western Pub.

Groves of Academe. Mary McCarthy. 240p. 1981. pap. 2.95 (ISBN 0-380-52522-4, 52522, Bard). Avon.

Grow a Plant Pet. Virginie Fowler Elbert. LC 76-56284. (gr. 7 up). 1977. PLB 6.95 (ISBN 0-385-11699-3). Doubleday.

Grow It Indoors. Richard W. Langer. (Illus.). 1976. pap. 2.50 (ISBN 0-446-91022-8). Warner Bks.

Grow Native Shrubs in Your Garden. F. M. Mooberry & Jane H. Scott. LC 80-69807. 1980. 5.95x. Brandywine Conserv.

Grow or Die: The Over-Population Myth. James A. Weber. 1977. 11.95 o.p. (ISBN 0-87000-367-4). Arlington Hse.

Grow Your Christian Life. Inter-Varsity Staff. pap. 3.50 (ISBN 0-87784-661-8). Inter-Varsity.

Grow Your Own Fruit & Vegetables. Lawrence D. Hills. 1974. 14.00 (ISBN 0-571-04830-7). Transatlantic.

Grow Your Roots Anywhere, Anytime. Ronald R. Raymond, Jr. et al. Date not set. 12.95. Wyden.

Growers Weed Identification Handbook. Bill Fischer et al. (Illus.). 183p. 1978. 40.00x (ISBN 0-931876-43-5, 4030). Ag Sci Pubns.

Growing & Cooking Beans. John Withee. Ed. by Georgia Orcutt. LC 79-57179. 144p. (Orig.). 1980. pap. 7.95 (ISBN 0-911658-05-X, 3070). Yankee Bks.

Growing & Cooking Potatoes. Ed. by Mary Cornog. LC 80-52993. 1981. pap. 7.95 (ISBN 0-911658-15-7, 3076). Yankee Bks.

Growing & Declining Urban Areas: A Fiscal Comparison. Thomas Muller. (Institute Paper). 121p. 1975. pap. 3.50 (ISBN 0-87766-154-5, 13400). Urban Inst.

Growing & Sharing: The Catechist Formation Book. David Sork et al. 128p. (Orig.). 1981. pap. 6.95 (ISBN 0-8091-2365-7). Paulist Pr.

Growing & Storing Herbs. Brian Walkden & Mary Walkden. 1979. pap. 3.95 o.s.i. (ISBN 0-7225-0508-6). Newcastle Pub.

Growing & Thinking Slim. 2nd expd. ed. Wilma Bower & Hildegard Willard. (Illus., Orig.). 1978. pap. text ed. 10.00 (ISBN 0-686-12310-7). Willard-Bower.

Growing As Jesus Grew. Jane Buerger. LC 80-17187. (Illus.). 32p. (ps-2). 1980. PLB 4.95 (ISBN 0-89565-173-4). Childs World.

Growing Beautiful Flowers Indoors. Jack Kramer. (Illus.). 1980. 24.95 (ISBN 0-312-35120-8). St Martin.

Growing Better Brighter Children. Daisy R. Mante & Bonnie W. Mathisen. 160p. (Orig.). Date not set. pap. price not set (ISBN 0-931310-02-4). Jifunza Educ.

Growing Brain: Childhood's Crucial Years. John Brierley. (General Ser.). (Illus., Orig.). 1976. pap. text ed. 10.75x (ISBN 0-85633-099-X, NFER). Humanities.

Growing by Discipling Pastor's Handbook. rev. ed. Churches Alive, Inc. (Illus.). 150p. 1980. pap. text ed. 8.00 (ISBN 0-934396-09-4). Churches Alive.

Growing California Native Plants. Marjorie G. Schmidt. 400p. 1980. 15.95 (ISBN 0-520-03761-8). U of Cal Pr.

Growing Child: Introduction to Child Development. J. F. Travers. 1977. 19.95x (ISBN 0-471-88500-2); study guide 6.95x. Wiley.

Growing Economy: The Principles of Political Economy, Vol.2. J. E. Meade. 1968. pap. text ed. 14.95x (ISBN 0-04-330122-3). Allen Unwin.

Growing Flowers. Michael Crooks. (Practical Gardening Ser.). (Illus.). 112p. (Orig.). 1979. pap. 10.50 (ISBN 0-589-01241-X, Pub. by Reed Bks Australia). C E Tuttle.

Growing Flowers. H. C. Thompson & Fred Bonnie. LC 74-18642. (Illus.). 1975. 7.95 o.p. (ISBN 0-8487-0391-X). Oxmoor Hse.

Growing Food. D. J. Edwards. LC 69-18748. (Finding Out About Science Ser). (Illus.). (gr. 3-6). 1969. PLB 7.89 (ISBN 0-381-99835-5, A31710, JD-J). John Day.

Growing Food Under Glass: One-Thousand & One Questions Answered. Adrienne Oldale & Peter Oldale. 1978. 11.95 (ISBN 0-7153-7334-X). David & Charles.

Growing for Showing. George Whitehead. (Illus.). 176p. 1981. pap. 7.95 (ISBN 0-571-11706-6, Pub. by Faber & Faber). Merrimack Bk Serv.

Growing from Word Play into Poetry. Buff Bradley. LC 76-29235. (Learning Handbooks Ser.). 1976. pap. 3.95 (ISBN 0-8224-1904-1). Pitman Learning.

Growing Fruits, Berries & Nuts in the South. George McEachern. LC 77-99266. (Illus.). 1978. pap. 3.95 (ISBN 0-88415-299-5). Pacesetter Pr.

Growing Herbs. Lorna Rowland. (Practical Gardening Ser.). (Illus.). 112p. (Orig.). 1979. pap. 10.50 (ISBN 0-589-01244-4, Pub. by Reed Bks Australia). C E Tuttle.

Growing Herbs for the Kitchen. Betty E. Jacobs. (Illus.). 1972. 6.95 (ISBN 0-910458-14-6). Select Bks.

Growing in Christ. Gerald Dye. (Double Trouble Puzzles Ser.). 48p. (Orig.). (gr. 6 up). 1981. pap. 1.25 (ISBN 0-87239-447-6, 2837). Standard Pub.

Growing in English Language Skills. Mary Finocchiaro & Violet Lavanda. 1977. pap. text ed. 4.75 (ISBN 0-685-79304-4); cassettes 25.00 (ISBN 0-88345-299-5); answer key 1.00 (ISBN 0-685-79305-2). Regents Pub.

Growing in Faith. Steve B. Clark. (Living As a Christian Ser.). 1972. pap. 1.50 (ISBN 0-89283-004-2). Servant.

Growing in Faith with Your Child. Archdiocese of Newark. Ed. by Thomas P. Ivory. 48p. (Orig.). pap. 2.50 (ISBN 0-697-01693-5). Wm C Brown.

Growing in the Priesthood: Messages of Inspiration & Motivation with Personal Records of Fulfillment. Ellvert H. Himes. LC 75-17103. (Illus.). 128p. 1975. 5.95 (ISBN 0-88290-052-8). Horizon Utah.

Growing into Christ: A Workbook for Confirmation. Virginia M. Malterner. (Illus.). 96p. (Orig.). (gr. 7). 1975. pap. 3.50x o.p. (ISBN 0-8192-4061-3); tchrs. ed. 4.75x o.p. (ISBN 0-8192-4062-1). Morehouse.

Growing Marijuana for Home Medical Use. Stevens & Perillo. (Illus.). 1981. perfect bdg. 5.95 (ISBN 0-686-26920-9). Pacific Pipeline.

Growing Markets for Computer Storage. 1981. 750.00 (ISBN 0-89336-265-4, G-061). BCC.

Growing Natural. Janet Gillepsie. 224p. 1976. pap. 1.75 o.p. (ISBN 0-345-24872-4). Ballantine.

Growing New Hair! How to Keep What You Have & Fill in Where It's Thin, by Margo, for Men Only. Margo. LC 80-66699. (Illus.). 112p. 1980. 7.95 (ISBN 0-394-51417-3). Autumn Pr.

Growing of America: Seventeen Eighty-Nine to Eighteen Forty-Eight. Raymond Robinson. LC 78-67275. 1979. pap. text ed. 6.95x (ISBN 0-88273-112-2). Forum Pr MO.

Growing Old: A Social Perspective. Rainer Baum & Martha Baum. (Ser. in Sociology). (Illus.). 1980. pap. text ed. 10.95 (ISBN 0-13-367797-4). P-H.

Growing Old in America: The Bland-Lee Lectures Delivered at Clark University, Expanded Edition. David H. Fischer. 1978. pap. 4.95 (ISBN 0-19-502366-8, GB532, GB). Oxford U Pr.

Growing Old in Silence. Gaylene Becker. 160p. 1980. 10.00 (ISBN 0-520-03900-9). U of Cal Pr.

Growing Old: Years of Fulfillment. Robert Kastenbaum. (Life Cycle Ser.). 1979. pap. text ed. 4.95 scp (ISBN 0-06-384750-7, HarpC). Har-Row.

Growing Orchids at Your Window. Jack Kramer. 1979. pap. 4.50 (ISBN 0-8015-3175-6, Hawthorn). Dutton.

Growing Out of Poverty. Ed. by Elizabeth Stamp. (Illus.). 1977. 12.50x (ISBN 0-19-857529-7); pap. 8.95x (ISBN 0-19-857528-9). Oxford U Pr.

Growing Pains in the Classroom: A Guide for Teachers of Adolescents. Ronald Tyrrell et al. (Illus.). 368p. 1977. text ed. 11.95 (ISBN 0-87909-312-9). Reston.

Growing Point. Alfred Heidenreich. (Illus.). 15.75 (ISBN 0-903540-17-7, Pub. by Floris Books). St George Bk Serv.

Growing Points. Elizabeth Jennings. 94p. 1975. 7.50 o.p. (ISBN 0-8023-1262-4). Dufour.

Growing Points in Ethology. Ed. by P. P. Bateson & R. A. Hinde. LC 76-8291. (Illus.). 500p. 1976. 57.50 (ISBN 0-521-21287-1); pap. 16.95x (ISBN 0-521-29086-4). Cambridge U Pr.

Growing Season. Joy Cowley. LC 77-81785. 1978. 7.95 o.p. (ISBN 0-385-04449-6). Doubleday.

Growing Season. Martha W. Hickman. LC 80-68983. 128p. (Orig.). 1980. pap. write for info. (ISBN 0-8358-0411-9). Upper Room.

Growing Soft Fruits. Ray Edwards. 1980. pap. 4.50 (ISBN 0-7153-7903-8). David & Charles.

Growing Spiritually. E. Stanley Jones. 1953. 4.95 (ISBN 0-687-15967-9). Abingdon.

Growing Strong. R. V. Fodor & G. J. Taylor. LC 79-65073. (Illus.). (gr. 4 up). 1979. 7.95 (ISBN 0-8069-4142-1); PLB 7.49 (ISBN 0-8069-4143-X). Sterling.

Growing Stronger: Two - Two. Vera Groomer. (Come Unto Me Ser.: Year 2, Bk. 2). 32p. (ps). 1980. pap. 1.50 (ISBN 0-8127-0271-9). Southern Pub.

Growing Things. Tricia Springstubb. 228p. (gr. 6). 1981. 8.95 (ISBN 0-686-69141-5, Pub. by Atlantic). Little.

Growing Through Divorce. James J. Young. LC 79-90993. (Paths of Life Ser.). 60p. (Orig.). 1979. pap. 2.45 (ISBN 0-8091-2267-7). Paulist Pr.

Growing Through Play: Readings for Parents & Teachers. Robert D. Strom. LC 80-23729. 212p. (Orig.). 1980. pap. text ed. 9.95 (ISBN 0-8185-0423-4). Brooks-Cole.

Growing Trees & Shrubs. Hugh Redgrove. (Practical Gardening Ser.). (Illus.). 96p. (Orig.). 1979. pap. 10.50 (ISBN 0-589-01247-9, Pub. by Reed Bks Australia). C E Tuttle.

Growing Trees Indoors. D. J. Herda. LC 78-37164. 1979. 14.95 (ISBN 0-88229-346-X); pap. 7.95 (ISBN 0-686-66163-X). Nelson-Hall.

Growing Unusual Vegetables. Alan Wilbur. 1980. pap. 4.50 (ISBN 0-7153-7904-6). David & Charles.

Growing Up. 4th ed. Karl De Schweinitz. (Illus.). (gr. 2-5). 1968. 4.50g o.s.i. (ISBN 0-02-729170-7). Macmillan.

Growing up: A Study of Children. J. T. Gibson. 1978. 17.95 (ISBN 0-201-02914-6); wkbk. 4.95 (ISBN 0-201-02917-0). A-W.

Growing up Alive: Humanistic Education for the Pre-Teen. Tim Timmermann. LC 75-21159. (Mandala Series in Education). (Illus.). 232p. 1975. pap. text ed. 8.95x (ISBN 0-916250-01-6). Irvington.

Growing (up) at 37. Jerry Rubin. 1977. pap. 1.95 o.s.i. (ISBN 0-446-89315-3). Warner Bks.

Growing up Between the Wars. Francis Wilkins. (Growing Up Ser.). 1979. 16.95 (ISBN 0-7134-0775-1, Pub. by Batsford England). David & Charles.

Growing up Chimpanzee. Eugenia Alston. LC 74-12307. (Illus.). 32p. (gr. 1-4). 1975. 7.95 (ISBN 0-690-00015-4, TYC-J); PLB 7.89 (ISBN 0-690-00564-4). T Y Crowell.

Growing up During the Industrial Revolution. Penny Clarke. LC 79-56472. (Growing up Ser.). (Illus.). 72p. (gr. 7 up). 1980. text ed. 14.95 (ISBN 0-7134-3370-1, Pub. by Batsford England). David & Charles.

Growing up During the Norman Conquest. Frances Wilkins. LC 79-56440. (Growing up Ser.). (gr. 7-9). 1980. text ed. 14.95 (ISBN 0-7134-3360-4, Pub. by Batsford England). David & Charles.

Growing up Forgotten: A Review of Research & Programs Concerning Early Adolescence. Joan Lipsitz. LC 76-28621. 1976. 18.95 (ISBN 0-669-00975-X). Lexington Bks.

Growing up Free: Raising Your Kids in the 80's. Lottie C. Pogrebin. LC 80-13054. 528p. 1980. 15.95 (ISBN 0-07-050370-2, GB). McGraw.

Growing up in a Hurry. Winifred Madison. (YA) (gr. 7-9). 1975. pap. 1.50 (ISBN 0-671-29988-3). PB.

Growing up in a One Parent Family. Elsa Ferri. 144p. 1976. pap. text ed. 13.75x (ISBN 0-85633-087-6, NFER). Humanities.

Growing up in Ancient Britain. Amanda Clarke. (Growing up Ser.). (Illus.). 72p. (gr. 6 up). 1981. 14.95 (ISBN 0-7134-3557-7, Pub. by Batsford England). David & Charles.

Growing up in Ancient Egypt. Sheila Ferguson. LC 79-56471. (Growing up Ser.). (Illus.). 72p. (gr. 7 up). 1980. text ed. 14.95 (ISBN 0-7134-2683-7, Pub. by Batsford England). David & Charles.

Growing up in Ancient Greece. Philippa Stewart. LC 79-56475. (Growing up Ser.). (Illus.). 72p. (gr. 7 up). 1980. text ed. 14.95 (ISBN 0-7134-3376-0, Pub. by Batsford England). David & Charles.

Growing up in Ancient Rome. Brenda R. Lewis. LC 79-56455. (Growing up Ser.). (Illus.). 72p. (gr. 7 up). 1980. text ed. 14.95 (ISBN 0-7134-3374-4, Pub. by Batsford England). David & Charles.

Growing up in Aztec Times. Brenda R. Lewis. (Growing up Ser.). (Illus.). 72p. (gr. 7-9). 1981. 15.95 (ISBN 0-7134-2734-5, Pub. by Batsford England). David & Charles.

Growing up in Care: Ten People Talking. Barbara Kahan. (Practice of Social Work Ser.: Vol. 2). 201p. 1980. 29.00x (ISBN 0-631-12171-4, Pub. by Basil Blackwell); pap. 11.50x (ISBN 0-631-12161-7). Biblio Dist.

Growing up in Christ: A Guide for Families with Adolescents. Eugene H. Peterson. LC 76-12396. 1976. pap. 3.95 (ISBN 0-8042-2026-3). John Knox.

Growing up in Church. Thelma H. Bryant. LC 79-67524. 1980. 6.95 (ISBN 0-533-04474-X). Vantage.

Growing up in Edwardian Britain. Nance L. Fyson. LC 79-56456. (Growing up Ser.). (Illus.). 72p. (gr. 7-9). 1980. text ed. 14.95 (ISBN 0-7134-3372-8, Pub. by Batsford England). David & Charles.

Growing up in Elizabethan Times. Amanda Clarke. LC 79-56439. (Growing up Ser.). (Illus.). 72p. (gr. 7 up). 1980. text ed. 14.95 (ISBN 0-7134-3364-7, Pub. by Batsford England). David & Charles.

Growing up in Flathill: Social Environment & Cognitive Development. Marida Hollos. 165p. 1974. 20.50x (ISBN 8-200-08944-4, Dist. by Columbia U Pr). Universitet.

Growing up in Inca Times. Brenda R. Lewis. (Growing up Ser.). (Illus.). 72p. (gr. 7-9). 1981. 15.95 (ISBN 0-7134-2736-1, Pub. by Batsford England). David & Charles.

Growing up in New Guinea. Margaret Mead. 8.75 (ISBN 0-8446-2569-8). Peter Smith.

Growing up in New Zealand. Jane Ritchie & James Ritchie. LC 78-52238. 1978. text ed. 13.50x (ISBN 0-86861-104-2); pap. text ed. 7.50x o.p. (ISBN 0-86861-112-3). Allen Unwin.

Growing Up in Old New England. Marc Bernheim & Evelyne Bernheim. LC 75-151160. (Illus.). (gr. 5-9). 1971. 9.95 (ISBN 0-02-709060-4, CCPr). Macmillan.

Growing up in Polynesia. Jane Ritchie & James Ritchie. 1979. text ed. 13.50x (ISBN 0-86861-201-4); pap. text ed. 9.50x (ISBN 0-86861-209-X). Allen Unwin.

Growing up in Puritan Times. Amanda Clarke. LC 79-56452. (Growing up Ser.). (Illus.). 72p. (gr. 7 up). 1980. text ed. 14.95 (ISBN 0-7134-3366-3, Pub. by Batsford England). David & Charles.

Growing up in Regency England. Madeline Jones. LC 79-56451. (Growing up Ser.). (Illus.). 72p. (gr. 7 up). 1980. text ed. 14.95 (ISBN 0-7134-3368-X, Pub. by Batsford England). David & Charles.

Growing up in Roman Britain. Frances Wilkins. (Growing up Ser.). (Illus.). 72p. (gr. 7 up). 1980. text ed. 14.95 (ISBN 0-7134-0773-5, Pub. by Batsford England). David & Charles.

Growing up in Stuart Times. Madeline Jones. (Growing Up Ser.). 1979. 16.95 (ISBN 0-7134-0771-9, Pub. by Batsford England). David & Charles.

Growing up in the Dark Ages. Brenda R. Lewis. LC 79-56478. (Growing up Ser.). (Illus.). 72p. (gr. 7 up). 1980. text ed. 16.95 (ISBN 0-7134-3362-0, Pub. by Batsford England). David & Charles.

Growing up in the Eighteenth Century. Nance L. Fyson. (Growing Up Ser.). 1977. 14.95 (ISBN 0-7134-0481-7, Pub. by Batsford England). David & Charles.

Growing up in the Medieval Times. Penny Davies. (Growing Up Ser.). 1979. 14.95 (ISBN 0-7134-0483-3, Pub. by Batsford England). David & Charles.

Growing up in the Midwest. Clarence Andrews. 168p. 1981. 11.25 (ISBN 0-8138-0250-4). Iowa St U Pr.

Growing up in the Second World War. Nance L. Fyson. (Growing up Ser.). (Illus.). 72p. (gr. 6 up). 1981. 14.95 (ISBN 0-7134-3574-7, Pub. by Batsford England). David & Charles.

Growing up in Tudor Times. Francis Wilkins. (Growing up). 1977. 16.95 (ISBN 0-7134-0479-5, Pub. by Batsford England). David & Charles.

Growing up in Victorian Britain. Sheila Ferguson. (Growing Up Ser.). 1977. 16.95 (ISBN 0-7134-0281-4, Pub. by Batsford England). David & Charles.

Growing up in Viking Times. Sheila Ferguson. (Growing up Ser.). (Illus.). 72p. (gr. 6 up). 1981. 14.95 (ISBN 0-7134-2730-2, Pub. by Batsford England). David & Charles.

Growing up Masai. Tom Shachtman. LC 80-25017. (Illus.). 56p. (gr. 3-6). 1981. PLB 8.95 (ISBN 0-02-782550-7). Macmillan.

Growing up of Mary Elizabeth. Mary M. McBride. LC 66-10854. (Illus.). (gr. 5-9). 1966. 4.50 (ISBN 0-396-05436-6). Dodd.

Growing up Puerto Rican. Ed. by Paulette Cooper. 144p. (RL 10). 1973. pap. 1.25 o.p. (ISBN 0-451-61233-7, MY1233, Ment). NAL.

Growing up: Readings on the Study of Children. Janice T. Gibson & Phyllis Blumberg. LC 77-83026. (Education Ser.). 1978. 7.95 (ISBN 0-201-02915-4); instr's man. 4.00 (ISBN 0-201-02916-2). A-W.

Growing up Southern: Southern Exposure Looks at Childhood, Then & Now. Ed. by Chris Mayfield. (Illus.). 1981. 17.95 (ISBN 0-394-50913-7); pap. 7.95 (ISBN 0-394-74809-3). Pantheon.

Growing up Thin. Alvin N. Eden & Joan R. Heilman. pap. 1.50 o.p. (ISBN 0-425-03169-1). Berkley Pub.

Growing up to Be Violent: A Longitudinal Study of the Development of Agression. M. M. Lefkowitz et al. 1976. text ed. 18.15 (ISBN 0-08-019515-6); pap. 10.25 (ISBN 0-08-019514-8). Pergamon.

Growing up with Chico. Maxine Marx. LC 80-15387. 1980. 9.95 (ISBN 0-13-367821-0). P-H.

Growing up with the North American Indians. Pat Hodgson. (Illus.). 72p. (gr. 6-10). 1980. 16.95 (ISBN 0-7134-2732-9, Pub. by Batsford England). David & Charles.

Growing Vegetables. Eric Toleman. (Practical Gardening Ser.). (Illus.). 112p. (Orig.). 1979. pap. 10.50 (ISBN 0-589-01239-8, Pub. by Reed Bks Australia). C E Tuttle.

Growing Vegetables & Herbs. Roger Grounds. (Orig.). 1980. pap. 6.95x (ISBN 0-8464-1016-8). Beekman Pubs.

Growing Vegetables in Alaska: & Other Far North Climates. Ann Roberts. (Illus.). 200p. 1981. 10.95 (ISBN 0-918270-08-1). That New Pub.

Growing Vegetables in the Pacific Northwest. Jill Severn. LC 77-29260. (Illus.). 1978. pap. 4.95 (ISBN 0-914842-25-0). Madrona Pubs.

Growing Vegetables the Big Yield-Small Space Way. Duane Newcomb. (Illus.). 272p. 1981. pap. 7.95 (ISBN 0-87477-170-6). J P Tarcher.

Growing with God. Maureen Curley. (Children of the Kingdom Activities Ser.). (ps). 1976. 7.95 (ISBN 0-686-13680-2). Pflaum Pr.

Growing-with-Language Program, 10 readers. Tanyzer et al. (gr. 2-4). text ed. 3.60 ea. o.p.; laboratory manual 1.92 ea. o.p. Pitman Learning.

Growing with Television: A Study of Biblical Values & the Television Experience - Adult Leader's Guide. Ed. by Peggy J. West. 32p. 1980. pap. 2.95 (ISBN 0-8164-2272-9). Seabury.

Growing with Your Children. Herbert Kohl. 256p. 1981. pap. 2.95 (ISBN 0-553-13923-1). Bantam.

Growing Years, 1789-1829. Margaret L. Coit. LC 63-8572. (Life History of the United States). (Illus.). (gr. 5 up). 1974. PLB 8.67 o.p. (ISBN 0-8094-0552-0, Pub. by Time-Life). Silver.

Growing Your Trees. W. Youngman & C. Randall. Date not set. 33.50 (ISBN 0-686-26730-3, 37). Am Forestry.

Growl When You Say R. Muriel Stanek. Ed. by Kathy Pacini. LC 79-171. (Concept Bk.: Level II). (Illus.). (gr. k-3). 1979. 6.50g (ISBN 0-8075-3074-3). A Whitman.

Grown-up Day. Jack Kent. LC 70-7782. (Illus.). (gr. k-2). 1969. 5.95 o.s.i. (ISBN 0-8193-0287-2, Four Winds); PLB 5.41 o.s.i. (ISBN 0-8193-0288-0). Schol Bk Serv.

Grownups Cry Too: Los Adultos Tambien Lloran. 2nd ed. Nancy Hazen. Tr. by Martha P. Cotera. LC 78-71542. (Illus.). 25p. (ps-1). 1978. pap. 2.50 (ISBN 0-914996-19-3). Lollipop Power.

Growplan Vegetable Book: A Monthly Guide Vegetable Book. Peter Peskett. (Illus.). 1978. 14.95 (ISBN 0-7153-7621-7). David & Charles.

Growth. William J. Robbins et al. 1928. 29.50x (ISBN 0-685-89755-9). Elliots Bks.

Growth: A Handbook of Classroom Ideas to Motivate the Teaching of Elementary Health. (Spice Ser.). 1975. 6.50 (ISBN 0-89273-119-2). Educ Serv.

Growth & Change in Rural America. Glenn V. Fuguitt et al. LC 79-65329. (Management & Control of Growth Ser.). 101p. 1979. pap. text ed. 14.50 (ISBN 0-87420-586-7). Urban Land.

Growth & Decline of American Philosophy. Joseph R. Schlegel. (Illus.). 1980. 33.45 (ISBN 0-89266-225-5). Am Classical Coll Pr.

Growth & Development of Children. 2nd ed. Catherine Lee. LC 76-56438. 1977. pap. text ed. 7.95x (ISBN 0-582-48828-1). Longman.

Growth & Development of Mothers. Angela B. McBride. LC 72-9138. 250p. 1973. 9.95 o.s.i. (ISBN 0-06-012899-2, HarpT). Har-Row.

Growth & Development of the Brain: Nutritional, Genetic, & Environmental Factors. Ed. by M. A. Brazier. LC 75-14565. (International Brain Research Organization Ser.: Vol. 1). 412p. 1975. 39.00 (ISBN 0-89004-037-0). Raven.

Growth & Development of Trees, 2 Vols. T. T. Kozlowski. LC 70-127688. (Physiological Ecology Ser). 1971. Vol. 1. 48.00 (ISBN 0-12-424201-4); Vol. 2. 58.00 (ISBN 0-12-424202-2); Set. 86.50 (ISBN 0-685-03085-7). Acad Pr.

Growth & Development: The Child in Physical Activity. Lionard D. Zaichkowsky et al. LC 79-23443. 1980. pap. text ed. 10.95 (ISBN 0-8016-5663-X). Mosby.

Growth & Development: With Special Reference to Developing Economics. 2nd ed. A. P. Thirlwall. LC 77-8582. 1978. 24.95 (ISBN 0-470-99214-X); pap. 14.95 (ISBN 0-470-26988-X). Halsted Pr.

Growth & Diffentiation in Plants. 3rd ed. P. F. Wareing & I. D. Phillips. Orig. Title: The Control of Growth & Differentiation in Plants. (Illus.). 176p. 1981. 38.00 (ISBN 0-08-026351-8); pap. 19.00 (ISBN 0-08-026350-X). Pergamon.

Growth & Differentiation in Physarum Polycephalum. Ed. by W. F. Dove & H. P. Rusch. LC 79-3202. (Illus.). 240p. 1980. 25.00x (ISBN 0-691-08254-5). Princeton U Pr.

Growth & Financing of the Firm: Models of Firm Behavior Tested with Data from Swedish Industrial Firms. Goran Eriksson. LC 77-26840. 1978. 29.95 (ISBN 0-470-99230-1). Halsted Pr.

Growth & Income Distribution. L. L. Pasinetti. LC 74-76579. (Illus.). 180p. 1974. 29.95 (ISBN 0-521-20474-7); pap. 13.95x (ISBN 0-521-29543-2). Cambridge U Pr.

Growth & Nature of Drama. R. F. Clarke. 1965. 4.95x (ISBN 0-521-04672-6). Cambridge U Pr.

Growth & Reform in Centrally Planned Economics: The Lessons of the Bulgarian Experience. George R. Feiwel. LC 76-12849. 1977. text ed. 31.95 (ISBN 0-275-23330-8). Praeger.

Growth & Regulation of Animal Populations. Lawrence B. Slobodkin. (Illus.). 1980. pap. 6.00 (ISBN 0-486-63958-4). Dover.

Growth & Stability in a Mature Economy. John Cornwall. 1976. pap. 28.00x (ISBN 0-85520-100-2, Pub. by Martin Robertson England). Biblio Dist.

Growth & Structure in the Economy of Modern Italy. George H. Hildebrand. LC 65-24450. 1965. 20.00x (ISBN 0-674-36450-3). Harvard U Pr.

Growth & Structure of Elizabethan Comedy. Muriel C. Bradbrook. LC 79-2313. (History of Elizabethan Drama Ser.: Vol. 2). 1979. pap. 10.95 (ISBN 0-521-29526-2). Cambridge U Pr.

Growth & Structure of Elizabethan Comedy. Muriel C. Bradbrook. 1955. text ed. 15.75x (ISBN 0-391-00319-4). Humanities.

Growth Centres in Spatial Planning. Malcolm Moseley. LC 74-9962. 1974. text ed. 19.00 (ISBN 0-08-018055-8). Pergamon.

Growth Centres in the European Urban System. Peter Hall & Dennis Hay. 1980. 28.50 o.p. (ISBN 0-520-04198-4). U of Cal Pr.

Growth Chamber Manual: Environmental Control for Plants. Ed. by Robert W. Langhans. LC 77-90906. (Illus.). 240p. 1978. 19.50x (ISBN 0-8014-1169-6). Comstock.

Growth Control, Differentiation, & Aging of the Eye Lens. Ed. by O. Bonn Hockwin. (Journal: Ophthalmic Research, Vol. 11, No. 5-6, 1979). (Illus.). 242p. 1979. softcover 29.50 (ISBN 3-8055-0862-X). S Karger.

Growth, Development, & Pattern. Norman J. Berrill. LC 61-8356. (Illus.). 1961. 26.95x (ISBN 0-7167-0607-5). W H Freeman.

Growth Encounter: A Guide for Groups. Kurt Haas. LC 75-2180. 1975. 15.95 (ISBN 0-88229-225-0). Nelson-Hall.

Growth, Equality, & the Mexican Experience. Morris Singer. (Latin American Monographs: No. 16). (Illus.). 1969. 15.00 (ISBN 0-292-70011-3). U of Tex Pr.

Growth for Water Treatment Chemicals. 1981. 850.00 (ISBN 0-89336-065-1, C002R). BCC.

Growth Group Leader's Guide. rev. ed. Churches Alive, Inc. (Illus.). 110p. 1980. pap. 6.50 (ISBN 0-934396-10-8). Churches Alive.

Growth Group Member's Notebook. Churches Alive Inc. (Illus.). 105p. (Orig.). 1980. pap. text ed. 5.00 (ISBN 0-934396-11-6). Churches Alive.

Growth in Advanced Capitalist Economics: 1950-1970. T. F. Cripps & R. J. Tarling. LC 73-84317. (Dept. of Applied Economics, Occasional Papers: No. 40). (Illus.). 64p. 1973. 6.95x (ISBN 0-521-09828-9). Cambridge U Pr.

Growth in Animals. Lawrence. LC 79-41574. (SAFS). 1980. 52.95 (ISBN 0-408-10638-7). Butterworths.

Growth in Ministry. Ed. by Thomas E. Kadel. LC 79-8902. 180p. 1980. pap. 5.95 (ISBN 0-8006-1383-X, 1-1383). Fortress.

Growth in Open Economics. J. A. Hanson. (Lecture Notes in Economics & Mathematical Systems: Vol. 59). (Illus.). 135p. 1971. pap. 10.70 o.p. (ISBN 0-387-05671-8). Springer-Verlag.

Growth in Prayer. Jim Wilson. 1961. pap. 3.25 (ISBN 0-227-67475-8). Attic Pr.

Growth Mechanisms & Silicon Nitride. Wilcox. Date not set. price not set (ISBN 0-8247-1368-0). Dekker.

Growth Multiplier & a General Theory of Economic Growth. V. Mishra. 5.00x o.p. (ISBN 0-210-33999-3). Asia.

Growth, Nutrition & Metabolism of Cells in Culture. Ed. by George H. Rothblat & Vincent J. Christofalo. Vol. 1, 1972. 51.50 (ISBN 0-12-598301-8); Vol. 2, 1972. 51.50 (ISBN 0-12-598302-6); Vol. 3, 1977. 39.00 (ISBN 0-12-598303-4); Set. 122.50. Acad Pr.

Growth of a Party System in Ceylon. Calvin A. Woodward. LC 76-89465. (Illus.). 338p. 1969. 12.50x (ISBN 0-87057-115-X, Pub. by Brown U Pr). Univ Pr of New England.

Growth of a Prehistoric Time Scale, Based on Organic Evolution. William B. Berry. LC 68-14224. (Illus.). 1968. pap. 6.95x (ISBN 0-7167-0237-1). W H Freeman.

Growth of American Politics: A Modern Reader. Frank O. Gatell et al. Incl. Vol. 1. Through Reconstruction. o.p.; pap. 6.95x (ISBN 0-19-501545-2); Vol. 2. Since the Civil War. o.p.; pap. 6.95x (ISBN 0-19-501547-9). 1972. Oxford U Pr.

Growth of American State Constitutions. J. Q. Dealey. LC 75-124891. (American Constitutional & Legal History Ser). 308p. 1972. Repr. of 1915 ed. lib. bdg. 32.50 (ISBN 0-306-71985-1). Da Capo.

Growth of Bureaucratic Medicine: An Inquiry into the Dynamics of Patient Behavior & the Organization of Medical Care. David Mechanic. LC 75-29347. (Health, Medicine & Society Ser.). 368p. 1976. 19.95 o.p. (ISBN 0-471-59021-5, Pub. by Wiley-Interscience). Wiley.

Growth of Christian Faith. George Ferries. 385p. Repr. of 1905 ed. 3.50 (ISBN 0-567-02106-8). Attic Pr.

Growth of Cities. David Lewis. LC 70-171916. 1971. 32.95 (ISBN 0-471-53198-7). Halsted Pr.

Growth of Civilization in East Asia. Peter Lum. LC 73-77311. (Illus.). (gr. 8 up). 1969. 10.95 (ISBN 0-87599-144-0). S G Phillips.

Growth of Collective Economy, 2 vols. Francis E. Lawley. (Studies in International Economics: No. 1). Repr. of 1938 ed. Set. lib. bdg. 57.50x (ISBN 0-87991-850-0). Porcupine Pr.

Growth of Criminal Law in Ancient Greece. George M. Calhoun. LC 73-10874. 179p. 1974. Repr. of 1927 ed. lib. bdg. 15.00x (ISBN 0-8371-7043-5, CACL). Greenwood.

Growth of Crystals, Vol. 12. Ed. by A. A. Chernov. (Illus.). 400p. 1981. 47.50 (ISBN 0-306-18112-6, Consultants). Plenum Pub.

Growth of English Law. Being Studies in the Evolution of Law & Procedure in England. Edward S. Roscoe. viii, 260p. 1980. Repr. of 1911 ed. lib. bdg. 26.00x (ISBN 0-8377-1029-4). Rothman.

Growth of English Representative Government. George L. Haskins. 7.50 (ISBN 0-8446-2216-8). Peter Smith.

Growth of English Representative Government. George L. Haskins. pap. 3.95 o.p. (ISBN 0-498-04003-8, Prpta). A S Barnes.

Growth of European Mixed Economics 1945-1970: A Concise Study of the Economic Evolution of Six Countries. S. Lieberman. 347p. 1979. 22.95 (ISBN 0-470-99168-2). Halsted Pr.

Growth of Human Behavior. 3rd ed. Norman L. Munn. 512p. 1974. text ed. 20.95 (ISBN 0-395-17017-6). HM.

Growth of Industrial Britain: A Work Book & Study Guide in Social & Economic History. Ed. by J. A. Morris. (Illus.). 1971. text ed. 16.95x (ISBN 0-245-50324-2). Intl Ideas.

Growth of Latin American Cities. Walter D. Harris, Jr. LC 76-141378. (Illus.). xvii, 314p. 1971. 17.95x (ISBN 0-8214-0086-X). Ohio U Pr.

Growth of Medical Information Systems in the United States. Donald A. Lindberg. LC 79-1555. 208p. 1979. 21.95 (ISBN 0-669-02911-4). Lexington Bks.

Growth of Nursing Home Care. Burton D. Dunlop. LC 78-14715. 1979. 18.95 (ISBN 0-669-02704-9). Lexington Bks.

Growth of Philosophic Radicalism. 3rd ed. Elie Halevy. (Orig.). 1972. 13.95 (ISBN 0-571-04759-9, Pub. by Faber & Faber); pap. 6.95 (ISBN 0-571-09787-1). Merrimack Bk Serv.

Growth of Presidential Power: A Documented History, 3 vols. Ed. by William M. Goldsmith. LC 74-9623. 1981. Repr. of 1974 ed. 96.50 set (ISBN 0-87754-125-6). Chelsea Hse.

Growth of Public Employment in Canada. Richard M. Bird. 190p. 1979. pap. text ed. 12.95x (ISBN 0-920380-17-4, Pub. by Inst Res Pub Canada). Renouf.

Growth of Public Expenditure in the United Kingdom. Alan T. Peacock & Jack Wiseman. (University of York Studies in Economics). 1967. pap. text ed. 7.95x o.p. (ISBN 0-04-336011-4). Allen Unwin.

Growth of Reform Judaism: American & European Sources Until 1948. Ed. by W. Gunther Plaut. 1965. 10.00 (ISBN 0-8074-0086-6, 382780). UAHC.

Growth of Southern Civilization, 1790-1860. Clement Eaton. (New American Nation Ser). (Illus.). pap. 6.95x (ISBN 0-06-133040-X, TB3040, Torch). Har-Row.

Growth of the Biblical Tradition. Klaus Koch. 1968. lib. rep. ed. 17.50x (ISBN 0-684-14524-3, ScribT). Scribner.

Growth of the Child: Reflections on Human Development. Jerome Kagan. (Illus.). 1978 12.95 (ISBN 0-393-01173-9); pap. 5.95x, 1979 (ISBN 0-393-95084-0). Norton.

Growth of the Gospels. Neil J. McEleney. LC 79-90141. (Orig.). 1980. pap. 3.95 (ISBN 0-8091-2243-X). Paulist Pr.

Growth of the Law. Benjamin N. Cardozo. LC 73-8154. xvi, 145p. 1973. Repr. of 1963 ed. lib. bdg. 15.75x (ISBN 0-8371-6953-4, CAGL). Greenwood.

Growth of the State. Malcolm Yapp. Ed. by Margaret Killingray & Edmund O'Connor. (Greenhaven World History Ser.). (Illus.). 32p. (gr. 10). 1980. Repr. of 1977 ed. lib. bdg. 5.95 (ISBN 0-89908-229-7); pap. text ed. 1.95 (ISBN 0-89908-204-1). Greenhaven.

Growth of the Surface Area of the Human Body. Edith Boyd. LC 75-14249. (Univ. of Minnesota, the Institute of Child Welfare Monograph: No. 10). (Illus.). 145p. 1975. Repr. of 1935 ed. lib. bdg. 14.00x (ISBN 0-8371-8069-4, CWBS). Greenwood.

Growth of U. S. Population. Committee on Population. 1965. pap. 2.50 (ISBN 0-309-01279-1). Natl Acad Pr.

Growth Patterns & Sex Education: Bibliography. 1972. 2.50 (ISBN 0-917160-07-X). Am Sch Health.

Growth Patterns & Sex Education, K-12. 1967. 3.50 (ISBN 0-917160-06-1). Am Sch Health.

Growth Points in Nuclear Physics, Vol. 1. P. E. Hodgson. (Illus.). 1980. 21.00 (ISBN 0-08-023080-6); pap. 9.50 (ISBN 0-08-023079-2). Pergamon.

Growth Points in Nuclear Physics, Vol. 2. P. E. Hodgson. (Illus.). 1980. 21.00 (ISBN 0-08-023082-2); pap. text ed. 9.50 (ISBN 0-08-023081-4). Pergamon.

Growth Pole Strategy & Regional Development Policy: Asian Experiences & Alternative Approaches. Ed. by Lo Fu-Chen & K. Salih. (Illus.). 1978. text ed. 55.00 (ISBN 0-08-021984-5). Pergamon.

Growth Problems & Clinical Advances: Proceedings. Birth Defects Conference, Kansas City, Mo., May 1975. Ed. by Daniel Bergsma & R. Neil Schimke. LC 76-21714. (Birth Defects - Original Article Ser.: Vol. 12, No. 6). 340p. 1976. 35.00x (ISBN 0-8451-1005-5). A R Liss.

Growth, Productivity & Relative Prices. Anders Olgaard. (Institute of Economics Univ. of Copenhagen). 1966. text ed. 23.00x (ISBN 0-7204-3028-3, Pub. by North Holland). Humanities.

Growth, Profits & Property. Ed. by Edward J. Nell. LC 79-47192. (Illus.). 352p. 1980. 39.50 (ISBN 0-521-22396-2). Cambridge U Pr.

Growth Regulation by Ion Fluxes. Ed. by H. L. Leffert. LC 80-13986. (N.Y. Academy of Sciences Annals: Vol. 339). 340p. 60.00x (ISBN 0-89766-049-8). NY Acad Sci.

Growth Requirements of Vertebrate Cells in Vitro. Ed. by Charity Waymouth et al. (Illus.). 480p. Date not set. price not set (ISBN 0-521-23019-5). Cambridge U Pr.

Growth Theory: An Exposition. Robert M. Solow. (Illus.). 1970. 8.95x (ISBN 0-19-501295-X). Oxford U Pr.

Growth to Selfhood: The Sufi Contribution. A. Reza Arasteh. (Orig.). 1980. pap. 8.50 (ISBN 0-7100-0355-2). Routledge & Kegan.

Growth with Equity: Strategies for Meeting Human Needs. Ed. by Mary E. Jegen & Charles K. Wilbur. LC 78-70818. 242p. (Orig.). 1979. pap. 4.95. Paulist Pr.

Growth with Equity: The Taiwan Case. John Fei et al. 1980. 14.95x (ISBN 0-19-520115-9); pap. 5.95x (ISBN 0-19-520116-7). Oxford U Pr.

Growth with Self-Management: Yugoslav Industrialization 1952-1975. John H. Moore. LC 79-2464. (Publication Ser.: No. 220). (Illus.). 350p. 1980. 17.95 (ISBN 0-8179-7201-3). Hoover Inst Pr.

Growth Without Ecodisasters: Proceedings. International Conference on Environment Future, 2nd. Ed. by Nicholas Polunin. LC 78-26933. 1979. 49.95 (ISBN 0-470-26615-5). Halsted Pr.

Grub & Stakers Move a Mountain. Alisa Craig. LC 80-2074. (Crime Club Ser.). 192p. 1981. 9.95 (ISBN 0-385-17411-X). Doubleday.

Grub-Street Opera. Henry Fielding. Ed. by Edgar V. Roberts. LC 67-12642. (Regents Restoration Drama Ser). 1968. 9.95x (ISBN 0-8032-0360-8); pap. 2.95x (ISBN 0-8032-5359-1, BB 264, Bison). U of Nebr Pr.

Grudge. Paul Chevalier. 352p. 1981. 11.95 (ISBN 0-312-35190-9). St Martin.

Gruene Heinrich. Gottfried Keller. (Insel-Bibliothek). 874p. (Ger.). 1980. 104.00 (ISBN 3-458-04821-9, Pub. by Insel Verlag Germany); text ed. 44.20 (ISBN 3-458-04937-1). Suhrkamp.

Grumley the Grouch. Majorie W. Sharmat. LC 79-28290. (Illus.). 32p. (ps). 1980. PLB 7.95 (ISBN 0-8234-0410-2). Holiday.

Grundfragen Des Mathematikunterrichts. E. Wittmann. 202p. (Ger.). 1978. pap. 13.50 (ISBN 3-528-48332-6). Birkhauser.

Grundprobleme der Operngeschichte. Hermann J. Abert. LC 80-2253. 1981. Repr. of 1926 ed. 14.00 (ISBN 0-404-18800-1). AMS Pr.

Grundriss der Vergleichenden Grammatik der Indogermanischen Sprachen, 5 vols. Karl Brugmann & Berthold Delbrueck. (Ger). 1970. Repr. of 1893 ed. 576.00x (ISBN 3-11-000180-2). De Gruyter.

Grundzuege deutscher Sprachgeschichte: Band 1. Stefan Sonderegger. 1979. text ed. 52.00x (ISBN 3-11-003570-7). De Gruyter.

Grunfeld Defence. William R. Hartston. 1973. 17.50 (ISBN 0-7134-0377-2). David & Charles.

Gruppe 47: Ein Querschmitt. E. W. Trahan. 1969. text ed. 7.95x o.p. (ISBN 0-471-00595-9). Wiley.

Gryphon in Glory. Andre Norton. LC 80-24835. 132p. (gr. 7 up). 1981. 9.95 (ISBN 0-689-50195-1, McElderry Book). Atheneum.

GS 1 Skill booklet. Barbara J. Crane. (Crane Reading System - English Ser.). (Illus.). (gr. k-2). 1977. pap. text ed. 12.20 per 10 (ISBN 0-89075-041-6). Crane Pub Co.

GTO: A Source Book. Ed. by Thomas E. Bonsall. (Illus.). 142p. (Orig.). 1980. pap. 12.95 (ISBN 0-934780-03-X). Bookman Dan.

Guadalcanal. Edwin P. Hoyt. LC 80-5433. 320p. 1981. 14.95 (ISBN 0-8128-2735-X). Stein & Day.

Guadalupe Mountains of Texas, Vol 10. Alan Tennant. (Elma Dill Russell Spencer Foundation Ser: Vol. 10). (Illus.). 160p. Date not set. 29.95 (ISBN 0-292-72720-8). U of Tex Pr.

Guaianolides & Germacranolides. Frantisek Sorm & Ladislaw Dolejs. LC 66-16515. 1966. 20.00x (ISBN 0-8162-8261-7). Holden-Day.

Guale: The Golden Coast of Georgia. James Valentine & Robert Hanie. LC 74-17220. (Earth's Wild Places Ser). (Illus.). 143p. 1974. 25.00 o.s.i. (ISBN 0-913890-02-2). Friends Earth.

Guanghou Conference on Theoretical Particle Physics, 1980: Proceedings, 2 vols. 1980. text ed. 89.50 (ISBN 0-442-20273-3). Van Nos Reinhold.

Guano Islands of Peru. (Young Americans Ser). (Illus.). 1973. pap. 1.00 (ISBN 0-8270-4900-5). OAS.

Guardian. John C. Stephens. LC 79-57559. 112p. 1981. 13.50x (ISBN 0-8131-1422-5). U Pr of Ky.

Guardian of the Heart. Caroline Courtney. (Large Print Bks.). 1980. lib. bdg. 11.95 (ISBN 0-8161-3095-7). G K Hall.

Guardians. John Christopher. (gr. 6 up). 1970. 5.95g o.s.i. (ISBN 0-02-718370-X). Macmillan.

Guardians of the Flutes: Idioms of Masculinity. Gilbert H. Herdt. (Illus.). 1980. 17.95 (ISBN 0-07-028315-X). McGraw.

Guardians of Tradition: American Schoolbooks of the Nineteenth Century. Ruth M. Elson. LC 64-17219. (Illus.). 1972. pap. 3.25x (ISBN 0-8032-5755-4, BB 553, Bison). U of Nebr Pr.

Guarding of Cultural Property: Protection of the Cultural Heritage - Technical Handbooks for Museums & Monuments. (Illus.). 40p. 1978. pap. 4.75 (ISBN 92-3-101429-3, U813, UNESCO). Unipub.

Guarding the Treasured Lands: The Story of the National Park Service. Ann Sutton & Myron Sutton. LC 65-13436. (Illus.). (gr. 7-9). 1965. 4.95 o.p. (ISBN 0-397-30805-1). Lippincott.

Guards. Robert Armstrong. (Stars of the NBA Ser.). (Illus.). (gr. 4-12). 1977. PLB 7.95 (ISBN 0-87191-564-2). Creative Ed.

Guards. John de St. Jorre. 1981. 25.00 (ISBN 0-517-54376-1). Crown.

Guarneri: Story of a Genius. Leonard Wibberley. LC 74-8142. 160p. (gr. 7 up). 1974. 5.95 (ISBN 0-374-32822-6). FS&G.

Guatemala. Woodman B. Franklin. (World Bibliographical Ser.: No. 9). 1981. write for info. (ISBN 0-903450-24-0). Abc-Clio.

Guatemala Guide. Paul Glassman. (Orig.). 1982. pap. 12.95 (ISBN 0-930016-02-5). Passport Pr.

Guatemala Guide. Paul Glassman. LC 77-74034. (Illus.). 1978. 10.00 (ISBN 0-930016-00-9). Passport Pr.

Guatemala-Indios De Guatemala. G. E. Holton. (Illus.). 10.00 o.p. (ISBN 0-911268-08-1). Rogers Bk.

Guatemalan Backstrap Weaving. Norbert Sperlich & Elizabeth K. Sperlich. LC 79-56663. (Illus.). 275p. 1980. 25.00 (ISBN 0-8061-1571-8). U of Okla Pr.

Guatemalan Caudillo: The Regime of Jorge Ubica, Guatemala, 1931-1944. Kenneth J. Grieb. LC 78-14339. 384p. 1979. 18.00x (ISBN 0-8214-0379-6). Ohio U Pr.

Guatemalan Sociology. Miguel Asturias. Tr. by Maureen Ahern. LC 77-8270. 1977. 12.95x o.p. (ISBN 0-87918-035-8); pap. 7.95x (ISBN 0-87918-037-4). ASU Lat Am St.

Guatimala, or the Republic of Central America, in 1827-8: Being Sketches & Memorandums Made During a Twelve-Months Residence. Henry Dunn. LC 80-25556. 1981. Repr. of 1829 ed. 25.00 (ISBN 0-87917-073-5). Blaine Ethridge.

Gueri Du Cancer. Tr. by Jill Lawson. (French Bks.). (Fr.). 1979. 1.85 (ISBN 0-686-28820-3). Life Pubs Intl.

Gueridon & Lamp Cookery. 2nd ed. John Fuller. 1975. 21.95 (ISBN 0-685-88360-4). Radio City.

Guerilla. Jack Slade. (Lassiter Ser). 1976. pap. 1.25 (ISBN 0-505-51105-3). Tower Bks.

Guerillas & Terrorists. Richard Clutterbock. 1977. 10.95 (ISBN 0-571-11027-4, Pub. by Faber & Faber). Merrimack Bk Serv.

Guernica. Gordon Thomas & Max M. Witts. 1977. pap. 1.95 o.p. (ISBN 0-345-25454-6). Ballantine.

Guernica & Other Plays. Fernando Arrabal. Tr. by Barbara Wright from Fr. Incl. Labyrinth; Tricycle; Picnic on the Battlefield. 1969. pap. 4.95 (ISBN 0-394-17318-X, E521, Ever). Grove.

Guernica! Guernica! A Study of Journalism, Diplomacy, Propaganda, & History. Herbert R. Southworth. LC 74-82850. 1977. 25.00x (ISBN 0-520-02830-9). U of Cal Pr.

Guernica: Studies - Postscripts. Schapiro. Date not set. 20.00 (ISBN 0-8076-0983-8). Braziller.

Guernsey. G. W. Robinson. LC 76-58788. 1977. 14.95 (ISBN 0-7153-7341-2). David & Charles.

Guerre Est Finie. J. Semprun. Tr. by Richard Seaver. (Illus., Text for the film by Alain Resnais. Film editor Robert Hughes.). 5.75 (ISBN 0-8446-2906-5). Peter Smith.

Guerrilla Attack. Jon Hart. LC 80-71035. (Mercenaries Ser.). 128p. 1981. pap. 2.95 (ISBN 0-87754-243-0). Chelsea Hse.

Guerrilla Warfare. Bert Y. Levy. Ed. by Robert K. Brown. LC 64-6189. (Illus.). 119p. 1965. pap. 5.00 (ISBN 0-87364-020-9). Paladin Ent.

Guerrilla Warfare & Terrorism. Stephen Goode. (gr. 8 up). 1977. PLB 6.90 s&l o.p. (ISBN 0-531-00383-3). Watts.

Guerrillas & Terrorists. Richard Clutterbuck. LC 80-83219. 125p. 1980. 12.00x (ISBN 0-8214-0590-X); pap. 5.95x (ISBN 0-8214-0592-6). Ohio U Pr.

Guerrillas in the Bureaucracy: The Community Planning Experiment in the United States. Martin L. Needleman & Carolyn E. Needleman. LC 73-19806. (Urban Research Ser.). 384p. 1974. 22.95 (ISBN 0-471-63099-3, Pub. by Wiley-Interscience). Wiley.

Guess What Grasses Do. Barbara Rinkoff. LC 76-177316. (gr. k-3). 1972. 7.25 o.p. (ISBN 0-688-41592-X); PLB 6.96 o.p. (ISBN 0-688-51592-4). Lothrop.

Guess What I Am, Vol. 2. (Vegetable Puppets Ser.). (Illus.). 10p. (ps). 1979. 2.50 o.p. (ISBN 0-89346-117-2, Pub. by Froebel-Kan Japan). Heian Intl.

Guess What I Am Thinking of... Linda P. Silbert & Alvin J. Silbert. (Little Twirps, TM Creative Thinking Wkbks.). (Illus.). (gr. 2-6). 1977. wkbk. 2.25 (ISBN 0-89544-021-0, 021). Silbert Bress.

Guess Who's Coming to My Tea Party. Barbara Williams. LC 77-10548. (ps-1). 1978. 5.95 o.p. (ISBN 0-03-021541-2). HR&W.

Guess Who's Cooking Dinner: One Hundred & Fifty Recipes from the Famous, the Near Famous & the Super Famous. Maria A. Bell. (Illus.). 1979. 12.95 (ISBN 0-8027-0614-2); pap. 6.95 (ISBN 0-8027-7141-6). Walker & Co.

Guest. James Marshall. (gr. k-3). 1981. pap. 3.45x (ISBN 0-395-31127-6). HM.

Guest of the Soul. Samuel L. Brengle. 1978. pap. 3.25 (ISBN 0-86544-001-8). Salvation Army.

Guestward Ho. Patrick Dennis & Barbara Hooton. LC 56-5034. 1955. 8.95 (ISBN 0-8149-0086-0). Vanguard.

Guestworkers in Germany: Prospects for Pluralism. Ray C. Rist. LC 78-6282. (Praeger Special Studies). 1978. 27.95 (ISBN 0-03-040766-4). Praeger.

Guggenheim Museum Collection: Paintings 1880-1945, 2 vols. Angelica Z. Rudenstine. LC 75-37356. (Illus.). 1976. Set. 85.00x (ISBN 0-89207-002-1); pap. 40.00x (ISBN 0-685-70089-5). S R Guggenheim.

Guggenheim Museum: Justin K. Thannhauser Collection. new ed. Vivian E. Barnett. LC 78-66357. (Illus.). 1978. 24.50 (ISBN 0-89207-016-1); pap. 15.50 (ISBN 0-685-91431-3). S R Guggenheim.

Guia Chilton Pare la Diagnosis De Averias En el Automovil. Chilton's Automotive Editorial Department. (Illus.). 130p. (Span.). 1975. 8.95 (ISBN 0-8019-6353-2); pap. 8.95 (ISBN 0-8019-6176-9). Chilton.

Guia De Estudios Sobre Bases Biblicas De la Etica. Julian C. Bridges. 1978. Repr. of 1973 ed. 2.75 (ISBN 0-311-43505-X). Casa Bautista.

Guia De Estudios Sobre Estudios En el Nuevo Testamento. Carlos Allen. (Illus.). 96p. Date not set. pap. price not set (ISBN 0-311-43502-5). Casa Bautista.

Guia De las Fuentes En Hispanoamerica Para el Estudio De la Administracion Virreinal Espanola En Mexico y En el Peru 1535-1700. OAS General Secretariat. 523p. 1980. pap. 15.00 (ISBN 0-8270-1091-5). OAS.

Guia Para Padres Al a Montessori. Aline D. Wolf. (Illus., Sp.). 1979. 5.00 (ISBN 0-9601016-3-2). Parent-Child Pr.

Guia Pare la Reparacion y Afinacion Del Volkswagen 1, 1949-1971. 2nd ed. Chilton's Automotive Editorial Department. (Illus.). 222p. (Span.). 1975. 8.95 (ISBN 0-8019-6354-0); pap. 8.95 (ISBN 0-8019-6175-0). Chilton.

Guia Rapida de Poblacion del Population Reference Bureau. Arthur Haupt & Thomas T. Kane. LC 79-9639. (Illus.). 80p. (Orig., Span.). 1980. pap. 3.00 (ISBN 0-917136-05-5). Population Ref.

Guidance: A Behavioral Approach. Richard H. Byrne. (Illus.). 1977. lib. bdg. 17.95 (ISBN 0-13-368001-0). P-H.

Guidance & Control 1979. Ed. by Robert D. Culp. LC 57-43769. (Advances in the Astronautical Sciences: Vol. 39). lib. bdg. 45.00x (ISBN 0-87703-100-2); fiche suppl. 5.00 (ISBN 0-87703-128-2). Univelt Inc.

Guidance & Control 1980. Ed. by L. A. Morine. LC 57-43769. (Advances in the Astronautical Sciences: Vol. 42). (Illus.). 738p. 1980. lib. bdg. 60.00x (ISBN 0-87703-137-1); pap. 45.00x (ISBN 0-87703-138-X). Univelt Inc.

Guidance & Counseling Around the World. Victor J. Drapela. LC 79-64966. 344p. 1981. lib. bdg. 20.50 (ISBN 0-8191-1384-0); pap. text ed. 11.50 (ISBN 0-8191-0777-3). U Pr of Amer.

Guidance & Counselling in British Schools. 2nd ed. Ed. by Hugh Lytton & Maurice Craft. 1974. pap. 11.95x (ISBN 0-7131-1860-1). Intl Ideas.

Guidance & God's Will. Tom Stark & Joan Stark. (Fisherman Bible Study Guide Ser.). 1978. saddle stitch 1.95 (ISBN 0-87788-324-6). Shaw Pubs.

Guidance for Today & Tomorrow: A Selection from the Writings of Shoghi Effendi. Shoghi Effendi. 1953. pap. 5.00 (ISBN 0-900125-14-4, 7-08-27). Baha'i.

Guidance: Foundations, Principles & Techniques. 2nd ed. Edward C. Glanz. 1974. text ed. 15.95x o.s.i. (ISBN 0-205-04280-5, 224280X). Allyn.

Guidance Function: Research & Precptions. Alice Bruce. 1977. pap. 10.00 o.p. (ISBN 0-686-00909-6, D-105). Essence Pubns.

Guidance in the Homeroom. Ruth Fedder. LC 67-24642. 1967. pap. text ed. 5.00x (ISBN 0-8077-1308-2). Tchrs Coll.

Guidance in the Secondary School: An Annotated Bibliography of Literature, Materials & Tests. Margaret I. Reid & Robert J. McDowell. (Occasional Reports Ser.: No. 2). 1976. pap. text ed. 7.75x (ISBN 0-85633-102-3, NFER). Humanities.

Guidance in Today's Schools. 3rd ed. Donald Mortensen & Alan Schmuller. LC 75-35989. 1976. text ed. 24.95 (ISBN 0-471-61779-2). Wiley.

Guidance Manual to Providing Neighborhood Services. S. J. Fitzsimmons et al. LC 77-5225. 1977. PLB 12.50x (ISBN 0-89158-242-8). Westview.

Guidance of Exceptional Children. 2nd ed. John C. Gowan et al. LC 70-185135. 1980. pap. 10.95x (ISBN 0-582-28169-5, Pub. by MacKay). Longman.

Guidance of Young Children. Marion C. Marion. (Illus.). 226p. 1981. pap. text ed. 7.95 (ISBN 0-8016-3108-4). Mosby.

Guidance: Principles & Services. 3rd ed. Frank W. Miller et al. (Guidance Ser.). 1977. text ed. 18.95 (ISBN 0-675-08461-X). Merrill.

Guidance: Program Development & Management. 3rd ed. Herman J. Peters & Bruce Shertzer. (Education-Guidance & Counseling Ser.). 640p. 1974. text ed. 19.95x (ISBN 0-675-08825-9). Merrill.

Guidance Towards Self-Government in British Colonies: 1941-1971, Vol. 5. D. J. Morgan. (Official History of Colonial Development Ser.). 1980. text ed. cancelled (ISBN 0-391-01688-1). Humanities.

Guide & Compendium for the Lawyer's Secretary, No. 4. rev. ed. LC 75-1667. 1979. 26.50 (ISBN 0-915362-13-9). M K Heller.

Guide & Manual for History 17B at Imperial Valley College. Samson. 1976. pap. text ed. 3.95 o.p. (ISBN 0-8403-0721-7). Kendall-Hunt.

Guide Book for Teaching Composition. new ed. Gene Stanford & Marie Smith. 1977. pap. text ed. 18.95 (ISBN 0-205-05872-8). Allyn.

Guide Book for Teaching Creative Writing. new ed. Gene Stanford & Marie Smith. 1977. pap. text ed. 16.95 (ISBN 0-205-05873-6). Allyn.

Guide Book of Mexican Coins. T. V. Buttrey. (Whitman Coin Hobby Books). (Illus.). 1977. pap. 4.95 o.p. (ISBN 0-307-09098-1). Western Pub.

Guide Book of United States Coins. R. S. Yeoman. 1979. 4.95 (ISBN 0-307-09051-5, Golden Pr). Western Pub.

Guide De Demographie. Arthur Haupt & Thomas T. Kane. (Illus.). 80p. (Orig., Fr.). 1980. pap. 3.00 (ISBN 0-917136-06-3). Population Ref.

Guide Des Sources De l'Histoire Des Etats-Unis Dans les Archives Francaises. Jean Favier. (Orig., Fr.). 1977. pap. text ed. 35.00x o.p. (ISBN 0-8287-1378-2). Clearwater Pub.

Guide for a Review of a Financial Forecast. 1980. pap. 6.00. Am Inst CPA.

Guide for an English Curriculum for the Eighties. Allan A. Glatthorn. 1980. pap. 6.50 (ISBN 0-8141-1922-0). NCTE.

Guide for Authors: Manuscript, Proof & Illustration. 2nd ed. Payne E. Thomas. (Illus.). 96p. 1980. pap. 5.25 (ISBN 0-398-03443-5). C C Thomas.

Guide for Beginning Psychotherapists. Joan S. Zaro. LC 77-76080. 1977. 27.50 (ISBN 0-521-21687-7); pap. 7.95 (ISBN 0-521-29230-1). Cambridge U Pr.

Guide for Bridge Maintenance Management. 1980. 3.00. AASHTO.

Guide for Citizen Action. (Illus.). 1980. pap. 3.98 (ISBN 0-930698-12-6). Natl Audubon.

Guide for Collection, Analysis, & Use of Urban Stormwater Data: Proceedings. ASCE Urban Water Resources Research Council Conference, Nov. 1976. Compiled By American Society of Civil Engineers. 128p. 1977. pap. text ed. 5.75 (ISBN 0-87262-077-8). Am Soc Civil Eng.

Guide for Collectors of Oral Traditions & Folk Cultural Materials in Pennsylvania. MacEdward Leach & Henry Glassie. (Illus., Orig.). 1973. pap. 2.00 (ISBN 0-911124-60-8). Pa Hist & Mus.

Guide for Control & Cleanup of Hazardous Materials. 1975. 0.75. AASHTO.

Guide for Determining the Ability of an Absent Parent to Pay Child Support. Mignon Sauber & Edith Taittonen. 1977. 1.50 (ISBN 0-86671-037-X). Comm Coun Great NY.

Guide for Early Developmental Training. Wabash Center for the Mentally Retarded. 1977. pap. text ed. 18.95 (ISBN 0-205-05810-8). Allyn.

Guide for Field Testing of Bridges. Compiled by American Society of Civil Engineers. LC 80-69154. 72p. 1980. pap. text ed. 12.00 (ISBN 0-87262-255-X). Am Soc Civil Eng.

Guide for Field Workers in Folklore. Kenneth S. Goldstein. LC 64-24801. xx, 199p. Repr. of 1964 ed. 15.00 (ISBN 0-8103-5000-9); pap. 6.00 (ISBN 0-8103-5041-6). Gale.

Guide for Friends, Neighbors, & Relatives of Retarded Children. Mary Carson. (Illus.). 1977. pap. 2.45 (ISBN 0-89570-107-3). Claretian Pubns.

Guide for Helping the Child with Spina Bifida. Gary Myers et al. (Illus.). 352p. 1981. text ed. 19.75 (ISBN 0-398-04113-X). C C Thomas.

Guide for Hospital Participation in an Emergency Medical Communications System. American Hospital Association. LC 73-86669. 52p. 1973. pap. 8.75 (ISBN 0-87258-132-2, 1685). Am Hospital.

Guide for Motorist Aid System. 1974. 0.50. AASHTO.

Guide for Oral History Programs. Ed. by Richard D. Curtiss et al. 10.00 (ISBN 0-930046-03-X). CSUF Oral Hist.

Guide for Parents Who Aren't Sure What to Believe Anymore. Dennis J. Geaney. (Illus.). 40p. pap. 1.50 (ISBN 0-89570-096-4). Claretian Pubns.

Guide for Processing Black-&-White Motion Picture Films (H-7) Eastman Kodak Co. LC 79-55036. (Illus.). 1979. pap. 5.95 (ISBN 0-87985-229-1, CAT 143 9892). Eastman Kodak.

Guide for Recreation Leaders. Glenn Bannerman & Robert Fakkema. LC 74-28523. 120p. (Orig.). 1975. pap. 3.95 (ISBN 0-8042-2154-5). John Knox.

Guide for Single Parents: Transactional Analysis for People in Crisis. Kathryn Hallett. LC 73-92524. (Illus.). 96p. 1974. 7.95 (ISBN 0-912310-64-2); pap. 4.95 (ISBN 0-912310-55-3). Celestial Arts.

Guide for the Design of Steel Transmission Towers. Compiled By American Society of Civil Engineers. (Manual & Report on Engineering Practice Ser.: No. 52). 1971. pap. text ed. 5.00 (ISBN 0-87262-226-6). Am Soc Civil Eng.

Guide for the Elementary Social Studies Teacher. 3rd ed. W. Linwood Chase & Martha T. John. 1978. pap. text ed. 11.50 (ISBN 0-205-05938-4). Allyn.

Guide for the Perplexed. E. F. Schumacher. 1978. pap. 3.95 (ISBN 0-06-090611-1, CN 611, CN). Har-Row.

Guide for the Protection of Concrete Against Chemical Attack by Means of Coatings & Other Corrosion-Resistant Materials. ACI Committee 515. 1966. 20.65 (ISBN 0-685-85152-4, 515R-79). ACI.

Guide for the Study of British Caribbean History, 1763-1834, Including the Abolitions & Emancipation Movements. L. J. Ragatz. LC 71-75275. (Law, Politics, & History Ser). 1970. Repr. of 1932 ed. lib. bdg. 65.00 (ISBN 0-306-71308-X). Da Capo.

Guide for the Unemployed: Keeping Busy Until... Frieda Carrol. LC 80-70495. 103p. 1981. 16.95 (ISBN 0-9605246-5-7); pap. 12.95. Biblio Pr Ga.

Guide for Understanding School Law. Thomas J. Pepe. LC 76-19897. 1976. pap. 6.95x o.p. (ISBN 0-8134-1835-6, 1835). Interstate.

Guide for Using the Foreign Exchange & Market. T. Walker. LC 80-21975. 280p. 1981. 20.95 (ISBN 0-471-06254-5, Ronald Pr). Wiley.

Guide for Using the Foreign Exchange Market. Townsend Walker. 360p. 1981. 20.95 (ISBN 0-471-06254-5). Ronald Pr.

Guide for Waste Management in the Food Processing Industry, Vol. II. The Food Processors Institute. Ed. by Louis F. Warrick. 555p. 1979. pap. text ed. 15.00 (ISBN 0-937774-01-4). Food Processors.

Guide for Waste Management in the Food Processing Industry, Vol. 1. The Food Processors Institute. Ed. by Allen M. Katsuyama. LC 79-115086. 276p. 1979. pap. text ed. 50.00 (ISBN 0-937774-00-6). Food Processors.

Guide for Writing the History of a Church. LC 70-87728. pap. 1.50 (ISBN 0-8054-3504-2). Broadman.

GUIDE: Gathering up Information for Developmental Education for the TMR. E. Dick et al. 1979. spiral bound 16.95 (ISBN 0-87804-358-6). Mafex.

Guide on Citizen Participation in Transportation Planning. 1978. 7.00. AASHTO.

Guide Specifications for Highway Construction. 1979. 10.00. AASHTO.

Guide Terrestre, Ou La Terre et Ses Singes. Joseph F. Conroy. (Orig.). (gr. 7-12). 1975. pap. text ed. 4.58 (ISBN 0-87720-461-6). AMSCO Sch.

Guide Through C. S. Lewis' Space Trilogy. Martha C. Sammons. LC 80-68329. 1980. pap. 4.95 (ISBN 0-89107-185-7, Cornerstone Bks). Good News.

Guide Through the Theory of Knowledge. Adam Morton. 1977. pap. 9.95x (ISBN 0-8221-0195-5). Dickenson.

Guide to Academic Protocol. Mary K. Gunn. LC 70-76250. 1969. 15.00x (ISBN 0-231-03036-3). Columbia U Pr.

Guide to Achitecture in Washington State: An Environmental Perspective. Sally B. Woodbridge & Roger Montgomery. LC 80-51076. (Illus.). 500p. 1980. 25.00 (ISBN 0-295-95761-1); pap. 12.95 (ISBN 0-295-95779-4). U of Wash Pr.

Guide to Addiction & Its Treatment. M. M. Glatt. LC 74-8421. 346p. 1974. 17.95 o.p. (ISBN 0-470-30322-0). Halsted Pr.

Guide to Adirondack Trails: High Peak Region. 10th ed. Adirondack Mountain Club, Map & Guidebook Committee. LC 80-15403. (Illus.). 324p. 1980. pap. 9.00 (ISBN 0-935272-11-9). ADK Mtn Club.

Guide to African History. Basil Davidson. LC 70-164025. 3.75 o.p. (ISBN 0-385-04138-1); pap. 1.45 o.p. (ISBN 0-385-04922-6). Doubleday.

Guide to Air Traffic Control. Robert Smith. 1963. pap. 3.95 o.p. (ISBN 0-8306-2213-6, 2213). TAB Bks.

Guide to America-Holy Land Studies: Vol. 1, American Presence. Ed. by Nathan M. Kaganoff. LC 79-8575. (Illus.). 1980. lib. bdg. 20.00x (ISBN 0-405-12755-3). Arno.

Guide to Ancient Maya Ruins. C. Bruce Hunter. LC 74-5956. (Illus.). 300p. 1974. 14.95 (ISBN 0-8061-1214-X); pap. 6.95 (ISBN 0-8061-1215-8). U of Okla Pr.

Guide to Aquarium Fishes & Plants. Arne Schiotz. Tr. by Gwynne Vevers. LC 75-38541. 1977. pap. 3.95 o.s.i. (ISBN 0-397-01210-1). Lippincott.

Guide to Archery. Tom Foy. (Illus.). 176p. 1981. 14.95 (ISBN 0-7207-1245-9). Merrimack Bk Serv.

Guide to Arizona's Indian Reservations. Boye De Mente. 1978. pap. 3.95 (ISBN 0-914778-14-5). Phoenix Bks.

Guide to Atlases - World, Regional, National, Thematic: An International Listing of Atlases Published Since 1950. Gerald L. Alexander. LC 70-157728. 1971. 23.50 (ISBN 0-8108-0414-X). Scarecrow.

Guide to Atlases Supplement, World, Regional, National, Thematic: An International Listing of Atlases Published 1971 Through 1975 with Comprehensive Indexes. Gerard L Alexander. LC 76-157728. 1977. 17.00 (ISBN 0-8108-1011-5). Scarecrow.

Guide to Badminton. George Sullivan. LC 67-31525. (Illus.). 1968. 6.95 (ISBN 0-8303-0003-1). Fleet.

Guide to Baltimore Architecture. 2nd ed. John Dorsey & James D. Dilts. 1981. 3.95x (ISBN 0-87033-272-4, Pub by Tidewater). Cornell Maritime.

Guide to Barsoom. John F. Roy. 1976. pap. 1.75 o.p. (ISBN 0-345-24722-1). Ballantine.

Guide to Basic Information Sources in Chemistry. Arthur Antony. LC 79-330. (Information Resources Ser.). 1979. 15.95 (ISBN 0-470-26587-6). Halsted Pr.

Guide to Basic Information Sources in Engineering. Ed. by Ellis Mount. LC 75-43261. (Information Resources Ser.). 1976. 13.95x (ISBN 0-470-15013-0). Halsted Pr.

Guide to Basic Information Sources in the Visual Arts. Gerd Muehsam. LC 77-17430. 289p. 1980. 27.50 (ISBN 0-87436-278-4). ABC-Clio.

Guide to Basic Information Sources in the Visual Arts: Where to Find the Facts in Every Art Field. Gerd Muehsam. 276p. 1980. pap. 9.95 (ISBN 0-442-21200-3). Van Nos Reinhold.

Guide to BASIC Programming. 2nd ed. Donald D. Spencer. 1975. text ed. 13.95 (ISBN 0-201-07106-1). A-W.

Guide to Basic Reference Materials for Canadian Libraries. 6th ed. Diane Henderson. 1980. looseleaf 16.50x (ISBN 0-8020-2410-6). U of Toronto Pr.

Guide to Basic Riding Instruction. Anne Lewis. (Illus.). pap. 4.35 (ISBN 0-85131-218-7, Dist. by Sporting Book Center). J A Allen.

Guide to Bathroom & Kitchen Remodeling. (Home Improvement Ser.). 1980. pap. 3.95 (ISBN 0-07-045968-1). McGraw.

Guide to Bees & Honey. Ted Cooper. 1977. 10.95 o.p. (ISBN 0-87857-177-9). Rodale Pr Inc.

Guide to Bees & Honey. Ted Hopper. (Illus.). 260p. 1981. 12.50 (ISBN 0-7137-0782-8, Pub. by Blandford Pr England). Sterling.

Guide to Behavioral Analysis & Therapy. R. P. Liberman. 368p. 1972. text ed. 17.25 (ISBN 0-08-016645-8); pap. text ed. 9.25 (ISBN 0-08-016786-1). Pergamon.

Guide to Better Wine & Beer Making for Beginners. S. M. Tritton. 157p. 1969. pap. 2.50 (ISBN 0-486-22528-3). Dover.

Guide to Bicycle Repair & Maintenance. (Home Improvement Ser.). (Illus.). 112p. 1980. pap. 3.95 (ISBN 0-07-045965-7, GB). McGraw.

Guide to Big Water Canoeing. David A. Herzog. LC 77-91195. 1978. 8.95 o.p. (ISBN 0-8092-7689-5); pap. 4.95 o.p. (ISBN 0-8092-7688-7). Contemp Bks.

Guide to Birmingham & Central England. (Illus.). 1979. pap. 4.95 o.p. (ISBN 0-905522-41-9, ADON 8112-0, Pub. by R Nicholson). Barrie & Jenkins.

Guide to Book Publishing. Datus C. Smith, Jr. LC 66-23133. 244p. 1966. Spanish ed. 14.25 (ISBN 0-8352-0055-8). Bowker.

Guide to British Government Publications. Frank Rodgers. 1980. 35.00 (ISBN 0-8242-0617-7). Wilson.

Guide to British Topographical Collections. M. W. Barley. 160p. 1980. pap. 17.95x (ISBN 0-900312-24-6, Pub. by Coun Brit Arch England). Intl Schol Bk Serv.

Guide to British Topographical Prints. Ronald Russell. LC 79-53737. (Illus.). 1979. 32.00 (ISBN 0-7153-7810-4). David & Charles.

Guide to Business Research: Developing, Conducting & Writing Research Projects. Charles B. Smith. LC 79-22991. 200p. 1981. text ed. 16.95 (ISBN 0-88229-546-2); pap. text ed. 8.95 (ISBN 0-88229-750-3). Nelson-Hall.

Guide to Caring for & Coping with Aging Parents. John Gillies. 1981. pap. 4.95 (ISBN 0-8407-5772-7). Nelson.

Guide to Carpentry. (McGraw-Hill Paperbacks Home Improvement Ser.). (Illus.). 112p. Date not set. pap. 3.95 (ISBN 0-07-045966-5). McGraw.

Guide to Cats of the World. Howard Loxton. (Illustrated Natural History Guides). (Illus.). 1977. pap. 4.95 (ISBN 0-8467-0366-1, Pub. by Two Continents). Hippocrene Bks.

Guide to Cellular Energetics. Lynne C. Carter. LC 72-5397. (Illus.). 1973. pap. text ed. 6.95x (ISBN 0-7167-0598-2); tchr's manual avail. W H Freeman.

Guide to Champagne & Sparkling Wines. Pauline Wasserman et al. 128p. Date not set. pap. cancelled (ISBN 0-346-12502-2). Cornerstone.

Guide to Clinical Laboratory Diagnosis. 2nd. ed. John A. Koepke. (Illus.). 320p. 1979. pap. 15.50x (ISBN 0-8385-3518-6). ACC.

Guide to Commentaries. Charles H. Spurgeon. Date not set. 0.30 (ISBN 0-686-28947-1). Banner of Truth.

Guide to Commercial-Scale Ethanol Production & Financing. Solar Energy Research Institute (SERI) 305p. 1981. 34.50 (ISBN 0-89934-118-7). Solar Energy Info.

Guide to Community Energy Self-Reliance, Vol. 1. Ken Bossong. (Illus.). 100p. (Orig.). 1981. pap. 2.50 (ISBN 0-89988-023-1). Citizens Energy.

Guide to Composition in Italian. Toni Cerutti. 1966. text ed. 6.50x (ISBN 0-521-04593-2). Cambridge U Pr.

Guide to Contemporary Italian Literature: From Futurism to Neorealism. Sergio Pacifici. LC 72-5472. (Arcturus Books Paperbacks). 352p. pap. 9.95 (ISBN 0-8093-0593-3). S Ill U Pr.

Guide to Contentment. Fulton J. Sheen. 1970. pap. 1.95 (ISBN 0-385-02527-0, Im). Doubleday.

Guide to Corals & Fishes. Idaz Greenberg. (Illus.). 1977. saddlestitched 4.95 (ISBN 0-913008-08-7). Seahawk Pr.

Guide to Corporate Giving in the Arts. Ed. by Robert Porter. 1981. 29.95 (ISBN 0-915400-23-5). Am Council Arts.

Guide to Corporate Giving in the Arts. Ed. by Susan E. Wagner. LC 78-55696. 402p. (Orig.). 1978. pap. 7.50 (ISBN 0-915400-12-X). Am Council Arts.

Guide to Creative Action. rev. ed. Ruth B. Noller et al. LC 76-44541. 1977. pap. text ed. 12.95x (ISBN 0-684-14888-9, ScribC). Scribner.

Guide to Critical Reviews of United States Fiction, 1870-1910. Clayton L. Eichelberger. LC 77-149998. 1971. 13.50 (ISBN 0-8108-0380-1). Scarecrow.

Guide to Critical Reviews of U.S. Fiction, 1870-1910, Vol. 2. Clayton L. Eichelberger. LC 77-14998. 1974. 12.00 (ISBN 0-8108-0701-7). Scarecrow.

Guide to Critical Reviews, Part I: American Drama, 1909-1969. 2nd ed. James M. Salem. LC 73-3120. 1973. 20.50 (ISBN 0-8108-0608-8). Scarecrow.

Guide to Critical Reviews, Part II: The Musical, 1909-1974. 2nd ed. James M. Salem. LC 73-3120. 1976. 25.00 (ISBN 0-8108-0959-1). Scarecrow.

Guide to Critical Reviews: Part III. 2nd ed. James M. Salem. LC 73-3120. 448p. 1979. 22.50 (ISBN 0-8108-1226-6). Scarecrow.

Guide to Critical Reviews, Part IV: The Screenplay from the Jazz Singer to Dr. Strangelove, 2 Vols. James M. Salem. LC 66-13733. 1971. Set. 39.50 (ISBN 0-8108-0367-4). Scarecrow.

Guide to Culture in the Classroom. Muriel Saville-Troike. LC 78-61039. 67p. 1978. pap. 4.50 (ISBN 0-89763-000-9). Natl Clearinghse Bilingual Ed.

Guide to Current American Government Fall Nineteen Eighty. Congressional Quarterly Inc. Ed. by Congressional Quarterly Inc. 190p. 1980. pap. text ed. 6.95 (ISBN 0-87187-151-3). Congr Quarterly.

Guide to Current American Government: Spring 1981 Edition. Congressional Quarterly Staff. 160p. 1980. pap. text ed. 6.95 (ISBN 0-87187-159-9). Congr Quarterly.

Guide to Current Research. Jean Greenberg et al. (Resources in Bilingual Education Ser.). (Orig.). 1981. pap. write for info. (ISBN 0-89763-052-1). Natl Clearinghse Bilingual Ed.

Guide to Daily Prayer. William Barclay. LC 62-11473. 1974. pap. 3.95 (ISBN 0-06-060401-8, RD75, HarpR). Har-Row.

Guide to Dance in Films: A Guide to Information Sources. David L. Parker & Esther Siegel. LC 76-20339. (Performing Arts Information Guide Series: Vol. 3). 1978. 30.00 (ISBN 0-8103-1377-4). Gale.

Guide to Dermatohistopathology. 3rd ed. Herman Pinkus. 672p. 1981. 40.00 (ISBN 0-8385-3151-2). ACC.

Guide to Development of Protective Services for Older People. Gertrude H. Hall et al. 160p. 1973. 13.75 (ISBN 0-398-02604-1); pap. 8.75 (ISBN 0-398-02758-7). C C Thomas.

Guide to Doing Business on the Arabian Peninsula. Quentin W. Fleming. 225p. 1981. 29.95 (ISBN 0-8144-5666-9); comb-bound 29.95 (ISBN 0-8144-7012-2). Am Mgmt.

Guide to Domestic Central Heating Installation & Controls. Peter Burberry & Arthur Aldersey-Williams. LC 78-16062. 1979. 17.50 (ISBN 0-85139-207-5, Pub. by Architectural Pr). Nichols Pub.

Guide to Driving Horses: Pelham Horsemaster Ser. Sallie Walrond. (Illus.). 1978. 14.00 (ISBN 0-7207-1009-X). Transatlantic.

Guide to Drug Information. Winifred Sewell. LC 75-17156. 180p. (Orig.). 1976. 13.00 (ISBN 0-914768-21-2). Drug Intl Pubns.

Guide to Early Developmental Training. new ed. Wabash Center for the Mentally Retarded. 1977. 25.95 o.p. (ISBN 0-205-05811-6). Allyn.

Guide to Eating & Drinking in Eugene. new ed. Mike Helm. Ed. by Christine Helm. LC 79-65123. (Illus.). 1979. 3.25 (ISBN 0-931742-02-1). Rainy Day Oreg.

Guide to Economic Analysis. B. Wylie Anderson et al. 1978. pap. text ed. 8.95 (ISBN 0-8403-1827-8). Kendall-Hunt.

Guide to Educational Research. 2nd ed. David R. Cook & N. Kenneth LaFleur. 192p. 1975. pap. text ed. 12.50x (ISBN 0-205-04747-5, 224747X). Allyn.

Guide to Effective Management: Practical Applications from Behavioral Science. Leslie E. This. (Illus.). 288p. 1974. pap. text ed. 8.95 (ISBN 0-201-07559-8). A-W.

Guide to Effective Teaching. Ed. by Editors, Change Magazine. LC 78-64963. 1978. pap. 6.95 o.p. (ISBN 0-915390-18-3). Change Mag.

Guide to Electronic Measurements & Laboratory Practice. Stanley Wolf. (Illus.). 560p. 1973. ref. ed. 22.95 (ISBN 0-13-369587-5). P-H.

Guide to Electronic Music. Paul Griffiths. 1979. 11.95 (ISBN 0-500-01224-5). Thames Hudson.

Guide to Electronic Music. Paul Griffiths. 128p. pap. 6.95 (ISBN 0-500-27203-4). Thames Hudson.

Guide to Employee Stock Ownership Plans: A Revolutionary Method for Increasing Corporate Profits. Charles A. Scharf. 1976. 27.95 o.p. (ISBN 0-13-369447-X). P-H.

Guide to Energy Conservation in Agriculture, 6 vols. Federal Energy Administration. (Reprint Ser.: No. 1). 1980. pap. 29.50 (ISBN 0-89934-039-3). Solar Energy Info.

Guide to England's Industrial Heritage. Keith Falconer. LC 80-8027. (Illus.). 270p. 1980. text ed. 29.50x (ISBN 0-8419-0646-7). Holmes & Meier.

Guide to English & American Literature. 3rd ed. F. W. Bateson. 352p. 1977. pap. text ed. 13.95 (ISBN 0-582-48417-0). Longman.

Guide to Environmental Research on Animals. Agricultural Board - Division Of Biology And Agriculture. LC 76-609948. (Illus., Orig.). 1971. pap. 11.25 (ISBN 0-309-01869-2). Natl Acad Pr.

Guide to European Foundations. Agnelli Foundation. 350p. 1972. 25.00x (ISBN 0-231-03701-5). Columbia U Pr.

Guide to Exposed Concrete Finishes. Michael Gage. LC 72-552437. (Illus.). 161p. (Orig.). 1970. pap. 18.50x (ISBN 0-85139-263-6). Intl Pubns Serv.

Guide to Ezra Pound's "Personae" 1926. K. K. Ruthven. 1969. 17.95x (ISBN 0-520-01526-6). U of Cal Pr.

Guide to Ezra Pound's Selected Cantos. George Kearns. 1980. text ed. 22.00x (ISBN 0-8135-0886-X); pap. 6.95 (ISBN 0-8135-0887-8). Rutgers U Pr.

Guide to Fairs, Festivals & Fun Events. Janice Gale & Stephen Gale. (Illus.). 190p. 1981. pap. 6.95 (ISBN 0-937928-00-3). Sightseer.

Guide to Far Eastern Navies. Barry M. Blechman. LC 77-87942. 1978. 32.95 (ISBN 0-87021-235-4). Naval Inst Pr.

Guide to Federal Tax Elections. (Study in Federal Taxation Ser.: No. 3). 1980. pap. 12.50. Am Inst CPA.

Guide to Field Identification of Native Orchids of the U.S. & Canada. condensed ed. Carlyle A. Luer. 1981. 15.95 (ISBN 0-8120-5191-2); pap. 10.95 (ISBN 0-8120-0933-9). Barron. Postponed.

Guide to Fishing Boats & Their Gear. Carvel H. Blair & Willits D. Ansel. LC 68-19048. (Illus.). 1968. 6.00 (ISBN 0-87033-002-0). Cornell Maritime.

Guide to Florida. (Illus.). 1979. pap. 4.95 o.p. (ISBN 0-528-84250-1). Rand.

Guide to Florida. 5th ed. Rand McNally. LC 79-656302. (Illus.). 1979. pap. 4.95 (ISBN 0-528-84109-2). Rand.

Guide to Flower Arranging. Phyllis G. Shields. (Illus.). 1967. 4.00 o.p. (ISBN 0-8231-6017-3). Branford.

Guide to Folk Art & Folklore in Poland. Marian Pokropek. Tr. by Magdalena M. Paszkiewicz from Polish. (Illus.). 307p. 1980. 20.00x (ISBN 83-213-3014-2). Intl Pubns Serv.

Guide to Food Service Management. National Association of College & University Food Services. Ed. by Frances Cloyd. LC 72-75293. 188p. 1972. pap. 9.95 o.p. (ISBN 0-8436-0554-5). CBI Pub.

Guide to Foreign Language Courses & Dictionaries. Ed. by Alberto J. Walford & J. E. Screen. LC 77-26283. 1978. lib. bdg. 22.50 (ISBN 0-313-20100-5, WGL/). Greenwood.

Guide to Fortified Wines. Pauline Wasserman & Sheldon Wasserman. Ed. by Madelyn Larsen. 128p. (Orig.). Date not set. pap. cancelled (ISBN 0-346-12446-8). Cornerstone.

Guide to Fortran Four. Seymour V. Pollack. LC 65-8201. 1966. 17.50x (ISBN 0-231-02904-7). Columbia U Pr.

Guide to Fortran IV Programming. 2nd ed. Daniel D. McCracken. LC 72-4745. (Illus.). 256p. 1972. pap. 15.50 (ISBN 0-471-58281-6). Wiley.

Guide to Franchising. 2nd ed. M. Mendelsohn. LC 78-40961. 1978. 27.50 (ISBN 0-08-022466-0). Pergamon.

Guide to French Studies: Supplement, with Cumulative Indexes. Charles B. Osburn. LC 68-12638. 1972. 13.50 (ISBN 0-8108-0493-X). Scarecrow.

Guide to Geneological Sources at the Pennsylvania State Archives. Robert M. Dructor. (Illus.). 129p. (Orig.). pap. 5.00 (ISBN 0-89271-011-X). Pa Hist & Mus.

Guide to Global Giving. Philadelphia Working Party. 59p. 1976. pap. 1.50 (ISBN 0-86571-006-6). Movement New Soc.

Guide to Good Programming Practice. Ed. by Brian Meek & Patricia Heath. 181p. 1979. 29.95 (ISBN 0-470-26869-7). Wiley.

Guide to Government Agency Programs. Lance D. Potter & Alexis Mazzocco. LC 80-116020. 145p. (Orig.). 1979. pap. 3.50 (ISBN 0-89763-019-X). Natl Clearinghse Bilingual Ed.

Guide to Government-Loan Film 16mm. 5th ed. Ed. by Daniel Sprecher. 1978. pap. 12.95 o.p. (ISBN 0-685-73566-4). Serina.

Guide to Graduate Departments of Geography in the United States & Canada, 1980-1981. 13th ed. Ed. by Teresa A. Mulloy. LC 68-59269. 1980. pap. 6.00 (ISBN 0-89291-152-2). Assn Am Geographers.

Guide to Graduate Study in Economics & Agricultural Economics. 5th ed. Wyn F. Owen & George H. Antoine. 1980. 11.50x (ISBN 0-256-02540-1). Irwin.

Guide to Greeting Card Writing. Ed. by Larry Sandman. LC 80-19737. 256p. 1980. 10.95 (ISBN 0-89879-022-0). Writers Digest.

Guide to Group & IPA HMO's. Dustin Mackie & Douglas Decker. 250p. 1981. text ed. price not set (ISBN 0-89443-341-5). Aspen Systems.

Guide to Health & Hygiene in Agricultural Work. 309p. 1980. pap. 15.25 (ISBN 92-2-101974-8, ILO-141, ILO). Unipub.

Guide to Health & Hygiene in Agricultural Work. International Labour Office, Geneva. (Illus.). 317p. 1980. pap. 15.70 (ISBN 92-2-101974-8). Intl Labour Office.

Guide to Heraldry. Ottfried Neubecker. LC 79-13611. (Illus.). 1980. 9.95 (ISBN 0-07-046312-3). McGraw.

Guide to Hi-Fi. John Wasley & Ron Hill. 1977. 15.00 (ISBN 0-7207-0906-7). Transatlantic.

Guide to Historical Method. 3rd ed. Ed. by Robert J. Shafer. 1980. pap. 9.95x (ISBN 0-256-02313-1). Dorsey.

Guide to Home Air Conditioners & Refrigeration Equipment. Bernard Lamere. (Illus., Orig.). 1963. pap. 6.50 (ISBN 0-8104-0294-7). Hayden.

Guide to Home Renovation: For Those Without the Time or Inclination to Do It Themselves. Michael C. Miller. LC 80-70390. (Illus.). 136p. (Orig.). 1981. pap. 7.95 (ISBN 0-686-69518-6). Chilton.

Guide to Homebuilts. Peter Bowers. 1974. pap. 3.95 o.p. (ISBN 0-8306-2214-4, 2214). TAB Bks.

Guide to Horoscope Interpretation. Marc E. Jones. LC 41-26719. 1972. 10.50 o.p. (ISBN 0-87878-003-3, Sabian). Great Eastern.

Guide to Horses of the World. Caroline Silver. (Illustrated Natural History Guides). (Illus.). 1977. pap. 4.95 (ISBN 0-8467-0365-3, Pub. by Two Continents). Hippocrene Bks.

Guide to Human Relations in Business & Industry. Martin M. Bruce. LC 73-6907. 1969. pap. 11.05 (ISBN 0-935198-00-8). M M Bruce.

Guide to Hunting in Texas. John Wootters. LC 79-19642. 1979. pap. 5.95 (ISBN 0-88415-369-X). Pacesetter Pr.

Guide to I. V. Admixture Compatibility. 3rd ed. New England Deaconess Hospital. 1980. pap. 6.95 (ISBN 0-87489-248-1). Med Economics.

Guide to Identification of Marine & Estuarine Invertebates: From Cape Hatteras to the Bay of Fundy. K. L. Gosner. 693p. 1971. pap. 22.50 (ISBN 0-471-31901-5). Wiley.

Guide to Identifying & Classifying Yeasts. J. A. Barnett et al. LC 79-11136. (Illus.). 1979. 82.50 (ISBN 0-521-22762-3). Cambridge U Pr.

Guide to Illinois Real Estate License Preparation. G. Kuhn & D. Weiss. 1979. pap. 16.95 (ISBN 0-13-370254-5). P-H.

Guide to Improving Food Hygiene. Graham Aston & John Tiffney. (Illus.). 1977. pap. 11.95x (ISBN 0-7198-2644-6). Intl Ideas.

Guide to Indexed Periodicals in Religion. John J. Regazzi & Theodore C. Hines. LC 75-22277. 328p. 1975. 12.00 (ISBN 0-8108-0868-4). Scarecrow.

Guide to Infectious Diseases of Mice & Rats. Institute Of Laboratory Animal Resources. LC 72-611182. (Orig.). 1971. pap. text ed. 4.25 (ISBN 0-309-01914-1). Natl Acad Pr.

Guide to Inner Canyon Hiking: Grand Canyon National Park. rev. ed. Scott Thybony. (Illus.). pap. 1.75 (ISBN 0-938216-12-0). Grand Canyon.

Guide to Intelligent Investing. Jerome B. Cohen et al. LC 77-83590. 1978. 12.50 (ISBN 0-87094-152-6). Dow Jones-Irwin.

Guide to International Monetary Reform. George N. Halm. LC 74-28969. 1975. 15.95 (ISBN 0-669-98061-7). Lexington Bks.

Guide to Invertebrate Fossils. rev. ed. F. A. Middlemiss. (Illus.). 128p. 1972. pap. text ed. 3.75x (ISBN 0-09-108401-6, Hutchinson U Lib). Humanities.

Guide to Investigation of Structural Failures. Compiled by American Society of Civil Engineers. 88p. 1979. pap. text ed. 6.50 (ISBN 0-87262-184-7). Am Soc Civil Eng.

Guide to Irish Bibliographical Material: A Bibliography of Irish Bibliographies and Sources of Information. Alan R. Eager. LC 80-12368. xv, 502p. 1980. lib. bdg. 65.00 (ISBN 0-313-22343-2, EIB/). Greenwood.

Guide to Israel 1980. 21st ed. Zev Vilnay. LC 66-33490. (Illus.). 662p. 1979. 10.00x (ISBN 0-8002-2713-1). Intl Pubns Serv.

Guide to Issues in Indian Language Retention. James J. Bauman. 1980. pap. text ed. 5.50 (ISBN 0-87281-132-8). Ctr Appl Ling.

Guide to I.V. Admixture Compatibility. 1977. pap. text ed. 4.95 o.s.i. (ISBN 0-8273-1715-8). Delmar.

Guide to Japanese Culture. Ed. by Hyoe Murakami & E. G. Seidensticker. 224p. 1977. 16.50 (ISBN 0-87040-403-2). Japan Pubns.

Guide to Japanese Foreign Policy. Ed. by James W. Morley. (Studies of the East Asian Institute). 624p. 1973. 27.50x (ISBN 0-231-08966-X). Columbia U Pr.

Guide to Jewish Themes in American Fiction, 1940-1980. Murray Blackman. LC 80-24953. 271p. 1981. lib. bdg. 15.00 (ISBN 0-8108-1380-7). Scarecrow.

Guide to Korean Characters: Reading & Writing Hangul & Hanja. Bruce K. Grant. 400p. 1979. 15.50 (ISBN 0-930878-13-2). Hollym Intl.

Guide to Landscape & Lawn Care. (McGraw-Hill Paperbacks Home Improvement Ser.). (Illus.). 112p. 1980. pap. 3.95 (ISBN 0-07-045972-X). McGraw.

Guide to Language & Study Skills, for College Students of English As a Second Language. McChesney et al. 1977. pap. text ed. 9.50 (ISBN 0-13-370452-1). P-H.

Guide to Language Camps in the United States. Lois Vines. (Language in Education Ser.: No. 26). 1980. pap. text ed. 3.95 (ISBN 0-87281-114-X). Ctr Appl Ling.

Guide to Learning Anatomy & Physiology. Kathleen Prezbindowski. (Illus.). 1980. pap. text ed. 9.95 (ISBN 0-8016-4040-7). Mosby.

Guide to Leavenworth Rock Climbing Areas. Fred Beckey & Eric Bjorstad. (Illus.). 88p. (Orig.). 1973. pap. 3.50 o.p. (ISBN 0-916890-05-8). Mountaineers.

Guide to Legal Gambling. Harland B. Adams. LC 66-16484. (Funk & W Bk.). (Illus.). 1969. pap. 2.75 o.s.i. (ISBN 0-308-90102-9, F72, TYC-T). T Y Crowell.

Guide to Library Resources for Nursing. K. P. Strauch & D. J. Brundage. 509p. 1980. pap. 12.75 (ISBN 0-8385-3528-3). ACC.

Guide to Longplay Jazz Records. Frederick Ramsey, Jr. LC 77-9065. (Roots of Jazz Ser.). (Illus.). 1977. Repr. of 1954 ed. lib. bdg. 25.00 (ISBN 0-306-70891-4). Da Capo.

Guide to Manpower Planning. Angela Bowey. 1977. text ed. 13.50x (ISBN 0-333-15555-6). Verry.

Guide to Manuscripts & Documents in the British Isles Relating to the Far East. Noel Matthews & M. Doreen Wainwright. Ed. by J. D. Pearson. 1977. text ed. 59.00x (ISBN 0-19-713591-9). Oxford U Pr.

Guide to Manuscrpits & Documents in the British Isles Relating to the Middle East & North Africa. Ed. by Noel Matthews & Doreen M. Wainwrights. 500p. 1980. 148.00x (ISBN 0-19-713598-6). Oxford U Pr.

Guide to Marine Fishes. Alfred Perlmutter. LC 60-14491. (Illus.). 431p. 1961. 15.00x (ISBN 0-8147-0336-4); pap. 5.95 (ISBN 0-8147-6561-0). NYU Pr.

Guide to Marine Photography. Peter R. Smyth. (Illus.). 144p. 1974. 12.50 o.p. (ISBN 0-393-03182-9). Norton.

Guide to Marxism & Its Effects on Soviet Development. Peter H. Vigor. 1966. text ed. 8.00x (ISBN 0-391-00500-6). Humanities.

Guide to Marxist Literary Criticism. Chris Bullock & David Peck. LC 79-3627. 160p. 1980. 12.95x (ISBN 0-253-13144-8). Ind U Pr.

Guide to Marxist Philosophy: An Introductory Bibliography. Ed. by Joseph M. Bochenski et al. LC 76-188168. 1972. pap. 4.95x (ISBN 0-8040-0561-3). Swallow.

Guide to Marx's "Capital". Mike Roth & Michael Eldred. 1978. pap. text ed. 5.25x (ISBN 0-906336-11-2). Humanities.

Guide to Maryland Zoning Decisions: With 1979 Supplement. Stanley D. Abrams. LC 75-3716. 216p. 1975. 27.50 (ISBN 0-87215-166-2); 1979 suppl. 9.50 (ISBN 0-87215-241-3). Michie.

Guide to Maximizing Recovery of Loss & Damage Claims. Raynard F. Bohman, Jr. 1976. spiral 14.95 o.p. (ISBN 0-8436-1408-0). CBI Pub.

Guide to Meat Inspection in the Tropics. 95p. 1981. pap. 22.50 (ISBN 0-85198-456-8, CAB 10, CAB). Unipub.

Guide to Medical Laboratory Instruments. Clifford D. Ferris. LC 80-80585. 260p. 1980. text ed. 14.95 (ISBN 0-316-28127-1). Little.

Guide to Medical Mathematics. D. A. Franklin & G. B. Newman. LC 73-15859. (Illus.). 453p. 1973. 26.95 (ISBN 0-470-27520-0). Halsted Pr.

Guide to Medical Schools & Medical School Admission. Henry Wechsler. Date not set. write for info. (ISBN 0-88410-723-X). Ballinger Pub.

Guide to Metrication. M. J. Jones. 1969. pap. 7.00 (ISBN 0-08-006539-2). Pergamon.

Guide to Mexican Witchcraft. William Madsen & Claudia Madsen. (Illus.). 1979. pap. 4.00 (ISBN 0-912434-10-4). Ocelot Pr.

Guide to Microcomputers. Franz J. Frederick. Ed. by Assn Ed Comm Tech. LC 80-68716. (Orig.). 1980. pap. 11.50 (ISBN 0-89240-038-2). Assn Ed Comm T.

Guide to Microforms in Print: Author-Title 1980. Ed. by Ardis Carleton. LC 61-7082. 1980. 49.50 (ISBN 0-913672-35-1). Microform Rev.

Guide to Microforms in Print: Subject. 1980. Ed. by Ardis Carleton. LC 62-21624. 1980. 49.50 (ISBN 0-913672-36-X). Microform Rev.

Guide to Microforms in Print: Supplement 1980. new ed. Ed. by Ardis V. Carleton. 320p. 1980. text ed. 35.00x (ISBN 0-913672-39-4). Microform Rev.

Guide to Micrographic Equipment: RS15-1979. 7th ed. National Micrographics Assn. 1979. 30.00 (ISBN 0-89258-053-4). Natl Micrograph.

Guide to Microwave Catering. 3rd ed. Lewis Napleton. (Illus.). 1976. pap. 11.95x (ISBN 0-7198-2523-7). Intl Ideas.

Guide to Middle Earth. Robert Foster. 1975. pap. 1.95 o.p. (ISBN 0-345-24936-4). Ballantine.

Guide to Midwifery: Heart & Hands. Elizabeth Davis. (Illus., Orig.). 1981. pap. 9.00 (ISBN 0-912528-22-2). John Muir.

Guide to Modern Clothing. Mary M. Sturm & E. H. Grieser. (American Home & Family Ser.). (First ed. also avail. at same prices). (gr. 10-12). 1968. text ed. 13.20 (ISBN 0-07-062274-4, W); tchrs' manual 1.32 (ISBN 0-07-062226-4). McGraw.

Guide to Modern Meals. Shank et al. Ed. by Martha O'Neill. (Illus.). 640p. (gr. 10-12). 1980. 17.28 (ISBN 0-07-056416-7, W); tchrs. resource guide avail. (ISBN 0-07-047514-8). McGraw.

Guide to Money for College. Louis T. Scaringi & Joyce W. Scaringi. LC 79-83587. 132p. 1979. pap. 2.95 (ISBN 0-9602432-1-6). Anchorage.

Guide to Mushroom Growing. Fred C. Atkins. (Illus.). 1974. 12.95 o.p. (ISBN 0-571-10190-9, Pub. by Faber & Faber). Merrimack Bk Serv.

Guide to Music Festivals in America. Carol Rabin. LC 78-74201. 1979. pap. 5.95 o.p. (ISBN 0-912944-51-X). Berkshire Traveller.

Guide to Music Festivals in North America. rev., enl. ed. Carol Rabin. LC 78-74201. 260p. 1981. 6.95 (ISBN 0-912944-67-6). Berkshire Traveller.

Guide to Musical Acoustics. H. Lowery. 1956. 6.95 (ISBN 0-234-77220-4). Dufour.

Guide to Musical Thought. Ian Parrott. (Student's Music Library Ser). 1955. 6.95 (ISBN 0-234-77309-X). Dufour.

Guide to Nantucket. Polly Burroughs. LC 74-76535. (Illus., Orig.). 1980. pap. 4.95 (ISBN 0-87106-144-9). Globe Pequot.

Guide to National Practices in Western Europe. Parkland Research. 1973. 17.50 (ISBN 0-685-88894-0). CBI Pub.

Guide to Neurological Assessment. Howard S. Barrows. (Illus.). 144p. 1980. text ed. 9.95 (ISBN 0-397-52093-X). Lippincott.

Guide to Neuropathology. Asao Hirano. LC 80-83980. (Illus.). 1981. 60.00. Igaku-Shoin.

Guide to Non-Ferrous Metals & Their Markets. 2nd ed. Ed. by John Edwards & Peter Robbins. 250p. 1980. 43.50x (ISBN 0-89397-096-4). Nichols Pub.

Guide to North American Waterfowl. Paul A. Johnsgard. LC 78-20612. (Illus.). 288p. 1979. 15.95x (ISBN 0-253-12789-0). Ind U Pr.

Guide to Nursing Management. Ann Marriner. LC 79-24241. (Illus.). 1980. pap. 10.00 (ISBN 0-8016-3121-1). Mosby.

Guide to Nursing Management of Psychiatric Patients. 2nd ed. Sharon Dreyer et al. LC 78-31432. 1979. pap. text ed. 10.95 (ISBN 0-8016-0832-5). Mosby.

Guide to Nutrition. Velda L. Largen. LC 80-25186. (Illus.). 144p. 1981. text ed. 8.96 (ISBN 0-87006-312-X). Goodheart.

Guide to Oklahoma Museums. David C. Hunt. LC 80-5939. (Illus.). 250p. 1981. 17.50 (ISBN 0-8061-1567-X); pap. 9.95 (ISBN 0-8061-1752-4). U of Okla Pr.

Guide to Operation "F". 95p. 1973. 5.00 (APO23, APO). Unipub.

Guide to Orchids of Canada & the United States: Excluding the Tropicals of Florida & Hawaii & the Asiatics of Alaska. W. Petrie & M. Campbell. (Illus.). 1981. pap. price not set (ISBN 0-88839-089-0). Hancock Hse.

Guide to Organizing a Health Care Fiscal Services Division with Job Descriptions for Key Functions. 2nd ed. Russell A. Caruana. 80p. 1981. pap. write for info. (ISBN 0-930228-13-8). Hospital Finan.

Guide to Oriental Classics. 2nd ed. William T. De Bary & T. Embree. (Companions to Asian Studies). 1974. 12.50x (ISBN 0-231-03891-7); pap. 7.50x (ISBN 0-231-03892-5). Columbia U Pr.

Guide to Orthopaedics, Vol. 1: Trauma. Ed. by K. L. Mills. (Illus.). 280p. Date not set. text ed. 25.00x (ISBN 0-443-02018-3). Churchill.

Guide to Outdoor Britain: North of England. Automobile Association & British Tourist Authority. (Illus.). 160p. 1981. pap. write for info. (ISBN 0-7099-0385-5, Pub. by Auto Assn-British Tourist Authority England). Merrimack Bk Serv.

Guide to Outer Space. Franklyn M. Branley. LC 59-13620. (Illus.). (gr. 4-6). 1960. PLB 6.95 (ISBN 0-87396-002-5). Stravon.

Guide to Paddle Adventure: How to Buy Canoes & Kayaks & Where to Travel. Rick Kemmer. LC 75-386. 384p. 1975. 10.00 (ISBN 0-8149-0760-1); pap. 6.95 (ISBN 0-685-52406-X). Vanguard.

Guide to Patient Evaluation. 3rd ed. Ed. by Jacques L. Sherman, Jr. & Sylvia K. Fields. LC 78-50128. 1978. 17.50 (ISBN 0-87488-985-5); pap. 12.75. Med Exam.

Guide to Patterns & Usage in English. 2nd ed. A. S. Hornby. 256p. 1975. pap. text ed. 4.95x (ISBN 0-19-431318-2). Oxford U Pr.

Guide to Pediatric Nursing: A Clinical Reference. M. L. Evans & B. D. Hansen. 284p. 1980. pap. 14.95 (ISBN 0-8385-3533-X). ACC.

Guide to Peking. 1979. pap. 6.95 o.p. (ISBN 0-8351-0659-4). China Bks.

Guide to Periodicals in Education & Its Academic Disciplines. 2nd ed. William L. Camp & Bryan L. Schwark. LC 75-6784. 568p. 1975. 23.50 (ISBN 0-8108-0814-5). Scarecrow.

Guide to Personal Finance: A Lifetime Program of Money Management. 3rd ed. Richard Stillman. 1979. text ed. 19.95 (ISBN 0-13-370486-6). P-H.

Guide to Personal Risk Taking. Richard E. Byrd. (AMACOM Executive Books). 1978. pap. 5.95 (ISBN 0-8144-7505-1). Am Mgmt.

Guide to Pigeons of the World. Andrew McNeillie. (Illustrated Natural History Guides). (Illus.). 1977. pap. 4.95 (ISBN 0-8467-0367-X, Pub. by Two Continents). Hippocrene Bks.

Guide to PL-M Programming for Microcomputer Applications. Daniel D. McCracken. 1978. pap. text ed. 11.95 (ISBN 0-201-04575-3). A-W.

Guide to Places on the Colorado Prairie. Ray Shaffer. (Illus.). 1978. 16.95x o.s.i. (ISBN 0-87108-513-5). Pruett.

Guide to Plastic Surgery for Men. Reardon. 1981. write for info. Everest Hse.

Guide to Police Report Writing. Harry A. Squires. (Illus.). 104p. 1976. pap. 10.50 (ISBN 0-398-01831-6). C C Thomas.

Guide to Practical Speech Training. Gordon Luck. 1979. 8.50 o.p. (ISBN 0-214-20036-1, 8033, Dist. by Arco). Barrie & Jenkins.

Guide to Practicals in Electronics. T. Dwarakanath. 1968. pap. 4.50x (ISBN 0-210-26932-4). Asia.

Guide to Prayer for Busy People. Beryl & Michael Newman. (Jubilee Ser.). (Illus.). 48p. (Orig.). 1980. pap. 1.95 (ISBN 0-89570-196-0). Claretian Pubns.

Guide to Pregnancy & Parenthood for Women on Their Own. Patricia Ashdown-Sharp. 1977. pap. 3.95 (ISBN 0-394-72272-8, V-272, Vin). Random.

Guide to Prehistoric England. Nicholas Thomas. 1977. 30.00 (ISBN 0-7134-3267-5, Pub. by Batsford England); pap. 14.50 (ISBN 0-7134-3268-3, Pub. by Batsford England). David & Charles.

Guide to Prehistoric Ruins of the Southwest. Norman T. Oppelt. 200p. (Orig.). 1981. pap. 6.95 (ISBN 0-87108-587-9). Pruett.

Guide to Prehistoric Scotland. Richard Feachem. 1977. 19.95 (ISBN 0-7134-3264-0, Pub. by Batsford England). David & Charles.

Guide to Primary Police Management Concepts. Donald G. Hanna & William D. Gentel. (Illus.). 208p. 1971. 13.75 (ISBN 0-398-00773-X). C C Thomas.

Guide to Printed Books & Manuscripts Relating to English & Foreign Heraldry & Genealogy. George Gatfield. 1966. Repr. of 1892 ed. 26.00 (ISBN 0-8103-3121-7). Gale.

Guide to Private Schools: Eastern Ed. Kuller. 1981. pap. 4.95 (ISBN 0-8120-0837-5). Barron.

Guide to Problems & Practices in First Aid & Emergency Care. 4th ed. William T. Brennan & James W. Crowe. 192p. 1981. wire coil 7.95x (ISBN 0-697-07390-4). Wm C Brown.

Guide to Professional Benefit Plan Management & Administration. Lee F. Jost & C. Bruce Sutherland. 405p. (Orig.). 1980. pap. 35.00 (ISBN 0-89154-096-2). Intl Found Employ.

Guide to Professional Development Opportunities for College & University Administrators. rev. ed. Ed. by Sylvia Galloway et al. 1977. 5.75 o.p. (ISBN 0-685-77228-4). ACE.

Guide to Professional Organizations. Marta Torres-Reilly et al. LC 80-110700. 168p. (Orig.). 1979. pap. text ed. 3.50 (ISBN 0-89763-015-7). Natl Clearinghouse Bilingual Ed.

Guide to Psychiatric Diagnosis & Understanding for the Helping Professions. Martin Goldberg. LC 73-77747. 1973. 15.95 (ISBN 0-88229-104-1). Nelson-Hall.

Guide to Psychiatry: A Handbook on Psychiatry for Health Professionals. James Allen & Barbara A. Allen. 1978. 17.50 (ISBN 0-87488-985-5); pap. 12.75 (ISBN 0-87488-716-X). Med Exam.

Guide to Psychologists & Their Concepts. Vernon J. Nordby & Calvin S. Hall. LC 74-11165. (Psychology Ser.). (Illus.). 1974. pap. text ed. 6.95x (ISBN 0-7167-0759-4). W H Freeman.

Guide to Public Administration. Debbie Cutchin. LC 80-84211. 130p. 1981. pap. text ed. 4.95 (ISBN 0-87581-272-4). Peacock Pubs.

Guide to Public Speaking. William Stedman. LC 70-136283. (Illus.). 1971. pap. text ed. 9.95 (ISBN 0-13-370635-4). P-H.

Guide to Public Speaking. 2nd ed. William Stedman. (Illus.). 208p. pap. text ed. 9.95 (ISBN 0-13-370619-2). P-H.

Guide to Publishers & Distributors Serving Minority Languages. rev. ed. Harpreet Sandhu & Laura Bukkila. 176p. 1980. pap. 4.50 (ISBN 0-89763-051-3). Natl Clearinghse Bilingual Ed.

Guide to Publishers & Distributors Serving Minority Languages. Harpreet K. Sandhu & Jory H. Barone. 171p. (Orig.). 1979. pap. 4.50 o.p. (ISBN 0-89763-012-2). Natl Clearinghouse Bilingual Ed.

Guide to Pynchon's Gravity's Rainbow. Douglas Fowler. 1980. 17.50 (ISBN 0-88233-404-2); pap. 7.50 (ISBN 0-88233-405-0). Ardis Pubs.

Guide to Quality Control. Kaorn Ishikowa. (Industrial Engineering & Technology Ser.). (Illus.). 1976. 20.75 (ISBN 92-833-1035-7, APO24, APO). Unipub.

Guide to Rapid Revision. 2nd ed. Daniel Pearlman & Paula R. Pearlman. LC 73-20076. 1974. pap. text ed. 2.50 (ISBN 0-672-63300-0). Odyssey Pr.

Guide to Real Estate License Examinations. 2nd ed. Jack Ellis. LC 78-14423. (Illus.). 1979. pap. 15.95 (ISBN 0-13-371070-X). P-H.

Guide to Recent Criminal Legislation. C. F. Schoolbred. LC 68-22498. 1968. 15.00 (ISBN 0-08-012895-5); pap. 7.00 (ISBN 0-08-012894-7). Pergamon.

Guide to Records of Northern Pacific Branch Lines, Subsidiaries, & Related Companies in the Minnesota Historical Society. Compiled by Maureen J. Leverty. LC 77-227041. 1977. pap. 2.00 (ISBN 0-87351-117-4). Minn Hist.

Guide to Recreation & Leisure. Donald C. Weiskopf. 362p. 1975. text ed. 19.95x (ISBN 0-205-04589-8, 6245897). Allyn.

Guide to Reference Books for School Media Centers. Christine L. Wynar. LC 73-87523. 473p. 1973. lib. bdg. 19.50 (ISBN 0-87287-069-3). Libs Unl.

Guide to Reference Books: Supplement. 9th ed. Ed. by Eugene P. Sheehy. LC 79-20541. 316p. 1980. pap. 15.00 (ISBN 0-8389-0294-4). ALA.

Guide to Refinery Operating Costs. 3rd ed. W. L. Nelson. LC 74-125557. 126p. 1976. 30.00 (ISBN 0-87814-002-6). Pennwell Pub.

Guide to Regional Dissection: Study of the Human Body. 4th ed. R. C. Crafts & R. T. Binhammer. LC 79-14417. 324p. 13.50 (ISBN 0-471-05154-3). Wiley.

Guide to Research & Reference Works on Sub-Saharan Africa. Peter Duignan & Helen F. Conover. LC 76-152424. (Bibliographical Ser.: No. 46). 1972. 19.50 (ISBN 0-8179-2461-2); pap. 8.95 (ISBN 0-8179-2462-0). Hoover Inst Pr.

Guide to Research Materials in the North Carolina State Archives, Section B: County Records. 1979. 5.00 (ISBN 0-86526-133-4). NC Archives.

Guide to Resource Organizations. Marta T. Reilly et al. (Resources in Bilingual Education Ser.). (Orig.). 1981. pap. write for info. (ISBN 0-89763-053-X). Natl Clearinghse Bilingual Ed.

Guide to Restringing. John W. Travis. LC 61-9870. (Illus.). 1972. 13.50x (ISBN 0-9600394-0-6); pap. 10.95x (ISBN 0-9600394-1-4). Travis.

Guide to Reupholstering. (Home Improvement Ser.). (Illus.). 112p. 1980. pap. 3.95 (ISBN 0-07-045971-1, GB). McGraw.

Guide to Reviews of Books from & About Hispanic America, 1978: Guia a las Resenas De Libros De y Sobre Hispanoamerica, 1978. Antonio Matos. LC 66-96537. 1980. 80.00 (ISBN 0-87917-073-5). Blaine Ethridge.

Guide to Rogallo Flight. Bob Skinner & Richard Finley. 1974. pap. 2.50 (ISBN 0-911721-76-2). Aviation.

Guide to Rough Shooting. Arthur Cadman. LC 74-15791. (Illus.). 144p. 1975. 11.95 (ISBN 0-7153-6637-8). David & Charles.

Guide to Russian Reference Books. Karol Maichel. Incl. Vol. 1. General Bibliographies & Reference Books. (Bibliographical Ser.: No. 10). 92p. 1962. 7.00 (ISBN 0-8179-2101-X); pap. 5.00 (ISBN 0-8179-2102-8); Vol. 2. History, Auxiliary Historical Sciences, Ethnography, & Geography. (Bibliographical Ser.: No. 18). 297p. 1964. 12.00 (ISBN 0-8179-2181-8); Vol. 5. Science, Technology & Medicine. (Bibliographical Ser.: No. 22). 384p. 1967. 17.50 (ISBN 0-8179-2321-7). LC 62-14067. Hoover Inst Pr.

Guide to Satellite Communication. (Reports & Papers on Mass Communication, No. 66). 50p. (Orig.). 1973. pap. 2.50 (ISBN 92-3-100959-1, U275, UNESCO). Unipub.

Guide to Science & Index to Life Science Library. Ed. by Life Editors. LC 67-29962. (Life Science Library). (Illus.). (gr. 5 up). 1967. PLB 8.97 o.p. (ISBN 0-8094-0936-4, Pub. by Time-Life). Silver.

Guide to Science Fiction & Fantasy in the Library of Congress Classification Scheme. R. Reginald. LC 80-11418. (Borgo Reference Library: Vol. 8). 64p. 1981. lib. bdg. 8.95x (ISBN 0-89370-807-0); pap. 2.95x (ISBN 0-89370-907-7). Borgo Pr.

Guide to Shell Collecting in the Kwajalein Atoll. Fred B. Brost & Robert D. Coale. LC 78-130418. (Illus.). 1971. pap. 11.00 (ISBN 0-8048-0942-9). C E Tuttle.

Guide to Site & Environmental Planning. 2nd ed. Harvey M. Rubenstein. LC 79-16142. 1980. 27.50 (ISBN 0-471-04729-5, Pub. by Wiley-Interscience). Wiley.

Guide to Slurry Pipeline Systems. P. J. Baker & B. E. Jacobs. (Illus.). 58p. (Orig.). 1980. PLB 32.00 (ISBN 0-906085-38-1, Dist. by Air Science Co.). BHRA Fluid.

Guide to Small Business Management. Hollingsworth. 1979. 10.95. Dryden Pr.

Guide to Smoke-Free Dining: National Directory of Restaurants Catering to Non-Smokers. Michael B. Horwitz. LC 80-66634. 112p. 1980. pap. 5.00 (ISBN 0-936960-01-9). Environ Pr.

Guide to Soil Mechanics. Malcolm Bolton. 439p. 1980. 37.95x (ISBN 0-470-26929-4). Halsted Pr.

Guide to Solar Electricity. Solarex Corporation. 143p. 1979. pap. text ed. 6.95 (ISBN 0-686-65543-5). Solar Energy Info.

Guide to Sources in Educational Media & Technology. Dorothy T. Taggart. LC 74-26849. 1975. 10.00 (ISBN 0-8108-0781-5). Scarecrow.

Guide to Special Collections. University of California, Berkeley, Library. Ed. by Audrey E. Phillips. LC 73-9572. 1973. 10.00 (ISBN 0-8108-0657-6). Scarecrow.

Guide to Stability Design Criteria for Metal Structures. 3rd ed. Bruce G. Johnston. LC 75-40155. 1976. 45.00 (ISBN 0-471-44629-7, Pub. by Wiley-Interscience). Wiley.

Guide to State Education Agencies. 48p. (Orig.). 1980. pap. 3.50 (ISBN 0-89763-027-0). Natl Clearinghse Bilingual Ed.

Guide to Store Location Research: With Emphasis on Super Markets. William Applebaum. 1968. text ed. 23.95 (ISBN 0-201-00285-X). A-W.

Guide to Story Telling. Arthur Burrell. LC 74-23577. 1971. Repr. of 1926 ed. 20.00 (ISBN 0-8103-3764-9). Gale.

Guide to Strategic Planning for Hospitals. Joseph P. Peters. LC 79-10063. 148p. (Orig.). 1979. 16.00 (ISBN 0-87258-259-0, 1200). Am Hospital.

Guide to Successful Dog Training. 2nd ed. Margaret E. Pearsall. LC 76-6806. 1976. 11.95 o.p. (ISBN 0-87605-758-X). Howell Bk.

Guide to Successful Investing. Charles D'Ambrosio. 1969. pap. text ed. 10.95x (ISBN 0-13-370817-9). P-H.

Guide to Surgical Terminology. 3rd ed. F. Coleman. 1978. pap. 18.95 (ISBN 0-87489-191-4). Med Economics.

Guide to Symphonic Music. Edward Downes. LC 76-13813. Orig. Title: New York Philharmonic Guide to the Symphony. (Illus.). 1058p. pap. 14.95 (ISBN 0-8027-7178-5). Walker & Co.

Guide to Systems Engineering & Management. Stanley M. Shinners. LC 76-7289. (Illus.). 1976. 21.95 (ISBN 0-669-00680-7). Lexington Bks.

Guide to Taxes & Record Keeping for Performers, Designers & Directors. rev. ed. R. Brendan Hanlon. LC 79-25783. (Illus.). 96p. 1980. pap. text ed. 4.95x (ISBN 0-89676-032-4). Drama Bk.

Guide to Teaching Strings. 3rd ed. Norman Lamb. (Instrumental Technique Ser.). 225p. 1980. pap. text ed. 7.95 (ISBN 0-697-03603-0). Wm C Brown.

Guide to the Administration of Charitable Remainder Trusts. 3rd ed. Ed. by David W. Clark & Robert L. Kaiser. 1978. pap. 38.50 (ISBN 0-89964-018-4). CASE.

Guide to the Appalachian Trail & Side Trails in the Shenandoah National Park. 7th ed. Ed. by Dana Dalrymple & Helen Dalrymple. 1973. pap. 3.50 o.p. (ISBN 0-915746-05-0). Potomac Appalach.

Guide to the Appalachian Trail & Side Trails in the Shenandoah National Park. 8th ed. Ed. by Molly T. Denton. LC 76-17452. 265p. 1977. pap. 5.00 o.p. (ISBN 0-915746-07-7). Potomac Appalach.

Guide to the Appalachian Trail from the Susquehanna River to the Shenandoah National Park. 9th ed. Dana Dalrymple & Helen Dalrymple. 1974. pap. 3.50 o.p. (ISBN 0-915746-06-9). Potomac Appalach.

Guide to the Archivo Franciscano of the National Library of Mexico. Ignacio Del Rio. (Miscellaneous Ser.). 1975. 20.00 (ISBN 0-88382-257-1). AAFH.

Guide to the Assessment of Day Care Services & Needs at the Community Level. Richard B. Zamoff. 1971. pap. 3.00 o.p. (ISBN 0-87766-072-7, 70007). Urban Inst.

Guide to the Automobile Mechanics Certification Examination. James G. Hughes. (Illus.). 1978. ref. ed. 15.95; pap. 10.50 (ISBN 0-8359-2618-4). Reston.

Guide to the Best in Contemporary Piano Music: An Annotated List of Graded Solo Piano Music Published Since 1950, 2 vols. Stanley Butler. Incl. Vol. 1. Levels 1-5. 10.00 (ISBN 0-8108-0628-2); Vol. 2. Levels 6-8. 10.00 (ISBN 0-8108-0669-X). LC 73-5693. 1973. Set. 17.95 o.p. (ISBN 0-685-34675-7). Scarecrow.

Guide to the Birds of Alaska. Robert H. Armstrong & Alaska Magazine Editors. 320p. 1980. pap. 15.95 (ISBN 0-88240-143-2). Alaska Northwest.

Guide to the Birds of Ceylon. 2nd ed. G. M. Henry. (Illus.). 1971. 37.50x (ISBN 0-19-217629-3). Oxford U Pr.

Guide to the Bright Angel Trail. Alan Berkowitz. 1979. pap. 1.00 (ISBN 0-938216-09-0). GCNHA.

Guide to the British Cathedrals. Leighton Houghton. (Illus.). 128p. 1974. pap. 5.95 (ISBN 0-212-97007-0). Transatlantic.

Guide to the Check Sheet of International Biological Programme Areas. G. F. Peterken. (International Biological Program Handbook No. 4). (Illus.). 1967. pap. 3.50 (ISBN 0-632-04670-8, Blackwell). Mosby.

Guide to the Collection: Isabella Stewart Gardner Museum. 2nd, rev. ed. LC 76-4176. (Illus.). 112p. 1980. pap. 2.00 (ISBN 0-914660-02-0). I S Gardner Mus.

Guide to the Collision Avoidance Rules: International Regulations for Preventing Collision at Sea, 1972, in Force 1977 (1978) 2nd ed. A. N. Cockcroft & J. N. Lameijer. (Illus.). 1978. 12.50 (ISBN 0-540-07272-9). Heinman.

Guide to the Colorado Ghost Towns & Mining Camps. 4th ed. Philip Eberhart. LC 59-11061. (Illus.). 496p. 1969. pap. 11.95 (ISBN 0-8040-0140-5, SB). Swallow.

Guide to the Colorado Mountains. rev. ed. Robert M. Ormes. LC 72-115033. 1970. 7.95 o.s.i. (ISBN 0-8040-0139-1, SB). Swallow.

Guide to the Continental Divide Trail: Wyoming, Vol. 3. James R. Wolf. LC 76-17632. (Guide to the Continental Divide Trail Ser.). (Illus., Orig.). 1980. pap. 9.95 (ISBN 0-934326-03-7). Continent Divide.

Guide to the Costing of Water from Nuclear Desalination Plants. (Technical Reports Ser.: No. 80). (Illus., Orig.). 1967. pap. 4.50 (ISBN 92-0-145267-5, IAEA). Unipub.

Guide to the Costing of Water from Nuclear Desalination Plants. (Technical Reports Ser.: No. 151). (Illus.). 79p. (Orig.). 1974. pap. 5.50 (ISBN 92-0-145273-X, IAEA). Unipub.

Guide to the Diagnostic Teaching of Arithmetic. Fredricka K. Reisman. (Elementary Education Ser.). 1978. pap. text ed. 7.95x (ISBN 0-675-08397-4). Merrill.

Guide to the Dissection of Domestic Ruminants. rev. 3rd ed. Robert E. Habel. (Illus.). 165p. 1975. text ed. 4.00x (ISBN 0-9600444-1-8). Habel.

Guide to the Economic Laws of Japan, 2 vols. Ministry of Finance, Japan. (Studies in Japanese Law & Government). 1979. Repr. of 1950 ed. Set. 62.50 (ISBN 0-89093-220-4). U Pubns Amer.

Guide to the Float Fishing Streams of Kentucky. Bob Sehlinger & Wes Underwood. (Illus., Orig.). 1980. pap. 9.95 (ISBN 0-89732-006-9). Thomas Pr.

Guide to the Freshwater Sport Fishes of Canada. D. E. McAllister & E. J. Crossman. (Illus.). 1973. pap. 4.95 (ISBN 0-660-00048-2, 56365-0, Pub. by Natl Mus Canada). U of Chicago Pr.

Guide to the Gardens of Kyoto. Marc Treib & Ron Herman. (Illus.). 200p. 1979. 9.95 o.p. (ISBN 0-8048-1345-0). C E Tuttle.

Guide to the Gardens of Kyoto. Marc Treib & Ron Herman. 216p. 1980. pap. text ed. 9.95 (ISBN 0-89955-312-5, Pub. by Shufunotomo Japan). Intl Schol Bk Serv.

Guide to the Ghost Towns & Mining Camps of Nye County, Nevada. Shawn Hall. (Illus.). 156p. 1981. 9.95 (ISBN 0-396-07955-5). Dodd.

Guide to the Golden Gate National Recreation Area. Dorothy L. Whitnah. Ed. by Thomas Winnett. LC 76-57009. (Illus., Orig.). 1978. pap. 5.95 (ISBN 0-911824-54-5). Wilderness.

Guide to the Historical & Archaeological Publications of Societies in England & Wales, 1901-1933. E. L. Mullins. 1968. text ed. 47.50x (ISBN 0-485-11094-6, Athlone Pr). Humanities.

Guide to the Historical Geography of New Spain. P. Gerhard. (Latin America Studies: No. 14). 1972. 84.50 (ISBN 0-521-08073-8). Cambridge U Pr.

Guide to the History & Restoration of Antique Trunks. Phyllis Ryerse. (Illus.). 34p. 1974. pap. 2.50 o.p. (ISBN 0-9603388-0-2). Ryerse.

Guide to the History of Brazil: 1500 to 1822. Francis A. Dutra. LC 80-10933. 625p. 1980. lib. bdg. 52.50 (ISBN 0-87436-263-6). ABC Clio.

Guide to the History of Mexico. Alfonso T. Zabre. (Illus.). 9.50 o.p. (ISBN 0-8363-0039-4). Jenkins.

Guide to the Hoover Institution Archives. Compiled by Charles G. Palm & Dale Reed. (Bibliographical Ser.: No. 59). 430p. 1980. pap. 50.00 (ISBN 0-8179-2591-0). Hoover Inst Pr.

Guide to the I Ching. Carol K. Anthony. LC 79-93376. 184p. (Orig.). 1980. pap. 4.95 (ISBN 0-9603832-0-4). Anthony Pub Co.

Guide to the Iliad. James C. Hogan. LC 78-58757. 1979. pap. 4.95 (ISBN 0-385-14519-5, Anch). Doubleday.

Guide to the Indian Tribes of Oklahoma. Muriel H. Wright. (Civilization of the American Indian Ser.: No. 33). (Illus.). 1979. Repr. of 1951 ed. 12.50 (ISBN 0-8061-0238-1). U of Okla Pr.

Guide to the Jellyfish of Canadian Atlantic Waters. C. T. Shih. (Illus.). 1977. pap. text ed. 5.00x (ISBN 0-660-00017-2, 56366-9, Pub. by Natl Mus Canada). U of Chicago Pr.

Guide to the Jewel Island. B. Olschak & T. Wangyal. 10.00 o.p. (ISBN 0-685-57295-1). Weiser.

Guide to the Kenya National Archives. Robert G. Gregoy et al. (Foreign & Comparative Studies-Eastern African Bibliographic Ser.: No. 3). 452p. 1969. 16.00. Syracuse U Foreign Comp.

Guide to the Lectionary. Ann B. Bushong. 1978. pap. 5.95 (ISBN 0-8164-2156-0). Crossroad NY.

Guide to the Mammals of Ohio. Jack L. Gottschang. (Illus.). 276p. 1981. 35.00 (ISBN 0-8142-0242-X). Ohio St U Pr.

Guide to the Manuscript Collections of the Bancroft Library, Vols. 1 & 2. Incl. Vol. I. Pacific & Western Manuscripts (Except California) Ed. by Dale L. Morgan & George P. Hammond. 1963 (ISBN 0-520-00882-0); Vol. II. Mexican & Central American Manuscripts. Ed. by George P. Hammond. 1973 (ISBN 0-520-01991-1). 31.50x ea. U of Cal Pr.

Guide to the Manuscript Groups in the Pennsylvania State Archives. Harry E. Whipkey. 1977. 7.00 (ISBN 0-911124-84-5). Pa Hist & Mus.

Guide to the Maryland Hall of Records: Local Judicial & Administrative Records on Microform, Vol. 1. Edward C. Papenfuse et al. 231p. 1978. 9.00 (ISBN 0-686-27482-2). MD Hall Records.

Guide to the Measurement of Animal Bones from Archaeological Sites. Angela Von den Driesch. LC 76-49773. (Peabody Museum Bulletins Ser.: No. 1). (Illus.). 1976. pap. text ed. 8.00x (ISBN 0-87365-950-3). Peabody Harvard.

Guide to the Measurement of Marine Primary Production Under Some Special Conditions. (Monographs on Oceanographic Methodology, No. 3). (Illus.). 73p. (Orig.). 1973. pap. 4.75 (ISBN 92-3-101099-9, U278, UNESCO). Unipub.

Guide to the Microfilm Collections in the Pennsylvania State Archives. Roland Baumann & Diane S. Wallace. 117p. 1980. pap. 5.00 (ISBN 0-89271-013-6). Pa Hist & Mus.

Guide to the Microfilm Edition of The Frank B. Kellogg Papers. Deborah K. Neubeck. LC 73-63612. 56p. 1978. pap. 2.00 (ISBN 0-87351-126-3). Minn Hist.

Guide to the Microfilm of the Records of Pennsylvania's Revolutionary Governments, 1775-1790. Ed. by Roland M. Baumann. 10.00 (ISBN 0-911124-96-9); pap. 8.00 (ISBN 0-911124-95-0). Pa Hist & Mus.

Guide to the Microfilm of the Records of the Provincial Council: 1682-1776. 130p. 1966. 5.00; pap. 3.00. Pa Hist & Mus.

Guide to the National Electral Code R. T. Harmon & C. Allen. 1981. 21.95 (ISBN 0-13-370478-5). P-H.

Guide to the National Trust in Devon & Cornwall. Peter Laws. LC 77-91765. (Illus.). 1978. 14.95 (ISBN 0-7153-7581-4). David & Charles.

Guide to the National Wildlife Refuges. Laura Riley & William Riley. (Illus.). 672p. 1981. pap. 9.95 (ISBN 0-385-14015-0, Anch). Doubleday.

Guide to the Native Mammals of Australia. W. D. Ride. (Illus.). 1970. 32.00x (ISBN 0-19-550252-3). Oxford U Pr.

Guide to the Natural World & Index to the Life Nature Library. Time-Life Books Editors. LC 65-22668. (Life Nature Library). 1965. lib. bdg. 8.97 o.p. (ISBN 0-8094-0932-1, Pub. by Time-Life). Silver.

Guide to the Nineteen Seventy-Eight National Electrical Code. Roland E. Palmquist. 1978. 12.95 (ISBN 0-672-23308-8). Audel.

Guide to the North Kaibab Trail. Alan Berkowitz. 1980. pap. 1.00 (ISBN 0-938216-10-4). GCNHA.

Guide to the Northville-Placid Trail. Adirondack Mountain Club, Map & Guidebook Committee. LC 80-16626. (Illus.). 160p. (Orig.). 1980. pap. 5.00 (ISBN 0-935272-12-7). ADK Mtn Club.

Guide to the Nudibranchs of California. Gary R. McDonald & James W. Nybakken. Ed. by R. T. Abbott. (Illus.). 72p. (Orig.). 1981. pap. 13.50 (ISBN 0-915826-08-9). Am Malacologists.

Guide to the Origin of British Surnames. Cecil H. Ewen. LC 68-30596. 1969. Repr. of 1938 ed. 18.00 (ISBN 0-8103-3123-3). Gale.

Guide to the Periodic Inspection of Nuclear Reactor Steel Pressure Vessels. (Technical Reports Ser.: No. 99). (Orig.). 1969. pap. 4.50 (ISBN 92-0-155069-3, IAEA). Unipub.

Guide to the Personal Papers in the Manuscripts Collections of the Minnesota Historical Society, Guide No. 1. Compiled by Grace L. Nute & Gertrude Ackermann. LC 35-27911. 146p. 1935. pap. 2.00 (ISBN 0-87351-004-6). Minn Hist.

Guide to the Pilgrim Hymnal. Albert C. Ronander & Ethel K. Porter. LC 65-26448. 456p. 1966. 10.95 (ISBN 0-8298-0055-7). Pilgrim Pr.

Guide to the Published Archives of Pennsylvania. Henry H. Eddy & Martha L. Simonetti. LC 49-9973. 1976. 3.50 (ISBN 0-911124-09-8). Pa Hist & Mus.

Guide to the Purchase of Children's Ponies. British Horse Society & Pony Club. 1979. pap. 1.95 (ISBN 0-8120-0786-7). Barron.

Guide to the Reference Literature on Women in the Social Sciences, Humanities, and Sciences. Gail M. Schlachter. (Clio Reference Guide Ser.). 1982. price not set (ISBN 0-87436-313-6). ABC Clio. Postponed.

Guide to the Romanization of Chinese. David Jordan. 78p. 1980. 3.95 (ISBN 0-89955-156-4, Pub. by Mei Ya Pub Taiwan). Intl Schol Bk Serv.

Guide to the Safe Design, Construction & Use of Radioisotopic Power Generators for Certain Land & Sea Applications. (Safety Ser.: No. 33). (Orig.). 1970. pap. 3.25 (ISBN 92-0-123070-2, ISP246, IAEA). Unipub.

Guide to the Safe Handling of Radioactive Wastes at Nuclear Power Plants. (Technical Reports Ser.: No. 198). 84p. 1980. pap. 12.00 (ISBN 92-0-125080-0, IOC198, IAEA). Unipub.

Guide to the Selection, Combination & Cooking of Foods, 2 vols. Carl A. Rietz. Incl. Vol. 1. Selection & Combination. 1961. 28.00 o.p. (ISBN 0-87055-032-2); Vol. 2. Formulation & Cookery. 1965. 30.00 o.p. (ISBN 0-87055-033-0). (Illus.). AVI.

Guide to the Ski Touring Centers of New England. Rod Lousteau. LC 80-82792. (Illus.). 144p. (Orig.). 1980. pap. 5.95 (ISBN 0-87106-046-9). Globe Pequot.

Guide to the Slavonic Languages, 2 pts. rev., enl., 3rd ed. Reginald G. De Bray. Incl. Pt. 1. South. 399p. 24.95 (ISBN 0-89357-060-5); Pt. 2. West. 483p. 27.95 (ISBN 0-89357-061-3). 1980. Slavica.

Guide to the Slavonic Languages: Part 2. 3rd rev. ed. Reginald G. DeBray. 483p. 80. 27.95 (ISBN 0-89357-061-3). Slavica.

Guide to the Slavonic Languages: Pt. 1, Guide to the South Slavonic Languages. 3rd rev. ed. Reginald G. De Bray. 399p. 1980. 24.95 (ISBN 0-89357-060-5). Slavica.

Guide to the Slavonic Languages: Pt. 3, Guide to the East Slavonic Languages. 3rd rev. ed. Reginald G. De Bray. 254p. 1980. 22.95 (ISBN 0-89357-062-1). Slavica.

Guide to the Social Services 1978. 66th ed. Family Welfare Assn. 1978. pap. 8.50x o.p. (ISBN 0-7121-0728-2). Intl Pubns Serv.

Guide to the Sources of British Military History. Ed. by Robin Higham. LC 74-104108. 1971. 38.50x (ISBN 0-520-01674-2). U of Cal Pr.

Guide to the Sources of the History of Africa South of the Sahara in the Netherlands, Vol. 9. Ed. by Netherlands State Archives Service. (Guides to the Sources for the History of Nations Ser. II: Africa South of the Sahara). 241p. 1978. 36.00 (ISBN 0-89664-007-8, Pub. by K G Saur). Gale.

Guide to the Sources of U. S. Military History: Supplement. Ed. by Robin Higham. 1981. 37.50 (ISBN 0-208-01750-X, Archon). Shoe String.

Guide to the Study of Animal Populations. James T. Tanner. LC 77-13630. 1978. 9.95x (ISBN 0-87049-235-7). U of Tenn Pr.

Guide to the Study of Freshwater Biology. 5th ed. James G. Needham & Paul R. Needham. LC 62-20742. (Illus.). 1962. pap. 5.95x (ISBN 0-8162-6310-8). Holden-Day.

Guide to the Study of Freshwater Ecology. W. Andrews. 1971. 11.36 (ISBN 0-13-370866-7); pap. text ed. 7.36 (ISBN 0-13-370759-8). P-H.

Guide to the Study of Medieval History. rev. ed. Louis J. Paetow. LC 80-81364. Repr. of 1931 ed. 55.00 (ISBN 0-527-69101-1). Kraus Repr.

Guide to the Study of the Holiness Movement. Charles E. Jones. LC 74-659. (ATLA Bibliography Ser.: No. 1). 1974. 35.00 (ISBN 0-8108-0703-3). Scarecrow.

Guide to the Underworld. Gunnar Ekelof. Tr. by Rika Lesser from Swedish. LC 80-13181. 96p. 1980. cloth. 10.00 (ISBN 0-87023-306-8). U of Mass Pr.

Guide to the Use of Medications During Pregnancy. Richard L. Berkowitz et al. 1980. pap. write for info. (ISBN 0-316-09173-1). Little.

Guide to the Use of Waterproofing, Dampproofing, Protective & Decorative Barrier Systems for Concrete. 1979. 17.15 (515.1R-79); 12.30. ACI.

Guide to the Vascular Flora of Illinois. Robert H. Mohlenbrock. LC 75-22414. 506p. 1975. lib. bdg. 22.95x (ISBN 0-8093-0704-9); pap. 10.95x (ISBN 0-8093-0756-1). S Ill U Pr.

Guide to the Vietnam Conflict. 2nd ed. Richard D. Burns & Milton Leitenberg. LC 80-13246. (Peace Bibliography Ser.: No. 3). 1981. write for info. (ISBN 0-87436-310-1). ABC Clio.

Guide to the Whiskies of Scotland. Derek Cooper. 1979. 2.95 (ISBN 0-346-12425-5). Cornerstone.

Guide to the Wines of Germany. Hans Siegel. 1979. pap. 2.95 (ISBN 0-346-12426-3). Cornerstone.

Guide to the Wines of the United States. Dominick Abel. 1979. 2.95 (ISBN 0-346-12427-1). Cornerstone.

Guide to the Works of John Dewey. Ed. by Jo Ann Boydston. LC 70-112383. (Arcturus Books Paperbacks). 413p. 1972. pap. 7.95 (ISBN 0-8093-0561-5). S Ill U Pr.

Guide to Thermoformed Plastic Packaging: Sales Builder-Cost Cutter. Stanley E. Farnham. LC 72-156481. 1972. 19.95 (ISBN 0-8436-1206-1). CBI Pub.

Guide to Theses & Dissertations: An Annotated, International Bibliography of Bibliographies. Ed. by Michael M. Reynolds. LC 74-11184. 600p. 1975. 42.00 (ISBN 0-8103-0976-9). Gale.

Guide to Title Seven ESEA: Bilingual Education Programs 1979 to 1980. LC 80-80697. 126p. 1980. pap. 2.50 (ISBN 0-89763-024-6). Natl Clearinghse Bilingual Ed.

Guide to Title VII ESEA Bilingual Bicultural Projects: 1973-1974. Dissemination Center for Bilingual-Bicultural Education. Ed. by Francesco Cordasco. LC 77-90544. (Bilingual Bicultural Education in the U. S. Ser.). 1978. Repr. of 1974 ed. lib. bdg. 18.00x (ISBN 0-405-11084-7). Arno.

Guide to Tournament Chess. William Lombardy & David Daniels. 1977. 8.95 o.p. (ISBN 0-679-13049-7); pap. 4.95 o.p. (ISBN 0-679-14041-7). McKay.

Guide to Travel Agency Accounting. M. J. Batham. LC 78-60276. 1979. 12.00 o.p. (ISBN 0-916032-05-1). Merton Hse.

Guide to Trekking in Nepal. 4th ed. Stephen Bezruchka. (Illus.). 240p. 1981. pap. 8.95 (ISBN 0-89886-003-2). Mountaineers.

Guide to Trivial Names, Trade Names & Synonyms for Substances Used in Analytical Chemistry. Ed. by H. M. Irving. 1978. pap. text ed. 10.00 (ISBN 0-08-022382-6). Pergamon.

Guide to Typewriting. Louis Freeman. (Orig.). (gr. 7-12). 1974. wkbk 4.00 (ISBN 0-87720-401-2). AMSCO Sch.

Guide to Undergraduate Projective Geometry. A. F. Horadam. LC 71-110243. 1970. 27.00 (ISBN 0-08-017479-5). Pergamon.

Guide to Understanding Romans. Harold J. Brokke. 284p. 1980. pap. 3.95 (ISBN 0-87123-193-X, 210193). Bethany Fell.

Guide to U. S. Government Directories. Donna R. Larson. 1981. lib. bdg. 27.50x (ISBN 0-912700-63-7). Oryx Pr.

Guide to Using CSMP: The Continuous System Modeling Program - a Program for Simulating Physical Systems. Frank H. Speckhart & Walter L. Green. 1976. 18.95 (ISBN 0-13-371377-6); solutions manual 4.50 (ISBN 0-13-371351-2). P-H.

Guide to Vegetable Gardening & Food Preserving. (Home Improvement Ser.). (Illus.). 112p. 1980. pap. 3.95 (ISBN 0-07-045969-X, GB). McGraw.

Guide to Venture Capital Sources. 5th ed. Stanley E. Pratt. 1981. 49.50 (ISBN 0-914470-12-4). Capital Pub Corp.

Guide to Vintage Wine Prices: Nineteen Seventy-Nine to Nineteen-Eighty Edition. S. Jay Aaron. 1979. pap. 7.95 (ISBN 0-446-97232-0). Warner Bks.

Guide to Virginia. Don Higginbotham. LC 80-53941. 1981. pap. 7.95 (ISBN 0-528-84540-3). Rand.

Guide to Virginia Military Organizations, 1861-1865. Lee A. Wallace, Jr. (Illus.). 348p. 1964. 35.00x o.p. (ISBN 0-685-65088-X). Va Bk.

Guide to Visiting Vineyards. Anthony Hogg. (Illus.). 1978. 12.50 o.p. (ISBN 0-7181-1560-0). Transatlantic.

Guide to Welsh Literature, Vol. 1. Ed. by A. O. Jarman & G. R. Hughes. 1976. text ed. 15.50x (ISBN 0-7154-0124-6). Humanities.

Guide to Welsh Literature, Vol. 2. Ed. by A. O. Jarman & G. R. Hughes. 1980. text ed. 23.50x (ISBN 0-7154-0457-1). Humanities.

Guide to Wisconsin's State Parks, Forests, & Trails. Jim Umhoefer. (Illus.). 160p. (Orig.). 1981. pap. 7.95 (ISBN 0-915024-26-8). Tamarack Edns.

Guide to Women's Art Organizations. Cynthia Navaretta. LC 79-83876. (Illus., Orig.). 1979. pap. text ed. 5.00 (ISBN 0-9602476-0-2, Pub. by Women's Artist News). Midmarch Assocs.

Guide to World Screw Threads. Peter Sidders. 292p. 1972. 19.50 (ISBN 0-8311-1092-9). Indus Pr.

Guide to Writing & Publishing in the Social & Behavioral Sciences. Carolyn J. Mullins. LC 77-1153. 1977. pap. 13.50 (ISBN 0-471-02708-1, Pub. by Wiley-Interscience). Wiley.

Guide to Writing Term Papers. Albert A. Theriault, Jr. (Orig.). (gr. 11-12). 1971. pap. text ed. 4.58 (ISBN 0-87720-350-4). AMSCO Sch.

Guidebook for Nutrition Counselors. Virginia Aronson & Barbara Fitzgerald. 448p. 1980. 19.50 (ISBN 0-8158-0387-7). Chris Mass.

Guidebook for Social Scientists. David Bartholomew. 148p. 1981. 34.50 (ISBN 0-471-27932-3, Pub. by Wiley-Interscience); pap. 19.95 (ISBN 0-471-27933-1). Wiley.

Guidebook for Teaching About the English Language. new ed. John Cormican & Gene Stanford. 1978. pap. text ed. 19.95 (ISBN 0-205-06119-2). Allyn.

Guidebook for Teaching English As a Second Language. Beverly Wattenmaker & Virginia Wilson. 224p. 1980. text ed. 19.95 (ISBN 0-205-06976-2). Allyn.

Guidebook for Teaching Foreign Language: Spanish, French, & German. Beverly Wattenmaker & Virginia Wilson. 312p. 1980. text ed. 17.95 (ISBN 0-205-06846-4). Allyn.

Guidebook for Teaching Literature. new ed. Raymond J. Rodrigues & Dennis Badaczewski. 1978. pap. text ed. 17.95 (ISBN 0-205-06068-4). Allyn.

Guidebook for Teaching United States History: Earliest Times to the Civil War. Tedd Levy & Donna C. Krasnow. 1979. pap. text ed. 18.95 (ISBN 0-205-06503-1). Allyn.

Guidebook for Teaching United States History: Mid-Nineteenth Century to Present. Tedd Levy & Donna C. Krasnow. 1979. pap. text ed. 18.95 (ISBN 0-205-06496-5). Allyn.

Guidebook for the Smart Investor: How to Analyze Real Estate Investment Returns. Walter N. Boyko. Ed. by Elizabeth H. Rand. LC 80-52879. (Illus.). 72p. (Orig.). 1981. pap. 6.95 (ISBN 0-914488-24-4). Rand-Tofua.

Guidebook for the Volunteer Reading Teacher. Lenore Sleisenger. LC 65-28685. (Orig.). 1965. pap. text ed. 3.00x (ISBN 0-8077-2167-0). Tchrs Coll.

Guidebook for Writers. Robert M. Frew et al. 200p. (gr. 9-12). 1981. pap. text ed. 6.95 (ISBN 0-917962-69-9). Peek Pubns.

Guidebook on Nuclear Techniques in Hydrology. (Technical Reports Ser.: No. 91). (Illus., Orig.). 1968. pap. 13.50 (ISBN 92-0-145068-0, IAEA). Unipub.

Guidebook to Better English, Bks. 1-4. Incl. Bk. 1 (ISBN 0-8332-1150-1); Bk. 2 (ISBN 0-8332-1151-X); Bk. 3 (ISBN 0-8332-1152-8); Bk. 4 (ISBN 0-8332-1153-6). 1978. pap. text ed. 2.49 ea.; dupl masters 18.60 ea.; tchr's handbook 1.17 (ISBN 0-8332-1154-4). Economy Co.

Guidebook to Better Reading: Levels 6-Adult. John Rambeau. (Guidebook to Better Reading Ser.). 1976. text ed. 2.67 (ISBN 0-87892-560-0); tchr's manual 2.67 (ISBN 0-87892-561-9). Economy Co.

Guidebook to Biochemistry. rev. 4th ed. Michael Yudkin & Robin Offord. LC 79-41606. (Illus.). 200p. 1980. 53.50 (ISBN 0-521-23084-5); pap. 15.95 (ISBN 0-521-29794-X). Cambridge U Pr.

Guidebook to Biochemistry: A New Edition of a Guidebook to Biochemistry by K. Harrison. 3rd ed. M. Yudkin & R. Offord. LC 70-153012. (Illus.). 1971. 32.50 (ISBN 0-521-08195-5); pap. text ed. 11.95x (ISBN 0-521-09654-5). Cambridge U Pr.

Guidebook to Dating, Waiting & Choosing a Mate. Norman Wright & Marvin Inmon. LC 78-26913. 1978. pap. 3.95 (ISBN 0-89081-150-4, 1504). Harvest Hse.

Guidebook to Mathematics. Blanche Laughlin. (Remedial). (gr. 7 up). 1967. pap. text ed. 2.19 (ISBN 0-87892-611-9); tchrs' handbook 2.19 (ISBN 0-87892-612-7). Economy Co.

Guidebook to Microscopical Methods. A. V. Grimstone & R. J. Skaer. LC 70-182027. (Illus.). 150p. 1972. 29.95 (ISBN 0-521-08445-8); pap. 8.95x (ISBN 0-521-09700-2). Cambridge U Pr.

Guidebook to North Carolina Taxes. Commerce Clearing House. 1981. pap. 9.00 (ISBN 0-685-39507-3). Commerce.

Guidebook to Nuclear Reactors. Anthony V. Nero, Jr. (Cal. Ser.: No. 393). 1979. 27.50x (ISBN 0-520-03482-1); pap. 9.95 (ISBN 0-520-03661-1). U of Cal Pr.

Guidebook to Ohio Taxes: 1981. Commerce Clearing House. 1981. pap. 9.00 (ISBN 0-685-39506-5). Commerce.

Guidebook to Stereochemistry. F. D. Gunstone. LC 75-12762. (Illus.). 128p. 1975. pap. text ed. 10.95x (ISBN 0-582-44170-6). Longman.

Guidebook to the Freedom of Information & Privacy Acts. Ed. by Robert F. Bouchard. LC 79-27406. 1980. 35.00 (ISBN 0-87632-310-7). Boardman.

Guidebook to the True Secret of the Heart, 2 vols. M. R. Bawa Muhaiyaddeen. (Illus.). 1976. pap. 4.95 ea. Vol. 1, 224p (ISBN 0-914390-07-4). Vol. 3, 223p (ISBN 0-914390-08-2). Fellowship Pr PA.

Guidebook to Wisconsin Taxes: 1981. Commerce Clearing House. 1981. pap. 9.00 (ISBN 0-685-39504-9). Commerce.

Guided Engineering Design: An Introduction to Engineering Calculations. Charles E. Wales et al. 432p. 1974. pap. text ed. 12.95 (ISBN 0-8299-0001-2); instrs.' manual avail. (ISBN 0-8299-0005-5). West Pub.

Guided Engineering Design: An Introduction to Engineering Calculations. 2nd ed. Charles E. Wales et al. (Illus.). 330p. 1980. pap. text ed. 13.95 (ISBN 0-8299-0353-4); Project Bk. 10.95 (ISBN 0-8299-0378-X). West Pub.

Guided Observations in Child Development. Jean Mercer. LC 79-88267. 1979. pap. text ed. 9.00 (ISBN 0-8191-0768-9). U Pr of Amer.

Guided Study in Forkner Shorthand. Gloria Hansen Weber & Edwin J. Weber. 1974. pap. 5.32x (ISBN 0-912036-21-4). Forkner.

Guided Weapon Control Systems. P Garnell & D. J. East. LC 76-40061. 1977. text ed. 33.00 o.p. (ISBN 0-08-019691-8). Pergamon.

Guidelines for a Corporate Law Office Manual. American Bar Association, Corporate, Banking & Business Law Committee of the Young Lawyers Div. LC 79-88508. 75p. (Orig.). 1980. pap. text ed. 35.00 (ISBN 0-89707-023-2). Prof Educ IL.

Guidelines for a Local Employment Study. Barrie Needham. 1978. text ed. 23.00x (ISBN 0-566-00241-8, Pub. by Gower Pub Co England). Renouf.

Guidelines for Appraisal Office Policies & Procedures. 69p. (Orig.). 1981. pap. 8.00 (ISBN 0-911780-49-1). Am Inst Real Estate Appraisers.

Guidelines for Better Platemaking. Ed. by Eastman Kodak Co. (Illus., Orig.). 1976. pap. 3.95 o.s.i. (ISBN 0-87985-065-5, Q213). Eastman Kodak.

Guidelines for Developing a Bridge Maintenance Program. 28p. 10.00 (ISBN 0-917084-17-9). Am Public Works.

Guidelines for Fiduciaries of Taft-Hartley Trusts: An ERISA Manual. Noel A. Levin. 137p. 1980. 25.00 (ISBN 0-89154-135-7). Intl Found Employ.

Guidelines for Field Studies in Environmental Perception. (MAB Technical Notes: No. 5). 1978. pap. 9.25 (ISBN 92-3-101483-8, U783, UNESCO). Unipub.

Guidelines for Graded Exercise Testing & Exercise Prescription. 2nd ed. Ed. by American College of Sports Medicine. LC 80-19484. (Illus.). 151p. 1980. pap. 6.50 (ISBN 0-8121-0769-1). Lea & Febiger.

Guidelines for High School Students on Conducting Research in the Sciences. Laurie A. Lyon. 1980. 1.25 (ISBN 0-87716-114-3). Moore Pub Co.

Guidelines for Improving Articulation Between Junior & Senior Colleges. Joint Committee on Junior & Senior Colleges. 1966. pap. 2.50 10 copies o.p. (ISBN 0-685-32623-3). ACE.

Guidelines for Integrated Control of Maize Pests. (FAO Plant Production & Protection Paper Ser.: No. 18). 98p. 1980. pap. 6.00 (ISBN 92-5-100875-2, F1942, FAO). Unipub.

Guidelines for Management Consultants in Asia. John E. Walsh, Jr. LC 73-83083. 205p. 1973. 15.00 (ISBN 92-833-1028-4, APO29, APO). Unipub.

Guidelines for Marriage in the Orthodox Church. S. Harakas. 1980. pap. 1.25 (ISBN 0-937032-21-2). Light&Life Pub Co MN.

Guidelines for Personnel in the Education of Exceptional Children. Jean R. Hebeler & Maynard C. Reynolds. LC 76-6728. 1976. pap. text ed. 3.50x o.p. (ISBN 0-86586-038-6). Coun Exc Child.

Guidelines for Productivity Measurement & Analysis for APO Member Countries. 52p. 1980. pap. 13.25 (ISBN 92-833-1463-8, APO 87, APO). Unipub.

Guidelines for School Nurse in School Health Program. 1974. members 1.50. Am Sch Health.

Guidelines for Selected Personnel Practices in Catholic Schools II. 58p. 1977. 3.75. Natl Cath Educ.

Guidelines for Selecting Basic & Life Skills Tests. 1980. pap. 4.25 (ISBN 0-89354-830-8). Northwest Regional.

Guidelines for Selecting Bias-Free Textbooks & Storybooks. Council on Interracial Books for Children, Inc. LC 80-165903. 105p. 1980. pap. 6.95 (ISBN 0-930040-33-3). CIBC.

Guidelines for Teaching Mathematics. 2nd ed. Donovan A. Johnson & Gerald R. Rising. 560p. 1972. 17.95x (ISBN 0-534-00189-0). Wadsworth Pub.

Guidelines for the Development of Continuing Education Offerings for Nurses. Eileen K. Austin. 176p. 1981. pap. 11.00 (ISBN 0-8385-3524-0). ACC.

Guidelines for the Development of Employment & Manpower Information Programmes in Developing Countries. 87p. 1980. pap. 8.00 (ISBN 92-2-102176-9, ILO148, ILO). Unipub.

Guidelines for the Development of Employment & Manpower Information Programmes in Developing Countries: A Practical Manual. International Labour Office, Geneva. (Illus.). 87p. (Orig.). 1979. pap. 7.15 (ISBN 9-22-102176-9). Intl Labour Office.

Guidelines for the Layout & Contents of Safety Reports for Stationary Nuclear Power Plants. (Safety Ser.: No. 34). (Orig.). 1970. pap. 4.50 (ISBN 92-0-123170-9, ISP272, IAEA). Unipub.

Guidelines for the Preparation of Radiopharmaceuticals in Hospitals. 1980. 10.00x (Pub. by Brit Inst Radiology). State Mutual Bk.

Guidelines for Women's Groups in the Congregation. Oscar E. Feucht. 1981. pap. 3.95 (ISBN 0-570-03828-6, 12-2793). Concordia.

Guidelines for Writers of SI Metric Standards & Other Documents. Ed. by Lou Perica & Len Boselovic. 1975. pap. text ed. 8.00 (ISBN 0-916148-04-1). Am Natl.

Guidelines, Informal Controls, & the Market Place. Ed. by George P. Shultz & Robert Z. Aliber. LC 66-23699. (Orig.). 1966. 12.00x o.s.i. (ISBN 0-226-75597-5); pap. 3.95 o.s.i. (ISBN 0-226-75598-3). U of Chicago Pr.

Guidelines on Statistics of Tangible Assets. (Statistical Papers Ser. M: No. 68). 63p. 1980. pap. 6.00 (ISBN 0-686-68959-3, UN80/17/2, UN). Unipub.

Guidelines on the Operation of Subscription Bus Services. Ronald F. Kirby & Kiran U. Bhatt. 76p. 1975. pap. 3.00 o.p. (ISBN 0-87766-141-3, 11100). Urban Inst.

Guidelines on the Provision of Adequate Reception Facilities in Ports, Part II: Residues & Mixtures Containing Noxious Liquid Substances. 14p. 1980. pap. 6.00 (ISBN 9-2801-1098-5, IMCCO 61, IMCO). Unipub.

Guidelines on the Provision of Adequate Reception Facilities in Ports: Oily Wastes, Pt. 1. 16p. 1976. 7.00 (IMCO). Unipub.

Guidelines on the Provision of Adequate Reception Facilities in Ports: Sewage, Pt. 3. 27p. 1978. 7.00 (IMCO). Unipub.

Guidelines on the Provision of Adequate Reception Facilities in Ports: Garbage, Pt. 4. 27p. 1978. 7.00 (IMCO). Unipub.

Guidelines to Assess Computerized General Ledger & Financial Reporting Systems for Use in CPA Firms. 1980. pap. 6.50. Am Inst CPA.

Guidelines to Assess Computerized Time & Billing Systems for Use in CPA Firms. 1980. pap. 6.50. Am Inst CPA.

Guidelines to Problems of Education in Brazil: A Review & Selected Bibliography. Malvina R. McNeill. LC 76-120599. 1970. text ed. 6.00x (ISBN 0-8077-1789-4). Tchrs Coll.

Guidelines to Professional Employment for Engineers & Scientists. Date not set. 1.00 (511-78). AAES.

Guidellines for Skid Resistant Pavement Design. 1976. 1.50. AASHTO.

Guideposts to the Stars: Exploring the Skies Through the Year. Leslie C. Peltier. LC 72-187797. (Illus.). (gr. 7 up). 1972. 9.95 (ISBN 0-02-770600-1). Macmillan.

Guideposts Treasury of Hope. Ed. by Guidepost Magazine. 320p. 1980. pap. 2.50 (ISBN 0-553-13678-X). Bantam.

Guideposts Treasury of Hope. Guideposts Associates. LC 78-22228. (Illus.). 1979. 9.95 (ISBN 0-385-14975-1). Doubleday.

Guideposts Treasury of Inspirational Classics. 1981. pap. 2.95 (ISBN 0-553-14271-2). Bantam.

Guideposts Treasury of Love. Guidepost Associates. (Illus.). 352p. 1981. 12.95 (ISBN 0-385-14973-5). Doubleday.

Guides to Creative Motion Musicianship. Margaret Allen. 136p. 1979. 6.95 (ISBN 0-8059-2616-X). Dorrance.

Guides to Straight Thinking, with Thirteen Common Fallacies. Stuart Chase. 1956. 10.00 o.s.i. (ISBN 0-06-010710-3, HarpT). Har-Row.

Guiding Children to Mathematical Discovery. 3rd ed. Leonard M. Kennedy. 544p. 1979. text ed. 17.95x (ISBN 0-534-00757-0). Wadsworth Pub.

Guiding Children's Reading Through Experience. Roma Gans. LC 79-16407. 1979. pap. 6.50x (ISBN 0-8077-2569-2). Tchrs Coll.

Guiding Discovery to Elementary School Math. 2nd ed. C. Alan Riedesel. 1973. text ed. 19.95 (ISBN 0-13-371583-3). P-H.

Guiding the Physically Handicapped College Student. Herbert Rusalem. LC 62-14646. (Orig.). 1962. pap. 4.25x (ISBN 0-8077-2071-2). Tchrs Coll.

Guiding the Psychological & Educational Growth of Children. Jerry W. Willis et al. (Illus.). 232p. 1976. 15.50 (ISBN 0-398-03273-4); pap. 9.75 (ISBN 0-398-03274-2). C C Thomas.

Guiding Young Children to Music: A Resource Book for Teachers. B. Joan Haines & Linda L. Gerber. (Early Childhood Education Ser.: No. C24). 288p. 1980. pap. text ed. 12.95 spiral bdg. (ISBN 0-675-08161-0). Merrill.

Guiding Young Children's Learning. Sara Lundsteen & Norma Bernstein-Tarrow. (Illus.). 528p. 1981. text ed. 16.95 (ISBN 0-07-039105-X, C); instrs'. manual avail. (ISBN 0-07-039106-8). McGraw.

Guiding Your Child: A 60-Point Checklist for Parents. Elliott D. Landau & M. Winston Egan. LC 78-70361. 1978. pap. 2.95 (ISBN 0-88290-103-6). Horizon Utah.

Guiding Youth. Donald S. Aultman. 1977. pap. 3.50 (ISBN 0-87148-358-0). Pathway Pr.

Guido Cantelli: Portrait of a Maestro. Lawrence Lewis. LC 80-29385. (Illus.). 176p. 1981. 11.95 (ISBN 0-498-02493-8). A S Barnes.

Guidry. Ron Guidry & Peter Golenbock. LC 80-13732. 1980. 8.95 (ISBN 0-13-371609-0). P-H.

Guigo II: The Ladder of Monks & Twelve Meditations. Guigo II. Tr. by Edmund Colledge & James Walsh. (Cistercian Studies: No. 48). 1981. pap. write for info. (ISBN 0-87907-748-4). Cistercian Pubns.

Guilds. Neil Grant. LC 72-3616. (First Bks). (Illus.). 96p. (gr. 4-7). 1972. PLB 4.90 o.p. (ISBN 0-531-00771-5). Watts.

Guillaume Apollinaire. Scott Bates. (World Authors Ser.: France: No. 14). lib. bdg. 10.95 (ISBN 0-8057-2052-9). Twayne.

Guillaume Apollinaire. LeRoy C. Breunig. LC 79-92030. (Columbia Essays on Modern Writers Ser.: No. 46). 1969. pap. 2.00 (ISBN 0-231-02995-0). Columbia U Pr.

Guillaume Apollinaire. Roger Little. (Athlone French Poets Ser). 160p. 1976. text ed. 20.00x (ISBN 0-485-14608-8, Athlone Pr); pap. text ed. 10.00x (ISBN 0-485-12208-1). Humanities.

Guillaume De Machaut. Siegmund Levarie. LC 70-98309. (Music Ser). 1969. Repr. of 1954 ed. lib. bdg. 15.00 (ISBN 0-306-71831-6). Da Capo.

Guillaume De Palerne. Ed. by H. Michelant. 1876. 25.25 (ISBN 0-384-20400-7); pap. 23.00 (ISBN 0-685-13449-0). Johnson Repr.

Guillaume D'Orange: Four Twelfth-Century Epics. Tr. by Joan M. Ferrante from Fr. LC 74-4421. (Records of Civilization Ser). 312p. 1974. 18.50x (ISBN 0-231-03809-7). Columbia U Pr.

Guillaume Tell, 2 vols. Gioachino Rossini. Ed. by Phillip Gossett & Charles Rosen. LC 76-49192. (Early Romantic Opera Ser.: No. 17). 1980. lib. bdg. 82.00 (ISBN 0-8240-2916-X). Garland Pub.

Guillen de Castro. William E. Wilson. (World Authors Ser.: Spain: No. 253). 1973. pap. 10.95 (ISBN 0-8057-2202-5). Twayne.

Guilt, Anger, & God. C. Fitzsimons Allison. 1972. pap. 3.95 (ISBN 0-8164-2091-2). Crossroad NY.

Guilt Edged. W. J. Burley. 1981. pap. 2.25 (ISBN 0-440-13082-4). Dell.

Guilt Trips. Ann Cates. (Illus.). 100p. (Orig.). 1980. pap. 2.95 (ISBN 0-937768-00-6). Expressions TX.

Guilty As Charged. Elizabeth Hanley. 1979. pap. 1.75 (ISBN 0-505-51373-0). Tower Bks.

Guilty, O Lord: Yes, I Still Go to Confession. Basset, Bernard, S.J. LC 74-9475. 120p. 1976. pap. 1.45 o.p. (ISBN 0-385-11372-2, Im). Doubleday.

Guilty Ones. George G. Gilman. (Edge Ser.: No. 31). 1979. pap. 1.75 (ISBN 0-523-41313-0). Pinnacle Bks.

Guinea-Bissau: A Study of Political Mobilization. Lars Rudebeck. (Illus.). 277p. 1974. pap. text ed. 15.00x o.p. (ISBN 0-8419-9715-2). Holmes & Meier.

Guinea Journals: Journeys into Guinea-Conakry During the Sierra Leone Phase, 1800-1821. Ed. by Bruce L. Mouser. LC 79-62896. 1979. pap. text ed. 10.25 (ISBN 0-8191-0713-1). U Pr of Amer.

Guinea Pigs, All About Them. Alvin Silverstein & Virginia Silverstein. LC 74-148487. (Illus.). 96p. (gr. 3-7). 1972. 7.25 o.p. (ISBN 0-688-41664-0); PLB 6.96 (ISBN 0-688-51664-5). Lothrop.

Guinea Pigs for Beginners. Mervin F. Roberts. (Illus.). 1972. pap. 2.00 (ISBN 0-87666-198-3, M-541). TFH Pubns.

Guinea Pigs: Their Care & Breeding. Hutchinson. (Illus.). 104p. 1981. 3.95 (ISBN 0-903264-21-8, 5213-9, Pub. by K & R Bks England). Arco.

Guinevere. Sharan Newman. 256p. 1981. 10.95 (ISBN 0-312-35318-9). St Martin.

Guinevere's Gift. Nicole St. John. 1979. pap. 1.95 (ISBN 0-446-89881-3). Warner Bks.

Guinness Book of Amazing Achievements. Norris McWhirter & Ross McWhirter. LC 75-14502. (Guinness Illustrated Collection for Young People Ser.). (Illus.). 96p. (YA) 1975. 5.95 (ISBN 0-8069-0034-2); lib. bdg. 6.69 (ISBN 0-8069-0035-0). Sterling.

Guinness Book of Astounding Feats & Events. Norris McWhirter & Ross McWhirter. LC 75-14503. (Guinness Illustrated Collection for Young People Ser.). 96p. (YA) 1975. 5.95 (ISBN 0-8069-0036-9); lib. bdg. 6.69 (ISBN 0-8069-0037-7). Sterling.

Guinness Book of Daring Deeds & Fascinating Facts. Norris McWhirter & Ross McWhirter. LC 78-66312. (Illus.). (gr. 3 up). 1979. 5.95 (ISBN 0-8069-0158-6); PLB 6.69 (ISBN 0-8069-0159-4). Sterling.

Guinness Book of Dazzling Endeavors. Ross McWhirter & Norris McWhirter. LC 80-52330. (Guinness Illustrated Collection of World Records for Young Readers). (Illus.). 96p. (gr. 3 up). 1980. 5.95 (ISBN 0-8069-0194-2); PLB 6.69 (ISBN 0-8069-0195-0). Sterling.

Guinness Book of Exceptional Experiences. Ed. by Norris McWhirter & Ross McWhirter. LC 76-19801. (Guinness Illustrated Collection of World Records for Young People). (Illus.). 96p. (gr. 3 up). 1976. 5.95 (ISBN 0-8069-0042-3); PLB 6.69 (ISBN 0-8069-0043-1). Sterling.

Guinness Book of Extraordinary Exploits. Norris McWhirter & Ross McWhirter. LC 77-79505. (Guinness Illustrated Collection of World Records for Young Readers). (Illus.). (gr. 3 up). 1977. 5.95 (ISBN 0-8069-0118-7); PLB 6.69 (ISBN 0-8069-0119-5). Sterling.

Guinness Book of Phenomenal Happenings. Ed. by Norris McWhirter & Ross McWhirter. LC 76-1162. (Illus.). 96p. (gr. 4 up). 1976. 5.95 (ISBN 0-8069-0040-7); PLB 6.69 (ISBN 0-8069-0041-5). Sterling.

Guinness Book of Sports Records, Winners & Champions. Norris McWhirter et al. LC 79-91388. (Illus.). 320p. 1980. 10.95 (ISBN 0-8069-0182-9); lib. bdg. 9.89 (ISBN 0-8069-0183-7). Sterling.

Guinness Book of Startling Acts & Facts. Norris McWhirter & Ross McWhirter. LC 78-57791. (Guinness Illustrated Collection of World Records for Young Readers). (Illus.). (gr. 2 up). 1978. 5.95 (ISBN 0-8069-0128-4); PLB 6.69 (ISBN 0-8069-0129-2). Sterling.

Guinness Book of Superstunts & Staggering Statistics. Norris McWhirter. LC 79-91387. (Guinness Illustrated Collection of World Records for Young Readers Ser.). (Illus.). 96p. (gr. 3-12). 1980. 5.95 (ISBN 0-8069-0180-2); PLB 6.69 (ISBN 0-8069-0181-0). Sterling.

Guinness Book of Surprising Accomplishments. Norris McWhirter & Ross McWhirter. LC 76-51178. (Guinness Illustrated Collection of World Records for Young People Ser.). (gr. 3 up). 1977. 5.95 (ISBN 0-8069-0046-6); PLB 6.69 (ISBN 0-8069-0047-4). Sterling.

Guinness Book of Women's Sports Records. Norris McWhirter et al. LC 78-66315. (Illus.). 1979. 7.95 (ISBN 0-8069-0162-4); lib. bdg. 7.49 (ISBN 0-8069-0163-2). Sterling.

Guinness Book of World Records. 19th ed. Ed. by Norris McWhirter. 672p. 1981. pap. 3.50 (ISBN 0-553-14500-2). Bantam.

Guinness Book of World Records 1981. rev. ed. Norris McWhirter. LC 65-24391. (Illus.). 652p. 1980. 10.95 (ISBN 0-8069-0196-9); deluxe ed. 15.95 (ISBN 0-8069-0198-5); lib. bdg. 10.79 (ISBN 0-8069-0197-7). Sterling.

Guinness Book of Young Recordbreakers. Norris McWhirter & Ross McWhirter. LC 76-1161. (Illus.). 96p. (gr. 2-5). 1976. 5.95 (ISBN 0-8069-0038-5); PLB 6.69 (ISBN 0-8069-0039-3). Sterling.

Guinness Book of Young Recordbreakers. rev. ed. Ross McWhirter & Norris McWhirter. LC 76-1161. (Guinness Illustrated Collection of World Records for Young Readers). (Illus.). 96p. (gr. 3 up). 1981. 5.95 (ISBN 0-8069-0216-7); PLB 6.69 (ISBN 0-8069-0217-5). Sterling.

Guinness Game Book. Norris McWhirter & Norvin Pallas. LC 77-93311. (Illus.). (gr. 3 up). 1978. 5.95 (ISBN 0-8069-0122-5); PLB 5.89 (ISBN 0-8069-0123-3). Sterling.

Guinness Sports Record Book. 7th ed. Ed. by Norris McWirter. 192p. 1980. pap. 2.25 (ISBN 0-553-13238-5). Bantam.

Guinness Sports Record Book, 1979-1980. Norris McWhirter. LC 78-66316. (Illus.). 1979. 5.95 o.p. (ISBN 0-8069-0164-0); lib. bdg. 5.89 o.p. (ISBN 0-8069-0165-9). Sterling.

Guinness World Records Comprehension Module Program II. Mary J. Yunker. LC 78-730959. (gr. 4-8). 1978. pap. text ed. 175.00 (ISBN 0-89290-110-1, CM-72). Soc for Visual.

Guinness World Records Math Learning Module. Robert Rohm. LC 79-730909. (Illus.). (gr. 6-7). 1979. pap. text ed. 175.00 (ISBN 0-89290-091-1, CM-73). Soc for Visual.

Guitar: An Introduction to the Instrument. Thomas A. Hill. LC 73-4532. (Keynote Bks.). (gr. 5 up). 1973. PLB 4.90 o.p. (ISBN 0-531-02635-3). Watts.

Guitar Chord Encyclopedia. 256p. 1980. pap. 2.49 (ISBN 0-8256-3206-4, Quick Fox). Music Sales.

Guitar for a Singing Planet. Joseph Adler. 1976. pap. text ed. 9.95 (ISBN 0-8403-1428-0). Kendall-Hunt.

Guitar Music in Print. Joseph Rezits. LC 80-84548. 1000p. (Orig.). 1981. pap. 50.00 (ISBN 0-8497-7802-6, Pub. by Kjos West). Kjos.

Guitar Player Book. rev. ed. Ed. by Jim Crockett. LC 79-2350. (Illus.). 416p. 1979. pap. 9.95 (ISBN 0-394-17169-1, E739, Ever). Grove.

Guitar Repair: A Manual of Repair for Guitars & Fretted Instruments. Richard Pollack & Irving Sloane. 1973. 14.95 (ISBN 0-525-12002-5). Dutton.

Guitar Songbook. Frederick M. Noad. LC 69-16492. 1969. pap. 6.95 (ISBN 0-02-871730-9). Schirmer Bks.

Guitar Songbook with Instructions. Beverly McKeown. 1975. pap. text ed. 9.95 (ISBN 0-395-18648-X). HM.

Guitarrero Cave: Early Man in the Andes. Ed. by Thomas F. Lynch. LC 79-8868. (Studies in Archaeology). 1980. 20.00 (ISBN 0-12-460580-X). Acad Pr.

Guizer. Alan Garner. LC 75-42040. (Illus.). 224p. (gr. 7 up). 1976. 9.50 (ISBN 0-688-86001-X). Greenwillow.

Guizot in the Early Years of the Orleanist Monarchy. Elizabeth P. Brush. LC 74-2319. (University of Illinois Studies in the Social Sciences). 236p. 1975. Repr. of 1929 ed. 15.25 (ISBN 0-86527-090-2). Fertig.

Gujarati Language Course. H. M. Lambert. LC 68-23180. 1970. 44.00 (ISBN 0-521-07157-7). Cambridge U Pr.

Gulbadan: Portrait of a Rose Princess at the Mughal Court. Rumer Godden. LC 80-51752. (Illus.). 160p. 1981. 14.95 (ISBN 0-670-35756-1, Studio). Viking Pr.

Gulf Stream: A Physical & Dynamical Description. Henry Stommmel. (California Library Reprint Ser). 1977. Repr. of 1964 ed. 20.00x (ISBN 0-520-03307-8). U of Cal Pr.

Gulf Stream North. Earl Conrad. LC 80-50244. 256p. 1980. 15.95 (ISBN 0-933256-13-2); pap. 7.95 (ISBN 0-933256-17-5). Second Chance.

Gulf Telephone Directory 1980. 1980. 95.00x (Pub. by Parrish-Rogers England). State Mutual Bk.

Gull Number 737. Jean C. George. LC 64-16531. (Illus.). (gr. 5-10). 1964. 8.95 (ISBN 0-690-36171-8, TYC-J). T Y Crowell.

Gulliver & the Gentle Reader: Studies in Swift & Our Time. C. J. Rawson. 200p. 1973. 18.50x (ISBN 0-7100-7602-9). Routledge & Kegan.

Gulliver of Mars. Edwin P. Arnold. 1976. lib. bdg. 12.95x (ISBN 0-89968-173-5). Lightyear.

Gulliveriana, No. 1. Incl. Trip to the Moon. Murtagh McDermot. Repr. of 1728 ed; Trip to the Moon. Humphrey Lunatic. Repr. of 1764 ed. LC 73-133329. 220p. 1970. 25.00x (ISBN 0-8201-1084-1). Schol Facsimiles.

Gulliver's Travels. Harold G. Shane. Ed. by William Clark. (Hero Legends Bk). (Illus.). 16p. (gr. 3-5). 1980. pap. 22.00 ten bks & one cass. (ISBN 0-89290-083-0, BC15-6). Soc for Visual.

Gulliver's Travels. rev. ed. Jonathan Swift. Ed. by Robert A. Greenberg. (Critical Editions). (Annotated). (gr. 9-12). 1970. pap. text ed. 5.95x (ISBN 0-393-09941-5, 9941, NortonC). Norton.

Gulliver's Travels. Jonathan Swift. (Literature Ser). (gr. 10-12). 1970. pap. text ed. 3.58 (ISBN 0-87720-727-5). AMSCO Sch.

Gulliver's Travels. Jonathan Swift. Ed. by Martin Price. LC 62-21262. 1964. pap. 5.95 (ISBN 0-672-60968-1, LL3). Bobbs.

Gulliver's Travels. Jonathan Swift. (gr. 7-9). 1962. 5.25g o.s.i. (ISBN 0-02-788770-7). Macmillan.

Gulliver's Travels. Jonathan Swift. (World's Classics Ser: No. 20). 3.95 o.p. (ISBN 0-19-250020-1). Oxford U Pr.

Gulliver's Travels. Jonathan Swift. Ed. by Peter Dixon & J. Chalker. (English Library Ser.). 1967. pap. 2.25 (ISBN 0-14-043022-9). Penguin.

Gulliver's Travels. Jonathan Swift. LC 78-3394. (Raintree's Illustrated Classics). (Illus.). (gr. 5-8). 1978. PLB 9.65 (ISBN 0-8393-6207-2). Raintree Child.

Gulliver's Travels & Other Writings. Jonathan Swift. pap. 1.75. Bantam.

Gulliver's Travels, Annotated. Jonathan Swift. Ed. & intro. by Isaac Asimov. (Clarkson N. Potter Bks.: Clarkson N. Potter Book). (Illus.). 320p. 1980. 19.95 (ISBN 0-517-53949-7). Crown.

Gulliver's Travels with the Illustrarions of J. J. Grandville. Jonathan Swift. LC 80-22845. (Illus.). 544p. 1981. 37.50x (ISBN 0-915556-06-5). Great Ocean.

Gumbo. George Barlow. LC 80-2557. 96p. 1981. 8.95 (ISBN 0-385-17529-9); pap. 4.95 (ISBN 0-385-17530-2). Doubleday.

Gumdrop Posts a Letter. Val Biro. (Illus.). 24p. (gr. k-3). 1977. PLB 6.00 (ISBN 0-516-03596-7). Childrens.

Gun. C. S. Forester. 1978. 6.95 (ISBN 0-370-00681-X, Pub. by Chatto Bodley Jonathan). Merrimack Bk Serv.

Gun Care & Repair. Monte Burch. 1978. 12.95 (ISBN 0-87691-256-0). Winchester Pr.

Gun Control. Ed. by Philip J. Cook & Richard D. Lambert. (Annals of the American Academy of Political & Social Science Ser.: No. 455). 250p. 1981. 7.50x (ISBN 0-87761-262-5); pap. 6.00x (ISBN 0-87761-263-3). Am Acad Pol Soc Sci.

Gun Control: A Decision for Americans. Edward F. Dolan, Jr. LC 78-5576. (Impact Bks). (Illus.). (gr. 7 up). 1978. PLB 6.90 s&l (ISBN 0-531-02202-1). Watts.

Gun Control: A Written Record of Efforts to Eliminate the Private Possession of Firearms in America. Robert J. Kukla. LC 73-9505. 448p. 1973. pap. 4.95 (ISBN 0-8117-2057-8). Stackpole.

Gun Digest Book of Firearms Assembly: Centerfire Rifles, Pt. IV. J. B. Wood. 288p. 1980. pap. 8.95 (ISBN 0-695-81420-6). Follett.

Gun Digest Book of Firearms Assembly-Disassembly: Automatic Pistols, Pt. I. J. B. Wood. (Illus.). 320p. 1979. pap. 8.95 (ISBN 0-695-81315-3). Follett.

Gun Digest Book of Firearms Assembly-Disassembly: Part V, Shotguns. J. B. Wood. 1980. pap. 8.95 (ISBN 0-695-81510-5). DBI.

Gun Digest Book of Firearms Assembly-Disassembly: Revolvers, Pt. II. J. B. Wood. 320p. 1979. pap. 8.95 (ISBN 0-695-81316-1). Follett.

Gun Digest Book of Firearms Assembly-Disassembly: Rimfire Rifles, Pt. III. J. B. Wood. 288p. 1980. pap. 8.95 (ISBN 0-695-81419-2). Follett.

Gun Digest Book of Pistolsmithing. Jack Mitchell. 288p. 1980. pap. 8.95 (ISBN 0-695-81429-X). Follett.

Gun Digest Nineteen Eighty. 34th ed. Ed. by Ken Warner. (Illus.). 448p. 1979. pap. 9.95 o.p. (ISBN 0-695-81309-9). Follett.

Gun Digest of Gunsmithing Tools...& Their Uses. John E. Traister. 1980. pap. 7.95 (ISBN 0-695-81452-4). DBI.

Gun Digest Review of Custom Guns. Ed. by Ken Warner. 256p. 1980. pap. 8.95 (ISBN 0-910676-10-0). DBI.

Gun Digest 1981. 35th ed. Ed. by Ken Warner. 448p. 1980. pap. 10.95 (ISBN 0-910676-09-7). DBI.

Gun Digest's Book of Gun Accessories. The Editors of Gun Digest. Ed. by Joseph J. Schroeder. (Illus.). 288p. 1979. pap. 8.95 (ISBN 0-695-81313-7). Follett.

Gun Dog. Revolutionary Rapid Training Method. Richard A. Wolters. (Illus.). 1961. 11.95 (ISBN 0-525-12005-X). Dutton.

Gun Feud at Tiedown: Rogues Rendezvous. Nelson Nye. 160p. (Orig.). 1976. pap. 2.25 (ISBN 0-441-30798-1). Ace Bks.

Gun in America: The Origins of a National Dilemma. Lee Kennett & James L. Anderson. LC 74-5990. (Contributions in American History: No. 37). (Illus., Orig.). 1975. lib. bdg. 17.50 (ISBN 0-8371-7530-5, ARF/); pap. text ed. 3.95 (ISBN 0-8371-8715-X, ARF). Greenwood.

Gun Merchants: Politics & Policies of the Major Arms Suppliers. Ed. by Cindy Cannizzo. (Pergamon Policy Studies). 1980. 27.00 (ISBN 0-08-024632-X). Pergamon.

Gun-Runner. Arthur Stringer. 1976. lib. bdg. 16.70x (ISBN 0-89968-119-0). Lightyear.

Gun Runners. Sebastian Morales. 160p. (Orig.). 1975. pap. 0.95 o.p. (ISBN 0-445-00684-6). Popular Lib.

Gun Shy Kid. Barry Cord. 1979. pap. 1.25 (ISBN 0-505-51379-X). Tower Bks.

Gun Trader's Guide. 8th ed. Paul Wohl. (Stoeger Bks). (Illus.). 1977. pap. 7.95 o.p. (ISBN 0-695-80843-5). Follett.

Gun Vote at Valdoro. Richard Poole. 1979. pap. 1.50 (ISBN 0-505-51440-0). Tower Bks.

Gun-Whipped. Paul E. Lehman. 1979. pap. 1.25 (ISBN 0-505-51369-2). Tower Bks.

Gunboat Diplomacy in the Wilson Era: The U.S. Navy in Haiti, 1915-1916. David Healy. LC 75-32074. 1976. 21.50x (ISBN 0-299-06980-X). U of Wis Pr.

Gundog Training. Keith Eriandson. (Illus.). 1978. 22.00 (ISBN 0-214-20167-8). Transatlantic.

Gundog Training. Keith Erlandson. 1978. 11.95 o.p. (8028, Dist. by Arco). Barrie & Jenkins.

Gundogs: Questions & Answers. Peter Moxon. (Illus.). 96p. (Orig.). 1980. pap. 7.50x (ISBN 0-85242-734-4). Intl Pubns Serv.

Gunfighter: Man or Myth? Joseph G. Rosa. LC 68-31378. (Illus.). 1979. Repr. of 1969 ed. 9.95 (ISBN 0-8061-0825-8). U of Okla Pr.

Gunfighter: Man or Myth? Joseph G. Rosa. (Illus.). 229p. 1980. pap. 5.95 (ISBN 0-8061-1561-0). U of Okla Pr.

Gunfighters. Paul Trachtman. LC 74-80284. (Old West Ser.). (gr. 5 up). 1974. lib. bdg. 12.96 (ISBN 0-8094-1481-3, Pub. Time-Life). Silver.

Gunfighters. Paul Trachtman. (Old West Ser). (Illus.). 1974. 12.95 (ISBN 0-8094-1479-1). Time-Life.

Gunfighter's Choice. F. M. Dumas. 192p. (YA) 1976. 4.95 o.p. (ISBN 0-685-61053-5, Avalon). Bouregy.

Gunfighters Pay. William Hopson. (YA) 1973. 5.95 (ISBN 0-685-31776-5, Avalon). Bouregy.

Gunfire & Flame. Scott Siegel. (Orig.). 1980. pap. 1.75 (ISBN 0-532-23137-6). Manor Bks.

Gunga Your Din Din Is Ready & Pinocchio Was Nosey. Roy Doty. (gr. 3-5). 1978. pap. 1.50 (ISBN 0-671-29856-9). Archway.

Gunga, Your Din-Din Is Ready: Son of Puns, Gags, Quips & Riddles. Roy Doty. LC 75-24624. 64p. (gr. 4-7). 1976. PLB 4.95 (ISBN 0-385-11522-9). Doubleday.

Gunhilde & the Halloween Spell. Virginia Kahl. (Illus.). 32p. (gr. k-3). pap. 2.95 (ISBN 0-689-70490-9, A-117, Aladdin). Atheneum.

Gunlock. Wayne D. Overholser. 1980. pap. 1.95 o.s.i. (ISBN 0-440-13322-X). Dell.

Gunman. Archie Joscelyn. 256p. (YA) 1975. 5.95 (ISBN 0-685-51236-3, Avalon). Bouregy.

Gunman's Gold. Max Brand. 1974. pap. 1.95 (ISBN 0-446-88337-9). Warner Bks.

Gunn Effect. G. S. Hobson. (Monographs in Electrical & Electronic Engineering). (Illus.). 142p. 1974. 27.00x (ISBN 0-19-859318-X). Oxford U Pr.

Gunn-Effect Logic Devices. Hans L. Hartnagel. 1973. text ed. 19.50x o.p. (ISBN 0-435-71485-6). Heinemann Ed.

Gunner's Run. Rebecca Orr. LC 79-9613. 160p. (gr. 4-7). 1980. 8.95 (ISBN 0-06-024617-0, HarpJ); PLB 8.79 (ISBN 0-06-024618-9). Har-Row.

Gunniwolf. Ed. by Wilhelmina Harper. (Illus.). (ps-3). 1967. PLB 8.95 (ISBN 0-525-31139-4). Dutton.

Gunpowder & Galleys. J. F. Guilmartin, Jr. LC 73-83109. (Early Modern History Studies). (Illus.). 380p. 1975. 46.50 (ISBN 0-521-20272-8). Cambridge U Pr.

Guns & Ammo Annual 1980. Ed. by Ralph Glaze. LC 72-1758. (Illus.). 1979. pap. 6.95 o.p. (ISBN 0-8227-3015-4). Petersen Pub.

Guns & Ammo Annual, 1981. Ed. by Guns & Ammo Magazine Editors. (Illus.). 320p. 1980. pap. 6.95 (ISBN 0-8227-3017-0). Petersen Pub.

Guns & Other Arms. Ed. by William Guthman. (Illus.). 160p. 1980. pap. 7.95 (ISBN 0-8317-4182-1). Mayflower Bks.

Guns at Twilight. Jonathan Scofield. (Freedom Fighters Ser.: No. 4). (Orig.). 1981. pap. 2.75 (ISBN 0-440-02919-8). Dell.

Guns Illustrated. Ed. by Harold A. Murtz. (Illus.). 288p. 1979. pap. 7.95 (ISBN 0-695-81310-2). Follett.

Guns Illustrated 1981. 13th ed. Ed. by Harold A. Murtz. 288p. 1980. pap. 8.95 (ISBN 0-910676-12-7). DBI.

Guns in the Sky: The Air Gunners of World War Two. Chaz Bowyer. (Illus.). 1979. 14.95 (ISBN 0-684-16262-8, ScribT). Scribner.

Guns of August. Barbara W. Tuchman. (Illus.). (gr. 9 up). 1962. 16.95 (ISBN 0-02-620310-3). Macmillan.

Guns of Dorking Hollow. Max Brand. 1976. pap. 1.75 (ISBN 0-446-94204-9). Warner Bks.

Guns of Hammer. Barry Cord. 1979. pap. 1.25 (ISBN 0-505-51338-2). Tower Bks.

Guns of Harpers Ferry. Stuart E. Brown, Jr. LC 77-746. (Illus.). 157p. 1968. 20.00 o.p. (ISBN 0-685-65063-4). Va Bk.

Guns of the Hawk. Owen G. Irons. (YA) 1976. 5.95 (ISBN 0-685-69050-4, Avalon). Bouregy.

Guns of the Wild West. Elsie Hanauer. LC 74-124202. (Illus.). 112p. Date not set. 12.00 o.p. (ISBN 0-498-07462-5). A S Barnes. Postponed.

Guns off Gloucester. Joseph E. Garland. LC 75-21650. (Illus.). 1975. pap. 3.95 (ISBN 0-930352-06-8). Nelson B Robinson.

Guns, Sails & Empires: Technological Innovation & the Early Phases of European Expansion 1400-1700. Carlo M. Cipolla. (Funk & W Bk.). (gr. 9-12). pap. 1.95 o.s.i. (ISBN 0-308-60014-2, M14, TYC-T). T Y Crowell.

Guns up. Ernest Haycox. 1977. pap. 1.25 (ISBN 0-505-51125-8, BT51125). Tower Bks.

Guns, Value & Identification Guide. (Illus.). 2.95 o.p. (ISBN 0-89689-005-8). Wallace-Homestead.

Gunsmithing. Roy F. Dunlap. LC 63-21755. (Illus.). 748p. 1963. 19.95 (ISBN 0-8117-0770-9). Stackpole.

Gunsmith's Manual: A Complete Handbook for the American Gunsmith. Stelle & Harrison. (Illus.). Repr. of 1883 ed. 12.95 (ISBN 0-88227-002-8). Gun Room.

Gunsmoke. Nelson Nye. 1979. pap. 1.25 (ISBN 0-505-51377-3). Tower Bks.

Gunsmoke Bonanza. Chuck Martin. 1978. pap. 1.25 (ISBN 0-505-51276-9). Tower Bks.

Gunsmoke Graze. Peter Dawson. 224p. 1980. pap. 1.75 (ISBN 0-553-14179-1). Bantam.

Gunsmoke in Paradise. Burt Arthur. 1978. pap. 1.25 (ISBN 0-505-51246-7). Tower Bks.

Gunsmoke Mesa. Dan James. 256p. (YA) 1974. 5.95 (ISBN 0-685-49094-7, Avalon). Bouregy.

Gunsmoke Over Sabado. Paul Evan. 256p. (YA) 1974. 5.95 (ISBN 0-685-49199-4, Avalon). Bouregy.

Gunstock Finishing & Care. A. Donald Newell. (Illus.). 512p. 1949. 19.95 (ISBN 0-8117-0780-6). Stackpole.

Gunswift. Stewart Gordon. 1979. pap. 1.50 (ISBN 0-505-51347-1). Tower Bks.

Gunter Grass. W. Gordon Cunliffe. (World Authors Ser.: Germany: No. 65). 1969. lib. bdg. 10.95 (ISBN 0-8057-2400-1). Twayne.

Gunter Grass. Kurt L. Tank. Tr. by John Conway. LC 68-31458. (Modern Literature Ser.). 1969. 10.95 (ISBN 0-8044-2863-8); pap. 3.45 (ISBN 0-8044-6892-3). Ungar.

Gunter Grass: The Writer in a Pluralist Society. Michael Hollington. LC 79-56840. 192p. 1980. 15.00 (ISBN 0-7145-2678-9, Pub. by M Boyars). Merrimack Bk Serv.

Gunther Grass: The Literature of Politics. A. V. Subiotto. (German Literature & Society Ser.: Vol. 3). 1980. pap. text ed. write for info. (ISBN 0-85496-076-7). Humanities.

Gunther Heritage. Louisa Bronte. 384p. (Orig.). 1981. pap. 2.75 (ISBN 0-515-04311-7). Jove Pubns.

Guntur District 1788-1848: A History of Local Influence & Central Authority in South India. Robert E. Frykenberg. 1965. 24.95x (ISBN 0-19-821532-0). Oxford U Pr.

Guppies. Herbert R. Axelrod & Wilfred H. Whitern. (Orig.). pap. 2.00 (ISBN 0-87666-082-0, M505). TFH Pubns.

Guppy: Its Life Cycle. William White, Jr. LC 73-83441. (Colorful Nature Ser.). 64p. (gr. 5 up). 1974. 9.95 (ISBN 0-8069-3476-X); PLB 9.29 (ISBN 0-8069-3477-8). Sterling.

Gupta Sculpture: Indian Sculpture of the Fourth to the Sixth Centuries A.D. J. C. Harle. (Illus.). 76p. 1975. 28.50x (ISBN 0-19-817322-9). Oxford U Pr.

Gurdjieff & Mansfield. James Moore. (Illus.). 304p. 1980. 25.00 (ISBN 0-7100-0488-5). Routledge & Kegan.

Gurdjieff Seeker of the Truth. Kathleen R. Speeth & Ira Friedlander. LC 78-24696. (Illus.). 1979. pap. 5.95 (ISBN 0-06-090693-6, CN-693, CN). Har-Row.

Gurkha Rifles. J. B. Nicholson. LC 74-76623. (Men-at-Arms Ser). (Illus.). 40p. (Orig.). 1974. pap. 7.95 (ISBN 0-88254-235-4). Hippocrene Bks.

Gurnee Guide to American Caves. Russell Gurnee & Jeanne Gurnee. 1980. 9.95 (ISBN 0-914264-29-X); pap. 5.95 (ISBN 0-914264-30-3). Caroline Hse.

Guru Nanak & the Origins of Sikh Faith. Harbans Singh. 1970. 10.00x (ISBN 0-210-22311-1). Asia.

Gus & the Baby Ghost. Jane Thayer. LC 76-161874. (Illus.). 32p. (ps-3). 1972. PLB 7.44 (ISBN 0-688-31369-8). Morrow.

Gus Was a Christmas Ghost. Jane Thayer. LC 77-101707. (Illus.). (ps-3). 1970. 7.25 o.p. (ISBN 0-688-21370-7); PLB 7.44 (ISBN 0-688-31370-1). Morrow.

Gus Was a Friendly Ghost. Jane Thayer. (Illus.). (ps-3). 1962. PLB 7.44 (ISBN 0-688-31368-X). Morrow.

Gus Was a Mexican Ghost. Jane Thayer. (Illus.). 32p. (ps-3). 1974. 7.75 (ISBN 0-688-20104-0); PLB 7.44 (ISBN 0-688-30104-5). Morrow.

Gustav Klimt: Erotic Drawings. Hans H. Hofstatter. (Illus.). 88p. 1980. 145.00 (ISBN 0-686-62690-7, 1203-1). Abrams.

Gustav Landauer: Philosopher of Utopia. Ruth L. Hyman. LC 76-49585. 1977. 25.00 (ISBN 0-915144-27-1). Hackett Pub.

Gustav Mahler. Bruno Walter. Tr. by James Galston. LC 78-87691. (Music Ser). 1970. Repr. of 1941 ed. lib. bdg. 19.50 (ISBN 0-306-71701-8). Da Capo.

Gustav Mahler: Memories & Letters. 3rd ed. Alma Mahler. Ed. by Donald Mitchell & Knud Martner. LC 74-26502. (Illus.). 409p. 1968. pap. 7.95 (ISBN 0-295-95378-0). U of Wash Pr.

Gustav Mahler: The Wunderhorn Years. Donald Mitchell. 1980. pap. 10.95 (ISBN 0-520-04220-4, CAL 442). U of Cal Pr.

Gustav Vigeland: The Sculptor & His Works. Ragna Stang. Tr. by Ardis Grosjean from Norwegian. LC 79-254352. (Tokens of Norway Ser.). (Illus.). 190p. (Orig.). 1965. pap. 11.25x (ISBN 82-518-0152-4). Intl Pubns Serv.

Gustave Courbet: a Study of Style & Society. Linda Nochlin. LC 75-23803. (Outstanding Dissertations in the Fine Arts - 19th Century). (Illus.). 1976. lib. bdg. 41.00 (ISBN 0-8240-1998-9). Garland Pub.

Gustave Flaubert. Stratton Buck. (World Authors Ser.: France: No. 3). 1966. pap. 10.95 (ISBN 0-8057-2312-9). Twayne.

Gustave ou le Bal Masque, 2 vols. Daniel F. Auber. LC 76-49212. (Early Romantic Opera Ser.: Vol. 31). 1980. lib. bdg. 82.00 (ISBN 0-8240-2930-5). Garland Pub.

Gustavo Gutierrez. Robert M. Brown. LC 80-82185. (Makers of Contemporary Theology Ser.). 75p. 1981. pap. 3.45 (ISBN 0-8042-0651-1). John Knox.

Guten Tag: A German Language Course for Television. R. Schneider. 1974. pap. text ed. 6.50x (ISBN 0-685-47484-4). Schoenhof.

Guts to Win. Jane Blalock & Dwayne Nettind. LC 77-7311. (Illus.). 158p. 1977. 7.95 (ISBN 0-914178-12-1). Golf Digest Bks.

Guy & the Flowering Plum Tree. Robin Stemp. LC 80-67029. (Illus.). 32p. (ps-3). 1981. 8.95 (ISBN 0-689-50188-9, McElderry Bk). Atheneum.

Guy Buffet's Hawaii. Guy Buffet. LC 80-67292. 1981. 9.95 (ISBN 0-918684-11-0). Cameron & Co.

Guy Carleton: A Biography. Paul R. Reynolds. LC 80-81587. 192p. 1980. 10.95 (ISBN 0-688-03770-4). Morrow.

Guy de Maupassant. Albert H. Wallace. (World Authors Ser.: France: No. 265). 1973. lib. bdg. 9.95 (ISBN 0-8057-2602-0). Twayne.

Guy Lenny. Harry Mazer. LC 79-157839. (gr. 4-7). 1971. 4.95 (ISBN 0-440-03316-0); PLB 4.58 o.s.i. (ISBN 0-440-03313-6). Delacorte.

Guy Mannering. Walter Scott. 1954. 6.00x o.p. (ISBN 0-460-00133-7, Evman). Dutton.

Guyana Gold: The Story of Wesley Baird, Guyana's Greatest Miner. Wesley Baird. 210p. (Orig.). 1981. 18.00x (ISBN 0-89410-192-7); pap. 7.00x (ISBN 0-89410-193-5). Three Continents.

Guyanese Seed of Soul: How to Prepare West Indian Food. Yvonne A. John. Ed. by Mosezelle Nichols. (Orig.). 1980. pap. text ed. 8.95x (ISBN 0-936026-04-9). R&M Pub Co.

Guys Like Us. Tom Lorenz. 252p. 1980. 11.95 (ISBN 0-670-35815-0). Viking Pr.

Guzman, Hinde & Hannam Outstript: Being a Discovery of the Whole Art, Mistery & Antiquity of Theeves & Theeving. Carlos Garcia. LC 80-2480. 1981. Repr. of 1657 ed. 49.50 (ISBN 0-404-19114-2). AMS Pr.

Gwendeline. Jane Ashford. 1981. pap. 1.75 (ISBN 0-446-94247-2). Warner Bks.

Gwinnett County, Georgia, Families Eighteen Eighteen to Nineteen Sixty-Eight. LC 80-52845. 662p. 1980. 30.00 (ISBN 0-87797-053-X). Cherokee.

GWR Engines, Names, Numbers, Types & Classes: A Reprint of the Engine Books of 1911, 1928 & 1946 with Some Pages from That of 1938. (Illus.). 250p. 1971. 11.95 (ISBN 0-7153-5367-5). David & Charles.

GWR Stars Castle & Kings. O. S. Nock. LC 80-66419. (Illus.). 304p. 1980. 32.00 (ISBN 0-7153-7977-1). David & Charles.

GWR Stars, Castles & Kings. O. S. Nock. LC 80-66419. (Illus.). 304p. 1980. 29.95. Darby Bks.

GWR Stars, Castles & Kings: Part 1 1906-1930. O. S. Nock. LC 74-78254. (Locomotive Monographs). (Illus.). 1975. 16.95 (ISBN 0-7153-6681-5). David & Charles.

Gyascutus: Studies in Antebellum Southern Humorous & Sporting Writings. Ed. by James L. West. (Costerus New Ser.: No. 5-6). 1978. pap. text ed. 20.00x (ISBN 90-6203-522-1). Humanities.

Gymnastic Apparatus Exercises for Girls. Diane H. Babbitt & Werner Haas. (Illus.). 1964. 10.95 (ISBN 0-8260-0590-X). Wiley.

Gymnastics. Ross R. Olney. (First Bks.). (Illus.). 96p. (gr. 4-6). 1976. PLB 6.45 (ISBN 0-531-00849-5). Watts.

Gymnastics. Ross R. Olney. 1980. pap. 1.75 (ISBN 0-380-49213-X, 49213, Camelot). Avon.

Gymnastics. Graham B. Smither. (Illus.). 128p. 1981. pap. 7.95 (ISBN 0-906071-36-4). Proteus Pub NY.

Gymnastics & You: The Whole Story of the Sport. Michael Resnick. LC 77-8345. (Illus.). (gr. 5-9). 1977. pap. 3.95 (ISBN 0-528-87052-1). Rand.

Gymnastics for Girls. Cliff Temple & Peter Tatlow. (Pelham Pictorial Sports Instruction Ser.). (Illus.). 1978. 12.50 (ISBN 0-7207-1013-8). Transatlantic.

Gymnastics for Girls & Women. Ernestine R. Carter. (Illus.). 1968. text ed. 11.95 (ISBN 0-13-371781-X). P-H.

Gymnastics for Men: A Competitive Approach for Teacher & Coach. Eric L. Hughes. (Illus.). 1966. 15.95 (ISBN 0-8260-4460-3). Wiley.

Gymnastics Safety Manual: The Official Manual of the United States Gymnastics Safety Association. 2nd ed. Ed. by Eugene Wettstone. LC 79-65860. (Illus.). 1979. text ed. 11.95x (ISBN 0-271-00242-5); pap. text ed. 7.95x (ISBN 0-271-00244-1). Pa St U Pr.

Gyn-Ecology: The Metaethics of Radical Feminism. Mary Daly. LC 78-53790. 1979. 14.95 (ISBN 0-8070-1510-5, BP-601); pap. 7.95 (ISBN 0-8070-1511-3). Beacon Pr.

Gynecologic & Obstetric Urology. Herbert J. Buchsbaum & Joseph D. Schmidt. LC 76-41535. (Illus.). 1978. text ed. 38.00 (ISBN 0-7216-2176-7). Saunders.

Gynecologic Nursing. Jeanne L. Paletta et al. (Nursng Outline Ser.). pap. 9.50 (ISBN 0-87488-388-1). Med Exam.

Gynecologic Oncology. Felix Rutledge et al. LC 75-30951. 272p. 1976. 32.50 (ISBN 0-471-74720-3, Pub. by Wiley Medical). Wiley.

Gynecologic Oncology Case Studies. Samuel Lifshitz & Herbert Buchsbaum. 1978. spiral bdg. 14.75 (ISBN 0-87488-005-X). Med Exam.

Gynecologic Surgery: Errors, Safeguards, & Salvage. John H. Ridley. 430p. 1974. 27.00 o.p. (ISBN 0-683-07276-5). Williams & Wilkins.

Gynecologic Surgery: Treatment of Complications & Prevention of Injuries. Frans Uyttenbroeck. 288p. 1980. 29.50 (ISBN 0-89352-088-8). Masson Pub.

Gynecologic Urology & Urodynamics: Theory & Practice. Donald Ostergaard. (Illus.). 374p. 1980. lib. bdg. 40.00 (ISBN 0-683-06645-5). Williams & Wilkins.

Gynecological Cancer. International Cancer Congress, 12th, Buenos Aires 5-11 Oct. 1978. Ed. by N. Thatcher. LC 79-40719. (Illus.). 1979. 68.00 (ISBN 0-08-024391-6). Pergamon.

Gynecological Endocrinology. 3rd ed. Jay J. Gold & John B. Josimovich. (Illus.). 918p. 1980. pap. 62.50 (ISBN 0-06-140954-5, Harper Medical). Har-Row.

Gynecology & Obstetrics. Edwin Jameson. (Illus.). 1962. Repr. of 1936 ed. pap. 7.50 o.s.i. (ISBN 0-02-847150-4). Hafner.

Gynecology & Obstetrics. D. W. Roberts. (Operative Surgery Ser.). 1977. 49.95 (ISBN 0-407-00615-X). Butterworths.

Gynecology & Obstetrics: The Health Care of Women. 2nd ed. Ed. by Seymour Romney et al. (Illus.). 1980. text ed. 48.50 (ISBN 0-07-053582-5, HP). McGraw.

Gypsies. W. Cohn. 1973. pap. 5.95 (ISBN 0-201-11362-7, 11362). A-W.

Gypsies. Werner Cohn. 1973. pap. text ed. 5.95 (ISBN 0-8461-1362-7). Benjamin-Cummings.

Gypsies: The Hidden Americans. Anne Sutherland. LC 75-3762. 1975. Repr. 16.95 (ISBN 0-02-932200-6). Free Pr.

Gypsies: Waggon Time & After. Denis Harvey. (Illus.). 144p. 1980. 24.00 (ISBN 0-7134-1548-7, Pub. by Batsford England). David & Charles.

Gypsy. Al Nussbaum. (Pacesetters Ser.). (Illus.). 64p. (gr. 4 up). 1978. PLB 7.95 (ISBN 0-516-02170-2). Childrens.

Gypsy, 3 bks. Sharon Wagner. (gr. 9 up). Date not set. pap. 3.75 boxed set (ISBN 0-307-13619-1, Golden Pr). Western Pub.

Gypsy & Nimblefoot. Sharon Wagner. (Gypsy Bks.). (gr. 4 up). 1978. pap. 1.25 (ISBN 0-307-21545-8, Golden Pr). Western Pub.

Gypsy Bibliography. George F. Black. LC 74-149780. 1971. Repr. of 1914 ed. 18.00 (ISBN 0-8103-3708-8). Gale.

Gypsy Fires in America. Irving H. Brown. LC 74-1035. Repr. of 1924 ed. 18.00 (ISBN 0-8103-3942-0). Gale.

Gypsy from Nowhere. Sharon Wagner. (Gypsy Bks.). (gr. 4 up). 1978. pap. 1.25 (ISBN 0-307-21509-1, Golden Pr). Western Pub.

Gypsy Heiress. Ed. by Laura London. (Orig.). 1981. pap. 1.50 (ISBN 0-440-12960-5). Dell.

Gypsy Idyll: A Personal Experience Among the Romanies. Rowena Farre. LC 64-16254. (Illus.). 8.95 (ISBN 0-8149-0092-5). Vanguard.

Gypsy King. Charles Runyon, Jr. 1979. pap. 2.25 o.s.i. (ISBN 0-515-04041-X). Jove Pubns.

Gypsy Lifestyles. John B. McLaughlin. LC 80-7572. 1980. 14.95 (ISBN 0-669-03754-0). Lexington Bks.

Gypsy Moth: Its History in America. Robert M. McClung. LC 74-6245. (Illus.). (gr. 5-9). 1974. PLB 6.96 (ISBN 0-688-20124-5); PLB 6.00 o.p. (ISBN 0-688-30124-X). Morrow.

Gypsy Politics & Social Change. Thomas Acton. 1974. 20.00x (ISBN 0-7100-7838-2). Routledge & Kegan.

Gypsy Season. Steven Nickels. Date not set. 10.95 (ISBN 0-87949-187-6). Ashley Bks.

Gypsy Wagon. Armando R. Rodriguez. (Creative Ser: No. 2). 1974. pap. 3.50 (ISBN 0-89551-005-7). UCLA Chicano Stud.

Gyro! The Life & Times of Lawrence Sperry. William W. Davenport. LC 78-17826. (Illus.). 1978. 12.95 o.p. (ISBN 0-684-15793-4, ScribT). Scribner.

Gyroscopic Theory. George Greenhill. LC 66-30616. 17.50 (ISBN 0-8284-0205-1). Chelsea Pub.

Gyula Juhasz the Beard Sunner. Anton N. Nyerges. 117p. 1980. pap. 12.00 (ISBN 0-9600954-0-3). Nyerges.

H

H & R Block Family Budget Workbook. Susan Ungaro. (H & R Block Ser.). 160p. 1980. pap. 4.95 (ISBN 0-02-007320-8, Collier). Macmillan.

H. C. Branner. T. L. Markey. (World Authors Ser.: Denmark: No. 245). 1973. lib. bdg. 10.95 (ISBN 0-8057-2172-X). Twayne.

H. C. The Secret Menopause of H. C. Douglas. Will Howard. Ed. by Joy Parnell. LC 80-52018. 400p. 1980. 12.95 (ISBN 0-936430-77-X). Red Feather.

H. E. Armstrong & the Teaching of Science 1880-1930. Ed. by W. H. Brock. LC 72-87179. (Cambridge Texts & Studies in the History of Education: No. 14). 168p. 1973. 23.95 (ISBN 0-521-08679-5). Cambridge U Pr.

H-Eight Programming for Beginners. Ron Santore et al. 175p. 1981. pap. 8.95 (ISBN 0-918398-17-7). Dilithium Pr.

H-Function with Applications in Statistics & Other Disciplines. A. M. Mathai & R. K. Saxena. 1978. 12.95 (ISBN 0-470-26380-6). Halsted Pr.

H. G. J. Moseley: The Life & Letters of an English Physicist, 1887-1915. John L. Heilbron. 1974. 25.00x (ISBN 0-520-02375-7). U of Cal Pr.

H. G. Wells. Richard H. Costa. (English Authors Ser.: No. 43). 1966. lib. bdg. 9.95 (ISBN 0-8057-1568-1). Twayne.

H. G. Wells: Interviews & Recollections. Ed. by J. R. Hammond. LC 79-55529. (Interviews & Recollections Ser.). 121p. 1981. text ed. 26.00x (ISBN 0-06-492671-0). B&N.

H. G. Wells: The Critical Heritage. Ed. by Patrick Parrinder. (Critical Heritage Ser.). 1972. 29.00x (ISBN 0-7100-7387-9). Routledge & Kegan.

H. G. Wells's Literary Criticism. Ed. by Patrick Parrinder & Robert Philmus. 261p. 1980. 27.50x (ISBN 0-389-20035-2). B&N.

H Grade Questions in Physics. Lanarkshire Physics Group. 1972. pap. text ed. 4.95x o.p. (ISBN 0-435-68200-8). Heinemann Ed.

H. H. Munro (Saki) Charles H. Gillen. (English Authors Ser.: No. 102). lib. bdg. 9.95 (ISBN 0-8057-1408-1). Twayne.

H. J. C. Von Grimmelshausen. Kenneth Negus. (World Authors Ser.: No. 291). 1974. lib. bdg. 10.95 (ISBN 0-8057-2405-2). Twayne.

H. L. Davis. Paul T. Bryant. (United States Authors Ser.: No. 306). 1978. lib. bdg. 12.50 (ISBN 0-8057-7211-1). Twayne.

H. L. Mencken. W. H. Williams. (United States Authors Ser.: No. 297). 1977. lib. bdg. 10.95 (ISBN 0-8057-7200-6). Twayne.

H. L. Mencken Bibliography. Bernard H. Porter. Ed. by Bernard H. Porter. (Illus.). 28p. 1972. 8.50 o.p. (ISBN 0-911156-01-1). Porter.

H. L. Mencken, Literary Critic. William H. Nolte. LC 66-18117. 1966. lib. bdg. 17.50x (ISBN 0-8195-3063-8, Pub. by Wesleyan U Pr). Columbia U Pr.

H. P. Blavatsky & the Theosophical Movement. 2nd,rev. ed. Charles J. Ryan. Ed. by Grace F. Knoche. LC 75-4433. (Illus.). 1975. 9.00 (ISBN 0-911500-79-0); softcover 6.00 (ISBN 0-911500-80-4). Theos U Pr.

H. P. Blavatsky Collected Writings, Vol. XII. Helena P. Blavatsky. Ed. by Boris De Zirkoff. LC 80-53953. (Illus.). 849p. 1981. cloth 18.95 (ISBN 0-8356-0228-1). Theos Pub Hse.

H. P. Blavatsky, Tibet & Tulku. Geoffrey A. Barborka. (Illus.). 1974. 12.95 (ISBN 0-8356-7159-3). Theos Pub Hse.

H. P. Blavatsky to the American Conventions: 1888-1891, with a Historical Perspective. Helena P. Blavatsky. LC 78-74256. 1979. softcover 3.75 (ISBN 0-911500-88-X). Theos U Pr.

H. P. Lovecraft & Lovecraft Criticism: An Annotated Bibliography. S. T. Joshi. LC 80-84662. (Serif Ser.: No. 38). 1981. 27.50x (ISBN 0-87338-248-X). Kent St U Pr.

H. P. Lovecraft: Four Decades of Criticism. Ed. by S. T. Joshi. LC 80-11535. xvi, 247p. 1980. 15.00 (ISBN 0-8214-0442-3, 0442E). Ohio U Pr.

H. R. H. The Man Who Will Be King. Tim Heald & Mayo Mohs. 1980. pap. 2.75 (ISBN 0-425-04659-1). Berkley Pub.

Ha Poder Em Suas Palavras. Tr. by Henrrieta Mears. (Portugese Bks.). (Port.). 1979. write for info. (ISBN 0-8297-0659-3). Life Pubs Intl.

Ha-Rikud: The Jewish Dance. Ed. by Fred Berk. (Illus.). 112p. (Orig.). 1972. pap. 5.00 o.p. (ISBN 0-685-24136-X, 582040). UAHC.

Haakon. C. F. Griffin. LC 77-26043. 1978. 9.95 o.s.i. (ISBN 0-690-01703-0, TYC-T). T Y Crowell.

Hab-Piru. Moshe Greenberg. (American Oriental Ser.: Vol. 39). 1955. pap. 5.00x (ISBN 0-686-00020-X). Am Orient Soc.

Habilitation of the Mentally Retarded Individual. Joe E. Walthall & Harold D. Love. (Illus.). 224p. 1974. 13.75 (ISBN 0-398-02908-3). C C Thomas.

Habima--Israel's National Theater 1917-1977. Emanuel Levy. LC 79-12486. 1979. 25.00x (ISBN 0-231-04582-4). Columbia U Pr.

Habitat. Bob Arnold. (Orig.). 1980. pap. 5.00x sewn (ISBN 0-915316-75-7). Pentagram.

Habitat Asia: Issues & Responses, 3 vols. Ed. by R. P. Misra. Incl. Vol. 1. India (ISBN 0-391-01824-8); Vol. 2. Indonesia & the Philippines (ISBN 0-391-01825-6); Vol. 3. Japan & Singapore (ISBN 0-391-01827-2). 1979. text ed. 15.50 ea. Humanities.

Habitat, Economy & Society: A Study of the Dangis. A. N. Bhattacharya & R. N. Vyas. 1979. text ed. 12.50x (ISBN 0-391-01818-3). Humanities.

Habitat: Human Settlements in an Urban Age. Angus M. Gunn. 1978. text ed. 27.00 (ISBN 0-08-021487-8); pap. 15.00 (ISBN 0-08-021486-X); tchr's. ed. 9.25 (ISBN 0-08-022998-0). Pergamon.

Habitation of Dragons. Keith Miller. 1976. pap. 1.75 (ISBN 0-89129-209-8). Jove Pubns.

Habitations of Man in All Ages. Eugene E. Viollet-Le-Duc. Tr. by Benjamin Bucknall. LC 74-146922. 1971. Repr. of 1876 ed. 32.00 (ISBN 0-8103-3787-8). Gale.

Habits. Richard Stiller. 158p. 1980. pap. 3.95 (ISBN 0-346-12437-9). Cornerstone.

Habits & Virtues: A Philosophical Analysis. George P. Klubertanz. LC 65-23606. 1965. 27.50x (ISBN 0-89197-196-3). Irvington.

Habituation, 2 vols. Ed. by Harmon V. Peeke & Michael J. Herz. Incl. Vol. 1. Behavioral Studies. 1973. 40.50 (ISBN 0-12-549801-2); Vol. 2. Electrophysiological Substrates. 1973. 35.50 (ISBN 0-12-549802-0). Set. 61.00 (ISBN 0-685-40604-0). Acad Pr.

Hablemos Espanol. Mary Finocchiaro. 180p. (gr. 9 up). 1976. pap. text ed. 3.50 (ISBN 0-88345-261-8, 18425). Regents Pub.

Habsburg & Bourbon Europe, 1470-1720. Roger Lockyer. LC 75-328564. (Illus.). 1974. pap. text ed. 10.95x (ISBN 0-582-35029-8). Longman.

Habsburgs & Zaporozhian Cossacks: The Diary of Erich Lassota Von Steblau 1594. Ed. by Lubomyr R. Wynar. Tr. by Orest Subtelny from Ger. LC 75-15543. Orig. Title: Tagebuch des Erich Lassota Von Steblau. (Illus.). 152p. 1975. 15.00x (ISBN 0-87287-119-3). Ukrainian Acad.

Hacia la Felicidad: Como Vivir una Vida Victoriosa y Practicar la Terapia Espiritual. C. R. Salomon. 1979. 2.50 (ISBN 0-311-42060-5). Casa Bautista.

Hacia la Meta. Floyd Woodworth. (Spanish Bks.). 1977. 1.60 (ISBN 0-8297-0562-7). Life Pubs Intl.

Haciendas & Ranchos in the Mexican Bajio Leon 1700-1860. D. A. Brading. LC 77-90203. (Cambridge Latin American Studies: No. 32). (Illus.). 1979. 41.50 (ISBN 0-521-22200-1). Cambridge U Pr.

Hackney Jade & the War Horse. Fritz W. Faiss. LC 76-15322. (Illus.). 60p. 1977. ltd. ed. signed 18.50x (ISBN 0-916678-00-8); hand-colored 125.00x (ISBN 0-916678-01-6). Green Hut.

Hades in Manganese. Clayton Eshleman. 150p. (Orig.). 1981. pap. 5.00 (ISBN 0-87685-472-2); signed cloth ed. 20.00 (ISBN 0-87685-473-0). Black Sparrow.

Hadith: An Introduction. A. R. Doj. 1980. pap. 4.95 (ISBN 0-686-64661-4). Kazi Pubns.

Hadlock Hill. Melvin Kivley. LC 79-56885. 178p. 1981. 7.95 (ISBN 0-533-04545-2). Vantage.

Hadrian's Wall. Theo Bergstrom. (Illus.). 1978. pap. 4.95 (ISBN 0-8467-0502-8, Pub. by Two Continents). Hippocrene Bks.

Hadrokkosaurus Bradyi from the Upper Moenkopi Formation of Arizona with a Review of the Brachyopid Labyrinthodonts. S. P. Welles & Richard Estes. (U. C. Publ. in Geological Sciences: Vol. 84). 1969. pap. 7.50x (ISBN 0-520-09188-4). U of Cal Pr.

Hadronic Matter at Extreme Energy Density. Ed. by N. Cabibbo & L. Sertorio. (Ettore Majoana International Science Ser., Physical Sciences: Vol. 2). 365p. 1980. 42.50 (ISBN 0-306-40303-X, Plenum Pr). Plenum Pub.

Haematological Aspects of Systemic Disease. M. G. Israels & I. W. Delamore. LC 76-26782. (Illus.). 1976. text ed. 30.00 (ISBN 0-7216-5047-3). Saunders.

Haemoglobin & Myoglobin. G. Fermi & M. F. Perutz. (Atlas of Molecular Structures in Biology Ser.: No. 2). (Illus.). 100p. 1981. text ed. 45.00x (ISBN 0-19-854706-4). Oxford U Pr.

Haesel the Slave No. 2. Dael Forest. 1978. pap. 1.75 o.p. (ISBN 0-345-25671-9). Ballantine.

Hagakure: A Code to the Way of the Samurai. Yamamoto Tsunetomo. Tr. by Takao Mukoh from Japanese. xii, 182p. 1980. pap. 13.50 (ISBN 0-89346-169-5, Pub. by Hokuseido Pr). Heian Intl.

Hagakure: The Book of the Samurai. Tsunetomo Yamamoto. Tr. by William S. Wilson from Jap. LC 78-71315. 1978. 9.95 (ISBN 0-87011-378-X). Kodansha.

Hagan & Bruner's Infectious Diseases of Domestic Animals. 7th rev. ed. James H. Gillespie & John F. Timoney. LC 80-15937. (Illus.). 912p. 1981. 39.50x (ISBN 0-8014-1333-8). Cornell U Pr.

Hagar the Horrible: Born Leader. Dik Browne. 128p. (gr. 3 up). 1981. pap. 1.50 (ISBN 0-448-12653-2, Tempo). G&D.

Hagar the Horrible: Bring Em Back Alive. Dik Browne. 1981. pap. 1.50 (ISBN 0-448-12650-8, Tempo). G&D.

Hagar the Horrible: On the Rack, No. 5. Dik B. Browne. (Hagar the Horrible Cartoons). 128p. (gr. 8-12). 1981. pap. text ed. 1.50 (ISBN 0-448-12649-4, Tempo). G&D.

Hagarism. Patricia Crone & M. Cook. LC 75-41714. 1980. pap. 11.95 (ISBN 0-521-29754-0). Cambridge U Pr.

Hagarism: The Making of the Islamic World. Patricia Crone & M. Cook. LC 75-41714. 268p. 1977. 29.95 (ISBN 0-521-21133-6). Cambridge U Pr.

Hagar's Hoard. George K. Turner. LC 75-104762. (Novel As American Social History Ser.). 320p. 1970. 10.00x (ISBN 0-8131-1208-7); pap. 4.50 (ISBN 0-8131-0129-8). U Pr of Ky.

Haggadah. Illus. by Warner Prins. (Illus.). 10.00 o.p. (ISBN 0-498-06401-8, Yoseloff). A S Barnes.

Haggadah for Children. Jacob Rudin. 1973. 2.25x (ISBN 0-8197-0032-0). Bloch.

Haggai-Malachi. T. V. Moore. (Geneva Commentaries Ser.). 1974. 7.95 (ISBN 0-85151-079-5). Banner of Truth.

Haggai, Zachariah, Malachi. M. Dods. (Handbooks for Bible Classes Ser.). 153p. Repr. of 1956 ed. 3.50 (ISBN 0-567-08109-5). Attic Pr.

Haggai, Zechariah & Malachi. Irving Jensen. (Bible Self Study Guide Ser.). 1976. pap. 2.25 (ISBN 0-8024-1037-5). Moody.

Haggai, Zechariah, Malachi, & Jonah. H. G. Mitchell et al. LC 12-22008. (International Critical Commentary Ser.). 544p. Repr. of 1912 ed. 23.00x (ISBN 0-567-05020-3). Attic Pr.

Haggi, Malachi, & Zechariah. T. V. Moore. (Banner of Truth Geneva Series Commentaries). 1979. 10.95 (ISBN 0-85151-288-7). Banner of Truth.

Hague in Pen & Pencil: Den Haag in Pen en Penseel. C. H. Slechte. (Illus.). 120p. 1977. 25.00 (ISBN 90-247-2029-X). Heinman.

Haida Culture in Custody: The Masset Band. Mary Lee Stearns. LC 80-50862. (Illus.). 315p. 1980. 24.50 (ISBN 0-295-95763-8). U of Wash Pr.

Haiku, 4 vols. R. H. Blyth. Date not set. pap. 8.95 ea. Vol. 1 (ISBN 0-89346-158-X). Vol. 2 (ISBN 0-89346-159-8). Vol. 3 (ISBN 0-89346-160-1). Vol. 4 (ISBN 0-89346-161-X). Heian Intl.

Haiku Form. Joan Giroux. LC 73-86135. 176p. 1974. 6.50 o.p. (ISBN 0-8048-1110-5). C E Tuttle.

Haiku in Western Languages: An Annotated Bibliography (with Some Reference to Senryu) Gary L. Brower. LC 70-187878. 1972. 10.00 (ISBN 0-8108-0472-7). Scarecrow.

Haiku Journey. Photos by Dennis Stock. LC 74-24903. (Illus.). 111p. 1975. 22.50 (ISBN 0-87011-239-2). Kodansha.

Haiku Journey: Basho's Narrow Road to a Far Province. Matsuo Basho. Tr. by Dorothy G. Britton from Jap. LC 74-24903. 124p. 1980. pap. 3.95 (ISBN 0-87011-423-9). Kodansha.

Hail & Farewell. George Moore. Ed. by Richard Cave. (Illus.). 774p. 1980. text ed. 35.00x (ISBN 0-7705-1467-7). Humanities.

Hail Columbia. Patricia Beatty. (gr. 5-9). 1970. PLB 8.40 (ISBN 0-688-31371-X). Morrow.

Hail, Hail Camp Timberwood. Ellen Conford. (Illus.). (gr. 4-6). 1980. pap. 1.75 (ISBN 0-671-56066-2). PB.

Hail, Hail, Camp Timberwood. Ellen Conford. (Illus.). (gr. 4-6). 1980. pap. 1.95 (ISBN 0-671-42685-0). Archway.

Hail Mary: Woman, Wife, Mother of God. James Breig. (Today Paperback Ser.). (Illus.). 40p. (Orig.). 1980. pap. 1.95 (ISBN 0-89570-197-9). Claretian Pubns.

Hail the Conquering Hero. Frank Yerby. 1980. pap. 2.95 o.s.i. (ISBN 0-440-13456-0). Dell.

Haile Selassie I: Ethiopia's Lion of Judah. Peter Schwab. LC 79-9897. (Illus.). 1979. 14.95 (ISBN 0-88229-342-7). Nelson-Hall.

Hailstones & Halibut Bones. Mary O'Neill. LC 60-7138. (gr. k-12). 6.95a (ISBN 0-385-07911-7); pap. 1.95 (ISBN 0-385-07912-5); Softbound 1.95 (ISBN 0-385-05374-6). Doubleday.

Haim's English-Persian Dictionary, 2 vols. 1976. Set. 70.00x o.s.i. (ISBN 0-686-16855-0). Intl Learn Syst.

Hair Colour in the Horse. Reiner Geurts. Tr. by Anthony Dent from Dutch. (Illus.). pap. 8.75 (ISBN 0-85131-290-X). J A Allen.

Hair of Harold Roux. Thomas Williams. 384p. 1975. pap. 1.95 o.p. (ISBN 0-345-25300-0). Ballantine.

Hair, Trace Elements & Human Illness. Ed. by A. C. Brown & Robert G. Crounse. LC 80-10280. 320p. 1980. 42.95 (ISBN 0-03-055441-1). Praeger.

Hair Transplant Surgery. O'Tar T. Norwood. (Illus.). 148p. 1973. 14.75 (ISBN 0-398-02892-3). C C Thomas.

Hair Transplantation for the Treatment of Male Pattern Baldness. Charles P. Vallis. (Illus.). 608p. 46.75 (ISBN 0-398-04165-2). C C Thomas.

Haircutting. Patricia Brent. LC 75-34251. (Career Concise Guides Ser.). (Illus.). 72p. (gr. 7 up). 1976. PLB 6.45 (ISBN 0-531-01127-5). Watts.

Hairdresser's Memoirs. Elfreda M. Bigelow. 1981. 6.75 (ISBN 0-8062-1643-3). Carlton.

Hairy Cell Leukaemia. Ed. by J. C. Cawley et al. (Recent Results in Cancer Research Ser.: Vol. 72). (Illus.). 180p. 1980. 33.00 (ISBN 0-387-09920-4). Springer-Verlag.

Haiti & the Dominican Republic. Rayford W. Logan. (Royal Institute of International Affairs Ser.). 1968. 13.95x (ISBN 0-19-214966-0). Oxford U Pr.

Haiti Circle. Marilyn Ross. 256p. 1976. pap. 1.25 o.p. (ISBN 0-445-00397-9). Popular Lib.

Haiti Through Its Holidays. Eleanor W. Telemaque. LC 79-52858. (Illus.). 64p. (gr. 4-6). 1980. 7.50 (ISBN 0-914110-12-8). Blyden Pr.

Haitian Potential: Research & Resources of Haiti. Ed. by Vera Rubin & Richard Schaedel. LC 73-78672. 1975. text ed. 15.75x (ISBN 0-8077-2377-0). Tchrs Coll.

Haitian Revolution, 1789-1804. Thomas O. Ott. LC 72-85085. (Illus.). 1973. 12.50x (ISBN 0-87049-143-1). U of Tenn Pr.

Hajj Studies, Vol. 1. Ed. by Ziauddin Sardar & M. Zaki Badawi. (Illus.). 168p. 1978. 22.00x (ISBN 0-85664-681-4, Pub. by Croom Helm Ltd England). Biblio Dist.

Hakka Dialect. M. Hashimoto. LC 72-85438. (Princeton-Cambridge Studies in Chinese Linguistics: No. 5). (Illus.). 700p. 1973. 110.00 (ISBN 0-521-20037-7). Cambridge U Pr.

Hala Sultan Tekke Five. Ulla Obrink. (Studies in Mediterranean Archaeology XLV: No. 5). (Orig.). 1979. pap. text ed. 42.00x (ISBN 91-85058-91-2). Humanities.

Halbritter's Arms Through the Ages: An Introduction to the Secret Weapons of History. Kurt Halbritter. (Richard Seaver Bk). (Illus.). 1979. 9.95 o.p. (ISBN 0-670-35908-4). Viking Pr.

Halcyon Island. Anne Knowles. LC 80-7909. 128p. (gr. 5 up). 1981. 8.95 (ISBN 0-06-023203-X, HarpJ); PLB 8.79g (ISBN 0-06-023204-8). Har-Row.

Halcyon Way. Mark McShane. (Orig.). 1980. pap. 1.95 (ISBN 0-532-23148-1). Manor Bks.

Hale-Ano: A Legend of Hawaii. David Guard. LC 80-69773. (Illus.). 118p. (gr. 6). 1981. 9.95 (ISBN 0-89742-048-9). Dawne-Leigh.

Hale County, Facts & Folklore. Vera D. Wofford. 18.00 (ISBN 0-686-68989-5). Pioneer Bk Tx.

Haleakala: The Story Behind the Scenery. Jim Mack. Ed. by Gweneth R. DenDooven. LC 78-51407. (Illus.). 1979. 7.95 (ISBN 0-916122-54-9); pap. 3.50 (ISBN 0-916122-53-0). K C Pubns.

Half a World Away. Gloria Bevan. (Harlequin Romances Ser.). 192p. (Orig.). 1981. pap. 1.25 (ISBN 0-373-02377-4, Pub. by Harlequin). PB.

Half-Blood: A Cultural Symbol in Nineteenth Century American Fiction. William J. Scheick. LC 79-4012. 128p. 1979. 10.50x (ISBN 0-8131-1390-3). U Pr of Ky.

Half Breed. J. T. Edson. (Orig.). 1981. pap. 1.95 (ISBN 0-425-04736-9). Berkley Pub.

Half-Breed in Johsonville. Benjamin Poore. 1981. 5.75 (ISBN 0-8062-1579-8). Carlton.

Half Century of Polish Mathematics: Remembrances & Reflections. K. Kuratowski. (International Series in Pure & Applied Mathematics: Vol. 108). (Illus.). 212p. 1980. 26.00 (ISBN 0-08-023046-6). Pergamon.

Half-Heart. Amanda Preble. (Orig.). 1981. pap. 1.50 (ISBN 0-440-13442-0). Dell.

Half Hours with St. John. Steele. pap. 5.95 (ISBN 0-686-12871-0). Schmul Pub Co.

Half Hours with St. Paul. Steele. pap. 4.95 (ISBN 0-686-12872-9). Schmul Pub Co.

Half Lines & Repetitions in Virgil. John Sparrow. Ed. by Steele Commager. LC 77-70823. (Latin Poetry Ser.). 1978. lib. bdg. 15.50 (ISBN 0-8240-2979-8). Garland Pub.

Half Man, Half Beast, & Other Fantastic Combinations. Douglas M. Silente. (Odd Books for Odd Moments Ser.). (Illus.). 72p. (Orig.). 1981. pap. 3.95 (ISBN 0-938338-02-1). Winds World Pr.

Half Past Human. T. J. Bass. 288p. 1975. pap. 1.50 o.p. (ISBN 0-345-24635-7). Ballantine.

Half the Human Experience. 2nd ed. Janet Hyde & B. G. Rosenberg. 1980. pap. text ed. 9.95x (ISBN 0-669-02500-3); instrs'. manual (ISBN 0-669-02502-X). Heath.

Half-Way Covenant: Church Membership in Puritan New England. Robert G. Pope. LC 69-18067. 1969. 18.50 o.p. (ISBN 0-691-07156-X). Princeton U Pr.

Half-Way Generation: A Study of Asian Youth in Newcastle-Upon-Tyne. John H. Taylor. 1976. pap. text ed. 17.00x (ISBN 0-85633-081-7, NFER). Humanities.

Half Way with Roosevelt. Ernest K. Lindley. LC 75-8789. (FDR & the Era of the New Deal Ser.). x, 449p. 1975. Repr. of 1937 ed. lib. bdg. 32.50 (ISBN 0-306-70706-3). Da Capo.

Halfhyde & the Flag Captain. Philip McCutchan. 196p. 1981. 9.95 (ISBN 0-312-35684-6). St Martin.

Halfhyde Ordered South. Philip McCutchan. 1980. 9.95 (ISBN 0-686-58172-5). St Martin.

Halfhyde to the Narrows. Philip D. McCutchan. LC 77-72303. 1977. 7.95 o.p. (ISBN 0-312-35690-0). St Martin.

Halfmoons & Dwarf Parrots. William Allen. pap. 4.95 (ISBN 0-87666-424-9, PS647). TFH Pubns.

Halfway Down Paddy Lane. Jean Marzollo. LC 80-25854. 176p. (gr. 6 up). 1981. 9.75 (ISBN 0-8037-3329-1). Dial.

Halfway Houses. Robert Z. Apte. 125p. 1968. pap. text ed. 5.00x (ISBN 0-7135-1522-8, Pub. by Bedford England). Renouf.

Halfway Houses for the Mentally Ill: A Study of Programs & Problems. R. M. Glasscote et al. 244p. 1971. 7.50 (ISBN 0-685-24870-4, P203-0). Am Psychiatric.

Halfway Through the Door. Alan Arkin. 128p. 1981. pap. 2.50 (ISBN 0-553-13816-2). Bantam.

Halfway to Heaven. Peter Lappin. 240p. (Orig.). 1980. pap. write for info. (ISBN 0-89944-052-5). D Bosco Pubns.

Halfway to Nineteen Eighty-Four. Hubert Gladwyn. LC 66-27476. 1966. 10.00x (ISBN 0-231-02991-8). Columbia U Pr.

Halfway up the Mountain. Theo E. Gilchrist. LC 77-29020. (Illus.). (gr. k-2). 1978. 6.89 (ISBN 0-397-31805-7). Lippincott.

Hall Effect in Metals & Alloys. Colin M. Hurd. LC 76-157936. (International Cryogenics Monographs). 400p. 1972. 39.50 (ISBN 0-306-30530-5, Plenum Pr). Plenum Pub.

Hall J. Kelley on Oregon. Ed. by Fred W. Powell. LC 79-87635. (American Scene Ser). (Illus.). 412p. 1972. Repr. of 1932 ed. lib. bdg. 39.50 (ISBN 0-306-71796-4). Da Capo.

Hall Jackson & the Purple Foxglove: Medical Practice & Research in Revolutionary America, 1760-1820. J. Worth Estes. LC 79-63083. (Illus.). 309p. 1980. text ed. 20.00x (ISBN 0-87451-173-9). U Pr of New Eng.

Hallelujah Trail. Bill Gulick. 176p. 1976. pap. 1.25 o.p. (ISBN 0-445-00336-7). Popular Lib.

Halley's Bible Handbook. Henry H. Halley. 1976. 7.95 (ISBN 0-310-25720-4); kivar 10.95 (ISBN 0-310-25727-1); large print 15.95 (ISBN 0-310-41390-7). Zondervan.

Halliwell's Teleguide. Leslie Halliwell. 1979. 29.95 o.s.i. (ISBN 0-8464-0051-0). Beekman Pubs.

Hallmark Homes. Hiawatha T. Estes. (Illus.). 1981. 2.00 (ISBN 0-911008-20-9). H Estes.

Halloween. Helen Borten. LC 65-16184. (Holiday Ser.). (Illus.). (gr. 1-3). 1965. PLB 7.89 (ISBN 0-690-36314-1, TYC-J). T Y Crowell.

Halloween. Joyce K. Kessel. LC 80-15890. (Carolrhoda on My Own Bks.). (Illus.). 48p. (gr. k-3). 1980. PLB 5.95g (ISBN 0-87614-132-7). Carolrhoda Bks.

Halloween. Larry Racioppo. LC 80-19119. (Illus.). 32p. (gr. 1 up). 1980. 8.95 (ISBN 0-684-16708-5). Scribner.

Halloween. Ron Reese. Ed. by Alton Jordan. (Holidays Ser.). (Illus.). (gr. k-3). 1977. PLB 3.50 (ISBN 0-89868-023-9, Read Res); pap. text ed. 1.75 (ISBN 0-89868-056-5). ARO Pub.

Halloween. Cass R. Sandak. (gr. 2-4). 1980. PLB 7.90 (ISBN 0-531-04149-2). Watts.

Halloween Mystery. Joan L. Nixon. Ed. by Kathy Pacini. LC 79-166. (First Read-Alone Mysteries). (Illus.). (gr. 1-3). 1979. 5.50g (ISBN 0-8075-3136-7). A Whitman.

Hallowing. Fran P. Yariv. (Orig.). pap. 2.50 (ISBN 0-515-05192-6). Jove Pubns.

Halls of Fame. Ed. by Thomas C. Jones. LC 77-70330. (Illus.). 1977. 29.95 o.s.i. (ISBN 0-690-01397-3, TYC-T). T Y Crowell.

Hallucinations: Behavior, Experience, & Theory. Ed. by R. K. Siegel & L. J. West. LC 75-12670. 322p. 1975. 43.95 (ISBN 0-471-79096-6, Pub. by Wiley Medical). Wiley.

Hallucinogenic Drugs. F. Christine Brown. (Amer. Lec. Living Chemistry Ser.). (Illus.). 164p. 1972. 19.75 (ISBN 0-398-02249-6). C C Thomas.

Hallucinogens & Shamanism. Ed. by Michael J. Harner. (Illus.). 224p. 1973. 14.95 (ISBN 0-19-501650-5). Oxford U Pr.

HALO: A Data Base Management System. Joseph Bernard et al. 1981. pap. 12.95 (ISBN 0-8359-2720-2). Reston.

Halocarbons: Effects on Stratospheric Ozone. Panel on Atmospheric Chemistry, Committee on Impacts of Stratospheric Change, National Research Council. 1976. pap. 10.25 (ISBN 0-309-02532-X). Natl Acad Pr.

Halocarbons: Environmental Effects of Chlorofluoromethane Release. Committee on Impacts of Stratospheric Change, National Research Council. 1976. pap. 6.25 (ISBN 0-309-02529-X). Natl Acad Pr.

Halter-Broke. John Reese. 1978. pap. 1.50 o.s.i. (ISBN 0-515-04580-2). Jove Pubns.

Halyts'ko-Volyns'kyi Litopys, 2 vols. Tr. by T. Kostruba from Ukrainian. 258p. 1967. 17.50. Slavia Lib.

Ham & Japheth: The Mythic World of Whites in the Antebellum South. Thomas V. Peterson. LC 78-15716. (ATLA Monograph: No. 12). 1978. lib. bdg. 11.00 (ISBN 0-8108-1162-6). Scarecrow.

Ham Radio. Kenneth Ullyet. LC 76-54072. 1977. 14.95 (ISBN 0-7153-7247-5). David & Charles.

Ham Radio Incentive Licensing Guide. 2nd ed. Bert Simon. (Illus.). 1977. pap. 4.95 o.p. (ISBN 0-8306-7989-8, 989). TAB Bks.

Hamada, Potter. Bernard Leach. LC 75-11394. (Illus.). 305p. 1975. 60.00 (ISBN 0-87011-252-X). Kodansha.

Hamadsha: A Study in Moroccan Ethnopsychiatry. Vincent Crapanzano. LC 72-75529. 1973. 21.50x (ISBN 0-520-02241-6). U of Cal Pr.

Hambro Euromoney Directory, 1979. 8th ed. Ed. by Ian Swanton. LC 75-644094. (Orig.). 1979. pap. 42.50x o.p. (ISBN 0-903121-05-0). Intl Pubns Serv.

Hamburg-American Clock Company. 176p. 1980. soft cover 10.20 (ISBN 0-933396-10-4). Antique Clocks.

Hamburg Switch. Angus Ross. 192p. 1980. 9.95 o.s.i. (ISBN 0-8027-5418-X). Walker & Co.

Hamburger Book: All About Hamburgers & Hamburger Cookery. Lila Perl. LC 73-7173. (Illus.). 128p. (gr. 5 up). 1974. 7.95 (ISBN 0-395-28921-1, Clarion). HM.

Hamburger Cookbook. Myra Waldo. (Orig.). 1962. pap. 0.95 o.s.i. (ISBN 0-02-010710-2, Collier). Macmillan.

Hamburger Heaven. James Trivers. (YA) 1979. pap. 1.75 (ISBN 0-380-48355-6, 48355). Avon.

Hamilton Basso. Joseph R. Millichap. (United States Authors Ser.: No. 331). 1979. lib. bdg. 13.95 (ISBN 0-8057-7225-1). Twayne.

Hamilton County. MacKinlay Kantor. LC 70-101724. (Illus.). 1970. 9.95 o.s.i. (ISBN 0-02-560660-3). Macmillan.

Hamilton County. James W. Livingood. Ed. by Joy B. Dunn & Charles W. Crawford. (Tennessee County History Ser.: No. 33). 144p. 1981. 12.50 (ISBN 0-87870-120-6). Memphis St Univ.

Hamilton Duck. Arthur Getz. (Illus.). 32p. (ps-2). 1972. PLB 7.62 (ISBN 0-307-62055-7, Golden Pr). Western Pub.

Hamilton Duck's Springtime Story. Arthur Getz. (Illus.). 32p. (gr. k-3). 1974. PLB 7.62 (ISBN 0-307-62048-4, Golden Pr). Western Pub.

Hamiltonian Approach to Dynamic Economics. Ed. by David Cass & Karl Shell. (Economic Theory, Econometrics, & Mathematical Economics Ser.). 1976. 16.50 (ISBN 0-12-163650-X). Acad Pr.

Hamlet. Ed. by John R. Brown & Bernard Harris. (Stratford - Upon -Avon Studies: No. 5). 212p. 1963. pap. text ed. 10.75x (ISBN 0-8419-5812-2). Holmes & Meier.

Hamlet. Henry B. Charlton. 50p. 1980. Repr. of 1942 ed. lib. bdg. 6.00 (ISBN 0-8492-3865-X). R West.

Hamlet. Ed. by Bernard Lott. (New Swan Shakespeare Advanced Ser.). (Illus.). pap. text ed. 4.50x (ISBN 0-582-52741-4). Longman.

Hamlet. William Shakespeare. Ed. by John Jump. LC 78-127579. (Casebook Ser). 1970. pap. text ed. 2.50 o.s.i. (ISBN 0-87695-047-0). Aurora Pubs.

Hamlet. William Shakespeare. Ed. by Cyrus Hoy. (Critical Editions). (Annotated). (gr. 9-12). 1963. pap. text ed. 3.95x (ISBN 0-393-09591-6, 9591, NortonC). Norton.

Hamlet. William Shakespeare. Ed. by Arthur Quiller-Couch et al. (New Shakespeare Ser). 23.95 (ISBN 0-521-07531-9); pap. 4.50x (ISBN 0-521-09474-7). Cambridge U Pr.

Hamlet. William Shakespeare. Ed. by Maynard Mack & Robert W. Boynton. (Shakespeare Ser). (Illus.). (gr. 10-12). 1972. pap. text ed. 0.95x (ISBN 0-8104-6016-5). Hayden.

Hamlet. William Shakespeare. Ed. by R. C. Bald. LC 47-25585. (Crofts Classics Ser.). 1946. pap. text ed. 2.25x (ISBN 0-88295-073-3). AHM Pub.

Hamlet: Another Interpretation. Robert Marks. LC 80-50694. 1980. 12.00 (ISBN 0-9605486-0-2). Raven Pub Co.

Hamlet, Fables & Other Poems. Peter Herisch. Tr. by Herman Salinger. LC 78-64434. 7.50 (ISBN 0-685-39467-0). Charioteer.

Hamlet Problem & Its Solution. Emerson Venable. 107p. 1980. Repr. of 1912 ed. lib. bdg. 20.00 (ISBN 0-8492-2835-2). R West.

Hamlet Warning. Leonard Sanders. 1977. pap. 1.95 o.s.i. (ISBN 0-446-89370-6). Warner Bks.

Hamlet, with Reader's Guide. William Shakespeare. (Literature Program Ser). (gr. 10-12). 1970. pap. text ed. 4.58 (ISBN 0-87720-801-8); tchrs ed. 2.95 (ISBN 0-87720-901-4). AMSCO Sch.

Hamlin Garland. Joseph B. McCullough. (United States Authors Ser.: No. 299). 1978. lib. bdg. 9.95 (ISBN 0-8057-7203-0). Twayne.

Hamlyn French-English Dictionary. 1977. pap. 3.95 (ISBN 0-600-36563-8, 8086). Larousse.

Hamlyn French Phrase Book. pap. 2.95 (ISBN 0-600-33608-5, 8143). Larousse.

Hamlyn German-English Dictionary. 1977. pap. 3.95 (ISBN 0-600-36564-6, 8088). Larousse.

Hamlyn German Phrase Book. pap. 2.95 (ISBN 0-600-34052-X, 8145). Larousse.

Hamlyn Italian-English Dictionary. 1977. pap. 3.95 (ISBN 0-600-36566-2, 8089). Larousse.

Hamlyn Italian Phrase Book. pap. 2.95 (ISBN 0-600-34900-4, 8146). Larousse.

Hamlyn Pocket Dictionary of Wines. 1980 pap. 3.95. Larousse.

Hamlyn Spanish-English Dictionary. 1977. pap. 3.95 (ISBN 0-600-36565-4, 8087). Larousse.

Hamlyn Spanish Phrase Book. pap. 2.95 (ISBN 0-600-38245-1, 8144). Larousse.

Hammarskjold. Brian Urguhant. 1972. 12.50 o.p. (ISBN 0-394-47960-2). Knopf.

Hammers on Stone: The History of Cape Ann Granite. Barbara H. Erkkila. (Illus.). 208p. 1980. 18.95 (ISBN 0-931474-19-1). TBW Bks.

Hammerstrike. Walter Winward. 304p. 1981. pap. 2.95 (ISBN 0-553-13317-9). Bantam.

Hammerword Technique. Mary Spouse. (Orig.). 1980. pap. 2.25 (ISBN 0-505-51496-6). Tower Bks.

Hammet Equation. C. D. Johnson. LC 79-42670. (Cambridge Texts in Chemistry & Biochemistry). (Illus.). 196p. 1980. pap. 12.95 (ISBN 0-521-29970-5). Cambridge U Pr.

Hammett Equation. C. D. Johnson. LC 72-93140. (Chemistry Texts Ser). (Illus.). 180p. 1973. 28.95 (ISBN 0-521-20138-1). Cambridge U Pr.
Hammond Almanac of a Million Facts, Records & Forecasts 1979. Ed. by Martin A. Bacheller. (Illus.). 1978. 6.95 o.p. (ISBN 0-8437-4014-0). Hammond Inc.
Hammond Almanac of a Million Facts, Records, Forecasts--1981. 1980. pap. 4.50 (ISBN 0-451-82061-4, XE2050, Sig). NAL.
Hammond Almanac of a Million Facts, Records, Forecasts 1981. Ed. by Martin A. Bacheller. (Illus.). 1980. 7.95 (ISBN 0-8437-4021-3). Hammond Inc.
Hammond Large Type World Atlas. rev. ed. Hammond Incorporated. Ed. by Hammond Cartographers. (Illus.). (gr. 4-9). 1979. 19.95 (ISBN 0-8437-1246-5). Hammond Inc.
Hampshire & the Isle of Wight. A. Temple Patterson. 1976. 17.95 (ISBN 0-7134-3221-7, Pub. by Batsford England). David & Charles.
Hampstead: Building a Borough 1650-1964. F. M. Thompson. (Illus.). 470p. 1974. 37.00x (ISBN 0-7100-7747-5). Routledge & Kegan.
Hampton Heritage. Julie Ellis. 1979. pap. 2.25 o.p. (ISBN 0-449-24131-9, Crest). Fawcett.
Hamptons. Leonard Harris. 1981. 13.95 (ISBN 0-671-61000-7, Wyndham Bks). S&S.
Hamptons. Charles Rigdon. 1979. pap. 2.50 o.p. (ISBN 0-523-40232-5). Pinnacle Bks.
Hamster, Bk. 1. Eileen Everett. (gr. 3-7). 1976. pap. 1.00 o.p. (ISBN 0-08-016235-5). Pergamon.
Hamsters, Gerbils, Guinea Pigs, Pet Mice, & Pet Rats. James Hahn & Lynn Hahn. LC 77-1389. (Illus.). (gr. 4 up). 1977. PLB 6.45 (ISBN 0-531-01287-5). Watts.
Hamsters, Gerbils, Guinea Pigs, Pet Mice & Pet Rats. James Hahn & Lynn Hahn. 1980. pap. 1.75 (ISBN 0-380-49239-3, 49231, Camelot). Avon.
Han Agriculture: The Formation of the Early Chinese Agrarian Economy. Cho-yun Hsu. Ed. by Jack Dull. LC 79-4920. (Illus.). 404p. (Includes material translated from Chinese). 1980. 20.00 (ISBN 0-295-95676-3). U of Wash Pr.
Han Fei Tzu: Basic Writings. Han Fei Tzu. Tr. by Burton Watson. LC 64-13734. (Orig.). 1964. pap. 5.00x (ISBN 0-231-08609-1). Columbia U Pr.
Han Tombs No. 1 at Mawangtui, 2 vols. (Illus.). 1973. 125.00 (ISBN 0-8351-0102-9). China Bks.
Hand. Marc Brandel. 1981. pap. 2.50 (ISBN 0-425-04838-1). Berkley Pub.
Hand. Kathleen Elgin. LC 68-11205. (Human Body Ser). (gr. 4-6). PLB 4.90 o.p. (ISBN 0-531-01173-9). Watts.
Hand. 3rd ed. R. G. Pulvertaft. (Operative Surgery Ser.). 1977. 94.95 (ISBN 0-407-00618-4). Butterworths.
Hand, Pt. 2. Association of Bone & Joint Surgeons. Ed. by Marshall Urist. (Clinical Orthopaedics Ser.). (Illus.). 1959. 15.00. Lippincott.
Hand & the Glove. Joaquim M. Assis. Tr. by Albert I. Bagby, Jr. LC 74-111502. (Studies in Romance Languages: No. 2). 144p. 1970. 8.00x (ISBN 0-8131-1211-7). U Pr of Ky.
Hand Book. Moulton K. Johnson. (Illus.). 130p. 1973. 12.50 (ISBN 0-398-02595-9). C C Thomas.
Hand-Book of Games. Ed. by Henry G. Bohn. LC 73-84610. 1969. Repr. of 1850 ed. 20.00 (ISBN 0-8103-3570-0). Gale.
Hand Book of International Food Regulatory Toxicology, 2 vols. Gaston Vettorazzi. Incl. Vol. 1. Evaluations. 176p. 1980 (ISBN 0-89335-086-9); Vol. 2. Profiles. 256p. 1981. text ed. 30.00 ea. Spectrum Pub.
Hand-Book of Mottoes: Borne by the Nobility, Gentry, Cities, Public Companies. Charles N. Elvin. LC 79-122638. (Illus.). 1971. Repr. of 1860 ed. 15.00 (ISBN 0-8103-3387-2). Gale.
Hand, Hand, Fingers, Thumb. Al Perkins. LC 76-77841. (Bright & Early Bk.). (Illus.). (ps-1). 1969. 3.95 (ISBN 0-394-81076-7, BYR); PLB 4.99 (ISBN 0-394-91076-1). Random.
Hand in Glove. Ngaio Marsh. 1978. pap. 1.95 (ISBN 0-515-05763-0). Jove Pubns.
Hand in the Glove. Rex Stout. 1976. pap. 1.25 o.s.i. (ISBN 0-515-04149-1). Jove Pubns.
Hand Injuries. Beasley. (Illus.). 320p. 1981. text ed. write for info. (ISBN 0-7216-1607-0). Saunders.
Hand Lapidary Craft. Graham Geldart. LC 79-56446. (Illus.). 144p. 1980. 19.95 (ISBN 0-7134-1536-3, Pub. by Batsford England). David & Charles.
Hand-List of Anglo-Saxon Non-Runic Inscriptions. Elizabeth Okasha. LC 75-129934. (Illus.). 1971. 58.00 (ISBN 0-521-07904-7). Cambridge U Pr.
Hand Made Object & Its Maker. Michael O. Jones. LC 73-93055. (Illus.). 288p. 1975. 18.50 (ISBN 0-520-02697-7). U of Cal Pr.
Hand Me Another Brick. Charles Swindoll. 176p. 1981. pap. 2.25 (ISBN 0-553-14524-X). Bantam.
Hand-Me-Down-Dreams. Carol Peacock. LC 80-26048. 192p. 1981. 12.95x (ISBN 0-8052-3761-5); pap. 8.95 (ISBN 0-8052-0678-7). Schocken.
Hand-Me-Downs. Rhea Kohan. 1980. 11.95 (ISBN 0-394-51161-1). Random.
Hand of Destiny: The Folk-Lore & Superstition of Everyday Life. C. J. Thompson. LC 70-125600. 1970. Repr. of 1932 ed. 22.00 (ISBN 0-8103-3419-4). Gale.
Hand of Oberon. Roger Zelazny. 1977. pap. 1.75 (ISBN 0-380-01664-8, 51318). Avon.
Hand Puppet Show: Methods & Plays. rev ed. Victoria S. Morris. (gr. 1-8). 1976. pap. 4.50 o.p. (ISBN 0-914318-01-2). V S Morris.
Hand Shadows. A. Almoznino. LC 70-105956. (Illus.). 1969. 7.95 (ISBN 0-87396-026-2); pap. 3.95 (ISBN 0-87396-027-0). Stravon.
Hand Splinting: Principles & Methods. Elaine Fess et al. LC 80-17398. (Illus.). 318p. 1980. text ed. 27.50 (ISBN 0-8016-1569-0). Mosby.
Hand Surgery Review. Roy Meals & Malcolm A. Lesavoy. 184p. 1980. softcover 14.95 (ISBN 0-683-05899-1). Williams & Wilkins.
Hand Test: A New Projective Test with Special Reference to the Prediction of Overt Aggressive Behavior. Barry Bricklin et al. (American Lecture in Psychology Ser.). 112p. 1978. 12.75 (ISBN 0-398-00223-1). C C Thomas.
Hand Woolcombing & Spinning: A Guide to Worsteds from the Spinning Wheel. Peter Teal. (Illus.). 1979. 14.95 (ISBN 0-7137-0814-X, Pub. by Blandford Pr England). Sterling.
Hand-Woven Carpets Oriental & European. A. F. Kendrick & C. E. Tattersall. LC 73-77381. (Illus.). 256p. 1973. Repr. of 1922 ed. 8.00 (ISBN 0-486-20385-9). Dover.
Handball. Richard Nelson & H. Berger. (Prentice-Hall Sports Ser). 1971. pap. 4.95 ref. ed. (ISBN 0-13-372433-6). P-H.
Handball Basics. George J. Zafferano. LC 76-19798. 1977. 9.95 (ISBN 0-8069-4104-9); PLB 9.29 (ISBN 0-8069-4105-7). Sterling.
Handbook Dictionary of Parliamentary Prodecure. William R. Gondin. (Quality Paperback: No. 234). (Orig.). 1969. pap. 2.95 (ISBN 0-8226-0234-2). Littlefield.
Handbook for AACRZ. Margaret Maxwell. 700p. 1980. pap. text ed. 20.00 (ISBN 0-8389-0301-0). ALA.
Handbook for Aides. Mary Lound Brotherson. 1981. pap. write for info (ISBN 0-8134-2177-2, 2177). Interstate.
Handbook for Apartment Living. John Bingham. LC 80-70350. 288p. (gr. 11-12). 1981. 13.95 (ISBN 0-686-69519-4); pap. 8.95 (ISBN 0-686-69520-8). Chilton.
Handbook for Applied Mathematics. REA Staff. 800p. 1980. 16.85 (ISBN 0-87891-521-4). Res & Educ.
Handbook for Beach Strollers: From Maine to Cape Hatteras. Donald J. Zinn. LC 75-1921. (Illus.). 128p. 1975. pap. 5.95 (ISBN 0-87106-055-8). Globe Pequot.
Handbook for Boys: Reproduction of the Nineteen Eleven Handbook. John L. Alexander et al. (Illus.). (gr. 7-12). Repr. of 1911 ed. pap. 6.80x (ISBN 0-8395-3100-1). BSA.
Handbook for Cat People. Celia Heriot. 1978. pap. 1.95 (ISBN 0-441-31596-8). Charter Bks.
Handbook for Chairmen of Junior Tennis Tournaments. 43p. 1976. 1.50 (ISBN 0-938822-01-2). USTA.
Handbook for College Admissions. Thomas C. Hayden. LC 80-66009. 1981. 12.95 (ISBN 0-689-11095-2); pap. 6.95 (ISBN 0-686-69529-1). Atheneum.
Handbook for Community Professionals: An Approach for Planning & Action. Merlin Taber et al. (Illus.). 228p. 1972. text ed. 18.50 (ISBN 0-398-02426-X). C C Thomas.
Handbook for Contemporary Photography. 4th ed. Arnold H. Gassan. LC 77-14576. (Illus.). 1977. 14.95 (ISBN 0-87992-009-2); pap. 8.95x (ISBN 0-87992-008-4). Light Impressions.
Handbook for Dairymen. Anthony Coletti. (Illus.). 1963. 6.00x o.p. (ISBN 0-8138-0740-9). Iowa St U Pr.
Handbook for Data Processing Educators. Roger Sullivan. Ed. by Edwin F. Kerr. (Illus.). 191p. (Orig.). 1979. pap. 18.00 (ISBN 0-89435-038-2). QED Info Sci.
Handbook for Development Officers at Independent Schools. Ed. by Donald J. Whelan. 1979. pap. 21.50 (ISBN 0-89964-045-1). CASE.
Handbook for Diagnosing Basic Skills: A Handbook for Deciding What to Teach. Kenneth W. Howell et al. (Special Education Ser.). 393p. 1980. pap. text ed. 17.50 (ISBN 0-675-08130-0). Merrill.
Handbook for Differential Diagnosis of Neurologic Signs & Symptoms. Heilman. (Illus.). 1977. pap. text ed. 12.95 (ISBN 0-8385-3617-4). ACC.
Handbook for Effective Curriculum Development. Ross L. Neagley & D. Evans. 1967. 14.95 o.p. (ISBN 0-13-372607-X). P-H.
Handbook for Effective Supervision of Instruction. 3rd ed. Ross L. Neagley & N. Dean Evans. 1980. text ed. 18.95 (ISBN 0-13-372672-X). P-H.
Handbook for Elementary School Teachers. 2nd ed. Kenneth Hoover & Paul Hollingsworth. pap. text ed. 14.95 o.p. (ISBN 0-205-05953-8). Allyn.
Handbook for Elementary School Teachers. 2nd abr. ed. Kenneth Hoover & Paul Hollingsworth. 1978. pap. text ed. 10.95 (ISBN 0-205-06058-7). Allyn.
Handbook for Emergencies: Coming Out Alive. Anthony Greenbank. LC 74-25104. 192p. (gr. 7 up). 1976. 8.95 (ISBN 0-385-09842-1); pap. 3.95 (ISBN 0-385-09822-7). Doubleday.
Handbook for Environmental Planning: The Social Consequences of Environmental Change. Ed. by James McEvoy, III & Thomas Dietz. LC 76-57239. 1977. 32.00 (ISBN 0-471-58389-8, Pub. by Wiley-Interscience). Wiley.
Handbook for Evaluating & Selecting Curriculum Materials. Meredith D. Gail. 190p. 1981. pap. text ed. 9.95 (ISBN 0-205-07301-8, 2373017). Allyn.
Handbook for Faculty Development, Vol. 3. William H. Bergquist & Steven R. Phillips. Ed. by Gary H. Quehl & Jean B. Bernard. LC 80-69254. 1981. pap. 15.00 (ISBN 0-937012-11-4). Coun Advance Small Colleges.
Handbook for Flower Arrangers. Phyllis Page. (Color Ser.). (Illus.). 1965. 9.95 (ISBN 0-7137-0765-8, Pub by Blandford Pr England). Sterling.
Handbook for Followers of Jesus. Winkie Pratney. LC 76-44385. 1976. pap. 4.95 (ISBN 0-87123-378-9, 210378). Bethany Fell.
Handbook for Georgia Legislators. 8th ed. Edwin L. Jackson. 220p. 1980. pap. 10.00x (ISBN 0-89854-069-0). U of GA Inst Govt.
Handbook for Human Services for Older People. Ed. by Monica B. Holmes & Douglas Holmes. LC 78-27668. 1979. text ed. 19.95 (ISBN 0-87705-381-2). Human Sci Pr.
Handbook for Junior Tennis Tournament Players. 22p. 1976. 1.00 (ISBN 0-938822-02-0). USTA.
Handbook for Meat Chemists. Edward S. Koniecko. 1979. pap. text ed. 20.00 (ISBN 0-89529-097-9). Avery Pub.
Handbook for Modal Counterpoint. S. Roberts & I. Fischer. LC 67-19238. 1967. pap. text ed. 12.95 (ISBN 0-02-926560-6). Free Pr.
Handbook for Modern Educational Dance. rev. ed. Valerie Preston. (Movement & Creative Drama Ser.). 1980. pap. 10.95 (ISBN 0-8238-0247-7). Plays.
Handbook for New Heads: An Introduction to Independent School Administration. Dexter K. Strong. 1977. pap. 6.50 (ISBN 0-934338-27-2). NAIS.
Handbook for New Parents. Alvin Eden. 1979. pap. 2.50 (ISBN 0-425-04285-5). Berkley Pub.
Handbook for Organization & Conduct of Tennis Clinics & Teacher Training Workshops. Paul Xanthos. (Illus.). 39p. 1974. 2.95 (ISBN 0-938822-03-9). USTA.
Handbook for Planning & Conducting Tennis Tournaments. Lois H. Blackburn. (Illus.). 1979. pap. 4.50 (ISBN 0-938822-04-7). USTA.
Handbook for Prescribing Medications During Pregnancy. Richard L. Berkowitz et al. 1981. pap. text ed. write for info (ISBN 0-316-09173-1). Little.
Handbook for Prospective African Students to the U.S.A. H. Oziri Ubamadu. LC 78-53791. 1978. pap. text ed. 5.50x (ISBN 0-8191-0514-7). U Pr of Amer.
Handbook for Radio Engineering Managers. John F. Ross. 1000p. 1980. text ed. 94.95 (ISBN 0-408-00424-X). Butterworths.
Handbook for Radiologic Technologists & Special Procedures Nurses in Radiology. N. W. Powell. (Illus.). 104p. 1974. 11.75 (ISBN 0-398-03066-9). C C Thomas.
Handbook for Recreation. rev. 1959 ed. U. S. Children's Bureau. LC 74-174126. (Children's Bureau Publication Ser.: No. 231). (Illus.). x, 148p. 1975. Repr. of 1960 ed. 16.00 (ISBN 0-8103-4001-1). Gale.
Handbook for Satyagrahis. Narayan Desai. 1980. pap. 3.00 perfect bdg. (ISBN 0-86571-002-3). Movement New Soc.
Handbook for School Media Personnel. 2nd ed. Philip M. Turner. LC 80-21152. (Illus.). 132p. 1980. pap. text ed. 9.50x (ISBN 0-87287-225-4). Libs Unl.
Handbook for Scientific Photography. Alfred A. Blaker. LC 77-24661. (Illus.). 1977. text ed. 28.95x (ISBN 0-7167-0285-1). W H Freeman.
Handbook for Spies. Alexander Foote. 12.50x (ISBN 0-392-07888-0, SpS). Soccer.
Handbook for Staff Development Workshops in Indian Education. LC 76-27562. 1976. pap. 1.00 (ISBN 0-87281-051-8). Ctr Appl Ling.
Handbook for Technologists of Nuclear Medicine. Julia S. Hudak. (Illus.). 168p. 1971. 12.75 (ISBN 0-398-02178-3). C C Thomas.
Handbook for the Ballet Accompanist. Gerald R. Lishka. LC 78-2051. (Illus.). 256p. 1979. 15.00x (ISBN 0-253-32704-0). Ind U Pr.
Handbook for the Businessman as a Witness. 2nd ed. 1976. pap. 3.50 o.p. (ISBN 0-686-20594-4). US Trademark.
Handbook for the Differential Diagnosis of Infectious Diseases. Jonas Schulman. (Illus.). 1980. pap. 14.50 (ISBN 0-8385-3616-6). ACC.
Handbook for the Hearing-Impaired Older Adult. Joan M. Sayre. (Illus.). 80p. 1980. pap. 3.95x (ISBN 0-8134-2121-7). Interstate.
Handbook for the Humanistic Astrologer. Michael R. Meyer. LC 73-83657. 456p. 1974. pap. 5.95 (ISBN 0-385-05729-6, Anch). Doubleday.
Handbook for the Lectionary. Horace T. Allen, Jr. LC 80-19735. pap. 8.95. Geneva Pr.
Handbook for the Lectionary. Horace T. Allen, Jr. 1980. softcover 9.95 (ISBN 0-664-24347-9). Westminster.
Handbook for the Personal Orientation Inventory. Robert R. Knapp. LC 75-17256. 1976. text ed. 12.95 (ISBN 0-912736-17-8). EDITS Pubs.
Handbook for the Preparation of Research Reports & Theses. Kenneth E. Anderson & Oscar M. Haugh. LC 78-61395. 1978. pap. text ed. 4.75 (ISBN 0-8191-0597-X). U Pr of Amer.
Handbook for the Teaching of Social Studies. new ed. Association of Teachers of Social Studies in the City of New York. 1977. text ed. 18.95 (ISBN 0-205-05769-1). Allyn.
Handbook for the Young Athlete. Bob Gaillard et al. 1978. pap. 5.95 (ISBN 0-915950-18-9). Bull Pub.
Handbook for Transistors. John D. Lenk. (Illus.). 320p. 1976. 18.95 (ISBN 0-13-382259-1); pap. 7.95 (ISBN 0-13-382267-2). P-H.
Handbook for Typists. Ellen Pate & Barbara Spengler. 96p. 1980. 6.95 (ISBN 0-8403-2194-5). Kendall-Hunt.
Handbook for Typists: Operation of the Selectric Typewriter, Technical Information, Format Illustrations & Procedures. Ellen Pate & Barbara Spengler. 96p. (Orig.). 1980. pap. text ed. 6.95 o.p. (ISBN 0-8403-2194-5). Kendall-Hunt.
Handbook for Weight Reduction. Francis Dickinson & Lesley Monteith. (Creative Arts Communications Ser.). (Illus.). cancelled o.s.i. (ISBN 0-916870-20-0). Creative Arts Bk.
Handbook for Writing Graduate Theses. Gomer Pound. LC 77-80739. 1977. pap. text ed. 5.5000 (ISBN 0-8403-1767-0). Kendall-Hunt.
Handbook in Clinical Laboratory Science, CRC: Section H-Virology & Rickettsiology, 2 pts, Vol. 1. Gueh-Djen Hsiung & Robert H. Green. (Clinical Laboratory Science Ser.). (Illus.). 1979. Pt. 1, 488p. 62.95 (ISBN 0-8493-7061-2); Pt. 2, 448p. 62.95 (ISBN 0-8493-7062-0). CRC Pr.
Handbook in Clinical Laboratory Science, CRC: Section I-Hematology. Ed. by Robert M. Schmidt. 1979-80. 67.95 (ISBN 0-8493-7091-4). CRC Pr.
Handbook in Diagnostic-Prescriptive Teaching. 2nd ed. Philip H. Mann et al. 1979. pap. text ed. 28.50 (ISBN 0-205-06611-9). Allyn.
Handbook in Diagnostic Teaching: A Learning Disabilities Approach. abr. 2nd ed. Philip H. Mann & Patricia Suiter. 200p. 1974. pap. text ed. 12.50 o.p. (ISBN 0-205-04416-6). Allyn.
Handbook in Marine Science, CRC: Section A, Oceanography. Ed. by F. Walton Smith & F. A. Kalber. LC 73-88624. 640p. 1974. Vol. 1. 59.95 (ISBN 0-87819-389-8); Vol. 2, 390p. 53.95 (ISBN 0-87819-390-1). CRC Pr.
Handbook in Nutrition & Food, CRC: Section E-Nutritional Disorders, Vols. 2-3. Ed. by Miroslav Rechcigl. 1978. Vol. II, 548p. 69.95 (ISBN 0-8493-2797-0); Vol. III, 388p. 59.95 (ISBN 0-8493-2798-9). CRC Pr.
Handbook in Research & Evaluation. Stephen Isaac & William B. Michael. LC 70-14612. pap. text ed. 8.95 (ISBN 0-912736-12-7). EDITS Pubs.
Handbook of Active Filters. David E. Johnson et al. (Illus.). 1980. text ed. 21.95 (ISBN 0-13-372409-3). P-H.
Handbook of Adapted Physical Education Equipment & Its Use. Michael Sosne. (Illus.). 224p. 1973. text ed. 16.50 (ISBN 0-398-02782-X). C C Thomas.
Handbook of Adhesive Bonding. Charles V. Cagle. 1973. 43.50 o.p. (ISBN 0-07-009588-4, P&RB). McGraw.
Handbook of Adolescence: A Medical Guide for Parents & Teenagers. Marvin J. Gersh & Iris F. Litt. LC 77-151288. 256p. (Orig.). 1980. pap. 5.95 (ISBN 0-8128-6070-5). Stein & Day.
Handbook of Adolescent Psychology. Ed. by Joseph Adelson. LC 79-21927. (Personality Processes Ser.). 1980. 35.95 (ISBN 0-471-03793-1, Pub. by Wiley-Interscience). Wiley.
Handbook of Adult Education. Robert M. Smith et al. 1970. 17.95 (ISBN 0-02-896110-2). Macmillan.

Handbook of Adult Education in the United States. Ed. by Robert M. Smith. 1970. 17.25 (ISBN 0-88379-003-3). Adult Ed.

Handbook of Advanced Solid-State Troubleshooting. M. Ritter-Sanders. 1977. 18.95 (ISBN 0-87909-321-8). Reston.

Handbook of African Names. Ihechukwu Madubuike. LC 75-25943. (Illus.). 1976. 10.00 (ISBN 0-914478-13-3); pap. 5.00 (ISBN 0-89410-029-7). Three Continents.

Handbook of Agricultural Occupations. 3rd ed. Norman K. Hoover. LC 76-47431. (Illus.). (gr. 9-12). 1977. 15.35 (ISBN 0-8134-1893-3); text ed. 11.50x (ISBN 0-685-03897-1). Interstate.

Handbook of Air Conditioning, Heating & Ventilating. 3rd ed. Ed. by Eugene Stamper & Richard L. Koral. (Illus.). 1979. 59.00 (ISBN 0-8311-1124-0). Indus Pr.

Handbook of Alkaloids & Alkaloid-Containing Plants. Robert F. Raffauf. LC 73-113713. 1970. 105.00 (ISBN 0-471-70478-4, Pub. by Wiley-Interscience). Wiley.

Handbook of Amazon Parrots. A. E. Decoteau. (Illus.). 221p. 1980. 12.95 (ISBN 0-87666-892-9, H-1025). TFH Pubns.

Handbook of American Music & Musicians. Ed. by F. O. Jones. LC 76-155355. (Music Ser). 1971. Repr. of 1886 ed. lib. bdg. 19.50 (ISBN 0-306-70163-4). Da Capo.

Handbook of American Physical Education & Sport. Paula D. Welch & Harold A. Lerch. write for info. C C Thomas.

Handbook of Analysis of Organic Solvents. V. Sedivec & J. Flek. Tr. by Harry Sommernitz. LC 75-44239. (Ser. in Analytical Chemistry). 1976. 61.95 (ISBN 0-470-15010-6). Halsted Pr.

Handbook of Analytical Control of Iron & Steel Production. T. S. Harrison. LC 78-41222. (Series in Analytical Chemistry). 1979. 109.95 (ISBN 0-470-26538-8). Halsted Pr.

Handbook of Analytical Derivatization Reactions. Daniel R. Knapp. LC 78-12944. 1979. 45.00 (ISBN 0-471-03469-X, Pub. by Wiley-Interscience). Wiley.

Handbook of Anatomy for Art Students. 5th ed. Arthur Thomson. (Illus.). (YA) (gr. 9-12). 1929. pap. text ed. 5.00 (ISBN 0-486-21163-0). Dover.

Handbook of Ancient Hebrew Letters. Dennis Pardee. LC 79-22372. (Society of Biblical Literature, Sources for Biblical Study: 15). Date not set. 15.00x (ISBN 0-89130-359-6, 060315); pap. 10.50x (ISBN 0-89130-360-X). Scholars Pr CA.

Handbook of Animal Management Techniques. R. A. Battaglia & V. Mayrose. 608p. 1981. write for info. (ISBN 0-8087-2957-8). Burgess.

Handbook of Antibiotic Compounds, 4 vols. Ed. by Janos Berdy. Incl. Vol. 1. Carbohydrate Antibiotics. 59.95 (ISBN 0-8493-3451-9); Vol. 2. Macrocyclic Lactone (Lactam) Antibiotics. 64.95 (ISBN 0-8493-3452-7); Vol. 3. 59.95 (ISBN 0-8493-3453-5); Vol. 4, 2 pts. Pt. 1. 64.95 (ISBN 0-8493-3454-3); Pt. 2, 576p. 59.95 (ISBN 0-8493-3455-1). 1980. CRC Pr.

Handbook of Appellate Advocacy. rev. ed. UCLA Moot Court Honors Program. Ed. by Bruce Dizenfeld et al. LC 79-23768. 260p. 1980. pap. text ed. 6.95 (ISBN 0-8299-2068-4). West Pub.

Handbook of Applicable Mathematics: Probability, Vol. 2. E. Lloyd. (Handbook of Applicable Mathematics Ser.). 444p. 1980. 32.50 (ISBN 0-471-27821-1, Pub. by Wiley-Interscience). Wiley.

Handbook of Applicable Mathematics, Vol. 1: Algebra. Walter Ledermann. LC 79-42724. (Handbook of Applicable Mathematics Ser.). 1980. text ed. 85.00 (ISBN 0-471-27704-5, Pub. by Wiley-Interscience). Wiley.

Handbook of Applied Behavior Analysis: Social & Instructional Processes. Ed. by A. Charles Catania & T. A. Brigham. (Century Psychology Ser.). 1979. 39.50 (ISBN 0-470-99347-2). Halsted Pr.

Handbook of Arabic Music. Afif Bulos. pap. 6.95x (ISBN 0-685-88938-6). Intl Bk Ctr.

Handbook of Architectural Details for Commercial Buildings. Joseph DeChiars. 512p. 1980. 32.50 (ISBN 0-07-016215-8, P&RB). McGraw.

Handbook of Artificial Intelligence, 3 vols. Ed. by Avron Barr & Edward Feigenbaum. 1981. 90.00 set (ISBN 0-86576-004-7); 30.00 ea. Vol. 1 (ISBN 0-86576-005-5). Vol. 2 (ISBN 0-86576-006-3). Vol. 3 (ISBN 0-86576-007-1). W Kaufmann.

Handbook of Audio Circuit Design. Derek Cameron. (Illus.). 1978. text ed. 18.95 (ISBN 0-87909-362-5). Reston.

Handbook of Audiological Rehabilitation. Gail D. Chermak. (Illus.). 480p. 1981. 43.75 (ISBN 0-398-04170-9). C C Thomas.

Handbook of Auditory & Vestibular Research Methods. Ed. by C. A. Smith & J. A. Vernon. (Illus.). 610p. 1976. 57.50 (ISBN 0-398-03231-9). C C Thomas.

Handbook of Auditory Perceptual Training. Cora L. Reagan. 168p. 1973. 11.75 (ISBN 0-398-02885-0). C C Thomas.

Handbook of Australian Languages, Vol. 1. R. M. Dixon & B. J. Blake. 1200p. 1980. text ed. 49.50x (ISBN 9-0272-0512-4). Humanities.

Handbook of Australian Languages, Vol. 1. Ed. by R. M. Dixon & B. J. Blake. (Handbook of Australian Languages Ser.). 390p. (Orig.). 1980. pap. text ed. 23.95 (ISBN 0-7081-1201-3, 0435). Bks Australia.

Handbook of Basic Citizenship Competencies: Guidelines for Comparing Materials, Assessing Instruction & Setting Goals. Richard C. Remy. Ed. by Ronald S. Brandt. LC 79-56888. 109p. (Orig.). 1980. pap. 4.75 (ISBN 0-87120-098-8, 611-80196). Assn Supervision.

Handbook of Basic English Skills. 2nd ed. Richard M. Bossone & James M. Reid, Jr. LC 77-20017. 1977. pap. text ed. 10.95 (ISBN 0-471-02196-2); tchrs. manual avail. (ISBN 0-471-04048-7). Wiley.

Handbook of Basic Pharmacokinetics. 2nd ed. W. A. Ritschel. LC 79-90428. 1980. 19.50 (ISBN 0-914768-34-4). Drug Intl Pubns.

Handbook of Behavioral Assessment. Ed. by Anthony R. Ciminero et al. LC 76-54170. (Personality Processes Ser). 1977. 39.50 (ISBN 0-471-15797-X, Pub. by Wiley-Interscience). Wiley.

Handbook of Behavioral Interventions. Alan Goldstein & Edna B. Foa. LC 79-16950. (Ser. on Personality Processes). 1980. 30.95 (ISBN 0-471-01789-2, Pub. by Wiley-Interscience). Wiley.

Handbook of Bible Lands. Guy P. Duffield. LC 77-80446. 1969. pap. 2.75 (ISBN 0-8307-0073-0, 5001854). Regal.

Handbook of Biblical Criticism. Richard N. Soulen. LC 76-12398. 1976. pap. 7.95 (ISBN 0-8042-0044-0). John Knox.

Handbook of Biblical Hebrew, 3 vols. William S. LaSor. Set. 12.95x (ISBN 0-8028-2379-3). Eerdmans.

Handbook of Biochemistry & Molecular Biology, CRC: Nucleic Acids Section, 2 vols. 3rd ed. Ed. by Gerald D Fasman. LC 75-29514. (Handbook Ser.). 1976. Vol. 1. 69.95 (ISBN 0-87819-506-8); Vol. 2, 923p. 74.95 (ISBN 0-87819-507-6). CRC Pr.

Handbook of Biochemistry & Molecular Biology, CRC: Proteins Section, 3 vols. 3rd ed. Gerald D. Fasman. LC 75-29514. (Handbook Ser.). 1976. (ISBN 0-685-61396-8); Vol. 2, 790p. 59.95 (ISBN 0-87819-504-1); Vol. 3, 633p. 74.95 (ISBN 0-87819-505-X); Vol. 3. 69.95 (ISBN 0-87819-510-6). CRC Pr.

Handbook of Biological Psychiatry, Pt. 2. Van Praag et al. (Experimental & Clinical Psychology Ser.: Vol. 1). 544p. 1980. 46.50 (ISBN 0-8247-6892-2). Dekker.

Handbook of Biological Psychiatry, Vol. 3. Van Praag. 29.50 (ISBN 0-8247-6965-1). Dekker.

Handbook of Black Librarianship. Ed. by E. J. Josey & A. A. Shockley. LC 77-21817. 1977. 25.00x (ISBN 0-87287-179-7). Libs Unl.

Handbook of Bovine Obstetrics. V. Sloss & J. H. Dufty. (Illus.). 224p. 1980. lib. bdg. 29.95 (ISBN 0-683-07745-7). Williams & Wilkins.

Handbook of Budgeting: Systems & Controls for Financial Management. H. W. Sweeny & Robert Rachlin. 700p. 1981. 34.50 (ISBN 0-471-05621-9). Ronald Pr.

Handbook of California Birds. 3rd rev. ed. Vinson Brown et al. LC 73-6326. (Illus.). 1979. 11.95 (ISBN 0-911010-17-3); pap. 7.95 (ISBN 0-911010-16-5). Naturegraph.

Handbook of Canadian Film. 2nd ed. Eleanor Beattie. (Take One-PMA Film Ser). (Illus.). 1977. 16.95 o.p. (ISBN 0-88778-130-6); pap. 8.00 (ISBN 0-88778-131-4). NY Zoetrope.

Handbook of Canaries. Matthew M. Vriends. (Illus.). 351p. 1980. 9.95 (ISBN 0-87666-876-7, H-994). TFH Pubns.

Handbook of Cellular Chemistry. 2nd ed. Annabelle Cohen. LC 78-11881. (Illus.). 1979. pap. 11.00 (ISBN 0-8016-1006-0). Mosby.

Handbook of Chemical Microscopy, Vol. 2. 2nd ed. E. M. Chamot & C. W. Mason. 1940. 37.50 (ISBN 0-471-04122-X). Wiley.

Handbook of Chemically Resistant Masonry. W. L. Sheppard. 1977. 40.00. W. L. Sheppard.

Handbook of Child Abuse & Neglect. Alejandro Rodriguez. 1977. spiral bdg. 13.00 (ISBN 0-87488-648-1). Med Exam.

Handbook of Child & Adolescent Psychiatric Emergencies. Gordon K. Farley et al. 1979. pap. 12.50 (ISBN 0-87488-656-2). Med Exam.

Handbook of Child Nursing Care. M. J. Wallace. LC 75-134041. (Wiley Paperback Nursing Ser.). 138p. 1971. pap. 11.95 (ISBN 0-471-91850-4). Wiley.

Handbook of Choral Technique. Percy M. Young. (Student's Music Library Ser). 1953. 6.95 (ISBN 0-234-77213-1). Dufour.

Handbook of Christian Feasts & Customs. Francis X. Weiser. LC 58-10908. 1958. 9.50 o.p. (ISBN 0-15-138435-5). HarBraceJ.

Handbook of Christian Symbols & Stories of the Saints, As Illustrated in Art. Clara E. Clement. LC 70-159863. 1971. Repr. of 1886 ed. 24.00 (ISBN 0-8103-3288-4). Gale.

Handbook of Christian Theologians. Martin E. Marty & Dean G. Peerman. (Fount Paperback Ser). pap. 4.95 (ISBN 0-529-01988-4, M244, Pub. by Collins Pubs). Abingdon.

Handbook of Christian Theologians. Ed. by Martin E. Marty & Dean G. Peerman. 1967. pap. 3.95 o.p. (ISBN 0-452-00244-3, F244, Mer). NAL.

Handbook of Christian Theologians. Ed. by Martin E. Marty & Dean G. Peerman. 512p. 1980. pap. 6.95 (ISBN 0-687-16566-0). Abingdon.

Handbook of Christian Theology. Ed. by Arthur A. Cohen & Marvin Halverson. 382p. 1980. pap. 5.95 (ISBN 0-687-16567-9). Abingdon.

Handbook of Christian Theology. Marvin Halverson & Arthur Cohen. (Fount Paperback Ser.). pap. 4.95 (ISBN 0-529-02087-4, M361, Pub. by Collins Pubs). Abingdon.

Handbook of Chromatography, CRC, 2 vols. Ed. by Gunter Zweig & Joseph Sherma. LC 76-163067. (Handbook Ser). 400p. 1972. Vol. 1, 784p. 59.95 (ISBN 0-8493-0561-6); Vol. 2, 343p. 49.95 (ISBN 0-87819-562-9). CRC Pr.

Handbook of Circulation Management. Ed. by Barbara Love. 1980. 49.95 (ISBN 0-918110-02-5). Folio.

Handbook of Classical & Modern Mandaic. Rudolf Macuch. 1965. 123.55x (ISBN 3-11-000261-2). De Gruyter.

Handbook of Classical Mythology. George Howe & G. A. Harrer. LC 77-121209. 1970. Repr. of 1947 ed. 15.00 (ISBN 0-8103-3290-6). Gale.

Handbook of Clinical Dental Auxiliary Practice. 2nd ed. Ed. by Francis A. Castano & Betsey Alden. LC 79-18202. 290p. 1980. text ed. 17.50 (ISBN 0-397-54285-2). Lippincott.

Handbook of Clinical Dietetics. American Dietetic Association. LC 80-11317. 480p. 1981. text ed. 20.00x (ISBN 0-300-02256-5). Yale U Pr.

Handbook of Clinical Drug Data. rev. 4th ed. James E. Knoben et al. LC 77-89811. 1979. 16.00 (ISBN 0-914768-27-1). Drug Intl Pubns.

Handbook of Clinical Endodontics. 2nd ed. Richard Bence. LC 80-15722. (Illus.). 262p. 1980. pap. text ed. 16.95 (ISBN 0-8016-0587-3). Mosby.

Handbook of Clinical Engineering, Vol. 1. Ed. by Barry N. Feinberg. 304p. 1980. 59.95 (ISBN 0-8493-0244-7). CRC Pr.

Handbook of Clinical Neuropsychology. Susan B. Filskov & Thomas J. Boll. LC 80-15392. (Wiley Ser. on Personality Processes). 768p. 1980. 29.95 (ISBN 0-471-04802-X, Pub. by Wiley-Interscience). Wiley.

Handbook of Clinical Nuclear Medicine. Philip Matin. 1977. cancelled (ISBN 0-87488-610-4). Med Exam.

Handbook of Clinical Nutrition: Clinicians Manual for the Diagnosis & Management of Nutritional Problems. Roland L. Weinsier. (Illus.). 231p. 1980. pap. text ed. 10.95 (ISBN 0-8016-5406-8). Mosby.

Handbook of Clinical Pathology. Joseph A. Sisson. LC 75-21273. (Illus.). 1976. pap. text ed. 21.50 o.p. (ISBN 0-397-50346-6). Lippincott.

Handbook of Clinical Pedodontics. Kenneth D. Snawder. LC 79-19983. 1979. pap. text ed. 19.95 (ISBN 0-8016-2951-9). Mosby.

Handbook of Clinical Psychobiology & Pathology, Vol 1 & 2. Sanford I. Cohen & Robert Ross. LC 80-14321. (Clinical & Community Psychology Ser.). 1981. Set. text ed. 55.00 (ISBN 0-89116-172-4); Vol. 1. text ed. 25.00 (ISBN 0-89116-173-2); Vol. 2. text ed. 35.00 (ISBN 0-89116-174-0). Hemisphere Pub. Postponed.

Handbook of Clinical Ultrasound. M. DeVlieger et al. LC 78-14458. 1978. 122.00 (ISBN 0-471-02744-8, Pub. by Wiley Medical). Wiley.

Handbook of COBOL Techniques. Computer Partners, Inc. (Illus.). 86p. (Orig.). 1979. pap. 10.00 (ISBN 0-89435-037-4). QED Info Sci.

Handbook of Common Methods in Limnology. 2nd ed. Owen T. Lind. LC 78-21173. (Illus.). 1979. pap. text ed. 11.95 (ISBN 0-8016-3019-3). Mosby.

Handbook of Community Health. 2nd ed. Murray Grant. LC 74-3029. 1975. pap. 7.50 o.p. (ISBN 0-8121-0495-1). Lea & Febiger.

Handbook of Community Health. 3rd ed. Murray Grant. LC 80-26182. (Illus.). 368p. 1981. pap. write for info. (ISBN 0-8121-0760-8). Lea & Febiger.

Handbook of Community Mental Health Practices: The San Mateo Experience. Ed. by H. Richard Lamb et al. LC 72-92886. (Behavioral Sciences Ser). 1969. 18.95x o.p. (ISBN 0-87589-040-7). Jossey-Bass.

Handbook of Compressed Gases. 2nd ed. Compressed Gas Association. 1981. text ed. 44.50 (ISBN 0-442-25419-9). Van Nos Reinhold.

Handbook of Conducting. Herman Scherchen. Tr. by M. D. Calvocoressi. LC 77-26270. (Music Reprint, 1978). 1978. Repr. of 1935 ed. lib. bdg. 22.50 (ISBN 0-306-77564-6). Da Capo.

Handbook of Conducting. rev. ed. Karl Van Hoesen. (Eastman School of Music Ser.). (Illus.). 1950. 22.50x (ISBN 0-89197-205-6); pap. text ed. 8.95x (ISBN 0-89197-206-4). Irvington.

Handbook of Construction Resources & Support Services. Professional Publications. Ed. by Joseph A. MacDonald. (Orig.). 1980. pap. 49.50 (ISBN 0-932836-02-X). Prof Pubns NY.

Handbook of Consumer Education: A Guide for Teaching Process & Content. new ed. Fannie L. Boyd & Ruth Stovall. 1978. pap. text ed. 17.95 (ISBN 0-205-05890-6). Allyn.

Handbook of Contemporary Theology. Bernard Ramm. (Orig.). 1966. pap. 2.65 o.p. (ISBN 0-8028-1159-0). Eerdmans.

Handbook of Controls & Instrumentation. John D. Lenk. (Illus.). 1980. text ed. 19.95 (ISBN 0-13-377069-9). P-H.

Handbook of Conversion Factors. Ed. by A. M. Shaw. 24p. 1978. 3.00x (ISBN 0-934366-01-2). Intl Research Serv.

Handbook of Corrosion Resistant Piping. Philip A. Schweitzer. (Illus.). 1969. 35.00 o.p. (ISBN 0-8311-3016-4). Indus Pr.

Handbook of Criminal Justice Evaluation. Ed. by Malcolm W Klein & Katherine S. Teilmann. LC 80-16909. (Illus.). 693p. 1980. 39.95 (ISBN 0-8039-1052-5). Sage.

Handbook of Cross-Cultural Human Development. Ruth H. Munroe et al. LC 79-12028. 900p. 1980. lib. bdg. 75.00 (ISBN 0-8240-7045-3). Garland Pub.

Handbook of Cross-Cultural Psychology: Perspectives, 6 vols. Harry C. Triandis & William W. Lambert. 1979. Vols. I & II. text ed. 25.95x ea. Vol. I (ISBN 0-205-06497-3). Vol. II (ISBN 0-205-06498-1). Vols. III-VI. text ed. write for info. Vol. III (ISBN 0-205-06499-X). Vol. IV (ISBN 0-205-06500-7). Vol. V (ISBN 0-205-06501-5). Vol. VI (ISBN 0-205-06502-3). Allyn.

Handbook of Cross-Cultural Psychology: Psychopathology, Vol. 6. Triandis & Draguns. 410p. 1981. text ed. 25.95 (ISBN 0-205-06502-3, 796502-8). Allyn.

Handbook of Cross-National MMPI Research. James N. Butcher & Paolo Pancheri. LC 75-28919. 1976. 22.50x (ISBN 0-8166-0758-3). U of Minn Pr.

Handbook of Cryosurgery. R. J. Albin. (Science & Practice of Surgery: Vol. 1). 1980. 59.75 (ISBN 0-8247-6981-3). Dekker.

Handbook of Current English. 6th ed. Jim W. Corder. 1981. pap. text ed. 8.95x (ISBN 0-673-15425-4). Scott F.

Handbook of Data Analysis & Data Base Design. Richard C. Perkinson. 175p. 1981. pap. 29.50 (ISBN 0-89435-045-5). QED Info Sci.

Handbook of Data Processing for Libraries. 2nd ed. Robert M. Hayes & Joseph Becker. LC 74-9690. (Information Sciences Ser). 712p. 1974. 38.95 (ISBN 0-471-36483-5, Pub. by Wiley-Interscience). Wiley.

Handbook of Data Processing Management, 6 vols. Martin L. Rubin. 1971. Set. 175.00 (ISBN 0-442-80343-5). Van Nos Reinhold.

Handbook of Decomposition Methods in Analytical Chemistry. Rudolf Bock & Iain L. Marr. LC 78-70559. 1979. 79.95 (ISBN 0-470-26501-9). Halsted Pr.

Handbook of Diabetes Mellitus, 5 vols. Michael Brownlee. Incl. Vol. 1. Etiology-Hormone Physiology. 450p. lib. bdg. 65.00 (ISBN 0-8240-7030-5); Vol. 2. Islet Cell Function-Insulin Action. 250p. lib. bdg. 37.50 (ISBN 0-8240-7214-6); Vol. 3. Intermediary Metabolism & Its Regulation. 340p. lib. bdg. 50.00 (ISBN 0-8240-7215-4); Vol. 4. Biochemical Pathology. 325p. lib. bdg. 45.00 (ISBN 0-8240-7223-5); Vol. 5. Current & Future Therapies. 420p. lib. bdg. 60.00 (ISBN 0-8240-7224-3). LC 79-26703. 1980. Garland Pub.

Handbook of Diabetes Mellitus: Vol. 1, Etiology-Hormone Physiology. Michael Brownlee. LC 79-26703. 450p. 1980. lib. bdg. 65.00 (ISBN 0-8240-7030-5). Garland Pub.

Handbook of Diabetes Mellitus: Vol. 3, Intermidiary Metabolism & Its Regulation. Michael Brownlee. LC 79-26703. 340p. 1980. lib. bdg. 50.00 (ISBN 0-8240-7215-4). Garland Pub.

Handbook of Diabetes Mellitus: Vol. 5, Current & Future Therapies. Michael Brownlee. LC 79-26703. 420p. 1981. lib. bdg. 60.00 (ISBN 0-8240-7224-3). Garland Pub.

Handbook of Digital Electronics. John D. Lenk. (Illus.). 384p. 1981. text ed. 21.95 (ISBN 0-13-377184-9). P-H.

Handbook of Digital IC Applications. D. Heiserman. 1980. 22.95 (ISBN 0-13-372698-3). P-H.

Handbook of Dimensional Measurement. Francis T. Farago. (Illus.). 1968. 36.00 (ISBN 0-8311-1025-2). Indus Pr.

Handbook of Diseases of Laboratory Animals. Malcolm Hime. 1979. pap. text ed. 32.00 (ISBN 0-433-14723-7). Intl Ideas.

Handbook of Drafting Technology. John A. Nelson. 368p. 1981. text ed. 22.95 (ISBN 0-442-28661-9); pap. text ed. 14.95 (ISBN 0-442-28662-7). Van Nos Reinhold.

Handbook of Drug Interactions. 3rd ed. Edward A. Hartshorn. LC 76-27057. 225p. 1976. pap. 7.50 (ISBN 0-914768-23-9). Drug Intl Pubns.

Handbook of Drug Interactions. Gerald Swidler. 1971. 27.50 o.p. (ISBN 0-471-83975-2, Pub. by Wiley-Interscience). Wiley.

Handbook of Drug Therapy in Psychiatry. Jerold G. Bernstein. 1981. write for info. (ISBN 0-88416-323-7). PSG Pub.

Handbook of Dyes. Anne Bliss. (Illus.). 180p. 1980. 15.95 (ISBN 0-684-16502-3, ScribT). Scribner.

Handbook of Ear, Nose & Throat Emergencies. 2nd ed. Ed. by M. Haskell Newman et al. 1973. spiral bdg. 11.00 (ISBN 0-87488-639-2). Med Exam.

Handbook of Early American Decoration. Edith Cramer. 7.50 o.p. (ISBN 0-8231-7007-1). Branford.

Handbook of Educational Administration: A Guide for the Practitioner. Emery Stoops et al. 912p. 1975. text ed. 35.95x o.p. (ISBN 0-205-04469-7, 2244691). Allyn.

Handbook of Educational Supervision: A Guide for the Practioner. 2nd ed. James R. Marks et al. 1978. text ed. 27.95 (ISBN 0-205-06020-X). Allyn.

Handbook of Electrical Systems Design Practices. John E. Traister. (Illus.). 1978. ref. ed. 16.95 (ISBN 0-87909-348-X). Reston.

Handbook of Electronic Charts, Graphs & Tables. John D. Lenk. 1970. ref. ed. 18.95 (ISBN 0-13-377275-6). P-H.

Handbook of Electronic Circuit Design. John D. Lenk. (Illus.). 320p. 1976. 19.95 (ISBN 0-13-377309-4). P-H.

Handbook of Electronic Circuits. Graham J. Scoles. LC 74-13558. 370p. 1975. 49.95 (ISBN 0-470-76715-4). Halsted Pr.

Handbook of Electronic Components & Circuits. John D. Lenk. LC 73-11038. (Illus.). 224p. 1973. ref. ed. 18.95x (ISBN 0-13-377283-7). P-H.

Handbook of Electronic Filter Design. Arthur B. Williams. 1980. write for info. (ISBN 0-07-070430-9). McGraw.

Handbook of Electronic Materials, Vol. 1: Optical Materials Properties. A. J. Moses. LC 76-147312. 104p. 1971. 37.50 (ISBN 0-306-67101-8). IFI Plenum.

Handbook of Electronic Materials, Vol. 9: Electronic Properties of Composite Materials. M. A. Leeds. LC 76-147312. 103p. 1972. 37.00 (ISBN 0-306-67109-3). IFI Plenum.

Handbook of Electronic Meters: Theory & Application. John D. Lenk. 1969. ref. ed. 18.95 (ISBN 0-13-377358-2). P-H.

Handbook of Electronic Systems Design. new ed. Charles A. Harper. (Handbook Ser.). (Illus.). 832p. 1979. 35.00 (ISBN 0-07-026683-2, P&RB). McGraw.

Handbook of Electronic Test Equipment. John D. Lenk. LC 78-135753. 1971. ref. ed. 21.95 (ISBN 0-13-377366-3). P-H.

Handbook of Electrophoresis, CRC, 2 vols. Ed. by L. A. Lewis & J. J. Opplt. 1980. Vol. 1, 336p. 56.95 (ISBN 0-8493-0571-3); Vol. 2, 400p. 59.95 (ISBN 0-8493-0572-1). CRC Pr.

Handbook of Emergency Care & Rescue. rev. ed. Lawrence W. Erven. 1976. text ed. 14.95x (ISBN 0-02-472630-3). Macmillan.

Handbook of Emergency Drugs. Gail Walraven. 100p. 1978. pap. text ed. 7.95 (ISBN 0-87618-949-4). R J Brady.

Handbook of Emergency Toxicology. 3rd ed. Sidney Kaye. 544p. 1977. 28.00 o.p. (ISBN 0-398-00987-2). C C Thomas.

Handbook of Emergency Toxicology: A Guide for the Identification, Diagnosis, & Treatment of Poisoning. 4th ed. Sidney Kaye. (American Lectures in Public Protection). (Illus.). 596p. 1980. 54.75 (ISBN 0-398-03960-7). C C Thomas.

Handbook of Endocrinology: Diagnosis & Management of Endocrine & Metabolic Disorders. 2nd ed. Richard S. Dillon. LC 79-10531. (Illus.). 760p. 1980. text ed. 52.00 (ISBN 0-8121-0642-3). Lea & Febiger.

Handbook of Engineering in Medicine & Biology, CRC. Ed. by David G. Fleming & Barry N. Feinberg. LC 75-44222. (Handbook Ser.). 1976. Vol. 1. 57.95 (ISBN 0-87819-285-9). CRC Pr.

Handbook of Engineering Mechanics. Ed. by Wilhelm Flugge. 1962. 69.50 o.p. (ISBN 0-07-021392-5, P&RB). McGraw.

Handbook of English. Clarence Stratton. LC 74-19222. 1975. Repr. of 1940 ed. 26.00 (ISBN 0-8103-4112-3). Gale.

Handbook of Environmental Data & Ecological Parameters. rev. ed. Ed. by S. E. Jorgensen. LC 78-41207. (Enviromental Sciences & Applications Ser.: Vol. 6). (Illus.). 1100p. 1979. 225.00 (ISBN 0-08-023436-4). Pergamon.

Handbook of Environmental Education with International Case Studies. Ed. by Robert N. Saveland. LC 76-4659. 1976. 29.75 (ISBN 0-471-75535-4, Pub. by Wiley-Interscience). Wiley.

Handbook of Environmental Engineering: Vol. 2, Solid Waste Processing & Resource Recovery. Ed. by Lawrence K. Wang & Norman C. Pereira. LC 79-91087. 1980. 49.50 (ISBN 0-89603-008-3). Humana.

Handbook of Environmental Health & Safety: Principles & Practices. Herman Koren. 1980. 99.50 (ISBN 0-08-023900-5). Pergamon.

Handbook of Enzyme Biotechnology. Alan Wiseman. LC 75-2466. 275p. 1975. 68.95 (ISBN 0-470-95617-8). Halsted Pr.

Handbook of Essential Drug Therapy for Critical Care Nurses. John A. Romankiewicz et al. LC 79-90429. 211p. 1980. pap. text ed. 12.50 spiral bound (ISBN 0-914768-35-2). Drug Intl Pubns.

Handbook of Essential Formulae & Data on Heat Transfer for Engineers. H. Y. Wong. LC 77-5681. (Illus.). 1977. pap. text ed. 14.50x (ISBN 0-582-46050-6). Longman.

Handbook of Evaluation Research, 2 vols. Ed. by Elmer L. Struening & Marcia Guttentag. LC 74-15764. 1975. 27.50x ea. (ISBN 0-8039-0428-2). Vol. 1. Vol. 2 (ISBN 0-8039-0429-0). Set. 55.00x (ISBN 0-8039-0429-0). Sage.

Handbook of Experiential Learning & Change. Gordon A. Walter. 600p. 1981. 29.95 (ISBN 0-471-08355-0, Pub. by Wiley-Interscience). Wiley.

Handbook of Experimental Immunology: Application of Immunological Methods, Vol. 3. 3rd ed. Weir. 1978. pap. 45.25 (ISBN 0-632-00186-0, Blackwell Scientific). Mosby.

Handbook of Experimental Immunology: Cellular Immunology, Vol. 2. 3rd ed. Ed. by D. M. Weir. 1978. pap. 45.25 (ISBN 0-632-00176-3, Blackwell Scientific). Mosby.

Handbook of Family Therapy. Alan S. Gurman & David P. Kniskern. LC 80-20357. 800p. 1981. 39.95 (ISBN 0-87630-242-8). Brunner Mazel.

Handbook of Fiberglass & Advanced Plastics Composites. George Lubin. LC 75-1316. 912p. (Orig.). 1975. Repr. of 1969 ed. 44.00 (ISBN 0-88275-286-3). Krieger.

Handbook of Fictitious Names. Ralph Thomas. LC 70-90248. 1969. Repr. of 1868 ed. 18.00 (ISBN 0-8103-3145-4). Gale.

Handbook of Financial Markets: Securities, Options and Futures. Frank J. Fabozzi & Frank G. Zarb. 920p. 1981. 37.50 (ISBN 0-87094-216-6). Dow Jones-Irwin.

Handbook of Fine Needle Aspiration Biopsy Cytology. Tilde S. Kline. (Illus.). 210p. 1981. text ed. 27.50 (ISBN 0-8016-2701-X). Mosby.

Handbook of Food Additives, Vol. 2. 2nd ed. Ed. by Thomas E. Furia. (Handbook Ser.). 1980. 59.95 (ISBN 0-8493-0543-8). CRC Pr.

Handbook of Foreign Birds, Volumes 1 & 2. A. Rutgers. Incl. Vol. 1. The Small Seed-& Insect-Eating Birds. rev. ed. 1977. Repr. of 1964 ed (ISBN 0-7137-0815-8); Vol. 2. Larger Birds, Including Parrots & Parakeets. rev. ed. 1969. Repr. of 1965 ed (ISBN 0-7137-0769-0). (Color Ser.). (Illus.). 9.95 ea. (Pub. by Blandford Pr England). Sterling.

Handbook of Free Conversation. Colin Black. 48p. 1970. pap. text ed. 2.50x (ISBN 0-19-432773-6). Oxford U Pr.

Handbook of French Phonetics. William A. Nitze & Ernest H. Wilkins. 1945. pap. text ed. 12.95x (ISBN 0-89197-781-3). Irvington.

Handbook of Fundamental Nursing Techniques. Mildred L. Montag & Alice R. Rines. LC 76-5246. 200p. 1976. 13.95 (ISBN 0-471-01475-3, Pub. by Wiley Medical); Arabic Translation avail. (ISBN 0-471-04525-X). Wiley.

Handbook of General Psychology. Ed. by Benjamin B. Wolman. LC 74-166142. (Illus.). 1088p. 1973. ref. ed. 65.00 (ISBN 0-13-378141-0). P-H.

Handbook of Geographical Nicknames. Harold S. Sharp. LC 79-26860. 153p. 1980. lib. bdg. 10.00 (ISBN 0-8108-1280-0). Scarecrow.

Handbook of Grammar, Rhetoric, Mechanics & Usage. Newman P. Birk & Genevieve B. Birk. LC 71-179751. 148p. 1972. pap. text ed. 5.95 (ISBN 0-672-63275-6). Odyssey Pr.

Handbook of Graphic Presentation. 2nd ed. Calvin F. Schmid & Stanton E. Schmid. LC 78-13689. 1979. 16.50 (ISBN 0-471-04724-4, Pub. by Wiley-Interscience). Wiley.

Handbook of Graphic Reproduction Processes. Felix Brunner. (Visual Communication Bks.). (Illus.). 1962. 35.00 o.s.i. (ISBN 0-8038-2964-7). Hastings.

Handbook of Greek Art: A Survey of the Visual Arts of Ancient Greece. Gisela Richter. (Illus.). 432p. 1980. pap. 10.95 (ISBN 0-525-47651-2). Dutton.

Handbook of Gundogs. Joe Stetson. (Sportsman's Library of Gun Dogs, Vol. 1). (Orig.). 1965. pap. 2.00 (ISBN 0-87666-315-3, DS1139). TFH Pubns.

Handbook of Gynecologic Emergencies. Cynthia W. Cooke. 1975. spiral bdg. 10.00 o.s.i. (ISBN 0-87488-640-6). Med Exam.

Handbook of Health Assessment. Ellen Rudy & Ruth Gray. (Illus.). 184p. 1981. pap. text ed. 9.95 (ISBN 0-87619-843-4). R J Brady.

Handbook of Health Education. Ed. by Peter Lazes. LC 79-50. 1979. 29.95 (ISBN 0-89443-085-8). Aspen Systems.

Handbook of Heart Disease, Blood Pressure & Strokes. C. Anthony D'Alonzo. 1962. pap. 0.95 o.s.i. (ISBN 0-02-058670-1, Collier). Macmillan.

Handbook of Heating, Ventilating & Air Conditioning. 7th ed. J. Porges. Ed. by F. Porges. (Illus.). 1977. 40.00x (ISBN 0-408-00233-6). Transatlantic.

Handbook of Hebrew Calligraphy: The ABC's of the Alef-Bet. Cara G. Marks. (Illus.). 128p. 1981. 10.95 (ISBN 0-89961-010-2); pap. 5.95 (ISBN 0-89961-011-0). SBS Pub.

Handbook of Hematological & Blood Transfusion Technique. 2nd ed. J. W. Delaney & G. Garratty. (Illus.). 1969. pap. text ed. 11.95x (ISBN 0-407-72852-X). Butterworths.

Handbook of Hematology, 4 Vols. Harold Downey. (Illus.). 1965. Repr. of 1938 ed. Set. 192.50 o.s.i. (ISBN 0-02-843980-5). Hafner.

Handbook of Heraldry. John E. Cussans. LC 76-132520. 1971. Repr. of 1893 ed. 26.00 (ISBN 0-8103-3012-1). Gale.

Handbook of High Resolution Infrared Spectra of Gases of Atmospheric Interest. Ed. by David G. Murcray. 304p. 1981. 49.95 (ISBN 0-8493-2950-7). CRC Pr.

Handbook of Histopathological & Histochemical Techniques. 3rd ed. C. F. Culling. 1974. 53.95 (ISBN 0-407-72901-1). Butterworths.

Handbook of Hospital Safety. Ed. by Paul E. Stanley. 416p. 1981. 59.95 (ISBN 0-8493-0751-1). CRC Pr.

Handbook of Human Sexuality. Benjamon B. Wolman & John Money. (Illus.). 1980. text ed. 36.95 (ISBN 0-13-378422-3). P-H.

Handbook of Hypergeometric Integrals: Theory Applications, Tables, Computer Programs. Harold Exton. (Mathematics & Its Applications Ser.). 1978. 54.95 (ISBN 0-470-26342-3). Halsted Pr.

Handbook of Hypnosis for Professionals. Roy Udolf. 384p. 1981. text ed. 24.50 (ISBN 0-442-28881-6). Van Nos Reinhold.

Handbook of IC Circuit Projects. Jim Ashe. LC 72-94804. (Illus.). 224p. 1973. pap. 5.95 o.p. (ISBN 0-8306-2629-8, 629). TAB Bks.

Handbook of Immediate Overdentures. Robert M. Morrow. LC 78-16585. (Illus.). 1978. pap. text ed. 17.95 (ISBN 0-8016-3543-8). Mosby.

Handbook of Industrial Energy Analysis. I. Boustead & G. F. Hancock. LC 78-40636. 1979. 76.95 (ISBN 0-470-26492-6). Halsted Pr.

Handbook of Industrial Fire Protection & Security. Ed. by Trade & Technical Press Ltd. 105.00x (ISBN 0-85461-059-6). Intl Ideas.

Handbook of Industrial Lighting. Lyons. 1981. text ed. price not set. Butterworth.

Handbook of Industrial Lubrication. M. G. Billett. 1979. 28.00 (ISBN 0-08-024232-4). Pergamon.

Handbook of Industrial Materials: Ferrous & Non-Ferrous Metals, Non-Metallic Materials, Plastics, Adhesives. 1978. 105.00x (ISBN 0-85461-068-5). Intl Ideas.

Handbook of Industrial Waste Disposal. Richard A. Conway & Richard D. Ross. 576p. 1980. text ed. 32.50 (ISBN 0-442-27053-4). Van Nos Reinhold.

Handbook of Industrial Wastes Pretreatment. Jon C. Dyer. LC 79-25702. 300p. 1981. lib. bdg. 32.50 (ISBN 0-8240-7066-6). Garland Pub.

Handbook of Infant Development. Ed. by Joy D. Osofsky. LC 78-17605. (Personality Processes Ser.). 1979. 46.50 (ISBN 0-471-65703-4, Pub. by Wiley-Interscience). Wiley.

Handbook of Infectious Diseases. Stewart M. Brooks et al. 1980. 9.95 (ISBN 0-316-10968-1). Little.

Handbook of Infertility. International Planned Parenthood Federation. Ed. by Ronald L. Kleinman & Pramilla Senayake. (Illus.). 58p. (Orig.). 1979. pap. 6.50x (ISBN 0-86089-034-1). Intl Pubns Serv.

Handbook of Information Display Devices. Harry Thomas. 1981. 24.95 (ISBN 0-8359-2743-1). Reston.

Handbook of Innovative Marketing Techniques. David D. Seltz. LC 79-27415. 320p. 1981. text ed. 19.95 (ISBN 0-201-07617-9). A-W.

Handbook of Innovative Psychotherapies. Raymond Corsini. 1100p. 1981. 40.00 (ISBN 0-471-06229-4, Pub. by Wiley-Interscience). Wiley.

Handbook of Instructional Resources & References for Teaching the Gifted. Frances A. Karnes & Emily C. Collins. 1980. text ed. 16.95 (ISBN 0-205-06823-5, 246823-9). Allyn.

Handbook of Instruments & Instrumentation. Ed. by Trade & Technical Press Ltd. (Illus.). 105.00x (ISBN 0-85461-064-2). Intl Ideas.

Handbook of Integrated Circuits: For Engineers & Technicians. John D. Lenk. (Illus.). 1978. ref. 19.95 (ISBN 0-8359-2744-X). Reston.

Handbook of International Economic Institutions. Marcel A. Van Meerhaeghe. 472p. 1980. lib. bdg. 76.50 (ISBN 90-247-2357-4, Pub. by Martinus Nijhoff). Kluwer Boston.

Handbook of International Purchasing. 2nd ed. Paul H. Combs. LC 75-31560. 224p. 1976. 15.95 (ISBN 0-8436-1309-2). CBI Pub.

Handbook of Interpersonal Psychotherapy. Ed. by Jack C. Anchin & Donald J. Kiesler. (Pergamon General Psychology Ser.). 400p. Date not set. price not set (ISBN 0-08-025959-6). Pergamon.

Handbook of Interpretations for the Comrey Personality Scales. Andrew Comrey. LC 80-67424. 1980. 7.95 (ISBN 0-912736-23-2). EDITS Pubs.

Handbook of Irish Folklore. Sean O'Suilleabhain. LC 73-129100. 1970. Repr. of 1942 ed. 30.00 (ISBN 0-8103-3561-1). Gale.

Handbook of Iron Meteorites: Their History, Distribution, Composition & Structure. Vagn F. Buchwald. 1976. 225.00x (ISBN 0-520-02934-8). U of Cal Pr.

Handbook of I.V. Additive Reviews. Ed. by Donald E. Francke. Incl. 1970. (Illus.). 50p (ISBN 0-914768-03-4); 1971. (Illus.). 60p (ISBN 0-914768-04-2); 1972. (Illus.) (ISBN 0-914768-05-0); 1973. (Illus.). 68p (ISBN 0-914768-06-9). pap. 3.75 ea. Drug Intl Pubns.

Handbook of Jewish Thought. Aryeh Kaplan. 307p. 12.95 (ISBN 0-686-27547-0). Maznaim.

Handbook of Kidney Nomenclature & Nosology. International Committee for Nomenclature & Nosology of Renal Disease. LC 73-17665. 400p. 1975. text ed. 19.95 (ISBN 0-316-41920-6). Little.

Handbook of Laboratory Animal Science, CRC, 2 vols. Ed. by Edward C. Melby, Jr. & Norman H. Altman. LC 74-19795. (Handbook Ser.). Vol. 2, 1974, 523p. 59.95 (ISBN 0-8493-0341-9); Vol. 3. 64.95 (ISBN 0-8493-0342-7). CRC Pr.

Handbook of Landmower Repair. rev. ed. Ed. by Franklyn Peterson. LC 77-92313. (Illus.). 1978. pap. 5.95 (ISBN 0-8015-3256-6, Hawthorn). Dutton.

Handbook of Latin American Studies, Author Index to Numbers 1-28. Francisco J. Cardona & Maria E. Cardona. LC 36-32633. 1968. 32.50x (ISBN 0-8130-0265-6). U Presses Fla.

Handbook of Latin American Studies: No. 42, Humanities. Ed. by Dolores M. Martin. 720p. 1981. text ed. 55.00x (ISBN 0-292-73016-0). U of Tex Pr.

Handbook of Leadership: A Survey of Theory & Research. Ralph M. Stogdill. LC 73-6494. (Illus.). 1974. 25.00 (ISBN 0-02-931660-X). Free Pr.

Handbook of Learned Societies & Institutions: America. LC 66-20613. viii, 592p. 1966. Repr. of 1908 ed. 21.00 (ISBN 0-8103-3079-2). Gale.

Handbook of Learning & Cognitive Processes, 6 vols. Ed. by W. K. Estes. Incl. Vol. 1. Introduction to Concepts & Issues. LC 75-20113. 303p. 1975. o.p. (ISBN 0-470-24585-9); Vol. 2. Conditioning & Behavior Therapy. LC 75-20113. 350p. 1975. 18.50 (ISBN 0-470-24586-7); Vol. 3. Approaches to Human Learning & Motivation. LC 76-15010. 1976. 18.50 (ISBN 0-470-15121-8); Vol. 4. Attention & Memory. LC 76-26002. 1976. o.p. (ISBN 0-470-98908-4); Vol. 5. Human Information Processing. LC 78-3847. 1978. 26.50 (ISBN 0-470-26310-5); Vol. 6. Linguistic Functions in Cognitive Theory. 1978. 18.00 (ISBN 0-470-26311-3). Halsted Pr.

Handbook of Legal Medicine. 5th ed. Charles P. Hirsch et al. LC 79-16053. (Illus.). 1979. pap. text ed. 19.95 (ISBN 0-8016-3509-8). Mosby.

Handbook of Legendary & Mythological Art. Clara E. Clement. LC 68-26616. (Illus.). 1969. Repr. of 1881 ed. 26.00 (ISBN 0-8103-3175-6). Gale.

Handbook of Legumes of World Economic Importance. James A. Duke. (Illus.). 350p. 1981. 45.00 (ISBN 0-306-40406-0, Plenum Pr). Plenum Pub.

Handbook of Leprosy. 2nd ed. W. H. Jopling. (Illus.). 1978. pap. 13.50x (ISBN 0-433-17566-4). Intl Ideas.

Handbook of Local Anesthesia. Stanley F. Malamed. LC 80-17546. (Illus.). 249p. 1980. pap. text ed. 17.95 (ISBN 0-8016-3072-X). Mosby.

Handbook of Logic. Eric R. Emmet. (Quality Paperback: No. 178). 1974. pap. 4.95 (ISBN 0-8226-0178-8). Littlefield.

Handbook of Loss Prevention & Crime Prevention. Fennelly. 1981. text ed. price not set. Butterworth.

Handbook of Magazine Publishing. Ed. by Folio Magazine Editors. 1977. 59.95 (ISBN 0-918110-00-9). Folio.

Handbook of Management Tactics: Aggressive Strategies for Getting Things Done Your Way! Richard H. Buskirk. LC 77-70138. (Orig.). 1978. pap. 4.95 (ISBN 0-8015-3489-5, Hawthorn). Dutton.

Handbook of Managerial Tactics. Richard H. Buskirk. LC 76-991. 1976. 12.95 (ISBN 0-8436-0745-9). CBI Pub.

Handbook of Marital Therapy: A Positive Approach to Helping Troubled Relationships. R. P. Liberman et al. (Applied Clinical Psychology Ser.). (Illus.). 250p. 1980. 19.50 (ISBN 0-306-40235-1, Plenum Pr). Plenum Pub.

Handbook of Material Trade Names, with Supplements 1, 2, 3, & 4. O. T. Zimmerman & Irvin Lavine. 1953-65. 175.00 (ISBN 0-686-20569-3). Indus Res Serv.

Handbook of Maternity Care: A Guide for Nursing Practice. Margaret Jensen & Irene Bobak. LC 79-18163. 1980. pap. text ed. 9.95 (ISBN 0-8016-2490-8). Mosby.

Handbook of Mathematical Formulas, Tables, Functions, Graphs, Transforms. Research & Education Association Staff. LC 80-52490. (Illus.). 800p. (Orig.). pap. text ed. 16.85x (ISBN 0-87891-521-4). Res & Educ.

Handbook of Mathematical Functions. Ed. by Milton Abramowitz & Irene A. Stegun. LC 65-12253. 1965. lib. bdg. 24.50x (ISBN 0-88307-589-X). Gannon.

Handbook of Mathematics. L. Kuipers & R. Timman. 1969. 60.00 (ISBN 0-08-011857-7); pap. 21.00 (ISBN 0-08-018996-2). Pergamon.

Handbook of Mechanical & Electrical Systems for Buildings. H. E. Bovay, Jr. (Illus.). 1981. 49.50 (ISBN 0-07-006718-X). McGraw.

Handbook of Mechanical Power Drives. 2nd ed. Ed. by Trade & Technical Press Ltd. (Illus.). 1978. 105.00x (ISBN 0-85461-067-7). Intl Ideas.

Handbook of Medical, Educational, & Psychological Information for Teachers of Physically Handicapped Children. Harold D. Love & Joe E. Walthall. (Illus.). 232p. 1977. 16.75 (ISBN 0-398-03629-2). C C Thomas.

Handbook of Medical Emergencies. 2nd ed. Jay H. Sanders & Laurence B. Gardner. LC 78-50127. 1978. pap. 12.75 (ISBN 0-87488-635-X). Med Exam.

Handbook of Medical Emergencies in the Dental Office. Stanley F. Malamed. LC 77-17870. (Illus.). 1978. pap. text ed. 19.95 (ISBN 0-8016-3077-0). Mosby.

Handbook of Medical Hypnosis. 4th ed. G. Ambrose & G. Newbold. 1980. text ed. 25.95 (ISBN 0-02-857110-X). Macmillan.

Handbook of Medical Sociology. 3rd ed. Howard E. Freeman et al. 1979. 21.95 (ISBN 0-13-380253-1). P-H.

Handbook of Medical Specialities. Henry Wechsler. LC 74-19051. 1976. text ed. 24.95 (ISBN 0-87705-232-8); pap. text ed. 9.95 (ISBN 0-87705-292-1). Human Sci Pr.

Handbook of Mental Health & Aging. Ed. by James E. Birren & R. Bruce Sloane. (Illus.). 1980. text ed. 72.00 (ISBN 0-13-380261-2). P-H.

Handbook of Mental Retardation Syndromes. 3rd ed. Charles H. Carter. (Illus.). 432p. 1979. text ed. 26.25 (ISBN 0-398-03090-1). C C Thomas.

Handbook of Metallic Cartridge Reloading. Edward Matunas. (Illus.). 272p. 1981. 14.95 (ISBN 0-87691-320-6). Winchester Pr.

Handbook of Method in Cultural Anthropology. Ed. by Raoul Naroll & Ronald Cohen. 1973. 47.50x (ISBN 0-231-03731-7); pap. 20.00x (ISBN 0-231-03749-X). Columbia U Pr.

Handbook of Microbiology, CRC, Vol. 3: Amino Acids & Proteins. 2nd ed. Ed. by Allen I. Laskin & Hubert Lechevalier. LC 77-12460. 576p. 1981. 64.95 (ISBN 0-8493-7203-8). CRC Pr.

Handbook of Microbiology, CRC, Vol. 4: Carbohydrates, Lipids & Minerals. 2nd ed. Ed. by Allen I. Laskin & Hubert Lechevalier. 480p. 1981. 59.95 (ISBN 0-8493-7204-6). CRC Pr.

Handbook of Microprocessor Applications. John A. Kuecken. (Illus.). 308p. (Orig.). 1980. 14.95 (ISBN 0-8306-9935-X); pap. 8.95 (ISBN 0-8306-1203-3). Tab Bks.

Handbook of Microscopic Anatomy for the Health Sciences. Annabelle Cohen. LC 74-13572. (Illus.). 1975. pap. text ed. 8.95 (ISBN 0-8016-1012-5). Mosby.

Handbook of Middle American Indians: Guide to Ethnohistorical Sources, Vols. 14 & 15, Pts. 3 & 4. Ed. by Howard F. Cline et al. LC 64-10316. 1975. 60.00x set (ISBN 0-292-70154-3). U of Tex Pr.

Handbook of Military Institutions. Ed. by Roger W. Little. LC 78-127989. (Sage Ser. on Armed Forces & Society: Vol. 1). 1971. 27.50x (ISBN 0-8039-0078-3). Sage.

Handbook of Mime & Pantomine. David Alberts. Date not set. 10.95 (ISBN 0-8238-0246-9). Plays. Postponed.

Handbook of Minimal Brain Dysfunctions: A Critical View. Ed. by Herbert E. Rie & Ellen D. Rie. LC 78-25656. (Personality Processes Ser.). 1980. 44.50 (ISBN 0-471-02959-9, Pub. by Wiley-Interscience). Wiley.

Handbook of Modern Electrical Wiring. John E. Traister. (Illus.). 1979. text ed. 16.95 (ISBN 0-8359-2754-7). Reston.

Handbook of Modern Solid State Amplifiers. John D. Lenk. (Illus.). 400p. 1974. ref. ed 19.95 (ISBN 0-13-380394-5); pap. 7.95 (ISBN 0-13-380386-4). P-H.

Handbook of Motion Picture Production. William B. Adams. LC 76-51818. (Wiley Ser. on Human Communication). 1977. 26.50 (ISBN 0-471-00459-6, Pub. by Wiley-Interscience). Wiley.

Handbook of Multichannel Recording. Alton Everest. LC 75-20842. 322p. 1975. 10.95 (ISBN 0-8306-5781-9); pap. 9.95 (ISBN 0-8306-4781-3, 781). TAB Bks.

Handbook of Music & Music Literature: In Sets & Series. Sydney R. Charles. LC 71-143502. 1972. 17.95 (ISBN 0-02-905400-1). Free Pr.

Handbook of Music Terms. W. Parks Grant. LC 67-10187. 1967. 22.50 (ISBN 0-8108-0054-3). Scarecrow.

Handbook of Naturally Occurring Compounds, 2 vols. T. K. Devon & A. I. Scott. Incl. Vol. 1. Acetogenins, Shikimates & Carbohydrates. 1975. 51.50 (ISBN 0-12-213601-2); Vol. 2. Terpenes. 1972. 42.00 (ISBN 0-12-213602-0). Acad Pr.

Handbook of Neurochemistry, Vols. 1-7. Ed. by Abel Lajtha. Incl. Vol. 1. Chemical Architecture of the Nervous System. 484p. 1969 (ISBN 0-306-37701-2); Vol. 2. Structural Neurochemistry. 562p. 1969 (ISBN 0-306-37702-0); Vol. 3. Metabolic Reactions in the Nervous System. 590p. 1970 (ISBN 0-306-37703-9); Vol. 4. Control Mechanisms in the Nervous System. 516p. 1970 (ISBN 0-306-37704-7); Vol. 5A. Metabolic Turnover in the Nervous Systems. 438p. 1971 (ISBN 0-306-37705-5); Vol. 5B. Metabolic Turnover in the Nervous System. 399p. 1971 (ISBN 0-306-37715-2); Vol. 6. Alterations of Chemical Equilibrium in the Nervous System. 584p. 1971 (ISBN 0-306-37706-3); Vol. 7. Pathological Chemistry of the Nervous System. 675p. 1972 (ISBN 0-306-37707-1). LC 68-28097. 45.00 ea. (Plenum Pr). Plenum Pub.

Handbook of New Testament Greek: An Inductive Approach Based on the Greek Text of Acts, 2 vols. William S. LaSor. 1973. pap. text ed. 10.95x (ISBN 0-8028-2341-6). Eerdmans.

Handbook of Noise & Vibration. 4th ed. Ed. by Trade & Technical Press Ltd. (Illus.). 1978. 110.00x o.p. (ISBN 0-85461-073-1). Intl Ideas.

Handbook of Noninvasive Diagnostic Techniques. Bok Y. Lee. 352p. 1981. pap. 15.00 (ISBN 0-8385-3620-4). ACC.

Handbook of Nonprescription Drugs. 6th ed. LC 68-2177. 1979. 30.00 (ISBN 0-917330-27-7). Am Pharm Assn.

Handbook of North American Indians: California, Vol. 8. Ed. by Robert F. Heizer & William C. Sturtevant. LC 77-17162. (Illus.). 800p. 13.50 (ISBN 0-87474-188-2). Smithsonian.

Handbook of Nuclear Data for Neutron Activation Analysis. A. I. Aliev et al. 1972. 24.95 (ISBN 0-470-02260-4). Halsted Pr.

Handbook of Numerical & Statistical Techniques. J. M. Pollard. LC 76-27908. (Illus.). 1977. 48.00 (ISBN 0-521-21440-8); pap. 14.95 (ISBN 0-521-29750-8). Cambridge U Pr.

Handbook of Nutritional Requirements in a Functional Context. Ed. by Miloslav Rechcigl. 1981. Vol. 1. 72.95 (ISBN 0-686-69343-4); Vol. 2. 77.95 (ISBN 0-8493-3958-8). CRC Pr.

Handbook of Obstetric Emergencies. 2nd ed. Ed. by Richard H. Schwarz. 1977. 11.00 (ISBN 0-87488-634-1). Med Exam.

Handbook of Oceanographic Engineering Materials. Stephen C. Dexter. LC 78-26196. (Ocean Engineering Ser.). 1979. 28.95 (ISBN 0-471-04950-6, Pub. by Wiley-Interscience). Wiley.

Handbook of Oil Industry Terms & Phrases. 2nd ed. R. D. Langenkamp. LC 74-80034. 176p. 1977. 14.00 (ISBN 0-87814-034-4). Pennwell Pub.

Handbook of Old Church Slavonic, Pt. 1: Old Church Slavonic Grammar. Nandris. 1959. text ed. 26.25x (ISBN 0-485-17507-X, Athlone Pr). Humanities.

Handbook of Old Church Slavonic, Text & Glossary. Robert Auty. (London East European Ser.). 1977. pap. text ed. 17.50x (ISBN 0-485-17518-5, Athlone Pr). Humanities.

Handbook of Operant Behavior. Ed. by Werner K. Honig & J. Staddor. LC 76-26034. (Century Psychology Ser.). 1977. 46.95 (ISBN 0-13-380535-2). P-H.

Handbook of Operations Research, 2 vols. Ed. by Joseph J. Moder & Salah E. Elmaghraby. 1978. Vols. 1 & 2. 32.50 ea. Vol. 1 (ISBN 0-442-24595-5). Vol. 2 (ISBN 0-442-24596-3). Vol. 3. 59.50 (ISBN 0-442-24597-1). Van Nos Reinhold.

Handbook of Ophthalmologic Emergencies. 2nd ed. Ed. by George M. Gombos. LC 76-62573. (Illus.). 1977. pap. 13.75 (ISBN 0-87488-633-3). Med Exam.

Handbook of Ophthalmology for Developing Countries. 2nd ed. Geoffrey G. Bisley. (Illus.). 160p. 1981. pap. text ed. 13.95x (ISBN 0-19-261244-1). Oxford U Pr.

Handbook of Organic Analysis: Qualitative & Quantitative. 5th ed. H. T. Clarke. Ed. by B. Haynes. LC 74-83479. 1975. pap. 20.50x (ISBN 0-8448-0662-5). Crane-Russak Co.

Handbook of Oriental Collections in Finland: Manuscripts, Xylographs, Inscriptions & Russian Minority Literature. Harry Halen. (Scandinavian Institute of Asian Studies Monograph: No. 31). 1978. pap. 15.25x (ISBN 0-7007-0105-2). Humanities.

Handbook of Ornament. 4th ed. Franz S. Meyer. (Illus.). 1892. pap. 6.00 (ISBN 0-486-20302-6). Dover.

Handbook of Ornament. Michael Poage. 1979. pap. 7.50 (ISBN 0-686-25597-6); 30.00 o.p. (ISBN 0-686-25596-8). Black Stone.

Handbook of Orthoptic Principles. 4th ed. G. T. Cashell & I. M. Durran. (Illus.). 1981. pap. text ed. 13.75 (ISBN 0-443-02200-3). Churchill.

Handbook of Packaging Materials. Stanley Sacharow. (Illus.). 1976. text ed. 26.50 (ISBN 0-87055-207-4). AVI.

Handbook of Paleontology for Beginners & Amateurs: The Fossils, Pt. 1. Winifred Goldring. (Illus.). 1960. Repr. 6.75 (ISBN 0-87710-363-1). Paleo Res.

Handbook of Parapsychology. Benjamin B. Wolman. 1070p. 1981. pap. text ed. 17.95 (ISBN 0-442-26479-8). Van Nos Reinhold.

Handbook of Pediatric Primary Care. Marilyn P. Chow et al. LC 78-19731. 1979. 27.95 (ISBN 0-471-01771-X, Pub. by Wiley Medical). Wiley.

Handbook of Pediatric Surgical Emergencies. 2nd. ed. Ed. by Diller B. Groff. 1980. write for info. (ISBN 0-87488-642-2). Med Exam.

Handbook of Pedigree Cat Breeding. Dorothy S. Richards. (Illus.). 143p. 1980. pap. 14.95 (ISBN 0-7134-0422-1, Pub. by Batsford England). David & Charles.

Handbook of Perception. Ed. by Edward C. Carterette & Morton P. Friedman. Incl. Vol. 1. 1974. 40.00 (ISBN 0-12-161901-X); Vol. 2. 1974. 48.00 (ISBN 0-12-161902-8); Vol. 4. Hearing. 1978. 49.50 (ISBN 0-12-161904-4); Vol. 5. 1975. 48.00 (ISBN 0-12-161905-2); Vol. 6, 2 pts. 1978. Pt. A, Testing & Smelling. 30.00 (ISBN 0-686-62060-7); Pt. B, Feeling & Hurting. 30.00 (ISBN 0-12-161922-2); Vol. 7. 1975. 48.00 (ISBN 0-12-161907-9); Vol. 8. Perceptual Coding. 1978. 40.00, by subscription 35.00 (ISBN 0-12-161908-7); Vol. 9. Perceptual Processing. 1978. 31.50, by subscription 25.00 (ISBN 0-12-161909-5); Vol. 10. Perceptual Ecology. 1978. 43.00, by subscription 34.00 (ISBN 0-12-161910-9). Acad Pr.

Handbook of Perinatal Infections. John L. Sever et al. 1979. pap. text ed. 16.95 (ISBN 0-316-78170-3). Little.

Handbook of Pest Management in Agriculture. Ed. by David Pimentel. 1981. Vol. 1. 69.95 (ISBN 0-8493-3841-7); Vol. 2. 67.95 (ISBN 0-8493-3842-5); Vol. 3. 69.95 (ISBN 0-8493-3843-3). CRC Pr.

Handbook of Phycological Methods. J. A. Hellebust & J. S. Craigie. LC 73-79496. (Illus.). 1978. 39.95 (ISBN 0-521-21855-1). Cambridge U Pr.

Handbook of Phycological Methods. Ed. by Janet Stein. (Illus.). 512p. 1973. 44.95 (ISBN 0-521-20049-0); pap. 15.95 (ISBN 0-521-29747-8). Cambridge U Pr.

Handbook of Physical Distribution. Felix Wentworth. 1977. 36.00x o.p. (ISBN 0-8464-0470-2). Beekman Pubs.

Handbook of Physiology, Section 3: Respiration, 2 Vols. American Physiological Society. Ed. by Wallace O. Fenn & Hermann Rahn. 1964-65. Vol. 1. 32.00 (ISBN 0-683-03148-1); Vol. 2. 32.00 (ISBN 0-683-03149-X). Williams & Wilkins.

Handbook of Physiology, Section 5: Adipose Tissue. American Physiological Society. Ed. by Albert E. Renold & George F. Cahill, Jr. 1965. 28.00 (ISBN 0-683-07232-3). Williams & Wilkins.

Handbook of Plastic Surgery. Peter McKinney & Bruce L. Cunningham. (Illus.). 150p. 1981. price not set softcover (ISBN 0-683-05865-7). Williams & Wilkins.

Handbook of Political Conflict: Theory & Research. Ed. by Ted R. Gurr. LC 79-6145. (Free Press Ser. on Political Behavior). (Illus.). 1980. 39.95 (ISBN 0-02-912760-2). Free Pr.

Handbook of Political Science, 8 vols. F. I. Greenstein & N. W. Polsby. Incl. Vol. 1. Political Science: Scope & Theory. 18.95 (ISBN 0-201-02601-5); Vol. 2. Micropolitical Theory. 17.75 (ISBN 0-201-02602-3); Vol. 3. Macropolitical Theory. 22.95 (ISBN 0-201-02603-1); Vol. 4. Nongovernmental Politics. 17.95 (ISBN 0-201-02604-X); Vol. 5. Governmental Institutions & Processes. 21.95 (ISBN 0-201-02605-8); Vol. 6. Politics & Policymaking. 20.95 (ISBN 0-201-02606-6); Vol. 7. Strategies of Inquiry. 18.95 (ISBN 0-201-02607-4); Vol. 8. International Politics. 20.95 (ISBN 0-201-02608-2). 1975. Set With Index. boxed 160.00 (ISBN 0-201-02611-2). A-W.

Handbook of Political Socialization: Theory and Research. Ed. by Stanley A. Renshon. LC 76-55102. 1977. 25.00 (ISBN 0-02-926340-9). Free Pr.

Handbook of Politics, 4 Vols. Edward McPherson. LC 72-146558. (Law, Politics & History Ser.). 1973. Repr. of 1894 ed. lib. bdg. 45.00 ea.; Set. pap. 175.00. Da Capo.

Handbook of Politics & Economics. Thomas E. Watson. (Studies in Populism). 1980. lib. bdg. 75.00 (ISBN 0-686-68879-1). Revisionist Pr.

Handbook of Pottery & Porcelain Marks. 3rd ed. J. P. Cushion & W. B. Honey. (Illus.). 1965. 19.95 o.p. (ISBN 0-571-06372-1, Pub. by Faber & Faber). Merrimack Bk Serv.

Handbook of Pottery & Porcelain Marks. 4th, rev. ed. J. P. Cushion & W. B. Honey. (Illus.). 272p. 1980. 30.00 (ISBN 0-571-04922-2, Pub. by Faber & Faber). Merrimack Bk Serv.

Handbook of Practical Electronic Tests & Measurements. John D. Lenk. 1969. ref. ed. 19.95 (ISBN 0-13-380626-X). P-H.

Handbook of Practical Microcomputer Troubleshooting. John D. Lenk. (Illus.). 1979. text ed. 19.95 (ISBN 0-8359-2757-1). Reston.

Handbook of Practical Organic Micro-Analysis: Recommended Methods for Determining Elements & Groups. S. Bance. LC 80-40145. (Ellis Horwood Ser. in Analytical Chemistry). 200p. 1980. 58.95x (ISBN 0-470-26972-3). Halsted Pr.

Handbook of Practical Pharmacology. 2nd ed. Sheila A. Ryan & Bruce D. Clayton. LC 79-26035. (Illus.). 1980. pap. text ed. 10.95 (ISBN 0-8016-4240-X). Mosby.

Handbook of Practice Teaching. Samson O. Olaitan & Obiora N. Augusiobo. LC 80-40291. 192p. 1981. write for info. (ISBN 0-471-27805-X, Pub. by Wiley-Interscience); pap. write for info. (ISBN 0-471-27804-1). Wiley.

Handbook of Preschool Special Education: Programming, Curriculum, Training. Allen A. Mori & Jane E. Olive. LC 80-14199. 528p. 1980. 34.95 (ISBN 0-89443-276-1). Aspen Systems.

Handbook of Procedures for the Design of Instruction. Leslie J. Briggs & Walter W. Wager. LC 80-20920. 270p. pap. 19.95 (ISBN 0-87778-177-X). Educ Tech Pubns.

Handbook of Process Stream Analysis. Kenneth J. Clevett. LC 73-14416. (Ser. in Analytical Chemistry). (Illus.). 544p. 1974. 58.95 (ISBN 0-470-16048-9). Halsted Pr.

Handbook of Professional Telephone Selling. G. J. Ortland. 1981. write for info. (ISBN 0-201-05490-6). A-W.

Handbook of Protein Sequences: A Compilation of Amino Acid Sequences of Proteins. L. R. Croft. LC 79-41487. 608p. 1980. 105.00 (ISBN 0-471-27703-7). Wiley.

Handbook of Proton Ionization Heats. James J. Christensen & Lee D. Hansen. 286p. Repr. of 1976 ed. lib. bdg. write for info. (ISBN 0-89874-344-3). Krieger.

Handbook of Proton Ionization Heats & Related Thermodynamic Quantities. J. J. Christensen et al. LC 76-16511. 1976. 34.50 (ISBN 0-471-01991-7). Wiley.

Handbook of Pseudonyms & Personal Nicknames: First Supplement, 2 vols. Harold S. Sharp. LC 71-189886. 1403p. 1975. Set. 40.00 (ISBN 0-685-55387-6). Vol 1: A-j. Vol. 2: K-Z. (ISBN 0-8108-0807-2). Scarecrow.

Handbook of Pseudonyms & Personal Nicknames, 2 vols. Harold S. Sharp. LC 71-189886. 1972. Set. 35.00 (ISBN 0-8108-0460-3). Scarecrow.

Handbook of PSI Discoveries. Sheila Ostrander & Lynn Schroeder. (Illus.). 224p. 1974. 9.95 o.p. (ISBN 0-399-11288-X, Dist. by Putnam). Berkley Pub.

Handbook of Psychiatric Emergencies. 2nd. ed. Andrew E. Slaby et al. 1981. pap. write for info. (ISBN 0-87488-645-7). Med Exam.
Handbook of Psychotherapy & Behavior Change: An Empirical Analysis. 2nd ed. Sol L. Garfield & Allen E. Bergin. LC 78-8526. 1978. text ed. 47.95 (ISBN 0-471-29178-1). Wiley.
Handbook of Radiation Measurement & Protection, CRC: Selection A-General Scientific & Engineering Information, 2 vols. Allen Brodsky. Vol. 1, 1979. 74.95 (ISBN 0-8493-3756-9); Vol. 2, 1980, 448p. 54.95 (ISBN 0-8493-3757-7). CRC Pr.
Handbook of Random Number Generation & Testing with TESTRAND Computer Code. Edward J. Dudewicz & Thomas G. Ralley. LC 80-68286. (American Sciences Press Ser. in Mathematical & Management Sciences: Vol. 4). 1981. text ed. write for info. (ISBN 0-935950-01-X). Am Sciences Pr.
Handbook of Range Distributions for Energetic Ions in All Elements. U. Littmark & J. F. Ziegler. LC 79-27825. (Stopping & Ranges of Ions in Matter Ser.: Vol. 6). 490p. 72.00 (ISBN 0-08-023879-3). Pergamon.
Handbook of Rectifier Circuits. G. Scoles. LC 79-41814. (Ellis Horwood Series in Electrical & Electronic Engineering). 238p. 1980. 69.95x (ISBN 0-470-26950-2). Halsted Pr.
Handbook of Refractory Compounds. Gregory Samsonov & I. M. Vinitskii. 550p. 1980. 75.00 (ISBN 0-306-65181-5). IFI Plenum.
Handbook of Refrigerating Engineering, 2 vols. 4th ed. Willis R. Woolrich. Incl. Vol. 1. Fundamentals. 460p. 1965 (ISBN 0-87055-054-3); Vol. 2. Applications. 434p. 1966 (ISBN 0-87055-055-1). (Illus.). 29.00 ea. o.p. AVI.
Handbook of Regular Patterns: An Introduction to Symmetry in Two Dimensions. Peter S. Stevens. (Illus.). 384p. 1981. 37.50 (ISBN 0-262-19188-1). MIT Pr.
Handbook of Relay Switching Technique. J. T. Appels & B. H. Geels. (Illus.). 1966. 14.90 o.p. (ISBN 0-387-91005-0). Springer-Verlag.
Handbook of Remote Control & Automation Techniques. John Cunningham. 1979. 12.95 o.p. (ISBN 0-8306-9848-5); pap. 8.95 (ISBN 0-8306-1077-4, 1077). TAB Bks.
Handbook of Reporting Methods. Maxwell McCombs & David Grey. LC 75-31009. (Illus.). 1976. text ed. 14.95 (ISBN 0-395-18958-6); inst. manual 1.00 (ISBN 0-395-18957-8). HM.
Handbook of Research Design & Social Measurement. 3rd ed. Delbert C. Miller. LC 77-128. 1977. pap. 12.95x (ISBN 0-582-29007-4, Pub. by MacKay). Longman.
Handbook of Retail Promotion Ideas. Reuben Guberman. LC 80-12276. 192p. 1981. text ed. 24.95 (ISBN 0-201-02720-8). A-W.
Handbook of Retail Promotion Ideas. David D. Seltz. 1970. 19.95 (ISBN 0-910580-20-0). Farnswth Pub.
Handbook of Revolutionary Warfare. Kwame Nkrumah. (Orig.). 1969. pap. 1.95 (ISBN 0-7178-0226-4). Intl Pub Co.
Handbook of Rice Diseases in the Tropics. 58p. 1979. pap. 5.00 (R032, IRRI). Unipub.
Handbook of Romanesque Art. J. J. Timmers. (Icon Editions). (Illus.). 240p. 1976. pap. 5.95x o.s.i. (ISBN 0-06-430073-0, IN-73, HarpT). Har-Row.
Handbook of Rotating Electric Machinery. Ed. by Donald V. Richardson. (Illus.). 652p. 1980. text ed. 24.95 (ISBN 0-8359-2759-8). Reston.
Handbook of Russian Roots. Catherine Wolkonsky & Marianna Poltoratzky. LC 61-1403. (Columbia Slavic Studies). 1961. 25.00x (ISBN 0-231-02117-8). Columbia U Pr.
Handbook of Selling: Psychological, Managerial & Marketing Basis. Gary M. Grikscheit et al. LC 80-19371. (Marketing Management Ser.). 650p. 1981. 29.95 (ISBN 0-471-04482-2, Pub. by Ronald). Wiley.
Handbook of Showing. Glenda Spooner. (Illus.). pap. 9.65 (ISBN 0-85131-240-3, Dist. by Sporting Book Center). J A Allen.
Handbook of Skin & Hair. Gary Null. 1976. pap. 1.75 (ISBN 0-515-03619-6). Jove Pubns.
Handbook of Skits & Stunts. Helen Eisenberg & Larry Eisenberg. 1953. 5.95 o.p. (ISBN 0-8096-1086-8, Assn Pr). Follett.
Handbook of Small Appliance Troubleshooting & Repair. David L. Heiserman. LC 73-14989. (Illus.). 320p. 1974. 16.95x o.p. (ISBN 0-13-381749-0). P-H.
Handbook of Small Business Advertising. Michael Anthony. 192p. 1981. text ed. price not set (ISBN 0-201-00086-5). A-W.
Handbook of Small Group Research. 2nd ed. A. Paul Hare. LC 75-28569. (Illus.). 1976. 25.00 (ISBN 0-02-913840-X). Free Pr.
Handbook of Social Science of Sport. Ed. by Gunther Luschen & George Sage. 700p. 1981. text ed. 22.00 (ISBN 0-87563-191-6). Stipes.
Handbook of Sociology. Edward B. Reuter. 233p. 1980. Repr. of 1941 ed. lib. bdg. 30.00 (ISBN 0-89987-156-9). Darby Bks.
Handbook of Soviet Lunar & Planetary Exploration. Nicholas L. Johnson. (Science & Technology Ser.: Vol. 47). 276p. 1979. lib. bdg. 35.00 (ISBN 0-87703-130-4); pap. text ed. 25.00 (ISBN 0-87703-131-2). Univelt Inc.
Handbook of Soviet Social Science Data. Ed. by Ellen Mickiewicz. LC 72-86510. (Illus.). 1973. 25.00 (ISBN 0-02-921190-5). Free Pr.
Handbook of Spanish Verbs. Judith Noble & Jaime Lacosa. (gr. 9-12). 1980. pap. text ed. 18.95 (ISBN 0-8138-1095-7). Iowa St U Pr.
Handbook of Special Vocational Needs Education. Gary Meers et al. LC 80-17759. 383p. 1980. 26.95 (ISBN 0-89443-288-5). Aspen Systems.
Handbook of Specialty Elements in Architecture. Andrew Alpern. (Illus.). 448p. 1981. 32.50 (ISBN 0-07-001360-8, P&RB). McGraw.
Handbook of Spectroscopy, Vol. 3. J. W. Robinson. 432p. 1981. 64.95 (ISBN 0-8493-0333-8). CRC Pr.
Handbook of Spectroscopy, CRC, 2 vols. Ed. by J. W. Robinson. LC 73-77524. (Handbook Ser). 1974. Set. (ISBN 0-685-48941-8); Vol. 1, 913p. 69.95 (ISBN 0-87819-331-6); Vol. 2, 578p. 59.95 (ISBN 0-8493-0332-X). CRC Pr.
Handbook of Spinal Cord Medicine. D. C. Burke & D. D. Murray. 100p. 1975. pap. 8.84 (ISBN 0-89004-066-4). Raven.
Handbook of Standard Structural Details for Buildings. Milo S. Ketchum. 1956. text ed. 18.95 (ISBN 0-13-381822-5). P-H.
Handbook of Statistical Tables. Owen. 1962. 26.95 (ISBN 0-201-05550-3). A-W.
Handbook of Structured Experiences for Human Relations Training, 7 vols. Ed. by J. William Pfeiffer & John E. Jones. LC 73-92840. (Series in Human Relations Training). 1973-81. pap. 9.50 ea.; Vol. 1. Rev. Ed. (ISBN 0-88390-041-6); Vol. 2. Rev. Ed. (ISBN 0-88390-042-4); Vol. 3. Rev. Ed. (ISBN 0-88390-043-2); Vol. 4. (ISBN 0-88390-044-0). Vol. 5 (ISBN 0-88390-045-9). Vol. 6 (ISBN 0-88390-046-7). Vol. 7 (ISBN 0-88390-047-5). Vol.8 (ISBN 0-88390-048-3). Univ Assocs.
Handbook of Structured Experiences for Human Relations Training, Vol. VIII. Ed. by J. William Pfeiffer & John E. Jones. LC 73-92840. (Ser. in Human Relations Training). 154p. (Orig.). 1981. pap. 9.50 (ISBN 0-88390-048-3). Univ Assocs.
Handbook of Style in Music. 2nd ed. George S. Dickinson. LC 72-90211. (Music Reprint Ser). 1969. Repr. of 1965 ed. 18.50 (ISBN 0-306-71820-0). Da Capo.
Handbook of Sugars. 2nd ed. Harry M. Pancoast & W. Ray Junk. (Illus.). 1980. text ed. 47.50 (ISBN 0-87055-348-8). AVI.
Handbook of Sugars: For Processors, Chemists & Technologists. Ray Junk & Harry M. Pancoast. (Illus.). 304p. 1973. 26.50 o.p. (ISBN 0-87055-133-7). AVI.
Handbook of Systems Analysis. 2nd ed. John E. Bingham & Garth W. Davies. LC 77-28954. 1978. 18.95 o.p. (ISBN 0-470-99129-1). Halsted Pr.
Handbook of Systems Analysis. 2nd ed. John E. Bingham & Garth W. Davies. LC 77-28954. 229p. 1980. pap. text ed. 17.95x (ISBN 0-470-26997-9). Halsted Pr.
Handbook of Teaching & Coaching Points for Basic Physical Education Skills. L. Dowell. 288p. 1974. pap. 14.50 (ISBN 0-398-03194-0). C C Thomas.
Handbook of Technical Writing Practices, 2 vols. S. Jordan et al. 1971. Set. 83.50 (ISBN 0-471-45062-6); Vol. 1. 40.00 (ISBN 0-471-45060-X); Vol. 2. 43.50 (ISBN 0-471-45059-6). Wiley.
Handbook of Terms Used in Algebra & Analysis. A. G. Howson. LC 71-178281. (Illus.). 260p. 1972. 32.95 (ISBN 0-521-08434-2); pap. 11.50 (ISBN 0-521-09695-2). Cambridge U Pr.
Handbook of Texas. Ed. by Walter P. Webb & H. Bailey Carroll. Incl. 1952. 55.00 (ISBN 0-87611-013-8); Vol. 3. Ed. by Eldon S. Branda. (Vol. 3 is sold both as a part of the 3 vol. set & by itself). 1976. supplement 35.00 (ISBN 0-87611-027-8). LC 76-55058. Three Vol. Set. 85.00 (ISBN 0-87611-036-7). Tex St Hist Assn.
Handbook of Textile Fibers, Dyes, and Finishes. Howard L. Needles. LC 79-23188. 175p. 1980. lib. bdg. 27.50 (ISBN 0-8240-7046-1). Garland Pub.
Handbook of the Analytical Chemistry of Rare Elements. A. I. Busev. LC 75-104379. 1972. 34.95 (ISBN 0-470-12620-5). Halsted Pr.
Handbook of the Birds of Europe, the Middle East & North Africa: The Birds of Western Palearctic, Vol. 2, Hawks to Buzzards. Ed. by Stanley Cramp et al. (Illus.). 704p. 1980. text ed. 85.00x (ISBN 0-19-857505-X). Oxford U Pr.
Handbook of the Birds of India & Pakistan: Together with Those of Nepal, Sikkim, Bhutan, & Ceylon, 7 vols. Salim Ali & S. Dillon Ripley. Incl. Vol. 2. Megapodes to Crab Plover. 362p. 1969. 20.00 o.p. (ISBN 0-19-635262-2); Vol. 3. Stone Curlews to Owls. 342p. 1969. 23.75x (ISBN 0-19-635264-9); Vol. 4. Frogmouths to Pittas. 282p. 1970. 23.75x (ISBN 0-19-635275-4); Vol. 5. Larks to the Grey Hypocolius. 292p. 1972. 29.50x (ISBN 0-19-560166-1); Vol. 6. Cuckoo-Shrikes to Babaxes. 262p. 1971. 23.50x (ISBN 0-19-560101-7); Vol. 7. Laughing Thrushes to the Mangrove Whistler. 252p. 1972. 23.50x (ISBN 0-19-560263-3); Vol. 8. Warblers to Redstarts. 294p. 1973. 29.50x (ISBN 0-19-560291-9); Vol. 9. Robins to Wagtails. 322p. 1973. 29.50x (ISBN 0-19-560349-4); Vol. 10. Flowerpackers to Buntings. 1974. 29.50 (ISBN 0-19-560385-0). (Illus.), Oxford U Pr.
Handbook of the Birds of India & Pakistan, Vol. II: Megapodes to Crab Plover. Salim Ali & S. D. Ripley. (Illus.). 345p. 1981. 34.00 (ISBN 0-19-561201-9). Oxford U Pr.
Handbook of the Bond & Money Markets. David M. Darst. (Illus.). 320p. 1981. 29.95 (ISBN 0-07-015401-5, P&RB). McGraw.
Handbook of the Cleveland Museum of Art. Cleveland Museum of Art Staff. LC 76-54618. (Illus.). 456p. 1978. pap. 20.00x vinyl cover (ISBN 0-910386-31-5, Pub. by Cleveland Mus Art). Ind U Pr.
Handbook of the Collection of Musical Instruments in the United States National Museum. Frances Densmore. LC 79-155231. (Music Ser). 1971. Repr. of 1927 ed. lib. bdg. 25.00 (ISBN 0-306-70167-7). Da Capo.
Handbook of the Daily News Sweated Industries Exhibition: Nineteen Six. Ed. by Richard Mudie-Smith. LC 79-56964. (English Working Class Ser.). 1980. lib. bdg. 16.00 (ISBN 0-8240-0116-8). Garland Pub.
Handbook of the Hypothalmus, Vol. 1. P. Morgane & J. Panksepp. 1979. 95.00 (ISBN 0-8247-6834-5). Dekker.
Handbook of the Hypothalmus, Vol. 3, Pt. A. Morgane & Panksepp. 472p. 1980. 145.00 (ISBN 0-8247-6904-X). Dekker.
Handbook of the Law Under the Uniform Commercial Code. 2nd ed. James J. White & Robert S. Summers. LC 79-27189. (Hornbook Ser.). 1287p. 1980. text ed. 19.95 (ISBN 0-8299-2082-X). West Pub.
Handbook of the Martial Arts & Self-Defense. William Logan & Herman Petras. LC 74-26776. (Funk & W Bk.). (Illus.). 1975. 10.95 o.s.i. (ISBN 0-308-10104-9, TYC-T). T Y Crowell.
Handbook of the Museum of Fine Arts, Boston. rev. ed. (Illus.). 1975. pap. 3.50 (ISBN 0-87846-092-6). Mus Fine Arts Boston.
Handbook of the Nutritional Contents of Foods. U.S. Department of Agriculture. LC 75-2616. (Illus.). 192p. 1975. pap. text ed. 4.00 (ISBN 0-486-21342-0). Dover.
Handbook of the Pharmacology of Emergency Drugs for Paramedics. Joseph P. Ornato & John A. Romankiewicz. LC 77-89812. 1977. pap. 120.00 (ISBN 0-914768-36-0). Drug Intl Pubns.
Handbook of the World's Religions. Ed. by A. M. Zehavi. LC 73-9283. (gr. 7-12). 1973. PLB 9.90 o.p. (ISBN 0-531-02644-2). Watts.
Handbook of Thermochemical Data for Compounds & Aqueous Species. Herbert E. Barner & Richard V. Scheuerman. LC 77-20244. 1978. 26.95 (ISBN 0-471-03238-7, Pub. by Wiley-Interscience). Wiley.
Handbook of Thermodynamic Constants of Inorganic & Organic Compounds. M. Khand Karapet'Yants & M. L. Karapet'Yants. LC 72-122509. 1968. 39.95 (ISBN 0-470-45850-X). Halsted Pr.
Handbook of Toxic Fungal Metabolites. Ed. by Richard J. Cole & Richard H. Cox. 1981. write for info. (ISBN 0-12-179760-0). Acad Pr.
Handbook of Transportation & Marketing in Agriculture: Volume 1: Food Commodities. Ed. by Essex E. Finney, Jr. 317p. 1981. 59.95 (ISBN 0-8493-3851-4). CRC Pr.
Handbook of Treatment of Mental Disorders in Childhood & Adolescence. Ed. by Benjamin B. Wolman. LC 77-7928. (Illus.). 1978. ref. ed. 45.00 (ISBN 0-13-382234-6). P-H.
Handbook of Trees for the Midwest. Pamela S. Stava. (Illus.). 1978. pap. text ed. 14.95 (ISBN 0-8403-1851-0). Kendall-Hunt.
Handbook of Trout & Salmon Diseases. Ronald J. Roberts & C. Jonathan Shepherd. (Illus.). 172p. 21.25 (ISBN 0-85238-066-6, FN). Unipub.
Handbook of Tswana Law & Custom. Isaac Schapera. 328p. 1970. Repr. 28.50x (ISBN 0-7146-2481-0, F Cass Co). Biblio Dist.
Handbook of Ultrasonic B-Scanning in Medicine. R. M. Lunt. LC 77-22257. (Techniques of Measurement in Medicine Ser.: No. 1). (Illus.). 1978. 31.95 (ISBN 0-521-21753-9); pap. 8.50x (ISBN 0-521-29264-6). Cambridge U Pr.
Handbook of United States Coins. R. S. Yeoman. 1979. 3.50 (ISBN 0-307-09050-7, Golden Pr). Western Pub.
Handbook of Urinalysis & Urinary Sediment. Neil A. Kurtzman & Philip W. Rogers. (Illus.). 112p. 1974. 12.75 (ISBN 0-398-02918-0). C C Thomas.
Handbook of Urologic Emergencies. Robert Kessler & Rodney U. Anderson. 1976. spiral bdg. 11.00 (ISBN 0-87488-647-3). Med Exam.
Handbook of Urological Endoscopy. J. G. Gow & H. H. Hopkins. (Illus.). 1978. text ed. 35.00x (ISBN 0-443-01419-1). Churchill.
Handbook of Vacuum Physics. A. H. Beck. Vol. 2, Pt. 1 1965. pap. 19.50 (ISBN 0-08-010888-1); Vol. 3, Pts. 1-3. 1965. pap. 22.00 (ISBN 0-08-011051-7). Pergamon.
Handbook of Valves. Philip Schweitzer. 258p. 1972. 22.00 o.p. (ISBN 0-8311-3026-1). Indus Pr.
Handbook of Veterinary Procedures & Emergency Treatment. 3rd ed. Robert W. Kirk & Stephen I. Bistner. (Illus.). 928p. 1981. text ed. write for info. (ISBN 0-7216-5475-4). Saunders.
Handbook of Visual Perceptual Training. Susanne A. Cunningham & Cora L. Reagan. 120p. 1972. text ed. 14.75 (ISBN 0-398-02267-4). C C Thomas.
Handbook of Weather Folk-Lore: Being a Collection of Proverbial Sayings in Various Languages Relating to the Weather. Charles Swainson. LC 73-5513. xii, 275p. 1974. Repr. of 1873 ed. 18.00 (ISBN 0-8103-3980-3). Gale.
Handbook of Weed & Insect Control Chemicals for Forest Resource Management. Michael Newton. 160p. 1980. pap. 24.95x (ISBN 0-917304-25-X, Pub. by Timber Pr). Intl Schol Bk Serv.
Handbook of Well Log Analysis: For Oil & Gas Formation Evaluation. Sylvain J. Pirson. 1963. ref. ed. 31.95 (ISBN 0-13-382804-2). P-H.
Handbook of West European Archival & Library Resources. 1981. 75.00 (ISBN 0-686-69415-5, Dist. by Gale Research). K G Saur.
Handbook of Western Civilization: 1700 to Present. 2nd ed. Sidney A. Burrell. LC 76-37642. 1972. pap. text ed. 10.95 (ISBN 0-471-12516-4). Wiley.
Handbook of Wild Flower Cultivation. Kathryn S. Taylor & Stephen F. Hamblin. (Illus.). 1962. 12.95 (ISBN 0-02-616760-3). Macmillan.
Handbook of Winning Football. George Allen & Don Weiskopf. 1976. text ed. 16.95 (ISBN 0-205-05426-9); pap. text ed. 10.95 (ISBN 0-205-04880-3). Allyn.
Handbook of World Philosophy: Contemporary Developments Since 1945. Ed. by John R. Burr. LC 80-539. (Illus.). xxii, 639p. 1980. lib. bdg. 45.00 (ISBN 0-313-22381-5, BCD/). Greenwood.
Handbook of World Transport. Yvan Du Jonchay. 221p. 1980. 20.00 (ISBN 0-87196-393-0). Facts on File.
Handbook of X-Rays. Emmett F. Kaelble. LC 63-23535. 1120p. 1967. 54.50 o.p. (ISBN 0-686-65349-1). Krieger.
Handbook of Yoga for Modern Living. Eugene Rawls. (Orig.). pap. 1.50 (ISBN 0-515-00958-X). Jove Pubns.
Handbook of 20th Century Opera. May S. Teasdale. LC 76-4920. (Music Reprint Ser.). 1976. Repr. of 1938 ed. lib. bdg. 22.50 (ISBN 0-306-70783-7). Da Capo.
Handbook on Accident Prevention: Injury Control for Children & Youth. Matilda S. McIntire. (Illus.). 128p. 1980. pap. text ed. 7.95 (ISBN 0-06-141611-8, Harper Medical). Har-Row.
Handbook on Biotelemetry & Radio Tracking: International Conference: Biotelemetry & Radio Tracking in Biology & Medicine, Oxford, 20-22 March 1979. Ed. by C. Amlaner & D. Macdonald. LC 79-41234. (Illus.). 826p. 1980. 105.00 (ISBN 0-08-024928-0). Pergamon.
Handbook on Calibration of Radiation Protection Monitoring Instruments. (Technical Reports Ser.: No. 133). (Illus.). 95p. (Orig.). 1972. pap. 6.00 (ISBN 92-0-125071-1, IAEA). Unipub.
Handbook on Evidence for West Virginia Lawyers. Franklin D. Cleckley. 1978. 40.00, with 1979 suppl (ISBN 0-87215-202-2); 1979 suppl 15.00 (ISBN 0-87215-285-5). Michie.
Handbook on International Study for U. S. Nationals: Study in Europe, Vol. 1. 307p. 1976. 10.00 (IIE). Unipub.
Handbook on International Study for U. S. Nationals: Study in the American Republics Area, Vol. 2. 230p. 1976. 12.00 (IIE). Unipub.
Handbook on Medical Librarianship. Ed. by M. Carmel. 1980. 33.00x (ISBN 0-85365-502-2, Pub. by Lib Assn England). Oryx Pr.

Handbook on Old High German Literature. 2nd ed. J. Knight Bostock. Ed. by K. C. King & D. R. McLintock. (Illus.). 1976. 49.95x (ISBN 0-19-815392-9). Oxford U Pr.

Handbook on Percentages. Charles E. Shampaign. (Gamblers Book Shelf). 1965. pap. 2.95 (ISBN 0-911996-02-8). Gamblers.

Handbook on Professional Magazine Article Writing. Donald G. Romero. 1975. 3.95 (ISBN 0-87543-127-5). Lucas.

Handbook on Quantity Food Management. 2nd ed. E. Evelyn Smith & Vera C. Crusius. 1970. spiral bdg. 7.95 o.p. (ISBN 0-8087-1959-9). Burgess.

Handbook on Real Estate Finance Law. George E. Osborne et al. LC 79-284. (Hornbook Ser.). 885p. 1979. 18.95 (ISBN 0-8299-2034-X). West Pub.

Handbook on Secured Transactions Under the Uniform Commercial Code. 2nd ed. Ray D. Henson. LC 78-26098. (Hornbook Ser). 504p. 1979. text ed. 17.95 (ISBN 0-8299-2023-4). West Pub.

Handbook on Serials Librarianship. Ed. by R. Bourne. 1980. 33.00x (ISBN 0-85365-631-2, Pub. by Lib Assn England); pap. text ed. 15.95x (ISBN 0-85365-721-1). Oryx Pr.

Handbook on Stress & Anxiety: Contemporary Knowledge, Theory, & Treatment. Irwin L. Kutash et al. LC 80-8014. (Social & Behavioral Science Ser.). 1980. text ed. 27.95x (ISBN 0-87589-478-X). Jossey-Bass.

Handbook on the Bach Flower Remedies. Phillip Chancellor. LC 79-93435. 254p. (Orig.). 1980. pap. 5.95 (ISBN 0-87983-196-0). Keats.

Handbook on the Constitutions of the United States & Georgia. rev. ed. Merritt B. Pound & Albert B. Saye. LC 46-27121. 184p. 1975. pap. 2.00x (ISBN 0-8203-0216-3). U of Ga Pr.

Handbook on the Holy Spirit. James E. Cummings. LC 77-79551. 1977. pap. 3.50 (ISBN 0-87123-541-2, 200541). Bethany Fell.

Handbook on the Laboratory Mouse. Charles G. Crispens, Jr. 278p. 1975. pap. 14.75 spiral (ISBN 0-398-03403-6). C C Thomas.

Handbook on the Law of Agency & Partnership. Harold G. Reuschlein & William A. Gregory. LC 78-12853. (Hornbook Ser.). 625p. 1978. text ed. 17.95 (ISBN 0-8299-2016-1). West Pub.

Handbook on the Traditional Old Irish Dress. H. F. McClintock. (Illus.). 8.95. Dufour.

Handbook on Tongues, Interpretation & Prophecy. Don Basham. (Handbk. Ser.: No. 2). 1971. pap. 2.95 (ISBN 0-88368-004-1). Whitaker Hse.

Handbook on Torsional Vibration. Ed. by E. J. Nestorides. 1958. 86.50 (ISBN 0-521-04326-3). Cambridge U Pr.

Handbook on University & Polytechnic Librarianship. Ed. by J. F. Stirling. 1980. 33.00x (ISBN 0-85365-621-5, Pub. by Lib Assn England). Oryx Pr.

Handbook Series in Clinical Laboratory Science, CRC: Section F, Immunology, 2 pts, Vol. 1. Alexander Baumgarten & Frank F. Richards. 1978-79. Pt. 1. 63.95 (ISBN 0-8493-7021-3); Pt. 2, 480p. 62.95 (ISBN 0-8493-7022-1). CRC Pr.

Handbook Series in Zoonoses, CRC, Section C: Parasitic Zoonoses. Ed. by Primo Arambulo & James H. Steele. Date not set. 64.95 (ISBN 0-8493-2916-7). CRC Pr. Postponed.

Handbook Series in Zoonoses, CRR, Section A: Bacterial, Rickettsial & Mycotic Diseases, Vol. 2. Ed. by Herbert Stoenner et al. 1980. 69.95 (ISBN 0-8493-2907-8). CRC Pr.

Handbook Series in Zoonoses: Viral Zoonoses. Ed. by George Beran & James H. Steele. (CRC Handbook Ser. in Zoonoses). 1980. 64.95 (ISBN 0-8493-2911-6). CRC Pr.

Handbook: The Guggenheim Museum Collection, 1900-1980. Vivian E. Barnett. (Illus.). 1980. 14.85 (ISBN 0-89207-021-8). S R Guggenheim.

Handbook to BS 5337, 1976: The Structural Use of Concrete for Retaining Aqueous Liquids. A. W. Hill et al. (Viewpoint Publication Ser.). (Illus.). 60p. 1979. pap. text ed. 25.00x (ISBN 0-7210-1078-4, Pub. by C&CA London). Scholium Intl.

Handbook to Literature. 4th ed. C. Hugh Holman. LC 79-10061. 1980. 12.95 (ISBN 0-672-61477-4); pap. 8.95 (ISBN 0-672-61441-3). Bobbs.

Handbook to Marriage. rev. ed. Theodore Bovet. LC 74-82958. 1969. pap. 1.95 (ISBN 0-385-09505-8, C23, Dolp). Doubleday.

Handbook to the Families & Orders of Living Mammals. 2nd ed. Timothy E. Lawlon. (Illus.). 1979. 9.40x (ISBN 0-916422-16-X). Mad River.

Handbook to the Lutheran Hymnal. 3rd rev. ed. W. G. Polack. 1975. Repr. of 1942 ed. lib. bdg. 13.95 (ISBN 0-8100-0003-2, 03-0700). Northwest Pub.

Handbook to the Primates, 2 vols. Henry O. Forbes. LC 78-72715. Repr. of 1894 ed. Set. 84.50 (ISBN 0-404-18288-7). Vol. 1 (ISBN 0-404-18289-5). Vol. 2 (ISBN 0-404-18290-9). AMS Pr.

Handbuch der Lehre von der Verteilung der Primzahlen, 2 vols. in 1. 3rd ed. Edmund Landau. LC 73-21539. 1974. text ed. 39.50 (ISBN 0-8284-0096-2). Chelsea Pub.

Handcrafting Jewelry: Designs & Techniques. William E Garrison & Merle E. Dowd. LC 71-183815. (Illus.). 256p. 1973. 14.95 o.p. (ISBN 0-8092-8851-6). Contemp Bks.

Handcrafts for the Homebound Handicapped. Mildred K. Rich. (Illus.). 116p. 1960. photocopy ed. spiral 11.75 (ISBN 0-398-01585-6). C C Thomas.

Handed Down: The Artisan Tradition. Barbara Traisman. LC 80-67829. 1980. pap. 12.95 (ISBN 0-916860-07-8). Bean Pub.

Handel: A Documentary Biography. Otto Deutsch. LC 74-3118. (Music Ser.). 942p. 1974. Repr. of 1954 ed. lib. bdg. 55.00 (ISBN 0-306-70624-5). Da Capo.

Handel & His Orbit. Percy Robinson. (Music Reprint Ser.). 1979. Repr. of 1908 ed. lib. bdg. 27.50 (ISBN 0-306-79522-1). Da Capo.

Handel & the Opera Seria. Winton Dean. (Ernest Bloch Lectures). 1969. 23.75x (ISBN 0-520-01438-3). U of Cal Pr.

Handel's "Messiah" The Conducting Score. Handel. 460p. 1979. Repr. of 1974 ed. 75.00x (ISBN 0-85967-158-5, Pub. by Scolar Pr England). Biblio Dist.

Handfuls on Purpose, 5 vols. James Smith. 1943. 55.00 set (ISBN 0-8028-8139-4). Eerdmans.

Handguide to the Coral Reef Fishes of the Caribbean. F. Joseph Stokes. LC 79-27224. (Illus.). 160p. 1980. 9.95 (ISBN 0-690-01919-X). Lippincott & Crowell.

Handgun Competition. George C. Nonte. (Illus.). 1978. 14.95 (ISBN 0-87691-253-6). Winchester Pr.

Handgun Hunting. George C. Nonte, Jr. & Lee E. Jurras. (Illus.). 1975. 10.95 (ISBN 0-87691-211-0). Winchester Pr.

Handicapped Awareness. Boy Scouts of America & Boys Scout of America. (Illus.). 48p. (gr. 6-12). 1981. pap. 0.70x (ISBN 0-8395-3370-5, 3370). BSA.

Handicapped Child in the Regular Classroom. Bill R. Gearheart & Mel Weishahn. LC 75-31543. (Illus.). 272p. 1976. 15.50 o.p. (ISBN 0-8016-1764-2). Mosby.

Handicapped Child: Research Review, Visual Impairment, Hearing Impairment, Vol. 2. Rosemary Dinnage. (Studies in Child Development). (Illus.). 447p. 1972. text ed. 12.00x (ISBN 0-582-32452-1). Humanities.

Handicapped Children. 3rd ed. John D. Kershaw. 1973. 17.50x (ISBN 0-433-18381-0). Intl Ideas.

Handicapped Children in Residential Care: A Study of Policy Failure. Ann Shearer. 114p. 1980. pap. text ed. write for info. (ISBN 0-7199-1035-8, Pub. by Bedford England). Renouf.

Handicapped Librarian: A Study in Barriers. G. Garry Warren. LC 79-21811. 155p. 1979. 10.00 (ISBN 0-8108-1259-2). Scarecrow.

Handicapped School Leavers: Their Further Education Training & Employment. L. Tuckey et al. 1973. pap. text ed. 4.50x (ISBN 0-85633-017-5, NFER). Humanities.

Handicapped Speak. William Roth. LC 80-20297. 240p. 1981. lib. bdg. write for info (ISBN 0-89950-022-6). McFarland & Co.

Handicapped Student in the Regular Classroom. 2nd ed. Bill R. Gearheart & Mel W. Weishahn. LC 79-23706. 1980. text ed. 17.95 (ISBN 0-8016-1760-X). Mosby.

Handicapper. Robert Kalich. Ed. by Herbert Michelman. 384p. 1981. 12.95 (ISBN 0-517-54024-X). Crown.

Handicappers Guide to Dogtrack Astrology. Elmer E. Edwards. (Illus.). 104p. 1980. pap. 10.00 (ISBN 0-9604834-0-3). Elmer Edwards.

Handicapping America: Barriers to Disabled People. Frank Bowe. LC 77-11816. 1978. 14.95 (ISBN 0-06-010422-8, HarpT). Har-Row.

Handicrafts for Holidays. Janet D'Amato & Alex D'Amato. (Illus.). (gr. 1-4). 1967. PLB 7.21 (ISBN 0-87460-086-3). Lion.

Handicrafts of France As Recorded in the Description Des Arts et Metiers, 1761-1788. Arthur H. Cole & George B. Watts. (Kress Library of Business & Economics: No. 8). (Illus.). 1952. pap. 5.00x (ISBN 0-678-09903-0, Baker Lib). Kelley.

Handicrafts of India. 60.00 (ISBN 0-7069-0735-3, Pub. by Vikas India). Advent Bk.

Handkonkordanz Zum Grieschischen Neuen Testament. 15th ed. Ed. by A Schmoller. 1973. 12.85 (ISBN 3-438-05131-1, 56850). United Bible.

Handlin Criminal Appeals, Vol. 1. Jonathan Purver & Lawrence Taylor. LC 80-81271. 1980. 47.50. Lawyers Co-Op.

Handling Accident Cases: 1963-73, 7 vols. in 8 bks. Albert Averbach. LC 58-4149. 1973. Set. 320.00 (ISBN 0-686-14528-3); Vols. 1-2. 85.00; Vols. 3a-3b. 42.50 ea.; Vols. 4-5. 85.00; Vols. 6-7. 85.00. Lawyers Co-Op.

Handling & Storage of High-Level Radioactive Liquid Wastes - Required Cooling. (Technical Reports Ser.: No. 191). 1979. pap. 15.00 (ISBN 92-0-125479-2, IDC191, IAEA). Unipub.

Handling Consumer Credit Cases, 2 vols. Barkley Clark & John R. Fonseca. LC 76-166148. (Criminal Law Library). 738p. 1972. 85.00 (ISBN 0-686-14480-5). Lawyers Co-Op.

Handling Employment Discrimination Cases, Vol. 1. Lee Modjeska. LC 78-70830. 1980. 47.50. Lawyers Co-Op.

Handling Federal Estate & Gift Taxes, 3 vols. 2nd ed. Homer I. Harris & Joseph Rasch. LC 72-96007. 1972. 150.00 (ISBN 0-686-14503-8). Lawyers Co-Op.

Handling Misdemeanor Cases. new ed. F. Lee Bailey & Henry B. Rothblatt. LC 76-12668. (Criminal Law Library). 1976. 47.50 (ISBN 0-686-20648-7). Lawyers Co-Op.

Handling Narcotic & Drug Cases. F. Lee Bailey & Henry B. Rothblatt. LC 72-84855. (Criminal Law Library). 652p. 1972. 47.50 (ISBN 0-686-05452-0). Lawyers Co-Op.

Handling of Chemical Data. P. D. Lark et al. LC 66-17264. 1968. 32.00 (ISBN 0-08-011849-6). Pergamon.

Handling of Chromosomes. C. D. Darlington & F. L. La Cour. (Illus.). 1942. pap. text ed. 16.50x o.p. (ISBN 0-04-574014-3). Allen Unwin.

Handling of Chromosomes. 6th ed. C. D. Darlington & L. F. LaCour. LC 75-20130. 1976. 18.95 (ISBN 0-470-19527-4). Halsted Pr.

Handling of Nuclear Information. (Illus., Orig., Eng., Fr. & Rus.). 1970. pap. 44.50 (ISBN 92-0-070170-1, ISP254, IAEA). Unipub.

Handling of Radiation Accidents. (Illus., Orig., Eng., Fr. & Rus.). 1969. pap. 47.25 (ISBN 92-0-020269-1, ISP229, IAEA). Unipub.

Handling of Radiation Accidents 1977. (Proceedings Ser: II). (Illus.). 1978. pap. 69.75 (ISBN 92-0-020077-X, ISP463, IAEA). Unipub.

Handling of Words & Other Studies in Literary Psychology. Vernon Lee. LC 68-13649. 1968. pap. 4.95x o.p. (ISBN 0-8032-5118-1, 376, Bison). U of Nebr Pr.

Handling Radioactivity: A Practical Approach for Scientists & Engineers. Donald C. Stewart. LC 80-19258. 416p. 1981. 38.00 (ISBN 0-471-04557-8, Pub. by Wiley-Interscience). Wiley.

Handling, Transporation & Storage of Fruits & Vegetables, Vol. 1. 2nd ed. A. Lloyd Ryall & Werner J. Lipton. (Illus.). 1979. text ed. 45.00 (ISBN 0-87055-264-3). AVI.

Handling, Transportation & Storage of Fruits & Vegetables: Fruits & Tree Nuts, Vol. No. 2. A. L. Ryall & Wilbur T. Pentzer. (Illus.). 1974. lib. bdg. 45.00 (ISBN 0-87055-165-5). AVI.

Handling Your Own Dog--for Show Obedience & Field Trials. Martha C. Thorne. LC 73-81451. (Illus.). 1979. 17.95 (ISBN 0-385-07391-7). Doubleday.

Handlist of Italian Cookery Books 1475-1860. Lord Westbury. (Illus.). pap. 30.00x o.p. (ISBN 0-685-08674-7). Corner.

Handlist of the Washington University Gallery of Art Collection. (Illus.). 100p. 1981. 4.00 (ISBN 0-936316-00-4). Wash U Gallery.

Handloader's Digest Bullet & Powder Update. Ken Warner. 96p. 1980. pap. 4.95 (ISBN 0-695-81418-4). Follett.

Handloom Weavers. Duncan Bythell. LC 69-10487. (Illus.). 1969. 53.50 (ISBN 0-521-07580-7). Cambridge U Pr.

Handmade ABC: A Manual Alphabet. Linda Bourke. LC 80-27007. (Illus.). 64p. (gr. 1-9). 1981. PLB 6.95 (ISBN 0-201-00016-4, A-W Childrens); pap. 3.95 (ISBN 0-201-00015-6). A-W.

Handmade Furniture Book. Berthold Schmultzhart. (Illus.). 144p. 1981. 13.95 (ISBN 0-13-383638-X); pap. 5.95 (ISBN 0-13-383620-7). P-H.

Handmade Homes: The Natural Way to Build Houses. Barry Shapiro & Arthur Boericke. (Illus.). Date not set. 17.95 (ISBN 0-440-03340-3). Delacorte. Postponed.

Handmade Jewelry: Techniques & Design. Alison Richards. LC 76-4644. (Funk & W Bk.). (Illus.). 1976. 12.95 o.s.i. (ISBN 0-308-10263-0, TYC-T). T Y Crowell.

Handook on the Methodology for an Integrated Experiment-Survey on Rice Yield Constraints. 59p. 1978. pap. 6.00 (R130, IRRI). Unipub.

Hands. Linda Rose. 1980. 14.95 (ISBN 0-671-24944-4). S&S.

Hands. Jack Winder. Ed. by Alton Jordan. (Elephant Ser.). (Illus.). (gr. k-3). 1975. PLB 3.50 (ISBN 0-89868-020-4, Read Res); pap. text ed. 1.75 (ISBN 0-89868-053-0). ARO Pub.

Hands Are Handy. Gerald Rasch. 20p. (Orig.). 1981. pap. 3.50 (ISBN 0-86629-011-7). Sunrise MO.

Hands in Clay. Charlotte F. Speight. LC 78-22715. 1979. pap. text ed. 14.50 (ISBN 0-88284-080-0). Alfred Pub.

Hands of Glory. Jaan Kangilaski. 272p. (Orig.). 1981. pap. 2.25 (ISBN 0-345-28489-5, Del Rey). Ballantine.

Hands of the South. Vittorio Bodini. Tr. by Ruth Feldman & Brian Swann. LC 80-68879. 1980. 7.50 (ISBN 0-686-62253-7). Charioteer.

Hands Up: Or Twenty Years of Detective Life in the Mountains & on the Plains. D. J. Cook. (Western Frontier Library: No. 11). (Illus.). 1958. pap. 4.95 (ISBN 0-8061-0934-3). U of Okla Pr.

Handsome Man. Elissa H. Guest. LC 80-66247. 192p. (gr. 7 up). 1980. 7.95 (ISBN 0-590-07661-2, Four Winds). Schol Bk Serv.

Handsome Road. Gwen Bristow. LC 38-27336. 1968. 7.95 o.s.i. (ISBN 0-690-36810-0, TYC-T). T Y Crowell.

Handspinner's Handbook. 3rd rev. ed. Bette Hochberg. LC 76-12949. 1978. 5.95 o.p. (ISBN 0-9600990-1-8). B&B Hochberg.

Handspinner's Handbook. rev. ed. Bette Hochberg. LC 76-12949. (Illus.). 68p. 1980. pap. 5.95 (ISBN 0-9600990-5-0). B&B Hochberg.

Handstands. Robert B. Ruddell et al. (Pathfinder - Allyn & Bacon Reading Program: Level 14). (gr. 3-4). 1978. text ed. 8.40 (ISBN 0-205-05168-5, 545168X); tchr's ed. 12.20 (ISBN 0-205-05169-3, 5451698); 2.60. Allyn.

Handtool Handbook. R. J. DeCristoforo. LC 77-89289. (Illus.). 1977. pap. 5.95 (ISBN 0-912656-53-0). H P Bks.

Handweaver's Workbook. Heather G. Thorpe. (Illus.). 1966. 5.95 o.s.i. (ISBN 0-02-618500-8). Macmillan.

Handweaver's Workbook. Heather G. Thorpe. (Illus.). 1966. pap. 2.95 o.s.i. (ISBN 0-02-011970-4, Collier). Macmillan.

Handweaving: For Pleasure & Profit. Harriette J. Brown. (Illus.). 1952. 7.95 o.p. (ISBN 0-06-030990-3, HarpT). Har-Row.

Handwriting. pap. text ed. 2.25 incl. tchrs' guide (ISBN 0-8449-2860-7). Learning Line.

Handwriting: A Key to Personality. Klara G. Roman. 1977. pap. 5.95 (ISBN 0-394-73091-7). Pantheon.

Handwriting Analysis Self-Taught. Joel Engel. (Illus.). 1980. 10.95 (ISBN 0-525-66687-7); pap. 6.95 (ISBN 0-525-66697-4). Elsevier-Nelson.

Handwriting Analysis: The Science of Determining Personality by Graphoanalysis. M. N. Bunker. 12.95 (ISBN 0-911012-68-0). Nelson-Hall.

Handwriting for Today. Tom Gourdie. 1978. pap. 3.50 (ISBN 0-8008-3812-2, Pentalic). Taplinger.

Handwriting in Psychological Interpretations. Arthur G. Holt. (Illus.). 276p. 1974. text ed. 21.75 (ISBN 0-398-00864-7). C C Thomas.

Handwriting Made Easy: A Simple Modern Approach. Tom Gourdie. (Illus.). 64p. 1981. pap. 3.95 (ISBN 0-8008-4597-8). Taplinger.

Handwriting of the Kings & Queens of England. W. J. Hardy. LC 78-58182. 1979. Repr. of 1893 ed. lib. bdg. 30.00 o.p. (ISBN 0-89341-472-7). Longwood Pr.

Handwriting Workbook. Rayner W. Markley. (Welcome to English Ser.). 1977. pap. text ed. 2.50x (ISBN 0-19-520029-2). Oxford U Pr.

Handwrought Jewelry. Lois Franke & William L. Udell. (gr. 7 up). 1962. text ed. 16.00 (ISBN 0-87345-175-9). McKnight.

Handy & Systematic Catalog of NMR Spectra: Instruction Through Examples. Addison Ault & Margaret R. Ault. LC 79-57227. 425p. 1980. 15.00 (ISBN 0-935702-00-8). Univ Sci Bks.

Handy Boatman. Ed. by Time-Life Books. (Library of Boating Ser.). (Illus.). 1976. 14.95 (ISBN 0-8094-2140-2). Time-Life.

Handy Boatman. Time-Life Editors. LC 76-26732. (Time-Life Library of Boating). 1976. lib. bdg. 13.95 (ISBN 0-8094-2141-0). Silver.

Handy Book of American Authors. Louis H. Peet. LC 75-156928. 1971. Repr. of 1907 ed. 24.00 (ISBN 0-8103-3360-0). Gale.

Handy Book of Commonly Used American Idioms. Solomon Wiener. (gr. 9 up). 1958. pap. text ed. 1.95 (ISBN 0-88345-061-5, 17395). Regents Pub.

Handy Book of Curious Information, Comprising Strange Happenings in the Life of Men & Animals, Odd Statistics, Extraordinary Phenomena & Out of the Way Facts Concerning the Wonderlands of the Earth. William S. Walsh. LC 68-30583. 1970. Repr. of 1913 ed. 38.00 (ISBN 0-8103-3100-4). Gale.

Handy-Book of Literary Curiosities. William S. Walsh. LC 68-24370. 1966. Repr. of 1892 ed. 44.00 (ISBN 0-8103-0162-8). Gale.

Handy Farm & Home Devices. J. V. Bartlett. (Illus.). 320p. (Orig.). 1981. pap. price not set. MIT Pr.

Handy Grammar Reference. Robert L. Shurter. 1959. pap. 3.50 (ISBN 0-07-057345-X). McGraw.

Handy Guide to Grammar & Punctuation. Richard B. Baldauf. (Programmed Instruction - Communications Skills Ser.). 160p. (Prog. Bk.). 1973. pap. text ed. 8.95 (ISBN 0-201-00382-1). A-W.

Handy Lumber Table. pap. 0.25 (ISBN 0-686-65405-6). Bennett IL.

Handy Matrices of Unit Conversion Factors for Biology & Mechanics. C. J. Pennycuick. LC 74-26762. 47p. 1976. pap. 4.95 o.p. (ISBN 0-470-67948-4). Halsted Pr.

Handy Medical Guide for Seafarers: Fishermen, Trawlermen & Yachtsmen. R. W. Scott. (Illus.). 96p. 7.50 (ISBN 0-85238-007-0, FN). Unipub.

Handy Sportsman. Loring D. Wilson. 1976. 12.95 (ISBN 0-87691-213-7). Winchester Pr.

Handy Sportsman. Loring D. Wilson. (Stoeger Bks). 1977. pap. 5.95 o.p. (ISBN 0-695-80848-6). Follett.

Handyman's Guide to Home Remodeling. Stanley Schuler. 1978. 14.95 (ISBN 0-8359-2773-3). Reston.

Handyman's Guide to Home Weather Proofing. Peter Jones. 1981. 14.95 (ISBN 0-8359-2078-X); pap. text ed. 7.95 (ISBN 0-8359-2077-1). Reston.

Handyman's Primer. Alfred De Cicco. (Illus.). 192p. 1975. pap. 5.95 (ISBN 0-8473-1123-6). Sterling.

Hang Gliding. Dunstan Hadley. (Black's Picture Sports Ser.). (Illus.). 96p. 1979. 8.95 (ISBN 0-7136-1914-7). Transatlantic.

Hang Gliding. rev. ed. James Mrazek. (Illus.). 160p. 1981. 17.95 (ISBN 0-312-35912-8). St Martin.

Hang Gliding Manual with Log. 6th ed. Dan Poynter. LC 76-14105. (Illus.). 1980. pap. 1.50 (ISBN 0-915516-12-8). Para Pub.

Hang Gliding: The Basic Handbook of Skysurfing. 9th ed. Dan Poynter. LC 75-46185. (Illus.). 1979. 11.95 (ISBN 0-915516-08-X); pap. 6.95 (ISBN 0-915516-07-1). Para Pub.

Hang Loose. Glen Chase. (Cherry Delight Ser.: No. 18). 1974. pap. 1.25 o.p. (ISBN 0-685-47977-3, LB233ZK, Leisure Bks). Nordon Pubns.

Hang Me Up My Begging Bowl. Chad Walsh. LC 80-26136. 96p. 1981. 8.95 (ISBN 0-8040-0351-3); pap. 4.95 (ISBN 0-8040-0358-0). Swallow.

Hang of the Gaol. Howard Barker. 1981. pap. 4.50 (ISBN 0-7145-3769-1). Riverrun NY.

Hang Tough, Paul Mather. Alfred Slote. (gr. 7 up). 1973. 8.95 (ISBN 0-397-31451-5). Lippincott.

Hang Tough, Paul Mather. Alfred Slote. (gr. 3-5). 1975. pap. 1.75 (ISBN 0-380-00225-6, 54999, Camelot). Avon.

Hanged for a Sheep. Rosemary Gatenby. 1977. pap. 1.50 o.s.i. (ISBN 0-515-04418-0). Jove Pubns.

Hanged Man. David Harper. pap. 1.50 o.s.i. (ISBN 0-515-04425-3). Jove Pubns.

Hanger Eighteen. Robert Werevka, Jr. & Charles E. Seller. 176p. (Orig.). 1980. pap. 2.25 (ISBN 0-553-14473-1). Bantam.

Hangin' Out with Cici. Francine Pascal. (YA) (gr. 7-9). 1978. pap. 1.75 (ISBN 0-671-41057-1). PB.

Hanging in Sweetwater. Stephen Overholser. 224p. 1975. pap. 1.25 o.p. (ISBN 0-523-22655-1). Pinnacle Bks.

Hanging Plants for Modern Living. M. Jane Helmer. (Modern Living Ser.). (Illus.). 80p. (Orig.). 1975. pap. 2.95 (ISBN 0-89484-001-0, 10102). Merchants Pub Co.

Hanging Tree. Dorothy M. Johnson. 1977. pap. 1.95 (ISBN 0-345-28621-9). Ballantine.

Hanging Tree. Dorothy M. Johnson. (Western Fiction Ser.). 1980. lib. bdg. 9.95 (ISBN 0-8398-2616-8). Gregg.

Hangman's Crusade. James Barwick. 320p. 1981. 11.95 (ISBN 0-698-11037-4). Coward.

Hangman's Holiday. Dorothy L. Sayers. 1970. pap. 1.95 (ISBN 0-380-01240-5, 48959). Avon.

Hangman's Knot. Peter McCurtin. (Sundance Ser.: No. 33). 1980. pap. 1.75 (ISBN 0-8439-0764-9, Leisure Bks). Nordon Pubns.

Hangman's Range. Lee Floren. 1975. pap. 0.95 o.p. (ISBN 0-685-53131-7, LB279NK, Leisure Bks). Nordon Pubns.

Hangtree Range. William Hopson. 1978. pap. 1.25 (ISBN 0-505-51249-1). Tower Bks.

Hank Aaron: Superstars. Paul Deegan. LC 73-20300. 1974. PLB 5.95 (ISBN 0-87191-321-6); pap. 2.95 (ISBN 0-89812-172-8). Creative Ed.

Hank Aaron: The Man Who Beat the Babe - from Mobile to Immortality. Phil Musick. 192p. (Orig.). 1974. pap. 1.25 o.p. (ISBN 0-445-08258-5). Popular Lib.

Hanlin Academy: Training Ground for the Ambitious, 1644-1850. Adam Yuen-Chung Lui. (Illus.). 1980. write for info. (ISBN 0-208-01833-6, Archon). Shoe String.

Hannah. Betty Neels. (Harlequin Romances Ser.). 192p. 1981. pap. 1.25 (ISBN 0-373-02403-7, Pub. by Harlequin). FB.

Hannah. Robert L. Osmunson. LC 76-22295. (Destiny Ser). 1976. pap. 4.95 (ISBN 0-8163-0256-1, 08050-7). Pacific Pr Pub Assn.

Hannah Fowler. Janice H. Giles. 1980. lib. bdg. 16.95 (ISBN 0-8161-3051-5, Large Print Bks). G K Hall.

Hannah Is a Palindrome. Mindy W. Skolsky. LC 79-2009. (Illus.). 128p. (gr. 3-6). 1980. 8.95 (ISBN 0-06-025726-1, HarpJ); PLB 8.79 (ISBN 0-06-025727-X). Har-Row.

Hannah Massey. Catherine Cookson. 1973. pap. 1.50 (ISBN 0-451-06623-5, W6623, Sig). NAL.

Hannes Bok Sketchbook. Ed. by Gerry De La Ree & Gene Nigra. 1976. 7.50 o.p. (ISBN 0-938192-04-3). De La Ree.

Hannibal. (MacDonald Educational Ser.). (Illus., Arabic.). 3.50 (ISBN 0-686-53097-7). Intl Bk Ctr.

Hannibal: Invader from Carthage. Robert N. Webb. LC 68-10512. (Biography Ser). (gr. 7 up). 1968. PLB 5.90 o.p. (ISBN 0-531-00881-9). Watts.

Hannibal's Campaigns. Tony Bath. (Illus.). 160p. 1981. 31.95 (ISBN 0-85059-492-8). Aztex.

Hannis Taylor: The New Southerner As an American. Tennant S. McWilliams. LC 77-17124. 192p. 1978. 12.95 (ISBN 0-8173-5114-0). U of Ala Pr.

Hannon's Field Guide for Bass Fishing. Douglas Hannon & Horace Carter. LC 80-68668. (Illus.). 208p. (Orig.). 1981. pap. 5.95 (ISBN 0-937866-01-6). D Hannon.

Hanoverian London, 1714-1808. George Rude. LC 69-10590. (History of London Series). (Illus.). 1971. 20.00x (ISBN 0-520-01778-1). U of Cal Pr.

Hans Andersen the Man. Elith Reumert. Tr. by Jessie Brochner from Danish. LC 71-110811. (Tower Bks). (Illus.). 1971. Repr. of 1927 ed. 20.00 (ISBN 0-8103-3902-1). Gale.

Hans Arp: The Poet of Dadaism. R. W. Last. LC 79-84905. (Modern German Authors Texts & Contexts: Vol. 1). 8.95 (ISBN 0-8023-1227-6). Dufour.

Hans Baldung Grien: Prints & Drawings. Ed. by James H. Marrow & Alan Shestack. LC 80-52733. (Illus.). xiv, 282p. 1981. lib. bdg. 19.95 (ISBN 0-89467-013-1). Yale Art Gallery.

Hans Bethe: Prophet of Energy. Jeremy Bernstein. LC 80-50555. (Illus.). 224p. 1980. pap. 12.95 (ISBN 0-465-02903-5). Basic.

Hans Christian Andersen. Elias Bredsdorff. LC 75-23827. 344p. 1975. 10.00 o.p. (ISBN 0-684-14457-3, ScribT). Scribner.

Hans Christian Andersen: The Man & His Work. R. Spink. (Illus.). 64p. 1975. pap. 5.00x (ISBN 8-7142-7882-0, D-742). Vanous.

Hans Scharoun-A Monograph. Peter B. Jones. LC 79-307585. 1979. 30.50 (ISBN 0-900406-57-7, Pub by G Fraser). Intl Schol Bk Serv.

Hansel & Gretel. Grimm Brothers. (Illus.). (gr. k-3). 1976. PLB 5.00 (ISBN 0-307-60419-5, Golden Pr). Western Pub.

Hansel & Gretel. Grimm Brothers. LC 75-117296. (Illus.). (gr. k-3). 1971. 6.95 (ISBN 0-440-03465-5); PLB 6.46 o.s.i. (ISBN 0-440-03466-3). Delacorte.

Hansel & Gretel. (Ladybird Ser.). (Illus., Arabic.). 2.50x (ISBN 0-686-63576-0). Intl Bk Ctr.

Hansel & Gretel. Ed. by Linda Hayward. LC 73-16856. (Illus.). 32p. 1974. pap. 1.25 (ISBN 0-394-82811-9, BYR). Random.

Hansel & Gretel. Illus. by T. Izawa & S. Hijkata. (Puppet Storybooks). (Illus.). 18p. (gr. k-2). 1981. 3.50 (ISBN 0-448-09754-0). G&D.

Hansel & Gretel. William Wiesner. LC 78-154302. (Illus.). (gr. k-3). 1971. 6.50 (ISBN 0-395-28829-0, Clarion). HM.

Hansi. Tr. by Maria A. Hirschmann. (Portuguese Bks.). 1979. write for info. (ISBN 0-8297-0825-1). Life Pubs Intl.

Hansi. Tr. by Maria A. Hirschmann. (Spanish Bks.). (Span.). 1979. 1.90 (ISBN 0-8297-0563-5). Life Pubs Intl.

Hanta Yo: An American Saga. Ruth B. Hill. 1980. 9.95 (ISBN 0-446-96298-8); pap. 3.50 (ISBN 0-446-97857-4). Warner Bks.

Hanukah Money. Sholem Aleichem. LC 77-26693. (Illus.). (gr. k-3). 1978. 7.95 (ISBN 0-688-80120-X); PLB 7.63 (ISBN 0-688-84120-1). Greenwillow.

Hanukah Tooth. Jacqueline D. Greene. (Illus.). 24p. (ps-2). 1980. pap. 2.00 (ISBN 0-938836-00-5). Pascal Pubs.

Hanukkah. Norma Simon. LC 66-10065. (Holiday Ser.). (Illus.). (gr. k-3). 1966. PLB 7.89 (ISBN 0-690-36953-0, TYC-J). T Y Crowell.

Hanukkah: Eight Nights, Eight Lights. Malka Drucker. LC 80-15852. (Jewish Holidays Book). (Illus.). 96p. (gr. 5 up). 1980. PLB 8.95 (ISBN 0-8234-0377-7). Holiday.

Hanunoo Agriculture: A Report on an Integral System of Shifting Cultivation in the Phillipines Fao Forestry Development Paper No. 12. Harold C. Conklin. LC 75-28745. (Illus.). 209p. 1975. text ed. 14.50x scholars (ISBN 0-911830-22-7); pap. 24.50x institutions (ISBN 0-685-69785-1). Elliots Bks.

Hanya Holm: The Biography of an Artist. Walter Sorell. LC 69-17796. 1979. 15.00x (ISBN 0-8195-3096-4, Pub. by Wesleyan U Pr); pap. 8.00 (ISBN 0-8195-6060-X). Columbia U Pr.

Haphazard Amorist. Graham Jackson. 127p. 1981. text ed. 12.00 (ISBN 0-7022-1497-3); pap. 6.00 (ISBN 0-7022-1498-1). U of Queensland Pr.

Hapless Child. Edward Gorey. 1961. pap. 3.50 (ISBN 0-8392-1044-2). Astor-Honor.

Hapless Child. Edward Gorey. LC 61-6959. (Illus.). 64p. 1980. 5.95 (ISBN 0-396-07817-6). Dodd.

Haploids in Plant Breeding. Werner Nitzsche & Gerhard Wenzel. (Advances in Plant Breeding Ser.). (Illus.). 101p. 1977. pap. text ed. 28.00 (ISBN 3-489-75010-1). Parey Sci Pubs.

Happenings at North End School. Hila Colman. LC 77-117224. (gr. 7 up). 1970. 7.25 (ISBN 0-688-21374-X). Morrow.

Happiest Day. Ruth S. Odor. LC 79-12184. (Bible Story Bks.). (Illus.). (ps-3). 1979. PLB 5.50 (ISBN 0-89565-085-1). Childs World.

Happiest People on Earth. Demos Shakarian & Elizabeth Sherrill. 1975. 6.95 o.p. (ISBN 0-912376-14-7); pap. 3.95 (ISBN 0-912376-18-X). Chosen Bks Pub.

Happily Ever After: A Portrait of Frances Hodgson Burnett. Constance B. Burnett. LC 65-17370. (gr. 7 up). 6.95 (ISBN 0-8149-0283-9). Vanguard.

Happily Ever After: Readiness Teacher's Guide (Visual, Listening, Conceptual Development) Pleasant Rowland. (Addison-Wesley Reading Program Ser.). (ps-1). 1979. pap. text ed. 40.00 (ISBN 0-201-20389-8, Sch Div); dupe masters avail. (ISBN 0-201-20399-5). A-W.

Happiness. Elizabeth Telfer. LC 79-16373. 1980. cancelled (ISBN 0-312-36171-8). St Martin.

Happiness Is a Warm Fuzzy. Elizabeth D. Latham. (Illus.). 64p. 1981. 5.00 (ISBN 0-682-49682-0). Exposition.

Happiness Is Too Much Trouble. Sandra Hochman. 1977. pap. 1.75 o.p. (ISBN 0-345-25509-7). Ballantine.

Happiness Outside the State. Igmaz Maybaum. 128p. 1980. 25.00 (ISBN 0-85362-183-7). Routledge & Kegan.

Happiness Under One Roof. Reinhold R. Bietz. LC 76-62562. (Harvest Ser.). 1977. pap. 3.95 (ISBN 0-8163-0315-0, 08104-2). Pacific Pr Pub Assn.

Happinism: A Goal for All Humanity. Howard O. Eaton. 1976. 4.00 o.p. (ISBN 0-682-48540-3). Exposition.

Happinism Revisited. 2nd rev. & enlarged ed. Howard O. Eaton. 1978. 4.50 o.p. (ISBN 0-682-49012-1). Exposition.

Happy Adding. (Children's Library of Picture Bks.). (Illus.). 10p. (ps). 1979. 1.95 (ISBN 0-89346-175-X, TA61, Pub. by Froebel-Kan Japan). Heian Intl.

Happy Are You Who Affirm. Thomas A. Kane. (Illus.). 144p. 1980. pap. 5.00 (ISBN 0-89571-010-2). Affirmation.

Happy Bear's Day. Joanna Stubbs. (Illus.). (ps-2). 1979. PLB 6.50 (ISBN 0-233-96999-3). Andre Deutsch.

Happy Birthday Mystery. Joan L. Nixon. Ed. by Fay Ann. LC 79-18362. (First Read-Alone Mysteries). (Illus.). (gr. 1-3). 1980. 5.50g (ISBN 0-8075-3150-2). A Whitman.

Happy Birthday, Sam. Pat Hutchins. LC 78-1295. (Illus.). (gr. k-3). 1978. 7.95 (ISBN 0-688-80160-9); PLB 7.63 (ISBN 0-688-84160-0). Greenwillow.

Happy Christmas Carol. Brooks Frederick, pseud. (Writers Workshop Redbird Book Ser.). 35p. 1975. 9.00 (ISBN 0-88253-554-4); pap. text ed. 4.00 (ISBN 0-88253-553-6). Ind-US Inc.

Happy Days. H. L. Mencken. Repr. of 1955 ed. 6.95 o.p. (ISBN 0-394-42767-X). Knopf.

Happy Days. Christine Price. LC 77-95577. (Illus.). (gr. 3-6). 2.00 (ISBN 0-935738-02-9, 5004). US Comm UNICEF.

Happy Days. Craig Schumacher. (T.V. & Movie Tie-Ins Ser.). (Illus.). (gr. 4-12). 1979. PLB 5.95 (ISBN 0-87191-702-5); pap. 2.95 (ISBN 0-89812-034-9). Creative Ed.

Happy Dolphins. Samuel Carter, III. (Illus.). (YA) (gr. 7-9). 1972. pap. 1.25 (ISBN 0-671-29726-0). PB.

Happy Exercise: An Adventure into a Fit World. Don Jacobs. LC 80-23547. (Illus.). 48p. (Orig.). (ps-5). 1980. pap. 4.95 (ISBN 0-89037-170-9). Anderson World.

Happy Families. Ed. by Barbara Willard. LC 73-22433. (Illus.). 256p. (gr. 5 up). 1974. 6.95g o.s.i. (ISBN 0-02-793010-6). Macmillan.

Happy Families Are Homemade. Marjorie K. Garrison. LC 75-18922. 144p. (Orig.). 1976. pap. 1.50 o.p. (ISBN 0-912692-80-4). Cook.

Happy Fish Hooker: A Piscatorial Perpetration. Milford S. Poltroon. LC 77-5000. 1977. pap. 3.95 (ISBN 0-87691-242-0). Winchester Pr.

Happy Genius. Alan Feldman. LC 78-15577. 1978. pap. 4.00 (ISBN 0-915342-27-8). SUN.

Happy Golden ABC. Joan Allen. (Illus.). 24p. (gr. k-1). 1976. PLB 5.00 (ISBN 0-307-60344-X, Golden Pr). Western Pub.

Happy Halloween: Things to Make & Do. Robyn Supraner. LC 80-23889. (Illus.). 48p. (gr. 2-5). 1980. lib. bdg. 6.92 (ISBN 0-89375-420-X); pap. 1.75 (ISBN 0-89375-421-8). Troll Assocs.

Happy, Healthy Pooh Book. Mary Carey. (Look-Look Ser.). (Illus.). 1977. PLB 5.38 (ISBN 0-307-61832-3, Golden Pr); pap. 0.95 (ISBN 0-307-11832-0). Western Pub.

Happy Helper A B C. June Goldsborough. (Illus.). (ps-1). 1971. PLB 5.38 (ISBN 0-307-68925-5, Golden Pr). Western Pub.

Happy Helper One-Two-Three. Les Gray. (Illus.). (ps-2). 1971. PLB 5.38 (ISBN 0-307-68926-3, Golden Pr). Western Pub.

Happy Helper Preschool Workbooks, 6 bks. (ps-k). 4.50 (ISBN 0-307-13642-6, Golden Pr). Western Pub.

Happy Horse. Claudia Fregosi. LC 76-54894. (Illus.). (ps-3). 1977. 8.25 (ISBN 0-688-80087-4); PLB 7.92 (ISBN 0-688-84087-6). Greenwillow.

Happy Hunting Grounds. Stanley Vestal. 219p. 1980. pap. 4.95 (ISBN 0-8061-1543-2). U of Okla Pr.

Happy Hustler. Grant T. Saxon. (Illus.). 192p. (Orig.). 1975. pap. 1.95 o.s.i. (ISBN 0-446-89613-6). Warner Bks.

Happy Jack. Max Brand. 224p. 1972. pap. 1.95 (ISBN 0-446-90303-5). Warner Bks.

Happy Jack. Sharon Peters. (Illus.). 32p. (gr. k-2). 1980. PLB 2.96 (ISBN 0-89375-380-7); pap. 0.95 (ISBN 0-89375-280-0). Troll Assocs.

Happy Lioness. Fatio. 113p. Date not set. lib. bdg. 7.95 (ISBN 0-07-020069-6). McGraw.

Happy Man. Lachlan Mackenzie. 1979. 8.95 (ISBN 0-85151-282-8). Banner of Truth.

Happy Man: Studies in the Metamorphoses of a Classical Ideal, 1600-1700, Vol. 1. 2nd ed. Maren Sofie Rostvig. 1962. text ed. 17.00x (ISBN 0-685-84008-5, Dist. by Columbia U Pr). Universitet.

Happy Man: Studies in the Metamorphoses of a Classical Ideal, 1700-1760, Vol. 2. 2nd ed. Maren Sofie Rostvig. 1971. text ed. 17.00x (ISBN 0-391-00218-X, Dist. by Columbia U Pr). Universitet.

Happy Moments with God. Margaret J. Anderson. (Illus.). 192p. 1969. pap. 3.50 (ISBN 0-87123-212-X, 210212). Bethany Fell.

Happy Person. Harold Greenwald. LC 80-6154. 192p. 1981. 10.95 (ISBN 0-8128-2783-X). Stein & Day.

Happy Prince & Other Tales. Oscar Wilde. Ed. by Alison Lurie & Justin G. Schiller. Incl. House of Pomergranates. LC 75-32193. (Classics of Children's Literature 1621-1932 Ser.). PLB 38.00 (ISBN 0-8240-2304-8). Garland Pub.

Happy Prince & Other Tales. Oscar Wilde. LC 79-3512. (Illus.). 1980. pap. 6.95 (ISBN 0-394-73881-0). Shambhala Pubns.

Happy Trails. Roy Rogers & Dale Evans. 224p. 1981. 2.50 (ISBN 0-553-14253-4). Bantam.

Happy-Unfortunate: or the Female-Page. Elizabeth Boyd. LC 76-170583. (Foundations of the Novel Ser.: Vol. 56). lib. bdg. 50.00 (ISBN 0-8240-0568-6). Garland Pub.

Happy Valley. Max Brand. 240p. 1972. pap. 1.95 (ISBN 0-446-90304-3). Warner Bks.

Happy World of Strawberry Shortcake. Illus. by Michael A. Vaccaro. LC 80-53104. (Board Bks.). (Illus.). 14p. (ps). 1981. boards 2.95 (ISBN 0-394-84734-2). Random.

Hapsburg Empire in World War I. Ed. by R. A. Kann et al. (Monographs: No. 23). 1977. text ed. 14.00x o.p. (ISBN 0-914710-16-8, Dist. by Columbia U Pr). East Eur Quarterly.

Hapsburg Empire Seventeen Ninety to Nineteen Eighteen. C. A. Macartney. LC 69-12834. 1969. 19.95 (ISBN 0-02-577200-7). Macmillan.

Hapsburg Monarchy, 2 vols. Ed. by F. L. Carsten et al. (Studies in Russian & East European History Ser.). 1981. text ed. 25.00x ea. Vol. 1, Austria & Bohemia 1835-1918 (ISBN 0-06-490991-3). Vol. 2, Hungary 1835-1918. B&N.

Hapsburg Monarchy. Henry W. Steed. 1969. 19.00 (ISBN 0-86527-091-0). Fertig.

Harassed Worker. Carroll M Brodsky. LC 76-43115. 1976. 17.95 (ISBN 0-669-01041-3). Lexington Bks.

Harassment Therapy: A Case Study of Psychiatric Violence. Don Stannard-Friel. (University Books Ser.). 1981. lib. bdg. 16.95 (ISBN 0-8161-9030-5). G K Hall.

Harbinger. Michael Hinkemeyer. (Orig.). 1980. pap. write for info. (ISBN 0-671-82179-2). PB.

Harbinger Press Library. M. W. Farnsworth. (Illus.). 1978. text ed. 24.50 scp (ISBN 0-06-042003-0, HarpC). Har-Row.

Harbor. Ernest Poole. 1976. lib. bdg. 17.25x (ISBN 0-89968-099-2). Lightyear.

Harbor Heritage. new ed. Oliver Vickery. 1979. 15.00 (ISBN 0-89430-036-9). Morgan-Pacific.

Harbor Lights. Anne Duffield. 1973. pap. 1.25 o.p. (ISBN 0-425-02727-9, 22727, Medallion). Berkley Pub.

Harbor of Refuge. Stephen Jones. (Illus.). 1981. 16.95 (ISBN 0-393-01417-7). Norton.

Harbor of the Heart. Joan Thompson. 192p. 1981. pap. 2.25 (ISBN 0-345-28747-9). Ballantine.

Harbottle's Dictionary of Battles. 3rd rev. ed. George Bruce. 304p. 1981. 14.95 (ISBN 0-442-22336-6); pap. 7.95 (ISBN 0-442-22335-8). Van Nos Reinhold.

Harcourt Brace Intermediate Dictionary. LC 68-1860. (Illus.). (gr. 5-9). 1968. 7.50 o.p. (ISBN 0-15-233405-X, HJ). HarBraceJ.

Hard Boiled Virgin. Frances Newman. LC 80-16376. (Brown Thrasher Ser.). 300p. 1980. pap. 5.95 (ISBN 0-8203-0526-X). U of Ga Pr.

Hard Chains, Soft Women. J. D. Hardin. LC 80-83563. (Pinkerton Ser.). 224p. (Orig.). 1981. pap. 1.95 (ISBN 0-87216-799-2). Playboy Pbks.

Hard Choices: The American Free Enterprise System at Work. William Luker et al. (Illus.). (gr. 12). 1979. text ed. 9.95 (ISBN 0-88408-128-1); pap. text ed. 7.95 (ISBN 0-88408-123-0); tchrs.' manual avail. Sterling Swift.

Hard Core Crafts. Nancy Levine. (Illus.). 120p. 1976. pap. 7.95 o.p. (ISBN 0-345-24997-6). Ballantine.

Hard Corps: Studies in Leather & Sado Masochism. Michael Grumley & Ed Gallucci. LC 76-47487. (Illus.). 1977. pap. 7.95 o.p. (ISBN 0-525-47457-9). Dutton.

Hard Feelings. Don Bredes. 352p. 1981. pap. price not set. Bantam.

Hard Freight. Charles Wright. LC 73-6014. (Wesleyn Poetry Program: Vol. 69). 1973. pap. 4.95 (ISBN 0-8195-1069-6, Pub. by Wesleyan U Pr). Columbia U Pr.

Hard Head I & Other Outdoor Stories. Ray A. Heady. LC 80-83551. (Illus.). 312p. 1980. 12.95 (ISBN 0-913504-59-9). Lowell Pr.

Hard Hit. John Wainwright. 1979. pap. 1.95 o.p. (ISBN 0-425-04136-0). Berkley Pub.

Hard Hunting. Patrick Shaughnessy & Diane Swingle. 1978. 11.95 (ISBN 0-87691-270-6). Winchester Pr.

Hard Landscape in Brick. Cecil C. Handisyde. (Illus.). 1977. 16.00x (ISBN 0-85139-283-0, Pub. by Architectural Pr). Nichols Pub.

Hard Landscape in Concrete. Michael Gage & M. Vandenberg. LC 75-31700. 167p. 1975. 27.95 (ISBN 0-470-28913-9). Halsted Pr.

Hard Living on Clay Street. Joseph T. Howell. LC 73-79736. 440p. 1973. pap. 4.50 (ISBN 0-385-05317-7, Anch). Doubleday.

Hard Loving. Marge Piercy. LC 70-82544. (Wesleyan Poetry Program: Vol. 46). 1969. 10.00x (ISBN 0-8195-2046-2, Pub. by Wesleyan U Pr); pap. 4.95 (ISBN 0-8195-1046-7). Columbia U Pr.

Hard Luck Horse. Fern Brown. Ed. by Caroline Rubin. LC 75-31939. (Pilot Bks Ser). (Illus.). 128p. (gr. 4-7). 1975. 6.95g (ISBN 0-8075-3159-6). A Whitman.

Hard Men. Jon Burmeister. LC 77-9170. 1978. 8.95 o.p. (ISBN 0-312-36196-3). St Martin.

Hard Money Book: An Insider's Guide to Successful Investment in Currency, Gold, Silver, & Precious Stones. Steven K. Becky. (Illus.). 160p. 1980. 14.95 (ISBN 0-8015-3281-7, Hawthorn); pap. 7.95 (ISBN 0-8015-3282-5). Dutton.

Hard on the Road. Barbara Moore. LC 73-13091. 312p. 1974. 6.95 o.p. (ISBN 0-385-08191-X). Doubleday.

Hard Rain. Dinitia Smith. 207p. 1980. 9.95 (ISBN 0-8037-3409-3). Dial.

Hard Road to Klondike. Michael MacGowan. Tr. by Valentin Iremonger from Irish. 1973. pap. 6.95 (ISBN 0-7100-7686-X). Routledge & Kegan.

Hard Road West: Alone on the California Trail. Gwen Moffat. 1981. 12.95 (ISBN 0-670-36145-3). Viking Pr.

Hard Scrabble Harvest. Dahlov Ipcar. 32p. (gr. k-3). 1976. 6.95a (ISBN 0-385-00769-8); PLB (ISBN 0-385-00777-9). Doubleday.

Hard Scrabble: Observations on a Patch of Land. John Graves. 1976. autographed 6.95 o.p. (ISBN 0-685-77042-7). Encino Pr.

Hard Summer. Stephen Fugate. 224p. (Orig.). 1981. pap. 1.95 (ISBN 0-449-14389-9, GM). Fawcett.

Hard Times. Charles Dickens. 1954. 8.95x o.p. (ISBN 0-460-00292-9, Evman); pap. 2.50 o.p. (ISBN 0-460-01292-4). Dutton.

Hard Times. Charles Dickens. pap. 1.95. Bantam.

Hard Times & Arnie Smith. Clifton Adams. 1976. pap. 1.75 (ISBN 0-441-31721-9). Ace Bks.

Hard-To-Employ: European Programs. Beatrice G. Reubens. (Illus.). 1970. 20.00x (ISBN 0-231-03388-5). Columbia U Pr.

Hard to Kill. Laudia Leva. 1981. 6.95 (ISBN 0-533-04672-6). Vantage.

Hard Tomatoes, Hard Times: The Hightower Report. Jim Hightower et al. (Orig.). 1978. pap. 5.95 (ISBN 0-8467-0516-8, Pub. by Two Continents). Hippocrene Bks.

Hard Trade. Arthur Lyons. LC 80-19679. (Rinehart Suspense Novel Ser.). 264p. 1981. 10.95 (ISBN 0-686-69123-7). HR&W.

Hard Trail to Santa Fe. Tom West. 205p. (Orig.). 1980. pap. 1.95 (ISBN 0-89083-676-0). Zebra.

Hard Way Home. Richard Shaw. LC 76-54132. (gr. 6 up). 1977. Repr. 6.95 o.p. (ISBN 0-525-66529-3). Elsevier-Nelson.

Hard Words & Other Poems. Ursula LeGuin. LC 80-8210. 96p. 1981. 10.00 (ISBN 0-06-012579-9, HarpT); pap. 4.95 (ISBN 0-06-090848-3, CN 848). Har-Row.

Hardacre. C. L. Skelton. 1977. pap. 2.25 o.p. (ISBN 0-445-04026-2). Popular Lib.

Harder They Come. Michael Thelwell. 1980. pap. 7.95 (ISBN 0-394-17599-9, E749, Ever). Grove.

Hardest Lesson: Personal Stories of a School Desegregation Crisis. Pamela Bullard & Judith Stoia. 252p. (gr. 7 up). 1980. 8.95 (ISBN 0-316-11477-4). Little.

Hardinge of Penshurst: A Study in the Old Diplomacy. Briton C. Busch. (British Biography Ser.: Vol. 1). (Illus.). 381p. 1980. 19.50 (ISBN 0-208-01830-1). Shoe String.

Hardness Scale. Joyce Peseroff. LC 77-82224. 72p. 1977. pap. 4.95 (ISBN 0-914086-18-9). Alicejamesbooks.

Hardon. Ira Bruckner. (Illus.). 1980. pap. 6.00 (ISBN 0-916906-30-2). Konglomerati.

Hardpore Corn. Mukul Sharma. 1976. 9.00 (ISBN 0-89253-817-1); flexible cloth 4.80 (ISBN 0-89253-818-X). Ind-US Inc.

Hardships of a Woman Plant Worker. Shea J. Hovater. LC 79-66795. 71p. 1980. 5.95 (ISBN 0-533-04404-9). Vantage.

Hardtack Regiment: An Illustrated History of the 154th Regiment, New York State Infantry Volunteers. Mark H. Dunkelman & Michael J. Winey. LC 79-64502. (Illus.). 220p. 1981. 20.00 (ISBN 0-8386-3007-3). Fairleigh Dickinson.

Hardware-Software Design of Digital Systems. R. Bywater. 1981. 28.00 (ISBN 0-13-383950-8). P-H.

Hardwood County Rescue Squad. James O. Page. 132p. (Orig.). (gr. 8-12). 1980. pap. 5.75 (ISBN 0-936174-01-3). Backdraft.

Hardy: A Collection of Critical Essays. Ed. by A. Guerard. 1963. pap. 2.95 o.p. (ISBN 0-13-384065-4, Spec). P-H.

Hardy Boys. Mark Turner. (T.V. & Movie Tie-Ins Ser.). (gr. 4-12). 1979. PLB 5.95 (ISBN 0-87191-703-3); pap. 2.95 (ISBN 0-89812-035-7). Creative Ed.

Hardy Boys: Mystery of Smugglers Cove. Franklin W. Dixon. (Hardy Boys Ser.). 192p. (gr. 3-7). 1980. PLB 7.95 (ISBN 0-671-41117-9); pap. 1.95 (ISBN 0-671-41112-8). Wanderer Bks.

Hardy Boys: The Mummy Case. Franklin W. Dixon. (Hardy Boys Ser.). 192p. (gr. 3-7). 1980. PLB 7.95 (ISBN 0-671-41116-0); pap. 1.95 (ISBN 0-671-41111-X). Wanderer Bks.

Hardy Boys Who-Dunnit Mystery Book. Franklin W. Dixon. 64p. (gr. 3-7). 1980. pap. 3.95 (ISBN 0-671-95721-X). Wanderer Bks.

Hardy Holzman Pfeiffer. Michael Sorkin. 136p. 1981. 18.95 (ISBN 0-8230-7264-9, Whitney Lib). Watson-Guptill.

Hardy-Littlewood Method. R. C. Vaughan. (Cambridge Tracts in Mathematics: No. 80). 160p. Date not set. price not set (ISBN 0-521-23439-5). Cambridge U Pr.

Hardy Race of Men: America's Early Indians. Eileen T. Callan. LC 70-88111. (Curriculum Related Bks). (Illus.). (gr. 7 up). 1970. 4.95 o.p. (ISBN 0-15-233411-4, HJ). HarBraceJ.

Hardy's Poetry, Eighteen Sixty to Nineteen Twenty-Eight. Dennis Taylor. 256p. 1980. 20.00x (ISBN 0-231-05050-X). Columbia U Pr.

Hare & the Bear & Other Stories. Yasue Maiyagawa. LC 74-158840. (Illus.). (gr. k-3). 1971. 5.95 o.s.i. (ISBN 0-8193-0517-0, Four Winds); PLB 5.41 o.s.i. (ISBN 0-8193-0518-9). Schol Bk Serv.

Hare & the Tortoise: Clean Air Policy in the United States and Sweden. Lennart J. Lundqvist. 248p. 1980. 15.00 (ISBN 0-472-09310-X). U of Mich Pr.

Harian Creative Awards No. One: Featuring the Gospel According to Everyman by Baron Mikan. Ed. by Harry Barba. 220p. 1981. lib. bdg. 8.95 (ISBN 0-911906-09-6); pap. 2.95 (ISBN 0-911906-16-9). Harian Creative.

Harikhan Baba--Known, Unknown. Baba Hari Dass. LC 75-3838. (Illus.). 93p. (Orig.). 1975. pap. 1.95 (ISBN 0-918100-00-3). Sri Rama.

Harim & the Purdah: Studies of Oriental Women. Elizabeth Cooper. LC 68-23147. 1975. Repr. of 1915 ed. 20.00 (ISBN 0-8103-3167-5). Gale.

Hariyana: Part One,"the Yoga of Dejection". Harvey Meyers. LC 79-84779. (Illus.). 256p. (Orig.). 1979. pap. 6.00 (ISBN 0-934094-01-2). Omkara Pr.

Harlan Legacy. Jo Anne Creighton. 1977. pap. 1.50 o.p. (ISBN 0-445-03206-5). Popular Lib.

Harlan Miners Speak Report on Terrorism in the Kentucky Coal Fields. Theodore Dreiser et al. LC 70-107410. (Civil Liberties in American History Ser.). 1970. Repr. of 1932 ed. lib. bdg. 22.50 (ISBN 0-306-71889-8). Da Capo.

Harlem: A History of Broken Dreams. Warren J. Halliburton & Ernest Kaiser. LC 72-79392. 128p. 1974. pap. 2.50 (ISBN 0-385-05840-3, Zenith). Doubleday.

Harlem Gallery. Melvin Tolson. 1969. pap. 1.50 o.s.i. (ISBN 0-02-070910-2, Collier). Macmillan.

Harlem Globetrotters. Chuck Melville. (Illus.). 1978. 12.95 o.p. (ISBN 0-679-50803-1); pap. 6.95 o.p. (ISBN 0-679-50812-0). McKay.

Harlem Globetrotters Funniest Games. C. Gault & G. Gault. (ps-3). pap. 0.95 (ISBN 0-590-03000-0, Schol Pap). Schol Bk Serv.

Harlem: Its Origins & Early Annals. James Riker. LC 78-104551. Repr. of 1881 ed. lib. bdg. 38.50x (ISBN 0-8398-1759-2). Irvington.

Harlem Renaissance Remembered. Ed. by Arna Bontemps. LC 72-723. (Illus.). 1972. 6.95 o.p. (ISBN 0-396-06517-1). Dodd.

Harlem Summer. Mary E. Vroman. (gr. 4-6). 1968. pap. 1.25 o.p. (ISBN 0-425-03778-9, Highland). Berkley Pub.

Harlem: The Making of a Ghetto, 1890-1930. Gilbert Osofsky. LC 66-10913. 1966. 9.95 o.s.i. (ISBN 0-06-054962-9, HarpT). Har-Row.

Harlequin. Thelma Niklaus. 1960. 7.50 o.p. (ISBN 0-8076-0036-9). Braziller.

Harlequin & the Gift of Many Colors. Remy Charlip & Burton Supree. LC 76-136999. (Illus.). 48p. (ps-3). 1973. 7.95 (ISBN 0-590-17710-9, Four Winds); lib. bdg. 7.95 (ISBN 0-590-07710-4). Schol Bk Serv.

Harlequin Moth: Its Life Story. Millicent E. Selsam. LC 75-17862. (Illus.). 48p. (gr. 2-5). 1975. 8.25 (ISBN 0-688-22049-5); PLB 7.92 (ISBN 0-688-32049-X). Morrow.

Harley-Davidson Service--Repair Handbook: Sportster Series, 1959-1980. Clymer Publications. Ed. by Jeff Robinson. (Illus.). 1978. pap. 9.95 (ISBN 0-89287-126-1, M419). Clymer Pubns.

Harley-Davidson Service, Repair Handbook: All 74 Cu. in. Models, 1959-1979. 3rd ed. Ed. by Eric Jorgensen. (Illus.). 1977. pap. 9.95 (ISBN 0-89287-190-3, M420). Clymer Pubns.

Harlots, Rakes, & Bawds. Ed. by Walter H. Rubsamen. (Ballad Opera Ser.). 1974. lib. bdg. 50.00 (ISBN 0-8240-0902-9). Garland Pub.

Harlow's Modern Surgery for Nurses. 9th ed. Ed. by Selwyn Taylor. (Illus.). 1973. text ed. 28.50x (ISBN 0-433-32205-5). Intl Ideas.

Harmatan: A Poem. Paul Violi. LC 77-3648. 1977. pap. 4.00 (ISBN 0-915342-24-3). Sun.

Harmless Ruse. Alexandra Lord. (Orig.). 1981. pap. 1.50 (ISBN 0-440-13582-6). Dell.

Harmonic Analysis in Euclidean Spaces, 2 pts. Ed. by Guido Weiss & Steve Wainger. LC 79-12726. (Proceedings of Symposia in Pure Mathematics: Vol. 35). 1979. Set. 44.40 (ISBN 0-8218-1436-2); Pt. 1. 26.00 (ISBN 0-686-67540-1, PSPUM 35, 1); Pt. 2. pap. 24.00 (ISBN 0-8218-1438-9, PSPUM 35, 2). Am Math.

Harmonic Analysis of Functions of Several Complex Variable in the Classical Domains. rev. ed. L. K. Hua. LC 63-16769. 1979. 19.60 (ISBN 0-8218-1556-3, MMONO-6). Am Math.

Harmonic Material in Tonal Music: A Programmed Course, 2 vols. 3rd ed. Paul O. Harder. 1977. pap. text ed. 11.95 ea. o.s.i. Pt. 1 (ISBN 0-205-05708-X). Pt. 2 (ISBN 0-205-05711-X). Allyn.

Harmonic Materials in Tonal Music: A Programmed Course, Pts. 1 & 2. 4th ed. Harder. 320p. 1980. pap. 14.95 (5869250). Pt. 1 (ISBN 0-205-06925-8). Pt. 2 (ISBN 0-205-06945-2, 5869455). Allyn.

Harmonic Technique in the Rock Idiom. Richard Bobbitt. 1976. text ed. 16.95x o.p. (ISBN 0-534-00474-1); wkbk. 6.95x o.p. (ISBN 0-534-00478-4). Wadsworth Pub.

Harmonica for Fun & Profit. Hal Leighton. 1978. pap. 4.00 (ISBN 0-87980-354-1). Wilshire.

Harmonica Man. pap. 1.25 (ISBN 0-590-20799-7, Schol Pap). Schol Bk Serv.

Harmonica Man. Hans Zander. (gr. 1-3). 1977. pap. 1.50 (ISBN 0-590-10350-4, Schol Pap). Schol Bk Serv.

Harmonics of Nicomachus & the Pythagorean Tradition. Flora R. Levin. (American Philological Association, American Classical Studies). 1975. pap. 4.50 (ISBN 0-89130-241-7, 400401). Scholars Pr Ca.

Harmonics of Sound, Color & Vibration. William David. (Illus.). 160p. (Orig.). 1980. pap. 6.95 (ISBN 0-87516-411-0). De Vorss.

Harmonie der Gesichtszuege. Charles A. Baud. (Illus.). 1981. pap. 29.50 (ISBN 3-8055-0067-X). S Karger.

Harmonious Madness: A Study of Musical Metaphors in the Poetry of Coleridge, Shelley & Keats. Erland Anderson. (Salzburg Studies in English Literature, Romantic Reassessment Ser.: No. 12). 321p. 1975. pap. text ed. 25.00x (ISBN 0-391-01299-1). Humanities.

Harmonists: A Folk-Cultural Approach. Hilda A. Kring. (ATLA Monograph: No. 3). 1973. 10.00 (ISBN 0-8108-0603-7). Scarecrow.

Harmonium Manual. M. Harris & N. Leschot. LC 79-54823. (Illus., Orig.). Date not set. pap. cancelled (ISBN 0-89793-016-9). Hunter Hse.

Harmonization at the Piano. 4th ed. Arthur Frackenpohl. 275p. 1981. pap. text ed. write for info. (ISBN 0-697-03559-X). Wm C Brown.

Harmonization in the EEC. Ed. by Carol C. Twitchett. 1980. write for info. (ISBN 0-312-36309-5). St Martin.

Harmony. Heinrich Schenker. Ed. by Oswald Jonas. Tr. by Elizabeth M. Borgese. LC 54-11213. 396p. 1980. pap. 8.95 (ISBN 0-226-73734-9, P894, Phoen). U of Chicago Pr.

Harmony from Discords: A Life of Sir John Denham. Brendan O Hehir. LC 68-27162. 1968. 20.00x (ISBN 0-520-00953-3). U of Cal Pr.

Harmony in Horsemanship. J. Talbot-Ponsonby. (Illus.). 10.50 (ISBN 0-85131-169-5, Dist. by Sporting Book Center). J A Allen.

Harmony in Marriage. Leland Foster Wood. 1979. 3.95 (ISBN 0-8007-1087-8). Revell.

Harmony of Deeper Music: Posthumous Poems of Edgar Lee Masters. Ed. by Frank K. Robinson. LC 79-108963. (Tower Poetry Ser.: No. 10). 1976. commemorative ed. 15.00 (ISBN 0-87959-021-1); 7.50 (ISBN 0-87959-091-2); pap. 5.00 (ISBN 0-87959-096-3). U of Tex Hum Res.

Harmony of Maine. Supply Belcher. Ed. by H. Wiley Hitchcock. LC 77-169607. (Earlier American Music Ser: Vol. 6). 104p. 1972. Repr. of 1794 ed. lib. bdg. 18.50 (ISBN 0-306-77306-6). Da Capo.

Harmony of the Gospels. Ralph D. Heim. LC 47-2807. 228p. 1974. pap. 4.95 (ISBN 0-8006-1494-1, 1-1494). Fortress.

Harmony of the World: Chinese Poems. rev. & enl. ed. Tr. by David Lattimore. (Illus.). 1980. pap. 4.50 (ISBN 0-914278-31-2). Cooper Beech.

Harmony on the Connoquenessing: George Rapp's First American Harmony: 1803-1815. Karl J. Arndt. LC 80-828. (Documentary History of Rapp's Harmony Society, 1700-1916 Ser.). (Illus.). 1072p. (Eng. & Ger.). 1981. 38.00 (ISBN 0-937640-01-8). Harmony Soc.

Harness Makers' Illustrated Manual. William Fitz-Gerald. (Illus.). 1977. Repr. of 1875 ed. 15.00x (ISBN 0-88427-014-9, Dist. by Caroline House Pubs). North River.

Harness Maker's Illustrated Manual. William Fitz-Gerald. 15.00. Green Hill.

Harnessing Ocean Energies: Tapping Ocean Energies to Produce Inexhaustible, Pollution-Free Electricity. Roger Charlier. 1977. Repr. soft cover 8.00 (ISBN 0-686-21178-2). Maple Mont.

Harnessing the Sun: The Story of Solar Energy. David Knight. (Illus.). 128p. (gr. 5-9). 1976. PLB 6.96 (ISBN 0-688-32070-8). Morrow.

Harney Papers. Ed. by Frank G. Black & Renee M. Black. (Publications on Social History Ser: No. 5). 1969. text ed. 25.25x (ISBN 90-232-0270-8). Humanities.

Harold & the Purple Crayon. Crockett Johnson. LC 55-7683. (Trophy Picture Bks.). (Illus.). 64p. (ps-3). 1981. pap. 1.95 (ISBN 0-06-443022-7, Trophy). Har-Row.

Harold D. Lasswell on Political Sociology. Harold D. Lasswell. Ed. by Dwaine Marvick. LC 76-22961. (Heritage of Sociology Ser.). vi, 456p. 1980. pap. text ed. 7.00x (ISBN 0-226-46921-2). U of Chicago Pr.

Harold Lloyd: The King of Daredevil Comedy. Adam Reilly. (Illus.). 1977. 14.95 o.s.i. (ISBN 0-02-601940-X). Macmillan.

Harold Monro & the Poetry Bookshop. Joy Grant. 1967. 18.50x (ISBN 0-520-00512-0). U of Cal Pr.

Harold Pinter. Arnold P. Hinchcliffe. (English Authors Ser.: No. 51). lib. bdg. 9.95 (ISBN 0-8057-1448-0). Twayne.

Harold Pinter. rev. ed. Arnold P. Hinchliffe. (English Authors Ser.: No. 51). 1981. lib. bdg. 9.95 (ISBN 0-8057-6784-3). Twayne.

Harold Sets a Record. Thomas Woldum & Robert Gadbois. LC 77-1690. (Books by Children for Children). (Illus.). (gr. 2-5). 1977. PLB 6.45 (ISBN 0-87191-612-6). Creative Ed.

Harold, the Easter Rat. D. R. Brauer. 1981. 4.95 (ISBN 0-8062-1631-X). Carlton.

Harold Urey. Alvin Silverstein & Virginia Silverstein. LC 74-125573. (Great Men of Science Ser). (gr. 7-10). 1971. 4.50 o.p. (ISBN 0-381-99705-7, A32700, JD-J). John Day.

Harold's ABC. Crockett Johnson. LC 63-14444. (Trophy Picture Bks.). (Illus.). 64p. (ps-3). 1981. pap. 1.95 (ISBN 0-06-443023-5, Trophy). Har-Row.

Harold's Circus. Crockett Johnson. LC 59-5318. (Trophy Picture Bks.). (Illus.). 64p. (ps-3). 1981. pap. 1.95 (ISBN 0-06-443024-3, Trophy). Har-Row.

Harold's Trip to the Sky. Crockett Johnson. LC 57-9262. (Trophy Picture Bks.). (Illus.). 64p. (ps-3). 1981. pap. 1.95 (ISBN 0-06-443025-1, Trophy). Har-Row.

Harp: Its History, Technique & Repertoire. Roslyn Rensch. (Illus.). 246p. 1971. 40.00x (ISBN 0-7156-0467-8, Pub. by Duckworth England). Biblio Dist.

Harper & Row's Complete Field Guide to North American Wildlife: Eastern Edition. Ed. by Henry H. Collins, Jr. LC 80-8198. (Illus.). 810p. 1981. 17.50 (ISBN 0-690-01977-7, HarpT); flexible vinyl cover 12.95 (ISBN 0-690-01969-6). Har-Row.

Harper & Row's Complete Field Guide to North American Wildlife: Western Edition. Ed. by Jay E. Ransom. LC 79-2635. (Illus.). 910p. 1981. 17.50 o.p. (ISBN 0-690-01979-3, HarpT); flexible vinyl cover 12.95 o.p. (ISBN 0-690-01971-8). Har-Row.

Harper Anthology of Poetry. John F. Nims. (Illus.). 864p. 1980. text ed. write for info. (ISBN 0-06-044846-6, 0-06-44874, HarpC); pap. text ed. 10.50 scp (ISBN 0-06-044846-6). Har-Row.

Harper Handbook of College Composition. 4th ed. George S. Wykoff & Harry Shaw. LC 69-10552. (Illus.). 1969. text ed. 10.50 scp (ISBN 0-06-047261-8, HarpC); scp wkbk. 6.95 (ISBN 0-06-047262-6); instructor's guide & key to selected exercises avail. (ISBN 0-06-367263-4). Har-Row.

Harper's Encyclopaedia of United States History, from 458 A. D. to 1905: With Special Contributions Covering Every Phase of American History & Development by Eminent Authorities, 10 vols. new ed. Benson J. Lossing. LC 73-22093. (Illus.). 1974. Repr. of 1915 ed. 265.00 (ISBN 0-8103-3954-4). Gale.

Harper's Encyclopedia of Bible Life. rev ed. Madeleine S. Miller & J. Lane Miller. Ed. by Boyce M. Bennett, Jr. & David H. Scott. LC 78-4752. (Illus.). 1978. 16.95 (ISBN 0-06-065676-X, HarpR). Har-Row.

Harper's English Grammar. John B. Opdycke. 1977. pap. 1.95 (ISBN 0-445-08387-5). Popular Lib.

Harper's Ferry. Barrie Stavis. LC 67-23982. 1967. 7.95 o.p. (ISBN 0-498-06728-9). A S Barnes.

Harpers Ferry Armory & the New Technology: The Challenge of Change. Merritt R. Smith. 1980. 19.50 o.p. (ISBN 0-8014-0984-5); pap. 7.95 o.p. Cornell U Pr.

Harpers Ferry: Time Remembered. Martin Conway. Ed. by Deborah Mehrkam. 160p. 1980. 13.95 (ISBN 0-938634-00-3). Carabelle.

Harper's Introduction to the Bible. Gerald Hughes & Stephen Travis. LC 80-8607. (Illus.). 144p. (Orig.). 1981. pap. 9.95 (ISBN 0-06-064078-2). Har-Row.

Harper's World of the New Testament. Edwin Yamauchi. LC 80-8606. (Illus.). 144p. (Orig.). 1981. pap. 9.95 (ISBN 0-06-069708-3, HarpR). Har-Row.

Harpist in the Wind. Patricia McKillip. LC 78-11410. (Illus.). (gr. 6 up). 1979. 8.95 (ISBN 0-689-30687-3, Argo). Atheneum.

Harpoon. Olaf Ruhen. 1975. pap. 1.25 o.p. (ISBN 0-685-61046-2, LB316, Leisure Bks). Nordon Pubns.

Harps in the Wind: The Story of The Singing Hutchinsons. Carol Brink. (The Story of the Singing Hutchinsons). (Illus.). v, 312p. 1980. Repr. of 1947 ed. lib. bdg. 27.50 (ISBN 0-306-76024-X). Da Capo.

Harpsichord & Clavichord. Raymond Russell. (Illus.). 1980. 30.00 (ISBN 0-684-16466-3, ScribT). Scribner.

Harpstrings & Confessions: Machine-Style Politics in the Irish Republic. Mart Bax. 1977. pap. text ed. 23.25x (ISBN 90-232-1481-1). Humanities.

Harrap Opera Guide. Alexander F. Morley. 320p. 1971. 15.00 (ISBN 0-245-50509-1). Dufour.

Harrap's New German Grammar. Charles B. Johnson. 1971. pap. text ed. 13.50x (ISBN 0-245-52989-6). Intl Ideas.

Harried Leisure Class. Staffan B. Linder. LC 73-92909. 1970. 17.50x (ISBN 0-231-03302-8); pap. 6.00x (ISBN 0-231-08649-0). Columbia U Pr.

Harried Staffer's Guide to Current Welfare Reform Proposals. Frank Levy. (Welfare Reform Policy Analysis Ser.: No. 4). 83p. 1978. pap. 3.50 (ISBN 0-87766-231-2, 23400). Urban Inst.

Harriet. Joan Mellows. 1977. pap. 1.50 o.p. (ISBN 0-449-23209-3, Crest). Fawcett.

Harriet Beecher Stowe. John R. Adams. (U. S. Authors Ser.: No. 42). 1963. lib. bdg. 9.95 (ISBN 0-8057-0700-X). Twayne.

Harriet Dark: Branwell Bronte's Lost Novel. Barbara Rees. 1980. pap. 1.95 (ISBN 0-446-90356-6). Warner Bks.

Harriet Hanson Robinson & Her Family: A Chronicle of Nineteenth-Century New England Life. Claudia L. Bushman. LC 80-54470. 320p. 1981. 16.50 (ISBN 0-87451-193-3). U Pr of New Eng.

Harriet Lane, First Lady of the White House. Mary V. Shelly & Sandra H. Munro. LC 80-20151. (Illus.). 48p. (gr. 4-6). 1980. 6.95 (ISBN 0-915010-29-1). Sutter House.

Harriet Martineau: The Woman & Her Work, Eighteen Hundred & Two to Eighteen Seventy-Six. Valerie Pichanick. (Women & Culture Ser.). 336p. 1980. 15.00x (ISBN 0-472-10002-5). U of Mich Pr.

Harriet Monroe. Daniel J. Cahill. (U. S. Authors Ser.: No. 222). 1973. lib. bdg. 10.95 (ISBN 0-8057-0515-5). Twayne.

Harriet Said. Beryl Bainbridge. pap. 1.50 (ISBN 0-451-06058-X, W6058, Sig). NAL.

Harriet Tubman. Matthew G. Grant. LC 73-15849. 1974. PLB 5.95 (ISBN 0-87191-309-7). Creative Ed.

Harriet Tubman: Conductor on the Underground Railroad. Ann Petry. (gr. 6-9). 1971. pap. 1.95 (ISBN 0-671-42167-0). Archway.

Harriette Arnow. Wilton Eckley. (U. S. Authors Ser.: No. 245). 1974. lib. bdg. 10.95 (ISBN 0-8057-0023-4). Twayne.

Harris-Indiana Industrial Directory 1981. Ed. by Kathi Graeser. (Illus., Annual). 1981. 36.40 (ISBN 0-916512-26-6). Harris Pub.

Harris Michigan Industrial Directory. rev. ed. Ed. by Peggy Edmonds. (Illus., Annual). 1981. 58.75 (ISBN 0-916512-15-0). Harris Pub.

Harris Nineteen Seventy-Two American Women's Opinion Poll. Louis Harris & Associates, Inc. 1975. codebk. 12.00 (ISBN 0-89138-114-7). ICPSR.

Harris Postage Stamp Catalog: Fall-Winter 1980-1981. Ed. by Joseph M. Heery. (Illus.). 362p. (Orig.). 1980. pap. 2.95 (ISBN 0-937458-02-3). Harris & Co.

Harrison Affair. Gerald Seymour. 1981. pap. 2.95 (ISBN 0-440-13566-4). Dell.

Harrison Family Genealogy: Sixteen Seventy-Three to Nineteen Seventy-Six. Katherine E. Bundick. (Illus.). 1977. 27.50x (ISBN 0-685-89824-5). Va Bk.

Harrison's Principles of Internal Medicine. Kurt J. Isselbacher et al. 400p. 1981. text ed. 30.00 (ISBN 0-07-032131-0). McGraw.

Harrison's Principles of Internal Medicine. 9th ed. Ed. by Kurt J. Isselbacher et al. (Illus.). 1980. text ed. 45.00 1 vol. ed. (ISBN 0-07-032068-3); text ed. 55.00 2 vol. ed. (ISBN 0-07-032069-1); medical review bk. 25.00 (ISBN 0-07-051657-X). McGraw Pretest.

Harrison's Principles of Internal Medicine Patient Management Cases PreTest Self-Assessment & Review. Ed. by Alfred J. Bollet. (Illus.). 248p. (Orig.). 1980. 25.00 (ISBN 0-07-051647-2). McGraw Pretest.

Harrow Railway Disaster 1952. L. F. Coombs. 1977. 14.95 (ISBN 0-7153-7409-5). David & Charles.

Harry & Shellburt. Dorothy O. Van Woerkom. LC 77-5352. (Ready-to-Read Ser.). (Illus.). (gr. 1-4). 1977. 7.95 (ISBN 0-02-791290-6, 79129). Macmillan.

Harry & the Terrible Whatzit. Dick Gackenbach. LC 76-40205. (Illus.). (ps-2). 1977. 6.95 (ISBN 0-395-28795-2, Clarion). HM.

Harry & Tonto. Josh Greenfield & Paul Mazursky. 1974. pap. 1.25 o.p. (ISBN 0-445-00214-X). Popular Lib.

Harry Anderson: The Man Behind the Paintings. Raymond H. Woolsey & Ruth Anderson. LC 76-15700. (Illus.). 1976. 7.95 (ISBN 0-8280-0047-6). Review & Herald.

Harry Byrd & the Changing Face of Virginia Politics, 1945-1966. J. Harvie Wilkinson, 3rd. LC 68-22731. (Illus.). 410p. 1968. 10.95x (ISBN 0-8139-0239-8). U Pr of Va.

Harry Callahan: Color. Harry Callahan. Ed. by Robert Tow & Ricker Winsor. (Illus.). 144p. 1980. 85.00 (ISBN 0-936554-00-2). Matrix Pubns.

Harry Clarke: His Graphic Art. Nicola G. Bowe. (Illus.). 120p. 1980. text ed. 39.00x (ISBN 0-85105-359-9, Dolmen Pr). Humanities.

Harry Emerson Fosdick's Art of Preaching: An Anthology. Lionel Crocker. (Illus.). 296p. 1971. pap. 19.75 photocopy ed. spiral (ISBN 0-398-00368-8). C C Thomas.

Harry Four Eyes. Nancy Kelton. LC 76-44244. (When They Were Young Ser.). (Illus.). (gr. k-3). 1977. PLB 7.95 (ISBN 0-8172-0453-9). Raintree Pubs.

Harry Hosier: United Methodist Circuit Rider. Warren T. Smith. LC 80-54008. 64p. 1980. pap. 2.95x (ISBN 0-8358-0422-4). Upper Room.

Harry Is a Scaredy-Cat. Byron Barton. LC 73-6039. (Illus.). 32p. (ps-2). 1974. 5.95g o.s.i. (ISBN 0-02-708440-X, 70844). Macmillan.

Harry L. Russell & Agricultural Science in Wisconsin. Edward H. Beardsley. (Illus.). 1969. 20.00x (ISBN 0-299-05470-5). U of Wis Pr.

Harry S. Truman. John Hedley. Ed. by I. E. Cadenhead. LC 76-54969. (Shapers of History Ser.). 1979. pap. text ed. 16.95 (ISBN 0-8120-5136-X). Barron.

Harry S. Truman in Family. Margaret Truman. LC 80-70224. 256p. 1981. 12.95 (ISBN 0-87795-313-9). Arbor Hse.

Harry S. Truman: The Man Who Walked with Giants. David Melton. (Illus.). 128p. (gr. 5 up). 1980. 20.00 (ISBN 0-8309-0293-7). Independence Pr.

Harry Stottlemeier's Discovery. rev. ed. Matthew Lipman. 96p. (gr. 5-6). 1980. pap. 6.00 (ISBN 0-916834-06-9). Inst Adv Philo.

Harry the Hider. Carol Nicklaus. LC 78-10250. (Easy-Read Story Bks.). (Illus.). (gr. k-3). 1979. 3.95 (ISBN 0-531-02381-8); PLB 6.45 s&l (ISBN 0-531-02298-6). Watts.

Harry the Hider. Carol Nicklaus. (Illus.). (gr. k-3). 1980. pap. 1.50 (ISBN 0-380-49189-3, 49189, Camelot). Avon.

Harry Truman: Last of His Kind, an Informal Portrait. Charles Robbins. (Illus.). 1979. 10.95 (ISBN 0-688-03447-0). Morrow.

Harry y el Terrible Quiensabeque (Harry & the Terrible Whatzit) Gackenbach. (ps-3). pap. 1.95 (ISBN 0-590-12116-2, Schol Pap). Schol Bk Serv.

Harry's Game. Gerald Seymour. 1977. pap. 1.95 o.p. (ISBN 0-449-23019-8, Crest). Fawcett.

Hart Crane. Vincent Quinn. (U. S. Authors Ser.: No. 35). 1963. lib. bdg. 10.95 (ISBN 0-8057-0164-8). Twayne.

Hart Crane: A Collection of Critical Essays. Alan Trachtenberg. (Twentieth Century Views Ser.). 224p. 1981. 13.95 (ISBN 0-13-383935-4, Spec); pap. 5.95 (ISBN 0-13-383927-3). P-H.

Hart Crane: An Introduction to the Poetry. Herbert A. Leibowitz. LC 68-13559. 1968. 17.50x (ISBN 0-231-03014-2); pap. 5.00 (ISBN 0-231-08670-9). Columbia U Pr.

Hart Crane & Yvor Winters: Their Literary Correspondence. Thomas Parkinson. 1978. 12.95 (ISBN 0-520-03538-0). U of Cal Pr.

Hart Crane's Divided Vision: An Analysis of "The Bridge". Helge N. Nilsen. 192p. 1980. pap. 20.00x (ISBN 82-00-01938-1). Universitet.

Harter's Picture Archive for Collage & Illustration: Over 300 Nineteenth Century Cuts. Jim Harter. 1978. pap. 5.00 (ISBN 0-486-23659-5). Dover.

Harting's Hints on Hawks. James E. Harting. 12.95 o.p. (ISBN 0-8231-2019-8). Branford.

Hartree-Fock Method for Atoms: A Numerical Approach. Charlotte F. Fischer. LC 76-50115. 1977. 35.00 (ISBN 0-471-25990-X, Pub. by Wiley-Interscience). Wiley.

Hart's Bridge. Sherman Paul. LC 76-188133. 320p. 1972. 15.00 (ISBN 0-252-00257-1). U of Ill Pr.

Harvard Encyclopedia of American Ethnic Groups. Ed. by Stephan Thernstrom et al. 1980. 60.00 (ISBN 0-674-37512-2). Harvard U Pr.

Harvard Guide to American History, 2 vols. rev. ed. Ed. by Frank Freidel & Richard K. Showman. LC 72-81272. 1312p. 1974. 45.00x (ISBN 0-674-37560-2, Belknap Pr); pap. 12.50 one-vol. ed. (ISBN 0-674-37555-6). Harvard U Pr.

Harvard Lampoon: Big Book of College Life. Harvard Lampoon, Inc. LC 77-15165. 1978. pap. 5.95 (ISBN 0-385-13446-0, Dolp). Doubleday.

Harvard Lectures on the Vergilian Age. Robert S. Conway. LC 67-13861. 1928. 9.50x (ISBN 0-8196-0182-9). Biblo.

Harvard Studies in Classical Philology, Vol. 84. Ed. by D. Shackleton Bailey. LC 44-32100. 1980. text ed. 30.00x (ISBN 0-674-37931-4). Harvard U Pr.

Harvest & the Reapers: Oral Traditions of Kentucky. Kenneth Clarke & Mary Clarke. LC 74-7872. (Kentucky Bicentennial Bookshelf Ser.). 112p. 1974. 5.95 (ISBN 0-8131-0201-4). U Pr of Ky.

Harvest Feast. rev. ed. Ed. by Wilhelmina Harper. (Illus.). (gr. 5 up). 1967. PLB 7.95 o.p. (ISBN 0-525-31510-1). Dutton.

Harvest Mouse. Stephen Harris. (Mammal Society Ser.). (Illus.). 50p. 1980. 6.95 (ISBN 0-7137-0897-2, Pub. by Blandford Pr England). Sterling.

Harvest of Horrors: Classic Tales of the Macabre. Ed. by Eric Protter. LC 79-56028. (Illus.). 286p. 1980. 12.50 (ISBN 0-8149-0755-5). Vanguard.

Harvest of Russian Children's Literature. Ed. by Miriam Morton. (Illus.). (ps up). 1967. 27.50x (ISBN 0-520-00886-3); pap. 5.95 (ISBN 0-520-01745-5, CAL199). U of Cal Pr.

Harvest Yet to Reap: A History of Prairie Women. Ed. by Linda Rasmussen et al. (Illus.). 240p. 1976. pap. 12.50 (ISBN 0-88961-050-9). U of Nebr Pr.

Harvester. Gene S. Porter. 1977. 9.95x (ISBN 0-89967-004-0). Harmony & Co.

Harvester. Gene S. Porter. 560p. 1977. PLB 22.50x (ISBN 0-89966-225-0). Buccaneer Bks.

Harvesting & Handling California Table Grapes for Market. Klayton E. Nelson. LC 79-51948. (Illus.). 1979. pap. 6.00x (ISBN 0-931876-33-8, 4095). Ag Sci Pubns.

Harvey & the Oxford Physiologists: A Study of Scientific Ideas & Social Interaction. Robert G. Frank, Jr. (Illus.). 1981. 27.50x (ISBN 0-520-03906-8). U of Cal Pr.

Harvey Cushing: A Biography. John F. Fulton. Ed. by I. Bernard Cohen. LC 79-7961. (Three Centuries of Science in America Ser.). (Illus.). 1980. Repr. of 1946 ed. lib. bdg. 62.00x (ISBN 0-405-12542-9). Arno.

Harvey Fergusson. William T. Pilkington. (U. S. Authors Ser.: No. 257). 1975. lib. bdg. 10.95 (ISBN 0-8057-7157-3). Twayne.

Harvey Lectures. Harvey Society of New York. Incl. Ser. 47. 1951-1952. 1953 (ISBN 0-12-312047-0); Ser. 48. 1952-1953. 1954 (ISBN 0-12-312048-9); Ser. 49. 1953-1954. 1955 (ISBN 0-12-312049-7); Ser. 50. 1954-1955. 1956 (ISBN 0-12-312050-0); Ser. 51. 1955-1956. 1957 (ISBN 0-12-312051-9); Ser. 52. 1956-1957. 1958 (ISBN 0-12-312052-7); Ser. 53. 1957-1958. 1959 (ISBN 0-12-312053-5); Ser. 54. 1958-1959. 1960 (ISBN 0-12-312054-3); Ser. 55. 1959-1960. 1961 (ISBN 0-12-312055-1); Ser. 56. 1960-1961. 1961 (ISBN 0-12-312056-X); Ser. 57. 1961-1962. 1962 (ISBN 0-12-312057-8); Ser. 58. 1962-1963. 1963. 16.50 (ISBN 0-12-312058-6); Ser. 59. 1963-1964. 1965 (ISBN 0-12-312059-4); Ser. 60. 1964-1965. 1966. o.s.i. (ISBN 0-12-312060-8); Ser. 61. 1965-1966. 1967 (ISBN 0-12-312061-6); Ser. 62. 1966-1967. 1968 (ISBN 0-12-312062-4); Ser. 63. 1967-1968. 1969 (ISBN 0-12-312063-2); Ser. 64. 1968-1969. 1970 (ISBN 0-12-312064-0); Ser. 65. 1969-1970. 1971 (ISBN 0-12-312065-9); Ser. 66. 1970-1971. 1972 (ISBN 0-12-312066-7); Ser. 67. 1971-1972. 1973 (ISBN 0-12-312067-5); Ser. 68. 1972-1973. 1974. 21.50 (ISBN 0-12-312068-3); Ser. 69. 1973-1974. 1975. 20.00 (ISBN 0-12-312069-1); Ser. 70. 1974-1975. 1976. 17.50 (ISBN 0-12-312070-5); Ser. 71. 1978. 22.50 (ISBN 0-12-312071-3); Ser. 72. 1979. 25.50 (ISBN 0-12-312072-1); Ser. 73. 1979. 24.00 (ISBN 0-12-312073-X). unless otherwise indicated 17.00 ea. Acad Pr.

Harvey Lectures: Nineteen Seventy-Nine. Ed. by Donald M. Marcus. 1980. write for info. (ISBN 0-12-312075-6). Acad Pr.

Harvey's Hideout. Russell Hoban. LC 80-15292. (Illus.). 48p. (ps-3). 1980. Repr. of 1969 ed. 8.95 (ISBN 0-590-07767-8, Four Winds). Schol Bk Serv.

Harvey's Law of Real Property & Title Closings, 3 vols. rev. ed. David C. Harvey. Ed. by Elliot L. Biskind. LC 66-23512. 1966. looseleaf with 1980 suppl. 145.00 (ISBN 0-87632-058-2). Boardman.

Has God Given You up. Philip B. Knoche. (Uplook Ser). 1970. pap. 0.75 (ISBN 0-8163-0257-X, 08165-3). Pacific Pr Pub Assn.

Has Man a Future? Bertrand Russell. 1961. 8.95 (ISBN 0-04-327015-8). Allen Unwin.

Hasan. Piers Anthony. LC 77-24589. (Illus.). 1977. lib. bdg. 10.95x (ISBN 0-89370-115-7); pap. 4.95 (ISBN 0-89370-215-3). Borgo Pr.

Hashish & Mental Illness. J. J. Moreau et al. Ed. by H. Peters & G. Nahas. Tr. by G. J. Barnett from Fr. LC 76-107227. Orig. Title: Du Haschish et De l'Alienation Mentale. 1973. pap. 18.00 (ISBN 0-911216-14-6). Raven.

Hashish: Studies of Long-Term Use. Ed. by Stefanis et al. LC 76-19848. 1977. 15.50 (ISBN 0-89004-138-5). Raven.

Hashknife of Stormy River. Wilbur C. Tuttle. 252p. 1980. Repr. of 1936 ed. lib. bdg. 12.95x (ISBN 0-89968-132-8). Lightyear.

Hashknife of the Double Bar Eight. Wilbur C. Tuttle. 244p. 1980. Repr. of 1936 ed. lib. bdg. 12.95x (ISBN 0-89968-133-6). Lightyear.

Haskell County Texas. Rex Felker. (Illus.). 350p. 1975. 17.95 (ISBN 0-89015-097-4). Nortex Pr.

Hassan. James E. Flecker. LC 66-25895. (Orig.). 1968. 1.95x (ISBN 0-87830-054-6). Theatre Arts.

Hasselblad Manual. Ernst Wildi. (Illus.). 468p. 1980. 34.95 (ISBN 0-240-51042-9). Focal Pr.

Hasselblad System. R. Gordon Taylor. (Illus.). 64p. 1980. pap. 5.00 (ISBN 0-240-51087-9). Focal Pr.

Hastings Conspiracy. Alfred Coppel. LC 80-10366. 352p. 1980. 12.95 (ISBN 0-03-056058-6). HR&W.

Hasty Bunch. Robert McAlmon. 1978. pap. 1.95 o.p. (ISBN 0-445-04314-8). Popular Lib.

Hasyarnava-the Ocean of Laughter. Jagadishvhra Bhattacarya. Tr. by David Nelson & Ramdayal Munda. (Translated from Sanskrit). 1976. 8.00 (ISBN 0-89253-805-8); flexible cloth 4.80 (ISBN 0-89253-806-6). Ind-US Inc.

Hat. Tomi Ungerer. LC 78-999134. (Illus.). (gr. k-3). 1970. 5.95 o.s.i. (ISBN 0-8193-0378-X, Four Winds); PLB 5.41 o.s.i. (ISBN 0-8193-0379-8). Schol Bk Serv.

Hat Book. Alan Couldridge & Celia Dowell. 128p. 1981. 16.95 (ISBN 0-13-384222-3, Spec); pap. 8.95 (ISBN 0-13-384214-2). P-H.

Hat Book. Leonard Shortall. (Illus.). 24p. (gr. k-1). 1976. PLB 5.38 (ISBN 0-307-68976-X, Golden Pr). Western Pub.

Hat for the Queen. Joan C. Bacon. (Eager Readers Ser.). (Illus.). (gr. k-3). 1975. PLB 5.00 (ISBN 0-307-60802-6, Golden Pr). Western Pub.

Hat on the Bed. John O'Hara. 416p. 1975. pap. 1.50 o.p. (ISBN 0-445-03068-2). Popular Lib.

Hatcher's Notebook. rev. ed. Julian S. Hatcher. LC 62-12654. (Illus.). 1962. 19.95 (ISBN 0-8117-0795-4). Stackpole.

Hatchet Man. William Marshall. 1977. 6.95 o.p. (ISBN 0-03-016901-1). HR&W.

Hatchet Man. William Marshall. 1978. pap. 1.50 o.p. (ISBN 0-445-04146-3). Popular Lib.

Hatchett. Lee McGraw. 1976. pap. 1.50 o.p. (ISBN 0-345-25103-2). Ballantine.

Hateful Contraries: Studies in Literature & Criticism. William K. Wimsatt. LC 65-11823. 280p. 1965. 11.00x (ISBN 0-8131-1099-8); pap. 4.50 (ISBN 0-8131-0110-7, KP110). U Pr of Ky.

Hatha Yoga. Eva Ruchpaul. LC 68-23738. (Funk & W Bk.). 1969. 7.95 o.s.i. (ISBN 0-308-70418-5, TYC-T). T Y Crowell.

Hatha Yoga for Total Health: Handbook of Practical Programs. Sue Luby. (Illus.). 1977. pap. 13.50 (ISBN 0-13-384123-5). P-H.

Hathaways Twelve Hundred to Nineteen-Eighty. Elizabeth S. Versailles. 621p. (YA) 1980. lib. bdg. write for info. Versailles.

Hats Galore. W. G. Alton. (Make & Play Ser.). (Illus.). 48p. (gr. k-6). 1976. pap. 1.50 (ISBN 0-263-05936-7). Transatlantic.

Hattie, the Backstage Bat. Don Freeman. (Illus.). (gr. k-3). 1970. PLB 4.95 o.p. (ISBN 0-670-36253-0). Viking Pr.

Hattie the Backstage Bat. Don Freeman. (Illus.). (gr. k-1). 1973. pap. 0.95 o.p. (ISBN 0-670-05082-2, Puffin). Penguin.

Hatznea Lechet: Walk Humbly. Abraham Shumsky & Adaia Shumsky. Ed. by Jack D. Spiro. (Mah Tov Hebrew Teaching Ser.: Bk. 3). (Illus.). (gr. 4). 1971. text ed. 5.00 (ISBN 0-8074-0181-1, 405307); tchrs'. guide 3.50 (ISBN 0-8074-0182-X, 205308); wkbk. 3.50 (ISBN 0-8074-0183-8, 405306). UAHC.

Haulin' Philip Finch. 1977. pap. 1.75 o.p. (ISBN 0-345-25102-4). Ballantine.

Hauling Out & Winterizing. David MacLean. (Boatowners How-to Guides). (Illus.). 1977. pap. 5.95 (ISBN 0-8306-6944-2). TAB Bks.

Haunted. Judith St. George. 156p. (YA) (gr. 7-12). 1980. 7.95 (ISBN 0-399-20736-8). Putnam.

Haunted Computer & the Android Pope. Ray Bradbury. LC 80-2724. 128p. 1981. 8.95 (ISBN 0-394-51444-0). Knopf.

Haunted Derbyshire. Clarence Daniel. (Illus.). 80p. (Orig.). (gr. 6 up). 1975. pap. write for info. (ISBN 0-913714-40-2). Legacy Bks.

Haunted House. Peggy Parish. LC 71-119833. (Illus.). (gr. 2-4). 1971. 8.95 (ISBN 0-02-769960-9). Macmillan.

Haunted House. Peggy Parish. (gr. k-6). 1981. pap. 1.50 (ISBN 0-440-43459-9, YB). Dell.

Haunted House. Jan Pienkowski. (Illus.). (ps-3). 1979. 8.95 (ISBN 0-525-31520-9). Dutton.

Haunted Houses. Camille Flammarion. LC 76-159957. (Tower Bks). 1971. Repr. of 1924 ed. 20.00 (ISBN 0-8103-3911-0). Gale.

Haunted Houses. Larry Kettelkamp. (Illus.). (gr. 5-9). 1969. 7.25 (ISBN 0-688-21377-4); PLB 6.96 (ISBN 0-688-31377-9). Morrow.

Haunted Houses of Grand Rapids. Don W. Farrant, Jr. LC 79-55532. (Illus.). 72p. 1980. pap. 2.95 (ISBN 0-935604-00-6). Ivystone.

Haunted Houses: Tales of the Supernatural with Some Account of Hereditary Curses & Family Legends. Charles G. Harper. LC 79-164326. (Illus.). xvi, 283p. 1971. Repr. of 1907 ed. 24.00 (ISBN 0-8103-3928-5). Gale.

Haunted Inheritance. Lucy B. Robe. LC 79-56903. (Illus., Orig.). 1980. pap. 5.95 (ISBN 0-89638-042-4). Compcare.

Haunted Mind: A Psychoanalyst Looks at the Supernatural. Nandor Fodor. LC 59-15675. 5.00 o.p. (ISBN 0-912326-05-0). Garrett-Helix.

Haunted Shul. Carol K. Hubner. (Judaica Youth Series: Devorah Doresh Mysteries). (gr. 3-8). 1979. 5.95 (ISBN 0-910818-14-2); pap. 4.95 (ISBN 0-686-64803-X). Judaica Pr.

Haunted Souvenir Warehouse. David C. Knight. LC 77-76251. (gr. 3-7). 1978. PLB 5.95 (ISBN 0-385-12729-4). Doubleday.

Haunted Summer. Hope D. Jordan. (gr. 7-9). 1969. pap. 1.75 (ISBN 0-671-42063-1). Archway.

Haunted Summer. Hope D. Jordan. (YA) (gr. 7-9). 1967. pap. 1.50 (ISBN 0-671-29963-8). PB.

Haunted Universe. D. Scott Rogo. 1977. pap. 1.50 o.p. (ISBN 0-451-07508-0, W7508, Sig). NAL.

Haunted Wisconsin. Beth Scott & Michael Norman. LC 80-22151. (Illus.). 256p. (Orig.). 1980. pap. 9.95 (ISBN 0-88361-082-5). Stanton & Lee.

Haunted Woman. new ed. David Lindsay. LC 74-30384. (Forgotten Fantasy Library: Vol. 4). 176p. 1975. pap. 2.85 (ISBN 0-87877-103-4, F-104). Newcastle Pub.

Haunted Woman. David Lindsay. Ed. by R. Reginald & Douglas Menveille. LC 80-19459. (Newcastle Forgotten Fantasy Library: Vol. 4). 176p. 1980. Repr. of 1975 ed. lib. bdg. 9.95x (ISBN 0-89370-503-9). Borgo Pr.

Haunting Compulsion. Anne Mather. (Harlequin Presents Ser.). 192p. 1981. pap. 1.50 (ISBN 0-373-10429-4, Pub. by Harlequin). PB.

Haunting of Cliffside. Jennette Letton. LC 74-7668. 250p. 1975. 7.95 o.s.i. (ISBN 0-8027-5326-4). Walker & Co.

Haunting of the Green Bird. Lynn Hall. 64p. 1980. lib. bdg. 5.39 (ISBN 0-695-41466-6). Follett.

Haunting Tales of Nathaniel Hawthorne. Ed. by Michael Hayes. 1981. 10.95 (ISBN 0-7145-3809-4). Riverrun NY.

Haunting We Will Go: Ghostly Stories & Poems. Lee B. Hopkins. Ed. by Caroline Rubin. LC 76-45449. (Anthology). (Illus.). 128p. (gr. 3-6). 1977. 7.75 (ISBN 0-8075-0006-2). A Whitman.

Hauntings. Norah Lofts. 1977. pap. 1.75 o.p. (ISBN 0-449-23393-6, Crest). Fawcett.

Haunts, Haunts, Haunts. Helen Hoke. (Terrific Triple Titles Ser.). (Illus.). (gr. 4 up). 1977. PLB 7.90 s&l (ISBN 0-531-00098-2). Watts.

Hausa Ba Dabo Ba Ne: A Collection of Five Hundred Proverbs. Tr. by Anthony H. Kirk-Greene. 1966. 2.50x o.p. (ISBN 0-19-639390-6). Oxford U Pr.

Hausa Reader: Cultural Materials with Helps for Use in Teaching Intermediate & Advanced Hausa. Charles H. Kraft. 1974. pap. 22.75x (ISBN 0-520-02067-7). U of Cal Pr.

Hausdorff Measures. Claude A. Rogers. (Illus.). 1970. 28.95 (ISBN 0-521-07970-5). Cambridge U Pr.

Hautnebenwirkungen interner Arzneimittel: Cutaneous Side Effects of Systemic Drugs. K. Zuercher & A. Krebs. (Illus.). 1980. pap. 50.50 (ISBN 3-8055-0019-X). S Karger.

Havasu Canyon: Gem of the Grand Canyon. 3rd ed. Joseph Wampler et al. (Illus.). 125p. 1978. 6.00 (ISBN 0-686-11222-9). J Wampler.

Havasupai Indians. Robert A. Manners et al. Ed. by David A. Horr. (American Indian Ethnohistory Ser.). 1974. lib. bdg. 42.00 (ISBN 0-8240-0707-7). Garland Pub.

Have a Healthy Baby: Section on What to Eat After Your Baby Is Born. Linda Peavy. LC 76-46807. 1977. 9.95 (ISBN 0-8069-8376-0); PLB 8.29 (ISBN 0-8069-8377-9). Sterling.

Have a Very Merry Christmas. Mabel J. Gabbot. LC 80-83034. 56p. (Orig.). 1981. pap. 2.50 (ISBN 0-88290-163-X, 2044). Horizon Utah.

Have Atheists Proved There Is No God? Thomas B. Warren. 1974. 5.95 (ISBN 0-934916-33-0). Natl Christian Pr.

Have His Carcase. Dorothy L. Sayers. LC 59-10623. 1959. 12.95 o.s.i. (ISBN 0-06-013785-1, HarpT). Har-Row.

Have His Carcase. Dorothy L. Sayers. (Large Print Bks.). 1980. lib. bdg. 17.95 (ISBN 0-8161-3043-4). G K Hall.

Have It His Way. Opal Reddin. LC 78-73143. 1980. pap. 1.95 (ISBN 0-88243-717-8, 02-0717). Gospel Pub.

Have You Considered Accounting? 1978. pap. 2.95 o.s.i. (ISBN 0-89584-004-9). Hippocrene Bks.

Have You Considered Banking? 1978. pap. 2.95 o.s.i. (ISBN 0-89584-005-7). Hippocrene Bks.

Have You Considered Engineering? 1978. pap. 2.95 o.s.i. (ISBN 0-89584-006-5). Hippocrene Bks.

Have You Considered Finance? 1978. pap. 2.95 o.s.i. (ISBN 0-89584-007-3). Hippocrene Bks.

Have You Considered Government & Politics? 1978. pap. 2.95 o.s.i. (ISBN 0-89584-008-1). Hippocrene Bks.

Have You Considered Industrial Management? 1978. pap. 2.95 o.s.i. (ISBN 0-89584-009-X). Hippocrene Bks.

Have You Considered Insurance? 1978. pap. 2.95 o.s.i. (ISBN 0-89584-010-3). Hippocrene Bks.

Have You Considered Restaurant Management? 1978. pap. 2.95 o.s.i. (ISBN 0-89584-012-X). Hippocrene Bks.

Have You Considered Retail Management? 1978. pap. 2.95 o.s.i. (ISBN 0-89584-011-1). Hippocrene Bks.

Have You Considered Sales? 1978. pap. 2.95 o.s.i. (ISBN 0-89584-013-8). Hippocrene Bks.

Have You Felt Like Giving up Lately? David Wilkerson. 1980. pap. 4.95 (ISBN 0-8007-5042-X). Revell.

Have You Got the Energy? Proceedings. Junior Liaison Organization Annual Conference, London, 1974. 130p. 1975. pap. text ed. 23.00 (ISBN 0-08-019651-9). Pergamon.

Have You Seen Hyacinth Macaw: A Mystery. Patricia R. Giff. LC 80-68729. (Illus.). 128p. (gr. 4-7). 1981. 7.95 (ISBN 0-440-03467-1); PLB 7.45 (ISBN 0-440-03472-8). Delacorte.

Have You Seen My Cat? Eric Carle. LC 76-185324. (Illus.). 32p. (ps-2). 1973. PLB 5.95 o.p. (ISBN 0-531-02552-7). Watts.

Have You Seen My Puppy. Adelaide Holl. (Early Bird Bks). (Illus.). (ps-1). 1968. 2.50 o.p. (ISBN 0-394-81249-2, BYR); PLB 3.69 (ISBN 0-394-91249-7). Random.

Havelock Ellis: Philosopher of Sex. Vincent Brome. (Illus.). 1979. 24.00 (ISBN 0-7100-0019-7). Routledge & Kegan.

Haven's Raid. Greg Hunt. (Orig.). 1980. pap. 1.95 o.s.i. (ISBN 0-440-13557-5). Dell.

Having Fun. Judy Dunn. LC 70-128851. (Illus.). (gr. k-3). 1970. PLB 6.75 (ISBN 0-87191-067-5). Creative Ed.

Having Fun Being Yourself. Jim Keelan. 1975. Repr. 5.00 (ISBN 0-686-18725-3, Pub. by Professional Writers Group). Comm Unltd.

Having Good Feelings in the Magic Circle at School: A Human Development Program Book. Geraldine Ball. (Illus.). 1972. pap. 0.40 (ISBN 0-86584-015-6); pap. 3.95 set of 10 (ISBN 0-86584-015-6). Human Dev Train.

Havoc in Heaven, Pictures & Text from the Cartoon Film. 1979. 3.95 (ISBN 0-8351-0670-5). China Bks.

Hawaii. 23.00 (ISBN 0-89770-087-2). Curriculum Info Ctr.

Hawaii. James A. Michener. 1978. pap. 3.50 (ISBN 0-449-23761-3, Crest). Fawcett.

Hawaii. Ed. by Robert D. Shangle. LC 78-102325. (Illus.). 72p. 1976. 14.95 (ISBN 0-915796-16-3); pap. 7.95 (ISBN 0-915796-15-5). Beautiful Am.

Hawaii. Ruth Tabrah. (States of the Nation Ser.). (Illus.). 1980. 12.95 (ISBN 0-393-05680-5). Norton.

Hawaii. Robert Wallace. LC 73-179462. (American Wilderness Ser). (Illus.). (gr. 6 up). 1973. lib. bdg. 11.97 (ISBN 0-8094-1177-6, Pub. by Time-Life). Silver.

Hawaii. Robert Wallace. (American Wilderness Ser.). (Illus.). 1973. 12.95 (ISBN 0-8094-1176-8). Time-Life.

Hawaii at-a-Glance. Howard Hillman. LC 76-185131. (At-a-Glance Guides Ser). 1972. pap. 1.95 o.p. (ISBN 0-679-50132-0). McKay.

Hawaii: Cooking with Aloha. Elvira Monroe & Irish Margah. LC 80-52928. 120p. 1981. pap. 5.95 (ISBN 0-933174-10-1). Wide World.

Hawaii on Twenty-Five Dollars a Day: 1981-82 Edition. 1981. pap. 5.95 (ISBN 0-671-41457-7). Frommer-Pasmantier.

Hawaii Volcanoes: The Story Behind the Scenery. Glen Kaye. Ed. by Gweneth R. DenDooven. LC 76-23359. (Illus.). 1976. 7.95 (ISBN 0-916122-41-7); pap. 3.50 (ISBN 0-916122-18-2). K C Pubns.

Hawaiian Antiquities. David Malo. (Special Publication Ser: No. 2). 278p. 1971. Repr. 6.00 (ISBN 0-910240-15-9). Bishop Mus.

Hawaiian Legends. William H. Rice. LC 77-83648. (Bernice P. Bishop Museum Publications: No. 63). (Illus.). 164p. 1977. pap. 23.50 (ISBN 0-295-95729-8). U of Wash Pr.

Hawaiian Monk Seal. Alfred M. Bailey. (Museum Pictorial: No. 7). 1949. pap. 1.10 o.p. (ISBN 0-916278-36-0). Denver Mus Natl Hist.

Hawaiian Petroglyphs. Halley Cox & Edward Stasack. LC 78-111491. (Special Publication Ser.: No. 60). (Illus.). 1977. 7.50 (ISBN 0-910240-09-4). Bishop Mus.

Hawaiian Quilting Made Easy. Milly Singletary. (Illus.). 64p. 1980. pap. 5.00 (ISBN 0-9601256-8-X). Singletary.

Hawaiian Tramways. Robert Ramsay. (Illus.). 36p. 1976. pap. 4.00 o.p. (ISBN 0-87095-062-2). Golden West.

Hawaii's Precious Corals. Richard W. Grigg. LC 77-78113. (Illus.). 1977. 5.95 (ISBN 0-89610-068-5); pap. 4.95 (ISBN 0-89610-069-3). Island Her.

Hawaii's Super Shopper. Kathleen D. Wolgemuth. LC 80-83398. 128p. (Orig.). 1980. pap. 3.50 (ISBN 0-9604798-0-5). Island Writers.

Hawk: California Shakedown. Don Streib. (Hawk Ser.: No. 5). 192p. (Orig.). 1981. pap. 1.95 (ISBN 0-515-05300-7). Jove Pubns.

Hawk in the Rain. Ted Hughes. 1968. pap. 4.95 (ISBN 0-571-08614-4, Pub. by Faber & Faber). Merrimack Bk Serv.

Hawk of May. Gillian Bradshaw. 1981. pap. 2.75 (ISBN 0-451-09765-3, E9765, Sig). NAL.

Hawk: The Cargo Gods. Dan Streib. (Hawk Ser.: No. 10). (Orig.). 1981. pap. 1.95 (ISBN 0-515-05875-0). Jove Pubns.

Hawk: The Deadly Crusader. Dan Streib. (Hawk Ser.: No. 1). (Orig.). pap. 1.95 (ISBN 0-515-05234-5). Jove Pubns.

Hawk: The Death Riders. Dan Streib. (Hawk Ser.: No. 7). 208p. (Orig.). 1981. pap. 1.95 (ISBN 0-515-05872-6). Jove Pubns.

Hawk: The Enemy Within. Dan Streib. (Hawk Ser.: No. 8). 192p. (Orig.). 1981. pap. 1.95 (ISBN 0-515-05873-4). Jove Pubns.

Hawk: The Mind Twisters. Dan Streib. (Hawk Ser.: No. 2). pap. 1.95 (ISBN 0-515-05235-3). Jove Pubns.

Hawk: The Power Barons. Dan Streib. (Hawk Ser.: No. 3). (Orig.). pap. 1.95 (ISBN 0-515-05236-1). Jove Pubns.

Hawk: The Predators. Dan Streib. (Hawk Ser.: No. 4). (Orig.). pap. 1.95 (ISBN 0-515-05299-X). Jove Pubns.

Hawk: The Seeds of Evil. Dan Streib. (Hawk Ser.: No. 6). 224p. (Orig.). 1981. pap. 1.95 (ISBN 0-515-05301-5). Jove Pubns.

Hawken Rifles: The Mountain Man's Choice. John D. Baird. 15.00 (ISBN 0-88227-010-9). Gun Room.

Hawker Hunter: Biography of a Thoroughbred. Francis K. Mason. (Illus.). 244p. 1981. 43.95 (ISBN 0-85059-476-6). Aztex.

Hawker Hurricane. B. Robertson & G. Scarborough. (Illus.). 104p. 21.95 (ISBN 0-85059-124-4). Aztex.

Hawkes Nest. Jean Hayward. 1979. pap. 2.25 (ISBN 0-505-51443-5). Tower Bks.

Hawkfall, & Other Stories. George M. Brown. 1979. 8.95 (ISBN 0-7012-0391-9, Pub. by Chatto Bodley Jonathan). Merrimack Bk Serv.

Hawkins & the Soccer Solution. Barbara B. Wallace. LC 80-23016. 128p. (gr. 4-6). 1981. 7.95g (ISBN 0-687-16672-1). Abingdon.

Hawkridge. Jane Blackmore. 1976. pap. 1.95 (ISBN 0-441-31930-0). Ace Bks.

Hawkstone: A Tale of & for England in 184-, 1845. William Sewell. Ed. by Robert L. Wolff. LC 75-446. (Victorian Fiction Ser.). 1975. lib. bdg. 66.00 (ISBN 0-8240-1526-6). Garland Pub.

Hawkweed Passive Solar House Book. The Hawkweed Group. (Illus.). 192p. 1980. 14.95 (ISBN 0-528-81107-X); pap. 7.95 (ISBN 0-528-88034-9). Rand.

Haworth Harvest: The Story of the Brontes. Brysson N. Morrison. LC 78-89661. (Illus.). 1969. 8.95 (ISBN 0-8149-0670-2). Vanguard.

Hawthorne. Herbert S. Gorman. LC 66-13474. 1927. 9.50x (ISBN 0-8196-0170-5). Biblo.

Hawthorne. Henry James. 145p. (YA) (gr. 9-12). 1956. pap. 12.50x o.p. (ISBN 0-8014-0203-4). Cornell U Pr.

Hawthorne, Melville, Stephen Crane: A Critical Bibliography. Theodore L. Gross & S. Wertheim. LC 75-142364. 1971. 12.95 (ISBN 0-02-913220-7). Free Pr.

Hawthorne: The Critical Heritage. Ed. by J. Donald Crowley. 1971. 36.00 (ISBN 0-7100-6886-7). Routledge & Kegan.

Hawthorne's Imagery: The Proper Light & Shadow in the Major Romances. Richard H. Fogle. 8.95 o.p. (ISBN 0-8061-0855-X). U of Okla Pr.

Hay, How's Your Lawn? Harry E. Lorence. (Illus.). spiral bdg. 6.50 o.p. (ISBN 0-686-19186-2). Thomson Pub CA.

Hayburners. Gene Smith. LC 73-15677. (Illus.). 80p. (gr. 5-8). 1974. 5.95 o.s.i. (ISBN 0-440-03500-7); PLB 5.47 o.s.i. (ISBN 0-440-03501-5). Delacorte.

Hayden. Henry Raynor & H. Robbins Landon. (Great Composers Ser.). (Illus.). 1972. 8.95 (ISBN 0-571-08361-7, Pub. by Faber & Faber). Merrimack Bk Serv.

Hayden's Complete Tube Caddy, Tube Substitution Guidebook. 24th ed. Herman A. Middleton. 1979. pap. 5.50 (ISBN 0-8104-0809-0). Hayden.

Haydn: His Life & Times. Neil Butterworth. (Illus.). 1978. 16.95 (ISBN 0-8467-0417-X, Pub. by Two Continents); pap. 5.95 (ISBN 0-8467-0418-8). Hippocrene Bks.

Haydn in America. Irving Lowens. LC 79-92140. (Bibliographies in American Music Ser.: No. 5). 1980. 11.50 (ISBN 0-911772-99-5). Info Coord.

Haydn Studies. Ed. by Jens P. Larsen et al. 1981. 29.95 (ISBN 0-393-01454-1). Norton.

Haydn: Symphony No. One Hundred & Three in E-Flat Major (Drum Roll) Ed. & pref. by Karl Geiringer. LC 73-20231. (Illus.). 116p. 1974. pap. 4.95x (ISBN 0-393-09349-2). Norton.

Hayek's Social & Economic Philosophy. Norman P. Barry. 1979. text ed. 31.25x (ISBN 0-333-25618-2). Humanities.

Hayes-Tilden Election of 1876: A Disputed Election in the Gilded Age. Harold C. Vaughan. (Focus Books). (Illus.). 72p. (gr. 7 up). 1972. PLB 4.90 o.p. (ISBN 0-531-02452-0). Watts.

Haym Solomon: Patriot of Liberty. Irving Gerber. 1979. of six 6.75 set (ISBN 0-87594-182-6). Book Lab.

Haymarket Affair, Chicago, 1886: The Great Anarchist Riot & Trial. Corinne J. Naden. (Focus Bks). (Illus.). (gr. 7 up). 1968. PLB 4.90 o.p. (ISBN 0-531-01001-5); pap. 1.25 o.p. (ISBN 0-531-02332-X). Watts.
Hazard Control Policy in Britain. John C. Chicken. LC 75-12900. 204p. 1975. text ed. 27.00 (ISBN 0-08-019739-6). Pergamon.
Hazard of New Fortunes. W. D. Howells. Ed. by David J. Nordloh. LC 73-75402. (Selected Edition of W. D. Howells: Center for Editions of American Authors: Vol. 16). (Illus.). 592p. 1975. 20.00x (ISBN 0-253-32708-3). Ind U Pr.
Hazardous Chemicals: A Manual for Schools & Colleges. Ed. by Scottish Schools Science Equipment Research Centre. 1979. pap. 12.95xlab. manual (ISBN 0-05-003204-6). Longman.
Hazardous Chemicals Data Book. Ed. by G. Weiss. LC 80-21634. (Environmental Health Review: No. 4). 1188p. 1981. 64.00 (ISBN 0-8155-0831-X). Noyes.
Hazardous Materials. Leroy Schieler & Denis Pauze. LC 75-19526. 1976. pap. 9.20 (ISBN 0-8273-0593-1); instructor's guide 1.60 (ISBN 0-8273-0594-X). Delmar.
Hazardous Materials Handbook. James Meidl. (Fire Science Ser). 1972. pap. text ed. 7.95x (ISBN 0-02-476370-5, 47637). Macmillan.
Hazardous Products Litigation. Edward M. Swartz. LC 73-77826. 416p. 1973. 47.50 (ISBN 0-686-05457-1). Lawyers Co-Op.
Hazards & Errors in Anaesthesia. D. A. Hopkin. (Illus.). 296p. 1981. pap. 24.80 (ISBN 0-387-10158-6). Springer-Verlag.
Hazards in Construction. 1980. 60.00x (Pub. by Telford England). State Mutual Bk.
Hazards in Tunnelling & on Falsework. Thomas Telford Ltd, Editorial Staff. 130p. 1980. 40.00x (ISBN 0-7277-0013-8, Pub. by Telford England). State Mutual Bk.
Hazards of Being Male: Surviving the Myth of Masculine Privilege. Herb Goldberg. 1977. pap. 2.25 (ISBN 0-451-09437-9, E9437, Sig). NAL.
Hazards of Nuclear Energy: A Policy & Planning Approach. Gary Hammerstrom. (Learning Packages in Policy Issues: No. 3). (Illus.). 86p. (Orig.). 1977. pap. text ed. 4.00 (ISBN 0-936826-12-6). Pol Stud Assocs.
Hazards to Health. Reinhold L. Klingbeil. LC 78-17381. (Better Living Ser.). 1978. pap. 0.95 (ISBN 0-8127-0185-2). Southern Pub.
Hazel's People. Merle Good. 1975. pap. 1.25 (ISBN 0-89129-008-7). Jove Pubns.
Hazlitt at Table. Robert Ready. LC 79-22811. 128p. 1981. 13.50 (ISBN 0-8386-2414-6). Fairleigh Dickinson.
Hazlitt: Selected Essays. William Hazlitt. Ed. by John R. Nabholtz. LC 70-91403. (Crofts Classics Ser.). 1970. pap. text ed. 1.95x (ISBN 0-88295-042-8). AHM Pub.
Hazlitt: Selected Essays. Ed. by Geoffrey Keynes. (Nonesuch Library). 1978. 11.95 (ISBN 0-370-00511-2, Pub. by Chatto Bodley Jonathan). Merrimack Bk Serv.
He Ain't No Bum. O. A. Phillips & Ray Buck. 1980. pap. 1.95 (ISBN 0-451-09540-5, J9450, Sig). NAL.
He & I & the Elephants. Bernhard Grzimek. Tr. by Eva Figes. (Illus.). 1967. 5.00 o.p. (ISBN 0-8090-5435-3). Hill & Wang.
He & She: How Males & Females Behave. S. Carl Hirsch. LC 75-15983. (Illus.). 160p. (gr. 5-8). 1975. 8.95 o.p. (ISBN 0-397-31633-X). Lippincott.
He Is Everything to Me. Ian Barclay. LC 75-29735. 96p. 1976. 1.95 o.p. (ISBN 0-684-14543-X, SL628, ScribT). Scribner.
He Is Lord. George Holmes. LC 76-20891. (Radiant Life Ser.). 1977. pap. 1.25 (ISBN 0-88243-902-2, 02-0902); teacher's ed 2.50 (ISBN 0-88243-172-2, 32-0172). Gospel Pub.
He Is Nigh: Even at the Doors. Richard H. Akeroyd. (Illus.). 1981. 8.95 (ISBN 0-916620-53-0). Portals Pr.
He Leadeth Me. Walter J. Ciszek & Daniel Flaherty. 240p. 1975. pap. 2.95 (ISBN 0-385-02805-9, Im). Doubleday.
He Leadeth Me & Other Stories. Naomi Strubhar. Ed. by Rosalyn B. Strubhar. 1959. pap. 2.50x o.s.i. (ISBN 0-87813-202-3). Park View.
He Loves Forever. Thomas H. Olbricht. LC 80-52461. (Journey Bks). (Orig.). 1980. pap. 2.60 (ISBN 0-8344-0117-7). Sweet.
He Never Slept So Long. Shiv K. Joshi. (Writers Workshop Bluebird Book Ser.). 49p. 1975. 14.00 (ISBN 0-88253-556-0); pap. text ed. 4.80 (ISBN 0-88253-555-2). Ind-US Inc.
He Rambled! 'til Cancer Cut Him Down. Jan Scobey. LC 76-54444. (Illus.). 1976. 35.00 (ISBN 0-918104-01-7). Pal Pub.
He Rode Alone. Steve Frazee. 1979. pap. 1.75 o.p. (ISBN 0-449-14103-9, GM). Fawcett.
He Sent Leanness. David Head. 1959. 1.95 o.s.i. (ISBN 0-02-549630-1). Macmillan.
He Shall Be Like a Tree. Don Pate. (Horizon Ser.). 128p. 1981. pap. price not set (ISBN 0-8127-0315-4). Southern Pub.
He Shall Be Like a Tree: An Interpretation of the Seguoias. Leon Loofbourow. (Illus.). 1968. pap. 1.50 (ISBN 0-918634-27-X). D M Chase.
He Sings for Us: A Sociolinguistic Analysis of the Appalachian Subculture & of Jesse Stuart As a Major American Author. John H. Spurlock. LC 80-8297. (Illus.). 190p. 1980. lib. bdg. 16.50 (ISBN 0-8191-1271-2); pap. text ed. 8.75 (ISBN 0-8191-1272-0). U Pr of Amer.
He That Is Spiritual. Lewis S. Chafer. 1918. 6.95 (ISBN 0-310-22340-7, Pub. by Dunham). Zondervan.
He Took Bread & Broke It. John Meeter. 1981. 6.95 (ISBN 0-533-04729-3). Vantage.
He Who Lets Us Be: A Theology of Love. Geddes MacGregor. 210p. 1975. 8.95 (ISBN 0-8164-1202-2). Crossroad NY.
Head & Figure Modelling. J. W. Mills. 1977. 24.00 (ISBN 0-7134-3258-6, Pub. by Batsford England). David & Charles.
Head & Neck Anatomy Review. Sidney A. Cohn & Marvin I. Gottlieb. (Basic Science Review Bks.). 1976. spiral bdg. 8.50 (ISBN 0-87488-222-2). Med Exam.
Head & Neck Surgery. 2nd ed. P. M. Stell & A. G. Maran. LC 78-66407. 1979. 35.00 (ISBN 0-397-58241-2). Lippincott.
Head Hunters. James Lucano. 320p. 1980. pap. 2.25 (ISBN 0-345-28529-8). Ballantine.
Head in the Clouds. Ivan Southall. LC 72-85189. (Illus.). 108p. (gr. 3-7). 1973. 4.95 o.s.i. (ISBN 0-02-786100-7). Macmillan.
Head Injury. Louis Bakay & Franz E. Glasauer. 1980. text ed. 28.95 (ISBN 0-316-07774-7). Little.
Head Injury from Antiquity to the Present with Special Reference to Penetrating Head Wounds. E. S. Gurdjian. (Beaumont Lecture Ser.). (Illus.). 148p. 1973. 16.75 (ISBN 0-398-02689-0). C C Thomas.
Head Men: Destroyer No. 31. Warren Murphy. (Destroyer Ser.). 1977. pap. 1.75 (ISBN 0-523-40905-2). Pinnacle Bks.
Head of the Force. James Barnett. LC 78-19614. 1979. 8.95 o.p. (ISBN 0-312-36499-7). St Martin.
Head Over Wheels. Lee Kingman. (gr. 7 up). 1981. pap. 1.75 (ISBN 0-440-93129-0, LE). Dell.
Head Start, a Tragicomedy with Epilogue. J. S. Payne et al. LC 72-10924. (Illus.). 1973. 22.95 (ISBN 0-87705-099-6); pap. 9.95 (ISBN 0-87705-098-8). Human Sci Pr.
Head Start Through Reading. Barbara Crane. (Crane Reading System-English Ser.). (Illus.). (gr. k-2). 1977. pap. text ed. 20.20 (ISBN 0-89075-135-8). Crane Pub Co.
Headache. Neil H. Raskin & Otto Appenzeller. LC 79-66042. (Monograph in Major Problems in Internal Medicine: No. 19). (Illus.). 244p. 1980. 19.50 (ISBN 0-7216-7467-4). Saunders.
Headache Book. Edda Hanington. LC 80-52621. (Illus.). 226p. 1980. 12.50 (ISBN 0-87762-292-2). Technomic.
Headache: Understanding, Alleviation. James W. Lance. LC 75-11809. (Illus.). 1975. pap. 0.95 o.p. (ISBN 0-684-14372-0, ScribT); pap. 0.95 (ISBN 0-684-16373-X, SL657, ScribT). Scribner.
Headaches: The Lasting Way to Drugless Relief. Harry C. Ehrmantraut. LC 80-66697. (Illus.). 144p. 1980. 8.95 (ISBN 0-394-51393-2). Autumn Pr.
Headed in the Direction of Heaven. Ed. by Lindsey D. Warren. 1980. 2.25 (ISBN 0-934916-28-4). Natl Christian Pr.
Heading for Change: The Management of Innovation in the Large Secondary School. William Taylor. (Orig.). 1973. 11.25x (ISBN 0-7100-7426-3); pap. 6.50 (ISBN 0-7100-7427-1). Routledge & Kegan.
Heading Out. Virginia Linton. LC 80-23182. 1981. 8.95 (ISBN 0-87233-054-0). Bauhan.
Headlands. Ed. by David Brower & Richard Kauffman. (Gallery Format Ser.). (Illus.). 1976. 125.00 o.p. (ISBN 0-913890-15-4). Friends Earth.
Headless Roommate & Other Tales of Terror. Daniel Cohen. (Illus.). 128p. (gr. 8 up). 1980. 7.95 (ISBN 0-87131-327-8). M Evans.
Headline History of the Sixties. Richard Diprima. LC 80-71081. 73p. (Orig.). (gr. 6-12). pap. text ed. write for info. (ISBN 0-86652-011-2). Educ Indus.
Headliners: Billy Joel. Donald Myra. 192p. (Orig.). 1981. pap. 2.25 (ISBN 0-448-17175-9, Tempo). G&D.
Headlines & Deadlines. Koral April. 64p. (gr. 4-7). 1981. write for info. Messner.
Headlong. Emlyn Williams. LC 80-51775. 300p. 1981. 12.95 (ISBN 0-670-36439-8). Viking Pr.
Headman. Kin Platt. LC 75-11808. 192p. (gr. 7 up). 1975. PLB 7.92 (ISBN 0-688-84011-6). Greenwillow.
Heads of Religious Houses, England & Wales, 940-1216. Ed. by D. Knowles et al. LC 79-171676. 336p. 1972. 47.95 (ISBN 0-521-08367-2). Cambridge U Pr.
Head's Tasks: A Handbook of Secondary School Administration. Geoffrey Lyons. (General Ser.). (Orig.). 1976. pap. text ed. 31.25x (ISBN 0-85633-068-X, NFER). Humanities.
Heads Up, Heels Down. Clarence W. Anderson. (Illus.). (gr. 8 up). 1944. 5.95g o.s.i. (ISBN 0-02-704160-3). Macmillan.
Heads You Win, Tails I Lose. Isabelle Holland. LC 73-5811. 160p. (gr. 7-10). 1973. 9.95 (ISBN 0-397-31380-2). Lippincott.
Heads You Win, Tales You Win. Ray Dirks. 192p. 1980. pap. 2.75 (ISBN 0-553-13223-7). Bantam.
Heal the Sick. Reginald East. LC 77-80678. (Orig.). 1977. pap. 1.95 (ISBN 0-87123-232-4, 200232). Bethany Fell.
Heal Thyself. White Eagle. 1962. 3.95 (ISBN 0-85487-015-6). De Vorss.
Healer. Daniel P. Mannix. 1971. 6.95 o.p. (ISBN 0-525-12235-4). Dutton.
Healer. F. Paul Wilson. 1977. pap. 1.50 o.s.i. (ISBN 0-440-13569-9). Dell.
Healers, Gurus, Spiritual Guide. William Wolf. LC 76-2180. 1969. pap. 6.50 (ISBN 0-933900-07-4). Foun Human Under.
Healers on Horseback. R. H. Smythe. pap. 8.75 (ISBN 0-85131-282-9). J A Allen.
Healey's Eye. Denis Healey. (Illus.). 192p. 1981. 19.95 (ISBN 0-224-01793-4, Pub. by Chatto-Bodley-Jonathan). Merrimack Bk Serv.
Healing. Francis MacNutt. LC 74-81446. (Illus.). 336p. 1974. pap. 3.50 (ISBN 0-87793-074-0). Ave Maria.
Healing Alcoholism. Claude M. Steiner. LC 79-2320. 208p. 1981. pap. 3.95 (ISBN 0-394-17923-4, BC). Grove.
Healing & Religion in Rural Ghana. Kofi Appiah-Kubi. (Orig.). 1981. pap. 10.95 (ISBN 0-377-00114-7). Friend Pr.
Healing & Religion in Rural Ghana: A Sociological Study of Health Care Among the Akans. Kofi Appiah-Kubi. (Illus.). 224p. 1981. text ed. 25.00 (ISBN 0-86598-011-X). Allanheld.
Healing & the Mind World. Inayat Khan. (Sufi Message of Hazrat Inayat Khan Ser.: Vol. 4). 1979. 6.95 (ISBN 90-6077-952-5, Pub. by Servire BV Netherlands). Hunter Hse.
Healing & Wholeness. Genevieve Parkhurst. 5.95 (ISBN 0-910924-90-2). Macalester.
Healing Art of Clara Walter. 64p. (Orig.). 1981. pap. 2.95 (ISBN 0-932870-08-2). Alyson Pubns.
Healing Art of Glove Puppetry. Gisela Bittleston. 1978. 7.95 (ISBN 0-903540-15-0, Pub. by Floris Bks). St George Bk Serv.
Healing Art of Homeopathy. E. C. Hamlyn. 111p. 1980. 15.00x (Pub. by Beaconsfield England). State Mutual Bk.
Healing Art of Homeopathy: The Organon of Samuel Hahnemann. Edward Hamlyn. LC 80-82321. (Orig.). 1980. pap. 4.95 (ISBN 0-87983-228-2). Keats.
Healing Arts. Larry Kettelkamp. (gr. 4-6). 1978. 6.95 (ISBN 0-688-22161-0); PLB 6.67 (ISBN 0-688-32161-5). Morrow.
Healing at Home: A Guide to Health Care for Children. Mary Howell. LC 77-88329. (Illus.). 1979. 12.95 o.p. (ISBN 0-8070-2368-X); pap. 5.95 (ISBN 0-8070-2369-8, BP573). Beacon Pr.
Healing by the Spirit. Ivan Cooke. 1955. 12.00 (ISBN 0-85487-039-3). De Vorss.
Healing Continuum: Journeys in the Philosophy of Holistic Health. Patricia A. Flynn. (Illus.). 568p. 1980. 14.95 (ISBN 0-87619-670-9). R J Brady.
Healing: Divine Art. Manly P. Hall. 9.90 (ISBN 0-89314-390-1); pap. 4.95 (ISBN 0-686-68489-3). Philos Res.
Healing: Faith or Fraud. Wayne Judd. (Uplook Ser.). 1978. pap. 0.75 (ISBN 0-8163-0199-9, 08303-0). Pacific Pr Pub Assn.
Healing Family Hurts. Ed. by Jean M. Hiesberger. LC 79-90991. (Paths of Life Ser.). 124p. (Orig.). 1979. pap. 2.45 (ISBN 0-8091-2266-9). Paulist Pr.
Healing Gifts of the Spirit. Agnes Sanford. 1976. pap. 1.75 (ISBN 0-89129-188-1). Jove Pubns.
Healing Handbook. Jade Easter. (Illus.). 128p. (Orig.). 1981. pap. 6.95 (ISBN 0-913300-15-2). Unity Pr.
Healing in His Wings. Carolyn Rhea. LC 68-31348. 1977. pap. 4.50 (ISBN 0-8054-5150-1). Broadman.
Healing Life's Hurts. Dennis Linn & Matthew Linn. LC 77-14794. 1978. 7.95 (ISBN 0-8091-0231-5); pap. 4.95 (ISBN 0-8091-2059-3). Paulist Pr.
Healing Massage Techniques: A Study of Eastern & Western Methods. Frances Tappan. (Illus.). 1978. ref. ed. 15.95 (ISBN 0-8359-2821-7); pap. 6.95 (ISBN 0-8359-2819-5). Reston.
Healing of Our Damaged Emotions. David A. Seamands. 1981. pap. 3.95 (ISBN 0-88207-228-5). Victor Bks.
Healing Power of Christ. Emily G. Neal. 1972. pap. 4.50 (ISBN 0-8015-3348-1, Hawthorn). Dutton.
Healing Power of Grief. Jack S. Miller. 1978. 7.95 (ISBN 0-8164-0402-X). Crossroad NY.
Healing Power of the Bible. Agnes Sanford. 1976. pap. 1.75 (ISBN 0-89129-192-X). Jove Pubns.
Healing Presence. Leanne Payne. 176p. 1981. pap. 4.95 (ISBN 0-89107-215-2). Good News.
Healing Sea. George D. Ruggieri & Norman D. Rosenberg. LC 78-7333. (Illus.). 1978. 7.95 (ISBN 0-396-07449-9). Dodd.
Healing Through Colour. Theo Gimbel. 108p. 1980. 23.95x (ISBN 0-8464-1017-6). Beekman Pubs.
Healing Through the Power of Christ. Jim Wilson. 1969. pap. 3.25 (ISBN 0-227-67478-2). Attic Pr.
Healing Touch of Affirmation. Thomas A. Kane. LC 76-151154. 1976. 4.95 o.p. (ISBN 0-89571-001-3); pap. 2.95. Affirmation.
Healing with Mind Power. Richard Shames & Chuck Sterin. 1980. 8.95 (ISBN 0-87857-210-4); pap. 6.95 (ISBN 0-87857-293-7). Rodale Pr Inc.
Healing Without Medicine. LC 75-34860. (New Library of the Supernatural Ser.: Vol. 9). (Illus.). 144p. 1976. 8.95 o.p. (ISBN 0-385-11319-6). Doubleday.
Healing Yourself Through Okida Yoga. Masahiro Oki. LC 76-29339. 1977. pap. 7.95 (ISBN 0-87040-380-X). Japan Pubns.
Healings in the Gospels. Alfred Heidenreich. 1980. pap. 7.25 (ISBN 0-903540-36-3, Pub. Floris Books). St George Bk Serv.
Healings of the Bible. Compiled by Nellie B. Woods. 1975. pap. 1.95 o.p. (ISBN 0-8015-3349-X). Dutton.
Health, 5 pts. Incl. Pt. 1. General, 17 vols. Set. 1494.00x (ISBN 0-686-01159-7); Pt. 2. Food & Drugs, 5 vols. Set. 423.00x (ISBN 0-686-01160-0); Pt. 3. Infectious Diseases, 13 vols. Set. 1242.00x (ISBN 0-686-01161-9); Pt. 4. Medical Profession, 5 vols. Set. 342.00x (ISBN 0-686-01162-7); Pt. 5. Mental, 8 vols. Set. 558.00x (ISBN 0-686-01163-5). (British Parliamentary Papers Ser.). 1971 (Pub. by Irish Academic Pr Ireland). Biblio Dist.
Health. 2nd ed. John Laplace. 1976. pap. text ed. 12.95 o.p. (ISBN 0-13-385369-1). P-H.
Health. 3rd ed. John LaPlace. (Illus.). 1980. text ed. 13.95 (ISBN 0-13-385393-4); cloth 16.95 (ISBN 0-13-385427-2). P-H.
Health: A Consumer's Dilemma. Robert E. Kime. 1970. pap. 4.95x (ISBN 0-534-00661-2). Wadsworth Pub.
Health & Aging. Tom Hickey. LC 79-25033. (Social Gerontology Ser.). 1980. pap. text ed. 7.95 (ISBN 0-8185-0374-2). Brooks-Cole.
Health & Beauty Secrets from Hollywood. Linda Arden. LC 78-5591. (Illus.). 1978. softcover 12.95 o.p. (ISBN 0-686-66477-9). Future Shop.
Health & Development. Ed. by Kevin M. Cahill. LC 75-29504. 110p. 1976. 6.95x o.p. (ISBN 0-88344-178-0). Orbis Bks.
Health & Disease in Farm Animals: An Introduction to Farm Animal Medicine. 3rd ed. W. H. Parker. Date not set. 42.00 (ISBN 0-08-025900-6); pap. 13.25 (ISBN 0-08-025899-9). Pergamon. Postponed.
Health & Healing in Yoga. 1979. pap. 5.00 (ISBN 0-89744-958-4). Auromere.
Health & Health Care: Policies in Perspective. Anne R. Somers & Herman M. Somers. LC 77-76921. 1977. 29.95 (ISBN 0-912862-45-9); pap. text ed. 15.95 (ISBN 0-912862-49-1). Aspen Systems.
Health & Human Nature. Paul Snyder. 256p. 1980. pap. 10.95 (ISBN 0-8019-6798-8). Chilton.
Health & Medical Care Services: Current Critical Issues. Charles E. Lewis. LC 80-17126. (Collected Essay Ser.). 64p. 1981. pap. text ed. 6.95 (ISBN 0-917724-17-8). Haworth Pr.
Health & Medical Economics: A Guide to Information Sources. Ed. by Ted J. Ackroyd. LC 73-17567. (Economics Information Guide Ser.: Vol. 7). 1977. 30.00 (ISBN 0-8103-1390-1). Gale.
Health & Physical Well Being: The Essential Knowledge of the Basic Rules on Being Healthy, Staying Healthy & Live a Long & Happy Life Which Everyone, but Absolutely Everyone Ought to Possess for the Benefit & Success of His Existence. Vernon De Castille. (Essential Knowledge Ser. Books). (Illus.). 1978. plastic spiral bdg. 27.35 (ISBN 0-89266-121-6). Am Classical Coll Pr.
Health & Population in Developing Countries: Selected Papers from the 5th Bellagio Populaion Conference, Rockefeller Foundation, Bellagio, 1979. Ed. by S. J. Segal & B. Winikoff. 100p. 1980. 20.00 (ISBN 0-08-026101-9). Pergamon.
Health & Safety in the Canadian Mining Industry. G. W. Gibbs & P. Pintus. 249p. (Orig.). 1978. pap. text ed. 12.00x (ISBN 0-88757-003-8, Pub. by Ctr Resource Stud Canada). Renouf.

Health & Social Education. May V. Lea. 1975. pap. text ed. 8.95x (ISBN 0-435-60601-8). Heinemann Ed.

Health & the Community. Alfred H. Katz & J. S. Felton. LC 65-10188. 1965. text ed. 19.75 (ISBN 0-02-917280-2). Free Pr.

Health & the War on Poverty: A Ten-Year Appraisal. Karen Davis & Cathy Schoen. (Studies in Social Economics). 1978. 14.95 (ISBN 0-8157-1758-X); pap. 5.95 (ISBN 0-8157-1757-1). Brookings.

Health & Travel. Ed. by Felix Marti-Ibanez. 1955. 3.00 o.p. (ISBN 0-910922-02-0). MD Pubns.

Health & Wealth. Derek Heater & Gwyneth Owen. Ed. by Malcolm Yapp & Margaret Killingray. (World History Ser.). (Illus.). (gr. 10). 1980. Repr. of 1977 ed. lib. bdg. 5.95 (ISBN 0-89908-142-8); pap. text ed. 1.95 (ISBN 0-89908-117-7). Greenhaven.

Health & Wealth: An International Study of Health-Care Spending. Robert Maxwell. LC 80-8472. 1981. 22.95 (ISBN 0-669-04109-2). Lexington Bks.

Health Assessment. 2nd ed. Lois Malasanos. (Illus.). 753p. 1981. text ed. 26.95 (ISBN 0-8016-3073-8). Mosby.

Health Assessment for Professional Nursing: A Developmental Approach. Gloria Block & Joellen Nolan. 496p. 1981. 24.95 (ISBN 0-8385-3660-3). ACC.

Health Assessment in Clinical Practice. Kenneth R. Burns & Patricia J. Johnson. (Illus.). 1980. text ed. 26.95 (ISBN 0-13-385054-4). P-H.

Health Assistant. Caldwell & Hegner. LC 79-50661. (Illus.). 1980. pap. 8.60 (ISBN 0-8273-1337-3); instr's. guide 1.60 (ISBN 0-8273-1338-1). Delmar.

Health Assistant. Esther Caldwell & Barbara Hegner. 288p. 1981. text ed. 13.95 (ISBN 0-442-21850-8). Van Nos Reinhold.

Health, Beauty & Happiness. Joe Parkhill. spiral 5.95 (ISBN 0-88427-014-9). Green Hill.

Health, Behavior & the Community: An Ecological Perspective. Ralph Catalano. LC 78-23714. (Pergamon General Psychology Ser.: Vol. 76). (Illus.). 1979. text ed. 33.00 (ISBN 0-08-022972-7); pap. text ed. 11.00 (ISBN 0-08-022971-9). Pergamon.

Health Care Administration: A Guide to Information Sources. Ed. by Dwight A. Morris & Lynne D. Morris. LC 78-53431. (Health Affairs Information Guide Ser.: Vol. 1). 1978. 30.00 (ISBN 0-8103-1378-2). Gale.

Health Care Administration: A Selected Bibliography. Ed. by Samuel Levey & Narendra P. Loomba. LC 72-11486. 149p. 1973. pap. 4.00 o.p. (ISBN 0-397-52060-3). Lippincott.

Health Care & Industrial Relations: Costs, Conflicts & Controversy. Ed. by Robert Goldstone. 120p. 1981. price not set (ISBN 0-89215-112-9). U Cal LA Indus Rel.

Health Care & Society: Patients, Professions, Programs & Policies. Arnold Birenbaum. LC 80-67092. 350p. 1981. text ed. 28.50 (ISBN 0-916672-57-3). Allanheld.

Health Care & the Elderly. C. Carl Pegals. 300p. 1980. text ed. write for info. (ISBN 0-89443-333-4). Aspen Systems.

Health Care: Can There Be Equity? the United States, Sweden, & England. Odin W. Anderson. LC 72-7449. 1972. 22.95 (ISBN 0-471-02760-X, Pub by Wiley-Interscience). Wiley.

Health Care Careers. Eleanor Kay. LC 72-8881. (Career Concise Guides Ser.). (Illus.). 96p. (gr. 7 up). 1973. PLB 4.90 o.p. (ISBN 0-531-02607-8). Watts.

Health Care Cost Containment: The Managerial Approach. Ed. by Bureau of Business Research. 1978. 7.50 (ISBN 0-686-28414-3). Bur Busn Res U Nebr.

Health Care Costs & Financing: A Guide to Information Sources. Ed. by Rita M. Keintz. LC 80-23862. (Health Affairs Information Guide Ser.: Vol. 6). 400p. 1981. 30.00 (ISBN 0-8103-1482-7). Gale.

Health Care Delivery in the United States. 2nd ed. Steven Jonas. 512p. 1981. text ed. price not set (ISBN 0-8261-2072-5); pap. text ed. price not set (ISBN 0-8261-2073-3). Springer Pub.

Health Care Delivery Systems. J. C. Salloway. (Behavioral Sciences for Health Care Professionals Ser.). 128p. (Orig.). 1981. lib. bdg. 15.00x (ISBN 0-86531-016-5); pap. text ed. 6.00x (ISBN 0-86531-017-3). Westview.

Health Care Dilemma. 2nd ed. Aubrey C. McTaggart & Lorna M. McTaggart. 275p. 1976. pap. text ed. 11.95 (ISBN 0-205-05446-3, 7154461). Allyn.

Health Care Directory. C. T. Norback & P. Norback. 1977. 49.95 o.p. (ISBN 0-87489-079-9). Med Economics.

Health Care Economics. Paul J. Feldstein. LC 79-14268. (Health Services Ser.). 1979. 21.95 (ISBN 0-471-05361-9, Pub. by Wiley Medical). Wiley.

Health-Care Finance: An Analysis of Cost & Utilization Issues. Robert J. Buchanan. LC 80-8362. 1981. write for info. (ISBN 0-669-04035-5). Lexington Bks.

Health Care Financing in Mainland Tanzania. Manuel Gottlieb. LC 75-30548. (Foreign and Comparative Studies Eastern African Series XX). 104p. 1975. pap. text ed. 4.50x (ISBN 0-915984-17-2). Maxwell Schl Citizen.

Health Care for the People: Studies from Vietnam. Ed. by Joan McMichael. 352p. (Orig.). 1980. pap. 6.95 (ISBN 0-932870-04-X). Alyson Pubns.

Health Care Guidance: Commercial Health Insurance & National Health Policy. Carol K. Morrow. LC 76-14415. 1976. text ed. 21.50 (ISBN 0-275-56950-0). Praeger.

Health Care Guidelines for Use in Developing Countries. pap. 6.75 (ISBN 0-912552-22-0). MARC.

Health Care in the U. S. Equitable for Whom? LuAnn Aday et al. LC 79-21841. 1980. 25.00x (ISBN 0-8039-1373-7). Sage.

Health Care Labor Manual, 3 vols. Ed. by Martin E. Skoler. (Updated bimonthly). 1974. loose-leaf metal binding 275.00 (ISBN 0-912862-11-4). Aspen Systems.

Health Care Management: Perspectives for Today. Seth Goldsmith. 300p. 1981. text ed. price not set (ISBN 0-89443-336-9). Aspen Systems.

Health Care Management Review. Ed. by Montague Brown. LC 75-45767. annual subscription 44.50 (ISBN 0-912862-50-5). Aspen Systems.

Health Care Marketing: Issues & Trends. Philip Cooper. LC 79-18447. 1979. text ed. 27.95 (ISBN 0-89443-162-5). Aspen Systems.

Health Care Ministries. 2nd ed. Gerald Fath. 1980. pap. 7.50 (ISBN 0-87125-061-6). Cath Health.

Health Care of the Aging. Ed. by Harold B. Haley & Patricia A. Keenan. 450p. 1981. write for info. (ISBN 0-8139-0869-8). U Pr of Va.

Health Care of the Elderly: Strategies for Prevention & Intervention. Gari Lesnoff-Caravaglia. LC 79-19192. 1980. text ed. 22.95x (ISBN 0-87705-417-7); pap. text ed. 9.95x (ISBN 0-87705-486-X). Human Sci Pr.

Health Care of Women: A Nursing Perspective. Catherine I. Fogel & Woods. LC 80-17400. (Illus.). 394p. 1981. pap. text ed. 24.95 (ISBN 0-8016-1605-0). Mosby.

Health Care Policy in a Changing Environment. Ed. by Roger M. Battistella & Thomas G. Rundall. LC 78-57148. 1979. 23.50 (ISBN 0-8211-0131-5); text ed. 21.00 in ten or more copies (ISBN 0-686-67039-6). McCutchan.

Health Care Supervisor's Handbook. Norman Metzger. LC 78-12513. 1978. text ed. 21.50 (ISBN 0-89443-078-5). Aspen Systems.

Health Care Teams: An Annotated Bibliography. Monique K. Tichy. LC 74-14674. (Special Studies). 190p. 1974. text ed. 24.95 (ISBN 0-275-05750-X). Praeger.

Health Care Technology Evaluation. Ed. by J. Goldman. (Lecture Notes in Medical Informatics: Vol. 6). 1980. pap. 12.50 (ISBN 0-387-09561-6). Springer-Verlag.

Health Careers & Medical Sciences. George Milles. LC 74-79837. (Allied Health Ser). 1975. pap. 5.50 (ISBN 0-672-61384-0). Bobbs.

Health Communications. Stacey B. Day. LC 79-78888. (Foundation Publication Ser.). (Illus.). 356p. (Orig.). 1979. pap. 26.50 (ISBN 0-934314-00-4). Intl Found Biosocial Dev.

Health Conditions in the Ceramic Industry. C. N. Davies. 286p. 1970. 46.00 (ISBN 0-08-013347-9). Pergamon.

Health Controls Out of Control. David M. Kinzer. 194p. 9.75 (ISBN 0-686-68584-9, 14918). Hospital Finan.

Health Counseling. Lawrence Litwack et al. 290p. 1980. 13.50 (ISBN 0-8385-3665-4). ACC.

Health: Current Perspectives. 3rd ed. Brice W. Corder et al. 403p. 1981. pap. text ed. write for info. (ISBN 0-697-07388-2); instructor's manual avail. (ISBN 0-697-07389-0). Wm C Brown.

Health Data & Information Management. Gene E. Thompson & Ira Handelman. (Illus.). 1978. 29.95 (ISBN 0-409-95008-4). Butterworths.

Health Economics: An Introduction. Alan Sorkin. LC 73-11656. (Illus.). 160p. 1975. 16.95 (ISBN 0-669-93393-7). Lexington Bks.

Health Economics & Health Care: Irreconcilable Gap? Ed. by Frank W. Musgrave. LC 78-59166. 1978. pap. text ed. 9.25 (ISBN 0-8191-0546-5). U Pr of Amer.

Health Economics in Developing Nations. Alan Sorkin. LC 74-25059. 1976. 18.95 (ISBN 0-669-96875-7). Lexington Bks.

Health Education Curriculum: A Guide for Curriculum Development in Health Education. J. Keogh Rash & R. Morgan Pigg. LC 78-24493. 1979. text ed. 17.95 (ISBN 0-471-03765-6). Wiley.

Health Education in Schools. J. Cowley. 1981. text ed. 21.00 (ISBN 0-06-318178-9, Pub. by Har-Row England Ltd); pap. text ed. 11.90 (ISBN 0-06-318179-7). Har-Row.

Health Education in Secondary Schools. rev. ed. 3rd ed. Cyrus Mayshark & Roy A. Foster. LC 77-173431. (Illus.). 1972. text ed. 12.50 o.p. (ISBN 0-8016-3176-9). Mosby.

Health Education: The Search for Values. D. Read et al. 1977. 12.95 (ISBN 0-13-384511-7). P-H.

Health Effects Investigation of Oil Shale Development. Ed. by W. H. Griest et al. 1981. text ed. 29.50. Ann Arbor Science.

Health Effects of Asbestos & of Some Other Minerals & Fibres As Reflected in the World Literature: A Compendium of References, 1906-1979. Premysl U. Pelnar. 1981. 25.00 set (ISBN 0-930376-25-0). Pathotox Pubs.

Health Effects of Environmental Pollutants. 2nd ed. George L. Waldbott. LC 77-26880. (Illus.). 1978. pap. text ed. 16.95 (ISBN 0-8016-5331-2). Mosby.

Health Effects of Fossil Fuel Burning: Assessment & Mitigation. Richard Wilson. 1980. 30.00 (ISBN 0-88410-714-0). Ballinger Pub.

Health Foods: Facts & Fakes. Sidney Margolius. 256p. 1973. 6.95 o.s.i. (ISBN 0-8027-0375-5). Walker & Co.

Health from the Kitchen. Eric F. Powell. 64p. 1969. pap. 2.50x (ISBN 0-8464-1018-4). Beekman Pubs.

Health Games Students Play: Creative Strategies for Health Education. Ruth C. Engs et al. 1976. perfect bdg. 7.50 (ISBN 0-8403-1238-5). Kendall-Hunt.

Health Goals & Health Indicators: Policy, Planning & Evaluation. Ed. by Jack Elinson et al. LC 77-14044. (AAAS Selected Symposium Ser.: No. 2). 1978. lib. bdg. 18.50x (ISBN 0-89158-429-3). Westview.

Health Handbook: An International Reference on Care & Cure. Ed. by G. K. Chacko. 1979. 146.50 (ISBN 0-444-85254-9, North Holland). Elsevier.

Health Hazards & Pollution Control in Synthetic Liquid Fuel Conversion. Ed. by Perry Nowacki. LC 80-16694. (Pollution Tech. Review, No. 68; Environmental Health Review, No. 2; Chemical Tech. Review, No. 165; Energy Tech. Review: No. 57). 511p. (Orig.). 1980. 54.00 (ISBN 0-8155-0810-7). Noyes.

Health Hazards from Pigeons, Starlings & English Sparrows. Walter Weber. LC 79-55324. Date not set. 13.00 (ISBN 0-913702-10-2). Thomson Pub Ca.

Health Impacts of Polynuclear Aromatic Hydrocarbons. Ed. by A. W. Pucknat. LC 80-28039. (Environmental Health Review Ser.: No. 5). (Illus.). 271p. 1981. 39.00 (ISBN 0-8155-0840-9). Noyes.

Health-Impaired Miner Under Black Lung Legislation. Ed. by Leo Kramer & Ewan Clague. LC 73-9385. (Special Studies in U.S. Economic, Social & Political Issues). 1973. 28.50x (ISBN 0-275-28759-9); pap. text ed. 12.50x (ISBN 0-89197-783-X). Irvington.

Health Implications of New Energy Technologies. Ed. by William N. Rom & Victor E. Archer. (Illus.). 700p. 1980. 40.00 (ISBN 0-250-40361-7). Ann Arbor Science.

Health in the City: Environmental & Behavioral Influences. Malcolm S. Weinstein. (Habitat Text Ser.). (Illus.). 1980. 11.00 (ISBN 0-08-023375-9). Pergamon.

Health in the Elementary Schools. 5th ed. Harold J. Cornacchia & Wesley M. Staton. LC 78-21076. (Illus.). 1979. text ed. 15.95 (ISBN 0-8016-1062-1). Mosby.

Health in the Mexican-American Culture: A Community Study. 2nd ed. Margaret Clark. 1970. 16.50x (ISBN 0-520-01666-1); pap. 3.85 (ISBN 0-520-01668-8, CAL192). U of Cal Pr.

Health in Tropical Africa During the Colonial Period. Ed. by E. E. Saben-Clare et al. (Illus.). 256p. 1980. 42.00 (ISBN 0-19-858165-3). Oxford U Pr.

Health, Infection & Diseases. Harvey Zarren. (Illus.). 1975. pap. 7.95 (ISBN 0-87618-064-0). R J Brady.

Health Instruction: An Action Approach. R. Kime et al. 1977. text ed. 16.50 (ISBN 0-13-385252-0). P-H.

Health Instruction II: Guidelines for Planning Health Education Programs K-12. 1981. 4.00 (ISBN 0-917160-14-2). Am Sch Health.

Health Instruction: Suggestions for Teachers. 1973. 3.00 (ISBN 0-917160-08-8). Am Sch Health.

Health Instruction: Theory & Application. 3rd ed. John T. Fodor & Gus T. Dalis. LC 80-24484. (Illus.). 150p. 1981. text ed. write for info. (ISBN 0-8121-0776-4). Lea & Febiger.

Health Insurance Agent: Hospital, Accident, Health, Life. 4th ed. (Licensing Exam Ser). 1970. pap. 5.00 o.p. (ISBN 0-668-02153-5). Arco.

Health Insurance & Psychiatric Care: Utilization & Cost. Louis S. Reed et al. 412p. 1972. 8.00 (ISBN 0-685-31187-2, 217). Am Psychiatric.

Health Insurance for Mental Illness. Patricia Scheidemandel et al. 89p. 1968. pap. 3.00 (ISBN 0-685-24845-3, P195-0). Am Psychiatric.

Health Is a Question of Balance. Paul Brenner. 143p. 1980. pap. 4.95 (ISBN 0-87516-415-3). De Vorss.

Health Is a Question of Balance. Paul H. Brenner. 1978. 5.95 o.p. (ISBN 0-533-03513-9). Vantage.

Health Maintenance Organization: Dimensions of Performance. Harold S. Luft. LC 80-22420. (Health, Medicine & Society Ser.). 412p. 1981. 25.00 (ISBN 0-471-01695-0, Pub. by Wiley-Interscience). Wiley.

Health Maintenance Through Physical Conditioning. Ed. by Robert C. Cantu. LC 80-15622. 275p. 1981. 12.50 (ISBN 0-88416-312-1). PSG Pub.

Health Manpower: An Economic Perspective. Alan Sorkin. LC 75-17335. 1977. 17.95 (ISBN 0-669-00086-8). Lexington Bks.

Health, Migration & Development. Michael Beenstock. 192p. 1980. text ed. 27.75x (ISBN 0-566-00369-4, Pub. by Gower Pub Co England). Renouf.

Health Needs of Children. Roger Manela & Armand Lauffer. LC 78-26373. (Sage Human Services Guides: Vol. 9). 1979. pap. 6.50x (ISBN 0-8039-1217-X). Sage.

Health of Mexican - Americans in South Texas. LBJ School of Public Affairs. LC 79-88345. (Policy Research Project Report Ser.: No. 32). 1979. 6.00 (ISBN 0-89940-628-9). LBJ Sch Public Affairs.

Health of the Preschool Child. Edith H. Reinisch & Ralph E. Minear. LC 78-8743. 1978. text ed. 17.95 (ISBN 0-471-60800-9). Wiley.

Health Organizations of the United States & Canada: A Directory of Voluntary Associations, Professional Societies & Other Groups Concerned with Health & Related Fields. 5th ed. Ed. by Paul Wasserman. 500p. 1981. 36.00 (ISBN 0-8103-0466-X). Gale.

Health Organizations of the U.S., Canada & Internationally: A Directory of Voluntary Associations, Professional Societies & Other Groups Concerned with Health & Related Fields. 5th ed. Paul Wasserman & Jane Bossart. 500p. 1977. 42.00 (ISBN 0-686-64907-9). Gale.

Health Organizations of the U.S., Canada, & Internationally: A Directory of Voluntary Associations, Professional Societies & Other Groups Concerned with Health & Related Fields. 4th ed. Ed. by Paul Wasserman & Jane Bossart. LC 77-79000. 500p. 1977. 36.00 (ISBN 0-686-27874-7). Kruzas Assoc.

Health Organizations: Research & Assessment of Health Services. Arnold D. Kaluzny & James E. Veney. LC 78-71810. (Health Care Ser.). 1979. 23.50 (ISBN 0-8211-1017-9); text ed. 21.00 ten or more copies (ISBN 0-685-63682-8). McCutchan.

Health, Personal & Communal. 4th ed. John Gibson. (Illus.). 1976. 8.95 (ISBN 0-571-04908-7, Pub. by Faber & Faber); pap. 4.95 (ISBN 0-571-04909-5). Merrimack Bk Serv.

Health Personnel: Meeting the Explosive Demand for Medical Care. Harold M. Goldstein et al. LC 76-55042. 1977. text ed. 22.50 (ISBN 0-912862-36-X). Aspen Systems.

Health Physics: A Backward Glance. Ronald L. Kathren. 1980. text ed. 28.00 (ISBN 0-08-021531-9). Pergamon.

Health Planning: A Systematic Approach. Herbert H. Hyman. LC 75-37405. 460p. 1976. text ed. 27.50 (ISBN 0-912862-17-3). Aspen Systems.

Health Planning & Regulation: Decision-Making Process. Drew Altman et al. (Illus.). 350p. 1981. text ed. price not set (ISBN 0-914904-57-4). Health Admin Pr.

Health Policy. Congressional Quarterly. Ed. by Congressional Quarterly. 220p. 1980. pap. text ed. 6.95 (ISBN 0-87187-199-8). Congr Quarterly.

Health Policy & Nursing Practice. Ed. by Linda Aiken. (Illus.). 308p. 1980. pap. text ed. 6.95 (ISBN 0-07-000745-4, HP). McGraw.

Health Policy Making: The Fundamental Issues. Anne Crichton. (Illus.). 432p. 1981. text ed. write for info. (ISBN 0-914904-44-2). Health Admin Pr.

Health Preserver. Wilfrid E. Shute. LC 77-14086. 1977. 8.95 (ISBN 0-87857-189-2). Rodale Pr Inc.

Health Principles & Practice. rev. ed. 6th ed. C. L. Anderson. LC 74-106045. (Illus.). 1970. text ed. 12.50 o.p. (ISBN 0-8016-0239-4). Mosby.

Health Problems in Australia & New Zealand. Ed. by N. D. McGlashan. 180p. 1980. 20.00 (ISBN 0-08-026103-5). Pergamon.

Health Problems in the Prison Setting. Lloyd F. Novick & Mohamed S. Al-Ibrahim. (Illus.). 244p. 1977. 19.75 (ISBN 0-398-03664-0). C C Thomas.

Health Professions. Marcia V. Boyles et al. LC 77-11331. (Illus.). 465p. Date not set. price not set (ISBN 0-7216-1904-5). Saunders. Postponed.

Health Professions in Medicine's New Technology. Janet Z. Nassif. LC 80-22030. (Illus.). 256p. 1981. pap. 5.95 (ISBN 0-668-04436-5, 4436). Arco.

Health Program Evaluation. Stephen M. Shortell & William C. Richardson. LC 78-4866. (Issues & PrOblems in Health Care). 1978. pap. text ed. 8.95 (ISBN 0-8016-4595-6). Mosby.

Health Protection of Radiation Workers. W. Daggett Norwood. (Illus.). 468p. 1975. 37.50 (ISBN 0-398-03291-2). C C Thomas.

Health Quackery: Consumer's Union's Report on False Health Claims, Worthless Remedies & Unproved Therapies. Consumer Reports Editors. 252p. 1981. 13.95 (ISBN 0-03-058899-5); pap. 6.95x (ISBN 0-03-058898-7). HR&W.

Health Questions & Answers. Alan Nittler. 1976. pap. 1.75 o.s.i. (ISBN 0-515-03723-0). Jove Pubns.

Health Regulation: Certificate of Need & 1122. Herbert H. Hyman. LC 76-45524. 1977. 22.00 (ISBN 0-912862-34-3). Aspen Systems.

Health Restoration: Area I. Jack Rudman. (ACT Proficiency Examination Program Ser.: PEP-51). pap. 9.95 (ISBN 0-8373-5901-5). Natl Learning.

Health Restoration: Area II. Jack Rudman. (ACT Proficiency Examination Program Ser.: PEP-52). (Cloth bdg. avail. on request). pap. 9.95 (ISBN 0-8373-5902-3). Natl Learning.

Health Risks of Imprisonment. David A. Jones. LC 76-5620. (Illus.). 1976. 21.50 (ISBN 0-669-00651-3). Lexington Bks.

Health Robbers: How to Protect Your Money & Your Life. new ed. Ed. by Stephen Barrett & Gilda Knight. LC 76-22281. (Illus.). 352p. 1976. 10.50 o.p. (ISBN 0-89313-001-X). G F Stickley Co.

Health Sciences & Services: A Guide to Information Sources. Ed. by Lois F. Lunin. LC 77-80614. (Management Information Guide Ser.: No. 36). 1979. 30.00 (ISBN 0-8103-0836-3). Gale.

Health Sciences Information Sources. Ching-Chih Chen. 608p. 1981. text ed. 50.00x (ISBN 0-262-03074-8). MIT Pr.

Health Sciences Librarianship: A Guide to Information Sources. Ed. by Beatrice K. Basler & Thomas G. Basler. LC 74-11552. (Books, Publishing, & Libraries Information Guide Ser.: Vol. 1). 180p. 1977. 30.000 (ISBN 0-8103-1284-0). Gale.

Health Sciences Video Directory. Ed. by Lawrence Eidelberg. LC 76-29480. 1977. pap. 30.00 (ISBN 0-917226-00-3). Nord Media.

Health Sciences Video Directory: 1978 Supplement, 4 vols. Ed. by Lawrence Eidelberg. LC 76-29480. 1978. pap. 30.00 set (ISBN 0-917226-05-4); Vol. 1. (ISBN 0-917226-01-1); Vol. 2. (ISBN 0-917226-02-X); Vol. 3. (ISBN 0-917226-03-8); Vol. 4. (ISBN 0-917226-04-6). Nord Media.

Health Services. Elliott Jacques. (Brunel Institute of Organization & Social Studies Ser.). 1978. text ed. 39.95x (ISBN 0-435-82474-0). Heinemann Ed.

Health Services Administration Education, 2 vols. Ed. by K. Peterson. Incl. Vol. I. 46.00 (ISBN 0-914904-55-8); pap. text ed. price not set; Vol. II. text ed. price not set (ISBN 0-914904-56-6); pap. text ed. price not set. (Illus.). 350p. 1981. Health Admin Pr.

Health Services in Norway. Karl Evang. 1976. pap. 17.00x (ISBN 8-200-02373-7, Dist. by Columbia U Pr). Universitet.

Health Services in the U. S. rev. ed. Florence Wilson & Duncan Neuhauser. Date not set. price not set (ISBN 0-88410-713-2). Ballinger Pub.

Health Services Management: An Anthology. Ed. by Anthony R. Kovner & Duncan Neuhauser. LC 78-4567. 1978. text ed. 27.50 (ISBN 0-914904-17-5). Health Admin Pr.

Health Services Management in the Health Administration Curriculum. 1978. 5.00. Assn Univ Progs Hlth.

Health Services Research. Institute of Medicine. 1979. pap. text ed. 5.50 (ISBN 0-309-02875-2). Natl Acad Pr.

Health Services: The Local Perspective. Ed. by Arthur Levin. LC 77-73219. (Praeger Special Studies). 1977. text ed. 26.95 (ISBN 0-03-039731-6). Praeger.

Health Statistics: A Guide to Information Sources. Ed. by Frieda O. Weise. LC 80-12039. (Health Affairs Information Guide Ser.: Vol. 4). 1980. 30.00 (ISBN 0-8103-1412-6). Gale.

Health Status & Use of Medical Services: Evidence on the Poor, the Black, & the Rural Elderly. Lynn Paringer et al. (Institute Paper). 111p. 1979. pap. 7.50 (ISBN 0-87766-241-X, 24800). Urban Inst.

Health Surveys & Related Studies. Ed. by W. F. Maunder. LC 78-40963. (Reviews of United Kingdom Statistical Sources Ser.: Vol. IX). 1979. 55.00 (ISBN 0-08-022459-8). Pergamon.

Health Teaching in Elementary Schools. James H. Humphrey et al. (Illus.). 356p. 1975. 18.75 (ISBN 0-398-03356-0). C C Thomas.

Health Technology: Issues & Activities. University of Southern California Center for Health Services Research. LC 77-12491. 1977. pap. 8.25 o.p. (ISBN 0-87258-220-5, 1755). Am Hospital.

Health Through Discovery. George B. Dintiman & Jerrold S. Greenberg. LC 79-20714. (Illus.). 1980. pap. text ed. 14.95 (ISBN 0-201-01256-1). A-W.

Health Unto His Majesty. Jean Plaidy. 288p. 1973. pap. 1.75 o.p. (ISBN 0-449-22019-2, P2019, Crest). Fawcett.

Health Visiting Practice. M. Saunders. 1968. 11.25 (ISBN 0-08-012899-8); pap. 5.75 (ISBN 0-08-012898-X). Pergamon.

Health: What Is It Worth? Measures of Health Benefits. Ed. by Selma J. Mushkin & David W. Dunlop. (Pergamon Policy Studies). 1979. 19.25 (ISBN 0-08-023898-X). Pergamon.

Healthier Living Highlights. 2nd ed. Justus J. Schifferes & Louis J. Peterson. LC 74-24339. (Illus.). 289p. 1975. text ed. 15.50x (ISBN 0-471-76071-4); thcrs. manual avail. (ISBN 0-471-76072-2). Wiley.

Healthwise Handbook: A Guide to Responsible Health Care. Toni M. Roberts et al. LC 78-55852. 1979. 6.95 o.p. (ISBN 0-385-14339-7, Dolp). Doubleday.

Healthy Adolescent: A Parent's Manual. Barry Lauton & Arthur S. Freese. 224p. 1981. 10.95 (ISBN 0-684-16819-7). Scribner.

Healthy Body Handbook: A Basic Guide to Diet & Nutrition, Yoga for Health, & Natural Cures for a Healthy Body. Swami Harihar Das & Dee Ito. LC 79-2802. (Illus.). 1980. pap. 5.95 (ISBN 0-06-090730-4, CN 730, CN). Har-Row.

Healthy Children: Nature's Way. Ann Wigmore. 120p. pap. 1.95. Hippocrates.

Healthy Eating. Margaret Happel. Ed. by B. Machtiger. (Savers Ser.). (Illus.). 128p. pap. cancelled (ISBN 0-88421-152-5). Butterick Pub.

Healthy Foods: Markets, Trends. BCC Staff. 1981. 750.00 (ISBN 0-89336-245-X, GA-047). BCC.

Healthy Gourmet: Low Calorie-Low Cholesterol-Low Cost Cookery. Doreen Wayne. 1979. 14.95x (ISBN 0-8464-0055-3). Beekman Pubs.

Healthy Heart. Arthur Fisher. Ed. by Time-Life Bks. Eds. (Library of Health). (Illus.). 176p. 1981. 11.95 (ISBN 0-8094-3750-3). Time-Life.

Healthy Heart Program. Terence Kavanagh. 328p. 1981. pap. 6.95 (ISBN 0-442-29768-8). Van Nos Reinhold.

Healthy Plant Handbook. Louis L. Pyenson. (Illus.). 1981. lib. bdg. 15.00 (ISBN 0-87055-377-1). AVI.

Healthy Pregnancy the Yoga Way. Judi Thompson. LC 76-23818. 160p. 1977. pap. 3.95 o.p. (ISBN 0-385-11631-4, Dolp). Doubleday.

Healthy Taste of Honey: Bee People's Recipes, Anecdotes & Lore. Larry J. Lonik. Ed. by Jean Campbell. (Illus.). 1981. deluxe ed. write for info. (ISBN 0-89865-020-8). Donning Co.

Heap O'Living. Edgar Guest. 1976. lib. bdg. 10.95x (ISBN 0-89968-041-0). Lightyear.

Hear the Word of the Lord. Neely D. McCarter. (Illus., Orig.). (gr. 11-12). 1964. pap. 3.45 (ISBN 0-8042-9210-8); tchrs' guide pap. 2.60. John Knox.

Hear Your Heart. Paul Showers. LC 68-11067. (Let's Read & Find Out Science Bk). (Illus.). (gr. k-3). 1968. bds. 6.95 (ISBN 0-690-37378-3, TYC-J); PLB 7.89 (ISBN 0-690-37379-1); filmstrip with record 11.95 (ISBN 0-690-37380-5); film with cassette 14.95 (ISBN 0-690-37382-1). T Y Crowell.

Hear Your Heart. Paul Showers. LC 68-11067. (Crocodile Paperbacks Ser.). (Illus.). 40p. (gr. k-3). 1975. pap. 2.95 (ISBN 0-690-00636-5, TYC-J). T Y Crowell.

Heard 'round the World. Ed. by Harold Hyman & Allan Nevins. (Impact of the Civil War Ser, Vol. 3). 1969. 7.95 o.p. (ISBN 0-394-42802-1). Knopf.

Hearers of the Word. Karl Rahner. 1969. 9.50 (ISBN 0-8164-1041-0). Crossroad NY.

Hearing. Gelfano. 392p. Date not set. 29.75 (ISBN 0-8247-1189-0). Dekker.

Hearing Aid Assessment & Use in Audiologic Rehabilitation. 2nd ed. W. R. Hodgson & Paul Skinner. (Illus.). 343p. 1981. write for info. (ISBN 0-683-04092-8). Williams & Wilkins.

Hearing Aid Dispensing for Audiologists: A Guide for Clinical Service. Ed. by Angela M. Loavenbruck & Jane Madell. 1980. 16.50 (ISBN 0-8089-1323-9). Grune.

Hearing Aids. Maurice Miller. LC 72-190707. (Studies in Communicative Disorders Ser). 1972. pap. 2.50 (ISBN 0-672-61284-4). Bobbs.

Hearing Aids & You. Craig et al. 121p. (gr. 4 up). 3.95 (ISBN 0-86575-028-9). Dormac.

Hearing & Research Theory, Vol. I. Ed. by Jerry V. Tobias & Earl D. Schubert. (Serial Publication). 1980. 18.50 (ISBN 0-12-312101-9). Acad Pr.

Hearing Book. Diane Barrager & Rodney Perkins. Orig. Title: Come Again, Please... (Illus.). 128p. 1980. pap. 8.95 (ISBN 0-89106-016-2, 7274). Consulting Psychol.

Hearing Conservation. Joseph Sataloff & Paul Michael. (Illus.). 376p. 1973. 21.75 (ISBN 0-398-02822-2). C C Thomas.

Hearing His Voice. John P. Grace. LC 79-54696. (Illus.). 160p. (Orig.). 1979. pap. 3.50 (ISBN 0-87793-187-9). Ave Maria.

Hearing-Impaired Preschool Child: A Book for Parents. Jean Semple. 104p. 1970. pap. 7.50 spiral (ISBN 0-398-01724-7). C C Thomas.

Hearing: Its Function & Dysfunction. E. D. Schubert. (Disorders of Human Communications: Vol. 1). (Illus.). 200p. 1980. 29.50 (ISBN 0-387-81579-1). Springer-Verlag.

Hearing Levels of U. S. Youths 12-17 Years. Jean Roberts & Elizabeth Ahuja. LC 74-11318. (Data from Health Examination Survey Ser. 11: No. 145). 65p. 1975. pap. 0.75 (ISBN 0-8406-0024-0). Natl Ctr Health Stats.

Hearing Loss, Hearing Aids & Your Child. A. L. Miller. (Illus.). 112p. 1980. lexotone 7.50 (ISBN 0-398-03979-8). C C Thomas.

Hearing on Hypolipidemic Drugs. Ed. by Rodolfo Paoletti. 1981. text ed. price not set (ISBN 0-89004-649-2). Raven.

Hearing: Physiology & Psychophysics. W. Lawrence Gulick. (Illus.). 1971. 16.95x (ISBN 0-19-501299-2). Oxford U Pr.

Hearing Science. Gelfand. Date not set. price not set (ISBN 0-8247-1189-0). Dekker.

Hearing the Parables of Jesus. Pheme Perkins. 216p. (Orig.). 1981. pap. 6.95 (ISBN 0-8091-2352-5). Paulist Pr.

Hearst & the New Deal - The Progressive As Reactionary. Rodney P. Carlisle. Ed. by Frank Freidel. LC 78-62378. (Modern American History Ser.: Vol. 4). 1979. lib. bdg. 28.00 (ISBN 0-8240-3628-X). Garland Pub.

Hearst: Family & Empire, the Later Years. Lindsay Chaney & Michael Ciepi. 1981. 14.95 (ISBN 0-671-24765-4). S&S.

Hearsts. Chaney & Cieply. 1981. 16.95 (ISBN 0-671-24765-4). S&S.

Heart. Kathleen Elgin. (Human Body Ser). (Illus.). (gr. 4-6). 1968. PLB 6.90 (ISBN 0-531-01174-7). Watts.

Heart. rev. ed. (Agni Yoga Ser.). 1975. softcover 9.00x (ISBN 0-933574-08-8). Agni Yoga Soc.

Heart. J. Willis Hurst. (Update Ser.: No. 5). (Illus.). 352p. 1981. text ed. 30.00 (ISBN 0-07-031495-0, HP). McGraw.

Heart & the Aorta. H. Vaquez & E. Bordet. 1920. 49.50x (ISBN 0-685-69879-3). Elliots Bks.

Heart & the Scarab. Marquerite Kloepfer. 288p. 1981. pap. 2.50 (ISBN 0-380-77610-3). Avon.

Heart & the Vascular System in Ancient Greek Medicine: From Alcmaeon to Galen. C. R. Harris. (Illus.). 500p. 1971. 74.00x (ISBN 0-19-858135-1). Oxford U Pr.

Heart & Vascular Systems Basic Sciences. 2nd ed. William B. Wood & Frank D. Sticht. 1977. spiral bdg. 11.50 (ISBN 0-87488-212-5). Med Exam.

Heart Attack! Louis S. Levine. LC 75-30337. 128p. 1976. 6.95 o.p. (ISBN 0-06-012595-0, HarpT). Har-Row.

Heart Attack: A Question & Answer Book. Oscar Roth & Lawrence Galton. (Illus.). 1978. 8.95 o.s.i. (ISBN 0-397-01263-2). Lippincott.

Heart Attack: Are You a Candidate? Arthur Blumenfeld. (Illus.). 1971. pap. 1.50 o.s.i. (ISBN 0-515-04302-8). Jove Pubns.

Heart Attack Rareness in Thyroid-Treated Patients. Broda O. Barnes & Charlotte W. Barnes. 104p. 1972. pap. 11.75 photocopy ed. spiral (ISBN 0-398-02519-3). C C Thomas.

Heart Attack Survival Manual. Roger J. Seymour. 144p. 1981. 11.95 (ISBN 0-13-385740-9, Spec); pap. 5.95 (ISBN 0-13-385732-8). P-H.

Heart Attack: You Don't Have to Die. Christiaan Barnard. 1972. 6.95 o.s.i. (ISBN 0-440-03536-8). Delacorte.

Heart Attacks: Is Your Family a Risk Factor? Ann Rubinson. 1981. 8.95 (ISBN 0-533-04217-8). Vantage.

Heart-Beguiling Araby. Kathryn Tidrick. (Illus.). 256p. Date not set. price not set (ISBN 0-521-23483-2). Cambridge U Pr.

Heart Book. American Heart Association. (Illus.). 1980. 25.00 (ISBN 0-525-93056-6). Dutton.

Heart Creatin Kinase. William E. Jacobus & Joanne Ingwall. (Illus.). 216p. 1980. 39.00 (ISBN 0-683-04353-6). Williams & Wilkins.

Heart Disease. Marianne Tully & Alice Tully. (gr. 4 up). 1980. PLB 6.45 (ISBN 0-531-04163-8). Watts.

Heart Disease & Pregnancy. Paul Szekely & Linton Snaith. (Illus.). 208p. 1974. text ed. 27.50x (ISBN 0-443-01135-4). Churchill.

Heart Disease & Rehabilitation. Michael L. Pollock & Donald H. Schmidt. 1979. 45.00x (ISBN 0-89289-407-5). HM Prof Med Div.

Heart Disease in Infancy. James H. Moller & William A. Neal. 522p. 1980. 36.50x (ISBN 0-8385-3671-9). ACC.

Heart Disease in Infancy & Childhood. 3rd ed. John D. Keith et al. (Illus.). 1978. text ed. 58.00 (ISBN 0-02-362220-2). Macmillan.

Heart Divided. Ann Gabhart. (Orig.). 1980. pap. 2.50 (ISBN 0-446-91250-6). Warner Bks.

Heart Failures. Ursula Perrin. 1980. pap. 1.95 (ISBN 0-380-47589-8, 47589). Avon.

Heart Has Wings. Faith Baldwin. 1981. pap. price not set (ISBN 0-671-83094-5). PB.

Heart in Pilgrimage: Christian Guidelines for the Human Journey. Christopher Bryant. 208p. 1980. 9.95 (ISBN 0-8164-0457-7). Seabury.

Heart Is a Lonely Hunter. Carson Mc Cullers. (Literature Ser). (gr. 9-12). 1940. pap. text ed. 4.25 (ISBN 0-87720-753-4). AMSCO Sch.

Heart Is Like Heaven: The Life of Lydia Maria Child. Helene G. Baer. LC 64-10895. 1964. 10.00x o.p. (ISBN 0-8122-7442-3). U of Pa Pr.

Heart Is No Stranger. Luciano Comici. (Orig.). 1981. pap. 2.50 (ISBN 0-515-04801-1). Jove Pubns.

Heart: Its Function in Health & Disease. rev. ed. Arthur Selzer. (Perspectives in Medicine: No. 1). (YA) (gr. 9 up). 1968. 14.50 (ISBN 0-520-01162-7). U of Cal Pr.

Heart Listens. Helen Van Slyke. 576p. 1975. pap. 2.75 (ISBN 0-445-08520-7). Popular Lib.

Heart Never Forgets. Carolyn Thornton. 192p. (Orig.). 1980. pap. 1.50 (ISBN 0-671-57019-6). S&S.

Heart of Arabia, 2 vols. H. St. John Philby. 1980. Repr. Set. 55.00x (ISBN 0-7146-3072-1, F Cass Co). Biblio Dist.

Heart of Confucius: Interpretations of "Genuine Living" & "Great Wisdom". Archie J. Bahm. LC 76-83638. (Arcturus Books Paperbacks). (Illus.). 159p. 1977. pap. 4.95 (ISBN 0-8093-0828-2). S Ill U Pr.

Heart of Darkness. Joseph Conrad. 112p. Repr. of 1973 ed. lib. bdg. cancelled (ISBN 0-8376-0458-3). Bentley.

Heart of Darkness & the Secret Sharer. Joseph Conrad. 1978. Repr. of 1910 ed. lib. bdg. 12.50x (ISBN 0-89966-054-1). Buccaneer Bks.

Heart of Emerson's Journals. Ed. by Bliss Perry. 357p. 1980. Repr. of 1926 ed. lib. bdg. 30.00 (ISBN 0-89987-670-6). Darby Bks.

Heart of England: Shakespeare Country. rev. ed. British Tourist Authority. (Illus.). 122p. 1981. pap. write for info. (ISBN 0-86143-041-7, Pub. by Auto Assn-British Tourist Authority England). Merrimack Bk Serv.

Heart of Friendship. Muriel James & Louis Savary. LC 74-25702. 1978. pap. 4.95 (ISBN 0-06-064113-4, RD 254, HarpR). Har-Row.

Heart of Gold. Paul Williams. 1981. pap. 4.95 (ISBN 0-9601428-8-6); 9.95 (ISBN 0-934558-10-8). Entwhistle Bks.

Heart of Hebrew History. H. I. Hester. 1980. Repr. of 1949 ed. 8.95 (ISBN 0-8054-1217-4). Broadman.

Heart of Honor. Caroline Courtney. 1980. pap. 1.75 (ISBN 0-446-94294-4). Warner Bks.

Heart of Ice. Benjamin Appel. LC 76-4815. (Illus.). (gr. 1 up). 1977. 5.95 (ISBN 0-394-83245-0); PLB 6.99 (ISBN 0-394-93245-5). Pantheon.

Heart of Jazz. William Grossman & Jack Farrell. LC 76-75730. (Roots of Jazz Ser.). 1976. Repr. of 1956 ed. lib. bdg. 25.00 (ISBN 0-306-70811-6). Da Capo.

Heart of Life. W. H. Mallock. Ed. by Robert L. Wolff. LC 75-1538. (Victorian Fiction Ser.). 1975. Repr. of 1895 ed. lib. bdg. 66.00 (ISBN 0-8240-1610-6). Garland Pub.

Heart of Man: Its Genius for Good & Evil. Erich Fromm. LC 64-18053. 1980. pap. 3.95 (ISBN 0-06-090119-5, CN 795, CN). Har-Row.

Heart of Midlothian. Walter Scott. 1956. 10.50x (ISBN 0-460-00134-5, Evman); pap. 3.95 o.p. (ISBN 0-460-01134-0, EP1134). Dutton.

Heart of Standing Is You Cannot Fly. Raji Narasimhan. (Writers Workshop Greenbird Book Ser.). 131p. 1975. 14.00 (ISBN 0-88253-558-7); pap. text ed. 6.75 (ISBN 0-88253-557-9). Ind-US Inc.

Heart of Texas. Al Cody. 1981. pap. 1.95 (ISBN 0-8439-0861-0, Leisure Bks). Nordon Pubns.

Heart of the Clan. Barbara Cartland. (Barbara Cartland Ser.: No. 13). 192p. (Orig.). 1981. pap. 1.75 (ISBN 0-515-05929-3). Jove Pubns.

Heart of the Gospel. 2nd rev. ed. George Townshend. 5.50 (ISBN 0-85398-025-X, 7-31-16); pap. 1.75 (ISBN 0-85398-020-9, 7-31-17, Pub. by G Ronald England). Baha'i.

Heart of the Hunter. Laurens Van Der Post. LC 80-15539. 1980. pap. 4.95 (ISBN 0-15-640003-0, Harv). HarBraceJ.

Heart of the Matter. Diana Burke. (Orig.). 1980. pap. 1.50 o.s.i. (ISBN 0-440-14208-3). Dell.
Heart of the Matter. Graham Greene. 1981. 14.95 (ISBN 0-670-36459-2). Viking Pr.
Heart of the New Testament. H. I. Hester. 1980. Repr. of 1950 ed. 8.95 (ISBN 0-8054-1386-3). Broadman.
Heart of the Ribhu Gita with a Story by Sri Ramana Maharshi. Ed. by Franklin Jones. LC 73-88178. (Illus.). 1973. pap. 2.50 o.p. (ISBN 0-913922-03-X). Dawn Horse Pr.
Heart of the World. H. Rider Haggard. Ed. by R. Reginald & Douglas Menville. LC 80-19175. (Newcastle Forgotten Fantasy Library: Vol. 10). 347p. 1980. Repr. of 1976 ed. lib. bdg. 10.95x (ISBN 0-89370-509-8). Borgo Pr.
Heart of the World. Hans Urs Von Balthasar. Tr. by Erasmo Leiva from Ger. LC 79-84879. Orig. Title: Herz der Welt. 219p. (Orig.). 1980. pap. 5.95 (ISBN 0-89870-001-9). Ignatius Pr.
Heart of the World: An Introduction to Contemplative Christianity. Thomas Keating. 96p. 1981. 8.95 (ISBN 0-8245-0014-8). Crossroad NY.
Heart of Truth: Finney's Outlines of Theology. Charles G. Finney. LC 75-46128. Orig. Title: Skeletons of a Course of Theological Lectures. 1976. pap. 4.50 (ISBN 0-87123-226-X, 210226). Bethany Fell.
Heart of War. John Masters. LC 80-12491. (Loss of Eden Ser.). 608p. 1980. write for info. McGraw.
Heart on Holiday. Elaine F. Palencia. (Orig.). 1980. pap. 1.50 o.s.i. (ISBN 0-440-13476-5). Dell.
Heart-Organ: Part of My Body. Terry Kennedy. 1981. pap. 3.50 (ISBN 0-915016-30-3). Second Coming.
Heart Possessed. Elizabeth Borton De Trevino. LC 77-26523. 1978. 7.95 o.p. (ISBN 0-385-03536-5). Doubleday.
Heart Sings. Georgiana L. Lahr. 3.50 o.p. (ISBN 0-685-26028-3). Vantage.
Heart Talks on Holiness. Samuel L. Brengle. 1978. pap. 3.25 (ISBN 0-86544-002-6). Salvation Army.
Heart to Hand: A Calligraphy Manual. Kitty Maguire. (Illus.). 68p. 1980. text ed. 25.00 limited ed of 50 (ISBN 0-9604818-0-X); pap. 12.00 (ISBN 0-9604818-1-8). Anemone Edns.
Heartaches & Handicaps: An Irreverent Survival Manual for Parents. Gail Stigen. LC 74-74561. 1976. 5.95 o.p. (ISBN 0-8314-0040-4). Sci & Behavior.
Heartbreak Hotel. Anne Rivers Siddons. 1977. pap. 1.95 o.p. (ISBN 0-445-04027-0). Popular Lib.
Heartbreak House. George B. Shaw. Ed. by Stanley Weintraub & Anne Wright. LC 79-56710. (Bernard Shaw Early Texts: Play Manuscripts in Facsimile). 1981. lib. bdg. 50.00 (ISBN 0-8240-4585-8). Garland Pub.
Hearth & Eagle. Anya Seton. 1978. pap. 2.50 (ISBN 0-449-23641-2, Crest). Fawcett.
Hearth & Home: Images of Women in the Mass Media. Ed. by Gaye Tuchman et al. 1978. text ed. 16.95x (ISBN 0-19-502351-X); pap. text ed. 5.95x (ISBN 0-19-502352-8). Oxford U Pr.
Hearthside Scrapbook. Arnett Tackett. 53p. 1979. pap. 2.95 o.p. (ISBN 0-8059-2681-X). Dorrance.
Heartland. Stuart Legg. 1970. 8.95 o.p. (ISBN 0-374-16866-0). FS&G.
Heartland II: Poets of the Midwest. Ed. by Lucien Stryk. LC 74-12817. 255p. 1975. o.p 10.00 (ISBN 0-87580-050-5); pap. 5.00 (ISBN 0-87580-517-5). N Ill U Pr.
Heartland of Cities: Surveys of Ancient Settlement & Land Use on the Central Floodplain of the Euphrates. Robert M. Adams. LC 80-13995. (Illus.). 384p. 1981. lib. bdg. 35.00x (ISBN 0-226-00544-5). U of Chicago Pr.
Heartland: Ohio, Indiana, Illinois. rev. ed. Walter Havighurst. Ed. by Carl Cramer. LC 74-1815. (Regions of America). (Illus.). 432p. (YA) 1974. 12.50 o.s.i. (ISBN 0-06-011781-8, HarpT). Har-Row.
Hearts & Heart-Like Organs: Comparative Anatomy & Development, Vol. I. Ed. by Geoffrey H. Bourne. LC 80-760. 1980. 51.00 (ISBN 0-12-119401-9). Acad Pr.
Hearts & Heart-Like Organs, Vol. 2: Physiology. Ed. by Geoffrey H. Bourne. LC 80-18121. 1980. 57.00 (ISBN 0-12-119402-7). Acad Pr.
Hearts & Heart-Like Organs: Vol. 3, Physiology. Ed. by Geoffrey H. Bourne. 1980. 53.00 (ISBN 0-12-119403-5). Acad Pr.
Heart's Awakening. Rose Marie Ferris. (Candelight Romance Ser.). (Orig.). 1981. pap. 1.50 (ISBN 0-440-13519-2). Dell.
Heart's Crow. Carmine Dandrea. (Redbird Book). 27p. 1975. 8.00 (ISBN 0-88253-714-8); pap. text ed. 4.80 (ISBN 0-685-53424-3). Ind-US Inc.
Hearts, Cupids & Red Roses. Edna Barth. LC 73-7128. (Illus.). (gr. 2-6). 8.95 (ISBN 0-395-28841-X, Clarion). HM.
Heart's Desire. Emerson Hough. 1976. lib. bdg. 16.25x (ISBN 0-89968-045-3). Lightyear.
Heart's Events: The Victorian Poetry of Relationships. Patricia M. Ball. 240p. 1976. text ed. 21.50x (ISBN 0-485-11163-2, Athlone Pr). Humanities.
Heart's Witness: The Sufi Quatrains of Awhaduddin Kirmani. Tr. by Bernd M. Weischer & Peter L. Wilson. LC 78-72535. 1979. 11.50 (ISBN 0-87773-719-3). Great Eastern.
Heartsounds. Martha W. Lear. 1981. pap. price not set (ISBN 0-671-41986-2). PB.
Heat. Vicki Cobb. LC 68-17703. (First Bks). (Illus.). 72p. (gr. 5-8). 1973. PLB 4.90 o.p. (ISBN 0-531-00787-1). Watts.
Heat. Philip Parker. 1971. text ed. 8.50x o.p. (ISBN 0-435-68644-5). Heinemann Ed.
Heat. rev. ed. Harlan Wade. LC 78-20959. (Book About Ser.). (Illus.). (gr. k-3). 1979. PLB 7.30 (ISBN 0-8172-1536-0). Raintree Pubs.
Heat & Fluid Flow in Power System Components. Ed. by A. M. Rezk. (Heat & Mass Transfer: Vol. 3). (Illus.). 300p. 1980. 55.00 (ISBN 0-08-024235-9). Pergamon.
Heat & Mass Transfer. 2nd ed. E. R. Eckert. LC 81-359. 344p. 1981. Repr. lib. bdg. price not set (ISBN 0-89874-332-X). Krieger.
Heat & Mass Transfer in Metallurgical Systems: Proceedings of the International Center for Heat & Mass Transfer. Ed. by D. Brian Spalding & Naim H. Afgan. (Illus.). 800p. 1981. text ed. 85.50 (ISBN 0-89116-169-4). Hemisphere Pub.
Heat & Mass Transfers in Flows with Separated Regions. Ed. by Z. Zaric. LC 72-85858. 232p. 1975. pap. text ed. 29.00 (ISBN 0-08-017156-7). Pergamon.
Heat & Temperature. Jeanne Bendick. LC 73-19885. (Science Experiences Ser.). (Illus.). 72p. (gr. 3-6). 1974. PLB 4.90 o.p. (ISBN 0-531-01438-X). Watts.
Heat & Thermodynamics. 6th ed. Mark Zemansky & Richard Dittman. (Illus.). 560p. 1981. text ed. 22.95 (ISBN 0-07-072808-9, C). McGraw.
Heat Budget Atlas of the Tropical Atlantic & Eastern Pacific Oceans. Stefan Hastenrath & Peter J. Lamb. LC 77-91052. (Illus.). 1978. pap. text ed. 50.00x (ISBN 0-299-07584-2). U of Wis Pr.
Heat Conduction. M. Necati Ozisik. LC 79-990. 1980. 29.95 (ISBN 0-471-05481-X, Pub. by Wiley-Interscience). Wiley.
Heat Death. Stephen Dobyns. LC 79-55592. 1980. 10.00 (ISBN 0-689-11034-0); pap. 5.95 (ISBN 0-689-11063-4). Atheneum.
Heat Engines Through Theory & Examples. J. S. Arwikar & C. B. Mishra. pap. 15.00x (ISBN 0-210-31219-X). Asia.
Heat Exchange Fluids & Techniques. M. W. Ranney. LC 79-20336. (Energy Tech Review, No. 50, Chemical Review Ser.: No. 143). (Illus.). 1980. 42.00 (ISBN 0-8155-0778-X). Noyes.
Heat Exchanges - Thermohydraulic Fundamentals & Design, 2 vols. Ed. by Sadik Kakac et al. (Illus.). 1000p. 1981. Set. text ed. 95.00 (ISBN 0-89116-225-9). Hemisphere Pub.
Heat, Mass & Momentum Transfer. Warren M. Rohsenow & H. Choi. (Illus.). 1961. text ed. 27.95 (ISBN 0-13-385187-7). P-H.
Heat Pipes. P. D. Dunn & D. A. Reay. 1975. text ed. 24.20 o.p. (ISBN 0-08-019854-6); pap. text ed. 16.50 o.p. (ISBN 0-08-021240-9). Pergamon.
Heat Pipes. 2nd ed. P. D. Dunn & D. A. Reay. 1977. text ed. 45.00 (ISBN 0-08-022127-0); pap. text ed. 17.00 (ISBN 0-08-022128-9). Pergamon.
Heat Pump Technology. Hans L. Von Cube & Fritz Staimle. Tr. by E. G. Goodall. 1981. text ed. price not set (ISBN 0-408-00497-5, Newnes-Butterworth). Butterworth.
Heat Pump Technology: A Survey of Technical Developments, Market Prospects & Research Needs. Gordian Associates for the U. S. Department of Energy. 464p. 1980. 44.95 (ISBN 0-89934-016-4); pap. 29.95 (ISBN 0-89934-017-2). Solar Energy Info.
Heat Pumps & Electric Heating: Residential, Commercial, Industrial Year-Round Air Conditioning. E. R. Ambrose. LC 65-27664. 1966. 25.00 (ISBN 0-471-02530-5, Pub by Wiley-Interscience). Wiley.
Heat Pumps Their Contribution to Energy Conservation. Ed. by E. Camatini & T. Kester. 428p. 1976. 42.50x (ISBN 90-286-0056-6). Sijthoff & Noordhoff.
Heat Resistant Polymers. V. V. Korshak. 1969. 43.95 o.p. (ISBN 0-470-50426-9). Halsted Pr.
Heat-Resistant Polymers. V. V. Korshak. 43.95 o.p. (ISBN 0-87245-446-0). Textile Bk.
Heat Transfer. 5th ed. J. P. Holman. (Illus.). 672p. 1981. text ed. 27.95x (ISBN 0-07-029618-9, C); solutions manual 8.95 (ISBN 0-07-029619-7). McGraw.
Heat Transfer & Fluid Flow in Nuclear Systems. Ed. by Henri French. 300p. 1981. 30.01 (ISBN 0-08-027181-2). Pergamon.
Heat Transfer & Turbulent Buoyant Convection: Studies & Applications for Natural Environment, Buildings Engineering Systems, 2 vols. new ed. Ed. by D. Brian Spalding & N. Afgan. LC 77-1868. (Thermal and Fluids Engineering Ser.). (Illus.). 1977. text ed. 129.50 set (ISBN 0-89116-163-5, Co-Pub. by McGraw Intl). Hemisphere Pub.
Heat Transfer & Vulcanisation of Rubber. D. A. Hills. (Illus.). 1971. text ed. 22.30x (ISBN 0-444-20075-4, Pub. by Applied Science). Burgess-Intl Ideas.
Heat Transfer Calculations for Buildings. R. W. Muncey. (Illus.). 1979. 23.20x (ISBN 0-85334-852-9, Pub. by Applied Science). Burgess-Intl Ideas.
Heat Transfer Calculations Using Finite Difference Equations. David R. Croft & David G. Lilley. (Illus.). 1977. 55.90x (ISBN 0-85334-720-4, Pub. by Applied Science). Burgess-Intl Ideas.
Heat Transfer-Current Application of Air Conditioning. International Institute of Refrigeration. Ed. by A. Van Iherbeek. 1971. 90.00 (ISBN 0-08-016597-4). Pergamon.
Heat Transfer in Nuclear Reactor Safety: Proceedings of the International Centre for Heat & Mass Transfer. Ed. by S. George Bankoff et al. (International Centre for Heat & Mass Transfer). (Illus.). 1981. text ed. 95.00 (ISBN 0-89116-223-2). Hemisphere Pub.
Heat Transfer in Rod Bundles. 1968. pap. 8.50 o.p. (ISBN 0-685-06527-8, H00003). ASME.
Heat Transfer Textbook. John Lienhard. (Illus.). 480p. 1981. text ed. 24.95 (ISBN 0-13-385112-5). P-H.
Heath Handbook of Composition. 10th ed. Langdon Elsbree et al. 448p. 1981. text ed. 8.95 (ISBN 0-669-03352-9); pap. text ed. 7.95 (ISBN 0-669-03353-7); instr's guide with tests avail. (ISBN 0-669-03356-1); wkbk. 4.95 (ISBN 0-669-03456-8). Heath.
Heathcliff. George Gately. (Heathcliff Cartoon Ser.: No. 1). (Illus.). 128p. (gr. 5 up). 1981. pap. 1.50 (ISBN 0-448-12616-8, Tempo). G&D.
Heathcliff Rides Again. George Gately. 128p. 1981. pap. 1.50 (ISBN 0-448-12629-X, Tempo). G&D.
Heathen Days. H. L. Mencken. Repr. of 1955 ed. 8.95 o.p. (ISBN 0-394-42810-2). Knopf.
Heather. Cordia Byers. (Orig.). 1979. pap. 1.95 o.p. (ISBN 0-449-14272-8, GM). Fawcett.
Heather McKay's Complete Book of Squash. Heather McKay & Jack Batten. (Illus.). 1979. 5.95 (ISBN 0-345-28250-7); pap. 10.95 (ISBN 0-345-28271-X). Ballantine.
Heather Song. Nicole Norman. 1980. pap. 2.50 (ISBN 0-671-41463-1). PB.
Heather's Feathers. Leatie Weiss. LC 76-12624. (Easy-Read Storybooks). (Illus.). 32p. (gr. k-3). 1976. 3.95 o.p. (ISBN 0-531-02475-X); PLB 4.90 o.p. (ISBN 0-531-01204-2). Watts.
Heathers in Color. Brian Proudley & Valerie Proudley. (Color Ser.). (Illus.). 1974. 9.95 (ISBN 0-7137-0635-X, Pub by Blandford Pr England). Sterling.
Heaths & Heathers. Terry Underhill. 1975. 14.00 o.p. (ISBN 0-7153-4970-8). David & Charles.
Heating & Air-Conditioning Ducts Encased in & Under Concrete Slabs-On-Ground. Federal Housing Administration - Building Research Advisory Board. 1961. pap. 3.00 (ISBN 0-309-00838-7). Natl Acad Pr.
Heating & Cooling. Ed. by Time-Life Books. LC 77-80200. (Home Repair & Improvement Ser.). (Illus.). (gr. 7 up). 1977. lib. bdg. 11.97 (ISBN 0-685-77684-0, Pub. by Time-Life). Silver.
Heating & Cooling. Ed. by Time-Life Books. (Home Repair & Improvement Ser.). 1977. 10.95 (ISBN 0-8094-2378-2). Time-Life.
Heating & Cooling Load Calculations. P. G. Down. 1969. 26.00 (ISBN 0-08-013001-1). Pergamon.
Heating & Cooling Safety. V. Paul Lang. LC 76-24983. (gr. 9-12). 1977. pap. 3.80 (ISBN 0-8273-1011-0); instructor's guide 1.00 (ISBN 0-8273-1012-9). Delmar.
Heating & Hot Water Services for Technicians. Keith Moss. 1978. 20.00 (ISBN 0-408-00300-6). Transatlantic.
Heating & Hot Water Services in Buildings. D. Kut. 1968. 32.00 (ISBN 0-08-012218-3). Pergamon.
Heating Boilers. (Boilers & Pressure Vessel Code Ser.: Sec. 4). 1980. 65.00 (P00040); pap. 85.00 loose-leaf (V00040). ASME.
Heating in Toroidal Plasmas: Proceedings. Commission of the European Communities, Joint Varenna-Grenoble International Symposium on Heating in Toroidal Plasmas, Grenoble, July 1978. 1978. text ed. 125.00 (ISBN 0-08-023400-3). Pergamon.
Heating Service Design. Bronthon. 1981. text ed. 53.95 (ISBN 0-408-00380-4). Butterworth.
Heating, Ventilating & Air Conditioning Fundamentals. Raymond Havrella. LC 80-17155. (Contemporary Construction Ser.). (Illus.). 288p. (gr. 10-12). 1981. text ed. 16.95x (ISBN 0-07-027281-6, G); wkbk. avail. (ISBN 0-07-027283-2). McGraw.
Heating, Ventilating, & Air Conditioning Library, 3 vols. James Brumbaugh. LC 76-29155. (Illus.). 1976. 11.95 ea. Vol. 1 (ISBN 0-672-23248-0, 23248). Vol. 2 (ISBN 0-672-23249-9, 23249). Vol. 3 (ISBN 0-672-23250-2, 23250). 32.95, set of 3 vols. (ISBN 0-672-23227-8). Audel.
Heating with Coal. John W. Bartok. (Illus.). 160p. 1980. pap. 6.95 (ISBN 0-88266-243-0). Garden Way Pub.
Heaven. Ed. by Edward Schillebeeck & Van B. Iersel. (Concilium Ser.: Vol. 123). 1979. pap. 4.95 (ISBN 0-8164-2231-1). Crossroad NY.
Heaven & Hell. S. Foster Damon. Ed. by Catherine Brown. (Illus., Orig.). 1978. pap. 5.50 (ISBN 0-914278-17-7). Copper Beech.
Heaven & Hell. Emanual Swedenborg. 1976. pap. 1.95 (ISBN 0-89129-110-5). Jove Pubns.
Heaven & Hell & the Megus Factor. Robert Nathan. 128p. 1975. 6.95 o.p. (ISBN 0-440-04328-X). Delacorte.
Heaven, Earth, & Man in the Book of Changes: Seven Eranos Lectures. Hellmut Wilhelm. LC 76-7801. (Publications on Asia of the School of International Studies: No. 28). 248p. 1977. 15.00 (ISBN 0-295-95516-3); pap. 8.95 (ISBN 0-295-95692-5). U of Wash Pr.
Heaven Help the Home! Howard G. Hendricks. LC 73-78689. 1974. pap. 3.95 (ISBN 0-88207-240-4). Victor Bks.
Heaven in My Hand. Alice L. Humphreys. LC 50-3332. 1950. deluxe ed. 4.95 (ISBN 0-8042-2352-1). John Knox.
Heaven Makers. Frank Herbert. (Del Rey Bk.). 1977. pap. 1.50 o.p. (ISBN 0-345-25304-3). Ballantine.
Heaven on Earth, Family Style. J. Norman Charles & Sharon Charles. (Orig.). 1980. pap. 4.95 (ISBN 0-88270-495-8). Logos.
Heaven: The Heart's Deepest Longing. Peter J. Kreeft. LC 80-7747. 160p. 1980. 8.95 (ISBN 0-06-064776-0, HarpR). Har-Row.
Heaven to Betsy. Maud H. Lovelace. LC 45-9806. (Illus.). (gr. 5-11). 1945. 9.95 (ISBN 0-690-37449-6, TYC-J). T Y Crowell.
Heavenly Bits of Specialness. Marjorie L. Dodd. Ed. by Bobbie J. Van Dolson. (Illus.). (gr. k-3). 1976. pap. 1.50 (ISBN 0-8280-0048-4). Review & Herald.
Heavenly Computer. Adah Brown. 1979. 4.50 o.p. (ISBN 0-8062-1212-8). Carlton.
Heavenly Deception. Chris Elkins. 1980. pap. 3.95 (ISBN 0-8423-1402-4). Tyndale.
Heavenly Life for Earthly Living. C. E. Orr. 60p. 0.40; 3 copies. Faith Pub Hse.
Heavenly Zoo. Alison Lurie. LC 71-21263. (Illus.). 64p. (gr. k-4). 1980. 9.95 (ISBN 0-374-32910-9). FS&G.
Heavens Are Cleft Asunder. rev. ed. Huschmand Sabet. Tr. by Oliver Coburn from Ger. Orig. Title: Gespaltene Himmel. (Eng.). 1975. 6.25 (ISBN 0-85398-055-1, 7-32-14, Pub. by G Ronald England); pap. 4.90 o.s.i. (ISBN 0-85398-056-X, 7-32-15). Baha'i.
Heavens Blaze Forth. Amanda H. Douglass. 1978. pap. 1.75 (ISBN 0-505-51252-1). Tower Bks.
Heaven's My Destination. Thornton Wilder. pap. 2.50 (ISBN 0-380-00331-7, 49395, Bard). Avon.
Heavens on Earth: Utopian Communities in America 1680-1880. rev. ed. Mark Holloway. 1966. pap. 4.00 (ISBN 0-486-21593-8). Dover.
Heaven's Tableland: The Dust Bowl Story. Vance Johnson. LC 73-20453. (FDR & the Era of the New Deal Ser.). (Illus.). 288p. 1974. Repr. of 1947 ed. lib. bdg. 29.50 (ISBN 0-306-70606-7). Da Capo.
Heavens to Betsy & Other Curious Sayings. Charles E. Funk. LC 55-8053. (Illus.). 1955. 10.95 o.p. (ISBN 0-06-001740-6, HarpT). Har-Row.
Heavy Clay Technology. F. H. Clews. 1969. 29.00 o.s.i. (ISBN 0-12-176350-1). Acad Pr.
Heavy Construction Cost File, 1980: Unit Prices. Coert Engelsman. 286p. 1980. pap. text ed. 24.50 (ISBN 0-686-63073-4). Van Nos Reinhold.
Heavy Equipment. Jan Adkins. LC 80-15213. (Illus.). 32p. (gr. 1-4). 1980. 7.95 (ISBN 0-686-62530-7). Scribner.
Heavy Equipment Repair. Herbert L. Nichols, Jr. LC 64-22821. (Illus.). 1964. 15.00 o.p. (ISBN 0-911040-06-4). North Castle.
Heavy Horse at Work. Edward Hart. (Illus.). 64p. 1981. pap. 5.95 (ISBN 0-7134-3805-3, Pub. by Batsford England). David & Charles.
Heavy Horses Past & Present. Edward Hart. LC 75-31325. (Illus.). 112p. 1976. 14.95 (ISBN 0-7153-7146-0). David & Charles.
Heavy-Ion, High-Spin States & Nuclear Structure, 2 vols. (Illus.). 872p. 1975. Set. pap. 64.25 (ISBN 0-685-61024-1, IAEA). Unipub.

Heavy Minerals in the Wellborn Formation, Lee & Burleson Counties, Texas. C. A. Shelby. (Illus.). 54p. 1965. 1.25 (RI 55). Bur Econ Geology.

Heavy Nuclei, Superheavy Nuclei, & Neutron Stars. J. M. Irvine. (Oxford Studies in Nuclear Physics). (Illus.). 200p. 1975. 34.95x (ISBN 0-19-851510-3). Oxford U Pr.

Heavy Sand. Anatoli Rybakov. Tr. by Harold Shukman from Rus. 384p. 1981. 13.95 (ISBN 0-670-36499-1). Viking Pr.

Heavy Transition Elements. S. A. Cotton & E. A. Hart. 1975. 28.95 o.p. (ISBN 0-470-17681-4). Halsted Pr.

Heavy Water Lattices. (Illus., Orig.). 1960. pap. 4.50 (ISBN 92-0-151060-8, IAEA). Unipub.

Heavy Water Lattices: Second Panel Report. (Technical Reports Ser.: No. 20). (Illus., Orig.). 1963. pap. 23.75 (ISBN 92-0-051063-9, IAEA). Unipub.

Heavy-Water Power Reactors. (Illus., Orig., Eng. & Fr.). 1968. pap. 47.25 (ISBN 92-0-050268-7, IAEA). Unipub.

Heavy Weather. Michael E. Knerr. 1979. pap. 1.75 (ISBN 0-505-51426-5). Tower Bks.

Hebbel's Prose Tragedies. Mary Garland. LC 72-88621. (Anglica Germanica Ser.: No. 2). 364p. 1973. 60.00 (ISBN 0-521-20090-3). Cambridge U Pr.

Hebreo Biblico Ejercicios Programados: Tomo 2. 192p. (Span.). Date not set. pap. price not set (ISBN 0-311-42069-9, Edit Mundo). Casa Bautista.

Hebreo Biblico Texto Programado: Tomo 1. Moises Chavez. (Span.). Date not set. pap. price not set (ISBN 0-311-42068-0, Edit Mundo). Casa Bautista.

Hebrew & Chaldee Lexicon, Tregelles Translation. William Gesenius. 1949. 11.95 (ISBN 0-8028-8029-0). Eerdmans.

Hebrew & English Lexicon to the Old Testament. William Osbourn, Jr. 287p. 1981. pap. 5.95 (ISBN 0-310-20361-9). Zondervan.

Hebrew & Hellene in Victorian England: Newman, Arnold, & Pater. David J. DeLaura. 1969. 16.50x o.p. (ISBN 0-292-78404-X). U of Tex Pr.

Hebrew-Arabic Dictionary of the Bible Known As Kitab Jami-Al-Alfaz, 2 vols. Ed. by Solomon Skoss. (Yale Oriental Researches Ser.: No. XX, XXI). 1945. 50.00x ea.; 95.00x set (ISBN 0-686-57837-6). Elliots Bks.

Hebrew Ballads & Other Poems. Else Lasker-Schuler. 128p. 1980. 10.95 (ISBN 0-8276-0179-4, 460); pap. 6.95 (ISBN 0-8276-0180-8, 459). Jewish Pubn.

Hebrew Basic Course. Foreign Service Institute. 552p. (Hebrew.). 1980. 185.00x (ISBN 0-88432-040-5, H345); 24 audiocassettes incl. J Norton Pubs.

Hebrew Bible in Art. Jacob Leveen. LC 74-78239. (Illus.). 208p. 1974. Repr. 14.50 (ISBN 0-87203-045-8). Hermon.

Hebrew Deluge Story. Albert T. Clay. (Yale Oriental Researches Ser.: No. V, Pt. III). 1922. 19.50x (ISBN 0-685-69802-5). Elliots Bks.

Hebrew-English Old Testament. 1200p. (Heb. & Eng.). 24.95 (ISBN 0-310-20370-8). Zondervan.

Hebrew Fragments of Pseudo-Philo. Ed. & tr. by Daniel J. Harrington. LC 73-89170. (Society of Biblical Literature. Texts & Translation-Psuedepigrapha Ser.). 1974. pap. 4.50 (ISBN 0-88414-036-9, 060203). Scholars Pr Ca.

Hebrew Illuminated Manuscripts in the British Isles: A Catalogue Raisonne, Vol. I; Spanish & Portugese Manuscripts. Bezalel Narkiss. (Illus.). 492p. 1981. 125.00 (ISBN 0-686-69114-8) (ISBN 0-19-725977-4). Oxford U Pr.

Hebrew Kingdoms. Eric W. Heaton. (New Clarendon Bible Ser.). 1968. 8.95x (ISBN 0-19-836905-0). Oxford U Pr.

Hebrew Kings. Joan Comay. (Illus.). 1977. 8.95 o.p. (ISBN 0-688-03139-0). Morrow.

Hebrew Old Testament Slidaverb Tm Conjugation Chart. David E. Peterson. laminated plastic 3.95 o.p. (ISBN 0-310-31090-3). Zondervan.

Hebrew Passover from the Earliest Times to A.D. 70. Judah B. Segal. 1963. 24.95x (ISBN 0-19-713529-3). Oxford U Pr.

Hebrew Scriptures: An Introduction to Their Literature & Religious Ideas. Samuel Sandmel. 1978. pap. 9.95x (ISBN 0-19-502369-2). Oxford U Pr.

Hebrew Syntax. 3rd ed. A. B. Davidson. 248p. pap. text ed. 12.00x (ISBN 0-567-21007-3). Attic Pr.

Hebrew Thought Compared with Greek. Thorleif Boman. Tr. by Jules L. Moreau from Ger. 1970. pap. 4.95 (ISBN 0-393-00534-8, Norton Lib). Norton.

Hebrewisms of West Africa: From Nile to Niger with the Jews. Joseph J. Williams. LC 67-19534. (Illus.). 1930. 17.50x (ISBN 0-8196-0194-2). Biblo.

Hebrews. Keith L. Brooks. (Teach Yourself the Bible Ser). 1961. pap. 1.75 (ISBN 0-8024-3507-6). Moody.

Hebrews. John Brown. (Geneva Commentaries Ser.). 1976. 12.95 (ISBN 0-85151-099-X). Banner of Truth.

Hebrews. Juliana Casey. (New Testament Message Ser.). 10.95 (ISBN 0-89453-141-7); pap. 5.95 (ISBN 0-89453-206-5). M Glazier.

Hebrews. Gerald Dye. (Double Trouble Puzzles Ser.). (Illus.). 1977. pap. 1.25 (ISBN 0-87239-154-X, 2825). Standard Pub.

Hebrews. Irving L. Jensen. (Bible Self-Study Ser). 1970. pap. 2.25 (ISBN 0-8024-1058-8). Moody.

Hebrews. William G. Johnsson. LC 79-92068. (Knox Preaching Guides Ser.). 98p. (Orig., John Hayes series editor). 1980. pap. 4.50 (ISBN 0-686-60242-0). John Knox.

Hebrews. Geoffrey Wilson. 1976. pap. 3.95 (ISBN 0-85151-099-X). Banner of Truth.

Hebrews & Hermeneutics. G. Hughes. LC 77-84806. (Society for New Testament Studies Monographs: No. 36). 1980. 22.50 (ISBN 0-521-21858-6). Cambridge U Pr.

Hebrews & Titus. H. A. Ironside. Date not set. 5.25 (ISBN 0-87213-363-X). Loizeaux.

Hebridean Folksongs, Vol. 3. Ed. by J. L. Campbell & Francis Collinson. 420p. 1980. 49.95 (ISBN 0-19-815215-9). Oxford U Pr.

Hecate the Bandicoot. Janet Little. LC 80-69437. 32p. 1980. 5.95 (ISBN 0-396-07893-1). Dodd.

HechizoSpells. (Creative Ser: No. 4). (Illus.). 1976. o. p. 20.95x (ISBN 0-89551-006-5); pap. text ed. 10.00 (ISBN 0-89551-024-3). UCLA Chicano Stud.

Hechos De los Apostoles: Texto Programado. Weldon E. Viertel. 208p. (Span.). 1981. pap. write for info. (ISBN 0-311-04348-8). Casa Bautista.

Hechos el Uno Para el Otro. John W. Drakeford. Tr. by Dafne C. De Plou. (Sexo en la Vida Cristiana Ser.). 1977. pap. 2.75 (ISBN 0-311-46256-1). Casa Bautista.

Hechos Epistolas-El Mar De la Vida: 14 Lecciones. Bernice C. Jordan. (Pasos De Fe Ser.). (Span.). pap. text ed. 2.25 (ISBN 0-86508-415-7); figuras 7.95 (ISBN 0-86508-416-5). BCM Inc.

Hechos Epistolas-Vosotros sois Edificio de Dios: 14 Lecciones, Tomo 1. Bernice C. Jordan. (Pasos De Fe Ser.). (Span.). pap. text ed. 2.25 (ISBN 0-86508-413-0); figuras 7.95 (ISBN 0-86508-414-9). BCM Inc.

Hector & Christina. Louise Fatio. (Illus.). (ps-3). 1977. 7.95 o.p. (ISBN 0-07-020072-6, GB); PLB 7.95 o.p. (ISBN 0-07-020073-4). McGraw.

Hector Berlioz. Victor Seroff. (gr. 7 up). 1967. 4.95g o.s.i. (ISBN 0-02-781910-8). Macmillan.

Hedda Gabler. John Osborne. 1972. 5.95 o.p. (ISBN 0-571-09887-8, Pub. by Faber & Faber); pap. 3.95 (ISBN 0-571-09888-6). Merrimack Bk Serv.

Hedda Gabler & Other Plays. Henrik Ibsen. Tr. by Eva LeGallienne & Norman Ginsbury. (Illus.). 1976. pap. 2.95 (ISBN 0-460-01111-1, Evman). Dutton.

Hedge School. Seamus Heaney. (Fine Press Poetry Ser.). (Illus.). 1979. signed ltd. ed. 50.00 o.p. (ISBN 0-931356-03-2). Seluzicki Poetry.

Hedgehog. Angela Sheehan. LC 76-49574. (Illus.). (gr. 2-4). 1977. 6.45 (ISBN 0-531-09079-5); PLB 3.50 (ISBN 0-531-09054-X). Watts.

Hedgerow. John T. White. LC 80-81264. (Illus.). 48p. 1980. 13.95 (ISBN 0-688-03683-X). Morrow.

Hedgerow Book. Ron Wilson. LC 78-75251. 1979. 17.95 (ISBN 0-7153-7728-0). David & Charles.

Hedonistic Neuron: A Theory of Memory, Learning, & Intelligence. A. Harry Klopf. LC 80-16410. (Illus.). 112p. Date not set. pap. 14.95 (ISBN 0-89116-202-X). Hemisphere Pub. Postponed.

Heeere's Johnny: A Behind the Scenes Closeup of Johnny Carson & the Tonight Show. Craig Tennis. (Orig.). 1980. pap. write for info. (ISBN 0-671-41451-8). PB.

Heere Beginneth a Mery Jest of Dan Hew, Munk of Leicester. Dan Hew. LC 74-80186. (English Experience Ser.: No. 666). 1974. Repr. 3.50 (ISBN 90-221-0666-7). Walter J Johnson.

Hefner. Frank Brady. (Illus.). 300p. 1974. 8.95 o.s.i. (ISBN 0-02-514600-9). Macmillan.

Hegel. C. Taylor. LC 74-25642. 700p. 1975. 57.50 (ISBN 0-521-20679-0); pap. 14.95 (ISBN 0-521-29199-2). Cambridge U Pr.

Hegel & Modern Society. C. Taylor. LC 78-54727. (Modern European Philosophy). 1979. 28.95 (ISBN 0-521-22083-1); pap. 6.95 (ISBN 0-521-29351-0). Cambridge U Pr.

Hegel: Bibliography. Ed. by Kurt Steinhauer. 894p. 1980. 129.50 (ISBN 3-598-03184-X). Bowker.

Hegel: From Foundation to System. David Lamb. (Martinus Nijhoff Philosophy Library: No. 1). 252p. 1980. lib. bdg. 34.50 (ISBN 90-247-2359-0, Martinus Nijhoff Pubs). Kluwer Boston.

Hegel Kierkegaard Marx. Robert Heiss. 1975. 12.50 o.s.i. (ISBN 0-440-03526-0, Sey Lawr). Delacorte.

Hegel: On Tragedy. G. W. Hegel. Ed. by Anne Paolucci & Henry Paolucci. 448p. (Orig.). 1975. pap. 4.95x o.p. (ISBN 0-06-131869-8, TB1869, Torch). Har-Row.

Hegel: Phenomenology of Spirit. G. W. Hegel. Tr. by A. V. Miller & J. N. Findlay. 1977. 29.50x (ISBN 0-19-824530-0). Oxford U Pr.

Hegel: Texts & Commentary. Walter Kaufmann. Incl. Who Thinks Abstractly. LC 65-13982. 1966. pap. 2.50 o.p. (ISBN 0-385-04058-X, A528B, Anch). Doubleday.

Hegelianism: The Path Toward Dialectic Humanism, 1805 to 1841. John E. Toews. LC 80-16370. 512p. Date not set. 39.50 (ISBN 0-521-23048-9). Cambridge U Pr.

Hegel's Concept of Marriage & Family: The Origin of Subjective Freedom. Rudolf J. Siebert. LC 78-78401. 1979. pap. text ed. 7.50 (ISBN 0-8191-0710-7). U Pr of Amer.

Hegel's Development: Toward the Sunlight, 1770-1801. H. S. Harris. 606p. 1972. text ed. 48.00x (ISBN 0-19-824358-8). Oxford U Pr.

Hegel's First American Followers: The Ohio Hegelians. Loyd D. Easton. LC 66-20062. ix, 353p. 1966. 15.00 (ISBN 0-8214-0026-6). Ohio U Pr.

Hegel's Idea of Philosophy. Quentin Lauer. LC 74-152244. xii, 159p. 1971. 9.00 o.p. (ISBN 0-8232-0925-3). Fordham.

Hegel's Phenomenology: A Philosophical Introduction. Richard Norman. (Philosophy Now). 1980. text ed. write for info. (ISBN 0-391-01720-9); pap. text ed. 4.50x (ISBN 0-391-01721-7). Humanities.

Hegel's Phenomenology of Mind: Analysis & Commentary. C. V. Dudeck. LC 80-67258. 292p. 1981. lib. bdg. 19.75 (ISBN 0-8191-1406-5); pap. text ed. 10.25 (ISBN 0-8191-1407-3). U Pr of Amer.

Hegel's Philosophy of History: Theological, Humanistic & Scientific Elements. Rudolf J. Siebert. LC 78-66279. 1979. pap. text ed. 9.00 (ISBN 0-8191-0689-5). U Pr of Amer.

Hegel's Social & Political Thought: The Philosophy of Objective Spirit Proceedings of the 1976th Hegel Society of America. Hegel Society of America Conference, 1976. Ed. by Donald P. Verene. LC 77-26183. 1980. text ed. 17.50x (ISBN 0-391-00543-X). Humanities.

Hegel's Theory of the Modern State. Shlomo Avineri. LC 70-186254. (Cambridge Studies in the History & Theory of Politics Ser.). 266p. 1973. 32.50 (ISBN 0-521-08513-6); pap. 8.95x (ISBN 0-521-09832-7). Cambridge U Pr.

Hegemony & Revolution: Antonio Gramsci's Political & Cultural Theory. Walter L. Adamson. 320p. 1980. 20.00x (ISBN 0-520-03924-6). U of Cal Pr.

Heidegger & Wittgenstein: The Poetics of Silence. Steven L. Bindeman. LC 80-6066. 159p. 1980. lib. bdg. 15.75 (ISBN 0-8191-1350-6); pap. text ed. 7.50 (ISBN 0-8191-1351-4). U Pr of Amer.

Heidegger on the Divine: The Thinker, the Poet & God. James L. Perotti. LC 73-92904. x, 134p. 1974. 9.50x (ISBN 0-8214-0144-0). Ohio U Pr.

Heidelberg Catechism. Tr. by Allen O. Miller & M. Eugene Osterhaven. LC 62-20891. 1963. 2.25 (ISBN 0-8298-0059-X); pap. 2.00 (ISBN 0-8298-0060-3). Pilgrim NY.

Heidelberg Catechism with Scripture Texts. (Orig.). 1981. write for info. (ISBN 0-933140-21-5). Bd of Pubns CRC.

Heidi. (Illustrated Junior Library). (Illus.). 336p. 1981. pap. 4.95 (ISBN 0-448-11012-1). G&D.

Heidi. Joanna Spyri. (Illus.). 24p. (ps-3). 1954. PLB 5.00 (ISBN 0-307-60407-1, Golden Pr). Western Pub.

Heidi. Johanna Spyri. (Illus.). (gr. 2-6). 1962. 4.95g o.s.i. (ISBN 0-02-786550-9). Macmillan.

Heidi. Johanna Spyri. LC 78-5489. (Raintree's Illustrated Classics). (Illus.). (gr. 5-8). 1978. PLB 9.65 (ISBN 0-8393-6206-4). Raintree Child.

Heidi's Horse. Sylvia Fein. LC 74-76077. (Illus.). 1976. 10.00 (ISBN 0-917388-01-1). Exelrod Pr.

Heifetz. 2nd ed. Ed. by Herbert R. Axelrod. (Illus.). 507p. 1980. 20.00 (ISBN 0-87666-600-4, Z-24). Paganiniana Pubns.

Height & Weight of Children in Relation to Socioeconomic Status: Tunisia & the United States. Harben B. Young et al. Ed. by Audrey Shipp. 50p. Date not set. pap. text ed. 1.75 (ISBN 0-8406-0206-5). Natl Ctr Health Stats.

Heightened Consciousness, Cultural Revolution, & Curriculum Theory. William Pinar. LC 73-17615. 1974. 15.25 (ISBN 0-8211-1511-1); text ed. 13.75 (ISBN 0-685-42641-6). McCutchan.

Heights. A. Goetze. 3.00 (ISBN 0-8283-1438-1). Branden.

Heights of Rimring. Duff Hart-Davis. LC 80-69379. 1981. 12.95 (ISBN 0-689-11148-7). Atheneum.

Heilige: Novelle. Conrad F. Meyer. Ed. by W. A. Coupe. (Blackwell's German Texts Ser.). 1965. pap. 4.50x o.p. (ISBN 0-631-01700-3, Pub. by Basil Blackwell). Biblio Dist.

Heimaey. Thomas D. Redshaw. 40p. (Orig.). 1974. pap. text ed. 3.75x (ISBN 0-85105-258-4, Dolmen Pr). Humanities.

Heimito Von Doderer. Michael Bachem. (World Authors Ser.: No. 595). 1981. lib. bdg. 14.95 (ISBN 0-8057-6437-2). Twayne.

Heims Kringla, History of the Kings of Norway. Snorri Sturluson. Tr. by Lee M. Hollander from Old Norse. LC 64-10460. (Illus.). 1977. Repr. of 1964 ed. 27.50x (ISBN 0-89067-040-4). Am Scandinavian.

Heimskringla: From the Sagas of the Norse Kings. Snorri. Tr. by Erling Monsen. (Illus.). 398p. 1980. 35.00 (ISBN 0-906191-39-4, Pub. by Thule Pr England). Intl Schol Bk Serv.

Heimwehr & Austrian Politics. C. Earl Edmondson. LC 77-21924. 384p. 1978. 25.00x (ISBN 0-8203-0437-9). U of Ga Pr.

Heinecken. Robert F. Heinecken. Ed. & pref. by James L. Enyeart. LC 80-69559. (Illus.). 160p. 1981. 75.00 (ISBN 0-933286-19-8). Friends Photography.

Heinemann Australian Dictionary. Ed. by K. Harber. 1976. text ed. 10.95x (ISBN 0-686-65318-1, 00511). Heinemann Ed.

Heinemann English Dictionary. Ed. by K. Harber & G. Payton. 1979. text ed. 10.95x (ISBN 0-435-10378-4). Heinemann Ed.

Heinemann Guided Readers. Ed. by John Milne. Incl. Beginner Level. Rich Man, Poor Man. T. C. Jupp. 1976. pap. text ed. 1.25x (ISBN 0-435-27022-2); Beginner Level. Death of a Soldier. Philip Prowse. 1976. pap. text ed. 1.25x (ISBN 0-435-27036-2); Beginner Level. Marco. Mike Espien. 1976. pap. text ed. 1.25x (ISBN 0-435-27023-0); Dangerous Journey. Alwyn Cox. 1976. pap. text ed. 1.25x (ISBN 0-435-27021-4); Beginner Level. Money for a Motorbike. John Milne. 1976. pap. text ed. 1.25x (ISBN 0-435-27035-4); Beginner Level. Truth Machine. Norman Whitney. 1976. pap. text ed. 1.25x (ISBN 0-435-27037-0); Elementary Level. Road to Nowhere. John Milne. 1975. pap. text ed. 1.50x (ISBN 0-435-27013-3); Elementary Level. Black Cat. John Milne. 1975. pap. text ed. 1.50x (ISBN 0-435-27012-5); Elementary Level. Star for a Day. Philip Prowse. 1976. pap. text ed. 1.50x (ISBN 0-435-27034-6); Intermediate Level. Bristol Murder. Philip Prowse. pap. text ed. 1.75x (ISBN 0-435-27003-6); Intermediate Level. Smuggler. Piers Plowright. pap. text ed. 1.75x (ISBN 0-435-27005-2); Intermediate Level. Football. Duncan Forbes. pap. text ed. 1.75x (ISBN 0-435-27004-4); Intermediate Level. Woman Who Disappeared. Philip Prowse. 1975. pap. text ed. 1.75x (ISBN 0-435-27011-7); Intermediate Level. Raid. Glyn Frewer. 1976. pap. text ed. 1.75x (ISBN 0-435-27017-6); Upper Level. Money for Sale. Michael Hardcastle. 1975. pap. text ed. 1.95x (ISBN 0-435-27020-6); Upper Level. Story of Pop. John Byrne. 1975. pap. text ed. 1.95x (ISBN 0-435-27025-7); Upper Level. Olympic Games. Bruce Tulloh. 1976. pap. text ed. 1.95x (ISBN 0-435-27027-3). pap. text ed. 2.25x 1977 handbook (ISBN 0-435-27039-7). Heinemann Ed.

Heinkel. P. S. Turner. LC 70-136294. (Aircraft Album Ser No. 1). (Illus.). 1970. pap. 3.95 o.p. (ISBN 0-668-02414-3). Arco.

Heinrich August Marschner, Seventeen Ninety-Five to Eighteen Sixty-One: His Life & Stage Works. A. Dean Palmer. Ed. by George Buelow. (Studies in Musicology). 327p. 1981. 34.95 (ISBN 0-8357-1114-5, Pub. by UMI Res Pr). Univ Microfilms.

Heinrich Bullinger & the Covenant: The Other Reformed Tradition. J. Wayne Baker. LC 80-14667. xxvi, 300p. 1980. 18.95 (ISBN 0-8214-0554-3). Ohio U Pr.

Heinrich Pestalozzi. Robert B. Downs. (World Leaders Ser.). 1975. lib. bdg. 9.95 (ISBN 0-8057-3560-7). Twayne.

Heinrich Schliemann: Discoverer of Buried Treasure. George Selden. (Illus.). (gr. 1-5). 1964. 3.50 o.s.i. (ISBN 0-02-781770-9). Macmillan.

Heir of Grangerfjord Castle. Ruth M. Sears. (Orig.). 1975. pap. 0.95 o.p. (ISBN 0-685-53126-0, LB273NK, Leisure Bks). Nordon Pubns.

Heir of Redclyffe. Charlotte Yonge. Ed. by Robert L. Wolff. LC 75-476. (Victorian Fiction Ser.). 1975. Repr. of 1853 ed. lib. bdg. 66.00 (ISBN 0-8240-1554-1). Garland Pub.

Heir of Sea & Fire. Patricia McKillip. 1978. pap. 2.25 (ISBN 0-345-28882-3, Del Rey Bks). Ballantine.

Heir to Rowanlea. Sally James. 224p. 1981. pap. 1.95 (ISBN 0-449-50175-2, Coventry). Fawcett.

Heiress. Kristina Roy. Tr. by Martha Tenjack. LC 79-56301. 1979. pap. 3.95 o.p. (ISBN 0-89107-176-8). Good News.

Heiress: The Rich Life of Marjorie Merriweather Post. William Wright. LC 77-26168. (Illus.). 1978. 12.50 o.p. (ISBN 0-915220-36-9). New Republic.
Heirich Heine: Poetry & Politics. Nigel Reeves. (Oxford Modern Languages & Literature Monographs). 215p. 1974. 29.95x (ISBN 0-19-815524-7). Oxford U Pr.
Heirs Apparent: What Happens When Mao Dies? Dennis Bloodworth & Ching Ping. 272p. 1973. 7.95 (ISBN 0-374-16898-9). FS&G.
Heirs of Love. Barbara F. Johnson. 1980. 2.95 (ISBN 0-380-75739-7, 75739, 75739). Avon.
Heirs of the Kingdom. Zoe Oldenbourg. Tr. by Anne Carter from Fr. LC 70-147805. 1971. Repr. 8.95 o.s.i. (ISBN 0-394-46835-X). Pantheon.
Heirs Together of Life. Charles Ellis & Norma Ellis. pap. 4.95. Banner of Truth.
Helbeck of Bannisdale, 1898. Mary A. Ward. Ed. by Robert L. Wolff. LC 75-465. (Victorian Fiction Ser.). 1975. lib. bdg. 66.00 (ISBN 0-8240-1543-6). Garland Pub.
Held Captive by Indians: Selected Narratives, 1642-1836. Ed. by Richard VanDerBeets. LC 73-3448. (Illus.). 1973. 16.50x (ISBN 0-87049-145-8). U of Tenn Pr.
Held Fast for England: G. A. Henty, Imperialist Boys' Writer. Guy Arnold. 224p. 1980. 27.00 (ISBN 0-241-10373-8, Pub. by Hamish Hamilton England). David & Charles.
Helen. Georgette Heyer. 1976. Repr. of 1928 ed. lib. bdg. 14.65x (ISBN 0-89966-120-3). Buccaneer Bks.
Helen: A Courtship & Mississippi Poems--Early Poetru. William Faulkner. 75p. 1981. 89.95. Yoknapatawpha.
Helen & All. Frances Weissman. (Orig.). 1980. pap. 3.95 (ISBN 0-89260-192-2). Hwong Pub.
Helen & Teacher: The Story of Helen Keller & Anne Sullivan Macy. Joseph P. Lash. 1980. 17.95 (ISBN 0-440-03654-2). Delacorte.
Helen in Egypt. H. D., pseud. LC 74-8563. 320p. 1974. 4.95 (ISBN 0-8112-0543-6); pap. 3.25 (ISBN 0-8112-0544-4, NDP380). New Directions.
Helen in Exile. Ian McLachlan. 384p. 1980. 11.95 (ISBN 0-8037-3561-8). Dial.
Helen Keller. Eileen Bigland. LC 67-22810. (Illus.). (gr. 7-10). 1967. 9.95 (ISBN 0-87599-134-3). S G Phillips.
Helen Keller. Margaret Davidson. (Illus.). (gr. 2-4). 1970. PLB 5.95 o.p. (ISBN 0-8038-3015-7). Hastings.
Helen Keller. Stewart Graff & Polly A. Graff. (Illus.). (gr. 2-7). 1966. pap. 1.25 (ISBN 0-440-43566-8, YB). Dell.
Helen Oxenbury's ABC of Things. Helen Oxenbury. (Illus.). 64p. (ps-2). 1972. PLB 4.95 o.p. (ISBN 0-531-02020-7). Watts.
Helen Van Pelt Wilson's African Violet Book. Helen V. Wilson. 1970. 11.95 (ISBN 0-8015-3852-1, Hawthorn); pap. 5.95 (ISBN 0-8015-3858-0, Hawthorn). Dutton.
Helicopter. H. F. Gregory. LC 74-30720. (Illus.). 224p. 1976. 15.00 o.p. (ISBN 0-498-01670-6). A S Barnes.
Helicopter Dynamics. A. R. Bramwell. LC 76-4944. 1976. 59.95 (ISBN 0-470-15067-X). Halsted Pr.
Helicopter External Loads, Vol. 1. Robert J. Rechs. (Planning & Operation Ser.). (Illus.). 100p. (Orig.). 1981. pap. text ed. 5.00 (ISBN 0-937568-19-8). Rechs Pubns.
Helicopter External Loads, Vol. 2. Robert J. Rechs. (Certification & Training Ser.). 100p. 1980. pap. text ed. 5.00 (ISBN 0-937568-21-X). Rechs Pubns.
Helicopter Fundamentals. Joseph Schafer. (Aviation Technician Training Course Ser.). (Illus.). 400p. 1980. pap. text ed. 8.95 (ISBN 0-89100-118-2). Aviation Maintenance.
Helicopter: History, Piloting & How It Flies. John Fay. LC 76-54073. (Illus.). 1977. 15.95 (ISBN 0-7153-7249-1). David & Charles.
Helicopter in Civil Operations. E. M. Brown. 208p. 1981. 17.95 (ISBN 0-442-24528-9). Van Nos Reinhold.
Helicopter: Its Importance to Commerce & to the Public. Ann N. Davis & Robert A. Richardson. 138p. 1978. 10.00 (ISBN 0-911721-70-3, Pub. by Helicopter Assn). Aviation.
Helicopter Theory. Wayne Johnson. LC 79-83995. 1000p. 1980. 95.00x (ISBN 0-691-07971-4). Princeton U Pr.
Helicopter Utilization in Municipal Law Enforcement: Administrative Considerations. James R. Beall & Robert E. Downing. (Illus.). 96p. 1973. text ed. 14.75 (ISBN 0-398-02780-3). C C Thomas.
Helicopters. Susan Harris. (Easy-Read Fact Bks.). (Illus.). (gr. 2-4). 1979. s&l 6.45 (ISBN 0-531-02850-X). Watts.
Helium: A Public Policy Program. Helium Study Committee. 1978. pap. 10.50 (ISBN 0-309-02742-X). Natl Acad Pr.
Helium Four. Z. M. Galasiewicz. 1971. 25.00 (ISBN 0-08-015816-1). Pergamon.
Helium: Stopping Powers & Ranges in All Elemental Matter. Ed. by James F. Ziegler. LC 77-13219. 1977. text ed. 40.00 (ISBN 0-08-021606-4). Pergamon.
Helix. Desmond Ryan & Joel Shurkin. 1981. pap. 2.75 (ISBN 0-671-41006-7). PB.
Helix Herbal Album. Richard L. Roen et al. 1978. 8.95 (ISBN 0-394-50309-0). Random.
Hell Bay. Sam Llewellyn. 1981. pap. 2.50 (ISBN 0-345-29642-7). Ballantine.
Hell-Bound. Don Wilkerson & David Manuel. LC 78-60735. 199p. 1978. pap. 2.95 (ISBN 0-932260-03-9). Rock Harbor.
Hell-Holes & Hangings. Fred Harrison. 8.95 (ISBN 0-685-48825-X). Nortex Pr.
Hell in His Holsters. Charles N. Heckelmann. 1977. pap. 1.25 o.p. (ISBN 0-445-00447-9). Popular Lib.
Hell in Paradise Valley. Barry Cord. 1978. pap. 1.25 (ISBN 0-505-51316-1). Tower Bks.
Hell Is Too Crowded. Jack Higgins. 160p. 1977. pap. 1.95 (ISBN 0-449-14274-4, GM). Fawcett.
Hell on Horseback. J. L. Bouma. 1981. pap. 1.75 (ISBN 0-8439-0893-9, Leisure Bks). Nordon Pubns.
Hell Raiser. Ray Hogan. 1980. pap. 1.75 (ISBN 0-451-09489-1, E9489, Sig). NAL.
Hell Screen & Other Stories. Ryunosuke Akutagawa. Tr. by W. H. Norman. LC 78-98800. Repr. of 1948 ed. lib. bdg. 17.50x (ISBN 0-8371-3017-4, AKHS). Greenwood.
Hellas: The Civilization of Ancient Greece. Keith Branigan et al. LC 80-18306. (Illus.). 224p. 1980. 39.95 (ISBN 0-07-007229-9). McGraw.
Hellbound for Ballarat: Trouble at Quinn's Crossing. Nelson Nye. 160p. (Orig.). 1976. pap. 2.25 (ISBN 0-441-32727-3). Ace Bks.
Hellbox. John O'Hara. 176p. 1975. pap. 1.25 o.p. (ISBN 0-445-00233-6). Popular Lib.
Hellenic Perspectives: Essays in the History of Greece. Ed. by John T. Koumoulides. LC 80-5475. 398p. 1980. lib. bdg. 20.75 (ISBN 0-8191-1107-4); pap. text ed. 12.75 (ISBN 0-8191-1108-2). U Pr of Amer.
Hellenism & the Unfinished Revolution. Apostolos Makrakis. Ed. by Orthodox Christian Educational Society. Tr. by Archimandrite E. Stephanou from Hellenic. 191p. (Orig.). 1968. pap. 3.00x (ISBN 0-938366-26-2). Orthodox Chr.
Hellenism: The History of a Civilization. Arnold J. Toynbee. LC 80-27772. xii, 272p. 1981. Repr. of 1959 ed. lib. bdg. 25.00x (ISBN 0-313-22742-X, TOHM). Greenwood.
Hellenisme Primitif de la Macedoine Prouve par la Numismatique et l'Or Du Pangee. J. N. Svoronos. (Illus.). 1979. text ed. 50.00 (ISBN 0-916710-48-3). Obol Intl.
Hellenistic Art. Jean Charbonneaux et al. LC 72-89850. (Arts of Mankind Ser). 35.00 o.s.i. (ISBN 0-8076-0666-9). Braziller.
Hellenistic Art. rev. ed. Christine M. Havelock. (Illus.). 1981. pap. text ed. 10.95x (ISBN 0-393-95133-2). Norton.
Hellenistic Mystery-Religions. Richard Reitzenstein. Tr. by John E. Steely from Ger. LC 77-12980. (Pittsburgh Theological Monographs: No. 15). Orig. Title: Hellenistischen Mysterienreligionen Nach Ihren Arundgedanken und Wirkungen. 1978. pap. text ed. 12.95 (ISBN 0-915138-20-4). Pickwick.
Hellenistic Philosophy: Stoics, Epicureans, Sceptics. A. A. Long. (Classical Life & Letters Ser.). 262p. 1974. 40.50x (ISBN 0-7156-0667-0, 298, Pub. by Duckworth England). Biblio Dist.
Hellenistic Pottery: Athenian & Imported Moldmade Bowls. Susan I. Rotroff. (Athenian Agora: Results of Excavations Conducted by the American School of Classical Studies at Athens: Vol. XXII). 1981. price not set (ISBN 0-87661-222-2). Am Sch Athens.
Hellenistic Queens. Grace H. Macurdy. LC 75-16848. (Johns Hopkins University Studies in Archaeology: No. 14). (Illus.). 250p. 1975. Repr. of 1932 ed. lib. bdg. 19.50x (ISBN 0-8371-8271-9, MAHQ). Greenwood.
Hellenistic Religions: The Age of Syncretism. Ed. by Frederick C. Grant. 1953. 8.95 (ISBN 0-672-60342-X, LLA134). Bobbs.
Hellenistic Statues of Aphrodite: Studies in the History of Their Stylistic Development. Dericksen M. Brinkerhoff. LC 77-94688. (Outstanding Dissertations in the Fine Arts Ser.). 1978. lib. bdg. 24.00 (ISBN 0-8240-3217-9). Garland Pub.
Hellenistic Ways of Deliverance & the Making of the Christian Synthesis. John H. Randall. LC 74-137339. 1970. 17.50x (ISBN 0-231-03327-3). Columbia U Pr.
Heller with a Gun. Louis L'Amour. (Western Fiction Ser.). 1981. lib. bdg. 11.95 (ISBN 0-8398-2696-6). Gregg.
Hellfire. Jake Logan. LC 80-83591. (Jake Logan Ser.). 256p. (Orig.). 1981. pap. 1.95 (ISBN 0-87216-795-X). Playboy Pbks.
Hellfire Files of Jules De Grandin. Seabury Quinn. (Jules De Grandin Ser.: No. 5). pap. 1.25 o.p. (ISBN 0-445-00428-2). Popular Lib.
Hellgate. William C. MacDonald. 1978. pap. 1.25 (ISBN 0-505-51298-X). Tower Bks.
Hellinger's Law. Justin Barr et al. (Orig.). pap. 2.25 (ISBN 0-515-05809-2). Jove Pubns.
Hello, Aurora. Anne-Catherine Vestly. Tr. by Eileen Amos from Norwegian. LC 74-5008. (Illus.). 96p. (gr. 3-6). 1974. 7.95 o.p. (ISBN 0-690-00513-X, TYC-J). T Y Crowell.
Hello, Cat, You Need a Hat. Gelman. (ps-3). 1980. pap. 1.25 (ISBN 0-590-05793-6, Schol Pap). Schol Bk Serv.
Hello Equal Rights! Aron Breslow. 1981. 2.00 (ISBN 0-918430-01-1). Happy History.
Hello, Goodbye, I Love You. Arleen Lorrance. (Illus., Orig.). 1981. pap. price not set (ISBN 0-916192-18-0). L P Pubns.
Hello, I'm God & I'm Here to Help You. Miriam Cameron. (Orig.). 1980. pap. 1.95 (ISBN 0-446-90063-X). Warner Bks.
Hello, I'm Johnny Cash. Allan & Hartley. 0.49 (ISBN 0-8007-8527-4). Revell.
Hello My Love, Goodbye. Lenora M. Weber. LC 77-132306. (Stacy Belford Story Ser). (gr. 6 up). 1971. 10.95 (ISBN 0-690-37697-9, TYC-J). T Y Crowell.
Hello Sigmund, This Is Eric! Louis H. Forman & Janelle S. Ramsburg. 1978. 12.95 o.p. (ISBN 0-8362-0754-8); pap. 5.95 o.p. (ISBN 0-8362-5202-0). Andrews & McMeel.
Hello, Winnie-the-Pooh! Walt Disney Studios. (Boxed Golden Bks. Ser.). (Contains 2 Little Golden Books, 2 Tell-A-Tale Books, 1 Shape Book & an activity book.). (ps-2). 1977. 3.95 set (ISBN 0-307-13692-2, Golden Pr). Western Pub.
Hello World. pap. 1.50 (ISBN 0-915266-05-9). Awani Pr.
Hellraisers, Heroines, & Holy Women. Jean Blashfield. 256p. 1981. 14.95 (ISBN 0-312-36736-8); pap. 7.95. St Martin.
Hell's Angels. Hunter S. Thompson. 1975. pap. 2.75 (ISBN 0-345-29238-3). Ballantine.
Hell's Cartographers: Some Personal Histories of Science Fiction Writers. Ed. by Brian W. Aldiss & Harry Harrison. LC 75-25074. (Illus.). 256p. (YA) 1976. 8.95 o.p. (ISBN 0-06-010052-4, HarpT). Har-Row.
Hell's Ransom. Karl Meyer. (Orig.). 1980. pap. 2.25 (ISBN 0-532-23183-X). Manor Bks.
Helmets. James Dickey. LC 64-13610. (Wesleyan Poetry Program: Vol. 21). (Orig.). 1964. 10.00x (ISBN 0-8195-2021-7, Pub. by Wesleyan U Pr). Columbia U Pr.
Heloise & Abelard. Etienne Gilson. 1960. pap. 3.95 (ISBN 0-472-06038-4, 38, AA). U of Mich Pr.
Heloise & Abelard, 2 Vols. in One. George Moore. (Black & Gold Lib). 1945. 7.95 o.p. (ISBN 0-87140-871-6). Liveright.
Help for Bedwetting. Meadow. Date not set. pap. text ed. 2.75 (ISBN 0-443-02236-4). Churchill.
Help for the Bereaved. 2nd ed. Curtis A. Smith, Jr. 1972. pap. 1.50 (ISBN 0-686-09019-5). Ed Dev Assn.
Help for the Depressed. Samuel H. Kraines & Eloise S. Thetford. (Illus.). 272p. 1979. pap. 11.75 (ISBN 0-398-02335-2). C C Thomas.
Help for the Hard of Hearing: A Speech, Reading & Auditory Training Manual for Home & Professionally Guided Training. Olaf Haug & Scott Haug. 144p. 1977. 13.00 (ISBN 0-398-03674-8); pap. 8.75 (ISBN 0-398-03675-6). C C Thomas.
Help for the Lonely Child: Strengthening Social Perceptions. Rita Siegel & Ernest Siegel. (Illus.). 1978. 9.95 o.p. (ISBN 0-87690-289-1). Dutton.
Help for the Over-Weight Child: A Parent's Guide to Helping Children Lose Weight. Dewey Lipe & Jurgen Wolff. 1978. 8.95 (ISBN 0-8128-2507-1). Stein & Day.
Help for Today. Ernest Holmes & William H. Hornaday. 1969. pap. 6.50 (ISBN 0-911336-04-4). Sci of Mind.
Help from Beyond: How to Lead an Enriched Life Through Spiritual Communication. Henry L. Stern. LC 73-90380. 192p. 1974. 7.95 o.s.i. (ISBN 0-8027-0444-1). Walker & Co.
Help! from Heloise. Heloise. LC 80-70543. (Illus.). 500p. 1981. 12.95 (ISBN 0-87795-318-X). Arbor Hse.
Help from the Baron. John Creasey. 1977. 6.95 o.s.i. (ISBN 0-8027-5368-X). Walker & Co.
Help from the Governor & Locating Lenders: Two Contact Directories for Scholarships & Student Loans, 1980-1982. Robert Leider. 16p. (Orig.). 1980. pap. 1.00 (ISBN 0-917760-21-2). Octameron Assocs.
Help! I Believe in Tongues. K. Neill Foster. LC 75-2518. 160p. (Orig.). 1975. pap. 2.45 (ISBN 0-87123-211-1, 210211). Bethany Fell.
Help! I Want to Remodel My Home: The New Woman's Guide to Home Improvement. Ann S. Augustin. LC 74-28307. (Illus.). 230p. 1975. 12.95 (ISBN 0-88229-214-5). Nelson-Hall.
Help! I'm a Camp Counselor. Norman Wright. LC 68-18057. (Orig.). 1969. pap. 2.95 (ISBN 0-8307-0032-3, 50-015-28). Regal.
Help! I'm a Layman. Kenneth Chafin. LC 66-22155. 1966. pap. 0.95 o.p. (ISBN 0-87680-908-5, 90008). Word Bks.
Help! I've Just Given Birth to a Teenager. Pat Baker. 128p. (Orig.). 1981. pap. 4.95 (ISBN 0-8010-0799-2). Baker Bk.
Help Me Lord--I Hurt. Virginia Thompson. LC 78-55505. (Illus., Orig.). 1978. pap. 2.25 (ISBN 0-89081-145-8, 1458). Harvest Hse.
Help Me Remember, Lord--Help Me Forget. Marie Chapian & Robert Sadler. (Illus.). 256p. 1981. pap. 2.95 (ISBN 0-87123-203-0, 200203). Bethany Fell.
Help! The Basics of Borrowing Money. Robin Gross & Jean Cullen. 160p. 1980. 9.95 (ISBN 0-8129-0899-6). Times Bks.
Help the Patient Tell His Story. M. Wexler & L. Adler. 1971. pap. 7.95 (ISBN 0-87489-080-2). Med Economics.
Help! There's a Cat Washing in Here! Alison Smith. LC 80-25522. (Illus.). (gr. 4-6). 1981. 9.95 (ISBN 0-525-31630-2). Dutton.
Help Wanted: A Guide to Career Counseling in the Bay Area. Florence Lewis. 4.95 (ISBN 0-931018-03-X). Green Hill.
Help Wanted: Everything You Need to Get the Job You Deserve. Bert Fregly. pap. 9.95 (ISBN 0-88280-071-X). Chicago Review.
Help, Yelled Maxwell. James Stevenson & Edwina Stevenson. LC 77-21247. (Illus.). (gr. 3-5). 1978. 7.95 (ISBN 0-688-80133-1); PLB 7.63 (ISBN 0-688-84133-3). Greenwillow.
Help Your Child Learn the Three R's Through Active Play. James Humphrey & Joy Humphrey. 184p. 1980. 13.75 (ISBN 0-398-04106-7). C C Thomas.
Help Your Child to Read Better. James Schiavone. LC 76-29055. 1977. 11.95 (ISBN 0-88229-221-8); pap. 6.95 (ISBN 0-88229-464-4). Nelson-Hall.
Help Your Mate Lose Weight. Joan Walker & Morton Walker. 1978. pap. 1.50 o.s.i. (ISBN 0-515-03872-5). Jove Pubns.
Help Yourself to a Job, 3 pts. Yvette Dogin. (Illus.). (gr. 7 up). Set. text ed. 6.75 (ISBN 0-912486-00-7); Pt. 1, 1977. text ed. 2.25 (ISBN 0-912486-32-5); Pt. 2, 1976. text ed. 2.25 (ISBN 0-912486-02-3); Pt. 3, 1978. text ed. 2.25 (ISBN 0-912486-03-1). Finney Co.
Help Yourself to Understand Nineteen Eighty-One. Ellin Young. 1980. pap. 2.95 (ISBN 0-87728-512-8). Weiser.
Helpers with Hammers. Frances Andrews. (Home Mission Graded Ser.). (Illus.). (gr. 1-3). 1977. pap. 0.75 o.p. (ISBN 0-686-19020-3). Home Mission.
Helpful Hints & Tricks for New Moms & Dads (& Not So New) Nanci R. Weinfeld. LC 79-57188. (Illus.). 88p. (Orig.). 1980. pap. 3.95 (ISBN 0-9603964-0-3). DJD Prods.
Helpful Hints & Tricks for New Moms & Dads. Nanci R. Weinfeld. LC 80-53669. (Illus.). 96p. (Orig.). 1981. pap. 3.95 (ISBN 0-528-88041-1). Rand.
Helping a Child Understand Death. Linda J. Vogel. LC 74-26325. 96p. 1975. pap. 2.50 (ISBN 0-8006-1203-5, 1-1203). Fortress.
Helping Active and Passive Preschoolers Through Play. Charles F. Wolfgang. (Elementary Education Ser.). 1977. pap. text ed. 7.50 (ISBN 0-675-08550-0). Merrill.
Helping Adults Learn: Getting off to a Good Start. 1980. video tape 195.00 (ISBN 0-87771-014-7). Grad School.
Helping Adults Learn: Getting off to a Good Start. 1980. pap. 9.00 (ISBN 0-87771-015-5). Grad School.
Helping Adults Learn: Getting off to a Good Start. 1980. Set. 200.00 (ISBN 0-87771-020-1). Grad School.
Helping Adults Learn: How & Why Adults Learn. 1980. video tape 195.00 (ISBN 0-87771-016-3). Grad School.
Helping Adults Learn: How & Why Adults Learn. 1980. 9.00 (ISBN 0-87771-017-1). Grad School.
Helping Adults Learn: How & Why Adults Learn. 1980. Set. 200.00 (ISBN 0-87771-021-X). Grad School.
Helping As a Humanistic Process: Perspectives & Viewpoints. G. Donald Polenz. 1976. pap. text ed. 8.95x o.p. (ISBN 0-8191-0079-X). U Pr of Amer.
Helping Children Behave: A Handbook of Applied Learning Principles. Gary Nielsen. LC 73-94303. 224p. 1974. 14.95 (ISBN 0-911012-90-7). Nelson-Hall.
Helping Children Learn Earth-Space Science: A Selection of Articles Reprinted from "Science & Children". Compiled by William H. Matthews, III. 1971. pap. 5.00 (ISBN 0-87355-000-5). Natl Sci Tchrs.
Helping Children Learn Mathematics: A Competency Based Laboratory Approach. G. R. Baur & L. O. George. LC 75-16772. 1976. 17.95 (ISBN 0-8465-0408-1); instr's guide 3.95 (ISBN 0-8465-0409-X). Benjamin-Cummings.

Helping Children Meet Change. Robin Worthington. (Uplook Ser.). 1978. pap. 0.75 (ISBN 0-8163-0200-6, 08493-9). Pacific Pr Pub Assn.
Helping Children Overcome Learning Difficulties: A Step-by-Step Guide for Parents & Teachers. 2nd, rev. ed. Jerome Rosner. (Illus.). 377p. pap. 98.95 (ISBN 0-8027-7178-5). Walker & Co.
Helping Clumsy Children. Ed. by Neil Gordon & Ian McKinlay. (Illus.). 200p. 1980. pap. text ed. 16.00x (ISBN 0-443-01868-5). Churchill.
Helping Couples Change: A Social Learning Approach to Marital Therapy. Richard B. Stuart. (Guilford Family Therapy Ser.). 464p. 1980. 22.50 (ISBN 0-89862-604-8). Guilford Pr.
Helping Families to Change. Virginia Satir et al. LC 75-29697. 296p. 1976. 20.00x (ISBN 0-87668-238-7). Aronson.
Helping Hospital Trustees Understand Physicians. Richard E. Thompson. LC 79-21428. 96p. (Orig.). 1979. pap. 11.25 (ISBN 0-87258-287-6, 1347). Am Hospital.
Helping: Human Services for the 80's. Frank Baker & John E. Northman. 221p. 1981. pap. text ed. 8.75 (ISBN 0-8016-0424-9). Mosby.
Helping in Social Work. Bill Jordan. 1979. 14.95x (ISBN 0-7100-0126-6); pap. 8.95 (ISBN 0-7100-0127-4). Routledge & Kegan.
Helping in the Community: Behavioral Applications. Ed. by Gary L. Martin & J. Grayson Osborne. 430p. 1980. 22.50 (ISBN 0-306-40402-8, Plenum Pr). Plenum Pub.
Helping Insure Our Energy Future: A Program for Developing Synthetic Fuel Plants Now. Committee for Economic Development. (CED Statement on National Policy Ser.). 1979. lib. bdg. 6.00 (ISBN 0-87186-769-9); pap. 4.50 (ISBN 0-87186-069-4). Comm Econ Dev.
Helping Interview. 3rd ed. Alfred D. Benjamin. LC 80-81650. 208p. 1981. pap. text ed. 7.95 (ISBN 0-395-29648-X). HM.
Helping Maltreated Children: School & Community Involvement. Michael Halperin. LC 78-31527. 1979. pap. text ed. 9.50 (ISBN 0-8016-2020-1). Mosby.
Helping Muriel Make It Through the Night-Stories. Lee Zacharias. LC 75-18047. 128p. 1976. pap. 4.95 (ISBN 0-8071-0166-4); pap. 3.95 (ISBN 0-8071-0177-X). La State U Pr.
Helping Others. Anthony D'Augelli et al. LC 80-17819. 170p. 1980. pap. text ed. 8.95 (ISBN 0-8185-0401-3). Brooks-Cole.
Helping Ourselves: Local Responses to Global Problems. Bruce Stokes. 1981. 12.95 (ISBN 0-393-01362-6); pap. 4.95 (ISBN 0-393-00054-0). Norton.
Helping People Change. F. H. Kanfer & A. P. Goldstein. 1976. 18.50 o.p. (ISBN 0-08-018272-0); pap. 10.45 o.p. (ISBN 0-08-018271-2). Pergamon.
Helping People Change: A Textbook of Methods. 2nd ed. Ed. by Frederick H. Kanfer & Arnold P. Goldstein. LC 79-17929. 560p. 1980. 39.50 (ISBN 0-08-025098-X); pap. 13.95 (ISBN 0-08-025097-1). Pergamon.
Helping People Grow. Gary Collins. (Orig.). 1980. pap. 6.95 (ISBN 0-88449-069-6). Vision Hse.
Helping People: Karen Horney's Psychoanalytic Approach. Harold Kelman. LC 75-140098. 1971. 35.00x (ISBN 0-87668-039-2, 75-140098). Aronson.
Helping People: The Task-Centered Approach. Laura Epstein. LC 79-21084. (Illus.). 1980. pap. text ed. 9.50 (ISBN 0-8016-1509-7). Mosby.
Helping People Volunteer. Judy A. Rauner. LC 80-82556. (Illus.). 96p. (Orig.). 1980. pap. 10.50 (ISBN 0-9604594-0-5). Marlborough Pubns.
Helping Relationship: Process & Skills. 2nd ed. Lawrence M. Brammer. (P-H Ser. in Counseling & Human Development). (Illus.). 1979. ref. ed. 14.95 (ISBN 0-13-386268-2); pap. 9.95 ref. ed. (ISBN 0-13-386250-X). P-H.
Helping Relationship Source Book. 2nd ed. Donald L. Avila et al. 1977. pap. text ed. 10.50 (ISBN 0-205-05843-4). Allyn.
Helping Relationships: Basic Concepts for the Helping Professions. 2nd ed. Arthur W. Combs et al. 1978. pap. text ed. 10.50 (ISBN 0-205-05959-7). Allyn.
Helping Skills: A Basic Training Program. 2nd ed. Steve Danish et al. 226p. 1980. wkbk softcover 8.95x (ISBN 0-87705-484-3); lab manual softcover 4.95x (ISBN 0-87705-483-5); Set. 10.95x (ISBN 0-87705-474-6). Human Sci Pr.
Helping Skills for Human Resource Development: A Facilitator's Package. Dennis C. Kinlaw. 100p. (Orig.). 1980. pap. write for info. (ISBN 0-88390-163-3). Univ Assocs.
Helping Students Help Themselves: How You Can Put Behavior Analysis into Action in Your Classroom. Dwight L. Goodwin & Thomas J. Coates. (Illus.). 256p. 1976. 14.95 (ISBN 0-13-386490-1); pap. text ed. 9.95 (ISBN 0-13-386482-0). P-H.
Helping Students Learn: The Improvement of Higher Education. Harry E. Stanton. LC 78-70519. 1978. pap. text ed. 7.25 o.p. (ISBN 0-8191-0644-5). U Pr of Amer.
Helping Students Think & Value: Strategies for Teaching the Social Studies. J. Fraenkel. 1973. 16.95 (ISBN 0-13-386557-6). P-H.
Helping the Bereaved. Richard S. Dunlop. LC 78-13534. 188p. 1978. pap. 9.95 (ISBN 0-913486-91-4). Charles.
Helping the Child to Use Foster Family Care. Marie H. O'Connell. 39p. 1953. pap. 2.45 o.p. (ISBN 0-87868-046-2, E-10). Child Welfare.
Helping the Fearful Child: A Guide to Everyday & Problem Anxieties. Jonathan Kellerman. 1981. 13.95 (ISBN 0-393-01392-8). Norton.
Helping the Handicapped Child: In Day & Residential Care, No. 3. Jessie Parfit. (General Ser.). (Illus.). 48p. 1975. pap. text ed. 2.25x (ISBN 0-85633-060-4, NFER). Humanities.
Helping the Handicapped Child, No. 1: In the Family. Megan Jobling. (Illus.). 40p. 1975. pap. text ed. 2.50x (ISBN 0-85633-058-2, NFER). Humanities.
Helping the Handicapped Child, No. 2: At School. R. Gulliford. (Illus.). 40p. 1975. pap. text ed. 2.50x (ISBN 0-85633-059-0, NFER). Humanities.
Helping the Mentally Retarded Acquire Play Skills: A Behavioral Approach. Paul Wehman. (Illus.). 244p. 1977. 17.50 (ISBN 0-398-03604-7). C C Thomas.
Helping the Older Adult with an Acquired Hearing Loss. Joan M. Sayre. (Illus.). 72p. 1980. pap. 3.95x (ISBN 0-8134-2120-9). Interstate.
Helping the Severely Handicapped Child: A Guide for Parents & Teachers. Phyllis B. Doyle et al. LC 78-3300. (John Day Bk. in Special Education). (Illus.). 1979. 10.95 (ISBN 0-381-90063-0, TYC-T). T Y Crowell.
Helping the Stroke Patient to Talk. Marie C. Crickmay. (Illus.). 132p. 1977. pap. 11.75 (ISBN 0-398-03593-8). C C Thomas.
Helping the Troubled Child. Ed. by Stephen Murgatroyd. 1980. text ed. 18.35 (ISBN 0-06-318067-7, IntlDept); pap. text ed. 9.25 (ISBN 0-06-318068-5, IntlDept). Har-Row.
Helping the Troubled Employee. Joseph F. Follmann. 1979. 17.95 (ISBN 0-8144-5488-7). Am Mgmt.
Helping Women: A Guide to Counseling Women and Girls. Gloria J. Sklansky & Linda Algazi. 192p. 1981. 12.95 (ISBN 0-916068-15-3). Groupwork Today.
Helping Women: Readings in the Psychology & Counseling of Women. Ed. by Eileen T. Nickerson et al. LC 78-64371. 1978. pap. text ed. 11.00 o.p. (ISBN 0-8191-0631-3). U Pr of Amer.
Helping Young Children Grow: A Humanistic Approach to Parenting & Teaching. Susan E. Warrell. 240p. 1980. 12.95 (Spec); pap. 5.95. P-H.
Helping Your Child Appreciate the Mass & the Sacraments. Thomas Artz & Ruth M. Haley. 144p. (Orig.). 1980. pap. 2.95 (ISBN 0-89243-132-6). Liguori Pubns.
Helping Your Exceptional Baby: A Practical & Honest Approach to Raising a Mentally Handicapped Child. Cliff Cunningham & Patricia Sloper. (Illus.). 1981. pap. 6.95 (ISBN 0-394-73867-5). Pantheon.
Helping Your Teen-Age Student: What Parents Can Do to Improve Reading & Study Skills. Marvin Cohn. 1980. pap. 2.50 (ISBN 0-451-09502-2, E9502, Sig). NAL.
Helplessness: On Depression, Development & Death. Martin E. Seligman. 1980. Repr. of 1975 ed. text ed. 20.00x o.p. (ISBN 0-8290-0048-8). Irvington.
Helplessness: On Depression, Development, & Death. Martin E. Seligman. LC 74-23125. (Psychology Ser.). (Illus.). 1975. text ed. 17.95x (ISBN 0-7167-0752-7); pap. text ed. 9.95x (ISBN 0-7167-0751-9). W H Freeman.
Helpmann: The Authorised Biography. Elizabeth Salter. (Illus.). 247p. 1981. text ed. 18.50x (ISBN 0-87663-349-1). Universe.
Helps & Hints at Bible Study. Louis M. Perschke. 176p. 1981. 8.50 (ISBN 0-682-49733-9). Exposition.
Helps for Family Prayer. David Knight. (Illus.). 1977. 0.50 (ISBN 0-89570-109-X). Claretian Pubns.
Helps from Hebrews. Don E. Boatman. (Bible Study Textbook Ser.). (Illus.). 1960. 13.50 (ISBN 0-89900-044-4). College Pr Pub.
Helps to Holiness. Samuel L. Brengle. 1978. pap. 3.25 (ISBN 0-86544-003-4). Salvation Army.
Helps to Holy Living. C. E. Orr. 64p. pap. 0.40; pap. 1.00 3 copies. Faith Pub Hse.
Helter Skelter. Inger Hagerup & Joan Tate. (Illus.). 32p. (gr. k-8). 1981. 7.95 (ISBN 0-7207-1198-3). Merrimack Bk Serv.
Helter Skelter: The True Story of the Manson Murders. Vincent Bugliosi & Curt Gentry. (Illus.). 502p. 1974. 15.00 (ISBN 0-393-08700-X). Norton.
Hematologic & Reticuloendothelial Pathology & Pathophysiology Case Studies. Richert E. Goyette. 1976. spiral bdg. 12.00 o.p. (ISBN 0-87488-076-9). Med Exam.
Hematologic Diseases - New Directions in Therapy. 2nd ed. Peter C. Ungaro. 1979. pap. 15.50 (ISBN 0-87488-682-1). Med Exam.
Hematology. Arthur A. Topilow & Merlin R. Wilson. (Medical Examination Review Book: Vol. 32). 1974. spiral bdg. 15.00 o.s.i. (ISBN 0-87488-148-X). Med Exam.
Hematology Case Studies, Vol. 1. Ed. by John B. Harley et al. 1973. spiral bdg. 12.00 o.s.i. (ISBN 0-87488-020-3). Med Exam.
Hematology for Medical Technologists PreTest Self-Assessment & Review. Ed. by Barbara L. Garrick. LC 78-51704. (PreTest Self-Assessment & Review Ser.). (Illus.). 1979. pap. 9.95 (ISBN 0-07-051573-5). McGraw-Pretest.
Hematology for the House Officer. Larry Waterbury. (House Officer Ser.). (Illus.). 152p. 1981. softcover 10.95 (ISBN 0-683-08851-3). Williams & Wilkins.
Hematology: Physiopathologic Basis for Clinical Practice. Paul R. Reich. 1978. text ed. 22.95 (ISBN 0-316-73860-3); pap. text ed. 17.95 (ISBN 0-316-73861-1). Little.
Hematology: Principles & Procedures. 3rd ed. Barbara A. Brown. LC 80-16943. (Illus.). 358p. 1980. text ed. 22.00 (ISBN 0-8121-0707-1). Lea & Febiger.
Hematology: UCLA Postgraduate Medicine for the Internist. William G. Figueroa. (Illus.). 1981. price not set (ISBN 0-89289-377-X). HM.
Hematopoietic Agents. J. C. Dreyfus & B. Dreyfus. 1971. 55.00 (ISBN 0-08-016211-8). Pergamon.
Hemi-Inattention & Hemisphere Specialization. Ed. by Edwin A. Weinstein & Robert P. Friedland. LC 77-5278. (Advances in Neurology Ser.: Vol. 18). 1977. 15.50 (ISBN 0-89004-115-6). Raven.
Hemingway & Faulkner: Inventors-Masters. Linda W. Wagner. LC 75-23367. 1975. 13.50 (ISBN 0-8108-0862-5). Scarecrow.
Hemingway & Film. Gene D. Phillips. LC 80-7563. (Ungar Film Library). (Illus.). 250p. 1980. 10.95 (ISBN 0-8044-2695-3); pap. 5.95 (ISBN 0-8044-6644-0). Ungar.
Hemingway & Jake. Vernon Klimo & Will Oursler. 224p. 1973. pap. 1.25 o.p. (ISBN 0-445-00176-3). Popular Lib.
Hemingway & the Dead Gods: A Study in Existentialism. John Killinger. LC 60-15379. 128p. 1960. 9.00x (ISBN 0-8131-1055-6). U Pr of Ky.
Hemingway & the Movies. Frank M. Laurence. LC 79-1437. 336p. 1980. 20.00 (ISBN 0-87805-115-5). U Pr of Miss.
Hemingway in Germany. Wayne Kvam. LC 79-181689. x, 214p. 1973. 12.95x (ISBN 0-8214-0126-2). Ohio U Pr.
Hemingway Reader. Ernest Hemingway. 1953. lib. rep. ed. 25.00x (ISBN 0-684-15164-2, ScribT); pap. 7.95 o.p. (ISBN 0-684-71872-3, SL119, ScribT). Scribner.
Hemingway's Paris. Robert E. Gajdusek. LC 78-17214. (Illus.). 1978. 14.95 o.p. (ISBN 0-684-15799-3, ScribT). Scribner.
Hemingway's Reading, Nineteen Ten to Nineteen Forty: Commentary & Inventory. Michael S. Reynolds. LC 80-7549. 200p. 1980. 17.50 (ISBN 0-691-06447-4). Princeton U Pr.
Hemiplegic Cerebral Palsy in Children & Adults. (Clinics in Developmental Medicine Ser. No. 4). 209p. 1961. 4.50 o.p. (ISBN 0-685-24711-2). Lippincott.
Hemispheric Disconnection & Cerebral Function. Ed. by Marcel Kinsbourne & W. Lynn Smith. (Illus.). 316p. 1975. text ed. 29.75 (ISBN 0-398-02967-9). C C Thomas.
Hemodynamic Monitoring in the Critically Ill. Paul W. Armstrong & Ronald S. Baigrie. (Illus.). 250p. 1980. text ed. 14.95 (ISBN 0-06-140268-0, Harper Medical). Har-Row.
Hemodynamics & Ventricular Function During Exercise. Schmutzler et al. Ed. by Heiss. (Advances in Clinical Cardiology: Vol. 2). 250p. 1980. pap. 23.00x (ISBN 0-933682-01-8). G Witzstrock Pub Hse.
Hemoglobinopathies & Thalassemias. Virgil Fairbanks. 1980. 32.50. Thieme Stratton.
Hemoperfusion: Kidney & Liver Support Detoxification, Pt. 2. Ed. by Samuel Sideman & T. M. Chang. 1982. text ed. price not set (ISBN 0-89116-211-9). Hemisphere Pub. Postponed.
Hemophilia: A Manual of Outpatient Management. Ed. by David Green. (Illus.). 132p. 1973. 12.75 (ISBN 0-398-02853-2). C C Thomas.
Hemophilia in the Child. Hilgartner. Date not set. price not set. Masson Pub. Postponed.
Hemorheology: Proceedings of the First International Conference. Ed. by A. Copley. 1968. 130.00 (ISBN 0-08-013171-9). Pergamon.
Hemorrhagic Diseases & the Pathology of Hemostasis. Armand J. Quick. (Illus.). 404p. 1974. text ed. 33.50 (ISBN 0-398-02998-9). C C Thomas.
Hemosorption. Y. M. Lopukhin & M. N. Molodenkov. LC 79-1273. (Illus.). 1979. 35.00 (ISBN 0-8016-3029-0). Mosby.
Hemostasis, Prostaglandins & Renal Disease. Ed. by Giuseppe Remuzzi et al. (Monographs of the Mario Negri Institute for Pharmacological Research). 475p. 1980. text ed. 39.00 (ISBN 0-89004-484-8). Raven.
Hempstead Plan: Sensible Approach to Dieting & Nutrition. Grace DeJose. (Illus.). 1980. 7.50 (ISBN 0-682-49516-6). Exposition.
Henderson: The Rain King. Saul Bellow. 1976. pap. 2.50 (ISBN 0-380-00832-7, 54320). Avon.
Henderson's Dictionary of Biological Terms. 9th ed. Sandra Holmes. 521p. text ed. 29.95 (ISBN 0-442-24865-2). Van Nos Reinhold.
Hendrik Goltzius, Master Engraver: A Complete Pictorial Catalogue of His Engravings, Etchings, & Woodcuts. new ed. Walter L. Strauss. LC 76-22304. (Illus.). 768p. 1976. 120.00 (ISBN 0-913870-10-2). Abaris Bks.
Hendrik van Veldeke. John R. Sinnema. (World Authors Ser.: Netherlands: No. 223). lib. bdg. 10.95 (ISBN 0-8057-2936-4). Twayne.
Henny Penny. Galdone. (ps-3). 1980. pap. 1.50 (ISBN 0-590-08732-0, Schol Pap). Schol Bk Serv.
Henny Penny. Paul Galdone. LC 68-24735. (Illus.). (ps-2). 1968. 6.95 (ISBN 0-395-28800-2, Clarion). HM.
Henny Youngman's Bar Bets, Bar Jokes, Bar Tricks. Henny Youngman. LC 73-90951. (Illus.). 168p. 1974. 5.95 (ISBN 0-8065-0404-8). Citadel Pr.
Henny Youngman's Big Blue Bamboozle. Henny Youngman. 1978. pap. 1.95 o.p. (ISBN 0-523-40349-6). Pinnacle Bks.
Henny Youngman's Five Hundred All-Time Greatest One-Liners. Henny Youngman. 160p. (Orig.). 1981. pap. 1.95 (ISBN 0-523-41142-1). Pinnacle Bks.
Henri & the Crocodile. Louise Kantenwein. (Illus.). 32p. (gr. 7 up). 1981. 5.00 (ISBN 0-682-49732-0). Exposition.
Henri Cartier-Bresson: Photographer. Henri Cartier-Bresson. LC 79-88493. (Illus.). 1979. 60.00 (ISBN 0-8212-0756-3, 357715). NYGS.
Henri Michaux. Peter Broome. (Athlone French Poets Ser). 1977. text ed. 19.75x (ISBN 0-485-14605-3, Athlone Pr); pap. text ed. 11.75x (ISBN 0-485-12205-7). Humanities.
Henri Michaux. Virginia A. La Charite. (World Authors Ser.: No. 465). 1977. lib. bdg. 11.95 (ISBN 0-8057-6302-3). Twayne.
Henri Michaux: A Study of His Literary Works. Malcolm Bowie. (Illus.). 224p. 1973. 24.00x (ISBN 0-19-815740-1). Oxford U Pr.
Henrietta. Ann Fairfax. (Orig.). 1979. pap. 1.75 (ISBN 0-515-05128-4). Jove Pubns.
Henrietta, 2 vols. in 1. Charlotte Lennox. (Flowering of the Novel Ser, 1740-1775: Vol. 50). 1974. Repr. of 1758 ed. lib. bdg. 50.00 (ISBN 0-8240-1149-X). Garland Pub.
Henrietta. Margaret C. Self. LC 66-24003. (Illus.). (gr. 3-6). 1966. 5.95 (ISBN 0-8149-0385-1). Vanguard.
Henrietta & the Day of the Iguana. Winifred Rosen. LC 77-19047. (Illus.). 32p. (gr. k-3). 1978. 6.95 (ISBN 0-590-07471-7, Four Winds). Schol Bk Serv.
Henrietta & the Gong from Hong Kong. Winifred Rosen. LC 80-19526. (Illus.). 32p. (gr. k-3). 1981. 7.95 (ISBN 0-590-07657-4, Four Winds). Schol Bk Serv.
Henrietta, Circus Star. Syd Hoff. (Illus.). 48p. (ps-2). 1981. pap. 1.95 (ISBN 0-671-42661-3, Pub. by Windmill). S&S.
Henrietta the Early Bird. Syd Hoff. (Illus.). 48p. (ps-2). 1981. pap. 1.95 (ISBN 0-671-42659-1, Pub. by Windmill). S&S.
Henrietta, the Wild Woman of Borneo. Winifred Rosen. LC 74-31017. (Illus.). 48p. (gr. k-3). 1975. 5.95 (ISBN 0-590-07390-7, Four Winds). Schol Bk Serv.
Henrik Bsen's Theatre Hengel Highlights. Ed. by Wanda Orynski. 1960. 4.75 (ISBN 0-8022-1245-X). Philos Lib.
Henrik Ibsen: John Gabriel Borkman, an English Version. Inga-Stina Ewbank & Peter Hall. 96p. 1975. pap. text ed. 4.50x (ISBN 0-485-12100-X, Athlone Pr). Humanities.
Henrik Ibsen, Vol. 1: The Making of a Dramatist, 1864-1882. Ed. by Michael Meyer. 260p. 1980. text ed. 9.25x (ISBN 0-246-64457-5). Humanities.
Henrik Ibsen, Vol. 2: The Farewell to Poetry, 1864-1882. Ed. by Michael Meyer. 344p. 1980. text ed. 13.00x (ISBN 0-246-64001-4). Humanities.
Henrik Ibsen, Vol. 3: The Top of a Cold Mountain 1883-1906. Ed. by Michael Meyer. 368p. 1980. text ed. 14.50x (ISBN 0-246-64040-5). Humanities.

Henrik Ibsen's Theatre Aesthetic & Dramatic Art. Jane E. Tammany. LC 79-92436. (Illus.). 380p. 1980. 22.50 (ISBN 0-8022-2365-6). Philos Lib.

Henrik Pontoppidan. P. M. Mitchell. (World Authors Ser.: No. 524). 1979. lib. bdg. 14.95 (ISBN 0-8057-6366-X). Twayne.

Henry, a Man of Aroostook: Pioneer in Northern Maine. Milton T. Lufkin. LC 76-8088. (Illus.). 1976. 10.00 o.p. (ISBN 0-87027-173-3). Wheelwright.

Henry A. Wallace of Iowa: The Agrarian Years, 1910-1940. Edward L. Schapsmeier & Frederick H. Schapsmeier. (Illus.). 1969. 8.95 o.p. (ISBN 0-8138-1741-2). Iowa St U Pr.

Henry Adams. Ferman Bishop. (United States Authors Ser.: No. 293). 1979. lib. bdg. 10.95 (ISBN 0-8057-7257-X). Twayne.

Henry Adams. Ed. by R. P. Blackmur. LC 79-1812. 1980. 19.95 (ISBN 0-15-139997-2). HarBraceJ.

Henry Adams. James G. Murray. (World Leaders Ser.: No. 31). 1974. lib. bdg. 10.95 (ISBN 0-8057-3651-4). Twayne.

Henry Adams. Ernest Samuels. Incl. The Major Phase. LC 64-21790. xv, 687p. 1964. 22.50x (ISBN 0-674-38751-1); The Middle Years. LC 58-12975. xiv, 514p. 1958. o.p. (ISBN 0-674-38753-8); The Young Henry Adams. LC 48-10525. xvi, 378p. 1948. 17.50x (ISBN 0-674-96630-9). Belknap Pr). Harvard U Pr.

Henry Adams & the American Experiment. David R. Contosta. (American Biography Library: Library of American Biography). 176p. (Orig.). 1980. 10.95 (ISBN 0-316-15401-6); pap. 4.95 (ISBN 0-316-15400-8). Little.

Henry & Beezus. Beverly Cleary. (Illus.). (gr. 3-7). 1952. 8.25 (ISBN 0-688-21383-9); PLB 7.92 (ISBN 0-688-31383-3). Morrow.

Henry & Fowler. Sarah Garland. LC 76-42160. (Illus.). 1976. 6.95 (ISBN 0-684-14866-8, ScribJ). Scribner.

Henry & Ribsy. Beverly Cleary. (Illus.). (gr. 3-7). 1954. 8.25 (ISBN 0-688-21382-0); PLB 7.92 (ISBN 0-688-31382-5); pap. 1.50 (ISBN 0-688-25382-2). Morrow.

Henry & the Clubhouse. Beverly Cleary. (Illus.). (gr. 3-7). 1962. 7.75 (ISBN 0-688-21381-2); PLB 7.44 (ISBN 0-688-31381-7). Morrow.

Henry & the Paper Route. Beverly Cleary. (Illus.). (gr. 3-7). 1957. 8.25 (ISBN 0-688-21380-4); PLB 7.92 (ISBN 0-688-31380-9). Morrow.

Henry Barnard. Robert B. Downs. LC 77-1775. (World Leaders Ser.: No. 59). 1977. 9.95 (ISBN 0-8057-7710-5). Twayne.

Henry Barnard: American Educator. Vincent P. Lannie. LC 74-4827. 1974. text ed. 8.75 (ISBN 0-8077-2441-6); pap. text ed. 4.00 (ISBN 0-8077-2443-2). Tchrs Coll.

Henry Barnard's School Architecture. Ed. by Jean McClintock & Robert McClintock. LC 72-729262. (Illus.). 1970. text ed. 15.70 (ISBN 0-8077-1725-8); pap. text ed. 6.75x (ISBN 0-8077-1724-X). Tchrs Coll.

Henry Becque. Lois B. Hyslop. (World Authors Ser.: France: No. 180). pap. 10.95 (ISBN 0-8057-2128-2). Twayne.

Henry Brown: Outlaw Marshal. William O'Neal. LC 80-65457. 165p. 1981. 12.95 (ISBN 0-932702-09-0); collector's edtion 75.00 (ISBN 0-932702-10-4). Creative Texas.

Henry Brown: The Outlaw-Marshall. Bill O'Neal. (Illus.). 165p. 12.95; leatherbound collector's edition 75.00. Creative Pubns.

Henry Cabot Lodge & the Search for an American Foreign Policy. William C. Widenor. 1980. 18.50 (ISBN 0-520-03778-2). U of Cal Pr.

Henry Clay. Carl Schurz. LC 80-18659. (American Statesmen Ser.). 815p. 1981. Set. pap. 10.95 (ISBN 0-87754-180-9). Chelsea Hse.

Henry D. Thoreau. Franklin B. Sanborn. LC 80-2515. 1981. Repr. of 1910 ed. 37.50 (ISBN 0-404-19063-4). AMS Pr.

Henry David Thoreau. Joseph W. Krutch. LC 73-16724. 1974. pap. 4.75 (ISBN 0-688-06774-3). Morrow.

Henry David Thoreau. Joseph W. Krutch. LC 80-2511. 1981. Repr. of 1948 ed. 34.00 (ISBN 0-404-19059-6). AMS Pr.

Henry David Thoreau. James G. Murray. (World Leaders Ser). lib. bdg. 9.95 (ISBN 0-8057-3723-5). Twayne.

Henry David Thoreau. Frank B. Sanborn. LC 80-23945. (American Men & Women of Letters Ser.). 330p. 1981. pap. 5.95 (ISBN 0-87754-155-8). Chelsea Hse.

Henry David Thoreau: Essays, Journals & Poems. Henry D. Thoreau. Ed. by Dean Flower. 640p. (Orig.). 1975. pap. 2.50 o.p. (ISBN 0-449-22378-7, L2378, Crest). Fawcett.

Henry David Thoreau: What Manner of Man? Edward Wagenknecht. LC 80-23542. (New England Writers Ser.). 224p. 1981. lib. bdg. 12.50x (ISBN 0-87023-136-7); pap. 5.95 (ISBN 0-87023-137-5). U of Mass Pr.

Henry Demarest Lloyd. E. Jay Jernigan. LC 76-17104. (U.S. Authors Ser: No. 277). 1976. lib. bdg. 12.50 (ISBN 0-8057-7177-8). Twayne.

Henry Derozio: Poems. Henry Derozio. Ed. by P. Lal. 67p. 1975. 14.00 (ISBN 0-88253-716-4); pap. 6.75 (ISBN 0-88253-848-9). Ind-US Inc.

Henry E. Sigerist on the Sociology of Medicine. Henry E. Sigerist. Ed. by Milton I. Roemer. LC 60-6647. 1960. 6.75 o.p. (ISBN 0-910922-14-4). MD Pubns.

Henry Eighth. William Shakespeare. Ed. by Arthur Quiller-Couch et al. (New Shakespeare Ser). 1969. 23.95 (ISBN 0-521-07538-6); pap. 2.95x o.p. (ISBN 0-521-09481-X). Cambridge U Pr.

Henry Eighth & His Court. Neville Williams. Ed. by Ray Roberts. LC 70-125407. (Illus.). 1971. 12.95 o.s.i. (ISBN 0-02-629100-2). Macmillan.

Henry Fielding: An Annotated Bibliography. H. George Hahn. LC 79-4498. (Author Bibliographies Ser.: No. 41). 1979. 11.00 (ISBN 0-8108-1212-6). Scarecrow.

Henry Fielding & the Politics of Mid-Eighteenth-Century England. Brian McCrea. LC 80-14711. (South Atlantic Modern Language Association Award Study, 1979). 328p. 1981. 20.00x (ISBN 0-8203-0531-6). U of Ga Pr.

Henry Fifth. William Shakespeare. Ed. by Arthur Quiller-Couch et al. (New Shakespeare Ser). 23.95 (ISBN 0-521-07534-3); pap. 4.50x (ISBN 0-521-09477-1). Cambridge U Pr.

Henry Ford & the Jews. Albert Lee. LC 79-3694. 252p. 1980. 12.95 (ISBN 0-8128-2701-5). Stein & Day.

Henry Ford: Ignorant Idealist. David E. Nye. (National University Publications, American Studies). 1979. 12.50 (ISBN 0-8046-9242-4). Kennikat.

Henry Ford: The Wayward Capitalist. Carol Gelderman. (Illus.). 416p. 1981. 14.95 (ISBN 0-8037-3436-0). Dial.

Henry Fourth, Pt. 1. rev. ed. William Shakespeare. Ed. by James L. Sanderson. (Critical Editions Ser). (Annotated). (gr. 9-12). 1969. text ed. 5.00 (ISBN 0-393-04234-0); pap. text ed. 5.95x (ISBN 0-393-09554-1, 9554, NortonC). Norton.

Henry Fourth, Pts. 1 & 2. William Shakespeare. (Shakespeare Ser). (gr. 10 up). pap. 1.25 ea. Pt. 1 (ISBN 0-8049-1018-9, S18). Pt. 2. pap. 0.60 (ISBN 0-8049-1019-7, S19). Airmont.

Henry Fourth, Pt. 1. William Shakespeare. Ed. by Arthur Quiller-Couch et al. (New Shakespeare Ser). 23.95 (ISBN 0-521-07532-7); pap. 4.50x (ISBN 0-521-09475-5). Cambridge U Pr.

Henry Fourth, Pt. 2. William Shakespeare. Ed. by Arthur Quiller-Couch et al. (New Shakespeare Ser). 23.95 (ISBN 0-521-07533-5); pap. 4.50x (ISBN 0-521-09476-3). Cambridge U Pr.

Henry George. Henry George, Jr. Ed. by Daniel Aaron. (American Men & Women of Letters Ser.). Orig. Title: The Life of Henry George. 640p. 1981. pap. 8.95 (ISBN 0-87754-164-7). Chelsea Hse.

Henry George. Jacob Oser. (World Leaders Ser.). 1974. lib. bdg. 9.95 (ISBN 0-8057-3682-4). Twayne.

Henry George: Printer, Bookseller, Stationer, & Bookbinder. 69p. 1980. 13.50 (ISBN 0-913720-17-8). Sandstone.

Henry Green. Keith C. Odom. (English Authors Ser.: No. 235). 1978. lib. bdg. 9.95 (ISBN 0-8057-6706-1). Twayne.

Henry Green. Robert S. Ryf. LC 67-27360. (Columbia Ser.: No. 29). 1968. pap. 2.00 (ISBN 0-231-02897-0, MW29). Columbia U Pr.

Henry Handel Richardson. William D. Elliott. LC 75-12692. (World Authors Ser.: Australia: No. 366). 1975. lib. bdg. 12.50 (ISBN 0-8057-6217-5). Twayne.

Henry! Henry Aaron. James Hahn & Lynn Hahn. Ed. by Howard Schroeder. (Sports Legends Ser.). (Illus.). 48p. (gr. 3-5). 1981. PLB 5.95 (ISBN 0-89686-120-1); pap. text ed. 2.95 (ISBN 0-89686-135-X). Crestwood Hse.

Henry Hudson. Joan Joseph. LC 73-14704. (Visual Biography Ser). (Illus.). 64p. (gr. 4-5). 1974. PLB 4.90 o.p. (ISBN 0-531-01276-X). Watts.

Henry Huggins. Beverly Cleary. (Illus.). (gr. 3-7). 1950. 7.75 (ISBN 0-688-25385-7); PLB 7.44 (ISBN 0-688-31385-X). Morrow.

Henry Huntington & the Pacific Electric. pap. 10.00. Chatham Pub CA.

Henry Irving, Shakespearean. Allan Hughes. LC 79-54019. (Illus.). 304p. Date not set. 44.50 (ISBN 0-521-22192-7). Cambridge U Pr.

Henry IV, Pt. I. William Shakespeare. Ed. by Maynard Mack & Robert W. Boynton. (Shakespeare Ser). (Illus.). (gr. 10-12). 1972. pap. text ed. 0.95x (ISBN 0-8104-6017-3). Hayden.

Henry James. F. W. Dupee. LC 73-16722. 280p. 1974. pap. 2.95 (ISBN 0-688-06776-X). Morrow.

Henry James, 4 vols. Leon Edel. Incl. Vol. 2. The Conquest of London, 1870-1881. (Illus.). 350p. 1962; Vol. 3. The Middle Years: 1882-1895. (Illus.). 400p. 1962 (ISBN 0-397-00216-5); Vol. 4. The Treacherous Years: 1895-1901. (Illus.). 384p. 1969 (ISBN 0-397-00583-0). 10.00 ea. o.s.i. Lippincott.

Henry James. Bruce R. McElderry, Jr. (U. S. Authors Ser.: No. 79). 1965. lib. bdg. 10.95 (ISBN 0-8057-0404-3). Twayne.

Henry James. Michael Swan. Ed. by Bonamy Dobree et al. Bd. with D. H. Lawrence. Kenneth Young; Joseph Conrad. Oliver Warner. LC 63-63096. (British Writers & Their Work Ser: Vol. 10). 1967. pap. 2.65x (ISBN 0-8032-5660-4, BB 459, Bison). U of Nebr Pr.

Henry James: A Bibliography of Secondary Works. Beatrice Ricks. LC 75-22128. (Author Bibliographies Ser.: No. 24). 1975. 21.00 (ISBN 0-8108-0853-6). Scarecrow.

Henry James: A Reader's Guide. Samuel G. Putt. LC 66-17350. (YA) (gr. 9-12). 1967. pap. 4.95 (ISBN 0-8014-9027-8). Cornell U Pr.

Henry James: A Study in the Aesthetics of the Novel. Rama K. Asthana. 130p. 1980. Repr. of 1936 ed. text ed. 11.25 (ISBN 0-391-02180-X). Humanities.

Henry James & Impressionism. James J. Kirschke. LC 80-52732. 357p. 1981. 22.50x (ISBN 0-87875-206-4). Whitston Pub.

Henry James & John Hay: The Record of a Friendship. George Monteiro. LC 65-24094. 205p. 1965. 8.50x (ISBN 0-87057-091-9, Pub. by Brown U Pr). Univ Pr of New England.

Henry James & the Experimental Novel. Sergio Perosa. LC 77-16847. 1978. 12.95x (ISBN 0-8139-0727-6). U Pr of Va.

Henry James & the Visual Arts. Viola H. Winner. LC 73-109223. (Illus.). 202p. 1970. 10.95x (ISBN 0-8139-0285-1). U Pr of Va.

Henry James: The Critical Heritage. Ed. by Roger Gard. (Critical Heritage Ser.). 1976. Repr. of 1968 ed. 38.50x (ISBN 0-7100-6068-8). Routledge & Kegan.

Henry James: The Ibsen Years. Ed. by Michael Egan. 154p. 1972. text ed. 8.00x (ISBN 0-85478-242-7). Humanities.

Henry James: The Later Novels. Nicola Bradbury. 236p. 1979. text ed. 36.00x (ISBN 0-19-812096-6). Oxford U Pr.

Henry Kendall. William H. Wilde. LC 75-41479. (World Authors Ser.: Australia: No. 387). 1976. lib. bdg. 12.50 (ISBN 0-8057-6229-9). Twayne.

Henry Kissinger. Paula Taylor. LC 74-32470. (Creative Education Closeup Bk.). (Illus.). 32p. (gr. 3-6). 1975. PLB 5.95 (ISBN 0-87191-422-0). Creative Ed.

Henry Knox, a Soldier of the Revolution. Noah Brooks. LC 74-8496. (Era of the American Revolution Ser). (Illus.). xiv, 286p. 1974. Repr. of 1900 ed. lib. bdg. 25.00 (ISBN 0-306-70617-2). Da Capo.

Henry Mackenzie. Gerard A. Barker. (English Authors Ser.: No. 184). 1975. lib. bdg. 10.95 (ISBN 0-8057-6651-0). Twayne.

Henry Miller. Kingsley Widmer. (U. S. Authors Ser.: No. 44). 1963. lib. bdg. 10.95 (ISBN 0-8057-0504-X). Twayne.

Henry Miller: A Bibliography of Secondary Sources. Lawrence J. Shifreen. LC 78-12518. (Scarecrow Author Bibliographies: No. 38). 1979. lib. bdg. 22.50 (ISBN 0-8108-1171-5). Scarecrow.

Henry Miller & the Critics. Ed. by George Wickes. LC 63-14289. (Crosscurrents-Modern Critiques Ser.). 212p. 1963. 12.95 (ISBN 0-8093-0102-4). S Ill U Pr.

Henry Miller Dinner Chats. Ed. by Twinka Thiebaud. (Illus.). 128p. (Orig.). 1981. pap. 6.95 (ISBN 0-88496-166-4). Capra Pr.

Henry Moore: Bibliography & Reproductions Index. Edward H. Teague. LC 80-28048. (Illus.). 185p. 1981. lib. bdg. 21.00x (ISBN 0-89950-016-1). McFarland & Co.

Henry More: A Collections of Several Philosophical Writings, 2 vols. Henry More. Ed. by Rene Wellek. LC 75-11238. (British Philosophers & Theologians of the 17th & 18th Centuries Ser.). 1978. lib. bdg. 42.00 (ISBN 0-8240-1790-0). Garland Pub.

Henry Peachman. Alan R. Young. (English Authors Ser.: No. 251). 1979. lib. bdg. 10.95 (ISBN 0-8057-6732-0). Twayne.

Henry Purcell & the Restoration Theatre. Robert E. Moore. LC 73-15057. (Illus.). 223p. 1974. Repr. of 1961 ed. lib. bdg. 19.75x (ISBN 0-8371-7155-5, MOHQ). Greenwood.

Henry Reed Inc. Keith Robertson. (gr. 2-5). 1974. pap. 1.75 (ISBN 0-440-43552-8, YB). Dell.

Henry Reeds Baby Sitting Service. Keith Robertson. (gr. 2-5). 1974. pap. 1.75 (ISBN 0-440-43565-X, YB). Dell.

Henry Reed's Big Show. Keith Robertson. (Illus.). (gr. 4-6). 1970. PLB 9.95 (ISBN 0-670-36839-3). Viking Pr.

Henry Second. W. L. Warren. (English Monarchs Ser.). 1973. 31.50x (ISBN 0-520-02282-3); pap. 8.95 (ISBN 0-520-03494-5). U of Cal Pr.

Henry Sixth, Pt. 1. William Shakespeare. Ed. by Arthur Quiller-Couch et al. (New Shakespeare Ser). 1968. 23.95 (ISBN 0-521-07535-1); pap. 4.50x (ISBN 0-521-09478-X). Cambridge U Pr.

Henry Sixth, Pts. 1, 2 & 3. William Shakespeare. Ed. by S. Bevington et al. 1966. Pt. 1. pap. 1.95 (ISBN 0-14-071434-0, Pelican); Pt.2&3. pap. 2.95 (ISBN 0-14-071435-9, Pelican). Penguin.

Henry Sixth, Pt. 2. William Shakespeare. Ed. by Arthur Quiller-Couch et al. (New Shakespeare Ser). 1968. 23.95 (ISBN 0-521-07536-X); pap. 4.50x (ISBN 0-521-09479-8). Cambridge U Pr.

Henry Sixth, Pt. 3. William Shakespeare. Ed. by Arthur Quiller-Couch et al. (New Shakespeare Ser). 1968. 23.95 (ISBN 0-521-07537-8); pap. 4.50x (ISBN 0-521-09480-1). Cambridge U Pr.

Henry the Lion: The Lothian Historical Essay for 1912. LC 80-2008. 1981. Repr. of 1912 ed. 18.50 (ISBN 0-404-18586-X). AMS Pr.

Henry Thoreau Bachelor of Nature. Leon Bazalgette. Tr. by Wyck Van Brooks. LC 80-2679. 1981. Repr. of 1924 ed. 37.50 (ISBN 0-404-19076-6). AMS Pr.

Henry Thoreau the Cosmic Yankee. Brooks J. Atkinson. LC 80-2678. 1981. Repr. of 1927 ed. 22.50 (ISBN 0-404-19075-8). AMS Pr.

Henry V. William Shakespeare. 1967. pap. text ed. 3.95x o.p. (ISBN 0-471-00519-3). Wiley.

Henry Vaughan. Kenneth Friedenreich. (English Authors Ser.: No. 226). 1978. lib. bdg. 12.50 (ISBN 0-8057-6697-9). Twayne.

Henry Vaughan: Selected Poems. Henry Vaughan. Ed. by Robert B. Shaw. (Fyfield Ser.). 1979. pap. 3.95 o.s.i. (ISBN 0-85635-138-5, Pub. by Carcanet New Pr England); pap. 3.95 (ISBN 0-85635-139-3). Persea Bks.

Henry Vaughan: The Achievement of Silex Scintillans. Thomas O. Calhoun. LC 79-51851. 272p. 1980. 22.50 (ISBN 0-87413-165-0). U Delaware Pr.

Henry Vaughan: The Achievement of Silex Scintillans. Thomas O. Calhoun. LC 79-51851. 272p. Date not set. 22.50 (ISBN 0-87413-165-0). U Delaware Pr. Postponed.

Henry Vaughan: The Complete Poems. Ed. by Alan Rudrum. LC 80-53979. 718p. 1981. text ed. 30.00x (ISBN 0-300-02680-3); pap. 7.95x (ISBN 0-300-02687-0). Yale U Pr.

Henry VII. S. B. Chrimes. LC 72-78947. (English Monarch Ser.). (Illus.). 400p. 1973. 27.50x (ISBN 0-520-02266-1). U of Cal Pr.

Henry VII. Ed. by S. B. Chrimes. (English Monarch Ser.). 1981. pap. 8.95 (ISBN 0-520-04414-2, CAL 506). U of Cal Pr.

Henry VIII. J. J. Scarisbrick. (English Monarchs Series). (Illus.). 1968. 20.00x (ISBN 0-520-01129-5); pap. 6.95 (ISBN 0-520-01130-9, CAL195). U of Cal Pr.

Henry Wadsworth Longfellow. Cecil B. Williams. (U. S. Authors Ser.: No. 68). 1964. lib. bdg. 9.95 (ISBN 0-8057-0456-6). Twayne.

Henry Wallace: The Man & the Myth. Dwight Macdonald. Ed. by Frank Freidel. LC 78-66546. (History of the United States Ser.: Vol. 11). 188p. 1979. lib. bdg. 15.00 (ISBN 0-8240-9701-7). Garland Pub.

Henry Ward Beecher. Lyman Abbott. LC 80-19338. (American Men & Women of Letters Ser.). 475p. 1980. pap. 6.95 (ISBN 0-87754-163-9). Chelsea Hse.

Henry Wheaton: 1785-1848. Elizabeth F. Baker. LC 70-154698. (American Constitutional & Legal History Ser.). 1971. Repr. of 1937 ed. lib. bdg. 42.50 (ISBN 0-306-70152-9). Da Capo.

Henry Wilson, Practical Radical: A Portrait of a Politician. Ernest McKay. LC 70-139359. 1971. 17.00 (ISBN 0-8046-9010-3, Natl U Pub). Kennikat.

Henry Youle Hind, Eighteen Twenty-Three to Nineteen Eight. W. L. Morton. (Canadian Biographical Stud.). 1980. 7.50 (ISBN 0-8020-3278-8). U of Toronto Pr.

Henry's Awful Mistake. Robert Quackenbush. (Illus.). 48p. (ps-3). 1981. 4.95 (ISBN 0-8193-1039-5); PLB 5.95 (ISBN 0-8193-1040-9). Parents.

Henry's Probate Law & Practice. 7th ed. John S. Grimes. 5500p. Date not set. text ed. 125.00 (ISBN 0-672-83934-2). Michie.

Henslowe Papers, 2 vols. facsimile ed. Philip Henslowe. Repr. of 1977 ed. Set. 220.00x o.p. (ISBN 0-85967-355-3, Pub. by Scolar Pr England). Biblio Dist.

Heparin (& Related Polysaccharides) Structural & Functional Properties. W. D. Comper. 1981. price not set (ISBN 0-677-05040-2). Gordon.

Hepatic & Portal Surgery in the Rat. D. Castaing et al. (Illus.). 184p. 1980. 37.50 (ISBN 0-89352-101-9). Masson Pub.

Hepatic Encephalopathy. Frederick Steigmann & Bernard F. Clowdus, 2nd. (Illus.). 214p. 1971. text ed. 18.75 (ISBN 0-398-01841-3). C C Thomas.

Hepatic Support in Acute Liver Failure. Gustavo G. Kuster. (Illus.). 320p. 1976. 31.75 (ISBN 0-398-03539-3). C C Thomas.

Hepatica Hawks. Rachel Field. (gr. 4-6). 1964. 4.95 o.s.i. (ISBN 0-02-734740-0). Macmillan.

Hepaticae & Anthocerotae of North America East of the Hundredth Meridian, 3 vols, Vols. 1, 2 & 3. Rudolf M. Schuster. LC 66-14791. 1966-74. 45.00x ea. Vol. 1 (ISBN 0-231-08981-3). Vol. 2 (ISBN 0-231-08982-1). Vol. 3 (ISBN 0-231-03567-5). Columbia U Pr.

Hepatitis B Virus & Primary Liver Cancer. Ed. by J. L. Melnick & P. Maupas. (Progress in Medical Virology Ser.: Vol. 27). (Illus.). 250p. 1981. 90.00 (ISBN 3-8055-1784-X). S Karger.

Hepatobiliary System: Fundamental & Pathological Mechanisms. Ed. by W. Taylor. LC 76-2486. (NATO Advanced Study Institutes Ser., Ser. A: Life Sciences: Vol. 7). 654p. 1976. 49.50 (ISBN 0-306-35607-4, Plenum Pr). Plenum Pub.

Hepatocellular Carcinoma. Ed. by Kunio Okuda & Robert L. Peters. LC 76-6500. (Wiley Series on Diseases of the Liver). 512p. 1976. 64.95 (ISBN 0-471-65316-0, Pub. by Wiley Medical). Wiley.

Hepatotoxicity: The Adverse Effects of Drugs & Other Chemicals on the Liver. Hyman J. Zimmerman. (Illus.). 1978. 54.50 (ISBN 0-8385-3725-1). ACC.

Hepplewhite Furniture Designs. Ralph Edwards. 1972. 16.50 (ISBN 0-685-52079-X). Transatlantic.

Hepzibah. Peter Dickinson. LC 80-65425. (Illus.). 32p. 1980. 8.95 (ISBN 0-87923-334-6). Godine.

Her-Bak Egyptian Initiate. Isha Schwaller De Lubicz. Tr. by Ronald Fraser from Fr. (Illus.). 1978. pap. 8.95 (ISBN 0-89281-002-5). Inner Tradit.

Her-Bak: Egyptian Initiate, Vol. 2. Isha S. De Lubicz. 1978. pap. 8.95 (ISBN 0-685-62083-2). Weiser.

Her-Bak, the Living Face of Ancient Egypt. Isha Schwaller De Lubicz. Tr. by Charles E. Spague from Fr. (Illus.). 1978. pap. 8.95 (ISBN 0-89281-003-3). Inner Tradit.

Her-Bak: The Living Face of Ancient Egypt, Vol. 1. Isha S. De Lubicz. 1978. pap. 8.95 (ISBN 0-685-62082-4). Weiser.

Her Death by Cold. Ralph McInerny. LC 76-39728. 1977. 7.95 (ISBN 0-8149-0781-4). Vanguard.

Her Honor the Judge. Beverly B. Clopton. 240p. 1980. 15.95 (ISBN 0-8138-0565-1). Iowa St U Pr.

Her Life for His Friends: A Biography of Terry McHugh. Cecelia D. Johnson. LC 80-25996. 1980. pap. 7.95 (ISBN 0-8190-0640-8). Fides Claretian.

Her Mothers. E. M. Broner. pap. 1.75 o.p. (ISBN 0-425-03206-X). Berkley Pub.

Her Name. James B. Hall. 1980. 17.50x (ISBN 0-915316-64-1); pap. 5.00 (ISBN 0-915316-63-3). Pentagram.

Her Name Is Woman, 2 bks. Gien Karssen. LC 77-81186. Bk. 1, 1975. pap. 3.95 (ISBN 0-89109-420-2, 14209); Bk. 2, 1977. pap. 3.95 (ISBN 0-89109-424-5, 14241). NavPress.

Her Own Way, the Story of Lottie Moon. Helen A. Monsell. LC 58-9919. (gr. 4-8). 1958. 4.50 (ISBN 0-8054-4303-7). Broadman.

Her Poems: An Anniversaric Chronology. S. Diane Bogus. (Illus., Orig.). 1980. pap. cancelled (ISBN 0-934172-02-1). WIM Pubns.

Her Shining Splendor. Valerie Sherwood. (Orig.). 1980. pap. 2.75 (ISBN 0-446-85487-5). Warner Bks.

Her Side of It. Thomas Savage. Date not set. price not set. Little.

Her Storms: Selected Poems 1938-1977. Sheila Wingfield. 1977. text ed. 19.50x (ISBN 0-85105-335-1, Dolmen Pr). Humanities.

Heraclea: A Legend of Warrior Women. Bernard Evslin. LC 77-17967. (Illus.). 272p. 1978. 9.95 (ISBN 0-590-07405-9, Four Winds). Schol Bk Serv.

Heraclides of Pontus. H. B. Gottschalk. 192p. 1980. 37.50x (ISBN 0-19-814021-5). Oxford U Pr.

Heraclitean Fire. Erwin Chargaff. 1980. pap. 6.95 (ISBN 0-446-97659-8). Warner Bks.

Herakleitos & Diogenes. Heraclitus of Ephesius & Diogenes, the Cynic. Tr. by Guy Davenport from Gr. LC 78-17310. 1979. 10.00 (ISBN 0-912516-35-6); pap. 4.00 (ISBN 0-912516-36-4). Grey Fox.

Heraldik in Diensten der Shakespeare-Forschung. Alfred Von Mauntz. LC 68-57296. 1969. Repr. of 1903 ed. 18.00 (ISBN 0-8103-3886-6). Gale.

Heraldry & Floral Forms As Used in Decoration. Herbert Cole. LC 74-164180. (Tower Bks). (Illus.). 1971. Repr. of 1922 ed. 22.00 (ISBN 0-8103-3913-7). Gale.

Heraldry Book: A Guide to Designing Your Own Coat of Arms. Marvin Grosswirth. LC 78-22321. (Illus.). 240p. 1981. 11.95 (ISBN 0-385-14157-2). Doubleday.

Heraldry Index of the St. Louis Public Library. St. Louis Public Library. 1980. lib. bdg. 475.00 (ISBN 0-8161-0311-9). G K Hall.

Heraldry of the World. Carl A. Von Volborth. (Illus.). 251p. 1980. 12.95 (ISBN 0-7137-0647-3, Pub. by Blandford Pr England). Sterling.

Heraldry: The Armiger's News, 1979-1980. David P. Johnson. LC 80-70043. (Illus.). 55p. 1980. pap. 9.95 (ISBN 0-9605668-0-5). Am Coll Heraldry.

Heralds of Revolt. William Barry. LC 78-11333. 1971. Repr. of 1904 ed. 13.25 o.p. (ISBN 0-8046-1182-3). Kennikat.

Herb Buyers Guide. Richard Heffern. (Orig.). pap. 1.50 (ISBN 0-515-04635-3). Jove Pubns.

Herb Denenberg's Smart Shopper's Guide. Herb Dennenberg. LC 80-66978. 208p. Date not set. pap. 6.95 (ISBN 0-8019-7003-2). Chilton.

Herb for Presents. Althea. (ps-2). 1979. pap. 1.45 avail. in 5 pk. (ISBN 0-85122-179-3, Pub. by Dinosaur Pubns). Merrimack Bk Serv.

Herb Gardening. Claire Loewenfeld. (Illus.). 1964. 9.95 (ISBN 0-571-06024-2, Pub. by Faber & Faber); pap. 5.50 (ISBN 0-571-09475-9). Merrimack Bk Serv.

Herb Gardening at Its Best: Everything You Need to Know About Growing Your Favorite Herbs. Sal Gilbertie & Larry Sheehan. LC 77-23678. (Illus.). 1980. pap. 6.95 (ISBN 0-689-70595-6, 255). Atheneum.

Herb Gardening in Five Seasons. Adelma G. Simmons. 1977. pap. 6.95 (ISBN 0-8015-3395-3, Hawthorn). Dutton.

Herb Gardening in the South. Sol Meltzer. LC 76-52240. (Illus.). 1977. pap. 3.95 (ISBN 0-88415-366-5). Pacesetter Pr.

Herb Gardens Delight. Adelma Simmons. 1979. pap. 4.95 (ISBN 0-8015-3403-8, Hawthorn). Dutton.

Herb Growing Book. Rosemary Verey. (Illus.). 48p. (gr. 5 up). 1981. 9.95 (ISBN 0-316-89974-7). Little.

Herb-Lore for Housewives. Constance Romanne-James. LC 71-180978. (Illus.). 264p. 1974. Repr. of 1938 ed. 18.00 (ISBN 0-8103-3976-5). Gale.

Herb Olsen's Guide to Watercolor Landscapes. Herb Olsen. 128p. 1980. pap. 12.95 (ISBN 0-442-25784-8). Van Nos Reinhold.

Herb Tea Book. Dorothy Hall. LC 80-84436. (Pivot Original Health Bk.). (Illus.). 120p. 1981. pap. 2.25 (ISBN 0-87983-248-7). Keats.

Herb Tea Book. Dorothy Hall. LC 80-84436. (Pivet Original Health Bk.). (Illus.). 120p. 1981. pap. 2.25 (ISBN 0-87983-248-7). Keats.

Herbaceous Perennials. F. A. Giles. (Illus.). 1980. text ed. 15.95 (ISBN 0-8359-2822-5). Reston.

Herbaceous Plants. Steven Still. (Illus.). 210p. 1980. text ed. write for info. (ISBN 0-87563-185-1); pap. text ed. write for info. (ISBN 0-87563-184-3). Stipes.

Herbal Connection. Ethan Neblekopf. 1980. 12.95 (ISBN 0-89557-048-3). Bi World Indus.

Herbal Handbook for Farm & Stable. Juliette D. Levy. LC 76-2734. 1976. pap. 5.95 (ISBN 0-87857-115-9); 5.95 o.p. (ISBN 0-87857-120-5). Rodale Pr Inc.

Herbal Pharmacology in the People's Republic of China: A Trip Report of the American Herbal Pharmacology Delegation. Committee of Scholarly Communication with the People's Republic of China, National Research Council. LC 75-39772. v, 169p. 1975. pap. 8.00 (ISBN 0-309-02438-2). Natl Acad Pr.

Herbalist. Joseph E. Meyer. (Illus.). 304p. 1981. 10.95 (ISBN 0-8069-3902-8); lib. bdg. 9.89 (ISBN 0-8069-3903-6). Sterling.

Herbalist. rev. & updated ed. Joseph E. Meyer & Clarence Meyer. (Illus.). 1979. 9.95 (ISBN 0-916638-01-4). Meyerbooks.

Herball or General Historie of Plants, 2 vols. John Gerard. LC 74-80179. (English Experience Ser.: Nos. 660a-660b). 1974. Repr. of 1597 ed. Set. 214.00 (ISBN 90-221-0660-8). Walter J Johnson.

Herbert Austin: The British Motor Car Industry to 1941. Roy Church. (Europa Library of Business Biography: No. 4). (Illus.). 233p. 1979. 30.00x (ISBN 0-905118-29-4). Intl Pubns Serv.

Herbert Butterfield: The Ethics of History & Politics. Ed. by Kenneth W. Thompson. LC 79-5375. 1979. text ed. 12.00 (ISBN 0-8191-0875-8); pap. text ed. 7.25 (ISBN 0-8191-0876-6). U Pr of Amer.

Herbert Butterfield: Writings on Christianity & History. Herbert Butterfield. 1979. 14.95 (ISBN 0-19-502454-0). Oxford U Pr.

Herbert Feigl: Inquiries & Provocations, Selected Writings. 1929 to 1974. Ed. by Robert S. Cohen. (Vienna Circle Collection: No. 14). 450p. 1980. lib. bdg. 50.00 (ISBN 90-277-1101-1, Pub. by D. Reidel); pap. 23.50 (ISBN 90-277-1102-X). Kluwer Boston.

Herbert Ferber. C. Goossen. LC 80-66531. (Illus.). 1981. 75.00 (ISBN 0-89659-148-4). Abbeville Pr.

Herbert Hoover. Wilton Eckley. (United States Author Ser.). 1980. lib. bdg. 10.95 (ISBN 0-8057-7285-5). Twayne.

Herbert Hoover & the Great Depression. Harris G. Warren. 1967. pap. 5.95 o.p. (ISBN 0-393-00394-9, Norton Lib). Norton.

Herbert Hoover & the Great Depression. Harris G. Warren. LC 80-19603. x, 372p. 1980. Repr. of 1970 ed. lib. bdg. 28.75x (ISBN 0-313-22659-8, WAHO). Greenwood.

Herbert L. Fink: Graphic Artist. Compiled by Judith Q. Carter & Richard D. Carter. (Illus.). Date not set. price not set (ISBN 0-8093-1016-3). S Ill U Pr.

Herbert List: Metaphysical Photographs, 1930-1970. Gunter Metken. LC 80-51597. (Illus.). 168p. 1981. pap. 32.50 (ISBN 0-8478-0344-9). Rizzoli Intl.

Herbert Read: The Stream & the Source. George Woodcock. 1972. 11.95 (ISBN 0-571-08656-X, Pub. by Faber & Faber). Merrimack Bk Serv.

Herbert Spencer. James G. Kennedy. (English Author Ser.: No. 219). 1978. 9.95 (ISBN 0-8057-6688-X). Twayne.

Herbert Spencer on Education. Ed. by Andreas M. Kazamias. LC 66-17068. 1966. text ed. 9.75 (ISBN 0-8077-1602-2); pap. text ed. 4.25x (ISBN 0-8077-1599-9). Tchrs Coll.

Herbert, the Timid Dragon. Mercer Mayer. (Illus.). (ps-3). 1980. PLB 9.15 (ISBN 0-307-63732-8, Golden Pr); pap. 3.95 (ISBN 0-307-13732-5). Western Pub.

Herbert the Timid Dragon. Mercer Mayer. (Illus.). (gr. 4-8). 3.95 (ISBN 0-307-13732-5, Golden Pr). Western Pub.

Herbert W. Armstrong. rev. ed. Walter Martin. 1969. pap. 1.25 (ISBN 0-87123-213-8, 210213). Bethany Fell.

Herbicides. James R. Critser, Jr. (Ser. 12-77). 1978. 80.00 (ISBN 0-914428-48-9). Lexington Data.

Herbie's Troubles. Carol Chapman. LC 80-21848. (Illus.). (ps-1). 1981. PLB 9.95 (ISBN 0-525-31645-0). Dutton.

Herblock on All Fronts. Herb Block. 1981. pap. 7.95 (ISBN 0-452-25266-0, Z5266, Plume). NAL.

Herbs. Norma J. Lathrop. (Orig.). 1981. pap. 7.95 (ISBN 0-89586-077-5). H P Bks.

Herbs. Ogden Tanner. LC 76-51513. (Time-Life Encyclopedia for Gardening Ser.). (Illus.). (gr. 6 up). 1977. pap. text ed. 11.97 (ISBN 0-8094-2551-3, Pub. by Time-Life). Silver.

Herbs. Ed. by Time-Life Books. (Time-Life Encyclopedia of Gardening Ser.). 1977. 11.95 (ISBN 0-8094-2550-5). Time-Life.

Herbs & Fruit for Dieting. Ceres. LC 80-53452. (Everybodys Home Herbal Ser.). 64p. 1981. pap. 1.95 (ISBN 0-394-74837-9). Shambhala Pubns.

Herbs & Herb Gardening. Eleanour S. Rohde. LC 70-180975. (Illus.). 1976. Repr. of 1936 ed. 24.00 (ISBN 0-8103-4303-7). Gale.

Herbs & the Fragrant Garden. Margaret Brownlow. 1980. 30.00x (ISBN 0-232-51396-1, Pub. by Darton-Longman-Todd England). State Mutual Bk.

Herbs for Better Body Beauty. Alyson Huxley. (Living with Herbs Ser: Vol. 5). Date not set. pap. 2.50 (ISBN 0-87983-177-4). Keats. Postponed.

Herbs for Colds & Flu. Nalda Gosling. LC 80-53450. (Everybody's Home Herbal Ser.). (Illus.). 64p. (Orig.). 1981. pap. 1.95 (ISBN 0-394-74834-4). Shambhala Pubn.

Herbs for Feminine Ailments. Sarah Beckett. LC 80-53449. (Everybody's Home Herbal Ser.). (Illus.). 63p. (Orig.). 1981. pap. 1.95 (ISBN 0-394-74836-0). Shambhala Pubn.

Herbs for First-Aid & Minor Ailments. Ceres. LC 80-53453. (Everybodys Home Herbal Ser.). (Illus.). 64p. 1981. pap. 1.95 (ISBN 0-394-74925-1). Shambhala Pubns.

Herbs for Headaches & Migraine. Nalda Gosling. LC 80-50750. (Everybody's Home Herbal Ser.). (Illus.). 64p. (Orig.). 1980. pap. 1.95 (ISBN 0-394-73946-9). Shambhala Pubns.

Herbs for Health & Flavor. Donald Law. LC 76-28046. 1977. 5.95 o.p. (ISBN 0-312-36960-3). St Martin.

Herbs for Healthy Hair. Ceres. LC 80-50747. (Everybody's Home Herbal Ser.). (Illus.). 62p. (Orig.). 1980. pap. 1.95 (ISBN 0-394-73947-7). Shambhala Pubns.

Herbs for Indigestion. Ceres. LC 80-53451. (Everybody's Home Herbal Ser.). (Illus.). 63p. (Orig.). 1981. pap. 1.95 (ISBN 0-394-74833-6). Shambhala Pubn.

Herbs for Use & for Delight: An Anthology from The Herbarist. Ed. by Herb Society of America. LC 74-80287. (Illus.). 352p. 1974. pap. 4.50 (ISBN 0-486-23104-6). Dover.

Herbs, Hoecakes & Husbandry: The Daybook of a Planter of the Old South. Ed. by Weymouth T. Jordan. LC 60-63360. (Florida State Univ. Studies). 1960. 8.00 o.p. (ISBN 0-8130-0496-9). U Presses Fla.

Herbs: How to Grow. Sunset Editors. LC 73-181520. (Illus.). 80p. (Orig.). 1972. pap. 2.95 (ISBN 0-376-03322-3, Sunset Bks.). Sunset-Lane.

Herbs: How to Grow Them. Geoff Hamilton. 1980. pap. 4.50 (ISBN 0-7153-7897-X). David & Charles.

Herbs That Heal. William A. Thomson. LC 77-72361. (Encore Edition). (Illus.). 1977. pap. 1.95 (ISBN 0-684-16928-2, ScribT). Scribner.

Herbs to Grow Indoors. Adelma Simmons. 1969. pap. 4.50 (ISBN 0-8015-3416-X, Hawthorn). Dutton.

Herbs to Help You Sleep. Ceres. LC 80-50749. (Everybody's Home Herbal Ser.). (Illus.). 62p. (Orig.). 1980. pap. 1.95 (ISBN 0-394-73946-9). Shambhala Pubns.

Herbs to Soothe Your Nerves. Sarah Beckett. LC 80-53448. (Everybody's Home Herbal Ser.). (Illus.). 64p. (Orig.). 1981. pap. 1.95 (ISBN 0-394-74835-2). Shambhala Pubn.

Herculine Barbin: Being the Recently Discovered Memoirs of a Nineteenth-Century Hermaphrodite. Tr. by Richard McDougall. Intro. by Michel Foucault. 1980. 8.95 (ISBN 0-394-50821-1); pap. 4.95 (ISBN 0-394-73862-4). Pantheon.

Herdsmen & Hermits. Thomas C. Lethbridge. 1950. text ed. 4.25x (ISBN 0-391-01986-4). Humanities.

Here & Away. new ed. William D. Sheldon et al. (Sheldon Reading Ser). (preprimer 3). 1973. pap. text ed. 3.92 (ISBN 0-205-03517-5, 5235170); tchr's. guide 8.20 (ISBN 0-205-03518-3, 5235189); activity bk. 3.92 (ISBN 0-205-03519-1, 5235197); tchrs'. ed. activity bk. 3.92 (ISBN 0-205-03520-5, 5235200); independent activ. 28.00 (ISBN 0-205-03521-3, 5235219). Allyn.

Here & Hereafter. William Kramer. 1978. pap. 4.95 (ISBN 0-8100-0053-9, 15-0365). Northwest Pub.

Here & Hereafter. Ruth Montgomery. 1978. pap. 2.25 (ISBN 0-449-24166-1, Crest). Fawcett.

Here and Human: An Anthology of Contemporary Verse. Compiled by Fes Finn. 1977. pap. 7.50 (ISBN 0-7195-3306-6). Transatlantic.

Here Beginneth the Booke of Raynarde the Foxe. LC 72-230. (English Experience Ser.: No. 162). 1969. Repr. of 1550 ed. 35.00 (ISBN 90-221-0162-2). Walter J Johnson.

Here Begynneth a Lityll Treatise Spekynge of the Arte & Crafte to Knowe Well to Dye. Tr. by W. Caxton. LC 72-169. (English Experience Ser.: No. 221). 28p. Repr. of 1490 ed. 14.00 (ISBN 90-221-0221-1). Walter J Johnson.

Here Begynneth the Boke Intituled Eracles & Also Godefrey of Boloyne. Heraclius. Tr. by William Caxton. LC 73-6140. (English Experience Ser.: No. 604). 1973. Repr. of 1481 ed. 52.00 (ISBN 90-221-0604-7). Walter J Johnson.

Here Begynneth the Boke of the Fayt of Armes & of Chyualrye. Christine Du Castel. Tr. by William Caxton. LC 78-6332. (English Experience Ser.: No. 13). 1968. Repr. of 1489 ed. 49.00 (ISBN 90-221-0013-8). Walter J Johnson.

Here Begynneth the First Volum of Sir J. Froyssart. Jean Froissart. Tr. by J. Bourchier. LC 72-26004. (English Experience Ser.: No. 257). 644p. 1970. Repr. of 1523 ed. 104.00 (ISBN 90-221-0257-2). Walter J Johnson.

Here Come Raccoons. Ed. by Lillian Hoban. LC 76-25205. (Illus.). (gr. k-4). 6.95 (ISBN 0-03-017781-2); pap. 2.25 (ISBN 0-03-048951-2). HR&W.

Here Come the Bears. Alice E. Goudey. LC 54-5924. (Illus.). 96p. (gr. 1-5). 1954. 5.95 (ISBN 0-684-13365-2, ScribJ). Scribner.

Here Come the Clowns. Gale Brennan. (Illus.). 32p. (Orig.). (gr. 1-4). 1980. pap. 1.95 (ISBN 0-89542-931-4). Ideals.

Here Comes a Candle. Jane A. Hodge. 1978. pap. 1.95 o.p. (ISBN 0-449-23600-5, Crest). Fawcett.

Here Comes Alex Pumpernickel. Fernando Krahn. (Illus.). 32p. (ps up). 1981. 7.95 (ISBN 0-316-50311-8, Atlantic). Little.

Here Comes Charlie Brown: Selected Cartoons from "Good Ol' Charlie Brown", Vol. 2. Charles M. Schulz. (Peanuts Ser.). (Illus.). 1978. pap. 1.50 (ISBN 0-449-23710-9, Crest). Fawcett.

Here Comes Everybody: Bodymind & Encounter Culture. William C. Schutz. 1981. Repr. of 1971 ed. text ed. 16.50x (ISBN 0-8290-0044-5). Irvington.

Here Comes Jesus. Ed Stewart. 1977. pap. 1.95 (ISBN 0-8307-0553-8, S101-1-57). Regal.

Here Comes Snoopy: Selected Cartoons from "Snoopy", Vol. 1. Charles M. Schulz. (Peanuts Ser.). (Illus.). 1978. pap. 1.50 (ISBN 0-449-23947-0, Crest). Fawcett.

Here Comes Tagalong. Anne Mallett. LC 78-153790. (Illus.). (gr. k-2). 1971. 5.95 o.s.i. (ISBN 0-8193-0496-4, Four Winds); PLB 5.41 o.s.i. (ISBN 0-8193-0497-2). Schol Bk Serv.

Here Comes the Bus. Carolyn Haywood. (Illus.). (gr. 1-5). 1963. PLB 7.92 (ISBN 0-688-31843-6). Morrow.

Here Comes the Sun. Emilie Loring. 224p. 1980. pap. 1.95 (ISBN 0-553-14290-9). Bantam.

Here Comes Weezie. Sue F. Kerr. LC 67-26516. (Illus.). (ps-2). 1967. 4.95g o.p. (ISBN 0-8075-3237-1). A Whitman.

Here Endeth the Book Named the Dictes or Sayengis of the Philosophres. Tr. by A. Wydeville & Earl Rivers. LC 79-84100. (English Experience Ser.: No. 920). 160p. (Eng.). 1979. Repr. of 1477 ed. lib. bdg. 25.00 (ISBN 90-221-0920-8). Walter J Johnson.

Here I Am. 2nd ed. Walter J. Limbacher. (Dimensions of Personality Ser). (gr. 4). text ed. 4.75x o.p. (ISBN 0-686-66516-3); pap. text ed. 3.95x (ISBN 0-88320-637-4); tchrs' ed. pap. 5.95x (ISBN 0-88320-639-0); spirit masters 12.95x (ISBN 0-88320-640-4, 10198). Pflaum-Standard.

Here I Am--Send Aaron. Jill Briscoe. 1978. pap. 2.95 (ISBN 0-88207-767-8). Victor Bks.

Here I Am, Em B! 96p. 1981. pap. write for info. (ISBN 0-8280-0028-X). Review & Herald.

Here I Stand. Roland Bainton. (Festival Bks.). 1978. pap. 2.25 (ISBN 0-687-16894-5). Abingdon.

Here I Stand. Paul Robeson. LC 70-159847. 1971. pap. 4.95 (ISBN 0-8070-6407-6, BP410). Beacon Pr.

Here Is Genius. Ed. by Dottie Walters. (Illus.). 402p. 1980. 11.95 (ISBN 0-8119-0351-6). Fell.

Here Is Henri! Edith Vacheron & Virginia Kahl. LC 59-14326. (Illus.). 32p. (gr. k-3). 1959. 2.50 (ISBN 0-684-14661-4). Scribner.

Here Lies Our Sovereign Lord. Jean Plaidy. 288p. 1977. pap. 1.75 o.p. (ISBN 0-449-23256-5, Crest). Fawcett.

Here on the Island: Being an Account of a Way of Life Several Miles off the Maine Coast. Charles Pratt. LC 73-14282. (Illus.). 192p. 1974. 17.50 o.s.i. (ISBN 0-06-013409-7, HarpT). Har-Row.

Here the Country Lies: Nationalism & the Arts in Twentieth-Century America. Charles C. Alexander. LC 80-7681. 384p. 1980. 32.50x (ISBN 0-253-15544-4). Ind U Pr.

Here, There & Everywhere. Frederic Hamilton. 332p. 1980. Repr. of 1921 ed. lib. bdg. 20.00 (ISBN 0-8492-5273-3). R West.

Here, There & Everywhere. Charlott M. Kodyen. 1981. 4.95 (ISBN 0-8062-1571-2). Carlton.

Here We Go Again Lord. Minnie Hawthorne. 1981. 4.50 (ISBN 0-8062-1659-X). Carlton.

Heredia. W. N. Ince. (French Poets Ser.). 1979. text ed. 25.00x (ISBN 0-485-14607-X, Athlone Pr); pap. text ed. 11.25x (ISBN 0-485-12207-3). Humanities.

Hereditary Disorders of the Eye & Ocular Adnexa. Ed. by Frank W. Newell. (Illus.). 288p. 1980. text ed. 14.95 (ISBN 0-936820-00-4). Ophthalmic.

Heredity. Robert E. Dunbar. (First Bks.). (Illus.). (gr. 4 up). 1978. PLB 6.45 s&l (ISBN 0-531-01408-8). Watts.

Heredity & Development. rev. 2nd ed. John A. Moore. (Illus.). 1972. pap. text ed. 5.95x (ISBN 0-19-501478-2). Oxford U Pr.

Heredity & Human Affairs. 2nd ed. James J. Nagle. LC 78-27066. (Illus.). 1979. pap. text ed. 15.95 (ISBN 0-8016-3621-3). Mosby.

Heredity & Variation in Microorganisms: Proceedings, Vol. 11. Cold Spring Harbor Symposia On Quantitative Biology. Repr. of 1946 ed. 22.00 (ISBN 0-384-22475-X). Johnson Repr.

Heredity, Evolution, & Society. 2nd ed. I. Michael Lerner & William J. Libby. LC 75-33968. (Illus.). 1976. text ed. 22.95x (ISBN 0-7167-0576-1); tchr's manual avail. W H Freeman.

Heredity in Humans. rev. ed. Amram Scheinfeld. (Illus.). 1972. 9.95 (ISBN 0-397-00820-1). Lippincott.

Heredity in Mental Traits. N. N. Sen Gupta. 207p. 1980. Repr. of 1941 ed. lib. bdg. 50.00 (ISBN 0-89984-409-X). Century Bookbindery.

Herencia. Joaquin Calvo-Sotelo. Ed. by Richard B. Klein. 112p. 1976. pap. text ed. 3.25x (ISBN 0-88334-075-5). Ind Sch Pr.

Here's How to Handle "L". Carolyn Ansberger & Mary J. Green. 1980. 50.00 (ISBN 0-88450-709-2, 30598-B). Communication Bks.

Here's How to Handle "R". Carolyn Ausberger & Mary J. Green. 1975. 50.00 (ISBN 0-88450-707-6, 2023-B). Communication Skill.

Here's How to Handle "S". Carloyn Ausberger & Mary J. Green. 1979. 50.00 (ISBN 0-88450-708-4, 3057-B). Communications Skill.

Here's Johnny: A Close-up of Johnny Carson & the Tonight Show. Craig Tennis. (Illus.). pap. 2.50 (ISBN 0-686-68808-2). PB.

Here's New England: A Guide to Vacationland. Federal Writers' Project. 1939. Repr. 29.00 (ISBN 0-403-02207-X). Somerset Pub.

Here's to You, Charlie Brown: Selected Cartoons from "You Can't Win, Charlie Brown", Vol. 1. Charles M. Schulz. (Peanuts Ser.). (Illus.). 1978. pap. 1.50 (ISBN 0-449-23708-7, Crest). Fawcett.

Here's to You Honey: The Book That Takes Where the World of Honey Leaves off, Vol. 2. Joe M. Parkhill. 160p. 1980. spiral bdg 6.95. Country Bazaar.

Here's What's Stopping You. Billy B. Sharp et al. LC 79-64794. Date not set. pap. cancelled (ISBN 0-88453-020-5). Barrington.

Heresies Exposed. William C. Irvine. 1917. pap. 2.75 (ISBN 0-87213-401-6). Loizeaux.

Heresy & Authority in Medieval Europe. Ed. by Edward Peters. LC 79-5262. (Middle Ages Ser.). 384p. 1980. 25.00x (ISBN 0-8122-7779-1); pap. 11.95x (ISBN 0-8122-1103-0). U of Pa Pr.

Heresy & Obedience in Tridentine Italy: Cardinal Pole & the Counter-Reformation. D. Fenlon. LC 72-87177. 336p. 1973. 47.50 (ISBN 0-521-20005-9). Cambridge U Pr.

Heresy, Crusade, & Inquisition in Southern France, 1100-1250. Walter L. Wakefield. 1974. 24.50x (ISBN 0-520-02380-3). U of Cal Pr.

Heresy of Self-Love: A Study of Subversive Individualism. Paul Zweig. LC 79-5482. 288p. 1980. 17.50x (ISBN 0-691-06431-8); pap. 4.95 (ISBN 0-691-01371-3). Princeton U Pr.

Heresy of the Free Spirit in the Later Middle Ages. Robert E. Lerner. LC 78-145790. 1972. 20.00x (ISBN 0-520-01908-3). U of Cal Pr.

Heresy, Schism & Religious Protest. Ed. by D. Baker. LC 75-184899. (Studies in Church History: Vol. 9). 1972. 52.00 (ISBN 0-521-08486-5). Cambridge U Pr.

Heresy Trials in the Diocese of Norwich: 1428-31. Ed. by Norman P. Tanner. (Royal Historical Society: Camden Society Fourth Ser.: Vol. 20). 233p. 1977. 20.00x (ISBN 0-8476-3305-5). Rowman.

Heretical Songs. Curtis White. LC 79-3848. 1981. 9.95 (ISBN 0-914590-62-6); pap. 4.95 (ISBN 0-914590-63-4). Fiction Coll.

Heretics in Love. James Lees-Milne. 1976. pap. 1.50 o.p. (ISBN 0-445-03167-0). Popular Lib.

Heriberto Frias. James W. Brown. (World Authors Ser.: No. 486). 1978. lib. bdg. 12.50 (ISBN 0-8057-6327-9). Twayne.

Hering's Dictionary of Classical & Modern Cookery. 5th ed. Ed. by Walter Bickel. 1974. 27.95 (ISBN 3-8057-0232-9, Pub. by Virtuea Col Ltd. England). CBI Pub.

Hering's Dictionary of Classical & Modern Cookery. rev. ed. Richard Hering. Tr. by Walter Bickel from Ger. (Illus.). 1977. text ed. 29.95 (ISBN 0-685-01584-X). Radio City.

Heritage. Frances P. Keyes. 1977. pap. 1.75 o.p. (ISBN 0-449-23236-0, Crest). Fawcett.

Heritage & Challenge of History. Paul K. Conkin & Roland N. Stromberg. 1971. pap. text ed. 9.50 scp (ISBN 0-06-041342-5, HarpC). Har-Row.

Heritage from Mendel. Mendel Centennial Symposium - Fort Collins - 1965. Ed. by R. Alexander Brink & E. Derek Styles. (Illus., Orig.). 1967. 27.50 (ISBN 0-299-04270-7); pap. 10.95 (ISBN 0-299-04274-X). U of Wis Pr.

Heritage Hill Farm Cookbook. Anna O. Rotz. 96p. 1980. 6.00 (ISBN 0-9605108-0-X). Rotz.

Heritage Hobbycraft. Elma Waltner & Willard Waltner. LC 77-19087. 1978. lib. bdg. 7.95 (ISBN 0-8313-0105-8); pap. 7.95. Lantern.

Heritage of American Social Work: Readings in Its Philosophical & Institutional Development. Ed. by Ralph E. Pumphrey & Muriel W. Pumphrey. LC 61-8989. 1961. 22.50x (ISBN 0-231-02486-X); pap. 9.00x (ISBN 0-231-08619-9). Columbia U Pr.

Heritage of Dress: Being Notes on the History & Evolution of Clothes. Wilfred M. Webb. LC 70-141749. (Illus.). 1971. Repr. of 1912 ed. 18.00 (ISBN 0-8103-3398-8). Gale.

Heritage of Flowers. Eleanor Bourne. (Leprechaun Library). (Illus.). 64p. 1980. 3.95 (ISBN 0-399-12544-2). Putnam.

Heritage of Horror: The English Gothic Cinema, 1946-1972. David Pirie. 1975. pap. 2.95 (ISBN 0-380-00069-5, 20099). Avon.

Heritage of Imperialism: A Study in Historical & Economic Analysis. Mashood B. Danmole. c, 600p. 1974. 25.00x (ISBN 0-210-40547-3). Asia.

Heritage of Ireland. DeBreffny. Date not set. 12.98 (ISBN 0-517-53809-1). Bonanza.

Heritage of Music: The Music of the Jewish People. Judith K. Eisenstein. (Illus.). (YA) (gr. 7-11). 1972. 10.00 o.p. (ISBN 0-685-04887-X, 164043). UAHC.

Heritage of Musical Style. Donald H. Van Ess. LC 73-101138. (Illus.). text ed. 16.95x (ISBN 0-03-081241-0); listener's guide 3.95x (ISBN 0-03-081242-9). Irvington.

Heritage of New York: Historic-Landmark Plaques of the New York Community Trust. New York Community Trust. LC 69-13762. 1970. 25.00 o.p. (ISBN 0-8232-0825-7). Fordham.

Heritage of Nuclear Medicine. Ed. by Brucer et al. LC 79-65338. (Illus.). 1979. soft cover 17.00 (ISBN 0-932004-02-4). Soc Nuclear Med.

Heritage of Nurse O'Hara. Colleen L. Reece. (YA) 1977. 4.95 o.p (ISBN 0-685-74272-5, Avalon). Bouregy.

Heritage of Stars. Clifford D. Simak. LC 76-53742. 1977. 7.95 o.p. (ISBN 0-399-11946-9, Dist. by Putnam). Berkley Pub.

Heritage of Stone. Jim Garrison. pap. 1.50 o.p. (ISBN 0-425-02953-0). Berkley Pub.

Heritage of the Cathedral. Sartell Prentice. 328p. 1980. Repr. of 1936 ed. lib. bdg. 40.00 (ISBN 0-8495-4399-1). Arden Lib.

Heritage of the Desert. Zane Grey. 1976. lib. bdg. 12.95x (ISBN 0-89968-151-4). Lightyear.

Heritage of the Heart. Pamela D'Arcy. 176p. (Orig.). 1980. pap. 1.75 (ISBN 0-515-05201-9). Jove Pubns.

Heritage Restored: America's Wildlife Refuges. Robert Murphy. (Illus.). (gr. 7 up). 1969. PLB 9.95 o.p. (ISBN 0-525-31765-1). Dutton.

Herk, Hero of the Skies. Joseph E. Dabney. 12.95 (ISBN 0-932298-07-9). Green Hill.

Herman & the Bears Again. Bernice Myers. (Illus.). (gr. k-3). 1979. pap. 1.25 (ISBN 0-590-10243-5, Schol Pap); pap. 3.50 bk. & record (ISBN 0-590-20803-9). Schol Bk Serv.

Herman Cortes, Conquistador in Mexico. J. Wilkes. (Introduction to the History of Mankind Ser.). (Illus.). 48p. (gr. 5-11). 1974. pap. 3.95 (ISBN 0-521-20424-0). Cambridge U Pr.

Herman Hang-Ups. Jim Unger. 20p. (gr. 4 up). 1980. pap. 4.95 (ISBN 0-8362-1954-6). Andrews & McMeel.

Herman Hesse: Biography & Bibliography, 2 vols. Joseph Mileck. 1977. 70.00 (ISBN 0-520-02756-6). U of Cal Pr.

Herman Melville. Tyrus Hillway. LC 78-11937. (Twayne's U. S. Authors Ser.). 177p. 1979. pap. text ed. 4.95 (ISBN 0-672-61504-5). Bobbs.

Herman Melville. rev. ed. Tyrus Hillway. (United States Authors Ser.: No. 37). 1979. lib. bdg. 9.95 (ISBN 0-8057-7256-1). Twayne.

Herman Melville & the Critics: A Checklist of Criticism, 1900-1978. Jeanetta Boswell. LC 80-25959. (Author Bibliographies Ser.: No. 53). 259p. 1981. 13.50 (ISBN 0-8108-1385-8). Scarecrow.

Herman Sorgel. Richard B. Cathcart. (Architecture Ser.: Bibliography A-181). 61p. pap. 6.50. Vance Biblios.

Herman the Helper Cleans up. Robert Kraus. (Tubby Bks). (Illus.). 10p. (ps). 1981. vinyl 2.95 (ISBN 0-671-45555-2). Windmill Bks.

Hermanas Coloradas. Garcia Francisco & Pavon. (Easy Readers, C). 1979. pap. 3.75 (ISBN 0-88436-295-7). EMC.

Hermann Broch, Gedichte. Hermann Broch. Ed. by Paul M. Lutzeler. (Suhrkamp Taschenbuecher: Vol. 8). 240p. (Orig.). 1980. pap. text ed. 4.55 (ISBN 3-518-37072-3, Pub. by Insel Verlag Germany). Suhrkamp.

Hermann Broch: World Author Ser. Ernestine S. Bradley. 1978. 12.95 (ISBN 0-8057-6326-0). Twayne.

Hermann Hesse. Franz Baumer. Tr. by John Conway. LC 68-31446. (Modern Literature Ser.). 1969. 10.95 (ISBN 0-8044-2027-0). Ungar.

Hermann Hesse. George W. Field. (World Authors Ser.: Germany: No. 93). lib. bdg. 9.95 (ISBN 0-8057-2424-9). Twayne.

Hermann Hesse: A Pictorial Autobiography. Hermann Hesse. Tr. by Theodore Ziolkowski & Yetta Ziolkowski. 240p. 1975. 10.00 (ISBN 0-374-16988-8). FS&G.

Hermann Hesse: Life & Art. Joseph Mileck. 1978. 16.95 (ISBN 0-520-03351-5); pap. 5.95 (ISBN 0-520-04152-6). U of Cal Pr.

Hermeneutic of Dogma. Thomas B. Ommen. LC 75-29493. (American Academy of Religion. Dissertation Ser.). 1975. pap. 7.50 (ISBN 0-89130-039-2, 010111). Scholars Pr Ca.

Hermeneutic Philosophy & the Sociology of Art. Janet Wolff. (International Library of Sociology). 1975. 20.00x (ISBN 0-7100-8048-4). Routledge & Kegan.

Hermeneutic Philosophy & the Sociology of Art: An Approach to Some of the Epistemological Problems of the Sociology of Art & Literature. Janet Wolff. (International Library of Sociology). 150p. 1981. pap. 12.50 (ISBN 0-7100-0682-9). Routledge & Kegan.

Hermeneutica. Tr. by A. Lund & A. Luce. (Portuguese Bks.). 1979. 1.20 (ISBN 0-8297-0825-1). Life Pubs Intl.

Hermeneutica E Introduccion Biblica. Tr. by A. Lund & A. Luce. (Spanish Bks.). (Span.). 1978. 1.90 (ISBN 0-8297-0564-3). Life Pubs Intl.

Hermeneutica: El Arte de la Parafrasis Libre. Moises Chavez. 132p. (Orig., Span.). 1978. pap. 3.50 (ISBN 0-89922-142-4). Edit Caribe.

Hermeneutics & Social Science. Zygmunt Bauman. 1978. 17.50x (ISBN 0-231-04546-8). Columbia U Pr.

Hermeneutics & Unification Theology. Ed. by Darrol Bryant & Durwood Foster. LC 80-66201. (Conference Ser.: No. 5). (Illus., Orig.). 1980. pap. 7.95 (ISBN 0-932894-05-4). Unif Theol Seminary.

Hermeneutics: Principles & Processes of Biblical Interpretation. Henry A. Virkler. 200p. 1981. 12.95 (ISBN 0-8010-9282-5). Baker Bk.

Hermeneutics Reader. Kurt Muller-Vollmer. 1981. 20.00 (ISBN 0-916354-88-1); pap. 8.95 (ISBN 0-916354-89-X). Urizen Bks.

Hermes - Guide of Souls. Karl Kerenyi. 100p. 1974. pap. 7.00 (ISBN 0-88214-207-0). Spring Pubns.

Hermes Stone. Robert Eilers. (Orig.). 1980. pap. 1.95 (ISBN 0-532-23264-X). Manor Bks.

Hermetic & Alchemical Writings of Paracelsus, Vol. 1: Hermetic Chemistry. Paracelsus. Ed. by Arthur E. Waite. LC 75-40261. 394p. (Orig.). 1976. pap. 7.50 o.p. (ISBN 0-394-73184-0). Shambhala Pubns.

Hermetic & Alchemical Writings of Paracelsus, Vol. 2: Hermetic Medicine & Hermetic Philosophy. Paracelsus. Ed. & tr. by Arthur E. Waite. LC 75-40261. 396p. 1976. pap. 7.50 o.p. (ISBN 0-394-73185-9). Shambhala Pubns.

Hermetic Philosophy & Alchemy. Mary A. Atwood. LC 79-8592. Repr. of 1960 ed. 49.50 (ISBN 0-404-18446-4). AMS Pr.

Hermit. Eugene Ionesco. Tr. by Richard Seaver. (Seaver-Grove Bk.). 1980. pap. 4.95 o.p. (ISBN 0-394-17746-0). Grove.

Hermit. Eugene Ionesco. LC 80-52072. 169p. 1980. pap. 4.95 (ISBN 0-394-17746-0). Seaver Bks.

Hermit. Peter Longueville. LC 75-170572. (Foundations of the Novel Ser.: Vol. 51). lib. bdg. 50.00 (ISBN 0-8240-0563-5). Garland Pub.

Hermit. T. Lobsang Rampa. pap. 2.50 (ISBN 0-685-27226-5). Weiser.

Hermit & the Love-Thief. Tr. by Barbara S. Miller from Sanskrit. 1978. 15.00 (ISBN 0-231-04644-8); pap. 6.00x (ISBN 0-231-04645-6). Columbia U Pr.

Hermit Dan. Peggy Parish. LC 77-5748. (Illus.). (gr. 2-5). 1977. 8.95 (ISBN 0-02-769840-8, 76984). Macmillan.

Hermit Dan. Peggy Parish. (gr. k-6). 1981. pap. 1.50 (ISBN 0-440-43501-3, YB). Dell.

Hermit Kingdom: Ladakh. H. P. Ahluwalia. (Illus.). 180p. 1981. text ed. 50.00x (ISBN 0-7069-1022-2, Pub. by Vikas India). Advent Bk.

Hermit of Far End. Margaret Pedler. 1976. lib. bdg. 15.75x (ISBN 0-89968-216-2). Lightyear.

Hermit of Fog Hollow Station. David Roth. LC 80-22241. 160p. (gr. 7 up). 1980. 7.95 (ISBN 0-8253-0012-6). Beaufort Bks NY.

Hermitage. Hermitage Staff. 315p. 1980. 75.00 (ISBN 0-569-08426-1, Pub. by Collets Holdings England). Intl Schol Bk Serv.

Hermits & Anchorites of England. Rotha M. Clay. LC 68-21759. (Illus.). 1968. Repr. of 1914 ed. 18.00 (ISBN 0-8103-3424-0). Gale.

Hermit's Swing. Victor Kolupaev. Tr. by Helen S. Jacobson. (Best of Soviet Science Fiction Ser.). 174p. 1980. 9.95 (ISBN 0-02-566350-X). Macmillan.

Hermsprong; or, Man As He Is Not, 3 vols. Robert Bage. LC 78-60853. (Novel 1720-1805 Ser.: Vol. 13). 1980. Set. lib. bdg. 93.00 (ISBN 0-8240-3662-X). Garland Pub.

Hernan Cortes. (Span.). 8.95 (ISBN 84-241-5408-8). E Torres & Sons.

Hernando Cortes. William J. Jacobs. LC 73-9509. (Visual Biography Ser). (Illus.). 64p. (gr. 4-5). 1974. PLB 4.90 o.p. (ISBN 0-531-00974-2). Watts.

Hero. Darrell Stoddard. Ed. by Alton Jordan. (I Can Read Underwater Bks). (Illus.). (gr. k-3). 1974. PLB 3.50 (ISBN 0-89868-001-8); pap. 1.75 (ISBN 0-89868-034-4). ARO Pub.

Hero. Saul Wernick. (Orig.). 1981. pap. write for info. (ISBN 0-671-82689-1). PB.

Hero & Chief: Epic Literature from the Banyanga(Zaire Republic) Daniel Biebuyck. LC 76-50242. 1978. 25.00x (ISBN 0-520-03386-8). U of Cal Pr.

Hero & Heroine of Shelley's "the Revolt of Islam". Alicia Martinez. (Salzburg Studies in English Literature: Romantic Reassessment: No. 63). 109p. 1976. pap. text ed. 25.00x (ISBN 0-391-01474-9). Humanities.

Hero, Artist, Sage, or Saint? Richard W. Coan. LC 76-57751. 1977. 22.50x (ISBN 0-231-03806-2); pap. 9.00x (ISBN 0-231-08355-6). Columbia U Pr.

Hero from Otherwhere. Jay Williams. (YA) (gr. 7-9). pap. 1.75 (ISBN 0-671-56076-X). PB.

Hero in French Decadent Literature. G. R. Ridge. LC 61-17538. 5.00 (ISBN 0-910294-23-2). Brown Bk.

Hero in French Romantic Literature. G. R. Ridge. LC 59-14610. 5.00 (ISBN 0-910294-24-0). Brown Bk.

Hero in the Tower. Hans H. Kirst. 352p. 1973. pap. 1.50 o.p. (ISBN 0-523-00145-2). Pinnacle Bks.

Hero of Hamblett. Sal Murdocca. LC 80-11346. (Illus.). 48p. (gr. 3 up). 1980. PLB 8.44 (ISBN 0-440-04458-8); pap. 4.95 (ISBN 0-440-04457-X). Delacorte.

Hero of Hill House. Mabel Hale. 224p. pap. 2.00. Faith Pub Hse.

Hero of Our Time. Mihail Lermontov. pap. 4.95 (ISBN 0-385-09344-6, A133, Anch). Doubleday.

Hero on a Donkey. Miodrag Bulatovic. 2.75 o.p. (ISBN 0-452-25025-0, Z5025, Plume). NAL.

Hero, Two. LaRue Selman. Ed. by Alton Jordan. (Buppet Series). (Illus.). (gr. k-3). 1981. PLB 4.50 (ISBN 0-89868-089-1, Read Res); pap. text ed. 1.95 (ISBN 0-89868-100-6). ARO Pub.

Herod Conspiracy. Russell Rhodes. LC 80-15323. 350p. 1980. 11.95 (ISBN 0-396-07865-6). Dodd.

Herodes und Mariamne. Friedrich Hebbel. Ed. by Edna Purdie. 1965. pap. 5.00x o.p. (ISBN 0-631-01330-X, Pub. by Basil Blackwell). Biblio Dist.

Herodotus, Book 6: Erato. Herodotus. Ed. by E. S. Shuckburgh. text ed. 9.95x (ISBN 0-521-05248-3). Cambridge U Pr.

Heroes. D. Houston. 1980. pap. 3.95. Starlog Pr.

Heroes. Charles Kingsley. (New Children's Classics). (Illus.). (gr. 6 up). 1954. 4.95g o.s.i. (ISBN 0-02-750710-6). Macmillan.

Heroes & Beasts of Spain. Manuel C. Nogales. Ed. by D. C. Harding. Tr. by Luis De Baeza from Span. LC 79-53465. (Short Story Index Reprint Ser.). Date not set. Repr. of 1937 ed. 24.50x (ISBN 0-8486-5006-9). Core Collection. Postponed.

Heroes & Emperors in Circassian History. Shawkat Mufti. (Arab Background Ser.). 1972. 14.00x (ISBN 0-685-77100-8). Intl Bk Ctr.

Heroes & Heroines of Fiction, 2 vols. William S. Walsh. LC 66-29782. 1966. Repr. of 1915 ed. 22.00 ea.; Vol. 1, Classical. 18.00 (ISBN 0-8103-0167-9); Vol. 2, Modern. 14.00 (ISBN 0-8103-0163-6). Gale.

Heroes & Heroines of Many Lands. Compiled by Harriet Ross. (Illus.). 160p. 1981. PLB 7.95 (ISBN 0-87460-214-9). Lion.

Heroes & Monsters. Retold by James Reeves. (Illus., Orig.). 1978. pap. 2.95 (ISBN 0-8467-0539-7, Pub. by Two Continents). Hippocrene Bks.

Heroes Die Young. Rick Sandford. 1979. pap. 1.75 (ISBN 0-505-51361-7). Tower Bks.

Heroes in American Folklore. Irwin Shapiro. LC 62-10205. (Illus.). (gr. 5 up). 1962. PLB 6.29 o.p. (ISBN 0-671-32054-8). Messner.

Heroes of Battle Rock. 21p. Repr. of 1904 ed. pap. 1.50 (ISBN 0-8466-0067-6, SJS67). Shorey.

Heroes of Journalism. Elizabeth D. Squire. LC 76-161377. (Heroes of Ser.). (Illus.). 128p. (gr. 9 up). 1973. 7.95 (ISBN 0-8303-0114-3). Fleet.

Heroes of Polar Exploration. Ralph K. Andrist & George J. Dufek. LC 62-16256. (Horizon Caravel Bks). (Illus.). 153p. (gr. 6-12). 1962. 9.95 (ISBN 0-8281-0352-6, J023-0). Am Heritage.

Heroes of Pro Basketball. Phil Berger. (Pro Basketball Library: No. 1). (Illus.). (gr. 5-9). 1968. PLB 3.69 (ISBN 0-394-90871-6, BYR). Random.

Heroes of Pro Hockey. Stan Fischler. (Pro Hockey Library: No. 2). (Illus.). (gr. 5-9). 1971. PLB 3.69 (ISBN 0-394-92146-1, BYR). Random.

Heroes of Tennessee. Ed. by Billy M. Jones. LC 79-124288. (Tennessee Ser.: No. 1). (Illus.). 1979. 11.95 (ISBN 0-87870-051-X). Memphis St Univ.

Heroes Twilight. Bernard Bergonzi. 1980. text ed. write for info. (ISBN 0-391-01137-5). Humanities.

Heroic Deeds of Gargantua & Pantagruel, 2 Vols. Francois Rabelais. 1954. 5.00x (ISBN 0-460-00826-9, Evman); Vol 1 O.p. o.p. Vol. 2 (ISBN 0-460-00827-7). Dutton.

Heroic Efforts at Meteor Crater, Arizona: Selected Correspondence Between Daniel Moreau Barringer & Elihu Thomson. Harold J. Abrahams. LC 78-75170. 480p. 1981. 20.00 (ISBN 0-8386-2399-9). Fairleigh Dickinson.

Heroic Image in Chile: Arturo Prat, Secular Saint. William F. Sater. LC 70-189221. 1973. 17.95x (ISBN 0-520-02235-1). U of Cal Pr.

Heroic Japan: A History of the War Between China & Japan. Yosi-Aki Yamada & F. Warrington Eastlake. (Studies in Japanese History & Civilization). 1979. Repr. of 1897 ed. 40.50 (ISBN 0-89093-291-3). U Pubns Amer.

Heroic Poetry of the Basotho. D. P. Kunene. (Oxford Library of African Literature Ser). 1971. 14.95x (ISBN 0-19-815132-2). Oxford U Pr.

Heroic Women of the West: Comprising Thrilling Examples of Courage, Fortitude, Devotedness, & Self-Sacrifice, Among the Pioneer Mothers of the Western Country. John Frost. LC 75-7090. (Indian Captivities Ser.: Vol. 66). 1976. Repr. of 1854 ed. lib. bdg. 44.00 (ISBN 0-8240-1690-4). Garland Pub.

Heroin Addiction: Theory, Research, & Treatment. Jerome Platt & Christina Labate. LC 76-5794. (Personality Processes Ser.). 417p. 1976. 29.95 (ISBN 0-471-69114-3, Pub. by Wiley-Interscience). Wiley.

Heroin & Behaviour. Gerry V. Stimson. LC 73-174. 246p. 1973. 17.95 (ISBN 0-470-82530-8). Halsted Pr.

Heroin Use in the Barrio. Bruce Bullington. LC 76-40403. 1977. 19.95 (ISBN 0-669-01042-1). Lexington Bks.

Heroin Was My Best Friend. James Berry. LC 70-153761. (gr. 6-12). 1971. 4.95 o.s.i. (ISBN 0-02-709700-5, CCPr). Macmillan.

Heroin Was My Best Friend. James Berry. LC 70-153761. 160p. (gr. 7 up). 1974. pap. 0.95 o.s.i. (ISBN 0-02-041560-5, 04156, Collier). Macmillan.

Heroines of Seventy-Six. Elizabeth Anticaglia. LC 74-24583. (Illus.). (gr. 3-6). 1975. 5.95 o.s.i. (ISBN 0-8027-6210-7); PLB 6.83 o.s.i. (ISBN 0-8027-6209-3). Walker & Co.

Heroine's Sister. Frances Murray. 208p. 1976. pap. 1.25 o.p. (ISBN 0-345-25004-4). Ballantine.

Herondas. Frederic Will. (World Authors Ser.: Greece: No. 227). lib. bdg. 10.95 (ISBN 0-8057-2420-6). Twayne.

Hero's Children: A Report on the Post-War Generation in Eastern Europe. Paul Neuberg. 1973. 10.00 o.p. (ISBN 0-688-00138-6). Morrow.

Heros of Seventy-Six! They Aren't What They Used to Be, but Then They Never Were. Arthur W. Ritchie. LC 80-50612. (Illus.). 255p. 1981. 9.95 (ISBN 0-9604516-0-9). Sigma Pr.

Herpesviruses. Ed. by Albert S. Kaplan. 1974. 51.00 (ISBN 0-12-397050-4). Acad Pr.

Herpetic Infections of Man. Ed. by Miro Juretic et al. LC 77-75516. (Illus.). 1980. text ed. 13.50x (ISBN 0-87451-151-8). U Pr of New Eng.

Herr Biedermann und Die Brandstifter: Rip Van Winkle, Zwei Hoerspiele. Max Frisch. (Suhrkamp Taschenbucher: No. 599). 128p. 1980. pap. text ed. 3.25 (ISBN 3-518-37099-5, Pub. by Insel Verlag Germany). Suhrkamp.

Herr Raiffeisen Among Chinese Farmers. China International Famine Relief Commission. LC 78-74320. (Modern Chinese Economy Ser.: Vol. 22). 140p. 1980. lib. bdg. 16.50 (ISBN 0-686-62487-4). Garland Pub.

Herring-Gull. Date not set. 4.95 (ISBN 0-8120-5382-6). Barron. Postponed.

Herself Surprised. Joyce Cary. 275p. 1976. Repr. of 1948 ed. lib. bdg. 13.95x (ISBN 0-89244-070-8). Queens Hse.

Herself Surprised. Joyce Cary. 1980. pap. 4.95 (ISBN 0-7145-0270-7). Riverrun NY.

Herstory. 2nd ed. Sochen. 1981. 11.95 (ISBN 0-88284-115-7). Alfred Pub.

Herstory: A Woman's View of American History. 2nd ed. June Sochen. Incl. Vol. 1. 1600-1880. 220p. 6.95x o.p. (ISBN 0-88284-046-0); Vol. 2. From 1861. 227p. 6.95x o.p. (ISBN 0-88284-047-9), LC 74-80471. (Illus.). 448p. 1974. Set. 12.50 o.p. (ISBN 0-88284-017-7); Complete. pap. text ed. 11.95x (ISBN 0-88284-115-7). Alfred Pub.

Herta's Viennese Kitchen. Herta J. Ford. LC 78-71096. (Illus.). 160p. (Orig.). 1980. pap. 8.95 (ISBN 0-930048-06-7). Prologue.

Herzensergieszungen Eines Kunstliebenden Klosterbruders. 2nd ed. William H. Wackenroder & Ludwig Tiek. Ed. by A. Gillies. (Blackwell's German Text Ser.). 1966. pap. 4.50x o.p. (ISBN 0-631-01720-8, Pub. by Basil Blackwell). Biblio Dist.

He's My Baby, Now. Jeanette Eyerly. (gr. 7-9). 1980. pap. 1.95 (ISBN 0-671-41675-8). Archway.

He's My Brother. Joe Lasker. LC 73-7318. (Concept Bks.). (Illus.). 40p. (gr. 1-3). 1974. 6.95g (ISBN 0-8075-3218-5). A Whitman.

He's Never Heard of You, Either. G. B. Trudeau. (Doonesbury Ser.). (Illus., Orig.). 1981. pap. 4.95 (ISBN 0-03-049196-7). HR&W.

Hesburgh Papers: Higher Values in Higher Education. Theodore Hesburgh. 1979. 12.95 o.p. (ISBN 0-8362-5908-4). Andrews & McMeel.

Hesperides & Other Poems. Agnes Yarnall. LC 80-66609. (Illus.). 64p. 1978. 4.95 (ISBN 0-8059-2485-X). Dorrance.

Hessian. Howard Fast. 1980. pap. 2.25 (ISBN 0-440-13536-2). Dell.

Hessian Tapestry: The Hesse Family & British Royalty. David Duff. (Illus.). 1979. 28.00 (ISBN 0-7153-7838-4). David & Charles.

Hessians: Mercenaries from Hessen Kassel in the American Revolution. Rodney Atwood. LC 79-20150. 1980. 28.50 (ISBN 0-521-22884-0). Cambridge U Pr.

Hester. Byron Barton. LC 75-9668. (Illus.). 32p. (ps-3). 1975. 8.25 (ISBN 0-688-80009-2); PLB 7.92 (ISBN 0-688-84009-4). Greenwillow.

Hester-Roundtree Women, Bk. III. Margaret Lewerth. 1979. pap. 2.50 o.s.i. (ISBN 0-440-14884-7). Dell.

Heteroaromatic Nitrogen Compounds: The Azoles. K. Schofield et al. LC 74-17504. (Illus.). 500p. 1976. 85.00 (ISBN 0-521-20519-0). Cambridge U Pr.

Heterocycles in Organic Synthesis. A. I. Meyers. (General Heterocyclic Chemistry Ser.). 336p. 1974. 36.95 (ISBN 0-471-60065-2). Wiley.

Heterocyclic Antibiotics. Janos Berdy. (CRC Handbook of Antibiotic Compounds: Vol. 5). 640p. 1981. 62.95 (ISBN 0-8493-3456-X). CRC Pr.

Heterocyclic Chemistry. D. W. Young. LC 75-11739. (Illus.). 1976. pap. text ed. 12.50x (ISBN 0-582-44253-2). Longman.

Heterocyclic Chemistry of Phosphorus: Systems Based on the Phosphorus Carbon Bond. Louis D. Quin. LC 80-19721. 420p. 1981. 35.00 (ISBN 0-471-06461-0, Pub. by Wiley-Interscience). Wiley.

Heterogeneous Catalysis: Principles & Applications. new ed. G. C. Bond. (Oxford Chemistry Ser). 132p. 1978. pap. text ed. 11.50x (ISBN 0-19-855412-5). Oxford U Pr.

Het'man Ivan Mazepa. Wasyl Luciw. LC 59-19855. (Ukra.). 1954. text ed. 6.00 (ISBN 0-685-89027-9). Slavia Lib.

Hevajra Tantra, 2 Vols. David L. Snellgrove. 1959. 59.00x (ISBN 0-19-713516-1). Oxford U Pr.

Hewins Lectures, 1947-1962. Ed. by Siri Andrews. LC 63-21644. 1963. 11.00 (ISBN 0-87675-054-4); pap. 6.00 (ISBN 0-87675-056-0). Horn Bk.

Hewitt-Donln Catalog of U. S. Small Size Paper Money. 14th ed. Hudgeons. (Collector Ser.). (Illus.). 192p. 1981. pap. 3.50 (ISBN 0-87637-112-8, 112-08). Hse of Collectibles.

Hey, Dollface. Deborah Hautzig. LC 78-54685. (gr. 7-9). 1978. 7.95 (ISBN 0-688-80170-6); PLB 7.63 (ISBN 0-688-84170-8). Greenwillow.

Hey Dollface. Deborah Hautzig. 128p. (gr. 7-9). 1980. pap. 1.75 (ISBN 0-553-13555-4). Bantam.

Hey, Don't Do That! Irene Herz. LC 77-27054. (Illus.). 32p. 1978. 7.95 (ISBN 0-13-387365-X). P-H.

Hey, God, What Should I Do Now? Jess Lair & Jacqueline Lair. 240p. 1978. pap. 2.50 (ISBN 0-449-23586-6, Crest). Fawcett.

Hey Kid. Rita Gelman. (Easy-Read Storybooks). (Illus.). (gr. k-3). 1977. PLB 4.90 s&l o.p. (ISBN 0-531-00376-0); 3.95. Watts.

Hey Kids, Stay Well-Feel Good. Kathryn Smith. LC 78-50432. 1979. pap. 3.95 (ISBN 0-8163-0236-7). Pacific Pr Pub Assn.

Hey Lenny, Hey Jack. Alan Brody. LC 77-24389. 1976. 8.95 o.p. (ISBN 0-688-03249-4). Morrow.

Hey, Lover Boy. Thomas Rockwell. LC 80-68739. 160p. (YA) (gr. 8-12). 1981. 8.95 (ISBN 0-440-03583-X). Delacorte.

Hey Man!, Open Up & Live! Ken Olson. 1978. pap. 1.95 o.p. (ISBN 0-449-14038-5, GM). Fawcett.

Hey, Preach, You're Comin' Through. David Wilkerson. 1975. pap. 1.25 (ISBN 0-89129-064-8, PV064). Jove Pubns.

Hey Presto! You're a Bear! Janosch. (Illus.). 28p. (gr. 1-3). 1980. 8.95g (ISBN 0-316-45765-5, Pub. by Atlantic-Little Brown). Little.

Hey, Riddle Riddle. Ann Bishop. LC 66-16074. (Riddle Bk.). (Illus.). (gr. 2-4). 1968. 5.75g (ISBN 0-8075-3257-6). A Whitman.

Hey, That's My Soul You're Stepping on. Barbara Corcoran. (gr. 5-9). pap. 2.95 (ISBN 0-689-70486-0, A-113, Aladdin). Atheneum.

Heyday. Dore Schary. 1981. pap. 2.95 (ISBN 0-425-04805-5). Berkley Pub.

Heyday of Natural History. Lynn Barber. LC 79-6533. (Illus.). 324p. 1981. 17.95 (ISBN 0-385-12574-7). Doubleday.

Heyden Advances Library in EDP Management in Six Volumes. Ed. by Thomas A. Rullo. 1980. 159.00 (ISBN 0-85501-600-0). Heyden.

Heydenweldt und Ihrer Gotter: The Renaissance & the Gods. Johann Heroldt. Ed. by Stephen Orgel. LC 78-68202. (Philosophy of Images Ser.). 1980. lib. bdg. 66.00 (ISBN 0-8240-3676-X). Garland Pub.

Hi, All You Rabbits. Carl Memling. LC 78-117558. (Illus.). (ps-2). 1970. 5.95 o.s.i. (ISBN 0-8193-0430-1, Four Winds); PLB 5.41 o.s.i. (ISBN 0-8193-0431-X). Schol Bk Serv.

Hi & Lois: Beware Children at Play. Mort Walker & Dik Brown. (Hi and Lois Ser.). 128p. (gr. 5 up). pap. 1.50 (ISBN 0-448-14051-9). G&D.

Hi, Cat. Ezra J. Keats. LC 71-102968. (Illus.). (gr. k-3). 1970. 8.95g (ISBN 0-02-749600-7). Macmillan.

Hi Fella. Era Zistel. LC 77-8583. (Illus.). 1977. 6.95 o.p. (ISBN 0-397-01241-1). Lippincott.

Hi-Fi: From Edison's Phonograph to Quadrophonic Sound. W. E. Butterworth. LC 76-56704. (Illus.). (gr. 7-11). 1977. 9.95g o.s.i. (ISBN 0-590-07365-6, Four Winds). Schol Bk Serv.

Hi-Fi in the Home. John Crabbe. (Illus.). 1971. 9.95 (ISBN 0-7137-0589-2). Transatlantic.

Hi-Fi Loudspeakers & Enclosures. 2nd, rev. ed. Abraham Cohen. (Illus.). 1968. 10.60 (ISBN 0-8104-0721-3). Hayden.

Hi-Fi Stereo Installation Simplified. Derek Cameron. (Illus.). 1978. 15.95 (ISBN 0-8359-2842-X). Reston.

Hi, I'm Ann. Ann Kiemel. (Direction Bks). pap. 1.75 (ISBN 0-8010-5346-3). Baker Bk.

Hi Lo Country. Max Evans. (Western Fiction Ser.). 1980. lib. bdg. 10.95 (ISBN 0-8398-2685-0). Gregg.

Hi Tom. Nanda Ward. Date not set. 3.84 (ISBN 0-8038-2991-4). Hastings.

Hi, Word Bird. Jane B. Moncure. LC 80-15919. (Early-Bird Reader Ser.). (Illus.). 32p. (ps-2). 1980. PLB 5.50 (ISBN 0-89565-159-9). Childs World.

Hibernation & the Hypothalamus. Nicholas Mrosovsky. 287p. 1971. 22.50 (ISBN 0-306-50058-2, Plenum Pr). Plenum Pub.

Hibiscus Lagoon. Dorothy Dowdell. (Orig.). 1981. pap. 1.50 (ISBN 0-440-14494-9). Dell.

Hiboy: Young Devil Horse. Justin F. Denzel. LC 80-10578. 48p. (gr. 3). 1980. PLB 5.67 (ISBN 0-8116-4866-4). Garrard.

Hickmans of Oldswinford. M. V. Herbert. 196p. 1980. 37.50x (ISBN 0-7050-0061-3, Pub. by Skilton & Shaw England). State Mutual Bk.

Hid in My Heart: The Word of God in Times of Need. Florence M. Taylor. 1974. 5.95 (ISBN 0-8164-1186-7). Crossroad NY.

Hidalgo's Beard: A California Fantasy. Conger Beasley. 1979. 9.95 o.p. (ISBN 0-8362-6103-8); pap. 5.95 o.p. (ISBN 0-8362-6100-3). Andrews & McMeel.

Hidation of Cambridgeshire. C. R. Hart. (Occasional Papers in English Local History, New Ser: No. 6). (Illus.). 64p. 1973. pap. text ed. 3.75x (ISBN 0-7185-2030-0, Leicester). Humanities.

Hidden Bible. William Leary. 1955. 8.50 (ISBN 0-910140-07-3). Anthony.

Hidden Box Mystery. Florence P. Heide & Sylvia Van Clief. LC 72-13351. (Pilot Bks. - Spotlight Club Mysteries Ser.). (Illus.). 128p. (gr. 3-6). 1973. 6.95g (ISBN 0-8075-3270-3). A Whitman.

Hidden by the Pond. Tr. by Editions les Belle Images Staff. (Butterfly Bks). (Illus.). 16p. (Orig.). (ps-2). 1976. 1.50 o.p. (ISBN 0-8467-0224-X, Pub. by Two Continents). Hippocrene Bks.

Hidden Center: Spirituality & Speculative Christology in St. Bonaventure. Zachary Hayes. 224p. (Orig.). 1981. pap. 7.95 (ISBN 0-8091-2348-7). Paulist Pr.

Hidden Communion. Joost A. Meerloo. LC 64-24910. 1964. 4.75 o.p. (ISBN 0-912326-12-3). Garrett-Helix.

Hidden Corners of Britain. David Yeadon. (Illus.). 1981. 19.95 (ISBN 0-393-01460-6). Norton.

Hidden Corners of New England. David Yeadon. LC 75-42072. (Funk & W Bk.). (Illus.). 224p. 1976. 12.50 o.s.i. (ISBN 0-308-10240-1, TYC-T); pap. 6.95 o.s.i. (ISBN 0-308-10241-X, TYC-T). T Y Crowell.

Hidden Corners of the Mid-Atlantic States. David Yeadon. LC 76-30417. (Funk & W Bk.). (Illus.). 1977. 12.95 o.s.i. (ISBN 0-308-10286-X, TYC-T); pap. 6.95 o.s.i. (ISBN 0-308-10297-5, TYC-T). T Y Crowell.

Hidden Country: Nature on Your Doorstep. John Richards. LC 72-12745. (Illus.). 144p. (gr. 5-8). 1973. PLB 9.95 (ISBN 0-87599-195-5). S G Phillips.

Hidden Crisis in American Politics. Samuel Lubell. LC 69-17630. 1971. 5.95 (ISBN 0-393-05370-9); pap. text ed. 4.95x (ISBN 0-393-09886-9, NortonC). Norton.

Hidden Dimension. Edward T. Hall. LC 66-11173. (Illus.). 1969. pap. 3.50 (ISBN 0-385-08476-5, A609, Anch). Doubleday.

Hidden Durer. Peter Strieder. LC 78-50816. (Illus.). 1978. 19.95 o.p. (ISBN 0-528-81041-3). Rand.

Hidden Economy: The Context & Control of Borderline Crime. Stuart Henry. 194p. 1978. 29.50x (ISBN 0-85520-240-8, Pub by Martin Robertson England); pap. 8.95x (ISBN 0-85520-353-6). Biblio Dist.

Hidden Events: Incredible Life & Behavior of Insects. Lee. 1981. 12.95 (ISBN 0-8120-5340-0). Barron.

Hidden God. L. Boros. 132p. 1973. 5.95 (ISBN 0-8164-1042-9). Crossroad NY.

Hidden Harbor. Kathrene Pinkerton. LC 51-13350. (Illus.). (gr. 9 up). 1951. 3.95 o.p. (ISBN 0-15-233973-6, HJ). HarBraceJ.

Hidden Health Care System: Mediating Structures & Health. Lowell Levin & Ellen Idler. 1980. 19.00 (ISBN 0-88410-822-8). Ballinger Pub.

Hidden Heritage: History & the Gay Imagination, an Anthology. Ed. by Byrne R. Fone. 323p. 1979. 18.95 (ISBN 0-686-66021-8); pap. 9.95 (ISBN 0-8290-0401-7). Irvington.

Hidden Hippopotamus: Reappraisal in African History, the Early Colonial Experience. Gwyn Prins. LC 79-41658. (African Studies: No. 28). (Illus.). 320p. 1980. 45.00 (ISBN 0-521-22915-4). Cambridge U Pr.

Hidden Human Image. Maurice Friedman. 1974. 12.50 o.s.i. (ISBN 0-440-03509-0). Delacorte.

Hidden Images-Games of Perception: Anamorphic Art Illusion. Fred Leeman. LC 76-3736. (Illus.). 1976. pap. 9.85 o.p. (ISBN 0-8109-9019-9); Anamorphic Jigsaw Puzzle 9.00 o.p. (ISBN 0-685-73055-7). Abrams.

Hidden in Plain Sight: The Practice of Christian Meditation. Avery Brooke. LC 77-17548. (Illus., Orig.). 1978. pap. 5.95 (ISBN 0-8164-2176-5). Crossroad NY.

Hidden in the Meadow. Tr. by Editions des Belles Images Staff. (Butterfly Bks). (Illus.). 16p. (Orig.). (ps-2). 1976. pap. 1.50 o.p. (ISBN 0-8467-0223-1, Pub. by Two Continents). Hippocrene Bks.

Hidden in the Woods. Ed. by Editions les Belles Images Staff. (Butterfly Bks). (Illus., Orig.). (gr. 2-6). 1977. pap. 1.50 (ISBN 0-8467-0332-7, Pub. by Two Continents). Hippocrene Bks.

Hidden Key to Life. Martin Schonberger. 1978. pap. 7.95 (ISBN 0-88231-023-2). ASI Pubs Inc.

Hidden Laws of Earth. Juliet B. Ballard. 241p. (Orig.). 1979. pap. 5.95 (ISBN 0-87604-117-9). ARE Pr.

Hidden Leonardo. Marco Rosci. LC 77-70250. (Illus.). 1977. 19.95 o.p. (ISBN 0-528-81042-1). Rand.

Hidden Life. C. E. Orr. 112p. pap. 0.75. Faith Pub Hse.

Hidden Life of Prayer. David M. M'Intyre. 1962. pap. 2.50 (ISBN 0-87123-214-6, 200214). Bethany Fell.

Hidden Life of Prayer. David M. M'Intyre. (Summit Books Ser). 1979. pap. 1.95 (ISBN 0-8010-6071-0). Baker Bk.

Hidden Malpractice. Gena Corea. 1978. pap. 1.95 (ISBN 0-515-04522-5). Jove Pubns.

Hidden Meanings. Charlotte V. Allen. 224p. (Orig.). 1976. pap. 1.50 o.s.i. (ISBN 0-446-88188-0). Warner Bks.

Hidden Menace. Maurice Griffiths. 160p. 1980. 20.75x (ISBN 0-85177-186-6, Pub. by Conway Maritime England). State Mutual Bk.

Hidden Michelangelo. Roberto Salvini. LC 78-50815. (Illus.). 1978. 19.95 o.p. (ISBN 0-528-81043-X). Rand.

Hidden Mind of Freedom. Tarthang Tulku. Ed. by Sylvia Derman. 1981. pap. 6.95. Dharma Pub.

Hidden Order of Art: A Study in the Psychology of Artistic Imagination. Anton Ehrenzweig. (California Library Reprint Ser). 1976. 20.00x (ISBN 0-520-03181-4, CAL 418); pap. 6.95 (ISBN 0-520-03845-2). U of Cal Pr.

Hidden Patient. Sylvia Sherwood & Vincent Mor. Date not set. price not set prof. reference (ISBN 0-88410-722-1). Ballinger Pub. Postponed.

Hidden Persuaders. rev. ed. Vance Packard. 1981. pap. write for info. (ISBN 0-671-83572-6). PB.

Hidden Pictures. Walt Disney Productions. (Winnie-the-Pooh Hunny Pot Bks.). 24p. (ps-3). 1980. PLB 5.38 (ISBN 0-307-68873-9, Golden Pr). Western Pub.

Hidden Places, Secret Words. Ed. by Anita L. Anderson. LC 80-81307. 1980. 9.95 (ISBN 0-89002-158-9); pap. 2.95 (ISBN 0-89002-149-X). Northwoods Pr.

Hidden Power. Todd Otis. 150p. (Orig.). 1980. text ed. cancelled (ISBN 0-936106-02-6); pap. cancelled (ISBN 0-686-65870-1). River Basin.

Hidden Power for Human Problems. new rev. deluxe ed. Frederick W. Bailes. 1957. deluxe ed. 7.95 o.p. (ISBN 0-13-386953-9). P-H.

Hidden Question of God. Helmut Thielicke. Tr. by Geoffrey Bromiley. 1977. pap. 4.95 o.p. (ISBN 0-8028-1661-4). Eerdmans.

Hidden Rainbow. Christmas-Carol Kauffman. 1963. pap. 3.50 (ISBN 0-8024-3807-5). Moody.

Hidden Rembrandt. J. Bolten & H. Bolten-Rempt. LC 77-70249. (Illus.). 1977. 19.95 o.p. (ISBN 0-528-81044-8). Rand.

Hidden Seed. Jan D. Tissot. 8.00 (ISBN 0-89253-743-4); flexible cloth 4.80 (ISBN 0-89253-744-2). Ind-US Inc.

Hidden Society. Vilhelm Aubert. (Social Science Classics Ser.). 351p. 1982. 19.95 (ISBN 0-87855-327-4); pap. 6.95 (ISBN 0-87855-730-X). Transaction Bks. Postponed.

Hidden Thoreau. Allen B. Hovey. LC 80-2450. 1981. Repr. of 1966 ed. 22.75 (ISBN 0-404-19056-1). AMS Pr.

Hidden Treasure: Holy Mass. St. Leonard. 1971. pap. 2.00 (ISBN 0-89555-036-9, 111). TAN Bks Pubs.

Hidden Treasure: Public Sculpture in Providence, Rhode Island. Robert Freeman. (Illus.). 50p. (Orig.). 1981. pap. 4.95 (ISBN 0-917012-23-2). RI Pubns Soc.

Hidden Treasures. Beatrice Levin. LC 79-87530. 232p. 1981. 3.95 (ISBN 0-89896-049-5, Pub. by the Lindahl Press). Larksdale.

Hidden Treasures. Vezio Melegari. (International Library). (Illus.). 128p. (gr. 7 up). 1972. PLB 6.90 o.p. (ISBN 0-531-02109-2). Watts.

Hidden Treasures in the Psalms. Rudolf Frieling. 1967. Repr. of 1954 ed. 8.50 (ISBN 0-900285-02-8, Pub. by Floris Books). St George Bk Serv.

Hidden Waterfall. Marya Zaturenska. LC 73-91288. 72p. 1974. 6.95 (ISBN 0-8149-0738-5). Vanguard.

Hidden Wisdom in the Holy Bible, Vol. 3. Geoffrey Hodson. 1971. 7.95 (ISBN 0-8356-7493-2). Theos Pub Hse.

Hidden Wisdom in the Holy Bible, Vol. 4. Geoffrey Hodson. LC 67-8724. 375p. (Orig.). 1981. pap. 5.95 (ISBN 0-8356-0548-5, Quest). Theos Pub Hse.

Hidden Words of Baha'u'llah. rev. ed. Baha'u'llah. Tr. by Shoghi Effendi. LC 54-7328. 1954. 4.00 (ISBN 0-87743-007-1, 7-03-05); pap. 2.50 (ISBN 0-87743-002-0, 7-03-06). Baha'i.

Hidden World: Life Under a Rock. Laurence Pringle. LC 76-47641. (Exploring an Ecosystem Ser.). (Illus.). (gr. 3-7). 1977. 8.95 (ISBN 0-02-775340-9, 77534). Macmillan.

Hidden Worlds: An Asian Journey. Noel Howlett. Ed. by Amber Crest Bks. Staff. LC 77-94417. (Hidden World Ser.: Vol. 1). (Illus.). 320p. 1980. 14.50 (ISBN 0-86533-001-8). Amber Crest.

Hide & Defend. Kathleen Daly. (Look-Look Ser.). (Illus.). 1977. PLB 5.38 (ISBN 0-307-61837-4, Golden Pr); pap. 0.95 (ISBN 0-307-11837-1). Western Pub.

Hide-&-Seek. Katalin Szecsi. (gr. k-6). 5.50 (ISBN 9-6313-0515-5). Newbury Bks Inc.

Hide My Savage Heart. Gimone Hall. 1977. pap. 1.95 o.s.i. (ISBN 0-515-04058-4). Jove Pubns.

Hide the Baron. John Creasey. LC 77-91362. 1978. 7.95 o.s.i. (ISBN 0-8027-5383-3). Walker & Co.

Hider. Loren D. Estleman. LC 77-81786. 1978. 6.95 o.p. (ISBN 0-385-13627-7). Doubleday.

Hiding Game. Ben Shecter. LC 80-15291. (Illus.). 40p. (ps-3). 1980. Repr. of 1977 ed. 7.95 (ISBN 0-590-07765-1, Four Winds). Schol Bk Serv.

Hiding House. Judith Vigna. Ed. by Ann Fay. LC 79-17251. (Concept Bk.: Level I). (Illus.). 32p. (gr. 1-3). 1979. 6.95g (ISBN 0-8075-3275-4). A Whitman.

Hier a la Septieme Heure. Tr. by Jeanne Hale. (French Bks.). (Fr.). 1979. 1.80 (ISBN 0-686-28821-1). Life Pubs Intl.

Hier Begynneth the Table of the Rubrices of This Presente Volume Namde the Myrrour of the Worlde or Thymage of the Same. Bellovacensis Vincentius. Tr. by William Caxton from Fr. LC 79-84143. (English Experience Ser.: No. 960). 204p. (Eng.). 1979. Repr. of 1481 ed. lib. bdg. 30.00 (ISBN 90-221-0960-7). Walter J Johnson.

Hierarchies & Rank Orders in Distinctive Features. M. P. Van Den Broecke. (Illus., Orig.). 1976. pap. text ed. 19.00x (ISBN 90-232-1369-6). Humanities.

Hierarchomachia, or the Antibishop. Ed. by Suzanne Gossett. LC 78-75201. 300p. 1981. 14.50 (ISBN 0-8387-2151-6). Bucknell U Pr.

Hierarchy & Society: Anthropological Perspectives on Bureaucracy. Ed. by Gerald M. Britan & Ronald Cohen. LC 80-10835. 1980. text ed. 16.00x (ISBN 0-89727-009-6); pap. text ed. 6.95x (ISBN 0-89727-010-X). Inst Study Human.

Hierbas Al Rescate. LaDean Griffin. Orig. Title: Herbs to the Rescue. (Spa.). 2.00 (ISBN 0-89557-006-8). Bi World Indus.

Hieroglyph of Time: The Petrarchan Sestina. Marianne Shapiro. LC 80-10112. 344p. 1981. 22.50x (ISBN 0-8166-0945-4). U of Minn Pr.

Hieroglyphic Inscriptions & Monumental Art of Alter De Sacrificios. John A. Graham. LC 70-186984. (Peabody Museum Papers: Vol. 64, No. 2). 1972. pap. text ed. 15.00 (ISBN 0-87365-184-7). Peabody Harvard.

Hieroglyphica. Giovanni P. Valeriano Bolzani. LC 75-27864. (Renaissance & the Gods Ser.: Vol. 17). (Illus.). 1977. Repr. of 1602 ed. lib. bdg. 73.00 (ISBN 0-8240-2069-3). Garland Pub.

Hieroglyphiques. Giovanni P. Valeriano Bolzani. Tr. by I. de Montlyard. LC 75-27867. (Renaissance & the Gods Ser.: Vol. 23). (Illus., Fr.). 1977. Repr. of 1615 ed. lib. bdg. 73.00 (ISBN 0-8240-2072-3). Garland Pub.

Hieronymous Bosch. Walter S. Gibson. (World of Art Ser.). (Illus.). 1973. pap. 9.95 (ISBN 0-19-519945-6). Oxford U Pr.

Hieronymus Bosch & Alchemy: A Study on the St. Anthony Triptych. Madeleine Bergman. (Stockholm Studies in History of Art Ser.: No. 31). (Illus.). 139p. 1979. pap. text ed. 17.50x (ISBN 91-22-00292-8). Humanities.

Hieronymus Cock: Printmaker & Publisher. Timothy A. Riggs. LC 76-23706. (Outstanding Dissertations in the Fine Arts Ser.). 1977. lib. bdg. 73.00 (ISBN 0-8240-2724-8). Garland Pub.

High Action Reading for Comprehension, C. Pearl Neuman. Incl. Study Skills. Merrily Hansen. pap. text ed. 2.40 (ISBN 0-87895-325-6); Vocabulary. Barbara Christensen. pap. text ed. 2.40 (ISBN 0-87895-323-X). (Skillbooster Ser.). (gr. 3). 1979. pap. text ed. 2.40 (ISBN 0-87895-324-8). Modern Curr.

High Action Reading for Comprehension, D. Janet Garber. Incl. Study Skills. Merrily Hansen. pap. text ed. 2.40 (ISBN 0-87895-428-7); Vocabulary. Barbara Christensen. pap. text ed. 2.40 (ISBN 0-87895-426-0). (Skillbooster Ser.). (gr. 4). 1979. pap. text ed. 2.40 (ISBN 0-87895-427-9). Modern Curr.

High Action Reading for Comprehension, E. Janet Garber. Incl. Study Skills. Merrily Hansen. pap. text ed. 2.40 (ISBN 0-87895-531-3); Vocabulary. Barbara Christensen. pap. text ed. 2.40 (ISBN 0-87895-529-1). (Skillbooster Ser.). (gr. 5). 1979. pap. text ed. 2.40 (ISBN 0-87895-530-5). Modern Curr.

High Action Reading for Study Skills-F. Janet Garber. Incl. Study Skills. Merrily Hansen. pap. text ed. 2.40 (ISBN 0-87895-634-4); High Action Reading for Vocabulary. Barbara Christensen. pap. text ed. 2.40 (ISBN 0-87895-632-8). (Skillbooster Ser.). (gr. 6). 1979. pap. text ed. 2.40 (ISBN 0-87895-633-6). Modern Curr.

High Adventure. James N. Hall. 237p. 1980. Repr. of 1918 ed. lib. bdg. 30.00 (ISBN 0-89984-283-6). Century Bookbindery.

High Adventure. George Otis. pap. 1.95 (ISBN 0-89728-036-9, 533135). Omega Pubns OR.

High Adventure. George Otis. 1977. pap. 1.50 (ISBN 0-89129-014-1). Jove Pubns.

High Adventure: A Narrative of Air Fighting in France. James N. Hall. Ed. by James Gilbert. LC 79-7267. (Flight: Its First Seventy-Five Years Ser.). 1979. Repr. of 1918 ed. lib. bdg. 20.00x (ISBN 0-405-12177-6). Arno.

High Adventure Outdoor Pursuits: Organization & Leadership. Joel F. Meier et al. (Brighton Ser. in Recreation & Leisure). (Illus.). 240p. (Orig.). 1980. pap. 9.95 (ISBN 0-89832-019-4). Brighton Pub.

High Altitude Geocology. Ed. by Patrick J. Webber. (AAAS Selected Symposium Ser.: No. 12). (Illus.). 1979. lib. bdg. 21.50x (ISBN 0-89158-440-4). Westview.

High Altitude Physiology & Medicine I: Physiology of Adaptation. Ed. by W. Brendel & R. A. Zink. (Topics in Environmental Physiology & Medicine Ser.). (Illus.). 190p. 1981. 39.80 (ISBN 0-387-90482-4). Springer-Verlag.

High Alumina Cement Concrete. A. M. Neville. LC 75-14379. 1975. 28.95 (ISBN 0-470-63280-1). Halsted Pr.

High-Alumina Cements & Concretes. Thomas D. Robson. 1963. 12.95 (ISBN 0-471-72846-2). Halsted Pr.

High & Inside: The Complete Guide to Baseball Slang. Joseph McBride. 288p. (Orig.). 1981. pap. 2.50 (ISBN 0-446-91939-X). Warner Bks.

High & Mighty. (Illus., Orig.). (gr. 7-12). 1972. pap. text ed. 1.25 (ISBN 0-8374-3509-9). Xerox Ed Pubns.

High Cards. Bernard Gunther & Corita Kent. 4.95 o.p. (ISBN 0-06-061585-0, HarpR). Har-Row.

High Church. Frederick W. Robinson. Ed. by Robert L. Wolff. LC 75-498. (Victorian Fiction Ser.). 1975. Repr. of 1860 ed. lib. bdg. 66.00 (ISBN 0-8240-1573-8). Garland Pub.

High Contrast: Creative Imagemaking for Photographers, Designers & Graphic Artists. J. Seeley. 1980. 24.95 (ISBN 0-442-23888-6). Van Nos Reinhold.

High Cost of Education in Cities: An Analysis of the Purchasing Power of the Educational Dollar. Betsy Levin et al. 1973. pap. 2.50 o.p. (ISBN 0-87766-056-5, 31000). Urban Inst.

High Cost of Living. Marge Piercy. LC 77-6149. 1978. 10.00 o.s.i. (ISBN 0-06-013339-2, HarpT). Har-Row.

High Cost Oil & Gas Resources. J. A. Davis. 240p. 1981. 40.00x (ISBN 0-85664-588-5, Pub. by Croom Helm LTD England). Biblio Dist.

High Couch of Silistra. Janet Morris. 256p. (Orig.). 1981. pap. 2.50 (ISBN 0-553-14532-0). Bantam.

High Country. Peter Dawson. 144p. 1981. pap. 1.75 (ISBN 0-553-14537-1). Bantam.

High Country. Yva Momatiuk & John Eastcott. (Illus.). 128p. 1980. 25.00 (ISBN 0-589-01321-1, Pub. by Reed Bks Australia). C E Tuttle.

High Country Showdown. Ray Gaulden. 1979. pap. 1.50 (ISBN 0-505-51438-9). Tower Bks.

High Coupon Callable Bond Values Tables No. 74. Financial Publishing Co. 35.00 o.p. (ISBN 0-685-02549-7). Finan Pub.

High Courage. Clarence W. Anderson. (Illus.). (gr. 7 up). 1968. 6.95 (ISBN 0-02-704280-4). Macmillan.

High Crimes & Misdemeanors: The Impeachment & Trial of Andrew Johnson. Gene Smith. LC 76-9838. 320p. 1976. 10.00 o.p. (ISBN 0-688-03072-6). Morrow.

High Crusade. Poul Anderson. 1978. pap. 1.75 (ISBN 0-425-04307-X, Medallion). Berkley Pub.

High Deryni. Katherine Kurtz. 1976. pap. 2.25 (ISBN 0-345-28614-6). Ballantine.

High Design: English Renaissance Tragedy & the Natural Law. George C. Herndl. LC 78-111511. 352p. 1970. 14.00x (ISBN 0-8131-1217-6). U Pr of Ky.

High Diddle Diddle. Illus. by Robert A. Propper. LC 75-15062. (Illus.). (ps-3). 1975. 5.95 (ISBN 0-87070-377-3). Museum Mod Art.

High Dose-Rate Afterloading in the Treatment of Cancer of the Uterus. Ed. by T. D. Bates & R. J. Berry. 1980. 90.00x (Pub. by Brit Inst Radiology). State Mutual Bk.

High Drama. Hamish MacInnes. (Illus.). 224p. 1981. 11.95 (ISBN 0-89886-031-8). Mountaineers.

High Energy Astrophysics & Its Relation to Elementary Particle Physics. Kenneth Brecher & Ginancarlo Setti. LC 74-19794. 1974. 34.50x (ISBN 0-262-52035-4); pap. 12.50x o.p. (ISBN 0-262-52035-4). MIT Pr.

High Energy Collisions of Elementary Particles. R. J. Eden. LC 75-22560. (Illus.). 312p. 1975. pap. 16.95 (ISBN 0-521-29030-9). Cambridge U Pr.

High-Energy Diet for Dynamic Living. Max Novich & Ted Kaufman. 1977. pap. 1.95 o.p. (ISBN 0-345-25153-9). Ballantine.

High Energy Electron Scattering. Russell A. Bonham & Manfred Fink. LC 73-12400. (ACS Monograph: No. 169). 1974. 33.00 (ISBN 0-442-30891-4). Am Chemical.

High Energy Electrons in Radiation Therapy. Ed. by A. Zuppinger et al. (Illus.). 130p. 1980. pap. 28.40 (ISBN 0-387-10188-8). Springer-Verlag.

High Energy Hadron Physics. Martin L. Perl. LC 74-6348. 584p. 1974. 37.50 (ISBN 0-471-68049-4, Pub. by Wiley-Interscience). Wiley.

High-Energy Physics & Elementary Particles. (Illus., Orig.). 1965. pap. 35.00 (ISBN 92-0-530265-1, IAEA). Unipub.

High-Energy Physics in the Einstein Centennial Year. Ed. by Arnold Perlmutter et al. (Studies in the Natural Science: Vol. 16). 1979. 55.00 (ISBN 0-306-40297-1, Plenum Pr). Plenum Pub.

High Escape. Eve Cowen. (Sportellers Ser.). (Illus.). 64p. (gr. 5 up). 1981. PLB 7.95 (ISBN 0-516-02264-4). Childrens.

High Fantasy. Jeffery Dillow. 1981. 14.95 (ISBN 0-8359-2827-6). Reston.

High Flier. Steven Otfinoski. Ed. by Mary Verdick. (Beginning Pal Paperbacks Ser.). (Illus., Orig.). (gr. 7-12). 1977. pap. text ed. 1.25 (ISBN 0-8374-3459-9). Xerox Ed Pubns.

High Frequency Circuit Design. Jim Hardy. (Illus.). 1979. ref. 21.95 (ISBN 0-8359-2824-1); students manual avail. (ISBN 0-8359-2825-X). Reston.

High Frequency Lighting. Building Research Advisory Board. (Federal Construction Council Technical Report, No. 53). 1968. pap. 4.00 (ISBN 0-309-01610-X). Natl Acad Pr.

High Hills. John Lawson. (Illus.). 220p. (Orig.). 1981. pap. 4.95 (ISBN 0-938658-01-8). West SW Pub Co.

High History of the Holy Grail. Ed. by Sabastian Evans. (Illus.). 395p. 1969. 12.95 (ISBN 0-227-67727-7). Attic Pr.

High in America. Patrick Anderson. LC 80-51772. 360p. 1981. 13.95 (ISBN 0-670-11990-3). Viking Pr.

High Island: New & Selected Poems. Richard Murphy. LC 74-1838. 128p. 1975. pap. 2.95 o.s.i. (ISBN 0-06-013121-7, TD-205, HarpT). Har-Row.

High Jumps & Dumbbells: The Adventures of an Obedience Dog. Joan Simmons. LC 79-55024. (Illus.). (gr. 6-12). 1979. 7.95 (ISBN 0-931866-04-9). Alpine Pubns.

High-Level Languages for Microprocessor Projects. National Computing Centre. Ed. by David Taylor & Lyndon Morgan. (Illus.). 279p. (Orig.). 1980. pap. 37.50x (ISBN 0-85012-233-3). Intl Pubns Serv.

High Level Manpower in Iran: From Hidden Conflict to Crisis. Gail C. Johnson. LC 79-21419. (Praeger Special Studies Ser.). 136p. 1980. 24.50 (ISBN 0-03-055366-X). Praeger.

High Level Nuclear Waste from Past to Present: Policy & Prophecy. 1980. 3.25. Tech Info Proj.

High-Low Consensus. Helen E. Williams. LC 80-19794. 1980. pap. 15.50 (ISBN 0-87272-088-8). Brodart.

High Marks. Annette Sloan & Albert Capaccio. (Orig.). (gr. 9). 1981. pap. text ed. 4.75 (ISBN 0-87720-393-8). AMSCO Sch.

High Middle Ages. Edward Rice. 128p. 1963. 2.95 (ISBN 0-374-29520-4). FS&G.

High Middle Ages in England, 1154-1377. B. Wilkinson. LC 77-8490. (Conference on British Studies Bibliographical Handbooks). 1978. 15.50x (ISBN 0-521-21732-6). Cambridge U Pr.

High Middle Ages, 1000-1300. Ed. by Bryce Lyon. LC 64-21207. (Orig.). 1964. pap. text ed. 5.95 (ISBN 0-02-919480-6). Free Pr.

High Mountain. 2nd ed. LC 65-26326. 1978. 7.50 (ISBN 0-935490-03-5). Euclid Pub.

High Mountains & Cold Seas: A Biography of H. W. Tilman. J. R. Anderson. LC 80-81520. (Illus.). 364p. 1980. 20.00 (ISBN 0-89886-008-3). Mountaineers.

High Noon: A Screen Adaptation, Directed by Fred Zinneman. John M. Cunningham. Ed. by George P. Garrett et al. LC 71-135273. (Film Scripts Ser.). 1971. pap. text ed. 5.95x (ISBN 0-89197-788-0). Irvington.

High Performance Liquid Chromatography: Advances & Perspectives, Vol. 2. Ed. by Csaba Horvath. 1980. lib ed 39.50 (ISBN 0-12-312202-3). Acad Pr.

High Performance Liquid Chromatography. John H. Knox. 205p. 1981. pap. 17.00x (ISBN 0-85224-383-9, Pub. by Edinburgh U Pr Scotland). Columbia U Pr.

High-Performance Review: Audio Equipment & Recordings for the Perceptive Listener, Vol. 1. Ed. by David H. Tarumoto. (Illus.). 480p. 1981. pap. 24.00x (ISBN 0-88232-068-8). Delbridge Pub Co.

High Politics, Low Politics: Toward a Foreign Policy for Western Europe. Roger P. Morgan. LC 73-86712. (Washington Papers: No. 11). 1973. 3.50x (ISBN 0-8039-0284-0). Sage.

High Polymers, Vols. 5-7, 9 & 12. Incl. Vol. 5, Pts. 1 & 2. Cellulose. Ed. by E. Ott & H. M. Spurin. LC 53-7161. 1954. Pt. 1. o.p. (ISBN 0-470-39006-9); Pt. 2. o.p. (ISBN 0-470-39007-7); Vol. 5, Pts. 4 & 5. Cellulose & Cellulose Derivatives. Ed. by Norbert M. Bikales & Leon Segal. LC 79-136710. 1141p. 1971. Set. 130.00 (ISBN 0-471-39038-0); Vol. 6. Mechanical Behavior of High Polymers. Ed. by I. Alfrey, Jr. 595p. 1948. pap. o.p. (ISBN 0-470-39040-9); Vol. 7. Phenoplasts. Ed. by Thomas S. Carswell. 279p. 1947. o.p. (ISBN 0-470-39072-7); Vol. 9. Emulsion Polymerization. Ed. by Frank A. Bovey et al. LC 54-7992. 457p. 1955. o.p. (ISBN 0-470-39138-3); Vol. 12. Analytical Chemistry of Polymers. Ed. by Gordon M. Kline. LC 59-9298. 1962. Pt. 1. o.p. (ISBN 0-685-33506-2); Pt. 2. 39.50 (ISBN 0-470-39238-X). Pub. by Wiley-Interscience). Wiley.

High Polymers, Vols. 13-20. Incl. Vol. 13. Polyethers. Ed. by N. G. Gaylord. LC 62-15824. 1962-73. Pt. 1. o.p. (ISBN 0-470-39265-7); Pt. 2. o.p. (ISBN 0-471-39268-5); Pt. 3. 27.50 (ISBN 0-470-39270-3); Vol. 15. Radiation Chemistry of Polymeric Systems. Ed. by A. Chapiro. LC 61-16747. 728p. 1962. o.p. (ISBN 0-470-39285-1); Vol. 16, Pt. 2. Polyurethanes. Ed. by J. H. Saunders & K. C. Frisch. LC 62-18932. 1962. o.p. (ISBN 0-470-39292-4); Vol. 16, Pt. 3. Ed. by D. J. David & H. B. Staley. LC 68-8110. 627p. 1969. o.p. (ISBN 0-471-39293-6); Vol. 17. Configurational Statistics of Polymeric Chains. Ed. by M. V. Volkenstein. LC 63-17452. 562p. 1963. o.p. (ISBN 0-470-39295-9); Vol. 18. Copolymerization. Ed. by G. E. Ham. LC 64-17050. 940p. 1964. 51.50 (ISBN 0-470-39300-9); Vol. 19. Chemical Reactions of Polymers. Ed. by E. M. Fettes. LC 64-17054. 1304p. 1964. 90.00 (ISBN 0-470-39305-X); Vol. 20. Crystalline Olefin Polymers. Ed. by R. A. Raff & K. W. Doak. LC 64-12191. 1964-65. Pt. 1. o.p. (ISBN 0-470-39309-2); Pt. 2. o.p. (ISBN 0-470-39312-2). Pub. by Wiley-Interscience). Wiley.

High Polymers, Vols. 21-29. 2nd ed. Incl. Vol. 21. Macromolecules in Solution. Ed. by H. Morawetz. LC 74-26655. 495p. 1975. 38.00 (ISBN 0-471-39321-5); Vol. 22. Conformation of Macromolecules. Ed. by T. Birshstein & O. Ptitsyn. LC 65-26217. 350p. 1966. o.p. (ISBN 0-470-39325-4); Vol. 23. Polymer Chemistry of Synthetic Elastomers. Ed. by J. P. Kennedy & E. G. Tornquist. LC 67-13948. 1968-69. Pt. 1. 46.95 (ISBN 0-470-39326-2); Pt.2. 49.50 (ISBN 0-470-39327-0); Vol. 24. Vinyl & Diene Monomers. Ed. by E. C. Leonard. LC 77-94013. 1970. Pt. 1. o.p. (ISBN 0-471-39328-2); Pt. 2. o.p. (ISBN 0-471-39329-0); Vol. 25. Fluoropolymers. Ed. by L. A. Wall. LC 74-165023. 550p. 1972. o.p. (ISBN 0-471-39350-9); Vol. 26. Cyclic Monomers. Ed. by K. C. Frisch. LC 73-174769. 782p. 1972. o.p. (ISBN 0-471-39360-6); Vol. 27. Condensation Monomers. Ed. by J. K. Stille & T. W. Campbell. LC 72-1260. 745p. 1972. o.p. (ISBN 0-471-39370-3); Vol. 28. Allyl Compounds & Their Polymers. Ed. by C. E. Schildknecht. LC 72-1363. 1973. o.p. (ISBN 0-471-39380-0). Pub. by Wiley-Interscience). Wiley.

High Pressure Engineering. W. R. Manning & S. Labrow. 1972. text ed. 37.50x (ISBN 0-7114-3804-8); pap. text ed. 19.95x (ISBN 0-685-83587-1). Intl Ideas.

High Pressure Liquid Chromatography & Therapeutic Drug Monitoring. Benjamin Gerson & John P. Anhalt. LC 80-16443. (Illus.). 1980. pap. text ed. 35.00 (ISBN 0-89189-077-7, 45-2-037-00). Am Soc Clinical.

High Pressure Science & Technology: Proceedings. International AIRAPT Conference, Le Creuset, France, July 30-Aug. 3, 1979. Ed. by B. Vodar & P. Marteau. (Illus.). 1200p. 1980. 230.00 (ISBN 0-08-024774-1). Pergamon.

High Renaissance & Mannerism: Italy, the North, & Spain, 1500-1600. Linda Murray. (World of Art Ser.). (Illus.). 1978. pap. text ed. 9.95 (ISBN 0-19-519990-1). Oxford U Pr.

High-Resolution Electrocardiography: A Superior Diagnostic Modality. Lawrence H. Krohn. (Illus.). 304p. 1976. 37.50 (ISBN 0-398-03515-6). C C Thomas.

High-Resolution Infrared & Submillimetre Spectroscopy: A Selection of Papers Presented at a Workshop Held in Bonn, 1977. Ed. by G. Schultz & T. S. Moss. 1977. pap. text ed. 23.00 (ISBN 0-08-021675-7). Pergamon.

High Resolution Nuclear Magnetic Resonance Spectroscopy, 2 Vols. J. W. Emsley et al. 1966. 46.00 (ISBN 0-08-011824-0). Pergamon.

High Ride Gobbler: The Story of the American Wild Turkey. David Stemple. LC 78-24200. (Illus.). 1979. 7.95 (ISBN 0-529-05524-4). Philomel.

High Rise. J. G. Ballard. 1978. pap. 1.95 o.p. (ISBN 0-445-04181-1). Popular Lib.

High-Rise. J. G. Ballard. LC 76-29899. 1977. 6.95 o.p. (ISBN 0-03-020651-0). HR&W.

High Risk Child: A Guide for Concerned Parents. Phillip Deppe et al. 224p. 1981. 12.95 (ISBN 0-02-531010-0). Macmillan.

High Risk Newborn Infants. 3rd ed. Sheldon B. Korones. (Illus.). 350p. 1981. text ed. 16.95 (ISBN 0-8016-2738-9). Mosby.

High School. David Owen. 252p. 1981. 12.95 (ISBN 0-670-37149-1). Viking Pr.

High School Entrance Examinations. Jacqueline Robinson & Dennis M. Robinson. LC 80-22278. 512p. 1981. lib. bdg. 9.00 (ISBN 0-668-05149-3); pap. 6.50 (ISBN 0-668-05155-8). Arco.

High School Equivalency Test. Gary R. Gruber. (Exam Prep. Ser.). pap. 6.95 (ISBN 0-671-18998-0). Monarch Pr.

High School Equivalency Test Guide. Raymond W. Hodges. LC 75-2181. 95p. (Orig.). (gr. 9-12). 1975. pap. text ed. 5.00 (ISBN 0-913310-13-1). Par Inc.

High School Graduate Guide for Scoring High on Civil Service Tests. Solomon Wiener. 160p. (Orig.). (gr. 12). 1981. pap. 4.95 (ISBN 0-671-42776-8). Monarch Pr.

High School Hookers. Ruth Miller. 1979. pap. 1.75 (ISBN 0-505-51417-6). Tower Bks.

High School Seniors Cohort Study, Nineteen Sixty-Five & Nineteen Seventy-Three. M. K. Jennings. 1980. 14.00 (ISBN 0-89138-964-4). ICPSR.

High School Work Study Program for the Retarded: Practical Information for Teacher Preparation & Program Organization & Operation. Kenneth H. Freeland. (Illus.). 120p. 1974. text ed. 11.50 (ISBN 0-398-00611-3). C C Thomas.

High Sierra. Ezra Bowen. (American Wilderness Ser). (Illus.). 1972. 12.95 (ISBN 0-8094-1140-7). Time-Life.

High Sierra. Ezra Bowen. (American Wilderness Ser). (Illus.). (gr. 6 up). 1972. lib. bdg. 11.97 (ISBN 0-8094-1141-5, Pub. by Time-Life). Silver.

High Sierra Hiking Guide to Blackcap Mountain. 2nd ed. Thomas Winnett & Ed Roberts. LC 74-27684. (High Sierra Hiking Guide Ser: Vol. 3). (Illus., Orig.). 1976. pap. 3.95 (ISBN 0-911824-36-7). Wilderness.

High Sierra Hiking Guide to Hetch Hetchy. Ron Felzer. Ed. by Thomas Winnett. LC 72-89914. (High Sierra Hiking Guide Ser: Vol. 12). (Illus., Orig.). 1973. pap. 3.95 (ISBN 0-911824-24-3). Wilderness.

High Sierra Hiking Guide to Merced Peak. Robert Pierce & Margaret Pierce. Ed. by Thomas Winnett. LC 72-89915. (High Sierra Hiking Guide Ser: Vol. 11). (Illus., Orig.). 1973. pap. 3.95 (ISBN 0-911824-23-5). Wilderness.

High Sierra Hiking Guide to Mineral King. Ron Felzer. Ed. by Thomas Winnett. LC 70-186759. (High Sierra Hiking Guide Ser: Vol. 8). (Illus., Orig.). 1972. pap. 2.95 o.p. (ISBN 0-911824-19-7). Wilderness.

High Sierra Hiking Guide to Mt. Abbot. 2nd ed. Ed. by Thomas Winnett. LC 73-100114. (High Sierra Hiking Guide Ser: Vol. 2). (Illus., Orig.). 1973. pap. 3.95 (ISBN 0-911824-08-1). Wilderness.

High Sierra Hiking Guide to Mt. Goddard. 2nd ed. John W. Robinson. Ed. by Thomas Winnett. (High Sierra Hiking Guide Ser.: Vol. 10). (Illus., Orig.). 1980. pap. 3.95 (ISBN 0-89997-002-8). Wilderness.

High Sierra Hiking Guide to Silver Lake. 2nd ed. Joseph R. Grodin & Sharon Grodin. LC 78-50994. (High Sierra Hiking Guide Ser.: Vol. 17). (Illus., Orig.). 1970. pap. 3.95 (ISBN 0-911824-73-1). Wilderness.

High Sierra Hiking Guide to Tower Peak. Ken Fawcett. Ed. by Thomas Winnett. LC 74-27687. (High Sierra Hiking Guide Ser: Vol. 16). (Illus., Orig.). 1975. pap. 3.95 (ISBN 0-911824-37-5). Wilderness.

High Sierra Hiking Guide to Triple Divide Peak. Andrew Selters. Ed. by Thomas Winnett. LC 79-57596. (High Sierra Hiking Guide Ser.: No. 20). (Illus., Orig.). 1980. pap. 3.95 (ISBN 0-911824-94-4). Wilderness.

High Sierra: Mountain Wonderland. Joseph Wampler & Weldon F. Heald. (Illus.). 125p. 1967. 5.50 (ISBN 0-686-11221-0). J Wampler.

High Slaughter. Jon Hart. LC 80-71037. (Mercenaries Ser.). 128p. 1981. pap. 2.95 (ISBN 0-87754-229-5). Chelsea Hse.

High Solids Coatings Buyer's Guide. 1981. 21.00 (ISBN 0-686-28813-0). Tech Marketing.

High Sounds, Low Sounds. Franklyn M. Branley. LC 67-23662. (Let's-Read-&-Find-Out Science Bk). (Illus.). (gr. k-3). 1967. 6.95 o.p. (ISBN 0-690-38017-8, TYC-J); PLB 7.89 (ISBN 0-690-38018-6); filmstrip with record 11.95 (ISBN 0-690-38019-4); filmstrip with cassette 14.95 (ISBN 0-690-38021-6). T Y Crowell.

High Speed Can Manufacture, 2 vols. Ed. by G. F. Allard et al. (Engineering Craftsmen: No. H301). (Illus.). 1972. Set. spiral bdg. 39.95x (ISBN 0-85083-159-8). Intl Ideas.

High Speed Digital Memories & Circuits. H. J. Gray. LC 75-14790. (University of Pennsylvania Advances in Modern Engineering Ser.: Vol.5). (Illus.). 151p. 1976. pap. text ed. 8.95 (ISBN 0-201-02579-5). A-W.

High Speed Pulse Technique. J. A. Coekin. Ed. by P. Hammond. 263p. 1975. text ed. 27.00 (ISBN 0-08-018774-9); pap. text ed. 14.50 (ISBN 0-08-018773-0). Pergamon.

High Speed Pulse Technology, 4 vols. Frank Frungel. Incl. Vol. 1. Capacitor Discharges, Magneto-Hydrodynamics, X-Rays, Ultrasonics. 1965. 55.25, by subscription 47.50 o.s.i. (ISBN 0-12-269001-X); Vol. 2. Optical Pulses, Lasers, Measuring Techniques. 1965. 51.00, by subscription 44.00 (ISBN 0-12-269002-8); Vol. 3. 1975. 55.25, by subscription 47.50 (ISBN 0-12-269003-6); Vol. 4. 1978. write for info. (ISBN 0-12-269004-4). Acad Pr.

High Speed Sailing: A Study of High-Performance Multihull Yacht Design. Joseph Norwood, Jr. LC 79-87640. (Illus.). 1979. 14.95 (ISBN 0-396-07738-2). Dodd.

High Speed Silicon Planar-Epitaxial Switching Diodes. Miklos Kocsis. LC 75-19391. 1976. 34.95 (ISBN 0-470-49707-6). Halsted Pr.

High Starlight. L. P. Holmes. 1976. pap. 0.95 o.p. (ISBN 0-445-00708-7). Popular Lib.

High Steel. Richard Dillon et al. LC 78-72833. (Illus.). 1978. pap. 25.00 o.p. (ISBN 0-89087-239-2). Celestial Arts.

High Stick. Ted Green & Al Hirshberg. LC 77-179695. (Illus.). 1971. 5.95 (ISBN 0-396-06427-2). Dodd.

High Technology -- a Failure Analysis, Vol. 2. Brenda Harrison & P. Aarne Vesilind. LC 80-65508. (Design & Management for Resource Recovery Ser.). (Illus.). 250p. 1981. 29.95 (ISBN 0-250-40311-0). Ann Arbor Science.

High Temperature Alloys for Gas Turbines. Ed. by D. Coutsouradis et al. (Illus.). 1978. text ed. 91.00x (ISBN 0-85334-815-4, Pub. by Applied Science). Burgess-Intl Ideas.

High-Temperature Materials & Technology. Ivor E. Campbell & E. M. Sherwood. LC 67-13521. (Electrochemical Society Ser.). 1967. 52.95 o.p. (ISBN 0-471-13299-3, Pub. by Wiley-Interscience). Wiley.

High-Temperature Oxidation Resistant Coatings for Superalloys,Refractory Metals, & Graphite. National Materials Advisory Board. LC 78-606278. (Orig.). 1971. pap. text ed. 13.25 (ISBN 0-309-01769-6). Natl Acad Pr.

High-Temperature Plasma Technology Applications. Lester A. Ettlinger et al. LC 80-65507. (Electrotechnology Ser.: Vol. 6). (Illus.). 163p. 1980. 29.95 (ISBN 0-250-40376-5). Ann Arbor Science.

High-Temperature Water for Heating & Light Process Loads. Building Research Advisory Board - Federal Construction Council. 1960. pap. 3.00 (ISBN 0-309-00753-4). Natl Acad Pr.

High Terror. Irving Greenfield. 1978. pap. 1.95 o.p. (ISBN 0-445-04244-3). Popular Lib.

High Times Encyclopedia of Recreational Drugs. Ed. by High Times Magazine Editors. (Illus.). 1978. 19.95 (ISBN 0-88373-081-2); pap. 10.95 (ISBN 0-88373-082-0). Stonehill Pub Co.

High Times, Hard Times. Anita O'Day & George Eells. 320p. 1981. 12.95 (ISBN 0-399-12505-1). Putnam.

High Tower. John Tomevlin. 224p. (Orig.). 1980. pap. 2.25 (ISBN 0-553-02982-7). Bantam.

High Treason at Catfish Bend. Ben L. Burman. LC 76-52136. (Illus.). (gr. 6 up). 1977. 6.95 (ISBN 0-8149-0785-7). Vanguard.

High Uinta Trails. Mel Davis. (Illus.). 132p. 1974. pap. 3.50 (ISBN 0-915272-02-4). Wasatch Pubs.

High Valley. Kenneth E. Read. LC 65-20581. (Illus.). lib. rep. ed. 17.50x (ISBN 0-684-15134-0, ScribT). Scribner.

High-Velocity Forming of Metals. rev. ed. Ed. by E. J. Bruno. LC 68-23027. (Manufacturing Data Ser). 1968. pap. 10.75x (ISBN 0-87263-009-9). SME.

High Voltage. Thomas Chastain. 1981. pap. 2.50 (ISBN 0-425-04831-4). Berkley Pub.

High Voltage Engineering. Kuffel & M. Abdullah. 1970. text ed. 28.00 (ISBN 0-08-006383-7); pap. text ed. 11.25 (ISBN 0-08-006382-9). Pergamon.

High Wires & Wigs. Robert B. Ruddell et al. (Pathfinder - Allyn & Bacon Reading Program: Level 7). (gr. 1). 1978. pap. text ed. 3.28 (ISBN 0-205-05112-X, 5451124); 8.80 (ISBN 0-205-05127-8, 5451272). Allyn.

Highbrows. C. E. Joad. 256p. 1980. Repr. of 1922 ed. lib. bdg. 20.00 (ISBN 0-89987-449-5). Darby Bks.

Higher Animals: A Mark Twain Bestiary. Ed. by Maxwell Geismar. LC 76-6563. (Illus.). 1976. 8.95 o.s.i. (ISBN 0-690-01149-0, TYC-T). T Y Crowell.

Higher Calculus. Frank Bowman & F. A. Gerard. 1967. 48.00x (ISBN 0-521-04293-3). Cambridge U Pr.

Higher Civil Service: An Evaluation of Federal Personnel Practices. David T. Stanley. 1964. 8.95 (ISBN 0-8157-8104-0). Brookings.

Higher Cortical Functions in Man. rev. & expanded ed. Aleksandr R. Luria. 655p. 1980. 27.50 (ISBN 0-306-10966-2, Consultants Bureau). Plenum Pub.

Higher Education Alternatives. Ed. by Michael D. Stephens & Gordon W. Roderick. LC 77-21407. 1978. text ed. 18.00x (ISBN 0-582-48915-6). Longman.

Higher Education & Business Recruitment in Japan. Koya Azumi. LC 71-81593. 1969. pap. 5.75x (ISBN 0-8077-1042-3). Tchrs Coll.

Higher Education & Earnings: College As an Investment & a Screening Device. Carnegie Commission on Higher Education. Ed. by P. Taubman & T. Wales. 1974. 21.50 o.p. (ISBN 0-07-010121-3, P&RB). McGraw.

Higher Education & Employment: A Case Study of Israel. Arye Globerson. LC 78-60131. (Praeger Special Studies). 1979. 22.95 (ISBN 0-03-046226-6). Praeger.

Higher Education & Rural Development in Africa. Joyce L. Moock & Peter R. Moock. 42p. 1977. pap. 1.75 (ISBN 0-89192-228-8). Interbk Inc.

Higher Education & Social Change, Vol. 2. Ed. by Kenneth W. Thompson et al. 1977. pap. 7.50 o.p. (ISBN 0-275-23390-1). Interbk Inc.

Higher Education & Social Change: Promising Experiments in Developing Countries, Vol. I. Kenneth W. Thompson & Barbara R. Fogel. LC 76-14474. (Illus.). 1976. text ed. 17.50 o.p. (ISBN 0-275-23390-1). Praeger.

Higher Education & Social Change: Promising Experiments in Developing Countries, Vol. 2: Case Studies. Ed. by Kenneth W Thompson et al. LC 76-14474. 1976. text ed. 32.50 o.p. (ISBN 0-275-23390-1). Praeger.

Higher Education & the Law. Harry T. Edwards & Virginia D. Nordin. LC 79-88195. 844p. 1979. 25.00x (ISBN 0-934222-00-2). Inst Ed Management.

Higher Education & the Nation's Health: Policies for Medical & Dental Education. Carnegie Commission On Higher Education. 1970. 5.50 o.p. (ISBN 0-07-010021-7, P&RB). McGraw.

Higher Education & the Needs of Society. Erich Teichler et al. (NFER Ser.). 141p. 1980. pap. text ed. 11.00x (ISBN 0-85633-209-7, NFER). Humanities.

Higher Education & the New England Economy in the Nineteen-Eighties. Ed. by John C. Hoy. 160p. 1981. 10.00x (ISBN 0-87451-197-6). U Pr of New Eng.

Higher Education & the Unholy Crusade Against Governmental Regulation. Harry T. Edwards. LC 80-26334. 62p. (Orig.). 1980. pap. text ed. 5.95x (ISBN 0-934222-04-5). Inst Ed Management.

Higher Education Bibliography. Jane N. White & Collins W. Burnett. 1981. price not set (ISBN 0-912700-80-7). Oryx Pr.

Higher Education: Demand & Response. Ed. by W. Roy Niblett. LC 71-110637. (Higher Education Ser.). 1970. 14.95x o.p. (ISBN 0-87589-064-4). Jossey-Bass.

Higher Education in the United Kingdom: 1980-1982. The British Council. (Illus.). 308p. 1980. pap. 11.95 (ISBN 0-582-49710-8). Longman.
Higher Education in the United States & Latin America. Casimir J. Kowalski & Joseph P. Cangemi. 128p. (Orig.). 1981. 8.50 (ISBN 0-8022-2385-0). Philos Lib.
Higher Education: International Trends 1960-1970. (Statistical Reports & Studies). (Illus.). 254p. 1976. pap. 10.00 (ISBN 92-3-101205-3, U287, UNESCO). Unipub.
Higher Education Reform: Implications for Foreign Students. 172p. 1978. 12.00 (IIE). Unipub.
Higher Education Revisited. Lord Robbins. 230p. 1980. text ed. 34.00x (ISBN 0-8419-5082-2). Holmes & Meier.
Higher Education: Who Pays? Who Benefits? Who Should Pay? Carnegie Commission on Higher Education. LC 73-8856. (Illus.). 208p. 1973. 7.95 o.p. (ISBN 0-07-010079-9, P&RB). McGraw.
Higher Excited States of Polyatomic Molecules. Robin. Vol. 1. 1974. 48.50 (ISBN 0-12-589901-7); Vol. 2. 1975. 50.25 (ISBN 0-12-589902-5). Acad Pr.
Higher Ground. Dee Brestin & Steve Brestin. (Fisherman Bible Study Guide). 1978. pap. 1.95 saddle stitch (ISBN 0-87788-345-9). Shaw Pubs.
Higher Learning in Colorado: A Historical Study, 1860-1940. Michael McGiffert. LC 64-18746. 307p. 1964. 13.95 (ISBN 0-8040-0085-9). Swallow.
Higher Oil Prices & the World Economy: The Adjustment Problem. Ed. by Edward R. Fried & Charles L. Schultze. 1975. 14.95 (ISBN 0-8157-2932-4); pap. 5.95 (ISBN 0-8157-2931-6). Brookings.
Higher Powers of the Soul. George McHardy. (Short Course Ser.). 142p. Repr. of 1912 ed. text ed. 2.95 (ISBN 0-567-08321-7). Attic Pr.
Higher Schooling in the United States. Ashley C. Ellefson. LC 77-94531. (Orig.). 1978. pap. 4.95 (ISBN 0-8467-0455-2, Pub. by Two Continents). Hippocrene Bks.
Higher Transcendental Functions, 3 vols. Bateman Manuscript Project, Calif. Inst. Technology. Incl. Vol. 1. 316p. Repr. of 1953 ed (ISBN 0-89874-206-4); Vol. 2. 414p. Repr. of 1953 ed; Vol. 3. 310p. Repr. of 1955 ed (ISBN 0-89874-207-2). LC 79-26544. 1980. lib. bdg. write for info. Krieger.
Higher Transcendental Functions, Vol. 2. A. Erdelyi. 1980. Repr. of 1953 ed. lib. bdg. write for info. (ISBN 0-89874-069-X). Krieger.
Highest Balloon on the Common. Carol Carrick & Donald Carrick. LC 77-23309. (gr. k-3). 8.25 (ISBN 0-688-80100-5); PLB 7.92 (ISBN 0-688-84100-7). Greenwillow.
Highest Education: A Study of Graduate Education in Britain. Ernest Rudd. 1975. 14.00x (ISBN 0-7100-8307-6). Routledge & Kegan.
Highest Hit. Williard. (gr. 4-6). Date not set. pap. cancelled (ISBN 0-590-30051-2, Schol Pap). Schol Bk Serv.
Highest State of Consciousness. Ed. by John Warren. LC 70-171340. 1972. pap. 3.50 (ISBN 0-385-04532-8, Anch). Doubleday.
Highland Coontess. Helen Crampton. (Orig.). 1981. pap. 1.95 (ISBN 0-671-83493-2). PB.
Highland Dress, Arms & Ornament. A. Campbell. 1969. Repr. of 1899 ed. 15.00 o.p. (ISBN 0-7129-0380-1, Dist by Shoe String). Dawson Pub.
Highland Fire. Abigail Clements. 1977. pap. 1.50 o.p. (ISBN 0-449-13638-8, GM). Fawcett.
Highland Fling. May Mackintosh. 1975. 7.95 o.p. (ISBN 0-440-04564-9). Delacorte.
Highland Folk Ways. I. F. Grant. (Illus.). 1961. 22.50 (ISBN 0-7100-1466-X); pap. 11.95 (ISBN 0-7100-8064-6). Routledge & Kegan.
Highland Maya: Patterns of Life & Clothing in Indian Guatemala. Roland Bunch & Roger Bunch. LC 77-77864. 1977. 8.95 (ISBN 0-930740-01-7). Indigenous Pubns.
Highland Peoples of New Guinea. Paula Brown. LC 77-80830. (Illus.). 1978. 29.95 (ISBN 0-521-21748-2); pap. 7.95x (ISBN 0-521-29249-2). Cambridge U Pr.
Highland Rapture. Marion P. Rettke. (Orig.). 1979. pap. 1.75 (ISBN 0-515-05318-X). Jove Pubns.
Highland Rogue: The Memorable Actions of the Celebrated Robert Mac-Gregor, Commonly Called Rob-Roy. Bd. with Love Upon Tick: Implicit Gallantry. LC 75-170556; Matchless Rogue; or, an Account of the Contrivances, Cheats, Stratagems & Amours of Tom Merryman, Commonly Called Newgate Tom. LC 78-170554. LC 71-170555. (Foundations of the Novel Ser.: Vol. 40). lib. bdg. 50.00 (ISBN 0-8240-0552-X). Garland Pub.
Highland Scots of North Carolina. Duane Meyer. (Illus.). 1968. pap. 1.00 (ISBN 0-86526-081-8). NC Archives.
Highland Settler: A Portrait of the Scottish Gael in Nova Scotia. Charles W. Dunn. LC 53-7025. 1953. pap. 5.95 (ISBN 0-8020-6094-3). U of Toronto Pr.
Highlands & the Islands. F. Darling & J. Boyd. 1964. pap. 2.25 o.p. (ISBN 0-531-06011-X, Fontana Pap). Watts.
Highlights in Astronomy. Fred Hoyle. LC 75-1300. (Illus.). 1975. pap. text ed. 9.95x (ISBN 0-7167-0354-8). W H Freeman.
Highlights: National Survey of Personal Health Practices & Consequences, United States, 1979. Kathleen M. Danchik & Charlotte A. Schoenborn. Ed. by Mary Olmsted. (Ser. 10: No. 137). 50p. 1981. pap. 1.75 (ISBN 0-8406-0218-9). Natl Ctr Health Stats.
Highlights of American History, 2 bks. Joel Legunn. (Janus Stamp & Story Ser.). (Illus.). 64p. (gr. 7-12). 1979. Bk. 1 Before 1850. pap. text ed. 2.85 (ISBN 0-915510-31-6); Bk. 2 After 1850. pap. text ed. 2.85 (ISBN 0-915510-32-4). Janus Bks.
Highlights of Astronomy, Vol. 5. (International Astronomical Union Highlights Ser.: No. 5). 868p. 1980. 84.00 (ISBN 90-277-1146-1); pap. 39.50 (ISBN 90-277-1147-X). Kluwer Boston.
Highlights of College Football. John Durant & Les Etter. (gr. 7 up). 1970. 8.95 (ISBN 0-8038-3013-0). Hastings.
Highlights of Hebrew History. Charles W. Conn. 1975. 4.50 (ISBN 0-87148-402-1); pap. 3.50 (ISBN 0-87148-401-3); instrs. guide 4.50 (ISBN 0-87148-834-5). Pathway Pr.
Highlights of Tarot. rev. ed. Paul F. Case. 1970. 2.00 (ISBN 0-938002-02-3). Builders of Adytum.
Highlights of the Bible: New Testament. William L. Lane. LC 80-50543. 160p. 1980. pap. 2.50 (ISBN 0-8307-0676-3, S343118). Regal.
Highlights of the World Series. rev. 3rd ed. John Durant. (Illus.). 208p. (gr. 6 up). 1973. 6.95g o.s.i. (ISBN 0-8038-3028-9). Hastings.
Highliners. William B. McCloskey, Jr. 408p. 1981. pap. 5.95 (ISBN 0-07-044858-2). McGraw.
Highly Irregular: Biafran Relief Story. Bruce Hilton. 1969. 5.95 o.s.i. (ISBN 0-02-551670-1); pap. 1.95 o.s.i. (ISBN 0-02-085490-0). Macmillan.
Highly Selective Vagotomy. Louis F. Hollender & Alain Marrie. LC 78-61475. (Illus.). 144p. 1979. 22.50 (ISBN 0-89352-026-8). Masson Pub.
Highman - de Limur Hypotheses. Arthur Highman & Charles De Limur. LC 79-28660. (Illus.). 196p. 1980. 14.95 (ISBN 0-88229-702-3). Nelson-Hall.
Highway & the City. Lewis Mumford. LC 80-22641. viii, 246p. 1981. Repr. of 1953 ed. lib. bdg. 25.00x (ISBN 0-313-22747-0, MUHC). Greenwood.
Highway Drainage Guidelines, 6 vols. 1973. Set. pap. 5.00 o.p. (ISBN 0-686-24169-X, HDG-1-4). AASHTO.
Highway Engineering. Robert Ashworth. 1966. pap. text ed. 18.50x o.p. (ISBN 0-435-72302-2). Heinemann Ed.
Highway Engineering. 4th ed. P. H. Wright & Radnor J. Poquette. LC 78-13643. 1979. text ed. 30.95 (ISBN 0-471-07260-5); solutions manual avail. (ISBN 0-471-05981-1). Wiley.
Highway Holidays: Reading Lab 1 & 2, 2 pts. (gr. 1-6). 1976. pap. text ed. 3.54 ea., write for additional price info. Bowmar-Noble.
Highway Materials, Soils & Concretes. Atkins. (Illus.). 1980. text ed. 24.95 (ISBN 0-8359-2828-4). Reston.
Highway of God. H. R. MacIntosh. (Scholar As Preacher Ser.). 263p. Repr. of 1931 ed. text ed. 7.75 (ISBN 0-567-04424-6). Attic Pr.
Highway Planning Techniques: The Balance of Cost & Benefit. G. R. Wells. 150p. 1971. 35.00x (ISBN 0-85264-196-6, Pub. by Griffin England). State Mutual Bk.
Highway to the Sky: "The Frank O'Hara Award Series". Michael Brownstein. LC 79-93499. (Full Court Rebound Bk.). 1978. pap. 6.00 (ISBN 0-231-03339-7). Full Court NY.
Highwayman No. One: Society of the Dispossessed. Raymond Foxall. pap. 1.25 (ISBN 0-451-07216-2, Y7216, Sig). NAL.
Highways & the Environment. Institute of Civil Engineers, UK. 1980. pap. 15.00x (ISBN 0-7277-0065-0, Pub. by Telford England). State Mutual Bk.
Hijacked. J. M. Marks. (Alpha Books). (Illus.). 96p. (Orig.). 1979. pap. 2.25x (ISBN 0-19-424212-9). Oxford U Pr.
Hijaz Railroad. William Ochsenwald. LC 80-10505. 1980. 14.95x (ISBN 0-8139-0825-6). U Pr of Va.
Hijo De Paz. Tr. by Don Richardson. (Spanish Bks.). (Span.). 1977. 2.45 (ISBN 0-8297-0572-4). Life Pubs Intl.
Hijo Prodigo y Otros Dramas. Dominguez & Lemus. 1977. pap. 0.75 (ISBN 0-311-07602-5). Casa Bautista.
Hiker's Bible. Robert Elman. LC 74-175411. 160p. 1973. pap. 2.50 o.p. (ISBN 0-385-04551-4). Doubleday.
Hiker's Guide to Glacier National Park. Dick Nelson & Sharon Nelson. (Illus.). 112p. (Orig.). 1978. pap. 5.95 (ISBN 0-915030-24-1). Tecolote Pr.
Hikers' Guide to the Smokies. Dick Murlless & Constance Stallings. LC 72-83981. (Totebook Ser.). (Illus.). 374p. 1973. pap. 7.95 (ISBN 0-87156-068-2); Hiker's Map of the Smokies 1.95 (ISBN 0-87156-095-X). Sierra.
Hikes to Abandoned Homesites in Shenandoah National Park. Jack Reeder & Carolyn Reeder. LC 80-81761. 72p. (Orig.). 1980. pap. write for info. o.p. (ISBN 0-915746-13-1). Potomac Appalach.
Hiking. Boy Scouts Of America. LC 19-600. (Illus.). 36p. (gr. 6-12). 1962. pap. 0.70x (ISBN 0-8395-3380-2, 3380). BSA.
Hiking & Exploring. Paul Neimark. (Wilderness World Ser.). (Illus.). 64p. (gr. 3 up). 1981. PLB 9.25 (ISBN 0-516-02453-1). Childrens.
Hiking Back to Health. Calvin Rutstrum. LC 80-19803. (Illus.). 136p. (Orig.). 1980. pap. 5.95 (ISBN 0-934802-06-8). Ind Camp Supply.
Hiking Cape Cod. John H. Mitchell & Whit Griswold. LC 77-93759. (Illus.). 192p. 1978. lib. bdg. 9.25 o.p. (ISBN 0-914788-04-3). East Woods.
Hiking Hawaii. Robert Smith. Ed. by Thomas Winnett. LC 79-93247. (Wilderness Press Trail Guide Ser.). (Illus.). 112p. (Orig.). 1981. write for info. (ISBN 0-89997-000-1). Wilderness Pr.
Hiking Oahu. 2nd ed. Robert Smith. LC 80-53464. 122p. 1980. pap. 4.95 (ISBN 0-89997-006-0). Wilderness Pr.
Hiking Skill Book. (Illus.). 1977. pap. 0.30x tchrs' guide (ISBN 0-8395-6589-5). BSA.
Hiking the Back Country. Jackie J. Maughan & Ann Puddicombe. 224p. (Orig.). 1981. pap. 9.95 (ISBN 0-8117-2170-1). Stackpole.
Hiking the Bigfoot Country: Exploring the Wildlands of Northern California & Southern Oregon. John Hart. LC 75-1149. (Totebook Ser). (Illus.). 398p. 1975. pap. 8.95 (ISBN 0-87156-127-1). Sierra.
Hiking the Grand Canyon & Havasupai. Larry A. Morris. (Illus.). 96p. 1981. pap. 4.95 (ISBN 0-89404-053-7). Aztex.
Hiking the Yellowstone Backcountry. Orville E. Bach, Jr. LC 72-96121. (Totebook Ser.). (Illus.). 240p. 1973. pap. 7.95 (ISBN 0-87156-078-X). Sierra.
Hiking Trails of Southern Idaho. Sheldon Bluestein. LC 79-52543. (Illus.). 235p. (Orig.). 1981. pap. 7.95 (ISBN 0-87004-280-7). Caxton.
Hiking Trails of the San Juans. Paul Pixler. (Illus.). 120p. (Orig.). 1981. pap. 5.95 (ISBN 0-87108-579-8). Pruett.
Hiking Virginia's National Forests. Karin Wuertz-Schaefer. LC 77-70414. (Illus.). 204p. 1977. lib. bdg. 10.25 (ISBN 0-914788-05-1). East Woods.
Hilarious Adventures of Paddington. pap. 6.25 boxed set (ISBN 0-440-43668-0). Dell.
Hilarious Saints. Albert Shiphorst. 1981. 5.75 (ISBN 0-8062-1640-9). Carlton.
Hilbert's Papers on Invariant Theory. D. Hilbert et al. LC 78-17596. (LIE Groups: History Frontiers & Applications Ser.: No. 8). 1978. 35.00 (ISBN 0-915692-26-0). Math Sci Pr.
Hilbert's Third Problem. Vladimir G. Boltyanskiy. LC 77-19011. (Scripta Mathematics Ser.). 1978. 19.95 (ISBN 0-470-26289-3). Halsted Pr.
Hilda, the Hen Who Wouldn't Give up. Hilda Tomlinson. LC 79-3764. (Illus.). 96p. (gr. 1-5). 1980. Repr. of 1967 ed. 5.95 (ISBN 0-15-234455-1, HJ). HarBraceJ.
Hildilid's Night. Cheli D. Ryan. LC 75-146627. (Illus.). (gr. k-3). 1971. 4.50g o.s.i. (ISBN 0-02-777990-4). Macmillan.
Hilgard & Marquis' Conditioning & Learning. 2nd ed. Ed. by Gregory A. Kimble. 1961. 21.95 (ISBN 0-13-388876-2). P-H.
Hiligaynon Reference Grammar. E. P. Wolfenden. Ed. by Howard P. McKaughan. LC 79-152473. (PALI Language Texts: Philippines). (Orig.). 1971. pap. text ed. 6.00x o.p. (ISBN 0-87022-867-6). U Pr of Hawaii.
Hill-Caves of Yucatan: A Search for Evidence of Man's Antiquity in the Caverns of Central America. Henry C. Mercer. LC 75-12599. (Speleologia Ser). (Illus.). 256p. 1975. 11.95 (ISBN 0-914264-04-4); pap. 5.50 o.p. (ISBN 0-914264-05-2). Zephyrus Pr.
Hill Country: Stories About Hunting & Fishing & Dogs & Guns & Such. Gene Hill. 1978. 11.95 (ISBN 0-87690-297-2). Dutton.
Hill Country Women. Steven Schwartzman. (Illus., Orig.). 1980. pap. 9.00 (ISBN 0-937710-02-4). SunShine.
Hill Farms & Padi Fields: Life in Mainland Southeast Asia. Robbins Burling. (Illus., Orig.). 1965. pap. 2.95 o.p. (ISBN 0-13-388926-2). P-H.
Hill-Forts of Britain. A. H. Hogg. 1979. 29.95x (ISBN 0-8464-0100-2). Beekman Pubs.
Hill Housing: A Guide to Design & Construction. Derek Abbott & Kimball Pollit. 304p. 1981. 34.50 (ISBN 0-8230-7259-2, Whitney Lib). Watson-Guptill.
Hill of Pains. Gilbert Parker. 1976. lib. bdg. 9.95x (ISBN 0-89968-082-8). Lightyear.
Hill of Summer. Allen Drury. LC 80-1849. 504p. 1981. 14.95 (ISBN 0-385-00234-3). Doubleday.
Hill of the Dead. Andrew Quiller. LC 80-71033. (Gladiators Ser.). Orig. Title: Eagles: the Hill of the Dead. 128p. 1981. pap. 2.95 (ISBN 0-87754-226-0). Chelsea Hse.
Hill of the Dragon: An Enquiry into the Nature of Dragon Legends. Paul Newman. (Illus.). 275p. 1980. 18.50x (ISBN 0-8476-6228-4). Rowman.
Hill Shepherd. Edward Hart. 1977. 13.50 (ISBN 0-7153-7483-4). David & Charles.
Hill-Shuler Local Faunas of the Upper Trinity River, Dallas & Denton Counties, Texas. B. H. Slaughter et al. (Illus.). 75p. 1962. 2.50 (RI 48). Bur Econ Geology.
Hill Station & Other Stories. Nirmal Varma. (Writers Workshop Greenbird Book Ser.). 115p. 1975. 14.00 (ISBN 0-88253-560-9); pap. text ed. 4.80 (ISBN 0-88253-559-5). Ind-US Inc.
Hillary & Tenzing: Conquerors of Mt. Everest. Julian May. LC 72-85045. 40p. (gr. 2-5). 1972. PLB 5.90 (ISBN 0-87191-219-8). Creative Ed.
Hillel's Calendar. Mamie G. Gamoran. (Illus.). (gr. 1-3). 1960. text ed. 3.25 o.p. (ISBN 0-685-20740-4, 101610). UAHC.
Hills Aren't Black: Poetry of the Black Hills. Larry C. Nelson. (Illus.). 48p. (Orig.). 1980. pap. 3.00 (ISBN 0-917624-20-3). Lame Johnny.
Hills Beyond. Thomas Wolfe. 1941. 12.50 o.s.i. (ISBN 0-06-014700-8, HarpT). Har-Row.
Hills Beyond the Hills. 2nd ed. 6.95 o.p. (ISBN 0-932052-05-3). North Country.
Hills End. new ed. Ivan Southall. LC 63-15002. 192p. (gr. 6-8). 1974. 5.95g o.s.i. (ISBN 0-02-786120-1). Macmillan.
Hill's Equation. Wilhelm Magnus & Stanley Winkler. LC 78-74114. 1979. pap. text ed. 3.00 (ISBN 0-486-63738-7). Dover.
Hills of Home. Amy S. Fraser. (Illus.). 250p. 1973. 15.00 (ISBN 0-7100-7414-X). Routledge & Kegan.
Hillside Strangler: A Murderer's Mind. Ted Schwarz. LC 80-2435. 264p. 1981. 12.95 (ISBN 0-385-17337-7). Doubleday.
Hillslope Analysis. Ian Statham & Brian Finlayson. LC 80-40564. (Sources & Methods in Geography Ser.). 176p. 1980. pap. text ed. 8.95 (ISBN 0-408-10622-0). Butterworths.
Hillslope Form & Process. M. A. Carson & M. J. Kirkby. (Cambridge Geographical Studies). 49.50 (ISBN 0-521-08234-X). Cambridge U Pr.
Hillslope Hydrology. Ed. by M. J. Kirkby. LC 77-2669. (Landscape Systems-A Ser. in Geomorphology). 1978. 63.90 (ISBN 0-471-99510-X, Pub. by Wiley-Interscience). Wiley.
Hilltop. Emory Smith. 1977. pap. 2.95 (ISBN 0-918784-16-6). Legacy Pub Co.
Hilt of the Sword: The Career of Peyton C. March. Edward M. Coffman. (Illus.). 1966. 25.00 (ISBN 0-299-03910-2). U of Wis Pr.
Hilter's Spanish Legion: The Blue Division in Russia. Gerald R. Kleinfeld & Lewis A. Tambs. LC 78-15677. (Illus.). 446p. 1979. 25.95 (ISBN 0-8093-0865-7). S Ill U Pr.
Himalayan Confessions. Georges Bettembourg & Michael Brame. 12.95 (ISBN 0-932998-05-4). Noit Amrofer.
Himalayan Pilgrimage: A Study of Tibetan Religion. David Snellgrove. (Illus.). 326p. (Orig.). 1981. pap. 12.50 (ISBN 0-87773-720-7). Great Eastern.
Himalayas. Nigel Nicolson. (World's Wild Places Ser.). (Illus.). 1975. 13.95 (ISBN 0-8094-2021-X). Time-Life.
Himalayas. Nigel Nicolson. (World's Wild Places Ser.). (Illus.). 1978. lib. bdg. 11.97 (ISBN 0-686-51019-4). Silver.
Himnos De Gloria. 150p. pap. 0.75. Faith Pub Hse.
Himnos De Gloria y Triunfo. (Spanish Bks.). 1977. 3.75 (ISBN 0-8297-0567-8). Life Pubs Intl.
Himnos De Gloria y Triunfo; Sin Musica. (Spanish Bks.). 1977. 1.40 (ISBN 0-8297-0568-6). Life Pubs Intl.
Himnos De Juan Romero. Tr. by Juan Romero. (Spanish Bks.). (Span.). 1978. 1.60 (ISBN 0-8297-0878-2). Life Pubs Intl.
Himnos de la Vida Cristiana. Tr. by Ellen Eck from Eng. 1980. write for info. (ISBN 0-87509-277-2); pap. write for info. (ISBN 0-87509-275-6). Chr Pubns.
Hind Swaraj, or Indian Home Rule. Mohandas K. Gandhi. 110p. (Orig.). 1981. pap. 1.50 (ISBN 0-934676-25-9). Greenlf Bks.
Hinderers. Richard Thrift. LC 78-51481. 1978. 10.95 (ISBN 0-9604520-0-1). R Thrift.

Hindi-English - English-Hindi Illustrated Dictionary, 2 vols. Ed. by R. C. Pathak. (Illus.). 1978. Set. 25.00 (ISBN 0-686-68936-4). Vol. 1, Hindi-Eng., 1512pp. Vol. 2. Eng.-Hindi, 1432pp. Heinman.
Hindi-English Dictionary. small ed. 15.00 (ISBN 0-87557-033-X); large ed. 19.50 (ISBN 0-685-59369-X). Saphrograph.
Hindi English Dictionary. R. C. Pathak. 1979. 11.00 (ISBN 0-89744-969-X). Auromere.
Hindi on Trial. S. Dwivedi. 250p. 1980. text ed. 25.00x (ISBN 0-7069-1210-1, Pub by Vikas India). Advent Bk.
Hindi Short Stories. Ed. by Shrawan Kumar & Prabhar Machwe. Tr. by Shrawan Kumar & Prabhar Machwe. 175p. 1970. pap. 1.80 (ISBN 0-88253-053-4). Ind-US Inc.
Hindi Structures: Intermediate Level. Peter E. Hook. LC 79-53527. (Michigan Papers on South & Southeast Asia: No. 16). (Illus.). 338p. (Orig.). 1979. pap. 8.50x (ISBN 0-89148-016-1). Ctr S&SE Asian.
Hindsight. Charlotte Woolf. Ed. by Dennis Campbell. 312p. 1981. 20.00 (ISBN 0-89182-035-3). Charles River Bks.
Hindu Conception of the Deity. B. Kumarappa. 1979. text ed. 17.50x (ISBN 0-391-01848-5). Humanities.
Hindu Epics, Myths & Legends in Popular Illustrations. Vassilis G. Vitsaxis. (Illus.). 1978. 10.95x (ISBN 0-19-560971-9). Oxford U Pr.
Hindu Intellectual Tradition. P. Bowes. 1977. 12.50 (ISBN 0-8364-0121-2). South Asia Bks.
Hindu Interpretation of the Hand & Its Portents As Practiced by the Palmists of India. Satis B. Day & Stacey B. Day. LC 73-85296. 5.50 (ISBN 0-912922-25-7); pap. 2.50 (ISBN 0-912922-25-7). U of Minn Bell.
Hindu Moral Life & Action. Radhakrishnan. 1980. text ed. write for info. (ISBN 0-391-02011-0). Humanities.
Hindu-Muslim Relations in Bengal, 1905-1947. Hossainur Rahman. 1977. text ed. 12.50 (ISBN 0-210-40605-4). Asia.
Hindu Myths. Tr. by Wendy O'Flaherty. (Classics Ser). 360p. 1975. pap. 3.50 (ISBN 0-14-044306-1). Penguin.
Hindu Omens. C. D. Bijalwan. 176p. 1980. 8.95x (ISBN 0-89955-321-4, Pub. by Interprint India). Intl Schol Bk Serv.
Hindu Places of Pilgrimage in India: A Study in Cultural Geography. Surinder M. Bhardwaj. LC 73-174454. (Illus.). 1973. 24.50x (ISBN 0-520-02135-5). U of Cal Pr.
Hindu Polytheism. Alain Danielou. (Bollingen Ser.: Vol. 73). 1964. 20.00 o.p. (ISBN 0-691-09745-3). Princeton U Pr.
Hindu Psychology: Its Meaning for the West. Swami Akhilananda. 1971. Repr. of 1948 ed. 20.00 (ISBN 0-7100-1006-0). Routledge & Kegan.
Hindu Quest for the Perfection of Man. Troy W. Organ. LC 73-81450. 1970. 14.00 o.p. (ISBN 0-8214-0066-5). Ohio U Pr.
Hindu Quest for the Perfection of Man. Troy W. Organ. LC 73-81450. x, 439p. 1981. pap. 10.00x (ISBN 0-8214-0575-6). Ohio U Pr.
Hindu Religious Tradition. Thomas Hopkins. (The Religious Life of Man Ser). 1971. pap. text ed. 7.95x (ISBN 0-8221-0022-3). Dickenson.
Hindu Religious Tradition: A Philosophical Approach. Pratima Bowes. 1978. 24.00 (ISBN 0-7100-8668-7). Routledge & Kegan.
Hindu Scriptural Value System & the Economic Development of India. Arvind Sharma. x, 113p. 1980. text ed. 15.00x (ISBN 0-86590-004-3). Apt Bks.
Hindu Scriptures. Ed. by R. C. Zaehner. 1976. 8.95x (Evman); pap. 5.95 (Evman). Dutton.
Hindu Sound. William Corlett & John Moore. LC 79-15815. (Questions Ser.). 1980. 8.95 (ISBN 0-87888-151-4). Bradbury Pr.
Hindu View of Life. S. Radhakrishnan. (Unwin Paperbacks Ser.). 92p. 1980. pap. 4.95 (ISBN 0-04-294045-1, 9048). Allen Unwin.
Hinduism. A. C. Bouquet. 1949. pap. text ed. 5.25x (ISBN 0-09-030672-4, Hutchinson U Lib). Humanities.
Hinduism. I. G. Edmonds. (First Bks.). (Illus.). (gr. 4 up). 1979. PLB 6.45 s&l (ISBN 0-531-02943-3). Watts.
Hinduism. Ed. by Louis Renou. LC 61-15496. (Great Religions of Modern Man Ser). 1961. 8.95 o.s.i. (ISBN 0-8076-0164-0). Braziller.
Hinduism. Robert C. Zaehner. 1962. pap. 4.95 (ISBN 0-19-500383-7, GB172, GB). Oxford U Pr.
Hinduism: A Religion to Live by. Nirad C. Chaudhuri. 352p. 1980. pap. 4.95 (ISBN 0-19-520221-X, GB 612). Oxford U Pr.
Hinduism: Religion & Way of Life. Satyavrata Patel. 165p. 1980. text ed. 21.00x (ISBN 0-8426-1661-6). Verry.
Hindus of the Himalayas: Ethnography & Change. 2nd ed. Gerald D. Berreman. LC 73-156468. (Center for South & Southeast Asia Studies, UC Berkeley). 1972. 24.50x (ISBN 0-520-01423-5); pap. 6.95x (ISBN 0-520-02035-9, CAMPUS66). U of Cal Pr.
Hindustan Under Free Lances: Seventeen Seventy to Eighteen Twenty. H. G. Keene. (Illus.). 238p. 1972. Repr. of 1907 ed. 20.00x (ISBN 0-686-28319-8, Pub. by Irish Academic Pr). Biblio Dist.
Hindustan Yearbook, 1979. 47th ed. Ed. by S. Sarkar. 180p. 1979. plastic cover 12.50x (ISBN 0-8002-2212-1). Intl Pubns Serv.
Hines & Allied Families. Benjamin M. Hines. LC 80-67479. 360p. 1981. 25.00 (ISBN 0-8059-2748-4). Dorrance.
Hints & Tips for Plastic Modelers. Ed. by Burr Angle. (Illus.). 1980. pap. 3.95 (ISBN 0-89024-546-0). Kalmbach.
Hints for Ordinary Mathematics. L. Harwood Clarke. 1971. pap. text ed. 2.95x o.p. (ISBN 0-435-50212-3). Heinemann Ed.
Hints on Driving. C. Morley Knight. (Illus.). 12.25 (ISBN 0-85131-040-0, Dist. by Sporting Book Center). J A Allen.
Hints on Public Architecture. Robert D. Owen. (Architecture & Decorative Art Ser.). (Illus.). 1978. Repr. of 1849 ed. lib. bdg. 59.50 (ISBN 0-306-77545-X). Da Capo.
Hints on Public Architecture. Robert D. Owen. LC 77-17509. (Illus.). 119p. 1978. Repr. of 1849 ed. 49.50x (ISBN 0-87474-736-8). Smithsonian.
Hints to Philanthropists. W. Davis. 176p. 1971. Repr. of 1821 ed. 20.00x (ISBN 0-7165-1564-4, Pub. by Irish Academic Pr Ireland). Biblio Dist.
Hints Toward a Select & Descriptive Bibliography of Education. G. Stanley Hall & John M. Mansfield. LC 72-10907. xx, 332p. 1973. Repr. of 1886 ed. 24.00 (ISBN 0-8103-3176-4). Gale.
Hip Disorders in Children. G. C. Lloyd-Roberts & A. H. Ratliff. (Postgraduate Orthopedics Ser.). 1978. 57.95 (ISBN 0-407-00132-8). Butterworths.
Hip Disorders in Infants & Children. Ed. by Stanley M. Chung. (Illus.). 450p. 1981. text ed. price not set (ISBN 0-8121-0706-3). Lea & Febiger.
Hip, High Protein, Low-Cal Easy Does It Cookbook. Naura Hayden. 1981. pap. price not set (ISBN 0-671-42390-8). PB.
Hip Manifestations of Systemic Disease, Vol. 90. Association of Bone & Joint Surgeons. Ed. by Marshall Urist. (Clinical Orthopaedics & Related Research Ser.). 1973. 15.00 (ISBN 0-685-34611-0). Lippincott.
Hip Pocket Guide to Planning & Evaluation: Manual & Trainers Manual. Dorothy Craig. LC 77-13388. 1978. pap. text ed. write for info. (ISBN 0-89384-024-6). Learning Concepts.
Hip Society: The Hip, 8 vols. Hip Society. Incl. Vol. 1. 1973. text ed. 25.00 (ISBN 0-8016-0019-7); Vol. 2. 1974. text ed. 35.00 (ISBN 0-8016-0020-0); Vol. 3. 332p. 1975. text ed. 39.50 (ISBN 0-8016-0035-9); Vol. 4. Ed. by C. M. Evarts. 1976. text ed. 32.50 (ISBN 0-8016-0036-7); Vol. 5. 1977. text ed. 34.50 (ISBN 0-8016-0038-3); Vol. 6. 1978. text ed. 34.50 (ISBN 0-8016-0041-3); Vol. 7. 1979. text ed. 39.50 (ISBN 0-8016-0033-2); Vol. 8. 336p. 1980. text ed. 44.50 (ISBN 0-8016-0049-9). LC 73-7515. (Illus.). Mosby.
Hiparama of the Classics. Lord Buckley. 1980. pap. 3.00 (ISBN 0-87286-120-1). City Lights.
Hippocampus. Ed. by Robert L. Isaacson & Karl H. Pribram. Incl. Vol. 1. Structure & Development. 418p. 27.50 (ISBN 0-306-37535-4); Vol. 2. Neurophysiology & Behavior. 445p. 29.50 (ISBN 0-306-37536-2). (Illus.). 1975 (Plenum Pr). Plenum Pub.
Hippodrome. Cyrus Colter. 192p. 1976. pap. 1.50 o.p. (ISBN 0-445-03122-0). Popular Lib.
Hippodrome: A Novel. Cyrus Colter. LC 72-96164. 213p. 1973. 9.95 (ISBN 0-8040-0625-3). Swallow.
Hippolyta's View: Some Christian Aspects of Shakespeare's Plays. J. A. Bryant, Jr. LC 61-6555. 256p. 1961. 12.00x (ISBN 0-8131-1057-2). U Pr of Ky.
Hippolyte Taine. Leo Weinstein. (World Authors Ser.: France: No. 139). lib. bdg. 10.95 (ISBN 0-8057-2878-3). Twayne.
Hippolytus. Euripides. Tr. by Robert Bagg. (Greek Tragedy in New Translation Ser). 96p. 1973. 10.95 (ISBN 0-19-501740-4). Oxford U Pr.
Hippolytus. Euripides. Tr. by Gilbert Murray. 1902. pap. text ed. 3.95x (ISBN 0-04-882032-6). Allen Unwin.
Hippolytus in Drama & Myth. Euripides. Tr. by Donald Sutherland. LC 60-13112. 1960. pap. 3.50x (ISBN 0-8032-5195-5, BB 103, Bison). U of Nebr Pr.
Hiram Martin Chittenden: His Public Career. Gordan B. Dodds. LC 72-91664. 232p. 1973. 14.00x (ISBN 0-8131-1283-4). U Pr of Ky.
Hiram Powers & His Ideal Sculpture. Donald M. Reynolds. LC 76-23685. (Outstanding Dissertations in the Fine Arts - American). (Illus.). 1977. Repr. of 1975 ed. lib. bdg. 63.00 (ISBN 0-8240-2720-5). Garland Pub.
Hired Heart. Pamela D'Arcy. 1978. pap. 1.75 o.p. (ISBN 0-425-03768-1, Medallion). Berkley Pub.
Hired Nose. Ronald Koertge. 1980. 2.50 (ISBN 0-917554-15-9). Maelstrom.
Hiring & Training the Disadvantaged for Public Employment. Grace Aboud. (Key Issues Ser.: No. 11). 1973. pap. 2.00 (ISBN 0-87546-202-2). NY Sch Indus Rel.
Hiroshima: A Study in the Science, Politics, & the Ethics of War. Jonathan Harris. Ed. by Richard H. Brown & Van R. Halsey. (Amherst Ser). (gr. 10-12). 1970. pap. text ed. 4.52 (ISBN 0-201-02687-2, Sch Div); tchr's manual 1.92 (ISBN 0-201-02689-9). A-W.
Hiroshima Flows Through Us. Brown Miller. LC 77-22290. 1977. pap. 2.50x o.p. (ISBN 0-916156-23-0); pap. 12.50x signed ed (ISBN 0-916156-29-X). Cherry Valley.
Hirschfeld by Hirschfeld. Al Hirschfeld. LC 79-17023. 1979. 15.00 (ISBN 0-396-07777-3). Dodd.
His & Hers: A Passage Through Middle-Age Crazies. Ric Masten & Billie B. Masten. 1978. pap. 3.95 (ISBN 0-931104-01-7). Sunflower Ink.
His Burial Too. Catherine Aird. 208p. 1980. pap. 1.95 (ISBN 0-553-13949-5). Bantam.
His Chute Didn't Open. Mary Verdick. Ed. by Thomas Mooney. (Pal Paperbacks, Pal Skills Ser.). (Illus., Orig.). (gr. 7-12). 1978. pap. text ed. 1.25 (ISBN 0-8374-6710-1). Xerox Ed Pubns.
His Day Is Marching on: Memoirs of W. E. B. DuBois. Shirley G. DuBois. LC 71-14693. 1971. 10.00 (ISBN 0-89388-156-2); pap. 5.95 (ISBN 0-89388-157-0). Okpaku Communications.
His Essays on Love, Vol. 1. Walter Trobisch et al. LC 68-57741. pap. 2.95 o.p. (ISBN 0-87784-669-3). Inter-Varsity.
His Eye Is on the Sparrow. Ethel Waters & Charles Michel. 1972. pap. 2.25 (ISBN 0-515-05287-6). Jove Pubns.
His Family. Ernest Poole. 1976. lib. bdg. 14.75x (ISBN 0-89968-100-X). Lightyear.
His Fine Wit: A Study of Thomas Love Peacock. Carl Dawson. LC 78-97050. 1970. 14.50x (ISBN 0-520-01632-7). U of Cal Pr.
His First Piano Lesson. Josie Butera. 1981. 4.75 (ISBN 0-8062-1596-8). Carlton.
His Gentle Voice. Julie Wayner. 112p. 1976. 2.95 (ISBN 0-930756-18-5, 4230-WA1). Women's Aglow.
His Guide to Evangelism. Paul E. Little et al. LC 77-72523. 1977. pap. 2.50 o.p. (ISBN 0-87784-488-7). Inter-Varsity.
HIS Guide to Life on Campus. Stephen Board et al. LC 73-75893. 128p. 1973. pap. 1.75 o.p. (ISBN 0-87784-355-4). Inter-Varsity.
His Hour. Elinor Glyn. (Barbara Cartland's Library of Love: Vol. 2). 182p. 1979. 12.95x (ISBN 0-7156-1378-2, Pub. by Duckworth England). Biblio Dist.
His Irish Connection. Andre J. Kehoe. (Illus.). 1980. 8.50 (ISBN 0-682-49575-1, Banner). Exposition.
His Last Bow. Arthur Conan Doyle. (gr. 10 up). pap. 1.95 (ISBN 0-425-04870-5, Medallion). Berkley Pub.
His Maiesties Gracious Grant & Privilege to William Braithwaite, for the Sole Printing & Publishing Musicke, His Way. LC 73-6105. (English Experience Ser.: No. 573). 1973. Repr. of 1636 ed. 3.50 (ISBN 90-221-0573-3). Walter J Johnson.
His Majesties Commission & Further Declaration Concerning the Reparation of Saint Pauls Church. LC 75-171754. (English Experience Ser.: No. 379). 1971. Repr. of 1633 ed. 7.00 (ISBN 90-221-0379-X). Walter J Johnson.
His Majesties Commission to Enquire of the Decayes of the Cathedral Church of St. Paul. LC 72-185. (English Experience Ser.: No. 355). 1971. Repr. of 1631 ed. 8.00 (ISBN 90-221-0355-2). Walter J Johnson.
His Majesties Commission Touching the Creation of Baronets. LC 70-26416. (English Experience Ser.: No. 309). 1971. Repr. of 1611 ed. 8.00 (ISBN 90-221-0309-9). Walter J Johnson.
His Majesties Declaration Concerning His Proceedings with His Subjects of Scotland. LC 70-25707. (English Experience Ser.: No. 310). 1971. Repr. of 1640 ed. 9.50 (ISBN 90-221-0310-2). Walter J Johnson.
His Majesties Declaration of the Causes Which Moved Him to Dissolve the Last Parliament. LC 79-38175. (English Experience Ser.: No. 450). 1972. Repr. of 1628 ed. 7.00 (ISBN 90-221-0450-8). Walter J Johnson.
His Majesties Proclamation in Scotland with an Explanation of the Oath & Covenant. LC 74-80216. (English Experience Ser.: No. 692). 1974. Repr. of 1639 ed. 3.50 (ISBN 90-221-0692-6). Walter J Johnson.
His Name Was Jesus. Mary A. Jones. (Illus.). 1950. pap. 2.50 o.p. (ISBN 0-528-87763-1). Rand.
His New Steam Man in Mexico; or Hot Work Among the Greasers. Electric Air Canoe; or the Search for the Valley of Diamonds. E. F. Bleiler. (Frank Reade Library: Vol. 1). 1979. lib. bdg. 44.00 (ISBN 0-8240-3540-2). Garland Pub.
His Only Son. Leopoldo Alas. Tr. by Julie Jones from Span. LC 80-20837. 240p. 1981. 22.50x (ISBN 0-8071-0759-X). La State U Pr.
His Power in You. John Killinger. LC 77-90811. 1978. 5.95 o.p. (ISBN 0-385-12717-0, Galilee). Doubleday.
His Promise. Jane Coffey. 1980. 5.95 (ISBN 0-533-04403-0). Vantage.
His Second Wife. Ernest Poole. 1976. lib. bdg. 14.25x (ISBN 0-89968-101-8). Lightyear.
His Servants Speak: Statements by Latter-day Saint Leaders on Contemporary Topics. R. Clayton Brough. LC 75-17101. 298p. 1975. 8.95 (ISBN 0-88290-054-4). Horizon Utah.
His Son: A Child of the Fifties. Bill Henderson. 1981. 12.95 (ISBN 0-393-01439-8). Norton.
His Way Out. Bernard L. Ramm. LC 73-87284. (Orig.). 1974. pap. 2.95 (ISBN 0-8307-0277-6, S282-1-27). Regal.
Hiscox Guide for Baptist Churches. 5.75 o.p. (ISBN 0-686-12410-3). Church History.
Hispanic American Periodicals Index 1978. Ed. by Barbara G. Valk. LC 75-642408. 1981. lib. bdg. price not set (ISBN 0-87903-404-1). UCLA Lat Am Ctr.
Hispanic Americans in the United States: A Union List of Periodicals & Newspapers Held by the Library of the State Historical Society of Wisconsin & the Libraries of the University of Wisconsin-Madison. Neil E. Strache & James P. Danky. LC 79-26240. 1979. pap. 2.50x (ISBN 0-87020-192-1). State Hist Soc Wis.
Hispanic Contribution to the State of Colorado. Ed. by Jose De Onis. LC 76-7014. 1976. 17.50x o.p. (ISBN 0-89158-100-6). Westview.
Hispanic Culture & Health Care: Fact, Fiction, Folklore. Ed. by Ricardo A. Martinez et al. LC 77-26985. 1978. pap. text ed. 11.50 (ISBN 0-8016-3143-2). Mosby.
Hispanic Folk Music of New Mexico & the Southwest: A Self-Portrait of the People. John D. Robb. LC 78-21392. (Illus.). 1980. 35.00 (ISBN 0-8061-1492-4). U of Okla Pr.
Hispanic Folktales from New Mexico: Narratives from the R.D. Jameson Collection. Stanley Robe. (Publications in Folklore & Mythology: No. 30). 1977. pap. 10.50x o.p. (ISBN 0-520-09570-7). U of Cal Pr.
Hispanic Heritage: A Guide to Juvenile Books About Hispanic People & Cultures. Isabel Schon. LC 80-10935. 178p. 1980. lib. bdg. 10.00 (ISBN 0-8108-1290-8). Scarecrow.
Hispanic Lace & Lacemaking. Florence L. May. 1980. 12.00 (ISBN 0-87535-048-8). Hispanic Soc.
Hispanic Society of America: Catalogue of the Library, 10 vols. 1962. Set. 810.00 (ISBN 0-87535-131-X); first supplement, 1970. 4 vols 395.00 (ISBN 0-87535-132-8). Hispanic Soc.
Hispanization of the Philippines: Spanish Aims & Filipino Responses, 1565-1700. John L. Phelan. (Illus.). 1959. 21.50x (ISBN 0-299-01810-5). U of Wis Pr.
Hispano-Arabic Poetry: A Student Anthology. James T. Monroe. LC 72-103925. 1975. 30.00x (ISBN 0-520-01692-0). U of Cal Pr.
Hispano-Arabic Strophic Poetry. Samuel M. Stern. Ed. by L. P. Harvey. 268p. 1974. text ed. 29.95x (ISBN 0-19-815735-5). Oxford U Pr.
Hispano-Classical Translations. Theodore S. Beardsley, Jr. 188p. 1970. 7.95 (ISBN 0-89192-064-1). Interbk Inc.
Hispanoamerica y Sus Razas y Civilizaciones. E. Urbanski. 1973. 15.00 (ISBN 0-88303-014-4); pap. 10.95 (ISBN 0-685-73217-7). E Torres & Sons.
Hist Whist & Other Poems for Children. Ed. by E. E. Cummings & George J. Firmage. (Illus.). 1981. 9.95 o.p. (ISBN 0-686-67746-3). Liveright.
Hist Whist & Other Poems for Children. Ed. by E. E. Cummings & George J. Firmage. (Illus.). 1981. 9.95 (ISBN 0-87140-640-3). Liveright.
Histamine & Antihistamines. Ed. by M. Schachter. LC 72-10535. 196p. 1973. text ed. 31.00 (ISBN 0-08-016390-4). Pergamon.
Histamine: Mechanisms of Regulation of the Biogenic Amines Level in the Tissues with Special Reference to Histamine. Ed. by C. Maslinski. LC 72-95941. 370p. 1974. 32.00 (ISBN 0-12-787052-0). Acad Pr.

Histochemical Atlas of Tissue Oxidation in the Brain Stem of the Cat. Reinhard L. Friede. (Illus., Eng. & Ger.). 1961. 19.75 o.s.i. (ISBN 0-02-844860-X). Hafner.

Histochemical Technique. 2nd ed. J. D. Bancroft. 336p. 1975. 39.95 (ISBN 0-407-00033-X). Butterworths.

Histochemistry & Cell Biology of Autonomic Neurons: Sif Cells, & Paraneurons. Ed. by Olavi Eranko et al. (Advances in Biochemical Psychopharmacology: Vol. 25). 410p. 1980. text ed. 45.00 (ISBN 0-89004-495-3). Raven.

Histocompatibility Testing Nineteen Eighty, Vol. 1. Paul I. Terasaki. LC 80-36737. (Illus.). 1980. 59.00 (ISBN 0-9604606-0-8). UCLA Tissue.

Histoenzymology of the Endocrine Gland. L. Arvy. 1971. 64.00 (ISBN 0-08-015649-5). Pergamon.

Histoire. Claude Simon. Tr. by Richard Howard. LC 68-16109. 1968. 5.95 o.p. (ISBN 0-8076-0443-7). Braziller.

Histoire Abregee De la Musique et Des Musiciens. Laure Collin. (Music Reprint Series). (Fr.). 1977. Repr. of 1897 ed. lib. bdg. 29.50 (ISBN 0-306-70875-2). Da Capo.

Histoire De Calejava, ou De. Claude Gilbert. (Utopias in the Enlightenment Ser.). 332p. (Fr.). 1976. Repr. of 1700 ed. 47.50x o.p. (ISBN 0-8287-0376-0). Clearwater Pub.

Histoire De Canada, De Son Eglise et De Ses Missions. E. Ch. Brasseur De Bourbourg. (Canadiana Avant 1867: No. 4). 1968. 65.25x (ISBN 90-2796-333-9). Mouton.

Histoire de France illustree. J. Beauregard. 1968. 15.00 (ISBN 0-08-013198-0); pap. 7.00 (ISBN 0-08-013197-2). Pergamon.

Histoire De Guillaume le Conquerant: Le Duc De Normandie, Vol. 1. LC 80-2252. 1981. Repr. of 1936 ed. 39.00 (ISBN 0-404-18777-3). AMS Pr.

Histoire de la France. G. Duby. 1978. pap. text ed. 33.95 (ISBN 2-03-079951-3, 3916). Larousse.

Histoire De la Musique Des Origines a la Fin Du 14th Siecle. T. Gerold. LC 78-162869. (Music Ser). (Fr). 1971. Repr. of 1936 ed. lib. bdg. 49.00 (ISBN 0-306-70196-0). Da Capo.

Histoire de la Musique Dramatique en Frane Depuis Ses Origines Jusqua Nos Jours. Gustave Chouquet. LC 80-2265. 1981. Repr. of 1873 ed. 45.00 (ISBN 0-404-18818-4). AMS Pr.

Histoire De L'internationale Par un Bourgeois Republicain. (Commune De Paris en 1871). (Fr.). 1977. lib. bdg. 33.00x o.p. (ISBN 0-8287-0435-X); pap. text ed. 23.00x o.p. (ISBN 0-685-77011-7). Clearwater Pub.

Histoire des dictionnaires francais. G. Matore. (Langue Vivante Ser). (Fr). pap. 11.95 (ISBN 0-685-13937-9, 3625). Larousse.

Histoire Des Institutions Francaises Au Moyen Age, Publiee Sous la Direction De Ferdinand Lot et Robert Fawtier. Ed. by Ferdinand Vols. Lot. LC 80-2204. 1981. Repr. of 1957 ed. 110.00 (ISBN 0-404-18606-8). AMS Pr.

Histoire Du Canada et Des Canadiens Sous la Domination Anglaise. M. Bibaud. (Canadiana Avant 1867: No. 2). 1968. 38.25x (ISBN 90-2796-323-1). Mouton.

Histoire Du Canada Sous la Domination Francaise. M. Bibaud. (Canadiana Avant 1867: No. 3). 1968. 38.25x (ISBN 0-686-20918-4). Mouton.

Histoire Du Theatre De l'Academie Royale De Musique En France, Depuis Son Etablissement Jusqu' a Present, 2 vols. in 1. 2nd ed. Jacques B. Durey De Noinville. 1981. Repr. of 1757 ed. 47.50 (ISBN 0-404-18838-9). AMS Pr.

Histoire D'une Revanche. Ed. by Louise C. Seibert & Lester G. Crocker. (Orig., Fr.). 1963. pap. text ed. 6.95x (ISBN 0-684-41430-9, ScribC). Scribner.

Histoire Psychanalytique: Une Anthologie. Ed. by Alain Besancon. (Le Savoir Historique: No. 7). 1974. pap. 23.00x (ISBN 90-2797-326-1). Mouton.

Histoires Droles. Jean E. Peyrazat. (Illus.). 1972. pap. text ed. 2.75 (ISBN 0-88345-063-1, 18069); 2 tapes o.p. 15.00 (ISBN 0-685-59048-8, 58265); 2 cassettes 25.00 (ISBN 0-685-59049-6, 58422). Regents Pub.

Histoires et Idees. Maresa Fanelli. 1978. pap. text ed. 7.95x (ISBN 0-669-01532-6). Heath.

Histologic Variations of Meningiomas. Kepes. 1981. price not set. Masson Pub.

Histological & Cytological Typing of Neoplastic Diseases of Haematopoietic & Lymphoid Tissues. G. Mathe & A. Rappaport. (World Health Organization: International Histological Classification of Tumours Ser.). 1976. 49.50 (ISBN 92-4-176014-1, 70-0-014-20); incl. slides 132.00 (ISBN 92-4-176014-1, 70-1-014-00). Am Soc Clinical.

Histological & Histochemical Methods: Theory & Practice. K. A. Kiernan. (Illus.). 400p. Date not set. 63.01 (ISBN 0-08-024936-1); pap. 27.01 (ISBN 0-08-024935-3). Pergamon.

Histological Methods & Terminology. Frances M. Brimmer. (Orig., In Dictionary Form). 1979. pap. text ed. 14.95x (ISBN 0-934696-00-4). Mosaic Pr.

Histological Processing for the Neural Sciences. Eileen LaBossiere. (Illus.). 100p. 1976. pap. 10.75 (ISBN 0-398-03516-4). C C Thomas.

Histological Techniques. M. Gabe. Tr. by R. E. Blackith & A. Kovoor. (Illus.). 1976. 62.70 (ISBN 0-387-90162-0). Springer-Verlag.

Histological Typing of Bone Tumours. F. Schajowicz et al. (World Health Organization: International Histological Classification of Tumours Ser.). 1972. incl. slides 119.00 (ISBN 0-685-77236-5, 70-1-006-00). Am Soc Clinical.

Histological Typing of Breast Tumours. R. W. Scarff & H. Torloni. (World Health Organization: International Histological Classification of Tumours Ser.). 1977. 9.50 (ISBN 0-685-77229-2, 70-1-002-20). Am Soc Clinical.

Histological Typing of Female Genital Tract Tumours. (World Health Organization: International Histological Classification of Tumours Ser.). 1975. 66.00 (ISBN 92-4-176013-3, 70-0-013-20); incl. slides 160.50 (ISBN 92-4-176013-3, 70-0-013-00). Am Soc Clinical.

Histological Typing of Gastric Oesophageal Tumours. K. Oota. (World Health Organization: International Histological Classification of Tumours Ser.). (Illus.). 1977. text ed. 31.00 (ISBN 0-685-99115-6, 70-1-018-20); with slides 98.80 (ISBN 0-685-99116-4, 70-1-018-00). Am Soc Clinical.

Histological Typing of Intestinal Tumours. B. C. Morson. LC 70-101520. (International Histological Classification of Tumours (World Health Organization) Ser.). (Illus.). 69p. 1976. text ed. 53.00 (ISBN 92-4-176015-X); text & slides 142.00. Am Soc Clinical.

Histological Typing of Odontogenic Tumours, Jaw Cysts & Allied Lesions. J. J. Pindborg & I. R. Kramer. (World Health Organization: International Histological Classification of Tumours Ser.). 1971. incl. slides 112.50 (ISBN 0-685-77234-9, 70-1-005-00). Am Soc Clinical.

Histological Typing of Oral & Oropharyngeal Tumours. P. N. Wahl. (World Health Organization: International Histological Classification of Tumours Ser.). 1971. incl. slides 37.00 (ISBN 0-685-77232-2, 70-1-004-00). Am Soc Clinical.

Histological Typing of Ovarian Tumours. S. F. Serov & R. F. Scully. (World Health Organization: International Histological Classification of Tumours Ser.). 1973. 36.50 (ISBN 0-685-77242-X, 70-1-009-20); incl. slides 112.00 (ISBN 0-685-77243-8, 70-1-009-00). Am Soc Clinical.

Histological Typing of Salivary Gland Tumours. (World Health Organization: International Histological Classification of Tumours Ser.). 1972. 16.80 o.p. (ISBN 0-685-77238-1, 70-1-007-20). Am Soc Clinical.

Histological Typing of Skin Tumours. R. E. Ten Seldam & E. B. Helwig. (World Health Organization: International Histological Classification of Tumours Ser.). 1977. 70.00 (ISBN 92-4-176012-5, 70-1-012-20); incl. slides 158.50 (ISBN 92-4-176012-5, 70-1-012-00). Am Soc Clinical.

Histological Typing of Soft Tissue Tumours. (International Histological Classification of Tumours). 1969. incl. slides 102.00 o.p. (ISBN 0-685-77230-6, 70-1-003-00). Am Soc Clinical.

Histological Typing of Testis Tumours. F. K. Mostofi. (World Health Organization: International Histological Classification of Tumours Ser.). (Illus.). 1976. pap. text ed. 59.50 (ISBN 92-4-176016-8, 70-1-016-20); with slides 188.00 (ISBN 92-4-176016-8, 70-1-015-00). Am Soc Clinical.

Histological Typing of Thyroid Tumours. C. Hedinger. (World Health Organization: International Histological Classification of Tumours Ser.). 1974. 18.50 (ISBN 92-4-176011-7, 70-1-011-20); incl. slides 48.50 (ISBN 0-685-77247-0, 70-1-011-00). Am Soc Clinical.

Histological Typing of Tumors of the Liver, Biliary Tract & Pancreas. J. B. Gibson. (World Health Organization: International Histological Classification of Tumours Ser.). (Illus.). 1978. text ed. 40.00 (ISBN 92-4-176020-6, 70-0-020-20); text & slides 122.00 (ISBN 0-685-96476-0, 70-1-020-00). Am Soc Clinical.

Histological Typing of Upper Respiratory Tract Tumors. K. Shanmugaratnam. (World Health Organization: International Histological Classification of Tumours Ser.). (Illus.). 1978. text ed. 59.50 (ISBN 92-4-176019-2, 70-1-019-20); text & slides 182.00 (ISBN 0-685-96477-9, 70-1-019-00). Am Soc Clinical.

Histological Typing of Urinary Bladder Tumours. (World Health Organization: International Histological Classification of Tumours Ser.). 1973. 22.50 (ISBN 0-685-77244-6, 70-1-010-20); incl. slides 59.50 (ISBN 0-685-77245-4, 70-1-010-00). Am Soc Clinical.

Histology. 2nd ed. Ed. by Peter S. Amenta. (Medical Outline Ser.). 1978. spiral bdg. 10.75 (ISBN 0-87488-662-7). Med Exam.

Histology. 8th ed. Arthur W. Ham & David H. Cormack. LC 79-13185. 1979. text ed. 39.50 (ISBN 0-397-52089-1). Lippincott.

Histology. Thomas S. Leeson & C. Roland Leeson. 1981. text ed. price not set (ISBN 0-7216-5704-4). Saunders.

Histology & Cytology: Functional Medical Laboratory Manual. Stanley L. Lamberg & Robert Rothstein. (Illus.). 1978. lab. manual 10.50 (ISBN 0-87055-272-4). AVI.

Histology & Embryology Notes for Dental Assistants & Dental Hygienists. Alfredo R. Fonts. 1980. pap. text ed. 8.50 (ISBN 0-89669-029-6). Collegium Bk Pubs.

Histology & Histopathology of the Nervous System, 2 vols. Webb Haymaker & Raymond D. Adams. (Illus.). 3520p. 1980. Set. 295.00 (ISBN 0-398-03482-6). C C Thomas.

Histology & Human Microanatomy. 4th ed. Hans Elias et al. LC 78-9108. 1978. 27.50 (ISBN 0-471-04929-8, Pub. by Wiley Medical). Wiley.

Histology of the Vertebrates: A Comparative Text. Warren Andrew & Cleveland P. Hickman, Sr. LC 73-17378. 1974. text ed. 17.95 o.p. (ISBN 0-8016-0247-5). Mosby.

Histopathology of Non-Hodgkin Lymphomas: Kiel Classification. K. Lennert. (Illus.). 130p. 1981. 46.00 (ISBN 0-387-10445-3). Springer-Verlag.

Histopathology of the Bone Marrow. Arkadi M. Rywlin. LC 75-41570. (Series in Laboratory Medicine). 229p. 1976. text ed. 22.50 (ISBN 0-316-76369-1). Little.

Histoplasmosis: Proceedings. Libero E. Ajello et al. (American Lecture in Clinical Microbiology Ser.). (Illus.). 540p. 1971. 49.50 (ISBN 0-398-02216-X). C C Thomas.

Historia Constitucional De Puerto Rico, Vol. I. Jose Trias Monge. LC 79-15893. vi, 748p. (Sp.). 1980. 20.00 (ISBN 0-8477-0861-6). U of PR Pr.

Historia Da Igraja. Tr. by Lyman Hurlbut. (Portuguese Bks.). 1979. write for info. (ISBN 0-8297-0667-4). Life Pubs Intl.

Historia De la Isla De Cuba. Carlos M. Sterling & Manuel M. Sterling. (Illus.). 392p. (Span.). (gr. 12 up). 1976. pap. 8.95 (ISBN 0-88345-251-0). Regents Pub.

Historia De la Musica Teatral en Espana. Jose Subira. LC 80-2304. 1981. Repr. of 1945 ed. 27.50 (ISBN 0-404-18871-0). AMS Pr.

Historia de la Villa Imperial de Potosi, 3 vols. Bartolome Arzans de Orsua y Vela. Ed. by Gunnar Mendoza & Lewis Hanke. LC 63-13533. (Illus.). 1464p. 1965. Set. 60.00x (ISBN 0-87057-097-8, Pub. by Brown U Pr). Univ. Pr of New England.

Historia De los Bautistas Tomo I: Sus Bases y Principios. Justo C. Anderson. 1978. pap. 4.25 (ISBN 0-311-15036-5). Casa Bautista.

Historia de Maria. M. M. Brem. (Libros Arco Ser.). (Illus.). 32p. (Orig., Span.). (gr. 1-3). 1979. pap. 0.95 (ISBN 0-89922-145-9). Edit Caribe.

Historia De Puerto Rico: Siglo XIX, 6 vols. Lidio Cruz Monclava. Set. pap. 60.00 (ISBN 0-8477-0801-2). U of PR Pr.

Historia de un Amor. Justo Gonzalez. (Illus.). 168p. (Orig., Span.). 1979. pap. 3.50 (ISBN 0-89922-151-3). Edit Caribe.

Historia De una Escalera. Antonio Buero Vallejo. Ed. by Jose Sanchez. 196p. (Span.). 1955. pap. text ed. 6.95x (ISBN 0-684-41189-X, ScribC). Scribner.

Historia Del Ano 1887. 3rd ed. Lidio Cruz Monclava. 4.35 o.s.i. (ISBN 0-8477-0808-X); pap. 3.10 (ISBN 0-8477-0809-8). U of PR Pr.

Historia del Cristianismo, Tomo I. Kenneth S. Latourette. Tr. by Jaime C. Quarles & Lemuel C. Quarles. (Illus.). 1980. pap. 10.80 (ISBN 0-311-15010-1). Casa Bautista.

Historia Eclesiastica De Eusebio. Eusebio De Cesarea. Tr. by Luis M. De Cadiz. (Biblioteca Mundo Hispano de Obras Clasicas). (Span.). Date not set. pap. price not set (ISBN 0-311-15042-X, Edit Mundo). Casa Bautista.

Historia Histronica: An Historical Account of the English Stage. James Wright. Bd. with Roscius Anglicanus: An Historical Review of the Stage. John Downes. LC 70-170465. (English Stage Ser.: Vol. 38). lib. bdg. 50.00 (ISBN 0-8240-0621-6). Garland Pub.

Historia Vitae et Regni Ricardi Secundi. George B. Stow. LC 76-19937. (Haney Foundation Ser). (Orig., Latin.). 1977. 9.00x (ISBN 0-8122-7711-2). U of Pa Pr.

Historiae, 2 Vols. 3rd ed. Herodotus. Ed. by Karl Hude. (Oxford Classical Texts Ser). 1927. Vol. 1. 18.95x (ISBN 0-19-814526-8); Vol. 2. 18.95x (ISBN 0-19-814527-6). Oxford U Pr.

Historiae, 2 vols. Thucydides. Ed. by H. W. Jones. (Oxford Classical Texts Ser). 1942. Vol. 1 Bks.1-4. 18.95x (ISBN 0-19-814550-0); Vol. 2 Bks. 5-8. 18.95x (ISBN 0-19-814551-9). Oxford U Pr.

Historian & Film. Ed. by P. Smith. LC 75-19577. 235p. 1976. 24.95 (ISBN 0-521-20992-7). Cambridge U Pr.

Historian & the Believer: The Morality of Historical Knowledge & Christian Belief. Van A. Harvey. 1981. pap. price not set (ISBN 0-664-24367-3). Westminster.

Historian As Detective: Essays on Evidence. Ed. by Robin W. Winks. 1970. pap. 6.95x (ISBN 0-06-131933-3, TB1933, Torch). Har-Row.

Historian As Diplomat: Charles Kingsley Webster & the United Nations 1939-1946. P. A. Reynolds & E. J. Hughes. 198p. 1976. 36.00x (ISBN 0-85520-131-2, Pub. by Martin Robertson England). Biblio Dist.

Historian As Moralist: Reflections on the Study of Tudor England. Joel Hurstfield. (John Coffin Memorial Lectures 1974 Ser.). 37p. 1975. pap. text ed. 2.50x (ISBN 0-485-16209-1, Athlone Pr). Humanities.

Historian at Work. John Cannon. 216p. (Orig.). 1980. text ed. 25.00x (ISBN 0-04-901025-5, 2395); pap. text ed. 7.50x (ISBN 0-04-901026-3, 2396). Allen Unwin.

Historians & Eighteenth-Century Europe 1715-1789. M. S. Anderson. 1979. 37.50x (ISBN 0-19-822548-2). Oxford U Pr.

Historians & Historiography in the Italian Renaissance. Eric Cochrane. LC 80-16097. 1981. lib. bdg. 35.00x (ISBN 0-226-11152-0). U of Chicago Pr.

Historians & the Living Past: The Theory & Practice of Historical Study. Allan J. Lichtman & Valerie French. LC 77-86035. 1978. pap. text ed. 8.95x (ISBN 0-88295-773-2). AHM Pub.

Historian's Approach to Religion. 2nd ed. Arnold J. Toynbee. 1979. 19.95 (ISBN 0-19-215260-2). Oxford U Pr.

Historians at Work, Vol. 1. Ed. by Peter Gay & Gerald J. Cavanaugh. LC 75-123930. 1972. 20.00 o.s.i. (ISBN 0-06-011473-8, HarpT). Har-Row.

Historians at Work, Vol. 2. Ed. by Peter Gay & Victor G. Wexler. LC 75-123930. 1972. 20.00 o.s.i. (ISBN 0-06-011472-X, HarpT). Har-Row.

Historians at Work, Vol. 3. Ed. by Peter Gay & Victor G. Wexler. LC 75-123930. 1975. 20.00 o.s.i. (ISBN 0-06-011474-6, HarpT). Har-Row.

Historians at Work, Vol. 4. Ed. by Peter Gay & Gerald J. Cavanaugh. LC 75-123930. 1975. 20.00 o.s.i. (ISBN 0-06-011476-2, HarpT). Har-Row.

Historian's Fallacies. David Fischer. LC 69-15583. 1970. 10.00 o.s.i. (ISBN 0-06-050041-7, HarpT). Har-Row.

Historian's Handbook. Helen J. Poulton & Marguerite S. Howland. LC 71-165774. 300p. 1972. 15.95x o.p. (ISBN 0-8061-0985-8); pap. 7.95x (ISBN 0-8061-1009-0). U of Okla Pr.

Historian's Handbook: A Key to the Study & Writing of History. 2nd ed. Wood Gray et al. (Orig.). 1964. pap. text ed. 3.95 (ISBN 0-395-04537-1, 3-19750). HM.

Historians in the Middle Ages. Beryl Smalley. 1975. lib. rep. ed. 20.00x o.p. (ISBN 0-684-15879-5, ScribT). Scribner.

Historian's Introduction to Early American Music. Richard Crawford. (Illus.). 1980. pap. 4.00 (ISBN 0-912296-44-5, Dist. by U Pr of Va). Am Antiquarian.

Historians on the Homefront: American Propagandists for the Great War. George T. Blakey. LC 79-132825. 176p. 1970. 9.50x (ISBN 0-8131-1236-2). U Pr of Ky.

Historias Biblicas Favoritas. Ethel Barrett. Ed. by Benjamin Mercado. Tr. by Virginia P. De Lobo from Eng. 103p. (Span.). (gr. 3). 1979. pap. 1.80 (ISBN 0-8297-0871-5). Vida Pubs.

Historias Biblicas Para Ninos, Vol. 1. Ethel Barrett. Ed. by Benjamin Mercado. Tr. by Virginia P. De Lobo from Eng. 117p. (Span.). (gr. 3). 1979. pap. text ed. 2.10 (ISBN 0-8297-0872-3). Vida Pubs.

Historias Extranas de Brujeria. Roger Elwood. Tr. by George Lockward from Eng. Orig. Title: Strange Things Are Happening. 112p. (Orig., Span.). 1974. pap. 1.50 (ISBN 0-89922-028-2). Edit Caribe.

Historias Que Jesus Conto. Margaret Ralph. (Serie Jirafa). Orig. Title: Stories Jesus Told. 1979. 2.95 (ISBN 0-311-38537-0, Edit Mundo). Casa Bautista.

Historic Alphabets & Initials. Carol Grafton. (Dover Pictorial Archive Ser.). (Illus.). 1977. pap. 5.00 (ISBN 0-486-23480-0). Dover.

Historic Alpine Tunnel. Dow Helmers. (Illus.). 208p. 1978. 15.00 (ISBN 0-937080-02-0); pap. 8.50 (ISBN 0-937080-03-9). Century One.

Historic America Guide. 1978. pap. 6.95 o.p. (ISBN 0-528-84173-4). Rand.

Historic American Buildings Survey, Virginia Catalog: A List of Measured Drawings, Photographs, & Written Documentation in the Survey. Virginia Historic Landmarks Commission. LC 74-7402. (Illus.). 350p. 1975. 20.00x (ISBN 0-8139-0518-4); pap. 7.95x (ISBN 0-8139-0708-X). U Pr of Va.

Historic Annals of the National Academy of Design. Thomas S. Cummings. LC 71-87503. (Library of American Art). 1969. Repr. of 1865 ed. 39.50 (ISBN 0-306-71411-6). Da Capo.

Historic Bridges of Pennsylvania. W. H. Shank. 1980. 3.00 (ISBN 0-933788-17-7). Am Canal & Transport.

Historic Buildings. Colourmaster. (Travel in England Ser.). (Illus.). 64p. 1975. 7.95 (ISBN 0-85933-129-6). Transatlantic.

Historic Buildings of Centre County, Pennsylvania. Historic Restoration Project. Ed. by Gregory Ramsey. LC 79-29737. (Keystone Bks.). (Illus.). 256p. 1980. 15.00 (ISBN 0-271-00258-1). Pa St U Pr.

Historic Costume. rev. ed. Katherine Lester et al. (gr. 10-12). 1977. text ed. 12.00 (ISBN 0-87002-174-5). Bennett IL.

Historic Country Inns of California. Jim Crain. LC 77-727. 170p. 1980. pap. 5.95 (ISBN 0-87701-208-3). Chronicle Bks.

Historic Deerfield: Houses & Interiors. Samuel Chamberlain & Henry N. Flynt. Date not set. 16.95 (ISBN 0-8038-3027-0). Hastings.

Historic Devices, Badges, & War-Cries. Fanny M. Palliser. LC 68-18030. (Illus.). 1971. Repr. of 1870 ed. 26.00 (ISBN 0-8103-3381-3). Gale.

Historic Documents: Nineteen Seventy-Nine. Congressional Quarterly. Ed. by Congressional Quarterly. 1000p. 1980. 44.00 (ISBN 0-87187-197-1). Congr Quarterly.

Historic House Museums. Laurence V. Coleman. LC 71-175318. (Illus.). xii, 187p. 1973. Repr. of 1933 ed. 20.00 (ISBN 0-8103-3118-7). Gale.

Historic Houses of America Open to the Public: An American Heritage Guide. American Heritage Editors. Ed. by Beverly Da Costa. LC 79-149725. (Illus.). 320p. 1971. 6.95 (ISBN 0-686-65707-1, 22991, Pub. by Am Heritage). S&S.

Historic India. Lucille Shulberg. LC 68-22440. (Great Ages of Man Ser.). (gr. 6 up). 1968. PLB 11.97 (ISBN 0-8094-0381-1, Pub. by Time-Life). Silver.

Historic Kansas. Margaret Whittemore. 1954. pap. 5.95 (ISBN 0-686-14876-2). Flint Hills.

Historic Maps of Kentucky. Thomas D. Clark. LC 79-4003. (Illus.). 1979. 27.50 (ISBN 0-8131-0097-6). U Pr of Ky.

Historic Ninepins. John Timbs. LC 68-22057. 1969. Repr. of 1869 ed. 18.00 (ISBN 0-8103-3539-5). Gale.

Historic Note-Book. E. Cobham Brewer. LC 66-23191. 1966. Repr. of 1891 ed. 38.00 (ISBN 0-8103-0152-0). Gale.

Historic Organs in France, No.1. Ch. W. Lindow. Tr. by Homer D. Blanchard. (Little Organ Books Ser.). (Illus.). 1980. pap. 21.00 (ISBN 0-930112-03-2). Praestant.

Historic Place Names of Orange County. Don Meadows. (Illus.). 1966. 9.50 (ISBN 0-685-59751-2). Acoma Bks.

Historic Places Around the Outer Banks. Helen H. Miller. (Illus., Orig.). 1974. pap. 2.95 o.p. (ISBN 0-685-52518-X). McNally.

Historic Plane Models: Their Stories & How to Make Them. Frank Ross, Jr. LC 72-9361. (Illus.). 160p. (gr. 5-12). 1973. PLB 7.92 o.p. (ISBN 0-688-50046-3); pap. 2.95 (ISBN 0-688-45046-6). Lothrop.

Historic Pottery of the Pueblo Indians, 1600-1880. Larry Frank & Francis Harlow. LC 73-89957. (Illus.). 224p. 1975. 27.50 (ISBN 0-8212-0586-2, 365017). NYGS.

Historic Preservation. James M. Fitch. (Illus.). 448p. 1981. 24.95 (ISBN 0-07-021121-3, P&RB). McGraw.

Historic Preservation: A Guide to Information Sources. Ed. by Arnold L. Markowitz. LC 80-14313. (Art & Architecture Information Guide Ser.: Vol. 13). 220p. 1980. 30.00 (ISBN 0-8103-1460-6). Gale.

Historic Property Owner's Handbook. 2nd ed. Historic House Association of America. (Illus.). 96p. (Orig.). 1981. pap. 7.95 (ISBN 0-89133-094-1). Preservation Pr.

Historic Shreveport. Ed. by Bailey Thomson. LC 80-54715. (Illus.). 128p. (Orig.). 1980. pap. 6.95 (ISBN 0-939042-00-2). Shreveport Pub.

Historic Wisconsin Buildings: A Survey in Pioneer Architecture 1835-1870. 2nd ed. Richard W. Perrin. (Publication in History Ser.: No. 4). (Illus.). 150p. 1981. pap. 7.95. Milwaukee Pub.

Historical Account of Pharmacology to the Twentieth Century. Chauncey D. Leake. (Illus.). 224p. 1975. 16.00 (ISBN 0-398-03277-7); pap. 11.75 (ISBN 0-398-03278-5). C C Thomas.

Historical Account of the Belief in Witchcraft in Scotland. Charles K. Sharpe. LC 74-8196. 1974. Repr. of 1884 ed. 24.00 (ISBN 0-8103-3590-5). Gale.

Historical Account of the Navigable Rivers, Canals, & Railways Throughout Great Britain. Joseph Priestley. LC 67-19729. (Illus.). Repr. of 1831 ed. 32.50x (ISBN 0-678-05081-3). Kelley.

Historical Analysis: Contemporary Approaches to Clio's Craft. Richard E. Beringer. LC 77-10589. 1978. pap. text ed. 15.95 (ISBN 0-471-06996-5); pap. text ed. 12.95 o.p. (ISBN 0-686-67925-3). Wiley.

Historical & Critical Dictionary: Selections. Pierre Bayle. Tr. by Richard H. Popkin. LC 64-16703. (Orig.). 1965. pap. 11.50 (ISBN 0-672-60406-X, LLA175). Bobbs.

Historical & Cultural Dictionary of Afghanistan. M. Jamil Hanifi. LC 75-40249. (Historical & Cultural Dictionaries of Asia Ser.: No. 5). 1976. 10.00 (ISBN 0-8108-0892-7). Scarecrow.

Historical & Cultural Dictionary of Burma. Joel M. Maring & Ester G. Maring. LC 73-1477. (Historical & Cultural Dictionaries of Asia Ser.: No. 4). 1973. 10.00 (ISBN 0-8108-0596-0). Scarecrow.

Historical & Cultural Dictionary of India. George T. Kurian. LC 76-16186. (Historical & Cultural Dictionaries of Asia Ser.: No. 8). 1976. 14.50 (ISBN 0-8108-0951-6). Scarecrow.

Historical & Cultural Dictionary of Thailand. Harold E. Smith. (Historical & Cultural Dictionaries of Asia Ser.: No. 6). 1976. 10.00 (ISBN 0-8108-0926-5). Scarecrow.

Historical & Cultural Dictionary of Vietnam. Danny J. Whitfield. (Historical & Cultural Dictionaries of Asia Ser.: No. 7). 1976. 15.00 o.p. (ISBN 0-8108-0887-0). Scarecrow.

Historical & Cultural Dictionary of the Sultanate of Oman & the Emirates of Eastern Arabia. John D. Anthony. LC 76-42216. (Historical & Cultural Dictionaries of Asia Ser.: No. 9). 1976. 10.00 (ISBN 0-8108-0975-3). Scarecrow.

Historical & Patriotic Subjects. Ed. by Walter H. Rubsamen. (Ballad Opera Ser.). 1974. lib. bdg. 50.00 (ISBN 0-8240-0901-0). Garland Pub.

Historical & Pictorial Review of the 28th Division in WW II. LC 80-68725. (Divisional Ser.: No. 15). (Illus.). 204p. 1980. Repr. of 1946 ed. 25.00 (ISBN 0-89839-035-4). Battery Pr.

Historical & Semantic Study of the Term "Islam" As Seen in a Sequence of Qur'an Commentaries. Jane I. Smith. LC 75-22485. (Harvard Dissertations in Religion). 1975. 7.50 (ISBN 0-89130-020-1, 020101). Scholars Pr Ca.

Historical & Statistical Gazetteer of New York State. J. H. French. (Illus.). 782p. 1980. Repr. of 1860 ed. deluxe ed. 22.50 deluxe (ISBN 0-932334-31-8); pap. 17.50 (ISBN 0-932334-32-6). Heart of the Lakes.

Historical Archaeology: A Structural Approach in an African Culture. Peter R. Schmidt. LC 77-84758. (Contributions in Intercultural & Comparative Studies: No. 3). (Illus.). 1978. lib. bdg. 29.95 (ISBN 0-8371-9849-6, SSA/). Greenwood.

Historical Atlas of Arizona. Henry P. Walker & Don Bufkin. LC 78-58086. (Illus.). 1979. 14.95 (ISBN 0-8061-1489-4); pap. 7.95 (ISBN 0-8061-1490-8). U of Okla Pr.

Historical Atlas of California. Warren A. Beck & Ynez P. Haase. LC 74-5952. (Illus.). 240p. 1975. 12.50 (ISBN 0-8061-1211-5); pap. 7.95 (ISBN 0-8061-1212-3). U of Okla Pr.

Historical Atlas of Kansas. Homer Socolofsky & Huber Self. 1972. 11.95x (ISBN 0-8061-1022-8); pap. 7.95 (ISBN 0-8061-1032-5). U of Okla Pr.

Historical Atlas of New Mexico. Warren A. Beck & Ynez D. Haase. LC 68-31366. (Illus.). 1969. 9.95 o.p. (ISBN 0-8061-0819-3); pap. 6.95 (ISBN 0-8061-0817-7). U of Okla Pr.

Historical Atlas of the World. Oddvar Bjorklund et al. LC 64-26. (Illus.). 1972. pap. 10.00x (ISBN 0-06-490435-0). B&N.

Historical Aviation Album, Vol. XVI. Paul Matt et al. Ed. by Kenn Rust & Thomas Foxworth. (All American Ser.). (Illus.). 96p. (Orig.). 1980, pap. 10.00 (ISBN 0-911852-15-8). Hist Aviation.

Historical Background of Chemistry. Henry M. Leicester. LC 79-166426. (Illus.). 1971. pap. text ed. 3.50 (ISBN 0-486-61053-5). Dover.

Historical Background of Technology Transfer, Transportation, & Development in Japan. 39p. 1980. pap. 5.00 (ISBN 92-808-0048-5, TUNU 031, UNU). Unipub.

Historical Biogeography, Plate Tectonics, & the Changing Environment: Proceedings. Biology Colloquium, 37th, Oregon State University, 1976. Ed. by Jane Gray & Arthur J. Boucot. LC 78-31376. (Illus.). 512p. 1979. 59.75 (ISBN 0-87071-176-8). Oreg St U Pr.

Historical Biographical Dictionaries Master Index. Ed. by Barbara McNeil & Miranda C. Herbert. LC 80-10719. (Biographical Index Ser.: No. 7). 1980. 140.00 (ISBN 0-8103-1089-9). Gale.

Historical Catalogue of Printed Editions of the English Bible 1525-1961. rev. ed. Ed. by A. S. Herbert. 1968. 10.50 (ISBN 0-564-00130-9, 17066). United Bible.

Historical Changes & Related Coastal Processes, Gulf & Mainland Shorelines, Matagorda Bay Area, Texas. J. H. McGowen & J. L. Brewton. (Illus.). 72p. 1975. 6.00. Bur Econ Geology.

Historical Commentary on Arrian's History of Alexander, Vol. I: Bks. I-III. A. B. Bosworth. 416p. 1980. 89.00 (ISBN 0-19-814828-3). Oxford U Pr.

Historical Commentary on Polybius: Commentary on Books XIX-XL, Vol. 3. F. W. Walbank. 872p. 1979. text ed. 65.00x (ISBN 0-19-814011-8). Oxford U Pr.

Historical Commentary on Polybius: Vol. 1, Commentary Books I-IV, Vol. 1. F. W. Walbank. (Illus.). 804p. 1957. text ed. 49.00x (ISBN 0-19-814152-1). Oxford U Pr.

Historical Commentary on the Epistle to the Galatians. William H. Ramsay. 1978. 15.75 (ISBN 0-686-12953-9). Klock & Klock.

Historical Commentary on the Hellenica Cxyrhynchia. I. A. Bruce. (Cambridge Classical Studies). 1967. 19.95 (ISBN 0-521-04352-2). Cambridge U Pr.

Historical Commentary on Thucydides. A. W. Gomme. Incl. Vol. 1. Introduction & Commentary of Book 1. 1945. 36.95x (ISBN 0-19-814126-2); Vol. 2. The Ten Years' War, Bks. 2-3. 1956. 34.00x (ISBN 0-19-814003-7); Vol. 3. The Ten Years' War, Bks. 4-5. 1956. 28.00x (ISBN 0-19-814001-0). Oxford U Pr.

Historical Commentary on Thucydides, Volume V: Book VIII. Ed. by A. W. Gomme et al. (Illus.). 520p. 1981. 75.00 (ISBN 0-19-814198-X). Oxford U Pr.

Historical Commentary on Thucydides Vol. 4: Books 5-7 25. A. W. Gomme et al. 1970. 42.00x (ISBN 0-19-814178-5). Oxford U Pr.

Historical Development of Economic & Business Literature. Arthur H. Cole. (Kress Library of Business & Economics: No. 12). 1957. pap. 5.00x (ISBN 0-678-09907-3, Baker Lib). Kelley.

Historical Development of the Calculus. C. H. Edwards, Jr. (Illus.). 351p. 1980. 28.00 (ISBN 0-387-90436-0). Springer-Verlag.

Historical Development of the Philippine National Language. Ernest J. Frei. LC 77-86950. (Anthro Ser.). 104p. 1980. Repr. of 1959 ed. cancelled (ISBN 0-404-16710-1). AMS Pr.

Historical Dictionary of Algeria. Alf A. Heggoy & Robert R. Crout. LC 80-24126. (African Historical Dictionaries Ser.: No. 28). x, 247p. 1981. 13.50 (ISBN 0-8108-1376-9). Scarecrow.

Historical Dictionary of Argentina. Ione S. Wright & Lisa M. Nekhom. LC 78-7918. (Latin American Historical Dictionaries: No. 17). 1978. 37.50 (ISBN 0-8108-1144-8). Scarecrow.

Historical Dictionary of Bolivia. Dwight D. Heath. LC 73-172476. (Latin American Historical Dictionaries Ser.: No. 4). 1972. 12.00 (ISBN 0-8108-0451-4). Scarecrow.

Historical Dictionary of Brazil. Robert M. Levine. LC 78-10178. (Latin American Historical Dictionaries: No. 19). 1979. lib. bdg. 13.50 (ISBN 0-8108-1178-2). Scarecrow.

Historical Dictionary of Burundi. Warren Weinstein. LC 76-13594. (African Historical Dictionaries Ser.: No. 8). 1976. 18.00 (ISBN 0-8108-0962-1). Scarecrow.

Historical Dictionary of Cameroon. Victor T. Le Vine & Roger Nye. LC 74-901. (African Historical Dictionaries Ser.: No. 1). 1974. 10.00 (ISBN 0-8108-0707-6). Scarecrow.

Historical Dictionary of Chad. Samuel Decalo. LC 77-23585. (African Historical Dictionaries Ser.: No. 13). 1977. 19.50 (ISBN 0-8108-1046-8). Scarecrow.

Historical Dictionary of Chile. Salvatore Bizzarro. LC 72-3161. (Latin American Historical Dictionaries Ser.: No. 7). 1972. 10.00 (ISBN 0-8108-0497-2). Scarecrow.

Historical Dictionary of Colombia. Ed. by Robert H. Davis. LC 76-54245. (Latin American Historical Dictionaries Ser: No. 14). (Illus.). 1977. 13.50 (ISBN 0-8108-0999-0). Scarecrow.

Historical Dictionary of Costa Rica. Theodore S. Creedman. LC 77-6390. (Latin American Historical Dictionaries Ser.: No. 16). 1977. 12.00 (ISBN 0-8108-1040-9). Scarecrow.

Historical Dictionary of Dahomey. Samuel Decalo. LC 75-42168. (African Historical Dictionaries Ser.: No. 7). 1976. 11.00 (ISBN 0-8108-0833-1). Scarecrow.

Historical Dictionary of Ecuador. Albert W. Bork & Georg Maier. LC 73-11256. (Latin-American Historical Dictionaries Ser.: No. 10). 1973. 10.00 (ISBN 0-8108-0638-X). Scarecrow.

Historical Dictionary of El Salvador. Philip F. Flemion. LC 78-189546. (Latin American Historical Dictionaries Ser.: No. 5). 1972. 10.00 (ISBN 0-8108-0471-9). Scarecrow.

Historical Dictionary of Equatorial Guinea. Max Liniger-Goumaz. LC 79-15914. (African Historical Dictionaries Ser.: No. 21). 246p. 1979. 13.00 (ISBN 0-8108-1230-4). Scarecrow.

Historical Dictionary of Guatemala. rev. ed. Richard E. Moore. LC 73-2828. (Latin American Historical Dictionaries Ser.: No. 1). 1973. 10.00 (ISBN 0-8108-0604-5). Scarecrow.

Historical Dictionary of Guinea: Republic of Guinea-Conakry. Thomas E. O'Toole. LC 77-28145. (African Historical Dictionaries Ser.: No. 16). 1978. 9.50 (ISBN 0-8108-1112-X). Scarecrow.

Historical Dictionary of Haiti. Roland I. Perusse. LC 76-30264. (Latin American Historical Dictionaries Ser: No. 15). (Illus.). 1977. 10.00 (ISBN 0-8108-1006-9). Scarecrow.

Historical Dictionary of Haute Volta. Daniel M. McFarland. LC 77-14987. (African Historical Dictionaries Ser.: No. 14). (Illus.). 1978. 11.50 (ISBN 0-8108-1088-3). Scarecrow.

Historical Dictionary of Honduras. Harvey K. Meyer. LC 76-4539. (Latin American Historical Dictionaries Ser.: No. 13). 413p. 1976. 18.00 (ISBN 0-8108-0921-4). Scarecrow.

Historical Dictionary of Lesotho. Gordon Haliburton. LC 76-49550. (African Historical Dictionaries Ser.: No. 10). (Illus.). 1977. 12.00 (ISBN 0-8108-0993-1). Scarecrow.

Historical Dictionary of Mali. Ed. by Pascal J. Imperato. LC 76-55775. (African Historical Dictionaries Ser: No. 11). (Illus.). 1977. 12.00 (ISBN 0-8108-1004-2). Scarecrow.

Historical Dictionary of Morocco. William Spencer. LC 80-21328. (African Historical Dictionaries: No. 24). 195p. 1980. 11.00 (ISBN 0-8108-1362-9). Scarecrow.

Historical Dictionary of Nicaragua. Harvey K. Meyer. LC 72-2441. (Latin American Historical Dictionaries Ser.: No. 6). (Illus.). 1972. 16.50 (ISBN 0-8108-0488-3). Scarecrow.

Historical Dictionary of Niger. Samuel Decalo. LC 79-15704. (African Historical Dictionaries Ser.: No. 20). 376p. 1979. 19.00 (ISBN 0-8108-1229-0). Scarecrow.

Historical Dictionary of Panama. Basil C. Hedrick & Anne K. Hedrick. Ed. by A. Curtis Wilgus. (Latin American Historical Dictionaries Ser.: No. 2). 1970. 10.00 (ISBN 0-8108-0347-X). Scarecrow.

Historical Dictionary of Paraguay. Charles J. Kolinski. LC 72-13238. (Latin American Historical Dictionaries Ser.: No. 8). 1973. 10.00 (ISBN 0-8108-0582-0). Scarecrow.

Historical Dictionary of Peru. Marvin Alisky. LC 79-16488. (Latin American Historical Dictionaries Ser.: No. 20). 163p. 1979. 10.00 (ISBN 0-8108-1235-5). Scarecrow.

Historical Dictionary of Puerto Rico & the U.S. Virgin Islands. Kenneth R. Farr. LC 73-7603. (Latin American Historical Dictionaries Ser.: No. 9). 1973. 10.00 (ISBN 0-8108-0670-3). Scarecrow.

Historical Dictionary of Rhodesia-Zimbabwe. R. Kent Rasmussen. Ed. by A. Curtis Wilgus. LC 78-23671. (African Historical Dictionaries Ser.: No. 18). 1979. lib. bdg. 22.50 (ISBN 0-8108-1187-1). Scarecrow.

Historical Dictionary of Senegal. Lucie G. Colvin. LC 80-25466. (African Historical Dictionaries: No. 23). 355p. 1981. 17.50 (ISBN 0-8108-1369-6). Scarecrow.

Historical Dictionary of Sierra Leone. Cyril P. Foray. LC 77-3645. (African Historical Dictionaries Ser.: No. 12). 1977. 16.00 (ISBN 0-8108-1035-2). Scarecrow.

Historical Dictionary of Somalia. Margaret F. Castagno. LC 75-25681. (African Historical Dictionary Ser.: No. 6). 1975. 11.50 (ISBN 0-8108-0830-7). Scarecrow.

Historical Dictionary of Swaziland. John J. Grotpeter. LC 75-4734. (African Historical Dictionaries Ser.: No. 3). 265p. 1975. 12.00 (ISBN 0-8108-0805-6). Scarecrow.

Historical Dictionary of Tanzania. Laura S. Kurtz. LC 77-25962. (African Historical Dictionaries Ser.: No. 15). 1978. 18.00 (ISBN 0-8108-1101-4). Scarecrow.

Historical Dictionary of the Central African Republic. Pierre Kalck. Tr. by Thomas O'Toole. LC 80-21199. (African Historical Dictionaries: No. 27). 194p. 1980. 10.00 (ISBN 0-8108-1360-2). Scarecrow.

Historical Dictionary of the French & Netherlands Antilles. Albert Gastmann. LC 78-19070. (Latin American Historical Dictionaries Ser.: No. 18). 1978. lib. bdg. 10.00 (ISBN 0-8108-1153-7). Scarecrow.

Historical Dictionary of the Gambia. Harry A. Gailey. LC 75-5882. (African Historical Dictionaries Ser.: No. 4). 180p. 1975. 10.00 (ISBN 0-8108-0810-2). Scarecrow.

Historical Dictionary of the People's Republic of the Congo (Congo-Brazzaville) Virginia Thompson & Richard Adloff. LC 74-14975. (African Historical Dictionaries Ser.: No. 2). 1974. 10.00 (ISBN 0-8108-0762-9). Scarecrow.

Historical Dictionary of the Republic of Botswana. Richard P. Stevens. LC 75-16489. (African Historical Dictionaries Ser.: No. 5). 189p. 1975. 10.00 (ISBN 0-8108-0857-9). Scarecrow.

Historical Dictionary of the Republics of Guinea-Bissau & Cape Verde. Richard Lobban. LC 79-18227. (African Historical Dictionaries Ser.: No. 22). 209p. 1979. 11.00 (ISBN 0-8108-1240-1). Scarecrow.

Historical Dictionary of the Sudan. John Voll. LC 77-28798. (African Historical Dictionaries Ser.: No. 17). 1978. 10.00- (ISBN 0-8108-1115-4). Scarecrow.

Historical Dictionary of Togo. Samuel Decalo. LC 76-14926. (African Historical Dictionaries Ser.: No. 9). 261p. 1976. 12.00 (ISBN 0-8108-0942-7). Scarecrow.

Historical Dictionary of Uruguay. Jean Willis. LC 74-14630. (Latin American Historical Dictionaries Ser.: No. 11). 1974. 11.00 (ISBN 0-8108-0766-1). Scarecrow.

Historical Dictionary of Zambia. John J. Grotpeter. LC 79-342. (African Historical Dictionaries Ser.: No. 19). 1979. 18.50 (ISBN 0-8108-1207-X). Scarecrow.

Historical Dimensions of Rational Faith: The Role of History in Kant's Religious Thought. G. E. Michalson. 1977. 9.50 (ISBN 0-8191-0308-X). U Pr of Amer.

Historical Disciplines & Culture in Australasia. Ed. by John Moses. 1980. 23.50x (ISBN 0-7022-1295-4). U. of Queensland Pr.

Historical Encyclopedia of World War II. Marcel Baudot et al. Tr. by Jesse Dilson. 500p. 1980. 24.95 (ISBN 0-87196-401-5). Facts on File.

Historical Encyclopedia of World War II. Baydot. Date not set. 25.00 (ISBN 0-87196-401-5). Facts on File.

Historical Epic in France 1500-1700. David Maskell. (Oxford Modern Languages & Literature Monographs). 275p. 1974. 24.95x (ISBN 0-19-815525-5). Oxford U Pr.

Historical Essay on Modern Spain. Richard Herr. 1974. pap. 6.50x (ISBN 0-520-02534-2). U of Cal Pr.

Historical French Reader: Medieval Period. Paul Studer & E. G. Waters. 1924. 22.50x (ISBN 0-19-815327-9). Oxford U Pr.

Historical Geography of Detroit. Almon E. Parkins. LC 77-118422. 1970. Repr. of 1918 ed. 15.50 o.p. (ISBN 0-8046-1371-0). Kennikat.

Historical Geography of Europe, 450 Bc-1330 AD. N. J. Pounds. 1973. 59.50 (ISBN 0-521-08563-2); pap. 22.95x (ISBN 0-521-29126-7). Cambridge U Pr.

Historical Geography of the Ottoman Empire: From Earliest Times to the End of the Sixteenth Century. Donald E. Pitcher. (Illus.). 171p. 1972. Repr. of 1968 ed. text ed. 156.75x (ISBN 9-0040-3945-7). Humanities.

Historical Geography of Western Europe Before 1800. rev. ed. Clifford T. Smith. (Geographies for Advances Study Ser.). (Illus.). 1978. pap. text ed. 21.00x (ISBN 0-582-48986-5). Longman.

Historical Geology. 3rd ed. Carl O. Dunbar & Karl M. Waage. LC 72-89681. (Illus.). 1969. text ed. 23.95 (ISBN 0-471-22507-X). Wiley.

Historical Geology. 2nd ed. Leigh W. Mintz. (Physical Science Ser.). 1977. text ed. 20.95 (ISBN 0-675-08603-5). Merrill.

Historical Geology: The Science of a Dynamic Earth. 3rd ed. Leigh W. Mintz. (Illus.). 576p. 1981. text ed. 20.95 (ISBN 0-675-08028-2); tchr's. ed. 3.95 (ISBN 0-686-69492-9). Merrill.

Historical German Phonology & Morphology. Charles V. Russ. (History of the German Language Ser.). (Illus.). 1979. 27.00 (ISBN 0-19-815727-4). Oxford U Pr.

Historical Guide to Florence. John W. Higson, Jr. LC 72-91632. (Illus.). 1977. pap. 5.95 (ISBN 0-87663-951-1). Universe.

Historical Guide to the City of Dublin. 2nd ed. G. N. Wright. 260p. 1981. Repr. of 1825 ed. 20.00x (ISBN 0-906127-21-1, Pub. by Irish Academic Pr Ireland). Biblio Dist.

Historical Houses of America. American Heritage. pap. 4.95 (ISBN 0-686-60941-7, 24711). S&S.

Historical Interpretations, 3 vols. Gerald N. Grob & George A. Billias. Incl. Vol. 1. From Puritanism to the First Party System (ISBN 0-02-912900-1); Vol. 2. From Jacksonian Democracy to the Gilded Age. pap. text ed. o.s.i. (ISBN 0-02-912910-9); Vol. 3. From Progressivism to the Cold War. pap. text ed. o.s.i. (ISBN 0-02-912920-6). LC 67-12834. 1972. pap. text ed. 5.95 ea. Free Pr.

Historical Introduction to Library Education: Problems & Progress to 1951. Carl White. LC 75-28086. 1976. 13.50 (ISBN 0-8108-0874-9). Scarecrow.

Historical Introduction to the Economic Geography of Great Britain. Wilfred Smith & M. J. Wise. (Advanced Economic Geography Ser.). 1968. lib. bdg. 20.00x (ISBN 0-7135-1509-0). Westview.

Historical Introduction to the Philosophy of Science. John Losee. (Oxford Paperbacks University Ser.). (Illus.). 224p. (Orig.). 1972. pap. 5.95x o.p. (ISBN 0-19-888077-4). Oxford U Pr.

Historical Introduction to the Philosophy of Science. 2nd ed. John Losee. (Illus.). 256p. 1980. 14.95x (ISBN 0-19-219156-X); pap. 6.95x (ISBN 0-19-289143-X). Oxford U Pr.

Historical Introduction to the Study of Roman Law. 3rd ed. H. F. Jolowics. Ed. by B. Nicholas. LC 74-164452. 624p. 1972. 79.00 (ISBN 0-521-08253-6). Cambridge U Pr.

Historical Introduction to the Theory of Law. John W. Jones. Repr. of 1940 ed. lib. bdg. 17.50x (ISBN 0-8371-2810-2, JOTL). Greenwood.

Historical Journals: A Handbook for Writers & Reviewers. Ed. by Dale R. Steiner. 1981. price not set (ISBN 0-87436-312-8). ABC-Clio.

Historical Letters. Peter Lavrov. Tr. by James P. Scanlan. 1967. 25.00x (ISBN 0-520-01136-8). U of Cal Pr.

Historical Lights, 2 vols. 3rd ed. Charles E. Little. LC 68-27175. 1968. Repr. of 1886 ed. Set. 25.00 (ISBN 0-8103-3186-1). Gale.

Historical Linguistics. Theodora Bynon. LC 76-62588. (Cambridge Textbooks in Linguistics). (Illus.). 1977. 39.95 (ISBN 0-521-21582-X); pap. 8.95 (ISBN 0-521-29188-7). Cambridge U Pr.

Historical Manuscript Depositories in Pennsylvania. Irwin Richman. LC 65-65225. 1965. 2.50 (ISBN 0-911124-08-X). Pa Hist & Mus.

Historical Materialism & the Economics of Karl Marx. Benedetto Croce. (Social Science Classics). 1981. 19.95 (ISBN 0-87855-313-4); pap. text ed. 6.95 (ISBN 0-87855-695-8). Transaction Bks.

Historical Models & the Anticipation of the Future. Homer D. Shipman. (Illus.). 1979. deluxe ed. 47.50 (ISBN 0-930008-43-X). Inst Econ Pol.

Historical Morphology: Papers Prepared for the Conference, Held at Boszkovo, Poland, March 1978. Ed. by Jacek Fisiak. (Trends in Linguistics, Studies & Monographs: No. 17). 1980. text ed. 79.50 (ISBN 90-279-3038-4). Mouton.

Historical Narrative & Topographical Description of Louisiana & West Florida. Thomas Hutchins. Ed. by J. G. Tregle, Jr. LC 68-21657. (Floridiana Facsimile & Reprint Ser). 1968. Repr. of 1784 ed. 7.75 (ISBN 0-8130-0119-6). U Presses Fla.

Historical Novel & Other Essays. Brander Matthews. LC 68-30586. 1969. Repr. of 1901 ed. 15.00 (ISBN 0-8103-3218-3). Gale.

Historical Novel & Popular Politics in Nineteenth-Century England. Nicholas Rance. (Critical Studies Ser.). 176p. 1975. 13.50x (ISBN 0-06-495805-1). B&N.

Historical Patterns of Industrialization. Tom Kemp. LC 77-3574. (Illus.). 1978. text ed. 17.00x (ISBN 0-582-48922-9); pap. text ed. 8.95x (ISBN 0-582-48923-7). Longman.

Historical Perspective of Farm Machinery. Society of Automotive Engineers. 1980. 12.50 (ISBN 0-89883-241-1). Soc Auto Engineers.

Historical Perspectives on Homosexuality. Ed. by Salvatore J. Licata & Robert Petersen. LC 80-6262. 240p. 1981. 14.95 (ISBN 0-8128-2810-0). Stein & Day.

Historical Phonology of the Polish Language. Z. A. Stieber. (Illus.). 171p. 1973. 32.50 (ISBN 0-685-55680-8). Adler.

Historical Phraseology: Supplement to Written Arabic. Alfred F. Beeston. 1969. 12.50x (ISBN 0-521-09578-6). Cambridge U Pr.

Historical Plant Geography. Philip Stott. (Illus.). 192p. 1981. text ed. 30.00x (ISBN 0-04-580010-3, 2641-2); pap. text ed. 14.95x (ISBN 0-04-580011-1). Allen Unwin.

Historical Register for the Year 1736. Henry Fielding. Ed. by William W. Appleton. Bd. with Eurydyce Hissed. LC 67-12643. (Regents Restoration Dramas Ser). 1967. 6.50x (ISBN 0-8032-0361-6); pap. 1.65x (ISBN 0-8032-5360-5, BB 265). U of Nebr Pr.

Historical Relics Unearthed in New China. (Illus.). 1972. linen bdg. 25.00 (ISBN 0-8351-0106-1). China Bks.

Historical Research on Social Mobility. Hartmut Kaelble. Tr. by Ingrid Noakes. 1981. text ed. 22.50x (ISBN 0-231-05274-X). Columbia U Pr.

Historical Rhetoric: An Annotated Bibliography of Selected Sources in English. Ed. by Winifred B. Horner. 1980. lib. bdg. 35.00 (ISBN 0-8161-8191-8). G K Hall.

Historical Roots of Elementary Mathematics. Lucas N. H. Bunt & Phillip S. Jones. (Illus.). 352p. 1976. Ref. Ed. 16.95 (ISBN 0-13-389015-5). P-H.

Historical Sketch of General Custer. James H. Kidd. (Custer Monograph: No. 3). 1978. pap. 8.00x (ISBN 0-686-27938-7). Monroe County.

Historical Sketch of Pierre & Jean Lafitte, the Famous Smugglers of Louisiana. Charles Gayarre. pap. 4.50 wrappers (ISBN 0-685-13272-2). Jenkins.

Historical Sketch of the Cherokee. James Mooney. LC 75-20706. (Illus.). 265p. 1975. 12.50x o.p. (ISBN 0-87474-652-3); pap. 5.95x o.p. (ISBN 0-87474-653-1). Smithsonian.

Historical Sketches of the South Indian History, 4 vols. Mark Wilks & Murry Hammick. Incl. Vol. 1. 453p; Vol. 2. 397p; Vol. 3. 335p; Vol. 4. 482p. 1980. Repr. of 1817 ed. 24.50 (ISBN 0-89684-265-7, Pub. by Cosmo Pubns India). Orient Bk Dist.

Historical Society Architectural Publications: Vermont, Virginia, Washington, West Virginia, Wisconsin, Wyoming. Mary Vance. (Architecture Ser.: Bibliography A-178). 51p. 1980. pap. 5.50. Vance Biblios.

Historical Sources in Geography. Ed. by Michael Morgan & D. Briggs. (Sources & Methods in Geography Ser.). 1979. pap. 6.95 (ISBN 0-408-10609-3). Butterworths.

Historical Studies in Nursing. Ed. by M. Louise Fitzpatrick. LC 78-12192. 1978. text ed. 9.25x (ISBN 0-8077-2527-7). Tchrs Coll.

Historical Study in the West: France, Western Germany, Great Britain, the United States. Boyd C. Shafer et al. LC 68-19485. 1968. 22.00x (ISBN 0-89197-212-9); pap. text ed. 6.95x (ISBN 0-89197-213-7). Irvington.

Historical Study of African Religion. Ed. by T. O. Ranger & Isaria Kimambo. (Library Reprint Ser.). 1976. 24.75x (ISBN 0-520-03179-2). U of Cal Pr.

Historical Tales of Old Reynoldsburg: Selections from the First Five Years of the Courier. Cornelia M. Parkinson. (Illus.). 152p. (Orig.). 1980. pap. 7.50 (ISBN 0-938404-00-8). Hist Tales.

Historical Theology, 2 vols. William Cunningham. 1979. Set. 31.95; Vol. 1. (ISBN 0-85151-286-0); Vol. 2. (ISBN 0-85151-287-9). Banner of Truth.

Historical Theory of the Ruling Class. Vilfredo Pareto. (Most Meaningful Classics in World Culture Ser.). (Illus.). 1979. 49.75 (ISBN 0-89266-193-3). Am Classical Coll Pr.

Historical Tradition in the Fourth Gospel. Charles H. Dodd. 1975. 64.00 (ISBN 0-521-04847-8); pap. 14.95x (ISBN 0-521-29123-2). Cambridge U Pr.

Historical View of the Hindu Astronomy from the Earliest Dawn of That Science in India to the Present Time. John Bentley. LC 5-29507. 1970. Repr. of 1825 ed. 35.00x (ISBN 3-7648-0107-7). Intl Pubns Serv.

Historicity & Variation in Creole Studies. Ed. by Arnold R. Highfield & Albert Valdman. 210p. 1981. 14.50 (ISBN 0-89720-036-5); pap. 10.50 (ISBN 0-89720-037-3). Karoma.

Historie of Great Britannie - from the Romans First Entrance, Untill the Raigne of Egbert, the West-Saxon Prince. John Clapham. LC 74-28837. (English Experience Ser.: No. 719). 1975. Repr. of 1606 ed. 22.00 (ISBN 90-221-0719-1). Walter J Johnson.

Historie of Life & Death: With Observations Naturall & Experimentall. Francis Bacon. LC 68-54613. (English Experience Ser.: No.20). 324p. Repr. of 1638 ed. 21.00 (ISBN 90-221-0020-0). Walter J Johnson.

Historie of Man. John Banister. LC 74-26164. (English Experience Ser.: No. 122). (Illus.). 250p. 1969. Repr. of 1578 ed. 42.00 (ISBN 90-221-0122-3). Walter J Johnson.

Histories. Polybius. Ed. by E. Badian. 1966. text ed. 20.00x (ISBN 0-8290-0196-4). Irvington.

Histories & Historians. Ed. by Albert Fell. (History Today Ser). 1968. 5.00 (ISBN 0-05-001654-7); pap. 3.95 (ISBN 0-685-00927-0). Dufour.

Histories & Prophecies of Daniel. Robert D. Culver. 192p. (Orig.). 1980. pap. 4.95 (ISBN 0-88469-131-4). BMH Bks.

Histories, or Tales of Past Times. Charles Perrault. Ed. by Alison Lurie & Justin G. Schiller. LC 75-32139. (Classics of Children's Literature Ser.: 1621-1932). PLB 38.00 (ISBN 0-8240-2255-6). Garland Pub.

Historiography: A Bibliography. Lester D. Stephens. LC 75-17578. 1975. 11.00 (ISBN 0-8108-0856-0). Scarecrow.

Historiography in Modern India. R. C. Majumdar. 4.50x (ISBN 0-210-22273-5). Asia.

Historiography of Latin America: A Guide to Historical Writing, 1500-1800. A. Curtis Wilgus. 1975. 18.00 (ISBN 0-8108-0859-5). Scarecrow.

Historiography of Southern Africa. (General History of Africa Studies & Documents: No. 4). 112p. 1980. pap. 8.25 (ISBN 92-3-101775-6, U1026, UNESCO). Unipub.

Historiography of the Chinese Labor Movement. Ming K. Chan. LC 80-8323. (Bibliographical Ser.: No. 60). 1981. 35.00 (ISBN 0-8179-2601-1). Hoover Inst Pr.

History. Jack Rudman. (Undergraduate Program Field Test Ser.: UPFT-13). (Cloth bdg. avail. on request). pap. 9.95 (ISBN 0-8373-6013-7). Natl Learning.

History, a Novel. Elsa Morante. 1978. pap. 2.95 (ISBN 0-380-41889-4, 41889, Bard). Avon.

History: An Outline for the Intending Student. Ed. by Harold Perkin. (Outline Ser). 1970. cased 14.95 (ISBN 0-7100-6814-X); pap. 7.95 (ISBN 0-7100-6815-8). Routledge & Kegan.

History & Adventures of Gil Blas of Santillane. Alain R. Le Sage. LC 74-170537. (Foundations of the Novel Ser.: Vol. 27). Part 1. lib. bdg. 50.00 (ISBN 0-8240-0539-2). Garland Pub.

History & Adventures of Gil Blas of Santillane. Alain R. Le Sage. LC 71-170539. (Foundations of the Novel Ser.: Vol. 28). Part 2. lib. bdg. 50.00 (ISBN 0-8240-0540-6). Garland Pub.

History & American Society: The Essays of David Potter. David Potter. Ed. by Don E. Fehrenbacher. 448p. 1973. 15.95 (ISBN 0-19-501628-9). Oxford U Pr.

History & Bibliography of American Magazines: 1810-1820. Neal L. Edgar. LC 75-11882. 384p. 1975. 18.00 (ISBN 0-8108-0821-8). Scarecrow.

History & Bibliography of American Newspapers, 1690-1820, 2 vols. Clarence S. Brigham. LC 75-40215. (Special supplement of corrections & additions). 1976. Repr. of 1947 ed. Set. lib. bdg. 102.00x (ISBN 0-8371-8677-3, BRAN). Greenwood.

History & Crime: Implications for Criminal Justice Policy. Ed. by James A. Inciardi & Charles E. Faupel. LC 80-19532. (Focus Editions Ser.: Vol. 27). (Illus.). 288p. 1980. 18.95 (ISBN 0-8039-1410-5); pap. 9.95 (ISBN 0-8039-1411-3). Sage.

History & Criticism of the Marcan Hypothesis. Hans-Herbert Stoldt. Tr. by Donald L. Niewyk from Ger. LC 80-82572. xvi, 302p. 1980. 18.95 (ISBN 0-86554-002-0). Mercer Univ Pr.

History & Description of Roman Political Institutions. 3rd ed. Frank F. Abbott. LC 63-10766. 451p. (gr. 7 up). 1910. 10.50x (ISBN 0-8196-0117-9). Biblo.

History & Development of the Fourth Amendment to the United States Constitution. Nelson B. Lasson. LC 75-87389. (American Constitutional & Legal History Ser.). 1970. Repr. of 1937 ed. lib. bdg. 22.50 (ISBN 0-306-71532-5). Da Capo.

History & Events of the Early Nineteen Twenties. Bill Riley & Laura Leake. LC 79-56202. 1981. 8.95 (ISBN 0-533-04515-0). Vantage.

History & Future of Rice Cultivation in Hokkaido. 15p. 1980. pap. 5.00 (ISBN 92-808-0100-7, TUNU-007, UNU). Unipub.

History & Heartburn: The Saga of Australian Film, 1896-1978. Eric Reade. 353p. 1980. 40.00 (ISBN 0-8386-3082-0). Fairleigh Dickinson.

History & Human Existence: From Marx to Merleau-Ponty. James Miller. LC 78-51747. 1979. 20.00x (ISBN 0-520-03667-0). U of Cal Pr.

History & Identity. Sidney E. Mead. LC 78-26543. (American Academy of Religion. Studies in Religion: No. 19). 1979. 12.00 (ISBN 0-89130-274-3, 010019); pap. 7.50 (ISBN 0-89130-297-2). Scholars Pr Ca.

History & Law of Nursing. Ed. by Harriet Levine & Frances P. Minno. (Nursing Examination Review Books: Vol. 10). 1971. spiral bdg. 6.00 (ISBN 0-87488-510-8). Med Exam.

History & Literature of Surgery. John S. Billings. 1970. Repr. of 1895 ed. 15.00 (ISBN 0-87266-038-9). Argosy.

History & Mystery of Precious Stones. William Jones. LC 68-22031. 1968. Repr. of 1880 ed. 18.00 (ISBN 0-8103-3450-X). Gale.

History & Nature of Sociological Theory. Daniel Rossides. (Illus., LC 77-074382). 1978. text ed. 18.50 (ISBN 0-395-25059-5). HM.

History & Power of Mind. Richard Ingalese. LC 80-19897. 332p. 1980. Repr. of 1976 ed. lib. bdg. 11.95x (ISBN 0-89370-637-X). Borgo Pr.

History & Practice of Woodcarving. Frederick Oughton. (Illus.). 1976. Repr. 8.95 (ISBN 0-918036-03-8). Woodcraft Supply.

History & Present Condition of St. Domingo, 2 vols. Jonathan Brown. 1972. Repr. of 1837 ed. 65.00x (ISBN 0-7146-2704-6, F Cass Co). Biblio Dist.

History & Present State of Virginia. Robert Beverley. Ed. by Louis B. Wright. LC 68-58999. (Illus.). 366p. 1968. pap. 3.95 (ISBN 0-8139-0028-X). U Pr of Va.

History & Psychoanalysis. Saul Friedlander. Tr. by Susan Suleiman from Fr. LC 77-18524. 1978. text ed. 27.50x (ISBN 0-8419-0339-5); pap. text ed. 15.50x (ISBN 0-8419-0611-4). Holmes & Meier.

History and Religion of Israel. G. W. Anderson. (New Clarendon Bible Ser.). (Illus.). 222p. 1966. pap. 6.95x (ISBN 0-19-836915-8). Oxford U Pr.

History & Romance of the Horse. Arthur Vernon. LC 70-185379. (Illus.). xviii, 525p. 1975. Repr. of 1939 ed. 22.00 (ISBN 0-8103-3982-X). Gale.

History & Systems of Social Psychology. 2nd ed. William S. Sahakian. LC 80-2137. (Illus.). 624p. Date not set. text ed. 24.50 (ISBN 0-89116-179-1); pap. text ed. 16.95 (ISBN 0-89116-191-0). Hemisphere Pub.

History & the Homeric Iliad. Denys L. Page. (Sather Classical Lectures: Vol. 31). (Illus.). 1959. 15.75x (ISBN 0-520-03246-2). U of Cal Pr.

History & the Theology of Liberation. Enrique Dussel. Tr. by John Drury from Span. LC 75-21773. 205p. 1976. 8.95x o.p. (ISBN 0-88344-179-9). Orbis Bks.

History & Topography of Ireland. Giraldus Cambrensis. Tr. by John J. O'Meara. (Dolmen Texts: No. 4). 1980. text ed. 31.25 (ISBN 0-391-01166-9, Dolmen Pr). Humanities.

History & Trends of Professional Nursing. 8th ed. Grace L. Deloughery. LC 77-386. (Illus.). 1977. pap. 14.95 (ISBN 0-8016-1974-2). Mosby.

History & Will: Philosophical Perspectives of Mao Tse-Tung's Thought. Frederic Wakeman. 408p. 1976. pap. 7.95x (ISBN 0-520-02907-0). U of Cal Pr.

History As Neurosis: Paternalism and Machismo in Spanish America. Marvin Goldwert. LC 80-5640. 85p. 1980. lib. bdg. 12.50 (ISBN 0-8191-1226-7); pap. text ed. 6.50 (ISBN 0-8191-1227-5). U Pr of Amer.

History at a Glance: A Chronological Chart of European Civilization. Ernst C. Helmreich. LC 63-16881. (Orig.). (gr. 9 up). 1974. pap. text ed. 1.95 o.p. (ISBN 0-8120-0074-9). Barron.

History, Education, & Public Policy: Recovering the American Educational Past. Ed. by Donald R. Warren. LC 77-95251. (National Society for the Study of Education, Series on Contemp. Educ. Issues). 1978. 17.90 (ISBN 0-8211-2258-4); text ed. 16.20 ten copies (ISBN 0-685-04973-6). McCutchan.

History for the League for Industrial Rights. Walter Merrit. LC 76-120852. (Civil Liberties in Americana History Ser.). 1970. Repr. of 1925 ed. lib. bdg. 17.50 (ISBN 0-306-71961-4). Da Capo.

History from the Farm. Ed. by W. G. Hoskins. (Illus.). 1970. 6.95 o.p. (ISBN 0-571-09437-6, Pub. by Faber & Faber). Merrimack Bk Serv.

History, Guilt, & Habit. Owen Barfield. LC 79-65333. 1979. 12.50x (ISBN 0-8195-5038-8, Pub. by Wesleyan U Pr). Columbia U Pr.

History in Art. Ariane Ruskin. LC 73-5673. (Illus.). 320p. (gr. 7 up). 1974. PLB 14.90 o.p. (ISBN 0-531-01988-8). Watts.

History in Communist China. Ed. by Albert Feuerwerker. 1968. 15.00x o.p. (ISBN 0-262-06021-3); pap. 3.95 o.p. (ISBN 0-262-56006-2). MIT Pr.

History in English Words. Owen Barfield. (Orig.). 1962. pap. 2.95 o.p. (ISBN 0-571-06283-0, Pub. by Faber & Faber). Merrimack Bk Serv.

History in Ovid. Ronald Syme. 1979. 29.95x (ISBN 0-19-814825-9). Oxford U Pr.

History in the Teaching of Physics: Proceedings. International Working Seminar on the Role of the History of Physics in Physics Education. Ed. by Stephen G. Brush & Allen L. King. LC 71-188602. 128p. 1972. text ed. 7.50x (ISBN 0-87451-065-1). U Pr of New Eng.

History of a Literary Radical & Other Essays. Randolph Bourne. LC 69-17713. 1969. Repr. of 1920 ed. 12.00x (ISBN 0-8196-0225-6). Biblo.

History of a Town: Or, the Chronicle of Foolov. Mikhail Saltykov-Shchedrin. Tr. by Susan Brownsberger from Rus. (Illus.). 204p. 1981. 16.50 (ISBN 0-88233-610-X); pap. 8.50 (ISBN 0-88233-611-8). Ardis Pubs.

History of Accounting in America: An Historical Interpretation of the Cultural Significance of Accounting. Gary J. Previts & Barabara D. Merino. LC 79-616. 1979. 24.50 (ISBN 0-471-05172-1, Pub by Ronald Pr). Wiley.

History of Aden 1839-1872. Z. H. Kour. 1980. 29.50x (ISBN 0-7146-3101-9, F Cass Co). Biblio Dist.

History of Adult Education. J. W. Hudson. (Social History of Education Ser.: First Series, No. 5). 238p. 1980. Repr. of 1851 ed. 17.50x (ISBN 0-7130-0006-6, Woburn Pr England). Biblio Dist.

History of Advertising from the Earliest Times. Henry Sampson. LC 68-22049. 1974. Repr. of 1874 ed. 30.00 (ISBN 0-8103-3515-8). Gale.

History of Africa Eighteen-Forty to Nineteen-Fourteen, Vol. 1. Michael Tidg & Donald Leeming. (Illus.). 188p. 1981. pap. text ed. 14.24x (ISBN 0-686-69152-0, Africana). Holmes & Meier.

History of Africa: From Earliest Times to 1800, Vol. 1. Harry A. Gailey, Jr. LC 80-15898. (Illus., Orig.). 1980. pap. text ed. 9.95 (ISBN 0-89874-032-0). Krieger.

History of Africa: From 1800 to Present, Vol. 2. rev. ed. Harry A. Gailey, Jr. LC 80-15898. (Orig.). 1980. pap. text ed. 12.95 (ISBN 0-89874-033-9). Krieger.

History of African Christianity: 1950-1975. A. Hastings. LC 78-16599. (Illus.). 1979. 39.95 (ISBN 0-521-22212-5); pap. 11.95x (ISBN 0-521-29397-9). Cambridge U Pr.

History of African Civilization. E. Jefferson Murphy. (Illus.). 448p. 1972. 12.50 o.s.i. (ISBN 0-690-38194-8, TYC-T). T Y Crowell.

History of Agriculture in Ontario 1613-1880. Robert L. Jones. LC 47-27166. 1946. pap. 7.95 (ISBN 0-8020-6304-7). U of Toronto Pr.

History of Agriculture in the Northern United States: 1620-1860. Percy W. Bidwell. 12.50 (ISBN 0-8446-1075-5). Peter Smith.

History of Air Power. Basil Collier. LC 73-20991. (Illus.). 331p. 1974. 14.95 o.s.i. (ISBN 0-02-527170-9). Macmillan.

History of Alameda County, California. facsimile ed. M. W. Wood. (Illus.). 1000p. Repr. of 1883 ed. simulated lea. 22.50 (ISBN 0-910740-09-7). Holmes.

History of Albania: From Its Origins to the Present Day. Stefanaq Pollo & Arben Puto. (Illus.). 1980. 50.00x (ISBN 0-7100-0365-X). Routledge & Kegan.

History of American Archaeology. 2nd ed. Gordon R. Willey & Jeremy A. Sabloff. LC 79-23114. (Illus.). 1980. text ed. 16.95x (ISBN 0-7167-1122-2); pap. text ed. 8.95x (ISBN 0-7167-1123-0). W H Freeman.

History of American Ceramics: The Studio Potter. Paul S. Donhauser. (Illus.). 1978. text ed. 17.95 (ISBN 0-8403-1864-2). Kendall-Hunt.

History of American City Government. Ernest S. Griffith. LC 72-3615. (Law, Politics & History Ser.). Repr. of 1938 ed. lib. bdg. 42.50 (ISBN 0-306-70526-5). Da Capo.

History of American Education. Compiled by Jurgen Herbst. LC 76-178293. (Goldentree Bibliographies in American History Ser.). 172p. (Orig.). 1973. pap. 6.95x (ISBN 0-88295-531-4). AHM Pub.

History of American Education: A Guide to Information Sources. Ed. by Francesco Cordasco et al. LC 79-23010. (Education Information Guide Ser.: Vol. 7). 1979. 30.00 (ISBN 0-8103-1382-0). Gale.

History of American Labor. J. G. Rayback. 1959. 6.95 o.s.i. (ISBN 0-02-601140-9). Macmillan.

History of American Labor. Joseph G. Rayback. LC 59-5344. 1966. pap. text ed. 7.95 (ISBN 0-02-925850-2). Free Pr.

History of American Literature, 1607-1765. Moses C. Tyler. Frwd. by Howard M. Jones. 584p. 1966. 25.00x (ISBN 0-8014-0433-9). Cornell U Pr.

History of American Medicine. Ed. by Felix Marti-Ibanez. 1959. 4.00 o.p. (ISBN 0-910922-12-8). MD Pubns.

History of American Pediatrics. Thomas E. Cone, Jr. 1980. 18.95 (ISBN 0-316-15289-7). Little.

History of American Philosophy. Herbert W. Schneider. LC 63-14114. 1963. 12.50x (ISBN 0-231-08612-1). Columbia U Pr.

History of American Presidential Elections, 4 vols. Arthur M. Schlesinger, Jr. & F. L. Israel. 1971. 150.00 o.p. (ISBN 0-07-079786-2, P&RB). McGraw.

History of American Presidential Elections, 5 vols. Ed. by Arthur M. Schlesinger, Jr. & Fred L. Israel. 4000p. 1981. pap. write for info. (ISBN 0-87754-124-8). Chelsea Hse.

History of American Psychiatry: A Teaching & Research Guide. Ed. by Daniel Blain & Michael Barton. LC 78-78396. (Task Force Reports: 15). 44p. 1979. pap. 5.00 (ISBN 0-685-95863-9, P146-0). Am Psychiatric.

History of American Wars: From Colonial Times to World War I. T. Harry Williams. LC 80-2717. 512p. 1981. 20.00 (ISBN 0-394-51167-0). Knopf.

History of American Wars: From Colonial Times to World War I. T. Harry Williams. LC 80-2717. 1981. 20.00 (ISBN 0-394-51167-0). Knopf.

History of Ancient Geography. J. Oliver Thomson. LC 64-23024. 1948. 15.00x (ISBN 0-8196-0143-8). Biblo.

History of Ancient Geography. 2nd ed. Henry F. Tozer. LC 54-13396. 1897. 15.00x (ISBN 0-8196-0138-1). Biblo.

History of Ancient Geography: Among the Greeks & Romans from the Earliest Ages till the Fall of the Roman Empire, 2 vols. E. H. Bunbury. (Illus.). 1979. Repr. of 1879 ed. Set. text ed. 185.25x (ISBN 90-7026-511-7). Humanities.

History of Ancient India. L. P. Sharma. 400p. 1981. text ed. 22.50 (ISBN 0-7069-1113-X, Pub. by Vikas India). Advent Bk.

History of Ancient India. R. S. Tripathi. 1977. 11.50 (ISBN 0-89684-215-0); pap. 6.95 (ISBN 0-686-51747-4). Orient Bk Dist.

History of Anglican Liturgy. Geoffrey Cuming. (Illus.). 450p. 1980. Repr. of 1969 ed. text ed. 39.00x (ISBN 0-333-30661-9). Humanities.

History of Anthropological Thought. Edward Evans-Pritchard. Ed. by Andre Singer. LC 80-68955. 256p. 1981. 15.00 (ISBN 0-465-02998-1). Basic.

History of Anti-Semitism: From Voltaire to Wagner, Vol. 3. Leon Poliakov. LC 75-2826. 1975. 15.00 (ISBN 0-8149-0762-8). Vanguard.

History of Antibiotics: A Symposium. Ed. by John Parascandola. (Illus.). 137p. (Orig.). 1980. pap. 5.40 (ISBN 0-931292-08-5). Am Inst Pharmacy.

History of Arabia. Kamal S. Salibi. LC 80-11919. 1980. write for info. (ISBN 0-88206-036-8). Caravan Bks.

History of Arbaic Literature: Umayyad Period. K. A. Fariq. 1978. 15.00 (ISBN 0-7069-0661-6, Pub. by Vikas India). Advent Bk.

History of Arsaces, Prince of Betlis, 1774, 2 vols. in 1. Charles Johnstone. Ed. by Michael F. Shugrue. (Flowering of the Novel, 1740-1775 Ser: Vol. 106). 1974. lib. bdg. 50.00 (ISBN 0-8240-1205-4). Garland Pub.

History of Art. 2nd ed. Janson. 1977. 21.95 (ISBN 0-13-389296-4). P-H.

History of Art. 2nd ed. Jean A. Vincent. (Orig.). 1967. pap. 3.95 o.p. (ISBN 0-06-460095-5, 95, COS). Har-Row.

History of Art: A Student's Handbook. Marcia Pointon. (Illus.). 104p. 1980. text ed. 14.95x (ISBN 0-04-701010-X, 2573); pap. text ed. 7.50x (ISBN 0-04-701011-8, 2574). Allen Unwin.

History of Art & Music. H. Janson & Joseph Kerman. 1969. pap. text ed. 12.95 (ISBN 0-13-389312-X). P-H.

History of Art Criticism. Lionello Venturi. 1964. pap. 4.25 o.p. (ISBN 0-525-47123-5). Dutton.

History of Art for Young People. 2nd, rev., enl. ed. H. W. Janson & Samuel Cauman. Ed. by Anthony F. Janson. (Illus.). 440p. 1980. 18.50 o.p. (ISBN 0-686-62689-3, 0700-3). Abrams.

History of Assassination. Brian McConnell. LC 78-114781. 360p. 1974. 6.95 o.s.i. (ISBN 0-87695-027-6). Aurora Pubs.

History of Astronomy. Tr. by A. Pannekoek. 521p. 1961. 19.50x (ISBN 0-87471-365-X). Rowman.

History of Australian Exploration from 1788-1888: Compiled from State Documents, Private Papers & the Most Authentic Sources of Information. E. Favenc. (Illus.). 1967. Repr. of 1888 ed. text ed. 42.75x (ISBN 90-6041-095-5). Humanities.

History of Barbados. Robert H. Schomburgk. LC 68-21443. Repr. of 1848 ed. 35.00x (ISBN 0-678-05003-1). Kelley.

History of Barbados. 2nd ed. Ronald Tree. 1979. 14.95x (ISBN 0-8464-0105-3). Beekman Pubs.

History of Baylor County: Salt Pork to Sirloin. Baylor County Historical Society. 19.95 (ISBN 0-685-48790-3). Nortex Pr.

History of Betty Barnes, 2 vols. in 1. (Flowering of the Novel Ser, 1740-1775: Vol. 38). 1974. Repr. of 1753 ed. lib. bdg. 50.00 (ISBN 0-8240-1137-6). Garland Pub.

History of Binary & Other Nondecimal Numeration. Anton Glaser. LC 71-149293. (Illus., Orig.). 1971. 7.50 o.p. (ISBN 0-9600324-2-8); pap. 4.00 o.p. (ISBN 0-9600324-1-X). A Glaser.

History of Books & Printing: A Guide to Information Sources. Ed. by Paul A. Winckler. LC 79-13006. (Books, Publishing & Libraries Information Guide Ser.: Vol. 2). 1979. 30.00 (ISBN 0-8103-1408-8). Gale.

History of Booksellers, the Old & the New. Henry Curwen. LC 68-19656. (Illus.). 1968. Repr. of 1873 ed. 20.00 (ISBN 0-8103-3300-7). Gale.

History of Bourne, 1622-1937. Betsey D. Keene. LC 75-5093. (Illus.). 288p. 1975. Repr. of 1937 ed. 10.00x (ISBN 0-88492-006-2). W S Sullwold.

History of British Bus Services: The North East. David Holding. LC 79-52370. 1979. 17.95 (ISBN 0-7153-7813-9). David & Charles.

History of British Gardening. 3rd ed. Miles Hadfield. (Illus.). 1979. text ed. 26.00x (ISBN 0-7195-3644-8). Humanities.

History of British Trade Unions Since 1889 Vol. 1: 1889-1910. Hugh A. Clegg et al. 1964. 37.50x (ISBN 0-19-828229-X). Oxford U Pr.

History of British Transport 1700 to the Present. John Ray. 1969. pap. text ed. 4.95x o.p. (ISBN 0-435-31753-9). Heinemann Ed.

History of Bubonic Plague in the British Isles. J. F. Shrewsbury. LC 69-10197. (Illus.). 1970. 75.00 (ISBN 0-521-07083-X). Cambridge U Pr.

History of Buddhism in Nepal: AD 704-1396. Ram Rajendra. 1979. 17.50x o.p. (ISBN 0-89684-035-2). South Asia Bks.

History of Buddhist Thought. 2nd ed. Edward J. Thomas. (History of Civilization Ser.). 1963. Repr. of 1957 ed. 24.00 (ISBN 0-7100-4971-4). Routledge & Kegan.

History of Business, Vol. 2: From the Monopolists to the Organization Man. Miriam Beard. 298p. 1963. pap. 2.25 o.p. (ISBN 0-472-06076-7, 76, AA). U of Mich Pr.

History of California, 7 vols. Hubert H. Bancroft. LC 67-29422. Repr. of 1888 ed. Set. 100.00x (ISBN 0-914888-20-X). Bancroft Pr.

History of Calvary Church of the Brethren. J. Floyd Wine. LC 72-95960. (Illus.). 1972. pap. 3.95 (ISBN 0-9604350-1-8). J F Wine.

History of Canadian Wealth. Gustavus Myers. LC 68-9159. 1968. Repr. of 1914 ed. 15.00 (ISBN 0-87266-024-9). Argosy.

History of Caricature. Bohun Lynch. LC 74-6414. (Illus.). 126p. 1975. Repr. of 1927 ed. 15.00 (ISBN 0-8103-4044-5). Gale.

History of Cell Respiration & Cytochrome. David Keilin. 1966. 59.50 (ISBN 0-521-05470-2). Cambridge U Pr.

History of Central America, 3 vols. Hubert H. Bancroft. LC 67-29422. (Works of Hubert Howe Bancroft Ser.). 1967. Repr. of 1888 ed. Set. 75.00x (ISBN 0-914888-06-4). Bancroft Pr.

History of Charles Wentworth, Esq., 1770, 3 vols. Edward Bancroft. (Flowering of the Novel, 1740-1775 Ser: Vol. 93). 1974. lib. bdg. 50.00 ea (ISBN 0-8240-1192-9). Garland Pub.

History of Chelsea. F. C. Finn. 10.00x (ISBN 0-392-07888-0, SpS). Soccer.

History of Chicago, 3 vols. Bessie L. Pierce. Incl. Vol. 1. Beginning of a City. xxii, 488p. Repr. of 1937 ed (ISBN 0-226-66817-7); Vol. 2. From Town to City, 1848-1871. xviii, 582p. Repr. of 1940 ed (ISBN 0-226-66818-5); Vol. 3. Rise of a Modern City, 1871-1893. xvi, 612p. Repr. of 1957 ed (ISBN 0-226-66819-3). LC 75-24667. 1976. lib. bdg. 20.00x ea. U of Chicago Pr.

History of Childhood. Ed. by Lloyd DeMause. 1974. pap. 8.50x (ISBN 0-06-131848-5, TB1848, Torch). Har-Row.

History of Children's Literature: A Syllabus with Selected Bibliographies. Elva S. Smith & Margaret Hodges. LC 79-28323. 312p. 1980. 40.00 (ISBN 0-8389-0286-3). ALA.

History of Children's Reading & Literature. Alec Ellis. 1968. pap. 9.75 (ISBN 0-08-012586-7). Pergamon.

History of China. rev.,4th ed. Wolfram Eberhard. 1977. 20.00x (ISBN 0-520-03227-6); pap. 5.95x (ISBN 0-520-03268-3). U of Cal Pr.

History of China, Vol. 1. Witold Rodzinski. 1978. text ed. 52.00 (ISBN 0-08-021806-7). Pergamon.

History of China's Internal Loan Issues: Shanghai, 1934. Eduard A. Kann. Bd. with China's Currency Reform, 1941. Lin Yu Shen. LC 78-74317. (Modern Chinese Economy Ser.: Vol. 26). 288p. 1980. lib. bdg. 33.00 (ISBN 0-8240-4274-3). Garland Pub.

History of Chinese Civilization. Jacques Gernet. Tr. by J. R. Foster. (Illus.). 750p. (Orig.). 1980. lib. bdg. cancelled (ISBN 0-89158-992-9); pap. cancelled (ISBN 0-89158-995-3). Westview.

History of Christian Doctrine, 2 vols. William G. Shedd. 1978. 30.25 (ISBN 0-686-12956-3). Klock & Klock.

History of Christian Doctrines. Louis Berkhof. (Twin Brooks Ser). 288p. 1975. pap. 5.95 (ISBN 0-8010-0636-8). Baker Bk.

History of Christian Doctrines. Louis Berkhof. 1978. 11.95 (ISBN 0-85151-005-1). Banner of Truth.

History of Christian Education: Study Guide. Charles B. Eavey. 1.50 (ISBN 0-8024-3580-7). Moody.

History of Christian Names. Charlotte M. Yonge. 1966. Repr. of 1884 ed. 24.00 (ISBN 0-8103-3139-X). Gale.

History of Christian Spirituality, 3 vols. Louis Bouyer. 1977. Set. 45.00 (ISBN 0-8164-0349-X); Vol. 1. 17.50 (ISBN 0-8164-0325-2); Vol. 2. 19.50 (ISBN 0-8164-0326-0); Vol. 3. 12.50 (ISBN 0-8164-0327-9). Crossroad NY.

History of Christian Thought, 3 vols. Justo L. Gonzalez. 1975. Set. 43.95 (ISBN 0-687-17177-6). Abingdon.

History of Christian Thought, Vol. 3: From the Protestant Reformation to the Twentieth Century. Justo L. Gonzalez. LC 74-109679. 416p. 1975. 16.95 (ISBN 0-687-17176-8). Abingdon.

History of Christianity. rev. ed. Kenneth S. Latourette. Incl. Vol. 1. Beginnings to 1500. 758p (ISBN 0-06-064952-6, RD-93); Vol. 2. Reformation to the Present. 922p (ISBN 0-06-064953-4, RD-94). LC 74-25692. 1975. pap. 9.95 ea. (HarpR). Har-Row.

History of Christianity. Donald W. Treadgold. LC 78-78118. 277p. (Orig.). 1979. 22.50 (ISBN 0-913124-35-4); pap. 7.95 (ISBN 0-913124-35-4). Nordland Pub.

History of Christianity from the Birth of Christ to the Abolition of Paganism in the Roman Empire, 3 vols. Henry Milman. Repr. Set. 85.00 o.p. (ISBN 0-686-12344-1). Church History.

History of Christianity in the Apostolic Age. A. C. McGiffert. (International Theologica Library). 692p. Repr. of 1897 ed. text ed. 13.95x (ISBN 0-567-07207-X). Attic Pr.

History of Christianity, 1650-1950: Secularization of the West. James H. Nichols. 1956. 17.50 o.p. (ISBN 0-8260-6725-5). Wiley.

History of Civilization in England. abr ed. Henry T. Buckle. Ed. by Clement Wood. LC 64-15688. (Milestones of Thought Ser.). 8.50 (ISBN 0-8044-1125-5); pap. 3.45 (ISBN 0-8044-6062-0). Ungar.

History of Civilization: Prehistory to 1300. 5th ed. C. Brinton et al. (Illus.). 352p. 1976. pap. text ed. 12.95 (ISBN 0-13-389791-5). P-H.

History of Civilization: Thirteen Hundred to Eighteen-Fifteen. 5th ed. C. Brinton et al. (Illus.). 288p. 1976. pap. text ed. 12.95 (ISBN 0-13-389817-2). P-H.

History of Civilization: Vol. 1, Prehistory to 1715. 5th ed. Brinton et al. 1976. pap. 15.95 (ISBN 0-13-389007-4); study guide 5.95 (ISBN 0-13-389833-4). P-H.

History of Civilization: 1715 to Present. 5th ed. C. Brinton et al. (Illus.). 528p. 1976. pap. text ed. 15.95 (ISBN 0-13-389809-1). P-H.

History of Classical Scholarship: From the Beginning to the End of the Hellenistic Age. Rudolph Pfeiffer. 1968. 37.50x (ISBN 0-19-814342-7). Oxford U Pr.

History of Classical Scholarship from 1300 to 1850. Rudolf Pfeiffer. 1976. 32.50x (ISBN 0-19-814364-8). Oxford U Pr.

History of Clay County. William C. Taylor. LC 73-87679. (Illus.). 200p. 1973. 12.50 (ISBN 0-8363-0118-8). Jenkins.

History of Codes & Ciphers in the United States During World War I. Ed. by Wayne G. Barker. (Cryptographic Ser.). (Illus.). 1979. 19.60 (ISBN 0-89412-031-X). Aegean Park Pr.

History of Collage. Eddie Wolfram. (Illus.). 176p. 1976. 16.95 o.s.i. (ISBN 0-02-630870-3). Macmillan.

History of Colorado for Children. Vivian S. Epstein. (Illus.). 32p. (ps-4). 1977. pap. 2.95 (ISBN 0-9601002-1-0). V S Epstein.

History of Commerce & Industry in Western Australia. Ed. by Peter Firkens. 223p. 1980. 17.95x (ISBN 0-85564-150-9, Pub. by U of West Australia Pr Australia). Intl Schol Bk Serv.

History of Computing: From ENIAC to UNIVAC. Nancy Stern. (Illus.). 280p. 1981. 21.00 (ISBN 0-932376-14-2). Digital Pr.

History of Computing in the Twentieth Century. Ed. by N. Metropolis et al. LC 79-51683. 1980. 29.50 (ISBN 0-12-491650-3). Acad Pr.

History of Control Engineering, Eighteen Hundred to Nineteen Thirty. S. Bennett. (IEE Control Engineering Ser.: No. 8). (Illus.). 224p. 1979. 39.50 (ISBN 0-906048-07-9). Inst Elect Eng.

History of Cornelia, 1750. Sarah Scott. (Flowering of the Novel, 1740-1775 Ser: Vol. 29). 1974. lib. bdg. 50.00 (ISBN 0-8240-1128-7). Garland Pub.

History of Corporal Punishment: A Survey of Flagellation in Its Historical, Anthropological & Sociological Aspects. George R. Scott. LC 74-1088. (Illus.). 261p. 1974. Repr. of 1938 ed. 18.00 (ISBN 0-8103-3978-1). Gale.

History of Costume. Lavina M. Franck. 1977. spiral bdg. 9.95x (ISBN 0-916434-27-3). Plycon Pr.

History of Costume. Carl Kohler. (Illus.). 10.00 (ISBN 0-8446-2393-8). Peter Smith.

History of Counseling Psychology. John M. Whiteley. LC 79-23441. 1980. pap. text ed. 8.95 (ISBN 0-8185-0370-X). Brooks-Cole.

History of Creation & Origin of the Species: A Scientific Theological Viewpoint. Reuben L. Katter. 1967. 14.95 (ISBN 0-911806-01-6); pap. 9.95 (ISBN 0-911806-00-8). Theotes.

History of Criminal Syndicalism Legislation in the United States. Eldridge F. Dowell. LC 73-87517. (American History, Politics & Law Ser). 1969. Repr. of 1939 ed. 19.50 (ISBN 0-306-71426-4). Da Capo.

History of Crosby County, 1876-1977. Crosby County Historical Commission. 1978. write for info. Crosby County.

History of Dairying in Western Australia. Maurice Cullity. 488p. 1980. 35.00x (ISBN 0-85564-177-0, Pub. by U of West Australia Pr Australia). Intl Schol Bk Serv.

History of Dance. Mary Clarke et al. 1981. 35.00 (ISBN 0-517-54282-X). Crown.

History of Democratic Education in Modern China. Lu-Dzai Djung. (Studies in Chinese History & Civilization). 258p. 1977. Repr. of 1934 ed. 19.00 (ISBN 0-89093-080-5). U Pubns Amer.

History of Dentistry. Walter A. Hoffman-Axthelm. (Illus.). 400p. 1981. 46.00. Quint Pub Co.

History of Dentistry from the Most Ancient Times Until the End of the 18th Century. V. Guerini. 1967. Repr. of 1909 ed. text ed. 71.25x (ISBN 90-6041-129-3). Humanities.

History of Design from the Victorian Era to the Present. Ann Ferebee. 128p. 1980. pap. 7.95 (ISBN 0-442-23115-6). Van Nos Reinhold.

History of Detroit & Wayne County & Early Michigan: A Chronological Cyclopedia of the Past & Present. Silas Farmer. LC 68-26178. 1969. Repr. of 1890 ed. 38.00 (ISBN 0-8103-3326-0). Gale.

History of Dickens County: Ranches & Rolling Plains. Fred Arrington. 17.95 (ISBN 0-685-48795-4). Nortex Pr.

History of Doll Houses. Flora G. Jacobs. LC 65-24648. 1965. pap. 14.95 (ISBN 0-684-14538-3, SL630, ScribT). Scribner.

History of Dutchess County, New York: 1683-1882. James H. Smith. 720p. 1980. Repr. of 1882 ed. 35.00 (ISBN 0-932334-35-0). Heart of the Lakes.

History of Early Chinese Art, 4 vols. in 2. Osvald Siren. LC 74-78362. (Illus.). 1970. Repr. of 1929 ed. 150.00 o.p. (ISBN 0-87817-036-7). Hacker.

History of Early Modern Europe, 1500-1815. Herbert H. Rowen. 1960. pap. 12.95 (ISBN 0-672-60697-6). Bobbs.

History of Early Spotsylvania. James R. Mansfield. LC 77-87193. (Illus.). 1977. 10.75x (ISBN 0-685-89825-3). Va Bk.

History of East Africa. 4th ed. Zoe Marsh & G. W. Kingsnorth. LC 72-171677. (Illus.). 1972. 19.95 (ISBN 0-521-08346-X); pap. 7.95x (ISBN 0-521-09677-4). Cambridge U Pr.

History of East Africa, Vol. 3. Ed. by D. A. Low. 1976. 49.50x (ISBN 0-19-821680-7). Oxford U Pr.

History of East & Central Africa. Basil Davidson. LC 69-20103. pap. 2.50 (ISBN 0-385-00520-2, A677, Anch). Doubleday.

History of Eastern Christianity. Aziz S. Atiya. LC 80-232. 1980. Repr. lib. bdg. 52.00 (ISBN 0-527-03703-6). Kraus Repr.

History of Economic Analysis. William K. Hutchinson. LC 73-17578. (Economics Information Guide Ser.: Vol. 3). 1976. 30.00 (ISBN 0-8103-1295-6). Gale.

History of Economic Theory: Scope, Method & Content. Harry H. Landreth. LC 75-31003. (Illus.). 512p. 1976. text ed. 20.95 (ISBN 0-395-19234-X). HM.

History of Economic Thought. rev. 2nd ed. H. L. Bhatia. 1980. text ed. 25.00x (ISBN 0-7069-0585-7, Pub. by Vikas India). Advent Bk.

History of Economic Thought. Eric Roll. 1974. text ed. 15.95x o.p. (ISBN 0-256-01609-7). Irwin.

History of Economic Thought. Isaac I. Rubin. Tr. by Don Filtzer. 448p. 1980. text ed. 33.00x (ISBN 0-906133-16-5); pap. text ed. 15.50x (ISBN 0-906133-17-3). Humanities.

History of Economic Thought: A Critical Perspective. E. K. Hunt. 1979. pap. text ed. 19.95x (ISBN 0-534-00581-0). Wadsworth Pub.

History of Education in America. 2nd ed. John D. Pulliam. (Educational Foundations Ser.). 196p. 1976. pap. text ed. 9.50 (ISBN 0-675-08660-4). Merrill.

History of Education in Australia. W. F. Connell et al. 1981. write for info. (ISBN 0-686-16293-5, Pub. by Sydney U Pr). Intl Schol Bk Serv.

History of Education in the Twentieth Century World. W. F. Connell. 1981. text ed. 29.95x (ISBN 0-8077-8024-3). Tchrs Coll.

History of Egyptian Architecture -The Empire (the New Kingdom) From the 18th Dynasty to the End of the 20th Dynasty, 1580-1085 B. C. Alexander Badawy. 1968. 40.00x (ISBN 0-520-00057-9). U of Cal Pr.

History of el Dorado County, California. facsimile ed. Ed. by P. Sioli. 272p. Repr. of 1883 ed. quarto 35.00. Holmes.

History of Elizabeth, Queen of England. Jacob Abbott. 252p. 1980. Repr. lib. bdg. 20.00 (ISBN 0-8492-3226-0). R West.

History of Emily Montague, 1769, 4 vols. in 2. Frances Brooke. Ed. by Michael F. Shugrue. (Flowering of the Novel, 1740-1775 Ser: Vol. 85). 1974. lib. bdg. 50.00 ea. (ISBN 0-8240-1184-8). Garland Pub.

History of England. 3rd ed. Harold J. Schultz. LC 79-153052. 1979. pap. 5.95 (ISBN 0-06-460188-9, CO 188, COS). Har-Row.

History of England, 4 vols. 3rd ed. Ed. by Lacey B. Smith. Incl. Vol. 1. The Making of England, 55 B.C.-1399. C. W. Hollister. pap. text ed. 7.95x (ISBN 0-685-56522-X); Vol. 2. This Realm of England, 1399-1688. Lacey B. Smith. pap. text ed. 7.95x (ISBN 0-669-97949-X); Vol. 3. The Age of Aristocracy, 1688-1830. William B. Willcox. pap. text ed. 7.95x (ISBN 0-669-97956-2); Vol. 4. Britain Yesterday & Today, 1830 to the Present. Walter L. Arnstein. (Illus.). pap. text ed. 8.95x (ISBN 0-669-97964-3). 1975. Heath.

History of England & the Empire Commonwealth. 5th ed. W. P. Hall et al. 1971. text ed. 25.50 (ISBN 0-471-00225-9). Wiley.

History of England from Edward II to James I. Anthony Goodman. LC 76-51405. (Illus.). 1977. text ed. 21.00x (ISBN 0-582-48281-X); pap. text ed. 12.95x (ISBN 0-582-48282-8). Longman.

History of England: From Prehistoric Times to the End of World War Two. John Thorn et al. (Apollo Eds.). (YA) (gr. 9-12). pap. 4.50 o.s.i. (ISBN 0-8152-0070-6, A70, TYC-T). T Y Crowell.

History of England Under the Anglo-Saxon Kings, 2 vols. Johann M. Lappenberg. Rev. by & tr. by Benjamin Thorpe. LC 80-2209. 1981. Repr. of 1845 ed. 97.50 (ISBN 0-404-18740-4). AMS Pr.

History of English. Nelson Francis. (Orig.). 1963. pap. text ed. 2.95x (ISBN 0-393-09709-9, NortonC). Norton.

History of English & Irish Glass to 1969. W. A. Thorpe. 75.00x (ISBN 0-87556-334-1). Saifer.

History of English Costume. Iris Brooke. LC 72-85476. (Illus.). 1973. pap. 7.45 (ISBN 0-87830-569-6). Theatre Arts.

History of English Drama, 1660-1900, 6 vols. Allardyce Nicoll. Incl. Vol. 1. Restoration Drama. 62.00 (ISBN 0-521-05827-9); Vol. 2. Early Eighteenth Century Drama. 59.50 (ISBN 0-521-05828-7); Vol. 3. Late Eighteenth Century Drama. 57.50 (ISBN 0-521-05829-5); Vol. 4. Early Nineteenth Century Drama, 1800-1850. 72.00 (ISBN 0-521-05830-9); Vol. 5. Late Nineteenth Century Drama. 77.00 (ISBN 0-521-05831-7); Vol. 6. Alphabetical Catalogue of the Plays. 57.50 (ISBN 0-521-05832-5). 1959. 340.00 set (ISBN 0-521-08777-5). Cambridge U Pr.

History of English Law Before the Time of Edward First, 2 vols. Edward Pollock & Frederic W. Maitland. Vol. 2. 59.00 (ISBN 0-521-07062-7); Vol. 1. pap. 24.95x (ISBN 0-521-09515-8); Vol. 2. pap. 24.95x (ISBN 0-521-09516-6). Cambridge U Pr.

History of English Literature Sixteen Sixty-Eighteen Thirty-Seven. Martin S. Day. LC 63-18042. 1963. pap. 3.95 (ISBN 0-385-01372-8, U12, CCG). Doubleday.

History of English Literature to Sixteen Sixty. Martin S. Day. LC 63-7694. 1963. pap. 4.95 o.p. (ISBN 0-385-01371-X, U10, CCG). Doubleday.

History of English Lotteries. John Ashton. LC 67-23945. (Illus.). 1969. Repr. of 1893 ed. 18.00 (ISBN 0-8103-3250-7). Gale.

History of English Music. 3rd ed. Henry Davey. LC 69-15620. (Music Ser). 1969. Repr. of 1921 ed. lib. bdg. 35.00 (ISBN 0-306-71133-8). Da Capo.

History of English Parliamentary Privilege. Carl Wittke. LC 74-87623. (Law, Politics, & History Ser). 1969. Repr. of 1921 ed. lib. bdg. 25.00 (ISBN 0-306-71810-3). Da Capo.

History of English Prison Administration: 1750-1877. Sean McConville. 520p. 1981. price not set (ISBN 0-7100-0694-2). Routledge & Kegan.

History of Engraving & Etching: From the Fifteenth Century to the Year 1914. 3rd ed. Arthur M. Hind. (Illus.). 1923. pap. text ed. 6.00 (ISBN 0-486-20954-7). Dover.

History of Entomology. Edward O. Essig. (Illus.). 1965. Repr. of 1931 ed. 29.00 o.s.i. (ISBN 0-02-844340-3). Hafner.

History of Entomology. Ed. by Smith. LC 73-76435. 517p. 1973. 18.25 (ISBN 0-686-09298-8). Entomol Soc.

History of Ethiopia. Arnold H. Jones & Elizabeth Monroe. 1955. 14.95x (ISBN 0-19-821609-2). Oxford U Pr.

History of Europe. John Bowle. xii, 626p. 1981. lib. bdg. write for info. (06856-0, Pub. by Secker & Warburg). U of Chicago Pr.

History of Europe from Thirteen Seventy-Eight to Fourteen Ninety-Four. 3rd ed. LC 80-23759. (Methuen's History of Medieval & Modern Europe: IV). (Illus.). xiii, 545p. 1980. Repr. of 1949 ed. lib. bdg. 45.00x (ISBN 0-8371-8091-0, WAHEU). Greenwood.

History of Europe in the Twentieth Century. David E. Sumler. 1973. pap. text ed. 12.50x (ISBN 0-256-01421-3). Dorsey.

History of Europe Since Eighteen Fifteen. 21st ed. Henry W. Littlefield. 1963. pap. 3.95 (ISBN 0-06-460012-2, CO 12, COS). Har-Row.

History of Europe: 1648-1815. Maurice Ashley. (Illus.). 304p. 1973. pap. text ed. 12.95 (ISBN 0-13-390062-2). P-H.

History of Everyday Things in England, 5 vols. Marjorie Ovennell & C. H. Ovennell. Incl. Volume I, 1066-1499. 1969 (ISBN 0-7134-1650-5); Volume II, 1500-1799. 1976 (ISBN 0-7134-1651-3); Volume III, 1733-1851. 1977 (ISBN 0-7134-1652-1); Volume IV, 1851-1914. 1976 (ISBN 0-7134-1653-X); Volume V, 1914-1968. S. E. Ellan. 1977 (ISBN 0-7134-1654-8). 17.95 ea. (Pub. by Batsford England). David & Charles.

History of Factory Legislation. 3rd ed. Elizabeth L. Hutchins & Amy Harrison. LC 66-5599. 1981. Repr. of 1926 ed. lib. bdg. 25.00x (ISBN 0-678-05173-9). Kelley.

History of Fanny Burney. Joyce Hemlow. 1958. 37.50x (ISBN 0-19-811549-0). Oxford U Pr.

History of Far Eastern Art. rev. ed. Sherman E. Lee. 528p. 1974. text ed. 21.95 (ISBN 0-13-390088-6). P-H.

History of Farmers' Movements in Canada: The Origins & Development of Agrarian Protest, 1872-1924. Louis A. Wood. LC 73-91559. (Social History of Canada Ser.). 1975. pap. 6.50 (ISBN 0-8020-6193-1); pap. 6.50. U of Toronto Pr.

History of Feudalism. David Herlihy. (Documentary History of Western Civilization Ser). 1971. 15.00x o.s.i. (ISBN 0-8027-2024-2). Walker & Co.

History of Film. Jack C. Ellis. (Illus.). 1979. pap. 14.95 ref. ed. (ISBN 0-13-389460-6). P-H.

History of Firefighting. Evan Green-Hughes. 158p. 1980. 37.50x (ISBN 0-903485-61-3, Pub. by Mooreland England). State Mutual Bk.

History of Fishes. 3rd ed. P. H. Greenwood & J. R. Norman. 1976. pap. 18.95 (ISBN 0-470-99012-0). Halsted Pr.

History of Flight. John Ray. 1968. pap. text ed. 4.95x o.p. (ISBN 0-435-31750-4). Heinemann Ed.

History of Florida. Charlton W. Tebeau. LC 80-53678. (Illus.). 1971. pap. 19.95x (ISBN 0-87024-303-9). U of Miami Pr.

History of Folklore in Europe. Giuseppe Cocchiara. Tr. by John N. McDaniel from Ital. LC 80-17823. (Translations in Folklore Studies Ser.). 1981. text ed. 19.50x (ISBN 0-915980-99-1). Inst Study Human.

History of Formal Logic. 2nd ed. Innocenty M. Bochenski. LC 72-113118. 1970. text ed. 16.95 (ISBN 0-8284-0238-8). Chelsea Pub.

History of Four-Footed Beasts, & Serpents & Insects, 3 Vols. 2nd ed. Edward Topsell. LC 65-23391. 1967. Repr. of 1658 ed. Set. lib. bdg. 150.00 (ISBN 0-306-70923-6). Da Capo.

History of Friedrich 2nd of Prussia Called Frederick the Great. Thomas Carlyle. Ed. by John Clive. LC 79-82375. (Classic European Histories Ser). 1969. text ed. 12.00x o.s.i. (ISBN 0-226-09296-8). U of Chicago Pr.

History of Gambling in England. John Ashton. LC 68-21520. 1968. Repr. of 1899 ed. 15.00 (ISBN 0-8103-3501-8). Gale.

History of Gardening in England. Alicia A. Rockley. LC 68-21522. 1969. Repr. of 1896 ed. 18.00 (ISBN 0-8103-3845-9). Gale.

History of Gavelkind & Other Remarkable Customs in the County of Kent. Charles Sandys. xvi, 352p. 1981. Repr. of 1851 ed. lib. bdg. 35.00x (ISBN 0-8377-1117-7). Rothman.

History of German Literature. Ernst Rose. LC 60-9405. (Gotham Library). (Orig.). 1960. 12.00x (ISBN 0-8147-0362-3); pap. 6.00x (ISBN 0-8147-0363-1). NYU Pr.

History of German Literature: From the Accession of Frederick the Great to the Death of Goethe. W. Scherer et al. Ed. by F. M. Muller. Tr. by Mrs. F. C. Conybeare. 335p. 1980. Repr. of 1981 ed. lib. bdg. 45.00 (ISBN 0-8495-4898-5). Arden Lib.

History of German Literature, 1760-1805. Werner Kohlschmidt. Tr. by Ian Hilton from Ger. LC 74-32062. 420p. 1975. text ed. 35.00x (ISBN 0-8419-0195-3). Holmes & Meier.

History of German Resistance, Nineteen Thirty-Three to Nineteen Forty-Five. Peter Hoffmann. Tr. by Richard Barry from Ger. 1979. 25.00 (ISBN 0-262-08088-5); pap. 9.95 (ISBN 0-262-58038-1). MIT Pr.

History of Ghana. W. E. Ward. 1967. text ed. 18.95x o.p. (ISBN 0-04-966007-1). Allen Unwin.

History of Golf: Illustrated. Henry Cotton. LC 75-8530. (Illus.). 240p. 1975. 16.95 o.s.i. (ISBN 0-397-01092-3). Lippincott.

History of Greece to 322 B. C. 2nd ed. Nicholas G. Hammond. (Illus.). 1967. 19.50x o.p. (ISBN 0-19-814260-9). Oxford U Pr.

History of Greek Art, 2 vols. C. M. Robertson. LC 73-79317. 1976. Set. 115.00 (ISBN 0-521-20277-9). Cambridge U Pr.

History of Greek Literature. Moses Hadas. LC 50-7015. 1950. 17.50x (ISBN 0-231-01767-7); pap. 4.00x o.p. (ISBN 0-231-08539-7). Columbia U Pr.

History of Greek Mathematics, 2 vols. Thomas L. Heath. (Illus.). 1058p. 1981. pap. price not set. Vol. I (ISBN 0-486-24073-8). Vol. II (ISBN 0-486-24074-6). Dover.

History of Greek Philosophy, 5 vols. W. K. Guthrie. LC 62-52735. 1975. 68.50 ea. Vol. 1 (ISBN 0-521-05159-2). Vol. 2 (ISBN 0-521-05160-6). Vol. 3 (ISBN 0-521-07566-1). Vol. 4 (ISBN 0-521-20002-4). Vol. 5 (ISBN 0-521-20003-2). Cambridge U Pr.

History of Greek Political Thought. T. A. Sinclair. 1967. pap. 12.00 (ISBN 0-7100-4615-4). Routledge & Kegan.

History of Greenville County, South Carolina: Narrative & Biographical. James M. Richardson. LC 80-23330. 342p. 1980. Repr. of 1930 ed. 22.50 (ISBN 0-87152-343-4). Reprint.

History of GWR & Goods Wagons: Vol. 1, General. A. G. Atkins et al. LC 75-11. (Illus.). 96p. 1975. 15.95 o.p. (ISBN 0-7153-6532-0). David & Charles.

History of GWR Goods Wagons: Vol. 2, Detail. A. G. Atkins & W. Beard. LC 76-45508. 1977. 15.95 o.p. (ISBN 0-7153-7290-4). David & Charles.

History of Hand Made Lace: Dealing with the Origin of Lace, the Growth of the Great Lace Centres, Etc. Emily Jackson. LC 70-136558. (Tower Bks.). (Illus.). xiv, 245p. 1972. Repr. of 1900 ed. 28.00 (ISBN 0-8103-3935-8). Gale.

History of Hants & Dorset Motor Services. Colin Morris. 1973. 12.95 (ISBN 0-7153-6051-5). David & Charles.

History of Hardeman County: The Last Frontier. Bill Neal. 17.95 (ISBN 0-685-48798-9). Nortex Pr.

History of Harmonic Theory in the United States. David M. Thompson. LC 80-82202. (Illus.). 211p. 1980. 14.50x (ISBN 0-87338-246-3). Kent St U Pr.

History of Helpless Harry: To Which Is Added a Variety of Amusing & Entertaining Adventures. Avi. (Illus.). 1980. 8.95 (ISBN 0-394-84505-6). Pantheon.

History of Higher Education in Pennsylvania, 2 vols. Saul Sack. LC 65-7193. 1963. 13.00 (ISBN 0-911124-32-2). Pa Hist & Mus.

History of Highland Dress. Telfer Dunbar. (Illus.). 248p. 1980. 50.00 (ISBN 0-7134-1894-X, Pub. by Batsford England). David & Charles.

History of Historical Writing, 2 vols. J. W. Thompson. 35.00 (ISBN 0-8446-1448-3). Peter Smith.

History of Holliday, Texas. Jeannine G. Hodge. 7.95 (ISBN 0-685-48799-7). Nortex Pr.

History of Hong Kong. G. B. Endacott. (Illus.). 351p. 1974. pap. 14.50x (ISBN 0-19-519776-3). Oxford U Pr.

History of Hull. Ed. by Edward Gillett & Kenneth A. MacMahon. (Illus.). 448p. 1980. 45.00x (ISBN 0-19-713436-X). Oxford U Pr.

History of Hungarian Literature. Frederick Riedl. Tr. by C. A. Ginever. LC 68-26602. 1968. Repr. of 1906 ed. 18.00 (ISBN 0-8103-3221-3). Gale.

History of Hymn Singing As Told Through One Hundred & One Famous Hymns. LC 79-65287. (Illus.). 224p. 1981. 14.95 (ISBN 0-87319-016-5). C Hallberg.

History of Hysteria. George R. Wesley. LC 79-51464. 1979. pap. text ed. 9.00 (ISBN 0-8191-0751-4). U Pr of Amer.

History of Icelandic Literature. Stefan Einarsson. 1957. 20.00x (ISBN 0-89067-033-1). Am Scandinavian.

History of Ideas: A Bibliographical Introduction, 2 vols. Jeremy L. Tobey. 320p. 1975-76. Vol. 1 Classical Antiquity. text ed. 11.65 (ISBN 0-87436-143-5, LC 74-83160); Vol. 2 Medieval & Early Modern Europe. text ed. 28.75 o.p. (ISBN 0-87436-239-3, LC 76-8017). ABC-Clio.

History of Ideas: An Introduction. George Boas. LC 74-85278. 1969. 6.95 o.p. (ISBN 0-684-10032-0, ScribT). Scribner.

History of Ideas in Brazil: The Development of Philosophy in Brazil & the Evolution of National History. Joao Cruz Costa. Tr. by Suzette Macedo. 1964. 25.00x (ISBN 0-520-00282-2). U of Cal Pr.

History of Impressionism. John Rewald. LC 68-17468. (Illus.). 672p. 1980. 40.00 (ISBN 0-87070-369-2, 365149, Pub. by Museum Mod Art); pap. 19.95 (ISBN 0-87070-369-2). NYGS.

History of India Under the Two First Sovereigns of the House of Taimur: Baber & Humayun, 2 vols. William Erskine. 1162p. 1972. Repr. of 1854 ed. 70.00x (ISBN 0-7165-2118-0, Pub. by Irish Academic Pr Ireland). Biblio Dist.

History of India Under the Two First Sovereigns of the House of Taimur, Baber & Humayun, 2 vols. William Erskine. 1162p. 1980. Repr. 70.00x (ISBN 0-686-28827-0, Pub. by Irish Academic Pr). Biblio Dist.

History of Indian & Indonesian Art. A. K. Coomaraswamy. (Illus.). 432p. 1972. 25.00x o.p. (ISBN 0-8426-0393-X). Verry.

History of Indiana Literature: With Emphasis on the Authors of Imaginative Works Who Commenced Writing Prior to World War II. Arthur W. Shumaker. 624p. 1962. 15.00x (ISBN 0-253-37012-4). Ind U Pr.

History of Industrial Education in the United States. Melvin L. Barlow. 1967. pap. text ed. 23.44 (ISBN 0-87002-241-5). Bennett IL.

History of Ireland in the Eighteenth Century. abr. ed. W. E. Lecky. Ed. by L. P. Curtis, Jr. LC 78-184286. (Classics of British Historical Literature Ser). 576p. 1972. 15.00x o.s.i. (ISBN 0-226-46994-8). U of Chicago Pr.

History of Irrigation in Adams County. William C. Sole. 1969. pap. 1.95 (ISBN 0-934858-07-1). Adams County.

History of Islington. John Nelson. Ed. by Julia Melvin. (Illus.). 417p. 1980. Repr. of 1811 ed. 80.00x (ISBN 0-85667-104-5, Pub. by Sotheby Parke Bernet England). Biblio Dist.

History of Israel. 3rd ed. John Bright. LC 80-22774. Date not set. price not set (ISBN 0-664-21381-2). Westminster.

History of Israel. John J. Davis & John C. Whitcomb. 14.95 (ISBN 0-88469-061-X). BMH Bks.

History of Israel. 2nd rev. ed. H. Wheeler Robinson. (Studies in Theology). 1967. pap. 13.50x (ISBN 0-7156-0163-6, Pub. by Duckworth England). Biblio Dist.

History of Israel in Old Testament Times. Siegfried Herrmann. Tr. by John Bowden from Ger. LC 74-24918. 384p. 1975. 15.50x (ISBN 0-8006-0405-9, 1-405). Fortress.

History of Italian Fascism. Federico Chabod. Tr. by Muriel Grindrod from It. 192p. 1975. Repr. of 1963 ed. 15.50 (ISBN 0-86527-095-3). Fertig.

History of Italian Renaissance Art. 2nd ed. Frederick Hartt. (Illus.). 1980. text ed. 21.95 (ISBN 0-13-392043-7). P-H.

History of Italy. Francesco Guicciardini. Tr. by Sidney Alexander. (Illus.). 1969. 12.50 o.s.i. (ISBN 0-02-500830-7). Macmillan.

History of Italy. Francesco Guicciardini. Tr. by Sidney Alexander. 496p. 1972. pap. 3.95 o.s.i. (ISBN 0-02-032980-6, Collier). Macmillan.

History of James Lovegrove, Esq., 1761, 2 vols. in 1. James Ridley. (Flowering of the Novel, 1740-1775 Ser: Vol. 58). 1974. lib. bdg. 50.00 (ISBN 0-8240-1157-0). Garland Pub.

History of Japan. Richard Mason & John Caiger. LC 73-13581. 1973. 10.95 (ISBN 0-02-920290-6). Free Pr.

History of Japan: Compiled from the Records of the English East India Company at the Instance of the Court of Directors, 2 vols. Ed. by Peter Pratt. (Studies in Japanese History & Civilization). 1979. Repr. of 1931 ed. Set. 62.00 (ISBN 0-89093-261-1). U Pubns Amer.

History of Japanese Printing & Book Illustration. D. G. Chibbett. LC 76-9362. (Illus.). 264p. 1977. 55.00 (ISBN 0-87011-288-0). Kodansha.

History of Jazz in America. Barry Ulanov. LC 74-37324. 382p. 1972. Repr. of 1955 ed. lib. bdg. 25.00 (ISBN 0-306-70427-7). Da Capo.

History of Jemmy & Jenny Jessamy, 1753, 3 vols. Eliza Haywood. (Flowering of the Novel, 1740-1775 Ser: Vol. 39). 1974. lib. bdg. 50.00 (ISBN 0-8240-1138-4). Garland Pub.

History of Jewish Literature, 5 vols. in 6. Meyer Waxman. Set. boxed 50.00 o.p. (ISBN 0-498-08640-2, Yoseloff); 10.00 ea. o.p. Vol. 1 (ISBN 0-498-08913-4). Vol. 2 (ISBN 0-498-08921-5). Vol. 3 (ISBN 0-498-08917-7). Vol. 4, Pt. 1 (ISBN 0-498-08912-6). Vol. 4, Pt. 2 (ISBN 0-498-08922-3). Vol. 5 (ISBN 0-498-08885-5). A S Barnes.

History of Joseph. George Lawson. 7.95 o.p. (ISBN 0-686-12473-1). Banner of Truth.

History of Karnes County & Old Helena. Compiled by Hedwig K. Didear. LC 78-15120. (Illus.). 9.50 o.p. (ISBN 0-685-13274-9). Jenkins.

History of Kennebunkport. Bradbury. 10.00 o.s.i. (ISBN 0-911764-01-1). Durrell.

History of King County, Texas. King County Historical Survey Committee. (Illus.). 350p. 1975. 25.00 (ISBN 0-89015-106-7). Nortex Pr.

History of King Lear. Nahum Tate. Ed. by James Black. LC 74-82562. (Regents Restoration Drama Ser). xl, 111p. 1975. 8.95x (ISBN 0-8032-0382-9); pap. 2.65x (ISBN 0-8032-5382-6, BB 278, Bison). U of Nebr Pr.

History of King Richard the Third (1619) George Buck. Ed. by A. N. Kincaid. 512p. 1980. text ed. 60.50x (ISBN 0-904387-26-7). Humanities.

History of Korea. Woo-Keun Han. Ed. by Grafton K. Mintz. Tr. by Kyung-Shik Lee from Korean. (Illus.). 568p. 1971. 15.00 o.p. (ISBN 0-8248-0106-7, Eastwest Ctr); pap. text ed. 8.95x (ISBN 0-8248-0334-5). U Pr of Hawaii.

History of Korea. Takashi Hatada. Ed. by Warren W. Smith, Jr. & Benjamin H. Hazard. LC 69-20450. Orig. Title: Chosen Shi. 1969. pap. 2.50 (ISBN 0-87436-065-X). ABC-Clio.

History of Korea. William E. Henthorn. LC 75-143511. 1971. 14.95 (ISBN 0-02-914460-4); pap. text ed. 7.95 (ISBN 0-02-914610-0). Free Pr.

History of la Salle County, Texas. Annette Ludeman. (Illus.). 300p. 1975. 17.95 (ISBN 0-89015-100-8). Nortex Pr.

History of Lace. Fanny M. Palliser. LC 75-78219. (Illus.). x, 454p. 1972. Repr. of 1875 ed. 30.00 (ISBN 0-8103-3941-2). Gale.

History of Lace. Margaret Simeon. (Illus.). 144p. 1979. 32.50x (ISBN 0-8476-6263-2). Rowman.

History of Lancashire. rev. ed. John J. Bagley. (County History Ser.). (Illus.). 1961. 10.95 (ISBN 0-85208-047-6). Dufour.

History of Lancashire. P. J. Gooderson. (Illus.). 144p. 1980. 17.95 (ISBN 0-7134-2588-1, Pub. by Batsford England). David & Charles.

History of Lancashire County Council 1889-1974. Ed. by J. D. Marshall. 456p. 1977. bds. 36.00x (ISBN 0-85520-215-7, Pub. by Martin Robertson England). Biblio Dist.

History of Latin Literature. Moses Hadas. LC 52-7637. 1952. 27.50x (ISBN 0-231-01848-7); pap. 5.00x o.p. (ISBN 0-231-08556-7, 56). Columbia U Pr.

History of Lee County, Texas. Lee County Historical Survey Committee. (Illus.). 480p. 1974. 25.00 (ISBN 0-685-53907-5). Nortex Pr.

History of Letter Post Communication Between the United States & Europe 1845-1875. George E. Hargest. LC 75-1787. (Illus.). 256p. 1975. 35.00x (ISBN 0-88000-062-7). Quarterman.

History of Libraries. Alfred Hessel. LC 57-2485. 1955. 10.00 (ISBN 0-8108-0058-6). Scarecrow.

History of Libraries in the Western World. 3rd ed. Elmer D. Johnson & Michael H. Harris. LC 76-25422. 1976. 12.00 (ISBN 0-8108-0949-4). Scarecrow.

History of Lighthouses. Patrick Beaver. (Illus.). 158p. 1976. pap. 4.95 (ISBN 0-8065-0256-8). Citadel Pr.

History of Little Goody Two Shoes. Oliver Goldsmith. (Illus.). (gr. 2-4). 1924. 4.95 (ISBN 0-02-736280-9). Macmillan.

History of Little Goody Two-Shoes, Repr. Of 1765 Ed. John Newbery. Bd. with Fairing or a Golden Toy for Children. Pref. by Brian Alderson. Repr. of 1768 ed. LC 75-32141. (Classics of Children's Literature, 1621-1932: Vol. 8). 1976. PLB 38.00 (ISBN 0-8240-2257-2). Garland Pub.

History of Little Jack. Thomas Day. Bd. with Original Stories from Real Life. Mary Wollstonecraft. LC 75-32149. (Classics of Children's Literature, 1621-1932: Vol. 15). 1976. Repr. of 1788 ed. PLB 38.00 (ISBN 0-8240-2263-7). Garland Pub.

History of Local Government in the 20th Century. Bryan K. Lucas & Peter G. Richards. (New Local Government Ser.). 1978. text ed. 25.00x (ISBN 0-04-352070-7); pap. text ed. 9.95x (ISBN 0-04-352071-5). Allen Unwin.

History of Luminescence from the Earliest Times Until 1900. E. Newton Harvey. LC 57-8124. (Memoirs Ser.: Vol. 44). (Illus.). 1957. 9.00 o.s.i. (ISBN 0-87169-044-6). Am Philos.

History of M. A. O. College, Aligarh. S. K. Bhatnagar. 8.50 o.p. (ISBN 0-210-22303-0). Asia.

History of Macedonia: Volume II: 550-336 B.C. N. G. L. Hammond & G. T. Griffith. (Illus.). 1979. 79.00x (ISBN 0-19-814814-3). Oxford U Pr.

History of Magic. Eliphas Levi. 1980. pap. 7.95 (ISBN 0-87728-077-0). Weiser.

History of Magic & Experimental Science, 8 vols. Lynn Thorndike. Incl. Vols. 1 & 2. The First Thirteen Centuries. 1923. Vol. 1. (ISBN 0-231-08794-2); Vol. 2. (ISBN 0-231-08795-0); Vols. 3 & 4. Fourteenth & Fifteenth Centuries. Vol. 3. (ISBN 0-231-08796-9); Vol. 4. (ISBN 0-231-08797-7); Vols. 5 & 6. The Sixteenth Century. 1941. Vol. 5. (ISBN 0-231-08798-5); Vol. 6. (ISBN 0-231-08799-3); Vols. 7 & 8. The Eighteenth Century. 1958. Vol. 7. (ISBN 0-231-08800-0); Vol. 8. (ISBN 0-231-08801-9). LC 23-2984. 30.00x ea. Columbia U Pr.

History of Maine: A Collection of Readings on the History of Maine 1600-1976. 4th ed. Ronald F. Banks. (History Series). 1976. pap. text ed. 12.95 o.p. (ISBN 0-8403-0020-4). Kendall-Hunt.

History of Malvern. Brian S. Smith. 1964. text ed. 6.75x (ISBN 0-7185-1041-0, Leicester). Humanities.

History of Man-Powered Flight. David A. Reay. 1977. text ed. 23.00 (ISBN 0-08-021738-9). Pergamon.

History of Management Thought. 2nd ed. Claude S. George, Jr. 256p. 1972. pap. text ed. 11.95 (ISBN 0-13-390187-4). P-H.

History of Manual & Industrial Education, 2 Vols, Vol. 1. to 1870, Vol. 2. 1870-1917. Charles A. Bennett. Vol. 1. text ed. 18.00 (ISBN 0-87002-005-6); Vol. 2. text ed. 20.68 (ISBN 0-87002-006-4). Bennett IL.

History of Maria Kittle, Repr. Of 1797 Ed. Ann E. Bleecker. Bd. with Miscellanies in Prose & Verse. Thomas Morris. Repr. of 1791 ed. LC 75-7041. (Indian Captivities Ser.: Vol. 20). 1976. lib. bdg. 44.00 (ISBN 0-8240-1644-0). Garland Pub.

History of Marine Corps Aviation in World War Two. Robert Sherrod. 496p. 1980. Repr. 16.95 (ISBN 0-89141-111-9). Presidio Pr.

History of Marketing Thought. 2nd ed. Robert Bartels. LC 76-6015. (Marketing Ser.). 1976. text ed. 19.95 o.p. (ISBN 0-88244-085-3). Grid Pub.

History of Maryland from the Earliest Period to the Present Day, 3 vols. Thomas J. Scharf. LC 67-5141. (Illus.). 1967. Repr. of 1879 ed. incl. index 74.00 (ISBN 0-8103-5037-8); index only 5.00 (ISBN 0-8103-5038-6). Gale.

History of Mathematical Notations, 2 vols. Florian Cajori. Incl. Vol. 1. Notations in Elementary Mathematics. xvi, 451p. 1951. 22.50 (ISBN 0-87548-171-X); pap. 5.95 o.p. (ISBN 0-87548-154-X); Vol. 2. Notations Mainly in Higher Mathematics. xviii, 367p. 1952. 19.95 (ISBN 0-87548-172-8). (Illus.). Open Court.

History of Mathematics. Carl B. Boyer. LC 68-16506. 1968. 26.95 (ISBN 0-471-09374-2). Wiley.

History of Mathematics. new ed. Arthur Gittleman. 304p. 1975. text ed. 18.95x (ISBN 0-675-08784-8). Merrill.

History of Mathematics, 2 vols. David E. Smith. Incl. Vol. 1. General Survey of the History of Elementary Mathematics. Repr. of 1923 ed (ISBN 0-486-20429-4); Vol. 2. Special Topics of Elementary Mathematics. Repr. of 1925 ed (ISBN 0-486-20430-8). pap. text ed. 7.50 ea. Dover.

History of Mechanical Engineering. Aubrey F. Burstall. (Illus.). 1963. 13.95 (ISBN 0-571-05343-2, Pub. by Faber & Faber). Merrimack Bk Serv.

History of Medical Education. Ed. by C. D. O'Malley. LC 72-85449. (UCLA Forum in Medical Sciences: No. 12). (Illus.). 1970. 50.00x (ISBN 0-520-01578-9). U of Cal Pr.

History of Medieval Europe. R. H. C. Davis. (Illus.). 1971. pap. text ed. 10.50x (ISBN 0-582-48208-9). Longman.

History of Medieval India. L. P. Sharma. 450p. 1981. text ed. 25.00x (ISBN 0-7069-1115-6, Pub. by Vikas India). Advent Bk.

History of Medieval Islam. J. J. Saunders. 1966. Repr. of 1965 ed. 20.00x (ISBN 0-7100-2077-5). Routledge & Kegan.

History of Medieval Islam. J. J. Saunders. (Illus.). 1978. pap. 8.95 (ISBN 0-7100-0050-2). Routledge & Kegan.

History of Mehmed the Conqueror. Beg Tursun. LC 77-89803. 1978. 30.00x (ISBN 0-88297-018-6). Bibliotheca.

History of Mental Retardation: Collected Papers, 2 vols. Ed. by Marvin Rosen & Gerald R. Clark. (Illus.). 700p. 1975. 24.50 ea. (ISBN 0-8391-0827-3). Vol. 2 (ISBN 0-685-56047-3). Univ Park.

History of Mexico, 6 vols. Hubert H. Bancroft. LC 67-29422. (Works of Hubert Howe Bancroft Ser.). 1967. Repr. of 1888 ed. Set. 150.00x (ISBN 0-914888-10-2). Bancroft Pr.

History of Mexico, 2 vols. Francesco S. Clavigero. Ed. by Burton Feldman & Robert D. Richardson. LC 78-60908. (Myth & Romanticism Ser.: Vol. 7). (Illus.). 1979. Set. lib. bdg. 132.00 (ISBN 0-8240-3556-9). Garland Pub.

History of Mexico: From Pre-Columbia to Present. A. Mayo. 1978. 13.95 (ISBN 0-13-390203-X). P-H.

History of Middle Europe: From the Earliest Times to the Age of the World Wars. Leslie C. Tihany. LC 75-25945. 1976. 21.00 (ISBN 0-8135-0814-2). Rutgers U Pr.

History of Militarism. rev. ed. Alfred Vagts. LC 59-7194. 1967. pap. text ed. 8.95 (ISBN 0-02-933050-5). Free Pr.

History of Mineola. Lucille Jones. 7.95 (ISBN 0-685-48804-7). Nortex Pr.

History of Miss Betsy Thoughtless, 4 vols. Eliza Haywood. Ed. by Ronald Paulson. LC 78-60837. (Novel 1720-1805 Ser.: Vol. 4). 1979. Set. lib. bdg. 124.00 (ISBN 0-8240-3653-0). Garland Pub.

History of Miss Clarinda Cathcart and Miss Fanny Renton, 1765, 2 vols. in 1. Jean Marishall. (Flowering of the Novel, 1740-1775 Ser: Vol. 71). 1974. lib. bdg. 50.00 (ISBN 0-8240-1170-8). Garland Pub.

History of Mississippi Libraries. Ed. by Margaret Peebles & J. B. Howell. 437p. 1975. 10.00 (ISBN 0-88289-190-1). Pelican.

History of Modern Art. 2nd ed. H. Horvard Arnason. (Illus.). 1976. 21.95 (ISBN 0-13-390351-6). P-H.

History of Modern Britain 1815-1975. 3rd ed. H. L. Peacock. 1976. pap. text ed. 10.50x o.p. (ISBN 0-435-31710-5). Heinemann Ed.

History of Modern British Geography. T. W. Freeman. (Illus.). 288p. 1980. lib. bdg. 33.00 (ISBN 0-582-30030-4). Longman.

History of Modern Criticism: 1750-1950: Volume 1 - the Later Eighteenth Century. Rene Wellek. 358p. Date not set. pap. price not set (ISBN 0-521-28295-0). Cambridge U Pr.

History of Modern Criticism: 1750-1950: Volume 2 - the Romantic Age. Rene Wellek. 460p. Date not set. pap. price not set (ISBN 0-521-28296-9). Cambridge U Pr.

History of Modern English Romanticism. Harko Gerrit De Maar. 246p. 1980. Repr. of 1924 ed. lib. bdg. 30.00 (ISBN 0-8492-4217-7). R West.

History of Modern France. Alfred Cobban. LC 65-14605. 1965. 10.00 o.s.i. (ISBN 0-8076-0310-4). Braziller.

History of Modern Greek Literature. Linos Politis. 341p. 1973. 31.00x (ISBN 0-19-815721-5). Oxford U Pr.

History of Modern Ireland: With a Sketch of Earlier Times. Giovanni Costigan. LC 69-15699. (Illus.). 1970. 7.50 (ISBN 0-672-63547-X). Pegasus.

History of Modern Non-Marxian Economics. Antal Matyas. Tr. by Istvan Veges. (Illus.). 598p. 1980. 50.00x (ISBN 963-05-1894-5). Intl Pubns Ser.

History of Modern Norway, 1814-1972. T. K. Derry. (Illus.). 1973. 45.00x (ISBN 0-19-822503-2). Oxford U Pr.

History of Modern Psychology. 3rd ed. Duane Schultz. LC 80-616. 1980. lib ed 18.95 (ISBN 0-12-633060-3); write for info. (ISBN 0-12-633065-4). Acad Pr.

History of Modern Whaling. Arne Odd Johnsen & Joh. N. Tonnessen. 1980. 45.00 (ISBN 0-520-03973-4). U of Cal Pr.

History of Montana: From Wilderness to Statehood, 1805-1970. 2nd. rev. & enl. ed. James M. Hamilton. LC 74-92542. (Illus.). 1970. 15.00 (ISBN 0-8323-0018-7). Binford.

History of Monterey County, Eighteen Eighty One: With Illustrations, Descriptions of Its Scenery, Farms, Residences, Public Buildings, Etc. Elliott & Moore. (Illus.). 1979. Repr. of 1881 ed. 24.95 (ISBN 0-913548-69-3, Valley Calif). Western Tanager.

History of Montgomery & Fulton Counties, New York. 1979. Repr. of 1878 ed. 25.00 o.s.i. (ISBN 0-932334-14-8). Heart of the Lakes.

History of Montgomery County. Robin Montgomery. (Illus.). 333p. 1975. 12.50 o.p. (ISBN 0-8363-0129-3). Jenkins.

History of Mother Twaddle & the Marvelous Achievements of Her Son Jack. Illus. by Paul Galdone. LC 73-9726. (Illus.). (ps-2). 1974. 6.95 (ISBN 0-395-28801-0, Clarion). HM.

History of Music. Ernst C. Krohn. LC 65-23398. (Music Reprint Ser.). 1973. Repr. of 1958 ed. lib. bdg. 27.50 (ISBN 0-306-70595-8). Da Capo.

History of Music. A. Perceval. (Teach Yourself Ser.). 1974. pap. 3.95 o.p. (ISBN 0-679-10437-2). McKay.

History of Music for Those Who Don't Want to Know Too Much About Music History. Lester Abbey. LC 80-124026. 1981. pap. 3.00. RWS Bks.

History of Music in American Life, Vol. 1: The Formative Years, 1620-1865. Ronald L. Davis. LC 79-25359. 386p. 1981. lib. bdg. 17.50 (ISBN 0-89874-002-9). Krieger.

History of Music in American Life, Vol. 2: The Gilded Years, 1865-1920. Ronald L. Davis. LC 79-25359. 314p. 1980. lib. bdg. 14.25 (ISBN 0-89874-003-7). Krieger.

History of Music in American Life, Vol. 3: The Modern Era, 1920 to the Present. Ronald L. Davis. LC 79-25359. 522p. 1981. lib. bdg. 23.50 (ISBN 0-89874-004-5); lib. bdg. 49.50 (ISBN 0-686-66036-6). Krieger.

History of Music in England. 3rd ed. Ernest Walker. Ed. by J. A. Westrup. LC 78-4596. (Music Reprint 1978 Ser.). 1978. Repr. of 1952 ed. lib. bdg. 35.00 (ISBN 0-306-77570-0). Da Capo.

History of Music in Scotland. Henry G. Farmer. LC 70-100613. (Music Ser). (Illus.). 1970. Repr. of 1947 ed. lib. bdg. 29.50 (ISBN 0-306-71865-0). Da Capo.

History of Music in Sound, Vols. 1-3. Ed. by Gerald Abraham. Incl. Vol. 1. Ancient & Oriental Music. Ed. by Egon Wellesz. (Illus.). 42p. 1957 (ISBN 0-19-323100-X); Vol. 2. Early Medieval Music up to 1300. Ed. by Dom A. Hughes. 70p. 1953 (ISBN 0-19-323101-8); Vol. 3. Ars Nova & the Renaissance, - C. 1300-1540. Ed. by J. A. Westrup. 70p. 1954 (ISBN 0-19-323102-6). 6.00 ea. Oxford U Pr.

History of Music in Sound, Vols. 4-10. Ed. by Gerald Abraham. Incl. Vol 4. Age of Humanism, 1540-1630. Ed. by J. A. Westrup. 1954 (ISBN 0-19-323103-4); Vol 5. Opera & Church Music, 1630-1750. Ed. by J. A. Westrup. 1954 (ISBN 0-19-323104-2); Vol 6. Growth of Instrumental Music 1630-1750. Ed. by J. A. Westrup. 1954 (ISBN 0-19-323105-0); Vol 7. Symphonic Outlook, 1750-90. Ed. by Egon Wellesz. 1957 (ISBN 0-19-323106-9); Vol. 8. Age of Beethoven, 1790-1830. Ed. by Gerald Abraham. 1958 (ISBN 0-19-323107-7); Vol. 9. Romanticism, 1830-90. Ed. by Gerald Abraham. 1958 (ISBN 0-19-323108-5); Vol. 10. Modern Music, 1890-1950. Ed. by Gerald Abraham. 1959 (ISBN 0-19-323109-3). 6.00 ea. Oxford U Pr.

History of Music Theory. rev. ed. Hugo Riemann. Tr. by Raymond Haggh. LC 75-125060. (Music Ser.). 435p. 1974. Repr. of 1966 ed. lib. bdg. 35.00 (ISBN 0-306-70637-7). Da Capo.

History of Music to the Death of Schubert. John K. Paine. LC 78-127280. (Music Ser). (Illus.). 1970. Repr. of 1907 ed. lib. bdg. 27.50 (ISBN 0-306-70038-7). Da Capo.

History of Musical Americanism. Barbara A. Zuck. Ed. by George Buelow. (Studies in Musicology). 412p. 1980. 34.95 (ISBN 0-8357-1109-9, Pub. by UMI Res Pr). Univ Microfilms.

History of Muslim Historiography. Franz Rosenthal. 1968. text ed. 93.50x (ISBN 90-04019-06-5). Humanities.

History of My Life, Vols. 1 & 2. Giacomo Casanova. Tr. by Willard R. Trask. LC 66-22274. (Helen & Kurt Wolff Bk). (Illus.). 679p. 1967. slipcase 10.00 o.p. (ISBN 0-15-141080-1). HarBraceJ.

History of Myddle. Richard Gough. 1979. Repr. text ed. 19.50x (ISBN 0-686-58501-1). Humanities.

History of Myddle, 17th Century England. Richard Gough. 35.00 (ISBN 0-87556-105-5). Saifer.

History of Narrative Film. David A. Cook. (Illus.). 1981. 24.95 (ISBN 0-393-01370-7). Norton.

History of National League Baseball: Since 1876. Glenn Dickey. LC 80-6261. 336p. 1981. 13.95 (ISBN 0-8128-2818-6); pap. 9.95 (ISBN 0-8128-6101-9). Stein & Day.

History of Nebraska. 2nd ed. James C. Olson. LC 54-8444. (Illus.). xvi, 387p. 1966. 14.95 (ISBN 0-8032-0135-4); pap. 9.95 (ISBN 0-8032-5790-2, BB 579, Bison). U of Nebr Pr.

History of Nepal. Ed. by D. Wright. Tr. by M. S. Singh. 1972. Repr. of 1877 ed. 18.00 (ISBN 0-8426-0478-2). Verry.

History of Nepal. Ed. by Daniel Wright. 1972. 9.50x (ISBN 0-685-89512-2). Himalaya Hse.

History of Neuces County. Nueces County Historical Society. 224p. 1974. 9.50 o.p. (ISBN 0-8363-0122-6). Jenkins.

History of Neurology. Walther Riese. LC 58-10645. (Illus.). 1959. 4.00 o.p. (ISBN 0-910922-09-8). MD Pubns.

History of Nevada. Russell R. Elliott. LC 72-187809. (Illus.). 1973. 13.95x (ISBN 0-8032-0781-6). U of Nebr Pr.

History of New Lots, Brooklyn to Eighteen Eighty-Seven. Alter F. Landesman. LC 76-30367. 1977. 12.50 (ISBN 0-8046-9172-X). Kennikat.

History of Newfoundland from the English, Colonial & Foreign Records. D. W. Prowse. 1971. Repr. of 1895 ed. pap. text ed. 51.50x (ISBN 90-6041-084-X). Humanities.

History of Nigeria. Alan Burns. 1972. text ed. 17.95x o.p. (ISBN 0-04-966011-X); pap. text ed. 17.95x (ISBN 0-04-966014-4). Allen Unwin.

History of Normandy & England, 4 vols. Francis Palgrave. LC 80-2218. 1981. Repr. of 1919 ed. 345.00 (ISBN 0-404-18770-6). AMS Pr.

History of Norwegian Literature. Harald Beyer. Tr. by Einar Haugen. LC 56-6801. 1956. pap. 7.00x (ISBN 0-8147-1023-9). NYU Pr.

History of Nursery Rhymes. Percy B. Green. LC 68-31082. 1968. Repr. of 1899 ed. 18.00 (ISBN 0-8103-3481-X). Gale.

History of Ophelia. Sarah Fielding. Ed. by Michael F. Shugrue. (Flowering of the Novel Ser.: 1740-1775). Repr. of 1760 ed. lib. bdg. 50.00 (ISBN 0-8240-1154-6). Garland Pub.

History of Ophthalmology. George E. Arrington, Jr. LC 58-13433. 1959. 4.00 o.p. (ISBN 0-910922-10-1). MD Pubns.

History of Orange County, New York: 1683-1881, 2 vols. E. M. Ruttenber & L. H. Clark. 1112p. 1980. Repr. of 1881 ed. 45.00 (ISBN 0-932334-33-4). Heart of the Lakes.

History of Orchestration. Adam Carse. (Illus.). 1935. pap. 5.00 (ISBN 0-486-21258-0). Dover.

History of Our Lord As Exemplified in Works of Art; with That of His Type; St. John the Baptist; & Other Persons of the Old & New Testament, 2 vols. Anna B. Jameson. LC 92-167006. (Illus.). 1976. Repr. of 1890 ed. Set. 35.00 (ISBN 0-8103-4304-5). Gale.

History of Oxford University. V. H. Green. 1974. 28.00 (ISBN 0-7134-1132-5, Pub. by Batsford England). David & Charles.

History of Parliamentary Elections & Electioneering: From the Stuarts to Queen Victoria. Joseph Grego. LC 73-141755. (Illus.). 403p. 1974. Repr. of 1892 ed. 36.00 (ISBN 0-8103-4030-5). Gale.

History of Pennsylvania. 2nd enlarged ed. Philip S. Klein & Ari Hoogenboom. LC 79-1731. (Illus.). 620p. 1980. 17.50 (ISBN 0-271-00216-6). Pa St U Pr.

History of Persia Under Qajar Rule. Tr. by Heribert Busse. LC 74-183229. 1972. 27.50x (ISBN 0-231-03197-1). Columbia U Pr.

History of Philosophical Ideas in America. William H. Werkmeister. LC 80-24507. xvi, 599p. 1981. Repr. of 1949 ed. lib. bdg. 49.75x (ISBN 0-313-22743-8, WEHI). Greenwood.

History of Philosophy. economy ed. George L. Abernathy & Thomas A. Langford. 1975. pap. text ed. 13.95x (ISBN 0-8221-0223-4). Dickenson.

History of Philosophy, 7 vols. Emile Brehier. Incl. Vol. 1. Hellenic Age. Tr. by Joseph Thomas. LC 63-20912. 1963. pap. text ed. 5.00x (ISBN 0-226-07217-7); Vol. 2. Hellenistic & Roman Age. Tr. by Wade Baskin. LC 63-20913. 1965. pap. text ed. 7.00x (ISBN 0-226-07221-5, P199); Vol. 3. Middle Ages & the Renaissance. Tr. by Wade Baskin. LC 63-20912. 1965. pap. text ed. 5.00x (ISBN 0-226-07219-3); Vol. 4. Seventeenth Century. Tr. by Wade Baskin. LC 63-20912. 1966. pap. text ed. 5.00x (ISBN 0-226-07225-8); Vol. 5. Eighteenth Century. Tr. by Wade Baskin. LC 63-20912. 1971. pap. text ed. 5.00x (ISBN 0-226-07227-4); Vol. 6. Nineteenth Century: Period of Systems 1800-1850. Tr. by Wade Baskin. LC 63-20912. 1973. pap. text ed. 5.00x (ISBN 0-226-07229-0); Vol. 7. Contemporary Philosophy - Since 1850. Tr. by Wade Baskin. LC 63-20912. 1973. pap. text ed. 5.00x (ISBN 0-226-07231-2, P538). Phoen). U of Chicago Pr.

History of Philosophy. J. Lewis. (Teach Yourself Ser.). 1974. pap. 2.95 o.p. (ISBN 0-679-10440-2). McKay.

History of Philosophy. William S. Sahakian. (Orig.). 1968. pap. 4.95 (ISBN 0-06-460002-5, 2, COS). Har-Row.

History of Philosophy, 3 vols. Thomas Stanley. Ed. by Rene Wellek. LC 75-11254. (British Philosophers & Theologians of the 17th & 18th Centuries Ser.). 1978. Repr. of 1687 ed. lib. bdg. 42.00 (ISBN 0-8240-1804-4). Garland Pub.

History of Philosophy: Greece & Rome, 2 pts, Vol. 1. Frederick Copleston. Pt. 1. pap. 2.95 (ISBN 0-385-00210-6, D134A, Im); Pt. 2. pap. 2.95 (ISBN 0-385-00211-4, D134B). Doubleday.

History of Philosophy in the West: A Synopsis from Descartes to Nietzsche. Thomas F. McGann. LC 79-66477. 1979. pap. text ed. 9.00 (ISBN 0-8191-0833-2). U Pr of Amer.

History of Philosophy-Maine De Biran to Sartre: Part I, the Revolution to Henri Bergson, Vol. 9. Frederick J. Copleston. 1977. pap. 2.45 (ISBN 0-385-12910-6, Im). Doubleday.

History of Philosophy-Maine De Biran to Sartre: Part II Bengson to Sartre, Vol. 9. Frederick J. Copleston. 1977. pap. 2.45 (ISBN 0-385-12926-2, Im). Doubleday.

History of Photography. Johann Willsberger. LC 76-24894. 1977. 13.95 (ISBN 0-385-12664-6). Doubleday.

History of Physical Education & Sport. Ed. by Earle F. Zeigler. LC 78-9066. (P-H Foundations of Physical Education & Sport Ser.). (Illus.). 1979. ref. ed. 15.95 (ISBN 0-13-391656-1). P-H.

History of Pianoforte Music. Herbert Westerby. LC 78-87624. (Music Ser). 1970. Repr. of 1924 ed. lib. bdg. 29.50 (ISBN 0-306-71809-X). Da Capo.

History of Pianoforte-Playing & Pianoforte-Literature. C. F. Weitzmann. LC 74-90209. (Music Reprint Ser). 1969. Repr. of 1897 ed. lib. bdg. 29.50 (ISBN 0-306-71817-0). Da Capo.

History of Pickwick. Percy H. Fitzgerald. 1980. Repr. of 1891 ed. lib. bdg. 45.00 (ISBN 0-8492-4631-8). R West.

History of Pike County, Georgia, 1822-1932. Lizzie R. Mitchell. LC 80-23352. x, 162p. 1980. Repr. 15.00 (ISBN 0-87152-345-0). Reprint.

History of Piracy. Philip Gosse. LC 75-16396. (Illus.). xvi, 349p. 1976. Repr. of 1934 ed. 22.00 (ISBN 0-8103-4156-5). Gale.

History of Pleasant Hill, California. Vallie Whitfield. 1981. 15.00 (ISBN 0-930920-15-5). Whitfield.

History of Poland Since Eighteen Sixty-Three. R. F. Leslie. LC 78-73246. (Soviet & East European Studies). 528p. 1980. 45.00 (ISBN 0-521-22645-7). Cambridge U Pr.

History of Polish Literature. Julian Krzyzanowski. Tr. by Doris Ronowicz from Polish. (Illus.). 807p. 1979. 39.95x (ISBN 0-686-60390-7, Pub. by Polish Scientific Pubs Poland). Hippocrene Bks.

History of Polish Literature. Czeslaw Milosz. LC 69-10189. (Illus.). 1969. 14.95 o.s.i. (ISBN 0-02-585010-5). Macmillan.

History of Political Parties in the Province of New York, 1760-1776. Carl L. Becker. 1960. pap. 7.95x (ISBN 0-299-02024-X). U of Wis Pr.

History of Political Philosophy. 2nd ed. Leo Strauss & Joseph Cropsey. LC 80-26907. xii, 850p. 1981. pap. text ed. 14.00x (ISBN 0-226-77690-5). U of Chicago Pr.

History of Political Thought in Germany, 1789-1815. Reinhold Aris. 414p. 1965. Repr. 28.00x (ISBN 0-7156-1646-3, F Cass Co). Biblio Dist.

History of Pompey the Little; or, the Life & Adventures of a Lap-Dog, 1751. Francis Coventry. Ed. by Michael F. Shugrue. (Flowering of the Novel, 1740-1775 Ser: Vol. 32). 1974. lib. bdg. 50.00 (ISBN 0-8240-1131-7). Garland Pub.

History of Portugal. Antonia H. De Olivera Marques. Incl. Vol. 1. From Lusitania to Empire. 507p. 22.50x (ISBN 0-231-03159-9); Vol. 2. From Empire to Corporate State. 303p. 20.00x (ISBN 0-231-08700-4). LC 77-184748. 1972. pap. 15.00x (ISBN 0-686-66878-2) (ISBN 0-231-08353-X). Columbia U Pr.

History of Post War Southeast Asia: Independence Problems. John F. Cady. LC 74-82497. xxii, 720p. 1974. pap. 20.00x (ISBN 0-8214-0160-2); pap. 10.00x (ISBN 0-8214-0175-0). Ohio U Pr.

History of Post-War Soviet Writing. Grigory Svirski. Tr. by Dessaix & Ulman. (Illus.). 1981. 17.50 (ISBN 0-88233-449-2). Ardis Pubs.

History of Postwar Britain, 1945-74. C. J. Bartlett. LC 77-3000. 1977. pap. text ed. 12.95 (ISBN 0-582-48320-4). Longman.

History of Postwar Russia. Pethybridge. pap. 2.45 (ISBN 0-452-25011-0, Z5011, Plume). NAL.

History of Presidential Elections: From George Washington to Jimmy Carter. Eugene H. Roseboom & Alfred E. Eckes, Jr. 1979. 15.95 (ISBN 0-02-604890-6); pap. 9.95 (ISBN 0-02-036420-2, Collier). Macmillan.

History of Preventive Medicine. Harry Wain. 420p. 1970. text ed. 42.50 (ISBN 0-398-02000-0). C C Thomas.

History of Printing Ink, Balls & Tollers: 1440-1850. Colin H. Bloy. (Illus.). 17.50 (ISBN 0-913720-07-0). Sandstone.

History of Private Bill Legislation, 2 Vols. Frederick Clifford. LC 70-350284. Repr. of 1885 ed. 55.00x (ISBN 0-678-05163-1). Kelley.

History of Private Bill Legislation, 2 vols. Frederick Clifford. 1968. 75.00x (ISBN 0-7156-1563-7, F Cass Co). Biblio Dist.

History of Procedure in England from the Norman Conquest: The Norman Period (1066-1204) Melville M. Bigelow. LC 80-2235. 1981. Repr. of 1880 ed. 44.50 (ISBN 0-404-18752-8). AMS Pr.

History of Programming Languages. Ed. by Richard L. Wexelblat. LC 80-518. (ACM Monograph Ser.). 1980. write for info. (ISBN 0-12-745040-8). Acad Pr.

History of Protective Tariff Laws. R. W. Thompson. (Neglected American Economists Ser.). 1974. lib. bdg. 50.00 (ISBN 0-8240-1022-1). Garland Pub.

History of Providence As Explained in the Bible. Alexander Carson. (Summit Bks). 1977. pap. 2.95 (ISBN 0-8010-2402-1). Baker Bk.

History of Prussia. H. W. Koch. (Illus.). 1978. text ed. 25.00x (ISBN 0-582-48189-9); pap. text ed. 12.50x (ISBN 0-582-48190-2). Longman.

History of Psychoanalysis. Reuben Fine. LC 78-31425. 1979. 25.00 (ISBN 0-231-04208-6). Columbia U Pr.

History of Psychology. Thomas H. Leahey. (Illus.). 1980. text ed. 18.95 (ISBN 0-13-391755-X). P-H.

History of Psychology: A Guide to Information Sources. Ed. by Wayne Viney et al. LC 79-9044. (Psychology Information Guide Ser.: Vol. 1). 1979. 30.00 (ISBN 0-8103-1442-8). Gale.

History of Psychology in Autobiography, Vol. VII. Ed. by Gardner Lindzey. LC 30-20129. (Series of Books in Psychology). (Illus.). 1980. text ed. 24.95x (ISBN 0-7167-1119-2); pap. text ed. 15.95x (ISBN 0-7167-1120-6). W H Freeman.

History of Psychology in Autobiography, Vol. 6. Gardner Lindzey. 480p. 1974. Repr. text ed. 21.95 (ISBN 0-13-392274-X). P-H.

History of Public Accounting in the United States. James D. Edwards. Ed. by Gary J. Previts. LC 66-63369. 1978. pap. 11.95 (ISBN 0-8173-8903-2). U of Ala Pr.

History of Public Health. George Rosen. LC 58-8307. 1958. 9.95 (ISBN 0-910922-06-3). MD Pubns.

History of Public Libraries in Great Britain, 1845 to 1975. 2nd ed. T. Kelly. 1977. 34.00x (ISBN 0-85365-239-2, Pub. by Lib Assn England). Oryx Pr.

History of Punch. M. H. Spielmann. LC 69-16069. 1969. Repr. of 1895 ed. 28.00 (ISBN 0-8103-3553-0). Gale.

History of Radiotherapy. Gilbert H. Fletcher. (Illus.). 450p. 1981. 20.00 (ISBN 0-87527-145-6). Green. Postponed.

History of Recreation: America Learns to Play. 2nd ed. Foster R. Dulles. (Illus., Orig.). 1965. pap. text ed. 15.95 (ISBN 0-13-391953-6). P-H.

History of Refrigeration Throughout the World. 476p. 1979. 37.50 (ISBN 0-686-60075-4, IIR 64, IIR). Unipub.

History of Regulatory Taxation. R. Alton Lee. LC 73-80460. 240p. 1973. 16.00x (ISBN 0-8131-1303-2). U Pr of Ky.

History of Religions: China, Japan, Egypt, Babylonia, Assyria, India, Persia, Greece, Rome, Vol. I. G. F. Moore. (International Theological Library). 654p. 1914. text ed. 13.95x (ISBN 0-567-07202-9). Attic Pr.

History of Religions: Judaism, Christianity, Mohammedanism, Vol. II. G. F. Moore. (International Theological Library). 568p. 1920. text ed. 13.95x (ISBN 0-567-07203-7). Attic Pr.

History of Religious Education: Documents & Interpretations from the Judaeo - Christian Tradition. Robert Ulich. LC 68-29433. 1968. 15.00x (ISBN 0-8147-0420-4). NYU Pr.

History of Religious Ideas: From the Stone Age to the Eleusinian Mysteries, Vol. 1. Mircea Eliade. Tr. by Willard R. Trask from Fr. LC 77-16784. 1979. Repr. 20.00 (ISBN 0-226-20400-6); pap. 12.50 (ISBN 0-226-20401-4). U of Chicago Pr.

History of Religious Ideas, Vol. I: From the Stone Age to the Eleusinian Mysteries. Mircea Eliade. Tr. by Willard R. Trask from Fr. LC 77-16784. xviii, 490p. 1981. pap. 8.95 (ISBN 0-226-20401-4). U of Chicago Pr.

History of Reynoldsburg & Truro Township, Ohio. Cornelia M. Parkinson. (Illus.). 200p. 1981. 25.00 (ISBN 0-938404-02-4). Hist Tales.

History of Rhedi, the Hermit of Mount Ararat: An Oriental Tale, 1773. William Duff. (Flowering of the Novel, 1740-1775 Ser: Vol. 101). 1974. lib. bdg. 50.00 (ISBN 0-8240-1200-3). Garland Pub.

History of Roman Private Law, 3 vols in 4. Edwin C. Clark. Incl. Vol. 1. Source. 168p; Vol. 2. Jurisprudence, 2 vols. 1234p; Vol. 3. Regal. 634p. LC 64-13392. 2036p. 1906. 50.00x set (ISBN 0-8196-0146-2). Biblo.

History of Rome from Its Origins to 529 A.D. Moses Hadas. 7.25 (ISBN 0-8446-2182-X). Peter Smith.

History of Rome Through the Fifth Century, Vols. 1 & 2. Ed. by A. H. Jones. LC 68-13332. (Documentary History of Western Civilization Ser). 1969. 12.50x ea. o.s.i. Vol. 1 (ISBN 0-8027-2010-2). Vol. 2 (ISBN 0-8027-2011-0). Walker & Co.

History of Russia. Basil Dmytryshyn. (Illus.). 1977. 19.95 (ISBN 0-13-392134-4). P-H.

History of Russia. rev. 6th ed. Walther Kirchner. LC 72-5830. (Illus.). 403p. 1976. pap. 5.50 (ISBN 0-06-460169-2, 169, COS). Har-Row.

History of Russia. 3rd ed. Nicholas V. Riasanovsky. LC 76-42634. (Illus.). 1977. 27.50 (ISBN 0-19-502129-0); text ed. 17.95x (ISBN 0-19-502128-2). Oxford U Pr.

History of Russia & the Soviet Union. David MacKenzie & Michael Curran. 1977. 18.25x (ISBN 0-256-01934-7). Dorsey.

History of Russia: Peter the Great: the Great Reforms Being, Vol. 16. Sergei M. Soloviev. Tr. by K. A. Papmehl. 1981. 20.00 (ISBN 0-87569-042-4). Academic Intl.

History of Russia: Vol. 24, the Character of Old Russia. Ed. by S. M. Solovier. Tr. by Alexander V. Muller. 1980. 20.00 (ISBN 0-87569-034-3). Academic Intl.

History of Russian & Soviet Sea Power. Donald Mitchell. (Illus.). 400p. 1974. 19.95 (ISBN 0-02-585290-6). Macmillan.

History of Russian Literature from the Eleventh Century to the End of the Baroque. Dmytro Chyzhevskyi. LC 79-3074. (Illus.). 451p. 1981. Repr. of 1960 ed. 35.00 (ISBN 0-8305-0067-7). Hyperion Conn.

History of Russian Music. M. Montagu-Nathan. LC 76-82815. 1918. 12.00x (ISBN 0-8196-0251-5). Biblo.

History of St. Jospeh's Parish. 10.95 (ISBN 0-685-48800-4). Nortex Pr.

History of St. Tammany Parish. Frederick S. Ellis. (Illus.). Date not set. 19.95 (ISBN 0-88289-252-5). Pelican.

History of San Luis Obispo County, California, with Illustrations & Biographical Sketches of Its Prominent Men & Pioneers, 1883. Myron Angel. (Illus.). 1979. Repr. of 1883 ed. 25.00 o.p. (ISBN 0-913548-66-9, Pub. by Thompson & West). Western Tanager.

History of Sandford & Merton, 3 vols. in 1. Thomas Day. LC 75-32143. (Classics of Children's Literature, 1621-1932: Vol. 11). 1977. Repr. of 1789 ed. PLB 38.00 ea. (ISBN 0-8240-2260-2). Garland Pub.

History of Scepticism from Erasmus to Descartes. rev. ed. Richard H. Popkin. (Philosophical Texts & Studies). 1964. text ed. 28.50x (ISBN 9-0232-0438-7). Humanities.

History of Scepticism from Erasmus to Spinoza. Richard H. Popkin. 1979. 20.00x (ISBN 0-520-03827-4); pap. 6.95x (ISBN 0-520-03876-2, CAMPUS NO. 226). U of Cal Pr.

History of Science. William C. Dampier. 1965. pap. 19.95x (ISBN 0-521-09366-X, 366). Cambridge U Pr.

History of Science & Technology: A Select Bibliography. K. J. Rider. 1970. 13.75x (ISBN 0-85365-144-2, Pub. by Lib Assn England). Oryx Pr.

History of Science & Technology in India, 5 vols. O. P. Jaggi. Incl. Vol. 1. Dawn of Indian Technology-Pre-&-Proto-Historic Period. text ed. 18.00x (ISBN 0-8426-0743-9); Vol. 2. Dawn of Indian Science-Vedic & Upanishadic Period. text ed. 12.00x (ISBN 0-8426-0744-7); Vol. 3. Folk Medicine (India) text ed. 18.00x (ISBN 0-8426-0745-5); Vol. 4. Indian System of Medicine. text ed. 24.00x (ISBN 0-8426-0746-3); Vol. 5. Yogic & Tantric Medicine. text ed. 18.00x (ISBN 0-8426-0747-1). (Illus.). 1975. Set. text ed. 77.50x set o.p. (ISBN 0-8426-1314-5). Verry.

History of Science, Two: Hellenistic Science & Culture in the Last Three Centuries B.C. George Sarton. 1970. pap. 5.95 o.p. (ISBN 0-393-00526-7, Norton Lib). Norton.

History of Scientific & Technical Periodicals: The Origins & Development of the Scientific & Technical Press, 1665-1790. 2nd ed. David A. Kronick. LC 75-41487. 1976. 15.00 o.p. (ISBN 0-8108-0844-7). Scarecrow.

History of Scottish Literature. Maurice Lindsay. 1977. 22.50 (ISBN 0-7091-5642-1). Dufour.

History of Sea Warfare. Gervis Frere-Cook & Kenneth Macksey. (Illus.). 245p. 1980. 14.95 (ISBN 0-8069-9214-X, Pub by Guinness Superlatives England). Sterling.

History of Seafaring Based on Underwater Archaeology. Ed. by George F. Bass. LC 72-81455. (Illus.). 320p. 1972. 22.50 o.s.i. (ISBN 0-8027-0390-9). Walker & Co.

History of Servia & the Servian Revolution. Leopold Von Ranke. LC 78-126598. (Europe 1815-1945 Ser). 506p. 1973. Repr. of 1848 ed. lib. bdg. 45.00 (ISBN 0-306-70051-4). Da Capo.

History of Ships. Peter Kemp. (Illus.). 1978. 19.95 o.p. (ISBN 0-8467-0499-4, Pub. by Two Continents). Hippocrene Bks.

History of Shock Treatment. Ed. by Leonard R. Frank. LC 78-13550. (Illus.). 206p. 1978. 6.00 (ISBN 0-9601376-1-0). L R Frank.

History of Shoe Fashion. Eunice Wilson. LC 75-89994. (Illus.). pap. 8.95 (ISBN 0-87830-548-3). Theatre Arts.

History of Sir Charles Grandison, 3 vols. Samuel Richardson. Ed. by Jocelyn Harris. (Oxford English Novels Ser). (Illus.). 1720p. 1972. Set. boxed 47.00x o.p. (ISBN 0-19-255358-5). Oxford U Pr.

History of Slavery in Mauritius & the Seychelles, 1810-1875. Moses D. Nwulia. LC 79-15363. 280p. 1981. 18.50 (ISBN 0-8386-2398-0). Fairleigh Dickinson.

History of Smith & Wesson. Roy G. Jinks. (Illus.). 290p. 1977. 15.95 (ISBN 0-917714-14-8). Beinfeld Pub.

History of Sociological Analysis. Ed. by Tom Bottomore & Robert Nisbet. 717p. 1981. pap. text ed. 10.95x (ISBN 0-465-03024-6). Basic.

History of Song. rev. ed. Ed. by Denis Stevens. (Illus.). 1970. pap. 7.95 (ISBN 0-393-00536-4, Norton Lib). Norton.

History of South Africa, Social & Economic. C. W. DeKiewiet. 1941. pap. 14.95x (ISBN 0-19-821638-6). Oxford U Pr.

History of South & Central Africa. D. Wilson. 1975. pap. text ed. 8.95x (ISBN 0-521-20559-X). Cambridge U Pr.

History of South Dakota. 3rd, rev ed. Herbert S. Schell. LC 74-18431. (Illus.). xiv, 445p. 1975. pap. 6.50 (ISBN 0-8032-5820-8, BB 603, Bison). U of Nebr Pr.

History of Southeast Missouri. Ed. by Felix E. Snider. (Illus.). 1978. Repr. of 1888 ed. 35.00 o.p. (ISBN 0-911208-09-7). Ramfre.

History of Soviet Russia, 7 vols. Edward H. Carr. Incl. Vol. 1-3. The Bolshevik Revolution. 1951-53. 12.95 ea. Vol. 1 (52169). Vol. 2 (52175). Vol. 3 (52181); Vol. 4. The Interregnum. 1954. 12.95 (ISBN 0-685-22917-3, 52187); Vols. 5-6. Socialism in One Country. 1958-60. 12.95 ea. Vol. 5 (52193). Vol. 6 (52199); Vol. 7. Socialism in One Country. 1964. 14.95 (ISBN 0-685-22919-X). Pt. 2 (52202). Set. 29.95 (ISBN 0-686-66600-3, 52200). Macmillan.

History of Soviet Russia. M. K. Dziewanowski. LC 78-133392. (Illus.). 1979. pap. text ed. 15.95 (ISBN 0-13-392159-X). P-H.

History of Soviet Russia. 6th ed. Georg von Rauch. Tr. by Peter Jacobsohn & Annette Jacobsohn. LC 76-185777. 541p. 1972. pap. text ed. 7.95x. Praeger.

History of Spain & Portugal, 2 vols. Stanley G. Payne. LC 72-7992. (Illus.). 802p. 1973. text ed. 25.00 ea.; Vol. 1. (ISBN 0-299-06270-8); Vol. 2. (ISBN 0-299-06880-3); pap. text ed. 7.95 ea.; Vol. 1. (ISBN 0-299-06274-0); Vol. 2. (ISBN 0-299-06284-8). U of Wis Pr.

History of Spanish Piano Music. Linton E. Powell. LC 79-3761. 256p. 1980. 17.50x (ISBN 0-253-18114-3). Ind U Pr.

History of Standard Oil Company, 2 vols. in 1. Ida M. Tarbell. (Illus.). 15.00 (ISBN 0-8446-1441-6). Peter Smith.

History of Statistics & Probability. D. B. Owen. 1976. 37.55 (ISBN 0-8247-6390-4). Dekker.

History of Studies of Human Growth. J. M. Tanner. (Illus.). 500p. Date not set. price not set (ISBN 0-521-22488-8, 40485). Cambridge U Pr.

History of Surnames of the British Isles: A Concise Account of Their Origin, Evolution, Etymology & Legal Status. Cecil H. Ewen. LC 68-30597. 1968. Repr. of 1931 ed. 20.00 (ISBN 0-8103-3124-1). Gale.

History of Swedish Literature. Alrik Gustafson. LC 61-7722. (Illus.). 1961. 25.00x (ISBN 0-89067-035-8). Am Scandinavian.

History of Tamilnadu to A. D. 1336. N. Subrahmanian. (Illus.). 428p. 1974. text ed. 10.00 (ISBN 0-88253-434-3). Ind-US Inc.

History of Tattooing & Its Significance, with Some Account of Other Forms of Corporal Marking. Wilfrid D. Hambly. LC 73-174052. (Illus.). 346p. 1975. Repr. of 1925 ed. 26.00 (ISBN 0-8103-4024-0). Gale.

History of Taxation & Taxes in England, 4 Vols. 2nd ed. Stephen Dowell. LC 67-5737. Repr. of 1884 ed. 85.00x (ISBN 0-678-05167-4). Kelley.

History of Taxes on Knowledge: Their Origin & Repeal. Collet D. Collet. LC 75-142565. 1971. Repr. 18.00 (ISBN 0-8103-3615-4). Gale.

History of Technology, 5 vols. Incl. Vol. 1. From Early Times to Fall of Ancient Empires. Ed. by Charles Singer et al. 1954. 89.00x (ISBN 0-19-858105-X); Vol. 2. The Mediterranean Civilizations & the Middle Ages, c. 700 B.C. to c. A.D. 1500. Ed. by Charles Singer et al. 1956. 89.00x (ISBN 0-19-858106-8); Vol. 3. From the Renaissance to the Industrial Revolution, c. 1500-c. 1750. Ed. by Charles Singer et al. 1957. 89.00x (ISBN 0-19-858107-6); Vol. 4. The Industrial Revolution, c. 1750 to c. 1850. Ed. by Charles Singer et al. 1958. 89.00x (ISBN 0-19-858108-4); Vol. 5. The Late Nineteenth Century, c. 1850 to c. 1900. Ed. by Charles Singer et al. 1958. 89.00x (ISBN 0-19-858109-2); Vol. 6. The Twentieth Century, C. 1900 to C. 1950, Part I. Ed. by Trevor I. Williams. (Illus.). 716p. 1978. text ed. 65.00x (ISBN 0-19-858151-3); Vol. 7. The Twentieth Century, C. 1900 to C. 1950, Part II. Ed. by Trevor I. Williams. (Illus.). 860p. 1978. text ed. 69.00x (ISBN 0-19-858155-6). Oxford U Pr.

History of Technology & Invention Progress Through the Ages, Vol. 1: The Origins of Technological Civilization to 1450. Ed. by Maurice Daumas. 520p. 1980. 40.00x (ISBN 0-7195-3730-4, Pub. by Murray Pubs England). State Mutual Bk.

History of Technology & Invention Progress Through the Ages, Vol. 3: The Expansion of Mechanization 1725-1860. Ed. by Maurice Daumas. 700p. 1980. 40.00x (ISBN 0-7195-3732-0, Pub. by Murray Pubs England). State Mutual Bk.

History of Technology & Invention Through the Ages, Vol. 2: The First Stages of Mechanization 1450-1725. Ed. by Maurice Daumas. 694p. 1980. 40.00x (ISBN 0-7195-3731-2, Pub. by Murray Pubs England). State Mutual Bk.

History of Temple, N. H. 1768-1976. LC 76-20435. 1976. 29.50x (ISBN 0-87233-040-0). Bauhan.

History of Texas, from Sixteen Eighty-Five to Eighteen Ninety-Two, 2 vols. John H. Brown. (Illus.). Set. 45.00 (ISBN 0-8363-0045-9). Jenkins.

History of Textiles. Kax Wilson. (Illus.). 1979. lib. bdg. 30.00 (ISBN 0-89158-491-9); text ed. 18.00x (ISBN 0-89158-491-9). Westview.

History of the African People. 3rd ed. Robert W. July. LC 73-1348. 1980. 22.50 o.p. (ISBN 0-684-16291-1, ScribT). Scribner.

History of the African People. 3rd ed. Robert W. July. 832p. 1980. 22.50 (ISBN 0-684-16291-1); pap. text ed. 10.95 (ISBN 0-684-16411-6). Scribner.

History of the American Drama: From the Beginning to the Civil War. 2nd ed. Arthur H. Quinn. 1943. 29.50x (ISBN 0-89197-218-8). Irvington.

History of the American Drama: From the Civil War to the Present Day. rev ed. Arthur H. Quinn. 1946. 29.50x (ISBN 0-89197-219-6). Irvington.

History of the American People. (History of the American People Ser.). (gr. 7 up). pap. text ed. 9.28 o.p. (ISBN 0-88343-660-4); tchrs'. manual 3.00 o.p. (ISBN 0-88343-662-0). McDougal-Littell.

History of the American People: From the Beginnings to the Civil War, Vol. 1. (gr. 7 up). pap. text ed. 6.52 o.p. (ISBN 0-88343-663-9); tchrs'. manual 1.96 o.p. (ISBN 0-88343-664-7). McDougal-Littell.

History of the American People: Into the Twentieth Century, Vol. 2. (History of the American People Ser.). (gr. 7 up). text ed. 6.52 o.p. (ISBN 0-88343-665-5); tchrs'. manual 1.96 o.p. (ISBN 0-88343-666-3). McDougal-Littell.

History of the American Pianoforte. 2nd ed. Daniel Spillane. LC 68-16246. (Music Ser). 1968. Repr. of 1890 ed. lib. bdg. 22.50 (ISBN 0-306-71109-5). Da Capo.

History of the American School of Classical Studies at Athens, Nineteen Thirty-Nine to Nineteen Eighty. Lucy S. Meritt. 1981. price not set (ISBN 0-87661-942-1). Am Sch Athens.

History of the American Society of Mechanical Engineers. Bruce Sinclair. 304p. 1980. 15.00x (ISBN 0-8020-2380-0). U of Toronto Pr.

History of the American Working Class. 3rd ed. Anthony Bimba. LC 68-30818. (Illus.). 1968. Repr. of 1936 ed. lib. bdg. 25.00x (ISBN 0-8371-0020-8, BIWC). Greenwood.

History of the Amritime Closed-Cone Pines, Alta & Baja California. Daniel I. Axelrod. (U. C. Publications in Geological Sciences: Vol. 120). 1980. pap. 8.00 (ISBN 0-520-09620-7). U of Cal Pr.

History of the Anglo-Saxons from the Earliest Period to the Norman Conquest, 3 vols. 7th ed. Sharon Turner. LC 80-2207. 1981. Repr. of 1852 ed. 160.00 (ISBN 0-404-18790-0). AMS Pr.

History of the Anti-Corn-Law League, 2 Vols. Archibald Prentice. LC 68-21442. Repr. of 1853 ed. 32.50x (ISBN 0-678-05191-7). Kelley.

History of the Atchison, Topeka, & Santa Fe Railway. Keith L. Bryant, Jr. LC 74-8250. (Railroads of America Ser). (Illus.). 512p. 1975. 12.95 o.s.i. (ISBN 0-02-517920-9). Macmillan.

History of the Balkan Peoples. Rene Ristelhueber. Ed. & tr. by Sherman D. Spector. LC 78-147184. (Illus.). 470p. 1978. 28.50x (ISBN 0-8290-0176-X); pap. text ed. 12.50x (ISBN 0-8290-0177-8). Irvington.

History of the Baptists. William Sweet. Repr. 18.95 (ISBN 0-686-12350-6). Church History.

History of the Baptists in Missouri. R. S. Duncan. Date not set. Repr. of 1882 ed. price not set. Church History.

History of the Bemba: Political Growth & Change in North-Eastern Zambia Before 1900. Andrew O. Roberts. LC 73-5813. 408p. 1974. 30.00 (ISBN 0-299-06450-6). U of Wis Pr.

History of the Bible. Fred G. Bratton. 1959. pap. 5.25 o.p. (ISBN 0-8070-1353-6, BP239). Beacon Pr.

History of the Bible. P. J. Hunt. (Ladybird Ser.). 1975. pap. 1.49 (ISBN 0-87508-839-2). Chr Lit.

History of the Bolivian Labour Movement 1848-1971. G. Lora. Ed. by L. Whitehead. Tr. by Christine Whitehead. LC 76-22988. (Latin American Studies: No. 27). 1977. 44.50 (ISBN 0-521-21400-9). Cambridge U Pr.

History of the Book. 2nd ed. Svend Dahl. LC 68-12627. (Illus.). 1968. 10.00 (ISBN 0-8108-0057-8). Scarecrow.

History of the Boroughs & Municipal Corporations of the United Kingdom: From the Earliest to the Present Time, 3 vols. H. A. Merewether & J. A. Stephens. 1972. Repr. of 1835 ed. Set. text ed. 150.00x (ISBN 0-85527-402-6). Humanities.

History of the British Flora. 2nd ed. Harry Godwin. LC 73-84324. (Illus.). 500p. 1975. 125.00 (ISBN 0-521-20254-X). Cambridge U Pr.

History of the British Secret Service: Covers the Development of the Intelligence System from the Days of Henry VII to the Present. Richard Deacon. 6.50 (ISBN 0-686-28849-1). Academy Chi Ltd.

History of the Byzantine Empire: 324 AD to 1453 AD, 2 vols. Repr. 16.50 o.p. (ISBN 0-686-12367-0). Church History.

History of the Byzantine Empire, 324-1453, 2 Vols. Alexander A. Vasiliev. (Illus., Orig.). 1968. pap. 7.50x ea.; Vol. 1. (ISBN 0-299-80925-0); Vol. 2. (ISBN 0-299-80926-9). U of Wis Pr.

History of the Calculus of Variations in the Nineteenth Century. Isaac Todhunter. LC 61-18586. 15.95 (ISBN 0-8284-0164-0). Chelsea Pub.

History of the Calculus of Variations in the 18th Century. Robert Woodhouse. LC 64-20969. 7.95 (ISBN 0-8284-0177-2). Chelsea Pub.

History of the Calculus of Vatriations from the Seventeenth Through the Nineteenth Century. H. H. Goldstine. (Studies in the History of Mathematics & Physical Sciences Ser.: Vol. 5). (Illus.). 410p. 1981. 48.00 (ISBN 0-387-90521-9). Springer-Verlag.

History of the Cameroon. Tambi Eyongetah & Robert Brian. (Illus.). 192p. 1975. pap. text ed. 5.50x (ISBN 0-582-60254-8). Longman.

History of the Cannes Film Festival, 1946-1979. Andrew Sarris. (Illus.). 450p. 1981. 14.95 (ISBN 0-87754-224-4). Chelsea Hse.

History of the Care & Study of the Mentally Retarded. L. Kanner. (Illus.). 160p. 1974. pap. 7.50 (ISBN 0-398-03038-3). C C Thomas.

History of the Catnach Press. Charles Hindley. LC 67-27867. 1969. Repr. of 1887 ed. 20.00 (ISBN 0-8103-3259-0). Gale.

History of the Cheyenne People. Tom Weist. (Indian Culture Ser.). (Illus.). 1977. write for info. (ISBN 0-89992-506-5); pap. write for info. (ISBN 0-89992-507-3). Mt Coun Indian.

History of the Christian Church. Lyman Hurlbut & J. R. Flower. 1979. 3.35 (ISBN 0-8297-0575-9); pap. 2.35 (ISBN 0-8297-0574-0). Life Pubs Intl.

History of the Christian Church, 8 vols. Philip Schaff. Incl. Vol. 1. Apostolic Christianity. 14.95 (ISBN 0-8028-8047-9); Vol. 2. Ante-Nicene. 100-325. 14.95 (ISBN 0-8028-8048-7); Vol. 3. Nicene & Post-Nicene. 311-600. 14.95 (ISBN 0-8028-8049-5); Vol. 4. Medieval Christianity. 590-1073. 14.95 (ISBN 0-8028-8050-9); Vol. 5. Middle Ages. 1049-1294. 14.95 (ISBN 0-8028-8051-7); Vol. 6. Middle Ages. 1295-1517. 14.95 (ISBN 0-8028-8052-5); Vol. 7. German Reformation. 14.95 (ISBN 0-8028-8053-3); Vol. 8. Swiss Reformation. 14.95 (ISBN 0-8028-8054-1). 1960. Repr. 14.95 ea.; 119.60 (ISBN 0-8028-8046-0). Eerdmans.

History of the Christian Church, 3 vols. Phillip Schaff. Set. 49.95 (ISBN 0-8254-3708-3, RBDH). Kregel.

History of the Christian Church. Williston Walker. Repr. 17.95 (ISBN 0-686-12356-5). Church History.

History of the Christian Movement: The Development of Christian Institutions. A. Daniel Frankforter. LC 77-8071. 1978. text ed. 18.95 (ISBN 0-88229-292-7); pap. 8.95 (ISBN 0-88229-568-3). Nelson-Hall.

History of the Christmas Card. George Buday. LC 74-174012. (Tower Bks). (Illus.). xxiii, 304p. 1972. Repr. of 1954 ed. 26.00 (ISBN 0-8103-3931-5). Gale.

History of the Church, 7 vols. Intro. by B. H. Roberts. Incl. Vol 1 (1820-1834) 511p. 1974 (ISBN 0-87747-074-X); Vol. 2 (1834-1837) 543p. 1974 (ISBN 0-87747-075-8); Vol. 3 (1834-1839) 478p (ISBN 0-87747-076-6); Vol. 4 (1839-1842) 620p (ISBN 0-87747-077-4); Vol. 5 (1842-1843) 563p (ISBN 0-87747-078-2); Vol. 6 (1843-1844) 641p (ISBN 0-87747-079-0); Vol. 7 (period 2, The Apostolic Interregnum) 640p (ISBN 0-87747-080-4). 9.95 ea.; index 9.95 (ISBN 0-87747-291-2). Deseret Bk.

History of the Church, 8 vols. & Index. Joseph Smith. (Vol. 7 from the Manuscript History of Brigham Young). Set. pap. 12.95 (ISBN 0-87747-725-6); index 9.95 (ISBN 0-87747-291-2). Deseret Bk.

History of the Church in England. 3rd rev ed. John R. Moorman. 485p. 1973. 24.95 (ISBN 0-8192-1282-2). Morehouse.

History of the Church of Englande. Beda. (English Experience Ser.: No. 234). 382p. Repr. of 1565 ed. 55.00 (ISBN 90-221-0234-3). Walter J Johnson.

History of the Church of York, 1066-1127. Hugh The Chantor, pseud. Tr. & intro. by Charles Johnson. LC 80-2227. 1981. Repr. of 1961 ed. 34.50 (ISBN 0-404-18764-1). AMS Pr.

History of the Church, Vol. 5: Reformation & Counter-Reformation. Ed. by Hubert Jedin & John P. Dolan. 920p. 1980. 37.50 (ISBN 0-8164-0449-6). Crossroad NY.

History of the Churches in the United States & Canada. Robert T. Handy. 1979. pap. 6.95 (ISBN 0-19-502531-8, GB577, GB). Oxford U Pr.

History of the Circus. G. Speaight. LC 80-17376. 216p. 1980. 20.00 (ISBN 0-498-02470-9). A S Barnes.

History of the Co-Operative Movement in Israel: A Source Book in Seven Volumes. Harry Viteles. Incl. Bk. 1. Evolution of the Co-Operative Movement. 252p. 1966. (ISBN 0-85303-052-9); Bk. 2. Evolution of the Kibbutz Movement. 749p. 1967. (ISBN 0-85303-053-7); Bk. 3. Analysis of the Four Sectors of the Kibbutz Movement. 751p. 1968. (ISBN 0-85303-010-3); Bk. 4. Co-Operative Smallholders Settlements: The Moshav Movement. 405p. 1968. (ISBN 0-85303-012-X); Bk. 5. Workers Producers Transportation & Service Co-Operatives. 414p. 1968. (ISBN 0-85303-013-8); Bk. 6. Central Agricultural Co-Operatives. 750p. 1970. (ISBN 0-85303-031-6); Bk. 7. Consumers Co-Operative. 348p. 1970. 140.00x set (ISBN 0-686-23409-X). 100.00x set (ISBN 0-686-23407-3, Pub. by Vallentine Mitchell England); 20.00x ea. Biblio Dist.

History of the Colonial Agricultural Service. Geoffrey B. Masefield. 187p. 1972. 19.50x (ISBN 0-19-822336-6). Oxford U Pr.

History of the Common Law of Contract: The Rise of the Action of Assumpsit. A. W. Simpson. 660p. 1975. 65.00x (ISBN 0-19-825327-3). Oxford U Pr.

History of the Conquest of Egypt & North Africa & Spain Known As the Futuh Misr of Ibn'Abd Alhakam. Ed. by Charles C. Torrey. (Yale Oriental Researches Ser.: No. III). (Arabic.). 1922. 65.00x (ISBN 0-685-69878-5). Elliots Bks.

History of the Conquest of Mexico, 2 Vols. William H. Prescott. 1957. 6.00x ea. o.p. (Evman). Vol. 1 (ISBN 0-460-00397-6). Vol. 2 (ISBN 0-460-00398-4). Dutton.

History of the Countess of Dellwyn, 1759, 2 vols. in 1. Sarah Fielding. (Flowering of the Novel, 1740-1775 Ser: Vol. 53). 1974. lib. bdg. 50.00 (ISBN 0-8240-1152-X). Garland Pub.

History of the County for Sussex, Vol. 6, Pt. 1. (Victoria History of the Counties of England Ser.). (Illus.). 272p. 1980. 149.00 (ISBN 0-19-722753-8). Oxford U Pr.

History of the County of Chester, Vol. 3. Ed. by B. E. Harris. (Victoria History of the Counties of England Ser.). (Illus.). 260p. 1980. 149.00 (ISBN 0-19-722754-6). Oxford U Pr.

History of the County of Gloucester, Vol 7. Ed. by N. M. Herbert. (Victoria History of the Counties of England Ser.). (Illus.). 250p. 1980. 149.00 (ISBN 0-19-722755-4). Oxford U Pr.

History of the Cries of London. Charles Hindley. LC 67-23948. 1969. Repr. of 1884 ed. 15.00 (ISBN 0-8103-0156-3). Gale.

History of the Crusades, 3 vols. Steven Runciman. 65.00 ea.; Vol. 1. (ISBN 0-521-06161-X); Vol.2. (ISBN 0-521-06162-8); Vol. 3. (ISBN 0-521-06163-6); 165.00 set (ISBN 0-521-20554-9). Cambridge U Pr.

History of the Crusades, 2 vols. 2nd ed. Ed. by Kenneth M. Setton. Incl. Vol. 1. The First Hundred Years. Ed. by Marshall W. Baldwin. (Illus.). 740p. Repr. of 1955 ed (ISBN 0-299-04831-4); Vol. 2. The Later Crusades, 1189 to 1311. 2nd ed. Ed. by Robert L. Wolff & Harry W. Hazard. (Illus.). 896p. Repr. of 1962 ed (ISBN 0-299-04841-1). 1969. 40.00 ea. U of Wis Pr.

History of the Crusades, Vol. 3. Harry W. Hazard & Kenneth M. Setton. LC 68-9837. (Illus.). 752p. 1975. 40.00x (ISBN 0-299-06670-3). U of Wis Pr.

History of the Crusades, Vol. 4: The Art & Architecture of the Crusader States. Ed. by Harry W. Hazzard & Kenneth M. Setton. LC 68-9837. 1977. 40.00x (ISBN 0-299-06820-X). U of Wis Pr.

History of the Cumberland Valley Railroad. Paul J. Westhaeffer. LC 79-178. (Illus.). 1979. 21.50 (ISBN 0-933954-00-X). Natl Rail Hist Soc DC Corp.

History of the Czechs & Slovaks. R. W. Seton-Weston. 413p. 1980. Repr. of 1943 ed. lib. bdg. 50.00 (ISBN 0-8492-2974-X). R West.

History of the Dance: In Art & Education. Richard Kraus. LC 69-13716. 1969. ref. ed. 15.95 (ISBN 0-13-390054-1). P-H.

History of the Dance in Art & Education. 2nd ed. Richard Kraus & Sarah Charman. (Illus.). 432p. 1981. text ed. 15.95 (ISBN 0-13-390021-5). P-H.

History of the Development of Small Arms Ammunition, Vol. I: Martial Long Arms, Flintlock Through Rimfire. George A. Hoyem. LC 80-67532. (Illus.). 240p. 1981. 27.50x (ISBN 0-9604982-8-1). Armory Pubns.

History of the Diocese of Cork from Earliest Times to the Reformation. Evelyn Bolster. (Illus.). 548p. 1972. 27.00x (ISBN 0-686-28339-2, Pub. by Irish Academic Pr). Biblio Dist.

History of the Donner Party: A Tragedy of the Sierra. rev. ed. Charles F. McGlashan. Ed. by George H. Hinkle & Bliss M. Hinkle. (Illus.). 1947. 10.95 (ISBN 0-8047-0366-3); pap. 4.95 (ISBN 0-8047-0367-1, SP26). Stanford U Pr.

History of the Earth. Don Eicher & Lee McAlester. (Illus.). 1980. text ed. 21.95 (ISBN 0-13-390047-9). P-H.

History of the Eastern Mongols During the Ming Dynasty from 1368 to 1631. Dmitri Pokotilov & Rudolf Loewenthal. (Studies in Chinese History & Civilization). 148p. 1977. Repr. of 1947 ed. 17.00 (ISBN 0-89093-087-2). U Pubns Amer.

History of the Economic Analysis of the Great Depression in America. William E. Stoneman. Ed. by Frank Freidel. LC 78-62514. (Modern American History Ser.: Vol. 17). 1979. lib. bdg. 30.00 (ISBN 0-8240-3640-9). Garland Pub.

History of the Electric Locomotive. F. J. Haut. LC 76-103871. (Illus.). 224p. 1980. 20.00 (ISBN 0-498-02466-0). A S Barnes.

History of the Elementary School Contest in England. Ed. by Asa Briggs. Incl. Struggle for National Education. 1975. Repr. text ed. 45.00x o.p. (ISBN 0-8277-4327-0). British Bk Ctr.

History of the Emanuel Moor Double Keyboard Piano. Herbert A. Shead. LC 78-322797. (Illus.). 310p. (Orig.). 1978. pap. 37.50x (ISBN 0-9506023-0-2). Intl Pubns Serv.

History of the English Agricultural Labourer. Wilhelm Hasbach. Tr. by Ruth Kenyon. LC 67-2118. Repr. of 1908 ed. 20.00x (ISBN 0-678-05056-2). Kelley.

History of the English Constitution, 2 vols. Rudolph Gneist. Tr. by Philip A. Ashworth from Ger. 1980. Repr. of 1886 ed. Set. lib. bdg. 75.00x (ISBN 0-8377-0613-0). Rothman.

History of the English House. Nathaniel Lloyd. Date not set. 36.95 (ISBN 0-8038-0107-6). Hastings.

History of the English Language. G. L. Brook. (Andre Deutsch Language Library). 1977. lib. bdg. 20.50 o.p. (ISBN 0-233-95910-6). Westview.

History of the English Language. Oliver F. Emerson. LC 70-145520. 1971. Repr. of 1909 ed. 26.00 (ISBN 0-8103-3666-9). Gale.

History of the English Railway: Its Social Relations & Revelations 1820-1845, Vols. 1 & 2. J. A. Francis. 1972. Repr. of 1851 ed. 13.50 o.p. (ISBN 0-7153-4238-X). David & Charles.

History of the Eton College Hunt, 1857-1968. Ed. by M. F. Berry & C. M. Floyd. (Illus.). 12.25 (ISBN 0-85131-029-X, Dist. by Sporting Book Center). J A Allen.

History of the Excellence & Decline of the Constitution, Religion, Laws, Manners, & Genius of the Sumatrans, 1763, 2 vols. in 1. John Shebbeare. (Flowering of the Novel, 1740-1775 Ser: Vol. 66). 1974. lib. bdg. 50.00 (ISBN 0-8240-1165-1). Garland Pub.

History of the Expedition to Jerusalem, 1095-1127. Ed. by Henry S. Fink. Tr. by Sr. Frances R. Ryan. 1972. pap. text ed. 6.95x (ISBN 0-393-09423-5). Norton.

History of the Expedition to Jerusalem, 1095-1127. Fulcher Of Chartres. Ed. by Harold S. Fink. Tr. by Frances R. Ryan from Lat. LC 78-77847. 1969. 18.50x (ISBN 0-87049-097-4). U of Tenn Pr.

History of the Fairchild Family. Mary Sherwood. LC 75-32157. (Classics of Children's Literature, 1621-1932: Vol. 22). 1976. Repr. of 1818 ed. lib. bdg. 38.00 (ISBN 0-8240-2271-8). Garland Pub.

History of the First Bulgarian Empire. Steven Runciman. LC 80-2369. 1981. Repr. of 1930 ed. 48.50 (ISBN 0-404-18916-4). AMS Pr.

History of the Five Indian Nations. Cadwallader Colden. 181p. (YA) (gr. 9-12). 1958. pap. 4.95 (ISBN 0-8014-9086-3, CP86). Cornell U Pr.

History of the Former Han Dynasty, 3 vols. Pan Ku. Tr. by H. H. Dubs from Chinese. Incl. Vol. 1. 9.00x (ISBN 0-685-32338-2); Vol. 2. 10.00x (ISBN 0-87950-281-9); Vol. 3. 12.00x (ISBN 0-87950-282-7). LC 43-46839. 1980. Repr. of 1955 ed. Set. 25.00x (ISBN 0-87950-283-5). Spoken Lang Serv.

History of the Franks. Gregory - Bishop Of Tours. Tr. by Ernest Brehaut. (Columbia University Records of Civilization Ser). 1969. pap. 6.95x (ISBN 0-393-09845-1, NortonC). Norton.

History of the French Language. Peter Rickard. (Modern Languages Ser). 174p. 1974. text ed. 10.75x (ISBN 0-09-118740-0, Hutchinson U Lib); pap. text ed. 9.25x (ISBN 0-09-118741-9). Humanities.

History of the Gambia. rev. ed. Harry A. Gailey. 256p. 1980. text ed. 28.50x (ISBN 0-8290-0350-9); pap. text ed. 16.95x (ISBN 0-8290-0351-7). Irvington.

History of the German Army Since the Armistice. Jacques Benoist-Mechin. 345p. 1979. Repr. of 1939 ed. 22.50 (ISBN 0-86527-094-5). Fertig.

History of the German Baptist Brethren in Europe & America. Brumbaugh. Repr. 39.00 o.p. (ISBN 0-686-12346-8). Church History.

History of the German General Staff, 1657-1945. Walter Gorlitz. Tr. by Brian Battershaw from Ger. LC 75-3867. (Illus.). 508p. 1975. Repr. of 1953 ed. lib. bdg. 33.00x (ISBN 0-8371-8092-9, GOGG). Greenwood.

History of the German Novelle. rev. ed. E. K. Bennett. Rev. by H. M. Waidson. (Orig.). 1961. 47.50 (ISBN 0-521-04152-X); pap. 11.50 (ISBN 0-521-09152-7). Cambridge U Pr.

History of the Gothic Revival. 2nd ed. Charles Eastlake. Ed. by J. Mordaunt Crools. (Victorian Library). 1978. Repr. of 1872 ed. text ed. 44.25x (ISBN 0-7185-5033-1, Leicester). Humanities.

History of the Great American Crimes. Frank Triplett. (American Culture Library Bks.). (Illus.). 127p. 1981. 69.75 (ISBN 0-89901-031-8). Found Class Reprints.

History of the Great Trains. Christopher Cook. LC 77-73046. (Illus.). 1977. 14.95 o.p. (ISBN 0-15-140930-7). HarBraceJ.

History of the Great War, 1914-1918. 2nd ed. Charles R. Cruttwell. (Illus.). 1936. 36.00x o.p. (ISBN 0-19-821416-2). Oxford U Pr.

History of the Greek & Roman Theater. rev. ed. Margaret Bieber. (Illus.). 360p. 1980. 40.00x (ISBN 0-691-03521-0); pap. 15.00 (ISBN 0-691-00212-6). Princeton U Pr.

•**History of the Greek States, 700-388 BC.** Raphael Sealey. 1977. 22.75x (ISBN 0-520-03125-3); pap. 9.95x (ISBN 0-520-03177-6, CAMPUS 165). U of Cal Pr.

History of the Habsburg Empire, 1526-1918. Robert A. Kann. LC 72-97733. 1974. 36.50x (ISBN 0-520-02408-7). U of Cal Pr.

History of the Hapsburg Empire, 1526-1918. 2nd ed. Robert A. Kann. 662p. 1981. pap. 10.95x (ISBN 0-520-04206-9, CAMPUS 265). U of Cal Pr.

History of the Hartford Convention. Theodore Dwight. LC 77-99474. (American Constitutional & Legal History Ser). 1970. Repr. of 1833 ed. 45.00 (ISBN 0-306-71855-3). Da Capo.

History of the Harvard Law School & of Early Legal Conditions in America. Charles Warren. LC 72-112311. (American Constitutional & Legal History Ser). 1970. Repr. of 1908 ed. lib. bdg. 75.00 (ISBN 0-306-71913-4). Da Capo.

History of the Human Heart; or, the Adventures of a Young Gentleman, 1749. Ed. by Michael F. Shugrue. (Flowering of the Novel, 1740-1775 Ser: Vol. 26). 1974. lib. bdg. 50.00 (ISBN 0-8240-1125-2). Garland Pub.

History of the Hussite Revolution. Howard Kaminsky. 1967. 28.50x (ISBN 0-520-00625-9). U of Cal Pr.

History of the ICC from Panacea to Palliative. Ari Hoogenboom & Olive Hoogenboom. (Norton Essays in American History Ser.). 224p. 1976. text ed. 10.00x (ISBN 0-393-05565-5); pap. text ed. 3.95x (ISBN 0-393-09204-6). Norton.

History of the Indians of the United States. Angie Debo. LC 73-108802. (Civilization of the American Indian Ser.: Vol. 106). (Orig.). 1970. 13.50 (ISBN 0-8061-0911-4). U of Okla Pr.

History of the Institute of Marine Engineers. B. C. Curling. 242p. 1961. 3.00x (ISBN 0-900976-92-6, Pub. by Inst Marine Eng). Intl Schol Bk Serv.

History of the Insurrections in Massachusetts in 1786. G. R. Minot. LC 76-148912. (Era of the American Revolution Ser). 1971. Repr. of 1788 ed. lib. bdg. 22.50 (ISBN 0-306-70100-6). Da Capo.

History of the Irish Brigades in the Service of France. J. C. O'Callaghan. 674p. 1969. Repr. of 1870 ed. 35.00x (ISBN 0-7165-0068-X, Pub. by Irish Academic Pr Ireland). Biblio Dist.

History of the Irish Newspaper, Sixteen Eighty-Five - Seventeen Sixty. R. L. Munter. 49.50 (ISBN 0-521-05786-8). Cambridge U Pr.

History of the Irish Rebellion of Seventeen Ninety-Eight and Sequel. Charles H. Teeling. 1972. Repr. of 1876 ed. 14.00x o.p. (ISBN 0-7165-0014-0, Pub. by Irish Academic Pr Ireland). Biblio Dist.

History of the Islamic Peoples. C. Brockelmann. 1980. 15.00 (ISBN 0-7100-1118-0); pap. cancelled (ISBN 0-7100-0521-0). Routledge & Kegan.

History of the Island of Madagascar. Samuel Copland. LC 72-106856. Repr. of 1822 ed. 19.75x (ISBN 0-8371-3478-1). Negro U Pr.

History of the Issues & Problems Surrounding Goodwill in Accounting. Hugh P. Hughes. (Research Monograph: No. 80). 1981. pap. 15.00 postponed (ISBN 0-88406-119-1). Ga St U Busn Pub.

History of the Jew Since the First Century A.D. F. Schweitzer. 1971. 7.95 o.p. (ISBN 0-02-608160-1); pap. 1.95 (ISBN 0-02-089260-8). Macmillan.

History of the Jewish People. Max Margolis & Alexander Marx. LC 70-90074. (Temple Books). 1969. pap. text ed. 7.95x (ISBN 0-689-70134-9, T8). Atheneum.

History of the Jewish People in the Age of Jesus Christ (175 B.C.-A.D. 135, 2 vols. Emil Schurer. Ed. by Geza Vermes et al. Vol. 1, Repr. Of 1973 Ed., 632p. 42.00x (ISBN 0-567-02242-0); Vol. 2, Repr. Of 1979 Ed., 608p. 43.75x (ISBN 0-567-02243-9). Attic Pr.

History of the Jews in America. Deborah Pessin. (Illus.). 1957. pap. 4.95x (ISBN 0-8381-0189-5). United Syn Bk.

History of the Jews in England. 3rd ed. Cecil Roth. 1979. 13.50x (ISBN 0-19-822488-5). Oxford U Pr.

History of the Joint Chiefs of Staff: The Joint Chiefs of Staff & National Policy, 4 vols. Incl. Vol. 1. 1945-1947. James P. Schnabel; Vol. 2. 1947-1949. Kenneth W. Condit; Vol. 3. Korean War, 2 pts. James F. Schnabel & Robert J. Watson. Vol. 4, 1950-1952. 49.00. Set. 179.00 (ISBN 0-89453-148-4). M Glazier.

History of the Judiciary of Massachusetts. William Davis. LC 74-8535. (American Constitutional & Legal History Ser). xxiv, 446p. 1974. Repr. of 1900 ed. lib. bdg. 45.00 (ISBN 0-306-70613-X). Da Capo.

History of the Kimball Family in America from Sixteen Thirty-Four to Eighteen Ninety-Seven. Leonard A. Morrison & Stephen P. Sharples. 1978. Repr. of 1897 ed. 30.00x o.s.i. (ISBN 0-932334-02-4). Heart of the Lakes.

History of the Labor Movement in California. Ira B. Cross. (California Library Reprint Ser.). 1974. Repr. 22.50x (ISBN 0-520-02646-2). U of Cal Pr.

History of the Labor Movement in the United States, 4 vols. Philip S. Foner. Incl. Vol. 1. From Colonial Times to the Founding of the American Federation of Labor. 576p. 1947. 15.00 (ISBN 0-7178-0091-1); pap. 3.95 (ISBN 0-7178-0376-7); Vol. 2. From the Founding of the American Federation of Labor to the Emergence of American Imperialism. 480p. 1955. 15.00 (ISBN 0-7178-0092-X); pap. 4.95 (ISBN 0-7178-0388-0); Vol. 3. Policies & Practices of the A. F. of L. 1900-1909. 480p. 1964. 15.00 (ISBN 0-7178-0093-8); pap. 3.95 (ISBN 0-7178-0389-9); Vol. 4. Industrial Workers of the World. 608p. 1965. 15.00 (ISBN 0-7178-0094-6); pap. 4.95 (ISBN 0-7178-0396-1). LC 47-19381. Intl Pub Co.

History of the Labor Movement in the United States: The AFL in the Progressive Era (1910-1915, Vol. 5. Philip S. Foner. 15.00 (ISBN 0-7178-0570-0); pap. 4.95 (ISBN 0-7178-0562-X). Intl Pub Co.

History of the Labour Party: New Impression. G. D. Cole. 1978. Repr. of 1958 ed. 40.00x (ISBN 0-7100-6628-7). Routledge & Kegan.

History of the Later Roman Empire from the Death of Theodosius Eight to the Death of Justinian, 2 vols. J. B. Bury. 11.00 ea. (ISBN 0-8446-1785-7). Peter Smith.

History of the Law of Charity, 1532-1827. Gareth H. Jones. (Cambridge Studies in English Legal History). 1969. 45.00 (ISBN 0-521-07347-2). Cambridge U Pr.

History of the Lewis & Clark Expedition, 3 vols. Meriwether Lewis & William Clark. Ed. by Elliot Coues. (Illus.). 1508p. 1979. pap. 5.00 ea. Vol. 1 (ISBN 0-486-21268-8). Vol. 2 (ISBN 0-486-21269-6). Vol. 3 (ISBN 0-486-21270-X). Dover.

History of the Life & Adventures of Mr. Anderson. Edward Kimber. Ed. by Wilcomb E. Washburn. LC 75-7026. (Narratives of North American Indian Captivities: Vol. 7). 1975. lib. bdg. 44.00 (ISBN 0-8240-1631-9). Garland Pub.

History of the Life & Works of Rafaello. A. C. De Quincy. Ed. by Sydney J. Freedberg. LC 77-25764. (Connoisseurship Criticism & Art History Ser.: Vol. 19). (Illus.). 1980. lib. bdg. 52.00 (ISBN 0-8240-3277-2). Garland Pub.

History of the Life of the Squire Marcos de Obregon, 2 vols. in 1. Vincente Espinel. Tr. by Algernon Langton. LC 80-2578. 1981. Repr. of 1816 ed. 76.50 (ISBN 0-404-19110-X). AMS Pr.

History of the Lombards. Paul The Deacon. Tr. by William D. Foulke. LC 72-80382. (Middle Ages Ser). 1974. 15.00x (ISBN 0-8122-7671-X); pap. 4.95x (ISBN 0-8122-1079-4). U of Pa Pr.

History of the Long Captivity & Adventures of Thomas Pellow in South Barbary... Written by Himself. LC 75-170600. (Foundations of the Novel Ser.: Vol. 71). lib. bdg. 50.00 (ISBN 0-8240-0583-X). Garland Pub.

History of the Los Angeles Labor Movement, 1911-1941. Louis B. Perry & Richard S. Perry. 1963. 22.75x (ISBN 0-520-01002-7). U of Cal Pr.

History of the Louisville & Nashville Railroad. Maury Klein. (Railroads of America Ser.). (Illus.). 384p. 1972. 10.95 o.s.i. (ISBN 0-02-563890-4). Macmillan.

History of the Loves of Antiochus & Stratonice, in Which Are Intersper'd Some Accounts Relating to Greece & Syria. Lewis Theobald. LC 76-170540. (Foundations of the Novel Ser.: Vol. 29). lib. bdg. 50.00 (ISBN 0-8240-0541-4). Garland Pub.

History of the Lower Shenandoah Valley Counties of Frederick, Berkeley, Jefferson, & Clarke. J. E. Norris. (Illus.). 925p. Repr. of 1890 ed. 32.50 (ISBN 0-685-65082-0). Va Bk.

History of the Maghrib. 2nd ed. J. M. Abun-Nasr. LC 74-25653. (Illus.). 432p. 1975. 49.50 (ISBN 0-521-20703-7); pap. 16.95x (ISBN 0-521-09927-7). Cambridge U Pr.

History of the Mathematical Theory of Probability. Isaac Todhunter. LC 51-146. 1949. 15.95 (ISBN 0-8284-0057-1). Chelsea Pub.

History of the Mental Health Services. Kathleen Jones. (International Library of Social Policy). 422p. 1972. 30.00x (ISBN 0-7100-7452-2). Routledge & Kegan.

History of the Modern British Chemical Industry. D. W. Hardie & J. Davidson Pratt. 1966. 22.00 (ISBN 0-08-011687-6); pap. 10.75 (ISBN 0-08-011686-8). Pergamon.

History of the Modern Music of Western Europe: From the First Century of the Christian Era to the Present Day. Raphael G. Kiesewetter. LC 74-140375. (Music Ser). 354p. 1973. Repr. of 1848 ed. lib. bdg. 25.00 (ISBN 0-306-70089-1). Da Capo.

History of the Modern World. R. J. Unstead. Incl. World War One. LC 72-92427 (ISBN 0-382-06091-1); The Twenties. LC 72-92427 (ISBN 0-382-06094-6); The Thirties. LC 72-92430 (ISBN 0-382-06095-4); World War Two. LC 72-92428 (ISBN 0-382-06093-8); Turn of the Century. LC 74-26174 (ISBN 0-382-06096-2); The Forties & Fifties. LC 74-31819 (ISBN 0-382-06097-0); The Sixties. LC 75-18048 (ISBN 0-382-06098-9). (Illus.). (gr. 4 up). lib. bdg. 7.95 (ISBN 0-686-57850-3, Pub. by Macdonald Ed). Silver.

History of the Moderne Protestant Divines, Containing Their Parents, Countries, Education, with Register of Their Writings. Verheiden Jacobus. Tr. by D. Lupton from Latin. LC 79-84142. (English Experience Ser.: No. 959). 400p. 1979. Repr. of 1637 ed. lib. bdg. 28.00 (ISBN 90-221-0959-3). Walter J Johnson.

History of the Moghuls of Central Asia, Being the Tarikh-I-Rashidi. Mirza M. Haidar. Ed. by N. Elias. Tr. by E. D. Ross. (Records of Asian History). (Illus.). 1972. text ed. 17.00x (ISBN 0-7007-0021-8). Humanities.

History of the Mongol Conquests. J. J. Saunders. 1971. 25.00 (ISBN 0-7100-7073-X). Routledge & Kegan.

History of the Mongols: Based on Eastern & Western Accounts of the Thirteenth & Fourteenth Centuries. Bertold Spuler. Tr. by Helga Drummond. 1971. 21.75x (ISBN 0-520-01960-1). U of Cal Pr.

History of the Musical Box & of Mechanical Music. Alfred Chapuis. Ed. by Howard M. Fitch & Helen F. Fitch. Tr. by Joseph E. Roesch from Fr. LC 80-12449. (Illus.). xvi, 304p. 1980. 27.50 (ISBN 0-915000-01-6). Musical Box Soc.

History of the National Negro Labor Council. Mindy Thompson. (Occasional Papers: No. 27). 1978. 2.25 (ISBN 0-89977-022-3). Am Inst Marxist.

History of the National Resources Planning Board, 1933-1943. Philip W. Warken. Ed. by Frank Freidel. LC 78-66882. (Modern American History Ser.: Vol. 19). 1979. lib. bdg. 24.00 (ISBN 0-8240-3642-5). Garland Pub.

History of the Near East in Modern Times, 3 vols. George Arnakis & Vucinish. Incl. Vol. 1. Ottoman Empire & the Balkan States to 1900. (Illus.). 452p (ISBN 0-8363-0046-7); Vol. 2. Forty Crucial Years: 1900-1940 (ISBN 0-8363-0047-5). 15.00 ea. Jenkins.

History of the Nineteenth Century in Caricature. Arthur B. Maurice & Frederic T. Cooper. LC 79-136560. (Tower Bks). (Illus.). 1971. Repr. of 1904 ed. 28.00 (ISBN 0-8103-3909-9). Gale.

History of the North Olympic Peninsula. Patricia Campbell. Ed. by Frank Ducceschi. (Illus.). 72p. 1979. pap. 6.95 (ISBN 0-918146-17-8). Peninsula WA.

History of the North Wales Slate Industry. Jean Lindsay. 1974. 25.00 (ISBN 0-7153-6265-8). David & Charles.

History of the Northern Securities Case. Balthasar Henry Meyer. LC 70-124898. (American Constitutional & Legal History Ser). 136p. 1972. Repr. of 1906 ed. lib. bdg. 19.50 (ISBN 0-306-71989-4). Da Capo.

History of the Oberlin-Wellington Rescue. Jacob R. Shipherd. LC 77-127261. (Civil Liberties in American History Ser). 280p. 1972. Repr. of 1859 ed. lib. bdg. 32.50 (ISBN 0-306-71241-5). Da Capo.

History of the Opera: From Monteverdi to Donizetti, 2 vols. in one. Sutherland Edwards. LC 77-5587. 1977. Repr. of 1862 ed. lib. bdg. 49.50 (ISBN 0-306-77416-X). Da Capo.

History of the Organ in the United States. Orpha Ochse. LC 73-22644. (Illus.). 512p. 1975. 22.50x (ISBN 0-253-32830-6). Ind U Pr.

History of the Ottoman Empire & Modern Turkey. S. J. Shaw. LC 76-9179. (Illus.). 1977. Set. 82.00 (ISBN 0-521-08772-4); Vol. 1. 42.00 (ISBN 0-521-21280-4); Vol. 2. 54.00 (ISBN 0-521-21449-1); Set. pap. 27.50 (ISBN 0-521-08759-7); Vol. 1. pap. 15.95 (ISBN 0-521-29163-1); Vol. 2. pap. 17.95 (ISBN 0-521-29166-6). Cambridge U Pr.

History of the Ottoman Empire 1730. Ed. by M. A. Cook. LC 75-38188. (Illus.). 232p. 1976. 32.95 (ISBN 0-521-20891-2); pap. 10.50x (ISBN 0-521-09991-9). Cambridge U Pr.

History of the Past & Present State of the Labouring Population, 2 vols. J. D. Tuckett. 916p. 1971. Repr. of 1846 ed. 60.00x (ISBN 0-7165-1572-5, Pub. by Irish Academic Pr Ireland). Biblio Dist.

History of the Peace Conference of Paris, 6 vols. Ed. by H. W. Temperley. Incl. Vol. 1. 1920; Vol. 2. The Settlement with Germany; Vol. 3. Chronology, Notes & Documents; Vol. 4. 1921; Vol. 5. Economic Reconstruction & Protection of Minorities; Vol. 6. 1924. (Royal Institute of International Affairs Ser). 1924. 179.00x set (ISBN 0-19-821478-2). Oxford U Pr.

History of the People of Trinidad & Tobago. Eric E. Williams. 10.95 (ISBN 0-685-20593-2). Transatlantic.

History of the Philippines: From the Spanish Colonization to the Second World War. Renato Constantino. 459p. 1981. pap. 8.95 (ISBN 0-85345-579-1). Monthly Rev.

History of the Pianoforte. Edgar Brinsmead. LC 79-76136. (Music Story Ser). (Illus.). 1969. Repr. of 1879 ed. 18.00 (ISBN 0-8103-3559-X). Gale.

History of the Pianoforte & Pianoforte Players. 2nd ed. Oscar Bie. LC 66-28445. 1966. Repr. of 1899 ed. lib. bdg. 18.50 (ISBN 0-306-70938-4). Da Capo.

History of the Political & Military Transactions in India During the Administration of the Marquis of Hastings, 1813-1823, 2 vols. H. T. Prinsep. (Illus.). 988p. 1972. Repr. of 1825 ed. 84.00x (ISBN 0-7165-2134-2, Pub. by Irish Academic Pr Ireland). Biblio Dist.

History of the Queen's Park Rangers. F. C. Signy. 10.00x (ISBN 0-392-07910-0, SpS). Soccer.

History of the Railways. John Ray. 1969. pap. text ed. 4.95x o.p. (ISBN 0-435-31754-7). Heinemann Ed.

History of the RAVC, 1919-1961. J. Clabby. (Illus.). 19.25 (ISBN 0-85131-082-6, Dist. by Sporting Book Center). J A Allen.

History of the Reformation, 2 vols. Thomas Lindsay. Repr. 48.00 o.p. (ISBN 0-686-12348-4). Church History.

History of the Reformation: In Germany, Vol. 1. 2nd ed., T. M. Lindsay. (International Theological Library). 544p. 1907. text ed. 13.95x. Attic Pr.

History of the Reformation: In Lands Beyond Germany, Vol. 2. 2nd ed. T. M. Lindsay. (International Theological Library). 648p. 1908. text ed. 13.95x (ISBN 0-567-07212-6). Attic Pr.

History of the Reign of King Henry the Seventh. Francis Bacon. Ed. by Fritz J. Levy. LC 70-177471. (European Historiography Ser). 1972. 6.95 (ISBN 0-672-61420-0). Bobbs.

History of the Religion of Israel: From the Babylonian Captivity to the End of the Prophecy, Vol. 4. 35.00x (ISBN 0-685-56209-3). Ktav.

History of the Reorganized Church of Jesus Christ of Latter Day Saints Vol. 5: 1890-1902. F. Henry Edwards. 1969. 15.00 (ISBN 0-8309-0019-5). Herald Hse.

History of the Reorganized Church of Jesus Christ of Latter Day Saints, Vols. 6 & 7. F. Henry Edwards. Incl. Vol. 6. 1903-1914. 1970 (ISBN 0-8309-0030-6); Vol. 7. 1915-1925. 1973 (ISBN 0-8309-0075-6). 15.00 ea. Herald Hse.

History of the Reorganized Church of Jesus Christ of the Latter Day Saints, Vol. 8: 1926-1946. F. Henry Edwards. 1976. 15.00 (ISBN 0-8309-0157-4). Herald Hse.

History of the Ridiculous Extravagancies of Monsieur Oufle Occasion'd by His Reading Books Treating of Magick, the Black-Art Demoniacks... & Other Superstitious Practices. Abbe L. Bordelon. LC 76-170524. (Foundations of the Novel Ser.: Vol. 17). lib. bdg. 50.00 (ISBN 0-8240-0529-5). Garland Pub.

History of the Roman People. Fritz M. Heichelheim & C. A. Yeo. 1962. text ed. 19.95 (ISBN 0-13-392126-3). P-H.

History of the Romanian Communist Party. Robert R. King. (Publication Ser.: No. 206). 225p. (Orig.). 1980. pap. 8.95 (ISBN 0-8179-7332-X). Hoover Inst Pr.

History of the Russian Revolution. Leon Trotsky. 1980. pap. 14.95 (ISBN 0-913460-83-4). Monad Pr.

History of the Sailing Ship. Marshall Cavendish Editorial Board. LC 74-32633. (Illus.). 1975. 12.95 o.p. (ISBN 0-668-03780-6). Arco.

History of the St. Louis Car Company. Andrew D. Young & Eugene F. Provenzo, Jr. (Illus.). 304p. 1981. Repr. of 1978 ed. 27.50 (ISBN 0-8310-7114-1). A S Barnes.

History of the St. Louis Car Company. Andrew D. Young & Eugene F. Provenzo, Jr. (Illus.). 304p. 1981. Repr. of 1978 ed. 27.50 (ISBN 0-8310-7114-1). Howell-North.

History of the San Francisco Committee of Vigilance of 1851. Mary F. Williams. LC 71-87676. (American Scene Ser.). 1969. Repr. of 1921 ed. lib. bdg. 49.50 (ISBN 0-306-71716-6). Da Capo.

History of the Santee Sioux: United States Indian Policy on Trial. Roy W. Meyer. LC 80-11810. xviii, 434p. 1979. pap. 7.95 (ISBN 0-8032-8109-9, BB 751, Bison). U of Nebr Pr.

History of the Sciences. Stephen F. Mason. Orig. Title: Main Currents of Scientific Thought. 1962. pap. 6.95 (ISBN 0-02-093400-9, Collier). Macmillan.

History of the Sciences in Greco-Roman Antiquity. Arnold Reymond. Tr. by Ruth G. De Bray. LC 63-18046. 1963. 10.50x (ISBN 0-8196-0128-4). Biblo.

History of the Secret Societies of the Army, & of the Military Conspiracies Which Had As Their Object the Destruction of the Government of Bonaparte. Charles Nodier. LC 78-14740. 1978. Repr. of 1815 ed. 26.00x (ISBN 0-8201-1318-2). Schol Facsimiles.

History of the Sheffield Scientific School of Yale, 2 vols. Russel H. Chittenden. 1928. 150.00x (ISBN 0-685-69797-5). Elliots Bks.

History of the Sherman Law of the United States of America. Albert H. Walker. LC 80-12873. xiii, 320p. 1980. Repr. of 1910 ed. lib. bdg. 25.00x (ISBN 0-313-22475-7, WAHS). Greenwood.

History of the Siege of Boston & of the Battles of Lexington, Concord & Bunker Hill. Richard Frothingham. LC 77-115680. (Era of the American Revolution Ser). 1970. Repr. of 1903 ed. lib. bdg. 37.50 (ISBN 0-306-71932-0). Da Capo.

History of the Sixteen Karmapas of Tibet. Karma Thinley. Ed. by David Stott. LC 80-179. (Illus.). 1980. pap. 6.95 (ISBN 0-87773-716-9, Prajna). Great Eastern.

History of the Skyscraper. Francisco Mujica. LC 76-57764. (Architecture & Decorative Art Ser.). 1977. Repr. of 1929 ed. lib. bdg. 85.00 (ISBN 0-306-70862-0). Da Capo.

History of the Soccer World Cup. Brian Glanville. LC 73-8089. (Illus.). 256p. 1974. pap. 4.95 o.s.i. (ISBN 0-02-028840-9, Collier). Macmillan.

History of the Society of Jesus. William V. Bangert. LC 78-188687. (Original Studies Composed in English Ser.: No. 3). (Illus.). 570p. 1972. 14.75 o.s.i. (ISBN 0-912422-05-X); pap. 7.00; Smyth sewn 9.00 (ISBN 0-912422-23-8). Inst Jesuit.

History of the Southern Confederacy. Clement Eaton. 1954. pap. text ed. 3.95 (ISBN 0-02-908710-4). Free Pr.

History of the Southern Confederacy. Clement Eaton. 1954. 7.95 o.s.i. (ISBN 0-02-534730-6). Macmillan.

History of the Spirit Lake Massacre! 8th March, 1857 & of Miss Abigail Gardiner's 3 Month's Captivity Among the Indians. According to Her Own Account, As Given to L. P. Lee, Repr. Of 1857 Ed. Lorenzo P. Lee. Bd. with History of the Spirit Lake Massacre & Captivity of Miss Abbie Gardner. Abigail Sharp. Repr. of 1885 ed. LC 75-7097. (Indian Captivities Ser.: Vol. 72). 1976. lib. bdg. 44.00 (ISBN 0-8240-1696-3). Garland Pub.

History of the Sunnyside Community: This Land We Hold. Ernestine L. Bowden. 12.95 o.p. (ISBN 0-685-48808-X). Nortex Pr.

History of the Synoptic Tradition. 2nd ed. Rudolf Bultmann. Tr. by John Marsh. 1972. Repr. of 1968 ed. 48.00x (ISBN 0-631-11350-9, Pub. by Basil Blackwell). Biblio Dist.

History of the Telescope. Henry C. King. LC 79-87811. (Illus.). 480p. 1980. Repr. of 1979 ed. 16.50x (ISBN 0-938164-05-8). Vintage Bk Co.

History of the Theory of Numbers, 3 Vols. Leonard E. Dickson. LC 66-26932. 49.50 (ISBN 0-8284-0086-5). Chelsea Pub.

History of the Thirteen. Honore de Balzac. Tr. by Herbert J. Hunt from Fr. (Classics Ser). 1978. pap. 3.95 (ISBN 0-14-044301-0). Penguin.

History of the Thirty Years' Peace 1816-1846, 4 vols. Harriet Martineau. (Development of Industrial Society Ser.). 2007p. 1980. Repr. 160.00x (ISBN 0-7165-1753-1, Pub. by Irish Academic Pr). Biblio Dist.
History of the Town of Keene (N.H.), Seventeen Thirty-Two to Nineteen Hundred & Four. S. G. Griffinn & M. A. Whitcomb. (Illus.). 792p. (Orig.). 1980. Repr. of 1904 ed. 38.00 (ISBN 0-917890-21-3). Heritage Bk.
History of the Two Maids of More-Clacke. Robert Armin. Ed. by Alexander S. Liddie & Stephen Orgel. LC 78-66849. (Renaissance Drama Ser.). 1979. lib. bdg. 35.00 (ISBN 0-8240-9742-4). Garland Pub.
History of the Uniforms of the British Army, Vols. 1-2, 4-5. Cecil C. P. Lawson. Vol. 1. 18.00 o.p. (ISBN 0-498-09865-6); Vol. 2. 18.00 o.p. (ISBN 0-498-06080-2); Vol. 3. 18.00 o.p. (ISBN 0-498-01529-7); Vol. 4. 18.00 o.p. (ISBN 0-498-07562-1); Vol. 5. 18.00 o.p. (ISBN 0-498-06692-4). A S Barnes.
History of the United States Army. R. F. Weigley. 1967. 14.95 (ISBN 0-02-625640-1). Macmillan.
History of the United States Capitol, 2 Vols. in 1. Glenn Brown. LC 71-77734. (Architecture & Decorative Art Ser.: Vol. 34). (Illus.). 1970. Repr. of 1903 ed. lib. bdg. 75.00 (ISBN 0-306-71372-1). Da Capo.
History of the United States of America: A Guide to Information Sources. Ed. by Ernest Cassara. LC 73-17551. (American Studies Information Guide Series: Vol. 3). 1977. 30.00 (ISBN 0-8103-1266-2). Gale.
History of the Viola. Maurice W. Riley. LC 79-66348. 1979. 27.50 (ISBN 0-9603150-0-4); pap. 22.50 (ISBN 0-9603150-1-2). M W Riley.
History of the Virginia Convention of 1788, 2 Vols. Hugh B. Grigsby. LC 70-75319. (American History, Politics & Law Ser.). 1969. Repr. of 1890 ed. Set. lib. bdg. 65.00 (ISBN 0-306-71280-6). Da Capo.
History of the Waldenses: 1832 Ed, 2 vols. Adam Blair. Set. 185.00 (ISBN 0-686-12404-9). Church History.
History of the Western Boundary of the Louisiana Purchase, 1819-1841. T. M. Marshall. LC 73-87411. (American Scene Ser). (Illus.). 1970. Repr. of 1914 ed. lib. bdg. 27.50 (ISBN 0-306-71554-6). Da Capo.
History of the Western Educational Experience. Gerald L. Gutek. 448p. 1972. text ed. 13.95x (ISBN 0-394-31355-0, RanC). Random.
History of the Western National. R. C. Anderson & G. Frankis. LC 79-51082. (Illus.). 1979. 19.95 (ISBN 0-7153-7771-X). David & Charles.
History of the Western Railway 1863-1921. Clinker Macdermat. 19.25x (ISBN 0-392-07907-0, SpS). Soccer.
History of the World's Racing Cars. Richard Hough & M. Frostick. (Illus.). 1965. 15.00 o.s.i. (ISBN 0-06-002700-2, HarpT). Har-Row.
History of the Worsted Manufacture in England from the Earliest Times. John James. LC 68-93903. Repr. of 1857 ed. 25.00x (ISBN 0-678-05179-8). Kelley.
History of the Worthies of England, 3 vols. Thomas Fuller. 66.50 o.p. (ISBN 0-686-12340-9). Church History.
History of the Yorubas: From the Earliest Times to the Beginning of the British Protectorate. Samuel Johnson. 1969. Repr. of 1921 ed. 32.50 (ISBN 0-7100-1615-8). Routledge & Kegan.
History of the 508th Parachute Infantry. William G. Lord. (Airborne Ser.: No. 2). (Illus.). 1977. 20.00 o.p. (ISBN 0-89839-002-8); pap. 15.00 (ISBN 0-89839-001-X). Battery Pr.
History of Thoracic Surgery. Richard H. Meade. (Illus.). 960p. 1961. 89.75 (ISBN 0-398-01271-7). C C Thomas.
History of Thought on Economic Integration. Fritz Machlup. LC 76-54770. 1977. 22.50x (ISBN 0-231-04298-1). Columbia U Pr.
History of Tom Jones, a Foundling, 2 vols. Henry Fielding. Ed. by Fredson Bowers. LC 73-15009. (Wesleyan Edition of the Works of Henry Fielding Ser.). (Illus.). 1250p. 1974. Set. 50.00x (ISBN 0-8195-4068-4, Pub. by Wesleyan U Pr); pap. 7.50x (ISBN 0-8195-6048-0). Columbia U Pr.
History of Tom Jones the Foundling, in His Married State, 1750. Ed. by Michael F. Shugrue. (Flowering of the Novel, 1740-1775 Ser: Vol. 28). 1974. lib. bdg. 50.00 (ISBN 0-8240-1127-9). Garland Pub.
History of Tom Thumb. Ed. by Alison Lurie & Justin G. Schiller. Incl. Robin Hood's Garland; Pleasant & Delightful History of Jack & the Giants, 2 pts; Home Treasury. LC 75-32133. (Classics of Children's Literature 1621-1932 Ser.). PLB 38.00 (ISBN 0-8240-2250-5). Garland Pub.
History of Transfusion & Blood Banking Practices. A. Gottleib. Date not set. 25.00 (ISBN 0-8391-1468-0). Univ Park.
History of Travel. Winfried Loschburg. Tr. by Ruth Michaelis-Jena & Patrick Murray. LC 80-461783. (Illus.). 190p. 1979. 37.50x (ISBN 0-8002-2423-X). Intl Pubns Serv.
History of Tunnels. Patrick Beaver. (Illus.). 155p. 1976. pap. 4.95 (ISBN 0-8065-0527-3). Citadel Pr.
History of Ukrainian Literature from the 11th to the End of the 19th Century. Dmytro Cyzevs'Kyj. Tr. by D. Ferguson. LC 73-94029. 650p. 1975. lib. bdg. 30.00x (ISBN 0-87287-093-6); pap. text ed. 20.00 (ISBN 0-87287-170-3). Ukrainian Acad.
History of U. S. Foreign Policy. 3rd ed. Julius W. Pratt. LC 72-149978. (Illus.). 1972. ref. ed. 18.95 o.p. (ISBN 0-13-392316-9). P-H.
History of United States Foreign Policy. 4th ed. Julius W. Pratt et al. 1980. text ed. 19.95 (ISBN 0-13-392282-0). P-H.
History of U. S. Political Parties, 4 vols. Ed. by Arthur M. Schlesinger, Jr. LC 72-8682. 3600p. 1981. Repr. of 1973 ed. pap. 75.00 (ISBN 0-87754-134-5). Chelsea Hse.
History of Urban & Regional Planning. Anthony Sutcliffe. 300p. 1980. 35.00 (ISBN 0-87196-303-5). Facts on File.
History of Urban Form: Before the Industrial Revolutions. 2nd ed. A. E. Morris. 1979. 46.95x (ISBN 0-470-26614-7); pap. 18.95 (ISBN 0-470-26612-0). Halsted Pr.
History of Urology. Leonard J. Murphy. (Illus.). 548p. 1972. 44.75 (ISBN 0-398-02366-2). C C Thomas.
History of Utopian Thought. Joyce O. Hertzler. LC 65-22443. 321p. 1965. Repr. of 1923 ed. 28.50x (ISBN 0-8154-0113-2). Cooper Sq.
History of Valency. C. A. Russell. 1971. text ed. 18.00x (ISBN 0-391-00033-0, Leicester). Humanities.
History of Vanillo Gonzales, Surnamed the Merry Bachelor. Alain R. Le Sage. LC 80-2489. 1981. Repr. of 1881 ed. 48.00 (ISBN 0-404-19123-1). AMS Pr.
History of Violin Etude to About Eighteen Hundred. K. Marie Stolba. (Music Reprint Ser.). 1968. Repr. of 1869 ed. lib. bdg. 25.00 (ISBN 0-306-79544-2). Da Capo.
History of Visual Communication. 2nd ed. Josef Muller-Brockmann. (Illus.). 334p. 1981. pap. 29.50 (ISBN 0-8038-3059-9, Visual Communication). Hastings.
History of Wages in the United States from Colonial Times to 1928 with Supplement, 1929-1933. United States Bureau Of Labor Statistics. LC 67-13749. 1966. Repr. of 1934 ed. 25.00 (ISBN 0-8103-3363-5). Gale.
History of War & Weapons: 449 to 1660 (English Warfare from the Anglo-Saxons to Cromwell) A. V. Norman & Don Pottinger. 1967. 7.95 o.p. (ISBN 0-690-39366-0, TYC-T). T Y Crowell.
History of West Africa. 4th ed. J. D. Fage. LC 71-85742. (Illus.). 1969. 27.50 (ISBN 0-521-07406-1); pap. 8.95x (ISBN 0-521-09579-4). Cambridge U Pr.
History of West Africa, Vol. 1. 2nd ed. Ed. by J. F. Ajayi & Michael Crowder. 1976. 30.00x (ISBN 0-231-04102-0); pap. text ed. 17.50x (ISBN 0-231-04103-9). Columbia U Pr.
History of West Africa, Vol. 2. Ed. by J. F. Ajayi & Michael Crowder. 672p. 1974. 22.50x o.p. (ISBN 0-231-03737-6); pap. 12.50x o.p. (ISBN 0-231-03738-4). Columbia U Pr.
History of West Africa 1000-1800. Basil Davidson. Ed. by F. A. Buah & J. F. Ade Ajayi. (Growth of African Civilisation Ser.). (Illus.). 1978. pap. text ed. 7.50x (ISBN 0-582-60340-4). Longman.
History of Western Art. Michael Levey. (World or Art Ser.). (Illus.). 1968. pap. 9.95 (ISBN 0-19-519943-X). Oxford U Pr.
History of Western Civilization: A Handbook. rev. ed. William H. McNeill. LC 69-18121. 1969. text ed. 16.50x (ISBN 0-226-56137-2); pap. 8.95x (ISBN 0-226-56138-0). U of Chicago Pr.
History of Western Education. 11th ed. William Boyd & Edmund J. King. LC 65-789. 1980. pap. 13.50x (ISBN 0-389-20131-6). B&N.
History of Western Music. rev. ed. Donald J. Grout. (Illus.). 1973. text ed. 18.95x (ISBN 0-393-09416-2). Norton.
History of Western Music. rev. ed. Donald J. Grout. (Illus.). 540p. 1973. pap. text ed. 15.95x (ISBN 0-393-09358-1). Norton.
History of Western Music. Christopher Headington. LC 76-20883. 1977. 12.95 (ISBN 0-02-871090-8); pap. text ed. 8.95 (ISBN 0-02-871080-0). Schirmer Bks.
History of Western Oil Shale. Paul L. Russell. (Illus.). 176p. 1980. 49.50 (ISBN 0-686-61811-4). Ctr Prof Adv.
History of Western Ontology from Thales to Heidegger. Rodolfo Ahumada. LC 78-60794. 1978. pap. text ed. 9.50 (ISBN 0-8191-0507-4). U Pr of Amer.
History of Western Seapower: From the Campaign of Discovery to the Rise of England. Peter Padfield. (Illus.). Date not set. 14.95 o.p. (ISBN 0-679-51075-3). McKay.
History of Western Society. John P. McKay et al. LC 78-69592. (Illus.). 1979. pap. text ed. 17.95 1 vol. ed. (ISBN 0-395-27276-9); pap. text ed. 13.75 ea. 2 vol. ed.; pap. text ed. 11.95 ea. 3 vol. ed.; inst. manual 0.65 (ISBN 0-395-27421-4); wkbk. study guide 7.50 (ISBN 0-395-27420-6). HM.
History of Western Technology. Friedrich Klemm. (Illus.). 1964. pap. 9.95x (ISBN 0-262-61001-9). MIT Pr.
History of White Magic. 1979. pap. 6.95 (ISBN 0-87728-482-2). Weiser.
History of Whitgift School. F. H. Percy. 1976. 16.95 (ISBN 0-7134-3158-X, Pub. by Batsford England). David & Charles.
History of Wichita Falls. Jonnie Morgan. 9.95 (ISBN 0-685-48810-1). Nortex Pr.
History of Winchester Firearms, Eighteen Sixty-Six to Nineteen Eighty. rev. ed. Duncan Barnes. (Illus.). 272p. 1980. 21.95 (ISBN 0-87691-324-9). Winchester Pr.
History of Wine. 2nd ed. H. Warner Allen. (Illus.). 1962. 8.95 o.p. (ISBN 0-571-04409-3, Pub. by Faber & Faber). Merrimack Bk Serv.
History of Wise County: A Link with the Past. Wise County Historical Survey Committee. Ed. by Rosalie Gregg. (Illus.). 515p. 1974. 25.00 (ISBN 0-89015-076-1). Nortex Pr.
History of Witchcraft & Demonology. Montague Summers. (Illus.). 370p. 1973. 28.00 (ISBN 0-7100-4970-6); pap. 12.50 (ISBN 0-7100-7613-4). Routledge & Kegan.
History of Witchcraft: Sorcerers, Heretics & Pagans. Jeffrey B. Russell. (Illus.). 1980. 15.95 (ISBN 0-500-01225-3). Thames Hudson.
History of Wood-Engraving. George E. Woodberry. LC 69-17490. 1969. Repr. of 1883 ed. 15.00 (ISBN 0-8103-3890-4). Gale.
History of Wool in Britain. Shiela Lewenhak. (Jackdaw Ser: No. 96). (Illus.). 1972. 5.95 o.p. (ISBN 0-670-78213-0, Grossman). Viking Pr.
History of World Cinema. rev. ed. David Robinson. LC 80-51767. (Illus.). 512p. 1981. 14.95 (ISBN 0-8128-2747-3). Stein & Day.
History of World War 1 First Day Bombardment Group. Thomas Miller. 1970. pap. 1.95x o.p. (ISBN 0-685-55084-2, Pub. by WW). Aviation.
History of Yiddish Literature in the Nineteenth Century. Leo Wiener. LC 73-136773. 440p. 1973. Repr. of 1899 ed. 14.50 o.p. (ISBN 0-87203-032-6). Hermon.
History of York-Pullman Auto, 1903-1917. W. H. Shank. 1970. 2.50 (ISBN 0-933788-24-X). Am Canal & Transport.
History, People & Places Series. Incl. History, People & Places in Normandy. Barbara Whelpton. LC 75-314602. 144p. 1975. 11.50x (ISBN 0-902875-57-4); History, People & Places in Yorkshire. Arthur Gaunt. LC 75-331730. 160p. 1975. 11.50x (ISBN 0-902875-77-9); History, People & Places in New Oxfordshire. Frank Martin. 144p. 1975. 12.50x (ISBN 0-902875-53-1); History, People & Places in the Thames Valley. Frank Martin. LC 73-167149. 142p. 1972. 9.00x (ISBN 0-902875-15-9); History, People & Places in Chiltern Villages. Vera Burden. LC 73-174593. 136p. 1972. 9.00x (ISBN 0-902875-21-3); History, People & Places in the Cotwolds. J. Allan Cash. LC 75-307571. 160p. 1975. 11.50x (ISBN 0-902875-59-0). (Illus.). 1975. Intl Pubns Serv.
History, Philosophy & Culture in the Young Gramsci. Ed. by Pedro Cavalcanti & Paul Piccone. LC 74-82995. 160p. (Orig.). 1975. 9.50 (ISBN 0-914386-07-7); pap. 3.95 (ISBN 0-914386-05-0). Telos Pr.
History, Principles, & Practice of Symbolism in Christian Art. F. Edward Hulme. LC 68-18027. 1969. Repr. of 1891 ed. 20.00 (ISBN 0-8103-3214-0). Gale.
History, Self-Understanding of the Church: Concilium, Vol.67. Ed. by Roger Aubert. LC 75-168655. (Religion in the Seventies). 1971. pap. 4.95 (ISBN 0-8164-2523-X). Crossroad NY.
History Teaching & Historical Understanding. Ed. by A. K. Dickinson. P. J. Lee. LC 79-300044. 1978. pap. text ed. 10.95x (ISBN 0-435-80291-7). Heinemann Ed.
History: The Last Things Before the Last. Siegfried Kracauer. 1969. text ed. 16.95x (ISBN 0-19-500604-6). Oxford U Pr.
Histriomastix. William Prynne. LC 75-170418. (English Stage Ser: Vol. 13). lib. bdg. 50.00 (ISBN 0-8240-0596-1). Garland Pub.
Hit. Brian Garfield. LC 75-93719. (Cock Robin Mystery). 1970. 4.50 o.s.i. (ISBN 0-02-542640-0). Macmillan.
H.I.T. A Manual for the Classification, Filing, & Retrieval of Palmprints. Patricia A. Kolb. (Illus.). 112p. 1979. text ed. 16.50 spiral bdg. (ISBN 0-398-03855-4). C C Thomas.
Hit Me with a Rainbow. James Kirkwood. 1981. pap. 3.25 (ISBN 0-440-13622-9). Dell.
Hit the Bike Trail. Alice Sankey. LC 73-7315. (Pilot Book Ser.). (Illus.). 128p. (gr. 4-7). 1974. 6.95 (ISBN 0-8075-3320-3). A Whitman.
Hit the Sign & Win a Free Suit of Clothes from Harry Finklestein. Bert R. Sugar. 1978. 11.95 o.p. (ISBN 0-8092-7787-5). Contemp Bks.
Hit the Silk. Doddy Hay. LC 72-85004. (gr. 5-8). 1969. 8.95 (ISBN 0-87599-163-7). S G Phillips.
Hitchhike. Isabelle Holland. (YA) 1979. pap. 1.50 (ISBN 0-440-93663-2, LFL). Dell.
Hitchhike. Isabelle Holland. LC 77-7931. (gr. 5-9). 1977. 9.95 (ISBN 0-397-31751-4). Lippincott.
Hitchikers. Thompson. (Triumph Bks.). (gr. 6 up). 1980. PLB 6.90 (ISBN 0-531-04115-8, B17). Watts.
Hitchikers No. 2. Paul Thompson. (Hi Lo Ser.). 96p. (gr. 6 up). 1981. pap. 1.50 (ISBN 0-553-14619-X). Bantam.
Hite Report. Shere Hite. Date not set. pap. price not set (ISBN 0-440-13690-3). Dell.
Hite Report on Male Sexuality. Shere Hite. LC 80-2709. 1981. 17.95 (ISBN 0-394-41392-X). Knopf.
Hitler, a Study in Tyranny. rev. ed. Alan Bullock. (Illus.). pap. 8.95x (ISBN 0-06-131123-5, TB 1123, Torch). Har-Row.
Hitler & Mussolini. John Ray. 1970. pap. text ed. 2.95x (ISBN 0-435-31755-5). Heinemann Ed.
Hitler & the Forgotten Nazis. Bruce Pauley. LC 80-17006. 360p. 1981. 19.00x (ISBN 0-8078-1456-3). U of NC Pr.
Hitler File. C. A. Hills. (Leaders Ser.). (Illus.). 96p. (gr. 9-12). 1980. 14.95 (ISBN 0-7134-1919-9, Pub. by Batsford England). David & Charles.
Hitler: Legend, Myth & Reality. Werner Maser. Tr. by Peter Ross & Betty Ross. LC 72-9136. (Illus.). 448p. 1973. 12.50 o.s.i. (ISBN 0-06-012831-3, HarpT). Har-Row.
Hitler Movement: A Modern Millenarian Revolution. James M. Rhodes. LC 78-70391. (Publications Ser.: 213). 263p. 1980. 14.95 (ISBN 0-8179-7131-9). Hoover Inst Pr.
Hitler State: The Foundation & Development of the Internal Structure of the Third Reich. Martin Broszat. Tr. by John Hiden from Ger. (Illus.). 400p. 1981. text ed. 22.00x (ISBN 0-582-49200-9); pap. text ed. 12.95x (ISBN 0-582-48997-0). Longman.
Hitler: The Survival Myth. Donald M. McKale. LC 80-5405. (Illus.). 264p. 1980. 14.95 (ISBN 0-8128-2724-4). Stein & Day.
Hitler Trial: Before the People's Court in Munich. People's Court, Munich & Adolph Hitler. Tr. by H. Francis Freniere et al. 1976. 130.00 (ISBN 0-89093-050-3). U Pubns Amer.
Hitler Was My Friend. Ed. by Heinrich Hoffmann. Tr. by R. H. Stevens from Ger. 1978. pap. 4.50x (ISBN 0-911038-36-1). Noontide.
Hitler's Children: The Story of the Baader - Meinhof Terrorist Gang. Jillian Becker. LC 76-55730. (Illus.). 1977. 10.00 o.p. (ISBN 0-397-01153-9). Lippincott.
Hitler's Death Camps. Konnilyn G. Feig. (Illus.). 400p. 1981. 29.50x (ISBN 0-8419-0675-0); pap. 12.50x (ISBN 0-8419-0676-9). Holmes & Meier.
Hitler's First Foreign Minister: Constantin Freiherr von Neurath. John L. Heineman. 1980. 30.00x (ISBN 0-520-03442-2). U of Cal Pr.
Hitler's Last Gamble. Jacques Nobecourt. 1980. pap. 2.25 (ISBN 0-505-51474-5). Tower Bks.
Hitler's Letters & Notes. Werner Maser. Tr. by Arnold Pomerance from Ger. LC 73-10677. (Illus.). 400p. 1974. 12.50 o.s.i. (ISBN 0-06-012832-1, HarpT). Har-Row.
Hitler's Mein Kampf in Britain & America: A Publishing History, 1930-39. James J. Barnes & Patience P. Barnes. LC 79-54014. 1980. pap. 18.95 (ISBN 0-521-22691-0). Cambridge U Pr.
Hitler's Reich. Eileen Pearson. Ed. by Malcolm Yapp & Margaret Killingray. (World History Ser.). (Illus.). (gr. 10). 1980. Repr. of 1977 ed. lib. bdg. 5.95 (ISBN 0-89908-208-4); pap. text ed. 1.95 (ISBN 0-89908-233-5). Greenhaven.
Hitler's S. S. Federic Reider. (Illus.). 256p. 1981. 24.95 (ISBN 0-89404-061-8). Aztex.
Hitler's Secret Service. Walter Schellenberg. 1977. pap. 2.25 o.s.i. (ISBN 0-515-04481-4). Jove Pubns.
Hitler's Spies: German Military Intelligence in World War II. David Kahn. (Illus.). 1978. 19.95 (ISBN 0-02-560610-7). Macmillan.
Hitler's S.S. Frederic Reider. (Illus.). 256p. 1981. 24.95 (ISBN 0-89404-061-8). Aztex.
Hitler's Youth. Franz Jetzinger. Tr. by Lawrence Wilson from German. LC 75-36096. (Illus.). 1976. Repr. of 1958 ed. lib. bdg. 18.00x (ISBN 0-8371-8617-X, JEHY). Greenwood.
Hitopadesa: Fables & Proverbs from the Sanskrit. LC 68-17014. 1968. Repr. of 1787 ed. 29.00x (ISBN 0-8201-1050-7). Schol Facsimiles.
Hitters. Thomas Braun. LC 76-8422. (Stars of the Nl & Al Ser.). (Illus.). (gr. 4-12). 1976. PLB 7.95 (ISBN 0-87191-515-4). Creative Ed.

Hitting Our Stride: Good News About Women in Their Middle Years. Joan Cohen et al. 1980. 10.95 (ISBN 0-440-03656-9). Delacorte.

Hitting, Pitching & Running Maybe. Gary Paulsen. LC 76-18092. (Sports on the Light Side Ser.). (Illus.). 32p. (gr. 3-6). 1976. PLB 9.65 (ISBN 0-8172-0177-7). Raintree Pubs.

Hittite Dictionary of the Oriental Institute of the University of Chicago, Vol. 3, Fasc. 1, L. Ed. by Harry A. Hoffner, Jr. & Hans G. Guterbock. LC 79-53554. 1980. pap. 9.00x (ISBN 0-918986-27-3). Oriental Inst.

Hitty: Her First Hundred Years. Rachel Field. (gr. 4-6). 1937. 8.95 (ISBN 0-02-734840-7). Macmillan.

Hive & the Honey Bee. Ed. by Dadant & Sons. LC 63-15838. (Illus.). 3740p. 1976. 17.50 (ISBN 0-684-14790-4, ScribT). Scribner.

Hiway Sex: Women Equal the Greatest Thing on Earth. R. S. Hart, pseud. 125p. (Orig.). Date not set. pap. 5.95 (ISBN 0-9604226-1-7). R S Hart.

Hjalmar Bergman. Erik H. Linder. LC 74-23060. (World Authors Ser.: Sweden: No. 356). 1975. lib. bdg. 12.50 (ISBN 0-8057-2147-9). Twayne.

HMO Handbook. John R. Kress & James Singer. LC 75-18637. 206p. 1975. text ed. 22.00 (ISBN 0-912862-14-9). Aspen Systems.

HMOs & the Politics of Health System Reform. Joseph L. Falkson. LC 79-21932. 224p. (Orig.). 1980. casebound 12.75 (ISBN 0-87258-288-4, 1183); pap. 9.75 (ISBN 0-87258-276-0, 1182). Am Hospital.

H.M.S. Thing. W. C. Chalk. pap. text ed. 2.75x o.p. (ISBN 0-435-11225-2). Heinemann Ed.

Ho Chi Minh: Legend of Hanoi. Jules Archer. LC 79-151161. (gr. 7-12). 1971. 7.95 (ISBN 0-02-705630-9, CCPr). Macmillan.

Ho for California: Women's Overland Diaries from the Huntington Library. Ed. by Sandra L. Myres. LC 79-28115. (Illus.). 1980. 20.00 (ISBN 0-87328-103-9). Huntington Lib.

Hoax. Clifford Irving. 380p. 1981. 14.95 (ISBN 0-932966-14-4). Permanent Pr.

Hoax of Romance. Jo Loudin. (Transformation Ser.). 320p. 1981. 12.95 (ISBN 0-13-392456-4, Spec); pap. 6.95 (ISBN 0-13-392449-1). P-H.

Hoax of the Twentieth Century. A. R. Butz. LC 77-778964. (Illus.). 1977. 10.00 (ISBN 0-911038-23-X, Inst Hist Rev); pap. 6.00 (ISBN 0-911038-00-0). Noontide.

Hobberdy Dick. K. M. Briggs. LC 76-39896. (gr. 5-9). 1977. 8.25 (ISBN 0-688-80079-3); PLB 7.92 (ISBN 0-688-84079-5). Greenwillow.

Hobbes & Locke: Power & Consent. Ramon M. Lemos. LC 77-7482. 190p. 1978. 13.50x (ISBN 0-8203-0428-X). U of Ga Pr.

Hobbes's Science of Politics. M. M. Goldsmith. LC 66-18860. 1966. 17.50x (ISBN 0-231-02803-2). Columbia U Pr.

Hobbes's Science of Politics. M. M. Goldsmith. 1978. pap. 7.00x (ISBN 0-231-02804-0). Columbia U Pr.

Hobbits Journal: Being a Blank Book with Some Curious Illustrations of Friends & Foes of the Nine Companions. Illus. by Michael Green. LC 79-20203. (Illus.). 1979. lib. bdg. 12.90 (ISBN 0-89471-089-3); pap. 4.95 (ISBN 0-89471-090-7). Running Pr.

Hobbit's Travels: Being the Hitherto Unpublished Travel Sketches of Sam Gamgee with Space for Notes. Illus. by Michael Green. LC 78-15318. (Illus.). 1978. lib. bdg. 12.90 (ISBN 0-89471-041-9); pap. 4.95 (ISBN 0-89471-040-0). Running Pr.

Hobby Collections A-Z. Roslyn W. Salny. LC 65-18701. (Illus.). (gr. 5-9). 1965. 6.95 o.p. (ISBN 0-690-39508-6, TYC-J). T Y Crowell.

Hobby Crafts. Linda Hetzer. LC 77-28949. (Illustrated Crafts for Beginners). (Illus.). (gr. 3-7). 1978. PLB 9.95 (ISBN 0-8172-1180-2). Raintree Pubs.

Hobo: The Sociology of the Homeless Man. Nels Anderson. LC 23-10481. (Midway Reprint Ser). (Illus.). xxxii, 296p. 1975. pap. 11.50x o.s.i. (ISBN 0-226-01965-9). U of Chicago Pr.

Hoboken Chicken Emergency. D. Manus Pinkwater. LC 76-41910. (Illus.). (gr. 3-7). 1977. 7.95 (ISBN 0-13-392514-5). P-H.

Hoby & Stub. Mary C. Dunne. LC 80-18449. 168p. (gr. 5-9). 1981. PLB 9.95 (ISBN 0-689-30806-X). Atheneum.

Hochgebirgsflora Des Tropischen Afrikas. A. Engler. (Akad. D. Wissenschaften, Berlin Ser.). 461p. (Ger.). 1975. pap. text ed. 91.50x (ISBN 3-87429-088-3). Lubrecht & Cramer.

Hockey Defenseman. Sheldon Ilowite. (Illus.). (gr. 4-7). 1971. 4.95g o.s.i. (ISBN 0-8038-3018-1). Hastings.

Hockey Is for Me. Lowell A. Dickmeyer. LC 78-54362. (Sports for Me Bks). (Illus.). (gr. 2-5). 1978. PLB 5.95 (ISBN 0-8225-1080-4). Lerner Pubns.

Hockey Rules Illustrated. John Cadman. (Illus.). 112p. 1980. 18.00 (ISBN 0-7207-1112-6). Transatlantic.

Hockey Talk. Howard Liss. (gr. 4-6). pap. 0.95 (ISBN 0-686-68482-6). PB.

Hockey: The Sport's Playbook. Red Kelley & Martin Lader. LC 75-40731. (Illus.). 144p. 1976. pap. 2.95 o.p. (ISBN 0-385-06045-9). Doubleday.

Hockey, 77-78. 1977. pap. 1.95 o.p. (ISBN 0-345-25824-X). Ballantine.

Hockey's Great Rivalries. Stan Fischler. LC 74-4930. (Pro Hockey Library). (Illus.). 160p. (gr. 5 up). 1974. PLB 3.69 (ISBN 0-394-92830-X, BYR). Random.

Hocus-Focus. Hal Kaufman & Bob Schroeter. (Orig.). 1981. pap. 1.50 (ISBN 0-451-09781-5, J9781, Sig). NAL.

Hocus Focus: The World's Weirdest Cameras. Carl Glassman. (Illus.). 96p. (gr. 5 up). 1976. PLB 5.90 o.p. (ISBN 0-531-00350-7). Watts.

Hocus-Pocus of the Universe. Laura Gilpin. LC 76-2746. 1977. 7.95 o.p. (ISBN 0-385-11600-4). Doubleday.

Hodaka Service - Repair Handbook: 90-125cc Singles, 1964-1975. Brick Price. Ed. by Jeff Robinson. (Illus.). 168p. 1975. pap. text ed. 9.95 (ISBN 0-89287-005-2, M307). Clymer Pubns.

Hodge & His Masters. Richard Jefferies. 310p. 1980. pap. 4.95 (ISBN 0-7043-3259-0, Pub. by Quartet England). Horizon.

Hodgepodge Book: An Almanac of American Folklore. Duncan Emrich. LC 72-77811. (Illus.). 368p. (gr. 1 up). 1972. 14.95 (ISBN 0-590-07250-1, Four Winds). Schol Bk Serv.

Hodgkin's Disease. Ed. by Mortimer J. Lacher. LC 75-25644. 464p. 1976. 50.50 (ISBN 0-471-51149-8, Pub. by Wiley Medical). Wiley.

Hodgkin's Disease & Non-Hodgkin's Lymphomas. Ed. by Charles A. Coltman, Jr. & Harvey Golomb. (Seminars in Oncology Ser.). 1980. write for info. (ISBN 0-8089-1354-9). Grune.

Hodgkin's Disease & the Lymphomas. Cliver R Taylor. Ed. by D. F. Horrobin. LC 78-300154. (Annual Reviews Ser.: Vol. 4). 374p. 1980. 38.00 (ISBN 0-88831-089-7). Eden Med Res.

Hodgkin's Disease & the Lymphomas, Vol. 1. Clive R. Taylor. 1977. 24.00 (ISBN 0-904406-48-2). Eden Med Res.

Hodgkin's Disease & the Lymphomas, Vol. 2, 1977. Clive R. Taylor. LC 78-300154. 1978. 28.80 (ISBN 0-88831-015-3). Eden Med Res.

Hodgkin's Disease & the Lymphomas, Vol. 3. Clive R. Taylor. Ed. by D. F. Horrobin. LC 78-300154. (Annual Research Reviews). 1979. 31.20 (ISBN 0-88831-043-9). Eden Med Res.

Hodograph Equations: An Introduction to the Mathematical Theory of Plane Transonic Flow. A. P. Manwell. (University Mathematical Monograph Ser: No. 8). 1970. 30.25 o.s.i. (ISBN 0-02-848780-X). Hafner.

Hoe & the Horse on the Plains: A Study of Cultural Development Among North American Indians. Preston Holder. LC 70-98474. (Illus.). xiv, 176p. 1970. 9.95x (ISBN 0-8032-0730-1); pap. 3.75x (ISBN 0-8032-5809-7, BB 594, Bison). U of Nebr Pr.

Hoert Zu! M. E. Mountjoy. 1971. pap. text ed. 2.95x o.p. (ISBN 0-435-38600-X); tape 24.00x o.p. (ISBN 0-435-38601-8). Heinemann Ed.

Hofmannsthal's Festival Dramas. Brian Coghlan. 1964. 65.00 (ISBN 0-521-04682-3). Cambridge U Pr.

Hofmannsthals Weg Zur Oper, Die Frau Ohne Schatten: Ruecksichten und Einfluesse auf die Musik. Jakob Knaus. (Quellen und Forschungen zur Sprach-und Kulturgeschichte der germanischen Volker, N. F. 38). (Ger). 1971. 29.40 (ISBN 3-11-001865-9). De Gruyter.

Hog Book. William B. Hedgepeth. LC 76-23766. 1978. pap. 6.95 (ISBN 0-385-11666-7, Dolp). Doubleday.

Hog Meat & Hoecake: Food Supply in the Old South, 1840-1860. Sam B. Hilliard. LC 75-156778. 309p. 1972. 17.95x (ISBN 0-8093-0512-7). S Ill U Pr.

Hog Murders. William L. DeAndrea. 1979. pap. 1.95 (ISBN 0-380-47548-0, 47548). Avon.

Hogan, M. P. May L. Hartley. (Nineteenth Century Fiction Ser.: Ireland: Vol. 66). 916p. 1979. lib. bdg. 46.00 (ISBN 0-8240-3515-1). Garland Pub.

Hogar Que Dios Me Dio. Josie De Smith. 1979. pap. 1.65 (ISBN 0-311-46082-8). Casa Bautista.

Hogares de la Biblia. Luis Salem. 107p. (Orig., Span.). pap. 1.95 (ISBN 0-89922-079-7). Edit Caribe.

Hogarth. David Bindman. (World of Art Ser.). (Illus.). 288p. 1981. 17.95 (ISBN 0-19-520239-2); pap. 9.95 (ISBN 0-19-520240-6). Oxford U Pr.

Hogarth. Michael Rosenthal. (Oresko-Jupiter Art Bks). (Illus.). 96p. 1981. 17.95 (ISBN 0-933516-81-9, Pub. by Oresko-Jupiter England). Hippocrene Bks.

Hogboon of Hell & Other Strange Orkney Tales. Nancy Cutt & W. Towrie Cutt. (Illus.). (gr. 2-7). 1979. PLB 8.95 (ISBN 0-233-97020-7). Andre Deutsch.

Hoghead. Frederick C. Gamst. (Case Studies in Cultural Anthropology). 128p. 1980. pap. text ed. 4.95 (ISBN 0-03-052636-1, HoltC). HR&W.

Hohenzollern: Tragik & Koenigtum. Reinhold Schneider. (Suhrkamp Taschenbuecher: No. 590). 218p. 1980. pap. text ed. 5.85 (ISBN 3-518-37090-1, Pub. by Insel Verlag Germany). Suhrkamp.

Hoists, Cranes, & Derricks. Herbert S. Zim & James R. Skelly. LC 74-79098. (How Things Work Ser). (Illus.). (gr. 3-7). 1974. PLB 6.48 (ISBN 0-688-31395-7); pap. 1.25 (ISBN 0-688-26395-X). Morrow.

Hojo Shigetoki (Eleven Ninety-Eight to Twelve Sixty-One) & His Role in the History of Political & Ethical Ideas in Japan. Carl Steenstrup. (Scandinavian Institute of Asian Studies Monographs: No. 41). (Orig.). 1980. pap. text ed. 16.50x (ISBN 0-7007-0132-X). Humanities.

Hoke's Jokes Cartoons & Funny Things. Helen Hoke. LC 74-7459. (Illus.). (gr. 1-4). 1975. PLB 4.90 o.p. (ISBN 0-531-02682-5). Watts.

Hokus Pokus: Coin Tricks. Ib Permin. LC 77-79507. (Little Magic Books). (Illus.). (gr. 2 up). 1977. 6.95 (ISBN 0-8069-4574-5); PLB 6.69 (ISBN 0-8069-4575-3). Sterling.

Hokus Pokus: Rope & Scarf Tricks. Ib Permin. LC 77-79506. (Illus.). (gr. 2 up). 1977. 6.95 (ISBN 0-8069-4576-1); PLB 6.69 (ISBN 0-8069-4577-X). Sterling.

Hokus Pokus with Wands, Water & Glasses. Ib Permin. LC 77-93314. (Illus.). (gr. 4 up). 1978. 6.95 (ISBN 0-8069-4578-8); PLB 6.69 (ISBN 0-8069-4579-6). Sterling.

Holar Cato. Ed. by Halldor Hermannsson. 91p. 1958. 12.50x (ISBN 0-8014-0202-6); soft cover 9.50x (ISBN 0-8014-9822-8). Cornell U Pr.

Hold 'em Poker. David Sklansky. (Gambler's Book Shelf). (Illus.). 64p. 1976. pap. 2.95 (ISBN 0-89650-567-7). Gamblers.

Hold Fast. Kevin Major. LC 79-17544. (YA) (gr. 9-12). 1980. 8.95 (ISBN 0-440-03506-6). Delacorte.

Hold Fire: Selected Poems. Gary Elder. 96p. (Orig.). 1981. pap. 4.75 (ISBN 0-931896-02-9). Cove View.

Hold Me Fast. Cecile Gilmore. (YA) 1972. 5.95 (ISBN 0-685-28627-4, Avalon). Bouregy.

Hold Your Horses. James N. Selvidge. (Illus.). 176p. 1976. pap. 6.95 (ISBN 0-915700-01-8). Jacada Pubns.

Hold Your Horses. 2nd ed. James N. Selvidge. (Illus.). 176p. 1976. pap. 6.95. Jacada Pubns.

Holdfast. John Beatty & Patricia Beatty. LC 75-187902. 224p. (gr. 7-9). 1972. PLB 7.44 o.p. (ISBN 0-688-31434-1). Morrow.

Holding Patterns. Ellen Roddick. 224p. 1981. 10.95 (ISBN 0-312-38833-0). St Martin.

Holding Together. Penelope Jones. 160p. (gr. 3-5). 1981. 7.95 (ISBN 0-87888-177-8). Bradbury Pr.

Holdouts. William Decker. 1981. pap. price not set (ISBN 0-671-42081-X). PB.

Hole in Space. Larry Niven. (Orig.). 1976. pap. 1.95 (ISBN 0-345-29225-1). Ballantine.

Hole in the Dike. Retold by Norma Green. (Illus.). (gr. k-3). 1975. pap. 1.50 (ISBN 0-590-08127-6, Schol Pap); pap. 3.50 bk. & record (ISBN 0-590-20742-3). Schol Bk Serv.

Holes, Gaps & Cavities: Stages 1 & 2. Roy Richards. LC 77-82990. (Science 5-13 Ser.). (Illus.). 1977. pap. text ed. 9.30 (ISBN 0-356-04108-5). Raintree Child.

Holes in the Welfare Net. Maureen Oswin. 168p. 1978. text ed. 13.75x (ISBN 0-7199-0939-2, Pub. by Bedford England). Renouf.

Holgota... 120p. (Ukrainian.). 1980. pap. 5.00 (ISBN 0-686-63320-2). Slavia Lib.

Holiday. Joan Tate. pap. text ed. 1.95x o.p. (ISBN 0-435-11882-X). Heinemann Ed.

Holiday: A Handbook of Elementary Classroom Ideas to Motivate Teaching Through the Use of Holiday Art Activities. (Spice Ser.). 1978. 6.50 (ISBN 0-89273-127-3). Educ Serv.

Holiday at the Dew Drop Inn. Eve Garnett. LC 62-11218. (Illus.). (gr. 7 up). 1962. 5.95 (ISBN 0-8149-0304-5). Vanguard.

Holiday Book. Harry Bornstein. (Signed English Ser.). 48p. 1974. pap. 3.50 (ISBN 0-913580-30-9). Gallaudet Coll.

Holiday Cards for You to Make. Susan Purdy. LC 67-10375. (Illus.). (gr. 4-9). 1967. 7.89 (ISBN 0-397-31574-0). Lippincott.

Holiday Cook: Recipes & Shopping Away from Home. Carol Wright. LC 80-68682. (Illus.). 160p. 1981. 14.50 (ISBN 0-7153-8017-6). David & Charles.

Holiday Craft & Fun. Joseph Leeming. (Illus.). (gr. 7-9). 1950. 7.50 (ISBN 0-397-30168-5). Lippincott.

Holiday-Craft Kit for the Jewish Child. Tamar Grand. (Illus.). (ps). 1976. pap. text ed. 5.00 (ISBN 0-8074-0138-2, 103901). UAHC.

Holiday Entertaining. Ed. by Georgia Orcutt & Sandra Taylor. LC 80-52141. (Flavor of New England). 1980. pap. 8.95 (ISBN 0-911658-13-0, 3074). Yankee Bks.

Holiday for Mr. Muster. Lobel. (gr. 2-3). 1980. pap. 3.50 incl. record (ISBN 0-590-24003-X, Schol Pap). Schol Bk Serv.

Holiday Graphs. Beverly J. Mick. (Illus.). 64p. (For tchrs. of gr. 6-9). 1978. 5.95 (ISBN 0-932786-00-6). Bellefontaine.

Holiday Guide to Britain. Ed. by Holiday Editors. 1976. pap. 2.95 o.p. (ISBN 0-394-73190-5). Random.

Holiday Guide to Caribbean. Ed. by Holiday Editors. 1976. pap. 2.95 o.p. (ISBN 0-394-73191-3). Random.

Holiday Guide to France. Ed. by Holiday Editors. 1976. pap. 2.95 o.p. (ISBN 0-394-73192-1). Random.

Holiday Guide to Greece & the Aegean Islands. Ed. by Holiday Editors. 1976. pap. 2.95 o.p. (ISBN 0-394-73193-X). Random.

Holiday Guide to Hawaii. Ed. by Holiday Editors. 1976. pap. 2.95 o.p. (ISBN 0-394-73194-8). Random.

Holiday Guide to Ireland. Holiday Editors. 1976. pap. 2.95 o.p. (ISBN 0-394-73195-6). Random.

Holiday Guide to Israel. Ed. by Holiday Editors. 1976. pap. 2.95 o.p. (ISBN 0-394-73196-4). Random.

Holiday Guide to Italy. Holiday Editors. 1976. pap. 2.95 o.p. (ISBN 0-394-73197-2). Random.

Holiday Guide to London. Ed. by Holiday Editors. 1976. pap. 2.95 o.p. (ISBN 0-394-73198-0). Random.

Holiday Guide to Mexico. Ed. by Holiday Editors. 1976. pap. 2.95 o.p. (ISBN 0-394-73199-9). Random.

Holiday Guide to Paris. Ed. by Holiday Editors. 1976. pap. 2.95 o.p. (ISBN 0-394-73200-6). Random.

Holiday Guide to Rome. Ed. by Holiday Editors. 1976. pap. 2.95 o.p. (ISBN 0-394-73201-4). Random.

Holiday Guide to Scandinavia. Ed. by Holiday Editors. 1976. pap. 2.95 o.p. (ISBN 0-394-73202-2). Random.

Holiday Guide to Spain. Ed. by Holiday Editors. 1976. pap. 2.95 o.p. (ISBN 0-394-73203-0). Random.

Holiday Guide to West Germany. Ed. by Holiday Editors. 1976. pap. 2.95 o.p. (ISBN 0-394-73204-9). Random.

Holiday History of France. Ronald Hamilton. 1978. 8.95 (ISBN 0-7011-1686-2, Pub. by Chatto Bodley Jonathan). Merrimack Bk Serv.

Holiday Hobbycraft. Willard Waltner & Elma Waltner. (gr. 6 up). 1964. 6.70 o.p. (ISBN 0-8313-0093-0). Lantern.

Holiday House. Catherine Sinclair. LC 75-32159. (Classics of Children's Literature, 1621-1932: Vol. 24). 1976. Repr. of 1839 ed. lib. bdg. 38.00 (ISBN 0-8240-2273-4). Garland Pub.

Holiday Hullabaloo! Facts, Jokes, & Riddles. E. Richard Churchill. (Illus.). (gr. 4 up). 1977. PLB 7.90 (ISBN 0-531-00384-1). Watts.

Holiday Magazine Award Cookbook. LC 76-41562. (Illus.). 1976. 12.50 (ISBN 0-89387-002-1). Sat Eve Post.

Holiday Programs for Boys & Girls. rev. ed. Aileen Fisher. LC 52-11997. (gr. 2-7). 1980. 10.95 (ISBN 0-8238-0244-2). Plays.

Holiday Programs for Boys & Girls. rev. ed. Aileen Fisher. LC 52-11997. (gr. 2-7). 1980. 12.00 (ISBN 0-8238-0244-2). Plays.

Holiday Series, 10 bks. Bob Reese et al. Ed. by Alton Jordan. (Illus.). (gr. k-6). 1977. Set. PLB 35.00 (ISBN 0-89868-022-0); Set. pap. 17.50 (ISBN 0-89868-055-7). ARO Pub.

Holiday Work & Play. Joyce Fischman. 1961. pap. 2.00 o.p. (ISBN 0-685-02011-8, 101960). UAHC.

Holidays: Days of Significance for All Americans. Ed. by Trevor N. Dupuy. LC 65-21633. (gr. 9 up). 1965. PLB 6.90 (ISBN 0-531-01687-0). Watts.

Holiness Revival of the Nineteenth Century. Melvin E. Dieter. LC 80-17259. (Studies in Evangelicalism: No. 1). 366p. 1980. 17.50 (ISBN 0-8108-1328-9). Scarecrow.

Holiness Teachings. B. T. Roberts. pap. 2.95 o.p. (ISBN 0-686-12880-X). Schmul Pub Co.

Holist Pilgrimage. Kelvin Van Nuys. LC 80-84738. 1981. 19.95 (ISBN 0-8022-2383-4). Philos Lib.

Holistic Approaches to Offender Rehabilitation. Leonard Hippchen. 400p. 1981. price not set (ISBN 0-398-04448-1). C C Thomas.

Holistic Assessment of the Healthy Aged. Miriam M. Schrock. LC 80-10198. 1980. pap. 10.95 (ISBN 0-471-05597-2, Pub. by Wiley Med). Wiley.

Holistic Dentistry. John K. Char. Date not set. cancelled (ISBN 0-9601978-3-4). G A Eversaul.

Holistic Health Lifebook. Berkeley Holistic Health Center. (Illus.). 384p. 1980. soft cover 9.95 (ISBN 0-915904-53-5). And-Or Pr.

Holistic Health Lifebook. Compiled by Berkley Holistic Health Center. 384p. 1981. pap. 9.95 (ISBN 0-915904-53-5). And-or Pr.

Holistic Health: The Art & Science of Care. Patricia A. Flynn. (Illus.). 259p. 1980. pap. text ed. 12.95 (ISBN 0-87619-626-1). R J Brady.

Holistic Massage. rev. ed. Richard Jackson. LC 77-72393. (Illus.). 128p. 1980. pap. 5.95 (ISBN 0-8069-8382-5). Sterling.

Holistic Medicine: From Pathology to Optimum Health. Ed. by Kenneth R. Pelletier. (Merloyd Lawrence Bk.). 1979. 10.00 (ISBN 0-440-05288-2, Sey Lawr). Delacorte.

Holistic Mental Health for Tomorrow's Children: For Teachers & Mental Health Workers. write for info. (ISBN 0-398-04472-4). C C Thomas.

Holistic Nursing. Barbara Blattner. (Illus.). 400p. 1981. text ed. 15.95 (ISBN 0-13-392571-4); pap. text ed. 12.95 (ISBN 0-686-68605-5). P-H.

Holland. Margaret Hides. LC 74-29023. 1976. 12.95 o.p. (ISBN 0-684-14188-4, ScribT). Scribner.

Holland House. Leslie Mitchell. (Illus.). 320p. 1980. 32.00x (ISBN 0-7156-1116-X, Pub. by Duckworth England). Biblio Dist.

Holland in Pictures. Sterling Publishing Company Editors. LC 62-18637. (Visual Geography Ser). (Illus., Orig.). (gr. 6 up). 1962. PLB 4.99 (ISBN 0-8069-1033-X); pap. 2.95 (ISBN 0-8069-1032-1). Sterling.

Holland-Tide; or, Munster Popular Tales. Gerald Griffin. (Nineteenth Century Fiction Ser.: Ireland: Vol. 26). 382p. 1979. lib. bdg. 46.00 (ISBN 0-8240-3475-9). Garland Pub.

Hollander: A Comedy Written Sixteen Thirty-Five. Henry Glapthorne. LC 79-84112 (English Experience Ser.: No.931). 76p. 1979. Repr. of 1640 ed. lib. bdg. 9.50 (ISBN 90-221-0931-3). Walter J Johnson.

Hollanders Declaration of the Affaires of the East Indies. LC 72-187. (English Experience Ser.: No. 326). 12p. Repr. of 1622 ed. 7.00 (ISBN 90-221-0326-9). Walter J Johnson.

Holley Carburetors & Manifolds. rev. ed. Mike Urich & Bill Fisher. LC 73-187040. (Illus.). 1976. pap. 7.95 (ISBN 0-912656-48-4) H P Bks.

Hollow Detente: Anglo-German Relations in the Balkans, 1911-1914. Richard Crampton. (Illus.). 250p. 1980. text ed. 18.75x (ISBN 0-391-02159-1). Humanities.

Hollow Mountains. Oliver B. Patton. 384p. 1981. pap. 2.75 (ISBN 0-445-08462-6). Popular Lib.

Hollow Needle. Maurice LeBlanc. 325p. 1980. Repr. of 1910 ed. lib. bdg. 15.50x (ISBN 0-89968-203-0). Lightyear.

Holly Hathaway, Physical Therapist. Marilyn Austin. 192p. (YA) 1976. 4.95 o.p. (ISBN 0-685-64241-0, Avalon). Bouregy.

Holly Hobbie's Jumbo Activity Book. Holly Hobbie. (Illus.). (gr. 1-5). 1980. 3.95 (ISBN 0-525-69526-5, Gingerbread). Dutton.

Holly, Reindeer, & Colored Lights: The Story of the Christmas Symbols. Edna Barth. LC 71-157731. (Illus.). (gr. 2-5). 1971. 8.95 (ISBN 0-395-28842-8, Clarion). HM.

Hollywood & le Vine. Andrew Bergman. 192p. 1976. pap. 1.75 o.p. (ISBN 0-345-25006-0). Ballantine.

Hollywood Confidential. David Hanna. (Illus., Orig.). 1976. pap. 1.50 (ISBN 0-8439-0331-7, LB331DK, Leisure Bks). Nordon Pubns.

Hollywood Directors, 1941-1976. Ed. by Richard Koszarski. LC 76-51716. (Illus.). 1977. 19.95 (ISBN 0-19-502217-3). Oxford U Pr.

Hollywood Directors, 1941-1976. Ed. by Richard Koszarski. LC 76-51716. (Illus.). 1977. pap. 6.95 (ISBN 0-19-502218-1, GB 509, GB). Oxford U Pr.

Hollywood Emergency Diet. Frank Downing & O. Bardoff. 192p. 1981. 9.95 (ISBN 0-8119-0419-9, Pegasus Rex). Fell.

Hollywood Genres. Thomas Schatz. 320p. 1981. pap. text ed. 9.95 (ISBN 0-394-32255-X). Random.

Hollywood Goes to War. Colin Shindler. (Cinema & Society Ser.). (Illus.). 1979. 23.50 (ISBN 0-7100-0290-4). Routledge & Kegan.

Hollywood Gothic. Thomas Gifford. 1980. pap. 2.50 (ISBN 0-345-29084-4). Ballantine.

Hollywood Greats. Barry Norman. 1980. 12.95 (ISBN 0-531-09917-2, C22). Watts.

Hollywood in a Suitcase. Sammy Davis, Jr. LC 80-14792. (Illus.). 1980. 11.95 (ISBN 0-688-03736-4). Morrow.

Hollywood in the Forty's. Charles Higham & Joel Greenberg. 192p. 1981. pap. 5.95 (ISBN 0-498-06928-1). A S Barnes.

Hollywood in the Seventies. Les Keyser. LC 78-75313. (Illus.). 172p. 1981. pap. 5.95 (ISBN 0-498-02545-4). A S Barnes.

Hollywood Is a Four Letter Town. James Bacon. 1977. pap. 1.95 (ISBN 0-380-01671-0, 33399). Avon.

Hollywood Kids. Ed. by Leonard Maltin. (Film Ser.). 1978. pap. 2.25 o.p. (ISBN 0-445-04194-3). Popular Lib.

Hollywood: Land & Legend. Zelda Cini et al. (Illus.). 192p. 1980. 19.95 (ISBN 0-87000-486-7). Arlington Hse.

Hollywood Nineteen Eighty Crossword Puzzle. Ruth M. Gogna. 80p. (Orig.). (gr. 7 up). 9.95 (ISBN 0-686-64482-4). Alchemy Bks.

Hollywood on Record: The Film Stars' Discography. Michael R. Pitts & Louis H. Harrison. LC 77-17144. (Illus.). 1978. 19.50 (ISBN 0-8108-1093-X). Scarecrow.

Hollywood Squares. Compiled by Gail Sicilia. (Illus.). 160p. 1974. pap. 1.25 o.p. (ISBN 0-445-00221-2). Popular Lib.

Hollywood: The Movie Factory. Ed. by Leonard Maltin. 288p. 1976. pap. 1.50 o.p. (ISBN 0-445-03132-8). Popular Lib.

Hollywood Tragedy. William H. Carr. (Orig.). 1977. pap. 1.95 o.p. (ISBN 0-449-22889-4, Crest). Fawcett.

Hollywood Trivia. David P. Strauss & Fred L. Worth. 352p. (Orig.). 1981. pap. 2.75 (ISBN 0-446-95492-6). Warner Bks.

Hollywood Writers' Wars. Nancy Schwartz & Sheila Schwartz. LC 80-2728. (Illus.). 448p. 1981. 16.95 (ISBN 0-394-41140-4). Knopf. Postponed.

Hollywood's Great Love Teams. James R. Parish. (Illus.). 1974. 14.95 o.p. (ISBN 0-87000-245-7). Arlington Hse.

Hollywood's Irish Rose. Nora Bernard. 1978. pap. 1.95 (ISBN 0-380-41061-3, 41061). Avon.

Hollywood's Other Women. Alex Barris. LC 74-6933. (Illus.). 300p. 1975. 17.50 o.p. (ISBN 0-498-01488-6). A S Barnes.

Holmes Principles of Physical Geology. 3rd ed. Arthur Holmes & Doris L. Holmes. 1978. 27.95 (ISBN 0-471-07251-6). Halsted Pr.

Holmes-Sheehan Correspondence: The Letters of Justice Oliver W. Holmes, Jr. & Canon Patrick Augustine Sheehan. Oliver Wendell Holmes. Ed. by David H. Burton. 1976. 8.95 (ISBN 0-8046-9164-9, National University Pub). Kennikat.

Holocaust As Historical Experience. Ed. by Yehuda Bauer & Nathan Rotenstreich. 300p. 1981. text ed. 24.50x (ISBN 0-8419-0635-1); pap. text ed. 12.50x (ISBN 0-8419-0636-X). Holmes & Meier.

Holocaust II. R. L. Hymers. 1978. pap. 1.95 (ISBN 0-89728-005-9, 711269). Omega Pubns OR.

Holocene Tidal Sedimentation. Ed. by G. deVries Klein. (Benchmark Papers in Geology Ser.: Vol. 30). 432p. 1976. 46.50 (ISBN 0-12-786859-3). Acad Pr.

Holograms: How to Make & Use Them. Graham Saxby. (Illus.). 184p. 1980. 24.95 (ISBN 0-240-51054-2). Focal Pr.

Holograph Manuscript: "a Portrait of the Artist As a Young Man". James Joyce et al. Ed. by Michael Groden. LC 77-6230. (James Joyce Archive Ser.: Vols. 9 & 10). (Illus.). 1977. Repr. Vol. 9. lib. bdg. 104.00 (ISBN 0-8240-2808-2); Vol. 10. lib. bdg. 94.38 (ISBN 0-8240-2809-0). Garland Pub.

Holographic Mind, Holographic Vision: A New Theory of Vision in Art & Physics. Lawrence F. Berley. LC 79-92384. (Illus.). 1980. 14.95x (ISBN 0-9603706-0-9); pap. 9.95x (ISBN 0-9603706-1-7). Lakstun Pr.

Holography. H. Arthur Klein. Ed. by Helen Hale. LC 77-117232. (Introducing Modern Science Ser). (Illus.). (gr. 7 up). 1970. 8.95 o.p. (ISBN 0-397-31122-2). Lippincott.

Holography & Coherent Optics. L. M. Soroko. (Illus.). 650p. 1978. 59.50 (ISBN 0-306-40101-0, Plenum Pr). Plenum Pub.

Holography Book. Jeff Berner. Date not set. 12.95x o.s.i. (ISBN 0-440-03680-1). Delacorte. Postponed.

Holst. Imogen Holst. (Great Composers Ser.). (Illus.). 1974. 7.95 o.p. (ISBN 0-571-09967-X, Pub. by Faber & Faber). Merrimack Bk Serv.

Holy Bible for Church Pew Rack. 1972. sienna red 5.95 (ISBN 0-8054-1031-7); rust brown 5.95 (ISBN 0-8054-1032-5); blue gray 3.95 (ISBN 0-8054-1005-8); white 5.95 (ISBN 0-8054-1029-5); light green 4.25 (ISBN 0-8054-1025-2); light brown 4.25 (ISBN 0-8054-1023-6); dark brown 4.25 (ISBN 0-8054-1024-4); dark red 4.25 (ISBN 0-8054-1022-8); blue (ISBN 0-8054-1027-9) 4.25. Broadman.

Holy Bible: King James Version. pap. 3.95 (ISBN 0-515-05672-3). Jove Pubns.

Holy Bible: King James Version. 1980. pap. 4.95 (ISBN 0-452-00484-5, F484, Mer). NAL.

Holy Bible: Norman Rockwell Commemorative Edition. (Illus.). 1979. 39.95 (ISBN 0-89387-037-4). Sat Eve Post.

Holy Boldness. Charles E. Cerling, Jr. LC 80-65435. 160p. 1980. pap. 5.95 (ISBN 0-915684-67-5). Christian Herald.

Holy Company: Christian Heros & Heroines. Elliott Wright. 1980. 11.95 (ISBN 0-02-631590-4). Macmillan.

Holy-Days & Holidays: A Treasury of Historical Material, Sermons in Full & in Brief, Suggestive Thoughts & Poetry, Relating to Holy Days & Holidays. Ed. by Edward M. Deems. LC 68-17940. 1968. Repr. of 1902 ed. 34.00 (ISBN 0-8103-3352-X). Gale.

Holy Days & Holidays: Prayer Celebrations with Children. Gaynell B. Cronin. 1979. pap. 6.95 (ISBN 0-03-042761-4). Winston Pr.

Holy Disorders. Edmund Crispin. 240p. (Orig.). 1980. pap. 2.25 (ISBN 0-380-51508-3, 51508). Avon.

Holy Earth. Liberty H. Bailey. LC 80-27854. (Illus.). 124p. 1980. pap. 4.95 (ISBN 0-9605314-6-7). NY St Coll Ag.

Holy Eucharist: Rite Two a Devotional Commentary. Donald Parsons. 1976. pap. 3.95 (ISBN 0-8164-2129-3). Crossroad NY.

Holy Fire. Robert Payne. LC 79-27594. 328p. 1980. pap. 8.95 (ISBN 0-913836-61-3). St Vladimirs.

Holy Goof: A Biography of Neal Cassady. William Plummer. (Illus.). 150p. Date not set. 10.00 (ISBN 0-13-392605-2). P-H. Postponed.

Holy in Christ. Andrew Murray. 1969. pap. 3.95 (ISBN 0-87123-216-2, 210216). Bethany Fell.

Holy Island of Lindisfarne. Raymond Cartwright & Betty Cartwright. (Island Ser.). (Illus.). 144p. 14.50 o.p. (ISBN 0-7153-7137-1). David & Charles.

Holy Land: An Archaeological Guide from Earliest Times to 1700. Jerome Murphy-O'Connor. (Illus.). 1352p. 1980. 19.95 (ISBN 0-19-217689-7); pap. 9.95 (ISBN 0-19-285088-1). Oxford U Pr.

Holy Land Hymns. Carl Brumback. LC 73-93792. 1974. pap. 1.45 o.p. (ISBN 0-88270-087-1). Logos.

Holy Land in American Protestant Life, Eighteen Hundred to Nineteen Forty Eight: A Documentary History. Ed. by Robert T. Handy. LC 79-1052. (Illus.). 1980. lib. bdg. 20.00 (ISBN 0-405-13466-5). Arno.

Holy Nativity. Harvey B. Hatcher. LC 57-10298. (Orig.). 1957. pap. 0.60 (ISBN 0-8054-9702-1). Broadman.

Holy Nudges: Listening to God's Voice. Marguerite Reiss. 1976. 5.95 o.p. (ISBN 0-88270-185-1); pap. 2.95 o.p. (ISBN 0-88270-186-X). Logos.

Holy of Holies. Alan Williams. 1980. 12.95 (ISBN 0-89256-147-5). Rawson Wade.

Holy Orthodox Church. Apostolos Makrakis. Ed. by Orthodox Christian Educational Society. Tr. by M. I. Lisney & L. Krick. 298p. (Orig.). 1980. pap. 5.00x (ISBN 0-938366-34-3). Orthodox Chr.

Holy Place. Carlos Fuentes. Tr. by Suzanne J. Levine. 1978. pap. 3.95 o.p. (ISBN 0-525-47528-1). Dutton.

Holy Places of Christendom. Stewart Perowne. LC 76-9272. (Illus.). 1976. 14.95 (ISBN 0-19-519878-6). Oxford U Pr.

Holy Pretence. George L. Mosse. LC 68-14552. 1968. 14.25 (ISBN 0-86527-099-6). Fertig.

Holy Quran. A. Yusuf. (Arabic & Eng.). 14.95 (ISBN 0-686-63572-8). Intl Bk Ctr.

Holy Quran with English Translation. Ed. by M. M. Pickthall. 1976. Repr. 14.50x (ISBN 0-8364-0415-7). South Asia Bks.

Holy Roman Empire: A Dictionary Handbook. Ed. by Jonathan W. Zophy. LC 79-8282. (Illus.). xxvii, 551p. 1980. lib. bdg. 45.00 (ISBN 0-313-21457-3, ZHR/). Greenwood.

Holy Roman Republic: A Historic Profile of the Middle Ages. Giorgio Falco. Tr. by K. V. Kent from Italian. LC 80-19696. Orig. Title: Santa Romana Republica. 336p. 1980. Repr. of 1965 ed. lib. bdg. 35.00x (ISBN 0-313-22395-5, FAHR). Greenwood.

Holy Rosary. Josemaria E. De Balaguer. (Illus.). 49p. 1979. pap. 8.00x (ISBN 0-906127-15-7, Pub. by Irish Academic Pr). Biblio Dist.

Holy Scriptures: A Survey. Robert C. Dentan. (Orig.). 1949. pap. 3.95 (ISBN 0-8164-2031-9, SP1). Crossroad NY.

Holy Spirit. Billy Graham. 336p. 1980. pap. 2.75 (ISBN 0-446-95038-6). Warner Bks.

Holy Spirit. (Aglow Bible Study: Bk. E-3). 64p. 1980. pap. 1.95 (ISBN 0-930756-57-6, 4220-E). Women's Aglow.

Holy Spirit. (Aglow Bible Study Bk: No. E-3). (Illus.). 64p. (Orig.). 1980. pap. 1.95 (ISBN 0-930756-57-6, 4220-E3). Women's Aglow.

Holy Spirit. Arthur W. Pink. 1970. pap. 4.95 (ISBN 0-8010-7041-4). Baker Bk.

Holy Spirit. Charles C. Ryrie. (Bible Doctrine Handbook Ser). (Orig.). 1965. pap. 2.95 (ISBN 0-8024-3565-3); pap. 2.95 leader's guide (ISBN 0-8024-3564-5). Moody.

Holy Spirit. Eduard Schweizer. LC 79-8892. 144p. 1980. 9.95 (ISBN 0-8006-0629-9, 1-629). Fortress.

Holy Spirit & His Gifts. J. Oswald Sanders. (Contemporary Evangelical Perspectives Ser). kivar 4.95 (ISBN 0-310-32481-5). Zondervan.

Holy Spirit & Other Spirits. D. O. Teasley. 192p. pap. 1.75. Faith Pub Hse.

Holy Spirit & the Christian. James D. Bales. 3.75 o.p. (ISBN 0-89315-102-5); pap. 3.50 (ISBN 0-89315-103-3). Lambert Bk.

Holy Spirit Baptism & the Second Cleansing. R. R. Byrum. 108p. pap. 60.75; pap. 2.00 3 copies. Faith Pub Hse.

Holy Spirit: Common Sense & the Bible. Eric S. Fife. (Orig.). 1979. pap. 4.95 (ISBN 0-310-24341-6). Zondervan.

Holy Spirit in Salvation. Thomas Goodwin. 1979. 12.95 (ISBN 0-85151-279-8). Banner of Truth.

Holy Spirit in the Theology of Martin Bucer. W. D. Stephens. LC 79-96100. Orig. Title: Martin Bucer, a Theologian of the Spirit. 1970. 51.00 (ISBN 0-521-07661-7). Cambridge U Pr.

Holy Spirit in Today's World. W. A. Criswell. 192p. 1976. pap. text ed. 5.95 (ISBN 0-310-22852-2). Zondervan.

Holy Spirit, Lord & Life-Giver: A Biblical Introduction to the Doctrine of the Holy Spirit. John Williams. LC 79-27891. 1980. 8.50 (ISBN 0-87213-950-6); pap. 5.75 (ISBN 0-87213-951-4). Loizeaux.

Holy Spirit: Mission of, & Praying in. H. A. Ironside. Date not set. pap. 1.95 (ISBN 0-87213-366-4). Loizeaux.

Holy Spirit of God. Herbert Lockyer. 1981. 9.95 (ISBN 0-8407-5234-2). Nelson.

Holy Spirit: The Key to Supernatural Living. Bill Bright. 200p. 1980. 8.95 (ISBN 0-918956-67-6); pap. 4.95 (ISBN 0-918956-66-8). Campus Crusade.

Holy Table, Name & Thing, More Patiently, Properly, & Literally Used Under the New Treatment, Than That of an Altar. John Williams. LC 79-84146. (English Experience Ser.: No.962). 244p. 1979. Repr. of 1637 ed. lib. bdg. 22.00 (ISBN 90-221-0962-3). Walter J Johnson.

Holy Theatre: Ritual & the Avant Garde. Chritoper Innes. (Illus.). 280p. Date not set. price not set (ISBN 0-521-22542-6). Cambridge U Pr.

Holy Types: The Gospel in Leviticus. Joseph A. Seiss. Repr. of 1972 ed. 5.95 (ISBN 0-686-05045-2). St Thomas.

Holy Vessels & Furniture of the Tabernacle. Henry W. Soltau. LC 74-85428. (Illus.). 1973. 8.95 (ISBN 0-8254-3707-5). Kregel.

Holy War. John Bunyan. Ed. by Roger Sharrock & James F. Forrest. (Oxford English Texts Ser.). 344p. 1980. 72.00 (ISBN 0-19-811887-2). Oxford U Pr.

Holy Way. Yocum. pap. 5.95 (ISBN 0-686-12915-6). Schmul Pub Co.

Holy Week. Richard L. Jeske & Browne Barr. Ed. by Elizabeth Achtemeier et al. LC 79-7377. (Proclamation 2: Aids for Interpreting the Lessons of the Church Year, Ser. A). 64p. (Orig.). 1980. pap. 2.50 (ISBN 0-8006-4094-2, 1-4094). Fortress.

Holy Week. William C. McFadden & Reginald H. Fuller. LC 74-24932. (Proclamation 1: Aids for Interpreting the Lessons of the Church Year, Ser. B). 64p. 1975. pap. 1.95 (ISBN 0-8006-4074-8, 1-4074). Fortress.

Holy Week. Krister Stendahl. LC 74-76926. (Proclamation 1: Aids for Interpreting the Lessons of the Church Year, Ser. A: Ser. A). 64p. (Orig.). 1974. pap. 1.95 (ISBN 0-8006-4064-0, 1-4064). Fortress.

Holy Week. Daniel B. Stevick & Ben Johnson. LC 73-79351. (Proclamation 1: Aids for Interpreting the Lessons of the Church Year, Ser. C). 64p. 1973. pap. 1.95 (ISBN 0-8006-4054-3, 1-4054). Fortress.

Holy Wind in Navajo Philosophy. James K. McNeley. 1981. text ed. 14.95x (ISBN 0-8165-0710-4); pap. 6.95x (ISBN 0-8165-0724-4). U of Ariz Pr.

Homage to Frank O'Hara. Ed. by Bill Berkson & Joe LeSeuer. (Illus.). 250p. 1980. pap. 8.95 (ISBN 0-916870-29-4). Creative Arts Bk.

Homage to Guru Gobind Singh. Khushwant Singh & Suneet V. Singh. 1970. pap. 2.30 (ISBN 0-88253-088-7). Ind-US Inc.

Homage to Malthus. Jane S. Nickerson. 1975. 12.95 (ISBN 0-8046-9105-3, Natl U). Kennikat.

Homage to Mistress Bradstreet & Other Poems. John Berryman. LC 68-24596. 1968. pap. 3.50 (ISBN 0-374-50660-4, N337). FS&G.

Homage to P. G. Wodehouse. Ed. by Thelma Cazalet-Keir. (Illus.). 146p. 1973. text ed. 9.00x (ISBN 0-214-66880-0). Humanities.

Homage to Robert Penn Warren. Ed. by Frank Graziano. 80p. (Orig.). 1981. price not set (ISBN 0-937406-12-0); pap. price not set (ISBN 0-937406-11-2); price not set limited ed. (ISBN 0-937406-13-9). Logbridge-Rhodes.

Hombre. Elmore Leonard. 1974. pap. 1.75 (ISBN 0-345-28850-5). Ballantine.

Hombre como Varon y Hembra. Paul K. Jewett. Tr. by Ernesto S. Vilela from Eng. 205p. (Orig., Span.). 1979. pap. 4.95 (ISBN 0-89922-132-7). Edit Caribe.

Hombre en Transicion. Gary Collins. Tr. by Roberto Ingledew from Eng. 220p. (Orig., Span.). 1978. pap. 4.50 (ISBN 0-89922-124-6). Edit Caribe.

Hombre que se Bano Siete Veces. Joann Scheck. Tr. by J. Alfonso Lockward from Eng. (Libros Arco). (Illus.). 32p. (Orig., Span.). (gr. 1-3). 1975. pap. 0.95 o.s.i. (ISBN 0-89922-038-X). Edit Caribe.

Hombre, Si Que Tengo Problemas. Tr. by David Wilkerson. (Spanish Bks.). (Span.). 1978. 1.50 (ISBN 0-8297-0576-7). Life Pubs Intl.

Hombre Tragado por un Pez. M. M. Bremm. Tr. by Fernando Villalobos from Eng. (Libros Arco). (Illus.). 32p. (Orig., Span.). (gr. 1-3). 1970. pap. 0.95 o.s.i. (ISBN 0-89922-047-9). Edit Caribe.

Home Again, My Love. Zoe Dozier. (YA) 1978. 5.95 (ISBN 0-685-86408-1, Avalon). Bouregy.

Home & Building Maintenance. J. C. Woodin & Louis Hayes. 14.00 (ISBN 0-87345-466-9). McKnight.

Home & Child Life in Colonial Days. abr. ed. Alice M. Earle. Ed. by Shirley Glubok. LC 69-11295. (Illus.). (gr. 5 up). 1969. 9.95 (ISBN 0-02-733250-0). Macmillan.

Home & Community Influences on Young Children. Karen D. Vander Ven. LC 76-14092. 1977. pap. text ed. 7.80 (ISBN 0-8273-0569-9); instructor's guide 1.60 (ISBN 0-8273-0570-2). Delmar.

Home & School Partnerships in Exceptional Education. Carol T. Michaelis. 375p. 1980. text ed. 27.95 (ISBN 0-89443-330-X). Aspen Systems.

Home & Shop Math. Robert Scharff. LC 76-48585. (Popular Science Ser). (Illus.). 425p. 1981. 14.95 (ISBN 0-06-013784-3, HarpT). Har-Row.

Home & Workshop Guide to Sharpening. Harry Walton. (Everday Handbook Ser.). (Illus.). 160p. 1974. pap. 2.95 o.p. (ISBN 0-06-463418-3, 418, EH). Har-Row.

Home Appliances: Selection, Use & Repair. Jeannette T. Adams. LC 79-25773. (Illus.). 1132p. 1980. lib. bdg. 19.95 o.p. (ISBN 0-668-04530-2). Arco.

Home Aquarium. W. Simister. LC 76-20105. 1976. 8.95 (ISBN 0-7153-7255-6). David & Charles.

Home As God Would Have It & Contemporary Attacks Against It. Ed. by Thomas B. Warren & Garland Elkins. 1979. 19.95 (ISBN 0-934916-34-9). Natl Christian Pr.

Home at Sundown. Lucy Walker. 1976. pap. 1.25 o.p. (ISBN 0-345-25235-7). Ballantine.

Home Baked. Cecelia Scurfield & George Scurfield. (Illus., Orig.). 1971. pap. 3.95 (ISBN 0-571-09844-4, Pub. by Faber & Faber). Merrimack Bk Serv.

Home Baked: A Little Book of Bread Recipes. Georgia Scurfield & Cecila Scurfield. 1972. 8.95 (ISBN 0-571-06614-3); pap. 2.95 (ISBN 0-571-09844-4). Transatlantic.

Home-Based Services for Children & Families: Policy, Practice, & Research. Sheila Maybanks & Marvin Bryce. 384p. 1979. 22.50 (ISBN 0-398-03880-5). C C Thomas.

Home Below Hell's Canyon. Grace Jordan. LC 54-6332. (Illus.). 1962. 11.95x (ISBN 0-8032-0946-0); pap. 4.95 (ISBN 0-8032-5107-6, BB 143, Bison). U of Nebr Pr.

Home Book of Greek Cookery. Joyce Stubbs. 8.95 (ISBN 0-571-05477-3). Transatlantic.

Home Book of Greek Cookery. Joyce M. Stubbs. LC 64-35740. (Home Cookery Book Ser). 159p. 1967. 6.25x (ISBN 0-571-08187-8). Intl Pubns Serv.

Home Book of Greek Cookery. Joyce M. Stubbs. (Orig.). 1967. pap. 5.95 (ISBN 0-571-08187-8, Pub. by Faber & Faber). Merrimack Bk Serv.

Home Book of Indian Cookery. Sipra Das Gupta. 184p. 1979. pap. 6.95 (ISBN 0-571-11508-X, Pub by Faber & Faber). Merrimack Bk Serv.

Home Book of Indonesian Cookery. Sri Owen. 1976. 9.95 o.p. (ISBN 0-571-10850-4, Pub. by Faber & Faber). Merrimack Bk Serv.

Home Book of Italian Cookery. Beryl Gould-Marks. (Orig.). 1974. pap. 3.95 o.p. (ISBN 0-571-10590-4, Pub. by Faber & Faber). Merrimack Bk Serv.

Home Book of Jewish Cookery. Judy Jackson. 176p. 1981. 24.00 (ISBN 0-571-11697-3, Pub. by Faber & Faber); pap. 9.95 (ISBN 0-571-11737-6). Merrimack Bk Serv.

Home Book of Quotations. rev. ed. Ed. by Burton Stevenson. LC 67-13583. 1967. 40.00 (ISBN 0-396-02533-1). Dodd.

Home Book of Smoke-Cooking Meat, Fish & Game. Raymond Hull & Jack Sleight. LC 76-162445. (Illus.). 160p. 1971. 10.95 (ISBN 0-8117-0803-9). Stackpole.

Home Book of Smoke Cooking, Meat, Fish & Game. Jack Sleight & Raymond Hull. 1975. pap. 1.50 (ISBN 0-515-03638-2). Jove Pubns.

Home Book of Spanish Cookery. Marina Aznar. LC 67-94477. (Home Cookery Book Ser). 1967. 10.50x (ISBN 0-571-10655-2). Intl Pubns Serv.

Home Book of Taxidermy & Tanning. Gerald J. Grantz. LC 77-85651. (Illus.). 160p. 1970. 10.95 (ISBN 0-8117-0805-5). Stackpole.

Home Book of the Picturesque: Or American Scenery, Art, & Literature. LC 67-10179. 1967. Repr. of 1852 ed. 20.00x (ISBN 0-8201-1029-9). Schol Facsimiles.

Home Book of Verse. 10th ed. Burton E. Stevenson. 45.00 o.p. (ISBN 0-03-028035-4). HR&W.

Home Brewing: An Illustrated Guide. Albert Whitehouse. LC 80-68689. (Illus.). 1981. 12.95 (ISBN 0-7153-7985-2). David & Charles.

Home Brewing Without Failures. H. E. Bravery. LC 66-17178. (Orig.). 1967. pap. 0.95 o.p. (ISBN 0-668-01436-9). Arc Bks.

Home Built Aircraft. David B. Thurston. (McGraw-Hill Series in Aviation). (Illus.). 224p. 1981. 24.95 (ISBN 0-07-064552-3, P&RB). McGraw.

Home Buyer's Guide. Nancy R. Hess. (Illus.). 224p. 1981. pap. 5.95 (ISBN 0-13-392647-8, Spec). P-H.

Home Buying: The Complete Illustrated Guide. Henry S. Harrison & Margery B. Leonard. Ed. by Helene Berlin. (Illus.). 500p. (Orig.). 1980. pap. 14.95 (ISBN 0-913652-18-0, BK128). Realtors Natl.

Home Cabinetmaker: Building Fine Furniture, Built-Ins, Millwork. Monte Burch. LC 79-4747. (Popular Science Bk.). (Illus.). Date not set. 19.95 (ISBN 0-06-010349-3, HarpT). Har-Row. Postponed.

Home Canning. Sunset Editors. LC 74-20016. (Illus.). 96p. (Orig.). 1975. pap. 2.95 o.p. (ISBN 0-376-02212-4, Sunset Bks.). Sunset-Lane.

Home Canning & Preserving Book. Ann Seranne. 1975. pap. 4.95 (ISBN 0-06-463424-8, EH). Har-Row.

Home Canning of Fruits & Vegetables. U. S. Dept. of Agriculture. (Illus.). 31p. Repr. pap. 2.50. Shorey.

Home Care for the Elderly. Julie Trocchio. LC 80-19713. 176p. 1980. pap. 8.95 (ISBN 0-8436-0770-X). CBI Pub.

Home Carpentry. F. E. Sherlock. (Illus.). 1980. 14.50 (ISBN 0-7207-1243-2, Pub. by Michael Joseph). Merrimack Bk Serv.

Home Computer Handbook. Edwin Sclossberg et al. LC 77-95272. (Illus.). 1978. 12.95 (ISBN 0-8069-3096-9); lib. bdg. 11.69 (ISBN 0-8069-3097-7). Sterling.

Home Computers: A Beginners Glossary & Guide. Merl K. Miller & Charles J. Sippl. 1978. pap. 8.95 (ISBN 0-918398-02-9). Dilithium Pr.

Home Computers: A Manual of Possibilities. Richard Koff. 1979. 7.95 o.p. (ISBN 0-15-142163-3). HarBraceJ.

Home Computers: A Simple & Informative Guide. Scott Corbett. (Illus.). 128p. (gr. 5 up). 1980. 7.95 (ISBN 0-316-15658-2, Pub. by Atlantic Monthly Pr); pap. 4.95 (ISBN 0-316-15712-0). Little.

Home Computers Can Make You Rich. Joe Weisbecker. 1980. pap. 6.50 (ISBN 0-8104-5177-8). Hayden.

Home Computers: Two to the Tenth Questions & Answers, 2 vols. Rich Didday. 1977. Vol. I. 9.95 (ISBN 0-918398-00-2); Vol. II. 9.95 (ISBN 0-918398-01-0). Dilithium Pr.

Home Course in Nutrition. Eric F. Powell. 104p. 1978. pap. 7.50x (ISBN 0-8464-1019-2). Beekman Pubs.

Home Decorating. David Johnson. LC 78-74079. (Penny Pinchers Ser). 1979. 2.95 (ISBN 0-7153-7751-5). David & Charles.

Home Decorating Sewing Book. Elizabeth J. Musheno. 1978. 16.95 (ISBN 0-02-588190-6); pap. 7.95 (ISBN 0-02-011890-2). Macmillan.

Home Do-It Yourself Market. Ed. by Business Communications Co. 1980. 675.00 (ISBN 0-89336-232-8, GB-054). BCC.

Home Economics. Beryl Ruth. 1974. pap. text ed. 4.95x o.p. (ISBN 0-435-42262-6). Heinemann Ed.

Home Economics Assignments. Beryl Ruth. 1969. pap. text ed. 2.50 o.p. (ISBN 0-435-42701-6). Heinemann Ed.

Home Economics Careers. Gilda Berger. LC 77-837. (Career Concise Guides Ser.). (gr. 7 up). 1977. PLB 6.45 s&l (ISBN 0-531-01280-8). Watts.

Home Economics Education. Martha L. Blankenship & Barbara D. Moerchen. LC 78-69595. (Illus.). 1979. text ed. 16.95 (ISBN 0-395-26700-5); inst. manual 1.80 (ISBN 0-395-26699-8); self instruction module 9.25 (ISBN 0-395-26698-X). HM.

Home Economics Evaluation. Aleene Cross. LC 73-75679. 1973. text ed. 20.95x (ISBN 0-675-08933-6). Merrill.

Home Electrician's Bible. Len Hilts. (Illus.). 160p. 1976. pap. 2.95 o.p. (ISBN 0-385-11234-3). Doubleday.

Home Electronics. Fairchild Market Research Division. (Fairchild Fact File Ser.). 1979. pap. 10.00 (ISBN 0-87005-320-5). Fairchild.

Home Energy Management: Principles & Practices. Stephen J. Mecca & Joseph E. Robertshaw. (Illus.). 160p. 1981. 12.00 (ISBN 0-89433-146-9). Petrocelli.

Home Energy Saver. Consumer Guide Editors. (Orig.). 1979. pap. 1.95 (ISBN 0-449-80002-4). Fawcett.

Home Entertainment for All the Family. Gyles Brandreth. LC 76-50266. (Illus.). 1977. 10.00 o.p. (ISBN 0-8289-0297-6); pap. 5.95 (ISBN 0-8289-0298-4). Greene.

Home Fires Beneath the Northern Lights. Rachel Showalter. 260p. 1970. 5.70 o.p. (ISBN 0-686-05598-5). Rod & Staff.

Home Fires Burning: The History of Domestic Heating & Cooking. Lawrence Wright. 1964. 15.00 (ISBN 0-7100-2332-4). Routledge & Kegan.

Home Fix-It Secrets of the Pros. Tom Philbin. (Illus.). 1980. cancelled (ISBN 0-525-93118-X); pap. 6.95 (ISBN 0-525-93104-X). Dutton.

Home Food Systems: Rodale's Catalog of Methods & Tools for Producing, Processing & Preserving Naturally Good Foods. Ed. by Roger B. Yepsen, Jr. (Illus.). 512p. 1981. 18.95 (ISBN 0-87857-325-9); pap. 15.95 (ISBN 0-87857-320-8). Rodale Pr Inc.

Home for a Bunny. Margaret W. Brown. (Illus.). 32p. (ps-2). 1975. 1.95 (ISBN 0-307-10446-X, Golden Pr); PLB 7.62 (ISBN 0-307-60446-2). Western Pub.

Home for Jamie. Doris D. Piper. (N. H.-Vermont Historiettes). (Illus.). 58p. (Orig.). (gr. 3-4). 1976. 4.95x (ISBN 0-915892-08-1); pap. 1.45 (ISBN 0-915892-13-8). Regional Ctr Educ.

Home for Sale by Owner. Gerald M. Steiner. LC 77-85358. (Illus.). 1978. pap. 8.95 (ISBN 0-8015-3529-8, Hawthorn). Dutton.

Home for the Heart. Hope Goodwin. (Orig.). 1980. pap. 1.95 (ISBN 0-532-23135-X). Manor Bks.

Home Freezing of Fruits & Vegetables. U. S. Dept. of Agriculture. (Illus.). 48p. pap. 2.50 (ISBN 0-8466-6056-3). Shorey.

Home from Hawaii. Frances Holton. (YA) 5.95 (ISBN 0-685-19058-7, Avalon). Bouregy.

Home from Home. Susan Price. (gr. 6-8). 1978. 8.95 (ISBN 0-571-11022-3, Pub. by Faber & Faber). Merrimack Bk Serv.

Home from the Shore. Gordon R. Dickson. Ed. by James P. Baen. 1979. pap. 2.25 (ISBN 0-441-34256-6). Ace Bks.

Home Front. Margaret Craven. 252p. 1981. 11.95 (ISBN 0-686-69591-7). Putnam.

Home Front: Japan. (World War II Ser.). (Illus.). 1979. kivar bdg. 14.94 (ISBN 0-8094-2527-0). Silver.

Home Front: Japan. Time-Life Books Editors & Richard Halloran. (World War II Ser.). (Illus.). 208p. 1981. 13.95 (ISBN 0-8094-3415-6). Time-Life.

Home Front: U. S. A. Ronald Bailey. LC 77-87556. (World War II Ser.). (Illus.). 1977. lib. bdg. 14.94 (ISBN 0-686-51046-1). Silver.

Home Front: USA. Ronald Bailey. Ed. by Time Life Books. (World War II Ser.). (Illus.). 1978. 12.95 (ISBN 0-8094-2478-9). Time-Life.

Home Fruit & Vegetable Production. R. B. Flood. LC 78-4214. 1978. 10.00 (ISBN 0-8108-1132-4). Scarecrow.

Home Furnishing Self Help. C. B. O'Connell. LC 68-12618. 1968. 10.00 (ISBN 0-8108-0180-9). Scarecrow.

Home Furnishing with Antiques. F. Gordon Roe. (Illus.). 1965. 6.95 o.p. (ISBN 0-8038-2993-0). Hastings.

Home Furnishings. Barbara Kaplan. LC 74-19485. 1975. pap. text ed. 9.50 (ISBN 0-672-96412-0); tchr's manual 5.00 (ISBN 0-672-96832-0). Bobbs.

Home Ground. Cecelia Holland. LC 80-2710. 384p. 1981. 13.95 (ISBN 0-394-50405-4). Knopf.

Home Growing. Ed. by Edwin Steffel. LC 77-256. (Illus.). 1977. 19.95 (ISBN 0-312-38836-5). St Martin.

Home Grown Kids. Raymond Moore & Dorothy Moore. 1981. 9.95 (ISBN 0-8499-0270-3). Word Bks.

Home Guide to Cartridge Conversions. rev. ed. George Nonte. 15.00 (ISBN 0-88227-005-2). Gun Room.

Home Guide to Lawns & Landscaping. Bruce Cassiday. LC 75-40601. (Popular Science Skill Bk.). 224p. 1976. 6.95 o.s.i. (ISBN 0-06-010689-1, HarpT). Har-Row.

Home Guide to Lawns & Landscaping. Bruce Cassiday. LC 75-40601. (Popular Science Skill Bk). (Illus.). 1977. pap. 3.95 o.p. (ISBN 0-06-010697-2, TD-275, HarpT). Har-Row.

Home Gun Care & Repair. P. O. Ackley. LC 69-16147. 1974. pap. 6.95 (ISBN 0-8117-2028-4). Stackpole.

Home Gunsmithing: The Colt Single Action Revolvers. Loren W. Smith. (Illus.). 1971. 7.95 o.p. (ISBN 0-686-15791-5). Ray Riling.

Home Has a Heart. Thyra F. Bjorn. (Spire Bks). 1975. pap. 1.75 o.p. (ISBN 0-8007-8222-4). Revell.

Home Has a Heart. Thyra F. Bjorn. (Orig.). pap. 1.75 (ISBN 0-89129-033-8). Jove Pubns.

Home Health Care. Jane E. Stewart. LC 78-31116. (Illus.). 1979. pap. text ed. 10.95 (ISBN 0-8016-4801-7). Mosby.

Home Health Care & the Quality of Life. Ed. by Elizabeth R. Prichard et al. (Foundation of Thanatology Ser.). 1979. 20.00x (ISBN 0-231-04258-2). Columbia U Pr.

Home Health Care for the Aged: How to Help Older People Stay in Their Homes & Out of Institutions. Philip W. Brickner. (Illus.). 1978. 16.75 (ISBN 0-8385-3809-6). ACC.

Home Heating. B. J. King & J. E. Beer. (Teach Yourself Ser.). 1974. pap. 2.95 o.p. (ISBN 0-679-10470-4). McKay.

Home Heating with Coal. Steve Sherman. (Illus.). 192p. 1980. pap. 8.95 (ISBN 0-8117-2081-0). Stackpole.

Home Help. Janet Marks. 112p. 1975. pap. text ed. 7.50x (ISBN 0-7135-1842-1, Pub. by Bedford England). Renouf.

Home, How to Run Effectively-Save Money. Bogart. 1980. pap. cancelled (ISBN 0-8120-0685-2). Barron.

Home Improvement, Home Repair. Richard V. Nunn. Ed. by Shirley M. Horowitz. LC 80-66637. (Illus.). 256p. 1980. 14.95 (ISBN 0-932944-17-5). Creative Homeowner.

Home Improvement-Home Repair. Richard V. Nunn. Ed. by Shirley M. Horowitz. LC 80-66637. (Illus.). 256p. (Orig.). 1980. pap. 7.95 (ISBN 0-932944-18-3). Creative Homeowner.

Home in the Woods: Pioneer Life in Indiana. Howard Johnson. LC 77-74426. (Illus.). 104p. 1978. Repr. of 1951 ed. 8.95x (ISBN 0-253-32842-X). Ind U Pr.

Home Is Best Book. Kathleen Daly. Orig. Title: Nest Book. (Illus.). 24p. (ps-4). 1977. PLB 5.38 (ISBN 0-307-68919-0, Golden Pr). Western Pub.

Home Is Not a Home: Life Within a Nursing Home. Tr. by J. G. Tulloch. LC 75-28220. 142p. 1975. 6.95 (ISBN 0-8164-9269-7). Continuum.

Home Landscape Nineteen Eighty-One. Landscape Architecture Magazine. Ed. by Grady Clay & Norman Johnson. (Landscape Architecture Magazine Ser.). 168p. 1981. 7.95 (ISBN 0-07-036193-2). McGraw.

Home Landscape, 1980. Landscape Architecture Magazine. (Illus.). 1980. pap. 5.95 o.p. (ISBN 0-07-036192-4). McGraw.

Home Landscaping. (Illus.). 1974. pap. 6.95 (ISBN 0-88453-002-7). Countryside Bks.

Home Landscaping. (Countryside Bks). (Illus.). 1977. pap. 4.95 o.p. (ISBN 0-695-80787-0, 0206C). Follett.

Home Life. D. Rabinowitz & Y. Nielsen. Orig. Title: Would You Like to Come & Live Here. 1971. 5.95 o.s.i. (ISBN 0-02-600300-7). Macmillan.

Home Life in China. Isaac T. Headland. LC 79-177278. (Illus.). xii, 319p. 1971. Repr. of 1914 ed. 26.00 (ISBN 0-8103-3822-X). Gale.

Home Life in Colonial Days. Alice M. Earle. LC 74-11507. 470p. 1974. lib. bdg. 9.95 o.p. (ISBN 0-912944-23-4); pap. 5.95 (ISBN 0-912944-23-4). Berkshire Traveller.

Home-Made Cakes and Biscuits. 2nd ed. Cecelia Scurfield & George Scurfield. (Orig.). 1975. pap. 3.95 (ISBN 0-571-10699-4, Pub. by Faber & Faber). Merrimack Bk Serv.

Home Maintenance. Weiss. (gr. 9-12). 1978. text ed. 10.60 (ISBN 0-87002-199-0); student guide 2.60 (ISBN 0-87002-239-3); tchr's guide avail. Bennett IL.

Home Maintenance: A Guide to Taking Better Care of Your House. William Weiss. (Illus.). 1978. 12.95 o.p. (ISBN 0-684-15594-X, ScribT). Scribner.

Home Maintenance & Repair: Walls, Ceilings, & Floors. Gary D. Branson. (Illus.). 1977. pap. 6.95 (ISBN 0-672-23281-2, 23281). Audel.

Home Management. Phyllis Davidson. 1975. pap. 16.95 (ISBN 0-7134-3047-8, Pub. by Batsford England). David & Charles.

Home Management. University of Missouri - Home Economics Resource Unit. text ed. 2.75x spiral bdg. (ISBN 0-87543-024-4). Lucas.

Home of Science: The Role of the University. Carnegie Commission on Higher Education. Ed. by Dael Wolfle. LC 78-39642. 209p. 1972. 8.95 o.p. (ISBN 0-07-010044-6, P&RB). McGraw.

Home of the Heroes: The Aegean Before the Greeks. Sinclair Hood. 1967. pap. 3.95 o.p. (ISBN 0-07-029718-5, SP). McGraw.

Home of the Heroes: The Aegean Before the Greeks. Sinclair Hood. (Illus.). 144p. 1975. pap. 7.50 (ISBN 0-500-29009-1). Transatlantic.

Home; or, Family Cares & Family Joys. Fredrika Bremer. Tr. by M. Howitt from Swedish. LC 76-28470. 1978. Repr. of 1850 ed. 19.75 (ISBN 0-86527-259-X). Fertig.

Home Ownership Game & How to Win It. David Hammond. LC 80-68693. (Illus.). 112p. 1981. 13.50 (ISBN 0-7153-7710-8). David & Charles.

Home Pet Vet Guide: Dogs. Martin Green. 1980. 7.95 (ISBN 0-345-28944-7). Ballantine.

Home Pet Vet Guide for Cats. Martin Green. pap. cancelled (ISBN 0-686-68438-9, 43406). Avon.

Home Pet Vet Guide for Dogs. Martin Green. pap. cancelled (ISBN 0-686-68439-7, 43414). Avon.

Home Place. Wright Morris. LC 48-1792. (Illus.). xii, 178p. 1968. pap. 4.50 (ISBN 0-8032-5139-4, BB 386, Bison). U of Nebr Pr.
Home Place. Dorothy Thomas. LC 36-16925. (Illus.). 1966. pap. 1.70 (ISBN 0-8032-5197-1, BB 346, Bison). U of Nebr Pr.
Home Place: A Memory & a Celebration. Robert Drake. LC 80-24110. (Illus.). 192p. 1980. 14.95 (ISBN 0-87870-198-2). Memphis St Univ.
Home Pool Safety. Bert Jacobs & Isabel Jacobs. LC 77-26215. (Illus.). 1978. 13.95 (ISBN 0-88229-392-3); pap. 7.95 (ISBN 0-88229-509-8). Nelson-Hall.
Home Recording for Musicians. Craig Anderton. LC 77-87208. (Illus.). 184p. 1978. pap. 9.95 (ISBN 0-89122-011-9). Guitar Player.
Home Remedies: Fixing up Houses and Apartments, Mostly Old but Also Otherwise. Christopher Fahy. LC 74-32200. 1976. pap. 2.95 o.p. (ISBN 0-684-14695-9, SL663, ScribT). Scribner.
Home Remodeling Design & Plans. Herb Hughes. Ed. by Shirley M. Horowitz. LC 79-23347. (Illus.). 144p. (Orig.). 1979. 12.95 (ISBN 0-932944-11-6); pap. 4.95 (ISBN 0-932944-12-4). Creative Homeowner.
Home Renovation. Peter Jones. Ed. by K. Lawson. (Home Environment "HELP" Ser.). (Illus.). 144p. pap. cancelled (ISBN 0-88421-154-1). Butterick Pub.
Home Repair & Improvement. Robert G. Schipf. LC 73-88698. (Spare Time Guides Ser.: No. 3). 1974. lib. bdg. 7.50 o.p. (ISBN 0-37287-078-2). Libs Unl.
Home Repairs. Boy Scouts Of America. LC 19-600. (Illus.). 48p. (gr. 6-12). 1961. pap. 0.70x (ISBN 0-8395-3329-2, 3329). BSA.
Home Repairs Made Easy. Dick Demske. Ed. by Donald D. Wolf. LC 79-84283. (Illus.). 1979. pap. 9.95 (ISBN 0-8326-2240-0, 7725). Delair.
Home Rule in the District of Columbia: The First 500 Days. Duane R. Taylor. LC 78-58442. 1978. pap. text ed. 11.25 (ISBN 0-8191-0535-X). U Pr of Amer.
Home Run! George Sullivan. LC 76-53582. (gr. 5 up). 1977. 5.95 (ISBN 0-396-07402-2). Dodd.
Home Run Kings. Clare Gault & Frank Gault. LC 74-31903. (Illus.). (gr. 3-5). 1975. 4.95 (ISBN 0-8027-6217-4); PLB 4.85 o.s.i. (ISBN 0-8027-6216-6). Walker & Co.
Home School & Leisure in the Soviet Union. Ed. by Jenny Brine et al. (Illus.). 304p. 1980. text ed. 28.50x (ISBN 0-04-335040-2, 2537). Allen Unwin.
Home-School-Community Interaction: What We Know & Why We Don't Know More. Cynthia Wallat & Richard Goldman. 1979. text ed. 14.95 (ISBN 0-675-08281-1). Merrill.
Home Security. (Home Repair & Improvement Ser.). (Illus.). 1979. lib. bdg. 11.97 (ISBN 0-686-51040-2). Silver.
Home Smoking & Curing: How You Can Smoke-Cure, Salt, & Preserve Fish, Meat, Poultry & Game. Keith Erlandson. 1978. 9.95 o.p. (ISBN 0-214-20322-0, 8048, Dist. by Arco). Barrie & Jenkins.
Home Storage. Richard V. Nunn. LC 75-12122. (Family Guidebooks Ser.). (Illus.). 96p. 1975. pap. 2.95 (ISBN 0-8487-0386-3). Oxmoor Hse.
Home Style Japanese Cooking in Pictures. Sadako Kohno. (Illus., Orig.). 1978. pap. 8.95 (ISBN 0-87040-423-7). Japan Pubns.
Home-Style Learning: Activities for Young Children & Their Parents. P. Morse & T. Brand. 1981. pap. 5.95 (ISBN 0-13-392944-2); 10.95 (ISBN 0-13-392951-5). P-H.
Home Sweet Hassle. Wally Metts. LC 79-53293. (Orig.). 1981. pap. 2.95 (ISBN 0-89636-036-9). Accent Bks.
Home Sweet Home. Mike Graham-Cameron. (Illus.). 32p. 1980. pap. 1.60 ea. (Pub. by Dinosaur Pubns); pap. in 5 pk. avail. (ISBN 0-85122-174-2). Merrimack Bk Serv.
Home Sweet Home: A History of Housework. Eleanor Allen. (Junior Reference Ser.). (Illus.). 64p. (gr. 7 up). 7.95 (ISBN 0-7136-1927-9). Dufour.
Home Textiles. Fairchild Market Research Division. (Fairchild Fact Files Ser.). 90p. 1980. pap. 10.00 (ISBN 0-87005-353-1). Fairchild.
Home to My Island. David Hurd. (Illus.). 192p. 1981. 9.50 (ISBN 0-682-49727-4). Exposition.
Home to Our Valleys. Walter Utt. LC 75-30138. (Destiny Ser.). 1976. pap. 4.95 (ISBN 0-8163-0258-8, 08698-3). Pacific Pr Pub Assn
Home to the Mountain. Brenda Canary. LC 74-82167. 192p. 1975. 11.95 o.p. (ISBN 0-8027-0578-2); pap. 7.95 (ISBN 0-8027-0474-3). Walker & Co.
Home Tour Through the Manufacturing Districts of England in the Summer of 1835. George Head. LC 67-31559. Repr. of 1836 ed. 17.50x (ISBN 0-678-05057-0). Kelley.
Home Video Handbook. 2nd, rev. ed. Charles Bensinger. 1980. pap. 8.95 (ISBN 0-931294-02-9). Video-Info.
Home Video Tape-Disc Guide: Children's Program. 1980. pap. 12.95 (ISBN 0-452-25256-3, Z5256, Plume). NAL.
Home Windmills. Lawrence G. Moison. (Illus.). 60p. (Orig.). 1980. pap. text ed. 2.95. Mod Handcraft.
Home Winemaker's Handbook. Walter S. Taylor & Richard P. Vine. 1968. 10.95 o.p. (ISBN 0-06-115020-7, HarpT). Har-Row.
Home Wiring. R. Graf & G. Whalen. 1981. 14.95 (ISBN 0-13-392977-9). P-H.
Home Workshop. Time-Life Books Editors. (Home Repair & Improvement Ser.). (Illus.). 128p. 1980. 10.95 (ISBN 0-8094-3454-7, Silver Burdett). Time-Life.
Home Workshop Digest. Dean A. Grennell. 256p. 1981. pap. 7.95 (ISBN 0-910676-14-3). DBI.
Home Workshop Guns for Defense & Resistance: The Handgun, Vol. II. Bill Holmes. Ed. by Devon Christensen. (Illus.). 144p. (Orig.). 1979. pap. 6.00 (ISBN 0-87364-154-X). Paladin Ent.
Homebuyer's Cost Calculator: U.S. Department of Housing & Urban Development. 1980. pap. cancelled (ISBN 0-8120-0820-0). Barron.
Homecoming. Nicholas Brady. 1977. pap. 1.50 (ISBN 0-505-51216-5). Tower Bks.
Homecoming. Norah Lofts. 1977. pap. 1.95 o.p. (ISBN 0-449-23166-6, Crest). Fawcett.
Homecoming. C. P. Snow. LC 56-10199. 1956. lib. rep. ed. 17.50x (ISBN 0-684-15133-2, ScribT). Scribner.
Homecoming. Cynthia Voigt. LC 80-36723. 320p. (gr. 5 up). 1981. PLB 12.95 (ISBN 0-689-30833-7). Atheneum.
Homefront. Winston M. Estes. LC 76-17579. 1976. 10.00 o.p. (ISBN 0-397-01147-4). Lippincott.
Homegrown. George R. Nevin, Jr. (Orig.). 1980. pap. 2.50 (ISBN 0-532-23140-6). Manor Bks.
Homegrown Christian Education: Planning & Programming in the Local Congregation. Ed. by David W. Perry. (Orig.). 1979. pap. 4.95 (ISBN 0-8164-2212-5). Crossroad NY.
Homeless Borstal Boys. Roger Hood. 103p. 1966. pap. text ed. 5.00x (Pub. by Bedford England). Renouf.
Homem, Estou Cheio De Problemas. Tr. by David Wilkerson. (Portugese Bks.). (Port.). 1979. 1.40 (ISBN 0-8297-0815-4). Life Pubs Intl.
Homemade Natural Mixes. Nina Shandler & Michael Shandler. LC 80-51253. 256p. 1981. 12.95 (ISBN 0-89256-145-9); pap. 6.95 (ISBN 0-89256-150-5). Rawson Wade.
Homemaker-Home Health Aide. Helen Huber et al. LC 78-66616. 1980. pap. 8.80 (ISBN 0-8273-1704-2); instr's. guide 1.50 (ISBN 0-8273-1705-0). Delmar.
Homemakers. Leonard E. Fisher. LC 73-5692. (Colonial American Ser). (gr. 4-6). 1973. PLB 4.90 o.p. (ISBN 0-531-01047-3). Watts.
Homemaker's Book of Time & Money Savers. Jean Laird. 1980. pap. 2.50 (ISBN 0-446-91562-9). Warner Bks.
Homemaker's Response to Inflation. Judy Hammersmark. (Orig.). 1980. pap. 2.95 (ISBN 0-88270-454-0). Logos.
Homemakers: The Forgotten Workers. Rae Andre. LC 80-21258. 1981. 15.00not set (ISBN 0-226-01993-4). U of Chicago Pr.
Homemaking Executive. Laura Snyder. pap. 3.95 (ISBN 0-89036-140-1). Hawkes Pub Inc.
Homemaking for Teen-Agers, Bk. 2. rev. ed. Irene McDermottt et al. (gr. 9-12). 1976. text ed. 17.28 (ISBN 0-87002-171-0). Bennett IL.
Homemaking for Teenagers, Bk. 1. new ed. Irene E. Mc Dermott & Jeanne L. Nicholas. (gr. 7-12). 1975. Bk 1. 17.24 (ISBN 0-87002-070-6). Bennett IL.
Homenagem a Agostino Da Silva, Vol. 10. 250p. 1980. pap. 7.00 (ISBN 0-912788-09-7). Tulane Romance Lang.
Homeopathic Drug Pictures. Margaret L. Tyler. 885p. 1952. text ed. 29.95x (ISBN 0-8464-1020-6). Beekman Pubs.
Homeopathic Handbook. A. C. Nelson. (Orig.). Date not set. 9.95 (ISBN 0-87983-239-8); pap. 6.95 (ISBN 0-87983-240-1). Keats. Postponed.
Homeopathy for the First Aider. Dorothy Sheperd. 1980. text ed. 4.75x (ISBN 0-8464-1021-4). Beekman Pubs.
Homeopathy in Practice. D. M. Borland. Ed. by Kathleen Priestman. 230p. 1980. 25.00x (Pub. by Beaconsfield England). State Mutual Bk.
Homeostasis in Injury & Shock: Proceedings of a Satellite Symposium of the 28th International Congress of Physiological Sciences, Budapest, Hungary, 1980. Ed. by Z. Biro et al. LC 80-42104. (Advances in Physiological Sciences: Vol. 26). (Illus.). 360p. 1981. 40.00 (ISBN 0-08-027347-5). Pergamon.
Homeothermia of the Brain. Sz. Donhoffer. (Illus.). 140p. (Orig.). 1980. pap. 13.50x (ISBN 963-05-2405-8). Intl Pubns Serv.
Homeowner's Complete Outdoor Building Book. John B. Brimer. (Popular Science Bk.). (Illus.). 1971. 12.50 o.s.i. (ISBN 0-06-010473-2, HarpT). Har-Row.
Homeowner's Energy Guide: How to Beat the Heating Game. John A. Murphy. LC 77-106. (Illus.). 1977. 9.95 o.s.i. (ISBN 0-690-01486-4, TYC-T); pap. 6.95 o.s.i. (ISBN 0-690-01487-2). T Y Crowell.
Homeowner's Guide to Landscaping That Saves Energy Dollars. Ruth S. Foster. (Illus.). 1978. 10.95 o.p. (ISBN 0-679-50863-5); pap. 5.95 o.p. (ISBN 0-679-50866-X). McKay.
Homeowner's Guide to Plumbing, Heating & Air Conditioning. Peter Jones. (Illus.). 1980. text ed. 13.95 (ISBN 0-8359-2845-4). Reston.
Homeowner's Guide to Saving Energy. Billy L. Price & James Price. LC 76-24785. (Illus.). 1976. pap. 5.95 (ISBN 0-8306-5904-8, 904). TAB Bks.
Homeowner's Guide to Solar Heating & Cooling. William Foster. LC 76-24786. (Illus.). 1976. pap. 4.95 (ISBN 0-8306-5906-4, 906). TAB Bks.
Homeowner's Handbook of Plumbing & Repair. Kendall W. Sessions. LC 77-2133. 1978. text ed. 23.95x (ISBN 0-471-02550-X). Wiley.
Homeowner's Handbook of Power Tools. Len Buckwalter. LC 75-28061. (Funk & W Bk.). (Illus.). 256p. 1976. 9.95 o.s.i. (ISBN 0-308-10226-6, TYC-T). T Y Crowell.
Homeowner's Pest Extermination Handbook. Gene B. Williams. LC 77-4204. (Illus.). 1978. lib. bdg. 6.95 o.p. (ISBN 0-668-04316-4, 4316); pap. 2.95 o.p. (ISBN 0-668-04321-0, 4321). Arco.
Homeowner's Quick-Repair & Emergency Guide. Max Alth. LC 77-6558. (Popular Science Skill Bk.). (Illus.). 1978. pap. 3.95 o.s.i. (ISBN 0-06-010142-3, TD-296, HarpT). Har-Row.
Homeownership Effects of Alternate Mortgage Instruments. James Follain & Raymond Struyk. (Institute Paper). 95p. 1977. pap. 6.00 (ISBN 0-87766-193-6, 18900). Urban Inst.
Homer. Andre Michalopoulos. (World Authors Ser.: Greece: No. 4). 1966. lib. bdg. 9.95 (ISBN 0-8057-2432-X). Twayne.
Homer & Mycenae. Martin P. Nilsson. (Illus.). 1972. pap. 5.95x (ISBN 0-8122-1033-6, Pa. Paperbacks). U of Pa Pr.
Homer & the Epic. abr. ed. Geoffrey S. Kirk. Orig. Title: Songs of Homer, Il. pap. 8.50 (ISBN 0-521-09356-2, 356). Cambridge U Pr.
Homer & the Oral Tradition. G. S. Kirk. LC 76-7806. 1977. 28.50 (ISBN 0-521-21309-6). Cambridge U Pr.
Homer on Life & Death. Jasper Griffin. 248p. 1980. 37.50x (ISBN 0-19-814016-9). Oxford U Pr.
Homer the Hunter. Richard J. Margolis. LC 73-185220. (Illus.). (gr. k-3). 1972. 6.95 (ISBN 0-02-762290-8). Macmillan.
Homeric Dictionary for Schools & Colleges. Georg Autenrieth. Ed. by Isaac Flagg. Tr. by Robert P. Keep. (Illus.). (YA) (gr. 9 up). 1979. Repr. of 1958 ed. 7.95x (ISBN 0-8061-0394-9). U of Okla Pr.
Homeric Greek: A Book for Beginners. Clyde Pharr. (Illus.). (YA) (gr. 9 up). 1980. Repr. of 1959 ed. 7.95x (ISBN 0-8061-1275-1). U of Okla Pr.
Homeric Hymns. Tr. by Charles Boer from Gr. LC 73-132581. 184p. 1971. 9.00x (ISBN 0-8040-0524-9); pap. 3.95x o.s.i. (ISBN 0-8040-0525-7). Swallow.
Homeric Hymns. rev. ed. Tr. by Charles Boer from Gr. (Dunquin Ser.). 1979. pap. text ed. 8.50 (ISBN 0-88214-210-0). Spring Pubns.
Homeric Hymns: A Verse Translation. Tr. by Thelma Sargent. 96p. 1975. pap. 3.95 (ISBN 0-393-00788-X, Norton Lib). Norton.
Homeric Vocabularies: Greek & English Word-Lists for the Study of Homer. William B. Owen & Edgar J. Goodspeed. LC 68-31669. (Gr, & Eng). (YA) (gr. 9 up). 1969. pap. 2.95x (ISBN 0-8061-0828-2). U of Okla Pr.
Homer's Original Genius. K. Simonsuuri. LC 78-56758. (Illus.). 1979. 32.95 (ISBN 0-521-22198-6). Cambridge U Pr.
Homer's Readers: A Historical Introduction to the Iliad & the Odyssey. Howard Clarke. LC 78-66824. 328p. 1980. 26.50 (ISBN 0-87413-150-2). U Delaware Pr.
Homes. Gillian Youldon. (All A-Board Bks). (Illus.). 16p. (ps-2). 1981. 3.50 (ISBN 0-531-02539-X). Watts.
Homes by Hiawatha. Hiawatha T. Estes. (Illus.). 1981. 2.00 (ISBN 0-911008-21-7). H Estes.
Homes for Pleasant Living. 28th ed. W. D. Farmer. (Illus.). 1977. pap. 2.50 o.p. (ISBN 0-931518-05-9). W D Farmer.
Homes for Pleasant Living. 35th ed. W. D. Farmer. (Illus., Orig.). 1980. pap. 2.50 (ISBN 0-931518-12-1). W D Farmer.
Homes for Pleasant Living. 36th ed. W. D. Farmer. (Illus.). 72p. (Orig.). 1980. pap. 3.50 (ISBN 0-931518-13-X). W D Farmer.
Homes in Britain. Molly Harrison. 1975. text ed. 10.95x (ISBN 0-04-942132-8); pap. text ed. 5.95x (ISBN 0-04-942133-6). Allen Unwin.
Homes in the Earth. Design Concept Associates. (Illus.). 112p. 1980. pap. 7.95 (ISBN 0-87701-212-1). Chronicle Bks.
Homes of Other Days: A History of Domestic Manners & Sentiments in England During the Middle Ages. Thomas Wright. LC 67-23902. (Social History References Ser.). (Illus.). 1968. Repr. of 1871 ed. 15.00 (ISBN 0-8103-3263-9). Gale.
Homes on Wheels. Michael A. Rockland. 192p. 1980. 12.95 (ISBN 0-8135-0892-4). Rutgers U Pr.
Homes, Today & Tomorrow. rev. ed. (gr. 9-12). 1981. text ed. 15.92 (ISBN 0-87002-326-8). Bennett Co.
Homes, Today & Tomorrow. rev. ed. Ruth Sherwood & George Sherwood. (gr. 9-12). 1976. text ed. 15.92 (ISBN 0-87002-173-7); trans. master 13.32 (ISBN 0-685-65670-5); student guide 5.80 (ISBN 0-87002-127-3); trans. master 11.56 (ISBN 0-87002-151-6). Bennett IL.
Homespun Yarns of a Country Schoolmaster. Alice V. Miller. 3.50 o.p. (ISBN 0-685-48821-7). Nortex Pr.
Homestead Strike of Eighteen Ninety-Two. Arthur G. Burgoyne. LC 79-4702. (Illus.). 1979. 12.95 (ISBN 0-8229-3405-1); pap. 5.95 (ISBN 0-8229-5310-2). U of Pittsburgh Pr.
Homesteaders. Robert J. Stead. LC 73-82583. (Literature of Canada Ser.). 1973. pap. 6.50 (ISBN 0-8020-6196-6). U of Toronto Pr.
Homesteaders. Lee D. Willoughby. (Making of America Ser.). (Orig.). 1981. pap. 2.75 (ISBN 0-440-03628-3). Dell.
Homesteaders & Indians. Dorothy Levenson. LC 79-136832. (First Bks). (Illus.). (gr. 4-6). 1971. PLB 4.90 o.p. (ISBN 0-531-00734-0); pap. 1.25 o.p. (ISBN 0-531-02314-1). Watts.
Homesteading: A Practical Guide to Living off the Land. Patricia Crawford. LC 74-9826. 224p. 1975. 11.95 (ISBN 0-02-583820-2, 52879). Macmillan.
Homesteading in the City-a Survival Manual for Young People Living in Town or off Campus. Nancy Seligmann. (Illus.). 224p. 1975. pap. 5.95 o.p. (ISBN 0-695-80513-4). Follett.
Homesteading in Urban U. S. A. Anne Clark & Zelma Rivin. LC 77-2939. (Special Studies). 1977. text ed. 22.95 (ISBN 0-275-24060-6). Praeger.
Hometown, U. S. A. Katherine Lucas & Louise Lucas. (Illus., Orig.). 1980. pap. 4.95 (ISBN 0-914634-75-5, 8001). DOK Pubs.
Hometrics. Lorelle Young & Carole Bielefeld. (Illus.). (gr. 7 up). 1977. pap. 4.95 (ISBN 0-933358-01-6). Enrich.
Homeward & Beyond. Poul Anderson. 1979. pap. 1.75 (ISBN 0-425-03162-4). Berkley Pub.
Homeward the Arrow's Flight. Marion M. Brown. LC 80-11957. (Illus.). 176p. (gr. 7 up). 1980. 7.95g (ISBN 0-687-17300-0). Abingdon.
Homeward Winds the River. Barbara F. Johnson. 1980. pap. 2.50 (ISBN 0-686-69242-X, 42952). Avon.
Homework in Counseling & Psychotherapy. J. L. Shelton & J. M. Ackerman. (Illus.). 308p. 1976. pap. 17.75 (ISBN 0-398-03076-6). C C Thomas.
Homework One: Inside. (Illus.). 1979. 14.95 (ISBN 0-912336-81-1); pap. 6.95 (ISBN 0-912336-82-X). Structures Pub.
Homework Two: Outside. (Illus.). 1979. 14.95 (ISBN 0-912336-83-8); pap. 6.95 (ISBN 0-912336-84-6). Structures Pub.
Homicidal Threats. John M. Macdonald. (Illus.). 136p. 1968. 9.75 (ISBN 0-398-01178-8). C C Thomas.
Homicide & Survivors. Ed. by Bruce Danto et al. (Thanatology Service Ser.). 225p. 1980. pap. 9.95 o.p. (ISBN 0-686-64831-5). Highly Specialized.
Homicide Investigation: Practical Information for Coroners, Police Officers, & Other Investigators. 3rd ed. LeMoyne Snyder. (Illus.). 416p. 1977. 26.75 (ISBN 0-398-03632-2). C C Thomas.
Homicide: Investigative Techniques. Daniel J. Hughes. (Illus.). 376p. 1974. 22.50 (ISBN 0-398-02952-0). C C Thomas.
Homicide: Perspectives on Prevention. Nancy Allen. LC 79-11841. 192p. 1979. text ed. 15.95x (ISBN 0-87705-382-0); pap. text ed. 8.95x (ISBN 0-87705-412-6). Human Sci Pr.
Homiletica Practica. Tomas Hawkins. 1978. Repr. of 1975 ed. 1.50 (ISBN 0-311-42041-9). Casa Bautista.
Homiletical Plot: The Sermon As Narrative Art Form. Eugene Lowry. LC 79-92074. 100p. (Orig.). 1980. pap. 3.95 (ISBN 0-8042-1652-5). John Knox.
Homilies of St. John Chrysostom on the Letters of St. Paul to Titus & Philemon. Blake Goodall. (Univ. of California Publications in Classical Studies: Vol. 20). 1979. 11.00x (ISBN 0-520-09596-0). U of Cal Pr.
Homilies, 48-88. St. John Chrysostom. (Fathers of the Church Ser.: Vol. 41). 25.00 (ISBN 0-8132-0041-5). Cath U Pr.
Homing. Jeffrey Campbell. 256p. (Orig.). 1981. pap. 2.50 (ISBN 0-345-28793-2). Ballantine.

Homing. Elswyth Thane. (Williamsburg Ser.: No. 7). 1981. lib. bdg. 15.95 (ISBN 0-8161-3164-3, Large Print Bks). G K Hall.

Homing in the Presence: Meditations for Daily Living. Gerhard Frost. 1978. pap. 4.95 (ISBN 0-03-043921-3). Winston Pr.

Homing Pigeons. Herbert S. Zim. (Illus.). (gr. 3-7). 1949. PLB 6.48 (ISBN 0-688-31398-1). Morrow.

Hominid Fossils. 2nd ed. Norman J. Sauer & Terrell W. Phenice. 1977. wire coil bdg. 5.95x (ISBN 0-697-07552-4). Wm C Brown.

Hominy & His Blunt-Nosed Arrow. Miriam E. Mason. (gr. 2-4). 1967. 3.95g o.s.i. (ISBN 0-02-763720-4). Macmillan.

Homme En Societe Ou Nouvelles Vues Politiques et Economiques Pour Porter la Population Au Plus Haut Degre En France. H. De Goyon De La Plombanie. (Fr.). 1977. Repr. of 1763 ed. lib. bdg. 47.50x o.p. (ISBN 0-8287-0386-8). Clearwater Pub.

Homme et la mer. S. Groueff. (Collection maitrise du monde). 64.50x (ISBN 0-685-36200-0, 2278). Larousse.

Homme et le cosmos. new ed. S. Groueff & J. P. Cartier. Ed. by Raymond Cartier. (Collection maitrise du monde). (Illus.). 396p. (Fr.). 1975. 64.50x (ISBN 2-03-013369-8). Larousse.

Homme fossile de la Quina. Henri Martin. LC 78-72703. (Illus.). Repr. of 1923 ed. 41.00 (ISBN 0-404-18272-0). AMS Pr.

Homme Fossilede la Chapelle aux Saints. Marcellin Boule. LC 78-72692. 1980. Repr. of 1913 ed. 46.50 (ISBN 0-404-18263-1). AMS Pr.

Homme Ou Singe, Mr. Darwin? Tr. by Harold Hill. (French Bks.). (Fr.). 1979. 1.75 (ISBN 0-8297-0840-5). Life Pubs Intl.

Hommes de bonne volonte, 2 Vols. Jules Romains. (Documentation thematique). (Illus., Fr.). pap. 2.95 ea. Larousse.

Hommes et Choses du Temps de la Commune: Recits et Portraits Pour Servir a l'Histoire de la Premiere Revolution Sociale. Maxime Vuillaume. (Commune de Paris en 1871 Ser.). (Fr.). 1977. lib. bdg. 17.50x o.p. (ISBN 0-8287-0877-0); pap. text ed. 7.50x o.p. (ISBN 0-685-75750-1). Clearwater Pub.

Hommes et la Peste En France et Dans les Pays Europeens et Mediterraneens: Le Peste Dans L'mistoire, Tome 1. Jean N. Biraben. (Civilisations et Societies: No. 35). (Illus.). 451p. 1975. pap. text ed. 63.50 (ISBN 90-2797-555-8). Mouton.

Homo Erectus: Essays in Honor of Davidson Black. Ed. by Becky A. Sigmon & Jerome S. Cybulski. 336p. 1981. 30.00x (ISBN 0-8020-5511-7). U of Toronto Pr.

Homo Faber. Max Frisch. Ed. by Paul K. Ackermann. LC 72-9379. 300p. (Orig.). 1973. pap. text ed. 8.05 (ISBN 0-395-14402-7). HM.

Homo Faber: Technology & Culture in India, China & the West from 1500 to the Present Day. Claude A. Alvares. xvi, 275p. 1980. lib. bdg. 47.50 (ISBN 90-247-2283-7, Martinus Nijhoff Pubs). Kluwer Boston.

Homo Hierarchicus: The Caste System & Its Implications. rev. ed. Louis Dumont. Tr. by Basia Gulati. LC 80-16480. 1981. 27.50x (ISBN 0-226-16962-6); pap. 9.95 (ISBN 0-226-16963-4, P601, Phoen). U of Chicago Pr.

Homo Loquens. Dennis B. Fry. LC 77-5134. (Illus.). 1977. 24.50 (ISBN 0-521-21705-9); pap. 6.95x (ISBN 0-521-29239-5). Cambridge U Pr.

Homo Ludens: A Study of the Play Element in Culture. Jehan Huizinga. 256p. 1980. Repr. of 1949 ed. 18.50x (ISBN 0-7100-0578-4). Routledge & Kegan.

Homo Predmostensis, fosilni Clovek z Predmosti na Morave, 2 vols. Jindrich Matiegka. LC 78-72704. Repr. of 1938 ed. Set. 72.50 (ISBN 0-404-18273-9). Vol. 1 (ISBN 0-404-18274-7). Vol. 3 (ISBN 0-404-18275-5). AMS Pr.

Homo Sapiens: From Man to DemiGod. Bernhard Rensch. LC 72-80482. 1972. 17.50x (ISBN 0-231-03683-3). Columbia U Pr.

Homo Sapiens in Decline: A Reappraisal of Natural Selection. Gerhard Kraus. 189p. 1973. text ed. 8.00x (ISBN 0-7121-5601-1). Humanities.

Homo Viator: Introduction to a Metaphysic of Hope. Gabriel Marcel. Tr. by Emma Crauford. 7.50 (ISBN 0-8446-2529-9). Peter Smith.

Homoeopathic Prescribing. Noel Pratt. 96p. 1980. 25.00x (Pub. by Beaconsfield England). State Mutual Bk.

Homoeopathy in Epidemic Diseases. D. Sheperd. 1980. text ed. 5.75 o.p. (ISBN 0-8464-1022-2). Beekman Pubs.

Homogeneous Catalysis by Metal Complexes, 2 vols. M. M. Khan & Arthur E. Martell. Incl. Vol. 1. Activation of Small Inorganic Molecules. 58.50 (ISBN 0-12-406101-X); Vol. 2. Activation of Alkenes & Alkynes. 38.00 (ISBN 0-12-406102-8). 1974. 78.50 set (ISBN 0-685-72440-9). Acad Pr.

Homolka: An Eneolithic Site in Bohemia. Robert W. Ehrich & Emilie Pleslova-Stikova. LC 79-16861. (American School of Prehistoric Research Ser.). (Orig.). 1968. pap. text ed. 15.00 (ISBN 0-87365-525-7). Peabody Harvard.

Homological Groups Theory. Ed. by C. T. Wall. LC 78-74013. (London Mathematical Society Lecture Note: No. 36). 1980. pap. 42.95x (ISBN 0-521-22729-1). Cambridge U Pr.

Homology Theory. Peter J. Hilton & Shaun Wylie. 1961. 59.50 (ISBN 0-521-05266-1); pap. 20.50x (ISBN 0-521-09422-4, 422). Cambridge U Pr.

Homology Theory: An Introduction to Algebraic Topology. James W. Vick. (Pure & Applied Mathematics Ser., Vol. 54). 1973. text ed. 22.95 (ISBN 0-12-721250-7). Acad Pr.

Homosexual Behaviour: Therapy & Assessment. M. P. Feldman & M. J. Macculloch. 1971. 55.00 (ISBN 0-08-016244-4). Pergamon.

Homosexualities & French Literature: Cultural Contexts, Critical Texts. Ed. by George Stambolian & Elaine Marks. LC 78-25659. 1979. 22.50x (ISBN 0-8014-1186-6). Cornell U Pr.

Homosexuality: A Selective Bibliography of Over Three Thousand Items. William Parker. LC 71-163430. 1971. 11.00 o.p. (ISBN 0-8108-0425-5). Scarecrow.

Homosexuality: A Symbolic Confusion. Ruth T. Barnhouse. 1976. 8.95 (ISBN 0-8164-0303-1). Crossroad NY.

Homosexuality: A Symbolic Confusion. 2nd ed. Ruth T. Barnhouse. 1979. pap. 4.95 (ISBN 0-8164-2235-4). Crossroad NY.

Homosexuality & American Psychiatry: The Politics of Diagnosis. Ronald Bayer. LC 80-68182. (Illus.). 224p. 1980. 12.95 (ISBN 0-465-03048-3). Basic.

Homosexuality & Ethics. Ed. by Edward Batchelor. LC 80-10533. 1980. 10.95 (ISBN 0-8298-0392-0). Pilgrim NY.

Homosexuality Bibliography: Supplement, 1970-1975. William Parker. LC 77-1114. 1977. 15.00 (ISBN 0-8108-1050-6). Scarecrow.

Homotopy Equivalence of Three-Manifolds with Boundaries. K. Johannson. (Lecture Notes in Mathematics: Vol. 761). 303p. 1979. pap. 18.00 (ISBN 0-387-09714-7). Springer-Verlag.

Honda. LC 80-80769. (Saturday Mechanic Car Care Guides). (Illus.). 176p. 12.95 (ISBN 0-87851-935-1); pap. 6.95 (ISBN 0-87851-927-0). Hearst Bks.

Honda ATC-Seventy & ATC Ninety Singles: Service, Repair, Performance, 1970-79. Ray Hoy. Ed. by Eric Jorgensen. (Illus.). 1978. pap. 3.95 (ISBN 0-89287-214-4, M311). Clymer Pubns.

Honda CB Seven Fifty DOHC Fours: 1979-1980. Ed Scott. Ed. by Eric Jorgensen. (Illus.). 318p. (Orig.). 1980. pap. text ed. 9.95 (ISBN 0-89287-304-3, M337). Clymer Pubns.

Honda CX Five Hundred Twins 1978-1979 Service Repair Maintenance. Ed Scott. Ed. by Eric Jorgesen. (Illus.). 200p. (Orig.). 1979. pap. text ed. 9.95 (ISBN 0-89287-295-0, M335). Clymer Pubns.

Honda Express: 1977-1980 Service-Repair-Performance. Ed. by Eric Jorgensen. (Illus.). 128p. (Orig.). 1979. pap. text ed. 9.95 (ISBN 0-89287-194-6, M314). Clymer Pubns.

Honda: Four Fifty & Five Hundred cc Twins 1965-1977--Service, Repair, Performance. 7th ed. Eric Jorgensen. Ed. by Jeff Robinson. (Illus.). 1978. pap. 9.95 (ISBN 0-89287-242-X, M333). Clymer Pubns.

Honda: G L-One Thousand Fours, 1975-1979--Service, Repair, Performance. 2nd ed. Eric Jorgensen. Ed. by Jeff Robinson. (Illus.). 1978. pap. 9.95 (ISBN 0-89287-238-1, M340). Clymer Pubns.

Honda Hawk: Four Hundred cc Twins 1978-1980--Service, Repair, Performance. Edward Scott. Ed. by Eric Jorgensen. (Illus.). 1978. pap. 9.95 (ISBN 0-89287-234-9, M334). Clymer Pubns.

Honda Hawk (Motorcycle) Nineteen Seventy-Seven to Eighty Repair Tune-up Guide: Nineteen Seventy Seven to Eighty Repaair Tune-up Guide. LC 79-3245. (New Automotive Bks.). 192p. 1980. 8.95 (ISBN 0-8019-6868-2). Chilton.

Honda Kid. Ed. by Robert Vitarelli. (Pal Paperbacks Ser., Kit B). (Illus., Orig.). (gr. 7-12). 1973. pap. text ed. 1.25 (ISBN 0-8374-3512-9). Xerox Ed Pubns.

Honda Odyssey: 1977-1979 Service-Repair-Performance. Ed Scott. Ed. by Eric Jorgensen. (Illus.). 224p. (Orig.). 1980. pap. 9.95 (ISBN 0-89287-308-6, M316). Clymer Pubns.

Honda: One Hundred-Three Fifty cc Four-Stroke Singles 1970-1978--Service, Repair Performance. 5th ed. Ed. by Eric Jorgensen. (Illus.). 1979. pap. 9.95 (ISBN 0-89287-184-9, M315). Clymer Pubns.

Honda Service Repair Handbook: Accord, 1976-79. Jim Combs. Ed. by Eric Jorgensen. 1978. pap. 10.95 (ISBN 0-89287-201-2, A228). Clymer Pubns.

Honda Service-Repair Handbook: Civic, 1973-1979. Mike Bishop. Ed. by Eric Jorgensen. (Illus.). 1978. pap. 10.95 (ISBN 0-89287-216-0, A227). Clymer Pubns.

Honda Service-Repair Handbook: 250-305cc Twins, All Years. Clymer Publications Staff. (Illus.). 184p. 1971. pap. text ed. 9.95 (ISBN 0-89287-010-9, M331). Clymer Pubns.

Honda Service Repair Handbook: 350-550cc Fours,1972-1978. Eric Jorgensen. Ed. by Jeff Robinson. (Illus.). 1978. pap. 9.95 (ISBN 0-89287-287-X, M332). Clymer Pubns.

Honda Service, Repair Handbook: 50-90cc Singles, 1963-1978. Ed. by Eric Jorgensen. (Illus.). 1978. pap. 9.95 (ISBN 0-89287-187-3, M310). Clymer Pubns.

Honda Service-Repair Handbook: 750cc Fours, 1969-1978. Clymer Publications. Ed. by Eric Jorgensen. (Illus.). 1978. pap. 9.95 (ISBN 0-89287-167-9, M341). Clymer Pubns.

Honda Three-Fifty - Five-Fifty cc Fours 1972-1978 Service Repair Performance. Ed. by Eric Jorgensen. (Illus.). 208p. (Orig.). 1978. pap. text ed. 9.95 (ISBN 0-89287-287-X, M332). Clymer Pubns.

Honda Tune-up for Everybody. Paul Young. (Illus.). 144p. (Orig.). 1981. pap. 7.95 (ISBN 0-89815-031-0). Ten Speed Pr.

Honda Twinstar Nineteen Seventy-Eight to Nineteen Eighty: Service, Repair, Maintenance. Edward Scott. Ed. by Eric Jorgensen. (Illus.). 242p. (Orig.). 1980. pap. text ed. 9.95 (ISBN 0-89287-325-6, M324). Clymer Pubns.

Honda XR-Seventy Five Singles: Service, Repair, Performance, 1975-78. Ed Scott. Ed. by Eric Jorgensen. (Illus.). 1978. pap. 9.95 (ISBN 0-89287-215-2, M312). Clymer Pubns.

Honda XR-XL 250 & 500 Singles: 1978-1979 Service-Repair-Maintenance. Ed Scott. Ed. by Eric Jorgensen. (Illus.). 251p. (Orig.). 1980. pap. text ed. 9.95 (ISBN 0-89287-310-8, M319). Clymer Pubns.

Honda 125-200cc Twins, 1964-1977: Service, Repair, Performance. Ray Hoy. Ed. by Eric Jorgensen. (Illus.). 1978. pap. 9.95 (ISBN 0-89287-208-X, M321). Clymer Pubns.

Honda 125-250 Elsinores 1973-1978: Service, Repair, Performance. Mike Bishop. Ed. by Eric Jorgensen. (Illus.). 1977. pap. 9.95 (ISBN 0-89287-176-8, M317). Clymer Pubns.

Honda 1973-1980. Chilton's Automotive Editorial Dept. (Illus.). 1980. pap. 8.95 (ISBN 0-8019-6980-8). Chilton.

Honda 250 & 350cc Twins, 1964-1974: Service-Repair-Performance. Ray Hoy. Ed. by Eric Jorgensen. 1978. pap. 9.95 (ISBN 0-89287-209-8, M322). Clymer Pubns.

Honda 250 & 360cc Twins, 1974-1977: Service-Repair-Performance. Ray Hoy. Ed. by Eric Jorgensen. (Illus.). 1978. pap. 9.95 (ISBN 0-89287-210-1, M323). Clymer Pubns.

Honda 750 1969-1980. Chilton's Automotive Editorial Dept. (Illus.). 1980. pap. 8.95 (ISBN 0-8019-6968-9). Chilton.

Honest, Abe. Abe Burrows. (Illus.). 1980. 14.95 (ISBN 0-316-11771-4, Pub. by Atlantic-Little Brown). Little.

Honest Andrew. Gloria Sjurzynski. (Let-Me-Read Ser.). (Illus.). (gr. k-3). 1980. pap. 1.95 (ISBN 0-15-642152-6, VoyB). HarBraceJ.

Honest Money Now! Howard S. Katz. LC 78-75028. 1979. pap. 4.95 (ISBN 0-916728-22-6). Bks in Focus.

Honest Politican's Guide to Crime Control. Norval Morris & Gordon Hawkins. LC 76-101467. 272p. 1972. pap. text ed. 4.50 (ISBN 0-226-53902-4, P460, Phoen). U of Chicago Pr.

Honest Prayer. Elsie Gibson. LC 80-39570. (Orig.). 1981. pap. price not set (ISBN 0-664-24348-7). Westminster.

Honest Truth or Unfair Competition? (Illus.). 1963. pap. 1.00 (ISBN 0-686-20591-X). US Trademark.

Honesty. rev. ed. Jane B. Moncure. LC 80-39571. (What Is It? Ser.). (Illus.). 32p. (gr. k-3). 1981. PLB 5.50 (ISBN 0-89565-203-X). Childs World.

Honey. Cavanagh. (gr. 7-12). 1980. pap. 1.25 (ISBN 0-590-30002-4, Schol Pap). Schol Bk Serv.

Honey. Isha Mellor. (Illus.). 80p. 1981. 6.95 (ISBN 0-312-92306-6). St Martin.

Honey: A Comprehensive Survey. Eva Crane. LC 74-14447. 1975. 52.50x (ISBN 0-8448-0062-7). Crane-Russak Co.

Honey: A Consideration. Isha Mellor. (Illus.). 80p. 1981. 6.95 (ISBN 0-312-92306-6). Congdon & Lattes.

Honey & Salt. Carl Sandburg. LC 63-9836. 1967. pap. 2.95 (ISBN 0-15-642165-8, HPL15, HPL). HarBraceJ.

Honey Badger. Robert Ruark. 1976. pap. 2.25 o.p. (ISBN 0-449-22924-6, 2924, Crest). Fawcett.

Honey Bee Pests, Predators & Diseases. Ed. by Roger A. Morse. LC 78-58027. (Illus.). 1978. 32.50x (ISBN 0-8014-0975-6). Comstock.

Honey by the Water. Ian H. Finlay. 60p. (Orig.). 1972. pap. 3.00 o.p. (ISBN 0-87685-142-1). Black Sparrow.

Honey for a Child's Heart. Gladys Hunt. 1969. o. p. 6.95 (ISBN 0-310-26380-8); pap. 4.95 (ISBN 0-310-26381-6). Zondervan.

Honey-God's Gift-for Health & Beauty: Cooking & Canning with Honey, Food Value Versus Sugar. Joe M. Parkhill. 158p. 1980. spiral bdg 6.95 (ISBN 0-936744-03-0). Country Bazaar.

Honey, I Love: And Other Love Poems. Eloise Greenfield. LC 77-2845. (Illus.). (gr. 1-3). 1978. 7.95 (ISBN 0-690-01334-5, TYC-J); PLB 7.89 (ISBN 0-690-03845-3). T Y Crowell.

Honey Kitchen. Dadant & Sons, Inc. LC 80-66361. (Illus.). 208p. 1980. 6.95 (ISBN 0-915698-06-4). Dadant & Sons.

Honey of a Chimp. Norma Klein. LC 79-20951. (gr. 3-7): 1980. 6.95 (ISBN 0-394-84412-2); PLB 6.99 (ISBN 0-394-94412-7). Pahtheon.

Honey-Pot. Mira Stables. 1979. pap. 1.75 o.p. (ISBN 0-449-23915-2, Crest). Fawcett.

Honey Tree Song: Poems, Chants & Epics of Sarawak Dayaks. Carol Rubenstein. (Illus.). 700p. 1981. 26.95x (ISBN 0-8214-0413-X); pap. 14.95 (ISBN 0-8214-0425-3). Ohio U Pr.

Honey You've Been Dealt a Winning Hand. Marilyn Krysl. 140p. (Orig.). 1980. pap. 6.50 (ISBN 0-88496-154-0). Capra Pr.

Honeybee. Paula Z. Hogan. LC 78-21165. (Life Cycles Ser.). (Illus.). (gr. k-3). 1979. PLB 9.95 (ISBN 0-8172-1256-6). Raintree Pubs.

Honeybee & the Robber: A Moving Picture Book. Eric Carle. (Illus.). 16p. (gr. 4-8). 1981. 10.95 (ISBN 0-399-20767-8). Philomel.

Honeybee Cousin. Louise Louis. (Illus.). 88p. (gr. 4-11). 1979. PLB 5.99. Pen-Art.

Honeycomb. Don Asher. LC 78-75155. (Illus.). 1979. 3.95 (ISBN 0-89395-021-1). Cal Living Bks.

Honeymoon. Nagib Mahfouz. (Arabic). pap. 5.50 (ISBN 0-685-82831-X). Intl Bk Ctr.

Honeymoon, Bittermoon. Ramon Perez de Ayala. Tr. by Barry Eisenberg. LC 79-116667. 1972. 16.95x (ISBN 0-520-01727-7). U of Cal Pr.

Honeymoon Book: A Tribute to the Last Ritual of Sexual Innocence. Paula Scher. Ed. by Fred Graver. (Illus.). 200p. (Orig.). 1981. pap. 9.95 (ISBN 0-87131-339-1). M Evans.

Honeymoon for Life: How to Live Happily Ever After. Joanna Woolfolk. LC 77-15966. 252p. 1981. pap. 6.95 (ISBN 0-8128-6102-7). Stein & Day.

Honeymoon Handbook: A Guide to Life's Most Romantic Adventure. Marcia Powell & Lynn Graeme. (Illus.). 256p. 1980. 12.95 (ISBN 0-02-598520-5). Macmillan.

Honeymoon in Honolulu. Ethel Hamill. (YA) 1970. 5.95 (ISBN 0-685-03335-X, Avalon). Bouregy.

Honeymoon Is Over. Shirley Boone & Pat Boone. 192p. 1980. pap. 4.95 (ISBN 0-8407-5721-2). Nelson.

Honeyphants & Elebees. V. Gilbert Beers. (Christian Home Library). 32p. (ps-3). 1974. 4.95 (ISBN 0-8024-3612-9). Moody.

Honeysuckle Rose. Robert Alley. 208p. 1980. pap. 2.25 (ISBN 0-553-14332-8). Bantam.

Honfleur Decision. Alan Hunter. 1981. 9.95 (ISBN 0-8027-5437-6). Walker & Co.

Hong Kong. Robert Elegant. (Great Cities Ser.). (Illus.). 1977. lib. bdg. 14.94 (ISBN 0-686-51003-8). Silver.

Hong Kong. Robert Elegant. Ed. by Time-Life Books. (Great Cities Ser.). (Illus.). 1977. 14.95 (ISBN 0-8094-2286-7). Time-Life.

Hong Kong: A Study in Bureaucratic Politics. Peter Harris. 1979. pap. text ed. 8.95x (ISBN 0-686-60437-7, 00106). Heinemann Ed.

Hong Kong & Macau. Carol Clewlow. (Illus., Orig.). 1978. pap. 2.95 (ISBN 0-8467-0519-2, Pub. by Two Continents). Hippocrene Bks.

Hong-Kong in Pictures. rev. ed. LC 63-19163. (Illus.). 1979. lib. bdg. 4.99 o.p. (ISBN 0-8069-1219-7); pap. 2.95 (ISBN 0-8069-1218-9). Sterling.

Hong Kong: The Cultured Pearl. Nigel Cameron. (Illus.). 1978. text ed. 29.50x (ISBN 0-19-580404-X). Oxford U Pr.

Hong Kong 1978: A Review of 1977. Ed. by Philip Rees. LC 78-640270. (Illus.). 1978. 10.00x o.p. (ISBN 0-8002-1514-1). Intl Pubns Serv.

Honi & His Magic Circle. Phillis Gershator. (Illus.). (gr. k-4). 1979. 6.95 (ISBN 0-8276-0167-0). Jewish Pubn.

Honiton Bobbin Lace: Designs for Prickling from Traditional Pieces. Jules Kliot & Kaethe Kliot. 1979. pap. 8.95 (ISBN 0-916896-16-1). Lacis Pubns.

Honk the Moose. Phil Stong. LC 35-27382. (Illus.). (gr. 4-6). 1935. PLB 6.95 (ISBN 0-396-07358-1). Dodd.

Honker: The Story of a Wild Goose. Robert M. McClung. (Illus.). (gr. 3-7). 1965. PLB 6.96 (ISBN 0-688-31399-X). Morrow.

Honky Tonkin' A Travel Guide to American Music. 3rd ed. Richard Wootton. LC 80-503. (Illus.). 192p. 1980. lib. bdg. 10.25 o.p. (ISBN 0-914788-26-4). East Woods.

Honkytonk Man. Clancy Carlile. 1981. 12.95 (ISBN 0-671-41212-4). S&S.

Honolulu Zoo Riddles. Harriet Johnson. (Illus.). 1974. pap. 1.25 (ISBN 0-686-63590-6). Topgallant.

Honor Card & Other Poems. Betsy Colquitt. 100p. 1980. 9.50 (ISBN 0-936830-01-8); pap. 4.50 (ISBN 0-936830-02-6). Saurian Pr.

Honor, Commerce & Industry in Eighteenth-Century Spain. William J. Callahan. (Kress Library of Business & Economics: No. 22). 1972. pap. 5.00x (ISBN 0-678-09916-2, Baker Lib). Kelley.

Honor Grades on Fifteen Hours a Week. A. Tobias. 1969. pap. 1.25 o.s.i. (ISBN 0-02-082100-X, Collier). Macmillan.

Honor Thy Father. Gay Talese. 1978. pap. 2.95 (ISBN 0-449-23630-7, Crest). Fawcett.

Honor Thy Father. Gay Talese. 1981. pap. 3.25 (ISBN 0-440-13668-7). Dell.

Honor Thy Teen. Joe Cantinieri. 1977. 5.95 o.p. (ISBN 0-533-02870-1). Vantage.

Honor to the Bride Like the Pigeon That Guards Its Grain Under the Clove Tree. Jane Kramer. 1970. 5.95 o.p. (ISBN 0-374-17257-9). FS&G.

Honorable Men. William Colby. 1980. pap. write for info. PB.

Honorable Profession: A Tribute to Robert F. Kennedy. Ed. by Pierre Salinger et al. LC 68-55381. (Illus.). 1968. (ISBN 0-385-07159-0). Doubleday.

Honore De Balzac. Diane Festa-McCormick. (World Authors Ser.: No. 541). 1979. lib. bdg. 12.50 (ISBN 0-8057-6383-X). Twayne.

Honore De Balzac. E. J. Oliver. 1964. 3.95 o.s.i. (ISBN 0-02-592880-5). Macmillan.

Honors Teaching in American History. Lawrence A. Fink. LC 68-54673. 1969. text ed. 5.25x (ISBN 0-8077-1350-3). Tchrs Coll.

Honour, Family & Patronage: A Study of Institutions & Moral Values in a Greek Mountain Community. J. K. Campbell. (Illus.). 406p. 1973. 29.95x (ISBN 0-19-823122-9); pap. text ed. 5.95x (ISBN 0-19-519756-9). Oxford U Pr.

Honour of St Valery: The Story of an English Manor House. Nicholas Davenport. (Illus.). 168p. (Orig.). 1979. pap. 7.95 (ISBN 0-85967-463-0, Pub. by Scolar Pr England). Biblio Dist.

Hoodlum's Priest. Elizabeth Mulligan. 174p. 1979. 9.95 (ISBN 0-86629-000-1). Sunrise MO.

Hoodoo Hollerin Bebop Ghosts. Larry Neal. LC 73-88972. 144p. 1974. 6.95x (ISBN 0-88258-011-6). Howard U Pr.

Hood's Texas Brigade: A Compendium, Vol. 4. new ed. Harold B. Simpson. LC 77-91396. (Illus.). 1977. 12.50 (ISBN 0-912172-22-3). Hill Jr Coll.

Hoof Beats North & South: Horses & Horsemen of the Civil War. Sue Cottrell. 1975. 7.50 o.p. (ISBN 0-682-48280-3, University). Exposition.

Hoofbeats Along the Tigris. Judith E. Forbis. (Illus.). 14.00 (ISBN 0-85131-018-4, Dist. by Sporting Book Center). J A Allen.

Hoofed Mammals of the World. Ugo Mochi & T. Donald Carter. LC 75-169790. (Illus.). 1971. 9.95 o.p. (ISBN 0-684-12382-7, Scribt). Scribner.

Hoofmarks. Michael Wynne. LC 80-51728. 270p. Date not set. pap. price not set (ISBN 0-89526-673-3). Regnery-Gateway. Postponed.

Hook, Line & Sinker. Ray Gooque. 14.50x (ISBN 0-392-07163-0, SpS). Soccer.

Hooked on Books: Program & Proof. new ed. Daniel N. Fader & Elton B. McNeil. (Orig.). 1977. pap. 1.95 o.p. (ISBN 0-425-04328-2, S1508, Medallion). Berkley Pub.

Hooked on Mad. Mad Magazine Editors. (Mad Ser.: No.42). (Illus.). 192p. 1976. pap. 1.75 (ISBN 0-446-94587-0). Warner Bks.

Hooked Rug. William W. Kent. LC 78-172437. (Tower Bks). (Illus.). 1971. Repr. of 1941 ed. 18.00 (ISBN 0-8103-3914-5). Gale.

Hooked Rugs: A Historical Collector's Guide - How to Make Your Own. William C. Ketchum, Jr. LC 76-13880. 1976. 14.95 o.p. (ISBN 0-15-142168-4). HarBraceJ.

Hoop, 2 vols. Mark Dunster. 140p. (Orig.). 1980. Set. pap. 8.00 (ISBN 0-89642-070-1). Linden Pubs.

Hooray for Me! Remy Charlip & Lilian Moore. LC 80-15285. (Illus.). 40p. (ps-3). 1980. Repr. of 1975 ed. 8.95 (ISBN 0-590-07768-6, Four Winds). Schol Bk Serv.

Hooray for Pig! Carla Stevens. LC 73-17074. (Illus.). (ps-3). 1974. 5.95 (ISBN 0-395-28824-X, Clarion). HM.

Hoosier Caravan: A Treasury of Indiana Life & Lore. new ed. Ed. by R. E. Banta. LC 73-16521. 640p. 1975. limited ed. 10.95 (ISBN 0-253-13863-9); deluxe ed. 10.95 o.p. (ISBN 0-253-13862-0). Ind U Pr.

Hoosier Cookbook. Ed. by Elaine Lumbra. LC 75-31420. (Illus.). 344p. 1976. 10.95x (ISBN 0-253-13865-5). Ind U Pr.

Hoosier Schoolmaster. rev. ed. Edward Eggleston. Ed. by Robert J. Dixson. (American Classics Ser.: Bk. 6). (gr. 9 up). 1974. pap. text ed. 2.75 (ISBN 0-88345-202-2, 18125); cassettes 40.00 (ISBN 0-685-38929-4); tapes 40.00 (ISBN 0-685-38930-8). Regents Pub.

Hoosier State: A Documentary of Indiana, 2 vols. Ed. by Ralph D. Gray. LC 80-12496. 448p. 1981. Vol. 1. pap. 14.95 (ISBN 0-8028-1842-0); Vol. 2. pap. 14.95 (ISBN 0-8028-1843-9). Eerdmans.

Hoover, Roosevelt, and the Brains Trust: From Depression to New Deal. Elliot A. Rosen. LC 76-49976. 1977. 22.50x (ISBN 0-231-04172-1). Columbia U Pr.

Hoover's Dominican Diplomacy & the Origins of the Good Neighbor Policy. E. R. Curry. Ed. by Frank Freidel. LC 78-62379. (Modern American History Ser.: Vol. 5). 1979. lib. bdg. 30.00 (ISBN 0-8240-3629-8). Garland Pub.

Hop, Skip, & Jump. Lucile Jones. Ed. by Bobbie J. Van Dolson. 32p. 1981. pap. price not set (ISBN 0-8280-0038-7). Review & Herald.

Hope: A Loss Survived. Richard Meryman. 1980. 10.95 (ISBN 0-316-56786-8). Little.

Hope Abandoned, Vol. 2. Nadezhda Mandelstam. Tr. by Max Hayward from Rus. LC 76-871412. 1973. 13.95 (ISBN 0-689-10549-5); pap. 12.95 (ISBN 0-689-70608-1). Atheneum.

Hope & Help for Your Nerves. Claire Weekes. LC 69-12957. 1968. 8.95 o.p. (ISBN 0-8015-3576-X). Dutton.

Hope for the Family. A. DeGraaff et al. 1971. pap. 1.25 o.p. (ISBN 0-686-11978-9). Wedge Pub.

Hope for the Future? Youth & the Church. John Krump. (Orig.). 1979. pap. 4.95 (ISBN 0-88347-092-6). Thomas More.

Hope in Time of Abandonment. Jacques Ellul. 1978. pap. 4.95 (ISBN 0-8164-2138-2). Crossroad NY.

Hope Is an Open Door. Mary L. Tobin. LC 80-21414. (Journeys in Faith Ser). 1981. 7.95 (ISBN 0-687-17410-4). Abingdon.

Hope of Glory: Exploring the Mystery of Christ in You. John B. Coburn. 160p. 1976. 7.95 (ISBN 0-8164-1208-1); pap. 3.95 (ISBN 0-8164-2117-X). Crossroad NY.

Hope of Heaven. John O'Hara. 176p. 1973. pap. 1.25 o.p. (ISBN 0-445-00149-6). Popular Lib.

Hope: The Dynamics of Self-Fulfillment. Arnold A. Hutschnecker. 320p. 1981. 11.95 (ISBN 0-399-12589-2). Putnam.

Hopes & Fears for Art. William Morris. Ed. by Sydney J. Freedberg. LC 77-19374. (Connoisseurship Criticism & Art History Ser.: Vol. 12). 217p. 1979. lib. bdg. 23.00 (ISBN 0-8240-3270-5). Garland Pub.

Hopes & Fears: Or, Scenes from the Life of a Spinster, 2 vols. in 1. Charlotte M. Yonge. LC 79-8221. Repr. of 1860 ed. 44.50 (ISBN 0-404-62173-2). AMS Pr.

Hopes & Promises. Dusty Sang. 384p. (Orig.). 1981. pap. 2.95 (ISBN 0-932844-03-0). R H Sang & Son.

Hopf Algebras. E. Abe. LC 79-50912. (Cambridge Tracts in Mathematics Ser.: No. 74). 1980. 39.50 (ISBN 0-521-22240-0). Cambridge U Pr.

Hopi Indians. Incl. The Hopi: Their History & Use of Lands. Florence H. Ellis; Hopi History & Ethnobotany. Harold E. Colton; Findings of Fact, & Opinion. Indian Claims Commission. (American Indian Ethnohistory Ser: Indians of the Southwest). (Illus.). lib. bdg. 42.00 (ISBN 0-8240-0706-9). Garland Pub.

Hopi Kachina: Spirit of Life. Ed. by Dorothy Washburn. California Academy of Sciences. (Illus.). 160p. (Orig.). 1980. pap. 14.95 (ISBN 0-295-95751-4, Pub. by Calif Acad Sci). U of Wash Pr.

Hopi Katcinas Drawn by Native Artists. Jesse W. Fewkes. LC 62-20282. (Beautiful Rio Grande Classics Ser). lib. bdg. 20.00 o.s.i. (ISBN 0-87380-023-0). Rio Grande.

Hopkins of Dartmouth: The Story of Ernest Martin Hopkins & His Presidency of Dartmouth College. Charles E. Widmayer. LC 77-153864. (Illus.). 320p. 1977. text ed. 27.50x (ISBN 0-87451-145-3). U Pr of New Eng.

Hopping Mad. Mad Magazine Editors. (Mad Ser.). (Illus.). 192p. 1976. pap. 1.75 (ISBN 0-446-94588-9). Warner Bks.

Hora Novissima (Opus 30) Horatio Parker. LC 75-169652. (Earlier American Music Ser.: No. 2). 167p. 1972. Repr. of 1900 ed. lib. bdg. 25.00 (ISBN 0-306-77302-3). Da Capo.

Horace. Eduard Fraenkel. (Oxford Paperbooks Ser). 1957. 34.00x (ISBN 0-19-814310-9). Oxford U Pr.

Horace. Eduard Fraenkel. 478p. 1981. pap. 23.95 (ISBN 0-19-814376-1). Oxford U Pr.

Horace & His Lyric Poetry. L. P. Wilkinson. 1957. pap. 6.95 (ISBN 0-521-09527-1). Cambridge U Pr.

Horace Binney Wallace. George E. Hatvary. (United States Authors Ser.: No. 287). 1977. lib. bdg. 12.95 (ISBN 0-8057-7190-5). Twayne.

Horace Greeley. W. A. Linn. LC 80-26831. (American Men & Women of Letters Ser.). 275p. 1981. pap. 4.95 (ISBN 0-87754-165-5). Chelsea Hse.

Horace Greeley. William A. Linn. (American Newspapermen 1790-1933 Ser.). (Illus.). xiii, 267p. 1974. Repr. of 1903 ed. 16.00x o.s.i. (ISBN 0-8464-0015-4). Beekman Pubs.

Horace Greeley & the Tribune in the Civil War. Ralph R. Fahrney. LC 77-135663. (American Scene Ser). 1970. Repr. of 1936 ed. lib. bdg. 25.00 (ISBN 0-306-71120-6). Da Capo.

Horace Greeley: The Editor. Francis Zabriskie. (American Newspapermen 1790-1933 Ser.). 398p. 1974. Repr. of 1890 ed. 19.50x o.s.i. (ISBN 0-8464-0000-6). Beekman Pubs.

Horace His Arte of Poetrie, Pistles, & Satyrs Englished (1567) Quintus Horatius Flaccus. Tr. by Thomas H. Drant from Lat. LC 73-173753. 296p. 1972. Repr. of 1567 ed. 30.00x (ISBN 0-8201-1099-X). Schol Facsimiles.

Horace Mann. Robert B. Downs. (World Leaders Ser: No. 29). 1974. lib. bdg. 9.95 (ISBN 0-8057-3544-5). Twayne.

Horace, Odes & Epodes: A Study in Poetic Word-Order. Henry D. Naylor. (Latin Poetry Ser.: Vol. 9). (LC 77-070832). 1977. Repr. of 1922 ed. lib. bdg. 33.00 (ISBN 0-8240-2958-5). Garland Pub.

Horace Walpole. Dorothy M. Stuart. 229p. 1980. Repr. of 1927 ed. lib. bdg. 30.00 (ISBN 0-8492-8119-9). R West.

Horace Walpole & the Unconscious: An Experiment in Freudian Analysis. Betsy P. Harfst. Ed. by Devendra P. Varma. LC 79-8455. (Gothic Studies & Dissertations Ser.). 1980. lib. bdg. 25.00x (ISBN 0-405-12645-X). Arno.

Horace's Satires & Epistles. Tr. by Jacob Fuchs. 1980. pap. 3.95 (ISBN 0-393-04479-3). Norton.

Horacio Quiroga: Cuentos escogidos. Horacio Quiroga. Ed. by Jean Franco. 1968. 10.00 (ISBN 0-08-012792-4); pap. 6.25 (ISBN 0-08-012791-6). Pergamon.

Horae Synopticae: Contributions to the Study of the Synoptic Problem. 2nd ed. John C. Hawkins. 1909. 8.95x o.p. (ISBN 0-19-826621-9). Oxford U Pr.

Horae Viaticae. Charles Kelsall. LC 79-18052. 1979. Repr. of 1839 ed. 48.00 (ISBN 0-8201-1333-6). Schol Facsimiles.

Horan's Field & Other Reservations. Valentin Iremonger. 1972. pap. text ed. 4.25x (ISBN 0-85105-303-3, Dolmen Pr). Humanities.

Horary Art & It's Synthesis. Elsie M. Knapp. 1974. 5.00x (ISBN 0-686-17210-8). Sandollar Pr.

Horary Astrology & the Judgement of Events. Barbara Watters. 1973. 13.50 o.s.i. (ISBN 0-685-42026-4). Arcane Pubns.

Horary Astrology: Problem Solving. Marc E. Jones. LC 78-149643. 1971. 13.50 o.p. (ISBN 0-87878-004-1, Sabian). Great Eastern.

Horatia Nelson. Winifred Gerin. 1970. 19.50x (ISBN 0-19-822331-5). Oxford U Pr.

Horatii Emblemata. Otho Vaenius. Ed. by Stephen Orgel. LC 78-68200. (Philosophy of Images Ser.: Vol. 10). (Illus.). 1980. Repr. of 1612 ed. lib. bdg. 66.00 (ISBN 0-8240-3684-0). Garland Pub.

Horatio Alger: A Fancy of Hers-The Disagreeable Woman. Intro. by Ralph D. Gardner. 160p. 1981. 14.95 (ISBN 0-442-24716-8). Van Nos Reinhold.

Horatio Alger, Jr. Gary Scharnhorst. (United States Author Ser.: No. 363). 1980. lib. bdg. 9.95 (ISBN 0-8057-7252-9). Twayne.

Horatio Alger's Children: The Role of the Family in the Origin & Prevention of Drug Risk. Richard H. Blum et al. LC 72-186580. (Social & Behavioral Science Ser.). 1972. 15.95x o.p. (ISBN 0-87589-120-9). Jossey-Bass.

Horatio Greenough: The First American Sculptor. Nathalia Wright. LC 62-11261. 1963. 9.50x o.p. (ISBN 0-8122-7324-9). U of Pa Pr.

Horatio Parker. Isabel P. Semler. LC 72-8291. (Music Ser). 332p. 1973. Repr. of 1942 ed. lib. bdg. 32.50 (ISBN 0-306-70538-9). Da Capo.

Horatio Seymour of New York. Stewart Mitchell. LC 69-19475. (American Scene Ser). 1970. Repr. of 1938 ed. lib. bdg. 59.50 (ISBN 0-306-71252-0). Da Capo.

Horizon. Helen MacInnes. 1979. pap. 1.95 o.p. (ISBN 0-449-24012-6, Crest). Fawcett.

Horizon. Helen MacInnes. 192p. 1981. pap. 2.50 (ISBN 0-449-24012-6, Crest). Fawcett.

Horizon Book of the Age of Napoleon. J. Christopher Herold & Horizon Magazine Editors. (Illus.). 1963. 30.00 o.s.i. (ISBN 0-06-011835-0, HarpT). Har-Row.

Horizon Book of the Arts of China. Horizon Magazine Editors. Ed. by Thomas Froncek. LC 69-15082. (Illus.). 383p. 1969. deluxe ed. 23.00 (ISBN 0-8281-0025-X, BO27D). Am Heritage.

Horizon Book of the Renaissance. J. H. Plumb. Ed. by Richard M. Ketchum. LC 61-11489. (Illus.). 432p. 1961. deluxe ed. 19.95 o.p. (ISBN 0-8281-0285-6, BO97D1-16). Am Heritage.

Horizon Book of Vanishing Primitive Man. Timothy Severin. Ed. by Alvin M. Josephy, Jr. LC 73-7781. (Illus.). 384p. 1973. 22.00 (ISBN 0-8281-0273-2, Dist. by Scribner); deluxe ed. 25.00 slipcased (ISBN 0-8281-0274-0, Dist. by Scribner). Am Heritage.

Horizon Guide: Great Historic Places of Europe. Ed. by Horizon Magazine & Beverley Hilowitz. LC 74-10941. (Illus.). 384p. 1974. 10.00 (ISBN 0-8281-0275-9, Dist. by Scribner). Am Heritage.

Horizon History of Africa, 2 vols. A. Adu Boahen et al. Ed. by Alvin M. Josephy, Jr. LC 75-149732. (Illus.). 544p. 1971. 25.00 (ISBN 0-8281-0271-6, Dist. by Scribner); deluxe ed. 35.00 slipcased (ISBN 0-8281-0329-1, Dist. by Scribner). Am Heritage.

Horizons Circled: Reflections on My Music. Ernst Krenek. (Illus.). 1975. 15.75x (ISBN 0-520-02338-2). U of Cal Pr.

Horizons in Biochemistry & Biophysics, 3 vols. Ed. by E. Quagliariello et al. Incl. Vol. 1. cancelled o.s.i. (ISBN 0-201-02711-9); pap. cancelled o.s.i. (ISBN 0-201-02721-6); Vol. 2. cancelled o.s.i. (ISBN 0-201-02712-7); pap. cancelled o.s.i. (ISBN 0-201-02722-4); Vol. 3. cancelled o.s.i. (ISBN 0-201-02713-5); pap. cancelled o.s.i. (ISBN 0-201-02723-2). (Illus., Adv Bk Prog). A-W.

Horizons in Biochemistry & Biophysics, Vol. 4. E. Quagliariello et al. (Illus.). text ed. write for info. o.s.i. (ISBN 0-201-02714-3, Adv Bk Prog). A-W.

Horizons in Biochemistry & Biophysics, Vol. 5. E. Quagliariello et al. (Illus.). text ed. cancelled o.s.i. (ISBN 0-201-02715-1, Adv Bk Prog). A-W.

Horizons in Clinical Criminology. Benigno Di Tullio. (New York University Criminal Law Education & Research Center Monograph: No. 3). 232p. (Orig.). 1969. pap. 20.00x (ISBN 0-8377-0501-0). Rothman.

Horizons of Anthropology. 2nd ed. Ed. by Sol Tax & Leslie G. Freeman. LC 76-46247. (Illus.). 1977. text ed. 19.95x (ISBN 0-202-01157-7); pap. text ed. 11.95x (ISBN 0-202-01158-5). Aldine Pub.

Horizons of Assent: Modernism, Postmodernism, & the Ironic Imagination. Alan Wilde. LC 80-22576. 224p. 1981. text ed. 15.00x (ISBN 0-8018-2449-4). Johns Hopkins.

Horizons of Health. Ed. by Henry Wechsler et al. 1977. 18.50 (ISBN 0-674-40630-3); pap. 6.95 (ISBN 0-674-40631-1). Harvard U Pr.

Horizons of Love. Barbara Cartland. (Barbara Cartland Ser.). (Orig.). pap. 1.75 (ISBN 0-515-05569-7). Jove Pubns.

Horizontal Boring. 2nd ed. Ed. by J. R. Beaton et al. (Engineering Craftsmen: No. H28/2). (Illus.). 1976. spiral bdg. 16.50x (ISBN 0-85083-307-8). Intl Ideas.

Horkheimer's Critical Sociology of Religion: The Relative & the Transcendent. Rudolf J. Siebert. LC 78-66280. 1979. pap. text ed. 7.50 (ISBN 0-8191-0688-7). U Pr of Amer.

Hormesis with Ionizing Radiation. T. D. Luckey. 288p. 1980. 69.95 (ISBN 0-8493-5841-8). CRC Pr.

Hormonal Control of Lactation, Vol. 1. W. J. Fulkerson. Ed. by D. F. Horrobin. (Annual Research Reviews). 1980. 18.00 (ISBN 0-88831-061-7). Eden Med Res.

Hormonal Proteins & Peptides, 7 vols. Ed. by Choh H. Li. Incl. Vol. 1. 1973. 31.00 (ISBN 0-12-447201-X); Vol. 2. 1973. 37.50 (ISBN 0-12-447202-8); Vol. 3. 1975. 43.00 (ISBN 0-12-447203-6); Vol. 4. 1977. 33.00 (ISBN 0-12-447204-4); Vol. 5. Lipotropin & Related Peptides. 1978. 29.00 (ISBN 0-12-447205-2); Vol. 6. Thyroid Hormones. 1978. 48.50 (ISBN 0-12-447206-0); Vol. 7. Hypothalmic Hormones. 1979. 32.50 (ISBN 0-12-447207-9). LC 78-5444. Acad Pr.

Hormonal Regulation of Development I: Molcular Aspects of Plant Hormones. Ed. by J. Macmillan. (Encyclopedia of Plant Physiology Ser.: Vol. 9). (Illus.). 681p. 1981. 134.60 (ISBN 0-387-10161-6). Springer-Verlag.

Hormonal Regulation of Spermatogenesis. Ed. by Frank S. French et al. LC 75-32541. (Current Topics in Molecular Endocrinology Ser.: Vol. 2). 526p. 1975. 45.00 (ISBN 0-306-34002-X, Plenum Pr). Plenum Pub.

Hormonal Steroids, Biochemistry, Pharmacology, Therapeutics, 2 Vols. Ed. by L. Martini & A. Pecile. 1965. Vol. 1. 55.50 (ISBN 0-12-475301-9); Vol. 2. 55.50 (ISBN 0-12-475302-7). Acad Pr.

Hormonal Steroids: Proceedings. International Congress on Hormonal Steroids, 5th, New Delhi, Oct.-Nov. 1978 & V. H. T. James. LC 79-40734. 950p. 1980. 160.00 (ISBN 0-08-023796-7). Pergamon.

Hormonal Steroids: Proceedings of the Fourth International Congress. Ed. by V. H. James & J. R. Pasqualini. 1976. 160.00 (ISBN 0-08-019682-9). Pergamon.

Hormone Action, Vol. 2. Ed. by Bert W. O'Malley. 1978. 52.50 (ISBN 0-12-526302-3); by subscription 45.00 (ISBN 0-686-67867-2). Acad Pr.

Hormone Analysis, Vol. 1. G. W. Pennington & Sandra Naik. 304p. 1981. 69.95 (ISBN 0-8493-5539-7). CRC Pr.

Hormone & Antihormone, Action at the Target Cell, LSRR 3. Ed. by J. H. Clark et al. (Dahlem Workshop Reports Ser.). 1976. pap. 26.50 (ISBN 0-89573-087-1). Verlag Chemie.

Hormone Chemistry, 2 vols. 2nd ed. W. R. Butt. Incl. Vol. 1. Protein, Polypeptides & Peptide Hormones. 272p. 1975. 54.95 (ISBN 0-470-12770-8); Vol. 2. Steroids, Thyroid Hormones, Biogenic Amines & Prostaglandins. 1977. 44.95 (ISBN 0-470-98961-0). LC 75-16158. Halsted Pr.

Hormone Receptors. Ed. by David M. Klachko et al. LC 77-25856. (Advances in Experimental Medicine & Biology Ser.: Vol. 96). 224p. 1978. 27.50 (ISBN 0-306-32696-5, Plenum Pr). Plenum Pub.

Hormone Receptors in Digestion & Nutrition: Proceedings of the 2nd Int'l Symposium, France 797. Ed. by G. Rosselin et al. 520p. 1979. 66.00 (ISBN 0-444-80155-3, North Holland). Elsevier.

Hormone Therapy of the Menopause & Aging. Helen Z. Jern. (Illus.). 196p. 1973. text ed. 15.75 (ISBN 0-398-02744-7). C C Thomas.

Hormones. Alan E. Nourse. (Impact Ser.). (Illus.). (gr. 7 up). 1979. PLB 6.90 s&l (ISBN 0-531-02892-5). Watts.

Hormones, Adaptation & Evolution: International Symposium. Ed. by S. Ishii. 300p. 1980. 44.80 (ISBN 0-387-10033-4). Springer-Verlag.

Hormones & Aggression, Vol. I. Paul F. Brain. Ed. by D. F. Horrobin. (Hormone Research Review Ser.). 126p. 1980. Repr. of 1977 ed. 16.95x (ISBN 0-87705-963-2). Human Sci Pr.

Hormones & Atherosclerosis: Proceedings. Ed. by Gregory Pincus. 1959. 38.50 (ISBN 0-12-557050-3). Acad Pr.

Hormones & Cancer. Ed. by Stefano Iacobelli et al. (Progress in Cancer Research & Therapy Ser.). 589p. 1980. text ed. 49.00 (ISBN 0-89004-486-4). Raven.

Hormones & Hyacinths. Martic C. Rosner. LC 79-82087. 1980. 5.95 (ISBN 0-87212-126-7). Libra.

Hormones & the Kidney. Ed. by G. S. Stokes & J. H. Mahony. (Progress in Biochemical Pharmacology: Vol. 17). (Illus.). 250p. 1980. 75.00 (ISBN 3-8055-1090-X). S Karger.

Hormones, Behavior, & Psychopathology. Ed. by Edward J. Sachar. LC 75-16660. (American Psychopathological Association Ser.). 1976. 32.00 (ISBN 0-89004-094-X). Raven.

Hormones Book. M. A. Tribe & M. R. Eraut. LC 77-87396. (Basic Biology Course Ser.: No. 11). 1979. 35.50 (ISBN 0-521-21371-1); pap. 11.95x (ISBN 0-521-21370-3); film strip 19.95x (ISBN 0-521-22956-1). Cambridge U Pr.

Hormones, Drugs & Aggression, Vol. III. Paul F. Brain. (Hormone Research Review Ser.). 173p. 1980. Repr. of 1979 ed. 21.95x (ISBN 0-87705-959-4). Human Sci Pr.

Hormones in Blood, 2 Vols. 2nd ed. Ed. by Charles H. Gray & Alfred L. Bacharach. Vol. 1, 1967. 38.50 (ISBN 0-12-296101-3); Vol. 2, 1968. 42.00 (ISBN 0-12-296102-1). Acad Pr.

Hormones in Development. Ed. by Max Hamburgh & E. J. Barrington. LC 72-116424. 854p. 1971. 59.50 (ISBN 0-306-50028-0, Plenum Pr). Plenum Pub.

Hormones in Development & Aging. A. Verandakis. Date not set. text ed. price not set (ISBN 0-89335-140-7). Spectrum Pub.

Hormones: Physiology, Chemistry & Applications, 5 vols. Ed. by Gregory Pincus & Kenneth V. Thimann. Incl. Vol. 1. 1948. 72.50 (ISBN 0-12-557001-5); Vol. 2. 1950. 72.50 (ISBN 0-12-557002-3); Vol. 3. 1955. 72.50 (ISBN 0-12-557003-1); Vol. 4. Ed. by Gregory Pincus et al. 1964. 72.50 (ISBN 0-12-557004-X); Vol. 5. Ed. by Gregory Pincus et al. 1964. 72.50 (ISBN 0-12-557005-8). Set. 292.50 (ISBN 0-685-23215-8). Acad Pr.

Hormones, Receptors, & Breast Cancer. Ed. by William L. McGuire. LC 77-90595. (Progress in Cancer Research & Therapy Ser.: Vol. 10). 1978. 31.50 (ISBN 0-89004-261-6). Raven.

Hormornal Disorders in Gynecology. Paul J. Keller. (Illus.). 113p. 1981. pap. 16.50 (ISBN 0-387-10341-4). Springer-Verlag.

Horn Book Reflections on Children's Books & Reading. Ed. by Elinor W. Field. LC 75-89793. 1969. pap. 6.50 (ISBN 0-87675-033-1). Horn Bk.

Horn Book Sampler on Children's Books & Reading. Norma R. Fryatt. LC 59-15028. 1959. 9.50 (ISBN 0-87675-030-7); pap. 6.50 (ISBN 0-87675-031-5). Horn Bk.

Horn Crown. Andre Norton. 1981. pap. 2.50 (ISBN 0-87997-635-7, UE1635). DAW Bks.

Horn of Plenty: The Story of Louis Armstrong. Robert Goffin. LC 77-8050. (Roots of Jazz). 1977. Repr. of 1947 ed. lib. bdg. 25.00 (ISBN 0-306-77430-5). Da Capo.

Horn Technique. Gunther Schuller. (YA) (gr. 9 up). 1962. 7.75 (ISBN 0-19-318701-9). Oxford U Pr.

Horned Moses in Medieval Art & Thought. Ruth Mellinkoff. LC 77-85450. (California Studies in the History of Art: No. XIV). (Illus.). 1970. 22.50x (ISBN 0-520-01705-6). U of Cal Pr.

Horner of Illinois. Thomas B. Littlewood. LC 70-78329. 1969. 12.95x o.s.i. (ISBN 0-8101-0250-1). Northwestern U Pr.

Horns & Antlers. Wilfrid S. Bronson. LC 42-7882. (Illus.). (gr. 3-7). 1942. 4.95 o.p. (ISBN 0-15-235942-7, HJ). HarBraceJ.

Horns, Strings & Harmony. Arthur H. Benade. LC 60-10663. pap. 2.50 (ISBN 0-385-09471-X, S11). Doubleday.

Horoscope Cannot Lie & Other Stories. G. D. Khosla. 4.50x o.p. (ISBN 0-210-33991-8). Asia.

Horoscope Symbols. Robert Hand. 384p. (Orig.). 1980. pap. 14.95 (ISBN 0-914918-16-8). Para Res.

Horowitz & Mrs. Washington. Henry Denker. 1980. pap. 2.50 o.p. (ISBN 0-425-04657-5). Berkley Pub.

Horrid Cruelty of the Indians, Exemplified in the Life of Charles Saunders, Late of Charles-Town, in South Carolina, Repr. Of 1763 Ed. Bd. with History of the Life & Sufferings of Henry Grace...Being a Narrative of the Hardships He Underwent During Several Years Captivity Among the Savages in North America...in Which Is Introduced an Account of the Several Customs & Manners of the Different Nations of Indians. Repr. of 1764 ed; Adventure of a Young English Officer Among the Abenakee Savages. in: Bickerstaff's Boston Almanack, for the Year of Our Lord 1768. Repr. of 1767 ed; Brief Narration of the Captivity of Isaac Hollister. Repr. of 1767 ed; Account of the Captivity of William Henry in 1755 & of His Residence Among the Senneka Indians Six Years & Seven Months till He Made His Escape from Them. Repr. of 1768 ed; Narrative of an Extraordinary Escape Out of the Hands of the Indians, in the Gulph of St. Lawrence; Interspersed with a Description of the Coast, & Remarks on the Customs & Manners of the Savages There. Gamaliel Smethurst. Repr. of 1774 ed. LC 75-7030. (Indian Captivities Ser.: Vol. 10). 1976. lib. bdg. 44.00 (ISBN 0-8240-1634-3). Garland Pub.

Horror & Science Fiction Films: A Checklist. Donald C. Willis. LC 72-3682. 1972. 21.00 (ISBN 0-8108-0508-1). Scarecrow.

Horror & Supernatural Literature. Marshall B. Tymn. 320p. 1981. 22.50 (ISBN 0-8352-1341-2). Bowker.

Horror Chambers of Jules De Grandin. Seabury Quinn. (Jules De Grandin Ser.: No. 6). 1977. pap. 1.50 o.p. (ISBN 0-445-03183-2). Popular Lib.

Horror Film Stars. Michael R. Pitts. LC 80-11241. (Illus.). 333p. 1981. lib. bdg. 16.95x (ISBN 0-89950-003-X); pap. 12.95x (ISBN 0-89950-004-8). McFarland & Co.

Horror Holiday: Secrets of Vacation Survival. Jane Stern & Michael Stern. 144p. 1981. pap. 5.95 (ISBN 0-525-47655-5). Dutton.

Horror House. J. N. Williamson. LC 80-85113. 304p. (Orig.). 1981. pap. 2.95 (ISBN 0-87216-832-8). Playboy Pbks.

Horrors, Horrors, Horrors. Helen Hoke. LC 78-2350. (Terrific Triple Titles Ser.). (Illus.). 1978. lib. bdg. 7.90 s&l (ISBN 0-531-02211-0). Watts.

Horse. J. Warren Evans et al. LC 76-22686. (Animal Science Ser.). (Illus.). 1977. 27.95x (ISBN 0-7167-0491-9). W H Freeman.

Horse Anatomy. Peter Goody. (Illus.). 17.50 (ISBN 0-85131-230-6, Dist. by Sporting Book Center). J A Allen.

Horse & Buggy Age in New England. Edwin V. Mitchell. LC 74-7066. 1974. Repr. of 1937 ed. 15.00 (ISBN 0-8103-3657-X). Gale.

Horse & Buggy Doctor. Arthur E. Hertzler. LC 78-105646. (Illus.). 1970. 10.95x (ISBN 0-8032-0769-7); pap. 3.95 (ISBN 0-8032-5717-1, BB 517, Bison). U of Nebr Pr.

Horse & His Boy. C. S. Lewis. (Illus.). (gr. 4-6). 1954. 8.95 (ISBN 0-02-757670-1). Macmillan.

Horse & Horseman. Ed. by Peter Vischer. (Illus.). 15.75 o.p. (ISBN 0-85131-130-X, Dist. by Sporting Book Center). J A Allen.

Horse & Horsemanship. Tamas Flandorffer & Jozsef Hajas. Tr. by Eniko Kortvelyessy. (Illus.). 184p. 1979. 12.50x (ISBN 963-13-3701-4). Intl Pubns Serv.

Horse Book. Virginia Parsons. (Illus.). (ps-1). 1968. PLB 5.38 (ISBN 0-307-68937-9, Golden Pr). Western Pub.

Horse Breeding & Stud Management. Henry Wynmalen. (Illus.). 20.10 (ISBN 0-85131-139-3, Dist. by Sporting Book Center). J A Allen.

Horse by Horse. Diana R. Tuke. (Illus.). 19.25 (ISBN 0-85131-203-9, Dist. by Sporting Book Center); pap. 12.25 (ISBN 0-685-85287-3). J A Allen.

Horse Came Running. Meindert DeJong. LC 71-99119. (Illus.). (gr. 4 up). 1970. 8.95 (ISBN 0-02-726540-4). Macmillan.

Horse Came Running. Meindert DeJong. LC 71-99119. 192p. (gr. 5-7). 1972. pap. 1.25 o.s.i. (ISBN 0-02-042800-6, Collier). Macmillan.

Horse Care. Eric Baird. (Illus.). 1979. 11.95 (ISBN 0-87691-296-X). Winchester Pr.

Horse-Drawn Carriages: A Source Book. Ed. by John Thompson. (Illus.). 100p. (Orig.). 1980. pap. 8.50x (ISBN 0-906922-00-3). Intl Pubns Serv.

Horse Feeding & Nutrition. Tony J. Cunha. LC 80-531. (Animal Feeding & Nutrition Ser.). 1980. 26.50 (ISBN 0-12-196560-0). Acad Pr.

Horse Fever. William Murray. LC 76-12532. 1976. 7.95 (ISBN 0-396-07336-0). Dodd.

Horse-Flambeau. LaVada Weir. LC 74-860. (Laurie Newman Adventures Ser). 32p. 1974. 5.95 (ISBN 0-87191-335-6). Creative Ed.

Horse for Charlie. Ann Tompert. (Tell-a-Tale Reader Ser.). (Illus.). (gr. k-3). 1979. PLB 4.77 (ISBN 0-307-68411-3, Whitman). Western Pub.

Horse for X.Y.Z. Moeri. (gr. 4-6). 1980. pap. 1.25 (ISBN 0-590-30039-3, Schol Pap). Schol Bk Serv.

Horse for X.Y.Z. Louise Moeri. (Illus.). (gr. 3-6). 1977. PLB 7.50 (ISBN 0-525-32220-5). Dutton.

Horse: From Conception to Maturity. Peter D. Rossdale. 21.00 (ISBN 0-85131-198-9, Dist. by Sporting Book Center). J A Allen.

Horse Grows up. Richards. (ps-3). pap. 1.25 (ISBN 0-590-12090-5, Schol Pap). Schol Bk Serv.

Horse in Action. Henry Wynmalen. LC 73-78531. (Illus.). 64p. 1974. 10.00 o.p. (ISBN 0-668-03313-4). Arco.

Horse in Blackfoot Indian Culture. x ed. John C. Ewers. LC 55-60591. (Classics in Smithsonian Anthropology Ser.: No. 3). (Illus.). 374p. 1980. pap. text ed. 9.95x (ISBN 0-87474-419-9). Smithsonian.

Horse in Greek Art. Sidney D. Markman. LC 72-88057. (Illus.). 1969. Repr. of 1943 ed. 17.50x (ISBN 0-8196-0247-7). Biblo.

Horse Keepers Encyclopedia. H. Walter. LC 78-9000. 1979. pap. 2.95 o.p. (ISBN 0-668-04601-5). Arc Bks.

Horse Knows the Way. John O'Hara. 384p. 1975. pap. 1.50 o.p. (ISBN 0-445-03057-7). Popular Lib.

Horse Management. C. E. Hope. (Teach Yourself Ser.). 1977. pap. 2.95 o.p. (ISBN 0-679-10367-8). McKay.

Horse Mania. Ed Radlauer & Ruth Radlauer. LC 80-21550. (Mania Bks). (Illus.). 32p. (gr. k-5). 1981. PLB 7.95g (ISBN 0-516-07784-8, Elk Grove Bks). Childrens.

Horse of Course! Guide to Winning at Western Trail Riding. Lynda Bloom. LC 78-13541. (Illus.). 1980. 12.95 (ISBN 0-668-04569-8, 4569). Arco.

Horse of Darius. Justin Cartwright. 1981. pap. 3.50 (ISBN 0-440-13761-6). Dell.

Horse of Hurricane Hill. Clarence W. Anderson. (Illus.). (gr. 3-7). 1962. 4.95g o.s.i. (ISBN 0-02-704520-X). Macmillan.

Horse of the Americas. Robert M. Denhardt. LC 74-5955. (Illus.). 343p. 1981. pap. 8.95 (ISBN 0-8061-1724-9). U of Okla Pr.

Horse of Two Colors. Glenn Balch. LC 69-11079. (Illus.). (gr. 3-9). 1969. 7.95 o.p. (ISBN 0-690-40360-7, TYC-J). T Y Crowell.

Horse Owner's Concise Guide. Elsie V. Hanauer. LC 69-14880. (Illus.). 1978. pap. 3.50 (ISBN 0-668-04661-9, 4661). Arco.

Horse Packing in Pictures. Francis W. Davis. LC 75-946. 1975. 10.95 (ISBN 0-684-14259-7, ScribT). Scribner.

Horse Power & Magic. George E. Evans. (Illus.). 1979. 17.95 (ISBN 0-686-25059-1, Pub. by Faber & Faber). Merrimack Bk Serv.

Horse Racing. Peter Churchill. (Illus.). 168p. 1981. 12.95 (ISBN 0-7137-1016-0, Pub. by Blandford Pr England); pap. 6.95 (ISBN 0-7137-1115-9). Sterling.

Horse Riding. C. E. Hope. (Illus.). 4.50x o.p. (ISBN 0-392-03288-0, SpS). Soccer.

Horse Selection & Care for Beginners. George H. Conn. pap. 4.00 (ISBN 0-87980-193-X). Wilshire.

Horse Sense: Buying & Looking After Your First Horse. Ed. by Jane Starkey. (Illus.). 128p. 1981. 9.95 (ISBN 0-8069-3746-7); lib. bdg. 9.29 (ISBN 0-8069-3747-5). Sterling.

Horse Show. Jennifer Baker. (Illus.). 1977. 7.95 o.p. (ISBN 0-04-798001-X). Allen Unwin.

Horse: Structure & Movement. 2nd ed. R. H. Smythe. (Illus.). pap. 10.50 (ISBN 0-85131-242-X, Dist. by Sporting Book Center). J A Allen.

Horse Tales. Ed. by Suzanne Wilding. LC 76-13052. (Illus.). (YA) 1976. 7.95 (ISBN 0-312-39200-1). St Martin.

Horse-Tamer. Walter Farley. LC 58-9030. (Black Stallion Bks.). 160p. 1980. 3.95 (ISBN 0-394-80614-X, BYR); PLB 5.99 (ISBN 0-394-90614-4); pap. 1.95 (ISBN 0-394-84374-6). Random.

Horse, the Fox, & the Lion. Paul Galdone. LC 68-14085. (Illus.). (ps-1). 1968. 6.95 (ISBN 0-395-28802-9, Clarion). HM.

Horse Trader. Lynn Hall. 144p. (gr. 5 up). 1981. 8.95 (ISBN 0-684-16852-9). Scribner.

Horse We Lie Down in: Eight Poems. Frannie Lindsay. (Pikestaff Poetry Chapbooks: No. 1). 10p. 1980. pap. 1.00 (ISBN 0-936044-02-0). Pikestaff Pr.

Horse World Catalog. Compiled by Estelle Roberts et al. LC 76-21819. 1977. pap. 7.95 o.p. (ISBN 0-397-01026-5). Lippincott.

Horse World of London. W. J. Gordon. (Illus.). 7.00 (ISBN 0-85131-144-X, Dist. by Sporting Book Center). J A Allen.

Horse World of the Bluegrass, Vol. 1. Mary E. Wharton & Edward L. Bowen. Ed. by Bruce F. Denbo & Mary E. Wharton. 246p. 1980. 30.00 (ISBN 0-934554-00-5). Host Assoc.

Horseback Honeymoon. Dorothy Ballard. LC 75-15042. 1975. 8.95 (ISBN 0-89430-021-0). Morgan-Pacific.

Horseback Riding. Frederick L. Devereux, Jr. LC 75-34189. (First Bks.). (Illus.). 72p. (gr. 4-6). 1976. PLB 6.45 (ISBN 0-531-00844-4). Watts.

Horseback Riding Is for Me. Art Thomas & Emily Blackburn. (Sports for Me Bks.). (Illus.). (gr. 2-5). 1981. PLB 5.95 (ISBN 0-8225-1092-8). Lerner Pubns.

Horseback Riding Made Easy & Fun. Sue H. Coen. pap. 4.00 (ISBN 0-87980-194-8). Wilshire.

Horseclans Odyssey. Robert Adams. (Orig.). 1981. pap. 2.50 (ISBN 0-451-09744-0, E9744, Sig). NAL.

Horsefeathers & Other Curious Words. Charles E. Funk & Charles E. Funk, Jr. LC 58-8870. (Illus.). 1958. 10.95 o.p. (ISBN 0-06-001830-5, HarpT). Har-Row.

Horsekeeper's Handbook. Jeanne K. Posey. 1974. 9.95 (ISBN 0-87691-134-3). Winchester Pr.

Horseman's Bible. Jack Coggins. LC 66-17921. pap. 3.50 (ISBN 0-385-03167-X). Doubleday.

Horseman's Companion. Dorian Williams. 574p. 1980. 15.00 (ISBN 0-312-39217-6). St Martin.

Horseman's Manual. C. E. Hope. LC 73-9303. 1976. pap. 3.95 o.p. (ISBN 0-684-14612-6, SL 623, ScribT). Scribner.

Horseman's Word: A Novel. Georgess McHargue. LC 80-68736. 256p. (YA) (gr. 8-12). 1981. 9.95 (ISBN 0-440-04167-8). Delacorte.

Horsemanship. Boy Scouts Of America. LC 19-600. (Illus.). 56p. (gr. 6-12). 1974. pap. 0.70x (ISBN 0-8395-3298-9, 3298). BSA.

Horsemanship: A Guide to Information Sources. Ed. by Ellen B. Wells. LC 79-16046. (Sports, Games, & Pastimes Information Guide Ser.: Vol. 4). 1979. 30.00 (ISBN 0-8103-1444-4). Gale.

Horsemanship in Europe. Jane Kidd. (Illus.). 17.35 (ISBN 0-85131-243-8, Dist. by Sporting Book Center). J A Allen.

Horsemanship in Pictures. Susan Harris. 1975. pap. 4.95 o.p. (ISBN 0-684-14337-2, SL598, ScribT). Scribner.

Horsemen of the Americas & the Literature They Inspired. Edward L. Tinker. (Illus.). 1966. 20.00 (ISBN 0-292-73657-6). U of Tex Pr.

Horsemen of the Plains. Joseph A. Altsheler. (Illus.). (gr. 7 up). 1967. 5.95x o.s.i. (ISBN 0-02-700650-6). Macmillan.

Horses. Frederick L. Devereux, Jr. LC 75-4897. (Illus.). 72p. (gr. 4-6). 1975. PLB 3.90 o.p. (ISBN 0-531-00836-3). Watts.

Horses. Dean Morris. LC 77-8243. (Read About Animals Ser.). (Illus.). (gr. k-3). 1977. PLB 9.95 (ISBN 0-8393-0008-5). Raintree Child.

Horses. Blanche Perrin. (Illus.). 24p. (ps-4). 1962. PLB 5.00 (ISBN 0-307-60459-4, Golden Pr). Western Pub.

Horses: A Guide to Their Care & Enjoyment. J. Warren Evans. LC 80-29070. (Illus.). 1981. text ed. price not set (ISBN 0-7167-1253-9). W H Freeman.

Horses: A Pactical & Scientific Approach. Melvin Bradley. (Illus.). 560p. 1980. text ed. 19.95x. McGraw.

Horses, Airplanes, & Frogs. Mark Parker. LC 76-54805. (Illus.). (ps-3). 1977. 5.50 (ISBN 0-913778-71-0). Childs World.

Horses & Foals. Ellen Rabinowich. (Easy-Read Fact Bk.). (Illus.). (gr. 2-4). 1979. PLB 6.45 s&l (ISBN 0-531-02272-2). Watts.

Horses & Horse Sense: The Practical Science of Horse Husbandry. James Blakely. 1981. 17.95 (ISBN 0-8359-2887-X); text ed. 14.95 (ISBN 0-8359-2887-X); instr's. manual free (ISBN 0-8359-2888-8). Reston.

Horses & Horse Shows. Harlan C. Abbey. LC 78-55449. (Illus.). 1979. pap. 7.95 cancelled (ISBN 0-498-02372-9). A S Barnes.

Horses & Horse Shows. Harlan C. Abbey. LC 78-55449. (Illus.). 1980. 14.95 (ISBN 0-498-02247-1). A S Barnes.

Horses & Horsemanship. 5th ed. M. E. Ensminger. LC 76-45238. (Illus.). 1977. 23.35 (ISBN 0-8134-1888-7); text ed. 17.50x (ISBN 0-685-85664-X). Interstate.

Horses & Ponies on Small Areas. Neil Dougall. (Illus.). pap. 2.65 (ISBN 0-85131-273-X, Dist. by Sporting Book Center). J A Allen.

Horses & Ponies: Their Breeding, Feeding & Management. Marguerite De Beaumont. (Illus.). 10.50 o.p. (ISBN 0-85131-220-9, Dist. by Sporting Book Center). J A Allen.

Horses & Their Wild Relatives. Dorothy H. Patent. LC 80-23559. (Illus.). 128p. (gr. 5 up). 1981. 8.95 (ISBN 0-8234-0383-1). Holiday.

Horse's Body. Joanna Cole. LC 80-28147. (Illus.). 48p. (gr. k-3). 1981. 6.95 (ISBN 0-688-00362-1); PLB 6.67 (ISBN 0-688-00363-X). Morrow.

Horses in Japan. Vivienne Kenrick. (Illus.). 5.25 (ISBN 0-85131-084-2, Dist. by Sporting Book Center). J A Allen.

Horses in Suburbia. Joyce Taylor. (Illus.). 5.25 (ISBN 0-85131-085-0, Dist. by Sporting Book Center). J A Allen.

Horses of the Night. Irmelin S. Lilius. Tr. by Joan Tate from Swedish. LC 79-2105. (gr. 5 up). 1980. 7.95 (ISBN 0-440-04450-2, Sey Lawr); PLB 7.45 (ISBN 0-440-04451-0). Delacorte.

Horses of the World. rev. ed. Daphne M. Goodall. LC 73-7480. (Illus.). 272p. 1974. 14.95 (ISBN 0-02-544650-9). Macmillan.

Horseshoe-Nail Crafting. Hans Carlbom. LC 73-83450. (Little Craft Book Ser.). 48p. (gr. 7 up). 1973. 5.95 (ISBN 0-8069-5280-6); PLB 6.69 (ISBN 0-8069-5281-4). Sterling.

Horseshow Organization. new ed. L. C. Cooper. 1978. 15.75 (ISBN 0-85131-310-8, Dist. by Sporting Book Center). J A Allen.

Horsethief Canyon. Jerry Brucker. 1981. pap. 1.95 (ISBN 0-8439-0911-0, Leisure Bks). Nordon Pubns.

Horsing Around. E. Radlauer & R. S. Radlauer. LC 77-180241. (Sports Action Bks). (Illus.). 48p. (gr. 3 up). 1972. PLB 6.45 (ISBN 0-531-02034-7). Watts.

Horst Janssen: Master Drawings. Illus. by Horst Janssen. LC 79-92751. (Illus.). 50p. (Orig.). 1980. pap. 6.50 (ISBN 0-88397-026-0). Intl Exhibit Foun.

Horticultural Reviews, Vol. 1. Ed. by Jules Janick. 1979. lib. bdg. 33.00 (ISBN 0-87055-314-3). AVI.

Horticultural Reviews, Vol. 2. Jules Janick. (Illus.). 1980. lib. bdg. 33.00 (ISBN 0-87055-352-6). AVI.

Horticultural Reviews, Vol 3. Ed. by Jules Janick. (Illus.). 1981. lib. bdg. 33.00 (ISBN 0-87055-383-6). AVI.

Horticultural Science. 3rd ed. Jules Janick. LC 78-13053. (Illus.). 1979. text ed. 21.95x (ISBN 0-7167-1031-5). W H Freeman.

Horticulture: A Basic Awareness. Robert F. Baudendistel. (Illus.). 1978. pap. 15.95 ref. ed. (ISBN 0-8359-2891-8); instrs'. manual avail. Reston.

Horticulture for the Disabled & Disadvantaged. Damon R. Olszowy. 240p. 1978. 17.50 (ISBN 0-398-03691-8). C C Thomas.

Horticulture: Principles & Practical Applications. R. Poincelot. 1980. 19.95 (ISBN 0-13-394809-9). P-H.

Horvath: A Study. Ian Huish. 105p. 1980. 11.50x (ISBN 0-8476-6269-1). Rowman.

Hosea. D. David Garland. 128p. 1975. pap. 3.50 (ISBN 0-310-24843-4). Zondervan.

Hosea. Hans W. Wolff. Ed. by Paul D. Hanson. Tr. by Gary Stansell from Ger. LC 70-179634. (Hermeneia: a Critical & Historical Commentary on the Bible). Orig. Title: Dodekapropheton-Hosea. 292p. 1973. 19.95 (ISBN 0-8006-6004-8, 20-6004). Fortress.

Hosea: The Heart & Holiness of God. G. Campbell Morgan. (Morgan Library). 1974. pap. 3.95 (ISBN 0-8010-5952-6). Baker Bk.

Hoshanos. Avie Gold. (Art Scroll Mesorah Ser.). 160p. 1980. 8.95 (ISBN 0-89906-162-1); pap. 5.95 (ISBN 0-89906-163-X). Mesorah Pubns.

Hosie's Alphabet. Leonard Baskin et al. (Illus.). 64p. (gr. k-3). 1972. PLB 10.00 (ISBN 0-670-37958-1). Viking Pr.

Hospice. Jack Zimmerman. 300p. 1981. price not set (ISBN 0-8067-2211-8). Urban & S.

Hospice: A Caring Community. Koff. (Illus.). 192p. 1980. text ed. 13.95 (ISBN 0-87626-332-5); pap. text ed. 7.95 (ISBN 0-87626-331-7). Winthrop.

Hospice: Development & Administration. Ed. by Glen W. Davidson. LC 78-3836. 1978. text ed. 19.50 (ISBN 0-89116-103-1). Hemisphere Pub.

Hospice Means Hope. Kenneth B. Wentzel. 1980. 9.95 (ISBN 0-89182-020-5); pap. text ed. 4.95 (ISBN 0-89182-030-2). Charles River Bks.

Hospice: Prescription for Terminal Care. Kenneth P. Cohen. LC 79-13341. 1979. text ed. 27.95 (ISBN 0-89443-151-X). Aspen Systems.

Hospice Program. Ed. by Sylvia Lack. 1981. cancelled (ISBN 0-88416-298-2). PSG Pub.

Hospice Way of Death. Paul Dubois. LC 79-12326. 1979. text ed. 17.95 (ISBN 0-87705-415-0). Human Sci Pr.

Hospital. Bryan Ward. LC 78-61228. (Careers Ser.). (Illus.). 1978. lib. bdg. 7.95 (ISBN 0-686-51120-4). Silver.

Hospital Accounting Systems & Controls. Nitin H. Mehta & Donald J. Maher. 272p. 1977. 32.95 (ISBN 0-686-68586-5, 14919). Hospital Finan.

Hospital Acquired Infections. T. C. Polk, Jr. (Illus.). 1977. 19.50 (ISBN 0-8391-1102-9). Univ Park.

Hospital Administration Consultant. Jack Rudman. (Career Examination Ser.: C-2768). (Cloth bdg. avail. on request). 1980. pap. 12.00 (ISBN 0-8373-2768-7). Natl Learning.

Hospital Administration for Middle Management: A Practical Approach. Stanley J. Malsky. 320p. 1981. 27.50 (ISBN 0-87527-170-7). Green.

Hospital Admitting Department. American Hospital Association. LC 76-54284. (Illus.). 100p. (Orig.). 1977. pap. 13.75 (ISBN 0-87258-200-0, 1855). Am Hospital.

Hospital Admitting Department. 90p. 1977. 9.50 (ISBN 0-87258-200-0, 1855). Hospital Finan.

Hospital & Surgical Insurance Coverage United States 1974. C. S. Wilder. Ed. by Taloria Stevenson. (Ser.10, No. 117). 1977. pap. text ed. 1.50 (ISBN 0-8406-0109-3). Natl Ctr Health Stats.

Hospital & Welfare Library Services: An International Bibliography. Ed. by E. E. Cumming. 1977. 24.50 (ISBN 0-85365-139-6, Pub. by Lib Assn England). Oryx Pr.

Hospital Care of Children: A Review of Contemporary Issues. Geoffrey C. Robinson & Heather F. Clarke. 288p. 1980. 18.95x (ISBN 0-19-502673-X). Oxford U Pr.

Hospital Certificate-of-Need Controls: Impact on Investment, Costs, & Use. David Salkever & Thomas Bice. 1979. pap. 5.25 (ISBN 0-8447-3325-3). Am Enterprise.

Hospital Chaplains: Who Needs Them? Raymond G. Carey. 1974. pap. 6.00 (ISBN 0-87125-054-3). Cath Health.

Hospital Computer Systems Planning: Preparation of Request for Proposal. American Hospital Association. LC 80-18002. 124p. 1980. 25.00 (1445). Am Hospital.

Hospital Consumables: Reference for Medical Surgical Products. Ed. by E. J. Smith. (Illus.). 652p. 1980. text ed. 145.00 (ISBN 0-87619-715-2). R J Brady.

Hospital Cost Containment Through Operations Management, 2 pts. American Hospital Association. (Illus.). 1980. Instructor's Manual. loose-leaf 37.50 (ISBN 0-87258-304-X, 2435, 206 PAGES); Participant's Manual. loose-leaf 10.00 (ISBN 0-87258-305-8, 2436, 2434, 264 PAGES). Am Hospital.

Hospital Costs Containment Operations Management. 201p. 1979. 37.50 (ISBN 0-686-68595-4, 2435). Hospital Finan.

Hospital Crisis Management: A Casebook. A. Brent Garber & Leroy Sparks. LC 79-25691. 1978. text ed. 27.00 (ISBN 0-89443-079-3). Aspen Systems.

Hospital Dental Practice. James R. Hooley & Lowell G. Daun. LC 79-17206. (Illus.). 1979. text ed. 24.95 (ISBN 0-8016-2226-3). Mosby.

Hospital Design Checklist. American Hospital Association. 48p. 1965. 8.75 (ISBN 0-87258-016-4, 3310). Am Hospital.

Hospital Emergency Department. James H. Spencer et al. (Illus.). 388p. 1972. 29.75 (ISBN 0-398-02482-0). C C Thomas.

Hospital Energy Management Manual. 184p. 1980. text ed. 79.00 loose leaf binder (ISBN 0-89443-296-6). Aspen Systems.

Hospital Engineering Handbook. 3rd ed. American Society for Hospital Engineering. (Illus.). 348p. 1980. casebound 31.25 (ISBN 0-87258-311-2, 1820). Am Hospital.

Hospital Experience: A Complete Guide to Understanding & Participating in Your Own Care. Judith Nierenberg & Florence Janovic. LC 78-55658. (Illus.). 1978. 12.95 (ISBN 0-672-52372-8); pap. 9.95 (ISBN 0-672-52373-6). Bobbs.

Hospital Financial Accounting Theory & Practice. L. Vann Seawell. LC 74-27241. (Illus.). 569p. 1975. text ed. 19.95x (ISBN 0-930228-00-6, 1454); instr's manual 39.90. Hospital Finan.

Hospital Food Service Management Review. American Society for Hospital Food Service Administrators. LC 80-11834. 80p. (Orig.). 1980. 10.00 (ISBN 0-87258-323-6, 1410). Am Hospital.

Hospital Happy. Evelyn Barkins. 1976. pap. 3.95 (ISBN 0-8119-0376-1). Fell.

Hospital-Health Care Training Media Profiles, Vol. 8. Ed. by Walter J. Carroll. 1981. 85.00 (ISBN 0-88367-206-5). Olympic Media.

Hospital House Staff & Thanatology. Irene Seeland & A. H. Kutscher. (Thanatology Service Ser.). 125p. 1980. pap. 6.95 o.p. (ISBN 0-686-64836-6). Highly Specialized.

Hospital Housekeeping Handbook. 2nd ed. American Hospital Association. Orig. Title: Housekeeping Manual for Health Care. (Illus.). 1979. 18.75 (ISBN 0-87258-273-6, 2086). Am Hospital.

Hospital in Modern Society. Ed. by Eliot Freidson. LC 63-10648. (Illus.). 1963. 19.95 (ISBN 0-02-910690-7). Free Pr.

Hospital Infection Control. Mary Castle. LC 80-13424. 251p. 1980. 16.95 (ISBN 0-471-05395-3, Pub. by Wiley Med). Wiley.

Hospital Infection Control: Principles & Practices. M. Castle. LC 80-13424. 1980. 16.95 (ISBN 0-471-05395-3). Wiley.

Hospital Labor Relations. Richard U. Miller. (Wisconsin Business Monographs: No. 11). (Illus.). 104p. 1980. 7.50 (ISBN 0-86603-003-4). Bureau Busn Res U Wis.

Hospital Laboratory: Modern Concepts of Management, Operations, & Finance. Richard M. Shuffstall & Brecharr Hemmaplardh. LC 78-11877. (Illus.). 1979. 15.95 (ISBN 0-8016-4620-0). Mosby.

Hospital Law Manual: Administrator's & Attorney's Set, 6 vols. Health Law Center. LC 74-80713. 350.00 (ISBN 0-912862-05-X). Aspen Systems.

Hospital Law Manual: Administrator's Set, 3 vols. Health Law Center. (Updated quarterly). 1974. loose-leaf metal binding 295.00 (ISBN 0-912862-06-8). Aspen Systems.

Hospital Law Manual: Attorney's Set, 3 vols. Health Law Center. (Updated quarterly). 1974. loose-leaf metal binding 295.00 (ISBN 0-912862-05-X). Aspen Systems.

Hospital Libraries: Recommended Standards for Libraries in Hospitals. 1972. pap. 2.75x (ISBN 0-686-64057-8, Pub. by Lib Assn England). Oryx Pr.

Hospital: Life in a Medical Center. Paul Deegan & Bruce Larson. LC 76-156064. (gr. 5-9). 1970. PLB 6.95 (ISBN 0-87191-052-7). Creative Ed.

Hospital Literature Index: 1978, Vol. 34. American Hospital Association. 350p. 75.00 (ISBN 0-87258-347-3, 1389). Am Hospital.

Hospital Literature Index: 1979, Vol. 35. American Hospital Association. 736p. 1980. 75.00 (ISBN 0-87258-306-6, 1388). Am Hospital.

Hospital Literature Index: 1980 Cumulative Annual, Vol. 36. Ed. by Alice Dunlap et al. 704p. 1981. 72.00 (ISBN 0-87258-348-1). Am Hospital.

Hospital Literature Subject Headings. 2nd ed. Alice Dunlap. LC 77-519. 200p. 1977. pap. 20.00 (ISBN 0-87258-202-7, 1371). Am Hospital.

Hospital Literature Subject Headings Transition Guide to Medical Subject Headings. LC 78-14972. 236p. 1978. pap. text ed. 22.50 (ISBN 0-87258-242-6, 1858). Am Hospital.

Hospital Looks at Itself. Elisabeth Shoenberg. 1972. 8.95 (ISBN 0-571-81004-7, Pub. by Faber & Faber). Merrimack Bk Serv.

Hospital Management Systems: Multi-Unit Organization & Delivery of Health Care. Montague Brown & Howard L. Lewis. LC 76-15769. 1976. 25.95 (ISBN 0-912862-22-X). Aspen Systems.

Hospital Manpower Budget Preparation Manual. Stephen H. Lipson & Mary D. Hensel. LC 75-20992. 200p. 1975. pap. text ed. 15.00 (ISBN 0-914904-11-6). Health Admin Pr.

Hospital Manpower Budget Preparation Manual. Stephen H. Lipson & Mary D. Hensel. 200p. 1975. 12.00 (ISBN 0-686-68583-0, 14917). Hospital Finan.

Hospital Materiel Management. Charles E. Housley. LC 78-14526. (Illus.). 1978. text ed. 32.95 (ISBN 0-89443-046-7). Aspen Systems.

Hospital Medical Records: Guidelines for Their Use & the Release of Medical Information. American Hospital Association. LC 70-188799. 70p. 1972. pap. 7.50 (ISBN 0-87258-087-3, 1250). Am Hospital.

Hospital Medical Staff: Selected Readings, 1972-76. LC 77-5049. 1977. pap. 12.00 o.p. (ISBN 0-87258-213-2, 2165). Am Hospital.

Hospital Mergers in the Making. David Starkweather. (Illus.). 1981. text ed. write for info. (ISBN 0-914904-54-X). Health Admin Pr.

Hospital of Cardinal Tavera Toledo. Catherine Wilkinson. LC 76-23660. (Outstanding Dissertations in the Fine Arts Ser.). (Illus.). 1977. lib. bdg. 63.00x (ISBN 0-8240-2739-6). Garland Pub.

Hospital of Santo Spirito & Pope Sixtus IV. Eunice D. Howe. (Outstanding Dissertations in the Fine Arts Ser.). (Illus.). 1978. lib. bdg. 43.00x (ISBN 0-8240-3230-6). Garland Pub.

Hospital Organization. R. W. Rowbottom et al. 1973. 19.50x o.p. (ISBN 0-8448-0684-6). Crane-Russak Co.

Hospital Pharmacy. 4th ed. William E. Hassan, Jr. LC 80-20700. (Illus.). 525p. 1981. text ed. write for info. (ISBN 0-8121-0772-1). Lea & Febiger.

Hospital Pharmacy Journal Articles. 3rd ed. Marvin I. Lew. 1977. spiral bdg. 15.50 (ISBN 0-87488-799-2). Med Exam.

Hospital Production: A Linear Programming Approach. William L. Dowling. LC 74-14408. (Illus.). 1976. 17.95 (ISBN 0-669-93187-X). Lexington Bks.

Hospital Purchasing Guide: Nineteen Eighty-One. 5th ed. Ed. by Calvin Probst. (Annual Ser.). 1981. pap. text ed. 85.00 (ISBN 0-933916-05-1). Medical Busn.

Hospital Regulation: Report of the Special Committee on the Regulatory Process. Ed. by T. Stewart Hamilton. LC 77-6184. 1977. pap. 6.25 o.p. (ISBN 0-87258-218-3, 1835). Am Hospital.

Hospital Regulation Through State Rate Review: Mandated Interference or a Noble Intrusion. 116p. 1978. 7.90 (ISBN 0-686-68585-7, 14922). Hospital Finan.

Hospital Scares Me. Paula Z. Hogan & Kirk Hogan. LC 79-23886. (Life & Living from a Child's Point of View Ser.). (Illus.). (gr. k-5). 1980. PLB 9.65 (ISBN 0-8172-1351-1). Raintree Child.

Hospital Sector Inflation. David Salkever. (Illus.). 208p. 1979. 22.95 (ISBN 0-669-00704-8). Lexington Bks.

Hospital Security. Russell L. Colling. LC 75-46098. (Illus.). 384p. 1976. 19.95 (ISBN 0-913708-22-4). Butterworths.

Hospital Security. 2nd ed. Russell L. Colling. 1981. text ed. price not set. Butterworths.

Hospital Security & Safety. A. Michael Pascal. LC 77-14083. 1977. text ed. 28.00 (ISBN 0-89443-029-7). Aspen Systems.

Hospital Security Guard Training Manual. John A. Wanat. (Illus.). 192p. 1977. 21.75 (ISBN 0-398-03656-X). C C Thomas.

Hospital Special Care Facilities: Planning for User Needs. Harold Laufman. (Clinical Engineering Ser.). 1981. price not set (ISBN 0-12-437740-8). Acad Pr.

Hospital-Sponsered Ambulatory Care: The Governing Board's Role. Maryland Hospital Education Institute. LC 80-18004. 116p. (Orig.). 1980. pap. 18.75 (ISBN 0-87258-308-2, 1077). Am Hospital.

Hospital Station. James White. 1979. pap. 2.25 (ISBN 0-345-29613-3). Ballantine.

Hospital Statistics: Data from the American Hospital Association 1979 Annual Survey. American Hospital Association. 256p. 1980. pap. 18.75 (ISBN 0-87258-282-5, 2452). Am Hospital.

Hospital Trustee Reader: Selections from Trustee Magazine. American Hospital Association. LC 75-19443. 216p. 1975. pap. 13.75 (ISBN 0-87258-169-1, 1915). Am Hospital.

Hospitality for Sale: Techniques of Promoting Business for Hospitality Establishments. C. DeWitt Coffman. LC 79-28567. (Illus.). 339p. 1980. 17.56x (ISBN 0-86612-000-9); text ed. 21.95 (ISBN 0-686-28892-0). Educ Inst Am Hotel.

Hospitality: In the Spirit of Love. Peggy Simpson. 1980. pap. 3.45 o.p. (ISBN 0-89137-416-7). Quality Pubns.

Hospitality Industry Cooperative Training. Seymour Hertzson. LC 75-142506. 1971. pap. text ed. 13.95 (ISBN 0-672-96098-2); tchr's manual 6.67 (ISBN 0-672-96099-0). Bobbs.

Hospitality Management Accounting. Michael M. Coltman. LC 77-16670. (Illus.). 1978. 15.95 (ISBN 0-8436-2170-2); paper student wkbk. 6.95 (ISBN 0-8436-2180-X). CBI Pub.

Hospitality Management: Avoiding Legal Pitfalls. Lothar A. Kreck & Jon P. McConnell. 1976. 16.95 (ISBN 0-8436-2064-1). CBI Pub.

Hospitality Personnel Management. William J. Morgan, Jr. LC 78-22031. 1979. text ed. 14.95 (ISBN 0-8436-2138-9). CBI Pub.

Hospitalized Adolescent: A Guide to Managing the Ill & Injured Youth. Adele D. Hofmann et al. LC 76-1698. 1976. 17.95 (ISBN 0-02-914790-5). Free Pr.

Hospitalized Child: Communication Techniques for Health Personnel. Dennis Klinzing & Dene Klinzing. (Illus.). 1977. pap. text ed. 9.95 (ISBN 0-13-394817-X). P-H.

Hospitals & the Long-Stay Patient. D. Norton. 1967. 21.00 (ISBN 0-08-011053-3); pap. 9.75 (ISBN 0-08-011052-5). Pergamon.

Hospitals (Architecture) R. Aloi & C. Bassi. (Illus.). 1972. 50.00 (ISBN 0-685-30577-5). Heinman.

Hospitals Are Us. Robert R. Cadmus. 184p. (Orig.). 1979. 15.95 (ISBN 0-931028-12-4); pap. 12.95 (ISBN 0-931028-11-6). Teach'em.

Hospitals, Children & Their Families: The Report of a Pilot Study. Margaret Stacey et al. (Medicine, Illness & Society Ser). 1970. 14.00x o.p. (ISBN 0-7100-6783-6). Routledge & Kegan.

Hospitals: The Planning & Design Process. Owen B. Hardy & Lawrence P. Lammers. LC 77-76922. 1977. 38.50 (ISBN 0-912862-44-0). Aspen Systems.

Hospitals: What They Are & How They Work. Donald Snook. 250p. 1981. text ed. price not set (ISBN 0-89443-339-3). Aspen Systems.

Hospiz. Franz Boeni. (Edition Suhrkamp: Neue Folge). 100p. (Orig.). 1980. pap. text ed. 3.25 (ISBN 3-518-11004-7, Pub. by Insel Verlag Germany). Suhrkamp.

Host-Hostess. Ser-Vo-Tel Institute. (Foodservice Career Education Ser.). 1974. pap. 4.95 (ISBN 0-8436-2024-2). CBI Pub.

Host State & the Transnational Corporation. Juha Kuusi. 1980. text ed. 25.25x (ISBN 0-566-00249-3, Pub. by Gower Pub Co England). Renouf.

Hostage! James Hamilton-Paterson. LC 79-25114. 192p. (gr. 7-12). 1980. 8.95 (ISBN 0-529-05596-1). Philomel.

Hostage. rev. ed. Murray S. Miron & Arnold P. Goldstein. LC 77-16554. (Pergamon General Psychology Ser.: No. 79). 170p. 1979. 22.00 (ISBN 0-08-023875-0); pap. 8.75 (ISBN 0-08-023876-9). Pergamon.

Hostage: A Police Approach to a Contemporary Crisis. George F. Maher. (Illus.). 100p. 1977. 12.75 (ISBN 0-398-03698-5). C C Thomas.

Hostage Negotiation for Police: Officer Reference. Richard Gallagher & Charles Remsberg. 1977. 2.50 (ISBN 0-686-52997-9). MTI Tele.

Hostage of Zir. L. Sprague DeCamp. LC 77-10137. (YA) 1977. 7.95 o.p. (ISBN 0-399-12097-1, Dist. by Putnam). Berkley Pub.

Hostage of Zir. L. Sprague de Camp. 1978. pap. 1.75 o.p. (ISBN 0-425-03870-X, Dist. by Putnam). Berkley Pub.

Hostage Seekers: A Study of Childless & Adopting Couples. Michael Humphrey. (Studies in Child Development). (Orig.). 1969. pap. text ed. 4.50x (ISBN 0-582-32438-6). Humanities.

Hostage-Takers. 1st ed. H. H. Cooper. (Illus.). 100p. (Orig.). 1981. pap. 12.00 (ISBN 0-87364-209-0). Paladin Ent.

Hostage-Taking: Theory & Practice. Ronald D. Crelinsten & Denis Szabo. (Illus.). 1979. 16.95 (ISBN 0-669-02841-X). Lexington Bks.

Hostage to Khomeini. Robert Dreyfuss. LC 80-24288. (Illus.). 260p. (Orig.). 1981. pap. 3.95 (ISBN 0-933488-11-4). New Benjamin.

Hostages. Geoffrey Lomas. 1979. 8.95 o.p. (ISBN 0-684-16072-2, ScribT). Scribner.

Hostages: The Personal Testimony of a Soviet Jew. Grigory Svirsky. Tr. by Gordon Clough. 1976. 10.00 o.p. (ISBN 0-394-49368-0). Knopf.

Hosteling U. S. A. The Offical American Youth Hostels Handbook. rev. ed. Intro. by Michael Frome. (Illus.). 250p. (Orig.). 1981. pap. 6.95 (ISBN 0-914788-33-7). East Woods.

Hosteling U. S. A. The Official American Youth Hostels Handbook. American Youth Hostels Inc. LC 79-936. (Illus.). 224p. 1979. pap. 9.25 o.p. (ISBN 0-686-27149-1); pap. 5.95 o.p. (ISBN 0-914788-26-4). East Woods.

Hostile Butterflies & Other Paintings. Carroll Cloar. LC 77-7549. (Illus.). 216p. 1980. Repr. of 1977 ed. 39.95 (ISBN 0-87870-040-4). Memphis St Univ.

Hostiles & Horse Soldiers. Ed. by L. J. White. LC 72-80262. 1972. 10.95 o.p. (ISBN 0-87108-061-3). Pruett.

Hostility. Lester Sumrall. 1981. pap. 3.95 (ISBN 0-8407-5765-4). Nelson.

Hosts & Guests: The Anthropology of Tourism. Ed. by Valene L. Smith. LC 77-81447. 1977. 16.00 (ISBN 0-8122-7732-5). U of Pa Pr.

Hot-Air Ballooning. Charles Coombs. LC 80-26704. (Illus.). 128p. (gr. 4-6). 1981. 7.95 (ISBN 0-688-00364-8); PLB 7.63 (ISBN 0-688-00365-6). Morrow.

Hot Air Ballooning. Barry T. Wells. LC 80-80504. (Free Time Fun Ser.). (Illus.). 56p. (gr. 5 up). 1981. lib. bdg. 6.79 (ISBN 0-8178-0003-4). Harvey.

Hot & Cold. rev. ed. Irving Adler. LC 74-9357. (Illus.). 1975. PLB 7.89 (ISBN 0-381-99990-4, A34461, JD-J). John Day.

Hot As an Ice Cube. Philip Balestrino. LC 70-139092. (Let's-Read-&-Find-Out Science Bk). (Illus.). (gr. k-3). 1971. PLB 7.89 (ISBN 0-690-40415-8, TYC-J). T Y Crowell.

Hot Atom Chemistry Status Report: Proceedings, Vienna, 1974. (Illus.). 332p. 1976. pap. 24.75 (ISBN 92-0-141075-1, IAEA). Unipub.

Hot Birds & Cold Bottles. Edith Fink & Avenelle Day. 320p. 1972. 10.00 o.s.i. (ISBN 0-440-03750-6). Delacorte.

Hot-Blooded Dinosaurs. Adrian J. Desmond. (Illus.). 336p. 1977. pap. 2.50 o.s.i. (ISBN 0-446-81359-1). Warner Bks.

Hot Campus: The Politics That Impede Change in the Technoversity. G. Louis Heath. LC 73-8824. 1973. 13.50 (ISBN 0-8108-0648-7). Scarecrow.

Hot Dog! Robert Fischer. LC 80-201. (Illus.). 64p. (gr. 3-6). 1980. PLB 6.97g (ISBN 0-671-33045-4). Messner.

Hot Electrons in Semiconductors. International Conference on Hot Electrons in Semiconductors, Denton, TX, 6-8 Jul. 1977. Ed. by W. Crawford Dunlap. 1978. pap. text ed. 38.50 (ISBN 0-08-022692-2). Pergamon.

Hot Footsteps. Yuki Hartman. Ed. by Maureen Owen. LC 76-20487. (Illus.). 45p. (Orig.). 1976. pap. 1.50 (ISBN 0-916382-10-9). Telephone Bks.

Hot Irons. Oren Arnold & John P. Hale. LC 71-188637. 1972. Repr. of 1940 ed. lib. bdg. 11.00x (ISBN 0-8154-0416-6). Cooper Sq.

Hot l Baltimore. Lanford Wilson. (Mermaid Dramabook). 145p. 1973. 7.95 (ISBN 0-8090-5544-9); pap. 4.50 (ISBN 0-8090-1230-8). Hill & Wang.

Hot Lead. Dwight Bruckner. 1977. pap. 1.25 (ISBN 0-505-51217-3). Tower Bks.

Hot Line to Heaven. Frances Hunter. 1978. pap. 1.95 (ISBN 0-87162-117-7). Hunter Bks.

Hot Oil. Mitchell Carlton. (Orig.). 1980. pap. 1.75 (ISBN 0-505-51477-X). Tower Bks.

Hot on Ice. Jack Woolgar. LC 65-15106. (Pilot Book Ser). (Illus.). 128p. (gr. 3-5). 1965. 6.95g (ISBN 0-8075-3383-1). A Whitman.

Hot Peppers: Cajuns & Capsicum in New Iberia, la. Richard Schweid. LC 80-23160. 200p. 1980. 9.95 (ISBN 0-914842-50-1); pap. 6.95 (ISBN 0-914842-51-X). Madrona Pubs.

Hot Rod. Henry G. Felsen. (Literature Ser). (gr. 9-12). 1950. pap. text ed. 3.50 (ISBN 0-87720-754-2). AMSCO Sch.

Hot Rod Thunder. Joe Brennan. LC 62-8928. (gr. 6-9). 1962. 5.95 o.p. (ISBN 0-385-01650-6). Doubleday.

Hot Shots of Pro Basketball. Lou Sabin. LC 74-4932. (Pro Basketball Library). (Illus.). 160p. (gr. 5 up). 1974. 2.50 o.p. (ISBN 0-394-82901-8); PLB 3.69 (ISBN 0-394-92901-2). Random.

Hot Thirty. Jeannie Sakol. 1981. pap. 3.75 (ISBN 0-440-13429-3). Dell.

Hot Tips: One Thousand Real Life Fashion & Beauty Tricks. Frances P. Stein & Rochelle Udell. (Illus.). 224p. 1981. 12.95 (ISBN 0-399-12580-9). Putnam.

Hot Tubs, Spas & Home Saunas. Sunset Editors. LC 78-70274. (Illus.). 80p. 1979. pap. 3.95 o.p. (ISBN 0-376-01242-0). Sunset-Lane.

Hot Tubs, Spas & Home Saunas. Sunset Editors. LC 78-70274. (Illus.). 80p. 1979. pap. 3.95 (ISBN 0-376-01242-0, Sunset Bks). Sunset-Lane.

Hot Wire. William Butterworth. LC 80-84814. (Illus.). 128p. (gr. 7-9). 1981. lib. bdg. 5.89 (ISBN 0-8178-0018-2). Harvey.

Hotbed of Tranquility. Brooks Hays. 1968. 9.95 o.s.i. (ISBN 0-02-549530-5). Macmillan.

Hotel. Arthur Hailey. 416p. 1981. pap. 3.50 (ISBN 0-553-14778-1). Bantam.

Hotel. Ed. by Reese Williams. 320p. 1980. 12.95 (ISBN 0-934378-13-4); pap. 6.95 (ISBN 0-934378-00-2). Tanam Pr.

Hotel. Carol Wright. LC 78-61229. (Careers Ser.). (Illus.). 1979. lib. bdg. 7.95 (ISBN 0-686-51121-2). Silver.

Hotel Accounting. 4th ed. Ernest B. Horwath et al. LC 77-79169. 1978. 26.95 (ISBN 0-471-07247-8, Pub. by Wiley-Interscience). Wiley.

Hotel & Catering French: A New Approach for Advanced Students & Practitioners. David Atkinson. (Illus.). 1980. text ed. 26.00 (ISBN 0-08-023731-2); pap. text ed. 11.50 (ISBN 0-08-023730-4). Pergamon.

Hotel & Motel Careers. Ralph H. Peck. (Career Concise Guides Ser.). (Illus.). (gr. 6 up). 1977. PLB 6.45 s&l (ISBN 0-531-00374-4). Watts.

Hotel & Motel Management. Burstein. 200p. 1980. 29.50 (ISBN 0-8247-1002-9). Dekker.

Hotel & Motel Security Management. Walter J. Buzby & David Paine. LC 76-12555. 256p. 1976. 17.95 (ISBN 0-913708-24-0). Butterworths.

Hotel & Restaurant Business. 3rd ed. Donald E. Lundberg. LC 79-207. 1979. text ed. 16.95 (ISBN 0-8436-2142-7); pap. text ed. 14.95 (ISBN 0-8436-2175-3). CBI Pub.

Hotel & Restaurants in Britain, 1978-79. LC 52-21171. 1979. 7.50x o.p. (ISBN 0-85630-601-0). Intl Pubns Serv.

Hotel Destiny. Elizabeth Zachary. (Grand Hotel Ser.: No. 1). Orig. Title: Adlon, Berlin. (Orig.). 1981. pap. 2.75 (ISBN 0-515-06046-1). Jove Pubns.

Hotel, Hostel & Hospital Housekeeping. 3rd ed. Joan C. Branson & Margaret Lennox. (Illus.). 1976. pap. 12.95x (ISBN 0-7131-1974-8). Intl Ideas.

Hotel Information Systems: A Contemporary Approach to Front Office Procedures. Michael L. Kasavana. LC 78-9310. 1978. text ed. 16.95 (ISBN 0-8436-2131-1). CBI Pub.

Hotel-Motel (Architecture) G. Aloi. (Illus.). 1970. 40.00 (ISBN 0-685-12023-6). Heinman.

Hotel-Motel Marketing. David Hertzson. LC 76-142509. 1971. text ed. 14.50 (ISBN 0-672-96083-4); tchr's manual 5.90 (ISBN 0-672-96085-0); wkbk. 6.95 (ISBN 0-672-96084-2). Bobbs.

Hotel Nirvana: Selected Poems. Harold Norse. LC 73-93942. (Pocket Poets Ser.: No. 32). (Orig.). 1974. pap. 2.00 o.p. (ISBN 0-87286-078-7). City Lights.

Hotel Reception. 3rd ed. Paul B. White & Helen Beckley. (Illus.). 1978. pap. 12.95x (ISBN 0-7131-0191-1). Intl Ideas.

Hotel Security Management. Harvey Burstein. LC 74-14039. 138p. 1975. text ed. 22.95 (ISBN 0-275-09820-6). Praeger.

Hotels in England. Automobile Association - British Tourist Authority. 1979. pap. 8.95 (ISBN 0-686-24020-0, Pub. by B T a). Merrimack Bk Serv.

Hotels, Motels & Condominiums: Design, Planning & Maintenance. Fred Lawson. (Illus.). 1976. 49.95 (ISBN 0-8436-2109-5). CBI Pub.

Hothouse World. Fred MacIsaac. (YA) 1971. 5.95 (ISBN 0-685-23398-7, Avalon). Bouregy.

Hotline: The Crisis Intervention Directory. James L. Greenstone & Sharon Leviton. 350p. 1981. lib. bdg. 45.00 (ISBN 0-87196-373-6). Facts on File.

Hotshot. Alfred Slote. (Triumph Books). (Illus.). (gr. 4 up). 1977. PLB 6.90 s&l (ISBN 0-531-00330-2). Watts.

Hottentot Ossuary. James Tate. 1974. limited signed ed. o.p. 25.00 (ISBN 0-686-22817-0); pap. 2.95 (ISBN 0-686-22818-9). Temple Bar.

Houdini & Other Masters of Magic. Jan Fortman. LC 77-12638. (Myth, Magic & Superstition Ser.). (Illus.). (gr. 4-5). 1977. PLB 9.65 (ISBN 0-8172-1032-6). Raintree Pubs.

Houdini on Magic. Walter B. Gibson & Morris N. Young. LC 53-13518. 1953. lib. bdg. 11.50x (ISBN 0-88307-538-5). Gannon.

Houdini on Magic. Harry Houdini. Ed. by Walter Gibson & Morris Young. (Illus.). 1954. pap. 3.95 (ISBN 0-486-20384-0). Dover.

Houdini: The Man Who Walked Through Walls. William L. Gresham. LC 59-10470. (Illus.). 1959. 8.95 o.p. (ISBN 0-03-027260-2). HR&W.

Houdini: The Untold Story. Milbourne Christopher. LC 69-11829. (Illus.). 1969. 9.95 o.s.i. (ISBN 0-690-40431-X, TYC-T). T Y Crowell.

Houdini's Escapes & Magic. Walter B. Gibson. LC 75-30523. (Funk & W Bk.). (Illus.). 656p. 1976. 12.50 o.s.i. (ISBN 0-308-10220-7, TYC-T); pap. 6.95 o.s.i. (ISBN 0-308-10235-5, TYC-T). T Y Crowell.

Houghton Books in Literature. Ed. by Kenneth S. Lynn. Incl. Designs for Reading, 4 bks. pap. 4.80 ea.; tchr's guide 4.80 (ISBN 0-395-11195-1); Plays (ISBN 0-395-02790-X); Poems (ISBN 0-395-02786-1); Short Stories (ISBN 0-395-02780-2); Nonfiction Prose (ISBN 0-395-02788-8); Range of Literature, 4 bks. tchr's guide 4.80 (ISBN 0-685-59075-5); Drama. pap. 6.48 (ISBN 0-395-02782-9); Poetry. pap. 4.80 (ISBN 0-395-02784-5); Fiction. pap. 5.60 (ISBN 0-395-02792-6); Nonfiction Prose. pap. 5.60 (ISBN 0-395-02794-2); Level 3, 4 bks. tchr's guide 4.80 (ISBN 0-395-13709-8); Five Comedies. pap. 6.96 (ISBN 0-395-12049-7); Tunnel & the Light: Readings in Modern Fiction. pap. 7.52 (ISBN 0-395-13452-8); Twentieth Century Poetry. pap. 6.48 (ISBN 0-395-12357-7); Scene Seventy: Recent Non Fiction. pap. 7.52 (ISBN 0-395-12505-7). HM.

Houn' Dog. Mary Calhoun. (Illus.). (gr. k-3). 1959. 6.25 (ISBN 0-688-21406-1). Morrow.

Hound & Bear. Dick Gackenbach. LC 76-3525. (Illus.). 32p. (ps-3). 1976. 6.95 (ISBN 0-395-28796-0, Clarion). HM.

Hound-Dog Man. Fred Gipson. LC 49-7116. 1949. PLB 9.89 o.s.i. (ISBN 0-06-011540-8, HarpT); lib. bdg. 9.89 (ISBN 0-06-011541-6). Har-Row.

Hound-Dog Man. Fred Gipson. LC 80-10995. viii, 247p. 1980. pap. 4.95 (ISBN 0-8032-7005-4, BB 748, Bison). U of Nebr Pr.

Hound Finds a Friend. Walt Disney Productions. (Sturdy Shape Bks). 14p. (ps). 1981. 2.95 (ISBN 0-307-12264-6, Golden Pr). Western Pub.

Hound of Conscience: A History of the No-Conscription Fellowship, 1914-1919. Thomas C. Kennedy. 304p. 1981. text ed. 22.00x (ISBN 0-938626-01-9). U of Mo Pr.

Hound of the Baskervilles. Arthur Conan Doyle. (Classics Ser). (gr. 8 up). pap. 1.25 (ISBN 0-8049-0062-0, CL-62). Airmont.

Hound of the Baskervilles. Arthur Conan Doyle. (gr. 10 up). pap. 1.95 (ISBN 0-425-04421-1, Medallion). Berkley Pub.

Hound of the Baskervilles. Arthur Conan Doyle. (gr. 7-12). 1972. pap. 1.50 o.p. (ISBN 0-590-01355-6, Schol Pap). Schol Bk Serv.

Hound of the Baskervilles. Arthur C. Doyle. lib. bdg. 13.95x (ISBN 0-89966-229-3). Buccaneer Bks.

Hound of the Baskervilles. Doyle, Arthur Conan, Sir. LC 76-27103. 1977. 7.95 o.p. (ISBN 0-385-12282-9). Doubleday.

Hound of the Baskervilles: Student Activity Book. Marcia Sohl & Gerald Dackerman. (Now Age Illustrated Ser.). (gr. 4-12). 1976. 0.95 (ISBN 0-88301-288-X). Pendulum Pr.

Hounds & Jackals. Barbara Wood. LC 77-12888. (Romantic Suspense Ser.). 1978. 7.95 o.p. (ISBN 0-385-12972-6). Doubleday.

Hounds & Jackals. Barbara Wood. 1979. pap. 1.95 (ISBN 0-380-48538-9, 48538). Avon.

Hounds for a Pack. Elie De Vezins. Tr. by Lionel R. Woolner. (Illus.). 7.00 (ISBN 0-85131-210-1, Dist. by Sporting Book Center). J A Allen.

Hounds of Tinaldos: The Early Long. Frank B. Long. 1978. pap. 1.75 o.s.i. (ISBN 0-515-04655-8). Jove Pubns.

Hour of Our Death. Philippe Aries. LC 79-2227. (Illus.). 800p. 1981. 20.00 (ISBN 0-394-41074-2). Knopf.

Hour of Redemption. F. B. Johnson. 1978. pap. 2.50 (ISBN 0-532-25000-1). Manor Bks.

Hour of the Assassins. Andrew Kaplan. (Orig.). 1980. pap. 2.75 o.s.i. (ISBN 0-440-13530-3). Dell.

Hour of the Clown. Amos Aricha. (Orig.). 1981. pap. 2.95 (ISBN 0-451-09717-3, E9717, Sig). NAL.

Hour of the Wolf. Robert Charles. 192p. (Orig.). 1975. pap. 1.25 o.p. (ISBN 0-523-00638-1). Pinnacle Bks.

Hour Power: How to Have More Time for Work & Play. John W. Lee & Milton Pierce. LC 80-70146. 260p. 1981. 11.95 (ISBN 0-87094-186-0). Dow Jones-Irwin.

Hourglass Man. Carl Tiktin. 1978. pap. 1.75 o.p. (ISBN 0-451-08083-1, E8083, Sig). NAL.

Hours of Light. Janet Tanner. 518p. 1981. 13.95. St Martin.

Hours of Solitude: A Collection of Original Poems by Charlotte Dacre, Better Known by the Name Rosa Matilda, 2 vols. in 1. Charlotte Dacre. Ed. by Donald Reiman. LC 75-31190. (Romantic Context Ser.: Poetry 1789-1830: Vol. 42). 1979. Repr. of 1805 ed. lib. bdg. 47.00 (ISBN 0-8240-2141-X). Garland Pub.

Hours with Art & Artists. G. W. Sheldon. Ed. by H. Barbara Weinberg. LC 75-28873. (Art Experience in Late 19th Century America Ser.: Vol. 9). (Illus.). 1976. Repr. of 1882 ed. lib. bdg. 58.00 (ISBN 0-8240-2233-5). Garland Pub.

House & Garden's Book of Remodeling. Ed. by House & Garden Editors. (Illus.). 1979. 35.00 o.p. (ISBN 0-670-37974-3, Studio). Viking Pr.

House at Luxor. Florence Stevenson. pap. 1.25 (ISBN 0-451-07156-5, Y7156, Sig). NAL.

House at Stink Alley. F. N. Monjo. (gr. k-6). 1980. pap. 1.25 (ISBN 0-440-43376-2, YB). Dell.

House at Sunset. Norah Lofts. 1978. pap. 1.95 o.p. (ISBN 0-449-23676-5, Crest). Fawcett.

House at Twelve Rose Street. Mimi Brodsky. (gr. 4-6). 1969. pap. 0.95 (ISBN 0-671-29717-1). PB.

House Beautiful: Essays on Beds & Tables, Stools & Candlesticks. Clarence Cook. LC 80-10704. (Illus.). 336p. 1980. Repr. of 1878 ed. 30.00 (Dist. by Caroline House). North River.

House, Bridge, Fountain, Gate. Maxine Kumin. LC 75-1353. 1975. pap. 3.50 o.p. (ISBN 0-670-00592-4). Penguin.

House Builders Reference Book. Ed. by M. J. V. Powell. (Illus.). 1979. text ed. 84.95 (ISBN 0-408-00337-5). Butterworths.

House by Exmoor. Caroline Stafford. 1977. pap. 1.50 o.p. (ISBN 0-449-23058-9, Crest). Fawcett.

House by the Church-Yard. Joseph S. Le Fanu. (Nineteenth Century Fiction Ser.: Ireland: Vol. 60). 952p. 1979. lib. bdg. 46.00 (ISBN 0-8240-3509-7). Garland Pub.

House Church Evolving. Ed. by Arthur L. Foster. LC 76-4198. (Studies in Ministry & Parish Life). 126p. 1976. 12.95x (ISBN 0-913552-04-6); pap. 5.50x (ISBN 0-913552-05-4). Exploration Pr.

House Construction & Purchase: A Guide to Buying, Building & Living in Your Own House. W. Eric Kelsey. (Illus.). 1973. 9.95 o.p. (ISBN 0-7153-5735-2). David & Charles.

House for All Peoples: Ethnic Politics in Chicago, 1890-1936. John M. Allswang. LC 76-119810. (Illus.). 264p. 1971. 14.00x (ISBN 0-8131-1226-5). U Pr of Ky.

House for Little Red. new ed. Margaret Hillert. LC 75-85953. (Just Beginning-To-Read Ser). (Illus.). (ps). 1970. 2.50 o.p. (ISBN 0-695-80082-5); PLB 3.39 o.p. (ISBN 0-695-40082-7). Follett.

House Form & Culture. Amos Rapoport. LC 69-14550. (Geography Ser). 1969. pap. 6.95 ref. ed. (ISBN 0-13-395673-3). P-H.

House in Block E4, Block F3, the Roman Baths, Discoveries in the Temple of Artemis-Manaia, Arms & Armor, New & Revised Material from the Temple of Azzanathkona. Frank E. Brown. (Illus.). 1936. pap. 47.50x (ISBN 0-686-52157-9). Elliots Bks.
House in Half Moon Street, & Other Stories. Hector Bolitho. LC 79-53450. (Short Story Index in Reprint Ser.). Date not set. Repr. of 1936 ed. 23.75x (ISBN 0-8486-5005-0). Core Collection. Postponed.
House in Paris. Elizabeth Bowen. 1979. pap. 2.50 (ISBN 0-380-44602-2, 44602). Avon.
House in the City. W. J. Reader. 1979. 30.00 (ISBN 0-7134-1647-5, Pub. by Batsford England). David & Charles.
House in the Hills & Other Short Stories. Sujatha B. Subramanian. (Indian Short Stories Ser.). 123p. 1974. 6.85 (ISBN 0-88253-464-5). Ind-US Inc.
House in the Waves. James Hamilton-Paterson. LC 76-103043. (gr. 8 up). 1970. 9.95 (ISBN 0-87599-171-8). S G Phillips.
House in the Woods. Leslie Lance. 1980. pap. 1.95 (ISBN 0-441-34382-1). Ace Bks.
House Mottoes & Inscriptions. Sophia F. Caulfield. LC 68-21758. 1968. Repr. of 1908 ed. 15.00 (ISBN 0-8103-3322-8). Gale.
House Names Around the World. Joyce C. Miles. LC 72-12695. 135p. 1973. 14.00 (ISBN 0-8103-2009-6). Gale.
House Next Door. Anne R. Siddons. 1980. pap. 2.50 (ISBN 0-345-29330-4). Ballantine.
House of a Thousand Lanterns. Victoria Holt. 384p. 1978. pap. 2.25 (ISBN 0-449-23685-4, Crest). Fawcett.
House of Bisque & Sawdust. Connie Kidwell. (Orig.). 1980. pap. 1.95 (ISBN 0-532-23205-4). Manor Bks.
House of Bondage. Alfred Bercovici. 1978. pap. 1.75 o.p. (ISBN 0-445-04170-6). Popular Lib.
House of Breath. William Goyen. LC 74-23987. 1975. 8.95 (ISBN 0-394-49699-X); pap. 4.95 (ISBN 0-394-73053-4). Random.
House of Cards. Peter Cave. (Avengers Ser.). 1978. pap. 1.50 o.p. (ISBN 0-425-03993-5, Medallion). Berkley Pub.
House of Cards: Legalization & Control of Casino Gambling. Skolnick. (Orig.). 1981. pap. text ed. 7.95 (ISBN 0-316-79708-1). Little.
House of Christina. Ben Haas. 1981. pap. 2.95 (ISBN 0-440-13793-4). Dell.
House of Cobwebs. George Gissing. 300p. 1980. Repr. of 1914 ed. lib. bdg. 25.00 (ISBN 0-89760-315-X). Telegraph Bks.
House of Commons at Work. 9th ed. Eric Taylor. 1979. text ed. 18.25x (ISBN 0-333-23319-0). Humanities.
House of Commons in the Twentieth Century. Ed. by S. A. Walkland. 1979. 59.00x (ISBN 0-19-827193-X). Oxford U Pr.
House of Desdemona or the Laurels & Limitations of Historical Fiction. Lion Feuchtwanger. Tr. by Harold A. Basilius. LC 63-8063. (Waynebooks Ser: No. 12). (Orig.). 1963. pap. 3.95x o.p. (ISBN 0-8143-1218-7). Wayne St U Pr.
House of Dies Drear. Virginia Hamilton. LC 8-23059. (Illus.). (gr. 5 up). 1968. 8.95 (ISBN 0-02-742500-2). Macmillan.
House of God. Samuel Shem. 1980. pap. 2.95 (ISBN 0-440-13368-8). Dell.
House of Hanover England in the Eighteenth Century. Leon Garfield. LC 75-42422. (Illus.). (gr. 6 up). 1976. 8.95 (ISBN 0-395-28904-1, Clarion). HM.
House of Horror: The Story of Hammer Films. Ed. by A. Wyle Adkinson & N. Fry. LC 74-76299. 1974. 6.95 (ISBN 0-89388-163-5). Okpaku Communications.
House of Ideas. Bill Baker. LC 73-11734. (Illus.). 288p. 1974. 19.95 (ISBN 0-02-506280-8, 50628). Macmillan.
House of Imposters. Willo D. Roberts. (Orig.). 1977. pap. 1.50 o.p. (ISBN 0-445-04039-4). Popular Lib.
House of Incest. Anais Nin. LC 61-65487. 72p. 1958. pap. 3.95 (ISBN 0-8040-0148-0, 31). Swallow.
House of Laughs. Lisa Eisenberg. LC 79-52656. (Laura Brewster Mysteries Ser.). (Illus.). 64p. (gr. 4 up). 1980. PLB 7.95 (ISBN 0-516-02208-3). Childrens.
House of Lim: Study of a Chinese Farm Family. Wolfe. 1960. pap. text ed. 6.95 (ISBN 0-13-394973-7). P-H.
House of Lords & the Labour Government, 1964-1970. Janet P. Morgan. (Illus.). 270p. 1975. text ed. 37.50x (ISBN 0-19-827191-3). Oxford U Pr.
House of Many Shadows. Barbara Michaels. 1978. pap. 1.75 o.p. (ISBN 0-449-23720-6, Crest). Fawcett.
House of Medici: Its Rise & Fall. Christopher Hibbert. LC 74-15763. (Illus.). 352p. 1975. 12.50 o.p. (ISBN 0-688-00339-7); pap. 6.95 (ISBN 0-688-05339-4). Morrow.
House of Mirth. Edith Wharton. 1976. lib. rep. ed. 17.50x (ISBN 0-684-14658-4, ScribT); pap. 4.95 (ISBN 0-684-71928-2, SL 41, ScribT). Scribner.
House of Mirth. Edith Wharton. Ed. by R. W. B. Lewis. LC 77-77299. (Gotham Library). 335p. 1977. 15.00x (ISBN 0-8147-4976-3); pap. 6.00x (ISBN 0-8147-4977-1). NYU Pr.
House of Mirth. Edith Wharton. 1981. pap. 2.95 (ISBN 0-425-04611-7). Berkley Pub.
House of Mirth: The Play of the Novel. Ed. by Glenn Loney. LC 78-75192. 220p. 1981. 13.50 (ISBN 0-8386-2416-2). Fairleigh Dickinsonn.
House of Scorpions. Jory Sherman. (Chill Ser.: No. 6). 192p. 1980. pap. 1.95 (ISBN 0-523-40699-1). Pinnacle Bks.
House of Silence. Dorothy Daniels. (Orig.). 1980. pap. 1.75 (ISBN 0-451-09423-9, E9423, Sig). NAL.
House of Slammers: A Novel. Nathan Heard. 256p. 1981. 9.95 (ISBN 0-686-68675-6). Macmillan.
House of Special Purpose: An Intimate Portrait of the Last Days of the Russian Imperial Family. J. C. Trewin. LC 74-30457. 148p. 1981. pap. 8.95 (ISBN 0-8128-6119-1). Stein & Day.
House of the Burgesses. M. R. Burgess. LC 80-10759. 64p. 1981. lib. bdg. 8.95x (ISBN 0-89370-801-1); pap. 2.95x (ISBN 0-89370-901-8). Borgo Pr.
House of the Evening Star. Louise Bergstrom. 192p. (YA) 1976. 5.95 (ISBN 0-685-66574-7, Avalon). Bouregy.
House of the Prophet. Louis Auchincloss. (Large Print Bks.). 1980. lib. bdg. 14.95 (ISBN 0-8161-3133-3). G K Hall.
House of the Seven Gables. Nathaniel Hawthorne. Ed. by Seymour L. Gross. (Critical Editions). (Annotated). (gr. 9-12). 1967. pap. text ed. 4.95x (ISBN 0-393-09705-6, 9705, NortonC). Norton.
House of the Seven Gables. Nathaniel Hawthorne. (Literature Ser). (gr. 10-12). 1970. pap. text ed. 3.50 (ISBN 0-87720-728-3). AMSCO Sch.
House of the Seven Gables. Nathaniel Hawthorne. (Riverside Bookshelf Ser). (Illus.). (gr. 9 up). 1952. 7.95 (ISBN 0-395-07072-4). HM.
House of the Seven Gables: Student Activity Book. Marcia Sohl & Gerald Dackerman. (Now Age Illustrated Ser.). (Illus.). (gr. 4-12). 1976. 0.95 (ISBN 0-88301-289-8). Pendulum Pr.
House of the Seven Gabls. Nathaniel Hawthorne. pap. 2.25 (ISBN 0-671-41373-2). WSP.
House of the Seven Gabls. Nathaniel Hawthorne. 1972. pap. 4.95 (ISBN 0-460-01176-6, Evman). Dutton.
House of the Seven Gabls. rev. ed. Nathaniel Hawthorne. Ed. by Robert J. Dixson. (American Classics Ser.: Bk. 1). 113p. (gr. 9 up). 1973. pap. 2.75 (ISBN 0-88345-197-2, 18120); cassettes 40.00 (ISBN 0-685-38988-X); tapes 40.00 (ISBN 0-685-38989-8). Regents Pub.
House of the Seven Gabls. Nathaniel Hawthorne. pap. 1.50. Bantam.
House of the Twelve Caesars. large type ed. Phyllis Hastings. pap. 1.25 o.p. (ISBN 0-425-03092-X). Berkley Pub.
House of Thirty Cats. Mary Calhoun. (gr. 4-6). 1980. pap. 1.95 (ISBN 0-671-42064-X). Archway.
House of Time Travel. Sandra Turner. Date not set. 6.95 (ISBN 0-533-04100-7). Vantage.
House of Tudor. Alison Plowden. LC 76-6936. 272p. 1981. pap. 8.95 (ISBN 0-8128-6123-X). Stein & Day.
House of Zeor. Jacqueline Lichtenberg. LC 80-83565. 224p. 1981. pap. 2.25 (ISBN 0-87216-801-8). Playboy Pbks.
House on Charlton Street. Dola De Jong. LC 62-9644. (Illus.). (gr. 3-7). 1962. pap. 0.95 o.p. (ISBN 0-684-12802-0, SBF 20, ScribT). Scribner.
House on E Street. Karen Moore. 1979. pap. 1.75 (ISBN 0-505-51446-X). Tower Bks.
House on Hibiscus Hill. Juanita Tyree Osborne. (YA) 1977. 4.95 o.p. (ISBN 0-685-74266-0, Avalon). Bouregy.
House on Lime Street. W. E. D. Ross. 192p. (YA) 1976. 5.95 (ISBN 0-685-64245-3, Avalon). Bouregy.
House on Nauset Marsh. Wyman Richardson. (Illus.). 1980. pap. 5.95 (ISBN 0-85699-046-9). Chatham Pr.
House on Pendleton Block. Ann Waldron. (Illus.). 160p. (gr. 4-7). 1975. PLB 6.95 (ISBN 0-8038-3033-5). Hastings.
House on Prague Street. Hana Demetz. 1980. lib. bdg. 12.95 (ISBN 0-8161-3143-0, Large Print Bks). G K Hall.
House on the Borderland. W. H. Hodgson. 1976. lib. bdg. 12.95x (ISBN 0-89968-178-6). Lightyear.
House on the Hill. Jonathan Black. 1977. pap. 1.95 o.p. (ISBN 0-425-03648-0, Medallion). Berkley Pub.
House Plans Designed for Southern Families. W. W. Chromaster. LC 72-96463. (Illus.). 1973. pap. 2.95 o.p. (ISBN 0-8487-0242-5). Oxmoor Hse.
House Plant Identifier. Helmut Bechtel. LC 72-95203. (Identifier Bks.). (Illus.). 256p. (gr. 6 up). 1973. 6.95 (ISBN 0-8069-3056-X); PLB 6.69 (ISBN 0-8069-3057-8). Sterling.
House Plants for the Purple Thumb. Maggie Baylis. LC 72-94894. (Illus.). 192p. (Orig.). 1973. 4.95 (ISBN 0-912238-33-X); pap. 4.95 (ISBN 0-912238-32-1). One Hund One Prods.
House Plants: How to Grow. 3rd ed. Sunset Editors. LC 76-7660. (Illus.). 80p. 1976. pap. 3.95 (ISBN 0-376-03335-5, Sunset Bks). Sunset-Lane.
House Possessed. Charity Blackstock. 222p. 1976. Repr. of 1962 ed. lib. bdg. 12.95x (ISBN 0-89244-077-5). Queens Hse.
House That Grew. Jean Strathdee. (Illus.). 32p. (ps-3). 1980. 8.95 (ISBN 0-19-558041-9). Oxford U Pr.
House That Jack Built. Illus. by Caldecott. (Peter Possum Paperbacks Ser). 1967. pap. 0.95 o.p. (ISBN 0-531-05100-5). Watts.
House That Jack Built. George Farwell. (Australian Theatre Workshop Ser.). 1970. pap. text ed. 4.25x o.p. (ISBN 0-686-65319-X). Heinemann Ed.
House That Nature Built. Sigmund Kalina. LC 72-177323. (Illus.). 64p. (gr. 2-7). 1972. PLB 6.48 o.p. (ISBN 0-688-41353-6); PLB 6.48 (ISBN 0-688-51353-0). Lothrop.
House That Sailed Away. Pat Hutchins. LC 74-9823. (Illus.). 192p. (gr. 2-6). 1975. PLB 7.92 (ISBN 0-688-84013-2). Greenwillow.
House That Stood Still. A. E. Van Vogt. 1980. pap. write for info. (ISBN 0-671-80546-0). PB.
House That Wouldn't Go Away. Paul Gallico. LC 79-53599. 1980. 8.95 (ISBN 0-440-03496-5); PLB 8.44 (ISBN 0-440-03497-3). Delacorte.
House, the City & the Judge: The Growth of Moral Awareness in the Oresteia. Richard Kuhns. LC 61-18061. 1962. 20.00x (ISBN 0-672-51317-X). Irvington.
House-Tree-Person (H-T-P) Clinical Research Manual. Emanuel F. Hammer. 47p. (Orig.). 1964. pap. 6.50x (ISBN 0-87424-016-6). Western Psych.
House Warming. Bob Cummings. pap. 7.95 (ISBN 0-930096-08-8). G Gannett.
House Wiring. 4th ed. Roland E. Palmguist. LC 78-50216. (Illus.). 1978. 8.95 (ISBN 0-672-23315-0). Audel.
House Wiring Simplified. Floyd M. Mix. LC 80-2122. (Illus.). 384p. 1981. 8.00 (ISBN 0-87006-309-X). Goodheart.
House Within Me: An Anthology of Poems by Children from Little River School. Ed. by Lisa Creed. 64p. (Orig.). (ps). 1981. pap. 4.00 (ISBN 0-932112-10-2). Carolina Wren.
House Without a Christmas Tree. Gail Rock. 96p. (gr. 4-6). 1980. pap. 1.75 (Skylark). Bantam.
Houseboat Girl. Lois Lenski. (Regional Stories Ser.). (Illus.). (gr. 4-6). 1957. 7.95 o.p. (ISBN 0-397-30366-1). Lippincott.
Houseboat Mystery. Gertrude C. Warner. LC 67-26521. (Boxcar Children Mysteries-Pilot Bk.). (Illus.). 128p. (gr. 3-7). 1967. 6.95g (ISBN 0-8075-3412-9). A Whitman.
Housebreak & Train Your Dog. Arthur Liebers. (Orig.). 1958. pap. 2.00 (ISBN 0-87666-318-8, DS1020). TFH Pubns.
Housebuilding for Children. Les Walker. LC 76-47220. (Illus.). 176p. 1977. 10.95 (ISBN 0-87951-059-5). Overlook Pr.
Household & Family in Past Time. Ed. by P. Laslett & R. Wall. LC 77-190420. 608p. 1972. 49.95 (ISBN 0-521-08473-3); pap. 15.95x (ISBN 0-521-09901-3). Cambridge U Pr.
Household & Kin: Families in Flux. Ed. by Florence Howe & John A. Rothermich. (Women's Lives - Women's Work Ser.). 208p. (Orig.). Date not set. pap. text ed. 4.71 (ISBN 0-07-020427-6). Webster-McGraw.
Household & Kin: Families in Flux. Amy Swerdlow et al. (Women's Lives - Women's Work Ser.). (Illus.). 192p. (Orig.). (gr. 11-12). 1981. 14.95 (ISBN 0-912670-91-6); pap. 5.95 (ISBN 0-912670-68-1). Feminist Pr.
Household Book of Animal Medicine. Richard Vargoshe & Peter Steinberg. 208p. 1980. 12.95 (ISBN 0-13-395871-X, Spec); pap. 6.95 (ISBN 0-13-395863-9). P-H.
Household Book of Hints & Tips. Ed. by Diane Raintree. 272p. 1980. pap. 2.25 (ISBN 0-345-28927-7). Ballantine.
Household Dimension of the Family in India. A. M. Shah. LC 71-126757. 1974. 20.00x (ISBN 0-520-01790-0). U of Cal Pr.
Household Energy & the Poor in the Third World: Domestic Energy Consumption for Low-Income Groups in Development Areas. Elizabeth Cecelski et al. LC 79-4863. (Resources for the Future Ser.). 1979. 6.75x (ISBN 0-8018-2283-1). Johns Hopkins.
Household Energy Use & Conservation: How to Prepare an Energy Budget. John Luetzelschwab. 1980. 19.95x (ISBN 0-88229-476-8); pap. 11.95 (ISBN 0-88229-733-3). Nelson-Hall.
Household Environment & Chronic Illness: Guidelines for Constructing & Maintaining a Less Polluted Residence. Guy O. Pfeiffer & Casimir M. Nikel. (Illus.). 208p. 1980. text ed. 14.75 (ISBN 0-398-03961-5). C C Thomas.
Household Equipment. 8th ed. Louise J. Peet et al. LC 78-11749. 1979. text ed. 20.95 (ISBN 0-471-02694-8); tchrs. manual avail. (ISBN 0-471-04876-3). Wiley.
Household Equipment: Selection & Management. Patricia P. Wilson. LC 75-31023. (Illus.). 384p. 1976. text ed. 18.95 (ISBN 0-395-20596-4); resource manual 5.00 (ISBN 0-395-20597-2). HM.
Household Furniture & Bedding. Fairchild Market Research Division. (Fact Files Ser). 1978. pap. 10.00 (ISBN 0-87005-222-5). Fairchild.
Household Furniture & Bedding. Fairchild Market Research Division. (Fact File Ser.). (Illus.). 60p. 1980. pap. 10.00 (ISBN 0-87005-346-9). Fairchild.
Household Pests: A Guide to the Identification & Control of Insect, Rodent Damp & Fungoid Problems in the Home. Peter Bateman. (Illus.). 1979. 14.95 (ISBN 0-7137-0915-4, Pub by Blandford Pr England). Sterling.
Household Pollutant Guide. Center for Science in the Public Interest. Ed. by Al Fritsch. LC 77-76269. 1978. pap. 3.50 (ISBN 0-385-12494-5, Anch). Doubleday.
Household Saints. Francine Prose. 224p. 1981. 10.95 (ISBN 0-312-39341-5). St Martin.
Household Songs: Eighteen Forty-Four to Eighteen Sixty-Four. Stephen Foster. LC 76-169647. (Earlier American Music Ser.: No. 12). (Illus.). 1973. Repr. of 1862 ed. lib. bdg. 19.50 (ISBN 0-306-77312-0). Da Capo.
Householders Philosophie - the True Economia - of Housekeeping - Annexed a Dairie Booke for Huswives. Torquato Tasso. Tr. by T. Kyd. LC 74-28888. (English Experience Ser.: No. 765). 1975. Repr. of 1588 ed. 8.00 (ISBN 90-221-0765-5). Walter J Johnson.
Households of God. David Parry. (Cistercian Studies Ser.: No. 39). (Orig.). 1980. pap. 7.95 (ISBN 0-87907-939-8). Cistercian Pubns.
Housekeeping. Marilynne Robinson. 1981. 10.95 (ISBN 0-374-17313-3). FS&G.
Housekeeping Among Malay Peasants. 2nd ed. Rosemary Firth. (Monographs on Social Anthropology: No. 7). 1966. text ed. 18.75x (ISBN 0-485-19507-0, Athlone Pr). Humanities.
Housekeeping for Public Buildings. (Special Reports Ser: No. 32). 25p. 1968. 3.00 o.p. (ISBN 0-917084-18-7). Am Public Works.
Houses. Irving Adler & Ruth Adler. LC 64-20708. (Reason Why Ser). (Illus.). (gr. 3-6). 1965. PLB 7.89 (ISBN 0-381-99967-X, A35060, JD-J). John Day.
Houses. Joel Oppenheimer. 1981. 2.00 (ISBN 0-686-69560-7). White Pine.
Houses. R. J. Unstead. (Junior Reference Ser.). (Illus.). 96p. (gr. 7 up). 7.95 (ISBN 0-7136-1301-7). Dufour.
Houses in the Landscape: A Regional Study of Vernacular Building Styles in England & Wales. John Penoyre & Jane Penoyre. (Illus.). 1978. 18.95 (ISBN 0-571-11055-X, Pub. by Faber & Faber). Merrimack Bk Serv.
Houses of Gold. John C. Campbell. (Illus.). 228p. (Orig.). 1980. pap. 15.00 (ISBN 0-8310-7121-4). Howell North.
Houses of Ireland: Domestic Architecture from the Medieval Castle to the Edwardian Villa. Brian De Breffney & Rosemary Folliott. (Illus.). 240p. 1981. 19.95 (ISBN 0-500-24091-4). Thames Hudson.
Houses of Mexico: Origins & Traditions. Verna C. Shipway & Warren Shipway. 16.95 (ISBN 0-8038-0104-1). Architectural.
Houses of Parliament. James Pope-Hennessy. (Folio Miniature Ser.). 1975. 4.95 (ISBN 0-7181-1302-0, Pub. by Michael Joseph). Merrimack Bk Serv.
Houses of Parliament. Ed. by Michael Port. LC 76-3374. (Studies in British Art Ser.). 1976. 50.00x (ISBN 0-300-02022-8). Yale U Pr.
Houses of Sin, Repr. Of 1897 Ed. Vincent O'Sullivan. Ed. by Ian Fletcher & John Stokes. Bd. with Poems. Vincent Sullivan. LC 76-25930. (Decadent Consciousness Ser.: Vol. 33). 1977. lib. bdg. 38.00 (ISBN 0-8240-2783-3). Garland Pub.
Houses That James Built and Other Literary Studies. R. W. Stallman. LC 77-371844. 256p. 1977. 12.00x (ISBN 0-8214-0362-1); pap. 4.50x (ISBN 0-8214-0363-X). Ohio U Pr.
Housesitter. Lee Karr. 1980. pap. 2.25 (ISBN 0-686-69262-4, 76364). Avon.
Housewife. Ruth Jernick. 1981. 10.95 (ISBN 0-698-11081-1). Coward.

Housewife Hustlers. Linda DuBreiul. (Orig.). 1976. pap. 1.50 o.p. (ISBN 0-685-64009-4, LB334DK, Leisure Bks). Nordon Pubns.

Housewife's Guide to Women's Liberation. Elizabeth Anticaglia. LC 72-85889. 1972. 12.95 (ISBN 0-911012-69-9). Nelson-Hall.

Housewiring Simplified. Floyd M. Mix. LC 80-21122. (Illus.). 176p. 1981. text ed. 8.00 (ISBN 0-87006-309-X). Goodheart.

Housework. Joan Larkin. (Illus.). 1976. pap. 3.50 (ISBN 0-918314-02-X). Out & Out.

Housing. Ed. by S. Groak & O. H. Koenigsberger. 140p. 1980. pap. 32.00 (ISBN 0-08-026082-9). Pergamon.

Housing. Carol B. Meeks. (Illus.). 1980. text ed. 15.95 (ISBN 0-13-394981-8). P-H.

Housing Allowances for the Poor: A Social Experiment. M. G. Trend. LC 78-52057. (Westview Replica Edition Ser.). 1978. lib. bdg. 28.50 o.p. (ISBN 0-89158-057-3). Westview.

Housing & Economics: The American Dilemma. Ed. by Michael Stegman. 1971. 19.95x o.p. (ISBN 0-262-19081-8). MIT Pr.

Housing & Home Furnishing. University of Missouri - Home Economics Resource Unit. text ed. 2.75x spiral bdg. (ISBN 0-87543-025-2). Lucas.

Housing & Public Policy: A Role for Mediating Structures. John Egan et al. 160p. 1981. 16.50 (ISBN 0-88410-827-9). Ballinger Pub.

Housing & Social Justice. Gill Burke. 240p. 1981. pap. text ed. 12.95x (ISBN 0-582-29514-9). Longman.

Housing & Social Policy. Chester Hartman. (Ser. in Social Policy). 176p. 1975. ref. ed. 10.95 (ISBN 0-13-394999-0). P-H.

Housing & Social Services for the Elderly: Social Policy Trends. Elizabeth D. Huttman. LC 75-44932. (Special Studies). 1977. text ed. 29.95 (ISBN 0-275-23830-X). Praeger.

Housing & the Spatial Structure of the City. R. M. Pritchard. LC 75-3859. (Cambridge Geographical Studies). (Illus.). 403p. 1976. 41.50 (ISBN 0-521-20882-3). Cambridge U Pr.

Housing & Urban Affairs: A Bibliographic Guide to the 1978 Documents Update. 1980. pap. write for info. (ISBN 0-667-00574-9). Microfilming Corp.

Housing & Urban Affairs: A Bibliographic Guide to the 1979 Documents Update. 1980. pap. write for info. (ISBN 0-667-00611-7). Microfilming Corp.

Housing & Urban Affairs, Nineteen Sixty-Five to Nineteen Seventy-Six: A Bibliographic Guide to the Microform Collection. Ed. by Doreen B. Tilton. 342p. 1978. 50.00 (ISBN 0-667-00519-6). Microfilming Corp.

Housing As Human Habitat: Proceedings. International Conference on Housing, Planning, Financing, Construction, 2-7 December, 1979, Miami Beach, Florida. Ed. by Oktay Ural. (Pergamon Policy Studies Ser.). 1200p. 1980. Vol. 1. 165.00 (ISBN 0-08-025592-2); Vol. 2. 125.00 (ISBN 0-08-025593-0). Pergamon.

Housing Careers. Sidney Schwartz. (Home Economics Careers Ser.). (gr. 10-12). 1977. 6.36 (ISBN 0-13-392811-X); pap. text ed. 5.12 (ISBN 0-13-392803-9). P-H.

Housing Cooperatives in Developing Countries: A Manual for Self-Help in Low Cost Housing Schemes. A. C. Lewin. 192p. 1981. 35.75 (ISBN 0-471-27820-3, Pub. by Wiley-Intrscience); pap. write for info. (ISBN 0-471-27819-X). Wiley.

Housing Decisions. Evelyn L. Lewis. LC 80-19068. 1980. text ed. 13.20 (ISBN 0-87006-302-2). Goodheart.

Housing, Family, & Society. Earl W. Morris & Mary Winter. LC 77-24772. 1978. text ed. 16.95x (ISBN 0-471-61570-6); tchrs. manual 4.00 (ISBN 0-471-03939-X). Wiley.

Housing: Federal Policies & Programs. John C. Weicher. 1980. pap. 6.25 (ISBN 0-8447-3378-4). Am Enterprise.

Housing Finance Agencies: A Comparison Between State Agencies & Hud. Nathan S. Betnun. LC 76-2899. 1976. text ed. 32.95 (ISBN 0-275-56660-9). Praeger.

Housing for New Types of Students. 1977. pap. 4.00 (ISBN 0-89192-231-8). Interbk Inc.

Housing for Special Groups: Proceedings. United Nations Economic Commission for Europe. 1977. pap. text ed. 34.00 (ISBN 0-08-021985-3). Pergamon.

Housing for the Aged. Edgar Rose. 1978. 24.95 (ISBN 0-566-00217-5, 02175-X, Pub. by Saxon Hse England). Lexington Bks.

Housing for the Elderly: Evaluation of the Effectiveness of Congregate Projects. Irene K. Maluzemoff et al. 1978. lib. bdg. 30.00 o.p. (ISBN 0-89158-303-3). Westview.

Housing for the Elderly: New Trends in Europe. Leon Goldenberg & Harry Weese. 1981. lib. bdg. 29.50 (ISBN 0-8240-7139-5). Garland Pub.

Housing Form & Public Policy in the United States. Ed. by Richard Plunz. LC 77-22686. 264p. 1980. 29.95 (ISBN 0-03-056839-0). Praeger.

Housing from the Existing Stock: Comparative, Economic Analyses of Owner-Occupants & Landlords. Larry Ozanne & Raymond J. Struyk. (Institute Paper). 196p. 1976. pap. 5.50 (ISBN 0-87766-168-5, 14900). Urban Inst.

Housing Improvement & Social Inequality. Paul N. Balchin. 1979. text ed. 31.25x (ISBN 0-566-00274-4, Pub. by Gower Pub Co England). Renouf.

Housing in America: Problems & Perspectives. 2nd ed. Daniel R. Mandelker & Roger Montgomery. 600p. pap. 19.50 (ISBN 0-672-83699-8). Bobbs.

Housing in Arid Lands Design & Planning. Gideon Golany. LC 80-41108. 257p. 1980. 104.95 (ISBN 0-470-27055-1). Halsted Pr.

Housing in Capitalist Societies. Cedric Pugh. 320p. 1980. lib. bdg. 44.00 (ISBN 0-566-00336-8, Pub. by Gower Pub Co England). Renouf.

Housing Investment in the Inner City: The Dynamics of Decline: a Study of Baltimore Maryland, 1968-1970. Michael Stegman. 320p. 1972. 18.00 (ISBN 0-262-19103-2). MIT Pr.

Housing Market Performance in the United States. Charles J. Stokes & Ernest M. Fisher. LC 74-11605. (Special Studies). (Illus.). 175p. 1976. text ed. 16.95 o.p. (ISBN 0-275-05720-8). Praeger.

Housing of Nations: Analysis & Policy in a Comparative Framework. L. S. Burns & L. Grebler. LC 76-43023. 1977. 29.95 (ISBN 0-470-98970-X). Halsted Pr.

Housing Policies for the Urban Poor. Raymond J. Struyk et al. 153p. 1978. pap. 7.50 (ISBN 0-87766-230-4, 23500). Urban Inst.

Housing Policy & the Housing System. Alan Murle et al. (Urban & Regional Studies). 1976. text ed. 25.00x o.p. (ISBN 0-04-350051-X); pap. text ed. 10.95x o.p. (ISBN 0-04-350053-6). Allen Unwin.

Housing Policy for the Eighties. Ed. by Dale Marshall & Roger Montgomery. 1979. pap. 5.00 (ISBN 0-918592-36-4). Policy Studies.

Housing Programs & Income Distribution in Canada. George Fallis. (Ontario Economic Council Research Studies). 184p. 1980. pap. 8.50x. U of Toronto Pr.

Housing Rehabilitation Handbook. Barry Evans. (Illus.). 1980. 52.50 (ISBN 0-85139-293-8, Pub. by Architectural Pr). Nichols Pub.

Housing Subsidies in the United States & England. Mandelker. 1973. 13.50 (ISBN 0-672-81871-X, Bobbs-Merrill Law). Michie.

Housing Taxation. Walter A. Morton. 1955. 20.00x (ISBN 0-299-01240-9). U of Wis Pr.

Housing the Family. Design Bulletins. 1974. 19.95 (ISBN 0-8436-0129-9). CBI Pub.

Housing: The Social & Economic Elements. Wallace F. Smith. LC 71-86372. (California Studies in Urbanization & Environmental Design). (Illus.). 1970. 18.50x (ISBN 0-520-01561-4). U of Cal Pr.

Housing Turnover & Housing Policy: Case Studies of Vacancy Chains in New York State. Gary Sands & Lewis L. Bower. LC 76-12619. (Special Studies). (Illus.). 1976. text ed. 23.95 (ISBN 0-275-56690-0). Praeger.

Housing Urban America. 2nd ed. Ed. by Jon Pynoos et al. LC 80-12108. 1980. text ed. 37.95 (ISBN 0-202-32010-3); pap. text ed. 15.95 (ISBN 0-202-32011-1). Aldine Pub.

Housing Vouchers for the Poor: Lessons from a National Experiment. Ed. by Raymond J. Stryk & Mark Bendick, Jr. 1981. 25.00 (ISBN 0-87766-280-0). Urban Inst.

Housman's Land of Lost Content: A Critical Study of "A Shropshire Lad". B. J. Leggett. LC 71-100407. 172p. 1970. 10.00x (ISBN 0-87049-106-7). U of Tenn Pr.

Houston. William Shelton & Ann Kennedy. LC 76-57516. 1978. pap. 2.95 o.p. (ISBN 0-385-11405-2, Dolp). Doubleday.

Houston: A Pictorial History. Ann Q. Wilson. Ed. by Donna R. Friedman. (Illus.). 205p. Date not set. pap. price not set (ISBN 0-89865-087-9). Donning Co.

Houston: City of Destiny. Ed. by Uinbook. 176p. 1980. 19.95 (ISBN 0-02-620900-4). Macmillan.

Houston Downtown Flood. R. G. Taylor-Winniford. 75p. 1981. 6.95 (ISBN 0-87881-098-6). Mojave Bks.

Houston Oilers. Jim Rothaus. (NFL Today Ser.). (gr. 3-12). 1980. PLB 6.45 (ISBN 0-87191-796-3); pap. 2.95 (ISBN 0-89812-248-1). Creative Ed.

Houston Symphony Orchestra 1913-1971. Hubert Roussel. (Illus.). 1972. 12.50 (ISBN 0-292-73000-4). U of Tex Pr.

Hovercraft & Hoverports. C. A. O'Flaherty & I. Cross. (Illus.). 1975. 16.00x o.p. (ISBN 0-8464-0490-7). Beekman Pubs.

Hovering Giant: U. S. Responses to Revolutionary Change in Latin America. Cole Blasier. LC 75-9130. (Pitt Latin American Ser.). (Illus.). 1976. 15.95 (ISBN 0-8229-3304-7); pap. 6.95x (ISBN 0-8229-5264-5). U of Pittsburgh Pr.

How. Boyd. 32p. 1980. 8.95 (ISBN 0-87705-176-3). Human Sci Pr.

How a Law Is Made: The Story of a Bill Against Air-Pollution. Leonard A. Stevens. LC 74-101934. (Illus.). (gr. 5-9). 1970. 7.95 (ISBN 0-690-40609-6, TYC-J). T Y Crowell.

How a Piglet Crashed the Christmas Party. Boris Zakhoder. LC 70-155750. (Illus.). (gr. k-3). 1971. PLB 7.92 o.p. (ISBN 0-688-51622-X). Lothrop.

How a Seed Grows. Helene J. Jordan. LC 60-11541. (Let's-Read-&-Find-Out Science Bk). (Illus.). (gr. k-3). 1960. PLB 7.89 (ISBN 0-690-40645-2, TYC-J). T Y Crowell.

How About a Career in Real Estate? Jack Gale. 34p. (Orig.). 1979. pap. 2.95 (ISBN 0-88462-374-2). Real Estate Ed Co.

How About Birdwatching. Val Singleton & Arthur Gilpin. (How About Paperback Ser.). (Illus.). 96p. 1980. pap. 3.95 (ISBN 0-8069-9078-3, Pub. by EP Publishing England). Sterling.

How About Keeping Fish. Val Singleton & Dick Mills. (How About Paperback Ser.). 96p. 1980. pap. 3.95 (ISBN 0-8069-9086-4, Pub. by EP Publishing England). Sterling.

How About Railway Modelling. John Craven & John Cockroft. (How About Paperback Ser.). 96p. 1980. pap. 3.95 (ISBN 0-8069-9092-9, Pub. by EP Publishing England). Sterling.

How Am I Supposed to Love Myself? Phoebe Cranor. LC 79-14229. 1979. pap. 3.50 (ISBN 0-87123-236-7, 210236). Bethany Fell.

How Americans Use Time: A Social-Psychological Analysis of Everyday Behavior. John Robinson. LC 76-58838. (Special Studies). 1977. text ed. 24.95 (ISBN 0-275-24200-5). Praeger.

How Animals Hunt. J. H. Prince. (Illus.). 1980. 8.95 (ISBN 0-525-66688-5). Elsevier-Nelson.

How Animals Move. J. H. Prince. (Illus.). 160p. (YA) 1981. 10.95 (ISBN 0-525-66712-1). Elsevier-Nelson.

How Animals Tell Time. Millicent E. Selsam. (Illus.). (gr. 5-9). 1967. PLB 7.92 (ISBN 0-688-31407-4). Morrow.

How Animals Work. K. Schmidt-Nielsen. LC 77-174262. (Illus.). 100p. 1972. 17.95 (ISBN 0-521-08417-2); pap. 5.75x (ISBN 0-521-09692-8). Cambridge U Pr.

How Animals Work for Us. rev. ed. Robin Wild & Jocelyn Wild. LC 73-157991. (Finding-Out Book). (Illus.). 64p. (gr. 2-4). 1974. PLB 6.95 (ISBN 0-8193-0707-6). Enslow Pubs.

How Any Woman Can Get Rich Fast in Real Estate. Margaret Crispen. 1978. 9.95 o.p. (ISBN 0-8362-6402-9). Andrews & McMeel.

How Any Woman Can Get Rich Fast in Real Estate. Margaret Crispen. 1980. pap. 4.95. Warner Bks.

How Artists Work. Pierre Belves & Francois Mathey. Tr. by Alice Bach. (gr. 6 up). 1968. PLB 12.00 (ISBN 0-87460-101-0). Lion.

How Beastly! A Menagerie of Nonsense Poems. Jane Yolen. LC 79-22416. (Illus.). 48p. (gr. 4-6). 1980. 7.95 (ISBN 0-529-05421-3). Philomel.

How Beautiful God's Gifts. Jane B. Moncure. Ed. by Jane Buerger. (Illus.). 1980. 4.95 (ISBN 0-89565-172-6, 4923). Standard Pub.

How Beautiful God's Gifts. Jane B. Moncure. LC 80-1544. (Illus.). 32p. (ps-2). 1980. PLB 4.95 (ISBN 0-89565-172-6). Childs World.

How Big & Still Beautiful? Macro-Engineering Revisited. Ed. by Frank P. Davidson & C. Lawrence Meador. (AAAS Selected Symposium: No. 30). 383p. 1980. lib. bdg. 28.50x (ISBN 0-89158-792-6). Westview.

How Big Is Baby? Illus. by Eloise Wilkin. (Baby's First Golden Bks.). (Illus.). 8p. (ps). Date not set. 1.25 (ISBN 0-307-10756-6, Golden Pr). Western Pub.

How Big Is God? Kathryn Kuhlman. LC 74-12775. 96p. (Orig.). 1974. pap. 1.75 (ISBN 0-87123-222-7, 200222). Bethany Fell.

How Birds Learn to Sing. Barbara Ford. LC 74-28482. (Illus.). (gr. 4-6). 1975. PLB 5.79 o.p. (ISBN 0-671-32729-1). Messner.

How Black Is the Gospel? Thomas Skinner. 1976. pap. 1.25 (ISBN 0-89129-185-7). Jove Pubns.

How Brave a New World: Dilemmas in Bioethics. Richard A. McCormick. LC 80-921. 456p. 1981. 15.95 (ISBN 0-385-17179-X). Doubleday.

How Came the Bible. Edgar J. Goodspeed. 1976. pap. 1.75 (ISBN 0-89129-125-3). Jove Pubns.

How Can I Best Manage My Classroom? Martha M. McCarthy. (Teachers Education Ser.: No. 2). 1980. pap. 1.25 (ISBN 0-934402-05-1). Byls Pr.

How Carla Saw the Shalako God. Biloine W. Young & Mary Wilson. (Illus.). 28p. (gr. 1-4). 1972. 1.50 o.p. (ISBN 0-8309-0088-8). Independence Pr.

How Chemical Reactions Occur. Edward L. King. (Orig.). (YA) (gr. 9-12). 1963. pap. 8.95 (ISBN 0-8053-5401-8, 5401). Benjamin-Cummings.

How Children Fail. John Holt. pap. text ed. 1.95 (ISBN 0-440-33869-7). Dell.

How Christians Grow. Russell T. Hitt. 1979. 8.95 (ISBN 0-19-502558-X). Oxford U Pr.

How Christmas Came to the Sunday-Schools: The Observance of Christmas in the Protestant Church Schools of the United States. Katharine L. Richards. LC 70-159860. 1971. Repr. of 1934 ed. 18.00 (ISBN 0-8103-3793-2). Gale.

How Communist China Negotiates. Arthur Lall. LC 67-29051. 1968. 17.95x (ISBN 0-231-02958-6); pap. 7.50x (ISBN 0-231-08592-3). Columbia U Pr.

How Corporate & Municipal Debt Is Rated: An Inside Look at Standard & Poor's Rating System. Hugh C. Sherwood. LC 76-12099. 1976. 29.95 (ISBN 0-471-78585-7, Pub by Wiley-Interscience). Wiley.

How Could I Be Forgetting. Ben H. Lampman. (Illus.). 1980. pap. 4.95 (ISBN 0-8323-0379-8). Binford.

How Creative Are You? Eugene Raudsepp. 196p. 1981. pap. 4.95 (ISBN 0-686-69593-3, Perigee). Putnam.

How Deep the Cup. Jessyca R. Gaver. (Orig.). 1975. pap. 1.50 o.p. (ISBN 0-685-53125-2, LB280DK, Leisure Bks). Nordon Pubns.

How Democracies Vote. Enid Lakeman. 1974. 10.95 (ISBN 0-571-09690-5, Pub. by Faber & Faber). Merrimack Bk Serv.

How Democratic Is the Constitution? Ed. by Robert A. Goldwin & William A. Schambra. 1980. 12.25 (ISBN 0-8447-3400-4); pap. 5.25. Am Enterprise.

How Did Numbers Begin? Mindel Sitomer & Harry Sitomer. LC 75-11756. (Young Math Ser.). (Illus.). 40p. (gr. k-3). 1976. 7.89 (ISBN 0-690-00794-9, TYC-J). T Y Crowell.

How Did They Die? Norman Donaldson & Betty Donaldson. 1980. 12.95 (ISBN 0-312-39488-8). St Martin.

How Did We Find Out About Black Holes? Isaac Asimov. LC 73-4320. (How Did We Find Out Ser.). (Illus.). (gr. 5 up). 1978. 0.p. 6.95 (ISBN 0-8027-6336-7); PLB 6.85 (ISBN 0-8027-6337-5). Walker & Co.

How Did We Find Out About Coal? Isaac Asimov. LC 80-50448. (History of Science (How Did We Find Out About...?) Ser.). (Illus.). 64p. (gr. 5-8). 1980. 6.95 (ISBN 0-8027-6400-2); PLB 7.85 (ISBN 0-8027-6401-0). Walker & Co.

How Did We Find Out About Earthquakes. Isaac Asimov. LC 77-78984. (gr. 6 up). 1978. 5.95 o.p. (ISBN 0-8027-6305-7); PLB 7.85 (ISBN 0-8027-6306-5). Walker & Co.

How Did We Find Out About Nuclear Power? Isaac Asimov. LC 76-12067. (How Did We Find Out Ser.). (Illus.). (gr. 4 up). 1976. 6.95 o.s.i. (ISBN 0-8027-6265-4); PLB 6.85 (ISBN 0-8027-6266-2). Walker & Co.

How Did We Find Out About Outer Space? Isaac Asimov. 1977. 6.85 o.p. (ISBN 0-8027-6283-2); PLB 6.85 (ISBN 0-8027-6284-0). Walker & Co.

How Did We Find Out About Solar Power? Isaac Asimov. (History of Science Ser.). (Illus.). 64p. (gr. 4-7). 1981. 6.95 (ISBN 0-8027-6422-3); PLB 7.85 (ISBN 0-8027-6423-1). Walker & Co.

How Did We Find Out About Volcanoes? Isaac Asimov. (History of Science Ser.). (Illus.). 64p. (gr. 4-7). 1981. 6.95 (ISBN 0-8027-6411-8); PLB 7.85 (ISBN 0-8027-6412-6). Walker & Co.

How Did We Find Out the Earth Is Round? Isaac Asimov. Ed. by Millicent Selsam. LC 72-81378. (How Did We Find Out Ser.). (Illus.). 64p. (gr. 5-8). 1972. 4.95 o.p. (ISBN 0-8027-6121-6); PLB 5.85 (ISBN 0-8027-6122-4). Walker & Co.

How Did We Get Clocks & Calendars? Susan Perry. (Creative's Questions & Answers Library). (Illus.). 32p. (gr. 3-4). Date not set. PLB 5.75 (ISBN 0-87191-746-7); pap. 2.75 (ISBN 0-89812-215-5). Creative Ed. Postponed.

How Do I Feel. Norma Simon. LC 77-126430. (Concept Bks.). (Illus.). (ps-2). 1970. 6.95g (ISBN 0-8075-3414-5). A Whitman.

How Do I Teach Reading. Robert C. Aukerman & Louise R. Aukerman. LC 80-23380. 550p. 1981. text ed. 14.95 (ISBN 0-471-03687-0). Wiley.

How Do the Ducks Know. Eddie Ruth. 1980. pap. 3.00. Am Atheist.

How Do We Know There Is a God? John W. Montgomery. LC 73-16882. 96p. 1973. pap. 2.25 (ISBN 0-87123-221-9, 200221). Bethany Fell.

How Do You Feel? Childs World Editors. LC 73-4745. (Illus.). (ps-2). 1973. 5.95 (ISBN 0-913778-01-X). Childs World.

How Do You Handle Life? Fritz Ridenour. 1976. pap. 1.95 (ISBN 0-8307-0430-2, S104156). Regal.
How Do You Know It's Old? Harold L. Peterson. LC 74-13118. (Encore Edition). (Illus.). 1975. 6.95 o.p. (ISBN 0-684-15286-X, ScribT). Scribner.
How Does a Czar Eat Potatoes? Anne Rose. LC 72-5140. (Illus.). 32p. (ps-3). 1973. PLB 6.96 o.p. (ISBN 0-688-51531-2). Lothrop.
How Does a Poem Mean. 2nd ed. John Ciardi & Miller Williams. LC 74-11592. 432p. 1975. 10.95 (ISBN 0-395-18605-6). HM.
How Does It Feel to Be a Tree? Flo Morse. LC 75-19177. (Illus.). 40p. (ps-3). 1976. 5.95 o.s.i. (ISBN 0-8193-0829-3, Four Winds); PLB 5.41 o.s.i. (ISBN 0-8193-0830-7). Schol Bk Serv.
How Does It Feel to Be Deaf? Judith Richards. (Illus.). (gr. 4-7). Date not set. PLB price not set (ISBN 0-671-34030-1). Messner. Postponed.
How Does Language Work? Arlene Larson & Carolyn Logan. 208p. (Orig.). 1980. pap. text ed. 11.95 (ISBN 0-8403-2199-6). Kendall-Hunt.
How Does Your Garden Grow? Mary. (Illus.). 64p. 1980. 4.95 (ISBN 0-517-54027-4); ten copy pre-pack 49.50 (ISBN 0-517-54118-1). Potter.
How Effective Are Your Community Services: Procedures for Monitoring the Effectiveness of Municipal Services. Harry P. Hatry et al. 1977. pap. 10.00 (ISBN 0-87766-206-1, 19500). Urban Inst.
How Energy Affects the Economy. Ed. by A. Bradley Askin. LC 77-70084. 1978. 17.95 (ISBN 0-669-01365-X). Lexington Bks.
How English Really Works. Joe E. Pierce. LC 79-202. (Illus.). 1979. pap. 11.95 (ISBN 0-913244-18-X). Hapi Pr.
How English Really Works. Joe E. Pierce. 235p. pap. 12.95 (ISBN 0-913244-18-X). Hapi Pr.
How Executives Make Decisions. Alexander Hamilton Institute, Inc. Ed. by James M. Jenks. (Illus.). 79p. (Orig.). 1976. pap. 48.25 (ISBN 0-86604-005-6, A783159). Hamilton Inst.
How Far I Can Go. Lawrence O. Richards. (Answers for Youth Ser.). 1980. pap. 3.95 (ISBN 0-310-38951-8). Zondervan.
How Far to Bethlehem? Norah Lofts. 320p. 1977. pap. 1.95 o.p. (ISBN 0-449-23277-8, Crest). Fawcett.
How Far Will a Rubber Band Stretch? Mike Thaler. LC 73-23052. (Illus.). 40p. (ps-3). 1974. 5.95 o.s.i. (ISBN 0-8193-0766-1, Four Winds); PLB 5.41 o.s.i. (ISBN 0-8193-0767-X). Schol Bk Serv.
How Fletcher Was Hatched. Wende Devlin & Harry Devlin. LC 69-12614. (Illus.). (gr. k-3). 1969. 5.95 o.s.i. (ISBN 0-8193-0247-3, Four Winds); PLB 5.41 o.s.i. (ISBN 0-8193-0248-1). Schol Bk Serv.
How German Is It. Walter Abish. LC 80-20838. 256p. 1980. 14.95 (ISBN 0-8112-0775-7); pap. 5.95 (ISBN 0-8112-0776-5, NDP508). New Directions.
How God Can Use Nobodies. James M. Boice. LC 74-91026. 160p. 1974. pap. 1.95 o.p. (ISBN 0-88207-027-4). Victor Bks.
How Greek Science Passed to the Arabs. De Lacy O'Leary. 1979. 17.50 (ISBN 0-7100-1903-3). Routledge & Kegan.
How Green Was My Valley. Richard Llewellyn. (gr. 9 up). 1941. 15.95 (ISBN 0-02-573430-X); pap. 2.75 (ISBN 0-02-022550-4, 02255). Macmillan.
How Green Was My Valley. Richard Llewellyn. Date not set. Repr. lib. bdg. 18.65x (ISBN 0-88411-936-X). Amereon Ltd.
How Housing Allowances Work: Integrated Findings to Date from the Experimental Housing Allowance Program. David B. Carlson & John D. Heinberg. (Institute Paper). 95p. 1978. pap. 4.00 (ISBN 0-87766-215-0, 21300). Urban Inst.
How Human the Animals. Jean Pommery. LC 78-24613. 224p. 1981. pap. 6.95 (ISBN 0-8128-6086-1). Stein & Day.
How Hypnosis Can Help You. Arthur S. Freese. 1976. pap. 1.75 o.p. (ISBN 0-445-08540-1). Popular Lib.
How I Became a Holy Mother & Other Stories. Ruth P. Jhabvala. LC 76-9206. 224p. (YA) 1976. 9.95 o.s.i. (ISBN 0-06-012198-X, HarpT). Har-Row.
How I Became a Holy Mother: And Other Short Stories. Ruth P. Jhabvala. LC 76-9206. (Orig.). 1979. pap. 2.50 (ISBN 0-06-080474-2, P 474, PL). Har-Row.
How I Can Be Real. Lawrence O. Richards. (Answers for Youth Ser.). 1980. pap. 3.95 (ISBN 0-310-38971-2). Zondervan.
How I Can Experience God. Lawrence O. Richards. (Answers for Youth Ser.). 1980. pap. 3.95 (ISBN 0-310-38991-7). Zondervan.
How I Can Fit in. Lawrence O. Richards. (Answers for Youth Ser.). 1980. pap. 3.95 (ISBN 0-310-38961-5). Zondervan.
How I Conquered Cancer Naturally. Eydie Mae & Chris Loeffler. LC 75-29754. 1976. 9.95 (0362); pap. 3.95 (ISBN 0-89081-036-2). Harvest Hse.
How I Did My Own Legal Work for Our Adoption Book. Mike Helm. 1978. 4.00 (ISBN 0-931742-00-5). Rainy Day Oreg.
How I Faded Away. Janice M. Udry. Ed. by Caroline Rubin. LC 75-30863. (Concept Bks). (Illus.). 32p. (gr. 2-4). 1975. 6.95g (ISBN 0-8075-3416-1). A Whitman.
How I Found Freedom in an Unfree World. Harry Browne. 1974. pap. 2.75 (ISBN 0-380-00423-2, 47837). Avon.
How I Found Myself at the Fair. Pat R. Mauser. LC 80-12058. (Illus.). 64p. (gr. 2-5). 1980. 7.95 (ISBN 0-689-30780-2). Atheneum.
How I Got Faith. Willis M. Brown. 199p. 2.00. Faith Pub Hse.
How I Got Ovah: New & Selected Poems. Carolyn M. Rodgers. LC 74-12707. 81p. 1976. pap. 3.95 (ISBN 0-385-04673-1, Anch). Doubleday.
How I Got to Be Perfect. Jean Kerr. 1979. pap. 2.25 o.p. (ISBN 0-449-24039-8, Crest). Fawcett.
How I Know God Answers Prayer. Rosalind Goforth. pap. 1.50 (ISBN 0-8024-3593-9). Moody.
How I Learned to Meditate. Malcolm Smith. 1977. pap. 3.95 o.p. (ISBN 0-88270-253-X). Logos.
How I Made the Sale That Did the Most for Me: Fifty Great Sales Stories by Fifty Great Salespeople. J. Mel Hickerson. 400p. 1981. 10.95 (ISBN 0-471-07769-0, Pub. by Wiley-Interscience). Wiley.
How I Put My Mother Through College. Corinne Gerson. LC 80-21681. 144p. (gr. 4-8). 1981. PLB 8.95 (ISBN 0-689-30810-8). Atheneum.
How I Trained My Colt. Sandy Rabinowitz. LC 79-3162. (Reading-on-My-Own Bk.). (Illus.). 64p. (gr. 2). 1981. 4.95a (ISBN 0-385-15423-2); PLB (ISBN 0-385-15424-0). Doubleday.
How I Work As a Poet & Other Essays - Plays - Stories. Lew Welch. Ed. & intro. by Donald Allen. LC 73-84119. 66p. 1973. 5.00 (ISBN 0-912516-07-0); pap. 5.00 o.p. (ISBN 0-912516-06-2). Grey Fox.
How I Wrote Certain of My Books. 2nd rev. ed. Raymond Roussel. Tr. by Trevor Winkfield & Kenneth Koch. LC 77-3630. 1977. pap. 4.00 (ISBN 0-915342-05-7). SUN.
How in Parliamentary Procedure. 3rd ed. Kenneth L. Russell. LC 76-6837. (Illus.). (gr. 9-12). 1976. pap. text ed. 1.00x o.p. (ISBN 0-8134-1804-6, 1804). Interstate.
How in Parlimentary Procedure. 4th ed. Ed. by Kenneth L. Russell. (Illus.). (gr. 9-12). 1981. pap. text ed. 1.95 (ISBN 0-8134-2171-3, 2171). Interstate.
How in This World Can I Be Holy? Leader's Guide. Erwin W. Lutzer. (Leader's Guide Ser.). (Illus.). 1978. pap. 3.25 (ISBN 0-8024-3592-0). Moody.
How Indians Use Wild Plants for Food, Medicine & Crafts. Frances Densmore. Orig. Title: Use of Plants by the Chippewa Indians. (Illus.). 7.50 (ISBN 0-8446-5029-3). Peter Smith.
How Industrial Societies Use Energy: A Comparative Analysis. Joel Darmstadter et al. LC 77-83780. (Illus.). 300p. 1978. text ed. 18.50x (ISBN 0-8018-2041-3). Johns Hopkins.
How Intelligent Are You? Victor Serebriakoff. 128p. 1974. pap. 1.50 (ISBN 0-451-09295-3, E9295, Sig). NAL.
How Iowa Cooks. 1964. 4.25 (ISBN 0-686-15945-4); supplement incl. Tipton Woman.
How It All Began. O. C. Edwards. (Orig.). 1973. 5.95 (ISBN 0-8164-2082-3). Crossroad NY.
How It All Began: (Genesis 1-11) Ronald Youngblood. LC 80-50539. (Bible Commentary for Laymen Ser.). 160p. 1980. pap. 2.50 (ISBN 0-8307-0675-5, S342103). Regal.
How It All Began: Origins of the Christian Church New Edition with Study Guide. O. C. Edwards. 1978. pap. 3.95 (ISBN 0-8164-2164-1). Crossroad NY.
How It Feels When a Parent Dies. Jill Krementz. LC 80-8808. (Illus.). 128p. 1981. 9.95 (ISBN 0-394-51911-6). Knopf.
How It Happens. Walt Disney Productions. (ps-1). 1979. PLB 6.08 (ISBN 0-307-61078-0, Golden Pr). Western Pub.
How It Is. William Sheldon & Nina C. Woessner. (Orig.). (RL 5). 1972. pap. text ed. 4.96 (ISBN 0-205-03093-9, 5230934); tchrs'. manual 2.40 (ISBN 0-205-03094-7, 5230942). Allyn.
How It Was: The War & Post-War Reconstruction in the Soviet Union. Leonid I. Brezhnev. LC 78-41080. (Illus.). 1979. 13.25 (ISBN 0-08-023579-4); pap. 5.50 (ISBN 0-08-023578-6). Pergamon.
How It Works: Rockets. (Illus.). Arabic 2.50x (ISBN 0-685-82832-8). Intl Bk Ctr.
How Japan's Economy Grew So Fast: The Sources of Postwar Expansion. Edward F. Denison & William K. Chung. 1976. 14.95 (ISBN 0-8157-1808-X); pap. 5.95 (ISBN 0-8157-1807-1). Brookings.
How Japan's Metal Mining Industries Modernized. 65p. 1980. pap. 5.00 (ISBN 92-808-0083-3, TUNU089, UNU). Unipub.
How John Became a Man. Isabel Byrum. 64p. pap. 0.40; pap. 1.00 3 copies. Faith Pub Hse.
How Kittens Grow. Millicent Selsam. LC 74-13162. (Illus.). 32p. (gr. k-3). 1975. 5.95 (ISBN 0-590-07409-1, Four Winds). Schol Bk Serv.
How Kittens Grow. Millicent Selsam. (gr. k-3). 1977. pap. 1.25 (ISBN 0-590-04794-9, Schol Pap). Schol Bk Serv.
How Little, & How Much: A Book About Scales. Franklyn M. Branley. LC 75-43643. (Young Math Ser.). (Illus.). 40p. (gr. k-3). 1976. PLB 7.89 (ISBN 0-690-01058-3, TYC-J). T Y Crowell.
How Little Is Enough? SALT & Security in the Long Run. Francis P. Hoeber. (NSIC Strategy Paper Ser.: No. 35). 96p. 1981. pap. text ed. 5.95x (ISBN 0-8448-1383-4). Crane-Russak Co.
How Long Is Always? Lenora M. Weber. LC 75-1937. (gr. 7 up). 1970. 10.95 (ISBN 0-690-40680-0, TYC-J). T Y Crowell.
How Long Will I Live? And 434 Other Questions Your Doctor Doesn't Have Time to Answer & You Can't Afford to Ask. Lawrence Galton. LC 76-2440. 1976. 9.95 o.s.i. (ISBN 0-02-542390-8, 54239). Macmillan.
How Love Grows in Marriage. L. F. Wood. 1974. pap. 2.95 o.p. (ISBN 0-8015-3660-X). Dutton.
How Mad Tulloch Was Taken Away. John Morris. 1976. pap. 4.95 (ISBN 0-571-11020-7, Pub. by Faber & Faber). Merrimack Bk Serv.
How Mail Order Fortunes Are Made. A. L. Stern. 1977. 12.50 o.p. (ISBN 0-685-80653-7). Porter.
How Mammals Run: Anatomical Adaptations. P. R. Gambaryan. Tr. by H. Hardin from Rus. LC 74-16190. 367p. 1974. 39.95 (ISBN 0-470-29059-5). Halsted Pr.
How Man Began. Carla Greene. LC 73-172346. (gr. 2-6). 1972. 6.95 o.p. (ISBN 0-672-51612-8). Bobbs.
How Managers Manage. Joe Kelley. (Illus.). 1980. 14.95 (ISBN 0-13-423756-0, Spec); pap. 7.95 (ISBN 0-686-59488-6, Spec); study guide 5.95 (ISBN 0-13-423731-5). P-H.
How Many Children? Ann Cartwright. (Direct Editions Ser.). (Orig.). 1976. pap. 16.50x (ISBN 0-7100-8341-6). Routledge & Kegan.
How Many Miles to Babylon? Paula Fox. LC 79-25802. (Illus.). (gr. 5-7). 1980. 7.95 (ISBN 0-87888-164-6). Bradbury Pr.
How Many Miles to Sundown. Patricia Beatty. LC 73-10770. (Illus.). (gr. 5-9). 1974. PLB 7.92 (ISBN 0-688-30102-9). Morrow.
How Many Roads: The Seventies. Herman A. Estrin & Esther Lloyd-Jones. 416p. 1970. pap. text ed. 7.95x (ISBN 0-02-474380-1, 47438). Macmillan.
How Many Teeth. Paul Showers. LC 62-11004. (Let's-Read-&-Find-Out Science Bk). (Illus.). (gr. k-3). 1962. PLB 7.89 (ISBN 0-690-40716-5, TYC-J); filmstrip with record 11.95 (ISBN 0-690-40717-3); films with cassette 14.95 (ISBN 0-690-40719-X). T Y Crowell.
How Many Zen Buddhists Does It Take to Screw in a Light Bulb? Hoffman. (Illus.). 96p. 1980. pap. 3.95 (ISBN 0-312-39527-2); prepack 39.50 (ISBN 0-312-39528-0). St Martin.
How Musical Is Man? John Blacking. LC 72-6710. (John Danz Lecture Ser). (Illus.). 132p. 1973. 9.50 (ISBN 0-295-95218-0, WP72); pap. 5.95 (ISBN 0-295-95338-1); tapes 17.50 (ISBN 0-295-75510-5); c-60 cassette 17.50 (ISBN 0-295-75517-2). U of Wash Pr.
How Nations Behave. 2nd ed. Louis Henkin. LC 79-1015. 1979. 25.00x (ISBN 0-231-04756-8); pap. 10.00x (ISBN 0-231-04757-6). Columbia U Pr.
How New Life Begins. Esther Meeks & Elizabeth Bagwell. (gr. 4-6). 1969. lib. ed. 3.48 o.p. (ISBN 0-695-43855-7). Follett.
How-Not-to-Do-It Book. Peter P. Porges. (Mad Ser.). (Illus., Orig.). 1981. pap. 1.75 (ISBN 0-446-94190-5). Warner Bks.
How Not to Have a Heart Attack. Morton Walker. 1980. 9.95 o.p. (ISBN 0-531-09927-X); pap. 7.95 (ISBN 0-531-09919-9). Watts.
How Not to Raise Cain. Dave Holt & Pat Holt. 1978. pap. 1.95 (ISBN 0-88207-515-2). Victor Bks.
How Not to Ruin a Perfectly Good Marriage. Marlene S. La Roe & Lee Herrick. 208p. 1980. pap. 2.50 (ISBN 0-553-13818-9). Bantam.
How Not to Split up. Jane Appleton & Appleton, William, M.D. LC 77-89874. 1978. 7.95 (ISBN 0-385-13201-8). Doubleday.
How Not to Write. Rudy Ydur. 64p. 1981. 5.00 (ISBN 0-930592-06-9). Lumeli Pr.
How Numbers Lie: A Consumer's Guide to Numerical Hocus Pocus. Richard P. Runyon. (Illus.). 192p. 1981. 7.95 (ISBN 0-86616-000-0). Lewis Pub Co.
How Odd This Ritual of Harmony. Patti Renner-Tana. (Poetry Discovery Ser.). 50p. (Orig.). 1981. pap. 4.75 (ISBN 0-933906-19-6). Gusto Pr.
How Oft Shall Phoenix Rise. Catherine M. Krueger. Date not set. 5.95 (ISBN 0-533-04837-0). Vantage.
How Old Is the Earth. Patrick M. Hurley. LC 59-11599. 1959. pap. 1.45 (ISBN 0-385-09431-0, S5, Anch). Doubleday.
How Organizations Are Represented in Washington. Lewis Anthony Dexter. LC 69-15729. 1969. pap. 5.95 (ISBN 0-672-60748-4). Bobbs.
How Others See Us. Commission on Critical Choice. LC 75-44720. (Critical Choices for Americans Ser.: Vol. 3). 1976. 14.95 (ISBN 0-669-00420-0). Lexington Bks.
How Our Grandfathers Lived. Albert B. Hart & Annie B. Chapman. LC 78-164331. 1971. Repr. of 1921 ed. 20.00 (ISBN 0-8103-3795-9). Gale.
How Our Universe Works. Al Snyder. 150p. (Orig.). 1978. pap. 6.95 (ISBN 0-686-27926-3). Snyder Inst Res.
How Philosophy Uses Its Past. John H. Randall. LC 63-20464. (Matchette Foundation Lecture Ser.: No. 14). 1963. 15.00 o.p. (ISBN 0-231-02663-3). Columbia U Pr.
How Pictures Mean. Hans Hess. LC 74-26195. (Illus.). 1975. pap. 5.95 (ISBN 0-394-73057-7). Pantheon.
How Plants Get Their Names. Liberty H. Bailey. LC 73-30611. 1975. Repr. of 1933 ed. 15.00 (ISBN 0-8103-3763-0). Gale.
How Plants Grow. LC 80-7777. (Illus.). 96p. (gr. 3-7). 15.95 (ISBN 0-88332-139-4). Larousse.
How Puppies Grow. Millicent E. Selsam. LC 72-77803. (Illus.). 40p. (gr. k-3). 1972. 7.95 (ISBN 0-590-07190-4, Four Winds). Schol Bk Serv.
How Real Is Real? Paul Watzlawick. 1976. 10.00 o.p. (ISBN 0-394-49853-4). Random.
How Rules Eighteen & Eleven Can Succeed in Magnifying the Profit Potential of Commodity Futures Trading Operations. Jerome F. Addison. (Illus.). 129p. 1981. 39.85 (ISBN 0-918968-81-X). Inst Econ Fina.
How Sacraments Celebrate Our Story. Mary P. Ryan. LC 78-53635. (Journeys Ser). 1978. pap. text ed. 4.20x (ISBN 0-88489-104-6); tchrs. guide 2.60x (ISBN 0-88489-108-9). St Mary's.
How Safe Is Safe? The Design of Policy on Drugs & Food Additives. LC 74-5981. (Academy Forum Ser). 250p. 1974. pap. 8.75 (ISBN 0-309-02222-3). Natl Acad Pr.
How Safe Is the Food in Your Kitchen. Beatrice T. Hunter. 96p. 1981. 5.95 (ISBN 0-684-16752-2, ScribT). Scribner.
How Santa Claus Had a Long & Difficult Journey Delivering His Presents. Fernando Krahn. LC 72-122769. (Illus.). (ps-3). 1970. PLB 7.45 (ISBN 0-440-03887-1, Sey Lawr); 7.95 (ISBN 0-440-03886-3). Delacorte.
How Shall I Go to God? Horatius Bonar. (Summit Bks). 1977. pap. 1.95 (ISBN 0-8010-0713-5). Baker Bk.
How Silly Can You Be? A Book of Jokes. Compiled by William Wiesner. LC 74-4044. (gr. 2-6). 1974. 6.95 (ISBN 0-395-28830-4, Clarion). HM.
How Sodium Nitrite Can Affect Your Health. rev. ed. Michael F. Jacobson. 1979. pap. 2.00. Ctr Sci Public.
How Spanish Grew. Robert K. Spaulding. (YA) (gr. 9-12). 1943. pap. 5.95x (ISBN 0-520-01193-7, CAMPUS60). U of Cal Pr.
How Spider Saved Christmas. Robert Kraus. LC 80-13662. (Illus.). 40p. (ps-2). 1980. pap. 2.50 (ISBN 0-671-41201-9, Pub. by Windmill). S&S.
How Spider Saved Halloween. Robert Kraus. LC 80-16778. (Illus.). 40p. (ps-3). 1980. Repr. of 1973 ed. 7.95 (ISBN 0-590-07769-4, Four Winds). Schol Bk Serv.
How Spider Saved Halloween. Robert Kraus. LC 80-13661. (Illus.). 32p. (ps-2). 1980. pap. 2.50 (ISBN 0-671-96086-5, Pub. by Windmill). S&S.
How Sports Began. Don Smith. (Illus.). (gr. 5 up). 1977. PLB 7.90 (ISBN 0-531-00093-1). Watts.
How Spring Comes. Alice Notley. 56p. 1981. 25.00 (ISBN 0-915124-41-6, Bookslinger); pap. 6.00 (ISBN 0-915124-42-4). Toothpaste.
How Staff Rule: Structures of Authority in Two Community Schools. Peter Bramham. 213p. 1980. text ed. 29.50x (ISBN 0-566-00321-X, Pub. by Gower Pub Co England). Renouf.
How Sweet the Sound. James Hefley. 1981. pap. 2.95 (ISBN 0-8423-1449-0). Tyndale.
How the Animals Got Their Names. G. A. Pottebaum. (Little People's Paperbacks Ser.). pap. 0.99 (ISBN 0-8164-2240-0). Crossroad NY.

How the Body Works. Ron Wilson. LC 78-54636. (Illus.). (gr. 5-7). 1979. 8.95 (ISBN 0-88332-096-7, 8049). Larousse.

How the Chipmunk Got Its Stripes. Cleaver. (ps-3). pap. 1.25 (ISBN 0-590-11960-5, Schol Pap). Schol Bk Serv.

How the Cold War Is Taught: Six American History Textbooks Examined. Martin F. Herz. 82p. 1978. pap. 3.00 (ISBN 0-89633-009-5). Ethics & Public Policy.

How the Economy Works & Other Essays. F. W. Paish. 1970. text ed. 17.00x (ISBN 0-333-11067-6). Humanities.

How the Experts Buy & Sell Gold Bullion, Gold Stocks & Gold Coins. James E. Sinclair & Harry D. Schultz. 1975. 8.95 o.p. (ISBN 0-87000-309-7). Arlington Hse.

How the Great Religions Began. rev. ed. Joseph Gaer. pap. 1.75 (ISBN 0-451-07764-4, E7764, Sig). NAL.

How the Hare Told the Truth About His Horse. Barbara K. Walker. LC 73-174604. (Illus.). 40p. (gr. k-3). 1972. 5.95 o.s.i. (ISBN 0-8193-0561-8, Four Winds); PLB 5.41 o.s.i. (ISBN 0-8193-0562-6). Schol Bk Serv.

How the Indians Really Lived. Gordon C. Baldwin. (Science Survey Ser.). (Illus.). (gr. 5-9). 1967. 5.49 o.p. (ISBN 0-399-60268-2). Berkley Pub.

How the Internal Revenue Service Selects Individual Income Tax Returns for Audit. 1977. pap. 2.00 (ISBN 0-918734-16-9). Reymont.

How the Internal Revenue Service Selects Individual Income Tax Returns for Audit. U.S. General Accounting Office. 1980. pap. 5.00 (ISBN 0-89499-007-1). Bks Business.

How the Irish Became Americans. Joseph P. O'Grady. (Immigrant Heritage of America Ser). lib. bdg. 11.95 (ISBN 0-8057-3229-2). Twayne.

How the KKK Was Born in the South. Benjamin Hopkins. 1981. 5.75 (ISBN 0-8062-1691-3). Carlton.

How the Leopard Got His Spots. Rudyard Kipling. LC 72-81373. (Just So Ser.). (Illus.). 32p. (gr. 2 up). 1972. 7.95 (ISBN 0-8027-6111-9); PLB 7.85 o.s.i. (ISBN 0-8027-6112-7). Walker & Co.

How the Leopard Got His Spots & Other Stories. R. Kipling. (Peter Possum Paperbacks Ser). 1967. pap. 0.95 o.p. (ISBN 0-531-05124-2). Watts.

How the Pope Became Infallible: Pius IX & the Politics of Persuasion. August B. Hasler. Tr. by Peter Heinegg. LC 79-6851. (Illus.). 320p. 1981. 14.95 (ISBN 0-385-15851-3). Doubleday.

How the Rhinoceros Got His Skin. Rudyard Kipling. LC 73-76356. (Just So Ser.). (Illus.). 32p. (gr. 1 up). 1974. 7.95 (ISBN 0-8027-6149-6); PLB 7.85 o.s.i. (ISBN 0-8027-6150-X). Walker & Co.

How the Rooster Saved the Day. Arnold Lobel. LC 76-17602. (Illus.). (gr. k-3). 1977. 7.95 (ISBN 0-688-80063-7); PLB 7.92 (ISBN 0-688-84063-9). Greenwillow.

How the Rural Poor Got Power: Narrative of a Grass-Roots Organizer. Paul D. Wellstone. LC 77-22109. 240p. 1980. pap. text ed. 6.50x (ISBN 0-87023-139-1). U of Mass Pr.

How the Secrets of Economic Psychology May Double, Triple & Even Quadruple the Profits of Your Business. William W. Morgenstern. (International Council for Excellence in Management Library). (Illus.). 115p. 1980. 28.95 (ISBN 0-89266-248-4). Am Classical Coll Pr.

How the Small Taxpayer Can Take the IRS to Court. 16p. 1976. pap. text ed. 1.50 (ISBN 0-918734-17-7). Reymont.

How the Stars Were Born. Dan Lindholm. Tr. by Leo Twyman. 1975. 7.95 o.p. (ISBN 0-904822-01-X, Pub by Henry Goulden, Ltd). St George Bk Serv.

How the Sun Was Brought Back to the Sky: Adapted from a Slovenian Folk Tale. Mirra Ginsburg. LC 74-19060. (Illus.). 32p. (ps-2). 1975. 8.95 (ISBN 0-02-735750-3). Macmillan.

How the Tsar Drinks Tea. Benjamin Elkin. LC 79-136989. (Illus.). (gr. k-3). 1971. 5.95 o.s.i. (ISBN 0-8193-0455-7, Four Winds); PLB 5.41 o.s.i. (ISBN 0-8193-0456-5). Schol Bk Serv.

How the West Was Lost. Don Fletcher. (Illus.). 1969. pap. 2.00 (ISBN 0-87970-114-5). North Plains.

How the Wind Blows. Katherine D. Marko. LC 80-22754. 32p. (gr. 2-4). 1981. 5.95g (ISBN 0-687-17680-8). Abingdon.

How the Witch Got Alf. Cora Annett. LC 74-8808. (Illus.). 64p. (gr. 1-4). 1975. PLB 4.90 o.p. (ISBN 0-531-02791-0). Watts.

How the Word Became Flesh: Story Dramas for Education & Worship. Michael E. Moynahan. 1981. pap. 9.95 (ISBN 0-89390-029-X). Resource Pubns.

How the World Cooks Chicken. H. J. Muessen. LC 80-51608. 350p. 1980. 17.95 (ISBN 0-8128-2740-6). Stein & Day.

How the World Looks to a Georgian. Jimmy Morgan. 1978. 5.50 o.p. (ISBN 0-682-49062-8). Exposition.

How the World's First Cities Began. Arthur S. Gregor. (Illus.). (gr. 3-7). 1967. PLB 6.50 o.p. (ISBN 0-525-32417-8). Dutton.

How the Writer Works: Through the Composing Room. Roger H. Garrison. 112p. 1980. pap. 5.95 scp (ISBN 0-06-042276-9, HarpC); avail. Har-Row.

How They Do It. Robert Wallace. (Illus.). 1980. pap. 4.95 (ISBN 0-688-08718-3, Quill). Morrow.

How They Fared in Adoption. Benson Jaffee & David Fanshel. LC 79-132192. 1970. pap. 7.50 (ISBN 0-231-08642-3). Columbia U Pr.

How They Fared: The Impact of the Comprehensive School Upon the University. Guy Neave. 1975. 26.00x (ISBN 0-7100-7967-2). Routledge & Kegan.

How They Lived in Cities Long Ago. R. J. Unstead. (Illus.). 80p. (gr. 6 up). 1981. 9.95 (ISBN 0-668-05188-4, 5188). Arco.

How They Ran - S. A. Seventy Five. Huey Mahl. (Gambler's Book Shelf). 64p. 1975. pap. 2.95 (ISBN 0-89650-553-7). Gamblers.

How They Train, Vol. 2: Long Distances. 2nd ed. Ed. by Fred Wilt. LC 73-76248. (Illus.). 128p. (Orig.). 1973. 5.00 o.p. (ISBN 0-911520-58-9); pap. 4.00 o.p. (ISBN 0-911520-46-5). Tafnews.

How They Train, Vol.1: Middle Distances. 2nd ed. Ed. by Fred Wilt. LC 73-76247. (Illus.). 128p. 1973. pap. 4.00 (ISBN 0-911520-38-4). Tafnews.

How Things Began...in Rockland County & Places Nearby. Wilfred B. Talman. (Illus.). 1977. 12.50 (ISBN 0-89062-052-0); pap. write for info. Rockland County Hist.

How Things Get Done: The Nitty-Gritty of Parliamentary Procedure. Dena C. Bank. LC 79-1287. 1979. 3.95 (ISBN 0-87249-343-1). U of SC Pr.

How Things Work. Michael Pollard. LC 78-54638. (Illus.). (gr. 5-7). 1979. 8.95 (ISBN 0-88332-097-5, 8129). Larousse.

How Things Work in Your Home. 368p. 1975. 19.95 (ISBN 0-8094-1639-5). Time-Life.

How Things Work in Your Home. Time Life Bks Editors. LC 74-24853. 1975. lib. bdg. 16.95 o.p. (ISBN 0-8094-1640-9). Silver.

How Tickled I Am: A Celebration of Ken Dodd. Michael Billington. (Illus.). 11.95 (ISBN 0-241-89345-3, Pub. by Hamish Hamilton England). David & Charles.

How to. Peter Passell. 1977. pap. 1.75 o.p. (ISBN 0-345-25506-2). Ballantine.

How to Acquire a Million. N. H. Moos. pap. 1.25 (ISBN 0-912576-08-1). R Collier.

How to Add a Room to Your House. Tom Philbin & Fritz Koelbel. (Illus.). 192p. 1980. 14.95 (ISBN 0-684-16494-9, ScribT). Scribner.

How to Add an Extra Bathroom. rev. ed. Donald R. Brann. LC 68-18108. 1976. lib. bdg. 5.95 (ISBN 0-87733-082-4); pap. 5.95 (ISBN 0-87733-682-2). Easi-Bild.

How to Anticipate the Business Future Without the Need of Computers: The Laws of Inevitabilities in Economics, Sociology & History. new ed. Cornelius Donatus. (Illus.). 1977. 39.50 (ISBN 0-89266-060-0). Am Classical Coll Pr.

How to Anticipate the Business Future Without the Need of Computers: The Laws of Inevitabilities in Economics, Sociology & History. 1975. 57.50 (ISBN 0-918968-04-6). Inst Econ Finan.

How to Anticipate the Business Future Without the Use of Computers. Cornelius Donatus. (Illus.). 47p. 1974. 39.50 (ISBN 0-913314-27-7). Am Classical Coll Pr.

How to Apply Statistics to Physical Distribution. Harry J. Bruce & Frederick J. Burke. 1967. 12.95 (ISBN 0-8436-1402-1). CBI Pub.

How to Appraise Commercial Properties. Peter Robinson. 1971. 24.95 o.p. (ISBN 0-13-401828-1). P-H.

How to Assess Your Managerial Style. Charles Margerison. 167p. 1981. 12.95 (ISBN 0-8144-5632-4). Am Mgmt.

How to Automate Your Plant Successfully. Ed. by Roger W. Bolz. LC 80-67334. (Illus.). 184p. (Orig.). 1980. pap. 28.50 (ISBN 0-930220-03-X). Conquest.

How to Avoid a Nervous Breakdown. Frank S. Caprio & Frances S. Leighton. 1969. pap. 2.95 o.p. (ISBN 0-8015-3798-3). Dutton.

How to Avoid a Tax Audit. JK Lasser Tax Inst. 1979. pap. 2.95 (ISBN 0-346-12363-1). Cornerstone.

How to Avoid Divorce. Luciano L'Abate & Bess L'Abate. LC 76-12389. 1976. pap. 4.95 (ISBN 0-8042-1118-3). John Knox.

How to Avoid Estate Tax. Gilbert M. Cantor. LC 80-67503. 1980. 19.95 (ISBN 0-913864-57-9). Enterprise Del.

How to Avoid OSHA. Robert D. Moran. (Illus.). 256p. 1981. 49.95 (ISBN 0-87201-652-8). Gulf Pub.

How to Avoid People Problems & Increase Lab Productivity. A. J. Griffin. 112p. 1980. pap. 12.00 (ISBN 0-931386-17-9). Quint Pub Co.

How to Avoid Pitfalls & Pratfalls in English. Mario Zito. LC 79-3810. 1980. pap. text ed. 11.25 (ISBN 0-8191-0930-4). U Pr of Amer.

How to Avoid the Ten Biggest Home Buying Traps. Art Watkins. 1979. pap. 4.50 (ISBN 0-8015-3895-5, Hawthorn). Dutton.

How to Be a Better Mother-in-Law. Lou Beardsley. 176p. (Orig.). 1981. pap. 4.95 (ISBN 0-89081-281-0). Harvest Hse.

How to Be a Better Past Life Regression Receiver. Dick Sutphen. 1977. 2.50 o.p. (ISBN 0-911842-16-0). Valley Sun.

How to Be a Better-Than-Average In-Law. H. Norman Wright. 1981. pap. 3.95 (ISBN 0-88207-342-7). Victor Bks.

How to Be a Christian in an Unchristian World. rev. ed. Fritz Ridenour. LC 72-169603. (Orig.). 1972. pap. 1.95 (ISBN 0-8307-0611-9, S123150). Regal.

How to Be a Christian Without Being Religious. Fritz Ridenour. (Illus.). (gr. 9-12). 1967. pap. 1.95 (ISBN 0-8307-0435-3, S121158). Regal.

How to Be a Compleat Clown. Toby Sanders. LC 78-7520. (Illus.). 288p. 1980. pap. 7.95 (ISBN 0-8128-6090-X). Stein & Day.

How to Be a Confident Woman: A Bible Study Guide for Women. Susan J. Souter. LC 78-51904. 1978. pap. 2.50 (ISBN 0-89081-124-5, 1245). Harvest Hse.

How to Be a Consistent Winner in the Most Popular Card Games. John R. Crawford. pap. 2.95 (ISBN 0-385-09687-9, C180, Dolp). Doubleday.

How to Be a Couple & Still Be Free. Riley K Smith & Tina B. Tessina. LC 80-8669. 1980. lib. bdg. 11.95x (ISBN 0-89370-651-5). Borgo Pr.

How to Be a Couple & Still Be Free. Riley K. Smith & Tina B. Tessina. 1980. pap. 5.95 (ISBN 0-87877-051-8). Newcastle Pub.

How to Be a Flight Stewardess or Steward. 3rd, rev. ed. Johni Smith. LC 65-28387. 331p. 1978. 14.95 (ISBN 0-87219-009-9). Pan Am Nav.

How to Be a Gifted Parent: Realize Your Child's Full Potential. David Lewis. 1981. 14.95 (ISBN 0-393-01394-4). Norton.

How to Be a Good Communist. Liu Shao-Chi. LC 75-26943. 1967. Repr. of 1964 ed. 4.00 o.p. (ISBN 0-87364-079-9). Paladin Ent.

How to Be a Ham; Including Latest FCC Rules. Kenneth W. Sessions. LC 73-86768. 192p. 1974. 7.95 o.p. (ISBN 0-8306-4673-6); pap. 3.95 o.p. (ISBN 0-8306-3673-0, 673). TAB Bks.

How to Be a Liberated Christian. Ruth Truman. LC 80-27302. 160p. 1981. 7.95 (ISBN 0-687-17710-3). Abingdon.

How to Be a Minister's Wife & Love It. Alice Taylor. 1968. pap. 3.95 (ISBN 0-310-33131-5). Zondervan.

How to Be a More Productive Employee. R. E. Megill. LC 72-9445. 120p. 1973. 15.00 (ISBN 0-87814-140-5). Pennwell Pub.

How to Be a Motorist. W. Heath Robinson. (Illus.). 130p. 1975. 10.95 (ISBN 0-7156-1180-1, Pub. by Duckworth England). Biblio Dist.

How to Be a Movie Star. Chris Chase. 1979. pap. write for info. o.p. (ISBN 0-425-04194-8). Berkley Pub.

How to Be a People Helper. Gary Collins. (Orig.). 1976. pap. 4.95 (ISBN 0-88449-055-6). Vision Hse.

How to Be a Seminary Student-& Survive. Denise George. 1981. pap. 3.95 (ISBN 0-8054-6930-3). Broadman.

How to Be a Successful Inventor: Patenting, Protecting, Marketing & Selling Your Invention. Clarence R. Taylor. 1972. 6.50 o.p. (ISBN 0-682-47473-8, Banner). Exposition.

How to Be a Successful Songwriter. Ken McNeil & Mark Luther. LC 78-54699. (Illus.). 1978. 012.95 o.p. (ISBN 0-312-39586-8); pap. 5.95 (ISBN 0-312-39587-6). St Martin.

How to Be a Super Camp Counselor. Doreen Mangan & Terry Fehr. (Concise Guides Ser.). (Illus.). (gr. 7 up). 1979. PLB 6.45 s&l (ISBN 0-531-02893-3). Watts.

How to Be a Winner. Harold Hill & Irene Harrell. LC 76-12035. 1976. 5.95 o.p. (ISBN 0-88270-178-9); pap. 2.95 (ISBN 0-88270-179-7). Logos.

How to Be a Yogi. Swami Abhedananda. 4.95 o.p. (ISBN 0-87481-609-2). Vedanta Pr.

How to Be an Alien: England. George Mikes. (Illus.). 1946. 9.75 (ISBN 0-233-95500-3). Transatlantic.

How to Be an Effective Group Leader. Bill D. Schul. LC 74-31420. 208p. 1975. 13.95 (ISBN 0-911012-61-3); pap. 7.95 (ISBN 0-88229-497-0). Nelson-Hall.

How to Be an Inventor. Harvey Weiss. LC 79-7823. (Illus.). 96p. (gr. 5 up). 1980. 8.95 (ISBN 0-690-04052-0, TYC-J); PLB 8.79 (ISBN 0-690-04053-9). T Y Crowell.

How to Be Employed & Make a Spectacular Success in an Extra Business of Your Own: Which You Conduct in Your Spare Time. Edward F. Tabares. (International Council for Excellence in Management Library). (Illus.). 107p. 1980. plastic spiral bdg. 38.95 (ISBN 0-89266-245-X). Am Classical Coll Pr.

How to Be Food Self-Sufficient: Organically, of Course! Glenn Andrews. Ed. by Viola Andrews. 1978. 8.95 o.p. (ISBN 0-533-02913-9). Vantage.

How to Be Happy If You Marry Again. Carmel B. Reingold. 1977. pap. 2.50 (ISBN 0-06-080412-2, P412, PL). Har-Row.

How to Be Healthy: For Infants. pap. write for info. o.p. (ISBN 0-392-07051-0, SpS). Soccer.

How to Be Healthy, Wealthy & Wise. Constance Mellor. 112p. 1976. pap. 6.00x (ISBN 0-8464-1023-0). Beekman Pubs.

How to Be Healthy with Yoga. Sonya Richmond. LC 62-20294. (Illus., Orig.). 1966. pap. 1.50 o.p. (ISBN 0-668-01004-5). Arc Bks.

How to Be One Hundred Years Young. George B. Ticktin. LC 78-12702. 1979. 9.95 (ISBN 0-8119-0318-4). Fell.

How to Be Outrageously Successful with Women. John M. Carter & Lois Wyse. 160p. 1976. pap. 1.75 o.p. (ISBN 0-345-25206-3). Ballantine.

How to Be Parents of Happy Obedient Children. Roy Lessin. 1978. 6.95 (ISBN 0-89728-003-2, 702120); pap. 3.95 (ISBN 0-686-67298-4). Omega Pubns OR.

How to Be Really with It: Guide to the Good Life. Basset, Bernard, S.J. LC 70-89099. 1971. pap. 1.45 o.p. (ISBN 0-385-04227-2, Im). Doubleday.

How to Be Successful in the Antique Business. rev. ed. Ronald S. Barlow. (Illus.). 185p. 1981. 10.95 (ISBN 0-686-69481-3, ScribT). Scribner.

How to Be Young, Rich & Free All Your Life. Dan Lytle. LC 80-66441. (Illus.). 117p. 1980. pap. 4.95 (ISBN 0-936956-00-3). Am Quality.

How to Be Your Cat's Best Friend. Elizabeth Randolph. (Illus.). 224p. 1981. 11.95 (ISBN 0-316-73376-8). Little.

How to Be Your Own Astrologer. Sybil Leek. 1974. pap. 1.75 (ISBN 0-451-09426-3, E9426, Sig). NAL.

How to Be Your Own Best Friend. Mildred Newman & Bernard Berkowitz. 96p. 1974. pap. 1.95 (ISBN 0-345-28379-1). Ballantine.

How to Be Your Own Hairdresser for Fun or Profit. Jacques S. Goei. Date not set. 7.50 (ISBN 0-682-49128-4). Exposition. Postponed.

How to Be Your Own Power Company: The Low-Voltage Direct-Current, Power-Generating System. Jim Cullen. 142p. 1980. 16.95 (ISBN 0-442-24340-5); pap. 10.95 (ISBN 0-442-24345-6). Van Nos Reinhold.

How to Be Your Own Thin Self. Maxine T. Vaneven. 1981. pap. price not set (ISBN 0-916774-03-1). Tolvan Co.

How to Beat Fatigue. Linda Pembrook. 1975. pap. 1.75 (ISBN 0-380-00671-5, 29371). Avon.

How to Beat the Employment Game. David Noer. Date not set. pap. 4.95 (ISBN 0-913668-96-6). Ten Speed Pr.

How to Beat the SAT's. Michael Donner. (gr. 11-12). 1981. pap. 3.95 (ISBN 0-89480-154-6). Workman Pub.

How to Become a Better Reader. Paul Witty. 1962. text ed. 10.07 (ISBN 0-574-30086-4, 3-0086); pap. text ed. 10.07 (ISBN 0-574-30086-4, 3-0086); student record book 0.87 (ISBN 0-574-30089-9, 3-0089). SRA.

How to Become a Christian & Stay One. Patricia Maxwell. LC 79-4603. (Waymark Ser.). 1979. pap. 1.25 (ISBN 0-8127-0221-2). Southern Pub.

How to Become a Complete Golfer. Bob Toski et al. LC 77-92909. (Illus.). 288p. 1978. 14.95 (ISBN 0-914178-15-6, 24169). Golf Digest.

How to Become an Advertising Man. James W. Young. LC 79-56393. (Advertising Publications Ser). 100p. 1963. pap. text ed. 4.95 (ISBN 0-87251-001-8). Crain Bks.

How to Become Financially Successful by Owning Your Own Business. Albert J. Lowry. 1981. 11.95 (ISBN 0-671-41261-2). S&S.

How to Become the Person You Want to Be. Norman E. Hankins. LC 78-21596. 1979. 14.95 (ISBN 0-88229-297-8); pap. 7.95 (ISBN 0-88229-647-7). Nelson-Hall.

How to Begin an Evangelistic Bible Study. Ada Lum. pap. 1.95 (ISBN 0-87784-317-1). Inter-Varsity.

How to Begin the Christian Life. George Sweeting. 128p. 1976. pap. 1.50 (ISBN 0-8024-3626-9). Moody.

How to Begin the Christian Life: Leader's Guide. George Sweeting. (Leader's Guide Ser.). (Illus.). 1977. pap. 3.25 (ISBN 0-8024-3629-3). Moody.

How to Believe Again. Helmut Thielicke. Tr. by H. George Anderson from Ger. LC 72-75656. 224p. 1972. pap. 4.75 (ISBN 0-8006-0123-8, 1-123). Fortress.

How to Benefit from Stress. Nicola M. Tauraso & L. Richard Batzler. 1979. 10.95 (ISBN 0-935710-00-0). Hidden Valley.

How to Bet the Harness Races. Walter B. Gibson. (Gambler's Book Shelf). 80p. 1975. pap. 2.95 (ISBN 0-89650-557-X). Gamblers.

How-to Book: Loving God, Loving Others. Ed. by Jan P. Dennis. LC 76-17671. pap. 3.95 (ISBN 0-89107-145-8). Good News.

How-to Book of Floors & Ceilings. Don Geary. (Illus.). 1978. 8.95 o.p. (ISBN 0-8306-8998-2); pap. 5.95 (ISBN 0-8306-7998-7, 998). TAB Bks.

How to Borrow Money. Oliver G. Wood, Jr. & William C. Barksdale. 144p. 1981. text ed. 13.95 (ISBN 0-442-25204-8). Van Nos Reinhold.

How to Borrow Your Way to Real Estate Riches Using Government Money. 2nd ed. Tyler G. Hicks. 150p. 1981. pap. 15.00 (ISBN 0-914306-52-9). Intl Wealth.

How to Break into Motion Pictures, Television Commercials & Modeling. Nina Blanchard. 272p. 1979. pap. 2.50 (ISBN 0-380-47118-3, 47118). Avon.

How to Break into the Media Professions. Caroline Zimmerman. 216p. 1981. 11.95 (ISBN 0-385-15933-1). Doubleday.

How to Break into the Media Professions. Caroline Zimmerman. LC 79-6665. 1981. pap. 5.95 (ISBN 0-385-15934-X, Dolp). Doubleday.

How to Break Ninety - Consistently! Frank Chinnock. LC 76-22655. (Illus.). 1977. 8.95 o.p. (ISBN 0-397-01118-0). Lippincott.

How to Break Ninety Before You Reach It. Steve Brody. 4.95 (ISBN 0-88427-040-8). Green Hill.

How to Break Ninety Before You Reach It. 3rd ed. Steve Brody. LC 80-10704. 1980. pap. 4.95 (ISBN 0-88427-040-8, Dist. by Caroline Hse). North River.

How to Break Ninety Before You Reach It: A Collection of Verse About Golf & Other Sports. Steve Brody. 1980. pap. 4.95. Caroline Hse.

How to Breed & Whelp Dogs. Joseph H. Hansen. (Illus.). 280p. 1973. 13.75 (ISBN 0-398-02541-X). C C Thomas.

How to Bring Men to Christ. R. A. Torrey. LC 76-57111. 1977. pap. 2.25 (ISBN 0-87123-230-8, 200230). Bethany Fell.

How to Bring Men to Christ. R. A. Torrey. 128p. 1981. pap. 2.50 (ISBN 0-88368-098-X). Whitaker Hse.

How to Bring Out the Magic in Your Mind. Al Koran. 272p. 1976. pap. 4.95 o.s.i. (ISBN 0-88391-046-2). Fell.

How to Bring up a Child to Become a Financial Leader. Geral S. Webster. (Human Development Library Bk.). (Illus.). 113p. 1981. 31.75 (ISBN 0-89266-294-8). Am Classical Coll Pr.

How to Bring up a Child Without Spending a Fortune. Lee Edwards Benning. LC 75-25436. 320p. 1976. pap. 2.95 (ISBN 0-385-11513-X, Dolp). Doubleday.

How to Bring Up Two Thousand Teenagers. Ralph D. Rutenber. LC 78-24060. 1979. 11.95 (ISBN 0-88229-550-0). Nelson-Hall.

How to Build a Better Mousetrap Car -- & Other Experimental Science Fun. Al G. Renner. LC 76-48912. 1977. 5.95 (ISBN 0-396-07419-7). Dodd.

How to Build a Better Outdoors: The Action Manual for Fisherman, Hunters, Backpackers, Hikers, Canoeists, Birders, & All Nature Lovers. Bill Vogt. (Illus.). 1978. 9.95 o.p. (ISBN 0-679-50857-0); pap. 4.95 o.p. (ISBN 0-679-50867-8). McKay.

How to Build a Better Vocabulary. Maxwell Nurnberg & Morris Rosenblum. 1977. pap. 1.95 (ISBN 0-445-08386-7). Popular Lib.

How to Build a Coin Collection. Fred Reinfeld. (Illus.). 160p. 1973. pap. 4.95 (ISBN 0-02-081230-2, Collier). Macmillan.

How to Build a Coin Collection. Fred Reinfeld & Burton H. Hobson. LC 58-12544. (Illus.). (gr. 3 up). 1977. 7.95 (ISBN 0-8069-6068-X); PLB 7.49 (ISBN 0-8069-6069-8). Sterling.

How to Build a Computer-Controlled Robot. Tod Loofbourrow. (gr. 10 up). 1978. pap. 9.75 (ISBN 0-8104-5681-8); computer program tape no. 00100 (kim) 14.95 (ISBN 0-686-66680-1). Hayden.

How to Build a Flying Saucer: And Other Proposals in Specultive Engineering. T. Pawlicki. 1980. pap. 6.95 (ISBN 0-13-402461-3). P-H.

How to Build a Hot Tub. Carlton Hollander. (Illus.). 128p. 1980. 12.95 (ISBN 0-8069-0212-4); lib. bdg. 11.69 (ISBN 0-8069-0213-2); pap. 6.95 (ISBN 0-8069-8948-3). Sterling.

How to Build a House with an Architect. John M. Baker. LC 79-203. 1979. pap. 6.95 (ISBN 0-397-01325-6). Lippincott.

How to Build a House with an Architect. John M. Baker. LC 76-49974. (Illus.). 1977. 14.95 o.p. (ISBN 0-397-01124-5). Lippincott.

How to Build a Kayak. Donald R. Brann. LC 75-2652. 1978. pap. 5.95 (ISBN 0-87733-757-8). Easi-Bild.

How to Build a One Car Garage-Carport-Stable. rev. ed. Donald R. Brann. LC 72-88709. 1973. lib. bdg. 5.95 (ISBN 0-87733-800-0); pap. 5.95 (ISBN 0-87733-680-6). Easi-Bild.

How to Build a Patio, Porch, & Sundeck. Donald R. Brann. LC 78-55238. 1979. pap. 5.95 (ISBN 0-87733-781-0). Easi-Bild.

How to Build a Profitable Newspaper. Frank J. Romano. LC 72-14136. 1973. 19.50 o.p. (ISBN 0-912920-15-7). North Am Pub Co.

How to Build a Small Budget Recording Studio from Scratch: With 12 Tested Designs. F. A. Everest. (Illus.). 1979. 12.95 (ISBN 0-8306-9787-X); pap. 9.95 (ISBN 0-8306-1166-5, 1166). TAB Bks.

How to Build a Solar Heater. rev. ed. Ted Lucas. 1980. pap. 6.95 (ISBN 0-517-54056-8, Michelman Books). Crown.

How to Build a Stable & a Red Barn Tool House. Donald R. Brann. LC 72-88710. (Illus.). 1973. lib. bdg. 5.95 (ISBN 0-87733-079-4); pap. 5.95 (ISBN 0-87733-679-2). Easi-Bild.

How to Build a Working Digital Computer. Edward Alcosser et al. (gr. 7 up). 1967. pap. 7.75 (ISBN 0-8104-0748-5). Hayden.

How to Build & Enclose a Porch. rev. ed. Donald R. Brann. LC 65-18912. 1978. pap. 3.00 o.p. (ISBN 0-87733-613-X). Easi-Bild.

How to Build & Furnish a Log Cabin: The Easy-Natural Way Using Only 12 Hand Tools & the Woods Around You. W. Ben Hunt. (Illus.). 160p. 1974. 8.95 o.s.i. (ISBN 0-02-557440-X). Macmillan.

How to Build & Use Electronic Devices Without Frustration, Panic, Mountains of Money, or an Engineering Degree. 2nd ed. Stuart A. Hoenig. 1980. pap. 12.95 (ISBN 0-316-36808-3). Little.

How to Build & Use Greenhouses. Ed. by Ortho Books Editorial Staff. LC 78-57889. (Illus.). 1979. pap. 4.95 (ISBN 0-917102-74-6). Ortho.

How to Build Bars. Donald R. Brann. LC 67-15263. 1979. pap. 5.95 (ISBN 0-87733-690-3). Easi-Bild.

How to Build Bookcases & Stereo Cabinets. Donald R. Brann. LC 79-56769. (Illus.). 194p. 1980. pap. 5.95 (ISBN 0-87733-804-3). Easi-Bild.

How to Build Collectors' Display Cases. Donald R. Brann. LC 78-57773. (Illus.). 194p. 1979. pap. 6.95 (ISBN 0-87733-792-6). Easi-Bild.

How to Build Country Homes on a Budget. Paul Corey. LC 75-6854. (Funk & W Bk.). (Illus.). 245p. 1975. 8.95 o.s.i. (ISBN 0-308-10197-9, TYC-T); pap. 5.95 o.s.i. (ISBN 0-308-10198-7, F128, TYC-T). T Y Crowell.

How to Build Dioramas. Sheperd Paine. Ed. by Bob Hayden. LC 80-82164. (Illus.). 104p. (Orig.). 1980. pap. 8.95 (ISBN 0-89024-551-7). Kalmbach.

How to Build Fences, Gates & Walls. Stanley Schuler. (Illus.). 192p. 1976. pap. 6.95 o.s.i. (ISBN 0-02-000840-6, Collier). Macmillan.

How to Build Greenhouses - Walk-in, Window, Sun House, Garden Tool House. Donald R. Brann. LC 80-67650. 210p. 1980. pap. 5.95 (ISBN 0-87733-811-6). Easi-Bild.

How to Build Greenhouses, Garden Shelters & Sheds. Thomas H. Jones. LC 75-29779. (Popular Science Bk.). (Illus.). 1978. 11.95 o.s.i. (ISBN 0-06-012218-8, HarpT). Har-Row.

How to Build Log End Houses. Robert L. Roy. LC 77-72392. (Illus.). 1977. 12.95 o.p. (ISBN 0-8069-8828-2); PLB 10.39 o.p. (ISBN 0-8069-8829-0). Sterling.

How to Build Metal-Treasurer Locators. John E. Traister & Robert J. Traister. LC 77-7510. (Illus.). 1977. 7.95 o.p. (ISBN 0-8306-7909-X); pap. 3.95 (ISBN 0-8306-6909-4, 909). TAB Bks.

How to Build Model Ships. William Nordner. (Illus.). (gr. 4-6). 1969. 2.95 o.p. (ISBN 0-8015-3112-9, 7561). Dutton.

How to Build Outdoor Projects. Donald R. Brann. 210p. 1981. pap. 5.95 (ISBN 0-87733-807-8). Easi-Bild.

How to Build Patios & Decks. Richard Day. LC 75-31065. (Popular Science Skill Bk.). 192p. 1976. 6.95 o.p. (ISBN 0-06-011028-7, HarpT); pap. 3.95 o.p. (ISBN 0-06-011056-2, TD-282, HarpT). Har-Row.

How to Build Patios & Sundecks. rev. ed. Donald R. Brann. LC 66-24279. 1976. lib. bdg. 5.95 (ISBN 0-87733-031-X); pap. 3.50 o.p. (ISBN 0-87733-631-8). Easi-Bild.

How to Build Plastic Ship Models. Lester Wilkins. Ed. by Burr Angle. LC 80-82496. (Illus.). 64p. (Orig.). 1980. pap. 6.25 (ISBN 0-89024-552-5). Kalmbach.

How to Build Shaker Furniture. Thomas Moser. LC 76-46809. (Illus.). 1979. 14.95 (ISBN 0-8069-8394-9); PLB 12.49 (ISBN 0-8069-8395-7). Sterling.

How to Build Storage Units. rev. ed. Donald R. Brann. LC 65-19666. 1965. lib. bdg. 5.95 (ISBN 0-87733-034-4); pap. 3.00 o.p. (ISBN 0-87733-634-2). Easi-Bild.

How to Build Travel Trailers. Date not set. 12.95 o.s.i. (ISBN 0-87593-007-7). Trail-R.

How to Build Truck Campers. Date not set. 12.95 o.s.i. (ISBN 0-686-52309-1). Trail-R. Postponed.

How to Build with Stone, Brick, Concrete & Tile. Leo D. Maldon. (Illus.). 1977. 9.95 o.p. (ISBN 0-8306-7980-4); pap. 6.95x (ISBN 0-8306-6980-9, 980). TAB Bks.

How to Build Your Garage, or Carport. Robert Scharff. LC 80-5207. (Popular Science Skill Bks.). (Illus.). 192p. (Orig.). 1980. pap. 4.95 (ISBN 0-06-090822-X, CN 822, CN). Har-Row.

How to Build Your Own Boat from Scratch. John E. Traister. 1978. pap. 6.95 (ISBN 0-8306-7923-5, 923). TAB Bks.

How to Build Your Own Fine Doll Houses & Furnishings. Lewis H. Hodges. (Illus.). 1979. 14.95 (ISBN 0-8306-9853-1); pap. 9.95 (ISBN 0-8306-1102-9, 1102). TAB Bks.

How to Build Your Own Furniture. R. J. De Cristoforo. (Illus.). 176p. pap. 3.50 (ISBN 0-06-463352-7, EH 352, EH). Har-Row.

How to Build Your Own Stereo Speakers: Construction, Applications, Circuits & Characteristics. Christopher Robin. (Illus.). 1978. ref. ed. 16.95 (ISBN 0-87909-374-9); pap. 6.95 (ISBN 0-8359-2936-1). Reston.

How to Build Your Own Working Robot Pet. Frank DaCosta. (Illus.). 1979. 11.95 (ISBN 0-8306-9796-9); pap. 7.95 (ISBN 0-8306-1141-X, 1141). TAB Bks.

How to Burglar-Proof Your Home. Robert L. Robinson. LC 76-54352. 1978. 14.95 (ISBN 0-88229-245-5); pap. 7.95 (ISBN 0-88229-505-5). Nelson-Hall.

How to Buy a Car. James Ross. 160p. 1981. pap. 3.95 (ISBN 0-312-39546-9); prepack 39.50 (ISBN 0-312-39547-7). St Martin.

How to Buy a Country Business. Frank Kirkpatrick. 1981. 11.95 (ISBN 0-8092-5944-3). Contemp Bks.

How to Buy a Home While You Can Still Afford to. Michael C. Murphy. LC 79-91390. (Illus.). 160p. 1981. 12.95 (ISBN 0-8069-7154-1); lib. bdg. 9.89 (ISBN 0-8069-7155-X); pap. 6.95 (ISBN 0-8069-8912-2). Sterling.

How to Buy a Home While You Can Still Afford One. Michael C. Murphy. LC 79-91390. (Illus.). 160p. 1981. 10.95 o.p. (ISBN 0-8069-7154-1); lib. bdg. 9.89 o.p. (ISBN 0-8069-7155-X); pap. 5.95 o.p. (ISBN 0-8069-8912-2). Sterling.

How to Buy & Enjoy a Small Farm: Your Comprehensive Guide to the Country Life. George Laycock. (Illus.). 1978. 12.95 o.p. (ISBN 0-679-50858-9); pap. 5.95 (ISBN 0-679-50865-1). McKay.

How to Buy & Sell a Condominium. Robert G. Natelson. 160p. (Orig.). 1981. pap. 4.95 (ISBN 0-346-12537-5). Cornerstone.

How to Buy & Sell Business Opportunities. Wilfred F. Tetreault et al. LC 80-66117. (Illus.). 300p. 1980. text ed. 49.95 (ISBN 0-937152-00-5). Am Busn Consult.

How to Buy Furniture. D. Difloe. 1972. pap. 2.95 o.s.i. (ISBN 0-02-079750-8, Collier). Macmillan.

How to Buy Real Estate Without Getting Burned. Ruth Rejnis. LC 81-80094. 288p. (Orig.). 1981. pap. 3.50 (ISBN 0-87216-851-4). Playboy Pbks.

How to Buy Wine. Philip Seldon. LC 79-8504. (Illus., Orig.). 1981. pap. 8.95 (ISBN 0-385-14961-1, Dolp). Doubleday.

How to by Suzanne. Suzanne Taylor-Moore. 64p. 1981. pap. 3.00 (ISBN 0-686-28091-1). MTM Pub Co.

How to Calculate Drug Dosages. Pecherer & Vertuno. 1978. pap. text ed. 6.50 o.s.i. (ISBN 0-8273-1834-0). Delmar.

How to Calculate Drug Dosages. A. Pecherer & S. Vertuno. 1978. pap. 7.50 (ISBN 0-87489-140-X). Med Economics.

How to Calculate Statistics. Carol T. Fitz-Gibbon & Lynn L. Morris. LC 78-58659. (Program Evaluation Kit: Vol. 7). 1978. pap. 8.50x (ISBN 0-8039-1072-X). Sage.

How to Call Wildlife. Bryon Dalrymple. LC 74-33568. (Funk & W Bk.). (Illus.). 192p. 1975. 8.95 (ISBN 0-308-10208-8, TYC-T); pap. 4.50 o.s.i. (ISBN 0-308-10209-6, TYC-T). T Y Crowell.

How to Care for Works of Art on Paper. Francis W. Dolloff & Roy L. Perkinson. (Illus.). 1971. pap. 2.00 (ISBN 0-87846-136-1). Mus Fine Arts Boston.

How to Care for Your Dog. Jean Bethell. LC 67-23535. (Illus.). 64p. (gr. 2-5). 1967. 5.95 (ISBN 0-590-07076-2, Four Winds). Schol Bk Serv.

How to Care for Your Older Dog. Kathleen Berman & Bill Landesman. LC 78-19063. 1979. 9.95 (ISBN 0-8119-0280-3). Fell.

How to Cast Small Metal & Rubber Parts. Bill Cannon. (Illus.). 1979. 9.95 (ISBN 0-8306-9869-8); pap. 5.95 (ISBN 0-8306-1105-3, 1105). TAB Bks.

How to Catalogue Works of Art: A Guide for the Private Collector. Marilyn Pink. LC 72-86380. (Illus.). 54p. (Orig.). 1972. pap. 3.50x (ISBN 0-686-02501-6). Mus Sys.

How to Catch California Trout. Jim Freeman. (Illus.). 80p. 1972. pap. 1.95 o.p. (ISBN 0-87701-027-7). Chronicle Bks.

How to Catch Saltwater Fish. Bill Wisner. LC 72-89130. 600p. 1973. 10.00 o.p. (ISBN 0-385-07217-1). Doubleday.

How to Celebrate the Feasts. Martha Zimmerman. (Illus.). 160p. (Orig.). 1981. pap. 4.95 (ISBN 0-87123-228-6, 210228). Bethany Fell.

How to Choose a Career. Delmar W. Karger. LC 78-6294. (Career Concise Guides Ser.). (Illus.). (gr. 7 up). 1978. PLB 6.45 s&l (ISBN 0-531-02836-4). Watts.

How to Choose a Career After College. Gordon Miller. 128p. 1981. 4.95 (ISBN 0-346-12443-3). Cornerstone.

How to Choose a Mate. Mavis Klein. 160p. 1981. 12.00 (ISBN 0-7145-2727-0, Pub. by M. Boyars). Merrimack Bk Serv.

How to Choose & Use Child Care. Compiled by Jean K. Reynolds. LC 79-54920. (Orig.). 1980. pap. 2.50 (ISBN 0-8054-5275-3). Broadman.

How to Choose & Use Lumber, Plywood, Panelboards, & Laminates. Mel Marshall. LC 79-4710. 1980. pap. 4.95 (ISBN 0-06-090724-X, CN 724, CN). Har-Row.

How to Choose & Use the Right Therapist for You. Jean Erwin & Jim Erwin. 1978. pap. 3.95 o.p. (ISBN 0-8362-2601-1). Andrews & McMeel.

How to Climb Your Family Tree: Genealogy for Beginners. Harriet Stryker-Rodda. LC 77-24667. (YA) 1977. 5.95 o.s.i. (ISBN 0-397-01159-8); pap. 3.95 (ISBN 0-397-01243-8). Lippincott.

How to Clip Your Own Poodle. Ernest H. Hart. (Illus.). pap. 2.00 (ISBN 0-87666-358-7, DS1040). TFH Pubns.

How to Close a Medical Practice. G. Balliett. 1978. 21.50 (ISBN 0-87489-142-6). Med Economics.

How to Collect: A Complete Guide. Carole Rogers. 1981. 12.95 (ISBN 0-525-93190-2); pap. 6.95 (ISBN 0-525-47671-7). Dutton.

How to Collect Old & Rare Books & Make a Fortune Out of Them. Leslie Dean. (Illus.). 1979. 8.95 (ISBN 0-89266-188-7); plastic spiral bdg. 18.95 (ISBN 0-685-92187-5). Am Classical Coll Pr.

How to Collect Stamps. rev. ed. Intro. by Wesley P. Mann. (Illus.). 187p. (gr. 4 up). 1980. pap. 2.50 (ISBN 0-937458-00-7). Harris & Co.

How to Collect Your Overdue Bills: A Guide to Collection Techniques & Customer Relations. Milton Pierce. LC 80-66023. 1980. 19.95 (ISBN 0-87094-198-4). Dow Jones-Irwin.

How to Communicate in Optometric Practice. James R. Gregg. LC 69-17435. 1969. text ed. 5.95x o.p. (ISBN 0-8019-5374-X). Chilton.

How to Complete Job Application Forms. Strohmenger. (NVGA Bk.). 36p. 1975. pap. 5.00 pkg. of 5 o.p. (ISBN 0-686-11202-4). Am Personnel.

How to Completely Secure Your Home. Gerald Hall. (Illus.). 1978. 9.95 o.p. (ISBN 0-8306-7758-5); pap. 7.95 (ISBN 0-8306-6758-X, 758). TAB Bks.

How to Conduct a One-Day Conference on Death Education. Ellen Zinner & Joan McMahon. (Thanatology Service Ser.). 50p. 1980. 7.95 (ISBN 0-930194-04-7). Highly Specialized.

How to Conquer Fear. Don Gossett. Orig. Title: How You Can Rise Above Fear. 160p. 1981. pap. 2.95 (ISBN 0-88368-092-0). Whitaker Hse.

How to Conquer Suffering Without Doctors. Roy Masters. LC 76-489. 222p. 1976. pap. 6.50 (ISBN 0-933900-04-X). Foun Human Under.

How to Control & Use Photographic Lighting. David Brooks. (Orig.). 1980. pap. 7.95 (ISBN 0-89586-059-7). H P Bks.

How to Control Your Allergies. Robert Forman. 256p. (Orig.). 1979. pap. 1.95 (ISBN 0-915962-29-2). Larchmont Bks.

How to Control Your Drinking. W. R. Miller & Ricardo F. Munoz. (Illus.). 1976. 9.95 o.p. (ISBN 0-13-404392-8); pap. 3.95 o.p. (ISBN 0-13-404384-7). P-H.

How to Control Your Emotions. Roy Masters. Ed. & pref. by Melrose H. Tappan. LC 75-15708. 1975. pap. 6.50 (ISBN 0-933900-01-5). Foun Human Under.

How to Convert Gasoline Lawn Mower for Cordless Electric Mowing. Albert H. Brewster, Jr. LC 76-48500. (Illus.). 1979. pap. 10.00x o.p. (ISBN 0-918166-02-0). Amonics.

How to Convert Gasoline Lawn Mowers for Cordless Electric Mowing. 3rd ed. Albert H. Brewster, Jr. LC 76-48500. (Illus.). 1981. pap. 10.00x (ISBN 0-918166-03-9). Amonics.

How to Convert Salvage Auto Starter to Powerful DC Motor. Albert H. Brewster, Jr. LC 76-48495. (Illus.). 1977. pap. 6.00x o.p. (ISBN 0-918166-01-2). Amonics.

How to Convert Salvage Auto Starter to Powerful DC Motor. 2nd ed. Albert H. Brewster, Jr. (Illus.). 1981. pap. 6.00x (ISBN 0-918166-04-7). Amonics.

How to Convert to an Electric Car. Ted Lucas & Fred Riess. (Illus.). 192p. 1980. 10.00 (ISBN 0-517-54055-X); pap. 5.95 (ISBN 0-517-53990-X). Crown.

How to Convert Your Car, Van or Pickup to Diesel. Paul Dempsy. (Illus.). 1978. pap. 6.95 (ISBN 0-8306-7968-5, 968). TAB Bks.

How to Convert Your Vehicle to Propane. Mother Earth News Staff. Ed. by Robert Hoffman. 50p. (Orig.). 1981. pap. 7.50 (ISBN 0-938432-01-X). Mother Earth.

How to Cook His Goose. Karen Green & Betty Black. 1977. pap. 6.95 (ISBN 0-87691-229-3). Winchester Pr.

How to Cook His Goose: And Other Wild Games. Karen Green & Betty Black. 1973. 8.95 (ISBN 0-87691-106-8). Winchester Pr.

How to Cook with Miso. Aveline T. Kushi. (Orig.). 1979. pap. 7.95 (ISBN 0-87040-450-4). Japan Pubns.

How to Create the Illusion of a More Perfect Figure. Oleda Baker & Francey Petty. LC 77-22825. (Illus.). 1978. 8.95 o.p. (ISBN 0-13-404475-4). P-H.

How to Create Your Own Publicity for Names, Products or Services & Get It for Free. Steve Berman. LC 77-2736. 128p. 1977. pap. 4.95 (ISBN 0-8119-0378-8). Fell.

How to Custom Design Your Solid-State Equipment. M. J. Salvati. (Illus.). 160p. 1974. pap. 7.75 (ISBN 0-8104-5585-4). Hayden.

How to Cut Your Children's Medical Costs. James G. Mumford. LC 79-67043. 54p. 1980. 5.95 (ISBN 0-533-04430-8). Vantage.

How to Cut Your Electric Bill & Install Your Own Emergency Power System. Edward A. Lacy. (Illus.). 1978. pap. 2.95 (ISBN 0-8306-1036-7, 1036). TAB Bks.

How to Cut Your Energy Bill Thirty to Fifty Percent. Frank Attkisson. (Illus., Orig.). 1979. pap. 5.95 o.p. (ISBN 0-9602440-1-8). Jesus-First.

How to Cut Your Energy Bills. 2nd rev. ed. Ronald Derven & Carol Nichols. Ed. by Shirley Horowitz & Peggy Frohn. LC 80-13162. (Successful Series). (Illus.). 1980. 13.95 (ISBN 0-89999-004-5); pap. 6.95 (ISBN 0-89999-005-3). Structures Pub.

How to Cut Your Energy Bills. Carol Nichols & Ronald Derven. LC 76-28727. (Illus.). 1976. 12.00 o.p. (ISBN 0-912336-28-5); pap. 5.95 o.p. (ISBN 0-912336-29-3). Structures Pub.

How to Dance. 2nd ed. Thomas E. Parson. (Illus.). 1969. pap. 2.50 (ISBN 0-06-463202-4, EH 202, EH). Har-Row.

How to Deal with a Bureaucrat & Best Him, 2 vols. new ed. Henry Hadrian. 1979. Set. 77.50 (ISBN 0-89266-161-5). Am Classical Coll Pr.

How to Deal with a Bureaucrat & Best Him, 2 vols. 1975. 71.50. Inst Econ Finan.

How to Deal with Goals & Objectives. rev. ed. Lynn L. Morris & Carol T. Fitz-Gibbon. LC 78-57012. (Program Evaluation Kit Ser.: Vol. 2). (Illus.). 78p. 1978. pap. 4.50 (ISBN 0-8039-1065-7). Sage.

How to Deal with Lawyers. Harold H. Menzel. LC 76-27568. 1977. 15.00 o.p. (ISBN 0-931204-00-3). Caroline Hse.

How to Debug Your Personal Computer. Huffman & Bruce. 175p. 1980. pap. 7.95 (ISBN 0-8359-2924-8). Reston.

How to Decide: A Workbook for Women. Nellie Scholz et al. 1978. pap. 4.95 (ISBN 0-380-18985-2, 37309). Avon.

How to Decipher & Study Old Documents: Being a Guide to the Reading of Ancient Manuscripts, the Key to the Family Deed Chest. 2nd ed. Emma E. Cope. LC 73-18446. 1974. Repr. of 1903 ed. 20.00 (ISBN 0-8103-3701-0). Gale.

How to Deliver on Time. S. Paulden. 128p. 1977. text ed. 19.25x (ISBN 0-566-02075-0, Pub. by Gower Pub Co England). Renouf.

How to Design a Program Evaluation. Carol T. Fitz-Gibbon & Lynn L. Morris. LC 78-57011. (Program Evaluation Kit: Vol. 3). 1978. pap. 7.50x (ISBN 0-8039-1068-1). Sage.

How to Design & Build a Fireplace. Stanley Schuler. LC 77-3331. (Illus.). 1977. 14.95 (ISBN 0-02-607360-9). Macmillan.

How to Design & Build a Fireplace. Stanley Schuler. LC 77-3331. (Illus.). 1977. pap. 6.95 o.s.i. (ISBN 0-02-081860-2, Collier). Macmillan.

How to Design & Build a Solar Swimming Pool Heater: With Sample Calculations, 2 vols. Francis De Winter. (Illus.). 1978. pap. 8.65 set (ISBN 0-930978-07-2). Solar Energy Info.

How to Design & Make Wood Assemblages & Reliefs. Robert Skinner. (Illus.). 64p. (Orig.). Date not set. pap. price not set (ISBN 0-486-24057-6). Dover. Postponed.

How to Design, Build, Remodel & Maintain Your Home. Joseph D. Falcone. LC 76-42014. 1978. text ed. 24.95 (ISBN 0-471-05042-3). Wiley.

How to Design, Build, Remodel & Maintain Your Home. Joseph D. Falcone. 1980. pap. write for info. (Fireside). S&S.

How to Detect & Collect Antique Porcelain & Pottery. Will Theus. 1974. 8.95 o.s.i. (ISBN 0-394-49130-0). Knopf.

How to Develop a Better Speaking Voice. Marjorie Hellier. pap. 3.00 (ISBN 0-87980-056-9). Wilshire.

How to Develop a Millionaire's Mind. Arthur C. Simon. LC 78-55990. (Illus.). 1978. softcover 12.95 o.p. (ISBN 0-686-66476-0). Future Shop.

How to Develop a Super-Power Memory. Harry Lorayne. LC 57-7884. (gr. 9 up). 1956. 8.95 (ISBN 0-8119-0078-9). Fell.

How to Develop the Learning Powers of the Child & of the Teenager. Raphael Colman. (Illus.). 1977. 39.50 (ISBN 0-89266-086-4). Am Classical Coll Pr.

How to Develop the Power of Transcendental Experience. Burton R. Metheny. (Illus.). 117p. 1980. 39.45 (ISBN 0-89920-014-1). Am Inst Psych.

How to Develop Your ESP Power. new ed. Jane Roberts. LC 66-17331. 1980. pap. 5.95 (ISBN 0-8119-0354-0). Fell.

How to Dictate. Adele F. Schrag. LC 80-26747. (Illus.). 96p. 1981. pap. text ed. 3.60 (ISBN 0-07-055601-6). McGraw.

How to Dig for Dollars. 1979. pap. 2.50 (ISBN 0-918734-18-5). Reymont.

How to Disciple Your Children. Walter A. Henrichsen. 120p. 1981. pap. 3.95 (ISBN 0-88207-260-9). Victor Bks.

How to Discipline Children Without Feeling Guilty. rev. ed. Reynold Bean & Harris Clemes. (Whole Child Ser.). (Illus.). 80p. 1980. pap. 3.95 (ISBN 0-933358-77-6). Enrich.

How to Discipline Without Feeling Guilty. Susan Wheelan & Melvin Silberman. 1980. 10.95 (ISBN 0-8015-3645-6, Hawthorn). Dutton.

How to Dispose of Toxic Substances & Industrial Wastes. P. W. Powers. LC 76-2317. (Environmental Technology Handbook Ser.: No. 4). (Illus.). 1976. 48.00 o.p. (ISBN 0-8155-0615-5). Noyes.

How to Do a Bankruptcy. 2nd ed. Harry E. Rogers. 7.95. Green Hill.

How to Do a Bankruptcy. 2nd ed. Harry E. Rogers. 1980. pap. 7.95. Caroline Hse.

How to Do a Science Project. David Webster. LC 73-12214. (First Bks). (Illus.). 72p. (gr. 4 up). 1974. PLB 6.45 (ISBN 0-531-00817-7). Watts.

How to Do a Science Project & Report. Martin J. Gutnik. (gr. 7 up). 1980. PLB 6.45 (ISBN 0-531-04129-8). Watts.

How to Do Almost Everything. Bert Bacharach. 304p. 1975. pap. 1.50 o.p. (ISBN 0-445-03054-2). Popular Lib.

How to Do Beadwork. Mary White. (Illus.). 160p. 1972. pap. 3.00 (ISBN 0-486-20697-1). Dover.

How to Do Business in Japan. Boye De Mente. 1974. 12.00 (ISBN 0-914778-15-3). Phoenix Bks.

How to Do Business-Tax Free. Midas Malone. LC 75-45877. 1976. 14.95 o.p. (ISBN 0-913864-10-2). Enterprise Del.

How to Do Your Own Painting & Wall Papering. Jackson Hand. (Popular Science Skill Bk.). (Illus.). 1969. 5.95 o.s.i. (ISBN 0-06-002381-3, HarpT); pap. 3.95 2nd ed. 1976 (ISBN 0-06-011793-1, TD-283, HarpT). Har-Row.

How to Do Your Own Texas Divorce for Under Forty Dollars. Frank Gilstrap. 80p. (Orig.). 1980. pap. 7.95 (ISBN 0-938356-00-3). How-to Pr.

How to Double Your Child's Grades in School. rev. ed. Eugene Schwartz. LC 64-17293. 1975. 8.95 (ISBN 0-8119-0081-9). Fell.

How to Double Your Sex Drive. Daniel Boyd. 160p. 1980. 12.95 (ISBN 0-917224-09-4). Gregory Pubns.

How to Double Your Vocabulary. rev. ed. S. Stephenson Smith. (Funk & W Bk.). 352p. 1974. pap. 4.95 o.p. (ISBN 0-308-10099-9, F87, TYC-T). T Y Crowell.

How to Draw & Paint. Alexander Z. Kruse. (Orig.). 1962. pap. 2.95 o.p. (ISBN 0-06-463244-X, 244, EH). Har-Row.

How to Draw from Memory. Robert A. Catterson. (Illus.). 1980. 33.45 (ISBN 0-930582-58-6). Gloucester Art.

How to Draw Portraits: A Book for Beginners. Arthur Zaidenberg. LC 62-11216. (Illus.). (gr. 7-9). 5.95 (ISBN 0-8149-0442-4). Vanguard.

How to Draw with Pen & Brush. Arthur Zaidenberg. LC 65-17376. (Illus.). (gr. 6-9). 1965. 5.95 (ISBN 0-8149-0441-6). Vanguard.

How to Dress an Old-Fashioned Doll. Mary H. Morgan. LC 72-93612. Orig. Title: How to Dress a Doll. (Illus.). 96p. (gr. 5-8). 1973. pap. 1.75 (ISBN 0-486-22912-2). Dover.

How to Dress Well: A Complete Guide for Women. Priscilla H. Grumet. (Illus., Orig.). 1980. pap. 6.95 (ISBN 0-346-12510-3). Cornerstone.

How to Earn Money As a Consultant: Including Specimen Contracts. rev. & 5th ed. Ernest Goodryder. LC 78-58276. (Frontiers of Industry Ser.). (Illus.). 1978. pap. 31.00 (ISBN 0-931918-01-4). Busn Psych.

How to Earn Money As an Internal-Consultant: Including Employment Contract. rev. 2nd ed. Ernest Goodryder. (Frontiers of Industry Ser). 1977. pap. 27.00 (ISBN 0-931918-00-6). Busn Psych.

How to Earn Twenty-Five Thousand Dollars a Year or More Typing at Home. rev. ed. Anne Drouillard & Wiuliam F. Keefe. 176p. 1980. 9.95 (ISBN 0-8119-0222-6). Fell.

How to (Easily) Eliminate the Smoking Habit. rev. ed. Gordon E. Bayless. Ed. by Arthur F. Ide. (Studies in Health). (Illus.). 50p. 1981. pap. 16.95 (ISBN 0-86663-653-6). Ide Hse.

How to Eat a Poem & Other Morsels: A Collection of Food Poems for Children. Rose H. Agree. (Illus.). (gr. 2-5). 1967. PLB 4.99 o.s.i. (ISBN 0-394-91622-0). Pantheon.

How to Eat Cheap but Good. Gene Kowalski. 1977. pap. 1.75 o.p. (ISBN 0-445-08601-7). Popular Lib.

How to Eat, Exercise & Dress Like a Professional Model. Daniela. (Illus.). 1980. pap. 12.95 o.p. (ISBN 0-930490-19-3). Future Shop.

How to Eat Fried Worms. Thomas Rockwell. LC 73-4262. (gr. 4-6). 1973. PLB 7.90 (ISBN 0-531-02631-0). Watts.

How to Eat Fried Worms. Thomas Rockwell. 128p. 1975. pap. 1.50 (ISBN 0-440-44545-0, YB). Dell.

How to Eat Fried Worms: And Other Plays. Thomas Rockwell. LC 78-72854. (gr. 4-7). 1980. 7.95 (ISBN 0-440-03498-1); PLB 7.45 (ISBN 0-440-03499-X). Delacorte.

How to Eat Like a Child. Delia Ephron. 2.25 (ISBN 0-345-28504-2). Ballantine.

How to Eat Your ABC's: A Book About Vitamins. Hettie Jones. LC 75-41442. (Illus.). 96p. (gr. 2-5). 1976. 7.95 (ISBN 0-686-67313-1, Four Winds). Schol Bk Serv.

How to Enjoy a Better Life. Edward B. Fallon. LC 79-92719. 125p. 1980. 8.95 (ISBN 0-935976-01-9); pap. 8.95 (ISBN 0-686-28454-2). Midland Pub Co.

How to Enjoy Calculus. Eli S. Pine. LC 80-10974. 128p. 1980. lib. bdg. 7.95 (ISBN 0-668-04949-9); pap. 4.95 (ISBN 0-668-04951-0). Arco.

How to Enjoy Life & Not Feel Guilty. James L. Johnson. LC 79-85748. 176p. 1980. pap. 4.95 (ISBN 0-89081-121-0). Harvest Hse.

How to Enjoy Reading the Bible. John Havlik. 1981. 7.95 (ISBN 0-8054-1137-2). Broadman.

How to Establish a Jail & Prison Ministry. Duane Pederson. 132p. 1981. pap. 3.95 (ISBN 0-8407-5675-5). Nelson.

How to Establish a Successful Real Estate Brokerage. John Cyr & Joan M. Sobeck. 1981. 21.95 (ISBN 0-88462-359-9). Real Estate Ed Co.

How to Execute an Agency. E. Waterhouse Allen. LC 79-53977. (Illus., Orig.). 1980. pap. 4.95 (ISBN 0-9603338-1-9). Bark-Back.

How to Face Death Without Fear. St. Alphonsus Liguori. 1976. pap. 1.50 (ISBN 0-89243-029-X, 28376). Liguori Pubns.

How to Fast Successfully. Derek Prince. 1976. pap. 1.50 (ISBN 0-934920-19-2, B-28). Derek Prince.

How to Feel Younger, Longer. Jane Kinderlehrer. LC 74-13909. (Illus.). 228p. 1974. 8.95 (ISBN 0-87857-083-7); pap. 6.95 (ISBN 0-87857-278-3). Rodale Pr Inc.

How to Fiberglass Boats. Ken Hankinson. LC 74-27715. (Illus.). pap. 7.95 (ISBN 0-686-09424-7). Glen-L Marine.

How to Fight City Hall: Or, A Guide to Grassroots Politics. Mary E. Kersch. 1980. lib. bdg. 14.50 (ISBN 0-933474-15-6); pap. 5.95 (ISBN 0-933474-18-0). Minn Scholarly.

How to Fight Fair with Your Kids...& Win. Luree Nicholson & Laura Torbet. LC 79-1837. 1980. 12.95 o.p. (ISBN 0-15-142191-9); pap. 7.95 o.p. (ISBN 0-15-642191-7). HarBraceJ.

How to Finance Your Company. Cyril Aydon. 206p. 1976. text ed. 19.50x (ISBN 0-220-66309-2, Pub. by Busn Bks England). Renouf.

How to Finance Your Growing Business. Royce Diener. 416p. 1981. pap. 8.95 (ISBN 0-13-406546-8, Spec). P-H.

How to Finance Your Retirement. Martin Dunetz. (Illus.). 1979. 17.95 (ISBN 0-8359-2950-7). Reston.

How to Find a Job. Lewis. 1981. pap. 2.95 (ISBN 0-8120-2298-X). Barron.

How to Find a Job, Start a Business, Learn to Offer What Others Want to Buy. Donald R. Brann. LC 80-65878. 194p. 1981. pap. 6.95 (ISBN 0-87733-850-7). Easi-Bild.

How to Find a Job When Jobs Are Hard to Find. Donald R. German & Joan W. German. 387p. 1981. 14.95 (ISBN 0-8144-5677-4). Am Mgmt.

How to Find Freedom from the Power of Sin. T. A. Hegre. 1969. pap. 1.75 (ISBN 0-87123-217-0, 200217). Bethany Fell.

How to Find Fullness of Power. R. A. Torrey. Orig. Title: How to Obtain Fullness of Power. 1971. pap. 1.50 (ISBN 0-87123-219-7, 200219). Bethany Fell.

How to Find Music Easily for Good Times in Harmony. Elise Courtney & Emily Celeste. LC 80-51888. (Illus.). 317p. (Orig.). 1980. pap. 6.00 (ISBN 0-686-28899-8). Merk.

How to Find Out. rev. 4th ed. G. Chandler. 216p. 1974. text ed. 16.00 (ISBN 0-08-017781-6). Pergamon.

How to Find Out About Children's Literature. 3rd ed. Alec Ellis. 1973. 23.00 (ISBN 0-08-016970-8); pap. text ed. 8.50 (ISBN 0-08-018230-5). Pergamon.

How to Find Out About Engineering. S. A. Parsons. 285p. 1972. text ed. 21.00 (ISBN 0-08-016919-8). Pergamon.

How to Find Out About Iron & Steel. D. White. 1970. 16.00 (ISBN 0-08-015790-4); pap. 9.50 (ISBN 0-08-015789-0). Pergamon.

How to Find Out About Italy. F. S. Stych. LC 70-123271. 1970. 21.00 (ISBN 0-08-015810-2). Pergamon.

How to Find Out About Local Government. W. H. Snape. 1969. 16.50 (ISBN 0-08-013957-4); pap. 7.75 (ISBN 0-08-013956-6). Pergamon.

How to Find Out About Patents. F. Newby. 1967. 22.00 (ISBN 0-08-012333-3); pap. 10.75 (ISBN 0-08-012332-5). Pergamon.

How to Find Out About Physics. B. Yates. 1965. 15.00 (ISBN 0-08-011289-7); pap. 7.00 (ISBN 0-08-011288-9). Pergamon.

How to Find Out About the Chemical Industry. R. Brown & G. A. Campbell. 1969. pap. 14.00 (ISBN 0-08-013050-X). Pergamon.

How to Find Out About the Novel. 4th ed. G. Chandler. 1974. write for info. (ISBN 0-685-25212-4). Pergamon.

How to Find Out About the Social Sciences. Gillian Burrington. LC 75-5809. 148p. 1975. text ed. 15.00 (ISBN 0-08-018289-5). Pergamon.

How to Find Out About the United Kingdom Cotton Industry. B. Yates. 1967. 13.75 (ISBN 0-08-012360-0); pap. 6.25 (ISBN 0-08-012361-9). Pergamon.

How to Find Out About the Victorian Period. L. Madden. LC 74-116777. 1970. text ed. 22.00 (ISBN 0-08-015834-X); pap. text ed. 10.75 (ISBN 0-08-015833-1). Pergamon.

How to Find Out About the Wool Textile Industry. H. Lemon. 1969. 29.00 (ISBN 0-08-012984-6); pap. 14.00 (ISBN 0-08-012983-8). Pergamon.

How to Find Out in Chemistry. 2nd ed. C. R. Burman. 1966. 15.00 (ISBN 0-08-011881-X); pap. 7.00 (ISBN 0-08-011880-1). Pergamon.

How to Find Out in History. H. Hepworth. (How to Find Out Series). (Illus.). 1966. 16.00 (ISBN 0-08-011482-2). Pergamon.

How to Find Out in Mathematics. 2nd ed. J. E. Pemberton. 1970. 22.00 (ISBN 0-08-006824-3); pap. 10.75 (ISBN 0-08-006823-5). Pergamon.

How to Find Out in Philosophy & Psychology. D. H. Borchardt. 1968. 11.25 (ISBN 0-08-012596-4); pap. 5.75 (ISBN 0-08-012595-6). Pergamon.

How to Find Out in Psychiatry: A Guide to Sources of Mental Health Information. Ed. by Bette Greenberg. LC 78-16005. 1978. text ed. 14.75 (ISBN 0-08-021860-1). Pergamon.

How to Find Out What's Wrong with Your Car. Mitch Bronaugh. 160p. 1980. pap. 6.95 (ISBN 0-442-29731-9). Van Nos Reinhold.

How to Find Real Love & Keep It. Mary Bernard. Date not set. 8.50 (ISBN 0-533-04684-X). Vantage.

How to Find True Peace & Hapiness-Plus Inherit Eternal Life. Hughley Savage. (Orig.). 1980. pap. 2.00 (ISBN 0-9605150-0-3). Savage.

How to Find Valuable Old & Scarce Coins. 3rd ed. Don Bale, Jr. 1973. pap. 5.00 o.p. (ISBN 0-912070-15-3). Bale Bks.

How to Find Valuable Old & Scarce Coins. 4th, rev. ed. Don Bale, Jr. 1980. pap. 5.00. Bale Bks.

How to Firm Flabby Flesh. Dorie A. Erickson. (Illus.). 35p. (Orig.). 1981. pap. 3.95 (ISBN 0-937242-02-0). Scandia Pubs.

How to Fish: A Commonsense Approach. Mel Marshall. (Illus.). 1978. 11.95 (ISBN 0-87691-273-0). Winchester Pr.

How to Fish for Smallmouth Bass. Hank Andrews. 1979. 12.95 o.p. (ISBN 0-8092-7645-3); pap. 5.95 (ISBN 0-8092-7644-5). Contemp Bks.

How to Fish from Top to Bottom. Sid Gordon. (Illus.). 384p. 1978. 21.95 (ISBN 0-8117-0931-0); deluxed slipcased ed. 30.00 (ISBN 0-8117-0931-0). Stackpole.

How to Fish Good. Milford Poltroon. pap. 3.95 (ISBN 0-87691-051-7). Winchester Pr.
How to Fish in Salt Water. Vlad Evanoff. (Illus.). 1962. 7.95 o.p. (ISBN 0-498-08918-5). A S Barnes.
How to Fix Up Old Cars. rev. ed. LeRoi Smith. LC 80-10614. (Illus.). 260p. 1980. 7.95x (ISBN 0-396-07830-3); pap. 3.95x (ISBN 0-396-07831-1). Dodd.
How to Fly. Gordon Baxter. 288p. 1981. 12.95 (ISBN 0-671-44801-3). Summit Bks.
How to Fly Floats: Seaplane Flying. Jay J. Frey. (Illus.). Date not set. pap. 4.95x (ISBN 0-911721-71-1, Pub. by Edo-Aire). Aviation.
How to Forecast Interest Rates: A Guide to Profits for Consumers, Managers & Investors. Martin J. Pring. 192p. 1981. 14.95 (ISBN 0-07-050865-8, P&RB). McGraw.
How to Franchise Your Business. rev. ed. Mack O. Lewis. LC 74-8015. 1980. 3.50 (ISBN 0-87576-007-4). Pilot Bks.
How to Free Yourself in a Business of Your Own. Byron Lane. (Illus.). 176p. 1980. 11.95 (Spec); pap. 5.95. P-H.
How to Gain Financial Independence. Edward T. O'Toole. (Orig.). pap. 1.50 o.p. (ISBN 0-671-10344-X, Pub by S & S). Benjamin Co.
How to Get a Better Job. rev. ed. Austin Marshall. 1977. pap. 4.95 (ISBN 0-8015-3775-4, Hawthorn). Dutton.
How to Get a Better Job Quicker. Richard Payne. 1975. pap. 1.75 o.p. (ISBN 0-451-07327-4, E7327, Sig). NAL.
How to Get a Career Job. Vertie Lee Carter. 1978. pap. 4.00 o.p. (ISBN 0-682-49159-4). Exposition.
How to Get a Grant for Your Own Special Project. Ulysses Van Spiva. 1980. 7.75. TIS Inc.
How to Get a Job - with "No Experience" or "Not Enough". rev. ed. Ell Ell Diversified, Inc. Staff. LC 80-67678. (Illus.). 56p. 1980. pap. 7.95 (ISBN 0-937428-00-0). Ell Ell Diversified.
How to Get a Job with the Post Office. Stephen M. Good. LC 79-2240. 1980. pap. 4.95 (ISBN 0-06-463500-7, EH 500, EH). Har-Row.
How to Get a Man After You're Forty. Maxime Daley & Barbara Lochner. 1978. pap. 2.95 (ISBN 0-06-464026-4, BN 4026, BN). Har-Row.
How to Get Along in This World. Ed. by Robert E. Adams. pap. 5.95 (ISBN 0-911012-33-8). Nelson-Hall.
How to Get Along with Others. Ellen G. White. (Uplook Ser.). 1964. pap. 0.75 (ISBN 0-8163-0072-0, 08835-1). Pacific Pr Pub Assn.
How to Get Along with Your Stomach: A Complete Guide to the Prevention & Treatment of Stomach Distress. Nancy Nugent. 1979. pap. 3.95 (ISBN 0-385-14947-6, Anch). Doubleday.
How to Get Any Job You Really Want. Patrice M. Brooks. 1980. write for info. Unique Ent.
How to Get Big Results from a Small Advertising Budget. Cynthia S. Smith. 1973. pap. 4.50 (ISBN 0-8015-3649-9, Hawthorn). Dutton.
How to Get from January Through December in Powerboating. Ed. by Martin Levin. LC 77-11815. (Illus.). 1979. 14.95 o.s.i. (ISBN 0-06-012558-6, HarpT). Har-Row.
How to Get Happily Published: A Complete & Candid Guide. Judith Appelbaum & Nancy Evans. LC 77-3737. 1978. 10.95 (ISBN 0-06-010141-5, HarpT). Har-Row.
How to Get Help for Kids: A Reference Guide to Services for Handicapped Children. Ed. by Barbara Zang. 245p. 1980. pap. 29.95 (ISBN 0-915794-18-7). Gaylord Prof Pubns.
How to Get in Shape. Argie W. Post. (Illus.). 1977. 4.50 o.p. (ISBN 0-682-48548-9). Exposition.
How to Get into Law School. rev. ed. Rennard Strickland. LC 73-10885. 1977. pap. 4.95 (ISBN 0-8015-3767-3, Hawthorn). Dutton.
How to Get into Medical & Dental School. rev. ed. Gershon J. Shugar et al. LC 80-23397. 160p. 1981. lib. bdg. 8.00 (ISBN 0-668-05105-1); pap. 6.00 (ISBN 0-668-05112-4). Arco.
How to Get into Medical School: A Comprehensive Guide. Marvin Fogel & Mort Walker. 196p. 1981. pap. 6.95 (ISBN 0-8015-3670-7, Hawthorn). Dutton.
How to Get Invited to the White House & Other Tricky Maneuvers. James C. Humes. 1977. 7.95 o.s.i. (ISBN 0-690-01658-1, TYC-T). T Y Crowell.
How to Get Lucky: Stacking the Odds in Your Favor in Life, Love, & Work. Sidney Lecker. LC 80-681. 256p. 1980. 10.95 (ISBN 0-672-52660-3). Bobbs.
How to Get One Hundred Thousand Dollars Worth of Services Free, Each Year, from the U. S. Government. rev. ed. E. Joseph Cossman. 1975. 9.95 o.s.i. (ISBN 0-8119-0257-9). Fell.
How to Get Out If You're in Over Your Head. Ted Nicholas. LC 75-45878. 1977. 12.95 o.p. (ISBN 0-913864-22-6). Enterprise Del.
How to Get Out of Debt. Daniel Kaufman. 208p. (Orig.). 1981. pap. 2.50 (ISBN 0-523-41197-9). Pinnacle Bks.
How to Get Out of Debt. Ted Nicholas. (Illus.). 146p. 1980. 14.95 (ISBN 0-913864-60-9). Enterprise Del.
How to Get Out of Debt & Stay Out of Debt. Ann David. 160p. 1980. 5.95 (ISBN 0-346-12480-8). Cornerstone.
How to Get Results with Adults. Gilbert A. Peterson. 1977. pap. 1.45 (ISBN 0-88207-178-5). Victor Bks.
How to Get Rich in Mail Order. Melvin Powers. 1980. pap. 10.00 (ISBN 0-87980-373-8). Wilshire.
How to Get Rid of Wrinkles. rev ed. Clara E. Patterson. LC 79-27184. (Illus.). 1980. 7.95 (ISBN 0-688-06546-5, Quill); pap. 2.95 (ISBN 0-688-03673-2, Quill). Morrow.
How to Get Something for Almost Nothing & More. Frieda Carrol. LC 78-59909. 52p. (Orig.). 1981. pap. text ed. 5.00 (ISBN 0-9605246-0-6). Biblio Pr GA.
How to Get Started in Your Own Franchise Business. rev. ed. Ed. by David Seltz. LC 79-27945. 1980. 19.95 (ISBN 0-87863-172-0). Farnswth Pub.
How to Get Started When You Dont Know Where to Begin. Patricia Hoyt. LC 79-3762. (Illus.). 224p. (gr. 10 up). 1980. 8.95 (ISBN 0-15-232263-9, HJ). HarBraceJ.
How to Get Started with CP-M: Control Programs for Microcomputers. Carl Townsend. 200p. 1981. pap. 9.95 (ISBN 0-918398-32-0). Dilithium Pr.
How to Get the Job That's Right for You: A Career Guide for the 80's. rev. ed. Ben Greco. LC 79-56085. 210p. (Orig.). 1981. pap. 6.95 (ISBN 0-87094-194-1). Dow Jones-Irwin.
How to Get the Money to by Your New Home. Dennis Jacobe & James N. Kendall. 200p. 1981. 10.95 (ISBN 0-87094-258-1). Dow Jones-Irwin.
How to Get the Money to Pay for College. Gene R. Hawes & David M. Brownstone. 1978. 12.95 o.p. (ISBN 0-679-50848-1); pap. 6.95 (ISBN 0-679-50849-X). McKay.
How to Get the Most Out of Your Audio Recording & Playback. Robin. (Illus.). 128p. 1980. pap. 5.95 (ISBN 0-8359-2957-4). Reston.
How to Get the Most Out of Your Cruise to Alaska. Lois Kerr. 1978. pap. 4.95 (ISBN 0-88894-174-9, Pub. by Douglas & McIntyre). Madrona Pubs.
How to Get the Most Out of Your Low-Cost Electronic Calculator. Ronald Benrey. 1976. pap. 5.95 (ISBN 0-8104-5942-6). Hayden.
How to Get the Most Out of Your Tools. LC 74-1607. (Illus.). 180p. 1974. 8.95 o.p. (ISBN 0-685-50618-5). Jonathan David.
How to Get Thinner Once & for All. Morton B. Glenn. 1979. pap. 1.95 o.p. (ISBN 0-449-23849-0, Crest). Fawcett.
How to Get up When You're Down. Lowell Lundstrom. 1977. pap. 1.75 (ISBN 0-88207-502-0). Victor Bks.
How to Get Well. Paavo Airola. 1974. cloth 12.95 (ISBN 0-932090-03-6). Health Plus.
How to Get Well. Paavo Airola. 9.95 o.s.i. (ISBN 0-89557-036-X). Bi World Indus.
How to Get What You Want. Raymond Hull. 1973. pap. 6.50 (ISBN 0-8015-3780-0, Hawthorn). Dutton.
How to Get Work & Make Money in Commercials & Modeling. Cecily Hunt. 1981. pap. 12.95 (ISBN 0-938814-02-8). Barrington.
How to Get Your Child into Commercials & Modeling. Jane G. Patrick. LC 79-8031. (Illus.). 264p. 1981. 11.95 (ISBN 0-385-15317-1). Doubleday.
How to Get Your Children to Be Good Students-How to Get Your Students to Be Good Children. Bernard Schwartz & James M. Pugh. LC 80-27826. 150p. 1981. 8.95 (ISBN 0-13-409862-5). P-H.
How to Get Your Children to Do What You Want Them to Do. Paul Wood & Bernard Schwartz. LC 76-54846. 1977. 7.95 o.p. (ISBN 0-13-409797-1). P-H.
How to Get Your Fair Share of Foundation Grants. Manning M. Patillo, Jr. et al. 12.00 o.p. (ISBN 0-686-24212-2). Public Serv Materials.
How to Get Your Own Patent. Robert O. Richardson. LC 80-54340. (Illus.). 128p. 1981. 16.95 (ISBN 0-8069-5564-3); lib. bdg. 14.99 (ISBN 0-8069-5565-1); pap. 8.95 (ISBN 0-8069-8990-4). Sterling.
How to Give a Party. Jean Frame & Paul Frame. LC 74-183296. (First Bks). (Illus.). 96p. (gr. 4-7). 1972. PLB 4.90 o.p. (ISBN 0-531-00759-6). Watts.
How to Give a Speech. Henry Gilford. (gr. 7 up). 1980. PLB 6.45 (ISBN 0-531-04130-1). Watts.
How to Give Yourself a Raise in Selling. Howard Bonnell. LC 80-7845. 144p. 1980. 9.95 (ISBN 0-8119-0340-0). Fell.
How to Go Railway Modelling. Norman Simmons. (Illus.). 215p. 1975. 17.95 o.p. (ISBN 0-85059-167-3). Aztex.
How to Go Railway Modelling. 3rd ed. Norman Simmons. (Illus.). 215p. 1980. 31.95 (ISBN 0-85059-402-2). Aztex
How to Grandparent. Dodson. 1981. 8.95 (ISBN 0-686-69161-X). Lippincott & Crowell.
How to Grandparent. Fitzhugh Dodson. 1981. 10.95 (ISBN 0-690-01874-6, H&R). Lippincott.
How to Grandparent. Fitzhugh Dodson & Paula Ruben. LC 80-7849. 304p. 1981. 12.95 (ISBN 0-690-01874-6, HarpT). Har-Row.
How to Grow a Moneytree. Dave Glubetich. Ed. by Dave Wigginton. 1977. pap. 6.95 (ISBN 0-9601530-0-4). Impact Pub.
How to Grow a Moneytree. Dave Glubetich & Dave Wigginton. 112p. 1977. pap. 7.95 o.p. (ISBN 0-9601530-0-4). Impact Pub.
How to Grow & Use Herbs. Ann Bonar & Daphne MacCarthy. (Orig.). 1980. pap. 6.95x (ISBN 0-8464-1024-9). Beekman Pubs.
How to Grow Beautiful House Plants. T. H. Everett. 1978. pap. 1.95 o.p. (ISBN 0-449-13967-0, GM). Fawcett.
How to Grow Beautiful Houseplants. Thomas H. Everett. LC 76-21286. 1976. pap. 2.50 o.p. (ISBN 0-668-04015-7). Arco.
How to Grow House Plants. Millicent E. Selsam. (Illus.). (gr. 5-9). 1960. PLB 7.44 o.p. (ISBN 0-688-31410-4). Morrow.
How to Grow in the Christian Life. B. Charles Hostetter. 1960. pap. 0.95 (ISBN 0-8024-3603-X). Moody.
How to Grow Living Foods in Seven Days. Ann Wigmore. pap. text ed. write for info. Hippocrates.
How to Grow, Preserve & Store All the Food You Need. Eddy Rice. (Illus.). 1977. 10.95 (ISBN 0-87909-350-1). Reston.
How to Grow Science. Michael J. Moravcsik. LC 80-17469. (Illus.). 224p. (Orig.). 1980. text ed. 12.50x (ISBN 0-87663-344-0). Universe.
How to Handle Competition. Marvin H. Moore. LC 77-17494. (Better Living Ser.). 1977. pap. 0.95 (ISBN 0-8127-0145-3). Southern Pub.
How to Handle Life's Hurts. James A. Nelson. LC 80-65056. 160p. (Orig.). 1980. pap. 3.95 (ISBN 0-89636-046-6). Accent Bks.
How to Handle Major Customers Profitably. Alan V. Melkman. 1979. text ed. 34.50x (ISBN 0-566-02097-1. Pub. by Gower Pub Co England). Renouf.
How to Handle Your Divorce Step by Step. Harold Mitnick. LC 80-80875. 177p. 1981. 21.95; pap. 14.95 (ISBN 0-936550-00-7). Lone Oak.
How to Handle Your Imagination. Marvin Moore. LC 78-13660. (Flame Ser.). 1979. pap. 0.95 (ISBN 0-8127-0195-X). Southern Pub.
How to Handle Your Own Contracts. rev. ed. Christopher Neubert & Jack Withiam, Jr. (Illus.). 1979. pap. 7.95 (ISBN 0-8069-8868-1). Sterling.
How to Handle Your Own Public Relations. H. G. Lewis. LC 76-20710. 1976. 12.95 (ISBN 0-88229-319-2); pap. 8.95 (ISBN 0-88229-408-3). Nelson-Hall.
How to Have a Child & Keep Your Job. Jane Price. LC 79-16316. 1979. 10.95 (ISBN 0-312-39592-2). St Martin.
How to Have a Daily Quiet Time. Larry Christenson. 1979. saddle stitch 0.60 (ISBN 0-87123-235-9, 200235). Bethany Fell.
How to Have a Good Marriage. Mark W. Lee. LC 78-56974. 1978. 7.95 (ISBN 0-915684-39-X); pap. 5.95 (ISBN 0-915684-89-6). Christian Herald.
How to Have a Good Marriage. Mark W. Lee. LC 78-56794. 1981. pap. 5.95 (ISBN 0-915684-89-6). Christian Herald.
How to Have a Green Thumb Without an Aching Back. Ruth Stout. 160p. 1968. pap. 3.50 (ISBN 0-346-12126-4). Cornerstone.
How to Have a Perfect Wedding. rev. ed. Effie H. Hunt. LC 69-20380. 1980. pap. 4.95 (ISBN 0-8119-0353-2). Fell.
How to Have an Ideal Business Client in Four Months. Luanna C. Blagrove. (Illus.). 67p. (Orig.). 1981. pap. 9.95 (ISBN 0-9604466-6-4). Blagrove Pubns.
How to Have Fun Baking Cookies & Cakes. Creative Educational Society Editors. LC 73-10467. 1974. PLB 5.95 (ISBN 0-87191-260-0). Creative Ed.
How to Have Fun Building a Sailboat. Creative Educational Society Editors. LC 73-9707. 1974. PLB 5.95 (ISBN 0-87191-250-3). Creative Ed.
How to Have Fun Knitting. Creative Educational Society Editors. LC 73-12471. (Creative Craft Bks.). (Illus.). 32p. (gr. 2-5). 1973. PLB 5.95 (ISBN 0-87191-274-0) Creative Ed.
How to Have Fun Making a Kite. Creative Educational Society Editors. LC 73-12514. (Creative Craft Bks.). (Illus.). 32p. (gr. 2-5). 1973. PLB 5.90 (ISBN 0-87191-273-2). Creative Ed.
How to Have Fun Making a Rug. Sr. M. Albertine Borawska. LC 74-14521. (Creative Craft Bks). (Illus.). 32p. (gr. 2-6). 1974. PLB 5.25 o.p. (ISBN 0-87191-359-3). Creative Ed.
How to Have Fun Making Bird Feeders & Bird Houses. Creative Educational Society Editors. LC 73-10463. (Creative Craft Bks.). (Illus.). 32p. (gr. 2-5). 1973. PLB 5.25 o.p. (ISBN 0-87191-271-6). Creative Ed.
How to Have Fun Making Breakfast. Creative Educational Society Editors. LC 73-18257. (Creative Craft Bks.). (Illus.). 32p. (gr. 2-5). 1973. PLB 5.95 (ISBN 0-87191-291-0). Creative Ed.
How to Have Fun Making Cards. Sr. Emily Kovash. LC 74-10532. (Creative Craft Bks.). (Illus.). 32p. (gr. 2-6). 1974. PLB 5.95 (ISBN 0-87191-360-7). Creative Ed.
How to Have Fun Making Christmas Decorations. Creative Educational Society Editors. LC 73-20197. (Creative Craft Bks.). (Illus.). 32p. (gr. 2-5). 1973. PLB 5.95 (ISBN 0-87191-292-9). Creative Ed.
How to Have Fun Making Dinner. Creative Editors. LC 74-8612. (Creative Craft Bks.). (Illus.). 32p. (gr. 2-6). 1974. PLB 5.25 o.p. (ISBN 0-87191-358-5). Creative Ed.
How to Have Fun Making Easter Decorations. Lee Wagner. LC 74-10595. (Creative Craft Bks.). (Illus.). 32p. (gr. 2-6). 1974. PLB 5.95 (ISBN 0-87191-361-5). Creative Ed.
How to Have Fun Making Holiday Decorations. Lee Wagner. LC 74-112308. (Creative Craft Bks.). (Illus.). 32p. (gr. 2-6). 1974. PLB 5.95 (ISBN 0-87191-362-3). Creative Ed.
How to Have Fun Making Lunch. Creative Editors. LC 74-8459. (Creative Craft Bks.). (Illus.). 32p. (gr. 2-6). 1974. PLB 5.95 (ISBN 0-87191-357-7). Creative Ed.
How to Have Fun Making Mobiles. Creative Educational Society Editors. LC 73-18210. (Creative Craft Bks.). (Illus.). 32p. (gr. 2-5). 1973. PLB 5.95 (ISBN 0-87191-293-7). Creative Ed.
How to Have Fun Making Paper Air Planes. Creative Educational Society Editors. LC 73-19589. (Creative Craft Bks.). (Illus.). 32p. (gr. 2-5). 1973. PLB 5.95 (ISBN 0-87191-294-5). Creative Ed.
How to Have Fun Making Puppets. Creative Educational Society Editors. LC 73-18225. (Creative Craft Bks.). (Illus.). 32p. (gr. 2-5). 1973. PLB 5.95 (ISBN 0-87191-295-3). Creative Ed.
How to Have Fun Pressing Flowers. Lee Wagner. LC 74-8926. (Creative Craft Bks.). (Illus.). 32p. (gr. 2-6). 1974. PLB 5.75 o.p. (ISBN 0-87191-365-8). Creative Ed.
How to Have Fun Sewing. Creative Educational Society Editors. LC 73-10066. (Creative Craft Bks.). (Illus.). 32p. 1973. PLB 5.75 o.p. (ISBN 0-87191-252-X). Creative Ed.
How to Have Fun Weaving. Creative Educational Society Editors. LC 73-12467. (Creative Craft Bks). (Illus.). 32p. (gr. 2-5). 1973. PLB 5.75 o.p. (ISBN 0-87191-272-4). Creative Ed.
How to Have Fun with a Flower Garden. Creative Editors. LC 74-12442. (Creative Craft Bks.). (Illus.). 32p. (gr. 2-6). 1974. PLB 5.25 o.p. (ISBN 0-87191-364-X). Creative Ed.
How to Have Fun with a Vegetable Garden. Creative Editors. LC 74-12297. (Creative Craft Bks.). (Illus.). 32p. (gr. 2-6). 1974. PLB 5.95 (ISBN 0-87191-363-1). Creative Ed.
How to Have Fun with an Indoor Garden. Creative Educational Society Editors. LC 73-18258. (Creative Craft Bks.). (Illus.). 32p. (gr. 2-5). 1973. PLB 5.95 (ISBN 0-87191-297-X). Creative Ed.
How to Have Fun with Decoupage. Lee Wagner. LC 74-9829. (Creative Craft Bks.). (Illus.). 32p. (gr. 2-6). 1974. PLB 5.95 (ISBN 0-87191-366-6). Creative Ed.
How to Have Fun with Macrame. Creative Educational Society Editors. LC 73-19667. (Creative Craft Bks.). (Illus.). 32p. (gr. 2-5). 1973. PLB 5.95 (ISBN 0-87191-290-2). Creative Ed.
How to Have Fun with Needlepoint. Creative Educational Society Editors. LC 73-18226. (Creative Craft Bks.). (Illus.). 32p. (gr. 2-5). 1973. PLB 5.95 (ISBN 0-87191-296-1). Creative Ed.
How to Have Intercourse Without Getting Screwed. Jennifer Wear & King Holmes. LC 76-41190. 1976. pap. 4.95 (ISBN 0-914842-12-9). Madrona Pubs.
How to Heat & Eat with Woodburning Stoves. Willah Weddon. (Illus.). 128p. 1980. pap. 4.95 (ISBN 0-932296-06-8). Eberly Pr.
How to Help Children with Common Problems. Charles E. Schaefer & Howard L. Millman. 445p. 1980. 15.95 (ISBN 0-442-24506-8). Van Nos Reinhold.
How to Help the Christian Home. Wayne E. Rickerson. LC 77-94923. 1978. pap. 3.25 (ISBN 0-8307-0588-0, 54-083-18). Regal.

How to Help Your Child Have a Spiritual Life: Inner Development with or Without Organized Religion. Annette Hollander. LC 79-28074. (Illus.). 224p. 1980. 12.95 (ISBN 0-89479-061-7). A & W Pubs.

How to Help Your Child Start School. Bernard Ryan. 1980. 9.95. Caroline Hse.

How to Help Your Child Start School. Bernard Ryan, Jr. Ed. by Harold S. Longman. LC 80-50170. 180p. 1980. 9.95 (ISBN 0-934924-01-5). Soundview Bks.

How to Help Your Child Start School: A Practical Guide for Parents & Teachers of Four to Six Year Olds. Bernard Ryan, Jr. 166p. 1981. pap. 4.95 (ISBN 0-399-50539-3, Perigee). Putnam.

How to Help Yourself: The Art of Program Development. Robert R. Carkhuff. LC 74-18144. (Life Skills Ser.). (Illus.). 172p. 1974. pap. text ed. 8.50x (ISBN 0-914234-02-1). Human Res Dev Pr.

How to Hold a Garage Sale. James M. Ullman. LC 80-53812. (Illus.). 96p. (Orig.). 1981. pap. 3.95 (ISBN 0-528-88040-3). Rand.

How to Hold an Audience in the Hollow of Your Hand: Seven Techniques for Starting Your Speech, Eleven Techniques for Keeping It Rolling. Art Fettig. LC 79-14145. 1979. 9.95 (ISBN 0-8119-0322-2). Fell.

How to Hotrod Small-Block Chevys. rev. ed. Bill Fisher & Bob Waar. LC 73-173702. (Illus.). 192p. 1976. pap. 7.95 (ISBN 0-912656-06-9). H P Bks.

How to Hotrod Volkswagen Engines. Bill Fisher. LC 72-28084. (Illus.). 1970. pap. 5.95 o.p. (ISBN 0-912656-03-4). H P Bks.

How to Hypnotize. Bradford Chambers. LC 57-6582. (Illus.). 1957. 9.95 (ISBN 0-87396-004-1). Stravon.

How to Hypnotize Yourself & Others. Rachel Copelan. LC 80-70951. 386p. 1981. 10.95 (ISBN 0-8119-0418-0). Fell.

How to Identify English Silver Drinking Vessels. Douglas Ash. 15.00x (ISBN 0-392-07924-0, SpS). Soccer.

How to Identify Grasses & Grasslike Plants. H. D. Harrington. LC 76-17744. (Illus.). 142p. 1977. pap. 5.95x (ISBN 0-8040-0746-2). Swallow.

How to Identify Mushrooms (to Genus II): Field Identification of Genera. David L. Largent & H. Thiers. (Illus.). 1977. pap. 3.50x (ISBN 0-916422-08-9). Mad River.

How to Identify Mushrooms (to Genus IV) Keys to Families & Genera. Daniel Stuntz et al. (Illus.). 1977. pap. 5.50x (ISBN 0-916422-10-0). Mad River.

How to Identify Mushrooms (to Genus I) Macroscopic Features. 2nd ed. David Largent. (Illus.). 1977. pap. 4.85x (ISBN 0-916422-00-3). Mad River.

How to Identify Mushrooms (to Genus III) Microscopic Features. David Largent et al. (Illus.). 1977. pap. 8.25x (ISBN 0-916422-09-7). Mad River.

How to Identify Mushrooms to Genus V. Using Cultural & Developmental Features. Roy Watling. 1981. pap. price not set. Mad River.

How to Identify Plants. H. D. Harrington & L. W. Durrell. LC 57-4731. (Illus.). 203p. 1957. pap. 5.95x (ISBN 0-8040-0149-9, 16). Swallow.

How to Immigrate Without a Lawyer. Rod Williams. 200p. 1980. pap. 19.95 (ISBN 0-89260-198-1). Hwong Pub.

How to Improve Collections Without Really Trying. Charles H. Hoffman. 1977. pap. 2.75 (ISBN 0-934914-07-9). NACM.

How to Improve Human Performance: Behaviorism in Business & Industry. Thomas K. Connellan. 1978. text ed. 13.95 scp (ISBN 0-06-041349-2, HarpC). Har-Row.

How to Improve Your Bridge. H. W. Kelsey. 1979. 6.95 o.p. (ISBN 0-571-09726-X, Pub. by Faber & Faber); pap. 4.95 (ISBN 0-571-11438-5). Merrimack Bk Serv.

How to Improve Your Bridge. H. W. Kelsey. (Illus.). 1971. 6.95 o.p. (ISBN 0-571-09726-X, Pub. by Faber & Faber). Merrimack Bk Serv.

How to Improve Your Child's Behavior Through Diet. Laura J. Stevens & Rosemary B. Stoner. 1981. pap. 3.50 (ISBN 0-451-09812-9, E9812, Signet Bks). NAL.

How to Improve Your Comprehension. Bertha Davis & Susan Whitfield. (gr. 7 up). 1980. PLB 6.45 (ISBN 0-531-04132-8). Watts.

How to Improve Your Grammar. (gr. 7 up). 1980. PLB 6.45 (ISBN 0-531-04131-X). Watts.

How to Improve Your Memory. Dan Halacy. (Career Concise Guides Ser.). (Illus.). (gr. 7 up). 1977. PLB 6.45 s&l (ISBN 0-531-00094-X). Watts.

How to Improve Your Memory. James D. Weinland. (Orig.). 1957. pap. 3.50 (ISBN 0-06-463273-3, EH 273, EH). Har-Row.

How to Improve Your Speaking Voice. Georgiana Peacher. LC 66-10277. 1966. 9.95 (ISBN 0-8119-0090-8). Fell.

How to Improve Your Spelling & Vocabulary. Jessica Davidson. (gr. 7 up). 1980. PLB 6.45 (ISBN 0-531-04133-6). Watts.

How to Incorporate in Tax Free Nevada for Only Fifty Dollars. John L. Hayden. LC 80-85433. 50p. 1981. text ed. 14.95. Newport Beach.

How to Increase Reading Ability. 7th ed. Albert J. Harris & Edward R. Sipay. (Illus.). 736p. 1980. text ed. 18.95 (ISBN 0-582-28066-4). Longman.

How to Increase Reading Ability: A Guide to Developmental & Remedial Methods. 6th ed. Albert J. Harris & Edward R. Sipay. 1978. text ed. 16.95x o.p. (ISBN 0-582-28089-3). Longman.

How to Install Paneling, Make Valances, Cornices. Donald R. Brann. LC 65-25756. 1979. pap. 5.95 (ISBN 0-87733-605-9). Easi-Bild.

How to Install Protective Alarm Devices. rev ed. Donald R. Brann. LC 72-89141. (Illus.). 1975. lib. bdg. 5.95 (ISBN 0-87733-095-6); pap. 5.95 (ISBN 0-87733-695-4). Easi-Bild.

How to Install Your Own Home or Mobile Electric Power Plant. Edward Dowis. (Illus.). 1979. 8.95 o.p. (ISBN 0-8306-9861-2); pap. 5.95 o.p. (ISBN 0-8306-1063-4, 1063). TAB Bks.

How to Interpret the Warning Signals Which the Stock Market Emits Foretelling the Future Course of Security & Commodity Prices. George M. Tracy. (Illus.). 1980. 37.45 (ISBN 0-918968-49-6). Inst Econ Finan.

How to Interpret Your Dreams. Mark Thurston. 1978. pap. 4.95 (ISBN 0-87604-107-1). ARE Pr.

How to Interview & Hire Productive People. Jack McQuaig et al. LC 80-70952. 204p. 1981. 9.95 (ISBN 0-8119-0332-X). Fell.

How to Invest in Bonds. Hugh C. Sherwood. LC 74-81543. 192p. 1974. 7.95 o.s.i. (ISBN 0-8027-0466-2). Walker & Co.

How to Invest in Diamonds, Metals & Collectibles for Maximum Profits. Arthur C. Simon. (Illus.). 1980. pap. 12.95 o.p. (ISBN 0-930490-23-1). Future Shop.

How to Invest in Gold Coins. Donald J. Hoppe. LC 70-115342. (Dollar Growth Lib.). (Illus.). 1970. 8.95 o.p. (ISBN 0-87000-076-4). Arlington Hse.

How to Invest in Singles. rev. 3rd ed. Don Bale, Jr. 1975. pap. 5.00 o.p. (ISBN 0-912070-09-9). Bale Bks.

How to Invest in Singles. 4th, rev. ed. Don Bale, Jr. 1980. pap. 5.00. Bale Bks.

How to Invest in Uncirculated Singles. rev. 3rd ed. Don Bale, Jr. 1975. pap. 5.00 o.p. (ISBN 0-912070-10-2). Bale Bks.

How to Invest in Uncirculated Singles. 4th, rev. ed. Don Bale, Jr. 1980. pap. 5.00. Bale Bks.

How to Invest Your Money & Profit from Inflation. Morton Shulman. 1981. pap. 2.50 (ISBN 0-345-29740-7). Ballantine.

How to Judge a House. A. M. Watkins. 1972. pap. 3.50 (ISBN 0-8015-3732-0, Hawthorn). Dutton.

How to Judge a Nativity. Alan Leo. (Astrologer's Library). 1979. pap. 6.95 (ISBN 0-89281-177-3). Inner Tradit.

How to Keep a Secret. Elizabeth James & Carol Barkin. (gr. k-6). 1980. pap. 1.25 (ISBN 0-440-43483-1, YB). Dell.

How to Keep Score in Business: Accounting & Financial Analysis for the Non-Accountant. Robert Follett. 1980. pap. 2.50 (ISBN 0-451-61860-2, ME1860, Ment). NAL.

How to Keep Slim, Healthy & Young with Juice Fasting. Paavo Airola. 3.25 o.p. (ISBN 0-685-90565-9). Bi World Indus.

How to Keep the Money You Owe: One Hundred One (Legal(Ways to Confound Your Creditors. David Rathbone. (Illus.). 70p. (Orig.). 1981. pap. 10.00. Phoenix Laguna.

How to Keep Warm in Winter. Dave Ross. LC 79-6838. (Illus.). 32p. (Orig.). 1980. PLB 6.89 (ISBN 0-690-04077-6, TYC-J); pap. 3.95 (ISBN 0-690-04060-1). T Y Crowell.

How to Keep Your Corvair Alive. Richard Finch. LC 77-16221. (Illus.). 1977. pap. 5.95 o.p. (ISBN 0-912656-58-1). H P Bks.

How to Keep Your Hair on. 1980. 15.00x (ISBN 0-85032-191-3, Pub. by Daniel Co England). State Mutual Bk.

How to Keep Your Hair On. Donald Law. 70p. 1968. pap. 4.00x (ISBN 0-8464-1025-7). Beekman Pubs.

How to Keep Your Pet Healthy. Elizabeth Charles. LC 79-180464. (Illus.). 176p. 1974. pap. 1.50 o.s.i. (ISBN 0-02-062400-X, Collier). Macmillan.

How to Keep Your VW Rabbit Alive, a Manual of Step by Step Procedures for the Compleat Idiot. Richard Sealey. LC 79-91278. (Illus.). 416p. (Orig.). 1980. pap. 12.00 (ISBN 0-912528-17-6). John Muir.

How to Kick a Football. Edward J. Storey. (Illus.). 160p. (Orig.). 1981. pap. text ed. 5.95 (ISBN 0-918438-61-6). Leisure Pr.

How to Kill, Vol. III. John Minnery. (Illus.). 92p. (Orig.). 1979. pap. 6.00 (ISBN 0-87364-156-6). Paladin Ent.

How to Kill, Vol. IV. John Minnery. (Illus.). 92p. (Orig.). 1979. pap. 6.00 (ISBN 0-87364-162-0). Paladin Ent.

How to Kill, Vol. V. John Minnery. (Illus.). 86p. 1980. pap. 5.00 (ISBN 0-87364-201-5). Paladin Ent.

How to Know God's Will. Lloyd J. Ogilvie. LC 80-84824. 1981. pap. 4.95 (ISBN 0-89081-282-9). Harvest Hse.

How to Know If You're Really in Love. Charlie Sheed. 1981. pap. 2.25 (ISBN 0-671-82841-X). PB.

How to Know the Beetles. 2nd ed. Ross H. Arnett, Jr. et al. (Pictured Key Nature Ser.). 1980. text ed. 10.95x (ISBN 0-697-04777-6); wire coil 7.95x (ISBN 0-697-04776-8). Wm C Brown.

How to Know the Non-Gilled Mushrooms. Alex H. Smith et al. (Pictured Key Nature Ser). 440p. 1973. text ed. 9.95x (ISBN 0-697-04867-5); wire coil 7.95x (ISBN 0-697-04866-7). Wm C Brown.

How to Know the True Slime Molds. M. L. Farr. 200p. 1981. write for info. wire coil (ISBN 0-697-04779-2). Wm C Brown.

How to Know the Weeds. 3rd ed. R. E. Wilkinson & Harry E. Jaques. (Picture Key Nature Ser.). 256p. 1979. cloth ed. write for info. (ISBN 0-697-04764-4); wire coil bdg. write for info. (ISBN 0-697-04765-2). Wm C Brown.

How to Know Western Australian Wildflowers: A Key to the Flore of the Flora of the Extratropical Regions of Western Australia, Pt. IIIA. Ed. by B. J. Grieve & W. E. Blackall. 350p. 1980. 39.50x (ISBN 0-85564-160-6, Pub. by U of West Australia Pr Australia). Intl Schol Bk Serv.

How to Know When God Speaks. Helen K. Hosier. LC 79-84721. 160p. (Orig.). pap. 4.95 (ISBN 0-89081-197-0). Harvest Hse.

How to Know You Are Born Again. Richard Dugan. 1978. pap. 1.95 (ISBN 0-89728-037-7, 679385). Omega Pubns OR.

How to Lead a Soul to Christ. R. G. Lee. 448p. 1974. pap. 1.25 (ISBN 0-310-27461-3). Zondervan.

How to Learn Astrology. Marc E. Jones. LC 76-55119. (Illus.). 1977. pap. 3.95 (ISBN 0-394-73342-8). Shambhala Pubns.

How to Learn Astrology. Marc E. Jones. LC 69-19864. 1969. 10.50 o.p. (ISBN 0-87878-002-5, Sabian). Great Eastern.

How to Learn Spanish the Easy Way. Livia Kampe. LC 79-6769. 192p. 1980. pap. text ed. 9.00 (ISBN 0-8191-0950-9). U Pr of Amer.

How to Leave Home & Survive. Claudia A. Forbes. LC 76-56832. (Illus.). 1978. pap. 3.95 (ISBN 0-89430-031-8). Morgan-Pacific.

How to Lick Executive Stress. Robert C. Page. 1977. Repr. 4.95 (ISBN 0-346-12252-X). Cornerstone.

How to Lick Inflation Before It Licks You. Eugene J. Benge. LC 80-70954. 204p. 1981. 9.95 (ISBN 0-8119-0342-7). Fell.

How to Limit Government Spending. Aaron Wildavsky. 197p. 1980. 8.95 (ISBN 0-686-69040-0). U of Cal Pr.

How to Listen Assertively. Baxter Geeting & Corinne Geeting. (Illus.). 1978. 7.95 o.p. (ISBN 0-671-18365-6, Sovereign). Monarch Pr.

How to Listen Assertively. Baxter Geeting & Corinne Geeting. (Illus.). 1976. 8.95 (ISBN 0-671-18336-2); pap. 3.95 (ISBN 0-671-18336-2). Sovereign Bks.

How to Listen Assertively. Baxter Geeting & Corinne Geeting. (Illus.). 1978. pap. 3.95 (ISBN 0-671-18336-2). Monarch Pr.

How to Listen-How to Be Heard. Thomas G. Banville. LC 77-17961. 1978. 12.95 (ISBN 0-88229-332-X); pap. 7.95 (ISBN 0-686-68003-0). Nelson-Hall.

How to Live a Holy Life. C. E. Orr. 112p. 0.75; pap. 2.00 3 copies. Faith Pub Hse.

How to Live Cheap but Good: A Primer for People with High Tastes & Low Income. M. Poriss. 1971. 6.95 o.p. (ISBN 0-07-050522-5, GB). McGraw.

How to Live Creatively. Dorothy E. Stanley. LC 79-17841. (Orig.). 1980. pap. 4.95 (ISBN 0-89865-016-X, Unilaw). Donning Co.

How to Live Forever. John Phillips. (Teach Yourself the Bible Ser). 1964. pap. 1.75 (ISBN 0-8024-3700-1). Moody.

How to Live in Florida on Ten Thousand Dollars a Year, 1981-82. 224p. Date not set. pap. 7.95 (ISBN 0-671-41397-X). Frommer-Pasmantier.

How to Live in High Victory. Harold Hill. 1978. 1.90 (ISBN 0-8297-0863-4). Life Pubs Intl.

How to Live in the Woods on Pennies a Day. Bradford Angier. LC 70-140741. (Illus.). 192p. 1971. pap. 7.95 (ISBN 0-8117-2009-8). Stackpole.

How to Live Like a King's Kid. Harold Hill. LC 73-93002. 1974. pap. 2.95 (ISBN 0-88270-083-9). Logos.

How to Live Longer, Stronger, Slimmer. Kenneth S. Keyes, Jr. 1966. 7.95 o.p. (ISBN 0-8119-0093-2). Fell.

How to Live Rent Free in the 1980's: It's Not Too Late! Jim Anderson. 1980. write for info. (ISBN 0-932574-04-1). Brun Pr.

How to Live Separately Together: A Guide for Working Couples. Richard K. Irish. LC 78-22637. 264p. 1981. 11.95 (ISBN 0-385-14650-7, Anchor Pr). Doubleday.

How to Live the Bible Like a King's Kid. Harold Hill & Irene B. Harrell. 1980. pap. 3.95 (ISBN 0-8007-5051-9). Revell.

How to Live the Jesus Life. LeRoy Dugan. Orig. Title: Youth's Exciting Possibilities. 128p. (YA) 1973. pap. 1.50 (ISBN 0-87123-660-5, 200660). Bethany Fell.

How to Live the Victorious Life. pap. 1.75 (ISBN 0-310-33482-9). Zondervan.

How to Live Three Hundred and Sixty-Five Days a Year. John A. Schindler. 192p. 1978. pap. 2.25 (ISBN 0-449-23922-5, Crest). Fawcett.

How to Live Three Hundred Sixty-Five Days a Year. Schindler. pap. 3.95 (ISBN 0-13-416792-9, Parker). P-H.

How to Live Through Jr. High School. new ed. Eric W. Johnson. LC 75-829. 288p. 1975. 9.95 (ISBN 0-397-01076-1). Lippincott.

How to Live with a Pregnant Wife. Janet Patterson & Robert C. Patterson. LC 76-2014. 192p. 1976. pap. 3.95 o.p. (ISBN 0-8407-5603-8). Nelson.

How to Live with Hemophilia. James M. Vogel et al. (Illus.). 140p. (Orig.). 1972. pap. 2.75 o.p. (ISBN 0-913456-66-7). Interbk Inc.

How to Live with Hypoglycemia. Charles Weller & Brian R. Boylan. 1977. pap. 2.25 (ISBN 0-515-05979-X). Jove Pubns.

How to Live with Your Children. Don Fontenelle. LC 80-21261. (Illus.). 264p. (Orig.). 1981. write for info. (ISBN 0-930256-07-7); pap. 9.95. Almar.

How to Live with Yourself. David Seabury. 104p. 1972. pap. 3.95 (ISBN 0-911336-39-7). Sci of Mind.

How to Lobby Congress: A Guide for the Citizen Lobbyist. Donald Dekieffer. 228p. 1981. 12.95 (ISBN 0-396-07965-2); pap. 7.95 (ISBN 0-396-07969-5). Dodd.

How to Locate Reviews of Plays & Films: A Bibliography of Criticism from the Beginnings to the Present. Gordon Samples. LC 76-3509. 124p. 1976. 10.00 (ISBN 0-8108-0914-1). Scarecrow.

How to Look As Young As You Feel. Rae Lindsay. (Illus.). 320p. 1980. pap. 2.50 o.p. (ISBN 0-523-40843-9). Pinnacle Bks.

How to Look Ten Years Younger. Adrien Arpel. 1981. pap. 8.95 (ISBN 0-446-97823-X). Warner Bks.

How to Lose Weight the Action Way: Young Adult-Teen Edition. Francie M. Berg. (Illus.). 176p. (gr. 9 up). 1980. 12.95 (ISBN 0-918532-03-5); pap. 8.95 (ISBN 0-918532-04-3); leaders guide for action groups, 48p. 4.95 (ISBN 0-918532-05-1). Flying Diamond Bks.

How to Lose Your Fear of Flying. Perry Lafferty. (Illus., Orig.). 1980. pap. 2.95 (ISBN 0-8431-0654-9). Price Stern.

How to Make a Book. Ellen Geisler et al. LC 77-83346. 1978. pap. 10.00 o.s.i. (ISBN 0-930638-03-4). Cal-Syl Pr.

How to Make a Cloud. Jeanne Bendick. LC 74-134834. (Finding-Out Book). (Illus.). 64p. (gr. 2-3). PLB 6.95 (ISBN 0-8193-0441-7). Enslow Pubs.

How to Make a Fortune in Finders' Fees. rev. ed. Jack Payne. 1981. 10.95 (ISBN 0-8119-0346-X). Fell.

How to Make a Fortune Through Export Mail-Order Riches. 2nd ed. Tyler G. Hicks. 150p. 1981. pap. 17.50 (ISBN 0-914306-57-X). Intl Wealth.

How to Make a Habit of Success. Bernhard Haldane. 240p. 1981. pap. 2.50 (ISBN 0-446-91658-7). Warner Bks.

How to Make a Hit Record. Mike Jahn. LC 76-9939. 192p. 1976. 7.95 o.p. (ISBN 0-87888-106-9). Bradbury Pr.

How to Make a Million Dollars from a Fruit & Vegetables Roadside Market. Gilbert S. Watts. (Illus.). 1977. Repr. 39.75 (ISBN 0-89266-054-6). Am Classical Coll Pr.

How to Make a Million Dollars in the Stock Market—Automatically. Robert Lichello. (Orig.). 1977. pap. 1.95 o.p. (ISBN 0-451-07619-2, J7619, Sig). NAL.

How to Make a Million Dollars in the Stock Market - Automatically. rev. ed. Robert Lichello. 1980. pap. 2.25 (ISBN 0-451-09461-1, E9461, Sig). NAL.

How to Make a Violin. John Broadhouse. Repr. lib. bdg. 29.00 (ISBN 0-403-03872-3). Scholarly.

How to Make & Sell Original Crosswords & Other Puzzles. William Sunners. LC 80-52333. (Illus.). 256p. 1981. 12.95 (ISBN 0-8069-4632-6); lib. bdg. 11.69 (ISBN 0-8069-4633-4). Sterling.

How to Make & Sell Your Arts & Crafts. Lois Becker. LC 75-29939. (Illus.). 1975. 8.95 (ISBN 0-8119-0250-1); pap. 4.95 (ISBN 0-88391-056-X). Fell.

How to Make & Set Nets: The Technology of Netting. John Garner. (Illus.). 96p. 10.00 (ISBN 0-85238-031-3, FN). Unipub.

How to Make & Use Overhead Transparancies. Anna S. Darkes. (Illus.). 1977. pap. 2.50 (ISBN 0-8024-3652-8). Moody.

How to Make Bamboo Fly Rods. George W. Barnes. 1977. 11.95 (ISBN 0-87691-237-4). Winchester Pr.

How to Make Baskets. Mary White. LC 72-162523. Repr. of 1902 ed. 15.00 (ISBN 0-8103-3064-4). Gale.

How to Make Better Speeches. William G. Hoffman. LC 48-6985. (Funk & W Bk.). 1976. pap. 3.00 o.s.i. (ISBN 0-308-10251-7, TYC-T). T Y Crowell.

How to Make Big Improvements in the Small PR Shop. Compiled by R. Keith Moore. (Orig.). 1979. pap. text ed. 8.00 (ISBN 0-89964-046-X). CASE.

How to Make Cowboy Horse Gear. 2nd ed. Bruce Grant & Lee W. Rice. LC 56-10884. (Illus.). 1956. pap. 6.00 (ISBN 0-87033-034-9). Cornell Maritime.

How to Make Democracy Work. Leonard Orr. 1972. pap. 3.00 o.p. (ISBN 0-686-09763-7). L Orr.

How to Make Dolls' Houses. Audrey Johnson. (Illus.). 1975. pap. 5.50 (ISBN 0-8231-7008-X). Branford.

How to Make Federal Mandatory Special Education Work for You: A Handbook for Educators & Consumers. Robert Hagerty & Thomas Howard. 144p. 1978. 15.75 (ISBN 0-398-03822-8). C C Thomas.

How to Make Fish Mounts & Other Fish Trophies. 2nd ed. Edward C. Midgalski. 288p. 1981. 15.95 (ISBN 0-471-07990-1, Pub. by Wiley-Interscience). Wiley.

How to Make Fish Mounts & Other Fish Trophies. Edward C. Migdalski. (Illus.). 1960. 17.50 (ISBN 0-8260-6095-1). Ronald Pr.

How to Make Good Curries. Helen Lawson. (Illus.). 80p. 1980. 11.95 (ISBN 0-600-34408-8). Transatlantic.

How to Make Historic American Costumes. Mary Evans. LC 78-159952. (Illus.). xii, 178p. 1976. Repr. of 1942 ed. 24.00 (ISBN 0-8103-4141-7). Gale.

How to Make It in Hollywood. Wende Hyland & Roberta Haynes. LC 75-17523. 250p. 1975. 13.95 (ISBN 0-88229-239-0). Nelson Hall.

How to Make Knives. Richard W. Barney et al. Ed. by Wallace Beinfeld. 182p. 1977. 13.95 (ISBN 0-917714-13-X). Beinfeld Pub.

How to Make Love to a Man. Alexandra Penney. Ed. by Carol Southern. 160p. 1981. 10.00 (ISBN 0-517-54145-9). Potter.

How to Make Meetings Work. Micheal Doyle & Davis Straus. 240p. 1981. pap. 2.50 (ISBN 0-87216-614-7). Playboy Pbks.

How to Make Money. Karen O. Sweeney. LC 77-2406. (Career Concise Guides Ser.). (gr. 5-8). 1977. PLB 6.45 (ISBN 0-531-01278-6). Watts.

How to Make Money from Antiques. Mel Lewis. (Illus.). 160p. 1981. 12.50 (ISBN 0-7137-1084-5, Pub. by Blandford Pr England). Sterling.

How to Make Money in Wall Street. Louis Rukeyser. 288p. 1976. pap. 4.95 (ISBN 0-385-04652-9, Dolp). Doubleday.

How to Make Money in Wall Street Through the Intelligent Use of Price-Earnings Ratios. Lloyd A. Mitchell. (The New Stock Market Reference Library). (Illus.). 112p. 1981. 39.45 (ISBN 0-918968-93-3). Inst Econ Fina.

How to Make Money Listing Business Opportunities. Bertram Klein. 1981. 9.95 (ISBN 0-533-04710-2). Vantage.

How to Make Money Selling the Songs You Write. rev. ed. Henry Boye. LC 75-124473. 1975. pap. 4.95 (ISBN 0-8119-0381-8). Fell.

How to Make Money Trading Listed Puts. Lin Tso. LC 78-9295. 1978. 10.95 (ISBN 0-8119-0295-1). Fell.

How to Make Money with Your Micro-Computer. Carl Townsend & Merl Miller. LC 79-53477. 1979. pap. 9.95 (ISBN 0-89661-001-2). Robotics Pr.

How to Make Money Writing Greeting Cards. Lorraine Hardt. LC 68-18134. (Illus.). 1968. 8.95 (ISBN 0-8119-0096-7). Fell.

How to Make Money Writing Short Articles & Fillers. Marjorie M. Hinds. 1967. 6.95 o.s.i. (ISBN 0-8119-0097-5). Fell.

How to Make Money 24 Hours a Day. Elbert Lee. 140p. 1980. pap. 9.95 (ISBN 0-686-28038-5). Positive Pub.

How to Make More Money with Your Garage Sale. Ryan Petty. 96p. 1981. pap. 3.95 (ISBN 0-312-39602-3). St Martin.

How to Make One Hundred Thousand Dollars a Year Selling Residential Real Estate. Dan Ramsey. 297p. 1980. 14.95 (ISBN 0-13-423582-7, Busn). P-H.

How to Make People Listen to You. Dominick A. Barbara. 188p. 1971. pap. 9.75 photocopy ed. spiral (ISBN 0-398-02223-2). C C Thomas.

How to Make Possum's Honey Bread. Carla Stevens. LC 75-28183. 40p. (gr. 2-6). 1976. 6.50 (ISBN 0-395-28882-7, Clarion). HM.

How to Make Psychology Work for You. rev. ed. A. P. Sperling. Orig. Title: Psychology for the Millions. 192p. 1975. pap. 1.25 o.p. (ISBN 0-449-30642-9, P642, Prem). Fawcett.

How to Make Something Out of Practically Nothing: New Fashions from Old Clothes. Barbara Corrigan. LC 75-15774. 96p. (gr. 4-7). 1976. 5.95 o.p. (ISBN 0-385-11670-5). Doubleday.

How to Make the Most of the New You. Linda Fine. 224p. 1981. 10.95 (ISBN 0-668-04919-7); pap. 6.95 (ISBN 0-668-04923-5). Arco.

How to Make Things Go Your Way. Ralph Charell. 192p. 1981. pap. 4.95 (ISBN 0-346-12518-9). Cornerstone.

How to Make Wine in Your Own Kitchen. 12th ed. Mettja C. Roate. (Orig.). 1979. pap. 1.75 (ISBN 0-532-17241-8). Manor Bks.

How to Make Wire Jewelry. Duane Ferre. (Illus.). 192p. 1980. 13.95 (ISBN 0-8019-6859-3); pap. 7.95 (ISBN 0-8019-6860-7). Chilton.

How to Make Working Decoys. George R. Starr, Jr. (Illus.). 1978. 17.50 (ISBN 0-87691-260-9). Winchester Pr.

How to Make Your Car Last a Lifetime. Bob Fendell. LC 80-19759. (Illus.). 216p. 1981. 12.95 (ISBN 0-03-053661-8); pap. 6.95 (ISBN 0-03-053656-1). HR&W.

How to Make Your Car Run Better. Ross R. Olney & Mary Ann Duganne. LC 77-1566. (Career Concise Guides Ser.). 1977. 6.45 (ISBN 0-531-01296-4). Watts.

How to Make Your Child a Winner: Ten Keys to Rearing Successful Children. Victor B. Cline. 320p. 1980. 14.95 o.p. (ISBN 0-8027-0658-4); pap. 8.95 o.p. (ISBN 0-8027-7165-3). Walker & Co.

How to Make Your Life Work. Ken Keyes, Jr. & Bruce Burkan. 1976. pap. 3.95 (ISBN 0-346-12226-0). Cornerstone.

How to Make Your Life Work, or Why Aren't You Happy? Ken Keyes, Jr. & Bruce T. Burkan. LC 74-76803. (Illus.). 192p. 1974. pap. 2.00 (ISBN 0-9600688-5-6). Living Love.

How to Make Your Money Make Money. Arthur Levitt, Jr. LC 80-70617. 220p. 1981. 11.95 (ISBN 0-87094-236-0). Dow Jones-Irwin.

How to Make Your Own Books. Harvey Weiss. LC 73-17267. (Illus.). (gr. 5-12). 1974. 9.95 (ISBN 0-690-00400-1, TYC-J). T Y Crowell.

How to Make Your Own Lures & Flies. Mel Marshall. (Funk & W Bk.). (Illus.). 1977. 7.95 o.s.i. (ISBN 0-308-10290-8, TYC-T); pap. 4.50 (ISBN 0-308-10292-4, TYC-T). T Y Crowell.

How to Make Your Own Recreation & Hobby Rooms. rev. ed. Ralph Treves. LC 68-31229. (Popular Science Skill Books Ser.). (Illus.). 164p. 1976. pap. 3.95 o.s.i. (ISBN 0-06-014364-9, TD-268, HarpT). Har-Row.

How to Make Your Own Wedding Gown. Claudia Ein. LC 77-74299. 1978. pap. 8.95 o.p. (ISBN 0-385-11105-3). Doubleday.

How to Make Yourself Miserable. Dan Greenberg & Marcia Jacobs. 1976. pap. 3.95 (ISBN 0-394-73168-9). Random.

How to Manage.., 4 vols. Thomas E. Anastasi, Jr. Incl. How to Manage Your Writing. 123p (ISBN 0-932078-46-X); How to Manage Your Speaking. 128p (ISBN 0-932078-45-1); How to Manage Your Reading. 129p (ISBN 0-932078-44-3); Face to Face Communication. 198p (ISBN 0-932078-47-8). 1974. pap. 6.50 ea.; pap. 24.50 set of four (ISBN 0-932078-43-5). GE Tech Prom & Train.

How to Manage a Non-Profit Organization. John Fisher. 1978. 16.50 (ISBN 0-920432-00-X, Pub by Management & Fund Raising Ctr. Canada). Public Serv Materials.

How to Manage by Objectives. John W. Humble. (AMACOM Executive Bks). 1978. pap. 5.95 (ISBN 0-8144-7508-6). Am Mgmt.

How to Manage for More Profitable Results. George F. Truell. 1974. 55.50 o.p. (ISBN 0-85013-038-7). Dartnell Corp.

How to Manage the Sales Territory for Maximum Growth. Howard Berrian. (Illus.). 49.95 o.p. (ISBN 0-89846-031-X). Sales & Mktg.

How to Manage Your Boss. Christopher Hegarty & Philip Goldberg. 288p. 1981. 12.95 (ISBN 0-89256-142-4). Rawson Wade.

How to Manage Your Money. John Kirk. (Orig.). pap. 1.50 o.p. (ISBN 0-87502-007-0). Benjamin Co.

How to Manage Yourself. Med Serif. LC 65-23870. (gr. 9 up). 1965. 9.95 (ISBN 0-8119-0098-3). Fell.

How to Master the Art of Pottery Painting. John C. Sparkes. (Illus.). 101p. 1981. 39.75 (ISBN 0-930582-86-1). Gloucester Art.

How to Master the Art of Spiritual Intercourse. Kenneth Rosellemar. (Society of Psychic Research Library). (Illus.). 1981. 45.75 (ISBN 0-89920-025-7). Am Inst Psych.

How to Master the Forces of Your Imagination for the Pursuit of Your Scientific Objectives. Julian Dekker. (Illus.). 1978. deluxe ed. 37.50 (ISBN 0-930582-07-1). Gloucester Art.

How to Maximize Your Advertising Investment. Philip M. Johnson. LC 80-10997. 224p. 1980. 18.95 (ISBN 0-8436-0769-6). CBI Pub.

How to Measure Achievement. rev. ed. Lynn L. Morris & Carol T. Fitz-Gibbon. LC 78-58656. (Program Evaluation Kit Ser.: Vol. 6). (Illus.). 159p. 1978. pap. 7.50 (ISBN 0-8039-1067-3). Sage.

How to Measure Attitudes. Marlene E. Henerson et al. LC 78-57010. (Program Evaluation Kit: Vol. 5). 1978. pap. 7.95x (ISBN 0-8039-1070-3). Sage.

How to Measure Program Implementation. Lynn L. Morris & Carol T. Fitz-Gibbon. LC 78-58655. (Program Evaluation Kit Ser.: Vol. 4). (Illus.). 140p. 1978. pap. 6.95 (ISBN 0-8039-1066-5). Sage.

How to Measure Programmer Productivity. Girish Parikh. 86p. 1981. pap. 15.00 (ISBN 0-932888-02-X). Shetal Ent.

How to Meditate Without Leaving the World. Avery Brooke. 1976. pap. 4.95 (ISBN 0-8164-0906-4). Crossroad NY.

How to Meet Girls: A Guide for Nice Guys. Rick Pagliotti. (Illus.). 1979. saddle stitched 2.95 (ISBN 0-9602694-0-1). R Pagliotti.

How to Meet Men...and Be Successful with Them. Mara L. Shaw. 1981. 9.95 (ISBN 0-9605602-0-3). Shaw Inc.

How to Minister to Senior Adults in Your Church. Horace L. Kerr. 1980. 4.95 (ISBN 0-8054-3222-1). Broadman.

How to Modernize a Kitchen. rev. ed. Donald R. Brann. LC 67-16947. 1976. lib. bdg. 5.95 (ISBN 0-87733-008-5); pap. 3.50 (ISBN 0-87733-608-3). Easi-Bild.

How to Modify Your Datsun- Four & Six Cylinder. (Orig.). 1981. pap. 9.95 (ISBN 0-89586-092-9). H P Bks.

How to Motivate Others Through Feedback. Ron Van Houten. 1980. 3.25 (ISBN 0-89079-048-5). H & H Ent.

How to Motivate Today's Workers: Motivational Models for Managers & Supervisors. Ed. by Bernard L. Rosenbaum. (Illus.). 192p. 1981. 14.95 (ISBN 0-07-053711-9, P&RB). McGraw.

How to Motivate Your Child Toward Success. William S. McBirnie. 1979. pap. 2.95 (ISBN 0-8423-1528-4). Tyndale.

How to Mount Fish. Archie Phillips & Bubba Phillips. (Illus.). 144p. 1981. 19.95 (ISBN 0-8117-0787-3). Stackpole.

How to Navigate Today. 5th ed. M. R. Hart. LC 68-23169. (Illus.). 1970. pap. 4.00 (ISBN 0-87033-035-7). Cornell Maritime.

How to Negotiate the Labor Agreement. 8th ed. Bruce Morse. 1979. 8.85 (ISBN 0-9602426-0-0). Trends Pub.

How to Obtain Abundant Clean Energy. Linda B. McGown & John O'M. Bockris. 275p. 1980. 14.95 (ISBN 0-306-40399-4, Plenum Pr). Plenum Pub.

How to Obtain Financing & Make Your Best Deal with Any Bank, Finance or Leasing Company. James G. Simmons. (Illus.). 380p. (Orig.). 1980. pap. 19.95 (ISBN 0-937700-00-2). Cambrian.

How to Open a Swiss Bank Account. James Kelder. LC 75-34285. 324p. 1976. 9.95 o.s.i. (ISBN 0-690-01033-8, TYC-T). T Y Crowell.

How to Open & Operate a Restaurant. Ray Petteruto. LC 80-67823. (Food Service Ser.). 269p. 1981. pap. 8.60 (ISBN 0-8273-1966-5); instr's. guide 1.90 (ISBN 0-8273-1967-3). Delmar.

How to Operate & Maintain Your Car & Save Thousands of Dollars. Peter A. Janzen. 120p. (Orig.). 1981. pap. 4.95 (ISBN 0-9604458-0-3). P A Janzen.

How to Organise & Operate a Small Business in Australia. John English. 270p. 1981. text ed. 22.50x (ISBN 0-86861-282-0, 2648). Allen Unwin.

How to Organize a Local Collection. A. Lynes. (Grafton Books on Library Science). 1977. lib. bdg. 8.75x (ISBN 0-233-96452-5). Westview.

How to Organize & Maintain an Efficient Hospital Housekeeping Department. Charles B. Miller. (Illus.). 142p. (Orig.). 1980. pap. 18.75 (ISBN 0-87258-290-6, 1440). Am Hospital.

How to Organize & Manage Your Own Religious Cult. Duke McCoy. 1980. pap. 6.95. Loompanics.

How to Organize & Operate a Small Business. 6th ed. Clifford M. Baumback & Kenneth Lawyer. (Illus.). 1979. ref. ed. 18.95 (ISBN 0-13-425694-8); study guide & wkbk. 7.95 (ISBN 0-13-425686-7). P-H.

How to Organize & Raise Funds for Small Non-Profit Organizations. David F. Long. 283p. 1979. 19.95 (ISBN 0-916068-09-9); pap. 10.95 (ISBN 0-916068-12-9). Groupwork Today.

How to Organize & Run a Film Society. Janet Weiner. (Illus.). 192p. 1973. pap. 3.95 o.s.i. (ISBN 0-02-012900-9, Collier). Macmillan.

How to Organize Meetings: A Handbook for Better Workshop, Seminar and Conference Management. Martin Jones. LC 80-28310. 138p. 1981. pap. 5.95 (ISBN 0-8253-0011-8). Beaufort Bks NY.

How to Organize Your Work & Your Life. Robert Moskowitz. LC 80-1815. (Illus.). 312p. 1981. 12.95 (ISBN 0-385-17011-4). Doubleday.

How to Organize Your Work & Your Life. Robert Moskowitz. LC 80-1815. (Illus.). 312p. 1981. pap. 6.95 (ISBN 0-385-17011-4, Dolp). Doubleday.

How to Overcome a Bad Back. James R. Sherman. LC 79-90870. (Illus., Orig.). 1980. pap. 5.95 (ISBN 0-935538-00-3). Pathway Bks.

How to Overcome Rejection & Become a Better Person. Douglas Delaney. (Illus.). 1980. pap. 12.95 o.p. (ISBN 0-930490-22-3). Future Shop.

How to Paint Anything. H. Cobb. 1972. 6.95 o.s.i. (ISBN 0-02-526360-9). Macmillan.

How to Paint in Oil: A Book for Beginners. Arthur Zaidenberg. LC 56-7892. (Illus.). (gr. 7-9). 1954. 5.95 (ISBN 0-8149-0444-0). Vanguard.

How to Paint the Chinese Way. Jean Long. (Illus.). 1979. 14.95 (ISBN 0-7137-0999-5, Pub by Blandford Pr England). Sterling.

How to Paint with a Knife. Coulton Waugh. LC 70-145666. (Illus.). 1971. 21.95 (ISBN 0-8230-3880-7). Watson-Guptill.

How to Paint with Water Colors: A Book for Beginners. Arthur Zaidenberg. LC 66-28885. (Illus.). (gr. 5 up). 1968. 5.95 (ISBN 0-8149-0440-8). Vanguard.

How to Parent. Fitzhugh Dodson. 444p. 1973. pap. 2.95 (ISBN 0-451-09401-8, E9401, Sig). NAL.

How to Parent Alone: A Guide for Single Parents. Joan Bel Geddes. LC 74-8241. 192p. 1974. 8.95 o.p. (ISBN 0-8164-9243-3). Continuum.

How to Pass the California Bar Exam. Rockne Reburn. (Illus.). 141p. (Orig.). 1980. 14.00 (ISBN 0-9605672-0-8). Bar-None.

How to Pass Your California Real Estate Exam. Homer C. Davey & Abert Sharum. 350p. 1975. pap. text ed. 15.50 scp (ISBN 0-06-453608-4, HarpC). Har-Row.

How to Pepare Building & Construction Contracts. LC 80-65099. 1980. write for info. (ISBN 0-89648-078-X); pap. write for info. (ISBN 0-89648-079-8). Citizens Law.

How to Perform Instant Magic. Ed. by Jay Marshall. LC 79-55634. (Illus.). 1980. cancelled (ISBN 0-89196-044-9, Domus Bks); pap. 8.95 (ISBN 0-89196-043-0). Quality Bks IL.

How to Photograph Flowers, Plants & Landscapes. Derek Fell. (Photography Ser.). (Orig.). 1980. pap. 7.95 (ISBN 0-89586-068-6). H P Bks.

How to Photograph Weddings: Groups & Ceremonies. Tom Burk. (Orig.). 1980. pap. 7.95 (ISBN 0-89586-057-0). H P Bks.

How to Pick up Girls. Eric Weber. 1981. 4.95 (ISBN 0-914094-00-9). Green Hill.

How to Pick up Women in Discos. Don Diebel. LC 80-67924. (Illus.). 128p. 1981. pap. 6.95 (ISBN 0-937164-00-3). Gemini Pub Co.

How to Picture What You Want. Harold Sherman. 1978. pap. 1.75 o.p. (ISBN 0-449-14003-2, GM). Fawcett.

How to Plan & Build Your Workshop. David X. Manners. LC 77-76854. (Illus.). 1977. 4.95 (ISBN 0-668-04131-5); pap. 2.50 o. p. (ISBN 0-668-04142-0). Arco.

How to Plan & Finance Your Business. William R. Osgood. LC 79-28070. 224p. 1980. pap. 18.95 (ISBN 0-8436-0757-2). CBI Pub.

How to Plan & Install Electronic Burglar Alarms. Howard Bierman. (gr. 10 up). 1977. pap. 5.95 (ISBN 0-8104-5734-2). Hayden.

How to Plan & Operate a Restaurant. rev., 2nd ed. Peter Dukas. 1972. text ed. 15.45x (ISBN 0-8104-9461-2). Hayden.

How to Plan & Organize Year-Round Bible Ministries. Margaret M. Self. (Orig.). 1976. pap. 2.95 o.p. (ISBN 0-8307-0413-2, 54-029-05). Regal.

How to Plan & Organize Year-Round Bible Ministries. Ed. by Margaret M. Self. pap. 2.25 o.p. (ISBN 0-8307-0751-4). Regal.

How to Plan, Buy or Build Your Leisure Home. Harry Wicks. (Illus.). 544p. 1976. 12.95 (ISBN 0-87909-345-5). Reston.

How to Plan, Design & Build Outdoor Sports Facilities. LC 78-56959. (Illus.). 1978. pap. 5.95 (ISBN 0-8069-8546-1). Sterling.

How to Plan, Design & Implement a Bad System. Ronald B. Smith. (Illus.). 1981. 12.00 (ISBN 0-89433-148-5). Petrocelli.

How to Plan Your Own Home Landscape. Nelva M. Weber. LC 75-33535. (Illus.). 1979. pap. 10.95 (ISBN 0-672-52599-2). Bobbs.

How to Plan Your Own Home Landscape. Nelva M. Weber. LC 75-33535. (Illus.). 320p. 1976. 13.95 (ISBN 0-685-62625-3). Bobbs.

How to Play Backgammon. Susan Perry. (Creative Games, Activities, Projects Ser.). (Illus.). 40p. (gr. 4-8). 1980. PLB 5.95 (ISBN 0-87191-749-1); pap. 2.95 (ISBN 0-89812-218-X). Creative Ed.

How to Play Better Basketball. C. Paul Jackson. LC 68-13584. (Illus.). (gr. 4 up). 1968. 8.95 o.p. (ISBN 0-690-41425-0, TYC-J). T Y Crowell.

How to Play Better Football. C. Paul Jackson. LC 72-158707. (Illus.). (gr. 3-5). 1972. 8.79 (ISBN 0-690-41567-2, TYC-J). T Y Crowell.

How to Play Better Tennis. Bill Tilden. 144p. 1962. pap. 3.95 (ISBN 0-346-12349-6). Cornerstone.

How to Play Chess Like a Champion. Fred Reinfeld. 1977. pap. 1.75 o.p. (ISBN 0-449-23289-1, Crest). Fawcett.

How to Play Drums. Joel Rothman. Ed. by Caroline Rubin. LC 76-39937. (Music Involvement Series). (Illus.). 48p. (gr. 4-6). 1977. 6.50 (ISBN 0-8075-3420-X). A Whitman.

How to Play Five Point Pitch: A Card Game for Everyone. Mark Stevens. (Illus.). 51p. (Orig.). 1980. 10.95; pap. 5.95 (ISBN 0-686-28069-5). Clawson.

How to Play Girls' Softball. Arnold Madison. (Illus.). 128p. (gr. 4-6). 1981. PLB 7.29 (ISBN 0-686-69303-5). Messner.

How to Play Rugby Union. John Thornett. (Illus.). 157p. 1976. pap. 5.25 (ISBN 0-909950-09-1). Reed.

How to Play Rummy Card Games. Susan Perry. (Creative Games, Activities, Projects Ser.). (Illus.). 32p. (gr. 4-8). 1980. PLB 5.95 (ISBN 0-87191-777-7); pap. 2.95 (ISBN 0-89812-245-7). Creative Ed.

How to Play the Guitar. Jerry Silverman. LC 68-14557. 1968. pap. 5.95 (ISBN 0-385-09862-6, Dolp). Doubleday.

How to Play Third Base. Jim Auker & Ron Cey. 1977. pap. 2.50 o.p. (ISBN 0-695-80867-2). Follett.

How to Play Winning Doubles. George Lott & Jeffrey Bairstow. LC 77-92904. (Illus.). 1979. 10.95 (ISBN 0-914178-20-2, 24923, Pub. by Tennis Mag). Golf Digest.

How to Play Winning Doubles. George Lott & Jeffrey Bairstow. LC 77-92904. (Illus.). 144p. 1979. pap. 6.95 (ISBN 0-914178-30-X). Golf Digest.

How to Play Winning Solitaire. Walter B. Gibson. LC 63-7724. 160p. 1976. 8.95 (ISBN 0-8119-0268-4); pap. 4.95 (ISBN 0-8119-0382-6). Fell.

How to Play with Your Children: And When Not to. Brian Sutton-Smith. 1974. pap. 4.95 (ISBN 0-8015-3685-5, Hawthorn). Dutton.

How to Play Word Games. Pamela Espeland. (Creative Activities, Games, Projects Ser.). (Illus.). 32p. (gr. 4-8). 1981. PLB 5.95 (ISBN 0-87191-797-1); pap. 2.75 (ISBN 0-89812-249-X). Creative Ed.

How to Play Your Best Golf All the Time. Tommy Armour. 1978. pap. 1.50 o.p. (ISBN 0-449-23516-5, Crest). Fawcett.

How to Play Your Best Tennis All the Time. Jack Kramer & Larry Sheehan. LC 76-53402. (Illus.). 1978. pap. 6.95 (ISBN 0-689-70576-X). Atheneum.

How to Pray. Keith L. Brooks. (Teach Yourself the Bible Ser). 1961. pap. 1.75 (ISBN 0-8024-3708-7). Moody.

How to Pray. E. Stanley Jones. (Mini-Libraries Ser.). 1975. pap. 1.25 (ISBN 0-687-17922-X). Abingdon.

How to Pray. rev. ed. W. Graham Scroggie. LC 80-8076. (W. Graham Scroggie Library). 112p. 1981. pap. 2.95 (ISBN 0-8254-3736-9). Kregel.

How to Pray. Reuben A. Torrey. pap. 1.50 (ISBN 0-8024-3709-5). Moody.

How to Prepare a Marketing Plan. 2nd ed. John Stapleton. 162p. 1975. 17.50 o.s.i. (ISBN 0-7161-0251-X). Herman Pub.

How to Prepare & Process Export-Import Documents: A Fully Illustrated Guide. 2nd ed. Tyler G. Hicks. 320p. 1981. pap. 25.00 (ISBN 0-914306-51-0). Intl Wealth.

How to Prepare Effective Business Program Blueprints: A Management Handbook. David D. Seltz. 1981. text ed. price not set (ISBN 0-201-07618-7). A-W.

How to Prepare for Advanced Placement Examinations: English. rev. ed. Max Nadel & Arthur Sherrer, Jr. LC 80-15687. (gr. 11-12). 1980. pap. text ed. 4.95 (ISBN 0-8120-2070-7). Barron.

How to Prepare for Advanced Placement Examinations: Mathematics. rev. ed. Shirley O. Hockett. LC 77-149360. (gr. 11-12). 1977. pap. text ed. 8.50 (ISBN 0-8120-0354-3). Barron.

How to Prepare for American College Testing (ACT) rev. ed. Murray Shapiro et al. LC 79-20856. (gr. 11-12). 1980. pap. text ed. 5.50 (ISBN 0-8120-0636-4). Barron.

How to Prepare for College Board Achievement Tests -- Spanish. rev. ed. Juan E. Lopez & Louis Cabat. (gr. 11-12). 1982. pap. 3.95 (ISBN 0-8120-0978-9). Barron. Postponed.

How to Prepare for College Board Achievement Tests -- German. Rosemarie Walz. LC 79-21101. (gr. 11-12). 1980. pap. 4.50 (ISBN 0-8120-0977-0). Barron.

How to Prepare for College Board Achievement Test -- French. rev. ed. Pearl Warner. LC 75-151972. (gr. 11-12). 1981. pap. text ed. 3.25 (ISBN 0-8120-0941-X). Barron.

How to Prepare for College Board Achievement Tests: German. rev. ed. Maxim Newmark & Rosemary Walz. LC 61-18358. (gr. 11-12). 1980. pap. 4.50 (ISBN 0-8120-0977-0). Barron.

How to Prepare for College Board Achievement Test in English. Shostak. 1981. pap. 3.95 (ISBN 0-8120-2282-3). Barron.

How to Prepare for the CLEP Subject Examination: Analysis & Interpretation of Literature. Nadel & Sherrer. 1981. pap. 4.95 (ISBN 0-8120-0619-4). Barron.

How to Prepare for the College Board Achievement Tests -- Chemistry. Joseph Mascetta. LC 68-26713. (gr. 10-12). 1981. pap. text ed. 5.50 (ISBN 0-8120-0304-7). Barron.

How to Prepare for the College-Level Examination Program (CLEP) rev. ed. W. C. Doster et al. LC 78-32129. (gr. 9-12). 1979. pap. text ed. 6.50 (ISBN 0-8120-2011-1). Barron.

How to Prepare for the College Level Examination Program (CLEP) Evarts Prescott, Jr. 1980. pap. 6.95 (ISBN 0-07-019764-4, SP). McGraw.

How to Prepare for the Dental Admission Test. 1981. pap. 4.95 (ISBN 0-8120-2162-2). Barron.

How to Prepare for the Graduate Record Examination (GRE) in Psychology. Edward L. Palmer. LC 77-12747. 1978. pap. 6.95 (ISBN 0-8120-0530-9). Barron.

How to Prepare for the High School Equivalency Examination: The Science Test. Farley. 1981. pap. 4.25 (ISBN 0-8120-2055-3). Barron.

How to Prepare for the High School Equivalency Examination: Vol. III the Reading Skills Test. Eugene J. Farley. LC 79-28101. (gr. 11-12). 1980. pap. text ed. 3.95 (ISBN 0-8120-2057-X). Barron.

How to Prepare for the High School Equivalency Examination, Vol. II: The Social Studies Test. Eugene J. Farley. (gr. 11-12). 1980. pap. text ed. 3.95 (ISBN 0-8120-2056-1). Barron.

How to Prepare for the LSAT: Canadian Edition. Shostak et al. LC 77-80603. 1977. pap. text ed. 6.95 (ISBN 0-8120-0864-2). Barron.

How to Prepare for the Real Estate Licensing Examination -- Salesman & Broker. J. Bruce Lindeman & Jack P. Friedman. LC 78-17332. 1979. pap. text ed. 7.95 (ISBN 0-8120-0771-9). Barron.

How to Prepare for the Regents Competency Examination in Mathematics. Wieland. 1981. pap. 6.95 (ISBN 0-8120-2246-7). Barron.

How to Prepare for the Regents Competency Exam in Reading. Barbara E. Lipner & Robert F. Fredericks. 340p. (gr. 9-12). 1981. pap. text ed. 6.95 (ISBN 0-8120-2287-4). Barron.

How to Prepare for the Registered Nurse Licensing Examination. Sutton et al. 1981. pap. 4.95 (ISBN 0-8120-2301-3). Barron.

How to Prepare for the Texas Real Estate Exam. 2nd ed. David F. Distelhorst. 248p. (Orig.). 1980. pap. 14.95 (ISBN 0-88462-270-3). Real Estate Ed Co.

How to Prepare Stamp Exhibits. C. E. Foster. LC 75-14662. 1970. 21.00 o.s.i. (ISBN 0-917922-04-2); plastic binding 12.00 (ISBN 0-917922-06-9); pap. 10.50 (ISBN 0-917922-05-0). Hobby Pub Serv.

How to Present an Evaluation Report. rev. ed. Lynn L. Morrris & Carol T. Fitz-Gibbon. LC 78-58657. (Program Evaluation Kit Ser.: Vol. 8). (Illus.). 80p. 1978. pap. 4.50 (ISBN 0-8039-1069-X). Sage.

How to Print T-Shirts for Fun & Profit. Ed. by Scott O. Fresener & Patricia A. Fresener. (Illus.). 176p. (Orig.). 1979. pap. text ed. 19.95 (ISBN 0-9603530-0-3). Southwest Screen Print.

How to Probate an Estate. new rev. ed. William J. Moody. 1981. pap. 3.95 (ISBN 0-346-12350-X). Cornerstone.

How to Profit from Condominium Conversions. Paul Bullock. 1981. 17.95 (ISBN 0-913864-64-1). Enterprise Del.

How to Profit from Your Arts & Crafts. Albert Lee. 1978. 9.95 o.p. (ISBN 0-679-50831-7); pap. 4.95 o.p. (ISBN 0-679-50868-6). McKay.

How to Profit from Your Personal Computer: Professional, Business, & Home Applications. T. G. Lewis. 1978. pap. 10.75 (ISBN 0-8104-5761-X). Hayden.

How to Profitably Buy & Sell Land. Rene A. Henry, Jr. LC 76-22522. (Real Estate for Professional Practitioners: a Wiley Ser.). 1977. 19.95 (ISBN 0-471-37291-9, Pub by Wiley-Interscience). Wiley.

How to Program a Computer (Using Fortran IV) Francis D. Tuggle. LC 74-31654. (Computer Science Ser.). 1975. pap. text ed. 10.95 o.p. (ISBN 0-88244-082-9). Grid Pub.

How to Program & Interface the 6800. Andrew C. Staugaard, Jr. LC 80-50050. 1980. pap. 15.95 (ISBN 0-672-21684-1). Sams.

How to Pronounce the Names in Shakespeare. Theodora U. Irvine. LC 74-7114. 1974. Repr. of 1919 ed. 22.00 (ISBN 0-8103-3653-7). Gale.

How to Prosper During the Coming Bad Years. rev. ed. Howard J. Ruff. 1981. pap. 3.50 (ISBN 0-446-96952-4). Warner Bks.

How to Prosper in the Coming Apocalypse. Richard Curtis. (Illus.). 96p. 1981. pap. 3.95 (ISBN 0-312-39611-2); prepack 39.50 (ISBN 0-312-39612-0). St Martin.

How to Prosper in Your Own Business: Getting Started & Staying on Course. Brian Smith. 352p. 1980. 20.00 (ISBN 0-8289-0408-1). Greene.

How to Protect Your Faith. Norvel Hayes. 1978. pap. 2.25 (ISBN 0-917726-19-7). Hunter Bks.

How to Protect Your Home & Family. Betsy Myers. 110p. 1981. pap. cancelled (ISBN 0-686-68067-7). Cornerstone.

How to Publish Your Own Book Successfully. Lee Howard. 80p. 1980. pap. 10.00 (ISBN 0-912584-00-9). Selective.

How to Put on a Horse Show. T. W. Carrithers. LC 70-124197. (Illus.). 1971. 8.95 o.p. (ISBN 0-668-04204-4). Arco.

How to Put Your Book Together & Get a Job in Advertising. Maxine Paetro. LC 79-81012. (Illus.). 1979. write for info. o.p. (ISBN 0-685-97191-0). Executive Comm.

How to Quit the Rat Race - Successfully! John F. Edwards. LC 80-82676. (Illus.). 159p. (Orig.). 1981. 9.95 (ISBN 0-937590-00-2, Dist. by Caroline Hse.); pap. 5.95 (ISBN 0-937590-01-0). New Era.

How to Quit the Rat Race-Successfully. John F. Edwards. 1981. 9.95 (ISBN 0-937590-00-2); pap. 5.95 (ISBN 0-937590-01-0). Green Hill.

How to Quit the Rat Race-Successfully! John F. Edwards. LC 80-82676. (Illus.). 110p. (Orig.). 1980. write for info. (ISBN 0-937590-00-2, New Era); pap. write for info. (ISBN 0-937590-01-0). World Merch Import.

How to Raise a Successful Daughter. Barbara Powell. LC 78-16975. 1979. 12.95 (ISBN 0-88229-457-1); pap. 6.95 (ISBN 0-88229-679-5). Nelson-Hall.

How to Raise & Train a Basenji. Jack D. Shofer. 1966. pap. 2.00 (ISBN 0-87666-239-4, DS1051). TFH Pubns.

How to Raise & Train a Basset Hound. Arthur Liebers & Dorothy Hardy. pap. 2.00 (ISBN 0-87666-240-8, DS1003). TFH Pubns.

How to Raise & Train a Beagle. Mary A. Ward & Sara M. Barbaresi. 1966. pap. 2.00 (ISBN 0-87666-242-4, DS1004). TFH Pubns.

How to Raise & Train a Bedlington Terrier. Elinore W. Young. (Orig.). 1966. pap. 2.00 (ISBN 0-87666-245-9, DS1052). TFH Pubns.

How to Raise & Train a Belgian Sheepdog. Frank E. Dyke. (Orig.). pap. 2.00 (ISBN 0-87666-246-7, DS1054). TFH Pubns.

How to Raise & Train a Bloodhound. Hylda F. Owen. (Orig.). pap. 2.00 (ISBN 0-87666-248-3, DS1058). TFH Pubns.

How to Raise & Train a Border Terrier. Seymour N. Weiss. (Illus., Orig.). pap. 1.79 o.p. (ISBN 0-87666-249-1, DS1060). TFH Pubns.

How to Raise & Train a Borzoi. Gail C. McRae. (Illus., Orig.). pap. 2.00 (ISBN 0-87666-250-5, DS1043). TFH Pubns.

How to Raise & Train a Boston Terrier. Evelyn Miller. (Illus.). pap. 2.00 (ISBN 0-87666-251-3, DS1005). TFH Pubns.

How to Raise & Train a Bouvier Des Flandres. Gerene C. Leggett. (Orig.). 1965. pap. 2.00 (ISBN 0-87666-252-1, DS1061). TFH Pubns.

How to Raise & Train a Boxer. Sara M. Barbaresi. pap. 2.00 (ISBN 0-87666-253-X, DS1006). TFH Pubns.

How to Raise & Train a Brittany Spaniel. Edwin E. Rosenblum. (Orig.). pap. 2.00 (ISBN 0-87666-257-2, DS1063). TFH Pubns.

How to Raise & Train a Brussels Griffon. 1966. pap. 2.00 (ISBN 0-87666-258-0, DS1064). TFH Pubns.

How to Raise & Train a Bull Terrier. Edwin E. Rosenblum. (Orig.). pap. 2.00 (ISBN 0-87666-261-0, DS1066). TFH Pubns.

How to Raise & Train a Bulldog. Evelyn Miller. (Illus.). pap. 2.00 (ISBN 0-87666-259-9, DS1007). TFH Pubns.

How to Raise & Train a Bullmastiff. Mary A. Prescott. (Orig.). pap. 2.00 (ISBN 0-87666-260-2, DS1065). TFH Pubns.

How to Raise & Train a Cairn Terrier. Erliss McCormack. pap. 2.00 (ISBN 0-87666-262-9, DS1068). TFH Pubns.

How to Raise & Train a Cardigan Welsh Corgi. Mrs. Henning Nelms & Mrs. Michael Pym. (Orig.). pap. 2.00 (ISBN 0-87666-263-7, DS1067). TFH Pubns.

How to Raise & Train a Cavalier King Charles Spaniel. Elizabeth C. Spalding. (Orig.). pap. 1.79 o.p. (ISBN 0-87666-264-5, DS1142). TFH Pubns.

How to Raise & Train a Chesapeake Bay Retriever. Stan Henschel. (Orig.). 1965. pap. 2.00 (ISBN 0-87666-265-3, DS1069). TFH Pubns.

How to Raise & Train a Chihuahua. Estelle Ferguson & Sara M. Barbaresi. pap. 2.00 (ISBN 0-87666-266-1, DS1008). TFH Pubns.

How to Raise & Train a Chow Chow. Clifford Shryock. (Orig.). pap. 2.00 (ISBN 0-87666-268-8, DS1070). TFH Pubns.

How to Raise & Train a Cocker Spaniel. Evelyn Miller. pap. 2.00 (ISBN 0-87666-269-6, DS1009). TFH Pubns.

How to Raise & Train a Collie. Sara M. Barbaresi. pap. 2.00 (ISBN 0-87666-272-6, DS1010). TFH Pubns.

How to Raise & Train a Coonhound. Stan Henschel. (Orig.). pap. 2.00 (ISBN 0-87666-274-2, DS1057). TFH Pubns.

How to Raise & Train a Dachshund. Lois Meistrell & Sara M. Barbaresi. pap. 2.00 (ISBN 0-87666-276-9, DS1011). TFH Pubns.

How to Raise & Train a Doberman Pinscher. Natalie Stebbins & Sara M. Barbaresi. (Illus.). pap. 2.00 (ISBN 0-87666-282-3, DS1013). TFH Pubns.

How to Raise & Train a Fox Terrier. Evelyn Miller. (Illus.). pap. 2.00 (ISBN 0-87666-294-7, DS1038). TFH Pubns.

How to Raise & Train a German Shepherd. Sara M. Barbaresi. pap. 2.00 (ISBN 0-87666-296-3, DS1017). TFH Pubns.

How to Raise & Train a German Short-Haired Pointer. Arthur Liebers. pap. 2.00 (ISBN 0-87666-301-3, DS1016). TFH Pubns.

How to Raise & Train a German Wirehaired Pointer. Newton L. Compere. 1966. pap. 1.79 o.p. (ISBN 0-87666-304-8, DS1080). TFH Pubns.

How to Raise & Train a Giant Schnauzer. Arthur S. Lockley. (Orig.). pap. 1.79 o.p. (ISBN 0-87666-305-6, DS1081). TFH Pubns.

How to Raise & Train a Golden Retriever. Evelyn Miller. (Illus.). pap. 2.00 (ISBN 0-87666-306-4, DS1018). TFH Pubns.

How to Raise & Train a Gordon Setter. Bart King. (Orig.). 1965. pap. 2.00 (ISBN 0-87666-307-2, DS1082). TFH Pubns.

How to Raise & Train a Great Dane. Lina Basquette. (Illus.). pap. 2.00 (ISBN 0-87666-308-0, DS1019). TFH Pubns.

How to Raise & Train a Great Pyrenees. Edith K. Smith. (Orig.). pap. 2.00 (ISBN 0-87666-311-0, DS1084). TFH Pubns.

How to Raise & Train a Greyhound. Georgiana Mueller. (Illus.). 1965. pap. 2.00 (ISBN 0-87666-312-9, DS1083). TFH Pubns.

How to Raise & Train a Keeshond. William D. Westcott. (Orig.). pap. 2.00 (ISBN 0-87666-326-9, DS1091). TFH Pubns.

How to Raise & Train a Kerry Blue Terrier. Frederick Schioeppe. (Illus., Orig.). pap. 1.79 o.p. (ISBN 0-87666-327-7, DS1092). TFH Pubns.

How to Raise & Train a Komondor. Oscar Beregi & Leslie M. Benis. (Orig.). 1966. pap. 1.79 o.p. (ISBN 0-87666-328-5, DS1093). TFH Pubns.

How to Raise & Train a Kuvasz. 1966. pap. 1.79 o.p. (ISBN 0-87666-329-3, DS1094). TFH Pubns.

How to Raise & Train a Labrador Retriever. Stan Henschel. (Illus.). pap. 2.00 (ISBN 0-87666-330-7, DS1095). TFH Pubns.

How to Raise & Train a Lakeland Terrier. Seymour N. Weiss. (Orig.). 1966. pap. 2.00 (ISBN 0-87666-333-1, DS1096). TFH Pubns.

How to Raise & Train a Lhasa Apso. Patricia Chenoweth & Thomas Chenoweth. (Orig.). pap. 2.00 (ISBN 0-87666-334-X, DS1097). TFH Pubns.

How to Raise & Train a Maltese. Arthur Liebers. pap. 2.00 (ISBN 0-87666-335-8, DS1025). TFH Pubns.

How to Raise & Train a Mastiff. Marie A. Moore. (Orig.). pap. 2.00 (ISBN 0-87666-336-6, DS1099). TFH Pubns.

How to Raise & Train a Miniature Pinscher. Evelyn Miller. (Illus.). pap. 2.00 (ISBN 0-87666-337-4, DS1039). TFH Pubns.

How to Raise & Train a Miniature Schnauzer. Leda B. Martin & Sara M. Barbaresi. (Orig.). pap. 2.00 (ISBN 0-87666-338-2, DS1026). TFH Pubns.

How to Raise & Train a Mixed or Pedigreed Puppy. Arthur Liebers. pap. 2.00 (ISBN 0-87666-370-6, DS1027). TFH Pubns.

How to Raise & Train a Newfoundland. Kitty Drury & Bill Lynn. (Orig.). pap. 2.00 (ISBN 0-87666-341-2, DS1100). TFH Pubns.

How to Raise & Train a Norwegian Elkhound. Glenna C. Crafts. (Orig.). pap. 2.00 (ISBN 0-87666-342-0, DS1101). TFH Pubns.

How to Raise & Train a Pekingese. Alice Scott. (Illus.). pap. 2.00 (ISBN 0-87666-346-3, DS1028). TFH Pubns.

How to Raise & Train a Pembroke Welsh Corgi. Ria Niccoli. (Illus.). pap. 2.00 (ISBN 0-87666-349-8, DS1106). TFH Pubns.

How to Raise & Train a Pointer. Ernest H. Hart. (Illus., Orig.). 1966. pap. 2.00 (ISBN 0-87666-350-1, DS1107). TFH Pubns.

How to Raise & Train a Pomeranian. Arthur Liebers & Georgie M. Sheppard. (Illus.). pap. 2.00 (ISBN 0-87666-352-8, DS1029). TFH Pubns.

How to Raise & Train a Poodle. Evelyn Miller. pap. 2.00 (ISBN 0-87666-355-2, DS1030). TFH Pubns.

How to Raise & Train a Pug. Evelyn Miller. (Illus.). pap. 2.00 (ISBN 0-87666-364-1, DS1031). TFH Pubns.

How to Raise & Train a Puli. Eleanor Anderson. (Orig.). pap. 1.79 o.p. (ISBN 0-87666-367-6, DS1108). TFH Pubns.

How to Raise & Train a Rottweiler. Joan R. Klem & P. G. Rodemacher. (Orig.). pap. 2.00 (ISBN 0-87666-373-0, DS1110). TFH Pubns.

How to Raise & Train a Saint Bernard. Lillian P. Buell. (Orig.). pap. 2.00 (ISBN 0-87666-374-9, DS1125). TFH Pubns.

How to Raise & Train a Saluki. Virginia M. Burch. (Illus.). 1965. pap. 2.00 (ISBN 0-87666-377-3, DS1112). TFH Pubns.

How to Raise & Train a Samoyed. Vera Kroman. (Orig.). pap. 2.00 (ISBN 0-87666-378-1, DS1113). TFH Pubns.

How to Raise & Train a Schipperke. Darwin J. Martin. (Orig.). pap. 2.00 (ISBN 0-87666-381-1, DS1114). TFH Pubns.

How to Raise & Train a Scottish Deerhound. Audrey M. Benbow. (Orig.). pap. 1.79 o.p. (ISBN 0-87666-382-X, DS1115). TFH Pubns.

How to Raise & Train a Scottish Terrier. Robert Gannon. (Illus.). pap. 2.00 (ISBN 0-87666-383-8, DS1032). TFH Pubns.

How to Raise & Train a Shetland Sheepdog. Evelyn Miller. (Illus.). pap. 2.00 (ISBN 0-87666-386-2, DS1033). TFH Pubns.

How to Raise & Train a Shih Tzu. Reginald H. Smythe. (Orig.). pap. 2.00 (ISBN 0-87666-388-9, DS1117). TFH Pubns.

How to Raise & Train a Siberian Husky. Lorna B. Demidoff. (Orig.). pap. 2.00 (ISBN 0-87666-391-9, DS1118). TFH Pubns.

How to Raise & Train a Skye Terrier. Seymour N. Weiss. (Orig.). pap. 1.79 o.p. (ISBN 0-87666-395-1, DS1119). TFH Pubns.

How to Raise & Train a Staffordshire Terrier. Edwin E. Rosenblum. (Orig.). pap. 2.00 (ISBN 0-87666-399-4, DS1123). TFH Pubns.

How to Raise & Train a Standard Schnauzer. Hamilton Hertz & Joan Hertz. (Orig.). pap. 2.00 (ISBN 0-87666-400-1, DS1124). TFH Pubns.

How to Raise & Train a Toy Fox Terrier. 1966. pap. 2.00 (ISBN 0-87666-295-5, DS1127). TFH Pubns.

How to Raise & Train a Viszla. 1966. pap. 1.79 o.p. (ISBN 0-87666-403-6, DS1129). TFH Pubns.

How to Raise & Train a Weimaraner. Arthur Liebers & Paul Jeffries. pap. 2.00 (ISBN 0-87666-405-2, DS1035). TFH Pubns.

How to Raise & Train a Welsh Terrier. Elizabeth D. Fryman. (Illus.). 1960. pap. 1.79 o.p. (ISBN 0-87666-407-9, DS1036). TFH Pubns.

How to Raise & Train a West Highland White Terrier. Florence J. Sherman. (Orig.). pap. 2.00 (ISBN 0-87666-408-7, DS1133). TFH Pubns.

How to Raise & Train a Whippet. Christine Cormany. (Orig.). pap. 2.00 (ISBN 0-87666-409-5, DS1131). TFH Pubns.

How to Raise & Train a Yorkshire Terrier. Arthur Liebers & Dana Miller. (Illus.). pap. 2.00 (ISBN 0-87666-410-9, DS1037). TFH Pubns.

How to Raise & Train an Afghan. Sunny Shay & Sara M. Barbaresi. (Orig.). pap. 2.00 (ISBN 0-87666-232-7, DS1001). TFH Pubns.

How to Raise & Train an Airedale. Evelyn Miller. (Illus.). pap. 2.00 (ISBN 0-87666-233-5, DS1002). TFH Pubns.

How to Raise & Train an Akita. Edita Delfosse. (Orig.). pap. 2.00 (ISBN 0-87666-234-3, DS1041). TFH Pubns.

How to Raise & Train an Alaskan Malamute. Charles J. Berger. (Orig.). pap. 2.00 (ISBN 0-87666-235-1, DS1042). TFH Pubns.

How to Raise & Train an Australian Terrier. Nell N. Fox. (Orig.). pap. 2.00 (ISBN 0-87666-238-6, DS1050). TFH Pubns.

How to Raise & Train an English Cocker Spaniel. Robert Gannon. pap. 2.00 (ISBN 0-87666-291-2, DS1014). TFH Pubns.

How to Raise & Train an English Setter. Susan S. Maire. (Illus.). pap. 2.00 (ISBN 0-87666-292-0, DS1074). TFH Pubns.

How to Raise & Train an English Springer Spaniel. Arthur Liebers. pap. 2.00 (ISBN 0-87666-398-6, DS1034). TFH Pubns.

How to Raise & Train an Irish Setter. Robert Gannon. (Illus.). pap. 2.00 (ISBN 0-87666-319-6, DS1024). TFH Pubns.

How to Raise & Train an Irish Terrier. pap. 1.79 o.p. (ISBN 0-87666-322-6, DS1087). TFH Pubns.

How to Raise & Train an Irish Wolfhound. Frederic Westover & Margaret Westover. (Orig.). pap. 2.00 (ISBN 0-87666-324-2, DS1089). TFH Pubns.

How to Raise & Train an Old English Sheepdog. Mona Berkowitz. pap. 2.00 (ISBN 0-87666-344-7, DS1103). TFH Pubns.

How to Raise & Train Gerbils. pap. 2.00 (ISBN 0-87666-195-9, M524). TFH Pubns.

How to Raise & Train Pigeons. enl. ed. William H. Allen, Jr. LC 58-7602. (Illus.). 160p. (gr. 10 up). 1972. 9.95 (ISBN 0-8069-3706-8); PLB 9.29 (ISBN 0-8069-3707-6). Sterling.

How to Raise & Train Rhodesian Ridgeback. 1966. pap. 2.00 (ISBN 0-87666-372-2, DS1109). TFH Pubns.

How to Raise Beautiful Comb Honey. Richard Taylor. LC 77-74619. (Illus.). 1977. 7.95 (ISBN 0-9603288-3-1); pap. 3.95 (ISBN 0-686-19087-4). Linden Bks.

How to Raise Children's Self-Esteem. rev. ed. Reynold Bean & Harris Clemes. (Whole Child Ser.). (Illus.). 80p. 1980. pap. 3.95 (ISBN 0-933358-75-X). Enrich.

How to Raise Good Kids. Barbara Cook. LC 78-7844. 1978. pap. 3.50 (ISBN 0-87123-233-2, 210233). Bethany Fell.

How to Raise Hamsters. Mervin F. Roberts. pap. 2.00 (ISBN 0-87666-205-X, M508). TFH Pubns.

How to Raise Rabbits for Fun & Profit. Milton I. Faivre. LC 73-81277. 1973. 14.95 (ISBN 0-911012-47-8); pap. 8.95 (ISBN 0-88229-493-8). Nelson-Hall.

How to Raise, Store & Sell Nighcrawlers. Charlie Morgan. 1975. pap. 2.50 (ISBN 0-686-65538-9). Shields WI.

How to Raise Teenagers' Self-Esteem. rev. ed. Reynold Bean et al. (Whole Child Ser.). (Illus.). 96p. 1980. pap. 3.95 (ISBN 0-933358-76-8). Enrich.

How to Raise Your Children for Christ. Andrew Murray. LC 75-29344. 1975. pap. 3.95 (ISBN 0-87123-224-3, 210224). Bethany Fell.

How to Read a Book for Pleasure & for Profit. (YA) 27.75 (ISBN 0-913314-20-X). Am Classical Coll Pr.

How to Read a Film: The Art, Technology, Language, History & Theory of Film & Television. James Monaco. (Illus.). 1977. 17.95 (ISBN 0-19-502227-0); pap. text ed. 9.95x (ISBN 0-19-502178-9). Oxford U Pr.

How to Read a Film: The Art, Technology, Language, History, & Theory of Film & Media. rev. ed. James Monaco. (Illus.). 576p. 1981. 25.00 (ISBN 0-19-502802-3); pap. 11.95 (ISBN 0-19-502806-6). Oxford U Pr.

How to Read a Financial Report: Wringing Cash Flow & Other Vital Signs Out of the Numbers. John A. Tracy. LC 79-18853. 1980. 14.95 (ISBN 0-471-05712-6, Pub. by Wiley-Interscience). Wiley.

How to Read a Financial Statement: Adapted Especially to Needs of Credit Men, Bankers & Investors. Herbert G. Stockwell. 443p. 1980. Repr. of 1925 ed. lib. bdg. 30.00 (ISBN 0-8495-5049-1). Arden Lib.

How to Read a Financial Statement for Better Stock Market Performance. 1976. 49.75 (ISBN 0-913314-33-1). Inst Econ Finan.

How to Read a Person Like a Book. Gerard I. Nierenberg & Henry H. Calero. 180p. 1972. pap. 3.95 (ISBN 0-346-12283-X). Cornerstone.

How to Read a Wine Label. Jeffrey Pogash. (Illus., Orig.). 1978. pap. 5.95 o.p. (ISBN 0-8015-3742-8). Dutton.

How to Read an ECG. Blowers & Smith. 1977. pap. 6.00 (ISBN 0-8273-1307-1). Delmar.

How to Read & Pray Saint Paul. Marilyn Norquist. (Handbook of the Bible Ser.). 1979. pap. 1.50 (ISBN 0-89243-110-5). Liguori Pubns.

How to Read & Write in College: A Complete Course, 5 forms. Richard H. Dodge. (Orig.). pap. text ed. 10.95 scp ea. (ISBN 0-686-66443-4, HarpC); Form 2. pap. text ed. (ISBN 0-06-041661-0); Form 3. pap. text ed. (ISBN 0-06-041662-9); Form 4. pap. text ed. (ISBN 0-06-041663-7); Form 5. pap. text ed. (ISBN 0-06-041664-5). Form 6 (ISBN 0-06-041657-2). Part 1. achievement tests & short quizzes avail. (ISBN 0-06-361687-4). Part 2 (ISBN 0-06-361688-2). Har-Row.

How to Read & Write Poetry. Anna Cosman. (First Bks.). (Illus.). (gr. 5-8). 1979. PLB 6.45 s&l (ISBN 0-531-02261-7). Watts.

How to Read Donald Duck: Imperialist Ideology in the Disney Comic. Ariel Dorfman & Armand Mattelart. Tr. by David Kunzle from Span. Orig. Title: Para Leer Al Pato Donald. (Illus.). 112p. (Orig.). 1975. pap. 4.25 (ISBN 0-88477-003-6). Intl General.

How to Read Electronic Circuit Diagrams. Robert M. Brown & Paul Lawrence. LC 72-105970. 1970. 9.95 (ISBN 0-8306-0510-X); pap. 7.95 (ISBN 0-8306-9510-9, 510). TAB Bks.

How to Read Factual Literature. Walter Pauk. LC 70-113589. 1970. Bk. 1, Levels 7-8. pap. text ed. 5.95 (ISBN 0-574-17061-8, 13-0061); Bk. 2, Levels 9-10. instr's guide avail. (ISBN 0-574-17062-6, 13-0062); Bk. 3, Levels 11-12. pap. text ed. 5.95 (ISBN 0-574-17063-4, 13-0063); instr's guide 1.50 (ISBN 0-574-17065-0, 13-0065). SRA.

How to Read for Speed & Comprehension. Gordon R. Wainwright. (Illus.). 1978. 12.95 (ISBN 0-13-430769-0); pap. 4.95 (ISBN 0-13-430751-8). P-H.

How to Read Lips for Fun & Profit. Edward Nitchie. 1979. pap. 3.95 (ISBN 0-8015-3740-1, Hawthorn). Dutton.

How to Read Palms. Litzka R. Gibson. LC 77-2290. 1977. 7.95 o.p. (ISBN 0-8119-0278-1); pap. 4.95 (ISBN 0-8119-0278-1). Fell.

How to Read Tarot Cards. Doris C. Doane et al. LC 67-19976. (Funk & W Bk.). (Illus.). 1968. pap. 2.95 o.p. (ISBN 0-308-90086-3, F57, TYC-T). T Y Crowell.

How to Read the Aura, Practice Psychometry, Telepathy, & Clairvoyancy. William Butler & Warner Destiny. 2.25 (ISBN 0-446-82751-7). Inner Tradit.

How to Read the Financial News. 10th ed. C. Norman Stabler. 239p. 1972. pap. 2.95 (ISBN 0-06-463327-6, EH 327, EH). Har-Row.

How to Read the Sciences. W. Royce Adams. 1970. pap. 6.50x o.p. (ISBN 0-673-05864-6). Scott F.

How to Read Your Opponent's Cards: The Bridge Experts' Way to Locate Missing High Cards. Michael Lawrence. LC 73-7820. 176p. 1973. 7.95 o.p. (ISBN 0-13-431122-1); pap. 3.95 (ISBN 0-13-431114-0). P-H.

How to Really Love Your Child. D. Ross Campbell. 1977. pap. 3.50 (ISBN 0-88207-751-1). Victor Bks.

How to Really Love Your Wife. Dean Merrill. 196p. 1980. pap. 4.95 (ISBN 0-310-35321-1, 10685). Zondervan.

How to Really Save Money & Energy in Cooling Your Home. George S. Garton. pap. 9.95 (ISBN 0-931624-00-2). Green Hill.

How to Rebuild Small Block Chevys. David Vizard. LC 78-52275. (Illus.). 1978. pap. 7.95 (ISBN 0-912656-66-2). H P Bks.

How to Rebuild Small-Block Mopar. (Orig.). 1981. pap. 7.95 (ISBN 0-89586-091-0). H P Bks.

How to Rebuild Your Ford V-8. Tom Monroe. (Orig.). 1980. pap. 7.95 (ISBN 0-89586-036-8). H P Bks.

How to Rebuild Your Small-Block Ford. Tom Monroe. LC 78-74545. (Illus.). 1979. pap. 7.95 (ISBN 0-912656-89-1). H P Bks.

How to Recognize the Antichrist. Arthur E. Bloomfield. LC 75-29424. 1975. pap. 3.50 (ISBN 0-87123-225-1, 210225). Bethany Fell.

How to Reconquer Your Lost Youth. Vernon De Castille. (Science of Man Library Bk). (Illus.). 67p. 1975. 27.95 (ISBN 0-913314-57-9); lib. bdg. 33.35 (ISBN 0-685-52671-2). Am Classical Coll Pr.

How to Recover Your Medical Expenses. Kal Waller. 96p. 1981. pap. 5.95 (ISBN 0-02-098940-7, Collier). Macmillan.

How to Redesign Your Yard & Garden. Stanley Schuler. 1977. pap. 4.95 o.p. (ISBN 0-8015-3746-0). Dutton.

How to Rehabilitate an Abandoned Building, Bk. 685. Donald R. Brann. LC 73-87513. 258p. 1974. lib. bdg. 6.95 (ISBN 0-87733-085-9); pap. 5.95 o.p. (ISBN 0-87733-685-7). Easi-Bild.

How to Relax: A Holistic Approach to Stress Management. Jack Curtis & Richard Detert. 190p. (Orig.). 1981. pap. text ed. price not set (ISBN 0-87484-527-0). Mayfield Pub.

How to Relax & Enjoy... Jerry Teplitz & Shelly Kellman. LC 77-74655. (Illus.). 1977. pap. 6.95 o.p. (ISBN 0-87040-402-4). Japan Pubns.

How to Relieve or Eliminate Chronic Pains - Discomforts Acquired During Sleep: A Doctor's Solution to Your Sleeping Problems. Israel Perlstein. (Illus.). 64p. (Orig.). 1981. pap. 1.95 (ISBN 0-8326-2252-4, 7445). Delair.

How to Remodel & Enlarge Your Home. M. E. Daniels. LC 77-15443. 1978. pap. 8.95 (ISBN 0-672-52585-2). Bobbs.

How to Remodel Your Attic or Basement. Richard Day. LC 69-19821. 1977. 4.95 o.p. (ISBN 0-668-01876-3); pap. 2.50 o.p. (ISBN 0-668-04068-8). Arco.

How to Remove Pollutants & Toxic Materials from Air & Water: A Practical Guide. M. Sittig. LC 77-71309. (Pollution Technology Review Ser.: No. 32). (Illus.). 1977. 48.00 o.p. (ISBN 0-8155-0654-6). Noyes.

How to Renovate Townhouses & Brownstones. 2nd ed. William H. Edgerton. 156p. 1980. text ed. 14.95 (ISBN 0-442-24841-5). Van Nos Reinhold.

How to Repair & Dress Old Dolls. Audrey Johnson. 128p. 1967. pap. 6.95 o.p. (ISBN 0-8231-3026-6). Branford.

How to Repair Briggs & Stratton Engines. Paul Dempsey. (Illus.). 1978. 8.95 (ISBN 0-8306-9873-6); pap. 4.95 (ISBN 0-8306-1087-1, 1087). TAB Bks.

How to Repair Home & Auto Air Conditioners. Wayne Lemons & Bill Price. LC 74-120384. 1970. pap. 5.95 (ISBN 0-8306-9520-6, 520). TAB Bks.

How to Repair Home Kitchen Appliances. Ben Gaddis. LC 76-45052. (Illus.). 1976. 8.95 o.p. (ISBN 0-8306-6885-3); pap. 5.95 (ISBN 0-8306-5885-8, 885). TAB Bks.

How to Repair Old-Time Radios. Clayton L. Hallmark. (Illus.). 1980. 12.95 (ISBN 0-8306-9737-3); pap. 7.95 (ISBN 0-8306-1148-7, 1148). TAB Bks.

How to Repair Small Gasoline Engines. 2nd ed. Paul Dempsey. LC 76-45056. 1976. 12.95 (ISBN 0-8306-6917-5); pap. 9.95 (ISBN 0-8306-5917-X, 917). TAB Bks.

How to Repair Violins. Alfred F. Common. Repr. lib. bdg. 19.00 (ISBN 0-403-03871-5). Scholarly.

How to Resist the Devil. F. J. Perryman. pap. 0.50. Faith Pub Hse.

How to Run a Railroad: Everything You Need to Know About Model Trains. Harvey Weiss. LC 76-18128. (Illus.). (gr. 5 up). 1977. 9.95 (ISBN 0-690-01304-3, TYC-J). T Y Crowell.

How to Run a Restaurant. H. Beal. 1978. 16.50 o.p. (ISBN 0-685-04998-1, 0-911156-27-6). Porter.

How to Run a School Newspaper. Enid A. Goldberg. LC 74-101898. (Illus.). (gr. 7 up). 1970. 8.95 o.p. (ISBN 0-397-31124-9). Lippincott.

How to Run a Small Box Office. Kirsten Beck. 1980. pap. 4.95 (ISBN 0-933750-01-3). Off off Broadw.

How to Run a Stately Home. George Mikes. (Illus.). 125p. 1972. 6.95 (ISBN 0-233-95848-7). Transatlantic.

How to Run a Successful Specialty Food Store. D. L. Brownstone. 124p. 1978. pap. 5.95 (ISBN 0-471-04031-2). Wiley.

How to Run Faster: A Do-It-Yourself Book for Athletes in All Sports. George B. Dintiman. LC 76-54436. (Illus.). 60p. 1979. text ed. 3.25. Champion Athle.

How to Run Your House. Ed. by Jean Gilles. LC 72-97091. 1973. 7.95 (ISBN 0-89795-007-0). Farm Journal.

How to Run Your Own Rock & Roll Band. Bill Henderson. (Orig.). 1977. pap. 1.50 o.p. (ISBN 0-445-04043-2). Popular Lib.

How to Safeguard Your Health & Beauty with the Simple Pressure of a Finger. Roger Dalet. LC 80-5497. (Illus.). 160p. 1981. 10.95 (ISBN 0-8128-2742-2). Stein & Day.

How to Save Lots of Money on Your Phone Bill. Howard Strange. 128p. (Orig.). 1981. pap. 1.95 (ISBN 0-345-29373-8). Ballantine.

How to Save Money on Almost Everything. Neil Gallagher. LC 78-19113. 1978. pap. 2.95 (ISBN 0-87123-234-0, 210234). Bethany Fell.

How to Save Money on Car Repairs. Shel Hochman. LC 76-6960. (Illus.). 1976. 5.95 (ISBN 0-396-07322-0). Dodd.

How to Save Money on Your Auto Insurance. James A. Kohl. LC 79-84203. (Illus.). 88p. 1980. pap. 10.00 (ISBN 0-935674-00-4). Jaks Pub Co.

How to Save or Make Thousands When You Buy or Sell Your House. Jens Nielsen & Jackie Nielson. LC 78-62635. 1979. Repr. of 1971 ed. 6.95 (ISBN 0-385-13522-X, Dolp). Doubleday.

How to Save Tax Dollars When You Sell Your House. 4th ed. Rich Robinson. 1980. pap. 1.95 (ISBN 0-88462-372-6). Real Estate Ed Co.

How to Save the World: Strategy for World Conservation. Robert Allen. (Illus.). 144p. 1981. pap. 4.95 (ISBN 0-8226-0366-7). Littlefield.

How to Save the World: Strategy for World Conservation. Robert Allen. (Illus.). 150p. 1980. 12.95x (ISBN 0-389-20011-5). B&N.

How to Save Urban America. W. Caldwell. pap. 1.50 (ISBN 0-451-05559-4, W5559, Sig). NAL.

How to Save Your Own Street. Racquel Ramati & Urban Design Group of the Department of City Planning, New York. LC 78-14709. (Illus.). 176p. 1981. pap. 19.95 (ISBN 0-385-14814-3, Dolp). Doubleday.

How to Say No to a Rapist - and Survive. Frederic Storaska. 224p. 1976. pap. 1.95 o.s.i. (ISBN 0-446-89277-7). Warner Bks.

How to Say No to a Stubborn Habit. Erwin W. Lutzer. 1979. pap. 3.50 (ISBN 0-88207-787-2). Victor Bks.

How to Screen Print on Cylindrical & Contoured Surfaces. rev. ed. Thomas Gilson. (Illus.). 1970. pap. 5.00 (ISBN 0-911380-10-8). Signs of Times.

How to Search for Information: A Beginner's Guide to the Literature of Psychology. Larry Greenwood. LC 80-53708. (Basic Tools Ser.: No. 1). 50p. (Orig.). 1980. pap. text ed. 3.95 (ISBN 0-938376-00-4). Willowood Pr.

How to Secure Help for Those Who Need It. pap. 0.50 (ISBN 0-86671-068-X). Comm Coun Great NY.

How to See Your Health: The Book of Oriental Diagnosis. Michio Kushi. LC 79-89346. (Illus.). 208p. (Orig.). 1980. pap. 9.95 (ISBN 0-87040-467-9). Japan Pubns.

How to Select an Advanced Communications System. 60p. 1979. pap. text ed. 18.75 (ISBN 0-686-60191-2, SM89179). Natl Ret Merch.

How to Select & Care for Shrubs & Hedges. Joseph E. Howland. Ed. by Ortho Books Staff. LC 80-66346. (Illus.). 96p. (Orig.). 1980. pap. 4.95 (ISBN 0-917102-88-6). Ortho.

How to Select & Care for Shrubs & Hedges. Joseph E. Howland. Ed. by Ortho Books Editorial Staff. LC 80-66346. (Illus.). 96p. (Orig.). 1981. pap. 4.95 (Ortho Bks). Chevron Chem.

How to Select & Install Antennas. 2nd ed. Lon Cantor. 1978. pap. 5.95 (ISBN 0-8104-5745-8). Hayden.

How to Select & Install Your Own Speakers. Norman H. Crowhurst. (Illus.). 1979. 9.95 (ISBN 0-8306-9823-X); pap. 6.95 (ISBN 0-8306-1034-0, 1034). TAB Bks.

How to Select & Use Hi-Fi & Stereo Equipment. Murray P. Rosenthal. 1979. pap. 9.85 (ISBN 0-8104-0424-9). Hayden.

How to Select & Use Hi-Fi & Stereo Equipment, Vol. 2. Murray P. Rosenthal. (Illus.). 1969. pap. 4.55 o.p. (ISBN 0-8104-0341-2). Hayden.

How to Select & Use Minolta SLR Cameras. Carl Shipman. (Orig.). 1980. pap. 9.95 (ISBN 0-89586-044-9). H P Bks.

How to Select & Use Nikon SLR Cameras. Carl Shipman. LC 78-52274. (Illus.). 1978. pap. 9.95 (ISBN 0-912656-77-8). H P Bks.

How to Select & Use Olympus Slr Cameras. Carl Shipman. LC 79-84702. (Illus.). 1979. pap. 9.95 (ISBN 0-89586-015-5). H P Bks.

How to Select & Use Photographic Gadgets. Carl Holzman & Phoebe Holzman. (Illus.). 1980. pap. 7.95 (ISBN 0-89586-043-0). H P Bks.

How to Select & Use Record Players. Murray P. Rosenthal. 1979. pap. 6.50 (ISBN 0-8104-0833-3). Hayden.

How to Select Reinforcers. R. Vance & Marilyn C. Hall. 1980. pap. 3.25 (ISBN 0-89079-052-3). H & H Ent.

How to Self-Publish Your Own Book & Make It a Best Seller. 2nd ed. Ted Nicholas. LC 75-33601. 1976. 14.95 o.p. (ISBN 0-913864-11-0). Enterprise Del.

How to Sell a Dealership. Elmer H. West. 64p. (Orig.). 1980. pap. 7.95 (ISBN 0-682-49645-6). Exposition.

How to Sell Anything to Anybody. Joe Girard & Stanley H. Brown. 240p. 1979. pap. 2.75 (ISBN 0-446-95810-7); pap. 4.95 (ISBN 0-446-97719-5). Warner Bks.

How to Sell Banquets. rev. ed. Derek Taylor. 224p. 1981. 16.95 (ISBN 0-8436-2198-2). CBI Pub.

How to Sell Fashion. 2nd ed. Annalee Gold. LC 78-51903. (Illus.). 1978. 12.50 (ISBN 0-87005-201-2). Fairchild.

How to Sell New Ideas: Your Company's & Your Own. Eugene Raudsepp & Joseph C. Yeager. (Illus.). 224p. 1981. 15.95 (ISBN 0-13-432427-7, Spec); pap. 6.95. P-H.

How to Sell to the Government: A Step by Step Guide to Success. William A. Cohen. LC 80-2297. 375p. 1981. 14.95 (ISBN 0-471-08103-5, Pub. by Ronald Pr). Wiley.

How to Sell to the People's Republic of China. Sal T. Massimino. LC 80-18997. (Illus.). 176p. 1980. 16.95 (ISBN 0-444-00454-8, Thomond Pr). Elsevier.

How to Sell Your Crafts. Ruth Wucherer. (Illus.). 192p. 1975. pap. 4.95 o.p. (ISBN 0-8069-8406-6). Sterling.

How to Sell Your Own Home Without a Real Estate Agent & Save Thousands of Dollars. Joseph M. Gardner, Jr. 1975. 6.50 o.p. (ISBN 0-682-48180-7, Banner). Exposition.

How to Sell Your Own House: Without a Broker! Harley Bjelland. 1979. pap. 4.95 (ISBN 0-346-12381-X). Cornerstone.

How to Sell Your Product Through (Not to) Wholesalers. William Friday. LC 79-90315. (Illus.). 1980. 14.50 (ISBN 0-934432-05-8). Prudent Pub Co.

How to Sell Your Product to Mail Order Houses by the Thousands. Duane Shinn. 1976. 19.95 (ISBN 0-912732-23-7). Duane Shinn.

How to Sell Yourself. Joe Girard. 352p. 1981. pap. 5.95 (ISBN 0-446-97336-X). Warner Bks.

How to Serve Your Dog. John B. Kubisz. LC 79-56249. (Illus.). 1980. 7.95 o.s.i. (ISBN 0-931866-05-7). Alpine Pubns.

How to Service & Repair Your Own Car. rev. ed. Richard Day. LC 72-97173. (Popular Science Ser.). (Illus.). 1980. 14.95 (ISBN 0-06-010985-8, HarpT). Har-Row.

How to Set up a Business Office: The Complete Guide to Locating, Outfitting & Staffing. Norma A. Morris. (Illus.). 210p. 1981. 14.95 (ISBN 0-913864-62-5). Enterprise Del.

How to Set up a Small Scale Industry. R. K. Vepa. 250p. 1980. text ed. 25.00 (ISBN 0-7069-1276-4, Pub by Vikas India). Advent Bk.

How to Share Your Faith Without Being Offensive. Joyce Neville. (Orig.). 1979. pap. 4.95 (ISBN 0-8164-2228-1). Crossroad NY.

How to Show Your Dog & Win. Kurt Unkelbach. LC 75-40179. (Illus.). 144p. (gr. 6 up). 1976. PLB 6.90 o.p. (ISBN 0-531-02622-1). Watts.

How to Sing-Art of Singing, 2 vols. in 1. Enrico Caruso & Louisa Tetrazzini. LC 74-23417. 1975. Repr. of 1909 ed. lib. bdg. 19.50 (ISBN 0-306-70674-1). Da Capo.

How to Single Out Your Mate: A Guide for Twogetherness in the 80's. Jim Soules. 140p. 1980. pap. 4.95 (ISBN 0-936890-05-3). Singles World.

How to Size up People. John E. Gibson. 1980. pap. write for info. (ISBN 0-671-83334-0). PB.

How to Sketch from Nature. Newton Fielding. (Illus.). 1980. deluxe ed. 36.45 (ISBN 0-930582-66-7). Gloucester Art.

How to Skyrocket Your Income: The Businessman's Guide to Making Money. James Sheeran. LC 75-45137. 192p. 1976. 9.95 (ISBN 0-8119-0263-3). Fell.

How to Slay a Dragon. Wauneta Hackleman. LC 80-65676. 1980. 9.95 (ISBN 0-89754-019-0); pap. 2.95 (ISBN 0-89754-018-2). Dan River Pr.

How to Solarize Your House. Thomas Scott Dean & Jay W. Hedden. (Illus.). 192p. 1980. 20.00 (ISBN 0-684-16295-4, ScribT). Scribner.

How to Solve Conflicts: Leader's Guide. David R. Douglass. (Leader's Guide Ser.). (Illus.). 1978. pap. 4.95 (ISBN 0-8024-3657-9). Moody.

How to Solve General Chemistry Problems. 6th ed. Robert S. Boikess & C. Harvey Sorum. (Illus.). 1981. pap. text ed. 10.95 (ISBN 0-13-434126-0). P-H.

How to Solve General Chemistry Problems. 5th ed. Boikess Sorum. (Illus.). 320p. 1976. pap. text ed. 10.95 (ISBN 0-13-434100-7). P-H.

How to Solve Problems: Elements of the Theory of Problems & Problem Solving. Wayne E. Wickelgren. LC 73-15787. (Psychology Ser.). (Illus.). 1974. pap. text ed. 8.95x (ISBN 0-7167-0845-0). W H Freeman.

How to Solve the Mismanagement Crisis: Diagnosis & Treatment of Management Problems. Ichak Adizes. 300p. Repr. of 1979 ed. 16.00. Irvington.

How to Spy on the U. S. Alexander Steele. 1974. 7.95 o.p. (ISBN 0-87000-278-3). Arlington Hse.

How to Stand up & Speak Well in Business. Frank Snell. 1968. 3.95 (ISBN 0-346-12307-0). Cornerstone.

How to Star in Soccer. Hubert Vogelsinger. LC 67-23549. (Illus.). 64p. (gr. 5-10). 1967. 4.95 (ISBN 0-590-07052-5, Four Winds). Schol Bk Serv.

How to Start a Bible Institute. Jackie Mallis. 1978. pap. 2.75 (ISBN 0-89265-051-6). Randall Hse.

How to Start a Business & Make It Grow. Arthur C. Simon. LC 78-55987. (Illus.). 1978. softcover 12.95 o.p. (ISBN 0-930490-04-5). Future Shop.

How to Start a Business in Your Home & Gro. Bud Witt. LC 47-332. 208p. (Orig.). (gr. 12). 1980. pap. text ed. 12.00 (ISBN 0-9604932-0-4). B Witt.

How to Start a Homestead Mail Order Business. Lewis Watson & Sharon Watson. (Illus.). pap. cancelled o.s.i. (ISBN 0-686-02631-4). Stonehouse.

How to Start a Jukebox & Pinball Business with Little or No Money: Part-Time, Full-Time or Absentee: A Guide to the Electronic Amusement Game Business. Glenn Perry & Joseph Fiorenza. LC 80-83931. (Illus., Orig.). 1981. 20.95 (ISBN 0-9602586-5-5); pap. 16.95 (ISBN 0-9602586-4-7). Perry Omega.

How to Start a Sideline Business of Your Own & Make a Success Out of It. Colin F. McPeters. (Illus.). 1980. 32.75 (ISBN 0-918968-57-7). Inst Econ Finan.

How to Start an Audiovisual Collection. Ed. by Myra Nadler. LC 78-1993. 1978. 10.00 (ISBN 0-8108-1124-3). Scarecrow.

How to Start & Operate a Business Manual. Luanna C. Blagrove. (Illus.). 175p. 1981. 24.95 (ISBN 0-9604466-4-8). Blagrove Pubns.

How to Start & Operate a Mail Order Business. 2nd ed. Julian L. Simon. (Illus.). 448p. 1976. 23.50 o.p. (ISBN 0-07-057409-X, P&RB). McGraw.

How to Start & Run a Successful Mail Order Business. Sean Martyn. 1971. 12.95 (ISBN 0-679-50259-9). McKay.

How to Start & Succeed in a Business of Your Own. John R. Taylor. 1978. ref. ed. 15.95 (ISBN 0-8359-2927-2); instrs'. manual avail. Reston.

How to Start & Succeed in Your Own Business. Wilfred F. Tetreault & Robert W. Clements. LC 80-66118. (Illus.). 210p. 1980. 16.95 (ISBN 0-937152-01-3). Am Busn Consult.

How to Start & Sustain a Literary Magazine: Practical Strategies for Publications of Lasting Value. Joseph Bruchac. LC 80-80568. 150p. (Orig.). 1980. pap. 12.95 (ISBN 0-935446-01-X). Provision.

How to Start Counseling. William E. Hulme. (Abingdon Reprint Library). 1971. pap. 2.95 (ISBN 0-687-17940-8). Abingdon.

How to Start, Finance & Manage Your Own Small Business. Joseph R. Mancuso. LC 77-14303. (Illus.). 1978. 18.95 (ISBN 0-13-434928-8); pap. 8.95 (ISBN 0-13-434910-5). P-H.

How to Start in Photography. Helen L. Kraas. (Illus.). 88p. (Orig.). 1981. pap. 4.95 (ISBN 0-934616-08-6). Valkyrie Pr.

How to Start Your Own Magazine. W. P. Williams & Joseph H. Van Zandt. 1979. 12.95 o.p. (ISBN 0-8092-7444-2); pap. 4.95 (ISBN 0-8092-7443-4). Contemp Bks.

How to Start Your Own Mail Order Business. rev. ed. Ken Alexander. (Illus.). 1960. 6.95 (ISBN 0-87396-000-9). Stravon.

How to Start Your Own Preschool Playgroup. Harriet Watts. LC 72-91198. (Illus.). 160p. 1973. 5.00x o.p. (ISBN 0-87663-177-4). Universe.

How to Start Your Own Small Business, Vol. 1. 272p. 1973. 5.95 (ISBN 0-8069-8410-4). Sterling.

How to Stay Healthy a Lifetime Without Medicines. Betty Y. Ho. LC 77-86248. 1979. pap. 10.00 (ISBN 0-9600148-3-7). Juvenescent.

How to Stay Healthy While Traveling: A Guide to Today's World Traveler. Bob Young. LC 80-5320. (Illus.). 119p. (Orig.). 1980. pap. 4.95 (ISBN 0-915520-31-1). Ross-Erikson.

How to Stay in College: A Learning Guide for Students. Ed. by Robert S. Kay & Robert A. Terry. LC 78-61683. 1978. pap. text ed. 6.75 (ISBN 0-8191-0623-2). U Pr of Amer.

How to Stay Out of the Hospital. Nathaniel W. Boyd, III. LC 76-39730. 1979. pap. 4.95 (ISBN 0-8119-0404-0). Fell.

How to Stencil & Decorate Furniture & Tinware. Nancy Richardson. 1956. 12.95 o.p. (ISBN 0-8260-7445-6). Ronald Pr.

How to Stick Together During Times of Tension: Directives for Christian Black Unity. Walter A. McCray. 200p. (Orig.). 1981. pap. 4.95 (ISBN 0-933176-03-1). Black Light Fellow.

How to Stop Smoking. Herbert Brean. LC 73-156224. (Rev, Ed). 1958. 5.95 (ISBN 0-8149-0027-5). Vanguard.

How to Stop the Porno Plague. Neil Gallagher. LC 77-21992. (Illus.). 1977. pap. 3.50 (ISBN 0-87123-231-6, 210231). Bethany Fell.

How to Strategically Negotiate the Consulting Contract. Howard L. Shenson. 107p. 1980. pap. text ed. 24.00 (ISBN 0-930686-10-1). Bermont Bks.

How to Stretch Your Dollar. Adele W. Fletcher. (Orig.). pap. 1.50 o.p. (ISBN 0-87502-001-1). Benjamin Co.

How to Study. Harry Maddox. 1978. pap. 2.25 (ISBN 0-449-30831-6, Prem). Fawcett.

How to Study. Ralph C. Preston & Morton Botel. 1974. pap. text ed. 6.00 (ISBN 0-574-51295-0, 5-1295); instr's guide avail. (ISBN 0-574-51296-9, 5-1296); specimen set 7.47 (ISBN 0-574-51299-3, 5-1299). SRA.

How to Study. 4th ed. Ralph C. Preston & Morton Botel. 176p. 1981. pap. 6.95 (ISBN 0-574-19625-0, 13-3625); instr's. guide avail. (ISBN 0-574-19626-9, 13-3626). SRA.

How to Study. Thomas F. Staton. 1959. pap. text ed. 1.35 (ISBN 0-913476-07-2). Am Guidance.

How to Study & Learn. Janet Wikler. (First Bks.). (Illus.). (gr. 4-6). 1978. PLB 6.45 s&l (ISBN 0-531-01409-6). Watts.

How to Study Better & Get Higher Marks. 2nd, rev. ed. Eugene Ehrlich. LC 76-41684. (Illus.). 1976. 10.95 (ISBN 0-690-01181-4, TYC-T). T Y Crowell.

How to Study Better & Get Higher Marks. Eugene H. Ehrlich. LC 61-14527. (Apollo Eds.). 1969. pap. 3.25 o.s.i. (ISBN 0-8152-0225-3, A225, TYC-T). T Y Crowell.

How to Study in College. 2nd ed. Walter Pauk. LC 72-7923. 1974. pap. text ed. 7.50 (ISBN 0-395-17815-0). HM.

How to Succeed in Business: A Resource Unit on Understanding Business & Getting Ahead in the Business World. Tom Rose. LC 74-33827. 1975. 4.95 (ISBN 0-686-10503-6); pap. 1.95 (ISBN 0-686-10504-4). American Ent Texas.

How to Succeed in Real Estate...in Ten Minutes...Twice a Day! Jess Mason. (Illus.). 160p. 1981. 12.50 (ISBN 0-682-49728-2). Exposition.

How to Succeed in Tennis Without Really Trying. Shepherd Mead. 1977. 8.95 o.p. (ISBN 0-679-50749-3). McKay.

How to Succeed in the Business of Finding a Job. Phoebe Taylor. LC 74-17812. 230p. 1975. 13.95 (ISBN 0-88229-162-9); pap. 7.95 (ISBN 0-88229-494-6). Nelson-Hall.

How to Succeed in the Christian Life. Reuben A. Torrey. pap. 3.25 (ISBN 0-8024-3659-5). Moody.

How to Succeed in Your Own Business. William R. Park & Sue Chapin-Park. LC 77-28955. 1978. 19.95 (ISBN 0-471-03189-5, Pub. by Wiley-Interscience). Wiley.

How to Succeed with Your Money. George M. Bowman. pap. 1.95 (ISBN 0-8024-3656-0). Moody.

How to Succeed with Your Money: Leader's Guide. Dennis Becker & Nancy Becker. (Leader's Guide Ser.). (Illus.). 1978. text ed. 3.25 (ISBN 0-8024-3661-7). Moody.

How to Survive a Roommate. James Comer. 240p. 1980. 7.95 (ISBN 0-531-09938-5). Watts.

How to Survive a Second Marriage. Alice Edelman & Roz Stuzin. 1980. 11.95 (ISBN 0-8184-0307-1). Lyle Stuart.

How to Survive a Tax Audit. 1974. pap. 2.00 (ISBN 0-918734-19-3). Reymont.

How to Survive a Tax Audit: What to Do Before & After You Hear from the IRS. Mary L. Sprouse. LC 80-1127. (Illus.). 288p. 1981. 11.95 (ISBN 0-385-17260-5). Doubleday.

How to Survive Being Alive. Donald L. Dudley & Elton Welke. LC 76-50763. 1977. 6.95 o.p. (ISBN 0-385-12107-5). Doubleday.

How to Survive Being Committed to a Mental Hospital. Doug Cameron. LC 79-66488. 143p. 1980. 7.95 (ISBN 0-533-04399-9). Vantage.

How to Survive Belonging to a Club. Dorothy Christen. 1979. pap. 1.95 (ISBN 0-916774-02-3). Tolvan Co.

How to Survive Hard Times. Fred E. Jayne. pap. 1.95 (ISBN 0-89036-146-0). Hawkes Pub Inc.

How to Survive in the Free Lance Jungle. Barbara Gordon & Elliott Gordon. (Illus.). 150p. 1980. pap. write for info. (ISBN 0-917168-06-2). Executive Comm.

How to Survive in Your Liberal School. James K. Fitzpatrick. (Illus.). 1975. 7.95 o.p. (ISBN 0-87000-323-2). Arlington Hse.

How to Survive Modern Technology. Charles T. McGee. LC 80-82327. (Orig.). 1981. pap. 2.95 (ISBN 0-87983-230-4). Keats.

How to Survive Stress (In This Mad Mad World) Ed. by William G. West. (Illus.). 108p. (Orig.). 1980. pap. 6.00 (ISBN 0-914778-35-8). Phoenix Bks.

How to Survive the Money Crash. 9.95 (ISBN 0-89081-174-1). Harvest Hse.

How to Survive Without Meat. Sabine Van Dessel. 1981. 6.95 (ISBN 0-533-04833-8). Vantage.

How to Survive Your Child's Rebellious Teens: New Solutions for Troubled Parents. Myron Brenton. 1979. 9.95 (ISBN 0-397-01340-X). Lippincott.

How to Survive Your Doctor's Care. L. Roy Clark & Sam Locke. (Illus.). 96p. 1981. pap. 4.95 (ISBN 0-87786-005-X). Gold Penny.

How to Take & Sell Erotic Photographs: Secrets of the Masters. Victor Wild. 126p. (Orig.). 1981. pap. 9.95 (ISBN 0-938444-00-X). Wildfire Pub.

How to Take Care of Your Paintings: The Art Owner's Guide to Preservation & Restoration. Caroline K. Keck. (Illus.). 1978. pap. 5.95 (ISBN 0-684-15552-4, ScribT). Scribner.

How to Take Care of Yourselves Naturally. 4th ed. John Barton & Margaret Barton. LC 77-80393. Orig. Title: Flow Lines to Health. (Illus.). 158p. 1980. pap. 8.00 (ISBN 0-937216-04-6). J & M Barton.

How to Take Minutes. 8th ed. H. Graham-Helwig. 136p. 1975. 6.95x o.p. (ISBN 0-8464-0496-6). Beekman Pubs.

How to Take Simple Tests for Civil Service Jobs & Score Higher. Solomon Wiener. 160p. (Orig.). 1981. pap. 4.95 (ISBN 0-671-42777-6). Monarch Pr.

How to Take Tests. W. Pauk & J. Millman. 1969. pap. 3.50 (ISBN 0-07-048915-7, SP). McGraw.

How to Take the Worry Out of Witnessing. George E. Worrell. LC 76-13342. 96p. 1976. pap. 2.75 (ISBN 0-8054-5568-X). Broadman.

How to Take Yourself Apart & Put Yourself Together Again. Harold Sherman. 1979. pap. 1.75 o.p. (ISBN 0-449-14182-9, GM). Fawcett.

How to Talk Back to the Telephone Company: Playing Tthe Telephone Game to Win. Louis J. Sirico, Jr. pap. 20.00 (ISBN 0-9603466-0-0). NCCB.

How to Talk Country. Ed. by Doug Todd. 64p. (Orig.). 1980. pap. 1.50 (ISBN 0-553-14346-8). Bantam.

How to Talk So Kids Will Listen & Listen So Kids Will Talk. Adele Faber & Elaine Mazlish. LC 80-51248. (Illus.). 256p. 1980. 11.95 (ISBN 0-89256-140-8). Rawson Wade.

How to Talk to the Birds & the Beasts. Jacques LeComte & Dorothee Koechlin-Schwartz. LC 79-54013. (Illus.). 1980. 9.95 (ISBN 0-87795-252-3). Arbor Hse.

How to Tape Instant Oral Biographies: Instant Oral Biographies. William Zimmerman. LC 79-56828. (Illus.). 96p. (Orig.). 1981. pap. price not set (ISBN 0-935966-00-5, 100). Guarionex Pr.

How to Teach a Foreign Language. Otto Jespersen. 1904. text ed. 13.50x o.p. (ISBN 0-04-407001-2). Allen Unwin.

How to Teach About Values: An Analytic Approach. Jack R. Fraenkel. (Illus.). 176p. 1977. text ed. 11.95x (ISBN 0-13-435446-X); pap. text ed. 8.95x (ISBN 0-13-435453-2). P-H.

How to Teach an Old Dog New Tricks. Kurt Unkelbach. LC 78-22430. (Illus.). 1979. 6.95 (ISBN 0-396-07669-6). Dodd.

How to Teach Children Responsibility. rev. ed. Reynold Bean & Harris Clemes. (Whole Child Ser.). (Illus.). 80p. 1980. pap. 3.95 (ISBN 0-933358-78-4). Enrich.

How to Teach Children to Draw, Paint and Use Color. Barbara Tuch & Harriet Judy. 1975. 13.95 o.p. (ISBN 0-685-73737-3). P-H.

How to Teach Foreign Languages Effectively. rev. ed. Theodore Huebener. LC 65-13880. 1965. 10.00x (ISBN 0-8147-0209-0). NYU Pr.

How to Teach Reading: A Competency-Based Program. Albert J. Harris & Edward R. Sipay. LC 77-17722. 1979. pap. text ed. 14.95x (ISBN 0-582-28048-6). Longman.

How to Teach School & Make a Living at the Same Time. Patrick H. Crowe. 1978. 9.95 o.p. (ISBN 0-8362-2605-4); pap. 5.95 o.p. (ISBN 0-8362-2600-3). Andrews & McMeel.

How to Teach Your Baby How to Read. Glenn Doman. 160p. 1975. pap. 3.50 (ISBN 0-385-11161-4, Dolp). Doubleday.

How to Teach Your Baby to Read. rev. ed. Glenn Doman. (Gentle Revolution Ser.). 166p. 1979. Repr. of 1964 ed. 9.50 (ISBN 0-936676-01-9). Better Baby.

How to Teach Your Child to Spell: A Guide for Parents. Barbara Hurtekant. LC 80-24308. 1980. pap. 7.95 (ISBN 0-937838-40-3); tchr's ed. 7.95 (ISBN 0-937838-41-1). Open Roads.

How to Teach Your Children About Sex. Stan Berenstain & Jan Berenstain. 1980. pap. 2.95. Ballantine.

How to Tell Stories to Children. Sara C. Bryant. LC 72-12693. 1973. Repr. of 1924 ed. 18.00 (ISBN 0-8103-3740-1). Gale.

How to Tell the Truth. Richard W. Dehaan. 1977. pap. 2.50 (ISBN 0-88207-750-3). Victor Bks.

How to Test Almost Everything Electronic. Jack Darr. LC 66-30560. 1967. 8.95 (ISBN 0-685-24819-4); pap. 4.95 (ISBN 0-8306-6132-8, 132). TAB Bks.

How to Think Ahead in Chess. I. A. Horowitz & Fred Reinfeld. (Illus., Orig.). 1972. pap. 3.50 o.p. (ISBN 0-571-09912-2, Pub. by Faber & Faber). Merrimack Bk Serv.

How to Think & Write. H. Edward Richardson. 1970. pap. 7.95x (ISBN 0-673-05289-3). Scott F.

How to Think Straight. James D. Weinland. (Quality Paperback: No. 81). (Orig.). 1975. pap. 3.95 (ISBN 0-8226-0081-1). Littlefield.

How to Tie Freshwater Flies. Kenneth E. Bay & Matthew M. Vinciguerra. 1974. 10.00 o.p. (ISBN 0-87691-148-3). Winchester Pr.

How to Trace Your Family History. Bill R. Linder. 1979. pap. 2.25 o.p. (ISBN 0-445-04508-6). Popular Lib.

How to Trace Your Family Tree. American Genealogical Research Institute Staff. LC 73-88881. 200p. 1975. pap. 2.95 (ISBN 0-385-09885-5, Dolp). Doubleday.

How to Trace Your Family Tree. David Poteet. LC 79-84344. 1979. pap. 3.50 (ISBN 0-87123-209-X, 210209). Bethany Fell.

How to Track & Find Game. Clyde Ormond. (Funk & W Bk.). (Illus.). 160p. 1975. 8.95 (ISBN 0-308-10210-X, TYC-T); pap. 4.50 (ISBN 0-308-10211-8, TYC-T). T Y Crowell.

How to Train Your Dog in Six Weeks. Kathleen Berman & Bill Landesman. LC 75-45459. 224p. 1976. 9.95 (ISBN 0-8119-0266-8). Fell.

How to Train Your Horse. Anthony Amaral. (Illus.). 1977. 10.95 (ISBN 0-87691-193-9). Winchester Pr.

How to Transform a Garage into Living Space, Bk. 684. Donald R. Brann. LC 72-92125. (Illus.). 128p. 1974. lib. bdg. 5.95 (ISBN 0-87733-084-0); pap. 5.95 (ISBN 0-87733-684-9). Easi-Bild.

How to Troubleshoot a Color TV Receiver. J. Richard Johnson. 1978. pap. 9.50 (ISBN 0-8104-0820-1). Hayden.

How to Troubleshoot & Repair Microcomputers. Lenk. 304p. 1980. pap. 7.95 (ISBN 0-8359-2981-7). Reston.

How to Troubleshoot & Repair Your Stereo System. Hershal Gardner. (Illus.). 240p. 1976. 17.95 (ISBN 0-87909-349-8); pap. 6.95 (ISBN 0-8359-2976-0). Reston.

How to Turn Down into up. E. E. Wakin. (gr. 9). 1980. pap. 1.25 (ISBN 0-590-31263-4, Schol Pap). Schol Bk Serv.

How to Understand Dreams. Elizabeth Lowe. 1979. 1.50 (ISBN 0-686-28862-9). Dreams Unltd.

How to Understand Music. Oscar Thompson. 347p. 1980. Repr. of 1935 ed. lib. bdg. 30.00 (ISBN 0-89984-453-7). Century Bookbindery.

How to Understand the Bible. rev. ed. W. Robert Palmer. 112p. 1980. pap. 2.95 (ISBN 0-89900-140-8). College Pr Pub.

How to up Your Potassium. Corinne Krause. 5.95 (ISBN 0-9604104-0-6). Green Hill.

How to Use ESP to Win the American Daily Lottery. Edward Marshall. LC 80-69615. (Illus.). 64p. (Orig.). 1981. price not set (ISBN 0-938284-00-2). Inner Circle.

How to Use Interest Rate Futures Contracts. Edward W. Schwarz. LC 79-51781. 1979. 19.95 (ISBN 0-87094-180-1). Dow Jones-Irwin.

How to Use Life & Health Insurance in Business & Estate Planning. 2nd ed. Edward A. Stoeber. LC 79-87867. 1979. pap. 15.00 o.p. (ISBN 0-87218-402-1). Natl Underwriter.

How to Use Mushrooms for Color. rev. ed. Miriam C. Rice. (Illus.). 145p. 1980. pap. 7.95 (ISBN 0-916422-19-4). Mad River.

How to Use Overcorrection. Nathan H. Azrin & V. A. Besalel. 1980. 3.25 (ISBN 0-89079-047-7). H & H Ent.

How to Use Planned Ignoring. R. Vance Hall & Marilyn C. Hall. 1980. 3.25 (ISBN 0-89079-045-0). H & H Ent.

How to Use Reference Materials. Bernice Macdonald. (gr. 7 up). 1980. PLB 6.45 (ISBN 0-531-04134-4). Watts.

How to Use Reprimands. Ron Van Houten. 1980. pap. 3.25 (ISBN 0-89079-051-5). H & H Ent.

How to Use Shaping. Marion V. Panyan. 1980. pap. 3.25 (ISBN 0-89079-050-7). H & H Ent.

How to Use Systematic Attention & Approval. R. Vance Hall & Marilyn C. Hall. 1980. 3.25 (ISBN 0-89079-044-2). H & H Ent.

How to Use the Modern Ephemeris. Elbert Benjamine. 1940. pap. 1.00 (ISBN 0-933646-08-9). Aries Pr.

How to Use the Power of Mind in Everyday Life. Craig Carter. 96p. 1976. pap. 3.50 (ISBN 0-911336-65-6). Sci of Mind.

How to Use the Power of Your Word. Stella T. Mann. 173p. 1975. pap. 2.95 o.p. (ISBN 0-87516-207-X). De Vorss.

How to Use the School Library. Daniel D. Stuhlman. (Teacher Education Ser.: No. 3). (Orig.). Date not set. pap. 1.25 (ISBN 0-934402-06-X). BYLS Pr. Postponed.

How to Use the Tremendous Power of Creative Prayer. Leland F. Gipson. 120p. (Orig.). 1981. pap. 3.95x (ISBN 0-9605014-0-1). Levada.

How to Use Time Out. R. Vance Hall & Marilyn C. Hall. 1980. 3.25 (ISBN 0-89079-046-9). H & H Ent.

How to Use Type. Ken Rodmell. 120p. 1981. pap. 7.95 (ISBN 0-442-29801-3). Van Nos Reinhold.

How to Use Your Apple II Computer. J. R. Weber. LC 80-70465. (IDM's How to Use Your Microcomputer Ser.). 250p. (gr. 10-12). 1981. 19.95 (ISBN 0-938862-02-2); pap. 14.95 (ISBN 0-938862-03-0). Five Arms Corp.

How to Use Your PET Computer. J. R. Weber. (IDM's How to Use Your Microcomputer Ser.). 250p. (gr. 10-12). 1981. 14.95 (ISBN 0-9604892-7-4); pap. 12.95 (ISBN 0-9604892-8-2). Five Arms Corp.

How to Use Your Time to Get Things Done. Edwin B. Feldman. LC 68-18138. 1968. 9.95 (ISBN 0-8119-0110-6). Fell.

How to Use Your TRS-80 Model II Computer. J. R. Weber. LC 80-70467. (IDM's How to Use Your Microcomputer Ser.). 250p. (gr. 10-12). 1981. 19.95 (ISBN 0-938862-00-6); pap. 14.95 (ISBN 0-938862-01-4). Five Arms Corp.

How to Vertical Fish for Great Lakes Salmon & Trout. Nick Ganzer. (Orig.). 1981. pap. write for info. (ISBN 0-9602648-1-7). Merganzer Pr. Postponed.

How to Visit Colleges. rev ed. American Personnel & Guidance Assn. 1972. pap. text ed. 3.75 pkg. of 5 o.p. (ISBN 0-686-04989-6). Am Personnel.

How to Wait for Jesus. Wayne Judd. LC 78-13975. (Nugget Ser.). 32p. 1979. pap. 0.65 (ISBN 0-8127-0206-9). Southern Pub.

How to Wake up the Financial Genius Inside of You. Mark O. Haroldsen. 192p. 1980. pap. 2.50 (ISBN 0-553-14427-8). Bantam.

How to Walk with God. David Winter. LC 99-78727. Orig. Title: Now What. (Illus.). 1969. pap. 1.95 (ISBN 0-87788-594-X). Shaw Pubs.

How to Wear Colors: With Emphasis on Dark Skins. 5th ed. Charleszine W. Spears. LC 73-89010. 1974. pap. text ed. 5.50 o.p. (ISBN 0-8087-1927-0). Burgess.

How to Weave Fine Cloth. James D. Scarlett. 208p. 1981. 14.95 (ISBN 0-8359-2987-6); pap. 7.95 (ISBN 0-8359-2986-8). Reston.

How to Weigh Less for the Rest of Your Life. Larry Adcock. 1980. pap. 2.25 (ISBN 0-446-92084-3). Warner Bks.

How to Win Arguments. William A. Rusher. LC 79-6874. 264p. 1981. 10.95 (ISBN 0-385-15255-8). Doubleday.

How to Win at Blackjack. Charles Einstein. (Gambler's Book Shelf). 64p. 1979. pap. 2.95 (ISBN 0-89650-552-9). Gamblers.

How to Win at Checkers. Fred Reinfeld. pap. 3.00 (ISBN 0-87980-068-2). Wilshire.

How to Win at Cribbage. Joseph P. Wergin. 1980. 10.95 (ISBN 0-87691-304-4). Winchester Pr.

How to Win at Duplicate Bridge. rev. ed. Marshall Miles. 1962. pap. 1.95 o.s.i. (ISBN 0-02-029280-5, Collier). Macmillan.

How to Win at Gin Rummy. Harold Hart. (Gambler's Book Shelf Ser.). 64p. 1972. pap. 2.95 (ISBN 0-89650-528-6). Gamblers.

How to Win at Gin Rummy. Oswald Jacoby. (Illus.). 1978. pap. 3.95 (ISBN 0-03-042886-6). HR&W.

How to Win at Ladies Doubles. Allegra Charles. LC 75-3780. (Illus.). 1975. pap. 2.95 o.p. (ISBN 0-668-03794-6). Arco.

How to Win at Othello. Goro Hasegawa & Maxine Brady. LC 77-5259. (Illus.). 1977. pap. 2.95 o.p. (ISBN 0-15-642215-8, Harv). HarBraceJ.

How to Win at Pocket Billiards. Knuchell. pap. 4.00 (ISBN 0-87980-069-0). Wilshire.

How to Win at Poker. John Moss. LC 55-7025. 1955. pap. 2.95 (ISBN 0-385-00094-4, Dolp). Doubleday.

How to Win at Poker. Terence Reese & A. T. Watkins. pap. 3.00 (ISBN 0-87980-070-4). Wilshire.

How to Win at Stud Poker. James M. Wickstead. (Gamblers Book Shelf). 1968. pap. 2.95 (ISBN 0-89650-509-X). Gamblers.

How to Win Chess Games Quickly. Fred Reinfeld. 1963. pap. 2.95 (ISBN 0-06-463269-5, EH 269, EH). Har-Row.

How to Win Customers. Heinz Goldman. pap. 4.95 (ISBN 0-8015-3898-X, Hawthorn). Dutton.

How to Win Over Yourself and Other People, Assertiveness Techniques and Traits. David Whiteside & Robert L. Whisteside. LC 76-16856. 1976. 7.95 (ISBN 0-8119-0270-6). Fell.

How to Win Productivity in Manufacturing. Wm. E. Sandman & John P. Hayes. (Illus.). 224p. (Orig.). 1980. pap. 14.95 (ISBN 0-9604612-0-5). Yellow Bk PA.

How to Win Souls Today. Jack Exum. 3.95 o.p. (ISBN 0-89315-106-8). Lambert Bk.

How to Win the Meeting. Frank Snell. 1979. 8.95 (ISBN 0-8015-3896-3, Hawthorn); pap. 4.95 (ISBN 0-8015-3897-1, Hawthorn). Dutton.

How to Win the Small Business Game. Paul M. German. (Illus.). 182p. (Orig.). 1981. 16.95 (ISBN 0-9605436-1-9); pap. 12.95 (ISBN 0-9605436-0-0). Small Busn Pubns.

How to Win Votes: The Politics of Nineteen Eighty. Edward N. Costikyan. LC 79-3892. 1980. 12.95 (ISBN 0-15-142221-4). HarBraceJ.

How to Win with Information or Lose Without It. Andrew Garvin & Hubert Bermont. (Bermont Bks.). 196p. 1980. 26.00 (ISBN 0-89696-110-9). Everest Hse.

How to Win Your Family to Christ. Nat Olson. LC 77-81561. pap. 2.95 (ISBN 0-89107-149-0). Good News.

How to Witness Successfully - Leader's Guide. Joe Ragont. 1979. pap. 3.25 (ISBN 0-8024-3793-1). Moody.

How to Wrap Five More Eggs: Traditional Japanese Packaging. Hideyuki Oka. LC 74-23690. (Illus.). 216p. 1975. 18.75 (ISBN 0-8348-0108-6). Weatherhill.

How to Write. Gertrude Stein. LC 74-17880. 416p. 1975. pap. text ed. 4.00 (ISBN 0-486-23144-5). Dover.

How to Write a Book: The Essential Knowledge Which Everyone, but Abolutely Everyone Should Possess on the Art of Writing for Fame & Profit. Alexander Aldrich. (Essential Knowledge Ser. Books). (Illus.). 1978. plastic spiral bdg. 28.45 (ISBN 0-89266-123-2). Am Classical Coll Pr.

How to Write a Book Which the Millions Will Want to Read. Valerious Marlowe. (Illus.). 1977. 28.45 (ISBN 0-89266-027-9). Am Classical Coll Pr.

How to Write a Composition. Elizabeth I. Kearney. (gr. 9-12). pap. text ed. 1.25x (ISBN 0-87543-535-1). Lucas.

How to Write a Good Advertisement. Victor O. Schwab. 1962. 9.95x o.p. (ISBN 0-06-111560-6, HarpT). Har-Row.

How to Write a Narrative Investigation Report. William Dienstein. (Police Science Ser.). 128p. 1975. 11.75 (ISBN 0-398-00454-4). C C Thomas.

How to Write a Poem. Lawrence J. Dessner. LC 78-65447. 1979. 11.00x (ISBN 0-8147-1766-7); pap. 5.95 (ISBN 0-8147-1767-5). NYU Pr.

How to Write a Report. Gerald Newman. (gr. 7 up). 1980. PLB 6.45 (ISBN 0-531-04135-2). Watts.

How to Write a Research Paper. R. Berry. 1969. pap. 6.50 (ISBN 0-08-006392-6). Pergamon.

How to Write a Research Paper. John A. Dwight & Dana C. Speer. LC 79-3012. (gr. 11-12). 1979. pap. text ed. 6.95 (ISBN 0-934902-01-1); tchr's ed. 30.00 (ISBN 0-934902-02-X); work pad 1.50 (ISBN 0-934902-03-8). Learn Concepts OH.

How to Write a Research Paper Step-by-Step. Phyllis Cash. (How to Ser.). 128p. 1975. pap. 2.50 (ISBN 0-671-18752-X). Monarch Pr.

How to Write a Term Paper. Elizabeth James & Carol Barkin. LC 80-13734. 96p. (gr. 7 up). 1980. PLB 6.67 (ISBN 0-688-51951-2); pap. 3.95 (ISBN 0-688-45025-3). Lothrop.

How to Write Advertisements. V. A. Schwab. 230p. 1981. 28.50 o.p. (ISBN 0-686-68303-X). Porter.

How to Write an Essay. Enid A. Goldberg. 1981. pap. text ed. 8.95x (ISBN 0-673-15181-6). Scott F.

How To Write an Operations Manual: A Guide for Apartment Management. Institute of Real Estate Management Staff. Ed. by Nancye J. Kirk. LC 78-61862. 1978. pap. text ed. 18.95 (ISBN 0-912104-35-X). Inst Real Estate.

How to Write & Publish a Scientific Paper. Robert Day. 1979. pap. 8.95 (ISBN 0-89495-006-1); 15.00 (ISBN 0-89495-008-8). ISI Pr.

How to Write & Sell a Book of Your Intimate Thoughts & of Your Personal Adventures. Wilson Ketterer. (Illus.). 1980. deluxe ed. 27.25 (ISBN 0-89266-233-6). Am Classical Coll Pr.

How to Write Anything. Robert Adleman. LC 80-81879. 1981. pap. 6.95 (ISBN 0-933350-37-6). Morse Pr.

How to Write Better Business Letters. 4th ed. Earle A. Buckley. (Illus.). 1957. 10.95 o.p. (ISBN 0-07-008778-4, P&RB); pap. 3.95 o.p. (ISBN 0-07-008779-2). McGraw.

How to Write Creatively. Riley Hughes. (gr. 7 up). 1980. PLB 6.45 (ISBN 0-531-04128-X). Watts.

How to Write Dumb Poems. Gus Kilthau. LC 79-88250. (Orig.). 1981. price not set (ISBN 0-89896-013-4). Larksdale.

How to Write Fillers & Short Features That Sell. 2nd ed. Louise Boggess. LC 80-8682. 256p. 1981. 10.95 (ISBN 0-06-010492-9, HarpT). Har-Row.

How to Write for Children. rev. ed. Jane Fitz-Randolph. LC 79-2747. (Everyday Handbook Ser.). 288p. 1980. pap. 4.95 (ISBN 0-06-463491-4, EH 491, EH). Har-Row.

How to Write Music Manuscript (in Pencil) A Workbook in the Basics of Music Notation. Gerald Warfield. LC 76-58400. (Music Ser.). 1977. pap. text ed. 9.95 (ISBN 0-679-30332-4, Pub. by MacKay). Longman.

How to Write Reports. J. Mitchell. 1975. pap. 1.50 o.p. (ISBN 0-531-06068-3, Fontana Pap). Watts.

How to Write the History of a Family: A Guide for the Genealogist. W. P. Phillimore. LC 70-179653. (Illus.). viii, 206p. 1972. Repr. of 1876 ed. 22.00 (ISBN 0-8103-3117-9). Gale.

How to Write What. Harry E. Chandler. 1978. 10.95 (ISBN 0-87170-001-8). ASM.

How Two: A Handbook for Office Workers. 2nd ed. James L. Clark & Lyn Clark. 1979. pap. text ed. 7.95x (ISBN 0-534-00635-3). Wadsworth Pub.

How We Chose A President. 5th ed. Lee L. Gray. 1980. 8.95 (ISBN 0-312-39411-X). St Martin.

How We Got Our Bible. W. Griffith Thomas. 1926. pap. 1.50 (ISBN 0-8024-3796-6). Moody.

How We Got Our First Cat. Tobi Tobias. (gr. 1-3). 1980. 5.95 (ISBN 0-531-02870-4, G35); PLB 7.90 (ISBN 0-531-04173-5, F20). Watts.

How We Know. Martin Goldstein & Inge Goldstein. (Da Capo Quality Paperbacks Ser.). (Illus.). 376p. 1981. pap. 8.95 (ISBN 0-306-80140-X). Da Capo.

How We Learn. Lee Edson. (Human Behavior Ser). 176p. 1975. 9.95 (ISBN 0-8094-1916-5); lib. bdg. avail. (ISBN 0-685-52491-4). Time-Life.

How We Learn. Lee Edson. LC 74-33050. (Human Behavior Ser.). (Illus.). 1975. lib. bdg. 9.99 o.p. (ISBN 0-686-51076-3). Silver.

How We Live. L. Rust Hills & Penny C. Hills. 1968. 12.50 o.s.i. (ISBN 0-02-551570-5). Macmillan.

How We Lived: A Documentary History of Immigrant Jews in America, Eighteen Eighty-Nineteen Thirty. Irving Howe & Kenneth Libo. 1981. pap. 6.95 (ISBN 0-452-25269-5, Z5269, Plume Bks). NAL.

How We Lived: Reminiscences, Stories, Speeches, & Songs of California Indians. Malcolm Margolin. 1981. 10.95 (ISBN 0-930588-03-7); pap. 5.95 (ISBN 0-930588-04-5). Heyday Bks.

How We Started Students on Successful Foodservice Careers. Herman A. Breithaupt. LC 72-75296. 256p. 1972. 11.95 (ISBN 0-8436-0544-8). CBI Pub.

How We Will Reach the Stars. John W. Macvey. 1969. pap. 1.25 o.s.i. (ISBN 0-02-093450-5, Collier). Macmillan.

How Wild Animals Fight. Dorothy E. Shuttlesworth. LC 75-19144. 96p. (gr. 2-5). 1976. 5.95 o.p. (ISBN 0-385-08596-6); PLB write for info. o.p. (ISBN 0-385-08599-0). Doubleday.

How Women Stay Slim. Robert L. Holt. LC 80-92693. 1980. 12.95x (ISBN 0-930926-04-8); pap. 7.95x (ISBN 0-930926-05-6). Calif Health.

How Would You Like to See the Slides of My Mission. Larry Nielson. LC 80-82708. (Illus.). 80p. (Orig.). 1980. pap. 4.95 (ISBN 0-88290-153-2, 2040). Horizon Utah.

How You Can Be Prepared. Jim McKeever. 246p. (Orig.). 1980. 14.95 (ISBN 0-931608-12-0); pap. 12.95 (ISBN 0-931608-13-9). Alpha Omega.

How You Can Get Straight A's in College by Beating the System. Dale Rich. 123p. (Orig.). 1981. 9.95 (ISBN 0-89896-099-1). Larksdale.

How You Can Influence Congress: The Complete Handbook for the Citizen Lobbyist. George Alderson & Everett Sentman. 1979. 15.95 o.p.; pap. 9.95 (ISBN 0-87690-320-0). Dutton.

How You Can Learn to Live with Computers. Harry Kleinberg. 1977. 8.95 o.p. (ISBN 0-397-01226-8). Lippincott.

How You Can Make Twenty Thousand Dollars a Year Writing: No Matter Where You Live. Nancy E. Hanson. LC 79-22725. 280p. 1980. 10.95x (ISBN 0-89879-011-5); pap. 6.95 (ISBN 0-89879-025-5). Writers Digest.

How You Can Use Inflation to Beat IRS: All the Legal Ways to Keep Your Money for Yourself & Your Family... Without Getting in Trouble with the IRS. B. Ray Anderson. LC 80-8429. (Illus.). 416p. 1981. 12.95 (ISBN 0-06-014825-X, HarpT). Har-Row.

How You Talk. Paul Showers. LC 66-15766. (Let's-Read-&-Find-Out Science Bk). (Illus.). (ps-3). 1967. 7.89 (ISBN 0-690-42136-2, TYC-J); filmstrip with record 11.95 (ISBN 0-690-42137-0); films with cassette 14.95 (ISBN 0-690-42139-7). T Y Crowell.

How You Too Can Make at Least One Million Dollars (But Probably Much More) in the Mail-Order Business. Gerardo Joffe. LC 77-92067. 1979. 19.95 (ISBN 0-930992-02-4, HarpT). Har-Row.

How Your Mind Can Keep You Well. 4th ed. Roy Masters. Ed. by Dorothy Baker. Orig. Title: Your Mind Can Keep You Well. 1976. pap. 6.50 (ISBN 0-933900-08-2). Foun Human Under.

How Your Mind Can Keep You Well. Roy Masters. 1977. pap. 1.75 o.p. (ISBN 0-449-23079-1, Crest). Fawcett.

How Your Muscles Work: Featuring Nautilus Training Equipment. Ellington Darden. Ed. by Ellington Darden. LC 77-75757. (Physical Fitness & Sports Medicine Ser.). (Illus.). 1977. pap. 3.95 (ISBN 0-89305-010-5). Anna Pub.

Howard, E. Watch Company, 1909. 48p. 1981. pap. 4.00 (ISBN 0-915706-01-6). Am Reprints.

Howard J. Stoddard: Founder of the Michigan National Bank. Richard D. Poll. (Illus.). x, 260p. 1980. 17.50x (ISBN 0-87013-220-2). Mich St U Pr.

Howard Mumford Jones: An Autobiography. Howard M. Jones. LC 78-65013. 1979. 21.50 (ISBN 0-299-07770-5). U of Wis Pr.

Howard Pyle. Willard S. Morse & Gertrude Brinckle. LC 68-31099. 1969. Repr. of 1921 ed. 15.00 (ISBN 0-8103-3493-3). Gale.

Howard University Bibliography of African & Afro-American Religious Studies: With Locations in American Libraries. Ethel L. Williams & Clifton F. Brown. LC 76-5604. 1977. 29.00 (ISBN 0-8420-2080-2). Scholarly Res Inc.

Howard W. Sams Crash Course in Microcomputers. Louis E. Frenzel, Jr. LC 79-65750. 1980. pap. 17.50 (ISBN 0-672-21634-5, 21634). Sams.

Howards End. E. M. Forster. Ed. by Oliver Stallybrass. (Abinger Edition of E. M. Forster Ser.). 1978. text ed. 20.50x (ISBN 0-8419-5806-8). Holmes & Meier.

Howdy: Stories About the Uncommon West Texans. Jeanne Lively. Ed. by Linda Roy. (Illus.). 70p. 1974. 5.50 o.p. (ISBN 0-89015-070-2). Nortex Pr.

Howell Book of Dog Care & Training. 2nd ed. Elsworth S. Howell et al. LC 63-14239. (Illus.). 1963. 5.95 o.p. (ISBN 0-87605-574-9). Howell Bk.

Howie Helps Himself. Joan Fassler. LC 74-12284. (Concept Bks). (Illus.). 32p. (gr. 1-3). 1975. 6.95g (ISBN 0-8075-3422-6). A Whitman.

Howl Like the Wolves: Growing up in Nazi Germany. Max Von Der Grun. Tr. by Jan Van Heurck from Ger. LC 80-19144. Orig. Title: Wie War das Eigentlich? (Illus.). 288p. (gr. 7-9). 1980. 9.95 (ISBN 0-688-22252-8); PLB 9.55 (ISBN 0-688-32252-2). Morrow.

Howling Mad. Mad Magazine Editors. (Mad Ser.). (Illus.). 192p. 1974. pap. 1.75 (ISBN 0-446-94367-3). Warner Bks.

How's It Made? A Photo Tour of Seven Small Factories. Stephen Lewis. LC 77-5485. (gr. 1-5). 1977. 8.25 (ISBN 0-688-80111-0); PLB 7.92 (ISBN 0-688-84111-2). Greenwillow.

Hoyle's Card Games. Edmund Hoyle. 1979. pap. 6.95 (ISBN 0-7100-0115-0). Routledge & Kegan.

Hoyle's Games. 20th. rev ed. Edmund Hoyle. 1967. Repr. of 1950 ed. 14.00 (ISBN 0-7100-1566-6). Routledge & Kegan.

Hoyle's Modern Encyclopedia of Card Games, Rules of All the Basic Games & Popular Variations. Walter B. Gibson. LC 73-163085. 408p. 1974. pap. 5.95 (ISBN 0-385-07680-0, Dolp). Doubleday.

Hoyles Rules of Games. Ed. by Morehead et al. (RL 7). 1973. pap. 2.25 (ISBN 0-451-09001-2, E9001, Sig). NAL.

Hoyt Collection Catalogue, Vol. 1. Hsien-Chi Teng. 1964. 20.00 (ISBN 0-87846-022-5). Mus Fine Arts Boston.

Hoyt Collection Catalogue, Vol. 2. 1972. 35.00 (ISBN 0-87846-059-4). Mus Fine Arts Boston.

Hoyt's New Cyclopedia of Practical Quotations. rev. ed. Ed. by Kate L. Roberts. LC 40-13383. (Funk & W Bk.). (YA) (gr. 9 up). 1940. thumb-indexed 10.95 o.p. (ISBN 0-308-40054-2, 429090, TYC-T). T Y Crowell.

Hrs. Cooper's Boardinghouse. Joan Lindau. 1980. lib. bdg. write for info. (Large Print Bks). G K Hall.

Hsi-Yu Chi. Glen Dudbridge. LC 71-85718. (Studies in Chinese History, Literature & Institutions). (Illus.). 1970. 42.00 (ISBN 0-521-07632-3). Cambridge U Pr.

Hsiao Hung. Howard Goldblatt. LC 75-30650. (World Authors Ser.: China: No. 386). 1976. lib. bdg. 12.50 (ISBN 0-8057-6228-0). Twayne.

Hsin Hsing, Taiwan: A Chinese Village in Change. Bernard Gallin. 1966. 19.50x (ISBN 0-520-00451-5). U of Cal Pr.

Hua: A Papuan Language of the Eastern Highlands of New Guinea. John Haiman. (Studies in Language Companion: No. 5). 1980. text ed. 55.00x (ISBN 90-272-3004-8). Humanities.

Huadong: The Story of a Chinese People's Commune. Gordon Bennett. (Westview Special Studies on China & East Asia Ser.). 1978. lib. bdg. 21.50x (ISBN 0-89158-094-8); pap. text ed. 8.75 (ISBN 0-89158-095-6). Westview.

Huai-nan-tzu, Book Eleven: Behavior, Culture, & the Cosmos. Benjamin E. Wallacker. (American Oriental Ser.: Vol. 48). 1962. pap. 4.00x (ISBN 0-686-00028-5). Am Orient Soc.

Hualapai Indians, Vol. 1: Prehistoric Indian Occupation Within the Eastern Area of the Yuman Complex: a Study in Applied Archaeology. Henry F. Dobyns. (American Indian Ethnohistory Ser: Indians of the Southwest). (Illus.). lib. bdg. 42.00 (ISBN 0-8240-0722-0). Garland Pub.

Hualapai Indians, Vol. 2: An Ethnological Report on the Hualapai (Walapai) Indians of Arizona. Robert A. Manners. (American Indian Ethnohistory Ser: Indians of the Southwest). (Illus.). lib. bdg. 42.00 (ISBN 0-8240-0723-9). Garland Pub.

Huan-Ying: Workers' China. Janet Goldwasser & Stuart Dowty. LC 74-7790. 400p. 1975. 12.50 o.p. (ISBN 0-85345-337-3, CL3373). Monthly Rev.

Hub. Robert Herring. 1981. 12.95 (ISBN 0-670-38552-2). Viking Pr.

Hub: Champion of the Cutting Horses. Robert Williams. (Illus.). 64p. 1975. 7.95 (ISBN 0-89015-104-0). Nortex Pr.

Hubble Atlas of Galaxies. Allan Sandage. LC 60-16568. (Illus.). 141p. 1961. pap. 17.00 (ISBN 0-87279-629-9, 618). Carnegie Inst.

Hubert H. Humphrey: The Happy Warrior. Ellen Erlanger. LC 79-1367. (Achievers Ser.). (Illus.). (gr. 4 up). Date not set. PLB 5.95g (ISBN 0-8225-0476-6). Lerner Pubns. Postponed.

Huck Scarry's Steam Train Press-Outs. Huck Scarry. (Illus.). 32p. (Orig.). (gr. 2-5). 1980. pap. 4.95 (ISBN 0-529-05588-0). Philomel.

Huckleberry Finn. Corbin S. Carnell. (Graded Readers for Students of English Ser.). (Illus.). 1979. pap. text ed. 3.50x o.p. (ISBN 0-89285-151-1). English Lang.

Huckleberry Finn. (Illustrated Junior Library). (Illus.). 384p. 1981. pap. 4.95 (ISBN 0-448-11000-8). G&D.

Huckleberry Finn. Gail R. Rosensfit. (Living Literature Workbook Ser.). (Orig.). (gr. 7). Date not set. pap. 1.50 (ISBN 0-671-09248-0). Monarch Pr. Postponed.

Huckleberry Hound Takes a Trip. Leslie Max. (Play & Learn Shape Board Bks). 14p. (gr. k-3). 1981. bds. 2.95 comb bdg. (ISBN 0-89828-105-9, 6006, Ottenheimer Pubs Inc). Tuffy Bks.

Hucklebug. Steve Cosgrove. (Serendipity Bks). (Illus.). (gr. k-4). 1978. PLB 6.95 (ISBN 0-87191-657-6). Creative Ed.

Hucksters in the Classroom: A Review of Industry Propaganda in Schools. Sheila Harty. (Illus., Orig.). 1980. pap. 10.00 o.p. (ISBN 0-686-28457-7). Ctr Responsive Law.

Hucksters in the Classroom: A Review of Industry Propaganda in Schools. Sheila Harty. (Illus.). 190p. 1979. individuals 10.00 (ISBN 0-936758-01-5); institutions 20.00 (ISBN 0-686-28151-9). Ctr Responsive Law.

Hud. Larry McMurtry. Orig. Title: Horseman, Pass by. 144p. 1974. pap. 0.95 o.p. (ISBN 0-445-08318-2). Popular Lib.

Hudibras. Samuel Butler. Ed. by John Wilders. (Oxford English Texts Ser.). (Illus.). 1967. 54.00x (ISBN 0-19-811844-9). Oxford U Pr.

Hudson-Meng Site: An Alberta Bison Kill in the Nebraska High Plains. Larry D. Agenbroad. LC 78-57606. (Illus.). 1978. pap. text ed. 10.00 (ISBN 0-8191-0530-9). U Pr of Amer.

Hudson River. Carl Carmer. 1974. pap. 4.95 o.p. (ISBN 0-03-089387-9). HR&W.

Hudson River Ecology: Fourth Symposium. 1976. pap. text ed. 11.50x (ISBN 0-89062-090-3, Pub by Hres). Pub Ctr Cult Res.

Hudson River Houses: Edwin Whitefield's the Hudson River & Rail Road Illustrated. Edwin Whitefield. LC 80-22371. (Illus.). 96p. 1981. 14.50 (ISBN 0-88427-043-2, Dist. by Caroline Hse). North River.

Hudson River Houses: Edwin Whitefield's the Hudson River & Railroad Illustrated. Edwin Whitefield. 1980. 14.95 (ISBN 0-88427-043-2). Caroline Hse.

Hug a Teddy: And One Hundred & Seventy-One Other Ways to Keep Safe & Secure. Jim Erskine & Goerge Moran. 1980. 5.95 (ISBN 0-517-54215-3, 542153); 10 copy prepack 59.50 (ISBN 0-517-54239-0). Potter.

Huge Season. Wright Morris. LC 54-10858. viii, 306p. 1975. pap. 2.95 (ISBN 0-8032-5805-4, BB 590, Bison). U of Nebr Pr.

Hugh Downs' The Best Years Book: How to Plan for Fulfillment, Security, & Happiness in the Retirement Years. Hugh Downs & Richard J. Roll. 1981. 14.95 (ISBN 0-440-04064-7, E Friede). Delacorte.

Hugh Gaitskell: A Political Biography. Philip M. Williams. 1979. 47.50x (ISBN 0-389-20032-8). B&N.

Hugh MacLennan: A Writers Life. Elspeth Cameron. 424p. 1981. 25.00 (ISBN 0-8020-5556-7). U of Toronto Pr.

Hugo & His Grandma. Catherine Storr. (Illus.). 24p. 1980. pap. 1.60 ea. (Pub. by Dinosaur Pubns); pap. in 5 pk. avail. (ISBN 0-85122-136-X). Merrimack Bk Serv.

Hugo & Josephine. Maria Gripe. Tr. by Paul B. Austin from Swedish. LC 79-18438. (Illus.). (gr. 4-6). 1970. 4.95 o.s.i. (ISBN 0-440-04283-6, Sey Lawr). Delacorte.

Hugo & Josephine. Maria Gripe. Tr. by Paul B. Austin from Swedish. LC 69-18438. (Illus.). (gr. 4-6). 1969. 4.95 o.s.i. (ISBN 0-440-03929-0, Sey Lawr). Delacorte.

Hugo Black & the Judicial Revolution. Gerald T. Dunne. 1977. text ed. 22.50x (ISBN 0-8290-0344-4). Irvington.

Hugo Riemann's Theory of Harmony. Ed. & tr. by William C. Mickelsen. Bd. with History of Music Theory, Book III. LC 76-15366. 1977. 15.00x (ISBN 0-8032-0891-X). U of Nebr Pr.

Hugo Von Hofmannsthal. Lowell A. Bangerter. LC 76-20408. (Modern Literature Ser.). 1977. 10.95 (ISBN 0-8044-2028-9). Ungar.

Hugo Winners, Vol. 1. Isaac Asimov. 320p. 1977. pap. 2.25 (ISBN 0-449-23917-9, Crest). Fawcett.

Huguenot Silver in England, 1688-1727. J. F. Hayward. 1959. 26.00 (ISBN 0-571-04551-0, Pub. by Faber & Faber). Merrimack Bk Serv.

Huguenots, 2 vols. Giacomo Meyerbeer. Ed. by Charles Rosen & Philip Gossett. LC 76-49196. (Early Romantic Opera Ser.: Vol. 20). 1980. lib. bdg. 82.00 (ISBN 0-8240-2919-4). Garland Pub.

Hugues Salel: His Life & Works. Howard Kalwies. Ed. by David J. Parent. LC 79-27150. (Applied Literature Press Medieval Studies: Vol. 4). 286p. 1979. 22.00 (ISBN 0-8357-0500-5, IS-00104, Pub by Applied Lit Pr). Univ Microfilms.

Huile. Harlan Wade. Tr. by Claude Potvin & Rose-Ella Potvin. (Book About Ser.). Orig. Title: Oil. (Illus., Fr.). (gr. k-3). 1979. PLB 7.30 (ISBN 0-8172-1460-7). Raintree Pubs.

Huits Journees De Mai Derriere les Barricades. H. Lissagaray. (Commune De Paris En 1871 Ser). 332p. (Fr.). 1977. lib. bdg. 20.00x o.p. (ISBN 0-8287-0549-6); pap. text ed. 10.00x o.p. (ISBN 0-685-75631-9). Clearwater Pub.

Huk Rebellion: A Study of Peasant Revolt in the Philippines. Benedict J. Kerkvliet. 1977. 22.00x (ISBN 0-520-03106-7). U of Cal Pr.

Hullo Sun. Joan Hodgson. (Illus.). (ps-3). 1972. 6.95 (ISBN 0-85487-019-9). De Vorss.

Human Action & Its Psychological Investigation. Gauld & Shotter. 1977. 16.00 (ISBN 0-7100-8568-0). Routledge & Kegan.

Human Action & Its Psychological Investigation. Alan Gauld & John Shotter. 248p. 1980. pap. 12.95 (ISBN 0-7100-0589-X). Routledge & Kegan.

Human Activity Patterns in the City: Things People Do in Time & in Space. F. Stuart Chapin, Jr. LC 74-5364. (Urban Research Ser). 272p. 1974. 21.95 (ISBN 0-471-14563-7, Pub. by Wiley-Interscience). Wiley.

Human Adaptation: A Functional Interpretation. A. Roberto Frisancho. LC 78-31913. (Illus.). 1979. text ed. 14.95 (ISBN 0-8016-1693-X). Mosby.

Human Adaptation & Its Failures. Leslie Phillips. LC 68-14646. (Personality & Psychopathology Ser.: Vol. 3). 1968. 32.50 o.p. (ISBN 0-12-553850-2). Acad Pr.

Human Adaptation & Population Growth: A Non-Malthusian Perspective. David S. Kleinman. LC 78-59176. 296p. 1980. text ed. 23.50 (ISBN 0-916672-18-2). Allanheld.

Human Adaption: Coping with Life Stresses. Ed. by Rudolf H. Moos. 464p. 1976. 19.95 (ISBN 0-669-00390-5). Lexington Bks.

Human Aggression & Conflict: Interdisciplinary Perspectives. Claude S. Fischer et al. (Illus.). 352p. 1975. pap. 11.95 ref. ed. (ISBN 0-13-444620-8). P-H.

Human Almanac: People Through Time. Richard Burrill. LC 79-92820. (Illus., Orig.). 1980. pap. cancelled (ISBN 0-915190-23-0). Jalmar Pr.

Human Anatomical Dissections: Laboratory Exercises for the Health Professions. E. K. Sauerland & B. A. Sauerland. (Illus.). 152p. 1980. pap. 13.95 (ISBN 0-683-07558-6). Williams & Wilkins.

Human Anatomy. Ruth Ashley. LC 76-65. (Self-Teaching Guides Ser.). 1976. pap. text ed. 6.95 (ISBN 0-471-03508-4). Wiley.

Human Anatomy. Charles E. Tobin. LC 75-78589. (Allied Health Ser). 1975. pap. 7.65 (ISBN 0-672-61375-1). Bobbs.

Human Anatomy. Doris B. Wilson & Wilfred Wilson. (Illus.). 1978. 21.95x (ISBN 0-19-502310-2). Oxford U Pr.

Human Anatomy & Physiology. 2nd ed. John W. Hole, Jr. 880p. 1981. text ed. 21.60 (ISBN 0-697-04597-8); write for info. instr's. manual (ISBN 0-697-04647-8); write for info. transparencies; study guide avail. (ISBN 0-697-04640-0). Wm C Brown.

Human Anatomy & Physiology. Alvin Silverstein. LC 79-13053. 1980. text ed. 27.95x (ISBN 0-471-79166-0); tchrs.' manual avail. (ISBN 0-471-03121-6); experiments avail. (ISBN 0-471-79164-4) (ISBN 0-471-07781-X). Wiley.

Human Anatomy & Physiology. Alexander Spence & Elliott Mason. LC 78-57266. (Illus.). 1979. text ed. 22.95 (ISBN 0-8053-6990-2); instr's resource package 150.00 (ISBN 0-8053-6991-0); transparencies 150.00 (ISBN 0-8053-6992-9). Benjamin-Cummings.

Human Anatomy & Physiology Laboratory Manual with Cat Dissections. Robert C. Wittrup. (Orig.). 1981. write for info. (ISBN 0-8087-2384-7). Burgess.

Human Anatomy: Introductory Laboratory Guide. Julia Guy. 1980. wire coil bdg. 7.95 (ISBN 0-88252-091-1). Paladin Hse.

Human Anatomy Laboratory Textbook. Kent Van de Graaff. 300p. 1981. pap. text ed. write for info. (ISBN 0-697-04598-6). Wm C Brown.

Human Anatomy Made Simple: A Comprehensive Course for Self-Study & Review. Murray, I. MacKay, M.D. LC 68-22473. 1969. pap. 3.50 (ISBN 0-385-01116-4, Made). Doubleday.

Human Ancestors: Readings from Scientific American. Intro. by Glynn Isaac. LC 79-4486. (Illus.). 1979. text ed. 15.95x (ISBN 0-7167-1100-1); pap. text ed. 7.95x (ISBN 0-7167-1101-X). W H Freeman.

Human (& Anti-Human) Values in Children's Books. Council on Interracial Books for Children, Inc. LC 76-11665. (Content Rating Instrument for Educators & Concerned Parents Ser.). 280p. 1976. 14.95 o.s.i. (ISBN 0-930040-00-7); pap. 7.95 (ISBN 0-930040-01-5). CIBC.

Human & Artificial Intelligence. Ed. by Frederick J. Crosson. LC 78-131431. (Orig.). 1970. pap. text ed. 6.95x (ISBN 0-89197-220-X). Irvington.

Human & Ecologic Effects of Nuclear Power Plants. Ed. by Leonard A. Sagan. (Illus.). 560p. 1974. 47.75 (ISBN 0-398-02929-6). C C Thomas.

Human & Economic Geography. Brian French & Stan Squire. (Illus.). 216p. (Orig.). 1973. pap. text ed. 4.50x (ISBN 0-19-519769-0). Oxford U Pr.

Human Anti-Human Gammaglobulins: Their Specificity & Function. R. Grubb & G. Samuelsson. 240p. 1971. 42.00 (ISBN 0-08-016451-X). Pergamon.

Human Artificial Insemination & Semen Preservation. Ed. by Georges David & Wendel S. Price. 620p. 1980. 65.00 (ISBN 0-306-40547-4, Plenum Pr). Plenum Pub.

Human Aspects of Urban Form: Towards a Man-Environment Approach to Urban Form & Design. Amos Rapoport. 1977. text ed. 36.00 (ISBN 0-08-017974-6). Pergamon.

Human Be-Ing: How to Have a Creative Relationship Instead of a Power Struggle. William V. Pietsch. 1975. pap. 1.95 (ISBN 0-451-08784-4, J8784, Sig). NAL.

Human Be-Ing: How to Have a Creative Relationship Instead of a Power Struggle. William V. Pietsch. LC 73-20379. 256p. 1974. 7.95 o.p. (ISBN 0-88208-042-3). Lawrence Hill.

Human Behavior & Adaptation, Vol. 18. Ed. by N. Blurton-Jones & V. Reynolds. (Symposium of the Society for the Study of Human Biology). 1979. 39.95x (ISBN 0-470-26578-7). Halsted Pr.

Human Behavior & Brain Function. Harvey J. Widroe. (Illus.). 132p. 1975. 10.75 (ISBN 0-398-03271-8). C C Thomas.

Human Behavior & Environment - Advances in Theory & Research, Vol. 4: Environment & Culture. Ed. by Ifrwin Altman et al. (Illus.). 368p. 1980. 25.00 (ISBN 0-306-40367-6, Plenum Pr). Plenum Pub.

Human Behavior & Environment: Children & the Environment. Ed. by Irwin Altman & J. F. Wohlwill. (Advances in Theory & Environment Ser.: Vol. 3). (Illus.). 316p. 1978. 18.95 (ISBN 0-306-40090-1, Plenum Pr). Plenum Pub.

Human Behavior & Life Insurance. George H. Russell & Kenneth Black. 1963. ref. ed. 10.95 (ISBN 0-13-444687-9). P-H.

Human Behavior & Public Policy - Political Psychology. M. H. Segall. 1977. 27.50 (ISBN 0-08-017087-0); pap. 12.50 (ISBN 0-08-017853-7). Pergamon.

Human Behavior & Wall Street. John L. King. LC 71-189196. 226p. 1972. 11.95 (ISBN 0-8040-0562-1). Swallow.

Human Behavior at Work. 6th ed. Keith Davis. (Management Ser.). (Illus.). 576p. 1981. text ed. 18.95x (ISBN 0-07-015516-X, C); instrs'. manual & test file avail. (ISBN 0-07-015517-8); study guide avail. (ISBN 0-07-015535-6) (ISBN 0-686-68262-9). McGraw.

Human Behavior in Educational Administration: A Behavioral Science Interpretation. Clarence A. Newell. (Illus.). 1978. ref. ed. 16.95 (ISBN 0-13-444638-0). P-H.

Human Behavior in Illness. Lynn Gillis. 1972. pap. text ed. 4.95 o.p. (ISBN 0-571-04788-2, Pub. by Faber & Faber). Merrimack Bk Serv.

Human Behavior in Illness: Psychology & Interpersonal Relationships. 3rd ed. Lynn Gillis. 224p. 1980. pap. 9.95 (ISBN 0-571-18025-6, Pub. by Faber & Faber). Merrimack Bk Serv.

Human Behavior in Organizations. Charles R. Milton. (Illus.). 432p. 1981. text ed. 18.95x (ISBN 0-13-444596-1). P-H.

Human Behavior in Organizations. Leonard Sayles & G. Strauss. 1966. ref. ed. 19.95 (ISBN 0-13-444703-4). P-H.

Human Behavior in the Social Environment. 2nd ed. Ralph E. Anderson & Irl Carter. LC 77-95322. 1978. text ed. 15.95x (ISBN 0-202-36021-0); pap. text ed. 7.50x (ISBN 0-202-36022-9). Aldine Pub.

Human Being & Citizen: Essays on Virtue, Freedom & the Common Good. new ed. George Anastaplo. LC 75-21909. xiv, 332p. 1975. 16.95 (ISBN 0-8040-0677-6). Swallow.

Human Being & Citizen: Essays on Virtue, Freedom & the Common Good. George Anastaplo. LC 75-21909. 1978. pap. 7.95 (ISBN 0-8040-0678-4). Swallow.

Human Biochemistry. 9th ed. James M. Orten & Otto W. Neuhaus. LC 74-19436. 1975. text ed. 26.95 (ISBN 0-8016-3729-5). Mosby.

Human Biology. 3rd ed. John R. Gibson. 1979. pap. 7.50 (ISBN 0-571-04974-5, Pub. by Faber & Faber). Merrimack Bk Serv.

Human Biology-an Exhibition of Ourselves. British Museum. LC 76-53266. (Illus.). 1977. 18.95 (ISBN 0-521-21589-7); pap. 5.95 (ISBN 0-521-29193-3). Cambridge U Pr.

Human Biology & Behavior. 3rd ed. Weiss & Mann. 1981. text ed. 16.95 (ISBN 0-316-92891-7); training manual free (ISBN 0-316-92892-5). Little.

Human Biology & Ecology. Albert Damon. LC 77-559. (Illus.). 1977. pap. text ed. 8.95x (ISBN 0-393-09103-1). Norton.

Human Biology of Circumpolar Populations. Ed. by F. A. Milan. LC 79-322. (International Biological Programme Ser.: No. 21). (Illus.). 1980. 90.00 (ISBN 0-521-22213-3). Cambridge U Pr.

Human Biology of Environmental Change. Ed. by D. J. Vorster. 1972. pap. text ed. 14.95x (ISBN 0-685-83590-1). Intl Ideas.

Human Body. Jonathan Rutland. LC 77-917. (Illus.). (gr. 5-12). 1977. PLB 4.90 s&l o.p. (ISBN 0-531-09057-4). Watts.

Human Body: Structure & Function in Health & Disease. 2nd ed. Brooks & Brooks. LC 79-24085. (Illus.). 1980. pap. text ed. 17.95 (ISBN 0-8016-0808-2). Mosby.

Human Bond: Introduction to Social Psychology. Elbert W. Stewart. LC 77-9002. 1978. pap. text ed. 18.95x (ISBN 0-471-82479-8); tchrs. manual avail. (ISBN 0-471-82481-X). Wiley.

Human Brain. Nedzad Gluhbegovic & Terence H. Williams. (Illus.). 176p. 1980. text ed. 27.50 (ISBN 0-06-140945-6, Harper Medical). Har-Row.

Human Brain in Dissection. Donald G. Montemurro & J. Edward Bruni. 1981. text ed. price not set (ISBN 0-7216-6438-5). Saunders.

Human Brain: Its Capacities & Functions. Isaac Asimov. pap. 2.25 (ISBN 0-451-61901-3, ME1901, Ment). NAL.

Human Capability Assessment. Ed. by Marvin D. Dunnette & Edwin A. Fleishman. (Human Performance & Productivity Ser.: Vol. 3). 336p. 1981. professional ref. text 19.95 (ISBN 0-89859-085-X). L Erlbaum Assocs.

Human Capital Formation & Manpower Development. R. A. Wykstra. LC 71-153077. 1971. 13.95 o.s.i. (ISBN 0-02-935630-X). Free Pr.

Human Capital: The Settlement of Foreigners in Russia, 1762-1804. R. P. Bartlett. LC 78-68337. 1980. 53.00 (ISBN 0-521-22205-2). Cambridge U Pr.

Human Cardiovascular System: Facts & Concepts. Ed. by J. T. Shepherd & P. M. Vanhoutte. 1979. 27.00 (ISBN 0-89004-367-1); softcover 15.95 (ISBN 0-686-52359-8). Raven.

Human Chromosomes. E. H. Ford. 1973. 54.00 o.s.i. (ISBN 0-12-262150-6). Acad Pr.

Human Chromosomes. E. Therman. (Illus.). 235p. 1981. 19.80 (ISBN 0-387-90509-X). Springer-Verlag.

Human Circle: An Existential Approach to the New Group Therapies. Carl Goldberg & Merle C. Goldberg. LC 73-75523. 1973. 16.95 (ISBN 0-911012-67-2). Nelson-Hall.

Human Cognition: Learning, Understanding & Remembering. John D. Bransford. 1979. pap. text ed. 12.95x (ISBN 0-534-00699-X). Wadsworth Pub.

Human Comedy. rev. ed. William Saroyan. LC 43-51036. (Illus.). (gr. 10 up). 1944. 10.95 (ISBN 0-15-142299-0). HarBraceJ.

Human Communication. 2nd ed. Stewart L. Tubbs & Sylvia Moss. 1977. text ed. 11.95x o.p. (ISBN 0-685-86655-6). Random.

Human Communication: An Interpersonal Introduction. Thomas Steinfatt. LC 76-18065. 1977. pap. 9.95 (ISBN 0-672-61359-X). Bobbs.

Human Communication: Elements & Contexts. Philip Emmert & William Donaghy. LC 80-17595. (Speech Ser.). (Illus.). 46p. 1981. text ed. 12.95 (ISBN 0-201-03597-9). A-W.

Human Communication Handbook: Simulations & Games, Vol. 1. Brent D. Ruben & Richard W. Budd. (Illus.). 1975. pap. text ed. 10.75 (ISBN 0-8104-5524-2). Hayden.

Human Communication Handbook: Simulations & Games, Vol. 2. Brent Ruben. 1978. pap. text ed. 10.75 (ISBN 0-8104-5765-2). Hayden.

Human Communication: The Process of Relating. G. Borden & J. Stone. LC 75-27821. 1976. 8.95 (ISBN 0-8465-0615-7). Benjamin-Cummings.

Human Communication Theory: History of a Paraigm. Nancy Harper. 320p. 1979. pap. 9.95x (ISBN 0-8104-6091-2). Hayden.

Human Condition: An Ecological & Historical View. William H. McNeill. LC 80-7547. 100p. 1980. 8.50 (ISBN 0-691-05317-0). Princeton U Pr.

Human Connection & the New Media. Ed. by Barry Schwartz. (Human Futures Ser). (Illus.). 1973. pap. 2.45 o.p. (ISBN 0-13-444745-X). P-H.

Human Context: Environmental Determinants of Behavior. Rudolf H. Moos. LC 75-26870. 444p. 1976. 28.95 (ISBN 0-471-61504-8, Pub. by Wiley-Interscience). Wiley.

Human Cytogenetics, 2 vols. John L. Hamerton. 1970-71. Vol. 1. 49.00 (ISBN 0-12-321001-1); Vol. 2. 52.75 (ISBN 0-12-321002-X). Acad Pr.

Human Cytogenetics, Vol. 7. ICN-UCLA Symposia on Molecular & Cellular Biology. Ed. by Robert S. Sparkes et al. (ICN-UCLA Symposia on Molecular & Cellular Biology Ser.). 1977. 26.00 (ISBN 0-12-656350-0). Acad Pr.

Human Development. T. G. Bower. LC 78-27223. (Psychology Ser.). (Illus.). 1979. text ed. 18.95x (ISBN 0-7167-0058-1). W H Freeman.

Human Development. 2nd ed. Grace J. Craig. (Illus.). 1980. text ed. 18.95 (ISBN 0-13-444984-3); study guide 6.95 (ISBN 0-13-445015-9). P-H.

Human Development. Hugh V. Perkins. 1975. text ed. 13.95x (ISBN 0-534-00383-4). Wadsworth Pub.

Human Development. 2nd ed. Eric Rayner. 1977. text ed. 25.00x (ISBN 0-04-155009-9); pap. text ed. 9.95x (ISBN 0-04-155008-0). Allen Unwin.

Human Development. 2nd ed. James W. Zanden. 665p. 1981. text ed. 16.95 (ISBN 0-394-32370-X); wkbk. 6.95 (ISBN 0-394-32371-8). Knopf.

Human Development & Learning. 2nd ed. Hugh V. Perkins. 1974. 17.95x (ISBN 0-534-00345-1). Wadsworth Pub.

Human Development in an Urban Age. Theron Alexander. (Illus.). 384p. 1973. ref. ed. 16.95 (ISBN 0-13-444786-7). P-H.

Human Development in Western Culture. 5th ed. Harold W. Bernard. 1978. text ed. 17.95x o.p. (ISBN 0-205-05911-2); instr's man. avail. o.p. (ISBN 0-205-05933-3). Allyn.

Human Development Program for Institutionalized Teenagers. Compiled by John Jensen. 1974. 9.95 (ISBN 0-86584-034-2). Human Dev Train.

Human Development Program Supplementary Idea Guide. rev. ed. Leif Fearn et al. 1975. 7.95 (ISBN 0-86584-008-3). Human Dev Train.

Human Development: The Span of Life. 2nd ed. George Kaluger & Merieum F. Kaluger. LC 78-12022. (Illus.). 1979. 17.95 (ISBN 0-8016-2610-2). Mosby.

Human Dilemma. Herbert Tonne. LC 80-81391. (Library of Liberal Religion). 240p. 1980. 13.95 (ISBN 0-87975-135-5). Prometheus Bks.

Human Dilemmas of Leadership. Abraham Zaleznik. LC 66-11480. 1966. 10.00x o.p. (ISBN 0-06-037160-9, HarpT). Har-Row.

Human Dimension: Experiences in Policy Research. Hadley Cantril. 1967. 13.50 (ISBN 0-8135-0538-0). Rutgers U Pr.

Human Direction: An Evolutionary Approach to Social & Cultural Anthropology. 3rd ed. J. Peacock & A. Kirsch. 1980. pap. 11.95 (ISBN 0-13-444851-0). P-H.

Human Diseases: A Systemic Approach. Mary L. Mulvihill. LC 79-23053. (Illus.). 399p. 1980. pap. text ed. 13.95 (ISBN 0-87619-623-7). R J Brady.

Human Diseases in Color. C. C. Smith. (Illus.). 1978. 32.95 (ISBN 0-87489-188-4). Med Economics.

Human Diversity. Alexander Alland. LC 79-138293. 1971. 17.50x (ISBN 0-231-03227-7). Columbia U Pr.

Human Document, 1892. W. H. Mallock. Ed. by Robert L. Wolff. LC 75-1537. (Victorian Fiction Ser.). 1975. lib. bdg. 66.00 (ISBN 0-8240-1609-2). Garland Pub.

Human Documents of Adam Smith's Time. Ed. by Royston E Pike. 1973. pap. text ed. 9.95x (ISBN 0-04-942119-0). Allen Unwin.

Human Documents of the Industrial Revolution in Britain. Ed. by Royston E. Pike. 1966. text ed. 13.50x o.p. (ISBN 0-04-942059-3); pap. text ed. 12.50x (ISBN 0-04-942060-7). Allen Unwin.

Human Documents of the Lloyd George Era. Royston E. Pike. (Illus.). 272p. 1972. text ed. 9.95x (ISBN 0-04-942098-4, 9095). Allen Unwin.

Human Documents of the Victorian Golden Age. Ed. by Royston E. Pike. 1967. text ed. 12.50x o.p. (ISBN 0-04-942068-2); pap. text ed. 9.50x (ISBN 0-04-942136-0). Allen Unwin.

Human Dynamics in Psychology & Education: Selected Readings. 3rd ed. Don E. Hamachek. 1977. pap. text ed. 12.50x (ISBN 0-205-05583-4). Allyn.

Human Ecology & Susceptibility to the Chemical Environment. Theron G. Randolph. (Illus.). 160p. 1978. 12.50 (ISBN 0-398-01548-1). C C Thomas.

Human Ecology in the Tropics: Symposia of the Society for the Study of Human Biology, Vol. 16. J. P. Garlick & R.. Keay. LC 76-18781. 1977. 15.95 (ISBN 0-470-15165-X). Halsted Pr.

Human Ecology: Problems & Solutions. Paul R. Ehrlich et al. LC 72-12828. (Illus.). 1973. pap. 10.95x (ISBN 0-7167-0595-8). W H Freeman.

Human Embryonic & Fetal Death. Ed. by Ian H. Porter & Ernest B. Hook. LC 80-19011. (Birth Defects Institute Symposium X Ser.). 1980. 27.00 (ISBN 0-12-562860-9). Acad Pr.

Human Endocrinology: A Developmental Approach. Dorothy B. Villee. LC 73-91280. (Illus.). 479p. 1975. 20.00 (ISBN 0-7216-9041-6). Saunders.

Human Engineering Guide for Equipment Designers. 2nd rev ed. Wesley E. Woodson & Donald W. Conover. (Illus.). 1965. 30.00x (ISBN 0-520-01363-8). U of Cal Pr.

Human Evolution: An Introduction to Man's Adaptations. 2nd ed. Bernard Campbell. LC 72-140006. 404p. 1974. lib. bdg. 19.95x (ISBN 0-202-02012-6); pap. text ed. 11.95x (ISBN 0-202-02013-4). Aldine Pub.

Human Evolution: Biosocial Perspectives. Sherwood L. Washburn & Elizabeth McCown. LC 76-27931. (Perspectives on Human Evolution). 1978. text ed. 22.95 (ISBN 0-8053-9517-2). Benjamin-Cummings.

Human Evolutionary Trees. E. A. Thompson. LC 75-2739. (Illus.). 160p. (Orig.). 1975. pap. 23.95x (ISBN 0-521-09945-5). Cambridge U Pr.

Human Experience of Space & Place. Anne Buttimer & David Seaman. LC 80-12173. (Illus.). 1980. write for info. (ISBN 0-312-39910-3). St Martin.

Human Experience of Time: The Development of Its Philosophic Meaning. Ed. by Charles M. Sherover. LC 74-21659. 1975. 25.00x (ISBN 0-8147-7759-7); pap. 12.50x (ISBN 0-8147-7766-X). NYU Pr.

Human Experience: Readings in Sociocultural Anthropology. Ed. by David H. Spain. 1975. pap. text ed. 9.95 o.p. (ISBN 0-256-01708-5). Dorsey.

Human Experimentation & the Law. Nathan Hershey & Robert D. Miller. LC 76-2179. 1976. 27.50 (ISBN 0-912862-19-X). Aspen Systems.

Human Factor. Graham Greene. 1978. pap. 2.75 (ISBN 0-380-41491-0, 50302). Avon.

Human Factors-Ergonomics for Building & Construction. Martin Helander. (Construction Management & Engineering Ser.). 400p. 1981. 35.00 (ISBN 0-471-05075-X, Pub. by Wiley-Interscience). Wiley.

Human Factors in Health Care. Thomas Triggs & Ronald Pickett. LC 74-16935. 288p. 1975. 23.95 (ISBN 0-669-95885-9). Lexington Bks.

Human Factors in Lighting. P. R. Boyce. (Illus.). xiii, 420p. 1981. 52.00x (ISBN 0-686-28903-X). Burgess-Intl Ideas.

Human Factors in Long-Duration Space Flight. Space Science Board. LC 70-189063. (Illus.). 288p. 1972. pap. 6.75 (ISBN 0-309-01947-8). Natl Acad Pr.

Human Factors in Work Design & Production. Ed. by H. G. Maule & J. S. Weiner. 1977. 26.95 (ISBN 0-470-99074-0). Halsted Pr.

Human Factors: Theory & Practice. David Meister. LC 77-148505. (Human Factors Ser). 1971. 36.95 (ISBN 0-471-59190-4, Pub. by Wiley-Interscience). Wiley.

Human Fertility Control: The Theory & Practice. M. G. Elder & D. F. Hawkins. 1979. text ed. 61.95 (ISBN 0-407-00127-1). Butterworths.

Human Fertility in India: Social Components & Policy Perspectives. David G. Mandelbaum. 1974. 14.50x (ISBN 0-520-02551-2). U of Cal Pr.

Human Fetal & Neonatal Circulation: Function & Structure. S. Zoe Walsh et al. (American Lectures in Cerebral Palsy Ser.). (Illus.). 368p. 1974. 21.75 (ISBN 0-398-02662-9). C C Thomas.

Human Figure As an Art Object. David E. Martindale. (Illus.). 1980. deluxe ed. 37.75 (ISBN 0-930582-52-7). Gloucester Art.

Human Figure in Motion. Eadweard Muybridge. (Illus.). 1955. 13.95 (ISBN 0-486-20204-6). Dover.

Human Function & Structure. Dorothy S. Luciano et al. (Illus.). 1978. text ed. 19.95 (ISBN 0-07-038942-X, C); study guide 6.95 (ISBN 0-07-038944-6); inst's manual 5.95 (ISBN 0-07-038943-8). McGraw.

Human Gene Mapping 4, Vol. 4. Ed. by Daniel Bergsma. LC 78-61294. (S. Karger Ser.: Vol. 14, No. 4). 1978. 50.00. March of Dimes.

Human Genetics. 2nd ed. Victor McKusick. (Foundations of Modern Genetics Ser). 1969. pap. 10.95x ref. ed. (ISBN 0-13-445106-6). P-H.

Human Genetics. Edward Novitski. (Illus.). 1977. text ed. 16.95 (ISBN 0-02-388550-5). Macmillan.

Human Genetics. Norman V. Rothwell. (Illus.). 1977. text ed. 19.95 (ISBN 0-13-445080-9). P-H.

Human Genetics. 3rd ed. A. M. Winchester. 1979. pap. text ed. 7.95 (ISBN 0-675-08314-1). Merrill.

Human Genetics: An Introduction to the Principles of Heredity. Sam Singer. LC 78-82. (Biology Ser.). (Illus.). 1978. pap. text ed. 7.95x (ISBN 0-7167-0054-9); tchr's resource bk. 2.95x. W H Freeman.

Human Genetics Notes. M. M. Green. LC 74-28814. (Illus.). 240p. 1975. text ed. 8.95 (ISBN 0-201-02599-X). A-W.

Human Genetics: Possibilities & Realities. Ciba Foundation. LC 79-10949. (Ciba Foundation Symposium Ser.: No. 66). 1979. 51.25 (ISBN 0-444-90064-0, Excerpta Medica). Elsevier.

Human Genetics: Readings on the Implications of Genetic Engineering. Thomas R. Mertens. LC 74-30471. 320p. 1975. text ed. 10.95x (ISBN 0-471-59628-0). Wiley.

Human Geography. 2d ed. Aime V. Perpillou. LC 76-55302. (Geographies for Advanced Study Ser.). (Illus.). 1977. text ed. 21.00x (ISBN 0-582-48571-1); pap. text ed. 15.95x (ISBN 0-582-48572-X). Longman.

Human Geography: Culture, Society, & Space. Harm J. De Blij. LC 76-25994. 1977. text ed. 20.95 (ISBN 0-471-20047-6); study guide 7.95x (ISBN 0-471-01932-1). Wiley.

Human Ground: Sexuality, Self & Survival. Stanley Keleman. LC 75-12453. 1975. pap. 4.95 o.p. (ISBN 0-8314-0047-1). Sci & Behavior.

Human Growth & Development. Robert W. McCammon. (Illus.). 308p. 1970. text ed. 12.75 (ISBN 0-398-01245-8). C C Thomas.

Human Growth & Development: Psychological Maturation & Socialization. Frank Wesley & Edith Sullivan. LC 79-21929. 1980. text ed. 19.95x (ISBN 0-87705-445-2); pap. text ed. 9.95x (ISBN 0-87705-446-0). Human Sci Pr.

Human Growth & Development: The Wolfson College Lectures, 1976. Ed. by Jerome S. Bruner & Alison Garton. (Illus.). 1978. pap. text ed. 8.95x (ISBN 0-19-857518-1). Oxford U Pr.

Human Growth & the Development of Personality. 2nd ed. J. H. Kahn. 264p. 1972. text ed. 21.00 (ISBN 0-08-015818-8); pap. text ed. 9.75 (ISBN 0-08-015817-X). Pergamon.

Human Growth & the Development of Personality. 3rd ed. Jack Kahn & Susan Wright. (Pergamon International Library, Mental Health & Social Medicine Division). Date not set. 36.00 (ISBN 0-08-023383-X); pap. 15.50 (ISBN 0-08-023382-1). Pergamon.

Human Guinea Pigs. Kenneth Mellanby. 1973. pap. 3.00 o.p. (ISBN 0-686-23495-2, Merlin Pr). Carrier Pigeon.

Human Hair Growth in Health & Disease. David Ferriman. (American Lectures in Living Chemistry Ser.). (Illus.). 76p. 1971. 11.75 (ISBN 0-398-00560-5). C C Thomas.

Human Health, Biology & Hygiene. David T. Hughes & P. T. Marshall. LC 79-128501. (Illus.). 1970. text ed. 8.50x (ISBN 0-521-07731-1). Cambridge U Pr.

Human Heart: A Guide to Heart Disease. 4th ed. Brendan Phibbs. LC 79-17665. 1979. pap. text ed. 14.95 (ISBN 0-8016-3917-4). Mosby.

Human Helplessness: Theory & Applications. Ed. by Judy Garber & Martin E. Seligman. LC 79-6773. 1980. 18.50 (ISBN 0-12-275050-0). Acad Pr.

Human Heredity & Birth Defects. E. Peter Volpe. LC 75-124674. (Science & Society Ser). (Illus.). 1971. pap. 4.95 (ISBN 0-672-63549-6). Pegasus.

Human Histological Atlas. Mohini Kaul et al. 200p. 1980. text ed. 50.00 (ISBN 0-7069-1055-9, Pub. by Vikas India). Advent Bk.

Human Histology: A Textbook in Outline Form. 4th ed. Leslie B. Arey. LC 73-88256. (Illus.). 338p. 1974. text ed. 19.00 (ISBN 0-7216-1392-6). Saunders.

Human History & the Word of God. James M. Connolly. 1965. 6.50 o.s.i. (ISBN 0-02-527360-4). Macmillan.

Human Hope & the Death Instinct: An Exploration of Psychoanalytical Theories of Human Nature & Their Implications for Culture & Education. David Holbrook. 1976. Repr. of 1971 ed. 26.00 (ISBN 0-08-015798-X). Pergamon.

Human Imperative. Alexander Alland, Jr. LC 77-183227. 160p. 1972. 17.00x (ISBN 0-231-03228-5); pap. 6.00x (ISBN 0-231-08301-7, 132). Columbia U Pr.

Human Inference: Strategies & Shortcomings in Social Judgement. Richard Nisbett & Lee Ross. (Century Psychology Ser.). (Illus.). 1980. text ed. 15.95 (ISBN 0-13-445130-9). P-H.

Human Influences in African Pastureland Environments. 89p. 1981. pap. 6.00 (ISBN 92-5-100874-4, F2076, FAO). Unipub.

Human Information Processing: An Introduction to Psychology. 2nd ed. Peter H. Lindsay & Donald A. Norman. 1977. 18.95 (ISBN 0-12-450960-6); test bklet. avail. Acad Pr.

Human Inquiry: A Sourcebook of New Paradigm Research. Peter Reason & John Rowan. 1981. price not set (ISBN 0-471-27936-6, Pub. by Wiley Interscience). Wiley.

Human Intelligence: Perspectives on Its Theory & Measurement. Ed. by Robert J. Sternberg & Douglas K. Detterman. LC 79-17994. 1979. 14.95 (ISBN 0-89391-030-9). Ablex Pub.

Human Interaction in Education. Gene Stanford & Albert E. Roark. 320p. 1974. pap. text ed. 8.95 o.p. (ISBN 0-205-03854-9, 2238543). Allyn.

Human Intimacy: Marriage, the Family & Its Meaning. Frank D. Cox. (Illus.). 1978. text ed. 16.95 (ISBN 0-8299-0152-3); instrs.' manual avail. (ISBN 0-8299-0473-5). West Pub.

Human Intimacy: Marriage, the Family & Its Meaning. 2nd ed. Frank D. Cox. (Illus.). 475p. 1981. text ed. 13.56 (ISBN 0-8299-0367-4). West Pub.

Human Joints & Their Artificial Replacements. Peter S. Walker. (Illus.). 528p. 1978. 64.75 (ISBN 0-398-03615-2). C C Thomas.

Human Judgement & Decision Making: Theories, Methods & Procedures. Kennneth R. Hammond et al. 272p. 1980. 25.95 (ISBN 0-03-057567-2). Praeger.

Human Judgement & Social Interaction. Ed. by Leon Rappoport & David Summers. LC 72-84872. 1973. 28.50x (ISBN 0-03-085870-4). Irvington.

Human Jurisprudence: Public Law As Political Science. Glendon Schubert. LC 74-78862. 416p. 1975. text ed. 16.00x (ISBN 0-8248-0294-2). U Pr of Hawaii.

Human Labor & Birth. 3rd ed. Oxorn. (Illus.). 1975. pap. text ed. 15.50 o.p. (ISBN 0-8385-3938-6). ACC.

Human Landscape: Geography & Culture. Chester Zimolzak & Charles Stansfield. 1979. text ed. 19.95 (ISBN 0-675-08290-0); instructor's manual 3.95 (ISBN 0-685-96155-9). Merrill.

Human Larynx: A Functional Study. B. Raymond Fink. LC 74-80536. 1975. 19.00 (ISBN 0-911216-86-3). Raven.

Human Learning. David L. Horton & Thomas W. Turnage. (P-H Series in Experimental Psychology). (Illus.). 464p. 1976. Ref. Ed. 19.95 (ISBN 0-13-445312-3). P-H.

Human Life: Controversies & Concerns. Ed. by Bruce W. Bohle. (Reference Shelf Ser.). 1979. 6.25 (ISBN 0-8242-0636-3). Wilson.

Human Life Styling: Keeping Whole in the Twentieth Century. John C. McCamy & James Presley. LC 73-14271. 206p. (YA) 1975. 12.95 o.s.i. (ISBN 0-06-012894-1, HarpT). Har-Row.

Human Like Me, Jesus. Malcolm Boyd. 1973. pap. 1.25 (ISBN 0-89129-148-2). Jove Pubns.

Human Listening. Carl H. Weaver. LC 75-182878. (Speech Communication Ser.). 1972. pap. text ed. 4.50 (ISBN 0-672-61234-8, SC18). Bobbs.

Human Lung. rev. enl. ed. H. von Hayek. 1960. 20.75 o.s.i. (ISBN 0-02-845850-8). Hafner.

Human Lymphoid Cell Cultures: The Fundamentals. Glick. Date not set. 22.50 (ISBN 0-8247-6988-0). Dekker.

Human Memory & Amnesia. Laird S. Cermack. 400p. 1981. ref. ed. 24.95 (ISBN 0-89859-095-7). L Erlbaum Assocs.

Human Memory: Contemporary Readings. Ed. by John G. Seamon. (Illus.). 464p. 1980. text ed. 19.95x (ISBN 0-19-502738-8); pap. text ed. 11.95x (ISBN 0-19-502739-6). Oxford U Pr.

Human Memory: Theory, Research & Individual Differences. Michael W. Eysenck. 1977. text ed. 18.25 (ISBN 0-08-020405-8). Pergamon.

Human Migration: A Guide to Migration Literature in English, 1955-1962. J. J. Mangalam. LC 67-23777. (Illus.). 200p. 1968. 18.50x (ISBN 0-8131-1170-6). U Pr of Ky.

Human Migration: Patterns & Policies. William H. McNeill & Ruth S. Adams. LC 77-23685. 1978. 22.50x (ISBN 0-253-32875-6). Ind U Pr.

Human Monsters in the Cinema. Michael H. Price & George E. Turner. LC 78-75327. (Illus.). Date not set. cancelled 17.50 (ISBN 0-498-02360-5). A S Barnes. Postponed.

Human Motivation. Magdalen D. Vernon. LC 69-14396. 1969. 27.50 (ISBN 0-521-07419-3); pap. 8.95x (ISBN 0-521-09580-8, 580). Cambridge U Pr.

Human Motivation: A Guide to Information Sources. rev. ed. Ed. by Charles N. Cofer. (Psychology Information Guide Ser.: Vol. 4). 175p. 1980. 30.00 (ISBN 0-8103-1418-5). Gale.

Human Motivation & Emotion. Ross W. Buck. LC 75-37893. 1976. text ed. 21.95 (ISBN 0-471-11570-3); instructor's manual avail. (ISBN 0-471-02468-6). Wiley.

Human Multiple Reproduction. Ian MacGillivray et al. LC 75-21750. (Illus.). 238p. 1975. text ed. 25.00 (ISBN 0-7216-5974-8). Saunders.

Human Nature: An Introduction to Cultural Anthropology. James F. Downs. LC 72-86791. 350p. 1973. text ed. 10.95x (ISBN 0-02-474090-X). Macmillan.

Human Nature & History: A Response to Sociobiology. Kenneth Bock. 192p. 1980. 18.95 (ISBN 0-231-05078-X). Columbia U Pr.

Human Nature & the Social Order. E. L. Thorndike. 1019p. 1980. Repr. of 1940 ed. lib. bdg. 100.00 (ISBN 0-89987-812-1). Darby Bks.

Human Nature, Class, & Ethnicity. Milton M. Gordon. (Illus.). 1978. 14.95 (ISBN 0-19-502236-X); pap. 4.95 (ISBN 0-19-502237-8). Oxford U Pr.

Human Nature Club. Edward Thorndike. 231p. 1980. Repr. of 1900 ed. lib. bdg. 25.00 (ISBN 0-8492-8410-4). R West.

Human Nature in Its Fourfold State. Thomas Boston. 1964. pap. 4.45 (ISBN 0-686-12519-3). Banner of Truth.

Human Nature of Christ: Growth & Perfection. Apostolos Makrakis. Ed. by Orthodox Christian Educational Society. Tr. by D. Cummings from Hellenic. 52p. (Orig.). 1965. pap. 1.00x (ISBN 0-938366-28-9). Orthodox Chr.

Human Needs & Politics. Ed. by Ross Fitzgerald. 1977. text ed. 26.00 (ISBN 0-08-021402-9); pap. text ed. 14.50 (ISBN 0-08-021401-0). Pergamon.

Human Needs & the Security of Nations. Lester R. Brown. LC 78-51516. (Headline Ser.: 238). (Illus.). 1978. pap. 2.00 (ISBN 0-87124-045-9). Foreign Policy.

Human Needs in Housing: An Ecological Approach. Karen Nattrass & Bonnie M. Morrison. 1977. pap. text ed. 9.00x (ISBN 0-8191-0094-3). U Pr of Amer.

Human Nervous System. David Jensen. 416p. 1980. pap. text ed. 14.95x (ISBN 0-8385-3944-0). ACC.

Human Nervous System: Basic Principles of Neurobiology. 3rd ed. Charles Noback & Robert Demarest. (Illus.). 1980. text ed. 24.00 (ISBN 0-07-046851-6, HP). McGraw.

Human Neurological Organization. Edward B. Le Winn. (Illus.). 244p. 1977. 14.75 (ISBN 0-398-01122-2). C C Thomas.

Human Nutrition, a Comprehensive Treatise: Vol. 3B, Nutrition & the Adult-Micronutrients. Ed. by Roslyn Alfin-Slater & David Kritchevsky. (Illus.). 444p. 1980. 39.50 (ISBN 0-306-40288-2, Plenum Pr). Plenum Pub.

Human Nutrition & Diet. Ed. by G. H. Bourne. (World Review of Nutrition & Dietetics Ser.: Vol. 36). (Illus.). x, 226p. 1980. 115.00 (ISBN 3-8055-1347-X). S Karger.

Human Nutrition & Nutrition & Pesticides in Cattle, Vol. 35. Ed. by G. H. Bourne. (World Review of Nutrition & Dietetics: Vol. 35). (Illus.). 238p. 1980. 115.00 (ISBN 3-8055-0442-X). S Karger.

Human Nutrition in Tropical Africa. (Food & Nutrition Ser: No. 11). 286p. 1980. pap. 19.25 (ISBN 92-5-100412-9, F2049, FAO). Unipub.

Human Nutrition: Its Physiological, Medical & Social Aspects,A Series of 82 Essays. Jean Mayer. (Illus.). 740p. 1979. 23.75 (ISBN 0-398-02359-X). C C Thomas.

Human Nutrition: Readings from Scientific American. Intro. by Norman Kretchmer. LC 78-17367. (Illus.). 1978. pap. text ed. 10.95x (ISBN 0-7167-0182-0). W H Freeman.

Human Nutrition Research. Ed. by Gary R. Beecher. LC 79-91006. (Beltsville Symposia in Agricultural Research Ser.: No. 4). (Illus.). 400p. 1980. text ed. 32.50 (ISBN 0-916672-48-4). Allanheld.

Human Nutrition the Value of Herbs. John Heineman. Date not set. cancelled (ISBN 0-89557-018-1). Bi World Indus.

Human Odds & Ends. George Gissing. Ed. by Ian Fletcher & John Stokes. LC 76-20076. (Decadent Consciousness Ser.). 1978. lib. bdg. 38.00 (ISBN 0-8240-2759-0). Garland Pub.

Human Option: An Autobiographical Notebook. Norman Cousins. (Illus.). 1981. 9.95 (ISBN 0-393-01430-4). Norton.

Human Organism in the Light of Anthropasaphy. Eugen Kolisko. 1980. pap. 1.95x (ISBN 0-906492-11-4, Pub. by Kolisko Archives). St George Bk Serv.

Human Orgasm. (Illus.). pap. 5.00 (ISBN 0-910550-38-7). Centurion Pr.

Human Patient. Naomi Remen. LC 77-16941. 264p. 1980. 10.95 (ISBN 0-385-13251-4, Anchor Pr). Doubleday.

Human Pax. Ted Sas. LC 79-67757. 1981. 5.95 (ISBN 0-533-04481-2). Vantage.

Human Person. Ed. by George F. McLean. LC 80-66375. (Proceedings: Vol. 53). 1980. pap. 8.00 (ISBN 0-918090-13-X). Am Cath Philo.

Human Physical Growth & Maturation: Methodologies & Factors. Ed. by F. E. Johnston et al. (NATO Advanced Study Institute Series, Series A: Life Sciences: Vol. 30). 375p. 1980. 42.50 (ISBN 0-306-40420-6, Plenum Pr). Plenum Pub.

Human Physiology. 2nd ed. Robert I. Macey. (Illus.). 224p. 1975. pap. 11.95 ref. ed. (ISBN 0-13-445288-7). P-H.

Human Physiology. 3rd ed. Arthur Vander et al. (Illus.). 736p. 1980. text ed. 20.95 (ISBN 0-07-066961-9, C); instructor's manual 4.95 (ISBN 0-07-066955-4); wkbk. study guide 7.95 (ISBN 0-07-066963-5). McGraw.

Human Physiology & the Environment in Health & Disease: Readings from Scientific American. Intro. by Arthur J. Vander. LC 76-1923. (Illus.). 1976. 19.95x (ISBN 0-7167-0527-3); pap. text ed. 9.95x (ISBN 0-7167-0526-5). W H Freeman.

Human Physiology: Mechanism of Functions & Clinical Co-Relates. Shushil Dua-Sharma & K. N. Sharma. 560p. Date not set. text ed. 50.00x (ISBN 0-7069-1232-2, Pub. by Vikas India). Advent Bk.

Human Plasma Proteins: Their Investigation in Pathological Conditions. J. W. Keyser. LC 79-1089. 1979. 60.00 (ISBN 0-471-27598-0, Pub. by Wiley-Interscience). Wiley.

Human Population: A Scientific American Book. Scientific American Editors. LC 74-19465. (Illus.). 147p. 1974. 15.95x (ISBN 0-7167-0515-X); pap. text ed. 7.95x (ISBN 0-7167-0514-1). W H Freeman.

Human Population Control Mechanisms. D. Stott. 1981. cancelled (ISBN 0-685-32564-4). Univ Park.

Human Portrait: An Introduction to Cultural Anthropology. John Friedl. (Illus.). 464p. 1981. pap. text ed. 13.95 (ISBN 0-13-445353-0); pap. 5.95 (ISBN 0-13-445387-5). P-H.

Human Possibilities: Mind Exploration in the USSR & Eastern Europe. Stanley Krippner. LC 80-953. 360p. 1980. 14.95 (ISBN 0-385-12805-3, Anchor Pr). Doubleday.

Human Predicament: Dissolution & Wholeness. George W. Morgan. LC 68-23791. 348p. 1971. Repr. of 1968 ed. 12.50 (ISBN 0-87057-111-7, Pub. by Brown U Pr). Univ Pr of New England.

Human Problem Solving. Allen Newell & Herbert Simon. LC 79-152528. (Illus.). 1972. 28.95 (ISBN 0-13-445403-0). P-H.

Human Psyche. J. Eccles. (Illus.). 300p. 1980. 25.00 (ISBN 0-387-09954-9). Springer-Verlag.

Human Quality. Aurelio Peccei. 216p. 1977. text ed. 19.50 (ISBN 0-08-021479-7); pap. text ed. 9.25 (ISBN 0-08-021480-0). Pergamon.

Human Races. 3rd ed. Stanley M. Garn. 216p. 1971. pap. 14.75 photocopy ed. spiral (ISBN 0-398-00646-6). C C Thomas.

Human Reflex: Behavioral Psychology in Biblical Perspective. Rodger K. Bufford. LC 80-8900. (Illus.). 256p. 1981. 12.95 (ISBN 0-06-061165-0). Har-Row.

Human Relations. Ann Ellenson. (Illus.). 304p. 1973. ref. ed. 16.95 (ISBN 0-13-445643-2). P-H.

Human Relations: A Job-Oriented Approach. 2nd ed. Andrew DuBrin. 300p. 1981. text ed. 16.95 (ISBN 0-8359-3002-5); cancelled (ISBN 0-8359-3006-8); instr's. manual avail. (ISBN 0-8359-3003-3). Reston.

Human Relations: A Job Oriented Approach. Andrew J. DuBrin. (Illus.). 1978. text ed. 15.95 (ISBN 0-87909-371-4); instrs'. manual avail. Reston.

Human Relations & Cooperative Planning in Education & Management. Anthony Marinaccio & M. Maxine Marinaccio. 1978. pap. text ed. 7.95 (ISBN 0-8403-0921-X). Kendall-Hunt.

Human Relations & Your Career: A Guide to Interpersonal Skills. David W. Johnson. (Illus.). 1978. 13.95 (ISBN 0-13-445601-7). P-H.

Human Relations Development: A Manual for Educators. 2nd ed. George M. Gazda et al. 1977. text ed. 14.95x (ISBN 0-205-05566-4); pap. text ed. 9.95x (ISBN 0-685-71782-8). Allyn.

Human Relations for the Educational Environment. E. K. Waters. LC 78-54601. 1978. pap. text ed. 6.75x (ISBN 0-8191-0510-4). U Pr of Amer.

Human Relations: From Theory to Practice. George Henderson. LC 73-19387. (Illus.). 450p. 1981. pap. 9.95 (ISBN 0-8061-1709-5). U of Okla Pr.

Human Relations in Administration. 4th ed. Robert Dubin. (Illus.). 640p. 1974. ref. ed. 19.95 (ISBN 0-13-446435-4). P-H.

Human Relations in Adult Corrections. Norman Fenton. 224p. 1973. 14.75 (ISBN 0-398-02837-0). C C Thomas.

Human Relations in Agribusiness: Career Preparation for Agriculture-Agribusiness. John Hillison & John Crunkilton. Ed. by R. Moore. (Illus.). 128p. (gr. 9-12). 1980. pap. text ed. 5.00 (ISBN 0-07-028904-2); activity guide 3.00 (ISBN 0-686-64659-2); tchrs. manual & key 3.70 (ISBN 0-07-028906-9). McGraw.

Human Relations in Handling Insurance Claims. Willis P. Rokes. 1967. text ed. 12.00x (ISBN 0-256-00467-6). Irwin.

Human Relations in Old Age. 1967. 6.95 (ISBN 0-571-08151-7, Pub. by Faber & Faber). Merrimack Bk Serv.

Human Relations in Organizations. Dan L. Costley & Ralph Todd. (Management Ser.). (Illus.). 1978. pap. text ed. 13.95 (ISBN 0-8299-0211-2); instrs.' manual avail. (ISBN 0-8299-0471-9). West Pub.

Human Relations: The Theory & Practice of Organizational Behavior. 2nd ed. Aubrey Sanford. (Business Ser.). 1977. text ed. 18.95 (ISBN 0-675-08505-5); instructor's manual 3.95 (ISBN 0-685-74283-0). Merrill.

Human Reproduction. Intro. by Arthur Campos Da Paz et al. (Illus.). 1974. 18.00 o.p. (ISBN 0-89640-012-3). Igaku-Shoin.

Human Reproduction. Janet Sadow et al. 224p. 1980. 50.00x (ISBN 0-85664-878-7, Pub. by Croom Helm England). State Mutual Bk.

Human Reproduction & Development. James L. Mariner. (Illus.). 155p. (Orig.). (gr. 9-12). 1979. pap. text ed. 3.95x (ISBN 0-88334-118-2). Ind Sch Pr.

Human Reproduction: Biology & Social Change. Harold D. Swanson. (Illus.). 300p. 1974. text ed. 12.95x (ISBN 0-19-501772-2); pap. text ed. 9.95x (ISBN 0-19-501771-4). Oxford U Pr.

Human Reproduction: Conception & Contraception. 2nd ed. E. S. Hafez. (Illus.). 932p. 1980. text ed. 47.50 (ISBN 0-06-141066-7, Harper Medical). Har-Row.

Human Reproduction: Essentials of Obstetrics, Gynecology, & Reproductive Medicine. Ernest W. Page et al. 1981. text ed. price not set (ISBN 0-7216-7053-9). Saunders.

Human Reproductive System. Matt Newman & Nita K. Lemay. (Illus.). (gr. 5-8). 1980. pap. text ed. 88.00 (ISBN 0-89290-101-2, A794-SATC). Soc for Visual.

Human Resource Accounting. Eric Flamholtz. LC 73-92477. 1974. text ed. 17.95 (ISBN 0-8221-0129-7). CBI Pub.

Human Resource Development in the Organization: A Guide to Information Sources. Ed. by Jerome L. Franklin. LC 76-28289. (Management Information Guide Ser.: No. 35). 1978. 30.00 (ISBN 0-8103-0835-5). Gale.

Human Resource Development: The New Trainer's Guide. Les Donaldson & Edward Scannell. 1978. pap. text ed. 8.95 (ISBN 0-201-03081-0). A-W.

Human Resource Function: Its Emergence & Character. (AMACOM Reprint Collection). 1978. pap. 8.95 o.p. (ISBN 0-686-67221-6). Am Mgmt.

Human Resource Management: An ROI Approach. Ray A. Killian. LC 76-7058. (Illus.). 208p. 1976. 14.95 (ISBN 0-8144-5415-1). Am Mgmt.

Human Resources & African Development. Ukandi G. Damachi & Victor P. Diejomaoh. LC 78-19133. (Praeger Special Studies). 1978. 34.95 (ISBN 0-03-022826-3). Praeger.

Human Resources & Economic Welfare. Ed. by Ivar E. Berg, Jr. LC 72-8331. 200p. 1972. 17.00x (ISBN 0-231-03710-4). Columbia U Pr.

Human Resources & Income Distribution. Ed. by Barry R. Chiswick & June O'Neill. 1977. 12.50 (ISBN 0-393-05623-6); pap. 5.95x (ISBN 0-393-09131-7). Norton.

Human Resources in Canadian Mining: A Preliminary Analysis. J. A. Macmillan et al. 176p. (Orig.). 1977. pap. 8.50x (ISBN 0-88757-004-6, Pub. by Ctr Resource Stud Canada). Renouf.

Human Resources Management: A Behavioral Systems Approach. Lawrence A. Klatt et al. 1978. text ed. 18.95x (ISBN 0-256-02045-0). Irwin.

Human Resources Management: An Information Systems Approach. Wayne F. Cascio & Elias M. Awad. 450p. 1981. text ed. 19.95 (ISBN 0-8359-3008-4); student activities guide 7.95 (ISBN 0-8359-3010-6); instr's. manual avail. (ISBN 0-8359-3009-2). Reston.

Human Resources Planning: A Guide to Data. 2nd ed. Ed. by Patricia J. Snider. LC 80-67468. 392p. 1980. pap. 21.00 (ISBN 0-937856-00-2). Equal Employ.

Human Response to Crowding. Ed. by Andrew Baum & Yakov M. Epstein. LC 78-6875. (Environmental Psychology Ser.). 1978. 24.95 (ISBN 0-470-26374-1). Halsted Pr.

Human Revolution. rev. ed. Daisaku Ikeda. Tr. by Richard L. Gage from Japanese. LC 72-79121. (Human Revolution Ser: Vol. 2). (Illus.). 272p. 1974. 9.50 (ISBN 0-8348-0087-X). Weatherhill.

Human Rights. F. E. Dowrick. 1979. text ed. 23.00x (ISBN 0-566-00281-7, Pub. by Gower Pub Co England). Renouf.

Human Rights. A. I. Melden. 1970. pap. 7.95x (ISBN 0-534-00220-X). Wadsworth Pub.

Human Rights. Ed. by J. Roland Penrock & John W. Chapman. (Nomos Ser.: Vol. 22). 336p. 1980. 19.50x (ISBN 0-8147-6578-5). NYU Pr.

Human Rights: Amintaphil, IVR-Northam, Vol. 1. Ervin H. Pollack. LC 70-173834. 1971. lib. bdg. 32.50 (ISBN 0-930342-65-8). W S Hein.

Human Rights & Foreign Policy. Hans J. Morgenthau. LC 79-53084. (First Distinguished CRIA Lecture on Morality & Foreign Policy Ser.). 1979. pap. 4.00 (ISBN 0-87641-216-9). Coun Rel & Intl.

Human Rights & Human Liberties. Tibor R. Machan. LC 74-26864. 318p. 1975. 15.95 (ISBN 0-88229-159-9). Nelson-Hall.

Human Rights & International Co-Operation. N. Singh. LC 70-904156. 1969. 12.50x (ISBN 0-8002-0907-9). Intl Pubns Serv.

Human Rights & State Sovereignty. Richard A. Falk. 180p. 1981. text ed. 24.00x (ISBN 0-8419-0619-X); pap. text ed. 9.75x (ISBN 0-8419-0620-3). Holmes & Meier.

Human Rights & the Legal System in Iran. William J. Butler & Georges Levasseur. 80p. (Orig.). 1976. pap. text ed. 2.50 (ISBN 0-89192-084-6). Interbk Inc.

Human Rights & U. S. Foreign Policy. Barry M. Rubin & Elizabeth P. Spiro. 1979. lib. bdg. 26.50x (ISBN 0-89158-476-5). Westview.

Human Rights & U. S. Foreign Policy: Principles & Applications. Principles & Applications. Ed. by Peter G. Brown & Douglas MacLean. 1979. 18.95 (ISBN 0-669-02807-X); pap. 10.95 (ISBN 0-669-04326-5). Lexington Bks.

Human Rights & World Order. Ed. by Abdul A. Said. LC 78-62438. 1978. 22.95 (ISBN 0-03-046341-6). Praeger.

Human Rights Book. Milton Meltzer. LC 79-13017. 272p. (gr. 6 up). 1979. 9.95 (ISBN 0-374-33514-1). FS&G.

Human Rights Casefinder 1953-1969: The Warren Court Era. Ed. by Ann Ginger. 1972. 17.50x o.p. (ISBN 0-913876-02-X). Meiklejohn Civil Lib.

Human Rights: Cultural & Ideological Perspectives. Ed. by Adamantia Pollis & Peter Schwab. LC 78-19771. (Praeger Special Studies). 1979. 22.95 (ISBN 0-03-046631-8); pap. 9.95 (ISBN 0-03-046631-8). Praeger.

Human Rights Day. Aileen Fisher & Olive Rabe. LC 65-25907. (Holiday Ser.). (Illus.). (gr. k-3). 1966. PLB 6.89 o.p. (ISBN 0-690-42349-7, TYC-J). T Y Crowell.

Human Rights in the World Society: The Commitments, the Reality, the Future. Asbjorn Eide. 300p. 1981. text ed. 25.00 (ISBN 0-930576-39-X). E M Coleman Ent.

Human Rights, International Law & the Helsinki Accord. Ed. by Thomas Buergenthal. LC 77-11762. 215p. 1978. text ed. 17.00x (ISBN 0-916672-91-3). Allanheld.

Human Rights: The International Petition System, Release 1. M. Tardu. 1980. 35.00 (ISBN 0-379-20252-2). Oceana.

Human Rights Today: Evolution or Revolution? Edward J. Schuster. LC 80-84737. 1981. 12.00 (ISBN 0-686-68868-6). Philos Lib.

Human Sacrifice: In History & Today. Nigel Davies. LC 80-21981. (Illus.). 320p. 1981. 13.95 (ISBN 0-688-03755-0). Morrow.

Human Scandals. Brad Holland. LC 76-57759. (Illus.). 1977. 12.95 o.s.i. (ISBN 0-690-01466-X, TYC-T). T Y Crowell.

Human Search: An Introduction to Philosophy. Ed. by John Lachs & Charles E. Scott. 528p. 1981. pap. text ed. 10.95x (ISBN 0-19-502675-6). Oxford U Pr.

Human Senses. Jeanne Bendick. (Science Experiences Ser). (Illus.). (gr. 4-6). PLB 4.90 o.p. (ISBN 0-531-01431-2); pap. 1.25 o.p. (ISBN 0-531-01884-9). Watts.

Human Senses. 2nd ed. Frank A. Geldard. LC 72-37432. 1972. text ed. 30.95 (ISBN 0-471-29570-1). Wiley.

Human Service Organizations: A Book of Readings. Ed. by Yeheskel Hasenfeld & Richard A. English. 1974. text ed. 15.00 c.p. (ISBN 0-472-08985-4); pap. text ed. 7.95x (ISBN 0-472-08986-2). U of Mich Pr.

Human Services: An Introduction. Alice Collins. LC 72-10176. Orig. Title: People to People - an Introduction to the Human Services. 1973. pap. 5.50 (ISBN 0-672-63081-8). Odyssey Pr.

Human Services & Social Work Responsibility. Ed. by Willard C. Richan. LC 72-108195. 382p. 1969. pap. 10.00 (ISBN 0-87101-053-4, CBO-058-C). Natl Assn Soc Wkrs.

Human Services: Concepts & Intervention Strategies. Mehr. 1979. text ed. 15.95 (ISBN 0-205-06807-3). Allyn.

Human Services for Older Adults. Anita S. Harbert & Leon H. Ginsberg. 1979. pap. text ed. 13.95x (ISBN 0-534-00607-8). Wadsworth Pub.

Human Services: New Careers & Roles in the Helping Professions. Robert J. Wicks. (Illus.). 248p. 1978. 15.50 (ISBN 0-398-03777-9). C C Thomas.

Human Services Technology. Ronald F. Holler & George M. DeLong. LC 73-1441. 1973. text ed. 11.75 o.p. (ISBN 0-8016-2227-1). Mosby.

Human Services: The Third Revolution in Mental Health. Walter Fisher et al. LC 74-75481. (Illus.). 1974. 14.50x (ISBN 0-88284-013-4). Alfred Pub.

Human Services Today. Eriksen. 1977. text ed. 12.95 (ISBN 0-87909-336-6). Reston.

Human Services Today. 2nd ed. Karin Eriksen. 192p. 1981. text ed. 12.95 (ISBN 0-8359-3004-1). Reston.

Human Settlements, an Annotated Bibliography. International Institute for Environment & Development (I.I.E.D.) Compiled by Mary Anglemyer & Signe R. Ottersen. LC 76-10832. 1976. pap. text ed. 37.00 (ISBN 0-686-67630-0). Pergamon.

Human Settlements & Energy: A Seminar of the United Nations Economic Commission for Europe. Ed. by C. I. Jackson. 1978. text ed. 23.00 (ISBN 0-08-022427-X); pap. text ed. 11.25 (ISBN 0-08-022411-3). Pergamon.

Human Settlements in the Arctic: An Account of the ECE Symposium on Human Settlements Planning & Development in the Arctic, Godthab, Greenland, Aug. 18-25, 1978. United Nations Economic Commission for Europe, Geneva, Switzerland. LC 79-42797. (ECE Seminars & Symposia). (Illus.). 122p. 1980. 26.00 (ISBN 0-08-023448-8). Pergamon.

Human Sex & Sexuality: With a Dictionary of Sexual Terms. Edwin B. Steen & James H. Price. LC 76-21654. (Illus.). 1977. 17.95x (ISBN 0-471-82101-2). Wiley.

Human Sex-Role Behavior. Alfred B. Heilbrun, Jr. (Pergamon General Psychology Ser.). 250p. 1981. 23.01 (ISBN 0-08-025974-X). Pergamon.

Human Sexual Behavior. P. Feldman & M. MacCulloch. LC 79-41220. 226p. 1980. 34.50 (ISBN 0-471-27676-6, Pub. by Wiley-Interscience). Wiley.

Human Sexual Behavior: A Book of Readings. Ed. by Bernhardt Lieberman. LC 70-162422. 1971. pap. text ed. 13.95x o.p. (ISBN 0-471-53423-4). Halsted Pr.

Human Sexual Ecology. Robert E. Joyce. LC 79-6727. 421p. 1981. lib. bdg. 22.75 (ISBN 0-8191-1359-X); pap. text ed. 12.00 (ISBN 0-8191-0937-1). U Pr of Amer.

Human Sexualities. John H. Gagnon. 1977. pap. 12.95x (ISBN 0-673-15033-X). Scott F.

Human Sexuality. Ed. by C. R. Austin & R. V. Short. LC 78-18959. (Reproduction in Mammals Ser.: Bk. 8). (Illus.). 110p. 1980. 24.95 (ISBN 0-521-22361-X); pap. 7.95 (ISBN 0-521-29461-4). Cambridge U Pr.

Human Sexuality. Raymond Rosen & Linda R. Rosen. 576p. 1981. text ed. 17.95 (ISBN 0-394-32028-X). Random.

Human Sexuality. David A. Schulz. (Illus.). 1979. pap. 15.95 ref. ed. (ISBN 0-13-447557-7). P-H.

Human Sexuality: A Nursing Perspective. Rosemarie Hogan. 768p. 1980. pap. text ed. 13.95 (ISBN 0-8385-3955-6). ACC.

Human Sexuality: A Text with Readings. 2nd ed. Wilson et al. 1980. pap. text ed. 11.16 (ISBN 0-8299-0328-3); study guide 4.95 (ISBN 0-8299-0322-4); instrs.' manual avail. (ISBN 0-8299-0584-7). West Pub.

Human Sexuality & Personhood. 200p. (Orig.). 1981. pap. price not set (ISBN 0-935372-09-1). Pope John Ctr.

Human Sexuality & Rehabilitation Medicine: Sexual Functioning Following Spinal Cord Injury. Ami Sha'Ked. (Illus.). 228p. 1981. write for info. (7749-X). Williams & Wilkins.

Human Sexuality & Social Work. Ed. by Harvey L. Gochros & Leroy G. Schultz. LC 71-129436. 1972. 9.95 o.p. (ISBN 0-8096-1808-7, Assn Pr). Follett.

Human Sexuality & the Mentally Retarded. Ed. by F. De La Cruz & G. D. LaVeck. LC 72-92057. 1973. 12.50 (ISBN 0-87630-063-8). Brunner-Mazel.

Human Sexuality: Essentials. Bryan Strong et al. (Illus.). 1978. pap. text ed. 10.50 (ISBN 0-8299-0154-X); test manual avail. (ISBN 0-8299-0576-6). West Pub.

Human Sexuality for Health Professionals. Martha U. Barnard et al. LC 77-84663. (Illus.). 1978. pap. text ed. 10.95 (ISBN 0-7216-1544-9). Saunders.

Human Sexuality in Health & Illness. 2nd ed. Nancy F. Woods. LC 78-11511. (Illus.). 1979. pap. 10.95 (ISBN 0-8016-5619-2). Mosby.

Human Sexuality in Our Time. Ed. by George Kelly. 1979. 4.00 (ISBN 0-8198-0610-2); pap. 3.00 (ISBN 0-8198-0611-0). Dghtrs St Paul.

Human Sexuality: Nursing Implications. (Contemporary Nursing Ser.). 276p. 1973. 6.50 o.p. (ISBN 0-686-08731-3, C08). Am Journal Nurse.

Human Sexuality: Sense & Nonsense. Herant Katchadourian. (Illus.). 160p. 1979. pap. text ed. 3.95x (ISBN 0-393-95017-4). Norton.

Human Side of Accident Prevention: Psychological Concepts & Principles Which Bear on Industrial Safety. Bruce L. Margolis & William H. Kroes. (Illus.). 160p. 1975. 15.50 (ISBN 0-398-03253-X). C C Thomas.

Human Side of Human Beings: Spanish Translation. Harvey Jackins. Tr. by Emma Ramos-Diaz & Azril Bacal. (Span.). 1980. pap. 3.00 (ISBN 0-911214-27-5). Rational Isl.

Human Side of Human Beings: The Theory of Re-Evaluation Counseling. Harvey Jackins. 1965. 3.00 o.p. (ISBN 0-911214-00-3); pap. 2.00 o.p. (ISBN 0-911214-01-1). Rational Isl.

Human Side of Management. James H. Morrison. (Business Ser). (Illus.). 1971. pap. text ed. 8.95 (ISBN 0-201-04839-6). A-W.

Human Side of Music. Charles W. Hughes. LC 70-107871. (Music Ser). 1970. Repr. of 1948 ed. lib. bdg. 32.50 (ISBN 0-306-71895-2). Da Capo.

Human Skeletal Remains: Excavation, Analysis, Interpretation. Douglas H. Ubelaker. (Aldine Manuals on Archeology). (Illus.). 1978. 12.50 o.p. (ISBN 0-202-33037-0). Beresford Bk Serv.

Human Skeletal Remains: Excavation, Analysis, Interpretation. Douglas H. Ubelaker. LC 77-95323. (Manuals on Archeology: No. 2). (Illus.). xi, 116p. 1980. Repr. of 1978 ed. 18.00x (ISBN 0-9602822-1-1). Taraxacum.

Human Skeletal Remains of Altar De Sacrificios: An Osteobiographic Analysis. Frank P. Saul. LC 72-91442. (Peabody Museum Papers: Vol. 63, No. 2). 1972. pap. text ed. 15.00 (ISBN 0-87365-181-2). Peabody Harvard.

Human Skeleton in Forensic Medicine. Wilton M. Krogman. (Illus.). 364p. 1978. 19.75 (ISBN 0-398-01054-4). C C Thomas.

Human Skills. Dennis H. Holding. (Studies in Human Performance Ser.). 304p. 1981. 39.95 (ISBN 0-471-27838-6, Pub. by Wiley-Interscience). Wiley.

Human Societies: An Introduction to Sociology. Geoffrey Hurd. 228p. 1973. cased 18.50x (ISBN 0-7100-7611-8); pap. 8.95 (ISBN 0-7100-7612-6). Routledge & Kegan.

Human Society in Ethics & Politics. Bertrand Russell. 1954. text ed. 18.50x (ISBN 0-04-172004-0). Allen Unwin.

Human Somesthetic Thalamus: With Maps for Physiological Target Localization During Stereotactic Neurosurgery. Raimond Emmers & Ronald R. Tasker. LC 74-80534. 1975. 70.00 (ISBN 0-911216-72-3). Raven.

Human Stereopsis: A Psychophysical Approach. W. Lawrence Gulick & Robert B. Lawson. (Illus.). 320p. 1976. text ed. 16.95x (ISBN 0-19-501971-7). Oxford U Pr.

Human Thing: The Speeches & Principles of Thucydides' History. Marc Cogan. LC 80-24226. (Chicago Original Paperback Ser.). 248p. 1981. lib. bdg. 19.00x (ISBN 0-226-11194-6). U of Chicago Pr.

Human Touch. Don Rutledge & Elaine S. Furlow. LC 75-2365. (Human Touch Ser.). (Illus.). 1975. 5.95 (ISBN 0-937170-13-5). Home Mission.

Human Tumors: Histology, Diagnosis, & Technique. Pierre Masson. Tr. by Sidney D. Kobernick from Fr. LC 70-83489. (Illus.). 1970. text ed. 45.00x (ISBN 0-8143-1405-8). Wayne St U Pr.

Human Types. Raymond Firth. (Illus.). pap. 1.25 o.p. (ISBN 0-451-61121-7, MY1121, Ment). NAL.

Human Use of Human Resources. 1st ed. Marvin Karlins. (Illus.). 208p. (Orig.). 11.95 (ISBN 0-07-033298-3); pap. text ed. 6.95 (ISBN 0-07-033297-5). McGraw.

Human Use of the Earth. Philip L. Wagner. LC 60-7092. 1964. 7.95 o.s.i. (ISBN 0-02-933560-4); pap. text ed. 3.00 (ISBN 0-02-933570-1). Free Pr.

Human Values in a Secular World. Ed. by Robert Z. Apostol. 1970. text ed. 7.50x (ISBN 0-391-00120-5). Humanities.

Human Values in Education. Rudolf Steiner. 190p. 1971. 9.75 o.p. (ISBN 0-85440-250-0). Anthroposophic.

Human Variation. Hermann K. Bleibtreu & James F. Downs. (gr. 4-9). 1971. pap. text ed. 7.95x (ISBN 0-02-473200-1). Macmillan.

Human Variation: An Introduction to Physical Anthropology. 2nd ed. James F. Downs & Hermann Bleibtreu. 1972. text ed. 10.95x (ISBN 0-02-474490-5, 47449). Macmillan.

Human Variation & Human Microevolution. Jane H. Underwood. (Illus.). 1979. pap. 10.95 (ISBN 0-13-447573-9). P-H.

Human Viral, Bedsonial & Rickettsial Diseases: A Diagnostic Handbook for Physicians. Abbas M. Behbehani. (Illus.). 370p. 1972. text ed. 37.50 (ISBN 0-398-02228-3). C C Thomas.

Human Vitamin B-Six Requirements. Food & Nutrition Board. 1978. pap. 13.25 (ISBN 0-309-02642-3). Natl Acad Pr.

Human Vocal Anatomy. David R. Dickson & Wilma M. Maue. (Illus.). 172p. 1977. 18.75 (ISBN 0-398-00449-8). C C Thomas.

Human Warmth & Other Stories. Daniel Curzon. LC 80-23270. 144p. 1981. 12.00 (ISBN 0-912516-53-4); pap. 4.95 (ISBN 0-912516-54-2). Grey Fox.

Human Zero: The Science Fiction Stories of Erle Stanley Gardner. Ed. by Martin H. Greenberg & Charles G. Waugh. 432p. Date not set. 12.95 (ISBN 0-688-00122-X). Morrow.

Humane Biology Projects. 3rd ed. Animal Welfare Institute. (Illus.). 57p. 1977. pap. text ed. 2.00 (ISBN 0-938414-05-4). Animal Welfare.

Humane Technologist. D. S. Davies et al. (Science & Engineering Policy Ser.). (Illus.). 1976. 15.95x (ISBN 0-19-858325-7). Oxford U Pr.

Humanism & Behaviorism: Dialogue & Growth. Abraham Wandersman et al. 400p. 1976. text ed. 42.00 (ISBN 0-08-019589-X); pap. text ed. 12.75 (ISBN 0-08-019588-1). Pergamon.

Humanism & Christianity. Claude Geffre. (Concilium Ser.: Religion in the Seventies: Vol. 86). 156p. 1973. pap. 4.95 (ISBN 0-8164-2542-6). Crossroad NY.

Humanism & Social Order in Tudor England. Fritz Caspari. LC 68-29071. 1968. 9.40 o.p. (ISBN 0-8077-1149-7); pap. text ed. 5.25x (ISBN 0-8077-1146-2). Tchrs Coll.

Humanism & Terror. Maurice Merleau-Ponty. LC 71-84797. 1969. pap. 5.95x (ISBN 0-8070-0277-1, BP342). Beacon Pr.

Humanism & Terror: An Essay on the Communist Problem. Maurice Merleau-Ponty. Tr. by John O'Neill from Fr. LC 80-21672. xlvii, 189p. 1980. Repr. of 1969 ed. lib. bdg. 25.00x (ISBN 0-313-22748-9, MEHU). Greenwood.

Humanism in Sociology: Its Historical Roots & Contemporary Problems. Aleksander Gella. LC 78-61394. 1978. pap. text ed. 10.25 (ISBN 0-8191-0598-8). U Pr of Amer.

Humanist & Scholastic Poetics, 1250-1500. Concetta C. Greenfield. LC 76-49779. 341p. 1981. 22.50 (ISBN 0-8387-1991-0). Bucknell U Pr.

Humanist Funeral Service. Corliss Lamont. LC 77-76001. 48p. 1977. 6.95 (ISBN 0-87975-093-6); pap. 2.95 (ISBN 0-87975-090-1). Prometheus Bks.

Humanist Papers, 4 vols, Vols. 1 & 2. Robert Kneeter. pap. write for info. (ISBN 0-938722-00-X). Word Ent.

Humanist Wedding Service. Corliss Lamont. 32p. pap. 2.95 saddle bdg. (ISBN 0-87975-000-6). Prometheus Bks.

Humanistic Botany. Oswald Tippo & William L. Stern. (Illus.). 1977. text ed. 14.95x (ISBN 0-393-09126-0); tchrs. manual gratis (ISBN 0-393-09130-9). Norton.

Humanistic Education. Ed. by Richard Weller. LC 77-71196. 1977. 19.50x (ISBN 0-685-78478-9); text ed. 17.50x (ISBN 0-8211-2256-8). McCutchan.

Humanistic Education for Business Executives. Morse Peckham. LC 60-9884. 1960. 10.00x (ISBN 0-8122-7177-7). U of Pa Pr.

Humanistic Education Sourcebook. Donald C. Read & Sidney B. Simon. (Illus.). 480p. 1975. ref. ed. 16.95 (ISBN 0-13-447714-6); pap. 12.50 (ISBN 0-13-447706-5). P-H.

Humanistic Education: Visions & Realities; Proceedings. Symposium on Educational Research,14th. Ed. by Richard H. Weller. LC 77-71196. 1977. 12.25 (ISBN 0-8211-2256-8, Co-Pub with McCutchan); pap. 10.00 (ISBN 0-87367-704-8, Pub with McCutchan). Phi Delta Kappa.

Humanistic Existentialism: The Literature of Possibility. Hazel E. Barnes. LC 59-11732. 1962. pap. 3.95 (ISBN 0-8032-5229-3, BB 145, Bison). U of Nebr Pr.

Humanistic Geography & Literature: Essays on the Experience of Place. Ed. by Douglas Pocock. 224p. 1981. 27.00x (ISBN 0-389-20158-8). B&N.

Humanistic Issues in Child Abuse. Ed. by Don Harkness. 100p. (Orig.). 1981. pap. 3.50 (ISBN 0-934996-13-X). Am Stud Pr.

Humanistic Nursing. Josephine G. Paterson & Loretta T. Zderad. LC 75-40431. 1976. 15.50 (ISBN 0-471-66946-6, Pub. by Wiley Medical). Wiley.

Humanistic Philosophy in Poland & Yugoslavia Today. Howard L. Parsons. (Occasional Papers Ser.: No. 4). 1968. pap. 1.00 (ISBN 0-89977-021-5). Am Inst Marxist.

Humanistic Pragmatism: The Philosophy of F. C. S. Schiller. Ed. by Reuben E. Abel. (Orig.). 1966. pap. text ed. 4.95 (ISBN 0-02-900120-X). Free Pr.

Humanistic Psychiatry: From Oppression to Choice. Roy D. Waldman. 1971. 12.00 (ISBN 0-8135-0681-6). Rutgers U Pr.

Humanistic Psychology. John B. Shaffer. LC 77-15044. (Foundations of Modern Psychology Ser.). (Illus.). 1978. ref. ed. 15.95 (ISBN 0-13-447698-0); pap. text ed. 9.95 (ISBN 0-13-447680-8). P-H.

Humanistic Psychology: A Guide to Information Sources. Ed. by Gloria B. Gottsegen & Abby J. Gottsegen. (Psychology Information Guide Ser.: Vol. 6). 175p. 1980. 30.00 (ISBN 0-8103-1462-2). Gale.

Humanistic Psychology & the Research Tradition: Their Several Virtues. Irvin L. Child. LC 72-6595. 256p. 1973. text ed. 17.95 o.p. (ISBN 0-471-15570-5). Wiley.

Humanistic Psychology & the Research Tradition: Their Several Virtues. Irvin L. Child. 220p. 1981. Repr. of 1973 ed. text ed. write for info. (ISBN 0-89874-277-3). Krieger.

Humanistic Sociology: Readings. Ed. by Claude C. Bowman. LC 72-13116. 1973. pap. text ed. 6.95x (ISBN 0-89197-221-8). Irvington.

Humanistic Teaching for Exceptional Children: An Introduction to Special Education. Ed. by William C. Morse. (Illus.). 344p. 1979. 18.00x (ISBN 0-8156-2199-X); pap. 8.95x (ISBN 0-8156-2215-5). Syracuse U Pr.

Humanists & Technocrats: Political Conflict in Contemporary China. Kurt Y. Kuriyama. LC 79-66648. 1979. pap. text ed. 9.50 (ISBN 0-8191-0846-4). U Pr of Amer.

Humanitarianism or Control? A Symposium on Nineteenth-Century Social Reform in Britain & America. David Rothman et al. Ed. by Martin Wiener. (Rice University Studies: Vol. 67, No. 1). (Orig.). 1981. pap. 5.50x (ISBN 0-89263-248-8). Rice Univ.

Humanitarians & the Ten Hour Movement in England. Raymond G. Cowherd. (Kress Library of Business & Economics: No. 10). (Illus.). 1956. pap. 5.00x (ISBN 0-678-09905-7, Baker Lib). Kelley.

Humanities: A Selective Guide to Information Sources. 2nd ed. A. Robert Rogers. LC 79-25335. (Library Science Text Ser.). 1980. lib. bdg. 25.00 (ISBN 0-87287-206-8); pap. text ed. 14.50 (ISBN 0-87287-222-X). Libs Unl.

Humanity & Culture: An Intro to Anthropology. Oriol Pi-Sunyer & Zdenek Salzmann. LC 77-76336. (Illus.). 1978. text ed. 19.95 (ISBN 0-395-25051-X); inst. manual 0.65 (ISBN 0-395-26239-9). HM.

Humanity & Divinity of Christ. John Knox. (Orig.). 18.95 (ISBN 0-521-05486-9); pap. 5.50x (ISBN 0-521-09414-3). Cambridge U Pr.

Humanity & Personhood: Personal Reaction to a World in Which Children Can Die. Jan Van Eys. write for info. (ISBN 0-398-04467-8). C C Thomas.

Humanity & Self-Cultivation Essays in Confucian Thought. Tu Wei-Ming. 1980. text ed. 22.50 (ISBN 0-89581-600-8, Asian Humanities). Lancaster-Miller.

Humanity of God. Karl Barth. Tr. by Thomas Weiser & John N. Thomas. LC 60-3479. 1960. pap. 3.95 (ISBN 0-8042-0612-0). John Knox.

Humanity's Three Major Contemporary False Prophets & Their Influence Upon the Decline & Chaos of Western Civilization. Alexander Verneuil. (Illus.). 1976. 47.80 (ISBN 0-89266-014-7). Am Classical Coll Pr.

Humanizing Health Care: Alternative Future for Medicine. Robert F. Rushmer. LC 75-1399. (Illus.). 211p. 1975. 15.50x (ISBN 0-262-18075-8); pap. 4.95x (ISBN 0-262-68032-7). MIT Pr.

Humanizing Nursing Education. Virginia King & Norma Gerwig. LC 80-83678. (Nursing Dimensions Education Ser.). 200p. 1981. text ed. 15.95 (ISBN 0-913654-69-8). Nursing Res.

Humanizing Social Psychology. M. Brewster Smith. LC 73-21076. (Social & Behavioral Science Ser.). 358p. 1974. 15.95x (ISBN 0-87589-229-9). Jossey-Bass.

Humanoid Touch. 2nd ed. Jack Williamson. 224p. 1981. pap. 2.25 (ISBN 0-553-14598-3). Bantam.

Humans & Animals. Ed. by John S. Baky. (Reference Shelf Ser.). 1980. 6.25 (ISBN 0-8242-0647-9). Wilson.

Humans Developing: A Lifespan Perspective. Robert Kastenbaum. 1979. text ed. 18.50x (ISBN 0-205-06513-9); instr's man. avail. (ISBN 0-205-06536-8); student guide avail. (ISBN 0-205-06535-X). Allyn.

Humans of Ziax II: The Drought on Ziax II. Morressy. (gr. 3-5). 1980. pap. 1.25 (ISBN 0-590-30382-1, Schol Pap). Schol Bk Serv.

Humanscale, Vols. 4-9. Niels Diffrient. 1981. Vols. 4-6. 37.50 (ISBN 0-686-69225-X); Vols. 7-9. 50.00 (ISBN 0-262-04061-1). MIT Pr.

Humanscale Four-Five-Six. Niels Diffrient. Date not set. price not set. MIT Pr.

Humanscale Seven-Eight-Nine. Niels Diffrient. Date not set. price not set. MIT Pr.

Humble on Wall Street. Martin T. Sosnoff. 1975. 8.95 o.p. (ISBN 0-87000-330-5). Arlington Hse.

Humblepuppy: And Other Stories for Telling. Ed. by Eileen Colwell. (Illus.). 176p. (gr. 3-5). 1980. 9.95 (ISBN 0-370-30127-7, Pub. by Chatto, Bodley Head & Jonathan). Merrimack Bk Serv.

Humboldt: The Life & Times of Alexander Humboldt. Helmut De Terra. LC 78-27653. 386p. 1979. Repr. of 1955 ed. lib. bdg. 24.00x (ISBN 0-374-92134-2). Octagon.

Humboldt Years: 1930-39. Beverly W. Brace. 1977. pap. 3.50 (ISBN 0-686-19169-2). B W Brace.

Humbug: The Art of P. T. Barnum. Neil Harris. LC 80-26944. xiv, 338p. 1981. pap. 8.95 (ISBN 0-226-31752-8). U of Chicago Pr.

Humbug Witch. Lorna Balian. (Illus.). (gr. k-2). 1965. 7.95 (ISBN 0-687-18023-6). Abingdon.

Humbugs of the World. Phineas T. Barnum. LC 68-21755. 1970. Repr. of 1865 ed. 15.00 (ISBN 0-8103-3580-8). Gale.

Hume. A. J. Ayer. 108p. 1980. 7.95 (ISBN 0-8090-5615-1); pap. 2.95 (ISBN 0-8090-1409-2). Hill & Wang.

Hume. Barry Stroud. (The Arguments of the Philosophers Ser.). 1977. 22.00x (ISBN 0-7100-8601-6). Routledge & Kegan.

Hume. Barry Stroud. (Arguments of the Philosophers Ser.). 292p. 1981. pap. 10.00 (ISBN 0-7100-0667-5). Routledge & Kegan.

Hume & the Problem of Causation. Tom L. Beauchamp & Alexander Rosenberg. 352p. 1981. 22.50. Oxford U Pr.

Hume's Intentions. 3rd ed. John Passmore. 180p. 1980. 26.50x (ISBN 0-7156-0918-1, Pub. by Duckworth England). Biblio Dist.

Hume's Philosophical Politics. D. Forbes. LC 75-9282. 400p. 1975. 47.95 (ISBN 0-521-20754-1). Cambridge U Pr.

Hume's Philosophy of Belief. Antony G. Flew. (International Library of Philosophy & Scientific Method). 1961. pap. text ed. 26.25x (ISBN 0-7100-1370-1). Humanities.

Hume's Theory of the Understanding. Ralph W. Church. LC 79-55608. 238p. 1980. Repr. of 1935 ed. lib. bdg. 19.75x (ISBN 0-313-20651-1, CHHU). Greenwood.

Humidification of Anesthetic Gases. Jack Chalon et al. (Illus.). 120p. 1981. price not set (ISBN 0-398-04461-9). C C Thomas.

Humility of Heart. Cajetan Mary da Bergamo. Tr. by Herbert C. Vaughan. 240p. 1978. pap. 3.00 (ISBN 0-89555-067-9, 117). Tan Bks Pubs.

Hummel. Berta Hummel. (Illus.). 78p. 1972. 11.00 (ISBN 0-686-68935-6). Heinman.

Hummel Art. John F. Hotchkiss. (Illus.). 1978. 17.95 o.p. (ISBN 0-87069-184-8); softbound o.p. 13.95 o.p. (ISBN 0-87069-249-6). Wallace-Homestead.

Hummel Art & Hummel Art Price Guide & Supplement. John Hotchkiss. (Illus.). 22.90 o.p. (ISBN 0-87069-298-4). Wallace-Homestead.

Humming Top. Dorothy Spicer. LC 68-31176. (gr. 7-11). 1968. 9.95 (ISBN 0-87599-147-5). S G Phillips.

Hummingbirds in the Garden. Roma Gans. LC 69-11083. (Let's Read- & Find-Out Science Bk). (Illus.). (gr. k-3). 1969. PLB 7.89 (ISBN 0-690-42562-7, TYC-J). T Y Crowell.

Humor & Humanity. Stephen Leacock. 232p. 1980. Repr. of 1938 ed. lib. bdg. 35.00 (ISBN 0-89984-322-0). Century Bookbindery.

Humor & Social Change in Twentieth-Century America. Joseph Boskin. pap. 8.00 (ISBN 0-89073-061-X). Boston Public Lib.

Humor & Social Change in Twentieth Century America. Joseph Boskin. pap. 8.00 (ISBN 0-89073-061-X). Boston Public Lib.

Humor in American Song. Arthur Loesser. LC 79-181804. (Illus.). 317p. 1975. Repr. of 1942 ed. 18.00 (ISBN 0-8103-4040-2). Gale.

Humor in Gospel Living. Roy A. Cheville. LC 77-27889. 1978. pap. 5.25 o.p. (ISBN 0-8309-0198-1). Herald Hse.

Humor in the American Pulpit from George Whitefield Through Henry Ward Beecher. rev. ed. Doug Adams. 1981. 6.95 (ISBN 0-686-22745-X). Sharing Co.

Humor: Its Origin & Development. Paul E. McGhee. LC 79-15401. (Psychology Ser.). (Illus.). 1979. text ed. 15.95x o.p. (ISBN 0-7167-1095-1); pap. text ed. 8.95x (ISBN 0-7167-1096-X). W H Freeman.

Humor of Christ. Elton Trueblood. LC 75-12280. 128p. 1975. pap. 4.95 (ISBN 0-06-068631-6, RD 298, HarpR). Har-Row.

Humor of the American Cowboy. Stan Hoig. LC 58-5328. (Illus.). 1970. pap. 2.45 (ISBN 0-8032-5719-8, BB 520, Bison). U of Nebr Pr.

Humor of the Old Southwest. 2nd ed. Ed. by Hennig Cohen & William B. Dillingham. LC 74-13512. 455p. 1975. pap. text ed. 7.95x (ISBN 0-8203-0358-5). U of Ga Pr.

Humor Power: How to Get It, Give It & Gain. Herb True & Anna Mang. LC 79-55370. 240p. 1980. 9.95 (ISBN 0-385-14618-3). Doubleday.

Humoral Control of Growth & Differentiation, 2 vols. Ed. by Joseph LoBue & Albert S. Gordon. Incl. Vol. 1. Vertebrate Regulatory Factors. 1973. 52.50 (ISBN 0-12-453801-0); Vol. 2. Nonvertebrate Neuroendocrinology & Ageing. 1974. 45.00 (ISBN 0-12-453802-9). Set. 79.00 (ISBN 0-686-66930-4). Acad Pr.

Humorous Courtier. James Shirley. Ed. by Marvin Morillo & Stephen Orgel. LC 78-66821. (Renaissance Drama Ser.). 1979. lib. bdg. 25.00 (ISBN 0-8240-9738-6). Garland Pub.

Humorous Look at Love & Marriage. Bob Phillips. LC 80-83841. 128p. 1981. pap. 2.25 (ISBN 0-89081-268-3). Harvest Hse.

Humorous Monologues for Teen-Agers. Robert Fontaine. (YA) 1975. Repr. 8.95 (ISBN 0-8238-0125-X). Plays.

Humour & Humanism in Chemistry. John Read. LC 79-8621. Repr. of 1947 ed. 38.00 (ISBN 0-404-18487-1). AMS Pr.

Humour in the Works of Proust. Maya Slater. (Oxford Modern Languages & Literature Monographs). 200p. 1979. text ed. 22.00x (ISBN 0-19-815534-4). Oxford U Pr.

Humour, Wit & Satire of the Seventeenth Century. John Ashton. LC 67-24350. (Social History Reference). 1968. Repr. of 1883 ed. 15.00 (ISBN 0-8103-3251-5). Gale.

Humours of Golf. W. Heath Robinson. (Illus.). 96p. 13.50 (ISBN 0-7156-0915-7, Pub. by Duckworth England). Biblio Dist.

Humphrey Lyttelton's Jazz & Big Band Quiz. Humphrey Lyttleton. 1979. 14.95 (ISBN 0-7134-2011-1, Pub. by Batsford England). David & Charles.

Hump's First Case. Ralph Dennis. (Hardman Ser.: No. 10). 1977. pap. 1.25 o.p. (ISBN 0-685-76989-5). Popular Lib.

Humpty Dumpty & Other Nursery Rhymes. Illus. by Rod Ruth. (Tell-a-Tale Reader). 32p. (ps-3). 1980. PLB 4.77 (ISBN 0-307-68415-6, Golden Pr). Western Pub.

Humpty Dumpty's Bedtime Stories. Ed. by Alvin Tresselt. LC 79-136997. (Illus.). (gr. k-3). 1971. 5.95 o.s.i. (ISBN 0-8193-0502-2, Four Winds); PLB 5.41 o.s.i. (ISBN 0-8193-0503-0). Schol Bk Serv.

Humpty Dumpty's Holiday Stories. Ed. by Alvin Tresselt. LC 72-8116. (Illus.). 72p. (gr. k-3). 1973. 5.95 o.s.i. (ISBN 0-8193-0644-4, Four Winds); PLB 5.41 o.s.i. (ISBN 0-8193-0645-2). Schol Bk Serv.

Hunchback of Notre Dame. Victor Hugo. 1953. 17.95x (ISBN 0-460-00422-0, Evman). Dutton.

Hunchback of Notre Dame. Victor Hugo. (Arabic.). pap. 7.95x (ISBN 0-686-63547-7). Intl Bk Ctr.

Hundred Best Restaurants in the Valley of the Sun: 1981. 4th ed. John Bogert & Joan Bogert. LC 77-79784. 160p. 1980. pap. 2.25 (ISBN 0-937974-00-5). ADM Co.

Hundred Camels in the Courtyard. Paul Bowles. (Orig.). 1962. pap. 2.00 (ISBN 0-87286-002-7). City Lights.

Hundred Glories of French Cooking. Robert Courtine. 1973. 15.00 o.p. (ISBN 0-374-17357-5). FS&G.

Hundred Islands. Mavis T. Clark. LC 77-5353. (gr. 6-9). 1977. 8.95 (ISBN 0-02-718900-7, 71890). Macmillan.

Hundred Merry Tales: Shakespeare's Jest Book: an Edition of a Hundred Mery Talys, 1526. LC 70-133328. 1970. 20.00x (ISBN 0-8201-1083-3). Schol Facsimiles.

Hundred Percent Black Steinway Grand. Laurel Speer. Ed. by M. Karl Kulikowski. (Gusto Press Short Story Discovery Ser.). (Orig.). 1979. pap. 6.95 (ISBN 0-933906-10-2). Gusto Pr.

Hundred Plus Ideas for Drama. Anna Scher & Charles Verrall. 1975. pap. text ed. 4.50x (ISBN 0-435-18799-6). Heinemann Ed.

Hundred Things Japanese. Japanese Culture Institute. (Illus.). 216p. 1976. 15.00 (ISBN 0-87040-364-8). Japan Pubns.

Hundredth Chance. Ethel M. Dell. (Barbara Cartland's Library of Love: Vol. 5). 306p. 1980. 12.95x (ISBN 0-7156-1381-2, Pub. by Duckworth England). Biblio Dist.

Hung Gar Kung-Fu Chinese Art of Self-Defense. Bucksam Kong & Eugene H. Ho. Ed. by John Scurra. LC 73-75551. (Ser. 310). 1973. pap. text ed. 6.95 (ISBN 0-89750-038-5). Ohara Pubns.

Hung Up to Die. Michael Meyers. (Hardy Ser.: No. 4). 192p. 1976. pap. 1.25 o.p. (ISBN 0-445-00378-2). Popular Lib.

Hungarian Cinema Today: History Must Answer to Man. Graham Petrie. (Illus.). 284p. (Orig.). 1980. pap. 8.95 (ISBN 9-6313-0485-X). NY Zoetrope.

Hungarian Classical Ballads & Their Folklore. Ninon A. Leader. 1967. 72.00 (ISBN 0-521-05526-1). Cambridge U Pr.

Hungarian Concise Dictionary: English-Hungarian. 9th ed. Laszlo Orszagh. 1979. 20.00x (ISBN 963-05-1883-X, H-269). Vanous.

Hungarian Concise Dictionary: Hungarian-English, Vol. 2. 7th ed. Laszlo Orszagh. 1976. 20.00x (ISBN 9-6305-0612-2, H268). Vanous.

Hungarian Cookery-Book: One Hundred Forty Hungarian Specialities. 10th rev. ed. Gundel Karoly. (Illus.). 103p. 1980. 7.50x (ISBN 963-13-0949-5). Intl Pubns Serv.

Hungarian Dances. 2nd rev. ed. Andor Czompo. LC 74-11041. (Illus.). 1980. pap. text ed. 5.95 (ISBN 0-935496-01-7). AC Pubns.

Hungarian Deluxe Dictionary: English-Hungarian, 2 vols. 4th ed. Orszagh. 1974. 60.00x (ISBN 963-05-0554-1, H-331). Vanous.

Hungarian-English - English-Hungarian Dictionary, 2 vols. 11th, rev. ed. Laszlo Orszagh. 1977. Set. 15.00 (ISBN 0-686-68937-2). Vol. 1, Hung.-Eng., 464pp (ISBN 963-05-1255-6). Vol. 2, Eng.-Hung., 608pp (ISBN 963-05-1256-4). Heinman.

Hungarian Folk Art. T Hofer & E. Fel. (Illus.). 1979. 35.00 (ISBN 0-19-211448-4). Oxford U Pr.

Hungarian Folk Designs for Embroiderers & Craftsmen. Anne Szalavary. (Illus.). 160p. (Orig.). 1980. pap. 4.00 (ISBN 0-486-23969-1). Dover.

Hungarian Foreign Policy, 1919-1945. rev. ed. Gyula Juhasz. Tr. by Sandor Simon from Hungarian. LC 80-468278. Orig. Title: Magyarorszag Kulpolitikaja, 1919-1945. 356p. 1979. 30.00x (ISBN 963-05-1882-1). Intl Pubns Serv.

Hungarian Language. Ed. by Lorand Benko & Samu Imre. (Janua Linguarum, Ser. Practica: No. 134). (Illus.). 377p. (Orig.). 1972. pap. text ed. 64.70x (ISBN 90-2792-075-3). Mouton.

Hungarian Language & General Linguistics. Ed. by Ferenc Kiefer. (Linguistic & Literary Studies in Eastern Europe Ser.: No. 4). 580p. 1980. text ed. 68.50x (ISBN 90-272-1508-1). Humanities.

Hungarian Prose & Verse. Ed. by G. F. Cushing. (London East European Ser.). 1956. text ed. 13.25x (ISBN 0-485-17501-0, Athlone Pr). Humanities.

Hungarian Soviet Republic. Tibor Hajdu. Tr. by Etelka De Laczay & Rudolph Fischer. LC 80-468236. (Studia Historica Academiae Scientiarum Hungaricae Ser.: No. 131). (Illus.). 172p. 1979. 20.00x (ISBN 963-05-1990-9). Intl Pubns Serv.

Hungarians in America. Desi K. Bognar. LC 72-97113. (East-European Biographies & Studies Ser.: No. 3). 240p. 1972. 8.50x (ISBN 0-912460-01-6). AFI Pubns.

Hungarians in America: A Biographical Directory of Professionals of Hungarian Origin. rev. ed. Ed. by Desi K. Bognar. LC 79-53801. (East European Biographies & Studies Ser: Nos. 4 & 5). 1979. 25.00 (ISBN 0-685-71858-1). AFI Pubns.

Hungary. Thomas Kabdebo. (World Bibliographical Ser.: No. 15). 236p. 1980. 31.50 (ISBN 0-903450-28-3). ABC-Clio.

Hungary. Diana McNair-Wilson. 1976. 24.00 (ISBN 0-7134-3199-7). David & Charles.

Hungary: A Guidebook. rev. 6th ed. Ivan Boldizsar. (Illus.). 1969. 6.95 o.p. (ISBN 0-8038-3006-8). Hastings.

Hungary: A Profile. Ivan Volgyes. (Nations of Contemporary Eastern Europe). (Illus.). 128p. 1981. lib. bdg. 16.50x (ISBN 0-89158-929-5). Westview.

Hungary: An Economic Geography. Gyorgy Enyedi. Ed. by Stephen Fischer-Galati. LC 76-3742. (Special Studies on Contemporary Eastern Europe Ser). 1976. 31.50x (ISBN 0-89158-030-1). Westview.

Hungary in the Late Eighteenth Century. Bela K. Kiraly. LC 69-19459. (East Central European Studies). (Illus.). 1969. 20.00x (ISBN 0-231-03223-4). Columbia U Pr.

Hunger. Whitley Strieber. LC 80-21355. 320p. 1981. write for info. (ISBN 0-688-03757-7). Morrow.

Hunger: Basic Mechanisms & Clinical Implications. Ed. by D. Novin et al. LC 75-14563. 510p. 1976. 39.00 (ISBN 0-89004-059-1). Raven.

Hunger Disease: Studies by the Jewish Physicians in the Warsaw Ghetto. Myron Winick. LC 78-26397. (Current Concepts in Nutrition Ser.: Vol. 7). 1979. 20.50 (ISBN 0-471-05003-2, Pub. by Wiley-Interscience). Wiley.

Hunger for Experience: Vital Religious Communities in America Today. John E. Biersdorf. 160p. 1975. 7.95 (ISBN 0-8164-1198-0). Crossroad NY.

Hunger, Politics & Markets: The Real Issues in the Food Crisis. Ed. by Sartaj Aziz. LC 75-34674. 130p. 1975. 10.00x (ISBN 0-8147-0559-6); pap. 5.00x (ISBN 0-8147-0560-X). NYU Pr.

Hunger Signs in Crops. 3rd ed. Ed. by Howard B. Sprague. LC 64-20015. 1977. 19.95x (ISBN 0-679-30106-2, Pub. by MacKay). Longman.

Hunger: The World Food Crisis, An NSTA Environmental Materials Guide. Kathryn M. Fowler. 1977. pap. 2.50 (ISBN 0-87355-005-6). Natl Sci Tchrs.

Hungry As the Sea. Wilbur Smith. 1981. pap. 3.50 (ISBN 0-451-09599-5, E9599, Sig). NAL.

Hungry for God. Ralph Martin. 1976. pap. 1.50 (ISBN 0-89129-040-0). Jove Pubns.

Hungry Forties: Life Under the Bread Tax. J. C. Unwin. 288p. Date not set. Repr. of 1904 ed. 24.00x (ISBN 0-686-28338-4, Pub. by Irish Academic Pr). Biblio Dist.

Hungry Ghosts: Seven Allusive Comedies. Joyce Carol Oates. 200p. (Orig.). 1978. 14.00 (ISBN 0-87685-204-5); pap. 5.00 (ISBN 0-87685-203-7). Black Sparrow.

Hungry Gun. Charles R. Pike. LC 80-68158. (Jubal Cade Westerns Ser.). 112p. 1980. pap. 2.95 (ISBN 0-87754-232-5). Chelsea Hse.

Hungry Hill. Daphne Du Maurier. LC 78-184732. 416p. 1971. Repr. of 1945 ed. lib. bdg. 12.50x (ISBN 0-8376-0414-1). Bentley.

Hungry Leprechaun. Mary Calhoun. (Illus.). (gr. k-3). 1962. PLB 7.44 (ISBN 0-688-31713-8). Morrow.

Hungry Sharks. John F. Waters. LC 72-7563. (Let's-Read-&-Find-Out Science Bk). (Illus.). 40p. (ps-3). 1974. PLB 7.89 (ISBN 0-690-01121-0, TYC-J). T Y Crowell.

Hungry World. Elaine Israel. LC 77-24424. (Illus.). 64p. (gr. 3 up). 1977. PLB 6.97 (ISBN 0-671-32821-2). Messner.

Hunk of Skin. Pablo Picasso. LC 68-8390. (Pocket Poet Ser.: No. 25). (Orig., Span. & Eng.). 1969. pap. 1.00 o.p. (ISBN 0-87286-040-X). City Lights.

Hunt. A. Alvarez. 288p. 1981. pap. 2.75 (ISBN 0-553-13115-X). Bantam.

Hunt. John G. Mitchell. LC 80-7621. 320p. 1980. 11.95 (ISBN 0-394-50684-7). Knopf.

Hunt & Other Poems. Ira De. 8.00 (ISBN 0-89253-467-2); flexible cloth 4.00 (ISBN 0-89253-468-0). Ind-US Inc.

Hunt Close! Jerome B. Robinson. (Illus.). 1978. 12.95 (ISBN 0-87691-259-5). Winchester Pr.

Hunt for the Mastodon. Georgianne Ensign. LC 78-157749. (gr. 4 up). 1971. PLB 4.90 o.p. (ISBN 0-531-01994-2). Watts.

Hunt with the Hounds. Mignon G. Eberhart. 192p. 1974. pap. 0.95 o.p. (ISBN 0-445-00527-0). Popular Lib.

Hunted. Jeremy Scott. 1981. 13.95 (ISBN 0-671-42187-5, Wyndham Bks). S&S.

Hunted Mammals of the Sea. Robert McClung. (Illus.). (gr. 7 up). 1978. 8.95 (ISBN 0-688-22146-7); PLB 8.59 (ISBN 0-688-32146-1). Morrow.

Hunter. Hugh Fosburgh. 1977. pap. 1.50 (ISBN 0-505-51182-7). Tower Bks.

Hunter & Habitat in the Central Kalahari Desert. G. B. Silberbauer. LC 80-16768. (Illus.). 288p. Date not set. 39.50 (ISBN 0-521-23578-2); pap. 14.95 (ISBN 0-521-28135-0). Cambridge U Pr.

Hunters. Clark Howard. 1978. pap. 1.95 o.s.i. (ISBN 0-515-04710-4). Jove Pubns.

Hunters. Daniel Jacobson. LC 74-963. (Indians of North America Ser). 96p. (gr. 4-7). 1974. PLB 5.90 (ISBN 0-531-02725-2). Watts.

Hunters. Elman R. Service. (Illus.). 1966. pap. 3.95 ref. ed. o.p. (ISBN 0-13-448076-7). P-H.

Hunters & the Hunted. Aldo Cocchia. Tr. by M. Gwyer. LC 79-6106. (Navies & Men Ser.). (Illus.). 1980. Repr. of 1958 ed. lib. bdg. 16.00x (ISBN 0-405-13035-X). Arno.

Hunters & the Hunted: Surviving in the Animal World. Dorothy H. Patent. LC 80-23559. (Illus.). 64p. (gr. 4-8). 1981. PLB 7.95 (ISBN 0-8234-0386-6). Holiday.

Hunter's Bible. William K. Merrill. 1968. 3.50 (ISBN 0-385-01533-X). Doubleday.

Hunter's Blood. Jere Cunningham. 1977. pap. 1.75 o.p. (ISBN 0-449-13794-5, GM). Fawcett.

Hunters, Farmers, & Civilizations: Old World Archaeology: Readings from Scientific American. Intro. by C. C. Lamberg-Karlovsky. LC 78-27049. (Illus.). 1979. text ed. 19.95x (ISBN 0-7167-1073-0); pap. text ed. 9.95x (ISBN 0-7167-1074-9). W H Freeman.

Hunter's Fireside Book: Tales of Dogs, Ducks, Birds & Guns. Gene Hill. (Illus.). 1972. 11.95 (ISBN 0-87691-076-2). Winchester Pr.

Hunters, Fishers & Farmers of Eastern Europe, 6000-3000 B.C. Ruth Tringham. 1971. text ed. 8.00x (ISBN 0-09-108790-2, Hutchinson U Lib). Humanities.

Hunter's Folly. Lee E. Caster. (Orig.). 1979. pap. 1.95 (ISBN 0-532-23288-7). Manor Bks.

Hunter's Game Cookbook. Jacqueline E. Knight. (Illus.). 1978. 12.95 (ISBN 0-87691-252-8). Winchester Pr.

Hunters, Gatherers & First Farmers Beyond Europe: An Archaeological Survey. Ed. by J. V. Megaw. (Illus.). 250p. 1976. pap. text ed. 15.00x (ISBN 0-7185-1136-0, Leicester). Humanities.

Hunters of Space. Joseph E. Kelleam. (YA) 5.95 (ISBN 0-685-07436-6, Avalon). Bouregy.

Hunters of the Northern Forest: Designs for Survival Among the Alaskan Kutchin. Richard K. Nelson. 1973. 10.50x (ISBN 0-226-57177-7). U of Chicago Pr.

Hunters of the Red Moon. Marion Bradley. (Science Fiction Ser). pap. 1.75 (ISBN 0-87997-407-9, UE1568). DAW Bks.

Hunters of the Whale, an Adventure in Northwest Coast Archaeology. Ruth Kirk & Richard D. Daugherty. LC 73-17317. (Illus.). 160p. (gr. 5-9). 1974. 7.92 (ISBN 0-688-30109-6); 8.25 (ISBN 0-688-20109-1). Morrow.

Hunters, Pastoralists & Ranchers. Tim Ingold. LC 78-73243. (Cambridge Studies in Social Anthropology: No. 28). (Illus.). 1980. 27.50 (ISBN 0-521-22588-4). Cambridge U Pr.

Hunters, Seamen & Entrepreneurs: The Tuna Seinermen of San Diego. Michael K. Orbach. (Illus.). 1978. 15.75x (ISBN 0-520-03348-5). U of Cal Pr.

Hunter's Stew & Hangtown Fry. Lila Perl. LC 77-5366. (gr. 6 up). 1977. 8.95 (ISBN 0-395-28922-X, Clarion). HM.

Hunting. Tom McNally. LC 77-125023. (All Star Sports Bk). (Illus.). 128p. (gr. 4 up). 1972. 3.95 o.p. (ISBN 0-695-80194-5); lib. ed. 5.97 o.p. (ISBN 0-695-40194-7). Follett.

Hunting America's Game Animals & Birds. Robert Elman. (Illus.). 384p. 1980. 12.95 (ISBN 0-87691-172-6). Winchester Pr.

Hunting & Fishing. Cecil F. Clotfelter. LC 73-90569. (Spare Time Guides Ser.: No. 2). 1974. lib. bdg. 7.50 o.p. (ISBN 0-87287-079-0). Libs Unl.

Hunting & Stalking Deer Throughout the Ages. Kenneth Whitehead. LC 79-56462. (Illus.). 241p. 1980. 53.00 (ISBN 0-7134-2083-9, Pub. by Batsford England). David & Charles.

Hunting Annual 1981. Ed. by Hunting Magazine Eds. (Illus.). 320p. 1980. pap. 6.95 (ISBN 0-8227-3016-2). Petersen Pub.

Hunting Dog Know-How. Dave Duffey. (Illus.). 1972. 9.95 (ISBN 0-87691-081-9). Winchester Pr.

Hunting Dogs: An Outdoor Life Book. rev. ed. F. Philip Rice & John I. Dahl. LC 67-14555. (Funk & W Bk.). (Illus.). 1978. 7.95 o.s.i. (ISBN 0-308-10324-6, TYC-T); pap. 4.50 o.s.i. (ISBN 0-308-10325-4, TYC-T). T Y Crowell.

Hunting for Fossils. Marian Murray. 1967. 11.95 (ISBN 0-02-588150-7). Macmillan.

Hunting Gun. Yasushi Inoue. LC 61-8740. 1977. pap. 3.95 (ISBN 0-8048-0257-2). C E Tuttle.

Hunting Hounds: How to Choose, Train & Handle America's Trail & Tree Hounds. Dave Duffey. (Illus.). 1972. 8.95 (ISBN 0-87691-062-2). Winchester Pr.

Hunting in Ireland. Collin A. Lewis. (Illus.). 26.25 (ISBN 0-85131-213-6, Dist. by Sporting Book Center). J A Allen.

Hunting of Leviathan. Samuel I. Mintz. 1962. 35.50 (ISBN 0-521-05736-1). Cambridge U Pr.

Hunting of the Buffalo. E. Douglas Branch. LC 62-8408. (Illus.). 1962. pap. 4.25 (ISBN 0-8032-5021-5, BB 130, Bison). U of Nebr Pr.

Hunting of the Hare. Ed. by Lionel R. Woolner. (Illus.). 6.10 (ISBN 0-85131-122-9, Dist. by Sporting Book Center). J A Allen.

Hunting of the Snark: Annotated by Martin Gardner. Lewis Carroll. Ed. by Martin Gardner. (Illus.). Date not set. 14.00 (ISBN 0-913232-98-X); collector's ed. 350.00 (ISBN 0-913232-98-X). W Kaufmann.

Hunting Peoples. Carleton S. Coon. (Illus.). 1979. 10.95 (ISBN 0-224-00685-1, Pub. by Chatto Bodley Jonathan). Merrimack Bk Serv.

Hunting Rifle. Jack O'Connor. (Illus.). 1970. 12.95 (ISBN 0-87691-007-X). Winchester Pr.

Hunting Shack. Gunnard Landers. 1980. pap. 2.50 (ISBN 0-440-13300-9). Dell.

Hunting the Clean Boot: The Working Bloodhound. Brian Lowe. (Illus.). 240p. 1981. 22.50 (ISBN 0-7137-0950-2). Sterling.

Hunting the Divine Fox. Robert F. Capon. 1977. pap. 3.95 (ISBN 0-8164-2137-4). Crossroad NY.

Hunting the Uplands with Rifle & Shotgun. Luther A. Anderson. (Illus.). 1977. 12.95 (ISBN 0-87691-191-2). Winchester Pr.

Hunting the Whitetailed Deer. rev. ed. Russell Tinsley. LC 65-14986. (Funk & W Bk.). (Illus.). 1977. 9.95 (ISBN 0-308-10326-2, TYC-T); pap. 4.50 (ISBN 0-308-10327-0, TYC-T). T Y Crowell.

Hunting the Yahoos. Gregory Fitzgerald. (Illus.). 100p. (Orig.). 1981. pap. 4.50 (ISBN 0-934996-14-8). Am Stud Pr.

Hunting Variety. Richard Flanagan. 224p. 1975. pap. 1.25 o.p. (ISBN 0-445-00315-4). Popular Lib.

Hunting with Bow & Arrow. George Laycock & Erwin Bauer. LC 65-28519. 1965. lib. bdg. 3.95 o.p. (ISBN 0-668-01417-2). Arco.

Hunting with Flushing Dogs. Joe Stetson. (Sportsman's Library of Gun Dogs, Vol. 2). (Orig.). 1965. pap. 2.00 (ISBN 0-87666-293-9, DS1137). TFH Pubns.

Hunting with Pointing Dogs. Joe Stetson. (Sportsman's Library of Gun Dogs, Vol. 3). (Orig.). 1965. pap. 1.79 o.p. (ISBN 0-87666-351-X, DS1138). TFH Pubns.

Hunting with Retrievers. Joe Stetson. (Sportsman's Library of Gun Dogs, Vol. 4). (Orig.). pap. 2.00 (ISBN 0-87666-371-4, DS1136). TFH Pubns.

Hunting with Scenthounds. Stetson. (Sportsman's Library off Gun Dogs Vol 5). 1965. pap. 1.79 o.p. (ISBN 0-87666-380-3, DS1140). TFH Pubns.

Huntingdon Plays: A Critical Edition with Introduction and Notes, of "The Downfall & The Death of Robert Earl of Huntington. John A. Meagher. Ed. by Stephen Orgel. LC 79-54352. (Renaissance Drama Second Ser.). 583p. 1980. lib. bdg. 55.00 (ISBN 0-8240-4469-X). Garland Pub.

Huntington's Chorea: Advances in Neurology, Vol. 1. Ed. by A. Barbeau et al. LC 72-93317. 1973. 73.50 (ISBN 0-911216-40-5). Raven.

Huntington's Disease. Ed. by Thomas N. Chase et al. LC 78-68608. (Advances in Neurology Ser.: Vol. 23). 1979. text ed. 41.00 (ISBN 0-89004-374-4). Raven.

Huntsman of Our Time. Kenneth Lingertwood. 15.00x (ISBN 0-392-07938-0, SpS). Soccer.

Hurdy-Gurdy. Susann Palmer & Samuel Palmer. LC 79-56052. (Illus.). 192p. 1980. 45.00 (ISBN 0-7153-7888-0). David & Charles.

Hurlbut's Story of the Bible. Jesse L. Hurlbut. pap. 1.95 o.s.i. (ISBN 0-89129-116-4). Jove Pubns.

Hurok of the Stone Age. Lin Carter. 1981. pap. 1.75 (ISBN 0-87997-597-0, UE1597). Daw Bks.

Hurrah! Selected Poems. Irving Stettner. (Illus.). 124p. (Orig.). 1980. pap. 3.50 (ISBN 0-917402-13-8). Downtown Poets.

Hurray for a Dutch Birthday. Antonia Ridge et al. (Illus.). (ps-5). 1964. 6.95 (ISBN 0-571-06025-0, Pub. by Faber & Faber). Merrimack Bk Serv.

Hurray for B.C. Johnny Hart. (B.C. Ser.). (Illus.). 1978. pap. 1.50 (ISBN 0-449-13625-6, GM). Fawcett.

Hurray for Captain Jane. Sam Reavin. LC 79-153793. (Illus.). (gr. k-3). 1971. 5.95 o.s.i. (ISBN 0-8193-0511-1, Four Winds); PLB 5.41 o.s.i. (ISBN 0-8193-0512-X). Schol Bk Serv.

Hurray for Pippa! Betty Boegehold. LC 79-19105. (Illus.). 64p. (gr. k-3). 1980. 4.95 (ISBN 0-394-84067-4); PLB 5.99 (ISBN 0-394-94067-9). Knopf.

Hurrell Style. George Hurrell. Ed. by Whitney Stine. LC 76-15396. (John Day Bk.). (Illus.). 1976. 16.95 o.s.i. (ISBN 0-381-98293-9, TYC-T); pap. 9.95 o.s.i. (ISBN 0-381-98299-8, TYC-T). T Y Crowell.

Hurrican Zoe & Other Sailing. Mike Peyton. 96p. 1980. 9.00x (ISBN 0-245-53132-7, Pub. by Nautical England). State Mutual Bk.

Hurricane. Gardner Fox. 1976. pap. 1.50 o.p. (ISBN 0-685-69510-7, LB375DK, Leisure Bks). Nordon Pubns.

Hurricane & Its Impact. Robert H. Simpson & Herbert Riehl. LC 80-13911. (Illus.). 448p. 1981. 20.00 (ISBN 0-8071-0688-7). La State U Pr.

Hurricane Hunters. Ivan R. Tannehill. LC 55-9480. (Illus.). (gr. 9 up). 1955. 4.50 (ISBN 0-396-03789-5). Dodd.

Hurricane Wake. Rosalind Ashe. 1978. pap. 1.95 o.s.i. (ISBN 0-446-89448-6). Warner Bks.

Hurricane Wake. Rosalind Ashe. LC 77-71366. 1977. 7.95 o.p. (ISBN 0-03-021366-5). HR&W.

Hurrish: A Study. Emily Lawless. Ed. by Robert L. Wolff. (Ireland Nineteenth Century Fiction - Ser. Two: Vol. 71). 584p. 1979. lib. bdg. 32.00 (ISBN 0-8240-3520-8). Garland Pub.

Hurry Gringo. Kenneth Farrar. Ed. by Sylvia Ashton. LC 78-31374. Date not set. 12.95 (ISBN 0-87949-143-4). Ashley Bks.

Hurting. Dan Day. (Uplook Ser.). 1978. pap. 0.75 (ISBN 0-8163-0088-7, 08889-8). Pacific Pr Pub Assn.

Hurting Parent. Margie M. Lewis & Gregg Lewis. 160p. (Orig.). 1980. pap. 3.95 (ISBN 0-310-41731-7). Zondervan.

Husband. Catherine Cookson. 1976. pap. 1.75 (ISBN 0-451-07858-6, E7858, Sig). NAL.

Husband/Coached Childbirth. 3rd ed. Robert A. Bradley. LC 80-8683. (Illus.). 256p. 1981. 9.95 (ISBN 0-06-014850-0, HarpT). Har-Row.

Husband in Boarding School. Giovanni Guareschi. 1967. 4.50 o.p. (ISBN 0-374-17392-3). FS&G.

Husband-Wife Equality. Herbert J. Miles & Fern H. Miles. 1978. 7.95 o.p. (ISBN 0-8007-0906-3). Revell.

Husbands & Wives: The Dynamics of Married Living. Robert O. Blood, Jr. & D. M. Wolfe. LC 59-6824. 1965. pap. text ed. 5.95 (ISBN 0-02-904070-1). Free Pr.

Husband's Notes About Her. Eve Merriam. LC 75-25973. 96p. 1976. 9.95 o.s.i. (ISBN 0-02-584350-8, 58435). Macmillan.

Husband's Notes About Her. Eve Merriam. LC 75-25970. 104p. 1976. pap. 2.95 o.s.i. (ISBN 0-02-070120-9, Collier). Macmillan.

Hush Little Baby. Aliki. (Illus.). (ps-1). 1968. PLB 7.95 (ISBN 0-13-448167-4); pap. 2.50 (ISBN 0-13-448175-5). P-H.

Hush Up! Jim Aylsworth. LC 79-2137. (Illus.). 32p. (gr. k-2). 1980. 6.95 (ISBN 0-03-054841-1). HR&W.

Hush, Winifred Is Dead. Audrey P. Johnson. 192p. (YA) 1976. 4.95 o.p. (ISBN 0-685-67082-1, Avalon). Bouregy.

Husqvarna Service - Repair Handbook: 125-450cc Singles, 1966-1975. Brick Price. Ed. by Jeff Robinson. (Illus.). 168p. 1976. pap. text ed. 9.95 (ISBN 0-89287-014-1, M423). Clymer Pubns.

Husserl, Intentionality & Cognitive Science. Ed. by Hubert L. Dreyfus & Harrison Hall. 1981. text ed. write for info. (ISBN 0-89706-010-5). Bradford Bks.

Husserl: Shorter Works. Ed. by Peter McCormick & Frederick A. Elliston. LC 80-53178. 440p. 1981. text ed. 26.00 (ISBN 0-268-01703-4); pap. text ed. 10.95 (ISBN 0-268-01077-3). U of Notre Dame Pr.

Hussite King: Bohemia in European Affairs, 1440-1471. Otakar Odlozilik. 1965. 22.00 (ISBN 0-8135-0497-X). Rutgers U Pr.

Hustle Won't Bring the Kingdom of God: Jesus' Parables Interpreted for Today. Brian A. Nelson. 1978. pap. 2.95 (ISBN 0-8272-1417-0). Bethany Pr.

Hustler. Walter Tevis. (Alpha Books). 94p. (Orig.). 1979. pap. text ed. 2.25x (ISBN 0-19-424209-9). Oxford U Pr.

Hustlers, Beats & Others. Ned Polsky. 1969. pap. 2.50 o.p. (ISBN 0-385-03400-8, A656, Anch). Doubleday.

Hut Hopping in the Austrian Alps. William E. Reifsnyder. LC 73-77290. (Totebook Ser). (Illus.). 224p. 1973. pap. 5.95 (ISBN 0-87156-081-X). Sierra.

Hutchinson's Clinical Methods. 16th ed. R. R. Bomford et al. (Illus.). 362p. 1975. 9.25 o.p. (ISBN 0-397-58154-8). Lippincott.

Hutchinson's Clinical Methods. 17th ed. Stuart Mason & Michael Swash. (Illus.). 495p. 1980. 14.50 (ISBN 0-397-58270-6). Lippincott.

Hutchinson's Clinical Methods. 17th ed. Stuart Mason & Michael Swash. 495p. 1980. 14.50 (ISBN 0-397-58270-6). Lippincott.

Hutterite Age Differences in Body Measurements. W. W. Howells & Hermann K. Bleibtreu. LC 78-115048. (Museum Papers 57, No. 2). (Orig.). 1970. pap. text ed. 10.00 (ISBN 0-87365-168-5). Peabody Harvard.

Huxley: His Life & Work. Gerald Leighton. 94p. 1980. Repr. lib. bdg. 15.00 (ISBN 0-8492-1649-4). R West.

Huxley: Selections from the Essays. Thomas H. Huxley. Ed. by Alburey Castell. LC 48-5544. (Crofts Classics Ser.). 1948. pap. text ed. 2.95x (ISBN 0-88295-043-6). AHM Pub.

HVAC Control Systems. Raymond K. Schneider. 400p. 1981. text ed. 19.95 (ISBN 0-471-05180-2). Wiley.

Hwa-Rang & Chung-Mu of Tae Kwon Do Hyung. Jhoon Rhee. LC 77-163382. (Ser. 109). (Illus.). 1971. pap. text ed. 5.95 (ISBN 0-89750-004-0). Ohara Pubns.

HWA Rang Do. Joo B. Lee. LC 78-52313. (Ser. 131). 1979. pap. 6.95 (ISBN 0-89750-070-9). Ohara Pubns.

Hwa Rang Do II, No. 134. Joo Bang Lee. 1980. pap. 6.95 (ISBN 0-89750-066-0). Ohara Pubns.

Hyacinths to Feed the Soul. Carol Amen. LC 74-33850. (Better Living Ser.). 64p. 1975. pap. text ed. 0.95 (ISBN 0-8127-0094-5). Southern Pub.

Hyaluronidase & Cancer. E. Cameron. 1966. 15.95 o.p. (ISBN 0-08-011480-6). Pergamon.

Hybridization Among the Subspecies of the Plethodontid Salamander Ensatina Eschscholtzi. Charles W. Brown. (U. C. Publ. in Zoology: Vol. 98). pap. 9.00x (ISBN 0-520-09442-5). U of Cal Pr.

Hybrids of Plants & Ghosts. Jorie Graham. LC 79-3210. (Princeton Series of Contemporary Poets). 1980. 8.75x (ISBN 0-691-06421-0); pap. 3.95 (ISBN 0-691-01335-7). Princeton U Pr.

Hyde Place. Virginia Coffman. 1977. pap. 1.75 o.p. (ISBN 0-449-23351-0, Crest). Fawcett.

Hydra-CMMP: An Experimental Computer System. W. A. Wulf et al. (Advanced Computer Science Ser.). (Illus.). 351p. 1980. text ed. 29.95 (ISBN 0-07-072120-3, C). McGraw.

Hydra Conspiracy. Philip Kirk. (Butler Ser.: No. 1). 1979. pap. 1.75 (ISBN 0-8439-0655-3, Leisure Bks). Nordon Pubns.

Hydra Head. Carlos Fuentes. Tr. by Margaret S. Peden from Sp. 292p. 1978. 9.95 (ISBN 0-374-17397-4); pap. 6.95 (ISBN 0-374-51563-8). FS&G.

Hydra-Matic Transmissions. Ron Sessions. (Orig.). 1981. pap. 9.95 (ISBN 0-89586-051-1). H P Bks.

Hydrabyss Red. William Tedford. (Timequest Ser.: No. 2). 1981. pap. 2.25 (ISBN 0-8439-0887-4, Leisure Bks). Nordon Pubns.

Hydration & Intermolecular Interaction: Infrared Investigations with Polyelectrolyte Membranes. George Zundell. 1970. 48.00 (ISBN 0-12-782850-8). Acad Pr.

Hydraulic & Pneumatic Cylinders. R. Brunell. (Illus.). 27.95x o.p. (ISBN 0-85461-049-9). Intl Ideas.

Hydraulic & Pneumatic Power & Control: Design, Performance, Application. F. Yeaple. 1966. 29.50 o.p. (ISBN 0-07-072257-9, P&RB). McGraw.

Hydraulic Behaviour of Estuaries. D. M. McDowell & B. A. O'Connor. 1977. 34.95x (ISBN 0-470-98922-X). Halsted Pr.

Hydraulic Cement Pastes, Their Structure & Properties: Proceedings. Univ. of Sheffield 8-9 April 1976 Conference. (Illus.). 1976. pap. 27.50 (ISBN 0-7210-1047-4). Scholium Intl.

Hydraulic Circuits & Control Systems. J. R. Fawcett. (Illus.). 32.500x o.p. (ISBN 0-685-90201-3). Intl Ideas.

Hydraulic Control Systems. Herbert E. Merritt. LC 66-28759. 1967. 39.00 (ISBN 0-471-59617-5, Pub. by Wiley-Interscience). Wiley.

Hydraulic Design of Pump Sumps & Intakes. M. J. Prosser. (Illus.). 1977. pap. 34.00 (ISBN 0-86017-027-6, Dist. by Air Science Co.). BHRA Fluid.

Hydraulic Engineering & the Environment. Compiled by American Society of Civil Engineers. 480p. 1973. pap. text ed. 12.50 (ISBN 0-87262-054-9). Am Soc Civil Eng.

Hydraulic Handbook. 7th ed. Ed. by Trade & Technical Press Ltd. (Illus.). 110.00 o.p. (ISBN 0-85461-074-X). Intl Ideas.

Hydraulic Machinery & Advanced Hydraulics. M. Manohar & P. Krishnamachar. 600p. Date not set. text ed. 37.50 (ISBN 0-7069-1194-6, Pub. by Vikas India). Advent Bk.

Hydraulic Machines Through Theory & Examples. C. B. Mishra. x, 318p. (Orig.). 1980. pap. text ed. 10.00x (ISBN 0-210-33860-1). Asia.

Hydraulic Modelling. J. J. Sharp. 1981. text ed. price not set (ISBN 0-408-00482-7). Butterworth.

Hydraulic Modelling: Theory & Practice. J. J. Sharp. 1981. text ed. price not set (Fnewnes-Butterworth). Butterworths.

Hydraulic Servo Mechanisms & Their Applications. J. R. Fawcett. (Illus.). 1970. 24.95x (ISBN 0-85461-026-X). Intl Ideas.

Hydraulic Technical Data, Vol. 4. Ed. by Trade & Technical Press Ltd. 21.00x (ISBN 0-85461-066-9). Intl Ideas.

Hydraulic Transport of Solids by Pipelines. A. G. Bain & S. T. Bonnington. 1971. text ed. 31.00 o.p. (ISBN 0-08-015778-5). Pergamon.

Hydraulics for off-the Road Equipment. Harry L. Stewart. LC 77-93790. 1978. 8.95 (ISBN 0-672-23306-1). Audel.

Hydraulics for the Fire Service: Hydraulic Field Equations, Vol. VI. National Fire Protection Association. Ed. by Paul R. Lyons. LC 78-50007. (Illus.). 72p. (Orig.). 1980. pap. text ed. 42.50 (ISBN 0-87765-171-X, SL-60). Natl Fire Prot.

Hydraulics in the Coastal Zone. Compiled by American Society of Civil Engineers. 376p. 1977. pap. text ed. 19.75 (ISBN 0-87262-085-9). Am Soc Civil Eng.

Hydraulics of Ground Water. Jacob Bear. (Water Resources & Environmental Engineering Ser.). (Illus.). 1980. text ed. 48.95 (ISBN 0-07-004170-9). McGraw.

Hydraulics of Multiple Mains. Goldman. 8.50 o.p. (ISBN 0-686-00161-3). Columbia Graphs.

Hydrides for Energy Storage: Proceedings of an International Symposium Held in Norway, Aug. 1977. Ed. by A. F. Andresen & A. Maeland. 1978. text ed. 90.00 (ISBN 0-08-022715-5). Pergamon.

Hydro-Electric Energy: Past - or Future? Robert V. Nelson. Ed. & illus. by Arthur F. Ide. (E Equals MC Squared Ser.: Vol. 14). (Illus.). 60p. 1980. 10.00 (ISBN 0-86663-802-4); pap. 6.95 (ISBN 0-86663-803-2). Ide Hse.

Hydro-Electric Engineering Practice: Mechanical & Electrical Engineering, Vol. 2. 2nd ed. Ed. by J. Guthrie Brown. (Illus.). 1970. 95.00x (ISBN 0-216-89056-X). Intl Ideas.

Hydro for the Eighties: Bringing Hydroelectric Power to Poor People. Ruben S. Brown. (Orig.). 1980. 15.00 (ISBN 0-936130-01-6). Intl Sci Tech.

Hydro-Power: The Use of Water As an Alternative Source. Charles Simeons. (Illus.). 560p. 1980. 89.00 (ISBN 0-08-023269-8). Pergamon.

Hydrobiology: A Text for Engineers & Scientists. Dietrich Uhlmann. LC 77-24258. 1979. 51.95 (ISBN 0-471-99557-6, Pub. by Wiley-Interscience). Wiley.

Hydrocarbon Fuels: Production Properties & Performance of Liquids & Gases. E. M. Goodger. LC 74-30837. 270p. 1975. 15.95 o.p. (ISBN 0-470-31365-X). Halsted Pr.

Hydrocarbons & Halogenated Hydrocarbons in the Aquatic Environment. Ed. by B. K. Afghan & D. Mackay. LC 79-26462. (Environmental Science Research Ser.: Vol. 16). 602p. 1980. 59.50 (ISBN 0-306-40329-3, Plenum Pr). Plenum Pub.

Hydrodynamic & Hydromagnetic Stability. S. Chandrasekhar. (Illus.). 704p. pap. write for info. (ISBN 0-486-64071-X). Dover.

Hydrodynamic Instabilities & the Transition to Turbulence. Ed. by H. L. Swinney & J. P. Gollup. (Topics in Applied Physics Ser.: Vol. 45). (Illus.). 320p. 1981. 56.60 (ISBN 0-387-10390-2). Springer-Verlag.

Hydrodynamic Stability. P. Drazin & W. Reid. LC 80-40273. (Cambridge Monographs on Mechanics & Applied Mathematics). (Illus.). 600p. Date not set. 77.00 (ISBN 0-521-22798-4). Cambridge U Pr.

Hydrodynamic Superposability. R. Ballabh. pap. 3.75x o.p. (ISBN 0-210-26873-5). Asia.

Hydrodynamics. 6th ed. Horace Lamb. (Illus.). 1932. pap. text ed. 8.95 (ISBN 0-486-60256-7). Dover.

Hydrodynamics of Micturition. Frank Hinman, Jr. (Illus.). 436p. 1971. 36.25 (ISBN 0-398-00839-6). C C Thomas.

Hydroelasticity of Ships. R. E. Bishop & W. G. Price. LC 78-67297. 1980. 90.00 (ISBN 0-521-22328-8). Cambridge U Pr.

Hydroelectricity Prospects in the New Energy Situation: Proceedings of a Symposium of the Committee on Electric Power of the United Nations Commission for Europe, Athens, Greece, 5-9 Nov. 1979. United Nations Economic Commission for Europe, Geneva, Switzerland. LC 80-40819. 530p. Date not set. price not set (ISBN 0-08-025702-X). Pergamon.

Hydrogen Bonding by C-H Groups. R. D. Green. LC 74-11310. 207p. 1974. 39.95 (ISBN 0-470-32478-3). Halsted Pr.

Hydrogen Energy Economy: A Realistic Appraisal of Prospects & Impacts. Edward M. Dickson et al. LC 76-56807. (Special Studies). 1977. text ed. 31.95 (ISBN 0-275-24290-0). Praeger.

Hydrogen Energy Progress: Proceedings, 4 vols. World Hydrogen Energy Conference, 3rd, Tokyo, Japan 23-26 June 1980 et al. Ed. by T. N. Veziroglu et al. LC 80-40559. (Advances in Hydrogen Energy: 2). (Illus.). 2500p. 1981. 385.00 set (ISBN 0-08-024729-6). Pergamon.

Hydrogen Energy System: Proceedings, 4 vols. World Hydrogen Energy Conference, 2nd, Zurich, Aug. 1978. Ed. by T. N. Veziroglu & W. Seifritz. LC 78-40507. 1978. Set. text ed. 410.00 (ISBN 0-08-023224-8). Pergamon.

Hydrogen: Its Technology & Implications, Vols. 2-5. Ed. by Kenneth E. Cox & Kenneth D. Williamson, Jr. Incl. Vol. 2. Transmission & Storage of Hydrogen. 144p. 1977. 44.95 (ISBN 0-8493-5122-7); Vol. 3. Hydrogen Properties. 336p. 1975. 67.95 (ISBN 0-8493-5123-5); Vol. 4. Utilization of Hydrogen. 256p. 1979. 59.95 (ISBN 0-8493-5124-3); Vol. 5. Implications of Hydrogen Energy. 144p. 1979. 44.95 (ISBN 0-8493-5125-1). LC 74-29484. (Uniscience Ser.). CRC Pr.

Hydrogen Power: An Introduction to Hydrogen Energy & Its Applications. L. O. Williams. LC 80-40434. (Illus.). 200p. 1980. 27.00 (ISBN 0-08-024783-0); pap. 11.00 (ISBN 0-08-025422-5). Pergamon.

Hydrogen Stopping Powers & Ranges in All Elements. Ed. by Hans H. Andersen & James F. Ziegler. LC 77-3068. 1977. text ed. 40.00 (ISBN 0-08-021605-6). Pergamon.

Hydrologic Cycle & the Wisdom of God: A Theme in Geoteleology. Yi-Fu Tuan. 1980. Repr. of 1968 ed. 20.00x (ISBN 0-8020-7112-0). U of Toronto Pr.

Hydrologic Information Systems. Ed. by G. W. Whetstone & V. J. Grigoriev. LC 72-90686. (Studies & Reports in Hydrology). (Illus.). 72p. (Orig.). 1973. pap. 9.25 (ISBN 92-3-100957-5, U289, UNESCO). Unipub.

Hydrologic Inventory of the Great Salt Lake Desert Area. Gary L Foote et al. 1971. 2.50 o.p. (ISBN 0-87421-062-3). Utah St U Pr.

Hydrological Maps: A Contribution to the International Hydrological Decade. (Studies & Reports in Hydrology: No. 20). (Illus.). 1977. pap. 22.50 (ISBN 92-3-101260-6, U292, UNESCO). Unipub.

Hydrology. A. J. Raudkivi. 1979. 68.00 (ISBN 0-08-024261-8). Pergamon.

Hydrology. 2nd ed. Chester O. Wisler & E. F. Brater. LC 59-14981. 1959. 23.95 (ISBN 0-471-95634-1). Wiley.

Hydrology & Quality of Water Resources. Mark J. Hammer & Kenneth A. Mackichan. LC 80-209. 400p. 1981. text ed. 19.95 (ISBN 0-471-02681-6). Wiley.

Hydrometry: Principles & Practices. R. W. Herschy. LC 78-4101. 1978. 81.00 (ISBN 0-471-99649-1, Pub. by Wiley-Interscience). Wiley.

Hydrophobic Effect: Formation of Micelles & Biological Membranes. Charles Tanford. 200p. 1973. 18.50 o.p. (ISBN 0-471-84460-8). Wiley.

Hydrophobic Interactions. Arieh Ben-Naim. LC 79-510. (Illus.). 325p. 1980. 32.50 (ISBN 0-306-40222-X, Plenum Pr). Plenum Pub.

Hydrophthalmia & Its Treatment: A General Study Based on 630 Cases in the Netherlands. F. G. Van Der Helm. 1963. 4.75 o.s.i. (ISBN 0-02-854100-6). Hafner.

Hydroponic Food Production: A Definitive Guide to Soilless Culture. Howard M. Resh. LC 78-23468. (Illus.). 1978. text ed. 14.95 (ISBN 0-912800-54-2). Woodbridge Pr.

Hydroponic Gardening: The Magic of Hydroponics for the Home Gardener. Raymond Bridwell. LC 72-86151. (Illus.). 224p. 1972. 7.95 (ISBN 0-912800-00-3); pap. 5.95 (ISBN 0-912800-09-7). Woodbridge Pr.

Hydroponics - the Food Farm of the Future: (a Guide to Modern Plant and Vegetable Care) (Illus.). 1980. pap. 12.95 o.p. (ISBN 0-930490-33-9). Future Shop.

Hydroponics for the Home Gardener: An Easy to Follow Step-by-Step Guide for Growing Healthy Vegetables, Herbs & House Plants Without Soil. Stewart Kenyon. 158p. 1980. pap. 6.95 (ISBN 0-442-29702-5). Van Nos Reinhold.

Hydroponics: Growing Without Soil. rev. ed. Dudley Harris. (Illus.). 160p. 1975. 22.50 (ISBN 0-7153-6397-2). David & Charles.

Hydrostatic Transmission Systems. J. Korn. 1970. pap. 10.00 (ISBN 0-7002-0189-0). Transatlantic.

Hydrotransport Bibliography. Ed. by Wendy A. Thornton. 1970. text ed. 25.00 (ISBN 0-900983-09-4, Dist. by Air Science Co.). BHRA Fluid.

Hydrotransport Seven: Papers Presented at the Seventh International Conference on the Hydraulic Transport of Solids in Pipes. Ed. by H. S. Stephens & L. Gittins. (Illus., Orig.). 1980. pap. 112.00. BHRA Fluid.

Hydrotransport Six: Proceedings, 2 vols. International Conference on the Hydraulic Transport of Solids in Pipes, 6th. Ed. by H. S. Stephens. 400p. 1979. Set. pap. 112.00 lib. ed. (ISBN 0-906085-21-7, Dist. by Air Science Co.). BHRA Fluid.

Hygenic Design & Operation of Food Plant. Ed. by R. Jowitt. (Illus., American edition). 1980. pap. text ed. 22.50 (ISBN 0-87055-345-3). AVI.

Hygiene. Jane E. Kozuszek. (First Bks.). (Illus.). (gr. 4 up). 1978. PLB 6.45 s&l (ISBN 0-531-01410-X). Watts.

Hygiene of the Brain & Nerves & the Cure of Nervousness. Martin L. Holbrook. LC 78-72799. Repr. of 1878 ed. 27.50 (ISBN 0-404-60862-0, RC351). AMS Pr.

Hygiene Standards of Chrysotile Asbestos Dust. British Occupational Hygiene Society. 1968. pap. text ed. 3.05 o.p. (ISBN 0-08-012995-1). Pergamon.

Hygienic System: Orthotrophy (Food & Feeding, Vol. 2. 8.25 o.p. (ISBN 0-686-20582-0). H M Shelton.

Hymenopterorum Catalogus. R. D. Shenfelt. (Hymenopterorum Catalogus Ser.: No. 16). 573p. 1980. pap. 137.00 (ISBN 0-686-28664-2, Pub. by Dr. W. Junk). Kluwer Boston.

Hymms to St. Geryon & Dark Brown. Michael McClure. LC 79-18173. 104p. 1980. pap. 5.95 (ISBN 0-912516-33-X). Grey Fox.

Hymn of the Universe. Pierre Teilhard De Chardin. LC 65-10375. 1969. pap. 3.95x (ISBN 0-06-131910-4, TB1910, Torch). Har-Row.

Hymnbook for Christian Worship. red 3.95 (ISBN 0-8170-9018-5); blue 3.95 (ISBN 0-8170-9019-3); beige 3.95 (ISBN 0-8170-9020-7); per 100 (red,blue or beige) 325.00; leather binding 12.50 (ISBN 0-8170-9022-3); organ ed. 4.95 (ISBN 0-8170-9021-5). Judson.

Hymnic Affirmation of Divine Justice. James L. Crenshaw. LC 75-22349. (Society of Biblical Literature. Dissertation Ser.). 180p. 1975. pap. 7.50 (ISBN 0-89130-016-3, 060124). Scholars Pr Ca.

Hymnology of the Eastern Orthodox Church. Savas J. Savas. 1977. pap. text ed. 9.00x (ISBN 0-8191-0161-3). U Pr of Amer.

Hymnos De Gloria; Sin Musica. (Spanish Bks.). 1977. 1.10 (ISBN 0-8297-0566-X). Life Pubs Intl.

Hymnos De Gloria y Triunfo; Sin Musica. (Spanish Bks.). 1977. 1.75 (ISBN 0-8297-0569-4). Life Pubs Intl.

Hymnos De Gloria y Triunfo; Sin Musica. (Spanish Bks.). 1977. 2.60 (ISBN 0-8297-0726-3). Life Pubs Intl.

Hymns & Tunes: An Index. Katharine S. Diehl. LC 66-13743. 1242p. 1979. lib. bdg. 45.00 (ISBN 0-8108-0062-4). Scarecrow.

Hymns As Poetry. Ed. by Sam Carr. 1980. 17.95 (ISBN 0-7134-3447-3). David & Charles.

Hymns for Choirs. Ed. by David Willcocks. 1976. pap. 5.00 (ISBN 0-19-353556-4). Oxford U Pr.

Hymns for Worship. 5.95 (ISBN 0-686-12671-8, BE-30); organist copy 15.00 (ISBN 0-686-12672-6). Evangel Indiana.

Hymns for Youth. National Union Of Christian Schools. (Illus.). 1966. pap. 3.95 o.p. (ISBN 0-8028-9002-4, Pub. by NUCS). Eerdmans.

Hymns from the Holy Granth. Ed. & tr. by Gobin S. Mansukhani. 1976. pap. 2.75 (ISBN 0-89253-063-4). Ind-US Inc.

Hymns II. Ed. by Paul Beckwith et al. LC 76-47503. 1976. text ed. 9.50 (ISBN 0-87784-898-X); pap. text ed. 5.95 (ISBN 0-87784-783-5); pap. text ed. 5.95 spiral text (ISBN 0-87784-750-9). Inter-Varsity.

Hymns in Prose for Children, Repr. Of 1781 Ed. Anna L. Barbauld. Bd. with Cheap Repository Tracts: The Shepherd of Salisbury Plain, the Two Wealthy Farmers, History of Tom White the Postilion, Black Giles the Poacher, & the History of Tawny Rachel the Fortune Teller, Black Giles' Wife. Hannah More. Repr. of 1797 ed. LC 75-32144. (Classics of Children's Literature, 1621-1932: Vol. 10). 1976. PLB 38.00 (ISBN 0-8240-2259-9). Garland Pub.

Hymns of Sankaras. T. M. Mahadevan. (Illus.). 188p. 1980. text ed. 16.50 (ISBN 0-8426-1652-7). Verry.

Hymns of the Atharva-Veda, Vol. 42. Ed. by F. Max Mueller. Tr. by Bloomfield. (Sacred Books of the East Ser.). 15.00x (ISBN 0-8426-1401-X). Verry.

Hymns That Live. Frank Colquhoun. 320p. 1981. pap. 6.95 (ISBN 0-87784-473-9). Inter Varsity.

Hymns to the Night & Other Writings. Novalis. Tr. by Charles Passage. LC 60-9556. 1960. pap. 2.95 (ISBN 0-672-60316-0, LLA115). Bobbs.

Hypatia; or, New Foes with an Old Face: 1853. Charles Kingsley. Ed. by Robert L. Wolff. (Victorian Fiction Ser.). 1975. lib. bdg. 66.00 (ISBN 0-8240-1571-1). Garland Pub.

Hyperactive Child. Domeena C. Renshaw. LC 73-86936. 1974. 13.95 (ISBN 0-911012-76-1). Nelson-Hall.

Hyperactive Child in the Classroom. Frank P. Alabiso & James C. Hansen. 336p. 1977. pap. 20.00 spiral (ISBN 0-398-03550-4). C C Thomas.

Hyperactivity: Research & Treatment Alternatives. Annette Geier. 1978. pap. 9.50 o.p. (ISBN 0-686-00910-X, D-112). Essence Pubns.

Hyperactivity: Research, Theory & Action. Dorothea M. Ross & Sheila A. Ross. LC 76-5227. (Personality Processes Ser.). 480p. 1976. 29.95 (ISBN 0-471-73678-3, Pub. by Wiley-Interscience). Wiley.

Hyperbolic Functions. V. G. Shervatov. (Topics in Mathematics Ser). 1963. pap. text ed. 2.95x o.p. (ISBN 0-669-19620-7). Heath.

Hypergraphics: Visualizing Complex Relationships in Art, Science & Technology. David W. Brisson. (Illus.). 1979. lib. bdg. 22.00x (ISBN 0-89158-292-4). Westview.

Hyperion. Friedrich Hoelderlin. (Insel-Bibliothek). 228p. 1980. leather bnd 46.80 (ISBN 3-458-04942-8, Pub. by Insel Verlag Germany); text ed. 18.20 (ISBN 3-458-04935-5). Suhrkamp.

Hypersonic & Planetary Entry Flight Mechanics. Nguyen X. Vinh et al. 376p. 1980. 29.95x (ISBN 0-472-10004-1). U of Mich Pr.

Hypersonic Flow Theory, Vol. 1: Inviscid Flows. 2nd ed. Ed. by Wallace D. Hayes & Ronald F. Probstein. (Applied Mechanics & Mathematics Ser.: Vol. 5). 1966. 48.75 (ISBN 0-12-334361-5). Acad Pr.

Hypertension. Julian T. Hart. (Library of General Practice Ser.). 296p. 1980. text ed. 18.75x (ISBN 0-443-01665-8). Churchill.

Hypertension. Herman Villarreal. (Becker-Perspectives in Nephrology & Hypertension Ser.). 448p. 1981. 35.00 (ISBN 0-471-07900-6, Pub. by Wiley Med). Wiley.

Hypertension: A Practitioner's Guide to Therapy. James C. Hutchinson. 1975. spiral bdg. 13.00 (ISBN 0-87488-709-7). Med Exam.

Hypertension & Cognitive Processes. Ed. by Merrill F. Elias & David H. Streeten. LC 80-22618. 165p. 1980. pap. text ed. 10.00 (ISBN 0-933786-04-2); 20.00 (ISBN 0-933786-04-2). Beech Hill.

Hypertension Control: A Manual for Nurses & Other Allied Health Professionals. Mahendra S. Kochar & Linda M. Daniels. LC 78-3750. 1978. pap. text ed. 11.95 (ISBN 0-8016-2717-6). Mosby.

Hypertension in Children & Adolescents. Ed. by G. Giovanelli et al. 364p. 1981. text ed. 33.00 (ISBN 0-89004-523-2). Raven.

Hypertension: Mechanisms & Management. Ed. by T. Philip & A. Distler. 279p. 1981. pap. 42.00 (ISBN 0-387-10171-3). Springer-Verlag.

Hypertension of Adults Twenty-Five to Seventy-Four Years of Age: United States, 1971-1975. Michael Rowland. Ed. by Audrey Shipp. (Ser. 11, No. 221). 50p. Date not set. text ed. price not set (ISBN 0-8406-0207-3). Natl Ctr Health Stats.

Hypertensions in Pregnancy. Norman F. Gant & Richard Worley. 224p. 1980. 18.50x (ISBN 0-8385-4002-3). ACC.

Hypertensive Heart Disease. B. E. Strauer. (Illus.). 106p. 1980. pap. 16.60 (ISBN 0-387-10041-5). Springer-Verlag.

Hypertention Research: Methods & Models. Radzialowski. Date not set. price not set (ISBN 0-8247-1344-3). Dekker.

Hypertrophic Ecosystems. Ed. by J. Barica & L. Mur. (Developments in Hydrobiology Ser.: No. 2). 330p. 1981. PLB 87.00 (ISBN 90-6193-752-3, Pub. by Dr. W. Junk). Kluwer Boston.

Hyphomycetes: Their Perfect-Imperfect Connexions. K. Tubaki. 300p. 1981. lib. bdg. 20.00x (ISBN 3-7682-1267-X). Lubrecht & Cramer.

Hypnerotomachia Poliphili. Francesco Colonna. LC 75-27842. (Renaissance & the Gods Ser.: Vol. 1). 1976. Repr. of 1499 ed. lib. bdg. 73.00 (ISBN 0-8240-2050-2). Garland Pub.

Hypnerotomachia: The Strife of Love in a Dreame. Francesco Colonna. Tr. by R. Dallington. LC 73-6347. (English Experience Ser.: No. 87). 200p. 1969. Repr. of 1592 ed. 28.50 (ISBN 90-221-0087-1). Walter J Johnson.

Hypnerotomachia, the Strife of Love in a Dreame. Francesco Colonna. LC 75-27858. (Renaissance & the Gods Ser.: Vol. 15). (Illus.). 1976. Repr. of 1592 ed. lib. bdg. 73.00 (ISBN 0-8240-2064-2). Garland Pub.

Hypnosis: A Clinical Study. S. Sunder Das. 1968. 5.50x (ISBN 0-210-22697-8). Asia.

Hypnosis: A Journey into the Mind. Anita Anderson-Evangelista. LC 79-27817. (Illus.). 256p. 1980. 10.95 (ISBN 0-668-04908-1, 4908-1). Arco.

Hypnosis: A Social Psychological Analysis of Influence Communication. Theodore R. Sarbin & William C. Coe. LC 72-185784. 1980. Repr. of 1972 ed. 21.00x (ISBN 0-8290-0388-6). Irvington.

Hypnosis & Behavior Therapy. Edward Dengrove. (Illus.). 428p. 1976. 36.75 (ISBN 0-398-03336-6). C C Thomas.

Hypnosis & Relaxation: Modern Verification of an Old Equation. William E. Edmonston. LC 80-22506. (Personality Processes Ser.). 280p. 1981. 21.00 (ISBN 0-471-05903-X, Pub. by Wiley Interscience). Wiley.

Hypnosis & Suggestibility: An Experimental Approach. Clark L. Hull. LC 33-30268. (Century Psychology Ser.). (Illus.). 1933. pap. text ed. 12.95x (ISBN 0-89197-223-4). Irvington.

Hypnosis at Its Bicentennial: Selected Papers. Ed. by F. H. Frankel & H. Zamansky. LC 78-16605. 320p. 1978. 27.50 (ISBN 0-306-40029-4, Plenum Pr). Plenum Pub.

Hypnosis Between Biology & Psychoanalysis. Leon Chertok. 220p. cancelled (ISBN 0-87630-244-4). Brunner-Mazel.

Hypnosis: Developments in Research & New Perspectives. 2nd ed. Erika Fromm & Ronald E. Shor. LC 79-89279. (Illus.). 1979. 42.95 (ISBN 0-202-26085-2). Aldine Pub.

Hypnosis, Imagination & Human Potentialities. Theodore X. Barber et al. LC 73-19539. 1974. 23.00 (ISBN 0-08-017932-0). Pergamon.

Hypnosis in Criminal Investigation. Frank J. Monoghan. (Orig.). 1980. pap. text ed. 6.95 (ISBN 0-8403-2132-5). Kendall-Hunt.

Hypnosis in Skin & Allergic Diseases. Michael Scott. (Illus.). 164p. 1960. pap. 8.00 spiral (ISBN 0-398-01703-4). C C Thomas.

Hypnosis in the Psychoses. W. Earl Biddle. 152p. 1967. pap. 12.75 photocopy ed. spiral (ISBN 0-398-00152-9). C C Thomas.

Hypnosis Induction Techniques. Myron Teitelbaum. 200p. 1980. 12.50 (ISBN 0-398-01907-X). C C Thomas.

Hypnosis Nineteen Hundred Seventy-Nine. Ed. by G. D. Burrows et al. LC 79-16095. 354p. 1979. 58.75 (ISBN 0-444-80142-1, North Holland). Elsevier.

Hypnosis: The Psychobiological Crossroads. Leon Chertok. 224p. 1981. 36.00 (ISBN 0-08-026793-9); pap. 18.00 (ISBN 0-08-026813-7). Pergamon.

Hypnosis: the Wakeful Sleep. Larry Kettelkamp. LC 75-17605. (Illus.). 96p. (gr. 5-9). 1975. 7.25 (ISBN 0-688-22045-2); PLB 6.96 (ISBN 0-688-32045-7). Morrow.

Hypnosis with Friends & Lovers. Freda Morris. LC 78-360. (Orig.). 1979. pap. 5.95 (ISBN 0-06-250600-5, RD 286, HarpR). Har-Row.

Hypnotherapy: An Exploratory Casebook. Milton Erickson & Ernest L. Rossi. LC 78-23839. 1979. 34.50 o.p. (ISBN 0-470-26595-7). Halsted Pr.

Hypnotic Realities: The Induction of Clinical Hypnosis & Forms of Indirect Suggestion. Milton H. Erickson et al. LC 76-20636. 1976. 24.95x (ISBN 0-8290-0112-3); two audio cassetes avail. Irvington.

Hypnotism. rev. ed. George H. Estabrooks. 1959. pap. 3.95 (ISBN 0-525-47038-7). Dutton.

Hypnotism. Carl Sextus. pap. 5.00 (ISBN 0-87980-076-3). Wilshire.

Hypodermic Injection: A Programed Unit. Elizabeth A. Krueger. LC 66-17379. (Orig.). 1965. pap. 7.50x (ISBN 0-8077-1650-2). Tchrs Coll.

Hypoglycemia: A Better Approach. Paavo Airola. 4.95 o.s.i. (ISBN 0-89557-040-8). Bi World Indus.

Hypolitus Earl of Douglas... with the Secret History of Mack-Beth King of Scotland. Marie C. Aulnoy. Bd. with Island of Content: A New Paradise Discovered. LC 70-170517. LC 76-170516. (Foundations of the Novel Ser.: Vol. 12). lib. bdg. 50.00 (ISBN 0-8240-0524-4). Garland Pub.

Hypothalamic Hormones, Vol. 1. Ed. by E. S. Hafez & J. R. Reel. LC 74-28654. (Perspectives in Human Reproduction Ser.). (Illus.). 1975. 24.00 (ISBN 0-250-40089-8). Ann Arbor Science.

Hypothalamic Hormones: Chemistry, Physiology & Clinical Applications. Derek Gupta & Wolfgang Voelter. (Illus.). 1978. 75.30 (ISBN 3-527-25712-8). Verlag Chemie.

Hypothalamic Hormones: Structure, Synthesis, & Biological Activity. Derek Gupta & Wolfgang Voelter. (Illus.). 1975. 34.20 (ISBN 3-527-25589-3). Verlag Chemie.

Hypothalamic Releasing Factors, Vol. 1. Wayne Watkins. 1977. 19.20 (ISBN 0-88831-002-1). Eden Med Res.

Hypothalamic Releasing Factors, Vol. 2, 1977. Wayne B. Watkins. Ed. by David F. Horrobin. (Annual Research Reviews Ser.). 1978. 21.60 (ISBN 0-88831-033-1). Eden Med Res.

Hypothalamo-Pituitary Control of the Ovary. J. S. Hutchinson. Ed. by D. F. Horrobin. (Annual Research Reviews Ser.: Vol. 2). 215p. 1980. 28.00 (ISBN 0-88831-091-9). Eden Med Res.

Hypothalamus. Ed. by L. Martini et al. 1971. 61.75 (ISBN 0-12-475550-X). Acad Pr.

Hypothalamus, Vol. 56. Ed. by Seymour Reichlin et al. LC 77-83691. (Association for Research in Nervous & Mental Disease Research Publications). 1978. 43.50 (ISBN 0-89004-167-9). Raven.

Hypothalamus & Central Levels of Autonomic Function: Proceedings, Vol. 20. Association For Research In Nervous And Mental Disease. (Illus.). 1966. Repr. of 1940 ed. 32.75 o.s.i. (ISBN 0-02-846330-7). Hafner.

Hypothalamus & Endocrine Functions. Ed. by Fernand Labrie et al. LC 76-13912. (Current Topics in Molecular Endocrinology Ser.: Vol. 3). 508p. 1976. 42.50 (ISBN 0-306-34003-8, Plenum Pr). Plenum Pub.

Hypothalamus & Pituitary in Health & Disease. Ed. by William Locke & Andrew V. Schally. (Illus.). 624p. 1972. 41.75 (ISBN 0-398-02526-6). C C Thomas.

Hypothalamus, Pituitary & Aging. Arthur V. Everitt & John A. Burgess. (Illus.). 808p. 1976. 67.50 (ISBN 0-398-03346-3). C C Thomas.

Hypothesis, Prediction, & Implication in Biology. Jeffrey J. Baker & Garland E. Allen. LC 68-30687. (Biology Ser). (Illus., Orig.). 1968. pap. 6.95 (ISBN 0-201-00482-8). A-W.

Hypothyroidism. John F. Hennessy. (Discussions in Patient Management Ser.). 1978. spiral 10.00 (ISBN 0-87488-898-0). Med Exam.

Hypothyroidism: The Unsuspected Illness. Broda Barnes & Lawrence Galton. LC 75-29251. 224p. 1976. 10.95 (ISBN 0-690-01029-X, TYC-T). T Y Crowell.

Hypovalemic Anemia of Trauma: The Missing Blood Syndrome. C. Robert Valeri & Mark D. Altschule. 224p. 1981. 64.95 (ISBN 0-8493-5389-0). CRC Pr.

Hysteria, Hypnosis, & Healing: The Work of J. M. Charcot. A. R. Owen. LC 75-88055. (Illus.). 1970. 7.50 o.p. (ISBN 0-912326-25-5). Garrett-Helix.

I

I A H S International Symposium on Housing Problems, 1976: Proceedings, 2 vols. P. F. Rad. Ed. by P. F. Rad et al. 1977. pap. 76.00 (ISBN 0-08-022121-1). Pergamon.

I Almost Burned in Hell. Peggy Joan Fontenot. 1978. 5.50 o.p. (ISBN 0-682-49078-4). Exposition.

I Almost Feel Thin. Albert J. Stunkard. LC 77-70403. 1977. pap. 5.95 o.p. (ISBN 0-915950-11-1). Bull Pub.

I Always Look up the Word "Egregious". Maxwell Nurnberg. 196p. 1981. 10.00 (ISBN 0-13-448720-6). P-H.

I Am - I Can. Daniel C. Steere. 128p. 1973. 4.95 o.p. (ISBN 0-8007-0618-8). Revell.

I Am a Dancer. Lynn Haney. (Illus.). 64p. (gr. 10 up). 1981. 8.95 (ISBN 0-399-20724-4); pap. 4.95 (ISBN 0-399-20792-9). Putnam.

I Am a Daughter of the Church. Marie Eugene. Tr. by M Verda Clare. 1981. pap. cancelled (ISBN 0-87061-050-3). Chr Classics.

I Am a Nymphomaniac. L. T. Woodward. 1975. pap. 1.50 o.p. (ISBN 0-685-52177-X, LB254DK, Leisure Bks). Nordon Pubns.

I Am: A Study of E. E. Cummings' Poems. Gary Lane. LC 75-38757. (Illus.). 144p. 1976. pap. 4.00x (ISBN 0-7006-0142-2). Regents Pr Ks.

I Am a Woman. Viveca Lindfors & Paul Austin. LC 76-740002. (Orig.). pap. 4.95 (ISBN 0-916840-01-8). Slohm Assoc.

I Am a Woman. Ella M. Miller. (Orig.). 1967. pap. 1.50 (ISBN 0-8024-3925-X). Moody.

I Am Blind & My Dog Is Dead. S. Gross. LC 77-7314. 1977. 7.95 (ISBN 0-396-07473-1). Dodd.

I Am Chrystie. Chrystie Jenner. LC 77-77949. (Illus.). 1977. pap. 4.95 o.p. (ISBN 0-89087-925-7). Les Femmes Pub.

I Am Curious (Yellow) Vilgot Sjoman. 1969. pap. 1.75 (ISBN 0-394-17133-0, B184, BC). Grove.

I Am Eyes. Ni Macho. Leila Ward. LC 78-1314. (Illus.). (gr. k-3). 1978. 8.95 (ISBN 0-688-80161-7); PLB 8.59 (ISBN 0-688-84161-9). Greenwillow.

I Am Happy. Maryann Dotts. (Illus.). (gr. k-2). 1971. 3.50 o.p. (ISBN 0-687-18203-4). Abingdon.

I Am Here: Yo estoy acqui. Rose Blue. LC 79-117183. (Illus.). (gr. k-3). 1971. PLB 4.33 o.p. (ISBN 0-531-01943-8). Watts.

I Am, I Can. Daniel C. Steere. 1976. pap. 1.50 (ISBN 0-89129-216-0). Jove Pubns.

I Am Learning to Live Because You Must Die: A Hospital Diary. Cordula Zickgraf. Tr. by David L. Scheidt from Ger. LC 80-2371. 144p. 1981. pap. 6.95 (ISBN 0-8006-1434-8, 1-1434). Fortress.

I Am Not Sure What You're Saying but I Can Relate. Steven A. Simon. 1980. pap. 3.95 (ISBN 0-9605594-0-X). Monkey Man.

I Am of Ireland. Cyril Reilly & Renee Reilly. (Illus.). 60p. (Orig.). 1981. pap. 6.95 (ISBN 0-03-059058-2). Winston Pr.

I Am of the Fourth Gospel: A Study in Johannine Usage & Thought. Philip B. Harner. Ed. by John Reumann. LC 72-123506. (Facet Bks.). 72p. (Orig.). 1970. pap. 1.00 (ISBN 0-8006-3060-2, 1-3060). Fortress.

I Am Persuaded. D. H. Read. (Scholar As Preacher Ser.). 190p. Repr. of 1961 ed. text ed. 7.75 (ISBN 0-567-04430-0). Attic Pr.

I Am That: The Science of Hamsa from Vijnana Bhairava, Vol. 24. Swami Muktananda. (Illus., Orig.). 1978. pap. 3.50 (ISBN 0-914602-27-6). SYDA Found.

I Am the Cat. Rosemary Kutak. 1964. pap. 0.95 o.s.i. (ISBN 0-02-022030-8, Collier). Macmillan.

I Am the Darker Brother: An Anthology of Modern Poems by Negro Americans. Ed. by Arnold Adoff. LC 68-12077. (gr. 7 up). 1968. 8.95 (ISBN 0-02-700080-X); pap. text ed. 2.12 (ISBN 0-02-296520-3). Macmillan.

I Am the Gate: Initiation & Discipleship. Bhagwan S. Rajneesh. (Orig.). 1977. pap. 4.95 (ISBN 0-06-090573-5, CN-573, CN). Har-Row.

I Am the Greatest. William D. Koller. (Pal Paperbacks, - Pal Skills II Ser.). (Illus.). (gr. 5-12). 1980. pap. text ed. 1.25 (ISBN 0-8374-6813-2). Xerox Ed Pubns.

I Am Worth It. Jan D. Kelley & Barbara J. Winship. LC 78-26111. 1979. 10.95 (ISBN 0-88229-291-9). Nelson-Hall.

I & My True Love. Helen MacInnes. 1978. pap. 2.25 (ISBN 0-449-23798-2, Crest). Fawcett.

I. Asimov: The Foundations of His Science Fiction. George E. Slusser. LC 78-1042. (Milford Ser.: Popular Writers of Today: Vol. 15). Date not set. lib. bdg. 8.95x (ISBN 0-89370-122-X); pap. 2.95 (ISBN 0-89370-222-6). Borgo Pr. Postponed.

I Believe. T. Rampa. pap. 2.50 (ISBN 0-685-88125-3). Weiser.

I Believe Because. Batsell B. Baxter. 1971. pap. 5.95 (ISBN 0-8010-0548-5). Baker Bk.

I Believe in God. 52p. 1975. 3.00. Natl Cath Educ.

I Believe in Miracles. Kath Kuhlman. 1975. pap. 1.50 (ISBN 0-89129-003-6). Jove Pubns.

I Believe in Miracles. Kathryn Kuhlman. 1969. pap. 1.95 o.s.i. (ISBN 0-515-04684-1). Jove Pubns.

I Believe in the Church. Watson. pap. 4.95. Eerdmans.

I Believe in the Holy Spirit. Michael Green. (I Believe Ser). 224p. 1975. pap. 3.95 (ISBN 0-8028-1609-6). Eerdmans.

I Believe in the Holy Spirit. Maynard James. LC 23-9036. Orig. Title: I Believe in the Holy Ghost. 176p. 1965. pap. 1.95 (ISBN 0-87123-241-3, 200241). Bethany Fell.

I Bought Me a Dog. Leonard Roberts. (Illus.). 1976. pap. 1.25. Pikeville Coll.

I Buried Hickok, the Memoirs of White Eye Anderson. Ed. by William Secrest. LC 80-65455. 300p. 1980. 17.50 (ISBN 0-932702-07-4); collector's edition 75.00 (ISBN 0-932702-08-2). Creative Texas.

I Called Him Babe: Elvis Presley's Nurse Remembers. Marian J. Cocke. LC 79-124443. (Twentieth Century Reminiscences Ser.). (Illus.). 160p. 1979. 10.95 (ISBN 0-87870-053-6); deluxe ed. 25.00 (ISBN 0-87870-056-0). Memphis St Univ.

I Came to Love You Late. Joyce Landorf. 1981. pap. 2.50 (ISBN 0-451-09897-8, E9897, Sig). NAL.

I Came to the City: Essays & Comments on the Urban Scene. Michael Eliot Hurst. 1975. pap. text ed. 10.95 (ISBN 0-395-17016-8). HM.

I Can--Can You, 4 bks. Peggy Parish. LC 79-26041. (Illus.). (ps). 1980. Set. 4.95 (ISBN 0-688-80279-6); write for info. pre-pack set. Greenwillow.

I Can Do It by Myself. Illus. by June Goldsborough. (Golden Sturdy Shape Bk.). (Illus.). 22p. 1981. 3.50 (ISBN 0-307-12123-2, Golden Pr). Western Pub.

I Can Do It by Myself. Lessie J. Little & Eloise Greenfield. LC 77-11554. (Illus.). (gr. k-2). 1978. 8.95 (ISBN 0-690-01369-8, TYC-J); PLB 7.89 (ISBN 0-690-03851-8). T Y Crowell.

I Can Do It: Manipulative Books. Beth Clure & Helen Rumsey. Incl. Come with Me (ISBN 0-8372-2169-2); Can You Guess (ISBN 0-8372-2170-6); What's Inside (ISBN 0-8372-2171-4); Sailor Said (ISBN 0-8372-2172-2); Matching Hands (ISBN 0-8372-2173-0); Surprise Boxes (ISBN 0-8372-2174-9); What Can It Be (ISBN 0-8372-2175-7); Mirror Magic (ISBN 0-8372-2176-5); Things I Like to Do (ISBN 0-8372-0367-8); Me (ISBN 0-8372-0363-5); Cowboy Can (ISBN 0-8372-0372-4); Where Is Home (ISBN 0-8372-0364-3); Through the Day (ISBN 0-8372-0366-X); Telling Tails (ISBN 0-8372-0365-1). (Illus.). (gr. k-2). 1976. text ed. 6.24 ea.; text ed. 75.00 set o.p. (ISBN 0-8372-3721-1, 2168); tchr's guide 6.00 (ISBN 0-8372-9130-5). Bowmar-Noble.

I Can Do It Myself. Emily P. Kingsley. (Sesame Street Starter Bks). (Illus.). 32p. (ps). 1981. 3.50 (ISBN 0-307-11604-2, Golden Pr). Western Pub.

I Can Draw Animals. Tony Tallarico. Ed. by Channa Taub. (I Can Draw Ser.). 80p. (Orig.). (gr. 3-7). 1980. pap. 2.50 (ISBN 0-671-41375-9). Wanderer Bks.

I Can Draw Cars, Trucks, & Other Wheels. Tony Tallarico. Ed. by Meg Scheider. (I Can Draw Ser.). 80p. (Orig.). (gr. 3-7). 1981. pap. 2.75 (ISBN 0-671-42535-8). Wanderer Bks.

I Can Eat an Elephant. Nancy Reese. Ed. by Alton Jordan. (Elephant Ser.). (Illus.). (gr. k-3). 1975. PLB 3.50 (ISBN 0-89868-012-3, Read Res); text ed. 1.75 softbd. (ISBN 0-89868-045-X). ARO Pub.

I Can Heal Myself & I Will. new ed. Cushing Smith. LC 62-14344. 1980. pap. 5.95 (ISBN 0-8119-0384-2). Fell.

I Can Lick Thirty Tigers Today! & Other Stories. Dr. Seuss. LC 71-86940. (Dr. Seuss Paperback Classics Ser.). (Illus.). 64p. (gr. k-3). 1980. pap. 2.95 (ISBN 0-394-84543-9). Random.

I Can Only Touch You Now. R. Levy. 1973. ref. ed. 13.95 (ISBN 0-13-448746-X); pap. text ed. 10.95 (ISBN 0-13-448738-9). P-H.

I Can Read, 8 bks. Sullivan Assoc. pap. text ed. 1.75 ea. Learning Line.

I Can Read French. Ed. by Penrose Colyer. LC 73-8788. 128p. (gr. 2 up). 1974. 6.90 o.p. (ISBN 0-531-02655-8); PLB 4.95 o.p. (ISBN 0-531-02654-X). Watts.

I Can Read Spanish. Penrose Colyer. LC 76-6136. (Illus.). 118p. (gr. 2 up). 1976. 4.95 o.p. (ISBN 0-531-02437-7); PLB 6.90 o.p. (ISBN 0-531-00333-7). Watts.

I Can Read Underwater Series, 10 bks. Bob Reese et al. Ed. by Alton Jordan. (Illus.). (gr. k-6). 1974. Set. PLB 35.00 (ISBN 0-89868-000-X); Set. pap. 17.50 (ISBN 0-89868-033-6). ARO Pub.

I Can Sell You Anything. Carl P. Wrighter. 1975. pap. 2.25 (ISBN 0-345-28462-3). Ballantine.

I Can Swim, You Can Swim. Tom Cuthbertson & Lee Cole. (Illus., Orig.). (gr. 4-8). 1978. pap. 4.00 (ISBN 0-913668-79-6). Ten Speed Pr.

I Can Use Tools. Judi R. Kesselman & Franklynn Peterson. (Illus.). 32p. (gr. 1-4). 1981. 5.95 (ISBN 0-525-66725-3). Elsevier-Nelson.

I Can Wait. Patricia Linn. (Orig.). 1980. pap. 2.25 (ISBN 0-505-51526-1). Tower Bks.

I Can Write - by Me, Myself. Theodore Le Sieg. (Illus.). (ps-1). 1971. 3.95 (ISBN 0-394-82323-0, BYR). Random.

I Cannot Go Back. Jimmy Snow & James Hefley. 1977. 5.95 o.p. (ISBN 0-88270-193-2); pap. 2.95 o.p. (ISBN 0-88270-194-0). Logos.

I Can't Always Hear You. Joy Zelonky. LC 79-23891. (Life & Living from a Child's Point of View Ser.). (Illus.). (gr. k-5). 1980. PLB 9.65 (ISBN 0-8172-1355-4). Raintree Child.

I-Can't-Draw Book. Jerry Warshaw. LC 73-165824. (Activity Bks.). (Illus.). 32p. (gr. 2 up). 1971. 6.50g (ISBN 0-8075-3502-8). A Whitman.

I Can't Stand Cindy, Lord. Barbara Bush. 1976. 4.95 o.p. (ISBN 0-310-22150-1). Zondervan.

I Care About Animals. Belton P. Mouras. LC 76-58590. (Illus.). 1977. cloth 9.95 (ISBN 0-498-02195-5); pap. 5.95 (ISBN 0-498-02195-5). A S Barnes.

I Cart. Michael Schnessel. Ed. by Jane West. 1981. 12.95 (ISBN 0-517-54399-0). Potter.

I Carve Stone. Joan Fine. LC 79-63798. (Illus.). (gr. 4-7). 1979. 7.95 (ISBN 0-690-03985-9, TYC-J); PLB 7.89 (ISBN 0-690-03986-7). T Y Crowell.

I Change Worlds. Anna L. Strong. LC 79-23128. (Illus.). 468p. 1979. pap. 7.95 (ISBN 0-931188-05-9). Seal Pr WA.

I, Charlotte Forten, Black & Free. Polly Longsworth. LC 79-109901. (gr. 5-8). 1970. 8.95 (ISBN 0-690-42869-3, TYC-J). T Y Crowell.

I Ching & Mankind. Diana F. Hook. 1975. 12.95 (ISBN 0-7100-8058-1). Routledge & Kegan.

I Ching, the Book of Change. Tr. by John Blofeld. 1968. pap. 3.95 (ISBN 0-525-47212-6). Dutton.

I Ching: The Book of Changes. I Ching. Tr. by James Legge. (Sacred Books of the East Ser.). 8.75 (ISBN 0-8446-2291-5). Peter Smith.

I-Ching: The Hexagrams Revealed. Gary G. Melyan & Wen-Kaung Chu. LC 76-6029. 1976. 8.75 (ISBN 0-8048-1182-2). C E Tuttle.

I Ching Workbook. R. L. Wing. LC 77-15142. 1979. pap. 7.95 (ISBN 0-385-12838-X). Doubleday.

I, Cleopatra. William Bostock. 1977. pap. 2.50 o.p. (ISBN 0-446-81379-6). Warner Bks.

I Confess. the Sacrament of Penance Today. Francis J. Buckley. LC 72-80971. (Illus.). 96p. 1972. pap. 1.25 o.p. (ISBN 0-87793-048-1). Ave Maria.

I Dare You! Judith Conaway. LC 76-46432. (Moods & Emotions Ser.). (Illus.). (gr. k-3). 1977. PLB 8.95 (ISBN 0-8172-0062-2). Raintree Pubs.

I, David. Harold Lakey. Ed. by Deborah Platt & Keith Wiesley. 250p. 1980. 10.95 (ISBN 0-934506-03-5). Westminster Comm & Pubns.

I David: Double Murder on Capitol Hill. H. L. Lakey. Ed. by Deborah Platt. 186p. 1981. 12.50 (ISBN 0-934506-03-5). Westminster Comm Pubns.

I Did It. Harlow Rockwell. LC 73-19059. (Ready-to-Read Ser.). (Illus.). 64p. (gr. 1-4). 1974. 6.95 (ISBN 0-02-777550-X). Macmillan.

I Didn't Know That. Douglas Leroy. 1973. pap. 1.75 (ISBN 0-87148-425-0). Pathway Pr.

I Didn't Know That: An Exhibition of First Happenings in Maryland. Edgar Heyl. LC 73-85764. (Illus.). 1973. 3.00 (ISBN 0-938420-07-0). Md Hist.

I Didn't Want to Be Nice. Penelope Jones. LC 76-57907. (Illus.). (ps-2). 1977. 7.95 (ISBN 0-87888-111-5). Bradbury Pr.

I Do Best Alone at Night. Gunnar Ekelof. Tr. by Robert Bly. 1977. 7.50 (ISBN 0-685-88901-7). Charioteer.

I Don't Believe in Elves. Jane Thayer. LC 74-32045. (Illus.). 32p. (ps-3). 1975. 7.25 o.p. (ISBN 0-688-22030-4); PLB 7.44 (ISBN 0-688-32030-9). Morrow.

I Don't Care. Marjorie W. Sharmat. LC 76-48251. (Illus.). (ps-1). 1977. 8.95 (ISBN 0-02-782290-7, 78229). Macmillan.

I Don't Want a Thunderbird Anymore: And New Poems. 2nd ed. Ilse Juergensen. 60p. 1980. pap. 5.00 (ISBN 0-934996-10-5). Am Stud Pr.

I Don't Want Much from Life - I Want More! Joan Kennedy. 204p. 1980. 9.95 (ISBN 0-8119-0335-4). Fell.

I Don't Want to Be Brave Anymore. Ruth T. Kaminska. LC 78-17417. (Illus.). 1978. 10.95 o.p. (ISBN 0-915220-42-3). New Republic.

I Don't Want to Go to School. Elizabeth Bram. LC 76-51274. (Illus.). (ps-3). 1977. 6.25 (ISBN 0-688-80095-5); PLB 6.00 (ISBN 0-688-84095-7). Greenwillow.

I Dreamed a College. Peter Sammartino. LC 76-1140. 9.95 (ISBN 0-498-01926-8). A S Barnes.

I E E E Four Eighty-Eight Interface Parts Handbook. C. W. Jensen & Eugene Fisher. 280p. (Orig.). 1980. pap. 6.99 (ISBN 0-931988-50-0). Osborne-McGraw.

I (EE), Bk. 7, Crystal. Helen Luster. (Illus.). 1979. 7.00 (ISBN 0-912662-22-0); pap. 5.00 (ISBN 0-912662-21-2). Fur Line Pr.

I Found a Feather. Paul Ricchiuti. LC 67-24371. (Hello World Ser.). 1967. pap. 1.65 (ISBN 0-8163-0309-6, 09020-9). Pacific Pr Pub Assn.

I Found Cleopatra. Thomas Kelley. LC 80-20507. 100p. 1980. Repr. of 1977 ed. lib. bdg. 11.95x (ISBN 0-89370-027-4). Borgo Pr.

I Found Cleopatra. Thomas P. Kelley. LC 77-87563. 1977. 5.95 (ISBN 0-913960-18-7). Fax Collect.

I Found the Key to the Heart of God. M. Basilea Schlink. LC 75-23920. 416p. 1975. pap. 3.95 (ISBN 0-87123-239-1, 200239). Bethany Fell.

I Giovedi Della Signora Giulia. Piero & Chiara. (Easy Readers, B). 1979. pap. 3.75 (ISBN 0-88436-292-2). EMC.

I Give Thee My Daughter: A Study on Marriage & Hierarchy Among the Anvil Brahmans of South Gujarat. K. W. Van Der Veen. (Studies in Developing Countries: No. 13). 336p. 1972. text ed. 24.50x (ISBN 0-685-23725-7). Humanities.

I Had the Craziest Dream Last Night: A Psychiatrist Helps You Interpret Your Dreams. Marion A. Steele & Ronald M. Armstrong. LC 73-169125. 1971. 11.95 (ISBN 0-911012-16-8). Nelson-Hall.

I Had Trouble in Getting to Solla Sollew. Dr. Seuss. LC 65-23994. (Dr. Seuss Paperback Classics Ser.). (Illus.). 64p. (gr. k-3). 1980. pap. 2.95 (ISBN 0-394-84542-0). Random.

I Had Wild Jack for a Lover. Meredith Marsh. 1978. pap. 1.95 o.p. (ISBN 0-449-23749-4, Crest). Fawcett.

I Hardly Knew You. Edna O'Brien. 1979. pap. 1.95 (ISBN 0-380-45138-7, 45138). Avon.

I Hate Boys - I Hate Girls. Paula Z. Hogan. LC 79-24056. (Life & Living from a Child's Point of View Ser.). (Illus.). (gr. k-5). 1980. PLB 9.65 (ISBN 0-8172-1358-9). Raintree Child.

I Hate Charades & Forty-Nine Other New Games. Phil Wiswell. LC 80-54341. (Illus.). 128p. 1981. 5.95 (ISBN 0-8069-4582-6); lib. bdg. 6.69 (ISBN 0-8069-4583-4). Sterling.

I Hate It. Miriam Schlein. Ed. by Caroline Rubin. LC 78-1744. (Self-Starter Bks.). (Illus.). (ps-2). 1978. 6.50 (ISBN 0-8075-3505-2). A Whitman.

I Hate Mondays! Brant Parker et al. 1978. pap. 1.25 o.p. (ISBN 0-449-13978-6, GM). Fawcett.

I Hate to Cook Almanack. Peg Bracken. 1977. pap. 2.50 (ISBN 0-449-23370-7, Crest). Fawcett.

I Hate to Go to Bed. Judi Barrett. LC 77-1583. (Illus.). 32p. (gr. k-3). 1977. 5.50 (ISBN 0-590-07472-5, Four Winds). Schol Bk Serv.

I Hate to Housekeep Book. Peg Bracken. 1977. pap. 1.75 o.p. (ISBN 0-449-23358-8, Crest). Fawcett.

I Hate to Take a Bath. Judi Barrett. LC 75-6955. (Illus.). 32p. (gr. k-3). 1975. 5.95 (ISBN 0-590-07429-6, Four Winds). Schol Bk Serv.

I Have a Ghetto in My Heart. James Steele. 1973. pap. 2.25 (ISBN 0-87148-428-5). Pathway Pr.

I Have a Horse of My Own. Charlotte Zolotow. (gr. 4-7). 7.95 (ISBN 0-690-04046-6). T Y Crowell.

I Have a Question, God. Jeannette W. Dward. (gr. 3-7). 4.95 (ISBN 0-8054-4265-0). Broadman.

I Have Abandoned My Search for Truth, & Am Now Looking for a Good Fantasy. Ashleigh Brilliant. LC 80-22852. (Illus.). 160p. (Orig.). 1980. 8.95 (ISBN 0-912800-66-6); pap. 4.95 (ISBN 0-912800-90-9). Woodbridge Pr.

I Have Been Thinking About You. Nita A. Jones. Date not set. 4.95 (ISBN 0-533-04784-6). Vantage.

I Have Believed: A Bishop Talks About His Faith. Earl G. Hunt, Jr. LC 80-50240. 175p. 1980. 6.95 (ISBN 0-8358-0401-1); pap. 4.50x (ISBN 0-8358-0403-8). Upper Room.

I Have Considered the Days. Cyrus Adler. (Illus.). 1969. 8.00x (ISBN 0-8381-3110-7). United Syn Bk.

I Have Loved You Already. Princess Orelia Benskina. 1975. 3.50 o.p. (ISBN 0-682-47871-7). Exposition.

I Have No Son. Gary Trudeau. (Doonesbury Ser.). (Illus.). 1975. pap. 1.75 (ISBN 0-445-08323-9). Popular Lib.

I Have Spoken: American History Through the Voices of the Indians. Ed. by Virginia I. Armstrong. LC 74-150755. xxii, 260p. 1971. 10.00 o.p. (ISBN 0-8040-0529-X, SB); pap. 5.95 (ISBN 0-8040-0530-3, Sb). Swallow.

I Have Two Families. Doris W. Helmering. LC 80-22392. 48p. (gr. 1-3). 1981. 8.95g (ISBN 0-687-18507-6). Abingdon.

I Haven't a Thing to Wear. Judith Keith. LC 76-57886. (Illus.). 1980. 12.95 (ISBN 0-913024-11-2). Tandem Pr.

I, He, We & They: A Literary Approach to Isaiah Fifty-Three. David J. Clines. (JSOT Supplement Ser.: No. 1). 65p. 1976. pap. text ed. 8.50x (ISBN 0-905774-00-0, Pub. by JSOT Pr England). Eisenbrauns.

I Hear Them Calling My Name: A Journey Through the New South. Chet Fuller. 320p. 1981. 12.95 (ISBN 0-395-30528-4). HM.

I Heard a Scream in the Street: Poetry by Young People in the City. Ed. by Nancy Larrick. LC 79-122820. (Illus.). 144p. (gr. 5 up). 1970. 7.95 (ISBN 0-87131-064-3). M Evans.

I Heard Singing. Molly K. Rankin. LC 74-27533. (Destiny Ser.). 1976. pap. 4.95 (ISBN 0-8163-0227-8, 09035-7). Pacific Pr Pub Assn.

I Heard the Owl Call My Name. Margaret Craven. LC 73-10800. 144p. 1973. 6.95 (ISBN 0-385-02586-6). Doubleday.

I Heard the Trumpet. M. E. Johnson. 5.95 o.p. (ISBN 0-8062-0940-2). Carlton.

I Hid in a Basket. Geoffrey Bull. (Hide & Seek Bks). 1975. 1.49 (ISBN 0-87508-881-3). Chr Lit.

I Hope I Get a Purple Ribbon. Ed. by Hal Lier & Howard Peterson. LC 80-50645. (Illus.). 110p. 1980. pap. text ed. 7.95 (ISBN 0-9604162-0-X). US Ski.

I, Juan De Pareja. Elizabeth B. De Trevino. LC 65-19330. 192p. (gr. 7 up). 1965. 8.95 (ISBN 0-374-33531-1). FS&G.

I Just Wanted Someone to Know. Bette Craig & Joyce Kornbluh. 1981. pap. price not set (ISBN 0-918266-16-5). Smyrna.

I Kept on Praying. Thomas Kilgore, Jr. (Prayer in My Life Ser.: Ser. II). 1974. pap. 1.00x (ISBN 0-8358-0315-5). Upper Room.

I Knew You'd Come! The Miracles of Jesus, Ser. A. Richard C. Hoefler. 80p. (Orig.). 1980. pap. text ed. 4.65 (ISBN 0-89536-444-1). CSS Pub.

I Know a Story. Charlotte Huber et al. (Wonder-Story Books Ser). (gr. 1). text ed. 7.60 (ISBN 0-06-517501-8, SchDept). Har-Row.

I Know an Old Lady Who Swallowed a Fly. Nadine B. Westcott. (gr. k-3). 32p. (ps-3). 1980. 8.95 (ISBN 0-316-93128-4, Pub. by Atlantic Monthly Pr); pap. 4.95 (ISBN 0-316-93127-6). Little.

I Know More About You Than You Ever Dreamed Possible. Verne Faust. LC 79-88004. 1980. 13.95 (ISBN 0-934162-00-X). Thomas Paine Pr.

I Know What I Like. Norma Simon. LC 76-165822. (Concept Bks.). (Illus.). (ps-2). 1971. 6.50g (ISBN 0-8075-3507-9). A Whitman.

I Know What It's Like to Die. Jonathan Ross. 1978. 8.95 o.s.i. (ISBN 0-8027-5386-8). Walker & Co.

I Know What You Did Last Summer. Lois Duncan. (gr. 7-9). 1975. pap. 1.95 (ISBN 0-671-41676-6). Archway.

I Know What You Did Last Summer. Lois Duncan. (gr. 7-9). 1975. pap. 1.75 (ISBN 0-671-56080-8). PB.

I Know You Cheated. Valjean McLenighan. LC 77-8623. (Moods & Emotions Ser.). (Illus.). (gr. k-3). 1977. PLB 8.95 (ISBN 0-8172-0962-X). Raintree Pubs.

I Learn to Read About Jesus: Primer. Leilah Runyon. (Basic Bible Readers Ser.). (Illus.). (gr. k-1). 1962. pap. 3.50 (ISBN 0-87239-257-0, 2754). Standard Pub.

I Learn to Write: 1978 Ed, 9 bks. Bell. Incl. Bk. A. (gr. k). pap. text ed. 2.92 (ISBN 0-8009-0255-6); tchr's. ed. 4.40 (ISBN 0-8009-0257-2); Bks. B-I. (gr. 1-8). pap. text ed. 2.44 ea. Bk. B (ISBN 0-8009-0259-9). Bk. C (ISBN 0-8009-0263-7). Bk. D (ISBN 0-8009-0269-6). Bk. E (ISBN 0-8009-0274-2). Bk. F (ISBN 0-8009-0278-5). Bk. G (ISBN 0-8009-0282-3). Bk. H (ISBN 0-8009-0288-2). Bk. I (ISBN 0-8009-0292-0); Bks. B-I, Tchr's. Eds. pap. 3.88 ea. Bk. B (ISBN 0-8009-0261-0). Bk. C (ISBN 0-8009-0265-3). Bk. D (ISBN 0-8009-0272-6). Bk. E (ISBN 0-8009-0276-9). Bk. F (ISBN 0-8009-0280-7). Bk. G (ISBN 0-8009-0286-6). Bk. H (ISBN 0-8009-0290-4). Bk. I (ISBN 0-8009-0294-7); Bks. C-G, Texas Edition. (gr. 2-6). Bk. C, Transition. pap. text ed. 2.00 (ISBN 0-8009-0250-5); Bks. D-G. pap. text ed. 2.20 ea. Bk. D (ISBN 0-8009-0240-8). Bk. E (ISBN 0-8009-0242-4). Bk. F (ISBN 0-8009-0244-0). Bk. G (ISBN 0-8009-0246-7). tchr's. ed. for Bk. C 3.88 (ISBN 0-8009-0252-1); Helping the Left-Handed Child. pap. 0.44 (ISBN 0-8009-0305-6); How Parents Help Pre-School Children Write. pap. 0.64 (ISBN 0-8009-0302-1); Learn Manuscript Writing - Student Bk. pap. 2.32 (ISBN 0-8009-0300-5); Transition - When? pap. 0.044 (ISBN 0-8009-0307-2). (gr. k-8). ABC reference & desk cards, charts, practice paper, pencils & pens avail.; 1968 & 1973 eds. of texts & tchr's. bks. also avail. Write for further info. McCormick-Mathers.

I Learned About Flying from That! Ed. by Editors of Flying Magazine. 1976. 10.95 (ISBN 0-440-04041-8, E Friede). Delacorte.

I Lift My Lamp. Alberta Smith. 1938. Repr. 3.50 o.p. (ISBN 0-685-88271-3). Metaphysical.

I Like Being Alone. Betty R. Wright. LC 80-25513. (Life & Living from a Child's Point of View Ser.). (Illus.). (gr. k-5). 1981. PLB 9.65 (ISBN 0-8172-1367-8). Raintree Child.

I Like Hats. Drawson. (ps-3). pap. 1.50 (ISBN 0-590-05800-2, Schol Pap). Schol Bk Serv.

I Like Jazz. Donald Myrus. (gr. 7 up). 1964. 3.95g o.s.i. (ISBN 0-02-768020-7). Macmillan.

I Like School. Michaela Muntean. (Sesame Street Early Bird Bks). (Illus.). 32p. (ps). 1981. 3.50 (ISBN 0-307-11602-6, Golden Pr). Western Pub.

I Like Things. Margaret Hillert. (Just Beginning-to-Read Ser.). (Illus.). (gr. 1-6). 1981. 4.39 (ISBN 0-695-41554-9); pap. 1.50 (ISBN 0-695-31554-4). Follett.

I Like to See: A Book About the Five Senses. Jean Tymms. (Tell-a-Tale Readers). (Illus.). (gr. k-2). 1973. pap. 4.77 (ISBN 0-307-68443-1, Whitman). Western Pub.

I Like Trains: Great Reading from THE Magazine of Railroading. Ed. by David P. Morgan. LC 80-84023. (Illus.). 104p. (Orig.). 1981. 6.50 (ISBN 0-89024-553-3). Kalmbach.

I Live in the City: A B C. Lou Moore. (Tell-a-Tale Readers). (Illus.). (ps-1). 1969. PLB 4.77 (ISBN 0-307-68554-3, Whitman). Western Pub.

I Live in the South of My Heart. Norman Moser. Ed. by Bill Herron. 60p. 1980. 2.00. Illuminations Pr.

I Looked Over Jordan & Other Stories. Ernie Brill. LC 80-51042. 344p. (Orig.). 1980. 15.00 (ISBN 0-89608-118-4); pap. 6.00 (ISBN 0-89608-117-6). South End Pr.

I Lost Everything in the Post-Natal Depression. Erma Bombeck. 1978. pap. 2.25 (ISBN 0-449-23785-0, Crest). Fawcett.

I Lost Them All but One. R. S. Hart. LC 80-81241. (Illus.). 200p. (Orig.). 1981. pap. 5.95 (ISBN 0-9604226-9-2). R S Hart.

I Love God - & My Husband. Marion Stroud. 96p. 1976. pap. 1.95 (ISBN 0-88207-734-1). Victor Bks.

I Love My Foster Grandparents. Beverly Amstutz. (Illus.). 204p. (gr. k-7). 1981. pap. 2.50 (ISBN 0-937836-06-0). Precious Res.

I Love My Grandma. Steven Palay. LC 76-46601. (Interaction 2 Ser.). (Illus.). (gr. k-3). 1977. PLB 7.95 o.p. (ISBN 0-8172-0067-3, Raintree Editions). Raintree Pubs.

I Love My Love with an A. Diana Ross. (Illus.). (ps-5). 1972. 6.95 (ISBN 0-571-09340-X, Pub. by Faber & Faber). Merrimack Bk Serv.

I Love New York Guide, 1981. Compiled by Marilyn Appleberg. (Illus.). 208p. 1981. pap. 3.95 (ISBN 0-02-097220-2, Collier). Macmillan.

I Love: The Story of Vladimir Mayakovsky & Lili Brik. Ann Charters & Samuel Charters. 432p. 1979. 17.50 (ISBN 0-374-17406-7). FS&G.

I Love to Tell the Story. Joseph Bayly. 1978. pap. 1.50 o.p. (ISBN 0-89191-162-6). Cook.

I Love You. Muktananda. (Illus.). 22p. (Orig.). 1975. pap. text ed. 1.25 (ISBN 0-914602-58-6). SYDA Found.

I Love You, I Hear You. Craig Massey. 160p. 1980. text ed. 6.95 (ISBN 0-8024-3957-8). Moody.

I Love You, Ugly Old Hag! Earlene G. Evans. 1981. 4.50 (ISBN 0-533-04488-X). Vantage.

I Loved a Girl. Walter Trobisch. LC 75-12281. (Jubilee Bks.). 128p. 1975. pap. 3.95 (ISBN 0-06-068443-7, RD 352, HarpR). Har-Row.

I Loved You Wednesday. David Marlow. 1976. pap. 1.75 o.p. (ISBN 0-345-24950-X). Ballantine.

I Married a Best Seller. Sheila Hailey. LC 77-76235. 1978. 8.95 o.p. (ISBN 0-385-12337-X). Doubleday.

I Married You. Walter Trobisch. LC 78-148437. (Jubilee Bks.). 144p. 1975. pap. 3.95 (ISBN 0-06-068452-6, RD 351, HarpR). Har-Row.

I May Not Be Totally Perfect, but Parts of Me Are Excellent. Ashleigh Brilliant. LC 79-10052. (Illus.). 1979. 7.95 (ISBN 0-912800-66-6); pap. 4.95 (ISBN 0-912800-67-4). Woodbridge Pr.

I, Me, My, We: From the Orient to a Kansas Ranch & Chick Hatchery, with Much Fun Along the Way. Edith H. Stewart. (Illus.). 151p. 1963. 3.95 (ISBN 0-8040-0084-0). Swallow.

I. N. L. Ira L. Swett. Ed. by Mark Effle. (Extra Three Ser.). 1978. pap. 13.00 (ISBN 0-916374-34-3). Interurban.

I Need a Hug. Bil Keane. (Family Circus Ser.). (Illus., Orig.). 1978. pap. 1.50 (ISBN 0-449-14147-0, GM). Fawcett.

I Need Help! 1977. pap. 3.50 (ISBN 0-911336-68-0). Sci of Mind.

I Need to Have You Know Me. Roland Larson & Doris Larson. (Orig.). 1980. pap. 7.95 (ISBN 0-03-053431-3). Winston Pr.

I Never Said I Didn't Love You. Robert Griffin. LC 76-24442. (Emmuas Book Ser.). 1977. pap. 1.95 (ISBN 0-8091-1989-7). Paulist Pr.

I Never Say I'm Thankful, but I Am. Jane B. Moncure. LC 78-21577. (Illus.). (ps-3). 1979. PLB 5.95 (ISBN 0-89565-023-1). Childs World.

I Never Walked Alone. Jessie Hickford. LC 76-10556. 1977. 6.95 o.p. (ISBN 0-312-40250-3). St Martin.

I Never Win! Judy Delton. LC 80-27618. (Carolrhoda on My Own Bk). (Illus.). 32p. (gr. k-3). 1981. PLB 5.95 (ISBN 0-87614-139-4). Carolrhoda Bks.

I-O Design: Data Management in Operating Systems. Donald E. Freeman & Olney R. Perry. (Illus.). 1977. text ed. 19.95x (ISBN 0-8104-5789-X). Hayden.

I Once Knew a Man. Franz Brandenberg. (Illus.). (gr. k-2). 1970. 4.95g o.s.i. (ISBN 0-02-711900-9). Macmillan.

I Once Spoke in Tongues. Wayne Robinson. pap. 1.50 (ISBN 0-89129-013-3). Jove Pubns.

I Only Work Here. 15.00; pap. 7.95. Primary Pr.

I-Opener. R. Platt. 1976. pap. 11.95 (ISBN 0-13-448779-6). P-H.

I Owe My Life to Jesus -- You Also? An Autobiography Charismatic. H. Winky-Lotz. (Illus.). 210p. 1980. 11.95 (ISBN 0-936112-00-X); pap. 7.95 (ISBN 0-936112-01-8). Willyshe Pub.

I Pick up Hitchhikers. Edwin T. Dahlberg. LC 77-25498. 1978. pap. 2.95 o.p. (ISBN 0-8170-0774-1). Judson.

I Pledge You My Troth: Marriage, Family, Friendship. James Olthuis. LC 74-25695. 160p. 1975. 4.95 (ISBN 0-06-066394-4, RD-155, HarpR). Har-Row.

I, Priscilla. Evelyn A. Hammett. (Illus.). (gr. 4-6). 1960. 3.00 o.s.i. (ISBN 0-02-742550-9). Macmillan.

I Promise You My Love. Ed. by Susan P. Schutz. (Illus.). 64p. (Orig.). 1981. pap. 4.95 (ISBN 0-88396-129-6). Blue Mtn Pr CO.

I Promise You Tomorrow. Freda Delphine. LC 73-91782. (Illus.). 112p. 1974. 5.95 (ISBN 0-88415-660-5). Pacesetter Pr.

I R R I Annual Report for Nineteen Seventy-Five. 479p. 1976. pap. 37.50 (R090, IRRI). Unipub.

I R R I Annual Report for Nineteen Seventy-Six. 418p. 1977. pap. 43.00 (R089, IRRI). Unipub.

I R R I Annual Report for Nineteen Seventy-Seven. 548p. 1978. pap. 43.00 (R088, IRRI). Unipub.

I Ran Away from Home Last Week. Katie Tonn. (Uplook Ser.). 1975. pap. 0.75 (ISBN 0-8163-0174-3, 09107-4). Pacific Pr Pub Assn.

I Read About God's Gifts. Carol Ferntheil. (Basic Bible Readers Ser.). (Illus.). (gr. 2). 1962. kivar 4.50 (ISBN 0-87239-259-7, 2756). Standard Pub.

I Read About God's Love. Carol Ferntheil. (Basic Bible Readers Ser.). (Illus.). (gr. 1). 1962. pap. 4.50 (ISBN 0-87239-258-9, 2755). Standard Pub.

I Realized God Via Mathematics. David Ferriz. Tr. by Patrick Norris from Span. 300p. (Orig.). 1980. pap. 5.95 (ISBN 0-89260-191-4). Hwong Pub.

I Really Should Be Practicing. Gary Graffman. LC 80-1119. 288p. 1980. 14.95 (ISBN 0-385-15559-X). Doubleday.

I Remain: The Letters of Lew Welch with the Correspondence of His Friends, Volume 2. Lew Welch. Ed. by Donald Allen. LC 79-21574. 208p. 1980. 12.00 (ISBN 0-912516-41-0); pap. 5.95 (ISBN 0-912516-42-9). Grey Fox.

I Remain, Your Uncle Ambrogio. Gene Horwitz. 1977. pap. 1.50 o.p. (ISBN 0-445-03197-2). Popular Lib.

I Remember. Joe Brainard. LC 75-23153. 1975. 14.95 (ISBN 0-916190-02-1); pap. 6.00 (ISBN 0-916190-03-X). Full Court NY.

I Remember America. Eric Sloane. (Funk & W Bk.). (Illus.). 1971. 14.95 o.p. (ISBN 0-308-70041-4, TYC-T). T Y Crowell.

I Remember My Brother Morris. Irving Klein. 1978. 4.50 o.p. (ISBN 0-682-48992-1). Exposition.

I Remember Root River. David Kherdian. LC 77-80201. 72p. 1978. 10.00 (ISBN 0-87951-065-X). Overlook Pr.

I Remember Root River. David Kherdian. LC 77-80201. 72p. Date not set. pap. 6.95 (ISBN 0-87951-127-3). Overlook Pr.

I Remember: Sketch for an Autobiography. Boris Pasternak. Tr. by David Magarshack. (Illus., With an essay "Translating Shakespeare"). 8.00 (ISBN 0-8446-2710-0). Peter Smith.

I Remember the Room Was Filled with Light. Judith Hemschemeyer. LC 72-11055. (Wesleyan Poetry Program: Vol. 66). 72p. 1973. pap. 4.95 (ISBN 0-8195-1066-1, Pub. by Wesleyan U Pr). Columbia U Pr.

I Ricordi Di Firenze. Bernard H. Porter. 60p. 1981. lib. bdg. 28.50 (ISBN 0-686-68872-4). Porter.

I, Roberta. Elizabeth G. Vining. LC 67-26611. 1967. 4.95 o.s.i. (ISBN 0-397-00468-0). Lippincott.

I, Robot. Isaac Asimov. LC 63-6943. 6.95 o.p. (ISBN 0-385-05048-8). Doubleday.

I. S. Q. D. (Identification System for Questioned Documents) Billy P. Bates. (Illus.). 112p. 1970. text ed. 9.75 (ISBN 0-398-00108-1). C C Thomas.

I. S. Turgenev: Dvoryanskoye Gnezdo. Ed. by P. Waddington. 1969. 22.00 (ISBN 0-08-012923-4); pap. 10.75 (ISBN 0-08-012922-6). Pergamon.

I Saw a Ship A-Sailing. Janina Domanska. LC 75-185147. (Illus.). (ps-3). 1972. 8.95 (ISBN 0-02-732940-2). Macmillan.

I Saw Booth Shoot Lincoln. W. J. Ferguson. LC 70-20379. (Illus.). 8.50 (ISBN 0-8363-0052-1). Jenkins.

I Saw Heaven Opened: The Message of Revelation. M. Wilcock. LC 74-31845. (Bible Speaks Today Ser.). 1975. pap. 5.25 (ISBN 0-87784-774-6). Inter-Varsity.

I Saw the World End: A Study of Wagner's Ring. Deryck Cooke. 1979. 19.95 (ISBN 0-19-315316-5). Oxford U Pr.

I Say! Arthur Marshall. 1978. 14.95 (ISBN 0-241-89682-7, Pub. by Hamish Hamilton England). David & Charles.

I See a Child: Learning About Learning. Cindy Herbert. LC 72-96280. 112p. 1974. pap. 2.95 (ISBN 0-385-04158-6, Anch). Doubleday.

I See a Song. Eric Carle. LC 72-9249. (Illus.). (ps-2). 1973. PLB 9.79 (ISBN 0-690-43307-7, TYC-J). T Y Crowell.

I See the Wind. James A. Wright. LC 74-81875. 70p. 1974. pap. 5.00 o.p. (ISBN 0-8283-1574-4). Branden.

I See You Burned the Cold Cuts Again. Bill Hoest. (Lockhorns No. 5). (Orig.). 1981. pap. 1.50 (ISBN 0-451-09711-4, J9711, Sig). NAL.

I Shall Not Want. Robert T. Ketcham. 1953. pap. 1.50 (ISBN 0-8024-0130-9). Moody.

I Shall Return: Jesus. Jerry Vines. 1977. pap. 2.50 (ISBN 0-88207-702-3). Victor Bks.

I Share God's Special Meal: My First Communion Book. Catherine Winter. 1977. 6.95 o.p. (ISBN 0-03-021251-0, 892). Winston Pr.

I Should Be Glad to Help You, Madame. Vienna I. Curtiss. LC 78-58850. 6.00 (ISBN 0-9602742-1-9). Collectors Choice.

I Should Have Seen It Coming When the Rabbit Died. Teresa Bloomingdale. 208p. 1980. pap. 2.25 (ISBN 0-553-13744-1). Bantam.

I Should Have Sold Petunias. Don Honig. (Orig.). 1977. pap. 1.50 o.s.i. (ISBN 0-515-04357-5). Jove Pubns.

I Should Worry, I Should Care. Miriam Chaikin. (gr. k-6). 1981. pap. price not set (ISBN 0-440-44149-8, YB). Dell.

I Shoulda Been Home Yesterday. David Harris. 1976. 7.95 o.s.i. (ISBN 0-440-04156-2, Sey Lawr). Delacorte.

I Sing the Song of Myself: An Anthology of Autobiographical Poems. Ed. by David Kherdian. LC 78-5807. (gr. 7-9). 1978. 8.95 (ISBN 0-688-80172-2); PLB 8.59 (ISBN 0-688-84172-4). Greenwillow.

I Take This Woman. Rajinder S. Bedi. Tr. by Khushwant Singh. 103p. 1967. pap. 2.25 (ISBN 0-88253-014-3). Ind-US Inc.

I Tell a Lie Every So Often. Bruce Clements. LC 73-22356. 160p. (gr. 7 up). 1974. 9.95 (ISBN 0-374-33619-9, 374-33619-9). FS&G.

I That Was Born in Wales: A New Selection from the Poems of Vernon Watkins. Vernon Watkins. Ed. by Gwen Watkins & R. Pryor. 1976. bds. 8.00 (ISBN 0-7083-0615-2). Verry.

I, the Jury. Mickey Spillane. 1972. pap. 1.75 (ISBN 0-451-08309-1, E9067, Sig). NAL.

I: The Story of the Self. Michal J. Eastcott. LC 80-51552. (Illus.). 201p. (Orig.). 1980. pap. 5.50 (ISBN 0-8356-0541-8, Quest). Theos Pub Hse.

I Thessalonians, II Thessalonians, Philippians, Philomen. Ernest W. Saunders. Ed. by John H. Hayes. (Preaching Guides Ser.). (Orig.). 1981. pap. 4.50 (ISBN 0-8042-3241-5). John Knox.

I Think...I Know: A Poster Book About God. Joan Hutson. (Illus.). 32p. (Orig.). (gr. 2-4). 1979. pap. 1.95 (ISBN 0-87793-186-0). Ave Maria.

I Thought of It First. Russel C. Alexander. (Illus.). 102p. (Orig.). pap. 6.95 (ISBN 0-918146-21-6). Peninsula Pub WA.

I, Tom Horn. Will Henry. LC 74-23407. 1975. 7.95 o.s.i. (ISBN 0-397-01073-7). Lippincott.

I Too Am Here. Ed. by Alan Simpson & Mary Simpson. LC 76-11093. (Illus.). 1977. 26.50 (ISBN 0-521-21304-5). Cambridge U Pr.

I, Too, Sing America: Black Voices in American Literature. Barbara D. Stanford. (gr. 10). 1971. text ed. 6.85x o. p. (ISBN 0-8104-5864-0); pap. text ed. 5.95x (ISBN 0-8104-5863-2). Hayden.

I Touch the Earth, the Earth Touches Me. Hugh Prather. LC 72-79420. 160p. 1972. pap. 3.95 (ISBN 0-385-05063-1). Doubleday.

I Tried to Run a Railway. G. F. Fiennes. pap. text ed. 14.95x (ISBN 0-392-07972-0, SpS). Soccer.

I, Tut: The Boy Who Became Pharaoh. Miriam Schlein. LC 78-15603. (Illus.). 48p. 1979. 8.95 (ISBN 0-590-07571-3, Four Winds). Schol Bk Serv.

I, Victoria. Sam Dodson. 1979. pap. 1.95 o.p. (ISBN 0-449-14152-7, GM). Fawcett.

I Want a Brother or Sister. Astrid Lindgren. Tr. by Barbara Lucas from Swedish. (Illus.). 32p. (ps-3). 1981. 7.95 (ISBN 0-15-239387-0, HJ). HarBraceJ.

I Want Happiness Now! Henry Brandt & Phil Landrum. 1978. 6.95 (ISBN 0-310-21640-0); pap. 4.95 (ISBN 0-310-21641-9). Zondervan.

I Want My Mummy. Alfred Hitchcock. 1981. pap. 2.25 o.s.i. (ISBN 0-440-13985-6). Dell.

I Want My Sunday, Stranger. Patricia Beatty. (gr. 7 up). 1977. 9.25 (ISBN 0-688-22118-1); PLB 8.88 (ISBN 0-688-32118-6). Morrow.

I Want to Be a Postal Clerk. Eugene Baker. LC 75-38520. (I Want to Be Bks.). (Illus.). 32p. (gr. k-4). 1976. PLB 7.95 o.p. (ISBN 0-516-01738-1). Childrens.

I Want to Be a Service Station Attendant. Eugene Baker. LC 70-178495. (I Want to Be Books). (Illus.). 32p. (gr. k-4). 1972. PLB 7.95 o.p. (ISBN 0-516-01797-7). Childrens.

I Want to Be Me. Bastien. (gr. 7-12). pap. 0.95 o.p. (ISBN 0-686-68467-2, Schol Pap). Schol Bk Serv.

I Want to Change, but I Don't Know How. Tom Rusk & Randy Read. 1979. pap. 7.95 (ISBN 0-915520-19-2). Ross-Erikson.

I Want to Change, but I Don't Know How. rev. & enl. 2nd ed. Tom Rusk & Randy Read. 367p. 1980. pap. 7.95 (ISBN 0-915520-19-2). Comm Creat.

I Want to Enjoy My Children. Henry Brandt & Phil Landrum. 160p. 1975. 5.95 (ISBN 0-310-21630-3); pap. 4.95 (ISBN 0-310-21631-1). Zondervan.

I Want to Know About the United States Senate. Percy, Charles, Senator. 96p. (gr. 3-7). 1976. 5.95 o.p. (ISBN 0-385-00192-4). Doubleday.

I Want to Read. Betty R. Wright. (Illus.). (ps-2). 1965. 1.95 (ISBN 0-307-10879-1, Golden Pr); PLB 7.62 (ISBN 0-307-60879-4). Western Pub.

I Want to See God. Marie Eugene. Tr. by M. Verda Clare. 1981. pap. cancelled (ISBN 0-87061-051-1). Chr Classics.

I Want to Talk: A Child Model of American Sign Language. Harry W. Hoemann & Rosemarie Lucafo. 189p. 1981. pap. text ed. 7.95x (ISBN 0-913072-41-9). Natl Assn Deaf.

I Wanted to See. Borghild Dahl. 1967. 8.95 (ISBN 0-02-529380-X). Macmillan.

I Was a Kamikaze. Ruyji Nagatsuka. LC 72-11281. (Illus.). 224p. 1974. 6.95 o.s.i. (ISBN 0-02-588280-5). Macmillan.

I Was a Male War Bride. Henri Rochard. (Illus.). 1977. Repr. lib. bdg. 5.00 (ISBN 0-686-21179-0). Maple Mont.

I Was a Stranger. Susan Davis. LC 78-58077. (Destiny Ser.). 1979. pap. 4.95 (ISBN 0-8163-0237-5). Pacific Pr Pub Assn.

I Was Quisling's Secretary. Franklin Knudsen. 192p. 1967. 6.00 (ISBN 0-911038-96-5, 351, Inst Hist Rev). Noontide.

I Was Quisling's Secretary. Franklin Knudsen. 192p. 1967. 6.00 (351, Pub. by Britons England). Inst Hist Rev.

I Was So Mad! Norma Simon. LC 73-22425. (Concept Bks.). (Illus.). 40p. (gr. k-2). 1974. 6.50g (ISBN 0-8075-3520-6). A Whitman.

I Watch Lois. Laurence Klavan. 192p. (Orig.). 1981. pap. 1.95 (ISBN 0-523-41318-1). Pinnacle Bks.

I, Weapon. Charles Runyon. pap. 1.50 o.p. (ISBN 0-445-04127-7). Popular Lib.

I Welcome You All with Love. Swami Muktananda. (Illus., Orig.). 1978. pap. 1.25 (ISBN 0-914602-59-4). SYDA Found.

I Will Be Called John. Lawrence Elliott. 1974. pap. 1.75 o.p. (ISBN 0-425-02735-X, Medallion). Berkley Pub.

I Will Fight No More Forever. Merrill D. Beal. 1975. pap. 2.50 (ISBN 0-345-28461-5). Ballantine.

I Will Fight No More Forever: Chief Joseph & the Nez Perce War. Merrill D. Beal. LC 62-13278. (Illus.). 384p. 1963. pap. 6.95 (ISBN 0-295-74009-4). U of Wash Pr.

I Will Not Go to Market Today. Harry Allard. LC 78-72474. (Illus.). 32p. (ps-2). 1981. pap. 2.75 (ISBN 0-8037-4178-2, Pied Piper Bk). Dial.

I Will Tell You About God. Hans Froer. Tr. by E. Theodore Bachmann from Ger. LC 78-14666. 80p. (gr. k up). 1979. pap. 3.50 (ISBN 0-8006-1350-3, 1-1350). Fortress.

I Wish I Could Give My Son a Wild Raccoon. Ed. by Eliot Wigginton. LC 76-5343. 1976. pap. 4.95 (ISBN 0-385-11391-9, Anchor Pr). Doubleday.

I Wish I Had Known. Symposium. 0.95 o.p. (ISBN 0-310-33122-6). Zondervan.

I Wish I Was Sick, Too. Franz Brandenberg. LC 75-46610. (Illus.). (gr. k-3). 1976. 8.25 (ISBN 0-688-80047-5); PLB 7.92 (ISBN 0-688-84047-7). Greenwillow.

I Won't Go Without a Father. Muriel Stanek. LC 78-188435. (Concept Bks.). (Illus.). 32p. (gr. 1-4). 1972. 6.50g (ISBN 0-8075-3524-9). A Whitman.

I Would Have Searched Forever. Sandra K. Musser. (Orig.). 1980. pap. 4.95 (ISBN 0-88270-487-7). Logos.

IAEA Laboratory Activities: 1st Report. (Technical Reports Ser.: No. 25). (Illus., Orig.). 1964. pap. 3.25 (ISBN 92-0-175064-1, IAEA). Unipub.

IAEA Laboratory Activities: 2nd Report. (Technical Reports Ser.: No. 41). (Illus., Orig.). 1965. pap. 2.75 (ISBN 92-0-175065-X, IAEA). Unipub.

IAEA Laboratory Activities: 3rd Report. (Technical Reports Ser.: No. 55). (Illus., Orig.). 1966. pap. 2.75 (ISBN 92-0-175166-4, IAEA). Unipub.

IAEA Laboratory Activities: 4th Report. (Technical Reports Ser.: No. 77). (Illus., Orig.). 1967. pap. 2.75 (ISBN 92-0-175167-2, IAEA). Unipub.

IAEA Laboratory Activities: 5th Report. (Technical Reports Ser.: No. 90). (Illus., Orig.). 1968. pap. 2.75 (ISBN 92-0-175168-0, IAEA). Unipub.

IAEA Laboratory Activities: 6th Report. (Technical Reports Ser.: No. 98). (Illus., Orig.). 1969. pap. 9.75 (ISBN 92-0-175169-9, IAEA). Unipub.

IAEA Laboratory Activities: 7th Report. (Technical Reports Ser.: No. 103). (Illus., Orig.). 1970. pap. 6.00 (ISBN 92-0-175070-6, IAEA). Unipub.

IAEA Research Contracts: 10th Annual Report. (Technical Reports Ser.: No. 105). (Orig.). 1970. pap. 12.00 (ISBN 92-0-175170-2, IAEA). Unipub.

IAEA Research Contracts: 11th Annual Report. (Technical Reports Ser.: No. 125). (Orig.). 1971. pap. 16.25 (ISBN 92-0-175071-4, IAEA). Unipub.

IAEA Research Contracts: 12th Annual Report. (Technical Reports Ser.: No. 134). 191p. (Orig.). 1972. pap. 14.00 (ISBN 92-0-175072-2, IDC134, IAEA). Unipub.

IAEA Research Contracts: 13th Annual Report. (Technical Reports Ser.: No. 144). 237p. (Orig.). pap. 18.75 (ISBN 92-0-175073-0, IAEA). Unipub.

IAEA Research Contracts: 14th Annual Report. (Technical Reports Series, No. 154). 184p. (Orig.). 1974. pap. 12.50 (ISBN 92-0-175074-9, IAEA). Unipub.

Iaia Garcia. Joaquim M. Assis. Tr. by Albert I. Bagby, Jr. LC 76-24338. (Studies in Romance Languages: No. 17). 192p. 1977. 15.50x (ISBN 0-8131-1353-9). U Pr of Ky.

Ialy in the Making, 3 vols. C. F. Berkeley. Incl. Vol. 1. Eighteen Fifteen to Eighteen Forty-Six. Repr. of 1932 ed. 38.50 (ISBN 0-521-07427-4); Vol. 2. Eighteen Forty-Six to Eighteen Forty-Eight. Repr. of 1936 ed. 44.50 (ISBN 0-521-07428-2); Vol. 3. January 1, Eighteen Forty-Eight to November 16, Eighteen Forty-Eight. Repr. of 1940 ed. 53.50 (ISBN 0-521-07429-0). (Illus.). 1969. Cambridge U Pr.

Ian Ramsey: To Speak Responsibly of God. Jerry H. Gill. 1976. text ed. 16.95x (ISBN 0-04-230014-2). Allen Unwin.

Iatrogenic Problems in Otorlaryngology. L. B. Jongkees. 1981. text ed. write for info. (ISBN 0-443-08050-X). Churchill.

Iban & Their Religion. Erik Jensen. (Oxford Monographs on Social Anthropology). (Illus.). 220p. 1975. 29.95x (ISBN 0-19-823179-2). Oxford U Pr.

Iban of Sarawak. Vinson H. Sutlive, Jr. Ed. by Walter Goldschmidt. LC 77-86045. (Worlds of Man Ser.). (Illus.). 1978. text ed. 11.50x (ISBN 0-88295-616-7); pap. text ed. 5.75x (ISBN 0-88295-617-5). AHM Pub.

Iberian Villages: Spain & Portugal. Norman Carver. 26.95 (ISBN 0-932076-02-5); pap. 17.95 (ISBN 0-932076-03-3). Morgan.

Ibizan Hounds. Joan Brearley. (Illus.). 128p. 1980. 2.95 (ISBN 0-87666-694-2, KW-060). TFH Pubns.

IBM Disk Storage Technology. G. V. Harries. (IBM Product Design & Development Ser.). (Illus.). 103p. 1980. pap. text ed. 3.80 (ISBN 0-933186-02-9, GA-26-1665-0). IBM Armonk.

IBM MVS. 1979. pap. text ed. 42.00x (ISBN 0-903796-38-4, Pub. by Online Conferences England). Renouf.

IBM Series One Design Decisions: Architecture. M. I. Davis. (Illus.). 48p. (Orig.). 1979. pap. text ed. 4.40 (ISBN 0-933186-01-0, G360-0066). IBM Armonk.

IBM Series 1: Small Computer Concept. James D. Schoeffler. 1980. pap. text ed. 10.95 (ISBN 0-574-21330-9, 13-4330). SRA.

IBM: Small Systems. 1979. text ed. 42.00x (ISBN 0-903796-47-3, Pub. by Online Conferences England). Renouf.

IBM System-38: Technical Developments. B. G. Utley. (IBM Systems Design & Development Ser.). (Illus.). 109p. 1980. pap. 5.50 (ISBN 0-933186-03-7, G-580-0237-1). IBM Armonk.

IBM: Teleprocessing - SNA & Distributed Processing. 1979. pap. text ed. 48.00x (ISBN 0-903796-40-6, Pub. by Online Conferences England). Renouf.

IBM: VM-CMS. 1979. pap. text ed. 42.00x (ISBN 0-903796-43-0, Pub. by Online Conferences England). Renouf.

IBM 360 Assembler Language Programming. Gopal K. Kapur. LC 76-12572. 1971. 23.50 (ISBN 0-471-45840-6). Wiley.

Ibn Al-Haytham's Optics: A Study of the Origins of Experimental Science. Saleh Beshara Omar. LC 76-42611. (Studies in Islamic Philosophy & Science). (Illus.). 1977. 25.00x (ISBN 0-88297-015-1). Bibliotheca.

Ibn Battuta in Black Africa. Ibn Battuta. Tr. by Said Hamdun & Noel King. 99p. (Orig.). 1978. pap. 5.00x (ISBN 0-901720-57-7, Dist. for Rex Collings, London). Three Continents.

Ibn Kammuna's Examination of the Three Faiths: A Thirteenth-Century Essay in the Comparative Study of Religion. Ed. & tr. by Moshe Perlmann. LC 73-102659. 1971. 20.00 (ISBN 0-520-01658-0). U of Cal Pr.

Ibn Khaldun: A Re-Interpretation. A. Azmeh. 1981. 25.00x (ISBN 0-7146-3140-X, F Cass Co). Biblio Dist.

Ibn Khaldun in Egypt: His Public Functions & His Historical Research, (1382-1406); A Study in Islamic Historiography. Walter J. Fischel. 1967. 17.50x (ISBN 0-520-00414-0). U of Cal Pr.

Ibn Khallikan's Biographical Dictionary: Wafayat Al-a Yan, 4 vols. B. MacGuckin Slane. 90.00x (ISBN 0-685-72046-2). Intl Bk Ctr.

Ibn Sina & the Muslim World. Malcolm Yapp. Ed. by Margaret Killingray & Edmund O'Connor. (World History Ser.). (Illus.). 1980. lib. bdg. 5.95 (ISBN 0-89908-037-5); pap. text ed. 1.95 (ISBN 0-89908-012-X). Greenhaven.

Iboland: A Century of Conflict with Britain 1860-1960. Nwabara. (Illus.). 1978. pap. text ed. 14.50x (ISBN 0-391-00552-9). Humanities.

IBP Survey of Conservation Sites: An Experimental Study. Ed. by A. R. Clapham. LC 79-50233. (International Biological Programme Ser.: No. 24). (Illus.). 500p. 1980. 57.50 (ISBN 0-521-22697-X). Cambridge U Pr.

Ibsen. Harold Clurman. (Masters of World Literature). 1977. 12.95 (ISBN 0-02-526420-6). Macmillan.

Ibsen: A Critical Study. J. Northam. LC 72-80297. (Major European Authors Ser.). 240p. 1973. 38.50 (ISBN 0-521-08682-5); pap. 11.50x (ISBN 0-521-09733-9). Cambridge U Pr.

Ibsen: A Dissenting View. R. Gray. LC 77-5653. 1977. 28.50 (ISBN 0-521-21702-4). Cambridge U Pr.

Ibsen & the Theatre: The Dramatist in Production. Ed. by Errol Durbach. LC 79-47995. 1980. 25.00x (ISBN 0-8147-1773-X). NYU Pr.

Ibsen: The Critical Heritage. Ed. by Michael Egan. (Critical Heritage Ser). 1972. 38.50 (ISBN 0-7100-7255-4). Routledge & Kegan.

Ibsen the Romantic: Analogues of Paradise in the Later Plays. Errol Durbach. 192p. 1981. lib. bdg. 19.00x (ISBN 0-8203-0554-5). U of Ga Pr.

Ibsen's Dramatic Technique. P. F. Tennant. 1965. Repr. of 1948 ed. text ed. 10.00x (ISBN 0-391-00471-9). Humanities.

Ibsen's Peer Gynt. Wilhelm Reich. 74p. 1975. 10.00 (ISBN 0-374-17416-4). FS&G.

IC Array Cookbook. Walter G. Jung. 208p. 1980. pap. 8.85 (ISBN 0-8104-0762-0). Hayden.

IC Master. 1250p. 1980. 75.00x (ISBN 0-89047-048-0). Herman Pub.

IC Op-Amp Cookbook. 2nd ed. Walter G. Jung. LC 73-90289. (Illus.). 1980. pap. 14.95 (ISBN 0-672-21695-7). Sams.

ICA Street Sights. LC 80-84550. (Illus.). 1980. write for info. (ISBN 0-88454-056-1). U of Pa Contemp Art.

Icart. S. Michael Schnessel. (Illus.). 1976. 25.00 (ISBN 0-517-52498-8, Dist. by Crown). Potter.

ICCH Commodities Yearbook 1980-81. G. T. Gemmill. 304p. 1980. 75.00x (ISBN 0-85941-071-4, Pub. by Woodhead-Faulkner England). State Mutual Bk.

Ice. Tristan Jones. 1980. pap. 2.75 (ISBN 0-686-69264-0, 50757). Avon.

Ice. Anna Kavan. 208p. 1974. pap. 0.95 o.p. (ISBN 0-445-00538-6). Popular Lib.

Ice Ages: Ancient & Modern; Geological Journal Special Issue, No. 6. A. E. Wright & F. Moseley. (Liverpool Geological Society & the Manchester Geological Association). 320p. 1980. 51.95 (ISBN 0-471-27753-3, Pub. by Wiley-Interscience). Wiley.

Ice & Iron. Wilson Tucker. 192p. 1975. pap. 1.50 o.p. (ISBN 0-345-24660-8). Ballantine.

Ice Brothers. Sloan Wilson. 1981. pap. 2.95. Avon.

Ice Brothers. Sloan Wilson. 544p. 1981. pap. 2.95 (ISBN 0-380-53611-0, 53611). Avon.

Ice Carving Made Easy. J. Amendola. (Illus.). pap. 12.00x (ISBN 0-685-47434-8). Corner.

Ice Cream. 3rd ed. Wendell S. Arbuckle. (Illus.). 1977. lib. bdg. 26.50 (ISBN 0-87055-256-2). AVI.

Ice Cream Cone. Mildred W. Willard. (Beginning to Read Ser). (Illus.). 32p. (gr. 1-3). 1973. 2.50 o.p. (ISBN 0-695-80418-9); PLB 3.39 o.p. (ISBN 0-695-40418-0). Follett.

Ice-Cream Cone Coot & Other Rare Birds. Arnold Lobel. LC 80-15290. (Illus.). 48p. (ps-3). 1980. Repr. of 1971 ed. 9.95 (ISBN 0-686-65811-6, Four Winds). Schol Bk Serv.

Ice Cream Service Handbook. W. S. Arbuckle. (Illus.). 1976. pap. text ed. 7.50 (ISBN 0-87055-211-2). AVI.

Ice Experience. Jeff Lowe. 1979. 12.95 o.p. (ISBN 0-8092-7512-0); pap. 6.95 (ISBN 0-8092-7511-2). Contemp Bks.

Ice Physics. Peter V. Hobbs. (Illus.). 782p. 1975. 105.00x (ISBN 0-19-851936-2). Oxford U Pr.

Ice Schooner. Michael Moorcock. 1978. pap. 1.75 o.s.i. (ISBN 0-440-14445-0). Dell.

Ice Schooner. Michael Moorcock. LC 76-47249. 1977. 9.95 o.p. (ISBN 0-06-013006-7, HarpT). Har-Row.

Ice Skating Fundamentals. Marilyn G. House. (Illus.). 1978. pap. text ed. 4.25 (ISBN 0-8403-1285-7, 40128502). Kendall-Hunt.

ICE Yearbook 1980. Institute of Civil Engineers. 848p. 1980. pap. 69.00 (ISBN 0-7277-0081-2, Pub. by Telford England). State Mutual Bk.

Iceberg! Bunting. Orig. Title: High Tides for the Labrador. (gr. 5-6). Date not set. pap. cancelled (ISBN 0-590-30880-7, Schol Pap). Schol Bk Serv.

Iceberg & Its Shadow. Jan Greenberg. 132p. 1980. 8.95 (ISBN 0-374-33624-5). FS&G.

Iceberg Hermit. Arthur Roth. LC 74-7435. 208p. (gr. 7 up). 1974. 7.95 (ISBN 0-590-07301-X, Four Winds). Schol Bk Serv.

Iceberg Utilization: Proceedings. International Iceberg Utilization Conference, 1st Ames, Iowa. Ed. by A. A. Husseiny. LC 78-5119. (Illus.). 780p. 1978. 73.00 (ISBN 0-08-022916-6); pap. 49.00 (ISBN 0-08-022915-8). Pergamon.

Icebergs. Roma Gans. LC 64-18163. (Let's-Read-&-Find-Out Science Bk). (Illus.). (gr. k-3). 1964. PLB 7.89 (ISBN 0-690-42775-1, TYC-J). T Y Crowell.

Icebergs. Husseiny. 350p. Date not set. text ed. price not set (ISBN 0-08-023911-0). Pergamon.

Icebergs & Their Voyages. Gwen Schultz. LC 75-9958. (Illus.). 96p. (gr. 7-9). 1975. PLB 6.96 (ISBN 0-688-32047-3). Morrow.

Icecraft. Norman Kingsley. (Illus.). 120p. 1975. wrappers 4.95 (ISBN 0-910856-59-1). La Siesta.

Icelandic Church Saga. John C. Hood. LC 79-8720. (Illus.). xii, 241p. 1981. Repr. of 1946 ed. lib. bdg. 27.50x (ISBN 0-313-22194-4, HOIC). Greenwood.

Icelandic-English - English-Icelandic Dictionary, 2 vols. 3rd ed. Angrimur Sigurdsson & Sigurdur O. Bogason. 1980. Set. 130.00 (ISBN 0-686-68938-0). Vol. 1, Icelandic-Eng., 942pp. Vol. 2, Eng.-Icelandic, 862pp. Heinman.

Icelandic-English Dictionary. 2nd ed. Ed. by Richard Cleasby & Gudbrand Vigfusson. 1957. 65.00x (ISBN 0-19-863103-0). Oxford U Pr.

Icelandic Enterprise: Economy & Commerce in the Middle Ages. Bruce E. Gelsinger. LC 80-26116. (Illus.). 1981. text ed. 19.50 (ISBN 0-87249-405-5). U of SC Pr.

Icelandic Saga. Peter Hallberg. Tr. by Paul Schach. LC 62-7873. (Illus.). 1962. 9.95x o.p. (ISBN 0-8032-0064-1); pap. 2.35x (ISBN 0-8032-5082-7, BB 136, Bison). U of Nebr Pr.

Iceman. Weldon Hill. LC 76-15607. 320p. 1976. 8.95 o.p. (ISBN 0-688-03071-8). Morrow.

Iceman Cometh. Eugene O'Neill. 1957. pap. 1.95 (ISBN 0-394-70018-X, Vin). Random.

Icerigger. Alan D. Foster. 1978. pap. 2.25 (ISBN 0-345-29454-8, Del Rey Bks). Ballantine.

Ich Lausche Dem Leben. Ed. by Hildegard R. Boeninger & D. Pietschmann. (Orig., Ger.). 1963. pap. 6.95x (ISBN 0-393-09558-4, NortonC); tapes 30.00 (ISBN 0-393-09911-3). Norton.

Ich Ohne Gewaehr: Gegenwartsautoren Aus der Schweiz. Gerda Zeltner. (Ger.). 1980. pap. 13.00 (ISBN 3-288-04743-8, Pub. by Insel Verlag Germany). Suhrkamp.

Ich und Er: First & Third-Person Self-Reference & Problems of Identity in Three Contemporary German-Language Novels. Paul F. Botheroyd. (De Proprietatibus Litterarum Series Practica: No.67). 143p. (Orig.). 1976. pap. text ed. 28.25x (ISBN 90-2793-214-X). Mouton.

Ichneumonidae of America North of Mexico: Subfamily Diplazontinae. Clement E. Dasch. (Memoirs Ser: No. 3). (Illus.). 1964. 20.00 (ISBN 0-686-00422-1). Am Entom Inst.

Ichneumonidae of America North of Mexico: Subfamily Gelinae, Tribe Hemigasterini. Henry Townes & Virendra K. Gupta. (Memoirs Ser: No. 2). (Illus.). 20.00 (ISBN 0-686-00421-3). Am Entom Inst.

Ichneumonidae of America North of Mexico: Subfamily Mesochorinae. Clement E. Dasch. (Memoirs Ser: No. 16). (Illus.). 376p. 1971. 30.00 (ISBN 0-686-01269-0). Am Entom Inst.

ICITA Equalant I & Equalant II: Oceanographic Atlas & Chemical & Biological Oceanography, Vol. 2. (Illus.). 1977. 81.00 (ISBN 0-685-86033-7, M76, UNESCO). Unipub.

ICITA Oceanographic Atlas, Equalant One & Equalant Two, Vol. 1: Physical Oceanography. (Illus.). 1974. 59.00 (ISBN 92-3-099996-2, M75, UNESCO). Unipub.

Icones Plantarum: On Orchids, Vols. 21 & 22. W. J. Hooker. (Ser. 4). 1967. Vol. 21. 30.00 ea. Vol. 22 (ISBN 3-7682-0853-2) (ISBN 3-7682-0854-0). Lubrecht & Cramer.

Iconographie Generale Des Ophidens: 1860-61, 3vols. in 1. G. Jan & F. Sordelli. 1961. 100.00 o.p. (ISBN 3-7682-0044-2). Lubrecht & Cramer.

Iconography of Minor Hindu & Buddhist Deities. Bhagwant Sahai. LC 75-904218. (Illus.). 1975. 26.00x o.p. (ISBN 0-88386-610-2). South Asia Bks.

Iconography of Religions: An Introduction. Albert C. Moore. LC 76-62598. 344p. 1977. 25.00 (ISBN 0-8006-0488-1, 1-489). Fortress.

Iconography of the English History Play. Martha H. Fleischer. (Salzburg Studies in English Literature, Elizabethan & Renaissance Studies: No. 10). 363p. 1974. pap. text ed. 25.00x (ISBN 0-391-01376-9). Humanities.

Iconography of the Facade of Saint-Gilles-Du-Gard. Carra F. O'Meara. LC 76-23668. (Outstanding Dissertations in the Fine Arts - Medieval). (Illus.). 1977. Repr. of 1975 ed. lib. bdg. 52.00 (ISBN 0-8240-2717-5). Garland Pub.

Iconography of Time. Narmadeshwar Prasad. (Redbird Bk.). 1976. flexible bdg. 4.80 (ISBN 0-89253-093-6). Ind-US Inc.

Iconologie. J. B. Boudard. LC 75-27888. (Renaissance & the Gods Ser.: Vol. 43). (Illus.). 1976. Repr. of 1766 ed. lib. bdg. 73.00 (ISBN 0-8240-2092-8). Garland Pub.

Iconologie. Cesare Ripa. Tr. by Jean Baudouin. LC 75-27874. (Renaissance & the Gods Ser.: Vol. 29). (Illus., Fr.). 1976. Repr. of 1644 ed. lib. bdg. 73.00 (ISBN 0-8240-2078-2). Garland Pub.

Iconology, 2 vols. George Richardson. Ed. by Stephen Orgel. LC 78-68201. (Philosophy of Images Ser.: Vol. 20). (Illus.). 1980. Set. lib. bdg. 132.00 (ISBN 0-8240-3694-8). Garland Pub.

Icons & Their History. David Rice & Tamara T. Rice. LC 74-78136. (Illus.). 192p. 1974. 45.00 (ISBN 0-87951-021-8). Overlook Pr.

Icons of Justice: Iconography & Thematic Imagery in Book Five of the Faerie Queen. Jane Aptekar. LC 79-79189. (Illus.). 1969. 17.50x (ISBN 0-231-03246-3). Columbia U Pr.

Icons of the Community, a Study of the Fine Arts & the Appraisal Process. LC 78-114860. (ASA Monograph: No. 3). 1970. 5.00 (ISBN 0-937828-12-2). Am Soc Appraisers.

ICS Nineteen Eighty-One: Proceedings of the International Computing Symposium on Systems Architecture. 1981. pap. text ed. price not set (ISBN 0-86103-050-8, Westbury Hse). Butterworth.

Icy Fire: Four Studies in European Petrarchism. Leonard W. Forster. LC 71-77288. (Illus.). 1969. 29.50 (ISBN 0-521-07495-9); pap. 8.95x (ISBN 0-521-29521-1). Cambridge U Pr.

I'd Rather Be Flying. Donna Vasko. (Illus.). 100p. 1980. spiral bdg. 6.00. Aviation.

I'd Rather Be Flying. Donna M. Vasko. 100p. (Orig.). 1980. pap. 5.95 (ISBN 0-9604308-0-6). Calligraphy Donna.

I'd Rather Be in Philadelphia. Oscar Shefler. 304p. (Orig.). 1981. pap. 2.75 (ISBN 0-523-41152-9). Pinnacle Bks.

I'd Rather Be Me. Laura Dayton. LC 78-72137. (Illus.). (gr. k-3). Date not set. price not set (ISBN 0-89799-115-X); pap. price not set (ISBN 0-89799-062-5). Dandelion Pr. Postponed.

I'd Rather Do It Myself, If You Don't Mind. Shirley Schwarzrock & C. Gilbert Wrenn. (Coping with Ser.). (Illus.). 39p. (gr. 7-12). 1970. pap. text ed. 1.30 (ISBN 0-913476-31-5). Am Guidance.

I'd Rather Stay Home. Carol Barkin & Elizabeth James. LC 75-19481. (Moods & Emotions Ser.). (Illus.). 32p. (gr. k-2). 1975. PLB 8.95 (ISBN 0-8172-0030-4). Raintree Pubs.

Ida: Life with My Handicapped Child. Ulla Bondo. (Illus.). 128p. 1981. 23.00 (ISBN 0-571-11589-6, Pub. by Faber & Faber); pap. 8.95 (ISBN 0-571-11590-X). Merrimack Bk Serv.

Ida M. Tarbell. Mary E. Tomkins. LC 73-2293. (U. S. Authors Ser.: No. 247). 184p. 1974. lib. bdg. 10.95 (ISBN 0-8057-0714-X). Twayne.

Ida Makes a Movie. Kay Chorao. LC 73-20147. (Illus.). 48p. (gr. 1-4). 1974. 5.95 (ISBN 0-395-28782-0, Clarion). HM.

Ida Rolf Talks About Rolfing & Physical Reality. Ed. by Rosemary Feitis. LC 78-2126. (Illus.). 1978. 8.95 o.s.i. (ISBN 0-06-011258-1, HarpT). Har-Row.

Idaho. 23.00 (ISBN 0-89770-088-0). Curriculum Info Ctr.

Idaho: A Bicentennial History. F. Ross Peterson. (State & the Nation Ser.). 1976. 12.95 (ISBN 0-393-05600-7, Co-Pub by AASLH). Norton.

Idaho: A Guide in Word & Picture. Federal Writers' Project. 1937. Repr. 45.00 (ISBN 0-403-02163-4). Somerset Pub.

Idaho & Only the Brave. Paul E. Lehman. 1979. pap. 2.25 (ISBN 0-505-51429-X). Tower Bks.

Idaho Chronology & Factbook, Vol. 12. R. I. Vexler. 1978. 8.50 (ISBN 0-379-16137-0). Oceana.

Idaho Industrial Minerals. 1975. 14.50. Minobras.

Idaho Official Code, 23 vols. 1947. write for info (ISBN 0-672-83888-5, Bobbs-Merrill Law); write for info 1980 suppl. (ISBN 0-672-84159-2). Michie.

Idaho Rules of Civil Procedure, 1 Vol. 1958. with 1979 suppl. 20.00 o.p. (ISBN 0-672-83889-3, Bobbs-Merrill Law); 1979 suppl 6.00 o.p. (ISBN 0-672-83783-8). Michie.

Idaho Statistical Abstract, 1980. 3rd ed. S. M. Ghazanfar. 1980. 30.00x (ISBN 0-686-28924-2). Ctr Bus Devel.

Idaho Supplement for Modern Real Estate Practice. 3rd ed. Ruth D. Silverman. 140p. 1981. pap. 7.95 (ISBN 0-88462-291-6). Real Estate Ed Co.

Idalia's Project ABC-Proyecto ABC. Idalia Rosario. LC 80-21013. (Illus.). 32p. (ps-2). 1981. 6.95 (ISBN 0-03-044141-2). HR&W.

Idanre & Other Poems. Wole Soyinka. LC 68-30761. 88p. 1968. 3.95 (ISBN 0-8090-5725-5); pap. 1.75 (ISBN 0-8090-1352-5). Hill & Wang.

Idea & Experience: Edmund Husserl's Project of Phenomenology in Ideas, I. Erazim Kohak. LC 78-661. xvi, 250p. 1980. pap. 5.95 (ISBN 0-226-45020-1, P901, Phoen). U of Chicago Pr.

Idea File of Harold Adam Innis. Ed. by William Christian. 1980. 20.00x (ISBN 0-8020-2350-9); pap. 7.50 (ISBN 0-8020-6382-9). U of Toronto Pr.

Idea Invaders. George N. Gordon et al. (Communication Arts Bks.). 1963. 4.95 o.p. (ISBN 0-8038-3338-5). Hastings.

Idea of a Christian Philosophy. H. Dooyeweerd et al. 1973. pap. 6.95x (ISBN 0-686-11979-7). Wedge Pub.

Idea of a Party System: The Rise of Legitimate Opposition in the United States, 1780-1840. Richard Hofstadter. LC 76-82377. (Jefferson Memorial Lectures). 1969. 15.75x (ISBN 0-520-01389-1); pap. 3.95 (ISBN 0-520-01754-4, CAL196). U of Cal Pr.

Idea of a Social Science & Its Relation to Philosophy. Peter Winch. LC 77-112410. (Studies in Philosophical Psychology). 1970. pap. text ed. 5.25x (ISBN 0-391-00061-6). Humanities.

Idea of a University. John H. Newman. 1979. pap. 10.50 o.p. (ISBN 0-87061-023-6). Chr Classics.

Idea of an Historical Education. Geoffrey Partington. 257p. 1981. pap. text ed. 20.75x (ISBN 0-85633-202-X, NFER). Humanities.

Idea of Being. S. D. Philaretos. Ed. by Orthodox Christian Educational Society. Tr. by D. Cummings from Hellenic. 287p. 1963. 3.00x (ISBN 0-938366-09-2). Orthodox Chr.

Idea of Biblical Poetry: Parallelism & Its History. James L. Kugel. LC 80-25227. 320p. 1981. 27.50x (ISBN 0-300-02474-6). Yale U Pr.

Idea of Fraternity in America. Wilson C. McWilliams. LC 73-101339. 1973. 21.50x (ISBN 0-520-01650-5); pap. 4.95 (ISBN 0-520-02772-8). U of Cal Pr.

Idea of Freedom: Essays in Honour of Isaiah Berlin. Ed. by Alan Ryan. 1979. 17.95x (ISBN 0-19-215859-7). Oxford U Pr.

Idea of Historical Recurrence in Western Thought: From Antiquity to the Reformation. G. W. Trompf. 1979. 22.75x (ISBN 0-520-03479-1). U of Cal Pr.

Idea of History. Robin G. Collingwood. Ed. by T. M. Knox. 1956. pap. 5.95 (ISBN 0-19-500205-9, 1, GB). Oxford U Pr.

Idea of Justice & the Problems of Argument. Chaim Perelman. (International Library of Philosophy & Scientific Method). 1963. text ed. 13.75x (ISBN 0-7100-3610-8). Humanities.

Idea of Landscape & the Sense of Place, 1730-1840: An Approach to the Poetry of John Clare. John Barrell. LC 77-160092. (Illus.). 1972. 39.50 (ISBN 0-521-08254-4). Cambridge U Pr.

Idea of Man. Floyd W. Matson. 1976. 8.95 (ISBN 0-440-04038-8). Delacorte.

Idea of Peace in Antiquity. Gerardo Zampaglione. Tr. by Richard Dunn from Italian. Orig. Title: Idea Della Pace Nel Mondo Antico. 344p. 1973. text ed. 20.00x (ISBN 0-8290-0341-X). Irvington.

Idea of Perfection in Christian Theology: An Historical Study of the Christian Ideal for the Present Life. R. Newton Flew. 1968. Repr. of 1934 ed. pap. text ed. 15.00x (ISBN 0-391-00507-3). Humanities.

Idea of Progress Since the Renaissance. Ed. by W. Warren Wagar. LC 76-81337. (Major Issues in History Ser.). 1969. pap. text ed. 6.95x o.p. (ISBN 0-471-91351-0). Wiley.

Idea of Race. Michael Banton. 1979. lib. bdg. 22.00x (ISBN 0-89158-719-5). Westview.

Idea of Revelation in Recent Thought. John Baillie. LC 56-8158. 1956. 12.00x (ISBN 0-231-02142-9); pap. 5.00x (ISBN 0-231-08554-0, 54). Columbia U Pr.

Idea of the Canterbury Tales. Donald R. Howard. LC 74-81433. 400p. 1976. 20.00x (ISBN 0-520-02816-3); pap. 5.95 (ISBN 0-520-03492-9). U of Cal Pr.

Idea of the City in Nineteenth-Century Britain. Ed. by B. I. Coleman. (Birth of Modern Britain Ser). 256p. 1973. 16.00 (ISBN 0-7100-7591-X); pap. 7.95 (ISBN 0-7100-7592-8). Routledge & Kegan.

Idea of the Clerisy, in the Nineteenth Century. B. Knights. LC 77-80840. 1978. 42.00 (ISBN 0-521-21798-9). Cambridge U Pr.

Idea of the Garden in the Renaissance. Terry Comito. 1978. 19.00 (ISBN 0-8135-0841-X). Rutgers U Pr.

Idea of the Holy: An Inquiry into the Non-Rational Factor in the Idea of the Divine & Its Relation to the Rational. 2nd ed. Rudolf Otto. Tr. by John W. Harvey. 1950. 10.95 o.p. (ISBN 0-19-501331-X). Oxford U Pr.

Idea of the Symbol: Some Nineteenth Century Comparisons with Coleridge. M. Jadwiga Swiatecka. LC 70-19802. 220p. 1980. 26.95 (ISBN 0-521-22362-8). Cambridge U Pr.

Idea People. Lee Taylor. LC 74-17805. 224p. 1975. 17.95 (ISBN 0-88229-149-1). Nelson-Hall.

I.D.E.A. Power for Reading Comprehension. L. V. Kolzow. 336p. 1976. pap. text ed. 9.95 (ISBN 0-13-450551-4). P-H.

Idea to Delivery: A Handbook of Oral Communication. 3rd ed. Dwight L. Garner. 1979. pap. 7.95x (ISBN 0-534-00599-3). Wadsworth Pub.

Ideal City. Canon Barnett. Ed. by Helen Meller. (Victorian Library). 1979. text ed. 16.25 (ISBN 0-7185-5061-7, Leicester). Humanities.

Ideal Communist City. Alexei Gutnov. LC 75-129358. (I Press Ser). 1970. 6.95 o.p. (ISBN 0-8076-0576-X); pap. 2.95 o.p. (ISBN 0-8076-0575-1). Braziller.

Ideal Imperfection. Gregory Tarbox. 1979. 4.75 o.p. (ISBN 0-8062-1185-7). Carlton.

Ideal Life: Fifty & Over. Gordon Elliott & Mary Elliot. (Illus., Orig.). 1980. pap. 5.95 (ISBN 0-89542-081-3). Ideals.

Ideal of the Practical: Colombia's Struggle to Form a Technical Elite. Frank Safford. (Latin American Monographs: No. 39). 290p. 1975. 20.00 (ISBN 0-292-73803-X). U of Tex Pr.

Ideal Theory. Douglas G. Northcott. (Cambridge Tracts in Mathematics & Mathematical Physics: No. 42). 1953. 20.50 (ISBN 0-521-05840-6). Cambridge U Pr.

Idealism Debased: From Volkisch Ideology to National Socialism. Roderick Stackelberg. LC 80-84663. (Illus.). 220p. 1981. 18.00x (ISBN 0-87338-252-8). Kent St U Pr.

Idealismus und Faktizitaet. Gerd Wolandt. 287p. 1971. 41.75x (ISBN 3-11-002375-X). De Gruyter.

Idealist View of Life. S. Radhakrishnan. (Unwin Bks.). 1961. pap. 2.95 o.p. (ISBN 0-04-141005-X). Allen Unwin.

Idealist View of Life. S. Radhakrishnan. (Paperbacks Ser.). 288p. 1980. pap. 6.75 (ISBN 0-04-141009-2, 1614). Allen Unwin.

Idealogical Training in Communist Education. Martin J. Croghan & Penelope P. Croghan. LC 79-47986. 209p. 1980. text ed. 17.75 (ISBN 0-8191-0992-4); pap. text ed. 9.50 (ISBN 0-8191-0993-2). U Pr of Amer.

Ideals & Ideologies: Communism, Socialism & Capitalism. rev. ed. Harry B. Ellis. (Illus.). 326p. (RL 7). 1972. pap. 1.25 o.p. (ISBN 0-451-61124-1, MY1124, Ment). NAL.

Ideals & Realities of Academic Advising. Don Martindale. (Intercontinental Series in Sociology: No. 3). 207p. 1980. lib. bdg. 14.95 (ISBN 0-933142-02-1). Intercont Press.

Ideals & Realities of Ph.D Advising. Don Martindale. (Intercontinental Series in Sociology: No. 3). 14.95 (ISBN 0-933142-02-1). Intercont Press.

Ideals & Realities: Some Problem Areas of Professional Social Science. Don Martindale & Raj P. Mohan. (Intercontinental Series in Sociogy: No. 2). 250p. 1980. lib. bdg. 14.95 (ISBN 0-933142-01-3). Intercont Press.

Ideals & Reality: An Analysis of the Debate Over Viet-Nam. Stephen A. Garrett. LC 78-59852. 1978. pap. text ed. 10.00 (ISBN 0-8191-0555-4). U Pr of Amer.

Ideals Farmhouse Cookbook. Ed. by James Kuse & Ralph D. Luedke. 1978. pap. 2.95 o.p. (ISBN 0-89542-609-9). Ideals.

Ideals in Art. Walter Crane. Ed. by Peter Stansky & Rodney Shewan. LC 76-17775. (Aesthetic Movement & the Arts & Crafts Movement Ser.). 1978. Repr. of 1905 ed. lib. bdg. 44.00x (ISBN 0-8240-2480-X). Garland Pub.

Ideals in Collision. Leonard Silk & Raleigh Warner, Jr. 1979 7.50 (ISBN 0-915604-33-7). Columbia U Pr.

Ideas. rev. ed. Harlan Wade. LC 78-26632. (Book About Ser.). (Illus.). (gr. k-3). 1979. PLB 7.30 (ISBN 0-8172-1530-1). Raintree Pubs.

Ideas. Harlan Wade. Tr. by Mamie M. Contreras from Eng. LC 78-26714. (Book About Ser.). (Illus., Sp.). (gr. k-3). 1979. PLB 7.30 (ISBN 0-8172-1481-X). Raintree Pubs.

Ideas About Measuring & Accounting. John E. Maher. LC 73-8977. (Ideas About Ser). (Illus.). 48p. (gr. 1-4). 1974. PLB 5.90 (ISBN 0-531-02657-4). Watts.

Ideas About Money. John E. Maher. LC 77-115412. (Ideas About Ser). (gr. k-3). 1970. PLB 4.33 o.p. (ISBN 0-531-01947-0). Watts.

Ideas About Taxes. John Maher. LC 79-182292. (Ideas About Ser). (Illus.). 48p. (gr. 1-3). 1972. PLB 3.90 o.p. (ISBN 0-531-02021-5). Watts.

Ideas & Concept. Julius R. Weinberg. (Aquinas Lectures Ser). 1970. 6.95 (ISBN 0-87462-135-6). Marquette.

Ideas & Data: The Process & Practice of Social Research. Sheldon R. Olson. 1976. text ed. 17.50x (ISBN 0-256-01809-X). Dorsey.

Ideas & Men: The Story of Western Thought. 2nd ed. Crane Brinton. 1963. ref. ed. 17.95 (ISBN 0-13-449249-8). P-H.

Ideas & the Novel. Mary McCarthy. 7.95 (ISBN 0-15-143682-7). HarBraceJ.

Ideas for a Better America. Natty Bumppo & Natalie Bumppo. LC 80-66966. (Illus.). 80p. 1980. pap. 3.95 (ISBN 0-9604894-0-1). Borf Bks.

Ideas for Art Teachers. Peter H. Gooch. 1972. pap. 16.95 (ISBN 0-7134-2304-8, Pub. by Batsford England). David & Charles.

Ideas for Canvas Work. Mary Rhodes. (Illus.). 1969. 13.50 (ISBN 0-8231-4014-8). Branford.

Ideas for Making Your Home Accessible. Ed. by Betty Garee. (Illus.). 1979. 6.50 (ISBN 0-915708-08-6). Cheever Pub.

Ideas for Patchwork. Suzy Ives. (Illus.). 112p. 1974. 7.95 o.p. (ISBN 0-8231-5042-9). Branford.

Ideas for Prayer. Hubert Van Zeller. 1973. pap. 3.95 (ISBN 0-87243-046-4). Templegate.

Ideas for Promoting Safety. 1976. 7.50 o.p. (ISBN 0-8144-6948-5). Am Mgmt.

Ideas for Teaching English in the Junior High & Middle School. Ed. by Candy Carter & Zora Rashkis. LC 80-25921. 320p. 1980. 15.00 (ISBN 0-8141-2253-1). NCTE.

Ideas for Teaching History. Sean Healy. 1974. 14.95 (ISBN 0-7134-2166-5, Pub. by Batsford England). David & Charles.

Ideas for Training Managers & Supervisors. Patrick Suessmuth. LC 77-93408. 328p. 1978. pap. 17.50 (ISBN 0-88390-143-9). Univ Assocs.

Ideas for Woodturning. Anders Thorlin. (Creative Handcrafts Ser.). (Illus.). 128p. 1980. 12.95 (ISBN 0-13-450361-9, Spec); pap. 5.95 (ISBN 0-13-450353-8). P-H.

Ideas from Chemistry. Tom Thomson. (Science Modules Ser.). (gr. 7-8). 1973. pap. text ed. 6.44 (ISBN 0-201-07578-4, Sch Div); tchr's manual 2.84 (ISBN 0-201-07579-2). A-W.

Ideas in Barotse Jurisprudence. Max Gluckman. (Institute for African Studies). (Illus.). 299p. (Orig.). text ed. 17.50x (ISBN 0-7190-1030-6); pap. text ed. 16.75x (ISBN 0-7190-1031-4). Humanities.

Ideas in the Drama. Ed. by John Gassner. LC 64-21201. 1964. 12.50x (ISBN 0-231-02733-8). Columbia U Pr.

Ideas Literarias en Espana entre 1840 y 1850. Salvador Garcia. (U. C. Publ. in Modern Philology: Vol. 98). (Span). 1971. pap. 7.50x (ISBN 0-520-09365-8). U of Cal Pr.

Ideas of Einstein. David E. Fisher. LC 80-10423. (Illus.). 64p. (gr. 3-5). 1980. 8.95 (ISBN 0-03-046516-8). HR&W.

Ideas of Order in Literature & Film: Selected Papers. Florida State University Conference on Literature & Films, Fourth. Ed. by Peter Ruppert et al. LC 80-2601. xiii, 135p. (Orig.). 1981. pap. 8.00 (ISBN 0-8130-0699-6). U Presses Fla.

Ideas of Religion: A Prolegomenon to the Philosophy of Religion. John E. Sullivan. LC 79-66230. 1979. pap. text ed. 9.50 (ISBN 0-8191-0808-1). U Pr of Amer.

Ideas of Space: Euclidean, Non-Euclidean & Relativistic. Jeremy Gray. (Illus.). 1980. 28.50x (ISBN 0-19-853352-7). Oxford U Pr.

Ideas of Statistics. J. Leroy Folks. LC 80-14723. 352p. 1981. text ed. 15.95 (ISBN 0-471-02099-0); tchr's ed. avail. (ISBN 0-471-07969-3); write for info. study guide (ISBN 0-471-07972-3). Wiley.

Ideas of the Great Economists. rev ed. John W. McConnell. (No. 511). 224p. 1980. pap. 4.95 (ISBN 0-06-463511-2, EH 511, EH). Har-Row.

Ideas of the Great Economists. George H. Soule. 1955. pap. 1.25 o.p. (ISBN 0-451-61475-5, MY1475, Ment). NAL.

Ideas of the Great Philosophers. William S. Sahakian & Mabel L. Sahakian. (Orig.). 1966. pap. 3.95 (ISBN 0-06-463218-0, EH 218, EH). Har-Row.

Idea's of the Woman's Suffrage Movement 1880-1920. Aileen S. Kraditor. 1980. pap. 6.95 (ISBN 0-393-00039-7). Norton.

Ideas Plus Dollars: Research Methodology & Funding. Harold Zallen & Eugenia M. Zallen. LC 75-46502. (Illus.). 387p. 1976. 17.25 (ISBN 0-915582-00-7); microfiche 12.00 (ISBN 0-915582-01-5). Academic World.

Ideas Plus Dollars: Research Methodology & Funding. 2nd ed. Harold Zallen & Eugenia M. Zellen. LC 79-55737. (Illus.). 1980. 12.95. Academic World.

Ideas That Become Big Business. Ed. by F. N. Beam. 1981. 28.50 o.p. (ISBN 0-686-68304-8). Porter.

Ideas to Make Your Days Easier: A Potpourri of Helpful Hints. Elenora Strand. 1977. 4.00 o.p. (ISBN 0-682-48813-5). Exposition.

Ideas y Motivos De Conversacion y Composicion En Espanol. Mireya Camurati & Dorothy Rosenberg. 1974. 14.95x o.p. (ISBN 0-669-90845-2). Heath.

Idee und Methode der Philosophie: Leitgedanken fuer eine Theorie der Vernunft. Iso Kern. xiv, 441p. (Ger.). 1975. 54.10x (ISBN 3-11-004843-4). De Gruyter.

Idees. Harlan Wade. Tr. by Claude Potvin & Rose-Ella Potvin. (Book About Ser.). Orig. Title: Ideas. (Illus., Fr.). (gr. k-3). 1979. PLB 7.30 (ISBN 0-8172-1456-9). Raintree Pubs.

Idelogie Reciste: Genese et Langage Actuel. Colette Guillaumin. (Publications De L'institut D'etudes et De Recherches Interethniques et Interculturelles: No. 2). 1972. pap. 17.75x (ISBN 90-2796-993-0). Mouton.

Identification & Registration of Firearms. Vaclav Krcma. (Illus.). 200p. 1971. 19.75 (ISBN 0-398-02336-0). C C Thomas.

Identification & System Parameter Estimation: Proceedings of the Fifth IFAC Symposium, Darmstadt, Federal Republic of Germany, 24-28 Sept. 1979, 2 vols. Ed. by R. Isermann. LC 79-42935. (IFAC Prodeedings Ser.). 1394p. 1980. Set. 225.00 (ISBN 0-08-024451-3). Pergamon.

Identification of Flowering Plant Families. P. H. Davis & J. Cullen. LC 78-8125. (Illus.). 1979. 21.50 (ISBN 0-521-22111-0); pap. 5.95x (ISBN 0-521-29359-6). Cambridge U Pr.

Identification of Microforms: ANSI-NMA MS19-1978. National Micrographics Assn. 1978. 4.50 (ISBN 0-89258-051-8). Natl Micrograph.

Identification of Modern Tertiary Woods. A. C. Barefoot & Frank W. Hankins. (Illus.). 220p. 1981. 54.00x (ISBN 0-19-854378-6). Oxford U Pr.

Identification of Molecular Spectra. 4th ed. R. W. Pearse & A. G. Gaydon. LC 76-18734. 407p. 1976. text ed. 53.95x o.p. (ISBN 0-412-14350-X, Pub. by Chapman & Hall). Methuen Inc.

Identification of Molecular Spectra. 4th ed. R. W. Pearse & A. G. Gaydon. LC 76-18734. 1976. 53.95 o.p. (ISBN 0-470-15164-1). Halsted Pr.

Identification of Myeloma Proteins. Ed. by Ted Davis. LC 75-10803. (Illus.). 1975. pap. text ed. 17.00 perfect bdg. (ISBN 0-89189-027-0, 45-A-002-00). Am Soc Clinical.

Identification of Plastics & Rubbers. K. J. Saunders. 1966. pap. 2.95 o.p. (ISBN 0-470-75511-3). Halsted Pr.

Identification of the Gifted. Elizabeth Hagen. Ed. by Abraham J. Tannenbaum. (Perspectives on Gifted & Talented Education Ser.). (Orig.). 1980. pap. text ed. 5.50x (ISBN 0-8077-2588-9). Tchrs Coll.

Identification Technologies: Computer, Optical, & Chemical Aids to Personal ID. George H. Warfel. (Illus.). 200p. 1979. text ed. 19.50 (ISBN 0-398-03889-9). C C Thomas.

Identifying American Architecture: A Pictorial Guide to Styles & Terms, 1600-1945. rev. ed. John J. Blumenson. (Illus.). 1981. 12.95 (ISBN 0-393-01428-2). Norton.

Identifying & Collecting Rocks & Minerals. Henry Lepp. LC 78-69632. (Illus.). 1979. 14.50 o.p. (ISBN 0-498-02208-0). A S Barnes.

Identifying & Solving Problems: A System Approach. 2nd ed. Roger Kaufman. LC 76-5702. 134p. 1979. pap. 10.00 (ISBN 0-88390-050-5). Univ Assocs.

Identifying Handicapped Children. Ed. by Lee Cross & Kenneth Goin. LC 76-52246. (First Chance Ser.). 1977. 8.95 o.s.i. (ISBN 0-8027-9041-0); pap. 7.95 (ISBN 0-8027-7111-4). Walker & Co.

Identifying Hyperactive Children: A Study in the Medicalization of Deviant Behavior. Peter F. Conrad. LC 75-44559. (Illus.). 1976. 15.95 (ISBN 0-669-00499-5). Lexington Bks.

Identifying the Talented & Gifted. Richard Bagley et al. (Ser. on Talented & Gifted Education). (Illus., Orig.). 1979. 2.95 (ISBN 0-89354-125-7). Northwest Regional.

Identite au Travail: Les effets culturels de l'organisation. Renaud Sainsaulieu. 1977. lib. bdg. 40.00x (ISBN 2-7246-0386-9); pap. text ed. 32.50x (ISBN 2-7246-0385-0). Clearwater Pub.

Identities. W. R. Moses. LC 65-14051. (Wesleyan Poetry Program: Vol. 26). (Orig.). 1965. 10.00x (ISBN 0-8195-2026-8, Pub. by Wesleyan U Pr); pap. 4.95 (ISBN 0-8195-1026-2). Columbia U Pr.

Identities & Interactions. rev. ed. George J. McCall & J. L. Simmons. LC 77-99093. 1978. 16.95 (ISBN 0-02-920630-8); pap. text ed. 9.95 (ISBN 0-02-920620-0). Free Pr.

Identities in the Lesbian World: The Social Construction of Self. Barbara Ponse. LC 77-84763. (Contributions in Sociology: No. 28). 1978. lib. bdg. 18.95x (ISBN 0-8371-9889-5, PLW/). Greenwood.

Identities of Persons. Ed. by Amelie O. Rorty. LC 75-13156. (Topics in Philosophy: Vol. 3). 1976. 15.75 o.p. (ISBN 0-520-03030-3); pap. 5.95x (ISBN 0-520-03309-4, CAMPUS 180). U of Cal Pr.

Identity & Anxiety. Ed. by Maurice R. Stein et al. LC 60-7091. 1965. pap. text ed. 6.95 o.s.i. (ISBN 0-02-930920-4). Free Pr.

Identity & Essence. Baruch A. Brody. LC 80-7511. 1980. 16.50 (ISBN 0-691-07256-6); pap. 5.95 (ISBN 0-691-02013-2). Princeton U Pr.

Identity & Individuation. Ed. by Milton K. Munitz. LC 73-124530. (Studies in Contemporary Philosophy). 1971. 15.00x o.p. (ISBN 0-8147-5352-3); pap. 7.00x (ISBN 0-8147-5375-2). NYU Pr.

Identity & Intimacy. William K. Kilpatrick. 272p. 1975. 8.95 o.p. (ISBN 0-440-04373-5). Delacorte.

Identity Crisis in Higher Education. Ed. by Harold L. Hodgkinson & Myron B. Bloy, Jr. LC 78-110644. (Higher Education Ser.). 1971. 11.95x o.p. (ISBN 0-87589-085-7). Jossey-Bass.

Identity Group Psychotherapy with Adolescents. Arnold W. Rachman. 336p. 1975. 23.50 (ISBN 0-398-03255-6). C C Thomas.

Identity Management in Lesbian Women. Alice E. Moses. (Praeger Special Studies). 1978. 21.95 (ISBN 0-03-047641-0). Praeger.

Identity of the New Testament, Text. Wilbur Pickering. LC 77-1559. 1977. 7.95 o.p. (ISBN 0-8407-5113-3). Nelson.

Ideologies & Utopias. Arthur A. Ekirch, Jr. pap. text ed. 2.95x (ISBN 0-8290-0342-8). Irvington.

Ideology & Consciousness: Spring 1978, No. 3. Ed. by Diana Adlam et al. 1978. pap. text ed. 3.25x (ISBN 0-391-01215-0). Humanities.

Ideology & Crime. Leon Radzinowicz. LC 66-15724. (James S. Carpentier Fund Lecture Ser). 1966. 15.00x (ISBN 0-231-02926-8). Columbia U Pr.

Ideology & Curriculum. Michael W. Apple. (Education Bks.). 1979. 18.00x (ISBN 0-7100-0136-3). Routledge & Kegan.

Ideology & Discontent. Ed. by David E. Apter. LC 64-20305. 1964. 17.95 (ISBN 0-02-900760-7). Free Pr.

Ideology & Foreign Policy: A Global Perspective. Ed. by George Schwab. 226p. 1981. Repr. of 1978 ed. pap. text ed. 10.95x (ISBN 0-8290-0393-2). Irvington.

Ideology & Imagination. F. Inglis. LC 74-82220. 240p. 1975. 27.50 (ISBN 0-521-20540-9); pap. 8.95x (ISBN 0-521-09886-6). Cambridge U Pr.

Ideology & Imagination. Geoffrey C. Kabat. 1978. 15.50x (ISBN 0-231-04422-4). Columbia U Pr.

Ideology & Insanity - Essays on the Psychiatric Dehumanization of Man. Szasz, Thomas S., M.D. LC 72-84397. 1970. pap. 2.95 (ISBN 0-385-02033-3, A704, Anch). Doubleday.

Ideology & Method in Economics. Homa Katouzian. LC 79-3301. 1981. cUSA 22.50x (ISBN 0-8147-4574-1); pap. 12.50x cUSA (ISBN 0-8147-4575-X). NYU Pr.

Ideology & Organization in Communist China. 2nd enl ed. Franz Schurmann. LC 68-26124. (Center for Chinese Studies, UC Berkeley). (Illus.). 1968. 25.00x (ISBN 0-520-01151-1); pap. 7.95 (ISBN 0-520-01153-8, CAL172). U of Cal Pr.

Ideology & Politics: The Socialist Party of France. George A. Codding, Jr. & William Safran. (Westview Special Studies in European Politics & Society). 1978. lib. bdg. 24.50 (ISBN 0-89158-182-0). Westview.

Ideology & Shopfloor Industrial Relations. J. F. Goodman et al. 224p. 1981. 37.50x (ISBN 0-7099-0465-7, Pub. by Croom Helm Ltd England). Biblio Dist.

Ideology & Social Character. Jon H. Huer. LC 78-56917. 1978. pap. write for info. (ISBN 0-8191-0522-8). U Pr of Amer.

Ideology & Social Knowledge. H. Bershady. LC 73-5337. 178p. 1973. 13.95 (ISBN 0-470-07155-9). Halsted Pr.

Ideology & Social Order. Eric Carlton. (International Library of Sociology). 1976. 27.50 (ISBN 0-7100-8474-9). Routledge & Kegan.

Ideology & the Development of Sociological Theory. Irving Zeitlin. 1968. text ed. 17.95 (ISBN 0-13-449561-6). P-H.

Ideology & the Development of Sociological Theory. 2nd ed. Irving M. Zeitlin. (P-H Ser. in Sociology). (Illus.). 336p. 1981. text ed. 17.95 (ISBN 0-13-449769-4). P-H.

Ideology & Utopia in the United States, 1956-1976. Irving L. Horowitz. 1977. pap. text ed. 7.95 (ISBN 0-19-502107-X, 477, GB). Oxford U Pr.

Ideology of Fascism. A. J. Gregor. LC 69-16920. 1969. 13.95 o.s.i. (ISBN 0-02-913030-1). Free Pr.

Ideology of Form. David Schuman. LC 77-15815. 1978. 19.90 (ISBN 0-669-02059-1). Lexington Bks.

Ideology of-in the Natural Sciences. Hilary Rose & Steven Rose. 363p. 1980. pap. text ed. 11.25x (ISBN 0-87073-881-X). Schenkman.

Ideology of Power & the Power of Ideology. Goran Therborn. 144p. 1981. 12.50x (ISBN 0-8052-7095-7, Pub. by NLB England); pap. 5.50 (ISBN 0-8052-7094-9). Schocken.

Ideology of Social Problems. Reasons & Purdue. 15.95 (ISBN 0-88284-110-6). Alfred Pub.

Ides of Mad. Mad Magazine Editors. (Mad Ser.). (Illus.). 192p. 1974. pap. 1.50 (ISBN 0-446-88747-1). Warner Bks.

Ides of March Conspiracy. Clyde Matthews. LC 80-83593. 320p. 1981. pap. 2.75 (ISBN 0-87216-789-5). Playboy Pbks.

Ides of Tomorrow: Original Science Fiction Tales of Horror. Ed. by Terry Carr. (gr. 7-12). 1976. 7.95 (ISBN 0-316-12970-4). Little.

Idi Amin's Rise to Power: The Inside Story. P. A. Olk-Apire. 192p. (Orig.). 1981. 15.95 (ISBN 0-905762-68-1, Pub. by Zed Pr); pap. 6.95 (ISBN 0-905762-67-3). Lawrence Hill.

Idiom Book of New Testament Greek. 2nd ed. Charles F. Moule. 1959. 36.00 (ISBN 0-521-05774-4); pap. text ed. 9.95x (ISBN 0-521-09237-X). Cambridge U Pr.

Idiom of Night. Pierre J. Jouve. Tr. by Keith Bosley. (Poetry Europe Ser.: No. 9). 80p. 1969. 6.95 (ISBN 0-8040-0150-2). Swallow.

Idiot. Fyodor Dostoevsky. pap. 2.25. Bantam.

Idiot. Fyodor Dostoyevsky. (Classic Ser.). 1969. pap. 2.25 (ISBN 0-451-51374-6, CE1874, Sig Classics). NAL.

Idle Hands. William O'Rourke. 1981. 12.95 (ISBN 0-440-04064-7). Delacorte.

Idle Haven: Community Building Among the Working-Class Retired. Sheila K. Johnson. LC 72-145786. (California Studies in Urbanization & Environmental Studies). 1971. 17.50x (ISBN 0-520-01909-1). U of Cal Pr.

Idle Weeds: The Life of a Sandstone Ridge. David R. Wallace. LC 79-21447. (Illus.). 192p. 1980. 12.95 (ISBN 0-87156-271-5). Sierra.

Idlewild: Special Issue 4. Stanley Nelson. pap. 1.00 (ISBN 0-912292-21-0). The Smith.

Idol for Others. Gordon Merrick. 1977. pap. 2.50 (ISBN 0-380-00971-4, 44842). Avon.

Idol Hunter. Barry Unsworth. 1980. 10.95 (ISBN 0-671-25357-3). S&S.

Idols. Dennis Cooper. 1979. pap. 4.95 (ISBN 0-686-28355-4). Sea Horse.

Idols Behind Altars. Anita Brenner. LC 67-19527. (Illus.). 1929. 18.00x (ISBN 0-8196-0190-X). Biblo.

Idylls of the King. Alfred Tennyson. (Classics Ser). (gr. 10 up). 1968. pap. 1.95 (ISBN 0-8049-0180-5, CL-180). Airmont.

Idylls of the King & a Selection of Poems. Alfred Tennyson. pap. 1.95 (ISBN 0-451-51382-7, CJ1382, Sig Classics). NAL.

IE in Japanese Steel Industry. 144p. 1973. 7.75 (APO30, APO). Unipub.

IES Lighting Handbook-1981: Application Volume. 5th ed. Ed. by John E. Kaufman. (Illus.). 532p. 1981. 50.00 (ISBN 0-87995-008-0). Illum Eng.

IES Lighting Handbook-1981: Reference Volume. 5th ed. Ed. by John E. Kaufman. (Illus.). 488p. 1981. 50.00 (ISBN 0-87995-007-2). Illum Eng.

If. Amy W. Carmichael. (Illus.). 64p. 1980. kivar 3.95 (ISBN 0-310-42202-7). Zondervan.

If. Rudyard Kipling. pap. 2.50 (ISBN 0-385-04217-5, Dolp). Doubleday.

If a Black Were President of the USA. Farghaneh Nejand. 1977. 4.00 o.p. (ISBN 0-682-48853-4). Exposition.

If a Dinosaur Came to Dinner. Jane B. Moncure. LC 77-12957. (Creative Dramatics Ser.). (Illus.). (ps-3). 1978. PLB 5.50 (ISBN 0-89565-008-8); pap. 2.50 (ISBN 0-89565-041-X). Childs World.

If a Divination: Communication Between Gods & Men in West Africa. William Bascom. LC 69-10349. (Illus.). 604p. 1969. 35.00x (ISBN 0-253-32890-X). Ind U Pr.

If a Poem Bothers You. Ed. by Mary Neville. (Illus.). 64p. (Orig.). 1980. pap. 3.75x (ISBN 0-913678-14-7). New Day Pr.

If All Else Fails... Craig Strete. LC 79-7117. (Doubleday D Science Fiction Ser.). 192p. 1980. 8.95 (ISBN 0-385-15237-X). Doubleday.

If All the Seas Were One Sea. Janina Domanska. (Illus.). (gr. k-3). 1971. 8.95 (ISBN 0-02-732930-5). Macmillan.

If an Auk Could Talk. Bernard L. Gordon & Esther S. Gordon. (Illus.). (gr. k-3). 1977. 5.95 o.p. (ISBN 0-8098-0002-0). Walck.

If Being a Christian Is So Great, Why Do I Have the Blahs? John A. Dobbert. LC 79-65420. 160p. 1980. pap. 3.95 (ISBN 0-8307-0729-8, 5413206). Regal.

If Christ Is the Answer, What Are the Questions? Tom Skinner. 192p. 1974. pap. 4.95 (ISBN 0-310-32821-7). Zondervan.

If Dragon Flies Made Honey: Poems. Ed. by David Kherdian. LC 77-3730. (Illus.). (gr. 1-5). 1977. 8.25 (ISBN 0-688-80101-3); PLB 7.92 (ISBN 0-688-84101-5). Greenwillow.

If Dreams Came True. (Illus.). 4.95 (ISBN 0-910550-39-5). Centurion Pr.

If God Loves Me, Why Can't I Get My Locker Open? Lorraine Peterson. 192p. (Orig.). (gr. 6-12). 1980. pap. 3.95 (ISBN 0-87123-251-0, 210251). Bethany Fell.

If He Hollers, Let Him Go. Chester Himes. 1971. pap. 0.95 (ISBN 0-451-04846-6, Q4846, Sig). NAL.

If He's My Brother. B. Williams. 1980. pap. 2.50 (ISBN 0-13-450627-8). P-H.

If I Built a Village... Kazue Mizumura. LC 77-140645. (Illus.). (gr. k-3). 1971. 7.95 (ISBN 0-690-42903-7, TYC-J); PLB 7.89 o.p. (ISBN 0-690-42904-5). T Y Crowell.

If I Can, You Can. Betty L. Esses. 128p. 1974. pap. 2.75 o.p. (ISBN 0-88368-040-8). Whitaker Hse.

If I Drove a Tractor. Miriam Young. LC 72-5142. (Illus.). 32p. (gr. k-3). 1973. 7.75 (ISBN 0-688-41338-2); PLB 7.44 o.p. (ISBN 0-688-51338-7). Lothrop.

If I Drove a Train. Miriam Young. LC 70-177317. (Illus.). 32p. (gr. k-3). 1972. PLB 7.44 (ISBN 0-688-51601-7). Lothrop.

If I Flew a Plane. Miriam Young. LC 79-101481. (Illus.). (gr. k-3). 1970. PLB 7.44 o.p. (ISBN 0-688-51043-4). Lothrop.

If I Ran the Circus. Dr. Seuss. LC 56-9469. (Dr. Seuss Paperback Classics Ser.). (Illus.). 64p. (gr. k-3). 1980. pap. 2.95 (ISBN 0-394-84546-3). Random.

If I Ran the Zoo. Dr. Seuss. LC 50-10185. (Illus.). 64p. (gr. k-3). 1980. pap. 2.95 (ISBN 0-394-84545-5). Random.

If I Take the Wings of the Morning. Elizabeth Beckwith. 1979. 2.00 (ISBN 0-686-28780-0). Forward Movement.

If I Were a Horse. Elizabeth Bridgman. LC 77-6079. (Illus.). (gr. 3-6). 1977. PLB 5.95 (ISBN 0-396-07464-2). Dodd.

If I Were a Mother... Kazue Mizumura. LC 67-23668. (Illus.). (gr. k-3). 1968. PLB 7.89 o.p. (ISBN 0-690-42917-7, TYC-J). T Y Crowell.

If I Were a Word, I'd Be a Song. Bill Staines. 96p. 1980. pap. 6.95 (ISBN 0-686-27977-8). Folk-Legacy.

If I'm the Better Player, Why Can't I Win? Allen Fox & Richard Evans. LC 79-63332. 160p. 1979. 8.95 (ISBN 0-914178-28-8, 24924, Pub. by Tennis Mag). Golf Digest.

If I'm the Better Player, Why Can't I Win. Allen Fox & Richard Evans. LC 79-63332. (Tennis Magazine Bks.). 160p. 1979. 8.95. Golf Digest Bks.

If It Doesn't Pan Out: How to Cope with Cooking Disasters. Barbara Bloch. LC 80-26508. 1981. 8.95 (ISBN 0-934878-02-1). Dembner Bks.

If It's Raining, This Must Be the Weekend. Nancy Stahl. 1979. 7.95 o.p. (ISBN 0-8362-1114-6). Andrews & McMeel.

If on a Winter's Night a Traveler. Italo Calvino. Tr. by William Weaver from It. LC 80-8741. (Helen & Kurt Wolff Bk.). 288p. 1981. 12.95 (ISBN 0-15-143689-4). HarBraceJ.

If Once You Have Lived in Alaska. Marie Blood. 1981. 6.95 (ISBN 0-533-04715-3). Vantage.

If the Devil Wrote a Bible. Kent Philpott. 1975. pap. 1.95 o.p. (ISBN 0-88270-105-3). Logos.

If the Earth Falls In. Mavis T. Clark. LC 75-4781. 176p. (gr. 6 up). 1975. 6.95 (ISBN 0-395-28900-9, Clarion). HM.

If the South Won Gettysburg. Mark Nesbitt. LC 80-52561. (Illus.). 200p. (Orig.). 1980. pap. 2.50 (ISBN 0-937740-01-2). Reliance Pub.

If the Stars Are Gods. Gregory Benford & Gordon Eklund. 1978. pap. 1.75 o.p. (ISBN 0-425-03761-4, Medallion). Berkley Pub.

If the Stars Are Gods. Gregory Benford & Gordon Eklund. LC 76-28692. (YA) 1977. 7.95 o.p. (ISBN 0-686-57865-1). Berkley Pub.

If There Be Thorns. V. C. Andrews. Date not set. pap. price not set. PB.

If There Is a God, Why Are There Atheists? R. C. Sproul. LC 74-13762. Orig. Title: Psychology of Atheism. 1974. pap. 2.95 (ISBN 0-87123-238-3, 200238). Bethany Fell.

If Thou Shalt Confess. rev. ed. Jan K. Van Baalen. 1962. 2.95 o.p. (ISBN 0-8028-3279-2). Eerdmans.

If We Dream Too Long. Goh Poh Seng. (Writing in Asia Ser.). 1972. text ed. 5.50x (ISBN 0-686-60439-3, 00225). Heinemann Ed.

If Ye Continue. Guy Duty. LC 82-2314. 1966. pap. 4.95 (ISBN 0-87123-243-X, 210243). Bethany Fell.

If You Ask Me...! Alice P. Morgan. LC 78-62901. (Illus.). 1978. 7.95 (ISBN 0-916624-23-4). TSU Pr.

If You Can Walk, You Can Ski. Frank Day. 1966. pap. 1.50 o.s.i. (ISBN 0-02-028320-2, Collier). Macmillan.

If You Can't Say Something Nice... Political Cartoons by Marlette. Douglas N. Marlette. LC 78-73463. (Orig.). 1978. pap. 4.95 o.s.i. (ISBN 0-89284-002-1). Graphic Pr.

If You Feel Like Singing: American Folksongs & Activities for Students of English. Alice H. Osman & Jean McConochie. (Illus.). 1979. pap. text ed. 3.95x (ISBN 0-582-79724-1); cassettes 11.50x (ISBN 0-582-79725-X); cassette & book 13.50x (ISBN 0-582-78310-0). Longman.

If-You Form an Israelite Law. Harry Gilmer. LC 75-23136. (Society of Biblical Literature. Dissertation Ser.). 140p. 1975. pap. 7.50 (ISBN 0-89130-004-X, 060115). Scholars Pr Ca.

If You Had Been in Bethlehem: Diorama Book. Carol Ferntheil. (gr. k-3). 1977. 3.25 (ISBN 0-87239-166-3, 3605). Standard Pub.

If You Listen. Charlotte Zolotow. LC 79-2688. (Ursula Nordstrom Bk.). (Illus.). 32p. (ps-3). 1980. 8.95 (ISBN 0-06-027049-7, HarpJ); PLB 8.79 (ISBN 0-06-027050-0). Har-Row.

If You Lived with the Sioux Indians. Ann McGovern. LC 74-7327. (Illus.). 96p. (gr. 2-4). 1974. 5.95 (ISBN 0-590-07340-0, Four Winds). Schol Bk Serv.

If You Love Me... Kenneth D. Barney. LC 75-22611. (Radiant Life Ser). 1977. pap. 1.50 (ISBN 0-88243-889-1, 02-0889); teacher's ed 2.50 (ISBN 0-88243-163-3, 32-0163). Gospel Pub.

If You Love Your Kids, Don't Let Them Grow up to Be Jerks. Stephen Pileggi. LC 80-16882. (Open Mind Bk.). 64p. (Orig.). 1980. pap. 4.95 (ISBN 0-916392-58-9). Oak Tree Pubns.

If You Read Me, Rock the Tower! Bob Stevens. LC 80-66159. (Illus.). 144p. 1980. write for info. (ISBN 0-8168-6505-1). Aero.

If You Think Your Child Is Gifted. P. M. Pickard. (Illus.). 160p. (Orig.). 1976. pap. 6.75 o.p. (ISBN 0-04-370072-1). Allen Unwin.

If You Were a Ballet Dancer. Gross. (gr. 3). 1979. pap. 1.50 (ISBN 0-590-05746-4, Schol Pap). Schol Bk Serv.

If Young Adult Is the Answer, What Is the Question? Jan Ballard. (Neal-Schuman Professional Bk.). Date not set. cancelled (ISBN 0-912700-14-9). Oryx Pr.

If Your Child Is Drinking... What You Can Do to Fight Alcohol Abuse at Home, at School, & in the Community. Nancy H. Woodward. 360p. 1981. 11.95 (ISBN 0-399-12457-8). Putnam.

If You're Afraid of the Dark Remember the Night Rainbow. Cooper Edens. (Illus.). 1981. 10.95 (ISBN 0-914676-26-1, Star & Elephant Bk); pap. 6.95 (ISBN 0-914676-27-X). Green Tiger.

IFLA Annual 1977: Proceedings. Ed. by Willem R. Koops et al. (IFLA Annual 1977). 275p. 1978. text ed. 31.25 (ISBN 3-7940-4303-0, Pub. by K G Saur). Shoe String.

IFLA Annual 1978: Proceedings. IFLA Council Meeting, 44th, Strbske, Pleso et al. Ed. by Willem R. Koops & Peter Harvard-Williams. 197p. Date not set. text ed. 30.00 (ISBN 0-89664-112-0). K G Saur.

IFR by the Book: Techniques of Instrument Flight. J. R. Williams. (Illus.). 1980. pap. 5.95 (ISBN 0-911721-83-5, Pub. by Gen. Avn. Press). Aviation.

IFR Pilot Exam-O-Grams. Federal Aviation Administration & Aviation Book Company Editors. (Illus.). 96p. 1980. pap. 2.95 (ISBN 0-911721-79-7). Aviation.

Ifugao Bibliography. Harold C. Conklin. (Bibliography: No. 11). vi, 75p. 1980. 4.00 (ISBN 0-686-63731-3). Yale U Pr.

IG for Management of Word Processing Operations. Paula B. Cecil. 1980. 3.95 (ISBN 0-8053-1762-7). Benjamin Cummings.

Iglook's Seal. Bernard Wiseman. LC 76-23410. (gr. 1-4). 1977. 5.95 (ISBN 0-396-07396-4). Dodd.

Ignacio de Luzan. Ivy L. McClelland. (World Authors Ser.: Spain: No. 221). lib. bdg. 10.95 (ISBN 0-8057-2552-0). Twayne.

Ignacio Manuel Altamirano. Chris N. Nacci. (World Authors Ser.: Mexico: No. 124). lib. bdg. 12.50 (ISBN 0-8057-2040-5). Twayne.

Ignacy Paderewski. Wladyslaw Duleba & Zofia Sokolowska. Tr. by Wiktor Litwinski from Polish. (Library of Polish Studies: Vol. VII). (Illus.). text ed. 8.95 (ISBN 0-917004-14-0). Kosciuszko.

Ignatius Donnelly. David D. Anderson. (United States Author Ser.: No. 362). 1980. lib. bdg. 14.50 (ISBN 0-8057-7303-7). Twayne.

Igneous Rocks of the British Isles. D. S. Sutherland. 560p. 1981. 94.00 (ISBN 0-471-27810-6, Pub. by Wiley-Interscience). Wiley.

Ignorance of Certainty. Ashley Montagu & Edward Darling. LC 78-123955. 1970. 8.95 o.s.i. (ISBN 0-06-012997-2, HarpT). Har-Row.

Ignorance of Social Intervention. Ed. by Digby C. Anderson. 163p. 1980. 27.50x (ISBN 0-7099-0270-0, Pub. by Croom Helm Ltd England). Biblio Dist.

Ihara Saikaku: Worldy Mental Calculations. Ben Befu. (Publications in Occasional Papers: No. 5). 1976. pap. 13.50x (ISBN 0-520-09406-9). U of Cal Pr.

I'Isniyatam. Katherine S. Saubel & Anne Galloway. 1978. 2.00 (ISBN 0-686-25514-3). Malki Mus Pr.

Ikebana in Quick & Easy Series. Koho Hihara et al. (Illus., Orig.). 1978. pap. 3.95 (ISBN 0-8048-1335-3, Pub. by Shufunotomo Co Ltd Japan). C E Tuttle.

Ikebana: Spirit & Technique. Shusul Komoda & Horst Pointer. (Illus.). 224p. 1980. 15.95 (ISBN 0-7137-1040-3, Pub. by Blandford Pr England). Sterling.

Ike's Spies: Eisenhower & the Espionage Establishment. Stephen E. Ambrose & Richard H. Immerman. LC 80-1117. (Illus.). 384p. 1981. 14.95 (ISBN 0-385-14493-8). Doubleday.

Ikons. John Stuart. 1975. 48.00 (ISBN 0-571-08846-5, Pub. by Faber & Faber). Merrimack Bk Serv.

Ikons, & Other Poems. 2nd ed. Lawrence Durrell. LC 80-17105. (Mediterranean Culture Ser.). (Illus.). 64p. 1981. 15.00x (ISBN 0-933806-01-9). Black Swan CT.

Il Prime Libre de' Madrigali Italiani et Canzoni Francese a due Voci: Masters & Monuments of the Renaissance, Vol. 1. Ihan Gero. Ed. by Lawrence F. Bernstein & James Haar. xliv, 213p. 1980. 35.00x (ISBN 0-8450-7301-X). Broude.

Il Principe (De Principatibus) Niccolo Machiavelli. Ed. & intro. by Brian Richardson. 153p. (Orig., Ital.). 1979. pap. 5.95x (ISBN 0-7190-0742-9, Pub. by Manchester England). S F Vanni.

Il Settimo Libro de, Madrigali a Cinque Voci 1595: Luca Marenzio, the Secular Works, 14. Luca Marenzio. Tr. by Patricia Myers. (Illus.). xxxv, 224p. 1980. 35.00x (ISBN 0-8450-7114-9). Broude.

Ilahita Arapesh: Dimensions of Unity. Donald F. Tuzin. 1976. 26.75x (ISBN 0-520-02860-0). U of Cal Pr.

Ilene, the Superstitious. Katheryn Kimbrough. (Saga of the Phenwick Women: No. 14). 1977. pap. 1.50 o.p. (ISBN 0-445-03181-6). Popular Lib.

Ileostomy Care. Marshall Sparberg. (Illus.). 176p. 1971. 14.50 (ISBN 0-398-02620-3). C C Thomas.

Ileostomy: Surgery, Physiology & Management. Graham L. Hill. LC 75-44116. (Illus.). 208p. 1976. 25.50 (ISBN 0-8089-0928-2). Grune.

Ileostomy, Surgery, Physiology, & Management. Graham L. Hill. 1976. 25.50 (ISBN 0-8089-0928-2). Grune.

Iliad. Homer. LC 80-15669. (Raintree Short Classics). (Illus.). 48p. (gr. 4 up). 1981. PLB 9.95 (ISBN 0-8172-1663-4). Raintree Pubs.

Iliad & the Odyssey, 2 vols. Tr. by Robert Fitzgerald & Robert Fitzgerald. 1080p. 1975. boxed set 27.50 o.p. (ISBN 0-385-11066-9, Anchor Pr). Doubleday.

Iliad of Homer. Homer. Tr. by Ennis Rees. LC 76-56428. (Library of Liberal Arts Ser.). 1977. pap. text ed. 7.95 (ISBN 0-672-61414-6). Bobbs.

Iliad of Homer. Tr. by Richard Lattimore. 63p. pap. 3.95 (ISBN 0-226-46940-9). U of Chicago Pr.

Iliad or the Poem of Force. Simone Weil. LC 57-6026. 1956. pap. 1.25x (ISBN 0-87574-091-X). Pendle Hill.

Iliada. Homer. (Span.). 7.95 (ISBN 84-241-5415-0). E Torres & Sons.

Iliada. 5th ed. Homero. (Biblioteca Basica De Cultura Ser.). (Span.). pap. 6.25 (ISBN 0-8477-0708-3). U of PR Pr.

I'll Be Seeing You. Larry Fagin. LC 77-28219. 1978. 14.95 (ISBN 0-916190-10-2); pap. 6.00 (ISBN 0-916190-11-0). Full Court NY.

I'll Be Your Best Friend. Linda P. Silbert & Alvin J. Silbert. (Little Twirps, TM Understanding People Books). (Illus.). (gr. k-4). 1978. pap. 2.25 (ISBN 0-89544-056-3). Silbert Bress.

I'll Cry Tomorrow. Lillian Roth. 1977. pap. 4.95 (ISBN 0-8119-0385-0). Fell.

I'll Eat Anything If I Can Make It Myself. Mouse Stori. (Illus.). 176p. spiral bdg. 7.95. Chicago Review.

Ill Feeling in the Era of Good Feeling. James A. Kehl. LC 56-6425. 1956. 4.00 (ISBN 0-910294-25-9). Brown Bk.

I'll Get By. Elizabeth Byrd. 204p. (gr. 7up). 1981. 9.95 (ISBN 0-670-39134-4). Viking Pr.

I'll Get Even. Judith Conaway. LC 77-23455. (Moods & Emotions Ser.). (Illus.). (gr. k-3). 1977. PLB 8.95 (ISBN 0-8172-0964-6). Raintree Pubs.

I'll Never Be Fat Again. Carole Livingston. 224p. 1981. pap. 2.50 (ISBN 0-345-28659-6). Ballantine.

I'll Never Lie to You: Jimmy Carter in His Own Words. Robert W. Turner. (Orig.). 1976. pap. 1.75 o.p. (ISBN 0-345-25702-2). Ballantine.

I'll Protect You from the Jungle Beasts. Martha Alexander. LC 73-6015. (Illus.). 31p. (ps-2). 1980. Repr. of 1973 ed. pap. 1.95 (ISBN 0-8037-3900-1, Pied Piper Bk.). Dial.

I'll Quit Tomorrow. rev. ed. Vernon E. Johnson. LC 79-3759. 192p. 1980. 9.95 (ISBN 0-06-250430-4, HarpR). Har-Row.

I'll See You in Court. Godfrey Isaac & Richard Kleiner. LC 79-51021. 1979. 9.95 o.p. (ISBN 0-8092-7399-3). Contemp Bks.

I'll Skip the Appetizer--I Ate the Flowers. Arnie Levin. 1980. pap. 4.95 (ISBN 0-452-25242-3, 25242, Plume). NAL.

I'll Stop Tomorrow. Barbara Tamasi. 450p. (Orig.). 1980. pap. 5.95 (ISBN 0-932260-06-3). Rock Harbor.

I'll Tell You Why. Chip Sale. 1975. Repr. 5.00 (ISBN 0-911416-01-3). Specialist.

I'll Throw the Book at You. Mort Walker. Ed. by Wendy Wallace. (Beetle Bailey Ser.: No. 8). 128p. (gr. 2 up). pap. 1.50 (ISBN 0-448-12635-4, Tempo). G&D.

Illabakan (Niger) Une Tribu Touaregue Sahelienne et Son Aire De Nomadisation. Edmond Bernus. (Atlas Des Structures Agraires Au Sud Du Sahara: No. 10). 1974. 44.10x (ISBN 90-2797-535-3). Mouton.

Illegal but Not Criminal: Business Crime in America. John Conklin. LC 77-7621. 1977. 8.95 o.p. (ISBN 0-13-450890-4); pap. 3.95 o.p. (ISBN 0-13-450882-3). P-H.

Illegal Man. Patrick Dearen. 1981. pap. 2.25 (ISBN 0-8439-0872-6, Leisure Bks). Nordon Pubns.

Illegal Mexican Aliens in the United States: A Teaching Manual on Impact Dimensions & Alternative Futures. Kenneth F. Johnson & Nina M. Ogle. LC 78-62177. 1978. pap. text ed. 9.25 (ISBN 0-8191-0575-9). U Pr of Amer.

Illegitimacy. Shirley F. Hartley. LC 73-83057. 1975. 15.75x (ISBN 0-520-02533-4). U of Cal Pr.

Illegitimacy, Sexuality & the Status of Women. Derek Gill. 1977. 36.00x (ISBN 0-631-17020-0, Pub. by Basil Blackwell). Biblio Dist.

Illiac IV: The First Super Computer. R. Michael Hord. (Illus.). 1981. text ed. price not set (ISBN 0-914894-71-4). Computer Sci.

Illinois. 33.00 (ISBN 0-89770-089-9). Curriculum Info Ctr.

Illinois: A Descriptive & Historical Guide. Federal Writers Project. LC 72-145010. (Illus.). 1971. Repr. of 1947 ed. 59.00 (ISBN 0-403-01292-9). Somerset Pub.

Illinois: A History. Richard J. Jensen. (States & the Nation Ser.). (Illus.). 1978. 12.95 (ISBN 0-393-05596-5, Co-Pub by AASLH). Norton.

Illinois Chronology & Factbook, Vol. 13. R. I. Vexler. 1978. 8.50 (ISBN 0-379-16138-9). Oceana.

Illinois Divorce, Separate Maintenance & Annulment, with Forms. 2nd ed. Meyer Weinberg. 1969. with suppl. 25.00 (ISBN 0-672-82919-3, Bobbs-Merrill Law); 1976 suppl. 10.00 (ISBN 0-672-82804-9). Michie.

Illinois: Government & Institutions. new ed. Carlson. (gr. 9-12). 1973. pap. text ed. 4.20 o.p. (ISBN 0-205-03645-7, 7636458). Allyn.

Illinois! Illinois! An Annotated Bibliography of Fiction. Thomas L. Kilpatrick & Patsy Rose Hoshiko. LC 79-13011. 627p. 1979. 30.00 (ISBN 0-8108-1222-3). Scarecrow.

Illinois in the Second World War: Vol. 2, The Production Front. Mary Watters. 1952. 5.00 (ISBN 0-912154-19-5). Ill St Hist Lib.

Illinois Legislature: Structure & Process. Samuel K. Gove et al. LC 76-21238. 203p. 1976. pap. 5.95 (ISBN 0-252-00621-6). U of Ill Pr.

Illinois Lobbyists Study, 1964. 2nd ed. Samuel Patterson. LC 75-38490. 1975. Repr. of 1969 ed. codebk 8.00 (ISBN 0-89138-006-X). ICPSR.

Illinois Supplement for Real Estate Principles & Practices. Patricia Carlon et al. (Business & Economics Ser.). 112p. 1976. 4.95 (ISBN 0-675-08583-7). Merrill.

Illinois Women's Directory: A Comprehensive Guide to Women's Organizations & Programs Throughout Illinois and Northwestern Indiana. Kathleen M. Ligare. LC 78-66125. (Illus.). 168p. 1978. pap. 5.95 (ISBN 0-8040-0802-7). Swallow.

Illiterate Digest. Will Rogers. LC 77-145720. (Illus.). 351p. 1975. Repr. of 1924 ed. 24.00 (ISBN 0-8103-3975-7). Gale.

Illness & Healing Among the Sakhalin Ainu: A Symbolic Interpretation. Emiko Ohnuki-Tierney. LC 80-24268. (Illus.). 272p. Date not set. price not set (ISBN 0-521-23636-3). Cambridge U Pr.

Illness, Immunity & Social Interaction. Gordon E. Moss. 298p. 1981. Repr. of 1973 ed. text ed. price not set (ISBN 0-89874-266-8). Krieger.

Illness, Immunity & Social Interaction: The Dynamics of Biosocial Resonation. Gordon E. Moss. LC 72-11782. 352p. 1973. 24.50 o.p. (ISBN 0-471-61925-6, Pub. by Wiley-Interscience). Wiley.

Illnesses of Our Time. Koenig. 1980. pap. 3.25x (ISBN 0-906492-36-X, Pub. by Kolisko Archives). St George Bk Serv.

Illuminated Alphabet. Ted Menten. (Illus.). 1978. pap. 1.50 (ISBN 0-486-22745-6). Dover.

Illuminated Blake. Ed. by David V. Erdman. LC 74-3702. 416p. 1974. pap. 8.95 (ISBN 0-385-06053-X, Anch). Doubleday.

Illuminati Papers. Robert A. Wilson. LC 80-16641. 160p. 1980. pap. 7.95 (ISBN 0-915904-52-7). And-Or Pr.

Illumination & Polarization of the Sunlit Sky on Rayleigh Scattering. S. Chandrasekhar & Donna D. Elbert. LC 54-12909. (Transactions Ser.: Vol. 44, Pt. 6). (Illus.). 1954. pap. 1.00 o.p. (ISBN 0-87169-446-8). Am Philos.

Illumination Engineering for Energy Efficient Luminous Environments. R. Helms. 1980. 28.95 (ISBN 0-13-450809-2). P-H.

Illumination-Fruits. 1974. 2.00 o.p. (ISBN 0-88497-148-1). Aum Pubns.

Illuminations. Arthur Rimbaud. Ed. by N. Osmond. (French Poets Ser.). (Illus.). 192p. 1976. text ed. 27.50x (ISBN 0-485-14710-6, Athlone Pr); pap. text ed. 13.00x (ISBN 0-485-12710-5, Athlone). Humanities.

Illuminations of the Stavelot Bible. Wayne Dynes. LC 77-94693. (Outstanding Dissertations in the Fine Arts Ser.). (Illus.). 1979. lib. bdg. 36.00 (ISBN 0-8240-3225-X). Garland Pub.

Illusion & Reality in Indian Secondary Education. G. K. Verma et al. 1979. text ed. 21.50x (ISBN 0-566-00292-2, Pub. by Gower Pub Co England). Renouf.

Illusion of Democracy in Dependent Nations: Vol. 3 of Politics of Change on Venezuela. Jose A. Silva-Michelena. 1971. 20.00x (ISBN 0-262-19069-9). MIT Pr.

Illusion of Immortality. 4th ed. Corliss Lamont. LC 65-25140. 1965. pap. 4.45 (ISBN 0-8044-6377-8). Ungar.

Illusion of Life: American Realism As a Literary Form. Harold H. Kolb, Jr. LC 76-93186. 1969. 9.95x (ISBN 0-8139-0286-X). U Pr of Va.

Illusion of Power. Stephen Orgel. LC 73-80827. (Quantum Bks). (Illus.). 1975. 11.95x (ISBN 0-520-02505-9); pap. 4.95 (ISBN 0-520-02741-8). U of Cal Pr.

Illusion of Power in Tudor Politics. Joel Hurstfield. (Creighton Lectures in History 1978 Ser.). (Orig.). 1979. pap. text ed. 4.75x (ISBN 0-485-14123-X, Athlone Pr). Humanities.

Illusion of the Epoch: Marxism-Leninism As a Philosophical Creed. H. B. Acton. 1955. cased 20.50 o.p. (ISBN 0-7100-1003-6). Routledge & Kegan.

Illusion of the Epoch: Marxism-Leninism As a Philosophical Creed. H. B. Acton. 286p. 1973. pap. 8.95 (ISBN 0-7100-7657-6). Routledge & Kegan.

Illusionists. Wolf Rilla. 1978. pap. 1.95 o.s.i. (ISBN 0-515-04560-8). Jove Pubns.

Illusionless Man: Some Fantasies & Meditations on Disillusionment. Allen Wheelis. 1971. pap. 2.95x o.p. (ISBN 0-06-131927-9, TB1927, Torch). Har-Row.

Illusions. Richard Bach. 1978. gift ed. 12.95 o.s.i. (ISBN 0-440-04105-8, E Friede). Delacorte.

Illusions. E. Lanners. 1977. 12.95 o.p. (ISBN 0-03-020891-2); pap. 6.95 o.p. (ISBN 0-03-020886-6). HR&W.

Illusions. Andre Maurois. LC 68-29043. 1968. 12.50x (ISBN 0-231-03171-8). Columbia U Pr.

Illusions of Justice. Lennox S. Hinds. LC 79-19318. 432p. (Orig.). 1979. pap. 6.50 (ISBN 0-934936-00-5). U of Iowa Sch Soc Wk.

Illusions of Power: The Fate of a Reform Government. Michael Sexton. 1979. text ed. 21.00x (ISBN 0-86861-265-0); pap. text ed. 11.50x (ISBN 0-86861-273-1). Allen Unwin.

Illusions of Progress. Georges Sorel. Tr. by John Stanley & Charlotte Stanley. LC 69-16511. 1969. 19.50x (ISBN 0-520-01531-2); pap. 3.25 (ISBN 0-520-02256-4, CAL251). U of Cal Pr.

Illustrated Atlas of the Middle East. 48p. 1975. 10.00 o.s.i. (ISBN 0-528-83077-5). Rand.

Illustrated Baseball Dictionary for Young People. Henry Walker. (Illus.). 1978. pap. 2.50 (ISBN 0-13-450924-2). P-H.

Illustrated Basic Crochet & Knit. Ondori Publishing Company Staff. (Illus.). 48p. 1977. pap. 2.95 (ISBN 0-87040-389-3). Japan Pubns.

Illustrated Basketball Dictionary for Young People. Steve Clark. (Illus.). 1978. pap. 2.50 (ISBN 0-13-450940-4). P-H.

Illustrated Basketball Rules. Edward S. Steitz. LC 75-44526. 2.50 (ISBN 0-385-11407-9, Dolp). Doubleday.

Illustrated Biology, 2 pts. Maud Jepson. Incl. Pt. 1. Plants (ISBN 0-7195-0735-9); Pt. 2. Animals (ISBN 0-7195-0734-0). (Illus.). (gr. 8-12). 6.95x ea. Transatlantic.

Illustrated Bird Watcher's Dictionary. Donald S. Heintzelman. 1980. 11.95 (ISBN 0-87691-314-1). Winchester Pr.

Illustrated Book of Baseball Folklore. Tristram P. Coffin. LC 75-9968. (Illus.). 250p. 1975. 14.95 o.p. (ISBN 0-8164-9262-X). Continuum.

Illustrated Book of World History. Margaret Shaman & Derek Wilson. (Illus.). 1978. 14.95 (ISBN 0-8467-0532-X, Pub. by Two Continents). Hippocrene Bks.

Illustrated Catalogue of the Rothschild Collection of Nycteribiidae (Diptera) in the British Museum (Natural History) Oskar Theodor. (Illus.). viii, 506p. 1967. 66.50x (ISBN 0-565-00655-X, Pub. by British Mus Nat Hist England). Sabbot-Natural Hist Bks.

Illustrated Catechism. Redemptorist Pastoral Publication. 112p. (Orig.). 1981. pap. 3.95 (ISBN 0-89243-135-0). Liguori Pubns.

Illustrated Dictionary of Bible Manners & Customs. A. Van Deursen. (Illus.). 1967. pap. 4.75 (ISBN 0-8022-1762-1). Philos Lib.

Illustrated Dictionary of British History. Ed. by Arthur Marwick et al. (Illus.). 320p. 1981. 19.95 (ISBN 0-500-25072-3). Thames Hudson.

Illustrated Dictionary of Impressionism. Raymond Cognia & Frank Elgar. (Illus.). (gr. 10-12). 1979. pap. 3.95 (ISBN 0-8120-0986-X). Barron.

Illustrated Dictionary of Jewellery. Anita Mason & Diane Packer. LC 73-11590. (Illus.). 400p. 1974. 15.95 o.s.i. (ISBN 0-06-012818-6, HarpT). Har-Row.

Illustrated Dictionary of Photography. pap. 18.95 o.p. (ISBN 0-85242-094-3, Pub. by Fountain). Morgan.

Illustrated Dictionary of Surrealism. Jose Pierre. (Illus.). (gr. 10-12). 1978. pap. 3.95 (ISBN 0-8120-0987-8). Barron.

Illustrated Dictionary of Terminology Microcomputer. Michael Hordeski. (Illus.). 1978. 12.95 (ISBN 0-8306-9875-2); pap. 8.95 (ISBN 0-8306-1088-X, 1088). TAB Bks.

Illustrated Edgar Allan Poe. Satty. (Illus.). 1977. pap. 7.95 o.s.i. (ISBN 0-446-87203-2). Warner Bks.

Illustrated Emmanuelle. Emmanuelle Arsan. LC 80-999. 144p. 1980. 25.00 (ISBN 0-8021-0206-9, GP837); pap. 9.95 (ISBN 0-8021-4316-4, E765 EVER). Grove.

Illustrated Encyclopedia of Archaology. Ed. by Glyn Daniel. LC 77-4817. (Illus.). 1977. 17.95 o.s.i. (ISBN 0-690-01473-2, TYC-T). T Y Crowell.

Illustrated Encyclopedia of Astronomy & Space. Ed. by Ian Ridpath. LC 76-3577. (Illus.). 1976. 17.95 (ISBN 0-690-01132-6, TYC-T). T Y Crowell.

Illustrated Encyclopedia of Boating. Alan Lucas. LC 78-9809. (Illus.). 1978. 12.95 o.p. (ISBN 0-684-15900-7, ScribT). Scribner.

Illustrated Encyclopedia of Medeival Civilization. Ayreh Grabois. (Illus.). 752p. 1980. 25.00 (ISBN 0-7064-0856-X). Mayflower Bks.

Illustrated Encyclopedia of Military Vehicles. Ivan V. Hogg & John Weeks. LC 80-8006. 1980. 30.00 (ISBN 0-13-450817-3). P-H.

Illustrated Encyclopedia of Mysticism & the Mystery Religions. John Ferguson. LC 76-55812. (Illus.). 1976. 14.95 (ISBN 0-8164-9310-3). Continuum.

Illustrated Encyclopedia of Ships, Boats, Vessels & Other Water-Borne Craft. Graham Blackburn. LC 78-16565. (Illus.). 1978. 17.95 (ISBN 0-87951-082-X). Overlook Pr.

Illustrated Encyclopedia of the Classical World. Ed. by Michael Avi Yonah & Israel Shatzman. LC 73-14245. (Illus.). 510p. 1976. 20.00 o.p. (ISBN 0-06-010178-4, HarpT). Har-Row.

Illustrated Encyclopedia of World Theater. Ed. by Martin Esslin. (Illus.). 320p. 1981. pap. 12.95 (ISBN 0-500-27207-7). Thames Hudson.

Illustrated Family Hymn Book. Ed. by Tony Jasper. (Illus.). 192p. 1980. 19.50 (ISBN 0-8164-0143-8); pap. 9.95 (ISBN 0-8164-2051-3). Seabury.

Illustrated Football Dictionary for Young People. Joseph Olgin. (Treehouse Illustrated Sports Dictionaries Ser.). (Illus.). 1978. pap. 2.50 (ISBN 0-13-450874-2). P-H.

Illustrated Gaelic-English Dictionary. 8th ed. Dwelly. (Illus.). 35.00x (ISBN 0-686-00868-5). Colton Bk.

Illustrated Glossary of Architecture: Eight Fifty to Eighteen Thirty. John Harris & Jill Lever. (Illus.). 1979. 15.95 (ISBN 0-571-06883-9, Pub. by Faber & Faber); pap. 9.95 (ISBN 0-571-09074-5). Merrimack Bk Serv.

Illustrated Glossary of Environmental & Ecological Terms. Arthur Torrie. (Illus.). 1977. pap. text ed. 6.50x o.p. (ISBN 0-435-59896-1). Heinemann Ed.

Illustrated Golden Bough. Frazer, James George, Sir. LC 78-3229. 1978. 14.95 o.p. (ISBN 0-385-14515-2). Doubleday.

Illustrated Guide to Bombers of World War II. Bill Gunston. LC 80-67628. (Illustrated Military Guides). (Illus.). 4094p. 1981. 7.95 (ISBN 0-668-05094-2, 5094). Arco.

Illustrated Guide to Collecting Bottles. Cecil Munsey. 1977. pap. 10.95 (ISBN 0-8015-3940-4, Hawthorn). Dutton.

Illustrated Guide to Food Preparation. 3rd ed. Margaret McWilliams. LC 76-13996. (Illus.). 1976. spiral bdg. 11.95x (ISBN 0-916434-17-6). Plycon Pr.

Illustrated Guide to Food Preparation. 4th rev. ed. Margaret McWilliams. 1981. pns (ISBN 0-8087-3409-1). Burgess.

Illustrated Guide to Foreign & Fancy Foods. Mary Kramer. LC 75-20972. (Illus.). 1975. pap. 1.95x spiral bdg. (ISBN 0-916434-14-1). Plycon Pr.

Illustrated Guide to Fossil Collecting. rev. ed. Richard L. Casanova & Ronald P. Ratkevich. (Illus.). 212p. 1981. lib. bdg. 9.95 (ISBN 0-87961-112-X); pap. 5.95 (ISBN 0-87961-113-8). Naturegraph.

Illustrated Guide to German, Italian & Japanese Fighters of World War II. Bill Gunston. LC 80-67627. (Illustrated Military Guides). (Illus.). 160p. 1981. 7.95 (ISBN 0-668-05093-4, 5093). Arco.

Illustrated Guide to Ghosts & Mysterious Occurrences in the Old North State. Bruce Roberts & Nancy Roberts. LC 59-14157. (Orig.). 5.95 (ISBN 0-87461-954-8); pap. 4.50 (ISBN 0-87461-955-6). McNally.

Illustrated Guide to Modern Fighters & Attack Aircraft. Bill Gunston. LC 80-65164. (Illustrated Military Guides Ser.). (Illus.). 160p. 1980. 7.95 (ISBN 0-668-04964-2, 4964-2). Arco.

Illustrated Guide to Modern Tanks & Fighting Vehicles. Christopher F. Foss. LC 80-65165. (Illustrated Military Guides Ser.). (Illus.). 160p. 1980. 7.95 (ISBN 0-668-04965-0, 4965-0). Arco.

Illustrated Guide to Modern Warships. Hugh Lyon. LC 80-65166. (Illustrated Military Guides Ser.). (Illus.). 160p. 1980. 7.95 (ISBN 0-668-04966-9, 4966-9). Arco.

Illustrated Guide to Pollen Analysis. P. D. Moore & J. A. Webb. LC 77-8822. 1978. 24.95x (ISBN 0-470-99218-2). Halsted Pr.

Illustrated Guide to Scotland. 1978. pap. 2.50 o.p. (ISBN 0-905522-11-7, 8014, Pub. by R. Nickelson). Barrie & Jenkins.

Illustrated Guide to Textiles. 2nd ed. Marjory Joseph & Audrey Gieseking. (Illus.). 1972. pap. 7.50x (ISBN 0-916434-02-8). Plycon Pr.

Illustrated Guide to Textiles. 2nd ed. Marjory Joseph & Audrey G. Gieseking. 1981. 8.95 (ISBN 0-8087-3400-8). Burgess.

Illustrated Guide to the Genera of the Staphylinidae of America North of Mexico. Ian Moore & E. F. Legner. (Illus.). 1979. pap. 10.00x (ISBN 0-931876-31-1, 4093). Ag Sci Pubns.

Illustrated Guide to the International Standard Bibliographic Description for Monographs. John L. Sayre & Roberta Hamburger. (Illus., Orig.). 1975. pap. 6.50x o.p. (ISBN 0-912832-12-6). Seminary Pr.

Illustrated Guide to the Legendary Trees of Santa Monica Bay. Fred E. Basten. LC 80-83609. (Illus.). 128p. (Orig.). 1980. pap. 10.95 (ISBN 0-937536-01-6). Graphics Calif.

Illustrated Guide to Trees & Shrubs. rev. ed. Arthur H. Graves. 1956. 12.95x o.p. (ISBN 0-06-070870-0, HarpT). Har-Row.

Illustrated Guide to X-Ray Technics. John E. Cullinan & Angeline M. Cullinan. 1980. text ed. write for info. o.p. (ISBN 0-397-50425-X). Lippincott.

Illustrated Guidebook to Japanese Painting. Innocent De La Salle. (Illus.). 1978. 49.50 (ISBN 0-89266-138-0). Am Classical Coll Pr.

Illustrated Guidebook to the Frescoes in the Sistine Chapel. Evelyn M. Phillips. (Illus.). 124p. 1981. Repr. of 1901 ed. 49.85 (ISBN 0-89901-029-6). Found Class Reprints.

Illustrated Gymnastics Dictionary for Young People. Ila Guraedy. LC 79-93357. (Illustrated Dictionary Ser.). (Illus.). 120p. (gr. 4 up). 1980. lib. bdg. 6.79 (ISBN 0-8178-0002-6). Harvey.

Illustrated Gymnastics Dictionary for Young People. Ila Guraedy. (Illus., Orig.). pap. 2.50 (ISBN 0-13-450932-3). P-H.

Illustrated Handbook of Vernacular Architecture. new ed. R. W. Brunskill. (Illus.). 1979. 17.50 (ISBN 0-571-08636-5, Pub. by Faber & Faber); pap. 8.95 (ISBN 0-571-11244-7). Merrimack Bk Serv.

Illustrated Herbal Handbook. Adelma G. Simmons. 120p. 1972. pap. 2.95 (ISBN 0-8015-3960-9, Hawthorn). Dutton.

Illustrated Historical Atlas of the County of Wayne, Michigan. (Illus.). 400p. 1967. Repr. of 1876 ed. 20.00 (ISBN 0-8103-3348-1). Gale.

Illustrated History of Civil Engineering. Neil Upton. LC 76-41092. 1976. 17.50x (ISBN 0-8448-1032-0). Crane-Russak Co.

Illustrated History of Country Music. Country Music Magazine Editors. Ed. by Patrick Carr. LC 77-82936. (Illus.). 1979. 14.95 (ISBN 0-385-11601-2); pap. 8.95 (ISBN 0-385-15385-6). Doubleday.

Illustrated History of England. G. M. Trevelyan. (Illus.). 824p. 1974. text ed. 31.00x (ISBN 0-582-48471-5). Longman.

Illustrated History of Indian Baskets & Plates. Viola Roseberry. (Illus.). 1974. pap. 2.50 o.s.i. (ISBN 0-913668-73-7). Ten Speed Pr.

Illustrated History of Poland. Mateusz Siuchninski. Tr. by Stanislaw Tarnowski from Pol. LC 80-460137. (Illus.). 228p. 1979. 13.50x (ISBN 0-8002-2293-8). Intl Pubns Serv.

Illustrated History of the Chinese in America. Ruthanne L. McCunn. LC 79-50114. (Illus.). 136p. 1979. 11.95 (ISBN 0-932538-01-0); pap. 6.95 (ISBN 0-932538-02-9). Design Ent SF.

Illustrated History of the Herbals. Frank J. Anderson. LC 77-8821. (Illus.). 1977. 20.00x (ISBN 0-231-04002-4). Columbia U Pr.

Illustrated History of the Jewish People. LC 72-94297. 1973. 6.95 (ISBN 0-89388-078-7). Okpaku Communications.

Illustrated History of the Rothschild Collection of Fleas (siphonaptera) in the British Museum (Natural History) Vol. Six. Pygiopsyllidae. D. K. Mardon. (Illus.). 296p. 1981. 100.00x (ISBN 0-565-00820-X, Pub. by Brit Mus Nat Hist England). Sabbot-Natural Hist Bks.

Illustrated Hockey Dictionary for Young People. Henry Walker. (Treehouse Illustrated Sports Dictionaries Ser.). (Illus.). 1978. pap. 2.50 (ISBN 0-13-451138-7). P-H.

Illustrated Horseback Riding Dictionary for Young People. E. Vansteenwyk. 1980. pap. 2.50 (ISBN 0-13-450908-0). P-H.

Illustrated Human Embryology, 3 vols. H. Tuchmann-Duplessis et al. Tr. by L. S. Hurley. Incl. Vol. 1. Embryogenesis. 1972. pap. 7.10 (ISBN 0-387-90018-7); Vol. 2. Organogensis. 1972. pap. 11.20 (ISBN 0-387-90019-5); Vol. 3. Nervous System & Endocrine Glands. 1973. pap. 12.40 (ISBN 0-387-90020-9). LC 72-177236. Springer-Verlag.

Illustrated Ice Hockey Rules. Bill Chadwick. LC 76-2834. 160p. 1976. pap. 2.50 (ISBN 0-385-11408-7, Dolp). Doubleday.

Illustrated Magic Dictionary. Geoffrey Lamb. (Illus.). 160p. 1980. 7.95 (ISBN 0-525-66689-3). Elsevier-Nelson.

Illustrated Manual of California Shrubs. Howard E. McMinn. 1939. 25.00x (ISBN 0-520-00847-2). U of Cal Pr.

Illustrated Manual of Pacific Coast Trees. Howard E. McMinn & Evelyn Maino. 1981. pap. 6.95 (ISBN 0-520-04364-2). U of Cal Pr.

Illustrated Night Before Christmas. Alicia Austin. (Illus.). 96p. (gr. k-5). 1980. pap. 1.95 (ISBN 0-448-14151-5, Tempo). G&D.

Illustrated Odyssey: Translated from Homer. Homer. Tr. by E. V. Tieu from Greek. (Illus.). 256p. 1981. 17.95 (ISBN 0-89479-076-5). A & W Pubs.

Illustrated Reference on Cacti & Other Succulents in 5 Volumes. Edgar Lamb & Brian Lamb. Incl. Vol. 1. 1955 (ISBN 0-7137-0681-3); Vol. 2. 1959 (ISBN 0-7137-0623-6); Vol. 3. 1963 (ISBN 0-7137-0009-2); Vol. 4. 1966 (ISBN 0-7137-0691-0). (Illus.). 20.95 ea. (Pub. by Blandford Pr England). Sterling.

Illustrated Reference on Cacti & Succulents, Vol. 5. Edgar Lamb & Brian Lamb. (Illus.). 1978. 20.95 (ISBN 0-7137-0852-2, Pub. by Blandford Pr England). Sterling.

Illustrated Riding Dictionary for Young People. Elizabeth Van Steenwyk. LC 80-81789. (Illustrated Dictionaries). (Illus.). 128p. (gr. 5 up). 1981. PLB 6.89 (ISBN 0-8178-0015-8). Harvey.

Illustrated Science & Invention Encyclopedia: How It Works, 21 vols. 1976. 146.58 (ISBN 0-87475-800-9). Stuttman.

Illustrated Skating Dictionary for Young People. C. Van Steenwyk. (Illus.). 1979. pap. 2.50 (ISBN 0-13-451260-X). P-H.

Illustrated Skating for Young People. Elizabeth Van Steenwyk. LC 79-53149. (Illustrated Dictionaries Ser.). (Illus.). 128p. (gr. 4 up). 1969. PLB 6.79 (ISBN 0-8178-6285-4). Harvey.

Illustrated Skiing Dictionary for Young People. C. Walter. 1980. pap. 2.50 (ISBN 0-13-450858-0). P-H.

Illustrated Skiing Dictionary for Young People. Claire Walter. LC 80-81790. (Illustrated Dictionaries). (Illus.). 128p. (gr. 4 up). 1981. PLB 6.89 (ISBN 0-8178-0017-4). Harvey.

Illustrated Soccer Dictionary for Young People. (Illus.). 1978. pap. 2.50 (ISBN 0-13-451146-8). P-H.

Illustrated Speech Anatomy. 3rd ed. William M. Shearer. (Illus.). 152p. 1979. 19.75 (ISBN 0-398-03817-1). C C Thomas.

Illustrated Sporting Books. John H. Slater. LC 71-75800. 1969. Repr. of 1899 ed. 15.00 (ISBN 0-8103-3889-0). Gale.

Illustrated Standard of the Dairy Goat. Nancy L. Owen. Date not set. 10.00 (ISBN 0-686-26679-X). Dairy Goat.

Illustrated Step-by-Step Beginner's Cookbook. Paul C. Huang. LC 79-18829. (Illus.). 96p. (gr. 3 up). 1980. 9.95 (ISBN 0-590-07476-8, Four Winds). Schol Bk Serv.

Illustrated Swimming, Diving & Surfing Dictionary for Young People. Diana C. Gleasner. LC 79-93358. (Illustrated Dictionary Ser.). (Illus.). 128p. (gr. 4 up). 1980. lib. bdg. 6.79 (ISBN 0-8178-0001-8). Harvey.

Illustrated Swimming, Diving & Surfing Dictionary for Young People. Diana C. Gleasner. (Illus.). (gr. 9 up). pap. 2.50 (ISBN 0-13-451195-6). P-H.

Illustrated Technical German for Builders-Bautechnisches Englisch Im Bild. W. K. Killer. LC 76-467695. 1977. pap. 12.50x (ISBN 3-7625-0898-4). Intl Pubns Serv.

Illustrated Tennis Dictionary for Young People. K. Sweeney. 1979. pap. 2.50 (ISBN 0-13-451278-2). P-H.

Illustrated Textbook of Dog Diseases. James Herriott. (Illus.). 284p. 1980. 7.95 (ISBN 0-87666-733-7, PS-770). TFH Pubns.

Illustrated Treasury of Cultivated Flowers. Frank J. Anderson. LC 79-64989. (Illus.). 160p. 1980. 17.95 (ISBN 0-89659-066-6). Abbeville Pr.

Illustrated Treasury of Orchids. Frank J. Anderson. LC 79-88367. (Illus.). 160p. 1980. 17.95 (ISBN 0-89659-067-4). Abbeville Pr.

Illustrated Tumor Nomenclature. 2nd ed. H. Hamperl & L. V. Ackermann. (Illus., Eng. Span, Fr, Ger. & Rus.). 1969. 37.10 (ISBN 0-387-04567-8). Springer-Verlag.

Illustrated T.V. Dictionary. Carolyn H. Miller. LC 78-73761. (Illustrated Dictionaries Ser.). (Illus.). (gr. 4 up). 1980. PLB 6.79 (ISBN 0-8178-6220-X). Harvey.

Illustrated Who's Who in British Films. Denis Gifford. (Illus.). 1980. 32.00 (ISBN 0-7134-1434-0). David & Charles.

Illustrated Wine Making Book. Ralph Auf Der Heide. LC 72-90968. pap. 1.50 o.p. (ISBN 0-385-06939-1, Dolp). Doubleday.

Illustration & the Novels of Thomas Hardy. Arlene M. Jackson. (Illus.). 168p. 1981. 25.00x (ISBN 0-8476-6275-6). Rowman.

Illustration Index. 3rd ed. Roger C. Greer. LC 72-10918. 1973. 10.00 (ISBN 0-8108-0568-5). Scarecrow.

Illustration, Its Technique & Application to the Sciences. 2nd ed. Carl D. Clarke. (Illus.). 258p. 1949. 18.00 (ISBN 0-685-25473-9). Standard Arts.

Illustration of an Epic: The Earliest Shahnama Manuscripts. Marianna S. Simpson. LC 78-74379. (Outstanding Dissertations in the Fine Arts, Fourth Ser.). (Illus.). 1979. lib. bdg. 47.00 (ISBN 0-8240-3966-1). Garland Pub.

Illustration of Books: A Manual for the Use of Students. Joseph Pennell. LC 78-146921. 1971. Repr. of 1896 ed. 18.00 (ISBN 0-8103-3641-3). Gale.

Illustrations Collection: Its Formation, Classification & Exploitation. Edmund V. Corbett. LC 72-164185. (Illus.). 1971. Repr. of 1941 ed. 18.00 (ISBN 0-8103-3786-X). Gale.

Illustrations from the Works of Andreas Vesalius of Brussels. Andreas Vesalius. Ed. by J. B. Saunders & Charles D. O'Malley. 13.50 (ISBN 0-8446-4830-2). Peter Smith.

Illustrations in Applied Network Theory. F. E. Rogers. LC 72-75949. 1973. 17.50x (ISBN 0-8448-0165-8). Crane-Russak Co.

Illustrations of Accounting for Joint Ventures. (Financial Report Survey Ser.: No. 21). 1980. pap. 8.00. Am Inst CPA.

Illustrations of Auditors' Reports on Comparitve Financial Statements. (Financial Report Survey Ser.: No. 18). 1979. pap. 9.50. Am Inst CPA.

Illustrations of Contra Costa County, California with Historical Sketch: 1879. Smith & Elliott. (Illus.). 1979. Repr. 19.95 (ISBN 0-913548-68-5, Valley Calif). Western Tanager.

Illustrations of Old Testament History. R. D. Barnett. (British Museum Publications). 1978. 9.95 o.p. (ISBN 0-374-83335-4); pap. 4.95 o.p. (ISBN 0-374-84336-8). FS&G.

Illustrations of Selected Proxy Information. (Financial Report Survey Ser.: No. 20). 1979. pap. 8.00. Am Inst CPA.

Illustrations of the Nervous System: Atlas Three. Louis Hausman. (Illus.). 208p. 1971. 18.75 (ISBN 0-398-00800-0). C C Thomas.

Illustrations of William Makepeace Thackeray. John Buchanan-Brown. (Illus.). 192p. 1980. 25.00 (ISBN 0-7153-7811-2). David & Charles.

Illustrations on the Moral Sense. Francis Hutcheson. Ed. by Bernard Peach. LC 71-135545. 1971. 10.00x (ISBN 0-674-44326-8, Belknap Pr). Harvard U Pr.

Illustrative Strategies for Research on Psychopathology in Mental Health, Vol. 3. Group for the Advancement of Psychiatry. (Symposium No. 2). 1956. pap. 1.00 o.p. (ISBN 0-87318-041-0). Adv Psychiatry.

Illustrator Illustrated: Art Directors Index to Illustrators. (Illustrator Illustrated Ser.: No. 2). (Illus.). 1981. 55.00 (ISBN 2-88046-004-2, Pub. by Roto-Vision). Norton.

Illustrators: No. 21. a Visual Communication Bk. 35.00 (ISBN 0-8038-3427-6). Hastings.

Illustrator's Notebook. Ed. by Lee Kingman. LC 77-20028. (Illus.). 1978. 28.00 (ISBN 0-87675-013-7). Horn Bk.

Illustrators of Books for Young People. 2nd ed. Martha E. Ward & Dorothy A. Marquardt. LC 75-9880. 223p. 1975. 10.00 (ISBN 0-8108-0819-6). Scarecrow.

Illustrators of Children's Books: 1744-1945, Vol. 1. Ed. by Bertha E. Mahony et al. (Illus.). 1947. 28.00x (ISBN 0-87675-015-3). Horn Bk.

Illustrators of Children's Books: 1946-1956, Vol. 2. Miller et al. LC 57-31264. (Illus.). 1958. 28.00 (ISBN 0-87675-016-1). Horn Bk.

Illustrators of Children's Books: 1957-1966, Vol. 3. Ed. by Lee Kingman et al. LC 47-31264. (Illus.). 1968. 28.00 (ISBN 0-87675-017-X). Horn Bk.

Illustrators of Children's Books: 1967-1976, Vol. 4. Ed. by Lee Kingman et al. LC 78-13759. (Illus.). 1978. 35.00 (ISBN 0-87675-018-8). Horn Bk.

Illustrators Twenty Two: The 22nd Annual of American Illustration. Ed. by Gerald McConnell. (Illus.). 368p. 1981. 37.50 (ISBN 0-8038-3433-0, Visual Communication). Hastings.

Illustrious Evidence: Approaches to Early Seventeenth-Century Literature. Ed. by Earl Miner. 1975. 15.75x (ISBN 0-520-02782-5). U of Cal Pr.

Illustrious House of Ramires. Eca de Queiroz. Tr. by Ann Stevens from Port. LC 68-29766. 310p. (Port). 1969. 12.00x (ISBN 0-8214-0044-4). Ohio U Pr.

Illustrious Lady: A Biography of Barbara Villiers, Countess of Castlemaine & Duchess of Cleveland. Elizabeth Hamilton. (Illus.). 248p. 1980. 38.00 (ISBN 0-241-10310-X, Pub. by Hamish Hamilton England). David & Charles.

Ilongot Headhunting, 1883-1974: A Study in Society & History. Renato Rosallo. LC 79-64218. (Illus.). 1980. 18.50x (ISBN 0-8047-1046-5). Stanford U Pr.

Ilse Aichinger. J. C. Alldridge. (Modern German Authors: Texts & Contexts Vol. 2). 8.95 (ISBN 0-8023-1235-7). Dufour.

Ilya Ehrenburg: Selections from People, Years & Life. Ed. by C. Moody. LC 73-128339. 312p. 1972. pap. text ed. 12.75 (ISBN 0-08-006354-3). Pergamon.

I'm a Good Man, But. Fritz Ridenour. LC 75-96702. 1969. pap. 1.95 (ISBN 0-8307-0429-9, S102153). Regal.

I'm an Endangered Species: The Autobiography of a Free Enterpriser. D. H. Byrd. LC 78-62614. 1978. 6.95 (ISBN 0-88415-258-8). Pacesetter Pr.

Im Anderen Deutschland: Reader 3. Rita M. Walbruck. LC 80-22199. (Auf Heisser Spur Ser.). (gr. 9-12). 1981. pap. 1.95 (ISBN 0-88436-852-1). EMC.

I'm Busy, Too. Norma Simon. Ed. by Kathleen Tucker. LC 79-18374. (Concept Bk.: Level I). (Illus.). (gr. k-1). 1980. 6.50g (ISBN 0-8075-3464-1). A Whitman.

I'm Cherry, Fly Me. Glen Chase. 1976. pap. 1.25 o.p. (ISBN 0-685-69160-8, LB368ZK, Leisure Bks). Nordon Pubns.

I'm Dancing! Albert D. McCarter & Glenn Reed. (Illus.). 32p. (gr. k-3). 1981. 9.95 (ISBN 0-686-69284-5). Scribner.

I'm Eve. Chris C. Sizemore & Elen S. Pittillo. 1978. pap. 2.25 (ISBN 0-515-04656-6). Jove Pubns.

I'm Frank Hamer: The Life of a Texas Peace Officer. H. Gordon Frost & John H. Jenkins. LC 68-31953. (Illus.). 12.50 (ISBN 0-8363-0051-3); limited ed. 150.00 (ISBN 0-685-13275-7). Jenkins.

I'm Free. Hildreth Scott. (Uplook Ser.). 31p. 1973. pap. 0.75 (ISBN 0-8163-0073-9, 09340-1). Pacific Pr Pub Assn.

I'm from Missouri. Robert F. Karsch. (gr. 7-9). 1978. pap. text ed. 3.50x saddle stitched (ISBN 0-87543-107-0). Lucas.

I'm Glad I'm Little. Kathleen Wulf. LC 76-16535. (Illus.). (ps-2). 1976. 5.50 (ISBN 0-913778-53-2). Childs World.

I'm Glad You Asked That. Rita Bennett. 207p. 4.95 (ISBN 0-930756-56-8, 4290-BE6, Pub. by Logos). Women's Aglow.

I'm Going to the Ocean. Eleanor Schick. (gr. k-1). 1966. 3.95g o.s.i. (ISBN 0-02-781190-5). Macmillan.

I'm Gonna Make You Love Me: The Story of Diana Ross. James Haskins. LC 79-3586. (Illus.). 160p. (gr. 6 up). 1980. 8.95 (ISBN 0-8037-4213-4). Dial.

I'm Gonna Right a Book: Teaching for Successful Living & Learning. Mary E. Murphy. 1981. pap. write for info (ISBN 0-914562-06-1). Merriam Eddy.

I'm Here for an Education...Really, I Am. A. David Shane. 72p. (Orig.). 1980. pap. 2.50 (ISBN 0-9604862-0-8). Westlake.

I'm Hiding. Myra C. Livingston & Erik Blegvad. LC 61-6119. (Illus.). (gr. k-2). 1961. 4.50 o.p. (ISBN 0-15-238090-6, HJ). HarBraceJ.

I'm Late. Barbara J. Crane. (Crane Reading System-English Ser.). (Illus.). (gr. k-2). 1977. pap. text ed. 2.95 (ISBN 0-89075-099-8). Crane Pub Co.

I'm Listening Lord, Keep Talking. Robert J. Baker. 200p. 1981. pap. 6.95 (ISBN 0-8361-1953-3). Herald Pr.

I'm My Mommy-I'm My Daddy. Daniel Wilcox. 24p. (ps). 1975. 1.95 (ISBN 0-307-10499-0, Golden Pr); PLB 7.62 (ISBN 0-307-60499-3). Western Pub.

I'm Nobody! Who Are You? Poems of Emily Dickinson for Children. Emily Dickinson. LC 78-6828. (Illus.). (gr. 1 up). 1978. 11.95 (ISBN 0-916144-21-6); pap. 5.95 (ISBN 0-916144-22-4). Stemmer Hse.

I'm Nobody, Who Are You: The Story of Emily Dickinson. Edna Barth. LC 72-129211. (Illus.). (gr. 3-7). 1971. 6.95 (ISBN 0-395-28843-6, Clarion). HM.

I'm Not a Women's Libber, but... Anne B. Follis. 128p. 1981. 7.95 (ISBN 0-687-18687-0). Abingdon.

I'm Not Going. Nancy Mack. LC 76-12457. (Moods & Emotions Ser.). (Illus.). 32p. (gr. k-3). 1976. PLB 8.95 (ISBN 0-8172-0011-8). Raintree Pubs.

I'm Not Mad at God. David Wilkerson. 1967. pap. 2.25 (ISBN 0-87123-245-6, 200245). Bethany Fell.

I'm Not Moving. Penelope Jones. LC 79-13062. (Illus.). (ps-2). 1980. 8.95 (ISBN 0-87888-156-5). Bradbury Pr.

I'm Not Your Laughing Daughter. Ellen Bass. LC 73-79503. 96p. 1973. 8.00x (ISBN 0-87023-128-6); pap. 3.95 (ISBN 0-87023-129-4). U of Mass Pr.

I'm O. K. - You're a Jerk. Gregory C. Hill. 144p. 1980. 9.95 (ISBN 0-917224-08-6). Gregory Pubns.

I'm OK-You're OK. Thomas Harris. 1973. pap. 2.50 (ISBN 0-380-00772-X, 46268). Avon.

I'm OKay, You're Not So Hot. Dolph Sharp. 1975. pap. 1.50 o.s.i. (ISBN 0-446-98176-1). Warner Bks.

I'm Radcliff Fly Me! Liva Baker. 1976. 12.95 (ISBN 0-02-506310-3). Macmillan.

I'm Running Away. Ann Helena. LC 77-19138. (Moods & Emotions Ser.). (Illus.). (gr. k-3). 1978. PLB 8.95 (ISBN 0-8172-1154-3). Raintree Pubs.

I'm Running to Win. Ann Kiemel. 1980. 6.95 (ISBN 0-8423-1736-8). Tyndale.

I'm Saved, You're Saved--Maybe. Jack R. Presseau. LC 76-12401. 1977. 6.95 (ISBN 0-8042-0832-8). John Knox.

I'm Still Me. Betty J. Lifton. LC 80-24372. 224p. (YA) 1981. 8.95 (ISBN 0-394-84783-0); PLB 8.99 (ISBN 0-394-94783-5). Knopf.

I'm Taggarty Toad. Peter Pavey. LC 80-16696. (Illus.). 32p. (ps-2). 9.95 (ISBN 0-87888-172-7). Bradbury Pr.

I'm Taking a Nap. Bil Keane. 1978. pap. 1.50 (ISBN 0-449-14144-6, GM). Fawcett.

I'm Terrific. Marjorie W. Sharmat. LC 76-9094. (ps-3). 1977. reinforced bdg. 7.95 (ISBN 0-8234-0282-7). Holiday.

I'm Too Busy Cook Book: Recipes for Busy People Who Love to Cook. Estelle Carlson. (Illus.). 59p. (Orig.). 1981. pap. write for info. Pot of Gold.

I'm Too Small: You're Too Big. Ed. by Judi Barrett. LC 80-23883. (Illus.). 32p. (ps-1). 1981. PLB 9.95 (ISBN 0-689-30800-0). Atheneum.

Image. Charlotte Paul. (Orig.). 1980. pap. 2.75 (ISBN 0-446-95145-5). Warner Bks.

Image. Pamela Townley. 360p. (Orig.). 1981. pap. 2.75 (ISBN 0-345-29115-8). Ballantine.

Image & Environment: Cognitive Mapping & Spatial Behavior. Ed. by Robert M. Downs & David Stea. LC 72-78215. 438p. 1973. 23.95x (ISBN 0-202-10058-8). Aldine Pub.

Image & Illusion: Anglo-Irish Literature & Its Contexts. Ed. by Maurice Harmon. 174p. 1979. text ed. 26.00x (ISBN 0-905473-42-6). Humanities.

Image & Immortality: A Study of Tristram Shandy. William V. Holtz. LC 79-118582. (Illus.). 175p. 1970. 8.00x (ISBN 0-87057-121-4, Pub. by Brown U Pr). Univ Pr of New England.

Image & Pilgrimage in Christian Culture. Victor Turner & Edith Turner. (Lectures on the History of Religions Ser.). 1978. 17.50x (ISBN 0-231-04286-8). Columbia U Pr.

Image & Reality in World Politics. Ed. by John C. Farrell & Asa P. Smith. LC 68-18994. (Orig.). 1968. pap. 5.00x (ISBN 0-231-08588-5). Columbia U Pr.

Image & Structure in Chamber Music. Donald N. Ferguson. LC 77-5586. (Music Reprint Ser.). 1977. Repr. of 1964 ed. lib. bdg. 25.00 (ISBN 0-306-77415-1). Da Capo.

Image & Symbol in Joseph Conrad's Novels. F. A. Inamdar. 1980. text ed. 15.50x (ISBN 0-391-01916-3). Humanities.

Image & the Word. Ed. by Joseph Gutmann. LC 77-23470. (American Academy of Religion & Society of Biblical Literature. Religion & the Arts Ser.: Vol. 4). 1977. 9.00 (ISBN 0-89130-142-9, 090104); pap. 7.50 (ISBN 0-89130-143-7). Scholars Pr Ca.

Image Breaking - Image Building. Linda Clark et al. 148p. (Orig.). 1981. pap. 7.95 (ISBN 0-8298-0407-2). Pilgrim NY.

Image Decade: Television Documentary 1965-1975. Charles Hammond. 256p. 1981. 16.95 (ISBN 0-8038-3431-4, Communication Arts); pap. 9.95 (ISBN 0-8038-3432-2). Hastings.

Image Formation & Cognition. 2nd ed. Horowitz. (Illus.). 1978. 24.50 (ISBN 0-8385-4274-3). ACC.

Image Impact. Jacquelin Thompson. (Illus.). 288p. 1981. 10.95 (ISBN 0-89479-072-2). A & W Pubs.

Image in Form: Selected Writings of Adrian Stokes. Adrian Stokes. Ed. by Richard Wollheim. LC 72-84750. (Icon Editions Ser.). (Illus.). 384p. 1972. 10.00 o.p. (ISBN 0-06-438540-X, HarpT); pap. 4.95x o.s.i. (ISBN 0-06-430028-5, IN-28, HarpT). Har-Row.

Image: Knowledge in Life & Society. Kenneth E. Boulding. 1956. pap. 4.50 (ISBN 0-472-06047-3, AA). U of Mich Pr.

Image Makers: A Bibliography of American Presidential Campaign Biographies. William Miles. LC 79-19472. 272p. 1979. 13.50 (ISBN 0-8108-1252-5). Scarecrow.

Image, Object, & Illusion: Readings from Scientific American. Intro. by Richard Held. LC 74-11012. (Illus.). 1974. pap. text ed. 7.95x (ISBN 0-7167-0504-4). W H Freeman.

Image of Africa: British Ideas & Action, 1780-1850, 2 vols. in 1. Philip D. Curtin. (Illus.). 1964. 37.50x (ISBN 0-299-03020-2); Vol. 1. pap. 6.95 (ISBN 0-299-83025-X); Vol. 2. pap. 6.95 (ISBN 0-299-83026-8). U of Wis Pr.

Image of an Oracle: A Report on Research into the Mediumship of Eileen J. Garrett. Ira Progoff. LC 64-24081. 1964. 7.50 o.p. (ISBN 0-912326-11-5). Garrett-Helix.

Image of Bothe Curhces, After the Moste Wonderfull & Heavenly Revelation of Sainct John the Evangelist. John Bale. LC 72-5965. (English Experience Ser.: No. 498). 872p. 1973. Repr. of 1548 ed. 51.00 (ISBN 90-221-0498-2). Walter J Johnson.

Image of China. William Alexander. (Oresko-Jupiter Art Bks). (Illus.). 96p. 1981. 17.95 (ISBN 0-933516-82-7, Pub. by Oresko-Jupiter England). Hippocrene Bks.

Image of Eternity: Roots of Time in the Physical World. David Park. 1981. pap. 5.95 (ISBN 0-452-00551-5, F551, Mer). NAL.

Image of George Washington: Studies in Mid-Nineteenth-Century History Painting. Mark Thistlethwaite. LC 78-74384. (Fine Arts Dissertations, Fourth Ser.). (Illus.). 1980. lib. bdg. 38.00 (ISBN 0-8240-3970-X). Garland Pub.

Image of Lincoln in the South. Michael Davis. LC 73-158115. 1971. 11.50x (ISBN 0-87049-133-4). U of Tenn Pr.

Image of Ourselves: Women with Disabilities Talking. Ed. by Jo Campling. 160p. 1981. price not set (ISBN 0-7100-0821-X); pap. price not set (ISBN 0-7100-0822-8). Routledge & Kegan.

Image of Progress: Alabama Photographs, 1872-1917. Melton A. McLaurin & Michael V. Thomason. LC 80-11441. (Illus.). 240p. (Orig.). 1980. pap. 19.95 (ISBN 0-8173-0043-0). U of Ala Pr.

Image of the American City in Popular Literature: 1820 to 1870. Adrienne Siegel. (National University Publications, Interdisciplinary Urban Ser.). 210p. 1981. 15.00 (ISBN 0-8046-9271-8). Kennikat.

Image of the Buddha. Ed. by David Snellgrove. LC 77-75964. (Illus.). 1978. 60.00 (ISBN 0-87011-302-X). Kodansha.

Image of the King: A Biography of Charles I & Charles II. Richard Ollard. LC 79-50965. (Illus.). 1979. 12.95 (ISBN 0-689-11006-5). Atheneum.

Image of Thomas Jefferson in the Public Eye: Portraits for the People, 1800-1809. Noble E. Cunningham, Jr. LC 80-22757. (Illus.). 1981. write for info. (ISBN 0-8139-0821-3). U Pr of Va.

Image of Women. Thomas Boslooper. LC 79-57637. (Illus.). 228p. 1980. 19.95 (ISBN 0-932894-04-6). Unif Theol Seminary.

Image Pattern & Moral Vision in John Webster. Floyd L. Goodwyn, Jr. (Salzburg Studies in English Literature: Jacobean Drama Ser: 71). 1977. pap. text ed. 25.00x (ISBN 0-391-01389-0). Humanities.

Image Reconstruction from Projections: The Fundamentals of Computerized Tomography. Gabor H. Herman. LC 79-6785. (Computer Science & Applied Mathematics Ser.). 1980. 29.50 (ISBN 0-12-342050-4). Acad Pr.

Imagery. Ed. by Ned J. Block. LC 81-24732. 192p. 1981. text ed. 15.00 (ISBN 0-89706-006-7); pap. text ed. 7.50 (ISBN 0-89706-007-5). Bradford Bks.

Imagery & Verbal Processes. Allan Paivio. LC 73-150787. 596p. 1979. text ed. 29.95 (ISBN 0-89859-069-8). L Erlbaum Assocs.

Imagery: Its Many Demensions & Applications. Ed. by Joseph B. Shorr et al. 405p. 1980. 32.50 (ISBN 0-306-40456-7, Plenum Pr). Plenum Pub.

Imagery of John Donne's Sermons. Winfried Schleiner. LC 70-91655. 254p. 1970. 10.00x (ISBN 0-87057-116-8, Pub. by Brown U Pr). Univ Pr of New England.

Imagery of Lord Byron's Plays. B. G. Tandon. (Salzburg Studies in English Literature: Poetic Drama & Poetic Theory: No. 31). (Illus.). 298p. (Orig.). 1976. pap. text ed. 25.00x (ISBN 0-391-01545-1). Humanities.

Images. Philostratus. Tr. by Blaise De Vigenere. LC 75-27866. (Renaissance & the Gods Ser.: Vol. 22). (Illus., Fr.). 1977. Repr. of 1614 ed. lib. bdg. 73.00 (ISBN 0-8240-2071-5). Garland Pub.

Images: A Unified View of Diffraction & Image Formation with All Kinds of Radiation. Charles A. Taylor. LC 77-94101. (Wykeham Science Ser: No. 46). (Illus.). 1978. pap. 14.50x (ISBN 0-8448-1379-6). Crane-Russak Co.

Images & Ideas in American Culture: The Functions of Criticism - Essays in Memory of Philip Rahv. Ed. by Arthur Edelstein. LC 78-63584. 232p. 1979. text ed. 12.50x (ISBN 0-87451-164-X). U Pr of New Eng.

Images & Impressions. G. S. Amur. 1980. text ed. 11.00x (ISBN 0-391-01917-1). Humanities.

Images & Policies in Senate Debates on Middle Eastern Issues. Jamil E. Jreisat. 1976. pap. 3.00 (ISBN 0-934484-07-4). Inst Mid East & North Africa.

Images & Reflections. Harold Sims. 1981. 4.95 (ISBN 0-533-04370-0). Vantage.

Images & Self-Images. Daisy H. Dwyer. (Illus.). 1978. 13.00x (ISBN 0-231-04302-3); pap. 5.50x (ISBN 0-231-04303-1). Columbia U Pr.

Images & the Imageless: A Study in Religious Consciousness & Film. Thomas M. Martin. LC 79-57611. 200p. 1981. 20.00 (ISBN 0-8387-5005-2). Bucknell U Pr.

Images Chez John Webster, Tome 1 & 2. Isabel M. Damisch. (Salzburg Studies in English Literature: Jacobean Drama Studies: No. 66 & 67). (Fr.). 1977. pap. text ed. 25.00x; Tome 1. pap. text ed. (ISBN 0-391-01355-6); Tome 2. pap. text ed. (ISBN 0-391-01356-4). Humanities.

Images for Self-Recognition: The Christian As Player, Sufferer, Vandal. David B. Harned. 1977. 10.95 (ISBN 0-8164-0334-1). Crossroad NY.

Images from the Bible: The Paintings of Shalom of Safed, the Words of Elie Wiesel. Elie Wiesel. LC 79-51032. (Illus.). 1980. 35.00 (ISBN 0-87951-107-9); limited, signed 400.00 (ISBN 0-87951-108-7). Overlook Pr.

Images from Within, the Photographs of Edmund Teske. Edmund Teske. Ed. by James Alinder. LC 80-67614. (Untitled Ser.: No. 22). (Illus.). 88p. (Orig.). 1980. pap. 15.00 (ISBN 0-933286-18-X). Friends Photography.

Images, Heroes & Self Perceptions: The Struggle for Identity from Maskwearing to Authenticity. L. Benson. 1974. 17.95 (ISBN 0-13-451187-5). P-H.

Images, Images, Images: The Book of Programmed Multi-Image Production. rev. ed. Eastman Kodak Company. (Illus.). 264p. (Orig.). 1980. pap. 19.95 (ISBN 0-87985-285-2, S-12). Eastman Kodak.

Images in a Crystal Ball: World Futures in Novels for Young People. Lillian B. Wehmeyer. 1981. lib. bdg. 18.50x (ISBN 0-87287-219-X). Libs Unl.

Images in the Margins of Gothic Manuscripts. Lilian M. Randall. (California Studies in the History of Art: No. IV). 1966. 60.00x (ISBN 0-520-01047-7). U of Cal Pr.

Images of a Queen: Mary Stuart in Sixteenth-Century Literature. James E. Phillips. 1964. 20.00x (ISBN 0-520-01007-8). U of Cal Pr.

Images of Africa. Aidan Higgins. 1980. pap. 3.95 (ISBN 0-7145-0775-X). Riverrun NY.

Images of Age. Michael Jacques. LC 80-69225. (Illus.). 146p. 1980. 30.00 (ISBN 0-89011-550-8). Abt Assoc.

Images of Alcoholism. Ed. by Jim Cook & Mike Lewington. (BFI Ser.). (Orig.). 1980. pap. 7.95 (ISBN 0-85170-091-8). NY Zoetrope.

Images of American Society: A History of the United States, 2 vols. G. D. Lillibridge. LC 75-31017. (Illus.). 736p. 1976. pap. text ed. 10.75 ea.; Vol. 1. pap. text ed. (ISBN 0-395-21873-X); Vol. 2. pap. text ed. (ISBN 0-395-21874-8); inst. manual 2.25 (ISBN 0-395-20371-6). HM.

Images of an Era: The American Poster 1945-1975. Smithsonian Institution, National Collection of Fine Arts (NCFA) LC 75-34602. 1976. 29.95 o.p. (ISBN 0-685-69547-6); pap. 12.50 o.p. (ISBN 0-262-64015-5). MIT Pr.

Images of Crime: Offenders & Victims. Ed. by Terence P. Thornberry & Edward Sagarin. LC 73-21460. (Special Studies). (Illus.). 150p. 1974. text ed. 24.95 (ISBN 0-275-08640-2). Praeger.

Images of Deviants: Stereotypes & Their Importance for Labeling Deviant Behavior. Gregory R. Staats. LC 78-52338. 1978. pap. text ed. 7.25x o.p. (ISBN 0-8191-0489-2). U Pr of Amer.

Images of Healing. Ann Novotny & Carter Smith. (Illus.). 144p. 1980. 16.95 (ISBN 0-02-590820-0). Macmillan.

Images of Horror & Fantasy. Gert Schiff. (Illus.). 160p. 1980. 19.95 (ISBN 0-8109-1062-4, 1062-4); pap. 9.95 (ISBN 0-8109-2192-8, 2192-8). Abrams.

Images of Information: Still Photography in the Social Sciences. Ed. by Jon Wagner. LC 79-16894. (Sage Focus Editions: Vol. 13). (Illus.). 1979. 18.95x (ISBN 0-8039-1088-6); pap. 9.95x (ISBN 0-8039-1089-4). Sage.

Images of Jesus: Exploring the Metaphors in Matthew's Gospel. Daniel O'Connor & Jacques Jimenez. (Orig.). 1977. pap. 6.95 o.p. (ISBN 0-03-021326-6). Winston Pr.

Images of Labor. Moe Foner. (Illus.). 96p. 1981. 25.00 (ISBN 0-8298-0433-1); pap. 12.95 (ISBN 0-8298-0452-8). Pilgrim NY.

Images of Love. Anne Mather. (Harlequin Presents Ser.). 192p. 1980. pap. 1.50 (ISBN 0-373-10402-2, Pub. by Harlequin). PB.

Images of Maharashhtra: A Regional Profile in India. Ed. by N. K. Wagle. 160p. 1980. pap. text ed. 10.50 (ISBN 0-7007-0144-3). Humanities.

Images of Man. Ed. by C. Wright Mills. LC 60-8989. 1960. 10.00 o.p. (ISBN 0-8076-0114-4). Braziller.

Images of Man: A Critique of the Contemporary Cinema. Donald Drew. LC 74-20099. (Illus.). 144p. 1974. pap. 2.95 o.p. (ISBN 0-87784-482-8). Inter-Varsity.

Images of Michigan. Mary L. Wermuth. LC 80-80509. (gr. 6-8). 1981. text ed. 15.65 (ISBN 0-910726-12-4). Hillsdale Educ.

Images of Our Roots: Photographic, Oral, & Written Documents of the San Francisco Bay Area's Black Pioneers, 1850-1930. Douglas H. Daniels. (National History Ser.). (Illus.). 1981. 22.50 (ISBN 0-89482-054-0); pap. 12.50 (ISBN 0-89482-055-9). Stevenson Pr.

Images of Religion in America. Jerald C. Brauer. Ed. by Richard C. Wolf. LC 67-22984. (Facet Bks). 48p. 1967. pap. 1.00 (ISBN 0-8006-3040-8, 1-3040). Fortress.

Images of Rural Texas. Terry Smith. LC 80-54842. (Illus.). 128p. 1981. 18.95 (ISBN 0-938898-11-6). Red River.

Images of the American City in the Arts. Joel C. Mickelson. 1978. pap. text ed. 8.95 (ISBN 0-8403-1858-8). Kendall-Hunt.

Images of the Ohio Valley: A Historical Geography of Travel. John A. Jakle. (Illus.). 1977. text ed. 14.95 (ISBN 0-19-502240-8); pap. text ed. 6.95x (ISBN 0-19-502241-6). Oxford U Pr.

Images of the Urban Environment. Douglas Pocock & Ray Hudson. LC 77-14371. (Illus.). 1978. 15.00 (ISBN 0-231-04502-6). Columbia U Pr.

Images of the U.S.A. A High School History Reader from Textbooks in Other Lands. William K. Medlin et al. 203p. (gr. 10-12). 1969. pap. text ed. 3.50x o.p. (ISBN 0-89039-101-7). Ann Arbor Pubs.

Images of Women in Literature. 2nd ed. Mary Ann Ferguson. LC 76-13098. (Illus.). 1976. pap. text ed. 9.95 (ISBN 0-395-24481-1). HM.

Images of Women in Literature. 3rd ed. Mary Anne Ferguson. LC 80-82761. (Illus.). 528p. 1981. pap. text ed. 10.50 (ISBN 0-395-29113-5). HM.

Images of Women in the Works of Thomas Heywood. Marilyn L. Johnson. (Salzburg Studies in English Literature, Jacobean Drama Studies: No. 42). 178p. 1974. pap. text ed. 25.00x (ISBN 0-391-01438-2). Humanities.

Imaginary Friend. Michael Young. LC 77-9925. (Moods & Emotions Ser.). (Illus.). (gr. k-3). 1977. PLB 8.95 (ISBN 0-8172-0960-3). Raintree Pubs.

Imaginary Music. Tom Johnson. 1974. pap. 5.95 (ISBN 0-938690-00-0). Two Eighteen.

Imaginary Radishes. James Magorian. LC 79-53857. 32p. 1980. 5.00 (ISBN 0-930674-03-0). Black Oak.

Imaginary Timber. James Galvin. LC 79-6746. 96p. 1980. pap. 4.95 (ISBN 0-385-15776-2). Doubleday.

Imaginary View Scenes of Antonio Canaletto. William L. Barcham. LC 76-23603. (Outstanding Dissertations in the Fine Arts - 18th Century). (Illus.). 1977. Repr. of 1974 ed. lib. bdg. 63.00 (ISBN 0-8240-2677-2). Garland Pub.

Imaginary Witness: The Critical Theory of Herbert Marcuse. Morton Schoolman. LC 80-640. 1980. 19.95 (ISBN 0-02-928040-0). Free Pr.

Imagination. Rhodri Jones. pap. text ed. 2.95x o.p. (ISBN 0-435-14481-2); tchr's ed 1.50x o.p. (ISBN 0-435-14485-5). Heinemann Ed.

Imagination. Mary Warnock. LC 75-22663. 1976. 20.00x (ISBN 0-520-03115-6); pap. 3.95 (ISBN 0-520-03115-6). U of Cal Pr.

Imagination: A Psychological Critique. Jean-Paul Sartre. Tr. by Forrest Williams from Fr. 1972. pap. 5.95 (ISBN 0-472-06185-2, 185, AA). U of Mich Pr.

Imagination: A Psychological Critique. Jean-Paul Sartre. Tr. by Forrest Williams. LC 62-7235. 1962. 3.95 o.p. (ISBN 0-472-80666-1). U of Mich Pr.

Imagination: A Way Toward Western Nirvana. Roberts Avens. LC 78-68693. 1979. pap. text ed. 8.25 (ISBN 0-8191-0697-6). U Pr of Amer.

Imagination & Language. Alison Fairlie. LC 80-40307. (Illus.). 400p. Date not set. 72.00 (ISBN 0-521-23291-0). Cambridge U Pr.

Imagination & Me Book. Joe Wayman & Don Mitchell. (gr. k-8). 1976. 5.95 (ISBN 0-916456-02-1, GA54). Good Apple.

Imagination & the Growth of Science. A. M. Taylor. LC 67-14963. 1970. 3.95x (ISBN 0-8052-3108-0); pap. 1.75 (ISBN 0-8052-0257-9). Schocken.

Imagination & the Life of the Spirit: An Introduction to the Study of Religion & Literature. Lynn Ross-Bryant. LC 79-28464. (Scholars Press General Ser.: Vol. 2). 13.50x (ISBN 0-89130-377-4, 00 03 02); pap. 9.00x (ISBN 0-89130-378-2). Scholar Pr CA.

Imagination Is Reality. rev. ed. Robert Avens. Ed. by Bedford A. Severson. 128p. 1979. pap. 7.00 (ISBN 0-88214-311-5). Spring Pubns.

Imagination on Trial: Conversations with the British & American Novelists. Alan Burns & Charles Sugnet. 192p. 1981. 16.95x (ISBN 0-8052-8084-7); pap. 7.95 (ISBN 0-8052-8083-9). Schocken.

Imaginative Canvas Embroidery. Nancy Hobbs. (Imaginative Craft Ser.). (Illus.). 1977. 12.95x o.p. (ISBN 0-8464-0500-8). Beekman Pubs.

Imaginative Man. Robert S. Hichens. LC 76-24387. (Decadent Consciousness Ser.: Vol. 15). 1977. Repr. of 1895 ed. lib. bdg. 38.00 (ISBN 0-8240-2763-9). Garland Pub.

Imaginative Management Control. Roland Ogden. (British Library of Business Studies). (Orig.). 1969. text ed. 12.75x (ISBN 0-7100-6584-1). Humanities.

Imaginative Printmaking. Roger Marsh & Glenda Marsh. (Illus.). 132p. 1975. 12.00x o.p. (ISBN 0-8464-0502-4). Beekman Pubs.

Imaginative Sex. John Norman. (Orig.). 1975. pap. 2.25 (ISBN 0-87997-146-0, UE1546). DAW Bks.

Imagine That! It's Modern Dance. D. Sorine. LC 80-19232. (Illus.). 48p. (ps-3). 1981. PLB 4.99 (ISBN 0-394-84474-2); PLB 8.95 (ISBN 0-394-94474-7). Knopf.

Imagined City: San Francisco in the Minds of Its Writers. John Van Der Zee & Boyd Jacobson. Ed. by Gail Larrick. LC 80-65977. (Illus.). 96p. (Orig.). 1980. pap. 4.95 (ISBN 0-89395-043-2). Cal Living Bks.

Imagined Past. Alan Holder. LC 78-75202. 298p. 1980. 22.50 (ISBN 0-8387-2319-5). Bucknell U Pr.

Imagined World: A Story of Scientific Discovery. June Goodfield. LC 79-1664. (Illus.). 288p. 1981. 12.95 (ISBN 0-06-011641-2, HarpT). Har-Row.

Imagineering for Health. Serge King. LC 80-53949. 154p. (Orig.). 1980. pap. 4.95 (ISBN 0-8356-0546-9, Quest). Theos Pub Hse.

Imagineering: How to Profit from Your Creative Powers. Michael LeBoeuf. LC 80-13232. 240p. 1980. 9.95 (ISBN 0-07-036952-6). McGraw.

Imagineering: How to Think & Act Creatively. LeBoeuf. 88p. Date not set. 9.95 (ISBN 0-07-036952-6). McGraw.

Imagines Demostrandae: Dentists Guide. (Illus.). 76p. 1978. 120.00 (ISBN 3-87652-031-2). Quint Pub Co.

Imaging for Medicine: Volume 1, Nuclear Medicine, Ultrasonics & Thermography. Ed. by Sol Nudelman & Dennis D. Patton. (Illus.). 494p. 1980. 49.50 (ISBN 0-306-40384-6, Plenum Pr). Plenum Pub.

Imaging Systems: Mechanism & Applications of Established & New Photosensitive Processes. K. I. Jacobson & R. E. Jacobson. LC 76-23144. 1976. 34.95 (ISBN 0-470-98905-X). Halsted Pr.

Imagini...Degli Dei. Vincenzo Cartari. LC 75-27855. (Renaissance & the Gods Ser.: Vol. 12). (Illus.). 1976. Repr. of 1571 ed. lib. bdg. 73.00 (ISBN 0-8240-2061-8). Garland Pub.

Imagism & Imagists: A Study in Modern Poetry. Glenn Hughes. 1973. Repr. of 1931 ed. 15.00x (ISBN 0-8196-0282-5). Biblo.

IMAS Seventy-Three: Proceedings. Institute of Marine Engineers, International Marine & Shipping Conference, 1973. Incl. Boilers, Main Steam Turbines & Gearing. 76p. Group 1. 9.00 (ISBN 0-900976-16-0); Ship Operation & Management: Ship & Propulsion Systems. 60p. Group 2. 9.00 (ISBN 0-900976-17-9); Fuel, Lubrication & Fire. 22p. Group 3. 6.00 (ISBN 0-900976-18-7); Marine Pollution - Noise, Sewage & Oil. 66p. Group 4. 9.00 (ISBN 0-686-11943-6); Training & Manning. 30p. Group 5. 6.00 (ISBN 0-900976-20-9); Radio Communications & Navigational Aids. 34p. Group 6. 6.00 (ISBN 0-900976-21-7); Ocean Engineering. 16p. Group 7. 6.00 (ISBN 0-900976-22-5); Marine Diesel Engines. 66p. Group 8. 9.00 (ISBN 0-900976-23-3); Stern Gear, Shafting & Propellers. 70p. Group 9. 9.00 (ISBN 0-900976-24-1). 434p. 1973. Set Of Parts. 89.00 (ISBN 0-900976-25-X, Pub. by Inst Marine Eng); Bound Volume. 36.00 (ISBN 0-686-11942-8). Intl Schol Bk Serv.

Imbroglio. Richard O. Collin. 288p. 1980. 13.95 (ISBN 0-312-40938-9). St Martin.

IMCO Grain Rules. 35p. 1977. 7.00 (IMCO). Unipub.

IMCO-ILO Guidelinesfor Training in the Packing of Cargo in Freight Containers. (Illus.). 21p. 1978. 7.00 (IMCO). Unipub.

Iminium Salts in Organic Chemistry. Ed. by H. Bohme & H. G. Viehe. LC 76-16155. (Advances in Organic Chemistry Ser: Vol. 9, Pt. 1). 544p. 1976. 65.00 (ISBN 0-471-90692-1, Pub. by Wiley-Interscience). Wiley.

Imitation & Praise in the Poems of Ben Jonson. Richard S. Peterson. LC 80-26261. (Illus.). 280p. 1981. 18.50x (ISBN 0-300-02586-6). Yale U Pr.

Imitation of Christ. Thomas A. Kempis. 1976. 5.00x (ISBN 0-460-00484-0, Evman); pap. 2.95 (ISBN 0-460-01484-6). Dutton.

Imitation of Christ. Thomas a Kempis. Tr. by E. M. Blaiklock. 228p. 1981. pap. 4.95 (ISBN 0-8407-5760-3). Nelson.

Imitation of the Sacred Heart of Jesus. Peter J. Arnoudt. LC 79-112463. 1974. pap. 7.50 (ISBN 0-89555-012-1, 149). TAN Bks Pubs.

Immaculate Murders. Kate Brooks. (Orig.). 1979. pap. 1.95 (ISBN 0-532-23268-2). Manor Bks.

Immanentists Anthology: Art of the Superconscious. Ed. by Duane Locke. LC 72-96447. (Illus.). 120p. 1973. pap. 2.50 (ISBN 0-912292-30-X). The Smith.

Immanuel Kant, Seventeen Hundred Twenty-Four to Nineteen Twenty-Four. Emil C. Wilm. 88p. 1980. Repr. of 1925 ed. lib. bdg. 20.00 (ISBN 0-8482-7062-2). Norwood Edns.

Immediacy: The Development of a Critical Concept from Addison to Coleridge. Wallace Jackson. LC 72-93571. 129p. (Orig.). 1973. pap. text ed. 14.25x (ISBN 0-391-01991-0). Humanities.

Immediate Care of the Acutely Ill & Injured. 2nd ed. Hugh E. Stephenson & Robert S. Kimpton. (Illus.). 1978. pap. text ed. 15.95 (ISBN 0-8016-4783-5). Mosby.

Immediate Care of the Sick & Injured Child. Ed. by Shiv K. Dube & Sophie H. Pierog. LC 78-763. 1978. pap. 24.50 (ISBN 0-8016-1459-7). Mosby.

Immediate Critical Reception of Ernest Hemingway. Frank L. Ryan. LC 79-6026. 77p. 1980. text ed. 12.75 (ISBN 0-8191-0970-3); pap. text ed. 6.50 (ISBN 0-8191-0971-1). U Pr of Amer.

Immediate Origins of the War. Pierre Renouvin. LC 68-9591. 1969. 19.50 (ISBN 0-86527-101-1). Fertig.

Immense Majesty: A History of Rome & the Roman Empire. Thomas W. Africa. LC 73-14536. 1974. 14.75x (ISBN 0-88295-700-7). AHM Pub.

Immensee. Theodor Storm. Ed. by E. H. Zeydel. (Illus., Ger.). 1926. text ed. 11.95x (ISBN 0-89197-226-9); pap. text ed. 3.95x (ISBN 0-89197-227-7). Irvington.

Immigrant City: Lawrence, Massachusetts Eighteen Forty Five to Nineteen Twenty One. Donald B. Cole. LC 63-39156. 257p. 1980. Repr. of 1963 ed. 13.50x (ISBN 0-8078-0876-8). U of NC Pr.

Immigrant Experience in America. Thomas J. Curran & Frank J. Coppa. (Immigrant Heritage of America Ser). 1977. lib. bdg. 9.95 (ISBN 0-8057-8406-3). Twayne.

Immigrant Professionals in the United States: Discrimination in the Scientific Labor Market. Bradley W. Parlin. LC 75-3409. (Special Studies). 96p. 1976. text ed. 22.95 (ISBN 0-275-01050-3). Praeger.

Immigrant Pupils in England: The L. E. A. Response. H. E. Townsend. (Research Reports). 1971. text ed. 13.75x (ISBN 0-901225-67-3, NFER). Humanities.

Immigrant School Learner: A Study of Pakistani Pupils in Glasgow. L. Dickinson et al. (General Ser.). 161p. 1975. pap. text ed. 18.25x (ISBN 0-85633-062-0, NFER). Humanities.

Immigrant Speaks. Anne B. Lous. 1981. 12.95 (ISBN 0-533-04294-1). Vantage.

Immigrant-Survivors: Post-Holocaust Consciousness in Recent Jewish-American Literature. Dorothy S. Bilik. 295p. 1981. 19.95x (ISBN 0-8195-5046-9). Wesleyan U Pr.

Immigrant Upraised: Italian Adventurers & Colonists in an Expanding America. Andrew F. Rolle. LC 68-10302. (Illus.). 1968. 17.95x (ISBN 0-8061-0810-X); pap. 6.95x o.p. (ISBN 0-8061-1204-2). U of Okla Pr.

Immigrant Women. Ed. by Maxine S. Seller. 325p. 1980. 17.50x (ISBN 0-87722-190-1); pap. text ed. 8.95 (ISBN 0-87722-191-X). Temple U Pr.

Immigrants. Reginald Massey & Jamila Massey. (Orient Paperbacks Ser.). 172p. (Orig.). 1973. pap. 2.50 (ISBN 0-88253-243-X). Ind-US Inc.

Immigrants' Influence on Wilson's Peace Policies. Ed. by Joseph P. O'Grady. LC 67-23776. 340p. 1967. 12.50x (ISBN 0-8131-1140-4). U Pr of Ky.

Immigrants Speak: The Italian Americans Tell Their Story. Ed. by Salvatore J. LaGumina. (Illus.). 200p. 1979. lib. bdg. 14.95x (ISBN 0-913256-37-4). Ctr Migration.

Immigrants to Freedom: Jewish Communities in Rural New Jersey Since 1882. Joseph Brandes & Martin Douglas. LC 76-122384. 1971. 15.00x (ISBN 0-8122-7620-5). U of Pa Pr.

Immigration & Defense. 2nd ed. National Lawyers Guild. LC 79-9735. 1979. 60.00 (ISBN 0-87632-109-0). Boardman.

Immigration & Ethnicity: A Guide to Information Sources. John D. Buenker & Nicholas C. Burckel. LC 74-11515. (American Government & History Information Guide Ser.: Vol. 1). 1977. 30.00 (ISBN 0-8103-1202-6). Gale.

Immigration & Industrialization: Ethnicity in an American Mill Town, 1870-1940. John Bodnar. LC 77-74549. 1977. 11.95 (ISBN 0-8229-3348-9). U of Pittsburgh Pr.

Immigration & Nationality Law Review: 1976-77, 3 vols. Bernard D. Reams, Jr. & Donald J. Dunn. 1977. Vol. 1. lib. bdg. 32.50 (ISBN 0-930342-08-9); Vol. 2, 1978-79. lib. bdg. 32.50 (ISBN 0-930342-67-4); Vol. 3. lib. bdg. 32.50 (ISBN 0-89941-061-8). W S Hein.

Immigration & Social Policy in Britain. Catherine Jones. 275p. 1977. pap. 9.95 (ISBN 0-422-74680-0, 6363). Methuen Inc.

Immigration & the American Tradition. Moses Rischin. (AHS Ser: No. 79). 512p. 1976. pap. 9.95 (ISBN 0-672-60130-3). Bobbs.

Immigration Laws of the United States. 3rd ed. Auerbach & Harper. 756p. 1975. 44.00, with 1979 suppl (ISBN 0-672-83703-X, Bobbs-Merrill Law); 1978 suppl. 9.00 (ISBN 0-672-83691-2). Michie.

Imminium Salts in Organic Chemistry. H. Bohme & H. G. Viehe. LC 76-16155. (Advances in Organic Chemistry Ser.: Vol. 9, Pt. 2). 1979. 85.00 (ISBN 0-471-90693-X, Pub. by Wiley-Interscience). Wiley.

Immobilized Enzymes: An Introduction & Applications in Biotechnology. Michael D. Trevan. LC 80-40502. 1980. write for info. (ISBN 0-471-27826-2, Pub. by Wiley-Interscience); pap. write for info. (ISBN 0-471-27825-4). Wiley.

Immobilized Enzymes for Food Processing. Wayne H. Pitcher, Jr. 256p. 1980. 63.95 (ISBN 0-8493-5345-9). CRC Pr.

Immobilized Enzymes in Analytical & Clinical Chemistry: Fundamentals & Applications. Peter Carr & Larry D. Bowers. LC 80-13694. (Chemical Analysis: a Series of Monographs on Analytical Chemistry & Its Applications). 454p. 1980. 45.00 (ISBN 0-471-04919-0, Pub. by Wiley-Interscience). Wiley.

Immobilized Enzymes: Research & Development. Ed. by Ichiro Chibata. LC 78-13266. 1978. 42.95 (ISBN 0-470-26531-0). Halsted Pr.

Immobilized Patient. Ffranz U. Steinberg. LC 79-25903. (Topics in Bone & Mineral Disorders Ser.). (Illus.). 160p. 1980. 16.50 (ISBN 0-306-40372-2, Plenum Pr). Plenum Pub.

Immoderate Past. C. Hugh Holman. LC 76-28927. 118p. 1977. 8.00x (ISBN 0-8203-0419-0). U of Ga Pr.

Immortal Wife. Irving Stone. 504p. 1972. pap. 2.50 (ISBN 0-451-08499-3, E8499, Sig). NAL.

Immortalist. Heathcote Williams. 1980. pap. 3.95 (ISBN 0-7145-3714-4). Riverrun NY.

Immortality & Resurrection. Ed. by Pierre Benoit & Roland Murphy. LC 71-129759. (Concilium Ser.: Religion in the Seventies: Vol. 60). 1970. pap. 4.95 (ISBN 0-8164-2516-7). Crossroad NY.

Immortality of the Soul. St. Augustine. (Fathers of the Church Ser.: Vol. 4). 24.00 (ISBN 0-8132-0004-0). Cath U Pr.

Immortality Principle: Continuum. Kay Croissant & Catherine Dees. 1978. pap. 4.75 (ISBN 0-934704-00-7, Pub. by Palm Publications Pr.). Theos U Pr.

Immortals. Nancy Freedman. 1977. pap. 2.25 o.s.i. (ISBN 0-446-82271-X). Warner Bks.

Immortals of Science Fiction. (Illus.). 120p. 1980. pap. 11.95 (ISBN 0-8317-4880-X). Mayflower Bks.

Immroth's Guide to the Library of Congress Classification. 3rd ed. John P. Immroth & Lois Mai Chan. LC 80-16981. (Library Science Text Ser.). 1980. lib. bdg. 25.00x (ISBN 0-87287-224-6); pap. text ed. 14.50 (ISBN 0-87287-235-1). Libs Unl.

Immunbiology of the Major Histocompatibility Complex. International Convocation on Immunology, 7th, Niagra Falls, N. Y., July 1980 et al. Ed. by M. B. Zaleski & K. Kano. (Illus.). xii, 390p. 1981. 90.00 (ISBN 3-8055-1896-X). S Karger.

Immune Modulation & Control of Neoplasia by Adjuvant Therapy. Ed. by Michael A. Chirigos. LC 76-5665. (Progress in Cancer Research & Therapy: Vol. 7). 1978. 48.50 (ISBN 0-89004-220-9). Raven.

Immune Reactivity of Lymphocytes: Development, Expression, & Control. Ed. by Michael Feldman & Amiela Globerson. LC 75-42123. (Advances in Experimental Medicine & Biology Ser.: Vol. 66). 732p. 1976. 49.50 (ISBN 0-306-39066-3, Plenum Pr). Plenum Pub.

Immune Recognition: Proceedings. Leukocyte Culture Conference, 9th. Ed. by Alan S. Rosenthal. 1975. 43.50 (ISBN 0-12-597850-2). Acad Pr.

Immune System: Festschrift in Honor of Niels Kaj Jerne, on the Occasion of His 70th Birthday, Vol. 1. Ed. by C. M. Steinberg & I. Lefkovits. (Illus.). x, 390p. 1981. 118.75 (ISBN 3-8055-3407-8). S Karger.

Immune System: Festschrift in Honor of Niels Kaj Jerne, on the Occasion of His 70th Birthday, 2 vols, Vols. 1 & 2. Ed. by C. M. Steinberg & I. Lefkovits. (Illus.). xx, 780p. 1981. 237.50 set (ISBN 3-8055-3409-4). S Karger.

Immune System: Festschrift in Honor of Neils Kaj Jerne, on the Occasion of His 70th Birthday, Vol. 2. Ed. by C. M. Steinberg & I. Lefkovits. (Illus.). x, 390p. 1981. 118.75 (ISBN 3-8055-3408-6). S Karger.

Immune System of Secretion. T. B. Tomasi. (Foundation of Biology Ser.). (Illus.). 176p. 1976. ref. ed. 22.95x (ISBN 0-13-451609-5). P-H.

Immunisation. George Dick. (Illus.). 1978. text ed. 12.50x (ISBN 0-906141-10-9, Pub. by Update Pubns England). Kluwer Boston.

Immunite Franque. Maurice Kroell. LC 80-2021. 1981. Repr. of 1910 ed. 39.50 (ISBN 0-404-18573-8). AMS Pr.

Immunization: Benefit Versus Risk Factors. Ed. by W. Hennessen & C. Huygelen. (Developments in Biological Standardization: Vol. 43). (Illus.). 1979. pap. 60.00 (ISBN 3-8055-2816-7). S Karger.

Immunization for Japanese Encephalitis. Ed. by William M. Hammon et al. (Illus.). 1971. 21.25 (ISBN 0-89640-005-0). Igaku-Shoin.

Immunoassays: Clinical Laboratory Techniques for the 1980's. Ed. by R. Nakamura et al. LC 80-21230. (Laboratory & Research Methods in Biology & Medicine: Vol. 4). 482p. 1980. 58.00 (ISBN 0-8451-1653-3). A R Liss.

Immunobiology & Transplantation, Cancer & Pregnancy. Ed. by Ray. 500p. Date not set. text ed. price not set (ISBN 0-08-025994-4). Pergamon.

Immunobiology for the Clinician. H. R. Barber. LC 76-23386. 1977. 38.95 (ISBN 0-471-04785-6). Wiley.

Immunobiology of Gametes. Ed. by M. Edinin & M. H. Johnson. LC 76-49952. (Clinical & Experimental Immunoreproduction Ser.: No. 4). (Illus.). 1977. 57.50 (ISBN 0-521-21441-6). Cambridge U Pr.

Immunobiology of Mammalian Reproduction. Alan E. Beer & Rupert E. Billingham. (Illus.). 275p. 1976. 22.95x (ISBN 0-13-451666-4). P-H.

Immunobiology of Neisseria Gonorrhoeae. Ed. by G. F. Brooks et al. (Illus.). 1978. text ed. 15.00 (ISBN 0-914826-18-2). Am Soc Microbio.

Immunobiology of the Erythrocyte. Ed. by S. Gerald Sandler & Jacob Nusbacher. LC 80-81465. (Progress in Clinical & Biological Research Ser.: Vol. 43). 360p. 1980. 40.00 (ISBN 0-8451-0043-2). A R Liss.

Immunobiology of the Prostate. Richard J. Ablin. 320p. 1981. 27.50 (ISBN 0-87527-178-2). Green.

Immunobiology of Trophoblast. Ed. by R. G. Edwards et al. LC 74-31800. (Clinical & Experimental Immunoreproduction Ser.: No. 1). (Illus.). 300p. 1975. 39.50 (ISBN 0-521-20636-7). Cambridge U Pr.

Immunochemistry. M. W. Steward. LC 74-4104. (Outline Studies in Biology). 64p. (Orig.). 1974. pap. 5.95x o.p. (ISBN 0-412-12450-5, Pub. by Chapman & Hall). Methuen Inc.

Immunochemistry. M. W. Steward. LC 74-4104. (Outline Studies in Biology). (Orig.). 1974. pap. text ed. 4.95 o.p. (ISBN 0-470-82470-0). Halsted Pr.

Immunochemistry of Enzymes & Their Antibodies. Ed. by Milton R. Salton. 240p. 1980. Repr. of 1977 ed. lib. bdg. write for info. (ISBN 0-89874-165-3). Krieger.

Immunochemistry of Proteins, 3 vols. Ed. by M. Z. Atassi. LC 76-2596. (Illus.). 1979. Vol. 1, 485p, 1977. 44.50 (ISBN 0-306-36221-X, Plenum Pr); Vol. 2, 438p, 1977. 44.50 (ISBN 0-306-36222-8); Vol. 3, 339p, 1979. 35.00 (ISBN 0-306-40131-2). Plenum Pub.

Immunocytochemistry. 2nd ed. Ludwig A. Sternberger. LC 78-13263. (Basic & Clinical Immunology Ser.). 1979. 35.50 (ISBN 0-471-03386-3, Pub. by Wiley Medical). Wiley.

Immunodeficient Animals for Cancer Research. Ed. by Stephen Sparrow. (Illus.). 230p. 1980. text ed. 39.50 (ISBN 0-19-520220-1). Oxford U Pr.

Immunodermatology. Ed. by Bijan Safai & Robert A. Good. (Comprehensive Immunology Ser.: Vol. 7). (Illus.). 625p. 1981. 49.50 (ISBN 0-306-40380-3, Plenum Pr). Plenum Pub.

Immunoglobulins: Biologic Aspects & Clinical Uses. (Illus.). 1971. 10.25 (ISBN 0-309-01850-1). Natl Acad Pr.

Immunologia Inmunopatologia. Stewart Sell. (Span.). 1980. pap. text ed. 16.50 (ISBN 0-06-317151-1, Pub. by HarLA Mexico). Har-Row.

Immunologic Diseases of the Mucous Membranes: Pathology, Diagnosis, & Treatment. Ed. by Richard C. O'Connor. LC 80-82050. (Illus.). 176p. 1980. 29.50 (ISBN 0-89352-102-7). Masson Pub.

Immunologic Tolerance & Macrophage Function: Proceedings. Meeting of the Midwest Autumn Immunology Conference, 7th, Michigan, Nov. 1978. Ed. by R. Baram et al. LC 79-243. (Developments in Immunology Ser.: Vol. 4). 1979. 40.00 (ISBN 0-444-00316-9, North Holland). Elsevier.

Immunological Aspects of Food. Nicholas Catsimpoolas. (Illus.). 1977. lib. bdg. 38.50 (ISBN 0-87055-203-1). AVI.

Immunological Aspects of Kidney Disease. John Verrier-Jones. (Illus.). Date not set. text ed. write for info. (ISBN 0-443-08023-2). Churchill. Postponed.

Immunological Aspects of Neurological Diseases. J. A. Aarli & O. Toender. (Monographs in Neural Sciences: Vol. 6). (Illus.). xiv, 190p. 1980. pap. 58.75 (ISBN 3-8055-0814-X). S Karger.

Immunological Disorders of the Nervous System. Ed. by Lewis P. Rowland. LC 72-139827. (ARNMD Research Publications Ser: Vol. 49). 1971. 31.50 (ISBN 0-683-00243-0). Raven.

Immunological Investigation of Renal Disease. Ed. by A. R. McGiven. (Practical Methods in Clinical Immunology Ser.: Vol. 1). (Illus.). 160p. 1980. text ed. 39.50 (ISBN 0-443-01899-5). Churchill.

Immunological Investigation of Tropical Parasitic Disease. Ed. by Vaclav Houba. (Practical Methods in Clinical Immunology Ser.: Vol. 2). (Illus.). 225p. 1980. text ed. 40.00x (ISBN 0-443-01900-2). Churchill.

Immunological Methods, Vol. 2. Ed. by Ivan Lefkovits. 1981. write for info. (ISBN 0-12-442702-2). Acad Pr.

Immunology. 2nd ed. Ed. by Jean F. Bach. 950p. 1981. 62.50 (ISBN 0-471-08044-6, Pub. by Wiley Med). Wiley.

Immunology. Ed. by Jean-Francois Bach. LC 77-12139. 1978. 55.00 (ISBN 0-471-01760-4, Pub. by Wiley Medical). Wiley.

Immunology. R. M. Hyde & Robert Patnode. (Illus.). 1978. text ed. 11.95 (ISBN 0-87909-385-4); pap. text ed. 10.95 (ISBN 0-8359-3853-0); instrs'. manual avail. Reston.

Immunology. 2nd ed. (Illus.). 259p. 1980. text ed. 16.50 (ISBN 0-06-140781-X, Harper Medical). Har-Row.

Immunology: A Programmed Text. Wayne J. Streilein & John D. Hughes. 1977. pap. text ed. 11.95 (ISBN 0-316-81919-0, Little Med Div). Little.

Immunology, Aging, & Cancer. F. M. Burnet. LC 76-16166. (Illus.). 1976. pap. text ed. 8.95x (ISBN 0-7167-0489-7). W H Freeman.

Immunology & Development. Ed. by Matteo Adinolfi. (Illus.). 1970. 18.95x (ISBN 0-685-83591-X). Intl Ideas.

Immunology & Immunopathology of Domestic Animals. Richard G. Olsen & Steven Krakowka. (Illus.). 320p. 1979. text ed. 29.75 (ISBN 0-398-03815-5). C C Thomas.

Immunology & Immunopathology of the Eye. Arthur M. Silverstein & G. Richard O'Connor. LC 79-84781. 416p. 1979. 57.25 (ISBN 0-89352-042-X). Masson Pub.

Immunology & Immunopathology of the Gastrointestinal Tract. David F. Keren. LC 80-11922. (Illus.). 128p. 1980. pap. text ed. 18.00 (ISBN 0-89189-076-9, 45-1-001-00). Am Soc Clinical.

Immunology & the Skin. LC 75-133174. (Advances in Biology of Skin Ser.: Vol. 11). 396p. 1971. 32.50 (ISBN 0-306-50055-8, Plenum Pr). Plenum Pub.

Immunology Examination Review Book, Vol. 1. 2nd ed. Julius M. Cruse. 1975. spiral bdg. 12.00 o.p. (ISBN 0-87488-424-1). Med Exam.

Immunology, Immunopathology & Immunity. 3rd ed. Stewart Sell. (Illus.). 600p. 1980. pap. text ed. 25.00 (ISBN 0-06-142369-6, Harper Medical). Har-Row.

Immunology in Medicine: A Comprehensive Guide to Clinical Immunology. Ed. by E. J. Holborow & W. G. Reeves. 1977. 57.00 (ISBN 0-8089-1028-0). Grune.

Immunology of Aging. William H. Alder & Albert A. Nordin. 240p. 1981. 59.95 (ISBN 0-8493-5809-4). CRC Pr.

Immunology of Breast Milk. Ed. by P. L. Ogra & Delbert H. Dayton. LC 79-64434. 1979. 30.00 (ISBN 0-89004-387-6). Raven.

Immunology of Human Infection. Ed. by Andre J. Nahmias & Richard O'Reilly. Incl. Pt. 1, Bacteria, Mycoplasmae, Chlamydiae, & Fungi. 49.50 (ISBN 0-306-40257-2); Pt. 2, Viruses & Parasites Immunodiagnosis & Presentation of Infectious Disease. 45.00 (ISBN 0-306-40258-0). (Comprehensive Immunology Ser.: Vols. 8 & 9). 1981 (Plenum Pr). Plenum Pub.

Immunology of Malignant Disease. 2nd ed. Jules E. Harris & Joseph G. Sinkovics. LC 75-42474. (Illus.). 1976. 46.00 o.p. (ISBN 0-8016-2067-8). Mosby.

Immunology of Parasitic Infections. Sydney Cohen & Elvio H. Sadun. (Blackwell Scientific Pubns.). (Illus.). 1976. 48.75 (ISBN 0-632-00097-X). Mosby.

Immunology: Readings from Scientific American. Intro. by F. M. Burnet. LC 75-19356. (Illus.). 1976. text ed. 19.95x (ISBN 0-7167-0525-7); pap. text ed. 9.95x (ISBN 0-7167-0524-9). W H Freeman.

Immunology 1978. Ed. by J. Gergely. (Illus.). 532p. 1978. 45.00x (ISBN 963-05-1878-3). Intl Pubns Serv.

Immunopathology of Insulin: Clinical & Experimental Studies. K. Federlin. LC 71-154799. (Monographs on Endocrinology: Vol. 6). (Illus.). 1971. 31.10 (ISBN 0-387-05408-1). Springer-Verlag.

Immunopathology of the Skin. 2nd ed. E. H. Beutner et al. LC 78-24139. 1979. 47.50 (ISBN 0-471-03514-9, Pub. by Wiley Medical). Wiley.

Immunopharmacologic Effects of Radiation Therapy. Ed. by J. B. Dubois. (European Organization for Research on Treatment of Cancer (EORTC) Monographs: Vol. 8). 475p. 1981. 45.00 (ISBN 0-89004-531-3). Raven.

Immunostimulation. Ed. by L. Chedid. (Illus.). 236p. 1981. 22.50 (ISBN 0-387-10354-6). Springer-Verlag.

Immunotherapy of Cancer in Man: Scientific Basis & Current Status. Evan M. Hersh et al. (Illus.). 152p. 1973. 13.75 (ISBN 0-398-02678-5). C C Thomas.

Immunotherapy of Cancer: Present Status of Trials in Man. Ed. by William D. Terry & Dorothy Windhorst. LC 77-83696. (Progress in Cancer Research & Therapy Ser.: Vol. 6). 1978. 61.50 (ISBN 0-89004-182-2). Raven.

Immunotherapy of Human Cancer: Proceedings. Annual Clinical Conference on Cancer, 22nd. Ed. by M. D. Anderson Hospital & Tumor Institute. LC 77-17701. (Illus.). 1978. 41.00 (ISBN 0-89004-263-2). Raven.

Imogen Cunningham: Photographs. Imogen Cunningham. LC 71-117733. (Illus.). 128p. 1970. 20.00 (ISBN 0-295-95080-3); pap. 10.95 (ISBN 0-295-95452-3). U of Wash Pr.

Imogen! Imogen Cunningham Photographs 1910-1973. Imogen Cunningham. LC 74-2490. (Index of Art in the Pacific Northwest Ser.: No. 7). (Illus.). 112p. 1974. 20.00 (ISBN 0-295-95332-2); pap. 10.95 (ISBN 0-295-95333-0). U of Wash Pr.

Impact American Beer Market Review & Forecast: Nineteen-Eighty-One Edition. 2nd ed. Marvin R. Shanken. (Illus.). 60p. 1981. pap. price not set (ISBN 0-918076-15-3). Tasco.

Impact American Beer Market Review & Forecast. Marvin R. Shanken. (Illus.). 1980. pap. 75.00 (ISBN 0-918076-09-9). Tasco.

Impact American Distilled Spirits Market Review & Forecast. 4th ed. Marvin R. Shanken. (Illus.). 1979. pap. 65.00 (ISBN 0-918076-04-8). Tasco.

Impact American Distilled Spirits Market Review & Forecast. 5th ed. Marvin R. Shanken. (Illus.). 1980. pap. 75.00 (ISBN 0-918076-08-0). Tasco.

Impact American Distilled Spirits Market Review & Forecast. 2nd ed. Ed. by Marvin R. Shanken. (Illus.). 1977. 75.00 (ISBN 0-918076-05-6). Tasco.

Impact American Distilled Spirits Market Review & Forecast. Ed. by Marvin R. Shanken. (Illus.). 1976. 50.00 (ISBN 0-918076-10-2). Tasco.

Impact American Distilled Spirits Market Review & Forecast: Nineteen-Eighty-One Edition. 6th ed. Marvin R. Shanken. (Illus.). 60p. 1981. pap. price not set (ISBN 0-918076-14-5). Tasco.

Impact American Distilled Spirits Review & Forecast. 3rd ed. Marvin R. Shanken. 1978. 50.00 (ISBN 0-918076-02-1). Tasco.

Impact American Wine Market Review & Forecast: Nineteen-Eighty-One Edition. 7th ed. Marvin R. Shanken. (Illus.). 60p. 1981. pap. price not set (ISBN 0-918076-13-7). Tasco.

Impact American Wine Market Review & Forecast. 4th ed. Marvin R. Shanken. 1978. 50.00 (ISBN 0-918076-00-5). Tasco.

Impact American Wine Market Review & Forecast. Marvin R. Shanken. (Illus.). 1975. 50.00 (ISBN 0-918076-12-9). Tasco.

Impact American Wine Market Review & Forecast. 6th ed. Marvin R. Shanken. (Illus.). 1980. pap. 75.00 (ISBN 0-918076-07-2). Tasco.

Impact American Wine Market Review & Forecast. 3rd ed. Ed. by Marvin R. Shanken. (Illus.). 1977. 50.00 (ISBN 0-918076-06-4). Tasco.

Impact American Wine Market Review & Forecast. 2nd ed. Ed. by Marvin R. Shanken. (Illus.). 1976. 50.00 (ISBN 0-918076-11-0). Tasco.

Impact American Wine Review & Forecast. 5th ed. Marvin R. Shanken. (Illus.). 1979. pap. 50.00 (ISBN 0-918076-03-X). Tasco.

Impact & Change: A Study of Counseling Relationships. Bill L. Kell & William J. Mueller. (Orig.). 1966. pap. 8.95 (ISBN 0-13-451799-7). P-H.

Impact & Explosion Cratering--Planetary & Terrestrial Implications: Proceedings. Symposium on Planetary Cratering Mechanics, Flagstaff, Ariz., 1976. Ed. by D. J. Roddy et al. LC 77-24753. 900p. 1978. 150.00 (ISBN 0-08-022050-9). Pergamon.

Impact & Response: Federal Education Programs & State Agencies. Mike M. Milstein. LC 76-14887. 1976. text ed. 13.95 (ISBN 0-8077-2502-1); pap. 8.25x (ISBN 0-8077-2501-3). Tchrs Coll.

Impact Modifiers P-057: How Much? Where? 1981. 950.00 (ISBN 0-89336-257-3). BCC.

Impact of a Metropolitan City on the Surrounding Region. C. D. Deshpande et al. (Illus.). 167p. 1980. pap. text ed. 8.00x (ISBN 0-391-02206-7). Humanities.

Impact of Absolutism in France: National Experience Under Richelieu, Mazarin, & Louis XIV. William F. Church. 1969. pap. text ed. 8.95x o.p. (ISBN 0-471-15633-7). Wiley.

Impact of Aerospace Technology on Studies of the Earth's Atmosphere. A. K. Oppenheim. LC 74-5410. 1974. text ed. 23.00 (ISBN 0-08-018131-7). Pergamon.

Impact of Air-Pollution Regulations on Design Criteria for Boiler Plants at Federal Facilities. Building Research Advisory Board. (Illus.). 62p. 1972. pap. 5.00 (ISBN 0-309-02107-3). Natl Acad Pr.

Impact of Annexation on City Finances: A Case Study in Richmond, Virginia. Thomas Muller & Grace Dawson. 1973. pap. 1.75 o.p. (ISBN 0-685-40588-5, 41000). Urban Inst.

Impact of Beltways on Central Business Districts: A Case Study of Richmond. Thomas Muller et al. 101p. 1978. pap. 5.50 (ISBN 0-87766-216-9, 21500). Urban Inst.

Impact of Cesarean Childbirth. Dyanne D. Affonso. 1981. write for info. (ISBN 0-8036-0034-8). Davis Co.

Impact of Collective Bargaining on Hospitals. Richard V. Miller et al. 1979. 26.50 (ISBN 0-03-051346-4). Praeger.

Impact of Collective Bargaining on Management. Sumner H. Slichter et al. 1960. 18.95 (ISBN 0-8157-7984-4). Brookings.

Impact of Computers on the Practice of Structural Engineering in Concrete. 1972. pap. 15.75 o.p. (ISBN 0-685-85108-7, SP-33); pap. 11.75 members o.p. (ISBN 0-685-85109-5). ACI.

Impact of Demographic Change on the Distribution of Earned Income & the AFDC Program: 1979-1985. Richard F. Wertheimer, II & Sheila R. Zedlewski. (Institute Paper). 96p. 1977. pap. 3.50 (ISBN 0-87766-179-0, 16200). Urban Inst.

Impact of Electric Power Transmission Line Easements on Real Estate Values. F. H. Treadway, Jr. 1972. 7.00 (ISBN 0-911780-29-7). Am Inst Real Estate Appraisers.

Impact of Family Planning Programs on Fertility: The U. S. Experience. Phillips Cutright & Fredericks S. Jaffe. LC 76-12847. 1977. text ed. 22.95 (ISBN 0-275-23350-2). Praeger.

Impact of Federal Legislation & Programs on Private Land in Urban & Metropolitan Development. Joseph L. Stevens. LC 73-5229. (Special Studies in U.S. Economic, Social & Political Issues). 1973. 28.50x (ISBN 0-275-28728-9). Irvington.

Impact of Fertilizer Storage: Focus on Asia. Symposium on Interrelationship Between Agricultural Input Industry & Agriculture. (APO Project SYP-I-74 Ser.). (Illus.). 1976. pap. 16.50 (ISBN 92-833-2001-8, APO31, APO). Unipub.

Impact of Hitler: British Politics & British Policy 1933-1940. M. Cowling. LC 74-12968. (Studies in the History & Theory of Politics). 448p. 1975. 59.50 (ISBN 0-521-20582-4). Cambridge U Pr.

Impact of Inflation on U.S. Productivity & International Competiveness. Michael Boskin et al. LC 80-83144. 69p. 1980. 7.00 (ISBN 0-89068-055-8). Natl Planning.

Impact of International Economic Disturbances on the Soviet Union & Eastern Europe. Ed. by Egon Neuberger & Laura D. Tyson. (Pergamon Policy Studies). 60.00 (ISBN 0-08-025102-1). Pergamon.

Impact of Marine Pollution. Ed. by Douglas J. Cusine & John P. Grant. LC 80-670. 336p. 1980. text ed. 32.50 (ISBN 0-916672-54-9). Allanheld.

Impact of Mass Media. Pearl Aldrich. 192p. (gr. 10-12). 1975. pap. text ed. 6.95 (ISBN 0-8104-6000-9). Hayden.

Impact of Microelectronics: A Review of the Literature. J. R. Bessant et al. LC 80-54414. (Illus.). 174p. 1981. text ed. 25.00 (ISBN 0-87663-729-2, Pica Special Studies). Universe.

Impact of Microprocessors on British Business. National Computing Centre. LC 80-478324. 72p. (Orig.). 1979. pap. 15.00x (ISBN 0-85012-232-5). Intl Pubns Serv.

Impact of Negro Voting: The Role of the Vote in the Quest for Equality. William R. Keech. LC 80-26518. (American Politics Research Series). ix, 113p. 1981. Repr. of 1968 ed. lib. bdg. 19.75x (ISBN 0-313-22774-8, KEIN). Greenwood.

Impact of Negro Voting: The Role of the Vote in the Quest for Equality. William R. Keech. LC 80-26518. (American Politics Research Ser.). ix, 113p. 1981. Repr. of 1968 ed. lib. bdg. 19.75x (ISBN 0-313-22774-8, KEIN). Greenwood.

Impact of New Military Technolgy. Ed. by Jonathan Alford. LC 80-67839. (Adelphi Library: Vol. 4). 140p. 1981. text ed. 29.50 (ISBN 0-916672-74-3). Allanheld.

Impact of New Technologies on the Arms Race. Ed. by Bernard T. Feld et al. 1971. 16.00x o.p. (ISBN 0-262-06042-6); pap. 4.95x (ISBN 0-262-56010-0). MIT Pr.

Impact of Noise Pollution: A Socio-Technological Introduction. George Bugliarello et al. 475p. 1976. text ed. 39.50 (ISBN 0-08-018166-X). Pergamon.

Impact of Nuclear Releases into the Aquatic Environment. (Illus.). 1976. pap. 47.25 (ISBN 92-0-020375-2, ISP406, IAEA). Unipub.

Impact of Physical Illness & Related Mental Health Concepts. Vickie A. Lambert & Clinton E. Lambert, Jr. (Illus.). 1979. pap. 11.95 ref. ed. (ISBN 0-13-451732-6). P-H.

Impact of Policy Change on Decisions in the Mineral Industry. Brian E. Owen & W. J. Kops. 116p. (Orig.). 1979. pap. text ed. 7.00x (ISBN 0-88757-015-1, Pub. by Ctr Resource Stud Canada). Renouf.

Impact of Price Uncertainty: A Study of Brazilian Exchange Rate Policy. Donald V. Coes. LC 78-75067. (Outstanding Dissertations in Economics Ser.). 1979. lib. bdg. 30.00 (ISBN 0-8240-4143-7). Garland Pub.

Impact of Product Substitution & New Technologies on the Pulp, Paper & Board Industry. Robert A. Higham. (Illus.). 1977. 400.00 o.p. (ISBN 0-87930-100-7). Miller Freeman.

Impact of Rule 10b-5, 3 vols. Arnold S. Jacobs. LC 74-27270. 1974. looseleaf with 1979 rev. pages 165.00 (ISBN 0-87632-093-0). Boardman.

Impact of School Resources on the Learning of Inner City Children. Richard J. Murnane. LC 75-4663. 144p. 1975. text ed. 16.50 o.p. (ISBN 0-88410-161-4). Ballinger Pub.

Impact of Science & Technology on Regional Economic Development. Executive Offices Of The National Academy Of Sciences - National Academy Of Engineering. LC 74-601605. (Orig.). 1969. pap. 5.00 (ISBN 0-309-01731-9). Natl Acad Pr.

Impact of Science on Technology. Ed. by Aaron W. Warner. LC 65-19445. (Seminar on Technology & Social Change Ser). 1965. 20.00x (ISBN 0-231-02823-7). Columbia U Pr.

Impact of Soviet Policies in Armenia, Nineteen Twenty to Nineteen Thirty-Six: A Study of Planned Cultural Transformation. Mary A. Matossian. LC 79-2910. 239p. 1981. Repr. of 1962 ed. 21.50 (ISBN 0-8305-0080-4). Hyperion Conn.

Impact of Technology on Geophysics. Geophysics Research Board. xii, 121p. 1979. pap. 10.25 (ISBN 0-309-02887-6). Natl Acad Pr.

Impact of the Cold War: Reconsiderations. Joseph M. Siracusa & Barclay St. John. 12.50 (ISBN 0-8046-9158-4); pap. text ed. 6.95 (ISBN 0-8046-9182-7). Kennikat.

Impact of the Federal Safe Drinking Water Act on Texas. LC 78-50660. (Policy Research Project Ser.: No. 21). 1978. 4.00 (ISBN 0-89940-614-9). LBJ Sch Public Affairs.

Impact of the Geosciences on Critical Energy Resources. Ed. by Creighton A. Burk & Charles Drake. 1978. lib. bdg. 17.00x (ISBN 0-89158-293-2). Westview.

Impact of the Great Depression on the Army. John W. Killigrew. Ed. by Frank Freidel. LC 78-62385. (Modern American History Ser.: Vol. 11). 1979. lib. bdg. 25.00 (ISBN 0-8240-3634-4). Garland Pub.

Impact of the Microelectronics Industry on the Structure of the Canadian Economy. J. Michael McLean. 50p. 1979. pap. text ed. 3.00x (ISBN 0-920380-22-0, Pub. by Inst Res Pub Canada). Renouf.

Impact of the Mining Industries on the Canadian Economy. R. W. Boadway & J. M. Treddenick. 117p. (Orig.). 1977. pap. text ed. 4.50x (ISBN 0-686-63141-2, Pub. by Ctr Resource Stud Canada). Renouf.

Impact of the Social Sciences. Kenneth E. Boulding. (Brown & Haley Lecture Ser.). 1966. 8.00 (ISBN 0-8135-0525-9). Rutgers U Pr.

Impact of Tokyo Round Agreements on U. S. Export Competitiveness, Vol. II. Thomas Graham. LC 80-67709. (Significant Issues Ser.: No. 10). 30p. 1980. 5.95 (ISBN 0-89206-024-7). CSI Studies.

Impact of Town Centre Shopping Schemes in Britain: Their Impact on Traditional Retail Environments. D. J. Bennison & R. L. Davies. (Progress in Planning Ser.: Vol. 14, Part 1). (Illus.). 104p. 1980. pap. 13.50 (ISBN 0-08-026789-0). Pergamon.

Impact of Toxiology on Food Processing. Ed. by John C. Ayres & John C. Kirschman. (Institute of Food Technologists Basic Symposia Ser.). (Illus.). 1981. lib. bdg. price not set (ISBN 0-87055-388-7). AVI.

Impact of U. S. Foreign Direct Investment on U. S. Export Competitiveness in Third World Markets, Vol. II. Jack Behrman & Raymond Mikesell. LC 80-65189. (Significant Issues Ser.: No. 1). 34p. 1980. 5.95 (ISBN 0-89206-014-X). CSI Studies.

Impact of U. S. Foreign Direct Investment on U. S. Export Competitiveness in Third World Markets. (Significant Issues Ser.: Vol. II, No. 1). 25p. 1980. pap. 5.00 (ISBN 0-89206-014-X, CSIS009, CSIS). Unipub.

Impact of Urbanization on Land Use in the Rural-Urban Fringe: A Case Study of Patna. M. M. Sinha. 258p. 1980. text ed. 18.00x (ISBN 0-391-02141-9). Humanities.

Impact of Welfare Reform on Benefits for the Poor: A Comparison of Eligibility Requirements & Benefit Levels Under the Proposed "Program for Better Jobs & Income" & the Current System. Margaret B. Sulvetta. (Welfare Reform Policy Analysis Ser.: No. 3). 52p. 1978. pap. 3.50 (ISBN 0-87766-218-5, 21700). Urban Inst.

Impact: The Religion of the Twenty-First Century. Walter A. Dawes. (Illus.). 79p. (Orig.). 1980. pap. text ed. 8.95 (ISBN 0-938792-05-9). New Capernaum.

Impacto Hispanico: Lectures Contemporaneas. Ernest J. Wilkins. LC 78-14336. 1979. pap. text ed. 8.95 (ISBN 0-471-03537-8). Wiley.

Impacts of Program Evaluation on Mental Health Care. Emil J. Posovac. (Westview Special Studies in Health Care). 1979. lib. bdg. 22.50x (ISBN 0-89158-271-1). Westview.

Impaired Vision in Childhood: Proceedings. Jerusalem Conference on Impaired Vision in Childhood, May 1977. Ed. by I. Nawratzki & S. Merin. (Illus.). 1979. text ed. 82.50 (ISBN 0-08-024416-5). Pergamon.

Impala Social Behavior: Territory, Hierarchy, Mating, & the Use of Space. Martha V. Jarman. (Advances in Ethology Ser.: Vol. 21). (Illus.). 96p. (Orig.). 1979. pap. text ed. 33.00 (ISBN 3-489-60936-0). Parey Sci Pubs.

Impartial Account of the Late Expedition Against St. Augustine Under General Oglethorpe. James Killpatrick. LC 78-21956. (Bicentennial Floridiana Facsimile & Reprint Ser). 1978. Repr. of 1742 ed. 6.00 (ISBN 0-8130-0420-9). U Presses Fla.

Impartial Critick. John Dennis. Bd. with Miscellaneous Letters & Essays. Charles Gildon. LC 72-170436. (English Stage Ser.: Vol. 21). lib. bdg. 50.00 (ISBN 0-8240-0604-6). Garland Pub.

Impartial Secret History of Arlus, Fortunatus, & Odolphus, Ministers of State to the Empress Ofgrand-Insula. Bd. with History of the Proceedings of the Mandarins & Proatins of the Britomartian Empire. LC 79-170522; Adventures of Five Englishmen from Pub Condoro, a Factory of the New Company in the East-Indies Who Were Shipwreckt Upon the Little Kingdom of Jehore. Walter Vaughan. LC 75-170521. (Foundations of the Novel Ser.: Vol. 16). lib. bdg. 50.00 (ISBN 0-8240-0528-7). Garland Pub.

Impasse of European Communism. Carl Boggs. 1981. lib. bdg. 20.00x (ISBN 0-89158-784-5). Westview.

Impassioned. Richard Posner. 352p. (Orig.). 1980. pap. 2.75 (ISBN 0-515-04624-8). Jove Pubns.

Impeachment & Parlimentary Judicature in Early Stuart England. C. G. Tite. (University of London Historical Studies: No. 37). 256p. 1974. text ed. 30.00x (ISBN 0-485-13137-4, Athlone Pr). Humanities.

Impeachment & Trial of Andrew Johnson. Michael L. Benedict. (Norton Essays in American History Ser). 224p. 1973. 6.95x (ISBN 0-393-05473-X); pap. text ed. 3.95x (ISBN 0-393-09418-9). Norton.

Impeachment: The Constitutional Problems. Raoul Berger. LC 72-75428. (Studies in Legal History). 360p. 1973. 16.00 (ISBN 0-674-44475-2); pap. 5.95x (ISBN 0-674-44476-0). Harvard U Pr.

Impedance Measurements in Biological Cells. Otto F. Schanne & E. Ruiz-P-Ceretti. LC 77-17434. 1978. 36.95 o.p. (ISBN 0-471-76530-9, Pub. by Wiley-Interscience). Wiley.

Impending Drama. Fernando Chaij. LC 78-22061. (Horizon Ser.). 1979. pap. 4.50 (ISBN 0-8127-0208-5). Southern Pub.

Imperfect Markets in Agricultural Trade. Ed. by Alix F. McCalla & Timothy E. Josling. LC 80-67393. 182p. 1981. text ed. 28.00 (ISBN 0-916672-68-9). Allanheld.

Imperfections & Impurities in Semiconductor Silicon. K. V. Ravi. LC 80-21978. 425p. 1981. 32.50 (ISBN 0-471-07817-4, Pub. by Wiley-Interscience). Wiley.

Imperial Bureaucrat: The Colonial Administrative Service in the Gold Coast,1920-1939. Henrika Kuklick. LC 79-2463. (Publications Ser.: No. 217). 256p. 1979. 10.95 (ISBN 0-8179-7171-8). Hoover Inst Pr.

Imperial Carnival Glass. Bill Edwards. (Illus.). 1980. pap. 9.95 (ISBN 0-89145-138-2). Collector Bks.

Imperial Church from Constantine to the Early Middle Ages. Ed. by Hubert Jedin & John P. Dolan. (History of the Church: Vol. 2). 1980. 37.50 (ISBN 0-8164-0444-5). Crossroad NY.

Imperial Cities: The Capitals of Japan from the Oldest Times Until 1229. Richard A. Ponsonby-Fane. (Studies in Japanese History & Civilization). 1979. 21.50 (ISBN 0-89093-251-4). U Pubns Amer.

Imperial Civil Service of Rome. Harold Mattingly. LC 79-1638. 1981. Repr. of 1910 ed. 16.50 (ISBN 0-88355-940-4). Hyperion Conn.

Imperial Experience in Sub-Saharan Africa. Henry S. Wilson. LC 76-9489. (Europe & the World in the Age of Expansion: Vol. 8). 1977. 20.00x (ISBN 0-8166-0797-4); pap. 3.45x (ISBN 0-8166-0854-7). U of Minn Pr.

Imperial Frontier. James Barber. LC 70-14208. (Illus.). 1968. 9.00x (ISBN 0-8002-1279-7). Intl Pubns Serv.

Imperial Germany & the Industrial Revolution. Thorstein Veblen. 1966. pap. 2.65 o.p. (ISBN 0-472-06114-3, 114, AA). U of Mich Pr.

Imperial Impact: Studies in the Economic History of Africa & India. Clive Dewey & A. G. Hopkins. (Commonwealth Papers Ser.: No.21). 1978. text ed. 41.75x (ISBN 0-485-17621-1, Athlone Pr). Humanities.

Imperial India: Dr. John Murray of Agra. John Fraser. (Oresko-Jupiter Art Bks). (Illus.). 96p. 1981. 17.95 (ISBN 0-933516-89-4, Pub. by Oresko-Jupiter England). Hippocrene Bks.

Imperial Order. Robert G. Wesson. 1967. 32.50x (ISBN 0-520-01325-5). U of Cal Pr.

Imperial Republic: The United States & the World 1945-1973. R. Aron. 1975. 9.95 (ISBN 0-13-451781-4). P-H.

Imperial Restoration in Medieval Japan. H. Paul Varley. LC 73-124573. (Studies of the East Asian Institute of Col. Univ.). 1971. text ed. 17.50x (ISBN 0-231-03502-0). Columbia U Pr.

Imperial Rome. Moses Hadas. (Great Ages of Man Ser). (Illus.). 1965. 12.95 (ISBN 0-8094-0342-0); lib. bdg. avail. (ISBN 0-685-20548-7). Time-Life.

Imperial Rome. Moses Hadas. LC 65-24363. (Great Ages of Man Ser.). 1965. lib. bdg. 11.97 (ISBN 0-8094-0364-1). Silver.

Imperial Rome. Patricia Vanags. (Civilization Library). (Illus.). (gr. 5-8). 1979. PLB 6.90 s&l (ISBN 0-531-01445-2). Watts.

Imperial Russia in Frontier America: The Changing Geography of Supply of Russian America, 1784-1867. James R. Gibson. (Andrew H. Clark Ser in the Historical Geography of North America). (Illus.). 300p. 1976. text ed. 10.95x (ISBN 0-19-501876-1); pap. text ed. 7.95x (ISBN 0-19-501875-3). Oxford U Pr.

Imperial San Francisco: Politics & Planning in an American City, 1897-1906. Judd Kahn. LC 79-9096. (Illus.). xiv, 263p. 1980. 17.95x (ISBN 0-8032-2702-7). U of Nebr Pr.

Imperial Stars. E. E. Smith. (Family Lambert Ser.: No. 1). (Orig.). 1976. pap. 1.50 o.s.i. (ISBN 0-515-03839-3). Jove Pubns.

Imperial Style: Fashions of the Hapsburg Era. Ed. by Polly Cone. (Illus.). 168p. 1980. 25.00 (ISBN 0-87099-232-5). Metro Mus Art.

Imperial Twilight: The Palaiologos Dynasty & the Decline of Byzantium. Constance Head. LC 76-26527. (Illus.). 1977. 14.95 (ISBN 0-88229-368-0). Nelson-Hall.

Imperial Years: The United States Since 1939. Alonzo L. Hamby. LC 76-5799. 1978. text ed. 16.95 (ISBN 0-582-28023-0); pap. 10.95x (ISBN 0-582-28101-6). Longman.

Imperialism. Peter Amey. Ed. by Malcolm Yapp et al. (World History Ser.). (Illus.). (gr. 10). 1980. Repr. of 1977 ed. lib. bdg. 5.95 (ISBN 0-89908-226-2); pap. text ed. 1.95 (ISBN 0-89908-201-7). Greenhaven.

Imperialism. Hannah Arendt. LC 66-22273. Orig. Title: Origins of Totalitarianism Pt. 2. (2). 1968. pap. 4.95 (ISBN 0-15-644200-0, HB132, Harv). HarBraceJ.

Imperialism. Ed. by Philip D. Curtin. LC 75-142853. (Documentary History of Western Civilization Ser.). 368p. 1972. 15.00x o.s.i. (ISBN 0-8027-2046-3). Walker & Co.

Imperialism. John A. Hobson. 1965. pap. 5.95 (ISBN 0-472-06103-8, 103, AA). U of Mich Pr.

Imperialism. Vladimir I. Lenin. 1965. pap. 1.95 (ISBN 0-8351-0113-4). China Bks.

Imperialism & Chinese Politics. Sheng Hu. (Studies in Chinese Government & Law). 308p. 1977. Repr. of 1955 ed. 19.50 (ISBN 0-89093-054-6). U Pubns Amer.

Imperialism & Religion: Assyria, Judah and Israel in the Eighth and Seventh Centuries B.C.E. Morton Cogan. LC 73-83723. (Society of Biblical Literature. Monograph). 1974. 9.00 (ISBN 0-89130-330-8, 060019); pap. 7.50 (ISBN 0-89130-331-6). Scholars Pr Ca.

Imperialism & Revolution: An Essay for Radicals. Bernard S. Morris. LC 73-81164. (Midland Bks.: No. 170). 96p. 1973. pap. 1.95x (ISBN 0-253-20170-5). Ind U Pr.

Imperialism & the Dilemma of Power. Thomas Buffinton. Ed. by Richard H. Brown & Van R. Halsey. (Amherst Ser). (gr. 9-12). 1975. pap. text ed. 4.52 (ISBN 0-201-00757-6, Sch Div); tchr's. manual 1.92 (ISBN 0-201-00772-X). A-W.

Imperialism & Underdevelopment. Dave Elliot. 1978. 24.50 o.p. (ISBN 0-685-85434-5). Porter.

Imperialism & World Economy. Nicolai Bukharin. 1966. 15.50 (ISBN 0-86527-102-X). Fertig.

Imperialism in East Africa: Vol. II: Imperialism & Exploitation. Dan W. Nabudere. 240p. (Orig.). 1981. 18.95 (ISBN 0-905762-05-3, Pub. by Zed Pr); pap. 7.95 o.p. (ISBN 0-905762-06-1). Lawrence Hill.

Imperialism in East Africa: Vol. 1: Imperialism & Integration. Dan W. Nabudere. 240p. (Orig.). 1981. 18.95 (ISBN 0-905762-99-1, Pub. by Zed Pr); pap. 7.95 o.p. (ISBN 0-905762-86-X). Lawrence Hill.

Imperialism in the Ancient World. Ed. by P. D. Garnsey & C. R. Whittaker. LC 77-85699. (Cambridge Classical Studies). (Illus.). 1979. 42.50 (ISBN 0-521-21882-9). Cambridge U Pr.

Imperialism in the Twentieth Century. A. P. Thornton. LC 77-81211. 1978. 22.50x (ISBN 0-8166-0820-2). U of Minn Pr.

Imperialism in the Twentieth Century. A. P. Thornton. LC 77-81211. xii, 363p. 1980. pap. 10.95x (ISBN 0-8166-0993-4). U of Minn Pr.

Imperialism: Pioneer of Capitalism. Bill Warren. 296p. 1981. 19.50x (ISBN 0-8052-7089-2, Pub. by NLB England); pap. 8.50 (ISBN 0-8052-7088-4). Schocken.

Imperialism Today: An Evaluation of Major Issues & Events of Our Time. Gus Hall. LC 72-90500. 384p. 1972. 2.50 o.p. (ISBN 0-7178-0303-1); pap. 3.50 (ISBN 0-7178-0304-X). Intl Pub Co.

Imperialisme Francais d'Avant 1914: Recueil De Textes. Jean Bouvier & Rene Girault. (Savoir Historique Ser.: No. 10). (Fr.). 1976. pap. text ed. 34.10x (ISBN 90-279-7992-8). Mouton.

Imperishable. Helen Mellor. 1979. 8.95 o.p. (ISBN 0-533-03962-2). Vantage.

Imperium. Yockey. 1962. 20.00 (ISBN 0-911038-52-3); pap. 6.00 (ISBN 0-911038-10-8). Noontide.

Implant & Transplant Surgery. Kenneth Cowan. 1972. pap. 6.75 (ISBN 0-7195-2249-8). Transatlantic.

Implantable Telemetry Systems Based on Integrated Circuits. H. P. Kimmich. (Biotelemetry & Patient Monitoring: Vol. 6, No. 3). (Illus.). 1979. pap. 16.25 (ISBN 3-8055-0358-X). S Karger.

Implementation, Change, in the Federal Bureaucracy: School Desegregation Policy in HEW, 1964-1968. Beryl Radin. LC 76-58320. 1977. pap. text ed. 10.95x (ISBN 0-8077-2522-6). Tchrs Coll.

Implementation; How Great Expectations in Washington Are Dashed in Oakland: Or Why It's Amazing That Federal Programs Work at All, This Being the Saga of the Economic Development Administration As Told to by Two Sympathetic Observers Who Seek to Build Morals on Ruined Hopes. 2nd, exp. ed. Jeffrey L. Pressman & Aaron Wildavsky. (Oakland Project). 1979. 15.75x (ISBN 0-520-03959-9); pap. 3.95x (ISBN 0-520-03946-7, CAMPUS NO. 247). U of Cal Pr.

Implementation of Complex Information Systems. Andrew E. Wessel. LC 79-9892. (Information Sciences Ser.). 1979. 23.95 (ISBN 0-471-02661-1, Pub. by Wiley-Interscience). Wiley.

Implementation of Long-Term Environmental Radiation Standards? The Issue of Verification. Committee on Radioactive Waste Management. ix, 65p. 1979. pap. text ed. 5.50 (ISBN 0-309-02879-5). Natl Acad Pr.

Implementation of Project Management: The Professional's Handbook. Ed. by Linn C. Stuckenbruck. LC 80-14898. 304p. 1981. text ed. price not set (ISBN 0-201-07260-2). A-W.

Implementation of Soviet Economic Reforms: Political, Organizational & Social Processes. Karl W. Ryavec. LC 75-3627. (Special Studies). (Illus.). 380p. 1975. text ed. 34.50 (ISBN 0-275-05240-0). Praeger.

Implementation Perspctive: A Guide for Mananging Social Service Delivery Programs. Walter Williams. 1980. 11.50 (ISBN 0-520-04054-6); pap. 3.95 (ISBN 0-520-04063-5). U of Cal Pr.

Implementation Procedures for Pricing Urban Roads. Kiran U. Bhatt et al. (Institute Paper). 49p. 1976. pap. 2.00 (ISBN 0-87766-178-2, 16400). Urban Inst.

Implementation: The Key to Successful Information Systems. Henry C. Lucas, Jr. LC 80-27009. 224p. 1981. 30.00x (ISBN 0-231-04434-8). Columbia U Pr.

Implementing Change: Alcoholism Policies in Work Organizations. Janice M. Beyer & Harrison M. Trice. LC 78-54127. 1978. 17.95 (ISBN 0-02-903460-4). Free Pr.

Implementing Change in Nursing. Ingeborg G. Mauksch & Michael H. Miller. LC 80-16576. (Illus.). 195p. 1980. pap. text ed. 10.95 (ISBN 0-8016-3476-8). Mosby.

Implementing Highway Safety Improvements. Compiled by American Society of Civil Engineers. LC 79-93190. 320p. 1980. pap. text ed. 22.50 (ISBN 0-87262-009-3). Am Soc Civil Eng.

Implementing Patient Education in the Hospital. American Hospital Association. LC 79-4292. (Illus.). 316p. 1979. pap. 34.25 (ISBN 0-87258-274-4, 1488). Am Hospital.

Implementing Public Policy. Ruth Levitt. 256p. 1981. 30.00x (ISBN 0-7099-0068-6, Pub. by Croom Helm Ltd England). Biblio Dist.

Implementing Public Policy. Dennis J. Palumbo & Marvin A. Harder. LC 80-8597. (Policy Studies Organization Bks.). 1981. price not set (ISBN 0-669-04305-2). Lexington Bks.

Implementing Software for Non-Numeric Applications. William M. Waite. (Automatic Computation Ser). (Illus.). 400p. 1973. ref. ed. 24.95x (ISBN 0-13-451898-5). P-H.

Implementing Teacher Competencies: Positive Approaches to Personalizing Education. Ed. by J. Weigand. 1977. pap. text ed. 11.95 (ISBN 0-13-451930-2). P-H.

Implements in Their Places. W. S. Graham. 1978. pap. 4.95 o.p. (ISBN 0-571-10955-1, Pub. by Faber & Faber). Merrimack Bk Serv.

Implication of the International Rice Blast Nursery Data to the Genetics of Resistance. (IRRI Research Paper Ser.: No. 40). 19p. 1979. pap. 5.00 (R080, IRRI). Unipub.

Implications in Indian Agriculture. S. S. Husain. 1980. text ed. write for info. (ISBN 0-391-01836-1). Humanities.

Implications of Environmental Regulations for Energy Production & Consumption. Board on Energy Studies. 1977. pap. 8.25 (ISBN 0-309-02632-6). Natl Acad Pr.

Implications of Soviet & Cuban Activities in Africa for U. S. Policy, Vol. 1. Michael A. Samuels et al. LC 79-90797. (Significant Issues Ser.: No. 5). 73p. 1979. write for info. (ISBN 0-89206-010-7). CSI Studies.

Implicit Meanings: Essays in Anthropology. Mary Douglas. (Illus.). 1978. pap. 8.95 (ISBN 0-7100-0047-2). Routledge & Kegan.

Implicit Meanings: Essays in Anthropology. Mary Douglas. (Illus.). 220p. 1975. 17.95x o.s.i. (ISBN 0-7100-8226-6). Routledge & Kegan.

Implicit Psychology: An Introduction to Social Cognition. Daniel M. Wegner & Robin R. Vallacher. (Illus.). 1978. 7.95x (ISBN 0-19-502228-9); pap. text ed. 6.95x (ISBN 0-19-502229-7). Oxford U Pr.

Implied Reader: Patterns of Communication in Prose Fiction from Bunyan to Beckett. Wolfgang Iser. LC 73-20075. 1978. text ed. 16.00x o.p. (ISBN 0-8018-1569-X); pap. text ed. 5.95 (ISBN 0-8018-2150-9). Johns Hopkins.

Import Liberalization & Employment: The Effects of Unilateral Reductions in U.S. Import Barriers. Walter S. Salant & Beatrice N. Vaccara. 1961. 12.95 (ISBN 0-8157-7696-9). Brookings.

Importance of Being Earnest. Oscar Wilde. pap. 2.00 (ISBN 0-8283-1442-X, 13, IPL). Branden.

Importance of Being Oscar. 2nd ed. Michael MacLiammoir. 1978. pap. text ed. 6.25x (ISBN 0-85105-348-3, Dolmen Pr). Humanities.

Importance of Feeling Inferior. Marie B. Ray. LC 80-19319. 266p. 1980. Repr. of 1971 ed. lib. bdg. 9.95x (ISBN 0-89370-606-X). Borgo Pr.

Importance of Fundamental Principles in Drug Evaluation. Ed. by David H. Tedeschi & Ralph E. Tedeschi. LC 68-56046. (Illus.). 1968. 31.50 (ISBN 0-911216-05-7). Raven.

Importance of Language. Ed. by Max Black. 1968. pap. 4.95 (ISBN 0-8014-9077-4, CP77). Cornell U Pr.

Importance of Techmer's Internationale Zeitschrift Fur Allgemeine Sprachwissenschaft in the Development of General Linguistics. E. F. Koerner. (Studies in the History of Linguistics: No. 1). 1973. pap. 17.25x (ISBN 0-391-01661-X). Humanities.

Important Dates in Afro-American History. Lee B. Hopkins. LC 73-83648. (Illus.). (gr. 4-6). 1969. PLB 5.90 (ISBN 0-531-01897-0). Watts.

Important Decision. Paul J. Deegan. LC 74-14514. (Dan Murphy Sports Ser.). (Illus.). 40p. (gr. 3-6). 1975. PLB 5.95 (ISBN 0-87191-401-8); pap. 2.95 (ISBN 0-89812-154-X). Creative Ed.

Important Moral Issues. Ed. by A. W. Hastings & E. Hastings. LC 66-78349. 128p. Repr. of 1966 ed. pap. text ed. 4.95 (ISBN 0-567-22302-7). Attic Pr.

Important Office of Immense Love: A Handbook for Eucharistic Ministers. Joseph M. Champlin. LC 80-80085. 128p. (Orig.). 1980. pap. 2.95 (ISBN 0-8091-2287-1). Paulist Pr.

Important Thing About. Joy T. Friedman. LC 80-83936. (Illus.). 96p. (gr. k-2). 1981. PLB 10.15 (ISBN 0-448-13947-2); pap. 3.95 (ISBN 0-448-14754-8). G&D.

Importing: Practical Tips & Ideas. Allan J. Siposs. (Illus.). 1979. 25.00x (ISBN 0-686-59709-5). Intl Comm Serv.

Importing Technology into Africa: Foreign Investment and the Supply of Technological Innovations. D. Babatunde Thomas. LC 74-11606. (Praeger Special Studies Ser.). 224p. 1976. text ed. 22.95 o.p. (ISBN 0-275-05740-2). Praeger.

Imports & Politics. David R. Protheroe. 170p. 1980. pap. text ed. 8.95x (ISBN 0-920380-45-X, Pub. by Inst Res Pub Canada). Renouf.

Imposition of Method: A Study of Descartes & Locke. Peter A. Schouls. 282p. 1980. text ed. 37.50x (ISBN 0-19-824613-7). Oxford U Pr.

Impossible Appetites. James Fetler. LC 80-17200. (Iowa School of Letters Award for Short Fiction Ser.: No. 11). 176p. 1980. 9.95 (ISBN 0-87745-101-X); pap. 5.95 (ISBN 0-87745-102-8). U of Iowa Pr.

Impossible Dream? Financing Community College's Evolving Mission. Richard C. Richardson, Jr. & Larry L. Leslie. (Horizon Issues Monograph Ser.). 52p. (Orig.). 1980. pap. 5.00 (ISBN 0-87117-105-8). Am Assn Comm Jr Coll.

Impossible Dreams. Pati Hill. LC 76-4419. 142p. 1976. pap. 4.95 (ISBN 0-914086-13-8). Alicejamesbooks.

Impossible Friendship: Boswell & Mrs. Thrale. Mary Hyde. LC 72-88127. (Illus.). 200p. 1972. 10.00x (ISBN 0-674-44541-4). Harvard U Pr.

Impossible Observer: Reason & the Reader in Eighteenth-Century Prose. Robert W. Uphaus. LC 79-4014. 176p. 1979. 14.50x (ISBN 0-8131-1389-X). U Pr of Ky.

Impossible Proof. Hans E. Nossack. Tr. by M. Lebeck. 1968. 5.95 o.p. (ISBN 0-374-17532-2). FS&G.

Impostors & Their Imitators. Philip Ward. (Oleander Modern Poets Ser.: Vol. 7). 1977. pap. 4.95 (ISBN 0-900891-22-X). Oleander Pr.

Impot Foncier et la Capitation Personnelle Sous le Bas-Empire et a l'epoque Franque. Ferdinand Lot. LC 80-2018. 1981. Repr. of 1928 ed. 21.50 (ISBN 0-404-18576-2). AMS Pr.

Impotence in the Male. 1971. pap. 3.95 (ISBN 0-686-64125-6). Liveright.

Impregnated Fibrous Materials. (Illus., Orig.). 1968. pap. 20.00 (ISBN 92-0-161168-4, IAEA). Unipub.

Impression Management: The Self-Concept, Social Identity, & Interpersonal Relations. Barry R. Schlenker. LC 80-15047. 250p. 1980. text ed. 14.95 (ISBN 0-8185-0398-X). Brooks-Cole.

Impression Management Theory & Social Psychological Research. Ed. by James T. Tedeschi. 1981. price not set (ISBN 0-12-685180-8). Acad Pr.

Impressionism. B. Denvir. LC 77-80177. (Modern Movements in Art Ser.). 1978. pap. 1.95 (ISBN 0-8120-0879-0). Barron.

Impressionism. Phoebe Pool. (World of Art Ser.). (Illus.). 1967. pap. 9.95 (ISBN 0-19-519930-8). Oxford U Pr.

Impressionism & Modern Art: The Season at Sotheby Parke Bernet 1973-74. Ed. by Michel Strauss. (Illus.). 288p. 1974. 40.00x (ISBN 0-85667-008-1, Pub. by Sotheby Parke Bernet England). Biblio Dist.

Impressionism & Post-Impressionism, 1874-1904: Sources in Documents. L. Nochlin. 1966. pap. 10.95 (ISBN 0-13-452003-3). P-H.

Impressionism in Perspective. Ed. by Barbara E. White. LC 77-21780. (Artists in Perspective Ser.). (Illus.). 1978. 10.95 o.p. (ISBN 0-13-452037-8); pap. 5.95 o.p. (ISBN 0-13-452029-7). P-H.

Impressionist Group Exhibitions. Ed. by Theodore Reff. (Modern Art in Paris 1855 to 1900 Ser.). 157p. 1981. lib. bdg. 44.00 (ISBN 0-8240-4723-0). Garland Pub.

Impressionists & Impressionism. Godfrey Blunden & Maria Blunden. (Illus.). 1980. pap. 14.95 (ISBN 0-686-68748-5). Rizzoli Intl.

Impressions. Lakshmi Kannan. flexible cloth 4.00 (ISBN 0-89253-504-0). Ind-US Inc.

Impressions of Africa. Raymond Roussel. 1967. 17.95x (ISBN 0-520-01096-5). U of Cal Pr.

Impressions of Lenin. Angelica Balabanoff. Tr. by Isotta Cesari. pap. 1.75 o.p. (ISBN 0-472-06133-X, 133, AA). U of Mich Pr.

Imprint Catalog in the Rare Book Division: The Research Libraries of the New York Public Library. The Research Libraries of the New York Public Library. (Library Catalogs-Bib. Guides). 1979. lib. bdg. 1848.00 (ISBN 0-8161-0092-6). G K Hall.

Imprinting. Ed. by Eckhard H. Hess & S. B. Petrovich. (Benchmark Papers in Animal Behavior: Vol. 5). 1977. 37.00 (ISBN 0-12-786658-2). Acad Pr.

Imprints Sixteen Hundred Eight to Nineteen Eighty, Hamilton, Allied Families. Sr. Mary Louise Donnelly. LC 80-84574. (Illus.). 660p. 1980. 38.00. Donnelly.

Imprisoned Mind: Guru Shisya Tradition in Indian Culture. Akhileshwar Jha. 1980. 18.50x (ISBN 0-8364-0665-6, Pub. by Ambika India). South Asia Bks.

Imprisonment in Medieval England. Ralph B. Pugh. LC 68-12061. (Illus.). 54.50 (ISBN 0-521-06005-2). Cambridge U Pr.

Improbable Fiction: The Life of Mary Roberts Rinehart. Jan Cohn. LC 79-3997. 1980. 16.95 (ISBN 0-8229-3401-9). U of Pittsburgh Pr.

Improbable Furniture. Suzanne Delehanty & Robert Pincus-Witten. (Illus.). 48p. 1977. pap. 7.00 (ISBN 0-88454-022-7). U of Pa Contemp Art.

Improbable Puritan. Ruth Spaulding. (Illus.). 1975. 12.95 o.p. (ISBN 0-571-10626-9, Pub. by Faber & Faber). Merrimack Bk Serv.

Impromptu Magic from the Castle. Leo Behnke. LC 79-57654. (Wizards of the Magic Castle Ser.: Vol. 1). (Illus.). 235p. 1980. 11.95 (ISBN 0-87477-135-8). J P Tarcher.

Improve Your Chess Fast. Alberic O'Kelly de Galway. 1978. pap. 9.95 (ISBN 0-7134-1054-X). David & Charles.

Improve Your Dressmaking. Ann Ladbury. 1978. 17.95 (ISBN 0-7134-0031-5, Pub. by Batsford England). David & Charles.

Improve Your Game (and Learn About) the Superstars of Golf. Nick Seitz. 192p. 1981. pap. 4.95 (ISBN 0-346-12477-8). Cornerstone.

Improve Your Gardening with Backyard Research. Lois Levitan. (Illus.). 1980. 12.95 (ISBN 0-87857-306-2); pap. 6.95 (ISBN 0-87857-267-8). Rodale Pr Inc.

Improve Your Handwriting. Tom Gourdie. (Illus.). 80p. 1975. 8.95x (ISBN 0-8464-0505-9); pap. 7.50x (ISBN 0-686-60815-1). Beekman Pubs.

Improve Your Own Spelling. Eric W. Johnson. (gr. 6-9). 1977. pap. text ed. 2.95 (ISBN 0-88334-093-3). Ind Sch Pr.

Improve Your Riding: Dressage, Jumping, Cross-Country. Albert Brandl. 116p. 1980. 12.95 (ISBN 0-8069-9120-8, Pub. by EP Publishing England). Sterling.

Improved Keelboat Performance. Fox Geen. (Illus.). 224p. 1976. 7.95 (ISBN 0-370-10318-1); pap. 7.95 (ISBN 0-370-10342-4). Transatlantic.

Improvement of Food Quality by Irradiation. (Illus.). 188p. (Orig.). 1974. pap. 12.00 (ISBN 92-0-011174-2, IAEA). Unipub.

Improvement of Productivity: Myths & Realities. Ed. by John E. Ullmann. 24.95 (ISBN 0-03-055301-6). Praeger.

Improvement of the Estate: A Study of Jane Austen's Novels. Alistair M. Duckworth. LC 75-161839. 264p. 1972. 16.50x o.p. (ISBN 0-8018-1269-0). Johns Hopkins.

Improving Academic Management: A Handbook of Planning & Institutional Research. Paul Jedamus et al. LC 80-8009. (Higher Education Ser.). 1980. text ed. 29.95x (ISBN 0-87589-477-1). Jossey-Bass.

Improving Access to Library Resources. Richard M. Dougherty & Laura L. Blomquist. LC 73-20482. (Illus.). 1974. 10.00 (ISBN 0-8108-0637-1). Scarecrow.

Improving & Arranging on the Keyboard. James Oestereich & Earl Pennington. (Illus.). 208p. 1981. 16.95 (ISBN 0-13-453563-4, Spec); pap. 7.95 (ISBN 0-13-453555-3). P-H.

Improving Assessment of Schoolchildren: A Guide to Evaluating Cognitive, Emotional & Physical Problems. LC 80-26130. (Social & Behavioral Science Ser.). 1981. text ed. write for info. (ISBN 0-87589-488-7). Jossey-Bass.

Improving Cattle by the Millions: NAAB & the Development & Worldwide Application of Artificial Insemination. Harry A. Herman. LC 80-25899. 352p. 1981. text ed. 30.00x (ISBN 0-8262-0320-5). U of Mo Pr.

Improving College English Skills. rev. ed. Leslie Wilbur et al. 448p. 1972. pap. 8.95x (ISBN 0-673-07655-5). Scott F.

Improving College Information for Prospective Students. Ed. by David W. Chapman. 70p. 1980. pap. 10.50 (ISBN 0-89964-162-8). CASE.

Improving College Study Skills: A Guide & Workbook. Theodore F. Simms. (Illus., Orig.). 1970. pap. text ed. 5.95x (ISBN 0-02-478180-0, 47818). Macmillan.

Improving Compliance with International Law. Roger Fisher. LC 80-14616. (Procedural Aspects of International Law Ser.: Vol. 14). 1981. 20.00x (ISBN 0-8139-0859-0). U Pr of Va.

Improving Credit Practice. Donald E. Miller & Donald B. Relkin. LC 70-119384. 1971. 24.95 o.p. (ISBN 0-8144-5222-1). Am Mgmt.

Improving Degree Programs: A Guide to Curriculum Development, Administration, & Review. Paul L. Dressel. LC 80-82376. (Higher Education Ser.). 1980. text ed. 15.95x (ISBN 0-87589-486-0). Jossey-Bass.

Improving Discussion Leadership. Ronald Hyman. 154p. (Orig.). 1980. pap. 9.95x (ISBN 0-8077-2610-9). Tchrs Coll.

Improving Doctor Performance: A Study in the Use of Information & Organizational Change. Steven Kelman. LC 79-21211. 352p. 1980. 24.95x (ISBN 0-87705-444-4). Human Sci Pr.

Improving Education for Disadvantaged Children: Some Belgian Studies. P. Osterrieth et al. LC 79-4086. 1979. 28.00 (ISBN 0-08-024265-0). Pergamon.

Improving Effectiveness & Reducing Costs in Mental Health. B. T. Yates. (Illus.). 240p. 1980. 19.75 (ISBN 0-398-03971-2). C C Thomas.

Improving Evaluations. Ed. by Lois-Ellin Datta & Robert Perloff. LC 79-13627. (Sage Focus Editions: Vol. 12). (Illus.). 1979. 18.95x (ISBN 0-8039-1240-4); pap. 9.95x (ISBN 0-8039-1241-2). Sage.

Improving Guidance Programs. N. Gysbers & E. Moore. 1981. 12.95 (ISBN 0-13-452656-2). P-H.

Improving Health Care Management: Organization Development & Organization Change. George F. Wieland. (Illus.). 528p. 1981. text ed. write for info. (ISBN 0-914904-49-3). Health Admin Pr.

Improving In-Service Education: Proposals & Procedures for Change. Louis J. Rubin. 1971. text ed. 12.95x o.s.i. (ISBN 0-205-03126-9, 2231263). Allyn.

Improving Leadership Effectiveness: The Leader Match Concept. Fred E. Fiedler et al. LC 76-20632. (Self-Teaching Guides). 1976. pap. text ed. 8.95 (ISBN 0-471-25811-3). Wiley.

Improving Learning Ability Through Compensatory Physical Education. James H. Humphrey. (Illus.). 160p. 1976. 14.75 (ISBN 0-398-03561-X). C C Thomas.

Improving Management in Criminal Justice. Ed. by Alvin W. Cohn & Benjamin Ward. LC 80-18331. (Sage Research Progress Ser. in Criminology: Vol. 17). (Illus.). 159p. 1980. 12.95 (ISBN 0-8039-1515-2); pap. 6.50 (ISBN 0-8039-1516-0). Sage.

Improving Management Performance in Health Care Institutions: A Total Systems Approach. Addison C. Bennett. LC 78-8010. (Illus., Orig.). 1978. casebound 26.00 (ISBN 0-87258-246-9, 1066); pap. 25.00 (ISBN 0-87258-229-9, 1056). Am Hospital.

Improving Middle School Guidance: Procedures for Counselors, Teachers, & Administrators. new ed. Martin L. Stamm & Blossom S. Nissman. 1979. text ed. 18.95 (ISBN 0-205-06449-3). Allyn.

Improving Performance & Productivity: Why Won't They Do What I Want Them to Do? Jared F. Harrison. (Illus.). 1978. pap. text ed. 8.95 (ISBN 0-201-02956-1). A-W.

Improving Personnel Selection Through Effective Interviewing: Essentials for Management. Benjamin Balinsky. LC 77-94944. (Orig.). 1979. true bindery 8.13 (ISBN 0-935198-04-0); pap. 7.74 saddle stitch (ISBN 0-935198-05-9). M M Bruce.

Improving Plant Protein by Nuclear Techniques. (Illus., Orig., Eng., Fr., Rus. & Span.). 1970. pap. 26.75 (ISBN 92-0-010170-4, IAEA). Unipub.

Improving Police Department Management Through Problem Solving Task Forces: A Case in Organization Development. M. Weisbord et al. 1974. 7.95 (ISBN 0-201-04122-7). A-W.

Improving Policy Analysis. Ed. by Stuart S. Nagel. LC 79-23019. (Sage Focus Editions: Vol. 16). (Illus.). 1980. 18.95x (ISBN 0-8039-1390-7); pap. 9.95x (ISBN 0-8039-1391-5). Sage.

Improving Productivity & the Quality of Work Life. Thomas G. Cummings & Edmond S. Molloy. LC 76-24348. (Praeger Special Studies). 1977. text ed. 29.95 (ISBN 0-275-56870-9); pap. 10.95 (ISBN 0-03-022601-5). Praeger.

Improving Productivity Through People Skills. Robert Lefton et al. 1980. 22.50 (ISBN 0-88410-498-2). Ballinger Pub.

Improving Prosecution? The Inducement & Implementartion of Innovations for Prosecution Management. David L. Weimer. LC 79-6190. (Contributions in Political Science: No. 49). (Illus.). xv, 237p. 1980. lib. bdg. 25.00 (ISBN 0-313-22247-9, WEP/). Greenwood.

Improving Reading Ability. 3rd ed. James B. Stroud et al. (Illus.). 1970. pap. text ed. 9.95 (ISBN 0-13-453605-3). P-H.

Improving Reading in Every Class: A Sourcebook for Teachers. 2nd ed. Ellen L. Thomas & H. Alan Robinson. 480p. 1972. text ed. 21.95x (ISBN 0-205-05590-7, 2255901); pap. 8.95x abr. ed. (ISBN 0-205-05716-0, 2257165). Allyn.

Improving Sentences: A Diagnostic Approach. Marian C. Bashinski. 200p. 1980. tchrs. ed. 7.95 (ISBN 0-89892-034-5). Contemp Pub Co Raleigh.

Improving Spoken English. Joan Morley. LC 76-49151. 1979. pap. text ed. 9.95x (ISBN 0-472-08660-X). U of Mich Pr.

Improving the Human Condition - Quality & Stability in Social Systems: Proceedings, Silver Anniversary International Meeting, London, England, August 20-24, 1979. Ed. by R. F. Ericson. LC 79-66355. 1979. 68.20 (ISBN 0-387-90442-5). Springer-Verlag.

Improving the Long-Term Effects of Psychotherapy. Paul Karoly & John Steffen. LC 79-18430. 1979. 27.95x (ISBN 0-470-26854-9). Halsted Pr.

Improving the Outside of Your Home. Joseph F. Schram. LC 77-28008. 1978. 13.95 (ISBN 0-912336-64-1); pap. 6.95 (ISBN 0-912336-65-X). Structures Pub.

Improving the Quality of Life: The Case of Norway. Bjorn Gustavson & Gerry Hunius. 112p. 1981. pap. 25.00x (ISBN 82-00-05525-6). Universitet.

Improving the Quality of Urban Management. Ed. by Willis Hawley & David Rogers. LC 72-98108. (Urban Affairs Annual Reviews: Vol. 8). 1974. 25.00x (ISBN 0-8039-0292-1). Sage.

Improving the Reading Program. 5th ed. Delwyn G. Schubert & Theodore L. Torgerson. 1981. pap. text ed. 8.95x (ISBN 0-697-06186-8). Wm C Brown.

Improving the Teaching of Reading. 2nd ed. Emerald Dechant. 1970. ref. ed. 18.95 (ISBN 0-13-453415-8). P-H.

Improving Total Productivity: MBO Strategies for Business, Government & Not-for-Profit Organizations. Paul Mali. LC 77-26191. 1978. 27.95 (ISBN 0-471-03404-5, Pub. by Wiley-Interscience). Wiley.

Improving Urban Management. abridged ed. Willis Hawley. Ed. by David Rogers. LC 76-4682. (Urban Affairs Annual Reviews: Vol. 8). 1976. pap. 8.95x (ISBN 0-8039-0693-5). Sage.

Improving Voice & Articulation. 2nd ed. Hilda B. Fisher. 1975. text ed. 17.50 (ISBN 0-395-19232-3). HM.

Improving Work Groups: A Practical Manual for Team Building. Dave Francis & Don Young. LC 78-64978. 262p. 1979. pap. 16.95 (ISBN 0-88390-149-8). Univ Assocs.

Improving Work Methods in Small Hospitals. American Hospital Association. LC 75-32509. (Illus.). 88p. 1975. pap. 12.50 (ISBN 0-87258-165-9, 1910). Am Hospital.

Improving Your Chess. Peter Griffiths. (Illus.). 72p. 1980. pap. 6.95 (ISBN 0-8069-9024-4, Pub. by EP Publishing England). Sterling.

Improving Your Chess. Fred Reinfeld. 1963. pap. 3.50 (ISBN 0-06-463267-9, EH 267, EH). Har-Row.

Improving Your Chess. Fred Reinfeld. (Illus., Orig.). 1970. pap. 2.95 o.p. (ISBN 0-571-09393-0, Pub. by Faber & Faber). Merrimack Bk Serv.

Improving Your Clock Repairing Skills. Harold C. Kelly. (Illus.). 1976. pap. 5.50 o.p. (ISBN 0-8096-1907-5, Assn Pr). Follett.

Improving Your Health with Vitamin A. Ruth Adams & Frank Murray. (Larchmont Preventive Health Library). 125p. (Orig.). 1978. pap. 1.25 (ISBN 0-915962-24-1). Larchmont Bks.

Improving Your Squash. 2nd ed. R. B. Hawkey. (Illus.). 1972. 7.95 (ISBN 0-571-04783-1, Pub. by Faber & Faber); pap. 3.95 (ISBN 0-571-09949-1). Merrimack Bk Serv.

Improving Your Tennis Game. Barbara B. Gordon. 1973. pap. 2.95 o.p. (ISBN 0-8015-3978-1). Dutton.

Improving Your Tennis: Strokes & Techniques. C. M. Jones & Mike Harring. (Illus.). 132p. 1973. 7.50 o.p. (ISBN 0-571-10148-8). Transatlantic.

Improving Your Vocabulary. Mildred C. Carter & Dorothy H. Dlugacz. (gr. 7-12). 1980. pap. text ed. 5.95 (ISBN 0-671-18432-6). Monarch Pr.

Improvisation, Dance, & Movement. Barbara Haselbach. Tr. by Margaret Murray from Ger. Orig. Title: Improvisation, Tanz, Bewegung. 1980. Repr. of 1976 ed. pap. 19.00 (ISBN 0-918812-15-1). Magnamusic.

Improvisation Through Keyboard Harmony. Sol Berkowitz. (Illus.). 288p. 1975. pap. 14.50 (ISBN 0-13-453472-7). P-H.

Improvised Modified Firearms, Vol. 1. J. David Truby & John Minnery. Ed. by Peder C. Lund. (Illus.). 140p. 1975. 9.95 o.p. (ISBN 0-685-52026-9). Paladin Ent.

Improvised Modified Firearms, Vol. 2. new ed. J. David Truby & John Minnery. Ed. by Peder C. Lund. (Illus.). 140p. 1975. 9.95 o.p. (ISBN 0-87364-030-6). Paladin Ent.

Improvised News: A Sociological Study of Rumor. Tamotsu Shibutani. (Orig.). 1966. pap. 6.50 (ISBN 0-672-60823-5). Bobbs.

Improvised News: A Sociological Study of Rumor. Tamotsu Shibutani. LC 66-29399. 1966. 24.50x (ISBN 0-672-51148-7). Irvington.

Improvising Blues Guitar. Straw Dog. LC 70-143775. (Green Note Musical Publications Ser.). (Illus.). 1975. 10.95 (ISBN 0-02-871290-0); pap. 6.95 (ISBN 0-02-870980-2). Schirmer Bks.

Improvising Blues Guitar, Vol. 2. Green Note Music Publications Staff. (Guitar Transcription Ser.). 1980. pap. 7.25 (ISBN 0-912910-11-9). Green Note Music.

Improvising Blues Guitar: A Programmed Manual of Instruction. Cecilia Heinz & Straw Dog. LC 70-143775. (Contemporary Guitar Styles Ser.). (Illus.). 84p. (Prog. Bk.). 1970. pap. 6.95 (ISBN 0-912910-01-1). Green Note Music.

Improvising Rock Guitar, Vol. 2. Green Note Music Publications Staff. (Guitar Transcription Ser.). 1980. pap. 7.25 (ISBN 0-912910-08-9). Green Note Music.

Improvising Rock Guitar, Vol. 3. Green Note Music Publications Staff. (Guitar Transcription Ser.). 1980. pap. 7.25 (ISBN 0-912910-09-7). Green Note Music.

Imprudent Lady. Joan Smith. (Regency Romance Ser.). 1978. pap. 1.75 o.p. (ISBN 0-449-23663-3, Crest). Fawcett.

Imram: Vol. II of the Blessing Trilogy. William Barnwell. (Orig.). 1981. pap. 2.95 (ISBN 0-671-41272-8). PB.

In a Bind. Glen Chase. (Cherry Delight Ser: No. 19). (Orig.). 1975. pap. 1.25 o.p. (ISBN 0-685-52171-0, LB242ZK, Leisure Bks). Nordon Pubns.

In a Bottle with a Cork on Top. Gloria Skurzynski. LC 75-29466. (Illus.). (gr. 2-5). 1976. 5.95 (ISBN 0-396-07277-1). Dodd.

In a Certain Kingdom: Twelve Russian Fairy Tales. Tr. by Thomas P. Whitney from Rus. LC 79-165106. (gr. 3-6). 1972. 5.95 o.s.i. (ISBN 0-02-792680-X). Macmillan.

In a Class by Herself. Linda Crawford. 1978. pap. 1.95 o.p. (ISBN 0-445-04218-4). Popular Lib.

In a Dark Garden. Frank G. Slaughter. 1976. Repr. of 1946 ed. lib. bdg. 16.70 (ISBN 0-89190-289-9). Am Repr-Rivercity Pr.

In a Dusty Light. John M. Haines. LC 77-153718. 1978. pap. 5.00 o.p. (ISBN 0-915308-12-6). Graywolf.

In a Flea's Navel: A Critic's Love Affair with Television. Don Freeman. LC 80-16781. 224p. 1980. 8.95 (ISBN 0-498-05030-0). A S Barnes.

In a Free State. V. S. Naipaul. 1977. pap. 2.95 (ISBN 0-14-003711-X). Penguin.

In a Fugitive Season. Robert Dana. LC 79-64294. 80p. 1980. 8.95 (ISBN 0-8040-0804-3); pap. 5.95 (ISBN 0-8040-0805-1). Swallow.

In a Herb Garden. George Jones. (Illus.). 98p. 1977. 12.95 (ISBN 0-85475-049-5). Dufour.

In a Lick of a Flick of a Tongue. Linda Hirschmann. LC 80-12632. (Illus.). 48p. (gr. 1-4). 1980. PLB 6.95 (ISBN 0-396-07833-8). Dodd.

In a Pig's Eye. Robert Siegel. LC 80-13313. (University of Central Florida Contemporary Poetry Ser.). 73p. 1980. 6.95 (ISBN 0-8130-0679-1). U Presses Fla.

In a Time Meant for Love. Alex Sawyer. LC 80-65678. 1980. 9.95 (ISBN 0-89754-017-4); pap. 2.95 (ISBN 0-89754-016-6). Dan River Pr.

In a Word: --Answers to 1001 Questions Parents Ask About Their Brain-Injured Children. Glenn Doman et al. LC 75-36620. 8.95 o.p. (ISBN 0-385-09401-9). Doubleday.

In Absolute Confidence. William G. Johnsson. LC 79-1387. (Anvil Ser.). 1979. pap. 5.95 (ISBN 0-8127-0225-5). Southern Pub.

In Accord-Let Us Worship. Justo Gonzalez & Catherine Gonzalez. (Orig.). 1981. pap. 3.95 (ISBN 0-377-00111-2). Friend Pr.

In All Your Ways: A Study of Proverbs. Andrew W. Blackwood, Jr. 1980. pap. 3.95 (ISBN 0-8010-0770-4). Baker Bk.

In an Eastern Rose Garden. Inayat Khan. (Sufi Message of Hazrat Inayat Khan Ser.: Vol. 7). 1979. 6.95 (ISBN 90-6325-096-7, Pub. by Servire BV Netherlands). Hunter Hse.

In & About English: Authentic Texts for Developing Reading Skills. Ian Dunlop & Heinrich Schrand. LC 80-40438. 96p. 1980. pap. 4.91 (ISBN 0-08-024570-6). Pergamon.

In & Around Albany: A Guide for Residents, Students & Visitors. Susanne Dumbleton & Anne Older. (Illus.). 183p. (Orig.). 1980. pap. 4.50 (ISBN 0-9605460-0-6). Wash Park.

In & Out of School: The ROSLA Community Education Project. Roger White & Dave Brockington. 1978. 15.00 (ISBN 0-7100-8888-4). Routledge & Kegan.

In & Out of Your Mind. Michael T. Brown. LC 78-55992. (Illus.). 1978. softcover 7.95 o.p. (ISBN 0-930490-09-6). Future Shop.

In & Out the Windows: Happy Poems for Children. Ivy O. Eastwick. LC 73-90841. (Illus.). (ps-3). 1969. 6.25 (ISBN 0-87486-007-5). Plough.

In Anger: British Culture in the Cold War, 1945-60. Robert Hewison. (Illus.). 212p. 1981. 19.95 (ISBN 0-19-520238-4). Oxford U Pr.

In Black & White. Kristin Morrison. LC 70-171566. 1972. pap. text ed. 4.50 o.s.i. (ISBN 0-02-921980-9). Free Pr.

In Black & White, 2 vols. 3rd ed. Ed. by Mary M. Spradling. 1980. Set. 65.00 (ISBN 0-8103-0438-4). Gale.

In Brief Authority. Francis Biddle. LC 76-5432. (Illus.). 494p. 1976. Repr. of 1962 ed. lib. bdg. 19.75x (ISBN 0-8371-8807-5, BIIB). Greenwood.

In Canon. Erling Bisgaard & Tossi Aaron. 1978. pap. 5.00 (ISBN 0-918812-03-8). Magnamusic.

In-Car Instruction: Methods & Content. 2nd ed. William G. Anderson. (Illus.). 1977. pap. text ed. 13.95 (ISBN 0-201-00217-5). A-W.

In Case I'm Found Unconscious, the Ups & Downs of Diabetes. Albert E. Stock & Bettyan Hargrave. (Illus.). 52p. (Orig.). 1972. 7.00 (ISBN 0-910584-26-5); pap. 2.00 (ISBN 0-910584-75-3). Filter.

In Christ's Place: Christian Ministry in Today's World. Ronald E. Osborn. Orig. Title: In Christ's Place. 256p. 1977. pap. 2.50 (ISBN 0-8272-1605-X). Bethany Pr.

In Cold Blood. Truman Capote. 1966. 8.95 (ISBN 0-394-43023-9). Random.

In Common Cause. rev. ed. John W. Gardner. 1974. o.p. (ISBN 0-393-06403-4); pap. write for info. Norton.

In Conflict & Order: Understanding Society. D. Stanley Eitzen. 1978. pap. text ed. 15.95 (ISBN 0-205-06063-3); instr's man. avail. (ISBN 0-205-06064-1); tests avail. (ISBN 0-205-06065-X). Allyn.

In Connection with Kilshaw. Peter Driscoll. LC 90-20288. 1974. 7.95 o.s.i. (ISBN 0-397-00985-2). Lippincott.

In Connection with Kilshaw. Peter Driscoll. 288p. 1975. pap. 1.75 o.p. (ISBN 0-445-08366-2). Popular Lib.

In Contempt of All Authority: Rural Artisans & Riot in the West of England. Buchanan Sharp. 1980. 19.50x (ISBN 0-520-03681-6). U of Cal Pr.

In Days to Come. Ashtar. (Illus.). 1975. pap. 3.95 o.p. (ISBN 0-685-59370-3). Saucerian.

In Deacon's Orders, 1895. Walter Besant. Ed. by Robert L. Wolff. Bd. with Red Pottage, 1899. Mary Cholmondely. LC 75-1541. (Victorian Fiction Ser). 1975. lib. bdg. 66.00 (ISBN 0-8240-1612-2). Garland Pub.

In Defence of Canada, Vol. I: From the Great War to the Great Depression. James Eayrs. LC 66-3834. (Studies in the Structure of Power). 1964. pap. 5.00 (ISBN 0-8020-6072-2). U of Toronto Pr.

In Defence of Canada, Vol. II: Appeasement & Rearmament. James Eayrs. LC 66-3834. (Studies in the Structure of Power). 1965. 12.50x (ISBN 0-8020-1485-2); pap. 5.00 (ISBN 0-8020-6076-5). U of Toronto Pr.

In Defence of the National Interest. rev. ed. Hans J. Morgenthau. 354p. 1980. cancelled (ISBN 0-935764-04-6). Ark Hse NY.

In Defense of Animals. J. J. McCoy. LC 76-58508. (Illus.). (gr. 3-6). 1978. 8.95 (ISBN 0-395-28864-9, Clarion). HM.

In Defense of Fascism: A New Critical Evaluation of the Fascist Experience in Modern History. Harrison Osborne. (Science of Man Library Bk.). 1978. 51.75 (ISBN 0-89266-128-3). Am Classical Coll Pr.

In Defense of Liberalism. Kavalam M. Panikkar. 1962. 6.50x (ISBN 0-210-34059-2). Asia.

In Defense of Mothers: How to Bring up Children in Spite of the More Zealous Psychologists. Leo Kanner. (Illus.). 176p. 1962. pap. 16.75 photocopy ed., spiral (ISBN 0-398-00968-6). C C Thomas.

In Defense of People. Richard J. Neuhaus. 1971. 6.95 o.s.i. (ISBN 0-02-588830-7). Macmillan.

In Defense of People. Richard J. Neuhaus. 1971. pap. 1.95 o.s.i. (ISBN 0-02-088730-2, Collier). Macmillan.

In Defense of Pretribulationism. John A. Sproule. 56p. (Orig.). 1980. pap. 2.95 (ISBN 0-88469-133-0). BMH Bks.

In Defense of Public Order: The Emerging Field of Sanction Law. Richard Arens & Harold D. Lasswell. LC 61-7946. 1961. 22.00x (ISBN 0-231-02430-4). Columbia U Pr.

In Defense of Raymond Sebond. Michel De Montaigne. Tr. by Arthur H. Beattie. LC 59-15521. (Milestones of Thought Ser.). 1959. 6.50 (ISBN 0-8044-5694-1); pap. 2.45 (ISBN 0-8044-6519-3). Ungar.

In Defense of Reason. Yvor Winters. LC 47-2236. 611p. 1947. pap. 12.95x (ISBN 0-8040-0151-0, 69). Swallow.

In Defense of the Alien: Proceedings, Vol. 1. Annual Legal Conference on the Representation of Aliens 1978. Ed. by Austin L. Fragomen & Lydio F. Tomasi. (In Defense of the Alien Ser.). 144p. 1979. lib. bdg. 25.00x (ISBN 0-913256-41-2). Ctr Migration.

In Defense of the American Public School. Ed. by Arthur J. Newman. LC 78-19570. 1979. 16.60 (ISBN 0-8211-1307-0); text ed. 15.00 ten or more copies (ISBN 0-685-59769-5). McCutchan.

In Defense of the Corporation. Robert Hessen. LC 78-24743. (Publications 207 Ser.). 1979. 7.95 (ISBN 0-8179-7071-1). Hoover Inst Pr.

In Defense of the Ukrainian Cause. Roman Rakhmanny. Ed. by Stephen D. Olynyk. 256p. 1979. 12.95 (ISBN 0-8158-0385-0). Chris Mass.

In Defiance of the Law: The Standing-Army Controversy, the Two Constitutions, & the Coming of the American Revolution. John P. Reid. LC 80-14002. (Studies in Legal History). 295p. 1981. 20.00x (ISBN 0-8078-1449-0). U of NC Pr.

In Dubious Battle. John Steinbeck. 1979. pap. 2.95 (ISBN 0-14-004888-X). Penguin.

In Enemy Hands: The Destroyer No. 26. Warren Murphy. (Destroyer Ser.). 1977. pap. 1.75 (ISBN 0-523-40251-1). Pinnacle Bks.

In English Ways: The Movement of Societies & the Transferal of English Local Law & Custom to Massachusetts Bay in the Seventeenth Century. David G. Allen. LC 80-13198. (Institute of Early American History & Culture Ser.). xxi, 312p. 1981. 27.00x (ISBN 0-8078-1448-2). U of NC Pr.

In Ethiopia with a Mule. Dervla Murphy. 1970. 9.95 (ISBN 0-7195-1830-X). Transatlantic.

In Every Person Who Hopes... James Goff & Margaret Goff. (Orig.). 1980. pap. 3.75 (ISBN 0-377-00096-5). Friend Pr.

In Evil Hour. Gabriel G. Marquez. 1980. pap. 2.75 (ISBN 0-686-69253-5, 52167, Bard). Avon.

In Extremity. John Robinson. LC 77-77725. 176p. 1980. 23.95 (ISBN 0-521-21690-7); pap. 7.95 (ISBN 0-521-29730-3). Cambridge U Pr.

In Fashion: Dress in the Twentieth Century. Prudence Glynn. (Illus.). 252p. 1978. 22.50 (ISBN 0-04-391003-3). Allen Unwin.

In Fear of Each Other: Studies of Dangerousness in America. John P. Conrad & Simon Dinitz. LC 77-286. (The Dangerous Offender Project). 1977. 15.95 (ISBN 0-669-01478-8). Lexington Bks.

In Focus: A Guide to Using Films. Linda Blackaby et al. (Cine Information Ser.). 1980. 20.00 o.p. (ISBN 0-918432-23-5); pap. 9.95 (ISBN 0-918432-22-7). NY Zoetrope.

In Focus: A Rated Guide to the Best in Photographic Equipment. Simon Nathan. LC 80-7600. (Illus.). 224p. 1980. 9.95 (ISBN 0-06-014028-3, HarpT). Har-Row.

In for a Penny: A Prospect of Kew Gardens. Wilfrid Blunt. (Illus.). 1978. 24.00 (ISBN 0-241-89823-4, Pub. by Hamish Hamilton England). David & Charles.

In Front of the Camera. Bernard Sandler & Steve Posner. 1981. 12.95 (ISBN 0-525-93176-7); pap. 7.95 (ISBN 0-525-93177-5). Dutton.

In Front of the Table & Behind It. Shirley Schwarzrock & C. Gilbert Wrenn. (Coping with Ser.). (Illus.). 41p. (gr. 7-12). 1971. pap. text ed. 1.30 (ISBN 0-913476-24-2). Am Guidance.

In Good Shape: Style in Industrial Products Nineteen Hundred to Nineteen Sixty. Stephen Bayley. 225p. 1979. pap. text ed. 12.95 (ISBN 0-442-26333-3). Van Nos Reinhold.

In Good Taste. Tina Jencks. 150p. (Orig.). 1980. pap. 4.95 (ISBN 0-89581-020-4). Lancaster-Miller.

In Grandma's Attic. Arleta Richardson. LC 74-75541. 112p. (Orig.). (gr. 4-8). 1974. pap. 1.95 (ISBN 0-912692-32-4). Cook.

In Harmony with Nature. Christain Bruyere & Robert Inwood. LC 74-22581. (Illus.). 200p. 1979. pap. 7.95 (ISBN 0-8069-8432-5). Sterling.

In Harmony with Nature. Robert Inwood & Christian Bruyere. LC 80-54351. (Illus.). 224p. 1981. pap. 7.95 (ISBN 0-8069-7504-0). Sterling.

In Her Garden. Jon Godden. LC 80-19849. 192p. 1981. 10.95 (ISBN 0-394-51361-4). Knopf.

In Her Own Image: Women Working in the Arts. Elaine Hedges & Ingrid Wendt. (Women's Lives-Women's Work Ser.). (Illus.). 336p. 1980. 16.95 (ISBN 0-912670-73-8); pap. 6.95 (ISBN 0-912670-62-2). Feminist Pr.

In Her Shadow. Suzanne Taylor-Moore. (Illus.). 1981. pap. 12.95 (ISBN 0-686-28089-X). MTM Pub Co.

In High Places. Dougal Haston. (Illus.). 176p. 1973. 9.95 (ISBN 0-02-548980-1). Macmillan.

In His Garden: The Anatomy of a Murderer. Leo Damore. LC 79-54008. (Illus.). 1981. 14.95 (ISBN 0-87795-250-7). Arbor Hse.

In His Image: The Cloning of a Man. David M. Rorvik. LC 78-5226. 1978. 8.95 o.p. (ISBN 0-397-01255-1). Lippincott.

In His Light: A Path into Catholic Belief. William Anderson. 216p. 1979. pap. 4.95 (ISBN 0-697-01716-8). Wm C Brown.

In His Native Habitat: Characteristics of the Science-Fiction Writer. R. Reginald & Dan Lewis. LC 80-11207. (Borgo Reference Library: Vol. 1). 64p. 1981. lib. bdg. 8.95x (ISBN 0-89370-810-0); pap. text ed. 2.95x (ISBN 0-89370-910-7). Borgo Pr.

In His Steps. Charles Sheldon. (Family Library). 1973. pap. 1.25 o.s.i. (ISBN 0-89129-178-4). Jove Pubns.

In His Steps. Charles Sheldon. deluxe ed. 4.95 o.p. (ISBN 0-8007-0501-7); pap. 1.75 (ISBN 0-8007-8022-1, Spire Bks). Revell.

In His Strength. Gwen Wilkerson & Betty Schonauer. LC 77-92619. 1978. pap. 3.45 (ISBN 0-8307-0619-4, 54-089-03). Regal.

In Hoc Signo? A Brief History of Catholic Parochial Education in America. Glen Gabert, Jr. LC 72-89992. 1973. 9.95 (ISBN 0-8046-9028-6, Natl U). Kennikat.

In Hostile Red. Joseph Altsheler. 1976. lib. bdg. 15.80x (ISBN 0-89968-003-8). Lightyear.

In Iron Years. Gordon R. Dickson. LC 73-20509. (Doubleday Science Fiction Ser.). 256p. 1980. 9.95 (ISBN 0-385-01555-0). Doubleday.

In Irrer Gesellschaft: Verstaendigungstexte Zur Psychtherapie und Selbsterfahrung. Ed. by Kurt Kreiler & Peter Sloterdijk. (Edition Suhrkamp: No. 435). 528p. (Orig.). 1980. pap. text ed. 10.40 (ISBN 0-686-64715-7, Pub. by Insel Verlag Germany). Suhrkamp.

In Job's Balances: On the Sources of the Eternal Truths. Lev Shestov. Tr. by Camilla Coventry & C. A. Macartney. LC 73-92902. l, 379p. (Eng.). 1975. 16.00x (ISBN 0-8214-0143-2). Ohio U Pr.

In L. Calpurnium Pisonem. Cicero. Ed. by R. G. Nisbet. (Lat). 1961. 17.95x (ISBN 0-19-814427-X). Oxford U Pr.

In Light of Genesis. Pamela White Hadas. 128p. 1980. 10.95 (ISBN 0-8276-0177-8, 462); pap. 6.95 (ISBN 0-8276-0178-6, 461). Jewish Pubn.

In Limbo: The Story of Stanley's Rear Column. Tony Gould. (Illus.). 269p. 1980. 27.00 (ISBN 0-241-10125-5, Pub. by Hamish Hamilton England). David & Charles.

In Love & in Trouble. Laurel Trivelpiece. (Orig.). 1981. pap. 1.95 (ISBN 0-671-41274-4). PB.

In Love, in Vienna. Daisy Thomson. (Orig.). 1977. pap. 1.25 o.s.i. (ISBN 0-515-04417-2). Jove Pubns.

In Memoriam. Alfred L. Tennyson. Ed. by Robert H. Ross. LC 73-13041. (Critical Editions Ser.). 261p. 1974. 8.95 (ISBN 0-393-04365-7); pap. 3.95x (ISBN 0-393-09379-4). Norton.

In Memory of David Archer. George Barker. 1973. 6.50 (ISBN 0-571-10398-7, Pub. by Faber & Faber). Merrimack Bk Serv.

In My Father's House. Min S. Yee & Thomas N. Layton. 384p. 1981. 13.95 (ISBN 0-03-053396-1). HR&W.

In My Garden: Learning to Count. Tr. by Editions les Belles Images Staff. (Butterfly Bks). (Illus.). 16p. (Orig.). (ps-2). 1976. pap. 1.50 (ISBN 0-8467-0219-3, Pub. by Two Continents). Hippocrene Bks.

In My Lady's Chamber. John Hawkesworth. Bd. with Upstairs Downstairs Two; Tv-Tie-in. 1974. pap. 1.25 o.s.i. (ISBN 0-440-14166-4). Dell.

In My Own Key. Elisabeth Soderstrom. (Illus.). 102p. 1980. 18.95 (ISBN 0-241-10318-5, Pub. by Hamish Hamilton England). David & Charles.

In My Sister's Eyes. Grace Posner. LC 80-20781. 160p. (gr. 7 up). 1980. 7.95 (ISBN 0-8253-0013-4). Beaufort Bks NY.

In My Town. Richard Scarry. (Golden Look-Look Bks.). (Illus.). (ps-1). 1976. PLB 5.38 (ISBN 0-307-61828-5, Golden Pr); pap. 0.95 (ISBN 0-307-11828-2). Western Pub.

In No Time at All. Carl Hamilton. 1974. 6.95 (ISBN 0-8138-0825-1). Iowa St U Pr.

In Noah's Wake. Allan Block. 1972. 5.95 o.p. (ISBN 0-87233-025-7). Bauhan.

In Old New England. Hezekiah Butterworth. LC 73-19716. 1974. Repr. of 1895 ed. 15.00 (ISBN 0-8103-3686-3). Gale.

In Old Southampton. 3rd ed. Abigail Halsey. (Illus.). 1968. pap. 3.95 (ISBN 0-911660-05-4). Yankee Peddler.

In Olde Connecticut. Charles B. Todd. LC 68-26612. 1968. Repr. of 1906 ed. 15.00 (ISBN 0-8103-3540-9). Gale.

In Olde Massachusetts: Sketches of Old Times & Places During the Early Days of the Commonwealth. Charles B. Todd. LC 77-99060. 1971. Repr. of 1907 ed. 15.00 (ISBN 0-8103-3775-4). Gale.

In One Door & Out the Other: A Book of Poems. Aileen Fisher. LC 70-81949. (Illus.). (gr. 1-4). 1969. 7.89 o.p. (ISBN 0-690-43555-X, TYC-J). T Y Crowell.

In Orbit. Wright Morris. LC 75-14359. 153p. 1976. 8.50x (ISBN 0-8032-0882-0); pap. 2.45 (ISBN 0-8032-5830-5, BB 612, Bison). U of Nebr Pr.

In Other Words. L. G. Alexander & C. Wilson. 1974. pap. text ed. 3.00x (ISBN 0-582-55200-1). Longman.

In Our Infancy: An Autobiography, Pt. 1, 1882-1912. Helen Corke. LC 74-31799. (Illus.). 250p. 1975. 32.50 (ISBN 0-521-20797-5). Cambridge U Pr.

In Our Own Interest: A Handbook for the Citizen Lobbyist in State Legislatures. Dorothy Smith. LC 78-10625. 144p. 1979. pap. 4.95 (ISBN 0-914842-33-1). Madrona Pubs.

In Our Time. Ernest Hemingway. 1930. Hudson River Edition. 15.00x (ISBN 0-684-16480-9); pap. 2.95 (ISBN 0-684-71802-2, SL56, ScribT). Scribner.

In Our Time. Eric Hoffer. LC 75-23887. 128p. 1976. 8.95 o.s.i. (ISBN 0-06-011922-5, HarpT). Har-Row.

In Our Time. Tom Wolfe. (Illus.). 1980. 12.95 (ISBN 0-374-17576-4). FS&G.

In Parenthesis. David Jones. 1972. pap. 8.95 (ISBN 0-571-10127-5, Pub. by Faber & Faber). Merrimack Bk Serv.

In Patagonia. Bruce Chatwin. LC 78-885. 1978. 8.95 (ISBN 0-671-40045-2); pap. 4.95 (ISBN 0-671-44857-9). Summit Bks.

In Peace & War: Interpretations of American Naval History, 1775-1978. Ed. by Kenneth J. Hagan. LC 77-91108. (Contributions in Military History: No. 16). (Illus.). 1978. lib. bdg. 18.95 (ISBN 0-313-20039-4, HPW/). Greenwood.

In-Pile Dosimetry. (Technical Reports Ser.: No. 46). (Illus., Orig.). 1965. pap. 5.50 (ISBN 92-0-055065-7, IAEA). Unipub.

In Praise of Ale, or Songs, Ballads, Epigrams & Anecdotes Relating to Beer Malt, & Hops. W. T. Marchant. LC 68-22038. 1968. Repr. of 1888 ed. 24.00 (ISBN 0-8103-3511-5). Gale.

In Praise of Chocolate. Paul A. Lawrence. (Illus.). 60p. (Orig.). 1981. pap. 6.95 (ISBN 0-938034-03-0). PAL Pr.

In Praise of Constantine: A Historical Study of Eusebius' Tricennial Orations. H. A. Drake. (Library Reprint Ser.: No. 93). 1978. 14.50x (ISBN 0-520-03694-8). U of Cal Pr.

In Praise of Darkness. Jorge L. Borges. Tr. by Norman T. Di Giovanni. LC 73-79553. 1974. 8.95 o.p.; pap. 4.95 (ISBN 0-525-03635-0). Dutton.

In Praise of Dollhouses: The Story of a Personal Collection. Catherine D. Callicott & Lawson Holderness. LC 78-17316. (Illus.). 1978. 14.95 (ISBN 0-688-03328-8). Morrow.

In Praise of Jesus. Richard Weaver. 1981. 4.95 (ISBN 0-8062-1711-1). Carlton.

In Praise of Seasons. Alan H. Olmstead. LC 76-23515. (Illus.). 1977. 6.95 o.s.i. (ISBN 0-06-013284-1, HarpT). Har-Row.

In Praise of the Baal Shem Tov (Shivhei ha-Besht) The Earliest Collection of Legends About the Founder of Hasidism. Ed. by Dan Ben-Amos & Jerome R. Mintz. Tr. by Dan Ben-Amos & Jerome R. Mintz. LC 76-98986. (Illus.). 384p. 1970. 15.00x (ISBN 0-253-14050-1); pap. 5.95x (ISBN 0-253-14051-X). Ind U Pr.

In Praise of the Common Man. Jason Alexander. 86p. (Orig.). 1981. pap. price not set (ISBN 0-931826-02-0). Sitnalta Pr.

In Praise of Women: A Christian Approach to Love, Marriage, & Equality. Robina Drakeford & John W. Drakeford. LC 79-3000. 160p. 1980. 8.95 (ISBN 0-06-062063-3). Har-Row.

In Preparation for College Chemistry. 2nd ed. William S. Seese & Guido H. Daub. (Illus.). 1980. pap. text ed. 9.95 (ISBN 0-13-453670-3). P-H.

In Prison. Ed. by James E. Trupin. (Orig.). 1975. pap. 2.50 o.p. (ISBN 0-451-61437-2, ME1437, Ment). NAL.

In Progress. Suzanne Taylor-Moore. 1978. 8.95 (ISBN 0-686-10295-9); pap. 4.95 (ISBN 0-686-10296-7). MTM Pub Co.

In Pursuit of Awareness: The College Student in the Modern World. Ed. by Esther Kronovet & Evelyn Shirk. LC 67-14573. (Orig.). 1967. pap. text ed. 10.95x (ISBN 0-89197-229-3). Irvington.

In Pursuit of Equality of Educational Opportunity: A Selective Bibliography & Guide to the Research Literature. Richard H. Quay. LC 76-52691. 200p. 1978. lib. bdg. 23.00 (ISBN 0-8240-9872-2). Garland Pub.

In Pursuit of Excellence. Robert A. Stein. (Illus.). 545p. 1980. 24.50 (ISBN 0-917126-13-0). Mason Pub.

In Pursuit of Peace: Speeches of the Sixties. Ed. by Donald W. Zacharias. 6.00 (ISBN 0-8446-0298-1). Peter Smith.

In Pursuit of Perfection: Courtly Love in Medieval Literature. Ed. by Joan M. Ferrante & George D. Economou. LC 74-80596. 1975. 15.00 (ISBN 0-8046-9092-8, Natl U). Kennikat.

In Pursuit of Poetry. Robert S. Hillyer. 1971. pap. 2.95 o.p. (ISBN 0-07-028923-9, SP). McGraw.

In Pursuit of the English. Doris Lessing. 1979. 16.95x (ISBN 0-8464-0089-8). Beekman Pubs.

In Quest. Sigmund Diamond. LC 79-26717. (Illus.). 1980. 14.95 (ISBN 0-231-04842-4). Columbia U Pr.

In Quest & Crisis: Emperor Joseph I & the Habsburg Monarchy. LC 77-88358. 278p. 1979. 12.95 (ISBN 0-911198-53-9). Purdue.

In Quest of Freedom: American Political Thought & Practice. Alpheus T. Mason & Richard H. Leach. LC 80-5749. 432p. 1981. pap. text ed. 12.00 (ISBN 0-8191-1473-1). U Pr of Amer.

In Quest of Man. P. Alsberg. 1970. text ed. 14.50 (ISBN 0-08-015680-0). Pergamon.

In Quest of Music. Irving Kolodin. LC 78-22336. (Illus.). 360p. 1980. 14.95 (ISBN 0-385-13061-9). Doubleday.

In Quest of Quasars: An Introduction to Stars & Starlike Objects. Ben Bova. (Surveyor Books Ser). (Illus.). (gr. 7 up). 1970. 7.95g o.s.i. (ISBN 0-02-711750-2, CCPr). Macmillan.

In Quest of Telescopes. Martin Cohen. (Illus.). 131p. 1980. 10.95 (ISBN 0-933346-25-5, 6255). Sky Pub.

In Quest of the Shared Life. Bob Benson. 168p. 1981. pap. 4.95 (ISBN 0-914850-55-5). Impact Tenn.

In Radical Pursuit. W. D. Snodgrass. 1977. pap. 3.95 o.p. (ISBN 0-06-090575-1, CN 575, CN). Har-Row.

In Re Alger Hiss, Vol. 2. Victor Rabinowitz. Ed. by Edith Tiger. 1981. pap. 9.95 (ISBN 0-8090-0150-0). Hill & Wang.

In Remembrance of Creation: Evolution of Art & Scholarship in the Medieval & Renaissance Bible. David S. Berkowitz. LC 68-28658. (Illus.). 324p. 1968. 20.00 (ISBN 0-87451-059-7). U Pr of New Eng.

In Remembrance of Me. Frank W. Lemons. 1975. 3.95 (ISBN 0-87148-430-7); pap. 2.95 (ISBN 0-87148-431-5). Pathway Pr.

In Response to Aggression: Controls & Alternatives. Arnold P. Goldstein et al. (Pergamon General Psychology Ser.). 500p. Date not set. 42.51 (ISBN 0-08-025580-9); pap. 14.91 (ISBN 0-08-025579-5). Pergamon.

In Retrospect: Remembrance of Things Past. F. F. Bruce. 272p. 1980. 13.95 (ISBN 0-8028-3537-6). Eerdmans.

In Retrospect: The History of a Historian. Arthur M. Schlesinger. LC 63-15318. 1963. 4.50 o.p. (ISBN 0-15-144490-0). HarBraceJ.

In Ruins: The Once Great Houses of Ireland. Duncan McLaren. LC 80-7662. (Illus.). 96p. 1980. 22.50 (ISBN 0-394-51095-X). Knopf.

In Scarlet & Grey. Florence Henniker. Ed. by Ian Fletcher & John Stokes. LC 76-20067. (Decadent Consciousness Ser.). 1977. lib. bdg. 38.00 (ISBN 0-8240-2762-0). Garland Pub.

In School Learning in Four Languages. Esther Hautzig. LC 69-18236. (Illus., Span, Eng, Fr. & Rus.). (gr. k-3). 1969. 4.95g o.s.i. (ISBN 0-02-743360-9). Macmillan.

In Search for Community. Ed. by Kurt W. Back. LC 77-90415. (AAAS Selected Symposium Ser.: No. 4). 1978. lib. bdg. 20.00x (ISBN 0-89158-431-5). Westview.

In Search of a Character. Graham Greene. 112p. 1981. pap. 2.50 (ISBN 0-14-002822-6). Penguin.

In Search of a Father. James Robinson & Jimmie Cox. 1979. pap. write for info. (ISBN 0-8423-1634-5). Tyndale.

In Search of a New World Economic Order. Ed. by H. Corbet & R. Jackson. LC 73-22724. 238p. 1974. 24.95 (ISBN 0-470-17221-5). Halsted Pr.

In Search of a Stranger. Warren E. Siegmond. Ed. by Irene Zola et al. LC 80-69803. 472p. (Orig.). 1981. pap. 5.95 (ISBN 0-937868-01-9). Cameo Pr.

In Search of Beauty in Music: A Scientific Approach to Musical Esthetics. Carl E. Seashore. LC 80-25447. (Illus.). xvi, 389p. 1981. Repr. of 1947 ed. lib. bdg. 29.50x (ISBN 0-313-22758-6, SEIS). Greenwood.

In Search of Christopher Marlowe: A Pictorial Biography. A. D. Wraight & Virginia Stern. LC 65-20820. (Illus.). 1965. 15.00 (ISBN 0-8149-0213-8). Vanguard.

In Search of Cultural History. E. H. Gombrich. 1969. pap. 5.95x (ISBN 0-19-817168-4). Oxford U Pr.

In Search of Cumorah. David S. Palmer. LC 80-83866. (Illus.). 300p. 1981. 7.75 (ISBN 0-88290-169-9, 1063). Horizon Utah.

In Search of Dracula. Radu Florescu & Raymond T. McNally. (Illus.). 256p. 1973. pap. 2.50 (ISBN 0-446-91630-7). Warner Bks.

In Search of Eden. Ed. by Leo Hamalian. (Orig.). 1981. pap. 3.50 (ISBN 0-451-61912-9, ME1912, Ment). NAL.

In Search of Ghosts. Hans Holzer. (Orig.). 1979. pap. 2.25 (ISBN 0-532-23272-0). Manor Bks.

In Search of Global Patterns. James N. Rosenau. LC 75-20950. (Illus.). 1976. 19.95 (ISBN 0-02-927050-2). Free Pr.

In Search of God & Self: Renaissance & Reformation Thought. Donald J. Wilcox. 1975. pap. text ed. 9.25 (ISBN 0-395-17178-4). HM.

In Search of Gods Ideal Woman: A Personal Examination of the New Testament. Dorothy R. Pape. LC 75-21453. 366p. (Orig.). 1976. pap. 5.95 (ISBN 0-87784-854-8). Inter-Varsity.

In Search of Harmony, Vol. 1. David L. Brandlen. 1980. cancelled (ISBN 0-87881-092-7). Mojave Bks.

In Search of Harmony, Vol. 2. David Brandlen. 112p. 1980. pap. text ed. cancelled (ISBN 0-87881-093-5). Mojave Bks.

In Search of Heffalumps. Uni V. Anholt. (Illus.). 88p. (Orig.). pap. 5.95 (ISBN 0-9601996-0-8). Beeberry Bks.

In Search of History. Theodore H. White. 720p. 1981. pap. cancelled (ISBN 0-446-96729-7). Warner Bks.

In Search of Humanity. Alfred Cobban. LC 60-13305. 1960. 6.00 o.p. (ISBN 0-8076-0119-5). Braziller.

In Search of Identity. A. C. Paranjpe. LC 75-257. 1976. 17.95 (ISBN 0-470-65856-8). Halsted Pr.

In Search of Identity: An Autobiography. Anwar Sadat. LC 77-3767. (Illus.). 1979. pap. 5.95 (ISBN 0-06-090705-3, CN705, CN). Har-Row.

In Search of Lake Monsters. Peter Costello. 1975. pap. 1.75 o.p. (ISBN 0-425-02935-2, Medallion). Berkley Pub.

In Search of Liberty. Frederick Macaskill. LC 78-74587. 1979. 12.95 (ISBN 0-916728-24-2). Bks in Focus.

In Search of Liberty. Frederick Macaskill. 1980. pap. cancelled (ISBN 0-916728-25-0). Bks in Focus.

In Search of Literary Theory. Ed. by Morton W. Bloomfield & Max Black. (Studies in Humanities Ser.). 272p. 1972. 16.50x o.p. (ISBN 0-8014-0714-1). Cornell U Pr.

In Search of Margaret Fuller: A Biography. Abby Slater. LC 77-86335. (gr. 7 up). 1978. 7.50 (ISBN 0-440-03944-4). Delacorte.

In Search of Meaning: From Freud to Teilhard De Chardin (an Analysis of the Classic Statements) John H. Morgan. 1977. 7.50 (ISBN 0-8191-0251-2). U Pr of Amer.

In Search of Omar Khayyam. Ali Dashti. Tr. by L. P. Elwell-Sutton from Persian. LC 77-168669. (Persian Studies Monographs). 276p. 1972. 20.00x (ISBN 0-231-03188-2). Columbia U Pr.

In Search of Origins: The Experiences of Adopted People. John Triseliotis. 190p. 1973. 17.00x (ISBN 0-7100-7534-0). Routledge & Kegan.

In Search of Ourselves: An Introduction to Physical Anthropology. 3rd rev. ed. Frank E. Poirier. 1981. pap. text ed. price not set (ISBN 0-8087-1666-2). Burgess.

In Search of Philosophic Understanding. E. A. Burtt. LC 65-26869. 350p. 1980. lib. bdg. 18.50 (ISBN 0-915145-06-5); pap. text ed. 6.95 (ISBN 0-915145-07-3). Hackett Pub.

In Search of Political Stability: A Comparative Study of New Brunswick & Northern Ireland. Edmund A. Aunger. 238p. 1981. 21.95x (ISBN 0-7735-0366-8). McGill-Queens U Pr.

In Search of Population Policy: Views from the Developing World. Office of the Foreign Secretary, National Research Council Commission on International Relations. LC 74-10125. ix, 108p. 1974. pap. 5.75 (ISBN 0-309-02242-8). Natl Acad Pr.

In Search of Saveopotomas. Steve Cosgrove. (Serendipity Bks). (Illus.). (gr. k-4). 1978. PLB 6.95 (ISBN 0-87191-661-4). Creative Ed.

In Search of Southeast Asia: A Modern History. David J. Steinberg et al. LC 70-121850. (Illus.). 522p. 1971. pap. 9.95x (ISBN 0-275-88390-6). Praeger.

In Search of Taylor Caldwell. Jess Stearn. LC 80-6150. 224p. 1981. 12.95 (ISBN 0-8128-2791-0). Stein & Day.

In Search of the Beyond. Carlo Carretto. LC 78-2048. 1978. pap. 2.45 (ISBN 0-385-14411-3, Im). Doubleday.

In Search of the Castaways. Hettie Jones. (gr. 5-7). pap. 1.50 o.s.i. (ISBN 0-671-81936-4). Archway.

In Search of the Constitution: Reflections on State & Society in Britain. Nevil Johnson. LC 76-43316. 1977. text ed. 23.00 (ISBN 0-08-021379-0). Pergamon.

In Search of the Healing Energy. Mary Coddington & Warner Destiny. 2.25 (ISBN 0-446-82575-1). Inner Tradit.

In Search of the New Working Class. D. Gallie. LC 77-80834. (Studies in Sociology: No. 9). (Illus.). 1978. 36.00 (ISBN 0-521-21771-7); pap. 10.95x (ISBN 0-521-29275-1). Cambridge U Pr.

In Search of the Primitive. Stanley Diamond. 387p. 1981. pap. 9.95 (ISBN 0-87855-582-X). Transaction Bks.

In Search of the Promised Land: Essays in Black Urban History. Ed. by Theodore Kornweibel, Jr. (National University Publications, Interdisciplinary Urban Ser.). 237p. 1981. 17.50 (ISBN 0-8046-9267-X). Kennikat.

In Search of the Red Ape. new ed. John MacKinnon. LC 73-15457. (Illus.). 256p. 1974. 8.95 o.p. (ISBN 0-03-012496-4). HR&W.

In Search of the Red Ape. John MacKinnon. 248p. 1975. pap. 1.95 o.p. (ISBN 0-345-24525-3). Ballantine.

In Search of the Saveopotomas. (gr. 1-6). 1974. pap. 1.50 (ISBN 0-8431-0557-7). Serendipity Pr.

In Search of the Scrounger. Alan Deacon. 110p. 1976. pap. text ed. 7.50x (ISBN 0-7135-1992-4, Pub. by Bedford England). Renouf.

In Search of the Silent South: Southern Liberals & the Race Issue. Morton Sosna. LC 77-4965. (Contemporary American History Ser.). 1977. 17.50x (ISBN 0-231-03843-7). Columbia U Pr.

In Search of Truth. Abel J. Jones. 207p. 1980. Repr. of 1946 ed. lib. bdg. 25.00 (ISBN 0-89984-259-3). Century Bookbindery.

In Search of Twilight. Colleen L. Reece. (YA) 1978. 5.95 (ISBN 0-685-84748-9, Avalon). Bouregy.

In Search of Wagner. Theodor Adorno. 160p. 1981. 14.50 (ISBN 0-8052-7087-6, Pub. by NLB England). Schocken.

In Search of World Records. George Worthington. LC 80-82032. (gr. 10-12). 1980. 12.95 (ISBN 0-938282-01-8); pap. 9.95 (ISBN 0-938282-02-6). Hang Gliding.

In Season & Out. Bruce Clanton. LC 80-54272. 80p. 1981. pap. 6.25 (ISBN 0-89390-025-7). Resource Pubns.

In-Service Casework Training. Elizabeth Nicholds. LC 65-20775. 1966. 20.00x (ISBN 0-231-02741-9). Columbia U Pr.

In Service Education & Teachers' Centers. Elizabeth Adams. 264p. 1975. text ed. 32.00 (ISBN 0-08-018291-7); pap. text ed. 21.00 (ISBN 0-08-018290-9). Pergamon.

In-Service Education of Teachers: Trends, Processes & Prescriptions. Louis Rubin. 1978. text ed. 19.95 (ISBN 0-205-06022-6). Allyn.

In-Service Inspection for Nuclear Power Plants. (Saftey Ser.: No. 50-Sg-02). 47p. 1980. pap. 7.25 (ISBN 92-0-123180-6, IAEA). Unipub.

In-Service: School Library - Media Workshops & Conferences. Nancy Polette. LC 73-12095. 1973. 11.50 (ISBN 0-8108-0658-4). Scarecrow.

In Session with Herb Ellis. 7.98 o.p. (ISBN 0-8256-9514-7). Guitar Player.

In Shelly's Leg. Sara Vogan. LC 80-20390. 256p. 1981. 10.95 (ISBN 0-394-51451-3). Knopf.

In Sickness & in Health: Social Dimensions of Medical Care. Ralph Hingson et al. 300p. 1981. pap. text ed. 12.50 (ISBN 0-8016-4411-9). Mosby.

In Situ Investigation in Soils & Rocks. 328p. 1980. 80.00x (ISBN 0-901948-30-6, Pub. by Telford England). State Mutual Bk.

In Situ Measurement of Soil Properties. Compiled by American Society of Civil Engineers. 1975. pap. text ed. 28.00 (ISBN 0-87262-156-1). Am Soc Civil Eng.

In Situ Uranium Mining & Ground Water Restoration. Ed. by W. J. Schlitt & D. A. Shock. LC 79-52217. (Illus.). 137p. 1979. pap. 15.00x (ISBN 0-89520-267-0). Soc Mining Eng.

In Six Days. Charles H. McGowen. pap. 2.95 (ISBN 0-89728-039-3, 658621). Omega Pubns OR.

In Small Things Forgotten: The Archaeology of Early American Life. James Deetz. LC 76-50760. 1977. pap. 2.50 (ISBN 0-385-08031-X, Anch). Doubleday.

In Solitary Witness: The Life & Death of Franz Jagerstatter. Gordon C. Zahn. 1981. Repr. of 1964 ed. 18.95x (ISBN 0-03-047535-X). Irvington.

In Spite of My Resistance, I've Learned from Children. Thomas C. Lovitt. (Special Education Ser.). 1977. pap. text ed. 8.95 (ISBN 0-675-08528-4). Merrill.

In-Stability: The Shape & Space of Claudel's Art Criticism. Lynne L. Gelber. Ed. by Donald B. Kuspit. (Studies in Fine Arts: Criticism: Vol. 15). 99p. 1980. 19.95 (ISBN 0-8357-1090-4, Pub. by UMI Res Pr). Univ Microfilms.

In Stalin's Time. Vera S. Dunham. LC 75-10238. 368p. 1976. 36.00 (ISBN 0-521-20949-8); pap. 9.95 (ISBN 0-521-29650-1). Cambridge U Pr.

In Summertime It's Tuffy. Judie Angell. LC 76-57810. (gr. 5-7). 1977. 8.95 (ISBN 0-87888-117-4). Bradbury Pr.

In Sunshine & Shadows. 2nd ed. Mabel O'Donnell. (Design for Reading Ser). (Illus.). (gr. 2-1). 1972. text ed. 8.56 (ISBN 0-06-516005-3, SchDept); tchr's ed. 14.28 (ISBN 0-06-516203-X); wkbk. 3.20, (ISBN 0-06-506304-4) tchr's ed. 6.36 (ISBN 0-06-516404-0); phonics wkbk. 2.68, (ISBN 0-06-516313-3) tchr's ed 5.36 (ISBN 0-06-516413-X); cupl. masters a & b with ans. key 22.52 ea.; mastery test pkg. of 30 14.48 (ISBN 0-06-516613-2); 5 Transition paperbacks 2.52 ea.; tchrs' ed. of Transition bks 14.20 (ISBN 0-685-02892-5); wkbk. 2.56, tchrs' wkbk. for Transition bks. 4.88 (ISBN 0-685-02893-3). Har-Row.

In the Air. Eugene Booth. LC 77-7984. (Raintree Spotlight Book). (Illus.). (gr. k-3). 1977. PLB 8.25 (ISBN 0-8393-0105-7). Raintree Child.

In the Arena. Isobel Kuhn. 1960. pap. 3.50 (ISBN 0-85363-023-2). OMF Bks.

In the Arresting Eye: The Rhetoric of Imagism. John T. Gage. LC 80-24893. 208p. 1981. 17.95x (ISBN 0-8071-0790-5). La State U Pr.

In the Bar of the Tokyo Hotel & Other Plays. Tennessee Williams. LC 78-159743. (Theatre of Tennessee Williams: Vol. VII). 352p. 1981. 17.95 (ISBN 0-8112-0795-1). New Directions.

In the Beginning. Isaac Asimov & Carole Baron. 1981. 10.95 (ISBN 0-517-54336-2). Crown.

In the Beginning. 4th ed. Brian M. Fagan. 1981. text ed. 16.95 (ISBN 0-686-68258-0). Little.

In the Beginning. E. J. Young. 1976. pap. 2.45 (ISBN 0-85151-235-6). Banner of Truth.

In the Beginning There Were the Parents: Discussion Guide. Dolores Curran. 1980. pap. 2.95 (ISBN 0-03-056978-8). Winston Pr.

In the Beginning There Were the Parents. Dolores Curran. 1978. pap. 4.95 (ISBN 0-03-042766-5). Winston Pr.

In the Cannon's Mouth. P. J. Campbell. 1979. 16.95 o.p. (ISBN 0-241-10166-2, Pub. by Hamish Hamilton England). David & Charles.

In the Castle of Cats. Betty Boegehold. LC 80-22144. (Illus.). (ps-5). 1981. PLB 9.95 (ISBN 0-525-32541-7). Dutton.

In the Cattle Country: History of Potter County, 1887-1966. Della T. Key. 11.95 (ISBN 0-685-48805-5). Nortex Pr.

In the Center: Kareem Abdul Jabbar. Alida Thacher. LC 76-11011. (Sports Profiles Ser.). (Illus.). 48p. (gr. 4-11). 1976. PLB 8.50 (ISBN 0-8172-0148-3). Raintree Pubs.

In the Children's Aid: J. J. Kelso & Child Welfare in Ontario. Andrew Jones & Leonard Rutman. 256p. 1981. 17.50 (ISBN 0-8020-5491-9). U of Toronto Pr.

In the Chinese Customs Service: A Personal Record of Forty-Seven Years. Paul King. LC 78-74327. (Modern Chinese Economy Ser.). 299p. 1980. lib. bdg. 33.00 (ISBN 0-8240-4254-9). Garland Pub.

In the Christian Spirit. Louis Evely. 120p. 1975. pap. 1.45 (ISBN 0-385-06266-4, Im). Doubleday.

In the Chutes. Nolan Zavoral & Peter Sanders. LC 75-22008. (Venture Ser, a Reading Incentive Program). (Illus.). 76p. (gr. 7-12,RL 4.5-6.5). 1975. text ed. 23.25 ea. pack of 5 (ISBN 0-8172-0243-9, Raintree Editions). Follett.

In the City. Eugene Booth. LC 77-7949. (Raintree Spotlight Book). (Illus.). (gr. k-3). 1977. PLB 8.25 (ISBN 0-8393-0109-X). Raintree Child.

In the Claws of the KGB: Memoirs of a Double Agent. Rupert Sigl. 248p. 1978. 7.95 (ISBN 0-8059-2520-1). Dorrance.

In the Cockpit. Ed. by Anthony Robinson. (Illus.). 316p. 1979. 29.95 (ISBN 0-87165-051-7, ZD Bks). Ziff-Davis Pub.

In the Common Cause: American Response to the Coercive Acts of 1774. David Ammerman. LC 74-2417. 1974. 10.95x (ISBN 0-8139-0525-7). U Pr of Va.

In the Common Cause: American Response to the Coercive Acts of 1775. David Ammerman. 184p. pap. 2.95 (ISBN 0-393-00787-1, Norton Lib). Norton.

In the Company of a Siddha: Interviews & Conversations with Swami Muktananda. Swami Muktananda. LC 78-65085. 1978. 4.50 (ISBN 0-685-94386-0). SYDA Found.

In the Company of Eagles. Ernest K. Gann. 240p. (Orig.). 1981. pap. 2.50 (ISBN 0-515-05484-4). Jove Pubns.

In the Company of Others. Jory Graham. LC 78-22252. 288p. 1981. 10.95 (ISBN 0-15-144642-3). HarBraceJ.

In the Company of the Holy Mother. Orig. Title: At Holy Mother's Feet. 382p. 1980. pap. 5.95 (ISBN 0-87481-208-9). Vedanta Pr.

In the Conquest of True Freedom. Suratano Bhikkhu. LC 78-63079. 100p. 1980. 5.95 (ISBN 0-533-03965-7). Vantage.

In the Country of the Skin. Peter Redgrove. 1973. 12.00 (ISBN 0-7100-7514-6). Routledge & Kegan.

In the Court of Public Opinion. Alger Hiss. 448p. 1972. pap. 3.95x o.p. (ISBN 0-06-090293-0, CN293, CN). Har-Row.

In the Days of the Dinosaurs. Roy C. Andrews. (Gateway Ser.: No. 11). (Illus.). (gr. 3-5). 1959. 3.50 (ISBN 0-394-80111-3, BYR); PLB 5.99 (ISBN 0-394-90111-8). Random.

In the Days of the Pilgrim Fathers. Mary C. Crawford. LC 74-129572. 1970. Repr. of 1921 ed. 20.00 (ISBN 0-8103-3470-4). Gale.

In the Empire of Ice. Olga Cabral. LC 80-53808. (Illus.). 88p. (Orig.). 1980. pap. 3.25 (ISBN 0-931122-19-8). West End.

In the Eye. Aaron Miller. 8.00 (ISBN 0-89253-700-0); flexible cloth 4.80 (ISBN 0-89253-701-9). Ind-US Inc.

In the Eye of the Law. Lorinda Hagen. 1979. pap. 1.75 (ISBN 0-505-51392-7). Tower Bks.

In the Eye of the Typhoon. Ruth E. La & Katherine S. Kinderman. LC 80-7937. (Illus.). 288p. 1980. 12.95 (ISBN 0-15-144374-2). HarBraceJ.

In the Face of the Nations. Thomas Tekoah. 1976. 10.00 (ISBN 0-8074-0087-4, 382600). UAHC.

In the Fog of the Season's End. A. La Guma. LC 72-93381. 1973. 8.95 (ISBN 0-89388-058-2). Okpaku Communications.

In the Footprints of the Lamb. G. Steinberger. Tr. by Bernard Christensen. LC 78-73416. 1979. pap. 1.95 (ISBN 0-87123-237-5, 200237). Bethany Fell.

In the Footsteps of Pope John Paul II. John M. Szostak & Frances S. Leighton. LC 80-20258. 1980. 11.95 (ISBN 0-13-476002-6). P-H.

In the Footsteps of the Prophets. Moshe Pearlman. LC 75-11965. (Illus.). 1975. 19.95 o.p. (ISBN 0-690-00962-3, TYC-T). T Y Crowell.

In the Forest of the Golden Dragon. Pierre Mornand. LC 73-76776. (Fr. & Eng.). 1973. 20.00 (ISBN 0-933652-04-6). Domjan Studio.

In the Fourth World: Poems. Sandra Gilbert. LC 78-11144. 80p. 1979. 7.95 o.p. (ISBN 0-8173-8528-2); pap. 3.95 (ISBN 0-8173-8527-4). U of Ala Pr.

In the Garden. Eugene Booth. LC 77-7628. (Raintree Spotlight Book). (Illus.). (gr. k-3). 1977. PLB 8.25 (ISBN 0-8393-0115-4). Raintree Child.

In the Hands of God. William Barclay. LC 80-25261. 1981. pap. price not set (ISBN 0-664-24362-2). Westminster.

In the Heart of the Heart of the Country. William Gass. LC 68-11820. 1968. 10.00 o.s.i. (ISBN 0-06-011468-1, HarpT). Har-Row.

In the Heart of the Heart of the Country. William H. Gass. 1981. pap. 7.95 (ISBN 0-87923-374-5). Godine.

In the Heavenlies: Ephesians. H. A. Ironside. 6.95 (ISBN 0-87213-367-2). Loizeaux.

In the Hour Before Midnight. Jack Higgins. 1978. pap. 2.25 (ISBN 0-449-13954-9, GM). Fawcett.

In the Hours of Night. William B. Huie. 352p. 1975. 8.95 o.p. (ISBN 0-440-04367-0). Delacorte.

In the House of Stone & Light. Donald Hughes. LC 77-93502. 137p. 1978. pap. 7.50 (ISBN 0-938216-00-7). GCNHA.

In the Human Grain. Walter J. Ong. 1967. 9.95 (ISBN 0-02-593340-X). Macmillan.

In the Image & Likeness of God. Vladimir Lossky. LC 76-383878. 232p. 1974. pap. 5.95 (ISBN 0-913836-13-3). St Vladimirs.

In the Image of God: Art Projects with Eight Years-Old & up. Marge Tuthill. LC 75-42050. (Illus.). 1976. pap. 2.95 (ISBN 0-8091-1926-9). Paulist Pr.

In the Jungle. Eugene Booth. LC 77-7947. (Raintree Spotlight Book). (Illus.). (gr. k-3). 1977. PLB 8.25 (ISBN 0-8393-0104-9). Raintree Child.

In the Labyrinths of Language: A Mathematician's Journey. V. V. Nalimov. Ed. by Robert G. Colodny. (Illus.). 246p. 1981. 22.50 (ISBN 0-89495-007-X). ISI Pr.

In the Land of Enchantment: A Panorama of Fairy Tales. Eros Keith. LC 75-654436. (Illus.). (ps-3). 1972. 7.95 (ISBN 0-87888-046-1). Bradbury Pr.

In the Land of Head-Hunters. Edward S. Curtis. (Illus.). Date not set. 7.95 (ISBN 0-913668-48-6); pap. 3.95 (ISBN 0-913668-47-8). Ten Speed Pr.

In the Land of Sniggl-dee Sloop. Gale Brennan. (Illus.). 1980. 7.95g (ISBN 0-516-09172-7). Childrens.

In the Land of Sniggle-Dee-Bloop. Gale Brennan. (Illus.). 48p. (Orig.). (ps-3). 1980. pap. 2.95 (ISBN 0-89542-936-5). Ideals.

In the Land of the Grasshopper Song: Two Women in the Klamath River Indian Country in 1908-09. Mary E. Arnold & Mabel Reed. LC 80-12556. (Illus.). iv, 330p. 1980. 17.95x (ISBN 0-8032-1804-4); pap. 5.95 (ISBN 0-8032-6703-7, BB 740, Bison). U of Nebr Pr.

In the Last Analysis. Amanda Cross. 176p. 1981. pap. 1.95 (ISBN 0-380-54510-1). Avon.

In the Magic Land of Peyote. Fernando Benitez. 1976. pap. 1.95 o.s.i. (ISBN 0-446-89306-4). Warner Bks.

In the Manner of Jesus. Rueben Hilde. LC 76-14727. (Dimension Ser.). 1976. pap. 5.95 (ISBN 0-8163-0259-6, 09415-1). Pacific Pr Pub Assn.

In the Matter of J. Robert Oppenheimer. Ed. by United States Atomic Energy Commission. 1971. 23.00x (ISBN 0-262-21003-7); pap. 5.95x (ISBN 0-262-71002-1). MIT Pr.

In the Matter of Karen Quinlan, Vol. 1: The Complete Legal Briefs, Court Proceedings, & Decision in the Superior Court of New Jersey. New Jersey Supreme Court. 575p. 1975. 29.50 (ISBN 0-89093-100-3). U Pubns Amer.

In the Matter of Karen Quinlan: Volume 2, The Complete Briefs, Oral Agruments, & Opinion in the New Jersey Supreme Court. New Jersey Supreme Court et al. 1976. 22.50 (ISBN 0-89093-114-3). U Pubns Amer.

In the Midst of a Revolution. David Hawke. LC 80-23581. 235p. 1980. Repr. of 1961 ed. lib. bdg. 23.50x (ISBN 0-313-22604-0, HAIT). Greenwood.

In the Midst of Life. Emily G. Neal. 1974. pap. 2.95 (ISBN 0-8015-3980-3, Hawthorn). Dutton.

In the Minister's Workshop. Halford E. Luccock. (Notable Books on Preaching). 1977. pap. 3.95 o.p. (ISBN 0-8010-5571-7). Baker Bk.

In the Mirror. Ajit Khullar. 8.00 (ISBN 0-89253-693-4); flexible cloth 4.80 (ISBN 0-89253-694-2). Ind-US Inc.

In the Money. William C. Williams. LC 40-35170. (Stecher Trilogy: Vol. 2). 1967. pap. 2.45 (ISBN 0-8112-0231-3, NDP240). New Directions.

In the Moons of Borea. Brian Lumley. (Orig.). 1979. pap. 1.75 (ISBN 0-515-05125-X). Jove Pubns.

In the Morning Mist. Eleanor J. Lapp. Ed. by Kathy Pacini. LC 77-28442. (Self-Starter Bks.). (Illus.). (gr. k-3). 1978. 6.50g (ISBN 0-8075-3634-2). A Whitman.

In the Name of a Woman. Arthur W. Marchmont. 1976. lib. bdg. 16.30x (ISBN 0-89968-065-8). Lightyear.

In the Name of God. Irving Lehrman. LC 79-51518. 1979. 12.00x (ISBN 0-8197-0467-9). Bloch.

In the Name of God. Marietta D. Moskin. LC 80-12319. (Illus.). 192p. (gr. 5 up). 1980. 10.95 (ISBN 0-689-30783-7). Atheneum.

In the Name of Money: A Professional's Guide to the Federal Reserve, Interest Rates & Money. Paul DeRosa & Gary H. Stern. (Illus.). 192p. 1980. 16.95 (ISBN 0-07-016521-1, P&RB). McGraw.

In the Nature of Materials: The Buildings of Frank Lloyd Wright, 1887-1941. Henry-Russell Hitchcock. LC 72-75322. (Architecture & Decorative Arts Ser). 1973. Repr. of 1942 ed. lib. bdg. 29.50 (ISBN 0-306-71283-0). Da Capo.

In the Neighborhoods. Susan Shepard & Robert Levering. (Orig.). 1981. pap. 6.95 (ISBN 0-87701-144-3). Chronicle Bks.

In the Night. Paul Showers. LC 61-6138. (Let's-Read-&-Find-Out Science Bk). (Illus.). (gr. k-3). 1961. PLB 7.89 (ISBN 0-690-44621-7, TYC-J). T Y Crowell.

In the Night Season. C. Barnard. 1978. 8.95 o.p. (ISBN 0-13-453654-1). P-H.

In the Old South with Brer Rabbit & His Neighbors. F. Roy Johnson. 1977. 4.95 (ISBN 0-930230-35-3). Johnson NC.

In the Park. Eugene Booth. LC 77-7622. (Raintree Spotlight Book). (Illus.). (gr. k-3). 1977. PLB 8.25 (ISBN 0-8393-0106-5). Raintree Child.

In the Park: An Excursion in Four Languages. Esther Hautzig. LC 68-10067. (Illus., Fr, Rus, Span & Eng.). (gr. 1-3). 1968. 7.95 (ISBN 0-02-743450-8). Macmillan.

In the Peanut Butter Colony. Louis Ross. (Illus.). (ps-3). 1979. 1.95 (ISBN 0-525-69022-0, Gingerbread Bks); PLB 5.95 (ISBN 0-525-69023-9, Gingerbread Bks). Dutton.

In the Pine: Selected Kentucky Folksongs. 2nd ed. Leonard W. Roberts & C. Buell Agey. LC 78-56599. 1979. 12.50 (ISBN 0-933302-25-8); pap. 7.95 (ISBN 0-933302-26-6). Pikeville Coll.

In the Presence of Mothers. Judith Minty. LC 80-5259. (Pitt Poetry Ser.). 1981. 9.95 (ISBN 0-8229-3427-2); pap. 4.50 (ISBN 0-8229-5321-8). U of Pittsburgh Pr.

In the Public Interest: The Governmental Role in Academic Institutions. Ed. by Editors, Change Magazine. LC 78-64964. 1980. cancelled (ISBN 0-915390-19-1). Change Mag.

In the Queens' Parlor & Other Leaves from the Editors' Notebook. Ellery Queen. LC 70-79516. 1969. Repr. of 1957 ed. 12.00x (ISBN 0-8196-0238-8). Biblo.

In the Ravine & Other Stories. Anton Chekhov. Tr. by Ronald Wilks. Date not set. pap. 4.95 (ISBN 0-14-044336-3). Penguin. Postponed.

In the Running: The New Woman Candidate. Ruth B. Mandel. LC 80-24190. 304p. 1981. 12.95 (ISBN 0-89919-027-8). Ticknor & Fields.

In the Sea of Sterile Mountains: The Chinese in British Columbia. James Morton. (Illus.). 294p. 1980. pap. 7.95 (ISBN 0-295-95724-7). U of Wash Pr.

In the Shadow of a Bell. Donna D. De La Torriente. 112p. 1981. 7.95 (ISBN 0-87881-100-1). Mojave Bks.

In the Shadow of Giants: Mountain Ascents Past & Present. Tom King. LC 77-84572. (Illus.). 1981. 14.95 (ISBN 0-498-02186-6). A S Barnes.

In the Shadow of Hammer & Sickle. Peter Wawrzkowicz. Date not set. 6.95 (ISBN 0-8062-1657-3). Carlton.

In the Shadow of History. Ed. by J. Frank Dobie et al. (Texas Folklore Society Publication Ser.: No. 25). 192p. 1980. Repr. of 1939 ed. 6.95 (ISBN 0-87074-173-X). SMU Press.

In the Shadow of Organization. Robert B. Denhardt. LC 80-23775. 168p. 1981. 17.50x (ISBN 0-7006-0210-0). Regents Pr KS.

In the Shadow of the Enlightenment: Occultism & Renaissance Science in Eighteenth-Century America. Herbert Leventhal. LC 75-13762. 336p. 1976. 17.50x (ISBN 0-8147-4965-8). NYU Pr.

In the Shadow of the Factory: Social Change in a Finnish Community. Patricia S. Lander. LC 75-37634. 198p. 1976. text ed. 12.50 o.p. (ISBN 0-470-01379-6); pap. text ed. 5.95 (ISBN 0-470-01380-X). Halsted Pr.

In the Shadow of the Tower. Ruth M. Sears. 1975. pap. 0.95 o.p. (ISBN 0-685-52179-6, LB251NK, Leisure Bks). Nordon Pubns.

In the Shadow of the White Plague: A Memoir. Elizabeth Mooney. LC 78-3311. 1979. 9.95 o.s.i. (ISBN 0-690-01696-4, TYC-T). T Y Crowell.

In the Shadow of Tomorrow. J. Huizinga. 6.50 (ISBN 0-8446-0717-7). Peter Smith.

In the Spell of the Past. S. R. Van Iterson. LC 74-31022. 192p. (gr. 7 up). 1975. PLB 6.96 (ISBN 0-688-32023-6). Morrow.

In the Spirit, in the Flesh. Kennedy, Eugene C., M.M. LC 72-157604. 160p. 1972. pap. 1.45 o.p. (ISBN 0-385-02126-7, Im). Doubleday.

In the Spirit of Enterprise from the Rolex Awards. Ed. by Gregory B. Stone. LC 78-23479. (Illus.). 1978. pap. 9.95x (ISBN 0-7167-1034-X). W H Freeman.

In the Strong Woods. Paul Lehmberg. 160p. 1981. pap. 4.95 (ISBN 0-312-41173-1). St Martin.

In the Teeth of the Evidence. Dorothy L. Sayers. pap. 1.50 (ISBN 0-380-01280-4, 35998). Avon.

In the Tennessee Mountains. Mary N. Murfree. LC 78-100406. (Tennesseana Editions Ser.). (Illus.). 1970. 9.50 (ISBN 0-87049-105-9). U of Tenn Pr.

In the Twilight of Christendom: Hegel Vs. Kierkegaard on Faith & History. Stephen Crites. LC 77-188905. (American Academy of Religion. Studies in Religion). 1972. pap. text ed. 7.50 (ISBN 0-89130-154-2, 010002). Scholars Pr Ca.

In the Twilight of My Memory: Windows to the Past. Walter E. Barton. 100p. 1981. 5.00 (ISBN 0-8059-2762-X). Dorrance.

In the Upper Room. D. J. Burrell. (Short Course Ser.). 146p. 1913. text ed. 2.95 (ISBN 0-567-08317-9). Attic Pr.

In the Valley of the Little Big Horn. rev. ed. Robert C. Kain. (Illus.). 117p. 1978. 7.95 (ISBN 0-917714-16-4). Beinfeld Pub.

In the Wake of Naxalbari: A History of the Naxalite Movement in India. Sumanta Banerjee. 436p. 1980. text ed. 22.50 (ISBN 0-8426-1656-X). Verry.

In the Wake of the "Wake". Ed. by David Hayman & Elliott Anderson. 1978. 18.50 (ISBN 0-299-07600-8). U of Wis Pr.

In the Wake of the Whale. John A. Barbour. LC 69-11397. (Surveyor Books Ser). (Illus.). (gr. 7-10). 1969. 3.95g o.s.i. (ISBN 0-02-708330-6, CCPr). Macmillan.

In the Way of the Whale: The Whaling Journal of John F. Martin, 1841 to 1844. John F. Martin. Ed. by Kenneth R. Martin. LC 80-66462. (Illus.). 224p. 1981. 15.00 (ISBN 0-87923-350-8). Godine.

In the Web. Saralyn Daly. 1978. pap. 1.95 o.p. (ISBN 0-449-14043-1, GM). Fawcett.

In the Witch's Kitchen: Poems for Halloween. John E. Brewton et al. LC 79-7822. (Illus.). 96p. (gr. 2-5). 1980. 8.95 (ISBN 0-690-04061-X, TYC-J); PLB 8.79 (ISBN 0-690-04062-8). T Y Crowell.

In the Words of Napoleon. Daniel S. Gray. LC 77-71468. 1977. pap. 8.50 (ISBN 0-916624-07-2). TSU Pr.

In the World. G. Leslie DeLapp. LC 73-75884. 1973. 7.50 o.p. (ISBN 0-8309-0099-3). Herald Hse.

In the Year of the Strike. Remco Campert. Tr. by John Scott & Graham Martin. (Poetry Europe Ser.: No. 8). 60p. 1969. 4.95 o.p. (ISBN 0-8040-0163-4). Swallow.

In Their Own Words: A History of the American Negro. Milton Meltzer. Incl. 1619-1865. LC 64-22541. 1964. 2.95 (ISBN 0-8152-0348-9); 1865-1916. LC 65-23778. 1965. 1.65 (ISBN 0-8152-0349-7); 1916-1966. LC 66-1439. 1967. 1.65 (ISBN 0-8152-0350-0). (Illus.). (gr. 5 up). pap. (AE-J). Apollo Eds.

In Their Own Words: Lyrics & Lyricists, 1955-74. Bruce Pollock. 224p. 1975. pap. 4.95 o.s.i. (ISBN 0-02-061420-9, Collier). Macmillan.

In Their Own Words: Lyrics & Lyricists, 1955-74. Bruce Pollock. 224p. 1975. 10.95 (ISBN 0-02-597950-7). Macmillan.

In Their Place: White America Defines Her Minorities, 1850-1950. Ed. by Lewis H. Carlson & George A. Colburn. LC 70-177881. 1972. pap. 9.95x o.p. (ISBN 0-471-13489-9). Wiley.

In This Boke Are Conteyened These Statutes,...Whiche to Put in Execution, the Justices of Peace...Ware Admonished. LC 79-84105. (English Experience Ser.: No.924). 68p. 1979. Repr. of 1538 ed. lib. bdg. 7.00 (ISBN 90-221-0924-0). Walter J Johnson.

In This Corner. J. R. Price & Valerie F. Putney. (Orig.). 1981. pap. 2.95 o.s.i. (ISBN 0-440-13970-8). Dell.

In This Corner: Muhammad Ali. F. M. Milverstedt. LC 75-42338. (Sports Profiles Ser.). (Illus.). 48p. (gr. 4-11). 1976. 7.49 o.p. (ISBN 0-8172-0130-0). Raintree Pubs.

In This Sign. Joanne Greenberg. 1972. pap. 1.95 (ISBN 0-380-38414-0, 38414). Avon.

In This Tretyse That Is Cleped Gouernayle of Helthe. LC 72-200. (English Experience Ser.: No. 192). 1969. Repr. of 1489 ed. 11.50 (ISBN 90-221-0192-4). Walter J Johnson.

In Times Like These. Vance Havner. 1969. 6.95 (ISBN 0-8007-0160-7). Revell.

In Times Like These. Nellie McClung. LC 70-163829. (Social History of Canada Ser.). 160p. 1972. pap. 4.95 (ISBN 0-8020-6125-7). U of Toronto Pr.

In Times of Sickness. Norman Autton. 1978. 1.40 (ISBN 0-686-28781-9). Forward Movement.

In Touch. Paul R. Malte & Wayne Saffen. pap. 1.95 (ISBN 0-933350-02-3). Morse Pr.

In Touch: A New American Series. Oscar Castro. Incl. students bk. 1, 1979 (ISBN 0-582-79742-X); tchr's manual 1 (ISBN 0-582-79743-8); workbook 1 (ISBN 0-582-79744-6); cassette 1; students bk. 2 (ISBN 0-582-79746-2); tchr's manual 2 (ISBN 0-582-79747-0); workbook 2 (ISBN 0-582-79748-9); cassette 2 (ISBN 0-582-79749-7); students bk. 3 (ISBN 0-582-79750-0); tchr's manual 3 (ISBN 0-582-79753-5); workbook 3 (ISBN 0-582-79752-7); cassette 3 (ISBN 0-582-79751-9). (Illus.). 1980. pap. text ed. 3.50x ea. student bk.; tchr's manual 4.50x ea.; wkbk. 1.95x ea.; cassette 18.95 ea. Longman.

In Vitro Aspects of Erythropoiesis. Ed. by M. J. Murphy, Jr. LC 78-16104. (Illus.). 1978. 37.30 (ISBN 0-387-90320-8). Springer-Verlag.

In Vitro Epithelia & Birth Defects: Proceedings. Ed. by B. Shannon Danes et al. LC 80-7693. (Birth Defects: Original Article Ser.: Vol. XVI, No. 2). 390p. 1980. 46.00x (ISBN 0-8451-1036-5). A R Liss.

In Vitro Procedures with Radioisotopes in Medicine. (Illus., Orig., Eng., Fr. & Span.). 1970. pap. 49.25 (ISBN 92-0-010070-8, IAEA). Unipub.

In Vivo Neutron Activation Analysis. (Illus.). 242p. (Orig.). 1974. pap. 16.25 (ISBN 92-0-111173-8, IAEA). Unipub.

In What Book. Ruth Harshaw & Hope H. Evans. LC 73-99122. (gr. k-12). 1970. 5.95 o.s.i. (ISBN 0-02-742780-3). Macmillan.

In Wicklow, West Kerry & Connemara. J. M. Synge. (Illus.). 166p. 1980. 19.50x (ISBN 0-8476-6260-8). Rowman.

In Winter. Michael K. Ryan. LC 80-19799. (National Poetry Ser.). 64p. 1981. 8.95 (ISBN 0-03-058942-8); pap. price not set (ISBN 0-03-058941-X). HR&W.

In Worlds Apart-Professionals & Their Clients in the Welfare State. Tim Robinson. 87p. 1978. pap. text ed. 4.90x (ISBN 0-7199-0942-2, Pub. by Bedford England). Renouf.

In Your Midst: Perspectives on Christian Mission. Sheila D. Collins & John A. Collins. (Orig.). 1980. pap. 3.25 (ISBN 0-377-00101-5). Friend Pr.

Inaccessible Earth. G. C. Brown & A. E. Mussett. (Illus.). 272p. 1981. text ed. 41.00x (ISBN 0-04-550027-4, 2538); pap. text ed. 22.50x (ISBN 0-04-550028-2, 2539). Allen Unwin.

Inbetween Yesterday. 2nd ed. Susan E. Barrett. LC 77-74036. (Illus.). 1976. pap. 4.00 (ISBN 0-89430-001-6). Morgan-Pacific.

Inboard Motor Installations. 2nd rev. ed. Glen L. Witt & Ken Hankinson. (Illus.). 1978. text ed. 13.95 (ISBN 0-686-08739-9). Glen-L Marine.

Inborn Disorders of Sphingolipid Metabolism. Ed. by S. M. Aronson & B. W. Volk. 1967. 64.00 (ISBN 0-08-012038-5). Pergamon.

Inborn Errors of Metabolism. Ed. by Roland Ellis. 112p. 1980. 30.00x (Pub. by Croom Helm England). State Mutual Bk.

Inc. Yourself. Judith H. McQuown. 1981. pap. 5.95 (ISBN 0-446-97817-5). Warner Bks.

Inca Architecture. Graziano Gasparini & Luise Margolies. Tr. by Patricia J. Lyon from Sp. LC 79-3005. (Illus.). 352p. 1980. 32.50x (ISBN 0-253-30443-1). Ind U Pr.

Inca Garcilaso de la Vega. Donald G. Castanien. (World Authors Ser.: Peru: No. 61). lib. bdg. 10.95 (ISBN 0-8057-2928-3). Twayne.

Inca: Indians of the Andes. Sonia Bleeker. (Illus.). (gr. 3-6). 1960. PLB 6.67 (ISBN 0-688-31417-1). Morrow.

Incandescent Ones. Fred Hoyle & Geoffrey Hoyle. LC 76-47254. 1977. 8.95 o.s.i. (ISBN 0-06-011956-X, HarpT). Har-Row.

Incarnations: Poems 1966-1968. Robert P. Warren. LC 68-28529. 1968. 7.95 (ISBN 0-394-40368-1); pap. 4.95 (ISBN 0-394-73935-3); lmtd. ed. 15.00 (ISBN 0-394-51305-3). Random.

Incas. Cottie Burland. LC 78-61225. (Peoples of the Past Ser.). (Illus.). 1979. lib. bdg. 7.95 (ISBN 0-686-51158-1). Silver.

Incas. Garcilasco De La Vega. 1964. pap. 3.50 (ISBN 0-380-01269-3, 45542, Discus). Avon.

Incas. Anne Millard. (Warwick Press Ser.). (gr. 5 up). 1980. PLB 6.90 (ISBN 0-531-09171-6, F23). Watts.

Incas & Other Men: Travels in the Andes. George Woodcock. (Illus., Orig.). 1965. pap. 4.95 (ISBN 0-571-06118-4, Pub. by Faber & Faber). Merrimack Bk Serv.

Ince Affair. Edward Epstein & Joseph Morella. (Orig.). 1978. pap. 1.75 o.p. (ISBN 0-451-08177-3, E8177, Sig). NAL.

Incense & Iconoclasm. Charles L. Moore. 343p. 1980. Repr. of 1915 ed. lib. bdg. 30.00 (ISBN 0-89987-573-4). Century Bookbindery.

Incentive: How the Conditions of Reinforcement Affect the Performance of Rats. Frank A. Logan. 1960. 42.50x (ISBN 0-686-51403-3). Elliots Bks.

Incentives & Productivity in Public Enterprises. J. Satyanarayana. 153p. 1975. 11.00 o.p. (ISBN 0-89253-007-3). InterCulture.

Incentives in the New Industrial Order. John A. Hobson. LC 79-51860. 1981. Repr. of 1922 ed. 16.00 (ISBN 0-88355-953-6). Hyperion Conn.

Incest & Human Love. R. Stein. LC 73-82641. 1973. 8.95 (ISBN 0-89388-090-6). Okpaku Communications.

Inchon: Macarthur's Last Triumph. Michael Langley. 1979. 24.00 (ISBN 0-7134-3346-9, Pub. by Batsford England). David & Charles.

Incidence & Economic Costs of Major Health Impairments: A Comparative Analysis of Cancer,Motor-Vehicle Injuries, Coronary Heart Disease, & Stroke. Nelson S. Hartunian et al. LC 80-8189. 1981. price not set (ISBN 0-669-03975-6). Lexington Bks.

Incidence of Emigration During the French Revolution. Donald Greer. 1951. 7.00 (ISBN 0-8446-1210-3). Peter Smith.

Incidence of Income Taxes. Duncan Black. LC 66-76596. Repr. of 1939 ed. 21.00x (ISBN 0-678-05156-9). Kelley.

Incident at Bloody Axe. Glenn R. Vernam. 1979. pap. 1.50 (ISBN 0-505-51451-6). Tower Bks.

Incident at Eagle Ranch: Man & Predator in the American West. Donald G. Schueler. LC 80-13588. 320p. 1980. 12.95 (ISBN 0-87156-230-8). Sierra.

Incident at Exeter. John G. Fuller. 272p. Date not set. pap. 1.95 (ISBN 0-425-03929-3). Berkley Pub.

Incident at Horado City. William C. MacDonald. 1978. pap. 1.25 (ISBN 0-505-51288-2). Tower Bks.

Incident on the Way to a Killing. Michael Hammonds. 176p. 1980. pap. 1.75 (ISBN 0-515-04681-7). Jove Pubns.

Incidents & Experiences in the Life of Thomas W. Parsons from 1826 to 1900. Thomas W. Parsons. Ed. by Frank F. Mathias. LC 74-7878. (Illus.). 1975. 14.00x (ISBN 0-8131-1319-9). U Pr of Ky.

Incidents in Modern Business. new ed. Bernard Deitzer & Karl Shilliff. 200p. 1975. pap. text ed. 10.95x (ISBN 0-675-08785-6). Merrill.

Incidents in the Life of Joseph Grimaldi. Giles Neville. (Illus.). 64p. 1981. 10.95 (ISBN 0-224-01869-8, Pub. by Chatto-Bodley-Jonathan). Merrimack Bk Serv.

Incidents of Border Life Illustrative of the Times & Condition of the First Settlements in Parts of the Middle & Western States... Compiled from Authentic Sources. Joseph Pritts. LC 75-7080. (Indian Captivities Ser.: Vol. 57). 1977. Repr. of 1839 ed. lib. bdg. 44.00 (ISBN 0-8240-1681-5). Garland Pub.

Incidents of Travel in Central America, Chiapas & Yucatan, 2 Vols. John Stephens. (Illus.). 1969. pap. 5.00 (ISBN 0-685-09122-8); Vol. 1. pap. 5.00 ea. (ISBN 0-486-22404-X); Vol. 2. pap. (ISBN 0-486-22405-8). Dover.

Incidents of Travel in Yucatan. John L. Stephens. Ed. by Victor W. Von Hagen. LC 62-10771. (American Exploration & Travel Ser.: Vol. 37). (Illus.). 1962. 32.50 (ISBN 0-8061-0528-3). U of Okla Pr.

Incinerator Plant Maintenance Foreman. Jack Rudman. (Career Examination Ser.: C-2773). (Cloth bdg. avail. on request). 1980. pap. 12.00 (ISBN 0-8373-2773-3). Natl Learning.

Incised Effigial Slabs, 2 vols. Frank Greenhill. 1976. Set. 98.00 (ISBN 0-571-10880-6, Pub. by Faber & Faber); Vol. 1. (ISBN 0-571-10741-9); Vol. 2. Merrimack Bk Serv.

Incitement to Nixonicide & Praise for the Chilean Revolution. 2nd ed. Pablo Neruda. Tr. by Steve Kowit from Spanish. (Illus.). 82p. 1980. pap. 5.00 (ISBN 0-686-68219-X). Quixote.

Incline. William Mayne. (gr. 5 up). 1972. PLB 6.95 o.p. (ISBN 0-525-32550-6). Dutton.

Income & Employment in the Southeast: A Study in Cyclical Behavior. L. Randolph McGee. LC 67-17849. (Illus.). 152p. 1967. 9.00x (ISBN 0-8131-1141-2). U Pr of Ky.

Income & Ideology: An Analysis of the American Political Formula. Joan Huber & William H. Form. LC 73-2128. (Illus.). 1973. 12.95 (ISBN 0-02-915330-1). Free Pr.

Income Approach to Property Valuation. Andrew Baum & David Mackmin. 1979. pap. 12.00 (ISBN 0-7100-0018-9). Routledge & Kegan.

Income Approach to Property Valuation. rev. ed. Andrew Baum & David Mackmin. 216p. (Orig.). 1981. pap. 14.95 (ISBN 0-7100-0833-3). Routledge & Kegan.

Income Conditioned Programs & Their Clients: A Research Agenda. Marc Bendick, Jr. & D. Lee Bawden. (Institute Paper). 96p. 1977. pap. 4.00 o.p. (ISBN 0-685-99486-4, 19600). Urban Inst.

Income Determination Theory: An Accounting Framework. Bedford. 1976. 17.95 (ISBN 0-201-00460-7). A-W.

Income Distribution & Economic Inequality. Ed. by Zvi Griliches et al. 1978. 34.95 (ISBN 0-470-26331-8). Halsted Pr.

Income Distribution & Growth in the Less-Developed Countries. Ed. by Charles R. Frank, Jr. & Richard C. Webb. LC 77-86494. 1977. pap. 13.95 (ISBN 0-8157-2915-4). Brookings.

Income Distribution in Latin America. Ed. by A. Foxley. LC 75-20835. 1976. 35.50 (ISBN 0-521-21029-1). Cambridge U Pr.

Income Distribution, Structure of Economy & Employment: A Comparative Study for Four Asian Countries. Felix Paukert et al. 176p. 1981. 35.00x (ISBN 0-7099-2006-7, Pub. by Croom Helm LTD England). Biblio Dist.

Income Distribution: The Limits to Redistribution. David Collard et al. 267p. 1981. 34.95 (ISBN 0-470-27099-3). Halsted Pr.

Income Distribution Theory. Martin Bronfenbrenner. LC 77-131045. (Treatises in Modern Economics Ser). 1971. 31.95x (ISBN 0-202-06037-3). Aldine Pub.

Income-Distributional Consequences of Roadway Pricing. Damian J. Kulash. 32p. 1974. pap. 2.50 o.p. (ISBN 0-87766-126-X, 84000). Urban Inst.

Income, Employment & Economic Growth. 4th ed. Wallace C. Peterson. Incl. Macroeconomics: Problems, Concepts & Self Tests. Harold R. Williams. 1978. pap. text ed. 9.95x wkbk. (ISBN 0-393-09058-2). 1978. text ed. 15.95x (ISBN 0-393-09069-8). Norton.

Income Equity Among U. S. Workers: The Bases & Consequences of Deprivation. Richard T. Curtin. LC 76-24349. (Praeger Special Studies). 1977. 22.95 (ISBN 0-275-23780-X). Praeger.

Income, Expense Analysis: Apartments. Ed. by Kenneth Anderson. 1979. lib. bdg. 45.00 o.p. (ISBN 0-912104-39-2). Inst Real Estate.

Income-Expense Analysis: Apartments. Inst. of Real Estate Management. Ed. by Kenneth Anderson. (Orig.). 1980. lib. bdg. 49.00 (ISBN 0-912104-48-1). Inst Real Estate.

Income, Expense Analysis: Suburban Office Buildings. Ed. by Kenneth Anderson. 1979. lib. bdg. 30.00 o.p. (ISBN 0-912104-40-6). Inst Real Estate.

Income-Expense Analysis: Suburban Office Buildings. Institute of Real Estate Management. Ed. by Kenneth A. Anderson. (Orig.). 1980. lib. bdg. 35.00 (ISBN 0-912104-47-3). Inst Real Estate.

Income in Sales-Marketing Management. Steven Langer. 1981. pap. 85.00 (ISBN 0-916506-58-4). Abbott Langer Assocs.

Income Inequality & Poverty: Methods of Estimation & Policy Applications. Nanak Kakwani. (World Bank Research Publications). (Illus.). 1980. 19.95x (ISBN 0-19-520126-4); pap. 8.95x (ISBN 0-19-520227-9). Oxford U Pr.

Income Inequality: Trends & International Comparisons. John R. Moroney. LC 79-4726. 192p. 1979. 20.95 (ISBN 0-669-03058-9). Lexington Bks.

Income Property Appraisal & Analysis. Jack Friedman & Nicholas Ordway. 300p. 1981. text ed. 17.95 (ISBN 0-8359-3057-2); instr's. manual free (ISBN 0-8359-3058-0). Reston.

Income Redistribution & the Welfare State. Adrian L. Webb. 125p. 1971. pap. text ed. 6.25x (Pub. by Bedford England). Renouf.

Income Stabilization for a Developing Democracy. Ed. by Max F. Millikan. 1953. 75.00x (ISBN 0-685-69843-2). Elliots Bks.

Income Support: Conceptual & Policy Issues. Ed. by Peter G. Brown et al. (Maryland Studies in Public Philosophy Ser.). 400p. 1981. 27.50x (ISBN 0-8476-6969-6). Rowman.

Income Tax & Business Decisions: An Introductory Tax Text. 4th ed. William L. Raby. LC 77-25840. (Illus.). 1978. ref. ed. 21.00 (ISBN 0-13-454363-7). P-H.

Income Tax Handbook for Ministers & Religious Workers: 1981 Edition for Preparing 1980 Returns. B. J. Worth. 60p. (Orig.). 1980. pap. 2.95 (ISBN 0-8010-9642-1). Baker Bk.

Income Tax Law for Ministers & Religious Workers. B. H. Worth. 1979. pap. 2.95 o.p. (ISBN 0-8010-9631-6). Baker Bk.

Income Tax Planning Model for Small Businesses. David H. Butler. Ed. by Gunter Dufey. (Research for Business Decisions). 178p. 1981. 24.95 (ISBN 0-8357-1131-5, Pub. by UMI Res Pr). Univ Microfilms.

Income Tax Treaty Between the U. S. & Japan. John Huston. (Asian Law Ser: 8). 1981. price not set o.p. U of Wash Pr.

Income Taxation of Estates & Trusts. 10th ed. Arthur M. Michaelson. 1978. text ed. 25.00 o.p. (ISBN 0-685-86796-X, J1-1422). PLI.

Income Taxation of Estates & Trusts. 11th ed. Arthur M. Michaelson. LC 80-83758. 220p. 1980. text ed. 35.00 (ISBN 0-686-69169-5, J1-1434). PLI.

Income Taxation of Estates & Trusts 1979. (Tax Law & Estate Planning Course Handbook Ser. 1979-80: Vol. 106). 1979. pap. 20.00 (ISBN 0-685-92233-2, D4-5123). PLI.

Income Transfers & Family Structure. Isabel V. Sawhill et al. (Institute Paper). 211p. 1975. pap. 8.50 (ISBN 0-87766-156-1, 13100). Urban Inst.

Incomes Policies, Inflation & Relative Pay. Ed. by J. L. Fallick & R. F. Elliot. (Illus.). 304p. 1981. text ed. 29.95x (ISBN 0-04-331077-X, 2578); pap. text ed. 12.95x (ISBN 0-04-331078-8, 2579). Allen Unwin.

Incomes Policy & the Public Sector. Campbell Balfour. 1972. 22.00x (ISBN 0-7100-7306-2). Routledge & Kegan.

Incomes Policy for the United States: New Approaches. Michael P. Claudon & Richard Cornwall. 240p. 1980. lib. bdg. 18.00 (ISBN 0-89838-048-0). Kluwer Boston.

Incomparable Max. Jerome Lawrence & Robert E. Lee, 1972. pap. 2.45 o.p. (ISBN 0-8090-1227-8, Mermaid). Hill & Wang.

Incomparable Story. Ralph W. Harris. (Radiant Life Ser.). 1977. pap. 1.50 (ISBN 0-88243-907-3, 02-0907); tchr's ed. 2.50 (ISBN 0-88243-177-3, 32-0177). Gospel Pub.

Incompatability in Fungi: A Symposium. International Congress of Botany, Edinburgh, 1964. Ed. by J. R. Raper & K. Esser. (Illus.). viii, 124p. 1965. pap. 25.80 (ISBN 0-387-03334-3). Springer Verlag.

Incompatible Destinies. Karl Kiseli. 1980. 10.95 (ISBN 0-533-04518-5). Vantage.

Incompleat Board: The Unfolding of Corporate Governance. Robert K. Mueller. LC 80-8639. 1981. 29.95 (ISBN 0-669-04339-7). Lexington Bks.

Incomplete Adult. Margaret J. Lundberg. LC 74-67. (Illus.). 245p. 1974. lib. bdg. 16.95 (ISBN 0-8371-7362-0, LUA/). Greenwood.

Incomplete Block Design. John. 112p. 1980. 17.75 (ISBN 0-8247-6995-3). Dekker.

Incomplete Guide to the Future. Willis W. Harman. 176p. 1979. pap. text ed. 4.95 (ISBN 0-393-95006-9). Norton.

Incongruities, Inconsistencies, Absurdities in Hegel's Conception of the Universe. Gerald H. Watson. (Illus.). 1980. 37.75 (ISBN 0-89266-220-4). Am Classical Coll Pr.

Inconsistant Lady by Arthur Wilson: An Edition with Introduction and Notes. Linda V. Itzoe. Ed. by Stephen Orgel. LC 79-54345. (Renaissance Drama Second Ser.). 300p. 1980. lib. bdg. 33.00 (ISBN 0-8240-4462-2). Garland Pub.

Inconsistent Ethic? Teachings of the American Catholic Bishops. Kenneth R. Overberg. LC 80-512. 220p. 1980. lib. bdg. 17.75 (ISBN 0-8191-1318-2); pap. text ed. 9.75 (ISBN 0-8191-1319-0). U Pr of Amer.

Incontinence & Its Management. Ed. by Dorothy Mandelstam. (Illus.). 233p. 1980. bds. 25.00x (ISBN 0-7099-0088-0, Pub. by Croom Helm Ltd England). Biblio Dist.

Incontro Con l'Italiano: Primo Corso. F. J. Bosco & F. Lolli. 1967. text ed. 16.95 (ISBN 0-471-00040-X); tapes avail. (ISBN 0-471-00041-8). Wiley.

Incorporating Your Business. Professional Report Editors & John Kirk. (Illus.). 1981. 15.00 (ISBN 0-8092-5903-6). Contemp Bks.

Increase Your Child's Learning Capacity: Through Hobbies, Exercise & Nutrition. Dorie A. Erickson. 200p. 1981. pap. 5.95 (ISBN 0-937242-06-3). Scandia Pubs.

Increase Your Knowledge Thru Fun. Dorie Erikson. 100p. 1981. pap. 5.95 (ISBN 0-937242-00-4). Scandia Pubs.

Increased Profits Through Control of Work in Process. Gue. (Illus.). 1980. text ed. 18.95 (ISBN 0-8359-3062-9). Reston.

Increasing Lodging Revenues & Restaurant Checks. Bruce H. Axler. 1974. pap. 3.95 (ISBN 0-672-96121-0). Bobbs.

Increasing Managerial Effectiveness: Keys to Management & Motivation. Norman C. Hill. LC 78-62547. 1979. pap. text ed. 8.95 (ISBN 0-201-02888-3). A-W.

Increasing Motor Carrier Productivity: An Empirical Analysis. Grant M. Davis & John E. Dillard, Jr. LC 77-7821. (Praeger Special Studies). 1977. text ed. 20.95 (ISBN 0-03-022641-4). Praeger.

Increasing Productivity in Foodservice. Ed. by Raymond B. Pedderson et al. LC 73-84798. 1973. 14.95 (ISBN 0-8436-0560-X). CBI Pub.

Increasing Productivity Through Performance Appraisal. Gary P. Latham & Kenneth N. Wexley. (Managing Human Resources Ser.). 175p. 1980. pap. 6.95 (ISBN 0-201-04217-7). A-W.

Increasing Programmer's Production Through Logic Development. Gloria H. Swann. (Illus.). 1978. text ed. 12.50 (ISBN 0-89433-065-9). Petrocelli.

Increasing Your Self Esteem: How to Feel Better About Yourself. Dean C. Dauw. (Illus.). 128p. 1980. pap. text ed. 4.95x (ISBN 0-917974-43-3). Waveland Pr.

Incredible Atlantic Herring. Joseph J. Cook. LC 78-24540. (Illus.). (gr. 4 up). 1979. 5.95 (ISBN 0-396-07647-5). Dodd.

Incredible Church. J. W. Stevenson. 2.50 o.p. (ISBN 0-227-67490-1). Attic Pr.

Incredible Coincidence: The Baffling World of Synchronicity. Alan Vaughn. 256p. 1980. pap. 2.25 (ISBN 0-451-09349-6, E9349, Sig). NAL.

Incredible Conditions of the World in the Year 2000: An Astonishing Forecast. Thomas A. Wollaston. (Illus.). 131p. 1981. 67.85 (ISBN 0-930008-74-X). Inst Econ Pol.

Incredible Crimes. Linda Atkinson. (Triumph Bks.). (gr. 5 up). 1980. PLB 6.90 (ISBN 0-531-04170-0, F21). Watts.

Incredible Detectives. Don Caufield & Joan Caufield. 1980. pap. 1.50 (ISBN 0-380-01282-0, 50443, Camelot). Avon.

Incredible Dr. Matrix. Martin Gardner. LC 76-16860. (Illus.). 265p. 1977. 8.95 o.p. (ISBN 0-684-14669-X, ScribT). Scribner.

Incredible Ghosts of Old Monterey's Hotel Del Monte. Randall A. Reinstedt. (Illus.). 48p. pap. 2.95 (ISBN 0-933818-07-6). Ghost Town.

Incredible Great White Fleet. Samuel Carter, 3rd. LC 77-129747. (Illus.). (gr. 7 up). 1971. 4.95 o.s.i. (ISBN 0-02-717770-X, CCPr). Macmillan.

Incredible Illustrated Tool Book. Ed. by Stephen Clark & Daniel Lyman. (Illus.). 415p. Date not set. price not set (ISBN 0-89196-082-1, Domus Bks). Quality Bks IL. Postponed.

Incredible Journey. Sheila Burnford. (Illus.). 1961. 8.95 (ISBN 0-316-11714-5, Pub. by Atlantic Monthly Pr). Little.

Incredible Journey: Through the Hole-in-the-Rock. Lee Reay. Ed. by Ranier Hechtle. (Illus.). 128p. (Orig.). 1981. 5.95 (ISBN 0-934826-05-6); pap. 3.95 (ISBN 0-934826-06-4). Meadow Lane.

Incredible Life: A Handbook of Biological Mysteries. William R. Corliss. LC 80-53971. (Illus.). 1050p. 1981. 22.50 (ISBN 0-915554-07-0). Sourcebook.

Incredible Mind-Blowing Trial of Jack Smith. Helmut Bakaitis. (Australian Theatre Workshop Ser.). 1973. pap. text ed. 4.25x (ISBN 0-686-65320-3, 00524). Heinemann Ed.

Incredible Shrinking Dream: An Illustrated People's History of the United States. Estelle Carol & Bob Simpson. (Illus.). 180p. (Orig.). 1981. pap. 6.95 (ISBN 0-932870-07-4). Alyson Pubns.

Incredible Shrinking Woman. Ed. by Jody Sibert. 160p. (Orig.). 1981. pap. 2.50 (ISBN 0-515-05753-3). Jove Pubns.

Incredible Swimfants! Lana E. Whitehead. LC 77-75712. 1979. 9.95 (ISBN 0-9604096-0-2). Family YMCA Stanislaus.

Incredible Television Machine. Lee Polk & Eda LeShan. LC 77-6247. (Illus.). (gr. 5 up). 1977. 8.95 (ISBN 0-02-774700-X, 77470). Macmillan.

Incredible Voyage. Tristan Jones. 1980. pap. 2.95 (ISBN 0-380-49999-1, 49999). Avon.

Incredible Voyage. Keith Knoche. (Uplook Ser.). 1975. pap. 0.75 (ISBN 0-8163-0184-0, 09446-6). Pacific Pr Pub Assn.

Incredible 305th. Wilbur H. Morrison. 1977. pap. 1.50 (ISBN 0-505-51154-1). Tower Bks.

Incredibly Foolish & Tragic Foreign Policy of the United States in the Middle East. new ed. Victor Marx. (Illus.). 1977. 39.15 (ISBN 0-89266-084-8). Am Classical Coll Pr.

Incubus. Ray Russell. Date not set. pap. price not set (ISBN 0-440-14129-X). Dell.

Incubus & Ideal: Ecclesiastical Figures in Chaucer & Langland. Peter S. Taitt. (Salzburg Studies in English Literature, Elizabethan & Renaissance Studies Ser.: No. 44). 228p. (Orig.). 1975. pap. text ed. 25.00x (ISBN 0-391-01544-3). Humanities.

Indaba My Children. Vusamazulu C. Mutwa. 1971. pap. text ed. 18.25x (ISBN 0-900707-07-0). Humanities.

Inde. Ed. by Daniel Moreau. (Collection monde et voyages). 159p. (Fr.). 1973. 21.00x (ISBN 2-03-053119-7). Larousse.

Indebtedness of Handel to Works by Other Composers. Sedley Taylor. (Music Reprint Ser.). 1979. Repr. of 1906 ed. lib. bdg. 22.50 (ISBN 0-306-79513-2). Da Capo.

Indecent Exposure. John M. Macdonald. 180p. 1973. 11.75 (ISBN 0-398-02598-3). C C Thomas.

Indecent Pleasures. William Targ. LC 75-15991. (Illus.). 448p. 1975. 14.95 o.s.i. (ISBN 0-02-619700-6, 61970). Macmillan.

Indentity & the Sacred. Hans J. Mol. LC 76-27153. 1977. 19.95 (ISBN 0-02-921600-1). Free Pr.

Independence & Opportunity: Political Change in Ahafo. J. Dunn & A. F. Robertson. LC 73-79303. (African Studies, No. 8). (Illus.). 420p. 1974. 36.00 (ISBN 0-521-20270-1). Cambridge U Pr.

Independence of Georgia in International Politics, 1918-1920. Zurab D. Avalov. LC 79-2890. 286p. 1981. Repr. of 1940 ed. 23.50 (ISBN 0-8305-0059-6). Hyperion Conn.

Independence Without Freedom. Ed. by Agrippah I. Mugomba. Mougo Nyaggah. Ed. by Peter Merkl. LC 80-154. (International & Comparative Politics Ser.: No. 13). 289p. 1980. 27.50 (ISBN 0-87436-293-8). ABC Clio.

Independent Iraq, Nineteen Thirty-Two to Nineteen Fifty-Eight: A Study in Iraqi Politics. 2nd ed. Majid Khadduri. LC 80-1919. 1981. Repr. of 1960 ed. 41.50 (ISBN 0-404-18972-5). AMS Pr.

Independent Journey: The Life of William O. Douglas. James F. Simon. LC 79-2637. (Illus.). 464p. 1980. 16.95 (ISBN 0-06-014042-9, HarpT). Har-Row.

Independent Living: Being on Your Own. Craig M. Pearson et al. LC 79-16892. (Independent Living Ser.). (Illus.). 464p. (gr. 11-12). 1979. text ed. 13.32 (ISBN 0-07-049061-9); tchrs. manual & key 3.00 (ISBN 0-07-049063-5); student wkbk. 5.28 (ISBN 0-07-049062-7). McGraw.

Independent Living for the Handicapped & the Elderly. Elizabeth E. May et al. 1974. text ed. 17.95 (ISBN 0-395-18108-9). HM.

Independent Living Rehabilitation for Severely Handicapped People: A Preliminary Appraisal. Ed. by Robert Counts. (Institute Paper). 67p. 1978. pap. 3.50 (ISBN 0-87766-228-2, 22600). Urban Inst.

Independent Local Politics in England. Wyn Grant. (Illus.). 1977. 19.95 (ISBN 0-566-00183-7, 01608-X, Pub. by Saxon Hse England). Lexington Bks.

Independent Marketing-Selling. Frank Lebell. 288p. 1980. 19.95 (ISBN 0-9600762-3-9). Herman Pub.

Independent Reading Grades One Through Three: An Annotated Bibliography with Reading Levels. Gale S. Jacob. LC 78-26607. 1975. pap. 4.50 o.p. (ISBN 0-87272-064-0). Brodart.

Independent Reading, K-Three. Helen E. Williams. LC 80-20423. 1980. pap. 17.25 (ISBN 0-87272-089-6). Brodart.

Independent School Trustee Handbook. 4th ed. 1980. pap. 6.50 (ISBN 0-934338-44-2). NAIS.

Independent Study: A New Interpretation of Concepts, Practices, & Problems. Paul L. Dressel & Mary M. Thompson. LC 73-50. (Higher Education Ser.). 1973. 11.95x o.p. (ISBN 0-87589-169-1). Jossey-Bass.

Independent Vietnamese: Vietnamese Communism Between Russia & China, 1959 to 1969. W. R. Smyser. (Southeast Asia Ser., Ohio University Center for International Studies). 143p. (Orig.). 1980. pap. 12.75 (ISBN 0-89680-105-5, 80-18308). Ohio U Ctr Intl.

Independent Woman. Rae Wisely & Gladys Sanders. 192p. 1981. 9.95 (ISBN 0-87477-176-5). J P Tarcher.

Independent Woman in the Restoration Comedy of Manners. Margaret L. McDonald. (Salzburg Studies in English Literature: Poetic Drama & Poetic Theory: No. 32). 255p. 1976. pap. text ed. 25.00x (ISBN 0-391-01478-1). Humanities.

Indeterminacy in Education. Ed. by John E. McDermott. LC 76-2987. 1976. 17.90x (ISBN 0-8211-1251-1); text ed. 16.20x (ISBN 0-685-71411-X). McCutchan.

Indeterminate Structural Analysis. J. S. Kinney. 1957. 22.95 (ISBN 0-201-03695-9). A-W.

Index. in gift box 9.95 (ISBN 0-932398-03-0). Good Food Bks.

Index Guide to Treaties, Vol. 1. C. Parry. 1979. 75.00 (ISBN 0-379-13002-5). Oceana.

Index Hepaticarum: An Index to the Liverworts of the World. C. E. Bonner. Incl. Pt. 2. Achiton to Balantiopsis. 37.50 (ISBN 3-7682-0092-2); Pt. 3. Barbilophozia to Ceranthus. 37.50 (ISBN 3-7682-0093-0); Pt. 4. Ceratolejeunea to Crystolejeunea. 37.50; Pt. 5. Delavayella to Geothallus. 50.00; Pt. 6. Goebelliella to Jubula. 37.50 (ISBN 3-7682-0096-5). 1963-66. Lubrecht & Cramer.

Index Kewensis Plantarum Phanerogamarum (Linnaeus to the Year 1885, 2 vols. Ed. by J. D. Hooker & B. D. Jackson. 1977. Repr. text ed. 530.00x set (ISBN 0-686-22706-9). Vol. 1. Vol. 2 (ISBN 3-87429-117-0). Lubrecht & Cramer.

Index Kewensis Supplements. Ed. by B. D. Jackson et al. Incl. Vol. 1. 1866-1895. Ed. by T. Durand & B. D. Jackson. 1901-06. 49.00x (ISBN 0-19-854310-7); Vol. 4. 1906-1910. Ed. by D. Prain. 1913. 49.00x (ISBN 0-19-854313-1); Vol. 6. 1916-1920. Ed. by A. W. Hill. 1926. 49.00x (ISBN 0-19-854315-8); Vol. 7. 1921-1925. Ed. by A. W. Hill. 1929. 49.00x (ISBN 0-19-854316-6); Vol. 8. 1926-1930. Ed. by A. W. Hill. 1933. 49.00x (ISBN 0-19-854317-4); Vol. 10. 1936-1940. Ed. by A. W. Hill & E. J. Salisbury. 1947. 34.95x (ISBN 0-19-854319-0); Vol. 12. 1951-1955. Ed. by George Taylor. 1959. 39.95x (ISBN 0-19-854321-2); Vol. 13. 1956-1960. Ed. by George Taylor. 1966. 43.50x (ISBN 0-19-854354-9); Vol. 14. 1961-1965. Ed. by George Taylor. 1970. 45.00x (ISBN 0-19-854370-0); Vol. 15. 1966-1970. Compiled by J. Heslop-Harrison. 156p. 1973. 45.00x (ISBN 0-19-854382-4); Vol. 16. 1971-1976. Ed. by J. P. Brenan. 250p. 1980. 42.00 (ISBN 0-19-854531-2). Oxford U Pr.

Index Libycus: A Cumlative Index to Bibliography of Libya,Nineteen Fifteen to Nineteen Seventy-Five. Hans Schuter & Kurt Magar. (Reference Books Ser.). 1981. 25.00 (ISBN 0-8161-8534-4). G K Hall.

Index Nordicus: A Cumulative Index to English-Language Periodicals on Scandinavian Studies. American Scandinavian Foundation. 1979. lib. bdg. 80.00 (ISBN 0-8161-0080-2). G K Hall.

Index Numbers in Theory & Practice. R. G. D. Allen. LC 75-7612. 304p. 1975. 34.95x (ISBN 0-202-06071-3). Aldine Pub.

Index of American Design. Erwin O. Christensen. (Illus.). 1950. 19.95 (ISBN 0-02-525240-2). Macmillan.

Index of American Periodical Verse, 1971. Sander W. Zulauf & Irwin H. Weiser. LC 73-3060. 1973. 20.00 (ISBN 0-8108-0606-1). Scarecrow.

Index of American Periodical Verse 1972. Sander W. Zulauf & Irwin H. Weiser. LC 73-3060. 1974. 20.00 (ISBN 0-8108-0698-3). Scarecrow.

Index of American Periodical Verse: 1973. Sander W. Zulauf & Irwin H. Weiser. LC 73-3060. 1975. 20.00 (ISBN 0-8108-0778-5). Scarecrow.

Index of American Periodical Verse: 1974. Sander W. Zulauf & Irwin H. Weiser. LC 73-3060. 1976. 20.00 (ISBN 0-8108-0872-2). Scarecrow.

Index of American Periodical Verse: 1975. Sander W. Zulauf & Irwin H. Weiser. LC 73-3060. 1977. 20.00 (ISBN 0-8108-0965-6). Scarecrow.

Index of American Periodical Verse: 1976. Sander W. Zulauf & Edward M. Cifelli. LC 73-3060. 1978. 20.00 (ISBN 0-8108-1082-4). Scarecrow.

Index of American Periodical Verse: 1977. Sander W. Zulauf & Edward M. Cifelli. LC 73-3060. 1979. lib, bdg. 20.00 (ISBN 0-8108-1169-3). Scarecrow.

Index of Economic Articles, Vol. 14,1972. Ed. by Mark Perlman et al. LC 61-8020. 1977. 50.00x (ISBN 0-917290-03-8). Irwin.

Index of Economic Articles, Vol. 15, 1978. Ed. by Mark Perlman et al. LC 61-8020. 1978. 50.00x (ISBN 0-917290-04-6). Irwin.

Index of Mathematical Papers. Incl. Vol. 1. July-December, 1970. 1972. 30.00 (ISBN 0-8218-4001-0, IMP-1); Vol. 2, 2 pts. 1972. Set. 60.00 (IMP-2); Jan-June, 1971 (ISBN 0-8218-4002-9); July-Dec., 1971 (ISBN 0-8218-4003-7); Vol. 3, 2 pts. 1973. Set. 80.00 (IMP-3); Jan.-June, 1972 (ISBN 0-8218-4004-5); July-Dec., 1972 (ISBN 0-8218-4005-3); Vol. 4, 2 pts. 1973-74. Set. 80.00 (IMP-4); Jan.-June, 1973 (ISBN 0-8218-4006-1); July-Dec., 1973 (ISBN 0-8218-4007-X); Vol. 5. Index to Mathematical Reviews for 1973. Date not set. 80.00 (ISBN 0-8218-4008-8, IMP-5); Vol. 6. Index to Mathematical Reviews for 1974. 80.00 (ISBN 0-8218-4009-6, IMP-6); Vol. 7. Index to Mathematical Reviews for 1975. 95.00 (ISBN 0-8218-4010-X, IMP-7); Vol. 8. Index to Mathematical Reviews for 1976. 120.00 (ISBN 0-8218-4011-8, IMP-8); Vol. 11. Index to Mathematical Reviews for 1979. 120.00 (ISBN 0-8218-4014-2, IMP-11); Cumulative Index (Author & Subject Index of Mathematical Reviews, 1973-1979) 1070.00 (ISBN 0-8218-0035-3, MREVIN-73-79). Am Math.

Index of Mathematical Papers, Vols. 9 & 10. (Lectures in Mathematics in the Life Sciences). 1979. 120.00 ea. o.p. Vol. 9 (ISBN 0-8218-4012-6). Vol. 10 (ISBN 0-8218-4013-4). Am Math.

Index of Model Periodicals: 1971 Through 1975. Paul Cardwell, Jr. LC 77-1737. 1977. 32.50 (ISBN 0-8108-1027-1). Scarecrow.

Index of Musical Wind-Instrument Makers. 6th, rev. enl. ed. L. G. Longwill. (Illus.). 1980. 50.00 (ISBN 0-686-64771-8). Heinman.

Index of Paramedical Vocabulary. J. E. Schmidt. (Illus.). 324p. 1974. pap. 10.75 (ISBN 0-398-02833-8). C C Thomas.

Index of Proper Names in French Arthurian Verse Romances, 1150-1300. G. D. West. LC 70-443975. (Romance Ser). 1969. 15.00x o.p. (ISBN 0-8020-5226-6). U of Toronto Pr.

Index of Stolen Art: Nineteen Seventy-Seven. Bonnie Burnham. (Illus.). 72p. (Orig.). 1978. pap. 25.00x (ISBN 0-89062-082-2, Pub. by Intl Found Art Res). Pub Ctr Cult Res.

Index of "Substantial Hazard" Reports to the Consumer Product Safety Commission. Product Safety Letter Staff. 1979. 45.00 (ISBN 0-914176-14-5). Wash Busn Info.

Index of the Spells on Egyptian Middle Kingdom Coffins & Related Documents. Leonard H. Lesko. LC 79-66500. (Orig.). 1979. pap. text ed. 6.00x (ISBN 0-930548-02-7). B C Scribe.

Index on Trademarks of German-Austrian-Swiss-French Industrialized Clockmakers. Ed. by K. Kochmann. 240p. 1980. softcover 10.50 (ISBN 0-686-12238-0). Antique Clocks.

Index to All Books, 1979. LC 74-17540. 600p. 17.50 (ISBN 0-8379-1408-6); of six indexes 1974 through 1979 94.50 set (ISBN 0-8379-1409-4). Marquis.

Index to American Author Bibliographies. Patricia P. Havlice. LC 73-163870. 1971. 10.00 (ISBN 0-8108-0426-3). Scarecrow.

Index to American Genealogies: With Supplement. 5th ed. 1966. Repr. of 1908 ed. 30.00 (ISBN 0-8103-3127-6). Gale.

Index to American Reference Books Annual, 1975-79: A Cumulative Index of Subjects, Authors & Titles. Christine L. Wynar. 1979. lib. bdg. 35.00x (ISBN 0-87287-199-1). Libs Unl.

Index to American Women Speakers, Eighteen Twenty-Eight to Nineteen Seventy-Eight. Beverley Manning. LC 79-26928. viii, 672p. 1980. lib. bdg. 30.00 (ISBN 0-8108-1282-7). Scarecrow.

Index to Architecture Series Bibliography: No. a-155 to A-396, Jan. 1980 to Dec. 1980, No. A-155 To A-396, Jan. 1980 To Dec. 1980. Vance Bibliographies. (Architecture Ser.: Bibliography: A-397). 50p. 1981. pap. 7.50. Vance Biblios.

Index to Art Reproductions in Books. Compiled by Professional Staff of Hewlett-Woodmere Public Library. Ed. by Elizabeth Thomson. LC 74-1286. 1974. 15.00 (ISBN 0-8108-0711-4). Scarecrow.

Index to Arthur Miller Criticism. 2nd ed. Tetsumaro Hayashi. LC 76-10893. (Author Bibliographies Ser.: No. 3). 165p. 1976. 10.00 (ISBN 0-8108-0947-8). Scarecrow.

Index to Artistic Biography, 2 vols. Patricia P. Havlice. LC 72-6412. 1973. Set. 45.00 (ISBN 0-8108-0540-5). Scarecrow.

Index to Biographical Material in Chin & Yuan Literary Works - Third Series. I. De Rachwiltz & M. Wang. LC 78-52594. (Faculty of Asian Studies Oriental Monograph: No. 20). 341p. 1980. pap. text ed. 19.95 (ISBN 0-7081-0179-8, 0556). Bks Australia.

Index to Biographies of Contemporary Composers. Storm Bull. LC 64-11781. 1964. 15.50 (ISBN 0-8108-0065-9). Scarecrow.

Index to Biographies of Contemporary Composers, Vol. 2. Storm Bull. LC 64-11781. 1974. 22.50 (ISBN 0-8108-0734-3). Scarecrow.

Index to Book Reviews in Historical Periodicals 1977. John W. Brewster & Deborah Gentry. LC 75-18992. 411p. 1979. 22.00 (ISBN 0-8108-1192-8). Scarecrow.

Index to Book Reviews in Historical Periodicals, 1973. John W. Brewster & Joseph A. McLeod. LC 75-18992. 1976. 18.00 (ISBN 0-8108-0893-5). Scarecrow.

Index to Book Reviews in Historical Periodicals 1972. John W. Brewster & Joseph A. McLeod. LC 75-18992. 393p. 1976. 15.50 (ISBN 0-8108-0894-3). Scarecrow.

Index to Book Reviews in Historical Periodicals 1975. John W. Brewster & Joseph A. McLeod. LC 75-18992. 1977. 27.50 (ISBN 0-8108-0977-X). Scarecrow.

Index to Book Reviews in Historical Periodicals 1974. John W. Brewster & Joseph A. McLeod. LC 75-18992. 1975. 21.00 (ISBN 0-8108-0818-8). Scarecrow.

Index to Book Reviews in Historical Periodicals 1976. John W. Brewster & Joseph A. McLeod. LC 75-18992. 1977. 22.00 (ISBN 0-8108-1078-6). Scarecrow.

Index to Business Indices. Donald H. Davenport. LC 70-153015. 1971. Repr. of 1937 ed. 18.00 (ISBN 0-8103-3706-1). Gale.

Index to Changes of Name. W. P. Phillimore & E. A. Fry. LC 68-27180. 1969. Repr. of 1905 ed. 18.00 (ISBN 0-8103-3132-2). Gale.

Index to Characters in the Performing Arts: Pt. 1. Non-Musical Plays, 2 vols. Harold Sharp & Marjorie Z. Sharp. LC 71-189886. 1966. Set. 45.00 (ISBN 0-8108-0066-7). Scarecrow.

Index to Characters in the Performing Arts: Pt. 2. Operas, & Musical Productions. Harold S. Sharp & Marjorie Z. Sharp. LC 66-13744. 1969. 37.50 (ISBN 0-8108-0075-6). Scarecrow.

Index to Characters in the Performing Arts: Pt. 3. Ballets A to Z & Symbols. Harold S. Sharp & Marjorie Z. Sharp. 1972. 13.50 (ISBN 0-8108-0486-7). Scarecrow.

Index to Characters in the Performing Arts: Pt. 4. Radio & Television. Harold S. Sharp & Marjorie Z. Sharp. LC 66-13744. 1973. 20.50 (ISBN 0-8108-0605-3). Scarecrow.

Index to Children's Literature in English Before 1900: Catalog of the Baldwin Library of the University of Florida at Gainesville. The Baldwin Library of Childrens Literature, Universityof Florida, Gainesville. (Supplements). 1981. lib. bdg. 325.00 (ISBN 0-686-69555-0). G K Hall.

Index to Children's Plays in Collections. 2nd ed. Barbara A. Kreider. LC 76-49666. 1977. 11.50 (ISBN 0-8108-0992-3). Scarecrow.

Index to Children's Poetry. John E. Brewton & Sara W. Brewton. 1942. 22.00 (ISBN 0-8242-0021-7); first suppl. 1954 12.00 (ISBN 0-8242-0022-5); second suppl. 1965. 12.00 (ISBN 0-8242-0023-3). Wilson.

Index to 'Chinese Literature' Hans J. Hinrup. (Scandinavian Institute of Asian Studies Monographs: No. 38). 1978. pap. text ed. 15.75x (ISBN 0-7007-0122-2). Humanities.

Index to Criticisms of British & American Poetry. Gloria S. Cline & Jeffrey A. Baker. LC 73-15542. 1973. 12.00 (ISBN 0-8108-0684-3). Scarecrow.

Index to Dental Literature. American Dental Association - Bureau of Library & Indexing Service. 1980. annual cumulative 100.00 (ISBN 0-685-77438-4); quarterly cumulative 125.00. Am Dental.

Index to Dental Literature, Nineteen Seventy-Nine. American Dental Association-Bureau of Library Services. 1979. 100.00 (ISBN 0-685-96599-6). Am Dental.

Index to Educational Overhead Transparencies. 6th ed. National Information Center for Educational Media. LC 79-89661. 1980. pap. 61.00 (ISBN 0-89320-032-8). Univ SC Natl Info.

Index to Educational Records. 5th ed. National Information Center for Educational Media. LC 79-89688. 1980. pap. 54.00 (ISBN 0-89320-034-4). Univ SC Natl Info.

Index to Educational Slides. 4th ed. National Information Center for Educational Media. LC 79-66599. 1980. pap. 49.00 (ISBN 0-89320-035-2). Univ SC Natl Info.

Index to Educational Video Tapes. 5th ed. National Information Center for Educational Media. LC 79-89686. 1980. pap. 34.00 (ISBN 0-89320-036-0). Univ SC Natl Info.

Index to Eight-mm Motion Cartridges. 6th ed. National Information Center for Educational Media. LC 79-89662. 1980. pap. 54.00 (ISBN 0-89320-031-X). Univ SC Natl Info.

Index to Environmental Studies - Multimedia. 2nd ed. National Information Center for Educational Media. LC 79-66630. 1980. pap. 40.00 (ISBN 0-89320-041-7). Univ SC Natl Info.

Index to Genealogical Periodical Literature, 1960-1977. Kip Sperry. LC 79-9407. (Gale Genealogy & Local History Ser.: Vol. 9). 1979. 30.00 (ISBN 0-8103-1403-7). Gale.

Index to Health & Safety Education - Multimedia. 4th ed. National Information Center for Education Media. LC 79-66629. 1980. pap. 55.00 (ISBN 0-89320-040-9). Univ SC Natl Info.

Index to Illustrations of the Natural World Outside of North America. Lucille T. Munz & Nedra Slauson. 1980. write for info. (ISBN 0-208-01857-3, Archon). Shoe String.

Index to Illustrations of the Natural World: Where to Find Pictures of the Living Things of North America. Ed. by Nedra Slauson. 265p. 1981. 29.95 (ISBN 0-208-01911-1, Lib Prof Pubns). Shoe String.

Index to Illustrations of the Natural World: Where to Find Pictures of the Living Things of North America. Ed. by Nedra Slauson & John W. Thompson. 265p. 1981. Repr. of 1980 ed. 29.95 (ISBN 0-208-01911-1, Lib Prof Pubns). Shoe String.

Index to International Public Opinion: Nineteen Seventy-Nine to Nineteen Eighty. Ed. by Elizabeth H. Hastings & Philip K. Hastings. LC 80-643917. 510p. 1981. lib. bdg. 75.00 (ISBN 0-313-22535-4, IN80). Greenwood.

Index to Legal Periodicals. 1952-70. Vols. 10-15. 85.00 ea. (ISBN 0-685-22250-0); Vols. 16 To Date. 170.00 ea. (ISBN 0-686-66572-4). Wilson.

Index to Literary Biography, 2 vols. Patricia P. Havlice. LC 74-8315. 1975. Set. 47.50 (ISBN 0-8108-0745-9). Scarecrow.

Index to Literature in the New Yorker, 1925-194, Vols. 1-15. Robert O. Johnson. LC 71-7740. 1969. 20.50 (ISBN 0-8108-0272-4). Scarecrow.

Index to Literature in the New Yorker, 1940-195, Vol. 16-30. Robert O. Johnson. 1970. 13.50 (ISBN 0-8108-0314-3). Scarecrow.

Index to Literature in the New Yorker, 1955-1970, Vols. 31-45. Robert O. Johnson. LC 71-7740. 1971. 20.50 (ISBN 0-8108-0413-1). Scarecrow.

Index to Literature in the New Yorker, 1970-75, Vol. 46-50. Robert O. Johnson. LC 71-7740. 1976. 10.00 (ISBN 0-8108-0905-2). Scarecrow.

Index to Little Magazines, 6 vols. Incl. Vol. 1. Nineteen-Forty-Three to Nineteen-Forty-Seven (ISBN 0-8040-0152-9); Vol. 2. Nineteen-Forty-Nine to Nineteen-Fifty-Two (ISBN 0-8040-0154-5); Vol. 3. Nineteen-Fifty-Three to Nineteen-Fifty-Five (ISBN 0-8040-0155-3); Vol. 4. Nineteen-Fifty-Six to Nineteen-Fifty-Seven (ISBN 0-8040-0156-1); Vol. 7. Nineteen-Sixty-Two to Nineteen-Sixty-Three (ISBN 0-8040-0159-6); Vol. 9. Nineteen-Sixty-Six to Nineteen-Sixty-Seven (ISBN 0-8040-0161-8). LC 51-4490. 20.00x ea. Swallow.

Index to Mathematics of Computation, 1943-1969. Y. L. Luke et al. 1972. 20.00 (ISBN 0-8218-4000-2, MCOMIN-1). Am Math.

Index to Model Making & Miniatures. Compiled by Mary L. Lathrop & Norman M. Lathrop. 1980. pap. 15.00 (ISBN 0-910868-20-4). Lathrop.

Index to Nineteenth-Century Fiction: 1945-1975, Vols. 1-30. Compiled by G. B. Tennyson & Elizabeth J. Tennyson. 1978. 17.50x (ISBN 0-520-03334-5). U of Cal Pr.

Index to Nutrition & Health. Joseph Sprug. (Useful Reference Ser. of Library Books: Vol. 119). 1981. write for info. (ISBN 0-87305-125-4). Faxon.

Index to Opera, Operetta & Musical Comedy Synopses in Collections & Periodicals. Jeanette M. Drone. LC 77-25822. 1978. 10.00 (ISBN 0-8108-1100-6). Scarecrow.

Index to Periodical Articles, Nineteen Seventy-Three to Nineteen Seventy-Eight, in the Library of the Royal Institute of International Affairs. The Royal Institute of International Affairs, London. (Library Catalogs-Bib. Guides). 1979. lib. bdg. 125.00 (ISBN 0-8161-0281-3). G K Hall.

Index to Periodical Articles Related to Law: Five Year Cumulation,(1969-1973) Ed. by Roy M. Mersky et al. LC 65-29677. 428p. 1974. lib. bdg. 35.00 (ISBN 0-87802-051-9). Glanville.

Index to Periodical Fiction in English, 1965-69. Ed. by Douglas Messerli & Howard N. Fox. LC 76-42288. 1977. 35.00 (ISBN 0-8108-0952-4). Scarecrow.

Index to Pickwick. Charles M. Neale. 75p. 1980. Repr. of 1897 ed. lib. bdg. 12.50 (ISBN 0-89987-603-X). Darby Bks.

Index to Playboy: Belles-Lettres, Articles & Humor, December, 1953 to December, 1969. Mildred L. Miles. LC 68-25183. 1970. 10.00 (ISBN 0-8108-0327-5). Scarecrow.

Index to Plays in Periodicals. rev. & expanded ed. Dean H. Keller. LC 79-962. 836p. 1979. 37.50 (ISBN 0-8108-1208-8). Scarecrow.

Index to Producers & Distributors. 5th ed. National Information Center for Educational Media. LC 79-66600. 1980. pap. 24.00 (ISBN 0-89320-037-9). Univ SC Natl Info.

Index to Profiles in the New Yorker. Robert O. Johnson. LC 71-186947. 1972. 10.00 (ISBN 0-8108-0473-5). Scarecrow.

Index to Psychology - Multimedia. 4th ed. National Information Center for Educational Media. LC 79-66627. 1980. pap. 55.00 (ISBN 0-89320-038-7). Univ SC Natl Info.

Index to Public Administration Series Bibliography: No. P-394 to P-636, Jan. 1980 to Dec. 1980, No. P-394 To P-636, Jan. 1980 To Dec. 1980. Vance Bibliographies. (Public Administration Ser.: Bibliography: P-637). 81p. 1981. pap. 7.50. Vance Biblios.

Index to Record & Tape Reviews: A Classical Music Buying Guide for 1979. Antoinette O. Maleady. 1980. 52.50 (ISBN 0-917600-05-3). Chulainn Press.

Index to Reproductions of American Paintings. Lyn W. Smith & Nancy D. Moure. LC 77-14498. 1977. 50.00 (ISBN 0-8108-1084-0). Scarecrow.

Index to Reviews of Bibliographical Publications, Nineteen Seventy-Seven, Vol. 2. Bibliographic Society of Northern Illinois. Ed. by Terry Oggel. (Reference Bks.). 1979. lib. bdg. 20.50 (ISBN 0-8161-8477-1). G K Hall.

Index to Rolls-Royce & Bentley Periodicals. Ed. by Tom C. Clarke. 43p. 1974. pap. 5.95 o.p. (ISBN 0-87938-023-3, Pub. by Transport Bkman England). Motorbooks Intl.

Index to Sixteen-mm Educational Films. 7th ed. National Information Center for Educational Media. LC 79-89659. 1980. pap. 126.00 (ISBN 0-89320-029-8). Univ SC Natl Info.

Index to Sociology Readers, 1960-1965, 2 vols. Harold J. Abramson & Nicholas Sofios. LC 73-977. 1973. Set. 35.00 (ISBN 0-8108-0592-8). Scarecrow.

Index to Song Books. Robert Leigh. LC 72-8344. (Music Ser). 242p. 1973. Repr. of 1964 ed. lib. bdg. 18.50 (ISBN 0-306-70553-2). Da Capo.

Index to South Carolina Land Grants, 1794-1800. Ronald V. Jackson & Gary R. Teeples. LC 77-86082. (Illus.). Date not set. lib. bdg. price not set (ISBN 0-89593-134-6). Accelerated Index.

Index to Speech, Language & Hearing Journal Titles, 1954-78. Paul H. Ptacek et al. LC 79-20058. 328p. 1979. text ed. 25.00 (ISBN 0-933014-54-6). College-Hill.

Index to the Biographees in Nineteenth Century California County Histories. Ed. by J. Carlyle Parker. LC 79-11900. (Genealogy & Local History Ser.: Vol. 7). 1979. 30.00 (ISBN 0-8103-1406-1). Gale.

Index to the Briefs, Transcripts & GAO Reports Before the Indian Claims Commission. Norman A. Ross. (Library of American Indian Affairs). 192p. 1981. 18.00x (ISBN 0-88354-108-4). Clearwater Pub.

Index to the Decisions of the Indian Claims Commission, 1948-1972. Ed. by Norman A. Ross. LC 72-13850. (Library of American Indian Affairs). 168p. 1973. lib. bdg. 18.00 (ISBN 0-88354-101-7). Clearwater Pub.

Index to the Described Life Histories, Early Stages & Hosts of the Macrolepidoptera of the Continental United States & Canada, 2 vols. Harrison M. Tietz. iv, 1041p. 1972. text ed. 25.00x (ISBN 0-913492-01-9). Entomological Repr.

Index to the Diaries of Beatrice Webb 1873-1943. Compiled by Routledge Associates. 1978. lib. bdg. 60.00x (ISBN 0-914146-60-2). Somerset Hse.

Index to the Eighteen Eighty-One Ruttenber & Clark History of Orange County, New York. Orange County Genealogical Society. LC 79-84908. 1980. 20.00 (ISBN 0-9604116-1-5). Orange County Genealog.

Index to the Expert Testimony Presented Before the Indian Claims Commission. Ed. by Norman A. Ross. LC 72-13851. (Library of American Indian Affairs). 112p. 1973. lib. bdg. 18.00 (ISBN 0-88354-102-5). Clearwater Pub.

Index to the Films of Charles Chaplin. Theodore Huff. (Gordon Press Film Ser.). 1980. lib. bdg. 59.95 (ISBN 0-8490-3090-0). Gordon Pr.

Index to the Guide to the Microfilm of the Records of Pennsylvania's Revolutionary Governments. 77p. 1980. pap. 3.50 (ISBN 0-89271-012-8). Pa Hist & Must.

Index to the Literature of American Economic Entomology, Vols 3-18. 1959. 60.00 set o.p. (ISBN 0-686-09296-1). Entomol Soc.

Index to the Literature of Semiconductor Detectors. National Academy Of Sciences. 1969. pap. 5.00 (ISBN 0-309-00093-9). Natl Acad Pr.

Index to the London Stage, 1660-1800. Compiled by Ben R. Schneider, Jr. 960p. 1979. 60.00x (ISBN 0-8093-0907-6). S Ill U Pr.

Index to the Poems of Ogden Nash. Lavonne B. Axford. LC 72-7266. 1972. 10.00 (ISBN 0-8108-0547-2). Scarecrow.

Index to the Proceedings of the British Academy, Vols. 1 - 63. Ed. by Michael Hope. 88p. 1981. 65.00 (ISBN 0-19-725999-5). Oxford U Pr.

Index to the Proceedings of the Lunar & Planetary Science Conferences, Houston, Texas, 1970-1978. Ed. by Amanda R. Masterson. LC 79-20109. (Illus.). 325p. 1979. 33.00 (ISBN 0-08-024620-6). Pergamon.

Index to the Sayings of Hazrat Inayat Khan. Ed. by Munir Graham & Laura De La Torre Bueno. (Collected Works of Hazrat Inayat Khan). 144p. (Orig.). 1981. pap. 3.95 (ISBN 0-930872-23-1, 1009P). Sufi Order Pubns.

Index to the Secret Doctrine. The Theosophy Company. x, 172p. 1939. 6.00 (ISBN 0-938998-02-1). Theosophy.

Index to the Sierra Club Bulletin, 1950-1976. Ed. by Edward Brazee. (Bibliographic Ser.: No. 16). 1978. pap. 4.00 (ISBN 0-87071-136-9). Oreg St U Pr.

Index to the Spanish American Biography: The Andean Countries, Vol. 1. Sara De Mundo Lo. (Reference Bks.). 1981. lib. bdg. 60.00 (ISBN 0-8161-8181-0). G K Hall.

Index to the Story of My Days. Edward G. Craig. 320p. Date not set. price not set (ISBN 0-521-23609-6); pap. price not set (ISBN 0-521-28070-2). Cambridge U Pr.

Index to the Waverley Novels. Philip Bradley. LC 75-6838. 695p. 1975. 30.00 (ISBN 0-8108-0812-9). Scarecrow.

Index to Thirty-Five-mm Filmstrips. 7th ed. National Information Center for Educational Media. LC 79-89660. 1980. pap. 99.00 (ISBN 0-89320-030-1). Univ SC Natl Info.

Index to Translations Selected by the American Mathematical Society, Vol. 1. 1966. 7.20 (ISBN 0-8218-0042-6, TRAN2I-1-50). Am Math.

Index to Translations Selected by the American Mathematical Society, Vol. 2. 1973. 14.00 (ISBN 0-8218-0059-0, TRAN2I-51). Am Math.

Index to Two-Dimensional Art Works, 2 vols. Yala H. Korwin. LC 80-25002. 1519p. 1981. 69.50 (ISBN 0-8108-1381-5). Scarecrow.

Index to Vocational & Technical Education - Multimedia. 4th ed. National Information Center for Educational Media. LC 79-66628. 1980. pap. 55.00 (ISBN 0-89320-039-5). Univ SC Natl Info.

Index to Well Samples. rev. ed. D. E. Feray & J. L. Starnes. 148p. 1950. 1.65 (PUB 5015). Bur Econ Geology.

Index to Writings of Ellen G. White, 3 vols. LC 62-14313. 1962. 14.95 ea. (ISBN 0-8163-0108-5); V0l. 1. (ISBN 0-8163-0107-7, 09551-3). Vol. 2 (ISBN 0-8163-0337-1, 09552-1). Vol. 3. (ISBN 0-8163-0338-X, 09553-9); Set. 43.95 (ISBN 0-8163-0108-5, 09550-5). Pacific Pr Pub Assn.

Index Translationium Twenty-Nine. 1006p. 1980. pap. 104.00 (ISBN 92-3-001596-2, U 1011, UNESCO). Unipub.

Index Verborum Catullianus. Monroe N. Wetmore. 1912. 37.50x (ISBN 0-685-89758-3). Elliots Bks.

Indexation of Pension & Other Benefits. Robert J. Myers. 1979. 11.00 (ISBN 0-256-02118-X). Irwin.

Indexation of the Tax Laws for Inflation. (Statement of Tax Policy: No. 6). 1980. pap. 3.00. Am Inst CPA.

Indexing & Abstracting: A Guide to International Sources. Ed. by Hans H. Wellisch. LC 80-11907. 398p. 1980. 22.75 (ISBN 0-87436-300-4). Abc-

Indexing Your Book: A Practical Guide for Authors. 2nd ed. Sina K. Spiker. 1963. pap. 2.50x (ISBN 0-299-01173-9). U of Wis Pr.

India. 2nd rev. ed. Jean Bothwell. Ed. by Jane Whipple. LC 78-2511. (First Bks). (Illus.). (gr. 4-6). 1978. PLB 6.45 s&l (ISBN 0-531-02229-3). Watts.

India. (gr. 6-8). Complete Pack. pap. text ed. 60.00x (ISBN 0-435-31505-6); Folder A-D. 6.50 ea. Folder A: Food (ISBN 0-435-31506-4). Folder B: Work (ISBN 0-435-31507-2). Folder C: Family (ISBN 0-435-31508-0). Folder D: Village (ISBN 0-435-31509-9). Heinemann Ed.

India. rev. ed. Hyman Kublin. LC 72-3351. (Illus.). 228p. (gr. 9-12). 1973. pap. text ed. 6.60 (ISBN 0-395-13928-7, 2-31034). HM.

India. Beatrice P. Lamb. (Illus.). (gr. 7 up). 1965. 4.95 o.s.i. (ISBN 0-02-751340-8). Macmillan.

India. rev. ed. T. A. Raman. LC 78-54252. (World Cultures Ser). (Illus.). (gr. 6 up). 1980. 1-4 copies 9.95 (ISBN 0-88296-127-6); 5 or more 7.96 (ISBN 0-685-14487-9); tchrs'. guide 8.94 (ISBN 0-88296-369-4). Fideler.

India: A Political Economy of Stagnation. Prem S. Jha. (Illus.). 330p. 1980. 13.95x (ISBN 0-19-561153-5). Oxford U Pr.

India: A Rising Middle Power. John W. Mellor. (Special Studies on South & Southeast Asia). 1979. lib. bdg. 27.50x (ISBN 0-89158-298-3). Westview.

India: a Study in Futurism. S. P. Gupta. LC 76-904615. 1976. 6.75x o.p. (ISBN 0-88386-824-5). South Asia Bks.

India: An Area Study. S. N. Chopra. 1977. 26.00x (ISBN 0-7069-0494-X, Pub by Croom Helm Ltd. England). Biblio Dist.

India & Africa. R. H. Ramchandani. 314p. 1980. text ed. 16.50x (ISBN 0-391-01796-9). Humanities.

India & Anglo-Soviet Relations. C. S. Samra. 1959. 4.50x o.p. (ISBN 0-210-33665-X). Asia.

India & Bangla Desh: Selected Speeches & Statements, March-December, 1971. Indira Gandhi. 200p. 1972. text ed. 4.50x (ISBN 0-391-00508-1). Humanities.

India & British Portraiture Seventeen Seventy to Eighteen Twenty-Five. Mildred Archer. (Illus.). 536p. 1979. 105.00x (ISBN 0-85667-054-5, Pub by Sotheby Parke Bernet England). Biblio Dist.

India & Indology. W. Norman Brown. Ed. by Rosane Rocher. 1979. 52.00x (ISBN 0-8364-0362-2). South Asia Bks.

India & Other Poems. V. K. Agnihotri. (Writers Workshop Redbird Book Ser.). 39p. 1975. 8.00 (ISBN 0-88253-562-5); pap. text ed. 4.00 (ISBN 0-88253-561-7). Ind-US Inc.

India & Pakistan in the Twentieth Century. Richard Tames. (Twentieth Century World History Ser.). (Illus.). 96p. (gr. 6 up). 1981. 15.95 (ISBN 0-7134-3415-5, Pub. by Batsford England). David & Charles.

India & Southeast Asia. T. A. Raman et al. LC 78-54253. (World Cultures Ser). (Illus.). (gr. 6 up). 1979. text ed. 12.43 1-4 copies o.p. (ISBN 0-88296-160-8); text ed. 9.94 5 or more o.p. (ISBN 0-685-14493-3); tchr's guide skills manual incl. 8.94 o.p. (ISBN 0-88296-369-4). Fideler.

India & the European Economic Community. Dharma Kumar. 1967. 8.50x (ISBN 0-210-27182-5). Asia.

India & the Greek World: A Study in the Transmission of Culture. Jean W. Sedlar. (Illus.). 381p. 1980. 30.00x (ISBN 0-8476-6173-3). Rowman.

India & the International System: A Selection from the Major Writings of Sisir Gupta. Ed. by M. S. Rajan & Shivaji Ganguly. 400p. 1981. text ed. 40.00x (ISBN 0-7069-1072-9, Pub. by Vikas India). Advent Bk.

India & the Nagas. Neville Maxwell. (Minority Rights Group: No. 17). 1973. pap. 2.50 (ISBN 0-89192-103-6). Interbk Inc.

India & the United Nations. Dhiraj R. Chamling. 1979. text ed. 15.00x (ISBN 0-210-40617-8). Asia.

India As a Secular State. Donald E. Smith. 1963. 27.00 o.p. (ISBN 0-691-03027-8, 76). Princeton U Pr.

India-China Comparative Research: Technology & Science for Development. Ed. by Erik Baark & Jon Sigurdson. (Studies on Asian Topics: No. 3). 180p. 1980. pap. text ed. 10.50x (ISBN 0-7007-0138-9). Humanities.

India, China, Tibet Triangle. Ram Gopal. 1966. pap. 2.00 (ISBN 0-88253-139-5). Ind-US Inc.

India: Emergent Power? Stephen P. Cohen & Richard L. Park. LC 78-50920. (NSIC Strategy Paper Ser.). 1978. 7.50x o.p. (ISBN 0-8448-1351-6). Crane-Russak Co.

India in Ceylonese History, Society & Culture. 2nd ed. M. D. Raghavan. 1970. 10.00x (ISBN 0-210-31211-4). Asia.

India in English Fiction, 1800-1970: An Annotated Bibliography. Brijen K. Gupta. LC 73-4194. 1973. 10.00 (ISBN 0-8108-0612-6). Scarecrow.

India in Transition. Ed. by Robert McLean. 1981. 15.00x (ISBN 0-8364-0011-9). South Asia Bks.

India: Mixed Enterprise & Western Business: Experiments in Controlled Change for Growth & Profit. Daniel L. Spencer. LC 79-1592. 1981. Repr. of 1959 ed. 21.00 (ISBN 0-88355-897-1). Hyperion Conn.

India, Nepal & Sri Lanka. Barbie Engstrom. (Engstrom's Travel Experience Guides Ser.). (Illus., Orig.). 1981. pap. 14.50 (ISBN 0-916588-06-8). Kurios Pr.

India, Pakistan, Ceylon. rev. ed. Ed. by W. Norman Brown. LC 61-15205. (Illus.). 1964. 10.00x o.p. (ISBN 0-8122-7428-8). U of Pa Pr.

India: People & Places. Richard Lannoy. (Illus.). 1955. 17.50 o.s.i. (ISBN 0-8149-0139-5). Vanguard.

India: Selected Readings. rev. ed. Hyman Kublin. LC 72-7637. 230p. (gr. 9-12). 1973. pap. text ed. 6.60 (ISBN 0-395-13929-5, 2-31040). HM.

India Today. Frank Moraes. 1960. 4.50 o.s.i. (ISBN 0-02-586350-9). Macmillan.

Indian Affairs in Georgia, 1732-1756. John P. Corry. LC 76-43685. 1977. Repr. of 1936 ed. 21.50 (ISBN 0-404-15518-9). AMS Pr.

Indian Agriculture: Problems, Progress & Prospects. A. N. Agrawal. 1980. text ed. 25.00x (ISBN 0-7069-0683-7, Pub. by Vikas India). Advent Bk.

Indian-American Joint Ventures: Business Policy Relationships. John I. Reynolds. LC 77-18587. 1978. pap. text ed. 10.50x (ISBN 0-8191-0403-5). U Pr of Amer.

Indian & His Horse. Robert Hofsinde. (Illus.). (gr. 3-7). 1960. PLB 6.48 (ISBN 0-688-31421-X). Morrow.

Indian & the Buffalo. Robert Hofsinde. (Illus.). (gr. 3-7). 1961. PLB 6.67 (ISBN 0-688-31420-1). Morrow.

Indian Antiquities of the Kennebec Valley. Charles C. Willoughby. Ed. by Arthur E. Spiess. (Occasional Publications in Mane Archaeology: No. 1). (Illus.). 160p. 1980. 22.00 (ISBN 0-913764-13-2). Maine St Mus.

Indian Antiquities of the Kennebec Valley. Charles C. Willoughby. (Illus.). 1980. 22.00 (ISBN 0-913764-13-2). Maine St Mus.

Indian Army: Its Contribution to the Development of a Nation. Stephen P. Cohen. LC 77-111421. 1971. 20.00x (ISBN 0-520-01697-1). U of Cal Pr.

Indian Art: From the George P. Bickford Collection. Stanislaw Czuma. LC 74-29377. (Illus.). 136p. 1975. 10.00x o.p. (ISBN 0-910386-21-8, Pub. by Cleveland Mus Art); pap. 5.00x (ISBN 0-910386-50-1). Ind U Pr.

Indian Arts. Robert Hofsinde. LC 73-137100. (Illus.). (gr. 3-7). 1971. PLB 6.48 (ISBN 0-688-31617-4). Morrow.

Indian Atomosm: History & Sources. Mrinalkanti Gangopadhyaya. 384p. 1980. pap. text ed. write for info. (ISBN 0-391-02177-X). Humanities.

Indian Atrocities: Affecting & Thrilling Anecdotes Respecting the Hardships & Sufferings of Our Brave & Venerable Forefathers, Etc, Repr. Of 1846. Bd. with Indians: Or, Narrative of Massacres & Depredations on the Frontier in Wawasink & Its Vicinity During the American Revolution. Abraham G. Bevier. Repr. of 1846 ed; Three Years Among the Indians & Mexicans. Thomas James. Repr. of 1846 ed. LC 75-7084. (Indian Captivities Ser.: Vol. 61). 1977. lib. bdg. 44.00 (ISBN 0-8240-1685-8). Garland Pub.

Indian Awakening in Latin America. Ed. by Yves Materne. (Orig.). 1980. pap. 5.95 (ISBN 0-377-00097-3). Friend Pr.

Indian Bead Stringing & Weaving. Ruth Scholz-Peters. LC 75-14524. (Illus.). 64p. 1975. 5.95 o.p. (ISBN 0-8069-5334-9); lib. bdg. 6.69 o.p. (ISBN 0-8069-5335-7). Sterling.

Indian Beadwork. Robert Hofsinde. (Illus.). (gr. 5-9). 1958. PLB 6.48 (ISBN 0-688-31575-5). Morrow.

Indian Boyhood. Charles Eastman. LC 76-46274. (Beautiful Rio Grande Classics Ser). 1976. lib. bdg. 10.00 o.p. (ISBN 0-87380-139-3). Rio Grande.

Indian Boyhood. Charles A. Eastman. (Illus.). 7.25 (ISBN 0-8446-0085-7). Peter Smith.

Indian Captive: A Narrative of the Adventures & Sufferings of Matthew Brayton, in His 34 Years of Captivity Among the Indians of North-Western America, Repr. Of 1860 Ed. Bd. with Indian Captives: In: Oquawka Spectator, III., V. 3, No. 16, May 17, 1860. Larsena A. Page. Repr. of 1860 ed; Short Narrative of James Kimball, 11 Years a Captive Among the Snake Indians. Repr. of 1861 ed; Life of Joseph Persinger Who Was Taken by the Shawnee Indians When an Infant: With a Short Account of the Indian Troubles in Missouri; & a Sketch of the Adventures of the Author. Repr. of 1861 ed; In Captivity. the Experience, Privations & Dangers of Sam'l J. Brown, & Others, While Prisoners of the Hostile Sioux, During the Massacre & War of 1862. Repr. of 1862 ed; Abenteuer Unter Den Indianern: Oder, Ina's Gefangenschaft Unter Den Wilden und Ihre Wunderbare Befreiung. Repr. of 1863 ed. LC 75-7101. (Indian Captivities Ser.: Vol. 76). 1977. lib. bdg. 44.00 (ISBN 0-8240-1700-5). Garland Pub.

Indian Captive: The Story of Mary Jemison. Lois Lenski. LC 41-51956. (Illus.). (gr. 7-9). 1941. 9.79 (ISBN 0-397-30072-7). Lippincott.

Indian Captivities: Being a Collection of the Most Remarkable Narratives of Persons Taken Captives by the North American Indians. Samuel G. Drake. LC 75-7077. (Indian Captivities Ser.: Vol. 55). 1976. Repr. of 1839 ed. lib. bdg. 44.00 (ISBN 0-8240-1679-3). Garland Pub.

Indian Captivity: A True Narrative of the Capture of the Rev. O. M. Spencer by the Indians in the Neighborhood of Cincinnati. LC 75-7075. (Indian Captivities Ser.: Vol. 53). 1976. Repr. of 1835 ed. lib. bdg. 44.00 (ISBN 0-8240-1677-7). Garland Pub.

Indian Caste, 2 vols. John Wilson. 1976. Repr. of 1877 ed. Set. 30.00x o.p. (ISBN 0-88386-914-4). South Asia Bks.

Indian Christ, the Indian King: The Historical Substrate of Maya Myth & Ritual. Victoria R. Bricker. (Illus.). 624p. 1981. text ed. 45.00x (ISBN 0-292-73824-2). U of Tex Pr.

Indian Contract Act: Vol. 1. Atul C. Patra. 1967. Vol. 1. 20.00x (ISBN 0-210-27073-X). Asia.

Indian Cookery. E. P. Veerasawmy. 1970. pap. 2.75 (ISBN 0-88253-197-2). Ind-US Inc.

Indian Cooking. 2nd ed. Savitri Chowdhary. 1976. pap. 3.25 (ISBN 0-89253-070-7). Ind-US Inc.

Indian Cooking, with Useful Hints on Good Housekeeping. Kala Primlani. Tr. by R. V. Ramchandani from Sindhi. 166p. 1975. pap. 2.40 (ISBN 0-88253-748-2). Ind-US Inc.

Indian Costumes. Robert Hofsinde. LC 68-11895. (Illus.). (gr. 3-7). 1968. PLB 6.48 (ISBN 0-688-31614-X). Morrow.

Indian Crafts. Janet D'Amato & Alex D'Amato. (Illus.). (gr. 1-4). PLB 7.95 (ISBN 0-87460-088-X). Lion.

Indian Dances: Their History & Growth. Reginald Massey & Rina Singha. LC 67-20736. 1967. 12.50 o.s.i. (ISBN 0-8076-0427-5). Braziller.

Indian Dancing. Mrinalini Sarabhai. 1967. pap. 2.00 (ISBN 0-88253-334-7). Ind-US Inc.

Indian Days of Long Ago. Edward S. Curtis. (Illus.). Date not set. 8.95 (ISBN 0-913668-46-X); pap. 3.95 (ISBN 0-913668-45-1). Ten Speed Pr.

Indian Drawings & Painted Sketches: 16th Through 19th Centuries. Stuart C. Welch. LC 75-29780. (Illus.). 144p. 1976. 17.50 (ISBN 0-87848-046-3). Asia Soc.

Indian Drinking: Navajo Practices & Anglo-American Theories. Jerrold E. Levy & Stephen J. Kunitz. LC 73-17173. 320p. 1974. 20.95 o.p. (ISBN 0-471-53163-4, Pub. by Wiley-Interscience). Wiley.

Indian Economic Policy & Performance: A Framework for a Progressive Society. Jagdish N. Bhagwati. (Working Papers on Development Ser.: No. 1). 1975. pap. 1.25x (ISBN 0-87725-401-X). U of Cal Intl St.

Indian-English Prose: An Anthology. Ed. by D. Ramakrishna. 1981. text ed. write for info. (ISBN 0-391-02190-7). Humanities.

Indian Exodus: Texas Indian Affairs. Kenneth F. Neighbours. 6.95 (ISBN 0-685-48786-5). Nortex Pr.

Indian Extradition Law. R. C. Hingorani. 10.00x (ISBN 0-210-98127-X). Asia.

Indian Fairy Tales. 2nd. ed. Mulk R. Anand. (Illus.). 166p. 1966. 4.00 (ISBN 0-88253-333-9). Ind-US Inc.

Indian Famine, Nineteen Sixty-Seven: A Study in Crisis & Change. K. Suresh Singh. LC 75-903386. 1975. 11.00 o.p. (ISBN 0-88386-602-1). South Asia Bks.

Indian Fights & Fighters. Cyrus T. Brady. LC 74-156373. (Illus.). 1971. 16.50x (ISBN 0-8032-1152-X); pap. 6.50 (ISBN 0-8032-5743-0, BB 538, Bison). U of Nebr Pr.

Indian Film. 2nd ed. Erik Barnouw & S. Krishnaswamy. (Illus.). 1980. 15.95 (ISBN 0-19-502682-9, 592); pap. 5.95 (ISBN 0-19-502683-7). Oxford U Pr.

Indian Finance in the Days of the Company. Pramathanath Banerjea. (Perspectives in Asian History: No. 5). Repr. of 1928 ed. lib. bdg. 25.00x (ISBN 0-87991-820-9). Porcupine Pr.

Indian Financial System. M. Y. Khan. LC 80-904855. 464p. 1980. text ed. 27.50x (ISBN 0-7069-1101-6, Pub. by Vikas India). Advent Bk.

Indian Fishing & Camping. Robert Hofsinde. (Illus.). (gr. 4-7). 1963. PLB 6.48 (ISBN 0-688-31797-9). Morrow.

Indian Fishing: Early Methods on the Northwest Coast. Hilary Stewart. LC 77-950. (Illus.). 136p. 1981. pap. 15.00 (ISBN 0-295-95803-0). U of Wash Pr.

Indian Foe, Indian Friend. Jules Archer. LC 72-93280. (Illus.). (gr. 7-12). 1970. 6.95 (ISBN 0-02-705650-3, CCPr). Macmillan.

Indian Foreign Policy: An Analysis. Baljit Singh. 111p. 1979. pap. 4.95 (ISBN 0-210-40570-8). Asia.

Indian Foreign Policy in Cambodia, Laos & Vietnam, 1947-1964. D. R. SarDesai. 1969. 21.75x (ISBN 0-520-01119-8). U of Cal Pr.

Indian Games & Crafts. Robert Hofsinde. (Illus.). (gr. 5-9). 1957. PLB 6.67 (ISBN 0-688-21607-2). Morrow.

Indian Government & Politics. D. C. Gupta. 1978. 20.00 (ISBN 0-7069-0521-0, Pub. by Vikas India). Advent Bk.

Indian Heart of Carrie Hodges. Katy Peake. (Illus.). 128p. (gr. 7 up). 1972. PLB 4.95 o.p. (ISBN 0-670-39788-1). Viking Pr.

Indian Herbs. Raymond Stark. Ed. by Margaret Campbell. (Illus.). 50p. 1981. pap. 4.95 (ISBN 0-88839-077-7). Hancock Hse.

Indian Heritage. 3rd ed. Humayun Kabir. 1970. pap. 4.50x (ISBN 0-210-33672-2). Asia.

Indian Hill. Clyde R. Bulla. LC 63-15085. (Illus.). (gr. 2-5). 1963. 7.95 (ISBN 0-690-43626-2, TYC-J). T Y Crowell.

Indian Hunting. Robert Hofsinde. (Illus.). (gr. 4-7). 1962. PLB 6.48 (ISBN 0-688-31608-5). Morrow.

Indian Idealism. Surendranath Dasgupta. 1962. 26.95 (ISBN 0-521-04783-8); pap. 7.95x (ISBN 0-521-09194-2, 194). Cambridge U Pr.

Indian in American History. Virgil V. Vogel. 1968. pap. 1.25 (ISBN 0-685-38480-2). Integrated Ed Assoc.

Indian in the Spanish-American Novel. John R. Tapia. LC 80-6182. 120p. (Orig.). 1981. lib. bdg. 16.25 (ISBN 0-8191-1428-6); pap. text ed. 7.75 (ISBN 0-8191-1438-3). U Pr of Amer.

Indian Jewelry Making, Vol. 1. O. T. Branson. (Illus.). 1977. pap. 7.95 (ISBN 0-918080-15-0). Treasure Chest.

Indian Killer. Harold Kalin. 1976. pap. 1.25 o.p. (ISBN 0-685-74569-4, LB425ZK, Leisure Bks). Nordon Pubns.

Indian Knoll. William S. Webb. LC 73-18473. (Illus.). 280p. 1974. Repr. of 1946 ed. 14.50x (ISBN 0-87049-150-4). U of Tenn Pr.

Indian Legal System. Indian Law Institute. 1979. 28.00 (ISBN 0-379-20368-5). Oceana.

Indian Legends of the Pacific Northwest. Ella E. Clark. (Illus.). (YA) (gr. 9-12). 1953. pap. 3.95 (ISBN 0-520-00243-1, CAL18). U of Cal Pr.

Indian Literature: A Guide to Information Sources. Ed. by Armitjit Singh et al. LC 74-11532. (American Literature, English Literature & World Literatures in English Information Guide Ser.: Vol 36). 450p. 1981. 30.00 (ISBN 0-8103-1238-7). Gale.

Indian Lore. Boy Scouts Of America. LC 19-600. (Illus.). 96p. (gr. 6-12). 1959. pap. 0.70x (ISBN 0-8395-3358-6, 3358). BSA.

Indian Masks & Myths of the West. Joseph H. Wherry. (Apollo Eds.). 288p. 1974. pap. 3.50 o.s.i. (ISBN 0-8152-0358-6, A358, TYC-T). T Y Crowell.

Indian Medicine Man. Robert Hofsinde. (Illus.). (gr. 3-7). 1966. PLB 6.48 (ISBN 0-688-31618-2). Morrow.

Indian Mosaic. R. H. Lesser. (Writers Workshop Greybird Book Ser.). 41p. 1975. 12.00 (ISBN 0-88253-564-1); pap. text ed. 4.80 (ISBN 0-88253-563-3). Ind-US Inc.

Indian Music: A Perspective. Ed. by Gowry Kuppuswamy. 1980. 32.50x (ISBN 0-8364-0629-X, Pub. by Sundeep). South Asia Bks.

Indian Music Makers. Robert Hofsinde. (Illus.). (gr. 3-7). 1967. PLB 6.48 (ISBN 0-688-31616-6). Morrow.

Indian Muslims: A Political History 1858-1947. R. Gopal. 10.00 (ISBN 0-210-33673-0). Asia.

Indian Nations of America. P. Jacauin. (Illus.). 1980. cancelled (ISBN 0-686-65197-9). Atheneum.

Indian Ocean in Global Politics. Ed. by Larry W. Bowman & Ian Clark. (Westview Special Studies in International Relations). 270p. 1980. lib. bdg. 25.00x (ISBN 0-86531-038-6); pap. 12.00x (ISBN 0-86531-191-9). Westview.

Indian Paths of Pennsylvania. Paul A. W. Wallace. LC 66-4482. 1971. 9.00 (ISBN 0-685-19109-5). Pa Hist & Mus.

Indian Peoples of Eastern America: A Documentary History of the Sexes. Ed. by James Axtell. (Illus.). 232p. 1981. text ed. 11.95x (ISBN 0-19-502740-X); pap. text ed. 6.95 (ISBN 0-19-502741-8). Oxford U Pr.

Indian Philosophy, 2 Vols. Sarvepelli Radhakrishnan. (Muirhead Library of Philosophy). 1962. Set. text ed. 36.00x (ISBN 0-04-181009-0). Humanities.

Indian Philosophy of Education. Humayuh Kabir. 1971. pap. 6.00x (ISBN 0-685-06519-7, 210-33880-6). Asia.

Indian Philosophy Since Independence. D. Riepe. (Philosophical Currents Ser.: No. 25). 403p. 1980. text ed. 34.25x (ISBN 90-6032-113-8). Humanities.

Indian Picture Writing. Robert Hofsinde. (Illus.). (gr. 5-9). 1959. PLB 6.48 (ISBN 0-688-31609-3). Morrow.

Indian Pirates. R. N. Saletore. 200p. 1980. pap. text ed. 11.25x (ISBN 0-391-02183-4, Pub. by Concept India). Humanities.

Indian Place-Names: Their Origin, Evolution, & Meanings, Collected in Kansas from the Siouan, Algonquian, Shoshonean, Caddoan, Iroquoian, & Other Tongues. John Rydjord. LC 68-10303. (Illus.). 380p. 1981. 19.95 (ISBN 0-8061-0801-0). U of Okla Pr.

Indian Poetry in English: A Literary History & Anthology. A. N. Dwivedi. 159p. 1980. text ed. 9.50x (ISBN 0-391-01789-6). Humanities.

Indian Poetry in English Today. Ed. by Pritish Nandy. (Indian Poetry Ser.). 140p. (Orig.). 1974. 2.00 (ISBN 0-88253-312-6). Ind-US Inc.

Indian Political Movements, 1919-1971: A Systematic Bibliography. Arun Ghosh. 1976. 36.00x o.p. (ISBN 0-88386-697-8). South Asia Bks.

Indian Politics & the Role of the Press. Sharad Karkhanis. 224p. 1981. text ed. 20.00x (ISBN 0-7069-1278-0, Pub. by Vikas India). Advent Bk.

Indian Politics & the Role of the Press. Sharad Karkhanis. 200p. 1980. write for info. (Pub. by Vikas India). Asia Bk Corp.

Indian Politics Since the Mutiny: Being an Account of the Development of Public Life & Political Institutions of Prominent Local Political Personalities. Sir Shirroavoore Y. Chintamani. LC 79-4911. 1981. Repr. of 1947 ed. 19.50 (ISBN 0-88355-961-7). Hyperion Conn.

Indian Population of New England in the 17th Century. S. F. Cook. (Publ. in Anthropology Ser: Vol. 12). 1977. pap. 6.75x o.p. (ISBN 0-520-09553-7). U of Cal Pr.

Indian Princess, 2 vols in 1. John N. Barker & John Bray. LC 77-169587. (Earlier American Music Ser.: No. 11). Repr. of 1808 ed. 19.50 (ISBN 0-306-77311-2). Da Capo.

Indian Prison. Indra J. Singh. 1979. text ed. 13.50x (ISBN 0-391-01849-3). Humanities.

Indian Running. Peter Nabokov. (Illus.). 160p. (Orig.). 1981. pap. 7.95 (ISBN 0-88496-162-1). Capra Pr.

Indian Sculpture in the Philadelphia Museum of Art. Stella Kramrisch. LC 60-14837. 1961. 12.00x o.p. (ISBN 0-8122-7276-5). U of Pa Pr.

Indian Shakers: A Messianic Cult of the Pacific Northwest. Homer Barnett. LC 72-5482. (Arcturus Books Paperbacks). (Illus.). 383p. 1972. pap. 7.95 (ISBN 0-8093-0595-X). S Ill U Pr.

Indian Shipping in Perspective. H. M. Trivedi. 540p. 1981. 40.00x (ISBN 0-7069-1202-0, Pub. by Vikas India). Advent Bk.

Indian Sign Language. Robert Hofsinde. (Illus.). (gr. 5 up). 1956. PLB 6.48 (ISBN 0-688-31610-7). Morrow.

Indian Sign Language. William Tomkins. Orig. Title: Universal Indian Sign Language of the Plains Indians of North America. (Illus.). 1969. pap. 2.00 (ISBN 0-486-22029-X). Dover.

Indian Signs & Signals. George Fronval & Daniel Dubois. Tr. by E. W. Egan. LC 78-57792. (Illus.). (gr. 3 up). 1978. 14.95 (ISBN 0-8069-2720-8); PLB 13.29 (ISBN 0-8069-2721-6). Sterling.

Indian Silver: Navajo & Pueblo Jewelers. Margery Bedinger. LC 72-94659. 1976. pap. 8.95 o.p. (ISBN 0-8263-0416-8). U of NM Pr.

Indian Songs & Legends. Guy C. Earl. LC 80-67271. 80p. (gr. 4-12). 1980. 10.00g (ISBN 0-87062-135-1). A H Clark.

Indian Studies Abroad. Ed. by C. H. Philips et al. 1964. 6.50x o.p. (ISBN 0-210-33635-8). Asia.

Indian Summer. Ann Deagon. LC 74-31937. (Illus.). 32p. 1975. 15.00 (ISBN 0-87775-078-5); pap. write for info. (ISBN 0-87775-107-2). Unicorn Pr.

Indian Summer & More. Robert E. Witt. 64p. 1981. 5.00 (ISBN 0-682-49668-5). Exposition.

Indian Tales of North America: An Anthology for the Adult Reader. Ed. by Tristram P. Coffin. LC 61-11866. (American Folklore Soc. Bibliographical & Special Ser.: No. 13). 1961. pap. 4.00 (ISBN 0-292-73506-5). U of Tex Pr.

Indian Temple Forms. M. A. Dhaky. 1977. 28.00x (ISBN 0-8364-0060-7). South Asia Bks.

Indian Theogony: Comparative Study of Indian Mythology from the Vedas to the Puranas. rev. ed. Sukumari Bhattacharji. 1978. Repr. of 1970 ed. 18.50x (ISBN 0-8364-0160-3). South Asia Bks.

Indian Thought: An Introduction. Ed. & pref. by D. H. Bishop. LC 73-13206. 1975. 10.95 (ISBN 0-470-07580-5). Halsted Pr.

Indian Thought & Its Development. Albert Schweitzer. 1962. 8.25 (ISBN 0-8446-2893-X). Peter Smith.

Indian Tipi: Its History... Reginald Laubin & Gladys Laubin. (Illus.). 288p. 1976. pap. 1.95 o.p. (ISBN 0-345-25034-6). Ballantine.

Indian Trade Guns. Ed. by T. M. Hamilton. 10.95 (ISBN 0-913150-43-6). Pioneer Pr.

Indian Traders. Frank McNitt. LC 62-16469. 393p. 1962. 16.95 (ISBN 0-8061-0531-3). U of Okla Pr.

Indian Two Feet & His Horse. Margaret Friskey. (Illus.). (gr. 2-3). pap. 1.25 (ISBN 0-590-08056-3, Schol Pap); pap. 3.95 indian two feet & witch next door (2 bks.) & record (ISBN 0-590-04394-3). Schol Bk Serv.

Indian Two Feet & the Wolf Cubs. Margaret Friskey. (Illus.). 64p. (gr. k-3). 1971. PLB 7.95 (ISBN 0-516-03501-0). Childrens.

Indian Verse in English 1970. Ed. by Shiv K. Kumar. (Writers Workshop Redbird Ser.). 1977. flxible bdg. 6.75 (ISBN 0-89253-752-3); text ed. 15.00 (ISBN 0-89253-751-5). Ind-US Inc.

Indian War of 1864. Eugene F. Ware. Ed. by Clyde C. Walton. LC 60-13875. (Illus.). 1963. pap. 4.95 (ISBN 0-8032-5212-9, BB 173, Bison). U of Nebr Pr.

Indian Warriors & Their Weapons. Robert Hofsinde. (Illus.). (gr. 4-7). 1965. PLB 6.48 (ISBN 0-688-31613-1). Morrow.

Indian Wars in North Carolina, 1663-1763. E. Lawrence Lee. (Illus.). 1968. pap. 1.00 (ISBN 0-86526-084-2). NC Archives.

Indian Water Rights. Richard L. Foreman. 1980. pap. text ed. 8.95x (ISBN 0-8134-2160-8, 2160). Interstate.

Indian Women. Devaki Jain. 312p. 1975. pap. 3.75x (ISBN 0-89253-538-5). Ind-US Inc.

Indian Women & Patriarchy. Maria Mies. 311p. 1980. text ed. 17.00x (ISBN 0-391-02126-5). Humanities.

Indian Women of the Western Morning: Their Life in Early America. John Upton Terrell & Donna M. Terrell. 200p. 1976. pap. 2.95 (ISBN 0-385-11038-3, Anch). Doubleday.

Indian Woodcarver. (Sharazad Stories Ser.). (Illus., Arabic.). pap. 3.50 (ISBN 0-686-53108-6). Intl Bk Ctr.

Indian Writing in English. David McCutchion. (Writers Workshop Greybird Ser.). 142p. 1975. 12.00 (ISBN 0-89253-596-2); pap. text ed. 8.00 (ISBN 0-88253-726-1). Ind-US Inc.

Indiana. 28.00 (ISBN 0-89770-090-2). Curriculum Info Ctr.

Indiana. George Sand. Tr. by G. B. Ives from Fr. LC 75-25896. xxi, 327p. 1975. Repr. of 1900 ed. 17.00 (ISBN 0-86527-260-3). Fertig.

Indiana: A Guide to the Hoosier State. Federal Writers' Project. 564p. 1941. Repr. 49.00 (ISBN 0-403-02165-0). Somerset Pub.

Indiana, a History. Howard H. Peckham. (States & the Nation Ser.). (Illus.). 1978. 12.95 (ISBN 0-393-05670-8, Co-Pub by AASLH). Norton.

Indiana: A History. William E. Wilson. LC 66-22445. (Illus.). 256p. 1966. 12.50x (ISBN 0-253-14150-8); pap. 6.95x (ISBN 0-253-28305-1). Ind U Pr.

Indiana Appellate Practice & Procedure, 2 vols. Bobbitt. 1972. 59.50, with 1977 suppl (ISBN 0-672-81526-5, Bobbs-Merrill Law); 1977 suppl 10.00 (ISBN 0-672-82813-8). Michie.

Indiana Banking & Related Laws. 3rd ed. Publisher's Editorial Staff. LC 78-15745. 1977. 50.00, with 1978 suppl (ISBN 0-672-83720-X, Bobbs-Merrill Law); 1978 suppl. 10.00 (ISBN 0-672-83721-8). Michie.

Indiana Chronology & Factbook, Vol. 14. R. I. Vexler. 1978. 8.50 (ISBN 0-379-16139-7). Oceana.

Indiana Dialects in Their Historical Setting. Marvin Carmony. (Illus.). 51p. 1979. pap. 2.95 (ISBN 0-936640-00-6). Sagamore Pr.

Indiana Experience: An Anthology. Ed. by Arnold L. Lazarus. LC 76-50528. 448p. 1977. 15.00x (ISBN 0-253-14156-7); pap. text ed. 4.95x (ISBN 0-253-32986-8). Ind U Pr.

Indiana Folklore: A Reader. Ed. by Linda Degh. LC 79-2970. (Illus.). 320p. 1980. 20.00x (ISBN 0-253-10986-8); pap. 7.95x (ISBN 0-253-20239-6). Ind U Pr.

Indiana Home. Logan Esarey. LC 76-12384. (Illus.). 136p. 1976. 10.00x (ISBN 0-253-32989-2); pap. 3.95x (ISBN 0-253-28325-6). Ind U Pr.

Indiana Pattern Jury Instructions - Criminal. Indiana Judges Association. 250p. 1980. 50.00 (ISBN 0-87215-353-3). Michie.

Indiana Place Names. Ronald L. Baker & Marvin Carmony. LC 74-17915. 224p. 1976. 7.95x o.p. (ISBN 0-253-14167-2); pap. 3.95x (ISBN 0-253-28340-X). Ind U Pr.

Indiana Politics during the Civil War. Kenneth M. Stampp. LC 77-23629. 320p. 1978. Repr. of 1949 ed. 12.50x (ISBN 0-253-37022-1). Ind U Pr.

Indiana Small Claims. Robert G. Whitinger. 180p. 1980. 20.00 (ISBN 0-87215-326-6). Michie.

Indiana State Industrial Directory, 1981. State Industrial Directories Corp. Date not set. pap. price not set (ISBN 0-89910-046-5). State Indus D.

Indiana Supplement for Modern Real Estate Practice. James A. Gorzelany & Violet Reus. 128p. (Orig.). 1980. pap. 7.95 (ISBN 0-88462-379-3). Real Estate Ed Co.

Indiana to Eighteen Sixteen: The Colonial Period. John D. Barnhart & Dorothy L. Riker. 536p. 1971. 15.00x (ISBN 0-253-37018-3). Ind U Pr.

Indiana University: Midwestern Pioneer, 3 vols. Thomas D. Clark. Incl. Vol. 1. The Early Years. (Illus.). 352p. 1970. 12.50x (ISBN 0-253-14170-2); Vol. 2. In Mid-Passage. (Illus.). 448p. 1973. 17.50x (ISBN 0-253-32995-7); Vol. 3. Years of Fulfillment. 704p. 1977. 19.95x (ISBN 0-253-32996-5). LC 74-126207. (Illus.). Set. 42.50x (ISBN 0-253-32997-3). Ind U Pr.

Indianapolis Collects & Cooks. Ed. by Cookbook Committee, 1979. (Illus.). 208p. 1980. pap. text ed. 11.75 (ISBN 0-936260-00-9). Ind Mus Art.

Indianapolis Five Hundred. Julian May. LC 75-8502. (Sports Classics Ser.). (Illus.). 48p. (gr. 4-6). 1975. PLB 8.95 o.p. (ISBN 0-87191-441-7). Creative Ed.

Indianapolis Five Hundred Yearbook: 1980. Carl Hungness et al. (Illus.). 224p. 1980. lib. bdg. 13.95 (ISBN 0-915088-24-X); pap. 7.95 (ISBN 0-915088-23-1). C Hungness.

Indianola: The Mother of Western Texas. Brownson Malsch. (Illus.). 300p. 1977. 15.00 (ISBN 0-88319-033-8). Shoal Creek Pub.

Indians. B. Capps. LC 72-93991. (Old West Ser). (Illus.). (gr. 5 up). 1973. 12.96 o.p. (ISBN 0-8094-1455-4, Pub. by Time-Life). Silver.

Indians. Ben Capps. (Old West Ser.). (Illus.). 1973. 12.95 (ISBN 0-8094-1454-6). Time-Life.

Indians & Pioneers: The Story of the American Southwest Before 1830. Grant Foreman. (Civilization of the American Indian Ser.: No. 14). (Illus.). 1967. 15.95 (ISBN 0-8061-0057-5); pap. 8.95 (ISBN 0-8061-1262-X). U of Okla Pr.

Indians & the Strangers. Johanna Johnston. LC 72-1447. (Illus.). (gr. 2 up). 1972. 5.95 (ISBN 0-396-06610-0). Dodd.

Indians at Home. Robert Hofsinde. (Illus.). (gr. 3-7). 1964. PLB 6.48 (ISBN 0-688-31611-5). Morrow.

Indians, Bureaucrats, & Land: The Dawes Act & the Decline of Indian Farming. Leonard A. Carlson. LC 80-1709. (Contributions in Economics & Economic History Ser.: No. 36). 280p. 1981. lib. bdg. 29.95 (ISBN 0-313-22533-8, CDA/). Greenwood.

Indians in Malaysia & Singapore. Sinnappah Arasaratnam. 1980. pap. 8.95x (ISBN 0-19-580427-9). Oxford U Pr.

Indians in Maryland & Delaware: A Critical Bibliography. Frank W. Porter. LC 79-2460. (Newberry Library Center for the History of the American Indian Bibliographical Ser.). 128p. 1980. pap. 4.95x (ISBN 0-253-30954-9). Ind U Pr.

Indians in Pennsylvania. Paul A. Wallace. LC 61-63955. (Illus., Orig.). 1970. 7.00 (ISBN 0-911124-41-1); pap. 4.00 (ISBN 0-911124-40-3). Pa Hist & Mus.

Indians in Seventhteenth Century Virginia. Ben C. McCary. 93p. 1980. pap. 1.95x (ISBN 0-8139-0142-1). U Pr of Va.

Indians in the Fur Trade: Their Role As Trappers, Hunters, & Middle Man in the Lands Southwest of Hudson Bay, 1660-1860. Arthur J. Ray. LC 73-89848. (Illus.). 1974. pap. 7.50 (ISBN 0-8020-6226-1). U of Toronto Pr.

Indians of Illinois & Indiana: Illinois, Kickapoo & Potawatomi Indians. Joseph Jablow. Ed. by David A. Horr. (American Indian Ethnohistory Ser.: North Central & Northeastern Indians). 1974. lib. bdg. 42.00 (ISBN 0-8240-0805-7). Garland Pub.

Indians of Illinois & Northwestern Indiana. Incl. Reports on the Kickapoo, Illinois & Potawatomi Indians. David B. Stout; Anthropological Report on the Chippewa, Ottowa, & Potawatomi Indians in Southwest Michigan. Erminie Wheeler-Voegelin. (American Indian Ethnohistory Ser: North Central & Northeastern Indians). (Illus.). lib. bdg. 42.00 (ISBN 0-8240-0804-9). Garland Pub.

Indians of North America. Geoffrey Turner. (Illus.). 261p. 1980. pap. 6.95 (ISBN 0-7137-1122-1, Pub. by Blandford Pr England). Sterling.

Indians of North & South America: A Bibliography Based on the Collection at the Willard E. Yager Library-Museum Hartwick College, Oneonta, N.Y. Carolyn E. Wolf & Karen R. Folk. LC 77-1759. 1977. 27.50 (ISBN 0-8108-1026-3). Scarecrow.

Indians of Northeastern Illinois. Incl. Anthropological Report on the Chippewa, Ottawa & Potawatomi Indians in Northeastern Illinois. David A. Baerreis et al; Identity of the Mascontens. David A. Barraeis et al. (American Indian Ethnohistory Ser: North Central & Northeastern Indians). (Illus.). lib. bdg. 42.00 (ISBN 0-8240-0803-0). Garland Pub.

Indians of Northern Ohio & Southeastern Michigan. Incl. An Ethnohistorical Report on the Wyandot, Ottawa, Chippewa, Munsee, Delaware, Shawnee, & Potawatomi of Ohio & Southeastern Michigan. Erminie Wheeler-Voegelin; The Location of Indian Tribes in Southeastern Michigan & Northern Ohio, 1700-1817. Helen H. Tanner. (American Indian Ethnohistory Ser: North Central & Northeastern Indians). (Illus.). lib. bdg. 42.00 (ISBN 0-8240-0800-6). Garland Pub.

Indians of Northwest Ohio: An Ethnohistorical Report on the Wyandot, Potawatomi, Ottawa & Chippewa of Northwest Ohio. Erminie Wheeler-Voegelin. Ed. by David A. Horr. (North Central & Northeastern Indians - American Indian Ethnohistory Ser.). 1974. lib. bdg. 42.00 (ISBN 0-8240-0799-9). Garland Pub.

Indians of Ohio & Indiana Prior to 1795, 2 vols. Incl. The Greenville Treaty, Seventeen Ninety-Five. Helen H. Tanner; Ethnohistory of Indian Use & Occupancy in Ohio & Indiana Prior to 1795. Erminie Wheeler-Voegelin. (American Indian Ethnohistory Ser: North Central & Northeastern Indians). (Illus.). Set. lib. bdg. 76.00 (ISBN 0-8240-0798-0); lib. bdg. 42.00 ea. Garland Pub.

Indians of Ohio, Indiana, Illinois, Southern Michigan & Southern Wisconsin: Findings of Fact & Opinion, 3 vols. Ed. by David A. Horr. (North Central & Northeastern Indians - American Indian Ethnohistory Ser.). 1974. Set. lib. bdg. 99.00 (ISBN 0-8240-0807-3); lib. bdg. 42.00 ea. Garland Pub.

Indians of Pennsylvania Workshop. Lucille Wallower. LC 76-12651. (gr. 3-4). 1976. pap. 3.50 (ISBN 0-931992-01-X). Penns Valley.

Indians of the American Southwest. Bertha P. Dutton. 336p. 1981. 17.50 (ISBN 0-8263-0551-2); pap. 8.95 (ISBN 0-8263-0552-0). U of NM Pr.

Indians of the Americas. abr. ed. John Collier. (Orig.). 1952. pap. 1.95 (ISBN 0-451-61886-6, MJ1886, Ment). NAL.

Indians of the Eastern Woodlands. Sally Sheppard. LC 74-13609. (Illus.). 96p. (gr. 5 up). 1975. PLB 3.90 o.p. (ISBN 0-531-00825-8). Watts.

Indians of the Great Lakes Region. W. Vernon Kinietz. 1965. pap. 4.95 (ISBN 0-472-06107-0, 107, AA). U of Mich Pr.

Indians of the Longhouse. Sonia Bleeker. (Illus.). (gr. 3-6). 1950. PLB 6.67 (ISBN 0-688-31453-8). Morrow.

Indians of the Oaks. rev. ed. Melicent H. Lee. (Illus.). 1978. pap. 6.95 (ISBN 0-916552-17-9). Acoma Bks.

Indians of the Pacific Northwest. Vine Deloria, Jr. LC 74-18789. (gr. 6-9). 1977. PLB 6.95 (ISBN 0-385-09791-3). Doubleday.

Indians of the Pacific Northwest: A History. Robert H. Ruby & John A. Brown. LC 80-5946. (Civilization of the American Indian Ser.: Vol. 158). (Illus.). 400p. 1981. 24.95 (ISBN 0-8061-1731-1). U of Okla Pr.

Indians of the Plains. Eugene Rachlis & John C. Ewers. LC 60-6402. (American Heritage Junior Library). (Illus.). 153p. (gr. 5 up). 1960. 9.95 (ISBN 0-8281-0385-2, J001-0). Am Heritage.

Indians of the Plains. Sally Sheppard. (First Bks. Ser.). (Illus.). 72p. (gr. 5 up). 1976. PLB 6.45 (ISBN 0-531-00847-9). Watts.

Indians of the Rio Grande Valley. Adolph F. Bandelier & Edgar L. Hewett. LC 72-95268. (Illus.). 274p. 1973. Repr. of 1939 ed. lib. bdg. 16.50x (ISBN 0-8154-0462-X). Cooper Sq.

Indians of the Southwest: A Critical Bibliography. Henry F. Dobyns. LC 80-8036. (Newberry Library Center for the History of the American Indian Bibliographical Ser.). 176p. 1980. pap. 4.95x (ISBN 0-253-35110-3). Ind U Pr.

Indians of the Subarctic: A Critical Bibliography. June Helm. LC 76-12373. (Newberry Library Center for the History of the American Indian Bibliographical Ser.). 104p. 1976. pap. 3.95x (ISBN 0-253-33004-1). Ind U Pr.

Indians of the United States: Four Centuries of Their History & Culture. Clark Wissler. LC 66-12215. 1966. 7.95 (ISBN 0-385-00757-4); pap. 2.95 o.p. (ISBN 0-385-02019-8). Doubleday.

Indians of the Western Great Lakes, 1615-1760. W. Vernon Kinietz. 1965. 8.95 (ISBN 0-472-09107-7). U of Mich Pr.

Indians of the Woodlands: From Prehistoric Times to 1725. George E. Hyde. (Civilization of the American Indian Ser.: No. 64). (Illus.). 1962. pap. 6.95 (ISBN 0-8061-1058-9). U of Okla Pr.

Indians of Western Illinois & Southern Wisconsin. Incl. Anthropological Report on the Chippewas, Ottawas, & Potawatomi Residing on the Illinois & Milwaukee Rivers on the Southwestern Parts of Lake Michigan. Erminie Wheeler-Voegelin et al; Anthropological Report on the Chippewa, Ottawa & Potawatomi Indians of Southwest Wisconsin & Northeast Illinois. J. A. Jones. (American Indian Ethnohistory Ser: North Central & Northeastern Indians). (Illus.). lib. bdg. 42.00 (ISBN 0-8240-0802-2). Garland Pub.

Indians on the Move. Robert Hofsinde. (Illus.). (gr. 3-7). 1970. PLB 6.48 (ISBN 0-688-31615-8). Morrow.

Indians: The First Americans. Kathryn F. Ernst. LC 78-13742. (Easy-Read Fact Bk.). (Illus.). (gr. 2-4). 1979. PLB 6.45 s&l (ISBN 0-531-02273-0). Watts.

Indians: The First Americans. Patricia Miles Martin. LC 70-99132. (Finding-Out Books for Science & Social Studies, Grades 1-4). (Illus.). (gr. 1-4). 1970. PLB 5.41 o.p. (ISBN 0-8193-0359-3). Enslow Pubs.

India's Aid Diplomacy in the Third World. Dewan C. Vohra. 256p. 1980. text ed. 22.50 (ISBN 0-7069-1058-3, Pub. by Vikas India). Advent Bk.

India's Constitution. 3rd rev. ed. M. V. Pylee. (Illus.). ix, 471p. (Orig.). 1980. pap. text ed. 11.95x (ISBN 0-210-33709-5). Asia.

India's Democracy. A. H. Hanson & Janet Douglas. (Introductions to Comparative Government Ser). 236p. 1972. 7.95x (ISBN 0-393-05469-1); pap. 4.95x (ISBN 0-393-09908-3). Norton.

India's Economic Relations with the USSR & Eastern Europe, 1953-54 to 1969-70. Asha L. Datar. LC 76-178285. (Soviet & East European Studies Ser). (Illus.). 1972. 42.50 (ISBN 0-521-08219-6). Cambridge U Pr.

India's Freedom. Jawajarial Nehru. (Unwin Bks.). 1962. pap. 2.95 o.p. (ISBN 0-04-320028-1). Allen Unwin.

India's Nuclear Bomb. Shyam Bhatia. 1980. text ed. 13.95x (ISBN 0-7069-0972-0, Pub. by Vikas India). Advent Bk.

India's Nuclear Option: Atomic Diplomacy & Decision Making. Ashok Kapur. LC 75-23974. (Illus.). 280p. 1976. text ed. 29.95 (ISBN 0-275-56100-3). Praeger.

India's Policy in the United Nations. T. Ramakrishna Reddy. LC 67-26816. 1968. 12.50 (ISBN 0-8386-6755-4). Fairleigh Dickinson.

India's Revolution: Gandhi & the Quit India Movement. Francis G. Hutchins. LC 72-96630. 384p. 1973. 17.50x (ISBN 0-674-45025-6). Harvard U Pr.

India's Security in Resurgent Asia. Ajit S. Sarhadi. viii, 338p. 1980. text ed. 22.50x (ISBN 0-86590-003-5). Apt Bks.

India's Wars Since Independence: Defence of the Western Front, Vol. II. Sukhwant Singh. 350p. 1981. text ed. 35.00 (ISBN 0-7069-1277-2, Pub by Vikas India). Advent Bk.

India's Water Wealth. rev. ed. K. L. Roa. 1980. 11.00x (ISBN 0-8364-0580-3, Pub. by Orient Longman). South Asia Bks.

Indications & Alternatives in X-Ray Diagnosis: A Guide to the Effective Employment of Roentgenologic Studies in the Solution of Diagnostic Problems. 2nd ed. Melvyn H. Schreiber. (Illus.). 192p. 1974. pap. 16.75 (ISBN 0-398-03027-8). C C Thomas.

Indicative Past: A Hundred Years of the Girls' Public Day School Trust. Josephine Kamm. 1971. text ed. 12.50x o.p. (ISBN 0-04-373002-7). Allen Unwin.

Indicators. E. Bishop. 756p. 1973. text ed. 105.00 (ISBN 0-08-016617-2). Pergamon.

Indicators of Child Health & Welfare: Development of the DIPOV Index. Leonard S. Kogan & Shirley Jenkins. LC 74-16402. 176p. 1974. 17.50x (ISBN 0-231-03951-4). Columbia U Pr.

Indicators of Environmental Quality & Quality of Life. (Reports & Papers in the Social Sciences Ser.: No. 38). 1979. pap. 4.75 (ISBN 92-3-101539-7, U862, UNESCO). Unipub.

Indicators of the Quality of U. S. Housing. Jeanne E. Goedert & John L. Goodman, Jr. (Institute Paper). 55p. 1977. pap. 5.50 (ISBN 0-87766-204-5, 20200). Urban Inst.

Indice Analitico: No. 3, Enero-Diciembre, Vol. 4-12. Incl. Vol. 4. 1963 (ISBN 0-8270-0130-4); Vol. 5. 1964 (ISBN 0-8270-0135-5); Vol. 6. 1965 (ISBN 0-8270-0140-1); Vol. 7. 1966 (ISBN 0-8270-0145-2); Vol. 8. 1967 (ISBN 0-8270-0150-9); Vol. 9. 1968 (ISBN 0-8270-0155-X); Vol. 10. 1969 (ISBN 0-8270-0160-6); Vol. 11. 1970. 178p. 1970 (ISBN 0-8270-0165-7); Vol. 12. 1971 (ISBN 0-8270-0170-3). (Documentos Officiales Ser.). (Span.). Vol. 1-9 & 11-12. pap. 2.00 ea.; Vol. 10. pap. 1.00 (ISBN 0-686-65025-5). OAS.

Indice Universal De la Obra De Jose Marti. Carlos Ripoll. 1971. 15.00 (ISBN 0-88303-009-8); pap. 10.95 (ISBN 0-685-73213-4). E Torres & Sons.

Indice y Lista General Vol. 2: Enero-Diciembre, 1961. (Documentes Oficiales Ser.). (Span.). pap. 2.00 o.p. (ISBN 0-685-02439-3). OAS.

Indices of Heat Stress. N. C. Mazumdar. 132p. 1980. 4.95x (ISBN 0-89955-318-4, Pub. by Interprint India). Intl Schol Bk Serv.

Indigenous Anthropology in Non-Western Countries. Hussein Fahim. 276p. 1980. lib. bdg. write for info. (ISBN 0-89089-197-4); pap. text ed. write for info (ISBN 0-89089-198-2). Carolina Acad Pr.

Indigenous Architecture Worldwide: A Guide to Information Sources. Ed. by Lawrence Wodehouse. LC 79-26580. (Art & Architecture Information Guide Ser.: Vol. 12). 1980. 30.00 (ISBN 0-8103-1450-9). Gale.

Indigenous Economics: A Cultural Approach. Chinyamata Chipeta. (Illus.). 64p. 1980. 12.50x (ISBN 0-682-49657-X). Exposition.

Indigent Rich: A Theory of General Equilibrium in a Keynesian System. J. W. Cumes. 224p. 1972. 16.50 (ISBN 0-08-017534-1). Pergamon.

Indigestible Mad. Mad Magazine Editors. (Mad Ser.: No. 24). (Illus.). 1975. pap. 1.75 (ISBN 0-446-94368-1). Warner Bks.

Indira Gandhi. Dom Moraes. 340p. 1980. 14.95 (ISBN 0-316-58191-7). Little.

Indira Gandhi Returns. Khushwant Singh. 1980. 10.00x (ISBN 0-8364-0655-9, Pub. by Vision India). South Asia Bks.

Indira Gandhi: Rose of India. Carol B. Church. Ed. by David L. Bender & Gary E. McCuen. (Focus on Famous Women Ser). (gr. 3-9). 1976. 6.95 (ISBN 0-912616-43-1); read-along cassette 9.95 (ISBN 0-89908-242-4). Greenhaven.

Indira Ghandi's India: The Political System Reappraised. Ed. by Henry C. Hart. LC 76-5433. (Special Studies on South & Southeast Asia Ser). 1976. 26.50x (ISBN 0-89158-042-5); pap. text ed. 10.00 o.p. (ISBN 0-89158-109-X). Westview.

Indirections. Charles Brasch. (Illus.). 450p. 1980. 33.00x (ISBN 0-19-558050-8). Oxford U Pr.

Indirections for Those Who Want to Write. Sidney Cox. 1981. pap. 8.95 (ISBN 0-87923-389-3). Godine.

Indiscretions. Evelyn Konrad. 1980. pap. 2.50 o.s.i. (ISBN 0-440-14079-X). Dell.

Indispensable Enemy: Labor & the Anti-Chinese Movement in California. Alexander Saxton. 1971. 21.50x (ISBN 0-520-01721-8); pap. 3.95 (ISBN 0-520-02905-4). U of Cal Pr.

Indispensable Rousseau. John H. Mason. 352p. (Orig.). 1980. 17.50 (ISBN 0-7043-2190-4, Pub. by Quartet England); pap. 7.95 (ISBN 0-7043-3220-5). Horizon.

Indispensables of Piano Playing. Abby Whiteside. LC 61-18671. 12.50 (ISBN 0-684-10653-1, ScribT). Scribner.

Individual. Paul Good. (Human Behavior Ser.). 1974. 9.95 (ISBN 0-8094-1904-1); lib. bdg. avail. (ISBN 0-685-50285-6). Time-Life.

Individual. Paul Good. LC 74-83977. (Human Behavior Ser.). (Illus.). 1974. lib. bdg. 9.99 o.p. (ISBN 0-686-51077-1). Silver.

Individual & Community Response to Energy Facility Siting: An Annotated Bibliography. Christopher Cluett et al. (Public Adminstration Ser.: Bibliography P-493). 50p. 1980. pap. 5.50. Vance Biblios.

Individual & State in Ancient China: Essays on Four Chinese Philosophers. Vitaly A. Rubin. Tr. by Steven I. Levine from Rus. 200p. 1976. 15.00x (ISBN 0-231-04064-4). Columbia U Pr.

Individual & the Cosmos in Renaissance Philosophy. Ernst Cassirer. Tr. by Mario Domandi. 1972. pap. 6.95x (ISBN 0-8122-1036-0, Pa. Paperbacks). U of Pa Pr.

Individual & the Future of Organizations, Vol. 9. Ed. by Michael H. Mescon & Carl A. Bramlette, Jr. (Franklin Foundation Lecture Ser.). 1980. pap. 3.75 (ISBN 0-88406-139-6). GA St U Busn Pub.

Individual & the Future of Organizations, Vol. 10. Ed. by Michael H. Mescon & Carl A. Bramlette, Jr. (Franklin Foundation Lecture Ser.). 1981. pap. 3.75 (ISBN 0-88406-144-2). GA St U Busn Pub.

Individual & the Future of Organizations, Vol. 11. Ed. by Michael H. Mescon & Carl A. Bramlette, Jr. (Franklin Foundation Lecture Ser.). 1981. pap. 3.75 (ISBN 0-88406-145-0). GA St U Busn Pub.

Individual & the Nature of Mass Events: A Seth Book. Jane Roberts & Robert F. Butts. LC 80-22600. 336p. 1981. 11.95 (ISBN 0-13-457259-9). P-H.

Individual & the Political Order: An Introduction to Social & Political Philosophy. Norman E. Bowie & R. L. Simon. 1977. pap. text ed. 11.95 (ISBN 0-13-457143-6). P-H.

Individual & the State. M. C. Chagla. 4.50x o.p. (ISBN 0-210-33676-5). Asia.

Individual, Business & Society. Jeffrey Barach. (Illus.). 1977. 16.95 (ISBN 0-13-458075-3); pap. text ed. 13.95x (ISBN 0-13-458067-2). P-H.

Individual Change Through Small Groups. Ed. by Paul H. Glasser et al. LC 73-14113. (Illus.). 1974. 16.95 (ISBN 0-02-911810-7); pap. text ed. 9.95 (ISBN 0-02-911800-X). Free Pr.

Individual Development & Social Experience. Sonja Hunt & Jennifer Hilton. (Illus.). 296p. 1981. pap. text ed. 12.50x (ISBN 0-04-150077-6, 2623). Allen Unwin.

Individual Differences & Universals in Language Learning Aptitude. Karl C. Diller. (Orig.). 1981. pap. text ed. 15.95 (ISBN 0-88377-164-0). Newbury Hse.

Individual Differences in Children. Ed. by Jack C. Westman. LC 72-10131. (Personality Processes Ser.). 368p. 1973. 31.00 (ISBN 0-471-93690-1, Pub. by Wiley-Interscience). Wiley.

Individual Identification & the Law Enforcement Officer. Donald J. Nash. (Illus.). 176p. 1978. 16.75 (ISBN 0-398-03708-6). C C Thomas.

Individual in a Social World: Essays & Experiments. Stanley Milgram. (Social Psychology Ser.). (Illus.). text ed. 9.95 (ISBN 0-201-04382-3). A-W.

Individual in Cultural Adaptation: A Study of Four East African Peoples. Robert B. Edgerton. LC 73-117948. 1971. 21.50 (ISBN 0-520-01730-7). U of Cal Pr.

Individual Income Tax. rev. ed. Richard Goode. (Studies of Government Finance). 1976. 15.95 (ISBN 0-8157-3198-1); pap. 6.95 (ISBN 0-8157-3197-3). Brookings.

Individual Liberty & the Law. Z. Cowan. 1977. 10.00 (ISBN 0-379-00597-2). Oceana.

Individual, Marriage & the Family. 4th ed. Lloyd Saxton. 672p. 1980. text ed. 17.95x (ISBN 0-534-00799-6); study guide 5.95x (ISBN 0-534-00800-3). Wadsworth Pub.

Individual Performance Assessment: An Approach to Criterion-Referenced Test Development. Robert W. Swezey. 1981. text ed. 16.95 (ISBN 0-8359-3066-1). Reston.

Individual Processes in Organizational Behavior. Jak Jabes. Ed. by Kenneth D. MacKenzie. LC 77-86012. (Organizational Behavior Ser.). 1978. pap. text ed. 9.95x (ISBN 0-88295-450-4). AHM Pub.

Individual Psychology of Alfred Adler: A Systematic Presentation in Selections from His Writings. Alfred Adler. Ed. by Heinz L. Ansbacher & Rowena R. Ansbacher. pap. 6.95x (ISBN 0-06-131154-5, TB1154, Torch). Har-Row.

Individual Psychotherapy & the Science of Psychodynamics. David H. Malan. LC 78-40691. (Postgraduate Psychiatic Ser.). 1979. 18.95 (ISBN 0-407-00088-7). Butterworths.

Individual Rights & the State in Foreign Affairs: An International Compendium. Elihu Lauterpacht & John G. Collier. LC 77-8010. (Praeger Special Studies). 1977. text ed. 52.95 (ISBN 0-275-24350-8). Praeger.

Individual, Society, & Health Behavior. Andie L. Knutson. 533p. (Orig.). 1982. pap. 6.95 (ISBN 0-87855-685-0). Transaction Bks. Postponed.

Individual, the Enterprise & the State. Ed. by R. I. Tricker. LC 77-78350. 1977. 18.95 (ISBN 0-470-99211-5). Halsted Pr.

Individual Values & Global Sharing. Earl R. Brubacker. 192p. 1980. 17.50x (ISBN 0-8147-1031-X). NYU Pr.

Individualism. Steven Lukes. 1973. pap. text ed. 9.95x (ISBN 0-631-18750-2, Pub. by Basil Blackwell). Biblio Dist.

Individualism & the Philosophy of the Social Sciences. Murray N. Rothbard. (Cato Papers Ser.: No. 4). 1979. pap. 2.00 (ISBN 0-932790-03-8). Cato Inst.

Individuality & the New Society. Ed. by Abraham Kaplan. LC 72-103294. (Washington Paperback Ser.: No. 59). 190p. 1970. 9.50 (ISBN 0-295-95057-9); pap. 2.95 (ISBN 0-295-95140-0). U of Wash Pr.

Individualized Arts & Crafts Lessons for the Elementary School. Elizabeth H. Penn. 1975. 13.95 o.p. (ISBN 0-685-73741-1). P-H.

Individualized Assessment & Treatment for Autistic & Developmentally Disabled Children. E. Schopler. Incl. Vol. I. Psycho-Educational Profile. 1978. 29.50 (ISBN 0-8391-1521-0); Vol. II. Teaching Strategies for Parents & Professionals. 1979. 19.95 (ISBN 0-685-97001-9). Univ Park.

Individualized Biology, 13 units. M. Druger. Incl. Unit 1. Microscope & Measurement. pap. 1.25 (ISBN 0-201-01371-1); Unit 2. Visit to the Great Barrier Reef. pap. 1.50 (ISBN 0-201-01372-X); Unit 3. How to Make Sense Out of the Diversity of Life. pap. 1.25 (ISBN 0-201-01373-8); Unit 4. Evolution & the Past Diversity of Life. pap. 1.50 (ISBN 0-201-01374-6); Unit 5. Unity of Life & Adaptation. pap. 1.50 (ISBN 0-201-01375-4); Unit 6. Microscopy & the Electron Microscope. pap. 1.25 (ISBN 0-201-01377-0); Unit 7. Architecture of Cells. pap. 1.50 (ISBN 0-201-01378-9); Unit 8. How Substances Get in & Out of Cells. pap. 1.50 (ISBN 0-201-01379-7); Unit 9. Chemicals of Life. pap. 1.95 (ISBN 0-201-01381-9); Unit 10. Proteins & Enzymes. pap. 1.25 (ISBN 0-201-01382-7); Unit 11. Origin of Life. pap. 1.25 (ISBN 0-201-01383-5); Unit 12. Cell Reproduction. pap. 1.75 (ISBN 0-201-01384-3); Unit 13. Animal Development. pap. 1.50 (ISBN 0-201-01444-0). 1971-74. A-W.

Individualized Biology, Unit XV: Energy & Life. Marvin Druger. 1978. pap. text ed. 1.95 (ISBN 0-201-01388-6). A-W.

Individualized Biology, Vol.14: Genetics - Script. Marvin Druger. (Life Sciences Ser.). 74p. 1976. pap. 1.95 (ISBN 0-201-01387-8). A-W.

Individualized Education for Preschool Exceptional Children. John Neisworth. LC 80-12722. 250p. 1980. text ed. 22.95 (ISBN 0-89443-285-0). Aspen Systems.

Individualized Instruction & Learning. Ed. by Ronald E. Hull & Madan Mohan. LC 73-89605. 1974. 19.95 (ISBN 0-88229-113-0). Nelson-Hall.

Individualized Instruction: Every Child a Winner. Gertrude Noar. LC 71-179420. 1972. pap. text ed. 7.50x o.p. (ISBN 0-471-64157-X). Wiley.

Individualized Instruction Game. James Neujahr. LC 75-22491. 1976. text ed. 8.00x (ISBN 0-8077-2485-8). Tchrs Coll.

Individualized Instruction in Mathematics. Sam Duker. LC 72-5739. 1972. 13.50 (ISBN 0-8108-0533-2). Scarecrow.

Individualized Instruction: Teaching Strategies Focusing on the Learner. G. Ray Musgrave. 189p. 1975. text ed. 11.95 o.p. (ISBN 0-205-04709-2); pap. 7.95x o.p. (ISBN 0-205-04779-3, 2247798). Allyn.

Individualized Instructional Programs in Archery, Badminton, Bowling, Golf & Tennis, 5 bklts. A. Annarino. 1973. pap. 12.95 o.p. (ISBN 0-13-457093-6); instructor's guide 1.95 o.p. (ISBN 0-13-457127-4). P-H.

Individualized Learning Program for En Camino! Virginia Benmaman & Suzanne Moore. 1981. pap. text ed. 4.95x (ISBN 0-673-15392-4). Scott F.

Individualized Mathematics Algebra 1: A Versatile Approach. L. Manlius Sargent, Jr. et al. (gr. 8-10). 1974. pap. text ed. 10.00x o.p. (ISBN 0-88334-064-X). Ind Sch Pr.

Individualized Reading. Sam Duker. 288p. 1971. pap. 22.50 photocopy ed. spiral (ISBN 0-398-02274-7). C C Thomas.

Individualized Related Instruction for Succeeding in the World of Work. Grady Kimbrell & Ben S. Vineyard. pap. 4.64 (ISBN 0-87345-547-9). McKnight.

Individualized Staff Development Programs for Competency Development: A Systematic Approach. Robert A. Roth. LC 80-8258. 123p. 1980. pap. text ed. 7.50 (ISBN 0-8191-1326-3). U Pr of Amer.

Individualized Typing Series, Pt. II, Intermediate. Shirley Hewitt. 1973. student guide 6.55 (ISBN 0-89420-036-4, 118100); pap. text ed. 234.85 cassette recordings (ISBN 0-89420-151-4, 118000). Natl Book.

Individualized Typing Series, Pt. III, Advanced. Shirley Hewitt. 1972. student guide 7.55 (ISBN 0-89420-088-7, 119100); cassette recordings 240.90 (ISBN 0-89420-152-2, 119000). Natl Book.
Individualized Typing Series: Pt. I, Beginning. Shirley Hewitt. 1972. student guide 6.05 (ISBN 0-89420-048-8, 117100); cassette recordings 234.60 (ISBN 0-89420-150-6, 117000). Natl Book.
Individualizing Instruction. C. M. Charles. LC 75-22246. (Illus.). 304p. 1976. pap. text ed. 11.50 o.p. (ISBN 0-8016-0967-4). Mosby.
Individualizing Instruction. 2nd ed. C. M. Charles. LC 79-26645. (Illus.). 1980. pap. 11.95 (ISBN 0-8016-0974-7). Mosby.
Individualizing the System: Current Issues in Higher Education 1976. Ed. by Dyckman W. Vermilye. LC 76-11947. (Higher Education Ser.). 1976. 12.95x o.p. (ISBN 0-87589-288-4). Jossey-Bass.
Individually Guided Mathematics. Thomas A. Romberg. LC 75-40905. (Leadership Ser in Indiv. Guided Ed.). 160p. 1976. pap. text ed. 7.95 (ISBN 0-201-19411-2); instr's guide 2.95 (ISBN 0-201-19421-X). A-W.
Individually Guided Science. R. E. Haney & J. S. Sorenson. 1977. pap. 7.95 (ISBN 0-201-19511-9). A-W.
Individuals & World Politics. Isaak. 265p. (Orig.). 1980. pap. text ed. 6.95 (ISBN 0-87872-274-2). Duxbury Pr.
Individuals in Thucydides. H. D. Westlake. LC 68-23918. 1968. 49.50 (ISBN 0-521-07246-8). Cambridge U Pr.
Individuals with Physical Disabilities: An Introduction for Educators. Gary A. Best. LC 78-1206. (Illus.). 1978. text ed. 16.50 (ISBN 0-8016-0665-9). Mosby.
Individuated Self: Cervantes & the Emergence of the Individual. John G. Weiger. LC 78-13019. xvi, 183p. 1979. 12.95x (ISBN 0-8214-0396-6). Ohio U Pr.
Individuation in Fairytales. Marie-Louise Von Franz. 1976. pap. 9.00 (ISBN 0-88214-112-0). Spring Pubns.
Indo-American Relations Between 1940-1974. Tripta Desai. 1977. pap. text ed. 9.00x (ISBN 0-8191-0155-9). U Pr of Amer.
Indo-Anglian Creed. S. Mokashi-Punekar. (Writers Workshop Greybird Ser.). 72p. 1975. 14.00 (ISBN 0-88253-566-8); pap. text ed. 4.80 (ISBN 0-88253-565-X). Ind-US Inc.
Indo-Australian Species of Xanthopimpla - Ichneumonidae. Henry Townes & Shui-Chen Chiu. (Memoirs Ser: No. 14). (Illus.). 372p. 1970. 25.00 (ISBN 0-686-17147-0). Am Entom Inst.
Indo-European. William F. Wyatt, Jr. LC 73-83140. (Haney Foundation Ser). 1970. 7.50x (ISBN 0-8122-7594-2). U of Pa Pr.
Indo-European Philology: Historical & Comparative. W. B. Lockwood. 1968. pap. text ed. 7.00x (ISBN 0-09-095581-1, Hutchinson U Lib). Humanities.
Indo-Europeans in the Fourth & Third Millennia: Proceedings. Conference on Indo-European Studies, U. of Texas, Austin, Feb. 4-5, 1980. Ed. by Edgar C. Polome. (Linguistica Extranea: Studia: No. 14). (Illus.). 245p. 1981. text ed. 21.50 (ISBN 0-89720-041-1). Karoma.
Indo-Pacific Fishery Commission Working Party of Experts on Central & Western Pacific Skipjack. (FAO Fisheries Report Ser.: No. 224). 12p. 1980. pap. 7.50 (ISBN 92-5-100843-4, F 1892, FAO). Unipub.
Indo-US Relations: 1947-1976. S. C. Tewari. 1977. text ed. 12.50x (ISBN 0-391-01001-8). Humanities.
Indochina War: Why Our Policy Failed. Ed. by David L. Bender & Gary E. McCuen. (Opposing Viewpoints Ser.: Vol. 11). (Illus.). 1975. lib. bdg. 8.95 (ISBN 0-912616-36-9); pap. text ed. 3.95 (ISBN 0-912616-17-2). Greenhaven.
Indoctrination & Education. I. A. Snook. (Students Library of Education). 1972. 15.00x (ISBN 0-7100-7222-8). Routledge & Kegan.
Indoctrination & Education. I. A. Snook. (Students of Library Education). 1975. pap. 7.95 (ISBN 0-7100-8163-4). Routledge & Kegan.
Indomitable Irishery: Paul Vincent Carroll: Study & Interviews. Marion Sitzman. (Salzburg Studies in English Literature, Romantic Reassessment Ser.: No. 29). (Illus.). 180p. 1975. pap. text ed. 25.00x (ISBN 0-391-01528-1). Humanities.
Indonesia. D. W. Fryer & James C. Jackson. LC 76-3707. (Nations of the Modern World Ser). 1977. 29.75x (ISBN 0-89158-028-X). Westview.
Indonesia. Leslie H. Palmier. (Nations & Peoples Library). (Illus.). 1966. 8.50x o.s.i. (ISBN 0-8027-2108-7). Walker & Co.
Indonesia: An Alternative History. Caldwell & Utrecht. 1978. 24.50 o.p. (ISBN 0-685-85435-3). Porter.
Indonesia & India, Fifteen Forty-Five to Fifteen Forty-Nine. 726p. (Orig.). 1980. 33.00 (ISBN 0-8294-0356-6). Loyola.
Indonesia & the Philippines: American Interests in Island Southeast Asia. Robert Pringle. LC 80-13474. (Illus.). 296p. 1980. 30.00x (ISBN 0-231-05008-9); pap. 8.00x (ISBN 0-231-05009-7). Columbia U Pr.
Indonesia: The Underdeveloped Freedom. S. Tas. LC 73-23034. 1974. 10.95 o.p. (ISBN 0-672-53655-2); pap. 8.95 (ISBN 0-672-63655-7). Pegasus.
Indonesian Economy. Ed. by Gustav F. Papanek. LC 80-18752. 300p. 1981. 26.95 (ISBN 0-03-057429-3). Praeger.
Indonesian Economy, Nineteen Fifty to Nineteen Sixty-Five: A Bibliography. George L. Hicks & Geoffrey McNicoll. (Bibliography: No. 9). x, 248p. 1967. 4.25 o.p. (ISBN 0-686-63733-X). Yale U Pr.
Indonesian Economy, Nineteen Fifty to Nineteen Sixty-Seven: Bibliographic Supplement. George L. Hicks & Geoffrey McNicoll. (Bibliography: No. 10). xii, 211p. 1968. 5.25 o.p. (ISBN 0-686-63732-1). Yale U Pr.
Indonesian-English Dictionary. 2nd ed. John M. Echols & Hassan Shadily. 431p. 1963. 25.00x (ISBN 0-8014-0112-7). Cornell U Pr.
Indonesian Food & Cooking. rev. ed. Sri Owen. (Illus.). 256p. 1980. pap. 10.95x (ISBN 0-907325-00-9, Pub. by Prospectengland). U Pr of Va.
Indonesian Kitchen. Marks Copeland & Mintari Soeharjo. LC 80-69385. 1981. write for info. (ISBN 0-689-11142-8). Atheneum.
Indonesian Manuscripts in Great Britain: A Catalogue of Manuscripts in Indonesian Languages in British Public Collections. M. C. Ricklefs & P. Voorhoeve. (London Oriental Bibliographies 5). 1977. 55.00x (ISBN 0-19-713592-7). Oxford U Pr.
Indonesian Revival: Why Two Million Came to Christ. Avery T. Willis, Jr. LC 77-12811. (Illus.). 1977. pap. 6.95 (ISBN 0-87808-428-2). William Carey Lib.
Indonesian Society in Transition: A Study of Social Change. Willem F. Wertheim. LC 78-14150. 1981. Repr. of 1959 ed. 27.50 (ISBN 0-88355-823-8). Hyperion Conn.
Indonesian Society in Transition: A Study of Social Change. Willem F. Wertheim. LC 80-19660. (Illus.). xiv, 394p. 1980. Repr. of 1959 ed. lib. bdg. 29.75x (ISBN 0-313-22578-8, WEIO). Greenwood.
Indonesian Tragedy. Brian May. (Illus.). 1978. 27.50x (ISBN 0-7100-8834-5). Routledge & Kegan.
Indoor Cat: How to Understand, Enjoy & Care for House Cats. Patricia Curtis. (Illus.). 192p. 1981. 10.95 (ISBN 0-385-15368-6). Doubleday.
Indoor Climate. D. A. McIntyre. (Illus.). xix, 442p. 1980. 65.00x (ISBN 0-85334-868-5). Intl Ideas.
Indoor Games Book. Andrew Pennycock. (Illus.). 1973. 10.95 (ISBN 0-571-09970-X, Pub. by Faber & Faber). Merrimack Bk Serv.
Indoor Garden: Design, Construction & Furnishing. Margaret K. Hunter & Edgar H. Hunter. LC 77-20942. 1978. 24.50 (ISBN 0-471-03016-3, Pub. by Wiley-Interscience). Wiley.
Indoor Gardening. D. X. Fenten. LC 74-3278. (First Bks). (Illus.). 72p. (gr. 4-10). 1974. PLB 4.90 o.p. (ISBN 0-531-02731-7). Watts.
Indoor Plants: Decorating with. Sunset Editors. LC 79-90333. (Illus.). 80p. 1980. pap. 3.95 (ISBN 0-376-03341-X, Sunset Bks). Sunset-Lane.
Indoor Sports. Max Brodnick. 1976. pap. 1.25 o.p. (ISBN 0-685-73455-2, LB396, Leisure Bks). Nordon Pubns.
Indoor Trees. Jack Kramer. 1980. 25.00x (ISBN 0-232-51399-6, Pub. by Darton-Longman-Todd England). State Mutual Bk.
Indoor Water Gardener's How to Handbook. H. Peter Loewer. 5.95 o.s.i. (ISBN 0-8027-0404-2). Walker & Co.
Indoor Water Gardener's How-to Handbook. Peter Loewer. 1976. pap. 1.25 o.p. (ISBN 0-445-08270-4). Popular Lib.
Indoors. Maureen Roffey. (Illus.). (ps). 1979. 1.25 (ISBN 0-370-02006-5, Pub. by Chatto Bodley Jonathan). Merrimack Bk Serv.
Induced Mutations Against Plant Diseases. (Proceedings Ser). (Illus.). 1978. pap. 50.50 (ISBN 92-0-010277-8, IAEA). Unipub.
Induced Mutations & Plant Improvement. (Illus.). 554p. (Orig., Eng. & Span.). 1972. pap. 34.25 (ISBN 92-0-011072-X, IAEA). Unipub.
Induced Mutations for Disease Resistance in Crop Plants. (Illus.). 193p. (Orig.). 1974. pap. 13.00 (ISBN 92-0-011274-9, IAEA). Unipub.
Induced Mutations in Cross-Breeding. (STI-PUB-447). (Illus.). 1977. pap. 25.75 (ISBN 92-0-111676-4, ISP447, IAEA). Unipub.
Induced Mutations in Plants. (Illus., Orig., Eng., Fr. & Span.). 1969. pap. 39.75 (ISBN 92-0-010369-3, IAEA). Unipub.
Induced Mutations in Vegetatively Propagated Plants. (Illus.). 222p. (Orig.). 1974. pap. 14.50 (ISBN 92-0-111473-7, IAEA). Unipub.
Induced Task Competence & Effects on Problem Solving Behavior. Don D. Davis. (Illus.). 52p. (Orig.). 1980. pap. text ed. 3.00 (ISBN 0-907152-00-7). Prytaneum Pr.
Induction. Nicholas Rescher. LC 80-52598. xii, 225p. 1981. 34.95 (ISBN 0-8229-3431-0). U of Pittsburgh Pr.
Induction & Deduction: A Study in Wittgenstein. Ilham Dilham. 1973. 29.75x (ISBN 0-631-14640-7, Pub. by Basil Blackwell England). Biblio Dist.
Indus Civilization. 3rd ed. Mortimer Wheeler. LC 22-11272. (Illus.). 1968. 32.50 (ISBN 0-521-06958-0); pap. 8.50x (ISBN 0-521-09538-7). Cambridge U Pr.
Industrial Accident Prevention: A Safety Management Approach. 5th rev. ed. Herbert W. Heinrich et al. (Illus.). 1980. text ed. 23.95 (ISBN 0-07-028061-4); instructor's manual 10.95 (ISBN 0-07-028062-2). McGraw.
Industrial Action in Australia. Ed. by Stephen J. Frenkel. 184p. 1981. text ed. 24.95x (ISBN 0-86861-122-0, 2513); pap. text ed. 12.50x (ISBN 0-86861-130-1, 2514). Allen Unwin.
Industrial Activity & Economic Geography: A Study of the Forces Behind the Geographical Location of Productive Activity in Manufacturing Industry. 3rd rev. ed. R. C. Estall & R. Olgilvie Buchanan. 1973. text ed. 13.50x (ISBN 0-09-117310-8, Hutchinson U Lib); pap. text ed. 11.25x (ISBN 0-09-117311-6, Hutchinson U Lib). Humanities.
Industrial Administration & Management. 4th ed. J. Batty et al. (Illus.). 592p. 1979. pap. 16.95x (ISBN 0-7121-0954-4, Pub. by Macdonald & Evans England). Intl Ideas.
Industrial Advertising & Publicity. Norman A. Hart. 1978. 24.95 (ISBN 0-470-99375-8). Halsted Pr.
Industrial Air Pollution Engineering. Compiled By Chemical Engineering Magazine. LC 80-12609. 304p. 1980. pap. 24.50 (ISBN 0-07-606664-9, Chem Eng). McGraw.
Industrial & Commercial Wiring. 2nd ed. Kennard C. Graham. (Illus.). 1963. 12.50 o.p. (ISBN 0-8269-1500-0). Am Technical.
Industrial & Economic Impacts of Improving Automobile Fuel Efficiency: An Input-Output Analysis. Melvyn D. Cheslow. (Institute Paper). 77p. 1976. pap. 3.50 (ISBN 0-87766-163-4, 14200). Urban Inst.
Industrial & Specialty Papers: Their Technology, Manufacture, & Use, 2 vols. Ed. by R. H. Mosher & D. S. Davis. (Illus.). 16.50 ea. (ISBN 0-8206-0222-1). Vol. 1. Vol. 4 (ISBN 0-8206-0223-X). Chem Pub.
Industrial Applications of Microbiology. J. Riviere. Ed. by J. Smith & M. Moss. Tr. by J. Smith & M. Moss. LC 77-22815. 1978. 27.95 (ISBN 0-470-99265-4). Halsted Pr.
Industrial Archaeology of Cornwall. A. C. Todd & Peter Laws. (Industrial Archaeology of the British Isles Ser). (Illus.). 288p. 1973. 14.95 (ISBN 0-7153-5590-2). David & Charles.
Industrial Archaeology of Farming in England & Wales. Nigel Harvey. (Illus.). 224p. 1980. 45.00 (ISBN 0-7134-1845-1, Pub. by Batsford England). David & Charles.
Industrial Archaeology of North-East England, 2 vols. Frank Atkinson. LC 74-81052. (Industrial Archaeology of British Isles Ser). (Illus.). 342p. 1974. Vol. 1. 5.95 (ISBN 0-7153-5911-8); Vol. 2, The Sites. 5.95 (ISBN 0-7153-6740-4). David & Charles.
Industrial Archaeology of Wales. D. Morgan Rees. LC 74-82832. (Industrial Archaeology of the British Isles Ser.). (Illus.). 288p. 1975. 22.50 (ISBN 0-7153-6819-2). David & Charles.
Industrial Arts for Elementary Classrooms. Swierkos et al. 1973. pap. text ed. 6.60 (ISBN 0-87002-116-8). Bennett IL.
Industrial Arts in General Education. 4th ed. Gordon O. Wilber & Norman C. Pendered. 1973. text ed. 20.50 scp (ISBN 0-685-51244-4, HarpC). Har-Row.
Industrial Arts of the Anglo-Saxons. J. De Baye. 1980. Repr. of 1893 ed. lib. bdg. 40.00 (ISBN 0-89341-380-1). Longwood Pr.
Industrial Arts Plastics. rev. ed. Lauton Edwards. (gr. 10-12). 1974. 11.28 (ISBN 0-87002-146-X). Bennett IL.
Industrial Arts Teacher's Handbook: Techniques, Principles & Methods. Donald Maley. 1978. text ed. 15.95 o.p. (ISBN 0-205-05952-X). Allyn.
Industrial Arts Woodworking. John L. Feirer. (gr. 9-12). 1977. text ed. 13.28 (ISBN 0-87002-195-8); wkbk 2.88 (ISBN 0-87002-284-9). Bennett IL.
Industrial Behavior Modification: A Learning Based Approach to Industrial-Organizational Problems. Ed. by Richard M. O'Brien et al. (Pergamon General Psychology Ser.). 300p. Date not set. price not set (ISBN 0-08-025558-2). Pergamon.
Industrial Bibliography. Michael Ahn. LC 74-82273. (Research Report Ser.: No. 22). 1974. 6.00 (ISBN 0-87420-322-8). Urban Land.
Industrial Britain Under the Regency. Ed. by William O. Henderson. LC 67-30258. (Illus.). 1968. 19.50x (ISBN 0-678-05058-9). Kelley.
Industrial Catering Management. D. S. Coates. 1971. 13.95x o.p. (ISBN 0-8464-0508-3). Beekman Pubs.
Industrial Change: Industrial Experience & Public Policy. Ed. by F. E. Hamilton. (Illus.). 1978. pap. text ed. 11.95x (ISBN 0-582-48593-2). Longman.
Industrial Chemistry, Pt. 1. R. Das. pap. 5.00x (ISBN 0-210-22520-3). Asia.
Industrial Coatings: New Trends, Markets, C-017. Ed. by Business Communications. 1979. 650.00 (ISBN 0-89336-221-2). BCC.
Industrial Concentration: The New Learning. Ed by Harvey J. Goldschmid et al. 1974. pap. 7.95 (ISBN 0-316-31941-4). Little.
Industrial Conflict in Modern Britain. James E. Cronin. 242p. 1979. 25.00x (ISBN 0-8476-6188-1). Rowman.
Industrial Control Equipment for Gaseous Pollutants, 2 vols. new ed. Anthony Buonicore & Louis Theodore. LC 74-25260. (Uniscience Ser). 1975. Vol. 1, 209p. 49.95 (ISBN 0-87819-067-8); Vol. 2, 168p. 39.95 (ISBN 0-87819-068-6). CRC Pr.
Industrial Crafts. LC 77-73248. 64p. (gr. 7-9). 1978. pap. text ed. 3.64 (ISBN 0-02-820450-6). Glencoe.
Industrial Democracy & Labour Market Policy in Sweden. John A. Fry. 1979. 35.00 (ISBN 0-08-022462-8); pap. 17.75 (ISBN 0-08-022498-9). Pergamon.
Industrial Design. John Heskett. (World of Art Ser.). (Illus.). 300p. 1980. 17.95 (ISBN 0-19-520217-1); pap. 9.95 (ISBN 0-19-520218-X). Oxford U Pr.
Industrial Design in Britain. Noel Carrington. 1976. text ed. 25.00x (ISBN 0-04-745006-1). Allen Unwin.
Industrial Development: A Practical Handbook for Planning & Implementing Development Programs. Richard S. Kaynor & Konrad F. Schultz. LC 72-76450. (Special Studies in International Economics & Development). 1973. 29.50x (ISBN 0-275-28683-5). Irvington.
Industrial Development & Industrial Policy: Proceedings. Internaional Conference on Industrial Economics, 2nd. Ed. by Zoltan Roman. 1979. 43.00 (ISBN 0-9960016-3-8, Pub. by Kiado Hungary). Heyden.
Industrial Development Handbook. ULI Industrial Council. Ed. by Frank H. Spink, Jr. LC 75-37218. (Community Builders Handbook Ser.). (Illus.). 256p. 1975. 29.00 (ISBN 0-87420-562-X). Urban Land.
Industrial Development in Europe. (Illus.). 327p. 1975. pap. 22.50 o.p. (ISBN 0-7161-0239-0, Gower). Unipub.
Industrial Development of Poland. Rosa Luxemburg. Tr. by Tessa DeCarlo. LC 77-2338. 1977. pap. 3.95 (ISBN 0-918388-00-7, Univ Edns). New Benjamin.
Industrial Dynamics. Jay W. Forrester. (Illus.). 1961. pap. 19.95x (ISBN 0-262-56001-1). MIT Pr.
Industrial Education Facilities: A Handbook for Organization & Management. Robert D. Brown. 1979. text ed. 19.95 (ISBN 0-205-06171-0). Allyn.
Industrial Electricity. Miller. (gr. 9-12). 1978. text ed. 15.00 (ISBN 0-87002-200-8); student guide 2.60 (ISBN 0-87002-244-X). Bennett IL.
Industrial Electronics: Atext-Lab Manual. 3rd ed. Electronic Industries Association & Paul B. Zbar. (Illus.). 320p. Date not set. 12.95x (ISBN 0-07-072793-7, G). McGraw.
Industrial Electronics: Design & Application. Charles Davis. LC 72-92570. 1973. text ed. 21.95x (ISBN 0-675-09010-5); instructors manual 3.95 (ISBN 0-686-66861-8). Merrill.
Industrial Electronics: Principles & Practice. Alfred Haas. LC 78-178690. 10.95d (ISBN 0-8306-1583-0, 583). TAB Bks.
Industrial Energy Conservation: A Handbook for Engineers & Managers. 2nd ed. D. A. Reay. (Illus.). 1979. 60.00 (ISBN 0-08-023273-6). Pergamon.
Industrial Estates: A Tool for the Development of Backward Areas. 57p. 1973. 2.75 (APO32, APO). Unipub.
Industrial Fasteners Handbook. Ed. by Trade & Technical Press. (Illus.). 115.00x (ISBN 0-85461-062-6). Intl Ideas.
Industrial Fire Hazards. Ed. by Paul Tasner et al. LC 79-66427. (Illus.). 1979. 30.00 (ISBN 0-87765-155-8, SPP-57). Natl Fire Prot.
Industrial Flood Losses: Damage Estimation in the Lehigh Valley. Robert W. Kates. LC 65-22713. (Research Papers Ser.: No. 98). 76p. 1965. pap. 8.00 (ISBN 0-89065-011-X). U Chicago Dept Geog.
Industrial Foodservice & Cafeteria Management. Mickey Warner. LC 72-92378. 1973. 16.95 (ISBN 0-8436-0563-4). CBI Pub.

Industrial Furnaces, 2 vols. W. Trinks. Incl. Vol. 1. Principals of Design & Operation. 5th ed. 1961 (ISBN 0-471-89034-0); Vol. 2. Fuels, Furnace Types & Furnace Equipment: Their Selection & Influence Upon Furnace Operation. 4th ed. 1967 (ISBN 0-471-89068-5). LC 61-11493. 39.95 ea. (Pub. by Wiley-Interscience). Wiley.

Industrial Gas Cleaning. 2nd, rev. ed. Werner Strauss. LC 74-8066. 632p. 1976. text ed. 82.00 (ISBN 0-08-017004-8); pap. 24.00 (ISBN 0-08-019933-X). Pergamon.

Industrial Gases. Norman Booth. LC 72-10293. 1973. pap. text ed. 9.25 (ISBN 0-08-016860-4). Pergamon.

Industrial Geology. Ed. by J. L. Knill. (Illus.). 1979. 29.95x (ISBN 0-19-854520-7). Oxford U Pr.

Industrial Growth & World Trade. Alfred Maizels. 44.50 (ISBN 0-521-05662-4); pap. 11.95x (ISBN 0-521-09527-1). Cambridge U Pr.

Industrial Hazard & Safety Handbook. Ralph W. King & John Magid. (Illus.). 1979. 74.95 (ISBN 0-408-00304-9). Butterworths.

Industrial Health. Jack E. Peterson. (Illus.). 1977. ref. ed. 26.95 (ISBN 0-13-459552-1). P-H.

Industrial History of Dean: With an Introduction to Its Industrial Archaeology. Cyril Hart. (Illus.). 466p. 1971. 22.50 (ISBN 0-7153-5288-1). David & Charles.

Industrial Housing Systems, an Evaluation: Proceedings of the IAHS Cairo Workshop, 1976. A. Fareed & M. El-Hifnawi. (Illus.). 1979. text ed. 60.00 (ISBN 0-08-024236-7). Pergamon.

Industrial Hygiene. A. W. Hart & M. Ells. (Illus.). 400p. 1976. 19.95x (ISBN 0-13-461202-7). P-H.

Industrial Hygiene & Toxicology, 2 vols. 2nd ed. F. A. Patty. LC 58-9220. 1958. Vol. 1, General Principles. o.p.; Vol. 2, Toxicology. 85.00 (ISBN 0-470-67188-2, Pub. by Wiley-Interscience). Wiley.

Industrial Imperialism in Italy, 1908-1915. Richard A. Webster. LC 74-76393. 480p. 1975. 31.50x (ISBN 0-520-02724-8). U of Cal Pr.

Industrial Innovation & Regional Economic Development. Ed. by J. B. Goddard. 120p. 1980. pap. 15.60 (ISBN 0-08-026102-7). Pergamon.

Industrial Invasion of NonMetropolitan America: A Quarter Century of Experience. Ed. by Gene F. Summers et al. LC 75-25026. (Special Studies). 1976. text ed. 26.50 (ISBN 0-275-56080-5). Praeger.

Industrial, Labor & Community Relations. Strong. LC 68-59238. 144p. 1974. pap. 5.40 (ISBN 0-8273-0371-8); instructor's guide 1.60 (ISBN 0-8273-0372-6). Delmar.

Industrial Labor in the USSR. Arcadius Kahan & Blair A. Ruble. (Pergamon Policy Studies). 1979. 42.00 (ISBN 0-08-023701-0); pap. 13.00 (ISBN 0-08-023899-8). Pergamon.

Industrial Location: An Economic Geographical Analysis. 2nd ed. David M. Smith. LC 80-19231. 450p. 1981. text ed. 22.95 (ISBN 0-471-06078-X). Wiley.

Industrial Location & Air Quality Control: A Planning Approach. Jean-Michel Guldmann & Daniel Shefer. LC 80-15380. (Environmental Science & Technology Monograph). 225p. 1980. 32.00 (ISBN 0-471-05377-5, Pub. by Wiley-Interscience). Wiley.

Industrial Location & Regional Systems: Spatial Organization in the Economic Sector. Ed. by John Rees et al. (Illus.). 320p. 1981. text ed. 24.95x (ISBN 0-89789-008-6). J F Bergin.

Industrial Location Processes & Employment Growth. G. Gudgin. 352p. 1978. text ed. 30.75x (ISBN 0-566-00144-6, Pub. by Gower Pub Co England). Renouf.

Industrial Management & Market Research-Conceptual Framework. S. Ranganadha. 1969. 5.50x o.p. (ISBN 0-8426-0061-2). Verry.

Industrial Marketing. B. F. Dodge. 1970. text ed. 18.95 o.p. (ISBN 0-07-017301-X, C). McGraw.

Industrial Marketing. 4th ed. Richard M. Hill et al. 1975. text ed. 19.50 (ISBN 0-256-00010-7). Irwin.

Industrial Marketing: An Analytical Approach to Planning & Execution. 2nd ed. Lawrence Fisher. 270p. 1976. text ed. 29.50x (ISBN 0-220-66292-4, Pub. by Busn Bks England). Renouf.

Industrial Marketing for Results. Richard C. Berry. LC 80-18222. (Illus.). 144p. 1981. text ed. 19.95 (ISBN 0-201-00075-X). A-W.

Industrial Marketing Management. Michael D. Hutt & Thomas W. Speh. LC 80-65803. 576p. 1981. text ed. 18.95 (ISBN 0-03-052656-6). Dryden Pr.

Industrial Microbiology. L. E. Casida. LC 68-22302. 1968. 35.95 (ISBN 0-471-14060-0). Wiley.

Industrial Model Building. Gary Lamit. (Illus.). 528p. 1981. text ed. 38.00 (ISBN 0-13-461566-2). P-H.

Industrial Movement & Regional Development: The British Case. M. E. Sant. 268p. 1975. text ed. 23.00 (ISBN 0-08-017965-7). Pergamon.

Industrial Movement: Experience in the United States & the United Kingdom. Peter Townroe. 1979. text ed. 38.65x (ISBN 0-566-00279-5, Pub. by Gower Pub Co England). Renouf.

Industrial New Product Development: A Manual for the 1980's. J. W. Carson & T. Rickards. LC 79-65781. 1979. 32.95x (ISBN 0-470-26821-2). Halsted Pr.

Industrial Noise Control. Bruce Fader. 320p. 1981. 29.95 (ISBN 0-471-06007-0, Pub. by Wiley Interscience). Wiley.

Industrial Noise Control Handbook. Paul N. Cheremisinoff & Peter P. Cheremisinoff. LC 76-46023. 1977. 37.50 (ISBN 0-250-40144-4). Ann Arbor Science.

Industrial Order & Social Policy. R. Peterson. 1973. pap. 8.95 ref. ed. (ISBN 0-13-464297-X). P-H.

Industrial Organic Chemicals in Perspective: Technology, Formulation & Use, Pt. 2. Harold Wittcoff & Bryan G. Reuben. 1980. 45.00 (ISBN 0-471-05780-0, Pub. by Wiley-Interscience). Wiley.

Industrial Organization & Prices. 2nd ed. James V. Koch. (Illus.). 1980. text ed. 17.95 (ISBN 0-13-462481-5). P-H.

Industrial Organization in Japan. Richard E. Caves & Masu Uekusa. 1976. 10.95 (ISBN 0-8157-1324-X); pap. 4.95 (ISBN 0-8157-1323-1). Brookings.

Industrial Organization: Theory & Practice. 2nd ed. Joan Woodward. (Illus.). 324p. 1981. 42.00 (ISBN 0-19-874122-7); pap. 20.00 (ISBN 0-19-874123-5). Oxford U Pr.

Industrial Peacemaking. Ann Douglas. LC 62-14463. (Illus.). viii, 675p. 1962. 27.50x (ISBN 0-231-02487-8). Columbia U Pr.

Industrial Plant Location. James E. Rowe. (Public Administation Ser.: Bibliography P-575). 52p. 1980. pap. 5.50. Vance Biblios.

Industrial Plastics. Ronald J. Baird. LC 75-139249. (Illus.). 1976. text ed. 10.86 (ISBN 0-87006-213-1). Goodheart.

Industrial Policies & Technology Transfers Between East & West. Ed. by C. T. Saunders. (East-West European Economic Interaction,Workshop Paper: Vol 3). (Illus.). 1978. pap. 33.70 o.p. (ISBN 0-387-81456-6). Springer-Verlag.

Industrial Policies in Western Europe. Ed. by Steven J. Warnecke & Ezra N. Suleiman. LC 75-23998. 266p. 1975. text ed. 32.50 (ISBN 0-275-01670-6). Praeger.

Industrial Politics. Robert Currie. LC 78-40480. 1979. 37.50x (ISBN 0-19-827419-X). Oxford U Pr.

Industrial Pollution Control: Vol. 1, Agro-Industries. E. J. Middlebrooks. LC 79-10573. (Environmental Science & Technology: Texts & Monographs: Vol. 1). 1979. 27.00 (ISBN 0-471-04779-1, Pub. by Wiley-Interscience). Wiley.

Industrial Price Policies & Economic Progress. Edwin G. Nourse & Horace B. Drury. (Brookings Institution Reprint Ser). (Illus.). Repr. of 1938 ed. lib. bdg. 29.50x (ISBN 0-697-00177-6). Irvington.

Industrial Pricing in the United Kingdom. K. Coutts et al. LC 77-8976. (Applied Economics Monograph: No. 26). (Illus.). 1978. 31.50 (ISBN 0-521-21725-3). Cambridge U Pr.

Industrial Process Control Systems. Dale R. Patrick & Stephen W. Fardo. LC 79-65744. 1979. pap. 13.95 (ISBN 0-672-21625-6). Sams.

Industrial Production: Historical Statistics, 1960-1975. 1976. 10.00 o.p. (ISBN 92-64-01562-0). OECD.

Industrial Products Master Catalog. write for info. Herman Pub.

Industrial Psychology. J. M. Fraser. 1962. 16.50 (ISBN 0-08-009649-2); pap. 7.75 (ISBN 0-08-009648-4). Pergamon.

Industrial Psychology. 6th ed. Ernest J. McCormick & Joseph Tiffin. (Psychology Ser.). 624p. 1974. ref. ed. 17.95 o.p. (ISBN 0-13-463125-0). P-H.

Industrial Psychology: Its Theoretical & Social Foundations. 3rd ed. Milton L. Blum & James C. Naylor. 1968. text ed. 22.95 scp o.p. (ISBN 0-06-040781-6, HarpC); tchrs' manual avail. o.p. (ISBN 0-06-360781-6). Har-Row.

Industrial Radiology Techniques. R. Halmshaw. (Wykeham Technology Ser.: No. 3). 1971. 14.00x (ISBN 0-8448-1174-2). Crane Russak Co.

Industrial Relations. B. Cooper & A. Bartlett. 1976. pap. 14.95x (ISBN 0-434-90261-6). Intl Ideas.

Industrial Relations, 44 vols. (British Parliamentary Papers Ser.). 1971. Set. 3789.00x (ISBN 0-7165-1451-6, Pub. by Irish Academic Pr Ireland). Biblio Dist.

Industrial Relations & Personnel Management: Selected Information Sources. Martha Soltow & Jo A. Sokkar. LC 78-31795. 294p. 1979. lib. bdg. 12.00 (ISBN 0-8108-1203-7). Scarecrow.

Industrial Relations & the Library Manager. M. Wallis. Ed. by A. Wilson. (Library Association Management Pamplet Ser.). 1980. pap. 8.95x (ISBN 0-85365-542-1, Pub. by Lib Assn Ehgland). Oryx Pr.

Industrial Relations in Construction. W. S. Hilton. 1969. 22.00 (ISBN 0-08-013040-2); pap. 10.75 (ISBN 0-08-013039-9). Pergamon.

Industrial Relations in Fleet Street. Keith Sisson. 1975. 17.50x o.p. (ISBN 0-631-16530-4, Pub. by Basil Blackwell). Biblio Dist.

Industrial Relations in Nigeria: Development & Practice. Tayo Fashoyin. (Illus.). 208p. 1981. pap. text ed. 11.95 (ISBN 0-582-64250-7). Longman.

Industrial Relations in Nineteenth Century Britain. P. S. Bagwell. 106p. 1974. 15.00x (ISBN 0-7165-2215-2, Pub. by Irish Academic Pr Ireland). Biblio Dist.

Industrial Relations in the Chemical Industry. Colin Gill et al. 1978. text ed. 30.00x (ISBN 0-566-00215-9, Pub. by Gower Pub Co England). Renouf.

Industrial Relations in the Public Sector: The Firemen. N. F. Dufty. (Illus.). 1980. 24.25x (ISBN 0-7022-1408-6). U of Queensland Pr.

Industrial Relations in the San Francisco Bay Area, 1900-1918. Robert E. Knight. (Institute of Industrial Relations, UC Berkeley). 1960. 28.50x (ISBN 0-520-00658-5). U of Cal Pr.

Industrial Relations Systems. John T. Dunlop. LC 77-24354. (Arcturus Books Paperbacks). 412p. 1977. pap. 8.95x (ISBN 0-8093-0850-9). S Ill U Pr.

Industrial Resources of Ireland. Robert J. Kane. 456p. Date not set. Repr. of 1845 ed. 31.00x (ISBN 0-686-28342-2, Pub. by Irish Academic Pr). Biblio Dist.

Industrial Revolution. Neil Grant. LC 73-5705. (First Bks). (Illus.). (gr. 7-12). 1973. PLB 4.90 o.p. (ISBN 0-531-00808-8). Watts.

Industrial Revolution, 5 pts. Incl. Pt. 1. Children's Employment, 15 vols. Set. 1143.00x (ISBN 0-686-01154-6); Pt. 2. Design, 4 vols. Set. 342.00x (ISBN 0-686-01155-4); Pt. 3. Factories, 31 vols. Set. 2548.00x (ISBN 0-686-01156-2); Pt. 4. Textiles, 10 vols. Set. 783.00x (ISBN 0-686-01157-0); Pt. 5. Trade, 5 vols. Set. 351.00x (ISBN 0-686-01158-9). (British Parliamentary Papers Ser.). 1971 (Pub. by Irish Academic Pr Ireland). Biblio Dist.

Industrial Revolution. Diana Knox. Ed. by Malcolm Yapp et al. (World History Ser.). (Illus.). (gr. 10). pap. text ed. 1.95 (ISBN 0-89908-133-9); pap. text ed. 2.75 (ISBN 0-89908-108-8). Greenhaven.

Industrial Revolution & British Overseas Trade. Ralph Davis. (Illus.). 1978. text ed. 20.50x (ISBN 0-391-00925-7, Leicester); pap. text ed. 9.75x (ISBN 0-391-00927-3). Humanities.

Industrial Rheology. P. Sherman. 1970. 58.50 o.s.i. (ISBN 0-12-639950-6). Acad Pr.

Industrial Robots: Applications, Vol. II. Ed. by William Tanner. LC 78-71001. (Manufacturing Update Ser). 1979. text ed. 29.00x (ISBN 0-87263-046-3). SME.

Industrial Robots: Fundamentals, Vol. I. new ed. Ed. by William Tanner. LC 78-71001. (Manufacturing Update Ser.). (Illus.). 1978. text ed. 29.00x (ISBN 0-87263-045-5). SME.

Industrial Safety. 3rd ed. Roland P. Blake. 1963. ref. ed. 15.95 (ISBN 0-13-463133-1). P-H.

Industrial Safety Techniques. R. A. Cole. 1975. 23.95 o.p. (ISBN 0-471-01424-9). Wiley.

Industrial Security for Strikes, Riots & Disasters. Raymond M. Momboisse. 516p. 1977. 24.75 (ISBN 0-398-01325-X). C C Thomas.

Industrial Security Management. Harvey Burstein. LC 77-12762. 1977. 25.95 (ISBN 0-275-24050-9). Praeger.

Industrial Slavery in the Old South. Robert S. Starobin. LC 72-112894. 1970. 14.95 (ISBN 0-19-500113-3). Oxford U Pr.

Industrial Society: Structures, Roles & Relations. Edward B. Harvey. 1975. text ed. 18.50x (ISBN 0-256-01685-2). Dorsey.

Industrial Structure & Market Conduct. J. F. Pickering. 335p. 1974. bds. 36.00x (ISBN 0-85520-040-5, Pub by Martin Robertson England); pap. 14.95x (ISBN 0-85520-039-1). Biblio Dist.

Industrial Systems: Planning, Analysis, Control. David D. Bedworth. 510p. 1973. 25.95 (ISBN 0-8260-0867-4). Wiley.

Industrial Technology Transfer. M. J. Certon & H. F. Davidson. 480p. 1977. 45.50x (ISBN 90-286-0426-X). Sijthoff & Noordhoff.

Industrial Triangle. Colvin. 5.50 o.p. (ISBN 0-686-00167-2). Columbia Graphs.

Industrial Uses of Large Radiation Sources, 2 vols. (Illus., Eng., Fr. & Rus.). 1963. Vol. 1. 16.25 (ISBN 92-0-060263-0, IAEA); Vol. 2. 11.00 (ISBN 92-0-060363-7). Unipub.

Industrial Uses of Starch & Its Derivatives. Ed. by J. A. Radley. 1976. 63.30x (ISBN 0-85334-691-7). Intl Ideas.

Industrial Waste Water & Solid Waste Engineering. Compiled By Chemical Engineering. LC 80-12608. 376p. 1980. pap. 23.50 (ISBN 0-07-010694-0, Chem Eng). McGraw.

Industrial Waste Water Management. Ed. by S. E. Jorgensen. (Studies in Environmental Science: Vol. 5). 388p. 1979. 46.50 (ISBN 0-686-62655-9). Elsevier.

Industrial Water Pollution: Origins, Characteristics & Treatment. Nelson L. Nemerow. LC 76-46612. 1978. text ed. 28.95 (ISBN 0-201-05246-6). A-W.

Industrial Waxes, 2 vols. H. Bennett. Incl. Vol. 1. Natural Waxes; Synthetic Waxes (ISBN 0-8206-0224-8); Vol. 2. Compounded Waxes; Technology (ISBN 0-8206-0225-6). 1975. 30.00 ea. (ISBN 0-686-67154-6). Chem Pub.

Industrial Welding Procedures. Frank R. Schell & Bill Matlock. LC 77-80481. 1979. text ed. 12.00 (ISBN 0-8273-1696-8); instructor's guide 1.60 (ISBN 0-8273-1697-6). Delmar.

Industrialisation & the Basis for Trade. R. A. Batchelor et al. LC 79-41582. (Economic & Social Studies: No. 32). 350p. 1980. 39.50 (ISBN 0-521-23302-X). Cambridge U Pr.

Industrialised Embayments & Their Environmental Problems: a Case Study of Swansea Bay: Proceedings of an Interdisciplinary Symposium Held at University College, Swansea, 26-28 Sept. 1979. Ed. by M. B. Collins et al. LC 80-40507. (Illus.). 608p. 1980. 84.00 (ISBN 0-08-023992-7). Pergamon.

Industrialism. Barry Turner. LC 73-94222. (Aspects of Modern Sociology Ser). 1975. text ed. 10.95x o.p. (ISBN 0-582-48058-2). Longman.

Industrialization & Developing Countries. 4th rev. ed. Alan B. Mountjoy. 1975. text ed. 11.75x (ISBN 0-09-123620-7, Hutchinson U Lib); pap. text ed. 6.50x (ISBN 0-09-123621-5, Hutchinson U Lib). Humanities.

Industrialization in a Latin American Common Market. Martin Carnoy. LC 73-161596. 1972. 11.95 (ISBN 0-8157-1294-4). Brookings.

Industrialization in Concrete Building Construction. 1975. pap. 21.25 (ISBN 0-685-85128-1, SP-48) (ISBN 0-685-85129-X). ACI.

Industrialization in Indonesia: Developments & Prospects. Peter McCawley. (Development Studies Centre - Occasional Paper: No. 13). (Orig.). 1980. pap. text ed. 3.95 (ISBN 0-7081-1593-4, 0412, Pub. by ANUP Australia). Bks Australia.

Industrialization in Nineteenth Century Europe. Tom Kemp. 1969. pap. text ed. 12.50x (ISBN 0-582-48025-6). Humanities.

Industrialization of Egypt 1939-1973: Policy & Performance. Robert Mabro. 1976. 29.95x (ISBN 0-19-828405-5). Oxford U Pr.

Industrialization of Japan. John Roberts. LC 75-158425. (First Bks). (Illus.). (gr. 5-7). 1971. PLB 4.90 o.p. (ISBN 0-531-00747-2). Watts.

Industrialization of Russia: An Historical Perspective. William L. Blackwell. LC 79-107304. (AHM Europe Since 1500 Ser.). 1970. pap. 5.95x (ISBN 0-88295-703-1). AHM Pub.

Industrie Photographique en France. Bernard Engrand. Ed. by Peter C. Bunnell & Robert A. Sobieszek. LC 78-67656. (Sources of Modern Photography Ser.). (Fr.). 1979. Repr. of 1934 ed. lib. bdg. 15.00x (ISBN 0-405-09897-9). Arno.

Industry & Labour: Class Struggle at Work & Monopoly Capitalism. Andrew L. Friedman. 1977. text ed. 26.00x (ISBN 0-333-23031-0); pap. text ed. 12.50x (ISBN 0-333-23032-9). Humanities.

Industry & the Photographic Image: One Hundred & Sixty Five Great Prints from 1845 to the Present. Jack F. Hurley. (Illus.). 160p. 1980. pap. 7.95 (ISBN 0-486-23980-2). Dover.

Industry in Crisis: Mexican-United States Cooperation in the Control of Foot-And-Mouth Disease. Manuel A. Machado, Jr. (U. C. Publ. in History: Vol. 80). 1968. pap. 6.50x (ISBN 0-520-09191-4). U of Cal Pr.

Industry Influence in Federal Regulatory Agencies. Paul J. Quirk. LC 80-8571. 264p. 1981. 18.50x (ISBN 0-691-09388-1); pap. 4.95x (ISBN 0-691-02823-0). Princeton U Pr.

Industry: People & the Machine. The Educational Research Council. (Concepts & Inquiry Ser). (gr. 4). 1975. pap. text ed. 7.24 (ISBN 0-205-04438-7, 8044384); tchrs'. guide 7.24 (ISBN 0-205-04439-5, 8044392). Allyn.

Industry, Prices & Markets. W. Duncan Reekie. LC 79-14543. 166p. 1979. 18.95x (ISBN 0-470-26709-7). Halsted Pr.

Industry Survey of the Need for a Federal Grant-Assisted Geothermal Demonstration Power Plant. Edgar Butler. (Illus.). 36p. 1978. pap. 3.50 (ISBN 0-934412-75-8). Geothermal.

Industry's Democratic Revolution. Charles Levinson. (Ruskin House Ser in Trade Union Studies). 1974. text ed. 13.50x o.p. (ISBN 0-04-331062-1). Allen Unwin.

Indy Five Hundred. Ron Dorson. 1974. 9.95 (ISBN 0-87880-025-5). Norton.

Indy: The World's Fastest Carnival Ride. Dan Gerber. LC 76-28812. (Illus.). 1977. pap. 8.95 o.p. (ISBN 0-13-464156-6). P-H.

Inelastic Light Scattering: Proceedings. U. S.-Japan Seminar or Inelastic Light Scattering, Santa Monica, California. January 22-25, 1979. Ed. by E. Burstein & H. Kawamura. 124p. 1980. 23.00 (ISBN 0-08-025425-X). Pergamon.

Inelastic Scattering of Neutrons in Solids & Liquids: 1962, 2 vols. (Illus., Eng., Fr. & Rus.). 1963. Vol. 1. 22.00 (ISBN 92-0-030363-3, ISP62-1, IAEA); Vol. 2. 23.75 (ISBN 92-0-030463-X, ISP62-2). Unipub.

Inelastic Scattering of Neutrons: 1964, 2 vols. (Illus., Eng., Fr. & Rus.). 1965. Vol. 1. 18.75 (ISBN 92-0-030365-X, IAEA); Vol. 2. 22.00 (ISBN 92-0-030465-6). Unipub.

Inelastic Steel Structures. Stuart R. Daniels. LC 65-25460. (Illus.). 1966. 12.50x (ISBN 0-87049-064-8). U of Tenn Pr.

Inequalities. 2nd ed. Godfrey H. Hardy et al. 1952. 42.00 (ISBN 0-521-05206-8). Cambridge U Pr.

Inequality Among Men. Andre Beteille. (Pavilion Ser.). 1977. 36.00x (ISBN 0-631-17410-9, Pub. by Basil Blackwell); pap. 12.00x (ISBN 0-631-17420-6, Pub. by Basil Blackwell). Biblio Dist.

Inequality & Economic Development in Malaysia. Donald R. Snodgrass. (East Asian Social Science Monographs). (Illus.). 340p. 1981. 34.95 (ISBN 0-19-580431-7); pap. 17.95 (ISBN 0-19-580442-2). Oxford U Pr.

Inequality & Heterogeneity: A Primitive Theory of Social Structure. Peter M. Blau. LC 77-70272. (Illus.). 1977. 15.95 (ISBN 0-02-903660-7). Free Pr.

Inequality & Stratification in the U. S. Robert A. Rothman. (P-H Ser. in Sociology). (Illus.). 1978. pap. 10.95 ref. ed. (ISBN 0-13-464305-4). P-H.

Inequality: Essays on the Political Economy of Social Welfare. Ed. by Allan Moscovitch & Glenn Drover. (Studies in the Political Economy of Canada). 408p. 1981. 30.00x (ISBN 0-8020-2403-3); pap. 10.00 (ISBN 0-8020-6426-4). U of Toronto Pr.

Inequality in an Age of Decline. Paul Blumberg. 250p. 1980. 15.95 (ISBN 0-19-502804-X). Oxford U Pr.

Inequality in Classroom Learning: Schooling & Democratic Citizenship. Edward P. Morgan. LC 77-5577. (Special Studies). 1977. text ed. 26.50 (ISBN 0-275-24510-1). Praeger.

Inequality in Local Government Services: A Case Study of Neighborhood Roads. Andrew Boots et al. 1972. pap. 1.50 o.p. (ISBN 0-87766-063-8, 15000). Urban Inst.

Inequality of Man. H. J. Eysenck. 1975. 10.95 (ISBN 0-912736-16-X). EDITS Pubs.

Inequality of Pay. E. H. Phelps Brown. LC 76-7768. 23.75x (ISBN 0-520-03380-9). U of Cal Pr.

Inequality: Privilege & Poverty in America. J. Turner & C. Starnes. 1976. 12.95 (ISBN 0-87620-419-1); pap. text ed. 9.95 (ISBN 0-685-93530-2). P-H.

Inert Gases: Model Systems for Science. B. L. Smith & J. P. Webb. (Wykeham Science Ser: No. 16). 1971. 9.95x (ISBN 0-8448-1118-1). Crane Russak Co.

Inertia of Fear. Valentin Turchin. Tr. by Guy Daniels from Russian. LC 80-36818. 336p. 1981. 16.95 (ISBN 0-231-04622-7). Columbia U Pr.

Inertia of the Vacuum: A New Foundation for Theoretical Physics. Donald R. McGregor. 96p. 1981. 6.00 (ISBN 0-682-49722-3). Exposition.

Inertial Navigation Systems Analysis. Kenneth R. Britting. LC 70-168635. 1971. 27.50 (ISBN 0-471-10485-X, Pub. by Wiley-Interscience). Wiley.

Inexpensive Justice: Self Representation in the Small Claims Court. Robert L. Spurrier, Jr. (National University Publications, Multi-Disciplinary Ser. in the Law). 1980. 9.95 (ISBN 0-8046-9262-9). Kennikat.

Inextinguishable Flame: Shelley Poetic & Creative Practice. Dharni D. Baskiyar. (Salzburg Studies in English Literature: Romantic Reassessment Ser.: No. 68). 1977. pap. text ed. 25.00x (ISBN 0-391-01315-7). Humanities.

Infa Press & Advertisers Year Book 1979. 17th ed. 318p. 1979. 25.00x (ISBN 0-8002-2737-9). Intl Pubns Serv.

Infamous Army. Georgette Heyer. 1977. pap. 1.75 o.p. (ISBN 0-449-23263-8, Crest). Fawcett.

Infamous Woman: The Life of George Sand. Joseph Barry. LC 76-5335. 1978. pap. 5.95 o.p. (ISBN 0-385-13366-9, Anchor Pr). Doubleday.

Infancy & Caregiving. Janet Gonzalez-Mena & Dianne W. Eyer. LC 79-91838. (Illus.). 163p. (Orig.). 1980. pap. text ed. 6.95 (ISBN 0-87484-515-7). Mayfield Pub.

Infancy & Childhood Development & Its Contexts. Barbara M. Newman & Philip R. Newman. LC 77-10455. 1978. text ed. 21.95x (ISBN 0-471-02212-8); tchrs. manual avail. (ISBN 0-471-03802-4). Wiley.

Infant & Child Feeding. Ed. by Jenny T. Bond et al. (Nutrition Foundation Ser.). 1981. write for info. (ISBN 0-12-113350-8). Acad Pr.

Infant Communication: Cry & Early Speech. Ed. by Thomas Murry & John Murry. (Illus.). 342p. 1980. text ed. 28.95 (ISBN 0-933014-62-7). College-Hill.

Infant Crafts for School & Home. Margaret Norton. (Illus.). 1975. 8.50 (ISBN 0-7137-0671-6, Pub by Blandford Pr England). Sterling.

Infant Cry: A Spectographic & Auditory Analysis. O. Wasz-Hoeckert et al. (Clinics in Developmental Medicine Ser. No. 29). 42p. 1968. 12.00 (ISBN 0-685-24737-6). Lippincott.

Infant Culture. Jane F. Jackson & Joseph Jackson. LC 78-4351. 1978. 9.95 o.s.i. (ISBN 0-690-01670-0, TYC-T). T Y Crowell.

Infant Death: An Analysis by Maternal Risk & Health Care. Health Services Research Study, Institute of Medicine. Orig. Title: Maternal & Infant Health Services. (Illus.). 192p. 1973. pap. 8.50 (ISBN 0-309-02119-7). Natl Acad Pr.

Infant Education. Ed. by Bettye Caldwell & Donald Stedman. 1977. 9.95 (ISBN 0-8027-9042-9); pap. 8.95 (ISBN 0-8027-7110-6). Walker & Co.

Infant Social Cognition: Empirical & Theoretical Considerations. Ed. by Michael E. Lamb & Lonnie R. Sherrod. LC 80-21137. 438p. 1981. text ed. 29.95 (ISBN 0-89859-058-2). L Erlbaum Assocs.

Infanticide & the Value of Life. Ed. by Marvin Kohl. LC 77-26376. 252p. 1978. 15.95 (ISBN 0-87975-100-2). Prometheus Bks.

Infantile Autism: Proceedings. Don W. Churchill. (Illus.). 360p. 1971. pap. 29.50 photocopy ed. (ISBN 0-398-00307-6). C C Thomas.

Infantile Autism: The Syndrome & Its Implications for a Neural Theory of Behavior. Bernard Rimland. (Century Psychology Ser.). 1981. Repr. of 1964 ed. text ed. 18.50x (ISBN 0-8290-0061-5). Irvington.

Infantile Autistic Behaviour & Experience: A New Clinical Picture. J. J. Prick. (Modern Approaches to the Diagnosis & Instruction of Multi-Handicapped Children: Vol. 1). 102p. 1971. text ed. 21.50 (ISBN 90-237-4101-3, Pub. by Swets Pub Serv Holland). Swets North Am.

Infantile Disorder? The Crisis & Decline of the New Left. Nigel Young. LC 76-30272. 1978. lib. bdg. 27.50x (ISBN 0-89158-549-4). Westview.

Infantile Spasms. P. M. Jeavons & B. D. Bower. (Clinics in Developmental Medicine Ser. No. 15). 82p. 1964. 4.50 o.p. (ISBN 0-685-24736-8). Lippincott.

Infantile Spasms. Joseph R. Lacy & J. Kiffin Penry. LC 76-25378. 1976. pap. 15.50 (ISBN 0-89004-018-4). Raven.

Infantry Regiments of the US Army. James A. Sawicki. LC 80-53362. (Illus.). 500p. 1981. 24.95 (ISBN 0-9602404-3-8); pap. 16.95 (ISBN 0-9602404-4-6). Wyvern.

Infantry Uniforms of Britain & the Commonwealth in Color, 1855-1939. Robert Wilkinson-Latham & Christopher Wilkinson-Latham. LC 79-95304. (World Uniforms in Color Ser). 1971. 8.90 (ISBN 0-02-628730-7). Macmillan.

Infantry Weapons Nineteen Eighty to Nineteen Eighty-One. Archer. 1980. 135.00 (ISBN 0-531-03936-6). Watts.

Infantry Weapons Nineteen Seventy-Nine to Nineteen Eighty. Archer. 1980. 89.50 (ISBN 0-531-03905-6). Watts.

Infants', Girls', & Boys' Wear. Fairchild Market Research Division. (Fairchild Fact File Ser.). 1979. pap. 10.00 (ISBN 0-87005-326-4). Fairchild.

Infants, Mothers, & Doctors. Eugene B. Gallagher. LC 78-2071. 1978. 19.95 (ISBN 0-669-02269-1). Lexington Bks.

Infants of the Spring: A Novel. Wallace Thurman. LC 78-16906. (Lost American Fiction Ser.). 314p. 1979. Repr. of 1932 ed. 13.95 (ISBN 0-8093-0864-9). S Ill U Pr.

Infaquatics: A Parents Guide to Swimmimg. John L. Murray. LC 80-82072. (Illus.). 248p. (Orig.). 1980. pap. text ed. 6.95 (ISBN 0-918438-59-4). Leisure Pr.

Infaquatics: Teaching Kids to Swim. John L. Murray. (Illus.). 224p. 1981. Repr. of 1980 ed. pap. 6.95 (ISBN 0-688-00476-8, Quill). Morrow.

Infection & Immunology in the Rheumatic Diseases. D. C. Dumonde & M. R. Path. (Blackwell Scientific Pubns.). (Illus.). 1976. 95.00 (ISBN 0-397-60361-4). Mosby.

Infection & the Compromised Host: Clinical Correlations & Therapeutic Approaches. 2nd ed. (Illus.). 281p. 1981. 29.00 (ISBN 0-686-69563-1, 0072-1). Williams & Wilkins.

Infection Control in the Hospital. 4th ed. LC 79-9862. (Illus.). 256p. 1979. pap. 16.25 (ISBN 0-87258-262-0, 2117). Am Hospital.

Infection Control Manual. 2nd ed. C. Meshelany. 1979. 49.95 (ISBN 0-87489-232-5). Med Economics.

Infection in Surgery: Basic & Clinical Aspects. Watts. 1981. text ed. 65.00 (ISBN 0-443-02246-1). Churchill.

Infection in Surgery: Basic & Clinical Aspects. J. McK. Watts et al. (Symposium Ser.). (Illus.). 488p. 1981. lib. bdg. 65.00 (ISBN 0-443-02246-1). Churchill.

Infection: Prevention & Control. 2nd ed. Elaine C. Dubay & Reba D. Grubb. LC 77-9512. (Illus.). 1978. 11.50 (ISBN 0-8016-1463-5). Mosby.

Infections in Cancer Chemotherapy. Ed. by J. Klastersky. 1976. text ed. 27.50 (ISBN 0-08-019964-X). Pergamon.

Infections in Obstetrics & Gynecology. Lester T. Hibbard. LC 80-18670. (Discussions in Patient Management Ser.). 1980. pap. 8.00 (ISBN 0-87488-896-4). Med Exam.

Infections of the Fetus & the Newborn Infant: Proceedings. Symposium by the New York University Medical Center & the National Foundation-March of Dimes, New York City, Mar. 1975. Ed. by Saul Krugman & Anne A. Gershon. LC 75-13856. (Progress in Clinical & Biological Research: Vol. 3). 204p. 1975. 23.00x (ISBN 0-8451-0003-3). A R Liss.

Infections of the Gastrointestinal Tract: Microbiology, Pathophysiology & Clinical Features. Herbert L. Dupont & Larry K. Pickering. (Current Topics in Infectious Disease Ser.). (Illus.). 266p. 1980. 24.50 (ISBN 0-306-40409-5, Plenum Med Bk). Plenum Pub.

Infectious & Parasitic Diseases of the Intestine - Discussions in Patient Management. Hobart A. Reimann & Kerrison Juniper, Jr. 1977. spiral bdg. 8.50 (ISBN 0-87488-880-8). Med Exam.

Infectious Disease for the House Officer. James C. Allen. (House Officer Ser.). (Illus.). 200p. 1981. price not set softcover (ISBN 0-683-00069-1). Williams & Wilkins.

Infectious Disease Reviews, Vol VI. Ed. by William J. Holloway. LC 78-50693. (Illus.). 192p. 1981. monograph 23.75 (ISBN 0-87993-151-5). Futura Pub.

Infectious Diseases. Martin J. Raff. (Medical Examination Review Bks.: Vol. 30). 1974. spiral bdg. 16.50 (ISBN 0-87488-147-1). Med Exam.

Infectious Diseases Case Studies. 2nd ed. C. Glenn Cobbs & Frank M. Griffin, Jr. 1974. spiral bdg. 14.00 (ISBN 0-87488-011-4). Med Exam.

Infectious Diseases: Epidemiology & Clinical Practice. 3rd ed. A. B. Christie. (Illus.). 1981. text ed. 95.00 (ISBN 0-443-02263-1). Churchill.

Infectious Diseases: Focus on Clinical Diagnosis. Haragopal Thadepalli. pap. 24.50 (ISBN 0-87488-830-1). Med Exam.

Infectious Diseases in Obstetrics & Gynecology. Ed. by Gilles R. Monif. (Illus.). 1974. text ed. 37.00x (ISBN 0-06-141795-5, Harper Medical). Har-Row.

Infectious Diseases of Children. 7th ed. Saul Krugman. LC 80-24696. (Illus.). 607p. 1980. text ed. 39.95 (ISBN 0-8016-2796-6). Mosby.

Infectious Diseases of the Central Nervous System. Ed. by Richard A. Thompson & J. R. Green. LC 74-79192. (Advances in Neurology Ser: Vol. 6). 1974. 34.50 (ISBN 0-911216-82-0). Raven.

Infectious Diseases of Wild Mammals. 2nd ed. Ed. by John W. Davis et al. 436p. 1981. text ed. 35.00 (ISBN 0-8138-0445-0). Iowa St U Pr.

Inferences of Patients' Pain & Psychological Distress: Studies of Nursing Behaviors. Joel R. Davitz & Lois L. Davitz. (Illus.). 1980. text ed. 25.00 (ISBN 0-8261-3360-6). Springer Pub.

Inferential Statistics: A Contemporary Approach. Richard P. Runyon. LC 76-23991. (Illus.). 1977. pap. 7.95 (ISBN 0-201-06653-X). A-W.

Inferential Statistics for Geographers: An Introduction. G. B. Norcliffe. LC 77-9427. 1977. 24.95 (ISBN 0-470-99206-9). Halsted Pr.

Inferential Statistics for Sociologists: An Introduction. Herman J. Loether & Donald G. McTavish. 304p. 1974. pap. text ed. 10.45x (ISBN 0-205-03737-2, 8137374). Allyn.

Inferior Olivary Nucleus: Anatomy & Physiology. Ed. by Jacques Courville et al. 407p. 1980. text ed. 49.00 (ISBN 0-89004-414-7). Raven.

Infernal Paradise: Mexico & the Modern English Novel. Ronald G. Walker. LC 75-46046. 1978. 20.00x (ISBN 0-520-03197-0). U of Cal Pr.

Inferno! Fourteen Fiery Tragedies of Our Time. Hall Butler. (Illus.). 240p. 1975. 9.95 o.p. (ISBN 0-8092-8352-2). Contemp Bks.

Infertile Couple. Ed. by R. J. Pepperell et al. (Illus.). 320p. 1980. text ed. 25.00x (ISBN 0-443-01727-1). Churchill.

Infertility, a Practical Guide for the Physician. University of North Carolina at Chapel Hill, Dept. of OB-GYN. Ed. by Mary G. Hammond & Luther M. Talbert. LC 80-84920. (Illus.). 128p. (Orig.). 1981. 14.95x (ISBN 0-938938-00-2, 810-M*O-001). Health Sci Consort.

Infidel Doctor of Salem. Effie M. Williams. 52p. pap. 0.40; pap. 1.00 3 copies. Faith Pub Hse.

Infield Flash. Robert S. Bowen. LC 69-14320. (gr. 7-12). 1969. 6.75 o.p. (ISBN 0-688-41007-3); PLB 6.48 (ISBN 0-688-51007-8). Lothrop.

Infielders. Jay H. Smith. LC 76-8465. (Stars of the Nl & Al Ser.). (Illus.). (gr. 4-12). 1976. PLB 7.95 (ISBN 0-87191-517-0). Creative Ed.

Infiltration: The SS & German Armament. Albert Speer. Tr. by Joachim Neugrosschel. 604p. 1981. 15.00 (ISBN 0-02-612800-4). Macmillan.

Infinite-Dimensional Lie Algebras. R. K. Amayo & I. Stewart. 436p. 1974. 62.50x (ISBN 90-286-0144-9). Sijthoff & Noordhoff.

Infinite Dreams. Joe Haldeman. 1979. pap. 2.25 (ISBN 0-380-47605-3, 47605). Avon.

Infinite Loop Spaces. J. Frank Adams. (Annals of Mathematics Studies Ser.: No. 90). 1978. 15.50x (ISBN 0-691-08207-3); pap. 5.50 (ISBN 0-691-08206-5). Princeton U Pr.

Infinite Power for Richer Living. Murphy. pap. 3.95 (ISBN 0-13-464396-8, Parker). P-H.

Infinite Sequences & Series. Konrad Knopp. Tr. by Frederick Bagemihl. 1956. pap. text ed. 3.00 (ISBN 0-486-60153-6). Dover.

Infinite Summer. Christopher Priest. 1981. pap. 2.75 (ISBN 0-440-14067-6). Dell.

Infinite Turbulence. Henri Michaux. 1980. 12.95 (ISBN 0-7145-1018-1). Riverrun NY.

Infinite Worlds of Giordano Bruno. Antoinette M. Paterson. (Amer. Lec. in Philosophy Ser.). (Illus.). 240p. 1970. 19.75 (ISBN 0-398-01452-3). C C Thomas.

Infinitely Happy. G. Arthur Keough. LC 78-21952. (Horizon Ser.). 1978. pap. 4.50 (ISBN 0-8127-0213-1). Southern Pub.

Infinity Box: A Collection of Speculative Fiction. Kate Wilhelm. LC 74-15894. 318p. (YA) 1975. 8.95 o.s.i. (ISBN 0-06-014653-2, HarpT). Har-Row.

Infinity I. (Agni Yoga Ser.). 1956. flexible cover 9.00x (ISBN 0-933574-05-3). Agni Yoga Soc.

Infinity II. (Agni Yoga Ser.). 1957. flexible cover 9.00x (ISBN 0-933574-06-1). Agni Yoga Soc.

Inflammation Mechanisms & Their Impact on Therapy. Ed. by I. L. Bonta et al. (Agents & Actions Supplements: No. 3). (Illus.). 192p. 1977. pap. text ed. 60.00 (ISBN 3-7643-0913-X). Birkhauser.

Inflammatory & Neoplastic Disease of the Gastrointestinal Tract, No. 18. Ed. by John H. Yardley & Basil C. Morson. International Academy of Pathology. 1977. 26.00 (ISBN 0-683-09317-7). Williams & Wilkins.

Inflammatory Bowel Disease. 2nd ed. Joseph B. Kirsner. Ed. by Roy G. Shorter. LC 79-8884. (Illus.). 693p. 1980. 74.00 (ISBN 0-8121-0698-9). Lea & Febiger.

Inflammatory Bowel Diseases. Ed. by Burton I. Korelitz. 332p. 1981. text ed. 27.50 (ISBN 0-88416-310-5). PSG Pub.

Inflated Self: Human Illusions and the Biblical Call to Hope. David G. Myers. 176p. 1980. 9.95 (ISBN 0-8164-0459-3). Seabury.

Inflation. Else M. Fleissner. Ed. by D. Steve Rahmas. LC 72-89225. (Topics of Our Times Ser.: No. 3). 32p. (Orig.). (gr. 7-12). 1973. lib. bdg. 2.75 incl. catalog cards (ISBN 0-87157-803-4); pap. 1.50 vinyl laminated covers (ISBN 0-87157-303-2). SamHar Pr.

Inflation. John Flemming. (Illus.). 144p. 1976. 17.95x (ISBN 0-19-877085-5); pap. 4.95x (ISBN 0-19-877086-3). Oxford U Pr.

Inflation. James Forman. (gr. 6 up). 1977. PLB 7.90 s&l (ISBN 0-531-00392-2). Watts.

Inflation. Michael Jefferson et al. 1979. 11.95 (ISBN 0-7145-3539-7); pap. 4.95 (ISBN 0-7145-3547-8). Riverrun NY.

Inflation: A Management Guide to Company Survival. Christopher J. West. 155p. 1976. 26.50 (ISBN 0-470-15087-4). Halsted Pr.

Inflation: A Study in Stability. J. W. Cumes. 202p. 1976. text ed. 16.75 (ISBN 0-08-018167-8). Pergamon.

Inflation: A World-Wide Disaster. 2nd ed. Irving S. Friedman. 320p. 1980. write for info.; pap. 5.95 (ISBN 0-395-29847-4). HM.

Inflation & Business Policy. David Hussey. LC 76-7065. (Business Strategy & Planning Ser.). (Illus.). 1976. text ed. 22.00x (ISBN 0-582-45073-X). Longman.

Inflation & Development: Some Reflections. D. R. Samant. 128p. 1976. 7.50 o.p. (ISBN 0-89253-056-1). InterCulture.

Inflation & the Income Tax. Ed. by Henry J. Aaron. LC 76-28669. (Studies of Government Finance). 1976. 15.95 (ISBN 0-8157-0024-5); pap. 6.95 (ISBN 0-8157-0023-7). Brookings.

Inflation & the Money Supply in the United States, 1956-1977. Peter I. Berman. LC 78-4344. 1978. 14.95 (ISBN 0-669-02346-9). Lexington Bks.

Inflation & the Use of Indexing in Developing Countries. Gustav D. Jud. LC 76-12859. (Praeger Special Studies). 1978. 25.95 (ISBN 0-275-23840-7). Praeger.
Inflation & Unemployment. 2nd ed. Morley. 1979. pap. 6.95 (ISBN 0-03-041016-9). Dryden Pr.
Inflation & Unemployment in France: A Quantitative Analysis. Jan Marczewski. LC 77-25490. (Praeger Special Studies). 1978. 23.95 (ISBN 0-03-040921-7). Praeger.
Inflation, Deflation, Reflation: Managemnent & Accounting in Economic Uncertainty. J. P. Wilson. 345p. 1980. text ed. 36.75x (ISBN 0-220-67015-3, Pub. by Busn Bks England). Renouf.
Inflation, Depression & Economic Policy in the West. Ed. by Anthony S. Courakis. LC 79-55497. 1980. text ed. 32.50x (ISBN 0-06-491293-0). B&N.
Inflation, Exchange Rates, & the World Economy: Lectures on International Monetary Economics. W. M. Corden. (Business & Society Studies). 1980. pap. write for info. (ISBN 0-226-11584-4). U of Chicago Pr.
Inflation Fighter's Big Book: Beat the High Cost of Operating Your Home. Carmen Waschek & Brownlee Waschek. (Illus.). 1979. 13.95 (ISBN 0-8359-3068-8). Reston.
Inflation Fighters' Preserving Guide. Allan Swenson. 1977. pap. 1.75 o.p. (ISBN 0-345-25159-8). Ballantine.
Inflation Fighter's Victory Garden. Allan A. Swenson. 288p. (Orig.). 1975. pap. 1.50 o.p. (ISBN 0-345-24288-2). Ballantine.
Inflation in the United Kingdom. Ed. by Michael Parkin & Michael T. Sumner. 1978. 25.00x o.p. (ISBN 0-8020-2321-5). U of Toronto Pr.
Inflation in the United States 1940-1948. Lester Chandler. (Fdr & the Era of the New Deal). 1976. Repr. of 1951 ed. lib. bdg. 29.50 (ISBN 0-306-70804-3). Da Capo.
Inflation, Interest, & Growth: A Synthesis. Hans Brems. LC 78-19226. 192p. 1980. 18.95 (ISBN 0-669-02466-X). Lexington Bks.
Inflation Management in Motor Transport Operations. Peter N. Cooke. 192p. 1978. text ed. 25.25x (ISBN 0-566-02056-4, Pub. by Gower Pr England). Renouf.
Inflation Management: One Hundred Practical Techniques for Business & Industry. Howe C. Stidger & W. Ruth. LC 80-11271. 448p. 1980. Repr. of 1976 ed. lib. bdg. 19.95 (ISBN 0-89874-132-7). Krieger.
Inflation Management: 100 Practical Techniques for Business & Industry. Howe C. Stidger & Ruth W. Stidger. LC 76-8927. 400p. 1976. 19.95 o.p. (ISBN 0-471-82485-2, Pub. by Wiley-Interscience). Wiley.
Inflation of House Prices: Its Extent, Causes & Consequences. Leo Grebler & Frank G. Mittelbach. LC 78-20272. (Special Ser. in Real Estate & Urban Land Economics). 1979. 25.95 (ISBN 0-669-02708-1). Lexington Bks.
Inflation, Policy & Unemployment Theory. Edmund S. Phelps. (Illus.). 1972. 15.95x (ISBN 0-393-09395-6). Norton.
Inflation Protection for Workers' Compensation Claimants in Michigan: A Simulation Study. H. Allan Hunt. LC 80-28834. 125p. (Orig.). 1981. pap. text ed. write for info. (ISBN 0-911558-77-2). Upjohn Inst.
Inflation, Stock Price, & Housing Cost: Empirical Studies. Kilman Shin. LC 77-84026. 1978. text ed. 20.00 (ISBN 0-686-12043-4). Ctr Econ Analysis.
Inflation Survival Book: A Jobs, Investment, Survival Guide. Jon B. Utley. 300p. 1981. 12.95 (ISBN 0-89803-042-0). Caroline Hse.
Inflation, Taxes & Other Economic Mysteries. Ken Davis et al. LC 79-25124. (Illus., Orig.). (gr. 6-10). 1980. pap. write for info. (ISBN 0-916392-46-5). Oak Tree Pubns.
Inflation Theory & Anti-Inflation Policy. Eric Lundberg. LC 76-30902. (International Economic Association Ser.). 1977. lib. bdg. 46.00 o.p. (ISBN 0-89158-729-2). Westview.
Inflation Under Pass-Along Management. Byung Y. Hong. 1979. 20.95 (ISBN 0-03-051331-6). Praeger.
Inflation-Wise: How to Do Almost Everything for Less. Christopher A. McLachlan. 1981. pap. 4.95 (ISBN 0-380-76836-4). Avon.
Inflationary Price Trends in India Since 1939. 2nd ed. D. Bright Singh. 10.00x (ISBN 0-210-33682-X). Asia.
Inflectional Morphology: A Theoretical Study Based on Aspects of Latin Verb Conjugation. P. H. Matthews. LC 76-171678. (Studies in Linguistics Ser., No. 6). (Illus.). 500p. 1972. 49.50 (ISBN 0-521-08372-9); pap. 14.95x (ISBN 0-521-29065-1). Cambridge U Pr.
Influence, Choice & Drugs: Toward a Systematic Approach to the Prevention of Substance Abuse. Martin Shain et al. LC 77-5230. 1977. 16.95 (ISBN 0-669-01597-0). Lexington Bks.
Influence of Angus Snead MacDonald & the Snead Bookstack on Library Architecture. Charles H. Baumann. LC 74-171928. (Illus.). 1972. 11.50 (ISBN 0-8108-0390-9). Scarecrow.
Influence of Border Troubles on Relations Between the United States & Mexico, 1876-1910. Robert S. Gregg. LC 72-98181. (American Scene Ser). 1970. Repr. of 1937 ed. lib. bdg. 25.00 (ISBN 0-306-71833-2). Da Capo.
Influence of Culture on Visual Perception. Marshall H. Segall et al. LC 64-16721. (Illus., Orig.). 1966. pap. 6.95 (ISBN 0-672-60825-1). Bobbs.
Influence of East Europe & the Soviet West on the USSR. Ed. by Roman Szporluk. LC 75-3752. (Special Studies). (Illus.). 272p. 1976. text ed. 25.95 (ISBN 0-275-07500-1). Praeger.
Influence of Fat Crystals in the Oil Phase of Stability of Oil-in-Water Emulsions. (Agricultural Research Report: No. 901). 1981. pap. 18.75 (ISBN 0-686-69540-2, PDC 216, Pudoc). Unipub.
Influence of Indiviual Differences in Health & Illness. Linas A. Bieliauskas. (Behavioral Sciences for Health Care Professionals). 128p. (Orig.). 1981. lib. bdg. 15.00x (ISBN 0-86531-004-1); pap. text ed. 6.00x (ISBN 0-86531-005-X). Westview.
Influence of Law on Sea Power. D. P. O'Connell. LC 75-21922. 1976. 15.50x (ISBN 0-87021-834-4). Naval Inst Pr.
Influence of Matthew Baillie's Morbid Anatomy: Biography, Evaluation & Reprint. Alvin E. Rodin. (American Lectures in History of Medicine & Science Ser.). (Illus.). 304p. 1973. 13.50 (ISBN 0-398-02781-1). C C Thomas.
Influence of Pantomime & Harlequinade. Ed. by Walter H. Rubsamen. (Ballad Opera Ser.). 1974. lib. bdg. 50.00 (ISBN 0-8240-0908-8). Garland Pub.
Influence of Photography on American Landscape Painting, 1839-1880. Elizabeth Lindquist-Cock. LC 76-23608. (Outstanding Dissertations in the Fine Arts - 2nd Series - American). (Illus.). 1977. Repr. of 1967 ed. lib. bdg. 48.00 (ISBN 0-8240-2680-2). Garland Pub.
Influence of Rome's Antique Monumental Sculptures on the Great Master's of the Renaissance. Edit Pogany-Balas. Tr. by Arpad Debreczeni. (Illus.). 115p. 1980. 25.00x (ISBN 963-05-1682-9). Intl Pubns Serv.
Influence of Seapower in History. A. Mahan & A. Preston. 29.95 (ISBN 0-13-464537-5). P-H.
Influence of Teeth, Diet & Habits on the Human Face. David Davies. 1972. 16.00x (ISBN 0-8448-0743-5). Crane-Russak Co.
Influence of the Bible on Civilization. E. Von Dobschutz. 200p. Repr. of 1914 ed. text ed. 2.95 (ISBN 0-567-02093-2). Attic Pr.
Influence of the Mongols of Russia: A Dimensional History. Paul Harrison Silfen. LC 74-76040. 1974. 7.00 o.p. (ISBN 0-682-47969-1, University). Exposition.
Influence of the Planet Pluto, Including an Ephemeris of Pluto 1840-1960. Elbert Benjamine. 1968. pap. 1.00 (ISBN 0-933646-09-7). Aries Pr.
Influence of the Sea on the Political History of Japan. G. A. Ballard. 312p. 1972. Repr. of 1921 ed. 25.00x (ISBN 0-7165-2048-6, Pub. by Irish Academic Pr Ireland). Biblio Dist.
Influence of William Godwin on the Novels of Mary Shelley. Katherine R. Powers. Ed. by Devendra P. Varma. LC 79-7469. (Gothic Studies & Dissertations Ser.). 1980. lib. bdg. 17.00x (ISBN 0-405-12657-3). Arno.
Influences of Hormones in Tumor Development, 2 vols. John A. Kellen & Russell Hilf. 1979. Vol. 1, 192p. 51.99 (ISBN 0-8493-5351-3); Vol. 2, 224p. 54.95 (ISBN 0-8493-5352-1). CRC Pr.
Influences of Measures Designed to Restrict the Use of Certain Transport Modes. 42nd roundtable ed. 59p. 1979. 4.50 (ISBN 92-821-1055-9). OECD.
Influences of Pancreatic Tumors on the Stomach. Robert M. Zollinger & David W. Coleman. (Beaumont Lecture Ser.). (Illus.). 224p. 1974. text ed. 22.50 (ISBN 0-398-02683-1). C C Thomas.
Influences of Rudolph Laban. John Foster. 1978. 16.95 (ISBN 0-86019-015-3). Transatlantic.
Influential Theologians on Wo-Man. William E. Phipps. LC 79-5431. 1980. pap. text ed. 7.50 (ISBN 0-8191-0880-4). U Pr of Amer.
Influenza: Proceedings. Royal Society et al. (Royal Society Ser.). (Illus.). 172p. 1980. lib. bdg. 50.00x (ISBN 0-85403-138-3, Pub. by Royal Soc London). Scholium Intl.
Influx: Essays on Literary Influence. Ed. by Ronald Primeau. (Literary Criticism Ser). 1977. 14.50 (ISBN 0-8046-9151-7, Natl U). Kennikat.
Informal Diagnostic Assessment of Children. Theodore S. Fremont et al. (Illus.). 176p. 1977. 16.75 (ISBN 0-398-03646-2). C C Thomas.
Informal Groups: An Introduction. Stephen R. Wilson. (P-H Ser. in Sociology). 1978. ref. ed. 17.95 (ISBN 0-13-464636-3). P-H.
Informal Learning in Elementary Schools. Danny G. Fulks. LC 78-61303. 1978. pap. text ed. 7.50 (ISBN 0-8191-0606-2). U Pr of Amer.
Informal Logic: The First International Symposium. Ed. by J. Antony Blair & Ralph H. Johnson. LC 80-67674. 175p. (Orig.). 1980. pap. 9.95 (ISBN 0-918528-09-7). Edgepress.
Informal Meeting, Steel Box Girder Bridges. Thomas Telford Ltd. Editorial Staff. 118p. 1980. pap. 25.00x (Pub. by Telford England). State Mutual Bk.
Informal Reading Diagnosis: A Practical Guide for the Classroom Teacher. Thomas C. Potter & Gwenneth R. Rae. LC 72-4727. (Illus.). 336p. 1973. pap. 11.95 ref. ed. (ISBN 0-13-464453-0). P-H.
Informal Reading Diagnosis: A Practical Guide for the Classroom Teacher. 2nd ed. G. Rac & T. Potter. 1981. 14.95 (ISBN 0-13-464628-2); pap. 10.95 (ISBN 0-13-464610-X). P-H.
Information: A Preservation Sourcebook. Ed. by National Trust for Historic Preservation. 1979. ring binder 15.00 (ISBN 0-89133-084-4). Preservation Pr.
Information: A Scientific American Book. Scientific American Editors. LC 66-29386. (Illus.). 1966. 14.95x (ISBN 0-7167-0967-8); pap. text ed. 7.95x (ISBN 0-7167-0966-X). W H Freeman.
Information Age: Its Development, Its Impact. Ed. by Donald P. Hammer. LC 76-10603. 1976. 11.00 o.p. (ISBN 0-8108-0945-1). Scarecrow.
Information: An Essential Factor in Educational Planning & Policy. 303p. 1981. pap. 18.75 (ISBN 92-3-101668-7, U1056, UNESCO). Unipub.
Information Analysis. Joel S. Demski. LC 78-184156. 1972. pap. text ed. 4.95 o.p. (ISBN 0-201-01477-7). A-W.
Information Analysis. 2nd ed. Joel S. Demski. LC 80-15971. (A-W Paperback Series in Accounting). 200p. 1980. pap. text ed. 6.50 (ISBN 0-201-01231-6). A-W.
Information Analysis & Retrieval. Allen Kent. LC 70-155120. (Information Science Ser). 1971. 29.95 (ISBN 0-471-46995-5). Wiley.
Information Analysis in Management Accounting. Donald L. Anderson & Donald L. Raun. LC 77-14938. (Accounting & Information Systems Ser.). 1978. pap. text ed. 24.50 (ISBN 0-471-02815-0); tchrs. manual 6.00 (ISBN 0-471-05664-2). Wiley.
Information Analysis Products: 1967-1972. Educational Resources Information Center. 1973. 14.95 o.s.i. (ISBN 0-02-468820-7). Macmillan Info.
Information & Advice Services. Rosalind Brooke. 181p. 1972. pap. text ed. 5.65x (ISBN 0-7135-1709-3, Pub. by Bedford England). Renouf.
Information & Behavior in a Sikh Village: Social Organization Reconsidered. Murray J. Leaf. LC 78-172390. (Illus.). 300p. 1972. 20.00x (ISBN 0-520-02115-0). U of Cal Pr.
Information & Coordination: Essays in Macroeconomic Theory. Axel Leijonhufvud. (Illus.). 320p. 1981. text ed. 15.95x (ISBN 0-19-502814-7); pap. text ed. 9.95x (ISBN 0-19-502815-5). Oxford U Pr.
Information & Instructions for Pediatric Patients. H. Winter Griffith et al. LC 80-51712. 320p. 1980. 35.00 (ISBN 0-938372-00-9). Winter Pub Co.
Information & Library Science Source Book: Supplement to Documentation Source Book. Gertrude Schutze. LC 72-1157. 1972. 16.50 (ISBN 0-8108-0466-2). Scarecrow.
Information Computer Communications Policy (ICCP) 4. OECD. 233p. (Orig.). 1980. pap. 14.50 (ISBN 92-64-12035-1, 93-80-01-1). OECD.
Information-Control Problems in Manufacturing Technology: Proceedings of the Second IFAC/IFIP Symposium, Stuttgart, Federal Republic of Germany, 22-24 October, 1979. Ed. by U. Rembold. LC 80-49945. (IFAC Proceedings Ser.). (Illus.). 330p. 1980. 75.00 (ISBN 0-08-024452-1). Pergamon.
Information Economics & Accounting Research: A Workshop Conducted by Joel S. Demski. Ed. by Gerald Lobo & Michael Maher. (Michigan Business Papers: No. 65). (Illus.). 240p. 1980. 9.00 (ISBN 0-87712-204-0). U Mich Busn Div Res.
Information for Action: From Knowledge to Wisdom. Ed. by Manfred Kochen. (Library & Information Science Ser.). 256p. 1975. 20.00 o.s.i. (ISBN 0-12-417950-9). Acad Pr.
Information for Decision-Making: Quantitative & Behavioral Dimensions. 2nd ed. Alfred Rappaport. (Illus.). 384p. 1975. ref. ed. 19.95 (ISBN 0-13-464388-7). P-H.
Information for Playwrights. Ed. by Michael Earley. 54p. 1979. pap. 4.00 (ISBN 0-930452-09-7, Pub. by Theatre Comm). Pub Ctr Cult Res.
Information Industry Market Place 1980-81. 2nd ed. 350p. 1981. pap. 32,50 (ISBN 0-8352-1291-2). Bowker.
Information Linkage Between Applied Mathematics & Industry II. Ed. by A. L. Schoenstadt et al. LC 80-17975. 1980. 20.00 (ISBN 0-12-628750-3). Acad Pr.
Information-Lossless Automata of Finite Order. A. A. Kurmit. Tr. by D. Louvish. LC 74-8183. 186p. 1974. 37.95 (ISBN 0-470-51099-4). Halsted Pr.
Information Management: An Executive Approach. Neil Duffy & Mike Assad. (Illus.). 224p. 1981. 34.50 (ISBN 0-19-570190-9). Oxford U Pr.
Information Market Place, 1978-1979: A Directory of Information Products & Services. Ed. by James B. Sanders. 1978. pap. 21.50 o.p. (ISBN 0-8352-1079-0, Pub. by Learned Information, Europe Ltd.). Bowker.
Information on Music: A Handbook of Reference Sources in European Languages Vol. 1, Basic & Universal Sources. Guy A. Marco. LC 74-32132. 1975. lib. bdg. 17.50x (ISBN 0-87287-096-0). Libs Unl.
Information on Music: A Handbook of Reference Sources in European Languages, Vol. 2, The Americas. Guy Marco et al. LC 74-32132. 1977. lib. bdg. 22.50x (ISBN 0-87287-141-X). Libs Unl.
Information on the Application of Meteorological Satellite Data in Routine Operations & Research: Abstracts, Annual Summaries & Bibliographies, Suppl. No. 3. (Global Observing System & Satellite Sub-System Ser.). 110p. 1980. pap. 5.00 (ISBN 0-686-62999-X, W-455, WMO). Unipub.
Information on the Renunciation of War 1927-1928. J. W. Wheeler-Bennett. LC 72-89272. 192p. 1973. Repr. of 1928 ed. 15.50 (ISBN 0-8046-1761-9). Kennikat.
Information Processing & Decision Making. Ed. by William C. Howell & Edwin A. Fleishman. (Human Performance & Productivity Ser.: Vol. 2). 1981. professional ref. text 19.95 (ISBN 0-89859-090-6). L Erlbaum Assocs.
Information Processing in the Nervous System. Ed. by Harold Pinsker & William D. Willis, Jr. 378p. 1980. text ed. 38.00 (ISBN 0-89004-422-8). Raven.
Information Processing in the United States: A Quantitative Summary. Ed. by Philip S. Nyborg & Pender M. McCarter. (Illus.). vii, 55p. 1977. saddle-stitch 6.00 (ISBN 0-686-68785-X). AFIPS Pr.
Information Processing in the Visual Systems of Arthropods. Ed. by R. Wehner. LC 72-91887. 340p. 1973. pap. 25.10 (ISBN 0-387-06020-0). Springer-Verlag.
Information Processing Models of Teaching: Expanding Your Teaching Repertoire. Marsha Weil & Bruce Joyce. LC 77-5414. (Illus.). 1978. ref. ed. 14.95 (ISBN 0-13-464552-9); pap. text ed. 10.95 (ISBN 0-13-464545-6). P-H.
Information Processing Systems. 2nd ed. William S. Davis. LC 79-26775. (First Course in Computers: Lo7). (Illus.). 480p. 1981. text ed. price not set (ISBN 0-201-03183-3). A-W.
Information Processing Systems: An Introduction to Modern Computer-Based Information Systems. William S. Davis. LC 77-76115. (Illus.). 1978. text ed. 14.95 o.p. (ISBN 0-201-00999-4); wkbk. 5.95 o.p. (ISBN 0-201-01113-1); instr's man. 2.95 o.p. (ISBN 0-201-01000-3). A-W.
Information Processing Theory of Consumer Choice. James R. Bettman. LC 78-52496. (Advances in Marketing). 1979. text ed. 16.95 (ISBN 0-201-00834-3). A-W.
Information, Representation & Manipulation in a Computer. 2nd ed. E. S. Page & L. B. Wilson. (Computer Science Texts Ser.). (Illus.). 1978. 40.75 (ISBN 0-521-22088-2); pap. 12.95x (ISBN 0-521-29357-X). Cambridge U Pr.
Information Resources on Industrial Maintenence & Repair. (UNIDO Guides to Information Sources Ser.: No.36). 86p. 1980. pap. 4.00 (UNID-236, UN). Unipub.
Information Retrieval & Processing. L. B. Doyle. LC 75-1179. (Information Science Ser.). 1975. 29.95 (ISBN 0-471-22151-1, Pub. by Wiley-Interscience). Wiley.
Information Retrieval on-Line. F. W. Lancaster & E. G. Fayen. LC 73-9697. (Information Sciences Ser.). 512p. 1973. 29.95 (ISBN 0-471-51235-4, Pub. by Wiley-Interscience). Wiley.
Information Retrieval Systems: Characteristics, Testing & Evaluation. 2nd ed. F. W. Lancaster. LC 78-11078. (Information Sciences Ser.). 1979. 23.95 (ISBN 0-471-04673-6, Pub. by Wiley-Interscience). Wiley.
Information Science: Theory & Practice. B. C. Vickery & A. Vickery. 1981. text ed. price not set. Butterworth.

Information Seekers: An International Study of Consumer Information & Advertising Image. Hans Thorelli et al. LC 74-9635. 288p. 1975. text ed. 20.00 o.p. (ISBN 0-88410-265-3). Ballinger Pub.
Information Services: Economics, Management, & Technology. Ed. by Robert M. Mason & John E. Crepps. (Westview Special Studies in Information Management). 200p. 1980. lib. bdg. 26.50x (ISBN 0-89158-938-4). Westview.
Information Services for Academic Administration. JB Lon Hefferlin & Ellis L. Phillips, Jr. LC 76-148659. (Higher Education Ser.). 1971. 9.95x o.p. (ISBN 0-87589-096-2). Jossey-Bass.
Information Societies: Comparing the Japanese & American Experiences. Alex S. Edelstein et al. LC 78-71366. 314p. (Orig.). 1979. pap. 10.95 (ISBN 0-295-95667-4, Pub. by Intl Communication Ctr). U of Wash Pr.
Information Sources in Agriculture & Food Science. Lilley. (Butterworths Guides to Information Sources Ser.). 1981. text ed. price not set (ISBN 0-408-10612-3). Butterworth.
Information Sources in Education & Work. James Tomlinson & Kenneth Dibden. LC 80-41801. (Butterworths Guides to Information Sources Ser.). 168p. 1980. text ed. 22.95 (ISBN 0-408-70923-5). Butterworths.
Information Sources in Geographical Science. Goddard. (Butterworths Guides to Information Sources Ser.). 1981. text ed. price not set (ISBN 0-408-10690-5). Butterworth.
Information Sources in Transportation, Material Management, & Physical Distribution: An Annotated Bibliography & Guide. Ed. by Bob J. Davis. LC 75-23864. (Orig.). 1976. lib. bdg. 45.00 (ISBN 0-8371-8379-0, DBT/). Greenwood.
Information Sources of Political Science, 5 vols. 2nd, rev. ed. Frederick L. Holler. LC 74-80344. 440p. 1975. Set. text ed. 12.00 (ISBN 0-87436-190-7); text ed. 8.75 ea.; Set. pap. text ed. 21.75 (ISBN 0-685-93193-5); pap. text ed. 1.75 ea.; Vol. 1. pap. text ed. (ISBN 0-87436-181-8); Vol. 2. pap. text ed. (ISBN 0-87436-183-4); Vol. 3. pap. text ed. (ISBN 0-87436-185-0); Vol. 4. pap. text ed. (ISBN 0-87436-187-7); Vol. 5. pap. text ed. (ISBN 0-87436-189-3). ABC-Clio.
Information Sources of Political Science. 3rd, rev. ed. Frederick L. Holler. 288p. 1980. 65.00 (ISBN 0-87436-179-6). ABC-Clio.
Information Sources on Bioconversion of Agricultural Wastes. (UNIDO Guide to Information Sources Ser.: No.33). 84p. 1980. pap. 4.00 (UNID-228, UN). Unipub.
Information Sources on Leather & Leather Products Industries. (UNIDO Guides to Information Sources Ser.: No. 3). 85p. 1980. pap. 4.00 (UNID 226, UN). Unipub.
Information Sources on the Foundry Industry. rev. ed. (UNIDO Guides to Information Sources Ser.: No.5). 87p. pap. 4.00 (UN). Unipub.
Information Sources on the Natural & Synthetic Rubber Industry. (UNIDO Guides to Information Sources Ser.: No.34). 108p. 1980. pap. 4.00 (UNIDO230, UN). Unipub.
Information Sources on the Utilization of Agricultural Residues for the Production of Panels, Pulp, & Paper. (UNIDO Information Sources Ser.: No.35). 99p. 1980. pap. 4.00 (UN). Unipub.
Information Soures: An International Selective Guide. K. Umapathy Setty. 1978. 12.50 (ISBN 0-7069-0628-4, Pub. by Vikas India). Advent Bk.
Information Storage & Retrieval: Tools, Elements & Theories. Joseph Becker & Robert M. Hayes. LC 62-12279. (Information Science Ser.). 1963. 28.95 (ISBN 0-471-06129-8, Pub by Wiley-Interscience). Wiley.
Information Strategies: New Pathways to Corporate Power. C. Goldhaber. 1979. 18.95 (ISBN 0-13-464651-7). P-H.
Information Systems Analysis: Theory & Application. Milton J. Alexander. LC 73-89599. (Illus.). 432p. 1974. text ed. 18.95 (ISBN 0-574-19100-3, 13-2100); instr's guide avail. (ISBN 0-574-19101-1, 13-2101). SRA.
Information Systems Developement: A Systematic Approach. M. Sundburg & G. Goldkuhl. 1981. 24.50 (ISBN 0-13-464677-0). P-H.
Information Systems for Agriculture. Ed. by M. J. Blackie & J. B. Dent. (Illus.). 1979. 28.50x (ISBN 0-85334-829-4). Intl Ideas.
Information Systems for Management Planning & Control. 3rd ed. Thomas R. Prince. 1975. text ed. 20.50 (ISBN 0-256-01647-X). Irwin.
Information Systems for Modern Management. 2nd ed. Robert G. Murdick & Joel E. Ross. (Illus.). 640p. 1975. ref. ed. 21.95 (ISBN 0-13-464602-9). P-H.
Information Systems for Panning & Control: Concepts & Cases. J. C. Higgins. 1976. 29.95x (ISBN 0-7131-3375-9); pap. 15.95x (ISBN 0-7131-3376-7). Intl Ideas.
Information Systems for Strategic Decisions. K. J. Radford. (Illus.). 1978. ref. ed. 14.95 (ISBN 0-87909-389-7). Reston.
Information Systems in Management. K. J. Radford. LC 73-80911. 1973. 15.95 (ISBN 0-87909-352-8). Reston.
Information Systems in Management. James A. Senn. 1978. text ed. 22.95x (ISBN 0-534-00563-2). Wadsworth Pub.
Information Systems, Services & Centers. Herman M. Weisman. LC 72-1156. (Information Sciences Ser.). 265p. 1972. 22.95 (ISBN 0-471-92645-0, Pub. by Wiley-Interscience). Wiley.
Information Systems: Technology, Economics, Applications, Management. 2nd ed. Chris Mader. LC 78-13048. 1979. text ed. 17.95 (ISBN 0-574-21150-0, 13-4150); instr's guide avail. (ISBN 0-574-21151-9, 13-4151). SRA.
Information Systems: Their Interconnection & Compatibility. (Illus.). 470p. 1975. pap. 34.25 (ISBN 92-0-070075-6, IAEA). Unipub.
Information Technology & Health Care: The Critical Issues. Ed. by Karen Duncan. 200p. 1980. write for info. (ISBN 0-88283-031-7). AFIPS Pr.
Information Technology Serving Society. Robert L. Chartrand & James W. Morentz. (Illus.). 1979. 35.00 (ISBN 0-08-021979-9). Pergamon.
Information Technology Serving Society. Ed. by Robert Lee Chartrand & James W. Morentz, Jr. 1979. 25.00 (ISBN 0-08-021979-9). Chartrand.
Information Theory. R. B. Ash. LC 65-24284. (Pure & Applied Mathematics Ser.). 1965. 33.50 (ISBN 0-470-03445-9, Pub by Wiley-Interscience). Wiley.
Information Theory & the Living System. Lila L. Gatlin. LC 76-187030. (Molecular Biology Ser.). 208p. 1972. 16.00x (ISBN 0-231-03634-5). Columbia U Pr.
Information Theory & Urban Spatial Structure. M. J. Webber. 394p. 1979. 80.00x (ISBN 0-85664-665-2, Pub. by Croom Helm Ltd England). Biblio Dist.
Information Theory for Systems Engineers. rev ed. L. P. Hyvaerinen. (Lecture Notes in Operations Research & Mathematical Systems: Vol. 5). 1968. pap. 14.70 o.p. (ISBN 0-387-04254-7). Springer-Verlag.
Information Through the Printed Word. Fritz Machlup & Kenneth W. Leeson. Incl. Vol. 1. Book Publishing. 28.95 (ISBN 0-03-047401-9); Vol. 2. Journals. 30.95 (ISBN 0-03-047406-X); Vol. 3. Libraries. 25.95 (ISBN 0-03-047411-6). LC 78-19460. 1978. Praeger.
Information to Authors: Editorial Guidelines Reprinted from 200 Medical Journals. Ed. by Harriet Meiss & Doris Jaeger. LC 80-19712. 1980. pap. 26.00 (ISBN 0-8067-1251-1). Urban & S.
Information to Be Submitted in Support of Licensing Applications for Nuclear Power Plants. (Safety Ser.: No. 50-Sg-02). 1979. pap. 6.50 (ISBN 92-0-123279-9, ISP515, IAEA). Unipub.
Information Transfer in Engineering. Hedvah L. Shuchman. (Illus.). 300p. (Orig.). 1981. pap. 45.00 (ISBN 0-9605196-0-2). Futures Group.
Information Utility & Social Choice. Ed. by Harold Sackman & Norman Nie. LC 78-129364. (Illus.). 310p. 1970. 9.00 (ISBN 0-88283-019-8). AFIPS Pr.
Information Work with Unpublished Reports. A. H. Holloway et al. LC 76-43366. (Institute of Information Scientists Monograph Ser.). (Illus.). 1978. lib. bdg. 28.50x (ISBN 0-89158-717-9). Westview.
Informational Bioelectromagnetics. David A. Copson. 650p. 1981. text ed. 24.95 (ISBN 0-916460-09-6). Matrix Pubns.
Informational Guides for Groups, Communication, Living & Change, Set-GL. rev. ed. Russell E. Mason. 1975. pap. 25.00x (ISBN 0-89533-019-9); tape-2, t-16, t-17 incl., notes, clinical applications 1979, H.E.S.T-a, set. F I Comm.
Informational Interviews & Questions. Thomas P. Slavens. LC 77-18502. 1978. 10.00 (ISBN 0-8108-1102-2). Scarecrow.
Informations Systems: An Introduction to Computers in Organizations. Taggart. 608p. 1980. text ed. 20.95 (ISBN 0-205-06908-8, 2069083). Allyn.
Informe Anual De la Comision Interamericana De Derechos Humanos a la Asamblea General Correspondiente a 1976. 1977. Span. Ed. 1976. pap. 2.00 (ISBN 0-8270-2535-1); Eng. Ed. pap. 2.00 (ISBN 0-8270-2560-2); Span. Ed., 1977. pap. 2.00 (ISBN 0-8270-2540-8); Span. Ed., 1978. pap. 2.00 (ISBN 0-8270-2545-9); Eng. Ed., 1978. pap. 6.00 (ISBN 0-8270-1046-X). OAS.
Informe Anual Del Secretario-General. 1971 ed. 3.50 (ISBN 0-8270-5000-3); 1972 ed. 3.50 (ISBN 0-8270-5010-0); 1973 ed. 3.50 (ISBN 0-8270-5020-8). OAS.
Informe Anual Del Secretario-General. (Span & Eng.). 1974. ea Eng. & Span. eds 5.00. Eng. Ed (ISBN 0-8270-5035-6). OAS.
Informe De la Comision Interamericana De Mujeres A la Conferenci A Mundial Del Decenio De las Naciones Unidas Para la Mujer: Iqualdad, Desarrollo Y Paz. OAS General Secretariat Inter-American Commission of Women. (Inter-American Commission of Women). 40p. 1980. 2.00 o.p. (ISBN 0-8270-1163-6). OAS.
Informe Sobre la Situacion De los Derechos Humanos En Haiti. OAS General Secretariat Inter-American Commision of Human Rights. (Human Rights Ser.). 77p. 1980. text ed. 5.00 (ISBN 0-8270-1095-8). OAS.
Informed Consent. James E. Ludlam. LC 78-24495. 96p. (Orig.). 1978. 8.75 (ISBN 0-87258-243-4, 1160). Am Hospital.
Informed Consent: A Guide for Health Care Providers. Arnold J. Rosoff. 300p. 1981. text ed. 37.50 (ISBN 0-89443-293-1). Aspen Systems.
Informed Heart: Autonomy in a Mass Age. Bruno Bettelheim. 1960. 12.95 (ISBN 0-02-903200-8). Free Pr.
Informed Sources. Lawrence Kamarck. Date not set. pap. 2.25 (ISBN 0-440-13750-0). Dell.
Informed Writer. Charles Bazerman. LC 80-68140. 320p. 1981. pap. text ed. 9.50 (ISBN 0-395-29715-X); instr's manual 0.50 (ISBN 0-395-29716-8). HM.
Informer. Liam O'Flaherty. pap. 1.25 o.p. (ISBN 0-451-50949-8, CY949, Sig Classics). NAL.
Informing the People: A Public Information Handbook. Ray Hiebert et al. (Longman Public Communication Ser.). (Illus.). 512p. 1981. 24.95 (ISBN 0-582-28200-4). Longman.
Infrared Absorption Spectroscopy. 2nd ed. Koji Nakanishi & Philippa H. Solomon. LC 76-27393. 1977. pap. 15.95x (ISBN 0-8162-6251-9). Holden-Day.
Infrared & Millimeter Waves, Vol. 3: Submillimeter Techniques. Ed. by Kenneth J. Button. 1980. 50.00 (ISBN 0-12-147703-7). Acad Pr.
Infrared & Raman Spectra of Crystals. G. Turrell. 1972. 53.00 o.s.i. (ISBN 0-12-705050-7). Acad Pr.
Infrared Characteristic Group Frequencies. G. Socrates. LC 79-1406. 1980. 72.00 (ISBN 0-471-27592-1, Pub. by Wiley-Interscience). Wiley.
Infrared Handbook. Ed. by W. L. Wolfe & G. J. Zissis. LC 77-90786. (Illus.). 1978. 25.00 (ISBN 0-9603590-0-1). Environ Res Inst.
Infrared Spectra of Surface Compounds. A. V. Kiselev & V. I. Lygin. Ed. by D. Slutzkin. Tr. by N. Kaner from Rus. LC 75-15866. 384p. 1975. 59.95 (ISBN 0-470-48905-7). Halsted Pr.
Infrared: The New Astronomy. David Allen. LC 75-16584. 228p. 1976. 15.95 (ISBN 0-470-02334-1). Halsted Pr.
Infrasound & Low Frequency Vibration. Ed. by W. Tempest. 1977. 50.50 (ISBN 0-12-685450-5). Acad Pr.
Ingenious Dr. Franklin: Selected Scientific Letters of Benjamin Franklin. Ed. by Nathan G. Goodman. LC 74-81751. 256p. 1974. 14.00 (ISBN 0-8122-7680-9); pap. 3.95x (ISBN 0-8122-1067-0). U of Pa Pr.
Ingenious Mechanisms for Designers & Inventors, Vols. 1-4, 1930-67. Franklin D. Jones et al. (Illus.). Set. 70.00 (ISBN 0-685-12543-2); Vol. 1. 20.00 (ISBN 0-8311-1029-5); Vol. 2. 20.00 (ISBN 0-8311-1030-9); Vol. 3. 20.00 (ISBN 0-8311-1031-7); Vol. 4. 20.00 (ISBN 0-8311-1032-5). Indus Pr.
Ingenious Yankees. Joseph Gies & Frances Gies. (Illus.). 1976. 12.95 o.s.i. (ISBN 0-690-01150-4, TYC-T). T Y Crowell.
Ingenue Among the Lions: The Letters of Emily Clark to Joseph Hergesheimer. Emily Clark. Ed. by Gerald Langford. 1965. 12.50x (ISBN 0-292-73274-0). U of Tex Pr.
Inglenook Cookbook. 416p. (Contributions of Recipes from Women of The Church of the Brethren). 1970. 6.95 (ISBN 0-87178-421-1); pap. o.p. (ISBN 0-87178-422-X). Brethren.
Ingles En Accion. Robert J. Dixson. (Illus.). 1977. pap. text ed. 3.50 (ISBN 0-88345-295-2); records 60.00 (ISBN 0-685-77024-9); cassettes 60.00 (ISBN 0-685-77025-7). Regents Pub.
Ingles En Accion: See It& Say It in English. Robert Dixon. pap. 1.75 (ISBN 0-451-08060-2, E8060, Sig). NAL.
Ingles EN Twenty Lecciones. The R. D. Cortina Company. 384p. 1980. pap. 4.95 (ISBN 0-06-463608-9, EH 608, EH). Har-Row.
Ingles Practico Sin Maestro, 2 vols. Robert J. Dixson. (gr. 9 up). 1972. One-vol. Ed. pap. text ed. 5.95 (ISBN 0-88345-068-2, 17382); Vol. 1. pap. text ed. 3.50 (ISBN 0-88345-069-0); Vol. 2. pap. text ed. 3.50 (ISBN 0-88345-070-4); records ea. level 18.00 (ISBN 0-685-04774-1); 60.00 ea.tapes o.p.; ea cassettes 60.00. Regents Pub.
Ingmar Bergman: The Cinema As Mistress. Philip Mosley. 192p. 1981. 15.00 (ISBN 0-7145-2644-4, Pub. by M. Boyars). Merrimack Bk Serv.
Ingratiation: A Social Psychological Analysis. Edward E. Jones. LC 64-25812. (Century Psychology Ser.). 1964. 22.50x (ISBN 0-89197-230-7); pap. text ed. 9.50x (ISBN 0-89197-795-3). Irvington.
Ingredient X. L. C. Schroeter. 1970. 17.25 (ISBN 0-08-015866-8). Pergamon.
Ingres. Jon Whitely. (Illus.). 15.95 (ISBN 0-8467-0250-9, Pub. by Two Continents); pap. text ed. 9.95 (ISBN 0-8467-0249-5). Hippocrene Bks.
Ingrid Bergman: My Story. Ingrid Bergman & Alan Burgess. 1980. 14.95 (ISBN 0-440-03299-7). Delacorte.
Ingrid und Maria. M. E. Mountjoy. (German Through Reading Ser.: Stage 1). (Illus.). 1977. pap. text ed. 2.50x (ISBN 0-435-38608-5). Heinemann Ed.
Inhalation Risks from Radioactive Contaminants. (Technical Reports Ser.: No. 142). (Illus.). 146p. (Orig.). 1973. pap. 12.00 (ISBN 92-0-125073-8, IAEA). Unipub.
Inherit My Heart. Lynna Cooper. (Orig.). 1981. pap. 1.95 (ISBN 0-451-09782-3, J9782, Sig). NAL.
Inherit the Earth. Maureen Duffy. (Illus.). 192p. 1980. 19.95 (ISBN 0-241-10205-7, Pub. by Hamish Hamilton England). David & Charles.
Inherit the Mirage. Julia Thatcher. 1976. pap. 1.25 o.p. (ISBN 0-345-25209-8). Ballantine.
Inherit the Stars. James P. Hogan. (Del Rey Bk.). 1978. pap. 1.95 (ISBN 0-345-28907-2). Ballantine.
Inheritance. Owen Brooks. 1981. pap. write for info. (ISBN 0-671-41398-8). PB.
Inheritance & the Inequality of Material Wealth. John A. Brittain. LC 77-91814. (Studies in Social Economics). 1978. 9.95 (ISBN 0-8157-1084-4); pap. 3.95 (ISBN 0-8157-1083-6). Brookings.
Inheritance of Creative Intelligence. John L. Karlsson. LC 77-19297. 1978. text ed. 16.95 (ISBN 0-88229-391-5); pap. text ed. 8.95 (ISBN 0-88229-607-8). Nelson-Hall.
Inheritance of Economic Status. John A Brittain. LC 76-56369. (Studies in Social Economics). 1977. 11.95 (ISBN 0-8157-1082-8); pap. 4.95 (ISBN 0-8157-1081-X). Brookings.
Inherited Ataxias: Biochemical, Viral, & Pathological Studies. Ed. by Pieter Kark et al. LC 77-92490. (Advances in Neurology Ser.: Vol. 21). 1978. 45.50 (ISBN 0-89004-268-3). Raven.
Inherited Bride. Rebecca Stratton. (Harlequin Romances). 192p. 1981. pap. 1.25 (ISBN 0-373-02399-5, Pub. by Harlequin). PB.
Inherited Deception. Gail MacMillan. 192p. (YA) 1976. 5.95 (ISBN 0-685-62626-1, Avalon). Bouregy.
Inheritors. William G. Golding. LC 62-16724. 1963. pap. 3.95 (ISBN 0-15-644379-1, HB64, Harv). HarBraceJ.
Inheritors. Christopher Nicole. (Haggard Ser.: No. 2). (Orig.). 1981. pap. 2.95 (ISBN 0-451-09763-7, E9763, Sig). NAL.
Inheritors of Earth. Gordon Eklund & Poul Anderson. 1979. pap. 1.75 (ISBN 0-515-04496-2). Jove Pubns.
Inhibitors of DNA & RNA Polymerases. Ed. by Prem S. Sarin & Robert C. Gallo. (International Encyclopedia of Pharmacology & Therapeutics: Section 103). (Illus.). 1980. 69.00 set (ISBN 0-08-024932-9). Pergamon.
Inhibitors of Nucleic Acid Synthesis: Biophysical & Biochemical Aspects. H. Kersten & W. Kersten. (Molecular Biology Biochemistry & Biophysics Ser.: Vol. 18). (Illus.). ix, 184p. 1974. 33.70 (ISBN 0-387-06825-2). Springer-Verlag.
Inhomogeneous Optical Waveguides. M. S. Sodha & A. K. Ghatak. (Optical Physics & Engineering Ser.). (Illus.). 281p. 1977. 35.00 (ISBN 0-306-30916-5, Plenum Pr). Plenum Pub.
Inimitable Jeeves. P. G. Wodehouse. 224p. 1975. pap. 2.95 (ISBN 0-14-000933-7). Penguin.
INIS: Authority List for Corporate Entries & Report Number Prefixes. 1979. pap. 25.75 (ISBN 92-0-178379-5, IN6/R12, IAEA). Unipub.
INIS: Authority List for Corporate Entries & Report Number Prefixes. 472p. 1980. pap. 29.75 (ISBN 92-0-178280-2, IN6-R13, IAEA). Unipub.
INIS: Authority List for Journal Titles. 1978. pap. 9.75 (ISBN 92-0-178578-X, IN11-R7, IAEA). Unipub.
INIS: Authority List for Journal Titles. (INIS-11(Rev.9)). 228p. 1981. pap. 14.00 (ISBN 0-686-69441-4, IN11R9, IAEA). Unipub.
INIS: Authority List for Journal Titles. (INIS-11: Revision 8). 211p. 1980. pap. 13.00 (ISBN 92-0-178479-1, IN11-R8, IAEA). Unipub.
INIS: Descriptive Cataloguing Rules. (Illus.). 1978. pap. 4.50 (ISBN 92-0-178178-4, IN 1-R4, IAEA). Unipub.
INIS: Descriptive Cataloguing Rules. 72p. 1980. pap. 5.50 (ISBN 92-0-178180-6, IAEA). Unipub.

INIS Reference Series, 16 vols. International Atomic Energy Agency. (Orig.). 1969-1974. pap. 72.25 (ISBN 0-685-02939-5, IAEA). Unipub.

INIS: Subject Categories & Scope Descriptions. 1979. pap. 5.00 (ISBN 92-0-178678-6, IN3-R5, IAEA). Unipub.

INIS: Thesaurus. (INIS-Thirteen Ser.: Rev. 18). 748p. 1980. pap. 45.00 (ISBN 92-0-178080-X, IAEA). Unipub.

INIS: Thesaurus. (INIS Ser.: No. 13, Rev. 19). 748p. 1980. pap. 45.00 (ISBN 92-0-178480-5, IN13/R19, IAEA). Unipub.

Initial Consonants. Carole Horlock. (Illus.). 44p. (gr. 1-3). 1980. pap. 5.95 (ISBN 0-933358-60-1). Enrich.

Initial Effects of Ionizing Radiations on Cells. Ed. by Robert J. Harris. 1963. 43.00 (ISBN 0-12-327162-2). Acad Pr.

Initial Skills in Bricklaying: A Practical Guide. LC 80-41756. (Illus.). 100p. 1981. 18.00 (ISBN 0-08-025424-1); pap. 10.00 (ISBN 0-08-025423-3). Pergamon.

Initial Studies in American Letters. Henry A. Beers. 291p. 1980. Repr. of 1895 ed. lib. bdg. 30.00 (ISBN 0-89987-063-5). Darby Bks.

Initial Vowels. Carole Horlock. (Illus.). 24p. (gr. 1-3). 1980. pap. 3.95 (ISBN 0-933358-61-X). Enrich.

Initiate in the New World. C. Scott. pap. 4.95 (ISBN 0-87728-363-X). Weiser.

Initiates. Paul Virdell. LC 80-70225. 288p. 1981. 11.95 (ISBN 0-87795-314-7). Arbor Hse.

Initiation. Elisabeth Haich. (Illus.). 1965. 13.50 o.s.i. (ISBN 0-04-133001-3). Allen Unwin.

Initiation. Elisabeth Haitch. 1980. pap. write for info. PB.

Initiation a la Compatibilite Financiere et Administrative. 2nd canadienne francaise ed. William W. Pyle et al. 1980. text ed. 26.85x (ISBN 0-256-02517-7); practice set 8.30x (ISBN 0-256-02541-X). Irwin.

Initiation, Human & Solar. Alice A. Bailey. 1977. 11.25 (ISBN 0-85330-010-0); pap. 4.75 (ISBN 0-85330-110-7). Lucis.

Initiation of the Heartbeat. 2nd ed. Denis Noble. 1977. 19.95x (ISBN 0-19-857177-1); pap. text ed. 9.95x (ISBN 0-19-857178-X). Oxford U Pr.

Initiative Fur Morgen: Strategian in Wettbewerb der 80er Jahre. 247p. (Orig., Ger.). 1980. pap. text ed. 22.50 (ISBN 3-7184-1002-8). Interbk Inc.

Injection-Mould Design Fundamentals. A. B. Glanvill & E. N. Denton. (Illus.). 1965. 18.00 (ISBN 0-8311-1033-3). Indus Pr.

Injective Modules. D. W. Sharpe & P. Vamos. (Cambridge Tracts in Mathematics & Mathematical Physics: No. 63). (Illus.). 250p. 1972. 32.95 (ISBN 0-521-08391-5). Cambridge U Pr.

Injuries Following Rear-End Automobile Collisions. William D. De Gravelles & John H. Kelley. (Illus.). 256p. 1969. photocopy ed. spiral 22.75 (ISBN 0-398-00414-5). C C Thomas.

Injuries Following Rear-End Automobile Collisions. William D. Degravelles, Jr. & John H. Kelley. 256p. 1969. pap. 16.00 spiral o.p. (ISBN 0-398-00418-8). C C Thomas.

Injuries to the Ankle. J. Grant Bonnin. (Illus.). Repr. of 1970 ed. 25.25 o.s.i. (ISBN 0-02-841630-9). Hafner.

Injuries to the Ankle. Isadore G. Yablon. (Illus.). 320p. 1981. lib. bdg. 30.00 (ISBN 0-443-08095-X). Churchill.

Injury Control in Traffic Safety. Norman W. Heimstra. 256p. 1970. 12.75 (ISBN 0-398-00823-X). C C Thomas.

Injustice to Tou O Yuan: A Study & Translation. Chung-Wen Shih. LC 74-155585. (Princeton-Cambridge Studies in Chinese Linguistics, No. 4). 480p. 1973. 49.50 (ISBN 0-521-08228-5); pap. 19.95x (ISBN 0-521-09739-8). Cambridge U Pr.

Inks & Printing Chemicals: New Developments, C-025. Ed. by Business Communications. 1981. 800.00 (ISBN 0-89336-212-3). BCC. Postponed.

Inkwells to Lace. Time-Life Books Editors. (Encyclopedia of Collectibles Ser.). (Illus.). 1979. lib. bdg. 10.98 (ISBN 0-686-50979-X). Silver.

Inland & Maritime Transportation of Unitized Cargo. 1963. pap. 5.00 (ISBN 0-309-01135-3). Natl Acad Pr.

Inland Chumash Archaeological Investigations. Ed. by David S. Whitley et al. (Monographs: Vol. XV). (Illus.). 258p. 1980. pap. 7.00 (ISBN 0-917956-18-4). UCLA Arch.

Inland Empire in the Pacific Northwest: The Historical Essays & Sketches of Ceylon S. Kingston. Ceylon S. Kingston. 1981. price not set (ISBN 0-87770-186-5). Ye Galleon.

Inland Transport Statistics Great Britain, 1900-1970. D. L. Munby. Ed. by A. H. Watson. LC 78-40311. (Railways, Public Road Passenger Transport, London's Transport: Vol. I). (Illus.). 1978. 65.00x (ISBN 0-19-828409-8). Oxford U Pr.

Inland Tribes of South Africa. Peter Becker. 1980. text ed. 39.00x (ISBN 0-246-10926-2). Humanities.

Inland Tribes of Southern Africa. Peter Becker. 1979. 44.95x (ISBN 0-8464-0058-8). Beekman Pubs.

Inland Waterways. Charles Hadfield. (Leisure & Travel Ser.). 1978. 7.50 o.p. (ISBN 0-7153-7502-4). David & Charles.

Inmante Society: Legs, Half-Pants & Gunmen, a Study of Inmate Guards. William L. McWhorter. LC 80-69327. 140p. 1981. perfect bdg. 11.95 (ISBN 0-86548-047-8). Century Twenty One..

Inmenso Amor De Dios. Jose Borras. 96p. (Span.). Date not set. pap. price not set (ISBN 0-311-43038-4). Casa Bautista.

Inn of the Clowns. Paula G Paul. 192p. (YA) 1976. 5.95 (ISBN 0-685-67081-3, Avalon). Bouregy.

Inn Perspective: A Guide to New England Country Inns. Jane Anderson. LC 74-1785. (Illus.). 288p. 1976. 12.50 o.p. (ISBN 0-06-010138-5, HarpT); pap. 4.95 (ISBN 0-06-010137-7, TD-223, HarpT). Har-Row.

Innards & Other Variety Meats. Jana Allen & Margaret Gin. LC 73-91942. (Illus.). 144p. 1974. 7.95 (ISBN 0-912238-49-6); pap. 4.95 o.p. (ISBN 0-912238-48-8). One Hund One Prods.

Innate Ideas. Ed. by Stephen P. Stich. 1975. 18.50x (ISBN 0-520-02822-8); pap. 5.95x (ISBN 0-520-02961-5). U of Cal Pr.

Inner American: Life, Work, & Mental Health from 1957-1976. Joseph Veroff et al. LC 80-68187. 492p. 1981. 30.00 (ISBN 0-465-03293-1). Basic.

Inner Cat: A New Approach to Cat Behavior. Carole C. Wilbourn. LC 77-20189. (Illus.). 204p. 1980. pap. 4.95 (ISBN 0-8128-6081-0). Stein & Day.

Inner Contradictions of Rigorous Research. Chris Argyris. LC 79-6792. (Organizational & Occupational Psychology Ser.). 1980. 16.00 (ISBN 0-12-060150-8). Acad Pr.

Inner Door. Nergis Dalal. 144p. 1975. pap. 1.85 (ISBN 0-89253-028-6). Ind-US Inc.

Inner Eye of Love: Mysticism & Religion. Wiliam Johnston. LC 78-4428. 1978. 9.95 (ISBN 0-06-064195-9, HarpR). Har-Row.

Inner Fire. Allen W. Brown. 1977. 3.95 o.p. (ISBN 0-87680-516-0, 80516). Word Bks.

Inner Game of Tennis. W. Timothy Gallwey. 1974. 8.95 (ISBN 0-394-49154-8). Random.

Inner Growth-Outer Change: An Educational Guide to Church Renewal. John H. Westerhoff, III. (Orig.). pap. 4.95 (ISBN 0-8164-2213-3). Crossroad NY.

Inner Harbour. Fleur Adcock. 55p. 1981. pap. 8.95 (ISBN 0-19-211888-9). Oxford U Pr.

Inner Healing Through Healing of Memories. Betty Tapscott. 1975. pap. 2.95 (ISBN 0-917726-29-4). Hunter Bks.

Inner History of the Chinese Revolution. Leang-Li T'Ang. (Studies in Chinese Government & Law). 391p. 1977. Repr. of 1930 ed. 23.50 (ISBN 0-89093-066-X). U Pubns Amer.

Inner Life. Inayat Khan. (Sufi Message of Hazrat Inayat Khan Ser.: Vol. 1). 1979. 6.95 (ISBN 90-6325-094-0, Pub. by Servire BV Netherlands). Hunter Hse.

Inner Limits of Mankind: Heretical Reflections on Today's Values, Culture & Politics. Ervin Laszlo. LC 77-30732. 1978. text ed. 21.00 (ISBN 0-08-023013-X); pap. text ed. 9.75 (ISBN 0-08-023012-1). Pergamon.

Inner Parent: Raising Ourselves, Raising Our Children. Susan Isaacs & Marti Keller. 1979. 9.95 o.p. (ISBN 0-15-144423-4). HarBraceJ.

Inner Planets. Clark R. Chapman. LC 76-58914. (Illus.). 1977. 9.95 (ISBN 0-684-14898-6, ScribT). Scribner.

Inner Sanctuary. Charles Ross. 1967. pap. 2.45 (ISBN 0-686-12520-7). Banner of Truth.

Inner Shooting. Barbara Yochem & Peggy Shelby. 128p. 1981. 6.95 (ISBN 0-938826-03-4); pap. 3.95 (ISBN 0-938826-02-6). By by Products.

Inner Signature. LC 58-5810. 1977. 5.00 (ISBN 0-935490-04-3). Euclid Pub.

Inner Source. Michael Emmons. 1978. pap. cancelled (ISBN 0-8431-0472-4). Impact Tenn.

Inner Space: The Wonders of You. rev. ed. Judith Geller. (Student Scientist Ser.). (Illus.). (gr. 7-12). 1979. PLB 7.97 (ISBN 0-8239-0446-6). Rosen Pr.

Inner Way: With Prayers from Psalms. Robert A. Smith. 1977. 5.50 (ISBN 0-912128-09-7); pap. 3.50 (ISBN 0-912128-10-0). Pubns Living.

Inner World: A Psycho-Analytic Study of Hindu Childhood & Society. Sudhir Kakar. (Illus.). 1978. 12.95x (ISBN 0-19-560888-7). Oxford U Pr.

Inner World of the Middle-Aged Man. Peter Chew. LC 76-7455. 1976. 8.95 o.s.i. (ISBN 0-02-525000-0, 52500). Macmillan.

Innerchange Career Education Resource Set for Senior High. Geraldine Ball. 1977. 95.00 (ISBN 0-86584-022-9). Human Dev Train.

Innerchange Career Educational Resource Set for Junior High. Geraldine Ball. 1977. 95.00 (ISBN 0-86584-027-X). Human Dev Train.

Innerchange Conflict Mgt. Resources Set for Sr. High. Geraldine Ball. 95.00 (ISBN 0-86584-023-7). Human Dev Train.

Innerchange Drug Abuse Prevention Resource Set for Jr. High. Geraldine Ball. 95.00 (ISBN 0-86584-029-6). Human Dev Train.

Innerchange Experiences: Reproducible Masters for Senior High. Geraldine Ball. 1977. 24.95 (ISBN 0-86584-018-0). Human Dev Train.

Innerchange Experiences: Reproduction Masters for Junior High. 1977. 24.95 (ISBN 0-86584-019-9). Human Dev Train.

Innerchange for Junior High. Geraldine Ball. 1977. 175.00 (ISBN 0-86584-021-0). Human Dev Train.

Innerchange for Senior High. Geraldine Ball. 1977. 175.00 (ISBN 0-86584-020-2). Human Dev Train.

Innerchange Language Arts Resource Ser for Junior High. Geraldine Ball. 1977. 95.00 (ISBN 0-86584-031-8). Human Dev Train.

Innerchange Language Arts Resource Set for Senior High. Geraldine Ball. 1977. 95.00 (ISBN 0-86584-026-1). Human Dev Train.

Innerchange Leader's Manual. Geraldine Ball. 1977. 12.95 (ISBN 0-86584-017-2). Human Dev Train.

Innere Bezirk: Roman in Drei Buechern. Hermann Lenz. 680p. (Ger.). 1980. write for info. (Pub. by Insel Verlag Germany). Suhrkamp.

Innerworld of the Outerworld of the Innerworld. Peter Handke. Tr. by Michael Roloff from Ger. LC 73-17875. 128p. 1974. 8.95 (ISBN 0-8164-9194-1); pap. 4.50 (ISBN 0-8164-9195-X, Continuum). Continuum.

Innocence & Experience: An Introduction to Blake. E. D. Hirsch, Jr. LC 74-22905. (Midway Reprint Ser). xvi, 336p. 1975. pap. 12.00x (ISBN 0-226-34238-7). U of Chicago Pr.

Innocent Abroad. Chay Blyth & Maureen Blyth. 196p. 1980. 6.00x (Pub. by Nautical England). State Mutual Bk.

Innocent Abroad: Belgium at the Paris Peace Conference of 1919. Sally Marks. LC 80-13698. (Illus.). 456p. 1980. 26.00x (ISBN 0-8078-1451-2). U of NC Pr.

Innocent Art. Ed. by David Larkin. (Gift Bks). (Illus.). 96p. (Orig.). 1974. pap. 4.95 o.p. (ISBN 0-345-24244-0). Ballantine.

Innocent Blood. P. D. James. 352p. 1981. pap. 3.50 (ISBN 0-445-04630-9). Popular Lib.

Innocent Bystander: Scene from the Seventies. L. E. Sissman. LC 75-25144. 1975. 7.95 (ISBN 0-8149-0769-5). Vanguard.

Innocent Erendira & Other Stories. Gabriel Garcia-Marquez. Tr. by Gregory Rabassa from Span. LC 74-15873. 1979. pap. 3.95 (ISBN 0-06-090701-0, CN 701, CN). Har-Row.

Innocent Fire. Brooke Hastings. 192p. (Orig.) 1980. pap. 1.50 (ISBN 0-671-57026-9). S&S.

Innocent Heart. Nina Pykare. (Orig.). 1981. pap. 1.50 (ISBN 0-440-14475-2). Dell.

Innocent Heiress, No. 15. Barbara Cartland. 1979. pap. 1.50 o.p. (ISBN 0-685-63662-3, 04880-1). Jove Pubns.

Innocent Thoughts, Harmless Intentions. John Heuer. Date not set. pap. 2.50 (ISBN 0-686-69001-X). Dramatists Play.

Innocent Victorian: The Satiric Poetry of Arthur Hugh Clough. Michael Timko. LC 66-11301. xvi, 198p. 1966. 12.00x (ISBN 0-8214-0016-9). Ohio U Pr.

Innocents Abroad. Mark Twain. (Illus.). Repr. of 1869 ed. 12.95x o.s.i. (ISBN 0-06-014380-0, HarpT). Har-Row.

Innocents Abroad. Mark Twain. pap. 2.50 (ISBN 0-451-51142-5, CE1379, Sig Classics). NAL.

Innokenty of Alaska. L. Puhalo. 1977. pap. 5.00 (ISBN 0-913026-86-7). St Nectarios.

Innovation. William Kingston. 1979. 11.95 (ISBN 0-7145-3540-0); pap. 4.95 (ISBN 0-7145-3611-3). Riverrun NY.

Innovation: A Study of Technological Policy. Arthur Gerstenfeld. 1976. pap. text ed. 9.75x (ISBN 0-8191-0037-4). U Pr of Amer.

Innovation & Employment. David Foster. 1980. 27.00 (ISBN 0-08-022500-4); pap. 11.25 (ISBN 0-08-022499-7). Pergamon.

Innovation & Implementation in Public Organizations. Richard R. Nelson & Douglas T. Yates. LC 74-16938. 1977. 21.95 (ISBN 0-669-95596-5). Lexington Bks.

Innovation & New Product Marketing. David Midgley. LC 76-50052. 1978. pap. 17.95x o.p. (ISBN 0-470-26517-5). Halsted Pr.

Innovation & Public Policy: The Case of Personal Rapid Transit. Catherine G. Burke. LC 79-2410. (Illus.). 416p. 1979. 23.95 (ISBN 0-669-03167-4). Lexington Bks.

Innovation & Social Process: A National Experiment in Implementing Social Technology. Louis G. Tornatzky. LC 80-36809. (Pergamon Policy Studies on Politics, Policy & Modeling). 150p. 1980. 25.00 (ISBN 0-08-026303-8). Pergamon.

Innovation & the American Economy. The Fourth Franklin Conference. 140p. 1980. pap. text ed. 8.95 (ISBN 0-89168-033-0). Franklin Inst Pr.

Innovation & U. S. Research: Problems & Recommendations. Ed. by W. Novis Smith & C. F. Larson. LC 80-16192. (ACS Symposium Ser.: No. 129). 1980. 26.75 (ISBN 0-8412-0561-2). Am Chemical.

Innovation, Competition & Government Policy in the Semiconductor Industry. Robert W. Wilson et al. LC 80-8317. 1980. 21.95 (ISBN 0-669-03995-0). Lexington Bks.

Innovation in Access to Higher Education: Ontario, Canada,England, Wales, & Sweden. Ed. by Robert M. Pike et al. (Access to Higher Education Ser.: No. 5). 336p. 1978. pap. 10.00 (ISBN 0-89192-217-2, Pub. by Intl Coun Ed Dev). Interbk Inc.

Innovation in Communist Systems. Ed. by Andrew Gyorgy & James A. Kuhlman. LC 77-29048. (Westview Special Studies on the Soviet Union & Eastern Europe Ser.). 1978. lib. bdg. 24.50x (ISBN 0-89158-418-8). Westview.

Innovation in Education. Ed. by Matthew B. Miles. LC 64-15445. 1964. text ed. 16.50x (ISBN 0-8077-1803-3). Tchrs Coll.

Innovation in Health Policy & Service Delivery: A Cross-National Perspective, 3vols, Vol. 3. Ed. by Christa Altenstetter. LC 80-39617. 256p. 1981. lib. bdg. 25.00 (ISBN 0-89946-078-X). Oelgeschlager.

Innovation in Higher Education. Ed. by K. G. Collier. (General Ser.). 140p. 1974. pap. text ed. 12.50x (ISBN 0-85633-032-9, NFER). Humanities.

Innovation in Reading in Britain. Judith Goyen & Hugh Philip. LC 73-77398. (Experiments & Innovations in Education Ser., No. 3). 52p. (Orig.). 1973. pap. 2.50 (ISBN 92-3-101112-X, U312, UNESCO). Unipub.

Innovation in Rural India. Kivlin. 1975. 10.00 (ISBN 0-87972-169-3). Bowling Green Univ.

Innovation Process in the Energy Industry. G. F. Ray & L. Uhlmann. LC 78-17064. (National Institute of Economic & Social Research, Occasional Papers Ser.: No. 30). 1979. 21.95 (ISBN 0-521-22371-7). Cambridge U Pr.

Innovation Research & Public Policy. Ed. by John A. Agnew. LC 80-12054. (Syracuse Geographical Ser.: No. 5). (Illus.). 310p. (Orig.). 1980. pap. 19.75 (ISBN 0-8357-0510-2, IS-00109, Pub. by Syracuse U Dept Geog). Univ Microfilms.

Innovation: The Management Connection. Robert O. Burns. 160p. 1975. 17.95 (ISBN 0-669-00084-1). Lexington Bks.

Innovation Without Renovation in the Elementary School. Jane Morton & Richard J. Morton. LC 74-79466. 192p. 1974. pap. text ed. 3.95 (ISBN 0-590-09582-X, Citation). Schol Bk Serv.

Innovations & Organizations. Gerald Zaltman et al. LC 73-5873. 224p. 1973. 18.95 (ISBN 0-471-98129-X, Pub. by Wiley-Interscience). Wiley.

Innovations for Future Cities. Gideon Golany. LC 75-36410. (Illus.). 1976. text ed. 28.95 (ISBN 0-275-22860-6). Praeger.

Innovations in Client-Centered Therapy. David A. Wexler & Laura N. Rice. LC 74-10538. (Personality Processes Ser). 1974. 34.95 (ISBN 0-471-93715-0, Pub. by Wiley-Interscience). Wiley.

Innovations in Community Health Nursing: Health Care Delivery in Shortage Areas. Ed. by Anne R. Warner. LC 77-20114. 1978. pap. text ed. 9.50 (ISBN 0-8016-5350-9). Mosby.

Innovations in Education: Reformers & Their Critics. 2nd ed. John M. Rich. 1978. pap. text ed. 8.95x o.p. (ISBN 0-205-06059-5). Allyn.

Innovations in Education: Reformers & Their Critics. 3rd ed. John M. Rich. 350p. 1980. pap. text ed. 10.50 (ISBN 0-205-07141-4, 237141-3). Allyn.

Innovations in Patient Care. D. Towell & C. Harries. 224p. 1980. 30.00x (ISBN 0-85664-692-X, Pub. by Croom Helm England). State Mutual Bk.

Innovations of the Roman Church. Apostolos Makrakis. 82p. (Orig.). 1966. pap. 1.50x (ISBN 0-938366-39-4). Orthodox Chr.

Innovative Design with an Introduction to Design Graphics. Warren J. Luzadder. (Illus.). 496p. 1975. 21.95 (ISBN 0-13-465641-5). P-H.

Innovative Furniture in America: From 1800 to the Present. David Hanks. (Illus.). 250p. 1981. text ed. 30.00 (ISBN 0-8180-0450-9). Horizon.

Innovative Idea Bank. Herbert E. Phillips. LC 80-65052. 192p. 1980. pap. 15.00 (ISBN 0-8408-0501-2). Carrollton Pr.

Innovative Machine Quilting. Hettie Risinger. LC 79-91393. (Illus.). 164p. 1980. 14.95 (ISBN 0-8069-5398-5); lib. bdg. 13.29 (ISBN 0-8069-5399-3). Sterling.

Innovative Numerical Analysis for the Engineering Sciences. Ed. by R. Shaw et al. LC 80-14005. 1980. 40.00x (ISBN 0-8139-0867-1). U Pr of Va.

Innovative Spirit. Algo D. Henderson. LC 78-128698. (Higher Education Ser.). 1970. 14.95x o.p. (ISBN 0-87589-073-3). Jossey-Bass.

Inns and Their Signs: Fact and Fiction. Eric R. Delderfield. LC 75-10564. (Illus.). 96p. 1975. 11.95 (ISBN 0-7153-7112-6). David & Charles.

Inorganic & Analytical Chemistry. Ed. by F. Boschke et al. LC 51-5497. (Topics in Current Chemistry: Vol. 14, Pt. 1). (Illus.). 1970. pap. 27.20 (ISBN 0-387-04816-2). Springer-Verlag.

Inorganic Chemistry. J. Bassett. 1965. text ed. 23.00 (ISBN 0-08-011207-2); pap. text ed. 9.75 o.p. (ISBN 0-08-011206-4). Pergamon.

Inorganic Chemistry, 2 vols. C. S. Phillips & R. J. Williams. Incl. Vol. 1. Principles & Non-Metals. 1965 (ISBN 0-19-501021-3, OxfordC); Vol. 2. Metals. 1966 (ISBN 0-19-501022-1). 12.95x ea. Oxford U Pr.

Inorganic Chemistry in Biology & Medicine. Arthur E. Martell. LC 80-23248. (ACS Symposium Ser.: No. 140). 1980. 39.50 (ISBN 0-8412-0588-4). Am Chemical.

Inorganic Chemistry in Nonaqueous Solvents. A. K. Holliday & A. G. Massey. 1965. 16.50 (ISBN 0-08-011335-4); pap. 7.25 (ISBN 0-08-011334-6). Pergamon.

Inorganic Chemistry of Biological Processes. 2nd ed. M. N. Hughes. 336p. 1981. pap. 24.50 (ISBN 0-471-27815-7, Pub. by Wiley-Interscience). Wiley.

Inorganic Hydrides. B. L. Shaw. 1967. 19.50 (ISBN 0-08-012110-1); pap. 9.75 (ISBN 0-08-012109-8). Pergamon.

Inorganic Nomenclature: A Programmed Approach. Wesley E. Lingren. (Illus.). 1980. pap. text ed. 8.95 (ISBN 0-13-466607-0). P-H.

Inorganic Pigments: Manufacturing Processes. Ed. by M. H. Gutcho. LC 80-16319. (Chemical Technology Review No. 166). 488p. 1980. 54.00 (ISBN 0-8155-0811-5). Noyes.

Inorganic Plant Nutrition. Hugh Gauch. LC 72-76542. 528p. 1972. 40.00 (ISBN 0-12-786518-7). Acad Pr.

Inorganic Reaction Chemistry: Reactions of the Elements, Vol. 2. D. T. Burns & A. Townshend. Ed. by A. H. Carter. (Ser. in Analytical Chemistry). 410p. 1981. 97.50 (ISBN 0-470-27105-1). Halsted Pr.

Inorganic Reaction Chemistry: Systematic Chemical Separation, Vol. 1. D. T. Burns et al. LC 79-42957. 248p. 1980. 57.50x (ISBN 0-470-26895-6). Halsted Pr.

Inorganic Reaction Mechanisms, Vol. 1, Pt. 2. Ed. by John O. Edwards. LC 72-105386. (Progress in Inorganic Chemistry Ser.). 1972. 52.50 o.p. (ISBN 0-471-23317-X, Pub. by Wiley Interscience). Wiley.

Inorganic Syntheses, Vol. 15. G. W. Parshall. (Inorganic Synthesis Ser.). 1974. 25.95 o.p. (ISBN 0-07-048521-6, P&RB). McGraw.

Inorganic Syntheses, Vol. 20. Daryle H. Busch. (Inorganic Synthesis Ser.). 1980. 29.95 (ISBN 0-471-07715-1, Pub. by Wiley-Interscience). Wiley.

Inorganic Synthesis, Vol. 16. F. Basolo. 1976. 27.50 o.p. (ISBN 0-07-004015-X, P&RB). McGraw.

Inpatient Health Facilities Statistics United States, 1978. Geneviene W. Strahan. Ed. by Mary Olmsted. (Ser. 14, No. 24). 50p. 1980. pap. text ed. 1.75 (ISBN 0-8406-0204-9). Natl Ctr Educ Broker.

Inpatient Utilization of Short-Stay Hospitals by Diagnosis: United States, 1974. Linda Glickman. Ed. by Taloria Stevenson. (Ser. 13: No. 32). 1977. pap. text ed. 1.50 (ISBN 0-8406-0002-X). Natl Ctr Health Stats.

Inpursuit of Price Stability: The Wage Price Freeze of 1971. Arnold R. Weber. LC 73-11346. (Studies in Wage-Price Policy: Studies in Wage Price Policy). 137p. 1973. 10.95 (ISBN 0-8157-9264-6); pap. 4.95 (ISBN 0-8157-9263-8). Brookings.

Input-Output Analysis of Large-Scale Interconnected Systems. M. Vidyasagar. (Lecture Notes in Control & Information Sciences Ser.: Vol. 29). 225p. 1981. pap. 16.50 (ISBN 0-387-10501-8). Springer-Verlag.

Input, Output & Marketing: Proceedings of the 1977 London Conference & the 1979 Toledo Ohio Workshop. Ed. by S. J. Gielnik & W. F. Gossling. (I.-O.P.C. Conference Ser.: No. 4). (Illus.). 400p. 1980. 50.00x (ISBN 0-904870-14-6, Pub. by Input-Output England). Kelley.

Input-Output Approaches in Global Modeling: Proceedings of the Fifth IIASA Symposium on Global Modeling, Sept. 26-29, 1977. Ed. by G. Bruckmann. (IIASA Proceedings: Vol. 9). (Illus.). 518p. 1980. 115.00 (ISBN 0-08-025663-5). Pergamon.

Input-Output Databases. Jay M. Gould. 1978. lib. bdg. 22.50 (ISBN 0-8240-7058-5). Garland Pub.

Input-Output Economics. Wassily W. Leontief. 1966. 19.95x (ISBN 0-19-500616-X). Oxford U Pr.

Inqua Field Guides, 16 vols. D. Q. Bowen. Incl. Vol. 1. East Anglia. Ed. by R. G. West; Vol. 2. English Midlands. Ed. by F. W. Shotton; Vol. 3. Isle of Man: Lancashire Coast & Lake District. Ed. by M. J. Tooley; Vol. 4. South East England & the Thames Valley. Ed. by E. R. Shepherd-Thorn & J. J. Wymer; Vol. 5. Yorkshire & Lincolnshire. Ed. by J. A. Catt; Vol. 6. South West England. Ed. by D. N. Mottershead; Vol. 7. Wales & the Cheshire Shropshire Lowland. Ed. by D. Q. Bowen; Vol. 8. Mid & North Wales. Ed. by E. Watson; Vol. 9. Northern Highlands of Scotland. Ed. by C. M. Clapperton; Vol. 10. Scottish Highlands. Ed. by J. B. Sissons; Vol. 11. Western Scotland I. Ed. by R. J. Price; Vol. 12. Western Scotland II. Ed. by J. H. Dickson; Vol. 13. South East Ireland. Ed. by D. Huddart; Vol. 14. South & Southwest Ireland. Ed. by C. A. Lewis; Vol. 15. Western Ireland. T. Finch; Vol. 16. Southern Shores of the North Sea. Ed. by R. Paepe. 1980. Set. pap. text ed. 112.00 (ISBN 0-686-64925-7, Pub. by GEO Abstracts England); pap. text ed. 8.00 ea. State Mutual Bk.

Inquest. Donald Freed. (Illus., Orig.). 1970. 4.50 o.p. (ISBN 0-8090-5845-6, New Mermaid); pap. 1.95 o.p. (ISBN 0-8090-1221-9, New Mermaid). Hill & Wang.

Inquilab. Asif Currimbhoy. 1970. 10.00 (ISBN 0-89253-784-1); pap. text ed. 4.80 (ISBN 0-88253-807-1). Ind-US Inc.

Inquire: A Handbook of Classroom Ideas to Motivate the Teaching of Intermediate Science. (Spice Ser.). 1976. 6.50 (ISBN 0-89273-121-4). Educ Serv.

Inquiries in Chemistry. A. Mason Turner & Curtis T. Sears. (gr. 9-12). 1974. text ed. 15.36 (ISBN 0-205-03373-3, 683373X); tchrs'. guide 7.56 (ISBN 0-205-03374-1, 6833748); lab ex. 6.20 (ISBN 0-205-03375-X, 6833756); tests & dup. masters 40.00 (ISBN 0-205-05401-3, 685401X). Allyn.

Inquiries in Sociology. rev. ed. Helen M. Hughes. (Sociological Resources for the Social Studies). (gr. 9-12). 1978. text ed. 15.36 (ISBN 0-205-05866-3, 8158665); tchr's guide 13.20 (ISBN 0-205-05867-1, 8158673). Allyn.

Inquiries into Chemistry. Michael R. Abraham & Michael J. Pavelich. (Illus.). 1979. 8.95x (ISBN 0-917974-32-8). Waveland Pr.

Inquiries into Human Faculty & Its Development. Francis Galton. 261p. 1980. Repr. lib. bdg. 20.00 (ISBN 0-89984-230-5). Century Bookbindery.

Inquiring Mind. Zechariah Chafee. LC 74-699. (American Constitutional & Legal History Ser.). 276p. 1974. Repr. of 1928 ed. lib. bdg. 27.50 (ISBN 0-306-70641-5). Da Capo.

Inquiry & Inspiration. Ruth McKinley. LC 79-54824. (Orig.). Date not set. pap. cancelled (ISBN 0-89793-021-5). Hunter Hse.

Inquiry by Design: Tools for Environment - Behavior. John Zeisel. LC 80-14292. (Basic Concepts in Environment & Behavior Ser.). (Orig.). 1980. pap. text ed. 8.95 (ISBN 0-8185-0375-0). Brooks-Cole.

Inquiry Concerning Human Understanding: An Abstract of a Treatise of Human Nature. David Hume. Ed. by Charles W. Hendel. LC 59-11685. 1955. pap. 5.50 (ISBN 0-672-60218-0, LLA49). Bobbs.

Inquiry Concerning the Principles of Morals: With a Supplement, a Dialogue. David Hume. Ed. by Charles W. Hendel. 1957. pap. 4.95 (ISBN 0-672-60236-9, LLA62). Bobbs.

Inquiry Handbooks. Ed. by Jules Davids. LC 74-21632. (41 vols. in 20). 1975. 795.00 (ISBN 0-8420-1798-4). Scholarly Res Inc.

Inquiry into Meaning & Truth. Bertrand Russell. 1940. text ed. 18.00x (ISBN 0-04-121007-7). Humanities.

Inquiry into the High Cost of Electricity in New England. William D. Shipman. LC 62-18344. (Illus.). 1962. 17.50x (ISBN 0-8195-3031-X, Pub. by Wesleyan U Pr). Columbia U Pr.

Inquiry into the Human Prospect. Robert L. Heilbroner. 1979. 8.95 (ISBN 0-393-01256-5). Norton.

Inquiry into the Nature & Causes of the Wealth of Nations, 2 vols. Adam Smith. Ed. by R. H. Campbell. (Glasgow Edition of the Works & Correspondence of Adam Smith). 1976. 98.00x (ISBN 0-19-828184-6). Oxford U Pr.

Inquiry into the Origin & Early History of Engraving Upon Copper & Wood, 2 vols. William Y. Ottley. Ed. by Sydney J. Freedberg. LC 77-25757. (Connoisseurship Criticism & Art History Ser.: Vol. 14). 835p. 1979. Set. lib. bdg. 80.00 (ISBN 0-8240-3272-1). Garland Pub.

Inquiry into the Relation of Cause & Effect. 4th ed. Thomas Brown. LC 77-16224. 1977. Repr. of 1835 ed. lib. bdg. 49.00 (ISBN 0-8201-1301-8). Schol Facsimiles.

Inquisition: A Tragic Mistake. John A. O'Brien. LC 73-1962. 192p. 1973. 6.95 o.s.i. (ISBN 0-02-591400-6). Macmillan.

Inquisitive Eye. Mark Fineman. (Illus.). 224p. 1981. pap. text ed. 7.95x (ISBN 0-19-502773-6). Oxford U Pr.

Inro & Other Miniature Forms of Japanese Lacquer Art. Melvin Jahss & Betty Jahss. LC 76-109406. 75.00 (ISBN 0-8048-0263-7). C E Tuttle.

Ins & Outs & Wins of Contract Bridge. Ira Martin. 1977. 6.00 o.p. (ISBN 0-682-48900-X). Exposition.

Ins & Outs of Ferry Flying. Don Downie & Julia L. Downie. (Modern Aviation Ser.). (Illus.). 288p. (Orig.). 1980. cancelled (ISBN 0-8306-9936-8, 2280); pap. 7.95 (ISBN 0-8306-2280-2). Tab Bks.

Ins & Outs of Gardening. D. X. Fenten. (Illus.). 128p. (YA) 1979. 8.95 o.p. (ISBN 0-87460-263-7). Lion.

Ins and Outs of Institutional Investing. Dean LeBaron. LC 76-40961. 176p. 1976. 14.95 (ISBN 0-88229-343-5). Nelson-Hall.

Insanity & the Criminal. John C. Goodwin. (Historical Foundations of Forensic Psychiatry & Psychology Ser.). 308p. 1980. Repr. of 1924 ed. lib. bdg. 29.50 (ISBN 0-306-76061-4). Da Capo.

Insanity & the Criminal Law. W. A. White. (Historical Foundations of Forensic Psychiatry & Psychology Ser.). 281p. 1980. Repr. of 1923 ed. lib. bdg. 25.00 (ISBN 0-306-76069-X). Da Capo.

Inscape & Landscape. Pierre Dansereau. 132p. 1975. 15.00x (ISBN 0-231-03991-3); pap. 5.00x (ISBN 0-231-03992-1). Columbia U Pr.

Inscape: Stories, Plays, & Poems. Ed. by Muriel Davis. LC 73-130272. 1971. pap. text ed. 5.95x o.p. (ISBN 0-397-47240-4); pap. instructor's manual avail. o.p. (ISBN 0-397-47241-2). Lippincott.

Inscribed Fibula Praenestina: Problems of Authenticity. Arthur E. Gordon. LC 75-620010. (Publications in Classical Studies: Vol. 16). 1975. 8.00x (ISBN 0-520-09537-5). U of Cal Pr.

Insearch. Frances Coe & Ivan Coe. 112p. 1981. 6.50 (ISBN 0-682-49713-4). Exposition.

Insearch. James Hillman. (Jungian Classics). 1979. pap. 7.50 (ISBN 0-88214-501-0). Spring Pubns.

Insect Allergy: Allergic & Toxic Reactions to Insects & Other Arthropods. 2nd ed. Claude A. Frazier. LC 67-30896. (Illus.). 508p. 1980-81. 26.50 (ISBN 0-87527-010-7). Green.

Insect Behavior. Robert W. Matthews & Janice R. Matthews. LC 78-7869. 1978. 28.50 (ISBN 0-471-57685-9, Pub. by Wiley-Interscience). Wiley.

Insect Biochemistry & Function. Ed. by D. J. Candy & B. A. Kilby. LC 74-26569. 314p. 1975. text ed. 29.95x o.p. (ISBN 0-412-21530-6, Pub. by Chapman & Hall). Methuen Inc.

Insect Biochemistry & Function. Ed. by D. J. Candy & B. A. Kilby. LC 74-26569. 314p. 1975. 32.50 o.p. (ISBN 0-470-13347-3). Halsted Pr.

Insect Biology in the Future: "VBW 80". Michael Locke & D. S. Smith. 1980. 50.00 (ISBN 0-12-454340-5). Acad Pr.

Insect Clocks. D. S. Saunders. 292p. 1976. text ed. 37.00 (ISBN 0-08-018211-9); pap. text ed. 13.75 (ISBN 0-08-024402-5). Pergamon.

Insect Colony. Charles R. Larson. LC 78-4701. 1978. 7.95 o.p. (ISBN 0-03-041896-8). HR&W.

Insect Control in the People's Republic of China: A Trip Report of the American Insect Control Delegation. Committee on Scholarly Communication with the People's Republic of China (CSCPRC) LC 76-52849. (CSCPRC Report: No. 2). 1977. pap. 11.25 (ISBN 0-309-02525-7). Natl Acad Pr.

Insect Cytogenetics. R. L. Blackman et al. (Royal Entomological Society of London Symposium Ser.). 272p. 1981. 69.95 (ISBN 0-470-27126-4). Halsted Pr.

Insect Development. P. A. Lawrence. LC 76-8196. (Royal Entomological Society of London Symposium Ser.). 1976. 30.95 (ISBN 0-470-15098-X). Halsted Pr.

Insect Ecology. Peter W. Price. LC 75-12720. 514p. 1975. 23.50 (ISBN 0-471-69721-4, Pub. by Wiley-Interscience). Wiley.

Insect Ecology & the Sterile-Male Technique. (Illus., Orig.). 1969. pap. 6.50 (ISBN 92-0-011269-2, IAEA). Unipub.

Insect Flight. R. C. Rainey. LC 75-22091. (Royal Entomological Society of London Symposium Ser.). 287p. 1976. 60.95 (ISBN 0-470-70550-7). Halsted Pr.

Insect Friends & Enemies. Margaret M. Anderson. (Illus.). 64p. 1981. 7.50 (ISBN 0-682-49689-8). Exposition.

Insect Fungus Symbiosis: Nutrition, Mutualism & Commensalism. Ed. by Lekh R. Batra. LC 78-20640. 288p. 1979. text ed. 27.50 (ISBN 0-470-26671-6). Allanheld.

Insect Hemocytes. A. P. Gupta. LC 78-10477. 1979. 95.00 (ISBN 0-521-22364-4). Cambridge U Pr.

Insect Hormones. V. B. Wigglesworth. (Illus.). 1970. text ed. 11.95x (ISBN 0-7167-0688-1). W H Freeman.

Insect Invasion. Ray Cummings. (YA) 4.95 o.p. (ISBN 0-685-07437-4, Avalon). Bouregy.

Insect Life. Boy Scouts Of America. LC 19-600. (Illus.). 64p. (gr. 6-12). 1973. pap. 0.70x (ISBN 0-8395-3353-5, 3353). BSA.

Insect Muscle. P. N. Usherwood. 1975. 84.50 (ISBN 0-12-709450-4). Acad Pr.

Insect Pathology: An Advanced Treatise, 2 Vols. Ed. by Edward A. Steinhaus. 1963. 55.25 ea. Vol. 1 (ISBN 0-12-665801-3). Vol. 2. (ISBN 0-12-665802-1). Acad Pr.

Insect Pests of Rice. 68p. 1977. pap. 5.00 (R005, IRRI). Unipub.

Insect Photoperiodism. Stanley Beck. 1968. 40.50 o.p. (ISBN 0-12-084350-1). Acad Pr.

Insect Phylogeny. Willi Hennig. 528p. 1981. price not set (ISBN 0-471-27848-3, Pub. by Wiley-Interscience). Wiley.

Insect Physiology. W. Mordue et al. LC 79-27743. 1981. pap. 16.95x (ISBN 0-470-26931-6). Halsted Pr.

Insect Population Control by the Sterile-Male Technique. Ed. by A. W. Lindguist. (Technical Reports Ser.: No. 21). (Illus., Orig.). 1963. pap. 2.75 (ISBN 92-0-115063-6, IAEA). Unipub.

Insect Thermoregulation. Bernd Heinrich. LC 80-19452. 312p. 1981. 27.50 (ISBN 0-471-05144-6, Pub. by Wiley-Interscience). Wiley.

Insect Travelers. John Kaufmann. (Illus.). 128p. (gr. 7 up). 1972. 7.75 (ISBN 0-688-20036-2); PLB 7.44 (ISBN 0-688-30036-7). Morrow.

Insect World of J. Henri Fabre. J. Henri Fabre. Ed. by Edwin W. Teale. (Nature Library Ser.). 352p. (Orig.). 1981. pap. 5.95 (ISBN 0-06-090806-8, CN 806, CN). Har-Row.

Insecticide, Herbicide, Fungicide Quick Guide, 1978. B. G. Page & W. T. Thomson. 1979. 10.00 o.p. (ISBN 0-686-19192-7). Thomson Pub CA.

Insecticides: Biochemical & Biological Methods, Natural Products. Ed. by R. Wegler. (Chemie der Pflanzenschutz und Schaedlingsbekaempfungsmittel). 500p. 1981. 152.30 (ISBN 0-387-10307-4). Springer-Verlag.

Insects. H. Angel. 1975. pap. 5.00 o.p. (ISBN 0-85242-402-7, Pub. by Fountain). Morgan.

Insects. Peter Farb. LC 62-21531. (Life Nature Library). (Illus.). (gr. 5 up). 1962. PLB 8.97 o.p. (ISBN 0-8094-0621-7, Pub. by Time-Life). Silver.

Insects. Alice Fields. (gr. 2-4). 1980. PLB 7.90 (ISBN 0-531-03244-2). Watts.

Insects. Ed. by Ross E. Hutchins. 336p. 1966. pap. 3.50 o.p. (ISBN 0-13-467423-5). P-H.

Insects. Url N. Lanham. LC 64-14235. (Illus.). 1967. 17.50x (ISBN 0-231-02603-X); pap. 5.00 (ISBN 0-231-08582-6, 82). Columbia U Pr.

Insects, 2 vols. Cecil J. Sharp. (Cambridge Natural History Ser.: Vols. 5 & 6). (Illus.). Set. 17.50 (ISBN 0-8446-0907-2). Peter Smith.

Insects & Allergy: And What to Do About Them. Claude A. Frazier & F. K. Brown. LC 79-6706. (Illus.). 350p. 1980. 14.95 (ISBN 0-8061-1518-1); pap. 8.95 (ISBN 0-8061-1706-0). U of Okla Pr.

Insects & Disease. Keith R. Snow. LC 73-15433. 208p. 1974. 9.95 (ISBN 0-470-81017-3, Pub. by Wiley). Krieger.

Insects & Diseases. Keith Snow. LC 73-15433. (Illus.). 208p. 1974. text ed. 16.95 (ISBN 0-470-81017-3). Halsted Pr.

Insects & Plants. Irving Adler & Ruth Adler. LC 62-19714. (Reason Why Ser). (Illus.). (gr. 3-6). 1962. PLB 7.89 (ISBN 0-381-99966-1, A38660, JD-J). John Day.

Insects & Plants: The Amazing Partnership. Elizabeth K. Cooper. LC 63-7893. (Illus.). (gr. 4-6). 1963. 6.95 o.p. (ISBN 0-15-238701-3, HJ). HarBraceJ.

Insects & Spiders. LC 76-58898. (Wild, Wild World of Animals Ser.). (Illus.). 1977. lib. bdg. 11.97 (ISBN 0-686-51170-0). Silver.

Insects & Their World. Harold Oldroyd. LC 60-50390. (Orig.). 1962. pap. 2.75 o.s.i. (ISBN 0-226-62636-9, P516, Phoen). U of Chicago Pr.

Insects Are Animals Too. Anthony Wooton. LC 77-91775. 13.50 (ISBN 0-7153-7534-2). David & Charles.

Insects Are Coming. Alan Landsburgh. (Illus., Orig.). 1978. pap. 2.25 o.s.i. (ISBN 0-446-82595-6). Warner Bks.

Insects: East Coast Edition. Ed. by Little, Brown Editors. (Explorer's Notebooks). (Illus.). 32p. (Orig.). (gr. 5 up). 1981. pap. 1.95 (ISBN 0-316-52771-8). Little.

Insects, Hygiene & History. J. R. Busvine. (Illus.). 1976. text ed. 23.75x (ISBN 0-485-11160-8, Athlone Pr). Humanities.

Insects in Color. N. D. Riley. (European Ecology Ser.). (Illus.). 1963. 9.95 (ISBN 0-7137-0144-7, Pub by Blandford Pr England). Sterling.

Insects in Relation to Plant Disease. 2nd ed. Walter Carter. LC 73-4362. 62.50 (ISBN 0-471-13849-5, Pub. by Wiley-Interscience). Wiley.

Insects of Hawaii: Diptera: Cyclorrhapha IV, Vol. 14. D. Elmo Hardy. LC 48-45482. (Illus.). 500p. (Orig.). 1981. pap. 35.00x (ISBN 0-686-69434-1). U Pr of Hawaii.

Insects of Nigeria. John T. Medler. (Memoir Ser.: No. 30). 919p. 1980. 68.00 (ISBN 0-686-27978-6). Am Entom Inst.

Insects: Readings from Scientific American. Intro. by Thomas Eisner & Edward O. Wilson. LC 77-23843. (Illus.). 1977. text ed. 19.95x (ISBN 0-7167-0047-6); pap. text ed. 9.95x (ISBN 0-7167-0046-8). W H Freeman.

Insects That Feed on Trees & Shrubs: An Illustrated Practical Guide. Warren T. Johnson & H. H. Lyon. (Illus.). 464p. 1976. 38.50x (ISBN 0-8014-0956-X). Comstock.

Insects That Live in Families. Dean Morris. LC 77-8254. (Read About Animals Ser.). (Illus.). (gr. k-3). 1977. PLB 9.95 (ISBN 0-8393-0001-8). Raintree Child.

Insects: West Coast Edition. Ed. by Little, Brown Editors. (Explorer's Notebooks). (Illus.). 32p. (Orig.). (gr. 5 up). 1980. pap. 1.95 (ISBN 0-316-52772-6). Little.

Insects You Have Seen. Lloyd Eighme. LC 79-24141. (Crown Ser.). (gr. 6 up). 1980. pap. 4.50 (ISBN 0-8127-0259-X). Southern Pub.

Insecure Heart & Other Poems. Wallace Weister. 1980. 4.00 o.p. (ISBN 0-8062-1127-X). Carlton.

Insei: Abdicated Sovereigns in the Politics of Late Heian Japan, 1086-1185. G. Cameron Hurst. 368p. 1976. 22.50x (ISBN 0-231-03932-8). Columbia U Pr.

Inserat Grotesk I: Special Issue 10. pap. 1.00 o.p. (ISBN 0-685-78400-2). The Smith.

Inshore Dinghy Fishing. E. J. Wood. (Leisure Plan Bks). pap. 2.95 (ISBN 0-600-40083-2). Transatlantic.

Inshore Fishing: Its Skills, Risks, Rewards. Stan Judd. (Illus.). 144p. 10.00 (ISBN 0-85238-096-8, FN). Unipub.

Inside & Out. Robert B. Ruddell et al. (Pathfinder - Allyn & Bacon Reading Program: Level 10). (gr. 1-2). 1978. text ed. 7.20 (ISBN 0-205-05115-4, 5451159); tchr's ed. 10.88 (ISBN 0-205-05130-8, 5451302); 3.28. Allyn.

Inside Bangladesh Today: An Eye-Witness Account. Basant Chatterjee. LC 73-906296. 159p. 1973. 6.00x (ISBN 0-8002-1568-0). Intl Pubns Serv.

Inside Baseball: Tips & Techniques for Coaches & Players. Dell Bethel. LC 69-17434. (Illus.). 1969. 7.95 (ISBN 0-8092-8871-0); pap. 4.95 o.p. (ISBN 0-8092-8870-2). Contemp Bks.

Inside Bohemian Grove: The Most Exclusive Men's Gathering in the World. Tom Moulin & Don DeNevi. LC 78-75157. (Illus.). 1979. cancelled (ISBN 0-89395-017-3); pap. cancelled (ISBN 0-89395-018-1). Cal Living Bks.

Inside Bowling for Women. Paula Sperber & Chuck Pezzano. LC 77-75852. (Inside Ser.). (Illus.). 1977. 7.95 o.p. (ISBN 0-8092-7995-9); pap. 4.95 (ISBN 0-8092-7980-0). Contemp Bks.

Inside China. Malcolm MacDonald. (Illus.). 208p. 1981. 19.95 (ISBN 0-316-54188-5). Little.

Inside Commercial Banking. Eric N. Compton. LC 80-13269. 191p. 1980. 19.95 (ISBN 0-471-07974-X, Pub. by Wiley-Interscience). Wiley.

Inside Computer Understanding: Five Programs Plus Miniatures. Roger C. Schank & Christopher K. Riesbeck. LC 80-18314. (Artificial Intelligence Ser.). 368p. 1981. profess. & reference 24.95 (ISBN 0-89859-071-X). L Erlbaum Assocs.

Inside Congress. 2nd ed. Congressional Quarterly. 1979. pap. text ed. 7.95 (ISBN 0-87187-177-7). Congr Quarterly.

Inside Death Valley. rev. 3rd ed. Chuck Gebhardt. LC 80-83123. (Illus.). 166p. 1980. pap. 5.95 (ISBN 0-9601410-1-4). C Gebhardt.

Inside Dope. Marvin Slobodkin. 1971. 5.50 o.p. (ISBN 0-525-13355-0). Dutton.

Inside Europe Today. rev. ed. John Gunther. LC 62-9889. 1962. 12.50 o.s.i. (ISBN 0-06-011670-6, HarpT). Har-Row.

Inside Folsom Prison: The TM-Sidhi Program. George A. Ellis. 1979. 13.95 o.p. (ISBN 0-88280-058-2); pap. 8.95 (ISBN 0-88280-059-0). ETC Pubns.

Inside Folsom Prison: Transcendental Meditation & the TM-Sidhi Program. George A. Ellis. LC 78-16774. 1979. 13.95 (ISBN 0-88280-059-0); pap. 7.95 (ISBN 0-685-94945-1). Chicago Review.

Inside Football. Mike Conklin. 1978. 9.95 o.p. (ISBN 0-685-25150-0); pap. 5.95 (ISBN 0-8092-7585-6). Contemp Bks.

Inside Golf for Women. Patty Berg & March Schiewe. LC 77-75715. (Inside Ser.). (Illus.). 1977. 7.95 o.p. (ISBN 0-8092-8041-8); pap. 4.95 (ISBN 0-8092-7738-7). Contemp Bks.

Inside Ice Skating. Einar Jonland & Jim Fitzgerald. 1978. 9.95 o.p. (ISBN 0-8092-7659-3); pap. 5.95 (ISBN 0-8092-7658-5). Contemp Bks.

Inside Jazz. L. Feather. LC 77-23411. (Roots of Jazz Ser.). (Illus.). 1977. lib. bdg. 17.50 (ISBN 0-306-77437-2); pap. 5.95 (ISBN 0-306-80076-4). Da Capo.

Inside Job. Stella Allan. 1980. pap. 2.25 (ISBN 0-380-50237-2, 50237). Avon.

Inside L. A. Art: A Guide to Museums & Galleries from Santa Barbara to San Diego. Deborah Ashin. LC 80-22527. (Illus.). 112p. (Orig.). 1980. pap. 6.95 (ISBN 0-87701-153-2). Chronicle Bks.

Inside Mao Tse-Tung's Thought: An Analytical Blueprint of His Actions by a Former Top Chinese Communist Leader. Yeh Ch'ing. Ed. by Stephen Pan. Tr. by T. H. Tsuan & Ralph Mortensen. 1975. 12.50 o.p. (ISBN 0-682-48339-7). Exposition.

Inside Moves. Todd Walton. (RL 5). 1979. pap. 2.25 o.p. (ISBN 0-451-08596-5, E8596, Sig). NAL.

Inside Nixon's Head. Arthur Woodstone. pap. 1.95 o.p. (ISBN 0-445-08576-2). Popular Lib.

Inside Organizational Communication. International Association of Business Communicators. (Longman Public Communication Ser.). 384p. (Orig.). 1981. text ed. 22.50 (ISBN 0-582-28235-7); pap. text ed. 12.50 (ISBN 0-582-28234-9). Longman.

Inside Outside. Philip J. Farmer. (Science Fiction Ser.). 1980. lib. bdg. 11.95 (ISBN 0-8398-2622-2). Gregg.

Inside Outward Bound. Renate Wlson. (Illus.). 208p. 1981. pap. 7.95 (ISBN 0-914788-41-8). East Woods.

Inside Passage Traveler. 3rd ed. Ellen Searby. (Illus.). 112p. 1980. 3.95 o.p. (ISBN 0-686-27648-5). Windham Bay.

Inside Passage Traveler: Getting Around in Southeastern Alaska. 4th ed. Ellen Searby. (Illus.). 128p. 1981. pap. 5.50 (ISBN 0-9605526-0-X). Windham Bay.

Inside R.A.W. The Story of India's Secret Service. Asoka Raina. 175p. 1981. 12.50x (ISBN 0-7069-1299-3, Pub. by Vikas India). Advent Bk.

Inside Red China. Helen Snow, pseud. 1974. lib. bdg. 27.50 (ISBN 0-306-70622-9); pap. 7.95 (ISBN 0-306-80110-8). Da Capo.

Inside Russia Today. new, rev. ed. John Gunther. LC 62-17196. 1962. 12.50 o.p. (ISBN 0-06-011685-4, HarpT). Har-Row.

Inside Russian Medicine. William A. Knaus. 1981. 14.95. Everest Hse.

Inside Skiing. Phil Byrne. LC 78-24074. 1979. 13.95 (ISBN 0-88229-455-5); pap. 7.95 (ISBN 0-88229-660-4). Nelson-Hall.

Inside Softball for Women. Sharron Backus. 1979. 9.95 o.p. (ISBN 0-8092-7491-4); pap. 5.95 (ISBN 0-8092-7490-6). Contemp Bks.

Inside Soviet Schools. Susan Jacoby. 1974. 8.95 o.p. (ISBN 0-8090-5846-4). Hill & Wang.

Inside Story: Personal Experiences of Faith. Nell Mohney. LC 79-67135. 1979. pap. 3.50x (ISBN 0-8358-0377-5). Upper Room.

Inside Tennis: A Season on the Pro Tour. Peter Bodo & June Harrison. (Illus.). 1979. 17.95 o.s.i. (ISBN 0-440-04297-6). Delacorte.

Inside Tennis for Women. Lesley Hunt. LC 77-91157. 1978. 8.95 o.p. (ISBN 0-8092-7715-8); pap. 4.95 (ISBN 0-8092-7713-1). Contemp Bks.

Inside the American Ballet Theatre. Clive Barnes. 1977. pap. 9.95 (Hawthorn). Dutton.

Inside the Australian Parliament. David Solomon. LC 77-78557. 1978. text ed. 15.95x (ISBN 0-86861-344-4); pap. text ed. 8.95x (ISBN 0-86861-352-5). Allen Unwin.

Inside the Big O. David Barker. 1980. 1.50 (ISBN 0-917554-03-5). Maelstrom.

Inside the Blood Factory. Diane Wakoski. LC 68-27104. 1968. Softbound 4.95 o.p. (ISBN 0-385-05299-5). Doubleday.

Inside the Brain. William H. Calvin & George A. Ojemann. (Illus., Orig.). 1980. pap. 2.50 (ISBN 0-451-61863-7, ME1863, Ment). NAL.

Inside the Bureaucracy: The View from the Assistant Secretary's Desk. Thomas Murphy et al. (Westview Special Studies in Public Policy & Public Systems Management). 1979. lib. bdg. 24.00x (ISBN 0-89158-154-5). Westview.

Inside the Cultural Revolution. Jack Chen. 512p. 1975. 15.95 o.s.i. (ISBN 0-02-524630-5). Macmillan.

Inside the Easter Egg. Marian Engel. (Anansi Fiction Ser.: No. 33). 172p. 1975. 14.95 (ISBN 0-88784-436-7, Pub. by Hse Anansi Pr Canada). U of Toronto Pr.

Inside the Family Business. Leon A. Danco. (A). 1980. 19.95x (ISBN 0-9603614-1-3). Univ Pr OH.

Inside the Fashion Business: Text & Readings. 3rd ed. Jeannette A. Jarnow. 450p. 1981. text ed. 20.95 (ISBN 0-471-06038-0). Wiley.

Inside the F.B.I. Andrew Tully. LC 80-14092. 240p. 1980. 12.95 (ISBN 0-07-065425-5, GB). McGraw.

Inside the Financial Futures Markets. Mark J. Powers & David J. Vogel. 260p. 1980. 23.95 (ISBN 0-471-08136-1). Ronald Pr.

Inside the Fourth Reich. Erich Erdstein & Barbara Bean. pap. 1.95 (ISBN 0-515-04897-6). Jove Pubns.

Inside the Great House: Planter Family Life in Eighteenth-Century Chesapeake Society. Daniel B. Smith. LC 80-14557. (Illus.). 368p. 1980. 17.50x (ISBN 0-8014-1313-3). Cornell U Pr.

Inside the Law Schools. Sally Goldfarb. 1980. pap. 8.95 (ISBN 0-525-47638-5). Dutton.

Inside the Movie Business. Compiled by Julian Schlossberg & Barry Yellen. LC 79-93082. 224p. Date not set. cancelled (ISBN 0-8069-0188-8); lib. bdg. cancelled (ISBN 0-8069-0189-6). Sterling.

Inside the North York Moors. Harry Mead. 1978. 17.95 (ISBN 0-7153-7699-3). David & Charles.

Inside the Occult: The True Story of Madame H. P. Blavatsky. Henry S. Olcott. LC 75-17044. Orig. Title: Old Diary Leaves. 1975. lib. bdg. 12.90 o.p. (ISBN 0-914294-31-8); pap. 3.95 o.p. (ISBN 0-914294-30-X). Running Pr.

Inside the Penn Central Crisis. Stephen Salsbury. (Illus.). 352p. 1980. 14.95 (ISBN 0-07-054483-2). McGraw.

Inside the SAS. Tony Geraghty. (Elite Unit Ser.: No. 2). (Illus.). 249p. 1981. 17.95 (ISBN 0-89839-039-7). Battery Pr.

Inside the Synagogue. Grace Freeman & Joan G. Sugarman. LC 62-19996. (Illus.). (gr. 3-5). 1963. 4.00 (ISBN 0-8074-0041-6, 301782). UAHC.

Inside the Third Reich. Albert Speer. (Illus.). 624p. 1981. 8.95 (ISBN 0-02-037500-X). Macmillan.

Inside the Third Reich: Memoirs of Albert Speer. Albert Speer. (Illus.). 1970. 24.95 (ISBN 0-02-612820-9). Macmillan.

Inside the Whale: Ten Personal Accounts of Social Research. Ed. by Colin Bell & Sol Encel. 1978. text ed. 29.00 (ISBN 0-08-022244-7); pap. text ed. 15.25 (ISBN 0-08-022243-9). Pergamon.

Inside the World of Miniatures & Dollhouses: A Comprehensive Guide to Collecting & Creating. Bernard Rosner & Jay Beckerman. LC 76-16458. (Illus.). 256p. 1976. 17.95 o.p. (ISBN 0-679-50617-9); pap. 9.95 (ISBN 0-679-50620-9). McKay.

Inside Track. Gerald Beyersdorff & Peter Sanders. LC 75-1204. (Venture Ser, a Reading Incentive Program). (Illus.). 80p. (gr. 7-12,RL 4.5-6.5). 1975. In Packs Of 5. text ed. 23.25 ea. pack (ISBN 0-8172-0214-5). Follett.

Inside View of Slavery: Or a Tour Among the Planters. C. G. Parsons. 1969. Repr. of 1855 ed. 15.00 (ISBN 0-87266-025-7). Argosy.

Inside Witchcraft. Hans Holzer. (Orig.). 1980. pap. 2.25 (ISBN 0-532-23220-8). Manor Bks.

Inside Wood. W. Harlow. Date not set. 6.50 (ISBN 0-686-26732-X, 27). Am Forestry.

Inside World Politics 1974. Diane P. Rogers et al. (gr. 9-12). 1974. text ed. 7.60 (ISBN 0-205-03480-2, 7634803); tchrs'. guide 3.12 (ISBN 0-205-03481-0, 7634811). Allyn.

Insiders. Rosemary Rogers. 1978. pap. 2.50 (ISBN 0-380-40576-8, 40576). Avon.

Insider's Banking & Credit Almanac. Mark Skousen. 14.95 (ISBN 0-932496-01-6). Green Hill.

Insiders' Guide to New Orleans. St. Leger M. Joynes & Jack Du'Arte. (Insiders' Guides Ser.). (Illus., Orig.). 1981. pap. 4.95 (ISBN 0-932338-03-8). Insiders Pub.

Insiders' Guide to Ocean City Maryland. rev. ed. St. Leger M. Joynes et al. (Insiders' Guides Ser.). (Illus., Orig.). 1981. pap. 3.95 (ISBN 0-932338-02-X). Insiders Pub.

Insiders' Guide to Southeastern Virginia. rev. ed. St. Leger Joynes et al. (Insiders' Guides Ser.). (Illus.). 1981. pap. 3.95 (ISBN 0-932338-00-3). Insiders Pub.

Insiders' Guide to the Outer Banks of North Carolina. rev. ed. Leger M. Joynes et al. (Insiders' Guides). (Illus.). 1981. pap. 3.95 (ISBN 0-932338-01-1). Insiders Pub.

Insidious Dr. Fu Manchu. Sax Rohmer. 1976. lib. bdg. 13.95x (ISBN 0-89968-143-3). Lightyear.

Insight: A Study of Human Understanding. Bernard J. Lonergan. LC 77-20441. 1977. pap. 11.95x (ISBN 0-06-065269-1, RD 251, HarpR). Har-Row.

Insight Authority & Power. P. Schouls. 1972. pap. 1.95 o.p. (ISBN 0-686-11990-8). Wedge Pub.

Insight Proverbs NASV. Compiled by Bryce Bartruff. LC 73-10830. 128p. 1973. pap. 1.25 (ISBN 0-87123-248-0, 200248). Bethany Fell.

Insight Through Fiction: Dealing Effectively with the Short Story. John Antico & Meredith K. Hazelrigg. LC 71-127360. (English Ser). (Orig.). 1970. pap. 4.95 o.p. (ISBN 0-8465-0253-4, 50253). Benjamin-Cummings.

Insights. Subhas C. Saha. (Writers Workshop Greybird Ser.). 109p. 1975. 8.00 (ISBN 0-88253-568-4); pap. text ed. 4.00 (ISBN 0-88253-567-6). Ind-US Inc.

Insights: A Contemporary Reader. Austin Flint. 192p. (Orig.). 1981. pap. text ed. 5.95 (ISBN 0-88377-185-3). Newbury Hse.

Insights for the Age of Aquarius. Gina Cerminara. LC 76-6173. 314p. 1976. pap. 5.75 (ISBN 0-8356-0483-7, Quest). Theos Pub Hse.

Insights into Human Behavior. 2nd ed. Stanley K. Fitch. 1974. pap. text ed. 14.95 o.p. (ISBN 0-205-06096-X, 7960964). Allyn.

Insights into Reality. Flower A. Newhouse et al. LC 75-36869. 1975. pap. 6.50 (ISBN 0-910378-10-X). Christward.

Insights of Sociology: An Introduction. Howard Boughey. 1978. pap. text ed. 11.95 (ISBN 0-205-06011-0); instr's man. avail. (ISBN 0-205-06012-9). Allyn.

Insights: Spirit Masters for Reading the New Testament. Religious Education Staff. (To Live Is Christ Ser.). 1978. 12.95 (ISBN 0-697-01674-9). Wm C Brown.

Insignium Armorum, Emblematum, Hieroglyphicorum et Symbolorum; Discours Ou Traicte Des Devises; The Art of Making Devises. Abraham Fraunce et al. Ed. by Stephen Orgel. LC 78-68183. (Philosophy of Images Ser.: Vol. 7). (Illus.). 1980. lib. bdg. 66.00 (ISBN 0-8240-3681-6). Garland Pub.

Insolubilized Enzymes. Ed. by M. Salmona et al. LC 74-80537. 1974. 27.00 (ISBN 0-911216-60-X). Raven.

Insoluble Problems of Crime. Robert P. Rhodes. LC 76-46275. 1977. text ed. 11.95 (ISBN 0-471-71799-1). Wiley.

Inspection & Enforcement by the Regulatory Body for Nuclear Power Plants. (Safety Ser.: No. 50-Sg-G4). 43p. 1980. pap. 7.00 (ISBN 0-686-68220-3, ISP557, IAEA). Unipub.

Inspection & Measurement. Ed. by S. Booth et al. (Engineering Craftsmen: No. H26). (Illus.). 1969. spiral bdg. 18.50x (ISBN 0-685-90149-1). Intl Ideas.

Inspection Machines: Measuring Systems & Instruments. H. C. Town & H. Moore. 1978. 22.50 (ISBN 0-7134-0795-6); pap. 13.50 (ISBN 0-7134-0796-4). David & Charles.

Inspection, Maintenance & Rehabilitation of Old Dams. Compiled by American Society of Civil Engineers. 960p. 1974. pap. text ed. 34.00 (ISBN 0-87262-061-1). Am Soc Civil Eng.

Inspector. Albert Bels. Tr. by Inara Cedrins from Latvian. 125p. Date not set. 13.50 (ISBN 0-931556-08-2); pap. 4.50 (ISBN 0-931556-09-0). Translation Pr. Postponed.

Inspector Mouse. Bernard Stone. LC 80-83772. (Illus.). (gr. k-2). 1981. 9.95 (ISBN 0-03-059113-9). HR&W.

Inspector Peckit. Don Freeman. (Viking Seafarer Ser.). (Illus.). (gr. 1-3). 1976. pap. 0.95 o.p. (ISBN 0-670-05101-2, Puffin). Penguin.

Inspectorates in British Government. Gerald Rhodes. (Royal Institute of Public Administration Ser.). (Illus.). 276p. 1981. text ed. 34.00x (ISBN 0-04-351056-6, 2596). Allen Unwin.

Inspector's Holiday: An Inspector Heimrich Mystery. new ed. Richard Lockridge. LC 79-134933. 1971. 4.95 o.p. (ISBN 0-397-00702-7). Lippincott.

Inspiration & Authority of the Bible. 2nd ed. Benjamin B. Warfield. 1948. 7.95 (ISBN 0-87552-527-X). Presby & Reformed.

Inspiration for All Time. Grant Wondersmith. LC 78-55989. (Illus.). 1978. softcover 12.95 o.p. (ISBN 0-930490-06-1). Future Shop.

Inspiration for Embroidery. Constance Howard. 240p. 1967. 15.50 (ISBN 0-8231-4017-2). Branford.

Inspirational Meditations for Sunday Church School Teachers. Richard Anderson. 1980. pap. 2.25 (ISBN 0-570-03810-3, 12-2919). Concordia.

Inspirational Series, 12 bks. Susan Powers. (Illus.). 1980. 2.95 ea. Mayflower Bks.

Inspirations from Isaiah. Nelle Vander Ark. (Good Morning Lord Ser.). 96p. 1980. 2.95 (ISBN 0-8010-9281-7). Baker Bk.

Inspired Principles of Prophetic Interpretation. John Wilmot. 1975. 9.95 o.p. (ISBN 0-685-54809-0). Reiner.

Inspired Talks, My Master & Other Writings. Swami Vivekananda. LC 58-13132. 280p. pocket ed. soft cover 3.50 (ISBN 0-911206-19-1). Ramakrishna.

Inspiring Boyhoods of Fifteen U. S. Presidents. Enos Perry. 1979. 6.00 o.p. (ISBN 0-8062-1190-3). Carlton.

Inspiring Stories for Young Latter-Day Saints. Compiled by Leon R. Hartshorn. LC 75-5178. 270p. 1975. 6.95 o.p. (ISBN 0-87747-547-4). Deseret Bk.

Instability of Agricultural Commodity Markets. OECD. (Agricultural Products & Markets Ser.). (Illus.). 237p. 1980. pap. text ed. 9.95x (ISBN 92-64-12041-6, 51-80-03-1). OECD.

Installing & Servicing Home Audio Systems. Jack Hobbs. LC 75-94452. (Orig. Ils Ser.). 1969. pap. 5.95 o.p. (ISBN 0-8306-8505-7, 505). TAB Bks.

Installing Solar Heating Systems. Gary Moselle. 224p. (Orig.). 1981. pap. 13.50 (ISBN 0-910460-83-3). Craftsman.
Instances of Accessory Art. Lewis F. Day. Ed. by Peter Stansky & Rodney Shewan. LC 76-17762. (Aesthetic Movement & the Arts & Crafts Movement Ser.: Vol. 18). 1978. Repr. of 1880 ed. lib. bdg. 44.00 (ISBN 0-8240-2467-2). Garland Pub.
Instant Astrology. Mort Gale. (Illus., Orig.). 1980. pap. 6.95 (ISBN 0-446-97355-6). Warner Bks.
Instant BASIC. Jerald Brown. LC 77-70966. (Illus., Orig.). 1977. pap. 10.95 (ISBN 0-918398-21-5). Dilithium Pr.
Instant Beauty. Robert A. Franklyn. LC 72-87046. 180p. 1973. pap. 1.45 o.p. (ISBN 0-668-02735-5). Arc Bks.
Instant Boats. Harold H. Payson. LC 78-64738. (Illus.). 1979. 15.00 (ISBN 0-87742-110-2). Intl Marine.
Instant Bridge. Victor Mollo. (Illus.). 1975. 12.95 (ISBN 0-571-10871-7, Pub. by Faber & Faber). Merrimack Bk Serv.
Instant Golf Lessons. Golf Digest Magazine Editors. LC 77-92907. (Instant Lesson Ser.). 225p. (Orig.). 1978. pap. 4.95 (ISBN 0-914178-16-4, 24167). Golf Digest.
Instant Home Repair Guide. Demski. (Career Institute Instant Reference Library). 1973. 2.95 (ISBN 0-531-02086-X). Watts.
Instant Image: Edwin Land & the Polaroid Experience. Mark Olshaker. LC 77-15965. (Illus.). 292p. 1980. pap. 8.95 (ISBN 0-8128-6093-4). Stein & Day.
Instant Japan. Masahiro Watanabe & Bruce Rogers. (Illus.). 202p. 1981. pap. 3.95 (ISBN 0-89346-181-4). Heian Intl.
Instant Japanese. Masahiro Watanabe & Kei Nagashima. (Illus.). 188p. 1981. pap. 3.95 (ISBN 0-89346-182-2). Heian Intl.
Instant Metric Conversion Tables. Editors of Hamlyn Publishing Group. LC 75-24712. 144p. 1979. 2.50 (ISBN 0-89196-001-5, Domus Bks). Quality Bks IL.
Instant Metric Reference: A Pocket Book of Conversion Tables. Compiled by Technical Staff of Barron's Educational Series. Date not set. pap. cancelled (ISBN 0-8120-0825-1). Barron.
Instant Mortgage-Equity: Extended Tables of Overall Rates. Irvin E. Johnson. LC 80-7729. (Lexington Books Real Estate & Urban Land Economics Special Ser.). 464p. 1980. 23.95 (ISBN 0-669-03808-3). Lexington Bks.
Instant Mortgage Equity Technique. Irvin E. Johnson. LC 72-6464. (Special Ser. in Real Estate & Urban Land Economics). 400p. 1972. 17.95 (ISBN 0-669-84749-6). Lexington Bks.
Instant Notetaking. Frances A. Greer. (Illus.). 1974. 7.95 o.p. (ISBN 0-911744-28-2). Intl Educ Systems.
Instant Oracle. Frank R. Kegan. 1980. pap. 2.00 (ISBN 0-933646-07-0). Aries Pr.
Instant Parliamentary Procedure. June A. McGlynn. (Illus.). 1976. pap. 3.25 (ISBN 0-9601350-1-4). McGlynn.
Instant Readers, 18 vols. Dorothy McMillan. Incl. Vol. 1. Farm Animals; Vol. 2. Round the House; Vol. 3. Grown Ups; Vol. 4. My Family; Vol. 5. Father; Vol. 7. Big Brother; Vol. 8. People We Know; Vol. 8. Where Are They Kept; Vol. 9. Animals at the Zoo; Vol. 10. Traffic; Vol. 11. Busy; Vo. 12. Me; Vol. 13. Mother; Vol. 14. Big Sister; Vol. 15. Baby; Vol. 16. In the Park; Vol. 17. We Like You; Vol. 18. Pets. (Illus.). (gr. k-4). 1976. Set Of 54 - 1 Copy Of 18 Titles. pap. text ed. 25.50 set large format (ISBN 0-8372-2184-6); small format-3 copies of 18 titles, 54 bks 28.50 (ISBN 0-8372-2203-6). Bowmar-Noble.
Instant Sermons for Busy Pastors. Russell E. Spray. (Sermon Outline Ser.). (Orig.). 1981. pap. 1.45 (ISBN 0-8010-8192-0). Baker Bk.
Instant Speaking Course. B. Lauren Lillis. 1981. pap. 1.50 (ISBN 0-8134-2176-4). Interstate.
Instant Spelling Power. Norman Lewis. (Orig.). 1976. wkbk 8.42 (ISBN 0-87720-952-9). AMSCO Sch.
Instant Tennis Lessons. Tennis Magazine Editors. (Tennis Magazine Bks-Instant Lesson Ser.). (Illus.). 191p. 1978. pap. 4.95 (ISBN 0-914178-18-0). Golf Digest Bks.
Instant Tennis Lessons. Tennis Magazine Editors. LC 77-92905. (Instant Lessons Ser.). (Illus.). 191p. 1978. pap. 4.95 (ISBN 0-914178-18-0, 24171, Pub. by Tennis Mag). Golf Digest.
Instant Vocabulary. Ida L. Ehrlich. pap. 2.95 (ISBN 0-671-42415-7). PB.
Instant Word Power. Norman Lewis. (Orig.). 1981. pap. text ed. price not set (ISBN 0-87720-963-4). AMSCO Sch.
Instant World Atlas. (Career Institute Instant Reference Library). 1971. 2.95 o.p. (ISBN 0-531-02010-X). Watts.
Instar. Ryder Brady. 1977. pap. 1.75 o.p. (ISBN 0-345-25658-1). Ballantine.
Instaurations: Essays in & Out of Literature, Pindar to Pound. D. S. Carne-Ross. 1979. 20.00x (ISBN 0-520-03619-0). U of Cal Pr.
Instead of Champagne. Inez H. Tilgner. 148p. 1979. 6.95 (ISBN 0-8059-2668-2). Dorrance.
Instead of Death: New & Expanded Edition. rev. ed. William Stringfellow. 1976. pap. 3.95 (ISBN 0-8164-2120-X). Crossroad NY.
Instead of the Thorn. Georgette Heyer. 1976. Repr. of 1923 ed. lib. bdg. 15.50x (ISBN 0-89966-119-X). Buccaneer Bks.
Instinct: A Study in Social Psychology. L. L. Bernard. 550p. 1980. Repr. of 1924 ed. lib. bdg. 40.00 (ISBN 0-89760-046-0). Telegraph Bks.
Instincts of the Herd in Peace & War. 2nd ed. Wilfred Trotter. LC 74-19217. 264p. 1975. Repr. of 1923 ed. 18.00 (ISBN 0-8103-4090-9). Gale.
Institute for Fund Advisors, Denver, May 10-12,1978: Proceedings. Ed. by Elizabeth Hieb. 1978. pap. 10.50 (ISBN 0-89154-083-0). Intl Found Employ.
Institute for Fund Advisors, Lake Tahoe, June, 1977: Proceedings. Ed. by Elizabeth Hieb. 1977. spiral bdg. 10.50 (ISBN 0-89154-067-9). Intl Found Employ.
Institute for Fund Advisors, Tahoe, Nevada, June 24-27, 1979: Proceedings. Ed. by Elizabeth Hieb. 97p. (Orig.). 1980. pap. text ed. 10.50 (ISBN 0-89154-115-2). Intl Found Employ.
Institute of Jamaica, Kingston, Jamaican National Bibliography, 1964-1974. Compiled by Rosalie I. Williams. LC 80-11767. 1981. lib. bdg. 120.00 (ISBN 0-527-45166-5). Kraus Intl.
Institute of the Laws of England: Or Laws of England in Their Natural Order According to Common Use. Thomas Wood. Ed. by David S. Berkowitz & Samuel E. Thorne. LC 77-86569. (Classics of English Legal History in the Modern Era Ser.: Vol. 71). 1979. lib. bdg. 55.00 (ISBN 0-8240-3058-3). Garland Pub.
Institute on Finite Groups, 1960: Proceedings, Vol. 6. Symposia in Pure Mathematics-Pasadena-1960. LC 50-1183. 1979. Repr. of 1961 ed. 14.80 (ISBN 0-8218-1406-0, PSPUM-6). Am Math.
Institute Supervision Training Program. Boyan. 1978. text ed. 10.95 (ISBN 0-675-08415-6); video 695.00 (ISBN 0-675-08350-8); 16 mm film 395.00 (ISBN 0-675-08414-8). Merrill.
Institutes of English Adjective Law (Procedure in Court) Embracing an Outline of the Law of Evidence & Measure of Damages. David Nasmith. xxii, 355p. 1980. Repr. of 1879 ed. lib. bdg. 30.00x (ISBN 0-8377-0904-0). Rothman.
Institutes of English Private Law: Embracing an Outline of the Substantive Branch of the Law of the Persons & Things, 2 vols. David Nasmith. 720p. 1980. Repr. of 1875 ed. Set. lib. bdg. 57.50x (ISBN 0-8377-0903-2). Rothman.
Institutes of English Public Law: Embracing an Outline of General Jurisprudence, the Development of the British Constitution, Public International Law, & the Public Municipal Law of England. David Nasmith. vi, 455p. 1980. Repr. of 1873 ed. lib. bdg. 35.00x (ISBN 0-8377-0905-9). Rothman.
Institutes of Moral Philosophy. 2nd rev. ed. Adam Ferguson. LC 75-11219. (British Philosophers & Theologians of the 17th & 18th Centuries Ser.: Vol. 22). 1978. Repr. of 1773 ed. lib. bdg. 42.00 (ISBN 0-8240-1773-0). Garland Pub.
Institutes of Vishnu, Vol. 7. Ed. by F. Max Mueller. Tr. by Jolly. (Sacred Books of the East Ser.). 15.00x (ISBN 0-8426-1402-8). Verry.
Institution & Outcome. L. P. Ullmann. 1967. 27.00 (ISBN 0-08-012205-1). Pergamon.
Institution of a Gentleman. LC 74-80193. (English Experience Ser.: No. 672). 200p. 1974. Repr. of 1555 ed. 20.00 (ISBN 90-221-0672-1). Walter J Johnson.
Institutional Adaptation of West Indian Immigrants to America: An Analysis of Rotating Credit Associations. Aubrey W. Bonnett. LC 80-69054. 160p. 1981. lib. bdg. 16.50 (ISBN 0-8191-1500-2); pap. text ed. 7.50 (ISBN 0-8191-1501-0). U Pr of Amer.
Institutional Analysis: An Approach to Implemental Problems in Medicaid. Lawrence M. Mead. (Institute Paper). 190p. 1977. pap. 4.50 o.p. (ISBN 0-685-99530-5, 46000). Urban Inst.
Institutional Arrangements for International Environmental Cooperation. Committee for International Environmental Programs. LC 72-188498. 80p. 1972. pap. 3.75 (ISBN 0-309-01946-X). Natl Acad Pr.
Institutional Change & American Economic Growth. Lance Davis & Douglass North. 1971. 27.50 (ISBN 0-521-08111-4). Cambridge U Pr.
Institutional Drive: A Study in Pluralistic Democracy. Carl G. Gustavson. LC 66-14029. 1966. 12.95x (ISBN 0-8214-0019-3). Ohio U Pr.
Institutional Imperative. Robert N. Kharasch. LC 72-95169. 1973. pap. 7.95x o.p. (ISBN 0-88327-039-0, Pub by McKay). Longman.
Institutional Imperative. Robert N. Kharasch. LC 72-95169. 1979. pap. 7.95x (ISBN 0-582-28106-7). Longman.
Institutional Issues in Public Accounting. Ed. by Robert R. Sterling. LC 73-86393. 1974. text ed. 20.00 (ISBN 0-914348-12-4). Scholars Bk.
Institutional Racism in America. Ed. by Louis Knowles & Kenneth Prewitt. 1969. pap. 3.95 o.p. (ISBN 0-13-467738-2). P-H.
Institutional Structure & Conflict in Nigeria. Ekwueme F. Okoli. LC 79-3425. 1980. pap. text ed. 7.75 (ISBN 0-8191-0888-X). U Pr of Amer.
Institutionalism & Schizophrenia. J. K. Wing & G. W. Brown. LC 75-118068. (Illus.). 1970. 32.50 (ISBN 0-521-07882-2). Cambridge U Pr.
Institutionalized Severely Retarded: A Study of Activity & Interaction. Richard H. Wills. (Illus.). 208p. 1973. 13.75 (ISBN 0-398-02755-2). C C Thomas.
Institutionalizing Innovation: A Study of Organizational Learning Systems. Mariann Jelinek. (Praeger Special Studies). 1979. 23.95 (ISBN 0-03-047031-5). Praeger.
Institutions in the Janata Phase. Arun Shourie. 300p. 1980. text ed. 18.00 (ISBN 0-8426-1678-0). Verry.
Institutions in Transition: A Profile of Change in Higher Education. Carnegie Commission on Higher Education. 1971. 10.95 o.p. (ISBN 0-07-010033-0, P&RB). McGraw.
Instrucciones En la Meditacion. Easwaran Eknath. 1980. pap. 1.00 (ISBN 0-915132-23-0). Nilgiri Pr.
Instrucciones Practicas Para Nuevos Creyentes. Rudolfo A. Cruz. LC 77-71308. 78p. (Orig., Span.). 1970. pap. text ed. 1.25 (ISBN 0-89922-002-9). Edit Caribe.
Instructional Alternatives for Exceptional Children. Ed. by Evelyn N. Deno. 194p. 1973. pap. 4.50 o.p. (ISBN 0-86586-044-0). Coun Exc Child.
Instructional Approaches to Slow Learning. William J. Younie. LC 67-21694. 1967. pap. text ed. 5.75x (ISBN 0-8077-2695-7). Tchrs Coll.
Instructional Design. 2nd ed. Jerrold E. Kemp. LC 77-140897. 1977. pap. 4.95 (ISBN 0-8224-3920-4). Pitman Learning.
Instructional Improvement: Principles & Processes. Jerry J. Bellon et al. 1978. pap. text ed. 5.95 (ISBN 0-8403-1838-3). Kendall-Hunt.
Instructional Materials Centers. LaMond F. Beatty. Ed. by James E. Duane. LC 80-21451. (Instructional Media Library: Vol. 5). (Illus.). 104p. 1981. 13.95 (ISBN 0-87778-165-6). Educ Tech Pubns.
Instructional Materials for Teaching the Use of the Library. Shirley L. Hopkinson. 1975. pap. 4.50x (ISBN 0-913860-03-4). Claremont House.
Instructional Methods in Occupational Education. Dennis C. Nystrom & Keith G. Bayne. LC 76-43204. 1977. 13.50 (ISBN 0-672-97111-9). Bobbs.
Instructional Objectives & Teacher's Guide, 1 bk. Sullivan Assoc. pap. text ed. 8.50 (ISBN 0-8449-2979-4). Learning Line.
Instructional Product Research, 8 vols. Southwest Regional Laboratory for Education Research & Development. Incl. Vol. 1. Classifying & Interpreting Educational Research Studies. pap. text ed. 1.95x (ISBN 0-442-27863-2); Vol. 2. Selecting Variables for Educational Research. pap. text ed. 1.95x (ISBN 0-442-27864-0); Vol. 3. Components of the Educational Research Proposal. pap. text ed. 1.50x (ISBN 0-442-27865-9); Vol. 4. pap. o.p.; Vol. 5. pap. o.p.; Vol. 6. Choosing an Appropriate Statistical Procedure. pap. text ed. 1.95x (ISBN 0-442-27868-3); Vol. 7. The Use of Library Computer Programs for Statistical Analysis. pap. text ed. 1.50x (ISBN 0-442-27869-1); Vol. 8. The Research Report. pap. text ed. 1.95x (ISBN 0-442-27870-5). 1972. Van Nos Reinhold.
Instructional Programming for the Handicapped Student. D. R. Anderson et al. (Illus.). 1024p. 1976. 49.75 (ISBN 0-398-03339-0); pap. 37.50 (ISBN 0-398-03340-4). C C Thomas.
Instructional Resources for Teachers of the Culturally Disadvantaged & Exceptional. Robert M. Anderson et al. (Illus.). 320p. 1971. text ed. 24.50 (ISBN 0-398-00045-X). C C Thomas.
Instructional Supervision: A Behavior System. 2nd ed. Firth N. Alfonso. 432p. 1980. text ed. 18.95 (ISBN 0-205-07142-2, 237142-1). Allyn.
Instructional Supervision Training Program. Norman Boyan & Willis Copeland. 1978. pap. text ed. 8.50 o.p. (ISBN 0-686-67368-9). Merrill.
Instructional Systems. Bela H. Banathy. LC 68-31771. 1968. pap. text ed. 3.32 o.p. (ISBN 0-8224-3930-1). Pitman Learning.
Instructional Technique. Ivor K. Davies. (Illus.). 352p. 1980. text ed. 14.95x (ISBN 0-07-015502-X, TD). McGraw.
Instructional Technology: An Annotated Bibliography. Zita M. Cantwell & Hortense A. Doyle. LC 74-7394. 1974. 15.00 (ISBN 0-8108-0729-7). Scarecrow.
Instructional Technology in Developing Countries: Decision Making Processes in Education. Stuart Wells. LC 76-24371. (Illus.). 1976. text ed. 23.95 (ISBN 0-275-23750-8). Praeger.
Instructions for Dental Patients. Thomas E. Lewis & H. Winter Griffith. LC 75-5052. (Illus.). 114p. 1975. pap. text ed. 24.00 o.p. (ISBN 0-7216-5760-5). Saunders.
Instructions for Fasting & Dieting. Arnold Ehret. 1980. pap. 2.95 (ISBN 0-87904-003-3). Lust.
Instructions for Practical Living, & Other Neo-Confucian Writings. Wing Tsit Chan. LC 62-16688. (Records of Civilization, Sources & Studies: No. 68). 1963. 22.50x (ISBN 0-231-02484-3). Columbia U Pr.
Instructions for the Defence. Jeremy Flint & David Greenwood. (Illus.). 125p. 1981. 12.50 (ISBN 0-370-30032-7, Pub. by Chatto-Bodley-Jonathan). Merrimack Bk Serv.
Instructions for the Selection & Presentation of Data for the International Register of Potentially Toxic Chemicals with Sixty Illustrative Chemical Data Profiles. (IRPTC Register Attribute Ser.: No. 2). 386p. 1979. pap. 40.00 (UNEP 41, UNEP). Unipub.
Instructions for Veterinary Clients. David L. Erlewein et al. LC 74-12908. (Illus.). 380p. 1975. pap. 42.00 (ISBN 0-7216-3400-1). Saunders.
Instructions for Viewing a Solar Eclipse. Dave Kelly. LC 78-184365. (Wesleyan Poetry Program: Vol. 61). 72p. (Orig.). 1972. 10.00x (ISBN 0-8195-2061-6, Pub. by Wesleyan U Pr); pap. 4.95 (ISBN 0-8195-1061-0). Columbia U Pr.
Instructions for Virginia & West Virginia, 3 vols. 2nd ed. Ed. by Earl L. Abbott & Erwin S. Solomon. 1962. with 1980 suppl. 75.00 (ISBN 0-87215-077-1); 1980 suppl. 25.00 (ISBN 0-87215-343-6). Michie.
Instructions in Ponymastership. Glenda Spooner. (Illus.). 1977. 9.10 (ISBN 0-85131-241-1, Dist. by Sporting Book Center). J A Allen.
Instructions of Saint Louis: A Critical Text. David O'Connell. (Romance Language Ser.). 104p. 1980. pap. 8.00 (ISBN 0-8078-9216-5). U of NC Pr.
Instructions to the British Ministers to the United States, 1791-1812. B. Mayo. LC 70-75280. (Law, Politics & History Ser). 1971. lib. bdg. 42.50 (ISBN 0-306-71303-9). Da Capo.
Instructions to Young Anglers. Shepherd. (Illus.). 9.75x (ISBN 0-392-06451-0, SpS). Soccer.
Instructions to Young Collectors. Guy Wiliams. 9.75x (ISBN 0-392-07941-0, SpS). Soccer.
Instructor for the Drum. John C. Moon. (Musick of the Fifes & the Drum: Vol. Iv). (Illus.). 56p. (Orig.). 1981. pap. 3.95 (ISBN 0-87935-059-8); record 5.95 (ISBN 0-686-69569-0); Set. pap. 8.95 (ISBN 0-87935-060-1). Williamsburg.
Instructor's Guide for the Teaching of Professional Cooking. rev. ed. Le Roi Folsom & Culinary Inst. of America. 272p. 1967. pap. 16.00 spiral bdg. (ISBN 0-8436-2048-X). CBI Pub.
Instructors' Handbook. British Horse Society & Pony Club. LC 76-55317. 1977. 5.75 (ISBN 0-8120-5125-4). Barron.
Instructor's Manual for Behavioral Neuroscience: An Introduction. Carl W. Cotman & Robert Jenson. 1979. 3.00 (ISBN 0-12-191655-3). Acad Pr.
Instructor's Manual for Linear Algebra & Its Applications. 2nd ed. W. Gilbert Strang. 1980. 3.00 (ISBN 0-12-673662-6). Acad Pr.
Instructor's Manual for Physics in the Modern World. 2nd ed. Jerry Marion. 1980. 2.00 (ISBN 0-12-472282-2). Acad Pr.
Instructor's Resource Manual to Accompany Human Anatomy & Physiology. Alexander P. Spence & Elliott B. Mason. 150.00 (ISBN 0-8053-6993-7, 800F00). Benjamin Cummings.
Instrument Fitting. Ed. by J. Barr et al. (Engineering Craftsmen: No. H24). (Illus.). 1969. spiral bdg. 15.95x (ISBN 0-85083-069-9). Intl Ideas.
Instrument Flying. Richard L. Taylor. 1978. 12.95 (ISBN 0-02-616670-4). Macmillan.
Instrument Flying Handbook. 3rd ed. Federal Aviation Administration. (Pilot Training Ser.). (Illus.). 274p. 1971. pap. 6.00 (ISBN 0-89100-164-6, E*A-A*C61-27B). Aviation Maintenance.
Instrument Flying Handbook: AC 61-27b. Federal Aviation Administration. pap. 6.00 (ISBN 0-685-46357-5, Pub. by Cooper). Aviation.
Instrument of Thy Peace. Alan Paton. 1967. 5.95 (ISBN 0-8164-0152-7). Crossroad NY.
Instrument of Thy Peace: The Prayer of St. Francis. A. Paton. (Illus., Orig.). 1976. pap. 4.95 (ISBN 0-8164-2596-5). Crossroad NY.
Instrument of Your Peace. St. Francis Of Assisi. LC 77-70404. 1977. pap. 2.95 o.p. (ISBN 0-385-13159-3). Doubleday.

Instrument Pilot Airplane Written Test Guide, Including Answers & Explanations. John King & Martha King. (Pilot Training Ser.). (Illus.). 290p. 1978. pap. 10.95 (ISBN 0-89100-196-4, E*A-A*C61-8D*G-1). Aviation Maintenance.

Instrument Rating. 22nd, rev. ed. LC 77-89942. 1979. soft bdg. 17.95 (ISBN 0-87219-002-1). Pan Am Nav.

Instrument Rating Course. (Pilot Training Ser.). 440p. 1982. write for info. (ISBN 0-88487-072-3, JS304907). Jeppesen Sanderson.

Instrument Rating Manual. 5th ed. (Pilot Training Ser.). (Illus.). 344p. 1981. pap. text ed. 17.95 (ISBN 0-88487-069-3, JS314299). Jeppesen Sanderson.

Instrument Rating Written Test Answer Book, with Explanations. Ed. by Wallace Manning. 1978. pap. 6.95 o.p. (ISBN 0-911721-39-8, Pub. by AvTest). Aviation.

Instrument Rating Written Test Guide. 5th ed. Federal Aviation Administration. (Pilot Bks.). (Illus.). 200p. 1977. pap. 3.75 (ISBN 0-89100-169-7, E*A-A*C61-8D). Aviation Maintenance.

Instrument Repair for the Music Teacher. Ed. by Burton Stanley. LC 78-11832. 154p. (Orig.). 1978. pap. 9.95x (ISBN 0-88284-075-4); pap. text ed. 9.95x (ISBN 0-686-64875-7). Alfred Pub.

Instrument Transducers: An Introduction to Their Performance & Design. 2nd ed. Hermann K. Neubert. (Illus.). 1976. 69.00x (ISBN 0-19-856320-5). Oxford U Pr.

Instrumental Analysis. Henry H. Bauer et al. 1978. text ed. 26.95 (ISBN 0-205-05922-8). Allyn.

Instrumental Methods of Analysis. 6th ed. Hobarth Willard et al. Date not set. text ed. price not set (ISBN 0-442-24502-5). D Van Nostrand.

Instrumental Methods of Food Analysis. A. J. MacLeod. LC 72-7618. (Illus.). 802p. 1973. 54.95 (ISBN 0-470-56308-7). Halsted Pr.

Instrumental Methods of Organic Functional Group Analysis. Ed. by Sidney Siggia. LC 77-168642. 1972. 40.50 o.p. (ISBN 0-471-79110-5, Pub. by Wiley-Interscience). Wiley.

Instrumental Music: A Conference, at Isham Memorial Library, Harvard University. Ed. by David G. Hughes. LC 70-166094. 152p. 1972. Repr. of 1959 ed. lib. bdg. 14.50 (ISBN 0-306-70273-8). Da Capo.

Instrumental Music Pedagogy. Daniel L. Kohut. (Illus.). 256p. 1973. ref. ed. 14.50 (ISBN 0-13-467944-X). P-H.

Instrumental Reasoning & Systems Methodology. Richard Mattessich. (Theory & Decision Library: No. 15). xvii, 396p. 1980. lib. bdg. 44.75 (ISBN 90-277-0837-1); pap. 19.95 (ISBN 90-277-1081-3). Kluwer Boston.

Instrumentation & Control Systems Engineering Handbook. Instrumentation Technology Magazine Editors. (Illus.). 1979. 22.95 (ISBN 0-8306-9867-1, 1035). TAB Bks.

Instrumentation for Coronary Care. Sue L. Grandis. (Techniques of Measurement in Medicine: No. 5). (Illus.). 150p. Date not set. price not set (ISBN 0-521-23548-0); pap. price not set (ISBN 0-521-28024-9). Cambridge U Pr.

Instrumentation for Ground Vibration & Earthquakes. 176p. 1980. pap. 65.00x (ISBN 0-7277-0052-9, Pub. by Telford England). State Mutual Bk.

Instrumentation for Neutron Inelastic Scattering Research. (Illus., Orig.). 1971. pap. 21.00 (ISBN 92-0-131070-6, ISP275, IAEA). Unipub.

Instrumentation for Psychology. Alan Cleary. LC 77-1250. 1978. 31.25 (ISBN 0-471-99483-9, Pub by Wiley Interscience). Wiley.

Instrumentation for the Operating Room: A Photographic Manual. Shirley M. Brooks. LC 78-3622. 1978. pap. text ed. 17.95 (ISBN 0-8016-0816-3). Mosby.

Instrumentation for Tomorrow's Crystallography. Ed. by Cole. pap. 7.50 (ISBN 0-686-60382-6). Polycrystal Bk Serv.

Instrumentation in Agriculture. S. W. Cox & D. E. Filby. 1972. 13.75 o.s.i. (ISBN 0-02-843290-8). Hafner.

Instrumentation in Human Relations Training, 2nd Ed. A Guide to 92 Instruments with Wide Application to the Behavioral Sciences. J. William Pfeiffer et al. LC 76-6621. 328p. 1976. pap. 17.50 (ISBN 0-88390-116-1). Univ Assocs.

Instrumentation Training Course: Electronic Instruments, 2 vols, Vol. 2. 2nd ed. Dale R. Patrick. LC 79-63866. 1979. pap. 11.95 (ISBN 0-672-21580-2, 21580); pap. 24.95 set (ISBN 0-672-21581-0). Sams.

Instrumentation Training Course: Pneumatic Instruments, Vol. 1. 2nd ed. Dale R. Patrick & Stephen Patrick. LC 79-63866. 1979. pap. 13.95 (ISBN 0-672-21579-9, 21579). Sams.

Instruments of Communication. P. Meredith. 1966. 56.00 (ISBN 0-08-010663-3). Pergamon.

Instruments of Flight. K. M. Siberry. LC 73-91533. (Illus.). 160p. 1974. 10.50x o.p. (ISBN 0-8448-0301-4). Crane-Russak Co.

Insulated Masonry Cavity Walls. National Academy Of Sciences. 1960. pap. 4.00 o.p. (ISBN 0-309-00793-3). Natl Acad Pr.

Insulating the Old House: A Handbook for the Owner. Ed. by Sally E. Nielsen. (Illus.). 1979. pap. 1.95 (ISBN 0-9600612-7-4). Greater Portland.

Insulation & Weatherstripping. Sunset Editors. LC 77-90718. (Illus.). 80p. 1978. pap. 4.95 (ISBN 0-376-01263-3, Sunset Bks). Sunset-Lane.

Insulin Action: Proceedings. Symposium on Insulin Action, Toronto, 1971. Ed. by Irving Fritz. 1973. 48.50 (ISBN 0-12-268750-7). Acad Pr.

Insulin: Chemistry, Structure & Function of Insulin & Related Hormones. Ed. by D. Brandenburg. text ed. 112.00 (ISBN 3-11-008156-3). De Gruyter.

Insulins, Growth Hormone, & Recombinant DNA Technology. Ed. by J. L. Gueriguian et al. 250p. 1981. 25.00 (ISBN 0-89004-544-5). Raven.

Insult & Society: Patterns of Comparative Interaction. Charles P. Flynn. 1976. 11.50 (ISBN 0-8046-9152-5, National University Pub). Kennikat.

Insuperable Opposition Between Catholicism & Liberalism. Martinius Vanderhofen. (Illus.). 107p. 1980. 39.75 (ISBN 0-930582-78-0). Gloucester Art.

Insurance Agency Advertising & Public Relations. George W. Nordhaus. (Illus.). 228p. 1964. 4.95 o.p. (ISBN 0-88245-002-6). Merritt Co.

Insurance & Third-Party-Payable Claims. A. Ziegler. (Illus.). 1979. pap. 12.00 (ISBN 0-87489-152-3). Med Economics.

Insurance for Nuclear Installations. (Legal Ser.: No. 6). (Illus., Orig., Eng. & Fr.). 1970. pap. 12.00 (ISBN 92-0-076070-8, ISP274, IAEA). Unipub.

Insurance Handbook for the Medical Office. 2nd ed. Marilyn T. Fordney. (Illus.). 475p. 1981. pap. text ed. price not set (ISBN 0-7216-3814-7). Saunders.

Insurance Information Sources. Ed. by Roy Thomas. LC 75-137575. (Management Information Guide Ser.: No. 24). 1971. 30.00 (ISBN 0-8103-0824-X). Gale.

Insurance Is a Funny Business. Ed. by George Nordhaus et al. (Illus.). 139p. 1971. 9.95 o.p. (ISBN 0-88245-003-4). Merritt Co.

Insurance Law Anthology, Vol. 1. Ed. by Phillip A. Garon. (National Law Anthology Ser.). 1981. text ed. 59.95. Intl Lib.

Insurance Pricing & Loss Prevention. Neil Doherty. 1976. 17.95 (ISBN 0-347-01097-0, 00308-5, Pub. by Saxon Hse). Lexington Bks.

Insurance Principles & Practices. Frederick G. Crane. LC 79-19510. 1980. text ed. 20.95 (ISBN 0-471-01763-9); tchr's ed. avail. (ISBN 0-471-01768-X). Wiley.

Insurance Principles & Practices: Property & Liability. 6th ed. R. Riegel & J. Miller. 1976. text ed. 20.95 (ISBN 0-13-468868-6). P-H.

Insurance Programs for Alumni. 1976. pap. 3.00 o.p. (ISBN 0-89964-006-0). CASE.

Insurance Valuations, Definitions, Derivations & Appraisals. LC 72-16891. (ASA Monograph: No. 4). 1971. 5.00 (ISBN 0-937828-13-0). Am Soc Appraisers.

Insurgency As a Strategic Problem. P. Kecskemeti. 1977. pap. 4.00 o.p. (ISBN 0-87364-097-7). Paladin Ent.

Insurgent Progressives in the United States Senate & the New Deal, 1933-1939. Ronald A. Mulder. Ed. by Frank Freidel. LC 78-62389. (Modern American History Ser.: Vol. 14). 1979. lib. bdg. 30.00 (ISBN 0-8240-3637-9). Garland Pub.

Integer Programming. Robert Garfinkel & George L. Nemhauser. LC 72-3881. (Decision & Control Ser.). 528p. 1972. 33.95 (ISBN 0-471-29195-1, Pub. by Wiley-Interscience). Wiley.

Integer Programming. Harvey M. Salkin. (Illus.). 450p. 1975. text ed. 21.95 (ISBN 0-201-06841-9). A-W.

Integer Programming & Network Flows. T. C. Hu. (Mathematics Ser). 1969. text ed. 19.95 (ISBN 0-201-03003-9). A-W.

Integers: Positive & Negative. Irving Adler. LC 78-162589. (Reason Why Ser.). (Illus.). 48p. (gr. 3-6). 1972. PLB 7.89 (ISBN 0-381-99988-2, A39160, JD-J). John Day.

Integral & Functional Differential Equations. Stech et al. Date not set. price not set (ISBN 0-8247-1354-0). Dekker.

Integral Bases. W. E. Berwick. (Cambridge Tracts in Mathematics & Mathematical Physics Ser.: No. 22). 1964. Repr. of 1927 ed. 9.75 o.s.i. (ISBN 0-02-841310-5). Hafner.

Integral Calculus, 2 Vols. Joseph W. Edwards. LC 55-234. 35.00 ea. Vol. 1 (ISBN 0-8284-0102-0). Vol. 2 (ISBN 0-8284-0105-5). Chelsea Pub.

Integral Calculus. Walter Ledermann. (Library of Mathematics). 1967. pap. 5.00 (ISBN 0-7100-4355-4). Routledge & Kegan.

Integral Equation Methods in Potential Theory & Elastostatics. M. A. Jaswon & G. T. Symm. 1978. 39.50 (ISBN 0-12-381050-7). Acad Pr.

Integral Equations. Benjamin L. Moiseiwitsch. LC 76-10282. (Longman Mathematical Texts). (Illus.). 1977. pap. text ed. 11.95x (ISBN 0-582-44288-5). Longman.

Integral Equations. Frank Smithies. (Cambridge Tracts in Mathematics & Mathematical Physics). 1958. 27.50 (ISBN 0-521-06502-X). Cambridge U Pr.

Integral Geometry & Inverse Problems for Hyperbolic Equations. V. G. Romanov. (Springer Tracts in Natural Philosophy: Vol. 26). (Illus.). 152p. 1974. 32.60 (ISBN 0-387-06429-X). Springer-Verlag.

Integral Humanism: Temporal & Spiritual Problems of a New Christendom. Jacques Maritain. Tr. by Joseph W. Evans from Fr. LC 73-12509. Orig. Title: Humanisme Integral. 328p. (Eng. & Fr.). 1973. text ed. 10.95x (ISBN 0-268-00516-8); pap. text ed. 3.95x (ISBN 0-268-00510-9). U of Notre Dame Pr.

Integral Operators in Potential Theory. J. Kral. (Lecture Notes in Mathematics Ser.: Vol. 823). 171p. 1981. pap. 11.80 (ISBN 0-387-10227-2). Springer-Verlag.

Integral Philosophy of Sri Aurobindo. Haridas Chaudhuri. Ed. by Frederic Spiegelberg. 350p. 1980. 6.00 (ISBN 0-89744-992-4, Pub. by Cultural Integration). Auromere.

Integral Representations of Functions & Imbedding Theorems, 2 vols. Oleg V. Besov et al. (Scripta Ser. in Mathematics). 1979. 19.95 ea. Vol. 1 (ISBN 0-470-26540-X). Vol. 2 (ISBN 0-470-26593-0). Halsted Pr.

Integrale Linguistik. Festschrift Fur Helmut Gipper. Ed. by Edeltraud Bulow & Peter Schmitter. 1979. text ed. 91.25x (ISBN 0-391-01264-9). Humanities.

Integralgleichungen. Ernst Hellinger & Otto Toeplitz. LC 54-2866. (Ger). 14.95 (ISBN 0-8284-0089-X). Chelsea Pub.

Integrals & Sums. P. C. Chakravarti. 1970. text ed. 22.50x (ISBN 0-485-11114-4, Athlone Pr). Humanities.

Integrated Approach to Curriculum Development in Primary Education in Sri-Lanka. (International Bureau of Education Ser: Experiments & Innovations in Education, No. 26). 25p. 1977. pap. 2.50 (ISBN 92-3-101373-4, U754, UNESCO). Unipub.

Integrated Basic Science. 4th ed. Stewart M. Brooks. LC 78-24430. (Illus.). 1979. 17.95 (ISBN 0-8016-0805-8). Mosby.

Integrated Circuit Engineering: Fabrication, Design, Application. Arthur Glaser & Gerald E. Subak-Sharpe. LC 77-73945. 1977. text ed. 28.95 (ISBN 0-201-07427-3, 0-201-07428). A-W.

Integrated Circuits. F. F. Mazda. LC 77-71418. (Illus.). 1978. 35.50 (ISBN 0-521-21658-3). Cambridge U Pr.

Integrated Circuits: A User's Handbook. Michael M. Cirovic. (Illus.). 1977. text ed. 21.00 (ISBN 0-87909-356-0); students manual avail. Reston.

Integrated Circuits: Making the Miracle Chip. Bill Pletsch. 80p. 1978. pap. 6.00 (ISBN 0-686-27006-1). Palmer-Pletsch.

Integrated Circuits: Theory & Applications. Charles F. Wojslaw. (Illus.). 1978. text ed. 18.95 (ISBN 0-87909-379-X); students manual avail. Reston.

Integrated Control of Insect Pests in the Netherlands. 304p. 1980. 52.75 (ISBN 90-220-0716-2, PDC 207, Pudoc). Unipub.

Integrated Cooperatives in the Industrial Society. Bartolke-Bergmann. 1980. text ed. 22.50x (ISBN 90-232-1772-1). Humanities.

Integrated Day in an American School. Betsye Sargent. (Illus.). 1972. pap. 5.75 (ISBN 0-934338-25-6). NAIS.

Integrated Development in Rural Ethiopia. Betru Gebregziabher. 1975. pap. text ed. 3.00 (ISBN 0-89249-029-2). Intl Development.

Integrated Devices in Digital Circuit Design. Gordon S. Hope. LC 80-17172. 335p. 1980. 24.00 (ISBN 0-471-07920-0, Pub. by Wiley-Interscience). Wiley.

Integrated Digital Electronics. Walter A. Triebel. (Illus.). 1979. ref. 19.95 (ISBN 0-13-468900-3). P-H.

Integrated Economic Accounting: Theory & Applications to National, Real, & Financial Economic Planning. Hector Correa. LC 76-17445. 1976. 26.95 (ISBN 0-669-00779-X). Lexington Bks.

Integrated Economic Planning. B. N. Juayl. 1980. text ed. write for info. (ISBN 0-391-01837-X). Humanities.

Integrated Electronics: How Cowboys & Longhorns Opened the Mid-Continent. R. B. Sorkin. 1970. 23.50 o.p. (ISBN 0-07-059738-3, P&RB). McGraw.

Integrated Environment in Building Design. Ed. by A. F. Sherratt. LC 74-22250. 281p. 1975. 44.95 (ISBN 0-470-78575-6). Halsted Pr.

Integrated Experimental Chemistry, 2 vols. David A. Aikens et al. Incl. Vol. 1. Principles & Techniques. text ed. 11.95x (ISBN 0-205-05923-6); Vol. 2. Laboratory Experiments. lab manual 12.95x (ISBN 0-205-05924-4). 1978. pap. text ed. 14.95 ea. Allyn.

Integrated Geophysics for Exploration Geologists. Thomas R. Lafehr. text ed. write for info. o.p. (ISBN 0-8087-3802-X, CEPCO); pap. text ed. write for info. o.p. (ISBN 0-8087-3803-8). Burgess.

Integrated Injection Logic. J. E. Smith. 424p. 1980. 34.00 (ISBN 0-471-08675-4, Pub. by Wiley-Interscience); pap. 22.00 (ISBN 0-471-08676-2). Wiley.

Integrated Injection Logic. Ed. by J. E. Smith. LC 80-18841. 1980. 34.95 (ISBN 0-87942-137-1). Inst Electrical.

Integrated Mathematics: Course I. Isidore Dressler & Edward P. Keenan. (Orig.). (gr. 9). 1980. text ed. 19.17 (ISBN 0-87720-249-4); pap. text ed. 12.09 (ISBN 0-87720-248-6). AMSCO Sch.

Integrated Pest Management: Rationale, Potential Needs & Implementation. E. W. Glass. 1975. 5.85 (ISBN 0-686-18864-0). Entomol Soc.

Integrated Plant Protection. Webster H. Sill, Jr. (Illus.). 328p. 1981. text ed. 25.00. Iowa St U Pr.

Integrated Principles of Zoology. 6th ed. Cleveland P. Hickman et al. LC 78-27064. (Illus.). 1979. text ed. 21.95 (ISBN 0-8016-2172-0). Mosby.

Integrated Science for Caribbean Schools, 2 bks. Florence Commissiong et al. 1976. Bk. 1. pap. text ed. 4.75x o.p. (ISBN 0-435-57579-1); Bk. 2. pap. text ed. 6.95x o.p. (ISBN 0-435-57580-5). Heinemann Ed.

Integrated Science for Health Students. 2nd ed. T. Randall Lankford. (Illus.). 1979. text ed. 18.95 (ISBN 0-8359-3103-X); pap. 7.95 lab manual (ISBN 0-8359-3105-6); instrs' manual avail. (ISBN 0-687-01281-3). Reston.

Integrated Science in the Junior Secondary Schools in Sri Lanka. (Experiments & Innovations 27 in Education, Asian Ser). (Illus.). 31p. 1977. pap. 2.50 (ISBN 92-3-101374-2, U314, UNESCO). Unipub.

Integrated Studies in Patient Care. Marion Glass & Evelyn Atchison. LC 76-46127. 1978. pap. text ed. 9.00 (ISBN 0-8273-1608-9); instructor's guide 1.60 (ISBN 0-8273-1609-7). Delmar.

Integrated Transformational Grammar of the English Language. Garland Cannon. (Costerus New Ser.: No. 8). 1978. pap. text ed. 34.25x (ISBN 90-6203-400-4). Humanities.

Integrating Jerusalem Schools. Zev Klein. (Quantitative Studies in Social Relations Ser.). 1980. 19.50 (ISBN 0-12-413250-2). Acad Pr.

Integrating Music with Other Studies. Mulligan. write for info. (ISBN 0-87628-218-4). Ctr Appl Res.

Integrating the Computer with Your Business: Accounting for Computer Charges. Jimathan Porter & Jonathan Chapple. LC 80-13930. 308p. 1980. pap. 29.95x (ISBN 0-470-26984-7). Halsted Pr.

Integrating the Individual & the Organization. Chris Argyris. LC 64-13209. 1964. 26.95 (ISBN 0-471-03315-4). Wiley.

Integrating the Organization: A Social Psychological Analysis. Ed. by Howard L. Fromkin & John J. Sherwood. LC 73-21306. (Illus.). 1974. 19.95 (ISBN 0-02-910920-5). Free Pr.

Integrating the Urban School. Ed. by Gordon J. Klopf & Israel Laster. LC 60-13467. (Orig.). 1963. pap. text ed. 4.25x (ISBN 0-8077-1632-4). Tchrs Coll.

Integrating Vocational & General Education. (UIE Case Studies: No. 1). 196p. 1980. pap. 4.00 (ISBN 92-820-1024-4, U935, Pub. by UNESCO). Unipub.

Integration & Conflict in Family Behavior, Vol. 6. GAP Committee on the Family. (Report No. 27A). 1968. pap. 2.00 (ISBN 0-87318-096-8). Adv Psychiatry.

Integration & Disintegration in East Africa. Ed. by Christian P. Potholm & Richard A. Fredland. LC 80-5914. 229p. 1980. lib. bdg. 17.75 (ISBN 0-8191-1298-4); pap. text ed. 9.75 (ISBN 0-8191-1299-2). U Pr of Amer.

Integration & Harmonic Analysis on Compact Groups. Ed. by R. E. Edwards. LC 77-190412. (London Mathematical Society Lecture Notes Ser.: No. 8). 228p. 1972. 20.50 (ISBN 0-521-09717-7). Cambridge U Pr.

Integration & Unequal Development. Ed. by Dudley Seers et al. (Studies in the Integration of Western Europe). 1981. write for info. (ISBN 0-312-41890-6). St Martin.

Integration of Developmentally Disabled Individuals into the Community. Ed. by Angela R. Novak & Laird W. Heal. LC 80-21082. (Illus.). 262p. 1980. pap. text ed. 12.95 (ISBN 0-933716-10-9). P H Brookes.

Integration of Handicapped Children in Society. Ed. by James Loring & Graham Burn. 172p. 1975. 16.00x (ISBN 0-7100-8269-X). Routledge & Kegan.

Integration of International Economic Relations. B. N. Ganguli. pap. 3.00x o.p. (ISBN 0-210-22217-4). Asia.

Integration of Science and Technology with Development: Caribbean and Latin American Problems in the Context of the United Nations Conference on Science and Technology for Development. Ed. by D. Babatunde Thomas & Miguel S. Wionczek. (Pergamon Policy Studies). 1979. 33.00 (ISBN 0-08-023881-5). Pergamon.

Integration of the Child into a Social World. Ed. by M. P. Richards. LC 73-82464. 320p. 1974. 35.00 (ISBN 0-521-20306-6); pap. 12.95x (ISBN 0-521-09830-0). Cambridge U Pr.

Integration of the European Economy Since 1815. Sidney Pollard. (Studies on Contemporary Europe: No. 4). 96p. 1981. text ed. 15.95x (ISBN 0-04-336069-6, 2615-6); pap. text ed. 6.95x (ISBN 0-04-336070-X). Allen Unwin.

Integration or Segregation for the Physically Handicapped Child? S. S. Dibner & A. S. Dibner. 228p. 1973. 14.75 (ISBN 0-398-02817-6). C C Thomas.

Integrative Preaching: The Pulpit at the Center. William H. Willimon. LC 80-39628. (Abingdon Preacher's Library). 112p. (Orig.). 1981. pap. 4.95 (ISBN 0-687-19129-7). Abingdon.

Integrity of Anglicanism. Stephen Sykes. 1978. 8.95 (ISBN 0-8164-0405-4). Crossroad NY.

Integrity of Frozen Spermatozoa. Commission on Sociotechnical Systems, National Research Council. LC 77-940301. (Illus.). 1978. pap. text ed. 9.75 (ISBN 0-309-02645-8). Natl Acad Pr.

Integrity of Life: Allegorical Imagery in the Plays of John Webster. Eloise K. Goreau. (Salzburg Studies in English Literature, Jacobean Drama Studies: No. 32). 194p. 1974. pap. text ed. 25.00x (ISBN 0-391-01390-4). Humanities.

Integument, a Textbook of Skin Biology. R. I. Spearman. LC 72-88612. (Biological Structure & Function Ser.: No. 3). (Illus.). 200p. 1973. 40.00 (ISBN 0-521-20048-2). Cambridge U Pr.

Intellectual & Manual Labour: A Critique of Epistemology. Alfred Sohn-Rethel. LC 77-12975. (Critical Social Studies). 1978. text ed. 25.00x (ISBN 0-391-00774-2); pap. text ed. 10.25x (ISBN 0-333-23046-9). Humanities.

Intellectual & Personality Characteristics of Children: Social-Class & Ethnic-Group Differences. Regina Yando & Victoria Seitz. 136p. 1979. profess./reference text 12.95 (ISBN 0-89859-001-9). Erlbaum Assocs.

Intellectual Capital of Michal Kalecki: A Study in Economic Theory & Policy. George R. Feiwel. LC 74-22487. 1975. 25.00x (ISBN 0-87049-161-X). U of Tenn Pr.

Intellectual Change & Political Development in Early Modern Japan: Ono Azusa, a Case Study. Sandra T. Davis. LC 76-14762. 1979. 24.50 (ISBN 0-8386-1953-3). Fairleigh Dickinson.

Intellectual Cowardice of the American Philosophers. Ernest V. Beaumont. (Illus.). 1980. deluxe ed. 49.75 (ISBN 0-89266-262-X). Am Classical Coll Pr.

Intellectual Design of John Dryden's Heroic Plays. Anne T. Barbeau. LC 71-81412. 1970. 18.50x o.p. (ISBN 0-300-01111-3). Yale U Pr.

Intellectual Development. new ed. Ed. by Pauline S. Sears. LC 73-146672. (Readings in Educational Research Ser.). 1971. 10 or more copies 25.00 19.50 (ISBN 0-471-76975-4); text ed. 22.50 (ISBN 0-686-67150-3). McCutchan.

Intellectual Evaluation of the Mentally Retarded Child: A Handbook. rev ed. Robert M. Allen & Sue P. Allen. LC 66-29865. 1975. pap. 8.75x o.p. (ISBN 0-87424-086-7). Western Psych.

Intellectual Experiments of the Greek Enlightenment. Friedrich Solmsen. LC 74-25629. 296p. 1975. 34.00x (ISBN 0-691-07201-9). Princeton U Pr.

Intellectual Freedom Primer. Ed. by Charles H. Busha. LC 77-7887. 1977. 20.00x (ISBN 0-87287-172-X). Libs Unl.

Intellectual History of Modern Europe. 2nd ed. Roland N. Stromberg. LC 74-22388. 595p. 1975. text ed. 19.95 (ISBN 0-13-469106-7). P-H.

Intellectual Life. A. D. Sertillanges. pap. 5.95 (ISBN 0-87061-053-8). Chr Classics.

Intellectual Life in Jefferson's Virginia, 1790-1830. Richard B. Davis. LC 64-13548. (Illus.). 524p. 1972. Repr. of 1964 ed. 14.50x (ISBN 0-87049-144-X). U of Tenn Pr.

Intellectual Origins of the Prague Spring: The Development of Reformist Ideas in Czechoslovakia, 1958-1967. Vladimir V. Kusin. (Soviet & East European Studies Monographs). 1971. 21.50 (ISBN 0-521-08124-6). Cambridge U Pr.

Intellectual Precursors of the Mexican Revolution, 1900-1913. James D. Cockcroft. (Latin American Monographs: No. 14). 1969. pap. 7.95x (ISBN 0-292-73808-0). U of Tex Pr.

Intellectual Property Law Review: Annual. Ed. by Gerald Rose. Incl. 1976 (ISBN 0-87632-142-2); 1977 (ISBN 0-87632-143-0); 1978 (ISBN 0-87632-144-9); 1979 (ISBN 0-87632-145-7). LC 79-88703. 42.50 ea. Boardman.

Intellectual Property Management - Law - Business - Strategy. Philip Sperber. LC 74-21479. 1974. with 1978 rev. pages 60.00 (ISBN 0-87632-150-3). Boardman.

Intellectual Revolution of the Seventeenth Century. Ed. by Charles Webster. (Past & Present Ser.). 452p. 1975. 25.00 (ISBN 0-7100-7844-7). Routledge & Kegan.

Intellectual Revolution: Selections from Euripides, Thucydides & Plato. Joint Association of Classical Teachers-Greek Course. LC 79-16754. (Illus.). 160p. 1980. pap. 9.95x (ISBN 0-521-22461-6). Cambridge U Pr.

Intellectuals & Politics. Robert J. Brym. (Controversies in Sociology Ser.: No. 9). (Orig.). 1980. text ed. 14.95x (ISBN 0-04-322005-3); pap. text ed. 6.95x (ISBN 0-04-322006-1). Allen Unwin.

Intellectuals on the Road to Class Power. George Konrad & Ivan Szelenyi. LC 77-92547. 1979. 10.00 (ISBN 0-15-177860-4). HarBraceJ.

Intelligence: An Introduction. David W. Pyle. (Illus.). 1979. 16.00x (ISBN 0-7100-0306-4); pap. 7.95 (ISBN 0-7100-0307-2). Routledge & Kegan.

Intelligence & Adaptation. Stanley I. Greenspan. LC 78-13893. (Psychological Issues Monograph: No. 47/48). (Illus.). 412p. 1980. text ed. 22.50x (ISBN 0-8236-2717-9, 002718); pap. 17.50x (ISBN 0-8236-2718-7). Intl Univs Pr.

Intelligence & Affectivity: Their Relationship During Child Development. Ed. by Mark R. Rosenzweig & T. A. Brown. Tr. by T. A. Brown & C. E. Kaegi. (Illus.). 1981. 8.00 (ISBN 0-8243-2901-5). Annual Reviews.

Intelligence & Aphasia. Yvan Lebrun & Richard Hoops. (Neurolinguistics Ser.: Vol. 2). 140p. 1974. pap. text ed. 15.75 (ISBN 90-265-0182-X, Pub. by Swets Pub Serv Holland). Swets North Am.

Intelligence & Experience. J. M. Hunt. (Illus.). 1961. 17.50 (ISBN 0-8260-4535-9). Wiley.

Intelligence & Motivation Among Day Release Students. Ethel C. Venables. (General Ser.). 168p. 1974. pap. text ed. 15.00x (ISBN 0-85633-047-7, NFER). Humanities.

Intelligence & Race: The Origins & Dimensions of the IQ Controversy. Douglas L. Eckberg. LC 79-19795. (Illus.). 298p. 1979. 27.95 (ISBN 0-03-052556-X). Praeger.

Intelligence, Creativity & Cognitive Style. George Shouksmith. 1970. 32.00 (ISBN 0-7134-0980-0, Pub. by Batsford England). David & Charles.

Intelligence, Creativity & Their Educational Implications. J. P. Guilford. LC 68-26627. 1968. pap. text ed. 8.95 (ISBN 0-912736-09-7). EDITS Pubs.

Intelligence, Espionage, Counterespionage & Covert Operations: A Guide to Information Sources. Paul W. Blackstock & Frank Schaf, Jr. LC 74-11567. (International Relations Information Guide Ser.: Vol. 2). 1978. 30.00 (ISBN 0-8103-1323-5). Gale.

Intelligence: Heredity & Environment. Philip E. Vernon. LC 78-11975. (Psychology Ser.). (Illus.). 1979. text ed. 17.50x o.p. (ISBN 0-7167-0738-1); pap. text ed. 10.95x (ISBN 0-7167-0737-3). W H Freeman.

Intelligence in Action: Physical Activities for Enhancing Intellectual Abilities. Bryant J. Cratty. (Illus.). 160p. 1973. ref. ed. 10.95 (ISBN 0-13-469049-4). P-H.

Intelligence: What Is It? Daniel Cohen. LC 73-80178. (Illus.). 160p. (gr. 5 up). 1974. 7.95 (ISBN 0-87131-127-5). M Evans.

Intelligent Anticipation of Stock Market Reversals for the Maximization of Speculative Profits. Timothy D. Vanderman. (The New Stock Market Reference Library). (Illus.). 116p. 1981. 41.75 (ISBN 0-918968-94-1). Inst Econ Fina.

Intelligent Guide to Book Distribution. Michael S. Cain. 250p. 1981. 12.50 (ISBN 0-913218-77-4); pap. 5.95 (ISBN 0-913218-78-2). Dustbooks.

Intelligent Investor's Guide to Real Estate. David W. Walters. LC 80-17718. (Professional Practitioners Ser.). 352p. 1980. 17.95 (ISBN 0-471-07874-3, Pub. by Ronald). Wiley.

Intelligent Life in the Universe. Carl Sagan & I. S. Shklovskii. LC 64-18404. 1978. pap. text ed. 12.50x (ISBN 0-8162-7913-6). Holden-Day.

Intelligent Testing with the WISC-R. Alan S. Kaufman. LC 78-31174. (Personality Processes Ser.). 1979. 24.95 (ISBN 0-471-04971-9, Pub. by Wiley-Interscience). Wiley.

Intelligent Understanding of Stained & Painted Glass. Sydney Eden. (Illus.). 131p. 1980. 49.85 (ISBN 0-930582-81-0). Gloucester Art.

Intelligent Woman's Guide to Socialism, Capitalism, Sovietism, & Fascism. George B. Shaw. 1981. pap. 3.95 (ISBN 0-14-040034-6). Penguin.

Intelligibility & the Philosophy of Nothingness. Kitaro Nishida. Tr. by Robert Schinzinger from Japanese. LC 72-12319. (Illus.). 251p. 1973. Repr. of 1958 ed. lib. bdg. 24.75x (ISBN 0-8371-6689-6, NIIP). Greenwood.

Intensity Interferometer: Its Application to Astronomy. R. Hanbury Brown. LC 74-14878. 184p. 1974. 26.95 (ISBN 0-470-10797-9). Halsted Pr.

Intensive Beef Production. 2nd ed. T. R. Preston & M. B. Willis. 1974. 24.00 (ISBN 0-08-018980-6); text ed. 40.00 (ISBN 0-08-017788-3). Pergamon.

Intensive Behavior Therapy. John C. Papajohn. (General Psychology Ser.). Date not set. 15.00 (ISBN 0-08-025544-2). Pergamon. Postponed.

Intensive Care. Janet Frame. LC 78-110305. 1970. 6.95 o.s.i. (ISBN 0-8076-0555-7). Braziller.

Intensive Care for Nurses. 2nd ed. Ed. by D. B. Clarke & A. D. Barnes. (Illus.). 208p. 1975. 22.50 (ISBN 0-632-00696-X, Blackwell). Mosby.

Intensive Care in the Newborn, Vol. III. Stern. 1981. write for info (ISBN 0-89352-114-0). Masson Pub.

Intensive Care in the Newborn. Leo Stern et al. LC 76-22262. 296p. 1977. 37.50 (ISBN 0-89352-000-4). Masson Pub.

Intensive Care Manual. T. Oh. (Illus.). 200p. 1980. text ed. 29.95 (ISBN 0-409-31380-7). Butterworths.

Intensive Care Nursing. Barbara J. Daly. LC 78-78019. (Current Clinical Nursing Ser.). 1979. pap. 13.50 (ISBN 0-87488-575-2). Med Exam.

Intensive Care Nursing Continuing Education Review. Janet A. Williamson et al. 1977. spiral bdg. 6.00 o.p. (ISBN 0-87488-399-7). Med Exam.

Intensive Care of the Newborn. G. Kelnar & D. Harvey. (Illus.). 1980. pap. text ed. 17.95 (ISBN 0-02-858020-6). Macmillan.

Intensive Care of the Newborn II. Leo Stern et al. LC 78-63400. (Newborn Ser.). (Illus.). 418p. 1979. 45.50 (ISBN 0-89352-022-5). Masson Pub.

Intensive Care Radiology: Imaging of the Critically Ill. Lawrence R. Goodman & Charles E. Putman. LC 78-64. 1978. text ed. 36.50 (ISBN 0-8016-1894-0). Mosby.

Intensive Care Therapeutics. Joseph M. Civetta. 400p. 1980. pap. 17.50x (ISBN 0-8385-4305-7). ACC.

Intensive Coronary Care: A Manual for Nurses. 3rd ed. L. E. Meltzer et al. LC 77-12120. (Illus.). 230p. 1977. 15.95 (ISBN 0-913486-79-5). Charles.

Intensive English for Communication, Bk. 1. Anne Lindell & M. Peter Hagiwara. LC 78-58152. (Illus.). 1979. pap. text ed. 6.95x (ISBN 0-472-08570-0, 08570); pap. text ed. 4.95x wkbk. (ISBN 0-472-08571-9). U of Mich Pr.

Intensive English for Communication: Book Two. Anne Lindell. (Illus.). 294p. 1980. pap. text ed. 6.95x (ISBN 0-472-08572-7). U of Mich Pr.

Intensive Foreign Language Courses. David P. Benseler & Renate A. Schultz. (Language in Education Ser.: No. 18). 55p. 1979. pap. 4.95 (ISBN 0-87281-104-2). Ctr Appl Ling.

Intensive Gardening Round the Year. Paul Doscher et al. (Illus.). 224p. 1981. pap. 15.00 (ISBN 0-8289-0399-9). Greene.

Intensive Multiple Cropping with Coconuts in India: Principles, Programmes & Prospects. P. K. Nair. (Advances in Agronomy & Crop Science Ser.: Vol. 6). (Illus.). 148p. (Orig.). 1979. pap. text ed. 28.00 (ISBN 3-489-71210-2). Parey Sci Pubs.

Intensive Therapy Unit & the Nurse. 2nd ed. Eric K. Gardner & Brenda Shelton. 1967. text ed. 3.95 o.p. (ISBN 0-571-08148-7, Pub. by Faber & Faber). Merrimack Bk Serv.

Intensivhaltung von Nutztieren aus ethischer, rechtlicher und ethologischer Sicht: Rechtlicher und Ethologischer Sicht. Ed. by Gotthard M. Teutsch & Eisenhart Von Loeper. (Tierhaltung-Animal Management: No. 8). (Ger.). 1979. pap. 18.00 (ISBN 3-7643-1119-3). Birkhauser.

Intention & Decision: A Philosophical Study. Richard M. Martin. LC 63-19620. 1963. 24.00x (ISBN 0-89197-231-5). Irvington.

Intention & Intentionality: Essays in Honour of G. E. M. Anscombe. Ed. by Cora Diamond & Jenny Teichman. LC 79-2478. (Illus.). 1980. 32.50x (ISBN 0-8014-1275-7). Cornell U Pr.

Intention der Verkuendigung Jesajas. Hans W. Hoffmann. LC 74-80632. (Beiheft 136 zur Zeitschrift fuer die alttestamentliche Wissenschaft). 125p. 1974. 37.10 (ISBN 3-11-004672-5). De Gruyter.

Intentional Community Movement: Building a New Moral World. Marguerite Bouvard. LC 74-80593. 1975. 15.00 (ISBN 0-8046-9100-2, Natl U). Kennikat.

Inter-Act: Using Interpersonal Communication Skills. 2nd ed. Rudolph F. Verderber & Kathleen S. Verderber. 368p. 1980. pap. text ed. 9.95x (ISBN 0-534-00785-6). Wadsworth Pub.

Inter-American Conventions on Women. (Treaty Ser.: No. 38). 10p. 1972. pap. 1.00 (ISBN 0-8270-0485-0). OAS.

Inter-American Development Bank: A Study in Development Financing. Sidney Dell. LC 70-185778. (Special Studies in International Economics & Development). 1972. 26.75x (ISBN 0-275-28606-1). Irvington.

Inter-American Development Bank & Political Influence: With Special Reference to Costa Rica. R. Peter DeWitt, Jr. LC 77-2929. (Special Studies). 1977. text ed. 24.95 (ISBN 0-275-24460-1). Praeger.

Inter-American Peace Treaties & Conventions. (Treaty Ser.: No. 16). (Eng., Span. & Port.). 1961. pap. 1.00 ea. Eng. Ed (ISBN 0-8270-0340-4). Span Ed (ISBN 0-8270-0345-5). Port. Ed (ISBN 0-8270-0445-1). OAS.

Inter-American Treaties & Conventions on Asylum & Extradition. (Treaty Ser.: No. 34). (Eng. & Span.). 1970. pap. 1.00 Eng. ed. (ISBN 0-8270-0440-0); pap. 1.00 Span ed. (ISBN 0-8270-0445-1). OAS.

Inter-American Treaties & Conventions: Signatures, Ratifications & Deposits with Explanatory Notes. (Treaty Ser.: No. 9). (Eng. Span.). 1980. Eng. ed. 15.00 (ISBN 0-8270-1158-X); span. ed. 15.00 (ISBN 0-8270-1159-8). OAS.

Inter-American Treaty of Reciprocal Assistance, Rio De Janeiro, 1947. (Treaty Ser.: No. 8). (Eng, Span, & Port.). 1961. pap. 1.00 ea. Eng. Ed (ISBN 0-8270-0305-6). Span. Ed (ISBN 0-8270-0310-2). Port. Ed (ISBN 0-8270-0315-3). OAS.

Inter-American Yearbook on Human Rights. (Inter-American Commission on Human Rights Ser.). (Eng. & Span.). 1960-67 15.00 (ISBN 0-8270-2640-4); 1968 15.00 (ISBN 0-8270-2645-5); 1969-1970 20.00 (ISBN 0-8270-2650-1). OAS.

Inter-City Wage & Salary Differentials 1980. 3rd ed. Steven Langer. 1980. pap. 50.00 (ISBN 0-916506-36-3). Abbott Langer Assocs.

Inter-City Wage & Salary Differentials, 1981. Ed. by Steven Langer. 1981. pap. 75.00 (ISBN 0-916506-62-2). Abbott Langer Assocs.

Inter-Economy Comparisons: A Case Study. Leonard A. Doyle. (Institute of Business & Economic Research, UC Berkeley). 1965. 18.00x (ISBN 0-520-00355-1). U of Cal Pr.

Inter-Governmental Relations in India: A Study in Indian Federalism. Amal Ray. 1967. 4.75x o.p. (ISBN 0-210-22719-2). Asia.

Inter Ice Age Four. Kobo Abe. Tr. by E. Dale Saunders from Jap. (Perigee Japanese Library). 240p. 1981. pap. 4.95 (ISBN 0-399-50519-9, Perigee). Putnam.

Inter-Urban Systems & Regional Economic Development. W. B. Stohr. LC 74-79829. (CCG Resource Papers Ser.: No. 26). (Illus.). 1974. pap. text ed. 4.00 (ISBN 0-89291-073-9). Assn Am Geographers.

Inter-War Economy: Britain 1919-1939. Derek H. Aldcroft. LC 70-20963. 1971. 21.50x (ISBN 0-231-03517-9). Columbia U Pr.

InterAct: Australia-U.S. George W. Renwick. LC 80-83910. (Country Orientation Ser.). 80p. 1980. pap. text ed. 10.00 (ISBN 0-933662-16-5). Intercult Pr.

InterAct: Mexico-United States. John C. Condon. Ed. by George W. Renwick. LC 80-83092. (Country Orientation Ser.). 80p. 1980. pap. text ed. 10.00 (ISBN 0-933662-13-0). Intercult Pr.

InterAct: Thailand-U.S. John Fieg. Ed. by George W. Renwick. LC 80-83909. (Country Orientation Ser.). 1980. pap. text ed. 10.00 (ISBN 0-933662-14-9). Intercult Pr.

Interact 2. Brent D. Ruben. 1977. wkbk. 7.95x (ISBN 0-89529-025-1). Avery Pub.

Interacting Binary Stars. J. Sahade & F. Wood. 1978. text ed. 30.00 (ISBN 0-08-021656-0). Pergamon.

Interacting Through Creative Arts Activities. Arden Rose. LC 76-29237. (Learning Handbooks Ser.). 1976. pap. 3.95 (ISBN 0-8224-1905-X). Pitman Learning.

Interaction. Ed. by Paul De Berker. 1969. 8.95 (ISBN 0-85181-016-0, Pub. by Faber & Faber). Merrimack Bk Serv.

Interaction Analysis: Theory, Research & Application. Edmund J. Amidon & John B. Hough. LC 67-23976. (Education Ser). (Illus., Orig.). 1967. pap. 9.95 (ISBN 0-201-00234-5). A-W.

Interaction in Everyday Life: Social Strategies. Ed. by John Lofland. LC 78-51495. (Sage Contemporary Social Science Anthologies Ser.: No. 1). 1978. pap. 5.50x (ISBN 0-8039-1035-5). Sage.

Interaction in Poetic Imagery. M. S. Silk. LC 73-90813. 304p. 1974. 42.00 (ISBN 0-521-20417-8). Cambridge U Pr.

Interaction in the Thai Bureaucracy: Structure, Culture, & Social Exchange. David F. Haas. (Westview Replica Edition Ser.). (Illus.). 1979. lib. bdg. 22.00x (ISBN 0-89158-578-8). Westview.

Interaction: Interpersonal Relationships in Organizations. Robert C. Sedwick. (Illus.). 240p. 1974. pap. 9.95 (ISBN 0-13-469155-5). P-H.

Interaction Models. N. L. Biggs. LC 77-80827. (London Mathematical Society Lecture Ser.: No. 30). (Illus.). 1977. 14.50x (ISBN 0-521-21770-9). Cambridge U Pr.

Interaction of Cancer & Host: Its Therapeutic Significance. Michael F. Woodruff. 1980. 46.50 (ISBN 0-8089-1265-8). Grune.

Interaction of Cultures. The Educational Research Council. (Human Adventure Concepts & Inquiry). (gr. 6). 1975. pap. text ed. 7.20 (ISBN 0-205-04458-1, 8044589); tchrs'. guide 5.20 (ISBN 0-205-04459-X, 8044597). Allyn.

Interaction of Economics & the Law. Bernard H. Siegan. LC 76-1223. 352p. 1977. 15.95 (ISBN 0-669-01340-4). Lexington Bks.

Interaction of Gases with Solid Surfaces. William A. Steele. LC 73-21747. 356p. 1974. text ed. 55.00 (ISBN 0-08-017724-7). Pergamon.

Interaction of Radiation & Anti-Tumor Drugs. Stanford Cade Memorial Symposium, Royal Institute, London, Sept. 1976. Ed. by Kurt Hellmann. (International Journal of Radiation Oncology, Biology, Physics: Vol. 4, No. 1-2 78--Special Issue). (Illus.). 1978. pap. text ed. 48.00 (ISBN 0-08-022666-3). Pergamon.

Interaction of Radiation with Condensed Matter, Vol. I. (Illus.). 1977. pap. 47.25 (ISBN 92-0-130377-7, ISP443-1, IAEA). Unipub.

Interaction of Radiation with Condensed Matter. (ICTP Ser: Vol. 2). (Illus.). 1978. pap. 47.25 (ISBN 92-0-130477-3, ISP-443-2, IAEA). Unipub.

Interaction Ritual: Essays on Face-To-Face Behavior. Erving Goffman. LC 67-22457. pap. 2.95 o.p. (ISBN 0-385-08850-7, A596, Anch). Doubleday.

Interactional View: Studies at the Mental Research Institute, Palo Alto, 1965-1974. Ed. by Paul Watzlawick & John H. Weakland. 1977. 18.95x (ISBN 0-393-01131-3). Norton.

Interactions Between Putative Neurotransmitters in the Brain. Ed. by S. Garattini et al. LC 77-83686. (Monographs of the Mario Negri Institute for Pharmacological Research). 1978. 34.50 (ISBN 0-89004-196-2). Raven.

Interactions of Energy & Climate. Ed. by Wilfrid Bach et al. 568p. 1980. lib. bdg. 58.00 (ISBN 90-277-1179-8, Pub. by D. Reidel); pap. 26.50 (ISBN 90-277-1177-1). Kluwer Boston.

Interactions of Mycotoxins in Animal Production. Board on Renewable Resources. 1979. pap. 9.25 (ISBN 0-309-02876-0). Natl Acad Pr.

Interactions: The Realm of Transference & Countertransference. Robert Langs. LC 80-68042. 575p. 1980. 30.00 (ISBN 0-87668-425-8). Aronson.

Interactions: Themes for Thoughtful Writing. Thelma Altschuler. 1972. pap. text ed. 6.95x (ISBN 0-02-473300-8, 47330). Macmillan.

Interactive Audio-Visual Programming: The Learning Wall Concept. Florence Schaefer. (Illus.). 172p. 1975. 15.50 (ISBN 0-398-03328-5). C C Thomas.

Interactive Computer Graphics. B. S. Walker et al. LC 74-24985. (Computer Systems Engineering Ser.). 1976. 19.50x (ISBN 0-8448-0650-1). Crane-Russak Co.

Interactive Computer Graphics in Science Teaching. Ed. by J. McKenzie et al. LC 78-40598. (Computers & Their Applications Ser.). 1979. 29.95 (ISBN 0-470-26419-5). Halsted Pr.

Interactive Data Analysis: A Practical Primer. Donald R. McNeil. LC 76-46571. 1977. text ed. 14.95 (ISBN 0-471-02631-X, Pub. by Wiley-Interscience). Wiley.

Interactive Incidents from Classroom, School & Community. Vincent Lunetta & Leon Zalewski. 1974. pap. 3.00 o.p. (ISBN 0-685-42403-0, 471-14668). Natl Sci Tchrs.

Interactive Processes in Reading. Ed. by Alan M. Lesgold & Charles A. Perfetti. LC 80-21048. 448p. 1981. professional reference text 24.95 (ISBN 0-89859-079-5). L Erlbaum Assocs.

Interactive Videotex. Dimitris Chorafas. (Illus.). 300p. 1981. text ed. 21.95 (ISBN 0-89433-127-2). Petrocelli.

Interavia ABC: World Dictionary of Aviation & Astronautics, 1980. 28th ed. Ed. by J. Didelot. 1126p. 1980. 107.50x (ISBN 0-8002-2697-6). Intl Pubns Serv.

Intercambios: An Activities Manual. Ronald G. Freeman. 209p. 1980. pap. text ed. 7.95 (ISBN 0-394-32425-0). Random.

Intercept. Ken Bernstein. 1978. pap. 1.50 o.p. (ISBN 0-523-40366-6, Dist. by Independent News Co.). Pinnacle Bks.

Intercept but Don't Shoot. Renato Vesco. 336p. 1981. pap. 2.50 (ISBN 0-553-13205-9). Bantam.

Interception Patrol: An Examination of the Theory of Random Patrol As a Municipal Police Tactic. J. F. Elliott. (Illus.). 88p. 1973. text ed. 11.75 (ISBN 0-398-02721-8). C C Thomas.

Interceptor Pilot. Kenneth Ganjemi. 128p. 1981. 11.50 (ISBN 0-7145-2699-1, Pub. by M. Boyars). Merrimack Bk Serv.

Intercessory Prayer of Our Lord Jesus Christ. John Brown. 1978. 10.50 (ISBN 0-686-12961-X). Klock & Klock.

Interchange of Bibliographic Information in Machine Readable Form. Ed. by R. E. Coward & M. Yelland. 1975. 8.95 (ISBN 0-85365-338-0, Pub. by Lib Assn England). Oryx Pr.

Intercity Differences in Costs of Living in March, 1935 - 59 Cities. Margaret L. Stecker. LC 79-165689. (FDR & the Era of the New Deal Ser). 1971. Repr. of 1937 ed. lib. bdg. 22.50 (ISBN 0-306-70344-0). Da Capo.

Intercity Transportation: Engineering & Planning. T. Rallis. 1978. 39.95 (ISBN 0-470-01394-X). Halsted Pr.

Intercollegiate Socialist Society, Nineteen Hundred Five to Nineteen Twenty-One: Origins of the Modern American Student Movement. Max Horn. LC 79-9404. (Westview Replica Edition Ser.). (Illus.). 1979. lib. bdg. 24.00x (ISBN 0-89158-584-2). Westview.

Intercomparison Procedures in the Dosimetry of Photon Radiation. 1978. pap. 16.25 (ISBN 92-0-115178-0, IDC 182, IAEA). Unipub.

Intercountry Income Distribution & Transnational Enterprises. Constantine V. Vaitsos. 192p. 1974. 24.00x (ISBN 0-19-828195-1). Oxford U Pr.

Intercultural & International Communication. Ed. by Fred L. Casmir. LC 78-61912. 1978. pap. text ed. 19.75 (ISBN 0-8191-0625-9). U Pr of Amer.

Intercultural Communication. L. E. Sarbaugh. (gr. 10 up). 1978. pap. text ed. 8.50x (ISBN 0-8104-6090-4). Hayden.

Intercultural Education. David S. Hoopes. LC 79-93119. (Fastback Ser.: No. 142). (Orig.). 1980. pap. 0.75 (ISBN 0-87367-142-2). Phi Delta Kappa.

Intercultural Sourcebook: Cross-Cultural Training Methodologies. Ed. by David S. Hoopes & Paul Ventura. LC 79-83667. 1979. pap. text ed. 7.50 (ISBN 0-933662-00-9). Intercult Pr.

Intercultural Theory & Practice: Perspectives on Education, Training & Research. Ed. by William G. Davey. LC 79-91280. (Orig.). 1980. pap. text ed. 6.50 o.p. (ISBN 0-933662-05-X). Intercult Pr.

Interdependence: A Handbook for Environmental Education. NAIS Teacher Services Committee. 1979. pap. 4.75 (ISBN 0-934338-23-X). NAIS.

Interdependence of Free Enterprise & Governments in the Global Marketplace. Raymond A. Robillard. LC 79-66832. 1979. pap. text ed. 9.00 (ISBN 0-8191-0852-9). U Pr of Amer.

Interdependence of Nations. Lester R. Brown. (Development Papers: No. 10). 70p. 1972. pap. 1.00 (ISBN 0-686-28679-0). Overseas Dev Council.

Interdisciplinary Analysis of Water Resource Systems. Compiled by American Society of Civil Engineers. 416p. 1975. pap. text ed. 21.00 (ISBN 0-87262-115-4). Am Soc Civil Eng.

Interdisciplinary Approach to American History, Vol. 2. Ed. by Ari Hoogenboom & Olive Hoogenboom. (Illus.). 416p. 1973. pap. text ed. 10.95 (ISBN 0-13-469221-7). P-H.

Interdisciplinary Approaches to Human Communication. Brent D. Ruben & Richard W. Budd. (gr. 12 up). 1979. pap. text ed. 8.50x (ISBN 0-8104-5125-5). Hayden.

Interdisciplinary Language Intervention Program for the Moderately & Profoundly Language-Retarded Child. Sol Adler et al. 1980. 19.50 (ISBN 0-8089-1301-8). Grune.

Interdisciplinary Methods: A Thematic Approach. Arthur Ellis et al. 1980. pap. text ed. write for info. (ISBN 0-8302-4387-9). Goodyear.

Interdisciplinary Studies in the Humanities: A Directory. Elizabeth Bayerl. LC 77-22960. 1977. 40.00 (ISBN 0-8108-1076-X). Scarecrow.

Interdisciplinary Team: A Handbook for the Education of Exceptional Children. Alex J. Ducanis & Anne K. Golin. 200p. 1981. text ed. price not set. Aspen Systems.

Interdiscplinary Approaches to Chemistry: An Instructional Program for High School Chemistry, 7 vols. Ed. by Marjorie Gardner & Henry Heikkinen. Incl. Delicate Balance: Environmental Chemistry Module. 4.00 (ISBN 0-06-561106-3); tchr's ed. 5.20 (ISBN 0-06-561215-9); tests 15.88 (ISBN 0-06-561606-5); Heart of Matter: Nuclear Chemistry Module; Molecules in Living Systems: Biochemistry Module. 4.00 (ISBN 0-06-561103-9); tchr's ed. 5.20 (ISBN 0-06-561213-2); tests 15.40 (ISBN 0-06-561604-9); Form & Function: An Organic Chemistry Module. 4.00 (ISBN 0-06-561102-0); tchr's ed. 5.20 (ISBN 0-06-561212-4); tests 14.80 (ISBN 0-06-561603-0); Diversity & Periodicity: An Inorganic Chemistry Module. 4.00 (ISBN 0-06-561101-2); tchr's ed. 5.20 (ISBN 0-06-561211-6); tests 15.88 (ISBN 0-06-561602-2); Reactions & Reason: An Introductory Chemistry Module. 4.00 (ISBN 0-06-561100-4); tchr's ed. 5.20 (ISBN 0-06-561210-8); tests 19.32 (ISBN 0-06-561601-4); Communities of Molecules: Physical Chemistry Module. 4.00 (ISBN 0-06-561107-1); tchr's ed. 5.20 (ISBN 0-06-561216-7); tests 15.40 (ISBN 0-06-561607-3). text ed. 25.88 set (ISBN 0-06-561110-1, SchDept). Har-Row.

Interest-Adjusted Index: Nineteen Eighty-One Edition. Ed. by Price Gaines. LC 76-6788. 410p. 1980. pap. 18.00 (ISBN 0-87218-012-3). Natl Underwriter.

Interest Amortization Tables. Jack C. Estes. (McGraw-Hill Paperbacks). 224p. (Orig.). 1976. pap. 4.95 (ISBN 0-07-019680-X, SP). McGraw.

Interest & Discipline in Education. P. S. Wilson. (Students Library of Education). 1971. 12.50x (ISBN 0-7100-7049-7); pap. 6.50 (ISBN 0-7100-7908-7). Routledge & Kegan.

Interest & Effort in Education. John Dewey. LC 74-18471. (Arcturus Books Paperbacks). 120p. 1975. pap. 6.95 (ISBN 0-8093-0716-2). S Ill U Pr.

Interest Groups in Norwegian Politics. Robert B. Kvavik. 1976. pap. 17.00x (ISBN 8-200-01477-0, Dist. by Columbia U Pr). Universitet.

Interest on Third Party Accounts: A Desk Top Primer. Frederic H. Karr. 160p. 1980. 18.95 (ISBN 0-03-058024-2). Praeger.

Interest Rates on Savings Deposits: Theory, Estimation, & Policy. M. B. Slovin & M. E. Sushka. LC 74-16931. (Illus.). 192p. 1975. 18.95 (ISBN 0-669-96453-0). Lexington Bks.

Interesting Narrative of the Sufferings of Mr. Joseph Barker & His Wife... Taken by a Scouting Party of British & Indians... in 1777, Repr. Of 1848 Ed. Bd. with Indian Tradition. No Fiction. the Traditionary History of a Narrow & Providential Escape of Some White Men from Being Tomahawked, Scalped, & Robbed by a Party of Taw-Way Indians. Repr. of 1848 ed; Dreadful Sufferings & Thrilling Adventures of an Overland Party of Immigrants to California, Their Terrible Conflicts with Savage Tribes of Indians!!! & Bands of Mexican Robbers!!! with Marriage, Funeral, & Other Interesting Ceremonies & Customs of Indian Life in Far West. George Adam. Repr. of 1850 ed; History of the Revolutionary War... Brief Account of the Captivity & Cruel Sufferings of Captain Deitz & John & Robert Brice. Repr. of 1851 ed; Life & Adventures of David C. Butterfield, a Northwestern Pioneer... Written by Himself, in His Wild Western Style. Repr. of 1851 ed. LC 75-7087. (Indian Captivities Ser.: Vol. 63). 1977. lib. bdg. 44.00 (ISBN 0-8240-1687-4). Garland Pub.

Interesting Times. Joan Thompson. 322p. 1981. 12.95 (ISBN 0-312-41914-7). St Martin.

Interests & Rights: The Case Against Animals. R. G. Frey. (Clarendon Library of Logic & Philosophy Ser.). 188p. 1980. 24.95x (ISBN 0-19-824421-5). Oxford U Pr.

Interests & the Growth of Knowledge. Barry Barnes. (Direct Editions Ser). (Orig.). 1977. pap. 11.00 (ISBN 0-7100-8669-5). Routledge & Kegan.

Interethnic Sensitivity Materials for Educators Who Want to Know. Judith A. Thomas. 1978. pap. text ed. 10.00 (ISBN 0-8191-0387-X). U Pr of Amer.

Interface Between the Psychodynamic & Behavioral Therapies. Ed. by Judd Marmor & Sherwyn M. Woods. LC 79-9197. (Critical Issues in Psychiatry Ser.). 397p. 1980. 22.50 (ISBN 0-306-40251-3, Plenum Pr). Plenum Pub.

Interface: Calculus & the Computer. David A. Smith. LC 75-25016. (Illus.). 288p. 1976. pap. text ed. 10.25 (ISBN 0-395-21875-6); instructors manual 2.25 (ISBN 0-395-21876-4). HM.

Interfaces Between Alcoholism & Mental Health. Ed. by Earl X. Freed. (NIAAA-RUCAS Alcoholism Treatment Ser.: No. 4). 1981. pap. 8.00 (ISBN 0-911290-50-8). Rutgers Ctr Alcohol.

Interfacial Chemistry: An Experimental Approach. E. Gileadi et al. 1975. text ed. 30.50 (ISBN 0-201-02398-9, Adv Bk Prog); pap. text ed. 18.50 (ISBN 0-201-02399-7). A-W.

Interfacial Segregation. Ed. by W. C. Johnson. 1979. 58.00 (ISBN 0-87170-004-2). ASM.

Interfacing to S-100 IEEE 696 Microcomputers. Soloman Libes. (Orig.). 1981. pap. text ed. 15.99 (ISBN 0-931988-37-3). Osborne-McGraw.

Interference Analysis of Communication. Ed. by P. Stavroulakis. LC 80-18464. 1980. 34.95 (ISBN 0-87942-135-5). Inst Electrical.

Interference Analysis of Communication Systems. Peter Stavroulakis. 472p. 1980. 38.00 (ISBN 0-471-08674-6, Pub. by Wiley-Interscience); pap. 25.75 (ISBN 0-471-08673-8). Wiley.

Interference Handbook. William R. Nelson. (Illus.). 240p. 1981. 8.95 (ISBN 0-933616-01-5). Radio Pubns.

Interference of Electromagnetic Waves. A. H. Cook. (International Series of Monographs on Physics). 264p. 1971. 25.75x o.p. (ISBN 0-19-851255-4). Oxford U Pr.

Interferences with Development. P. Malone. 1981. 25.00 (ISBN 0-685-32525-3). Univ Park.

Interferometry. William H. Steel. (Cambridge Monographs on Physics). 1967. 35.50 (ISBN 0-521-06547-X). Cambridge U Pr.

Interferon & Interfaron Inducers: Clinical Applications. Ed. by Stringfellow. 336p. 1980. 39.50 (ISBN 0-8247-6931-7). Dekker.

Interferon & Interferon Inducers. Permanent Section of Microbiological Standardization, 31st Symposium, Omstotite of Child Health, Ondon, 1969. Ed. by F. T. Perkins & R. H. Regamey. (Immunobiological Standardization: Vol. 14). 1970. 36.00 (ISBN 3-8055-0637-6). S Karger.

Interferon & Non-Specific Resistance. Alexander Yabrov. LC 80-13677. 376p. 1980. 39.95 (ISBN 0-87705-497-5). Human Sci Pr.

Interferons: A Primer. Robert M. Friedman. 1981. price not set (ISBN 0-12-268280-7). Acad Pr.

Intergalva 76: Proceedings. International Galvanizing Conference Madrid 1976. Ed. by Zinc Development Assoc., London. (Illus.). 272p. (Orig.). 1978. pap. 32.50x (ISBN 0-8002-2228-8). Intl Pubns Serv.

Intergenerational House-Sharing. Stephen R. McConnell & Carolyn E. Usher. LC 80-67436. (Andrus Papers). 52p. 1980. pap. 3.25 (ISBN 0-88474-098-6). USC Andrus Geron.

Intergenerational Occupational Mobility in the United States. Marshall Pomer. LC 80-20626. (University of Florida Social Science Monograph: No. 66). write for info. (ISBN 0-8130-0674-0). U Presses Fla.

Intergerini Parietis Septum (Eph. 2: 14) Essays Presented to Markus Barth on His 65th Birthday. Ed. by Dikran Y. Hadidian. (Pittsburgh Theological Monograph Ser.: No. 33). 1980. pap. 15.95 (ISBN 0-915138-42-5). Pickwick.

Intergovernmental Conference on Communication Policies in Asia & Oceania: Final Report. 87p. 1980. pap. 7.50 (ISBN 0-686-68811-2, U1022, UNESCO). Unipub.

Intergovernmental Conference on Environmental Education: Final Report. 101p. 1980. pap. 7.50 (ISBN 0-686-68812-0, U1021, UNESCO). Unipub.

Intergovernmental Conference on the Convention on the Dumping of Wastes at Sea. 36p. 1976. 8.25 (IMCO). Unipub.

Intergovernmental Fiscal Relations in the United States. George F. Break. (Studies of Government Finance). 14.95 (ISBN 0-8157-1074-7); pap. 5.95 (ISBN 0-8157-1073-9). Brookings.

Intergovernmental Relations & Australian Education. I. Birch et al. LC 79-55415. (Centre for Research on Federal Financial Relations - Research Monograph: No. 29). 107p. (Orig.). 1980. pap. text ed. 11.95 (ISBN 0-908160-46-1, 0566). Bks Australia.

Intergovernmental Relations in the European Community. R. A. Rhodes & C. Hull. 96p. 1977. text ed. 23.00x (ISBN 0-566-00191-8, Pub. by Gower Pub Co England). Renouf.

Intergroup Processes: A Micro-Macro Perspective. Hubert M. Blalock, Jr. & Paul H. Wilken. LC 78-19856. 1979. 24.95 (ISBN 0-02-903620-8). Free Pr.

Interim Radiation Protection Standards for the Design, Construction, Testing & Control of Radioisotopic Cardiac Pacemakers. Organization for Economic Cooperation & Development. 54p. 1974. 2.50 o.p. (ISBN 92-64-11246-4). OECD.

Interim Report on the Books Jesus & Christ. Edward Schillebeeckx. 160p. 1980. 12.95 (ISBN 0-8245-0477-1). Crossroad NY.

Interim Specifications - Bridges. 1980. 4.00. AASHTO.

Interim Specifications - Materials. 1980. 6.00. AASHTO.

Interim Specifications for Bridges. 1979. 4.00. AASHTO.

Interior Castle. St. Teresa of Avila. 1972. pap. 2.95 (ISBN 0-385-03643-4, Im). Doubleday.

Interior Decorating with Plants. Carla Wallach. (Illus.). 224p. 1976. pap. 8.95 o.s.i. (ISBN 0-02-012000-1, Collier). Macmillan.

Interior Design. Alice Waugh. 1967. spiral bdg. 5.95 o.p. (ISBN 0-8087-2305-7). Burgess.

Interior Design & Decoration: A Bibliography of Books. Mary Vance. (Architecture Ser.: Bibliography A-257). 75p. 1980. pap. 8.00. Vance Biblios.

Interior Design for Profit. Mary V. Knackstedt. Ed. by Laura J. Haney. 1980. 17.00 (ISBN 0-9604676-0-2). Kobro Pubns.

Interior Lighting for Environmental Designers. James L. Nuckolls. LC 75-40413. 371p. 1976. 32.50 (ISBN 0-471-65163-X, Pub. by Wiley-Interscience). Wiley.

Interior Planting in Large Buildings: A Handbook for Architects Interior Designers & Horticulturists. Steven Scrivens. LC 80-23565. 200p. 1981. 44.95 (ISBN 0-470-27067-5). Halsted Pr.

Interior Planting Line Art. Regina Kurtz & Susan Van Gieson. (Illus.). 1980. pap. text ed. 25.00 (ISBN 0-918436-13-3). Environ Design.

Interior Salish & Eastern Washington Indians, Vol. 1. Incl. Ethnological Field Investigation & Analysis of Historical Material Relative to Coeur D'alene Indian Aboriginal Distribution. Stuart A. Chalfant; The Coeur D'alene Country 1805-1892: an Historical Sketch. William N. Bischoff; Findings of Fact, & Opinion. Indian Claims Commission. (American Indian Ethnohistory Ser: Indians of the Northwest). (Illus.). lib. bdg. 42.00 (ISBN 0-8240-0752-2). Garland Pub.

Interior Salish & Eastern Washington Indians, Vol. 2. Incl. Aboriginal Territories of the Flathead, Pend D'oreille & Kutenai Indians of Western Montana. Stuart A. Chalfant; Economy & Land Use by the Indians of Western Montana. Carling Malouf; Historical Report Concerning Lands Ceded to the U.S. by Flathead, Pend D'oreille & Kutenai Indians. Merrill G. Burlingame. (American Indian Ethnohistory Ser: Indians of the Northwest). (Illus.). lib. bdg. 42.00 (ISBN 0-8240-0753-0). Garland Pub.

Interior Salish & Eastern Washington Indians, Vol. 3. Incl. The Confederated Salish & Kutenai Tribes of the Flathead Reservation, Montana. E. O. Fuller; Aboriginal Territory of the Kalispel Indians. Stuart A. Chalfant; History of the Confederated Salish & Kootenai Tribes of the Flathead Reservation, Montana. Paul C. Phillips; Flathead, Kutenai & Upper Pend D'oreille Genealogies. Carling Malouf & Paul C. Phillips; Findings of Fact, & Opinion. Indian Claims Commission. (American Indian Ethnohistory Ser: Indians of the Northwest). (Illus.). lib. bdg. 42.00 (ISBN 0-8240-0754-9). Garland Pub.

Interior Salish & Eastern Washington Indians, Vol. 4. Incl. Ethnohistorical Report on Aboriginal Land Use & Occupancy by Spokan Indians. Stuart A. Chalfant; Ethnohistory of the Spokane Indians. Angelo Anastasio; Ethnohistorical Report on Aboriginal Land Occupancy & Utilization by Palus Indians. Stuart A. Chalfant; Anthropological & Ethnohistorical Material Relative to Aboriginial Land Use & Occupancy by the Columbia Salish of Central Washington. Stuart A. Chalfant; Anthropological & Ethnohistorical Material Relative to Aboriginal Land Use & Occupancy by the Wenatchi Salish of Central Washington. Stuart A. Chalfant; Ethnological Notes on the Columbia, Chelan, Entiat & Wenatchee Tribes. Verne F. Ray; Findings of Fact, & Opinion. Indian Claims Commission. (American Indian Ethnohistory Ser: Indians of the Northwest). (Illus.). lib. bdg. 42.00 (ISBN 0-8240-0782-4). Garland Pub.

Interior Spaces Designed by Architects. 2nd ed. Architectural Record Magazine. (Architectural Record Ser.). (Illus.). 224p. 1981. 32.50 (ISBN 0-07-002354-9, P&RB). McGraw.

Interior Wiring. LC 78-7075. (Illus.). 1978. pap. 5.95 (ISBN 0-8069-8444-9). Sterling.

Interiors & Interior Details. William B. Tuthill. (Architecture & Decorative Arts Ser). (Illus.). 1975. Repr. of 1882 ed. lib. bdg. 35.00 (ISBN 0-306-70747-0). Da Capo.

Interiors Book of Shops & Restaurants. From the Pages of Interiors Magazine. 144p. 1981. 25.00 (ISBN 0-8230-7284-3, Whitney Lib). Watson-Guptill.

Interiors of the Planets. A. H. Cook. (Cambridge Planetary Science Ser.: No. 1). (Illus.). 360p. 1981. 59.50 (ISBN 0-521-23214-7). Cambridge U Pr.

Interlocking Directorates: Origins & Consequences of Connections Among Organizations' Boards of Directors. Johannes M. Pennings. LC 80-8001. (Social & Behavioral Science Ser.). 1980. text ed. 14.95x (ISBN 0-87589-469-0). Jossey-Bass.

Interlopers. Donald Hamilton. (Matt Helm Ser.). 1978. pap. 1.95 (ISBN 0-449-13994-8, GM). Fawcett.

Interlude. Michael Tarachow. (Illus.). 1979. signed ltd. ed. 7.50 (ISBN 0-915316-68-4); pap. 3.50 (ISBN 0-915316-67-6). Pentagram.

Interlude in Venice. Florence Bowes. LC 80-1720. (Starlight Romance Ser.). 192p. 1981. 9.95 (ISBN 0-385-17316-4). Doubleday.

Intermediary World & Patterns of Perfection in Philo & Hebrews. Lala Kalyan Kumar Dey. LC 75-22457. (Society of Biblical Literature. Dissertation Ser.). 1975. pap. 7.50 (ISBN 0-89130-022-8, 060125). Scholars Pr Ca.

Intermediate Accounting. 2nd ed. Sidney Davidson et al. LC 80-65795. 1088p. 1981. text ed. 24.95 (ISBN 0-03-058081-1). Dryden Pr.

Intermediate Accounting. W. Asquith Howe. (Illus.). 288p. (Orig.). 1974. pap. 4.50 (ISBN 0-06-460143-9, CO 143, COS). Har-Row.

Intermediate Accounting. Donald E. Kieso & Jerry J. Weygandt. 1290p. 1980. text ed. 25.95 (ISBN 0-471-04819-4); write for info. (ISBN 0-471-05580-8); write for info. (ISBN 0-471-06439-4); 9.95 (ISBN 0-471-04821-6); practice set 7.65 (ISBN 0-471-06441-6). Wiley.

Intermediate Accounting. Loren A. Nikolai et al. 1120p. 1980. text ed. 22.95x (ISBN 0-534-00786-4, Kent Pub.); guide 7.95xstudy (ISBN 0-534-00821-6); papers 9.95xworking (ISBN 0-534-00830-5). Kent Pub Co.

Intermediate Accounting. 5th ed. Glenn A. Welsch et al. (Illus.). 1979. text ed. 23.95 (ISBN 0-256-02178-3); pap. 6.50x working papers 1-14 (ISBN 0-256-02180-5); pap. 6.50x working papers 15-25 (ISBN 0-256-02181-3); pap. 4.95 study guide (ISBN 0-256-02179-1). Irwin.

Intermediate Accounting. Glenn A. Welsch et al. (Second canadian edition). 1978. text ed. 23.95 (ISBN 0-256-01984-3). Irwin.

Intermediate Accounts. 3rd ed. L. W. Owler. 400p. 1975. pap. text ed. 12.95x (ISBN 0-7121-0936-6, Pub. by Macdonald & Evans England). Intl Ideas.

Intermediate Aeronautical Language Manual. Deborah J. Balter. Date not set. pap. 14.95. Aviation.

Intermediate Algebra. Dennis Bila et al. LC 74-84642. (Illus.). xvii, 625p. (Prog. Bk.). 1975. text ed. 13.95x (ISBN 0-87901-038-X). Worth.

Intermediate Algebra. Steven J. Bryant et al. 368p. 1968. text ed. 12.95x (ISBN 0-02-473860-3, 47386). Macmillan.

Intermediate Algebra. Cohen & Cameron. 576p. 1980. pap. text ed. 17.80 (ISBN 0-205-07172-4, 5671728); free tchr's ed. (ISBN 0-205-07173-2). Allyn.

Intermediate Algebra. Richard J. Easton & George P. Graham. LC 72-4744. (Illus.). 305p. 1973. text ed. 17.95x (ISBN 0-471-22939-3); student wkbk. 9.95 (ISBN 0-471-22943-1). Wiley.

Intermediate Algebra. Tom Green & William Wooton. 608p. 1980. pap. text ed. 16.95x (ISBN 0-534-00788-0). Wadsworth Pub.

Intermediate Algebra. 2nd ed. Carol L. Johnston & Alden T. Willis. 1979. pap. text ed. 16.95x (ISBN 0-534-00595-0). Wadsworth Pub.

Intermediate Algebra. 3rd ed. Margaret L. Lial & Charles D. Miller. 1981. text ed. 15.95x (ISBN 0-673-15406-8). Scott F.

Intermediate Algebra. Charles P. McKeaugue. 494p. 1979. 16.95 (ISBN 0-12-484760-9); instr's. manual avail. Acad Pr.

Intermediate Algebra. new ed. Frances S. Mangan. (Mathematics Ser). (Illus.). 480p. 1975. pap. text ed. 16.95 (ISBN 0-675-08742-2); instructor's manual 3.95 (ISBN 0-686-67092-2). Merrill.

Intermediate Algebra. 2nd ed. John H. Minnick. (Illus.). 1978. ref. ed. 16.95 (ISBN 0-13-469569-0). P-H.

Intermediate Algebra. Francis J. Mueller. (Illus.). 1979. pap. 16.95 ref. (ISBN 0-13-469452-X). P-H.

Intermediate Algebra. 2nd ed. Mustafa Munem & William Tschirhart. LC 76-27388. (Illus.). 1977. text ed. 15.95x (ISBN 0-87901-064-9); study guide 6.95x (ISBN 0-87901-067-3). Worth.

Intermediate Algebra. Joseph Newmyer & Gus Klentos. LC 74-106504. 1970. text ed. 14.95 (ISBN 0-675-09352-X). Merrill.

Intermediate Algebra. 2nd ed. Joseph Newmyer, Jr. & Gus Klentos. Ed. by Kleinfeld. (Mathematics Ser). (Illus.). 416p. 1975. pap. text ed. 15.95 (ISBN 0-675-08744-9); instructors manual 3.95 (ISBN 0-685-50980-X); audio cassettes 140.00 (ISBN 0-685-50981-8); 2-6 90.00 ea. (ISBN 0-675-08717-1); 7 or more 60.00 (ISBN 0-686-67093-0). Merrill.

Intermediate Algebra. Marvin Schlichting. Date not set. text ed. price not set (ISBN 0-442-21214-3). D Van Nostrand.

Intermediate Algebra. Howard A. Silver. 512p. 1981. text ed. 17.95 (ISBN 0-13-469411-2). P-H.

Intermediate Algebra. Arnold J. Steffensen & L. M. Johnson. 1980. pap. text ed. 14.95 (ISBN 0-673-15369-X). Scott F.

Intermediate Algebra. 5th ed. William Wooton & Irving Drooyan. 1979. text ed. 17.95x (ISBN 0-534-00704-X); study guide 5.95x (ISBN 0-534-00787-2); solutions for students 4.95x (ISBN 0-534-00739-2). Wadsworth Pub.

Intermediate Algebra. new ed. D. Franklin Wright & Bill D. New. 450p. 1981. text ed. 16.75 (ISBN 0-205-07185-6, 567185-X); tchrs'. ed. avail. (ISBN 0-205-07186-4). Allyn.

Intermediate Algebra: A Clear Approach. Norman L. Siever. 1981. write for info. (ISBN 0-8302-4206-6). Goodyear.

Intermediate Algebra: A Programmed Approach. Anthony J. Pettofrezzo & Lee H. Armstrong. 1981. pap. text ed. 13.95 (ISBN 0-673-15315-0). Scott F.

Intermediate Algebra: A Text Workbook. Marion W. Keller. LC 74-171526. pap. text ed. 12.25 (ISBN 0-395-12644-4, 3-29361); test ans. & prob. pap. 2.95 (ISBN 0-685-02020-7, 3-29362). HM.

Intermediate Algebra: A Text-Workbook. Charles D. Miller & Margaret L. Lial. 1980. pap. text ed. 14.95x (ISBN 0-673-15271-5). Scott F.

Intermediate Algebra & Analytic Geometry Made Simple. William R. Gondin & Bernard Sohmer. 1959. pap. 3.50 (ISBN 0-385-00437-0, Made). Doubleday.

Intermediate Algebra for College Students. H. S. Bear. LC 72-104058. 1970. text ed. 12.95 o.p. (ISBN 0-8465-0420-0). Benjamin-Cummings.

Intermediate Algebra for College Students. Mary P. Dolciani et al. LC 71-146721. 1971. text ed. 15.70 (ISBN 0-395-12072-1); tchrs. ed. & key 5.80 (ISBN 0-395-12074-8). HM.

Intermediate Algebra for College Students. Isidore Dressler et al. 1977. pap. text ed. 10.00 (ISBN 0-87720-977-4). AMSCO Sch.

Intermediate Algebra for College Students. 5th ed. Thurman S. Peterson & Charles R. Hobby. 1980. text ed. 16.50 scp (ISBN 0-06-045184-X, HarpC); answer key avail. (ISBN 0-06-365152-1). Har-Row.

Intermediate Algebra for College Students. D. Franklin Wright & Kenneth E. Lindgren. LC 74-146711. (Illus.). 1971. text ed. 15.95x o.p. (ISBN 0-669-61754-7); instructor's manual free o.p. (ISBN 0-669-61762-8). Heath.

Intermediate Algebra Skills for College. Harry Lewis. (Orig.). Date not set. pap. text ed. price not set (ISBN 0-442-23163-6); price not set instr's. manual (ISBN 0-442-28663-5). D Van Nostrand.

Intermediate Analysis: An Introduction to Theory of Functions of One Real Variable. John M. Olmsted. LC 56-5844. (Illus.). 1956. 32.50x (ISBN 0-89197-796-1); pap. text ed. 18.50x (ISBN 0-8290-0385-1). Irvington.

Intermediate Anecdotes in American English. L. A. Hill. (Anecdotes in American English Ser.). (Illus.). 80p. 1980. pap. 2.50x (ISBN 0-19-502602-0). Oxford U Pr.

Intermediate Chemistry: Organic Chemistry. Holiday & Hunt. 1981. text ed. price not set (ISBN 0-408-70915-4). Butterworth.

Intermediate Chinese. John DeFrancis. 1964. text ed. 35.00x (ISBN 0-300-00412-5); pap. text ed. 8.95x (ISBN 0-300-00064-2). Yale U Pr.

Intermediate Chinese Reader, 2 Pts. John DeFrancis et al. text ed. 40.00x ea.; Pt. 1 1967. pap. 7.95x (ISBN 0-300-00413-3); Pt. 2 1968. pap. 8.50x (ISBN 0-300-00414-1); Pt. 1. pap. 8.95x (ISBN 0-300-00065-0); Pt. 2. pap. text ed. 8.95x (ISBN 0-300-00066-9). Yale U Pr.

Intermediate Christian Training. Jean Gibson. 1981. pap. 6.50 (ISBN 0-937396-60-5). Walterick Pubs.

Intermediate Classical Mechanics. Joseph Norwood, Jr. (Illus.). 1979. ref. 25.95 (ISBN 0-13-469635-2). P-H.

Intermediate Colloquial Arabic Course. Raja Nasr. 1974. 12.00x (ISBN 0-685-72047-0). Intl Bk Ctr.

Intermediate Composition Practice, Bk I. Linda L. Blanton. (Illus., Orig.). (gr. 7-12). 1981. pap. text ed. 5.95 (ISBN 0-88377-194-2). Newbury Hse.

Intermediate Economic Statistics, 2 vols. 2nd ed. Karl A. Fox & Tej K. Kaul. Incl. Vol. 1. Integration of Economic Theory & Statistical Methods. Repr. of 1968 ed. 23.50 (ISBN 0-88275-521-8); Vol. 2. Guide to Recent Developments & Literature, 1968-1978. 186p. 10.50 (ISBN 0-88275-987-6). LC 76-30914. 584p. 1980. 30.00 set (ISBN 0-686-64856-0). Krieger.

Intermediate English Practice Book. S. Pit Corder. 1974. pap. text ed. 4.25x (ISBN 0-582-52512-8); key 2.00x (ISBN 0-582-52513-6). Longman.

Intermediate Greek-English Lexicon. Compiled by H. G. Liddell & Robert Scott. 1959. text ed. 29.50x (ISBN 0-19-910206-6). Oxford U Pr.

Intermediate Mathematics. Irving Drooyan & William Wooten. 1971. 17.95x (ISBN 0-534-00095-9). Wadsworth Pub.

Intermediate Mathematics of Electromagnetics. D. C. Stinson. (Illus.). 320p. 1976. ref. ed 24.95 (ISBN 0-13-470633-1). P-H.

Intermediate Microeconomics. James P. Quirk. LC 75-34009. (Illus.). 448p. 1976. text ed. 18.50 (ISBN 0-574-19265-4, 13-2265); instr's guide avail. (ISBN 0-574-19266-2, 13-2266); mathematical notes 3.95 (ISBN 0-574-19267-0, 13-2267). SRA.

Intermediate Microeconomics & Application. 2nd ed. Walter Nicholson. LC 78-56197. 1979. text ed. 20.95 (ISBN 0-03-041481-4). Dryden Pr.

Intermediate Microeconomics with Applications. Aroop K. Mahanty. 1980. 17.95 (ISBN 0-12-465150-X). Acad Pr.

Intermediate Moisture Foods. R. Davies et al. (Illus.). 1976. 63.30x (ISBN 0-85334-702-6). Intl Ideas.

Intermediate Nepali Reader, 2 vols. M. K. Verma & T. N. Sharma. 1980. Vol.1. write for info. (ISBN 0-8364-0652-4, Pub. by Manohar India); Vol. 2. write for info. (ISBN 0-8364-0653-2); Set. 32.50 (ISBN 0-686-69016-8). South Asia Bks.

Intermediate Piano for Adults, Vol. 1. Helene Robinson. 1970. pap. 10.95x (ISBN 0-534-00210-2). Wadsworth Pub.

Intermediate Politometrics. Gordon Hilton. LC 74-43733. 336p. 1976. 17.00x (ISBN 0-231-03783-X). Columbia U Pr.

Intermediate Price Theory: Analysis, Issues & Applications. Micha Gisser. (Illus.). 608p. 1981. text ed. 17.95 (ISBN 0-07-023312-8, C); instructor's manual 4.95 (ISBN 0-07-023313-6). McGraw.

Intermediate Quantum Mechanics. 2nd ed. Hans A. Bethe & Roman W. Jackiw. LC 68-24363. (Lecture Notes & Supplements in Physics Ser.: No. 9). 1968. pap. 17.50 (ISBN 0-8053-0755-9, Adv Bk Prog). Benjamin-Cummings.

Intermediate Quantum Theory of Crystalline Solids. Alex O. E. Animalu. LC 76-16858. (Illus.). 1977. 27.95 (ISBN 0-13-470799-0). P-H.

Intermediate Racquetball Drills. Jean Sauser & Arthur Shay. (Illus., Orig.). 1981. pap. 3.95 (ISBN 0-8092-5926-5). Contemp Bks.

Intermediate Readings in Tagalog. Ed. by J. Donald Bowen. (Orig.). 1968. pap. 15.50x (ISBN 0-520-00157-5). U of Cal Pr.

Intermediate Science Bookshelf. (Classroom Libraries). (gr. 4-6). 103.44 o.p. (ISBN 0-531-00731-6). Watts.

Intermediate Sign Language. Louie J. Fant, Jr. (Illus.). 225p. (gr. 7 up). 1980. text ed. 17.95 (ISBN 0-917002-54-7). Joyce Media.

Intermediate Soccer Guide. Bobby Moffat. (Illus.). 160p. (Orig.). 1981. pap. write for info. (ISBN 0-89037-181-4). Anderson World.

Intermediate Spanish Review Grammar. Gino Parisi. 336p. Date not set. pap. text ed. 8.95 (ISBN 0-669-02632-8); wkbk. 3.95 (ISBN 0-669-02633-6). Heath. Postponed.

Intermediate Stories for Reproduction. Leslie A. Hill. 68p. 1965. pap. 2.50x (ISBN 0-19-432542-3). Oxford U Pr.

Intermediate Structure in Nuclear Reactions. Ed. by Hugh P. Kennedy & Rudolph Schrils. LC 67-29341. (Illus.). 232p. 1968. pap. 9.50x (ISBN 0-8131-1155-2). U Pr of Ky.

Intermediate Studies in Alchemy. new ed. Saint Germain. LC 74-82295. (Alchemy Ser.). (Illus.). 132p. 1975. pap. 3.95 (ISBN 0-916766-01-2). Summit Univ.

Intermetallic Semiconducting Films. H. H. Wieder. LC 76-80293. 1970. 50.00 (ISBN 0-08-013367-3). Pergamon.

Intermezzo. Jean Giraudoux. Ed. by John H. Reilly. LC 67-14570. (Fr.). 1967. pap. text ed. 6.95x (ISBN 0-89197-232-3). Irvington.

Intermission. Anne Baxter. 1978. pap. 2.50 (ISBN 0-345-29267-7). Ballantine.

Intermolecular Forces. T. Kihara. LC 77-12353. 1978. 30.25 (ISBN 0-471-99583-5, Pub. by Wiley-Interscience). Wiley.

Intermolecular Forces, Vol. 12. Ed. by Joseph O. Hirschfelder. 648p. 1967. 32.50 (ISBN 0-470-40067-6). Krieger.

Intermolecular Forces & Packing in Crystals. Ed. by Busing. pap. 5.00 (ISBN 0-686-60377-X). Polycrystal Bk Serv.

Intermolecular Interactions & Biomolecular Organization. A. J. Hopfinger. LC 76-26540. 1977. 37.50 (ISBN 0-471-40910-3, Pub by Wiley-Interscience). Wiley.

Intermountain Flora, Vol. 6. A. Cronquist et al. LC 73-134298. 1977. 60.00x (ISBN 0-231-04120-9). Columbia U Pr.

Internaional Shipping & Shipbuilding Directory. 1980. 95.00x (ISBN 0-686-27091-6). State Mutual Bk.

Internal Accounting Control: Evaluation & Auditor Judgment. (Auditing Research Monograph: No. 3). 1980. pap. 9.00. Am Inst CPA.

Internal Accounting Control: Report of The Special Advisory Committee. 1979. pap. 2.75. Am Inst CPA.

Internal Auditing for Hospitals. Seth Allcorn. LC 79-20072. 1979. text ed. 29.00 (ISBN 0-89443-163-3). Aspen Systems.

Internal Colonialism: The Celtic Fringe in British National Development. Michael Hechter. 1975. 22.75x (ISBN 0-520-02559-8); pap. 6.50x (ISBN 0-520-03512-7). U of Cal Pr.

Internal Combustion Engines, 2 vols. Rowland S. Benson & N. D. Whitehouse. LC 79-40359. (Thermodynamics & Fluid Mechanics for Mechanical Engineers). (Illus.). 1979. Set. 68.00 (ISBN 0-08-022717-1); Vol. 1. pap. 15.75 (ISBN 0-08-022718-X); Vol. 2. pap. 15.75 (ISBN 0-08-022720-1). Pergamon.

Internal Control & Audit. Kussel Smith & DePaula. 24.50x (ISBN 0-392-07955-0, SpS). Soccer.

Internal Control & Internal Auditing for Hospitals. 66p. 1969. 8.00 (ISBN 0-686-68592-X, 2025). Hospital Finan.

Internal Control in U. S. Corporations: The State of the Art. R. K. Mautz et al. LC 80-66623. 1980. 6.50 (ISBN 0-910586-33-0). Finan Exec.

Internal Controls for Computerized Systems. Jerry FitzGerald. LC 78-69677. (Illus.). 93p. 1978. pap. text ed. 11.15 (ISBN 0-932410-04-9). FitzGerald & Assocs.

Internal Development of Man in Dynamic Representational Expressions. Soren A. Kierkegaard. Ed. by Joseph R. Karlweiss. (Illus.). 107p. 1981. 49.75 (ISBN 0-89266-273-5). Am Classical Coll Pr.

Internal Fabric of the Atlantic Alliance. Ed. by Gregory A. Flynn et al. 350p. 1981. text ed. 32.50 (ISBN 0-86598-039-X). Allanheld.

Internal Fire: The Internal Combustion Engine, 1673-1900. C. Lyle Cummins, Jr. LC 75-40701. (Illus.). 1976. 20.00x (ISBN 0-917308-01-8). Carnot Pr.

Internal Friction & Ultrasonic Attentuation in Solids: Proceedings of the 3rd European Conference 18-20 July 1979, University of Manchester, England. Ed. by C. C. Smith. (Illus.). 400p. 1980. 50.00 (ISBN 0-08-024771-7); pap. 18.00 (ISBN 0-08-024770-9). Pergamon.

Internal Labor Markets & Manpower Analysis. Peter B. Doeringer & Michael J. Piore. 1971. 13.95 (ISBN 0-669-63529-4). Lexington Bks.

Internal Medicine Patient Management Cases: PreTest Self-Assessment & Review. Ed. by James Nordlund. LC 77-78730. (PreTest Self-Assessment & Review Ser.). (Illus.). 1977. pap. 20.00 o.p. (ISBN 0-07-079145-7). McGraw-Pretest.

Internal Medicine PreTest Self-Assessment & Review. Ed. by James Nordlund. (PreTest Self-Assessment & Review Ser.). (Illus.). 1977. pap. 20.00 o.p. (ISBN 0-07-050798-8). McGraw-Pretest.

Internal Medicine: PreTest Self-Assessment & Review. PreTest Service, Inc. (Illus.). 1977. pap. text ed. 25.00 o.p. (ISBN 0-07-050798-8, HP). McGraw.

Internal Medicine Review. Robert E. Pieroni. LC 75-21781. (Arco Medical Review Ser.). pap. text ed. 11.00 (ISBN 0-668-03881-0, 3881). Arco.

Internal Medicine Specialty Board Review. 6th ed. Ed. by Nathaniel Wisch et al. 1978. spiral bdg. 16.50 (ISBN 0-87488-303-2). Med Exam.

Internal Migration During Modernization in Late Nineteenth-Century Russia. Barbara A. Anderson. LC 80-7509. (Illus.). 248p. 1980. 18.00 (ISBN 0-691-09386-5). Princeton U Pr.

Internal Migration: The New World & the Third World. Ed. by Anthony Richmond & Daniel Kubat. LC 75-42537. (Sage Studies in International Sociology: Vol. 4). 1976. 18.00x (ISBN 0-8039-9960-7); pap. 9.95x (ISBN 0-8039-9974-7). Sage.

Internal Security & Subversion: Principal State Laws & Cases. United States Senate Committee On The Judiciary - 89th Congress - 1st Session. LC 70-167844. (Civil Liberties in American History Ser.). 1971. Repr. of 1965 ed. lib. bdg. 69.50 (ISBN 0-306-70121-9). Da Capo.

Internal Structure of the City: Readings on Space & Environment. Ed. by Larry S. Bourne. 1971. pap. text ed. 8.95x (ISBN 0-19-501321-2). Oxford U Pr.

Internal Theft: Investigation & Control. Ed. by Sheryl Leininger. LC 75-17137. 256p. (Anthology). 1975. 15.95 (ISBN 0-913708-21-6). Butterworths.

Internal War: Problems & Approaches. Ed. by Harry Eckstein. LC 80-23162. x, 339p. 1980. Repr. of 1964 ed. lib. bdg. 27.50x (ISBN 0-313-22451-X, ECIW). Greenwood.

International - Intercultural Education in the Four-Year College. (Occasional Publication Ser.: No. 22). 88p. 1976. pap. 3.00 (ISBN 0-89192-198-2). Interbk Inc.

International Acceptance of Irradiated Food: Legal Aspects. (Legal Ser.: No. 11). 1979. pap. 8.75 (ISBN 92-0-176079-5, ISP530, IAEA). Unipub.

International Accounting & Financial Reporting. Norlin G. Rueschhoff. LC 76-12871. (Special Studies). 1976. 24.95 (ISBN 0-275-23110-0). Praeger.

International Accounts. Cleona Lewis. (Brookings Institution Reprint Ser.). Repr. of 1927 ed. lib. bdg. 28.00x (ISBN 0-697-00163-6). Irvington.

International Adjudication: Procedural Aspects. V. S. Mani. 456p. 1980. text ed. 26.75x (ISBN 0-391-01952-X). Humanities.

International Administration: Its Evolution & Contemporary Applications. Ed. by Robert S. Jordan. 1971. pap. 6.95x (ISBN 0-19-501462-6). Oxford U Pr.

International Advances in Nondestructive Testing, Vol. 7. Ed. by W. McGonnagle. 348p. 1981. write for info. (ISBN 0-677-15700-2). Gordon.

International Advances in Surgical Oncology, Vol. 4. Ed. by Gerald P. Murphy. LC 78-51119. 365p. 1981. 46.00x (ISBN 0-8451-0503-5). A R Liss.

International Adventure Travelguide, 1979. American Adventures Association. 1979. pap. 9.95 (ISBN 0-394-73723-7). Random.

International Advertising. Bob Roth. 1981. price not set (ISBN 0-87251-058-1). Crain Bks.

International Advertising & Marketing. S. Watson Dunn & E. S. Lorimor. LC 78-6802. 1979. text ed. 22.50 (ISBN 0-88244-174-4). Grid Pub.

International Affairs, Eighteen Ninety to Nineteen Thirty Nine. R. N. Rundle. LC 79-12170. (Illus.). 1980. text ed. 27.75x (ISBN 0-8419-0516-9); pap. text ed. 12.95x (ISBN 0-8419-0601-7). Holmes & Meier.

International Affairs Nineteen Thirty-Nine to Nineteen Seventy-Nine. LC 80-22312. 1981. text ed. 24.00 (ISBN 0-8419-0677-7); pap. 12.00 (ISBN 0-8419-0678-5). Holmes & Meier.

International Aid & National Decisions: Developmental Programs in Malawi, Tanzania & Zambia. Leon Gordenker. (Center of International Studies). 200p. 1976. text ed. 16.00 (ISBN 0-691-05662-5). Princeton U Pr.

International Air Transport Conference. Compiled by American Society of Civil Engineers. 424p. 1977. pap. text ed. 28.00 (ISBN 0-87262-093-X). Am Soc Civil Eng.

International Almanac of Electoral History. Thomas T. Mackie & Richard Rose. LC 74-11577. 1974. 19.95 (ISBN 0-02-919640-X). Free Pr.

International & Area Studies Librarianship: Case Studies. Martin H. Sable. LC 73-5547. 1973. 10.00 (ISBN 0-8108-0622-3). Scarecrow.

International & Comparative Librarianship Group (CLG) Handbook. Ed. by A. Whatley. 1977. pap. 7.95x (ISBN 0-85365-790-4, Pub. by Lib Assn England). Oryx Pr.

International & Comparative Politics: A Handbook. Philip M. Burgess et al. 1978. pap. text ed. 13.60 (ISBN 0-205-06009-9). Allyn.

International & Regional Politics in the Middle East & North Africa: A Guide to Information Sources. Ed. by Ann T. Schulz. LC 74-11568. (International Relations Information Guide Ser.: Vol. 6). 1977. 30.00 (ISBN 0-8103-1326-X). Gale.

International Arbitration from Athens to Locarno. Jackson H. Ralston. LC 75-147737. (Library of War & Peace; Int'l. Organization, Arbitration & Law). 38.00 (ISBN 0-8240-0472-8). Garland Pub.

International Aspects of the Provision of Medical Care. Ed. by P. W. Kent. 1976. 25.00 (ISBN 0-85362-160-8, Oriel). Routledge & Kegan.

International Aspects of U. S. Income Taxation: Cases & Materials, Vol. III, Parts Four & Five. Elisabeth A. Owens. LC 80-18605. 512p. 1980. pap. text ed. 12.50x (ISBN 0-915506-24-6). Harvard Law Intl Tax.

International Atlas. rev. 2nd ed. Ed. by Paul Tiddens. LC 77-78100. 558p. 1977. 45.00 o.p. (ISBN 0-528-83046-5); leather binding 100.00 o.p. (ISBN 0-528-83044-9). Rand.

International Auditing Guidelines. 1980. pap. 2.75. Am Inst CPA.

International Auditing Standards. E. Stamp. 1979. 21.95 (ISBN 0-13-470948-9). P-H.

International Bank Regulation. James Baker. LC 76-19545. (Praeger Special Studies). 1978. 23.95 (ISBN 0-275-23570-X). Praeger.

International Banking & Finance. F. A. Lees. LC 73-11884. 419p. 1974. text ed. 32.95 (ISBN 0-470-52273-9). Halsted Pr.

International Banking & Finance: Vol. 1 - Comprehensive Overview. 5th ed. Robert D. Fraser. (Comprehensive Overview: Vol. 1). 700p. 1979. 26.00 (ISBN 0-686-66081-1). R & H Pubs.

International Banking & Finance: Vol. 2 - Global Funds Management of Assets Liabilities, Vol. 2. 1st ed. Robert D. Fraser. 500p. 1978. 35.00 (ISBN 0-686-66082-X). R & H Pubs.

International Behavior: A Social-Psychological Analysis. Ed. by Herbert C. Kelman. 1980. text ed. 38.50x (ISBN 0-8290-0027-5); pap. text ed. 18.50x (ISBN 0-8290-0028-3). Irvington.

International Bibliography of Azolla. 66p. 1979. pap. 34.50 (R129, IRRI). Unipub.

International Bibliography of Directories. 6th rev. ed. Ed. by Helga Lengenfelder. 1978. 72.00 (ISBN 0-89664-002-7, Pub. by K G Saur). Gale.

International Bibliography of Discographies: Classical Music and Jazz & Blues 1962-1972. David E. Cooper. LC 75-4516. (Keys to Music Bibliography Ser.: No. 2). 272p. 1975. lib. bdg. 13.50x o.p. (ISBN 0-87287-108-8). Libs Unl.

International Bibliography of Historical Sciences: 1976-1977, Vols. 45-46. Ed. by Michel Francois et al. 492p. 1980. 58.00 (ISBN 3-598-20402-7, Dist. by Gale Research Co.). K G Saur.

International Bibliography of Rice Research Cumulative Indexes Nineteen Seventy-One to Nineteen Seventy-Five. 232p. 1976. pap. 57.50 (R098, IRRI). Unipub.

International Bibliography of Rice Research Cumulative Indexes Nineteen Sixty-Six to Nineteen Seventy. 153p. 1972. pap. 21.50 (R091, IRRI). Unipub.

International Bibliography of Rice Research Nineteen Sixty-Eight Supplement. 348p. 1969. pap. 21.50 (R105, IRRI). Unipub.

International Bibliography of Rice Research Nineteen Seventy-Five Supplement. 452p. 1976. pap. 57.50 (R097, IRRI). Unipub.

International Bibliography of Rice Research Nineteen Seventy-Four Supplement. 386p. 1975. pap. 36.00 (R096, IRRI). Unipub.

International Bibliography of Rice Research Nineteen Sixty-Nine Supplement. 289p. 1970. pap. 21.50 (R106, IRRI). Unipub.

International Bibliography of Rice Research Nineteen Sixty-One Supplement. 164p. 1963. pap. 21.50 (R100, IRRI). Unipub.

International Bibliography of Rice Research Nineteen Seventy-One Supplement. 282p. 1972. pap. 21.50 (R093, IRRI). Unipub.

International Bibliography of Rice Research Nineteen Seventy Supplement. 1971. pap. 21.50 (R092, IRRI). Unipub.

International Bibliography of Rice Research: Ninteen Sixty-Seven Supplement. 353p. 1980. pap. 21.50 (ISBN 0-686-69536-4, R 104, IRRI). Unipub.

International Bibliography of Rice Research Nineteen Sixty-Six Supplement. 296p. 1967. pap. 21.50 (R103, IRRI). Unipub.

International Bibliography of Rice Research Nineteen Sixty-Seven Supplement. 143p. 1968. pap. 21.50 (R115, IRRI). Unipub.

International Bibliography of Rice Research Nineteen Seventy-Six Supplement. 470p. 1977. pap. 63.25 (R099, IRRI). Unipub.

International Bibliography of Rice Research Nineteen Sixty-Two Supplement. 164p. 1964. pap. 21.50 (RIOI, IRRI). Unipub.

International Bibliography of Rice Research Nineteen Seventy-Two Supplement. 295p. 1973. pap. 21.50 (R094, IRRI). Unipub.

International Bibliography of Rice Research Nineteen Sixty-Three Supplement. 213p. 1965. pap. 21.50 (R102, IRRI). Unipub.

International Bibliography of Rice Research Nineteen Seventy-Three Supplement. 321p. 1974. pap. 21.50 (R095, IRRI). Unipub.

International Bibliography of Rice Research 1978: Supplement. 598p. 1979. pap. 106.50 (R123, IRRI). Unipub.

International Bibliography of Rice Research 1977: Supplement. 556p. 1978. pap. 100.00 (R122, IRRI). Unipub.

International Bibliography of Specialized Dictionaries. (Handbook of International Documentation & Information: Vol. 4). 1979. 95.00 (ISBN 0-89664-061-2, Pub. by K G Saur). Gale.

International Bibliography of Standardized Vocabularies. Compiled by Helmut Felber. (International Bibliography of Infoterm Ser., Vol. 2). 1978. 95.00 (ISBN 0-89664-075-2, Pub. by K G Saur). Gale.

International Bibliography of Studies on Alcohol, 3 vols. Ed. by Mark Keller. Incl. Vol. 1. References, 1901-1950. Compiled by Sarah S. Jordy. 1966. 40.00x (ISBN 0-911290-34-6); Vol. 2. Indexes, 1901-1950. Vera Efron & Sarah S. Jordy. 1968. 35.00x (ISBN 0-911290-35-4); Vol. 3. References, 1951-1960; Indexes, 1951-1960. Sarah S. Jordy et al. 1980. 75.00x (ISBN 0-686-66592-9). LC 60-14437. Set Of Vols. 1 & 2. 65.00x (ISBN 0-911290-07-9). Rutgers Ctr Alcohol.

International Bibliography of the Book Trade & Librarianship 1976-79. Ed. by Helga Lengenfelder. (Handbook of International Documentation & Information Ser.: Vol. 2). 800p. 1981. 95.00 (ISBN 3-598-20504-X, Dist. by Gale Research). K G Saur.

International Bibliography on Burns, 1981 Supplement. I. Feller. 1981. pap. 12.00 (ISBN 0-917478-12-6). Natl Inst Burn.

International Bibliography on Cropping Systems Nineteen Seventy-Five. 195p. 1977. pap. 36.00 (R109, IRRI). Unipub.

International Bibliography on Cropping Systems Nineteen Seventy-Three to Nineteen Seventy-Four. 300p. 1976. pap. 36.00 (IRRI). Unipub.

International Bibliography on Cropping Systems 1976. 181p. 1977. pap. 36.00 (R124, IRRI). Unipub.

International Bibliograpy on Jewish Affairs: A Selected Annotated List of Books & Articles Published in the Diaspora, 1976-1977. Ed. by Elizabeth E. Eppler. 450p. 1981. lib. bdg. 35.00x (ISBN 0-86531-164-1). Westview.

International Bibliogrphy on Burns: 1980 Supplement. National Institute for Burn Medicine. Ed. by I. Feller. LC 71-94573. 144p. 1980. 12.00 (ISBN 0-917478-11-8). Natl Inst Burn.

International Bill of Human Rights. United Nations. 132p. 1981. 7.95 (ISBN 0-934558-06-X); pap. 2.95 (ISBN 0-934558-07-8). Entwhistle Bks.

International Biographical Dictionary of Central Emigres, 1933-1945. (Politics, Economics, & Public Life Ser.: Vol. I). 875p. 1980. 210.00 (ISBN 3-598-10088-4, Dist by Gale Research). K G Saur.

International Book of Christmas Carols. Walter Ehret & George K. Evans. LC 80-13105. (Illus.). 352p. 1980. pap. 12.95 (ISBN 0-8289-0378-6). Greene.

International Books in Print. 1979. 175.00 (ISBN 0-89664-050-7, Pub. by K G Saur). Gale.

International Books in Print 1980-81, 2 vols. 1251p. Set. text ed. 170.00 o.p. (ISBN 3-598-10201-1). K G Saur.

International Boundaries of Nigeria: The Framework of an Emergent African Nation. A. Anene. (Ibadan History Ser). 1970. text ed. 10.50x (ISBN 0-391-00080-2). Humanities.

International Broadcasting Convention. (IEE Conference Publications Ser.: No. 191). 354p. (Orig.). 1980. soft cover 59.50 (ISBN 0-85296-222-3). Inst Elect Eng.

International Bureaucracy: An Analysis of the Operation of Functional Global International Secretariats. Thomas G. Weiss. LC 75-2. 160p. 1975. 19.95x (ISBN 0-669-99341-7). Lexington Bks.

International Business. 2nd ed. R. Hal Mason et al. (Management & Administration Ser.). 500p. 1981. text ed. 21.95 (ISBN 0-686-69162-8). Wiley.

International Business: An Introduction to the World of the Multinational Firm. R. Hays et al. 1972. ref. ed. 19.95 (ISBN 0-13-472472-0). P-H.

International Business & Foreign Trade. Ed. by Lora J. Wheeler. LC 67-31263. (Management Information Guide Ser.: No. 14). 1968. 30.00 (ISBN 0-8103-0814-2). Gale.

International Business & Multinational Enterprises. rev ed. Stefan H. Robock et al. 1977. text ed. 20.95 (ISBN 0-256-01974-6). Irwin.

International Business Education: A Curriculum Survey of Australia & New Zealand. Ed. by Michael T. Skully. LC 77-670090. (Illus.). 1977. pap. 5.95 o.p. (ISBN 0-909162-05-0). Australiana.

International Business Enterprise. 2nd ed. E. Kolde. LC 78-37518. (Illus.). 672p. 1973. ref. ed. 21.95 (ISBN 0-13-472381-3). P-H.

International Business Finance. Raj Aggarwal. 1981. 19.95 (ISBN 0-03-047191-5). Praeger.

International Business Finance. Douglas Wood & James Byrne. LC 80-23951. 400p. 1981. text ed. 47.50x (ISBN 0-8419-0663-7). Holmes & Meier.

International Business in the Middle East: Case Studies. Ed. by Ashok Kapoor. (Special Studies in International Economics & Business). 1979. lib. bdg. 20.00x (ISBN 0-89158-257-6). Westview.

International Business in the Pacific Basin. Ed. by R. Hal Mason. LC 78-346. 1978. 19.95 (ISBN 0-669-02189-X). Lexington Bks.

International Business Management. 2nd ed. 1978. 20.95 (ISBN 0-03-040181-X). Dryden Pr.

International Business Prospects: Nineteen Seventy-Seven to Nineteen Ninety-Nine. Harold Van Zandt. LC 78-15745. (Key Issues Lecture Ser). 1978. 8.50 (ISBN 0-672-97221-2); pap. 5.50 (ISBN 0-672-97220-4). Bobbs.

International Business Transactions in a Nutshell. (Nutshell Ser.). 400p. 1981. pap. text ed. 7.95 (ISBN 0-8299-2119-2). West Pub.

International Cartels: Policy Implications for the United States. Charles River Assoc. 1979. write for info. o.p. Praeger.

International Casebook on Law & Psychiatry. David N. Weisstub & Larry O. Gostin. (Law & Psychiatry Ser.). Date not set. price not set (ISBN 0-08-023158-6). Pergamon.

International Cell Biology 1980 - 1981. Ed. by H. G. Schweiger. (Illus.). 1180p. 1981. 68.00 (ISBN 0-387-10475-5). Springer-Verlag.

International Championship Chess: A Complete Record of Fide Events. Bozidar Kazic. 1974. 19.95 (ISBN 0-7134-2795-7). David & Charles.

International Chili Society Official Chili Cookbook. Martina Neely & William Neely. (Illus.). 224p. 1981. 10.95 (ISBN 0-312-41988-0). St Martin.

International Circus: A Reproduction of the Antique Pop-up Book. Lothar Meggendorfer. LC 79-67737. (Illus.). (gr. k-3). 1980. 7.95 (ISBN 0-670-40011-4, Co-Pub. by Kestral Books). Viking Pr.

International Civil Service: Law & Management. Plantley. 1981. write for info. (ISBN 0-89352-103-5). Masson Pub.

International Classification & Mapping of Vegetation. LC 79-96442. (Ecology & Conservation Ser., No. 6). 93p. (Orig.). 1973. pap. 18.00 (ISBN 92-3-001046-4, UNESCO). Unipub.

International Clean Air Conference, 1981: Proceedings. Clean Air Society. International Clean Air Conference, 7th, Australia. 1981. text ed. 49.95 (ISBN 0-250-40415-X). Ann Arbor Science.

International Codata Conference on Generation, Compilation, Evaluation & Dissemination of Data for Science & Technology, 4th: Proceedings. Ed. by M. Bertrand Drefus. 160p. 1975. pap. 21.00 (ISBN 0-08-019850-3). Pergamon.

International Code Training System. International Teaching Systems Inc. LC 62-21976. (Illus., Orig.). (YA) (gr. 8 up). 1963. pap. 12.50 with records o.p. (ISBN 0-672-20138-0, 20138); pap. 12.95 with tape cassette (ISBN 0-672-20812-1, 20812). Sams.

International Commercial Banking Management. James L. Kammert. 336p. 1981. 19.95 (ISBN 0-8144-5680-4). Am Mgmt.

International Commercial Satellite Communications: Economic & Political Issues of the First Decade of Intelstat. Marcellus S. Snow. LC 75-8410. (Special Studies). (Illus.). 192p. 1976. text ed. 23.95 (ISBN 0-275-01150-X). Praeger.

International Commission on Radiation Units & Measurements. Methods of Assessment of Absorbed Dose in Clinical Use of Radionuclides. LC 79-90172. 11.00 (ISBN 0-913394-26-2). Intl Comm Rad Meas.

International Commodity Agreements: An Evaluation of the UNCTAD Integrated Commodity Programme. Jere R. Behrman. LC 77-90146. (Monographs: No. 9). 112p. 1977. 5.00 (ISBN 0-686-28686-3). Overseas Dev Council.

International Commodity Agreements & the Common Fund: A Legal & Financial Analysis. Paul Reynolds. LC 78-16265. (Praeger Special Studies). 1978. 26.95 (ISBN 0-03-044266-4). Praeger.

International Community & the Right of War. Luigi Sturzo. LC 68-9649. 1971. Repr. of 1929 ed. 16.00 (ISBN 0-86527-104-6). Fertig.

International Comparison of Nuclear Power Costs. (Illus., Orig., Eng. & Fr.). 1968. pap. 17.25 (ISBN 92-0-050368-3, IAEA). Unipub.

International Compendium of Numerical Data Projects. Committee On Data For Science And Technology Of The International Council Of Scientific Unions. 1969. 29.70 (ISBN 0-387-04570-8). Springer-Verlag.

International Competition & the Canadian Mineral Industries. 109p. (Orig.). 1978. pap. text ed. 5.00x (ISBN 0-88757-009-7, Pub. by Ctr Resource Stud Canada). Renouf.

International Conference on Differential Equation: Procedings. Ed. by H. A. Antosiewicz. 1975. 48.50 (ISBN 0-12-059650-4). Acad Pr.

International Conference on Limitation of Liability for Maritime Claims. 46p. 1977. 8.25 (IMCO). Unipub.

International Conference on Marine Pollution, 1973 - 1977 Edition. 168p. 1977. 13.75 (IMCO). Unipub.

International Conference on Maritime Search & Rescue, 1979. 38p. 1979. 9.25 (IMCO). Unipub.

International Conference on Medical & Sports Devices. Ed. by T. E. Shoup. 270p. 1980. 30.00 (H00160). ASME.

International Conference on Revision of the International Regulations for Preventing Collisions at Sea. 128p. 1974. 12.50 (IMCO). Unipub.

International Conference on Safety of Fishing Vessels. 204p. 1977. 18.00 (IMCO). Unipub.

International Conference on Safety of Life at Sea Nineteen Seventy-Four (Solas Nineteen Seventy-Four) 320p. 1975. pap. 20.75 (ISBN 0-686-64011-X, IMCO 4, IMCO). Unipub.

International Conference on Safety of Life at Sea, 1960. Incl. Supplement One. 185p. 1976. Repr. of 1970 ed. pap. 12.50 (ISBN 0-686-64930-3, IMCO 02); Supplement Two. 85p. 1978. Repr. of 1974 ed. pap. 11.00 (ISBN 0-686-64931-1, IMCO 03). 512p. 1976. pap. 22.00 (ISBN 0-686-64929-X, IMCO 01, IMCO). Unipub.

International Conference on Tanker Safety & Pollution Prevention. 106p. 1978. 18.00 (IMCO). Unipub.

International Conference on the Establishment of an International Maritime Satellite System, 1975-1976. 102p. 1976. 11.00 (IMCO). Unipub.

International Conference on the Future Supply of Nature-Made Petroleum & Gas: Proceedings. United Nations Institute for Training & Research. 1977. text ed. 76.00 (ISBN 0-08-021734-6); pap. text ed. 51.00 (ISBN 0-08-021735-4). Pergamon.

International Conference on Training & Certification of Seafarers, 1978. 146p. 1978. 22.00 (IMCO). Unipub.

International Conflicts & Collective Security: 1946-1977. Mark W. Zacher. LC 78-19775. (Praeger Special Studies). 1979. 25.95 (ISBN 0-03-044261-3). Praeger.

International Congress of Maritime Museums, 3rd Conference: Proceedings, 1978. Mystic Seaport Museum, Inc. LC 79-26650. 306p. (Orig.). 1979. pap. 20.00 (ISBN 0-913372-22-6, IS-00103, Pub. by Mystic Seaport). Univ Microfilms.

International Congress of Pharmacology, 7th, Paris, 1978: Abstracts. Ed. by J. R. Boissier et al. 1979. text ed. 150.00 (ISBN 0-08-023768-1). Pergamon.

International Congress of Phonetic Sciences, 9th Special Lectures. Copenhagen, August 1979. Ed. by Fischer-Jorgensen. (Journal: Phonetica Ser.: Vol. 37, No 1-2). (Illus.). 108p. 1980. pap. 19.75 (ISBN 3-8055-1414-X). S Karger.

International Congress of Pure & Applied Chemistry, XXVI: Chemistry for the Welfare of Mankind, Vol. 1. Ed. by T. Tsuruta. (IUPAC Symposia Ser.). 1979. text ed. 115.00 (ISBN 0-08-022007-X). Pergamon.

International Congress of Pure & Applied Chemistry, 27th. International Congress of Pure & Applied Chemistry, 27th, Helsinki, Finland, Aug. 27-31, 1979. Ed. by A. Varmavuori. LC 79-42639. 396p. 1980. 115.00 (ISBN 0-08-023936-6). Pergamon.

International Constitutional Law: International Law As Applied by International Courts & Tribunals, Vol. 3. George Schwarzenberger. LC 57-59355. 1976. lib. bdg. 97.50x (ISBN 0-89158-542-7). Westview.

International Construction. Sherratt & Urry. 160p. 1980. 38.00 (ISBN 0-86095-847-7, Construction Pr). Longman.

International Control of Marine Pollution, Vols. 1-2. Timagenis. 1980. 37.50 ea. Vol. 1 (ISBN 0-379-20685-4). Vol. 2 (ISBN 0-379-20686-2). Oceana.

International Convention for Safe Containers. 23p. 1977. 7.00 (IMCO). Unipub.

International Convention for the Prevention of Pollution of the Sea by Oil, 1954. 25p. 1978. 7.00 (IMCO). Unipub.

International Convention on Civil Liability for Oil Pollution Damage. 20p. 1977. 7.00 (IMCO). Unipub.

International Convention Relating to Intervention on the High Seas in Cases of Oil Pollution Casualties (1969) 25p. 1977. 7.00 (IMCO). Unipub.

International Conventions on Civil Liability for Nuclear Damage. (Legal Series: No. 4). (Orig.). 1976. pap. 25.25 (ISBN 0-685-74380-2, ISP430, IAEA). Unipub.

International Cooperation in Terminology. (Infoterm Ser.: Vol. 3). 333p. 1975. pap. text ed. 35.00 (ISBN 3-7940-5503-9, Pub. by K G Saur). Gale.

International Cooperative Information Systems. 111p. 1980. pap. 10.00 (ISBN 0-88936-252-1, IDRC156, IDRC). Unipub.

International Corrections. Robert J. Wicks. LC 77-8721. 1979. 21.00 (ISBN 0-669-01638-1). Lexington Bks.

International Council of Social Welfare: The Struggle for Equal Opportunity: Proceedings. International Conference on Social Welfare, 18th, San Juan, P.R. LC 77-5341. 1977. 20.00x (ISBN 0-231-04346-5). Columbia U Pr.

International Court of Justice: Its Role in the Maintenance of International Peace & Security. Oliver J. Lissitzyn. LC 78-2885. (Carnegie Endowment for International Peace, United Nations Studies: No. 6). 1978. Repr. of 1951 ed. lib. bdg. 15.25x (ISBN 0-313-20333-4, LICJ). Greenwood.

International Criminal Court: A Step Toward World Peace, 2 vols. Benjamin Ferencz. LC 80-10688. 1212p. 1980. Vol. 1. lib. bdg. 37.50 ea. (ISBN 0-379-20389-8). Vol. 2 (ISBN 0-379-20390-1). Oceana.

International Criminal Law. Gerhard O. Mueller & E. M. Wise. (New York University Criminal Law Education & Research Center Pubns: Vol. 2). 1965. 20.00x o.p. (ISBN 0-8377-0829-X). Rothman.

International Criminal Law: A Draft International Criminal Code. M. Cherif Bassiouni. LC 80-50452. 286p. 1980. 50.00x (ISBN 90-286-0130-9). Sijthoff & Noordhoff.

International Crises. Ed. by Charles F. Herman. LC 74-165102. 1973. 19.95 (ISBN 0-02-914560-0). Free Pr.

International Crisis & Crisis Management. Daniel Frei. LC 78-58474. 1978. 24.95 (ISBN 0-03-046346-7). Praeger.

International Currency Plans & Expansion of World Trade. K. Venkatagiri Gowda. 1964. 7.75x o.p. (ISBN 0-210-27039-X). Asia.

International Development Administration: Implementation Analysis for Development Projects. Ed. by George Honadle & Rudi Klaus. LC 79-65182. (Praeger Special Studies). 236p. 1979. 23.95 (ISBN 0-03-051041-4). Praeger.

International Development of China. rev. 2nd ed. Sun Yat-sen. LC 74-34490. (China in the 20th Century Ser). (Illus.). ix, 265p. 1975. Repr. of 1929 ed. lib. bdg. 29.50 (ISBN 0-306-70697-0). Da Capo.

International Dictionary of Building Construction: English-French-German-Italian. Angelo C. Schwicker. 1280p. 1975. lib. bdg. 60.00x (ISBN 0-87936-004-6). Scholium Intl.

International Dictionary of Consulting & Environmental Engineers. 2nd rev. ed. Ed. by A. M. Shaw. 1981. 10.00. Intl Research Serv.

International Dictionary of Education. Ed. by G. Terry Page et al. (Illus.). 1977. 25.00 (ISBN 0-89397-003-4). Nichols Pub.

International Dictionary of Education. Derek Rowntree. 1980. text ed. 15.70 (ISBN 0-06-318157-6, IntlDept). Har-Row.

International Dictionary of Geophysics, 2 vols. Ed. by S. K. Runcorn. 1968. Set. 300.00 (ISBN 0-08-011834-8). Pergamon.

International Diffusion of Technology: The Case of Semiconductors. John E. Tilton. LC 72-161593. (Studies in the Regulation of Economic Activity). 1971. 11.95 (ISBN 0-8157-8458-9). Brookings.

International Dimensions of Corporate Finance. David A. Ricks. LC 77-22693. (Foundations of Finance Ser.). (Illus.). 1978. pap. text ed. 10.95 (ISBN 0-13-471706-6). P-H.

International Direct Investment: Policies, Procedures & Practices in OECD Member Countries, 1979. Organization for Economic Cooperation & Development. 72p. (Orig.). 1980. pap. text ed. 4.25x (ISBN 92-64-12026-2, 21 80 02 1). OECD.

International Directory of Book Collectors 1978-1980: A Directory of Book Collectors in Britain, America & the Rest of the World. 2nd ed. Compiled by Roger Sheppard & Judith Sheppard. cancelled o.s.i. (ISBN 0-904929-18-3, Pub. by Trigon Press England). Bowker.

International Directory of Booksellers. Ed. by Michael Zils. 1978. 120.00 (ISBN 0-89664-014-0, Pub. by K G Saur). Gale.

International Directory of Certified Radioactive Materials. 1976. pap. 8.25 (ISBN 92-0-172075-0, IAEA). Unipub.

International Directory of Little Magazines & Small Presses. 16th ed. Ed. by Len Fulton & Ellen Ferber. (Dustbooks Small Press Info. Library). 580p. 1980. 17.95 (ISBN 0-913218-94-4); pap. 13.95 (ISBN 0-913218-93-6). Dustbooks.

International Directory of Medievalists, 2 vols. 5th ed. Ed. by Centre National De la Recherche Scientifique, Paris. 1979. 140.00 (ISBN 0-89664-046-9, Pub. by K G Saur). Gale.

International Directory of Psychology. Benjamin B. Wolman. LC 78-27868. (Illus.). 313p. 1979. 19.95 (ISBN 0-306-40209-2, Plenum Pr). Plenum Pub.

International Directory of Social Science Research Councils & Analogous Bodies 1978-79. Conference of National Social Science Councils & Analogous Bodies. 1979. pap. 22.00 (ISBN 0-89664-149-X, Pub. by K G Saur). Gale.

International Distributor Locator. A. Palmisano. LC 77-82718. 1977. pap. 35.00 o.p. (ISBN 0-917408-03-9). Intercontinental Pubns.

International Diversification & the Multinational Enterprise. Alan M. Rugman. (Illus.). 160p. 1979. 16.95 (ISBN 0-669-02772-3). Lexington Bks.

International Economic Co-Operation & the World Bank. Robert W. Oliver. 421p. 1975. text ed. 35.00x (ISBN 0-8419-5013-X). Holmes & Meier.

International Economic Development Law. Beverly M. Carl. (Praeger Special Studies). 1981. write for info. (ISBN 0-03-022321-0). Praeger.

International Economic Problems. 3rd ed. James C. Ingram. LC 77-11139. (Wiley Introduction to Economic Ser.). 1978. pap. text ed. 9.50 (ISBN 0-471-02182-2). Wiley.

International Economic Relations. Andrew Shonfield. LC 76-54540. (Washington Papers: No. 42). 1977. 3.50x (ISBN 0-8039-0790-7). Sage.

International Economic Relations of the Western World, 1959-71, Vol. 2: International Monetary Relations. Susan Strange. Ed. by Andrew Shonfield. 1976. 45.00x (ISBN 0-19-218317-6). Oxford U Pr.

International Economic Relations of the Western World 1959-1971, Vol. 1. Andrew Shonfield et al. Ed. by Andrew Shonfield. (Royal Institute of International Affairs Ser). 448p. 1976. 45.00x (ISBN 0-19-218314-1). Oxford U Pr.

International Economics. Herbert G. Grubel. 1977. 18.95x (ISBN 0-256-01793-X). Irwin.

International Economics. Roy Harrod. (Cambridge Economic Handbook Ser). 1957. pap. 10.95x (ISBN 0-521-08780-5). Cambridge U Pr.

International Economics. 6th ed. Charles P. Kindleberger & Peter Lindert. 1978. text ed. 19.25 (ISBN 0-256-02028-0). Irwin.

International Economics. M. A. Van Meerhaeghe. LC 72-90766. 259p. 1973. 19.50x (ISBN 0-8448-0150-X). Crane-Russak Co.

International Economics. 2nd ed. Ingo Walter. 1975. 23.95 (ISBN 0-471-06644-3). Wiley.

International Economics. 3rd ed. Ingo Walter. LC 80-21541. 528p. 1981. text ed. 19.95 (ISBN 0-471-04957-3). Wiley.

International Economics: A Policy Approach. 3rd ed. Mordechai E. Kreinin. 464p. 1979. text ed. 18.95 (ISBN 0-15-541540-9, HC). HarBraceJ.

International Economics: In an Integrated World. Laffer & Miles. 416p. 1981. pap. write for info. (ISBN 0-8302-4028-4). Goodyear.

International Economics: Theory & Practice. Alan Batchelder & Kanji Haitani. LC 70-21770. (Economics Ser.). 420p. 1981. text ed. 20.95 (ISBN 0-88244-231-7). Grid Pub.

International Economy: A Modern Approach. Ferdinand E. Banks. LC 77-26560. (Illus.). 1979. 17.95 (ISBN 0-669-01504-0). Lexington Bks.

International Economy & the National Interest. Irvin M. Grossack. LC 78-13817. (Illus.). 272p. 1980. 17.95x (ISBN 0-253-36775-1). Ind U Pr.

International Ecumenical Bibliography: 1973-1975, Vols. 12-14. LC 68-132921. Orig. Title: Internationale Oekumenische Bibliographie. 672p. 1980. 80.00x (ISBN 0-8002-2756-5). Intl Pubn Serv.

International Education: A Documentary History. Ed. by David G. Scanlon. LC 64-12575. (Orig.). 1960. text ed. 8.75 (ISBN 0-8077-2098-4); pap. 4.00x (ISBN 0-8077-2095-X). Tchrs Coll.

International Education Contacts on U. S. Campuses: A Directory. (World Studies Data Bank). 1974. pap. 5.00 o.p. (ISBN 0-89192-090-0). Interbk Inc.

International Education: The American Experience, A Bibliography, 2 pts, Vol. 2, Periodical Articles. rev. ed. Ed. by Agnes M. Tysse. Incl. Part 1. General; Part 2. Area Studies, & Indexes. LC 73-16429. 1977. 45.00 (ISBN 0-8108-1009-3). Scarecrow.

International Education: the American Experience a Bibliography: Vol. 1: Dissertations & Theses. Agnes N. Tysse. 1974. 10.00 (ISBN 0-8108-0686-X). Scarecrow.

International Educational Exchange: A Bibliography. 156p. 1970. 6.00 (IIE). Unipub.

International Electronic Music Catalog. Hugh Davies. 1968. 21.00x (ISBN 0-262-04012-3). MIT Pr.

International Encyclopedia of Dogs. 2nd ed. Ed. by Elsworth S. Howell & Stanley Dangerfield. LC 74-19842. 1971. 24.95 (ISBN 0-87605-623-0). Howell Bk.

International Encyclopedia of Music & Musicians. 10th, rev. ed. Oscar Thompson. Ed. by Bruce Bohle. LC 64-23285. (Illus.). 2600p. 1975. 49.95 (ISBN 0-396-07005-1). Dodd.

International Encyclopedia of the Social Sciences, 17 vols. Ed. by D. E. Sills. 1968. 55.00 ea. o.s.i. (89511-89527). Macmillan.

International Encyclopedia of the Social Sciences, 8 vols. Ed. by David L. Sills. LC 77-72778. (Illus.). 1977. 250.00 set (ISBN 0-02-895700-8). Free Pr.

International Energy Policy. Ed. by Robert M. Lawrence & Martin O. Heisler. LC 79-4748. (Policy Studies Organization Book). 240p. 1980. 23.95 (ISBN 0-669-02929-7). Lexington Bks.

International Energy Policy. Pachauri. 600p. 1980. 35.00 (ISBN 0-471-08984-2, Wiley-Interscience). Wiley.

International Energy Policy: Petroleum, Prices, Power & Payments. Nazli Choucri. (Illus.). 352p. 1981. text ed. 35.00x (ISBN 0-262-03075-6). MIT Pr.

International Energy Relations of China. Kim Woodard. LC 77-92949. (Illus.). 744p. 1980. 50.00x (ISBN 0-8047-1008-2). Stanford U Pr.

International Energy Strategies: Proceedings of the 1979 IAEE-RFF Conference. Ed. by Joy Dunkerley. LC 80-16503. 384p. 1980. text ed. 27.50 (ISBN 0-89946-039-9). Oelgeschlager.

International English. Virginia Haley. LC 75-28718. (Illus.). 1975. pap. 7.95 (ISBN 0-8048-1151-2). C E Tuttle.

International Environmental Law. Ed. by Ludwipk A. Teclaff & Albert E. Utton. LC 73-15198. (Special Studies). 262p. 1974. text ed. 25.00 (ISBN 0-275-08630-5). Praeger.

International Episodes. Henry James. Date not set. pap. write for info. (ISBN 0-14-004641-0). Penguin. Postponed.

International Equivalences in Access to Higher Education. W. D. Halls. (Studies on International Equivalences of Degrees). 137p. 1972. pap. 7.00 (ISBN 92-3-100909-5, U327, UNESCO). Unipub.

International Film Guide, 1977. Ed. by Peter Cowie. LC 64-1076. pap. 7.95 (ISBN 0-498-01907-1). A S Barnes.

International Film Guide 1981. Ed. by Peter Cowie. LC 64-1076. (Illus.). 512p. 1981. pap. 9.95 (ISBN 0-498-02530-6). A S Barnes.

International Film Necrology. William T. Stewart et al. LC 80-17636. (Garland Reference Library of Humanities). 350p. 1981. 35.00 (ISBN 0-8240-9552-9). Garland Pub.

International Finance: Cases & Simulation. Robert S. Carlson et al. LC 80-81213. 400p. 1980. pap. text ed. 6.95 (ISBN 0-201-00903-X). A-W.

International Finance: Text & Cases. new ed. George Feiger & Bertrand Jacquillat. 496p. 1980. text ed. 19.95 (ISBN 0-205-07137-6, 1071378); tchr's ed. avail. (ISBN 0-205-07138-4). Allyn.

International Financial Aid. Wolfgang G. Friedmann et al. LC 66-20494. 1966. 25.00x (ISBN 0-231-02953-5). Columbia U Pr.

International Financial Integration: The Limits of Sovereignty. David T. Llewellyn. 200p. 1980. 29.95x (ISBN 0-470-26960-X). Halsted Pr.

International Financial Management. 2nd ed. E. Eugene Carter & Rita M. Rodriguez. (Illus.). 1979. text ed. 21.95 (ISBN 0-13-472977-3). P-H.

International Financial Management. Charles N. Henning et al. (Illus.). 1978. text ed. 20.50x (ISBN 0-07-028175-0, C); instructor's manual 4.95 (ISBN 0-07-028176-9). McGraw.

International Financial Markets: Development of the Present System & Future Prospects. Francis A. Lees & Maximo Eng. LC 73-13345. (Special Studies). (Illus.). 576p. 1975. text ed. 32.95 o.p. (ISBN 0-275-28789-0); pap. text ed. 12.95 (ISBN 0-275-89180-1). Praeger.

International Folktales Series. Mollie Clark. Incl. Bird Catcher & the Crow-Peri: Turkey. LC 73-84508. (RL 3.7) (ISBN 0-8224-9300-4); Buffalo Stone: North America. LC 73-84505. (RL 3.4) (ISBN 0-8224-9302-0); Clever Jackal: India. LC 73-84503. (RL 3.3) (ISBN 0-8224-9304-7); Mac-the-Rascal from Mull: Scotland. LC 73-84504. (RL 3.3) (ISBN 0-8224-9306-3); Mink & the Fire: North America. LC 73-84501. (RL 3.2) (ISBN 0-8224-9308-X); Monkey & the Roaring Rakhas: India. LC 73-84506. (RL 3.6) (ISBN 0-8224-9310-1); Rabbit & Fox: Canada. LC 73-84500. (RL 2.9) (ISBN 0-8224-9312-8); Remarkable Rat: India. LC 73-84502. (RL 3.2) (ISBN 0-8224-9314-4); Three Marvelous Things: Italy. LC 73-84509. (RL 3.7) (ISBN 0-8224-9316-0); Wu & the Yellow Dragon: China. LC 73-84510. (RL 3.7) (ISBN 0-8224-9318-7). 1973. pap. text ed. 2.60 ea. Pitman Learning.

International Football Book, No. 22. Ed. by Eric G. Batty et al. (Illus.). 142p. (YA) 1980. text ed. 17.50x (ISBN 0-285-62445-8, SpS). Soccer.

International Foundation Directory. 2nd ed. Ed. by H. V. Hodson. LC 73-90303. 1980. 65.00 (ISBN 0-8103-2018-5, Europa Publication). Gale.

International Gallup Polls: Public Opinion, 1979. Ed. by George H. Gallup. LC 79-3844. 350p. 1981. lib. bdg. 49.50 (ISBN 0-8420-2180-9). Scholarly Res Inc.

International Games. Valjean McLenighan. LC 77-28069. (Games & Activities Ser.). (Illus.). (gr. k-3). 1978. PLB 9.30 (ISBN 0-8172-1162-4). Raintree Pubs.

International Geographic Encyclopedia & Atlas. Ed. by Fernando De Mello. 1024p. 1979. text ed. 55.00x (ISBN 3-11008-137-7). De Gruyter.

International Glossary of Technical Terms for the Pulp & Paper Industry. Ed. by Paul D. Van Derveer & Leonard E. Haas. LC 74-20168. (A Pulp & Paper Book). 238p. 1976. 35.00 (ISBN 0-87930-037-X). Miller Freeman.

International Gourmet Cooking with Microwave. Phe Laws. LC 76-12163. 1976. pap. 5.95 (ISBN 0-8256-3811-9, Hidden Hse). Music Sales.

International Government Finance & the Amsterdam Capital Market: 1740-1815. James C. Riley. LC 79-152. (Illus.). 1980. 37.50 (ISBN 0-521-22677-5). Cambridge U Pr.

International Guide to Educational Documentation, 1960-1965. 2nd ed. 575p. 1972. 41.00 (ISBN 0-685-26759-8, U331, UNESCO). Unipub.

International Guide to Library, Archival, & Information Science Associations. 2nd ed. Josephine R. Fang & Alice H. Songe. 400p. 1980. 32.50 (ISBN 0-8352-1285-8). Bowker.

International Gymnastics for Girls & Women. Tuovi S. Cochrane. LC 69-15372. (Illus., Orig.). 1969. 12.25 o.p. (ISBN 0-201-01144-1). A-W.

International Handbook of Industrial Relations: Contemporary Developments & Research. Ed. by Albert A. Blum. LC 79-8586. (Illus.). 640p. 1981. 45.00 (ISBN 0-313-21303-8, BLH/). Greenwood.

International Handbook on Local Government Reorganization: Contemporary Developments. Ed. by Donald C. Rowat. LC 79-54063. (Illus.). xv, 626p. 1980. lib. bdg. 45.00 (ISBN 0-313-21269-4, RHL/). Greenwood.

International Headache Congress, 1980. Ed. by Macdonald Critchley et al. 1980. write for info. Raven.

International History of City Development, 8 vols. Erwin A. Gutkind. Incl. Vol. 1. Urban Development in Central Europe. 1964 (ISBN 0-02-913250-9); Vol. 2. Urban Development in Alpine & Scandinavian Countries. 1965 (ISBN 0-02-913260-6); Vol. 3. Urban Development in Southern Europe; Spain & Portugal. 1967 (ISBN 0-02-913270-3); Vol. 4. Urban Development in Southern Europe; Italy & Greece. 1969 (ISBN 0-02-913280-0); Vol. 5. Urban Development in Western Europe; France & Belgium. 1970 (ISBN 0-02-913300-9); Vol. 6. Urban Development in Western Europe: The Netherlands & Great Britain. 1971 (ISBN 0-02-913310-6); Vol. 7. Urban Development in East-Central Europe: Poland, Czechoslavia, & Hungary. 1972 (ISBN 0-02-913320-3); Vol. 8. Urban Development in Eastern Europe: Bulgaria, Romania, & U.S.S.R. 1972 (ISBN 0-02-913330-0). LC 64-13231. 45.00 ea. Free Pr.

International Horseman's Dictionary. Zdzislaw Baranowski. (Illus.). 9.10 (ISBN 0-85131-262-4, Dist. by Sporting Book Center). J A Allen.

International Housing Policies: A Comparative Analysis. Chester C. McGuire. LC 80-8815. 1981. price not set (ISBN 0-669-04385-0). Lexington Bks.

International Human Rights: Law & Practice. Ed. by James C. Tuttle. LC 78-61659. (Professional Education Publications Ser.). 1978. pap. text ed. 15.00 (ISBN 0-89707-006-2). Amer Bar Assn.

International Hydrological Programme (IHP) Third Session of the Intergovernmental Council Final Report IHP-IC-III. 72p. 1981. pap. 10.00 (ISBN 0-686-69436-8, UNI 1051, UNESCO). Unipub.

International Implications of National Industrial Strategies. Ed. by John Pinder. 320p. 1981. text ed. 32.50 (ISBN 0-86598-040-3). Allanheld.

International Indebtedness & World Economic Stagnation. Miguel S. Wionczek. 135p. 1981. 17.50 (ISBN 0-08-024702-4). Pergamon.

International Investing. Douglas R. Casey. 1981. pap. 9.95. Everest Hse.

International Investing Made Easy. new ed. Martin J. Pring. 224p. 1980. 15.95 (ISBN 0-07-050872-0, P&RB). McGraw.

International ISBN Publishers' Directory. 1980 ed. Ed. by International ISBN Agency. 1433p. 1981. 95.00 (ISBN 3-88053-010-6). Bowker.

International Jew. Henry Ford. 1978. pap. 5.00x (ISBN 0-911038-45-0). Noontide.

International Joke Book, No. 2. Max Brodnick. 1976. pap. 1.25 o.p. (ISBN 0-685-69150-0, LB349ZK, Leisure Bks). Nordon Pubns.

International Journal of Psychoanalytic Psychotherapy, Vol. 8. Ed. by Robert Langs. LC 75-648853. 705p. 1980. 35.00 (ISBN 0-87668-428-2). Aronson.

International Labor Migration in Europe. Ronald E. Krane. LC 78-19746. (Praeger Special Studies). 1979. 24.95 (ISBN 0-03-022361-X). Praeger.

International Labour Documentation: Cumulative Edition 1970-71, 2 vols. International Labour Office, Central Library, Geneva. 1972. Set. lib. bdg. 210.00 (ISBN 0-685-24887-9). G K Hall.

International Law & National Behavior: A Behavioral Interpretation of Contemporary International Law & Politics. Ahmed Sheikh. LC 73-19922. 352p. 1974. pap. text ed. 13.95x (ISBN 0-471-78230-0). Wiley.

International Law & the Movement of Persons Between States. Guy S. Goodwin-Gill. 1978. 49.50x (ISBN 0-19-825333-8). Oxford U Pr.

International Law & the Resources of the Sea. Juraj Andrassy. LC 76-130960. (International Legal Studies). (Illus.). 1970. 16.00x (ISBN 0-231-03409-1). Columbia U Pr.

International Law & the United Nations. Quincy Wright. LC 74-27430. 1976. Repr. of 1960 ed. lib. bdg. 16.00x (ISBN 0-8371-7900-9, WRIL). Greenwood.

International Law & World Order: An Introductory Problem-Oriented Coursebook. Burns H. Weston et al. LC 80-15873. (American Casebook Ser.). 1195p. 1980. text ed. 23.95 (ISBN 0-8299-2097-8). West Pub.

International Law: Current & Classic. R. N. Swift. LC 68-23928. 1969. 22.95 o.p. (ISBN 0-471-83980-9). Wiley.

International Law for Seagoing Officers. 4th ed. Burdick H. Brittin. LC 80-81095. (Illus.). 624p. 1981. 22.95x (ISBN 0-87021-304-0). Naval Inst Pr.

International Law for Seagoing Officers. 3rd ed. Burdick H. Brittin & Liselotte B. Watson. LC 77-172513. 1972. 17.00x o.p. (ISBN 0-87021-303-2). Naval Inst Pr.

International Law in a Changing World. Edward Collins, Jr. 1970. text ed. 14.95 (ISBN 0-394-30098-X, RanC). Random.

International Law in Comparative Perspective. W. E. Butler. 324p. 1980. 42.50x (ISBN 90-286-0089-2). Sijthoff & Noordhoff.

International Law in the Twentieth Century. American Society Of International Law. Ed. by Leo Gross. LC 69-16894. (Orig.). 1969. pap. text ed. 18.95x (ISBN 0-89197-234-X). Irvington.

International Law of Pollution. James Barros & Douglas M. Johnston. LC 73-6491. 1974. text ed. 19.95 (ISBN 0-02-901910-9). Free Pr.

International Law of the Resources of the Sea. S. Oda. 144p. 1980. Repr. 17.50 (ISBN 90-286-0399-9). Sijthoff & Noordhoff.

International Legal Conference on Maritime Carriage of Nuclear Subtances, 1971. 39p. 1972. 8.25 (IMCO). Unipub.

International Legislation & Fiscality of Hydrocarbons, Parts 1-8. R. Brasseur. Incl. Pt. 1 (ISBN 0-87201-950-0); Pt. 2 (ISBN 0-87201-951-9); Pt. 3 (ISBN 0-87201-952-7); Pt. 4; Pt. 5 (ISBN 0-87201-954-3); Pt. 6 (ISBN 0-87201-955-1); Pt. 7 (ISBN 0-87201-956-X); Pt. 8 (ISBN 0-87201-957-8). write for info. Gulf Pub.

International Lending, Risk & the Euromarkets. Anthony Angelini et al. LC 79-10712. 213p. 1979. 21.95x (ISBN 0-470-26653-8). Halsted Pr.

International Lesson Annual, 1980-81. Ed. by Horace R. Weaver. (Orig.). 1980. pap. 4.50 o.p. (ISBN 0-687-19144-0). Abingdon.

International Lesson Annual 1981-1982. Ed. by Horace R. Weaver. 448p. (Orig.). 1981. pap. 4.50 (ISBN 0-687-19145-9). Abingdon.

International Library & Information Programmes. Ed. by D. Burnett & E. E. Cumming. 1979. pap. 11.50 (ISBN 0-85365-591-X, Pub. by Lib Assn England). Oryx Pr.

International Linguistics: Volume 5, Morphology & Morphosemant-Tics. Hans-Heinrich Leib. (Current Issues in Linguistic Theory Ser.: No. 17). 250p. 1981. text ed. 27.50x (ISBN 90-272-3508-2). Humanities.

International Linguistiics: Volume 4, Syntax & Semantics. Hans-Heinrich Lieb. (Current Issues in Linguistic Theory Ser.: No. 17). 250p. 1981. text ed. 27.50x (ISBN 90-272-3508-2). Humanities.

International Liquidity Issues. Thomas D. Willett. 1980. pap. 5.25 (ISBN 0-8447-3388-1). Am Enterprise.

International List of Geographical Serials. rev., 3rd ed. Chauncy D. Harris & Jerome D. Fellmann. LC 80-16392. (Research Papers: No. 193). 457p. 1980. pap. 8.00 (ISBN 0-89065-100-0). U Chicago Dept Geog.

International Literary Market Place 1981. 15th ed. Ed. by Peter Found. LC 77-70295. 500p. 1981. pap. 42.50 (ISBN 0-8352-1345-5). Bowker.

International Man. Douglas Casey. 19.95 (ISBN 0-932496-01-6). Green Hill.

International Management & Business Policy. Michael Z. Brooke & H. Lee Remmers. LC 78-69612. (Illus.). 1978. Repr. of 1977 ed. text ed. 20.95 (ISBN 0-395-26505-3). HM.

International Managerial Finance. J. Fred Weston & Bart W. Sorge. 1972. text ed. 18.95 (ISBN 0-256-01390-X). Irwin.

International Manual on Collective Bargaining for Public Employees. Ed. by Seymour P. Kaye & Arthur Marsh. LC 71-130530. (Special Studies in International Economics & Development). 1973. 39.50x (ISBN 0-275-28074-8). Irvington.

International Marine Science Affairs. Ocean Affairs Board. LC 74-183584. 104p. (Orig.). 1972. pap. text ed. 5.00 (ISBN 0-309-01937-0). Natl Acad Pr.

International Maritime Dangerous Goods Code: Annex 1: Packing Recommendations, Glossary of Packagings, Illustrations of Packagings, 1977 Edition. (Illus.). 196p. 1977. 16.50 (IMCO). Unipub.

International Maritime Dangerous Goods Code Amendments 16-78. 1978. 38.50 (IMCO). Unipub.

International Maritime Dangerous Goods Code: Amendments 14-76 & 15-77, 4 vols. 800p. 1978. 55.00 (IMCO). Unipub.

International Maritime Dangerous Goods Code: Brochure. (Illus.). 4p. 1975. 4.25 (IMCO). Unipub.

International Maritime Dangerous Goods Code. 1977. Vol. 1, 509. pap. 184.25 set (ISBN 0-686-64012-8, IMCO). Vol. 2, 499. Vol. 3, 412. Vol. 4, 425. Unipub.

International Marketing. 4th ed. Philip R. Cateora & John M. Hess. 1979. text ed. 19.50x (ISBN 0-256-02153-8). Irwin.

International Marketing. 2nd ed. Terpstra. 1978. 21.95 (ISBN 0-03-039296-9). Dryden Pr.

International Marketing. L. S. Walsh. 272p. 1978. pap. text ed. 11.95x (ISBN 0-7121-0943-9, Pub. by Macdonald & Evans England). Intl Ideas.

International Marketing. K. A. Yarker. 178p. 1976. text ed. 23.50x (ISBN 0-220-66298-3, Pub. by Busn Bks England). Renouf.

International Marketing: A Strategic Approach to World Markets. S. Majaro. LC 76-44628. 1977. 29.95 (ISBN 0-470-98936-X). Halsted Pr.

International Marketing Data & Statistics 1979-80. 1980. 115.00x (ISBN 0-686-60664-7, Euromonitor). Nichols Pub.

International Marketing of Nuclear Power Plants. Lee C. Nehrt. LC 65-24596. (Social Science Ser: No. 22). 1966. pap. 15.00x o.p. (ISBN 0-253-38422-2). Ind U Pr.

International Marketing Strategy. rev. ed. Ed. by Hans Thorelli & Helmut Becker. LC 80-14689. (Pergamon Policy Studies on Business). 400p. 1980. 40.00 (ISBN 0-08-025542-6); pap. 12.95 (ISBN 0-08-025543-4). Pergamon.

International Meat Science Dictionary. Donald M. Kinsman. (Illus.). 282p. (Orig.). 1979. pap. 9.95x (ISBN 0-89641-029-3). American Pr.

International Medical Who's Who, 2 vols. Francis Hodgson. 1300p. 1980. Set. text ed. 180.00x (ISBN 0-582-90107-3). Churchill.

International Migration & Dependence. Stephen Adler. 250p. 1980. text ed. 23.00x (ISBN 0-566-00202-7, Pub. by Gower Pub Co England). Renouf.

International Mineral Cartels & Embargoes: Policy Implications for the United States. Michael W. Klass et al. LC 80-11123. 350p. 1980. 22.95 (ISBN 0-03-044366-0). Praeger.

International Molybdenum Encyclopedia, 3 vols. Ed. by Alexander Sutulor. Incl. Vol. 1. Resources & Production. 402p. 1978; Vol. 2. Metallurgy & Processing. 375p. 1979; Vol. 3. Products, Uses & Trade. 341p. 1980. (Illus.). Set. text ed. 330.00 (ISBN 0-87930-098-1). Miller Freeman.

International Molybdenum Encyclopedia 1778-1978, 3 vols. Ed. by Alexander Sutulov. Incl. Vol. 1. Resources & Production. 402p; Vol. 2. Metallurgy & Processing. 375p; Vol. 3. Products, Uses & Trade. 1978-80. 330.00 (ISBN 0-87930-098-1). Miller Freeman.

International Monetary Chaos & a Positive Plan for the Monetary Reconstruction of the World. George C. Erlanger. (Illus.). 127p. 1981. 67.85 (ISBN 0-918968-90-9). Inst Econ Finan.

International Monetary Economics. H. Robert Heller. (Illus.). 256p. 1974. ref. ed. 17.95 (ISBN 0-13-473140-9). P-H.

International Monetary Issues & Development Policies. Xenophon Zolotas. LC 77-90142. 1977. 22.50x (ISBN 0-8147-9654-0). NYU Pr.

International Monetary Policy. W. M. Scammell. LC 74-26769. 1976. pap. 14.95 (ISBN 0-470-15197-8). Halsted Pr.

International Monetary Reform & the Developing Countries. William R. Cline. 1976. 9.95 (ISBN 0-8157-1476-9); pap. 3.95 (ISBN 0-8157-1475-0). Brookings.

International Monetary Reform & the Developing Countries: The Rule of Law Problem. Gilbert P. Verbit. LC 74-22362. (International Legal Research Program Ser). 336p. 1975. 22.50x (ISBN 0-231-03832-1). Columbia U Pr.

International Monetary System. Lawrence H. Officer & Thomas D. Willett. 4.50x (ISBN 0-87543-096-1). Lucas.

International Monetary System & the Less Developed Countries. Graham Bird. LC 78-65139. (Praeger Special Studies Ser.). 1979. 28.95 (ISBN 0-03-051211-5). Praeger.

International Monetary System: Beyond the First Stage of Reform. J. Carter Murphy. 1979. pap. 7.25 (ISBN 0-8447-3362-8). Am Enterprise.

International Money Market. Gunter Dufey & Ian H. Giddy. LC 78-1298. (Foundations of Finance Ser.). (Illus.). 1978. ref. ed. o.p. 13.95 (ISBN 0-13-470914-4). P-H.

International Mortality Statistics. Michael Alderson. 380p. 1981. lib. bdg. 55.00 (ISBN 0-87196-514-3). Facts on File.

International Music Guide, 1981. Ed. by Derek Elley. (Illus.). 1981. pap. 8.95 (ISBN 0-686-69099-0). A S Barnes.

International Mussel Watch. Environmental Studies Board. vi, 248p. 1980. pap. text ed. 11.50 (ISBN 0-309-03040-4). Natl Acad Pr.

International Mussel Watch. 1980. 11.50 (ISBN 0-309-03040-4). Natl Acad Pr.

International Needlework Designs. Mira Silverstein. LC 77-21189. (Encore Edition). (Illus.). 1978. 8.95 (ISBN 0-684-16925-8, ScribT). Scribner.

International Neutron Data System. (Technical Reports Ser.: No. 100). (Orig.). 1969. pap. 2.75 (ISBN 92-0-135069-4, IAEA). Unipub.

International News Agencies. Oliver Boyd-Barrett. LC 80-51779. (Communication & Society Ser.: Vol. 13). (Illus.). 284p. 1980. 25.00 (ISBN 0-8039-1511-X); pap. 12.50 (ISBN 0-8039-1512-8). Sage.

International Nomenclature of Constitutional Diseases of Bone Wih Bibliography. Ed. by David L. Rimoin. LC 79-54820. (March of Dimes Birth Defects Foundation Ser.: Vol. 15, No. 10). 1979. write for info. March of Dimes.

International Nuclear Fuel Cycle Evaluation. Incl. Report of INFCE Working Group 1 - Fuel & Heavy Water Availability. 314p. pap. 40.25 (ISBN 92-0-159180-2, ISP534-1); Report of INFCE Working Group 2 - Enrichment Availability. 157p. pap. 21.00 (ISBN 9-2015-9280-9, ISP534-2); Report of INFCE Working Group 3 - Assurances of Long-Term Supply of Technology, Fuel, & Heavy Water & Services in the Interest of National Needs Consistent with Non-Proliferation. 104p. pap. 14.00 (ISBN 92-0-159380-5, ISP534-3); Report of INFCE Working Group 4 - Reprocessing, Plutonium Handling, Recycle. 300p. pap. 36.25 (ISBN 9-2015-9480-1, ISP534-4); Report of INFCE Working Group 5 - Fast Breeders. 217p. pap. 28.75 (ISBN 92-0159-580-8, ISP534-5); Report of INFCE Working Group 6 - Spent Fuel Management. 113p. pap. 16.00 (ISBN 92-0-159680-4, ISP534-6); Report of INFCE Working Group 7 - Waste Management & Disposal. 287p. pap: 36.75 (ISBN 92-0-159780-0, ISP534-7); Report of INFCE Working Group 8 - Advanced Fuel Cycle & Reactor Concepts. 181p. pap. 23.75 (ISBN 9-2015-9880-7, ISP534-8); INFCE Summary Volume. 285p. pap. 35.00 (ISBN 9-2015-9980-3, ISP534-9). 1980 (IAEA). Unipub.

International Nuclear Proliferation: Multilateral Diplomacy & Regional Aspects. Ashde Kapur. LC 78-19744. (Praeger Special Studies). 1979. 29.95 (ISBN 0-03-046316-5). Praeger.

International Nursing. VeNeta Masson. 1981. text ed. price not set (ISBN 0-8261-3170-0); pap. text ed. price not set (ISBN 0-8261-3171-9). Springer Pub.

International Oil Policy. Arnold E. Safer. LC 79-7185. 192p. 1979. 14.95 (ISBN 0-669-02959-9). Lexington Bks.

International Oil Tanker & Terminal Safety Guide. 2nd ed. I. O. T. T. S. Group. LC 75-2371. 185p. 1975. 19.95 (ISBN 0-470-42807-4). Halsted Pr.

International Order & Foreign Policy: A Theoretical Sketch of Post-War Internaional Politics. Friedrich V. Kratochwil. LC 77-94107. (Westview Replica Edition Ser.). 1978. lib. bdg. 28.00 (ISBN 0-89158-065-4). Westview.

International Organization. S. J. Bilgrami. (Illus.). 1979. text ed. 17.50x (ISBN 0-7069-0548-2, Pub. by Vikas India). Advent Bk.

International Organization Documents for Translation from French. Ed. by J. Coveney. 93p. 1972. 16.00 (ISBN 0-08-016287-8); pap. 7.00 o.p. (ISBN 0-08-016286-X). Pergamon.

International Organization for Masoretic Studies, Proceedings & Papers. Harry M. Orlinsky. LC 74-16568. (Society of Biblical Literature, Masoretic Studies). 1974. 9.00 (ISBN 0-89130-308-1, 060501). Scholars Pr Ca.

International Organization: Politics & Process. Ed. by Leland M. Goodrich & David A. Kay. 1973. 25.00 (ISBN 0-299-06250-3); pap. 9.95x (ISBN 0-299-06254-6). U of Wis Pr.

International Organizations: A Guide to Information Sources. Ed. by Alexine L. Atherton. LC 73-17502. (International Relations Guide Ser.: Vol. 1). 1976. 30.00 (ISBN 0-8103-1324-3). Gale.

International Organizations in Europe & the Right to Health Care. Roscam H. Abbing. 1979. pap. 48.00 (ISBN 90-268-1077-6, Kluwer Law & Taxation). Kluwer Boston.

International Organizations in World Politics Yearbook, 1975. Ed. by Avi Shlaim. 1976. 26.25x (ISBN 0-89158-608-3). Westview.

International Payments, Debts & Gold: Collected Essays. 2nd ed. Fritz Machlup. LC 76-20371. 1976. pap. 9.00x (ISBN 0-8147-5412-0). NYU Pr.

International Payoffs: A Dilemma for Business. Yerachmiel Kugel & Gladys Gruenberg. LC 76-48404. 1977. 18.95 (ISBN 0-669-01150-9). Lexington Bks.

International Perceptions of the Superpower Military Balance. Ed. by Donald C. Daniel. LC 78-19456. 1978. 23.95 (ISBN 0-03-046471-4). Praeger.

International Perspectives in Rural Sociology. H. Newby. 220p. 1978. 38.25 (ISBN 0-471-99606-8). Wiley.

International Perspectives on Future Special Education. Albert H. Fink. LC 78-74018. 1979. text ed. 15.00 o.p. (ISBN 0-86586-046-7). Coun Exc Child.

International Perspectives on Social-Political Education. Ed. by Irving Morrissett. 1980. pap. write for info. (ISBN 0-89994-253-9). Soc Sci Ed.

International Poetry Festival. Ed. by Stanley H. Barkan & Eva Feiler. (International Poetry Festival Ser.: No. 1). (Illus.). 1972. pap. 5.00 o.p. (ISBN 0-89304-001-0, CCC100). Cross Cult.

International Political System. F. S. Northedge. 1976. 15.95 o.p. (ISBN 0-571-11008-8, Pub. by Faber & Faber); pap. 9.95 (ISBN 0-571-11009-6). Merrimack Bk Serv.

International Politics. Prakash Chandra. 1980. text ed. 12.50x (ISBN 0-7069-0773-6, Pub by Vikas India). Advent Bk.

International Politics: A Framework for Analysis. 3rd ed. Kalvei J. Holsti. (Illus.). 1977. 17.95 (ISBN 0-13-473371-1). P-H.

International Politics & the Sea: The Case of Brazil. Michael A. Morris. (Westview Replica Edition). 1979. lib. bdg. 27.00x (ISBN 0-89158-456-0). Westview.

International Politics in East Asia Since World War Two. Donald F. Lach & Edmund S. Wehrle. LC 75-58. (Illus.). 400p. 1975. text ed. 27.95 o.p. (ISBN 0-275-05420-9); pap. text ed. 8.95 o.p. (ISBN 0-275-89380-4). Praeger.

International Politics in the Atomic Age. John H. Herz. LC 59-6901. 1959. pap. 9.00x (ISBN 0-231-08534-6, 34). Columbia U Pr.

International Politics of Eastern Europe. Ed. by Charles Gati. LC 75-23963. (Illus.). 1976. text ed. 29.95 (ISBN 0-275-55960-2); pap. text ed. 10.95 (ISBN 0-275-89500-9). Praeger.

International Politics: Policymakers & Policymaking. Robert L. Wendzel. LC 80-36681. 500p. 1981. text ed. 16.95 (ISBN 0-471-05046-6). Wiley.

International Politics Since World War II: A Short History. 2nd ed. Charles L. Robertson. LC 74-23998. 448p. 1975. pap. text ed. 15.95x (ISBN 0-471-72744-X). Wiley.

International Population Assistance: the First Decade. Rafael M. Salas. 1979. 45.00 (ISBN 0-08-024701-6); pap. 21.00 (ISBN 0-08-024700-8). Pergamon.

International Portrait Gallery: Base Collection. (International Portrait Gallery Ser.: No. IPG-1). (Illus.). 1968. 225.00 (ISBN 0-8103-1525-4). Gale.

International Portrait Gallery: First General Supplement. (International Portrait Gallery Ser.: No. IPG-2). 1972. 150.00 (ISBN 0-8103-1526-2). Gale.

International Portrait Gallery: Juvenile Authors Supplement. (International Portrait Gallery Ser.: No. IPG-5). (Illus.). 1974. 150.00 (ISBN 0-8103-1529-7). Gale.

International Portrait Gallery: Literary Figures Supplement. (International Portrait Gallery Ser.: No. IPG-4). (Illus.). 1974. 150.00 (ISBN 0-8103-1528-9). Gale.

International Portrait Gallery: Media People Supplement. (International Portrait Gallery Ser.: No. IPG-8). (Illus.). 1978. 150.00 (ISBN 0-8103-1532-7). Gale.

International Portrait Gallery: Second General Supplement. (International Portrait Gallery Ser.: No. IPG-3). (Illus.). 1974. 150.00 (ISBN 0-8103-1527-0). Gale.

International Portrait Gallery: Second Literary Figures Supplement. (International Portrait Gallery Ser.: No. IPG-7). (Illus.). 1978. 150.00 (ISBN 0-8103-1529-7). Gale.

International Portrait Gallery: Third General Supplement. (Illus.). 1978. 150.00 (ISBN 0-8103-1530-0). Gale.

International Portrait Gallery: Vol. 12, Children's Authors & Illustrators Supplement. (Illus.). 64p. 1981. 35.00 (ISBN 0-686-69448-1, IPG-12). Gale.

International Portrait Gallery: Vol. 10, Film Directors & Producers Supplement. (Illus.). 64p. 1981. 35.00 (ISBN 0-686-69446-5, IPG-10). Gale.

International Portrait Gallery: Vol. 11, Second Media People Supplement. (Illus.). 64p. 1981. 35.00 (ISBN 0-686-69447-3, IPG-11). Gale.

International Portrait Gallery: Vol. 9, Writers for Young Adults Supplement. (Illus.). 64p. 1981. 35.00 (ISBN 0-686-69445-7, IPG-9). Gale.

International Price Indexation. J. D. Cuddy. (Illus.). 1977. 17.95 (ISBN 0-347-01140-3, 00684-X, Pub. by Saxon Hse England). Lexington Bks.

International Publications: An Annual Annotated Subject Bibliography 1980-1981. 4th ed. Intl. Pubns. Serv. LC 72-626822. 256p. 1981. pap. 7.50x (ISBN 0-8002-0140-X). Intl Pubns Serv.

International Redistribution of Wealth & Power: A Study of the Charter of Economic Rights & Duties of States. Robert F. Meagher. (Pergamon Policy Studies). 1979. text ed. 29.50 (ISBN 0-08-022478-4). Pergamon.

International Regime of River Navigation. B. Vitanyi. 406p. 1980. 57.50x (ISBN 90-286-0529-0). Sijthoff & Noordhoff.

International Regulation of Internal Resources: A Study of Law & Policy. Mahnoush H. Arsanjani. LC 80-21169. 1981. write for info. (ISBN 0-8139-0879-5). U Pr of Va.

International Regulation of Multinational Corporations. Don Wallace, Jr. LC 75-8411. (Special Studies). (Illus.). 1976. text ed. 24.95 (ISBN 0-275-05880-8). Praeger.

International Rehabilitation: Approaches & Programs. Richard Hardy et al. 200p. 1980. text ed. 22.50x (ISBN 0-8290-0399-1); pap. text ed. 10.95x (ISBN 0-8290-0247-2). Irvington.

International Relations. James Bryce. LC 66-21391. Repr. of 1922 ed. 8.50 (ISBN 0-8046-0053-8). Kennikat.

International Relations: A Transnational Policy Approach. Werner Feld. LC 77-25959. (Illus.). 1979. text ed. 14.50x (ISBN 0-88284-058-4). Alfred Pub.

International Relations Dictionary. 2nd ed. Jack Plano & Roy Olton. 1978. 6.50 o.p. (ISBN 0-932826-00-8). New Issues MI.

International Relations: New Approaches. Davis B. Bobrow. LC 72-77282. 1972. pap. text ed. 3.95 (ISBN 0-02-904370-0). Free Pr.

International Relations of Eastern Europe: A Guide to Information Sources. Ed. by Robin A. Remington. LC 73-17512. (International Relations Information Guide Ser.: Vol. 8). 1978. 30.00 (ISBN 0-8103-1320-0). Gale.

International Relations: Theories & Evidence. Michael P. Sullivan. (Illus.). 400p. 1976. 18.95 (ISBN 0-13-473470-X). P-H.

International Relations Theory: Western & Non-Western Perspectives. Ed. by K. P. Misra & Richard S. Beal. 272p. 1980. text ed. 27.50 (ISBN 0-7069-1087-7, Pub. by Vikas India). Advent Bk.

International Research in Early Education. Ed. by Maurice Chazan. (General Ser.). (Illus.). 1978. pap. text ed. 22.00x (ISBN 0-85633-143-0, NFER). Humanities.

International Review in Physical Chemistry. Buckingham. 1981. text ed. price not set (ISBN 0-408-12271-4). Butterworth.

International Review of Cytology. Ed. by G. H. Bourne & J. F. Danielli. Incl. Vol. 1. 1952. 49.50 (ISBN 0-12-364301-5); Vol. 2. 1953. 49.50 (ISBN 0-12-364302-3); Vol. 3. 1954. 49.50 (ISBN 0-12-364303-1); Vol. 4. 1955. 49.50 (ISBN 0-12-364304-X); Vol. 5. 1956. 49.50 (ISBN 0-12-364305-8); Vol. 6. 1957. 49.50 (ISBN 0-12-364306-6); Vol. 7. 1958. 49.50 (ISBN 0-12-364307-4); Vol. 8. 1959. 49.50 (ISBN 0-12-364308-2); Vol. 9. 1960. 49.50 (ISBN 0-12-364309-0); Vol. 10. 1960. 49.50 (ISBN 0-12-364310-4); Vol. 11. 1961. 49.50 (ISBN 0-12-364311-2); Vol. 12. 1961. 49.50 (ISBN 0-12-364312-0); Vol. 13. 1962. 49.50 (ISBN 0-12-364313-9); Vol. 14. 1963. 49.50 (ISBN 0-12-364314-7); Vol. 15. 1963. 49.50 (ISBN 0-12-364315-5); Vol. 16. 1964. 49.50 (ISBN 0-12-364316-3); 49.50 (ISBN 0-12-364317-1); Vol. 18. 1965. 49.50 (ISBN 0-12-364318-X); Vol. 19. 1966. 49.50 (ISBN 0-12-364319-8); Vol. 20. 1966. 49.50 (ISBN 0-12-364320-1); Vol. 21. 1967. 49.50 (ISBN 0-12-364321-X); Vol. 22. Ed. by K. Jeon. 1967. 46.50 (ISBN 0-12-364322-8); Vol. 23. 1968. 49.50 (ISBN 0-12-364323-6); Vol. 24. 1968. 49.50 (ISBN 0-12-364324-4); Vol. 25. 1969. 49.50 (ISBN 0-12-364325-2); Vol. 26. 1969. 49.50 (ISBN 0-12-364326-0); Vol. 27. 1970. 49.50 (ISBN 0-12-364327-9); Vol. 28. 1970. 49.50 (ISBN 0-12-364328-7); Vol. 29. 1970. 49.50 (ISBN 0-12-364329-5). Acad Pr.

International Review of Cytology. Ed. by G. H. Bourne & J. F. Danielli. Incl. Vol. 30. 1971. 49.50 (ISBN 0-12-364330-9); Vol. 31. 1971. 49.50 (ISBN 0-12-364331-7); Vol. 32. 1972. 49.50 (ISBN 0-12-364332-5); Vol. 33. 1972. 49.50 (ISBN 0-12-364333-3); Vol. 34. 1973. 49.50 (ISBN 0-12-364334-1); Vol. 35. 1973. 49.50 (ISBN 0-12-364335-X); Vol. 36. 1973. 49.50 (ISBN 0-12-364336-8); Vol. 37. 1974. 49.50 (ISBN 0-12-364337-6); Vol. 38. 1974. 49.50 (ISBN 0-12-364338-4); Vol. 39. 1974. 49.50 (ISBN 0-12-364339-2); Vol. 40. Ed. by R. N. Jones. 1975. 49.50 (ISBN 0-12-364340-6); Vol. 41. Ed. by Paul J. Leibowitz & Moselio Schaechter. 1975. 49.50 (ISBN 0-12-364341-4); Vol. 42. Ed. by Bismarck B. Lozzio & Carmen Lozzio. 1975. 49.50 (ISBN 0-12-364342-2); Vol. 43. Ed. by Henry R. Mahler & Rudolf A. Raff. 1975. 49.50 (ISBN 0-12-364343-0); Vol. 44. 1976. 49.50 (ISBN 0-12-364344-9); Vol. 45. 49.50 (ISBN 0-12-364345-7); Vol. 46. 1976. 52.50 (ISBN 0-12-364346-5); Vol. 47. 1976. 46.00 (ISBN 0-12-364347-3); Vol. 48. 1977. 52.75 (ISBN 0-12-364348-1); Vol. 49. 1977. 47.00 (ISBN 0-12-364349-X); Vol. 50. 1977. 44.00 (ISBN 0-12-364350-3). Acad Pr.

International Review of Cytology, Vol. 64. Ed. by Geoffrey H. Bourne & James F. Danielli. LC 52-5203. 1980. 36.50 (ISBN 0-12-364464-X). Acad Pr.

International Review of Cytology, Vol. 65. Ed. by Geoffrey H. Bourne & James F. Danielli. 1980. 39.50 (ISBN 0-12-364465-8). Acad Pr.

International Review of Cytology, Vol. 66. Ed. by Geoffrey H. Bourne & James F. Danielli. (Serial Pub.). 1980. 39.00 (ISBN 0-12-364466-6). Acad Pr.

International Review of Cytology, Vol. 68. Ed. by Geoffrey H. Bourne & James F. Danielli. 1980. 38.00 (ISBN 0-12-364468-2). Acad Pr.

International Review of Cytology, Vol. 69. G. H. Bourne & J. F. Danielli. (Serial Publications Ser.). 1981. 38.00 (ISBN 0-12-364469-0). Acad Pr.

International Review of Cytology, Vol. 70. Ed. by Geoffrey H. Bourne & James F. Danielli. (Serial Publication). 1981. price not set (ISBN 0-12-364470-4). Acad Pr.

International Review of Cytology, Vol. 71. Ed. by G. H. Bourne & J. F. Danielli. 1981. write for info. (ISBN 0-12-364471-2). Acad Pr.

International Review of Cytology, Vol. 72. Ed. by Geoffrey Bourne & James Danielli. (Serial Publication). 1981. price not set (ISBN 0-12-364472-0). Acad Pr.

International Review of Cytology: Supplement 12. Ed. by G. H. Bourne & Audrey L. Muggleton-Harris. (Serial Publication). 1981. price not set (ISBN 0-12-364373-2). Acad Pr.

International Review of Cytology: Supplement 11, Part A: Perspectives in Plant Cell & Tissue Culture. Ed. by Indra K. Vasil. (Serial Pub.). 1980. 29.50 (ISBN 0-12-364371-6). Acad Pr.

International Review of Experimental Pathology. Ed. by G. W. Richter & M. A. Epstein. Incl. Vol. 1. 1962. 52.00 (ISBN 0-12-364901-3); Vol. 2. 1963. 52.00 (ISBN 0-12-364902-1); Vol. 3. 1965. 52.00 (ISBN 0-12-364903-X); Vol. 4. 1965. 52.00 (ISBN 0-12-364904-8); Vol. 5. 1967. 52.00 (ISBN 0-12-364905-6); Vol. 6. 1968. 52.00 (ISBN 0-12-364906-4); Vol. 7. 1969. 52.00 (ISBN 0-12-364907-2); Vol. 8. 1969. 52.00 (ISBN 0-12-364908-0); Vol. 9. 1971. 52.00 (ISBN 0-12-364909-9); Vol. 10. 1972. 52.00 (ISBN 0-12-364910-2); Vol. 11. 1972. 52.00 (ISBN 0-12-364911-0); Vol. 12. 1973. 52.00 (ISBN 0-12-364912-9); Vol. 17. 1977. 43.50 (ISBN 0-12-364917-X); Vol. 18. 1978. 52.50 (ISBN 0-12-364918-8); Vol. 19. 1979. 29.50 (ISBN 0-12-364919-6). Acad Pr.

International Review of Experimental Pathology, Vol. 22. Ed. by G. W. Richter & M. A. Epstein. 1980. write for info. (ISBN 0-12-364922-6). Acad Pr.

International Review of General & Experimental Zoology, 4 vols. Ed. by William J. Felts & Richard J. Harrison. 1964-70. Vol. 1. 48.50, by subscription 40.00 (ISBN 0-12-368101-4); Vol. 2. 48.50, by subscription 40.00 (ISBN 0-12-368102-2); Vol. 3. 48.50, by subscription 40.00 (ISBN 0-12-368103-0); Vol. 4. 48.50, by subscription 40.00 (ISBN 0-12-368104-9); 160.00 (ISBN 0-686-66612-7). Set. Acad Pr.

International Review of Halogen Chemistry, 3 Vols. Ed. by Viktor Gutmann. LC 66-30147. (Illus.). Vol. 1, 1967. 64.50 (ISBN 0-12-310901-9); Vol. 2, 1967. 66.00 (ISBN 0-12-310902-7); Vol. 3, 1968. 64.50 (ISBN 0-12-310903-5). Acad Pr.

International Review of Neurobiology, Vol. 22. John R. Smythies & Ronald J. Bradley. (Serial Publication). 1980. write for info. (ISBN 0-12-366822-0). Acad Pr.

International Review of Tropical Medicine. Ed. by David R. Lincicome. Incl. Vol. 1. 1960 (ISBN 0-12-367501-4); Vol. 2. 1963 (ISBN 0-12-367502-2); Vol. 3. 1969 (ISBN 0-12-367503-0); Vol. 4. Ed. by David R. Lincicome & A. W. Woodruff. 1971 (ISBN 0-12-367504-9). 43.50 ea. Acad Pr.

International Schools & Their Role in the Field of International Education. R. J. Leach. 1969. 22.00 (ISBN 0-08-013037-2); pap. 10.75 (ISBN 0-08-013036-4). Pergamon.

International Seminar on Probabilistic & Extreme Load Design of Nuclear Plant Facilities. Compiled by American Society of Civil Engineers. 464p. 1979. pap. text ed. 27.00 (ISBN 0-87262-146-4). Am Soc Civil Eng.

International Social Welfare. Walter A. Friedlander. (Illus.). 256p. 1975. 16.95 (ISBN 0-13-470906-3). P-H.

International Society As a Legal Community. Hermann Mosler. LC 80-50454. (Collected Courses, the Hague Academy of International Law: Vol. 140, 1974-IV). 327p. 1980. pap. 27.50x (ISBN 90-286-0080-9). Sijthoff & Noordhoff.

International Solar Energy Congress: Proceedings Held May 28 to June 1,1979, Atlanta, Georgia. International Solar Energy Society. 1980. 360.00 (ISBN 0-08-025074-2); pap. 275.00 (ISBN 0-08-025075-0). Pergamon.

International Standardization of Fruit & Vegetables. Organization for Economic Cooperation & Development. Incl. Tomatoes, Cauliflowers, Lettuces, Curled-Leaved Endives & Broad-Leaved Endives. 200p. 1971; Onions, Apricots, Plums, Strawberries, Table Grapes. 150p. 1965. 3.25 o.p. (ISBN 0-686-14864-9); Artichokes, Cherries, Cabbages, Cucumbers, Asparagus. 148p. 1969. 6.50 o.p. (ISBN 0-686-14865-7); o.p. (ISBN 0-686-14866-5); Apples & Pears. 74p. 1971. 5.25 o.p. (ISBN 0-686-14867-3); Citrus Fruit. 72p. 1971. 5.25 o.p. (ISBN 0-686-14868-1). OECD.

International Standardization of Fruit & Vegetables: Apples & Pears, Tomatoes, Citrus Fruit, Shelling Peas, Beans, Carrots. 1977. 24.00 o.p. (ISBN 92-64-11578-1). OECD.

International Student Guide to United States Colleges & Universities. William F. Shanahan. LC 78-24772. 1981. pap. 5.95 (ISBN 0-671-18422-9). Monarch Pr.

International Study of Achievement in Mathematics, Vol 1 & 2. Ed. by Torsten Husen. (Orig.). 1967. 10.95 ea. o.p. (Pub. by Wiley). Vol. 1, 304 Pgs. Vol. 2, 368 Pgs. Wiley.

International Style of Eighteen Hundred: A Study in Linear Abstraction. Robert Rosenblum. LC 75-23813. (Outstanding Dissertations in the Fine Arts - 18th Century). (Illus.). 1976. lib. bdg. 37.50 (ISBN 0-8240-2006-5). Garland Pub.

International Supply of Medicines: Implications of U. S. Regulatory Reform. Ed. by Robert Helms. 1980. 14.25 (ISBN 0-8447-2190-5); pap. 6.25 (ISBN 0-8447-2191-3). Am Enterprise.

International Symposium on Hepatotoxicity. Ed. by M. Eliakim. 1974. 25.00 (ISBN 0-12-237850-4). Acad Pr.

International Symposium on Macromolecules. C. Overberger & H. Mark. (JPS Symposium: No. 62). 1978. 40.50 (ISBN 0-471-05602-2, Pub by Wiley-Interscience). Wiley.

International Symposium on Malignant Hyperthermia. Ed. by R. A. Gordon et al. (Illus.). 512p. 1973. 32.75 (ISBN 0-398-02549-5). C C Thomas.

International Symposium on Pain. Ed. by John J. Bonica. LC 72-93317. (Advances in Neurology Ser.: Vol. 4). 874p. 1974. 56.50 (ISBN 0-911216-57-X). Raven.

International Symposium on Pain of Advanced Cancer. Ed. by John J. Bonica & Vittorio Ventafridda. LC 78-55811. (Advances in Pain Research & Therapy Ser.: Vol. 2). 1979. text ed. 73.50 (ISBN 0-89004-271-3). Raven.

International Symposium on Patent Information & Documentation, May 16 to May 18, 1977, Munich. German Society for Documentation. 479p. 1978. 65.00 (ISBN 0-89664-047-7, Pub. by K G Saur). Gale.

International Symposium on Programming. Ed. by B. Robinet. (Lecture Notes in Computer Science: Vol. 83). 341p. 1980. pap. 19.50 (ISBN 0-387-09981-6). Springer-Verlag.

International Symposium on Stratified Flow. Compiled by American Society of Civil Engineers. 760p. 1973. pap. text ed. 32.50 (ISBN 0-87262-059-X). Am Soc Civil Eng.

International Symposium on Urban Storm Runoff: Proceedings. Ed. by R. William De Vore & R. R. Huffsey. LC 79-66289. (Illus., Orig.). 1979. pap. 33.50 (ISBN 0-89779-020-0, UKY BU118); microfiche 4.50 (ISBN 0-89779-023-5). OES Pubns.

International Symposium on Urban Storm Water Management: Proceedings. Ed. by R. William De Vore & Charles T. Haan. 1978. pap. text ed. 33.50 (ISBN 0-89779-002-2); microfiche 4.50 (ISBN 0-89779-003-0). OES Pubns.

International System for Human Cytogenetic Namenclature. Ed. by Daniel Bergsma. LC 78-61295. (S. Karger Ser.: Vol. 14, No. 8). 1978. 10.00. March of Dimes.

International Tapestries. Ed. by G. A. Chevallez. (Illus.). 1973. pap. 2.50 o.p. (ISBN 0-88397-054-6). Intl Exhibit Found.

International Technical Communication Conference, Dallas, 1978: Proceedings, Vol. 25. Ed. by Society for Technical Communication. 1978. 25.00 (ISBN 0-914548-29-8). Univelt Inc.

International Technical Conference on Slurry Transportation: Proceedings. 5th ed. Ed. by Charles W. Linderman. LC 79-92621. (Illus.). 296p. (Orig.). 1980. pap. 65.00 (ISBN 0-932066-05-4). Slurry Transport.

International Technology Transfer: Guidelines, Codes & a Muffled Quadrilogue. Howard V. Perlmutter & Tagi Sagafi-Nejad. (Pergamon Policy Studies on International Developement). (Illus.). 250p. 1981. 27.50 (ISBN 0-08-027519-2). Pergamon.

International Telex Directory, 1980: Incl. Touring Telex, 6 vols. 28th ed. 9300p. (Eng., Ger., & Fr.). 1980. 140.00x (ISBN 3-87810-016-7). Intl Pubns Serv.

International Terrorism & Political Crimes. M. Cherif Bassiouni. 624p. 1975. pap. 29.75 (ISBN 0-398-03296-3). C C Thomas.

International Terrorism & World Security. Ed. by D. Carlton & C. Schaerf. LC 75-16273. 1975. 24.95 (ISBN 0-470-13503-4). Halsted Pr.

International Terrorism: National, Regional, & Global Perspectives. rev. ed. Ed. by Yonah Alexander. LC 75-8396. 320p. 1981. text ed. 28.95 (ISBN 0-275-09480-4). Praeger.

International Theory & European Integration. Charles Pentland. LC 73-10832. 1973. 17.95 (ISBN 0-02-925210-5). Free Pr.

International Thermodynamic Tables of the Fluid State-5. Ed. by S. Angus. 1978. text ed. 60.00 (ISBN 0-08-021981-0). Pergamon.

International Thermodynamic Tables of the Fluid State-6. Ed. by S. Angus. 1979. text ed. 82.00 (ISBN 0-08-022372-9). Pergamon.

International Thermodynamic Tables of the Fluid State-7. Ed. by S. Angus. 1980. text ed. 100.00 (ISBN 0-08-022373-7). Pergamon.

International Thesaurus of Quotations. Ed. by Rhoda T. Tripp. LC 73-106587. 1970. 11.95 (ISBN 0-690-44584-9, TYC-T); thumb-indexed 12.95 (ISBN 0-690-44585-7). T Y Crowell.

International Tokamak Reactor: Zero Phase. (Panel Proceedings Ser.). 650p. 1980. pap. 81.50 (ISBN 92-0-131080-3, ISP556, IAEA). Unipub.

International Trade & Agriculture: Theory & Policy. Ed. by Jimmye S. Hillman & Andrew Schmitz. (Special Studies in International Economics & Business). 1979. lib. bdg. 28.50 (ISBN 0-89158-498-6). Westview.

International Trade & Central Planning: An Analysis of Economic Interactions. Ed. by Alan A. Brown & Egon Neuberger. 1968. 30.00x (ISBN 0-520-00187-7). U of Cal Pr.

International Trade & Development. Gerald M. Meier. LC 73-13405. 208p. 1975. Repr. of 1963 ed. lib. bdg. 19.50x (ISBN 0-8371-7061-3, MEIT). Greenwood.

International Trade & Development Theory. Ronald E. Findlay. LC 73-8623. 208p. 1973. 17.50x (ISBN 0-231-03546-2). Columbia U Pr.

International Trade & Finance. 2nd ed. Baldwin & Richardson. 1981. pap. text ed. 8.95 (ISBN 0-316-07922-7). Little.

International Trade & Finance. Ed. by P. B. Kenen. LC 75-2717. (Illus.). 580p. 1976. 32.50 (ISBN 0-521-20719-3). Cambridge U Pr.

International Trade & Payments. D. P. Whiting. (Illus.). 160p. 1978. pap. 11.95x (ISBN 0-7121-0952-8). Intl Ideas.

International Trade Arbitration. Ed. by Martin Domke. LC 73-11852. 320p. 1974. Repr. of 1958 ed. lib. bdg. 25.00x (ISBN 0-8371-7075-3, DOTA). Greenwood.

International Trade Credit Management: A Twenty-Two Country Survey of Effective Credit Practices. (Illus.). 192p. 1976. pap. 18.00 o.p. (ISBN 0-7161-0273-0, Gower). Unipub.

International Trade in Rhinoceros Products. 83p. 1980. pap. 7.50 (ISBN 2-88032-203-0, IUCN 86, IUCN). Unipub.

International Trade Instability. Joseph D. Coppock. 1977. 32.95 (ISBN 0-566-00154-3, 001276-9, Pub. by Saxon Hse). Lexington Bks.

International Trade, Investment & Payments. H. Peter Gray. LC 78-69573. (Illus.). 1979. text ed. 19.50 (ISBN 0-395-26659-9). HM.

International Trade Policy: Agriculture & Development. Vernon Sorenson. LC 74-620204. xix, 290p. 1975. 11.00 (ISBN 0-87744-127-8); pap. 6.00 (ISBN 0-87744-168-5). Mich St U Busn.

International Trade: Selected Readings. Ed. by Jagdish Bhagwati. 456p. 1981. text ed. 25.00x (ISBN 0-262-02160-9); pap. text ed. 9.95x (ISBN 0-262-52060-5). MIT Pr.

International Trade: Theory & Empirical Evidence. 2nd ed. R. Heller. 1973. 17.95 (ISBN 0-13-473918-3). P-H.

International Trade Unionism. Charles Levinson. (Ruskin House Series in Trade Union Studies). 1972. text ed. 15.95x (ISBN 0-04-331049-4). Allen Unwin.

International Trade 1979-80. 192p. 1981. pap. 18.00 (G144, GATT). Unipub.

International Training. Lucia Pierce & Lucia Pierce. 1981. pap. 7.95x (ISBN 0-915432-81-1). NE Conf Teach Foreign.

International Treasury Management for the 1980's: A Practical Approach to Treasury Management in the Multinatioanl Corporation. John B. Giannotti & Richard W. Smith. 600p. 1981. 39.50 (ISBN 0-471-08062-4, Pub. by Wiley Interscience). Wiley.

International Treaties Relating to Nuclear Control & Disarmament. (Legal Ser. No. 9). 78p. 1975. pap. 6.50 (ISBN 92-0-176075-2, IAEA). Unipub.

International Tune-up-Maintenance, Scouts, Wagons, Pickups, Through 1980. new ed. Mike Bishop. Ed. by Jeff Robinson. (Illus.). 1977. pap. 7.95 (ISBN 0-89287-137-7, A233). Clymer Pubns.

International Urban Growth Policies: New-Town Contributions. Gideon Golany. LC 77-28274. 1978. 40.00 (ISBN 0-471-03748-6, Pub. by Wiley-Interscience). Wiley.

International Value-International Prices. L. Zelko. LC 80-50648. 153p. 1980. 17.50 (ISBN 90-286-0040-X). Sijthoff & Noordhoff.

International Vegetarian Cookery. Sonya Richmond. LC 66-21124. 1965. 3.75 o.p. (ISBN 0-668-01510-1). Arco.

International Vegetarian Health Food Handbook. 208p. 1979. pap. 3.95x (ISBN 0-8464-1026-5). Beekman Pubs.

International Vocabulary of Town Planning & Architecture. LC 70-860237. (Illus.). 366p. (Fr. Ger. & Eng.). 1970. 55.00x (ISBN 0-8002-1582-6). Intl Pubns Serv.

International Weapon Developments: A Survey of Current Developments in Weapon Systems. 4th ed. Ed. by The Royal United Services Institute for Defence Studies. (Illus.). 203p. 1980. pap. 13.25 (ISBN 0-08-027028-X). Pergamon.

International Who's Who in Art & Antiques. 1st ed. (Illus.). 679p. 1972. 32.50x (ISBN 0-900332-21-2, Pub. by Intl Biog). Biblio Dist.

International Who's Who in Community Service. Ed. by Nina Watkins. 851p. 1974. 32.50x (ISBN 0-85649-012-1, Pub. by Intl Biog). Biblio Dist.

International Who's Who in Education. 2nd ed. 1981. 54.50x (ISBN 0-686-27373-7, Pub. by Intl Biog Ctr). Biblio Dist.

International Who's Who 1980-1981. 44th ed. LC 35-10257. 1409p. 1980. 90.00x (ISBN 0-905118-48-0). Intl Pubns Serv.

International Who's Who 1980-1981. 1385p. 1980. 90.00 (ISBN 0-905118-48-0, EUR021, Europa). Unipub.

International Yearbook of Education, Vol. XXXII, 1980. 242p. 1980. pap. 12.25 (ISBN 92-3-101634-2, U1039, UNESCO). Unipub.

International Yearbook of Educational & Instructional Technology 1980-81. Association for Educational & Training Technology. 500p. 1980. 36.00x (ISBN 0-89397-082-4). Nichols Pub.

International Yearbook of Foreign Policy Analysis, Vol. 2. Ed. by Peter Jones. LC 75-21728. 256p. 1976. 17.50x (ISBN 0-8448-0762-1). Crane-Russak Co.

Internationale Wagner - Bibliographie: 1967-1978. Ed. by Herbert Barth. LC 80-483676. 175p. (Orig.). 1979. pap. 12.50 (ISBN 3-921733-08-1). Intl Pubns Serv.

Internationale Wagner-Bibliographie, International Wagner Bibliography, 4 vols. Henrik Barth. Incl. Vol. 2. 1956-1960. Vol. 1. 7.50x (ISBN 3-921733-05-7); Vol. 2. 1956-1960. Vol. 2. 7.50x (ISBN 3-921733-05-7); 1961-1966. Vol. 3. 7.50 (ISBN 3-921733-06-5). LC 79-455691. Intl Pubns Serv.

Internationalism: Opposing Viewpoints. Ed. by Bruno Leone. (ISMS Ser.). (Illus.). (gr. 9-12). 8.95 (ISBN 0-912616-59-8); pap. 3.95 (ISBN 0-912616-58-X). Greenhaven.

Internationalism or Russification? A Study in the Soviet Nationalities Problem. 2nd ed. Ivan Dzyuba. Ed. by M. Davies. 1970. text ed. 9.50x (ISBN 0-297-17613-7). Humanities.

Internationalization to Prevent the Spread of Nuclear Weapons. SIPRI. LC 80-14962. 220p. 1980. 24.50x (ISBN 0-8448-1378-8). Crane-Russak Co.

Internationalize Your School. Ed. by Nais Committee for International & World Education. 1977. pap. 3.25 (ISBN 0-934338-22-1). NAIS.

Internships Nineteen Hundred Eighty-One. Ed. by Kirk Polking. (Orig.). 1981. pap. 6.95 (ISBN 0-89879-036-0). Writers Digest.

Interorganizational Relations. Ed. by William M. Evan. LC 77-25062. 1978. pap. 7.50x (ISBN 0-8122-7745-7). U of Pa Pr.

Interpersonal Attraction. 2nd ed. Ellen Berscheid & Elaine H. Walster. LC 77-77726. (Topics in Social Psychology). (Illus.). 1978. pap. text ed. 8.95 (ISBN 0-201-00569-7). A-W.

Interpersonal Behavior. A. Athos & J. Gabarro. 1978. 21.95 (ISBN 0-13-475004-7). P-H.

Interpersonal Behavior and Administration. A. N. Turner & G. F. Lombard. LC 69-11486. 1969. text ed. 16.95 (ISBN 0-02-932760-1). Free Pr.

Interpersonal Behavior & Health Care. Michael A. Counte & Luther Christman. (Behavioral Sciences for the Health Care Professional Ser.). 128p. (Orig.). 1981. lib. bdg. 15.00x (ISBN 0-86531-008-4); pap. text ed. 6.00x (ISBN 0-86531-009-2). Westview.

Interpersonal Behavior in Small Groups. Richard Ofshe. (Illus.). 816p. 1973. text ed. 21.95x (ISBN 0-13-475020-9). P-H.

Interpersonal Communication. Ed. by W. D. Brooks & R. A. Vogel. LC 76-44141. (Ser. in Speech Communication). 1977. pap. text ed. 5.95 (ISBN 0-8465-7603-1); instr's. guide 3.95 (ISBN 0-8465-7607-4). Benjamin-Cummings.

Interpersonal Communication. 2nd ed. William D. Brooks & Philip Emmert. 1980. pap. text ed. 9.95x (ISBN 0-697-04172-7); instr's manual 2.00 (ISBN 0-697-04180-8). Wm C Brown.

Interpersonal Communication. Kurt Danziger. 250p. 1976. text ed. 23.00 (ISBN 0-08-018757-9); pap. text ed. 14.00 (ISBN 0-08-018756-0). Pergamon.

Interpersonal Communication. 2nd ed. Stewart L. Tubbs & Sylvia Moss. 299p. 1981. pap. text ed. 10.95 (ISBN 0-394-32684-9). Random.

Interpersonal Communication: A Cross-Disciplinary Approach. Arthur Solomon et al. 120p. 1970. 12.75 (ISBN 0-398-01810-3). C C Thomas.

Interpersonal Communication: A Question of Needs. Michael D. Scott & William G. Powers. LC 77-76342. (Illus.). 1978. text ed. 12.95 (ISBN 0-395-25055-2); inst. manual 0.60 (ISBN 0-395-25056-0). HM.

Interpersonal Communication: A Relational Perspective. Ben W. Morse & Lynn A. Phelps. 1979. 15.95 (ISBN 0-8087-3963-8). Burgess.

Interpersonal Communication in Action: Basic Text & Readings. 2nd ed. Bobby R. Patton & Kim Giffin. (Auer Ser.). 1977. pap. text ed. 14.50 scp o.p. (ISBN 0-06-042316-1, HarpC); instructor's manual free o.p. (ISBN 0-06-364974-8). Har-Row.

Interpersonal Communication in Action: Basic Text & Readings. 3rd ed. Bobby R. Patton & Kim Giffin. (Illus.). 448p. 1980. pap. 12.95 scp (ISBN 0-06-045062-2, HarpC); avail. Har-Row.

Interpersonal Communication in Organizations. Richard C. Huseman et al. 1975. text ed. 15.95 (ISBN 0-205-04897-8, 484897-7). Allyn.

Interpersonal Communication in the Modern Organization. E. Bormann et al. 1969. text ed. 15.95 (ISBN 0-13-475038-1). P-H.

Interpersonal Communication Journal. Lynn Phelps & Sue Dewine. LC 76-3576. (Illus.). 200p. 1976. pap. text ed. 9.50 (ISBN 0-8299-0102-7); instrs.' manual avail. (ISBN 0-8299-0566-9). West Pub.

Interpersonal Communication: Roles, Rules, Strategies & Games. 2nd ed. R. Dennis Smith & L. Keith Williamson. 370p. 1981. pap. text ed. write for info. (ISBN 0-697-04182-4); instrs.' manual 2.00 (ISBN 0-697-04188-3). Wm C Brown.

Interpersonal Communications: Influences & Alternatives. new ed. J. Dan Rothwell & James I. Costigan. (Speech & Drama Ser.). 288p. 1975. pap. text ed. 8.95x o.p. (ISBN 0-675-08764-3); instructors manual 3.95 o.p. (ISBN 0-685-50547-2). Merrill.

Interpersonal Diagnosis of Personality: A Functional Theory & Methodology for Personality Evaluation. T. Leary. 518p. 1957. 24.95 (ISBN 0-471-06915-9). Wiley.

Interpersonal Diagnosis of Personality: A Functional Theory & Methodology for Personality Evaluation. Timothy Leary. (Illus.). 1957. 24.95 (ISBN 0-8260-5315-7). Ronald Pr.

Interpersonal Helping: Emerging Approaches for Social Work Practice. Ed. by Joel Fischer. (Illus.). 704p. 1973. pap. 13.75 (ISBN 0-398-02565-7). C C Thomas.

Interpersonal Influence. 2nd ed. Ladd Wheeler et al. 1978. pap. text ed. 10.95 (ISBN 0-205-06061-7). Allyn.

Interpersonal Interaction in Nursing. Virgil Parsons & Nancy Sanford. 1979. 7.95 (ISBN 0-201-05551-1, 05551, M&N Div). A-W.

Interpersonal Judgments in Education. Meriel Downey. 1977. text ed. 15.70 (ISBN 0-06-318051-0, IntlDept); pap. text ed. 7.80 (ISBN 0-06-318052-9, IntlDept). Har-Row.

Interpersonal Peacemaking: Confrontations & Third Party Consultation. Richard E. Walton. (Organization Development Ser). (Orig.). 1969. pap. text ed. 6.50 (ISBN 0-201-08435-X). A-W.

Interpersonal Processes in Groups & Organizations. Sara B. Kiesler. Ed. by Kenneth D. Mackenzie. LC 77-86018. (Organizational Behavior Ser.). 1978. pap. text ed. 9.95x (ISBN 0-88295-451-2). AHM Pub.

Interpersonal Psychotherapy. Arthur Burton. LC 74-29379. 172p. 1975. Repr. of 1972 ed. 10.00x (ISBN 0-87668-192-5). Aronson.

Interpersonal Relations: A Theory of Interdependence. Harold H. Kelley & John W. Thibaut. LC 78-164. 1978. 27.95 (ISBN 0-471-03473-8, Pub. by Wiley-Interscience). Wiley.

Interpersonal Relations & Education. David H. Hargreaves. (International Library of Sociology). 1972. 25.00x (ISBN 0-7100-7245-7). Routledge & Kegan.

Interpersonal Relations & Education. rev. ed. David H. Hargreaves. (International Library of Sociology). 1975. pap. 8.95 (ISBN 0-7100-8081-6). Routledge & Kegan.

Interpersonal Skills for Health Professionals. Brian Gerrard et al. (Illus.). 272p. 1980. text ed. 15.95 (ISBN 0-8359-3138-2); pap. text ed. 12.95 (ISBN 0-8359-3136-6). Reston.

Interpersonal Speech Communication: Principles & Practices. Ralph Webb, Jr. (Illus.). 320p. 1975. pap. text ed. 14.95 (ISBN 0-13-475103-5). P-H.

Interpersonal Strategies for Systems Management. Raymond G. Hunt. LC 73-85594. (Behavior Science in Industry Ser.). (Orig.). 1974. pap. text ed. 6.95 o.p. (ISBN 0-8185-0099-9). Brooks-Cole.

Interpeting Orthodoxy. M. Nissiotis. 1980. pap. 2.45 (ISBN 0-937032-23-9). Light&Life Pub Co MN.

Interplay. Jerome L. Jacobs. 1979. 10.00 (ISBN 0-07-032146-9). Readers Digest Pr.

Interplay: A Theory of Religion & Education. Gabriel Moran. LC 80-53203. 125p. (Orig.). 1981. pap. 5.95 (ISBN 0-88489-125-9). St Mary's.

Interpol. Michael Fooner. 1977. pap. 1.95 o.p. (ISBN 0-445-08580-0). Popular Lib.

Interpolation of Linear Operators. S. G. Krein et al. (Mathematical Monographs). 1981. cancelled (ISBN 0-8218-4504-7). Am Math.

Interpreatations of the ASME Boiler & Pressure Vessel Code. 1980. annual subscription 30.00 (E0098); special 3-yr. subscription 70.00. ASME.

Interpretacion De los Derechos Civiles En Puerto Rico. Julio J. Santa-Pinter. LC 77-25835. 1978. pap. 9.00 (ISBN 0-8477-3015-8). U of PR Pr.

Interpretating Religious Experience. Peter Donovan. 1979. pap. 3.95 (ISBN 0-8164-2209-5). Crossroad NY.

Interpretation: An Essay in the Philosophy of Literary Criticism. P. D. Juhl. LC 80-7534. 276p. 1980. 20.00 (ISBN 0-691-07242-6). Princeton U Pr.

Interpretation & Use of Rate Data: The Rate Concept. rev. ed. Stuart W. Churchill. LC 78-23365. (Illus.). 1979. text ed. 24.50 (ISBN 0-89116-133-3); solutions man. avl. 5.95. Hemisphere Pub.

Interpretation in Teaching. 2nd ed. I. A. Richards. 435p. 1973. text ed. 18.00x (ISBN 0-391-00282-1). Humanities.

Interpretation: Jungian Symbolism & Astrology, Pt. 1. Karen Hamaker-Zondag. 192p. 1981. 7.95 (ISBN 0-87728-523-3). Weiser.

Interpretation Klinisch-Chemischer Laborresultate. 2nd ed. R. C. Eastham. Tr. by E. Peheim. Ed. by J. P. Colombo. xii, 248p. 1981. pap. 17.00 (ISBN 3-8055-1879-X). S Karger.

Interpretation of Audiometric Results. Irving Hochberg. LC 72-85146. (Studies in Communicative Disorders Ser). 45p. 1973. pap. text ed. 2.50 (ISBN 0-672-61285-2). Bobbs.

Interpretation of Biblical History in the Antiquitates Judaicae of Flavius Josephus. Harold W. Attridge. LC 76-26597. (Harvard Theological Review, Dissertations in Religion). 1976. pap. 7.50 (ISBN 0-89130-081-3, 020107). Scholars Pr Ca.

Interpretation of Biochemical Multitest Profiles: An Analysis of 100important Conditions. Paul L. Wolf. LC 76-54053. (Illus.). 296p. 1977. 25.00 (ISBN 0-89352-002-0). Masson Pub.

Interpretation of Biopsy of Endometrium. Ancel Blaustein. (Biopsy Interpretation Ser.). 1979. text ed. 27.00 (ISBN 0-89004-370-1). Raven.

Interpretation of Christian Ethics. Reinhold Niebuhr. (Library of Contemporary Theology). 1979. pap. 6.95 (ISBN 0-8164-2206-0). Crossroad NY.

Interpretation of Electrocardiograms: A Self-Instructional Approach. Nora Laiken et al. (Illus.). 1978. 13.95 (ISBN 0-8385-4047-3). ACC.

Interpretation of Environmental Isotope and Hydrochemcal Data in Groundwater Hydrology: Proceedings. Advisory Group Meeting, Vienna, Jan. 27-31, 1975. (Panel Proceedings Ser.). (Illus., Orig.). 1976. pap. 18.25 (ISBN 92-0-141076-X, IAEA). Unipub.

Interpretation of Fundus Fluorescein Angiography. new ed. Howard Schatz et al. LC 77-19094. (Illus.). 1977. text ed. 84.50 (ISBN 0-8016-4343-0). Mosby.

Interpretation of Geological Phase Diagrams. Ernest G. Ehlers. LC 75-182129. (Illus.). 1972. text ed. 32.95x (ISBN 0-7167-0254-1). W H Freeman.

Interpretation of Historic Sites. William T. Alderson & Shirley P. Low. LC 75-33292. (Illus.). 1976. pap. 6.95 (ISBN 0-910050-19-8). AASLH.

Interpretation of Igneous Rocks. K. G. Cox et al. 1979. text ed. 45.00x (ISBN 0-04-552015-1); pap. text ed. 22.95x (ISBN 0-04-552016-X). Allen Unwin.

Interpretation of Immunoelectrophoretic Patterns. Gerald M. Penn & Judith Batya. LC 77-93640. (Atlas Ser.). (Illus.). 1978. text ed. 30.00 (ISBN 0-89189-036-X, 16-A-001-00); incl. slides 140.00 (ISBN 0-89189-098-X, 15-A-001-00). Am Soc Clinical.

Interpretation of Immunofluorescent Patterns in Renal Diseases. Rafael Valenzuela & Sharad D. Deodhar. (Illus.). 144p. 1981. text ed. 45.00 (ISBN 0-89189-079-3, 16-A-003-00); atlas & slides 140.00 (ISBN 0-89189-098-X, 15-A-003-00). Am Soc Clinical.

Interpretation of Language. rev. ed. Theodore Thass-Thienemann. Incl. Vol. 1. Understanding the Symbolic Meaning of Language. 512p. o.p. (ISBN 0-87668-087-2); Vol. 2. Understanding the Unconscious Meaning of Language. 448p (ISBN 0-87668-088-0). LC 73-79984. 1973. 17.50x ea. Aronson.

Interpretation of Mass Spectra. Fred W. McLafferty. Ed. by Nicholas J. Turro. LC 80-51179. (Organic Chemistry Ser.). 303p. 1980. text ed. 13.00x (ISBN 0-935702-04-0). Univ Sci Bks.

Interpretation of Multiple Observations. Marriott. 1974. 17.00 (ISBN 0-12-473450-2). Acad Pr.

Interpretation of Music. Thurston Dart. 1975. Repr. of 1967 ed. pap. text ed. 9.25x (ISBN 0-09-031683-5, Hutchinson U Lib). Humanities.

Interpretation of Narrative. Ed. by Mario J. Valdes & Owen J. Miller. LC 78-23683. 1978. 15.00x o.p. (ISBN 0-8020-5443-9). U of Toronto Pr.

Interpretation of Old English Poems. Stanley B. Greenfield. 1972. 16.00 (ISBN 0-7100-7340-2). Routledge & Kegan.

Interpretation of Ordinary Landscapes. Ed. by D. W. Meinig. (Illus.). 1979. pap. text ed. 5.95 (ISBN 0-19-502536-9). Oxford U Pr.

Interpretation of Otherness: Literature Religion & the American Imagination. Giles Gunn. 1979. 15.95 (ISBN 0-19-502453-2). Oxford U Pr.

Interpretation of Prophecy. Paul Lee Tan. 1975. 8.95 (ISBN 0-88469-000-8). BMH Bks.

Interpretation of Shakespeare. Hardin Craig. 1966. Repr. text ed. 5.95x perfect bdg. (ISBN 0-87543-005-8). Lucas.

Interpretation of Shear & Bond in Reinforced Concrete. Gustav Florin. (Structural Engineering Ser.: Vol. 1). (Illus.). 86p. 1980. pap. 24.00x (ISBN 0-87849-033-7). Trans Tech.

Interpretation of Symbolism. Ed. by Roy Willis. LC 75-4111. (Association of Social Anthropologists Studies: No. 2). 181p. 1975. 24.95 (ISBN 0-470-94920-1). Halsted Pr.

Interpretation of the Book of Revelation. Apostolos Makrakis. Ed. by Orthodox Christian Educational Society. Tr. by A. G. Alexander from Hellenic. 564p. 1972. 8.00x (ISBN 0-938366-12-2). Orthodox Chr.

Interpretation of the Entire New Testament (Revelation Not Included, 2 vols. Apostolos Makrakis. Ed. by Orthodox Christian Educational Society. Tr. by Albert G. Alexander from Hellenic. 2052p. (Vol. 1, 1127 pp.;vol. 2, 925 pp.). 1949. Set. 20.00x (ISBN 0-938366-08-4). Orthodox Chr.

Interpretation of the Fourth Gospel. Charles H. Dodd. 59.50 (ISBN 0-521-04848-6); pap. text ed. 13.95x (ISBN 0-521-09517-4, 517). Cambridge U Pr.

Interpretation of the Gospel Law. Apostolos Makrakis. Ed. by Orthodox Christian Educational Society. Tr. by Denver Cummings from Hellenic. 317p. 1955. 6.00x (ISBN 0-938366-10-6). Orthodox Chr.

Interpretation of the Halstead Reitan Neuropsychological Test Battery: A Casebook Approach. Charles A. Golden et al. 1980. 26.50 (ISBN 0-8089-1298-4). Grune.

Interpretation of the New Testament, 1861-1961. Stephen Neill. 1964. pap. 8.95x (ISBN 0-19-283005-8, OPB). Oxford U Pr.

Interpretation of the Scriptures. Arthur W. Pink. 1972. pap. 3.95 (ISBN 0-8010-7025-2). Baker Bk.

Interpretation of Therapeutic Drug Levels. Ed. by Daniel M. Baer & William R. Dito. (Illus.). 400p. 1981. text ed. 35.00 (ISBN 0-89189-080-7, 45-9-009-00). Am Soc Clinical.

Interpretations: Essays on Twelve English Poems. 2nd ed. Ed. by John Wain. 256p. 1972. 18.00x (ISBN 0-7100-7385-2); pap. 7.95 (ISBN 0-7100-7386-0). Routledge & Kegan.

Interpretations in Clinical Chemistry. Myrton F. Beeler. LC 77-95109. (Illus.). 1978. text ed. 35.00 binder (ISBN 0-89189-045-9, 45-2-036-00). Am Soc Clinical.

Interpretations in Shakespeare's Sonnets. Hilton Landry. LC 76-1901. (Perspectives in Criticism Ser.: No. 14). (Illus.). 185p. 1976. Repr. of 1963 ed. lib. bdg. 16.75x (ISBN 0-8371-8749-4, LAIS). Greenwood.

Interpretations of Plato: A Swarthmore Symposium. Ed. by Helen F. North. (Supplement Mnemosyne: No. 50). viii, 112p. 1980. text ed. 21.75x (ISBN 0-391-01138-3). Humanities.

Interpretations of Poetry & Religion. George Santayana. 8.25 (ISBN 0-8446-0893-9). Peter Smith.

Interprete English-French: A Language Travel Guide. pap. 3.95 (ISBN 2-03-070208-0, 3770). Larousse.

Interprete Larousse, francais-allemand et allemand-francais. Larousse And Co. pap. 3.95 (ISBN 0-685-13946-8, 3782). Larousse.

Interprete Larousse, francais-italien et italien-francais. Larousse And Co. (Fr. & It.). pap. 3.95 (ISBN 0-685-13947-6, 3787). Larousse.

Interprete Larousse, French-Spanish & Spanish-French. Larousse And Co. (Fr. & Span.). pap. 3.95 (ISBN 0-685-13948-4, 3777). Larousse.

Interpreter, Wherein Three Principal Terms of State Are Clearly Unfolded. Thomas Scott. LC 74-80194. (English Experience Ser.: No. 673). 1974. Repr. of 1624 ed. 3.50 (ISBN 90-221-0281-5). Walter J Johnson.

Interpreters & Critics of the Cold War. Kenneth W. Thompson. LC 78-57575. 1978. pap. text ed. 6.75 (ISBN 0-8191-0504-X). U Pr of Amer.

Interpreter's Bible, 12 vols. George A. Buttrick. Incl. Vol. 1. General Articles, Genesis, Exodus (ISBN 0-687-19207-2); Vol. 2. Leviticus - Samuel. 1953 (ISBN 0-687-19208-0); Vol. 3. Kings - Job. 1954 (ISBN 0-687-19209-9); Vol. 4. Psalms, Proverbs. 1955 (ISBN 0-687-19210-2); Vol. 5. Ecclesiates - Jeremiah. 1956 (ISBN 0-687-19211-0); Vol. 6. Lamentations - Malachi. 1956 (ISBN 0-687-19212-9); Vol. 7. General Articles, Matthew, Mark. 1951 (ISBN 0-687-19213-7); Vol. 8. Luke, John. 1952 (ISBN 0-687-19214-5); Vol. 9. The Acts, Romans. 1954 (ISBN 0-687-19215-3); Vol. 10. Corinthians, Ephesians. 1953 (ISBN 0-687-19216-1); Vol. 11. Philippians - Hebrews. 1955 (ISBN 0-687-19217-X); Vol. 12. James - Revelation. 1957 (ISBN 0-687-19218-8). 16.95; 185.00 (ISBN 0-687-19206-4). Abingdon.

Interpreters' Services & the Role of Health Care Volunteers. American Hospital Association. LC 74-77268. (Illus.). 74p. (Orig.). 1974. pap. 6.25 (ISBN 0-87258-149-7, 2880). Am Hospital.

Interpreting Automotive Systems. Harry G. Hill. LC 75-19527. 1977. pap. 10.36 (ISBN 0-8273-1057-9); instructor's guide 1.60 (ISBN 0-8273-1058-7). Delmar.

Interpreting Blake. Ed. by M. Phillips. LC 78-8322. (Illus.). 1979. 42.00 (ISBN 0-521-22176-5). Cambridge U Pr.

Interpreting Dental Radiographs. Brian Beeching. (Illus.). 142p. 1981. PLB 33.55 (ISBN 0-906141-20-6, Pub. by Update Books Ltd). Kluwer Boston.

Interpreting Earth History: A Manual in Historical Geology. 2nd ed. Morris S. Petersen & J. Keith Rigby. 202p. 1978. wire coil bdg. write for info. (ISBN 0-697-05080-7); instrs'. manual avail. Wm C Brown.

Interpreting Engineering Drawings. C. H. Jensen. LC 70-92052. 256p. 1972. 10.40 (ISBN 0-8273-0061-1); instructor's guide 1.60 (ISBN 0-8273-0062-X). Delmar.

Interpreting Engineering Drawings: Metric Edition. C. H. Jensen & R. D. Hines. LC 77-78175. 1979. pap. text ed. 10.60 (ISBN 0-8273-1061-7); instructor's guide 1.60 (ISBN 0-8273-1062-5). Delmar.

Interpreting Folklore. Alan Dundes. LC 79-2969. 304p. 1980. 25.00x (ISBN 0-253-14307-1); pap. 9.95x (ISBN 0-253-20240-X). Ind U Pr.

Interpreting Handwriting. Jane Paterson. 1977. 7.95 o.p. (ISBN 0-679-50700-0); pap. 4.95 o.p. (ISBN 0-679-50701-9). McKay.

Interpreting Hearing Aid Technology. Ed. by Kenneth Donnelly. (Illus.). 320p. 1974. text ed. 21.50 (ISBN 0-398-03087-1). C C Thomas.

Interpreting Religious Experience. Peter Donovan. (Orig.). 1979. pap. 3.95 (ISBN 0-8164-2209-5). Crossroad NY.

Interpreting the City: Urban Geography. Truman A. Hartshorn. LC 79-19544. 1980. text ed. 21.95x (ISBN 0-471-05637-5). Wiley.

Interpreting the Eclipses. Robert Jansky. 1979. pap. 5.95 (ISBN 0-917086-08-2, Pub. by Astro Comp Serv). Para Res.

Interpreting the Electrocardiagram. new ed. James Fleming. (Illus.). 1979. text ed. 16.50 (ISBN 0-906141-05-2, Pub. by Update Pubns, England). Kluwer Boston.

Interpreting the Environment. Ed. by Grant W. Sharpe. LC 76-4564. 505p. 1976. 22.95 (ISBN 0-471-77896-6). Wiley.

Interpreting the Gospels. Ed. by James L. Mays. LC 80-8057. 320p. 1981. pap. 13.50 (ISBN 0-8006-1439-9, 1-1439). Fortress.

Interpreting the Gospels for Preaching. D. Moody Smith. LC 79-8900. 132p. (Orig.). 1980. pap. 4.50 (ISBN 0-8006-1381-3, 1-1381). Fortress.

Interpreting the New Testament: A Practical Guide. Daniel J. Harrington. Ed. by Wilfrid Harrington & Donald Senior. (New Testament Message Ser.: Vol. 1). 1979. 9.00 (ISBN 0-89453-124-7); pap. 4.95 (ISBN 0-89453-189-1). M Glazier.

Interpreting the Universe. John MacMurray. 164p. 1980. Repr. lib. bdg. 25.00 (ISBN 0-89987-576-9). Darby Bks.

Interpreting the Weather: A Practical Guide for Householders, Gardners, Motorist and Sportsmen. Ingrid Holford. (Illus.). 1973. 13.50 (ISBN 0-7153-5800-6). David & Charles.

Interpreting Western Civilization, 2 vols. Ed. by Brison D. Gooch. Incl. Vol. 1. From Antiquity to the Sun King. pap. text ed. o.p. (ISBN 0-256-01094-3); Vol. 2. From the Enlightenment to the Present. pap. text ed. 9.95x (ISBN 0-256-01095-1). 1969. Dorsey.

Interpretive Analysis of Selected Papers from Changes in Rice Farming in Selected Areas of Asia. 825p. 1978. pap. 11.00 (R007, IRRI). Unipub.

Interpretive Atlas of Narragansett Bay. Steve Olsen et al. (Marine Bulletin Ser.: No. 40). 1980. 2.00 (ISBN 0-938412-16-7). URI MAS.

Interpretive Social Science: A Reader. Ed. by Paul Rabinow & William M. Sullivan. LC 77-85743. (Campus Ser.: No. 218). 1979. 24.50x (ISBN 0-520-03588-7); pap. 6.95x (ISBN 0-520-03834-7). U of Cal Pr.

Interracial Sex. (Illus.). pap. 5.00 guide (ISBN 0-910550-40-9). Centurion Pr.

Intercom: Readings in Organizational Communication. Stewart Ferguson & Sherry D. Ferguson. 432p. 1980. 12.95x (ISBN 0-8104-5127-1). Hayden.

Interregional Movements & Regional Growth. Ed. by William C. Wheaton. (Papers on Public Economics Ser.: Vol. 2). 253p. (Orig.). 1980. pap. 7.50 (ISBN 0-87766-257-6, 26600). Urban Inst.

Interregional Trade & Money Flows in Nigeria, 1964. Alan M. Hay & Robert H. Smith. (Nigerian Institute of Social & Economic Research Ser). 1970. 12.00x o.p. (ISBN 0-19-646029-8). Oxford U Pr.

Interregional Water Transfers: Projects & Problems: Proceedings of the Task Force Meeting, International Institute for Applied Systems Analysis, Laxenburg, Austria, Oct. 1977. Ed. by G. N. Golubev & A. K. Biswas. 1978. text ed. 27.00 (ISBN 0-08-022430-X). Pergamon.

Interrelated Arts in Leisure: Perceiving & Creating. Nellie D. Arnold. LC 75-30965. (Illus.). 224p. 1976. 10.50 o.p. (ISBN 0-8016-0328-5). Mosby.

Interrelated Intergrated Electronics Circuits for the Radio Amateur, Technicians, Hobbyist & CB'er. R. M. Mendelson. 128p. 1979. pap. 7.70 (ISBN 0-8104-0760-4). Hayden.

Interrogating the Oracle: A History of the London Browning Society. William A. Petersen. 290p. 1979. 4.40x (ISBN 0-686-64109-4, Pub. by Browning Inst). Pub Ctr Cult Res.

Interrogating the Oracle: A History of the London Browning Society. William S. Peterson. LC 69-15916. (Illus.). xii, 276p. 1970. 14.00x (ISBN 0-8214-0056-8). Ohio U Pr.

Interrupted Journey. John G. Fuller. 1980. pap. 2.50 (ISBN 0-686-62913-2). Berkley Pub.

Interrupted Time Series Analysis. David McDowall et al. LC 80-52761. (Quantitative Applications in the Social Sciences Ser.: No. 21). (Illus.). 96p. 1980. pap. 3.50 (ISBN 0-8039-1493-8). Sage.

Intersex Child. Ed. by Nathalie Josso. (Pediatric & Adolescent Endocrinology Ser.: Vol. 8). 300p. 1980. soft cover 54.00 (ISBN 3-8055-0909-X). S Karger.

Interspecific Relationships in the Genus Monarda (Labiatae) Rainer W. Scora. (U. C. Publ. in Botany: Vol. 41). 1967. pap. 6.50x (ISBN 0-520-09014-4). U of Cal Pr.

Interstate Relations in Australia. Richard H. Leach. LC 65-11828. 200p. 1965. 9.50x (ISBN 0-8131-1101-3). U Pr of Ky.

Interstate Road Atlas, 1981. pap. 2.95 (ISBN 0-528-89215-0). Rand.

Interstellar Communication: Scientific Perspectives. Ed. by Cyril Ponnamperuma & A. G. W. Cameron. (Illus.). 272p. 1974. pap. text ed. 11.50 (ISBN 0-395-17809-6). HM.

Interstellar Medium. S. A. Kaplan & S. B. Pikelner. LC 70-85076. (Illus.). 1970. 22.50x (ISBN 0-674-46075-8). Harvard U Pr.

Interstellar Molecules. Ed. by Bryan H. Andrew. (International Astronomical Union Symposia: No. 87). 500p. 1980. PLB 76.50 (ISBN 90-277-1160-7, Pub. by D. Reidel); pap. 34.00 (ISBN 90-277-1161-5). Kluwer Boston.

Intersystemare Phonologie: Exemplarisch an diastratisch-Diatopischen Differenzierungen im Deutschen. W. H. Veith. x, 310p. 1972. 53.00x (ISBN 3-11-004350-5). De Gruyter.

Intertidal Invertebrates of California. Robert H. Morris et al. LC 77-92946. (Illus.). 904p. 1980. 30.00x (ISBN 0-8047-1045-7). Stanford U Pr.

Interurban Railways of the Bay Area. 20.00. Chatham Pub CA.

Interurbans Without Wires. Ed Keilty. Ed. by Mac Sebree. LC 79-53961. (Special Ser.: No. 66). 1979. 23.95 (ISBN 0-916374-38-6). Interurban.

Interval Mathematics: 1980. Karl L. Nickel. LC 80-25009. 1980. lib ed 29.50 (ISBN 0-12-518850-1). Acad Pr.

Intervening in Disadvantage: A Challenge for Nursery Education. Martin Woodhead. (General Ser.). (Orig.). 1976. pap. text ed. 8.25x (ISBN 0-85633-095-7, NFER). Humanities.

Intervention & Dollar Diplomacy in the Carribean, Nineteen Hundred - Nineteen Hundred Twenty-One. Dana G. Munro. LC 80-14089. (Illus.). ix, 553p. 1980. Repr. of 1964 ed. lib. bdg. 42.25x (ISBN 0-313-22510-9, MUIN). Greenwood.

Intervention & Negotiation: The United States & the Dominican Revolution. Jerome Slater. LC 70-95985. (Illus.). 1970. text ed. 22.50x (ISBN 0-06-013924-2). Irvington.

Intervention & Reflection: Basic Issues in Medical Ethics. Ron Munson. 1979. text ed. 19.95x (ISBN 0-534-00608-6). Wadsworth Pub.

Intervention & Revolution. rev. ed. Richard J. Barnet. 336p. 1972. pap. 1.75 o.p. (ISBN 0-451-61156-X, ME 1156, Ment). NAL.

Intervention at Archangel: Allied Intervention & Russian Counter-Revolution in North Russia, 1918-1920. Leonid I. Strakhovsky. LC 74-80594. 1971. Repr. 17.50 (ISBN 0-86527-105-4). Fertig.

Intervention in Human Services. 2nd ed. Eveline D. Schulman. LC 77-15488. (Illus.). 1978. pap. text ed. 13.95 (ISBN 0-8016-4369-4). Mosby.

Intervention or Abstention: The Dilemma of American Foreign Policy. Ed. by Robin Higham. LC 74-18934. 232p. 1975. 15.50x (ISBN 0-8131-1317-2). U Pr of Ky.

Intervention Strategies for Specialized Secondary Education. new ed. David A. Sabatino & August J. Mauser. 1978. text ed. 19.95 (ISBN 0-686-52747-X). Allyn.

Intervention Theory & Method: A Behavioral Science View. Chris Argyris. LC 79-114331. (Business Ser). 1970. text ed. 18.95 (ISBN 0-201-00342-2). A-W.

Interventions: A Cold War Novel of Love & Death. Patrick Breslin. LC 79-6091. 264p. 1980. 10.95 (ISBN 0-385-15816-5). Doubleday.

Intervertebrate Structure & Function. 2nd ed. E. J. Barrington. 1979. 32.95 o.p. (ISBN 0-470-26502-7); pap. 18.95x (ISBN 0-470-26503-5). Halsted Pr.

Interview. Jug Suraiya. 10.00 (ISBN 0-89253-635-7); flexible cloth 5.00 (ISBN 0-89253-636-5). Ind-US Inc.

Interview in Staff Appraisal. W. E. Beveridge. 1975. text ed. 16.50x (ISBN 0-04-658212-6). Allen Unwin.

Interview with Alan Page. Larry Batson. (Interviews Ser.). (Illus.). (gr. 3-8). 1977. PLB 6.75 (ISBN 0-87191-569-3). Creative Ed.

Interview with Bobby Clarke. John Gilbert. (Interviews Ser.). (Illus.). (gr. 3-8). 1977. PLB 6.75 (ISBN 0-87191-573-1). Creative Ed.

Interview with Bobby Knight. Larry Batson. (Interviews Ser.). (Illus.). (gr. 3-8). 1977. PLB 6.75 (ISBN 0-87191-574-X). Creative Ed.

Interview with Bobby Unser. John Gilbert. (Interviews Ser.). (Illus.). (gr. 3-8). 1977. PLB 6.75 (ISBN 0-87191-572-3). Creative Ed.

Interview with Jim Plunkett. Larry Batson. (Interviews Ser.). (Illus.). (gr. 3-8). 1977. PLB 6.75 (ISBN 0-87191-570-7). Creative Ed.

Interview with Lynne Cox. Gary Libman. (Interviews Ser.). (Illus.). (gr. 3-8). 1977. PLB 6.75 (ISBN 0-87191-571-5). Creative Ed.

Interview with Rod Carew. Larry Batson. (Interviews Ser.). (Illus.). (gr. 3-8). 1977. PLB 5.95 o.p. (ISBN 0-87191-568-5). Creative Ed.

Interview with the Dalai Lama. John F. Avedon. LC 80-83015. (Illus.). 83p. (Orig.). 1980. pap. 6.95 (ISBN 0-937896-00-4). Littlebird.

Interviewing: A Guide for Health Professionals. 3rd ed. Lewis Bernstein & Rosalyn S. Bernstein. 1974. pap. 11.95 (ISBN 0-8385-4307-3). ACC.

Interviewing & Communication in Social Work. Ed. by Crispin P. Cross. (Library of Social Work). 192p. 1974. 16.00 (ISBN 0-7100-7879-X); pap. 6.00 (ISBN 0-7100-7880-3). Routledge & Kegan.

Interviewing & Counselling. Robert Bessell. 1976. 22.50 (ISBN 0-7134-0965-7, Pub. by Batsford England). David & Charles.

Interviewing & Patient Care. 2nd ed. Allen J. Enelow & Scott N. Swisher. 1979. text ed. 11.95x (ISBN 0-19-502545-8); pap. text ed. 5.95x (ISBN 0-19-502546-6). Oxford U Pr.

Interviewing for the Decisionmaker. Lawrence R. O'Leary. LC 75-44322. 144p. 1976. 12.95 (ISBN 0-88229-215-3); pap. 7.95 (ISBN 0-88229-512-8). Nelson-Hall.

Interviewing in Market & Social Research. Joan M. Smith. 1972. 14.75 o.p. (ISBN 0-7100-7196-5). Routledge & Kegan.

Interviewing Skills for Supervisory Personnel. Lawrence L. Steinmetz. (Business Ser). (Illus.). 1971. pap. text ed. 8.95 (ISBN 0-201-07280-7). A-W.

Interviewing: Strategy, Techniques & Tactics. 3rd ed. R. L. Gordon. 1980. 18.50x (ISBN 0-256-02370-0). Dorsey.

Interviewing the Patient. George L. Engel & W. L. Morgan, Jr. LC 73-81834. 1973. pap. 9.50 (ISBN 0-7216-3393-5). Saunders.

Interviewing the People of Pennsylvania: A Conceptual Guide to Oral History. Carl Oblinger. pap. 3.00 (ISBN 0-911124-94-2). Pa Hist & Mus.

Interviews. Edward Dorn. Ed. by Donald Allen. LC 78-6100. (Writing: 38). 126p. 1980. pap. 5.00 (ISBN 0-87704-038-9). Four Seasons Foun.

Interviews with Francis Bacon. rev., enl. ed. David Sylvester. (Illus.). 176p. 1981. pap. 9.95 (ISBN 0-500-27196-8). Thames Hudson.

Interviews with Jesus. Jerry Vines. 1981. 3.25 (ISBN 0-8054-5180-3). Broadman.

Interwar Britain: A Social & Economic History. Sean Glynn & John Oxborrow. 1976. pap. text ed. 9.95x o.p. (ISBN 0-04-942041-0, 1974). Allen Unwin.

Interworld. Isidore Haiblum. 1977. pap. 1.50 o.s.i. (ISBN 0-440-12285-6). Dell.

Interwoven: A Pioneer Chronicle. Sallie R. Matthews. (M. K. Brown Range Life Ser: No. 13). (Illus.). 226p. 1973. Repr. 15.00 (ISBN 0-292-73800-5). U of Tex Pr.

Intestinal Absorption & Malabsorption. Ed. by T. Z. Csaky. LC 74-80532. 1975. 27.00 (ISBN 0-89004-020-6). Raven.

Intestinal Helminths. Ed. by James W. Smith. (Atlases of Diagnostic Medical Parasitology: 3). (Illus.). 1976. slide atlas 76.50 (ISBN 0-89189-066-1, 15-7-008-00); microfiche ed. 22.00 (ISBN 0-89189-048-3, 17-7-008-00). Am Soc Clinical.

Intestinal Protozoa. Ed. by James W. Smith. (Atlases of Diagnostic Medical Parasitology: 2). (Illus.). 1976. 76.50 (ISBN 0-89189-067-X, 15-007-00); microfiche ed. 22.00 (ISBN 0-89189-047-5, 17-7-007-00). Am Soc Clinical.

Intestinal Stomas. Ed. by Ian P. Todd. 1979. 28.50x (ISBN 0-433-32501-1). Intl Ideas.

Intimacies: Stars Share Their Confidences & Feelings. Alan Ebert. (Orig.). 1980. pap. 2.95 o.s.i. (ISBN 0-440-13653-9). Dell.

Intimacy. Henri J. M. Nouwen. LC 80-8906. 160p. 1981. pap. 3.95 (ISBN 0-06-066323-5, HarpR). Har-Row.

Intimacy & Ritual: A Study of Spiritualism, Mediums & Groups. Vieda Skultans. 114p. 1974. 14.00x (ISBN 0-7100-7760-2). Routledge & Kegan.

Intimacy, Commitments & Marriage: Development of Relationships. J. Ross Eshleman & Juanne N. Clarke. 1978. pap. text ed. 12.55 (ISBN 0-205-05932-5); instr's manual (ISBN 0-205-05934-1). Allyn.

Intimacy: Pastoral Psychological Essays. rev. ed. Henri J. Nouwen. LC 79-79241. 1977. pap. 2.95 o.p. (ISBN 0-8190-0614-9). Fides Claretian.

Intimate Art of Writing Poetry. Ottone M. Riccio. 240p. 1980. 14.95 (ISBN 0-13-476846-9, Spec); pap. 5.95 (ISBN 0-686-65793-4). P-H.

Intimate Enemy: How to Fight Fair in Love & Marriage. George R. Bach & Peter Wyden. 384p. 1981. pap. 2.95 (ISBN 0-380-00392-9, 54452). Avon.

Intimate Friendships. J. Ramey. 1976. 9.95 o.p. (ISBN 0-13-476903-1); pap. 3.95 o.p. (ISBN 0-13-476895-7). P-H.

Intimate Journals. Charles Baudelaire. Tr. by Christopher Isherwood from Fr. LC 75-1454. 1977. Repr. of 1930 ed. 13.25 (ISBN 0-86527-262-X). Fertig.

Intimate Letters of Carl Schurz, 1841-1869. Carl Schurz. Ed. by Joseph Schafer. LC 73-106989. (American Public Figures Ser). 1970. Repr. of 1928 ed. lib. bdg. 49.50 (ISBN 0-306-71876-6). Da Capo.

Intimate Memoirs of Barbara, the Duchess of Cleveland. Gaston M. Lafranehe. (Great Women of History Library). (Illus.). 93p. 1981. 19.85 (ISBN 0-89266-276-X). Am Classical Coll Pr.

Intimate Memoirs of Louise Renee De Kerouaile, Duchess of Portsmouth & Aubigny. Gaston M. Lafranche. (Great Women of History Library). (Illus.). 94p. 1981. 19.85 (ISBN 0-89266-275-1). Am Classical Coll Pr.

Intimate Portraits of Women in the Bible. Lee Roddy. LC 80-65432. 256p. 1980. 9.95 (ISBN 0-915684-64-0). Christian Herald.

Intimate Psychology of Stock Market Action. Kenneth L. Rushing. (Illus.). 1980. deluxe ed. 49.75 (ISBN 0-918968-55-0). Inst Econ Finan.

Intimate Relations. Murray S. Davis. LC 73-1859. (Illus.). 1973. 12.95 (ISBN 0-02-907020-1); pap. 3.95 (ISBN 0-02-907200-X). Free Pr.

Intimate Relationships: An Introduction to Marriage & the Family. Dennis K. Orthner. LC 80-21527. (Sociology Ser.). (Illus.). 496p. 1981. text ed. 16.95 (ISBN 0-201-05519-8). A-W.

Intimate Relationships: Marriage, Family & Lifestyles Through Literature. Ed. by Rose M. Somerville. (Family & Consumer Science Ser.). (Illus.). 480p. 1975. ref. ed. 16.95 (ISBN 0-13-476861-2); pap. 10.95 (ISBN 0-13-476879-5). P-H.

Intimations of Immortality. R. Crookall. 157p. 1965. 10.75 (ISBN 0-227-67662-9). Attic Pr.

Intimidators. Donald Hamilton. (Matt Helm Ser.). 1978. pap. 1.95 (ISBN 0-449-14110-1, GM). Fawcett.

Into a Black Sun. Ken Kaiko. Tr. by Cecilia S. Seigle from Japan. LC 80-50500. 216p. 1980. 9.95 (ISBN 0-87011-428-X). Kodansha.

Into Action. Ed. by Peter Abbs. (Approacher Ser.: No. 1). 1974. pap. text ed. 2.95x o.p. (ISBN 0-435-10021-1). Heinemann Ed.

Into Film, 2 vols. Laurence Goldstein & Jay Kaufman. 1976. Set. pap. 12.95 (ISBN 0-525-47315-7). Dutton.

Into Passion's Dawn. Michele DuBarry. (Loves of Angela Carlyle Ser.: No. 1). 1981. pap. 2.50 (ISBN 0-8439-0902-1, Leisure Bks). Nordon Pubns.

Into Print. John Gough. 1979. 19.95 (ISBN 0-7134-0739-5, Pub. by Batsford England). David & Charles.

Into Television. Ed. by G. Moir. LC 68-8870. 1969. pap. 7.50 (ISBN 0-08-013032-1). Pergamon.

Into the Bright Oasis: The Great Knight Reason. Sean Bentley. 1976. 2.50 (ISBN 0-918116-01-5). Jawbone Pr.

Into the Dark: Hannah Arendt & Totalitarianism. Stephen J. Whitfield. 352p. 1980. 18.95 (ISBN 0-87722-188-X). Temple U Pr.

Into the Strong City. Patrick O'Connor. 1979. 16.95 (ISBN 0-241-10065-8, Pub. by Hamish Hamilton England). David & Charles.

Into the Twentieth Century (1880-1939) The Educational Research Council. (American Adventure Concepts & Inquiry Ser.). (Orig.). (gr. 8). 1977. pap. 9.40 (ISBN 0-205-04631-2, 804631X). Allyn.

Into the Unknown: Eleven Tales of Imagination. Ed. by Terry Carr. LC 73-7826. 192p. 1973. 7.95 o.p. (ISBN 0-525-66342-8). Elsevier-Nelson.

Into the Woods: Exploring the Forest Ecosystem. Laurence Pringle. LC 72-92448. (Illus.). 64p. (gr. 3-6). 1973. 7.95 (ISBN 0-02-775320-4). Macmillan.

Into Thin Air: People Who Disappear. Paul Begg. (Illus.). 1979. 17.95 (ISBN 0-7153-7724-8). David & Charles.

Into This Land: Centennial History of the Cleveland Poor Clare Monestary of the Blessed Sacrament. Mary C. Koester. (Illus.). 274p. 1980. write for info. (ISBN 0-934906-03-3); pap. write for info. (ISBN 0-934906-04-1). R J Liederbach.

Into Tibet: The Early British Explorers. George Woodcock. (Great Travellers Ser.). (Illus.). 1971. 6.95 o.p. (ISBN 0-571-08394-3, Pub. by Faber & Faber). Merrimack Bk Serv.

Intonation & Music: The Semantics of Czech Prosody. Duncan B. Gardiner. LC 79-67358. (Physsardt Series in Prague Linguistics: No. 2). (Illus.). 1980. pap. 10.00 (ISBN 0-916062-04-X). Physsardt.

Intonation, Perception, & Language. Philip Lieberman. LC 67-13392. (Press Research Monographs: No. 38). 1967. 16.00x (ISBN 0-262-12024-0); pap. 4.95x o.p. (ISBN 0-262-62031-6). MIT Pr.

Intra - Firm Trade & the Developing Countries. Gerald K. Helleiner. 1981. 25.00 (ISBN 0-312-42538-4). St Martin.

Intra-Asian International Relations. Ed. by George T. Yu. LC 77-24382. (Westview Special Studies on China & East Asia-South & Southeast Asia). 1978. lib. bdg. 20.00x (ISBN 0-89158-125-1). Westview.

Intra-Industry Trade. H. G. Grubel & P. J. Lloyd. LC 74-13576. 205p. 1975. 34.95 (ISBN 0-470-33000-7). Halsted Pr.

Intra Muros: My Dream of Heaven. Rebecca R. Springer. LC 78-67820. 1980. pap. 1.75 (ISBN 0-932484-01-8). Book Searchers.

Intra-National Transfer of Technology. (Illus.). 1976. 13.75 (ISBN 92-833-1038-1, APO33, APO). Unipub.

Intra Urban Market Geography: A Case Study of Patna. A. Sami. 219p. 1980. text ed. 15.75x (ISBN 0-391-02121-4). Humanities.

Intracellular Protein Catabolism, III. Ed. by Vito Turk et al. LC 77-72034. 368p. 1977. 35.00 (ISBN 0-306-31037-6, Plenum Pr). Plenum Pub.

Intracellular Transport. International Society For Cell Biology. Ed. by Katherine B. Warren. (Proceedings: Vol. 5). 1967. 49.00 (ISBN 0-12-611905-8). Acad Pr.

Intracity Residential Mobility in an Industrial City: A Case Study of Ludhiana. Sunita V. Auluck. 180p. 1980. text ed. 10.25x (ISBN 0-391-02134-6). Humanities.

Intracranial Pressure Two: Proceedings. International Symposium on Intracranial Pressure, 2nd. Ed. by N. Lundberg & U. Poten. (Illus.). 560p. 1975. 37.50 (ISBN 0-387-07199-7). Springer-Verlag.

Intrahepatic Cholestasis. Ed. by P. Gentilini et al. LC 75-10551. 199p. 1975. 24.50 (ISBN 0-89004-049-4). Raven.

Intramural Administration: Theory & Practice. James A. Peterson. 384p. 1976. 15.95 (ISBN 0-13-477232-6). P-H.

Intramural Director's Guide to Program Evaluation. Tyler Coulbourn. 104p. (Orig.). 1981. pap. price not set (ISBN 0-918438-67-5). Leisure Pr.

Intramural-Recreational Sports: Programming & Administration. 5th ed. Pat Mueller & John W. Reznik. LC 78-10122. 1979. text ed. 18.95 (ISBN 0-471-04911-5). Wiley.

Intramural Sports: Organization & Administration. Ronald W. Hyatt. LC 76-29694. (Illus.). 1977. pap. text ed. 10.95 (ISBN 0-8016-2320-0). Mosby.

Intramurals: Their Organization & Administration. 2nd ed. L. Means. 1973. ref. ed. 16.95 (ISBN 0-13-477216-4). P-H.

Intrance: Fundamental Psychological Problems of the Inner & Outer World. C. J. Schuurman. Tr. by Louise E. Boer-Hoff from Dutch. LC 78-70618. (Illus.). 1981. pap. 6.95 (ISBN 0-89793-023-1). Hunter Hse.

Intraocular Lens Manual. rev. 3rd ed. Ed. by Dennis D. Shepard. LC 80-51743. 464p. 1980. 40.00 (ISBN 0-9601234-2-3). D D Shepard.

Intraocular Lenses. Wilensky. (Illus.). 19.50 (ISBN 0-8385-4304-9). ACC.

Intraocular Light Scattering: Theory & Clinical Application. David Miller & George Benedek. (Illus.). 132p. 1973. text ed. 11.75 (ISBN 0-398-02665-3). C C Thomas.

Intrauterine Contraception, Vol 1. Max Elstein & Richard Sparks. Ed. by Michael Briggs. (Annual Research Reviews Ser.). 1978. 12.00 (ISBN 0-88831-021-8). Eden Med Res.

Intrauterine Devices Abstracts: A Guide to the Literature, 1976-1979. Helen K. Kolbe. (Population Information Library Ser.: Vol. 1). 575p. 1980. 75.00 (ISBN 0-306-65191-2, IFI). Plenum Pub.

Intravascular Catherization. Henry A. Zimmerman. (Illus.). 1304p. 1972. pap. 57.50 spiral (ISBN 0-398-02148-1). C C Thomas.

Intravenous Nutrition in the High Risk Infants. Robert W. Winters & Eileen G. Hasselmeyer. LC 74-26712. (Clinical Pediatrics, Maternal & Child Health Ser). 528p. 1975. 48.95 (ISBN 0-471-95500-0, Pub. by Wiley Medical). Wiley.

Intravenous Therapy: A Handbook for Practice. Charlene D. Coco. LC 79-19930. 1980. pap. text ed. 10.50 (ISBN 0-8016-0995-X). Mosby.

Intrepid Sailor. Samuel Sobel. LC 80-13026. (Illus.). 1980. 12.95 (ISBN 0-936082-04-6). Cresset Pubs.

Intrepretation of Electrophoretic Patterns of Serum Proteins, Lipoproteins, Isoenzymes, & Hemoglobins. Wolf. 1981. price not set (ISBN 0-89352-035-7). Masson Pub.

Intriguing Innocent. Rebecca Ashley. (Orig.). 1980. pap. 1.50 o.p. (ISBN 0-440-10258-8). Dell.

Intrinsic Inertia Universe. James R. Taylor. (Illus.). xii, 244p. 1971. 10.95 o.p. (ISBN 0-685-25833-5). Trend House.

Intrinsic Mutagenesis: A Genetic Approach to Aging. Macfarlane Burnet. LC 74-6978. 236p. 1974. 36.95 (ISBN 0-471-12440-0, Pub. by Wiley-Medical). Wiley.

Intrinsic Neuronal Organization of the Vestibular Nuclear Complex in the Cat: A Golgi Study. E. Hauglie-Hanssen. LC 64-20582. (Advances in Anatomy, Embryology & Cell Biology: Vol. 40, Pt. 5). (Illus.). 1968. pap. 25.40 o.p. (ISBN 0-387-04089-7). Springer-Verlag.

Intro Twelve. Ed. by Tony Ardizzone. (Intro Ser.). 244p. 1981. pap. 6.95 (ISBN 0-936266-02-3). Assoc Writing Progs.

Introd. Operations Research Models. Cooper. 1977. 18.95 (ISBN 0-7216-2688-2). Dryden Pr.

Introduccion a la Literatura Espanola. Francisco P. Rivera & Mario Hurtado. (gr. 11-12). 1976. pap. text ed. 7.95 (ISBN 0-88345-275-8). Regents Pub.

Introduccion a la Psicologia Fisiologica. Richard F. Thompson. (Span.). 1977. pap. text ed. 12.00 (ISBN 0-06-317100-7, IntlDept). Har-Row.

Introduccion Al Antiguo Testamento. C. T. Francisco. Tr. by Juan J. Lacue. Orig. Title: Introducing the Old Testament. 350p. (Span.). 1980. pap. 4.25 (ISBN 0-311-04010-1). Casa Bautista.

Introduccion Al Calculo Elemental. J. J. Del Grande & G. F. Duff. 1976. text ed. 7.20x (ISBN 0-06-310070-3, IntlDept). Har-Row.

Introduccion Al Estudio Del Nuevo Testamento. H. I. Hester. Tr. by Felix Benlliure from Eng. Orig. Title: Heart of the New Testament. 366p. (Span.). 1980. pap. 6.60 (ISBN 0-311-04330-5). Casa Bautista.

Introduccion E Historica De la Filosofia. 3rd ed. Humberto Pinera-Llera. LC 89-65885. (Coleccion Textos). (Illus.). 348p. (Span.). 1980. pap. 12.95 (ISBN 0-89729-254-5). Ediciones.

Introduccion Popular Al Estudio De las Sagradas Escrituras. A. R. Miles. Orig. Title: Introduction to the Bible. 234p. (Span.). 1970. pap. write for info o.p. (ISBN 0-89922-007-X). Edit Caribe.

Introducing Alcohol Education in the Elementary School, K-4. 1978. non-members 1.50 (ISBN 0-917160-11-8). Am Sch Health.

Introducing Astronomy. 2nd ed. J. B. Sidgwick. (Illus., Orig.). 1973. pap. 6.50 (ISBN 0-571-04823-4, Pub. by Faber & Faber). Merrimack Bk Serv.

Introducing Beads. Mary Seyd. 1973. 14.95 (ISBN 0-7134-2439-7, Pub. by Batsford England). David & Charles.

Introducing Buddhism. Kodo Matsunami. LC 75-28970. (Illus.). 304p. 1976. pap. 7.50 (ISBN 0-8048-1192-X). C E Tuttle.

Introducing C. B. Greenfield. Lucille Kallen. LC 80-25043. 363p. Repr. of 1979 ed. large print ed. 11.95 (ISBN 0-89621-260-2). Thorndike Pr.

Introducing Chemistry. Hazel Rossotti. 1975. pap. 3.95 (ISBN 0-14-021864-5, Pelican). Penguin.

Introducing Christian Ethics. Henlee H. Barnette. LC 61-5629. 1961. 6.50 (ISBN 0-8054-6102-7). Broadman.

Introducing Computers. G. F. Schaefler. LC 73-14925. 121p. 1974. 10.50x o.p. (ISBN 0-471-75695-4). Wiley.

Introducing Corporate Planning. 2nd ed. D. E. Hussey. (Pergamon International Library). 1979. 27.00 (ISBN 0-08-022491-1); pap. 17.75 (ISBN 0-08-022485-7). Pergamon.

Introducing Corporate Planning. David E. Hussey. 220p. 1976. text ed. 7.15 o.p. (ISBN 0-08-017793-X). Pergamon.

Introducing Cultural Geography. 2nd ed. J. E. Spencer & W. L. Thomas. LC 77-20230. 1978. text ed. 20.95x (ISBN 0-471-81631-0); tchrs.' manual avail. (ISBN 0-471-03422-3). Wiley.

Introducing Culture. 3rd ed. Ernest Schusky & T. Patrick Culbert. (P-H Anthropology Ser.). (Illus.). 1978. pap. 9.95 ref. (ISBN 0-13-477240-7). P-H.

Introducing Data Communications Standards. P. R. Scott. (Illus.). 226p. 1979. pap. 25.00x (ISBN 0-85012-220-1). Intl Pubns Serv.

Introducing David Jones. Ed. by John Matthias. 240p. 1980. 18.95 (ISBN 0-571-11526-8, Pub. by Faber & Faber); pap. 8.95 (ISBN 0-571-11525-X, Pub. by Faber & Faber). Merrimack Bk Serv.

Introducing Design in Embroidery. Betty Chicken. (Illus.). 1971. 7.50 o.p. (ISBN 0-8231-4028-8). Branford.

Introducing Drawing Techniques. Robin Capon. LC 73-14367. (Illus.). 96p. 1974. 7.50 o.p. (ISBN 0-8008-4174-3). Taplinger.

Introducing Eastern Wildflowers. E. B. Kavasch. (Northeast Color Ser.). (Illus.). 50p. 1981. pap. 3.95 (ISBN 0-88839-092-0). Hancock Hse.

Introducing Eavan Boland: Poems. Eavan Boland. LC 80-84833. (Ontario Review Press Poetry Ser.). 80p. 1981. 9.95 (ISBN 0-86538-009-0); pap. 4.95 (ISBN 0-86538-010-4). Ontario Rev NJ.

Introducing Expanded Polystyrene. Alan Barnsley. 1973. 14.95 (ISBN 0-7134-2442-7, Pub. by Batsford England). David & Charles.

Introducing Finger Painting. Guy Scott. 1973. 17.95 (ISBN 0-7134-2432-X, Pub. by Batsford England). David & Charles.

Introducing Geology. 2nd ed. D. V. Ager. (Illus.). 1975. 12.95 (ISBN 0-571-04857-9, Pub. by Faber & Faber); pap. 8.95 (ISBN 0-571-04858-7). Merrimack Bk Serv.

Introducing Graphic Techniques. Robin Capon. 1979. 17.95 (ISBN 0-7134-2435-4, Pub. by Batsford England). David & Charles.

Introducing Handbuilt Pottery. Tony Jolly. (Illus.). 96p. 1974. 9.95 o.p. (ISBN 0-8230-6194-9). Watson-Guptill.

Introducing India. Raj Thapar. 1966. pap. 2.50x (ISBN 0-210-22505-X). Asia.

Introducing Japan. Donald Richie. LC 77-75966. (Illus.). 1978. 14.95 (ISBN 0-87011-308-9). Kodansha.

Introducing Jewelry Making. John Crawford. LC 69-10796. (Introducing Ser). (Illus.). (gr. 1-4). 1969. 9.95 o.p. (ISBN 0-8230-6200-7). Watson-Guptill.

Introducing Macrame. 1974. pap. 13.50 (ISBN 0-7134-2446-X, Pub. by Batsford England). David & Charles.

Introducing Macrobiotic Cooking. Wendy Esko. LC 79-1957. (Illus.). 1979. pap. 8.95 (ISBN 0-87040-458-X). Japan Pubns.

Introducing Oil Painting. Michael Pope. 1977. pap. 16.95 (ISBN 0-7134-0238-5, Pub. by Batsford England). David & Charles.

Introducing Op Art. John Lancaster. LC 72-10428. (Illus.). 112p. 1973. 9.95 o.p. (ISBN 0-8230-6267-8). Watson-Guptill.

Introducing Op Art. John Lancaster. 1973. 16.95 (ISBN 0-7134-2438-9, Pub. by Batsford England). David & Charles.

Introducing Relief Printing. John O'Conner. LC 72-2115. 128p. 1973. 9.95 o.p. (ISBN 0-8230-6299-6). Watson-Guptill.

Introducing Root Locus. P. Dransfield & D. F. Haber. (Illus.). 150p. 1973. 12.95x (ISBN 0-521-20118-7). Cambridge U Pr.

Introducing Social Change: A Manual for Community Development. 2nd ed. Conrad M. Arensberg & Arthur H. Niehoff. LC 78-14936. 1971. 16.95x (ISBN 0-202-01072-4). Aldine Pub.

Introducing Social Policy. Ed. by David C. Marsh. 1979. 20.00x (ISBN 0-7100-0132-0); pap. 9.95 (ISBN 0-7100-0133-9). Routledge & Kegan.

Introducing Social Psychology. Sampson. 1980. 12.95 (ISBN 0-531-05413-6, BB02); pap. 9.95 (ISBN 0-531-05627-9, BB11, New Viewpoints). Watts.

Introducing Sociology. James M. Henslin. LC 74-12595. (Illus.). 1975. text ed. 12.95 (ISBN 0-02-914430-2); student's guide 3.95 (ISBN 0-02-914300-4). Free Pr.

Introducing Sociology: Selected Readings. Ed. by James M. Henslin. LC 74-16903. 1975. pap. text ed. 4.95 (ISBN 0-02-914650-X). Free Pr.

Introducing Southern Baptists. C. B. Hastings. 176p. (Orig.). 1981. pap. 6.95 (ISBN 0-8091-2364-9). Paulist Pr.

Introducing Statistics. Hyman Alterman. (Illus.). 1968. 8.95 o.p. (ISBN 0-571-08429-X, Pub. by Faber & Faber). Merrimack Bk Serv.

Introducing Structures. A. J. Francis. (International Series in Structure & Solid Body Mechanics). 1980. 34.00 (ISBN 0-08-022701-5); pap. 12.00 (ISBN 0-08-022702-3). Pergamon.

Introducing Systems Design. Enid Squire. LC 78-18651. 1979. pap. text ed. 13.95 (ISBN 0-201-07421-4). A-W.

Introducing the Alto Clef for Trombone. Reginald Fink. 1969. pap. 3.95 (ISBN 0-918194-04-0). Accura.

Introducing the Book of Common Prayer. Charles P. Price. LC 77-6125. 1977. pap. 1.75 (ISBN 0-8164-2171-4). Crossroad NY.

Introducing the Electronic Office. S. G. Price. (Illus.). 161p. 1979. pap. 22.50x (ISBN 0-85012-204-X). Intl Pubns Serv.

Introducing the Existentialists. Robert C. Solomon. (Philosophical Dialogues Ser.). 80p. 1981. lib. bdg. 9.50 (ISBN 0-915145-00-6); pap. text ed. 2.50 (ISBN 0-915145-01-4). Hackett Pub.

Introducing the German Idealists. Robert C. Solomon. (Philosophical Dialogue Ser.). 80p. 1981. lib. bdg. 9.50 (ISBN 0-915145-02-2); pap. text ed. 2.50 (ISBN 0-915145-03-0). Hackett Pub.

Introducing the Lessons of the Church Year: A Guide for Lay Readers & Congregations. Frederick Borsch. 1978. 8.95 (ISBN 0-8164-0396-1). Crossroad NY.

Introducing the Song Sheet. Helen Westin. LC 75-40331. (Illus.). 176p. 1976. 14.95 o.p. (ISBN 0-8407-4325-4). Nelson.

Introducing the Tenor Clef for Trombone. Reginald H. Fink. 1968. pap. 3.95 (ISBN 0-918194-03-2). Accura.

Introducing Tobacco Education in the Elementary School, K-4. 1978. non-members 1.50 (ISBN 0-917160-10-X). Am Sch Health.

Introducing Tom Wayman, Selected Poems 1973-80. Tom Wayman. LC 80-20260. (Ontario Review Press Poetry Ser.). 144p. 1980. 10.95 (ISBN 0-86538-003-1); pap. 5.95 (ISBN 0-86538-004-X). Ontario Rev NJ.

Introducing Visual Sociology. Timothy J. Curry & Alfred C. Clarke. (Illus.). 1978. pap. text ed. 6.50 (ISBN 0-8403-2267-4, 40226701). Kendall-Hunt.

Introducing Watercolour Painting. Michael Pope. 1973. 19.95 (ISBN 0-7134-2434-6, Pub. by Batsford England). David & Charles.

Introduction. William Hordern. (New Directios in Theology Today: Vol. 1). 1966. pap. 4.95 (ISBN 0-664-24706-7). Westminster.

Introduction a la linguistique. G. H. Gleason. (Sciences humaines et sociales). (Fr). pap. 20.95 (ISBN 2-03-070351-6, 3652). Larousse.

Introduction a la Poesie Francaise. H. A. Grubbs & J. W. Kneller. 1962. 14.95x (ISBN 0-471-00217-8). Wiley.

Introduction a la textologie: Verification...etablissement, edition des textes. R. Laufer. (Collection L). 160p. (Orig., Fr.). 1972. pap. 13.95 (ISBN 2-03-036006-6). Larousse.

Introduction & Geology, 2 vols. H. H. Read & Janet Watson. Incl. Vol. 1. Principles. 2nd ed. LC 76-50637. 1977. 27.95 (ISBN 0-470-99031-7); Vol. 2, 2 pts. LC 75-501. 1975; Pt. 1. Early Stages of Earth History. 221p. 19.95 (ISBN 0-470-71165-5); Pt. 2. Later Stages of Earth History. 371p. 24.95 (ISBN 0-470-71166-3). Halsted Pr.

Introduction & Guide: Japanese & Chinese Studies & Documents, Vol. 1. Ed. by Donald S. Detwiler & Charles B. Burdick. (War in Asia & the Pacific Ser., 1937 to 1949). 460p. 1980. lib. bdg. 60.50 (ISBN 0-8240-3285-3). Garland Pub.

Introduction & Guide to the Marine Bluegreen Algae. Harold J. Humm & Susanne B. Wicks. LC 79-24488. 1980. 23.50 (ISBN 0-471-05217-5, Pub. by Wiley Interscience). Wiley.

Introduction & Literature Guide to Mixing. Eugene T. Sweeney. (BHRA Fluid Engineering Ser., Vol. 5). 1978. pap. 21.00 (ISBN 0-900983-77-9, Dist. by Air Science Co.). BHRA Fluid.

Introduction Five: Stories by New Writers. 1974. 8.95 (ISBN 0-571-10478-9, Pub. by Faber & Faber). Merrimack Bk Serv.

Introduction Four: Stories by New Writers. 1971. 8.95 (ISBN 0-571-09535-6, Pub. by Faber & Faber). Merrimack Bk Serv.

Introduction into Physicke. Christopher Langton. LC 75-25797. (English Experience Ser.: No. 281). 1970. Repr. of 1550 ed. 16.00 (ISBN 90-221-0281-5). Walter J Johnson.

Introduction of Macromolecules into Viable Mammalian Cells. Ed. by Renato Baserga et al. LC 79-91743. (Wistar Symposium Ser.: Vol. 1). 354p. 1980. 26.00x (ISBN 0-8451-2000-X). A R Liss.

Introduction of Marine Environments. 2nd ed. Robert A. Zottoli. 1978. pap. text ed. 11.50 (ISBN 0-8016-5694-X). Mosby.

Introduction Quant. Meth. Dec. Marketing. 2nd ed. R. Trueman. 1977. 19.95 (ISBN 0-03-018391-X). Dryden Pr.

Introduction Seven: Stories by New Writers. 256p. 1981. 13.95 (ISBN 0-571-11680-9, Pub. by Faber & Faber). Merrimack Bk Serv.

Introduction to a Christian Psycho-Therapy. 2nd ed. J. A. Murray. 291p. 1947. text ed. 4.95 (ISBN 0-567-02202-1). Attic Pr.

Introduction to a Theological Theory of Language. Gerhard Ebeling. Tr. by R. A. Wilson from Ger. LC 72-87057. 224p. 1973. 6.50 (ISBN 0-8006-0256-0, 1-256). Fortress.

Introduction to a University Library Administration. 3rd rev. ed. James Thompson. 256p. 1979. 18.75 (ISBN 0-89664-407-3, Pub. by K G Saur). Shoe String.

Introduction to Abdominal Surgery: Fifty Clinical Studies. Clarence J. Schein. (Illus.). 416p. 1981. pap. text ed. write for info. (ISBN 0-06-142381-5, Harper Medical). Har-Row.

Introduction to Abstract Algebra. C. R. Clapham. (Library of Mathematics). 1969. pap. 5.00 (ISBN 0-7100-6626-0). Routledge & Kegan.

Introduction to Abstract Algebra. J. T. Moore. 1975. text ed. 20.95 (ISBN 0-12-505750-4). Acad Pr.

Introduction to Abstract Algebra. Thomas A. Whitelaw. (Illus.). 1978. pap. text ed. 16.95x (ISBN 0-216-90488-9). Intl Ideas.

Introduction to Abstract Algebra, Vol. 1. 2nd ed. F. M. Hall. LC 75-185565. 314p. 1972. 27.50x (ISBN 0-521-08484-9). Cambridge U Pr.

Introduction to Abstract Algebra, Vol. 1. 2nd ed. F. M. Hall. (Illus.). 314p. 1980. pap. 12.50x (ISBN 0-521-29861-X). Cambridge U Pr.

Introduction to Abstract Algebra, Vol. 2. F. M. Hall. LC 66-10040. (Illus.). 1969. text ed. 35.50x (ISBN 0-521-07055-4). Cambridge U Pr.

Introduction to Abstract Algebra, Vol. 2. F. M. Hall. (Illus.). 400p. 1980. pap. 15.95x (ISBN 0-521-29862-8). Cambridge U Pr.

Introduction to Abstract Mathematics. T. A. Bick. 1971. text ed. 18.50 o.p. (ISBN 0-12-095850-3). Acad Pr.

Introduction to Accounting: Economic Measurement for Decisions. W. J. Bruns. 1971. 16.95 (ISBN 0-201-00676-6); instructor's manual 2.95 (ISBN 0-201-00677-4). A-W.

Introduction to Accounting for Decision Making & Control. Edward L. Summers. 1974. text ed. 16.50x o.p. (ISBN 0-256-01499-X). Irwin.

Introduction to Acoustical Space Time Information Processing. Alan A. Winder & Charles J. Loda. (Illus.). 200p. 1980. pap. 14.95 (ISBN 0-932146-04-X). Peninsula.

Introduction to Acoustics. R. D. Ford. (Illus.). 1970. pap. text ed. 15.00x (ISBN 0-444-20078-9). Intl Ideas.

Introduction to Acupuncture Anesthesia. William C. Lowe. 1973. 6.00 o.p. (ISBN 0-87488-753-4). Med Exam.

Introduction to Administration for Social Workers. Joyce Warham. (Orig.). 1967. pap. text ed. 6.50x (ISBN 0-391-00394-1). Humanities.

Introduction to Advocacy: Brief Writing & Oral Argument in Moot Court Competition. 3rd ed. Harvard Law School Board of Student Advisers. 100p. 1980. text ed. write for info. (ISBN 0-88277-019-5). Foundation Pr.

Introduction to African Culture: General Aspects. 184p. 1980. pap. 7.00 (ISBN 92-3-101478-1, U936, Pub. by UNESCO). Unipub.

Introduction to African Literature. 2nd ed. Ulli Beier. 1979. pap. text ed. 9.95 (ISBN 0-582-64228-0). Longman.

Introduction to African Pastureland Production. 192p. 1981. pap. 11.00 (ISBN 92-5-100872-8, F2075, FAO). Unipub.

Introduction to Agri-Business Management. 2nd ed. Walter J. Wills. LC 78-62100. 1979. 14.65 (ISBN 0-8134-2055-5, 2055); text ed. 11.00x (ISBN 0-685-34807-5). Interstate.

Introduction to Agribusiness. N. Omri Rawlins. (Illus.). 1980. text ed. 11.95 (ISBN 0-13-477703-4). P-H.

Introduction to Agribusiness Management. Don L. Long et al. Ed. by Jasper S. Lee. (Careeer Preparation for Agriculture-Agribusiness). 1979. pap. text ed. 5.80x (ISBN 0-07-038665-X, G); activity guide 3.60x (ISBN 0-07-038666-8); tchrs manual & key 2.75x (ISBN 0-07-038667-6). McGraw.

Introduction to Agricultural Economic Analysis. Charles E. Bishop & W. D. Toussaint. LC 58-12715. (Illus.). 1958. 20.50 (ISBN 0-471-07557-4). Wiley.

Introduction to Agricultural Engineering. L. O. Roth et al. (Illus.). 1975. pap. text ed. 19.50 (ISBN 0-87055-302-X). AVI.

Introduction to Airline Economics. William E. O'Conner. LC 77-7809. (Praeger Special Studies). 1978. 18.95 (ISBN 0-03-022416-0). Praeger.

Introduction to Algebraic & Abelian Functions. Serge Lang. LC 72-1765. 1972. text ed. 16.50 (ISBN 0-201-04163-4, Adv Bk Prog). A-W.

Introduction to Algebraic Geometry. 3rd ed. Serge A. Lang. 1958. 16.50 (ISBN 0-201-04164-2, Adv Bk Prog). A-W.

Introduction to Algebraic Structures. Azriel Rosenfeld. LC 68-13895. 1968. 18.95x (ISBN 0-8162-7304-9). Holden-Day.

Introduction to Algebraic System Theory. Michael K. Sain. LC 80-522. (Mathematics in Science & Engineering Ser.). 1981. write for info. (ISBN 0-12-614850-3). Acad Pr.

Introduction to ALGOL. F. L. Bauer et al. 1964. ref. ed. 13.95 (ISBN 0-13-477828-6). P-H.

Introduction to Alkaloids: A Biogenetic Approach. Goeffrey A. Cordell. 1056p. 1981. 50.00 (ISBN 0-471-03478-9, Pub. by Wiley-Interscience). Wiley.

Introduction to American Archaeology, Vol. 1: North & Middle America. Gordon R. Willey. 1966. text ed. 26.95 (ISBN 0-13-477836-7). P-H.

Introduction to American Archaeology, Vol. 2: South America. Gordon R. Willey. (Illus.). 1971. text ed. 26.95 (ISBN 0-13-477851-0). P-H.

Introduction to American Business Enterprise: Introductory Text & Cases. 3rd ed. Jerry B. Poe. 1976. text ed. 16.95 o.p. (ISBN 0-256-01822-7); pap. 6.50x wkbk o.p. (ISBN 0-256-01823-5). Irwin.

Introduction to American Business Enterprises. 4th ed. Jerry B. Poe. 1980. 16.95x (ISBN 0-256-02280-1). Irwin.

Introduction to American Corrections. Paul Clare & John Kramer. 1976. text ed. 15.95 (ISBN 0-205-05465-X, 825465-6); instructor's manual free (ISBN 0-205-05466-8, 8254664). Allyn.

Introduction to American Criminal Procedure. abr. ed. Stephen A. Saltzburg. LC 80-52110. (American Casebook Ser.). 725p. 1980. pap. text ed. 13.95 (ISBN 0-8299-2106-0). West Pub.

Introduction to American Education: A Human Relations Approach. George Henderson. LC 77-18609. 1979. 13.95 (ISBN 0-8061-1458-4). U of Okla Pr.

Introduction to American Land Law: Cases & Materials. George Lefcoe. LC 74-2945. (Contemporary Legal Education Ser). 1974. text ed. 18.00 (ISBN 0-672-81893-0, Bobbs-Merrill Law). Michie.

Introduction to American Law. Timothy Walker. LC 79-172176. (American Constitutional & Legal History Ser). 672p. 1972. Repr. of 1837 ed. lib. bdg. 59.50 (ISBN 0-306-70224-X). Da Capo.

Introduction to American Literature. Jorge L. Borges. Ed. by Robert O. Evans & L. Clark Keating. Tr. by Robert O. Evans & L. Clark Keating. LC 73-147854. 108p. 1971. 8.00x (ISBN 0-8131-1247-8). U Pr of Ky.

Introduction to American Poetry & Prose. Ed. by Norman Foerster et al. LC 72-140999. 1971. text ed. 17.50 (ISBN 0-395-04457-X). HM.

Introduction to Analytic Geometry & Calculus. rev. ed. A. C. Burdette. 1973. text ed. 19.95 (ISBN 0-12-142252-6). Acad Pr.

Introduction to Analytic Geometry & Calculus. H. M. Dadourian. (Illus.). 1949. 15.95x o.p. (ISBN 0-8260-2285-5). Wiley.

Introduction to Analytic Geometry & the Calculus. H. M. Dadourian. 256p. 1981. Repr. of 1949 ed. lib. bdg. price not set (ISBN 0-89874-267-6). Krieger.

Introduction to Analytical Chemistry. 2nd ed. Schenk et al. 540p. 1981. text ed. 21.95 (ISBN 0-205-07236-4, 6872360); student's manual. Allyn.

Introduction to Ancient Egypt. T. G. James. (British Museum Bks.). 286p. 1979. 20.00 (ISBN 0-374-83343-5); pap. 8.95 (ISBN 0-374-84339-2). FS&G.

Introduction to Anesthesia: The Principles of Safe Practice. 5th ed. Robert D. Dripps et al. LC 76-51011. (Illus.). 1977. text ed. 19.95 (ISBN 0-7216-3193-2). Saunders.

Introduction to Anesthesiology. 1977. pap. text ed. 24.50 (ISBN 0-89147-047-6). CAS.

Introduction to Anglo-Saxon England. 2nd ed. P. H. Blair. LC 77-71404. (Illus.). 1977. 47.95 (ISBN 0-521-21650-8); pap. 10.95x (ISBN 0-521-29219-0). Cambridge U Pr.

Introduction to Animal Behavior: Ethology's First Century. 2nd ed. Peter H. Klopfer & Jack P. Hailman. (Biological Sciences Ser). (Illus.). 304p. 1974. 18.95x (ISBN 0-13-477935-5). P-H.

Introduction to Animal Husbandry. J. O. King. LC 78-4883. 1978. pap. 28.95 (ISBN 0-470-26338-5). Halsted Pr.

Introduction to Animal Husbandry in the Tropics. 3rd ed. G. Williamson & W. J. Payne. (Tropical Agriculture Ser.). (Illus.). 1978. text ed. 31.00x (ISBN 0-582-46813-2). Longman.

Introduction to Animal Physiology & Physiological Genetics. E. M. Pantelouris. 1966. text ed. 29.00 o.p. (ISBN 0-08-011722-8); pap. text ed. 15.50 o.p. (ISBN 0-08-018981-4). Pergamon.

Introduction to Anisotropic Elasticity Theory of Dislocations. J. W. Steeds. (Monographs on the Physics & Chemistry of Materials). (Illus.). 286p. 1973. 42.00x (ISBN 0-19-851341-0). Oxford U Pr.

Introduction to Anthropology, 2 vols. 3rd ed. Victor Barnouw. Incl. Vol. 1. Physical Anthropology & Archaeology (ISBN 0-256-02000-0); Vol. 2. Ethnology (ISBN 0-256-02001-9). 1978. pap. text ed. 12.95x ea. Dorsey.

Introduction to Anthropology. E. Miller & C. Weitz. 1979. 17.95 (ISBN 0-13-478008-6); study guide 6.95 (ISBN 0-13-478016-7). P-H.

Introduction to Antiques. Therle Hughes. (Illus.). 1978. 12.00 (ISBN 0-600-30346-2). Transatlantic.

Introduction to APL & Computer Programming. Edward Harms & Michael P. Zabinski. LC 76-20587. 1977. pap. text ed. 16.95 (ISBN 0-471-35201-2); instructor's manual 1.75 (ISBN 0-471-01940-2). Wiley.

Introduction to Applicable Mathematics: Elementary Analysis, Vol. 1. Fred A. Hinchey. LC 80-18569. 290p. 1981. 19.95 (ISBN 0-470-27041-1). Halsted Pr.

Introduction to Applied Drawing. rev. ed. E. M. Hale et al. (gr. 7 up). 1962. pap. 4.48 (ISBN 0-87345-051-5). McKnight.

Introduction to Applied Econometric Analysis. R. F. Wynn & K. Holden. LC 74-3665. 245p. 1974. text ed. 26.95 (ISBN 0-470-96898-2). Halsted Pr.

Introduction to Applied Economics. 3rd ed. J. L. Hanson. (Illus.). 512p. 1980. pap. text ed. 17.50x (ISBN 0-7121-0963-3). Intl Ideas.

Introduction to Applied Economics. G. Douglas Vaughan. 1974. 19.95x (ISBN 0-434-92190-4); pap. 12.95x (ISBN 0-434-92191-2). Intl Ideas.

Introduction to Applied Physics. Abraham Marcus & James R. Thrower. 450p. 1980. text ed. 17.95x (ISBN 0-534-00825-9, Breton Pubs). Wadsworth Pub.

Introduction to Applied Probability. Ed. by Paul E. Pfeiffer & David A. Schum. 1973. text ed. 20.95 (ISBN 0-12-553150-8); instrs' manual 3.00 (ISBN 0-12-553156-7). Acad Pr.

Introduction to Applied Probability & Random Processes. John B. Thomas. (Illus.). 1981. Repr. of 1971 ed. lib. bdg. write for info. (ISBN 0-89874-232-3). Krieger.

Introduction to Applied Solid State Physics: Topics on the Applications of Semiconductors, Superconductors, & the Nonlinear Optical Properties of Solids. Richard Dalven. (Illus.). 345p. 1980. 27.50 (ISBN 0-306-40385-4, Plenum Pr). Plenum Pub.

Introduction to Art Therapy: Studies of the "Free" Art Expression of Behavior Problem Children & Adolescents As a Means of Diagnosis & Therapy. rev. ed. Margaret Naumburg. LC 73-78074. (Illus.). 225p. 1973. text ed. 9.40 (ISBN 0-8077-2412-2); pap. text ed. 9.75x (ISBN 0-8077-2425-4). Tchrs Coll.

Introduction to Asepsis: A Programmed Unit in Fundamentals of Nursing. 2nd ed. Marie M. Seedor. (Nursing Education Monograph Ser No. 3). 1969. pap. 5.95 o.p. (ISBN 0-397-54095-7, Pub. by Columbia U Pr). Lippincott.

Introduction to Asian Politics. Lawrence Zifing & C. I. Kim. (Illus.). 1977. text ed. 16.95 (ISBN 0-13-478081-7). P-H.

Introduction to Astrology. William Lilly. LC 80-19691. 346p. 1980. Repr. of 1972 ed. lib. bdg. 11.95x (ISBN 0-89370-614-0). Borgo Pr.

Introduction to Astronomy. 9th ed. Laurence Fredrick & Robert Baker. 1980. text ed. 22.95 (ISBN 0-442-22422-2); instr's. manual 3.95 (ISBN 0-442-22421-4). D Van Nostrand.

Introduction to Astronomy. Ronald Oriti & William Starbird. 1977. text ed. 14.95x (ISBN 0-02-478560-1). Macmillan.

Introduction to Atmospheric Physics. 2nd ed. Robert G. Fleagle. LC 80-766. (International Geophysics Ser.). 1981. 29.50 (ISBN 0-12-260355-9). Acad Pr. Postponed.

Introduction to Atmospheric Radiation. Ed. by Kuo-Nan Liou. LC 80-769. (International Geophysics Ser.). 1980. 32.50 (ISBN 0-12-451450-2). Acad Pr.

Introduction to Atomic Physics. Harald A. Enge et al. LC 77-162464. 1972. text ed. 20.95 (ISBN 0-201-01871-3). A-W.

Introduction to Audiology. Frederick N. Martin. (Illus.). 496p. 1975. 19.95 (ISBN 0-13-478123-6). P-H.

Introduction to Audiology. 2nd ed. Frederick N. Martin. (Illus.). 480p. 1981. text ed. 19.95 (ISBN 0-13-478131-7). P-H.

Introduction to Augustine. Robert Meagher. LC 77-99085. 1978. 17.50x (ISBN 0-8147-5423-6). NYU Pr.

Introduction to Automata Theory, Languages, & Computation. John E. Hopcroft & Jeffrey D. Ullman. LC 78-67950. 1979. text ed. 21.95 (ISBN 0-201-02988-X). A-W.

Introduction to AV for Technical Assistants. Albert J. Casciero & Raymond G. Roney. (Illus.). 300p. 1981. lib. bdg. price not set (ISBN 0-87287-232-7). Libs Unl.

Introduction to Axiomatic Quantum Field Theory. Nikolai N. Bogolubov et al. Tr. by Stephen Fulling & Ludmila G. Popova. LC 72-5554. (Mathematical Physics Monographs: No. 18). 700p. 1975. text ed. 39.50 (ISBN 0-8053-0982-9, Adv Bk Prog). Benjamin-Cummings.

Introduction to Bacteria. U. Sinha & S. Srivastava. (Illus.). 180p. Date not set. text ed. 13.95x (ISBN 0-7069-1179-2, Pub. by Vikas India). Advent Bk.

Introduction to Basic. M. R. Eagle. 1977. pap. 11.95 o.p. (ISBN 0-7135-1928-2). Transatlantic.

Introduction to Basic Programming: A Structured Approach. Peter B. Worland. LC 78-56436. (Illus.). 1979. pap. text ed. 11.95 (ISBN 0-395-26775-7); solutions manual 0.60 (ISBN 0-395-26776-5). HM.

Introduction to Basic Speech. William K. Grasty & Mary T. Newman. (Illus., Orig.). 1969. text ed. 7.95x (ISBN 0-02-474180-9, 47418). Macmillan.

Introduction to Basic Supervision of People. Raymond J. Burby. 1966. pap. 8.95 (ISBN 0-201-00719-3). A-W.

Introduction to Behavioral Genetics. G. E. McClearn & J. C. DeFries. LC 73-8862. (Psychology Ser.). (Illus.). 347p. 1973. text ed. 21.95x (ISBN 0-7167-0835-3). W H Freeman.

Introduction to Benefit-Cost Analysis for Evaluating Public Programs. T. R. Durham. (Learning Packages in the Policy Sciences: No. 14). (Illus.). 70p. (Orig.). 1979. pap. text ed. 3.50 (ISBN 0-936826-03-7). Pol Stud Assocs.

Introduction to Benin Art & Technology. Philip J. Dark. (Illus.). 209p. 1973. 36.00x (ISBN 0-19-817191-9). Oxford U Pr.

Introduction to Bible Truths. Alexander C. De Jong. 1978. pap. 2.45 (ISBN 0-8010-2887-6). Baker Bk.

Introduction to Biblical Christian Education. Ed. by Werner Graendorf. 1981. text ed. 11.95 (ISBN 0-8024-4128-9). Moody.

Introduction to Biblical Hebrew. Thomas O. Lambdin. 1971. text ed. 17.95x (ISBN 0-684-41322-1, ScribC). Scribner.

Introduction to Biblical Literature. O. B. Davis. (Literature Ser.). 1976. pap. text ed. 6.65x (ISBN 0-8104-5834-9). Hayden.

Introduction to Bibliography for Literary Students. Ronald B. McKerrow. (Illus.). 1927. 24.95x (ISBN 0-19-818103-5). Oxford U Pr.

Introduction to Bioethics. Thomas A. Shannon & James DiGiacomo. LC 79-66585. 1979. pap. 3.95 (ISBN 0-8091-2257-X). Paulist Pr.

Introduction to Biological Membranes. Mahendra K. Jain & Roger C. Wagner. LC 79-16690. 1980. 32.50 (ISBN 0-471-03471-1, Pub. by Wiley-Interscience). Wiley.

Introduction to Biological Rhythms. David C. Saunders. (Tertiary Level Biology Ser). 1978. text ed. 17.95 (ISBN 0-470-99019-8). Halsted Pr.

Introduction to Biomechanics. Harold M. Frost. 160p. 1971. pap. 14.75 photocopy ed. spiral (ISBN 0-398-00622-9). C C Thomas.

Introduction to Biomedical Electronics. Edward J. Bukstein. LC 73-83370. (Orig.). 1973. pap. 7.50 (ISBN 0-672-21005-3). Sams.

Introduction to Biomedical Equipment Technology. Joseph J. Carr & John M. Brown. LC 80-6218. 448p. 1981. text ed. 23.95 (ISBN 0-471-04143-2); solutions manual avail. (ISBN 0-471-04144-0). Wiley.

Introduction to Biomedical Genetics. K. Mather & J. L. Jinks. LC 77-76809. 1978. 19.50x (ISBN 0-8014-1123-8). Cornell U Pr.

Introduction to Biomedical Instrumentation. 2nd ed. D. J. Dewhurst. 288p. 1975. text ed. 50.00 (ISBN 0-08-018755-2); pap. text ed. 31.00 (ISBN 0-08-018884-2). Pergamon.

Introduction to Biophysical Chemistry. Robert B. Martin. 1964. text ed. 23.00 o.p. (ISBN 0-07-040629-4, C). McGraw.

Introduction to Biophysical Plant Physiology. Park S. Nobel. LC 73-13696. (Illus.). 1974. text ed. 27.95x (ISBN 0-7167-0592-3). W H Freeman.

Introduction to Biostatistics. Robert R. Sokal & F. James Rohlf. LC 71-178257. (Illus.). 1973. text ed. 22.95x (ISBN 0-7167-0693-8). W H Freeman.

Introduction to Bivariate & Multivariate Statistics. Richard Lindeman et al. 1980. text ed. 19.95x (ISBN 0-673-15099-2). Scott F.

Introduction to Black Nonstandard English for Teachers. Mary L. Bronzo et al. Ed. by Donald E. Smith. (Michigan Learning Modules Ser.: No. 30). 56p. (Orig.). 1979. pap. text ed. 2.95 (ISBN 0-914004-33-6). Ulrich.

Introduction to Blood Banking. 3rd ed. Robert M. Greendyke. LC 79-91979. 1980. pap. 14.50 (ISBN 0-87488-975-8). Med Exam.

Introduction to Bookbinding. Lionel S. Darley. (Illus.). 1977. pap. 7.95 (ISBN 0-571-11082-7, Pub. by Faber & Faber). Merrimack Bk Serv.

Introduction to Boundary Value Problems. Stephen R. Bernfeld & V. Lakshmikantham. (Mathematics in Science & Engineering: A Series of Monographs & Textbooks, Vol. 109). 1974. 33.00 (ISBN 0-12-093150-8). Acad Pr.

Introduction to Brazil. rev ed. Charles Wagley. (Illus.). 1971. 20.00x (ISBN 0-231-03542-X); pap. 7.50x (ISBN 0-231-03543-8). Columbia U Pr.

Introduction to British Prehistory. Ed. by J. V. Megaw & D. D. Simpson. 1979. text ed. 47.50x (ISBN 0-7185-1122-0, Leicester). Humanities.

Introduction to Buddhist Esoterism. Benoytosh Bhattacharyya. 1980. Repr. of 1931 ed. 19.00x (ISBN 0-686-69019-2, Pub. by Motilal Banarsidas). South Asia Bks.

Introduction to Building Management. 4th ed. Calvert. 1981. text ed. price not set (ISBN 0-408-00520-3); pap. price not set. Butterworth.

Introduction to Business. 2nd ed. Richard M. Hodgetts. LC 76-12797. 1981. text ed. write for info. (ISBN 0-201-02897-2); write for info. resource guide; write for info. study guide (ISBN 0-201-03896-X). A-W.

Introduction to Business. 2nd ed. Richard M. Hodgetts. LC 80-21284. (Business Ser.). (Illus.). 600p. 1981. text ed. 15.95 (ISBN 0-201-03894-3). A-W.

Introduction to Business. Anthony F. McGann et al. LC 78-12146. 1979. text ed. 20.95 (ISBN 0-471-57240-3); tchrs. manual avail. (ISBN 0-471-57241-1); study guide avail. (ISBN 0-471-04864-X). Wiley.

Introduction to Business: A Contemporary View. 3rd ed. Reinecke. 704p. 1980. text ed. 17.95 (ISBN 0-205-06879-0, 0868795). Allyn.

Introduction to Business: A Programmed Approach. Belford E. Carver & Charles D. Cloud. 1975. pap. text ed. 9.50 o.p. (ISBN 0-8403-1125-7). Kendall-Hunt.

Introduction to Business: A Societal Approach. 3rd ed. Walter W. Perlick & Raymond V. Lesikar. 1979. 16.95x (ISBN 0-256-02086-8). Business Pubns.

Introduction to Business: A Systems Approach. Samuel D. Deep & William D. Brincklow. (Illus.). 576p. 1974. ref. ed. 18.95 (ISBN 0-13-478529-0); study guide 4.95 (ISBN 0-13-478552-5). P-H.

Introduction to Business Accounting for Managers. 3rd ed. W. C. Hartley. 1980. 28.00 (ISBN 0-08-024061-5); pap. 12.00 (ISBN 0-08-024062-3). Pergamon.

Introduction to Business: An Integrated Approach. Richard D. Brown & George J. Petrello. 1976. text ed. 14.95x (ISBN 0-02-471230-2). Macmillan.

Introduction to Business & Office Careers. Grady Kimbrall. (gr. 7-10). 1975. pap. text ed. 5.00 activity ed. (ISBN 0-87345-181-3). McKnight.

Introduction to Business Communication. Zane K. Quible et al. (Illus.). 496p. 1981. text ed. 16.95 (ISBN 0-13-479055-3). P-H.

Introduction to Business: Concepts & Applications. Steven L. Mandell et al. (Illus.). 580p. 1981. pap. text ed. 15.95 (ISBN 0-8299-0393-3). West Pub.

Introduction to Business Concepts & Applications: Test Bank. Steven L. Mandell et al. 1980. write for info. (ISBN 0-8299-0527-8). West Pub.

Introduction to Business: Concepts & Careers. F. Haner & S. Keiser. 1976. 16.95 (ISBN 0-87626-392-9); student guide 6.95 (ISBN 0-87626-391-0). P-H.

Introduction to Business Data Processing: With Basic, Fortran & Cobol Programming. 2nd ed. D. K. Carver. LC 78-19131. 1979. text ed. 21.95 (ISBN 0-471-03091-0); tchrs. manual (ISBN 0-471-03092-9); wkbk. 9.50 (ISBN 0-471-03998-5). Wiley.

Introduction to Business Finance. G. S. Hemingway. 1975. 19.95x (ISBN 0-434-90730-8); pap. 12.95x (ISBN 0-434-90731-6). Intl Ideas.

Introduction to Business Mathematics. John Ernest & Herbert M. Stein. LC 79-86252. 384p. 1969. pap. text ed. 11.95x (ISBN 0-02-474100-0, 47410); tests 13.95x (ISBN 0-02-474590-1, 47459). Macmillan.

Introduction to Business Statistics. Robert L. Brite. LC 76-17717. (Illus.). 1977. text ed. 13.95 (ISBN 0-201-00593-X). A-W.

Introduction to Business Translation: A Handbook in English - Spanish Contrastive Linguistics. Roman Perez & Carmen Ferrie. LC 80-18052. 196p. 1980. pap. write for info. (ISBN 0-8477-3328-9). U of PR Pr.

Introduction to Business: Workbook. 3rd ed. David P. Alexander & Walter W. Perlick. 1979. pap. 6.50x (ISBN 0-256-01691-7). Business Pubns.

Introduction to Calculus. S. W. Hockey. 1970. 8.50 (ISBN 0-08-012579-4). Pergamon.

Introduction to Calculus. Lynn H. Loomis. LC 74-30700. 804p. 1975. text ed. 20.95 (ISBN 0-201-04306-8). A-W.

Introduction to Calculus & Analysis, 2 vols. Richard Courant & Fritz John. LC 65-16403. 912p. 1975. Vol. 1. 33.95 (ISBN 0-470-17860-4); Vol. 2, 1974. 39.50 (ISBN 0-471-17862-4, Pub. by Wiley-Interscience). Wiley.

Introduction to Calculus for the Biological & Life Sciences. Rodney D. Gentry. LC 77-79470. (Illus.). 1978. text ed. 20.95 (ISBN 0-201-02477-2); instr's man. avail. (ISBN 0-201-02478-0); key avail. (ISBN 0-201-02479-9). A-W.

Introduction to Calculus One & Two. Alfred B. Willcox et al. 1971. lib. bdg. 24.95 (ISBN 0-395-05543-1, 3-60410). HM.

Introduction to California Plant Life. Robert Ornduff. (California Natural History Guides). (Illus.). 1974. 12.95x (ISBN 0-520-02583-0); pap. 4.95 (ISBN 0-520-02735-3). U of Cal Pr.

Introduction to Canadian Business. Brian E. Owen et al. 1980. 21.95 (ISBN 0-205-06998-3, 0869988); tchrs. ed. free (ISBN 0-205-07007-8, 0870072). Allyn.

Introduction to Cancer Medicine. Kenneth C. Calman & John Paul. LC 77-91854. 1978. 21.95 (ISBN 0-471-04274-9, Pub. by Wiley Medical). Wiley.

Introduction to Canoeing. Bradford Angier & Zack Taylor. (Illus.). 192p. (Orig.). 1981. pap. 8.95 (ISBN 0-8117-2010-1). Stackpole.

Introduction to Cardiology. Robert H. Eich. (Illus.). 304p. 1980. pap. text ed. 22.50 (ISBN 0-06-140770-4, Harper Medical). Har-Row.

Introduction to Cataloging & Classification. 5th ed. Mildred H. Downing. LC 80-20299. (Illus.). 240p. 1981. lib. bdg. 14.95x (ISBN 0-89950-017-X). McFarland & Co.

Introduction to Cataloging & Classification. 6th ed. Bohdan S. Wynar et al. LC 80-16462. (Library Science Text Ser.). 1980. lib. bdg. 25.00x (ISBN 0-87287-220-3); pap. text ed. 15.50x (ISBN 0-87287-221-1). Libs Unl.

Introduction to Catastrophe Theory. P. T. Saunders. LC 79-54172. (Illus.). 1980. 27.50 (ISBN 0-521-23042-X); pap. 8.95 (ISBN 0-521-29782-6). Cambridge U Pr.

Introduction to Categories, Homological Algebra & Sheaf Cohomology. J. R. Strooker. LC 77-80849. 1978. 47.50 (ISBN 0-521-21699-0). Cambridge U Pr.

Introduction to Cerebral Angiography. Anne G. Osborn. (Illus.). 424p. 1980. text ed. 42.50 (ISBN 0-06-141829-3, Harper Medical). Har-Row.

Introduction to Chain Indexing. T. D. Wilson. (Library & Information Science Ser.). 107p. 1971. 11.00 (ISBN 0-208-01069-6, Linnet). Shoe String.

Introduction to Chemical Engineering Computer Calculations. A. Myers & W. Seider. 1976. 27.95 (ISBN 0-13-479238-6). P-H.

Introduction to Chemical Equilibrium & Kinetics. L. Meites. (Pergamon Ser. on Analytical Chemistry: Vol. 2). 1981. 75.00 (ISBN 0-08-023802-5); pap. 19.95 (ISBN 0-08-023803-3). Pergamon.

Introduction to Chemical Metallurgy: In SI-Metric Units. 2nd ed. R. H. Parker. 1978. text ed. 52.00 (ISBN 0-08-022125-4); pap. text ed. 14.00 (ISBN 0-08-022126-2). Pergamon.

Introduction to Chemical Thermodynamics. R. P. Rastogi & R. R. Misra. 1978. 22.50 (ISBN 0-7069-0638-1, Pub. by Vikas India). Advent Bk.

Introduction to Chemical Thermodynamics. Reuben E. Wood. LC 79-84475. (Illus.). 1970. text ed. 34.50x (ISBN 0-89197-238-2); pap. text ed. 18.95x (ISBN 0-89197-798-8). Irvington.

Introduction to Chemistry. Gordon M. Barrow. 1976. text ed. 21.95x (ISBN 0-534-00326-5). Wadsworth Pub.

Introduction to Chemistry. 3rd ed. T. R. Dickson. LC 78-17406. 1979. text ed. 18.95x (ISBN 0-471-02223-3); tchrs. manual avail. (ISBN 0-471-04750-3); experiments 7.95x (ISBN 0-471-04747-3); transparencies avail. (ISBN 0-471-04757-0); study guide 7.50x (ISBN 0-471-04748-1). Wiley.

Introduction to Chemistry. Warren Hankins & Marie Hankins. LC 73-8600. (Illus.). 1974. text ed. 13.95 o.p. (ISBN 0-8016-2041-4). Mosby.

Introduction to Chemistry. 2nd ed. A. L. Williams et al. 1973. text ed. 18.95 o.p. (ISBN 0-201-08738-3); instr's manual o.p. 2.50 (ISBN 0-201-08744-8). A-W.

Introduction to Chemistry. 3rd ed. Arthur L. Williams et al. (Chemistry Ser.). (Illus.). 896p. 1981. text ed. 21.95 (ISBN 0-201-08726-X). A-W.

Introduction to Chemistry: Study Guide. Warren M. Hankins & Marie Hankins. (Illus.). 116p. 1975. 4.25 o.p. (ISBN 0-8016-2052-X). Mosby.

Introduction to Chess. Leonard Barden. 112p. 1968. pap. 4.95 (ISBN 0-7100-5221-9). Routledge & Kegan.

Introduction to Chess Moves & Tactics Simply Explained. Leonard Barden. (Illus., Orig.). 1959. pap. 2.00 (ISBN 0-486-21210-6). Dover.

Introduction to Chess Openings. V. Vainshtein. (Chess Player Ser.). 1977. pap. 3.95 o.p. (ISBN 0-906042-01-1, H-1276). Hippocrene Bks.

Introduction to Child Drama. Peter Slade. 1958. pap. 5.00x (ISBN 0-340-11881-4). Verry.

Introduction to Children's Literature. Mary J. Lickteig. 448p. 1975. text ed. 17.95x (ISBN 0-675-08716-3). Merrill.

Introduction to China. Innes Herdan. 1979. pap. 3.95 (ISBN 0-8351-0643-8). China Bks.

Introduction to Chinese Civilization. Ed. by John Meskill. LC 72-9410. 650p. 1973. 27.50x (ISBN 0-231-03649-3). Columbia U Pr.

Introduction to Chinese Literature. Liu Wu-hi. LC 66-12729. 332p. 1966. 12.50x (ISBN 0-253-33090-4); pap. 4.95x (ISBN 0-253-33091-2). Ind U Pr.

Introduction to Christian Camping. Ed. by Werner Graendorf & Lloyd Mattson. 1979. 6.95 (ISBN 0-8024-4131-9). Moody.

Introduction to Christian Education. Marvin J. Taylor. 412p. 1975. pap. 8.50 (ISBN 0-687-19498-9). Abingdon.

Introduction to Christian Faith. Walter Kasper. Tr. by David Smith from Ger. 224p. 1981. pap. 4.95 (ISBN 0-8091-2324-X). Paulist Pr.

Introduction to Christian Missions. Harold R. Cook. 1971. 7.95 o.p. (ISBN 0-8024-4132-7). Moody.

Introduction to Christianity. Joseph Ratzinger. 1970. 8.95 (ISBN 0-8164-2262-1). Crossroad NY.

Introduction to Cichlids. R. J. Goldstein. 1970. pap. 7.95 (ISBN 0-87666-019-7, PS-662). TFH Pubns.

Introduction to Circuit Analysis. John D. Ryder. (Illus.). 400p. 1973. ref. ed. 26.95 (ISBN 0-13-481101-1). P-H.

Introduction to Circuit Analysis. Timothy N. Trick. LC 77-10843. 1978. 26.95 (ISBN 0-471-88850-8); solutions manual 6.00 (ISBN 0-471-03041-4). Wiley.

Introduction to Classical & Modern Optics. Jurgen Meyer-Arendt. LC 71-157723. (Illus.). 1972. ref. ed. 23.95 (ISBN 0-13-479436-2). P-H.

Introduction to Classical Chinese. Raymond Dawson. 1978. pap. 13.95x (ISBN 0-19-815451-8). Oxford U Pr.

Introduction to Classical Ethiopic (Ge'ez) Thomas O. Lambdin. LC 78-12895. (Harvard Semitic Museum. Harvard Semitic Studies: No. 24). 1978. 15.00 (ISBN 0-89130-263-8, 040424). Scholars Pr Ca.

Introduction to Classical Real Analysis. Karl Stromberg. (Wadsworth International Mathematics Ser.). 576p. 1981. text ed. 29.95x (ISBN 0-686-69568-2). Wadsworth Pub.

Introduction to Classification & Number Building in Dewey. Marty Bloomberg & Hans Weber. LC 76-26975. 200p. 1976. lib. bdg. 18.50x (ISBN 0-87287-115-0). Libs Unl.

Introduction to Clay Colloid Chemistry. 2nd ed. H. Van Olphen. LC 77-400. 1977. 32.95 (ISBN 0-471-01463-X, Pub. by Wiley-Interscience). Wiley.

Introduction to Clinical Endocrinology. 2nd ed. John A. Thomson. (Churchill Livingstone Medical Text Ser.). (Illus.). 220p. 1981. text ed. 10.75 (ISBN 0-443-02307-7). Churchill.

Introduction to Clinical Scotometry. John M. Evans. 1938. 47.50x (ISBN 0-685-89759-1). Elliots Bks.

Introduction to Cognitive Psychology. Danny R. Moates & Gary M. Schumacher. 1979. text ed. 19.95x (ISBN 0-534-00724-4). Wadsworth Pub.

Introduction to Collective Bargining in Higher Education. A. W. J. Thomson. (Key Issues Ser.: No. 16). 1974. pap. 2.00 (ISBN 0-87546-250-2). NY Sch Indus Rel.

Introduction to College Engineering. Paul B. Daitch. LC 72-2651. 1973. pap. text ed. 10.95 (ISBN 0-201-01417-3). A-W.

Introduction to Colloid & Surface Chemistry. 2nd ed. D. J. Shaw. 248p. 1970. 12.95 (ISBN 0-408-70021-1). Butterworths.

Introduction to Colloid & Surface Chemistry. 3rd ed. D. J. Shaw. LC 80-49871. 256p. 1980. text ed. 14.95 (ISBN 0-408-71049-7). Butterworths.

Introduction to Combinatorial Analysis. J. Riordan. LC 80-337. 1980. 18.00 (ISBN 0-691-08262-6); pap. 6.95 (ISBN 0-691-02365-4). Princeton U Pr.

Introduction to Combinatorics. Gerald Berman & K. D. Fryer. 1972. text ed. 19.95 (ISBN 0-12-092750-0). Acad Pr.

Introduction to Combinatorics. Ioan Tomescu. Ed. by E. Keith Lloyd. Tr. by S. Rudeanu from Romanian. Orig. Title: Introducere in Combinatorica. (Illus.). 250p. 1975. text ed. 28.50x (ISBN 0-569-08057-6, Pub. by Collets England). Scholium Intl.

Introduction to Communication. Robert Kelley. Ed. by W. D. Brooks & R. A. Vogel. LC 76-39748. (Ser. in Speech Communication). 1977. pap. text ed. 5.95 (ISBN 0-8465-7606-6). Benjamin-Cummings.

Introduction to Communication Command & Control Systems. David J. Morris. 1977. text ed. 45.00 (ISBN 0-08-020378-7). Pergamon.

Introduction to Communication Disorders. Thomas J. Hixon et al. (Illus.). 1979. text ed. 18.95 (ISBN 0-13-480186-5). P-H.

Introduction to Communication Systems. Ferrel G. Stremler. LC 76-12803. (Electrical Engineering Ser.). 1977. text ed. 25.95 (ISBN 0-201-07244-0); sol. man. avail. (ISBN 0-201-07245-9). A-W.

Introduction to Communications Careers. Hauenstein & Bachmeyer. (gr. 9-10). 1975. pap. text ed. 5.00 activity ed. (ISBN 0-87345-183-X). McKnight.

Introduction to Communications Engineering. Robert Gagliardi. LC 77-18531. 1978. 34.00 (ISBN 0-471-03099-6, Pub. by Wiley-Interscience). Wiley.

Introduction to Community Work. Fred Milson. 168p. 1974. 14.00x (ISBN 0-7100-7840-4); pap. 5.25 (ISBN 0-7100-7841-2). Routledge & Kegan.

Introduction to Commutative Algebra. Michael F. Atiyah & I. G. Macdonald. 1969. text ed. 17.95 (ISBN 0-201-00361-9). A-W.

Introduction to Company Law. James A. Hornby. (Repr. of 1957 ed). 1970. text ed. 5.75 (ISBN 0-09-020713-0, Hutchinson U Lib); pap. text ed. 3.75 (ISBN 0-09-020714-9, Hutchinson U Lib). Humanities.

Introduction to Comparative Literature. Francois Jost. LC 73-19849. 1974. 14.95 (ISBN 0-672-63657-3). Pegasus.

Introduction to Comparative Philosophy. P. T. Raju. LC 62-7870. (Arcturus Books Paperbacks). 376p. 1970. pap. 9.95 (ISBN 0-8093-0419-8). S Ill U Pr.

Introduction to Comparative Politics. Sam C. Sarkesian & James H. Buck. Ed. by John Stout. LC 78-12083. (Illus.). 1979. text ed. 15.95 (ISBN 0-88284-067-3). Alfred Pub.

Introduction to Comparative Politics: Thirteen Nation States. 2nd ed. Marion D. Irish & Elke Frank. LC 77-22021. (Illus.). 1978. ref. ed. 17.95 (ISBN 0-13-500991-X). P-H.

Introduction to Comparative Psychology. C. Lloyd Morgan. (Contributions to the History of Psychology D, II Comparative Psychology Ser.). 1978. Repr. of 1894 ed. 30.00 (ISBN 0-89093-171-2). U Pubns Amer.

Introduction to Complex Analysis. P. L. Walker. LC 74-24686. 141p. 1974. 18.95 (ISBN 0-470-91807-1). Halsted Pr.

Introduction to Complex Variables. Edward A. Grove & Gerasimbs E. Ladas. 1974. 19.50 (ISBN 0-395-17087-7). HM.

Introduction to Composite Materials. Stephen W. Tsai & H. Thomas Hahn. LC 80-51965. 475p. 1980. 35.00 (ISBN 0-87762-288-4). Technomic.

Introduction to Computability. Fred Hennie. LC 76-12796. (Illus.). 1977. text ed. 24.95 (ISBN 0-201-02848-4). A-W.

Introduction to Computational Combinatorics. E. S. Page & L. B. Wilson. LC 78-54722. (Computer Science Texts Ser.). (Illus.). 1979. 32.95 (ISBN 0-521-22427-6); pap. 10.95x (ISBN 0-521-29492-4). Cambridge U Pr.

Introduction to Computational Fluid Mechanics. Chuen-Yen Chow. LC 78-27555. 1979. text ed. 25.95 (ISBN 0-471-15608-6). Wiley.

Introduction to Computer Architecture. 2nd, rev. ed. Harold S. Stone. 640p. 1980. text ed. 25.95 (ISBN 0-574-21225-6, 13-4225). SRA.

Introduction to Computer-Based Information Systems. J. Daniel Couger & Fred R. McFadden. LC 74-28437. 655p. 1975. text ed. 25.95 (ISBN 0-471-17736-9). Wiley.

Introduction to Computer Design & Implementation. S. I. Ahmad & Kwok Fung. (Illus.). 1981. text ed. 19.95 (ISBN 0-914894-11-0). Computer Sci.

Introduction to Computer Logic. H. T. Nagel et al. (Illus.). 544p. 1975. ref. ed. 27.95 (ISBN 0-13-480012-5). P-H.

Introduction to Computer Music. Wayne Bateman. LC 79-26361. 314p. 1980. 24.95 (ISBN 0-471-05266-3, Pub. by Wiley-Interscience). Wiley.

Introduction to Computer Organization. Ivan Tomek. (Illus.). 200p. 1981. text ed. 21.95 (ISBN 0-914894-08-0). Computer Sci.

Introduction to Computer Organization Workbook. Ivan Tomek. (Illus., Orig.). 1981. pap. text ed. price not set (ISBN 0-914894-70-6). Computer Sci.

Introduction to Computer Programming. F. H. George. (Illus.). 1968. 12.10 o.p. (ISBN 0-08-012394-5); pap. 5.50 o.p. (ISBN 0-08-012393-7). Pergamon.

Introduction to Computer Programming - Basic Fortran IV: A Practical Approach. William J. Keys & Thomas J. Cashman. (Illus.). 1972. pap. text ed. 10.95x (ISBN 0-88236-151-1). Anaheim Pub Co.

Introduction to Computer Programming & Data Structures Using MACRO-11. Harry Lewis. 188p. 1981. text ed. 18.95 (ISBN 0-8359-3143-9); soln. manual avail. (ISBN 0-8359-3144-7). Reston.

Introduction to Computer Programming for Chemists: BASIC Version. Isenhour et al. 16.95 o.p. (ISBN 0-205-04392-5, 6943926). Allyn.

Introduction to Computer Programming for Chemists: Fortran. 2nd ed. Thomas L. Isenhour & Peter C. Jurs. 1979. text ed. 17.95 (ISBN 0-205-05897-3). Allyn.

Introduction to Computer Programming Structured Cobol. Gary B. Shelly & Thomas J. Cashman. LC 77-89824. 1977. pap. 14.95x (ISBN 0-88236-111-2). Anaheim Pub Co.

Introduction to Computer Science. Peter M. Banks & Joseph Doupnik. LC 75-20407. 384p. 1976. text ed. 21.95 (ISBN 0-471-04710-4); instructors manual avail. (ISBN 0-471-01552-0). Wiley.

Introduction to Computer Science. G. W. Gear. LC 72-86105. 1975. text ed. 15.95 (ISBN 0-574-18045-1, 13-4035); instr's guide avail. (ISBN 0-574-18471-6, 13-1471); transparency masters 46.00 (ISBN 0-574-18472-4, 13-1472). SRA.

Introduction to Computer Science. Terry M. Walker. Incl. BASIC Language Programming. o.p. (ISBN 0-205-03590-6, 2035901); COBOL Language Programming. o.p. (ISBN 0-205-03998-7, 2039982); FORTRAN Language Programming (ISBN 0-205-03578-7, 2035782). 6.95x ea. o.p. Allyn.

Introduction to Computer Science: A Structured Approach. Neill Graham. (Illus.). 1979. text ed. 18.50 (ISBN 0-8299-0187-6); instrs.' manual avail. (ISBN 0-8299-0482-4). West Pub.

Introduction to Computer Science: An Algorithmic Approach, Short Edition. Jean-Paul Tremblay & Richard B. Bunt. Ed. by Charles E. Stewart. (Illus.). 432p. 1980. text ed. 16.95 (ISBN 0-07-065167-1, C). McGraw.

Introduction to Computer Science: An Interdisciplinary Approach. Terry Walker. 840p. 1972. text ed. 18.95x o.p. (ISBN 0-205-03451-9, 2034514). Allyn.

Introduction to Computer Science Mathematics. Robert V. Jamison. LC 70-39901. (Illus.). 256p. 1972. text ed. 14.95 o.p. (ISBN 0-07-032276-7, G); answer key 1.50 o.p. (ISBN 0-07-032281-3). McGraw.

Introduction to Computer Simulation. A. Wayne Bennett. LC 74-4509. 480p. 1974. text ed. 20.95 (ISBN 0-8299-0017-9); solutions manual avail. (ISBN 0-8299-0459-X). West Pub.

Introduction to Computers. Thomas V. Gemmer. 1975. coil bdg. 5.95 o.p. (ISBN 0-88252-036-9). Paladin Hse.

Introduction to Computers. Alton R. Kindred. 1976. 19.95 (ISBN 0-13-480087-7). P-H.

Introduction to Computers & Computer Science. 2nd ed. Richard Dorf. LC 77-81994. (Illus.). 1977. text ed. 15.95x (ISBN 0-87835-061-6). Boyd & Fraser.

Introduction to Computers & Computer Programming. Samuel Bergman & Steven Bruckner. LC 72-140834. 1972. text ed. 17.95 (ISBN 0-201-00552-2); instructor's guide & soultions manuals 2.50 (ISBN 0-201-00553-0). A-W.

Introduction to Computers & Data Processing. Daniel D. Benice. (Applied Mathematics Ser). 1970. ref. ed. 16.95 (ISBN 0-13-479543-1). P-H.

Introduction to Computers & Data Processing. Gary B. Shelly & Thomas J. Cashman. (Illus.). 1980. pap. text ed. 15.95x (ISBN 0-88236-115-5); wkbk 5.95x (ISBN 0-88236-116-3). Anaheim Pub Co.

Introduction to Computers & Information Processing. Don Cassel & Martin Jackson. (Orig.). 1980. study guide 7.95 (ISBN 0-8359-3154-4). Reston.

Introduction to Computers & Information Processing: Language Free Editon. Don Cassel & Martin Jackson. 1981. text ed. 17.95 (ISBN 0-8359-3155-2); study guide 7.95 (ISBN 0-8359-3157-9); instrs'. manual avail. (ISBN 0-8359-3156-0). Reston.

Introduction to Computers & Programming. Jessica Hellwig. LC 71-85919. 1969. 15.00x (ISBN 0-231-03263-3). Columbia U Pr.

Introduction to Computers in Business. Elias M. Awad. (Illus.). 512p. 1977. text ed. 19.95 (ISBN 0-13-479378-1); student guide 7.95 (ISBN 0-13-479360-9). P-H.

Introduction to Computers in Information Science. 2nd ed. Susan B. Artandi. LC 68-12643. (Illus.). 1972. 10.00 (ISBN 0-8108-0485-9). Scarecrow.

Introduction to Computing: Problem-Solving Algorithms & Data Structures. Daniel U. Wilde. LC 72-5754. (Illus.). 448p. 1973. ref. ed. 18.95 (ISBN 0-13-479519-9). P-H.

Introduction to Concepts & Theories in Physical Science. 2nd ed. Gerald J. Holton. LC 72-2787. 1973. text ed. 19.95 (ISBN 0-201-02971-5). A-W.

Introduction to Conservation of Orbital Symmetry: A Programmed Text. A. J. Bellamy. 160p. (Orig.). 1974. pap. text ed. 8.95x (ISBN 0-582-44089-0). Longman.

Introduction to Construction. Mark W. Huth. LC 78-60838. (Construction Ser.). (YA) (gr. 9-12). 1980. pap. text ed. 14.52 (ISBN 0-8273-1737-9); instr's manual 2.00 (ISBN 0-8273-1738-7). Delmar.

Introduction to Construction Careers. Don Lux. (gr. 7-10). 1975. pap. text ed. 5.00 activity ed. (ISBN 0-87345-187-2). McKnight.

Introduction to Consumer Behavior. James U. McNeal. LC 72-6717. (Marketing Ser.). (Illus.). 400p. 1973. text ed. 19.95x o.p. (ISBN 0-471-58700-1). Wiley.

Introduction to Contemporary Business. J. Diamond & G. Pintel. 1975. 15.95 (ISBN 0-13-487991-0); study guide 5.95 (ISBN 0-13-488015-3). P-H.

Introduction to Contemporary Civilization in the West, 2 Vols. 3rd ed. Columbia College - Contemporary Civilization Staff. LC 60-16650. 1960-61. Vol. 1. text ed. 22.50x (ISBN 0-231-02423-1); Vol. 2. text ed. 22.50x (ISBN 0-231-02477-0). Columbia U Pr.

Introduction to Contemporary Psychoanalysis. Anne E. Bernstein & Gloria Warner. LC 80-70246. 300p. 1981. 25.00 (ISBN 0-87668-442-8). Aronson.

Introduction to Contemporary Psychology. Edmund J. Fantino & George S. Reynolds. LC 74-23201. (Illus.). 1975. text ed. 21.95x (ISBN 0-7167-0761-6); 4.00 o.p.study guide (ISBN 0-686-67086-8); test items avail. W H Freeman.

Introduction to Contemporary Statistics. Koopmans. (Illus.). 500p. 1981. text ed. 20.95. Duxbury Pr.

Introduction to Continuum Mechanics. Morton E. Gurtin. (Mathematics in Science & Engineering Ser.). 1981. write for info. (ISBN 0-12-309750-9). Acad Pr.

Introduction to Continuum Mechanics. W. M. Lai et al. LC 72-10904. 1974. text ed. 24.20 o.p. (ISBN 0-08-017622-4). Pergamon.

Introduction to Continuum Mechanics: In SI-Metric Units. rev. ed. W. M. Lai et al. 1978. text ed. 45.00 (ISBN 0-08-022698-1); pap. text ed. 19.75 (ISBN 0-08-022699-X). Pergamon.

Introduction to Control System Analysis & Design. Francis J. Hale. (Illus.). 400p. 1973. ref. ed. 25.95 (ISBN 0-13-479824-4). P-H.

Introduction to Control Systems. D. K. Anand. LC 72-12834. 1974. text ed. 31.00 (ISBN 0-08-017104-4); pap. text ed. 17.60 (ISBN 0-08-019005-7). Pergamon.

Introduction to Control Systems Performance Measurements. K. C. Garner. 1968. 23.00 (ISBN 0-08-012499-2); pap. 11.25 (ISBN 0-08-012498-4). Pergamon.

Introduction to Control Systems Technology. 2nd ed. Bateson. (Technology Ser.). 560p. 1980. text ed. 23.95 (ISBN 0-675-08255-2); instructor's manual 3.95 (ISBN 0-686-63341-5). Merrill.

Introduction to Control Theory. O. L. Jacobs. 378p. 1974. 29.95x (ISBN 0-19-856108-3). Oxford U Pr.

Introduction to Control Theory, Including Optimal Control. D. N. Burghes & M. A. Graham. 400p. 67.95x (ISBN 0-470-26998-7). Halsted Pr.

Introduction to Controlled Thermonuclear Fusion. M. O. Hagler & M. Kristiansen. LC 74-33596. 1977. 19.95 (ISBN 0-669-99119-8). Lexington Bks.

Introduction to Correctional Rehabilitation. Ed. by Richard E. Hardy & John G. Cull. (American Lectures in Social & Rehabilitation Psychology Ser.). 288p. 1975. 16.75 (ISBN 0-398-02649-1). C C Thomas.

Introduction to Corrections. Clemens Bartollas. (Illus.). 496p. 1981. text ed. 18.50 scp (ISBN 0-06-040516-3, HarpC); avail. instrs manual. Har-Row.

Introduction to Corrections. 2nd ed. Vernon B. Fox. (Illus.). 1977. text ed. 17.95 (ISBN 0-13-479485-0). P-H.

Introduction to Creative Supervision. Raymond J. Burby. LC 79-13802. 1980. pap. text ed. 8.95 (ISBN 0-201-00836-X). A-W.

Introduction to Criminal Investigation. Richard A. Ward. LC 74-19703. 368p. 1975. text ed. 13.95 (ISBN 0-201-08523-2). A-W.

Introduction to Criminal Justice. Robert Pursley. 1977. text ed. 14.95x (ISBN 0-02-477540-1). Macmillan.

Introduction to Criminal Justice. Joseph J. Senna & Larry J. Siegel. (Criminal Justice Ser.). (Illus.). 1978. text ed. 16.95 (ISBN 0-8299-0170-1); instrs.' manual avail. (ISBN 0-8299-0600-2). West Pub.

Introduction to Criminal Justice. 2nd ed. Joseph J. Senna & Larry J. Siegel. (Criminal Justice Ser.). (Illus.). 550p. 1981. text ed. 16.95 (ISBN 0-8299-0409-3). West Pub.

Introduction to Criminal Justice: Police, Courts, Corrections. George E. Berkley et al. 1976. text ed. 16.95 (ISBN 0-205-05448-X, 825448-6); instr's manual free (ISBN 0-205-04993-1, 825449-4). Allyn.

Introduction to Criminalistics: The Application of the Physical Sciences to the Detection of Crime. rev. ed. Charles E. O'Hara & James W. Osterburg. LC 49-11434. 736p. 1972. Repr. of 1949 ed. 17.50x (ISBN 0-253-33103-X). Ind U Pr.

Introduction to Criminology. 2nd ed. Barlow. 1981. text ed. 16.95 (ISBN 0-316-08115-9); tchrs'. manual free (ISBN 0-316-08116-7). Little.

Introduction to Criminology. Vernon Fox. (Illus.). 416p. 1976. 17.95 (ISBN 0-13-480053-2). P-H.

Introduction to Criminology. Stephen Schafer. 352p. 1976. 14.95 (ISBN 0-87909-390-0). Reston.

Introduction to Critical Theory: Horkheimer to Habermas. David Held. 497p. 1980. 32.50x (ISBN 0-520-04121-6); pap. 12.75x (ISBN 0-520-04175-5, CAMPUS 261). U of Cal Pr.

Introduction to Crop Husbandry. rev. 3rd ed. J. A. Lockhart & A. J. Wiseman. LC 74-10000. 1975. text ed. 23.10 o.p. (ISBN 0-08-018115-5); pap. text ed. 9.90 o.p. (ISBN 0-08-018105-8). Pergamon.

Introduction to Crop Husbandry. 4th ed. J. A. Lockhart & A. J. Wiseman. 1978. text ed. 45.00 (ISBN 0-08-022653-1); pap. text ed. 14.00 (ISBN 0-08-022652-3). Pergamon.

Introduction to Crop Physiology. 2nd ed. F. L. Milthorpe & J. Moorby. LC 78-26380. (Illus.). 1980. 42.50 (ISBN 0-521-22624-4); pap. 12.50x (ISBN 0-521-29581-5). Cambridge U Pr.

Introduction to Crystal Chemistry. 2nd ed. Robert C. Evans. (Illus.). 1964. pap. text ed. 19.95x (ISBN 0-521-09367-8, 367). Cambridge U Pr.

Introduction to Crystallography. 4th ed. F. C. Phillips. 1979. pap. text ed. 25.95 (ISBN 0-470-26347-4). Halsted Pr.

Introduction to Cultural Anthropology. E. Miller. 1979. pap. 13.95 (ISBN 0-13-480236-5); study guide & wkbk. 5.95 (ISBN 0-13-480244-6). P-H.

Introduction to Cultural Geography. 2nd ed. Samuel N. Dicken & Forrest R. Pitts. 1970. text ed. 19.50x o.p. (ISBN 0-471-00117-1). Wiley.

Introduction to Curriculum Studies. P. H. Taylor & C. M. Richards. (General Ser.). 1979. pap. text ed. 10.50x (ISBN 0-85633-164-3, NFER). Humanities.

Introduction to Data Analysis. Bruce D. Bowen & Herbert F. Weisberg. LC 79-27870. (Illus.). 1980. text ed. 15.95x (ISBN 0-7167-1173-7); pap. text ed. 7.95x (ISBN 0-7167-1174-5). W H Freeman.

Introduction to Data Analysis & Statistical Inference. Carl Morris & John Rolph. (Illus.). 416p. 1981. pap. text ed. 13.95. P-H.

Introduction to Data Base Design. John K. Lyon. LC 75-155904. (Communigraph Business Data Processing Ser). 1971. 24.50 (ISBN 0-471-55735-8, Pub. by Wiley-Interscience). Wiley.

Introduction to Data Management. William D. Haseman & Andrew B. Whinston. 1977. 19.95x (ISBN 0-256-01949-5). Irwin.

Introduction to Data Processing. 3rd ed. Carl Feingold. 1980. pap. text ed. 17.95x (ISBN 0-697-08136-2); pap. wkbk. 7.95x (ISBN 0-697-08143-5); pap. instr's man. 6.00x (ISBN 0-686-60814-3). Wm C Brown.

Introduction to Data Processing. Gary Popkin & Arthur Pike. LC 76-10893. (Illus.). 1977. pap. text ed. 17.95 (ISBN 0-395-20628-6); inst. manual 1.25 (ISBN 0-395-20629-4). HM.

Introduction to Data Processing. 3rd ed. Andrew Vazsonyi. 1980. 18.95x (ISBN 0-256-02343-3). Irwin.

Introduction to Data Processing for Business. Robert J. Thierauf & John F. Niehaus. LC 79-20568. 1980. text ed. 21.95 (ISBN 0-471-03439-8); tchrs' manual avail. (ISBN 0-471-03440-1); study guide avail. (ISBN 0-471-07870-0). Wiley.

Introduction to Data Processing for the New Age: Syllabus. Hempel & Solem. 1977. pap. text ed. 7.95 (ISBN 0-89420-034-8, 223020); cassette recordings 139.65 (ISBN 0-89420-138-7, 223000). Natl Book.

Introduction to Data Processing with BASIC. 2nd ed. Gary S. Popkin & Arthur M. Pike. (Illus.). 592p. 1981. text ed. 17.50 (ISBN 0-395-29483-5); wkbk 6.95 (ISBN 0-395-29485-1); write for info. instr's manual (ISBN 0-395-29484-3). HM.

Introduction to Data Structures & Non-Numeric Computation. Doron J. Cohen & Peter C. Brillinger. (Illus.). 656p. 1972. ref. ed. 22.95 (ISBN 0-13-479899-6). P-H.

Introduction to Database Systems. 2nd ed. C. J. Date. LC 76-55633. (IBM Systems Programming Series). 1977. text ed. price not set (ISBN 0-201-14456-5). A-W.

Introduction to Database Systems. 3rd ed. C. J. Date. LC 80-17603. (IBM Systems Programming Ser.). (Illus.). 704p. 1981. text ed. 20.95 (ISBN 0-201-14471-9). A-W.

Introduction to Debate. John Pacilio, Jr. & William H. Stites. LC 67-25696. (gr. 10-12). 1967. pap. text ed. 7.95 o.p. (ISBN 0-87108-140-7). Pruett.

Introduction to Decision Theory. J. Morgan Jones. 1977. 20.95 (ISBN 0-256-01950-9). Irwin.

Introduction to DECsystem 20: Assembly Language Programming. Ralph E. Gorin. 1981. pap. 21.00 (ISBN 0-932376-12-6). Digital Pr.

Introduction to Deductive Logic. Gary Iseminger. LC 68-14984. (Century Philosophy Ser.). (Illus., Orig.). 1968. pap. text ed. 5.95x (ISBN 0-89197-239-0). Irvington.

Introduction to Deepwater Floating Drilling Operations. new ed. L. M. Harris. LC 72-76603. 256p. 1972. 21.00 (ISBN 0-87814-011-5). Pennwell Pub.

Introduction to Defense Radar Systems Engineering. James N. Constant. (Illus.). 1972. text ed. 22.95x (ISBN 0-8104-9194-X, 0-8104-9194-X). Hayden.

Introduction to Defensive Bidding. Ronald P. Von Der Porten. LC 67-25630. (Illus.). 1968. 5.95 o.p.; pap. 3.95 (ISBN 0-13-479808-2). P-H.

Introduction to Dental Statistics. Roger Weinberg & Shu L. Cheuk. LC 80-36706. 185p. (Orig.). 1980. 18.00 (ISBN 0-8155-0813-1). Noyes.

Introduction to Design & Analysis: A Student's Handbook. Geoffrey Keppel & William H. Saufley, Jr. LC 79-26166. (Psychology Ser.). (Illus.). 1980. text ed. 27.95x (ISBN 0-7167-1142-7); pap. text ed. 15.95x (ISBN 0-7167-1143-5). W H Freeman.

Introduction to Designing & Conducting Research. 2nd. ed. Clifford J. Drew. LC 79-25403. (Illus.). 1980. 14.95 (ISBN 0-8016-1460-0). Mosby.

Introduction to Designing Research & Evaluation. Clifford J. Drew. LC 75-20115. (Illus.). 224p. 1976. text ed. 13.95 o.p. (ISBN 0-8016-1464-3). Mosby.

Introduction to Developmental Biology. Donald A. Ede. LC 78-16359. (Tertiary Level Biology Ser.). 1978. text ed. 19.95 (ISBN 0-470-26469-1). Halsted Pr.

Introduction to Diagnostic Microbiology. Orten C. Skinner. LC 75-78591. (Allied Health Ser). 1975. pap. 12.05 (ISBN 0-672-61391-3). Bobbs.

Introduction to Diagnostic Radiology. M. H. Schreiber. (Illus.). 368p. 1980. 29.50 (ISBN 0-398-04026-5). C C Thomas.

Introduction to Diagnostic Radiology: A Correlated Approach to Imaging. Richard H. Daffner. LC 78-5680. 1978. pap. text ed. 16.95 (ISBN 0-8016-1203-9). Mosby.

Introduction to Diagnostic Sonography. Arthur C. Fleischer & A. Everette James. LC 79-19065. 1980. 27.50 (ISBN 0-471-05473-9, Pub. by Wiley-Medical). Wiley.

Introduction to Difference Equations: With Illustrative Examples from Economics, Psychology & Sociology. Samuel Goldberg. LC 58-10223. (Illus.). 1958. pap. 14.50 (ISBN 0-471-31051-4). Wiley.

Introduction to Differential Equations. H. S. Bear. (Illus.). 490p. 1981. pap. text ed. 19.50 (ISBN 0-9605502-0-8). Manoa Pr.

Introduction to Differential Equations. William E. Boyce & Richard C. DiPrima. 1970. text ed. 18.50x (ISBN 0-471-09338-6). Wiley.

Introduction to Differential Equations. R. Creighton Buck & Ellen Buck. LC 75-25009. (Illus.). 416p. 1976. text ed. 19.50 (ISBN 0-395-20654-5). HM.

Introduction to Differential Geometry. Abraham Goetz. (Intermediate Mathematics Ser). 1970. text ed. 18.95 (ISBN 0-201-02431-4). A-W.

Introduction to Differential Geometry. T. J. Willmore. (Illus.). 1959. 19.50x (ISBN 0-19-853125-7). Oxford U Pr.

Introduction to Digital Board Testing. R. G. Bennetts. (Computer Systems Engineering Ser.). 1981. text ed. price not set (ISBN 0-8448-1385-0). Crane-Russak Co.

Introduction to Digital Computer Technology. 2nd ed. Louis Nashelsky. LC 76-42245. 1977. text ed. 22.95 (ISBN 0-471-02094-X). Wiley.

Introduction to Digital Computing. F. H. George. 1966. pap. 7.75 (ISBN 0-08-011280-3). Pergamon.

Introduction to Digital Techniques. Dan I. Porat & Arpad Barna. LC 78-17696. (Electronic Technology Ser.). 1979. text ed. 23.95x (ISBN 0-471-02924-6); solutions manual (ISBN 0-471-04351-6). Wiley.

Introduction to Dinghy Sailing. Nicolette M. Walker. (Illus.). 104p. 1981. 14.95 (ISBN 0-7153-8022-2). David & Charles.

Introduction to Discourse Analysis. Malcolm Coulthard. (Applied Linguistics & Language Study). 1978. pap. text ed. 9.00x (ISBN 0-582-55087-4). Longman.

Introduction to Discrete-Time Signal Processing. Steven A. Tretter. LC 76-25943. 1976. text ed. 32.95 (ISBN 0-471-88760-9). Wiley.

Introduction to Dislocations. 2nd ed. Derek Hull. 280p. 1976. text ed. 27.00 (ISBN 0-08-018129-5); pap. text ed. 14.00 (ISBN 0-08-018128-7). Pergamon.

Introduction to Distributed Data Processing. Harry Katzan, Jr. LC 78-27323. (Illus.). 242p. 1979. text ed. 20.00 (ISBN 0-89433-061-6). Petrocelli.

Introduction to Distributed Systems & Fields. B. V. Sonnerup. 1978. 25.00 o.p. (ISBN 0-08-017101-X). Pergamon.

Introduction to Dogmatic Theology. E. A. Litton. 1960. 16.00 (ISBN 0-227-67501-0). Attic Pr.

Introduction to Dynamic Programming. George L. Nemhauser. (Series in Decision & Control). 1966. 23.95 o.p. (ISBN 0-471-63150-7, Pub. by Wiley-Interscience). Wiley.

Introduction to Dynamic Systems. James Reswick & Charles Taft. 1967. ref. ed. 23.95 (ISBN 0-13-479907-0). P-H.

Introduction to Dynamic Systems: Theory, Models & Applications. David G. Luenberger. LC 78-12366. 1979. 24.95 (ISBN 0-471-02594-1); solutions manual avail. (ISBN 0-471-06081-X). Wiley.

Introduction to Dynamics. Bruce H. Karnopp. LC 73-3741. 1974. text ed. 22.95 (ISBN 0-201-03614-2). A-W.

Introduction to Dynamics & Control. R. J. Richards. 1979. text ed. 45.00 (ISBN 0-582-44182-X); pap. text ed. 24.00 (ISBN 0-582-44183-8). Longman.

Introduction to Early Greek Philosophy. John M. Robinson. LC 68-1065. 1968. pap. text ed. 10.95 (ISBN 0-395-05316-1). HM.

Introduction to Earth & Man: A Systematic Geography. Donald Steila et al. LC 80-19689. 600p. 1981. text ed. 19.95 (ISBN 0-471-04221-8). Wiley.

Introduction to Ecology. Paul A. Colinvaux. LC 72-3788. 621p. 1973. text ed. 25.95 (ISBN 0-471-16498-4). Wiley.

Introduction to Econometric Forecasting & Forecasting Models. Ed. by Lawrence R. Klein & Richard M. Young. LC 79-1542. (Wharton Econometric Forecasting Studies: No. 3). 176p. 1980. 18.95 (ISBN 0-669-02896-7). Lexington Bks.

Introduction to Econometrics. 2nd ed. Oskar Lange. 1963. text ed. 9.65 (ISBN 0-08-009759-6); pap. text ed. 8.00 (ISBN 0-08-013560-9). Pergamon.

Introduction to Econometrics. M. J. Surrey. (Illus.). 88p. 1974. text ed. 12.50x (ISBN 0-19-877048-0). Oxford U Pr.

Introduction to Econometrics. Henri Theil. LC 77-14972. (Illus.). 1978. ref. 22.95 (ISBN 0-13-481028-7). P-H.

Introduction to Econometrics. A. A. Walters. 1970. text ed. 12.95x (ISBN 0-393-09931-8, NortonC). Norton

Introduction to Econometrics: Principles & Applications. 2nd ed. Harry H. Kelejian & Wallace E. Oates. (Illus.). 384p. 1980. text ed. 10.50 scp (ISBN 0-06-043618-2, HarpC). Har-Row.

Introduction to Economic Cybernetics. Oskar Lange. Ed. by Antoni Banasinski. Tr. by Jozef Stadler. LC 73-106449. 1970. 19.50 (ISBN 0-08-006652-6). Pergamon.

Introduction to Economics. 5th ed. Cairncross. 1973. pap. 7.95 (ISBN 0-408-70518-3). Butterworths.

Introduction to Economics. Kenneth Long. (Illus.). Date not set. text ed. price not set (ISBN 0-442-23894-0). D Van Nostrand.

Introduction to Educational Administration. 5th ed. Roald F. Campbell et al. 1977. text ed. 17.95 (ISBN 0-205-05678-4). Allyn.

Introduction to Educational Computing. N. J. Rushby. 224p. 1980. 30.00x (Pub. by Croom Helm England). State Mutual Bk.

Introduction to Educational Gerontology. new ed. Ed. by R. H. Sherron & D. B. Lumsden. LC 78-13292. (Illus.). 1978. pap. text ed. 17.00 (ISBN 0-89116-101-5). Hemisphere Pub.

Introduction to Egyptian Arabic. Ernest T. Abdel-Massih. LC 75-24784. 1974. pap. text ed. 7.00 (ISBN 0-932098-09-6). Ctr for NE & North African Stud.

Introduction to Eighty-Eighty, Eighty Eighty-Five Assembly Language Programming. Judi Fernandez & Ruth Ashley. 300p. 1981. pap. text ed. 8.95 (ISBN 0-471-08009-8). Wiley.

Introduction to Electric Circuit Analysis. Ronald J. Tocci. 1973. text ed. 22.95x (ISBN 0-675-08985-9); instructor's manual 3.95 (ISBN 0-686-66873-1). Merrill.

Introduction to Electric Instrumentation & Measurement. B. A. Gregory. LC 80-22869. 435p. 1981. pap. 29.95 (ISBN 0-470-27092-6). Halsted Pr.

Introduction to Electrical Engineering. Muller-Schwarz. 1980. write for info. (ISBN 0-85501-259-5). Heyden.

Introduction to Electrical Machines & Transformers. George McPherson. 544p. 1981. text ed. 22.95 (ISBN 0-471-05586-7); tchrs.' ed. avail. (ISBN 0-471-07954-5). Wiley.

Introduction to Electricity. L. T. Agger. 1971. 29.95x (ISBN 0-19-859306-6). Oxford U Pr.

Introduction to Electricity & Electronics. Orla Loper et al. LC 77-78174. 1979. text ed. 15.80 (ISBN 0-8273-1160-5); instructor's guide 2.25 (ISBN 0-8273-1162-1). Delmar.

Introduction to Electrochemical Science. J. Bockris et al. (Wyckeham Science Ser.: Vol. 29). pap. 8.30 o.p. (ISBN 0-387-91116-2). Springer Verlag.

Introduction to Electrochemical Science. J. Bockris et al. (Wykeham Science Ser.: No.29). 1974. 9.95x (ISBN 0-8448-1156-4). Crane Russak Co.

Introduction to Electromagnetic Theory. P. C. Clemmow. LC 73-77174. (Illus.). 320p. 1973. 42.00 (ISBN 0-521-20239-6); pap. 14.50x (ISBN 0-521-09815-7). Cambridge U Pr.

Introduction to Electron & Electromechanical Devices. D. Yeager & R. Gourley. 1976. 20.95 (ISBN 0-13-481408-8). P-H.

Introduction to Electron Microscopy. 2nd ed. Cecil E. Hall. LC 80-39788. 410p. 1981. Repr. of 1966 ed. lib. bdg. price not set (ISBN 0-89874-302-8). Krieger.

Introduction to Electron Microscopy. 2nd ed. S. Wischnitzer. LC 77-93757. 1970. 19.50 (ISBN 0-08-006944-4). Pergamon.

Introduction to Electron Microscopy. 3rd ed. Saul Wischnitzer. LC 80-15266. 320p. 1980. 19.75 (ISBN 0-08-026298-8). Pergamon.

Introduction to Electronic Analogue Computers. 2nd ed. C. A. Wass & K. C. Garner. 1965. 22.00 (ISBN 0-08-011071-1); pap. 10.75 (ISBN 0-08-013655-9). Pergamon.

Introduction to Electronic Computing. R. L. Boyes et al. 1971. 17.00 (ISBN 0-471-09380-7, Pub. by Wiley). Krieger.

Introduction to Electronic Data Processing. rev ed. Andrew Vazsonyi. 1977. text ed. 16.95x o.p. (ISBN 0-256-01834-0); study guide 5.95 o.p. (ISBN 0-256-01844-8). Irwin.

Introduction to Electronic Technology. Richard J. Romanek. (Illus.). 480p. 1975. ref. ed. 19.95 (ISBN 0-13-468801-5). P-H.

Introduction to Electronics. Theodore Korneff. 1966. text ed. 19.95 (ISBN 0-12-421150-X). Acad Pr.

Introduction to Electronics. 2nd ed. H. A. Romanowitz & R. E. Puckett. LC 75-23060. 531p. 1976. text ed. 24.95x (ISBN 0-471-73264-8); instructor's manual avail. (ISBN 0-471-01509-1). Wiley.

Introduction to Electronics & Instrumentation. John W. McWane. 1981. text ed. 19.95 (ISBN 0-534-00938-7, Breton Pubs). Wadsworth Pub.

Introduction to Electronics for Technologists. John P. Hoffman. LC 77-74381. (Illus.). 1978. text ed. 17.95 (ISBN 0-395-25115-X); solutions manual 1.25 (ISBN 0-395-25819-7). HM.

Introduction to Elementary Particle Theory. Yuri V. Novozhilov. Tr. by Jonathon L. Rosner. 1974. text ed. 64.00 (ISBN 0-08-017954-1). Pergamon.

Introduction to Elementary Vector Analysis. John C. Tallack. 1966. text ed. 16.95x (ISBN 0-521-07999-3). Cambridge U Pr.

Introduction to Enamelling. Pam Patterson. (Illus.). 1978. 14.50 (ISBN 0-589-50050-3, Pub by Reed Books Australia). C E Tuttle.

Introduction to Energy Conversion, 3 vols. V. Kadambi & Manchar Prasad. Incl. Vol. 1. Basic Thermodynamics. 1976. o.p. (ISBN 0-470-50925-2); Vol. 2. Energy Conversion Cycles. 1974 (ISBN 0-470-50926-0); Vol. 3. Principles of Turbomachinery. 1978 (ISBN 0-470-99157-7). LC 74-13881. 13.95 ea. Halsted Pr.

Introduction to Engineering. Robert M. Glorioso & F. S. Hill, Jr. (Illus.). 448p. 1975. ref. ed. 21.95x (ISBN 0-13-482398-2). P-H.

Introduction to Engineering Design. T. T. Woodson. 1966. text ed. 17.00 o.p. (ISBN 0-07-071760-5, C); instructor's manual 1.50 o.p. (ISBN 0-07-071761-3). McGraw.

Introduction to Engineering Design with Design Projects. T. Shoup et al. 1981. pap. 15.95 (ISBN 0-13-482364-8); pap. 8.95 wkbk. (ISBN 0-13-716274-X). P-H.

Introduction to Engineering Economics. 192p. 1980. 21.00x (Pub. by Telford England). State Mutual Bk.

Introduction to Engineering Including Fortran Programming. L. S. Fletcher & T. E. Shoup. (Illus.). 1978. pap. 14.95 ref. ed. (ISBN 0-13-501858-7). P-H.

Introduction to Engineering Measurements. A. Richard Graham. (Illus.). 224p. 1975. ref. ed 19.95 (ISBN 0-13-482406-7). P-H.

Introduction to Engineering: Methods, Concepts & Issues. Edward V. Krick. LC 75-41432. 351p. 1976. text ed. 17.95x (ISBN 0-471-50750-4); instructor's manual avail. (ISBN 0-471-01912-7). Wiley.

Introduction to Engineering Systems. Samuel Seely. 548p. 1972. text ed. 31.00 (ISBN 0-08-016821-3); pap. text ed. 15.50 (ISBN 0-08-018998-9). Pergamon.

Introduction to Engineering Thermodynamics. Howard Silver & John Nydahl. LC 76-3601. (Illus.). 500p. 1977. text ed. 22.95 (ISBN 0-8299-0053-5); solutions manual avail. (ISBN 0-8299-0573-1). West Pub.

Introduction to English Language Teaching. John Haycraft. (Longman Handbooks for Language Teachers). (Illus.). 1979. pap. text ed. 7.25x (ISBN 0-582-55604-X). Longman.

Introduction to English Literature. Jorge L. Borges. Ed. by Robert O. Evans & L. Clark Keating. Tr. by Robert O. Evans & L. Clark Keating. LC 73-86401. 88p. 1974. 7.00x (ISBN 0-8131-1307-5). U Pr of Ky.

Introduction to English Mediaeval Architecture. 2nd ed. Hugh Braun. 1968. 14.95 o.p. (ISBN 0-571-08331-5, Pub. by Faber & Faber). Merrimack Bk Serv.

Introduction to English Transformational Syntax. Rodney Huddleston. (English Language Ser.). (Illus.). 304p. 1975. text ed. 19.95x (ISBN 0-582-55061-0); pap. text ed. 13.50x (ISBN 0-582-55062-9). Longman.

Introduction to Entomology. 9th ed. John H. Comstock. 1093p. 1940. text ed. 35.00x (ISBN 0-8014-0083-X). Comstock.

Introduction to Environmental Microbiology. Ralph Mitchell. (Illus.). 400p. 1974. ref. ed. 26.95x (ISBN 0-13-482489-X). P-H.

Introduction to Environmental Science. Joseph M. Moran et al. LC 79-19007. (Illus.). 1980. text ed. 19.95x (ISBN 0-7167-1020-X); instr's manual & transparency masters avail. W H Freeman.

Introduction to Epidemiology: A Programmed Text. Fisher. (Illus.). 1975. pap. 15.50 o.p. (ISBN 0-8385-0091-9). ACC.

Introduction to Equilibrium Thermodynamics. Bernard Morrill. 1973. text ed. 32.00 (ISBN 0-08-016891-4); pap. text ed. 17.60 (ISBN 0-08-019003-0); manual 0.50 (ISBN 0-686-67231-3). Pergamon.

Introduction to Error-Correcting Codes. Shu Lin. LC 76-124417. 1970. ref. ed. 24.95 (ISBN 0-13-482810-0). P-H.

Introduction to Estates & Trusts. Institute for Paralegal Training. Ed. by Steven Stern & Caroline S. Laden. LC 78-27574. (Paralegal Ser). 697p. 1979. text ed. 18.95 (ISBN 0-8299-2025-0). West Pub.

Introduction to Existentialism. Robert G. Olson. (Orig.). 1962. pap. text ed. 3.50 (ISBN 0-486-20055-8). Dover.

Introduction to Experimental Astronomy: Preliminary Edition. Roger B. Culver. (Illus.). 1974. pap. text ed. 8.95x (ISBN 0-7167-0347-5). W H Freeman.

Introduction to Experimental Ecology. Trevor Lewis & L. R. Taylor. 1967. 30.50 o.p. (ISBN 0-12-447150-1). Acad Pr.

Introduction to Experimental Psychology. Eva Conrad & Terry Maul. 350p. 1981. text ed. 16.95 (ISBN 0-471-06005-4). Wiley.

Introduction to Experimentation. Ernest Rabinowicz. LC 72-93989. 1970. pap. 7.95 (ISBN 0-201-06481-2). A-W.

Introduction to Exploration Economics. 2nd ed. R. E. Megill. LC 75-153985. 160p. 1979. 23.00 (ISBN 0-87814-004-2). Pennwell Pub.

Introduction to Factor Analysis: What It Is & How to Do It. Jae-On Kim & Charles Mueller. LC 79-103006. (University Papers Ser.: Quantitive Applications in the Social Sciences No. 13). 1978. pap. 3.50x (ISBN 0-8039-1165-3). Sage.

Introduction to Family Medicine. Ian R. McWhinney. (Illus.). 224p. 1981. text ed. 16.95x (ISBN 0-19-502807-4); pap. text ed. 9.95 (ISBN 0-19-502808-2). Oxford U Pr.

Introduction to Farm Organisation & Mamagement. M. Buckett. (Illus.). 280p. 1981. 50.00 (ISBN 0-08-024433-5); pap. 21.00 (ISBN 0-08-024432-7). Pergamon.

Introduction to Fashion Merchandising. Evelyn Grace. LC 78-1318. (Illus.). 1978. ref. ed. 16.95 (ISBN 0-13-483206-X). P-H.

Introduction to Fastening Systems. D. H. Chaddock. (Engineering Design Guides Ser.). (Illus.). 1974. pap. 5.95x o.p. (ISBN 0-19-859128-4). Oxford U Pr.

Introduction to Federal Taxation: 1981 Edition. Victor H. Tidwell & William L. Raby. (Illus.). 480p. 1981. text ed. 21.00 (ISBN 0-13-483404-6); pap. 9.95 study guide (ISBN 0-13-483446-1). P-H.

Introduction to Feeding Farm Livestock. 2nd ed. R. H. Nelson. 1979. text ed. 28.00 (ISBN 0-08-023757-6); pap. text ed. 9.75 (ISBN 0-08-023756-8). Pergamon.

Introduction to Feynman Diagrams. S. M. Bilenky. LC 73-21657. 1974. text ed. 37.00 (ISBN 0-08-017799-9). Pergamon.

Introduction to Field Biology. 2nd ed. Donald P. Bennett & David A. Humphries. 1974. pap. text ed. 13.50x (ISBN 0-7131-2458-X). Intl Ideas.

Introduction to Field Quantization. Y. Takahashi. 1969. 32.00 (ISBN 0-08-012824-6). Pergamon.

Introduction to Film. Thomas Sobchack & Vivian C. Sobchack. (Illus.). 512p. 1980. pap. text ed. 11.95 (ISBN 0-316-80250-6); instructor's manual free (ISBN 0-316-80251-4). Little.

Introduction to Filter Theory. David E. Johnson. (Illus.). 336p. 1976. 24.95 (ISBN 0-13-483776-2). P-H.

Introduction to Financial Accounting. C. Horngren. 1981. 21.00 (ISBN 0-13-483743-6); practice set 6.95, (ISBN 0-13-483701-0); working papers 6.95 (ISBN 0-13-483727-4); student guide 6.95 (ISBN 0-13-483750-9). P-H.

Introduction to Financial Accounting. 5th ed. Charles T. Horngren. (Ser. in Accounting). 672p. 1981. text ed. 21.95 (ISBN 0-686-69276-4). P-H.

Introduction to Financial Accounting. Levis D. McCullers & Relmond P. Van Daniker. LC 74-23261. (Management, Accounting & Information Systems Ser.). 1975. text ed. 23.95x (ISBN 0-471-58365-0). Wiley.

Introduction to Financial Accounting. Chris Nobes. (Illus.). 272p. 1980. text ed. 27.50x (ISBN 0-04-332071-6, 2363); pap. text ed. 11.50x (ISBN 0-04-332072-4, 2364). Allen Unwin.

Introduction to Financial Economics. E. L. Furness. 1972. pap. 13.95x (ISBN 0-434-90596-8). Intl Ideas.

Introduction to Financial Management. O. Maurice Joy. 1977. 17.50x o.p. (ISBN 0-256-01880-4). Irwin.

Introduction to Financial Management. rev. ed. O. Maurice Joy. 1980. 19.95x (ISBN 0-256-02340-9). Irwin.

Introduction to Fire Prevention. James C. Robertson. (Fire Science Ser.). 1975. text ed. 14.95x (ISBN 0-02-477080-9). Macmillan.

Introduction to Fire Science. Loren S. Bush & James McLaughlin. Ed. by Harvey Gruber. (Fire Science Ser.). 1970. text ed. 13.95x (ISBN 0-02-473900-6). Macmillan.

Introduction to Fishery Sciences. William F. Royce. 351p. 1972. text ed. 22.50 (ISBN 0-12-600950-3). Acad Pr.

Introduction to Floriculture. Roy A. Larson. 1980. text ed. 29.50 (ISBN 0-12-437650-9). Acad Pr.

Introduction to Fluid & Particle Mechanics. S. J. Michell. 1970. 41.00 (ISBN 0-08-013313-4); pap. 14.00 (ISBN 0-08-013312-6). Pergamon.

Introduction to Fluid Dynamics. George K. Batchelor. (Illus.). 634p. 1967. 71.50 (ISBN 0-521-04118-X); pap. 19.95x (ISBN 0-521-09817-3). Cambridge U Pr.

Introduction to Fluid Logic. E. C. Fitch & J. B. Surjaatmadja. (McGraw-Hill-Hemisphere in Fluids & Thermal Engineering Ser.). (Illus.). 1978. text ed. 26.50 (ISBN 0-07-021126-4, C). McGraw.

Introduction to Fluid Mechanics. 2nd ed. Robert W. Fox & Alan T. McDonald. LC 77-20839. 1978. text ed. 25.95 (ISBN 0-471-01909-7); solutions manual 15.00 (ISBN 0-471-03681-1). Wiley.

Introduction to Fluid Mechanics. R. W. Henke. 1966. 15.95 (ISBN 0-201-02809-3). A-W.

Introduction to Fluid Mechanics. 2nd ed. J. John & W. Haberman. 1980. 25.95 (ISBN 0-13-483941-2). P-H.

Introduction to Fluid Mechanics & Heat Transfer. 3rd. rev. ed. J. M. Kay & R. M. Nedderman. LC 74-77383. 300p. 1975. 44.50 (ISBN 0-521-20533-6); pap. 17.50x (ISBN 0-521-09880-7). Cambridge U Pr.

Introduction to Fluid Mechanics & Heat Transfer. J. D. Parker et al. (Engineering Ser). 1969. text ed. 25.95 (ISBN 0-201-05710-7). A-W.

Introduction to Folklore. David C. Laubach. 192p. (gr. 10-12). 1980. pap. 6.25 (ISBN 0-8104-6039-4). Hayden.

Introduction to Food Rheology. H. G. Muller. LC 72-81532. 260p. 1973. 19.50x (ISBN 0-8448-0013-9). Crane-Russak Co.

Introduction to Food Science. George Stewart & Maynard Amerine. (Food Science & Technology Ser). 1973. text ed. 18.95 (ISBN 0-12-670250-0). Acad Pr.

Introduction to Forensic Sciences. William G. Eckert. LC 80-10864. (Illus.). 1980. pap. text ed. 9.95 (ISBN 0-8016-1489-9). Mosby.

Introduction to Forest Biology. Harold W. Hocker, Jr. LC 78-26878. 1979. text ed. 25.95 (ISBN 0-471-01978-X). Wiley.

Introduction to Forest Genetics. Jonathan W. Wright. 1976. 29.50 (ISBN 0-12-765250-7). Acad Pr.

Introduction to Formal Language Theory. Michael A. Harrison. LC 77-81196. 1978. text ed. 24.95 (ISBN 0-201-02955-3). A-W.

Introduction to Fortran: A Program for Self-Instruction. S. C. Plumb. 1964. pap. text ed. 13.50 o.p. (ISBN 0-07-050350-8, C). McGraw.

Introduction to Free Radical Chemistry. William A. Pryor. (Illus.). 1966. pap. 9.95 ref. ed. (ISBN 0-13-484154-9). P-H.

Introduction to French Classical Tragedy. C. J. Gossip. 1981. 29.50x (ISBN 0-389-20163-4). B&N.

Introduction to Functional Analysis. Nachbin. 200p. 1981. 19.75 (ISBN 0-8247-6984-8). Dekker.

Introduction to Fundamental & Applied Physics. Duane Roller, Sr. & Ronald Blum. 1200p. 1980. Vols. I & II. 28.95 (ISBN 0-8162-7282-4). Holden-Day.

Introduction to Fungi. H. C. Dube. 400p. 1980. 24.00x (Pub. by Croom Helm England). State Mutual Bk.

Introduction to Fungi. 2nd ed. John Webster. LC 79-52856. (Illus.). 1980. 79.50 (ISBN 0-521-22888-3); pap. 21.95x (ISBN 0-521-29699-4). Cambridge U Pr.

Introduction to Furniture Making. John R. Trussell. LC 73-3299. (Illus.). 1973. pap. 5.95 (ISBN 0-8069-8448-1). Sterling.

Introduction to General Pathology. 2nd ed. (Churchill Livingstone Medical Text). (Illus.). 320p. 1981. pap. text ed. 12.50 (ISBN 0-443-01970-3). Churchill.

Introduction to General Relativity. S. K. Bose. LC 80-19150. 120p. 1981. pap. 9.95 (ISBN 0-470-27054-3). Halsted Pr.

Introduction to General Topography. Paul E. Long. LC 71-138370. 1971. text ed. 17.95 (ISBN 0-675-09253-1). Merrill.

Introduction to Genetic Analysis. David T. Suzuki & A. J. Griffiths. LC 75-29480. (Illus.). 1976. 20.95x (ISBN 0-7167-0574-5); answers to problems 0.75 (ISBN 0-7167-0362-9). W H Freeman.

Introduction to Genetic Analysis. 2nd ed. David T. Suzuki & Anthony J. F. Griffiths. LC 80-24522. (Illus.). 1981. text ed. price not set (ISBN 0-7167-1263-6); instrs.' guide avail.; solutions manual avail. W H Freeman.

Introduction to Genetics. 3rd ed. D. J. Mackean. 1978. pap. text ed. 8.95 (ISBN 0-7195-3346-5). Transatlantic.

Introduction to Genetics & Cytogenetics. Herbert P. Riley. (Illus.). 1967. Repr. of 1948 ed. 19.50 o.s.i. (ISBN 0-02-850960-9). Hafner.

Introduction to Genetics & Evolution. James L. Mariner. (Illus.). (gr. 10-12). 1977. pap. text ed. 4.25 (ISBN 0-88334-092-5). Ind Sch Pr.

Introduction to Geographic Field Methods & Techniques. John F. Lounsbury & Frank T. Aldrich. 1979. pap. text ed. 11.95 (ISBN 0-675-08304-4). Merrill.

Introduction to Geological Maps. 2nd rev ed. J. A. Thomas. (Illus.). 1977. pap. text ed. 4.95x (ISBN 0-04-550018-5). Allen Unwin.

Introduction to Geological Structures & Maps: Metric. 3rd ed. G. M. Bennison. (Illus.). 1975. pap. text ed. 9.95x (ISBN 0-7131-2513-6). Intl Ideas.

Introduction to Geology: Physical & Historical. 2nd ed. William L. Stokes et al. LC 77-21570. 1978. text ed. 20.95 (ISBN 0-13-484352-5). P-H.

Introduction to Geometry. 2nd ed. H. S. Coxeter. LC 72-93909. 1969. 27.95 (ISBN 0-471-18283-4). Wiley.

Introduction to Geotechnical Engineering. William D. Kovacs & Robert D. Holtz. (Illus.). 720p. 1981. text ed. 28.95 (ISBN 0-13-484394-0). P-H.

Introduction to Geotechniical Engineering. W. Kovaco & R. Holtz. 1981. 28.95 (ISBN 0-13-484394-0). P-H.

Introduction to Global Analysis: Pure & Applied Mathematics Ser. Donald W. Kahn. LC 79-8858. 1980. 34.50 (ISBN 0-12-394050-8). Acad Pr.

Introduction to Grain Marketing. Walter J. Wills. LC 74-155289. 155p. 1972. 11.65 (ISBN 0-8134-1299-4, 1299); text ed. 8.75x (ISBN 0-685-25881-5). Interstate.

Introduction to Group Characters. W. Ledermann. LC 76-46858. (Illus.). 1977. 47.00 (ISBN 0-521-21486-6); pap. 12.95 (ISBN 0-521-29170-4). Cambridge U Pr.
Introduction to Hamiltonian Optics. Hans A. Buchdahl. LC 69-19372. (Cambridge Monographs on Physics). (Illus.). 1970. 44.50 (ISBN 0-521-07516-5). Cambridge U Pr.
Introduction to Harmonic Analysis. Yitzhak Katznelson. 264p. 1976. pap. text ed. 4.00 (ISBN 0-486-63331-4). Dover.
Introduction to Harmonic Analysis on Reductive P-Adic Groups. Allan J. Silberger. LC 79-19020. (Mathematical Notes Ser.: 23). 376p. 1979. pap. 11.00x (ISBN 0-691-08246-4). Princeton U Pr.
Introduction to Head Injuries. Asoke K. Bagchi. (Illus.). 1981. text ed. 12.95x (ISBN 0-19-561151-9). Oxford U Pr.
Introduction to Health Careers. Joan M. Birchenall & Mary E. Streight. LC 77-26305. 1978. text ed. cancelled (ISBN 0-397-54215-1); pap. text ed. 6.95x (ISBN 0-397-54210-0). Lippincott.
Introduction to Health Careers. Mary E. Kimbrall. (gr. 7-10). 1975. pap. text ed. 5.00 activity ed (ISBN 0-87345-179-1). McKnight.
Introduction to Health Professions. 3rd ed. Anne S. Allen. LC 79-26136. (Illus.). 1980. pap. text ed. 11.50 (ISBN 0-8016-0113-4). Mosby.
Introduction to Health Services & Community Health Systems. new ed. John T. Gentry. LC 77-78899. 1978. text ed. 20.50 (ISBN 0-8211-0612-0); text ed. 18.00 in ten or more copies (ISBN 0-685-48956-6). McCutchan.
Introduction to Heat Engines, Vol. 1. 2nd ed. K. P. Roy. pap. 7.50x (ISBN 0-210-31186-X). Asia.
Introduction to Hebrew. Moshe Greenberg. 1964. text ed. 14.95 (ISBN 0-13-484469-6). P-H.
Introduction to Herpetology. 3rd ed. Coleman J. Goin et al. LC 77-13554. (Illus.). 1978. text ed. 20.95x (ISBN 0-7167-0020-4). W H Freeman.
Introduction to High Energy Physics. Donald H. Perkins. LC 74-137836. (Advanced Physics Ser). 1972. text ed. 20.95 (ISBN 0-201-05785-9). A-W.
Introduction to Higher Algebra. J. Mostowski & M. Stark. 1964. 25.00 (ISBN 0-08-010152-6). Pergamon.
Introduction to Hilbert Space. 2nd ed. Sterling K. Berberian. LC 75-29231. 206p. 1976. text ed. 9.95 (ISBN 0-8284-0287-6). Chelsea Pub.
Introduction to Hilbert Space. 2nd ed. Paul R. Halmos. LC 57-12834. 7.95 (ISBN 0-8284-0082-2). Chelsea Pub.
Introduction to Historical Linguistics. Anthony Arlotto. LC 80-6309. 284p. 1981. lib. bdg. 19.75 (ISBN 0-8191-1459-6); pap. text ed. 10.25 (ISBN 0-8191-1460-X). U Pr of Amer.
Introduction to Homeopathic Medicine. Hamish Boyd. 240p. 1980. 49.00x (Pub. by Beaconsfield England). State Mutual Bk.
Introduction to Homer. W. A. Camps. 128p. 1980. 17.50x (ISBN 0-19-872099-8); pap. 7.50x (ISBN 0-19-872101-3). Oxford U Pr.
Introduction to Homotopy Theory. Peter J. Hilton. (Cambridge Tracts in Mathematics & Mathematical Physics: No. 43). 1953. 21.50 (ISBN 0-521-05265-3). Cambridge U Pr.
Introduction to Hospital Accounting. rev. ed. L. Vann Seawell. LC 77-74543. (Illus.). 508p. 1977. text ed. 14.95x (ISBN 0-930228-05-7); Practice Set (1978) 7.00 (ISBN 0-930228-08-1); Solutions Manual (1977) 29.90 (ISBN 0-930228-06-5). Hospital Finan.
Introduction to Hospitality - Recreation Careers. Judi Evert. (gr. 7-10). 1975. pap. text ed. 5.00 activity ed. (ISBN 0-87345-185-6). McKnight.
Introduction to Hp Spaces. P. J. Koosis. LC 80-65175. (London Mathematical Society Lecture Note Ser.: No. 40). (Illus.). 380p. (Orig.). 1980. pap. 23.95 (ISBN 0-521-23159-0). Cambridge U Pr.
Introduction to Human Anatomy. 7th ed. Carl C. Francis & Alexander H. Martin. LC 75-2455. (Illus.). 1975. text ed. 19.95 (ISBN 0-8016-1646-8). Mosby.
Introduction to Human Anatomy. J. H. Green & P. H. Silver. (Illus.). 400p. 1981. pap. text ed. 16.95x (ISBN 0-19-261196-8). Oxford U Pr.
Introduction to Human Geography. J. H. Lebon. 1966. text ed. 5.50x (ISBN 0-09-031612-6, Hutchinson U Lib). Humanities.
Introduction to Human Physiology. 4th ed. John H. Green. (Illus.). 1976. pap. text ed. 16.50x (ISBN 0-19-263328-7). Oxford U Pr.
Introduction to Human Services. William Lyon & Bill Duke. (Illus.). 320p. 1981. pap. text ed. 14.95 (ISBN 0-8359-3216-8). Reston.
Introduction to Huna. Max F. Long. 3.00 (ISBN 0-89861-004-4). Esoteric Pubns.
Introduction to Hunting. John Williams. (Illus.). pap. 5.25 (ISBN 0-85131-200-4, Dist. by Sporting Book Center). J A Allen.
Introduction to Hydrometeorology. J. P. Bruce & R. H. Clark. 1966. 25.00 (ISBN 0-08-011715-5); pap. 12.00 (ISBN 0-08-011714-7). Pergamon.
Introduction to I-O Concepts & Job Control Language for the IBM Operating System 360. Gordon P. Ashby & Robert L. Heilman. 1971. pap. 13.95x (ISBN 0-8221-0004-5). Dickenson.
Introduction to IBM Direct Access Storage Devices. Marilyn Bohl. 320p. 1981. text ed. 12.95t (ISBN 0-574-21140-3, 13-4140). SRA.
Introduction to Immunohematology. Neville J. Bryant. LC 75-25269. (Illus.). 320p. 1976. text ed. 14.95 (ISBN 0-7216-2170-8). Saunders.
Introduction to Indian Thought. A. L. Herman. (Illus.). 375p. 1976. pap. text ed. 11.95 (ISBN 0-13-484477-7). P-H.
Introduction to Individual Appraisal. George P. Robb & Ann P. Williamson. (Illus.). 360p. write for info. (ISBN 0-398-04473-2); pap. write for info. (ISBN 0-398-04474-0). C C Thomas.
Introduction to Industrial Drying Operations. R. B. Keey. LC 77-30467. 396p. 1978. 52.00 (ISBN 0-08-020594-1); pap. 15.00 (ISBN 0-08-020593-3). Pergamon.
Introduction to Information & Communication Theory. Fred Haber. (Advances in Modern Engineering Ser.). (Illus.). 224p. 1974. text ed. 8.95 (ISBN 0-201-02669-4). A-W.
Introduction to Information, Data & File Structuring. Joanc. Veim. 200p. 1981. pap. 13.00x (ISBN 82-00-05322-9). Universitet.
Introduction to Information Processing. 2nd ed. Donald D. Spencer. (Business Ser.). 1977. text ed. 17.95 (ISBN 0-675-08520-9); student guide 6.95 (ISBN 0-675-08519-5); instructor's manual 3.95 (ISBN 0-686-67522-3); transparencies 3.95 (ISBN 0-686-67523-1). Merrill.
Introduction to Information Processing. 3rd ed. Donald D. Spencer. 650p. 1981. text ed. 17.95 (ISBN 0-675-08073-8). Merrill.
Introduction to Information Theory: Symbols, Signals & Noise. 2nd, rev. ed. J. R. Pierce. 320p. pap. write for info. (ISBN 0-486-24061-4). Dover.
Introduction to Insurance. Mark S. Dorfman. LC 77-22029. (Illus.). 1978. ref. 18.95 (ISBN 0-13-485359-8). P-H.
Introduction to Intercultural Communication. John C. Condon & Fathi S. Yousef. LC 74-14633. (No. 19). 326p. 1975. 7.50 (ISBN 0-672-61328-X, SC19). Bobbs.
Introduction to International Economics. 7th ed. Delbert A. Snider. 1979. text ed. 18.95x (ISBN 0-256-02176-7). Irwin.
Introduction to International Financial Management. Suk H. Kim. LC 80-5203. 302p. 1980. pap. text ed. 10.75 (ISBN 0-8191-1054-X). U Pr of Amer.
Introduction to International Financial Management. Suk H. Kim. LC 80-5203. 272p. 1980. 13.50 o.p. U Pr of Amer.
Introduction to International Law. Ronald B. Kirkemo. LC 73-81677. 1974. 15.95 (ISBN 0-88229-118-1). Nelson-Hall.
Introduction to International Politics. Robert D. Cantor. LC 75-17314. (Illus.). 1976. text ed. 12.95 (ISBN 0-87581-189-2, 189). Peacock Pubs.
Introduction to International Politics. 3rd ed. William D. Coplin. (Illus.). 1980. text ed. 16.95 (ISBN 0-13-485383-0). P-H.
Introduction to International Relations. 2nd ed. P. A. Reynolds. 352p. 1980. pap. text ed. 12.95 (ISBN 0-582-29502-5). Longman.
Introduction to International Relations: Power & Justice. James H. Wolfe & Theo. A. Couloumbis. (Illus.). 1978. text ed. 16.95 (ISBN 0-13-485300-8). P-H.
Introduction to Interpersonal Communication. Sarah A. Barnhart. 1967. pap. text ed. 6.50 scp (ISBN 0-690-00855-4, HarpC). Har-Row.
Introduction to Interpersonal Communication. James C. McCroskey et al. LC 71-126966. 1971. text ed. 14.95x (ISBN 0-13-485425-X). P-H.
Introduction to Invariant Imbedding. Richard Bellman & Milton G. Wing. LC 74-18455. (Pure & Applied Mathematics Ser.). 288p. 1975. 30.50 o.p. (ISBN 0-471-06416-5, Pub. by Wiley-Interscience). Wiley.
Introduction to Investment Management. R. Ronald Sprecher. 1975. text ed. 20.50 (ISBN 0-395-18706-0); instructor's manual pap. 1.50 (ISBN 0-395-18784-2). HM.
Introduction to Islamic Civilization. Ed. by R. M. Savory. LC 74-25662. 220p. 1976. 36.00 (ISBN 0-521-20777-0); pap. 9.95 (ISBN 0-521-09948-X). Cambridge U Pr.
Introduction to Islamic Law. Joseph Schacht. 1964. 24.95x (ISBN 0-19-825161-0). Oxford U Pr.
Introduction to Islamic Theology & Law. Ignaz Goldziher. Ed. by Bernard Lewis. Tr. by Andras Hamori & Ruth Hamori. LC 80-7523. (Modern Classics in Near Eastern Studies). 325p. 1981. 22.50 (ISBN 0-691-07257-4); pap. 9.95 (ISBN 0-691-10099-3). Princeton U Pr.
Introduction to Italian. Gifford Orwen. 1971. 7.75 (ISBN 0-913298-11-5). S F Vanni.
Introduction to Japan. 2nd ed. Herschel Webb. LC 57-9552. 1957. pap. 5.00x (ISBN 0-231-08505-2). Columbia U Pr.
Introduction to Japanese Civilization. Ed. by Arthur E. Tiedemann. 626p. 1974. 27.50x (ISBN 0-231-03651-5). Columbia U Pr.
Introduction to Javanese Law. M. C. Hoadley & M. B. Hooker. LC 80-26636. (Monographs of the Association for Asian Studies: No. XXXVII). 1981. text ed. 9.95x (ISBN 0-8165-0727-9). U of Ariz Pr.
Introduction to Jewelry Casting. Illus. by Robert Wald. 1974. pap. 7.95 o.p. (ISBN 0-8096-1885-0, Assn Pr). Follett.
Introduction to Judaism. Joseph Kalir. LC 79-6758. 170p. 1980. text ed. 17.50 (ISBN 0-8191-0948-7); pap. text ed. 8.50 (ISBN 0-8191-0949-5). U Pr of Amer.
Introduction to Juristic Psychology. Prabodh C. Bose. (Historical Foundations of Forensic Psychiatry & Psychology Ser.). 426p. 1980. Repr. of 1917 ed. lib. bdg. 39.50 (ISBN 0-686-68561-X). Da Capo.
Introduction to Kinetic Theory. T. Koga. LC 76-93474. 1970. 82.00 (ISBN 0-08-006538-4); pap. 27.00 (ISBN 0-08-018993-8). Pergamon.
Introduction to Kinship & Social Organization. Burton Pasternak. (Illus.). 208p. 1976. Ref. Ed. pap. 8.95 (ISBN 0-13-485466-7). P-H.
Introduction to Labor. Ed. by James W. Robinson et al. 1975. pap. 9.95 (ISBN 0-13-485490-X). P-H.
Introduction to Laboratory Chemistry. 9th ed. L. Earle Arnow. (Illus.). 102p. 1976. pap. text ed. 8.50 (ISBN 0-8016-0325-0). Mosby.
Introduction to Laboratory Chemistry: General. 2nd ed. Arthur L. Williams et al. LC 77-79451. (Chemistry Ser.). 1978. pap. text ed. 8.50 (ISBN 0-201-08458-9). A-W.
Introduction to Laboratory Chemistry: Organic & Biochemistry. 2nd ed. Arthur L. Williams et al. LC 77-81204. (Chemistry Ser.). 1978. pap. text ed. 8.50 (ISBN 0-201-08459-7). A-W.
Introduction to Lalique Glass. Katherine M. McClinton. (Illus.). 1978. 17.95 (ISBN 0-87069-238-0). Wallace-Homestead.
Introduction to Lasers & Their Applications. Donald C. O'Shea et al. (Physics Ser.). 1977. text ed. 20.95 (ISBN 0-201-05509-0). A-W.
Introduction to Latin American Politics: The Structure of Conflict. Martin C. Needler. LC 77-23222. 1977. text ed. 16.95 (ISBN 0-13-486043-8). P-H.
Introduction to Lattice Dynamics. A. K. Ghatak & L. S. Kothari. 1972. 22.50 (ISBN 0-201-02363-6, Adv Bk Prog). A-W.
Introduction to Law. Phil Harris. (Law in Context Ser.). 288p. 1980. 31.00x (ISBN 0-297-77826-9, Pub. by Weidenfeld & Nicolson England). Rothman.
Introduction to Law & the Legal Process. 3rd ed. Bernard F. Cataldo et al. LC 79-13193. 1980. 26.50 (ISBN 0-471-14082-1); tchr's manual avail. (ISBN 0-471-02267-5). Wiley.
Introduction to Law & the Legal System. 2nd ed. Harold J. Grilliot. LC 78-69579. (Illus.). 1979. text ed. 18.50 (ISBN 0-395-26866-4); inst. manual 0.80 (ISBN 0-395-26865-6). HM.
Introduction to Law Enforcement & Criminal Justice. rev. ed. A. C. Germann et al. (Illus.). 400p. 1980. 11.75 (ISBN 0-398-03799-X). C C Thomas.
Introduction to Law Enforcement & Criminal Justice. Henry M. Wrobleski & Karen M. Hess. (Criminal Justice Ser.). (Illus.). 1979. text ed. 17.95 (ISBN 0-8299-0250-3); instrs.' manual avail. (ISBN 0-8299-0602-9). West Pub.
Introduction to Law in Contemporary Africa. 100p. 1976. pap. 15.00 (ISBN 0-914970-18-6, CM 002, Conch Mag). Unipub.
Introduction to Learning Disabilities. Kim Reid & Wayne Hresko. (Illus.). 448p. Date not set. text ed. 16.95x (ISBN 0-07-051768-1, C). McGraw.
Introduction to Learning Disabilities: The Psycho-Behavioral Approach. D. Hallahan & J. Kauffman. 1976. 17.95 (ISBN 0-13-485524-8). P-H.
Introduction to Lecithin. Howard E. Hill. 1976. pap. 1.25 o.s.i. (ISBN 0-515-04219-6). Jove Pubns.
Introduction to Legal Typing. Berniece Craft. LC 78-2421. 1978. pap. 8.55 (ISBN 0-672-97097-X); tchr's manual 3.33 (ISBN 0-672-97313-8). Bobbs.
Introduction to Library Research in French Literature. Robert K. Baker. LC 77-18074. (Westview Special Study Ser.). 1978. lib. bdg. 22.50x (ISBN 0-89158-060-3); pap. text ed. 9.00 (ISBN 0-89158-082-4). Westview.
Introduction to Library Science: Basic Elements of Library Services. Jesse H. Shera. LC 76-21332. (Library Science Text Ser.). 1976. lib. bdg. 13.50x (ISBN 0-87287-173-8). Libs Unl.
Introduction to Library Technical Services. Frances S. Bernhardt. 1979. 15.00 (ISBN 0-8242-0637-1). Wilson.
Introduction to Lie Algebras & Representation Theory. J. E. Humphreys. LC 72-85951. (Graduate Texts in Mathematics: Vol. 9). (Illus.). 170p. 1978. 18.80 (ISBN 0-387-90053-5). Springer-Verlag.
Introduction to Ligand Fields. B. N. Figgis. 351p. 1966. 33.95 (ISBN 0-470-25880-2). Wiley.
Introduction to Linear Algebra. Philip W. Gillett. 1975. text ed. 19.50 (ISBN 0-395-18574-2); solutions manual 3.00 (ISBN 0-395-18809-1). HM.
Introduction to Linear Algebra. Lee W. Johnson & R. Dean Riess. LC 80-19984. (Mathematics Ser.). (Illus.). 352p. 1981. text ed. 16.95 (ISBN 0-201-03392-5). A-W.
Introduction to Linear Algebra. Serge A. Lang. LC 77-100872. (Mathematics Ser). 1970. pap. 10.95 (ISBN 0-201-04206-1). A-W.
Introduction to Linear Algebra. Peter V. O'Neil. 1979. text ed. 19.95x (ISBN 0-534-00606-X). Wadsworth Pub.
Introduction to Linear Algebra for Social Scientists. Gordon Mills. 1969. text ed. 18.95x o.p. (ISBN 0-04-512008-0); pap. text ed. 8.95x o.p. (ISBN 0-04-512009-9). Allen Unwin.
Introduction to Linear Analysis. Donald L. Kreider et al. 1966. 22.95 (ISBN 0-201-03949-4). A-W.
Introduction to Linear & Nonlinear Programming. David G. Luenberger. LC 72-186209. 1973. text ed. 19.50 (ISBN 0-201-04347-5). A-W.
Introduction to Linear Models. J. Ward, Jr. & E. Jennings. 1973. ref. ed. 21.95x (ISBN 0-13-486175-2). P-H.
Introduction to Linear Programming & Game Theory. Paul R. Thie. LC 78-15328. 1979. text ed. 20.95 (ISBN 0-471-04248-X); tchr's. manual avail. (ISBN 0-471-04267-6). Wiley.
Introduction to Linear Programming & the Theory of Games. S. Vajda. 76p. 1963. pap. text ed. 4.95x o.p. (ISBN 0-412-20310-3, Pub. by Chapman & Hall). Methuen Inc.
Introduction to Linear Programming & the Theory of Games. S. Vajda. 1963. pap. 4.95 o.p. (ISBN 0-470-89782-1). Halsted Pr.
Introduction to Linear Regression & Correlation. Allen L. Edwards. LC 75-38811. (Illus.). 1976. pap. text ed. 9.95x (ISBN 0-7167-0561-3). W H Freeman.
Introduction to Linguistics. Crane et al. 320p. (Orig.). 1981. pap. text ed. 11.95 (ISBN 0-316-16015-6). Little.
Introduction to Linguistics. Bruce L. Liles. 368p. 1975. ref. ed. 14.50 (ISBN 0-13-486134-5); pap. text ed. 9.95 (ISBN 0-13-486126-4). P-H.
Introduction to Literature. 7th ed. Barnet et al. 1981. pap. text ed. 9.95 (ISBN 0-316-08211-2); tchrs'. manual free (ISBN 0-316-08212-0). Little.
Introduction to Literature. Seyler & Wilan. 1981. 10.95 (ISBN 0-88284-113-0). Alfred Pub.
Introduction to Literature & the Fine Arts. J. F. Taylor et al. (Illus.). 418p. 1950. text ed. 10.00x (ISBN 0-87013-037-4). Mich St U Pr.
Introduction to Literature in Brazil. Alfranio Coutinho. Tr. by Gregory Rabassa. LC 69-15569. 1969. 20.00x (ISBN 0-231-02993-4). Columbia U Pr.
Introduction to Liturgical Theology. Alexander Schmemann. LC 66-69197. 170p. 1966. pap. 5.95 (ISBN 0-913836-18-4). St Vladimirs.
Introduction to Livestock Production: Including Dairy & Poultry. 2nd ed. Ed. by H. H. Cole. LC 66-16377. (Illus.). 1966. 26.95x (ISBN 0-7167-0812-4). W H Freeman.
Introduction to Logic. Andrew H. Bachhuber. (Illus.). 1957. text ed. 11.95 (ISBN 0-13-487280-0). P-H.
Introduction to Logic. Charles W. Kegley & Jacquelyn A. Kegley. (Philosophy Ser.). 1978. text ed. 15.95 (ISBN 0-675-08358-3); media pkg. 75.00 (ISBN 0-675-08357-5); instructor's manual 3.95 (ISBN 0-686-67979-2). Merrill.
Introduction to Logic. David Mitchell. 1967. text ed. 9.00x (ISBN 0-09-064633-9, Hutchinson U Lib); pap. text ed. 5.25x (ISBN 0-09-064634-7, Hutchinson U Lib). Humanities.
Introduction to Logic: Mastering the Powers of Logical Thinking. Alexius Rodman. (Illus.). 1980. deluxe ed. 37.75 (ISBN 0-89266-228-X). Am Classical Coll Pr.
Introduction to Logic: Predicate Logic. Howard Pospesel. (Illus.). 224p. 1976. text ed. 9.95 (ISBN 0-13-486225-2). P-H.
Introduction to Logic: Propositional Logic. Howard Pospesel. (Illus.). 224p. 1974. pap. text ed. 8.95 (ISBN 0-13-486217-1). P-H.
Introduction to Logical Design of Digital Circuits. C. M. Reeves. LC 77-182029. (Computer Science Texts Ser: No. 1). (Illus.). 200p. 1972. text ed. 11.95x (ISBN 0-521-09705-3). Cambridge U Pr.
Introduction to Macro-Economics. J. Harvey & M. Johnson. 320p. 1971. text ed. 13.00x (ISBN 0-333-12509-6); pap. text ed. 6.00x (ISBN 0-333-12511-8). Humanities.

Introduction to Magnetic Materials. Berrard D. Cullity. LC 71-159665. 1972. text ed. 27.95 (ISBN 0-201-01218-9). A-W.

Introduction to Management. Joseph A. Litterer. LC 77-23820. (Ser. in Management & Administration). 1978. text ed. 20.95 (ISBN 0-471-54100-1); tchrs. manual avail. Wiley.

Introduction to Management. Gerald A. Silver. (Illus.). 525p. 1981. text ed. 16.95 (ISBN 0-8299-0415-8). West Pub.

Introduction to Management: A Contingency Approach. Fred Luthans. 1975. text ed. 18.95x (ISBN 0-07-039125-4, C); instructors' manual 4.95 (ISBN 0-07-039126-2). McGraw.

Introduction to Management Accounting. 4th ed. Charles T. Horngren. LC 77-14973. 1978. ref. ed. 19.95 (ISBN 0-13-487595-8). P-H.

Introduction to Management Accounting. 5th ed. Charles T. Horngren. (Ser. in Accounting). (Illus.). 848p. 1981. text ed. 21.00 (ISBN 0-13-487652-0); wkbk. by Dudley W. Curry 8.95 (ISBN 0-13-487785-3). P-H.

Introduction to Management Accounting: Student Guide. 4th ed. Dudley W. Curry. (Illus.). 1978. pap. text ed. 8.95 ref. (ISBN 0-13-487587-7). P-H.

Introduction to Management in the Hospitality Industry. Thomas F. Powers. LC 78-23205. (Service Management Ser.). 1979. text ed. 17.95c (ISBN 0-471-03128-3); tchrs. manual (ISBN 0-471-05355-4). Wiley.

Introduction to Management Information Systems. Robert C. Murdick & Joel E. Ross. (Illus.). 1977. 18.95 (ISBN 0-13-486233-3). P-H.

Introduction to Management Science. A. Victor Cabot & Donald L. Hartnett. LC 76-20024. (Illus.). 1977. text ed. 18.95 (ISBN 0-201-02746-1). A-W.

Introduction to Management Science. Thomas M. Cook & Robert A. Russell. 1977. text ed. 19.95 (ISBN 0-13-486084-5). P-H.

Introduction to Management Science. 2nd ed. Thomas M. Cook & Robert A. Russell. (Illus.). 640p. 1981. text ed. 22.95 (ISBN 0-13-486092-6). P-H.

Introduction to Management Science: Quantitative Approaches to Decision Making. 2nd ed. Anderson et al. 1979. text ed. 19.95 (ISBN 0-8299-0193-0); study guide 7.50 (ISBN 0-8299-0283-X); instrs.' manual avail. (ISBN 0-8299-0451-4); transparency masters avail. (ISBN 0-8299-0452-2). West Pub.

Introduction to Management Science: Quantitative Approach to Managerial Decisions. Billy M. Thornton & Paul Preston. (Business Ser.). 1977. text ed. 18.95 (ISBN 0-675-08518-7); instructor's manual 3.95 (ISBN 0-686-67524-X); card deck 3.95 (ISBN 0-686-67525-8); transparencies 3.95 (ISBN 0-686-67526-6). Merrill.

Introduction to Managerial Economics. Christopher I. Savage & John R. Small. 1967. text ed. 6.50x (ISBN 0-09-084092-5, Hutchinson U Lib). Humanities.

Introduction to Managerial Economics. William F. Sharpe. LC 73-7950. 128p. 1973. 15.00x (ISBN 0-231-03693-0); pap. 6.00x (ISBN 0-231-03786-4). Columbia U Pr.

Introduction to Managerial Finance. Harold Bierman, Jr. & Jerome Haas. 1973. text ed. 12.95x (ISBN 0-393-09353-0). Norton.

Introduction to Manufacturing Careers. Willis Ray. (gr. 7-10). 1975. pap. text ed. 5.00 activity ed. (ISBN 0-87345-177-5). McKnight.

Introduction to Marine Biology. 3rd ed. Bayard H. McConnaughey. LC 77-25826. (Illus.). 1978. text ed. 23.50 (ISBN 0-8016-3258-7). Mosby.

Introduction to Marine Biology (a Laboratory Text) Jules M. Crane. LC 73-76466. 1973. pap. text ed. 11.95 (ISBN 0-675-08954-9); instructor's manual 3.95 (ISBN 0-686-66860-X). Merrill.

Introduction to Marine Geology. M. J. Keen. 1968. 27.00 (ISBN 0-08-012506-9); pap. 9.25 (ISBN 0-08-012505-0). Pergamon.

Introduction to Marine Geology & Geomorphology. Cuchlaine King. LC 74-81340. 336p. 1975. pap. 19.50x (ISBN 0-8448-0401-0). Crane-Russak Co.

Introduction to Marine Science. P. S. Meadows & J. I. Campbell. LC 78-6738. (Tertiary Level Biology Ser.). 1978. pap. text ed. 19.95x (ISBN 0-470-26379-2). Halsted Pr.

Introduction to Marketing. D. Amarchand & B. Varadharajan. 1980. text ed. 15.00x (ISBN 0-7069-0699-3, Pub. by Vikas India). Advent Bk.

Introduction to Marketing Management. 3rd. ed. Stewart H. Rewoldt et al. 1977. text ed. 19.95 (ISBN 0-256-01928-2). Irwin.

Introduction to Mass Communications & Mass Media. William E. Francois. LC 76-46059. (Advertising & Journalism Ser.). 1977. pap. text ed. 14.95 (ISBN 0-88244-141-8). Grid Pub.

Introduction to Mass Spectrometry: Biomedical, Environmental & Forensic Applications. J. Throck Watson. LC 74-21989. 1976. 27.00 (ISBN 0-89004-056-7). Raven.

Introduction to Materials & Structure of Music. William Christ & Richard P. Delone. (Illus.). 390p. 1975. pap. text ed. 13.95 (ISBN 0-13-485532-9). P-H.

Introduction to Materials Science & Engineering. Kenneth Ralls et al. LC 76-10813. 608p. 1976. text ed. 26.95 (ISBN 0-471-70665-5); solution manual avail. (ISBN 0-471-02397-3). Wiley.

Introduction to Materials Science: S. I. Edition. B. R. Schlenker. LC 73-16682. 364p. 1974. 22.95 (ISBN 0-471-76177-X). Wiley.

Introduction to Mathematical Analysis. C. R. Clapham. (Library of Mathematics). (Illus.). 92p. 1973. pap. 5.00 (ISBN 0-7100-7529-4). Routledge & Kegan.

Introduction to Mathematical Analysis with Applications to Problems of Economics. Paul H. Daus & William M. Whyburn. 1958. 13.95 (ISBN 0-201-01445-9). A-W.

Introduction to Mathematical Biology. S. I. Rubinow. LC 75-12520. 386p. 1975. 34.50 (ISBN 0-471-74446-8, Pub. by Wiley-Interscience). Wiley.

Introduction to Mathematical Concensus Theory. Kim & Roush. 192p. 1980. 25.00 (ISBN 0-8247-1001-0). Dekker.

Introduction to Mathematical Control Theory. Stephen Barnett. (Oxford Applied Mathematics & Engineering Sciences Ser). (Illus.). 280p. 1975. 21.00x (ISBN 0-19-859618-9). Oxford U Pr.

Introduction to Mathematical Economics. Anthony L. Ostrosky, Jr. & James V. Koch. LC 78-69569. (Illus.). 1979. text ed. 18.95 (ISBN 0-395-27052-9); solutions manual 1.10 (ISBN 0-395-27053-7). HM.

Introduction to Mathematical Economics: Matrix Algebra & Linear Economic Models. Richard H. Puckett. LC 70-142830. (Illus.). 276p. text ed. 8.95x o.p. (ISBN 0-669-49783-5). Heath.

Introduction to Mathematical Fluid Dynamics. Richard E. Meyer. LC 75-158527. (Pure & Applied Mathematics Ser.: No. 24). 1971. 25.95 o.p. (ISBN 0-471-60050-4, Pub. by Wiley-Interscience). Wiley.

Introduction to Mathematical Methods in Economics. J. Colin Glass. 352p. 1980. text ed. 18.95 (ISBN 0-07-084116-0, C). McGraw.

Introduction to Mathematical Methods of Physics. Lorella M. Jones. LC 78-57377. 1979. text ed. 21.95 (ISBN 0-8053-5130-2). Benjamin-Cummings.

Introduction to Mathematical Modeling. Edward A. Bender. LC 77-23840. 1978. 22.95 (ISBN 0-471-02951-3, Pub by Wiley-Interscience); solutions manual 4.50 (ISBN 0-471-03407-X). Wiley.

Introduction to Mathematical Models in the Social & Life Sciences. Michael Olinick. LC 77-77758. (Illus.). 1978. text ed. 22.95 (ISBN 0-201-05448-5). A-W.

Introduction to Mathematical Philosophy. Bertrand Russell. (Muirhead Library of Philoaophy Ser.). Repr. of 1963 ed. text ed. 19.50x (ISBN 0-04-510020-9). Humanities.

Introduction to Mathematical Risk Theory. Hans U. Gerber. LC 79-89749. (S. S. Huebner Foundation Monographs: No. 8). (Illus.). 1980. pap. 15.95 (ISBN 0-918930-08-1). Huebner Foun Insur.

Introduction to Mathematical Sociology. James S. Coleman. 1964. 19.95 (ISBN 0-02-906520-8). Free Pr.

Introduction to Mathematical Statistics & Its Applications. R. Larsen & M. Marx. 1981. 22.95 (ISBN 0-13-487744-6). P-H.

Introduction to Mathematics, 2 bks. 1980. pap. text ed. 3.00 ea. Bk. 1 (ISBN 0-8428-9341-5). Cambridge Bk.

Introduction to Mathematics. 4th ed. Bruce E. Merserve & Max A. Sobel. (Illus.). 1978. text ed. 17.95 (ISBN 0-13-487553-2). P-H.

Introduction to Mathematics. V. Dean Turner & Howard L. Prouse. 1972. 13.95x o.p. (ISBN 0-673-05960-X). Scott F.

Introduction to Mathematics for Business Analysis. R. C. Meier & S. H. Archer. 1960. text ed. 15.95 o.p. (ISBN 0-07-041332-0, C); answers 4.95 o.p. (ISBN 0-07-041333-9). McGraw.

Introduction to Mathematics for Life Scientists. 2nd ed. E. Batschelet. LC 75-11755. (Biomathematics Ser.: Vol. 2). (Illus.). 643p. 1975. 29.00 o.p. (ISBN 0-387-07293-4); pap. text ed. 13.20 o.p. (ISBN 0-387-07350-7). Springer-Verlag.

Introduction to Matrices & Linear Transformations. 3rd ed. Daniel T. Finkbeiner, 2nd. LC 78-18257. (Mathematical Sciences Ser.). (Illus.). 1978. text ed. 21.95x (ISBN 0-7167-0084-0). W H Freeman.

Introduction to Matrices, Vectors & Linear Programming. 2nd ed. Hugh G. Campbell. LC 76-22757. (Illus.). 1977. text ed. 15.95 (ISBN 0-13-487439-0). P-H.

Introduction to Matrix & Finite Elements in Civil Engineering. G. N. Smith. (Illus.). 1971. text ed. 18.60x (ISBN 0-85334-502-3). Intl Ideas.

Introduction to Measure & Integration. S. J. Taylor. LC 73-84325. 272p. 1975. pap. text ed. 15.50x (ISBN 0-521-09804-1). Cambridge U Pr.

Introduction to Measure & Probability. John F. Kingman & S. J. Taylor. 1966. 44.50 (ISBN 0-521-05888-0). Cambridge U Pr.

Introduction to Measurement in Physical Education. Henry J. Montoye. 1978. text ed. 19.95 (ISBN 0-205-05787-X, 6257879); instr's man. avail. (ISBN 0-205-05789-6); lab manual avail. (ISBN 0-205-05796-9). Allyn.

Introduction to Measurement Theory. Mary J. Allen & Wendy M. Yen. LC 78-25821. 1979. text ed. 16.95 (ISBN 0-8185-0283-5). Brooks-Cole.

Introduction to Mechanical Drawing. new ed. Earl W. Harman. (gr. 7-12). 1979. pap. text ed. 6.40 (ISBN 0-205-06580-5, 3265803). Allyn.

Introduction to Mechanics. 2nd ed. Irving J. Levinson. 1968. text ed. 18.95 (ISBN 0-13-487660-1). P-H.

Introduction to Mechanics of Continua. William Prager. 6.75 o.p. (ISBN 0-8446-4797-7). Peter Smith.

Introduction to Mechanics of Solids. Egor P. Popov. 1968. ref. ed. 24.95 (ISBN 0-13-487769-1). P-H.

Introduction to Medical Chemistry. D. MacLean Evans & John Bowen Jones. 288p. 1976. text ed. 20.50 o.p. (ISBN 0-06-041921-0, HarpC). Har-Row.

Introduction to Medical Laboratory Technology. 5th ed. F. J. Baker & R. E. Silverton. 1976. 29.95 (ISBN 0-407-73251-9). Butterworths.

Introduction to Medical Malpractice. Jerry Lubliner & Mary W. Bednarski. (Learning Packages in Policy Issues: No. 1). 52p. 1976. pap. text ed. 3.00 (ISBN 0-936826-10-X). Pol Stud Assocs.

Introduction to Medical Microbiology. C. W. Potter et al. 1968. 8.95 (ISBN 0-407-56500-0). Butterworths.

Introduction to Medical Physics. Edwin A. Aird. (Illus.). 1975. 22.50x (ISBN 0-433-00350-2). Intl Ideas.

Introduction to Medical Statistics. H. O. Lancaster. LC 73-11323. (Ser. in Probability & Mathematical Statistics). 1974. 34.50 (ISBN 0-471-51250-8, Pub. by Wiley-Interscience). Wiley.

Introduction to Medicine: 100 Topics. J. G. Lewis. (Illus.). 1975. 17.95x (ISBN 0-433-19253-4). Intl Ideas.

Introduction to Membrane Noise. Louis J. DeFelice. 440p. 1981. 39.50 (ISBN 0-306-40513-X, Plenum Pr). Plenum Pub.

Introduction to Mennonite History. C. J. Dyck. 400p. 1981. pap. 9.95 (ISBN 0-8361-1955-X). Herald Pr.

Introduction to Mental Retardation - a Programmed Text. 2nd ed. Walter H. Ehlers & Curtis H. Krishef. (Special Education Ser.). 1977. pap. text ed. 14.95 (ISBN 0-675-08526-8). Merrill.

Introduction to Metallurgical Laboratory Techniques. P. G. Ormandy. LC 68-18530. 1968. 11.25 (ISBN 0-08-012560-3). Pergamon.

Introduction to Metallurgy. Alan Cottrell. LC 75-21731. 1975. pap. 19.50x (ISBN 0-8448-0767-2). Crane-Russak Co.

Introduction to Metaphysics. 2nd ed. Henri Bergson. Tr. by T. E. Hulme. LC 49-3135. 1955. pap. 1.95 (ISBN 0-672-60171-0, LLA10). Bobbs.

Introduction to Metaphysics. C. H. Whiteley. LC 77-1892. (Repr. of 1950 ed.). 1977. text ed. 13.00x (ISBN 0-391-00711-4). Humanities.

Introduction to Metaphysics: The Creative Mind. Henri Bergson. (Quality Paperback: No. 164). 1975. pap. 3.95 (ISBN 0-8226-0164-8). Littlefield.

Introduction to Meteorology. 3rd ed. Franklyn W. Cole. LC 79-1212. 1980. text ed. 20.95 (ISBN 0-471-04705-8); tchr's manual avail. (ISBN 0-471-06224-3). Wiley.

Introduction to Metric & Topological Spaces. Wilson A. Sutherland. (Illus.). 196p. 1975. 19.95x (ISBN 0-19-853155-9); pap. 12.50x (ISBN 0-19-853161-3). Oxford U Pr.

Introduction to Metropolitan Washington, 1968: Annual Meeting Field Trip Guide. pap. 1.00 o.p. (ISBN 0-89291-095-X). Assn Am Geographers.

Introduction to Microbiology. 2nd ed. Anderson & Sobieski. LC 79-20560. 1980. pap. 17.95 (ISBN 0-8016-0206-8). Mosby.

Introduction to Microcomputers. 1979. pap. text ed. 42.00x (ISBN 0-903796-44-9, Pub. by Online Conferences England). Renouf.

Introduction to Microcomputers & Microprocessors. Arpad Barna & Dan I. Porat. LC 75-31675. 1976. 15.00 (ISBN 0-471-05051-2, Pub. by Wiley-Interscience). Wiley.

Introduction to Microcomputers: Some Real Microprocessors. Adam Osborne & Jerry Kane. (Intro. to Microcomputers Ser.: Vol. 2). (Orig.). 1978. pap. text ed. 30.00 (ISBN 0-931988-15-2). Osborne-McGraw.

Introduction to Microcomputers: Some Real Support Devices. Adam Osborne & Jerry Kane. 1978. pap. text ed. 20.00 (ISBN 0-931988-18-7). Osborne-McGraw.

Introduction to Microcomputers: Vol. 1, Basic Concepts. rev. ed. Adam Osborne. 1980. pap. 12.99 (ISBN 0-931988-34-9). Osborne-McGraw.

Introduction to Microeconomics. Edward Nevin. 300p. 1974. text ed. 10.00x o.p. (ISBN 0-85665-018-8). Verry.

Introduction to Microelectronics. 2nd ed. D. Roddy. 1978. text ed. 30.00 (ISBN 0-08-022687-6); pap. text ed. 14.00 (ISBN 0-08-022688-4). Pergamon.

Introduction to Microprocessors. Herb Brunner. 1981. text ed. 17.95 (ISBN 0-8359-3247-8); instr's. manual free (ISBN 0-8359-3248-6). Reston.

Introduction to Microprocessors. Charles M. Gilmore. LC 80-26115. (Basic Skills in Electricity & Electronics). 320p. 1981. pap. 14.96. McGraw.

Introduction to Microprocessors: Activities Manual. Charles M. Gilmore. (Basic Skills in Electricity & Electronics Ser.). 96p. 1981. lab manual 8.96 (ISBN 0-07-023302-0). McGraw.

Introduction to Microprocessors: Software, Hardware, Programming. Lance A. Leventhal. LC 78-7800. (Illus.). 1978. ref. ed. 27.95 (ISBN 0-13-487868-X). P-H.

Introduction to Microwave Theory. rev. ed. Harry A. Atwater. Repr. of 1962 ed. lib. bdg. write for info. (ISBN 0-89874-192-0). Krieger.

Introduction to Microwaves. Gershon Wheeler. (Illus.). 1963. ref. ed. 18.95 (ISBN 0-13-487843-4). P-H.

Introduction to Middle School Teaching. Larry L. Sale. 1979. text ed. 15.95 (ISBN 0-675-08279-X). Merrill.

Introduction to Minicomputers & Microcomputers. Martha E. Sloan. LC 78-74693. 1980. text ed. 23.95 (ISBN 0-201-07279-3). A-W.

Introduction to Minimax. V. Demyanov & V. N. Malozemov. Tr. by D. Louvish from Rus. LC 74-8156. 1974. 32.95 (ISBN 0-470-20850-3). Halsted Pr.

Introduction to Mining: Exploration, Feasibility, Extraction, Rock Mechanics. L. J. Thomas. LC 73-14857. 1977. pap. 19.95 (ISBN 0-470-99220-4). Halsted Pr.

Introduction to Modern Abstract Algebra. D. M. Burton. 1967. 19.95 (ISBN 0-201-00722-3). A-W.

Introduction to Modern Accounting. 3rd ed. Ronald J. Thacker. (Illus.). 1977. pap. text ed. 19.95 (ISBN 0-13-487736-5); study guide 8.95 (ISBN 0-13-487710-1); working papers 9.95 (ISBN 0-13-488064-1). P-H.

Introduction to Modern Algebra. 3rd ed. Neal McCoy. 296p. 1975. text ed. 22.00x (ISBN 0-205-04545-6, 564545X). Allyn.

Introduction to Modern Approaches in Visual Perception. Terry Caelli. LC 80-40167. (Illus.). 200p. 1981. 38.51 (ISBN 0-08-024420-3); pap. 18.71 (ISBN 0-08-024419-X). Pergamon.

Introduction to Modern Behaviorism. 2nd ed. Howard Rachlin. LC 76-1151. (Illus.). 1976. text ed. 17.95x (ISBN 0-7167-0493-5); pap. text ed. 9.95x (ISBN 0-7167-0492-7). W H Freeman.

Introduction to Modern Biochemistry. 4th ed. P. Karlson. Tr. by Charles Doering from Ger. 1975. 24.95 (ISBN 0-12-399764-X). Acad Pr.

Introduction to Modern Biology. 2nd ed. Paul C. Bailey & K. A. Wagner. LC 72-183720. 1972. pap. text ed. 18.50 scp (ISBN 0-7002-2361-4, HarpC). Har-Row.

Introduction to Modern Business: Issues & Environment. 8th ed. Vernon A. Musselman & Eugene Hughes. (Illus.). 640p. 1981. text ed. 17.95 (ISBN 0-13-488072-2); pap. 7.95 study guide (ISBN 0-13-488080-3). P-H.

Introduction to Modern Business: Issues and Environment: Issues & Environment. 7th ed. Vernon Musselman. (Illus.). 1977. text ed. 18.95 (ISBN 0-13-488148-6); study guide & wkbk. 7.95 (ISBN 0-13-488130-3). P-H.

Introduction to Modern Chemistry. Eugene Meyer. (Illus.). 1979. text ed. 19.95 (ISBN 0-13-488320-9); student manual 6.95 (ISBN 0-13-488338-1). P-H.

Introduction to Modern Criminal Investigation: With Basic Laboratory Techniques. S. S. Krishnan. (Illus.). 440p. 1978. 29.75 (ISBN 0-398-03722-1); pap. 22.00 (ISBN 0-398-03723-X). C C Thomas.

Introduction to Modern Criminal Law in China. Marinus J. Meijer. (Studies in Chinese Government & Law). 1977. Repr. of 1950 ed. 20.00 (ISBN 0-89093-057-0). U Pubns Amer.

Introduction to Modern Economic Theory. Basil J. Moore. LC 77-96708. 1973. text ed. 16.95 (ISBN 0-02-921960-4). Free Pr.

Introduction to Modern Electronics. Julien C. Sprott. 512p. 1981. text ed. 22.95 (ISBN 0-471-05840-8). Wiley.

Introduction to Modern France. Robert Mandrou. 1977. pap. 5.95x (ISBN 0-06-131627-X, TB1627, Torch). Har-Row.

Introduction to Modern Genetics. Donald I. Patt & Gail R. Patt. LC 74-12803. (Life Sciences Ser.). (Illus.). 384p. 1975. text ed. 19.95 (ISBN 0-201-05743-3); sol. manual 2.50 (ISBN 0-201-05742-5). A-W.

Introduction to Modern Greek Literature. Ed. by Mary P. Gianos. LC 67-30722. 1969. text ed. 29.50x (ISBN 0-8057-3125-3); pap. text ed. 16.50x (ISBN 0-89197-801-1). Irvington.

Introduction to Modern Liquid Chromatography. 2nd ed. L. R. Snyder & J. J. Kirkland. LC 79-4537. 1979. 33.95 (ISBN 0-471-03822-9, Pub. by Wiley-Interscience). Wiley.

Introduction to Modern Literary Arabic. David Cowan. 1958. pap. 11.95x (ISBN 0-521-09240-X, 240). Cambridge U Pr.

Introduction to Modern Mathematics. 2nd ed. Elbridge P. Vance. 1968. text ed. 17.95 (ISBN 0-201-08015-X). A-W.

Introduction to Modern Mathematics Series 1. Hancock. (gr. 8-12). 1972. pap. text ed. 7.50 each incl. 5 texts, 1 tchrs' manual & test (ISBN 0-8449-0210-1). Learning Line.

Introduction to Modern Mathematics Series 2. Hancock. (gr. 8-12). 1972. pap. text ed. 7.50 each incl. 4 texts, 1 tchrs' manual & test (ISBN 0-8449-0220-9). Learning Line.

Introduction to Modern Microscopy. H. N. Southworth & R. A. Hull. LC 74-32488. (Wykeham Science Ser.: No.34). 1975. 8.60x (ISBN 0-8448-1161-0). Crane-Russak Co.

Introduction to Modern Network Synthesis. M. E. Van Valkenburg. LC 60-10328. 1960. 30.95 (ISBN 0-471-89991-7). Wiley.

Introduction to Modern Physics. John D. McGervey. 1971. text ed. 22.95 (ISBN 0-12-483550-3). Acad Pr.

Introduction to Modern Police Firearms. Willis J. Roberts & Allen P. Bristow. Ed. by Douglas Gourley. (Criminal Justice Ser). (Illus.). 1969. text ed. 10.95x (ISBN 0-02-477000-0, 47700). Macmillan.

Introduction to Modern Polish Literature. Ed. by Adam Gillon & Ludwik Krzyzanowski. 480p. 1981. pap. 6.95 (ISBN 0-88254-516-7, Pub. by Ars Polona Poland). Hippocrene Bks.

Introduction to Modern Political Theory. Norman P. Barry. 1980. write for info. (ISBN 0-312-43098-1). St Martin.

Introduction to Modern Virology. S. B. Primrose. LC 74-23739. (Basic Microbiology Ser.: No. 2). 1975. pap. text ed. 10.95 o.p. (ISBN 0-470-70038-6). Halsted Pr.

Introduction to Modern Virology. 2nd ed. S. B. Primrose & N. J. Dimmock. (Basic Microbiology Ser.: Vol. 2). 251p. 1980. pap. text ed. 19.95x (ISBN 0-470-26941-3). Halsted Pr.

Introduction to Molecular Structure & Spectroscopy. William A. Guillory. 1977. text ed. 27.95 (ISBN 0-205-05718-7). Allyn.

Introduction to Monetary Theory & Policy. 2nd ed. Dwayne Wrightsman. LC 75-22767. (Illus.). 1976. 14.95 o.s.i. (ISBN 0-02-935510-9); pap. text ed. 9.95 (ISBN 0-02-935560-5). Free Pr.

Introduction to Moroccan Arabic. Ernest T. Abdel-Massih. LC 72-154239. 1977. pap. text ed. 7.00 (ISBN 0-932098-80-0). Ctr for NE & North African Stud.

Introduction to Mortgage-Equity Capitalization. Charles B. Akerson. 1970. 3.00 (ISBN 0-911780-35-1). Am Inst Real Estate Appraisers.

Introduction to Motor Behavior: A Neuro-Psychological Approach. 2nd ed. George H. Sage. LC 76-14660. (A-W Physical Ed Ser.). 1977. text ed. 21.95 (ISBN 0-201-06766-8). A-W.

Introduction to Multinational Management. S. Benjamin Prasad & Y. Krishna Shetty. (Illus.). 256p. 1976. 11.95 (ISBN 0-13-489203-8). P-H.

Introduction to Music. Hugh M. Miller. (Illus., Orig.). 1978. pap. 4.50 (ISBN 0-06-460177-3, CO 177, COS). Har-Row.

Introduction to Music Fundamentals. 4th ed. J. Austin Andrews & Jeanne Wardian. 1978. pap. text ed. 13.95 (ISBN 0-13-489575-4). P-H.

Introduction to Music Reading: Concepts & Applications. 2nd ed. William E. Thomson. 320p. 1980. pap. text ed. 12.95x (ISBN 0-534-00817-8). Wadsworth Pub.

Introduction to Music Theory. 2nd ed. A. Winold & J. Rehm. 1979. pap. 15.95 (ISBN 0-13-489666-1). P-H.

Introduction to Mysticism. Margaret Smith. 1977. pap. 5.95 (ISBN 0-19-519956-1). Oxford U Pr.

Introduction to Myth. Peter R. Stillman. (Literature Ser.). (gr. 10 up). 1977. pap. text ed. 6.40x (ISBN 0-8104-5890-X). Hayden.

Introduction to National Accounts Statistics. Roy Allen. 125p. 1980. text ed. 43.50x (ISBN 0-8419-5079-2). Holmes & Meier.

Introduction to Natural Science, Pt. 2, The Life Sciences. V. L. Parsegian. 1970. text ed. 21.50 (ISBN 0-12-545202-0); lab. suppl. 5.50 (ISBN 0-12-545256-X); tchrs' guide 5.00 (ISBN 0-12-545257-8). Acad Pr.

Introduction to Nature & Management of Hypertension. Edward C. Freis. (Illus.). 1974. pap. 16.95 (ISBN 0-87618-030-6). R J Brady.

Introduction to Naval Engineering. Edward F. Gritzen. LC 79-90773. 448p. 1980. text ed. 13.95x (ISBN 0-87021-319-9). Naval Inst Pr.

Introduction to Neo-Colonialism. Jack Woddis. (Orig.). 1968. pap. 1.95 (ISBN 0-7178-0102-0, LNW). Intl Pub Co.

Introduction to Nepal. Rishikesh Shaha. (Illus.). 1976. 8.50x (ISBN 0-685-89510-6). Himalaya Hse.

Introduction to Nepali. N. Clark. 1977. 22.00x (ISBN 0-88386-385-5). South Asia Bks.

Introduction to Nervous Systems. Theodore H. Bullock et al. LC 76-3735. (Illus.). 1977. pap. text ed. 23.95x (ISBN 0-7167-0030-1). W H Freeman.

Introduction to Neutron Kinetics of Nuclear Power Reactors. J. G. Tyror & R. I. Vaughan. LC 76-94936. 1970. 25.00 (ISBN 0-08-006667-4). Pergamon.

Introduction to New Testament Literature. Donald Juel et al. LC 77-18036. (Illus.). 1978. 13.95 (ISBN 0-687-01360-7); pap. 9.50 (ISBN 0-687-01361-5). Abingdon.

Introduction to Newton's Principia. I. Bernard Cohen. LC 76-28770. 1971. 30.00 o.p. (ISBN 0-674-46175-4); pap. 10.00x (ISBN 0-674-46193-2). Harvard U Pr.

Introduction to Nineteenth Century Germany. Eda Sagarra. (Illus.). 1981. text ed. 14.95x (ISBN 0-582-35138-3); pap. text ed. 6.95x (ISBN 0-582-35137-5). Longman.

Introduction to Nonharmonic Fourier Series. Robert M. Young. LC 79-6807. (Pure & Applied Ser.). 1980. 32.00 (ISBN 0-12-772850-3). Acad Pr.

Introduction to Nonlinear Differential & Integral Equations. Harold T. Davis. 1960. pap. 7.50 (ISBN 0-486-60971-5). Dover.

Introduction to Nonlinear Oscillations. Ronald E. Mickens. LC 80-13169. (Illus.). 320p. Date not set. text ed. price not set (ISBN 0-521-22208-7). Cambridge U Pr.

Introduction to Nonprofit Organization Accounting. Emerson O. Henke. 464p. 1979. text ed. 19.95x (ISBN 0-534-00742-2). Wadsworth Pub.

Introduction to Normative Economics. E. J. Mishan. (Illus.). 576p. (Orig.). 1981. pap. text ed. 14.95x (ISBN 0-19-502791-4). Oxford U Pr.

Introduction to Nuclear Engineering. John R. Lamarsh. LC 74-4718. (Nuclear Science & Engineering Ser.). (Illus.). 600p. 1975. text ed. 26.95 (ISBN 0-201-04160-X). A-W.

Introduction to Nuclear Physics. Harald A. Enge. 1966. 24.95 (ISBN 0-201-01870-5). A-W.

Introduction to Nuclear Physics & Chemistry. 2nd ed. Bernard G. Harvey. 1969. ref. ed. 26.95 (ISBN 0-13-491159-8). P-H.

Introduction to Nuclear Reactor Theory. J. R. Lamarsh. 1966. 26.95 (ISBN 0-201-04120-0). A-W.

Introduction to Nuclear Techniques in Agronomy & Plant Biology. P. B. Vose. (Illus.). 1980. 53.00 (ISBN 0-08-024924-8); pap. 29.00 (ISBN 0-08-024923-X). Pergamon.

Introduction to Number Theory. Trygve Nagell. 309p. 1981. 14.95 (ISBN 0-8284-0163-2). Chelsea Pub.

Introduction to Numerical Analysis. Kendall E. Atkinson. LC 78-6706. 1978. text ed. 26.95 (ISBN 0-471-02985-8); solutions manual 5.00 (ISBN 0-471-03749-4). Wiley.

Introduction to Numerical Analysis. F. Stummel & K. Hainer. 276p. 1980. 15.00x (ISBN 0-7073-0130-0, Pub. by Scottish Academic Pr). Columbia U Pr.

Introduction to Numerical Linear Algebra. Leslie Fox. (Monographs on Numerical Analysis Ser.). 1965. 12.95x (ISBN 0-19-500325-X). Oxford U Pr.

Introduction to Numerical Mathematics. E. L. Stiefel. Tr. by W. C. Rheinboldt. 1963. text ed. 18.95 (ISBN 0-12-671150-X); problem bklt. free (ISBN 0-685-05133-1). Acad Pr.

Introduction to Nursing: An Adaptation Model. Sr. Callista Roy. LC 75-43612. (Illus.). 400p. 1976. ref. ed. 16.95 (ISBN 0-13-491290-X). P-H.

Introduction to Nursing Essentials: A Handbook. Helen Readey et al. LC 76-41198. (Illus.). 1977. pap. text ed. 9.50 (ISBN 0-8016-4099-7). Mosby.

Introduction to Oceanography. 2nd ed. David Ross. LC 76-17838. (Illus.). 1977. text ed. 19.95 (ISBN 0-13-491332-9). P-H.

Introduction to Old Javanese Language and Literature: A Kawi Prose Anthology. Mary S. Zurbuchen. LC 76-16235. (Michigan Series in South & Southeast Asian Languages & Linguistics: No. 3). 150p. 1976. pap. 5.00x (ISBN 0-89148-053-6). Ctr S&SE Asian.

Introduction to Old Norse. 2nd ed. Eric V. Gordon. Ed. by A. R. Taylor. 1957. 17.95x (ISBN 0-19-811105-3). Oxford U Pr.

Introduction to Operating System Design. new ed. A. N. Habermann. LC 75-34073. (Computer Science Ser.). (Illus.). 480p. 1976. text ed. 25.95 (ISBN 0-574-21075-X, 13-4075). SRA.

Introduction to Operational Research & Data Management. R. Bandyopadhyay & S. M. Padwal. 400p. 1981. text ed. 25.00x (ISBN 0-7069-1234-9, Pub. by Vikas India). Advent Bk.

Introduction to Operations Research. 3rd ed. Frederick S. Hillier & Gerald J. Lieberman. 848p. 1980. text ed. 28.95 (ISBN 0-8162-3867-7); solutions manual 7.50 (ISBN 0-8162-3868-5). Holden-Day.

Introduction to Operations Research Techniques. Hans G. Daellenbach & John A. George. 1978. text ed. 26.95 (ISBN 0-205-05755-1); answer book (ISBN 0-205-05756-X). Allyn.

Introduction to Opinion & Attitude Measurement. Hermann H. Remmers. LC 74-138127. 437p. 1972. Repr. of 1954 ed. lib. bdg. 29.75x (ISBN 0-8371-4166-4, REOA). Greenwood.

Introduction to Optimization Methods. P. R. Adby & M. A. Dempster. LC 74-4109. (Mathematics Ser.). 204p. 1974. pap. text ed. 11.95 (ISBN 0-412-11040-7, Pub. by Chapman & Hall). Methuen Inc.

Introduction to Optimization Methods. P. R. Adby & M. A. Dempster. LC 74-4109. (Mathematics Ser.). 204p. 1974. pap. text ed. 11.95 (ISBN 0-470-00830-X). Halsted Pr.

Introduction to Optimization Practice. Lucas Pun. 1969. 29.50 o.p. (ISBN 0-471-70233-1, Pub. by Wiley-Interscience). Wiley.

Introduction to Oral Medicine. Derrick M. Chisholm et al. (Illus.). 1979. text ed. 18.00 (ISBN 0-7216-2593-2). Saunders.

Introduction to Oral Preventive Medicine. Hans R. Muhlemann. (Illus.). 253p. 1976. 22.00. Quint Pub Co.

Introduction to Ordinary Differential Equations. Earl A. Coddington. 1964. ref. ed. 19.95 (ISBN 0-13-491316-7). P-H.

Introduction to Ordinary Differential Equations. 2nd ed. Albert Rabenstein. 538p. 1972. 20.95 (ISBN 0-12-573957-5). Acad Pr.

Introduction to Ore Deposits. Ludwig Baumann. LC 74-26527. 163p. 1976. 19.95 (ISBN 0-470-05937-0). Halsted Pr.

Introduction to Organic & Biological Chemistry. 3rd ed. Stuart J. Baum. Date not set. 19.50 (ISBN 0-686-65087-5); pap. 2.95 answer bk. (ISBN 0-02-306580-X). Macmillan. Postponed.

Introduction to Organic Chemistry. 2nd ed. Charles H. DePuy & Kenneth L. Rinehart. LC 74-19442. 323p. 1975. text ed. 22.95 (ISBN 0-471-20350-5). Wiley.

Introduction to Organic Chemistry. H. Lowther. 1964. text ed. 11.25 (ISBN 0-08-010819-9); pap. text ed. 5.75 (ISBN 0-08-010818-0). Pergamon.

Introduction to Organic Chemistry. William Reusch. LC 76-50855. 1977. text ed. 27.50 (ISBN 0-8162-7161-5); study guide 9.95 (ISBN 0-686-28568-9). Holden Day.

Introduction to Organizational Behavior: A Situational Approach. Robin Stuart-Kotze. (Illus.). 1980. text ed. 17.95 (ISBN 0-8359-3259-1). Reston.

Introduction to Organizational Behavior: Text & Readings. L. L. Cummings & Randall B. Dunham. 1980. pap. 14.95x (ISBN 0-256-02043-4). Irwin.

Introduction to Ornithology. 3rd ed. George J. Wallace & Harold D. Mahan. (Illus.). 1974. text ed. 18.95 (ISBN 0-02-423980-1). Macmillan.

Introduction to p-Adic Numbers & Their Function. Kurt Mahler. (Tracts in Mathematics & Mathematical Physics: No. 64). 19.95 (ISBN 0-521-20001-6). Cambridge U Pr.

Introduction to Paint Chemistry. G. P. Turner. 1967. pap. 7.50 o.p. (ISBN 0-470-89311-7). Halsted Pr.

Introduction to Paradise Lost. John Broadbent. (Milton for Schools & Colleges Ser). (Illus.). 1971. 28.50 (ISBN 0-521-08068-1); pap. 7.95x (ISBN 0-521-09639-1). Cambridge U Pr.

Introduction to Parasitology. A. W. Jones. 1967. 19.95 (ISBN 0-201-03365-8). A-W.

Introduction to Parasitology: With Special References to the Parasites of Man. 10th ed. Asa C. Chandler & C. P. Read. LC 61-5670. 1961. 29.95 (ISBN 0-471-14487-8). Wiley.

Introduction to Pareto: His Sociology. George C. Homans & Charles P. Curtis, Jr. LC 68-9664. 1970. Repr. 17.00 (ISBN 0-86527-106-2). Fertig.

Introduction to PASCAL. Henry Davis. (Pascal Notebook Ser.: Vol. 1). 150p. 1981. pap. 9.95 (ISBN 0-918398-43-6). Dilithium Pr.

Introduction to PASCAL. Neil Graham. 272p. 1980. pap. text ed. 10.95 (ISBN 0-8299-0334-8). West Pub.

Introduction to Pascal. J. Welsh & J. Elder. 1979. 15.95 (ISBN 0-13-491522-4). P-H.

Introduction to Pascal for Scientists. James W. Cooper. 304p. 1981. 17.50 (ISBN 0-471-08785-8, Pub. by Wiley-Interscience). Wiley.

Introduction to Patient Care. 3rd ed. Beverly W. Du Gas. LC 76-58601. (Illus.). 1977. text ed. 16.95 (ISBN 0-7216-3226-2). Saunders.

Introduction to Perception. S. Howard Bartley. (Illus.). 1980. pap. 18.95 scp (ISBN 0-06-040514-7, HarpC). Har-Row.

Introduction to Persian Literature. Reuben Levy. LC 68-8876. 194p. 1969. 17.50x (ISBN 0-231-03177-7). Columbia U Pr.

Introduction to Personality. 2nd ed. Donn Bryne. LC 73-17157. (Personality, Clinical & Social Psychology Ser). (Illus.). 624p. 1974. ref. ed. 18.95 (ISBN 0-13-491597-6). P-H.

Introduction to Perturbation Techniques. Ali H. Nayfeh. LC 80-15233. 475p. 1980. 24.95 (ISBN 0-471-08033-0, Pub. by Wiley Interscience). Wiley.

Introduction to Petroleum Production Operations, Vol. 1. David R. Skinner. 200p. 1981. 12.95 (ISBN 0-87201-767-2). Gulf Pub.

Introduction to Petrology. Brian Bayly. 1968. text ed. 23.95 (ISBN 0-13-491621-2). P-H.

Introduction to Pharmaceutical Dosage Forms. 3rd ed. Howard C. Ansel. LC 80-16842. (Illus.). 408p. 1981. text ed. write for info. (ISBN 0-8121-0771-3). Lea & Febiger.

Introduction to Phenomenological Psychology. Dreyer Kruger. LC 80-29203. 212p. 1981. pap. text ed. 8.95 (ISBN 0-8207-0150-5). Duquesne.

Introduction to Philosophical Analysis. 2nd ed. John Hospers. 1967. lib. bdg. 17.95 (ISBN 0-13-491688-3). P-H.

Introduction to Philosophical Logic. Tony Grayling. (Harvester Studies in Philosophy Ser.: No. 15). 1980. text ed. write for info. (ISBN 0-391-01791-8). Humanities.

Introduction to Philosophy. rev. ed. Daniel J. Sullivan. 1964. 7.95 (ISBN 0-02-829320-7). Macmillan.

Introduction to Philosophy: A Case Study Approach. Jack B. Rogers & Forrest Baird. LC 80-8344. (Case Study Ser.). 240p. (Orig.). 1981. pap. text ed. 8.95x (ISBN 0-06-066997-7, RD 346, HarpR). Har-Row.

Introduction to Philosophy: From Wonder to World View. Donald Scherer et al. (Illus.). 1979. text ed. 17.95 (ISBN 0-13-491860-6). P-H.

Introduction to Philosophy of History. W. H. Walsh. 1981. pap. text ed. 9.75x (ISBN 0-391-02163-X, Hutchinson U Lib). Humanities.

Introduction to Philosophy of History. 3rd rev. ed. William H. Walsh. 1967. text ed. 7.50x (ISBN 0-391-00672-X); pap. text ed. 7.50x (ISBN 0-391-02163-X). Humanities.

Introduction to Phonetics. L. F. Brosnahan & B. Malmberg. LC 75-26277. (Illus.). 243p. 1975. 34.50 (ISBN 0-521-21100-X); pap. 9.95x (ISBN 0-521-29042-2). Cambridge U Pr.

Introduction to Phonology. Clarence Sloat et al. LC 77-23100. (Illus.). 1978. ref. 12.95 (ISBN 0-13-492207-7). P-H.

Introduction to Phosphorus Chemistry. H. Goldwhite. LC 79-27141. (Cambridge Texts in Chemistry & Biochemistry). 175p. Date not set. 30.00 (ISBN 0-521-22978-2); pap. text ed. 12.95 (ISBN 0-521-29757-5). Cambridge U Pr.

Introduction to Photo-Offset Lithography. Hird. 1981. text ed. price not set (ISBN 0-87002-336-5). Bennett Co.

Introduction to Photographic Theory: The Silver Halide Process. B. H. Carroll et al. LC 79-26802. 1980. 29.50 (ISBN 0-471-02562-3, Pub. by Wiley Interscience). Wiley.

Introduction to Photography. Wakefield. 8.95 o.p. (ISBN 0-85242-050-1, Pub. by Fountain). Morgan.

Introduction to Photography: A Self Directing Approach. Marvin J. Rosen. LC 75-31013. (Illus.). 384p. 1976. pap. text ed. 14.25 (ISBN 0-395-20471-2); inst. manual 3.25 (ISBN 0-395-20472-0). HM.

Introduction to Physical & Biological Oceanography. Cuchlaine King. LC 74-81339. 1974. pap. 19.50x (ISBN 0-8448-0400-2). Crane-Russak Co.

Introduction to Physical Anthropology & Archaeology. C. Weitz. 1979. pap. 13.95 (ISBN 0-13-492637-4); pap. 5.95 study guide & wkbk. (ISBN 0-13-492645-5). P-H.

Introduction to Physical Anthropology. Harry Nelson & Robert Jurmain. (Illus.). 1979. pap. text ed. 16.50 (ISBN 0-8299-0240-6); study guide 4.95 (ISBN 0-8299-0285-6); instrs.' manual avail. (ISBN 0-8299-0563-4). West Pub.

Introduction to Physical Diagnosis. Ed. by Mark H. Swartz. Date not set. text ed. price not set (ISBN 0-89004-562-3). Raven.

Introduction to Physical Education: A Humanistic Perspective. Leonard H. Kalakian & Myra F. Goldman. 224p. 1976. text ed. 15.95x (ISBN 0-205-05475-7). Allyn.

Introduction to Physical Education: Concepts of Human Movement. John T. Cheffers & Thomas Evual. (Illus.). 1978. text ed. 16.50 (ISBN 0-13-493031-2). P-H.

Introduction to Physical Oceanography. William S. Von Arx. (Illus.). 1962. 26.50 (ISBN 0-201-08174-1, Adv Bk Prog). A-W.

Introduction to Physical Organic Chemistry. Richard D. Gilliom. LC 75-99483. (Chemistry Ser). 1970. text ed. 20.95 (ISBN 0-201-02375-X). A-W.

Introduction to Physical Science. David M. Riban. (Illus.). 656p. 1981. text ed. 21.95 (ISBN 0-07-052140-9, C); instr's manual 4.95 (ISBN 0-07-052141-7). McGraw.

Introduction to Physical Science. 3rd ed. James T. Shipman et al. 1979. text ed. 19.95x (ISBN 0-669-01720-5); inst. manual free (ISBN 0-669-01723-X); lab. manual 6.95x (ISBN 0-669-01722-1); student guide 6.95x (ISBN 0-669-01721-3). Heath.

Introduction to Physics. H. E. Gauss. LC 66-12756. (Illus.). 1966. pap. 1.65 o.p. (ISBN 0-668-01411-3). Arc Bks.

Introduction to Physics in Nursing. 7th ed. Hessel H. Flitter. (Illus.). 294p. 1976. pap. 13.95 (ISBN 0-8016-1597-6). Mosby.

Introduction to Physics, Vol. 1: Mechanics, Hydrodynamics, Thermodynamics. P. Frauenfelder & P. Huber. 1966. text ed. 27.00 (ISBN 0-08-011603-5); pap. 21.00 (ISBN 0-08-013521-8). Pergamon.

Introduction to Physiological Plant Ecology. Peter Bannister. LC 76-16743. 1978. pap. text ed. 18.95 (ISBN 0-470-99389-8). Halsted Pr.

Introduction to Physiological Psychology: Information Processing in the Nervous System. Jackson Beatty. LC 74-17631. (Illus.). 1975. text ed. 15.95x o.p. (ISBN 0-8185-0123-5). Brooks-Cole.

Introduction to Physiological Psychology. 3rd ed. Francis Leukel. LC 75-33031. (Illus.). 1976. text ed. 17.95 (ISBN 0-8016-2974-8). Mosby.

Introduction to Piecewise-Linear Topology. C. P. Rourke & B. J. Sanderson. LC 72-85229. (Ergebnisse der Mathematik und Ihrer Grenzgebiete: Vol. 69). (Illus.). 140p. 1972. 17.60 o.p. (ISBN 0-387-05800-1). Springer-Verlag.

Introduction to PL-1 Programming for Library & Information Science. Thomas H. Mott, Jr. et al. (Library & Information Science Ser.). 239p. 1972. text ed. 19.95 (ISBN 0-12-508750-0). Acad Pr.

Introduction to Plane Geometry. H. F. Baker. LC 70-141879. 1971. text ed. 14.95 (ISBN 0-8284-0247-7). Chelsea Pub.

Introduction to Plant Biochemistry. T. W. Goodwin & E. I. Mercer. 1972. 18.00 (ISBN 0-08-016223-1). Pergamon.

Introduction to Plant Nematology. Victor H. Dropkin. LC 80-13556. 336p. 1980. 36.00 (ISBN 0-471-05578-6, Pub. by Wiley Interscience). Wiley.

Introduction to Plant Science: A Humanistic & Ecological Approach. Norman Russell. LC 75-1445. (Illus.). 302p. 1975. pap. text ed. 12.95 (ISBN 0-8299-0043-8); instrs.' manual avail. (ISBN 0-8299-0603-7). West Pub.

Introduction to Plasma Physics. 2nd ed. William B. Thompson. 1964. text ed. 27.00 o.p. (ISBN 0-08-011180-7). Pergamon.

Introduction to Pl360 Programming. Richard L. Guertin. 1977. pap. text ed. 13.95x (ISBN 0-534-00524-1). Wadsworth Pub.

Introduction to Police-Community Relations: A Guide for the Pre-Service Student & Practicing Police Officer. Ralph A. Olmos. 128p. 1974. 10.50 (ISBN 0-398-02941-5). C C Thomas.

Introduction to Policy Analysis in Science & Technology. (Science Policy Studies & Documents: No. 46). 93p. 1979. pap. 4.75 (ISBN 92-3-101725-X, U955, UNESCO). Unipub.

Introduction to Polish. Gerald Stone. 128p. 1980. 11.50x (ISBN 0-19-815802-5). Oxford U Pr.

Introduction to Political Philosophy. A. R. Murray. 1968. Repr. of 1953 ed. 18.50 (ISBN 0-7100-1873-8). Routledge & Kegan.

Introduction to Political Science. Leon Hurwitz. LC 79-11293. (Illus.). 1979. text ed. 16.95 (ISBN 0-88229-321-4); pap. text ed. 8.95 (ISBN 0-88229-677-9). Nelson-Hall.

Introduction to Political Science. rev. ed. Rais A. Khan et al. 1977. text ed. 14.95x (ISBN 0-256-01785-9). Dorsey.

Introduction to Political Science Methods. Robert A. Bernstein & James A. Dyer. (Illus.). 1979. pap. 10.95 ref. ed. (ISBN 0-13-493304-4). P-H.

Introduction to Political Science: People, Politics, & Perception. H. Van Dallen & L. Zeigler. 1977. pap. 10.95 (ISBN 0-13-493205-6). P-H.

Introduction to Political Sociology. Phillip Althoff & Michael Rush. LC 77-180276. 1972. pap. 4.95 (ISBN 0-672-61311-5). Bobbs.

Introduction to Political Sociology: The Social Anatomy of Body Politics. Anthony M. Orum. (P-H Ser. in Sociology). (Illus.). 1978. ref. ed. 17.95 (ISBN 0-13-491381-7). P-H.

Introduction to Polo. Marco. (Illus.). 26.25 (ISBN 0-85131-142-3, Dist. by Sporting Book Center). J A Allen.

Introduction to Polymer Chemistry. D. Margerison & G. C. East. 1966. 25.00 (ISBN 0-08-011891-7); pap. 12.75 (ISBN 0-08-011890-9). Pergamon.

Introduction to Polymer Painting. Harold Workman. (Illus.). 1967. 4.50 o.p. (ISBN 0-8231-7027-6). Branford.

Introduction to Polymer Science. L. R. Treloar & W. F. Archenhold. (Wykeham Science Ser.: No. 9). 1970. pap. 9.95x (ISBN 0-8448-1347-8). Crane-Russak Co.

Introduction to Polymer Viscoelasticity. Ed. by John J. Aklonis et al. LC 72-473. 256p. 1972. 27.50 (ISBN 0-471-01860-0, Pub by Wiley-Interscience). Wiley.

Introduction to Population Geography. W. F. Hornby & M. Jones. LC 78-74536. (Illus.). 1980. pap. 11.50 (ISBN 0-521-21395-9). Cambridge U Pr.

Introduction to Population Studies: A Sociological Approach. Judah Matras. (Illus.). 1977. text ed. 18.95 (ISBN 0-13-493122-X). P-H.

Introduction to Positive Philosophy. August Comte. Ed. by Frederick Ferre. LC 73-84164. (Library of Liberal Arts Ser). (Orig.). 1970. pap. 3.05 o.p. (ISBN 0-672-60284-9, LLA94). Bobbs.

Introduction to Potential Theory. N. Du Plessis. (University Mathematical Monographs Ser.: No. 7). 1970. 13.75 o.s.i. (ISBN 0-02-844130-3). Hafner.

Introduction to Powder Surface Area. S. Lowell. LC 79-15878. 1979. 22.95 (ISBN 0-471-04771-6, Pub. by Wiley-Interscience). Wiley.

Introduction to Praise. Ruth Collingridge & JoAnne Sekowsky. (Workshop Ser.). (Orig.). 1980, pap. write for info. (ISBN 0-930756-60-6, 4235-PW1). Women's Aglow.

Introduction to PRECIS for North American Usage. Phyllis A. Richmond. 340p. 1981. lib. bdg. 25.00x (ISBN 0-87287-240-8). Libs Unl.

Introduction to Principles of Electromagnetism. Walter Hauser. (Physics Ser). 1971. text ed. 20.95 (ISBN 0-201-02821-2). A-W.

Introduction to Printing. Herbert Simon. 1968. 4.95 o.p. (ISBN 0-571-08408-7, Pub. by Faber & Faber). Merrimack Bk Serv.

Introduction to Printing: The Craft of Letterpress. Herbert Simon. (Illus.). 1980. pap. 7.50 (ISBN 0-571-11528-4, Pub. by Faber & Faber). Merrimack Bk Serv.

Introduction to Probability. James Huneycutt. LC 72-97005. (gr. 9-12). 1973. text ed. 16.95 (ISBN 0-675-08960-3). Merrill.

Introduction to Probability. Frederick Williams & J. E. Holstein. 1967. text ed. 3.00x spiral bdg (ISBN 0-87543-061-9). Lucas.

Introduction to Probability & Statistics: Concepts & Principles. Harry Frank. LC 73-19852. 448p. 1974. 19.95 o.p. (ISBN 0-471-27500-X). Wiley.

Introduction to Probability & Statistics from a Bayesian Viewpoint: Pt. 1 Probability. D. V. Lindley. (Illus.). 270p. 1980. pap. 15.50x (ISBN 0-521-29867-9). Cambridge U Pr.

Introduction to Probability & Statistics from a Bayesian Viewpoint: Pt. 2: Inference. D. V. Lindley. (Illus.). 300p. 1980. pap. 15.50x (ISBN 0-521-29866-0). Cambridge U Pr.

Introduction to Probability & Statistics from a Bayesian Viewpoint, 2 Pts. Dennis V. Lindley. Pt. 1. Probability. text ed. 34.95x (ISBN 0-521-05562-8); Pt. 2. Inference. text ed. 34.95 (ISBN 0-521-05563-6). Cambridge U Pr.

Introduction to Probability & Statistics in Engineering & Management Science. 2nd ed. William W. Hines & Douglas C. Montgomery. LC 79-26257. 1980. text ed. 22.95 (ISBN 0-471-04759-7); write for info. solutions manual (ISBN 0-471-05006-7). Wiley.

Introduction to Probability & Statistics. 6th ed. Henry L. Alder & Edward B. Roessler. LC 76-13643. (Illus.). 1977. text ed. 19.95x (ISBN 0-7167-0467-6); answer book avail. W H Freeman.

Introduction to Probability & Stochastic Processes. James L. Melsa & Andrew P. Sage. (Illus.). 448p. 1973. ref. ed. 26.95 (ISBN 0-13-034850-3). P-H.

Introduction to Probability Models. Sheldon M. Ross. (Probability & Mathematical Statistics Ser.). 1972. text ed. 20.95 (ISBN 0-12-598450-2). Acad Pr.

Introduction to Probability Theory. Paul Hoel et al. LC 74-136173. 1971. text ed. 19.50 (ISBN 0-395-04636-X, 3-25650). HM.

Introduction to Probability Theory & Its Applications, Vol. 1. 3rd ed. William Feller. LC 68-11708. (Probability & Mathematical Statistics Ser.). 1968. 26.95 (ISBN 0-471-25708-7). Wiley.

Introduction to Probability Theory with Computing. J. Laurie Snell. (Illus.). 288p. 1975. pap. 13.95x ref. ed. (ISBN 0-13-493445-8). P-H.

Introduction to Probation & Parole. 2nd ed. Alexander B. Smith & Louis Berlin. (Criminal Justice Ser.). (Illus.). 1979. text ed. 14.95 (ISBN 0-8299-0235-X); instrs.' manual avail. (ISBN 0-8299-0601-0). West Pub.

Introduction to Programming & Problem Solving with Pascal. G. Michael Schneider et al. 394p. 1978. 16.95 (ISBN 0-471-02542-9). Wiley.

Introduction to Programming Languages. W. Wesley Peterson. 1974. 21.95 (ISBN 0-13-493486-5). P-H.

Introduction to Project Planning. Jack Gido. 1974. pap. 6.75 (ISBN 0-932078-48-6). GE Tech Prom & Train.

Introduction to Proprietor & Partnership Businesses. Luanna C. Blagrove. 160p. 1981. 24.95; pap. 19.95. Blagrove Pubns.

Introduction to Pseudodifferential & Fourier Integral Operators. J. F. Treves. Incl. Vol. 1. Pseudodifferential Operators. 300p (ISBN 0-306-40403-6); Vol. 2. Fourier Integral Operators. 340p (ISBN 0-306-40404-4). (Univeristy Ser. in Mathematics). 1980. 29.95 ea. (Plenum Pr). Plenum Pub.

Introduction to Psychoanalytic Theory of Motivation. W. Toman. 1960. text ed. 18.75 (ISBN 0-08-009485-6). Pergamon.

Introduction to Psychohistory: Theories & Case Studies. Salvatore Prisco, III. LC 80-8245. 190p. 1980. lib. bdg. 17.50 (ISBN 0-8191-1335-2); pap. text ed. 9.00 (ISBN 0-8191-1336-0). U Pr of Amer.

Introduction to Psychology. Eugene De La Fronde. (Library of Scientific Psychology). (Illus.). 1979. 27.45 (ISBN 0-89266-178-X). Am Classical Coll Pr.

Introduction to Psychology. 4th ed. L. Dodge Fernald & Peter S. Fernald. LC 77-78911. (Illus.). 1978. text ed. 18.95 (ISBN 0-395-25815-4); inst. manual 1.15 (ISBN 0-395-25816-2); student guidebk. 6.95 (ISBN 0-395-25817-0); test item manual 2.00 (ISBN 0-395-25818-9). HM.

Introduction to Psychology Exploration & Application. 2nd ed. Dennis L. Coon. (Illus.). 1980. text ed. 17.95 (ISBN 0-8299-0303-8). study guide 5.95 (ISBN 0-8299-0304-6); instrs.' manual avail. (ISBN 0-8299-0467-0). West Pub.

Introduction to Psychopathology. 3rd ed. D. Russell Davis. 180p. 1973. pap. text ed. 5.95x o.p. (ISBN 0-19-264417-3). Oxford U Pr.

Introduction to Psychopharmacology. Ed. by R. Rech & K. E. Moore. LC 78-116995. 1971. 15.50 (ISBN 0-911216-12-X). Raven.

Introduction to Psychotherapy. David G. Martin. LC 75-145969. (Orig.). 1971. pap. text ed. 6.95 o.p. (ISBN 0-8185-0010-7). Brooks-Cole.

Introduction to Pteridophyta. A. Rashid. 1976. 12.50 (ISBN 0-7069-0447-8, Pub. by Vikas India). Advent Bk.

Introduction to Qualitative Analysis. 2nd ed. Durwood C. Layde & Daryle H. Busch. (Illus.). 1968. pap. text ed. 12.95x (ISBN 0-205-02334-7, 6823343). Allyn.

Introduction to Qualitative Genetics. 2nd ed. D. S. Falconer. (Illus.). 1981. pap. text ed. 25.00x (ISBN 0-582-44195-1). Longman.

Introduction to Qualitative Research Methods: A Phenomenological Approach to the Social Sciences. Robert Bogdan & Steven J. Taylor. LC 75-19407. 266p. 1975. 21.95 (ISBN 0-471-08571-5, Pub. by Wiley-Interscience). Wiley.

Introduction to Quality Control. Archibald Jamieson. 1981. text ed. 16.95 (ISBN 0-8359-3264-8); instr's. manual free (ISBN 0-8359-3265-6). Reston.

Introduction to Quantitative Business Analysis. 2nd ed. Ira Horowitz. (Illus.). 352p. 1972. text ed. 19.95 (ISBN 0-07-030398-3); solutions to problems 2.75 (ISBN 0-07-030399-1). McGraw.

Introduction to Quantitative Methods: A Managerial Emphasis. Harish L. Verma & Charles W. Gross. LC 77-21089. 1978. text ed. 24.95 (ISBN 0-471-02610-7); tchrs. manual avail. (ISBN 0-471-02495-3, Pub. by Wiley-Hamilton). Wiley.

Introduction to Quantitative Methods for Business Decisions: Text & Cases. Barry Shore. (Illus.). 1978. text ed. 19.95 (ISBN 0-07-057050-7, C); instructor's manual 6.95 (ISBN 0-07-057051-5). McGraw.

Introduction to Quantitative Research Methods for Librarians. 2nd ed. Taverekere Srikantaiah & Herbert H. Hoffman. 223p. 1978. pap. 8.00x (ISBN 0-89537-002-6). Headway Pubns.

Introduction to Quantum Electronics. P. Hlawiczka. 1972. 38.50 (ISBN 0-12-349950-X). Acad Pr.

Introduction to Quantum Electronics. P. A. Lindsay. LC 75-15696. 202p. 1975. 27.95 (ISBN 0-470-53891-0). Halsted Pr.

Introduction to Quantum Electronics. H. G. Unger. LC 76-86534. 1970. 19.50 (ISBN 0-08-006368-3). Pergamon.

Introduction to Quantum Mechanics. Robert H. Dicke & J. P. Wittke. 1960. 22.95 (ISBN 0-201-01510-2). A-W.

Introduction to Radiation Dosimetry, No. 4. S. Lovell. LC 78-67261. (Techniques of Measurement in Medicine Ser.). (Illus.). 1979. 21.95 (ISBN 0-521-22436-5); pap. 6.50x (ISBN 0-521-29497-5). Cambridge U Pr.

Introduction to Radiation Protection. 2nd ed. Alan Martin & Samuel A. Harbison. LC 79-42847. 1980. pap. text ed. 15.00x o.p. (ISBN 0-412-20960-8, Pub. by Chapman & Hall). Methuen Inc.

Introduction to Radiation Protection. 2nd ed. Alan Martin & Samuel A. Harbison. LC 79-42847. 1980. 22.95x o.p. (ISBN 0-470-26761-5); pap. 12.95x o.p. (ISBN 0-470-26877-8). Halsted Pr.

Introduction to Radiochemistry. David J. Malcombe-Lawes. LC 79-18096. 145p. 1980. 26.95x (ISBN 0-470-26783-6). Halsted Pr.

Introduction to Radiographic Technique. Patricia A. Myers. 1980. 12.95 (ISBN 0-03-056654-1). Praeger.

Introduction to Real Analysis. Derek S. Ball. LC 72-84200. (Mathematical Topics). (Illus.). 324p. 1973. text ed. 23.00 o.p. (ISBN 0-08-016936-8); pap. text ed. 9.90 o.p. (ISBN 0-08-016937-6). Pergamon.

Introduction to Real Estate Law. The Institute for Paralegal Training. Ed. by Russell C. Bellavance & Caroline S. Laden. LC 78-7930. (Paralegal Ser.). 466p. 1978. text ed. 17.95 (ISBN 0-8299-2006-4). West Pub.

Introduction to Real Estate Law. University of Southern Main - Center for Real Estate Education. 250p. (Orig.). 1981. pap. 14.95 (ISBN 0-88462-428-5). Real Estate Ed Co.

Introduction to Reference Sources in the Health Sciences. Fred Roper & JoAnne Boorkman. 256p. 1980. text ed. 18.00 (ISBN 0-912176-08-3). Med Lib Assn.

Introduction to Reformed Dogmatics. Auguste Lecerf. Tr. by S. Leigh-Hunt. (Twin Brooks Ser.). 408p. (Orig.). 1981. pap. 9.95 (ISBN 0-8010-5603-9). Baker Bk.

Introduction to Regge Theory & High-Energy Physics. P. D. Collins. LC 76-2233. (Cambridge Monographs on Mathematical Physics). (Illus.). 1977. 97.50 (ISBN 0-521-21245-6). Cambridge U Pr.

Introduction to Regional Science. Walter Isard. (Illus.). 544p. 1975. ref. ed. 21.95 (ISBN 0-13-493841-0). P-H.

Introduction to Research Procedure in Social Sciences. 2nd ed. M. H. Gopal. 1970. pap. 6.00x o.p. (ISBN 0-210-27013-6). Asia.

Introduction to Respiratory Care. 2nd ed. Stanton Belinkoff. LC 76-1045. 1976. text ed. 10.95 o.p. (ISBN 0-316-08802-1). Little.

Introduction to Respiratory Physiology. 2nd ed. Harold A. Braun et al. 1980. pap. 9.95 (ISBN 0-316-10699-2). Little.

Introduction to Rhetorical Communication. 3rd ed. James McCroskey. 1977. pap. 14.95 (ISBN 0-13-495432-7). P-H.

Introduction to Risk Management. Neil Crockford. 112p. 1980. 27.00x (ISBN 0-85941-116-8, Pub. by Woodhead-Faulkner England). State Mutual Bk.

Introduction to Risk Management. Neil Crockford. 112p. 1980. 17.50x. Herman Pub.

Introduction to Roman Legal & Constitutional History. 2nd ed. Wolfgang Kunkel. Tr. by J. M. Kelly. 1973. 22.50x (ISBN 0-19-825317-6). Oxford U Pr.

Introduction to Romance Linguistics. D. Lincoln Canfield & J. Cary Davis. LC 74-34260. (Illus.). 230p. 1975. 13.95x (ISBN 0-8093-0677-8). S Ill U Pr.

Introduction to RPG: RPG II Programming. Robert A. Fisher. LC 74-9537. 393p. 1975. pap. 21.95 (ISBN 0-471-26001-0). Wiley.

Introduction to Rural Settlements. R. B. Mandal. 1979. text ed. 18.50x (ISBN 0-391-01817-5). Humanities.

Introduction to Satire. facsimile ed. Leonard Feinberg. 293p. (gr. 11 up). 1967. pap. 7.50x o.p. (ISBN 0-8138-2410-9). Iowa St U Pr.

Introduction to Scholarship in Modern Languages & Literatures. Winfred P. Lehmann et al. Ed. by Joseph Gibaldi. 160p. 1981. 10.50x (ISBN 0-87352-092-0); pap. 6.00x (ISBN 0-87352-093-9). Modern Lang.

Introduction to Science for Catering & Homecraft Students. 3rd ed. O. F. Kilgour. (Illus.). 1976. pap. text ed. 15.95x (ISBN 0-434-91057-0). Intl Ideas.

Introduction to Scientific Reasoning in Geography. Douglas Amedeo & Reginald G. Golledge. LC 75-1411. 437p. 1975. text ed. 29.95 (ISBN 0-471-02537-2). Wiley.

Introduction to Security. 2nd ed. Gion Green & Raymond C. Farber. LC 78-7318. 1978. 15.95 (ISBN 0-913708-31-3). Butterworths.

Introduction to Security & Crime Prevention Surveys. A. A. Kingsbury. (Illus.). 384p. 1973. 16.75 (ISBN 0-398-02836-2); pap. 11.95 (ISBN 0-398-02893-1). C C Thomas.

Introduction to Security: Principles & Practices. 3rd ed. Gion Green & Raymond C. Farber. 1981. text ed. 17.95 (ISBN 0-409-95036-X). Butterworth.

Introduction to Seed Technology. J. R. Thomson. LC 79-4412. 252p. 1979. 49.95 (ISBN 0-470-26644-9). Halsted Pr.

Introduction to Semiconductor Devices. F. J. Balley. 1972. pap. text ed. 9.50x o.p. (ISBN 0-04-621017-2). Allen Unwin.

Introduction to Semiconductor Physics. Richard B. Adler et al. (S. E. E. C. Ser.). (Illus.). pap. 14.95 (ISBN 0-471-00887-7). Wiley.

Introduction to Semimicro Qualitative Analysis. 5th ed. Henry Sorum & Joseph J. Lagowski. LC 76-51795. (Illus.). 320p. 1977. pap. text ed. 11.95 (ISBN 0-13-496059-9). P-H.

Introduction to Sensation-Perception. D. McBurney & Collings. (Experimental Psychology Ser.). 1977. 18.95 (ISBN 0-13-496000-9). P-H.

Introduction to Sensory Processes. Jacqueline Ludel. LC 77-16785. (Psychology Ser.). (Illus.). 1978. text ed. 21.95x (ISBN 0-7167-0032-8); pap. text ed. 12.95 (ISBN 0-7167-0031-X). W H Freeman.

Introduction to Separation Science. Barry L. Karger et al. LC 73-4016. 586p. 1973. 32.50 (ISBN 0-471-45860-0, Pub. by Wiley-Interscience). Wiley.

Introduction to Set Theory. J. Donald Monk. LC 79-21279. 206p. 1980. Repr. lib. bdg. 14.50 (ISBN 0-89874-006-1). Krieger.

Introduction to Set Theory & Topology. 2nd, rev. ed. K. Kuratowski. 356p. 1972. text ed. 19.50 (ISBN 0-08-016160-X). Pergamon.

Introduction to Short Fiction & Criticism. Ed. by Emil Hurtik & Robert Yarber. LC 73-138096. (Orig.). 1971. pap. text ed. 12.95 (ISBN 0-471-00273-9). Wiley.

Introduction to Simulation & Slam. A. Alan Pritsker & Claude D. Pegden. LC 78-23385. 1978. 28.95 (ISBN 0-470-26588-4). Halsted Pr.

Introduction to Social Administration in Britain. Muriel Brown. 1969. text ed. 4.00x (ISBN 0-09-110271-5, Hutchinson U Lib); pap. text ed. 2.75x (ISBN 0-09-084093-3, Hutchinson U Lib). Humanities.

Introduction to Social Anthropology. 2nd ed. Lucy Mair. 576p. 1972. pap. text ed. 5.95x (ISBN 0-19-874011-5). Oxford U Pr.

Introduction to Social Anthropology. D. N. Majumdar & T. N. Madan. x, 304p. 1981. pap. text ed. 8.95x (ISBN 0-210-33687-0). Asia.

Introduction to Social Epidemiology. J. C. Salloway. (Behavioral Science for Health Care Professionals Ser.). 128p. (Orig.). 1981. lib. bdg. 15.00x (ISBN 0-86531-014-9); pap. text ed. 6.00x (ISBN 0-86531-015-7). Westview.

Introduction to Social Geography. Emrys Jones & John Eyles. 1977. text ed. 29.95x (ISBN 0-19-874062-X); pap. 8.95x (ISBN 0-19-874063-8). Oxford U Pr.

Introduction to Social Medicine. 2nd ed. Thomas McKeown & C. R. Lowe. (Illus.). 356p. 1974. 20.00 (ISBN 0-397-60221-9, Dist. by Mosby). Lippincott.

Introduction to Social Policy. Elizabeth D. Huttman. Ed. by Nelson W. Black. (Illus.). 368p. 1980. text ed. 14.95x (ISBN 0-07-031548-5). McGraw.

Introduction to Social Problems. Leonard Glick & Daniel E. Hebding. LC 78-67953. (Sociology Ser.). 1980. pap. text ed. 12.95 (ISBN 0-201-02600-7). A-W.

Introduction to Social Psychology. 3rd ed. Henry C. Lindgren & John H. Harvey. (Illus.). 500p. 1981. text ed. 17.95 (ISBN 0-8016-3038-X). Mosby.

Introduction to Social Psychology. David J. Schneider. LC 75-18160. (Social Psychology Ser.). (Illus.). 656p. 1976. text ed. 18.95 (ISBN 0-201-06728-5); instr's manual 2.75 (ISBN 0-201-06724-2). A-W.

Introduction to Social Psychology. David Stang. LC 80-19469. 570p. 1981. text ed. 17.95 (ISBN 0-8185-0427-7). Brooks-Cole.

Introduction to Social Science. 2nd ed. Alfred Apsler. 1976. text ed. 13.95 o.p. (ISBN 0-394-31974-5). Random.

Introduction to Social Science. 3rd ed. Alfred Apsler. 541p. 1981. text ed. 16.95 (ISBN 0-394-32534-6). Random.

Introduction to Social Science. Ernest L. Schusky. (Illus.). 512p. 1981. pap. text ed. 15.95 (ISBN 0-13-496703-8). P-H.

Introduction to Social Statistics. Vanderlyn R. Pine. (Methods of Social Science Ser.). (Illus.). 1977. text ed. 18.95 (ISBN 0-13-496844-1). P-H.

Introduction to Social Welfare. 5th ed. Walter A. Friedlander & Robert Z. Apte. (Illus.). 1980. text ed. 17.95 (ISBN 0-13-497032-2). P-H.

Introduction to Social Welfare & Social Work: Structure, Function, & Process. Beulah R. Compton. 1980. 17.95x (ISBN 0-256-02093-0). Dorsey.

Introduction to Social Welfare Institutions: Social Problems, Services, & Current Issues. Charles H. Zastrow. 1978. 17.95x (ISBN 0-256-02090-6). Dorsey.

Introduction to Social Welfare Policy. Joseph Heffernan. LC 78-61882. 1979. text ed. 12.95 (ISBN 0-87581-241-4). Peacock Pubs.

Introduction to Social Work. 2nd ed. R. A. Skidmore & Milton G. Thackeray. (Illus.). 464p. 1976. ref. ed. 17.95 (ISBN 0-13-497024-1). P-H.

Introduction to Social Work: A Primer. rev. ed. Betty Piccard. 1979. pap. text ed. 7.95x (ISBN 0-256-02109-0). Dorsey.

Introduction to Social Work Practice. Neil Gilbert et al. (P-H Ser. in Social Work Practice). (Illus.). 1980. text ed. 16.95 (ISBN 0-13-479105-3). P-H.

Introduction to Sociology. 3rd ed. Mavis Biesanz & John Biesanz. (Illus.). 1978. text ed. 17.95 (ISBN 0-13-497412-3); study guide 4.95 (ISBN 0-13-497404-2). P-H.

Introduction to Sociology. 2nd ed. J. E. Goldthorpe. LC 73-83107. (Illus.). 200p. 1974. text ed. 29.95 (ISBN 0-521-20338-4); pap. text ed. 8.95x (ISBN 0-521-09826-2). Cambridge U Pr.

Introduction to Sociology. B. S. Green & E. A. Johns. 1966. 11.25 (ISBN 0-08-012155-1); pap. 6.25 (ISBN 0-08-012154-3). Pergamon.

Introduction to Sociology. 4th ed. Cathy Greenblat & David Dressler. 592p. 1981. pap. text ed. 15.95 (ISBN 0-394-32656-3); wkbk 6.95 (ISBN 0-394-32711-X). Knopf.

Introduction to Sociology. 2nd ed. Daniel E. Hebding & Leonard Glick. (Sociology Ser.). (Illus.). 480p. 1981. pap. text ed. 12.95 (ISBN 0-201-03997-4). A-W.

Introduction to Sociology: Situations & Structures. Ed. by Jack D. Douglas. LC 75-163608. 1973. text ed. 14.95 (ISBN 0-02-907540-8). Free Pr.

Introduction to Soil Mechanics & Foundations. 3rd ed. (Illus.). xi, 405p. 1980. pap. text ed. 22.50x (ISBN 0-85334-873-1). Intl Ideas.

Introduction to Soil Microbiology. 2nd ed. Martin Alexander. LC 77-1319. 460p. 1977. text ed. 24.95 (ISBN 0-471-02179-2); arabic translation avail. Wiley.

Introduction to Soil Science. E. A. FitzPatrick. (Ecology Ser). (Illus.). 176p. 1974. pap. text ed. 7.50x (ISBN 0-05-002777-8). Longman.

Introduction to Solid Mechanics. Irving H. Shames. (Illus.). 688p. 1975. ref. ed. 25.95 (ISBN 0-13-497503-0). P-H.

Introduction to Solid State Physics. 5th ed. Charles Kittel. LC 75-25936. 560p. 1976. text ed. 28.95 (ISBN 0-471-49024-5). Wiley.

Introduction to Spanish-American Literature. Jean Franco. LC 69-12927. 1969. 42.00 (ISBN 0-521-07374-X); pap. 9.95x (ISBN 0-521-09891-2). Cambridge U Pr.

Introduction to Spatial Allocation Analysis. A. J. Scott. LC 71-173661. (CCG Resource Papers Ser.: No. 9). (Illus.). 1971. pap. text ed. 4.00 (ISBN 0-89291-056-9). Assn Am Geographers.

Introduction to Special Education. Blackhurst & Berdine. 1981. text ed. 15.95 (ISBN 0-316-09060-3); tchrs'. manual free (ISBN 0-316-09061-1). Little.

Introduction to Special Relativity. R. Resnick. 1972. pap. 10.95x (ISBN 0-471-71725-8). Wiley.

Introduction to Spectroscopic Methods for the Identification of Organic Compounds, Vol. 1. F. Scheinmann. LC 76-99991. 1970. text ed. 18.75 (ISBN 0-08-006661-5); pap. text ed. 9.25 (ISBN 0-08-006662-3). Pergamon.

Introduction to Spectroscopic Methods for the Identification of Organic Compounds, Vol. 2. F. Scheinmann. LC 76-99991. 368p. 1974. text ed. 25.00 (ISBN 0-08-016719-5); pap. text ed. 12.75 (ISBN 0-08-016720-9). Pergamon.

Introduction to Speech Communication. John F. Cragan & David W. Wright. 400p. 1980. pap. text ed. 9.95x (ISBN 0-917974-45-X). Waveland Pr.

Introduction to Speech Communication. 2nd ed. Gerald R. Miller. LC 78-173982. 1972. pap. text ed. 3.95 (ISBN 0-672-61298-4, SC7). Bobbs.

Introduction to Statics. Helen Plants & Wallace Venable. LC 74-32425. (Illus.). 1045p. 1975. text ed. 19.50 (ISBN 0-8299-0023-3); tchrs' ed. avail. (ISBN 0-8299-0568-5); notebook avail. (ISBN 0-8299-0047-0). West Pub.

Introduction to Statistical Communication Theory. John B. Thomas. LC 68-8108. 1969. 35.95 (ISBN 0-471-85893-5). Wiley.

Introduction to Statistical Method. B. C. Brookes & W. F. Dick. 1969. pap. text ed. 7.50x o.p. (ISBN 0-435-53124-7). Heinemann Ed.

Introduction to Statistical Methods. 2nd ed. Donald L. Harnett. LC 74-10353. (Illus.). 500p. 1975. text ed. 18.50 (ISBN 0-201-02752-6). A-W.

Introduction to Statistical Models in Geology. William C. Krumbein & F. A. Graybill. (International Ser.in the Earth & Planetary Sciences). 1965. text ed. 21.95 o.p. (ISBN 0-07-035555-X, C). McGraw.

Introduction to Statistical Science in Agriculture. 4th ed. D. J. Finney. 1972. 27.95 (ISBN 0-470-25900-0). Halsted Pr.

Introduction to Statistical Theory. Paul Hoel et al. LC 70-136172. 1971. text ed. 19.75 (ISBN 0-395-04637-8, 3-25652). HM.

Introduction to Statistical Thermodynamics. Terrell L. Hill. 1960. 22.95 (ISBN 0-201-02840-9). A-W.

Introduction to Statistical Time Series. Wayne A. Fuller. LC 76-6954. (Probability & Mathematical Statistics Ser.). 1976. 32.95 (ISBN 0-471-28715-6, Pub. by Wiley-Interscience). Wiley.

Introduction to Statistics. Bennett et al. LC 77-21394. write for info. o.p. (ISBN 0-87618-920-6). R J Brady.

Introduction to Statistics. Lincoln L. Chao. LC 79-13686. 1979. text ed. 17.95 (ISBN 0-8185-0321-1); study guide 6.95 (ISBN 0-8185-0410-2). Brooks-Cole.

Introduction to Statistics: A Nonparametric Approach. 2nd ed. Gottfried E. Noether. LC 75-19532. (Illus.). 336p. 1976. text ed. 18.25 (ISBN 0-395-18578-5); solutions manual 1.50 (ISBN 0-395-18789-3). HM.

Introduction to Statistics: An Applications Approach. David R. Anderson Sweeney & Thomas A. Williams. (Illus.). 750p. text ed. 14.36 (ISBN 0-8299-0361-5). West Pub.

Introduction to Statistics & Probability. Edward J. Dudewicz. LC 75-26827. 1976. text ed. 22.95 (ISBN 0-03-086688-X); solns. manual o.p. 20.00 (ISBN 0-03-089629-0). Am Sciences Pr.

Introduction to Statistics for Business Decisions. Robert Schlaifer. 1961. text ed. 20.95 (ISBN 0-07-055308-4, C); solutions manual 4.95 (ISBN 0-07-055305-X). McGraw.

Introduction to Stellar Atmospheres & Interiors. Eva Novotny. 680p. 1973. text ed. 22.95x (ISBN 0-19-501588-6). Oxford U Pr.

Introduction to Steroid Chemistry. J. R. Hanson. 1968. 16.50 (ISBN 0-08-012809-2); pap. 7.75 (ISBN 0-08-012808-4). Pergamon.

Introduction to Still Life & Flower Painting. Barbara Dorf. (Illus.). 184p. 1976. 15.95 (ISBN 0-7207-0885-0). Transatlantic.

Introduction to Stochastic Processes. 3rd ed. M. S. Bartlett. LC 76-57094. (Illus.). 404p. Date not set. pap. 17.95 (ISBN 0-521-28085-0). Cambridge U Pr.

Introduction to Stochastic Processes. E. Cinlar. (Illus.). 448p. 1975. ref. ed. 22.95 (ISBN 0-13-498089-1). P-H.

Introduction to Stochastic Processes. Paul Hoel et al. LC 79-105035. (Illus.). 1972. text ed. 19.75 (ISBN 0-395-12076-4, 3-25656). HM.

Introduction to Stochastic Processes. J. P. Medhi. 320p. 1981. 19.95 (ISBN 0-470-27000-4). Halsted Pr.

Introduction to Stochastic Processes with Special Reference to Methods & Applications. 3rd ed. M. S. Bartlett. LC 76-57094. (Illus.). 1978. 57.50 (ISBN 0-521-21585-4). Cambridge U Pr.

Introduction to Structural Design: Concrete Bridges, No. 1. Derrick Beckett. (Illus.). 240p. 1975. 18.00x (ISBN 0-903384-01-9). Transatlantic.

Introduction to Structural Design: Timber. Derrick Beckett & Paul Marsh. (Illus.). 1974. 22.50x (ISBN 0-903384-02-7). Intl Ideas.

Introduction to Structural Design: Timber, No. 2. Derrick Beckett & Paul Marsh. (Illus.). 216p. 1975. 18.00x (ISBN 0-903384-02-7). Transatlantic.

Introduction to Structural Equation Models. Otis D. Duncan et al. (Studies in Population Ser.). 1975. 20.00 (ISBN 0-12-224150-9). Acad Pr.

Introduction to Superconductivity. A. C. Rose-Innes. 244p. 1975. text ed. 26.40 o.p. (ISBN 0-08-013469-6); pap. 16.50 o.p. (ISBN 0-08-019011-1). Pergamon.

Introduction to Superconductivity. 2nd ed. A. C. Rose-Innes & E. H. Rhoderick. 1977. text ed. 45.00 (ISBN 0-08-021651-X); pap. 24.00 (ISBN 0-08-021652-8). Pergamon.

Introduction to Superconductivity. Michael Tinkham. (International Ser. in Pure & Applied Physics). (Illus.). 320p. 1975. text ed. 23.00 o.p. (ISBN 0-07-064877-8, C). McGraw.

Introduction to Survey Research & Data Analysis. Herbert F. Weisberg & Bruce D. Bowen. LC 76-39975. (Illus.). 1977. text ed. 18.95x (ISBN 0-7167-0485-4); pap. text ed. 9.95x (ISBN 0-7167-0484-6). W H Freeman.

Introduction to Surveys & Interviews. Lawrence P. Clark. (Learning Packages in the Policy Sciences: No. 12). (Illus.). 56p. (Orig.). 1978. pap. text ed. 3.00 (ISBN 0-936826-01-0). Pol Stud Assocs.

Introduction to Switching Theory & Logical Design. 3rd ed. Frederick J. Hill & Gerald R. Peterson. LC 80-20333. 640p. 1981. text ed. 27.95 (ISBN 0-471-04273-0). Wiley.

Introduction to Symbolic Logic. 3rd ed. Susanne K. Langer. 1953. pap. text ed. 5.00 (ISBN 0-486-60164-1). Dover.

Introduction to Synergetics: Nonequilibrium Phase Transitions & Self-Organization in Physics, Chemistry & Biology. H. Haken. LC 76-54243. (Illus.). 1977. 33.30 o.p. (ISBN 0-387-07885-1). Springer-Verlag.

Introduction to Synthesis Using Organocopper Reagents. Gary H. Posner. LC 80-13538. 140p. 1980. 23.50 (ISBN 0-471-69538-6, Pub. by Wiley-Interscience). Wiley.

Introduction to System Design Using Integrated Circuits. B. S. Sonde. 261p. 1981. 24.95 (ISBN 0-470-27110-8). Halsted Pr.

Introduction to System Dynamics. L. S. Shearer et al. 1967. 24.95 (ISBN 0-201-07017-0). A-W.

Introduction to Systems Analysis. Gerald A. Silver & Joan B. Silver. (Illus.). 1976. 17.95x (ISBN 0-13-498683-0). P-H.

Introduction to Systems Engineering: Deterministic Models. Tung Au & Thomas E. Stelson. (Civil Engineering Ser). (Illus.). 1969. text ed. 22.95 (ISBN 0-201-00363-5); instructor's manual 3.00 (ISBN 0-201-00364-3). A-W.

Introduction to Systems for the Educational Administrator. Glenn L. Immegart & Francis J. Pilecki. LC 72-1939. 1973. text ed. 13.95 (ISBN 0-201-03175-2). A-W.

Introduction to T-Bug. Don Inman & Kurt Inman. LC 79-67461. 1979. pap. 7.95 (ISBN 0-918398-33-9). Dilithium Pr.

Introduction to Tacitus. Herbert W. Benario. LC 73-85025. 184p. 1975. text ed. 7.50x o.p. (ISBN 0-8203-0328-3); pap. text ed. 5.00x (ISBN 0-8203-0361-5). U of Ga Pr.

Introduction to Tantra Shastra. John Woodroffe. 7.50 (ISBN 0-89744-114-1, Pub. by Ganesh & Co. India). Auromere.

Introduction to Technical Drawing: Metric Edition. Norman Stirling. LC 79-56653. 370p. 1981. pap. text ed. 15.00 (ISBN 0-8273-1939-8). Delmar.

Introduction to Technical Mathematics: A Calculator Approach. Herman R. Hyatt et al. LC 78-17016. 1979. text ed. 17.95x (ISBN 0-471-22240-2); tchrs. manual avail. (ISBN 0-471-04053-3). Wiley.

Introduction to Technical Mathematics. Daniel R. Peterson & Gilbert M. Peter. 416p. 1974. 12.95x (ISBN 0-673-07784-5). Scott F.

Introduction to Technical Mathematics. 2nd ed. Allyn J. Washington. LC 77-85502. 1978. 19.95 (ISBN 0-8053-9525-3). Benjamin-Cummings.

Introduction to Technical Services for Library Technicians. 3rd ed. Marty Bloomberg & G. Edward Evans. LC 76-43294. (Library Science Text Ser.). 1976. lib. bdg. 15.00x (ISBN 0-87287-125-8). Libs Unl.

Introduction to Technical Services for Library Technicians. 4th ed. Marty Bloomberg & G. Edward Evans. (Library Science Text Ser.). (Illus.). 325p. 1981. lib. bdg. 19.50 (ISBN 0-87287-228-9); pap. text ed. 14.50x (ISBN 0-87287-248-3). Libs Unl.

Introduction to Teleprocessing. James Martin. (Illus.). 1972. ref. ed. 21.95 (ISBN 0-13-499814-6). P-H.

Introduction to Tensegrity. Anthony Pugh. LC 75-5951. 150p. 1976. 14.50x (ISBN 0-520-02996-8); pap. 4.95 (ISBN 0-520-03055-9, CAL 325). U of Cal Pr.

Introduction to Terrariums. Barbara J. Grubman. (Illus.). 128p. 1973. pap. 1.50 o.p. (ISBN 0-445-08488-X). Popular Lib.

Introduction to the Administration of Criminal Justice: An Overview of the Justice System & Its Components. 2nd ed. Thomas F. Adams. (Ser. in Criminal Justice). (Illus.). 1980. text ed. 15.95 (ISBN 0-13-477794-8). P-H.

Introduction to the Administration of Justice. 2nd ed. C. A. Foster et al. LC 78-13498. 347p. 1979. 17.50 (ISBN 0-471-04079-7). Wiley.

Introduction to the Administrative History of Mediaeval England. 3rd ed. S. B. Chrimes. 1966. 36.00x (ISBN 0-631-09170-X, Pub. by Basil Blackwell). Biblio Dist.

Introduction to the Algae. Ian Morris. (Orig.). 1967. pap. text ed. 7.50x (ISBN 0-09-080713-8, Hutchinson U Lib). Humanities.

Introduction to the Algae: Structure & Reproduction. Harold C. Bold & Michael J. Wynne. (P-H Biology Ser.). (Illus.). 1978. ref. ed. 28.95 (ISBN 0-13-477786-7). P-H.

Introduction to the American Legal System: A Supplement to Higher Education & the Law. Harry T. Edwards & Virginia D. Nordin. LC 80-82033. 76p. (Orig.). 1980. pap. text ed. 5.95 (ISBN 0-934222-02-9). Inst Ed Manage.

Introduction to the Analysis of Educational Concepts. 2nd rev. ed. Jonas F. Soltis. LC 77-79465. (Education Ser.). (Illus.). 1978. pap. text ed. 6.95 (ISBN 0-201-06989-X). A-W.

Introduction to the Anatomy & Physiology of the Speech Mechanisms. Charles F. Diehl. (Illus.). 192p. 1968. pap. 14.75 photocopy ed. spiral (ISBN 0-398-00452-8). C C Thomas.

Introduction to the Anglo-American Legal System, Readings & Cases. Edgar Bodenheimer et al. LC 80-18757. (American Casebook Ser.). 185p. 1980. pap. text ed. 6.95 (ISBN 0-8299-2103-6). West Pub.

Introduction to the Apocrypha. Bruce M. Metzger. 1957. pap. 5.95 (ISBN 0-19-502340-4). Oxford U Pr.

Introduction to the Approximation of Functions. Theodore J. Rivlin. 160p. 1981. pap. price not set (ISBN 0-486-64069-8). Dover.

Introduction to the Art & Science of Collecting Butterflies. Clarence M. Weed. (Illus.). 1980. Repr. of 1917 ed. 41.75 (ISBN 0-89901-003-2). Found Class Reprints.

Introduction to the Art Song. Barbara Meister. LC 79-66640. 1980. 11.95 (ISBN 0-8008-4203-0, Crescendo). Taplinger.

Introduction to the Atmosphere Lab Manual. Alan Cole. 1980. loose leaf shrink wrapped 4.75 (ISBN 0-88252-110-1). Paladin Hse.

Introduction to the Bible. H. J. Flanders & B. C. Cresson. 1973. 17.95 (ISBN 0-8260-3125-0). Wiley.

Introduction to the Biochemistry & Pharmacology of Antibiotics. R. A. D. Williams & Z. L. Kruk. 128p. 1980. 25.00x (ISBN 0-85664-857-4, Pub. by Croom Helm England). State Mutual Bk.

Introduction to the Biological Bases of Behavior for the Health Professions. Alfred W. Kaszniak. (Behavioral Sciences for Health Care Professionals Ser.). 128p. (Orig.). 1981. lib. bdg. 15.00x (ISBN 0-86531-010-6); pap. text ed. 6.00x (ISBN 0-86531-011-4). Westview.

Introduction to the Biological Basis of Feeding: Essential Biological Ideas Necessary to a Study of Living Beings from the Evolutionary Standpoint. Faustino Cordon. LC 79-40933. (Illus.). 250p. 1980. pap. 34.00 (ISBN 0-08-025484-5). Pergamon.

Introduction to the Botany of Tropical Crops. 2nd ed. L. S. Cobley. LC 76-7447. (Longman Text Ser.). (Illus.). 1977. pap. text ed. 17.95x (ISBN 0-582-44153-6). Longman.

Introduction to the Chemical Aspects of Nursing Science. O. F. Kilgour. (Illus.). 1972. 19.95x (ISBN 0-433-18471-X). Intl Ideas.

Introduction to the Chemistry of Benzenoid Components. M. Tomlinson. 1971. 22.00 (ISBN 0-08-015659-2); pap. 9.75 (ISBN 0-08-016921-X). Pergamon.

Introduction to the Chemistry of Life: Biochemistry. 2nd ed. Harold J. Debey. 272p. 1976. text ed. 8.95 (ISBN 0-201-01474-2). A-W.

Introduction to the Chemistry of Life. 2nd ed. Harland D. Embree & Harold J. Debey. 1975. text ed. 16.95 (ISBN 0-201-01886-1). A-W.

Introduction to the Chemistry of Life: Organic Chemistry. Harland D. Embree. 1968. 9.50 (ISBN 0-201-01868-3). A-W.

Introduction to the Child's Conception of Geometry. G. E. Holloway. (Illus.). 1967. pap. text ed. 1.50x (ISBN 0-7100-1543-7). Humanities.

Introduction to the Clinical History. 2nd ed. Ed. by Iver F. Small. 1971. spiral bdg. 4.00 o.p. (ISBN 0-87488-729-1). Med Exam.

Introduction to the Computer: An Integrative Approach. Jeffrey Frates & William Moldrup. (Illus.). 1980. text ed. 18.95 (ISBN 0-13-480301-9); pap. 5.95 study guide (ISBN 0-13-480285-3). P-H.

Introduction to the Computer: The Tool of Business. 2nd ed. William M. Fuori. (Illus.). 1977. text ed. 18.95 (ISBN 0-13-480103-2). P-H.

Introduction to the Computer: The Tool of Business. 3rd ed. William M. Fuori. (Illus.). 720p. 1981. text ed. 17.95 (ISBN 0-13-480343-4); pap. 5.95 study guide (ISBN 0-13-480368-X). P-H.

Introduction to the Criminal Justice System. 2nd ed. Hazel B. Kerper & Jerold H. Israel. (Criminal Justice Ser.). (Illus.). 1979. text ed. 15.95 (ISBN 0-8299-0276-7); pap. study guide 5.95 (ISBN 0-8299-0260-0); instrs.' manual avail. (ISBN 0-8299-0593-6). West Pub.

Introduction to the DEC System Ten Assembler Language Programming. M. Singer. LC 78-8586. 1978. 12.95 (ISBN 0-471-03458-4). Wiley.

Introduction to the Devout Life. rev. ed. St. Francis de Sales. 1972. pap. 2.45 (ISBN 0-385-03009-6, Im). Doubleday.

Introduction to the Devout Life. Saint Francis De Sales. Tr. by M. Day. 1961. 10.50x (ISBN 0-460-00324-0, Evman). Dutton.

Introduction to the Economic History of Ethiopia. Richard Pankhurst. 1961. text ed. 12.50x (ISBN 0-391-01992-9). Humanities.

Introduction to the Elastic Stability of Structures. George J. Simitses. (Illus.). 288p. 1976. 27.95 (ISBN 0-13-481200-X). P-H.

Introduction to the Electron Theory of Solids. J. Stringer. 1967. 23.00 (ISBN 0-08-012219-1); pap. 9.75 (ISBN 0-08-012220-5). Pergamon.

Introduction to the English Novel, 2 vols. Arnold Kettle. Incl. Vol. 1. Up to George Eliot. text ed. o.p. (ISBN 0-09-031603-7); pap. text ed. 9.00x (ISBN 0-09-031604-5); Vol. 2. Henry James to the Present. text ed. o.p. (ISBN 0-09-048543-2); pap. text ed. 8.50x (ISBN 0-09-048544-0). 1974 (Hutchinson U Lib). Humanities.

Introduction to the Episcopal Church. rev ed. Joseph B. Bernardin. (Orig.). 1978. pap. 3.75 (ISBN 0-8192-1231-8). Morehouse.

Introduction to the Essay. Edmund Fuller & O. B. Davis. (Introduction to Ser.). 1972. pap. 7.15x (ISBN 0-8104-5824-1). Hayden.

Introduction to the Evaluation of Measurement Data in Physical Education. Thomas J. Sheehan. LC 78-137837. (Physical Education Ser). 1971. text ed. 14.95 (ISBN 0-201-07007-3). A-W.

Introduction to the Foundations of American Education. 3rd ed. James A. Johnson et al. 560p. 1976. text ed. 13.95x o.s.i. (ISBN 0-205-05018-2); instr's manual free o.s.i. (ISBN 0-205-05019-0). Allyn.

Introduction to the Foundations of American Education. 4th ed. James A. Johnson et al. 1979. text ed. 16.95 (ISBN 0-205-06566-X); instr's man. avail. (ISBN 0-205-06567-8). Allyn.

Introduction to the Foundations of Mathematics. Raymond L. Wilder. LC 80-12446. 346p. 1980. Repr. of 1965 ed. pap. 19.50 (ISBN 0-89874-170-X). Krieger.

Introduction to the Fundamentals of Financial Analysis for Business Students. James W. Thomson. LC 79-8512. 1979. pap. text ed. 12.25 (ISBN 0-8191-0872-3). U Pr of Amer.

Introduction to the Gothic Language. 4th, rev. ed. William H. Bennett. Ed. by Winfred P. Lehmann. LC 79-87574. (Introductions to the Older Languages of Europe Ser.: No. 2). xvii, 190p. 1981. 18.50x (ISBN 0-87352-290-7). Modern Lang.

Introduction to the Historical Grammar of the Tamil Language. K. Zvelebil. (Oriental Institute Czechoslovakia Dissertationes Orientales, Vol. 25). 1970. 6.00x o.p. (ISBN 0-685-27140-4). Paragon.

Introduction to the History of Christian Spirituality. Urban T. Holmes. 176p. 1980. 8.95 (ISBN 0-8164-0141-1). Crossroad NY.

Introduction to the History of English Medieval Towns. Susan Reynolds. (Illus.). 1977. text ed. 27.00x (ISBN 0-19-822455-9). Oxford U Pr.

Introduction to the History of Mycology. G. C. Ainsworth. LC 75-21036. (Illus.). 350p. 1976. 47.50 (ISBN 0-521-21013-5). Cambridge U Pr.

Introduction to the History of Plant Pathology. G. C. Ainsworth. LC 80-40476. 220p. Date not set. price not set (ISBN 0-521-23032-2). Cambridge U Pr.

Introduction to the History of the Land Law. Alfred W. Simpson. 1961. 29.50x (ISBN 0-19-825150-5). Oxford U Pr.

Introduction to the History of the Revolt of the American Colonies, 2 Vols. George Chalmers. LC 75-119049. (Era of the American Revolution Ser). 1971. Repr. of 1845 ed. lib. bdg. 65.00 (ISBN 0-306-71948-7). Da Capo.

Introduction to the History of the Science of Politics. Frederick Pollock. 6.00 o.p. (ISBN 0-8446-2750-X). Peter Smith.

Introduction to the History of Virology. A. P. Waterson & L. Wilkinson. LC 77-17892. (Illus.). 1978. 38.50 (ISBN 0-521-21917-5). Cambridge U Pr.

Introduction to the Hospitality Industry. Nathan Kalt. LC 71-142505. 1971. text ed. 13.50 (ISBN 0-672-96086-9); tchr's manual 5.90 (ISBN 0-672-96088-5); wkbk. 6.50 (ISBN 0-672-96087-7). Bobbs.

Introduction to the Human Services: Developing Knowledge, Skills, & Sensitivity. Charlotte Epstein. (Illus.). 368p. 1981. text ed. 15.95 (ISBN 0-686-69277-2). P-H.

Introduction to the Humanities: Painting, Sculpture, Architecture, Music & Literature. Doris Van De Bogart. LC 67-29656. (Orig.). 1968. pap. 4.95 (ISBN 0-06-463277-6, EH 277, EH). Har-Row.

Introduction to the Interpretation of Fairy Tales. Marie-Louise Von Franz. Ed. by James Hillman. (Seminar Ser.). 159p. 1970. pap. text ed. 7.50 (ISBN 0-88214-101-5). Spring Pubns.

Introduction to the Interpretation of the Electrocardiogram. Louis N. Katz et al. LC 52-14734. (Illus.). 1952. pap. 4.50x o.s.i. (ISBN 0-226-42590-8). U of Chicago Pr.

Introduction to the Ionosphere & Magnetosphere. J. A. Ratcliffe. LC 74-171680. (Illus.). 200p. 1972. 35.50 (ISBN 0-521-08341-9); pap. 11.50x (ISBN 0-521-09970-6). Cambridge U Pr.

Introduction to the Laboratory Study of the Ear. David M. Lipscomb. (Illus.). 296p. 1974. 26.75 (ISBN 0-398-02938-5). C C Thomas.

Introduction to the Laplace Transform. Dio L. Holl et al. LC 59-7720. (Century Mathematics Ser.). (Illus.). 1959. 28.50 (ISBN 0-89197-247-1). Irvington.

Introduction to the Law of Industrial Disputes. R. F. Rustamji. 1968. pap. 7.25x (ISBN 0-210-98198-9). Asia.

Introduction to the Law Relative to Trials at Nisi Prius. Francis Buller. Ed. by David S. Berkowitz & Samuel E. Thorne. LC 77-89211. (Classics of English Legal History in the Modern Era Ser.: Vol. 60). 670p. 1979. lib. bdg. 40.00 (ISBN 0-8240-3159-8). Garland Pub.

Introduction to the Literature of the New Testament. 3rd ed. James Moffatt. (International Theological Library). 704p. Repr. of 1918 ed. 13.95x (ISBN 0-567-07213-4). Attic Pr.

Introduction to the Literature of the Old Testament. 9th ed. S. R. Driver. (International Theological Library). 640p. Repr. of 1913 ed. 13.95x (ISBN 0-567-07205-3). Attic Pr.

Introduction to the Living World. Sol. A. Karlin. 1974. pap. text ed. 10.95 (ISBN 0-917962-33-8); lab manual 4.50 (ISBN 0-917962-29-X). Peek Pubns.

Introduction to the Magnetic Properties of Solids. A. S. Chakravarty. LC 80-12793. 736p. 1980. 65.00 (ISBN 0-471-07737-2, Pub. by Wiley-Interscience). Wiley.

Introduction to the Mathematical Theory of Finite Elements. J. T. Oden & J. N. Reddy. LC 76-6953. (Pure & Applied Mathematics Ser.). 429p. 1976. 35.00 (ISBN 0-471-65261-X, Pub. by Wiley-Interscience). Wiley.

Introduction to the Mathematics of Finance. rev. ed. A. H. Pollard. 1978. pap. 7.00 (ISBN 0-08-021796-6). Pergamon.

Introduction to the Mathematics of Population - with Revisions. Nathan C. Keyfitz. LC 76-17718. 496p. 1977. 23.95 (ISBN 0-201-03649-5). A-W.

Introduction to the Mechanics of a Continuous Medium. Lawrence E. Malvern. 1969. ref. ed. 27.95 (ISBN 0-13-487603-2). P-H.

Introduction to the Mechanics of Plastic Forming Metals. W. Szczepinski. 378p. 1979. 60.00x (ISBN 90-286-0126-0). Sijthoff & Noordhoff.

Introduction to the Mechanics of Solids. Martin A. Eisenberg. LC 78-74682. (Illus.). 1980. text ed. 24.95 (ISBN 0-201-01934-5). A-W.

Introduction to the Metaphysical Poets. Patricia Beer. 1972. 7.50x o.p. (ISBN 0-87471-134-7). Rowman.

Introduction to the Microbial World. Roger Stanier et al. (Illus.). 1979. ref. ed. 19.95 (ISBN 0-13-488049-8); lab. manual 8.95 (ISBN 0-13-488031-5). P-H.

Introduction to the Morphology of the Cellular Elements of the Blood. Necheles. 1975. pap. 17.95 o.p. (ISBN 0-8385-4350-2). ACC.

Introduction to the Natural History of the San Francisco Bay Region. Arthur C. Smith. (California Natural History Guides: No. 1). (Illus.). 1959. 12.95x (ISBN 0-520-03099-0); pap. 3.95 (ISBN 0-520-01185-6). U of Cal Pr.

Introduction to the New Testament. Robert W. Crapps et al. LC 72-75637. (Illus.). 566p. 1969. 18.95 (ISBN 0-8260-2225-1, Pub. by Wiley Medical). Wiley.

Introduction to the New Testament, 3 vols. Theodor Zahn. 1977. 48.00 (ISBN 0-686-12975-X). Klock & Klock.

Introduction to the Old Testament Prophets. Hobart Freeman. 10.95 (ISBN 0-8024-4145-9). Moody.

Introduction to the Parables Through Programmed Instruction. William R. Stegner. 1977. pap. text ed. 6.50x o.p. (ISBN 0-8191-0132-X). U Pr of Amer.

Introduction to the Peoples & Cultures of Indonesia & Malaysia. R. M. Koentjaraningrat. LC 75-4078. 1975. pap. 6.95 (ISBN 0-8465-1670-5). Benjamin-Cummings.

Introduction to the Peoples & Cultures of Melanesia. 2nd ed. Ann Chowning. LC 76-7651. 1977. pap. 4.95 o.p. (ISBN 0-8465-0931-8). Benjamin-Cummings.

Introduction to the Phenomenological Theory of Ferroelectricity. J. Grindlay. LC 72-90455. 1970. 36.00 (ISBN 0-08-006362-4). Pergamon.

Introduction to the Philosophy of Education. James Gribble. 1969. pap. text ed. 7.95x o.p. (ISBN 0-205-02397-5, 222397X). Allyn.

Introduction to the Philosophy of Education. 2nd ed. George F. Kneller. LC 78-168637. 1971. pap. text ed. 7.25 (ISBN 0-471-49515-8). Wiley.

Introduction to the Philosophy of Law. William H. Bruening. LC 78-62249. 1978. pap. text ed. 9.00 (ISBN 0-8191-0570-8). U Pr of Amer.

Introduction to the Philosophy of Law. rev. ed. Roscoe Pound. (Storrs Lectures Ser.). 1954. 14.50x (ISBN 0-300-00839-2); pap. 4.95 1959 (ISBN 0-300-00188-6, Y10). Yale U Pr.

Introduction to the Philosophy of Mind: Readings from Descartes to Strawson. Harold Morick. 1970. 12.95x o.p. (ISBN 0-673-05973-1); pap. 9.95x o.p. (ISBN 0-673-05193-5). Scott F.

Introduction to the Philosophy of Science. rev. 2nd ed. Karel Lambert & Gordon G. Brittan, Jr. 1979. lib. bdg. 22.00 (ISBN 0-917930-37-1); pap. text ed. 7.50x (ISBN 0-917930-17-7). Ridgeview.

Introduction to the Phonetics of American English. 2nd ed. Charles K. Thomas. (Illus.). 1958. 15.50 (ISBN 0-8260-8630-6). Wiley.

Introduction to the Physical Properties of Large Molecules in Solution. E. G. Richards & S. D. Dover. LC 79-41583. (IUPAB Biophysics Ser.: No. 3). (Illus.). 200p. 1980. 29.50 (ISBN 0-521-23110-8); pap. 9.95 (ISBN 0-521-29817-2). Cambridge U Pr.

Introduction to the Physics & Psychophysics of Music. J. G. Roederer. LC 72-97698. (Heidelberg Science Library: Vol. 16). (Illus.). xii, 164p. 1973. pap. 7.10 o.p. (ISBN 0-387-90063-2). Springer-Verlag.

Introduction to the Physics of Electronics. Myron F. Uman. 1974. 25.95 (ISBN 0-13-492702-8). P-H.

Introduction to the Physics of Fluids & Solids. James S. Trefil. 320p. 1976. text ed. 28.00 (ISBN 0-08-018104-X). Pergamon.

Introduction to the Pierpont Morgan Library. Frederick B. Adams. Ed. by Charles Ryskamp. LC 64-21147. 54p. 1974. pap. 4.00 (ISBN 0-87598-032-5). Pierpont Morgan.

Introduction to the Play: In the Theater of the Mind. rev., 2nd ed. Robert W. Boynton & Maynard Mack. (Series in Literature). 1976. pap. text ed. 6.10x (ISBN 0-8104-5731-8); tchr's guide 1.75 (6048). Hayden.

Introduction to the Poem. rev. 2nd ed. Ed. by Robert W. Boynton & Maynard Mack. (Introduction to Ser.). (gr. 10-12). 1972. text ed. 8.50x o.p. (ISBN 0-8104-5517-X); pap. text ed. 7.45x (ISBN 0-8104-5516-1). Hayden.

Introduction to the Poetry of Robert Browning. William J. Alexander. 210p. 1980. Repr. of 1889 ed. lib. bdg. 22.50 (ISBN 0-89987-006-6). Darby Bks.

Introduction to the Poetry of Yvor Winters. Elizabeth Isaacs. LC 80-17013. 240p. 1981. 15.00x (ISBN 0-8040-0353-X). Swallow.

Introduction to the Primates: Living & Fossil. S. Rosen. 1974. pap. 9.95 (ISBN 0-13-493478-4). P-H.

Introduction to the Principles & Practice of Homoeopathy. C. E. Whiiler & J. D. Kenyon. 371p. 1957. 17.95x (ISBN 0-8464-1027-3). Beekman Pubs.

Introduction to the Principles & Practice of Soil Science. R. E. White. LC 79-14361. 198p. 1979. pap. 22.95x (ISBN 0-470-26717-8). Halsted Pr.

Introduction to the Principles of Communication Theory. John C. Hancock. (Electrical & Electronic Engineering Ser.). 1961. text ed. 19.95 o.p. (ISBN 0-07-025980-1, C). McGraw.

Introduction to the Principles of Disease. John B. Walter. LC 76-27063. (Illus.). 1977. text ed. 18.95 (ISBN 0-7216-9114-5). Saunders.

Introduction to the Principles of Mechanics. Walter Hauser. 1965. 20.95 (ISBN 0-201-02806-9). A-W.

Introduction to the Principles of Morals & Legislation. Jeremy Bentham. Ed. by J. H. Burns & H. L. Hart. (Collected Works of Jeremy Bentham Ser.). 1970. text ed. 47.00x (ISBN 0-485-13211-7, Athlone Pr). Humanities.

Introduction to the Principles of Psychology. 2nd ed. B. R. Bugelski. LC 73-323. 640p. 1973. pap. text ed. 4.95 (ISBN 0-672-61266-6); wkbk 4.65 (ISBN 0-672-61344-1). Bobbs.

Introduction to the Principles of Surface Chemistry. R. Aveyard & D. A. Haydon. LC 72-89802. (Illus.). 200p. 1973. 42.50 (ISBN 0-521-20110-1); pap. 15.95x (ISBN 0-521-09794-0). Cambridge U Pr.

Introduction to the Principles of Transformational Syntax. Adrian Akmajian & Frank Heny. 448p. 1980. text ed. 20.00x (ISBN 0-262-01043-7); pap. text ed. 10.00x (ISBN 0-262-51022-7). MIT Pr.

Introduction to the Principles of Transformational Syntax. Adrian Akmajian & Frank W. Heny. LC 74-3054. 544p. 1975. 18.00x (ISBN 0-262-01043-7); pap. 10.00x (ISBN 0-262-51022-7). MIT Pr.

Introduction to the Pronunciation of English. 3rd ed. A. C. Gimson. 352p. 1980. 19.00x (Pub. by Arnold Pubs England). State Mutual Bk.

Introduction to the Properties of Crystal Surfaces. Jack Blakely. 1973. text ed. 22.00 (ISBN 0-08-017641-0). Pergamon.

Introduction to the Psychoanalysis of Mallarme. Charles Mauron. Tr. by Will McLendon & Archibald Henderson, Jr. (Perspectives in Criticism: No. 10). 1963. 18.50x (ISBN 0-520-00833-2). U of Cal Pr.

Introduction to the Psychology of Adolescence. Barbara W. Newman & Philip R. Newman. 1979. 17.95x (ISBN 0-256-02188-0). Dorsey.

Introduction to the Psychology of Religion. 3rd ed. R. H. Thouless. LC 76-184142. 160p. 1972. pap. 29.50 (ISBN 0-521-08149-1); pap. 7.95x (ISBN 0-521-09665-0). Cambridge U Pr.

Introduction to the Psychotherapies. Ed. by Sidney Bloch. 1979. pap. text ed. 11.95x (ISBN 0-19-261217-4). Oxford U Pr.

Introduction to the Reading of Hegel: Lectures on the "Phenomenology of Spirit". Alexandre Kojeve. Ed. by Allan Bloom. LC 70-78467. (Cornell Paperbacks Ser.). 304p. 1980. pap. 7.95 (ISBN 0-8014-9203-3). Cornell U Pr.

Introduction to the Realestate Profession: Guide to Real Estatelicense Examination. J. Ellis. 1981. pap. 8.24 (ISBN 0-13-494005-9). P-H.

Introduction to the Reprint of Pursh's Flora Americae Septentrionalis. J. Ewan. 118p. 1980. pap. text ed. 18.00 (ISBN 3-7682-1272-6). Lubrecht & Cramer.

Introduction to the Science of Comparative Mythology & Folklore. George W. Cox. LC 68-20124. 1968. Repr. of 1883 ed. 18.00 (ISBN 0-8103-3425-9). Gale.

Introduction to the Short Story. rev. 2nd ed. Robert W. Boynton & Maynard Mack. (Introduction to Ser.). 304p. (gr. 10-12). 1972. text ed. 10.20x (ISBN 0-8104-5051-8); pap. text ed. 6.70x (ISBN 0-8104-5050-X). Hayden.

Introduction to the Skill of Musick. John Playford & Henry Purcell. LC 67-27551. (Music Reprint Ser.). 282p. 1972. Repr. of 1694 ed. lib. bdg. 29.50 (ISBN 0-306-70937-6). Da Capo.

Introduction to the Social Sciences. John J. Bonstingl. (gr. 7-12). 1980. text ed. 16.96 (ISBN 0-205-05886-8, 8058865); tchrs'. guide 12.00 (ISBN 0-205-05887-6). Allyn.

Introduction to the Sociologies of Everyday Life. Douglas et al. 1980. text ed. 12.95 (ISBN 0-205-06813-8, 816813X). Allyn.

Introduction to the Sociology of Education. Karl Mannheim & W. A. Stewart. (International Library of Sociology & Social Reconstruction). 1970. text ed. 10.50x (ISBN 0-7100-3416-4); pap. text ed. 3.75x (ISBN 0-7100-6897-2). Humanities.

Introduction to the Sociology of Language. Fernando Penalosa. 320p. (Orig.). 1981. pap. text ed. 13.95 (ISBN 0-88377-183-7). Newbury Hse.

Introduction to the Sociology of Learning. Sarane S. Boocock. LC 72-7924. (Illus.). 1972. text ed. 17.50 o.p. (ISBN 0-395-12565-0, 3-04930). HM.

Introduction to the Soil Ecosystem. B. N. Richards. LC 73-85688. (Illus.). 160p. (Orig.). 1974. pap. text ed. 16.95x (ISBN 0-582-44130-7). Longman.

Introduction to the Solar Wind. John C. Brandt. LC 75-89919. (Illus.). 1970. text ed. 20.95x (ISBN 0-7167-0328-9). W H Freeman.

Introduction to the Statistical Analysis of Data. T. W. Anderson & Stanley L. Sclove. LC 77-78890. (Illus.). 1978. text ed. 18.50 (ISBN 0-395-15045-0); sol. manual 0.75 (ISBN 0-395-15046-9). HM.

Introduction to the Statistical Theory of Classical Simple Dense Fluids. G. H. Cole. 1967. 45.00 (ISBN 0-08-010397-9). Pergamon.

Introduction to the Study of Beetles. 2nd ed. 1979. write for info. o.p. (ISBN 0-916846-03-2). World Natural Hist.

Introduction to the Study of Disease. 8th ed. William Boyd & Huntington Sheldon. LC 80-23487. (Illus.). 660p. 1980. 19.75 (ISBN 0-8121-0729-2). Lea & Febiger.

Introduction to the Study of Fabrics of Geological Bodies. B. Sander. 1970. 94.00 (ISBN 0-08-006660-7). Pergamon.

Introduction to the Study of Political Economy. Luigi Cossa. Tr. by Louise Dyer from It. LC 79-1576. 1981. Repr. of 1893 ed. 37.50 (ISBN 0-88355-882-3). Hyperion Conn.

Introduction to the Study of Programming Languages. D. W. Barron. LC 76-11070. (Cambridge Computer Science Texts Ser.: No. 7). (Illus.). 1977. 22.50 (ISBN 0-521-21317-7); pap. 8.95x (ISBN 0-521-29101-1). Cambridge U Pr.

Introduction to the Talmud & Midrash. Hermann L. Strack. LC 59-7191. (Temple Books). 1969. pap. text ed. 5.95x (ISBN 0-689-70189-6, T10). Atheneum.

Introduction to the Talmud Study. Ed. by B. Haskelevich. 400p. (Rus.). 1981. pap. 6.00 (ISBN 0-938666-01-0). CHAMH.

Introduction to the Teaching of Dance. Elizabeth R. Hayes. LC 80-15371. 350p. 1980. Repr. of 1964 ed. lib. bdg. 14.50 (ISBN 0-89874-227-7). Krieger.

Introduction to the Teaching of Home Economics. Samson O. Olaitan & Obiora N. Agusiobo. 320p. 1981. write for info. (ISBN 0-471-27807-6, Pub. by Wiley-Interscience); pap. write for info. (ISBN 0-471-27806-8). Wiley.

Introduction to the Teaching of Writing. Stephen N. Judy & Susan J. Judy. 225p. 1981. pap. text ed. 10.95 (ISBN 0-471-06222-7). Wiley.

Introduction to the Technology of Pottery. P. Rado. LC 79-90454. 1969. 22.00 (ISBN 0-08-006458-2); pap. 9.25 (ISBN 0-08-006457-4). Pergamon.

Introduction to the Theatre. 4th ed. Frank M Whiting. 1978. text ed. 18.50 scp (ISBN 0-06-047089-5, HarpC). Har-Row.

Introduction to the Theories of Personality. B. R. Hergenhahn. (Illus.). 1980. 18.95 (ISBN 0-13-498766-7). P-H.

Introduction to the Theory & Application of Differential Equations with Deviating Arguments. L. E. Elsgolts & S. B. Norkin. 1973. 31.50 (ISBN 0-12-237750-8). Acad Pr.

Introduction to the Theory & Context of Accounting. 2nd ed. R. Sidebotham. 1970. pap. 7.15 o.p. (ISBN 0-08-015620-7). Pergamon.

Introduction to the Theory of Algebraic Functions of One Variable. Claude C. Chevalley. LC 51-4714. (Mathematical Surveys Ser.: No. 6). 1979. Repr. of 1971 ed. 18.40 (ISBN 0-8218-1506-7, SURV-6). Am Math.

Introduction to the Theory of Atomic Spectra. I. I. Sobel'man. 632p. 1972. text ed. 81.00 (ISBN 0-08-016166-9). Pergamon.

Introduction to the Theory of Computation. Erwin Engeler. (Computer Science & Applied Mathematics Ser). 1973. text ed. 21.95 (ISBN 0-12-239250-7). Acad Pr.

Introduction to the Theory of Diffraction. C. J. Ball. 1971. text ed. 25.00 (ISBN 0-08-015787-4); pap. text ed. 12.75 (ISBN 0-08-015786-6). Pergamon.

Introduction to the Theory of Distributions. Jose Barros-Neto. LC 80-11323. 234p. 1980. Repr. of 1973 ed. lib. bdg. write for info. (ISBN 0-89874-128-9). Krieger.

Introduction to the Theory of Finance: Asset Holder Behaviour Under Uncertainty. Basil J. Moore. LC 68-12033. (Orig.). 1968. pap. text ed. 7.95 (ISBN 0-02-921950-7). Free Pr.

Introduction to the Theory of Fourier Integrals. 2nd ed. Edward C. Titchmarsh. 1948. 48.00x (ISBN 0-19-853320-9). Oxford U Pr.

Introduction to the Theory of Functions of a Complex Variable. E. T. Copson. (Illus.). 1935. pap. 19.95x (ISBN 0-19-853145-1). Oxford U Pr.

Introduction to the Theory of Heavy-Ion Collisions. W. Norenberg & H. A. Weidenmuller. (Lecture Notes in Physics: Vol. 51). (Illus.). 1976. soft cover 13.10 o.p. (ISBN 0-387-07801-0). Springer-Verlag.

Introduction to the Theory of Liquid Metals. T. E. Faber. LC 76-184903. (Cambridge Monographs in Physics). (Illus.). 600p. 1972. 71.50 (ISBN 0-521-08477-6). Cambridge U Pr.

Introduction to the Theory of Macro-Economic Policy. 3rd ed. G. K. Shaw. 208p. 1977. bds. 30.50x (ISBN 0-85520-183-5, Pub. by Martin Robertson England); pap. 12.50x (ISBN 0-85520-182-7). Biblio Dist.

Introduction to the Theory of Magnetism. D. Wagner. 290p. 1972. text ed. 28.00 (ISBN 0-08-016595-8). Pergamon.

Introduction to the Theory of Mechanics. 8th ed. K. E. Bullen. 1971. 35.50 (ISBN 0-521-08291-9). Cambridge U Pr.

Introduction to the Theory of Molecular Vibrations & Vibrational Spectroscopy. L. A. Woodward. (Illus.). 370p. 1972. 37.50x (ISBN 0-19-855352-8). Oxford U Pr.

Introduction to the Theory of Music. Howard Boatwright. (Illus.). 1956. 16.95x (ISBN 0-393-02057-6, NortonC). Norton.

Introduction to the Theory of Numbers. Ralph Archibald. LC 76-118978. 1970. text ed. 17.95 (ISBN 0-675-09351-1). Merrill.

Introduction to the Theory of Numbers. 4th ed. Ivan Niven & Herbert S. Zuckerman. LC 79-24869. 355p. 1980. text ed. 19.95 (ISBN 0-471-02851-7); solutions manual avail. (ISBN 0-471-06394-0). Wiley.

Introduction to the Theory of Plasma Turbulence. V. N. Tsytovich. 142p. 1972. text ed. 30.00 (ISBN 0-08-016587-7). Pergamon.

Introduction to the Theory of Relativity. Francis W. Sears & Robert W. Brehme. 1968. 16.95 (ISBN 0-201-06890-7). A-W.

Introduction to the Theory of Seismology. K. E. Bullen. LC 79-7707. (Illus.). 1979. 44.50 (ISBN 0-521-04367-0); pap. 15.95x (ISBN 0-521-29686-2). Cambridge U Pr.

Introduction to the Theory of Shells. Clive L. Dym. LC 73-13563. 172p. 1974. text ed. 27.00 o.p. (ISBN 0-08-017784-0); pap. text ed. 17.50 o.p. (ISBN 0-08-017785-9). Pergamon.

Introduction to the Theory of Similarity. A. A. Gukhman. 1965. 33.50 o.p. (ISBN 0-12-305450-8). Acad Pr.

Introduction to the Theory of Solid Surfaces. F. Garcia-Moliner & F. Flores. LC 78-17617. (Cambridge Monographs on Physics). (Illus.). 1979. 71.50 (ISBN 0-521-22294-X). Cambridge U Pr.

Introduction to the Theory of Space-Charge Optics. G. A. Nagy & M. Szilagyi. LC 76-39107. 1974. 31.95 o.p. (ISBN 0-471-62867-0). Halsted Pr.

Introduction to the Theory of Special Divisors on Algebraic Curves. Phillip A. Griffiths. LC 80-16415. (Conference Board of Mathematical Sciences Ser.). 1980. 5.60 (ISBN 0-8218-1694-2). Am Math.

Introduction to the Theory of Thermal Neutron Scattering. G. L. Squires. LC 77-85682. (Illus.). 1978. 57.50 (ISBN 0-521-21884-5). Cambridge U Pr.

Introduction to the Tiberian Masorah. Israel Yeivin. LC 79-24755. (Society of Biblical Literature Masoretic Studies: No. 5). pap. 10.50x (ISBN 0-89130-374-X, 06 05 05). Scholars Pr Ca.

Introduction to the Uralic Languages. Bjorn Collinder. 1965. 20.00x (ISBN 0-520-00256-3). U of Cal Pr.

Introduction to the Use of the Public Records. Vivian H. Galbraith. 1934. 12.95x (ISBN 0-19-821221-6). Oxford U Pr.

Introduction to the Uses of Computers. M. Laver. LC 75-23535. (Cambridge Computer Science Texts Ser.). (Illus.). 187p. 1976. 11.95x (ISBN 0-521-29035-X). Cambridge U Pr.

Introduction to the World Around You: Student Tutor, Alternate Edition. Dennis J. Weidenaar & Emanuel T. Weiler. (Economics Ser.). pap. text ed. 7.95 (ISBN 0-201-08518-6). A-W.

Introduction to the Yoga Philosophy. Srisa Vasu. 1976. Repr. 6.50x o.p. (ISBN 0-685-71772-0). South Asia Bks.

Introduction to Theatre: A Mirror to Nature. O. I. Holtan. (Theatre & Drama Ser.). (Illus.). 240p. 1976. ref. ed. 14.95 (ISBN 0-13-498741-1). P-H.

Introduction to Theology. Marianne H. Micks. 1967. pap. 3.95 (ISBN 0-8164-2036-X, SP40). Crossroad NY.

Introduction to Theoretical Linguistics. John Lyons. (Illus., Orig.). 1968. 49.50 (ISBN 0-521-05617-9); pap. text ed. 13.95x (ISBN 0-521-09510-7). Cambridge U Pr.

Introduction to Theories of Learning. B. R. Hergenhahn. (Illus.). 352p. 1976. 18.95 (ISBN 0-13-498733-0). P-H.

Introduction to Theories of Personality. Robert B. Ewen. 1980. 17.95 (ISBN 0-12-245150-3). Acad Pr.

Introduction to Thermodynamics. 2nd ed. Kurt A. Rolle. 1980. text ed. 22.95 (ISBN 0-675-08268-4); instructor's manual 3.95 (ISBN 0-686-63342-3). Merrill.

Introduction to Thermodynamics. Kurt C. Rolle. LC 72-95278. 1973. text ed. 18.95x o.p. (ISBN 0-675-08994-8); instructor's manual 3.95 o.p. (ISBN 0-686-66872-3). Merrill.

Introduction to Thermodynamics. Robert S. Silver & James Watt. LC 79-138380. (Illus.). 1971. 21.50 (ISBN 0-521-08064-9). Cambridge U Pr.

Introduction to Thermodynamics. D. C. Spanner. (Experimental Botany Ser.: Vol. 1). 1965. 23.50 o.p. (ISBN 0-12-656050-1). Acad Pr.

Introduction to Thermodynamics & Heat Transfer. David A. Mooney. 1955. text ed. 26.95 (ISBN 0-13-499681-X). P-H.

Introduction to Thermonuclear Engineering. Paulinus S. Shieh & Inam-Ur-Rahman. LC 80-13153. Date not set. text ed. cancelled o.p. (ISBN 0-88275-973-6). Krieger.

Introduction to TI BASIC. Don Inman et al. 300p. (gr. 10-12). 1980. pap. 10.95 (ISBN 0-8104-5185-9). Hayden.

Introduction to Tonal Theory. Peter Westergaard. 448p. 1976. pap. text ed. 16.00x (ISBN 0-393-09342-5). Norton.

Introduction to Tool Marks, Firearms & the Striagraph. John E. Davis. 302p. 1958. pap. 24.50 photocopy ed. spiral (ISBN 0-398-00402-1). C C Thomas.

Introduction to Topological Groups. P. J. Higgins. LC 74-82222. (London Mathematical Society Lecture Note Ser.: No. 15). 100p. 1974. 12.95 (ISBN 0-521-20527-1). Cambridge U Pr.

Introduction to Topological Groups. Taqdir Husain. 230p. 1981. Repr. of 1966 ed. lib. bdg. write for info. (ISBN 0-89874-193-9). Krieger.

Introduction to Topology. 3rd ed. Bert Mendelson. 1975. text ed. 15.95x o.s.i. (ISBN 0-205-04495-6, 564495X). Allyn.

Introduction to Traditional Art of Western Africa: Representative Examples from Various Regions. E. V. Asihene. (Illus.). 96p. 1972. 14.50x o.p. (ISBN 0-8448-0077-5). Crane-Russak Co.

Introduction to Transfusion Therapy: A Programmed Text. Duke O. Kasprisin & Christina A. Kasprisin. LC 80-17972. 1980. pap. 10.50 (ISBN 0-87488-822-0). Med Exam.

Introduction to Transportation. Donald J. Bowersox et al. 1981. 14.95 (ISBN 0-02-313030-X). Macmillan.

Introduction to Transportation Engineering. 2nd ed. William W. Hay. LC 77-9293. 1977. text ed. 29.95 (ISBN 0-471-36433-9); tchr's manual avail. (ISBN 0-471-04712-0). Wiley.

Introduction to Transportation Engineering: Highways & Transit. Everett Carter & Wolfgang S. Homburger. (Illus.). 1978. ref. ed. 21.95 (ISBN 0-87909-388-9). Reston.

Introduction to Tribology. J. Halling. (Wykeham Technology Ser.: Vol. 5). 1975. pap. 9.50 o.p. (ISBN 0-387-91128-6). Springer-Verlag.

Introduction to Tribology. J. Halling & W. E. Smith. LC 75-19385. (Wykeham Technology Ser.: No. 5). 1975. 6.50x (ISBN 0-8448-1126-2). Crane-Russak Co.

Introduction to Tropical Grassland Husbandry. 2nd ed. Robert J. McIlroy. 1972. pap. 13.95x (ISBN 0-19-859427-5). Oxford U Pr.

Introduction to TRS-Eighty Graphics. Don Inman. LC 78-24835. 175p. 1979. pap. 9.95 (ISBN 0-918398-18-5). Dilithium Pr.

Introduction to Turbulence & Its Measurements. P. Bradshaw. Ed. by W. A. Woods. 218p. 1975. text ed. 25.00 (ISBN 0-08-016620-2); pap. text ed. 13.25 (ISBN 0-08-016621-0). Pergamon.

Introduction to Twentieth Century Music. 4th ed. Peter S. Hansen. 1978. pap. text ed. 16.95 (ISBN 0-205-05921-X). Allyn.

Introduction to Type. 3rd ed. Isabel B. Myers. 18p. 1980. Repr. of 1970 ed. pap. 0.75 (ISBN 0-935652-06-X). Ctr Applications Psych.

Introduction to Ukrainian History, Vol. 1. Nicholas L. Chirovsky. LC 79-84848. 1981. 19.95 (ISBN 0-8022-2248-X). Philos Lib.

Introduction to U. S. Public Documents. 2nd ed. Joe Morehead. LC 78-16866. (Library Science Text). (Illus.). 1978. lib. bdg. 22.50x (ISBN 0-87287-186-X); pap. text ed. 13.50x (ISBN 0-87287-190-8). Libs Unl.

Introduction to University Physics, 2 vols. Joseph Morgan. LC 77-12757. 1978. Repr. of 1969 ed. Set. 30.00 (ISBN 0-88275-617-6); Vol. 1 560p. lib. bdg. 17.50 (ISBN 0-88275-617-6); Vol. 2 512p. lib. bdg. 17.00 (ISBN 0-88275-874-8). Krieger.

Introduction to Urban Economics. Douglas M. Brown. 301p. 1974. tchrs' ed. 17.95 (ISBN 0-12-136650-2). Acad Pr.

Introduction to V-STOL Airplanes. David L. Kohlman. (Illus.). 1981. write for info. (ISBN 0-8138-0660-7). Iowa St U Pr.

Introduction to Variational Methods in Control Engineering. A. R. Noton. 1965. text ed. 11.75 o.p. (ISBN 0-08-011365-6); pap. text ed. 7.50 o.p. (ISBN 0-08-013584-6). Pergamon.

Introduction to Vector Analysis. 4th ed. Harry F. Davis & Arthur D. Snider. LC 78-27618. 1979. text ed. 21.55 (ISBN 0-205-06598-8). Allyn.

Introduction to Vector Analysis for Radio & Electronic Engineers. William D. Day. 14.00x (ISBN 0-685-20598-3). Transatlantic.

Introduction to Vector & Tensor Analysis. Robert C. Wrede. 418p. 1972. pap. text ed. 6.00 (ISBN 0-486-61879-X). Dover.

Introduction to Vergil's Bucolics. E. Coleiro. 1979. pap. text ed. 46.00x (ISBN 90-6032-117-0). Humanities.

Introduction to Virgil's Aeneid. W. A. Camps. 174p. (Orig.). 1969. pap. 9.95x (ISBN 0-19-872024-6). Oxford U Pr.

Introduction to Viruses. S. B. Biswas & Anita Biswas. 1976. 12.50 (ISBN 0-7069-0411-7, Pub. by Vikas India). Advent Bk.

Introduction to Viscous Flow. William F. Hughes. LC 78-14471. (Illus.). 1979. text ed. 24.95 (ISBN 0-07-031130-7, C). McGraw.

Introduction to VLSI Systems. Carver Mead & Lynn Conway. LC 78-74688. 1979. text ed. 29.95 (ISBN 0-201-04358-0). A-W.

Introduction to Vocational Rehabilitation. James A. Bitter. LC 78-24530. (Illus.). 1979. text ed. 16.95 (ISBN 0-8016-0693-4). Mosby.

Introduction to Voice Pathology: Functional & Organic. P. H. Damste & J. W. Lerman. (Illus.). 120p. 1975. pap. 14.75 photocopy ed. spiral (ISBN 0-398-03289-0). C C Thomas.

Introduction to Waldorf Education: Curriculum & Methods. Ed. by Earl J. Ogletree. LC 78-65425. 1978. pap. text ed. 16.25 (ISBN 0-8191-0665-8). U Pr of Amer.

Introduction to Wallace Stevens. Henry W. Wells. LC 75-45395. 218p. 1976. Repr. of 1964 ed. lib. bdg. 18.75x (ISBN 0-8371-8736-2, WEWS). Greenwood.

Introduction to Wargaming. John Sandars. 11.95 (ISBN 0-7207-0861-3, Pub. by Michael Joseph). Merrimack Bk Serv.

Introduction to Welding. I. G. Edmonds & Ronald F. Gonzales. 1975. pap. text ed. 14.95 scp (ISBN 0-06-453303-4, HarpC); tchr's ed. avail. (ISBN 0-685-66883-5). Har-Row.

Introduction to Welding & Brazing. D. R. Milner & R. L. Apps. 1968. text ed. 19.50 (ISBN 0-08-012306-6); pap. text ed. 8.50 (ISBN 0-08-013342-8). Pergamon.

Introduction to Western Music. F. E. Kirby. LC 69-15248. 1970. text ed. 12.95 (ISBN 0-02-917360-4). Free Pr.

Introduction to Western Philosophy: Ideas & Argument from Plato to Sartre. Antony Flew. LC 74-142179. 1971. 13.50 (ISBN 0-672-51523-7); pap. 11.95 (ISBN 0-672-61221-6). Bobbs.

Introduction to Western Philosophy: Pre-Socratics to Mill. student economy ed. George L. Abernathy & Thomas A. Langford. 1976. pap. text ed. 11.95x (ISBN 0-8221-0179-3). Dickenson.

Introduction to Wholesale Distribution. William P. Dannenberg et al. (Illus.). 1978. 18.50 (ISBN 0-13-500777-1); stud. ed. 16.95 (ISBN 0-685-85447-7). P-H.

Introduction to Wittgenstein's Tractatus. G. E. Anscombe. 1971. pap. 5.95x (ISBN 0-8122-1019-0, Pa Paperbks). U of Pa Pr.

Introduction to Wittgenstein's Tractatus. 3rd ed. G. E. Anscombe. 1967. pap. text ed. 4.00 (ISBN 0-09-051131-X, Hutchinson U Lib). Humanities.

Introduction to Wolfram's Parzival. Hugh Sacker. 1963. 42.50 (ISBN 0-521-06180-6). Cambridge U Pr.

Introduction to Women's Gymnastics. Blanche J. Drury & Andrea B. Schmid. 1976. pap. 3.50 (ISBN 0-8015-4084-4, Hawthorn). Dutton.

Introduction to Woodland Ecology. John Cousens. (Ecology Ser). (Illus.). 155p. (gr. 1-6). 1974. pap. text ed. 6.00x (ISBN 0-05-002775-1). Longman.

Introduction to Working with Metal. LC 77-88953. (Drake Home Craftsman Ser.). (Illus.). 1978. pap. 5.95 (ISBN 0-8069-8452-X, 019720). Sterling.

Introduction to World Politics: A Conceptual & Developmental Perspective. Donald M. Snow. LC 80-5851. 230p. 1981. lib. bdg. 18.25 (ISBN 0-8191-1398-0); pap. text ed. 9.75 (ISBN 0-8191-1399-9). U Pr of Amer.

Introduction to X-Ray Crystallography. M. M. Woolfson. LC 69-16289. (Illus.). 1970. 57.50 (ISBN 0-521-07440-1); pap. 17.50x (ISBN 0-521-29343-X). Cambridge U Pr.

Introduction to Yachting. L. Francis Herreshoff. LC 61-18278. (Illus.). 1980. Repr. of 1963 ed. 30.00 (ISBN 0-911378-14-6). Sheridan.

Introduction to Yoga. Annie Besant. 1972. 3.25 (ISBN 0-8356-7120-8). Theos Pub Hse.

Introduction to Zen Buddhism. Daisetz T. Suzuki. 1964. pap. 2.95 (ISBN 0-394-17474-7, B341, BC). Grove.

Introductions East & West. Thomas Merton. (Illus.). 175p. 1981. 19.95 (ISBN 0-87775-139-0); pap. 9.95 (ISBN 0-87775-140-4). Unicorn Pr.

Introductions, Notes & Commentaries to Texts in the Dramatic Works of Thomas Dekker, 2 vols. Cyrus Hoy. Ed. by Fredson Bowers. LC 77-80838. 1980. 57.50 ea. Vol. 1 (ISBN 0-521-21786-5). Vol. 2 (ISBN 0-521-21894-2). Set. 97.50 (ISBN 0-521-23647-9). Cambridge U Pr.

Introductory Accounting: An Audio-Tutorial Approach. Charles F. Grant. (Business Ser.). 1977. pap. text ed. 15.95 (ISBN 0-675-08502-0); audio cassettes 140.00 (ISBN 0-675-08501-2); 2-5 sets 90.00, 6 or more sets 60.00 (ISBN 0-685-74284-9); instructor's manual 3.95 (ISBN 0-686-67615-7). Merrill.

Introductory Accounting: Part One, Syllabus. Marvin W. Hempel. 1972. pap. text ed. 9.95 (ISBN 0-89420-024-0, 351004); cassette recordings 201.10 (ISBN 0-89420-154-9, 351100). Natl Book.

Introductory Accounting: Part Two Syllabus. Marvin W. Hempel. (gr. 8-12). 1973. pap. text ed. 10.75 (ISBN 0-89420-027-5, 351006); cassette recordings 248.15 (ISBN 0-89420-155-7, 351125). Natl Book.

Introductory Algebra. Dennis Bila et al. LC 74-84641. (Illus.). xviii, 610p. (Prog. Bk.). 1975. text ed. 13.95x (ISBN 0-87901-037-1). Worth.

Introductory Algebra. 3rd ed. Milton D. Eulenburg et al. LC 74-24338. 384p. 1975. text ed. 18.50 (ISBN 0-471-24686-7). Wiley.

Introductory Algebra. 3rd ed. Mervin L. Keedy & Marvin L. Bittinger. LC 78-55821. (Illus.). 1979. pap. text ed. 14.95 (ISBN 0-201-03874-9); instr's man. 3.50 (ISBN 0-201-03875-7); answer book 3.50 (ISBN 0-201-03876-5); student sol. manual 3.50 (ISBN 0-201-03877-3). A-W.

Introductory Algebra. Arnold R. Steffensen & L. Murphy Johnson. 1980. pap. text ed. 14.95x (ISBN 0-673-15368-1). Scott F.

Introductory Algebra. 3rd ed. June Wood. (Mathematics Ser.). 1977. text ed. 17.95 (ISBN 0-675-08511-X); instr's manual 3.95 (ISBN 0-686-67527-4). Merrill.

Introductory Algebra. Wright & New. 298p. 1981. text ed. 16.95 (ISBN 0-205-07310-7, 5673100); free tchr's ed. (ISBN 0-205-07311-5); free student's guide (ISBN 0-205-07312-3). Allyn.

Introductory Algebra & Related Topics for Technicians. K. King. 1979. pap. 11.95 (ISBN 0-13-501585-5). P-H.

Introductory Algebra for College Students. Isidore Dressler & Robert Dressler. (Orig.). 1976. pap. text ed. 10.00 (ISBN 0-87720-975-8). AMSCO Sch.

Introductory ALGOL Sixty-Eight Programming. D. F. Brailsford & A. N. Walker. LC 79-40241. 1979. 34.95x (ISBN 0-470-26746-1); pap. text ed. 17.95x (ISBN 0-470-26799-2). Halsted Pr.

Introductory Analytical Chemistry. Alexander I. Popov & R. T. Pflaum. 1966. text ed. 12.95x o.p. (ISBN 0-669-25239-5). Heath.

Introductory & Publications Photography. 3rd ed. C. William Horrell & Robert A. Steffes. 1976. 5.50x (ISBN 0-9603876-0-9). Kenilworth.

Introductory Animal Science. George Brant. 1980. perfect binding 7.95 (ISBN 0-88252-112-8). Paladin Hse.

Introductory Anthropology. Joseph B. Aceves & H. Gill King. 1979. text ed. 15.95x (ISBN 0-673-15303-7). Scott F.

Introductory Approach to Operations Research. Robert J. Thierauf. LC 77-23031. (Ser. on Management & Administration). 1978. text ed. 25.95 (ISBN 0-471-03125-9). Wiley.

Introductory Astronomy. E. G. Ebbighausen. LC 73-89492. 1974. pap. 14.95x (ISBN 0-675-08843-7). Merrill.

Introductory Atlas: Economics, Commerce & Administration, a Visual Analysis, Vol. 1. N. Skene Smith. 1966. 14.50 (ISBN 0-08-010966-7). Pergamon.

Introductory Biology. Kenneth C. Jones & Anthony J. Gaudin. LC 76-45648. 1977. text ed. 20.95x (ISBN 0-471-44875-3); instr's manual avail. (ISBN 0-471-02381-7); study guide avail. Wiley.

Introductory Biology Laboratory Manual. Carole D. Ross & Aileen Kennedy. 1979. pap. text ed. 6.95 o.p. (ISBN 0-8403-2086-8). Kendall-Hunt.

Introductory Biomechanics. 2nd ed. Jeanne M. Schenck & F. David Cordova. (Illus.). 173p. 1980. 13.95 (ISBN 0-8036-7733-2). Davis Co.

Introductory Biophysics. F. R. Hallett & P. A. Speight. LC 76-21809. 1977. pap. text ed. 16.95 (ISBN 0-470-15195-1). Halsted Pr.

Introductory Calculus: Second Edition with Analytic Geometry & Linear Algebra. A. Wayne Roberts. 1972. text ed. 20.95 (ISBN 0-12-589756-1); answer bk 3.00 (ISBN 0-12-589758-8). Acad Pr.

Introductory Calculus with Applications. 2nd ed. Jogindar Ratti & Manoug Manougian. LC 76-13096. (Illus.). 1977. pap. text ed. 17.50 (ISBN 0-395-24545-1); inst. manual 1.75 (ISBN 0-395-24544-3). HM.

Introductory Chemistry. John H. Bedenbaugh & J. Emory Howell. 1978. lib. bdg. 17.95 (ISBN 0-205-05943-0); instr's man. avail. (ISBN 0-205-05945-7); programmed supplement 5.95 (ISBN 0-205-05944-9). Allyn.

Introductory Chemistry: A New View. Peter Hamlet. 272p. 1975. pap. text ed. 7.95x o.p. (ISBN 0-669-83600-1); instr's manual free o.p. (ISBN 0-669-94532-3). Heath.

Introductory Chemistry: A Survey of General, Organic, & Biological Chemistry. Karl F. Kumli. (Illus.). 608p. 1974. text ed. 20.95 (ISBN 0-13-501668-1); study guide pap. 4.95 (ISBN 0-13-501684-3). P-H.

Introductory Chemistry: General, Organic, Biological. Spencer L. Seager & Michael R. Slabaugh. 1979. text ed. 19.95x (ISBN 0-673-15026-7); study guide 6.95x (ISBN 0-673-15215-4). Scott F.

Introductory Chemistry: Models & Basic Concepts. John R. Amend. LC 76-41820. 1977. text ed. 16.95 o.p. (ISBN 0-471-02533-X); study guide 5.95 o.p. (ISBN 0-471-97715-2); experimental chemistry 7.95 o.p. (ISBN 0-471-02534-8). Wiley.

Introductory Clinical Pharmacology. Jeanne Scherer. LC 75-4606. 300p. 1975. pap. 11.95 o.p. (ISBN 0-397-54168-6). Lippincott.

Introductory Cobol. Dennie L. VanTassel. 1979. pap. text ed. 14.95 (ISBN 0-8162-9133-0). Holden-Day.

Introductory College Mathematics. 2nd ed. Adele Leonhardy. LC 63-12284. 1963. text ed. 22.95 (ISBN 0-471-52736-X). Wiley.

Introductory College Mathematics: With Linear Algebra & Finite Mathematics. H. Flanders & Justin J. Price. 1973. text ed. 19.95 (ISBN 0-12-259660-9). Acad Pr.

Introductory Discourse to the Canterbury Tales. Thomas Tyrwhitt. 52p. 1980. Repr. of 1778 ed. lib. bdg. 15.00 (ISBN 0-8495-5161-7). Arden Lib.

Introductory Dynamic Oceanography. G. L. Pickard & S. Pond. LC 77-4427. 1978. text ed. 45.00 (ISBN 0-08-021614-5); pap. text ed. 12.50 (ISBN 0-08-021615-3). Pergamon.

Introductory Econometrics. 2nd ed. Mark B. Stewart & Wallis F. Kenneth. 352p. 1981. 24.95 (ISBN 0-470-27132-9). Halsted Pr.

Introductory Economic Statistics. David G. Mayes & Anne C. Mayes. LC 73-14378. 248p. 1976. 28.50 (ISBN 0-471-58031-7); pap. 15.95 (ISBN 0-471-58111-9, Pub. by Wiley-Interscience). Wiley.

Introductory Economics. 4th ed. Sanford D. Gordon & George G. Dawson. 1980. text ed. 14.95x (ISBN 0-669-02425-2); instrs' manual avail. (ISBN 0-669-02427-9); study guide 5.95 (ISBN 0-669-02426-0); test file avail. (ISBN 0-669-02429-5). Heath.

Introductory Electric Circuit Analysis. D. Johnson & J. Johnson. 1981. 21.00 (ISBN 0-13-500835-2). P-H.

Introductory Electronics. Aldert Van Der Ziel. (Illus.). 416p. 1974. ref. ed. 25.95 (ISBN 0-13-501700-9). P-H.

Introductory Electronics for Scientists & Engineers. Robert Simpson. 600p. 1974. text ed. 25.95x (ISBN 0-205-03845-X, 7338457). Allyn.

Introductory Engineering Electromagnetics. Branko D. Popovic. (Engineering Ser). 1971. text ed. 25.95 (ISBN 0-201-05871-5). A-W.

Introductory Experiments in Digital Electronics & 8080a Microcomputer Programming & Interfacing. Peter R. Rony et al. Incl. Vol. 1. pap. 14.95 (ISBN 0-672-21550-0); Vol. 2. pap. 13.50 (ISBN 0-672-21551-9). 1978. 2 vol. set 25.50 (ISBN 0-672-21552-7). Sams.

Introductory Finite Mathematics with Computing. William S. Dorn & Daniel D. McCracken. LC 75-30647. 449p. 1976. text ed. 19.95 (ISBN 0-471-21917-7); instructor's manual (ISBN 0-471-01539-3). Wiley.

Introductory Food Chemistry. Ira D. Garard. (Illus.). 1976. lib. bdg. 27.00 (ISBN 0-87055-206-6); pap. text ed. 17.00 (ISBN 0-87055-288-0). AVI.

Introductory Foods: A Laboratory Manual of Food Preparation & Evaluation. 3rd ed. Mary L. Morr & Theodore F. Irmiter. (Illus.). 1980. pap. text ed. 8.95 (ISBN 0-02-384120-6). Macmillan.

Introductory French Program, 2 Bks. Walter M. Hayes & Veronica A. Killeen. (Prog. Bk.). (gr. 9-12). 1970. Set. pap. 13.00 (ISBN 0-8294-0197-0); 15 tapes s.p. 85.00 (ISBN 0-685-04188-3). Loyola.

Introductory Functional Analysis with Applications. Debra Mandrigues. LC 77-2560. 1978. text ed. 30.95 (ISBN 0-471-50731-8); answer bklt. avail. (ISBN 0-471-02872-X). Wiley.

Introductory General Chemistry: Laboratory Manual. 2nd ed. Victor S. Krimsley et al. (Illus.). 114p. 1976. pap. text ed. 5.50 o.p. (ISBN 0-8016-2744-3). Mosby.

Introductory Guide to Central Labour Legislation. W. A. Dawson. 10.00x (ISBN 0-210-27188-4). Asia.

Introductory Guide to Research in Librarianship & Information Studies in the U. K. Ed. by P. L. Ward & J. Burkett. (Pamphlet Ser.: No. 37). 1975. pap. 7.95x (ISBN 0-85365-058-6, Pub. by Lib Assn England). Oryx Pr.

Introductory Hausa. Charles H. Kraft & Marguerite G. Kraft. LC 79-92676. 1974. 22.75x (ISBN 0-520-01988-1). U of Cal Pr.

Introductory Hearing Science: Physical & Psychological Concepts. Sanford E. Gerber. LC 73-89177. (Illus.). 305p. 1974. text ed. 17.00 (ISBN 0-7216-4104-0). Saunders.

Introductory Hebrew Grammar, with Progressive Exercises in Reading & Writing. 26th ed. A. B. Davidson. Ed. by John Mauchline. 336p. 1966. text ed. 14.50x (ISBN 0-567-01005-8). Attic Pr.

Introductory Hindi Readings. Ernest Bender & Theodore Riccardi, Jr. LC 75-133202. 1971. text ed. 12.00x (ISBN 0-8122-7626-4). U of Pa Pr.

Introductory Horticulture. H. Edward Reiley & Carroll L. Shry, Jr. LC 77-81006. 1979. pap. text ed. 22.00 (ISBN 0-8273-1893-6); instructor's guide 1.60 (ISBN 0-8273-1645-3). Delmar.

Introductory Laboratory Exercises for Medical Technologists. Shauna C. Anderson. LC 77-8819. (Illus.). 1978. pap. text ed. 8.50 (ISBN 0-8016-0173-8). Mosby.

Introductory Lectures on General Semantics. Francis P. Chisholm. 1971. Repr. of 1944 ed. 5.00x (ISBN 0-910780-05-6). Inst Gen Semantics.

Introductory Macroeconomics. Michael Veseth. 432p. 1980. 12.95 (ISBN 0-12-719550-5); instrs' manual 3.00 (ISBN 0-12-719555-6). Acad Pr.

Introductory Macroeconomics, 1980-81: Readings on Contemporary Issues. Ed. by Peter D. McClelland. LC 80-66907. (Illus.). 224p. (Orig.). 1980. pap. 8.95x (ISBN 0-8014-9873-2). Cornell U Pr.

Introductory Manual of Flying Training, Vol. 1. N. H. Birch & A. E. Bramson. (Flight Briefing for Pilots Ser.). (Illus.). 1978. 6.95 o.p. (ISBN 0-685-59601-X, Flying-Zd). Ziff-Davis Pub.

Introductory Mass Spectrometry. Stephen R. Shrader. 1971. pap. 10.95x o.p. (ISBN 0-205-02914-0, 6829147). Allyn.

Introductory Mathematical Analysis. 5th ed. Edgar D. Eaves & J. H. Carruth. 1978. text ed. 22.00 (ISBN 0-205-05991-0, 5659914); instr's man. avail. (ISBN 0-205-05992-9); student study guide avail. (ISBN 0-205-05993-7). Allyn.

Introductory Mathematical Statistics: Principles & Methods. Erwin Kreyszig. LC 70-107583. 1970. 26.95 (ISBN 0-471-50730-X). Wiley.

Introductory Mathematics for Economic Analysis. Thomas K. Kim. 1971. 14.95x o.p. (ISBN 0-673-05144-7). Scott F.

Introductory Mathematics for the Clinical Laboratory. Kanai L. Mukherjee. LC 78-10915. (Illus.). 1979. pap. text ed. 20.00 (ISBN 0-89189-069-6, 45-9-006-00). Am Soc Clinical.

Introductory Microbiology. P. Tauro et al. 432p. Date not set. text ed. 27.50 (ISBN 0-7069-1181-4, Pub. by Vikas India). Advent Bk.

Introductory Modern Algebra. Elwyn Davis. LC 73-87837. 1974. text ed. 16.95x (ISBN 0-675-08872-0). Merrill.

Introductory Multivariate Analysis (for Educational Psychological and Social Research) Ed. by Daniel J. Amick & Herbert Walberg. LC 74-30754. (Illus.). 275p. 1975. 17.90 (ISBN 0-8211-0013-0); text ed. 16.20 in ten or more copies (ISBN 0-685-52138-9). McCutchan.

Introductory Musical Acoustics. Michael Wagner. (Illus.). 1978. pap. text ed. 10.00 (ISBN 0-89892-025-6). Contemp Pub Co of Raleigh.

Introductory Mycology. 3rd ed. Constantine J. Alexopoulos & Charles W. Mims. LC 79-12514. 1979. text ed. 25.95 (ISBN 0-471-02214-4). Wiley.

Introductory Nutrition. 4th ed. Helen Guthrie. LC 78-16649. (Illus.). 1979. text ed. 19.95 (ISBN 0-8016-2001-5). Mosby.

Introductory Oceanography. 2nd ed. Harold V. Thurman. 1978. text ed. 19.95 (ISBN 0-675-08428-8); instructor's manual 3.95 (ISBN 0-686-67980-6). Merrill.

Introductory Oceanography. 3rd ed. Harold V. Thurman. (Illus.). 596p. 1981. text ed. 19.95 (ISBN 0-675-08058-4); tchr's. ed. 3.95 (ISBN 0-686-69493-7). Merrill.

Introductory Organic & Biochemistry: A New View. Peter Hamlet. 416p. 1975. text ed. 14.95x o.p. (ISBN 0-669-83618-4); instructors' manual free o.p. (ISBN 0-669-94532-3). Heath.

Introductory Philosophy. Ed. by Robert P. Wolff. 1979. text ed. 17.50 (ISBN 0-13-500876-X). P-H.

Introductory Physical Chemistry. Arthur R. Knight. 1969. text ed. 20.95 (ISBN 0-13-502203-7). P-H.

Introductory Physics. K. H. Channappa et al. 1977. 12.50 (ISBN 0-7069-0571-7, Pub. by Vikas India). Advent Bk.

Introductory Physics. Mashuri L. Warren. LC 78-22089. (Illus.). 1979. text ed. 21.95x (ISBN 0-7167-1008-0); tchr's manual avail. W H Freeman.

Introductory Physics: A Model Approach. Robert Karplus. 1969. 16.95 (ISBN 0-8053-5216-3). Benjamin-Cummings.

Introductory Physics: A Problem-Solving Approach. Jesse D. Wall. 1977. text ed. 15.95x (ISBN 0-669-00188-0). Heath.

Introductory Physics: Syllabus. Norman H. Crowhurst. 1974. pap. text ed. 9.35 (ISBN 0-89420-084-4, 230330); cassette recordings 164.70 (ISBN 0-89420-158-1, 230000). Natl Book.

Introductory Plant Physiology. Fritz Noggle. (Illus.). 592p. 1976. ref. ed. 23.95 (ISBN 0-13-502187-1). P-H.

Introductory Plant Science. 3rd ed. Henry T. Northen. (Illus.). 586p. 1968. 28.95 (ISBN 0-8260-6770-0); instr's manual avail. (ISBN 0-471-07522-1). Wiley.

Introductory Problems in Spectroscopy. R. C. Banks et al. 1980. pap. 12.95 (ISBN 0-8053-0572-6). A-W.

Introductory Psychology, 7 vols. 2nd ed. John S. Abma. Incl. Vol. 1-Introductory to Psychology (ISBN 0-86589-007-2); Vol. 2-Learning (ISBN 0-86589-008-0); Vol. 3-the Physiological Bases of Behavior (ISBN 0-86589-009-9); Vol. 4-Individual Differences & Group Processes (ISBN 0-86589-010-2); Vol. 5-Motivation & Stress (ISBN 0-86589-011-0); Vol. 6-Mental Health (ISBN 0-86589-012-9); Vol. 7-Measurements, Statistics & Analysis (ISBN 0-86589-013-7). 1973. Set. 16.75 (ISBN 0-86589-006-4). Individual Learn.

Introductory Psychology. Jonathan L. Freedman. LC 76-15461. 1978. text ed. 17.95 (ISBN 0-201-05788-3); instr's manual o.p. avail. (ISBN 0-201-05791-3); tests o.p. 4.00 (ISBN 0-685-85890-1). A-W.

Introductory Psychology. Morris K. Holland. 688p. 1981. text ed. 17.95 (ISBN 0-669-03347-2); instr's. guide with test avail. (ISBN 0-669-03346-4); student guide 5.95 (ISBN 0-669-03347-2). Heath.

Introductory Psychology. Marvin L. Schroth & Derald W. Sue. 1975. pap. text ed. 12.95x (ISBN 0-256-01710-7). Dorsey.

Introductory Readings in Aesthetics. John Hospers. LC 69-15921. 1969. pap. text ed. 8.95 (ISBN 0-02-915260-7). Free Pr.

Introductory Readings in Ethics. William K. Frankena & John T. Granrose. 496p. 1974. text ed. 18.95 (ISBN 0-13-502112-X). P-H.

Introductory Readings in Metaphysics. Richard Taylor. 1979. pap. text ed. 10.95 (ISBN 0-13-502302-5). P-H.

Introductory Readings in the Philosophy of Science. Ed. by E. D. Klemke et al. LC 80-65940. 373p. 1980. pap. text ed. 11.95 (ISBN 0-87975-134-7). Prometheus Bks.

Introductory Real Analysis. Marshall E. Munroe. 1965. 17.95 (ISBN 0-201-04905-8). A-W.

Introductory Report of the Normandy Reservoir Salvage Project: Environmental Setting, Typology & Survey. Charles H. Faulkner & Major C. McCollough. (Illus.). 1973. pap. 11.00x o.p. (ISBN 0-87049-174-1). U of Tenn Pr.

Introductory Russian Grammar. 2nd ed. Galina Stilman et al. LC 75-179421. (Illus.). 576p. (Rus.). 1972. text ed. 18.95x (ISBN 0-471-00738-2) (ISBN 0-471-00740-4). wkbk. 4.50x (ISBN 0-471-00906-7); o.p. (ISBN 0-685-99773-1); tapes avail. (ISBN 0-471-00741-2). Wiley.

Introductory Sociology: Lectures, Readings & Exercises. Gordon D. Morgan. LC 80-65606. 145p. 1981. perfect bdg. 10.50 (ISBN 0-86548-049-4). Century Twenty One.

Introductory Spanish. Donald D. Walsh. 1946. 5.95x (ISBN 0-393-09454-5, NortonC). Norton.

Introductory Statistical Analysis. 2nd ed. D. L. Harnett & J. L. Murphy. 1980. 19.95 (ISBN 0-201-02758-5); student's wkbk. 5.95 (ISBN 0-201-02859-X); instructor's manual 2.95 (ISBN 0-201-02759-3). A-W.

Introductory Statistics. John A. Ingram. LC 73-90820. 1974. text ed. 18.95 (ISBN 0-8465-2640-9). Benjamin-Cummings.

Introductory Statistics. 2nd ed. M. H. Quenouille. 1968. pap. text ed. 11.25 (ISBN 0-08-013783-0). Pergamon.

Introductory Statistics. James A. Twaite & Jane A. Monroe. 1979. text ed. 17.95x (ISBN 0-673-15097-6). Scott F.

Introductory Statistics. Neil Weiss & Matthew Hassett. LC 80-23520. (Statistics Ser.). (Illus.). 672p. 1981. text ed. 17.95 (ISBN 0-201-09507-6). A-W.

Introductory Statistics. 3rd ed. Thomas H. Wonnacott & Ronald J. Wonnacott. (Wiley Ser. in Probability & Mathematical Statistics). 1977. text ed. 24.95 (ISBN 0-471-95982-0). Wiley.

Introductory Statistics: A New Approach for Behavioral Science Students. Louis S. Berger. LC 79-2484. 350p. 1981. text ed. 24.95 (ISBN 0-8236-2775-6). Intl Univs Pr.

Introductory Statistics: A Service Course. A. H. Pollard. 1973. pap. 12.00 (ISBN 0-08-017352-7). Pergamon.

Introductory Statistics & Probability: A Basis for Decision-Making. David W. Blakeslee & William G. Chinn. (gr. 11-12). 1975. text ed. 16.28 (ISBN 0-395-19992-1); instrs' guide 5.44 (ISBN 0-395-19991-3). HM.

Introductory Statistics for Business Economics. Iver F. Bradley & John B. South. LC 80-65789. 640p. 1981. text ed. 18.95 (ISBN 0-03-053026-1). Dryden Pr.

Introductory Statistics for Business & Economics. 2nd ed. Thomas H. Wonnacott & Ronald J. Wonnacott. LC 76-55773. (Probability & Mathematical Statistics Ser.). 1977. text ed. 24.50 (ISBN 0-471-95980-4, Pub. by Wiley-Hamilton). Wiley.

Introductory Statistics for Psychology. 2nd ed. Chester A. Insko & Douglas A. Schoeninger. 1977. text ed. 19.95 (ISBN 0-205-05514-1); test manual free (ISBN 0-685-71781-X); student guide avail. (ISBN 0-205-05516-8). Allyn.

Introductory Statistics for Psychology. Thorne. LC 79-10613. 1980. text ed. 14.95 (ISBN 0-87872-222-X). Duxbury Pr.

Introductory Statistics for Psychology: The Logic & the Methods. Gustav Levine. LC 80-81254. 1981. write for info. (ISBN 0-12-445480-1). Acad Pr.

Introductory Statistics for the Behavioral Sciences. Joan Welkowitz et al. 316p. 1976. 15.95 (ISBN 0-12-743260-4); wkbk. 5.95 (ISBN 0-12-743267-1); ans. key 2.00 (ISBN 0-12-743268-X). Acad Pr.

Introductory Statistics with Applications. Wayne W. Daniel. LC 76-10897. (Illus.). 1977. text ed. 17.95 (ISBN 0-395-24430-7); inst. guide with solutions 3.00 (ISBN 0-395-24431-5); study guide 7.75 (ISBN 0-395-24843-4). HM.

Introductory Structural Analysis with Matrix Methods. Wang Chu-Kia. LC 72-667. 240p. 1973. ref. ed. 26.95 (ISBN 0-13-501650-9). P-H.

Introductory Structured Cobol Programming. Gary Popkin. (Orig.). 1980. pap. text ed. 16.95 (ISBN 0-442-23166-0); instr's. manual 4.95 (ISBN 0-442-26773-8). D Van Nostrand.

Introductory Structured COBOL Programming. Gary S. Popkin. 496p. 1981. text ed. 18.95 (ISBN 0-442-26771-1). Van Nos Reinhold.

Introductory Theology. Zoltan Alszeghy & Maurizio Flick. LC 79-88517. 1981. pap. text ed. cancelled (ISBN 0-87973-589-9). Our Sunday Visitor.

Introductory Transformational Grammar. Bruce L. Liles. LC 70-122388. (Illus.). 1971. pap. text ed. 8.95x (ISBN 0-13-502286-X). P-H.

Introductory Treatise on Lie's Theory. John R. Campbell. LC 65-28441. 14.95 (ISBN 0-8284-0183-7). Chelsea Pub.

Introductory View of Management. Peter F. Drucker. 1978. text ed. 19.50 scp (ISBN 0-06-166402-2, HarpC); scp casebk 9.50 (ISBN 0-06-166403-0); inst. manual avail. (ISBN 0-685-88069-9). Har-Row.

Introductory Zoology. David A. Nunnally & Burton J. Bogitsh. LC 72-7415. 441p. 1973. 18.00 (ISBN 0-471-65188-5, Pub. by Wiley). Krieger.

Introdution to Software Quality Control. Chin-Kuei Cho. LC 80-15241. (Business Data Processing Ser.). 445p. 1980. 29.95 (ISBN 0-471-04704-X, Pub. by Wiley-Interscience). Wiley.

Introspection-Panacea or Pitfall? Robert E. Birdsong. (Aquarian Academy Supplementary Lecture No. 1: No. 1). 1975. pap. 0.75 (ISBN 0-917108-16-7). Sirius Bks.

Intruder. Brooke Leimas. (Orig.). 1980. pap. 2.50 (ISBN 0-451-09524-3, E9524, Sig). NAL.

Intruder in the Dust. William Faulkner. 1948. 8.95 (ISBN 0-394-43074-3). Random.

Intruders. Pat Montandon. 1977. pap. 1.95 o.p. (ISBN 0-449-22963-7, Crest). Fawcett.

Intrusion Detection Systems. Robert L. Barnard. 300p. 1981. text ed. 21.95 (ISBN 0-409-95026-2). Butterworths.

Intrusions. Ursula Hegi. 288p. 1981. 12.95 (ISBN 0-670-40065-3). Viking Pr.

Intuition & Ego States: The Origins of Transactional Analysis. Eric Berne. LC 76-57549. 1977. 8.95 o.p. (ISBN 0-06-060784-X, HarpR). Har-Row.

Intuitive IC Electronics: A Sophisticated Primer for Engineers & Technicians. Thomas M. Fredericksen. (Illus.). 208p. 1981. 18.50 (ISBN 0-07-021923-0, P&RB). McGraw.

Intuitive Journey & Other Works. Russell Edson. LC 75-30331. 188p. 1976. 10.00 o.p. (ISBN 0-06-011118-6, HarpT); pap. 4.95 o.p. (ISBN 0-06-011121-6, TD-254, HarpT). Har-Row.

Intussusception in Infants & Children. Mark M. Ravitch. 156p. 1981. 28.50 (ISBN 0-87527-169-3). Green. Postponed.

Invader. Albert F. Hill & David C. Hill. 304p. (Orig.). 1981. pap. 2.75 (ISBN 0-515-05415-1). Jove Pubns.

Invasion Nineteen Forty-Four: Rommel & the Normandy Campaign. Hans Speidel. LC 79-147223. (Illus.). 1971. Repr. of 1950 ed. lib. bdg. 18.75x (ISBN 0-8371-5988-1, SPIN). Greenwood.

Invasion of Canada: 1812-1813. Pierre Berton. 320p. 1980. 17.50 (ISBN 0-686-62570-6, An Atlantic Monthly Press Book). Little.

Invasion of Czechoslovakia: August, 1968. Tad Szulc. LC 73-12072. (World Focus Bks). (Illus.). 72p. (gr. 7 up). 1974. PLB 4.47 o.p. (ISBN 0-531-02172-6). Watts.

Invasion of Privacy. William Zelermyer. LC 59-15386. 1956. 10.00x (ISBN 0-8156-0017-8). Syracuse U Pr.

Invasion of the Brain Sharpeners. Curtis. LC 80-21434. (Capers Ser.). (Illus.). 128p. (gr. 3-6). 1981. PLB 4.99 (ISBN 0-394-84676-1); pap. 1.95 (ISBN 0-394-94676-6). Knopf.

Invasion: The German Invasion of Britain-July 1940. Kenneth Macksey. (Illus.). 224p. 1981. 12.95 (ISBN 0-02-578030-1). Macmillan.

Inventario Del Potencial Cientifico-Tecnologico a Nivel Nacional. (Span.). 1975. pap. 1.50 o.p. (ISBN 0-685-65432-X). OAS.

Invention & Design: Rhetorical Reader. 3rd ed. Forest D. Burt & E. Cleve Want. 406p. 1981. pap. text ed. 8.95 (ISBN 0-394-32557-5). Random.

Invention of Culture. rev., exp. ed. Roy W. Wagner. 1981. lib. bdg. 21.00x (ISBN 0-226-86933-4); pap. 5.95 (ISBN 0-226-86934-2). U of Chicago Pr.

Invention of Ordinary Things. Don L. Wulffson. LC 80-17498. (Illus.). 96p. (gr. 3 up). 1981. 6.95 (ISBN 0-688-41978-X); PLB 6.67 (ISBN 0-688-51978-4). Morrow.

Invention of Printing. Theodore L. DeVinne. LC 68-17971. 1969. Repr. of 1876 ed. 24.00 (ISBN 0-8103-3302-3). Gale.

Invention of the Self: The Hinge of Consciousness in the Eighteenth Century. John O. Lyons. LC 77-27103. (Illus.). 277p. 1978. 15.95x (ISBN 0-8093-0815-0). S Ill U Pr.

Invention Protection for Practicing Engineers. Tom Arnold & Frank S. Vaden. LC 73-133266. 1971. 10.95 (ISBN 0-8436-0312-7); pap. 8.95 (ISBN 0-8436-0313-5). CBI Pub.

Inventions, 2 vols. (British Parliamentary Papers Ser.). 1971. Set. 171.00x (ISBN 0-7165-1450-8, Pub. by Irish Academic Pr Ireland). Biblio Dist.

Inventions & Discoveries. Brian Williams. (Skylark Bks.). (Illus.). (gr. 5 up). 1979. 4.95 (ISBN 0-685-65720-5); PLB 7.90 s&l (ISBN 0-531-09112-0). Watts.

Inventions of Leonardo Da Vinci. Margaret Cooper. (Illus.). (gr. 7 up). 1968. 9.95 (ISBN 0-02-724490-3). Macmillan.

Inventions of Leonardo Da Vinci. Charles Gibbs-Smith. LC 77-94117. (Illus.). 1978. pap. 7.95 o.p. (ISBN 0-684-15746-2, ScribT). Scribner.

Inventions Wanted. Harry Goff. 1981. 5.95 (ISBN 0-914960-24-5). Green Hill.

Inventions Wanted! Harry Goff. LC 79-56695. (Illus.). 160p. (Orig.). 1980. text ed. 8.95 (ISBN 0-914960-27-X, Dist. by Caroline Hse); pap. 5.95 (ISBN 0-914960-24-5). Academy Bks.

Inventive Activity in the Asian & the Pacific Region. 152p. 1981. pap. 26.00 (WIPO66, WIPO). Unipub.

Inventories: Control, Costing, & Effect Upon Income & Taxes. 2nd ed. Raymond A. Hoffman & Henry Gunders. LC 75-128350. 420p. 1970. 29.95 (ISBN 0-8260-4205-8, 49781). Ronald Pr.

Inventors. Egon Lehrburger. LC 68-2276. (Pegasus Books: No. 5). (Illus.). 1965. 7.50x (ISBN 0-234-77841-5). Intl Pubns Serv.

Inventors & Inventions of the Ancient World. Gordon C. Baldwin. LC 73-76461. (Illus.). 256p. (gr. 7-11). 1973. 7.95 (ISBN 0-590-07164-5, Four Winds). Schol Bk Serv.

Inventor's Guide in a Series of Four Parts: How to Protect, Search, Compile Facts & Sell Your Invention. Charles L. Cook. (Illus.). 1979. 11.95 (ISBN 0-9604670-0-9). C L Cook.

Inventor's Guide in a Series of Four Parts: How to Protect, Search, Compile Facts & Sell Your Invention. rev. ed. Chester L. Cook. (Illus.). 52p. 1981. Repr. of 1979 ed. saddle stitch 11.95 (ISBN 0-9604670-1-7). C L Cook.

Inventorum Natura. Una Woodruff. LC 79-63799. (Illus.). 128p. 1981. pap. 8.95 (ISBN 0-06-090815-7, CN 815, CN). Har-Row.

Inventory Control for the Financial Executive. Thomas S. Dudick & Ross Cornell. LC 79-10699. (Systems & Controls for Financial Management Ser.). 1979. 28.95 (ISBN 0-471-01503-2). Ronald Pr.

Inventory Management for Small Computers. Chuck Atkinson. 140p. 1981. pap. 16.95 (ISBN 0-918398-48-7). Dilithium Pr.

Inventory of Educational Improvement Efforts in the New York City Public Schools. David Rogers. LC 77-10481. 1977. pap. text ed. 12.75x (ISBN 0-8077-2531-5). Tchrs Coll.

Inventory of Major Research Facilities in the European Community, 2 vols. Ed. by Commission for the European Communities, Directorate-General for Research, Science & Education. 1561p. 1977. text ed. 120.00 (ISBN 3-7940-3019-2, Pub. by K G Saur). Gale.

Inventory of Marriage & Family Literature, Vol. 5. Ed. by David H. Olson. LC 67-63014. 1979. 60.00x (ISBN 0-8039-1232-3); pap. 29.95x (ISBN 0-8039-1233-1). Sage.

Inventory of Marriage & Family Literature, Vol. 6. Ed. by David H. Olson. LC 67-63014. (Illus.). 390p. 60.00 (ISBN 0-8039-1474-1); pap. 29.95 (ISBN 0-8039-1475-X). Sage.

Inventory of Published Letters to & from Physicists: 1900-1950. LC 80-51581. (Berkeley Papers in History of Science: No. VI). (Orig.). 1981. pap. write for info. (ISBN 0-918102-06-5). U Cal Hist Sci Tech.

Inventory of Teacher Knowledge of Reading. Sterl Artley. (Lucas Text Ser). text ed. 1.35x saddle stitched (ISBN 0-87543-102-X). Lucas.

Inventory of the Records of the National Lawyers Guild, 1936-1976, & an Index to NIG Periodicals, 1936-1979. Compiled by Richard N. Katz et al. LC 80-81943. pap. 10.00 (ISBN 0-913876-12-7). Meiklejohn Civil Lib.

Inventory Systems. Eliezer Naddor. LC 65-26850. 1966. 25.95 (ISBN 0-471-62830-1). Wiley.

Inverse Scattering Problems in Optics. Ed. by H. P. Baltes. (Topics in Current Physics: Vol. 20). (Illus.). 313p. 1980. 42.00 (ISBN 0-387-10104-7). Springer-Verlag.

Inversion Methods in Atmospheric Remote Sounding. Ed. by Adarsh Deepak. 1977. 40.00 (ISBN 0-12-208450-0). Acad Pr.

Inversions. Scott Kim. 200p. 1980. pap. 8.95 (ISBN 0-07-034546-5). McGraw.

Invertebrata. 4th ed. L. A. Borradaile & F. A. Potts. 1961. text ed. 29.95x (ISBN 0-521-04285-2). Cambridge U Pr.

Invertebrate Neuropharmacology. Lucy D. Leake & Robert J. Walker. LC 79-21390. 358p. 1980. 64.95x (ISBN 0-470-26857-3). Halsted Pr.

Invertebrate Palaeontology & Evolution. E. N. Clarkson. (Illus.). 1979. text ed. 40.00x (ISBN 0-04-560007-4); pap. text ed. 19.95x (ISBN 0-04-560008-2). Allen Unwin.

Invertebrate Pathology: Noncommunicable Diseases. Albert K. Sparks. 1972. 48.50 (ISBN 0-12-656450-7). Acad Pr.

Invertebrate Spain. Jose Ortega y Gasset. LC 73-16212. iv, 212p. 1974. Repr. of 1937 ed. 12.00 (ISBN 0-86527-107-0). Fertig.

Invertebrates. R. McNeill Alexander. LC 78-6275. (Illus.). 1979. 65.50 (ISBN 0-521-22120-X); pap. 17.95x (ISBN 0-521-29361-8). Cambridge U Pr.

Inverted World. Christopher Priest. 256p. 1975. pap. 1.25 o.p. (ISBN 0-445-00309-X). Popular Lib.

Invest in You. Helen Shearer. 1981. 5.75 (ISBN 0-8062-1600-X). Carlton.

Investigacion Social En Puerto Rico. Ed. by Ronald J. Duncan. LC 80-23445. 350p. 1980. text ed. 13.00 (ISBN 0-913480-45-2); pap. 8.00 (ISBN 0-913480-44-4). Inter Am U Pr.

Investigating Behavior: Principles of Psychology. Otello Desiderato et al. (Illus.). 672p. 1976. text ed. 19.50 scp o.p. (ISBN 0-06-041614-9, HarpC); instructor's manual free o.p. (ISBN 0-06-361630-0); scp wkbk. & study guide 6.50 o.p. (ISBN 0-06-041618-1); pamphlet of test items free o.p. (ISBN 0-685-66557-7). Har-Row.

Investigating Chemistry. L. Davies et al. 1973. pap. text ed. 9.95x o.p. (ISBN 0-435-64164-6); tchr's notes 7.50 o.p. (ISBN 0-435-64161-1). Heinemann Ed.

Investigating Crimes: An Introduction. Alfred R. Stone & Stuart M. Deluca. LC 79-88446. (Illus.). 1980. text ed. 19.50 (ISBN 0-395-28525-9); inst. manual 1.00 (ISBN 0-395-28526-7). HM.

Investigating Psychics: Five Life Histories. Larry Kettelkamp. (Illus.). (gr. 5-9). 1977. 7.25 (ISBN 0-688-22123-8); PLB 6.96 (ISBN 0-688-32123-2). Morrow.

Investigating School Mathematics, 6 bks. Robert E. Eicholz et al. (ISM Ser.). (gr. 1-6). 1973. Bk. 1. pap. text ed. 5.44 o.p. (ISBN 0-201-01310-X, Sch Div); tchrs' manual o.p. 12.60 o.p. (ISBN 0-201-01311-8); wkbk. 2.52 o.p. (ISBN 0-201-01317-7); dittomasters o.p. 33.80 o.p. (ISBN 0-201-01318-5). A-W.

Investigating School Mathematics. Robert E. Eicholz et al. pap. text ed. 5.16 o.p. (ISBN 0-201-01303-7); Bk. 2, Gr. K-2. pap. text ed. 5.16 o.p. (ISBN 0-201-01304-5). A-W.

Investigating School Mathematics, 6 bks. 2nd ed. Robert E. Eicholz et al. (ISM Ser.). (ps-6). 1976. text ed. 3.52 primary ext o.p. (ISBN 0-201-01290-1, Sch Div); text ed. 6.08 grade 1 (ISBN 0-201-09510-6); text ed. 6.08 grade 2 (ISBN 0-201-09520-3); text ed. 10.24 grade 3 (ISBN 0-201-09530-0); text ed. 10.24 grade 4 (ISBN 0-201-09540-8); text ed. 10.24 grade 5 (ISBN 0-201-09550-5); text ed. 10.24 grade 6 (ISBN 0-201-09560-2). A-W.

Investigating School Mathematics. Ed. by Robert E. Eicholz et al. Phares G. O'Daffer & Charles R. Fleenor. Incl. Unit P (ISBN 0-201-01293-6); Unit R (ISBN 0-201-01294-4). (Investigating School Mathematics Ser). (gr. k). pap. text ed. 8.04 ea. o.p. (Sch Div). A-W.

Investigating School Mathematics, Bk. 8. Robert E. Eicholz et al. (ISM Ser.). (gr. 8). 1974. text ed. 12.32 (ISBN 0-201-01280-4, Sch Div); tchr's ed. 16.00 (ISBN 0-201-01281-2); wkbk. 3.52 (ISBN 0-201-01282-0). A-W.

Investigating School Mathematics Primer. Robert E. Eicholz et al. (Investigating School Math Ser.). (gr. 1-6). 1973. pap. text ed. 3.92 (ISBN 0-201-01290-1, Sch Div); tchr's. ed. 11.84 (ISBN 0-201-01291-X). A-W.

Investigating Social Mobility. L. Broom et al. (ANU Department of Sociology Monograph: No. 1). (Illus.). 220p. (Orig.). 1980. pap. text ed. 11.95 (ISBN 0-909851-32-8, 1561). Bks Australia.

Investigating the Unexplained: A Compendium of Mysteries of the Natural World. Ivan T. Sanderson. LC 78-157765. (Illus.). 1972. pap. 4.95 (ISBN 0-13-503169-9). P-H.

Investigating UFO's. Larry Kettelkamp. LC 77-155993. (Illus.). (gr. 5-9). 1971. PLB 6.96 (ISBN 0-688-31768-5). Morrow.

Investigating Your Environment Ser. Biological Science Curriculum Study. Incl. Bk. 1. Environment: Some Viewpoints. pap. text ed. 3.92 (ISBN 0-201-00933-1); Bk. 2. Price of Progress. pap. text ed. 4.52 (ISBN 0-201-00934-X); Bk. 3. Food for Humanity. pap. text ed. 4.52 (ISBN 0-201-00935-8); Bk. 4. Human Population. pap. text ed. 4.52 (ISBN 0-201-00936-6); Bk. 5. Solid Waste. pap. text ed. 4.52 (ISBN 0-201-00937-4); Bk. 6. Pesticides. pap. text ed. 4.52 (ISBN 0-201-00938-2); Bk. 7. Land Use. pap. text ed. 4.52 (ISBN 0-201-00939-0); Bk. 8. Water Quality. pap. text ed. 4.52 (ISBN 0-201-00940-4). (gr. 10-12). 1975. pap. text ed. 8.80 student hndbk. (ISBN 0-201-00931-5, Sch Div); tchr's hndbk. 8.00 (ISBN 0-201-00932-3). A-W.

Investigation into the Powers of the Conscious, the Subconscious & of the Unconscious. Bruce D. Hertzfelt. (Illus.). 1980. 37.55 (ISBN 0-89920-005-2). Am Inst Psych.

Investigation of Fires. C. Roblee & A. McKechnie. 1981. 14.95 (ISBN 0-13-503169-9). P-H.

Investigation of Nazi Crimes, Nineteen Forty-Five to Nineteen Seventy-Eight: A Documentation. Adalbert Ruckerl. 145p. 1980. 15.00 (ISBN 0-208-01883-2, Archon). Shoe String.

Investigation of Safe & Money Chest Burglary. Donald G. Webb. (Illus.). 124p. 1975. 16.75 (ISBN 0-398-03270-X). C C Thomas.

Investigation of Separated Flow Model in Annular Gas-Liquid Two-Phase Flows. John C. Dallman. LC 78-75007. (Outstanding Dissertations on Energy Ser.). 1979. lib. bdg. 20.00 (ISBN 0-8240-3988-2). Garland Pub.

Investigation of the Administration of Louis F. Post, Assistant Secretary of Labor in the Matter of Deportation of Aliens. United States Congress. LC 72-124850. (Civil Liberties in American History Ser). Repr. of 1921 ed. lib. bdg. 29.50 (ISBN 0-306-71962-2). Da Capo.

Investigation of the Conceptual & Qualitative Impact of Employment Tax Credits. Gary C. Fethke et al. LC 78-14292. 1978. pap. 2.50 (ISBN 0-911558-00-4). Upjohn Inst.

Investigation of the Laws of Thought. George Boole. 9.50 (ISBN 0-8446-1699-0). Peter Smith.

Investigation of the Physical World. G. Toraldo Di Francia. LC 80-12791. (Illus.). 480p. Date not set. price not set (ISBN 0-521-29925-X); pap. price not set (ISBN 0-521-23338-0). Cambridge U Pr.

Investigation of Vascular Disorders. A. N. Nicolaides & James T. Yao. (Illus.). 1981. text ed. 40.00 (ISBN 0-443-08020-8). Churchill. Postponed.

Investigation of Violent & Sudden Death: A Manual for Medical Examiners. Robert C. Hendrix. (Illus.). 104p. 1972. 9.75 (ISBN 0-398-02474-X). C C Thomas.

Investigations, Pts. 1 & 2. Margaret Collis. LC 77-83013. (Using the Environment). (Illus.). 1977. Pt. 1. pap. text ed. 9.30 (ISBN 0-356-04354-1); Pt. 2. pap. text ed. 9.30 (ISBN 0-356-04355-X). Raintree Child.

Investigations in a Shi'a Village in Bahrain. Henny H. Hansen. (Ethnographical Ser.: No. 12). (Illus.). 1968. pap. text ed. 28.75x (ISBN 87-480-7202-8). Humanities.

Investigations in Animal Physiology. John Simpkins. (Investigations in Biology Ser.). 1973. pap. text ed. 3.95x o.p. (ISBN 0-435-60285-3). Heinemann Ed.

Investigations in General Biology. Kenneth B. Armitage. 1970. text ed. 9.50 (ISBN 0-12-062460-5). Acad Pr.

Investigations in Southwest Yukon, Vol. 6. F. Johnson et al. 1964. 12.50 (LIBSN 0-686-21691-1). Northland Pubns WA.

Investigations on the Theory & Applications of Differentiable Functions of Several Variables, 4: Proceedings. Steklov Institute of Mathematics, No. 117. Ed. by S. M. Nikolsky. LC 68-1677. 403p. 1974. 43.60 o.p. (ISBN 0-8218-3017-1, STEKLO-117). Am Math.

Investigative Guidelines & Procedures, No. 1. Mouzakis. 1981. text ed. 43.95 (ISBN 0-409-95016-5). Butterworth.

Investigative Methods. James D. Scott. (Illus.). 1978. ref. ed. 14.95 (ISBN 0-87909-392-7); instrs'. manual avail. Reston.

Investigative Reporting & Editing. Paul N. Williams. LC 77-4855. (Illus.). 1978. 14.50 (ISBN 0-13-504662-9). P-H.

Investigator-Inspector. 3rd ed. Arco Editorial Board. LC 67-22816. (Orig.). 1967. lib. bdg. 7.50 (ISBN 0-668-01711-2); pap. 5.00 o. p. (ISBN 0-668-01670-1). Arco.

Investing in Japan. Nomura Research Institute. (Illus.). 208p. 1980. 25.00x (ISBN 0-85941-067-6). Herman Pub.

Investing in Natural Resources. 2nd ed. Walter Youngquist. LC 80-67667. 264p. 1980. 14.95 (ISBN 0-87094-221-2). Dow Jones-Irwin.

Investing in New Jersey. Ronald W. Dickey & Wolodymyr Klachko. LC 79-93331. 1980. 14.95 (ISBN 0-686-64291-0). W H Wise.

Investing in Old Buildings. Ed. by Sally E. Nielsen. (Illus.). 1980. pap. 3.95. Greater Portland.

Investing in Real Estate. Fred E. Case. LC 78-3486. (Illus.). 1978. 15.95 o.p. (ISBN 0-13-503219-9); pap. 6.95 o.p. (ISBN 0-13-503201-6). P-H.

Investing in Residential Real Estate: A Guide to Increasing Your Income & Profit. Paul Lyons. (Illus.). 1981. text ed. 16.95 (ISBN 0-8359-3304-0). Reston. Postponed.

Investing in Securities: A Handbook for Today's Market. Richard A. Haft. 1975. pap. 5.95 o.p. (ISBN 0-13-502708-X). P-H.

Investing in Securities: An Efficient Markets Approach. Seha M. Tinic & Richard R. West. LC 78-55833. 1979. text ed. 20.95 (ISBN 0-201-07631-4); instr's manual avail. (ISBN 0-201-07632-2). A-W.

Investing in Value. D. Warburton-Brown. 164p. 1975. 13.00 (ISBN 92-833-1031-4, APO35, APO). Unipub.

Investmensts Institute, Miami, April 1978: Proceedings. Ed. by Elizabeth A. Hieb. 1978. pap. 7.50 (ISBN 0-89154-079-2). Intl Found Employ.

Investment. W. L. Fairweather. (Teach Yourself Ser.). 1973. pap. 2.95 o.p. (ISBN 0-679-10473-9). McKay.

Investment Activities of Life Insurance Companies. J. David Cummins. 1977. 16.00x (ISBN 0-256-01974-6). Irwin.

Investment Analysis & Management. Stanley Huang. (Illus.). 500p. 1981. text ed. 19.95 (ISBN 0-87626-453-4). Winthrop.

Investment Analysis & Portfolio Management. 3rd ed. Jerome B. Cohen et al. 1977. text ed. 18.95x (ISBN 0-256-01883-9). Irwin.

Investment Analysis & Portfolio Management. F. Reily. LC 78-56196. 1979. 20.95 (ISBN 0-03-013576-1). Dryden Pr.

Investment Analysis & Portfolio Management. Ed. by Basil Taylor. 1970. 39.95 o.p. (ISBN 0-236-17611-0, Pub. by Paul Elek). Merrimack Bk Serv.

Investment Analysis: The Techniques of Appraising the British Stock Market. Michael A. Firth. 1975. 23.65 (ISBN 0-06-318028-6, IntlDept). Har-Row.

Investment & Divestment Policies of Multinationals in Europe. B. Martens. (Praeger Special Studies). 1979. 22.95 (ISBN 0-03-046196-0). Praeger.

Investment & Portfolio Analysis. Haim Levy & Marshall Sarnat. LC 74-175793. (Ser. in Finance). 568p. 1972. 26.50 (ISBN 0-471-53152-9). Wiley.

Investment & the Value of Capital. Andrew B. Abel. LC 78-75063. (Outstanding Dissertations in Economics Ser.). 1979. lib. bdg. 22.00 (ISBN 0-8240-4139-9). Garland Pub.

Investment & Unit Trust in Britain & America. H. Burton & D. C. Corner. 1970. 39.95 o.p. (ISBN 0-236-17603-X, Pub. by Paul Elek). Merrimack Bk Serv.

Investment Banking in America: A History. Vincent P. Carosso. Ed. by Martin V. Sears & Irving Katz. LC 70-99515. (Studies in Business History: No. 25). 1970. 20.00x (ISBN 0-674-46574-1). Harvard U Pr.

Investment Decision of Firms. S. J. Nickell. LC 78-73957. (Economic Handbooks Ser.). 1975. 42.50 (ISBN 0-521-22465-9); pap. 13.95x (ISBN 0-521-29511-4). Cambridge U Pr.

Investment Decisions & Capital Costs. James T. Porterfield. (Illus.). 1965. pap. 10.95 ref. ed. (ISBN 0-13-502617-2). P-H.

Investment Decisions in the Nationalized Fuel Industries. R. W. Bates & N. M. Fraser. LC 74-76575. (Illus.). 208p. 1974. 29.50 (ISBN 0-521-20455-0). Cambridge U Pr.

Investment Efficiency in a Socialist Economy. H. Fiszel. 1966. 13.75 (ISBN 0-08-011760-0). Pergamon.

Investment for Production: Managing the Plant Investment Process. Paul Lowe. LC 79-143. 1979. 29.95x (ISBN 0-470-26646-5). Halsted Pr.

Investment Guide to Home & Land Purchase. Fred E. Case. LC 77-24751. (Illus.). 1977. 9.95 o.p. (ISBN 0-13-502674-1); pap. 3.95 o.p. (ISBN 0-13-502666-0). P-H.

Investment in Human Capital. T. W. Schultz. LC 77-122273. 1971. 14.95 (ISBN 0-02-928220-9). Free Pr.

Investment Information: A Detailed Guide to Selected Sources. Ed. by James B. Woy. LC 79-118791. (Management Information Guides Ser.: No. 19). 1970. 30.00 (ISBN 0-8103-0819-3). Gale.

Investment Institute Hollywood, Florida, April 27 to 30, 1980: Proceedings. Ed. by Mary E. Brennan & Elizabeth A. Heib. 137p. 1980. pap. 10.00 (ISBN 0-89154-134-9). Intl Found Employ.

Investment, Interest, & Capital. Jack Hirshleifer. (Finance Ser). 1970. text ed. 16.95x (ISBN 0-13-502955-4). P-H.

Investment Laws of the World, Binder 10. International Center for Settlement of Investment Disputes. 1979. 75.00 (ISBN 0-379-00650-2). Oceana.

Investment Management. 4th ed. Harry C. Sauvain. 592p. 1973. ref. ed. 19.95x (ISBN 0-13-503094-3). P-H.

Investment Policies of National Oil Companies: A Comparative Study of Sonatrach, Nioc & Pemex. Abderrahmane Megateli. LC 80-12841. 344p. 1980. 31.95 (ISBN 0-03-052736-8). Praeger.

Investment Portfolio Decision-Making. Ed. by James L. Bicksler & Paul A. Samuelson. LC 73-1561. 1974. 19.95 (ISBN 0-669-86215-0). Lexington Bks.

Investment Principles. Timothy E. Johnson. LC 77-13345. (Illus.). 1978. ref. 18.95 (ISBN 0-13-504506-1). P-H.

Investment Railways in Britain, 1820-1844: A Study in the Development of the Capital Market. M. C. Reed. (Illus.). 240p. 1975. write for info. (ISBN 0-19-821852-4). Oxford U Pr.

Investment, Valuation & the Managerial Theory of the Firm. Alan J. Baker. 336p. 1978. text ed. 25.25x (ISBN 0-566-00192-6, Pub. by Gower Pub Co England). Renouf.

Investments. 2nd ed. W. Sharpe. 1981. 19.95 (ISBN 0-13-504613-0). P-H.

Investments. William F. Sharpe. LC 77-8880. (Illus.). 1978. ref. ed. 21.00 (ISBN 0-13-504605-X). P-H.

Investments: Analysis & Management. 3rd ed. Douglas A. Hayes & W. Scott Bauman. (Illus.). 1976. text ed. 19.95 (ISBN 0-02-352710-2). Macmillan.

Investments Institute, April 1976, Palm Springs, California: Proceedings. Ed. by James J. Neitzel. 1976. spiral bdg. 10.50 (ISBN 0-89154-051-2). Intl Found Employ.

Investments Institute, New Orleans, May, 1977: Proceedings. Ed. by James J. Neitzel. 1977. spiral bdg. 12.50 (ISBN 0-89154-066-0). Intl Found Employ.

Investor & the Securities Act. Homer V. Cherrington. LC 78-173651. (FDR & the Era of the New Deal Ser.). 266p. 1973. Repr. of 1942 ed. lib. bdg. 27.50 (ISBN 0-306-70371-8). Da Capo.

Investor-Owned Hospitals & Their Role in the Changing U. S. Health Care System. Ekaterini Siafaca. (Health Care Economics & Technology Ser.). 192p. 1981. 32.95x (ISBN 0-86621-000-8). F&S Pr.

Investor Relations Handbook. Ed. by Arthur R. Roalman. LC 73-85192. 240p. 1974. 17.95 (ISBN 0-8144-5349-X). Am Mgmt.

Investor Relations That Work. A. R. Roalman. 148p. 1981. 34.95 (ISBN 0-8144-5620-0). Am Mgmt.

Investors Bond Values, 2 vols. Incl. Vol. 1, No. 194. Coupons-2 per cent to 6 per cent; Vol. 2, No. 294. Coupons-6 per cent to 10 per cent. Set. 50.00 (ISBN 0-685-26872-1); 30.00 ea. Finan Pub.

Investors Can Beat Inflation. Thurman L. Smith. LC 79-52816. 150p. 1980. pap. 5.95 (ISBN 0-89709-018-7). Liberty Pub.

Investor's Guide to American Convertible & Special-Interest Automobiles, 1946-1976. Charles Webb. LC 77-84592. (Illus.). 1979. 25.00 (ISBN 0-498-02183-1). A S Barnes.

Investor's Guide to Investing in Multiple Dwellings. Robert S. Wilson. LC 76-4381. 1976. 16.95x (ISBN 0-669-00648-3). Lexington Bks.

Investors Legal Guide. 2nd ed. S. L. Kaufman. 1979. 5.95 (ISBN 0-379-11126-8). Oceana.

Investor's Quotient: The Psychology of Successful Investing in Commodities & Stock. Jacob Bernstein. LC 80-17127. 296p. 1980. 16.95 (ISBN 0-471-07849-2). Wiley.

Invincibles. Frank O'Connor & Hugh Hunt. (Abbey Theatre Ser.). pap. 2.95 (ISBN 0-912262-67-2). Proscenium.

Invisible Additives: Environmental Contamination of Food. Linda Pim. 195p. 1981. 9.95 (ISBN 0-385-17001-7); pap. 6.95 (ISBN 0-385-17002-5). Doubleday.

Invisible Alcoholics: Women & Alcohol Abuse in America. Marian Sandmaier. 324p. 1981. pap. 4.95 (ISBN 0-07-054661-4). McGraw.

Invisible Armies: The Impact of Disease on American History. Howard N. Simpson. LC 80-682. 300p. 1980. 12.95 (ISBN 0-672-52659-X). Bobbs.

Invisible Chain: Diseases Passed on by Inheritance. Elizabeth Jolly. LC 72-80166. 1972. 12.95 (ISBN 0-911012-26-5). Nelson-Hall.

Invisible City: A New York Sketchbook. Pete Hamill. LC 80-5276. (Illus.). 1980. 8.95 (ISBN 0-394-50377-5). Random.

Invisible Colleges: A Profile of Small, Private Colleges with Limited Resources. Carnegie Commission on Higher Education. Ed. by A. Astin & C. Lee. 1971. 8.95 o.p. (ISBN 0-07-010037-3, P&RB). McGraw.

Invisible Death. Lin Carter. (Zarkon Ser.: No. 2). 1978. pap. 1.50 o.p. (ISBN 0-445-04256-7). Popular Lib.

Invisible Epidemic: A Documented Study of the UFO Abduction Experience. Budd Hopkin. 256p. 1981. 12.95 (ISBN 0-399-90102-7). Marek.

Invisible Giant: The California State Colleges. Donald R. Gerth & James O. Haehn. LC 79-173855. (Higher Education Ser.). 1971. 14.95x o.p. (ISBN 0-87589-110-1). Jossey-Bass.

Invisible Government. 3rd ed. Dan Smoot. 1977. pap. 3.95 o.p. (ISBN 0-88279-125-7). Western Islands.

Invisible Green. John Sladek. 1979. 7.95 o.s.i. (ISBN 0-8027-5404-X). Walker & Co.

Invisible Hand. Jay I. Olnek. 1980. 14.95 (ISBN 0-938538-00-4). N Stonington.

Invisible Land: A Study of the Artistic Imagination of Iurii Olesha. Elizabeth K. Beaujour. LC 71-130959. 1970. 20.00x (ISBN 0-231-03428-8). Columbia U Pr.

Invisible Mad. Mad Magazine Editors. (Mad Ser.: No. 37). (Illus.). 1974. pap. 1.75 (ISBN 0-446-94369-X). Warner Bks.

Invisible Man. H. G. Wells. pap. 1.25 o.p. (ISBN 0-445-08417-0). Popular Lib.

Invisible Man: A Fantastic Sensation. H. G. Wells. LC 80-10547. 279p. 1981. Repr. lib. bdg. 10.00x (ISBN 0-8376-0457-5). Bentley.

Invisible Minority: Urban Appalachians. Ed. by William W. Philliber & Clyde B. McCoy. LC 79-4008. (Illus.). 192p. 1981. 15.50x (ISBN 0-8131-1395-4). U Pr of Ky.

Invisible Outlaw. Max Brand. 1974. pap. 1.75 (ISBN 0-446-94343-6). Warner Bks.

Invisible Partners. John Sanford. LC 79-56604. (Orig.). 1980. pap. 5.95 (ISBN 0-8091-2277-4). Paulist Pr.

Invisible Picture: A Study of Psychic Experiences. Louisa E. Rhine. LC 80-10545. (Illus.). 275p. 1981. lib. bdg. 15.95x (ISBN 0-89950-015-3). McFarland & Co.

Invisible Present: African Art & Literature. Dennis Duerden. LC 74-25153. (Icon Editions). (Illus.). 184p. 1975. 10.00x o.s.i. (ISBN 0-06-432000-6, HarpT). Har-Row.

Invisible Scar: The Great Depression, & What It Did to American Life, from Then Until Now. Caroline Bird. LC 65-24266. (gr. 10 up). 1978. pap. 9.95x (ISBN 0-582-28016-8). Longman.

Invisible University: Postdoctoral Education in the United States. National Research Council. LC 70-601489. (Illus., Orig.). 1969. pap. 13.75 (ISBN 0-309-01730-0). Natl Acad Pr.

Invisible War. Donald G. Barnhouse. 288p. 1980. pap. 6.95 (ISBN 0-310-20481-X). Zondervan.

Invisible World. Stanley L. Weinberg & Herbert J. Stoltze. (Action Biology Ser.). (gr. 9-12). 1974. pap. text ed. 3.20 (ISBN 0-205-04145-0, 6741452). Allyn.

Invisible World. Robert H. West. 275p. 1980. Repr. of 1939 ed. lib. bdg. 30.00 (ISBN 0-8482-7063-0). Norwood Edns.

Invisible Writing. Arthur Koestler. LC 70-85782. (Danube Edition Ser). 1970. 10.95 o.s.i. (ISBN 0-02-565190-0). Macmillan.

Invisibles, Two. Larry Evans. (Illus.). 40p. (Orig.). 1981. pap. 2.50 (ISBN 0-89844-028-9). Troubador Pr.

Invitacion al Ingles. Madrigal & Meyer. (gr. 9 up). 1965. pap. text ed. 3.50 (ISBN 0-88345-072-0, 17398); cassettes 40.00 (ISBN 0-685-48113-1); tapes o.p. 22.50 (ISBN 0-685-48114-X); records o.p. 9.95 (ISBN 0-685-48115-8); ans. key 1.00 (ISBN 0-686-67015-9). Regents Pub.

Invitacion del Rey. Virginia Mueller. Tr. by Fernando Villalobos from Eng. (Libros Arco). (Illus.). 32p. (Orig., Span.). (gr. 1-3). 1970. pap. 0.95 o.s.i. (ISBN 0-89922-039-8). Edit Caribe.

Invitation System. Iain Murray. 1973. pap. 0.50 (ISBN 0-85151-171-6). Banner of Truth.

Invitation to a Dynamite Party. Peter Lovesey. (Crime Ser.). 176p. 1981. pap. 3.50 (ISBN 0-14-004029-3). Penguin.

Invitation to a Hanging. Walt Coburn. 1977. pap. 1.25 (ISBN 0-505-51196-7). Tower Bks.

Invitation to Biology. 2nd ed. Helena Curtis. LC 76-50677. (Illus.). 1977. 15.95x o.p. (ISBN 0-87901-072-X); study guide 5.95x o.p. (ISBN 0-87901-073-8). Worth.

Invitation to Biology. 3rd ed. Helena Curtis & N. Sue Barnes. 1981. text ed. write for info. (ISBN 0-87901-131-9); write for info. study guide (ISBN 0-87901-139-4). Worth.

Invitation to Chinese Philosophy. Ed. by Arne Naess & Alistair Hannay. 1972. pap. 19.00x (ISBN 82-00-02264-1, Dist. by Columbia U Pr). Universitet.

Invitation to Critical Sociology: Involvement, Criticism, Exploration. Donald E. Hansen. LC 75-5234. (Illus.). 1976. pap. text ed. 7.95 (ISBN 0-02-913750-0). Free Pr.

Invitation to Danger. Pat Phillips. 192p. (YA) 1976. 4.95 o.p. (ISBN 0-685-64246-1, Avalon). Bouregy.

Invitation to Flying. Robert S. Hunter. (Illus.). 1978. 12.95 (ISBN 0-87165-032-0, Flying-Zd). Ziff-Davis Pub.

Invitation to Forth. Harry Katzan, Jr. (Illus.). 240p. 1981. 17.50 (ISBN 0-89433-173-6). Petrocelli.

Invitation to Hinduism. M. Bannerjee. 1979. pap. 5.95 (ISBN 0-89684-081-6, Pub. by Arnold Heinemann India). Orient Bk Dist.

Invitation to Indian Philosophy. T. M. Mahadevan. (Orig.). 1979. pap. 5.95 (ISBN 0-89684-090-5, Pub. by Arnold Heinemann India). Orient Bk Dist.

Invitation to Japanese Civilization. Robert S. Ellwood, Jr. (Illus.). 1980. pap. text ed. 6.95 (ISBN 0-87872-237-8). Duxbury Pr.

Invitation to John: A Commentary on the Gospel of John with Complete Text from the Jerusalem Bible. Macrae, George W., S.J. LC 77-91559. 1978. pap. 2.95 (ISBN 0-385-12212-8, Im). Doubleday.

Invitation to Listening. 2nd ed. Richard L. Wink & Lois Williams. LC 75-31007. (Illus.). 352p. 1976. text ed. 14.95 (ISBN 0-395-18651-X); instructor's manual 1.25 (ISBN 0-395-18778-8); of six LP records 18.75 set (ISBN 0-395-19372-9). HM.

Invitation to Luke: A Commentary on the Gospel of Luke with Complete Text from the Jerusalem Bible. Karris, Robert J., Rev. LC 77-73331. 1977. pap. 3.50 (ISBN 0-385-12209-8, Im). Doubleday.

Invitation to Mark: A Commentary on the Gospel of Mark with Complete Text from the Jerusalem Bible. Paul J. Achtemeier. LC 77-91555. 1978. pap. 2.95 (ISBN 0-385-12213-6, Im). Doubleday.

Invitation to Mathematics. Norman Gowar. (Illus.). 214p. 1979. text ed. 27.50x (ISBN 0-19-853002-1); pap. 11.50x (ISBN 0-19-853001-3). Oxford U Pr.

Invitation to Matthew: A Commentary on the Gospel of Matthew with Complete Text from the Jerusalem Bible. Donald Senior. LC 77-73337. 1977. pap. 2.95 (ISBN 0-385-12211-X, Im). Doubleday.

Invitation to Music. Elie Siegmeister. LC 61-15658. (Illus.). (gr. 8-12). 1961. PLB 6.27 (ISBN 0-8178-3182-7). Harvey.

Invitation to Philosophy. 3rd ed. Stanley M. Honer & Thomas C. Hunt. 1978. pap. 9.95x (ISBN 0-534-00564-0). Wadsworth Pub.

Invitation to Physics. Jay M. Pasachoff & Marc L. Kutner. 1980. text ed. 16.95x (ISBN 0-393-95164-2); tchr's manual & test bank free (ISBN 0-393-95167-7). Norton.

Invitation to Psychology. John P. Houston & Victor Benassi. 741p. 1979. text ed. 17.95 (ISBN 0-12-356860-9); instrs'. manual 2.00 (ISBN 0-12-356862-5); study guide 6.95 (ISBN 0-12-356864-1); test blank 1.00 (ISBN 0-12-356861-7); test bklt. 2.00 (ISBN 0-12-356863-3); test tape bank (ISBN 0-12-356865-X). Acad Pr.

Invitation to Shabbat. Rosalyn Moss & David Moss. (Illus.). 160p. 1981. 12.95 (ISBN 0-89961-013-7); pap. 6.95 (ISBN 0-89961-014-5). SBS Pub.

Invitation to Sociology: A Humanistic Perspective. Peter L. Berger. LC 63-8758. 1963. pap. 2.95 (ISBN 0-385-06529-9, A346, Anch). Doubleday.

Invitation to the Book of Revelation: A Commentary on the Apocalypse with Complete Text from the Jerusalem Bible. Elizabeth S. Fiorenza. LC 79-6744. 224p. 1981. pap. 3.95 (ISBN 0-385-14800-3, Im). Doubleday.

Invitation to the Butterfly Ball. Jane Yolen. LC 75-19191. (Illus.). 40p. (ps-3). 1976. 5.95 o.s.i. (ISBN 0-8193-0799-8, Four Winds); PLB 5.41 o.s.i. (ISBN 0-8193-0800-5). Schol Bk Serv.

Invitation to the New Testament. W. D. Davies. LC 65-17223. 1969. pap. 4.95 (ISBN 0-385-04767-3, A013, Anch). Doubleday.

Invitation to the New Testament Epistles IV: A Commentary on Hebrews, James, 1 & 2 Peter, 1, 2 & 3 John & Jude, with Complete Text from the Jerusalem Bible. Frederick W. Danker. LC 79-6743. 256p. (Orig.). 1980. pap. 3.95 (ISBN 0-385-14799-6, Im). Doubleday.

Invite a Bird to Dinner: Simple Feeders You Can Make. Beverly C. Crook. LC 78-8657. (Illus.). (gr. 3-7). 1978. 6.95 (ISBN 0-688-41849-X); PLB 6.67 (ISBN 0-688-51849-4). Lothrop.

Invite Me Again. Illus. by Mary Gibbons. 300p. (Orig.). 1979. pap. 6.95x plastic cone spine (ISBN 0-9605174-0-5). IMA Ed.

Inviting the Mystic, Supporting the Prophet: The Dynamics of Spiritual Direction. L. Patrick Carroll & Katharine M. Dyckman. 128p. (Orig.). 1981. pap. 4.95 (ISBN 0-8091-2378-9). Paulist Pr.

Involuntary Journey to Siberia, Russian Edition. Andrei Amalrik. LC 75-118829. (Rus). 1970. 10.00 (ISBN 0-15-145503-1). HarBraceJ.

Involution Ocean. Bruce Sterling. (Orig.). 1978. pap. 1.50 o.s.i. (ISBN 0-515-04301-X). Jove Pubns.

Involved. Wilfred M. Hillock. LC 77-78102. (Anvil Ser.). 1977. pap. 7.95 (ISBN 0-8127-0140-2). Southern Pub.

Inward Hunger: The Education of a Prime Minister. Eric E. Williams. LC 70-170729. 352p. 1972. 10.00x (ISBN 0-226-89920-9). U of Chicago Pr.

Inward Journey: Art As Therapy for You. Margaret F. Keyes. LC 74-10070. (Illus.). 1974. pap. 4.95 o.p. (ISBN 0-912310-81-2). Celestial Arts.

Inward Vision: Imaginative Writing. John B. Ogden & Barbara Pannwitt. (gr. 9-11). 1971. pap. text ed. 4.50x (ISBN 0-88334-038-0). Ind Sch Pr.

Inwrought with Figures Dim: A Reading of Milton's Lycidas. David S. Berkeley. (De Proprietatibus Litterarum Ser. Didactica: No. 2). 1974. pap. text ed. 22.35x (ISBN 90-2792-605-0). Mouton.

Io Sono (I Am) Florence Slobodkin & Louis Slobodkin. LC 62-11219. (Illus.). (gr. 3 up). 1962. 4.95 (ISBN 0-8149-0392-4). Vanguard.

Ioann Skot Erigena. A. I. Brilliantor. LC 80-2358. 1981. Repr. of 1898 ed. 64.50 (ISBN 0-404-18904-0). AMS Pr.

Iolaus: An Anthology of Friendship. 3rd ed. Edward Carpenter. LC 76-174018. 1971. Repr. of 1920 ed. 15.00 (ISBN 0-8103-3790-8). Gale.

Ion. Euripides. Tr. by Gilbert Murray. 1954. pap. text ed. 3.95x (ISBN 0-04-882034-2). Allen Unwin.

Ion. Liviu Rebreau. Ed. by Ralph M. Aderman. LC 67-25190. 1967. 16.95x (ISBN 0-8057-5695-7). Irvington.

Ion Chambers for Neutron Dosimetry Workshop, Rijswijk, the Netherlands, Sept. 1979. Ed. by J. J. Broerse. (European Applied Research Reports Special Topics). 351p. 1980. 57.00 (ISBN 0-686-63373-3). Harwood Academic.

Ion Exchange for Pollution Control, 2 vols. C. Calmon & H. Gold. 1979. Vol. 1, 272p. 64.95 (ISBN 0-8493-5153-7); Vol. 2, 288p. 69.95 (ISBN 0-8493-5154-5). CRC Pr.

Ion Implantation & Ion Beam Analysis Techniques in Corrosion Studies. Ed. by J. C. Scully. 1977. pap. text ed. 16.00 (ISBN 0-08-021420-7). Pergamon.

Ion Implantation of Semiconductors. G. Carter & W. A. Grant. LC 76-13558. (Contemporary Electrical Engineering Ser.). 1976. 24.50x o.p. (ISBN 0-470-15125-0). Halsted Pr.

Ion Implantation Range & Energy Deposition Distributions, Vol. 1: High Incident Ion Energies. David K. Brice. LC 74-34119. 590p. 1975. 79.50 (ISBN 0-306-67401-7). IFI Plenum.

Ion Implementation & Ion Beam Analysis Techniques in Corrosion: Selected Papers Presented at the Conference at the Corrosion & Protection Centre, UMIST, Manchester, 28-30 June 1978. Ed. by J. C. Scully. 148p. 1980. 16.00 (ISBN 0-08-026135-3). Pergamon.

Ion-Molecule Reactions, 2 vols. Ed. by J. L. Franklin. LC 77-179758. 1972. Vol. 1, 362p. 42.50 (ISBN 0-306-30551-8, Plenum Pr); Vol. 2. 42.50 (ISBN 0-306-30552-6). Plenum Pub.

Ion Selective Electrode Methodology, 2 vols. Ed. by A. K. Covington. 1979. Vol. 2, 144p. 59.95 (ISBN 0-8493-5247-9); Vol. 2. 42.95 (ISBN 0-8493-5248-7). CRC Pr.

Ion Selective Electrodes. J. Koryta. LC 75-9090. (Physical Chemistry Monographs). (Illus.). 250p. 1975. 42.50 (ISBN 0-521-20569-7). Cambridge U Pr.

Ion-Selective Electrodes. Pungor. 1977. 18.50 (ISBN 0-9960003-5-6, Pub. by Kaido Hungary). Heyden.

Ion-Selective Electrodes in Analytical Chemistry, Vol. 2. Ed. by Henry Freiser. (Modern Analytical Chemistry Ser.). (Illus.). 290p. 1980. 35.00 (ISBN 0-306-40500-8, Plenum Pr). Plenum Pub.

Ion Transport & Cell Structure in Plants. D. Clarkson. LC 74-7132. 1974. text ed. 32.95 (ISBN 0-470-15985-5). Halsted Pr.

Ion Transport in Heart. L. J. Mullins. 125p. 1981. 15.00 (ISBN 0-89004-645-X). Raven.

Ionesco. Allan Lewis. (World Authors Ser.: France: No. 239). lib. bdg. 10.95 (ISBN 0-8057-2452-4). Twayne.

Ionesco: A Collection of Critical Essays. Ed. by Rosette C. Lamont. (Twentieth Century Views Ser). (Illus.). 192p. 1973. 10.95 o.p. (ISBN 0-13-504977-6); pap. 1.95 o.p. (ISBN 0-13-504969-5). P-H.

Ionians & Hellenism: A Study of the Cultural Achievement of the Early Greek Inhabitants of Asia Minor. C. J. Emlyn-Jones. (States & Cities of Ancient Greece Ser.). (Illus.). 256p. 1980. 30.00 (ISBN 0-7100-0470-2). Routledge & Kegan.

Ionic Equilibria. J. E. Prue. 1966. 15.00 (ISBN 0-08-011344-3). Pergamon.

Ionic Equilibrium. James N. Butler. (Illus.). 1964. 20.95 (ISBN 0-201-00730-4). A-W.

Ionic Liquids. Ed. by Douglas Inman & David G. Lovering. 445p. 1981. 49.50 (ISBN 0-306-40412-5, Plenum Pr). Plenum Pub.

Ionic Polymers. Ed. by L. Holliday. LC 74-11509. 416p. 1975. 53.95 (ISBN 0-470-40640-2). Halsted Pr.

Ionisation Constants of Organic Acids in Aqueous Solution. Ed. by E. P. Serjeant & B. Dempsey. (Chemical Data Ser.: Vol. 23). (Illus.). 1979. text ed. 190.00 (ISBN 0-08-022339-7). Pergamon.

Ionisation of Carbon Acids. J. R. Jones. 1974. 32.00 (ISBN 0-12-389750-5). Acad Pr.

Ionizing Radiation: Neural Function & Behavior. Donald J. Kimeldorf & Edward L. Hunt. (Atomic Energy Commission Monographs). 1965. 19.00 o.p. (ISBN 0-12-406950-9). Acad Pr.

Ionophores & Their Structure. Max Dobler. 350p. 1981. 35.00 (ISBN 0-471-05270-1, Pub. by Wiley-Interscience). Wiley.

Iowa. 28.00 (ISBN 0-89770-091-0). Curriculum Info Ctr.

Iowa. Joseph F. Wall. (States & the Nation Ser.). (Illus.). 1978. 12.95 (ISBN 0-393-05671-6, Co-Pub by AASLH). Norton.

Iowa: A Guide to the Hawkeye State. Federal Writers' Project. 583p. 1938. Repr. 48.00 (ISBN 0-403-02166-9). Somerset Pub.

Iowa Chronology & Factbook, Vol. 15. R. I. Vexler. 1978. 8.50 (ISBN 0-379-16140-0). Oceana.

Iowa Takes to the Air: 1845-1918, Vol. 1. Ann H. Pellegreno. LC 79-55458. (Illus.). (YA) 1981. 14.95 (ISBN 0-935092-01-3). Aerodrome Pr.

Iowa Writers' Workshop: Origins, Emergence & Growth. Stephen Wilbers. LC 80-20190. 148p. 1981. 12.50 (ISBN 0-87745-098-6); pap. 7.95 (ISBN 0-87745-105-2). U of Iowa Pr.

IPC: Interpersonal Communication Skills for Correctional Management. John Blakeman et al. 118p. (Orig.). 1977. pap. text ed. 8.95x (ISBN 0-914234-69-2); Trainer Guide. pap. text ed. 12.95x (ISBN 0-914234-70-6). Human Res Dev Pr.

Ipcress File. Len Deighton. 1976. pap. 1.95 (ISBN 0-345-28439-9). Ballantine.

Iphigeneia at Aulis. Euripides. Tr. by W. S. Merwin & George E. Dimock, Jr. (Greek Tragedy in New Translations). 1978. 10.95 (ISBN 0-19-502272-6). Oxford U Pr.

Iphigeneia at Tauris. Euripides. Tr. by Richmond Lattimore. (Greek Tragedy in New Translation Ser). 112p. 1973. 10.95 (ISBN 0-19-501736-6). Oxford U Pr.

Iphigenia in Tauris. Euripides. Tr. by Gilbert Murray. 1910. pap. text ed. 3.95x (ISBN 0-04-882036-9). Allen Unwin.

IPS Notebook. rev. ed. P. Nowlan. (Illus.). 128p. 1980. pap. 3.52 (ISBN 0-913688-02-9). Pawnee Pub.

IPS Research Guide to Current Military & Strategic Affairs. William Arkin. 160p. 1981. pap. 5.95 (ISBN 0-89758-025-7). Inst Policy Stud.

IQ & Mental Testing. B. H. Evans & B. A. Waites. 1980. text ed. 30.00x (ISBN 0-391-01911-2); pap. text ed. 13.00x (ISBN 0-391-01912-0). Humanities.

I.Q. Game: A Methodological Inquiry into the Heredity-Environment Controversy. Howard F. Taylor. 300p. 1980. 19.50 (ISBN 0-8135-0902-5). Rutgers U Pr.

IQ, Heritability & Racism. James Lawler. 1978. 12.00 o.p. (ISBN 0-7178-0499-2); pap. 3.95 (ISBN 0-7178-0554-9). Intl Pub Co.

IQ: Race, Social Class & Individual Differences. Sandra W. Scarr. 500p. 1981. profess. & reference 30.00 (ISBN 0-89859-055-8). L Erlbaum Assocs.

Iqbal, Jinnah, & Pakistan: The Vision & the Reality. Ed. by C. M. Naim. LC 79-25477. (Foreign & Comparative Studies-South Asian Ser: No. 5). 216p. (Orig.). 1979. pap. text ed. 6.50x (ISBN 0-915984-81-4). Syracuse U Foreign Comp.

Iqbal: Poet-Philosopher of Pakistan. Ed. by Hafeez Malik. LC 75-135475. (Studies in Oriental Culture Ser.: No. 7). 1971. 20.00x (ISBN 0-231-03320-6). Columbia U Pr.

IR & Roman Spectoscopy of Polymers. Siesler & Holland-Moritz. 440p. 1980. 47.50 (ISBN 0-8247-6935-X). Dekker.

IR Forty-Two: A Rice Type for Small Farmers of South & Southeast Asia. (IRRI Research Paper Ser.: No. 44). 10p. 1979. pap. 5.00 (R084, IRRI). Unipub.

Iracema, the Honey-Lips: A Legend of Brazil. Jose M. De Alencar. LC 75-44268. 1977. Repr. of 1886 ed. 12.50 (ISBN 0-86527-263-8). Fertig.

Iran. Emil Lengyel. LC 72-180169. (First Bks). (Illus.). 72p. (gr. 6-9). 1972. PLB 6.45 (ISBN 0-531-00760-X). Watts.

Iran. rev. ed. Emil Lengyel. (First Bks). (Illus.). (gr. 4-6). 1978. PLB 6.45 s&l (ISBN 0-531-02242-0). Watts.

Iran: A People in Revolution. Bob Saibel. (Illus.). 352p. 1981. 21.95 (ISBN 0-916650-14-6); pap. 6.95 (ISBN 0-916650-15-4). Banner Pr IL.

Iran & Islam. Geo Widengren. (Jordon Lectures in Comparative Religion Ser: No. 10). 160p. 1979. cancelled (ISBN 0-485-17410-3, Athlone Pr). Humanities.

Iran Crisis. R. Douglas Wead. (Orig.). 1980. pap. 2.95 (ISBN 0-88270-433-8). Logos.

Iran: Quest for Security. K. R. Singh. 421p. 1980. text ed. 37.50x (ISBN 0-7069-1259-4, Pub. by Vikas India). Advent Bk.

Iran: Religion, Politics & Society--Collected Essays. Nikki R. Keddie. 243p. 1980. pap. 9.95x (ISBN 0-7146-4031-X, F Cass Co). Biblio Dist.

Iran, Saudi Arabia, & the Law of the Sea: Political Interaction and Legal Development in the Persian Gulf. Charles G. MacDonald. LC 79-6186. (Contributions in Political Science: No. 48). xv, 226p. 1980. lib. bdg. 28.50 (ISBN 0-313-20768-2, MLS/). Greenwood.

Iran: The Illusion of Power. Robert Graham. LC 78-65258. (Illus.). 272p. 1980. 17.95x (ISBN 0-312-43587-8); pap. 6.95 (ISBN 0-312-43589-4). St Martin.

Iran Under the Safavids. Roger M. Savory. LC 78-73817. (Illus.). 300p. 1980. 34.50 (ISBN 0-521-22483-7). Cambridge U Pr.

Iranian Christian. Nasser Lotfi. 160p. 1980. 8.95 (ISBN 0-8499-0275-4). Word Bks.

Iranians: How They Live & Work. John Abbot. 168p. 1978. text ed. 8.95 (ISBN 0-03-042496-8, HoltC). HR&W.

Iran's Quest for Security: U. S. Arms Transfers & the Nuclear Option. Alvin J. Cottrell & James E. Dougherty. LC 77-80298. (Foreign Policy Reports Ser.). 1977. 5.00 (ISBN 0-89549-004-8). Inst Foreign Policy Anal.

Iran's Revolutionary Upheaval: An Interpretive Essay. new ed. Sepehr Zabih. LC 79-53696. (Orig.). 1979. 9.95x (ISBN 0-931290-18-X); pap. 5.95x (ISBN 0-686-66195-8). Alchemy Bks.

Iraq. George Fichter. (First Bks). (Illus.). (gr. 4-6). 1978. PLB 6.45 s&l (ISBN 0-531-02236-6). Watts.

Iraq: Economics, Oil & Politics. Edith Penrose & E. F. Penrose. LC 77-16007. (Nations of the Modern World Ser.). 1978. lib. bdg. 38.50x (ISBN 0-89158-804-3). Westview.

Iraq Nineteen Hundred to Nineteen Fifty. Stephen Longrigg. (Arab Background Ser.). 1968. 15.00x (ISBN 0-685-77098-2). Intl Bk Ctr.

Ireland. O. R. Orme. (The World's Landscapes Ser.). (Illus.). 1970. pap. text ed. 8.50x o.p. (ISBN 0-582-31155-1). Longman.

Ireland. Lillian F. Quigley. (Illus.). (gr. 7 up). 1964. 2.95 o.s.i. (ISBN 0-02-775690-4). Macmillan.

Ireland Before the Normans. Donncha O'Corrain. (Gill History of Ireland: Vol. 2). (Illus.). 222p. 1972. pap. 6.95 (ISBN 0-7171-0559-8). Irish Bk Ctr.

Ireland Before the Vikings. Gearoid MacNiochaill. (Gill History of Ireland: Vol. 1). (Illus.). 184p. 1972. pap. 6.95 (ISBN 0-7171-0558-X). Irish Bk Ctr.

Ireland, Eighteen Hundred to Nineteen Seventy. M. E. Collins. (Illus.). 1976. pap. text ed. 6.95x (ISBN 0-582-22140-4). Longman.

Ireland: From Colony to Nation State. Lawrence J. McCaffrey. 1979. 14.95 (ISBN 0-13-506196-2); pap. 11.95 (ISBN 0-13-506188-1). P-H.

Ireland from Old Photographs. M. Gorham. 1979. pap. 11.95 (ISBN 0-7134-2195-9, Pub. by Batsford England). David & Charles.

Ireland in Early Medieval Europe. Ed. by Dorothy Whitlock et al. LC 80-40325. (Studies in Memory of Kathleen Hughes). (Illus.). 400p. Date not set. price not set (ISBN 0-521-23547-2). Cambridge U Pr.

Ireland in Fiction. Stephen Brown. 382p. Repr. of 1919 ed. 13.00x (ISBN 0-686-28347-3, Pub. by Irish Academic Pr). Biblio Dist.

Ireland in Pictures. rev. ed. Sterling Publishing Company Editors. LC 62-12600. (Visual Geography Ser). (Illus., Orig.). (gr. 6 up). 1978. PLB 4.99 o.p. (ISBN 0-8069-1025-9); pap. 2.95 (ISBN 0-8069-1024-0). Sterling.

Ireland in Prehistory. Michael Herity & George Eogan. (Illus.). 1976. 30.00 (ISBN 0-7100-8413-7). Routledge & Kegan.

Ireland in the Eighteenth Century. Edith M. Johnston. (Gill History of Ireland: Vol. 8). 224p. 1974. pap. 6.95 (ISBN 0-7171-0565-2). Irish Bk Ctr.

Ireland in the Nineteenth Century: A Breviate of Official Publications. Arthur Maltby & Jean Maltby. (Guides to Official Publications Ser.: Vol. 4). (Illus.). 1979. 55.00 (ISBN 0-08-023688-X). Pergamon.

Ireland on Fifteen Dollars a Day, 1979-80. 320p. pap. 4.95 (ISBN 0-671-41421-6). Frommer-Pasmantier.

Ireland: The Land & the People. Donald Cowie. LC 74-9279. (Illus.). 240p. 1976. 12.00 o.p. (ISBN 0-498-01499-1). A S Barnes.
Ireland: The Union & Its Aftermath. Oliver MacDonagh. 1977. text ed. 25.00x (ISBN 0-04-941004-0); pap. text ed. 8.95x (ISBN 0-04-941005-9). Allen Unwin.
Ireland Through Tudor Eyes. Edward M. Hinton. 111p. 1980. Repr. of 1935 ed. lib. bdg. 22.50 (ISBN 0-89987-362-6). Darby Bks.
Ireland Under the Union: Varieties of Tension. Ed. by F. S. Lyons & R. A. Hawkins. (Illus.). 348p. 1980. 42.00x (ISBN 0-19-822469-9). Oxford U Pr.
Ireland's Hope. Philip Streeter. LC 73-75961. 190p. (Orig.). 1973. pap. 1.95 o.p. (ISBN 0-88270-027-8). Logos.
Irenic Apocalypse: Some Uses of Apocalyptic in Dante, Petrarch & Rebelais. Dennis Costa. (Stanford French & Italian Studies: Vol. 21). 160p. 1980. pap. 20.00 (ISBN 0-915838-18-4). Anma Libri.
Iridology: How the Eyes Reveal Your Health & Personality. Dorothy Hall. LC 80-84439. (Illus.). 256p. (Orig.). 1981. pap. 8.95 (ISBN 0-87983-241-X). Keats.
Iris Murdoch. Frank Baldanza. (English Authors Ser.: No. 169). 169p. 1974. lib. bdg. 10.95 (ISBN 0-8057-1410-3). Twayne.
Iris Murdoch. Rubin Rabinovitz. LC 68-19756. (Columbia Essays on Modern Writers Ser.: No. 34). (Orig.). (gr. 9 up). 1968. pap. 2.00 (ISBN 0-231-03000-2, MW34). Columbia U Pr.
Iris Murdoch & Muriel Spark: A Bibliography. Thomas T. Tominaga & Wilma Schneidermeyer. LC 76-909. (Author Bibliographies Ser.: No. 27). 253p. 1976. 12.00 (ISBN 0-8108-0907-9). Scarecrow.
Irish. Arnold Dobrin. LC 75-10053. (Illus.). 64p. (gr. 2-5). 1976. 6.95 o.s.i. (ISBN 0-8027-6225-5); PLB 6.85 o.s.i. (ISBN 0-8027-6230-1). Walker & Co.
Irish Affair. Andrea Harris. LC 78-59970. 1978. pap. 1.50 o.p. (ISBN 0-87216-492-6). Playboy Pbks.
Irish Album. Robin Skelton. 1969. 6.50 (ISBN 0-85105-003-4). Dufour.
Irish-American Fiction: Essays in Criticism. Ed. by Daniel J. Casey & Robert E. Rhodes. 1978. 24.50 (ISBN 0-404-16037-9); pap. 7.95 (ISBN 0-686-67216-X). AMS Pr.
Irish Art in the Romanesque Period (1020-1170 A.D) Francoise Henry. LC 76-82117. (Illus.). 386p. 1969. 30.00x (ISBN 0-8014-0526-2). Cornell U Pr.
Irish Ballad Operas & Burlesques 1. Ed. by Walter H. Rubsamen. (Ballad Opera Ser.). 1974. lib. bdg. 50.00 (ISBN 0-8240-0921-5). Garland Pub.
Irish Ballad Operas & Burlesques 2. Ed. by Walter H. Rubsamen. (Ballad Opera Ser.). 1974. 50.00 (ISBN 0-8240-0922-3). Garland Pub.
Irish Blood: Northern Ireland and the American Conscience. Dennis J. Clark. LC 76-21808. (National University Publications Ser. in American Studies). 1977. 11.00 (ISBN 0-8046-9163-0). Kennikat.
Irish Book: A Miscellany of Facts & Fancies, Folklore & Fragments, Poems & Prose to Do with Ireland & Her People. Ronald M. Douglas. LC 74-164227. xxvi, 393p. 1972. Repr. of 1936 ed. 20.00 (ISBN 0-8103-3166-7). Gale.
Irish Border As a Cultural Divide: A Contribution of the Study of Regionalism in the British Isles. M. R. Heslinga. 1980. pap. text ed. 18.75x (ISBN 90-232-0864-1). Humanities.
Irish Cattle Bills: A Study in Restoration Politics. Carolyn A. Edie. LC 76-111461. (Transactions Ser.: Vol. 60, Pt. 2). 1970. pap. 1.00 o.p. (ISBN 0-87169-602-9). Am Philos.
Irish Chronicle Fifteen Seventy-Seven: The Historie of Ireland from the First Inhabitation Thereof, Unto the Years 1509. Holinshed. LC 78-12424. (Dolemen Edition: No. XXVIII). 1979. Repr. of 1577 ed. text ed. 96.75x (ISBN 0-391-00562-6, Dolmen Pr). Humanities.
Irish Comic Tradition. Vivian Mercier. 1969. pap. 4.95 (ISBN 0-19-500297-0, 284, GB). Oxford U Pr.
Irish Constitutional Revolution in the Sixteenth Century. Brendan Bradshaw. LC 78-58785. 1979. 41.50 (ISBN 0-521-22206-0). Cambridge U Pr.
Irish Derby: Eighteen Sixty-Six to Nineteen Seventy-Nine. Guy St. John Williams & Francis Hyland. (Illus.). 432p. 1980. 40.00 (ISBN 0-85131-358-2). J A Allen.
Irish Diaspora in America. Lawrence J. McCaffrey. LC 75-23894. (Midland Bks.: No. 215). 224p. 1978. 8.50x o.p. (ISBN 0-253-33166-8); pap. 3.95x (ISBN 0-253-20215-9). Ind U Pr.
Irish Drama of Europe from Yeats to Beckett. Katharine Worth. LC 78-18909. 1978. text ed. 32.50x (ISBN 0-391-00891-9, Athlone Pr). Humanities.
Irish Elegies. 4th ed. Padraic Colum. 1976. text ed. 11.75x (ISBN 0-85105-315-7, Dolmen Pr). Humanities.
Irish: Emigration, Marriage, & Fertility. Robert E. Kennedy, Jr. LC 70-187740. 304p. 1973. 20.00x (ISBN 0-520-01987-3); pap. 4.95x (ISBN 0-520-02896-1). U of Cal Pr.
Irish-English, English-Irish Dictionary. Talbot Press. 9.50x o.s.i. (ISBN 0-686-05263-3). Colton Bk.
Irish Erotic Art. Seamus Cork. 96p. 1981. 5.95 (ISBN 0-312-43601-7). St Martin.
Irish Fairy Tales. James Stephens. LC 20-21207. (Illus.). (gr. 4 up). 1968. Repr. of 1920 ed. 9.95g (ISBN 0-02-788000-1). Macmillan.
Irish Family Names. Patrick Kelly. LC 68-26580. 1975. Repr. of 1939 ed. 24.00 (ISBN 0-8103-4146-8). Gale.
Irish Flora. D. A. Webb. (Illus.). 14.95. Dufour.
Irish Folkways. E. Estyn Evans. (Illus.). 1966. 20.00 (ISBN 0-7100-1344-2); pap. 11.95 (ISBN 0-7100-2888-1). Routledge & Kegan.
Irish Ghost Stories. Ed. by Joseph Hone. 1978. 17.95 (ISBN 0-241-89680-0, Pub. by Hamish Hamilton England). David & Charles.
Irish Giant. G. Frankcom & J. H. Musgrave. (Illus.). 128p. 1976. 15.50x (ISBN 0-7156-1021-X, Pub. by Duckworth England). Biblio Dist.
Irish Harp. 2nd ed. Joan Rimmer. (Irish Life & Culture Series). (Illus.). 1977. pap. 3.95 (ISBN 0-85342-151-X). Irish Bk Ctr.
Irish: How They Live & Work. Martin Wallace. (How They Live & Work Ser.). (Illus.). 1974. 11.95 (ISBN 0-7153-5492-2). David & Charles.
Irish in America. Carl Wittke. LC 68-9259. 1968. pap. 2.95 (ISBN 0-8077-2345-2). Tchrs Coll.
Irish Journals of Elizabeth Smith Eighteen Forty to Eighteen Fifty. Elizabeth Smith. Ed. by David Thomson & Moyra McGusty. (Illus.). 352p. 1980. 29.00x (ISBN 0-19-822471-0). Oxford U Pr.
Irish Land & British Politics: Tenant-Right & Nationality, 1865-1870. E. D. Steele. LC 73-91618. (Illus.). 352p. 1974. 41.00 (ISBN 0-521-20421-6). Cambridge U Pr.
Irish Language. David Greene. (Irish Life & Culture). 1977. pap. 2.25 o.p. (ISBN 0-85342-283-4). Irish Bk Ctr.
Irish Language: Great Languages. David Green. 1980. text ed. write for info. (ISBN 0-391-01135-9). Humanities.
Irish Legacy. Kay P. Presson. 1978. 4.50 (ISBN 0-533-03573-2). Vantage.
Irish Life in the Seventeenth Century. Edward MacLysaght. 324p. 1979. 15.00x (ISBN 0-7165-2343-4, Pub. by Irish Academic Pr); pap. 7.50x (ISBN 0-7165-2342-6, Pub. by Irish Academic Pr). Biblio Dist.
Irish Literature, Eighteen Hundred-Eighteen Seventy-Five: A Guide to Information Sources. Ed. by Brian McKenna. LC 74-11540. (American Literature, English Literature & World Literatures in English Information Guide Ser.: Vol. 13). 1978. 30.00 (ISBN 0-8103-1250-6). Gale.
Irish Literature in English: The Romantic Period (1789-1850, Vol. II, Pts. IV, Bibliography. Patrick Rafroidi. 1980. text ed. write for info. (ISBN 0-391-01033-6). Humanities.
Irish Literature in English: The Romantic Period (1789-1850, Vol. I, Pts. 1, 2 & 3. Patrick Rafroidi. (Illus.). 1980. text ed. write for info. (ISBN 0-391-01032-8). Humanities.
Irish Nature: The Book of Plant & Animal Life. Norman Hickin. (Illus.). 224p. 1981. 29.50x (ISBN 0-8476-6291-8). Rowman.
Irish Novelists, 1800-1850. Thomas J. Flanagan. LC 76-21874. 362p. 1976. Repr. of 1959 ed. lib. bdg. 25.00x (ISBN 0-8371-9004-5, FLIN). Greenwood.
Irish Official Publications: A Guide to Republic of Ireland Papers, with a Breviate of Reports 1922-1972. Arthur Maltby & Brian McKenna. (Guides to Official Publications Ser.: Vol. 7). 388p. 1981. 54.00 (ISBN 0-08-023703-7). Pergamon.
Irish Poems for Young People; Wolfhound Book of. Bridie Quinn & Seamus Cashman. (Illus.). (gr. 6-12). 1976. 9.95 (ISBN 0-9503454-3-1). Irish Bk Ctr.
Irish Poems, from Cromwell to the Famine: A Miscellany. Ed. & tr. by Joan Keefe. LC 76-755. 1976. 12.00 (ISBN 0-8387-1887-6). Bucknell U Pr.
Irish Poetry: An Essay in Irish with Translation in English. Douglas Hyde. LC 77-94587. 1979. Repr. of 1902 ed. lib. bdg. cancelled o.p. (ISBN 0-89341-189-2). Longwood Pr.
Irish Poetry from Moore to Yeats. Robert Welch. 248p. 1980. text ed. 23.25x (ISBN 0-901072-93-1). Humanities.
Irish Political Elite. A. S. Cohan. (Studies in Irish Political Culture). 128p. 1972. pap. 3.75 o.p. (ISBN 0-7171-0538-5). Irish Bk Ctr.
Irish Priests in Penal Times. William P. Burke. 508p. 1968. Repr. of 1914 ed. 19.00x (ISBN 0-7165-0034-5, Pub. by Irish Academic Pr Ireland). Biblio Dist.
Irish Question. Schools Councils History 13-16 Project. (Modern World Problems Ser.). (Illus.). 1979. lib. bdg. 9.95 (ISBN 0-912616-72-5); pap. text ed. 4.45 (ISBN 0-912616-71-7). Greenhaven.
Irish Question, Eighteen Hundred to Nineteen Twenty-Two. Lawrence J. McCaffrey. LC 68-12962. 202p. 1968. pap. 4.00x (ISBN 0-8131-0117-4). U Pr of Ky.
Irish Red. Jim Kjelgaard. 192p. (gr. 4-6). 1981. pap. 1.95 (ISBN 0-553-15008-1, Skylark). Bantam.
Irish Renaissance Annual I. Ed. by Zack Bowen. (Irish Renaissance Annual Ser.). 192p. 1980. 8.00 (ISBN 0-87413-168-5). U Delaware Pr.
Irish Renaissance Annual II. Ed. by Zack Bowen. 192p. 1981. 12.00 (ISBN 0-87413-185-5). U Delaware Pr.
Irish Sea Cruising Guide. Robert Kemp. 1979. 47.95x (ISBN 0-8464-0076-6). Beekman Pubs.
Irish Setters. rev. ed. Jack Baird. (Illus.). 128p. 1974. pap. 2.95 o.p. (ISBN 0-87666-321-8, HS 1055). TFH Pubns.
Irish Shop Prints. John Murphy. (Illus.). 72p. 1981. pap. cancelled (ISBN 0-312-43623-8). St Martin.
Irish Short Story. Patrick Rafroidi & Terence Brown. 1979. text ed. 29.25x (ISBN 0-391-01703-9). Humanities.
Irish Silver in the Rococo Period. Kurt Ticher. 142p. 1972. 20.00x (ISBN 0-7165-0039-6, Pub. by Irish Academic Pr Ireland). Biblio Dist.
Irish: Sinners, Saints, Gamblers, Gentry, Priests, Maoists, Rebels, Tories, Orangemen, Dippers, Heroes, Villains & Other Proud Natives of the Fabled Isle. Thomas J. O'Hanlon. LC 74-1843. (Illus.). 334p. (YA) 1975. 13.95 o.p. (ISBN 0-06-013238-8, HarpT). Har-Row.
Irish Song Tradition. 2nd ed. Sean O. Boyle. (Illus.). 1976. 12.95 (ISBN 0-9505173-0-5); pap. 4.95 (ISBN 0-9505173-1-3). Irish Bk Ctr.
Irish Spinning Dyeing & Weaving. Lillias Mitchell. (Illus.). 1978. 12.95 (ISBN 0-85221-101-5). Dufour.
Irish Standard Guage Railways. Tom Middlemass. LC 80-68690. (Illus.). 96p. 1981. 16.50 (ISBN 0-7153-8007-9). David & Charles.
Irish Strategies. J. L. Borges. (Dolmen Editions: No. XXI). (Illus.). 87p. 1975. text ed. 39.00x (ISBN 0-85105-277-0, Dolmen Pr). Humanities.
Irish Struggle: Nineteen Seventy to Nineteen Eighty. Bernadette D. McAliskey. 1981. lib. bdg. 25.00 (ISBN 0-913460-80-X); pap. 6.95 (ISBN 0-913460-79-6). Monad Pr. Postponed.
Irish Studies, Vol. 1. P. J. Drudy. LC 80-40084. 192p. Date not set. 27.50 (ISBN 0-521-23336-4). Cambridge U Pr.
Irish Town: An Approach to Survival. Patrick Shaffrey. (Illus.). 1976. 15.95 o.p. (ISBN 0-9502046-5-X). Irish Bk Ctr.
Irish Wonders: The Ghosts, Giants, Pookas, Demons, Leprechauns, Banshees, Fairies, Witches, Widows, Old Maids, & Other Marvels of the Emerald Isle. Popular Tales As Told by the People. David R. McAnally. LC 79-175738. (Illus.). xii, 218p. 1971. Repr. of 1888 ed. 22.00 (ISBN 0-8103-3818-1). Gale.
Irishman in Canada. N. F. Davin. 718p. Repr. of 1877 ed. 30.00x (ISBN 0-686-27787-2, Pub. by Irish Academic Pr Ireland). Biblio Dist.
Iron. James D. Cook. (Methods in Hematology Ser.: Vol. 1). (Illus.). 224p. 1980. 32.00 (ISBN 0-443-08118-2). Churchill.
Iron Age. Arlene W. Weiner. Ed. by Stephen Orgel. LC 78-66846. (Renaissance Drama Ser.). 1979. lib. bdg. 35.00 (ISBN 0-8240-9728-9). Garland Pub.
Iron Age & Roman Riverside Settlements at Farmoor, Oxfordshire. George Lambrick & Mark Robinson. 160p. 1980. pap. 54.00x (ISBN 0-900312-57-2, Pub. by Coun Brit Arch England). Intl Schol Bk Serv.
Iron Age Communities in Britain. 2nd ed. Barry Cunliffe. (Archaeology of Britain Ser). (Illus.). 1978. 42.00 (ISBN 0-7100-8725-X). Routledge & Kegan.
Iron Age Cultures in Zambia, Vol. 2: Dambwa, Ingombe Illede & the Tonga. Brian M. Fagan. (Robins Ser.: No. 6). 1969. text ed. 17.00x (ISBN 0-391-01993-7). Humanities.
Iron Age Farming. P. Reynolds. (Cambridge Introduction to the History of Mankind Ser.). 48p. 1976. pap. 3.95 (ISBN 0-521-21084-4). Cambridge U Pr.
Iron Age Settlement of Arctic Norway, Vol. II. Thorleif Sjovold. 1974. pap. text ed. 27.00x (ISBN 82-00-06157-4, Dist. by Columbia U Pr). Universitet.
Iron Age to Independence: A History of Central Africa. D. E. Needham. (Illus.). 208p. 1974. pap. text ed. 5.95x (ISBN 0-582-60298-X). Longman.
Iron Arm: The Mechanization of Mussolini's Army, 1920-1940. John J. Sweet. LC 79-6825. (Contributions in Military History: No. 23). (Illus.). xxi, 217p. 1980. lib. bdg. 25.00 (ISBN 0-313-22179-0, SWM/). Greenwood.
Iron Blast Furnace: Theory & Practice. J. G. Peacey & W. G. Davenport. 1979. text ed. 41.00 (ISBN 0-08-023218-3); pap. text ed. 16.25 (ISBN 0-08-023258-2). Pergamon.
Iron Bridge: Symbol of the Industrial Revolution. Neil Cossons & Barrie Trinder. (Illus.). 1979. text ed. 23.50 (ISBN 0-239-00187-7). Humanities.
Iron Cage. Andre Norton. 1976. pap. 1.954 (ISBN 0-441-37291-0). Ace Bks.
Iron Deposits: Origin, Evolution, & Present Characteristics. J. H. Tatsch. LC 76-28095. (Illus.). Date not set. text ed. 180.00 (ISBN 0-912890-12-6). Tatsch.
Iron Dream. Norman Spinrad. 1978. pap. 1.95 o.s.i. (ISBN 0-685-54629-2, 04741-4). Jove Pubns.
Iron Fist & the Velvet Glove: An Analysis of the U. S. Police. 2nd ed. Tony Platt et al. (Illus.). 1977. pap. text ed. 3.50 (ISBN 0-917404-02-5). Ctr Res Criminal.
Iron Heel. rev. ed. Jack London. 228p. 1980. pap. 4.95 (ISBN 0-88208-118-7). Lawrence Hill.
Iron Heel. Jack London. (Arabic.). pap. 7.95x (ISBN 0-686-63557-4). Intl Bk Ctr.
Iron Horses to Promontory Railroad: Central Pacific Union Pacific. Gerald M. Best. LC 69-20447. (Illus.). 1969. 18.95 (ISBN 0-87095-001-0). Golden West.
Iron Jehu. Ray Hogan. LC 76-10518. 1976. 5.95 o.p. (ISBN 0-385-12409-0). Doubleday.
Iron Lily. Barbara Willard. LC 74-7195. 176p. (gr. 5-7). 1974. PLB 5.95 o.p. (ISBN 0-525-32592-1). Dutton.
Iron Lion. Peter Dickinson. 48p. 1973. pap. 4.50 o.p. (ISBN 0-04-823108-8). Allen Unwin.
Iron Lords. Andrew J. Offutt. 1979. pap. 1.75 (ISBN 0-515-04600-0). Jove Pubns.
Iron Man. W. C. Chalk. 1971. pap. text ed. 2.95x o.p. (ISBN 0-435-11195-7). Heinemann Ed.
Iron Marshal. Louis L'Amour. 1980. pap. 8.95 (ISBN 0-8161-3101-5, Large Print Bks). G K Hall.
Iron Marshal: A Biography of Louis N. Davout. John G. Gallaher. LC 75-37956. 432p. 1976. 24.95x (ISBN 0-8093-0691-3). S Ill U Pr.
Iron Metabolism & Thalassemia: Proceedings. Conference Sponsored by National Foundation-March of Dimes, Key Biscayne, Florida, Nov. 1975. Ed. by Daniel Bergsma et al. LC 76-25835. (Birth Defects Original Article Ser.: Vol. 12, No. 8). 212p. 1976. 26.00x (ISBN 0-8451-1006-3). A R Liss.
Iron Mustang. Jake Logan. LC 78-54989. (Jake Logan Ser.: No. 15). 1978. pap. 1.75 (ISBN 0-87216-740-2). Playboy Pbks.
Iron-On T-Shirt Transfers for Hand Coloring. Ed Sibbett, Jr. (Illus., Orig.). 1976. pap. 1.75 (ISBN 0-486-23395-2). Dover.
Iron-on Transfers from a Treasury of Needlework Designs: Ready-to-Use Patterns for Needlepoint & Embroidery. Martha R. Zimikes. 96p. 1981. pap. 9.95 (ISBN 0-442-23119-9). Van Nos Reinhold.
Iron Ore to Iron Lace. Emily S. Van Antwerp. (Illus.). 150p. 1980. 10.00 (ISBN 0-914334-07-7). Museum Mobile.
Iron Road: A Portrait of American Railroading. Richard Snow. LC 78-5388. (Illus.). 96p. (gr. 5 up). 1978. 9.95 (ISBN 0-590-07523-3, Four Winds). Schol Bk Serv.
Iron Road to the West: American Railroads in the 1850's. John F. Stover. LC 78-9588. (Illus.). 1978. 17.50x (ISBN 0-231-04046-6). Columbia U Pr.
Iron Sceptre. John White. (Illus.). 404p. (Orig.). (gr. 4-7). 1981. pap. 7.95 (ISBN 0-87784-589-1). Inter-Varsity.
Iron-Sulfur Proteins, 3 vols. Ed. by Walter Lovenberg. Incl. Biological Properties. Vol. 1, 1973. 53.00 (ISBN 0-12-456001-6); Molecular Properties. Vol. 2, 1974. 49.00 (ISBN 0-12-456002-4); Vol. 3. 1977. 55.00 (ISBN 0-12-456003-2). 1973. 127.50 set (ISBN 0-685-40605-9). Acad Pr.
Iron Tiger. Jack Higgins. 1979. pap. 2.25 (ISBN 0-449-14225-6, GM). Fawcett.
Iron Trail to Stirrup. Lynn Westland. 192p. (YA) 1975. 5.95 (ISBN 0-685-55330-2, Avalon). Bouregy.
Ironbrand. John Morressey. LC 80-80999. 320p. (Orig.). 1980. pap. 2.25 (ISBN 0-87216-689-9). Playboy Pbks.
Ironclad. Seymour Reit. LC 76-50649. (gr. 4-6). 1977. 5.95 (ISBN 0-396-07403-0). Dodd.
Ironhead. Mel Ellis. pap. 0.75 (ISBN 0-671-29540-3). PB.
Ironhead. Gerald Rose. (Illus.). (ps-5). 1973. 6.95 (ISBN 0-571-10301-4, Pub. by Faber & Faber). Merrimack Bk Serv.
Ironic Discourse: An Interdisciplinary Approach. Edmund Wright. (Harvester Studies in Philosophy: No. 19). 1980. text ed. write for info. (ISBN 0-391-01807-8). Humanities.

Ironic Drama. P. Vellacott. LC 74-19522. 276p. 1975. 36.00 (ISBN 0-521-20590-5); pap. 10.50 (ISBN 0-521-09896-3). Cambridge U Pr.

Ironic Historian: The Narrator of Books 3 & 4 of the Faerie Queene. (Elizabethan Studies: No. 98). 1980. pap. text ed. 25.00x (ISBN 0-391-02186-9). Humanities.

Irony & Consciousness: American Historiography & Reinhold Niebuhr's Vision. Richard Reinitz. LC 77-92574. 232p. Date not set. 18.00 (ISBN 0-8387-2062-5). Bucknell U Pr.

Irony & Self-Knowledge in the Creation of Tragedy. Frances E. Bolen. (Salzburg Studies in English Literature, Elizabethan & Renaissance Studies: No. 18). 379p. 1973. pap. text ed. 25.00x (ISBN 0-391-01330-0). Humanities.

Irony in Shakespeare's Roman Plays. Michael Payne. (Salzburg Studies in English Literature, Elizabethan & Renaissance Studies: No. 19). 224p. 1976. pap. text ed. 25.00x (ISBN 0-391-01495-1). Humanities.

Irony in the Medieval Romance. D. H. Green. LC 78-14930. 1979. 69.00 (ISBN 0-521-22458-6). Cambridge U Pr.

Irony in the Mind's Life: Essays on Novels by James Agee, Elizabeth Bowen, & George Eliot. Robert Coles. LC 74-5260. (University of Virginia Page-Barbour Lecture Ser.). 1974. 12.95x (ISBN 0-8139-0550-8). U Pr of Va.

Irony of Apartheid: The Struggle for National Independence of Afrikaner Calvinism Against British Imperialism. Irving Hexham. (Texts & Studies in Religion: Vol. 8). 1981. soft cover 24.95x (ISBN 0-88946-904-0). E Mellen.

Irony of Democracy. Dye & Zeigler. 420p. 1981. pap. text ed. 12.95 (ISBN 0-87872-278-5). Duxbury Pr.

Irony of Vietnam: The System Worked. Leslie H. Gelb & Richard K. Betts. 1979. 16.95 (ISBN 0-8157-3072-1); pap. 7.95 (ISBN 0-8157-3071-3). Brookings.

Iroquois Indians, Vol. 2. Incl. Historical Report on the Niagara River to 1759. Donald H. Kent; Findings of Fact, & Opinion. Indian Claims Commission. (American Indian Ethnohistory Ser: North Central & Northeastern Indians). (Illus.). lib. bdg. 42.00 (ISBN 0-8240-0769-7). Garland Pub.

Iroquois Indians, Vol. 1: History of Pennsylvania Purchases from the Indians. Donald H. Kent. (American Indian Ethnohistory Ser: North Central & Northeastern Indians). (Illus.). lib. bdg. 42.00 (ISBN 0-8240-0768-9). Garland Pub.

IRP, Vol. III: Police Computer Technology. Kent W. Colton. LC 77-9137. (Irp Ser.). 1978. 24.95 (ISBN 0-669-01786-8). Lexington Bks.

Irradiation Effects in Crystalline Solids. J. Gittus. (Illus.). 1978. 102.60x (ISBN 0-85334-778-6). Intl Ideas.

Irradiation Facilities for Research Reactors. (Illus.). 478p. (Orig., Eng. & Fr.). 1973. pap. 30.00 (ISBN 92-0-050073-0, IAEA). Unipub.

Irrational Man. William Barrett. LC 58-8081. 1958. pap. 4.50 (ISBN 0-385-03138-6, A371, Anch). Doubleday.

Irrational Season. Madeleine L'Engle. 1977. 8.95 (ISBN 0-8164-0324-4). Crossroad NY.

Irreducible Tensor Methods: An Introduction for Chemists. B. L. Silver. 1976. 42.50 o.p. (ISBN 0-12-643650-9). Acad Pr.

Irregular Serials & Annuals. 6th ed. 1143p. 1980. 60.00 (ISBN 0-8352-1241-6). Bowker.

Irresistible Virgin: A Vision of Unrequited Love Within & Outside the Confines of a Closed World. Hugh B. Maya. (Intimate Life of Man Library Book). (Illus.). 1979. 27.75 (ISBN 0-89266-199-2). Am Classical Coll Pr.

IRRI Annual Report for 1978. 478p. 1979. pap. 43.00 (R128, IRRI). Unipub.

IRRI Computerized List System. (IRRI Research Paper Ser.: No. 51). 37p. 1981. pap. 5.00 (R134, IRRI). Unipub.

Irrigated Rice Production Systems. Jaw-Kai Wang & Ross E. Hagan. (Tropical Agriculture Ser.). 1980. lib. bdg. 35.00x (ISBN 0-89158-486-2). Westview.

Irrigation & Agricultural Development. S. S. Johl & C. De Clerq. LC 80-40435. (Illus.). 386p. 1980. 58.00 (ISBN 0-08-025675-9). Pergamon.

Irrigation & Drainage in an Age of Competition for Resources. Compiled by American Society of Civil Engineers. 560p. 1975. pap. text ed. 19.00 (ISBN 0-87262-123-5). Am Soc Civil Eng.

Irrigation & Drainage in the Nineteen Eighties. Compiled by American Society of Civil Engineers. 448p. 1979. pap. text ed. 27.00 (ISBN 0-87262-181-2). Am Soc Civil Eng.

Irrigation: Design & Practice. 2nd ed. Bruce Withers & Stanley Vipond. LC 80-66673. (Illus.). 300p. 1980. soft cover 12.95 (ISBN 0-8014-9874-0). Cornell U Pr.

Irrigation Equipment Manufacturers Directory. 2nd ed. Ed. by International Irrigation Information Center, Bet Dagan, Israel. LC 79-42940. (IIIC Publications: No. 5). 312p. 1980. 58.00 (ISBN 0-08-025512-4). Pergamon.

Irrigation: International Guide to Organizations & Institutions. Ed. by International Irrigation Information Center Bet Dagan, Israel. LC 80-49935. 165p. 1980. 46.00 (ISBN 0-08-026363-1). Pergamon.

Irrigation of Field & Orchard Crops Under Semi-Arid Conditions. Ed. by J. Shalhevet et al. (Illus.). 110p. 1980. pap. 10.50 (ISBN 0-08-025511-6). Pergamon.

Irrigation Planning for Intensive Cultivation. H. L. Sally. 8.00x o.p. (ISBN 0-210-22610-2). Asia.

Irrigation Policy & Management in Southeast Asia. 198p. 1978. pap. 16.00 (R009, IRRI). Unipub.

Irrigation Principles & Practices. 3rd ed. Orson W. Israelsen & Vaughn E. Hansen. LC 62-15179. 1962. 25.95 (ISBN 0-471-42999-6). Wiley.

Irrigation: Theory & Practice. A. M. Michael. 1978. text ed. 30.00 (ISBN 0-7069-0613-6, Pub. by Vikas India). Advent Bk.

Irrupcion Juvenil. Samuel Escobar. LC 77-17648. 96p. (Orig., Span.). 1978. pap. 1.95 (ISBN 0-89922-106-8). Edit Caribe.

Irvin S. Cobb. Fred G. Neuman. (American Newspapermen 1790-1933 Ser.). (Illus.). 275p. 1974. Repr. of 1934 ed. 16.50x o.s.i. (ISBN 0-8464-0011-1). Beekman Pubs.

Is a Job Really Worth It? Sue H. Boggs. 1979. pap. 2.25 (ISBN 0-89137-522-8). Quality Pubns.

Is American Democracy Exportable. Edward McGrath. Ed. by Fred Krinsky & Joseph Boskin. (Insight Series: Studies in Contemporary Issues). 128p. 1968. pap. text ed. 4.95x (ISBN 0-02-476350-0, 47635). Macmillan.

Is Anyone There? Answers About God. David Watson. 120p. 1981. pap. 3.50 (ISBN 0-87788-395-5). Shaw Pubs.

Is Blood Sugar Making You a Nutritional Cripple? rev. ed. Ruth Adams & Frank Murray. 174p. (Orig.). 1975. pap. 1.75 (ISBN 0-915962-11-X). Larchmont Bks.

Is Evolutionism the Answer. Ed. by Commission For Christian Literature. (Truth Unchanging Series). (Illus.). 1968. pap. 2.50 (ISBN 0-8100-0023-7, 12-0331). Northwest Pub.

Is Government the Source of Monopoly? And Other Essays. Yale Brozen. LC 80-14176. (Cato Paper Ser.: No. 9). 80p. 1980. pap. 2.00 (ISBN 0-932790-09-7). Cato Inst.

Is It Hard? Is It Easy? Mary M. Green. LC 60-50169. (ps-1). 1960. PLB 6.95 (ISBN 0-201-09243-3, A-W Childrens). A-W.

Is It Moral to Modify Man? Ed. by Claude A. Frazier. 252p. 1973. 15.75 (ISBN 0-398-02632-7). C C Thomas.

Is It Red? Is It Yellow? Is It Blue? Tana Hoban. LC 78-2549. (Illus.). (gr. k-3). 1978. 7.95 (ISBN 0-688-80171-4); PLB 7.63 (ISBN 0-688-84171-6). Greenwillow.

Is It the Sun, Philibert? Roch Carrier. Tr. by Sheila Fischman from Fr. LC 75-190705. (Anansi Fiction Ser.: No. 20). 100p. 1972. pap. 3.95 (ISBN 0-88784-321-2, Pub. by Hse Anansi Pr Canada). U of Toronto Pr.

Is James Bond Dead? Geraldine Woods & Harold Woods. LC 80-13633. (gr. 4-10). 1980. pap. 1.95 (ISBN 0-88436-763-0). EMC.

Is Man Incomprehensible to Man? Philip H. Rhinelander. (Illus.). 1974. text ed. 10.95x (ISBN 0-7167-0765-9); pap. text ed. 5.95x (ISBN 0-7167-0764-0). W H Freeman.

Is Marriage Necessary? Lawrence Casler. 256p. 1976. pap. 1.50 o.p. (ISBN 0-445-03125-5). Popular Lib.

Is Mormonism Christian? Gordon H. Fraser. 1977. pap. 2.50 (ISBN 0-8024-4169-6). Moody.

Is-Ought Problem: Its History, Analysis, & Dissolution. William H. Bruening. LC 77-18569. 1978. pap. text ed. 8.75x (ISBN 0-8191-0364-0). U Pr of Amer.

Is Probation Working: A Guide for Managers & Methodologists. Jay S. Albanese et al. LC 80-6311. 190p. 1981. lib. bdg. 17.75 (ISBN 0-8191-1507-X); pap. text ed. 8.75 (ISBN 0-8191-1508-8). U Pr of Amer.

Is Public Education Necessary. Samuel L. Blumenfeld. 1981. 10.00 (ISBN 0-8159-5826-9). Devin. Postponed.

Is Salvation Forever? Robert Gromacki. 1973. pap. 3.95 (ISBN 0-8024-7506-X). Moody.

Is Salvation Forever? Robert Gromacki. 1981. pap. 4.95 (ISBN 0-8024-7507-8). Moody.

Is Sexual Reproduction Necessary? Edythe B. Mayes. LC 79-92237. 1980. 15.00 (ISBN 0-89002-157-0); pap. 3.95 (ISBN 0-89002-156-2). Northwoods Pr.

Is Surgery Necessary. Siegfried J. Kra & Robert S. Boltax. 256p. 1981. 10.95 (ISBN 0-02-566560-X). Macmillan.

Is That in the Bible? Chas Potter. 1978. pap. 2.25 (ISBN 0-449-23540-8, Crest). Fawcett.

Is That Mother in the Bottle? Jessica Davidson. LC 72-1997. (Illus.). 128p. (gr. 9 up). 1972. PLB 4.90 o.p. (ISBN 0-531-02575-6). Watts.

Is That My Hook in Your Ear. R. Pearsall. 9.95x (ISBN 0-392-06563-0, SpS). Soccer.

Is the Cat Dreaming Your Dream. Margaret O. Hyde. LC 79-22684. (gr. 7-9). 1980. 7.95 (ISBN 0-07-031594-9). McGraw.

Is the Homosexual My Neighbor? Another Christian View. Letha Scanzoni & Virginia R. Mollenkott. LC 77-20445. 176p. 1980. pap. 4.95 (ISBN 0-06-067076-2, RD 337, HarpR). Har-Row.

Is the Panama Canal Still Essential to the Defense of the Uniited States & the Safety of the Free World? Alfred T. Mahan. (Illus.). 1977. 39.50 (ISBN 0-930008-01-4). Inst Econ Pol.

Is There a Chef in the Kitchen. Mary Barnes. (Illus., Orig.). 1969. pap. 7.50x (ISBN 0-392-06983-0, AUS68-2523, LTB). Soccer.

Is There a Doctor in the Zoo. David Taylor. LC 78-2595. (Illus.). 1978. 8.95 o.p. (ISBN 0-397-01284-5). Lippincott.

Is There an Answer to Death. Peter Kostenbaum. LC 76-1939. (Illus.). 224p. 1976. pap. 3.95 (ISBN 0-13-506097-4). P-H.

Is There Anything I Can Do for You? Dottie Rambo & Dave Huntsinger. (Creek Bank Kids Ser.: Vol. 5). (ps-8). 1979. 3.95 (ISBN 0-914850-74-1). Impact Tenn.

Is There Intelligent Life on Earth? Jack Catran. LC 80-80016. 240p. 1981. 12.95 (ISBN 0-936162-29-5, L42). Lidiraven Bks.

Is There Life After Housework. Don Aslett. (Illus.). 109p. (Orig.). 1980. pap. 4.50. Article One.

Is There Life After Sobriety. Mel B. 1980. pap. 4.95. Hazelden.

Is There Life on a Plastic Planet? Mildred Ames. 144p. (gr. 4-6). 1975. PLB 9.95 (ISBN 0-525-32594-8). Dutton.

Is This My Dinner? Irma S. Black. LC 72-83682. (Self Starter Bks.). (Illus.). 32p. (ps-2). 1972. 6.50g (ISBN 0-8075-3665-2). A Whitman.

Is This My Neighbor? The Union Gospel Mission. J. R. Braun. (Illus.). 60p. (Orig.). 1980. pap. text ed. 8.95 (ISBN 0-933656-08-4). Trinity Pub Hse.

Is Water Quality Enhancement Feasible. Compiled by American Society of Civil Engineers. 144p. 1970. pap. text ed. 11.75 (ISBN 0-87262-025-5). Am Soc Civil Eng.

Is Your Prescription Killing You? Richard Coleman. Ed. by Carolyn Richards. 1980. 9.95 (ISBN 0-87949-164-7). Ashley Bks.

Isa & Kena Upanisads. Upanisads. Tr. by Deb K. Das. (Translated from Sanskrit). 8.00 (ISBN 0-89253-515-6); flexible cloth 4.80 (ISBN 0-89253-499-0). Ind-US Inc.

Isaac & Jacob, God's Chosen Ones. Henri B. Gaubert. (Bible in History Ser.). Date not set. 5.95 o.p. (ISBN 0-8038-3356-3). Hastings.

Isaac & Rebekah. Gordon Lindsay. (Old Testament Ser.). 1.25 (ISBN 0-89985-127-4). Christ Nations.

Isaac Asimov Presents the Best Science Fiction of the 19th Century. Ed. by Isaac Asimov et al. LC 80-27721. 192p. 1981. 9.95 (ISBN 0-8253-0038-X). Beaufort Bks NY.

Isaac Asimov Presents the Great SF Stories, No. 5. Ed. by Isaac Asimov & Martin H. Greenberg. 1981. pap. 2.50 (ISBN 0-87997-604-7, UE1604). Daw Bks.

Isaac Asimov's Adventures of Science Fiction. Ed. by George Scithers. 1980. 9.95 (ISBN 0-8037-3533-2). Dial.

Isaac Asimov's Worlds of Science Fiction. Ed. by George A. Scithers. 288p. 1980. 9.95 (ISBN 0-8037-4192-8). Davis Pubns.

Isaac Babel. R. W. Hallett. LC 72-79939. (Modern Literature Ser.). 1973. 10.95 (ISBN 0-8044-2337-7). Ungar.

Isaac Babel, Russian Master of the Short Story. James E. Falen. LC 74-7169. 1974. 14.50x (ISBN 0-87049-156-3). U of Tenn Pr.

Isaac Bashevis Singer. Irving Malin. LC 73-185350. (Modern Literature Ser.). 128p. 1972. 10.95 (ISBN 0-8044-2588-4). Ungar.

Isaac Bashevis Singer & the Eternal Past. Irving H. Buchen. LC 68-29427. (Gotham Library). 1968. 15.00x (ISBN 0-8147-0062-4); pap. 3.95x (ISBN 0-8147-0063-2). NYU Pr.

Isaac Bashevis Singer Reader. Isaac B. Singer. 586p. 1971. 12.95 (ISBN 0-374-17747-3); pap. 7.95 (ISBN 0-374-64030-0). FS&G.

Isaac Collins: A Quaker Printer in 18th Century America. Richard F. Hixson. (Illus.). 1968. 16.00 (ISBN 0-8135-0570-4). Rutgers U Pr.

Isaac Newton. C. A. Ronan. (Clarendon Biography Ser.). (Illus.). 1976. pap. 3.50 (ISBN 0-912728-05-1). Newbury Bks Inc.

Isaac Newton: Mastermind of Science. David C. Knight. (Biography Ser). (Illus.). (gr. 7 up). 1961. PLB 5.90 o.p. (ISBN 0-531-00910-6). Watts.

Isabel la Catolica. (Span.). 7.50 (ISBN 84-241-5417-7). E Torres & Sons.

Isadora Duncan. Arnold Genthe. LC 79-5300. (Dance Ser.). (Illus.). 1980. Repr. of 1929 ed. lib. bdg. 24.00x (ISBN 0-8369-9306-3). Arno.

Isadora Duncan: The Russian Years. Ilya I. Schneider. Tr. by David Magarshack from Rus. (Da Capo Quality Paperbacks Ser.). (Illus.). 221p. 1981. pap. 6.95 (ISBN 0-306-80142-6). Da Capo.

Isaiah, Vol. I. Paul Butler. LC 75-328170. (Bible Study Textbook Ser.). (Illus.). 1975. 13.50 (ISBN 0-89900-020-7). College Pr Pub.

Isaiah. rev. ed. F. C. Jennings. LC 55-41748. 1935. 9.50 (ISBN 0-87213-420-2). Loizeaux.

Isaiah. John T. Willis. Ed. by David G. Jones. (Living Word Commentary - Old Testament Ser.). 465p. 1980. 13.95 (ISBN 0-8344-0115-0). Sweet.

Isaiah - Jeremiah. rev. ed. Ed. by Irving L. Jensen. (Bible Self-Study Ser). (Illus., Orig.). 1968. pap. 2.25 (ISBN 0-8024-1023-5). Moody.

Isaiah: A Commentary. Solomon Freehof. 1972. 15.00 (ISBN 0-8074-0042-4, 383015). UAHC.

Isaiah & Jeremiah. Gordon Lindsay. (Old Testament Ser.). 1.25 (ISBN 0-89985-155-X). Christ Nations.

Isaiah & the New Jerusalem. R. E. Clements. (Journal for the Study of the Old Testament, Supplement Ser.: No. 13). 1980. text ed. 16.95 (ISBN 0-905774-23-X, Pub. by JSOT Pr England). Eisenbrauns.

Isaiah: Chapters 1-39. G. Buchanan Gray. (International Critical Commentary Ser.). 576p. 1912. text ed. 23.00x (ISBN 0-567-05015-7). Attic Pr.

Isaiah Forty to Sixty-Six. R. N. Whybray. Ed. by Ronald E. Clements. (New Century Bible Commentary). 320p. (Orig.). 1981. pap. 7.95 (ISBN 0-8028-1884-6). Eerdmans.

Isaiah II. August Pieper. 1980. pap. 24.50 (ISBN 0-8100-0109-8). Northwest Pub.

Isaiah-Malachi. Matthew Henry. (Commentary on the Whole Bible Ser: Vol. 4). 12.00 (ISBN 0-8007-0200-X). Revell.

Isaiah Twenty-Four to Twenty-Seven & the Origin of Apocalyptic. William R. Millar. LC 76-3561. (Harvard Semetic Museum Ser.). 1976. 7.50 (ISBN 0-89130-102-X, 040011). Scholars Pr Ca.

Isaiah XXI: A Palimpsest. A. A. Macintosh. LC 79-41375. 160p. 1980. 29.50 (ISBN 0-521-22943-X). Cambridge U Pr.

Isaias W. Hellman & the Farmers & Merchants Bank. Robert G. Cleland & Frank B. Putnam. LC 65-12230. (Huntington Library Classics). 136p. 1980. Repr. of 1965 ed. softcover 4.00 (ISBN 0-87328-018-0). Huntington Lib.

Isak Dinesen's Aesthetics. Thomas R. Whissen. LC 73-83272. 144p. 1974. 10.00 (ISBN 0-8046-9059-6). Kennikat.

Isamu Noguchi: The Life of a Sculptor. Tobi Tobias. LC 72-7560. (Illus.). 48p. (gr. 2-5). 1974. 7.89 (ISBN 0-690-45014-1, TYC-J). T Y Crowell.

Ischemic Heart Disease. Igor K. Shkhvatsabaya. LC 78-31414. (Illus.). 1979. 37.50 (ISBN 0-8016-4624-3). Mosby.

Ischemic Myocardium & Antianginal Drugs. Ed. by Martin Winbury & Yasushi Abiko. (Perspectives in Cardiovascular Research Ser.: Vol. 3). 1979. 25.00 (ISBN 0-89004-380-9). Raven.

Isfahan: Pearl of Persia. Wilfrid Blunt. 1966. 21.95 (ISBN 0-236-31026-7, Pub. by Paul Elek). Merrimack Bk Serv.

Isha Upanishad. Sri Aurobindo. Tr. by Sri Aurobindo. 1979. pap. 2.00 (ISBN 0-89744-922-3). Auromere.

Ishah, la Mujer en la Biblia. Moises Chavez. LC 76-43123. 180p. (Orig., Span.). 1976. pap. 3.25 (ISBN 0-89922-078-9). Edit Caribe.

Ishikawa Takuboku. Yukihito Hijiya. (World Authors Ser.: No. 539). 1979. lib. bdg. 14.95 (ISBN 0-8057-6381-3). Twayne.

Ishkabibble! Dorothy Crayder. LC 75-30862. (Illus.). (gr. 4-6). 1976. 5.95 o.p. (ISBN 0-689-30499-4). Atheneum.

Isidore of Seville's History of the Goths, Vandals, & Suevi. 2nd, rev. ed. Isidore of Seville. Tr. by Gordon B. Ford, Jr. LC 70-509890. 1970. pap. 8.00 o.p. (ISBN 0-916760-00-6). Medieval Latin.

Isis Unveiled, 2 vols. Helena P. Blavatsky. LC 72-186521. 1976. Repr. of 1877 ed. Set. 17.00 (ISBN 0-911500-02-2); Set. softcover 12.50 (ISBN 0-911500-03-0). Theos U Pr.

Isis Unveiled: A Master-Key to the Mysteries of Ancient & Modern Science & Theology, 2 vols. in 1. Helena P. Blavatsky. (Illus.). xlix, 1260p. 1931. Repr. of 1877 ed. 12.50 (ISBN 0-938998-01-3). Theosophy.

Iskandarnamah: A Persian Medieval Alexander-Romance. Tr. by Minoo S. Southgate. LC 77-27047. 1978. 17.50x (ISBN 0-231-04416-X). Columbia U Pr.

Isla Negra. Pablo Neruda. Tr. by Alastair Reid. (Span. & Eng.). 1981. 12.95 (ISBN 0-374-17759-7). FS&G.

Islam. I. G Edmonds. LC 77-2664. (First Bks.). (gr. 5-8). 1977. PLB 6.45 s&l (ISBN 0-531-01288-3). Watts.

Islam, 2 vols. Bernard Lewis. 1976. 15.00 ea. o.s.i.; Vol. 1. (ISBN 0-8027-2023-4); Vol. 2. (ISBN 0-8027-2055-2). Walker & Co.

Islam. 2nd ed. Fazlur Rahman. LC 78-68547. 1979. pap. 6.50 (ISBN 0-226-70280-4); pap. 6.50 (ISBN 0-226-70281-2, P806, Phoen). U of Chicago Pr.

Islam. Edward D. Ross. LC 79-2880. 127p. 1981. Repr. of 1931 ed. 14.50 (ISBN 0-8305-0048-0). Hyperion Conn.

Islam & Capitalism. Maxime Rodinson. LC 73-17297. 1974. 10.00 (ISBN 0-394-46719-1). Pantheon.

Islam & Colonialism. Rudilph Peters. (Religion & Society Ser.). 1980. text ed. 37.50x (ISBN 90-279-3347-2). Mouton.

Islam & Development: Religion and Sociopolitical Change. Ed. by John L. Esposito. 1980. 18.00x (ISBN 0-8156-2229-5); pap. 9.95 (ISBN 0-8156-2230-9). Syracuse U Pr.

Islam & Development: Religion & Sociopolitical Change. Ed. by John L. Esposito. LC 80-25119. (Contemporary Issues in the Middle East Ser.). 292p. 1980. text ed. 22.00x (ISBN 0-8156-2229-5); pap. text ed. 9.95x (ISBN 0-8156-2230-9). Syracuse U Pr.

Islam & International Relations. Ed. by Jesse H. Procler. LC 80-1914. 1981. Repr. of 1965 ed. 27.50 (ISBN 0-404-18969-5). AMS Pr.

Islam & Politics in East Africa: The Sufi Order in Tanzania. August H. Nimtz, Jr. LC 80-429. (Illus.). 1980. 20.00x (ISBN 0-8166-0963-2). U of Minn Pr.

Islam & Social Order in Mauritania: A Case Study from the Nineteenth Century. C. C. Stewart & E. K. Stewart. (Oxford Studies in African Affairs Ser.). 1973. 24.00x (ISBN 0-19-821688-2). Oxford U Pr.

Islam & the Confluence of Religions in Uganda, 1840-1966. Ed. by Noel King. LC 73-85593. (American Academy of Religion. Studies in Religion). 1973. pap. 6.00 (ISBN 0-89130-157-7, 010006). Scholars Pr Ca.

Islam & the Integration of Society. W. Montgomery Watt. 1961. 13.95x o.s.i. (ISBN 0-8101-0240-4). Northwestern U Pr.

Islam & the Modern Age. Ilse Lichtenstadter. 228p. 1980. text ed. 21.00x (ISBN 0-8290-0179-4). Irvington.

Islam & the Plight of Modern Man. Seyyed H. Nasr. LC 75-29014. (World of Islam Ser.). 1976. text ed. 24.00x (ISBN 0-582-78053-5). Longman.

Islam & the Race Question. A. Abd-Al-Qadir Kamil. (Race Question & Modern Thought). (Orig.). 1970. pap. 2.50 (ISBN 92-3-100833-1, U342, UNESCO). Unipub.

Islam & Tribal Art in West Africa. R. A. Bravmann. (African Studies: No. 11). (Illus.). 180p. 1974. 36.00 (ISBN 0-521-20192-6). Cambridge U Pr.

Islam at the Cross Roads: A Brief Survey of the Present Position and Problems of the World of Islam. De Lacy O'Leary. LC 80-1916. 1981. Repr. of 1923 ed. 26.50 (ISBN 0-404-18983-0). AMS Pr.

Islam: Belief & Practices. Arthur S. Tritton. LC 79-2883. 200p. 1981. Repr. of 1954 ed. 18.00 (ISBN 0-8305-0051-0). Hyperion Conn.

Islam: Beliefs & Observances. rev. ed. Caesar E. Farah. LC 72-135505. (Orig.). (YA) 1970. text ed. op (ISBN 0-8120-6022-9); pap. 3.95 (ISBN 0-8120-0277-6). Barron.

Islam Contemporain. Roger Le Journeau. LC 80-1922. 1981. Repr. of 1950 ed. write for info. (ISBN 0-404-18975-X). AMS Pr.

Islam, Europe, & Empire. Norman Daniel. 1967. 35.00x (ISBN 0-85224-108-9, Pub. by Edinburgh U Pr Scotland). Columbia U Pr.

Islam, from the Prophet Muhammad to the Capture of Constantinople Vol. 1: Politics & War. Ed. by Bernard Lewis. (Documentary History of Western Civilization Ser.). 1973. pap. 6.95x (ISBN 0-06-131749-7, TB1749, Torch). Har-Row.

Islam in Egypt Today: Social & Political Aspects of Popular Religion. Morroe Berger. LC 70-113597. 1970. 23.95 (ISBN 0-521-07834-2). Cambridge U Pr.

Islam in India. Ja'Far Sharif. Ed. by William Crooke. Tr. by G. A. Herklots from Hindustani. (Illus.). 414p. 1972. Repr. of 1921 ed. text ed. 15.00x (ISBN 0-7007-0015-3). Humanities.

Islam in the Modern World. Elie Kedourie. 336p. 1981. 16.95 (ISBN 0-686-69288-8). HR&W.

Islam in Tropical Africa. 2nd ed. Ed. by I. M. Lewis. LC 79-3292. 352p. 1980. 25.00x (ISBN 0-253-14956-8); pap. 10.95x (ISBN 0-253-28514-3). Ind U Pr.

Islam in West Africa. John S. Trimingham. 1959. 22.50x (ISBN 0-19-826511-5). Oxford U Pr.

Islam: Its Meaning & Message. Ed. by Khurshid Ahmad. 279p. 1980. 17.50 (ISBN 0-86037-002-X, Pub. by Islamic Council of Europe England); pap. 8.95x (ISBN 0-86037-000-3). Intl Schol Bk Serv.

Islam: Legacy of the Past, Challenge of the Future. Don Peretz et al. 1981. 9.95 (ISBN 0-88427-048-3). Green Hill.

Islam: Legacy of the Past, Challenge of the Future. Don Peretz et al. 160p. 1981. 9.95 (ISBN 0-88427-048-3, Dist. by Caroline Hse). North River.

Islam: Muhammad & His Religion. Ed. by Arthur Jeffrey. LC 58-9958. 1958. pap. 5.75 (ISBN 0-672-60348-9, LLA137). Bobbs.

Islam Observed: Religious Development in Morocco & Indonesia. Clifford Geertz. 1971. pap. 3.95 (ISBN 0-226-28511-1, P439, Phoen). U of Chicago Pr.

Islam Observed: Religious Development in Morocco & Indonesia. Clifford Geertz. LC 68-27753. (Terry Lectures Ser). (Illus.). 1968. 10.00x o.p. (ISBN 0-300-00483-4). Yale U Pr.

Islam: Outline of a Classification Scheme. Ziauddin Sardar. 1979. 12.50 (ISBN 0-89664-408-1, Pub. by K G Saur). Shoe String.

Islam Under the Double Eagle: The Muslims of Bosnia & Hercegovina, 1878-1914. Robert J. Donia. (East Europan Monographs: No. 78). 256p. 1981. text ed. 17.50x (ISBN 0-914710-72-9). East Eur Quarterly.

Islamic Arms & Armour. Ed. by Robert Elgood. (Illus.). 252p. 1979. 175.00x (ISBN 0-85967-470-3, Pub. by Scolar Pr England). Biblio Dist.

Islamic Art. David T. Rice. (World of Art Ser.). (Illus.). 1975. pap. 9.95 (ISBN 0-19-519926-X). Oxford U Pr.

Islamic Art & Architecture. LC 76-14076. (Garland Library of the History of Art: XIII). 1977. lib. bdg. 50.00 (ISBN 0-8240-2423-0). Garland Pub.

Islamic Carpets & Textiles. Friedrich Spuhler. Tr. by George Wingfield Digby & Cornelia Wingfield Digby. (Illus.). 1978. 92.00 (ISBN 0-571-09783-9, Pub. by Faber & Faber). Merrimack Bk Serv.

Islamic City: Selected Papers from the Colloquium Held at the Middle East Centre. 210p. 1980. pap. 13.50 (ISBN 92-3-101665-2, U1033, UNESCO). Unipub.

Islamic Courts in Indonesia: A Study in the Political Bases of Legal Institutions. Daniel S. Lev. LC 78-182281. 304p. 1972. 21.50x (ISBN 0-520-02173-8). U of Cal Pr.

Islamic Dynasties. C. E. Bosworth. 245p. 1980. pap. 9.00x (ISBN 0-85224-402-9, Pub. by Edinburgh U Pr Scotland). Columbia U Pr.

Islamic Dynasties. C. E. Bosworth. 1967. 14.50x (ISBN 0-85224-110-0, Pub. by Edinburgh U Pr Scotland). Columbia U Pr.

Islamic History A. D. Six Hundred to Seven Fifty: New Interpretation I. M. A. Shaban. LC 79-145604. 1971. 37.50 (ISBN 0-521-08137-8); pap. 11.95 (ISBN 0-521-29131-3). Cambridge U Pr.

Islamic History: A.D. 750 to 1055, (A.H. 132 to 448) New Interpretation II, Vol. 2. M. A. Shaban. LC 75-39390. (Illus.). 190p. 1976. 37.50 (ISBN 0-521-21198-0); pap. 11.95 (ISBN 0-521-29453-3). Cambridge U Pr.

Islamic Iran & Central Asia (7th-12th Centuries) Richard N. Frye. 380p. 1980. 75.00x (ISBN 0-86078-044-9, Pub. by Variorum England). State Mutual Bk.

Islamic Metalwork of the Eighth to the Fifteenth Century. Geza Fehervari. 1976. 92.00 (ISBN 0-571-09740-5, Pub. by Faber & Faber). Merrimack Bk Serv.

Islamic Middle East 700-1900: Studies in Economic & Social History. Ed. by A. L. Udovitch. LC 79-52703. (Illus.). 832p. 1981. 24.95x (ISBN 0-87850-030-8). Darwin Pr.

Islamic Movement & the Threat to Western Civilization. Richard N. Sanderson. (Illus.). 141p. 1980. deluxe ed. 47.45 (ISBN 0-930008-59-6). Inst Econ Pol.

Islamic Painting & the Arts of the Book. B. W. Robinson et al. LC 76-15727. 1976. 95.00 o.p. (ISBN 0-684-14789-0, ScribT). Scribner.

Islamic Philosophy & Mysticism. Ed. by Parviz Morewedge. LC 80-14364. 1980. write for info. (ISBN 0-88206-302-2). Caravan Bks.

Islamic Political Thought. W. M. Watt. 186p. 1980. pap. 6.50x (ISBN 0-85224-403-7, Pub. by Edinburgh U Pr Scotland). Columbia U Pr.

Islamic Pottery. Robert J. Charleston. LC 78-55079. (Masterpieces of Western & Near Eastern Ceramics: Vol. IV). (Illus.). 1980. thru. sept. 1980 165.00 (ISBN 0-87011-345-3); thereafter 200.00 (ISBN 0-87011-345-3). Kodansha.

Islamic Pottery. Geza Fehervari. 1973. 45.00 o.p. (ISBN 0-571-09401-5, Pub. by Faber & Faber). Merrimack Bk Serv.

Islamic Society on the South Asian Frontier: The Mappilas of Malabar, 1498 - 1922. Stephen F. Dale. (Illus.). 352p. 1981. 49.00x (ISBN 0-19-821571-1). Oxford U Pr.

Islamic Space. William Corlett & John Moore. LC 79-15204. (Questions Ser.). 1980. 8.95 (ISBN 0-87888-154-9). Bradbury Pr.

Islamic State. Asgar Ali Engineer. 192p. 1980. text ed. 17.95x (ISBN 0-89891-002-1). Advent Bk.

Islamic Textiles. Serteant. 1972. 35.00x (ISBN 0-685-77132-6). Intl Bk Ctr.

Islamization Among the Upper Pokomo. 2nd ed. Robert L. Bunger. LC 80-242. (Foreign & Comparative Studies-African Ser.: No. XXXIII). 128p. (Orig.). 1979. pap. 8.00 (ISBN 0-915984-55-5). Syracuse U Foreign Comp.

Island. Marc Hudson. 1977. 2.50 (ISBN 0-918116-07-4). Jawbone Pr.

Island. Robert Russell. LC 72-83352. 368p. 1972. 9.95 (ISBN 0-8149-0721-0). Vanguard.

Island: A Native History of America's Costal Islands. Bill Thomas. (Illus.). 1980. 29.95 (ISBN 0-393-01373-1). Norton.

Island Adventure. Cleo M. Stephens. (YA) 5.95 (ISBN 0-685-07438-2, Avalon). Bouregy.

Island Bibliographies Supplement. Marie-Helene Sachet & F. Raymond Fosberg. LC 55-60007. 448p. 1971. text ed. 11.00 (ISBN 0-309-01932-X). Natl Acad Pr.

Island Biology. Sherwin Carlquist. LC 73-4643. (Illus.). 656p. 1974. 32.50x (ISBN 0-231-03562-4). Columbia U Pr.

Island Called Moreau. Brian W. Aldiss. 1981. 10.95 (ISBN 0-671-25453-7). S&S.

Island Conquest. Brooke Hastings. 192p. 1981. pap. 1.50 (ISBN 0-671-57067-6). S&S.

Island Destiny. Paula Fulford. 192p. (Orig.). 1980. pap. 1.50. S&S.

Island Destiny. Paula Fulford. (Sihouette Ser.: No. 20). pap. 1.50 (ISBN 0-686-68328-5). PB.

Island Ecology. M. Gorman. LC 79-41166. (Outline Studies in Ecology). 79p. 1979. pap. 5.95x o.p. (ISBN 0-412-15540-0, Pub. by Chapman & Hall). Methuen Inc.

Island Ecology. M. Gormán. LC 79-41166. 79p. 1979. pap. 4.95x o.p. (ISBN 0-470-26751-8). Halsted Pr.

Island Fiesta. Jane Corrie. (Harlequin Romances Ser.). 192p. (Orig.). 1981. pap. 1.25 (ISBN 0-373-02384-7, Pub. by Harlequin). PB.

Island Fighting. Rafael Steinberg. LC 78-52847. (World War II Ser.). (Illus.). 1978. lib. bdg. 14.94 (ISBN 0-686-51047-X). Silver.

Island Fighting. Rafael Steinberg & Time-Life Books Editors. (World War II Ser.). 1978. 12.95 (ISBN 0-8094-2486-X). Time-Life.

Island Flame. Karen Robards. 1981. pap. 2.50 (ISBN 0-8439-0868-8, Leisure Bks). Nordon Pubns.

Island for Dreams. Katrina Britt. (Harlequin Romances Ser.). 192p. 1980. pap. 1.25 (ISBN 0-373-02371-5, Pub. by Harlequin). PB.

Island Futures. Roy Gronneberg. 96p. 1980. pap. 5.95 (ISBN 0-686-68846-5, Pub. by Thule Pr England). Intl Schol Bk Serv.

Island Hopping Through the Indonesian Archipelago. Maurice Taylor. (Illus.). 1976. 19.95x o.p. (ISBN 0-905064-10-0). Intl Learn Syst.

Island in the Crossroads: The History of Puerto Rico. M. M. Brau. LC 68-17802. (gr. 6 up). 4.95 o.p. (ISBN 0-385-06170-6); pap. 2.50 o.p. (ISBN 0-385-06171-4). Doubleday.

Island in the Sky. Ernest K. Gann. 224p. 1981. pap. 2.50 (ISBN 0-515-05483-6). Jove Pubns.

Island Keeper. Harry Mazer. LC 80-39762. 192p. (gr. 6 up). 1981. PLB 8.95 (ISBN 0-440-03976-2). Delacorte.

Island Kingdom Passes. Kathleen D. Mellen. 1958. 7.95 (ISBN 0-8038-3357-1). Hastings.

Island Kingdom Passes: Hawaii Becomes American. new ed. (Kathleen Dickenson Mellen's Epic Saga of the Hawaiian Kingdom). 420p. 1980. pap. 7.95 o.p. (ISBN 0-8038-3429-2). Hastings.

Island Life. LC 77-95115. (Wild, Wild World of Animals Ser.). (Illus.). 1978. lib. bdg. 11.97 (ISBN 0-686-51171-9). Silver.

Island Life. Ed. by Time-Life Books. (Wild, Wild World of Animals). (Illus.). 1978. 10.95 (ISBN 0-913948-19-5). Time-Life.

Island of Bute. Ian S. Munro. (Islands Ser). (Illus.). 208p. 1973. 16.95 (ISBN 0-7153-6081-7). David & Charles.

Island of Doctor Moreau. H. G. Wells. LC 80-110. 1981. Repr. of 1960 ed. lib. bdg. 10.00x (ISBN 0-8376-0431-1). Bentley.

Island of Eden. Leona Morrison. LC 76-41021. 1977. 8.95 o.p. (ISBN 0-688-03151-X). Morrow.

Island of Gold. James Grant. 1978. 7.95 o.s.i. (ISBN 0-8027-5400-7). Walker & Co.

Island of Immunity: Health Secrets from the Andes. Paul Martin. (Illus.). 176p. 1981. 10.00 (ISBN 0-8159-5828-5). Devin.

Island of Isis. William Macquitty. LC 76-5574. (Encore Edition). (Illus.). 192p. 1976. 6.95 o.p. (ISBN 0-684-15694-6, ScribT). Scribner.

Island of One. Eve Bunting. (Science Fiction Ser.). (Illus.). (gr. 3-9). 1978. PLB 5.95 (ISBN 0-87191-626-6); pap. 2.95 (ISBN 0-89812-058-6). Creative Ed.

Island of Peril. John Creasey. 1976. pap. 1.25 o.p. (ISBN 0-445-00379-0). Popular Lib.

Island of Silence. Carolyn Norris. 1976. pap. 1.25 o.p. (ISBN 0-445-00411-8). Popular Lib.

Island of Terror. Elsie W. Strother. (YA) 1976. 4.95 o.p. (ISBN 0-685-68913-1, Avalon). Bouregy.

Island of the Blue Dolphins. Scott O'Dell. (gr. 7 up). 1960. 7.95 (ISBN 0-395-06962-9). HM.

Island of the Pelicans. John D. Mercer & Patricia Mercer. LC 75-39153. (Illus.). 1976. 6.00 (ISBN 0-916480-01-1). Creative Eye.

Island of the Seven Hills. Zoe Cass. 1975. pap. 1.25 o.p. (ISBN 0-445-00277-8). Popular Lib.

Island Ponies: An Environmental Study of Their Life on Assateague. Barbara Ford. LC 79-11026. (Illus.). (gr. 4-6). 1979. 7.50 (ISBN 0-688-22179-3); PLB 7.20 (ISBN 0-688-32179-8). Morrow.

Island Promise. (Orig.). Date not set. pap. 2.50 (ISBN 0-440-04139-2). Dell.

Island Refuge: Britain & Refugees from the Third Reich 1933-1939. A. J. Sherman. 1974. 20.00x (ISBN 0-520-02595-4). U of Cal Pr.

Island Sojourn. Elizabeth Arthur. LC 79-2611. (Illus.). 1980. 9.95 (ISBN 0-06-010156-3, HarpT). Har-Row.

Island Stallion. Walter Farley. (Illus.). (gr. 5-6). 1948. 3.95 (ISBN 0-394-80604-2, BYR); PLB 5.99 (ISBN 0-394-90604-7); pap. 1.95 (ISBN 0-394-84376-2). Random.

Island Stallion Races. Walter Farley. (Illus.). (gr. 4-6). 1965. 3.95 (ISBN 0-394-80611-5, BYR); PLB 5.99 (ISBN 0-394-90611-X); pap. 1.95 (ISBN 0-394-84375-4). Random.

Island Stallion's Fury. Walter Farley. (Illus.). (gr. 5-6). 1951. 3.95 (ISBN 0-394-90607-1, BYR); PLB 5.99 (ISBN 0-394-90607-1); pap. 1.95 (ISBN 0-394-84373-8). Random.

Island Steamers: A Chronology of Steam Transportation to & from the Offshore Islands of Martha's Vineyard & Nantucket. 2nd ed. Paul C. Morris & Joseph F. Morin. Ed. by Sumner A. Towne, Jr. LC 77-79090. (Illus.). 196p. 1977. pap. 11.95 (ISBN 0-686-28900-5). Nantucket Nautical.

Island Sunrise: Prehistoric Culture in the British Isles. Jill P. Walsh. LC 75-4666. (Illus.). 128p. (gr. 6-12). 1976. 8.95 (ISBN 0-395-28928-9, Clarion). HM.

Island Survivors: The Ecology of the Soay Sheep of St. Kilda. Ed. by A. P. Jewell et al. (Illus.). 400p. 1974. text ed. 40.00x (ISBN 0-485-11141-1, Athlone Pr). Humanities.

Island Time. Bette Lamont. LC 75-26998. (Illus.). (gr. k-3). 1976. 7.95 (ISBN 0-397-31568-6). Lippincott.

Island Waterfowl. new ed. Milton W. Weller. (Illus.). 144p. 1980. text ed. 11.95 (ISBN 0-8138-1310-7). Iowa St U Pr.

Islands & People. Leikur & Torshavn. 150p. 1980. 27.50 (ISBN 0-906191-22-X, Pub. by Thule Pr England). Intl Schol Bk Serv.

Islands in the Sky. Arthur C. Clarke. (RL 7). pap. 1.75 (ISBN 0-451-08382-2, E8382, Sig). NAL.

Islands in the Stream. Ernest Hemingway. LC 71-123834. 1970. Hudson River Edition. 20.00x (ISBN 0-684-16499-X); pap. 4.95 (ISBN 0-684-14642-8, ScribT). Scribner.

Islands of the Adriatic. Vladimir Kolar. (Illus.). 1978. 19.95 (ISBN 0-8467-0465-X, Pub. by Two Continents). Hippocrene Bks.

Islands of the Caribbean. Hans W. Hannau. Date not set. 6.45 o.p. (ISBN 0-8038-3395-4). Hastings.

Islands of the Mid-Maine Coast: Penobscot & Blue Hill Bays. Charles B. McLane. (Illus.). 576p. 1981. 35.00 (ISBN 0-933858-00-0, Pub by Kennebec River Pr); signed & numbered limited ed 100.00 (ISBN 0-933858-01-9). TBW Bks.

Islands of the South Pacific: Travel Guide. 3rd ed. Sunset Editiors. LC 79-88018. (Illus.). 128p. 1979. pap. 5.95 (ISBN 0-376-06385-8, Sunset Bks). Sunset-Lane.

Islands off Maine. Leslie Norris. (Illus., Ltd. ed. 50 boxed, 500 trade). 1977. boxed Gray Parrot Deluxe ed. 50.00 (ISBN 0-930954-16-5); pap. 8.50 o.p. (ISBN 0-930954-00-9); deluxe ed. avail. (ISBN 0-930954-16-5). Tidal Pr.

Islands: The Worlds of the Puerto Ricans. Stan Steiner. LC 72-9157. (Illus.). 448p. (YA) 1974. 12.50 o.s.i. (ISBN 0-06-014079-8, HarpT). Har-Row.

Isle of Arran. Robert McLellan. LC 74-20460. 256p. 1976. 13.50 (ISBN 0-7153-6946-6). David & Charles.

Isle of Man. H. S. Corran. (Islands Ser.). 1977. 13.50 (ISBN 0-7153-7417-6). David & Charles.

Isle of Man Railway Album. R. Preston Hendry. LC 75-28. (Illus.). 96p. 1976. 13.50 (ISBN 0-7153-6828-1). David & Charles.

Isle of Mull. P. A. Macnab. (Islands Ser.). (Illus.). 246p. 1974. 16.95 (ISBN 0-7153-4354-8). David & Charles.

Isle of Palms, & Other Poems. John Wilson. Ed. by Donald H. Reiman. LC 75-31275. (Romantic Context Ser.: Poetry 1789-1830: Vol. 121). 1978. Repr. of 1812 ed. lib. bdg. 47.00 (ISBN 0-8240-2221-1). Garland Pub.

Isle of Palms: Sketches of Hainan. American Presbyterian Mission. LC 78-74354. (Modern Chinese Economy Ser.: Vol. 21). 141p. 1980. lib. bdg. 16.50 (ISBN 0-8240-4269-7). Garland Pub.

Isle of the Dead. Roger Zelazny. (Science Fiction Ser.). 208p. 1976. Repr. of 1969 ed. lib. bdg. 11.00 (ISBN 0-8398-2346-0). Gregg.
Isle of the Dead. Roger Zelzany. 192p. 1976. pap. 1.95 (ISBN 0-441-37469-7). Ace Bks.
Isle of Wight. Brian Dicks. LC 75-74082. 1979. 14.95 (ISBN 0-7153-7657-8). David & Charles.
Isle of Wight Album. G. M. Kitchenside. 15.95x (ISBN 0-392-07972-0, SpS). Soccer.
Isle Royale Shipwrecks. 4th ed. (Illus.). 3.95 o.s.i. (ISBN 0-932212-08-5). Avery Color.
Isles of Scilly. Crispin Gill. LC 75-12. (Island Series). (Illus.). 208p. 1975. 16.95 (ISBN 0-7153-6957-1). David & Charles.
Ismaili Contributions to Islamic Culture. Ed. by Seyyed H. Nasr. 1978. 15.00 (ISBN 0-87773-731-2). Great Eastern.
Isn't It a Wonder! Carrie Lou Goddard. LC 75-15664. (Illus.). (gr. k-3). 1976. 7.95 (ISBN 0-687-19715-5). Abingdon.
Isn't It Time He Outgrew This? or A Training Program for Parents of Retarded Children. Victor L. Baldwin et al. (Illus.). 230p. 1980. 13.50 (ISBN 0-398-02636-X). C C Thomas.
Isobel. Jane Parkhurst. 1977. pap. 1.95 o.s.i. (ISBN 0-515-04334-6). Jove Pubns.
Isoelectric Focusing. Ed. by J. P. Arbuthnott & J. A. Beeley. 400p. 1976. 59.95 (ISBN 0-408-70659-7). Butterworths.
Isolated Liver Perfusion & Its Applications. Ed. by I. Bartosek et al. LC 72-95635. (Mario Negri Institute for Pharmacological Research Monographs). (Illus.). 1973. 25.00 (ISBN 0-911216-43-X). Raven.
Isolated Schools. C. Turney et al. 152p. 1980. pap. 8.50x (ISBN 0-424-00068-7, Pub. by Sydney U Pr Australia). Intl Schol Bk Serv.
Isolating Details & Recalling Specific Facts. Glenn R. Williston. (Comprehension Skills Ser.). (Illus.). 64p. (gr. 6-12). 1976. Middle Level. pap. text ed. 2.40x (ISBN 0-89061-072-X, CB9M); Advanced Level. pap. text ed. 2.40x (ISBN 0-89061-020-7, CB9A). Jamestown Pubs.
Isolation of Mechanical Vibration Impact & Noise, AMD Vol. I. Ed. by John C. Snowdon & Eric E. Ungar. 270p. 1973. pap. text ed. 25.00 o.p. (ISBN 0-685-38862-X, G00047). ASME.
Isolation of Plant Growth Substances. Ed. by J. R. Hillman. LC 77-83997. (Society for Experimental Biology Seminar Ser.: No. 4). (Illus.). 1978. 39.50 (ISBN 0-521-21866-7); pap. 13.95x (ISBN 0-521-29297-2). Cambridge U Pr.
Isolation or Interdependence? Ed. by Morton A. Kaplan. LC 74-32547. 1975. 15.95 (ISBN 0-02-916940-2). Free Pr.
Isometric Perspective Designs & How to Create Them. John Locke. (Illus.). 64p. (Orig.). 1981. pap. price not set (ISBN 0-486-24123-8). Dover.
Isometrics: The Static Way to Physical Fitness. Isadore Rossman & Victor Obeck. LC 66-24095. (Illus.). 1966. 7.95 (ISBN 0-87396-017-3); pap. 3.95 (ISBN 0-87396-018-1). Stravon.
Isophotometric Atlas of Comets, 2 pts. W. Hoegner & N. Richter. (Illus.). 1979. Pt. 1. 72.60 (ISBN 0-387-09171-8); Pt. 2. 52.00 (ISBN 0-387-09172-6). Springer-Verlag.
Isotope & Radiation Research on Animal Diseases & Their Vectors. (Proceedings Ser.). 468p. 1980. pap. 58.50 (ISBN 92-0-010080-5, ISP-525, IAEA). Unipub.
Isotope & Radiation Techniques in Soil Physics & Irrigation Studies. (Illus., Orig., Eng., Fr., Rus. & Span.). 1967. pap. 22.50 (ISBN 92-0-010467-3, IAEA). Unipub.
Isotope & Radiation Techniques in Soil Physics & Irrigation Studies - 1973. (Illus.). 517p. (Orig., Eng. & Fr.). 1974. pap. 32.25 (ISBN 92-0-010174-7, IAEA). Unipub.
Isotope Dilution Analysis. J. Tolgyessy et al. 196p. 1972. 27.00 (ISBN 0-08-015856-0). Pergamon.
Isotope Hydrology, 1970. (Illus., Orig., Eng., Fr., Rus. & Span.). 1971. pap. 51.50 (ISBN 92-0-040070-1, IAEA). Unipub.
Isotope Hydrology, 1978, 2 vols. 1979. Vol. 1. pap. 49.25 (ISBN 92-0-040079-5, ISP 493-1, IAEA); Vol. 2. pap. 56.00 (ISBN 92-0-040179-1, ISP 493-2, IAEA). Unipub.
Isotope Ratios As Pollutant Source & Behavior Indicators: Proceedings. Symposium. (Illus.). 489p. 1975. pap. 36.50 (ISBN 92-0-010375-8, IAEA). Unipub.
Isotope Studies on Rice Fertilization. (Technical Reports Ser: No. 181). 1978. pap. 13.00 (ISBN 92-0-115078-4, IDC 181, IAEA). Unipub.
Isotope Studies on the Nitrogen Chain. (Illus., Orig., Eng., Fr. & Rus.). 1968. pap. 21.00 (ISBN 92-0-010068-6, ISP161, IAEA). Unipub.
Isotope Studies on the Physiology of Domestic Animals. (Illus.). 412p. (Orig., Eng., Fr. & Rus.). 1973. pap. 26.75 (ISBN 92-0-010172-0, IAEA). Unipub.
Isotope Studies on Wheat Fertilization. (Illus.). 99p. (Orig.). 1975. pap. 6.50 (ISBN 92-0-115074-1, IAEA). Unipub.
Isotope Techniques for Hydrology. (Technical Reports Ser.: No. 23). (Orig.). 1964. pap. 2.75 (ISBN 92-0-145064-8, IAEA). Unipub.
Isotope Techniques for Studying Animal Protein Production from Non-Protein Nitrogen. (Technical Reports Ser.: No. 111). (Orig.). 1970. pap. 4.50 (ISBN 92-0-115470-4, IAEA). Unipub.
Isotope Techniques in Groundwater Hydrology, 1974, 2 vols. (Illus.). 1003p. (Orig.). 1975. Set. pap. 76.00 (ISBN 0-685-52196-6, ISP373, IAEA). Unipub.
Isotope Tracer Studies of Chemical Residues in Food & the Agricultural Environment. (Illus.). 156p. (Orig.). 1974. pap. 10.75 (ISBN 92-0-111274-2, IAEA). Unipub.
Isotopes & Radiation in Agricultural Research in the Soviet Union. (Study Tour Reports: No. 15). 108p. (Orig.). 1974. pap. 7.50 (ISBN 92-0-117173-0, IAEA). Unipub.
Isotopes & Radiation in Entomology. (Illus., Orig., Eng., Fr., Rus. & Span.). 1968. pap. 22.50 (ISBN 92-0-010168-2, IAEA). Unipub.
Isotopes & Radiation in Parasitology - 2. (Illus., Orig.). 1970. pap. 8.25 (ISBN 92-0-111170-3, IAEA). Unipub.
Isotopes & Radiation in Parasitology - 3. (Illus.). 206p. (Orig.). 1973. pap. 14.50 (ISBN 92-0-111273-4, IAEA). Unipub.
Isotopes & Radiation in Research on Soil-Plant Relationships. 657p. pap. 82.00 (ISBN 0-686-65377-7, ISP 501, IAEA). Unipub.
Isotopes & Radiation in Soil Organic-Matter Studies. (Illus., Orig., Eng., Fr., Rus. & Span.). 1968. pap. 30.00 (ISBN 92-0-010368-5, IAEA). Unipub.
Isotopes & Radiation in Soil-Plant Nutrition Studies. (Illus., Orig., Eng., Fr., Rus. & Span.). 1965. pap. 26.75 (ISBN 92-0-010265-4, IAEA). Unipub.
Isotopes & Radiation in Soil Plant Relationships Including Forestry. (Illus.). 674p. (Orig., Eng., Fr. & Rus.). 1972. pap. 41.75 (ISBN 92-0-010072-4, IAEA). Unipub.
Isotopes in Biological Dinitrogen Fixation. 1979. pap. 29.00 (ISBN 92-0-011078-9, ISP478, IAEA). Unipub.
Isotopes in Hydrology. (Illus., Orig., Eng., Fr. & Rus.). 1967. pap. 35.50 (ISBN 92-0-040067-1, ISP141, IAEA). Unipub.
Isotopes in Lake Studies. 290p. 1980. pap. 36.75 (ISBN 92-0-141179-0, ISP511, IAEA). Unipub.
Isotopes in Plant Nutrition & Physiology. (Illus., Orig., Eng., Fr., Rus. & Span.). 1967. pap. 35.00 (ISBN 92-0-010067-8, IAEA). Unipub.
Isotopes in Weed Research. (Illus., Orig.). 1966. pap. 10.75 (ISBN 92-0-010066-X, IAEA). Unipub.
Isotopic Tracers in Biology: An Introduction to Tracer Methodology. 3rd ed. Martin D. Kamen. (Organic & Biological Chemistry, Vol. 1). 1957. 40.50 (ISBN 0-12-394862-2). Acad Pr.
Isozymes: Current Topics in Biological & Medical Research, Vol. 3. Ed. by Mario C. Rattazzi et al. LC 77-12288. 1979. 22.00x (ISBN 0-8451-0252-4). A R Liss.
Isozymes: Current Topics in Biological & Medical Research, Vol. 4. Ed. by Mario C. Rattazzi et al. LC 77-12288. 218p. 1980. 26.00 (ISBN 0-8451-0253-2). A R Liss.
Israel. Joan Comay & Moshe Pearlman. (Illus.). (gr. 7 up). 1964. 3.95 o.s.i. (ISBN 0-02-724190-4). Macmillan.
Israel. Bill Harris. (Illus.). 1980. 24.95 (ISBN 0-686-68761-2). Mayflower Bks.
Israel. 2nd rev. ed. Nora B. Kubie. (First Bks). (Illus.). (gr. 4-6). 1978. PLB 6.45 s&l (ISBN 0-531-02239-0). Watts.
Israel. Ed. by Daniel Moreau. (Collection monde et voyages). 159p. (Fr.). 1973. 21.00x (ISBN 2-03-053120-0). Larousse.
Israel. Danah Zohar. LC 77-88352. (Countries Ser.). (Illus.). 1978. lib. bdg. 7.95 (ISBN 0-686-51152-2). Silver.
Israel! - Do You Know. L. Richards. 5.95 o.p. (ISBN 0-87747-124-X). Deseret Bk.
Israel: A Developing Society. Ed. by Asher Arian. 456p. 1980. pap. text ed. 14.25x (ISBN 90-232-1710-1). Humanities.
Israel Among the Nations. J. L. Talmon. Ed. by To Mandel. 1971. 11.95 (ISBN 0-02-616250-4). Macmillan.
Israel & Me. Morris Alexander. LC 76-40091. 1977. 10.00 (ISBN 0-8467-0265-7, Pub. by Two Continents). Hippocrene Bks.
Israel & South Africa. 2nd ed. Ed. by George Tomeh. 1973. pap. 1.95 o.p. (ISBN 0-911026-02-9). New World Press NY.
Israel & South Africa: The Progression of a Relationship. LC 76-47719. 1978. pap. 6.00 (ISBN 0-911026-03-7). New World Press NY.
Israel & the Nations in Prophecy. Richard W. De Haan. LC 68-22171. 1971. pap. 1.50 o.p. (ISBN 0-310-23512-X). Zondervan.
Israel and the Palestine Arabs. Don Peretz. LC 80-1915. 1981. Repr. of 1958 ed. 31.00 (ISBN 0-404-18984-9). AMS Pr.
Israel: Chaos & Challenge: Politics vs. Economics. Salomon J. Flink. 265p. 1980. 18.00x (ISBN 965-20-0027-2, Pub. by Turtledove Pr Israel). Intl Schol Bk Serv.
Israel Criminal Procedure Law. (American Series of Foreign Penal Codes: Vol. 13). 66p. 1967. 10.00x (ISBN 0-8377-0033-7). Rothman.
Israel Elihu & Cadwallader Washburn. Gaillard Hunt. LC 71-87440. (American Scene Ser). 1969. Repr. of 1925 ed. lib. bdg. 39.50 (ISBN 0-306-71510-4). Da Capo.
Israel in Europe. G. F. Abbott. Ed. & intro. by C. C. Aronsfeld. 556p. 1972. text ed. 17.00x o.p. (ISBN 0-391-00182-5). Humanities.
Israel in Pictures. rev. ed. Sterling Publishing Company Editors. LC 62-12601. (Visual Geography Ser). (Illus.). 64p. (gr. 5 up). 1974. PLB 4.99 (ISBN 0-8069-1027-5); pap. 2.95 (ISBN 0-8069-1026-7). Sterling.
Israel in Revolution, 6-74 C.E. A Political History Based on the Writings of Josephus. David M. Rhoads. LC 75-36452. 208p. 1976. 9.95 (ISBN 0-8006-0442-3, 1-442); pap. 5.95 (ISBN 0-8006-1442-9, 1-1442). Fortress.
Israel in the Book of Chronicles. H. G. Williamson. LC 76-11096. 1977. 34.00 (ISBN 0-521-21305-3). Cambridge U Pr.
Israel: Its Life & Culture, 4 bks. Johannes Pederson. Incl. Bks. 1 & 2. 1973. Repr. of 1926 ed. 59.00x (ISBN 0-19-647899-5); Bks. 3 & 4. 2nd ed. 1973. Repr. of 1964 ed. o.p. (ISBN 0-19-647900-2). Oxford U Pr.
Israel Jacobson: The Founder of the Reform Movement in Judaism. Jacob R. Marcus. 10.00 (ISBN 0-685-31435-9, Pub. by Hebrew Union). Ktav.
Israel on Twenty Dollars a Day: 1980-81 Edition. 344p. 1981. pap. 4.95 (ISBN 0-671-25490-1). Frommer-Pasmantier.
Israel: One Land, Two Peoples. Harry B. Ellis. LC 73-175104. (Illus.). 210p. 1972. 8.95 (ISBN 0-690-45028-1, TYC-T). T Y Crowell.
Israel: Pluralism & Conflict. Sammy Smooha. LC 74-76390. 1978. 28.50x (ISBN 0-520-02722-1). U of Cal Pr.
Israel Studies in Criminology, Vol. V. Ed. by S. Giora Shoham. 228p. 1980. 20.00x (ISBN 965-20-0026-4, Pub. by Turtledove Pr Israel). Intl Schol Bk Serv.
Israel: The Challenge of the Fourth Decade. Alon Ben-Meir. 224p. 1978. text ed. 12.95x (ISBN 0-8290-0392-4). Irvington.
Israel: The Eternal Idea. Irving Miller. 1955. 17.50x (ISBN 0-686-50046-6). Elliots Bks.
Israel, The Middle East & the Moral Conscience of the Western World. Robert L. Schuster. (Major Currents in Contemporary World History). (Illus.). 133p. 1981. 47.85 (ISBN 0-89266-301-4). Am Classical Coll Pr.
Israel Today. rev. ed. Harry Essrig & Abraham Segal. LC 77-7536. (Illus.). (YA) (gr. 8-10). 1977. text ed. 8.50 (ISBN 0-8074-0007-6, 142601); tchrs'. guide 5.00 (ISBN 0-8074-0050-5, 202601). UAHC.
Israel: Utopia Incorporated. Uri Davis. 182p. 1977. 10.00 (ISBN 0-905762-12-6, Pub. by Zed Pr); pap. 6.00 (ISBN 0-905762-13-4). Lawrence Hill.
Israel: Years of Challenge. David Ben-Gurion. 1963. 5.00 o.p. (ISBN 0-03-030985-9). HR&W.
Israeli Army. Edward Luttwak & Dan Horowitz. LC 73-14270. (Illus.). 480p. 1975. 15.00 o.p. (ISBN 0-06-012723-6, HarpT). Har-Row.
Israeli Dilemma: Essays on a Warfare State. G. R. Tamarin. (Publications of Polemological Centre of the Free University of Brussels: Vol. 2). 202p. 1973. pap. text ed. 16.00 (ISBN 90-237-6220-7, Pub. by Swets Serv Holland). Swets North Am.
Israeli Ecstacies - Jewish Agonies. Irving L. Horowitz. 240p. 1974. 12.95 (ISBN 0-19-501747-1). Oxford U Pr.
Israeli-Egyptian War of Attrition, Nineteen Sixty-Nine to Nineteen Seventy: A Case-Study of Limited Local War. Yaacov Bar-Siman-Tov. LC 80-11124. 256p. 1980. 19.50x (ISBN 0-231-04982-X). Columbia U Pr.
Israeli Fitness Strategy: Based on the Physical Training Program of the Israel Defense Forces. Amos Bar-Khama et al. LC 80-15443. (Illus.). 192p. 1980. 10.95 (ISBN 0-688-03628-7). Morrow.
Israeli Fitness Strategy: Based on the Physical Training Program of the Israel Defense Forces. Amos Bar-Khama et al. LC 80-17222. (Illus.). 192p. 1980. pap. 5.95 (ISBN 0-688-08628-4, Quill). Morrow.
Israeli Left: History, Problems, Documents. Peretz Merhav. LC 77-84578. 1980. 15.00 (ISBN 0-498-02184-X). A S Barnes.
Israeli Periodicals & Serials in English & Other European Languages: A Classified Bibliography. Ruth Tronik. LC 73-14901. 1974. 10.00 (ISBN 0-8108-0682-7). Scarecrow.
Israelis: How They Live & Work. Brian Dicks. LC 74-30350. 156p. 1975. text ed. 8.95 (ISBN 0-03-029706-0, HoltC). HR&W.
Israelites. LC 75-4101. (Emergence of Man Ser.). (gr. 6 up). 1975. PLB 9.63 o.p. (ISBN 0-8094-1295-0, Pub. by Time-Life). Silver.
Israelites. Norman Kotker. (Emergence of Man Ser.). (Illus.). 1975. 9.95 (ISBN 0-8094-1294-2); lib. bdg. avail. (ISBN 0-685-72431-X). Time-Life.
Israel's Black Hebrews: Black Americans in Search of Identity. Morris Lounds, Jr. LC 80-5651. 231p. 1981. lib. bdg. 18.25 (ISBN 0-8191-1400-6); pap. text ed. 9.75 (ISBN 0-8191-1401-4). U Pr of Amer.
Israel's Final Holocaust. Jack Van Impe & Roger F. Campbell. 1980. pap. 3.95 (ISBN 0-8407-9400-2). Nelson.
Israel's Oriental Immigrants & Druzes. Alfred Friendly. (Minority Rights Group: No. 12). 1972. pap. 2.50 (ISBN 0-89192-101-X). Interbk Inc.
Israel's Sacred Songs: A Study of Dominant Themes. Harvey H. Guthrie. 1978. pap. 4.95 (ISBN 0-8164-2178-1). Crossroad NY.
Israel's Wisdom Literature: Its Bearing on Theology & the History of Religions. O. S. Rankin. LC 36-33127. 288p. Repr. of 1936 ed. text ed. 7.50 (ISBN 0-567-02214-5). Attic Pr.
Issa Valley. Czeslaw Milosz. Tr. by Louis Iribarne. 1981. 12.95 (ISBN 0-374-17798-8). FS&G.
Issei & Nisei: The Internment Years. D. Kitagawa. 1967. pap. 3.95 (ISBN 0-8164-9244-1). Continuum.
Issues: An Overview of Primary Prevention. Ed. by George W. Albee & Justin M. Joffe. LC 76-53992. (Primary Prevention of Psychopathology Ser.: Vol. 1). (Illus.). 440p. 1977. text ed. 20.00x (ISBN 0-87451-135-6). U Pr of New Eng.
Issues and Concepts in Patient Education. Barbara K. Redman. (Patient Education Series). 160p. 1981. pap. 11.50 (ISBN 0-8385-4405-3). ACC.
Issues & Ideas in America. Ed. by Benjamin J. Taylor & Thurman J. White. LC 76-18769. 1976. 19.95x (ISBN 0-8061-1327-8); pap. 8.95 (ISBN 0-8061-1386-3). U of Okla Pr.
Issues & Prospects for New International Economic Order. William G. Tyler. LC 77-78367. (Illus.). 1977. 19.95 (ISBN 0-669-01445-1). Lexington Bks.
Issues & Trends in Afro-American Journalism. James S. Tinney & Justine J. Rector. LC 80-6074. 371p. 1980. lib. bdg. 20.75 (ISBN 0-8191-1352-2); pap. text ed. 12.50 (ISBN 0-8191-1353-0). U Pr of Amer.
Issues Before the Thirty-Fifth General Assembly of the United Nations. Ed. by Frederic Eckhard & Donald J. Puchala. 150p. 1980. text ed. 12.50x (ISBN 0-8147-2159-1). NYU Pr.
Issues Before the Thirty-Fourth U.N. General Assembly. Ed. by Frederick Eckhard & Donald J. Puchala. LC 76-43509. (UNA-USA Book). 132p. 1979. 11.00x (ISBN 0-8147-2158-3). NYU Pr.
Issues Before the Thirty-Third General Assembly of the United Nations. Ed. by Frederic Eckhard & Ronald H. Linden. LC 76-640166. 1978. 10.00x (ISBN 0-8147-2155-9); pap. 5.00x (ISBN 0-8147-2156-7). NYU Pr.
Issues Debates & Controversies: An Introduction to Sociology. Ritzer. 1972. 7.95x o.s.i. (ISBN 0-205-03499-3, 8134995); instr's manual free o.s.i. (ISBN 0-205-04467-0). Allyn.
Issues, Debates & Controversies: An Introduction to Sociology. 2nd ed. George Ritzer. LC 81-6721'4. 1980. pap. text ed. 10.45 (ISBN 0-205-06721-2, 8167214). Allyn.
Issues Four: Critical Questions for the '70s. L. Reichman & B. J. Wishart. 1972. pap. 7.95x (ISBN 0-02-476850-2, 47685). Macmillan.
Issues in Adolescent Psychology. 3rd ed. Rogers. 1977. pap. 12.95 (ISBN 0-13-506428-7). P-H.
Issues in Adult Basic Education & Other Adult Education: An Annotated Bibliography & Guide to Research. Darlene F. Russ-Eft et al. LC 80-16926. (Garland Bibliographies in Contemporary Educations, Vol. 1; Garland Reference Library of Social Science). 200p. 1981. 25.00 (ISBN 0-8240-9551-0). Garland Pub.
Issues in Adult Development. Dorothy Rogers. LC 79-26993. 1980. pap. text ed. 9.95 (ISBN 0-8185-0385-8). Brooks-Cole.
Issues in American Social Work. Alfred J. Kahn. LC 59-6701. 1959. 20.00x (ISBN 0-231-02239-5). Columbia U Pr.
Issues in American Society. Joseph Boskin. 1978. pap. text ed. 8.95 (ISBN 0-02-472330-4). Macmillan.
Issues in Business: An Introduction to American Enterprise. 3rd ed. Karl F. Price & James W. Walker. LC 76-30750. 1977. text ed. 20.95x (ISBN 0-471-69734-6); instructors manual avail. (ISBN 0-471-02613-1). Wiley.
Issues in Business & Society. 3rd ed. William T. Greenwood. LC 76-12021. (Illus.). 576p. 1976. pap. text ed. 12.75 (ISBN 0-395-21410-6). HM.

Issues in Canadian Nursing. B. Lasor & M. Elliot. 1977. 9.95 o.p. (ISBN 0-13-506220-9); pap. 9.25 (ISBN 0-13-506238-1). P-H.

Issues in Canadian-U. S. Transborder Computer Data Flows. W. E. Cundiff & Mado Reid. 89p. 1979. pap. text ed. 6.50x (ISBN 0-920380-12-3, Pub. by Inst Res Pub Canada). Renouf.

Issues in Child Psychology. 2nd ed. Dorothy Rogers. LC 76-28503. 1977. pap. text ed. 11.95 (ISBN 0-8185-0193-6); test items avail. (ISBN 0-685-74949-5). Brooks-Cole.

Issues in Community Psychology & Preventive Mental Health. American Psychological Association, Division 27. LC 75-140047. 161p. (Orig.). 1971. 14.95 (ISBN 0-87705-022-8); pap. 7.95 (ISBN 0-87705-027-9). Human Sci Pr.

Issues in Contemporary Corrections: Social Control & Conflict. Ed. by C. Ronald Huff. LC 77-81150. (Sage Research Progress Series in Criminology: Vol. 3). 1977. 12.95x (ISBN 0-8039-0914-4); pap. 6.50x (ISBN 0-8039-0909-8). Sage.

Issues in Controlled Substance Use. Committee on Substance Abuse & Habitual Behavior. Ed. by Deborah R. Maloff & Peter K. Levison. LC 80-81027. ix, 183p. 1980. pap. text ed. 8.25 (ISBN 0-309-03041-2). Natl Acad Pr.

Issues in Corrections: A Book of Readings. Edward Eldefonso. LC 73-7365. (Criminal Justice Ser). 320p. 1974. pap. text ed. 7.95x (ISBN 0-02-474110-8). Macmillan.

Issues in Developmental Disabilities. Ronald F. Jarman & J. P. Das. LC 80-12931. 136p. (Orig.). 1980. pap. 11.50 (ISBN 0-8357-0524-2, SS-00136). Univ Microfilms.

Issues in Digital Image Processing. Ed. by R. M. Hralick & J. C. Simon. LC 80-50682. (NATO Advanced Study Institute Ser.: No. 34). 356p. 1980. 40.75x (ISBN 90-286-0460-X). Sijthoff & Noordhoff.

Issues in Foreign Language & Biilingual Education. Adolph Caso. 125p. 1979. pap. 7.50 (ISBN 0-8283-1721-6). Dante U Am.

Issues in Global Politics. Ed. by Gavin Boyd & Charles Pentland. LC 80-69282. 1981. pap. text ed. 9.95 (ISBN 0-02-904470-7). Free Pr.

Issues in Health Care Regulation. Richard S. Gordon. (Regulation of American Business & Industry). (Illus.). 400p. 1980. 35.00 (ISBN 0-07-023780-8, C). McGraw.

Issues in Health Services. Stephen J. Williams. LC 79-22066. (Ser. in the Health Services). 1980. 17.95 (ISBN 0-471-04679-5, Pub. by Wiley-Med). Wiley.

Issues in Instructional Systems Development. Ed. by Harold F. O'Neil, Jr. 224p. 1979. 17.50 (ISBN 0-12-526640-5). Acad Pr.

Issues in International Economics. Ed. by Peter Oppenheimer. (Oxford International Symposia). 300p. 1980. 40.00 (ISBN 0-85362-186-1, Oriel). Routledge & Kegan.

Issues in Library Administration. Ed. by Warren Tsuneishi et al. 140p. 1974. 12.50x (ISBN 0-231-03818-6). Columbia U Pr.

Issues in Life-Span Human Development. Dorothy Rogers. LC 79-27550. 1980. pap. text ed. 9.95 (ISBN 0-8185-0390-4). Brooks-Cole.

Issues in Managerial Finance. 2nd ed. Eugene F. Brigham & Ramon E. Johnson. 1980. pap. text ed. 9.95 (ISBN 0-03-055241-9). Dryden Pr.

Issues in Microanalysis, Vol. 1. Ed. by Robert Dreeben & J. Alan Thomas. LC 79-62118. (Analysis of Educational Productivity Ser.: Vol. 1). 320p. 1980. reference 25.00 (ISBN 0-88410-191-6). Ballinger Pub.

Issues in Nursing Research. Ed. by Florence S. Downs & Juanita W. Fleming. LC 78-21914. 1979. 10.95 (ISBN 0-8385-4436-3). ACC.

Issues in Pacific-Asian American Health & Mental Health. Ed. by Alice K. Murata & Judith Farguhar. (Occasional Paper Ser.). (Orig.). 1981. pap. write for info. (ISBN 0-934584-12-5). Pacific-Asian.

Issues in Participant Observation: A Text & Reader. George J. McCall & J. L. Simmons. (Orig.). 1969. pap. text ed. 11.95 (ISBN 0-201-07027-8). A-W.

Issues in Pharmaceutical Economics. Ed. by Robert I. Chien. LC 78-19726. 1979. 18.95 (ISBN 0-669-02729-4). Lexington Bks.

Issues in Physical Education & Sports. Ed. by George H. McGlynn. LC 73-91388. 1974. pap. text ed. 7.95 (ISBN 0-87484-238-7). Mayfield Pub.

Issues in Police Administration. Harold K. Becker. LC 72-9389. 1970. 10.00 (ISBN 0-8108-0281-3). Scarecrow.

Issues in Police & Criminal Psychology. William Taylor & Michael Braswell. LC 78-61915. 1978. pap. text ed. 10.25 (ISBN 0-8191-0624-0). U Pr of Amer.

Issues in Political Economy: A Critical Approach. Ed. by Francis Green & Petter Nore. 294p. 1980. text ed. 31.25x (ISBN 0-333-25376-0). Humanities.

Issues in Public-Utility Pricing & Regulation. Ed. by Michael A. Crew. LC 79-6033. 1980. 22.95 (ISBN 0-669-03606-4). Lexington Bks.

Issues in Race & Ethnic Relations. Ed. by Jack Rothman. LC 76-9544. 1977. pap. text ed. 9.95 (ISBN 0-87581-193-0). Peacock Pubs.

Issues in Science & Religion. Ian G. Barbour. 1971. pap. 8.50x (ISBN 0-06-131566-4, TB1566, Torch). Har-Row.

Issues in Social Policy. Kathleen Jones et al. 1978. 16.00 (ISBN 0-7100-8972-4); pap. 10.00 (ISBN 0-7100-8973-2). Routledge & Kegan.

Issues in Socialist Economic Modernization. Jan S. Prybyla. 140p. 1980. 19.95 (ISBN 0-03-057962-7). Praeger.

Issues in the Classification of Children: A Sourcebook on Categories, Labels, & Their Consequences. Ed. by Nicholas Hobbs. LC 73-20966. (Social & Behavioral Science Ser.). 1104p. 1974. Set. 37.50x (ISBN 0-87589-426-7); Vol. 1. (ISBN 0-87589-244-2); Vol. 2. (ISBN 0-87589-245-0). Jossey-Bass.

Issues in the Sociology of Criminal Justice. Sheldon R. Olson. LC 74-31261. (Studies in Sociology Ser.). 58p. 1975. pap. text ed. 2.50 (ISBN 0-672-61348-4). Bobbs.

Issues of the Seventies: The Future of Higher Education. Ed. by Fred F. Harcleroad. LC 79-110639. (Higher Education Ser.). 1970. 11.95x o.p. (ISBN 0-87589-057-1). Jossey-Bass.

Issues of Theological Conflict. rev. ed. Richard J. Coleman. 1980. pap. 5.95 o.p. (ISBN 0-8028-1806-4); 12.95 (ISBN 0-8028-3185-0). Eerdmans.

Issues Past & Present: An American History Sourcebook, 2 vols. Ed. by Paludan et al. 1978. Vol. 1. pap. text ed. 6.95x (ISBN 0-669-00784-6); Vol. 2. pap. text ed. 6.95x (ISBN 0-669-00954-7). Heath.

Issues That Divide the Church. Robert Hoyt. 1968. 4.95 o.p. (ISBN 0-02-555190-6); pap. 1.45 (ISBN 0-02-085500-1). Macmillan.

Issunboshi. Ed. by Ruth Tabrah. LC 74-80514. (Illus.). (gr. 1-7). 1974. 5.95 (ISBN 0-89610-004-9). Island Her.

Istanbul. new ed. Colin Thubron. Ed. by Time-Life Books. (Great Cities). (Illus.). 1979. 14.95 (ISBN 0-8094-2335-9). Time-Life.

Istanbul. Colin Thubron. (Great Cities Ser.). (Illus.). 1978. lib. bdg. 14.94 (ISBN 0-686-51004-6). Silver.

Istanbul & the Civilization of the Ottoman Empire. Bernard Lewis. (Centers of Civilization Ser.: No. 9). (Illus.). 1972. 6.95x (ISBN 0-8061-0567-4); pap. 4.95x (ISBN 0-8061-1060-0). U of Okla Pr.

It. William Mayne. LC 78-1902. (gr. 5-9). 1978. 7.95 (ISBN 0-688-80173-0); PLB 7.63 (ISBN 0-688-84173-2). Greenwillow.

It All Adds Up to Love. Finney & Jepson. pap. 2.95 (ISBN 0-89728-040-7, 669881). Omega Pubns OR.

It All Began with Jane Eyre: Or, the Secret Life of Franny Dillman. Sheila Greenwald. (Illus.). (gr. 3-7). 1980. 7.95 (ISBN 0-316-32671-2, Pub. by Atlantic-Little Brown). Little.

It Can Happen to You. Ernest Holmes. Ed. by Willis Kinnear. 1959. pap. 3.50 (ISBN 0-911336-25-7). Sci of Mind.

It Changed My Life. Betty Friedan. 1977. pap. 2.25 o.s.i. (ISBN 0-440-13936-8). Dell.

It Could Always Be Worse: A Yiddish Folk Tale. Retold by & illus. by Margot Zemach. LC 76-53895. 32p. (ps-3). 1977. 7.95 (ISBN 0-374-33650-4). FS&G.

It Could Happen to Anyone. Margaret M. Craig. (gr. 7-10). 1970. pap. 0.95 o.p. (ISBN 0-425-02988-3, S2591, Highland). Berkley Pub.

It Depends: A Poet's Notebook. Eugenio Montale. Tr. by G. Singh from Ital. LC 80-16629. 192p. 1980. 12.95 (ISBN 0-8112-0773-0); pap. 4.95 (ISBN 0-8112-0774-9, NDP507). New Directions.

It Depends: Appropriate Interpersonal Communication. Gaw. 1981. 9.95 (ISBN 0-88284-124-6). Alfred Pub.

It Depends on How You Say It: Dialogues in Everyday Social English. Brita Haycraft & W. R. Lee. LC 80-41174. (Illus.). 128p. 1981. 12.00 (ISBN 0-08-025315-6); pap. 4.95 (ISBN 0-08-025314-8). Pergamon.

It Does Not Die. Maitreyi Devi. (Translated from Bengali). 15.00 (ISBN 0-89253-644-6); flexible cloth 11.00 (ISBN 0-89253-645-4). Ind-US Inc.

It Does Not Say Meow. Beatrice S. De Regniers. LC 72-75704. (Illus.). 40p. (ps-1). 1972. 5.95 (ISBN 0-395-28822-3, Clarion). HM.

It Doesn't Always Have to Rhyme. Eve Merriam. (Illus.). (gr. 5 up). 1964. PLB 5.95 o.p. (ISBN 0-689-20671-2). Atheneum.

It Happened in Chichipica. Francis Kalnay. LC 74-158004. (Illus.). 127p. (gr. 4-6). 1971. 4.95 o.p. (ISBN 0-15-239340-4, HJ). HarBraceJ.

It Happened in Pennsylvania. Eleanor S. Perrott. (gr. 4-5). 1952. pap. 3.50 (ISBN 0-931992-11-7). Penns Valley.

It Happened in Russia. Helene Scriabine. (Illus.). 140p. (Orig.). 1980. pap. 7.00x (ISBN 0-935090-02-9, Dist. by Almanac Press). Maxims Bks.

It Happened in Three Counties. Renee Rosen. 1981. 10.95 (ISBN 0-8062-1586-0). Carlton.

It Happened on Thursday. Judy Delton. Ed. by Kathy Pacini. LC 77-19086. (Concept Bks.). (Illus.). (gr. 1-3). 1978. 6.50 (ISBN 0-8075-3669-5). A Whitman.

It Happened One Day. Charlotte Huber et al. (Wonder-Story Books Ser). (gr. 2). text ed. 8.76 (ISBN 0-06-517502-6, SchDept). Har-Row.

It Happened This Way. Mabel O'Donnell. (Design for Reading Ser). (Illus.). (gr. 1). 1972. text ed. 7.96 (ISBN 0-06-516004-5, SchDept); tchrs' ed. 13.24 (ISBN 0-06-516202-1); wkbk. 2.92, (ISBN 0-06-516303-6) tchr's ed. 5.76 (ISBN 0-06-516403-2); phonics wkbk. 2.68, (ISBN 0-06-516312-5) tchr's ed 5.36 (ISBN 0-06-516412-1); dupl. masters a & b with ans. key 22.52 ea.; mastery test pkg. of 30 14.48 (ISBN 0-06-516612-4). Har-Row.

IT: Interval Training for Lifetime Fitness. Jeffrey Bairstow et al. (Illus.). 194p. 1980. 8.95 (ISBN 0-8037-4087-5). Dial.

It Is Never Too Late to Mend: A Matter-of-Fact Romance, 3 vols. in 2. Charles Reade. LC 80-2496. 1981. Repr. of 1857 ed. Set. 104.00 (ISBN 0-404-19130-4). Vol. 1 (ISBN 0-404-19131-2). Vol. 2 (ISBN 0-404-19132-0). AMS Pr.

It Is No Dream. LC 78-51766. 1978. pap. 3.95 (ISBN 0-915540-21-5). Friends Israel-Spearhead Pr.

It Is Not Lawful for Me to Fight. Jean-Michel Hornus. LC 79-26846. 376p. 1980. pap. 13.95 (ISBN 0-8361-1911-8). Herald Pr.

It Isn't Time That's Passing. Ruskin Bond. 8.00 (ISBN 0-89253-461-3); flexible cloth 4.00 (ISBN 0-89253-462-1). Ind-US Inc.

It May Come in Handy Someday. Ann Tompert. LC 74-19487. (Illus.). 48p. (gr. 4-6). 1975. 5.95 o.p. (ISBN 0-685-50951-6, GB); PLB 5.72 o.p. (ISBN 0-07-064933-2). McGraw.

It Must Be Magic. Charlotte Huber et al. (Wonder-Story Books Ser). (gr. 4). text ed. 5.16 (ISBN 0-06-517504-2, SchDept). Har-Row.

It Only Hurts Between Paydays. 2nd ed. Amy R. Mumford. 160p. 1981. pap. 2.25 (ISBN 0-89636-067-9). Accent Bks.

It Only Hurts Between Paydays. Amy R. Young. LC 75-17366. (Illus.). 1975. pap. 2.25 (ISBN 0-916406-09-1). Accent Bks.

It Only Hurts When I Serve: Best Tennis Humor. Ed. by David Wiltse & Tennis Magazine. LC 80-66687. (Tennis Magazine Bks.). (Illus.). 192p. 1980. 9.95 (ISBN 0-914178-37-7, 41419-4). Golf Digest.

It Seems I Am a Jew: A Samizdat Essay. Grigori Freiman. Ed. & tr. by Melvyn B. Nathanson. LC 80-404. (Science & International Affairs Ser.). 120p. 1980. 9.95 (ISBN 0-8093-0962-9). S Ill U Pr.

It Sounds Like Fun: How to Use & Enjoy Your Tape Recorder & Stereo. Edward F. Dolan, Jr. (Illus.). 192p. 1981. PLB price not set (ISBN 0-671-34053-0). Messner.

It Was a Short Summer, Charlie Brown. Schulz. (gr. 3-5). 1980. pap. 1.95 (ISBN 0-590-30059-8, Schol Pap). Schol Bk Serv.

It Was a Short Summer, Charlie Brown. Charles Schulz. pap. 1.25 (ISBN 0-451-07958-2, Y7958, Sig). NAL.

It Was a Wonderful Summer for Running Away. Charles N. Barnard. LC 78-17282. 1978. 8.95 (ISBN 0-396-07574-6). Dodd.

Italian. Holloway Staff. (Harper Phrase Books for the Traveler Ser.). (Orig.). 1977. pap. 1.00 (ISBN 0-8467-0312-2, Pub. by Two Continents). Hippocrene Bks.

Italian-American Folktales. Catherine H. Ainsworth. LC 76-52643. (Folklore Bks.). xii, 180p. 1980. 5.00 (ISBN 0-933190-03-4). Clyde Pr.

Italian-Americans. Luciano J. Iorizzo & Salvatore Mondello. (Immigrant Heritage of America Ser.). lib. bdg. 9.95 (ISBN 0-8057-3234-9). Twayne.

Italian Americans: A Guide to Information Sources. Ed. by Francesco Cordasco. LC 78-4833. (Ethnic Studies Information Guide Ser.: Vol. 2). 1978. 30.00 (ISBN 0-8103-1397-9). Gale.

Italian Ars Nova Music: A Bibliographic Guide to Modern Editions & Related Literature. 2nd, rev. ed. Viola L. Hagopian. LC 70-187748. 1973. 17.50x (ISBN 0-520-02223-8). U of Cal Pr.

Italian Art: Fourteen Hundred to Fifteen Hundred. C. Gilbert. 1980. pap. 10.95 (ISBN 0-13-507947-0). P-H.

Italian Baroque Stage: Documents by Giulio Troili, Andrea Pozzo, Ferdinando Galli-Bibiena, & Baldassare Orsini. Tr. by Dunbar H. Ogden. LC 75-7197. 1978. 25.75x (ISBN 0-520-03006-0). U of Cal Pr.

Italian Bronze Statuettes of the Renaissance. Wilhelm Bode. Ed. by James D. Draper. Tr. by William Gretor. LC 80-82165. (Illus.). 1980. 295.00 (ISBN 0-937370-00-2). MAS De Reinis.

Italian Campaign. Robert Wallace. Ed. by Time-Life Books. (World War II). (Illus.). 1978. 12.95 (ISBN 0-8094-2502-5). Time-Life.

Italian Campaign. Robert Wallace. LC 78-52857. (World War II Ser.). (Illus.). 1978. lib. bdg. 14.94 (ISBN 0-686-51048-8). Silver.

Italian Ceramics. Giuseppe Liverani. Ed. by Robert J. Charleston. LC 78-55079. (Masterpieces of Western & Near Eastern Ceramics Ser.: Vol. V). (Illus.). 308p. 1981. 200.00 (ISBN 0-87011-346-1); pre-April 1981 165.00 (ISBN 0-686-63472-1). Kodansha.

Italian Communist Party: Yesterday, Today, & Tomorrow. Ed. by Simon Serfaty & Lawrence Gray. LC 79-6833. (Contributions in Political Science: No. 46). (Illus.). xiii, 256p. 1980. lib. bdg. 29.95 (ISBN 0-313-20995-2, GIT/). Greenwood.

Italian Cookery-Home Style. rev. ed. Pauline N. Barrese. LC 74-82514. 1977. pap. 5.95 (ISBN 0-912656-69-7). H P Bks.

Italian Cooking for Beginners. Alice Schryver. LC 76-53442. (gr. 7 up). 1977. 6.95 (ISBN 0-396-07428-6). Dodd.

Italian Cotton Industry in the Later Middle Ages: Eleven Hundred to Sixteen Hundred. Maureen F. Mazzaoui. LC 80-41023. (Illus.). 272p. Date not set. price not set (ISBN 0-521-23095-0). Cambridge U Pr.

Italian Dictionary. John Purves. (Routledge Pocket Dictionaries Ser.). 862p. 1980. pap. 8.95 (ISBN 0-7100-0602-0). Routledge & Kegan.

Italian Drawings. Roseline Bacou. LC 68-23040. (Great Drawings of the Louvre Museum Ser: Vol. 2). (Illus.). 1968. 20.00 o.s.i. (ISBN 0-8076-0475-5). Braziller.

Italian Drawings of the Fifteenth, Sixteenth, & Seventeenth Centuries. The Art Institute of Chicago & Harold Joachim. LC 79-14276. (Chicago Visual Library: No. 31). (Illus.). 1979. text ed. 80.00 incl. microfiche (ISBN 0-226-68801-1). U of Chicago Pr.

Italian Drawings 1780-1890. Roberta J. Olson. LC 79-9648. (Illus.). 248p. 1980. 29.95x (ISBN 0-253-11963-4). Ind U Pr.

Italian Economy. Donald C. Templeman. 400p. 1981. 26.95 (ISBN 0-03-057612-1). Praeger.

Italian Element in Milton's Verse. F. T Prince. 183p. 1980. Repr. of 1954 ed. lib. bdg. 30.00 (ISBN 0-8492-2191-9). R West.

Italian-English, English-Italian Commercial Dictionary (1977) Giuseppe Ragazzini & Giancarlo Gagliardelli. 1978. 50.00 (ISBN 0-685-25202-7). Heinman.

Italian Experience in the United States. Silvano M. Tomasi & Madeline H. Engel. 1970. pap. 9.95x (ISBN 0-913256-01-3, Dist. by Ozer). Ctr Migration.

Italian Fascist Party in Power: A Study in Totalitarian Rule. Dante L. Germino. LC 74-80551. 1971. Repr. 16.50 (ISBN 0-86527-108-9). Fertig.

Italian First Year. Angelo Gimondo. (gr. 8-11). 1978. wkbk. 7.17 (ISBN 0-87720-593-0). AMSCO Sch.

Italian First Year. Angelo Gimondo. (Orig.). (gr. 7-12). 1975. pap. text ed. 6.00 (ISBN 0-87720-590-6). AMSCO Sch.

Italian for Beginners. 2nd rev ed. Charles Duff. 1959. pap. 3.95 (ISBN 0-06-463214-8, EH 214, EH). Har-Row.

Italian for Commerce. J. Popescu. 1968. 18.75 (ISBN 0-08-012454-2). Pergamon.

Italian Idioms with Proverbs. Vincent Luciani. 1964. 6.95 (ISBN 0-913298-15-8). S F Vanni.

Italian in America: The Progressive View, 1891-1914. rev. ed. Ed. by Lydio F. Tomasi. LC 72-80258. (Illus.). 221p. 1978. pap. text ed. 9.95x (ISBN 0-913256-03-X, Dist. by Ozer). Ctr Migration.

Italian Jokes. Joe Bonfanti. 1976. pap. 1.25 o.p. (ISBN 0-685-69147-0, LB356ZK, Leisure Bks). Nordon Pubns.

Italian Level Three, Comprehensive. Diego Coscarelli. LC 75-39381. (Regents Exams & Answers Ser.). 1977. pap. 3.95 (ISBN 0-8120-0663-1). Barron.

Italian Linguistics, Nineteen Seventy-Seven-One: Verbi 'modali' an Italiano, No. 3. Ed. by Vincenzo Cascio. 1977. pap. text ed. 8.75x (ISBN 0-391-01996-1). Humanities.

Italian Lordship: The Bishopric of Lucca in the Late Middle Ages. Duane J. Osheim. (UCLA Center for Medieval & Renaissance Studies: Vol. 11). 1977. 15.75x (ISBN 0-520-03005-2). U of Cal Pr.

Italian Made Simple. Eugene Jackson & Joseph LoPreato. 1960. pap. 3.50 (ISBN 0-385-00736-1, Made). Doubleday.

Italian Manpower 225 B.C.-A.D. 14. P. A. Brunt. 1971. 69.00x (ISBN 0-19-814283-8). Oxford U Pr.

Italian Mass Emigration: The Exodus of a Latin People--A Bibliographical Guide to the "Bollettino Dell'Emigrazione, 1902-1927. Francesco Cordasco. (Illus.). 307p. 1980. 47.50x (ISBN 0-8476-6283-7). Rowman.

Italian Merchant in the Middle Ages. Armando Sapori. 1970. pap. text ed. 3.95x (ISBN 0-393-09956-3, NortonC). Norton.

Italian Navy in World War II. Marc'Antonio Bragadin. Tr. by Gale Hoffman. LC 79-6102. (Navies & Man Ser.). (Illus.). 1980. Repr. of 1957 ed. lib. bdg. 32.00x (ISBN 0-405-13031-7). Arno.

Italian Opera in Transition, Eighteen Seventy-One to Eighteen Ninety-Three. Jay Nicolaisen. Ed. by George Buelow. (Studies in Musicology). 273p. 1980. 34.95 (ISBN 0-8357-1121-8, Pub. by UMI Res Pr). Univ Microfilms.

Italian Opera Librettos. Ed. by Howard M. Brown. LC 76-20993. (Italian Opera 1640-1770 Ser.: Vol. 52). 1979. lib. bdg. 75.00 (ISBN 0-8240-2651-9). Garland Pub.

Italian Opera Librettos. Ed. by Howard M. Brown. LC 76-20993. (Italian Opera Ser. 1640 to 1770: Vol. 60). 1979. lib. bdg. 75.00 (ISBN 0-8240-2659-4); lib. bdg. 3700.00 set of 60 vols. (ISBN 0-686-60104-1). Garland Pub.

Italian, Or, the Confessional of the Black Penitents. Ann Radcliffe. Ed. by Frederick Garber. (Oxford English Novels Ser). 1968. 17.95x (ISBN 0-19-255315-1). Oxford U Pr.

Italian Paintings from the Fourteenth to the Eighteenth Century in the Collection of the Baltimore Museum of Art. Ed. by Gertrude Rosenthal. LC 80-66714. 1981. pap. write for info. (ISBN 0-912298-51-0). Baltimore Mus.

Italian Panel Painting of the Fourteenth & Fifteenth Centuries. Miklos Boskovits. Tr. by Elisabeth Hoch from Hungarian. (Illus.). 70p. 1980. 25.00 (ISBN 0-937832-02-2). Dante Univ Bkshlf.

Italian Panel Paintings. Miklos Boskovits. (Illus.). 12.50x (ISBN 0-89918-309-3, H309). Vanous.

Italian Phonetics, Diction & Intonation. Pierina B. Castiglione. 103p. pap. 9.50x (ISBN 0-913298-48-4); castinglone tape set 20.00. S F Vanni.

Italian Popular Tales. Thomas F. Crane. LC 68-21762. 1968. Repr. of 1885 ed. 20.00 (ISBN 0-8103-3462-3). Gale.

Italian Porcelain. Arthur Lane. 1954. 19.95 o.p. (ISBN 0-571-05331-9, Pub. by Faber & Faber). Merrimack Bk Serv.

Italian Primitives at Yale University. Richard Offner. (Illus.). 1927. 75.00x (ISBN 0-685-89760-5). Elliots Bks.

Italian Publishing in the Seventies: An Exhibition (Catalog) pap. 3.00. Boston Public Lib.

Italian Renaissance Illuminations. Ed. by J. J. Alexander. LC 77-2841. (Magnificent Paperback Ser.). (Illus.). 1977. 19.95 (ISBN 0-8076-0863-7); pap. 9.95 (ISBN 0-8076-0864-5). Braziller.

Italian Renaissance in Its Historical Background. 2nd ed. Denys Hay. (Illus.). 1977. 33.50 (ISBN 0-521-21321-5); pap. 7.95 (ISBN 0-521-29104-6). Cambridge U Pr.

Italian Renaissance Studies. Ed. by E. F. Jacob. 1960. 24.95 o.p. (ISBN 0-571-06930-4, Pub. by Faber & Faber). Merrimack Bk Serv.

Italian Repatriation from the United States, 1900-1914. Betty B. Caroli. LC 73-85825. (Illus.). 117p. 1974. pap. 9.95x (ISBN 0-913256-10-2, Dist. by Ozer). Ctr Migration.

Italian School of Design; Being a Series of Facsimiles of Original Drawings by the Most Eminent Painters & Sculptors of Italy, 3 vols. William Y. Ottley. Ed. by Sydney J. Freedberg. LC 77-25758. (Connoisseurship Criticism & Art History Ser.: Vol. 15). (Illus.). 1980. Set. lib. bdg. 250.00 (ISBN 0-8240-3273-X). Garland Pub.

Italian Sculpture of the Renaissance: The Charles Eliot Norton Lectures for the Years 1927-1928. Eric R. Maclagan. LC 70-110272. (Illus.). 1971. Repr. of 1935 ed. lib. bdg. 25.75x (ISBN 0-8371-4498-1, MAIS). Greenwood.

Italian Stage from Goldoni to D'annunzio. Marvin Carlson. LC 80-10554. 225p. 1981. lib. bdg. write for info. (ISBN 0-89950-000-5). McFarland & Co.

Italian Story. Geoffrey Trease. LC 64-16262. (Illus.). 1964. 8.95 (ISBN 0-8149-0221-9). Vanguard.

Italian Straw Hat. Eugene M. Labiche. Tr. by Frederick Davies. Bd. with Spelling Mistakes. LC 67-28051. (Orig.). (gr. 8up). 1967. pap. 2.65x (ISBN 0-87830-543-2). Theatre Arts.

Italian Studies in the Philosophy of Science. Ed. by M. L. Chiara. Tr. by Carolyn Fawcett. (Boston Studies in the Philosophy of Science Ser.: No. 47). 525p. 1980. lib. bdg. 73.50 (ISBN 90-277-0735-9); pap. 34.00 (ISBN 90-277-1073-2). Kluwer Boston.

Italian Syntax. Ed. by A. Radford. LC 77-71424. (Cambridge Studies in Linguistics: No. 21). 1977. 42.50 (ISBN 0-521-21643-5). Cambridge U Pr.

Italian Textbook: Ci Divertiamo con la Famiglia Tatasure. Carmen P. Malandrino. LC 76-20046. (Illus.). 1977. text ed. 8.50 o.p. (ISBN 0-682-48608-6, University). Exposition.

Italian Townscape. Ivor De Wolfe. LC 66-10392. (Illus.). 1966. 12.50 o.p. (ISBN 0-8076-0350-3). Braziller.

Italian Two & Three Years. Paul D. Cincinnato & Joseph A. Tursi. (It.). (gr. 9-12). 1978. pap. text ed. 6.50 (ISBN 0-87720-594-9). AMSCO Sch.

Italian Villas & Their Gardens. Edith Wharton. LC 76-10659. (Architecture & Decorative Arts Ser.). 1976. lib. bdg. 39.50 (ISBN 0-306-70817-5); pap. 8.95 (ISBN 0-306-80048-9). Da Capo.

Italian Villas Today. Marco D. Bardeschi & Giulio Segoloni. (Eng, Fr, It. & Ger.). 25.00 (ISBN 0-685-20599-1). Transatlantic.

Italianissimo: Italian Cooking at Its Best. Pellegrino Artusi. Tr. by Elisabeth Abbott from It. 552p. 1975. 12.50 o.p. (ISBN 0-87140-596-2). Liveright.

Italians: How They Live & Work. Andrew Bryant. LC 75-27493. 164p. 1976. text ed. 8.95 (ISBN 0-03-028511-9, HoltC). HR&W.

Italians in America. rev. ed. Ronald Grossman. LC 66-10149. (In America Bks.). (Illus.). (gr. 5-11). 1979. PLB 5.95 (ISBN 0-8225-0202-X). Lerner Pubns.

Italians in Chicago, 1880-1930: A Study in Ethnic Mobility. Humbert S. Nelli. (Urban Life in America Ser.). (Illus.). 300p. 1973. 15.95 (ISBN 0-19-501283-6); pap. text ed. 4.50x (ISBN 0-19-501674-2). Oxford U Pr.

Italians of San Francisco, Eighteen Fifty to Nineteen Thirty: (Gli Italiani Di San Francisco, 1850 to 1930) dual language ed. Deanna P. Gumina. Tr. by Ennio T. Are. LC 77-89342. 1978. pap. text ed. 9.95x (ISBN 0-913256-28-5, Dist. by Ozer). Ctr Migration.

Italic & Romance: Studies in Historical & Descriptive Linguistics in Honor of Ernst Pulgram. Ed. by Herbert J. Izzo. (Current Issues in Linguistic Theory: Vol. 18). 400p. 1980. text ed. 42.75x (ISBN 90-272-3511-2, Pub. by Benjamins Holland). Humanities.

Italic Handwriting & Calligraphy for the Beginner: A Craft Manual. Charles Lehman. (Illus.). 160p. (Orig.). 1981. pap. 3.95 (ISBN 0-8008-4290-1, 80-53415, Pentalic). Taplinger.

Italie. Ed. by Daniel Moreau. (Collection monde et voyages). (Illus.). 159p. (Fr.). 1973. 21.00x (ISBN 2-03-053102-2, 3898). Larousse.

Italo Svevo. Naomi Lebowitz. 1978. 16.50 (ISBN 0-8135-0848-7). Rutgers U Pr.

Italo Svevo: The Man & the Writer. P. N. Furbank. 1966. 16.50x (ISBN 0-520-00436-1). U of Cal Pr.

Italy. Michael Leech. LC 75-44863. (Macdonald Countries). (Illus.). (gr. 6 up). 1976. PLB 7.95 (ISBN 0-382-06107-1, Pub. by Macdonald Ed). Silver.

Italy. Ed. by Ronald Steel. (Reference Shelf Ser: Vol. 35, No. 6). 1963. 6.25 (ISBN 0-8242-0078-0). Wilson.

Italy: A Modern History. rev. & enl. ed. Denis Mack Smith. LC 69-15851. (History of the Modern World Ser). (Illus.). 1969. 12.50x (ISBN 0-472-07051-7). U of Mich Pr.

Italy A to Z: A Grand Tour of the Classic Cities. Robert S. Kane. LC 76-16247. 1977. 7.95 o.p. (ISBN 0-385-11623-3). Doubleday.

Italy & English Literature: Seventeen Sixty-Four to Nineteen Thirty. Kenneth Churchill. LC 79-55524. 230p. 1980. text ed. 25.00x (ISBN 0-06-491130-6). B&N.

Italy & Spain: 1600-1750. Robert Enggass & Jonathan Brown. (Sources & Documents in the History of Art Ser). 1970. pap. 10.95 ref. ed. (ISBN 0-13-508101-7). P-H.

Italy & the Great War: Politics & Culture, 1870-1914. John A. Thayer. (Illus.). 1964. 37.50 (ISBN 0-299-03280-9). U of Wis Pr.

Italy from Napoleon to Mussolini. Rene Albrecht-Carrie. LC 49-50178. 1950. pap. 6.00x (ISBN 0-231-08508-7). Columbia U Pr.

Italy from Unification to 1919: Growth & Decay of a Liberal Regime. Salvatore Saladino. LC 75-101945. (AHM Europe Since 1500 Ser.). 1970. pap. text ed. 5.95x (ISBN 0-88295-762-7). AHM Pub.

Italy in Pictures. Sterling Publishing Company Editors. LC 66-16199. (Visual Geography Ser). (Illus., Orig.). (gr. 4-12). 1966. PLB 4.99 (ISBN 0-8069-1071-2); pap. 2.95 (ISBN 0-8069-1070-4). Sterling.

Italy in the Age of Dante & Petrarch: 1216-1380. John Larner. (Longman History of Italy Ser.). (Illus.). 288p. 1980. text ed. 43.00 (ISBN 0-686-27681-7). Longman.

Italy in Transition. William Arthur. 469p. 1980. Repr. of 1860 ed. lib. bdg. 50.00 (ISBN 0-89760-005-3). Telegraph Bks.

Italy in Transition: Conflict & Consensus. Ed. by Peter Lange & Sidney Tarrow. 186p. 1980. 25.00x (ISBN 0-7146-3147-7, F Cass Co). Biblio Dist.

Italy, the Least of the Great Powers. R. J. Bosworth. LC 78-18090. (Illus.). 532p. 1980. 69.50 (ISBN 0-521-22366-0). Cambridge U Pr.

Itard, Sequin & Kephart: Sensory Education, a Learning Interpretation. Thomas S. Ball. LC 70-154658. 1971. text ed. 7.95x (ISBN 0-675-09191-8). Merrill.

Itch, Sniffle & Sneeze: All About Asthma, Hay Fever & Other Allergies. Alvin Silverstein & Virginia Silverstein. LC 77-20791. (Illus.). 48p. (gr. 1-5). 1978. 7.95 (ISBN 0-590-07540-3, Four Winds). Schol Bk Serv.

Itching Parrot. Jose J. Fernandez De Lizardi. Tr. & intro. by Katherine A. Porter. LC 80-2479. (Span.). 1981. Repr. of 1942 ed. 39.50 (ISBN 0-404-19113-4). AMS Pr.

Item Banking. R. Wood & L. S. Skurnik. (General Ser.). (Illus.). 184p. 1969. pap. text ed. 15.00x (ISBN 0-901225-10-X, NFER). Humanities.

Iterative Methods for Solution of Operator Equations. N. S. Kurrel. LC 76-1711. (Translations of Mathematical Monographs: Vol. 46). 1976. 24.80 o.p. (ISBN 0-8218-1596-2, MMONO-46). Am Math.

Iterative Solution of Large Linear Systems. David M. Young. 1971. 49.90 o.s.i. (ISBN 0-12-773050-8). Acad Pr.

Ithaca: A Book of Photographs. Ed. by Andrea F. Clardy. (Illus.). 96p. (Orig.). 1980. pap. 8.95 (ISBN 0-935526-03-X). McBooks Pr.

Itinerant Ambassador: The Life of Sir Thomas Roe. Michael J. Brown. LC 77-94064. (Illus.). 324p. 1970. 12.00x (ISBN 0-8131-1192-7). U Pr of Ky.

Itinerant Townsmen: Friendship & Social Order in Urban Uganda. David Jacobson. LC 72-89137. 160p. 1973. pap. 5.95 (ISBN 0-8465-3751-6). Benjamin-Cummings.

Itinerario De la Pasion: Meditacion De la Semana Santa. Cecelio Arrastia. 1978. pap. 2.50 (ISBN 0-311-43036-8). Casa Bautista.

Itinerary of Prince Charles Edward Stuart. Walter B. Blaikie. 1976. 12.50x (ISBN 0-7073-0103-3, Pub. by Scottish Academic Pr Scotland). Columbia U Pr.

It's a Baby! George Ancona. LC 79-10453. (Illus.). (gr. k-3). 1979. PLB 8.95 (ISBN 0-525-32598-0). Dutton.

It's a Funny Thing Humour: The International Conference on Humor & Laughter. Antony J. Chapman & Hugh C. Foot. LC 76-53731. 400p. 1976. text ed. 45.00 (ISBN 0-08-021376-6). Pergamon.

It's a Funny World. Mary Verdick. Ed. by Thomas J. Mooney. (Beginning Pal Paperbacks Ser.). (Illus., Orig.). (gr. 7-12). 1977. pap. text ed. 1.25 (ISBN 0-8374-3458-0). Xerox Ed Pubns.

It's a Good Thing I'm Not Married. Marilyn Gratton. 1975. 1.95 o.p. (ISBN 0-686-17211-6). Sandollar Pr.

It's a Great World. Emilie Loring. 224p. 1980. pap. 1.75. Bantam.

It's a Long Way to Guacamole: The Tex-Mex Cookbook. Rue Judd & Ann Worley. (Illus.). 106p. (Orig.). 1978. pap. 6.00 (ISBN 0-9604842-0-5). J&W Tex-Mex.

It's a Mad Mad World. Paul S. Hagerman. LC 78-51065. (Illus.). 1978. 5.95 (ISBN 0-8069-0120-9); lib. bdg. 5.89 (ISBN 0-8069-0121-7). Sterling.

It's a New Day: Reflections of a House Husband. Hakon Torjesen. 1981. 7.95 (ISBN 0-9602790-6-7). The Garden.

It's a Special Day. Greta Lipson. (gr. k-4). tchrs. ed. 9.95 (ISBN 0-916456-25-0, GA87). Good Apple.

It's a World, World, World, World Mad. Mad Magazine Editors. (Mad Ser.). (Illus.). 1973. pap. 1.75 (ISBN 0-446-94370-3). Warner Bks.

It's a Ziggy World. Tom Wilson. (Alligator Bks). (Illus.). 96p. 1974. pap. 2.50 (ISBN 0-8362-0575-8). Andrews & McMeel.

It's About Love. Joyce Doiron. 1981. 4.95 (ISBN 0-8062-1610-7). Carlton.

It's Alive. Richard Woodley. 1977. pap. 1.95 (ISBN 0-345-27465-2). Ballantine.

It's Alive: The Classic Cinema Saga of Frankenstein. Gregory W. Mank. LC 80-26625. (Illus.). 176p. 1981. 15.00 (ISBN 0-498-02473-3). A S Barnes.

It's All in the Stars, Zolar. 1978. pap. 1.75 o.p. (ISBN 0-449-13566-7, GM). Fawcett.

It's All Relative: Einstein's Theory of Relativity. Necia H. Apfel. LC 80-28188. (Illus.). 144p. (gr. 5 up). 1981. 8.95 (ISBN 0-688-41981-X); PLB 8.59 (ISBN 0-688-51981-4). Morrow.

It's All There If You Want It: And Here Is the Map. Jack E. Blalock, Jr. LC 80-69519. 250p. (Orig.). 1980. 12.95 (ISBN 0-9605156-1-5); pap. 10.95 (ISBN 0-9605156-1-5). Better Am Corp.

It's an Odd World. Paul S. Hagerman. LC 76-51184. (Illus.). (gr. 6 up). 1977. 5.95 (ISBN 0-8069-0112-8); lib. bdg. 5.89 (ISBN 0-8069-0113-6). Sterling.

It's an Old State of Maine Custom. Edwin V. Mitchell. LC 78-8102. 1978. lib. bdg. 11.50 o.p. (ISBN 0-89621-007-3); pap. 4.95x (ISBN 0-89621-006-5). Thorndike Pr.

It's Better to Believe. John D. Verdery. LC 64-20780. 224p. 1964. 7.95 (ISBN 0-87131-009-0). M Evans.

It's Cold in Pongo-Ni. Edward Franklin. LC 65-17368. 1965. 6.95 (ISBN 0-8149-0100-X). Vanguard.

It's Easy to Become a Citizen. Carolyn Bain. LC 68-28131. 1968. pap. 3.50 (ISBN 0-8015-4134-4, Hawthorn). Dutton.

It's Easy to Cook - Favorite American Recipes. Betty L. Torre. LC 76-2826. (gr. 3 up). 1977. 5.95 o.p. (ISBN 0-385-11091-X); PLB write for info. o.p. (ISBN 0-385-11092-8). Doubleday.

It's Easy to Have a Snail Visit You. Ed. by Caroline O'Hagan. LC 79-3457. (Illus.). 24p. (gr. 1-4). 1980. 4.95 (ISBN 0-688-41948-8); PLB 4.76 (ISBN 0-688-51948-2). Lothrop.

It's Easy to Have a Worm Visit You. Ed. by Caroline O'Hagan. LC 79-3454. (Illus.). 24p. (gr. 1-4). 1980. 4.95 (ISBN 0-688-41946-1); PLB 4.76 (ISBN 0-688-51946-6). Lothrop.

It's Easy to Raise & Train a Puppy. Bob Becker. 1950. pap. 1.95 (ISBN 0-385-00102-9, Dolp). Doubleday.

It's Easy to Sew-Knit and Stretch Fabric. Kerstin Martensson. (Illus.). 1973. pap. text ed. 5.95 o.p. (ISBN 0-913212-03-2). Kwik Sew.

It's Easy to Sew Swimwear. Kerstin Martensson. (Illus.). 1971. pap. 5.95 o.p. (ISBN 0-913212-04-0). Kwik Sew.

It's Easy to Sew with Scraps & Remnants. Carol Inouye. LC 76-2784. (gr. 8-9). 1977. 6.95a (ISBN 0-385-11052-9); PLB Doubleday.

It's Everybody's Business: Study Guide & Readings for "Introduction to Business, Third Ed.". 3rd ed. Kathryn W. Hegar. (Illus.). 400p. 1981. 8.95 (ISBN 0-13-506659-X). P-H.

It's for You, Snoopy: Selected Cartoons from "Sunday's Fun Day, Charlie Brown", Vol. 1. Charles M. Schulz. (Peanuts Ser.). (Illus.). 1978. pap. 1.50 (ISBN 0-449-23807-5, Crest). Fawcett.

It's Going to Rain. Ada B. Litchfield. LC 80-12732. (Illus.). 32p. (ps-2). 1980. 8.95 (ISBN 0-689-30779-9). Atheneum.

Its Good to Be Alive. Roy Campanella. (RL 7). pap. 1.25 (ISBN 0-451-05952-2, Y5952, Sig). NAL.

It's Good to Be Black. Ruby B. Goodwin. LC 53-11462. (Arcturus Books Paperbacks). 256p. 1976. pap. 4.95 (ISBN 0-8093-0757-X). S Ill U Pr.

It's Halloween. Jack Prelutsky. (Illus.). 48p. 1980. Repr. pap. 1.50 (ISBN 0-590-03275-5, Schol Pap). Schol Bk Serv.

It's Halloween, Dear Dragon. Hillert. Date not set. lib. bdg. 4.39 (ISBN 0-695-41361-9). Follett.

It's Hard to Be Hip Over Thirty & Other Tragedies of Married Life. Judith Viorst. 1980. 4.95 (ISBN 0-453-00276-5, H276). NAL.

It's Hard to Leave While the Music's Playing. I. S. Cooper. 1978. pap. 1.95 o.p. (ISBN 0-445-04267-2). Popular Lib.

It's How You Say It. Al Berkman. 1977. 12.50 (ISBN 0-934972-04-4). Melrose Pub Co.

It's Just Too Much. Jean D. Okimoto. 128p. (YA) (gr. 5-12). 1980. 8.95 (ISBN 0-399-20737-6). Putnam.

It's Magic. Robert Lopshire. LC 78-78075. (Illus.). (gr. 1-4). 1969. 6.95 o.s.i. (ISBN 0-02-761430-1). Macmillan.

It's Magic? Robert Lopshire. LC 78-78075. (Illus.). 32p. (gr. k-3). 1973. pap. 1.25 o.s.i. (ISBN 0-02-044360-9, Collier). Macmillan.

It's Me & I'm Here: From West Point to Esalen: How a Rigid Overachiever Revolutionized His Life. Harold C. Lyon, Jr. 224p. 1974. 6.95 o.p. (ISBN 0-440-04355-7). Delacorte.

It's Me, O Lord: The Autobiography of Rockwell Kent. Rockwell Kent. LC 77-5590. (Graphic Arts Ser.). (Illus.). 1977. Repr. of 1955 ed. lib. bdg. 50.00 (ISBN 0-306-77412-7). Da Capo.

It's Nesting Time. Roma Gans. LC 64-10861. (Let's-Read-&-Find-Out Science Bk). (Illus.). (gr. k-3). 1964. PLB 6.89 o.p. (ISBN 0-690-45544-5, TYC-J); filmstrip with record 11.95 o.p. (ISBN 0-690-45545-3); filmstrip with cassette 14.95 o.p. (ISBN 0-690-45547-X). T Y Crowell.

It's Nesting Time. Roma Gans. LC 64-10861. (Crocodile Paperbacks Ser.). (Illus.). 33p. (gr. k-3). 1972. pap. 1.45 o.p. (ISBN 0-690-45549-6, TYC-J). T Y Crowell.

It's No Sin to Be Rich: A Defense of Capitalism. William Davis. LC 77-9527. 1977. 8.95 o.p. (ISBN 0-525-66560-9). Elsevier-Nelson.

It's Not Really Magic: Microwave Cooking for Young People. Marie C. Sanderson & Rosella J. Schroeder. LC 79-24795. (Doing & Learning Bks.). (Illus.). 104p. (gr. 5 up). 1981. PLB 7.95 (ISBN 0-87518-196-1). Dillon.

It's Not the End of the World. Judy Blume. LC 70-181739. 160p. (gr. 6-8). 1972. 8.95 (ISBN 0-87888-042-9). Bradbury Pr.
It's Not the End of the World. Judy Blume. (gr. 4-6). 1980. pap. 1.95 (ISBN 0-553-15090-1, Skylark). Bantam.
It's Not Too Late. Fred Carvell & Max Tadlock. 1971. pap. 4.95x (ISBN 0-02-472500-5, 47250). Macmillan.
It's Not Too Late for a Baby: For Men & Women Over Thirty Five. Sylvia P. Rubin. (Illus.). 272p. 1980. 14.95 (ISBN 0-13-507046-5, Spec); pap. 6.95 (ISBN 0-13-507038-4). P-H.
It's Ok If You Don't Love Me. Norma Klein. 1978. pap. 1.95 (ISBN 0-449-23526-2, Crest). Fawcett.
It's Only Rock & Roll. Bruce Pollock. (gr. 12 up). 1980. 7.95 (ISBN 0-395-29182-8). HM.
It's Perfectly True. Ed. by Alma Gilleo. LC 76-730153. (Hans Christian Andersen Cassette Bks). (Illus.). 16p. 1976. 10 bks. & one cassette 21.00 (ISBN 0-89290-001-6). Soc for Visual.
It's Possible. Robert Schuller. 1978. 6.95 o.p. (ISBN 0-8007-0927-6). Revell.
It's Possible. Robert H. Schuller. 1979. pap. 1.75 o.p. (ISBN 0-449-14094-6, GM). Fawcett.
It's Rock 'n' Roll. Gene Busnar. LC 79-10927. (Illus.). 256p. (gr. 7 up). 1979. PLB 9.29 (ISBN 0-671-32977-4). Messner.
It's Scary Sometimes. Tr. by Writers Collective. LC 77-17641. (gr. 4-8). 1978. 8.95 (ISBN 0-87705-366-9). Human Sci Pr.
It's Show Time, Snoopy: Selected Cartoons from "Speak Softly & Carry a Beagle", Vol. II. Charles Schulz. (Peanuts Ser.). (Illus.). 1978. pap. 1.50 (ISBN 0-449-23602-1, Crest). Fawcett.
Its Snowing. Margaret Cosgrove. LC 80-14254. (A Skylight Bk.). (Illus.). 48p. (gr. 2-5). 1980. PLB 5.95 (ISBN 0-396-07851-6). Dodd.
It's So Good, Don't Even Try It Once: Heroin in Perspective. Ed. by David E. Smith & George R. Gay. 224p. 1972. pap. 2.45 o.p. (ISBN 0-13-506584-4). P-H.
It's the A.B.C. Book. Illus. by Joyce Harada. (Illus.). 32p. (ps). Date not set. 6.95 (ISBN 0-89346-157-1). Heian Intl. Postponed.
It's the Family That Counts. Don Hayworth. 1976. 6.95 (ISBN 0-912598-14-X). Florham.
It's Time, My Love, It's Time. Vasiliy Aksyonov. LC 77-108294. 226p. 1974. 3.95 o.s.i. (ISBN 0-87695-026-8). Aurora Pubs.
It's Too Late for Sorry. Emily Hanlon. (gr. 7 up). Date not set. pap. 1.75 (ISBN 0-440-93905-4, LE). Dell.
It's Up to You. Ed. by Joanne Dresner. (Illus.). 1979. pap. text ed. 3.95x (ISBN 0-582-79727-6); cassette 8.95x (ISBN 0-582-79728-4); plastic tote (book & cassette) 10.95 (ISBN 0-582-79771-3). Longman.
It's up to You. Ernest Holmes. 95p. 1968. pap. 3.50 (ISBN 0-911336-34-6). Sci of Mind.
It's Wings That Make Birds Fly: The Story of a Boy. Sandra Weiner. LC 68-12658. (Illus.). (gr. 1-4). 1968. PLB 5.99 (ISBN 0-394-91266-7). Pantheon.
It's Women's Work, Too! Walter Oleksy. LC 80-10879. (Illus.). 192p. (gr. 7 up). 1980. PLB 8.29 (ISBN 0-671-33041-1). Messner.
It's Your Body - Know What the Doctor Ordered: Your Complete Guide to Medical Testing. M. Fox & T. Schnabel. 1979. 10.00 (ISBN 0-13-507624-2). P-H.
It's Your Death, Make the Most of It. Harold Billnitzer. LC 79-88402. 1979. pap. 6.95 (ISBN 0-933350-27-9). wkbk. 0.90 (ISBN 0-933350-28-7). Morse Pr.
It's Your Move: Expressive Movement in the Language Arts Reading Class. Gloria T. Blatt. (Orig.). 1981. pap. 8.95 (ISBN 0-8077-2640-0). Tchrs Coll.
It's Your World. Claudia Blocksom. (Illus.). 40p. (gr. 1-8). 1979. pap. 2.25 (ISBN 0-912300-19-1). Troubador Pr.
Ittki Pittki. Miriam Chaikin. LC 75-137000. (Illus.). (gr. k-3). 1971. 5.95 o.s.i. (ISBN 0-8193-0463-8, Four Winds); PLB 5.41 o.s.i. (ISBN 0-8193-0464-6). Schol Bk Serv.
Itumbiara Hydroelectric Project: Environmental Impact Reconnaissance. Robert Goodland. (Illus.). 1972. pap. 5.00 o.p. (ISBN 0-89327-217-5). NY Botanical.
IUCN Plant Red Data Book. 540p. 1978. pap. 20.00 (ISBN 2-88032-202-2, IUCN84, IUCN). Unipub.
Ivan & the Moscow Circus. Myrna Grant. (gr. 4-8). 1980. pap. write for info. (ISBN 0-8423-1843-7). Tyndale.
Ivan, Divan, & Zariman. Marta Koci. LC 76-25196. (Illus.). (gr. k-3). 1977. 5.95 o.s.i. (ISBN 0-8193-0893-5, Four Winds); PLB 5.41 o.s.i. (ISBN 0-8193-0894-3). Schol Bk Serv.
Ivan Goncharov. Alexandra Lyngstad & Sverre Lyngstad. (World Authors Ser.: Russia: No. 200). lib. bdg. 10.95 (ISBN 0-8057-2380-3). Twayne.
Ivan Krylov. Nikolai L. Stepanov. (World Authors Ser.: Russia: No. 247). lib. bdg. 10.95 (ISBN 0-8057-2504-0). Twayne.
Ivan Mauger's World Speedway Book. Juan Mauger & Peter Oakes. (Illus.). 1974. 9.95 (ISBN 0-7207-0725-0). Transatlantic.
Ivan Pavlov. Jeffrey A. Gray. (Modern Masters Ser.). 1981. pap. 3.95. Penguin.
Ivan the Terrible. Francis Carr. 1981. 18.50x (ISBN 0-389-20150-2). B&N.
Ivan the Terrible. R. G. Skrynnikov. Ed. by Hugh F. Graham. (Russian Ser.: No. 32). 1981. 15.00 (ISBN 0-87569-039-4). Academic Intl.
Ivanhoe. Walter Scott. (Literature Ser.). (gr. 7-12). 1970. pap. text ed. 3.83 (ISBN 0-87720-729-1). AMSCO Sch.
Ivanhoe. Walter Scott. 1962. pap. 0.95 o.s.i. (ISBN 0-02-053760-3, Collier). Macmillan.
I've Decided I Want My Seat Back. Bill Mauldin. LC 63-20294. (Illus.). 1965. 10.00 o.s.i. (ISBN 0-06-012845-3, HarpT). Har-Row.
I've Got This Problem with Sex... Dan Day. (Uplook Ser.). 32p. (YA) 1973. pap. 0.75 (ISBN 0-8163-0012-7, 09790-7). Pacific Pr Pub Assn.
I've Got to Talk to Somebody, God. Marjorie Holmes. LC 69-10938. 1969. 6.95 (ISBN 0-385-05209-X). Doubleday.
I've Heard Those Songs Before: The Weekly Top Ten Tunes from 1930 Through 1980. Elston Brooks. 448p. (Orig.). Date not set. 12.95 (ISBN 0-688-00379-6). Morrow.
I've Met Jesus Christ. Michel Quoist. LC 73-79643. 160p. 1975. pap. 1.95 (ISBN 0-385-02802-4, Im). Doubleday.
Ivies. Peter Q. Rose. (Illus.). 180p. 1980. 17.50 (ISBN 0-7137-0969-3, Pub. by Blandford Pr England). Sterling.
Ivory & Slaves in East Central Africa: Changing Patterns of International Trade to the Late Nineteenth Century. Edward A. Alpers. LC 73-93046. (Illus.). 1975. 20.00 (ISBN 0-520-02689-6). U of Cal Pr.
Ivory City: And Other Stories from India & Pakistan. Marcus Crouch. (Illus.). 192p. (gr. 8-12). 1981. 11.95 (ISBN 0-7207-1188-6). Merrimack Bk Serv.
Ivory Hammer I: 1962-63. 40.00x (ISBN 0-85667-078-2, Pub. by Sotheby Parke Bernet England). Biblio Dist.
Ivory Hammer II: 1963-64. 40.00x (ISBN 0-686-15551-3, Pub. by Sotheby Parke Bernet England). Biblio Dist.
Ivory Hammer III: 1964-65. 40.00x (ISBN 0-85667-079-0, Pub. by Sotheby Parke Bernet England). Biblio Dist.
Ivory Hammer IV: 1965-66. 40.00x (ISBN 0-85667-080-4, Pub. by Sotheby Parke Bernet England). Biblio Dist.
Ivy Book: The Growing & Care of Ivy & Ivy Topiary. Suzanne Pierot. LC 73-1855. (Illus.). 160p. 1974. 8.95 (ISBN 0-02-597500-5). Macmillan.
Ivy Compton-Burnett. Blake Nevius. LC 74-110600. (Columbia Essays on Modern Writers Ser.: No. 47). (Orig.). 1970. pap. 2.00 (ISBN 0-231-02988-8, MW47). Columbia U Pr.
Ivy Tree. Mary Stewart. 1978. pap. 2.25 (ISBN 0-449-23976-4, Crest). Fawcett.
Iwein. Von Aue Hartmann. Tr. by J. W. Thomas. LC 79-1139. 1979. 10.95x (ISBN 0-8032-4404-5). U of Nebr Pr.
Iwein. 2nd ed. Hartmann von Ave. Ed. by G. F. Benecke et al. Tr. & notes by Thomas Cramer. vi, 232p. (Ger.). 1974. 20.00x (ISBN 3-11-004860-4). De Gruyter.
Iwein: Eine Erzaehlung, 2 vols. 7th ed. Hartmann Von Aue. Ed. by G. F. Benecke et al. Incl. Vol. 1. Text. xii, 196p. 1968. 17.75x (ISBN 3-11-000329-5); Vol. 2. Handschriftenuebersicht: Anmerkungen und Lesarten. iv, 227p. 1968. 17.75 (ISBN 3-11-000330-9). (Ger.). De Gruyter.
Ixil Country: A Plural Society in Highland Guatemala. Benjamin N. Colby & Pierre L. Van Den Berghe. 1969. 18.50x (ISBN 0-520-01515-0). U of Cal Pr.
Iz Evreskikh Poetov. Vladislav Khodasevich. (Rus.). 1981. 10.50 (ISBN 0-88233-412-3); pap. 3.50 (ISBN 0-686-66059-5). Ardis Pubs.
Izbrannye Stikhi. Sergei Esenin. (Rus.). 1979. 11.00 o.p. (ISBN 0-88233-590-1); pap. 3.95 (ISBN 0-88233-574-X). Ardis Pubs.

J

J & P Switchgear Book. 7th ed. R. Lythall. LC 72-5777. 800p. 1972. 49.95 (ISBN 0-470-55790-7). Halsted Pr.
J & P Transformer Book. 10th ed. S. Austin Stigant & A. C. Franklin. Ed. by C. A. Worth. 770p. 1973. 76.95 (ISBN 0-470-82505-7). Halsted Pr.
J. B. Priestley: An Annotated Bibliography. Alan E. Day. LC 78-68251. (Garland Reference Library of the Humanities). 350p. 1980. lib. bdg. 35.00 (ISBN 0-8240-9798-X). Garland Pub.
J. B. Watson-the Founder of Behaviourism: A Biography. David Cohen. 1979. 22.00 (ISBN 0-7100-0054-5). Routledge & Kegan.
J-Black Bam & the Masquerades. Garth St. Omer. 1972. 3.95 o.p. (ISBN 0-571-09102-4, Pub. by Faber & Faber). Merrimack Bk Serv.
J. C. Fischer & His Diary of Industrial England, 1815-1841. William O. Henderson. LC 66-55759. (Illus.). 1966. 19.50x (ISBN 0-678-05059-7). Kelley.
J. D. Mari Evans. LC 72-89129. 64p. (gr. 4 up). 1973. PLB 6.95 o.p. (ISBN 0-385-00429-X). Doubleday.
J. D. Polson & the Liberty Head Dimme. Michael Bond. (Illus.). 48p. 1980. 6.95 (ISBN 0-7064-1381-4). Mayflower Bks.
J. D. Salinger. 2nd rev. ed. Warren French. (U. S. Author Ser.: No. 40). 1976. lib. bdg. 9.95 (ISBN 0-8057-7163-8). Twayne.
J. D. Salinger. Ed. by Warren French. (Twayne's U. S. Authors Ser.). 187p. 1963. pap. text ed. 4.95 (ISBN 0-672-61505-3). Bobbs.
J. D. Salinger. James Lundquist. LC 78-4301. (Modern Literature Ser.). 1978. 10.95 (ISBN 0-8044-2560-4); pap. 3.45 (ISBN 0-8044-6452-9). Ungar.
J. D. Salinger: A Thirty Year Bibliography,1938-1968. Kenneth Starosciak. 1971. 6.95 (ISBN 0-87018-072-X). Ross.
J. E. Buttersworth: Nineteenth Century Marine Painter. Rudolph J. Shaefer. LC 74-82666. 1975. 75.00x (ISBN 0-913372-12-9, Pub. by Wesleyan U Pr England). Columbia U Pr.
J. Edgar Thomson, Master of the Pennsylvania. James A. Ward. LC 79-6569. (Contributions in Economics & Economic History: No. 33). (Illus.). xviii, 265p. 1980. lib. bdg. 25.00 (ISBN 0-313-22095-6, WJE/). Greenwood.
J. Evetts Haley: Passing of the Old West. Chandler A. Robinson. Date not set. 12.50 (ISBN 0-8363-0160-9). Jenkins.
J. G. Herder on Social & Political Culture. Ed. by F. M. Barnard. LC 69-11022. (Cambridge Studies in the History & Theory of Politics). (Illus.). 1969. 39.95 (ISBN 0-521-07336-7). Cambridge U Pr.
J. Gresham Machen. Henry W. Coray. 128p. (Orig.). 1981. pap. 4.95 (ISBN 0-8254-2327-9). Kregel.
J. H. Shorthouse. F. J. Wagner. (English Authors Ser.). 1979. 14.50 (ISBN 0-8057-6729-0). Twayne.
J. H. Thomas: A Life for Unity. Gregory Blaxland. 14.95 (ISBN 0-392-07986-0, SpS). Soccer-
J. Hudson Taylor: God's Man in China. Howard Taylor & Mrs. Howard Taylor. 1977. pap. 6.95 (ISBN 0-8024-4225-0). Moody.
J. J. Griesbach. Ed. by D. B. Orchard & R. W. Longstaff. LC 77-27405. (Society for New Testament Studies Monographs: No. 34). 1979. 27.50 (ISBN 0-521-21706-7). Cambridge U Pr.
J. L. Austin: A Critique of Ordinary Language Philosophy. Keith Graham. 1977. text ed. 22.25x (ISBN 0-391-00747-5). Humanities.
J. L. Hobb's Local History & the Library. G. A. Carter. (Grafton Books on Library Science). (Illus.). 1977. lib. bdg. 17.75 o.p. (ISBN 0-233-95615-8). Westview.
J. M. Clark. C. Addison Hickman. (Essays on the Great Economists). 112p. 1975. 12.50x (ISBN 0-231-03187-4); pap. 5.00x (ISBN 0-231-03918-2). Columbia U Pr.
J. M. G. Leclezio. Jennifer R. Waelti-Walters. (World Author Ser.: No. 426). 1977. lib. bdg. 12.50 (ISBN 0-8057-6266-3). Twayne.
J. M. Jujol Architect. R. Saariste & V. Ligtelijn. (Archives d'Architecture Moderne). 150p. (Orig., Fr. & Eng.). 1980. write for info. (ISBN 0-8150-0923-2). Wittenborn.
J. M. Synge & the Western Mind. Weldon Thornton. (Irish Literary Studies: No. 4). 1979. text ed. 20.75x (ISBN 0-901072-89-3). Humanities.
J. M. Synge Centenary Papers, 1971. Ed. by Maurice Harmon. 1972. text ed. 13.25x (ISBN 0-85105-203-7, Dolmen Pr). Humanities.
J. Norman Heard's Bookman's Guide to Americana. 5th ed. Ed. by Robert A. Hamm. LC 67-10190. 1969. 15.00 (ISBN 0-8108-0182-5). Scarecrow.
J. R. McCulloch (1789-1864) Treatise or Taxation? Ed. by B. P. O'Brien. 1974. 30.00x (ISBN 0-7073-0189-0, Pub. by Scottish Academic Pr Scotland). Columbia U Pr.
J. R. R. Tolkien. Katharyn F. Crabbe. LC 80-53699. (Modern Literature Ser.). 200p. 1981. 9.95 (ISBN 0-8044-2134-X); pap. 4.95 (ISBN 0-8044-6091-4). Ungar.
J. Reuben Clark: The Public Years. Frank W. Fox. LC 80-17903. (Illus.). 702p. 12.95 (ISBN 0-87747-834-1). Deseret Bk.
J. Reuben Clark: The Public Years. Frank W. Fox. LC 80-17903. (J. Reuben Clark Three Vol. Ser.). (Illus.). 706p. 1980. 10.95 (ISBN 0-8425-1832-0). Brigham.
J. Robert Oppenheimer: Shatterer of Worlds. Peter Goodchild. (Illus.). 320p. 1981. 15.00 (ISBN 0-686-69049-4). HM.
J. S. Bach, 2 Vols. Albert Schweitzer. (Illus.). 1962. Set. pap. 9.95 (ISBN 0-8283-1733-X, 64); pap. 4.95 ea. Branden.
J. S. Bach, 2 vols. Albert Schweitzer. Tr. by Ernest Newman. Set. 22.00 (ISBN 0-8446-0902-1). Peter Smith.
J. S. Mill. Alan Ryan. (Routledge Author Guides). 1974. 18.00x (ISBN 0-7100-7954-0); pap. 10.95 (ISBN 0-7100-7955-9). Routledge & Kegan.
J. S. Sargent: Paintings, Drawings, Watercolors. Richard Ormond. LC 76-114743. (Illus.). 1970. 30.00 o.s.i. (ISBN 0-06-013249-3, HarpT). Har-Row.
Jacintha Point. Elizabeth Graham. (Harlequin Romances Ser.). 192p. 1980. pap. 1.25 (ISBN 0-373-02374-X, Pub. by Harlequin). PB.
Jack & Fred. Byron Barton. (Illus.). 32p. (gr. k-2). 1974. 8.95 (ISBN 0-02-708400-0, 70840). Macmillan.
Jack & Jill. Louisa M. Alcott. (gr. 5 up). 1879. 9.95 (ISBN 0-316-03092-9). Little.
Jack & Jill: A Study in Our Christian Names. Ernest Weekley. LC 74-148925. 1974. Repr. of 1939 ed. 15.00 (ISBN 0-8103-3649-9). Gale.
Jack & Mitie. George Ohsawa. Ed. by Sandy Rothman. Tr. by Ken Burns from Fr. Orig. Title: Jack et Madame Mitie En Occident. 224p. (Orig.). 1981. pap. 9.50 (ISBN 0-918860-36-9). G Ohsawa.
Jack & the Beanstalk. Illus. by T. Izawa & S. Hijkata. (Puppet Storybooks). (Illus.). 18p. (gr. k-2). 1981. 3.50 (ISBN 0-448-09758-3). G&D.
Jack & the Beanstalk. (Illus.). Arabic 2.50x (ISBN 0-685-82835-2). Intl Bk Ctr.
Jack & the Beanstalk. Bd. with Treasure Island; Bremen Town Musicians; Ugly Duckling; Pussin Boots; Thumbelina. (Pocket Pop-Ups Ser.). (Illus.). (ps-5). 1980. Set. 15.00 (ISBN 0-89346-165-2). Heian Intl.
Jack & the Beanstalk. Joseph Jacobs. Tr. by David Walser. LC 77-23586. (Jan Pienkowski Fairy Tale Lib.). (Illus.). (gr. 1 up). 1978. 2.95 o.p. (ISBN 0-690-03821-6, TYC-J). T Y Crowell.
Jack & the Beanstalk. William D. Johnson. (gr. 1-3). 1976. 6.95 (ISBN 0-316-46941-6). Little.
Jack & the Beanstalk. Stella W. Nathan. (Illus.). 24p. (gr. k-3). 1976. PLB 5.00 (ISBN 0-307-60454-3, Golden Pr). Western Pub.
Jack & the Beanstalk. Illus. by Ed Parker. LC 78-18072. (Illus.). (gr. 1-4). 1979. PLB 5.21 (ISBN 0-89375-125-1); pap. 1.50 (ISBN 0-89375-103-0). Troll Assocs.
Jack & the Beanstalk. Tony Ross. LC 80-67493. (Illus.). 32p. (gr. k-2). 1981. 8.95 (ISBN 0-440-04168-6); PLB 8.44 (ISBN 0-440-04174-0). Delacorte.
Jack & the Beanstalk & Other Stories. (Peter Possum Paperbacks Ser). 1967. pap. 0.95 o.p. (ISBN 0-531-05109-9). Watts.
Jack B. Yeats: A Centenary Gathering. Ed. by Roger McHugh. (Tower Series of Anglo Irish Studies). 1971. pap. text ed. 4.75x (ISBN 0-85105-205-3, Dolmen Pr). Humanities.
Jack Benny: An Intimate Biography. Irving A. Fein. LC 75-30975. (Illus.). 320p. (YA) 1976. 8.95 o.p. (ISBN 0-399-11640-0). Berkley Pub.
Jack Dawn & the Vanishing Horses. Joseph W. Coughlin. 140p. (Orig.). (gr. 5-8). 1980. pap. 2.25. BMA Pr.
Jack Dempsey: The Manassa Mauler. Randy Roberts. LC 80-992. (Illus.). 320p. 1980. pap. 6.95 (ISBN 0-394-17660-X, E759, Ever). Grove.
Jack Fairfax-Blakeborough: Memoirs. Ed. by Noel Fairfax-Blakeborough. 1978. 17.35 (ISBN 0-85131-269-1, Dist. by Sporting Book Center). J A Allen.
Jack Holborn. Leon Garfield. (Windward Bks.). (gr. 7 up). 1965. pap. 0.75 o.p. (ISBN 0-394-82115-0, BYR). Random.
Jack in the Beanstalk. Joanne Greenburg. (Illus.). 48p. (gr. 3 up). 1980. write for info. (ISBN 0-8299-1033-6). West Pub.
Jack Johnson in the Ring & Out. Jack Johnson. LC 72-162515. (Illus.). ix, 259p. 1975. Repr. of 1927 ed. 15.00 (ISBN 0-8103-4047-X). Gale.
Jack Kent's Twelve Days of Christmas. Jack Kent. LC 73-1823. (Illus.). 40p. (gr. 1 up). 1973. 5.95 o.s.i. (ISBN 0-8193-0696-7, Four Winds); PLB 5.41 o.s.i. (ISBN 0-8193-0697-5). Schol Bk Serv.
Jack Kerouac: An Annotated Bibliography of Secondary Sources, 1944-1979. Robert J. Milewski et al. LC 80-24477. (Author Bibliographies Ser.: No. 52). 237p. 1981. 12.50 (ISBN 0-8108-1378-5). Scarecrow.
Jack Lemmon: An Authorized Biography. Don Widener. (Illus.). 256p. 1975. 9.95 o.s.i. (ISBN 0-02-628200-3). Macmillan.
Jack London. Earle Labor. (U. S. Authors Ser.: No. 230). 184p. 1974. lib. bdg. 10.95 (ISBN 0-8057-0455-8). Twayne.
Jack London & Conan Doyle: A Literary Kinship. Dale L. Walker. LC 80-67698. (Sherlock Holmes Monograph). (Illus.). 70p. 1981. 8.95x (ISBN 0-934468-03-6). Gaslight.

Jack London As Poet & As Platform Man. William McDevitt. 32p. 1972. Repr. of 1947 ed. pap. 2.00 o.p. (ISBN 0-915046-03-2). Wolf Hse.

Jack London First Editions. James E. Sisson & Robert W. Martens. LC 78-63374. (Illus.). 1978. 24.50 (ISBN 0-932458-00-9). Star Rover.

Jack London in the High School Aegis. Jack London. Ed. by Jim Sisson. (Illus.). 125p. (Orig.). (gr. 7-12). 1980. pap. 3.95 (ISBN 0-932458-01-7). Star Rover.

Jack Nicholson: The Search for a Superstar. Norman Dickens. (Film Ser.). (Illus., Orig.). 1975. pap. 1.50 o.p. (ISBN 0-451-06726-6, W6726, Sig). NAL.

Jack Nicklaus' Lesson Tee. Jack Nicklaus & Ken Bowden. LC 76-46733. (Illus.). 160p. 1977. 10.95 (ISBN 0-914178-11-3). Golf Digest Bks.

Jack Nicklaus' Playing Lessons. Jack Nicklaus & Ken Bowden. (Illus.). 144p. 1981. 12.95 (ISBN 0-914178-42-3, 42901-9). Golf Digest Bks.

Jack of Shadows. Jack Zelazny. pap. 1.75 (ISBN 0-451-09370-4, E9370, Sig). NAL.

Jack O'Lantern. Edna Barth. LC 73-20194. (Illus.). 48p. (gr. 1-4). 1974. 6.95 (ISBN 0-395-28763-4, Clarion). HM.

Jack Parsley. Fritz K. Downey. 1981. 6.95 (ISBN 0-8062-1682-4). Carlton.

Jack Russell & His Terriers. Dan Russell. 1978. 10.35 (ISBN 0-85131-276-4, Dist. by Sporting Book Center). J A Allen.

Jack Smith: Paintings & Drawings, 1949 to 1976. 96p. 1980. pap. 10.95x (ISBN 0-904461-19-X, Pub. by Geolfrith Pr England). Intl Schol Bk Serv.

Jack Smith's L.A. Jack Smith. LC 80-13127. 224p. 1980. 9.95 (ISBN 0-07-058471-0, GB). McGraw.

Jack Sprat Cookbook: Good Eating on a Low-Cholesterol, Low-Saturated-Fat Diet. Polly Zane. LC 72-79701. 512p. 1980. pap. 6.95 (ISBN 0-06-090803-3, CN 803, CN). Har-Row.

Jack Sprat Cookbook, or Good Eating on a Low-Cholesterol Diet. Polly Zane. LC 72-79701. (Illus.). 510p. 1973. 12.95 o.p. (ISBN 0-06-014801-2, HarpT). Har-Row.

Jack Sprat's Legacy: The Science & Politics of Fat & Cholesterol. Patricia Hausman. 320p. 1981. 12.95 (ISBN 0-399-90111-6). Marek.

Jack Teagarden (Jazz) Jay D. Smith & Len Guffridge. 208p. 21.50 (ISBN 0-306-70813-2). Da Capo.

Jack: The Struggles of John F. Kennedy. Herbert S. Parmet. 1980. 14.95 (ISBN 0-8037-4452-8). Dial.

Jack the Wise & the Cornish Cuckoos. Mary Calhoun. LC 77-22714. (Illus.). (gr. k-3). 1978. 7.95 (ISBN 0-688-22132-7); PLB 7.63 (ISBN 0-688-32132-1). Morrow.

Jack Vance. Ed. by Tim Underhill & Chuck Miller. (Writers of the 21st Century Ser.). 1981. 12.95 (ISBN 0-8008-4294-4); pap. 5.95 (ISBN 0-8008-4295-2). Taplinger.

Jackal's Gold. Kenneth Fowler. 1981. pap. 1.95 (ISBN 0-440-14237-7). Dell.

Jackie Oh! Kitty Kelley. 1979. pap. 2.50 (ISBN 0-345-28327-9). Ballantine.

Jackie Robinson. Kenneth Rudeen. LC 75-139100. (Biography Ser). (Illus.). (gr. 2-5). 1971. PLB 7.89 (ISBN 0-690-45650-6, TYC-J); pap. 2.95 crocodile paperback ser. (ISBN 0-690-00208-4). T Y Crowell.

Jackie Stewart. Sam Hasegawa. LC 75-1357. (New Creative Education Superstar Bks.). (Illus.). 32p. (gr. 3-6). 1975. PLB 5.95 (ISBN 0-87191-437-9); pap. 2.95 (ISBN 0-89812-178-7). Creative Ed.

Jackie's Book of Household Charts. Jacqueline Hostage. LC 80-68361. (Illus.). 112p. (Orig.). 1981. plastic comb bdg. 5.95 (ISBN 0-932620-04-3). Betterway Pubns.

Jackie's Indoor-Outdoor Gardening Charts. Jacqueline Hostage. (Illus.). 128p. (Orig.). 1981. pap. 5.95 plastic comb bdg. (ISBN 0-932620-07-8). Betterway Pubns.

Jackpot: To the Casino by Bus. Maxine Schneider. (Gambler's Bookshelf). (Illus.). 1977. pap. 2.95 (ISBN 0-89650-577-4). Gamblers.

Jacks & Jack Games: Follow My Fancy. Marta Weigle. Ed. by Jessica H. Davis. LC 71-81735. (Orig.). (gr. 1-6). 1970. pap. 2.00 (ISBN 0-486-22081-8). Dover.

Jackson Five. Charles Morse & Ann Morse. LC 74-12248. (Rock 'n Pop Stars Ser.). (Illus.). 32p. (gr. 3-6). 1974. PLB 5.95 (ISBN 0-87191-389-5); pap. 2.95 (ISBN 0-89812-098-5). Creative Ed.

Jackson Hole. Frank Calkins. 1973. 7.95 o.p. (ISBN 0-394-47437-6). Knopf.

Jackson Hole, Wyoming: In the Shadow of the Tetons. David J. Saylor. (Illus.). 1971. pap. 4.95 (ISBN 0-8061-1424-X). U of Okla Pr.

Jacksonian America: Society, Personality, & Politics. rev. ed. Edward Pessen. (Orig.). 1978. pap. text ed. 10.25x (ISBN 0-256-01651-8). Dorsey.

Jacksonian America, 1815-1840: New Society, Changing Politics. Ed. by Frank O. Gatell & John M. McFaul. 1970. 5.95 o.p. (ISBN 0-13-509604-9); pap. 2.95 o.p. (ISBN 0-13-509596-4, S218). P-H.

Jacksonian Democracy in Mississippi. Edwin A. Miles. LC 78-107415. (American Scene Ser). 1970. Repr. of 1960 ed. lib. bdg. 25.00 (ISBN 0-306-71884-7). Da Capo.

Jacksonian Era: Eighteen Twenty-Eight to Eighteen Forty-Eight. Glyndon G. Van Deusen. (New American Nation Ser). 1959. 15.00x o.p. (ISBN 0-06-014485-8, HarpT). Har-Row.

Jacksonian Heritage: Pennsylvania Politics, 1833-1848. Charles M. Snyder. LC 59-9122. 1958. 8.00 (ISBN 0-911124-28-4). Pa Hist & Mus.

Jacksonian Jew: The Two Worlds of Mordecai Noah. Jonathan D. Sarna. LC 79-24379. 1981. text ed. 24.50x (ISBN 0-8419-0567-3). Holmes & Meier.

Jacksonian Panorama. Ed. by Edward Pessen. LC 75-20140. (AHS Ser: No. 85). 1976. pap. 8.95 (ISBN 0-672-60142-7). Bobbs.

Jacksonians Versus the Bank: Politics in the States After the Panic of 1837. James R. Sharp. LC 70-127783. 1970. 22.50x (ISBN 0-231-03260-9). Columbia U Pr.

Jacob A. Riis: The American City. Ed. by James B. Lane. LC 74-77650. 267p. 1974. 17.50 (ISBN 0-8046-9058-8, Natl U). Kennikat.

Jacob & His Son, Joseph. Gordon Lindsay. (Old Testament Ser.). 1.25 (ISBN 0-89985-129-0). Christ Nations.

Jacob Bidermann. Thomas W. Best. (World Authors Ser.: Germany: No. 314). 1974. lib. bdg. 12.50 (ISBN 0-8057-2154-1). Twayne.

Jacob Epstein. Lester & Levy. LC 78-50724. Date not set. price not set casebound (ISBN 0-916526-05-4). Maran Pub.

Jacob Hurd & His Sons, Silversmiths. Hollis French. LC 70-175722. (Architecture & Decorative Art Ser.: Vol. 39). 158p. 1972. Repr. of 1939 ed. lib. bdg. 32.50 (ISBN 0-306-70406-4). Da Capo.

Jacob N. Cardozo. M. Leiman. LC 66-27478. 1966. 20.00x (ISBN 0-231-09608-9). Columbia U Pr.

Jacob, The Supplanter Who Became a Prince with God. Gordon Lindsay. (Old Testament Ser.). 1.25 (ISBN 0-89985-128-2). Christ Nations.

Jacob Tonson, Kit-Cat Publisher. Kathleen M. Lynch. LC 77-111046. (Illus.). 256p. 1971. 15.00x (ISBN 0-87049-122-9). U of Tenn Pr.

Jacob Two: Me & My Human. Sven Hartmann & Thoman Hartner. Ed. by Jack Bernard. Tr. by Angelika Macri. 80p. (gr. k-6). 1981. pap. 7.95 (ISBN 0-8120-2391-9). Barron.

Jacob Two Two Meets the Hooded Fang. Mordecai Richler. 1981. pap. 2.50 (ISBN 0-686-68904-6). Bantam.

Jacobean Dramatic Perspectives. Arthur C. Kirsch. LC 70-180964. 1972. 7.50x o.p. (ISBN 0-8139-0390-4). U Pr of Va.

Jacobean Miscellany. James Hogg. (Jacobean Drama Ser.: No. 95). 1980. pap. text ed. 25.00x (ISBN 0-391-02144-3). Humanities.

Jacobite Rising in Britain Sixteen Eighty-Nine to Seventeen Forty-Six. Bruce Lenman. 1980. text ed. 34.00x (ISBN 0-8419-7004-1). Holmes & Meier.

Jacobite's Journal & Related Writings. Henry Fielding. Ed. by William Coley. LC 73-17020. (Wesleyan Edition of the Works of Henry Fielding Ser.). 1975. 27.50x (ISBN 0-8195-4072-2, Pub. by Wesleyan U Pr). Columbia U Pr.

Jacobowsky & der Oberst. Franz Werfel. Ed. by Gustave O. Arlt. (Illus., Orig., Ger.). 1961. pap. text ed. 3.95x (ISBN 0-89197-250-1). Irvington.

Jacobs Park Killings: A Police Procedural Mystery. William Camp. LC 78-57257. 1979. 8.95 (ISBN 0-8149-0803-9). Vanguard.

Jacopo Sansovino: Architecture & Patronage in Renaissance Venice. Deborah Howard. LC 75-8441. 208p. 1975. 30.00x (ISBN 0-300-01891-6). Yale U Pr.

Jacqueline Kennedy: A Woman for the World. Robert T. Harding & A. L. Holmes. (Illus.). 8.95 o.s.i. (ISBN 0-8149-0115-8). Vanguard.

Jacques Ellul: Interpretive Essays. Jacques Ellul et al. Ed. by Clifford G. Christians & Jay M. Van Hook. LC 80-12342. 340p. 1981. 24.95 (ISBN 0-252-00812-X). U of Ill Pr.

Jacques Hurtubise: Recent Works - Oeuvres Recentes. Mary-Venner Shee. (Illus.). 64p. (Fr. & Eng.). 1981. pap. 10.00 (ISBN 0-936270-16-0). Art Mus Gall.

Jacques Lacan. Anika Lemaire. Tr. by David Macey from Fr. 21.00 (ISBN 0-7100-8621-0). Routledge & Kegan.

Jacques Lipschitz & Cubism. Deborah A. Stott. LC 77-94717. (Outstanding Dissertations in the Fine Arts Ser.). 1978. lib. bdg. 33.00x (ISBN 0-8240-3251-9). Garland Pub.

Jacques-Louis David. Anita Brookner. LC 79-3386. (Icon Editions). (Illus.). 1981. 35.00 (ISBN 0-06-430507-4, HarpT). Har-Row.

Jacques Maritain. John M. Dunaway. (World Authors Ser.). 1978. lib. bdg. 12.50 (ISBN 0-8057-6315-5). Twayne.

Jacques Offenbach. Jacques Offenbach. 1981. 29.95 (ISBN 0-7145-3512-5); pap. 11.95 (ISBN 0-7145-3841-8). Riverrun NY.

Jacques Perk. Rene Breugelmans. LC 74-8658. (World Authors Ser.: Netherlands: No. 328). 1974. lib. bdg. 12.50 (ISBN 0-8057-2688-8). Twayne.

Jacques Tourneur. Edinburgh Festival. (EIFF Ser). 1978. pap. 4.00 (ISBN 0-918432-15-4). NY Zoetrope.

Jade. Lynn Devon. 1978. pap. 1.75 o.p. (ISBN 0-449-13941-7, GM). Fawcett.

Jade Alliance. Elizabeth Darrell. Date not set. pap. 2.95 (ISBN 0-440-14057-9). Dell.

Jade Bough, White Shadows. Sue McConkey. 1970. 5.00 o.p. (ISBN 0-87482-000-6). Wake-Brook.

Jade Pagoda. Betty H. Hyatt. LC 79-8433. (Romantic Suspense Ser.). 1980. 8.95 (ISBN 0-385-15746-0). Doubleday.

Jade Princess. Clarissa Ross. 1977. pap. 1.95 o.s.i. (ISBN 0-515-04033-9). Jove Pubns.

Jade: Stone of Heaven. Richard Gump. LC 62-12100. 1962. 10.95 (ISBN 0-385-01705-7). Doubleday.

Jades from the Cenote of Sacrifice, Chichen Itza, Yucatan. Tatiana Proskouriakoff. LC 74-77555. (Peabody Museum Memoirs: Vol. 10, No. 1). 1974. pap. text ed. 40.00 (ISBN 0-87365-682-2). Peabody Harvard.

Jagadis Chandra Bose. S. N. Basu. (National Biography Ser.). (Orig.). 1979. pap. 2.50 (ISBN 0-89744-205-9). Auromere.

Jaguar. 2nd rev. ed. Lord Montague. LC 80-27039. (Illus.). 240p. 1981. 19.95 (ISBN 0-498-02547-0). A S Barnes.

Jaguar E-Type Collector's Guide. Paul Skilleter. (Collector's Guide Ser.). (Illus.). 1979. 17.50 (ISBN 0-900549-46-7, Pub. by Motor Racing Pubns. England). Motorbooks Intl.

Jaguar E-Type 1966-1971. R. M. Clarke. (Brooklands Bks.). (Illus.). 100p. 1979. pap. 11.95 (ISBN 0-906589-58-4). Motorbooks Intl.

Jaguar E Type 1971-1975. R. M. Clarke. (Brooklands Bks). (Illus.). 100p. (Orig.). 1979. pap. 11.95 (ISBN 0-906589-77-0, Pub. by Enthusiast England). Motorbooks Intl.

Jaguar Service - Repair Handbook: All 3.8 & 4.2 E-Types. David Sales. Ed. by Jeff Robinson. (Illus.). 240p. 1975. pap. text ed. 10.95 (ISBN 0-89287-055-9, A225). Clymer Pubns.

Jaguar XJ Six & Twelve, Daimler, Vanden Plas, XJ-S. Chris Harvey. (AutoHistory Ser.). (Illus.). 128p. 1980. 12.95 (ISBN 0-85045-364-X, Pub. by Osprey England). Motorbooks Intl.

Jahrestagung der Oesterreichischen Gesellschaft fur Gynaekologie und Geburtshilfe, Juni 1980, Krems. Ed. by E. Reinhold. (Gynaekologische Rundschau: Vol. 20, Suppl. 2, 1981). (Illus.). vi, 294p. 1981. pap. 39.75 (ISBN 3-8055-2191-X). S Karger.

Jahrestagung der Oesterreichischen Gesellschaft Fur Gynaekologie und Geburtshilfe, Juni 1980, Krems. Ed. by E. Reinold. (Journal: Gynaekologische Rundschau: Vol. 20, Suppl. 2). 300p. 1980. pap. write for info. (ISBN 3-8055-2191-X). S Karger.

Jai Alai-Walls & Balls. Hal Coddon. 1978. pap. 2.95 (ISBN 0-89650-772-6, Gambler's Book Shelf). Gamblers.

Jail Management. E. Eugene Miller. LC 76-43590. 1978. 18.95 (ISBN 0-669-00959-8). Lexington Bks.

Jailbird. Kurt Vonnegut. 1980. pap. 8.95 (ISBN 0-8161-3022-1, Large Print Bks). G K Hall.

Jailbird. Kurt Vonnegut. 1980. pap. 3.25 (ISBN 0-440-15447-2). Dell.

Jails & Justice. Ed. by Paul F. Cromwell, Jr. (Illus.). 336p. 1975. 24.50 (ISBN 0-398-03144-4); pap. 17.50 (ISBN 0-398-03145-2). C C Thomas.

Jaime Torres Bodet. Sonja Karsen. (World Authors Ser.: Mexico: No. 157). lib. bdg. 10.95 (ISBN 0-8057-2156-8). Twayne.

Jaimie. John Becker. LC 80-65424. 176p. 1980. 10.00 (ISBN 0-87923-340-0). Godine.

Jaina Path of Purification. Padmanabh S. Jaini. LC 77-73496. 1979. 21.50x (ISBN 0-520-03459-7). U of Cal Pr.

Jaina Sutras. Cowell & Muller. Ed. by F. Max Muller. (Sacred Books of the East Ser.: Vols. 22 & 45). 15.00x ea.; Vol. 22. (ISBN 0-8426-1217-3); Vol. 45. (ISBN 0-8426-1218-1). Verry.

Jaina Sutras, Part One: The Akaranga Sutra, the Kapla Sutra. Tr. by Hermann Jacobi. (The Sacred Books of the East Ser.: Vol. 22). Date not set. 6.50 (ISBN 0-8446-0725-8). Peter Smith.

Jaina Sutras, Part Two: The Uttaradyayana Sutra, the Sutrakritanga Sutra, Vol. 45. Tr. by Hermann Jacobi. (The Sacred Books of the East Ser.). Date not set. 6.50 (ISBN 0-8446-0726-6). Peter Smith.

Jaina Theory of Perception. Pushpa Bothra. 1976. 7.50 (ISBN 0-89684-229-0). Orient Bk Dist.

Jajal Al-Din Al-Suywti, 2 vols. E. M. Sartain. Incl. Vol. 1. Biography & Background. 230p. 44.00 (ISBN 0-521-20547-6); Vol. 2. Al-Tahadduth bini'mat allah. 370p. 51.00 (ISBN 0-521-20546-8). LC 74-82226. (Oriental Publications Ser.: Nos. 23 & 24). 1975. Set. 86.00 (ISBN 0-521-20633-2). Cambridge U Pr.

Jake & Honeybunch Go to Heaven. Margot Zemach. (Illus.). 40p. (ps up). Date not set. 10.95 (ISBN 0-374-33652-0). FS&G.

Jake & Katie. Brad Solomon. 304p. (Orig.). 1980. pap. 2.50 (ISBN 0-380-52969-6, 52969). Avon.

Jake Claus, Santa's Brother. Swiftwater Jones. LC 79-56509. 1980. 5.95 (ISBN 0-533-04534-7). Vantage.

Jake Gaither, America's Most Famous Black Coach. George E. Curry. LC 76-50580. (Illus.). 1977. 7.95 (ISBN 0-396-07381-6). Dodd.

Jake O'Shawnasey. Steve Cosgrove. (Serendipity Bks). (Illus.). (gr. k-4). 1978. PLB 6.95 (ISBN 0-87191-654-1). Creative Ed.

Jake's Thing. Kingsley Amis. 1980. pap. 3.50 (ISBN 0-14-005096-5). Penguin.

Jaky or Dodo? Natalie S. Carlson. (Illus.). 96p. (gr. 1-4). 1978. 6.95 (ISBN 0-684-15340-8). Scribner.

Jalaluddin Rumi: Songbird of Sufism. Roy C. DeLamotte. LC 80-5884. 187p. 1980. lib. bdg. 16.75 (ISBN 0-8191-1286-0); pap. text ed. 8.75 (ISBN 0-8191-1287-9). U Pr of Amer.

Jamaa & the Church: A Bantu Catholic Movement in Zaire. Willy De Craemer. (Oxford Studies in African Affairs). 1977. 45.00x (ISBN 0-19-822708-6). Oxford U Pr.

Jamaica. Amanda H. Douglass. 1977. pap. 1.75 (ISBN 0-8439-0492-5, Leisure Bks). Nordon Pubns.

Jamaica Bay & Kennedy Airport: A Multidisciplinary Environmental Study, 2 vols. 1971. Set. 9.75 (ISBN 0-309-01871-4). Natl Acad Pr.

Jamaica Farewell: Jamaican Migrants in London. Nancy Foner. LC 77-80471. 1978. 20.00x (ISBN 0-520-03544-5). U of Cal Pr.

Jamaica in Pictures. Sterling Publishing Company Editors. LC 67-16016. (Visual Geography Ser). (Illus.). (gr. 4-12). 1967. PLB 4.99 (ISBN 0-8069-1085-2); pap. 2.95 (ISBN 0-8069-1084-4). Sterling.

Jamaican Leaders: Political Attitudes in a New Nation. Wendell Bell. 1964. 19.00x (ISBN 0-520-00103-6). U of Cal Pr.

Jambalaya. Junior League of New Orleans Inc. (Illus.). 256p. (Orig.). 1980. pap. 7.95 (ISBN 0-9604774-0-3). Jr League New Orleans.

Jamboo the African Elephant. Robert Hunt. LC 72-736441. (Adventures of Wild Animals Book). (Illus.). (gr. 2-5). 1978. 10 bks. & one cassette 21.00 (ISBN 0-89290-026-1). Soc for Visual.

Jamboree. Michael Upchurch. LC 80-18489. 192p. 1981. 9.95 (ISBN 0-394-51150-6). Knopf.

James. Martin Dibelius. Ed. by Helmut Koester. Tr. by Michael A. Willims. LC 74-80428. (Hermeneia: a Critical & Historical Commentary on the Bible). 252p. 1975. 16.95 (ISBN 0-8006-6006-4, 20-6006). Fortress.

James. Irving L. Jensen. (Bible Self-Study Ser). (Illus.). 1972. pap. 2.25 (ISBN 0-8024-1059-6). Moody.

James. Robert Johnstone. (Geneva Commentaries Ser.). 1977. 12.95 (ISBN 0-85151-257-7). Banner of Truth.

James. Curtis Vaughan. pap. 3.50 (ISBN 0-310-33553-1). Zondervan.

James A. Michener. 2nd ed. A. Grove Day. (U. S. Authors Ser.: No. 60). 1977. lib. bdg. 10.95 (ISBN 0-8057-7184-0). Twayne.

James, a Primer for Christian Living. Earl Kelly. 1973. kivar 3.95 o.p. (ISBN 0-934532-13-3). Presby & Reformed.

James Agee. Victor A. Kramer. LC 74-23882. (U. S. Authors Ser.: No. 252). 1975. lib. bdg. 9.95 (ISBN 0-8057-0006-4). Twayne.

James & Conrad. Elsa Nettels. LC 76-2897. (SAMLA Studies Award Ser.). 289p. 1977. 17.50x (ISBN 0-8203-0408-5). U of Ga Pr.

James & Nora: A Portrait of Joyce's Marraige. Edna O'Brien. 50p. 1981. limited signed edition 35.00 (ISBN 0-935716-09-2). Lord John.

James & the Giant Peach. Roald Dahl. 160p. (gr. 4-6). pap. 2.50 (ISBN 0-553-15113-4, Skylark). Bantam.

James at Fifteen. April Smith. 1977. pap. 1.50 o.s.i. (ISBN 0-440-14389-6). Dell.

James at Fifteen. April Smith. (gr. 7-12). 1980. pap. 1.50 (ISBN 0-440-94389-2, LFL). Dell.

James Baldwin. Louis H. Pratt. (United States Authors Ser.: No. 290). 1978. lib. bdg. 9.95 (ISBN 0-8057-7193-X). Twayne.

James Baldwin. Carolyn W. Sylvander. LC 80-5338. (Modern Literature Ser.). 160p. 1981. 10.95 (ISBN 0-8044-2848-4); pap. 4.95 (ISBN 0-8044-6891-5). Ungar.

James Baldwin: A Collection of Critical Essays. Ed. by Kenneth Kinnamon. LC 74-6175. (Twentieth Century Views Ser). 192p. 1973. 10.95 (ISBN 0-13-055566-5, Spec). P-H.

James Barr & the Bible: Critique of a New Liberalism. Paul R. Wells. 1980. pap. 12.00 (ISBN 0-87552-546-6). Presby & Reformed.

James Beard Cookbook. rev. ed. James Beard. 1970. 14.95 (ISBN 0-525-13621-5, Hawthorn). Dutton.

James Beard's American Cookery. James Beard. 1980. pap. 9.95 (ISBN 0-686-63303-2). Little.

James Beard's Casserole Cookbook. James Beard. 1977. pap. 1.50 o.p. (ISBN 0-449-13871-2, GM). Fawcett.

James Beard's Fish Cookery. James Beard. 1967. pap. 2.75 (ISBN 0-446-95680-5). Warner Bks.

James Beattie. Everard H. King. (English Authors Ser.: No. 206). 1977. lib. bdg. 10.95 (ISBN 0-8057-6653-7). Twayne.

James: Belief in Action. Keith L. Brooks. (Teach Yourself the Bible Ser). 1961. pap. 1.75 (ISBN 0-8024-4227-7). Moody.

James Bland Burges Baronet (1752-1824) Richard the First, a Poem: in Eighteen Books. 1801. James B. Burges. Ed. by Donald H. Reiman. LC 75-31172. (Romantic Context Ser.: Poetry 1789-1830). 1977. lib. bdg. 47.00 (ISBN 0-8240-2125-8). Garland Pub.

James Bond & Moonraker. Christopher Wood. (Orig.). 1979. pap. 2.25 (ISBN 0-515-05344-9). Jove Pubns.

James Bond in the Cinema. 2nd rev. ed. John Brosnan. LC 80-26573. (Illus.). 200p. 1981. 9.95 (ISBN 0-498-02546-2). A S Barnes.

James Boswell. A. Russell Brooks. (English Authors Ser.: No. 122). lib. bdg. 10.95 (ISBN 0-8057-1048-5). Twayne.

James Boswell & His World. David Daiches. LC 75-29826. 1976. 8.95 o.p. (ISBN 0-684-14549-9, ScribT). Scribner.

James Boyd. David E. Whisnant. (U. S. Authors Ser.: No. 199). lib. bdg. 10.95 (ISBN 0-8057-0080-3). Twayne.

James Branch Cabell. Carl Van Doren. 87p. 1980. Repr. of 1928 ed. lib. bdg. 10.00 (ISBN 0-89984-475-8). Century Bookbindery.

James Branch Cabell: A Reference Guide. Maurice Duke. (Reference Bks.). 1979. lib. bdg. 14.00 (ISBN 0-8161-7838-0). G K Hall.

James Burgh, Spokesman for Reform in Hanoverian England. Carla H. Hay. LC 79-89204. 1979. pap. text ed. 9.00 (ISBN 0-8191-0800-6). U Pr of Amer.

James Burnett, Lord Monboddo. E. L. Cloyd. (Illus.). 212p. 1972. 15.25x o.p. (ISBN 0-19-812437-6). Oxford U Pr.

James Burnett Monboddo (1714-1799) Antient Metaphysics, 6 Vol., 1779-99. Ed. by Rene Wellek. LC 75-11236. (British Philosophers & Theologians of the 17th & 18th Centuries Ser.). 1977. lib. bdg. 42.00 (ISBN 0-8240-1789-7). Garland Pub.

James Clarence Mangan. Henry J. Donaghy. (English Authors Ser.: No. 171). 1974. lib. bdg. 10.95 (ISBN 0-8057-1370-0). Twayne.

James Clerk Maxwell & Electromagnetism. Charles P. May. (Biography Ser). (Illus.). (gr. 7 up). 1962. PLB 5.90 o.p. (ISBN 0-531-00902-5). Watts.

James Connolly: Selected Writings. Ed. by P. Berresford Ellis. LC 73-90071. 320p. 1974. 11.50 o.p. (ISBN 0-85345-326-8, CL-3628). Monthly Rev.

James Craig. Patrick Buckland. (Gill's Irish Lives Ser.). 143p. 1980. 20.00 (ISBN 0-7171-1078-8, Pub. by Gill & Macmillan Ireland); pap. 6.50 (ISBN 0-7171-0984-4). Irish Bk Ctr.

James Dean Revisited. Dennis Stock. (Large Format Ser.). (Illus.). 1978. pap. 5.95 o.p. (ISBN 0-14-004939-8); pap. 15.00 o.p. (ISBN 0-670-40481-0). Penguin.

James Dickey: A Bibliography, Nineteen Forty-Seven to Nineteen Seventy-Four. Jim Elledge. LC 79-10405. (Author Bibliographies Ser.: No. 40). 1979. 13.00 (ISBN 0-8108-1218-5). Scarecrow.

James Earl Carter: The Man & the Myth. Peter Meyer. (Illus.). 1978. 9.95 o.p. (ISBN 0-8362-6605-6). Andrews & McMeel.

James Elroy Flecker. John M. Munro. LC 75-46531. (English Authors Ser.: No. 185). 1976. lib. bdg. 10.95 (ISBN 0-8057-6656-1). Twayne.

James Elroy Flecker: A Critical Study. Mary B. Davis. (Salzburg Studies in English Literature: Poetic Drama & Poetic Theory: No. 33). 1977. text ed. 25.00x (ISBN 0-391-01358-0). Humanities.

James: Faith in Action. Chuck Christensen & Winnie Christensen. LC 75-33442. (Fisherman Bible Study Guides). 1975. pap. 1.95 saddle stitched (ISBN 0-87788-421-8). Shaw Pubs.

James: Faith That Works. Harold L. Fickett, Jr. LC 76-169604. (Orig.). 1972. pap. 2.25 (ISBN 0-8307-0130-3, S254123). Regal.

James Fenimore Cooper. T. R. Lounsbury. LC 80-29308. (American Men & Women of Letters Ser.). 310p. 1981. pap. 4.95 (ISBN 0-87754-156-6). Chelsea Hse.

James Fenimore Cooper. Thomas R. Lounsbury. LC 67-23882. 1968. Repr. of 1882 ed. 20.00 (ISBN 0-8103-3037-7). Gale.

James Fenimore Cooper. Donald A. Ringe. (U. S. Authors Ser.: No. 11). 9.95 (ISBN 0-8057-0156-7). Twayne.

James Ford Bell Library: An Annotated Catalog of Original Source Materials Relating to the History of European Expansion, 1400-1800. James Ford Bell Library, University of Minnesota & University of Minnesota. (Library Catalogs). Date not set. lib. bdg. 95.00 (ISBN 0-8161-0361-5). G K Hall.

James Fraser. Alexander McPherson. 1968. 8.95 o.p. (ISBN 0-686-12484-7). Banner of Truth.

James G. Endicott: Rebel Out of China. Stephen Endicott. 1980. 18.95 (ISBN 0-8020-2377-0). U of Toronto Pr.

James Gordon Bennetts, Father & Son: Proprietors of the New York Herald. Don C. Seitz. (American Newspapermen 1790-1933). (Illus.). 405p. 1974. Repr. of 1928 ed. 20.00x o.s.i. (ISBN 0-8464-0008-1). Beekman Pubs.

James Gould Cozzens. Pierre Michel. (U. S. Authors Ser.: No. 237). 1974. 10.95 (ISBN 0-8057-0163-X). Twayne.

James Gould Cozzens: A Descriptive Bibliography. Matthew J. Bruccoli. LC 80-53553. (Pittsburgh Ser in Bibliography). (Illus.). 256p. 1981. 32.95x (ISBN 0-8229-3435-3). U of Pittsburgh Pr.

James Gould Cozzens: New Acquist of True Experience. Ed. by Matthew J. Bruccoli. LC 79-14581. (Crosscurrents-Modern Critiques-New Ser.). 158p. 1979. 17.95 (ISBN 0-8093-0930-0). S Ill U Pr.

James Graham Cooper: Pioneer Western Naturalist. Eugene Coan. LC 80-52313. (GEM Books-Historical & Natural History Ser.). (Illus.). 210p. (Orig.). 1981. pap. 11.95 (ISBN 0-89301-071-5). U Pr of Idaho.

James Harrington. Michael Downs. (English Authors Ser.: No. 188). 1977. lib. bdg. 12.50 (ISBN 0-8057-6693-6). Twayne.

James, Hebrews. James Moffatt. LC 24-21703. (International Critical Commentary Ser.). 336p. Repr. of 1924 ed. text ed. 17.50 (ISBN 0-567-05034-3). Attic Pr.

James Herriot's Yorkshire. James Herriot. 1979. 16.95 (ISBN 0-312-43970-9). St Martin.

James Herriot's Yorkshire. James Herriot. (Illus.). 224p. 1981. pap. 9.95 (ISBN 0-312-43971-7). St Martin.

James Hewat Mackenzie: Pioneer of Psychical Research. Muriel Hankey. 1963. 4.50 o.p. (ISBN 0-912326-07-7). Garrett-Helix.

James Hunt Against All Odds. Eoin Young & James Hunt. 1978. 9.95 o.p. (ISBN 0-525-13625-8). Dutton.

James Innes & His Brothers of the F.H.C. Jane Carson. LC 65-26594. (Williamsburg Research Studies). 171p. 1965. pap. 2.25x o.p. (ISBN 0-8139-0062-X). U Pr of Va.

James Jones. James R. Giles. (United States Authors Ser.: No. 366). 1981. lib. bdg. 9.95 (ISBN 0-8057-7293-6). Twayne.

James Joyce. Armin Arnold. LC 68-31445. (Modern Literature Ser.). 1969. 10.95 (ISBN 0-8044-2007-6); pap. 3.45 (ISBN 0-8044-6008-6). Ungar.

James Joyce. Peter Costello. (Gill's Irish Lives Ser.). 135p. 1980. 20.00 (ISBN 0-7171-1077-X, Pub. by Gill & Macmillan Ireland); pap. 6.50 (ISBN 0-7171-0986-0). Irish Bk Ctr.

James Joyce. A. Walton Litz. (English Authors Ser.: No. 31). 1966. lib. bdg. 9.95 (ISBN 0-8057-1300-X). Twayne.

James Joyce: A Student's Guide. Matthew Hodgart. 1978. 16.00x (ISBN 0-7100-8817-5); pap. 7.95 (ISBN 0-7100-8943-0). Routledge & Kegan.

James Joyce & the Common Reader. rev. ed. William P. Jones. LC 55-9624. 1970. 9.95x (ISBN 0-8061-0324-8); pap. 4.95 (ISBN 0-8061-0930-0). U of Okla Pr.

James Joyce & the German Novel - 1922-1933. Breon Mitchell. LC 75-36980. xvi, 194p. 1976. 12.95x (ISBN 0-8214-0192-0). Ohio U Pr.

James Joyce & the Mullingar Connection. Leo Daly. (Dolmen Editions: No. 20). 40p. (Demi quarto size). 1975. text ed. 22.50x (ISBN 0-391-00418-2, Dolmen Pr). Humanities.

James Joyce: Critical Heritage, 2 vols. Ed. by R. H. Deming. Incl. Vol. 1. 1907-1927; Vol. 2. 1928-1941. 1970. 35.00 ea. Routledge & Kegan.

James Joyce: The Critical Heritage, 2 vols. Ed. by Robert H. Deming. (Critical Heritage Ser.). 1970. Set. 65.00 (ISBN 0-7100-6747-X). Vol. 1, 1907-1927. Vol. 2, 1928-1941. Routledge & Kegan.

James Joyce's Dubliners. James R. Baker & Thomas F. Staley. 1969. pap. 4.95x o.p. (ISBN 0-534-00682-5). Wadsworth Pub.

James Joyce's Miltonic Affliction. John L. Lyons. 52p. 1980. Repr. of 1973 ed. lib. bdg. 7.50 (ISBN 0-8492-1632-X). R West.

James Joyce's Ulysses. Stuart Gilbert. 1955. pap. 2.95 (ISBN 0-394-70013-9, V13, Vin). Random.

James K. Baxter. Charles Doyle. LC 75-33781. (World Authors Ser.: New Zealand: No. 384). 1976. lib. bdg. 12.50 (ISBN 0-8057-6227-2). Twayne.

James Kent: A Study in Conservatism, 1763-1847. John T. Horton. LC 76-84189. (American Scene, Comments & Commentators Ser). 1969. Repr. of 1939 ed. lib. bdg. 35.00 (ISBN 0-306-71502-3). Da Capo.

James Knowles: Victorian Editor & Architect. Pricilla Metcalf. (Illus.). 414p. 1980. 44.00x (ISBN 0-19-812626-3). Oxford U Pr.

James Krenov Worker in Wood. James Krenov. (Illus.). 128p. 1981. 24.95 (ISBN 0-442-26336-8). Van Nos Reinhold.

James L. Orr & the Sectional Conflict. Roger P Leemhuis. LC 78-65850. 1979. pap. text ed. 9.75 (ISBN 0-8191-0679-8). U Pr of Amer.

James Larkin, Irish Labor Leader, 1876-1947. Emmett Larkin. (Illus.). 1977. Repr. of 1965 ed. 28.00x (ISBN 0-7100-8606-7). Routledge & Kegan.

James Longstreet: Soldier, Politician, Officeholder, & Writer. Donald B. Sanger & Thomas R. Hay. 10.00 (ISBN 0-8446-0890-4). Peter Smith.

James M. Landis: Dean of the Regulators. Donald A. Ritchie. LC 80-12828. 1980. text ed. 17.50x (ISBN 0-674-47171-7). Harvard U Pr.

James McCosh & the Scottish Intellectual Tradition: From Glasgow to Princeton. J. David Hoeveler, Jr. (Illus.). 384p. 1981. 25.00x (ISBN 0-691-04670-0). Princeton U Pr.

James Madison. Sydney H. Gay. LC 80-25344. (American Statesmen Ser.). 350p. 1981. pap. 5.95 (ISBN 0-87754-196-5). Chelsea Hse.

James Mill on Education. Ed. by W. H. Burston. LC 69-11268. (Cambridge Texts & Studies in Education: No. 6). 1969. 22.95 (ISBN 0-521-07414-2). Cambridge U Pr.

James Mill on Philosophy & Education. W. H. Burston. 256p. 1973. text ed. 22.50x (ISBN 0-485-11138-1, Athlone Pr). Humanities.

James Monroe. Daniel C. Gilman. LC 80-24500. (American Statesmen Ser.). 315p. 1981. pap. 4.95 (ISBN 0-87754-187-6). Chelsea Hse.

James Monroe: Public Claimant. L. Wilmerding, Jr. LC 60-11525. 1960. 4.00 (ISBN 0-910294-26-7). Brown Bk.

James Montgomery. Ed. by Donald H. Reiman. LC 75-31239. (Romantic Context Ser.: Poetry 1789-1830). 1978. lib. bdg. 47.00 (ISBN 0-8240-2188-6). Garland Pub.

James Montgomery (1771-1854) Ed. by Donald H. Reiman. Incl. Prison Amusements. Repr. of 1797 ed; Wanderer of Switzerland. Repr. of 1806 ed. LC 75-31235. (Romantic Context Ser.: Poetry 1789-1830). 1978. lib. bdg. 47.00 (ISBN 0-8240-2185-1). Garland Pub.

James Norman Hall. Robert Roulston. (United States Authors Ser.: No. 323). 1978. 12.50 (ISBN 0-8057-7255-3). Twayne.

James: Roadmap for Down-to-Earth Christians (Student & Teacher) Margaret Fromer & Carolyn Nystrom. (Young Fisherman Bible Studyguide). (Illus.). 80p. 1981. tchr.'s ed. 4.95 (ISBN 0-87788-420-X, 420-X); wkbk. 3.95 (ISBN 0-87788-419-6, 419-X). Shaw Pubs.

James Russell Lowell. Edward E. Hale. LC 80-20008. (American Men & Women of Letters Ser.). 310p. 1981. pap. 4.95 (ISBN 0-87754-168-X). Chelsea Hse.

James Russell Lowell. Claire McGlinchee. (U. S. Authors Ser.: No. 120). lib. bdg. 10.95 (ISBN 0-8057-0460-4). Twayne.

James Russell Lowell: His Life & Work. Ferris Greenslet. LC 77-77162. 1969. Repr. of 1905 ed. 18.00 (ISBN 0-8103-3893-9). Gale.

James Scott & William Scott, Bookbinders. F. H. Loudon. (Illus.). 1980. 65.00 (ISBN 0-89679-003-7). Moretus Pr.

James Shirleys Beitrag Zur Entwicklung der Comedy of Manners. Karl Roeloffs. (Salzburg Studies in English Literature, Poetic Drama & Poetic Theory Ser.: No. 37). 1978. pap. text ed. 25.00x (ISBN 0-391-01508-7). Humanities.

James Smith (Seventeen Seventy-Five to Eighteen Thirty-Nine) & Horatio (Horace) Smith (Seventeen Seventy-Nine to Eighteen Forty-Nine) James Smith & Horatio Smith. Ed. by Donald H. Reiman. LC 75-31254. (Romantic Context Ser.: Poetry 1789-1830). 1978. lib. bdg. 47.00 (ISBN 0-8240-2201-7). Garland Pub.

James Stirling: Buildings & Projects, 1950-1974. James Stirling. (Illus.). 184p. 1975. 30.00 o.p. (ISBN 0-19-519801-8). Oxford U Pr.

James Strange's Journal & Narrative of the Commercial Expedition from Bombay to the Northwest Coast of North America. (Illus.). 64p. pap. 5.00 (ISBN 0-8466-0137-0, SJS137). Shorey.

James T. Farrell - Literary Essays, 1954-1974. Ed. by Jack A. Robbins. (Literary Criticism Ser.). 1976. 11.50 (ISBN 0-8046-9125-8, Natl U). Kennikat.

James T. Farrell: The Revolutionary Socialist Years. Alan M. Wald. LC 77-84156. 1978. 15.00x (ISBN 0-8147-9179-4); pap. 5.00x (ISBN 0-8147-9180-8). NYU Pr.

James Thomson. Hilbert H. Campbell. (English Authors Ser.: No. 269). 1979. lib. bdg. 10.95 (ISBN 0-8057-6715-0). Twayne.

James Thomson, (B. V.): Beyond "The City". William D. Schaefer. (Perspectives in Criticism: No. 17). 1965. 19.50x (ISBN 0-520-01138-4). U of Cal Pr.

James Thurber. Robert E. Morsberger. (U. S. Authors Ser.: No. 62). 1964. lib. bdg. 10.95 (ISBN 0-8057-0728-X). Twayne.

James Tissot, Catalogue: Raisonne of His Prints. Michael J. Wentworth. (Illus.). 1978. 20.00 (ISBN 0-685-67986-1). Minneapolis Inst Arts.

James Van der Zee. new ed. Ed. by Liliane De Cock. LC 73-75105. (Morgan & Morgan Monographs). 160p. 1974. 14.00 o.p. (ISBN 0-87100-039-3). Morgan.

James Van der Zee: The Picture-Takin' Man. Jim Haskins. LC 78-22431. (Illus.). 1979. 8.95 (ISBN 0-396-07678-5). Dodd.

James Wallace, 3 vols. Robert Bage. Ed. by Ronald Paulson. LC 78-60847. (Novel 1720-1805 Ser.: Vol. 11). 1979. 31.00 ea. (ISBN 0-8240-3660-3). Garland Pub.

James Watt: Inventor of the Steam Engine. Robert N. Webb. LC 74-93767. (Biography Ser). (Illus.). (gr. 7 up). 1970. PLB 5.90 o.p. (ISBN 0-531-00940-8). Watts.

James Weldon Johnson. Ophelia S. Egypt. LC 73-9521. (Biographies Ser). (Illus.). 40p. (gr. 2-5). 1974. PLB 7.89 (ISBN 0-690-00215-7, TYC-J). T Y Crowell.

James Whatman, Father & Son. Thomas Balston. Ed. by John Bidwell. LC 78-74386. (Nineteenth-Century Book Arts & Printing History Ser.: Vol. 1). (Illus.). 1979. lib. bdg. 22.00 (ISBN 0-8240-3875-4). Garland Pub.

James Whitcomb Riley. Peter Revell. (U. S. Authors Ser.: No. 159). lib. bdg. 9.95 (ISBN 0-8057-0624-0). Twayne.

James White. Virgil Robinson. LC 75-16921. (Illus.). 1976. 7.50 (ISBN 0-8280-0049-2). Review & Herald.

Jamie Is My Heart's Desire. Alfred Chester. LC 57-12253. 3.50 (ISBN 0-8149-0465-3). Vanguard.

Jamie Reid. Gordon Ogilvie. 448p. (Orig.). 1981. pap. 2.75 (ISBN 0-380-76737-6, 76737). Avon.

Jamie, The Adventures of. Tom Bowie. LC 78-62815. (Illus.). 1978. 12.50 (ISBN 0-932508-00-6); pap. 3.95 (ISBN 0-932508-01-4). Seven Oaks.

Jamie the Saxt. Robert McLellan. 1981. pap. 3.95 (ISBN 0-7145-0307-X). Riverrun NY.

Jamie's Story. Wendy Watson. (Illus.). 32p. (gr. 1-4). 1981. 6.95 (ISBN 0-399-20789-9); lib. bdg. 6.99 (ISBN 0-399-61177-0). Philomel.

Jamieson, Fausset & Brown's Commentary on the Whole Bible. 1957. 18.95 (ISBN 0-310-26570-3). Zondervan.

Jan Both: Paintings, Drawings & Prints. James D. Burke. LC 75-23783. (Outstanding Dissertations in the Fine Arts - 17th Century). (Illus.). 1976. lib. bdg. 45.00 (ISBN 0-8240-1980-6). Garland Pub.

Jan in India. Otis A. Kline. LC 80-23787. 128p. 1980. Repr. of 1973 ed. lib. bdg. 10.95x (ISBN 0-89370-090-8). Borgo Pr.

Jan in India. Otis Adelbert Kline. LC 73-94035. (Illus.). 1974. pap. 5.00 (ISBN 0-87707-131-4). Fictioneer Bks.

Jane. Dee Wells. 1975. pap. 1.95 (ISBN 0-380-00222-1, 38356). Avon.

Jane Adams. Jane Adams. LC 73-15838. 1974. PLB 5.95 (ISBN 0-87191-304-6). Creative Ed.

Jane Addams. Gail F. Keller. LC 71-139098. (Biography Ser). (Illus.). (gr. 1-4). 1971. 7.95 (ISBN 0-690-45791-X, TYC-J). T Y Crowell.

Jane Austen. Douglas Bush. LC 73-18765. 256p. 1975. 10.95 (ISBN 0-02-519600-6, 51960). Macmillan.

Jane Austen. Douglas Bush. 256p. 1975. pap. 6.95 o.s.i. (ISBN 0-02-049250-2, Collier). Macmillan.

Jane Austen. Yasmine Gooneratne. LC 75-123669. (British Authors Ser.: Introductory Critical Studies). 1970. 28.50 (ISBN 0-521-07843-1); pap. 7.95x (ISBN 0-521-09630-8). Cambridge U Pr.

Jane Austen & Samuel Johnson. Peter L. De Rose. LC 78-7813. 133p. 1980. lib. bdg. 16.25 (ISBN 0-8191-1073-6); pap. text ed. 7.50 (ISBN 0-8191-1074-4). U Pr of Amer.

Jane Austen: Bicentenary Essays. Ed. by J. Halperin. 368p. 1975. 36.00 (ISBN 0-521-20709-6); pap. 11.50x (ISBN 0-521-09929-3). Cambridge U Pr.

Jane Austen Companion. rev. ed. F. B. Pinion. (Critical Survey & Reference Book). 1980. text ed. 31.25x (ISBN 0-333-12489-8). Humanities.

Jane Austen Household Book. Peggy Hickman. LC 77-89377. 1978. 10.50 (ISBN 0-7153-7324-2). David & Charles.

Jane Austen in a Social Context. Ed. by David Monaghan. 176p. 1981. 22.50x (ISBN 0-389-20007-7). B&N.

Jane Austen: Spatial Structure of Thematic Variations. Joseph Kestner. (Salzburg Studies in English Literature, Romantic Reassessment: No. 39). 145p. 1974. pap. text ed. 25.00x (ISBN 0-391-01443-9). Humanities.

Jane Austen Today. Ed. by Joel Weinsheimer. LC 75-11447. 187p. 1975. 13.00x (ISBN 0-8203-0382-8). U of Ga Pr.

Jane Austen's Letters to Her Sister Cassandra & Others. 2nd ed. Jane Austen. Ed. by R. W. Chapman. 716p. 1979. 45.00x (ISBN 0-19-212102-2). Oxford U Pr.

Jane Austen's "Sir Charles Grandison". Ed. by Brian Southam. (Illus.). 128p. 1981. 24.00 (ISBN 0-19-812637-9). Oxford U Pr.

Jane Austin & Some Contemporaries. Mona Wilson. 304p. 1980. Repr. of 1938 ed. lib. bdg. 20.00 (ISBN 0-8492-2973-1). R West.

Jane Brody's Nutrition Book: A Lifetime Guide to Good Eating for Better Health & Weight Conrol by the Personal Health Columnist for the New Yok Times. Jane Brody. (Illus.). 1981. 17.95 (ISBN 0-393-01429-0). Norton.

Jane Butel's Tex-Mex Cookbook. Jane Bitel. 224p. 1980. 10.95 (ISBN 0-517-53986-1, Harmony). Crown.

Jane Cable. George B. McCutcheon. 1976. lib. bdg. 15.25x (ISBN 0-89968-062-3). Lightyear.

Jane Eyre. Charlotte Bronte. Ed. by Richard J. Dunn. (Critical Editions Ser). (gr. 9-12). 1971. pap. text ed. 5.95x (ISBN 0-393-09966-0). Norton.

Jane Eyre. Charlotte Bronte. (Classics Ser). (gr. 9 up). 1964. pap. 1.95 (ISBN 0-8049-0017-5, CL-17). Airmont.

Jane Eyre. Charlotte Bronte. (Literature Ser). (gr. 7-12). 1969. pap. text ed. 3.75 (ISBN 0-87720-706-2). AMSCO Sch.

Jane Eyre. Charlotte Bronte. 1963. 10.50x (ISBN 0-460-00287-2, Evman); pap. 2.95 (ISBN 0-460-01287-8). Dutton.

Jane Eyre. Charlotte Bronte. (Illus.). (gr. 9 up). 1962. 6.95g o.s.i. (ISBN 0-02-714760-6). Macmillan.

Jane Eyre. Charlotte Bronte. Ed. by Jane Jack & Margaret Smith. (Clarendon Editions of the Novels of the Brontes Ser.). 1969. 45.00x (ISBN 0-19-811490-7). Oxford U Pr.

Jane Eyre. Charlotte Bronte. Ed. by Q. D. Leavis. (English Library Ser.). pap. 2.25 (ISBN 0-14-043011-3). Penguin.

Jane Eyre. Charlotte Bronte. (Zodiac Press Ser.). 1978. 9.95 (ISBN 0-7011-1239-5, Pub. by Chatto Bodley Jonathan). Merrimack Bk Serv.

Jane Eyre. Charlotte Bronte. LC 78-3388. (Raintree's Illustrated Classics). (Illus.). (gr. 5-8). 1978. PLB 9.65 (ISBN 0-8393-6202-1). Raintree Child.

Jane Eyre. Charlotte Bronte. pap. 1.75. Bantam.

Jane Eyre. Charlotte Bronte. LC 80-14426. (Raintree Short Classics). (Illus.). 48p. (gr. 4 up). 1981. PLB 9.95 (ISBN 0-8172-1661-8). Raintree Pubs.

Jane Eyre: Student Activity Book. Marcia Sohl & Gerald Dackerman. (Now Age Illustrated Ser.). (Illus.). (gr. 4-12). 1976. wkbk. 0.95 (ISBN 0-88301-290-1). Pendulum Pr.

Jane Fonda. Ellen Erlanger. (Achievers Ser.). (Illus.). (gr. 4-9). 1981. PLB 5.95 (ISBN 0-8225-0485-5). Lerner Pubns.

Jane Goodall: Living Chimp Style. Mary V. Fox. LC 80-27542. (Taking Part Ser.). (Illus.). 48p. (gr. 3 up). 1981. PLB 6.95 (ISBN 0-87518-204-6). Dillon.

Jane Grigson's Vegetable Book. Jane Grigson. 1981. pap. 6.95 (ISBN 0-14-046352-6). Penguin.

Jane Mander. Dorothea Turner. (World Authors Ser.: New Zealand: No. 178). lib. bdg. 10.95 (ISBN 0-8057-2576-8). Twayne.

Jane Talbot. Charles B. Brown. 237p. 1980. Repr. of 1857 ed. lib. bdg. 40.00 (ISBN 0-89987-062-7). Century Bookbindery.

Jane Taylor: Prose & Poetry. Intro. by F. V. Barry. 177p. 1980. Repr. of 1925 ed. lib. bdg. 30.00 (ISBN 0-89760-075-4). Telegraph Bks.

Jane's Adventures in & Out of the Book. Jonathan Gathorne-Hardy. LC 80-29185. (Illus.). 192p. 1981. 10.95 (ISBN 0-87951-122-2). Overlook Pr.

Jane's All in the World's Aircraft, Nineteen Nuneteen. Ed. by Fred T. Jane. LC 69-14964. (Illus.). Repr. 25.00x (ISBN 0-685-06493-X, Pub by Arco). Biblo.

Jane's All the World's Aircraft, 1938. facsimile ed. Ed. by C. G. Grey & Leonard Bridgeman. LC 10-8268. 1972. lib. bdg. 35.00 o.p. (ISBN 0-668-02646-4). Arco.

Jane's All the World's Aircraft 1976-77. Ed. by John W. Taylor. 1976. 72.50 o.p. (ISBN 0-531-03260-4). Watts.

Jane's Fighting Ships, 1914. facs. ed. Ed. by Fred T. Jane. LC 69-14519. (Illus.). 1969. 19.95 o.p. (ISBN 0-668-01873-9). Arco.

Jane's Fighting Ships, 1919. facsimile ed. Ed. by Fred T. Jane. LC 69-14519. (Illus.). 1970. lib. bdg. 25.00 o.p. (ISBN 0-668-02018-0). Arco.

Jane's Fighting Ships, 1939. Ed. by Francis E. McMurtrie. LC 69-14519. (Illus.). 1979. lib. bdg. 29.95 o.s.i. (ISBN 0-668-02431-3). Arco.

Jane's Freight Containers 1976-77. Ed. by Patrick Finlay. 1977. 72.50 o.p. (ISBN 0-531-03904-8). Watts.

Jane's Historical Aircraft from Nineteen Two to Nineteen Sixteen. Jane's Yearbooks. 96p. 1973. 4.95 o.p. (ISBN 0-385-01314-0). Doubleday.

Jane's Infantry Weapons: Nineteen Eighty. 1980. 125.00 (ISBN 0-686-64828-5). Watts.

Jane's Infantry Weapons 1977. Ed. by Denis Archer. 1977. 72.50 o.p. (ISBN 0-531-03905-6). Watts.

Jane's Pocket Book of Helicopters. Ed. by John W. Taylor. (Illus.). 260p. 1981. pap. 8.95 (ISBN 0-686-69548-8, Collier). Macmillan.

Jane's Pocket Book of Record Breaking Aircraft. Jane's Pocket Books. Ed. by John W. Taylor. (Jane's Pocket Book Ser.). 1981. pap. 6.95 (ISBN 0-02-080630-2, 08063, Collier). Macmillan.

Jane's Surface Skimmers 1976-77. Ed. by Roy McLeavy. 1976. 60.00 o.p. (ISBN 0-531-03266-3). Watts.

Jane's Surface Skimmers 1977-78: Hovercraft & Hydrofoils. Ed. by Roy McLeary. (Illus.). 1978. 60.00 (ISBN 0-531-03283-3). Watts.

Jane's Weapon Systems. Ed. by Ronald T. Pretty. 1976. 72.50 o.p. (ISBN 0-531-03267-1). Watts.

Jane's Weapon Systems: Nineteen Eighty to Eighty-One. 11th ed. 1980. 125.00 (ISBN 0-686-64829-3). Watts.

Jane's World Railways 1977. Ed. by Paul Goldsack. 1977. 72.50 o.p. (ISBN 0-531-03268-X). Watts.

Janet at School. Paul White. LC 77-26681. (John Day Bk.). (Illus.). (gr. k-4). 1978. PLB 7.89 (ISBN 0-381-99557-7, TYC-J). T Y Crowell.

Janet Frame. Patrick Evans. (World Authors Ser.). 1977. 9.95 (ISBN 0-8057-6254-X). Twayne.

Janet Guthrie: Foot to the Floor. Mary V. Fox. LC 80-28309. (Taking Part Bks.). (Illus.). 48p. (gr. 3 up). 1981. PLB 6.95 (ISBN 0-87518-202-X). Dillon.

Janet Reachfar & Chickabird. Jane Duncan. LC 77-12709. (gr. 1-5). 1978. 7.95 (ISBN 0-395-28788-X, Clarion). HM.

Janet Reachfar & the Kelpie. Jane Duncan. LC 75-44166. (Illus.). 32p. (gr. 1-4). 1976. 7.50 (ISBN 0-395-28789-8, Clarion). HM.

Janine. Michelle De Winter. 1979. pap. 1.95 o.p. (ISBN 0-449-14215-9, GM). Fawcett.

Janis Hall, Nurse Instructor. Lucy Bowdler. (YA) 1977. 4.95 o.p. (ISBN 0-685-73811-6, Avalon). Bouregy.

Janitor's Girl. Frieda Friedman. (Illus.). (gr. 3-7). 1956. PLB 7.44 (ISBN 0-688-31708-1). Morrow.

Janner's Compendium of Employment Law. Greville Janner. 759p. 1979. text ed. 45.50x (ISBN 0-220-66363-7, Pub. by Busn Bks England). Renouf.

Janner's Employment Forms. Greville Janner. 397p. 1979. text ed. 61.25x (ISBN 0-220-67027-7, Pub. by Busn Bks England). Renouf.

Janner's Product Liability. Greville Janner. 405p. 1979. text ed. 36.75x (ISBN 0-220-67008-0, Pub. by Busn Bks England). Renouf.

Jan's Consumer Savings. Jan Leasure. (Illus.). 175p. 1981. pap. write for info. (ISBN 0-930256-08-5). Almar.

January Thirty-First. Albert Goldbarth. LC 73-22534. 120p. 1974. pap. 5.95 (ISBN 0-385-05955-8). Doubleday.

Janus Imperative. Evelyn Anthony. 1981. pap. 2.95 (ISBN 0-451-09890-0, E9890, Sig). NAL.

Japan. Pat Barr. (Illus.). 160p. 1980. 24.00 (ISBN 0-7134-0578-3, Pub. by Batsford England). David & Charles.

Japan. Sophy Hoare. LC 75-44864. (Macdonald Countries). (Illus.). (gr. 7 up). 1976. PLB 7.95 (ISBN 0-382-06106-3, Pub. by Macdonald Ed). Silver.

Japan. Charles McNulty. (Orig.). (gr. 9-12). 1975. pap. text ed. 4.50 (ISBN 0-87720-616-3). AMSCO Sch.

Japan. rev. ed. Forrest R. Pitts. LC 77-87223. (World Cultures Ser.). (Illus.). 192p. (gr. 6 up). 1979. text ed. 9.95, 5 or more copies 7.96 ea. o.p. (ISBN 0-88296-119-5); tchrs'. guide 8.94 o.p. (ISBN 0-686-67105-8). Fideler.

Japan. E. W. Tomlin. (Nations & Peoples Library). 1973. 8.50x o.s.i. (ISBN 0-8027-2127-3). Walker & Co.

Japan: A Short Cultural History. rev. ed. George Sansom. LC 77-76152. (Illus.). 1952. 18.75x (ISBN 0-8047-0952-1); pap. 8.95 (ISBN 0-8047-0954-8, SP141). Stanford U Pr.

Japan: A Traveller's Companion. Lensey Namioka. LC 78-63639. (Illus.). 1979. 12.95 (ISBN 0-8149-0810-1); pap. 7.95 (ISBN 0-8149-0816-0). Vanguard.

Japan: Activities & Projects in Color. Claude Soleillant. LC 79-91394. (Illus.). 96p. (gr. 2-12). 1980. 9.95 (ISBN 0-8069-4556-7); PLB 9.29 (ISBN 0-8069-4557-5). Sterling.

Japan, America, & the Future World Order. Morton A. Kaplan & Kinhide Mushakoji. LC 76-15063. 1976. 15.95 (ISBN 0-02-916910-0). Free Pr.

Japan: An Economic Survey 1953-1973. Andrea Boltho. (Economies of the World). (Illus.). 220p. 1975. 24.00x (ISBN 0-19-877036-7). Oxford U Pr.

Japan & a New World Economic Order. Kiyoshi Kojima. LC 76-5808. 1977. 22.50 o.p. (ISBN 0-89158-607-5). Westview.

Japan & Its World: Two Centuries of Change. Marius B. Jansen. LC 80-7532. (Illus.). 120p. 1980. 9.50 (ISBN 0-691-05310-3). Princeton U Pr.

Japan & the Pacific Basin. Ed. by Arthur S. Hoffman. (Atlantic Papers Ser.: No. 40). 68p. 1980. write for info. (ISBN 0-86598-042-X). Allanheld.

Japan & the Soviet Union, Pt. 1. Ed. by Donald S. Detwiler & Charles B. Burdick. (War in Asia & the Pacific Ser., 1937 to 1949: Vol. 10). 670p. 1980. lib. bdg. 50.60 ea. (ISBN 0-8240-3294-2). Garland Pub.

Japan & the United States: Challenges & Opportunities. Ed. by William J. Barnds. LC 79-1551. 1979. 15.00x (ISBN 0-8147-1020-4); pap. 7.00x (ISBN 0-8147-1021-2). NYU Pr.

Japan & the United States: Economic & Political Adversaries. Ed. by Leon Hollerman. LC 79-18646. (Westview Special Studies in International Economics & Business). (Illus.). 245p. 1980. 23.50x (ISBN 0-89158-582-6). Westview.

Japan & the United States: The Early Encounters, 1791-1860. Alfred Tamarin. LC 78-99126. (Illus.). (gr. 9 up). 1970. 6.95 o.s.i. (ISBN 0-02-788810-X). Macmillan.

Japan As Number One: Lessons for America. Ezra F. Vogel. LC 79-24059. 1980. pap. 4.95 (ISBN 0-06-090791-6, CN 791, CN). Harper Row.

Japan at the Brink. Konosuke Matsushita. Tr. by Charles Terry from Japanese. LC 75-30180. 136p. 1975. 8.95 (ISBN 0-87011-270-8). Kodansha.

Japan Before Perry: A Short History. Conrad Totman. (Illus.). 275p. 1981. 20.00x (ISBN 0-520-04132-1). U of Cal Pr.

Japan Before Tokugawa: Political Consolidation & Economic Growth, 1500 to 1650. Ed. by John W. Hall et al. LC 80-7524. (Illus.). 400p. 1981. 32.50 (ISBN 0-691-05308-1). Princeton U Pr.

Japan by the Japanese: A Survey by Its Authorities, 2 vols. Ed. by Alfred Stead. (Studies in Japanese History & Civilization). 1979. Repr. of 1904 ed. 55.00 (ISBN 0-89093-264-6). U Pubns Amer.

Japan, China & the Modern World Economy. F. V. Moulder. LC 76-2230. (Illus.). 1977. 24.95 (ISBN 0-521-21174-3); pap. 7.95x (ISBN 0-521-29736-2). Cambridge U Pr.

Japan-China Phenomenon. Shuichi Kato. Tr. by David Chibbett. LC 75-11392. 103p. 1974. 8.75x (ISBN 0-87011-260-0). Kodansha.

Japan Destiny. Albert Axelbank. LC 73-1810. (Illus.). 160p. (gr. 7-12). 1973. PLB 5.88 o.p. (ISBN 0-531-02615-9). Watts.

Japan Diary. Mark Gayn. LC 80-51196. 530p. 1981. pap. 9.50 (ISBN 0-8048-1369-8). C E Tuttle.

Japan Directory, 1980, 3 vols. LC 62-46629. 1971p. 1980. Set. 180.00x (ISBN 0-8002-2687-9). Intl Pubns Serv.

Japan: Divided Politics in a Growth Economy. J. A. Stockwin. (Comparative Modern Government Ser). 320p. 1975. text ed. 10.00x (ISBN 0-393-05544-2); pap. text ed. 6.95x (ISBN 0-393-09233-X). Norton.

Japan: Economic Growth, Resource Scarcity, & Environmental Constraints. Edward A. Olsen. LC 77-28013. (Westview Replica Edition Ser.). 1978. lib. bdg. 18.50x (ISBN 0-89158-064-6). Westview.

Japan Electronics Buyers' Guide 1980. (Illus.). 1158p. 1980. pap. 65.00 (ISBN 0-8002-2285-7). Intl Pubns Serv.

Japan Fact Book, 1980: Who's Who in Electronics Industry, Almanac of Electronics Industry. (Illus.). 244p. (Orig.). 1980. pap. 30.00x (ISBN 0-8002-2347-0). Intl Pubns Serv.

Japan in Days of Yore. Walter Dening. (Illus.). 1978. 18.00 (ISBN 0-87773-748-7). Great Eastern.

Japan in Pictures. rev. ed. Sterling Publishing Company Editors. LC 60-14338. (Visual Geography Ser). (Orig.). (gr. 6 up). 1978. PLB 4.99 (ISBN 0-8069-1011-9); pap. 2.95 (ISBN 0-8069-1010-0). Sterling.

Japan in Story & Pictures. Lily Edelman. LC 53-9027. (Illus.). (gr. 4-6). 1953. 4.95 o.p. (ISBN 0-15-239701-9, HJ). HarBraceJ.

Japan in the Muromachi Age. Ed. by John W. Hall & Takeshi Toyoda. LC 74-22963. 1977. 24.00x (ISBN 0-520-02888-0); pap. 7.95x (ISBN 0-520-03214-4). U of Cal Pr.

Japan in Transition. Emil Lederer & Emy Lederer-Seidler. 1938. 32.50x o.p. (ISBN 0-685-69837-8). Elliots Bks.

Japan: Its Art, Architecture, & Art Manufacture. Christopher Dresser. LC 76-17752. (Aesthetic Movement & the Arts & Crafts Movement Ser.: Vol. 5). 1977. Repr. of 1882 ed. lib. bdg. 44.00 (ISBN 0-8240-2454-0). Garland Pub.

Japan, Korea & China. William Watts et al. LC 78-7128. 1979. 17.95 (ISBN 0-669-02470-8). Lexington Bks.

Japan Labor Code, 2 vols. Ministry of Labor, Japan. (Studies in Japanese Law & Government). 1979. Repr. of 1953 ed. Set. 56.00 (ISBN 0-89093-217-4). U Pubns Amer.

Japan Nineteen Forty-Eight to Nineteen Fifty-Four Through One American's Eyes. Betsy O'Hara. Ed. by Donald M. Scott. Tr. by Reiko Yamakawa. 72p. (Orig., English-Japanese.). 16.95x (ISBN 0-9604188-0-6); pap. 12.95x (ISBN 0-9604188-1-4). B O'Hara.

Japan: Patterns of Continuity. Fosco Maraini. LC 76-107610. (Illus.). 240p. 1971. 27.50 (ISBN 0-87011-106-X). Kodansha.

Japan: Profile of a Postindustrial Power. Ardath W. Burks. (Nations of Contemporary Asia Ser.). (Illus.). 250p. 1980. lib. bdg. 22.00x (ISBN 0-89158-786-1); pap. 9.50x (ISBN 0-86531-040-8). Westview.

Japan Quality Control Circles. LC 77-186288. 208p. 1973. 18.75 (ISBN 92-833-1021-7, APO39, APO). Unipub.

Japan Reader, 2 vols. Jon Livingston et al. LC 73-7015. 1974. Vol. 1. pap. 7.95 (ISBN 0-394-70668-4); Vol. 2. pap. 7.95 (ISBN 0-394-70669-2). Pantheon.

Japan: Regional Study. Hyman Kublin. (World Regional Studies). (gr. 7-12). 1973. pap. 6.60 (ISBN 0-395-13830-2, 2-31046). HM.

Japan: Selected Readings. rev. ed. Hyman Kublin. LC 72-84106. (Illus.). 228p. (gr. 6-9). 1973. pap. text ed. 6.60 (ISBN 0-395-13930-9, 2-31046). HM.

Japan Style. Ikko Tanaka. Tr. by Joe Earle from Japanese. LC 79-66243. (Illus.). 151p. 1980. text ed. 14.95 (ISBN 0-87011-400-X). Kodansha.

Japan the Beautiful & Myself. Yasunari Kawabata. Tr. by Edward G. Seidensticker. LC 75-90028. 1968. pap. 3.95 (ISBN 0-87011-088-8). Kodansha.

Japan: The New Superstate, a Portable Stanford. Nobutake Ike. pap. text ed. 4.95x (ISBN 0-393-95011-5). Norton.

Japan: The Story of a Nation. rev. ed. Edwin O. Reischauer. (Illus.). 428p. 1974. 11.95 (ISBN 0-394-49510-1); pap. text ed. 10.95. Knopf.

Japan Today. Clara Desiles. (Illus.). 1979. bds. 14.95 (ISBN 2-8525-8110-8, Pub. by Two Continents). Hippocrene Bks.

Japan Today. Ed. by Kenneth A. Grossberg. (Illus., Orig.). 1981. 12.95 (ISBN 0-89727-018-5); pap. 5.95 (ISBN 0-89727-019-3). Inst Study Human.

Japan: Tradition & Transformation. Edwin O. Reischauer & Albert M. Craig. LC 77-77979. (Illus.). 1978. text ed. 14.25 (ISBN 0-395-25814-6). HM.

Japanese Abacus Explained. Yozo Yoshino. (Illus.). pap. 3.50 o.p. (ISBN 0-486-21109-6). Dover.

Japanese Abacus: Its Use & Theory. Takashi Kojima. LC 55-3550. (Illus.). (YA) (gr. 7 up). 1955. pap. 3.75 (ISBN 0-8048-0278-5). C E Tuttle.

Japanese Aircraft of the Pacific War. Rene Francillon. (Illus.). 1980. 31.95 (ISBN 0-370-30251-6, Pub. by Chatto Bodley Jonathan). Merrimack Bk Serv.

Japanese & U.S. Research Libraries at the Turning Point: Proceedings. Japan-U.S. Conference on Libraries & Information Science in Higher Education, 3rd, Kyoto, Japan, Oct. 28-31, 1975. Ed. by Robert D. Stevens et al. LC 77-2535. 1977. 12.00 (ISBN 0-8108-1028-X). Scarecrow.

Japanese Architecture. William Alex. LC 63-7516. (Great Ages of World Architecture Ser). 1963. 7.95 o.s.i. (ISBN 0-8076-0211-6). Braziller.

Japanese Bamboo Baskets. Kazuyoshi Kudo. LC 78-71255. (Form & Function Ser.: Vol. 4). (Illus.). 80p. 1981. pap. 8.95 (ISBN 0-87011-394-1). Kodansha.

Japanese Blue Collar: The Changing Tradition. Robert E. Cole. LC 77-107656. 1971. 12.75 o.p. (ISBN 0-520-01681-5); pap. 7.95x (ISBN 0-520-02354-4, CAMPUS86). U of Cal Pr.

Japanese Border Designs. Ed. by Theodore Menten. LC 75-13124. (Pictorial Archive Ser). Orig. Title: Kodal Moshiki Zuko. (Illus.). 93p. 1975. pap. 2.50 (ISBN 0-486-23180-1). Dover.

Japanese Buddhist Prints. Ed. by Mosaku Ishida. LC 63-22012. (Illus.). 1964. 85.00 (ISBN 0-87011-005-5). Kodansha.

Japanese Business: A Research Guide with Annotated Bibliography. Yoshi Tsurumi. LC 78-70324. (Praeger Special Studies). 1978. 22.95 (ISBN 0-03-044251-6). Praeger.

Japanese Challenge: The Success & Failure of Economic Success. Herman Kahn & Herbert Passin. LC 78-69520. 1979. 10.95 (ISBN 0-690-01784-7, TYC-T). T Y Crowell.

Japanese Children's Books. 1972. pap. 1.00 o.p. (ISBN 0-87104-613-X, Branch Lib). NY Pub Lib.
Japanese Cockpit Interiors, Pt.2. Robert C. Mikesh. (Monogram Aircraft Close-up: No. 15). (Illus.). 1978. pap. 5.95 (ISBN 0-914144-15-4, Pub by Monogram). Aviation.
Japanese Cockpit Interiors: Pt. 1. Robert C. Mikesh. LC 76-6214. (Monogram Close-up: No. 14). (Illus.). 1976. pap. 5.95 (ISBN 0-914144-14-6, Pub. by Monogram). Aviation.
Japanese Colonization in Eastern Paraguay. Division Of Earth Sciences. 1967. pap. 9.00 o.p. (ISBN 0-309-01490-5). Natl Acad Pr.
Japanese Communist Movement, 1920-1966. Robert A. Scalapino. (Center for Japanese & Korean Studies, UC Berkeley). 1967. 17.50x o.p. (ISBN 0-520-01134-1). U of Cal Pr.
Japanese Company. Rodney Clark. 1979. 25.00x (ISBN 0-300-02310-3). Yale U Pr.
Japanese Company. Rodney Clark. LC 78-65480. 292p. 1981. pap. 7.95 (ISBN 0-300-02646-3). Yale U Pr.
Japanese Constitution & Politics. Niichiro Matsunami. (Studies in Japanese Law & Government). 577p. 1979. 38.75 (ISBN 0-89093-217-4). U Pubns Amer.
Japanese Cookbook. David Scott. (Illus.). 1978. 9.95 o.p. (ISBN 0-214-20576-2, 8069, Dist. by Arco). Barrie & Jenkins.
Japanese Cooking: A Simple Art. Shizuo Tsuji. LC 79-66244. (Illus.). 517p. 1980. 14.95 (ISBN 0-87011-399-2). Kodansha.
Japanese Crafts: Materials & Their Applications. Ed. by B. Hickman. (Illus.). 1978. 18.00 (ISBN 0-87773-749-5). Great Eastern.
Japanese Direct Foreign Investment. Sueo Sekiguchi. LC 78-59177. (Atlantic Institute for International Affairs Research Studies: Vol. 1). 171p. 1979. text ed. 20.00 (ISBN 0-916672-17-4). Allanheld.
Japanese Discovery of Europe, 1720-1830. rev. ed. Donald Keene. LC 69-13180. (Illus.). 1969. 10.00x (ISBN 0-8047-0668-9); pap. 5.95 (ISBN 0-8047-0669-7). Stanford U Pr.
Japanese Economic Development: A Short Introduction. Kunio Yoshihara. (Illus.). 168p. 1979. text ed. 9.95x (ISBN 0-19-580439-2). Oxford U Pr.
Japanese Economic System: An Institutional Overview. Kanji Haitani. LC 76-11972. 1976. 18.95 (ISBN 0-669-00716-1). Lexington Bks.
Japanese Education. Herbert Passin. LC 74-93507. 1970. pap. 5.75x (ISBN 0-8077-1879-3). Tchrs Coll.
Japanese Enlightenment. Carmen Blacker. (University of Cambridge Oriental Pubns). 1964. 32.50 (ISBN 0-521-04267-4). Cambridge U Pr.
Japanese Etiquette: An Introduction. Y. W. C. A. World Fellowship Committee - Tokyo. LC 59-9828. (Illus.). (gr. 7 up). 1959. pap. 4.75 (ISBN 0-8048-0290-4). C E Tuttle.
Japanese Factory. rev. ed. James C. Abegglen. LC 80-52878. 200p. 1981. pap. 6.25 (ISBN 0-8048-1372-8). C E Tuttle.
Japanese Feudal Law. Tr. by John C. Hall from Japanese. (Studies in Japanese Law & Government). (Illus.). 266p. 1979. Repr. of 1906 ed. 24.50 (ISBN 0-89093-211-5). U Pubns Amer.
Japanese Flower Arrangement. Wafu Teshigahara. LC 66-27558. (Illus.). 1966. 12.95 o.p. (ISBN 0-87011-036-5). Kodansha.
Japanese Flower Arrangement: A Complete Primer. rev. ed. Ellen G. Allen. LC 62-21731. (Illus.). 1963. Repr. 8.25 (ISBN 0-8048-0293-9). C E Tuttle.
Japanese Flower Arrangement in a Nutshell. Ellen G. Allen. (Illus., Orig.). pap. 4.50 (ISBN 0-8048-0295-5). C E Tuttle.
Japanese Food & Cooking. Stuart Griffin. LC 55-10617. 1955. pap. 5.25 (ISBN 0-8048-0299-8). C E Tuttle.
Japanese for Beginners. Yasuo Yoshida et al. (gr. 12). 1977. 19.95 (ISBN 0-8120-5189-0). Barron.
Japanese Foreign Policy, 1869-1942: Kasumigaseki to Miyakezaka. Ian Nish. (Foreign Policies of the Great Powers Ser.). 1976. 22.00 (ISBN 0-7100-8421-8). Routledge & Kegan.
Japanese Garden. 2nd ed. Teiji Ito. LC 72-75196. (Illus.). 1978. 29.50 o.p. (ISBN 0-87040-441-5). Japan Pubns.
Japanese Gardens. James U. Crockett & Wendy B. Murphy. (Time-Life Encyclopedia of Gardening Ser.). (Illus.). 1979. lib. bdg. 11.97 (ISBN 0-686-66220-2); kivar bdg. 8.95 (ISBN 0-686-66221-0). Silver.
Japanese Government Documents: (of the Meiji Era, 2 vols. Walter W. McLaren. (Studies in Japanese History & Civilization). 1979. Repr. of 1914 ed. Set. 52.50 (ISBN 0-89093-265-4). U Pubns Amer.
Japanese Imperial Institution in the Tokugawa Period. Herschel Webb. LC 68-11912. (East Asian Institute Ser). 1968. 17.50x (ISBN 0-231-03120-3). Columbia U Pr.
Japanese Industrial Estates for Small Business Development. 32p. 1973. 2.75 (APO37, APO). Unipub.
Japanese Industrialization & Its Social Consequences. Hugh Patrick. LC 75-7199. 1976. 27.50x o.p. (ISBN 0-520-03000-1); pap. 8.95x (ISBN 0-520-03285-3, CAMPUS 179). U of Cal Pr.
Japanese Inn. Oliver Statler. (Arena Bks). 1972. pap. 1.95 o.s.i. (ISBN 0-515-02780-4, Y2780). Jove Pubns.
Japanese Institutions. Ed. by Eva Kraft. 611p. (Japanese, Eng.). 1972. text ed. 42.00 (ISBN 3-7940-5041-X, Pub. by K G Saur). Gale.
Japanese International Negotiating Behavior. Michael Blaker. LC 77-8056. (Studies of the East Asian Institute). 1977. 17.50x (ISBN 0-231-04130-6). Columbia U Pr.
Japanese Journalists & Their World. Young C. Kim. LC 80-25720. 1981. price not set (ISBN 0-8139-0877-9). U Pr of Va.
Japanese Kana Workbook. P. G. O'Neill. 1957. pap. 4.95 (ISBN 0-87011-039-X). Kodansha.
Japanese Lacquer. Ann Yonemura. LC 79-19719. (Illus., Orig.). 1979. pap. 12.00 (ISBN 0-934686-35-1). Freer.
Japanese Lacquer, 1600-1900: Selections from the Charles A. Greenfield Collection. Andrew J. Pekarik. Ed. by Rosanne Wasserman. (Illus.). 146p. 1980. 19.95 (ISBN 0-87099-247-3). Metro Mus Art.
Japanese Landlords: The Decline of a Rural Elite. Ann Waswo. 1977. 15.75x (ISBN 0-520-03217-9). U of Cal Pr.
Japanese Language. Roy A. Miller. LC 67-16777. (History & Structure of Language Ser.). 1967. 17.50x o.s.i. (ISBN 0-226-52717-4). U of Chicago Pr.
Japanese Language. Roy A. Miller. LC 67-16777. (History & Structure of Languages Ser.). 496p. 1980. pap. 16.00x (ISBN 0-226-52718-2, Midway). U of Chicago Pr.
Japanese Law of Criminal Procedure. S. Dando. Tr. by B. J. George, Jr. (New York University Comparative Criminal Law Project, Pubns: Vol. 4). 1965. 25.00x (ISBN 0-8377-0500-2). Rothman.
Japanese Literature in Chinese: Poetry and Prose in Chinese by Japanese Writers, 2 vols. Tr. by Burton Watson. 132p. Vol. 1 1975. 12.50x (ISBN 0-231-03986-7); Vol. 2 1976. 15.00x (ISBN 0-231-04146-2). Columbia U Pr.
Japanese Love Poems. Ed. by Jean Bennett. LC 76-2753. 1976. 6.95 o.p. (ISBN 0-385-03085-1). Doubleday.
Japanese Manners & Ethics in Business. Boye De Mente. 1980. pap. 9.95 (ISBN 0-914778-00-5). Phoenix Bks.
Japanese Militarism: Past & Present. Harold H. Sunoo. LC 74-23366. 170p. 1975. 13.95 (ISBN 0-88229-217-X). Nelson-Hall.
Japanese Military Studies Nineteen Thirty-Seven to Nineteen Forty-Nine, Naval Armament Program & Naval Operations: Japanese & Chinese Studies & Documents, Vol. 4. Ed. by Donald S. Detwiler & Charles B. Burdick. (War in Asia & the Pacific Ser., 1937 to 1949). 550p. 1980. Part I. lib. bdg. 60.50 (ISBN 0-8240-3288-8); lib. bdg. 650.00 set of 15 vols. (ISBN 0-686-60107-6). Garland Pub.
Japanese Military Studies Nineteen Thirty-Seven to Nineteen Forty-Nine, Naval Armament Program & Naval Operations: Japanese & Chinese Studies & Documents, Vol. 5. Ed. by Donald S. Detwiler & Charles B. Burdick. (War in Asia & the Pacific Ser., 1937 to 1949). 520p. 1980. Part II. lib. bdg. 60.50 (ISBN 0-8240-3289-6); lib. bdg. 650.00 set 15 vols. (ISBN 0-686-60108-4). Garland Pub.
Japanese Military Studies: The Southern Area: Japanese & Chinese Studies & Documents, Vol. 7. Ed. by Donald S. Detwiler & Charles B. Burdick. (War in Asia & the Pacific Ser., 1937 to 1949). 420p. 1980. Part II. lib. bdg. 60.50 (ISBN 0-8240-3291-8); lib. bdg. 650.00 set of 15 vols. (ISBN 0-686-60114-9). Garland Pub.
Japanese Military Studies 1937-1949: Command, Administration, & Special Operations; Japanese & Chinese Studies & Documents. Ed. by Donald S. Detwiler & Charles B. Burdick. (War in Asia & the Pacific Ser., 1937 to 1949: Vol. 3). 660p. 1980. lib. bdg. 60.50 (ISBN 0-8240-3287-X); lib. bdg. 650.00 set of 15 vols. Garland Pub.
Japanese Military Studies 1937-1949: China, Manchuria, & Korea, Pt. 1. Ed. by Donald S. Detwiler & Charles B. Burdick. (War in Asia & the Pacific Ser., 1937 to 1949: Vol. 8). 630p. 1980. lib. bdg. 55.00 (ISBN 0-8240-3292-6); lib. bdg. 650.00 set of 15 vols. (ISBN 0-686-60097-5). Garland Pub.
Japanese Military Studies 1937-1949: China, Manchuria, & Korea, Pt. 2. Ed. by Donald S. Detwiler & Charles B. Burdick. (War in Asia & the Pacific Ser., 1937 to 1949: Vol. 9). 650p. 1980. lib. bdg. 55.00 (ISBN 0-8240-3293-4); lib. bdg. 60.50 set of 15 vols. Garland Pub.
Japanese Military Studies, 1937-1949: Political Background of the War: Japanese & Chinese Studies & Documents, Vol. 2. Ed. by Donald S. Detwiler & Charles B. Burdick. (War in Asia & the Pacific Ser., 1937 to 1949). 500p. 1980. lib. bdg. 60.50 (ISBN 0-8240-3286-1); lib. bdg. 650.00 set of 15 vols. Garland Pub.
Japanese Military Studies, 1937-1949: The Southern Area: Japanese & Chinese Studies & Documents, Vol. 6. Ed. by Donald S. Detwiler & Charles B. Burdick. (War in Asia & the Pacific Ser., 1937 to 1949). 530p. 1980. Part I. lib. bdg. 60.50 (ISBN 0-8240-3290-X); lib. bdg. 650.00 set of 15 vols. (ISBN 0-686-60113-0). Garland Pub.
Japanese Military Studies, 1937-1949: The Sino-Japanese & the Chinese Civil Wars, Pt. 1. Ed. by Donald S. Detwiler & Charles B. Burdick. (War in Asia & the Pacific Ser., 1937 to 1949: Vol. 13). 460p. 1980. lib. bdg. 60.50 (ISBN 0-8240-3297-7); lib. bdg. 650.00 set of 15 vols. (ISBN 0-686-60110-6). Garland Pub.
Japanese Military Studies, 1937-1949: The Sino-Japanese & the Chinese Civil Wars, Pt. 2. Ed. by Donald S. Detwiler & Charles B. Burdick. (War in Asia & the Pacific Ser., 1937 to 1949: Vol. 14). 610p. 1980. lib. bdg. 60.50 (ISBN 0-8240-3298-5); lib. bdg. 650.00 set of 15 vols. (ISBN 0-686-60111-4). Garland Pub.
Japanese Military Studies, 1939-1949: The Sino-Japanese & the Chinese Civil Wars, Pt. 3. Ed. by Donald S. Detwiler & Charles B. Burdick. (War in Asia & the Pacific Ser., 1937 to 1949: Vol. 15). 570p. 1980. lib. bdg. 60.50 (ISBN 0-8240-3299-3); lib. bdg. 650.00 set of 15 vols. (ISBN 0-686-60112-2). Garland Pub.
Japanese Mistress. Richard Neely. 1979. pap. 1.75 (ISBN 0-515-05164-0). Jove Pubns.
Japanese Motifs for Needlepoint. Sally Nicoletti. LC 80-22650. (Illus.). 136p. 1981. 14.95 (ISBN 0-688-00163-7). Morrow.
Japanese Names & How to Read Them: A Manual for Art-Collectors & Students. Albert J. Koop & Hogitaro Inada. 1972. 75.00 (ISBN 0-7100-1707-3). Routledge & Kegan.
Japanese Oligarchy & the Russo-Japanese War. Shumpei Okamoto. LC 74-114259. (Studies of the East Asian Institute of Col. Univ.). 1971. 20.00x (ISBN 0-231-03404-0). Columbia U Pr.
Japanese Optical & Geometrical Art. Hajime Ouchi. LC 77-82360. (Orig.). 1977. pap. 5.00 (ISBN 0-486-23553-X). Dover.
Japanese Patterns of Behavior. Takie S. Lebra. LC 76-110392. 1976. pap. text ed. 5.95x (ISBN 0-8248-0460-0, Eastwest Ctr). U Pr of Hawaii.
Japanese Poetic Diaries. Tr. by Earl Miner. (Center for Japanese & Korean Studies, UC Berkeley). (Illus.). 1969. 18.50x (ISBN 0-520-01466-9); pap. 3.95 (ISBN 0-520-03047-8). U of Cal Pr.
Japanese Police Establishment. Ralph J. Rinalducci. 388p. 1974. 26.75 (ISBN 0-398-03577-6). C C Thomas.
Japanese Politics, an Inside View: Readings from Japan. Ed. & tr. by Hiroshi Itoh. LC 72-12407. (Illus.). 248p. 1973. 19.50x (ISBN 0-8014-0735-4); pap. 6.95 (ISBN 0-8014-9138-X, CP138). Cornell U Pr.
Japanese Porcelain. Soame Jenyns. (Illus.). 1965. 65.00 (ISBN 0-571-06446-9, Pub. by Faber & Faber). Merrimack Bk Serv.
Japanese Portrait Sculpture. Hisashi Mori. Tr. by W. Chie Ishibashi. LC 76-9353. (Japanese Arts Library: Vol. 2). 1977. 16.95 (ISBN 0-87011-286-4). Kodansha.
Japanese Pottery. Soame Jenyns. 1971. 65.00 (ISBN 0-571-08709-4, Pub. by Faber & Faber). Merrimack Bk Serv.
Japanese Pottery Handbook. Penny Simpson & Kanji Sodeoka. LC 78-71314. 118p. 1979. pap. 8.95 (ISBN 0-87011-373-9). Kodansha.
Japanese Press, 1980. 32nd ed. Ed. by Osamu Asano & Mutsuko Ishiwata. Tr. by Century E. Henshu-sha & Shinbu Higashi. LC 49-25552. (Illus.). 172p. (Orig.). 1980. pap. 25.00x (ISBN 0-8002-2699-2). Intl Pubns Serv.
Japanese Prints & Western Painters. Frank Whitford. LC 76-45182. (Illus.). 1977. 35.00 (ISBN 0-02-627180-X, 62718). Macmillan.
Japanese Prints Today: Tradition with Innovation. Margaret K. Johnson & Dale K. Hilton. (Illus.). 256p. (Orig.). 1980. pap. 9.95 (ISBN 0-8048-1345-0, Pub. by Shufunotomo Co Ltd Japan). C E Tuttle.
Japanese Radicals Revisited: Student Protest in Postwar Japan. Ellis S. Krauss. 1974. 20.00x (ISBN 0-520-02467-2). U of Cal Pr.
Japanese Religion: Unity & Diversity. 2nd ed. H. Bryon Earhart. 1974. pap. text ed. 7.95x (ISBN 0-8221-0123-8). Dickenson.
Japanese Scientific & Technical Literature: A Subject Guide. Robert W. Gibson, Jr. & Barbara K. Kunkel. LC 80-39693. (Illus.). 480p. 1981. lib. bdg. 75.00 (ISBN 0-313-22929-5, GJS/). Greenwood.
Japanese Seizure of Korea, 1868-1910: A Study of Realism & Idealism in International Relations. Hilary Conroy. LC 60-6936. 544p. 1974. pap. 7.50x (ISBN 0-8122-1074-3). U of Pa Pr.
Japanese Society. Chie Nakane. LC 71-100021. (Center for Japanese & Korean Studies, UC Berkeley). 1970. 15.75x (ISBN 0-520-01642-4); pap. 4.50x (ISBN 0-520-02154-1, CAMPUS74). U of Cal Pr.
Japanese Sources on Korea in Hawaii. Ed. by Minako I. Song & Masato Matsui. LC 79-55927. (Occassional Papers Ser.: No. 10). 251p. (Orig.). 1980. pap. 8.00 (ISBN 0-917536-14-2). Ctr Korean U HI at Manoa.
Japanese-Soviet Relations. Young C. Kim. LC 74-27559. (Washington Papers: No. 21). 1975. 3.50x (ISBN 0-8039-0377-4). Sage.
Japanese Sponsored Regime in North China. George Taylor. LC 78-4330. (Modern Chinese Economy Ser.). 145p. 1980. lib. bdg. 16.50 (ISBN 0-8240-4287-5). Garland Pub.
Japanese Stencil Designs: One Hundred Outstanding Examples. Andrew W. Tuer. Orig. Title: Book of Delightful & Strange Designs Being One Hundred Facsimile Illustrations of the Art of the Japanese Stencil-Cutter, Il. pap. 4.00 (ISBN 0-486-21811-2). Dover.
Japanese Sword Blades. 3rd ed. Alfred Dobree. LC 72-161471. (Illus.). 71p. 1971. softbound 6.00 o.p. (ISBN 0-87387-034-4). Shumway.
Japanese Sword Guards. Emil Schnorr. (Illus.). Date not set. pap. cancelled (ISBN 0-8048-1186-5). C E Tuttle.
Japanese Swordsmanship. Donn F. Draeger. (Illus.). 1981. 19.95 (ISBN 0-8348-0146-9). Weatherhill.
Japanese Swordsmanship: Technique & Practice. Donn F. Draeger & Gordon Warner. (Illus.). 224p. Date not set. 19.95 (ISBN 0-8348-0146-9, Pub. by John Weatherhill Inc Japan). C E Tuttle.
Japanese Swordsmiths. rev. ed. 1100p. 1980. vinyl bdg. 75.00 (ISBN 0-686-65147-2, 910704-60). Hawley.
Japanese Tattoo. Donald Richie & Ian Burma. LC 79-26738. (Illus.). 120p. 1980. 23.50 (ISBN 0-8348-0149-3, Pub. by John Weatherhill Inc Japan). C E Tuttle.
Japanese Things: Being Notes on Various Subjects Connected with Japan. Basil H. Chamberlain. LC 76-87791. 1970. pap. 8.50 (ISBN 0-8048-0713-2). C E Tuttle.
Japanese Touch for Your Garden. Kiyoshi Seike & Masanobu Kudo. LC 79-66238. (Illus.). 80p. 1980. 14.95 (ISBN 0-87011-391-7). Kodansha.
Japanese Traditions of Christianity: Being Some Old Translations from the Japanese, with British Consular Reports of the Persecutions of 1868-1872. Ed. by Montague Paske-Smith. (Studies in Japanese History & Civilization). 1979. Repr. of 1930 ed. 17.50 (ISBN 0-89093-257-3). U Pubns Amer.
Japanese-Trained Armies in Southeast Asia: Independence & Volunteer Forces in World War 2. Joyce C. Lebra. LC 75-16116. 264p. 1977. 17.50x (ISBN 0-231-03995-6). Columbia U Pr.
Japanese Urbanism: Industry & Politics in Kariya, 1872-1972. Gary D. Allinson. LC 74-84141. 296p. 1975. 24.00x (ISBN 0-520-02842-2). U of Cal Pr.
Japan's Commission on the Constitution: The Final Report. Ed. by John M. Maki. LC 80-50869. (Asian Law Ser.: No. 7). 352p. 1980. 25.00 (ISBN 0-295-95767-0). U of Wash Pr.
Japan's Dependence on World Economy: An Approach Toward Economic Liberalization. Leon Hollerman. 1967. 17.00x o.p. (ISBN 0-691-05625-0). Princeton U Pr.
Japan's Economic Aid: Policy-Making & Politics. Alan G. Rix. 1980. write for info. (ISBN 0-312-44063-4). St Martin.
Japan's First General Election, Eighteen Ninety. R. H. Mason. LC 68-23915. (University of Cambridge Oriental Pubns.). 1969. 38.50 (ISBN 0-521-07147-X). Cambridge U Pr.
Japan's First Modern Novel. Tr. by Marleigh G. Ryan. LC 67-15896. 1971. 7.50x (ISBN 0-231-08666-0). Columbia U Pr.
Japan's Food Prospects & Policies. Fred Sanderson. 1979. pap. 3.95 (ISBN 0-8157-7701-9). Brookings.
Japan's Foreign Relations, Fifteen Forty-Two to Nineteen Thirty-Six: A Short History. Roy Akagi. (Studies in Japanese History & Civilization). (Illus.). 560p. 1979. Repr. of 1936 ed. 36.50 (ISBN 0-89093-260-3). U Pubns Amer.
Japan's Greatest East Asia Co-Prosperity Sphere in World War Two: Selected Readings & Documents. Ed. by Joyce C. Lebra. 234p. 1975. 27.50x (ISBN 0-19-638265-3). Oxford U Pr.
Japan's Longest Day. Ed. by Pacific War Research Society. LC 68-17573. (Illus.). 340p. 1980. pap. 4.95 (ISBN 0-87011-422-0). Kodansha.

Japan's Minorities: Burakumin, Koreans, Ainu. George A. De Vos & William O. Witherall. (Minority Rights Group: No. 3). 1974. pap. 2.50 (ISBN 0-89192-093-5). Interbk Inc.
Japan's Modern Century--from Perry to 1970. 2nd ed. Hugh Borton. 610p. 1970. 18.95 (ISBN 0-8260-1220-5). Wiley.
Japan's Modernization. Edmund O'Connor. Ed. by Malcolm Yapp & Marget Killingray. (World History Ser.). (Illus.). (gr. 10). 1980. Repr. of 1977 ed. lib. bdg. 5.95 (ISBN 0-89908-232-7); pap. text ed. 1.95 (ISBN 0-89908-207-6). Greenhaven.
Japan's New Middle Class: The Salary Man & His Family in a Tokyo Suburb. new enl. ed. Ezra F. Vogel. 1971. 19.50x (ISBN 0-520-02092-8); pap. 5.75x (ISBN 0-520-02100-2, CAMPUS72). U of Cal Pr.
Japan's Parliament: An Introduction. H. H. Baerwald. LC 73-90810. 200p. 1974. 19.95x (ISBN 0-521-20387-2). Cambridge U Pr.
Japan's Quest for Autonomy: National Security & Foreign Policy, 1930-1938. James B. Crowley. 1966. 22.50x o.p. (ISBN 0-691-03031-6). Princeton U Pr.
Japan's Role in Soviet Economic Growth: Transfer of Technology Since 1965. Raymond S. Mathieson. LC 78-19790. 1979. 21.95 (ISBN 0-03-046481-1). Praeger.
Japji (Adi Granth) Tr. by P. Lal from Punjabi. 38p. 1973. 4.80 (ISBN 0-88253-262-6); pap. text ed. 4.00 (ISBN 0-89253-788-4). Ind-US Inc.
Japon. new ed. Ed. by Daniel Moreau. (Collection monde et voyages). 159p. (Fr.). 1973. 21.00 (ISBN 2-03-053115-4, 2720). Larousse.
Jar Garden. Dorothy Weeks. LC 76-428. (Illus.). 64p. (Orig.). 1976. pap. 3.95 (ISBN 0-912800-26-7). Woodbridge Pr.
Jargonaphasia. Ed. by Jason W. Brown. (Perspectives in Neurolinguistics & Psycholinguistics Ser.). 1981. price not set (ISBN 0-12-137580-3). Acad Pr.
Jarm-How to Jog with Your Arms to Live Longer. Joseph D. Wassersug. 1981. 11.95 (ISBN 0-87949-197-3). Ashley Bks.
Jarrow March. Tom Pickard. (Illus.). 96p. 1981. 11.95 (ISBN 0-8052-8079-0, Pub. by Allison & Busby England); pap. 5.95. Schocken.
Jarry: Le Monstre et la marionette. new ed. (Collection themes et textes). 272p. (Orig., Fr.). 1973. pap. 6.75 (ISBN 0-685-39579-0, 2649). Larousse.
Jasmine Bride. Daphne Clair. (Harlequin Romance Ser.). (Orig.). 1980. pap. 1.25 o.p. (ISBN 0-373-02329-4, Pub. by Harlequin). PB.
Jason, Son of Jason. J. U. Giesy. (YA) 5.95 (ISBN 0-685-07439-0, Avalon). Bouregy.
Jason the Lobsterman. Hilda Bijur & Nancy Smith. LC 78-58577. 1978. write for info. o.p. (ISBN 0-932384-00-5). Tashmoo.
Jason's Quest. Margaret Laurence. 144p. 1981. pap. 2.50 (ISBN 0-686-68905-4). Bantam.
Jasper & the Hero Business. Betty Horvath. (Easy-Read Storybook Ser.). (Illus.). (gr. k-3). 1977. lib. bdg. 4.90 s&l o.p. (ISBN 0-531-01317-0). Watts.
Jasper County, Texas Cemeteries. Mildred S. Wright. LC 76-44116. (Illus.). 1979. pap. 22.75 (ISBN 0-917016-05-X). M S Wright.
Jasper F. Cropsey, Eighteen Twenty-Three to Nineteen Hundred. William S. Talbot. LC 76-23652. (Outstanding Dissertations in the Fine Arts - American). (Illus.). 1977. Repr. of 1972 ed. lib. bdg. 84.00 (ISBN 0-8240-2731-0). Garland Pub.
Jasper Johns: Prints 1970-1977. Richard S. Field. LC 77-93988. (Illus.). 1978. pap. 10.95 (ISBN 0-931266-00-9, Pub. by Wesleyan U Pr). Columbia U Pr.
Jataka Tales. Ellen C. Babbitt. (Illus.). (gr. 7-12). 1912. text ed. 6.50 (ISBN 0-13-509729-0). P-H.
Jataka Tales from the Ajanta Murals. Anjali Pal. (Illus.). 103p. (gr. 4-6). 1968. 1.00 (ISBN 0-88253-330-4). Ind-US Inc.
Jaubert Ring. Willo D. Roberts. 1978. pap. 1.50 o.p. (ISBN 0-445-04169-2). Popular Lib.
Jaufry the Knight & the Fair Brunissende: A Tale of the Times of King Arthur. Ed. by R. Reginald & Douglas Menville. LC 80-19436. (Newcastle Forgotten Fantasy Library: Vol. 21). 156p. 1980. Repr. of 1979 ed. lib. bdg. 10.95x (ISBN 0-89370-520-9). Borgo Pr.
Jaufry the Knight & the Fair Brunissende. LC 79-15119. (Forgotten Fantasy Library: Vol. 21). 1979. pap. write for info. Newcastle Pub.
Java Jack. Luqman Keele & Daniel Pinkwater. LC 79-7892. (Illus.). 160p. (gr. 5-12). 1980. 7.95 (ISBN 0-690-03995-6, TYC-J); PLB 7.89 (ISBN 0-690-03996-4). T Y Crowell.
Javanese Batiks. Susan M. Arensberg. LC 78-54015. (Illus.). 1978. pap. text ed. 5.50 (ISBN 0-87846-128-0). Mus Fine Arts Boston.
Javanese Batiks. Susan M. Arensberg. LC 78-54015. (Illus.). 64p. 1978. pap. 7.00 (Pub. by Mus Fine Arts Boston). C E Tuttle.
Javanese Silat: The Fighting Art of Perisai Diri. Donn F. Draeger & Quintin Chambers. LC 78-60969. (Illus.). 128p. 1979. pap. 7.95 (ISBN 0-87011-353-4). Kodansha.
Javits: The Autobiography of a Public Man. Jacob K. Javits & Rafael Steinberg. (Illus.). 1981. 16.95 (ISBN 0-395-29912-8). HM.
Jawaharlal Nehru. John B. Alphonso-Karkala. (World Authors Ser.: India: No. 345). 1975. lib. bdg. 10.95 (ISBN 0-8057-2649-7). Twayne.
Jawaharlal Nehru of India Eighteen Eighty-Nine to Nineteen Sixty-Four. Ian Copland. (Leaders of Asia Ser.). 53p. (Orig.). 1980. pap. 3.00x (ISBN 0-7022-1506-6). U of Queensland Pr.
Jawaharlal Nehru. the Brahman from Kashmir. Emil Lengyel. LC 68-17704. (Biography Ser). (Illus.). (gr. 7 up). 1968. PLB 5.90 o.p. (ISBN 0-531-00908-4). Watts.
Jawaharlal Nehru's Writings. A. K. Chakraborty. 1981. 15.00x (ISBN 0-685-59378-9). South Asia Bks.
Jay J. Armes, Investigator: The World's Most Successful Private Eye. Jay J. Armes. Ed. by Frederick Nolan. (Illus.). 1976. 8.95 o.s.i. (ISBN 0-02-503200-3). Macmillan.
Jay Treaty: Political Battleground of the Founding Fathers. Jerald A. Combs. LC 70-84044. 1970. 18.50x (ISBN 0-520-01573-8). U of Cal Pr.
Jazz. G. Collier. (Resources of Music Ser.). (Illus.). 200p. 1975. 19.95 (ISBN 0-521-20561-1); pap. 6.95 (ISBN 0-521-09887-4); tape 16.95 (ISBN 0-521-20560-3); record 11.95 (ISBN 0-521-20563-8). Cambridge U Pr.
Jazz. Andre Francis. LC 76-6983. (Roots of Jazz Ser.). 1976. Repr. of 1960 ed. lib. bdg. 19.50 (ISBN 0-306-70812-4). Da Capo.
Jazz. Dean Tudor & Nancy Tudor. LC 78-11737. (American Popular Music on Elpee). 1979. lib. bdg. 22.50 (ISBN 0-87287-148-7). Libs Unl.
Jazz: A People's Music. Sidney Finkelstein. LC 74-23386. (Roots of Jazz Ser). ix, 278p. 1975. Repr. of 1948 ed. lib. bdg. 22.50 (ISBN 0-306-70659-8). Da Capo.
Jazz Age. Ed. by Max Bogart. LC 69-11435. (American Character Ser). (Illus.). (gr. 9-12). 1969. pap. text ed. 5.95 (ISBN 0-684-51500-8, SSP18, ScribC). Scribner.
Jazz Band: My Life in Jazz. Max Kaminsky & V. E. Hughes. (Da Capo Quality Paperbacks Ser.). (Illus.). 242p. 1981. pap. 6.95 (ISBN 0-306-80135-3). Da Capo.
Jazz Cavalcade. Dave Dexter, Jr. LC 77-8035. (Roots of Jazz). (Illus.). 1977. Repr. of 1946 ed. lib. bdg. 22.50 (ISBN 0-306-77431-3). Da Capo.
Jazz Chants. Carolyn Graham. 1978. pap. text ed. 3.95 (ISBN 0-19-502407-9); cassette 6.95x (ISBN 0-19-502410-9); text & cassette 9.00x (ISBN 0-19-502429-X). Oxford U Pr.
Jazz Dance & Jazz Gymnastics. Uta Fischer-Munstermann. Ed. by Liz Williamson. LC 78-57794. (Illus.). 1978. 12.95 (ISBN 0-8069-4618-0); lib. bdg. 11.69 (ISBN 0-8069-4619-9); pap. 6.95 (ISBN 0-8069-4620-2). Sterling.
Jazz Ensemble. Robert E. Henry. (Illus.). 144p. 1981. 15.95 (ISBN 0-13-509992-7, Spec); pap. 7.95 (ISBN 0-13-509984-6). P-H.
Jazz: From the Congo to the Metropolitan. Robert Goffin. Tr. by Walter Schaap & Leonard G. Feather. LC 74-23384. (Roots of Jazz Ser). xii, 254p. 1975. Repr. of 1944 ed. lib. bdg. 22.50 (ISBN 0-306-70680-6). Da Capo.
Jazz Guitarists. Ed. by Guitar Player Magazine. (Illus.). 120p. 5.95 (ISBN 0-8256-9508-2). Guitar Player.
Jazz, Hot & Hybrid. new 3rd ed. Winthrop Sargeant. LC 74-20823. (Roots of Jazz Ser). 302p. 1975. lib. bdg. 22.50 (ISBN 0-306-70656-3); pap. 3.45 (ISBN 0-306-80001-2). Da Capo.
Jazz in Perspective. Iain Lang. LC 76-6985. (Roots of Jazz Ser.). 1976. lib. bdg. 18.50 (ISBN 0-306-70814-0). Da Capo.
Jazz: Its Evolution & Essence. rev. ed. Andre Hodeir. Tr. by David Noakes from French. LC 79-52101. (Illus.). 1980. pap. 3.95 (ISBN 0-394-17525-5, B436, BC). Grove.
Jazz: Its Evolution & Essence. Andre Hodeir. Tr. by David Noakes from Fr. LC 74-23387. (Roots of Jazz Ser). ix, 295p. 1975. Repr. of 1956 ed. lib. bdg. 22.50 (ISBN 0-306-70682-2). Da Capo.
Jazz Life. Nat Hentoff. LC 74-23383. (The Roots of Jazz Ser.). 1978. lib. bdg. 22.50 (ISBN 0-306-70681-4); pap. 5.95 (ISBN 0-306-80088-8). Da Capo.
Jazz Lives. Michael Ullman. (Illus.). 1980. 9.95 o.p. (ISBN 0-915220-51-2). New Republic.
Jazz Masters in Transition: 1957-1969. Martin Williams. (Roots of Jazz Ser.). 1980. Repr. of 1970 ed. 25.00 (ISBN 0-306-79612-0). Da Capo.
Jazz Masters of New Orleans. Martin Williams. (Roots of Jazz Ser.). 1978. Repr. of 1967 ed. lib. bdg. 22.50 (ISBN 0-306-77541-7). Da Capo.
Jazz Masters of the Fifties. Joe Goldberg. (Roots of Jazz Ser.). 246p. 1980. Repr. of 1965 ed. lib. bdg. 22.50 (ISBN 0-306-76031-2). Da Capo.
Jazz Masters of the Forties. I. Gitler. 1966. 5.95 o.p. (ISBN 0-02-543950-2). Macmillan.
Jazz Masters of the Thirties. Rex Stewart. (Roots of Jazz Ser.). 223p. 1980. Repr. of 1972 ed. lib. bdg. 22.50 (ISBN 0-306-76030-4). Da Capo.
Jazz Masters of the Twenties. Richard Hadlock. 1965. 5.95 o.p. (ISBN 0-685-15381-9); pap. 2.95 (ISBN 0-02-060770-9). Macmillan.
Jazz: New Perspectives on the History of Jazz. Nat Hentoff & Albert McCarthy. (Music Reprint Ser.). 1974. Repr. of 1959 ed. lib. bdg. 25.00 (ISBN 0-306-70592-3). Da Capo.
Jazz Panorama. Ed. by Martin Williams. (Roots of Jazz Ser.). 1979. Repr. of 1962 ed. lib. bdg. 22.50 (ISBN 0-306-79574-4). Da Capo.
Jazz Rock Fusion. Julie Coryell & Laura Friedman. 1978. 15.95 o.s.i. (ISBN 0-440-04187-2). Delacorte.
Jazz Scene. Francis Newton. LC 75-4748. (Roots of Jazz Ser). 303p. 1975. Repr. of 1960 ed. lib. bdg. 25.00 (ISBN 0-306-70685-7). Da Capo.
Jazz Singer. Ed. by Tino Balio. LC 78-53295. (Screenplay Ser.). (Illus.). 1979. 15.00 (ISBN 0-299-07660-1); pap. 5.95 (ISBN 0-299-07664-4). U of Wis Pr.
Jazz Singer. Richard Woodley. 192p. (Orig.). 1980. pap. 2.25 (ISBN 0-553-13236-9). Bantam.
Jazz Style in Kansas City & the Southwest. Ross Russell. 1971. 18.95x (ISBN 0-520-01853-2); pap. 3.45 o.p. (ISBN 0-520-02363-3, CAL258). U of Cal Pr.
Jazz Styles. Mark C. Gridley. (Illus.). 352p. 1978. text ed. 16.95 (ISBN 0-13-509885-8); pap. text ed. 11.95 (ISBN 0-13-509877-7). P-H.
Jazz Theory: A Creative Approach. Kenneth Stanton. LC 79-9651. 192p. (Orig.). Date not set. pap. 7.95 (ISBN 0-8008-4311-8, Crescendo). Taplinger.
Jazz Titans. Robert George Reisner. LC 76-58559. (Roots of Jazz Ser.). 1977. Repr. of 1960 ed. lib. bdg. 19.50 (ISBN 0-306-70866-3). Da Capo.
Jazzy. Margaret Doerkson. 272p. 1981. 11.95 (ISBN 0-8253-0039-8). Beaufort Bks NY.
JD & the Bee. LaRue Selman. Ed. by Alton Jordan. (Buppet Series). (Illus.). (gr. k-3). 1981. PLB 4.50 (ISBN 0-89868-093-X, Read Res); pap. text ed. 1.95 (ISBN 0-89868-104-9). ARO Pub.
Jealous. Sylvia R. Tester. (What Does It Mean Ser.). (Illus.). 1980. 7.35g (ISBN 0-516-06446-0). Childrens.
Jealousy in Marriage. (Illus.). pap. 5.00 (ISBN 0-910550-41-7). Centurion Pr.
Jean & Johnny. Beverly Cleary. (Illus.). (gr. 6-9). 1959. 8.75 (ISBN 0-688-21740-0); PLB 8.40 (ISBN 0-688-31740-5). Morrow.
Jean Anouilh. Alba della Fazia. (World Authors Ser.: France: No. 76). lib. bdg. 10.95 (ISBN 0-8057-2048-0). Twayne.
Jean Anouilh: An Annotated Bibliography. Kathleen W. Kelly. LC 73-960. (Author Bibliographies Ser.: No. 10). 1973. 10.00 (ISBN 0-8108-0593-6). Scarecrow.
Jean Anouilh: Five Plays, Vol. 2. Jean Anouilh. Incl. Ardele; Time Remembered; Mademoiselle Colombe; Restless Heart; Lark. 302p. (Orig.). 1959. pap. 6.95 (ISBN 0-8090-0713-4, Mermaid). Hill & Wang.
Jean Anouilh: Seven Plays, Vol. 3. Jean Anouilh. Incl. Thieves Carnival; Medea; Cecile (or the School for Fathers; Traveller Without Luggage; Orchestra; Episode in the Life of an Author; Catch As Catch Can. 379p. (Orig.). 1967. pap. 4.25 (ISBN 0-8090-0739-8, Mermaid). Hill & Wang.
Jean Anouilh: Stages in Rebellion. B. A. Lenski. LC 73-12687. 109p. 1974. text ed. 7.50x (ISBN 0-391-00323-2). Humanities.
Jean-Baptiste-Colbert. Andrew Trout. (World Leaders Ser.: No. 64). 1978. lib. bdg. 13.95 (ISBN 0-8057-7715-6). Twayne.
Jean-Baptiste Oudry (Sixteen Eighty-Six to Seventeen Fifty-Five) Hal N. Opperman. LC 76-23674. (Outstanding Dissertations in the Fine Arts Ser.). 1977. lib. bdg. 133.00 (ISBN 0-8240-2718-3). Garland Pub.
Jean Barois. Roger Du Gard. Ed. by Eugen Weber. 1969. pap. 7.95 (ISBN 0-672-60306-3). Bobbs.
Jean Cocteau. William Fifield. (Columbia Essays on Modern Writers Ser.: No. 70). 1974. pap. 2.00 (ISBN 0-231-03369-9). Columbia U Pr.
Jean Cocteau & Andre Gide: An Abrasive Friendship. Arthur K. Peters. LC 73-185393. 1973. 30.00 (ISBN 0-8135-0709-X). Rutgers U Pr.
Jean de la Bruyere. Edward Knox. (World Authors Ser.: France: No. 298). 1973. lib. bdg. 10.95 (ISBN 0-8057-2507-5). Twayne.
Jean de Vigo: Le Mal Francais Selections from Ancient Syphilographers. Wallace B. Hamby. Tr. by Alfred Fournier & Wallace Hamby. LC 78-50191. 124p. 1981. 15.00x (ISBN 0-87527-191-X). Green.
Jean Francois Milet. Jean-Jacques Leveque. 1977. pap. text ed. 5.95 (ISBN 0-8120-0712-3). Barron.
Jean Genet. Tom F. Driver. LC 66-26003. (Essays on Modern American Writers Ser.: No. 20). (Orig.). 1966. pap. 2.00 (ISBN 0-231-02942-X, MW20). Columbia U Pr.
Jean Giraudoux. John H. Reilly. (World Authors Ser.: No. 513 (France)). 1978. 12.50 (ISBN 0-8057-6354-6). Twayne.
Jean Henri Fabre's Insects. Jean H. Fabre. Ed. by David Black. (Encore Edition). (Illus.). 1979. 4.95 (ISBN 0-684-16820-0, ScribT). Scribner.
Jean-Jacques Rousseau, 2 vols. Jean Guehenno. Tr. by John Weightman & Doreen Weightman. LC 66-12112. 1966. Set. 35.00x (ISBN 0-231-08961-9). Columbia U Pr.
Jean-Jacques Rousseau. George R. Havens. (World Authors Ser.: No. 471). 1978. lib. bdg. 10.95 (ISBN 0-8057-6312-0). Twayne.
Jean-Jacques Rousseau: Authoritarian Libertarian? Ed. by Guy H. Dodge. LC 77-158944. (Problems in Political Science Ser.). 1971. pap. text ed. 2.95x o.p. (ISBN 0-669-74534-0). Heath.
Jean Jacques Rousseau: The Father of Romanticism. Robert N. Webb. LC 76-93947. (Biography Ser). (Illus.). (gr. 7 up). 1970. PLB 6.90 (ISBN 0-531-00941-6). Watts.
Jean-Jacques Rousseau: The Prophetic Voice, 1758-78. Lester G. Crocker. 384p. 1973. 10.95 o.s.i. (ISBN 0-02-528840-7). Macmillan.
Jean-Jacques Rousseau: The Quest, 1712-1758. Lester G. Crocker. LC 68-22818. 1968. 9.95 o.s.i. (ISBN 0-02-528830-X). Macmillan.
Jean-Juliem Lemordant: Ensemble of the Decorative Works of the Painter. Jean-Julien Lemordant. (Illus.). 1919. pap. 32.50x (ISBN 0-686-51409-2). Elliots Bks.
Jean Le Clerc. Samuel A. Golden. (World Authors Ser.: Netherlands: No. 209). lib. bdg. 10.95 (ISBN 0-8057-2232-7). Twayne.
Jean Mairet. William A. Bunch. (World Authors Ser.: France: No. 358). 1975. lib. bdg. 10.95 (ISBN 0-8057-2565-2). Twayne.
Jean Paul Friedrich Richter. Dorothea Berger. (World Authors Ser.: Germany: No. 192). lib. bdg. 10.95 (ISBN 0-8057-2762-0). Twayne.
Jean-Paul Sartre. Liselotte Richter. Tr. by Fred Wieck from Ger. LC 68-31456. (Modern Literature Ser.). 135p. 1970. 10.95 (ISBN 0-8044-2732-1); pap. 3.45 (ISBN 0-8044-6728-5). Ungar.
Jean-Paul Sartre: Contemporary Approaches to His Philosophy. Ed. by Hugh J. Silverman & Frederick A. Elliston. 425p. 1981. text ed. 22.50x (ISBN 0-391-01634-2); pap. 9.95x (ISBN 0-391-01635-0). Duquesne.
Jean-Paul Sartre: Philosopher Without Faith. Rene Marill-Alberes. LC 60-15950. 1960. 4.75 (ISBN 0-8022-0015-X). Philos Lib.
Jean-Paul Sartre: The Philosopher As a Literary Critic. Benjamin Suhl. LC 71-116377. 311p. 1973. 20.00x (ISBN 0-231-03338-9); pap. 7.50x (ISBN 0-231-08319-X). Columbia U Pr.
Jean-Paul Satre's "Les Temps Modernes". Alain D. Ranwez. LC 80-50077. 163p. 1980. 15.00x (ISBN 0-87875-191-2). Whitston Pub.
Jean Piaget. Margaret A. Boden. (Modern Masters Ser.). 1980. pap. 4.95 (ISBN 0-14-005327-1). Penguin.
Jean Racine. Claude Abraham. (World Authors Ser.: No. 458). 1977. lib. bdg. 12.50 (ISBN 0-8057-6295-7). Twayne.
Jean Renoir. Raymond Durgnat. LC 72-82221. (Illus.). 1975. 22.50 (ISBN 0-520-02283-1); pap. 4.95 (ISBN 0-520-02743-4). U of Cal Pr.
Jean Rhys: Woman in Passage. Helen Nebeker. 250p. 1981. price not set (ISBN 0-920792-04-9). Eden Women.
Jean Tinguely "Meta". K. G. Hulten. LC 73-80231. (Illus.). 364p. 1976. signed limited ed. 100.00 (ISBN 0-8212-0547-1, 459054). NYGS.
Jean Vigo. P. E. Salles Gomes. Tr. by Allan Francovich. 1972. 17.95x (ISBN 0-520-01676-9); pap. 5.95 (ISBN 0-520-02332-3, CAL252). U of Cal Pr.
Jeanne. Katherine Howard. 1979. pap. 1.95 (ISBN 0-505-51331-5). Tower Bks.
Jeanne d'Arc. Peter Wild. LC 78-13043. (Raccoon Book). 1980. pap. 4.95 signed ed (ISBN 0-918518-16-4); pap. 3.95 (ISBN 0-918518-12-1). St Luke TN.
Jeanne Jones Party Planner & Entertaining Diary. Jeanne Jones. (Illus.). 1979. 4.95 (ISBN 0-89286-156-8). One Hund One Prods.
Jeax Sont Faits. Ed. by J. Sartre & M. Stover. 1952. pap. 7.95 (ISBN 0-13-530675-2). P-H.
Jeddah Commercial Directory 1980. 1980. 95.00x (Pub. by Parrish-Rogers England). State Mutual Bk.

Jedediah Smith & the Opening of the West. Dale L. Morgan. LC 53-10550. (Illus.). 1964. pap. 4.50 (ISBN 0-8032-5138-6, BB 184, Bison). U of Nebr Pr.

Jeep All Models: 1969-1978, 4-Wheel Drive Maintenance. Mike Bishop. Ed. by Eric Jorgensen. (Illus.). 1978. pap. 7.95 (ISBN 0-89287-291-8, A234). Clymer Pubns.

Jeep Service, Repair Handbook: Covers Willy-Overland Model MB & Ford Model GPW. Clymer Publications. (Illus.). 1971. pap. 7.95 (ISBN 0-89287-250-0, A162). Clymer Pubns.

Jeeves. Northcote Parkinson. 192p. 1981. 8.95 (ISBN 0-312-44144-4). St Martin.

Jeff. P. B. Ricchiuti. 1973. pap. 0.65 o.p. (ISBN 0-8163-0105-0, 10130-3). Pacific Pr Pub Assn.

Jeff Milton: A Good Man with a Gun. J. Evetts Haley. (Illus.). 432p. 1981. 19.91 (ISBN 0-8061-0182-2); pap. 9.95 (ISBN 0-8061-1756-7). U of Okla Pr.

Jeff White: Young Woodsman. Lew Dietz. LC 79-22669. (Illus.). 224p. (gr. 6-10). 1979. pap. 4.95 (ISBN 0-89621-042-1). Thorndike Pr.

Jefferson & Madison: The Great Collaboration. Adrienne Koch. 1964. pap. 8.95 (ISBN 0-19-500420-5, GB). Oxford U Pr.

Jefferson & the American Revolutionary Ideal. Otto Vossler. Tr. by Catherine Philippon & Bernard Wishy. LC 79-6726. 1980. pap. text ed. 10.50 (ISBN 0-8191-0941-X); lib. bdg. 18.50 (ISBN 0-8191-0938-X). U Pr of Amer.

Jefferson & the Arts: An Extended View. Ed. by Howard Adams. LC 76-21951. 1976. 20.00x (ISBN 0-685-79644-2, National Gallery of Art). U Pr of Va.

Jefferson Davis. Clement Eaton. LC 77-2512. 1979. pap. text ed. 7.95 (ISBN 0-02-908740-6). Free Pr.

Jefferson Davis Gets His Citizenship Back. Robert P. Warren. LC 80-51023. 120p. 1980. Repr. of 1980 ed. 8.75 (ISBN 0-8131-1445-4). U Pr of Ky.

Jefferson Davis: The Sphinx of the Confederacy. Clement Eaton. LC 77-2512. 1977. 14.95 (ISBN 0-02-908700-7). Free Pr.

Jefferson Himself. Bernard Mayo. LC 70-87871. 7.50x o.p. (ISBN 0-8139-0284-3); pap. 5.95x (ISBN 0-8139-0310-6). U Pr of Va.

Jefferson Scandals. Virginius Dabney. (Illus.). 156p. 1981. 8.95 (ISBN 0-396-07964-4). Dodd.

Jeffersonian Persuasion: Evolution of a Party Ideology. Lance Banning. LC 77-14666. (Cornell Paperbacks Ser.). 328p. 1980. pap. 5.95 (ISBN 0-8014-9203-3). Cornell U Pr.

Jeffersonianism & the American Novel. Howard M. Jones. LC 66-28267. (Orig.). 1966. text ed. 6.50x (ISBN 0-8077-1593-X); pap. text ed. 4.50x (ISBN 0-8077-1590-5). Tchrs Coll.

Jefferson's Buildings at the University of Virginia: The Rotunda. William B. O'Neal. (Illus.). 1960. 10.00 o.p. (ISBN 0-8139-0189-8). U Pr of Va.

Jefferson's Fine Arts Library. W. B. O'Neal. 1976. 20.00 (ISBN 0-8139-0648-2). Brown Bk.

Jefferson's Gas Welding Manual. 4th ed. Ted B. Jefferson & D. T. Jefferson. (Monticello Bks). 140p. 1980. pap. 5.00. Jefferson Pubns.

Jefferson's Nephews: A Frontier Tragedy. Boynton Merrill. 1977. pap. 2.95 (ISBN 0-380-01837-3, 36277, Discus). Avon.

Jeffrey's Department Store: A Retailing Simulation-Employee's Guide. Jimmy Koeninger & Thomas Hephner. (Illus.). (gr. 11-12). 1978. pap. text ed. 6.96x (ISBN 0-07-035231-3, G); replacement forms 75.00x (ISBN 0-07-086511-6); general mgr's manual 6.95x (ISBN 0-07-035230-5); store box 150.00x (ISBN 0-07-086510-8). McGraw.

Jehol, City of Emperors. Sven Hedin. LC 79-2827. (Illus.). 278p. 1981. Repr. of 1933 ed. 23.50 (ISBN 0-8305-0005-7). Hyperion Conn.

Jehovah's Witnesses. Walter Martin. 1969. pap. 1.50 (ISBN 0-87123-270-7, 210270). Bethany Fell.

Jehovah's Witnesses in Central Africa. Tony Hodges. (Minority Rights Group Ser.: No. 29). 16p. (Orig.). 1976. pap. 2.50 (ISBN 0-89192-120-6). Interbk Inc.

Jelly Belly: A Novel. Robert K. Smith. LC 80-23898. (Illus.). 156p. (gr. 4-7). 1981. 8.95 (ISBN 0-440-04186-4); PLB 8.44 (ISBN 0-440-04190-2). Delacorte.

Jelly Was the Word. Donald L. Weismann. (Illus.). 8.50 o.p. (ISBN 0-8363-0124-2). Jenkins.

Jellybeans for Breakfast. Miriam Young. LC 68-21082. (Illus.). (gr. k-3). 1968. 5.95 o.s.i. (ISBN 0-8193-0339-9, Four Winds); PLB 5.41 o.s.i. (ISBN 0-8193-0340-2). Schol Bk Serv.

Jemmy. Jon Hassler. LC 79-23091. (gr. 7 up). 1980. 7.95 (ISBN 0-689-50130-7, McElderry Bk). Atheneum.

Jennifer. Zoa Sherburne. (gr. 7 up). 1959. 8.25 (ISBN 0-688-21744-3). Morrow.

Jennifer & Josephine. Bill Peet. (Illus.). (ps-3). 1980. pap. 3.45 (ISBN 0-395-29608-0, Sandpiper). HM.

Jennifer, Hecate, Macbeth, William McKinley, & Me, Elizabeh. E. L. Konigsburg. (gr. 3-6). 1967. pap. 2.95 (ISBN 0-689-70296-5, Aladdin). Atheneum.

Jennifer Jean, the Cross-Eyed Queen. Phyllis Naylor. LC 67-15701. (General Juvenile Bks). (Illus.). (gr. k-5). 1967. PLB 3.95 o.p. (ISBN 0-8225-0263-1). Lerner Pubns.

Jenny. Gene Inyart. (gr. 3-5). 1970. pap. 1.50 (ISBN 0-671-29917-4). PB.

Jenny. Patricia Phillips. (Histoical Romance Ser.). 432p. (Orig.). 1981. pap. 2.75 (ISBN 0-515-05538-7). Jove Pubns.

Jenny. Joan Tate. pap. text ed. 1.95x o.p. (ISBN 0-435-11876-5). Heinemann Ed.

Jenny & The Tennis Nut. Janet Schulman. (gr. k-6). 1981. pap. price not set (ISBN 0-440-44211-7, YB). Dell.

Jenny Doone, Office Nurse. Addie Adam. 192p. (YA) 1976. 4.95 o.p. (ISBN 0-685-62627-X, Avalon). Bouregy.

Jenny Kimura. Betty Cavanna. (gr. 7 up). 1964. PLB 7.92 (ISBN 0-688-31737-5). Morrow.

Jenny Lind & Her Listening Cat. Frances Cavanah. LC 61-15483. (Illus.). (gr. 3-6). 1961. 6.95 (ISBN 0-8149-0289-8). Vanguard.

Jenny Moves. Dawn Tutela. Ed. by Eli Newberger. (Jenny Ser.). (Illus.). (gr. 4-9). 1981. pap. 2.95 (ISBN 0-8326-2609-0, 7611). Delair.

Jenny Redbird Finds Her Friends. Biloine W. Young & Mary Wilson. (Illus.). 28p. (gr. 1-4). 1972. 1.50 o.p. (ISBN 0-8309-0087-X). Independence Pr.

Jenny's Cat. Miska Miles. LC 79-11501. (Illus.). (gr. 1-4). 1979. PLB 7.50 (ISBN 0-525-32746-0, Unicorn Bk.). Dutton.

Jenny's Corner. Frederic Bell. LC 73-18741. (Illus.). 72p. 1974. 3.95 (ISBN 0-394-82741-4); PLB 5.99 (ISBN 0-394-92741-9). Random.

Jenny's First Friend. Dawn Tutela. Ed. by Eli Newberger. (Jenny Ser.). (Illus.). (gr. 4-9). 1981. pap. 2.95 (ISBN 0-8326-2608-2, 7610). Delair.

Jensen's Bible Study Charts. Irving L. Jensen. 128p. 1981. pap. 19.95 (ISBN 0-8024-4296-X). Moody.

Jensen's Survey of the New Testament. Irving L. Jensen. 608p. 1981. text ed. 14.95 (ISBN 0-8024-4308-7). Moody.

Jensen's Survey of the Old Testament. Irving L. Jensen. 1978. text ed. 12.95 (ISBN 0-8024-4307-9). Moody.

Jephthah & Samson. Gordon Lindsay. (Old Testament Ser.). 1.25 (ISBN 0-89985-136-3). Christ Nations.

Jeppesen Instrument Rating Course (Mach 2) Jeppesen Sanderson. (Illus.). 1978. 35.95 (ISBN 0-88487-022-7, JE304907). Jeppesen Sanderson.

Jeppesen Instrument Rating Manual. Jeppesen Sanderson. (Flight Instruction Manuals Ser.). (Illus.). 1978. pap. text ed. 17.95 o.p. (ISBN 0-88487-021-9, JE314923). Jeppesen Sanderson.

Jeppesen Mach One Private Pilot Course. 10th ed. (Illus.). 1980. looseleaf bdg. 20.26 (ISBN 0-88487-063-4, JE304903). Jeppesen Sanderson.

Jeppesen Sanderson Aerospace Fundamentals Textbook. Jeppesen Sanderson. (Illus.). 1977. lib. bdg. 11.80 (ISBN 0-88487-043-X, SA315253). Jeppesen Sanderson.

Jeppesen Sanderson Aviation Yearbook. 1979 ed. (Yearbook Ser.). (Illus.). 1979. 14.95 o.p. (ISBN 0-88487-050-2). Jeppesen Sanderson.

Jeremiah: A Study Guide Commentary. F. B. Huey, Jr. (Study Guide Commentary Ser.). 144p. (Orig.). 1981. pap. 3.95 (ISBN 0-310-36063-3). Zondervan.

Jeremiah: A Study in Ancient Hebrew Rhetoric. Jack R. Lundbom. LC 75-15732. (Society of Biblical Literature. Dissertation Ser.). xiv, 195p. 1975. pap. 9.00 (ISBN 0-89130-011-2, 060118). Scholars Pr Ca.

Jeremiah Dummer: Colonial Craftsman & Merchant 1645-1718. Herman F. Clarke & Henry W. Foote. LC 75-87563. (Architecture & Decorative Art Ser). (Illus.). 1970. Repr. of 1935 ed. 27.50 (ISBN 0-306-71394-2). Da Capo.

Jeremiah, Eight Twenty. Carol Hill. 1970. 8.95 o.p. (ISBN 0-394-43119-7). Random.

Jeremiah, Meet the Twentieth Century. James W. Sire. LC 74-31846. 120p. 1975. pap. 2.50 o.p. (ISBN 0-87784-641-3). Inter-Varsity.

Jeremiah: Prophecy & Lamentations. H. A. Ironside. Date not set. 6.50 (ISBN 0-87213-371-0). Loizeaux.

Jeremiah: Spokesman Out of Time. William L. Holladay. LC 74-7052. 160p. 1974. pap. 3.95 (ISBN 0-8298-0283-5). Pilgrim NY.

Jeremiah Sullivan Black, a Defender of the Constitution & the Ten Commandments. William N. Brigance. LC 72-139196. (American Scene Ser). (Illus.). 1971. Repr. of 1934 ed. lib. bdg. 32.50 (ISBN 0-306-70078-6). Da Capo.

Jeremy Bentham & the Law, a Symposium. Ed. by George W. Keeton & Georg Schwarzenberger. Repr. of 1948 ed. lib. bdg. 15.00x (ISBN 0-8371-2832-3, KEJB). Greenwood.

Jeremy Poldark, No. 3. Winston Graham. (Poldark Ser). 1977. pap. 2.25 (ISBN 0-345-27733-3). Ballantine.

Jeremy Visick. David Wiseman. (gr. 5 up). 1981. 7.95 (ISBN 0-395-30449-0). HM.

Jericho Commandment. James Patterson. 1981. pap. 2.50 (ISBN 0-345-29241-3). Ballantine.

Jericho Man. John Lutz. LC 80-14988. 256p. 1980. 10.95 (ISBN 0-688-03719-4). Morrow.

Jerk. Steve Martin. (Illus., Orig.). 1979. pap. 2.25 (ISBN 0-446-92523-3). Warner Bks.

Jermiah Bacon. James A. Janke. (Orig.). 1980. pap. 1.95 (ISBN 0-440-15289-5). Dell.

Jerome Biblical Commentary. Ed. by Raymond E. Brown et al. 1969. 43.95 (ISBN 0-13-509612-X). P-H.

Jerome, Chrysostom, & Friends: Essays & Translations. Elizabeth A. Clark. LC 79-66374. (Studies in Women & Religion: Vol. 1). xi, 254p. 1979. soft cover 24.95x (ISBN 0-88946-548-7). E Mellen.

Jerome K. Jerome. Ruth M. Faurot. LC 73-15938. (English Authors Ser.: No. 164). 1974. lib. bdg. 10.95 (ISBN 0-8057-1291-7). Twayne.

Jerome Kern. Michael Freedland. (Illus.). 182p. 1978. 13.25x (ISBN 0-8476-3126-5). Rowman.

Jerome Kern: A Biography. Michael Freedland. LC 80-6160. 200p. 1981. 12.95 (ISBN 0-8128-2776-7). Stein & Day.

Jerry Ford Joke Book. George Lombardi. 1976. pap. 0.95 o.p. (ISBN 0-685-69157-8, LB365, Leisure Bks). Nordon Pubns.

Jerry N. Uelsmann. LC 74-125448. (Aperture Monograph). (Illus.). pap. 10.00 o.p. (ISBN 0-912334-15-0). Aperture.

Jerry N. Uelsmann Photographs from Nineteen Seventy-Five to Nineteen Seventy-Nine. Jerry N. Uelsmann. Ed. by Steven Klindt. (Illus.). 90p. (Orig.). 1980. pap. 7.95 (ISBN 0-932026-04-4). Chicago Contemp Photo.

Jerry the Newsboy. Leonard Shortall. LC 70-118273. (Illus.). (ps-3). 1970. PLB 7.44 (ISBN 0-688-31711-1). Morrow.

Jerry West: Superstars. Paul J. Deegan. LC 73-19525. 1974. PLB 5.95 o.p. (ISBN 0-87191-311-9). Creative Ed.

Jerry Works in a Service Station. Jewel M. Wade. (Illus., Special education ser. for slow learners). (gr. 7-12,RL 2.2). 1967. pap. 2.56 (ISBN 0-8224-4025-3); tchrs'. manual free (ISBN 0-8224-4024-5). Pitman Learning.

Jersey. Ward Rutherford. LC 75-31326. (Island Ser). (Illus.). 1976. 13.50 (ISBN 0-7153-7075-8). David & Charles.

Jersey Cattle. Ed. by Eric Boston. (Illus.). 1954. 8.50 o.p. (ISBN 0-571-02213-8, Pub. by Faber & Faber). Merrimack Bk Serv.

Jerusalem. John M. Oesterreicher & Anne Sinai. (Illus., Orig.). 1974. text ed. 5.95 o.p. (ISBN 0-381-98266-1). John Day.

Jerusalem. Colin Thubron. (Great Cities Ser.). (Illus.). 1976. 14.95 (ISBN 0-8094-2250-6). Time-Life.

Jerusalem. Colin Thubron. (The Great Cities Ser.). (Illus.). (gr. 6 up). 1976. 14.94 (ISBN 0-8094-2251-4, Pub by Time-Life). Silver.

Jerusalem & Rome: The Writings of Josephus. Josephus. Ed. by Nahum N. Glatzer. 8.00 (ISBN 0-8446-2341-5). Peter Smith.

Jerusalem: Bridging the Four Walls: a Geopolitical Perspective. Saul B. Cohen. LC 77-76665. (Illus.). 1978. lib. bdg. 12.00 o.p. (ISBN 0-685-91823-8). Westview.

Jerusalem: City of Jesus. Richard M. Mackowski. (Illus.). 224p. 1980. 29.95 (ISBN 0-8028-3526-0). Eerdmans.

Jerusalem Einstein Centennial Symposium. Ed. by Yuval Ne'Emann. (Illus.). 528p. 1980. text ed. 39.50 (ISBN 0-201-05289-X). A-W.

Jerusalem Fifteen Hundred. Alexandra W. Johnson. (Illus.). 1981. 12.95 (ISBN 0-930720-66-0). Liberator Pr.

Jerusalem History Atlas. Martin Gilbert. (Illus.). 1977. 12.95 (ISBN 0-02-543410-1). Macmillan.

Jerusalem in the Time of Jesus: An Investigation into Economic & Social Conditions During the New Testament Period. Joachim Jeremias. Tr. by F. H. Cave & C. H. Cave. LC 77-81530. 434p. 1975. pap. 5.95 (ISBN 0-8006-1136-5, 1-1136). Fortress.

Jerusalem Poker. Edward Whittemore. 1978. 10.95 o.p. (ISBN 0-03-018516-5). HR&W.

Jerusalem: Problems & Prospects. Ed. by Joel L. Kraemer. 256p. 1980. 25.95 (ISBN 0-03-057733-0); pap. 9.95 (ISBN 0-03-057734-9). Praeger.

Jerusalem Question: 1917-1968. H. Eugene Bovis. LC 73-149796. (Studies Ser.: No. 29). (Illus.). 175p. 1971. 6.95 (ISBN 0-8179-3291-7). Hoover Inst Pr.

Jerusalem: The Christian Herald Photoguide. Ed. by Dave Foster. LC 79-57167. (Illus.). 128p. 1980. 14.95 (ISBN 0-915684-60-8). Christian Herald.

Jerusalem Undivided. Saul B. Cohen. 1980. pap. 3.00 (ISBN 0-930832-58-2). Herzl Pr.

Jessamyn West. Alfred S. Shivers. (U. S. Authors Ser.: No. 192). lib. bdg. 10.95 (ISBN 0-8057-0784-0). Twayne.

Jesse. Ed. by Paul Neimark. Pul Neimark. Ed. by Benjamin Mercado. Tr. by Rhode Flores from Eng. 192p. (Span.). 1979. pap. 1.95 (ISBN 0-8297-0677-1). Vida Pubs.

Jesse. Jesse Owens & Paul Neimark. 1978. 6.95 o.p. (ISBN 0-88270-314-5). Logos.

Jesse & Abe. Rachel Isadora. LC 80-15584. (Illus.). 32p. (gr. k-4). 1981. 7.95 (ISBN 0-688-80302-4); PLB 7.63 (ISBN 0-688-84302-6). Greenwillow.

Jesse Comes Back. Clifton Snider. 1980. 1.50 (ISBN 0-917554-05-1). Maelstrom.

Jesse Hill Ford: An Annotated Checklist of His Published Works & of His Papers. Helen White. (Mississippi Valley Collection Bulletin, No. 7). (Illus.). 55p. 1974. pap. 5.95x (ISBN 0-87870-083-8). Memphis St Univ.

Jesse Jackson: I Am Somebody. Paul Westman. LC 80-20521. (Taking Part Ser.). 48p. (gr. 3 up). 1980. PLB 6.95 (ISBN 0-87518-203-8). Dillon.

Jesse Jackson: The Man, the Movement, the Myth. Barbara A. Reynolds. LC 74-17813. 416p. 1975. 14.95 (ISBN 0-911012-80-X). Nelson-Hall.

Jesse James. John Ernst. LC 76-10206. (Illus.). (gr. 4-7). 1976. PLB 6.95 (ISBN 0-13-509695-2); pap. 1.95 (ISBN 0-13-509661-8). P-H.

Jesse James: The Making of a Legend. Larry C. Bradley. LC 80-81622. (Illus.). 228p. (Orig.). 1980. pap. 8.95 (ISBN 0-9604370-0-2). Larren Pubs.

Jesse James Was His Name, or Fact & Fiction Concerning the Careers of the Notorious James Brothers of Missouri. William A. Settle, Jr. LC 65-22965. (Illus.). 1966. 11.00x o.p. (ISBN 0-8262-0052-4). U of Mo Pr.

Jesse James Was His Name: or, Fact & Fiction Concerning the Careers of the Notorious James Brothers of Missouri. William A. Settle, Jr. LC 76-56786. (Illus.). 1977. pap. 5.95 (ISBN 0-8032-5860-7, BB 640, Bison). U of Nebr Pr.

Jesse Stuart. Ruel E. Foster. LC 68-24298. (U. S. Authors Ser.: No. 140). 1968. lib. bdg. 10.95 (ISBN 0-8057-0704-2). Twayne.

Jesse Stuart: Essays on His Work. Ed. by J. R. Lemaster & Mary W. Clarke. LC 76-46032. 176p. 1977. 15.00x (ISBN 0-8131-1352-0). U Pr of Ky.

Jesse Stuart: Kentucky's Chronicler-Poet. J. R. LeMaster. LC 79-28224. 1980. 14.95x (ISBN 0-87870-049-8). Memphis St Univ.

Jesse's Dream Skirt. Bruce Mack. LC 79-89892. 36p. (ps-1). 1979. pap. 3.00 (ISBN 0-914996-20-7). Lollipop Power.

Jessie Fremont at Black Point. Lois Rather. (Illus.). 1974. ltd. ed. 15.00 o.p. (ISBN 0-686-20622-3). Rather Pr.

Jessie Redmon Fauset: Black American Writer. Carolyn W. Sylvander. LC 80-51050. (Illus.). 285p. 1980. 18.50x (ISBN 0-87875-196-3). Whitston Pub.

Jessie White Mario: Risorgimento Revolutionary. Elizabeth A. Daniels. LC 78-158178. (Illus.). vii, 199p. 1972. 12.95 (ISBN 0-8214-0103-3). Ohio U Pr.

Jessie Willcox Smith. S. Michael Schnessel. LC 77-3530. (Illus.). 1977. 22.95 o.s.i. (ISBN 0-690-01493-7, TYC-T). T Y Crowell.

Jesucristo, Roca Firme. Tr. by David Wilkerson. (Spanish Bks.). (Span.). 1978. 1.60 (ISBN 0-8297-0577-5). Life Pubs Intl.

Jesuit Education: An Essay on the Foundations of Its Ideas. John W. Donohue. LC 63-11902. 1963. 17.50 o.p. (ISBN 0-8232-0490-1). Fordham.

Jesuit Hacienda in Colonial Mexico: Santa Lucia, 1576-1767. Herman W. Konrad. LC 79-65518. (Illus.). 472p. 1980. 28.50x (ISBN 0-8047-1050-3). Stanford U Pr.

Jesuit Letters & Indian History 1542-1773. John Correia-Alfonso. 1969. pap. 7.25x o.p. (ISBN 0-19-635280-0). Oxford U Pr.

Jesuit Religious Life Today. Ed. by George E. Ganss. LC 77-78816. (Jesuit Primary Sources in English Translation Ser.: No. 3). 190p. 1977. pap. 3.00 (ISBN 0-912422-27-0); pap. 4.00 smyth sewn o.s.i. (ISBN 0-912422-29-7). Inst Jesuit.

Jesuits. David Mitchell. (Illus.). 320p. 1981. 17.50 (ISBN 0-531-09947-4). Watts.

Jesuits & Music. Thomas D. Cully. 1970. pap. 14.00 (ISBN 0-8294-0335-3). Jesuit Hist.

Jesus. Grace Dickerson. 1981. 5.50 (ISBN 0-533-03936-3). Vantage.

Jesus. Joe Maniscalco. (Bible Hero Stories). (Illus.). 48p. (Orig.). (gr. 3-6). 1975. pap. 2.00 o.p. (ISBN 0-87239-036-5, 2738). Standard Pub.

Jesus. Eduard Schweizer. LC 76-107322. 1979. pap. 4.95 (ISBN 0-8042-0331-8). John Knox.

Jesus. Edward W. H. Vick. LC 78-10253. (Anvil Ser.). 1979. pap. 4.95 (ISBN 0-8127-0220-4). Southern Pub.

Jesus: A Pictorial History of the New Testament. Eugene Weiler. (Illus.). 160p. 1980. pap. 10.95 (ISBN 0-8245-2287-7). Crossroad NY.

Jesus Alive! The Mighty Message of Mark. Thomas J. Smith. LC 73-81824. 1973. pap. 4.90x (ISBN 0-88489-015-5); tchr ed 2.60x (ISBN 0-88489-117-8). St Marys.

Jesus: An Experiment in Christology. Edward Schillebeeckx. 1979. 24.50. Crossroad NY.

Jesus & His Friends. (Children of the Kingdom Activities Ser.). (gr. k-4). 1974. 7.95 (ISBN 0-686-13683-7). Pflaum Pr.

Jesus & Logotherapy. Robert C. Leslie. LC 65-11077. (Series AD). 1968. pap. 2.25 (ISBN 0-687-19927-1, Apex). Abingdon.

Jesus & the Crippled Man. (Tell-a-Bible Story Ser.). (Illus.). 28p. bds. 0.69 (ISBN 0-686-68644-6, 3688). Standard Pub.

Jesus & the Future: Unsolved Questions on Eschatology. Richard H. Hisis. LC 80-82189. 1981. 16.50 (ISBN 0-8042-0341-5); pap. 9.95 (ISBN 0-8042-0340-7). John Knox.

Jesus & the Gospel, Vol. 1. P. Benoit. 264p. 1973. 9.75 (ISBN 0-8164-1055-0). Crossroad NY.

Jesus & the Language of the Kingdom: Symbol & Metaphor in New Testament Interpretation. Norman Perrin. LC 80-20822. 240p. 1980. pap. 8.95 (ISBN 0-8006-1432-1, 1-1432). Fortress.

Jesus & the New Age According to Saint Luke. Frederick W. Danker. LC 72-83650. 255p. 1980. pap. 12.00 (ISBN 0-915644-21-5). Clayton Pub Hse.

Jesus & the New Age: According to St. Luke, A Commentary on the Third Gospel. 3rd rev. ed. Frederick W. Danker. LC 72-83650. xxiv, 256p. 1974. pap. text ed. 9.00 o.p. (ISBN 0-915644-03-7). Clayton Pub Hse.

Jesus & the Pharisees. John Bowker. 240p. 1973. 32.00 (ISBN 0-521-20055-5). Cambridge U Pr.

Jesus & Woman: An Exciting Discovery of What He Offered Her. Lisa Sergio. LC 75-4365. 139p. 1980. pap. 4.95 (ISBN 0-914440-44-6). EPM Pubns.

Jesus As Friend. Salvatore Canals. 127p. 1979. 10.00x (ISBN 0-906127-11-4, Pub. by Irish Academic Pr). Biblio Dist.

Jesus Book: Short Ed. Ronald J. Wilkins. (To Live Is Christ Ser.). 112p. 1979. pap. 3.00 (ISBN 0-697-01695-1). Wm C Brown.

Jesus by the Sea of Galilee. Lucy Diamond. (Ladybird Ser). (Illus.). 1958. bds. 1.49 (ISBN 0-87508-840-6). Chr Lit.

Jesus Calls His Disciples. Lucy Diamond. (Ladybird Ser). (Illus.). 1959. bds. 1.49 (ISBN 0-87508-842-2). Chr Lit.

Jesus Calls Us His Sheep. Agnes Richardson. (Illus.). 1981. 4.95 (ISBN 0-8062-1636-0). Carlton.

Jesus Christ & Human Freedom. Ed. by Edward Schillebeeckx & B. Van Iersel. LC 73-17908. (Concilium Ser.: Religion in the Seventies: Vol. 93). 1974. pap. 4.95 (ISBN 0-8164-2577-9). Seabury.

Jesus Christ & Mythology. Rudolf Bultmann. 1958. 2.95 o.p. (ISBN 0-684-71727-1, ScribT). Scribner.

Jesus Christ & the Temple. George Barrois. LC 80-19700. 164p. 1980. pap. 5.95. St Vladimirs.

Jesus Christ & the Temple. Georges A. Barrois. LC 80-19700. 163p. (Orig.). 1980. pap. 5.95 (ISBN 0-913836-73-7, BS680 T4837). St Martin.

Jesus Christ in Matthew, Mark, & Luke. Jack D. Kingsbury. Ed. by Gerhard Krodel. LC 80-69755. (Proclamation Commentaries Ser.: The New Testament Witnesses for Preaching). 144p. (Orig.). 1981. pap. 4.25 (ISBN 0-8006-0596-9, 1-596). Fortress.

Jesus Christ Our Lord. John F. Walvoord. 318p. 1974. pap. text ed. 4.95 (ISBN 0-8024-4326-5). Moody.

Jesus Christ: Prophet-Priest. Andrew Murray. 64p. 1967. pap. 1.75 (ISBN 0-87123-271-5, 200271). Bethany Fell.

Jesus Christ: The Divine Executive. Reuben L. Katter. 1981. price not set (ISBN 0-685-96808-1). Theotes.

Jesus Christ: The God-Man. Bruce A. Demarest. 1978. pap. 3.95 (ISBN 0-88207-760-0). Victor Bks.

Jesus Christ University. Bob Summers. 1973. pap. 1.95 o.p. (ISBN 0-88270-051-0). Logos.

Jesus Cristo, a Rocha Firme. Tr. by David Wilkerson. (Portuguese Bks.). 1979. 1.40 (ISBN 0-8297-0669-0). Life Pubs Intl.

Jesus' Death As Saving Event the Background & Origin of a Concept. Sam K. Williams. LC 75-28341. (Harvard Dissertations in Religion). 1975. pap. 9.00 (ISBN 0-89130-029-5, 020102). Scholars Pr Ca.

Jesus, Dollars & Sense: An Effective Stewardship Guide for Clergy & Lay Leaders. Ed. by Oscar C. Carr, Jr. 1976. pap. 3.95 (ISBN 0-8164-2132-3). Crossroad NY.

Jesus Es el Senor. Ed. by Eadie Goodboy. Tr. by Todd H. Fast. Orig. Title: Jesus Is Lord. 113p. (Span.). 1979. pap. 3.50 (ISBN 0-930756-50-9, 4230-G01(S)). Women's Aglow.

Jesus Feeds Five Thousand. (Tell-a-Bible Story Ser.). (Illus.). 28p. bds. 0.69 (ISBN 0-686-68645-4, 3689). Standard Pub.

Jesus: Historias de su Vida. Margaret Ralph. Tr. by Teresa LaValle. (Serie Jirafa). Orig. Title: Life of Jesus. 1979. 2.95 (ISBN 0-311-38536-2, Edit Mundo). Casa Bautista.

Jesus in Danger. Jenny Robertson & Alan Parry. (Ladybird Bible Ser.). (Illus.). 32p. (ps-4). 1980. Repr. 1.95 (ISBN 0-310-42870-X). Zondervan.

Jesus in Exodus. Michael Esses. 1977. pap. 4.95 (ISBN 0-88270-196-7). Logos.

Jesus in Genesis. Michael Esses. LC 74-82565. 1975. pap. 4.95 (ISBN 0-88270-100-2). Logos.

Jesus in Gethsemane: The Early Church Reflects on the Suffering of Jesus. David M. Stanley. LC 80-80596. (Orig.). 1980. pap. 7.95 (ISBN 0-8091-2285-5). Paulist Pr.

Jesus in Our Affluent Society. Joseph B. Carl. 208p. 1981. 9.95 (ISBN 0-938234-01-3); pap. 5.95 (ISBN 0-938234-00-5). Ministry Pubns.

Jesus in the Church's Gospels: Modern Scholarship & the Earliest Sources. John Reumann. LC 68-10983. 564p. 1973. pap. 6.95 (ISBN 0-8006-1091-1, 1-1091). Fortress.

Jesus in the Qur'an. Geoffrey Parrinder. 1977. pap. 7.95 (ISBN 0-19-519963-4). Oxford U Pr.

Jesus in the Tide of Time: An Historical Study. John Ferguson. 224p. 1980. 35.00 (ISBN 0-7100-0561-X). Routledge & Kegan.

Jesus Incident. Frank Herbert & Bill Ransom. 1979. 10.95 o.p. (ISBN 0-399-12268-0). Berkley Pub.

Jesus Is Born. (Tell-a-Bible Story Ser.). (Illus.). 28p. bds. 0.69 (ISBN 0-686-68642-X, 3686). Standard Pub.

Jesus Is Coming Again. H. M. Riggle. 111p. pap. 1.00. Faith Pub Hse.

Jesus Is Lord. Ed. by Eadie Goodboy. 130p. 1977. 3.50 (ISBN 0-930756-27-4, 4230-G01). Women's Aglow.

Jesus, Lord & Savior. Archibald M. Hunter. 1978. pap. 3.95 o.p. (ISBN 0-8028-1755-6). Eerdmans.

Jesus, Lord & Savior. William M. Thompson. LC 80-80152. 288p. 1980. pap. 8.95 (ISBN 0-8091-2306-1). Paulist Pr.

Jesus Means Freedom. Ernst Kasemann. Tr. by Frank Clarke from Ger. LC 75-94357. 168p. (Orig.). 1972. pap. 2.95 (ISBN 0-8006-1235-3, 1-1235). Fortress.

Jesus Miracles. Maureen Curley. (Children of the Kingdom Acitivities Ser.). (gr. 4-7). 1973. 7.95 (ISBN 0-686-13689-6). Pflaum Pr.

Jesus Mystery: Of Lost Years & Unknown Travels. Janet L. Bock. LC 80-67420. (Illus.). 231p. (Orig.). 1980. pap. 6.95 (ISBN 0-937736-00-7). Aura Bks.

Jesus Nos Habla Por Medio De Sus Parabolas. Tomas R. De La Fuente. 1978. 2.40 (ISBN 0-311-04344-5). Casa Bautista.

Jesus Now. Malachi Martin. 320p. 1974. pap. 1.95 o.p. (ISBN 0-445-08309-3). Popular Lib.

Jesus of Faith: A Study in Christology. Micheal L. Cook. 192p. (Orig.). pap. 6.95 (ISBN 0-8091-2349-5). Paulist Pr.

Jesus of Nazareth. William Barclay. 1977. pap. 1.95 (ISBN 0-345-27253-6). Ballantine.

Jesus of Nazareth. William Barclay. 288p. 1981. pap. 10.95 (ISBN 0-8407-5759-X). Nelson.

Jesus of Nazareth. Gunther Bornkamm. LC 61-5256. 240p. 1975. pap. 6.95 (ISBN 0-06-060932-X, RD113, HarpR). Har-Row.

Jesus of Nazareth. Maureen Curley. (Children of the Kingdom Activities Ser.). (gr. 5-10). 1977. 7.95 (ISBN 0-686-13695-0). Pflaum Pr.

Jesus of Nazareth in New Testament Preaching. G. N. Stanton. LC 73-92782. (Society of New Testament Studies: No. 27). 228p. 1975. 34.00 (ISBN 0-521-20465-8). Cambridge U Pr.

Jesus of Nazareth: The Man & His Time. Herbert Braun. Tr. by Everett R. Kalin from Ger. LC 78-14664. 160p. 1979. 6.95 (ISBN 0-8006-0531-4, 1-531). Fortress.

Jesus: One of Us. Ed. by Chris Davies et al. 148p. 1981. pap. 3.95 (ISBN 0-87784-618-9). Inter Varsity.

Jesus Only. rev. ed. Vance Havner. 6.95 (ISBN 0-8007-0165-8). Revell.

Jesus Our Brother. Francis Schraff & Anne Schraff. 1968. pap. 1.95 o.p. (ISBN 0-89243-030-3, 46525). Liguori Pubns.

Jesus Party. Hugh J. Schoenfeld. 320p. 1974. 7.95 o.s.i. (ISBN 0-02-607280-7). Macmillan.

Jesus' Pattern of Prayer. John Macarthur, Jr. 200p. 1981. 7.95 (ISBN 0-8024-4961-1). Moody.

Jesus Performs Miracles. Judith Wolman. LC 78-64419. (Illus.). (gr. k-5). 1979. 3.50 (ISBN 0-89799-119-2); pap. 1.50 (ISBN 0-89799-034-X). Dandelion Pr.

Jesus Person Pocket Promise Book. Ed. by David Wilkerson. LC 72-86208. 96p. pap. 1.95 (ISBN 0-8307-0191-5, 50-078-01); gift ed. imitation leather 3.95. Regal.

Jesus Prayer. Per-Olof Sjogren. Tr. by Sydney Linton from Swedish. LC 75-18789. 96p. 1975. pap. 3.50 (ISBN 0-8006-1216-7, 1-1216). Fortress.

Jesus' Proclamation of the Kingdom of God. Johannes Weiss. Ed. by Leander E. Keck. Tr. by Richard H. Hiers & David L. Holland. LC 79-135267. (Lives of Jesus Ser). 160p. (Orig.). 1971. pap. 3.95 (ISBN 0-8006-0153-X, 1-153). Fortress.

Jesus, Prophecy & the Middle East. Anis A. Shorrosh. 1981. pap. 3.95 (ISBN 0-8407-5764-6). Nelson.

Jesus: Sketches for a Portrait. rev. & enl. ed. Mary C. Morrison. 1979. 2.00 (ISBN 0-686-28782-7). Forward Movement.

Jesus, Son of Mary: A Book for Children. Fulton J. Sheen. (Illus.). 32p. 1980. 7.95 (ISBN 0-8164-0470-4). Seabury.

Jesus Song. R. R. Knudson. LC 73-1067. (Illus.). 160p. (gr. 5-9). 1973. 5.95 o.s.i. (ISBN 0-440-04215-1). Delacorte.

Jesus: Stranger from Heaven & Son of God. Marinus De Jonge. Ed. by John E. Steely. LC 77-9984. (Soceity of Biblical Literature. Sources for Biblical Studies). 1977. pap. 7.50 (ISBN 0-89130-134-8, 060311). Scholars Pr Ca.

Jesus Tales, a Novel. Romulus Linney. 208p. 1980. 10.00 (ISBN 0-86547-020-0). N Point Pr.

Jesus, the Child. Jenny Robertson. (Ladybird Bible Ser.). (Illus.). 32p. (ps-4). 1980. Repr. 1.95 (ISBN 0-310-42820-3). Zondervan.

Jesus the Christ. James E. Talmage. 804p. pap. 2.95 (ISBN 0-87747-456-7). Deseret Bk.

Jesus: The Gift of Life. (Little People's Paperbacks Ser.). 1979. pap. 0.99 (ISBN 0-8164-2246-X). Crossroad NY.

Jesus the Jew: A Historian's Reading of the Gospels. Geza Vermes. LC 73-18516. 286p. 1974. 6.95 o.s.i. (ISBN 0-685-39615-0). Macmillan.

Jesus the Jew: A Historian's Reading of the Gospels. Geza Vermes. LC 80-2381. 288p. 1981. pap. 6.95 (ISBN 0-8006-1443-7, 1-1443). Fortress.

Jesus, the Leader. Jenny Robertson. (Ladybird Bible Ser.). (Illus.). 32p. (ps-4). 1980. Repr. 1.95 (ISBN 0-310-42830-0). Zondervan.

Jesus the Life Changer. Ada Lum. 40p. 1978. pap. 2.25 (ISBN 0-87784-316-3). Inter-Varsity.

Jesus: The Living Bread. limited ed. 14.95 o.p. (ISBN 0-88270-211-4); deluxe ed. 9.95 o.p. (ISBN 0-88270-199-1). Logos.

Jesus, the Man & the Myth. James P. Mackey. LC 78-61627. 1979. pap. 8.95 (ISBN 0-8091-2169-7). Paulist Pr.

Jesus: The Man, the Mission, & the Message. 2nd ed. C. Milo Connick. (Illus.). 512p. 1974. 17.95 (ISBN 0-13-509521-2). P-H.

Jesus, The Master Teacher. Lowell Bennion. 63p. 1980. 4.95 (ISBN 0-87747-833-3). Deseret Bk.

Jesus: the Story of His Life: A Modern Retelling Based on the Gospels. Walter Barnett. LC 75-28260. 1976. 13.95 (ISBN 0-88229-308-7). Nelson Hall.

Jesus, the Storyteller. Jenny Ronertson. (Ladybird Bible Ser.). (Illus.). 32p. (ps-4). 1980. Repr. 1.95 (ISBN 0-310-42840-8). Zondervan.

Jesus Touch. Richard Hogue. LC 72-79168. 128p. 1972. pap. 2.50 (ISBN 0-8054-5524-8, 42-5524). Broadman.

Jesus: 220 Names. George Otis. pap. 1.50 (ISBN 0-89728-041-5, 533144). Omega Pubns OR.

Jet Age: Forty Years of Jet Aviation. Ed. by Walter J. Boyne & Donald S. Lopez. LC 79-20216. (Illus.). 190p. 1979. 19.50 (ISBN 0-87474-248-X); pap. 8.95 (ISBN 0-87474-247-1). Smithsonian.

Jet Cutting Technology: A Bibliography. Ed. by Wendy A. Thornton & Christine A. Richardson. 1973. pap. 24.00 (ISBN 0-900983-22-1, Dist. by Air Science Co.). BHRA Fluid.

Jet Pilot. Henry B. Lent. (Illus.). (gr. 7-9). 1958. 4.50g o.s.i. (ISBN 0-02-756350-2). Macmillan.

Jet Propulsion. David Evans. 9.75x (ISBN 0-392-07180-0, LTB). Soccer.

Jet Pumps & Ejectors: A State of the Art Review & Bibliography. 2nd ed. Ed. by S. T. Bonnington & A. L. King. (BHRA Fluid Engineering Ser.: Vol. 1). 1977. pap. 36.00 (ISBN 0-900983-63-9, Dist. by Air Science Co.). BHRA Fluid.

Jet Stress: What It Is & How to Cope with It. Judith Goeltz. Ed. by Kurt W. Donsbach. LC 79-89366. 350p. 1980. 9.95 (ISBN 0-86664-000-2). Inst Pubs.

Jeunes Voix, Jeunes Visages. Yvone Lenard. (Verbal-Active French Ser.). text ed. 12.76 (ISBN 0-06-582100-9, SchDept); tchr's ed 22.32 (ISBN 0-06-582204-8); wkbk 4.00 (ISBN 0-06-582300-1); tests 3.56 (ISBN 0-06-582602-7); tchrs.' tests 3.56 (ISBN 0-06-582700-7); tapes 252.84 (ISBN 0-06-582801-1); study prints 48.08 (ISBN 0-06-582800-3). Har-Row.

Jeux Sont Faits. Ed. by J. Sartre & M. Storer. 1952. pap. 7.95 o.p. (ISBN 0-13-530675-2). P-H.

Jew & His Home. 10th ed. A. E. Kitov. Tr. by Nathan Bulman. LC 63-17660. 233p. 1976. 8.50 (ISBN 0-88400-004-4). Shengold.

Jew in American Sports. rev. ed. Harold U. Ribalow. 1980. 14.95 (ISBN 0-8197-0175-0). Bloch.

Jew in the Medieval Community. James W. Parkes. 456p. 1976. 14.95 o.p. (ISBN 0-87203-059-8); pap. 9.75 (ISBN 0-87203-060-1). Hermon.

Jew in the Modern World: A Documentary History. Paul R. Mendes-Flohr & Jehuda Reinharz. 1980. pap. text ed. 11.95x (ISBN 0-19-502632-2). Oxford U Pr.

Jew of Malta. Christopher Marlowe. Ed. by Richard W. Van Fossen. LC 63-14699. (Regents Renaissance Drama Ser). 1964. 8.50x (ISBN 0-8032-0270-9); pap. 3.95x (ISBN 0-8032-5270-6, BB 203, Bison). U of Nebr Pr.

Jewel Cave Adventure: Fifty Miles of Discovery Under South Dakota. Herb Conn & Jan Conn. (Speleologia Ser.). (Illus.). 240p. 1977. 12.95 o.s.i. (ISBN 0-914264-19-2, Dist. by Caroline Hse); pap. 6.95 o.s.i. (ISBN 0-914264-20-6). Zephyrus Pr.

Jewel in the Skull. Michael Moorcock. (Science Fiction Ser.). 1977. pap. 1.75 (ISBN 0-87997-419-2, UE1547). DAW Bks.

Jewel of Humility. Sri Chinmoy. (Illus.). 56p. (Orig.). 1980. pap. 2.00 (ISBN 0-88497-493-6). Aum Pubns.

Jewel Ornament of Liberation. SGam po pa. Tr. by Herbert V. Guenther from Tibetan. LC 72-146507. (Clear Light Ser.). 349p. 1981. pap. 9.95 (ISBN 0-87773-717-7). Great Eastern.

Jeweled Egg. Linda Szilvasy. (Illus.). 1976. pap. 9.95 o.p. (ISBN 0-8096-1916-4, Assn Pr). Follett.

Jewelers' Inventory Manual. Richard F. Laffin. 1981. 24.95 (ISBN 0-931744-04-0). Jewelers Circular.

Jewellery & Gemcraft. Glen Pownall. (New Crafts Books Ser.). 1980. 7.50 (ISBN 0-85467-018-1, Pub. by Viking Sevenseas New Zealand). Intl Schol Bk Serv.

Jewelry: Ancient to Modern. The Walters Art Gallery. 1980. 35.00 (ISBN 0-670-40697-X, Studio). Viking Pr.

Jewelry: Basic Technique & Design. Alice Sprintzen. 224p. Date not set. 15.95 (ISBN 0-8019-6828-3); pap. 9.95 (ISBN 0-8019-6830-5). Chilton.

Jewelry Book. Suzan St. Maur & Norbert Streep. (Illus.). 198p. 1981. 9.95 (ISBN 0-312-44230-0). St Martin.

Jewelry for Everyone: Soft Jewelry to Create at Home from Twine & Wool, Bone & Shell, Fur & Feather, Clay & Leather, Beads, Recyclables, Other Easy-to-Find Materials. Joan Gibbs. (Illus.). 128p. 1981. 15.95 (ISBN 0-916144-74-7); pap. 7.95 (ISBN 0-916144-73-9). Stemmer Hse.

Jewelry Making: A Guide for Beginners. Ted Foote. LC 80-67547. (Illus.). 112p. 1981. 14.95 (ISBN 0-87192-130-8). Davis Mass.

Jewelry Making by the Lost Wax Process. rev. ed. Greta Pack. 96p. 1979. pap. 4.95 (ISBN 0-442-25176-9). Van Nos Reinhold.

Jewelry Making for the Beginning Craftsman. Greta Pack. 78p. 1980. pap. 6.95 (ISBN 0-442-20173-7). Van Nos Reinhold.

Jewelry of the Prehistoric Southwest. E. Wesley Jernigan. LC 77-89436. (Southwestern Indian Arts Ser). (Illus.). 1978. 30.00x (ISBN 0-8263-0459-1). U of NM Pr.

Jewels of Formal Language Theory. Arto Salomaa. (Illus.). 1981. text ed. 24.95 (ISBN 0-914894-69-2). Computer Sci.

Jewels of the Qur'an: Al-Ghazali's Theory. M. A. Quasem. 244p. 1980. 13.95x (ISBN 0-89955-204-8, Pub. by M A Quasem Malaysia); pap. 7.95x (ISBN 0-89955-205-6). Intl Schol Bk Serv.

Jewels of the Wise. (Illus.). 1979. pap. 4.60 perfect bdg. (ISBN 0-916700-20-8). Epiphany Pr.

Jewett's Ceramic Art of Great Britain, 1800-1900. Geoffrey A. Godden. LC 76-184414. (Illus.). 300p. 1972. 25.00 o.p. (ISBN 0-668-02595-6). Arco.

Jewish Americana. 1954. 7.00 (ISBN 0-685-38410-1, Pub. by Hebrew Union). Ktav.

Jewish & Christian Self-Definition, Vol. 1: The Shaping of Christianity in the Second & Third Centuries. Ed. by E. P. Sanders. LC 79-7390. 336p. 1980. 15.95 (ISBN 0-8006-0578-0, 1-578). Fortress.

Jewish & Christian Self-Definition, Vol. 2: Aspects of Judaism in the Greco-Roman Period. Ed. by E. P. Sanders et al. LC 80-2391. 450p. 1981. 17.95 (ISBN 0-8006-0660-4, 1-660). Fortress.

Jewish Assimilation in Modern Times. Bela Vago. 300p. 1981. lib. bdg. 24.50x (ISBN 0-86531-030-0). Westview.

Jewish Book of Lists & Summaries, Vol. 2. Eliezer Wenger. (gr. 5 up). 1979. pap. 1.00 (ISBN 0-89655-141-5). BRuach HaTorah.

Jewish Ceremonial Art & Religious Observance. Abram Kanof. 32.50 (ISBN 0-8109-0178-1); pap. 12.50 (ISBN 0-8109-2199-5). Abrams.

Jewish Ceremonial Institutions & Customs. rev. ed. 3rd. ed. William Rosenau. LC 70-78222. (Illus.). 1971. Repr. of 1925 ed. 15.00 (ISBN 0-8103-3402-X). Gale.
Jewish Child Is Born. Nathan Gottlieb. LC 60-16833. 1976. pap. 4.95 (ISBN 0-8197-0017-7). Bloch.
Jewish Cookbook. Mildred G. Bellin. 1980. write for info. (ISBN 0-8197-0058-4). Bloch.
Jewish Cookbook for Children. Ronnie Steinkoler. LC 80-17428. (Illus.). 96p. (gr. 4-7). 1980. PLB 7.79 (ISBN 0-671-33093-4). Messner.
Jewish Dietary Laws, 2 vols. Grunfeld. 1973. Set. 31.50x (ISBN 0-685-32987-9). Bloch.
Jewish Education in the United States. Ed. by Lloyd P. Gartner. LC 73-112708. 1970. pap. text ed. 4.25x (ISBN 0-8077-1404-6). Tchrs Coll.
Jewish Festival Cookbook. Fannie Engle & Gertrude Blair. 1966. pap. 2.25 o.s.i. (ISBN 0-446-82514-X). Warner Bks.
Jewish Festivals: From Their Beginnings to Our Own Day. rev. ed. Hayyim Schauss. (Illus.). (YA) 1969. 8.00 (ISBN 0-8074-0095-5, 383202); course syll. 1.25 (ISBN 0-686-66555-4, 247330). UAHC.
Jewish-Gentile Courtships: An Exploratory Study of a Social Process. John E. Mayer. LC 80-16130. x, 240p. 1980. Repr. of 1961 ed. lib. bdg. 22.50x (ISBN 0-313-22465-X, MAJG). Greenwood.
Jewish History Atlas. Martin Gilbert. (Illus.). 1969. 11.95 (ISBN 0-02-543280-X). Macmillan.
Jewish Holiday Cookbook. Susan G. Purdy. (Holiday Cookbook Ser.). (Illus.). (gr. 4 up). 1979. s&l 7.90 (ISBN 0-531-02281-1); pap. 2.95 (ISBN 0-531-03430-5). Watts.
Jewish Info. Quiz Book. Alfred J. Kolatch. LC 66-30508. 250p. 1980. 9.95 (ISBN 0-8246-0248-X). Jonathan David.
Jewish Jurisprudence: Its Sources & Modern Applications, Vol. II. Emanuel B. Quint & Neil S. Hecht. (Jewish Jurisprudence Ser.). 1981. price not set (ISBN 3-7186-0064-1). Harwood Academic.
Jewish Jurisprudence Its Sources & Modern Applications, Vol. 1. Emanuel B. Quint & Neil S. Hecht. 268p. 1980. 28.00 (ISBN 3-7186-0055-2); pap. 10.00 (ISBN 3-7186-0054-4). Harwood Academic.
Jewish Law & Jewish Life, 8 bks. in 4 vols. Jacob Bazak. Ed. by Stephen M. Passamaneck. Incl. Bk. 1. Selected Rabbinical Response (ISBN 0-8074-0034-3, 180210); Bks. 2-4. Contracts, Real Estate, Sales & Usury (180211); Bks. 5-6. Credit, Law Enforcement & Taxation (180212); Bks. 7-8. Criminal & Domestic Relations (ISBN 0-8074-0037-8, 180213). 1978. pap. 12.50 complete vol. (ISBN 0-8074-0038-6, 180218); pap. 5.00 ea. UAHC.
Jewish Library. Leo Jung. Incl. Vol. 1. Faith. 9.50x (ISBN 0-685-23058-9); Vol. 2. Folk. 9.50x (ISBN 0-685-23059-7); Vol. 3. Women. 8.00x (ISBN 0-685-23060-0); Vol. 4. Judaism in a Changing World. 9.50x (ISBN 0-685-23061-9); Vol. 5. Panorama of Judaism: Part 1. 9.50x (ISBN 0-685-23062-7); Vol. 6. Panorama of Judaism: Part 2. 9.50x (ISBN 0-685-23063-5). Bloch.
Jewish Life. Mordecai Soloff et al. (Sacred Hebrew Ser.). (Illus.). 112p. (Orig.). 1980. pap. 3.50 (ISBN 0-86628-000-6). Ridgefield Pub.
Jewish Life in the Middle Ages: Illuminated Hebrew Manuscripts. Therese Metzger & Mendel Metzger. Tr. by Rowan Watson from Hebrew. (Illus.). 1981. 75.00 (ISBN 0-19-520168-X). Oxford U Pr.
Jewish Life on New York's Lower East Side: Drawings & Paintings, 1912-1962. Samuel Zagat. Ed. by I. R. Zagat. (Illus.). 1972. 25.00 (ISBN 0-911268-09-X). Rogers Bk.
Jewish Literature Between the Bible & the Mishnah: A Historical & Literary Introduction. George W. Nickelsburg. LC 80-16176. 352p. 1981. 19.95 (ISBN 0-8006-0649-3, 1-649). Fortress.
Jewish Minority in the Soviet Union. Thomas E. Sawyer. (Special Studies on the Soviet Union & Eastern Europe). 1979. lib. bdg. 27.50x (ISBN 0-89158-480-3). Westview.
Jewish Monotheism & Christian Trinitarian Doctrine. Pinchas Lapide & Jurgen Moltmann. Tr. by Leonard Swidler from Ger. LC 80-8058. 96p. 1981. pap. 4.50 (ISBN 0-8006-1405-4, 1-1405). Fortress.
Jewish Mystical Tradition. Ben Z. Bokser. 280p. 1981. 14.95 (ISBN 0-8298-0435-8); pap. 9.95 (ISBN 0-8298-0451-X). Pilgrim NY.
Jewish Mystical Tradition. Ben Zion Bokser. 1980. 15.00 (ISBN 0-88482-922-7); pap. 6.95 (ISBN 0-88482-923-5). Hebrew Pub.
Jewish New Year. Molly Cone. LC 66-10056. (Holiday Ser.). (Illus.). (gr. k-3). 1966. PLB 7.89 (ISBN 0-690-46041-4, TYC-J). T Y Crowell.
Jewish People & Jesus Christ After Auschwitz. Jakob Jocz. 172p. (Orig.). 1981. pap. 6.95 (ISBN 0-8010-5123-1). Baker Bk.
Jewish Physicians in the Netherlands Sixteen Hundred to Nineteen-Forty. Hindle S. Hes-Swartenberg. (Illus.). 1980. pap. text ed. 17.75x (ISBN 90-237-1743-0). Humanities.
Jewish Princedom in Feudal France 768-900. Arthur J. Zuckerman. LC 72-137392. (Studies in Jewish History, Culture, & Institutions: No. 2). 435p. 1972. 27.50x (ISBN 0-231-03298-6). Columbia U Pr.
Jewish Radicals 1875-1914: From Czarist Stetl to London Ghetto. William J. Fishman. LC 74-26194. 384p. 1975. Repr. 12.95 o.p. (ISBN 0-394-49764-3). Pantheon.
Jewish Reactions to German Anti-Semitism, 1870-1914. Ismar Schorsch. LC 74-190193. (Studies in Jewish History, Culture & Institutions). 288p. 1972. 20.00x (ISBN 0-231-03643-4). Columbia U Pr.
Jewish Resistance in Nazi-Occupied Eastern Europe: With a Historical Survey of the Jew As Fighter & Soldier in Diaspora. Reuben Ainsztein. LC 74-1759. 970p. 1974. 37.50x o.p. (ISBN 0-06-490030-4). B&N.
Jewish Responses to Nazi Persecution. Isaih Trunk. LC 78-6378. 384p. 1981. pap. 9.95 (ISBN 0-8128-6103-5). Stein & Day.
Jewish Revolution: Jewish Statehood. Israel Eldad. Tr. by Hannah Schmorak. LC 79-163739. 184p. 1971. 7.95 (ISBN 0-88400-037-0). Shengold.
Jewish Sects at the Time of Jesus. Marcel Simon. Tr. by James H. Farley from Fr. LC 66-25265. 192p. 1980. pap. 5.95 (ISBN 0-8006-0183-1, 1-183). Fortress.
Jewish Self-Government in Medieval Egypt: The Origins of the Office of Head of the Jews, ca. 1065-1126. Mark R. Cohen. LC 80-7514. (Princeton Studies on the Near East). 425p. 1980. 27.50 (ISBN 0-691-05307-3). Princeton U Pr.
Jewish War. Flavius Josephus. Tr. by Geoffrey A. Williamson. (Classics Ser.). (Orig.). 1959. pap. 3.95 (ISBN 0-14-044090-9). Penguin.
Jewish Way to Life. Nathan A. Barack. LC 74-19272. 216p. 1975. 7.95 o.p. (ISBN 0-685-53375-1). Jonathan David.
Jewish Writers of North America: A Guide to Information Sources. Ed. by Ira B. Nadel. (American Studies Information Guide Ser.: Vol. 8). 500p. 1980. 30.00 (ISBN 0-8103-1484-3). Gale.
Jewish Yoga: A System of Visualization & Movement Rooted in Genesis. Catherine De Segonzac. 208p. 1981. pap. 7.95 (ISBN 0-87728-529-2). Weiser.
Jews & Christians in Antioch in the First Four Centuries of the Common Era. Wayne A. Meeks & Robert L. Wilken. LC 78-3760. 1978. pap. 6.00 (ISBN 0-89130-331-6). Scholars Pr Ca.
Jews & Freemasons in Europe, 1723-1939. Jacob Katz. Tr. by Leonard Oschry from Heb. LC 71-115475. 1970. 16.00x (ISBN 0-674-47480-5). Harvard U Pr.
Jews & Greeks in Ancient Cyrene. Shimon Applebaum. (Illus.). 367p. 1980. text ed. 64.00x (ISBN 90-04-05970-9). Humanities.
Jews & Non-Jews Falling in Love. Sandford Seltzer. 1976. 4.00 (ISBN 0-8074-0098-X, 164050). UAHC.
Jews & the Crusaders: The Hebrew Chronicles of the First & Second Crusades. Ed. by Shlomo Eidelberg. 1977. 17.50 (ISBN 0-299-07060-3). U of Wis Pr.
Jews & the Left. Arthur Liebman. LC 78-20871. (Contemporary Religious Movements Ser.). 1979. 19.50 (ISBN 0-471-53433-1, Pub. by Wiley-Interscience). Wiley.
Jews, God & History. Max I. Dimont. 1972. pap. 2.50 (ISBN 0-451-07870-5, E8995, Sig). NAL.
Jews Helped Build America. Arlene H. Kurtis. LC 74-19114. (Illus.). (gr. 4-6). 1970. PLB 4.64 o.p. (ISBN 0-671-32707-0). Messner.
Jews in America. rev. ed. Frances Butwin. LC 68-31501. (In America Bks.). (Illus.). (gr. 5-11). 1980. PLB 5.95. Lerner Pubns.
Jews in Nazi Germany. American Jewish Committee. 1979. Repr. of 1935 ed. 11.50 (ISBN 0-86527-110-0). Fertig.
Jews in the Roman World. Michael Grant. LC 72-11118. 1973. lib. rep. ed. 20.00x (ISBN 0-684-15494-3, ScribT). Scribner.
Jews of Ireland. Louis Hyman. 422p. 1972. 15.00x (ISBN 0-7165-2082-6, Pub. by Irish Academic Pr Ireland). Biblio Dist.
Jews of Lancaster, Pennsylvania: A Story with Two Beginnings. David Brener. LC 79-21690. (Illus.). 200p. 1979. 18.00 (ISBN 0-686-28857-2); pap. 12.00 (ISBN 0-686-28858-0). Cong Shaarai.
Jews of Lancaster, Pennsylvania: A Story with Two Beginnings. David A. Brener. (Illus.). 188p. (Orig.). 1981. 18.00 (ISBN 0-9605482-1-1); pap. 12.00 (ISBN 0-9605482-0-3). Shaarai Shomayim.
Jews of Spain: Journey of Fifteen Centuries. Robert Sugar. 1973. 8.00 (ISBN 0-8074-0139-0, 561010); tchrs'. resource kit 10.00 (ISBN 0-8074-0140-4, 201010). UAHC.
Jews of the United States, 1790-1840: A Documentary History, 3 Vols. Ed. by Joseph L. Blau et al. LC 64-10108. 1964. Set. 75.50x (ISBN 0-231-02651-X). Columbia U Pr.
Jews Struggle for Religious & Civil Liberty in Maryland. E. Milton Altfeld. LC 78-99859. (Civil Liberties in American History Ser). 1970. Repr. of 1924 ed. lib. bdg. 25.00 (ISBN 0-306-71859-6). Da Capo.
Jews: Their Religious Beliefs & Practices. Alan Unterman. (Library of Religious Beliefs & Practices). 288p. 1980. write for info. (ISBN 0-7100-0743-4). Routledge & Kegan.
J.F.B. - Fausset Combination Set, 2 vols. Incl. Commentary on the Whole Bible. R. Jamieson et al; Fausset's Bible Dictionary. A. R. Fausset. Set. 30.90 (ISBN 0-310-35248-7). Zondervan.
JFCC Catalogue of Cultures. 3rd ed. Ikeda Yonisuke. 320p. 1980. 35.00x (ISBN 0-89955-221-8, Pub. by JSSP Japan). Intl Schol Bk Serv.
Ji-Nongo-Nongo Means Riddles. Verna Aardema. LC 78-4038. (Illus.). 40p. (gr. 3 up). 1978. 7.95 (ISBN 0-590-07474-1, Four Winds). Schol Bk Serv.
Jicaque (Torrupan) Indians of Honduras. Victor W. Von Hagen. LC 76-44796. (Illus.). 128p. 1980. Repr. of 1943 ed. 18.25 (ISBN 0-404-15743-2). AMS Pr.
Jig & Fixture Design, Vol.1. Edward G. Hoffman. LC 78-55901. 330p. pap. 8.00 (ISBN 0-8273-1694-1); instructor's guide 1.60 (ISBN 0-686-67378-6). Delmar.
Jig & Fixture Design & Detailing. John G. Nee. LC 78-71562. (Illus.). 1979. pap. 14.90x (ISBN 0-911168-41-9). Prakken.
Jig & Fixture Design Manual. Erik K. Henriksen. (Illus.). 308p. 1973. 35.00 (ISBN 0-8311-1098-8). Indus Pr.
Jig Boring. Ed. by F. T. Bright et al. (Engineering Craftsmen: No. H27). (Illus.). 1969. spiral bdg. 16.95x (ISBN 0-85083-043-5). Intl Ideas.
Jigalong Mob: Aboriginal Victors of the Desert Crusade. Robert Tonkinson. LC 73-85115. (Illus.). 166p. 1974. pap. 6.95 (ISBN 0-8465-7549-3). Benjamin-Cummings.
Jiggs. Mark Dunster. (Rin Ser.: Pt. 49). 82p. (Orig.). 1981. pap. 5.00 (ISBN 0-89642-076-0). Linden Pubs.
Jigs & Fixtures. Ed. by William E. Boyes. LC 79-64915. (Manufacturing Update Ser.). (Illus.). 1979. 29.00 (ISBN 0-87263-051-X). SME.
Jigsaw Man. Dorothea Bennett. 1977. pap. 1.95 o.s.i. (ISBN 0-446-89414-1). Warner Bks.
Jill Wins a Friend. Kay M. Rivers. LC 76-16021. (Kids in Sports Ser.). (Illus.). (gr. 1-3). 1976. PLB 4.95 (ISBN 0-913778-59-1); pap. 2.75 (ISBN 0-89565-123-8). Childs World.
Jilla. Elizabeth Richards. 1978. pap. 1.50 o.s.i. (ISBN 0-685-86425-1). Jove Pubns.
Jillions of Gerbils. Arnold Dobrin. LC 72-11502. (Fun-To-Read Bk.). (Illus.). (gr. 1-4). 1973. 6.95 o.p. (ISBN 0-688-40051-5); PLB 6.67 (ISBN 0-688-50051-X). Lothrop.
Jim. Ruth Bornstein. LC 77-12712. (Illus.). (ps-3). 1978. 7.95 (ISBN 0-395-28772-3, Clarion). HM.
Jim Anderson's How to Live Rent in the 1980's, Vol. 2. Jim Anderson. (Illus.). 324p. 1980. 25.00 (ISBN 0-932574-02-5); pap. 15.00 (ISBN 0-932574-03-3). Brun Pr.
Jim Beckwourth: Black Mountain Man & War Chief of the Crows. Elinor Wilson. 248p. 1980. pap. 6.95 (ISBN 0-8061-1555-6). U of Okla Pr.
Jim Boen--a Man of Opposites. Ann Redpath. 48p. (gr. 4-8). 1980. PLB 5.95 (ISBN 0-87191-744-0). Creative Ed.
Jim Bowie & Lost Mine. Herman Toepperwein. pap. text ed. 1.50 (ISBN 0-910722-08-0). Highland Pr.
Jim Bridger. J. Cecil Alter. (Illus.). 1979. Repr. of 1962 ed. 14.95 (ISBN 0-8061-0546-1). U of Okla Pr.
Jim Bridger. Matthew G. Grant. LC 73-10071. 1974. PLB 5.95 (ISBN 0-87191-254-6). Creative Ed.
Jim Bridger, Mountain Man. Stanley Vestal. LC 73-108790. (Illus.). 1970. pap. 3.95 (ISBN 0-8032-5720-1, BB 519, Bison). U of Nebr Pr.
Jim Corbett's India: Stories Selected by R. E. Hawkins. Jim Corbett. Ed. by R. E. Hawkins. (Illus.). 1979. 14.95 (ISBN 0-19-212968-6). Oxford U Pr.
Jim Crow in Boston: The Origin of the "Separate but Equal Doctrine". Ed. by Leonard W. Levy & Douglas L. Jones. LC 73-39622. (Civil Liberties in American History Ser). 1974. lib. bdg. 25.00 (ISBN 0-306-70157-X). Da Capo.
Jim Dine Figure Drawings, Nineteen Seventy Five-Nineteen Seventy Nine. Constance W. Glenn. LC 79-3060. (Icon Edns.). (Illus.). 1980. pap. 12.95 (ISBN 0-06-430102-8, HarpT). Har-Row.
Jim Fixx's Second Book of Running. James F. Fixx. 320p. 1980. 10.95 (ISBN 0-394-50898-X). Random.
Jim Hart Story. Thomas Barnidge & Douglas Grow. (Illus.). 1977. 6.95 (ISBN 0-8272-1705-6); pap. 4.95 (ISBN 0-8272-1704-8). Bethany Pr.
Jim Hunter International Spy Stories. Butterworth & Stockdale. (gr. 6-12). 1975-1978. pap. 30.00 boxed set of 12 books with teacher's gd. (ISBN 0-8224-3780-5). Pitman Learning.
Jim Love up to Now. Ed. by Dominique De Menil. LC 80-82000. (Illus.). 1980. pap. 8.00 (ISBN 0-914412-16-7). Inst for the Arts.
Jim Mundy. Robert H. Fowler. 1978. pap. 2.25 o.s.i. (ISBN 0-515-04707-4). Jove Pubns.
Jim Rice: Power Hitter. Maury Allen. LC 79-91490. (Star People Ser.). (Illus.). 72p. (gr. 4-9). 1980. PLB 5.79 (ISBN 0-8178-6265-X). Harvey.
Jim Silent. W. C. Chalk. 1971. pap. text ed. 2.95x o.p. (ISBN 0-435-11196-5). Heinemann Ed.
Jim Thorpe. Thomas Fall. LC 72-94793. (Crocodile Paperback Ser.). (Illus.). (gr. 2-5). 1970. pap. 2.95 (ISBN 0-690-46219-0, TYC-J). T Y Crowell.
Jim Thorpe - Althea Gibson. John N. Fago & Naunerle C. Farr. (Pendulum Illustrated Biography Ser.). (Illus.). (gr. 4-12). 1979. text ed. 4.50 (ISBN 0-88301-372-X); pap. text ed. 1.45 (ISBN 0-88301-360-6); wkbk. 0.95 (ISBN 0-88301-384-3). Pendulum Pr.
Jim Thorpe, All American. Saul Levitt. (Orig.). 1980. playscript 2.50 (ISBN 0-87602-237-9). Anchorage.
Jim Thorpe: The World's Greatest Athlete. Robert W. Wheeler. LC 78-58080. (Illus.). 320p. 1981. pap. 5.95 (ISBN 0-8061-1745-1). U of Okla Pr.
Jimi Hendrix: Voodoo Child of the Aquarian Age. David Henderson. LC 76-56299. 1978. 13.95 (ISBN 0-385-07357-7). Doubleday.
Jimmie the Kid: The Life of Jimmie Rodgers. Mike Paris & Chris Comber. (Da Capo Quality Paperbacks Ser.). (Illus.). 211p. 1981. pap. 6.95 (ISBN 0-306-80133-7). Da Capo.
Jimmy Carter's Odyssey to Black Africa: Part One. Stan Grant. (Illus.). 9.50. Courier Pr FL.
Jimmy Doolittle: Master of the Calculated Risk. Carroll V. Glines. 208p. 1980. pap. 4.95 (ISBN 0-442-23102-4). Van Nos Reinhold.
Jimmy Trilogy. Jacques Poulin. Tr. by Sheila Fischman from Fr. (Anansi Fiction Ser.: No. 39). 250p. (Orig.). 1979. pap. 8.95 (ISBN 0-88784-074-4, Pub. by Hse Anansi Pr Canada). U of Toronto Pr.
Jimmy Walker-the Dyn-O-Mite Kid. Cohen. (gr. 3-5). pap. 1.25 (ISBN 0-590-10268-0, Schol Pap). Schol Bk Serv.
Jingala. Legson Kayira. 160p. (Orig.). (gr. 10up). 1979. pap. 5.00 (ISBN 0-582-64268-X, Drum Beat). Three Continents.
Jinx Glove. Matt Christopher. (Illus.). 48p. (gr. 1-3). 1974. 6.95 (ISBN 0-316-13965-3). Little.
Jiunior Miss. Sally Benson. (YA) (gr. 7-9). 1969. pap. 1,50 (ISBN 0-671-29981-6). PB.
Jo, Flo & Yolanda. Carol De Poix. 35p. (ps-1). 1973. pap. 2.50 (ISBN 0-914996-04-5). Lollipop Power.
Jo Grimond: Memoirs. (Illus.). 316p. 1980. text ed. 27.50x (ISBN 0-8419-6106-9). Holmes & Meier.
Jo-Jo. Ella Anderson. 1975. pap. 1.25 (ISBN 0-87508-693-4). Chr Lit.
Jo Stern. David R. Slavitt. LC 77-11548. 1978. 8.95 o.p. (ISBN 0-06-013994-3, HarpT). Har-Row.
Joachim du Bellay. L. Clark Keating. (World Authors Ser.: France: No. 162). lib. bdg. 10.95 (ISBN 0-8057-2132-0), Twayne.
Joan Didion. Mark R. Winchell. (United States Authors Ser.: No. 370). 1980. lib. bdg. 8.95 (ISBN 0-8057-7308-8). Twayne.
Joan Miro, Lithographs, Vol. 1. Michael Leiris & Fernand Mourlot. (Illus.). 231p. 1972. 150.00x (ISBN 0-8148-0494-2, Pub. by Tudor). Hennessey.
Joan Miro: The Development of a Sign Language. Sidra Stich. LC 80-80078. (Illus.). 72p. pap. 6.00x o.p. (ISBN 0-936316-00-4). Wash U Gallery.
Joan of Arc. Maurice Boutet de Monvel. LC 80-5169. (Illus.). 64p. (gr. 7). 1980. Repr. of 1897 ed. 12.95 (ISBN 0-670-40735-6, Studio). Viking Pr.
Joan of Arc in History, Legend & Literature. Ingvald Raknem. (Scandinavian University Books). 284p. 1972. 22.00x (ISBN 8-200-02247-1, Dist. by Columbia U Pr). Universitet.
Joan of Arc: Maid of Orleans. Jeanette Struchen. LC 67-12557. (Biography Ser). (gr. 7 up). 1967. PLB 5.90 o.p. (ISBN 0-531-00889-4). Watts.
Joan of Arc: The Image of Female Heroism. Marina Warner. LC 80-2720. (Illus.). 1981. 17.95 (ISBN 0-394-41145-5). Knopf.

Joan of Arc: The Legend & the Reality. Frances Gies. LC 80-7900. (Illus.). 256p. 1981. 12.95 (ISBN 0-690-01942-4, HarpT). Har-Row.

Joan: The Reluctant Kennedy. Lester David. (Illus.). 256p. 1975. pap. 1.75 o.s.i. (ISBN 0-446-59761-9). Warner Bks.

Joan Walsh Anglund Storybook. Joan W. Anglund. LC 78-55913. (Illus.). (ps-2). 1978. 4.95 (ISBN 0-394-83803-3, BYR); PLB 5.99 (ISBN 0-394-93803-8). Random.

Joanjo, a Portuguese Tale. Jan Balet. LC 67-10705. (Illus.). (ps-2). 1967. 4.95 (ISBN 0-440-04236-4, Sey Lawr); PLB 4.58 o.s.i. (ISBN 0-440-04233-X, Sey Lawr). Delacorte.

Joanne, the Unpredictable. Katheryn Kimbrough. (Saga of the Phenwick Women Ser.: Bk. 8). 256p. 1976. pap. 1.25 o.p. (ISBN 0-445-00347-2). Popular Lib.

Joannes Secundus: The Latin Love Elegy in the Renaissance. Clifford W. Endres. 1981. 25.00 (ISBN 0-208-01832-8, Archon). Shoe String.

Joao Guimaraes Rosa. Jon S. Vincent. (World Authors Ser.: No. 506 (Brazil)). 1978. 13.50 (ISBN 0-8057-6347-3). Twayne.

Job. S. R. Driver & G. Buchanan Gray. LC 21-15647. (International Critical Commentary Ser.). 816p. Repr. of 1921 ed. 23.00x (ISBN 0-567-05010-6). Attic Pr.

Job. Norman C. Habel. Ed. by John Hayes. LC 80-82193. (Knox Preaching Guides). 96p. (Orig.). 1981. pap. 4.50 (ISBN 0-8042-3216-4). John Knox.

Job. Irving L. Jensen. (Bible Self Study Guide Ser.). 1975. pap. 2.25 (ISBN 0-8024-1018-9). Moody.

Job: A Study Guide Commentary. D. David Garland. 160p. 1971. pap. 2.95 (ISBN 0-310-24863-9). Zondervan.

Job: A Vision of God. Ward B. Ewing. 1976. 8.95 (ISBN 0-8164-0285-X). Crossroad NY.

Job Abroad. George Bartram. 224p. 1975. 7.95 o.s.i. (ISBN 0-02-521030-0). Macmillan.

Job Abroad. George Bartram. 1976. pap. 1.75 o.p. (ISBN 0-445-08482-0). Popular Lib.

Job Analysis Approach to Affirmative Action. Clement J. Berwitz. LC 75-11660. 327p. 1975. 34.50 (ISBN 0-471-07157-9, Pub. by Wiley-Interscience). Wiley.

Job Catalog: Where to Find That Creative Job in Washington D. C./Baltimore. 2nd ed. Dorothy O'Callaghan. LC 80-83443. 1980. pap. 6.00 (ISBN 0-914694-05-7). Mail Order.

Job Competancy: Adult Vocational Instruction. John Boulmetis. LC 80-82711. (CBE Forum Ser.: Bk.2). 1981. pap. 5.95 (ISBN 0-8224-4014-8). Pitman Learning.

Job Creation in the Community: An Evaluation of Locally Initiated Employment Projects in Massachusetts. Audrey Prager & Barry Gettleman. 1977. 17.50 (ISBN 0-89011-506-0, EMT 114). Abt Assoc.

Job Evaluation. 2nd ed. Jay L. Otis & R. H. Leukart. 1954. ref. ed. 19.95 (ISBN 0-13-509562-X). P-H.

Job Evaluation: A Manual for the Patterson Method, Vol. II. T. T. Patterson. 208p. 1978. text ed. 22.00x (ISBN 0-220-66844-2, Pub. by Busn Bks England). Renouf.

Job Evaluation: A Practical Guide for Managers. Ed. by Management Publications, Ltd. 1970. 11.95x (ISBN 0-8464-0538-5). Beekman Pubs.

Job Evaluation: A Systematic Approach. Dov Elizur. 188p. 1980. text ed. 37.25 (ISBN 0-566-02120-X, Pub. by Gower Pub Co England). Renouf.

Job Evaluation: An Analytical Review. Committee on Occupational Classification & Analysis. 1979. pap. 7.00 (ISBN 0-309-02882-5). Natl Acad Pr.

Job Evaluation-Wage & Salary Administration. Douglas Bartley. LC 80-21099. 272p. 1981. text ed. 14.95 (ISBN 0-201-00095-4). A-W.

Job Game. S. Figgins. 1980. 12.95 o.p. (ISBN 0-13-510099-2); pap. 6.95 o.p. (ISBN 0-13-510081-X). P-H.

Job Hunting Blueprint: How to Get the Job You Want. Ian Mitchell. (Orig.). 1981. pap. 5.95 (ISBN 0-938306-00-6). Shoreline Pub.

Job Hunting Guide. 2nd ed. Ed. by John A. Erdlen. LC 75-3824. (Career Guide Management Ser.). 160p. 1981. 12.95 (ISBN 0-89047-044-8); pap. 5.95 (ISBN 0-89047-043-X). Herman Pub.

Job Hunting Guide. Ed. by John D. Erdlen. LC 75-3824. (Career Management Guides Ser.). 160p. 1975. 11.95 o.p. (ISBN 0-89047-004-9); pap. 5.95 o.p. (ISBN 0-89047-005-7). Herman Pub.

Job Hunting Guide. condensed ed. Ed. by John D. Erdlen. 65p. 1981. pap. 2.95 (ISBN 0-89047-026-X). Herman Pub.

Job Hunting Handbook for the Municipal Executive. William E. Kirchnoff. (Illus.). 63p. 1980. pap. 8.50 (ISBN 0-9603848-0-4). Appellate Pub.

Job Hunting Secrets & Tactics. Kirby W. Stanat & Patrick Reardon. LC 76-49663. 1977. lib. bdg. 10.95 (ISBN 0-8172-0509-8); pap. 4.95 (ISBN 0-8172-0508-X). Follett.

Job: Interviews by Daniel Odier. William S. Burroughs. LC 73-20496. 212p. 1974. pap. 4.95 (ISBN 0-394-17870-X, E642, Ever). Grove.

Job Marketing. LC 80-67812. (Marketing Ser.). 1980. pap. 4.95 (ISBN 0-87251-050-6). Crain Bks.

Job of Sex. Ed. by National Lampoon Editors. (Illus.). 1974. pap. 2.25 (ISBN 0-446-92837-2). Warner Bks.

Job of the Congressman: An Introduction to Service in the U. S. House of Representatives. 2nd ed. Ed. by Donald G. Tacheron & Morris K. Udall. LC 77-140113. (Orig.). 1970. pap. 9.50 (ISBN 0-672-51416-8). Bobbs.

Job of the Federal Executive. Marver H. Bernstein. 1958. 10.95 (ISBN 0-8157-0918-8). Brookings.

Job Pay for Job Worth: Designing & Managing an Equitable Job Classification & Pay System. Richard I. Henderson et al. (Research Monograph: No. 86). 320p. 1981. pap. 24.00 (ISBN 0-88406-130-2). Ga St U Busn Pub.

Job Placement of the Emotionally Disturbed. Lawrence P. Blum & Richard K. Kujoth. LC 75-185399. 1972. 14.50 (ISBN 0-8108-0468-9). Scarecrow.

Job Power. Ralph Bugg. 1977. pap. 1.75 o.s.i. (ISBN 0-685-75871-0). Jove Pubns.

Job Redesign & Management Control. F. H. Blackler & C. A. Brown. LC 78-60430. 1978. 22.95 (ISBN 0-03-046210-X). Praeger.

Job Satisfaction. Bonnie Carroll. (Key Issues Ser.: No. 3). 1973. pap. 2.00 (ISBN 0-87546-206-5). NY Sch Indus Rel.

Job Satisfaction. Ed. by Michael M. Gruneberg. LC 75-43852. 1976. 29.95 (ISBN 0-470-32911-4). Halsted Pr.

Job Seeking Guide. Albert J. Pautler, Jr. LC 78-57903. 1979. pap. text ed. 3.80 (ISBN 0-8273-1771-9). Delmar.

Job Speaks. David Rosenberg. 101p. 1980. Repr. of 1977 ed. 3.95 (ISBN 0-934450-09-9). Unmuzzled Ox.

Job Stands Up: Play with Music & Lyrics. S. M. Gelber. (Orig.). 1975. pap. 6.00 (ISBN 0-8074-0189-7, 382660). UAHC.

Job to Song of Solomon. Matthew Henry. (Commentary on the Whole Bible Ser: Vol. 3). 12.00 (ISBN 0-8007-0199-2). Revell.

Jobbers. Francis Ford. (Illus.). 1980. pap. 9.95 o.p. (ISBN 0-930490-26-6). Future Shop.

Jobs. Williams Anderson. (gr. 10-12). 1972. pap. text ed. 8.50 incl. suppl. & tchrs' manual (ISBN 0-8449-3050-4). Learning Line.

Jobs & Agricultural Development. Robert D'A. Shaw. LC 79-145446. (Monographs: No. 3). 84p. 1970. 1.00 (ISBN 0-686-28692-8). Overseas Dev Council.

Jobs & Earnings for State Citizens: Monitoring the Outcomes of State Economic Development & Employment & Training Programs. Robert E. Winnie et al. (Institute Paper). 146p. 1977. pap. 4.00 (ISBN 0-87766-208-8, 19900). Urban Inst.

Jobs & Energy in Michigan: The Next Twenty Years. Mark R. Berg et al. LC 80-24884. (Illus.). 262p. 1981. 17.95 (ISBN 0-87944-264-6); pap. 11.95 (ISBN 0-87944-263-8). U of Mich Soc Res.

Jobs & Energy: The Employment & Economic Impacts of Nuclear Power, Conservation, & Other Energy Options. Council on Economic Priorities & Steven Buchsbaum. Ed. by Wendy C. Schwartz. LC 79-91065. 1979. 300.00 (ISBN 0-87871-011-6). CEP.

Jobs for Americans. Ed. by Eli Ginzberg. (American Assembly Ser.). 1976. pap. 4.50 (ISBN 0-13-510016-X, Spec) (ISBN 0-13-510016-X). P-H.

Jobs for Writers. Ed. by Kirk Polking. LC 80-16070. 256p. 1980. 10.95 (ISBN 0-89879-019-0). Writers Digest.

Job's Illness: Loss, Grief & Integration; a Psychological Interpretation. J. H. Kahn. 284p. 1975. text ed. 27.00 (ISBN 0-08-018087-6). Pergamon.

Jobs in Communications. Edward Wakin. LC 73-17470. (Exploring Careers Ser.). (Illus.). 96p. (gr. 5 up). 1974. 7.25 (ISBN 0-688-75006-0). Lothrop.

Jobs in Construction. Arthur Liebers. LC 73-4944. (Exploring Careers Ser.). (Illus.). 96p. (gr. 5 up). 1973. 7.25 o.p. (ISBN 0-688-75004-4). Lothrop.

Jobs, Jobs, Jobs for the College Graduate. U. S. Department of Labor. LC 77-23041. 1977. pap. 3.75 o.p. (ISBN 0-8120-0671-2). Barron.

Jobs People Do. Jane B. Moncure. LC 76-5452. (Illus.). (ps-3). 1976. 5.95 (ISBN 0-913778-37-0). Childs World.

Jobs '79. William N. Yeomans. 1979. pap. 3.95 o.p. (ISBN 0-425-04197-2). Berkley Pub.

Jobson's Mining Year Book, 1979. Ed. by E. Hughes. LC 66-2200. 305p. 1979. 50.00x (ISBN 0-8002-2224-5). Intl Pubns Serv.

Jock Tamson's Bairns: Essays on a Scots Childhood. Ed. by Trevor Royle. 1978. 19.95 (ISBN 0-241-89638-X, Pub. by Hamish Hamilton England). David & Charles.

Jockey-or Else. Fern G. Brown. Ed. by Kathy Pacini. LC 78-1715. (Pilot Bks.). (Illus.). (gr. 4-7). 1978. 6.95g (ISBN 0-8075-3944-9). A Whitman.

Jockey Poems. Ronald Koertge. 1980. 2.50 (ISBN 0-917554-12-4). Maelstrom.

Jock's Island. Elizabeth Coatsworth. (Viking Seafarer Ser). (Illus.). (gr. 7 up). 1969. pap. 0.65 o.p. (ISBN 0-670-05026-1, Puffin). Penguin.

Joe Camp's Benji: Fastest Dog in the West. Gina Ingoglia. (Big Picture Bk.). (Illus.). (ps-k). 1979. 1.95 (ISBN 0-307-10826-0, Golden Pr); PLB 7.62 (ISBN 0-307-60826-3). Western Pub.

Joe Chronicles Sacre Coeur. Rochelle Owens. 1981. pap. 4.95 (ISBN 0-915298-16-3). Sagarin Pr.

Joe D: On the Street with a Chicago Homicide Cop. Richard Whittingham. 288p. 1980. pap. 5.95 (ISBN 0-89505-040-4). Argus Comm.

Joe DiMaggio: An Informal Biography. George DeGregorio. LC 80-6159. 272p. 1981. 12.95 (ISBN 0-8128-2777-5). Stein & Day.

Joe Grimaldi: His Life & Theatre. R. Findlater. LC 78-7465. 1979. 42.00 (ISBN 0-521-22221-4); pap. 12.95x (ISBN 0-521-29407-X). Cambridge U Pr.

Joe Haldeman. Joan Gordon. LC 80-25936. (Starmont Reader's Guide: No. 4). 80p. 1980. Repr. lib. bdg. 9.95x (ISBN 0-89370-035-5). Borgo Pr.

Joe Hill. Wallace Stegner. LC 80-10760. 381p. 1980. 19.50x (ISBN 0-8032-4116-X); pap. 5.95 (ISBN 0-8032-9115-9, BB 728, Bison). U of Nebr Pr.

Joe Humphreys's Trout Tactics. Joe Humphreys. (Illus.). 192p. (Orig.). 1981. pap. 12.95 (ISBN 0-8117-2079-9). Stackpole.

Joe Meek, the Merry Mountain Man. Stanley Vestal. LC 52-5211. (Illus.). 1963. pap. 3.95 (ISBN 0-8032-5206-4, BB 154, Bison). U of Nebr Pr.

Joe Namath. James Olsen. LC 76-16187. 1974. PLB 5.95 (ISBN 0-87191-265-1); pap. 2.95 (ISBN 0-89812-165-5). Creative Ed.

Joe Namath: High-Flying Quarterback. Julian May. LC 74-31946. (Sports Close-up Ser.). (gr. 3-9). 1975. PLB 5.95 o.p. (ISBN 0-913940-17-8); pap. 2.50 o.p. (ISBN 0-913940-24-0). Crestwood Hse.

Joe Norwood's Golf-O-Metrics. Joe Norwood et al. LC 75-21238. 1978. 7.95 o.p. (ISBN 0-385-01823-1). Doubleday.

Joe Overstreet. Intro. by David Henderson. LC 72-85404. (Illus.). 1972. pap. 2.25 (ISBN 0-914412-02-7). Inst for the Arts.

Joe Pepper. Lee McElroy. 1976. pap. 1.25 o.p. (ISBN 0-505-50986-5, BT50986). Tower Bks.

Joe Petrosino. Arrigo Petacco. Tr. by Charles Lam Markmann. (Illus.). 192p. 1974. 5.95 o.s.i. (ISBN 0-02-595160-2). Macmillan.

Joel & Amos. Hans W. Wolff, Jr. Ed. by Dean McBride. Tr. by Waldemar Janzen from Fr. LC 75-76932. (Hermeneia: a Critical & Historical Commentary on the Bible). 416p. 1977. 22.95 (ISBN 0-8006-6007-2, 20-6007). Fortress.

Joel Chandler Harris. R. Bruce Bickley, Jr. (United States Authors Ser.: No. 308). 1978. lib. bdg. 12.50 (ISBN 0-8057-7215-4). Twayne.

Joel in Tananar. Robert M. Walton. (Illus.). 1981. 7.95 (ISBN 0-914598-05-8). Padre Prods.

Joey: A Loving Portrait of Alfred Perles Together with Some Bizarre Episodes Relating to the Other Sex. Henry Miller. (Book of Friends Ser.: Vol. 3). 1979. 8.95 (ISBN 0-88496-136-2); pap. 3.95 (ISBN 0-88496-137-0). Capra Pr.

Joey & DeVon. James Bruce Eure. 1976. 8.00 o.p. (ISBN 0-682-48414-8). Exposition.

Jog, Run, Race. Joe Henderson. LC 77-73651. (Illus.). 204p. 1977. pap. 3.95 (ISBN 0-89037-122-9); handbk. 4.95 (ISBN 0-89037-121-0). Anderson World.

Jogging. Shirley Zeleznak. Ed. by Howard Schroeder. (Back to Nature Ser.). (Illus.). (gr. 3-5). 1979. lib. bdg. 5.95 (ISBN 0-89686-068-X). Crestwood Hse.

Jogging & Running. Richard B. Lyttle. (Concise Guides Ser.). (gr. 5 up). 1979. PLB 6.45 s&l (ISBN 0-531-02949-2). Watts.

Jogjakarta Under Sultan Mangkubumi 1749-1792: A History of the Division of Java. M. C. Ricklefs. (London Oriental Ser: No. 30). 496p. 1974. text ed. 33.00x (ISBN 0-19-713578-1). Oxford U Pr.

Jogotherapy: Jogging As a Therapeutic Strategy. Frederick D. Harper. LC 79-55453. 1979. pap. 3.95 (ISBN 0-935392-00-9). Douglass Pubs.

Johan Borgen. Randi Birn. (World Authors Ser.: Norway: No. 311). 1974. lib. bdg. 10.95 (ISBN 0-8057-2167-3). Twayne.

Johan Ludvig Runeberg. Tore Wreto. (World Author Ser.: No. 503). 1981. lib. bdg. 14.95 (ISBN 0-8057-6344-9). Twayne.

Johann Georg Harmann. James C. Flaherty. (World Authors Ser.: No. 527). 1979. lib. bdg. 14.95 (ISBN 0-8057-6371-6). Twayne.

Johann Jakob Moser & the Holy Roman Empire of the German Nation. Mack Walker. LC 79-27720. 352p. 1980. 26.00x (ISBN 0-8078-1441-5). U of NC Pr.

Johann Ladislaus Dussek: Seine Sonaten und Seine Konzerte. Leo Schiffer. LC 79-168672. 136p. 1972. Repr. of 1914 ed. lib. bdg. 17.50 (ISBN 0-306-70266-5). Da Capo.

Johann Liss: A German Painter of the European Baroque. Ann T. Lurie et al. LC 75-34907. (Illus.). 192p. 1975. pap. 10.00x (ISBN 0-910386-25-0, Pub. by Cleveland Mus Art). Ind U Pr.

Johann Mattheson's der Vollkommene Capellmeister: A Revised Translation with Critical Commentary. Ernest C. Harriss. Ed. by George Buelow. (Studies in Musicology). 875p. 1981. 59.95 (ISBN 0-8357-1134-X, Pub. by UMI Res Pr). Univ Microfilms.

Johann Sebastian Bach: His Life, Art, & Work. Johann N. Forkel. LC 75-125044. (Music Ser). 1970. Repr. of 1920 ed. lib. bdg. 27.00 (ISBN 0-306-70010-7). Da Capo.

Johann Sebastian Bach: Revolutionary of Music. Carmel B. Reingold. LC 72-114927. (Biography Ser). (Illus.). (gr. 7 up). 1970. PLB 5.90 o.p. (ISBN 0-531-00956-4). Watts.

Johann Valentin Andreae's Christianopolis: An Ideal State of the Seventeenth Century. Johann V. Andrea. Tr. by Felix E. Held from Lat. (Illus.). x, 287p. 1981. Repr. of 1916 ed. lib. bdg. 20.00x (ISBN 0-87991-958-2). Porcupine Pr.

Johann Wolfgang Goethe. Liselotte Dieckmann. (World Authors Ser.: Germany: No. 292). 1974. lib. bdg. 10.95 (ISBN 0-8057-2378-1). Twayne.

Johannes Adelphus: Ausgewaehlte Schriften, 4 vols, Vol. 1, Barbarosssa. Johannes Adelphus. Ed. by Bodo Gotzkowsky. (Ausgaben Deutscher Literatur des XV Bis XVIII Jahrhunderts). 1974. 123.50x (ISBN 3-11-003382-8). De Gruyter.

Johannes Brahms: His Work & Personality. Hans Gal. Tr. by Joseph Stein from Ger. LC 76-55410. (Illus.). Repr. of 1963 ed. lib. bdg. 21.00x (ISBN 0-8371-9367-2, GABR). Greenwood.

Johannes Schwalm Historical Assn., Inc. M. A. Schwalm. (Monde D'outre-Mer Passe et Present: Etudes 38). (Illus.). 1972. 64.00x (ISBN 90-2797-052-1); pap. 50.00x (ISBN 0-686-21243-6). Mouton.

Johannes Schwalm the Hessian. (Illus.). 300p. 1976. 22.00 (ISBN 0-686-18265-0). Johannes Schwalm Hist.

Johannes Schwalm the Hessian, No. 3. (Illus.). 53p. 1979. 5.75. Johannes Schwalm Hist.

Johannes Schwalm the Hessian, No. 4. (Illus.). 72p. 1980. 6.50. Johannes Schwalm Hist.

Johannes von Apamea. Werner Strothmann. (Patristische Texte und Studien 11). 1972. 60.60x (ISBN 3-11-002457-8). De Gruyter.

Johannine Epistles. A. E. Brooke. LC 13-170. (International Critical Commentary Ser.). 336p. 1912. text ed. 17.50x (ISBN 0-567-05037-8). Attic Pr.

Johannine Epistles. Rudolf Bultmann. Ed. by Robert W. Funk. Tr. by R. Philip O'Hara et al from Gr. LC 75-171510. (Hermeneia: a Critical & Historical Commentary on the Bible). 158p. 1973. 14.95 (ISBN 0-8006-6003-X, 20-6003). Fortress.

Johannine Epistles. John R. Stott. (Tyndale Bible Commentaries). 1964. pap. 3.95 (ISBN 0-8028-1418-2). Eerdmans.

John. Floyd V. Filson. LC 59-10454. (Layman's Bible Commentary Ser: Vol. 19). 1963. 4.25 (ISBN 0-8042-3019-6). John Knox.

John. Don H. Hillis. (Teach Yourself The Bible Ser). 1962. pap. 1.75 (ISBN 0-8024-4306-0). Moody.

John. George Hutcheson. (Geneva Commentaries Ser.). 8.95 o.p. (ISBN 0-686-12457-X). Banner of Truth.

John. Irving L. Jensen. (Bible Self-Study Guide). 1970. pap. 2.25 (ISBN 0-8024-1043-X). Moody.

John. James McPolin. Ed. by Wilfrid Harrington & Donald Senior. (New Testament Message Ser.: Vol. 6). 244p. 1979. 10.95 (ISBN 0-89453-129-8); pap. 5.95 (ISBN 0-89453-194-8). M Glazier.

John. Guy N. Woods. 1981. 8.95 (ISBN 0-89225-207-3). Gospel Advocate.

John -- the Man Who Would Be President. LC 79-93341. 1979. 9.95 (ISBN 0-89387-040-4). Sat Eve Post.

John A. Williams: The Evolution of a Black Writer. E. A. Cash. LC 73-92796. 1974. 10.00 (ISBN 0-89388-142-2). Okpaku Communications.

John Adams, 2 vols. John Q. Adams. LC 80-24028. (American Statesmen Ser.). 920p. 1981. Set. pap. 13.95 (ISBN 0-87754-177-9). Chelsea Hse.

John Adams. Robert East. (World Leaders Ser.). 1979. lib. bdg. 13.50 (ISBN 0-8057-7723-7). Twayne.

John Adams: A Biography in His Own Words. John Adams. Ed. by James B. Peabody. LC 72-92141. (Founding Fathers Ser.). (Illus.). 416p. (YA) 1973. 15.00 o.p. (ISBN 0-06-013308-2, HarpT). Har-Row.

John Adams & the Diplomacy of the American Revolution. James H. Hutson. LC 79-57575. 208p. 1980. 13.00x (ISBN 0-8131-1404-7). U Pr of Ky.

John Alexander Dowie: A Life of Tragedies & Triumphs. Gordon Lindsay. 1980. 4.95 (ISBN 0-89985-985-2). Christ Nations.

John Amos Comenius on Education. Jean Piaget. LC 67-21499. 1968. text ed. 9.75 (ISBN 0-8077-1911-0); pap. text ed. 5.25x (ISBN 0-8077-1908-0). Tchrs Coll.

John & Mary J. Rife of Greene County Ohio: Their Ancestors & Descendants. John M. Rife & W. R. Rife. LC 80-83318. 1980. 5.00. Reiff Pr.

John & Michael (the O'hara Brothers) A Study of the Early Development of the Anglo-Irish Novel. Mark D. Hawthorne. (Salzburg Studies in English Literature: Romantic Reassessment Ser.: No. 50). 1976. pap. text ed. 25.00x (ISBN 0-391-01401-3). Humanities.

John Arden. Simon Trussler. (Columbia Essays on Modern Writers Ser.: No. 65). 1973. pap. 2.00 (ISBN 0-231-03533-0, MW65). Columbia U Pr.

John Ashbery: An Introduction to the Poetry. David Shapiro. LC 79-4420. (Columbia Introductions to Twentieth-Century American Poetry Ser.). 1979. 15.00 (ISBN 0-231-04090-3). Columbia U Pr.

John B. Connally: Portrait in Power. Ann F. Crawford & Jack Keever. (Illus.). 460p. 1974. 9.50 o.p. (ISBN 0-8363-0121-8). Jenkins.

John Barth: An Annotated Bibliography. Richard A. Vine. LC 76-55322. (Author Bibliographies Ser.: No. 31). 1977. 10.00 (ISBN 0-8108-1003-4). Scarecrow.

John Barth: The Comic Sublimity of Paradox. Jac Tharpe. LC 74-12263. (Arcturus Books Paperbacks). 146p. 1977. pap. 4.95 (ISBN 0-8093-0836-3). S Ill U Pr.

John Bell Seventeen Forty-Five to Eighteen Thirty-One, Bookseller, Printer, Publisher, Typefounder, Journalist, &C. Stanley Morison. LC 78-74416. (Nineteenth-Century Book Arts & Printing History Ser.: Vol. 13). 245p. 1980. lib. bdg. 44.00 (ISBN 0-8240-3887-8). Garland Pub.

John Berryman. J. M. Linebarger. (U. S. Authors Ser.: No. 244). 1974. lib. bdg. 10.95 (ISBN 0-8057-0054-4). Twayne.

John Berryman: A Checklist. Richard J. Kelly. LC 72-6332. (Author Bibliographies Ser.: No. 8). 1972. 10.00 (ISBN 0-8108-0552-9). Scarecrow.

John Berryman: An Introduction to the Poetry. Joel Conarroe. LC 77-8461. (Columbia Introductions to Twentieth-Century American Poetry). 1977. 15.00x (ISBN 0-231-03811-9). Columbia U Pr.

John Billington, Friend of Squanto. Clyde R Bulla. LC 56-9797. (Illus.). (gr. 2-5). 8.95 (ISBN 0-690-46253-0, TYC-J). T Y Crowell.

John Bright. Keith Robbins. (Illus.). 1979. 25.00x (ISBN 0-7100-8992-9). Routledge & Kegan.

John Brown. rev. ed. William E. Du Bois. LC 62-21668. (Orig.). 1962. pap. 2.25 (ISBN 0-7178-0112-8). Intl Pub Co.

John Brown of Haddington. Robert Mackenzie. 1964. pap. 2.25 (ISBN 0-686-12523-1). Banner of Truth.

John Brown, Rose & the Midnight Cat. Jenny Wagner. LC 77-76836. (Illus.). (ps-2). 1978. 9.95 (ISBN 0-87888-120-4). Bradbury Pr.

John Brown: The Sword & the Word. Barrie Stavis. LC 76-81676. (Illus.). 1969. 8.95 o.p. (ISBN 0-498-07520-6). A S Barnes.

John Brown's Journey: Notes & Reflections on His America & Mine. Albert Fried. LC 72-79388. 1978. 10.00 o.p. (ISBN 0-385-05511-0, Anchor Pr). Doubleday.

John Bull & the Papists; or, Passages in the Life of an Anglican Rector, 1846. A. H. Edgar. Ed. by Robert L. Wolff. (Victorian Fiction Ser.). 1975. lib. bdg. 66.00 (ISBN 0-8240-1527-4). Garland Pub.

John Bunyan. Frank M. Harrison. pap. 1.95 o.p. (ISBN 0-686-12524-X). Banner of Truth.

John Bunyan. Lynn Sadler. (English Authors Ser.: No. 260). 1979. lib. bdg. 10.95 (ISBN 0-8057-6757-6). Twayne.

John Bunyan: A Study in Narrative Technique. Charles W. Baird. LC 76-53813. (National University Publications in Literary Criticism Ser.). 1977. 12.00 (ISBN 0-8046-9162-2). Kennikat.

John Bunyan & Pilgrim's Progress. Erwin P. Rudolph. 1977. pap. 1.25 o.p. (ISBN 0-88207-505-5). Victor Bks.

John Bunyan, The Man & His Works. Henri A. Talon. 340p. 1980. Repr. of 1951 ed. lib. bdg. 35.00 (ISBN 0-89987-810-5). Darby Bks.

John Bunyan: Tinker of Bedford. William S. Deal. LC 77-81556. pap. 3.95 (ISBN 0-89107-153-9). Good News.

John Burroughs. Perry D. Westbrook. (U. S. Authors Ser.: No. 227). 1974. lib. bdg. 10.95 (ISBN 0-8057-0117-6). Twayne.

John Butler Yeats & John Sloan. Robert Gordon. (New Yeats Papers: Vol. 14). 1978. pap. text ed. 9.25x (ISBN 0-85105-322-X, Dolmen Pr). Humanities.

John Butler Yeats & the Irish Renaissance. James White. (New Yeats Papers Ser: No. 5). 1972. pap. text ed. 4.50x (ISBN 0-85105-234-7, Dolmen Pr). Humanities.

John C. Calhoun. Hermann E. Von Holst. LC 80-18653. (American Statesmen Ser.). 375p. 1980. pap. 5.95 (ISBN 0-87754-185-X). Chelsea Hse.

John C. Fremont & the Republican Party. Ruhl J. Bartlett. LC 73-87663. (American Scene Ser). 1970. Repr. of 1930 ed. lib. bdg. 19.50 (ISBN 0-306-71763-8). Da Capo.

John Cabot & Son. new ed. David Goodnough. LC 78-18054. (gr. 4-9). 1979. PLB 4.89 (ISBN 0-89375-172-3); pap. 1.75 (ISBN 0-89375-164-2). Troll Assocs.

John Cage. Ed. by Richard Kostelanetz. LC 70-12174. (Illus.). 1978. 12.50 (ISBN 0-932360-09-2); pap. 4.95 (ISBN 0-932360-10-6). RK Edns.

John Calvin: Selections from His Writings. Ed. by John Dillenberger. LC 75-26875. (American Academy of Religion. Aids for the Study of Religion). 590p. 1975. pap. 10.50 (ISBN 0-89130-025-2, 010302). Scholars Pr Ca.

John Calvin's Sermons on the Ten Commandments. John Calvin. Ed. by Benjamin W. Farley. 544p. 1980. 12.95 (ISBN 0-8010-2443-9). Baker Bk.

John Cam Hobhouse (Seventeen Eighty-Six to Eighteen Sixty-Nine) John C. Hobhouse. Ed. by Donald H. Reiman. LC 75-31220. (Romantic Context Ser.: Poetry 1789-1830). 1977. lib. bdg. 42.00 (ISBN 0-8240-2170-3). Garland Pub.

John Carter of Mars. Edgar R. Burroughs. 1973. pap. 1.95 (ISBN 0-345-27844-5). Ballantine.

John Cartwright. J. W. Osborne. LC 74-190422. (Conference on British Studies, Biographical Ser). 168p. 1972. 36.00 (ISBN 0-521-08537-3). Cambridge U Pr.

John Cassian. 2nd ed. Owen Chadwick. 1968. 26.50 (ISBN 0-521-04607-6). Cambridge U Pr.

John Chalk Claris. Ed. by Donald H. Reiman. LC 75-31179. (Romantic Context Ser.: Poetry 1789-1830). 1977. lib. bdg. 47.00 (ISBN 0-8240-2131-2). Garland Pub.

John Chalk Claris ("Arthur Brooke") (1797-1866) Ed. by Donald H. Reiman. LC 75-31178. (Romantic Context Ser.: Poetry 1789-1830). 1978. lib. bdg. 47.00 (ISBN 0-8240-2130-4). Garland Pub.

John Cheap, the Chapman's Library: The Scottish Chap Literature of the Last Century, Classified, 3 vols. LC 68-20126. Repr. of 1877 ed. 70.00 (ISBN 0-8103-3413-5). Gale.

John Cheever. Samuel Coale. LC 77-4829. (Modern Literature Ser.). 1977. 10.95 (ISBN 0-8044-2126-9). Ungar.

John Cheever. Lynne Waldeland. (United States Authors Series: No. 335). 1979. lib. bdg. 10.95 (ISBN 0-8057-7251-0). Twayne.

John Cheever: A Reference Guide. Francis J. Bosha. (Reference Books Ser.). 1981. 20.00 (ISBN 0-8161-8447-X). G K Hall.

John Chrysostom Saint: Discourses Against Judaizing Christians. Tr. by Paul W. Harkins from Gr. LC 77-8466. (Fathers of the Church Ser.: Vol. 68). Orig. Title: Logoi Kata Ioudaion. 366p. 1979. 24.00 (ISBN 0-8132-0068-7). Cath U Pr.

John Clancy Baking Book. John Clancy. 1975. pap. 3.95 o.p. (ISBN 0-445-08327-1). Popular Lib.

John Clare & Thomas Hardy. Peter Levi. (John Coffin Memorial Lecture Ser., 1975). 1976. pap. text ed. 2.50x (ISBN 0-485-16210-5, Athlone Pr). Humanities.

John Cleland: A Biography. William Epstein. 1974. 17.50x (ISBN 0-231-03725-2). Columbia U Pr.

John Cleveland. Lee A. Jacobus. (English Authors Ser.: No. 180). 1975. lib. bdg. 12.50 (ISBN 0-8057-1095-7). Twayne.

John Colet & Marsilio Ficino. Sears R. Jayne. LC 80-17262. (Illus.). 172p. 1980. Repr. of 1963 ed. lib. bdg. 18.75x (ISBN 0-313-22606-7, JACF). Greenwood.

John Constable. Conal Shields & Leslie Parris. (Tate Gallery: Little Art Book Ser.). (Illus.). 1977. pap. 1.95 (ISBN 0-8120-0860-X). Barron.

John Coulter. Geraldine Anthony. (World Authors Ser.: Canada: No. 400). 1976. lib. bdg. 10.95 (ISBN 0-8057-6240-X). Twayne.

John Crowe Ransom. Thornton H. Parsons. (U. S. Authors Ser.: No. 150). 1969. lib. bdg. 10.95 (ISBN 0-8057-0604-6). Twayne.

John Davidson. Carroll V. Peterson. (English Authors Ser.: No. 143). lib. bdg. 10.95 (ISBN 0-8057-1140-6). Twayne.

John Dee on Astronomy: Propaedeumata Aphoristica (1558 & 1568) Wayne Shumaker & J. L. Heilbron. LC 76-50254. 1978. 22.75x (ISBN 0-520-03376-0). U of Cal Pr.

John Dee: The World of an Elizabethan Magus. Peter J. French. 256p. 1980. 25.00 (ISBN 0-7100-7158-2). Routledge & Kegan.

John Deere Snowmobile Service-Repair: 1972-1977. David Sales. Ed. by Eric Jorgenson. (Illus.). 1977. pap. 8.95 (ISBN 0-89287-163-6, X950). Clymer Pubns.

John Denver. Charles Morse & Ann Morse. LC 74-14551. (Rock'n Pop Stars Ser.). (Illus.). 32p. (gr. 3-6). 1974. PLB 5.95 (ISBN 0-87191-392-5); pap. 2.95 (ISBN 0-89812-104-3). Creative Ed.

John Denver: Rocky Mountain Wonder Boy. Ed. by James M. Martin. (Illus., Orig.). 1977. pap. 1.50 o.p. (ISBN 0-523-40002-0). Pinnacle Bks.

John Dewey & the World View. Ed. by Douglas E. Lawson & Arthur E. Lean. LC 64-11170. 1964. lib. bdg. 6.00x o.p. (ISBN 0-8093-0130-X). S Ill U Pr.

John Dewey & the World View. Ed. by Douglas E. Lawson & Arthur E. Lean. LC 64-11170. (Arcturus Books Paperbacks). 168p. 1966. pap. 2.25 (ISBN 0-8093-0224-1). S Ill U Pr.

John Dewey Reconsidered. Ed. by R. S. Peters. (International Library of the Philosophy of Education Ser.). 1977. 16.50x (ISBN 0-7100-8623-7). Routledge & Kegan.

John Dewey: The Reconstruction of the Democratic Life. Jerome Nathanson. LC 66-26511. (Orig.). (gr. 11-12). 1967. text ed. 5.50 o.p. (ISBN 0-8044-6580-0); pap. 2.45 (ISBN 0-686-66560-0). Ungar.

John Dewey's Challenge to Education: Historical Perspectives on the Cultural Context. Oscar Handlin. 59p. 1972. Repr. of 1959 ed. lib. bdg. 11.75x (ISBN 0-8371-5602-5, HAJD). Greenwood.

John Dobson, Architect & Landscape Gardener. Lyall Wilkes. 144p. 1980. 30.00 (ISBN 0-85362-181-0). Routledge & Kegan.

John Donne & the New Philosophy. Charles M. Coffin. 1958. Repr. of 1937 ed. text ed. 12.50x (ISBN 0-391-00444-1). Humanities.

John Donne: Devotions Upon Emergent Occasions. Ed. by Anthony Raspa. 248p. 1976. 18.00x o.s.i. (ISBN 0-7735-0194-0). McGill-Queens U Pr.

John Donne: Language & Style. A. C. Partridge. (Andre Deutsch Language Library). 1979. lib. bdg. 26.50x (ISBN 0-233-97030-4). Westview.

John Donne: Life, Mind & Art. John Carey. 336p. 1981. 19.95 (ISBN 0-19-520242-2). Oxford U Pr.

John Donne: The Critical Heritage. Ed. by A. J. Smith. (Critical Heritage Ser.). 448p. 1975. 40.00x (ISBN 0-7100-8242-8). Routledge & Kegan.

John Donne Treasury. Erwin P. Rudolph. 1978. pap. 1.50 o.p. (ISBN 0-88207-514-4). Victor Bks.

John Donne's Poetry. Wilbur Sanders. LC 75-149436. 1971. 29.95 (ISBN 0-521-07968-3); pap. 8.95x (ISBN 0-521-09909-9). Cambridge U Pr.

John Donne's Sermons on the Psalms & Gospels: With a Selection of Prayers & Meditations. John Donne. Ed. & intro. by Evelyn M. Simpson. 1963. 14.00x (ISBN 0-520-00338-1); pap. 2.65 (ISBN 0-520-00340-3, CAL84). U of Cal Pr.

John Dos Passos. George J. Becker. LC 74-78437. (Modern Literature Ser.). 142p. 1974. 10.95 (ISBN 0-8044-2034-3). Ungar.

John Dos Passos. John H. Wrenn. (U. S. Authors Ser.: No. 9). 1961. lib. bdg. 10.95 (ISBN 0-8057-0208-3). Twayne.

John Dowland. Diana Poulton. 1972. 38.50x o.p. (ISBN 0-520-02109-6). U of Cal Pr.

John Dryden. George R. Wasserman. (English Authors Ser.: No. 14). 1964. lib. bdg. 10.95 (ISBN 0-8057-1176-7). Twayne.

John Duns Scotus: God & Creatures; the Quodlibetal Questions. Illus. by Felix Alluntis & Allan B. Wolter. Orig. Title: Quaestiones Quodlibetales. 548p. Repr. of 1975 ed. write for info. Cath U Pr.

John E. Fogarty: Political Leadership for Library Development. James S. Healey. LC 73-19661. 1974. 10.00 (ISBN 0-8108-0689-4). Scarecrow.

John Elias: Life & Letters. Edward Morgan. 1973. 11.95 (ISBN 0-85151-174-0). Banner of Truth.

John Eliot's Indian Dialogues: A Study in Cultural Interaction. Henry W. Bowden & James P. Ronda. Ed. by John Eliot. LC 80-542. (Contributions in American History: No. 88). (Illus.). 173p. 1980. lib. bdg. 22.95 (ISBN 0-313-21031-4, RID/). Greenwood.

John Evelyn. Jeanne K. Welcher. (English Authors Ser.: No. 144). lib. bdg. 10.95 (ISBN 0-8057-1184-8). Twayne.

John Evelyn & His Cracked World. John Bowle. (Illus.). 256p. 1981. price not set (ISBN 0-7100-0721-3). Routledge & Kegan.

John Evelyn & His Family Circle. W. G. Hiscock. 256p. 1980. Repr. of 1955 ed. lib. bdg. 35.00 (ISBN 0-8495-2374-5). Arden Lib.

John Evelyn & His Times. B. Saunders. 1976. 21.00 (ISBN 0-08-007118-X). Pergamon.

John F. Kennedy. Peter Schwab & J. Lee Shneidman. (World Leaders Ser: No. 28). 1974. lib. bdg. 9.95 (ISBN 0-8057-3696-4). Twayne.

John F. Kennedy: An Annotated Bibliography. Joan I. Newcomb. LC 77-7568. 1977. 10.00 (ISBN 0-8108-1042-5). Scarecrow.

John F. Kennedy & the Second Reconstruction. Carl M. Brauer. 1979. pap. 8.00x (ISBN 0-231-08367-X). Columbia U Pr.

John F. Kennedy & the Second Reconstruction. Carl M. Brauer. LC 76-57686. (Contemporary American History Ser.). 1977. 20.00x (ISBN 0-231-03862-3). Columbia U Pr.

John F. Kennedy: The Promise & the Performance. Lewis J. Paper. xi, 408p. 1980. pap. 7.95 (ISBN 0-306-80114-0). Da Capo.

John Fell, the University Press & the Fell Types. Stanley Morison. LC 78-74401. (Nineteenth-Century Book Arts & Printing History Ser.: Vol. 14). 315p. 1980. lib. bdg. 83.00 (ISBN 0-8240-3888-6). Garland Pub.

John Fiske. George P. Winston. (U. S. Authors Ser.: No. 197). lib. bdg. 10.95 (ISBN 0-8057-0256-3). Twayne.

John Ford. Donald K. Anderson, Jr. (English Authors Ser.: No. 129). lib. bdg. 10.95 (ISBN 0-8057-1204-6). Twayne.

John Ford. Joseph McBride & Michael Wilmington. LC 75-19281. (Theatre, Film & the Performing Arts Ser.). (Illus.). 234p. 1975. lib. bdg. 18.95 (ISBN 0-306-70750-0); pap. 4.95 (ISBN 0-306-80016-0). Da Capo.

John Ford & the Traditional Moral Order. Mark Stavig. 1968. 25.00x (ISBN 0-299-04680-X). U of Wis Pr.

John Ford Movie Mystery. Andrew Sarris. LC 75-37286. (Cinema One Ser.: No. 27). (Illus.). 192p. 1976. 8.95x (ISBN 0-253-33167-6). Ind U Pr.

John Foster Dulles: A Statesman & His Times. Michael A. Guhin. LC 72-5873. (Illus.). 435p. 1972. 22.50x (ISBN 0-231-03664-7). Columbia U Pr.

John Foster: The Politics of the Anglo-Irish Ascendancy. A. P. Malcomson. 1978. 55.00x (ISBN 0-19-920087-4). Oxford U Pr.

John Fowles. Barry N. Olshen. LC 78-3149. (Modern Literature Ser.). 1978. 10.95 (ISBN 0-8044-2665-1). Ungar.

John Foxe & the Elizabethan Church. V. Norskov Olsen. 1973. 22.75x (ISBN 0-520-02075-8). U of Cal Pr.

John Frederick Oberlin. rev. ed. John W. Kurtz. LC 76-25211. 1977. lib. bdg. 24.50 o.p. (ISBN 0-89158-118-9). Westview.

John G. Lake: Apostle to Africa. Gordon Lindsay. 1.50 (ISBN 0-89985-011-1). Christ Nations.

John G. Neihardt. Blair Whitney. LC 76-6543. (U. S. Authors Ser.: No. 270). lib. bdg. 10.95 (ISBN 0-8057-7170-0). Twayne.

John Gabriel Borkman. Henrik Ibsen. 1979. 7.95x (ISBN 0-8464-0092-8). Beekman Pubs.

John Galsworthy: An Annotated Bibliography of Writings About Him. Compiled by Earl E. Stevens & H. Ray Stevens. LC 78-60456. (Annotated Secondary Bibliography Ser. on English Literature in Transition, 1880-1920). 496p. 1980. 30.00x o.p. (ISBN 0-87580-073-4). N Ill U Pr.

John Galt. Ruth I. Aldrich. (English Authors Ser.: No. 231). 1978. lib. bdg. 12.50 (ISBN 0-8057-6657-X). Twayne.

John Garfield: His Life & Films. James N. Beaver, Jr. LC 75-38450. (Illus.). 1977. 17.50 o.p. (ISBN 0-498-01890-3). A S Barnes.

John Gibson Lockhart. Marian Lockhead. 324p. 1980. lib. bdg. 30.00 (ISBN 0-8482-1621-0). Norwood Edns.

John Gilpin's Ride. W. Cowper. (Peter Possum Paperbacks Ser). 1967. pap. 0.95 o.p. (ISBN 0-531-05125-0). Watts.

John Glenn. (gr. 1). 1974. pap. text ed. 2.80 (ISBN 0-205-03870-0, 8038708); tchrs'. guide 12.00 (ISBN 0-205-03866-2, 803866X). Allyn.

John Goldfarb, Please Come Home! William P. Blatty. 160p. (Orig.). 1980. pap. 2.25 (ISBN 0-553-14251-8). Bantam.

John Gordon: Invictus Georgia Love Story. Juliet C. Coleman. 1980. 8.95 (ISBN 0-533-04441-3). Vantage.

John Greenleaf Whittier. Lewis Leary. (U. S. Authors Ser.: No. 6). lib. bdg. 10.95 (ISBN 0-8057-0796-4). Twayne.

John Grierson: A Documentary Biography. Forsyth Hardy. LC 79-670273. (Illus.). 1979. 21.95 (ISBN 0-571-10331-6, Pub. by Faber & Faber). Merrimack Bk Serv.

John Grierson: Film Master. James Beveridge. LC 77-17799. 1978. 22.95 (ISBN 0-02-510530-2). Macmillan.

John Hamilton Reynolds. Ed. by Donald H. Reiman. LC 75-31251. (Romantic Context Ser.: Poetry 1789-1830). 1977. lib. bdg. 47.00 (ISBN 0-8240-2199-1). Garland Pub.

John Hamilton Reynolds. Ed. by Donald H. Reiman. Incl. Garden of Florence. Repr. of 1821 ed; Press, or Literary Chit-Chat. Repr. of 1822 ed; Odes & Addresses to Great People. Repr. of 1825 ed. LC 75-31252. (Romantic Context Ser.: Poetry 1789-1830). 1978. lib. bdg. 47.00 (ISBN 0-8240-2200-9). Garland Pub.

John Hamilton Reynolds. John H. Reynolds. Ed. by Donald H. Reiman. LC 75-31250. (Romantic Context Ser.: Poetry 1789-1830). 1978. lib. bdg. 47.00 (ISBN 0-8240-2198-3). Garland Pub.

John Hart: The Biography of a Signer of the Declaration of Independence. Cleon E. Hammond. LC 77-70992. (Illus.). 1977. 15.95x (ISBN 0-9603426-0-5). Pioneer VT.

John Hassell Lifestyle: A Biography of an Artist. David Cuppleditch. (Illus.). 140p. 1980. 25.00 o.p. (ISBN 0-8390-0250-5). Allanheld & Schram.

John Havlicek. Thomas Braun. LC 75-34489. (Sports Superstars Ser.). (Illus.). (gr. 3-9). 1976. PLB 5.95 o.p. (ISBN 0-87191-498-0). Creative Ed.

John Hawkes: An Annotated Bibliography. Carol A. Hryciw. LC 77-700. (Author Bibliographies Ser.: No. 32). 1977. 10.00 (ISBN 0-8108-1024-7). Scarecrow.

John Hawkes & the Craft of Conflict. John Kuehl. 1975. 14.00 (ISBN 0-8135-0802-9). Rutgers U Pr.

John Hay. Robert L. Gale. (United States Authors Ser.: No. 296). 1978. lib. bdg. 12.50 (ISBN 0-8057-7199-9). Twayne.

John Hay-Howells Letters: The Correspondence of John Milton Hay & William Dean Howells 1861-1905. Ed. by George Monteiro & Brenda Murphy. (American Literary Manuscripts Ser.). 1981. lib. bdg. 14.95 (ISBN 0-8057-9652-5). Twayne.

John Hedgecoe's Complete Course in Photographing Children. Ed. by John Hedgecoe. 1980. 14.95 (ISBN 0-671-41220-5). S&S.

John Hejduk: Seven Houses. Peter Eisenman & John Hejduk. Ed. by Kenneth Frampton. (IAUS Exhibition Catalogues Ser.). (Illus.). 112p. 1979. pap. 12.00 (ISBN 0-932628-03-6). IAUS.

John Hemphill: First Chief Justice of Texas. Rosalee M. Curtis. (Illus.). 1971. 9.50 (ISBN 0-8363-0054-8). Jenkins.

John Henry Bufford: American Lithographer. David Tatham. 22p. 1976. pap. 3.00x o.p. (ISBN 0-912296-33-X, Dist. by U Pr of Va). Am Antiquarian.

John Henry McCoy. Lillie D. Chaffin. (Illus.). 169p. (gr. 4-6). 1971. 4.95 o.s.i. (ISBN 0-02-717920-6). Macmillan.

John Henry Newman. Americo D. Lapati. (English Authors Ser.: No. 140). lib. bdg. 10.95 (ISBN 0-8057-1416-2). Twayne.

John Hills, Assistant Engineer: With a Collection of Plans of the Provinces of New Jersey. Peter J. Guthorn. LC 76-1497. 1977. pap. text ed. 24.75 (ISBN 0-916762-01-7). Portolan.

John Hopton. C. Richmond. (Illus.). 280p. Date not set. price not set (ISBN 0-521-23434-4). Cambridge U Pr.

John Hus at the Council of Constance. Tr. by Matthew Spinka. LC 65-11019. (Records of Civilzation, Sources & Studies: No. 73). 1965. 20.00x (ISBN 0-231-02742-7). Columbia U Pr.

John Huston. Axel Madsen. LC 78-55842. 1978. 10.00 o.p. (ISBN 0-385-11070-7). Doubleday.

John Inglesant. Joseph H. Shorthouse. Ed. by Robert L. Wolff. (Victorian Fiction Ser.). 1975. Repr. of 1880 ed. lib. bdg. 66.00 (ISBN 0-8240-1557-6). Garland Pub.

John Is Easy to Please: Encounters with the Written & Spoken Word. Ved Mehta. 256p. 1971. 7.50 (ISBN 0-374-17986-7). FS&G.

John James Audubon. Alice E. Ford. (Illus.). 1964. 24.95x (ISBN 0-8061-0630-1); pap. 9.95x o.p. (ISBN 0-8061-1115-1). U of Okla Pr.

John Jay. George Pellew. LC 80-19992. (American Statesmen Ser.). 342p. 1980. pap. 5.95 (ISBN 0-87754-193-0). Chelsea Hse.

John Jay: Founder of a State & Nation. Donald L. Smith. LC 68-57156. (gr. 12 up). 1968. text ed. 8.75x (ISBN 0-8077-2177-8). Tchrs Coll.

John Jay: The Nation & the Court. Richard B. Morris. LC 67-25933. 1967. 7.00x (ISBN 0-8419-8713-0, Pub. by Boston U Pr). Holmes & Meier.

John Keats. Douglas Bush. 1967. pap. 1.95 o.s.i. (ISBN 0-02-049260-X, Collier). Macmillan.

John Keats. Robin Mayhead. (British Authors Ser). (Orig.). 1967. 23.95 (ISBN 0-521-05706-X); pap. 7.95x (ISBN 0-521-09419-4). Cambridge U Pr.

John Kenneth Galbraith. John S. Gambs. (World Leaders Ser.: No. 37). 1975. lib. bdg. 9.95 (ISBN 0-8057-3681-6). Twayne.

John Knox. Iain Murray. 1976. pap. 0.50. Banner of Truth.

John Knox. Eustace Percy. LC 65-11937. 1965. 6.95 (ISBN 0-8042-0924-3). John Knox.

John Knox. Eustace Percy. 1964. 8.95 (ISBN 0-227-67510-X). Attic Pr.

John Knox, Bold One for God. Charles Edwards. LC 78-61733. (Destiny Ser.). 1979. pap. 4.95 (ISBN 0-8163-0238-3). Pacific Pr Pub Assn.

John Lafarge,A Memoir &A Study. Royal Cortissoz. LC 70-87508. (Library of American Art Ser). (Illus.). 1971. Repr. of 1911 ed. lib. bdg. 25.00 (ISBN 0-306-71405-1). Da Capo.

John Leech: His Life & Work, 2 Vols. William P. Frith. LC 69-17491. 1969. Repr. of 1891 ed. Set. 32.00 (ISBN 0-8103-3831-9). Gale.

John Leland. Ed. by Rene Wellek. LC 75-11232. (British Philosophers & Theologians of the 17th & 18th Centuries Ser.). 1978. lib. bdg. 42.00 (ISBN 0-8240-1785-4). Garland Pub.

John Lennon. ESE California. (Front Page News Book Ser.). 1981. lib. bdg. 12.95 (ISBN 0-912076-46-1); pap. 5.95 (ISBN 0-912076-45-3). ESE Calif.

John Lennon: One Day at a Time. A Personal Biography. 2nd ed. Anthony Fawcett. LC 76-14557. (Illus.). 192p. 1980. pap. 8.95 (ISBN 0-394-17754-1, E772, Ever). Grove.

John Locke. Geraint Parry. (Political Thinkers Ser.). 1978. text ed. 21.00x o.p. (ISBN 0-04-320130-X); pap. text ed. 8.95x (ISBN 0-04-320131-8). Allen Unwin.

John Locke. Mabel L. Sahakian & William S. Sahakian. (World Leaders Ser.: No. 40). 1975. lib. bdg. 9.95 (ISBN 0-8057-3539-9). Twayne.

John Locke. Kathleen Squadrito. (English Authors Ser.: No. 271). 1979. 10.95 (ISBN 0-8057-6772-X). Twayne.

John Locke: Empiricist, Atomist, Conceptualist & Agnostic. John L. Kraus. LC 68-22348. 1969. 4.95 o.p. (ISBN 0-8022-2257-9). Philos Lib.

John Locke on Education. Ed. by Peter Gay. LC 64-14307. 1964. text ed. 8.75 (ISBN 0-8077-1419-4); pap. text ed. 4.00x (ISBN 0-8077-1416-X). Tchrs Coll.

John Locke's of the Conduct of the Understanding. Ed. by Francis W. Garforth. LC 66-20498. 1966. text ed. 8.75 (ISBN 0-8077-1401-1); pap. text ed. 4.00x (ISBN 0-8077-1398-8). Tchrs Coll.

John Lyly. Joseph W. Houppert. LC 74-20932. (English Authors Ser.: No. 177). 1975. lib. bdg. 10.95 (ISBN 0-8057-1349-2). Twayne.

John McPhee Reader. Ed. by William L. Howarth. 1977. pap. 2.50 o.p. (ISBN 0-394-72113-6, Vin). Random.

John Madson: Out Home. John Madson. Ed. by Michael McIntosh. (Illus.). 1979. 11.95 (ISBN 0-87691-285-4). Winchester Pr.

John Marin. Mackinley Helm. LC 75-87484. (Library of American Art Ser.). (Illus.). 1970. Repr. of 1948 ed. lib. bdg. 29.50 (ISBN 0-306-71489-2). Da Capo.

John Marino's Bicycling Book. John Marino et al. (Illus.). 320p. 1981. 12.95 (ISBN 0-87477-131-5). J P Tarcher.

John Mark & the Origin of the Gospels: A Foundation Document Hypohasis. George F. Melick, Jr. LC 79-52095. 69p. 1979. 4.95 (ISBN 0-8059-2650-X). Dorrance.

John Marshall, 4 vols. Albert J. Beveridge. LC 80-24550. (American Statesmen Ser.). 2400p. 1981. Set. pap. 30.00 (ISBN 0-87754-178-7). Chelsea Hse.

John Marshall. James B. Thayer. LC 76-155923. (American Constitutional & Legal History Ser.). 157p. 1974. Repr. of 1901 ed. lib. bdg. 19.50 (ISBN 0-306-70287-8). Da Capo.

John Marshall: A Life in Law. Leonard Baker. LC 73-2751. (Illus.). 1974. 19.75 o.s.i. (ISBN 0-02-506360-X). Macmillan.

John Marshall: Defender of the Constitution. Frances N. Stites. (Library of American Biography). (Orig.). 1981. 11.95 (ISBN 0-316-81669-8); pap. text ed. 4.95 (ISBN 0-316-81667-1). Little.

John Marshall: Defender of the Constitution. Francis Stites. 208p. 1980. 11.95 (ISBN 0-316-81669-8). Little.

John Marston. R. W. Ingram. (English Authors Ser.: No. 216). 1978. 12.50 (ISBN 0-8057-6725-8). Twayne.

John Marston, Dramtist. Ejner J. Jensen. (Salzburg Institute for English Literature Jacobean Drama Studies). (Orig.). 1980. pap. text ed. 25.00x (ISBN 0-391-01717-9). Humanities.

John Marston's Plays: Themes, Images, Sources. George L. Geckle. LC 77-89977. 1979. 18.50 (ISBN 0-8386-2157-0). Fairleigh Dickinson.

John Marston's Theatrical Drama. John S. Colley. (Salzburg Studies in English Literature, Jacobean Drama Studies: No. 33). 202p. 1974. pap. text ed. 25.00x (ISBN 0-391-01347-5). Humanities.

John Masefield. Sanford Sternlicht. (English Authors Ser.: No. 209). 1977. lib. bdg. 10.95 (ISBN 0-8057-6678-2). Twayne.

John Maynard Keynes. Hyman P. Minsky. (Essays on the Great Economists). 192p. 1975. 17.50x (ISBN 0-231-03616-7); pap. 4.00x (ISBN 0-231-03917-4). Columbia U Pr.

John: Meditations. August Van Ryn. 1949. 3.00 (ISBN 0-87213-887-9). Loizeaux.

John Millington Synge. Donna Gerstenberger. (English Authors Ser.: No. 12). 1964. lib. bdg. 10.95 (ISBN 0-8057-1532-0). Twayne.

John Millington Synge: A Bibliography of Published Criticism. P. Levitt. 224p. 1974. 10.00x (ISBN 0-7165-2155-5, Pub. by Irish Academic Pr). Biblio Dist.

John Millington Synge, Eighteen Seventy-One to Nineteen Hundred & Nine: A Catalogue of an Exhibition Held at Trinity College Library, Dublin on the Occasion of the 50th Anniversary of His Death. Dublin University. 53p. 1980. Repr. of 1959 ed. lib. bdg. 8.50 (ISBN 0-8492-8117-2). R West.

John Milton. Flora Strousse. LC 62-13343. (gr. 7-11). 1960. 6.95 (ISBN 0-8149-0411-4). Vanguard.

John Milton & the English Revolution: A Study in the Sociology of Literature. Andrew Milner. 224p. 1981. 29.50x (ISBN 0-389-20123-5). B&N.

John Milton: Complete Poems & Major Prose. John Milton. Ed. by Merritt Y. Hughes. 1957. 18.95 (ISBN 0-672-63178-4). Odyssey Pr.

John Milton: Complete Shorter Poems. Ed. by John Carey. (Longman Annotated English Poets Ser.). (Illus.). 1971. pap. text ed. 12.50x (ISBN 0-582-48456-1). Longman.

John Milton Hay. Howard I. Kushner & Anne H. Sherrill. (World Leaders Ser.: No. 69). 1977. lib. bdg. 12.50 (ISBN 0-8057-7719-9). Twayne.

John Milton, His Life & Times, Religious & Political Opinions. Joseph Ivimey. 397p. 1980. Repr. of 1833 ed. lib. bdg. 40.00 (ISBN 0-8495-2619-1). Arden Lib.

John Milton: Introductions. Ed. by J. Broadbent. LC 72-93144. (Milton for Schools & Colleges Ser.). (Illus.). 350p. 1973. 42.00 (ISBN 0-521-20172-1); pap. 11.50 (ISBN 0-521-09799-1). Cambridge U Pr.

John Milton: Paradise Lost. Alastair Fowler. (Longman Annotated English Poets Ser.). (Illus.). 1974. pap. text ed. 9.95x (ISBN 0-582-48455-3). Longman.

John Milton: Poetry. David M. Miller. (English Authors Ser.: No. 242). 1978. 12.50 (ISBN 0-8057-6724-X). Twayne.

John Morley. Edward Alexander. (English Authors Ser.: No. 147). lib. bdg. 10.95 (ISBN 0-8057-1404-9). Twayne.

John Muir & His Legacy: The American Conservation Movement. Stephen R. Fox. (Illus.). 416p. 1981. 16.95 (ISBN 0-316-29110-2). Little.

John Muir-to Yosemite & Beyond: Writings from the Years 1863-1875. Robert Engberg & Donald Wesling. (Illus.). 192p. 1981. 17.50 (ISBN 0-299-08270-9); pap. 5.95 (ISBN 0-299-08274-1). U of Wis Pr.

John Muir's America. T. H. Watkins. (Illus.). 160p. 1981. pap. 12.95 (ISBN 0-912856-64-5). Graphic Arts Ctr.

John Muir's Longest Walk. John Earl. 1975. 7.95 o.p. (ISBN 0-385-09216-4). Doubleday.

John Nash & the Village Picturesque. Nigel Temple. (Illus.). 172p. 1980. text ed. 33.00x (ISBN 0-904387-24-0). Humanities.

John Neal. Donald A. Sears. (United States Authors Ser.). 1978. lib. bdg. 12.50 (ISBN 0-8057-7230-8). Twayne.

John of God: His Place in the History of Psychiatry & Medicine. Ruben D. Rumbaut. LC 77-91668. 1978. pap. 5.95 (ISBN 0-89729-198-0). Ediciones.

John Osborne. H. Ferrar. (Columbia Essays on Modern Writers Ser.: No. 67). pap. 2.00 (ISBN 0-231-03361-3, MW67). Columbia U Pr.

John P. Adams' Third Bottle Book. John P. Adams. LC 72-80183. (Illus.). 128p. 1972. pap. 5.95 (ISBN 0-912274-19-0). NH Pub Co.

John P. Holland: 1841-1914. Richard K. Morris. LC 79-6120. (Navies & Men Ser.). (Illus.). 1980. Repr. of 1966 ed. lib. bdg. 18.00x (ISBN 0-405-13048-1). Arno.

John P. Marquand. John J. Gross. (U. S. Authors Ser.: No. 33). 1962. lib. bdg. 10.95 (ISBN 0-8057-0476-0). Twayne.

John Paul II, Pilgrimage of Faith: The First Year of the New Pope & the Story of His Visit to the United States. Ed. by National Catholic News Serv. LC 79-23105. (Illus.). 278p. 1979. 17.50 (ISBN 0-8164-0109-8); pap. 8.95 (ISBN 0-8164-2014-9). Crossroad NY.

John Paul II: The Pope from Poland. 2nd, enl. ed. Tadeusz Karolak. Tr. by David Evans from Polish. LC 80-468695. (Illus.). 176p. 1979. 25.00x (ISBN 83-223-1845-6). Intl Pubns Serv.

John Paul Jones. Matthew G. Grant. LC 73-18212. 1974. PLB 5.95 (ISBN 0-87191-300-3). Creative Ed.

John Paul Jones. Susan Poole. LC 78-74129. (Illus.). (gr. 2-5). Date not set. price not set (ISBN 0-89799-180-X); pap. price not set (ISBN 0-89799-179-6). Dandelion Pr. Postponed.

John Paul Jones, Victory at Sea. Carole Charles. LC 75-33157. (Stories of the Revolution Ser.). (Illus.). (gr. 2-6). 1975. PLB 5.50 (ISBN 0-913778-21-4). Childs World.

John Penry & the Marprelate Controversy. Donald J. McGinn. 1966. 17.50 (ISBN 0-8135-0513-5). Rutgers U Pr.

John Peter Zenger. Livingstone Rutherford. LC 80-29427. (American Men & Women of Letters Ser.). (Illus.). 275p. 1981. pap. 4.95 (ISBN 0-87754-150-7). Chelsea Hse.

John Phoenix Esq., the Veritable Squibob, a Life of Captain George H. Derby, U. S. A. George R. Stewart. LC 75-87721. (American Scene Ser.). 1969. Repr. of 1937 ed. lib. bdg. 25.00 (ISBN 0-306-71669-0). Da Capo.

John Ploughman's Pictures. C. H. Spurgeon. 1975. pap. 2.25 (ISBN 0-686-10526-5). Pilgrim Pubns.

John Ploughman's Talk. C. H. Spurgeon. 1976. pap. 2.25 (ISBN 0-686-16833-X). Pilgrim Pubns.

John Prince, Seventeen Ninety-Six to Eighteen Seventy: A Collection of Documents. R. Alan Douglas. (Champlain Society Ontario Ser.). 350p. 1980. 20.00 (ISBN 0-8020-2378-9). U of Toronto Pr.

John Quincy Adams. John T. Morse, Jr. LC 80-20125. (American Statesmen Ser.). 335p. 1981. pap. 5.95 (ISBN 0-87754-182-5). Chelsea Hse.

John Quincy Adams & the Foundations of American Foreign Policy. Samuel F. Bemis. LC 80-23039. (Illus.). xix, 588p. 1981. Repr. of 1949 ed. lib. bdg. 49.75x (ISBN 0-313-22636-9, BEAD). Greenwood.

John Quincy Adams & the Union. Samuel Flagg Bemis. LC 80-20402. (Illus.). xv, 546p. 1980. Repr. of 1965 ed. lib. bdg. 45.00x (ISBN 0-313-22637-7, BEJQ). Greenwood.

John Randolph. Henry Adams. LC 80-24498. (American Statesmen Ser.). 310p. 1981. pap. 4.95 (ISBN 0-87754-186-8). Chelsea Hse.

John Rawls' Theory of Social Justice: An Introduction. Ed. by H. Gene Blocker & Elizabeth H. Smith. LC 80-11272. xxiii, 520p. 1980. 22.95x (ISBN 0-8214-0445-8, 0445E); pap. 11.95x (ISBN 0-8214-0593-4). Ohio U Pr.

John Reuben Thompson. Gerald R. Garmon. (United States Authors Ser.: No. 346). 1979. lib. bdg. 13.50 (ISBN 0-8057-7284-7). Twayne.

John Ruskin. Frederic Harrison. LC 72-78229. 1971. Repr. of 1902 ed. 15.00 (ISBN 0-8103-3719-3). Gale.

John Ruskin: A Bibliography, 1900-1974. Kirk H. Beetz. LC 76-13611. (Author Bibliographies Ser.: No. 28). 1976. 10.00 (ISBN 0-8108-0938-9). Scarecrow.

John S. Goodall's Theatre: The Sleeping Beauty. Illus. by John S. Goodall. Margaret K. McElderry. (Illus.). 1980. 3.95 (ISBN 0-689-50161-7, McElderry Bk). Atheneum.

John Sargent...with Reproductions from His Paintings & Drawings. Evan E. Charteris. LC 70-164163. (Illus.). xii, 308p. 1972. Repr. of 1927 ed. 24.00 (ISBN 0-8103-3946-3). Gale.

John Skelton. Anthony S. Edwards. (Critical Heritage Ser.). 300p. 1981. price not set (ISBN 0-7100-0724-8). Routledge & Kegan.

John Smilbert, Painter. Henry W. Foote. LC 78-87537. (Library of American Art Ser). 1969. Repr. of 1930 ed. lib. bdg. 29.50 (ISBN 0-306-71453-1). Da Capo.

John Smith: Jamestown Boy. Thomas F. Barton. (Childhood of Famous Americans Ser). (Illus.). (gr. 3-7). 1966. 3.95 (ISBN 0-672-50110-4). Bobbs.

John Smith of Virginia. Ronald Syme. (Illus.). (gr. 5-9). 1954. 6.95 (ISBN 0-688-21597-1). Morrow.

John Soane's Architectural Education, 1753-1780. Pierre De La Ruffiniere Du Prey. LC 76-23615. (Outstanding Dissertations in the Fine Arts Ser.). 1977. lib. bdg. 87.00x (ISBN 0-8240-2686-1). Garland Pub.

John Steinbeck. 2nd ed. Warren French. (U. S. Authors Ser.: No. 2). 1975. lib. bdg. 12.50 (ISBN 0-8057-0693-3). Twayne.

John Steinbeck. Ed. by Warren French. (Twayne's U. S. Authors Ser.). 189p. pap. text ed. 4.95 (ISBN 0-672-61501-0). Bobbs.

John Steinbeck. Paul McCarthy. LC 78-20929. (Modern Literature Ser.). 1980. 10.95 (ISBN 0-8044-2606-6). Ungar.

John Steinbeck: Nature & Myth. Peter Lisca. LC 77-11556. (Twentieth Century American Writers Ser.). (gr. 7 up). 1978. 7.95 (ISBN 0-690-01315-9, TYC-J); PLB 7.89 o.p. (ISBN 0-690-03835-6). T Y Crowell.

John Stewart Curry & Grant Wood: A Portrait of Rural America. Joseph S. Czestochowski. 240p. 1981. text ed. 26.00x (ISBN 0-8262-0336-1). U of Mo Pr.

John Stuart Mill. John B. Ellery. (English Authors Ser.: No. 5). 1964. lib. bdg. 10.95 (ISBN 0-8057-1392-1). Twayne.

John Stuart Mill. R. J. Halliday. (Political Thinkers Ser.). 1976. text ed. 21.00x (ISBN 0-04-320113-X); pap. text ed. 9.95x o.p. (ISBN 0-04-320114-8). Allen Unwin.

John Stuart Mill: A Selection of His Works. John S. Mill. Ed. by John M. Robson. LC 66-19868. (College Classics in English Ser). 1966. pap. 7.50 (ISBN 0-672-63062-1). Odyssey Pr.

John Stuart Mill & Representative Government. Dennis F. Thompson. 236p. 1976. text ed. 16.50 (ISBN 0-691-07582-4); pap. 4.95 (ISBN 0-691-02187-2). Princeton U Pr.

John Stuart Mill on Education. Ed. by Francis W. Garforth. LC 75-115230. 1971. text ed. 10.50 (ISBN 0-8077-1403-8); pap. 4.50x (ISBN 0-8077-1402-X). Tchrs Coll.

John Sullivan Dwight: A Biography. George W. Cooke. LC 79-90210. (Music Reprint Ser). 1969. Repr. of 1898 ed. 29.50 (ISBN 0-306-71818-9). Da Capo.

John Swett: California's Frontier Schoolmaster. Nicholas C. Polos. LC 78-69836. (Illus.). 1978. pap. text ed. 10.25 (ISBN 0-8191-0580-5). U Pr of Amer.

John Swinton: American Radical, 1829-1901. Sender Garlin. (Occasional Paper: No. 20). 1976. pap. 1.50 (ISBN 0-89977-022-3). Am Inst Marxist.

John Synge Comes Next. Maurice Good. 48p. (Orig.). 1973. pap. text ed. 3.75x (ISBN 0-85105-225-8, Dolmen Pr). Humanities.

John Taylor of Caroline: Pastoral Republican. Robert E. Shalhope. LC 80-12501. 314p. 1980. 19.50 (ISBN 0-87249-390-3). U of SC Pr.

John the Beloved: An Essene Understanding of the Book of Revelations. Elizabeth Clark. 1981. 6.95 (ISBN 0-533-04781-1). Vantage.

John: The Gospel of Belief. Merrill C. Tenney. 1948. 8.95 (ISBN 0-8028-3252-0). Eerdmans.

John, the Maverick Gospel. Robert Kysar. LC 76-12393. (Biblical Foundations Ser.). 1976. pap. 4.95 (ISBN 0-8042-0302-4). John Knox.

John Thelwall. Ed. by Doanld H. Reiman. Incl. Ode to Science. Repr. of 1791 ed; John Gildin's Ghost. Repr. of 1795 ed; Poems. Repr. of 1801 ed. LC 75-31261. (Romantic Context Ser.: Poetry 1789-1830). 1978. lib. bdg. 47.00 (ISBN 0-8240-2207-6). Garland Pub.

John Thorndykes Cases. R. Austin Freeman. 1976. lib. bdg. 12.95x (ISBN 0-89968-169-7). Lightyear.

John Travolta. Craig Schumacher. (Rock 'n Pop Stars Ser.). (Illus.). (gr. 4-12). 1979. PLB 5.95 (ISBN 0-87191-698-3); pap. 2.95 (ISBN 0-89812-094-2). Creative Ed.

John Trumbull. Victor E. Gimmestad. (U. S. Authors Ser.: No. 240). lib. bdg. 10.95 (ISBN 0-8057-0746-8). Twayne.

John Updike. Robert Detweiler. (U. S. Authors Ser.: No. 214). lib. bdg. 9.95 (ISBN 0-8057-0752-2). Twayne.

John Updike. Ed. by Robert Detweiler. LC 74-187611. (Twayne's U. S. Authors Ser.). 183p. 1972. pap. text ed. 4.95 (ISBN 0-672-61506-1). Bobbs.

John Updike. Suzanne H. Uphaus. LC 79-48076. (Modern Literature Ser.). 160p. 1980. 10.95 (ISBN 0-8044-2934-0); pap. 4.95 (ISBN 0-8044-6945-8). Ungar.

John Updike & the Three Great Secret Things: Sex, Religion, & Art. George Hunt. 176p. 1980. 13.95 (ISBN 0-8028-3539-2). Eerdmans.

John W. Campbell Letters, 3 vols. Incl. Vol. 1. Ed. by George Hay. write for info. (ISBN 0-931150-02-7); pap. write for info (ISBN 0-931150-03-5); lib. bdg. write for info. (ISBN 0-931150-04-3); Vol 2. Ed. by Perry A. Chapdelaine, Sr. write for info; pap. write for info (ISBN 0-931150-06-X); lib. bdg. write for info (ISBN 0-931150-07-8); Vol. 3. Ed. by A. E. Vogt. write for info (ISBN 0-931150-08-6); pap. write for info (ISBN 0-931150-09-4); lib. bdg. write for info (ISBN 0-931150-10-8). 1981. Authors Co Op.

John W. Foster: Politics & Diplomacy in the Imperial Era-1873-1917. Michael J. Devine. LC 80-17387. (Illus.). 200p. 1981. 14.95x (ISBN 0-8214-0437-7). Ohio U Pr.

John Wain. Dale Salwak. (English Authors Ser.: No. 316). 1981. lib. bdg. 11.95 (ISBN 0-8057-6806-8). Twayne.

John Wayne. David Paige. (Stars of Stage & Screen Ser.). (Illus.). (gr. 4-12). 1976. PLB 5.50 o.p. (ISBN 0-87191-551-0). Creative Ed.

John Wayne & the Movies. Allen Eyles. LC 73-13191. (Illus.). 320p. 1976. 17.50 o.p. (ISBN 0-498-01449-5). A S Barnes.

John Webster: A Classified Bibliography. William E. Mahaney. (Salzburg Studies in English Literature, Jacobean Drama Studies: No. 10). 319p. 1973. pap. text ed. 25.00x (ISBN 0-391-01471-4). Humanities.

John Webster Concordance, Vol. 2, Pt. 3. R. Corballis & J. M. Harding. (Jacobean Drama Studies: No. 70). 1979. pap. text ed. 25.00x (ISBN 0-391-01761-6). Humanities.

John Webster: Politics & Tragedy. Robert Griffin. (Salzburg Studies in English Literature, Jacobean Drama Studies: No. 12). 179p. 1972. pap. text ed. 25.00x (ISBN 0-391-01394-7). Humanities.

John Websters Tragodienstil Als Ausdruck der Leidenschaftlichkeit. Lutze. (Jacobean Ser.). (Ger.). 1980. pap. text ed. 25.00x (ISBN 0-391-02196-6). Humanities.

John Websters Tragodienstil Als Ausdruck der Leidenschaftlichkeit. Lotha Von Lutze. (Jacobean Drama Studies: No.84). 189p. (Orig.). 1980. 25.00 (ISBN 0-391-02196-6). Humanities.

John Welch. Ethel Barrett. 128p. (gr. 5-9). 1980. pap. 2.95 (ISBN 0-310-43151-4). Zondervan.

John Wesley. Stanley Ayling. 1979. 12.95 (ISBN 0-529-05688-7, RB5688, Pub. by Collins Pubs). Abingdon.

John Wesley. Stanley Ayling. 1980. Repr. 10.95 (ISBN 0-687-20376-7). Abingdon.

John Wesley. Basil Miller. 1969. pap. 2.25 (ISBN 0-87123-272-3, 200272). Bethany Fell.

John Wesley. Ed. by Albert Outler. 516p. 1980. pap. 9.95 (ISBN 0-19-502810-4). Oxford U Pr.

John Wesley. John Vickers. (Ladybird Ser.). 1977. 1.49 (ISBN 0-87508-841-4). Chr Lit.

John Wesley: A Theological Biography, Vol. 2, Pt. 1. Martin Schmidt. Tr. by Norman Goldhawk from Ger. 312p. 1973. 12.95 o.p. (ISBN 0-687-20481-X). Abingdon.

John Wesley & Authority: A Psychological Perspective. Robert L. Moore. LC 79-13709. (American Academy of Religion. Dissertation Ser.: No. 29). 1979. 12.00 (ISBN 0-89130-290-5, 010129); pap. 7.50 (ISBN 0-89130-291-3). Scholars Pr Ca.

John Wesley: His Life & Theology. Robert Tuttle. 1978. 11.95 (ISBN 0-310-36660-7). Zondervan.

John Wesley Treasury. Erwin P. Rudolph. 1979. pap. 1.95 (ISBN 0-88207-517-9). Victor Bks.

John Wilkins, 1614-1672: An Intellectual Biography. Barbara J. Shapiro. LC 73-84042. 1969. 23.75x (ISBN 0-520-01396-4). U of Cal Pr.

John Woolman: Child of Light. Catherine O. Peare. LC 54-6990. (gr. 7-9). 6.95 (ISBN 0-8149-0376-2). Vanguard.

Johnnie: The Barefoot Dreamer. David Summers. 1974. 1.50 (ISBN 0-88243-535-3, 02 0535). Gospel Pub.

Johnny Alleluia. Charles Causley. 1962. 4.95 (ISBN 0-246-63643-2). Dufour.

Johnny Bench. George Heaslip. LC 73-13862. (Creative Superstars Ser.). 1974. PLB 5.95 (ISBN 0-87191-289-9); pap. 2.95 (ISBN 0-89812-171-X). Creative Ed.

Johnny Carson. David Paige. (Stars of Stage & Screen Ser.). (Illus.). (gr. 4-12). 1977. PLB 5.95 (ISBN 0-87191-560-X). Creative Ed.

Johnny Cash. Paula Taylor. LC 74-14549. (Rock'n Pop Stars Ser.). (Illus.). 32p. (gr. 3-6). 1974. PLB 5.95 (ISBN 0-87191-391-7); pap. 2.95 (ISBN 0-89812-102-7). Creative Ed.

Johnny Crow's Garden. Leslie L. Brooke. (Peter Possum Paperbacks Ser.). 1967. pap. 0.95 o.p. (ISBN 0-531-05110-2). Watts.

Johnny Deadline Reporter: The Best of Bob Greene. Bob Greene. LC 76-6932. 1976. 14.95 (ISBN 0-88229-361-3). Nelson-Hall.

Johnny Hong of Chinatown. Clyde R. Bulla. LC 52-7859. (Illus.). (gr. 2-5). 1952. 8.95 (ISBN 0-690-46466-5, TYC-J); PLB 6.49 (ISBN 0-690-46467-3). T Y Crowell.

Johnny Horton-Your Singing Fisherman. Michael LeVine. Date not set. 10.95 (ISBN 0-533-04802-8). Vantage.

Johnny Osage. Janice H. Giles. 1980. lib. bdg. 15.95 (ISBN 0-8161-3053-1, Large Print Bks). G K Hall.

Johnny Reb Band from Salem. Harry H. Hall. (Music Reprint 1980 Ser.). (Illus.). xi, 118p. 1980. Repr. of 1963 ed. lib. bdg. 15.00 (ISBN 0-306-76014-2). Da Capo.

Johnny Still Can't Read...but You Can Teach Him at Home. 5th ed. Kathryn Diehl & G. K. Hodenfield. (Illus.). 75p. 1979. pap. 2.50 (ISBN 0-9603552-0-0). K Diehl.

Johnny the Clockmaker. Edward Ardizzone. (Illus.). 48p. (ps-3). 1981. pap. 4.95 (ISBN 0-19-272120-8). Oxford U Pr.

Johnny Unitas: And the Long Pass. Julian May. LC 72-77302. (Sports Close-Up Ser.). (gr. 3-9). 1972. PLB 5.95 o.p. (ISBN 0-87191-200-7); pap. 2.50 o.p. (ISBN 0-685-64985-7). Crestwood Hse.

Johnny's Egg. Earlene Long. LC 79-21248. (Illus.). 1980. 6.95 (ISBN 0-201-04153-7, 4153). A-W.

Johns Hopkins Atlas of Human Functional Anatomy. rev., 2nd ed. Ed. by George D. Zuidema. LC 79-25191. 1980. text ed. 17.50x (ISBN 0-8018-2363-3); pap. text ed. 10.95x (ISBN 0-8018-2364-1). Johns Hopkins.

Johns Hopkins Textual Studies. Glyph. 1980. No. 6, 224p. 14.50 (ISBN 0-8018-2296-3); pap. 3.95 (ISBN 0-8018-2297-1); No. 7 240p. 16.50 (ISBN 0-8018-2365-X); pap. 5.95 (ISBN 0-8018-2366-8). Johns Hopkins.

Johnson, Grant, & the Politics of Reconstruction. Martin E. Mantell. 225p. 1973. 15.00x (ISBN 0-231-03507-1). Columbia U Pr.

Johnson on Shakespeare. Ed. by R. W. Desai. 1979. text ed. 12.50x (ISBN 0-86131-120-5). Humanities.

Johnson Outboards, Forty to One Hundred & Forty HP: 1965-1977. (Illus.). 248p. 8.00 o.p. (ISBN 0-89287-219-5, B665). Western Marine Ent.

Johnson Outboards, One and One-Half to Thirty-Five HP: 1965-1978. (Illus.). 192p. 8.00 o.p. (ISBN 0-89287-230-6, B663). Western Marine Ent.

Johnsoniana, 25 vols. Incl. Vol. 1. Early Criticism (ISBN 0-8240-1279-8); Vol. 2, On Johnson's Shakespeare (ISBN 0-8240-1280-1); Vol. 3. Satire on Johnson's Dictionary (ISBN 0-8240-1281-X); Vol. 4. On the False Alarm, Etc (ISBN 0-8240-1282-8); Vol. 5. On Taxation No Tyranny 1 (ISBN 0-8240-1283-6); Vol. 6. On Taxation No Tyranny 2 (ISBN 0-8240-1284-4); Vol. 7. On the Journey to the Western Isles 1 (ISBN 0-8240-1285-2); Vol. 8. On the Journey to the Western Isles 2 (ISBN 0-8240-1286-0); Vol. 9. On the Journey to the Western Isles 3 (ISBN 0-8240-1287-9); Vol. 10. Johnsonian Testbook (ISBN 0-8240-1288-7); Vol. 11. On the Lives of the Poets 1 (ISBN 0-8240-1289-5); Vol. 12. On the Lives of the Poets 2 (ISBN 0-8240-1290-9); Vol. 13. On the Lives of the Poets 3 (ISBN 0-8240-1291-7); Vol. 14. On the Lives of the Poets 4 (ISBN 0-8240-1292-5); Vol. 15. Biography (ISBN 0-8240-1293-3); Vol. 16. Biography (ISBN 0-8240-1294-1); Vol. 17. Biography (ISBN 0-8240-1295-X); Vol. 18. Biography (ISBN 0-8240-1296-8); Vol. 19. Biography (ISBN 0-8240-1297-6); Vol. 20. Biography (ISBN 0-8240-1298-4); Vol. 21. Biography (ISBN 0-8240-1299-2); Vol. 22. Biography (ISBN 0-8240-1300-X); Vol. 23. Biography (ISBN 0-8240-1301-8); Vol. 24. Biography (ISBN 0-8240-1302-6); Vol. 25. Biography (ISBN 0-8240-1303-4). (Life & Times of Seven Major British Writers Ser). 1974. lib. bdg. 47.00 ea. Garland Pub.

Join the Dots. Isobel R. Beard. (Activity Fun Books). (Illus.). (ps-3). 1969. 0.99 o.p. (ISBN 0-695-90390-X). Follett.

Joining Together: Group Theory & Group Skills. David W. Johnson & Frank P. Johnson. LC 74-23698. (Illus.). 480p. 1975. pap. 12.95 (ISBN 0-13-510370-3). P-H.

Joint Acquisitions List of Africana: 1978. Northwestern University. 1980. lib. bdg. 90.00 (ISBN 0-8161-0329-1). G K Hall.

Joint Chiefs of Staff: The First 25 Years. Lawrence J. Korb. LC 75-16839. (Illus.). 224p. 1976. 10.95x (ISBN 0-253-33169-2). Ind U Pr.

Joint Custody: An Alternative for Divorcing Families. Mel Morgenbesser & Nadine Nehls. LC 80-22182. (Illus.). 176p. 1981. 13.95 (ISBN 0-88229-620-5). Nelson-Hall.

Joint Custody & Co-Parenting Handbook. rev. ed. Miriam Galper. 207p. 1980. lib. bdg. 12.90 (ISBN 0-89471-116-4); pap. 5.95 (ISBN 0-89471-117-2). Running Pr.

Joint Development: Making the Real Estate-Transit Connection. ULI Research Division & Gladstone Associates. LC 79-66189. (Illus.). 216p. 1979. pap. text ed. 25.75 (ISBN 0-87420-588-3). Urban Land.

Joint International Business Ventures. Ed. by Wolfgang Friedman & George Nalmanoff. LC 61-7173. 1961. 25.00x (ISBN 0-231-02465-7). Columbia U Pr.

Joint Statistical Papers of J. Neyman & E. S. Pearson. 299p. 1967. 25.00x (ISBN 0-85264-706-9, Pub. by Griffin England). State Mutual Bk.

Joint Trust Pension Plans. Daniel F. McGinn. 1979. 12.95x (ISBN 0-256-02105-8). Irwin.

Joints in Buildings. Bruce Martin. 1977. 54.95 (ISBN 0-470-99106-2). Halsted Pr.

Joke-a-Day Book. Gyles Brandreth. LC 78-66298. (Illus.). (gr. 3 up). 1979. 6.69 (ISBN 0-8069-4598-2); PLB 5.89 (ISBN 0-8069-4599-0). Sterling.

Joke Teller's Handbook or, One Thousand Nine Hundred Ninety-Nine Belly Laughs. Robert Orben. LC 66-12229. 1966. 5.95 o.p. (ISBN 0-385-04042-3). Doubleday.

Jokes & Fun. Helen Hoke. LC 72-2403. (Illus.). 48p. (gr. 1-4). 1973. PLB 3.90 o.p. (ISBN 0-531-02616-7). Watts.

Jokes & Riddles. Walt Disney Productions. (Winnie-the-Pooh Hunny Pot Bk.). 24p. (ps-3). 1980. PLB 5.38 (ISBN 0-307-68869-0, Golden Pr). Western Pub.

Jokes, Giggles & Guffaws. Helen Hoke. LC 75-6047. 160p. (gr. 3 up). 1975. 6.90 (ISBN 0-531-02844-5). Watts.

Jokes, Jokes, Jokes. Ed. by Helen Hoke. (Terrific Triple Titles Ser). (Illus.). (gr. 4-6). 1963. PLB 7.90 (ISBN 0-531-01704-4). Watts.

Jokes on You. Ed. by Dorothy Russell. (Pal Paperbacks Ser., Kit A). (Illus., Orig.). (gr. 7-12). 1974. pap. text ed. 1.25 (ISBN 0-8374-3479-3). Xerox Ed Pubns.

Jokes, Puns, & Riddles. David Allen Clark. LC 67-19070. (gr. 3-7). 1968. 5.95a (ISBN 0-385-09018-8); PLB (ISBN 0-385-09019-6). Doubleday.

Jolly Barnyard. Annie N. Bedford. (Illus.). (ps-1). 1950. PLB 5.00 (ISBN 0-307-60067-X, Golden Pr). Western Pub.

Jolly Christmas at the Patterprints. Vera Nyce. LC 76-153795. (Illus.). (gr. k-3). 1971. 5.95 o.s.i. (ISBN 0-8193-0521-9, Four Winds); PLB 5.41 o.s.i. (ISBN 0-8193-0522-7). Schol Bk Serv.

Jolly Time Party Book. Patricia F. Sheinhold. 6.95 (ISBN 0-916752-21-6). Green Hill.

Jomon Pottery: Prehistoric Japanese Arts. J. Edward Kidder. LC 68-17458. (Illus.). 308p. 1968. 85.00 (ISBN 0-87011-095-0). Kodansha.

Jonah. Denise Adler. 1980. pap. 1.98 (ISBN 0-8423-1948-4). Tyndale.

Jonah. Hugh Martin. (Banner of Truth Geneva Series Commentaries). 1978. 10.95 (ISBN 0-85151-115-5). Banner of Truth.

Jonah: An Old Testament Story. Beverly Brodsky. LC 77-5925. (gr. 3 up). 1977. 9.95 (ISBN 0-397-31733-6). Lippincott.

Jonah & the Big Fish. (Tell-a-Bible Story Ser.). (Illus.). 28p. bds. 0.69 (ISBN 0-686-68641-1, 3685). Standard Pub.

Jonah & the Great Fish. Clyde R. Bulla. LC 69-13636. (Illus.). (gr. k-4). 1970. 9.95 (ISBN 0-690-46430-4, TYC-J). T Y Crowell.

Jonah Complex. Andre Lacocque & Pierre Lacocque. LC 80-84649. 1981. 14.00 (ISBN 0-8042-0091-2); pap. 7.95 (ISBN 0-8042-0092-0). John Knox.

Jonah: His Life, Character, & Mission. Patrick Fairbairn. (Summit Bks.). 248p. 1980. pap. 3.95 (ISBN 0-8010-3498-1). Baker Bk.

Jonah Legend: A Suggestion of Interpretation. William Simpson. LC 72-177422. (Illus.). vi, 182p. 1971. Repr. of 1899 ed. 15.00 (ISBN 0-8103-3820-3). Gale.

Jonah, Messenger of the Eleventh Hour. Gerhard Hasel. LC 76-12907. (Dimension Ser.). 1976. pap. 5.95 (ISBN 0-8163-0260-X, 10440-6). Pacific Pr Pub Assn.

Jonah's Gourd Vine. Zora N. Hurston. LC 70-166496. 1971. 5.95 o.p. (ISBN 0-397-00754-X); pap. 2.95 o.p. (ISBN 0-397-00723-X, LP-45). Lippincott.

Jonas. Gordon Stowell. Tr. by S. D. de Lerin from English. (Libros Pescaditos Sobre Personajes Biblicos). (Illus.). 1978. pap. 0.40 (ISBN 0-311-38514-1, Edit Mundo). Casa Bautista.

Jonas Lie. Sverre Lyngstad. (World Authors Ser.: No. 434). 1977. lib. bdg. 12.50 (ISBN 0-8057-6274-4). Twayne.

Jonatan y el Corderito Travieso. Jane Latourette. Tr. by Ronald Ross from Eng. (Libros Arco). (Illus.). 32p. (Orig., Span.). (gr. 1-3). 1972. pap. 0.95 o.s.i. (ISBN 0-89922-040-1). Edit Caribe.

Jonathan Bing. Beatrice C. Brown. LC 68-14074. (gr. k-3). 1968. 5.75 (ISBN 0-688-40989-X); PLB 5.00 o.p. (ISBN 0-688-50989-4). Lothrop.

Jonathan David Dictionary of First Names. Kolatch. 1980. 19.95 (ISBN 0-8246-0234-X). Jonathan David.

Jonathan Edwards: Art & the Sense of the Heart. Terrence Erdt. LC 80-5380. (New England Writers Ser.). 144p. 1980. lib. bdg. 13.50x (ISBN 0-87023-304-1). U of Mass Pr.

Jonathan Edwards on God's Kingdom: Three Stages of Theological Development. M. Darrol Bryant. (Studies in American Religion: Vol. 4). 1981. soft cover 24.95x (ISBN 0-88946-908-3). E Mellen.

Jonathan Edwards: Pastor. Patricia Tracy. 288p. 1980. 14.95 (ISBN 0-8090-6195-3); pap. 5.95 (ISBN 0-8090-0149-7). Hill & Wang.

Jonathan Edwards, Seventeen Fifty-Six to Nineteen Seventy-Eight: Bibliographical Synopses. (Studies in American Religion: Vol. 3). 1981. soft cover 39.95x (ISBN 0-88946-907-5). E Mellen.

Jonathan Edwards to Aaron Burr, Jr. From Great Awakening to Democratic Politics. (Studies in American Religion: Vol. 1). 1981. soft cover 24.95x (ISBN 0-88946-906-7). E Mellen.

Jonathan Livingston Seagull. R. Bach. (Keith Jennison Large Type Ser). 8.95 o.p. (ISBN 0-531-00320-5). Watts.

Jonathan Livingston Seagull. Richard Bach. LC 75-119617. (Illus.). 1970. 8.95 (ISBN 0-02-504540-7). Macmillan.

Jonathan Swift. Nigel Dennis. 1965. 3.95 o.s.i. (ISBN 0-685-15394-0). Macmillan.

Jonathan Swift. D. Donoghue. LC 77-79053. 1969. 42.00 (ISBN 0-521-07564-5). Cambridge U Pr.

Jonathan Swift. Ed. by John Hayward. (Nonesuch Library). 1978. 11.95 (ISBN 0-370-00517-1, Pub. by Chatto Bodley Jonathan). Merrimack Bk Serv.

Jonathan Swift. Robert Hunting. (English Authors Ser.: No. 42). 1966. lib. bdg. 10.95 (ISBN 0-8057-1520-7). Twayne.

Jonathan Swift: A Biography. A. L. Rowse. LC 75-37779. (Encore Edition). 1976. 2.95 o.p. (ISBN 0-684-15447-1, ScribT). Scribner.

Jonathan Swift: Dean & Pastor. Robert W. Jackson. 185p. 1980. Repr. of 1939 ed. lib. bdg. 20.00 (ISBN 0-8492-1279-0). R West.

Jonathan Swift: Preacher & Jester. Peter Steele. 1979. 31.00x (ISBN 0-19-812088-5). Oxford U Pr.

Jonathan Swift: Selected Poems. Jonathan Swift. Ed. by C. H. Sisson. (Fyfield). 1979. pap. 3.95 (ISBN 0-85635-134-2, Pub. by Carcanet New Pr England). Persea Bks.

Jonathan Wild. Henry Fielding. Incl. Journal of a Voyage to Lisbon. 1958. 6.00x (ISBN 0-460-00877-3, Evman); pap. 5.95 (ISBN 0-460-01877-9, Evman). Dutton.

Jonathan: You Left Too Soon. David Biebel. 192p. 1981. 8.95 (ISBN 0-8407-5235-0). Nelson.

Jone Brent: Neurosurgeon. Jeanette Seletz. LC 78-50163. 1981. 12.50 (ISBN 0-87527-136-7). Green.

Jones. James E. Myers. 256p. 1981. 9.95 (ISBN 0-916392-77-5). Oak Tree Pubns.

Jones' Animal Nursing. 3rd. ed. D. R. Lane. (Illus.). Date not set. 67.50 (ISBN 0-08-024945-0); pap. 36.00 (ISBN 0-08-024944-2). Pergamon. Postponed.

Jones on Evidence, Civil & Criminal, 4 vols. 6th ed. Spencer A. Gard. LC 72-76892. 1972. Set. 170.00 (ISBN 0-686-14505-4). Lawyers Co-Op.

Jones Very: The Effective Years, 1833-1840. Edwin Gittleman. LC 67-16202. 1967. 22.50x (ISBN 0-231-03043-6). Columbia U Pr.

Jongkind. (Artists Ser.). (Illus.). 1979. pap. 5.95 (ISBN 0-8120-0716-6). Barron.

Joni. Joni Eareckson & Joe Musser. 1976. o. p. 6.95 (ISBN 0-310-23960-5); kivar, large print 4.95 (ISBN 0-310-23967-2); pap. 3.95 (ISBN 0-310-23961-3); pap. 2.95 (ISBN 0-310-23962-1). Zondervan.

Joni. Joni Eareckson & Joe Musser. (Illus.). 256p. 1980. pap. 2.95 (ISBN 0-310-23982-6). Zondervan.

Joni. Tr. by Joni Eareckson. (Portuguese Bks.). 1979. 1.40 (ISBN 0-8297-0800-6). Life Pubs Intl.

Joni. Tr. by Joni Eareckson. (Spanish Bks.). (Span.). 1977. 1.90 (ISBN 0-8297-0774-3). Life Pubs Intl.

Joni of Storm Hill. Lucile V. Stevens. 192p. (YA) 1976. 4.95 o.p. (ISBN 0-685-61054-3, Avalon). Bouregy.

Jonie Goes to Academy. Jo-An Ritchie. LC 78-21271. (Orion Ser.). (gr. 6-12). 1979. pap. 1.95 (ISBN 0-8127-0193-3). Southern Pub.

Jonie Graduates. Jo-An Ritchie. LC 78-27431. (Orion Ser.). (gr. 6-12). 1979. pap. 1.95 (ISBN 0-8127-0201-8). Southern Pub.

Jonie's Direct Line. Jo-An Ritchie. LC 75-44644. (Crown Ser.). 1976. pap. 4.50 (ISBN 0-8127-0110-0). Southern Pub.

Joplin: A Pictorial History. Kay Kirkman & Roger Stinnett. Ed. by Donna R. Friedman. (Illus.). 192p. 1980. pap. 13.95 (ISBN 0-89865-070-4). Donning Co.

Jordan. Frederick K. Poole. LC 73-14618. (First Bks). (Illus.). 72p. (gr. 5-8). 1974. PLB 6.45 (ISBN 0-531-00818-5). Watts.

Jordan. rev. ed. Frederick K. Poole. Ed. by Linda O'Brien. (First Bks). (Illus.). (gr. 4-6). 1978. PLB 6.45 s&l (ISBN 0-531-02241-2). Watts.

Jordan Fantosme's Chronicle. Ed. by R. C. Johnston. 256p. 1980. 60.00 (ISBN 0-19-815758-4). Oxford U Pr.

Jordan Intercept. J. Alexander McKenzie. (Canaan Trilogy Ser.). 266p. (Orig.). 1980. pap. 2.95 (ISBN 0-87123-269-3, 200269). Bethany Fell.

Jordan to Jerusalem: A Lenten Pilgrimage. Katie Elberfeld. 1979. 1.20 (ISBN 0-686-28783-5). Forward Movement.

Jordanus De Nemore, De Numeris Datis: A Critical Edition & Translation. Ed. by Barnabas E. Hughes. (Publications of the Center for Medieval & Renaissance Studies, UCLA). 200p. 1981. 40.00x (ISBN 0-520-04283-2). U of Cal Pr.

Jorge Carrera Andrade: Introduccion A Su Vida. Enriave Ojeda. 1972. 16.95 (ISBN 0-88303-003-9); pap. 12.95 (ISBN 0-685-73209-6). E Torres & Sons.

Jorge Isaacs. Donald McGrady. (World Authors Ser.: Colombia: No. 166). lib. bdg. 10.95 (ISBN 0-8057-2460-5). Twayne.

Jorge Luis Borges. Martin S. Stabb. (World Authors Ser.: Argentina: No. 108). lib. bdg. 10.95 (ISBN 0-8057-2168-1). Twayne.

Jorgito. Robert Bright. LC 76-23789. (ps-k). 1977. PLB 5.95 (ISBN 0-385-12005-2). Doubleday.

Jorgoto (Goergie) Bright. (ps-3). 1980. pap. 1.50 (ISBN 0-590-30048-2, Schol Pap). Schol Bk Serv.

Joris of the Rock: The Neustrian Cycle, Bk. 2. Leslie Barringer. Ed. by R. Reginald & Douglas Menville. LC 80-19241. (Newcastle Forgotten Fantasy Library: Vol. 9). 318p. 1980. Repr. of 1976 ed. lib. bdg. 10.95x (ISBN 0-89370-508-X). Borgo Pr.

Jorn, Vol. III. Guy Atkins. (Asger Jorn Complete Work Ser.). 250p. 1980. write for info. (ISBN 0-8150-0927-5). Wittenborn.

Jornado. E. R. Slade. (Orig.). 1979. pap. 1.95 (ISBN 0-532-23270-4). Manor Bks.

Jose. Armando P. Valdes. Ed. by J. Cano & E. Cameron. 1932. 5.50 (ISBN 0-672-73223-8). Odyssey Pr.

Jose & the Mexican Jumping Bean. Emilie Toepperwein & Fritz A. Toepperwein. (Illus.). (gr. 4-7). 1965. PLB 2.00 (ISBN 0-910722-05-6). Highland Pr.

Jose Asuncion Silva. Betty T. Osiek. (World Authors Ser.: No. 505 (Columbia)). 1978. 13.50 (ISBN 0-8057-6346-5). Twayne.

Jose Carlos Mariategui & the Rise of Modern Peru, 1890-1930. Jesus Chavarria. LC 78-21426. 1979. 14.95 (ISBN 0-8263-0507-5). U of NM Pr.

Jose De Escandon & the Founding of Nuevo Santander: A Study in Spanish Colonization. Lawrence F. Hill. (Perspectives in Latin American History Ser.). (Illus.). v, 149p. 1980. Repr. of 1926 ed. lib. bdg. 15.00x (ISBN 0-87991-086-0). Porcupine Pr.

Jose Donoso. George R. McMurray. (World Authors Ser.: No. 517). 1979. lib. bdg. 13.95 (ISBN 0-8057-6358-9). Twayne.

Jose M. Arguedas: Los Rios profundos. Ed. by William Rowe. LC 73-4524. 288p. 1973. text ed. 19.50 (ISBN 0-08-017014-5); pap. text ed. 12.75 (ISBN 0-08-017015-3). Pergamon.

Jose-Maria de Heredia. Alvin Harms. LC 74-22312. (World Authors Ser.: No. 347). 1975. lib. bdg. 12.50 (ISBN 0-8057-2421-4). Twayne.

Jose Maria Gironella. Ronald Schwartz. (World Authors Ser.: Spain: No. 164). lib. bdg. 10.95 (ISBN 0-8057-2372-2). Twayne.

Jose Maria Pereda: Selections from Sotileza & Penas Arriba. Jose M. Pereda. Ed. by Florence W. Talamantes. 1978. pap. text ed. 9.00x (ISBN 0-8191-0379-9). U Pr of Amer.

Jose Marti, Letras y Huellas Desconocidas. Carlos Ripoll. 1976. 10.95 (ISBN 0-88303-024-1); pap. 6.50 (ISBN 0-685-73013-1). E Torres & Sons.

Jose Marti y las Artes Plasticas. Cisneros F. Garcia. 1972. 9.95 (ISBN 0-88303-996-6); pap. 7.95 (ISBN 0-685-73207-X). E Torres & Sons.

Jose Ortega y Gasset. Franz Niedermayer. Tr. by Peter Tirner from Ger. LC 71-163150. (Modern Literature Ser.). 1973. 10.95 (ISBN 0-8044-2659-7). Ungar.

Joseph Addison's Sociable Animal: In the Market Place, On the Hustings, In the Pulpit. Edward A. Bloom & Lillian D. Bloom. LC 73-111455. (Illus.). 276p. 1971. 12.50x (ISBN 0-87057-120-6, Pub. by Brown U Pr). Univ Pr of New England.

Joseph & His Brethren. Gordon Lindsay. (Old Testament Ser.). 1.25 (ISBN 0-89985-130-4). Christ Nations.

Joseph & His Brethren in Genesis. George Lawson. LC 80-8071. 1981. 12.95 (ISBN 0-8254-3122-0). Kregel.

Joseph & His Brothers. Maud Petersham & Miska Petersham. (Illus.). (gr. 3-4). 1958. 4.95g o.s.i. (ISBN 0-02-772240-6). Macmillan.

Joseph & Koza, or the Sacrifice to the Vistula. Isaac B. Singer. LC 78-106398. (ps-3). 1970. 4.95 o.p. (ISBN 0-374-33795-0). FS&G.

Joseph Andrews. Henry Fielding. Ed. by Martin Battestin. LC 66-23917. (Works of Henry Fielding). 1967. 27.50x (ISBN 0-8195-3070-0, Pub. by Wesleyan U Pr). Columbia U Pr.

Joseph Banks in Newfoundland & Labrador, 1766: His Diary, Manuscripts & Collections. Ed. by A. M. Lysaght. LC 70-81800. (Illus.). 1971. 60.00 (ISBN 0-520-01780-3). U of Cal Pr.

Joseph Beuys, Multiples: Catalog Raisonne. Ed. by Jorg Schellmann & Bernd Kluser. LC 80-11593. (Illus.). 246p. 1981. 22.50x (ISBN 0-8147-7813-5); pap. 14.95 (ISBN 0-8147-7814-3). NYU Pr.

Joseph Brown: Or, the Young Tennessean Whose Life Was Saved by the Power of Prayer. an Indian Tale. Thomas O. Summers. Bd. with Narrative of a Captivity Among the Mohawk Indians, & a Description of New Netherland in 1642-3. Isaac Jogues. LC 75-7091. (Indian Captivities Ser.: Vol. 67). Repr. of 1856 ed. lib. bdg. 44.00 (ISBN 0-8240-1691-2). Garland Pub.

Joseph Conrad. Neville H. Newhouse. LC 69-16157. (Literary Critiques Ser.). (Illus.). 1969. Repr. lib. bdg. 4.95 o.p. (ISBN 0-668-01887-9). Arco.

Joseph Conrad. Robert S. Ryf. LC 74-110599. (Columbia Essays Ser.: No. 49). (Orig.). 1970. pap. 2.00 (ISBN 0-231-03264-1, MW49). Columbia U Pr.

Joseph Conrad. Roger Tennant. LC 80-69393. 1981. 12.95 (ISBN 0-689-11152-5). Atheneum.

Joseph Conrad. Martin Tucker. LC 75-37265. (Modern Literature Ser.). 1980. 10.95 (ISBN 0-8044-2928-6). Ungar.

Joseph Conrad: A Commemoration Papers from 1974 International Conference on Conrad. Ed. by Norman Sherry. LC 76-24069. 1979. Repr. of 1976 ed. text ed. 18.50x (ISBN 0-06-496233-4). B&N.

Joseph Conrad, a Pen Portrait. Anon. 24p. 1980. Repr. of 1913 ed. lib. bdg. 10.00 (ISBN 0-8482-1309-2). Norwood Edns.

Joseph Conrad & the West: Signs of Empire. Jacques Darras. 1981. 26.50x (ISBN 0-389-20071-9). B&N.

Joseph Conrad: Giant in Exile. Leo Gurko. 1979. 12.95 (ISBN 0-02-546700-X). Macmillan.

Joseph Conrad on Fiction. Joseph Conrad. Ed. by Walter F. Wright. LC 64-11355. (Regents Critics Ser). 1964. 11.95x (ISBN 0-8032-0452-3); pap. 3.45x (ISBN 0-8032-5452-0, BB 400, Bison). U of Nebr Pr.

Joseph Conrad: The Major Phase. Jacques Berthoud. LC 77-8242. (British Authors Ser.). 1978. 22.50 (ISBN 0-521-21742-3); pap. 8.95x (ISBN 0-521-29273-5). Cambridge U Pr.

Joseph Conrad: The Making of a Moralist. John E. Saveson. LC 72-83547. 195p. (Orig.). 1972. pap. text ed. 20.00x (ISBN 0-391-01998-8). Humanities.

Joseph Conrad-Times Remembered. John Conrad. LC 79-41596. (Illus.). 212p. Date not set. price not set (ISBN 0-521-22805-0). Cambridge U Pr.

Joseph Conrad's Letters to R. B. Cunninghame Graham. Ed. by C. T. Watts. LC 69-16288. (Illus.). 1969. 42.00 (ISBN 0-521-07213-1). Cambridge U Pr.

Joseph Cornell. Ed. by Kynaston McShine. (Illus.). 296p. 1980. 29.95 (ISBN 0-87070-271-8); pap. 13.50 (ISBN 0-87070-272-6). Museum Mod Art.

Joseph de Maistre. Charles M. Lombard. LC 76-13846. (World Authors Ser: No. 407). 1976. lib. bdg. 12.50 (ISBN 0-8057-6247-7). Twayne.

Joseph Glanvill: Scepsis Scientifica, or Confest Ignorance, the Way to Science, 1664. Joseph Glanvill. Ed. by Rene Wellek. LC 75-11222. (British Philosophers & Theologians of the 17th & 18th Centuries Ser.). 1978. lib. bdg. 42.00 (ISBN 0-8240-1776-5). Garland Pub.

Joseph: God's Man in Egypt. Leslie Flynn. 1979. pap. 2.50 (ISBN 0-88207-788-0). Victor Bks.

Joseph Hall. Leonard D. Tourney. (English Authors Ser.: No. 250). 1979. lib. bdg. 11.95 (ISBN 0-8057-6740-1). Twayne.

Joseph Jones, M.D. Scientist of the Old South. James O. Breeden. LC 73-80462. (Illus.). 320p. 1975. 17.00x (ISBN 0-8131-1296-6). U Pr of Ky.

Joseph Lancaster & the Monitorial School Movement: A Documentary History. Carl F. Kaestle. LC 72-97206. 1973. text ed. 12.00 (ISBN 0-8077-2375-4); pap. text ed. 5.50x (ISBN 0-8077-2380-0). Tchrs Coll.

Joseph Losey. Foster Hirsch. (Theater Arts Ser.). 1980. lib. bdg. 12.95 (ISBN 0-8057-9257-0). Twayne.

Joseph McKenna. Matthew McDevitt. LC 73-21874. (American Constitutional & Legal History Ser.). 250p. 1974. Repr. of 1946 ed. lib. bdg. 27.50 (ISBN 0-306-70632-6). Da Capo.

Joseph Nicollet & His Map. Martha C. Bray. LC 79-54278. (Memoirs Ser.: Vol. 140). 1980. 15.00 (ISBN 0-87169-140-X). Am Philos.

Joseph of Copertino. Angelo Pastrovicchi. LC 79-91298. 135p. 1979. Repr. of 1918 ed. pap. write for info. o.p. (ISBN 0-89555-135-7). Tan Bks Pubs.

Joseph Pennell's Sketches of Old New Orleans. E. C. Matthews. 64p. 1966. pap. 2.00 (ISBN 0-911116-85-0). Pelican.

Joseph Richardson & Family: Philadelphia Silversmiths. Martha G. Fales. LC 74-5911. (Illus.). 372p. 1974. 20.00 (ISBN 0-8195-4076-5, Pub. by Wesleyan U Pr). Columbia U Pr.

Joseph Schillinger: A Memoir. Frances Schillinger. LC 76-7575. (Music Reprint Ser.). 1976. Repr. of 1949 ed. lib. bdg. 22.50 (ISBN 0-306-70780-2). Da Capo.

Joseph Skipsey: Selected Poems. Ed. by Basil Bunting. 96p. pap. 5.95x (ISBN 0-904461-08-4, Pub. by Ceolfrith Pr England). Intl Schol Bk Serv.

Joseph Stalin. Robert D. Warth. (World Leaders Ser: No. 10). 1969. lib. bdg. 9.95 (ISBN 0-8057-3080-X). Twayne.

Joseph, the Border Guard. Kurt Bauman. LC 70-178743. (gr. k-3). 1972. 5.95 o.s.i. (ISBN 0-8193-0548-0, Four Winds); PLB 5.41 o.s.i. (ISBN 0-8193-0549-9). Schol Bk Serv.

Joseph: The Man Closest to Jesus. Joseph Filas. 1962. 7.75 (ISBN 0-8198-0070-8); pap. 6.50 o.s.i. (ISBN 0-8198-0071-6). Dghtrs St Paul.

Joseph von Eichendorff. Egon Schwarz. (World Authors Ser.: Germany: No. 163). lib. bdg. 10.95 (ISBN 0-8057-2296-3). Twayne.

Josephine. Josephine Baker & Jo Bouillon. LC 76-26212. (Illus.). 1977. 12.95 o.s.i. (ISBN 0-06-010212-8, HarpT). Har-Row.

Josephine. Hubert Cole. 1979. pap. 1.95 (ISBN 0-505-51351-X). Tower Bks.

Josephine. Dieter Kuehn. (Suhrkamp Taschenbuch: No. 587). 176p. 1980. pap. text ed. 3.90 (ISBN 3-518-37087-1, Pub. by Insel Verlag Germany). Suhrkamp.

Josephson Effect in Superconducting Tunneling Structures. I. O. Kulik & I. K. Yanson. Tr. by P. Gluck from Rus. LC 75-184438. 182p. 1972. 32.50 (ISBN 0-470-51050-1). Halsted Pr.

Josh. Ivan Southall. LC 75-187795. 192p. (gr. 7 up). 1972. 7.95g (ISBN 0-02-786080-9). Macmillan.

Josh Billings (Henry W. Shaw) David B. Kesterson. (U. S. Authors Ser.: No. 229). 1974. lib. bdg. 10.95 (ISBN 0-8057-0058-7). Twayne.

Josh Gibson: A Life in the Negro Leagues. William Brashler. LC 77-83861. (Illus.). 1978. 9.95 o.s.i. (ISBN 0-06-010446-5, HarpT). Har-Row.

Josh McDowell & Don Stewart Answer Tough Questions That Skeptics Ask About the Christian Faith. Josh McDowell & Don Stewart. 190p. (Orig.). 1980. pap. 4.95 o.p. (ISBN 0-918956-65-X). Campus Crusade.

Joshers. Humphrey Carpenter. (Illus.). 1977. 10.50 (ISBN 0-04-823142-8). Allen Unwin.

Joshua. H. A. Ironside. Date not set. 4.50 (ISBN 0-87213-374-5). Loizeaux.

Joshua. rev. ed. Ed. by Irving L. Jensen. (Bible Self-Study Ser). (Illus.). 80p. 1967. pap. 2.25 (ISBN 0-8024-1006-5). Moody.

Joshua, Conqueror of Canaan. Gordon Lindsay. (Old Testament Ser.). 1.25 (ISBN 0-89985-134-7). Christ Nations.

Joshua-Esther. Matthew Henry. (Commentary on the Whole Bible Ser: Vol. 2). 12.00 (ISBN 0-8007-0198-4). Revell.

Joshua: Fighter for Bar Kochba. Irena Narell. LC 78-55959. (gr. 6-12). 1979. pap. 8.95 (ISBN 0-934764-01-8). Akiba Pr.

Joshua Fortune. Cynthia D. Grant. LC 80-11983. 156p. (gr. 6-9). 1980. 8.95 (ISBN 0-689-30777-2). Atheneum.

Joshua in the Light of the New Testment. W. Graham Scroggie. LC 80-8074. (W. Graham Scroggie Library). 1981. pap. 2.50 (ISBN 0-8254-3734-2). Kregel.

Joshua Then & Now. Mordecai Richler. 384p. 1981. pap. 3.25 (ISBN 0-553-14583-5). Bantam.

Joshua's Day. 2nd ed. Sandra L Surowiecki. LC 77-20479. 27p. (ps-1). 1977. pap. 2.75 (ISBN 0-914996-18-5). Lollipop Power.

Josiah Conder. Ed. by Donald H. Reiman. LC 75-31183. (Romantic Context Ser.: Poetry 1789-1830). 1977. lib. bdg. 47.00 (ISBN 0-8240-2134-7). Garland Pub.

Josiah Gregg & His Vision of the Early West. Paul Horgan. 116p. 1979. 8.95 (ISBN 0-374-18017-2). FS&G.

Josiah Royce. Thomas F. Powell. (World Leaders Ser). lib. bdg. 10.95 (ISBN 0-8057-3713-8). Twayne.

Josiah W. Wilson & Lydia Melinda Wilson & Slasham Valley, St. Clair County, Alabama Kinfolk. Mildred S. Wright. LC 79-56809. (Illus.). 1979. 28.75 (ISBN 0-917016-14-9); pap. 18.75 (ISBN 0-917016-15-7). M S Wright.

Josiah Wedgewood. Samuel Smiles. LC 71-141603. 1971. Repr. of 1894 ed. 20.00 (ISBN 0-8103-3617-0). Gale.

Josiah Willard Gibbs-American Physicist Par Excellance. Raymond J. Seeger. (Men of Physics Ser.). 1975. 34.00 (ISBN 0-08-018013-2). Pergamon.

Josie Pearl. Alma A. Schulmerich. 1966. 4.95 (ISBN 0-913814-13-X). Nevada Pubns.

Josquin Des Prez. Ed. by Edward E. Lowinsky. (Illus.). 1977. incl. 3 seven inch discs 74.00x (ISBN 0-19-315229-0). Oxford U Pr.

Jottings of a Stock Market Jackass. 3rd ed. Jules Penn. 80p. (Orig.). 1973. pap. 5.00 o.p. (ISBN 0-912070-16-1). Bale Bks.

Journal & Letters of Samuel Curwen, an American in England, from 1775-1783. Samuel Curwen. Ed. by George A. Ward. LC 70-14720. (Era of the American Revolution Ser). 1970. Repr. of 1864 ed. lib. bdg. 65.00 (ISBN 0-306-71923-1). Da Capo.

Journal AWWA, Vol. 70, 1978. American Water Works Association. (Journal Bound Volumes). (Illus.). 788p. 1979. text ed. 36.50 (ISBN 0-89867-205-8). Am Water Wks Assn.

Journal AWWA, Vol. 71, 1979. American Water Works Association. (Journal Bound Volumes). (Illus.). 788p. 1980. lib. bdg. 28.80 (ISBN 0-89867-232-5); text ed. 36.50 (ISBN 0-686-68527-X). Am Water Wks Assn.

Journal de la Confederation. F. N. Babeuf. (Fr.). 1977. lib. bdg. 17.50x o.p. (ISBN 0-8287-0048-6); pap. text ed. 7.50x o.p. (ISBN 0-685-75752-8). Clearwater Pub.

Journal de la Liberte de la Presse, No. 1-22: Prospectus du Tribun du Peuple, le Tribun de Peuple ou le Defenseur des DrOits de l'Homme, No. 23-43, 2 vols. F. N. Babeuf. (Fr.). 1977. lib. bdg. 70.00x o.p. (ISBN 0-8287-0049-4); pap. text ed. 50.00x o.p. (ISBN 0-685-75754-4). Clearwater Pub.

Journal de l'annee: 1974-1975. new ed. Ed. by Maurice Barrois. (Illus.). 415p. (Fr.). 1975. 25.00x (ISBN 0-686-67325-5). Larousse.

Journal from an Obscure Place. Judith Miles. LC 78-60279. 1978. pap. 1.95 (ISBN 0-87123-273-1, 200273). Bethany Fell.

Journal Kept at Nootka Sound by John R. Jewitt, One of the Surviving Crew of the Ship Boston...Interspersed with Some Account of the Natives, Their Manners & Customs, Repr. Of 1807 Ed. Incl. Narrative of the Adventures & Sufferings of John R. Jewitt. Ed. by Richard Alsop. Repr. of 1815 ed. LC 75-7050. (Indian Captivities Ser.: Vol. 28). 1976. lib. bdg. 44.00 (ISBN 0-8240-1652-1). Garland Pub.

Journal Meiner Reise Im Jahr, 1769. 2nd, rev. ed. Johann G. Herder. Ed. by A. Gillies. (Blackwell's German Text Ser.). 1969. pap. 6.50x o.p. (ISBN 0-631-01830-1, Pub. by Basil Blackwell). Biblio Dist.

Journal, Nineteen Seventy-Three. Cimarron Valley Historical Society. 7.95 (ISBN 0-685-48813-6). Nortex Pr.

Journal of a Fur Trading Expedition on the Upper Missouri, 1812-1813. John C. Luttig. (Illus.). 1964. Repr. of 1920 ed. 12.50 (ISBN 0-87266-019-2). Argosy.

Journal of a London Playgoer. Henry Morley. (Victorian Library Ser.). 348p. 1974. Repr. of 1866 ed. text ed. 13.50x (ISBN 0-7185-5031-5, Leicester). Humanities.

Journal of a Neurosurgeon. Edgar A. Kahn. (Illus.). 182p. 1972. 12.75 (ISBN 0-398-02325-5). C C Thomas.

Journal of a Solitude. May Sarton. 1977. pap. 3.95 (ISBN 0-393-00853-3, N853, Norton Lib). Norton.

Journal of a Soul. Pope John XXIII. Tr. by Dorothy White. LC 79-7786. (Illus.). 504p. 1980. pap. 5.95 (ISBN 0-385-14842-9, Im). Doubleday.

Journal of a Trapper. Osborne Russell. Ed. by Aubrey L. Haines. LC 56-52. (Illus.). 1965. 13.50x (ISBN 0-8032-0897-9); pap. 3.50 (ISBN 0-8032-5166-1, BB 316, Bison). U of Nebr Pr.

Journal of African Languages & Linguistics 1979, Vol. 1, No. 1. Ed. by Paul Newman. 1979. pap. text ed. 14.25x (ISBN 0-686-59702-8). Humanities.

Journal of Beckett, Nos. 3 & 4. James Knowlson. 1978. pap. text ed. 8.00x (ISBN 0-685-59433-5). Vol. 3. Vol. 4. pap. text ed. 8.25x (ISBN 0-7145-3709-8). Humanities.

Journal of Beckett Studies. James Knowlson. 1975. pap. 5.00 (ISBN 0-7145-3669-5). Riverrun NY.

Journal of Captain William Pote, Jr., During His Captivity in the French & Indian War from May 1745 to August 1747. LC 75-7127. (Indian Captivities Ser.: Vol. 100). 1976. Repr. of 1896 ed. lib. bdg. 44.00 (ISBN 0-8240-1724-2). Garland Pub.

Journal of Charlotte L. Forten. Charlotte L. Forten. Ed. by Ray A. Billington. 286p. 1981. pap. 4.95 (ISBN 0-393-00046-X). Norton.

Journal of Debates & Proceedings. Massachusetts Constitutional Convention - 1820-21. LC 76-133169. (Law, Politics, & History Ser). 1970. Repr. of 1853 ed. lib. bdg. 69.50 (ISBN 0-306-70068-9). Da Capo.

Journal of Elder William Conrad: Pioneer Preacher. Lloyd W. Franks. 1976. pap. text ed. 6.50x o.p. (ISBN 0-8191-0054-4). U Pr of Amer.

Journal of Eugene Delacroix. Eugene Delacroix. Ed. by Sydney J. Freedberg. LC 77-19378. (Connoisseurship Criticism & Art History Ser.: Vol. 9). (Illus.). 1980. lib. bdg. 44.00 (ISBN 0-8240-3266-7). Garland Pub.

Journal of Glass Studies: Nineteen Seventy-Two, Vol. 22. (Illus.). 165p. 1980. 15.00x (ISBN 0-87290-022-3). Corning.

Journal of Jewish Art, Vol. 7. Ed. by B. Narkiss. (Illus.). 90p. 1981. pap. 15.00 (ISBN 0-8390-0271-8). Allanheld & Schram.

Journal of John Cardan. J. V. Cunningham. LC 64-16116. 56p. 1964. 2.50x (ISBN 0-8040-0173-1). Swallow.

Journal of Jules Renard. Jules Renard. Ed. by Louise Bogan. Tr. by Elizabeth Roget. LC 64-21767. 1964. 6.00 o.s.i. (ISBN 0-8076-0276-0). Braziller.

Journal of Katherine Mansfield. Katherine Mansfield. Ed. by John M. Murry. LC 74-14981. (Illus.). 292p. 1975. Repr. of 1927 ed. 24.00 (ISBN 0-86527-265-4). Fertig.

Journal of Madame Royale. Elizabeth Powers. LC 75-43990. (Illus.). 192p. (gr. 5 up). 1976. 7.50 o.s.i. (ISBN 0-8027-6251-4); PLB 7.39 (ISBN 0-8027-6252-2). Walker & Co.

Journal of Major George Washington. George Washington. Ed. by James R. Short & Thaddeus W. Tate, Jr. 1963. 2.50x o.p. (ISBN 0-8139-0402-1). U Pr of Va.

Journal of Notarial Acts & Recordkeeping Practices. 2nd ed. Editors of The National Notary Magazine of the National Notary Assn. LC 73-75903. 1979. 11.65 (ISBN 0-933134-01-0). Natl Notary.

Journal of Notarial Acts & Recordkeeping Practices. 8th ed. Editors of The National Notary Magazine of the National Notary Assn. LC 73-75903. 1979. sewn bdg. semi hard cover 6.85 (ISBN 0-933134-02-9). Natl Notary.

Journal of One Davey Wyatt. Donald Honig. LC 74-171901. (Illus.). 128p. (gr. 5 up). 1972. PLB 5.90 (ISBN 0-531-02040-1). Watts.

Journal of Practical Practice, Vol. 4, No. 2. Ed. by Jay E. Adams. 1980. pap. 5.00 (ISBN 0-87552-032-4). Presby & Reformed.

Journal of Prince Alexander Liholiho: Voyages Made to the United States, England, & France in 1849-50. Alexander Liholiho. Ed. by Jacob Adler. LC 67-27052. (Personal Diary, Photos, Index, Notes, 188p). 1967. 10.00 (ISBN 0-87022-009-8). U Pr of Hawaii.

Journal of the Fictive Life. Howard Nemerov. 1965. 12.00 o.p. (ISBN 0-8135-0493-7). Rutgers U Pr.

Journal of the New Alchemists, No. 7. Ed. by Nancy J. Todd. (Illus.). 184p. 1981. 15.95 (ISBN 0-8289-0405-7); pap. 9.95 (ISBN 0-8289-0406-5). Greene.

Journal of the Plague Year. Daniel Defoe. 1953. 10.50x (ISBN 0-460-00289-5, Evman); pap. 3.95 (ISBN 0-460-01289-4). Dutton.

Journal of the Proceedings of the Friends of Domestic Industry: In General Convention Met at the City of New York, October 26, 1831. Alexander Everett. Ed. by Michael Hudson. Bd. with British Opinions on the Protecting System. (Neglected American Economists Ser.). 1974. lib. bdg. 50.00 (ISBN 0-8240-1003-5). Garland Pub.

Journal of the Proceedings of the President: 1793 to 1797. Ed. by Dorothy Twohig. LC 80-17174. (Papers of George Washington). 1981. price not set (ISBN 0-8139-0874-4). U Pr of Va.

Journal of the Santa Fe Expedition Under Colonel Doniphan. Jacob S. Robinson. LC 75-87634. (American Scene Ser.). (Illus.). 96p. 1972. Repr. of 1932 ed. lib. bdg. 12.50 (ISBN 0-306-71798-0). Da Capo.

Journal of the Seasons on an Ozark Farm. Leonard Hall. LC 57-7800. (Illus.). 242p. 1980. pap. 6.95 (ISBN 0-8262-0317-5). U of Mo Pr.

Journal of the Southern Indian Mission: Diary of Thomas D. Brown. Ed. by Juanita Brooks. 1972. pap. 5.00 (ISBN 0-87421-047-X). Utah St U Pr.

Journal of the Sufferings & Hardships of Capt. Parker H. French's Overland Expedition to California. William Miles. 8.50 (ISBN 0-8363-0057-2); pap. 4.50 wrappers (ISBN 0-685-13276-5). Jenkins.

Journal of the Way. K. D. Katrak. 40p. 1975. 8.00 (ISBN 0-88253-570-6); pap. text ed. 4.80 (ISBN 0-88253-569-2). Ind-US Inc.

Journal of Travels into the Arkansas Territory During the Year 1819. Thomas Nuttall. Ed. by Savoie Lottinville. LC 79-4742. 1980. 25.00 (ISBN 0-8061-1598-X). U of Okla Pr.

Journal of William Scudder, an Officer in the Late New-York Line, Who Was Taken Capture by the Indians at Fort Stanwix. LC 75-7044. (Indian Captivities Ser.: Vol. 22). 1977. Repr. of 1794 ed. lib. bdg. 44.00 (ISBN 0-8240-1646-7). Garland Pub.

Journalism. Boy Scouts Of America. LC 19-600. (Illus.). 40p. (gr. 6-12). 1976. pap. 0.70x (ISBN 0-8395-3350-0, 3350). BSA.

Journalism. Ion Trewin. (Profession Ser.). 144p. 1976. 13.50 (ISBN 0-7153-6891-5). David & Charles.

Journalism, Communication & the Law. G. Adam. 1976. pap. 8.25 o.p. (ISBN 0-13-511170-6); 12.50 o.p. (ISBN 0-13-511188-9). P-H.

Journalism: Readings in the Mass Media. Ed. by Allen Kirschner & Linda Kirschner. LC 76-158976. 1971. pap. 7.95 (ISBN 0-672-73224-6). Odyssey Pr.

Journalist Biographies Master Index. 1st ed. Ed. by Alan E. Abrams. LC 77-9144. (Gale Biographical Index Ser.: No. 4). 1979. 52.00 (ISBN 0-8103-1086-4). Gale.

Journall & Relation of the Action Which E. Lord Cecil Did Vndertake Vpon the Coast of Spaine. Edward Cecil. LC 68-54643. (English Experience Ser.: No. 27). 1968. Repr. of 1625 ed. 7.00 (ISBN 90-221-0027-8). Walter J Johnson.

Journals, 2 Vols. George Sturt. Ed. by E. D. Mackerness. 1967. Set. 110.00 (ISBN 0-521-06569-0). Cambridge U Pr.

Journals & Letters of Fanny Burney (Madame D'Arblay), Eighteen Twelve to Eighteen Fourteen: Vol. VII, Letters 632-834. Fanny Burney. Ed. by Edward A. Bloom et al. (Illus.). 650p. 1978. 69.00x (ISBN 0-19-812468-6). Oxford U Pr.

Journals Kept in France & Italy from 1848 to 1852. Nassau W. Senior. LC 70-126608. (Europe 1815-1945 Ser.). 654p. 1973. Repr. of 1871 ed. lib. bdg. 59.50 (ISBN 0-306-70055-7). Da Capo.

Journals of Benjamin Henry Latrobe, 1799-1820. Ed. by Edward C. Carter et al. LC 79-19001. (Papers of Benjamin Henry Latrobe Ser. 1: Vol. 3). (Illus.). 432p. 1981. text ed. 65.00x (ISBN 0-300-02383-9). Yale U Pr.

Journals of Charles King Newcomb. Charles K. Newcomb. Ed. by Judith K. Johnson. (Brown University Studies: No. 10). (Illus.). 299p. 1946. 10.00x (ISBN 0-87057-025-0, Pub. by Brown U Pr). Univ Pr of New England.

Journals of Convention Assembled at the City of Austin on the Fourth of July, 1845 for the Purpose of Forming a Constitution for the State of Texas. Intro. by Mary B. Hart. LC 74-19564. 398p. 1975. Repr. of 1845 ed. 2.95 o.p. (ISBN 0-88319-019-2). Shoal Creek Pub.

Journals of David E. Lilienthal, 6 vols. David E. Lilienthal. Incl. Vol. 1. The TVA Years, 1939-45. 1964 (ISBN 0-06-012610-8); Vol. 2. The Atomic Energy Years, 1945-50. 1964. o.p. (ISBN 0-06-012611-6); Vol. 3. Venturesome Years, 1950-55. 1966 (ISBN 0-06-012612-4); Vol. 4. The Road to Change, 1955-59. 1969 (ISBN 0-06-012613-2); Vol. 5. The Harvest Years, 1959-63. 1971 (ISBN 0-06-012614-0); Vol. 6. Creativity & Conflict, 1964-1967. 1976. o.p. (ISBN 0-06-012619-1). LC 64-18056. (Illus.). 20.00 ea. o.s.i. (HarpT). Har-Row.

Journals of Dorothy Wordsworth. Dorothy Wordsworth. Ed. by Mary Moorman. (Oxford Paperbacks Ser). 1971. pap. 5.95x (ISBN 0-19-281103-7). Oxford U Pr.

Journals of Fanny Burney (Madam D'Arblay, 4 vols. Fanny Burney. Incl. Vol. 1. Seventeen Ninety-One to Seventeen Ninety-Two, Letters 1-39. Ed. by Joyce Hemlow et al. 1972. 34.95x (ISBN 0-19-811498-2); Vol. 2. Courtship & Marriage Seventeen Ninety-Three, Letters 40-121. Ed. by Joyce Hemlow & Althea Douglas. 1972. 34.95x (ISBN 0-19-812421-X); Vol. 3. Great Bookham, 1793-1797. Ed. by Joyce Hemlow et al. (Illus.). 376p. (Letters 122-250). 1973. 37.50x (ISBN 0-19-812419-8); Vol. 4. West Humble, 1797-1801. Ed. by Joyce Hemlow. (Illus.). 560p. (Letters 251-422). 1973. 42.00x (ISBN 0-19-812432-5); Vol. 5. West Humble & Paris 1801-1803, Letters 423-549. Ed. by Joyce Hemlon. 1975. 55.00x (ISBN 0-19-812467-8); Vol. 6. France, 1803-1812, Letters 550-631. Ed. by Joyce Hemlon. 1975. 49.50x (ISBN 0-19-812516-X). (Illus.). Oxford U Pr.

Journals of George Whitefield, 1737-1741. George Whitefield. LC 73-81363. (Illus.). 1969. Repr. of 1905 ed. 52.00x (ISBN 0-8201-1069-8). Schol Facsimiles.

Journals of Several Expeditions Made in Western Australia. 262p. 1980. 19.95x (ISBN 0-85564-185-1, Pub. by U of West Australia Pr Australia). Intl Schol Bk Serv.

Journals of Two Cruises Aboard the Privateer Yankee. W. V. Pratt. 1967. 4.95 o.s.i. (ISBN 0-02-598580-9). Macmillan.

Journey. Si Lewen. LC 80-67120. 88p. 1980. 15.00 (ISBN 0-87982-032-2). Art Alliance.

Journey Around My Room: The Autobiography of Louise Bogan. Ruth Limmer. LC 79-56279. (Illus.). 224p. 1980. 13.95 (ISBN 0-670-40942-1). Viking Pr.

Journey at Dawn. Nancy Dorer & Frances Dorer. (Orig.). 1980. pap. 1.95 (ISBN 0-532-23179-1). Manor Bks.

Journey Back: Escaping the Drug Trap. Albert J. Kastl & Lena Kastl. LC 74-20711. 176p. 1975. 11.95 (ISBN 0-88229-123-8). Nelson-Hall.

Journey Begins. Vern Rutsala. LC 76-12681. (Contemporary Poetry Ser.). 64p. 1977. 7.50 (ISBN 0-8203-0406-9). U of Ga Pr.

Journey Behind the Wind. Patricia Wrightson. LC 80-25005. (gr. 7 up). 1981. 8.95 (ISBN 0-689-50198-6, McElderry Bk). Atheneum.

Journey Beyond Tragedy: A Study of Modern Myth & Literature. Ted R. Spivey. LC 80-18348. 1980. 20.00 (ISBN 0-8130-0681-3). U Presses Fla.

Journey from the East. P. Krishna. pap. 0.50 o.p. (ISBN 0-87784-140-3). Inter-Varsity.

Journey from This World to the Next. Henry Fielding. 1976. pap. 2.50 o.p. (ISBN 0-460-01112-X, Evman). Dutton.

Journey Home: Some Words in Defense of the American West. Edward Abbey. 1977. 10.95 (ISBN 0-525-13753-X); pap. 5.95 (ISBN 0-525-03700-4). Dutton.

Journey in Faith. Wolf. pap. 6.95 (ISBN 0-8164-5646-1); leader's guide 0.95 (ISBN 0-8164-5645-3). Crossroad NY.

Journey in Nepal & Northern India. Cecil Bendall. (Illus.). 1975. 5.95x (ISBN 0-685-89508-4). Himalaya Hse.

Journey in North America. Joseph J. Gurney. LC 71-159795. (American Scene Ser.). 422p. 1973. Repr. of 1841 ed. lib. bdg. 39.50 (ISBN 0-306-70572-9). Da Capo.

Journey in North America, 1831. Sandor B. Farkas. Tr. by Arpad Kadarkay from Hung. LC 77-19145. 230p. 1978. text ed. 7.95 (ISBN 0-87436-270-9). ABC-Clio.

Journey into a Hollow Tree. Donald Perry & Sylvia Merschel. LC 80-14284. (Illus.). 64p. (gr. 4-12). 1980. PLB 7.95 (ISBN 0-89490-038-2). Enslow Pubs.

Journey into Another World: The Life Story of Arthur Prudden Coleman, Pioneer American Slavist, 3 pts. 5.00 ea. Alliance Coll.

Journey into Christ. Alan W. Jones. 1977. pap. 4.95 (ISBN 0-8164-0338-4). Crossroad NY.

Journey into Fear. Eric Ambler. 1977. pap. 1.95 (ISBN 0-345-28256-6). Ballantine.

Journey into Fear. Marianne Ruuth. 1977. pap. 1.50 (ISBN 0-505-51193-2). Tower Bks.

Journey into Fire. Patricia Wright. 1978. pap. 2.50 o.s.i. (ISBN 0-446-81525-X). Warner Bks.

Journey into Life. Ernest Holmes. 1967. pap. 4.50 (ISBN 0-911336-05-2). Sci of Mind.

Journey into Love's Past. Ruth Wagenblast. 1981. 5.95 (ISBN 0-533-04439-1). Vantage.

Journey into Mystery, Story of Explorers Burke & Wills. Ivan Southall. 10.00x (ISBN 0-392-08006-0). Soccer.

Journey into Northern Pennsylvania & the State of New York. Michel-Guillanme St. J. De Crevecoeur. Tr. by Clarissa S. Bostelmann. LC 63-14014. (Illus.). 1964. 15.00 o.p. (ISBN 0-472-25100-7). U of Mich Pr.

Journey into the Mind's Eye. Lesley Blanch. 1977. pap. 1.95 o.p. (ISBN 0-445-08581-9). Popular Lib.

Journey into the Word. Donald W. Barton. 130p. (Orig.). 1981. pap. 3.50 (ISBN 0-938736-00-0). Life Enrich.

Journey of Discovery: On Writing for Children. Ivan Southall. LC 75-31547. 108p. 1976. 6.95 o.s.i. (ISBN 0-02-786150-3, 78615). Macmillan.

Journey of Simon McKeever. Albert Maltz. 1979. pap. 2.25 (ISBN 0-380-45526-9, 45526). Avon.

Journey of the Three Jewels: Japanese Buddhist Paintings from Western Collections. John M. Rosenfield & Elizabeth Ten Grotenhuis. LC 79-15072. (Illus.). 1979. 19.95 (ISBN 0-87848-054-4). Asia Soc.

Journey South: Discovering the Americas. Mary Hoey. (gr. 4-6). 1980. pap. 3.50 (ISBN 0-377-00099-X). Friend Pr.

Journey Through Afghanistan: Amemonal. David Chaffetz. LC 80-51565. 350p. 1981. 13.00 (ISBN 0-89526-675-X). Regnery-Gateway.

Journey Through Dread. Arland Ussher. LC 68-54234. 1955. 9.00x (ISBN 0-8196-0221-3). Biblo.

Journey Through Texas: Or, a Saddle Trip on the Southwestern Frontier. Frederick L. Olmsted. LC 78-7028. (Barker Texas History Center Ser: No. 2). (Illus.). 1978. pap. 6.95 (ISBN 0-292-74008-5). U of Tex Pr.

Journey Through the Universe: An Introduction to Astronomy. Thomas L. Swihart. LC 77-76343. (Illus.). 1978. text ed. 19.95 (ISBN 0-395-25518-X); inst. manual 0.45 (ISBN 0-395-25519-8). HM.

Journey to Adventure. Lorena A. Olmsted. (YA) 1977. 5.95 (ISBN 0-685-74274-1, Avalon). Bouregy.

Journey to America. rev. ed. Alexis C. De Tocqueville. Ed. by J. P. Mayer. Tr. by George Lawrence from Fr. LC 80-22556. xvi, 424p. 1981. Repr. of 1971 ed. lib. bdg. 35.00x (ISBN 0-313-22712-8, TOJA). Greenwood.

Journey to Chaos: Samuel Beckett's Early Fiction. Raymond Federman. 1965. 18.00x (ISBN 0-520-00398-5). U of Cal Pr.

Journey to Damascus, Through Egypt, Nubia, Arabia Petroea, Palestine & Syria. Robert S. Londonderry. LC 80-1925. 1981. Repr. of 1947 ed. 69.50 (ISBN 0-404-18976-8). AMS Pr.

Journey to Flesh. Nick Yermakov. (Orig.). 1981. pap. 2.25 o.p. (ISBN 0-425-04588-9). Berkley Pub.

Journey to Great Salt-Lake City, 2 vols. Jules Remy & Julius Brenchley. LC 75-134399. (Illus.). 1124p. 1972. Repr. of 1861 ed. Set. write for info. (ISBN 0-404-08441-9). Vol. 1 (ISBN 0-404-08442-7). Vol. 2 (ISBN 0-404-08443-5). AMS Pr.

Journey to Jerusalem. Grace Halsell. 256p. 1981. 9.95 (ISBN 0-02-547590-8). Macmillan.

Journey to Khiva Through the Turkoman Country. Nikolay Murav'Yov. 1977. text ed. 25.50x (ISBN 0-905820-00-2). Humanities.

Journey to Lhasa & Central Tibet. Sarat C. Das. (Illus.). 1970. Repr. of 1902 ed. 12.00x o.p. (ISBN 0-685-19325-X). Paragon.

Journey to Love. Daisy Thomson. 1978. pap. 1.25 (ISBN 0-515-04479-2). Jove Pubns.

Journey to Mexico During the Years Eighteen Twenty-Six to Eighteen Thirty-Four, 2 vols. Jean L. Berlandier et al. Ed. by Sheila M. Ohlendorf & Josette Bigelow. LC 80-52705. (Illus.). 1980. boxed 75.00 (ISBN 0-87611-044-8); special limited ed. 150.00 (ISBN 0-87611-051-0). Tex St Hist Assn.

Journey to Paradise. Barbara Cartland. 1979. 7.95 o.p. (ISBN 0-525-13756-4). Dutton.

Journey to Quiet Waters. William Lavender. 496p. 1980. pap. 2.75 (ISBN 0-515-05389-9). Jove Pubns.

Journey to the Center of the Earth. Jules Verne. (Classics Ser). (gr. 6 up). pap. 1.50 (ISBN 0-8049-0060-4, CL-60). Airmont.

Journey to the End of the World: A Three-Year Adventure in the New Hebrides. Charlene Gourguechon. LC 76-46360. (Encore Edition). (Illus.). 1977. 3.95 o.p. (ISBN 0-684-16193-1, ScribT). Scribner.

Journey to the Green & Golden Lands: The Epic of Survival on the Wagon Trail. Raymond N. Doetsch. 1976. 11.50 (ISBN 0-8046-9142-8, Natl U). Kennikat.

Journey to the Lord of Power. Ibn Arabi. Tr. by Rabia Harris from Arab. (Illus.). 1981. 9.95 (ISBN 0-89281-024-6); pap. 7.95 (ISBN 0-89281-018-1). Inner Tradit.

Journey to the Moon. Erich Fuchs. LC 74-103151. (Illus.). (ps-3). 1970. 5.95 (ISBN 0-440-04277-1, Sey Lawr); PLB 5.47 o.s.i. (ISBN 0-440-04278-X, Sey Lawr). Delacorte.

Journey to the West, Vol. 3. Ed. by Anthony C. Yu. LC 75-27896. 1980. lib. bdg. 30.00x (ISBN 0-226-97147-3). U of Chicago Pr.

Journey to the World Underground, 1742. Ludwig Holberg. Ed. by Michael F. Shugrue. LC 74-18234. (Novel in England 1700-1775). 1974. lib. bdg. 50.00 (ISBN 0-8240-1105-8). Garland Pub.

Journey Toward the Roots. Hans Juergensen. LC 76-14366. (Illus.). 48p. 1976. 5.00 o.p. (ISBN 0-912760-23-0); pap. 2.50 (ISBN 0-685-67386-3). Valkyrie Pr.

Journey up. Maurice Collis. (Illus.). 1970. 9.95 (ISBN 0-571-09000-1, Pub. by Faber & Faber). Merrimack Bk Serv.

Journey Upward. Flower A. Newhouse. Ed. by Athene Bengtson. LC 78-74955. 1978. pap. 6.00 (ISBN 0-910378-15-0). Christward.

Journey with Job. Thomas J. Carlisle. LC 75-34230. 96p. 1976. pap. 2.25 o.p. (ISBN 0-8028-1617-7). Eerdmans.

Journeying Self: A Study in Philosophy & Social Role. Maurice Natanson. (Philosophy Ser). 1970. pap. text ed. 9.95 (ISBN 0-201-05249-0). A-W.

Journeys: An Introductory Guide to Jewish Mysticism. William E. Kaufman. LC 80-69017. 1980. 12.50 (ISBN 0-8197-0482-2); pap. 7.95. Bloch.

Journeys Down the Line: Building the Trans-Alaska Pipeline. Robert Douglas Mead. LC 77-92226. 1978. 12.95 o.p. (ISBN 0-385-11578-4). Doubleday.

Journey's Echo. Freya Stark. 16.95 (ISBN 0-7195-1336-7). Transatlantic.

Journeys of David Toback. Carole Malkin. LC 80-22962. 224p. 1981. 10.95 (ISBN 0-8052-3756-9). Schocken.

Journeys of Frodo. Barbara Strachey. 128p. (Orig.). 1981. pap. 7.95 (ISBN 0-345-29633-8). Ballantine.

Journeys on the Mississippi. Kay Cooper. (Illus.). 96p. (gr. 4-6). 1981. PLB 7.29 (ISBN 0-686-69304-3). Messner.

Journeys Out of the Body. Robert A. Monroe. LC 72-157612. 288p. 1977. pap. 6.50 (ISBN 0-385-00861-9, Anch). Doubleday.

Journeys Through the South. Fred Powledge. LC 77-93299. 1979. 10.00 (ISBN 0-8149-0796-2). Vanguard.

Journeys to Selfhood: Hegel & Kierkegaard. Mark C. Taylor. 264p. 1981. 22.50x (ISBN 0-520-04167-4); pap. 7.95 (ISBN 0-520-04176-3, CAL 483). U of Cal Pr.

Journeys to the Past. Norman Davis. 1980. 10.00 (ISBN 0-910286-83-3); pap. 6.95 (ISBN 0-910286-78-7). Boxwood.

Jovem Portugal: After the Revolution. Jason Laure & Ettagale Laure. LC 77-8127. (Illus.). 160p. (gr. 7 up). 1977. 8.95 (ISBN 0-374-33934-1). FS&G.

Jovial Crew. Richard Brome. Ed. by Ann Haaker. LC 68-10433. (Regents Renaissance Drama Ser). 1968. 9.50x (ISBN 0-8032-0254-7); pap. 2.45x (ISBN 0-8032-5255-2, BB 228, Bison). U of Nebr Pr.

Joy. 186p. 1980. 6.95 (ISBN 0-87747-819-8). Deseret Bk.

Joy & Sadness in Children's Sports. Ed. by Rainer Martens. LC 78-107073. (Illus.). 1978. 11.95x o.s.i. (ISBN 0-931250-10-2). Human Kinetics.

Joy & Sadness in Children's Sports. Ed. by Rainer Martens. 375p. 1978. pap. text ed. 9.95x (ISBN 0-931250-15-3). Human Kinetics.

Joy Comes with the Morning. William Kinnaird. 1979. pap. 4.95 (ISBN 0-8499-2874-5). Word Bks.

Joy: Expanding Human Awareness. William C. Schutz. 1981. Repr. of 1967 ed. text ed. 18.50x (ISBN 0-8290-0050-X). Irvington.

Joy in Exile. Eileen Early. LC 79-5429. 1980. pap. text ed. 7.50 (ISBN 0-8191-0878-2). U Pr of Amer.

Joy in the Morning. Betty Smith. 1976. pap. 1.75 (ISBN 0-06-080368-1, P368, PL). Har-Row.

Joy of Being a Vegetarian. Philip S. Chen. LC 76-44049. (Dimension Ser.). 1977. pap. 5.95 (ISBN 0-8163-0302-9, 10484-4). Pacific Pr Pub Assn.

Joy of Being a Woman. Ingrid Trobisch. LC 75-9324. (Jubilee Ser.). 144p. 1975. pap. 3.95 (ISBN 0-06-068453-4, RD 353, HarpR). Har-Row.

Joy of Breastfeeding. 2nd ed. Margaret B. Salmon. LC 77-73690. (Illus.). 1979. 8.95 (ISBN 0-918662-04-4); pap. 5.95 (ISBN 0-918662-03-6). Techkits.

Joy of Breeding Your Own Show Dog. Anne Seranne. LC 80-16081. (Illus.). 272p. 1980. 11.95 (ISBN 0-87605-413-0). Howell Bk.

Joy of Brewing. rev. ed. Charlie Papazian. (Illus.). 88p. 1980. pap. 4.50 (ISBN 0-9604130-0-6). Log Boom.

Joy of Caring. Gary Collins. 192p. 1980. pap. 5.95 (ISBN 0-8499-2928-8). Word Bks.

Joy of Cataloging. Sanford Berman. 1981. lib. bdg. 22.50 (ISBN 0-912700-51-3); pap. 16.50 (ISBN 0-912700-94-7). Oryx Pr.

Joy of Cheesecake. Jeremy Iggers & Dana Bovbjerg. (Illus.). 1980. 11.95 (ISBN 0-8120-5350-8). Barron.

Joy of Chinese Cooking. Doreen Y. Feng. (Illus., Orig.). 1964. pap. 3.95 o.p. (ISBN 0-571-05865-5, Pub. by Faber & Faber). Merrimack Bk Serv.

Joy of Christmas: A Selection of Carols by Edward Heath. Ed. by Edward Heath. (Illus.). 1978. 12.95 (ISBN 0-19-520080-2); pap. 3.95 (ISBN 0-19-520081-0). Oxford U Pr.

Joy of Coaching Youth Soccer. Graham Ramsay & Paul Harris. LC 79-54131. (Illus., Orig.). 1979. pap. 4.95 (ISBN 0-916802-15-9). Soccer for Am.

Joy of Cooking. Irma S. Rombauer & Marion R. Becker. pap. 5.95 (ISBN 0-451-07166-2, E8978, Sig). NAL.

Joy of Cooking. rev. ed. Irma S. Rombauer & Marion R. Becker. LC 75-10772. (Illus.). 930p. 1975. 14.95 (ISBN 0-672-51831-7); deluxe ed. 20.00 (ISBN 0-672-52385-X). Bobbs.

Joy of Cooking, Vol. 1. Marion R. Becker & Irma Rombauer. pap. 2.50 (ISBN 0-451-08625-2, E8625, Sig). NAL.

Joy of Cooking, Vol. 2. Marion R. Becker & Irma Rombauer. pap. 2.50 (ISBN 0-451-08072-6, E8691, Sig). NAL.

Joy of Eating French Food: Great French Dishes Made Easy. Renny Darling. 1980. pap. 8.95 (ISBN 0-930440-05-6). Royal Calif.

Joy of Expense Account Living (& the Pleasures of Executive Perks) Sidney Rutberg. LC 79-50990. 1979. 9.95 o.p. (ISBN 0-8092-7400-0). Contemp Bks.

Joy of Fellowship. J. Dwight Pentecost. 1977. pap. 4.95 (ISBN 0-310-30921-2). Zondervan.

Joy of Finding: An Exposition of Luke 15: 11-32. A. E. Garvie. (Short Course Ser.). 146p. 1914. text ed. 2.95 (ISBN 0-567-08313-6). Attic Pr.

Joy of Gardening. V. Sackville-West. LC 76-39685. (Illus.). 1977. 9.95 o.s.i. (ISBN 0-06-013741-X, HarpT). Har-Row.

Joy of Home Winemaking. Clem Stein, Jr. LC 72-6901. (Illus.). 96p. 1973. 7.95 (ISBN 0-87396-073-4). Stravon.

Joy of Learning. Peggy Eaton & Leslie Eiring. (Illus.). 10.50 (ISBN 0-86575-027-0, 106). Dormac.

Joy of Life Through Yoga. Eugene S. Rawls & Eve Diskin. 1976. pap. 1.25 o.s.i. (ISBN 0-446-76736-0). Warner Bks.

Joy of Living. J. Dwight Pentecost. 160p. 1973. pap. text ed. 5.95 (ISBN 0-310-30871-2). Zondervan.

Joy of Man's Desiring. Jean Giono. Tr. by Katherine A. Clarke from Fr. 464p. 1980. pap. 9.50 (ISBN 0-86547-015-4). N Point Pr.

Joy of Nature. Reader's Digest. (Illus.). 1977. 16.95 (ISBN 0-89577-036-9, Pub. by Reader's Digest). Norton.

Joy of Reading: A Personal Introduction to Great Books. Floyd Zulli. LC 75-171904. 192p. (gr. 7 up). 1972. PLB 5.88 o.p. (ISBN 0-531-00430-9). Watts.

Joy of Running. Thaddeus Kostrubala. LC 76-9835. 1976. 8.95 o.p. (ISBN 0-397-01110-5); pap. 4.95 o.p. (ISBN 0-397-01169-5). Lippincott.

Joy of Sleep: Facts, Fantasy, & Folklore Relating to the Mystery of Sleep with 22 Remedies for Insomniacs. Shirley M. Linde & Louis M. Savary. LC 73-7066. 192p. 1980. pap. 4.95 (ISBN 0-06-250515-7, BN 3002, HarpR). Har-Row.

Joy of Soaring: A Training Manual. Carle Conway. LC 73-98038. (Illus.). 134p. 1969. 14.95 (ISBN 0-911720-54-5, Pub. by Soaring). Aviation.

Joy of the Limerick Sex Manual: Sex for Sophisticates. Freude N. Slipp. 1979. 6.95 (ISBN 0-934622-01-9). Agora Pr.

Joy of the Plain Life. John C. Cooper. 200p. 1981. pap. 4.95 (ISBN 0-914850-62-8, 14015P). Impact Tenn.

Joy Six. rev. ed. Winston Press Editorial Staff. (Joy Religious Ser.). 1979. pap. 4.50 (ISBN 0-03-008331-1, 665); teacher's ed 5.95 (ISBN 0-03-049536-9). Winston Pr.

Joy Spartan & the Money Mix-Up. Ruth I. Johnson. (gr. 5-8). 1960. pap. 1.50 (ISBN 0-8024-4403-2). Moody.

Joy Spartan of Parsonage Hill. Ruth I. Johnson. (gr. 5-8). 1958. pap. 1.50 (ISBN 0-8024-4401-6). Moody.

Joy Sparton & Her Problem Twin. Ruth I. Johnson. (gr. 5-8). 1963. pap. 1.50 (ISBN 0-8024-4404-0). Moody.

Joy Sparton & the Mystery in Room Seven. Ruth I. Johnson. (Preteen Ser). 128p. (Orig.). (gr. 5-8). 1974. pap. 1.50 (ISBN 0-8024-4405-9). Moody.

Joy Sparton & the Vacation Mix-Up. Ruth I. Johnson. (gr. 5-8). 1959. pap. 1.50 (ISBN 0-8024-4402-4). Moody.

Joy Supplement Two: Descendants of Thomas Joy, Pt. 1. Helen B. Lee. LC 76-45277. (Illus.). 1976. pap. 2.50 (ISBN 0-87106-074-4). Globe Pequot.

Joy Supplement, Two: Descendants of Thomas Joy, Pt.2. Helen B. Lee. LC 76-45277. (Illus.). 1980. pap. write for info. (ISBN 0-87106-075-2). Globe Pequot.

Joy Three. rev. ed. Ed. by Winston Editorial Staff. (Joy Ser.). (gr. 3). 1977. pap. text ed. 4.50 (ISBN 0-03-017671-9); tchr's ed. 5.95 (ISBN 0-03-004196-1). Winston Pr.

Joy to the World: An Introduction to Kingdom Evangelism. Robert T. Henderson. LC 80-14597. 207p. (Orig.). 1980. pap. 6.95 (ISBN 0-8042-2096-4, 2096-4). John Knox.

Joy Way. Guy King. 1973. pap. 2.50 (ISBN 0-87508-280-7). Chr Lit.

Joy with Honey. Doris Mech. 135p. 1979. 3.95 (ISBN 0-930756-46-0, 4230-JH). Women's Aglow.

Joy Without a Cause: Selected Essays. Christopher Derrick. 9.95 (ISBN 0-89385-007-1). Green Hill.

Joyce & Dante: The Shaping Imagination. Mary T. Reynolds. LC 80-7550. (Illus.). 400p. 1981. 22.50x (ISBN 0-691-06446-6). Princeton U Pr.

Joyce Carol Oates. Joanne V. Creighton. (United States Authors Ser.: No. 321). 1979. lib. bdg. 10.95 (ISBN 0-8057-7212-X). Twayne.

Joyce Carol Oates. Ellen G. Friedman. LC 79-4828. (Modern Literature Ser.). 1980. 13.50 (ISBN 0-8044-2221-4). Ungar.

Joyce Cary. William V. O'Connor. LC 66-19552. (Columbia Essays on Modern Writers Ser.: No. 16). (Orig.). 1966. pap. 2.00 (ISBN 0-231-02680-3, MW16). Columbia U Pr.

Joyce Cary: Liberal Principles. Cornelia Cook. (Barnes & Noble Critical Studies). 240p. 1981. 28.50x (ISBN 0-389-20201-0). B&N.

Joyce Cary: The Writer & His Theme. Barbara Fisher. 1980. text ed. 25.50x (ISBN 0-391-01763-2). Humanities.

Joyce Chen Cook Book. Joyce Chen. (Illus.). 1963. 13.95 o.s.i. (ISBN 0-397-00285-8); pap. 6.95 o.s.i. (ISBN 0-397-01278-0). Lippincott.

Joyce, I Feel Like I Know You. Joyce Landorf. 1976. pap. 2.95 (ISBN 0-88207-742-2). Victor Bks.

Joyce in Nighttown: A Psychoanalytic Inquiry into Ulysses. Mark Shechner. 1974. 14.50x (ISBN 0-520-02398-6). U of Cal Pr.

Joyce's Benefictions. Helmut Bonheim. (Perspectives in Criticism: No. 16). 1964. 16.75x (ISBN 0-520-00147-8). U of Cal Pr.

Joyce's Cities: Archaeologies of the Soul. Jackson I. Cope. LC 80-8056. 176p. 1981. text ed. 12.95x (ISBN 0-8018-2543-1). Johns Hopkins.

Joyce's Ulysses & the Assault Upon Character. James H. Maddox, Jr. 1978. 17.50 (ISBN 0-8135-0851-7). Rutgers U Pr.

Joyce's Voices. Hugh Kenner. LC 76-38887. (Quantum Book Ser.). 1978. 8.95 (ISBN 0-520-03206-3, CAL 426); pap. 2.95 (ISBN 0-520-03935-1). U of Cal Pr.

Joyday for Jodi. Lucy Walker. 1976. pap. 1.25 o.p. (ISBN 0-345-25478-3). Ballantine.

Joyful Christian: 100 Readings from the Works of C. S. Lewis. C. S. Lewis. LC 77-21685. 1977. 8.95 (ISBN 0-02-570900-3). Macmillan.

Joyful Meeting: Sexuality in Marriage. Mike Grace & Joyce Grace. (Illus.). 100p. (Orig.). 1980. pap. 3.00 (ISBN 0-936098-14-7). Natl Marriage.

Joyful Nursery Rhymes. (Children's Library of Picture Bks.). (Illus.). 10p. (ps). 1979. 1.95 (ISBN 0-89346-179-2, TA63, Froebel-Kan Japan). Heian Intl.

Joyful Poems for Children. James W. Riley. LC 60-14663. (gr. 2-6). 1960. 5.95 o.p. (ISBN 0-672-50342-5). Bobbs.

Joyfully Expectant. Helen K. Hosier. 1977. pap. 1.50 o.p. (ISBN 0-8007-8296-8, Spire Bks). Revell.

Joyner's Guide to Official Washington for Doing Business Overseas. Ed. by Nelson T. Joyner, Jr. & Jackie Durham. LC 79-20957. (Pergamon Policy Studies). 400p. 1980. 99.50 (ISBN 0-08-025108-0). Pergamon.

Joyner's Guide to Official Washington for Doing Business Overseas. 364p. 1981. 95.00 (ISBN 0-08-025108-0, JOY 3, Joyner's). Unipub.

Joyous Vision: A Sourcebook for Elementary Art Appreciation. Al Hurwitz & Stanley Madeja. (Illus.). 320p. 1977. text ed. 16.95 (ISBN 0-13-511600-7). P-H.

Joyride. Betty Cavanna. LC 74-5930. 224p. (gr. 7 up). 1974. 8.25 (ISBN 0-688-20125-3); PLB 7.92 (ISBN 0-688-30125-8). Morrow.

Joys & Sorrows of Parenthood. Group for the Advancement of Psychiatry. LC 73-1365. 1975. pap. 2.95 o.p. (ISBN 0-684-14438-7, SL 609, ScribT). Scribner.

Joys & Teardrops. Kathleen Armstrong. 1976. pap. 2.95 (ISBN 0-917578-02-3). Eternal Ent.

Joys of Aging & How to Avoid Them. Phyllis Diller. LC 79-7863. (Illus.). 192p. 1981. 8.95 (ISBN 0-385-14555-1). Doubleday.

Joys of Chess. Fred Reinfeld. (Illus.). 288p. 1974. pap. 2.95 o.s.i. (ISBN 0-02-029730-0, Collier). Macmillan.

Joys of Chinese Cooking. Purobi Bubber. (Illus.). 1978. text ed. 10.00 (ISBN 0-7069-0553-9, Pub. by Vikas India). Advent Bk.

Joys of Italian Humor & Folklore. Ed. by Henry Spalding. LC 80-13750. 360p. 1980. 16.95 (ISBN 0-8246-0255-2). Jonathan David.

Joys of Woodstoves & Fireplaces. Mary Presper. LC 78-73323. pap. 6.95 (ISBN 0-448-14847-1). G&D.

Joy's Way: A Map for the Transformational Journey & an Introduction to the Potentials for Healing with Body Energies. W. Brugh Joy. LC 78-62795. (Illus.). 1979. 11.95 o.p. (ISBN 0-312-90644-7); pap. 6.95 o.p. (ISBN 0-312-90645-5). St Martin.

JU 87 Stuka. B. Robertson & G. Scarburough. (Illus.). 1976. 15.75 o.p. (ISBN 0-85059-193-7). Aztex.

Juan Boscan. David H. Darst. (World Authors Ser.: No. 475). 1978. lib. bdg. 11.95 (ISBN 0-8057-6316-3). Twayne.

Juan Carlos Onetti. Djelal Kadir. (World Authors Ser.: Peru: No. 469). 1977. lib. bdg. 12.50 (ISBN 0-8057-6310-4). Twayne.

Juan Colon Alias Christopher Columbus. Brother Nectario M. Ed. by Emanuel M. Josephson. LC 72-166573. (Blacked-Out History Ser.). 1971. pap. 5.00 (Pub. by Chedney). Alpine Ent.

Juan de la Cueva. Richard F. Glenn. (World Authors Ser.: Spain: No. 273). 1973. lib. bdg. 10.95 (ISBN 0-8057-2258-0). Twayne.

Juan De la Cueva's los Inventores De las Cosas: A Critical Edition & Study. Beno Weiss & Louis C. Perez. LC 80-83466. 220p. 1980. text ed. 17.50x (ISBN 0-271-00279-4). Pa St U Pr.

Juan de Mairena: Epigrams, Maxims, Memoranda, & Memoirs of an Apocryphal Professor. Antonio Machado. Tr. by Ben Belitt. (Illus.). 1963. 12.95x (ISBN 0-520-00792-1); pap. 1.50 (ISBN 0-520-00794-8, CAL89). U of Cal Pr.

Juan De Valdes Leal (Sixteen Twenty-Two to Sixteen Ninety) His Life & Work. Duncan T. Kinkead. LC 77-94700. (Outstanding Dissertations in the Fine Arts Ser.). 1978. lib. bdg. 72.50 (ISBN 0-8240-3232-2). Garland Pub.

Juan Del Encina. Henry W. Sullivan. LC 76-16068. (World Authors Ser.: Spain: No. 399). 1976. lib. bdg. 12.50 (ISBN 0-8057-6166-7). Twayne.

Juan Domingo Peron. Robert J. Alexander. 1979. lib. bdg. 20.00x (ISBN 0-89158-369-6). Westview.

Juan el Bautista. Gordon Stowell. Tr. by S. D. de Lerin from English. (Libros Pescaditos Sobre Personajes Biblicos). (Illus.). 1978. pap. 0.40 (ISBN 0-311-38515-X, Edit Mundo). Casa Bautista.

Juan Eugenio Hartzenbusch. Carmen Iranzo. (World Authors Ser.: No. 501 (Spain)). 1978. 12.95 (ISBN 0-8057-6342-2). Twayne.

Juan Godoy. Thomas E. Lyon. (World Authors Ser.: Chile: No. 189). lib. bdg. 10.95 (ISBN 0-8057-2376-5). Twayne.

Juan Huarte de San Juan. M. K. Read. (World Authors Ser.: No. 619). 1981. lib. bdg. 14.95 (ISBN 0-8057-6461-5). Twayne.

Juan Melendez Valdez. R. Merritt Cox. (World Authors Ser.: Spain: No. 302). 1974. lib. bdg. 10.95 (ISBN 0-8057-2918-6). Twayne.

Juan Pablo Forner. Gilbert Smith. LC 75-33832. (World Authors Ser.,: Spain: No. 377). 1976. lib. bdg. 12.50 (ISBN 0-8057-6170-5). Twayne.

Juan Perez De Montalvan. J. H. Parker. LC 74-23740. (World Authors Ser.: Spain: No. 352). 1975. lib. bdg. 12.50 (ISBN 0-8057-2625-X). Twayne.

Juan Rodriguez de la Camara. Martin S. Gilderman. (World Authors Ser.: No. 423). 1977. lib. bdg. 12.50 (ISBN 0-8057-6195-0). Twayne.

Juan Ruiz de Alarcon. Walter Poesse. (World Authors Ser.: Spain: No. 231). lib. bdg. 10.95 (ISBN 0-8057-2012-X). Twayne.

Juan Sebastian Elcano. (Span.). 7.50 (ISBN 84-241-5401-0). E Torres & Sons.

Juan Timoneda. John J. Reynolds. LC 75-9837. (World Author Ser.: Spain: No. 367). 1975. lib. bdg. 10.95 (ISBN 0-8057-6205-1). Twayne.

Juan Valera. Cyrus DeCoster. LC 74-3058. (World Authors Ser.: Spain: No. 316). 192p. 1974. lib. bdg. 12.50 (ISBN 0-8057-2919-4). Twayne.

Juan Valera: Pepita Jimenez. Ed. by R. E. Lott. 1974. 25.00 (ISBN 0-08-017918-5); pap. 10.75 (ISBN 0-08-017919-3). Pergamon.

Juan y Hechos: Tomo II. L. Bonnetty A. Schroeder. Tr. by A. Cativiela. 1977. Repr. of 1975 ed. 9.95 (ISBN 0-311-03051-3). Casa Bautista.

Juana De Ibarbourou: Oficio De Poesia. Ester F. Mendoza. LC 80-20020. (Mente y Palabra Ser.). (Illus.). xi, 370p. (Span.). 1980. 6.25 (ISBN 0-8477-0572-2); pap. 5.00 (ISBN 0-8477-0573-0). U of PR Pr.

Juarez, a Son of the People. Jean Rouverol. LC 72-81071. (Illus.). 192p. (gr. 7 up). 1973. 4.95g o.s.i. (ISBN 0-02-777820-7, CCPr). Macmillan.

Juba This & Juba That. Virginia A. Tashjian. LC 69-10666. (Illus.). (gr. 1-3). 1969. 7.95 (ISBN 0-316-83230-8). Little.

Jubilee College State Park: Retrospective by Way of Explanation. Charles Creed. 20p. 1980. pap. 2.50 (ISBN 0-933180-11-X). Spoon Riv Poetry.

Jubilee for Our Times: A Practical Program for Income Equality. Ed. by Alvin L. Schorr. LC 76-41824. 1977. 17.50x (ISBN 0-231-04056-3). Columbia U Pr.

Jubilee of a Ghost. March Cost. LC 68-8080. 1968. 7.95 (ISBN 0-8149-0048-8). Vanguard.

Jubilee Trail. Gwen Bristow. 1969. pap. 2.75 (ISBN 0-445-08306-9). Popular Lib.

Jubilee Trail. Gwen Bristow. LC 50-5268. 1969. 10.95 o.s.i. (ISBN 0-690-46750-8, TYC-T). T Y Crowell.

Judah. Allan Appel. 1976. pap. 1.75 o.p. (ISBN 0-685-74570-8, LB418KK, Leisure Bks). Nordon Pubns.

Judah P. Benjamin. Pierce Butler. LC 80-20134. (American Statesmen Ser.). 460p. 1981. pap. 6.95 (ISBN 0-87754-198-1). Chelsea Hse.

Judaic Law. William Corlett & John Moore. LC 79-16432. (Questions Ser.). 1980. 8.95 (ISBN 0-87888-152-2). Bradbury Pr.

Judaism. Ed. by Arthur Hertzberg. LC 61-15498. (Great Religions of Modern Man Ser.). 8.95 o.s.i. (ISBN 0-8076-0163-2). Braziller.

Judaism. Michael Kaniel. (Illus.). 1979. 14.95 (ISBN 0-7137-0972-3, Pub by Blandford Pr England). Sterling.

Judaism. Samuel T. Lachs & Saul P. Wachs. (Illus.). 1978. pap. 3.95 (ISBN 0-89505-023-4). Argus Comm.

Judaism. Seymour Rossel. LC 75-31561. (First Bks. Ser.). (Illus.). 72p. (gr. 4-8). 1976. PLB 6.45 (ISBN 0-531-00841-X). Watts.

Judaism. Jay G. Williams. LC 80-51551. 204p. 1981. pap. 5.50 (ISBN 0-8356-0540-X, Quest). Theos Pub Hse.

Judaism & Christian Beginnings. Samuel Sandmel. 25.00 (ISBN 0-19-502281-5); pap. 7.95x (ISBN 0-19-502282-3). Oxford U Pr.

Judaism & Hellenism: Studies in Their Encounter in Palestine During the Early Hellenistic Period. Martin Hengel. Tr. by John Bowden from Ger. 672p. 1981. Set. 19.95 (ISBN 0-8006-1495-X, 1-1495). Fortress.

Judaism & Psychical Phenomena. Jacob Bazak. LC 71-184295. 6.50 o.p. (ISBN 0-912326-27-1). Garrett-Helix.

Judaism & the Gentile Faiths: Comparative Studies in Religion. Joseph P. Schultz. LC 75-5250. 405p. 1981. 19.50 (ISBN 0-8386-1707-7). Fairleigh Dickinson.

Judaism & Zionism: Principles & Definitions. Neturei Karta. 1980. lib. bdg. 59.95 (ISBN 0-686-68745-0). Revisionist Pr.

Judaism in German Christian Theology Since 1945: Christianity & Israel Considered in Terms of Mission. Eva Fleischner. LC 75-22374. (ATLA Monograph: No. 8). 1975. 10.00 (ISBN 0-8108-0835-8). Scarecrow.

Judaism in the Greek Period, from the Rise of Alexander the Great to the Intervention of Rome. George H. Box. LC 73-109712. Repr. of 1932 ed. lib. bdg. 21.50x (ISBN 0-8371-4288-1, BOJG). Greenwood.

Judaism in Theory & Practice. 3rd rev. ed. Beryl D. Cohon. LC 68-57021. 1969. write for info. (ISBN 0-8197-0069-X). Bloch.

Judaism: Post Biblical & Talmudic Period. Ed. by Salo W. Baron & Joseph L. Blau. LC 55-1342. 1954. 5.25 o.p. (ISBN 0-672-60344-6, LLA135). Bobbs.

Judas Cross. Jeffrey M. Wallman. 1977. pap. 1.50 (ISBN 0-380-01846-2, 36426). Avon.

Judas Gene. Albert Klainer & Jo-Ann Klainer. 258p. 1981. pap. 2.95 (ISBN 0-441-39298-9). Charter Bks.

Judas Goat. Robert B. Parker. 1979. pap. 1.95 o.p. (ISBN 0-425-04204-9). Berkley Pub.

Judas Ship. Brian Callison. 1978. 7.95 o.p. (ISBN 0-525-13780-7). Dutton.

Judas Spy. (Nick Carter Ser.). 1978. pap. 1.75 (ISBN 0-441-41295-5). Charter Bks.

Jude the Obscure. Thomas Hardy. Ed. by F. R. Southerington. LC 76-140800. (Library of Literature Ser.: No. 35). 1972. pap. 8.50 (ISBN 0-672-61022-1, LL35). Bobbs.

Jude the Obscure. Thomas Hardy. Ed. by Norman Page. (Norton Critical Edition Ser.). 1978. 17.50 (ISBN 0-393-04473-4); pap. 5.95x (ISBN 0-393-09089-2). Norton.

Jude the Obscure. Thomas Hardy. pap. 1.75. Bantam.

Judge. Rebecca West. (Virago Modern Classic). 430p. 1981. pap. 6.95 (ISBN 0-8037-3996-6). Dial.

Judge. Harve Zemach. LC 79-87209. (Illus.). 48p. (ps-3). 1969. 9.95 (ISBN 0-374-33960-0). FS&G.

Judge & Jury in Imperial Brazil, 1808-1871: Social Control & Political Stability in the New State. Thomas Flory. 288p. 1981. text ed. 25.00x (ISBN 0-292-74015-8). U of Tex Pr.

Judge Horton & the Scottsboro Boys. Barbara Bauer & Robert Moss. 1977. pap. 1.75 o.p. (ISBN 0-345-25268-3). Ballantine.

Judge in a Communist State: A View from Within. Otto Ulc. LC 71-141382. xiv, 307p. 1972. 12.00x (ISBN 0-8214-0091-6). Ohio U Pr.

Judge Lynch: His First Hundred Years. Frank Shay. LC 70-75359. 1969. Repr. of 1938 ed. 12.00x (ISBN 0-8196-0231-0). Biblo.

Judge Me Not. John D. MacDonald. 1978. pap. 1.75 o.p. (ISBN 0-449-14057-1, GM). Fawcett.

Judge on Trial: Hearings on the Nomination of George Harrold Carswell: Proceedings. United States Senate, Committee on the Judiciary Ninety-First Congress, 2nd Session. LC 70-3962. (American Constitutional & Legal History Ser). 467p. 1974. Repr. of 1970 ed. lib. bdg. 27.50 (ISBN 0-306-70209-6). Da Capo.

Judge Roy Bean Almanac. pap. text ed. 1.50 (ISBN 0-910722-06-4). Highland Pr.

Judge Your Own Horsemanship. Neale Haley. LC 74-76850. (Illus.). 169p. 1974. pap. 1.95 o.p. (ISBN 0-668-03410-6). Arco.

Judgement. Barry Collins. (Orig.). 1974. pap. 3.95 o.p. (ISBN 0-571-10649-8, Pub. by Faber & Faber). Merrimack Bk Serv.

Judgement & Choice: Strategies for Decisions. Robin M. Hogarth. LC 79-42822. 250p. 1980. 23.95 (ISBN 0-471-27744-4, Pub. by Wiley-Interscience). Wiley.

Judgement House. Gilbert Parker. 1976. lib. bdg. 19.50x (ISBN 0-89968-080-1). Lightyear.

Judgement in St. Peters. Aaron N. Rotsstein. 256p. 1981. pap. 2.50 (ISBN 0-445-04651-1). Popular Lib.

Judgement in the Church. Ed. by William Bassett & Peter Huizing. (Concilium Ser.: Vol. 107). 1978. pap. 4.95 (ISBN 0-8164-2166-8). Crossroad NY.

Judgement Night. C. L. Moore. 1979. pap. 2.25 o.s.i. (ISBN 0-440-14442-6). Dell.

Judgement of the Synode at Dort Touching Conradus Vortius. (English Experience Ser.: No. 678). 1974. Repr. of 1619 ed. 10.50 (ISBN 90-221-0678-0). Walter J Johnson.

Judges. G. F. Moore. LC 25-19368. (International Critical Commentary Ser.). 528p. 1895. text ed. 23.00x (ISBN 0-567-05004-1). Attic Pr.

Judges: A Commentary. J. Alberto Soggin. Tr. by John Bowden from Ital. (Old Testament Library). 1981. text ed. price not set (ISBN 0-664-21368-5). Westminster.

Judges, Ruth. rev. ed. Ed. by Irving L. Jensen. (Bible Self-Study Ser). (Illus.). 96p. 1967. pap. 2.25 (ISBN 0-8024-1007-3). Moody.

Judging & Coaching Women's Gymnastics. 2nd ed. Carolyn O. Bowers et al. 360p. 1981. pap. text ed. price not set (ISBN 0-87484-391-X). Mayfield Pub.

Judging Delinquents: Context & Process in Juvenile Court. Robert M. Emerson. LC 70-75047. (Law in Action Ser). 1969. 17.95x (ISBN 0-202-23001-5). Aldine Pub.

Judging Horses & Ponies. Valerie Russel. (Pelham Horsemaster Ser.). (Illus.). 1979. 14.00 (ISBN 0-7207-1099-5). Transatlantic.

Judging Justice: An Introduction to Contemporary Political Philosophy. Philip Pettit. 192p. 1980. 25.00x (ISBN 0-7100-0563-6); pap. 11.95 (ISBN 0-7100-0571-7). Routledge & Kegan.

Judging the Dreamer. Sally L. Lillie. 52p. 1980. pap. 4.50x (ISBN 0-938564-00-5). P a Abbott.

Judgment by Peers. Barnaby C. Keeney. LC 80-2023. 1981. Repr. of 1949 ed. 25.00 (ISBN 0-404-18571-1). AMS Pr.

Judgment Day. Penelope Lively. LC 80-2749. 192p. 1981. 11.95 (ISBN 0-385-15814-9). Doubleday.

Judgment in Administration. Ray E. Brown. (Management Ser). 1966. 16.95 o.p. (ISBN 0-07-008175-1, C). McGraw.

Judgment of Whole Kingdoms & Nations. John Somers & Giles Jacob. Ed. by David S. Berkowitz & Samuel E. Thorne. LC 77-86589. (Classics of English Legal History in the Modern Era Ser.: Vol. 19). 467p. 1979. lib. bdg. 40.00 (ISBN 0-8240-3069-9). Garland Pub.

Judgment on Janus. Andre Norton. 1979. pap. 1.95 o.p. (ISBN 0-449-24214-5, Crest). Fawcett.

Judicial Administration in Canada. Perry S. Millar & Carl Baar. (Institute of Public Administration of Canada, Ipac Ser.). (Illus.). 550p. 1981. 35.95x (ISBN 0-7735-0367-6); pap. 18.95x (ISBN 0-7735-0368-4). McGill-Queens U Pr.

Judicial Administration: Text & Readings. R. Wheeler & H. Whitcomb. 1977. text ed. 15.95 (ISBN 0-13-511675-9). P-H.

Judicial Attitudes in Sentencing. Edward Green. LC 74-17589. (Cambridge Studies in Criminology: Vol. 15). 149p. 1975. Repr. of 1961 ed. lib. bdg. 15.00x (ISBN 0-8371-7834-7, GRJA). Greenwood.

Judicial Beginnings in New Hampshire, 1640-1700. Elwin L. Page. LC 59-3040. (Illus.). 278p. 1959. text ed. 10.00x (ISBN 0-915916-02-9). U Pr of New Eng.

Judicial Committee of the Privy Council: 1833-1876. P. A. Howell. LC 78-54326. (Cambridge Studies in English Legal History). (Illus.). 1979. 35.50 (ISBN 0-521-22146-3). Cambridge U Pr.

Judicial Conduct Organization. 2nd ed. Irene A. Tesitor & Dwight B. Sinks. 96p. 1980. pap. 3.75 (8567). Am Judicature.

Judicial Control of Administrative Action. Louis L. Jaffe. 704p. 1966. pap. 12.50 o.s.i. (ISBN 0-316-45604-7). Little.

Judicial Control of Administrative Action in India & Pakistan: A Comparative Study of Principles & Remedies. M. A. Fazal. 1961. 18.95x o.p. (ISBN 0-19-825186-6). Oxford U Pr.

Judicial Decision-Making. Ed. by Glendon A. Schubert. LC 63-8422. 1963. 14.95 (ISBN 0-02-928230-6). Free Pr.

Judicial Doctrines of Religious Rights in America. William G. Torpey. LC 78-132289. (Civil Liberties in American History Ser). 1970. Repr. of 1948 ed. lib. bdg. 39.50 (ISBN 0-306-70067-0). Da Capo.

Judicial Mind Revisited: Psychometric Analysis of Supreme Court Ideology. Glendon Schubert. (Science & Engineering Policy Ser). (Illus.). 208p. 1974. text ed. 10.95x (ISBN 0-19-501754-4); pap. text ed. 5.95x (ISBN 0-19-501753-6). Oxford U Pr.

Judicial Process Among the Barotse of Northern Rhodesia. Max Gluckman. (Rhodes Livingston Institute Bks). 1955. pap. text ed. 15.00x (ISBN 0-7190-1040-3). Humanities.

Judicial Process in a Nutshell. William L. Reynolds. LC 80-12730. (Nutshell Ser.). 322p. 1980. pap. text ed. 6.95 (ISBN 0-8299-2089-7). West Pub.

Judicial Retention Elections in the United States. Susan B. Carbon & Larry C. Berkson. LC 80-69565. 96p. (Orig.). 1980. pap. 4.00 (8566). Am Judicature.

Judicial Review & the Reasonable Doubt Test. Sanford B. Gabin. (National University Publications, Multi-Disciplinary Studies in the Law). 1980. 17.50 (ISBN 0-8046-9248-3). Kennikat.

Judicial Review in Mexico: A Study of the Amparo Suit. Richard D. Baker. (Latin American Monographs, No. 22). 304p. 1971. 13.50 (ISBN 0-292-70105-5). U of Tex Pr.

Judicial Review of Governmental Action & the Requirement of an Interest to Sue. P. Van Dijk. LC 80-51740. 618p. 1980. 100.00x (ISBN 90-286-0120-1). Sijthoff & Noordhoff.

Judicial Review of Legislation. R. Von Moschzisker. LC 78-153372. (American Constitutional & Legal History Ser.). 1971. Repr. of 1923 ed. lib. bdg. 19.50 (ISBN 0-306-70151-0). Da Capo.

Judicial Review Unmasked. Thomas J. Higgins. 1981. 14.95 (ISBN 0-8158-0405-9). Chris Mass.

Judicial Supremacy: The Supreme Court on Trial. Robert K. Dornan & Csaba Vedlik. LC 80-82300. (Nordland Series in Contemporary American Social Problems). 145p. (Orig.). 1980. pap. 5.95 (ISBN 0-913124-38-9). Nordland Pub.

Judiciary in a Democratic Society. Ed. by Leonard Theberge. LC 77-25740. 1979. 16.95 (ISBN 0-669-01508-3). Lexington Bks.

Judiciary: The Supreme Court in the Governmental Process. 5th ed. Abraham. 264p. 1980. pap. text ed. 7.95 (ISBN 0-205-06848-0, 7668481). Allyn.

Judiciary: The Supreme Court in the Governmental Process. 4th ed. Henry J. Abraham. 1977. pap. text ed. 5.95x o.p. (ISBN 0-205-05757-8). Allyn.

Judith. Brian Cleeve. 1979. pap. 2.25 o.p. (ISBN 0-425-04168-9). Berkley Pub.

Judith: Lyric Drama for Soli, Chorus, & Orchestra. George W. Chadwick. LC 70-169727. (Earlier American Music Ser.: Vol. 3). 176p. 1972. Repr. of 1901 ed. lib. bdg. 22.50 (ISBN 0-306-77303-1). Da Capo.

Judo. Sadaki Nakabayashi et al. LC 58-10422. (Athletic Institute Ser). (Illus.). 128p. (gr. 7 up). 1974. 6.95 (ISBN 0-8069-4316-5); PLB 7.49 (ISBN 0-8069-4317-3). Sterling.

Judo: A Gentle Beginning. Jeannette Bruce. LC 74-26503. (Illus.). 160p. (gr. 3 up). 1975. 8.95 (ISBN 0-690-00557-1, TYC-J). T Y Crowell.

Judo and Self-Defence for Women & Girls. Pat Butler & Karen Butler. (Illus.). 1968. 10.95 (ISBN 0-571-08238-6, Pub. by Faber & Faber). Merrimack Bk Serv.

Judo Complete. Pat Butler. (Illus.). 1971. 8.95 (ISBN 0-571-05397-1, Pub. by Faber & Faber); pap. 4.95 (ISBN 0-571-09725-1). Merrimack Bk Serv.

Judo: How to Become a Champ. John Goodbody. (Illus.). 1976. pap. 7.50 (ISBN 0-86002-128-9). Transatlantic.

Judo in Action: Throwing Techniques. Kazuzo Kudo. LC 67-20768. (Illus.). pap. 5.95 (ISBN 0-87040-073-8). Japan Pubns.

Judo: Self-Taught. Eric Dominy. (Everyday Handbook Ser.). (Illus.). 208p. 1976. pap. 1.95 o.p. (ISBN 0-06-463440-X). B&N.

Judo: Sport Techniques for Physical Fitness & Tournament. Bruce Tegner. LC 76-18090. (Illus.). 144p. 1976. pap. 2.95 (ISBN 0-87407-025-2, T25). Thor.

Judo Starbrook Style: Champion's Method. Dave Starbrook. (Illus.). 1978. pap. 9.95x (ISBN 0-8464-0540-7). Beekman Pubs.

Judo Yell. Alice Sankey. LC 74-165819. (Pilot Book Ser). (Illus.). (gr. 4-8). 1971. 6.95 (ISBN 0-8075-4095-1). A Whitman.

Judy's Journey. Lois Lenski. LC 47-4504. (Regional Stories Ser). (Illus.). (gr. 4-6). 1947. 9.79 (ISBN 0-397-30131-6). Lippincott.

Judy's Summer Adventure. Sally Scott. LC 60-6211. (Illus.). (gr. 1-5). 1960. 3.95 o.p. (ISBN 0-15-241133-X, HJ). HarBraceJ.

Jug & Related Stoneware of Bennington. Cornelius Osgood. LC 73-152111. (Illus.). 1971. 16.50 o.p. (ISBN 0-8048-0888-0). C E Tuttle.

Juggle with Me! Isle-Margret Vogel. (Illus.). (ps-1). 1970. PLB 5.00 (ISBN 0-307-60594-9, Golden Pr). Western Pub.

Juggler. Siv C. Fox & Bil Brauer. (Illus.). 1977. pap. 4.95 (ISBN 0-915298-08-2). Sagarin Pr.

Juggler. Arland Ussher. 88p. 1980. text ed. write for info. (ISBN 0-85105-374-2, Dolmen Pr). Humanities.

Juggling for the Complete Klutz. 2nd ed. John Cassidy & B. C. Rimbeaux. (Illus.). 1980. pap. 7.95 (ISBN 0-932592-00-7). Klutz Enterprises.

Jugs: A Collector's Guide. James Paton. (Illus.). 1977. 9.95 o.p. (ISBN 0-684-14885-4, ScribT). Scribner.

Jugtown Pottery: History & Design. Jean Crawford. LC 64-8376. (Illus.). 1964. 8.00 o.p. (ISBN 0-910244-39-1). Blair.

Juicing. Paul Reps. LC 77-82770. 1978. pap. 3.50 o.p. (ISBN 0-385-13250-6, Anch). Doubleday.

Juive, 2 vols. Jacques-Francois Halevy. Ed. by Philip Gossett & Charles Rosen. LC 76-49218. (Early Romantic Opera Ser.). 1980. 82.00 (ISBN 0-8240-2935-6). Garland Pub.

Juju Sheep & the Python's Moonstone. Miriam Schlein. LC 72-83686. (Folklore Ser.). (Illus.). 128p. (gr. 8-12). 1973. 5.95g o.p. (ISBN 0-8075-4050-1). A Whitman.

Jules Laforgue. Michael Collie. (Athlone French Poets Ser). 160p. 1977. text ed. 18.75x (ISBN 0-485-14606-1, Athlone Pr); pap. text ed. 6.25x (ISBN 0-485-12206-5). Humanities.

Jules Verne. new ed. Armand Goupil. Ed. by Pierre Barberis & Georges Jean. (Textes pour aujourd'hui). (Illus.). 191p. (Orig., Fr.). 1975. pap. 3.95 (ISBN 2-03-038006-7). Larousse.

Jules Verne & His Work. I. O. Evans. 188p. 1980. Repr. of 1965 ed. lib. bdg. 35.00 (ISBN 0-89760-224-2). Telegraph Bks.

Jules Verne: Inventor of Science Fiction. Peter Costello. LC 78-57528. (Illus.). 1978. 10.95 o.p. (ISBN 0-684-15824-8, ScribT). Scribner.

Julia. Susan Bright. Ed. by Joseph F. Lomax & J. Whitebird. (Illus.). 1977. pap. 3.00 (ISBN 0-930324-01-3). Wings Pr.

Julia, a Novel, 2 vols. Helen M. Williams. (Feminist Controversy in England, 1788-1810 Ser.). 1974. Set. lib. bdg. 76.00 (ISBN 0-8240-0887-1); lib. bdg. 50.00 ea. Garland Pub.

Julia Alpinula; with the Captive of Stamboul, & Other Poems, Repr. Of 1820 Ed. Jeremiah H. Wiffen. Ed. by Donald H. Reiman. Bd. with Echo of Antiquity. the Past & the Future. (Poems. LC 75-31273. (Romantic Context Ser.: Poetry 1789-1830: Vol. 119). 1979. lib. bdg. 47.00 (ISBN 0-8240-2219-X). Garland Pub.

Julia & the Bazooka. Anna Kavan. 1975. 6.95 o.p. (ISBN 0-394-49445-8). Knopf.

Julia & the Hand of God. Eleanor Cameron. LC 77-4507. (Illus.). 1977. PLB 8.95 (ISBN 0-525-32910-2). Dutton.

Julia & the Third Bad Thing. Barbara B. Wallace. LC 75-2965. (Illus.). 64p. (gr. 2-4). 1975. 5.95 o.p. (ISBN 0-695-80590-8); PLB 5.97 o.p. (ISBN 0-695-40590-X). Follett.

Julia Bulette & the Red Light Ladies of Nevada. Doug McDonald. (Illus.). 1980. 2.95 (ISBN 0-913814-29-6). Nevada Pubns.

Julia de Roubigne, 2 vols. Henry MacKenzie. Ed. by Ronald Paulson. LC 78-60840. (Novel 1720-1805 Ser.: Vol. 7). 1979. Set. lib. bdg. write for info. (ISBN 0-8240-3656-5); lib. bdg. 50.00 ea. Garland Pub.

Julia Margaret Cameron: Her Life & Photographic Work. Helmut Gernsheim. LC 73-85258. (Illus.). 128p. 1974. 25.00 o.p. (ISBN 0-912334-50-9); pap. 14.50 o.p. (ISBN 0-912334-51-7). Aperture.

Julia Peterkin. Thomas H. Landess. (U.S. Authors Ser.: No. 273). 1976. lib. bdg. 10.95 (ISBN 0-8057-7173-5). Twayne.

Julian Carroll of Kentucky. Charles P. Conn. (Illus.). 1977. 5.95 o.p. (ISBN 0-8007-0838-5). Revell.

Julian Green. Glenn S. Burne. (World Authors Ser.: France: No. 195). lib. bdg. 10.95 (ISBN 0-8057-2404-4). Twayne.

Julian Hooge: A Biography. Timothy O'Sullivan. 1981. price not set (ISBN 0-7100-0592-X). Routledge & Kegan.

Julian Huxley: Scientist & World Citizen, 1887-1975. 1979. pap. 7.00 (ISBN 92-3-101461-7, U894, UNESCO). Unipub.

Julian of Norwich, "Showings". Ed. by Edmund Colledge et al. (Classics of Western Spirituality). 1978. 11.95 (ISBN 0-8091-0234-X); pap. 7.95 (ISBN 0-8091-2091-7). Paulist Pr.

Juliana Horatia Ewing & Her Books. Horatia K. Eden. LC 71-77001. (Library of Lives & Letters). (Illus.). 1969. Repr. of 1896 ed. 18.00 (ISBN 0-8103-3897-1). Gale.

Julia's Book. Julia Corbit. Ed. by Iver Sonnack & Mike Hatchimonji. LC 79-66049. (Illus.). 1979. 14.95 (ISBN 0-934724-00-8). Xenos Bks.

Julia's Sister. Charlotte V. Allen. (Orig.). 1978. pap. 1.95 o.s.i. (ISBN 0-446-89357-9). Warner Bks.

Julie Eisenhower's Cookbook for Children. Julie Nixon Eisenhower. 96p. (gr. 5-7). 1975. 6.95 o.p. (ISBN 0-385-11432-X). Doubleday.

Juliette. Pierre Viallet. LC 76-56393. 1977. pap. 1.75 o.p. (ISBN 0-345-25250-0). Ballantine.

Julio Cortazar. Evelyn P. Garfield. LC 74-78440. (Modern Literature Ser.). 184p. 1975. 10.95 (ISBN 0-8044-2224-9). Ungar.

Julius Caesar. Peter David. LC 68-10817. (gr. 7 up). 1968. 3.50g o.s.i. (ISBN 0-02-726300-2, CCPr). Macmillan.

Julius Caesar. Shakespeare. LC 80-16406. (Raintree Short Classics). (Illus.). 48p. (gr. 4 up). 1981. PLB 9.95 (ISBN 0-8172-1664-2). Raintree Pubs.

Julius Caesar. William Shakespeare. Ed. by Arthur Quiller-Couch et al. (New Shakespeare Ser). 1968. 23.95 (ISBN 0-521-07539-4); pap. 4.50x (ISBN 0-521-09482-8). Cambridge U Pr.

Julius Caesar. William Shakespeare. Ed. by Maynard Mack & Robert W. Boynton. (Shakespeare Ser). (Illus.). (gr. 10-12). 1972. pap. text ed. 0.95x (ISBN 0-8104-6014-9). Hayden.

Julius Caesar & It's Sources. David C. Green. (Salzburg Institute for English Literature Jacobean Drama Studies: No. 86). (Orig.). 1980. pap. text ed. 25.00x (ISBN 0-391-01715-2). Humanities.

Julius Caesar, with Reader's Guide. William Shakespeare. (Literature Program). (gr. 10-12). 1970. pap. text ed. 4.00 (ISBN 0-87720-802-6); with model ans. s.p. 2.65 (ISBN 0-87720-902-2). AMSCO Sch.

Julius Erving. Thomas Braun. LC 75-37584. (Sports Superstars Ser.). (Illus.). (gr. 3-9). 1976. PLB 5.95 (ISBN 0-87191-499-9); pap. 2.95 (ISBN 0-89812-181-7). Creative Ed.

Julius Robert Mayer, Prophet of Energy. R. B. Lindsay. LC 72-8045. (Men of Physics Ser.). 1973. 22.00 (ISBN 0-08-016985-6). Pergamon.

July's People. Nadine Gordimer. LC 80-24877. 192p. 1981. 10.95 (ISBN 0-670-41048-9). Viking Pr.

Jumanji. Chris Van Allsburg. 1981. 9.95 (ISBN 0-395-30448-2). HM.

Jumble: No. 19. Henri Arnold & Bob Lee. (Orig.). 1981. pap. price not set (ISBN 0-451-09907-9, Sig). NAL.

Jumble: That Scrambled Word Game, No. 16. Henri Arnold. 128p. (Orig.). 1980. pap. 1.50 (ISBN 0-451-09311-9, W9311, Sig). NAL.

Jumble: That Scrambled Word Game, No. 17. Henri Arnold & Bob Lee. (Orig.). 1980. pap. 1.50 (ISBN 0-451-09492-1, W9492, Sig). NAL.

Jumble: That Scrambled Word Game, No. 18. Henri Arnold & Bob Lee. (Orig.). 1981. pap. 1.50 (ISBN 0-451-09740-8, W9240, Sig). NAL.

Jumeau Doll. Margaret Whitton. (Illus.). 96p. (Orig.). 1980. pap. 6.00 (ISBN 0-486-23954-3). Dover.

Jump Rope! Peter L. Skolnik. LC 75-8811. (Illus.). 160p. (Orig.). (gr. 2 up). 1974. pap. 3.95 (ISBN 0-911104-47-X). Workman Pub.

Jump Rope Verses Around the United States. Catherine H. Ainsworth. (Folklore Bks.). 24p. 1980. 2.00 (ISBN 0-933190-01-8). Clyde Pr.

Jump the Rope Jingles. Emma V. Worstell. (gr. k up). 1967. 4.95g o.s.i. (ISBN 0-02-793400-4). Macmillan.

Jump to Joy: Helping Children Grow Through Active Play. Maida L. Riggs. (Illus.). 176p. 1980. 12.95 (Spec); pap. 6.95. P-H.

Jump Your Horse Right. Frederick L. Devereux, Jr. LC 78-7734. (Illus.). (gr. 5 up). 1978. 6.50 (ISBN 0-396-07611-4). Dodd.

Jumping-off Place: American Drama of the 1960's. Gerald Weales. 1969. 6.95 o.s.i. (ISBN 0-02-624670-8). Macmillan.

Jumping off Place & Other Stories. Baine Kerr. LC 80-14023. 80p. 1981. text ed. 11.00x (ISBN 0-8262-0311-6). U of Mo Pr.

Jumps: Contemporary Theory, Technique & Training. Ed. by Fred Wilt. LC 73-189447. 160p. 1972. pap. 6.50 o.p. (ISBN 0-911520-35-X). Tafnews.

Junction. Jack Dann. (Orig.). 1981. pap. 2.50 (ISBN 0-440-14416-7). Dell.

Juncture. Ed. by Mark Arnoff & Mary-Louise Kean. (Studia Linguistica et Philologica: Ovol. 7). 144p. 1980. pap. 25.00 (ISBN 0-915838-46-X). Anma Libri.

June Brown's Guide to Let's Read. June B. Garner. 55p. 1980. pap. 2.50 (ISBN 0-8143-1667-0). Wayne St U Pr.

June Seven. Aliki. (gr. 1-5). 1972. 4.95g o.s.i. (ISBN 0-02-700400-7). Macmillan.

Jung & Politics: The Political & Social Ideas of C. G. Jung. Volodymyr Walter Odajnyk. LC 76-55153. 1976. 12.00x (ISBN 0-8147-6154-2). NYU Pr.

Jung & Tarot: An Archetypal Journey. Sallie Nichols. 1980. 25.00 (ISBN 0-87728-480-6); pap. 9.95 (ISBN 0-87728-515-2). Weiser.

Jung, Harold, Hesse: Contributions of C. G. Jung, Preston Harold & Hermann Hesse Toward a Spiritual Psychology. Winifred Babcock. 275p. 1981. 12.95 (ISBN 0-686-68720-5). World Authors.

Jung: Man & Myth. Vincent Brome. LC 80-25159. 327p. 1981. pap. 6.95 (ISBN 0-689-70588-3). Atheneum.

Jungian Psychoanalytic Interpretation of William Faulkner's "As I Lay Dying". Dixie M. Turner. LC 80-5582. 107p. 1981. lib. bdg. 16.50 (ISBN 0-8191-1451-0); pap. text ed. 7.50 (ISBN 0-8191-1452-9). U Pr of Amer.

Jungian Psychology in Literary Analysis: A Demonstration Using T. S. Eliot's Poetry. Joyce M. Jones. LC 79-66227. 1979. pap. text ed. 5.75 (ISBN 0-8191-0810-3). U Pr of Amer.

Jungian-Senoi Dreamwork Manual. Strephon K. Williams. 302p. (Orig.). 1980. pap. 14.95 o.p. (ISBN 0-918572-04-5). Journey Pr.

Jungle. (MacDonald Educational Ser.). (Illus., Arabic.). 3.50 (ISBN 0-686-53079-9). Intl Bk Ctr.

Jungle. Carroll R. Norden. LC 77-27590. (Read About Animals Ser.). (Illus.). (gr. k-3). 1978. PLB 9.95 (ISBN 0-8393-0078-6). Raintree Child.

Jungle. Upton Sinclair. LC 79-151835. 1971. Repr. of 1906 ed. lib. bdg. 12.50x (ISBN 0-8376-0400-1). Bentley.

Jungle. Upton Sinclair. (Literature Ser). (gr. 9-12). 1970. pap. text ed. 3.75 (ISBN 0-87720-730-5). AMSCO Sch.

Jungle Books. Rudyard Kipling. (gr. 5 up). 1964. 4.95g o.s.i. (ISBN 0-02-750800-5). Macmillan.

Jungle Journey. Bent A. Larsen. LC 76-7856. (Destiny Ser.). 1977. pap. 4.50 o.p. (ISBN 0-8163-0283-9). Pacific Pr Pub Assn.

Jungle of Stars. Jack L. Chalker. 1976. pap. 2.25 (ISBN 0-345-28960-9). Ballantine.

Jungle Oil: Hazardous Times. Ernest Avery. 1981. 8.95 (ISBN 0-533-04889-3). Vantage.

Jungle Pilot. Russell T. Hitt. 320p. 1973. pap. 3.50 (ISBN 0-310-26082-5). Zondervan.

Jungle Tales of Tarzan, No. 6. Edgar R. Burroughs. 192p. 1975. pap. 1.95 (ISBN 0-345-29478-5). Ballantine.

Jungle Trip. Ed. by Lee Mountain. (Attention Span Stories Ser). (Illus., Orig.). (gr. 6-10). 1978. pap. text ed. 3.20x (ISBN 0-89061-148-3, 584). Jamestown Pubs.

Jungleland Frieze. John Burningham. (Illus.). (ps-8). 1981. 4.95. Merrimack Bk Serv.

Jung's Psychology & Its Social Meaning. Ira Progoff. LC 72-97273. 320p. 1973. pap. 3.50 (ISBN 0-385-03273-0, Anch). Doubleday.

Juniata Valley. Virginia Cassel. LC 80-25173. 336p. 1981. 13.95 (ISBN 0-670-41085-3). Viking Pr.

Junior Bachelor Society. John A. Williams. LC 75-32297. 7.95 o.p. (ISBN 0-385-09455-8). Doubleday.

Junior Book of Authors. 2nd rev. ed. Ed. by Stanley J. Kunitz & Howard Haycraft. (Illus.). 1951. 12.00 (ISBN 0-8242-0028-4). Wilson.

Junior Chess Games. Raymond Bott & Stanley Morrison. 1966. 6.95 (ISBN 0-685-52088-9). Transatlantic.

Junior Chess Puzzles. Raymond Bott & Stanley Morrison. (Illus., Orig.). 1975. pap. 3.95 (ISBN 0-571-10688-9, Pub. by Faber & Faber). Merrimack Bk Serv.

Junior High School Art Curriculum. William S. Devall, Jr. LC 79-6770. 79p. 1980. pap. text ed. 6.50 (ISBN 0-8191-0951-7). U Pr of Amer.

Junior High School Library Catalog. 4th ed. 1980. 62.00 (ISBN 0-8242-0652-5). Wilson.

Junior History of the American Negro, 2 vols. M. C. Goodman. Incl. Vol. 1. Discovery to Civil War. 1969 (ISBN 0-8303-0072-4); Vol. 2. Civil War to Civil Rights War. LC 73-76026. 1970 (ISBN 0-8303-0073-2). (Illus.). (gr. 6-12). 6.50 ea.; text ed. avail. (ISBN 0-8303-0162-3); teaching manual 0.50 ea. Fleet.

Junior Impact. R. H. Poole & P. J. Shepherd. Incl. One. It's a Fact (ISBN 0-435-01736-5); Two. Senses (ISBN 0-435-01737-3); Three. Creatures (ISBN 0-435-01738-1); Four. Myth & Legend. 1976 (ISBN 0-435-01739-X). (gr. 6-9). 1976. pap. text ed. 3.95x ea. o.p.; pap. text ed. 8.50 tchrs' bk o.p. (ISBN 0-435-01740-3). Heinemann Ed.

Junior Jewish Encyclopedia. 9rev. ed. Ed. by Naomi Ben-Asher & Hayim Leaf. LC 79-66184. (Illus.). (gr. 9-12). 1979. 14.95 (ISBN 0-88400-066-4). Shengold.

Junior Judo. rev. ed. E. J. Harrison. LC 58-10422. (gr. 4 up). 1965. 6.95 (ISBN 0-8069-4430-7); PLB 6.69 (ISBN 0-8069-4431-5). Sterling.

Junior Karate. Russel Kozuki. (Illus.). (gr. 4-6). 1977. pap. 1.50 (ISBN 0-686-68483-4). PB.

Junior Karate. Russell Kozuki. LC 71-167665. (Illus.). (gr. 3 up). 1971. 6.95 (ISBN 0-8069-4446-3); PLB 6.69 (ISBN 0-8069-4447-1). Sterling.

Junior Karate. Russell Kozuki. (gr. 4-6). 1977. pap. 1.75 (ISBN 0-671-42065-8). Archway.

Junior Magic. Walter B. Gibson. LC 76-58624. (Illus.). (gr. 5 up). 7.95 (ISBN 0-8069-4546-X); PLB 7.49 (ISBN 0-8069-4547-8). Sterling.

Junior Miss. Sally Benson. (gr. 7-9). 1969. pap. 1.75 (ISBN 0-671-42066-6). Archway.

Junior Pears Encyclopaedia. 20th ed. Ed. by Edward Blishen. (Illus.). 704p. 1980. 11.95 (ISBN 0-7207-1263-7, Pub. by Michael Joseph). Merrimack Bk Serv.

Junior Pears Encyclopedia. 19th ed. Ed. by Edward Blishen. (Illus.). 704p. 1980. 9.95 o.p. (ISBN 0-7207-1158-4, Pub. by Michael Joseph). Merrimack Bk Serv.

Junior Soccer. John Jarman. (Illus.). 1976. 7.95 (ISBN 0-571-10846-6, Pub. by Faber & Faber); pap. 3.95 (ISBN 0-571-10847-4). Merrimack Bk Serv.

Junior Surprise Sermons with Handmade Objects, 2 bks. Set. pap. 6.00; No. 1. pap. 3.00 (ISBN 0-915398-18-4); No. 2. pap. 3.00 (ISBN 0-915398-19-2). Visual Evangels.

Junior Words, Phrases, Clauses: Exercises in Elementary Grammar. Edward J. Fox & Malcolm T. Moore. 89p. (Orig.). (gr. 4-6). 1980. pap. 3.25x (ISBN 0-88334-127-1). Ind Sch Pr.

Juniper Tree & Other Tales from Grimm, 2 vols. Jacob Grimm & Wilhelm Grimm. Tr. by Segal Lore & Randall Jarrell. LC 73-82698. 384p. (gr. 4 up). 1973. boxed set 15.00 (ISBN 0-374-18057-1). FS&G.

Juniper Waterway: A History of the Albemarle & Chesapeake Canal. Alexander Brown. LC 80-14093. 1981. price not set (ISBN 0-917376-35-8). U Pr of Va.

Junius & Philip Francis. David McCracken. (English Authors Ser.: No. 259). 1979. lib. bdg. 14.50 (ISBN 0-8057-6753-3). Twayne.

Junius Francais, Journal Politique. Jean - Paul Marat. 104p. (Fr.). 1977. lib. bdg. 22.50x o.p. (ISBN 0-8287-0569-0); pap. text ed. 12.50x o.p. (ISBN 0-685-75627-0). Clearwater Pub.

Junius Manuscript. Ed. by George P. Krapp. LC 31-8589. 1931. 17.50x (ISBN 0-231-08765-9). Columbia U Pr.

Junius Tracts. Calvin Colton. (Neglected American Economists Ser.). 1974. lib. bdg. 50.00 (ISBN 0-8240-1009-4). Garland Pub.

Junk Bonds. Charles A. Fracchia. (Illus.). 1980. 10.95 (ISBN 0-07-021766-1). McGraw.

Junk Food Alternative. Linda Burum. LC 80-17799. (Illus.). 168p. (Orig.). 1980. pap. 5.95 (ISBN 0-89286-163-0). One Hund One Prods.

Junk Food Cookbook. Lydia Saiger. (Orig.). 1979. pap. 2.50 (ISBN 0-515-05740-1). Jove Pubns.

Junk Food, Fast Food, Health Food What America Eats & Why. Lila Perl. 192p. (gr. 5 up). 1980. 9.95 (ISBN 0-395-29108-9, Clarion); pap. 4.95 (ISBN 0-395-30060-6). HM.

Junk Sculpture. Gregg LeFevre. LC 72-95204. (Little Craft Book Ser.). (Illus.). 50p. 1972. 4.95 o.p. (ISBN 0-8069-5258-X); lib. bdg. 5.89 o.p. (ISBN 0-8069-5259-8). Sterling.

Junk Treasures: A Sourcebook for Using Recycled Materials with Children. Mary J. Cliatt & Jean M. Shaw. (Illus.). 256p. 1981. pap. text ed. 14.95 (ISBN 0-13-512608-8). P-H.

Junker in the Prussian Administration Under William Second, 1888-1914. Lysbeth W. Muncy. LC 70-80574. 1970. Repr. of 1944 ed. 15.75 (ISBN 0-86527-112-7). Fertig.

Junkies & Straights. Ed. by Robert H. Coombs. LC 75-27250. (Illus.). 240p. 1975. 19.95 (ISBN 0-669-00320-4). Lexington Bks.

Junky. William S. Burroughs. 1977. pap. 2.95 (ISBN 0-14-004351-9). Penguin.

Jupiter Project. Gregory Benford. 1980. pap. 2.25 (ISBN 0-425-04569-2). Berkley Pub.

Jupiter's Travels. Ted Simon. 360p. 1981. pap. 4.95 (ISBN 0-14-005410-3). Penguin.

Jurassic Environments. A. Hallam. LC 74-80359. (Earth Science Ser.). (Illus.). 260p. 1975. 47.50 (ISBN 0-521-20555-7). Cambridge U Pr.

Jurchen in Twelfth-Century China: A Study of Sinicization. Jing-shen Tao. LC 76-7800. (Publications on Asia of the School of International Studies: No. 29). (Illus.). 236p. 1977. 12.50 (ISBN 0-295-95514-7). U of Wash Pr.

Juridical Studies in Ancient Indian Law, 2 vols. L. Sternbach. 1967. 24.00 set (ISBN 0-89684-232-0). Orient Bk Dist.

Jurisdiction in a Nutshell, State & Federal. 4th ed. Albert A. Ehrenzweig et al. LC 80-312. (Nutshell Ser.). 298p. 1980. pap. 6.95 (ISBN 0-8299-2086-2). West Pub.

Jurisprudence in the Middle Ages. Walter Ullmann. 390p. 1980. 75.00x (ISBN 0-86078-065-1, Pub. by Variorum England). State Mutual Bk.

Jurisprudence: Its American Prophets; a Survey of Taught Jurisprudence. Harold G. Reuschlein. LC 70-158741. 1971. Repr. of 1951 ed. lib. bdg. 29.75x (ISBN 0-8371-6180-0). Greenwood.

Jurisprudence of John Marshall. Robert K. Faulkner. LC 80-14281. xii, 307p. 1980. Repr. of 1968 ed. lib. bdg. 25.50x (ISBN 0-313-22508-7, FAJU). Greenwood.

Jurocracy: Government Lawyers, Agency Programs, & Judicial Decisions. Donald L Horowitz. LC 76-27921. 1977. 16.95 (ISBN 0-669-00986-5). Lexington Bks.

Jurors & Rape: A Study in Psychology & Law. Hubert S. Feild & Leign B. Bienen. LC 76-48473. (Illus.). 1980. 34.95x (ISBN 0-669-01148-7). Lexington Bks.

Jury: History of the Trial Jury. Lloyd Moore. 1973. 12.00 (ISBN 0-87084-576-4). Anderson Pub C.

Jury of One. Mignon G. Eberhart. 144p. 1974. pap. 0.95 o.p. (ISBN 0-445-00544-0). Popular Lib.

Jury Verdicts: The Role of Group Size & Social Decision Rule. Michael J. Saks. LC 76-44569. 1977. 16.95 (ISBN 0-669-01100-2). Lexington Bks.

Just a Bite: Egon Ronay's Lucas Guide 1979 for Gourmets on a Family Budget. Egon Ronay. 1979. pap. 3.95 o.p. (ISBN 0-14-005143-0). Penguin.

Just a Dog. Helen Griffiths. (gr. 5-7). 1976. pap. 1.95 (ISBN 0-671-42166-2). Archway.

Just a Dog. Helen Griffiths. (gr. 5-7). 1976. pap. 1.75 (ISBN 0-671-56036-0). PB.

Just a French Major from the Bronx: Selected Cartoons from "Still a Few Bugs in the System". G. B. Trudeau. (Doonesbury Ser.). (Illus.). 128p. 1981. pap. 1.75 (ISBN 0-445-00623-4). Popular Lib.

Just a Minute, Vol. 5. (Vegetable Puppets Ser.). (Illus.). 10p. (ps). 1979. 2.50 o.p. (ISBN 0-89346-120-2, Pub. by Froebel-Kan Japan). Heian Intl.

Just About Anything Can Be Moved. Richard Whittingham. LC 80-22669. (On the Move Ser.). 48p. (gr. 3-6). 1981. PLB 9.25 (ISBN 0-516-03889-3). Childrens.

Just Above My Head. James Baldwin. 1980. pap. 3.50 (ISBN 0-440-14777-8). Dell.

Just an Old Sweet Song. Melvin Van Peebles. 1976. pap. 1.50 (ISBN 0-345-28114-4). Ballantine.

Just As I Am. Eugenia Price. 1968. 4.95 o.p. (ISBN 0-397-10060-4, Holman). Lippincott.

Just As I Am. Eugenia Price. (Orig.). 1976. pap. 1.75 (ISBN 0-89129-187-3). Jove Pubns.

Just As the Boy Dreams of White Thighs Under Flowered Skirts. Michele Cusumano. (Backstreet Editions Ser.). 24p. (Orig.). 1980. pap. 2.00 (ISBN 0-935252-24-X); signed 5.00 (ISBN 0-686-63441-1). Street Pr.

Just Because They're Jewish: The Incredible, Ironic, Bizarre, Funny, & Provocative in the Way Jews Are Seen by Other People. M. Hirsh Goldberg. LC 78-6400. 264p. 1981. pap. 6.95 (ISBN 0-8128-6122-1). Stein & Day.

Just Because...I Needed to. Joe Shaffer. Ed. by M. Karl Kulikowski. (Gusto Press Poetry Discovery Ser.). (Orig.). 1979. pap. 4.25 (ISBN 0-933906-03-X). Gusto Pr.

Just Being at the Piano. Mildred P. Chase. LC 80-8999. 112p. (Orig.). 1981. 9.95 (ISBN 0-915238-44-6); pap. 5.95 (ISBN 0-915238-45-4). Peace Pr.

Just Between Us. Susan B. Pfeffer. LC 79-53606. (gr. 4-7). 1980. 7.95 (ISBN 0-440-07823-7); PLB 7.45 (ISBN 0-440-05046-4). Delacorte.

Just Causes. Malcolm McConnell. LC 80-23692. (Illus.). 384p. 1981. 13.95 (ISBN 0-670-41092-6). Viking Pr.

Just Complaint Against an Unjust Doer, Mr. J. Paget. John Davenport. LC 76-57376. (English Experience Ser.: No. 793). 1977. Repr. of 1634 ed. lib. bdg. 5.00 (ISBN 90-221-0793-0). Walter J Johnson.

Just David. Eleanor H. Porter. 1976. lib. bdg. 15.25x (ISBN 0-89968-107-7). Lightyear.

Just Deserts. Roderic Jeffries. 208p. 1981. 9.95 (ISBN 0-312-44942-9). St Martin.

Just Desserts. Tim Heald. LC 78-10856. 1979. 7.95 o.p. (ISBN 0-684-16098-6, ScribT). Scribner.

Just Dial a Number. Edith Maxwell. (gr. 7-9). 1972. pap. 1.95 (ISBN 0-671-42891-8). Archway.

Just Dial a Number. Edith Maxwell. (YA) (gr. 7-9). 1972. pap. 1.95 (ISBN 0-671-56103-0). PB.

Just Folks. Edgar Guest. 192p. 1980. Repr. of 1917 ed. lib. bdg. 11.95x (ISBN 0-89968-190-5). Lightyear.

Just Folks: Visitin' with Carolina People. Jerry Bledsoe. LC 80-36880. (Illus.). 208p. 1980. 9.95 (ISBN 0-914788-31-0). East Woods.

Just for Fun. Patricia Scarry. (Illus.). (ps-1). 1977. PLB 5.00 (ISBN 0-307-60264-8, Golden Pr). Western Pub.

Just for Kicks. Ed. by Mary Verdick. (Pal Paperbacks Ser., Kit B). (Illus., Orig.). (gr. 7-12). 1973. pap. text ed. 1.25 (ISBN 0-8374-3516-1). Xerox Ed Pubns.

Just for Kids: Things to Make, Do & See, Easy As 1-2-3. James Razzi. LC 73-13521. 64p. (ps-3). 1974. 5.95 o.s.i. (ISBN 0-8193-0723-8, Four Winds); PLB 5.41 o.s.i. (ISBN 0-8193-0724-6). Schol Bk Serv.

Just for Me Poems. Leona Lacroix. (gr. k-4). 1977. pap. text ed. 2.25x (ISBN 0-933892-02-0). Child Focus Co.

Just for Starters. Gloria Edwinn. LC 80-51771. 272p. 1981. 14.95 (ISBN 0-670-41093-4). Viking Pr.

Just for You: A Special Collection of Inspirational Verses. Helen Steiner Rice. LC 67-10385. 1967. 4.50 (ISBN 0-385-07721-1). Doubleday.

Just Friends: Friends and Lovers, Poems, 1959-1962. Joel Oppenheimer. LC 70-83559. 1980. 15.00 (ISBN 0-912330-26-0); pap. 7.50 (ISBN 0-912330-27-9). Jargon Soc.

Just Good Food. Paul Rubinstein. (Illus.). 1978. 9.95 o.p. (ISBN 0-684-15526-5, ScribT). Scribner.

Just Imagine: A Guide to Materialization Using Imagery. new ed. William Fezler. 144p. 1980. 9.95 (ISBN 0-934810-00-1). Laurida.

Just in Case: Disaster Preparedness & Emergency Self-Help. John Moir. LC 79-28435. (Orig.). 1980. pap. 4.95 (ISBN 0-87701-200-8). Chronicle Bks.

Just in Time: The Inner Game of Time Management. Robert D. Rutherford. 186p. 1981. 13.95 (ISBN 0-471-08434-4, Pub. by Wiley-Interscience). Wiley.

Just Like an Animal. Maurice Burton. (Illus.). 1979. 12.50 o.p. (ISBN 0-684-15911-2, ScribT). Scribner.

Just Like Everyone Else. Eve Bunting. (Young Romance Ser.). (Illus.). (gr. 3-9). 1978. PLB 5.95 (ISBN 0-87191-630-4); pap. 2.95 (ISBN 0-89812-062-4). Creative Ed.

Just Like Jenny. Sandy Asher. LC 80-27653. 160p. (gr. 7 up). 1981. 7.95 (ISBN 0-8253-0040-1). Beaufort Bks NY.

Just Mary. Efie M. Williams. 96p. pap. 0.75. Faith Pub Hse.

Just Me & My Dad. Mercer Mayer. (Look-Look Ser.). (Illus.). 1977. PLB 5.38 (ISBN 0-307-66839-8, Golden Pr); pap. 0.95 (ISBN 0-307-11839-8). Western Pub.

Just Measure of Pain: The Penitentiary in the Industrial Revolution, 1750-1850. Michael Ignatieff. (Morningside Bks.). 272p. 1980. pap. 6.50x (ISBN 0-231-05057-7, Pub. by Morningside). Columbia U Pr.

Just Momma & Me. Christine E. Eber. LC 75-30308. (Illus.). 40p. (Orig.). (ps-3). 1975. pap. 3.00 (ISBN 0-914996-09-6). Lollipop Power.

Just off Fifth. Edith Begner. 352p. 1981. pap. 2.95 (ISBN 0-380-77321-X, 77321). Avon.

Just One More. James L. Free. LC 77-86272. 1977. pap. 5.95 (ISBN 0-915950-12-X). Bull Pub.

Just One More. Los Angeles Press Photographers. (Illus.). 1981. lib. bdg. 14.95 (ISBN 0-912076-41-0); pap. 9.95 (ISBN 0-912076-45-3). ESE Calif.

Just Open a Book. P. K. Hallinan. LC 80-22099. (Self-Awareness Storybooks). (Illus.). 32p. (ps-3). 1981. PLB 7.95 (ISBN 0-516-03521-5). Childrens.

Just Peace. Peter Matheson. (Orig.). 1981. pap. 5.95 (ISBN 0-377-00107-4). Friend Pr.

Just Pick a Harricane? N. E. Chantz. 1.25 (ISBN 0-902675-11-7). Oleander Pr.

Just Representation: A James Gould Cozzens Reader. James G. Cozzens. Ed. & intro. by Matthew Bruccoli. LC 78-9357. 1978. pap. 6.95 (ISBN 0-15-646611-2, Harv). HarBraceJ.

Just Right for You. Cynthia Watts. (Hello World Ser.). 1977. pap. 1.65 (ISBN 0-8163-0284-7). Pacific Pr Pub Assn.

Just Sixteen. Terry Morris. 176p. (Orig.). (gr. 7 up). 1980. pap. 1.50 (ISBN 0-590-31341-X, Schol Pap). Schol Bk Serv.

Just So Stories. Rudyard Kipling. (Doubleday Classic). (Illus.). (gr. 1-6). 1946. 8.95a (ISBN 0-385-07352-6); PLB (ISBN 0-385-07110-8). Doubleday.

Just So Stories: Anniversary Edition. Rudyard Kipling. LC 79-170932. 112p. (gr. 2-5). 1972. 12.95a (ISBN 0-385-07225-2); PLB (ISBN 0-385-07443-3). Doubleday.

Just Society? Essays on Equity in Australia. Ed. by P. N. Troy. 192p. 1981. text ed. 22.50x (ISBN 0-86861-234-0, 2655). Allen Unwin.

Just Some Weeds from the Wilderness. Patricia Beatty. (gr. 7-9). 1978. 8.95 (ISBN 0-688-22137-8); PLB 8.59 (ISBN 0-688-32137-2). Morrow.

Just Talk to Me. Andre Bustanoby & Fay Bustanoby. 192p. (Orig.). 1981. pap. text ed. 5.95 (ISBN 0-310-22181-1). Zondervan.

Just Tammie. Dorothy Bryan & Marguerite Bryan. LC 51-13037. (Illus.). (gr. 1-3). 1951. 3.50 (ISBN 0-396-03314-8). Dodd.

Just the Beginning. Betty Miles. 1978. pap. 1.75 (ISBN 0-380-01913-2, 55004, Camelot). Avon.

Just the Right Place! Jane B. Moncure. LC 75-34176. (Illus.). (ps-3). 1976. 5.50 (ISBN 0-913778-36-2). Childs World.

Just the Same Today. J. Oswald Sanders. 1979. pap. 2.50 (ISBN 0-85363-105-0). OMF Bks.

Just the Thing for Geraldine. Ellen Conford. (Illus.). 32p. (gr. 1-3). 1974. 7.95 (ISBN 0-316-15304-4). Little.

Just This Once. Alice Schick & Joel Schick. LC 77-28871. (I-Like-to-Read Bks). (gr. k-2). 1978. 6.95 (ISBN 0-397-31803-0). Lippincott.

Just This Side of Madness: Creativity & the Drive to Create. Carol A. Morizot. LC 78-55258. (Illus.). 1978. pap. 6.95 o.p. (ISBN 0-930138-04-X). Harold Hse.

Just Vindication of Learning. Charles Blount et al. Ed. by David S. Berkowitz & Samuel E. Thorne. LC 77-86655. (Classics of English Legal History in the Modern Era Ser.: Vol. 39). 109p. 1979. lib. bdg. 40.00 (ISBN 0-8240-3088-5). Garland Pub.

Just Wait till You Have Children of Your Own! Erma Bombeck & Bil Keane. 1979. pap. 2.25 (ISBN 0-449-23786-9, Crest). Fawcett.

Just War in the Middle Ages. F. H. Russell. LC 74-25655. (Studies in Medieval Life & Thought). 360p. 1975. 51.00 (ISBN 0-521-20690-1); pap. 13.95 (ISBN 0-521-29276-X). Cambridge U Pr.

Justice: Alternative Political Perspectives. James P. Sterba. 272p. 1979. pap. text ed. 8.95x (ISBN 0-534-00762-7). Wadsworth Pub.

Justice & Consequences. John P. Conrad. LC 78-348. (Dangerous Offender Project Ser.). 1981. price not set (ISBN 0-669-02190-3). Lexington Bks.

Justice & Equality. Hugo Bedau. (Central Issues of Philosophy Ser). (Illus.). 1971. pap. 9.00 ref. ed. (ISBN 0-13-514125-7). P-H.

Justice & Her Brothers. Virginia Hamilton. LC 78-54684. (gr. 7 up). 1978. 8.95 (ISBN 0-688-80182-X); PLB 8.59 (ISBN 0-688-84182-1). Greenwillow.

Justice & Liberty. David Raphael. 1980. text ed. 40.00x (ISBN 0-485-11195-0, Athlone Pr). Humanities.

Justice & Older Americans. Ed. by Marlene A. Young Rifai. LC 76-52764. (Illus.). 1977. 19.95 (ISBN 0-669-01333-1). Lexington Bks.

Justice & the Mare's Ale: Law & Disorder in Seventeenth-Century England. Alan Macfarlane. (Illus.). 225p. Date not set. 19.95 (ISBN 0-521-23949-4). Cambridge U Pr.

Justice & Troubled Children Around the World, Vol. 1. Intro. by V. Lorne Stewart. LC 79-3154. 1981. 17.50 (ISBN 0-8147-7809-7). NYU Pr.

Justice As Fairness: Perspectives on the Justice Model. Ed. by David Fogel & Joe Hudson. 300p. 1981. pap. text ed. price not set (ISBN 0-87084-287-0). Anderson Pub Co.

Justice by the Book. new ed. Helene Schwartz. 1977. pap. 2.75x. Bloch.

Justice for Children. Alison Morris et al. 176p. 1980. text ed. 26.00x (ISBN 0-333-27486-5); pap. text ed. 9.95x (ISBN 0-686-64581-2). Humanities.

Justice for Juveniles: The Nineteen Hundred Sixty-Nine Children & Young Persons Act-A Case for Reform? Philip Priestley et al. (Library of Social Work). 1978. 13.00 (ISBN 0-7100-8703-9). Routledge & Kegan.

Justice for Our Children. Dennis A. Romig. LC 77-9154. 1978. 21.00 (ISBN 0-669-01787-6). Lexington Bks.

Justice Frankfurter & Civil Liberties. Clyde Jacobs. LC 74-1331. (Civil Liberties in American History Ser.). 265p. 1974. Repr. of 1961 ed. lib. bdg. 25.00 (ISBN 0-306-70585-0). Da Capo.

Justice Game. A. Engel et al. 1974. pap. 5.95 (ISBN 0-02-472590-0, 47259). Macmillan.

Justice, Human Nature, & Political Obligation. Morton A. Kaplan. LC 76-8145. 1976. 16.95 (ISBN 0-02-916890-2). Free Pr.

Justice in America. Ed. by William P. Lineberry. (Reference Shelf Ser: Vol. 44, No. 1). 200p. 1972. 6.25 (ISBN 0-8242-0464-6). Wilson.

Justice in Colonial Virginia. Oliver P. Chitwood. LC 72-87557. (American Constitutional & Legal History Ser). 1971. Repr. of 1905 ed. lib. bdg. 17.50 (ISBN 0-306-71388-8). Da Capo.

Justice in Jeopardy: Strategy to Revitalize the American Dream. Albert B. Logan. (Illus.). 260p. 1973. text ed. 12.50 (ISBN 0-398-02694-7); pap. text ed. 8.25 (ISBN 0-398-02764-1). C C Thomas.

Justice in Medieval Russia: Muscovite Judgment Characters (Pravye Gramoty) of the 15th & 16th Centuries. Ann M. Kleimola. LC 75-7171. (Transactions Ser: Vol. 65, Pt. 6). 1975. pap. 5.00 o.p. (ISBN 0-87169-656-8). Am Philos.

Justice in South Africa. Albie Sachs. (Perspectives on Southern Africa Ser., No. 12). 1973. 17.50x (ISBN 0-520-02417-6); pap. 3.25 (ISBN 0-520-02624-1). U of Cal Pr.

Justice in the Mountains: Stories & Tales by a Vermont Country Lawyer. Deane C. Davis. LC 80-82866. (Illus.). 192p. 1980. 9.95 (ISBN 0-933050-05-4); pap. 6.95 (ISBN 0-933050-06-2). New Eng Pr VT.

Justice, Law & Argument: Essays on Moral & Legal Reasoning. Chaim Perelman. (Synthese Library: No. 142). 175p. 1980. lib. bdg. 28.50 (ISBN 90-277-1089-9, Pub. by D. Reidel); pap. 10.50 (ISBN 90-277-1090-2). Kluwer Boston.

Justice Lion. Robert N. Peck. 264p. (gr. 7 up). 1981. 9.95 (ISBN 0-316-69658-7). Little.

Justice of Zeus. Hugh Lloyd-Jones. (Sather Classical Lectures: No. 41). 1971. 17.50x (ISBN 0-520-01739-0); pap. 3.45x (ISBN 0-520-02359-5). U of Cal Pr.

Justice Oliver Wendell Holmes, 2 vols. Mark D. Howe. Incl. Vol. 1. The Shaping Years, 1841-1870. (Illus.). 330p. 1957 (ISBN 0-674-49500-4); Vol. 2. The Proving Years, 1870-1882. (Illus.). 1963 (ISBN 0-674-49501-2). 16.50x ea. (Belknap Pr). Harvard U Pr.

Justice Oliver Wendell Holmes: His Book Notices & Uncollected Letters & Papers. Ed. by H. C. Shriver. LC 72-10336. (American Constitutional & Legal History Ser). 300p. 1973. Repr. of 1936 ed. lib. bdg. 29.50 (ISBN 0-306-70557-5). Da Capo.

Justice or Revolution. Leslie Snyder. LC 78-74594. 1979. 12.95 (ISBN 0-916728-20-X). Bks in Focus.

Justice or Tyranny? A Critique of John Rawls's "Theory of Justice". David L. Schaefer. (National Univ. Pubns. Political Science. Ser.). 1979. 12.50 (ISBN 0-8046-9221-1, National Univ. Pubns.). Kennikat.

Justice! Par un Officier De l'Armee De Paris. F. F. Borgella. (Commune De Paris En 1871). (Fr.). 1977. lib. bdg. 13.75x o.p. (ISBN 0-8287-0119-9); pap. text ed. 3.75x o.p. (ISBN 0-685-74928-2). Clearwater Pub.

Justice, Punishment, Treatment: The Correctional Process. Leonard Orland. LC 72-94014. 1973. text ed. 25.00 (ISBN 0-02-923440-9). Free Pr.

Justice Samuel Chase. Jane S. Elsmere. (Illus.). 1981. 14.95 (ISBN 0-937174-00-9). Janevar Pub.

Justice: Selected Readings. Joel Feinberg & Hyman Gross. (Philosophy of Law Ser.). 1977. pap. text ed. 9.95x (ISBN 0-8221-0201-3). Dickenson.

Justice with Faith Today: Selected Letters & Addresses--II. Pedro Arrupe. Ed. by Jerome Aixala. LC 80-81055. 336p. 1980. 8.00 (ISBN 0-912422-51-3); pap. 7.00 (ISBN 0-912422-50-5). Inst Jesuit.

Justice-Worm. Nadya Aisenberg. LC 80-53871. (Chapbook Ser.: No. 3). 64p. (Orig.). Date not set. pap. 4.95 (ISBN 0-937672-02-5). Rowan Tree.

Justices of the United States Supreme Court, 1789-1978, 5 vols. Ed. by Leon Friedman & Fred L. Israel. LC 69-13699. 1980. pap. 75.00 set (ISBN 0-87754-130-2). Chelsea Hse.

Justicia De Deus. 1980. pap. 1.90 (ISBN 0-686-69353-1). Vida Pubs.

Justicia De Dios. Tr. by Morris Williams. (Spanish Bks.). (Span.). 1977. 2.50 (ISBN 0-8297-0759-X). Life Pubs Intl.

Justiciarship in England 1066-1232. F. J. West. (Cambridge Studies in Medieval Life & Thought: No. 12). 1966. 42.95 (ISBN 0-521-06772-3). Cambridge U Pr.

Justification of Linguistic Hypotheses. Rudolf P. Botha. (Janua Linguarum Ser.Maior: No. 84). 1973. text ed. 57.65x (ISBN 90-2792-542-9). Mouton.

Justification of Man by Faith Only. Philipp Melanchthon. Tr. by Nicholas Lesse. LC 79-84123. (English Experience Ser.: No. 942). 204p. 1979. Repr. of 1548 ed. lib. bdg. 15.00 (ISBN 90-221-0942-9). Walter J Johnson.

Justification of Religious Belief. Basil Mitchell. LC 73-17904. 1974. 8.95 (ISBN 0-8164-1152-2). Crossroad NY.

Justification of the Law. Clarence Morris. LC 77-153424. 1971-72. 15.00 (ISBN 0-8122-7639-6); pap. 4.95x (ISBN 0-8122-1030-1, Pa Paperbacks). U of Pa Pr.

Justification: The Doctrine of Karl Barth & a Catholic Reflection. Hans Kung. LC 80-26001. 1981. pap. price not set (ISBN 0-664-24364-9). Westminster.

Justifying Research & Teaching Objectives in Universities. Graeme Norris. 1979. text ed. 26.50x (ISBN 0-566-00243-4, Pub. by Gower Pub Co England). Renouf.

Justifying Violence: Attitudes of American Men. Monica D. Blumenthal et al. LC 74-169101. (Orig.). 1972. cloth 12.00 (ISBN 0-87944-005-8); pap. 7.50 (ISBN 0-87944-004-X). U of Mich Soc Res.

Justin Martyr & the Mosaic Law. Theodore Stylianopoulos. LC 75-22445. (Society of Biblical Literature. Dissertation Ser.). 1975. pap. 7.50 (ISBN 0-89130-018-X, 060120). Scholars Pr Ca.

Justin Winsor: Scholar-Librarian. Ed. by Wayne Cutler & Michael H. Harris. LC 80-19310. (Heritage of Librarianship Ser.: No. 5). 196p. 1980. lib. bdg. 25.00x (ISBN 0-87287-200-9). Libs Unl.

Justine. Lawrence Durrell. 1957. 5.95 o.p. (ISBN 0-525-13807-2); pap. 3.75 (ISBN 0-525-47080-8). Dutton.

Justinian & the Later Roman Empire. John W. Barker. LC 66-11804. 336p. 1976. pap. text ed. 7.95 (ISBN 0-299-03944-7). U of Wis Pr.

Justinian Two of Byzantium. Constance Head. (Illus.). 1972. 19.50x (ISBN 0-299-06030-6). U of Wis Pr.

Justinus Kerners Weg Nach Weinsberg 1809-1819: Die Entpolitisierung eines Romantikers. Lee B. Jennings. LC 80-69125. (Studies in German Literature, Linusitics, & Culture: Vol. 3). (Illus.). 160p. 1981. text ed. 17.00x (ISBN 0-938100-00-9). Camden Hse.

Justo Sierra Y el Mar. Ellen L. Leeder. LC 78-58669. (Coleccion Polymita Ser.). 83p. (Orig., Span.). 1979. pap. 6.95 (ISBN 0-89729-202-2). Ediciones.

Juteopolis. William M. Walker. 570p. 1979. 20.00x o.p. (ISBN 0-7073-0252-8, Pub. by Scottish Academic Pr Scotland). Columbia U Pr.

Jutish Forest: A Study of the Weald of Kent from 450 to 1380 AD. K. P. Witney. (Illus.). 1976. text ed. 37.75x (ISBN 0-485-11165-9, Athlone Pr). Humanities.

Juvenile Adventures of David Ranger, Esq. 1757, 2 vols. in 1. Edward Kimber. LC 74-17443. (Novel in England, 1700-1775 Ser.). 1974. lib. bdg. 50.00 (ISBN 0-8240-1148-1). Garland Pub.

Juvenile Court Reform: Widening the Social Control Net. Thomas G. Blomberg. 256p. 1981. lib. bdg. 20.00 (ISBN 0-89946-087-9). Oelgeschlager.

Juvenile Delinquency: A Book of Readings. 3rd ed. Ed. by Rose Giallombardo. LC 75-35887. 1976. pap. text ed. 15.95 (ISBN 0-471-29726-7). Wiley.

Juvenile Delinquency: A Paradigmatic Perspective. Robert M. Rich. LC 78-53025. 1978. pap. text ed. 10.75x o.p. (ISBN 0-8191-0493-0). U Pr of Amer.

Juvenile Delinquency & Its Origins. R. E. Johnson. LC 78-67263. (ASA Rose Monograph). (Illus.). 1979. 19.95 (ISBN 0-521-22477-2); pap. 6.95 (ISBN 0-521-29516-5). Cambridge U Pr.

Juvenile Delinquency: Theory, Practice & Law. Larry J. Siegel & Joseph J. Senna. (Criminal Justice Ser.). (Illus.). 550p. 1981. text ed. 17.95 (ISBN 0-8299-0414-X). West Pub.

Juvenile Delinquents: Psychodynamic Assessment & Hospital Treatment. Richard C. Marohn et al. LC 80-18398. 300p. 1980. 22.50 (ISBN 0-87630-239-8). Brunner-Mazel.

Juvenile Hypertension. Ed. by Maria New & Lenore Levine. LC 76-51556. 1977. 20.00 (ISBN 0-89004-145-8). Raven.

Juvenile Justice. Willard A. Heaps. LC 74-4011. 1974. 7.95 (ISBN 0-395-28906-8, Clarion). HM.

Juvenile Justice & Injustice. Margaret O. Hyde. (gr. 7 up). 1977. lib. bdg. 7.90 s&l (ISBN 0-531-00122-9). Watts.

Juvenile Justice in America. Clifford E. Simonsen & Marshall S. Gordon. 1979. text ed. write for info. (ISBN 0-02-478350-1). Macmillan.

Juvenile Justice in America. Victor L. Streib. (National University Pubns. Multi-Disciplinary Studies in the Law). 1978. 12.50 (ISBN 0-8046-9212-2). Kennikat.

Juvenile Justice in Britain & the United States: The Balance of Needs & Rights. Phyllida Parsloe. (Library of Social Work). 1978. 21.50x (ISBN 0-7100-8772-1). Routledge & Kegan.

Juvenile Justice System. Ed. by Malcolm W. Klein. LC 75-14632. (Sage Criminal Justice System Annuals: Vol. 5). 1976. 20.00x (ISBN 0-8039-0450-9); pap. 9.95x (ISBN 0-8039-0451-7). Sage.

Juvenile Justice: System & Procedures. Kenneth R. McCreedy. LC 75-6061. 1975. pap. 9.60 (ISBN 0-8273-0437-4); instructor's guide 1.60 (ISBN 0-8273-0438-2). Delmar.

Juvenile Law & Procedure in California. 2nd ed. Ernest Kamm et al. (California Handbook Ser). 1971. pap. text ed. 7.95x (ISBN 0-02-474690-8, 47469). Macmillan.

Juvenile Offender & the Law: A Symposium. D. Hopson, Jr. et al. LC 79-146557. (Symposia on Law & Society Ser). 1968. Repr. lib. bdg. 22.50 (ISBN 0-306-70095-6). Da Capo.

Juvenile Offender: Control, Correction & Treatment. Clemens Bartollas & Stuart J. Miller. 1978. text ed. 17.95 (ISBN 0-205-06069-2, 826069-9). Allyn.

Juvenile Offenders. rev., 6th ed. Clyde B. Vedder. (Illus.). 368p. 1979. text ed. 14.25 (ISBN 0-398-03844-9). C C Thomas.

Juveniles Waiver of Righs: Legal & Psychological Competence. Thomas Grisso. (Perspectives in Law & Psychology Ser.: Vol. 3). 285p. 1981. 32.50 (ISBN 0-306-40526-1, Plenum Pr). Plenum Pub.

Juxtaposition, Encore! James B. Hogins & Gerald R. Bryant, Jr. LC 74-15169. (Illus.). 304p. 1975. pap. text ed. 11.95 (ISBN 0-574-17000-6, 13-5000); instr's guide avail. (ISBN 0-574-17001-4, 13-5001). SRA.

K

K. D. Dufford Hears. David Halliwell. 1970. pap. 4.95 (ISBN 0-571-09248-9, Pub. by Faber & Faber). Merrimack Bk Serv.

K G R A Special Bulletin 1979. (Bulletin: Vol. 8, No. 3). (Illus.). 25p. 1979. pap. 2.50 (ISBN 0-934412-41-3). Geothermal.

K-Speech News. Dianne S. Barad. (gr. 7-12). 1981. manual 15.00. Communication Skill.

K Two: Mountain of Mountains. Reinhold Messner. (Illus.). 176p. 1981. 35.00 (ISBN 0-19-520253-8). Oxford U Pr.

K-2-FDOS: A Floppy Disk Operating System for the 8080. Kenneth B. Welles. (Orig.). 1979. pap. 20.00 (ISBN 0-07-069206-8, BYTE Bks). McGraw.

Kabala of Numbers. Sepharial. LC 80-53342. 423p. 1980. Repr. of 1974 ed. lib. bdg. 12.95x (ISBN 0-89370-627-2). Borgo Pr.

Kabalah. Gershom Scholem. 1978. pap. 5.95 (ISBN 0-452-00483-7, F483, Mer). NAL.

Kabbalah. David S. Milton. LC 79-3360. 360p. 1980. 13.95 (ISBN 0-15-146608-4). HarBraceJ.

Kabbalah & Exodus. Z'ev Halevi. LC 80-50743. (Illus.). 234p. 1980. pap. 7.95 (ISBN 0-394-73950-7). Shambhala Pubns.

Kabbalah & Exodus. Z'Ev B. Halevi. LC 80-50743. 234p. Date not set. pap. 7.95 (ISBN 0-394-73950-7). Random.

Kabir: The Apostle of Hindu-Muslim Unity. Muhammad Hedayetullah. 1978. 14.95 (ISBN 0-89684-042-5, Pub. by Motilal Banarsidass India). Orient Bk Dist.

Kabuki. Masakatsu Gunji. LC 70-82658. (Illus.). 265p. 1965. 85.00 (ISBN 0-87011-090-X). Kodansha.

Kachina Doll Book 1. 1972. pap. 2.50 (ISBN 0-918858-00-3). Fun Pub.

Kachina Doll Book 2. 1973. pap. 2.50 (ISBN 0-918858-01-1). Fun Pub.

Kadin. Beatrice Small. 1977. pap. 2.25 (ISBN 0-380-01699-0, 43190). Avon.

Kadmos & the Possibility of a Semitic Presence in Halladic Greece. Jon C. Billigmeier. (Publications of the Henri Frankfort Foundation Ser.: No. 6). 1980. pap. text ed. write for info. (ISBN 90-6032-110-3). Humanities.

Kaethe Kollwitz. Galerie St. Etienne. (Illus.). 1976. pap. 7.00 (ISBN 0-910810-18-4). Johannes.

Kafka & the Yiddish Theater: Its Impact on His Work. Evelyn T. Beck. LC 75-143763. 1971. 19.50 (ISBN 0-299-05881-6). U of Wis Pr.

Kagok: A Traditional Korean Vocal Form. Coralie Rockwell. LC 72-87568. (D (Monographs), No. 3). (Illus.). 312p. (Orig.). 1972. pap. text ed. 7.50x (ISBN 0-913360-05-8). Asian Music Pub.

Kaguya Hime: The Shimmering Princess. Robert B. Goodman & Robert A. Spicer. Ed. by Victor Johnson. LC 75-18791. (Illus.). (gr. 1-7). 1974. 5.95 (ISBN 0-89610-005-7). Island Her.

Kahlil Gibran: Collection of His Famous Works. 19.00x. Intl Bk Ctr.

Kahlil Gibran Diary for Nineteen Eighty-One. Kahlil Gibran. LC 80-7662. (Illus.). 224p. 1980. ivory bdg. 5.95 (ISBN 0-394-51329-0); blue bdg. 5.95 (ISBN 0-394-51327-4); red bdg. 5.95 (ISBN 0-394-51328-2). Knopf.

Kahlil Gibran Diary for 1979. 1978. 5.00 ea. o.p.; Ivory. (ISBN 0-394-50214-0); Red. (ISBN 0-394-50215-9); Blue. (ISBN 0-394-50216-7). Knopf.

Kai Lung's Golden Hours. Ernest Bramah, pseud. LC 79-53463. (Short Story Index in Reprint Ser.). Date not set. Repr. of 1922 ed. 24.75x (ISBN 0-8486-5011-5). Core Collection. Postponed.

Kainic Acid As a Tool in Neurobiology. Ed. by Edith G. McGeer et al. LC 78-55812. 1978. 29.00 (ISBN 0-89004-279-9). Raven.

Kaiparowits Coal Project & the Environment. Electric Power Research Institute. 1980. text ed. 14.95 (ISBN 0-250-40399-4). Ann Arbor Science.

Kaiser's Memoirs, 1888-1918. Wilhelm. Tr. by Thomas R. Ybarra from Ger. LC 74-22349. 366p. 1977. Repr. of 1922 ed. 22.50 (ISBN 0-86527-113-5). Fertig.

Kalambo Falls Prehistoric Site, 2 vols. J. Desmond Clark. LC 68-25084. (Illus.). 1973. Vol. 1. 75.00 (ISBN 0-521-06962-9); Vol. 2. 125.00 (ISBN 0-521-20009-1). Cambridge U Pr.

Kalasamuddesa of Bhartrhari's Vakyapadiya. P. S. Sharma. 1972. 4.50 (ISBN 0-8426-0414-6). Orient Bk Dist.

Kaleidoscope. Lyman Andrews. LC 74-160170. 1979. 9.95 (ISBN 0-7145-1024-6, Pub. by M Boyars); pap. 5.95 (ISBN 0-7145-1025-4). Merrimack Bk Serv.

Kaleidoscope: A Book of Readings. 2nd ed. Kevin Ryan & James M. Cooper. 1975. pap. text ed. 9.00 o.p. (ISBN 0-395-18623-4); learning guide 6.75 o.p. (ISBN 0-395-19859-3). HM.

Kaleidoscope: A Variety of Short Stories. Ed. by Ralph E. West. (gr. 9-11). 1970. pap. text ed. 3.95x (ISBN 0-88334-030-5). Ind Sch Pr.

Kaleidoscope of Char-a-Bancs & Coaches. Stan Lockwood. (Illus.). 1980. 20.00x (ISBN 0-906116-02-3). Intl Pubns Serv.

Kaleidoscope of Motor Cycling. Dennis Howard. (Old Motor Kaleidoscopes Ser.). (Illus.). 1978. 12.50 o.p. (ISBN 0-906116-00-7, Pub. by Old Motor Magazine England). Motorbooks Intl.

Kaleidoscope of Steam Wagons. R. A. Whitehead. (Illus.). 1979. 15.00x (ISBN 0-906116-10-4). Intl Pubns Serv.

Kaleidoscope of Traction Engines. R. A. Whitehead. (Illus.). 1980. 20.00x (ISBN 0-906116-20-1). Intl Pubns Serv.

Kaleidoscope-Plus. Rosemary Cobham. 160p. 1980. 25.00x (ISBN 0-85683-046-1, Pub. by Shepheard-Walwyn England). State Mutual Bk.

Kaleidoscope: Readings in Education. 3rd ed. Kevin Ryan & James M. Cooper. LC 79-90056. (Illus.). 1980. pap. text ed. 9.50 (ISBN 0-395-28498-8). HM.

Kaleidoscope Series. 3rd ed. Incl. One Thing at Once. Wyatt & Bamman (ISBN 0-201-40867-8). tchr's ed. (ISBN 0-201-40868-6); Two Blades of Grass. Wyatt (ISBN 0-201-40869-4). tchr's ed. (ISBN 0-201-40870-8); Three O'clock Courage. Stowe & Bamman (ISBN 0-201-40871-6); Four Corners of the Sky. Stowe & Bamman (ISBN 0-201-40873-2). tchr's ed. (ISBN 0-201-40874-0); Five Words Long. Dawson (ISBN 0-201-40875-9). tchr's ed. (ISBN 0-201-40876-7); Six Impossible Things. Dawson & Bamman (ISBN 0-201-40877-5). tchr's ed. (ISBN 0-201-40878-3); Seven Is a Handy Figure. Belden & Bamman (ISBN 0-201-40879-1). tchr's ed. (ISBN 0-201-40880-5); Eighth Day of the Week. Belden & Bamman (ISBN 0-201-40881-3). tchr's ed. (ISBN 0-201-40882-1). (gr. 7-12). 1978. pap. text ed. 6.08 ea. (Sch Div); tchr's eds. 6.64 ea. A-W.

Kaleidoscopic Designs & How to Create Them. Norma Y. Finkel & Leslie G. Finkel. 1980. pap. 2.00 (ISBN 0-486-23935-7). Dover.

Kalendarium of Nicholas of Lynn. Ed. by Sigmund Eisner. Tr. by Gary MacEoin from Lat. LC 78-3532. (Chaucer Library Ser.: No. 2). 260p. 1979. 30.00x (ISBN 0-8203-0449-2). U of Ga Pr.

Kalender of Sheepehards. LC 79-11349. 1979. Repr. of 1502 ed. 25.00x (ISBN 0-8201-1329-8). Schol Facsimiles.

Kalevala or, The Land of Heroes, 2 vols. in 1. Elias Lonnrot. 1978. 15.50x (ISBN 0-460-00259-7, Evman). Dutton.

Kalila Wa Dimna: Fables from a Fourteenth Century Arabic Manuscript. Esin Atil. (Illus.). 96p. (Orig.). 1981. 17.50 (ISBN 0-87474-216-1); pap. 9.95 (ISBN 0-87474-215-3). Smithsonian.

Kalinga of Northern Luzon, Philippines. Edward P. Dozier. Ed. by George Spindler & Louise Spindler. (Case Studies in Cultural Anthropology). (Illus.). 112p. pap. text ed. 4.95x (ISBN 0-8290-0279-0). Irvington.

Kaliya Serpent. LC 79-4669. (Childhood Pastimes of Krishna). (Illus.). (gr. 3-6). pap. 2.95 (ISBN 0-89647-009-1). Bala Bks.

Kallias of Sphettos & the Revolt of Athens in 286 B.C. T. Leslie Shear, Jr. (Hesperia: Supplement 17). 1978. 10.00x (ISBN 0-87661-517-5). Am Sch Athens.

Kalman Mikszath. Steven C. Scheer. (World Authors Ser.: Hungary: No. 462). 1977. lib. bdg. 11.95 (ISBN 0-8057-6299-X). Twayne.

Kalu & the Wild Boar. Peter Hallard. LC 72-8916. (Illus.). 96p. (gr. 2-6). 1973. PLB 4.90 o.p. (ISBN 0-531-02600-0). Watts.

Kama Sutra of Vatsyayana. Ed. by Richard Burton. Tr. by F. F. Arbuthnot. 1963. 8.50 (ISBN 0-04-891008-2). Allen Unwin.

Kamala Das. Devindra Kohli. Ed. by C. D. Narasimhaiah. (Indian Writers Ser.). 128p. 1976. 8.50 (ISBN 0-89253-046-4). Ind-US Inc.

Kambuya's Cattle: The Legacy of an African Herdsman. Walter Goldschmidt. 1968. 19.50x (ISBN 0-520-01472-3). U of Cal Pr.

Kameas. Jack Hirschman. Date not set. 4.00 (ISBN 0-686-13974-7). Tree Bks. Postponed.

Kamilaroi & Kurnai: Group Marriage & Relationship, & Marriage by Elopement, the Kurnai Tribe: Their Customs in Peace & War. Lorimer Fison & Alfred W. Howitt. (Maps). 1967. pap. text ed. 15.50x (ISBN 90-6234-053-9). Humanities.

Kanchanjanga. Lawrence Bantleman. 8.00 (ISBN 0-89253-493-1); flexible cloth 4.00 (ISBN 0-89253-494-X). Ind-US Inc.

Kandinsky: The Development of an Abstract Style. Rose-Carol W. Long. (Studies in the History of Art & Architecture). (Illus.). 224p. 1980. 98.00 (ISBN 0-19-817311-3). Oxford U Pr.

Kandinsky: The Language of the Eye. Paul Overy. 1969. pap. 17.50 (ISBN 0-236-17770-2, Pub. by Paul Elek). Merrimack Bk Serv.

Kane & Abel. Jeffrey Archer. 480p. 1981. pap. 3.75 (ISBN 0-449-24376-1, Crest). Fawcett.

Kangaroo. Yuz Aleshkovsky. Tr. by Tamara Glenny from Rus. 1981. 12.95 (ISBN 0-374-18068-7). FS&G.

Kangaroo. Anita Townsend. LC 78-68536. (First Look at Nature Ser.). (Illus.). (gr. 2-4). 1979. 2.50 (ISBN 0-531-09141-4); PLB 6.45 s&l (ISBN 0-531-09152-X). Watts.

Kangaroo for Christmas. James Flora. LC 62-14243. (Illus.). (gr. k-3). 1962. 5.95 o.p. (ISBN 0-15-242026-6, HJ); PLB 4.95 o.p. (ISBN 0-15-242027-4). HarBraceJ.

Kangaroo in the Kitchen: And Other Adventures of an American Family Down Under. Ethel Sloan. LC 77-15437. 1978. 7.95 (ISBN 0-672-52378-7). Bobbs.

Kangaroos. Bernard Stonehouse. LC 77-60872. (Animals of the World Ser.). (Illus.). (gr. 4-8). 1978. PLB 10.65 (ISBN 0-8172-1079-2). Raintree Pubs.

Kangaroos & Other Animals with Pockets. Louis Darling. (Illus.). (gr. 3-7). 1958. PLB 6.48 (ISBN 0-688-31501-1). Morrow.

Kangaroos & Other Creatures from Down Under. LC 77-87164. (Wild, Wild World of Animals Ser.). (Illus.). 1978. lib. bdg. 11.97 (ISBN 0-686-51172-7). Silver.

Kangaroos & Other Creatures from Down Under. Time Life Books Editors. (Wild, Wild World of Animals). (Illus.). 1978. 10.95 (ISBN 0-913948-17-9). Time-Life.

Kangaroos, Koalas, & Other Marsupials. Ellen Rabinowich. LC 78-5805. (First Bks). (Illus.). (gr. 4-6). 1978. PLB 6.45 s&l (ISBN 0-531-01489-4). Watts.

Kangaroos, Opossums, & Other Marsupials. Marie M. Jenkins. LC 75-10798. (Illus.). 160p. (gr. 5 up). 1975. 7.95 o.p. (ISBN 0-8234-0264-9). Holiday.

Kanji ABC. Andrew Dykstra. LC 76-58964. (Illus.). 185p. 1977. pap. 7.95 (ISBN 0-913232-37-8). W Kaufmann.

Kanji & Kana: A Handbook & Dictionary of the Japanese Writing System. Wolfgang Hadamitzky & Mark Spahn. LC 81-50106. 384p. 1981. 11.50 (ISBN 0-8048-1373-6). C E Tuttle.

Kannada: A Cultural Introduction to the Spoken Styles of the Language. William McCormack & M. G. Krishnamurthi. 1966. text ed. 17.50 (ISBN 0-299-03840-8). U of Wis Pr.

Kano Eitoku. Tsuneo Takeda. Tr. by H. Mack Horton & Catherine Kaputa. LC 76-44155. (Japanese Arts Library: Vol. 3). 178p. 1977. 16.95 (ISBN 0-87011-295-3). Kodansha.

Kansas: A Bicentennial History. Kenneth S. Davis. (States & the Nation Ser). (Illus.). 1976. 12.95 (ISBN 0-393-05593-0, Co-Pub by AASLH). Norton.

Kansas: A Guide to the Sunflower State. Federal Writers' Project. 538p. 1939. Repr. 49.00 (ISBN 0-403-02167-7). Somerset Pub.

Kansas a Land of Contrast. rev ed. Robert Richmond. LC 74-77390. 1979. pap. text ed. 10.95x. Forum Pr MO.

Kansas, a Land of Contrasts. rev. ed. Robert W. Richmond. (Illus., Orig.). 1977. text ed. 10.95x o.p. (ISBN 0-88273-010-X); pap. text ed. 7.95x o.p. (ISBN 0-88273-025-8). Forum Pr MO.

Kansas Chronology & Factbook, Vol. 16. R. I. Vexler. 1978. 8.50 (ISBN 0-379-16141-9). Oceana.

Kansas City Catalog. Barbara Unell. 96p. (Orig.). (gr. 4 up). 1980. pap. 7.00 (ISBN 0-8309-0286-4). Independence Pr.

Kansas City Chiefs. Julian May. (NFL Today Ser.). (gr. 4-8). 1980. lib. bdg. 6.45 (ISBN 0-87191-729-7); pap. 2.95 (ISBN 0-89812-232-5). Creative Ed.

Kansas City Chiefs. Julian May. LC 74-2301. (Superbowl Champions Ser). 48p. 1974. PLB 6.45 (ISBN 0-87191-353-4); pap. 2.95 (ISBN 0-89812-087-X). Creative Ed.

Kansas in Turmoil, 1930-1936. Francis W. Schruben. LC 76-93048. 1969. 10.00x o.p. (ISBN 0-8262-0080-X). U of Mo Pr.

Kansas-Nebraska Bill: Party, Section, & the Origin of the Civil War. Gerald Wolff. 1980. lib. bdg. 69.95 (ISBN 0-87700-255-X). Revisionist Pr.

Kansas Prairie Wildflowers. Clenton E. Owensby. (Illus.). 1980. text ed. 15.00 (ISBN 0-8138-0850-2); pap. text ed. 6.95 (ISBN 0-8138-1160-0). Iowa St U Pr.

Kansas State Industrial Directory, 1980. State Industrial Directory Corp. 1980. pap. 35.00 (ISBN 0-89910-002-3). State Indus Dir.

Kant. Ralph C. Walker. (Arguments of the Philosophers Ser.). 1978. 22.00x (ISBN 0-7100-8994-5). Routledge & Kegan.

Kant: An Introduction. O. D. Broad. Ed. by C. Lewy. LC 77-80829. 1978. 47.50 (ISBN 0-521-21755-5); pap. 11.50 (ISBN 0-521-29265-4). Cambridge U Pr.

Kant & His English Critics: A Comparison of Critical & Empirical Philosophy. John Watson. Ed. by Lewis W. Beck. LC 75-32046. (Philosophy of Immanuel Kant Ser.: Vol. 10). 1977. Repr. of 1881 ed. lib. bdg. 37.00 (ISBN 0-8240-2334-X). Garland Pub.

Kanthapura. Raja Rao. LC 63-18637. 1967. Repr. 4.95 (ISBN 0-8112-0168-6). New Directions.

Kant's Aesthetic Theory. Donald W. Crawford. LC 73-15259. 1974. 19.50x (ISBN 0-299-06510-3, 651). U of Wis Pr.

Kant's Analytic. Jonathan Bennett. (Orig.). 1966. 35.50 (ISBN 0-521-04157-0); pap. 9.95x (ISBN 0-521-09389-9, 389). Cambridge U Pr.

Kant's Conception of God. F. E. England. Bd. with Nova Dilucidatio. 1968. Repr. of 1929 ed. text ed. 12.50x (ISBN 0-391-00636-3). Humanities.

Kant's Conceptions of the Categorical Imperative & the Will. Theodosius N. Pelegrinis. 236p. 1980. text ed. 12.50x (ISBN 0-391-01922-8). Humanities.

Kant's Dialectic. Jonathan Bennett. LC 73-89762. 290p. 1974. 38.50 (ISBN 0-521-20420-8); pap. 9.95x (ISBN 0-521-09849-1). Cambridge U Pr.

Kant's Moral Philosophy: An Interpretation of the Categorical Imperative. Viggo Rossvaer. 1979. pap. 23.00x (ISBN 82-00-01881-4, Dist. by Columbia U. Pr.). Universitet.

Kant's Pre-Critical Ethics. 2nd ed. Paul A. Schilpp. Ed. by Lewis W. Beck. LC 75-32043. (Philosophy of Immanuel Kant Ser.: Vol. 6). 1977. Repr. of 1960 ed. lib. bdg. 24.00 (ISBN 0-8240-2330-7). Garland Pub.

Kant's Principle of Personality. Hardy E. Jones. LC 70-157393. 1971. 17.50x (ISBN 0-299-06020-9). U of Wis Pr.

Kant's Theory of Freedom: A Metaphysical Inquiry. W. Michael Hoffman. LC 78-70860. 1978. pap. text ed. 7.50 (ISBN 0-8191-0651-8). U Pr of Amer.

Kant's Theory of Knowledge. H. A. Prichard. Ed. by Lewis W. Beck. LC 75-32042. (Philosophy of Immanuel Kant Ser.: Vol. 5). 1977. Repr. of 1909 ed. lib. bdg. 26.00 (ISBN 0-8240-2329-3). Garland Pub.

Kant's Theory of Knowledge: An Outline of One Central Argument in the Critique of Pure Reason. Graham Bird. (International Library of Philoaophy & Scientific Method Ser.). 1973. Repr. of 1962 ed. text ed. 10.00x (ISBN 0-391-00316-X). Humanities.

Kant's Theory of Mental Activity, a Commentary on the Transcendental Analytic of the Critique of Pure Reason. Robert P. Wolff. 8.00 (ISBN 0-8446-4054-9). Peter Smith.
Kao Shih. Marie Chan. (World Authors Ser.: No. 476). 1978. lib. bdg. 12.50 (ISBN 0-8057-6317-1). Twayne.
Kapalikas & Kalamukhas: Two Lost Saivite Sects. David N. Lorenzen. LC 70-138509. (Center for South & Southeast Asia Studies, UC Berkeley). 1972. 20.00x (ISBN 0-520-01842-7). U of Cal Pr.
Kapetanios: Partisans & Civil War in Greece, 1943-1949. Dominique Eudes. Tr. by John Howe from Fr. LC 72-92032. (Illus.). 400p. 1973. 11.50 o.p. (ISBN 0-85345-275-X, CL-275X). Monthly Rev.
Kaposi's Sarcoma. Ed. by Ch. L. Olweny et al. (Antibodies & Chemotherapy: Vol. 29). (Illus.). 200p. 1981. 72.00 (ISBN 3-8055-2076-X). S Karger.
Kappillan of Malta. Nicholas Monsarrat. 1974. 8.95 o.p. (ISBN 0-688-00243-9). Morrow.
Karaite Studies. Ed. by Philip Birnbaum. LC 76-136771. 1971. Repr. 12.50 o.p. (ISBN 0-87203-027-X). Hermon.
Karamazov Companion: Commentary on the Genesis, Language, & Style of Dostoevsky's Novel. Victor Terras. 400p. 1981. 30.00 (ISBN 0-299-08310-1); pap. text ed. 9.95 (ISBN 0-299-08314-4). U of Wis Pr.
Karamzin's Memoir on Ancient & Modern Russia. Richard Pipes. LC 59-6484. 1966. pap. text ed. 4.95x (ISBN 0-689-70157-8, 83). Atheneum.
Karari. Ismat H. Zulfo. xv, 252p. 1980. 10.50 (ISBN 0-208-09495-4, SSC) Shoe String.
Karate: Art of Empty Hand Fighting. Hidetaka Nishiyama & Richard C. Brown. LC 59-10409. (Illus.). (gr. 9 up). 1960. 22.50 (ISBN 0-8048-0340-4). C E Tuttle.
Karate: Basic Principles. A. Pfluger. 1970. pap. 2.95 (ISBN 0-06-463307-1, EH 307, EH). Har-Row.
Karate Breaking Techniques: With Practical Applications to Self-Defense. Jack Hibbard. LC 80-50893. (Illus.). 1981. 23.50 (ISBN 0-8048-1225-X). C E Tuttle.
Karate-Do-Kyohan: The Master Text. Gichin Funakoshi. Tr. by Tsutomu Oshima from Japanese. LC 72-90228. (Illus.). 370p. 1973. 22.50 (ISBN 0-87011-190-6). Kodansha.
Karate Experience: A Way of Life. Randall G. Hassell. LC 80-53429. 110p. 1981. 9.95 (ISBN 0-8048-1348-5). C E Tuttle.
Karate for Young People. Russell Kozuki. LC 73-93590. (Athletic Institute Ser.). (Illus.). 128p. (gr. 3 up). 1974. 6.95 (ISBN 0-8069-4074-3); PLB 6.69 (ISBN 0-8069-4075-1). Sterling.
Karate Kiai! Perfecting Your Power. A. Pfluger. Tr. by Manly Banister from Ger. LC 76-58748. (Illus.). 1977. 7.95 (ISBN 0-8069-4448-X); lib. bdg. 7.49 (ISBN 0-8069-4449-8). Sterling.
Karate Pratique, Vol. 2. Masatoshi Nakayama & Donn F. Draeger. (Illus., Orig., Fr.). 1965. pap. 2.75 o.p. (ISBN 0-8048-0338-2). C E Tuttle.
Karate: Self Defense & Traditional Sport Forms. Bruce Tegner. LC 73-9742. (Illus.). 160p. (Orig.). 1973. pap. 2.95 (ISBN 0-87407-023-6). Thor.
Karate: Self-Taught. Eric Dominy. (Everyday Handbook Ser.). (Illus.). 192p. 1976. pap. 1.95 o.p. (ISBN 0-06-463441-8). B&N.
Karate: The Energy Connection. Scott Russell. 1976. 7.95 o.s.i. (ISBN 0-440-04386-7). Delacorte.
Karate Within Your Grasp. Carlos Sampayo. LC 76-1170. (Illus.). 160p. (YA) 1976. 5.95 o.p. (ISBN 0-8069-4102-2); PLB 6.69 o.p. (ISBN 0-8069-4103-0). Sterling.
Karel Appel: Works on Paper. Ed. by Jean-Clarence Lambert. Tr. by Kenneth White. LC 79-92227. (Illus.). 256p. 1980. 65.00 (ISBN 0-89659-069-0); limited ed. 2500.00 (ISBN 0-89659-140-9). Abbeville Pr.
Karel Capek. William E. Harkins. LC 62-10148. 1962. 20.00x (ISBN 0-231-02512-2). Columbia U Pr.
Karel the Robot: A Gentle Introduction to the Art of Programming. Richard E. Pattis. 128p. 1981. pap. text ed. 8.95 (ISBN 0-471-08928-1). Wiley.
Karen. Marie Killilea. pap. 1.75 o.s.i. (ISBN 0-440-14376-4). Dell.
Kari, the Elephant. Dhan G. Mukerji. (Illus.). (gr. 5-7). 1922. PLB 7.95 o.p. (ISBN 0-525-33008-9). Dutton.
Karl Barth Letters: 1961 to 1968. Karl Barth. Tr. by Geoffrey W. Bromiley. LC 80-29140. 288p. 1981. 14.95 (ISBN 0-8028-3536-8). Eerdmans.
Karl Barth: Studies of His Theological Method. S. W. Sykes. 214p. 1979. text ed. 29.00x (ISBN 0-19-826649-9). Oxford U Pr.
Karl Hofer. Ida K. Rigby. LC 75-23811. (Outstanding Dissertations in the Fine Arts - 20th Century). (Illus.). 1976. lib. bdg. 45.00 (ISBN 0-8240-2005-7). Garland Pub.
Karl Knaths: Five Decades of Painting. Intro. by Charles Eaton. LC 73-82318. (Illus.). 160p. 1973. pap. 8.00 (ISBN 0-88397-056-2). Intl Exhibit Foun.
Karl Lark-Horovitz, Pioneer in Solid State Physics. V. A. Johnson. LC 77-91464. (Men of Physics Ser.). 1970. 22.00 (ISBN 0-08-006581-3); pap. 10.75 (ISBN 0-08-006580-5). Pergamon.
Karl Marx. Ed. by Tom Bottomore. 194p. 1979. 29.00x (ISBN 0-631-10961-7, Pub. by Basil Blackwell); pap. 10.50x (ISBN 0-631-11061-5). Biblio Dist.
Karl Marx. Michael Evans. (Political Thinkers). 1975. text ed. 17.95x (ISBN 0-04-921020-3); pap. text ed. 7.50x o.p. (ISBN 0-04-921021-1). Allen Unwin.
Karl Marx. Richard Olsen. (World Leaders Ser.: No. 70). 1978. lib. bdg. 11.95 (ISBN 0-8057-7678-8). Twayne.
Karl Marx. Julius Smulkstys. (World Authors Ser.: Germany: No. 296). 1974. lib. bdg. 10.95 (ISBN 0-8057-2595-4). Twayne.
Karl Marx. Murray Wolfson. 1969. pap. 3.00 (ISBN 0-231-03146-7, 108). Columbia U Pr.
Karl Marx. Allen Wood. (Arguments of the Philosophers Ser.). 280p. 1981. 25.00 (ISBN 0-7100-0672-1). Routledge & Kegan.
Karl Marx: An Intimate Biography. abr. ed. Saul K. Padover. (Illus.). 1980. pap. 3.50 (ISBN 0-451-61897-1, ME1897, Ment). NAL.
Karl Marx & Frederick Engels on Literature & Art. Karl Marx & Frederick Engels. Ed. by Lee Baxandall & Stefan Morawski. (Documents on Marxist Aesthetics: Vol.I). 192p. 1974. 10.00 (ISBN 0-88477-000-1); pap. 4.25 (ISBN 0-88477-001-X). Intl General.
Karl Marx & World Literature. S. S. Prawer. 1976. 39.95x (ISBN 0-19-815745-2). Oxford U Pr.
Karl Marx: As a Religious Type. Sergei Bulgakov. Ed. by Virgil Lang. Tr. by Luba Barna from Rus. LC 78-78117. 200p. 1980. 12.50 (ISBN 0-913124-34-6). Nordland Pub.
Karl Marx-Frederick Engels: Collected Works, Vol. 14. 1980. 8.50 (ISBN 0-7178-0514-X). Intl Pub Co.
Karl Marx-Frederick Engels: Collected Works, Vol. 16. (Illus.). 8.50 (ISBN 0-7178-0516-6). Intl Pub Co.
Karl Marx: The Roots of His Thought. Johan Van Der Hoeven. (Bidragen Tot De Filosophie: No. 8). (Orig.). 1976. pap. text ed. 14.00x (ISBN 90-232-1388-2). Humanities.
Karl Marx: The Roots of His Thought. Johan Van Der Hoeven. 1976. 6.95x (ISBN 0-88906-001-0). Wedge Pub.
Karl Marx's Philosophy of Man. John Plamenatz. 292p. 1975. 37.50x (ISBN 0-19-824551-3); pap. 13.95 (ISBN 0-19-824649-8). Oxford U Pr.
Karl Marx's Theory of Revolution, Part One: The State & Bureaucracy, 2 vols. Hal Draper. LC 76-26319. 1977. 28.50 set o.p. (ISBN 0-85345-387-X, CL-387-X). Monthly Rev.
Karl Rahner: An Introduction to His Theology. Karl-Heinz Weger. 1980. 10.95 (ISBN 0-8164-0127-6). Crossroad NY.
Karl Rahner: His Life, Thought & Work. Herbert Vorgrimler. Tr. by Edward Quinn. 1966. pap. 1.95 (ISBN 0-8091-1609-X, Deus). Paulist Pr.
Karl Rahner, S. J., Discoverer in Theology. William J. Kelly. 320p. 24.95 (ISBN 0-87462-521-1). Marquette.
Karl Schranz 7-Day Ski System. Karl Schranz. Tr. by Curtis W. Casewit. (Illus.). 112p. 1974. 6.95 o.s.i. (ISBN 0-02-607300-5). Macmillan.
Karl Shapiro. Joseph Reino. (United States Authors Ser.: No. 404). 1981. lib. bdg. 12.95 (ISBN 0-8057-7333-9). Twayne.
Karluk: The Great Untold Story of Arctic Exploration. William L. McKinley. (RL 10). 1978. pap. 1.95 o.p. (ISBN 0-451-08074-2, J8074, Sig). NAL.
Karma. 10th ed. Annie Besant. 1975. 3.25 (ISBN 0-8356-7035-X). Theos Pub Hse.
Karma. 2nd rev. ed. Ed. by Virginia Hanson. Rosemarie Stewart. 200p. 1980. pap. write for info. (ISBN 0-8356-0543-4). Theos Pub Hse.
Karma & Rebirth. Christmas Humphreys. (Wisdom of the East Ser.). 6.50 (ISBN 0-7195-0684-0). Paragon.
Karma & Rebirth in Classical Indian Traditions. Wendy D. O'Flaherty. 400p. 1980. 27.50x (ISBN 0-520-03923-8). U of Cal Pr.
Karma Kola. Gita Mehta. 1981. pap. 5.95 (ISBN 0-671-25084-1, Touchstone). S&S.
Karma Mimansa Sutras of Jaimini. Jaimini. 91p. 1980. pap. 5.50. KMS Pr Co.
Karma; Nirvana: Two Buddhist Tales. Paul Carus. LC 73-82781. (Illus.). 160p. 1973. 10.95 (ISBN 0-87548-249-X); pap. 4.95. Open Court.
Karmic Astrology: The Karma of the Now, Vol. 4. Martin Schulman. 1978. pap. 4.95 (ISBN 0-87728-288-9). Weiser.
Karmic Relationships. Martin Schulman. 1981. pap. 6.951311 (ISBN 0-686-69318-3). Weiser.
Karmic Relationships, 8 vols. Rudolf Steiner. Incl. Vol. 1. o.p. (ISBN 0-685-36127-6); Vol. 2. 12.50 (ISBN 0-685-36128-4); Vol. 3. 9.75 (ISBN 0-685-36129-2); Vol. 4. o.p. (ISBN 0-685-36130-6); Vol. 5. o.p. (ISBN 0-685-36131-4); Vol. 6. 9.75 (ISBN 0-685-36132-2); Vol. 7. 8.50 (ISBN 0-685-36133-0); Vol. 8. 8.50 (ISBN 0-685-36134-9). Anthroposophic.
Karna. Neela D'Souza. 105p. (gr. 6-8). 1969. 1.00 (ISBN 0-88253-328-2). Ind-US Inc.
Karna & Other Poems. Rohini Gupta. 1976. 8.00 (ISBN 0-89253-825-2); flexible cloth 4.80 (ISBN 0-89253-826-0). Ind-US Inc.
Karok Myths. A. L. Kroeber & E. W. Gifford. Ed. by Grace Buzaljko. 450p. 1980. 25.00 (ISBN 0-520-03870-3). U of Cal Pr.
Karpov-Korchnoi 1974. W. R. Hartston & R. D. Keene. (Illus.). 94p. 1975. pap. 3.95 o.p. (ISBN 0-19-217530-0). Oxford U Pr.
Karst Hydrogeology. Petar Milanovic. 1981. 29.00 (ISBN 0-918334-36-5). WRP.
Karst Hydrology & Physical Speleology & Physical Speleology. A. Boegli. (Illus.). 300p. 1980. 38.00 (ISBN 0-387-10098-9). Springer-Verlag.
Karst Landforms. Marjorie M. Sweeting. LC 72-172813. (Illus.). 380p. 1973. 30.00x (ISBN 0-231-03623-X). Columbia U Pr.
Kart Racing. Jerry Leonard. LC 79-26985. (Illus.). 160p. (gr. 7 up). 1980. PLB 7.79 (ISBN 0-671-34033-6). Messner.
Karting: Racing's Fast Little Cars. Rosemary G. Washington. LC 80-12385. (Superwheels & Thrill Sports Bks.). (Illus.). (YA) (gr. 4 up). 1980. PLB 6.95g (ISBN 0-8225-0435-9). Lerner Pubns.
Kartusch. Stephen Cosgrove. (Creative Fantasies Ser.). (Illus.). (gr. k-4). 1979. PLB 6.95 (ISBN 0-87191-689-4). Creative Ed.
Kashmir Story. Brij L. Sharma. 1967. 7.50x (ISBN 0-210-98107-5). Asia.
Kashmiri Passions. Clarissa Ross. (Orig.). 1978. pap. 2.25 o.s.i. (ISBN 0-446-82839-4). Warner Bks.
Kassel Manuscript of Bede's Historia Ecclesiastica Gentis Anglorum & Its Old English Material. T. J. Van Els. (Illus.). 280p. 1972. text ed. 30.25x (ISBN 0-685-27425-X, 90-232-0962-1). Humanities.
Kate. Brian Cleeve. 1978. pap. 2.25 o.p. (ISBN 0-425-03827-0, Medallion). Berkley Pub.
Kate Alone. Patricia L. Gauch. 112p. (YA) (gr. 5-12). 1980. 7.95 (ISBN 0-399-20738-4). Putnam.
Kate & Mona in the Jungle. Amy Aitken. LC 80-15110. (Illus.). 32p. (gr. k-2). 1980. 8.95 (ISBN 0-87888-167-0). Bradbury Pr.
Kate & the Island. Catherine Storr. (Illus.). 1978. 8.95 (ISBN 0-571-10119-4, Pub. by Faber & Faber). Merrimack Bk Serv.
Kate Chopin: A Critical Biography. Per Seyerstead. LC 77-88740. (Southern Literary Ser.). (Illus.). 256p. 1980. pap. 5.95 (ISBN 0-8071-0678-X). La State U Pr.
Kate Greenaway Book: A Collection of Illustration, Verse, & Text. Ed. by Bryan Holme. LC 76-7904. (Illus.). 144p. 1976. 8.95 o.p. (ISBN 0-670-41183-3, Studio). Viking Pr.
Kate Greenaway: Catalogue of an Exhibition of Original Artworks & Related Materials Selected from the Frances Hooper Collection at the Hunt Institute. Bernadette Callery et al. Compiled by Elizabeth Mosimann. (Illus.). 112p. 1981. 22.00x (ISBN 0-913196-33-9). Hunt Inst Botanical.
Kate Greenaway Paper Dolls. Kathy Allert. (Illus.). 32p. (Orig.). 1981. pap. price not set (ISBN 0-486-24153-X). Dover.
Kate Ryder. Hester Burton. LC 75-8576. (Illus.). 160p. (gr. 7 up). 1975. 8.95 (ISBN 0-690-00978-X, TYC-J). T Y Crowell.
Kate Shelley & the Midnight Express. Wesley Porter. (Illus.). 1979. (gr. 5-8) 2.95 (ISBN 0-531-02504-7); PLB 5.90 s&l (gr. k-3) (ISBN 0-531-04083-6). Watts.
Kate's Death: Poems. Emery George. 1980. 8.95 (ISBN 0-88233-583-9); pap. 3.95 (ISBN 0-88233-584-7). Ardis Pubs.
Kate's Secret Riddle Book. Sid Fleischman. (Easy-Read Story Books). (Illus.). (gr. k-3). 1977. PLB 6.45 s&l (ISBN 0-531-00377-9). Watts.
Katha Upanishad. Tr. by Swami Gambhirananda from Sanskrit. (Upanishads with Shankara's Commentary Ser.). 136p. pap. 2.95 (ISBN 0-87481-201-1). Vedanta Pr.
Katharine Tynan. Ann C. Fallon. (English Authors Ser.: No. 272). 1979. 13.50 (ISBN 0-8057-6754-1). Twayne.
Kathe Kollwitz - Jake Zeitlin: Jake Zeitlin Bookshop & Gallery-1937; The Art Museum & Galleries, California State University, Long Beach-1979. Ed. by Constance Glenn. (Illus.). 64p. (Orig.). 1979. pap. 8.00 (ISBN 0-936270-14-4). Art Mus Gall.
Katherine. Anya Seton. 640p. 1978. pap. 2.75 (ISBN 0-449-24052-5, Crest). Fawcett.
Katherine. Antonia Van-Loon. 320p. 1981. pap. 2.50 (ISBN 0-449-24381-8, Crest). Fawcett.
Katherine Anne Porter. John E. Hardy. LC 72-79929. (Modern Literature Ser.). 1973. 10.95 (ISBN 0-8044-2351-2). Ungar.
Katherine Anne Porter. George Hendrick. (U. S. Authors Ser.: No. 90). 1965. lib. bdg. 9.95 (ISBN 0-8057-0592-9). Twayne.
Katherine Anne Porter. E. H. Lopez. 352p. 1981. 14.95 (ISBN 0-316-53199-5). Little.
Katherine Mansfield. Saralyn R. Daly. (English Authors Ser.: No. 23). 1965. lib. bdg. 9.95 (ISBN 0-8057-1372-7). Twayne.
Katherine Tree. Nan Morrison. (YA) 5.95 (ISBN 0-685-07440-4, Avalon). Bouregy.
Kathie Webber's Book of Autumn Cooking. Kathie Webber. (Illus.). 1978. 14.95 (ISBN 0-241-89820-X, Pub. by Hamish Hamilton England). David & Charles.
Kathie Webber's Book of Spring Cooking. Kathie Webber. (Illus.). 1978. 14.95 (ISBN 0-241-89818-8, Pub. by Hamish Hamilton England). David & Charles.
Kathie Webber's Book of Summer Cooking. Kathie Webber. (Illus.). 1978. 14.95 (ISBN 0-241-89819-6, Pub. by Hamish Hamilton England). David & Charles.
Kathie Webber's Book of Winter Cooking. Kathie Webber. 1979. 14.95 (ISBN 0-241-89821-8, Pub. by Hamish Hamilton England). David & Charles.
Kathleen. Dianne Cannon. LC 76-13241. 1977. 8.95 (ISBN 0-87949-072-1). Ashley Bks.
Kathleen. Francine Rivers. 1979. pap. 2.25 (ISBN 0-515-04726-0). Jove Pubns.
Kathleen, Please Come Home. Scott O'Dell. (gr. 6-12). 1980. pap. 1.50 (ISBN 0-440-94283-7, LFL). Dell.
Kathmandu & the Kingdom of Nepal. 2nd ed. Praskah A. Raj. (Illus.). 1978. pap. 3.95 o.p. (ISBN 0-908086-01-6, Pub. by Two Continents). Hippocrene Bks.
Kathy. Charles P. Conn & Barbara Miller. 1981. pap. 2.50 (ISBN 0-425-04825-X). Berkley Pub.
Kathy Whitworth. Patricia M. Eldred. LC 75-1358. (New Creative Education Superstar Bks.). (Illus.). 32p. (gr. 3-6). 1975. PLB 5.50 o.p. (ISBN 0-87191-436-0). Creative Ed.
Katia: Wife Before God. Alexandre Tarsaidze. (Illus.). 1970. 12.95 (ISBN 0-02-616270-9). Macmillan.
Katie. Margaret A. Graham. 1981. pap. 2.95 (ISBN 0-8423-2028-8). Tyndale.
Katie. Clara B. Miller. 288p. 1974. pap. 2.95 (ISBN 0-8024-4524-1). Moody.
Katie: An Impertinent Fairy Tale. B. J. Chute. 1978. 7.95 o.p. (ISBN 0-525-13826-9). Dutton.
Katie John & Heathcliff. Mary Calhoun. LC 80-7770. 160p. (gr. 3-6). 1980. 8.95 (ISBN 0-06-020931-3, HarpJ); PLB 8.79 (ISBN 0-06-020932-1). Har-Row.
Katie John & Heathcliff. Mary Calhoun. LC 80-7770. 160p. (gr. 3-6). 1981. pap. 1.95 (ISBN 0-06-440120-0, Trophy). Har-Row.
Katie King: A Voice from Beyond. Gil Roller. 1976. pap. 1.50 o.p. (ISBN 0-445-03100-X). Popular Lib.
Katie McCrary & the Wiggins Crusade. Kathleen C. Phillips. (gr. 4-7). 1980. 9.95 (ISBN 0-525-66717-2). Elsevier-Nelson.
Katie Mulholland. Catherine Cookson. 512p. 1981. pap. 2.75 (ISBN 0-553-13935-5). Bantam.
Katie's Treasure. Eda Stertz. (Pathfinder Ser.). 144p. (gr. 2-6). 1980. pap. 2.50 (ISBN 0-310-37921-0, 0018P). Zondervan.
Katmandu Contract. Nick Carter. (Nick Carter Ser.). 176p. (Orig.). 1981. pap. 2.25 (ISBN 0-441-43201-8). Charter Bks.
Katsura: A Princely Retreat. Akira Naito. Tr. by Charles S. Terry from Jap. LC 75-30183. 182p. 1977. 55.00 (ISBN 0-87011-271-6). Kodansha.
Katy No-Pocket. Emmy Payne. (gr. 1-3). 1969. reinforced bdg. 9.95 (ISBN 0-395-17104-0). HM.
Katy Railroad & the Last Frontier. V. V. Masterson. (Illus.). 312p. 1981. 12.95 (ISBN 0-8061-0255-1). U of Okla Pr.
Katyn. Louis Fitzgibbon. (Illus.). 1979. Repr. of 1971 ed. 12.00 (ISBN 0-911038-25-6, Inst Hist Rev); pap. 8.00 (ISBN 0-911038-60-4). Noontide.
Kauai. Bob Krauss. LC 77-82233. (Illus.). 1978. pap. 4.95 (ISBN 0-89610-067-7). Island Her.
Kauai, & the Park Country of Hawaii. Robert Wenkam. Ed. by Kenneth Brower. (Illus.). 1969. pap. 3.95 o.p. (ISBN 0-345-21557-5). Ballantine.
Kauai: Hawaii's Garden Island. Robert Wenkam. (Illus.). 1979. 25.00 (ISBN 0-528-81040-5). Rand.
Kawaiisu Mythology: An Oral Tradition of South-Central California. Maurice L. Zigmond. (Anthropological Papers: No. 18). (Illus.). 252p. (Orig.). 1980. pap. 11.95 (ISBN 0-87919-089-2). Ballena Pr.
Kawasaki K2650 Fours Nineteen Seventy-Six to Nineteen Eighty Service, Repair, Performance. Ed. by Eric Jorgensen. (Illus.). 1979. pap. 9.95 (ISBN 0-89287-296-9, M358). Clymer Pubns.

Kawasaki Nine Hundred & 1000cc Four, 1973-1979: Includes Shaft Drive Service Repair Performance. Anton Vesely. Ed. by Eric Jorgensen. (Illus.). 324p. (Orig.). 1980. pap. text ed. 9.95 (ISBN 0-89287-321-3, M359). Clymer Pubns.

Kawasaki Service - Repair Handbook: 250 & 350cc Twins, All Years. Tim Lockwood. Ed. by Jeff Robinson. (Illus.). 144p. 1972. pap. text ed. 9.95 (ISBN 0-89287-016-8, M352). Clymer Pubns.

Kawasaki Service--Repair Handbook: 80-450cc Singles, 1966-1977. Ed. by Jeff Robinson. (Illus.). 1977. pap. 9.95 (ISBN 0-89287-152-0, M350). Clymer Pubns.

Kawasaki Service & Repair Handbook: Kz400 Twins, 1974-1979. Ed. by Jeff Robinson. (Illus.). 1979. pap. 9.95 (ISBN 0-89287-138-5, M355). Clymer Pubns.

Kawasaki Snowmobiles Nineteen Seventy-Six to Nineteen Eighty: Service, Repair, Maintenance. Mike Bishop. Ed. by Eric Jorgensen. (Illus.). 152p. (Orig.). 1980. pap. text ed. 8.95 (ISBN 0-89287-320-5, X995). Clymer Pubns.

Kawasaki: 250-750cc Triples 1969-1979--Service, Repair, Maintenance Handbook. 4th ed. Ed. by Eric Jorgensen. (Illus.). 1978. pap. 9.95 (ISBN 0-89287-192-X, M353). Clymer Pubns.

Kawasaki 900 & 1000cc Fours, 1973-1979: Service, Repair, Performance. Clymer Publications. Ed. by Jeff Robinson. (Illus.). 1978. pap. 8.50 (ISBN 0-89287-321-3, M359). Clymer Pubns.

Kawi Lexicon. Soewojo Wojowasito. Ed. by Roger F. Mills. LC 78-57221. (Michigan Papers on South & Southeast Asia: No. 17). 636p. (Orig.). 1980. pap. 13.00x (ISBN 0-89148-017-X). Ctr S&SE Asian.

Kay Price & Stella Pajunas: Work for a Poetry Context 1967-1969. Vito Acconci. LC 77-77011. 1981. pap. text ed. 10.95 (ISBN 0-915570-08-4). Oolp Pr.

K.C. A History of Kansas City, Missouri. A. Theodore Brown & Lyle W. Dorsett. (Western Urban History Ser.). (Illus.). 320p. 1980. pap. 6.95 (ISBN 0-87108-563-1). Pruett.

K.C. A History of Kansas City, Missouri. A. Theordore Brown & Lyle W. Dorsett. (Western Urban History Ser.). (Illus.). 1978. 13.50 (ISBN 0-87108-526-7); pap. 6.95 (ISBN 0-87108-563-1). Pruett.

Keaton. Rudi Blesh. 1971. pap. 3.95 o.s.i. (ISBN 0-02-012090-7, Collier). Macmillan.

Keaton: The Man Who Wouldn't Lie Down. Tom Dardis. 1980. pap. 4.95 (ISBN 0-14-005701-3). Penguin.

Keats: A Collection of Critical Essays. Ed. by Walter J. Bate. (Orig.). 1964. pap. 2.95 (ISBN 0-13-514745-X, STC43, Spec). P-H.

Keats & the Critics, 1848-1900. Thomas M. Harwell. (Salzburg Studies in English Literature, Romantic Reassessment: No. 2). 1972. pap. text ed. 25.00x (ISBN 0-391-01399-8). Humanities.

Keats Metaphors for the Poetic Imagination. Mario L. D'Avanzo. LC 67-17149. 1967. 12.75 o.p. (ISBN 0-8223-0043-5). Duke.

Keats-Poems of Eighteen Twenty. D. G. Gillham. 224p. 1969. pap. text ed. 9.95x (ISBN 0-7121-0141-1, Pub. by Macdonald & Evans England). Intl Ideas.

Keats Reviewed by His Contemporaries: A Collection of Notices for the Years 1816-1821. Lewis M. Schwartz. LC 72-12779. 1973. 13.50 (ISBN 0-8108-0577-4). Scarecrow.

Keats, Skepticism, & the Religion of Beauty. Ronald A. Sharp. LC 78-21463. 208p. 1979. 14.00x (ISBN 0-8203-0470-0). U of Ga Pr.

Keats: The Critical Heritage. Ed. by G. M. Matthews. 1971. 36.00x (ISBN 0-7100-7147-7). Routledge & Kegan.

Kedang: A Study of the Collective Thought of an Eastern Indonesian People. R. H. Barnes. (Oxford Monographs in Social Anthropology). (Illus.). 359p. 1974. 29.50x (ISBN 0-19-823185-7). Oxford U Pr.

Keelboat Age on Western Waters. Leland D. Baldwin. LC 41-10342. (Illus.). x, 264p. 1980. pap. 5.95 (ISBN 0-8229-5319-6). U of Pittsburgh Pr.

Keep Cooking: The Maine Way. Marjorie Standish. 8.95 (ISBN 0-930096-02-9). G Gannett.

Keep Cooking the Maine Way. 5th ed. Marjorie Standish. (Illus.). 260p. 1980. 8.95 (ISBN 0-930096-15-0). G Gannett.

Keep 'em Rolling. Stephen W. Meader. LC 67-17155. (Illus.). (gr. 7 up). 1967. 4.95 o.p. (ISBN 0-15-242195-5, HJ). HarBraceJ.

Keep Healthy Keep Active. William E. Jensen & Donna Winters. 1979. pap. 1.95 (ISBN 0-910286-73-6). Boxwood.

Keep in Touch. Herman C. Ahrens, Jr. (Illus.). 96p. (Orig.). (gr. 7-12). 1978. pap. 4.95 (ISBN 0-8298-0351-3). Pilgrim NY.

Keep in Touch. Al Bryant. 1981. 8.95. Word Bks.

Keep It Peaking. Hugh Fox. (Rockbottom Proseworks Ser.). Date not set. 15.00 o.p. (ISBN 0-930012-17-8, 79-87598); pap. 5.00 o.p. (ISBN 0-930012-16-X). Mudborn. Postponed.

Keep It Simple. Marion Burrows. 256p. 1981. 10.95 (ISBN 0-688-00450-4). Morrow.

Keep off the Grass: A Scientific Enquiry into the Biological Effects of Marijuana. Gabriel G. Nahas. (Illus.). 1979. 16.50 (ISBN 0-08-023779-7); pap. 9.95 (ISBN 0-08-023780-0). Pergamon.

Keep on Keeping on. Harold L. Fickett, Jr. LC 75-23517. 160p. (Orig.). 1977. pap. 2.25 (ISBN 0-8307-0371-3, S311-1-00). Regal.

Keep Running, Allen! Clyde R. Bulla. LC 77-23311. (Illus.). (gr. k-2). 1978. 6.95 (ISBN 0-690-01374-4, TYC-J); PLB 7.89 (ISBN 0-690-01375-2). T Y Crowell.

Keep Stompin' till the Music Stops. Stella Pevsner. LC 76-27845. (gr. 4-7). 1977. 6.95 (ISBN 0-395-28875-4, Clarion). HM.

Keep the Aspidistra Flying. George Orwell. LC 56-5326. 1969. pap. 4.95 (ISBN 0-15-646899-9, HPL38, HPL). HarBraceJ.

Keep the Last Bullet for Yourself: The True Story of Custer's Last Stand. new ed. Thomas B. Marquis. Ed. by Keith Irvine & Robert Faherty. LC 75-39093. (Illus.). 192p. 1976. 12.50 (ISBN 0-917256-02-6); pap. 5.95 (ISBN 0-917256-14-X). Ref Pubns.

Keep the Last Bullet for Yourself: The True Story of Custer's Last Stand. Thomas B. Marquis. Ed. by Keith Irvine & Robert Faherty. LC 75-39093. (Illus.). 1980. pap. 5.95 (ISBN 0-917256-14-X). Ref Pubns.

Keep to the Vascular Plants of Northwest California. J. P. Smith & J. O. Sawyer. 1981. pap. price not set. Mad River.

Keep Tropical Fish. Clifford W. Emmens. (Illus.). (YA) (gr. 7-10). 6.95 (ISBN 0-87666-091-X, H910). TFH Pubns.

Keep Up the Good Work, Charlie Brown. Charles M. Schulz. (Peanuts Ser.). (Illus.). 1979. pap. 1.50 (ISBN 0-449-23748-6, Crest). Fawcett.

Keep Your Face to the Sunshine: A Lost Chapter in the History of Woman Suffrage. Pauline Meyer. LC 80-68583. (Illus.). 64p. 1980. pap. 6.95 (ISBN 0-936998-00-8). Alcott Pr.

Keep Your Head Up, Mr. Putnam. Peter Putnam. LC 52-5468. 1952. lib. bdg. 9.87 o.s.i. (ISBN 0-06-013441-0, HarpT). Har-Row.

Keep Your Heart in Shape. Siegfried Heyden. 96p. (Orig.). 1981. pap. 1.95 (ISBN 0-8326-2249-4, 7446). Delair.

Keep Your Heart Running. Paul J. Kiell & Joseph Frelinghuysen. 1976. 11.95 (ISBN 0-87691-182-3). Winchester Pr.

Keep Your Pigeons Flying. 2nd ed. Leon F. Whitney. (Illus.). 1968. 9.95 o.p. (ISBN 0-571-04649-5, Pub. by Faber & Faber). Merrimack Bk Serv.

Keep Yourself Pure. B. Charles Hostetter. 1957. pap. 0.95 deluxe ed. (ISBN 0-8024-4521-7). Moody.

Keepers. B. M. Crouch. 368p. 1980. 24.75 (ISBN 0-398-03970-4). C C Thomas.

Keepers of the House. Shirley A. Grau. 1976. pap. 1.50 o.p. (ISBN 0-449-23031-7, Crest). Fawcett.

Keepers of the Springs: And Other Messages from Mister Jones, Meet the Master. Peter Marshall. (Inspirational Classics Ser). 1962. 4.95 (ISBN 0-8007-1011-8). Revell.

Keeping a Cow. Val Spreckley. LC 78-74083. 1979. 11.95 (ISBN 0-7153-7655-1). David & Charles.

Keeping a Family Cow. Joan S. Grohman. (Illus.). 192p. 1981. 9.95 (ISBN 0-684-16867-7, ScribT). Scribner.

Keeping a Spiritual Journal. Harry J. Cargas & Roger J. Radley. LC 80-2072. 128p. (gr. 6 up). 1981. pap. 2.75 (ISBN 0-385-17439-X, Im). Doubleday.

Keeping Alive. Stanley L. Weinberg & Herbert J. Stoltze. (Action Biology Ser.). (gr. 9-12). 1974. pap. text ed. 3.20 (ISBN 0-205-04141-8, 674141X). Allyn.

Keeping Amphibians & Reptiles As Pets. George S. Fichter. (First Bks.). (Illus.). (gr. 4-6). 1979. PLB 6.45 s&l (ISBN 0-531-02257-9). Watts.

Keeping Chickens. John Walters & Michael Parker. (Illus.). 1979. 8.95 (ISBN 0-7207-0882-6, Pub. by Michael Joseph). Merrimack Bk Serv.

Keeping Domestic Geese. Barbra Soames. (Illus.). 128p. 1980. 13.95 (ISBN 0-7137-1070-5, Pub. by Blandford Pr England). Sterling.

Keeping Ducks, Geese & Turkeys. John Walters & Michael Parker. (Gardening Farming Ser.). 1976. 8.95 (ISBN 0-7207-0932-6, Pub. by Michael Joseph). Merrimack Bk Serv.

Keeping Festival. Suzanne Toolan. 1979. pap. 4.95 (ISBN 0-89390-011-7). Resource Pubns.

Keeping Fit. Don Otis. 1979. pap. 2.25 (ISBN 0-89728-013-X). Omega Pubns OR.

Keeping Goats. Elizabeth Downing. (Pelham Ser.). (Illus.). 1976. 8.95 (ISBN 0-7207-0883-4, Pub. by Michael Joseph). Merrimack Bk Serv.

Keeping Healthy in an Unhealthy World. Linda Arden. (Illus.). 1980. pap. 12.95 o.p. (ISBN 0-930490-25-8). Future Shop.

Keeping Honey Bees. Judy Urquhart. LC 77-85028. (Penny Pinchers Ser.). 1978. 2.95 (ISBN 0-7153-7548-2). David & Charles.

Keeping in Shape. Nancy Lewis & Richard Lewis. LC 75-29267. (Career Concise Guides Ser.). (Illus.). 72p. (gr. 5-9). 1976. PLB 4.90 o.p. (ISBN 0-531-02848-8). Watts.

Keeping Insects As Pets. Ross Olney & Pat Olney. LC 78-2578. (First Bks). (Illus.). (gr. 4 up). 1978. PLB 6.45 s&l (ISBN 0-531-01490-8). Watts.

Keeping Kennedy's Promise: The Peace Corps: Unmet Hope of the New Frontier. Kevin Lowther & C. Payne Lucas. LC 77-21187. 1978. 18.00x (ISBN 0-89158-422-6). Westview.

Keeping Pace with the New Television- Public Television & Changing Technology. Sheila Mahony et al. 281p. 1980. pap. 3.25 (Pub Telecom). NAEB.

Keeping Parents Out of Trouble. Dan Kiley. (Orig.). 1981. 11.95 (ISBN 0-446-51221-4). Warner Bks.

Keeping Room. Betty Levin. LC 80-23931. 256p. (gr. 5 up). 1981. 8.95 (ISBN 0-688-80300-8). Greenwillow.

Keeping Score: Film Music 1972-1979. James L. Limbacher. LC 80-26474. 519p. 1981. 22.50 (ISBN 0-8108-1390-4). Scarecrow.

Keeping the Church Year. H. Boone Porter. 1978. pap. 3.95 (ISBN 0-8164-2161-7). Crossroad NY.

Keeping the Faith: Writings by Contemporary Black American Women. Ed. by Patricia C. Exum. 288p. (Orig.). 1974. pap. 1.75 o.p. (ISBN 0-449-30714-X, X714, Prem). Fawcett.

Keeping the Harvest. rev. ed. Nancy Chioffi & Gretchen Mead. (Illus.). 208p. 1980. pap. text ed. 7.95 (ISBN 0-88266-247-3). Garden Way Pub.

Keeping the Lock in Wedlock. Thomas B. Warren. 1980. pap. 10.95 (ISBN 0-934916-26-8). Natl Christian Pr.

Keeping Track: A Personal Medical Record System. Eleanor Laumark & Victoria Christianson. LC 80-22042. (Illus., Orig.). 1980. pap. 7.95 (ISBN 0-912800-79-8). Woodbridge Pr.

Keeping Warm with an Ax. D. Cook. LC 80-19295. (Illus.). 160p. 1981. 12.95x (ISBN 0-87663-347-5); pap. 6.50 (ISBN 0-87663-552-4). Universe.

Keeping Your Family Healthy Overseas. James P. Carter et al. 1971. 6.95 o.s.i. (ISBN 0-440-04429-4, Sey Lawr). Delacorte.

Keeping Your Personal Journal. George F. Simons. LC 77-99299. 1978. pap. 4.95 (ISBN 0-8091-2092-5). Paulist Pr.

Kein Schnaps Fur Tamara. Hansborg Martin. (Easy Readers, B). (Illus.). 1977. pap. text ed. 3.75 (ISBN 0-88436-282-5). EMC.

Keith County Journal. John Janovy, Jr. 1980. pap. 4.95 (ISBN 0-312-45124-5). St Martin.

Keithwood Directory of Hospital & Surgical Supply Dealers. 302p. 1980. 45.00 (ISBN 0-686-27082-7). Keithwood.

Kel, Part 1: Les. Mark Dunster. (Rin Ser.: Pt. 28). (Illus.). 60p. 1981. pap. 4.00 (ISBN 0-89642-075-2). Linden Pubs.

Keller Plan for Self-Paced Study Using Masterton & Slowinski's Chemical Principles. 2nd ed. Joseph L. Clouser. LC 76-20081. 1977. pap. text ed. 9.95 o.p. (ISBN 0-7216-2611-4). Saunders.

Kelly. E. C. Goossen. (Derriere le Miroir: No. 110). (Illus.). 1978. pap. 19.95 (ISBN 0-8120-2000-6). Barron.

Kelly Blue. William W. Johnson. LC 60-8875. 263p. 1974. pap. 2.95 (ISBN 0-8032-5795-3, BB 583, Bison). U of Nebr Pr.

Kellys & the OKelleys. Anthony Trollope. (World's Classics Ser: No. 341). 1975. 10.95 (ISBN 0-19-250341-3). Oxford U Pr.

Kellys & the O'Kellys. Anthony Trollope. Ed. by Robert L. Wolff. (Ireland Nineteenth Century Fiction - Ser. Two: Vol. 54). 888p. 1979. lib. bdg. 32.00 (ISBN 0-8240-3503-8). Garland Pub.

Kelly's Manufacturers & Merchants Directory, 1979-80. 93rd ed. LC 12-34808. 2260p. 1979. 65.00x (ISBN 0-610-00521-9). Intl Pubns Serv.

Kelp for Better Health & Vitality. Frank Wilson. 1979. pap. 1.95 o.s.i. (ISBN 0-7225-0367-9). Newcastle Pub.

Kelp, the Health Giver. Eric Powell. 1980. pap. 1.95 (ISBN 0-87904-041-6). Lust.

Kelp the Health Giver. Eric F. Powell. 1980. 2.25 (ISBN 0-8464-1028-1). Beekman Pubs.

Kelston Knoll. Catherine Dupre. 1981. pap. 2.75 (ISBN 0-451-09895-1, E9895, Sig). NAL.

Kelston Knoll. Catherine Dupre. 364p. 1980. 11.95 (ISBN 0-312-45137-7). St Martin.

Kemps British Clothing Industry Yearbook, 1979. 1979. pap. 36.50 (ISBN 0-905255-51-8, KEMPOO5, Kemps). Unipub.

Kemps Scrap & Reclamation Yearbook, 1979. 1979. pap. 29.75 (ISBN 0-905255-57-7, KEMP003, Kemps). Unipub.

Ken Rosewall on Tennis. Ken Rosewall. LC 78-18730. (Illus.). 1978. 9.95 (ISBN 0-8119-0334-6); pap. 4.95 (ISBN 0-8119-0386-9). Fell.

Ken Russell. Gene D. Phillips. (Theatrical Arts Ser.). 1979. lib. bdg. 10.95 (ISBN 0-8057-9266-X). Twayne.

Ken Stabler. William H. Feinberg. (Sports Superstars Ser). (Illus.). (gr. 3-9). 1978. PLB 5.95 (ISBN 0-87191-670-3); pap. 2.95 (ISBN 0-89812-170-1). Creative Ed.

Kena Upanishad. Sri Aurobindo. Tr. by Sri Aurobindo. 1979. pap. 2.50 (ISBN 0-89744-923-1). Auromere.

Kenguru. Yuz Aleshkovsky. 85p. (Rus.). 1980. 13.50 (ISBN 0-88233-566-9); pap. 5.00 (ISBN 0-88233-567-7). Ardis Pubs.

Kenilworth. Walter Scott. 1955. 12.95x (ISBN 0-460-00135-3, Evman). Dutton.

Kennedy. Elizabeth Campling. (Leaders Ser.). (Illus.). 80p. (gr. 9-12). 1980. 16.95 (ISBN 0-7134-1920-2, Pub. by Batsford England). David & Charles.

Kennedy. Theodore Sorensen. LC 65-14660. 1965. 17.50 o.s.i. (ISBN 0-06-013950-1, HarpT). Har-Row.

Kennedy & Sirhan, Why. Mohammad T. Mehdi. LC 68-57262. (Illus., Orig.). pap. 3.00 (ISBN 0-911026-04-5, KSW). New World Press NY.

Kennedy & the Berlin Wall Crisis: A Case Study in U. S. Decision Making. Honore M. Catudal. (Illus.). 358p. (Orig.). 1980. pap. 20.00x (ISBN 3-87061-160-X). Intl Pubns Serv.

Kennedy Brothers. Don Lawson. 160p. (gr. 8-12). 1981. 8.95 (ISBN 0-416-30731-0). Methuen Inc. Postponed.

Kennedy Case. Rita Dallas & Jeanira Ratcliffe. 368p. 1974. pap. 1.75 o.p. (ISBN 0-445-08259-3). Popular Lib.

Kennedy Corridos: A Study of the Ballads of a Mexican American Hero. Dan W. Dickey. (Mexican American Monographs: No. 4). (Illus.). 125p. 1978. pap. 4.25 (ISBN 0-292-74303-3, Pub by Ctr Mex Am Stud). U of Tex Pr.

Kennedy for the Defense. George V. Higgins. 224p. 1981. pap. 2.75 (ISBN 0-345-29315-0). Ballantine.

Kennedy Literature: A Bibliographical Essay on John F. Kennedy. James Tracy Crown. LC 68-29428. 1968. 12.00x (ISBN 0-8147-0109-4). NYU Pr.

Kennet & Avon Canal. Kenneth R. Clew. (Inland Waterways Histories Ser.). (Illus.). 1973. 16.95 (ISBN 0-7153-5939-8). David & Charles.

Kenneth Callahan: Universal Voyage. Ed. by Michael R. Johnson. LC 73-96. (Index of Art in the Pacific Northwest Ser: No. 6). (Illus.). 80p. 1973. 15.00 (ISBN 0-295-95270-9); pap. 7.50 (ISBN 0-295-95271-7). U of Wash Pr.

Kenneth Noland: A Retrospective. Diane Waldman. (Illus.). 1977. pap. 9.95 (ISBN 0-89207-009-9). S R Guggenheim.

Kenneth Patchen. Larry R. Smith. (United States Authors Ser.: No. 292). 1978. lib. bdg. 12.50 (ISBN 0-8057-7195-6). Twayne.

Kenneth Slessor. Herbert C. Jaffa. (World Authors Ser.: Australia: No. 145). lib. bdg. 10.95 (ISBN 0-8057-2838-4). Twayne.

Kenny's Stories. Kenny McGuire. 1981. 4.95 (ISBN 0-8062-1559-3). Carlton.

Kensim: A Systems Simulation of the Developing Kenyan Economy, 1970-1978. Charles C. Slater et al. LC 77-4141. 1977. lib. bdg. 23.50x (ISBN 0-89158-346-7). Westview.

Kent State Incident: Impact of Judicial Process on Public Attitudes. Thomas R. Hensley. LC 80-1712. (Contributions in Political Science Ser.: No. 56). 224p. 1981. lib. bdg. 27.50 (ISBN 0-313-21220-1, HKS/). Greenwood.

Kent State Ten Years After. Bettina Aptheker et al. Ed. by Scott Bills. (Illus.). 88p. (Orig.). 1980. pap. 3.95 (ISBN 0-933522-04-5). Kent Popular.

Kenton Year. Ruth Wallace-Brodeur. LC 80-13448. 104p. (gr. 4-7). 1980. 7.95 (ISBN 0-689-50186-2, McElderry Bk). Atheneum.

Kentuckians. John Fox. 1976. lib. bdg. 13.50x (ISBN 0-89968-038-0). Lightyear.

Kentucky. Steven A. Channing. (States & the Nation Ser.). (Illus.). 1977. 12.95 (ISBN 0-393-05654-6, Co-Pub by AASLH). Norton.

Kentucky. Thomas D. Clark. LC 65-23498. 1965. pap. 2.95 (ISBN 0-8077-1164-0). Tchrs Coll.

Kentucky. 28.00 (ISBN 0-89770-093-7). Curriculum Info Ctr.

Kentucky: A Guide to the Bluegrass State. Federal Writers' Project. 492p. 1939. Repr. 45.00 (ISBN 0-403-02168-5). Somerset Pub.

Kentucky Birds: A Finding Guide. Roger W. Barbour et al. LC 72-91662. (Illus.). 328p. 1973. 13.50 (ISBN 0-8131-1281-8). U Pr of Ky.

Kentucky Chronology & Factbook, Vol. 17. R. I. Vexler. 1978. 8.50 (ISBN 0-379-16142-7). Oceana.

Kentucky Coal Refuse Disposal & Utilization Seminar, Fourth: Proceedings. Ed. by J. G. Rose & R. W. De Vore. (Illus.). 1978. pap. text ed. 7.00 (ISBN 0-89779-010-3); microfiche 1.50 (ISBN 0-89779-011-1). OES Pubns.
Kentucky Derby. Julian May. LC 75-6976. (Sports Classics Ser.). (Illus.). 48p. (gr. 4-6). 1975. PLB 8.95 o.p. (ISBN 0-87191-442-5). Creative Ed.
Kentucky in Retrospect: Noteworthy Personages & Events in Kentucky History, 1792-1967. rev. ed. G. Glenn Clift et al. Ed. by Mrs. Wm. B. Ardery & Harry V. McChesney. (Illus.). 1967. 5.00 o.p. (ISBN 0-916968-00-6). Kentucky Hist.
Kentucky in the New Republic: The Process of Constitution Making. Joan W. Coward. LC 77-92920. (Illus.). 232p. 1979. 17.00x (ISBN 0-8131-1380-6). U Pr of Ky.
Kentucky: In Words & Pictures. Dennis Fradin. LC 80-25810. (Young People's Stories of Our States Ser.). 48p. (gr. 2-5). 1981. PLB 8.65g (ISBN 0-516-03917-2, Time Line). Childrens.
Kentucky: Land of Contrast. Thomas D. Clark. (Regions of America Ser). (YA) 1968. 11.95 o.s.i. (ISBN 0-06-010808-8, HarpT). Har-Row.
Kentucky Probate Methods with 1979 Supplement. Randolph Noe. 1976. 35.00 (ISBN 0-672-82532-5, Bobbs-Merrill Law); 1979 suppl 7.50 (ISBN 0-672-83978-4). Michie.
Kentucky Revised Statutes, 21 vols. 1971. write for info (ISBN 0-672-83035-3, Bobbs-Merrill Law); 1980 suppl. avail. (ISBN 0-87215-349-5). Michie.
Kentucky Sampler: Essays from the Filson Club History Quarterly, 1926 to 1976. Ed. by Lowell H. Harrison & Nelson L. Dawson. LC 77-76471. 452p. 1980. Repr. of 1977 ed. 16.00x (ISBN 0-8131-1360-1). U Pr of Ky.
Kentucky State Industrial Directory, Nineteen Eighty-One. State Industrial Directories Corp. Date not set. pap. price not set (ISBN 0-89910-042-2). State Indus D.
Kentucky Votes: U. S. House Primary & Genral Elections, 1920-1960. Malcolm E. Jewell. LC 63-12390. 104p. 1963. pap. 2.25x (ISBN 0-8131-0083-6). U Pr of Ky.
Kentucky's Age of Wood. Kenneth Clarke & Ira Kohn. LC 76-4432. (Kentucky Bicentennial Bookshelf Ser.). (Illus.). 88p. 1976. 5.95 (ISBN 0-8131-0225-1). U Pr of Ky.
Kentucky's Last Frontier. Henry P. Scalf. 565p. 1972. Repr. of 1966 ed. 12.00. Pikeville Coll.
Kenya: A Vacation Guide. rev. ed. Michael Tomkinson. LC 77-70382. (Illus.). 1977. 5.95 o.p. (ISBN 0-684-14911-7, SL696, ScribT). Scribner.
Kenya's Nomads. Ross-Larson. LC 71-190187. (Illus.). (gr. 4-8). 1972. PLB 5.95 o.p. (ISBN 0-87191-209-0). Creative Ed.
Kenyatta. Jeremy Murray-Brown. 1973. 12.50 o.p. (ISBN 0-525-13855-2). Dutton.
Kenzo Tange. Robin Boyd. LC 62-16267. (Makers of Contemporary Architecture Ser). 1962. 4.95 o.p. (ISBN 0-8076-0196-9). Braziller.
Kep. Zachary Ball. 208p. (gr. 7-9). 1961. 4.95 o.p. (ISBN 0-8234-0064-6). Holiday.
Kephala. John E. Coleman. LC 76-13187. (Keos Ser: Vol. 1). 1977. pap. 35.00x (ISBN 0-87661-701-1). Am Sch Athens.
Kepler's Dream: With the Full Text & Notes of Somnium Sive Astronomia Lunaris, Joannis Kepleri. John Lear. Tr. by Patrica F. Kirkwood. 1965. 15.75x (ISBN 0-520-00716-6). U of Cal Pr.
Kepone, Mirex, Hexachlorocyclopentadiene. Environmental Studies Board. 1978. pap. 5.75 (ISBN 0-309-02766-7). Natl Acad Pr.
Kept by the Power of God. I. Howard Marshall. LC 74-23996. 288p. 1975. pap. 5.95 (ISBN 0-87123-304-5, 210304). Bethany Fell.
Kept Men. Linda DuBreuil. (Orig.). 1976. pap. 1.50 o.p. (ISBN 0-685-64010-8, LB341DK, Leisure Bks). Nordon Pubns.
Kept Men? The First Century of Trade Union Representation in the British House of Commons, 1874-1975. William D. Muller. (Illus.). 1977. text ed. 39.75x (ISBN 0-85527-184-1). Humanities.
Keratins: Their Composition, Structure & Biosynthesis. R. D. Fraser et al. (Amer. Lec. Living Chemistry Ser.). (Illus.). 320p. 1972. 24.75 (ISBN 0-398-02283-6). C C Thomas.
Keresan Bridge: A Problem in Pueblo Ethnology. Robin Fox. (Monographs on Social Anthropology: No. 35). 1967. text ed. 20.75x (ISBN 0-485-19535-6, Athlone Pr). Humanities.
Kerkeosiris: An Egyptian Village in the Ptolemaic Period. Dorothy J. Crawford. LC 70-96083. (Classical Studies). (Illus.). 1971. 34.50 (ISBN 0-521-07607-2). Cambridge U Pr.
Kermanshah Transfer. Efrem Sigel. 224p. 1973. 6.95 o.s.i. (ISBN 0-02-610630-2). Macmillan.
Kermit the Hermit. Bill Peet. (Illus.). (gr. k-3). 1965. 8.95 (ISBN 0-395-15084-1). HM.
Kermit the Hermit. Bill Peet. (Illus.). (ps-3). 1980. pap. 3.45 (ISBN 0-395-29607-2, Sandpiper). HM.
Kerouac West Coast: A Bohemian Pilot, Detailed Navigational Instructions. John Montgomery. LC 76-40359. 1976. bds. 5.95 (ISBN 0-918704-02-2); pap. 1.95 (ISBN 0-918704-01-4). Fels & Firn.
Kerouacs Crooked Road: Development of a Fiction. Tim Hunt. 288p. 1981. 19.50 (ISBN 0-208-01871-9, Archon). Shoe String.
Kerr's Country Kitchen. Don Kerr & Vivian Kerr. (Illus.). 164p. 1981. pap. 6.95 (ISBN 0-933614-08-X). Peregrine Pr.
Kerry Blue Terrier. Edith Izant. LC 77-87764. (Other Dog Books). (Illus.). 1981. price not set (ISBN 0-87714-060-X). Denlingers.
Kes: A Play of the Novel. Barry Hines & Allan Stronach. 1976. pap. text ed. 2.95x (ISBN 0-435-23500-1). Heinemann Ed.
Kesselring: The Making of the Luftwaffe. Kenneth MacKsey. 1978. 27.00 (ISBN 0-7134-0862-6, Pub. by Batsford England). David & Charles.
Kessler Alliance. Thomas Horstman. 1980. pap. 2.25 (ISBN 0-505-51463-X). Tower Bks.
Kestrel & Other Poems of Past & Present. George Woodcock. 54p. 1980. signed ed 14.95x (ISBN 0-904461-40-8, Pub. by Ceolfrith Pr England); pap. 5.95x (ISBN 0-904461-39-4). Intl Schol Bk Serv.
Ketchup Pickles Sauces: 19th Century Food in Glass. Betty Zumwalt. (Illus.). 480p. 1980. 25.00x (ISBN 0-686-28760-6). M West Pubs.
Ketotifen in the Prophylactic Treatment of Bronchial Asthma. Ed. by H. Herzog. (Journal: Respiration: Vol. 39). (Illus.). 54p. 1980. pap. 24.00 (ISBN 3-8055-1171-X). S Karger.
Ketubah. new ed. Moses Gaster. LC 68-9532. (Illus.). 90p. 1974. 7.95 (ISBN 0-87203-029-6). Hermon.
Kewpie Designs. 1980. Vol. I. pap. 2.50 (ISBN 0-686-65151-0); Vol. II. pap. 2.50 o.p. (ISBN 0-87588-166-1); Vol. III. pap. 2.50 o.p. (ISBN 0-87588-167-X). Hobby Hse.
Key. Junichiro Tanizaki. Tr. by Howard Hibbett from Jap. (Perigee Japanese Library). 190p. 1981. pap. 4.95 (ISBN 0-399-50522-9, Perigee). Putnam.
Key into the Language of America. 5th ed. Roger Williams. LC 70-157500. Repr. of 1643 ed. 18.00 (ISBN 0-8103-3723-1). Gale.
Key Issues in Population & Food Policy: Capon Springs Public Policy Conference No. 2. Ed. by Eliot Glassheim & Charles Cargille. LC 78-63063. (Illus.). 1978. pap. text ed. 14.00 (ISBN 0-8191-0613-5). U Pr of Amer.
Key Issues in Population: Problems, Options, & Recommendations for Action. Capon Springs Public Policy Conference, No. 1. Ed. by Eliot Glassheim et al. LC 78-50770. 1978. pap. text ed. 14.00x (ISBN 0-8191-0467-1). U Pr of Amer.
Key Issues: Issues & Events of 1979. Ed. by Janet Byrne. LC 80-1717. (News in Print Ser.). (Illus.). 1980. lib. bdg. 24.95x (ISBN 0-405-12877-0). Arno.
Key of the Mysteries. Eliphas Levi. 1980. pap. 6.95 (ISBN 0-87728-078-9). Weiser.
Key of Truth. Fred C. Conybeare. 55.00 (ISBN 0-686-12403-0). Church History.
Key Papers in Information Science. Ed. by Belver C. Griffith. LC 79-24288. 439p. 1980. text ed. 25.00 (ISBN 0-914236-50-4, ASIS). Knowledge Indus.
Key Papers in the Economics of Information. Ed. by Donald W. King et al. 350p. 1980. text ed. 25.00 (ISBN 0-914236-62-8, ASIS). Knowledge Indus.
Key Problems of Sociological Theory. John Rex. (International Library of Sociology & Social Reconstruction). 1970. text ed. 11.25x o.p. (ISBN 0-7100-3409-1); pap. text ed. 4.50x o.p. (ISBN 0-391-00091-8). Humanities.
Key Punch. Jules Rosenblatt. 1969. wkbk. 10.50 (ISBN 0-672-96027-3); wkbk. & kit 29.95 (ISBN 0-672-96029-X). Bobbs.
Key Readings in Testing. Harley D. Christiansen. 96p. (Orig.). 1981. pap. text ed. 8.95 (ISBN 0-915456-06-0). P Juul Pr.
Key References in Internal Medicine. P. J. Blackshear. 1981. pap. text ed. write for info. (ISBN 0-443-08079-8). Churchill.
Key Soup. Illus. by Beverly S. Brown. LC 78-73538. (Illus.). (gr. 1-5). Date not set. price not set (ISBN 0-89799-155-9); pap. price not set (ISBN 0-89799-073-0). Dandelion Pr. Postponed.
Key System Album. 16.00. Chatham Pub CA.
Key System Album. Jim Walker. LC 78-55027. (Special Ser.: No. 68). (Illus.). 1978. 17.95 (ISBN 0-916374-31-9). Interurban.
Key to Accounting & Costing. J. A. Tainsh. 119p. 1959. 11.75x (ISBN 0-85264-062-5, Pub. by Griffin England). State Mutual Bk.
Key to Advanced Spanish Course. M. J. Lawrence & K. L. Mason. LC 78-122008. 1970. 4.80 (ISBN 0-08-016084-0); pap. 3.85 (ISBN 0-08-016083-2). Pergamon.
Key to Cribbage. William H. Green. (Gambler's Book Shelf). 1965. pap. 2.95 (ISBN 0-89650-501-4). Gamblers.
Key to Everything. Norman Grubb. 1975. pap. 3.50 (ISBN 0-8024-4545-4). Moody.
Key to Geometry Series, 8 bks. Newton Hawley & Patrick Suppes. Ed. by George Gearheart & Peter Rasmussen. Incl. Bk. 1. Lines & Segments. 56p. pap. 0.95 (ISBN 0-913684-71-6); Bk. 2. Circles. 56p. pap. 0.95 (ISBN 0-913684-72-4); Bk. 3. Constructions. 56p. pap. 0.95 (ISBN 0-913684-73-2); Bk. 4. Perpendiculars. 56p. pap. 0.95 (ISBN 0-913684-74-0); Bk. 5. Squares & Rectangles. 56p. pap. 0.95 (ISBN 0-913684-75-9); Bk. 6. Angles. 56p. pap. 0.95 (ISBN 0-913684-76-7); Bk. 7. Perpendiculars & Parallels, Chords & Tangents, Circles. 154p. pap. 2.85 (ISBN 0-913684-77-5); Bk. 8. Triangles, Parallel Lines, Similar Polygons. 139p. pap. 2.85 (ISBN 0-913684-78-3). (gr. 4 up). 1980. pap. Key Curr Project.
Key to Know Thyself. pap. 7.50 o.s.i. (ISBN 0-685-90824-0). Saphrograph.
Key to Latin Course for Schools, Part I. R. W. Wilding. 1966. 2.95 o.p. (ISBN 0-571-06632-1, Pub. by Faber & Faber). Merrimack Bk Serv.
Key to Latin Course for Schools, Part II. R. W. Wilding. 1966. 2.95 o.p. (ISBN 0-571-06633-X, Pub. by Faber & Faber). Merrimack Bk Serv.
Key to Laurels. March Cost. LC 72-90476. 7.95 (ISBN 0-8149-0723-7). Vanguard.
Key to Many Doors. Emilie Loring. 208p. 1980. pap. 1.95 (ISBN 0-553-14289-5). Bantam.
Key to Modern British Poetry. Lawrence Durrell. 1952. pap. 5.95 (ISBN 0-8061-0919-X). U of Okla Pr.
Key to Murder. Ralph Cross. (Orig.). 1980. pap. 1.95 (ISBN 0-505-51488-5). Tower Bks.
Key to Rebecca. Ken Follett. 1981. lib. bdg. 16.95 (ISBN 0-8161-3151-1, Large Print Bks). G K Hall.
Key to Rebecca. Ken Follett. LC 80-16760. 1980. 12.95 (ISBN 0-688-03734-8). Morrow.
Key to the Constitution of the United States. 6th ed. Robert B. Weaver & Henry B. Watson. LC 79-64230. 67p. 1979. pap. 1.00 (ISBN 0-912530-12-X). Patriotic Educ.
Key to the Exercises in the Introductory Hebrew Grammar. John Mauchline. 146p. Repr. of 1967 ed. 10.95x (ISBN 0-567-01006-6). Attic Pr.
Key to the Genera of Grasses of the Conterminous United States. J. P. Smith, Jr. 1981. pap. price not set. Mad River.
Key to the Genera of Grasses of the Conterminus United States. James P. Smith. (Illus.). 40p. 1975. pap. 2.00x o.p. (ISBN 0-916422-04-6). Mad River.
Key to the Genera of Grasses of the Coterminous United States. rev. ed. James P. Smith, Jr. 80p. 1980. pap. write for info. (ISBN 0-916422-22-4). Mad River.
Key to the Solar Compass. William A. Burt. 1978. pap. 8.50 (ISBN 0-686-25540-2, 512). CARBEN Survey.
Key to the Suite. John D. MacDonald. 1978. pap. 1.95 (ISBN 0-449-13995-6, GM). Fawcett.
Key to the Treasure. Peggy Parish. (gr. k-6). 1980. pap. 1.50 (ISBN 0-440-44438-1, YB). Dell.
Key to Theosophy. Helena P. Blavatsky. 12.25 o.p. (ISBN 0-7229-5006-3). Theos Pub Hse.
Key to Theosophy. Helena P. Blavatsky. xii, 310p. 1930. Repr. of 1889 ed. 6.00 (ISBN 0-938998-03-X). Theosophy.
Key to Theosophy: Verbatim with 1889 Edition. Helena P. Blavatsky. LC 72-95701. 1972. 8.00 (ISBN 0-911500-06-5); pap. 5.00 (ISBN 0-911500-07-3). Theos U Pr.
Key to Victory. Fernando Chaij. LC 79-548. (Horizon Ser). 1979. pap. 4.50 (ISBN 0-8127-0224-7). Southern Pub.
Key to Weaving. rev. ed. Mary E. Black. (Illus.). 1980. 24.95 (ISBN 0-02-511170-1). Macmillan.
Key to Your Own Nativity. Alan Leo. 1978. pap. 6.95 (ISBN 0-685-62086-7). Weiser.
Key West Connection. Randy Striker. (Dusky MacMorgan Ser.: No. 1). (Orig.). 1981. pap. 1.95 (ISBN 0-451-09567-7, J9567, Sig). NAL.
Key Words to Reading: The Language Experience Approach. 2nd ed. Veatch et al. (Elementary Reading Ser.). 1979. pap. text ed. 8.95 (ISBN 0-675-08363-X). Merrill.
Key Writings: Representative Selections. rev. ed. Edgar A. Poe. Ed. by Hardin Craig & Margaret Alterton. 7.50 o.p. (ISBN 0-8446-0225-6). Peter Smith.
Keyboard & Dictation Manual. Allen I. McHose & Donald F. White. (Eastman School of Music Ser.). 1949. 29.50x (ISBN 0-89197-255-2); pap. text ed. 18.50x (ISBN 0-89197-819-4). Irvington.
Keyboard Harmony Course, 2 bks. Angela Diller. 1937. pap. 2.95 ea. Bk. I (ISBN 0-02-870730-3). Bk. II (ISBN 0-02-870740-0). Schirmer Bks.
Keyboard Music from the Middle Ages to the Beginnings of the Baroque. 2nd ed. Gerald S. Bedbrook. LC 69-15605. (Music Ser). (Illus.). 1973. Repr. of 1949 ed. 19.50 (ISBN 0-306-71056-0). Da Capo.
Keyboarding for Information Processing. Robert N. Hanson & D. Sue Rigby. (Illus.). 96p. 1981. pap. text ed. 6.95 (ISBN 0-07-026105-9, G). McGraw.
Keyes Papers, Vol. 2. P. G. Halpern. (Illus.). 464p. 1980. text ed. 34.00x (ISBN 0-04-942165-4, 2282). Allen Unwin.
Keynes & the Bloomsbury Group. Ed. by Derek Crabtree & A. P. Thirlwall. 1980. text ed. 30.00x (ISBN 0-8419-5066-0). Holmes & Meier.
Keynes & the Economic Bankruptcy of the United States. Wilfred V. Langlois. (Illus.). 139p. 1980. deluxe ed. 49.85 (ISBN 0-918968-71-2). Inst Econ Finan.
Keynes, Keynesians, & Monetarists. Sidney Weintraub. LC 77-20307. (Illus.). 1978. pap. 9.95x (ISBN 0-8122-7741-4). U of Pa Pr.
Keynotes. George Egerton. Ed. by Ian Fletcher & John Stokes. LC 76-24384. (Decadent Consciousness Ser.). 1978. lib. bdg. 38.00 (ISBN 0-8240-2758-2). Garland Pub.
Keynotes to Modern Dance. 3rd ed. Dorothy E. Norris & Reva P. Shiner. LC 69-15426. 1969. pap. 8.95 o.p. (ISBN 0-8087-1411-2). Burgess.
Keypunching: A Basic Office Skill. Benjamin A. Micallef. LC 74-75692. (Data Processing Ser.). 160p. 1974. pap. 8.95 o.p. (ISBN 0-8465-4734-1, 54734). Benjamin-Cummings.
Keys of Hell. Jack Higgins. 160p. 1976. pap. 1.95 (ISBN 0-449-14298-1, GM). Fawcett.
Keys of Hell. Louise Osborne. 256p. 1975. pap. 1.25 o.p. (ISBN 0-445-00284-0). Popular Lib.
Keys, Species & Host List, & Bibliography for Nasal Mites of North American Birds (Acarina: Rhinonyssinae, Turbinoptinae, Speleognathinae, & Cytoditidae) Danny B. Pence. (Special Publications: No. 8). (Illus., Orig.). 1975. pap. 6.00 (ISBN 0-89672-033-0). Tex Tech Pr.
Keys to Chemistry: Metric. 2nd ed. Elaine Ledbetter & Jay Young. (gr. 11-12). 1977. text ed. 15.40 (ISBN 0-201-04361-0, Sch Div); tchr's ed. 5.28 (ISBN 0-201-04362-9); lab man. 5.72 (ISBN 0-201-04363-7). A-W.
Keys to Economic Understanding. Jeffrey M. Elliot & Francis Shieh. LC 76-13795. 1976. pap. text ed. 8.95 (ISBN 0-8403-1483-3). Kendall-Hunt.
Keys to Library Research on the Graduate Level: A Guide to Guides. Harvey R. Gover. LC 80-5841. 75p. 1981. pap. text ed. 5.75 (ISBN 0-8191-1370-0). U Pr of Amer.
Keys to Queenscourt. Jeanne Hines. 1976. pap. 1.75 o.p. (ISBN 0-445-08508-8). Popular Lib.
Keys to Spelling: Sounds & Syllables. Julie W. Sevastopoulos. 80p. (Orig.). 1981. pap. text ed. 5.95 (ISBN 0-88499-541-0). Inst Mod Lang.
Keys to the Deeper Life. A. W. Tozer. 56p. 1973. pap. 1.25 (ISBN 0-310-33362-8). Zondervan.
Keys to the Occult: Two Guides to Hidden Wisdom. Hereward Carrington & Willis F. Whitehead. LC 80-23835. 182p. 1980. Repr. of 1977 ed. lib. bdg. 10.95x (ISBN 0-89370-641-8). Borgo Pr.
Keys to the Vascular Plants of Northwest California. J. P. Smith & J. O. Sawyer. 1978. pap. 3.75x o.p. (ISBN 0-916422-11-9). Mad River.
Keys to the Vascular Plants of Northwest California. rev. ed. J. P. Smith & J. O. Sawyer. 160p. 1980. pap. text ed. write for info (ISBN 0-916422-23-2). Mad River.
Keys to Wisdom. Ernest Holmes. 1965. pap. 4.50 (ISBN 0-911336-06-0). Sci of Mind.
Keystone in the Democratic Arch: Pennsylvania Politics, 1800-1816. Sanford W. Higginbotham. LC 52-14646. (Orig.). 1952. 8.00 (ISBN 0-911124-27-6). Pa Hist & Mus.
Keywords: A Vocabulary of Culture & Society. Raymond William. 1976. pap. 4.95 (ISBN 0-19-519855-7, GB). Oxford U Pr.
Keywords: A Vocabulary of Culture & Society. Raymond Williams. 288p. 1976. Repr. 14.95 (ISBN 0-19-519854-9, 464). Oxford U Pr.
KGB. John Barron. 1979. pap. 2.50 (ISBN 0-88264-085-2). Diane Bks.
KGB: The Eyes of Russia. Harry Rositzke. LC 80-2063. 288p. 1981. 14.95 (ISBN 0-385-15390-2). Doubleday.
Khajuraho & Other Poems. Malithi Rao. 1976. 8.00 (ISBN 0-89253-821-X); flexible cloth 4.80 (ISBN 0-89253-822-8). Ind-US Inc.
Khan el Khalili. Nagib Mahfouz. pap. 5.50 arabic ed. (ISBN 0-685-82837-9). Intl Bk Ctr.
Khanskie Iarlyki Russkim Metropolitam. Mikhail D. Priselkov. LC 80-2364. 1981. Repr. of 1916 ed. 25.50 (ISBN 0-686-69404-X). AMS Pr.
Khedives and Pashas: Sketches of Contemporary Egyptian Rulers and Statesmen. by One Who Knows Them Well. Charles Frederic M. Bell. LC 80-2196. 1981. Repr. of 1884 ed. 30.00 (ISBN 0-404-18954-7). AMS Pr.

Khilafat Movement: Religious Symbolism & Political Mobilization in India. Gail Minault. 1981. text ed. 22.50x (ISBN 0-231-05072-0). Columbia U Pr.

Khmers, Tigers, & Talismans: From the History & Legends of Mysterious Cambodia. Jewell R. Coburn. LC 77-14887. (Illus.). 100p. 1978. 8.95 (ISBN 0-918060-02-8). Burn-Hart.

Khotanese Texts, 4 bks. Harold W. Bailey. 1961-1967. Vols. 1-3. 156.00 (ISBN 0-521-06961-0); Vol. 4. 75.00 (ISBN 0-521-04080-9); Vol. 5. 136.00 (ISBN 0-521-04081-7); Vol. 6. 150.00 (ISBN 0-521-07113-5). Cambridge U Pr.

Khowano, the Brave. (Sharazad Stories Ser.). (Illus., Arabic.). pap. 3.50 (ISBN 0-686-53107-8). Intl Bk Ctr.

Khrushchev: The Years in Power. Roy A. Medvedev & Zhores A. Medvedev. LC 76-19104. 240p. 1976. 15.00x (ISBN 0-231-03939-5). Columbia U Pr.

Khyber: The Story of an Imperial Migraine. Charles Miller. LC 77-6382. (Illus.). 1977. 12.95 o.s.i. (ISBN 0-02-584860-7). Macmillan.

Kiangsi Native Trade & Its Taxation. Stanley Wright. LC 78-74332. (Modern Chinese Economy Ser.). 201p. 1980. lib. bdg. 22.00 (ISBN 0-8240-4258-1). Garland Pub.

Kibbutz: Life in an Israeli Commune. Paul J. Deegan & Yair Shazar. LC 72-156063. (Illus.). 80p. (gr. 4-9). 1970. PLB 5.95 o.p. (ISBN 0-87191-053-5). Creative Ed.

Kibbutz: New a of Life. D. Leon. 1969. 16.50 (ISBN 0-08-013357-6); pap. 7.75 (ISBN 0-08-013356-8). Pergamon.

Kick a Stone Home. Doris B. Smith. LC 74-4209. (gr. 5 up). 1974. 8.95 (ISBN 0-690-00535-0, TYC-J). T Y Crowell.

Kickapoos: Lords of the Middle Border. Arrell M. Gibson. (Civilization of the American Indian Ser.: No. 70). (Illus.). 1976. pap. 6.95 (ISBN 0-8061-1264-6). U of Okla Pr.

Kicking Techniques. Roy Kurban. LC 79-65639. (Ser. 211). (Illus.). 1979. pap. 5.95 (ISBN 0-89750-065-2). Ohara Pubns.

Kicking Your Stress Habits: A Do-It-Yourself Guide for Coping with Stress. Donald A. Tubesing. LC 80-54046. (Orig.). 1981. pap. 10.00 (ISBN 0-938586-00-9). Whole Person.

Kickingbird Kids' Book Factory. Theodore L. Harris et al. (Keys to Reading Ser.). (Illus.). 160p. (gr. 4). 1975. pap. text ed. 2.97 (ISBN 0-87892-448-5); tchr's. ed. 2.97 (ISBN 0-87892-449-3); dupl. masters 15.51 (ISBN 0-87892-049-8). Economy Co.

Kickle Snifters & Other Fearsome Critters. Alvin Schwartz. LC 75-29048. (gr. k-4). 1976. 8.95 (ISBN 0-397-31645-3). Lippincott.

Kid. Pete Axthelm. (Illus.). 1978. 10.00 o.p. (ISBN 0-670-41296-1). Viking Pr.

Kid. John Baxter. LC 80-25042. 312p. 1981. 13.95 (ISBN 0-670-41297-X). Viking Pr.

Kid. Elizabeth B. Custer. (Custer Monograph: No. 2). (Illus.). 47p. 1978. Repr. of 1900 ed. limited ed. 8.00x (ISBN 0-686-28493-3). Monroe County Lib.

Kid Andrew Cody & Julie Sparrow. Tony Curtis. 1977. 8.95 o.p. (ISBN 0-385-12405-8). Doubleday.

Kid Comes Home. Leo Mailman. 1980. 2.00 (ISBN 0-916918-01-7, Pub. by Duck Down Press). Maelstrom.

Kid Crafts. Janet Dubane & Diane Friend. (Illus.). 64p. (Orig.). 1980. pap. 2.00 (ISBN 0-918178-23-1). Simplicity.

Kid Glove Charlie. John Cashman. LC 77-3786. 1978. 10.00 o.p. (ISBN 0-06-010698-0, HarpT). Har-Row.

Kid Power. Susan B. Pfeffer. LC 77-1975. (gr. 4-6). 1977. PLB 6.90 s&l (ISBN 0-531-00123-7). Watts.

Kid Who Only Hit Homers. Matt Christopher. (gr. 4-6). 1972. 6.95 (ISBN 0-316-13918-1). Little.

Kidnapped. Robert L. Stevensen. (Childrens Illustrated Classics Ser). (Illus.). 1974. Repr. of 1960 ed. 5.50x o.p. (ISBN 0-460-05045-1, Pub. by J. M. Dent England). Biblio Dist.

Kidnapped at Chowchilla. Gail Miller & Sandra Tompkins. 1977. pap. 1.95 o.p. (ISBN 0-88270-217-3). Logos.

Kidnapped at Christmas: A Play for Children. Willis Hall. (gr. 10). 1975. pap. text ed. 2.95x (ISBN 0-435-23368-8). Heinemann Ed.

Kidnapped for My Faith. Kent Levitt. 1978. pap. cancelled o.s.i. (ISBN 0-89728-006-7). Omega Pubns OR.

Kidnapped Saint & Other Stories by B. Traven. Ed. by Nina C. Klein & H. Arthur Klein. LC 74-9349. 1977. 8.95 (ISBN 0-88208-049-0); pap. 5.95 (ISBN 0-88208-074-1). Lawrence Hill.

Kidnapper. Kelley Roos. 1981. 9.95 (ISBN 0-8027-5436-8). Walker & Co.

Kidnapping Mr. Tubbs. Don Schellie. LC 78-6153. 192p. (gr. 7 up). 1978. 7.95 (ISBN 0-590-07542-X, Four Winds). Schol Bk Serv.

Kidnapping of Anna. Ruth Hooker & Carole Smith. Ed. by Kathy Pacini. LC 78-32051. (Pilot Bk.). (Illus.). (gr. 3-8). 1979. 6.95g (ISBN 0-8075-4176-1). A Whitman.

Kidnapping of Christina Lattimore. Joan L. Nixon. (gr. 7-12). 1980. pap. 1.50 (ISBN 0-440-94520-8, LFL). Dell.

Kidney, 2 vols. 2nd ed. Ed. by Barry M. Rector & Floyd C. Rector. 1981. Vol. 1. text ed. write for info. (ISBN 0-7216-1967-3); Vol. 2. text ed. write for info. (ISBN 0-7216-1968-1); Set. text ed. write for info. (ISBN 0-7216-1969-X). Saunders.

Kidney & Pregnancy. Ed. by G. M. Eisenbach & J. Brod. (Contributions to Nephrology Ser.: Vol. 25). (Illus.). vi, 144p. 1981. pap. 54.00 (ISBN 3-8055-1798-X). S Karger.

Kidney & Urinary Tract Physiology, Vol. III. K. Thurau. 1982. 39.50 (ISBN 0-685-32572-5). Univ Park. Postponed.

Kidney & Urinary Tract Physiology, II. K. Thurau. (International Review of Physiology: Vol. II). 1976. 29.50 (ISBN 0-8391-1060-X). Univ Park.

Kidney Disease Case Studies. 2nd. ed. Alvin E. Parrish. 1979. 14.75 (ISBN 0-87488-022-X). Med Exam.

Kidney Disease: Hematologic & Vascular Problems. R. M. McIntosh et al. LC 77-7529. (Perspectives in Nephrology & Hypertension Ser.). 1977. 34.50 (ISBN 0-471-01921-6, Pub. by Wiley Medical). Wiley.

Kidney in Pregnancy. Ed. by Russell R. De Alvarez. LC 76-13184. (Clinical Obstetrics & Gynecology Ser.). 1976. 33.95 (ISBN 0-471-20030-1, Pub. by Wiley Medical). Wiley.

Kidney: Morphology, Biochemistry, Physiology. Ed. by C. Rouiller & A. Muller. Incl. Vols. 1-2. 1969. 65.00. Vol. 1 (ISBN 0-12-598801-X). Vol. 2. 68.00 (ISBN 0-12-598802-8); Vols. 3-4. 1971. 52.00 ea. Vol. 3 (ISBN 0-12-598803-6). Vol. 4 (ISBN 0-12-598804-4). Set. 196.00 (ISBN 0-686-66787-5). Acad Pr.

Kidneys & the Internal Environment. R. J. Harvey. LC 74-2776. 167p. 1976. text ed. 10.95x o.p. (ISBN 0-412-12260-X, Pub. by Chapman & Hall). Methuen Inc.

Kidneys & the Internal Environment. R. J. Harvey. LC 74-2776. 1976. 10.95 o.p. (ISBN 0-470-35775-4). Halsted Pr.

Kids & Booze: What You Must Know to Help Them. Wilbur Cross. 1979. 10.95 o.p.; pap. 5.95 (ISBN 0-87690-314-6). Dutton.

Kids & Cash. Ken Davis & Tom Taylor. 320p. 1981. pap. 2.95 (ISBN 0-553-14152-X). Bantam.

Kids & Cash: Solving a Parent's Dilemma. Ken Davis & Tom Taylor. LC 79-13092. (Illus.). 1979. 8.95 (ISBN 0-916392-26-0). Oak Tree Pubns.

Kids & Dog Shows. Lynn Hall. LC 73-93558. 160p. (gr. 4-7). 1974. 5.95 o.p. (ISBN 0-695-80482-0); lib. bdg. 5.97 o.p. (ISBN 0-695-40482-2). Follett.

Kids Are God's Idea. Roy Lessin. (God's Idea Books Ser.). (Illus.). 32p. (ps-4). 1981. pap. 1.25 (ISBN 0-87123-178-6, 210178). Bethany Fell.

Kids Are Natural Cooks. Parents Nursery School. (Illus.). (ps-6). 1974. pap. 5.95 (ISBN 0-395-18521-1, Sandpiper). HM.

Kids at the Door: A Preventative Project on a Council Estate. Bob Holman. (Practical of Social Work Ser.: No. 8). 208p. 1981. 25.00x (ISBN 0-631-12586-8, Pub. by Basil Blackwell England); pap. 12.50x (ISBN 0-631-12587-6). Biblio Dist.

Kids' Book of Divorce. Fayerweather Street School. Ed. by Eric Rofes. 112p. 1981. 7.95 (ISBN 0-86616-003-5). Lewis Pub Co.

Kids, Brains, & Learning: What Goes Wrong-Prevention & Treatment. Ray C. Wunderlich, Jr. LC 76-79767. (Illus.). 534p. 1970. 13.75 (ISBN 0-910812-03-9); pap. 9.85 (ISBN 0-910812-04-7). Johnny Reads.

Kid's Code & Cipher Book. Nancy Garden. LC 80-10434. (Illus.). 176p. (gr. 5 up). 1981. 10.95 (ISBN 0-03-053856-4); pap. 4.95 (ISBN 0-03-059267-4). HR&W.

Kids Cooking Naturally. Catherine J. Frompovich. (Illus.). 32p. (gr. 2-5). 1979. pap. 1.29x (ISBN 0-935322-04-3). C J Frompovich.

Kids' Fifty-State Cookbook. Aileen Paul. LC 76-2812. (gr. 3-7). 1976. PLB 6.95 (ISBN 0-385-11228-9). Doubleday.

Kid's Guide. Ira Kamin. Ed. by Jan Leonard. LC 80-66586. (Savvy San Francisco Ser.). 64p. (Orig.). 1980. pap. 2.50 (ISBN 0-89395-046-7). Cal Living Bks.

Kids Having Kids. Janet Bode. (gr. 9 up). 1980. PLB 7.90 (ISBN 0-531-02882-8, B19). Watts.

Kids in the Kitchen. Nellie Edge & Pierr M. Leitz. Orig. Title: Kindergarten Cooks. (Illus.). 165p. (gr. k-6). 1979. pap. 6.95 (ISBN 0-918146-18-6). Peninsula WA.

Kids Indoor Gardening. Aileen Paul. (gr. 4-7). 1975. pap. 0.75 o.s.i. (ISBN 0-671-29608-6). Archway.

Kids' Indoor Gardening. Aileen Paul. (gr. 4-7). pap. 0.75 (ISBN 0-671-29608-6). PB.

Kids' Kitchen Takeover. Sara Stein. LC 75-20382. (Parents & Children Together Ser.). (Illus.). 208p. (gr. 4 up). 1975. 9.95 (ISBN 0-911104-45-3); pap. 5.95 (ISBN 0-911104-46-1). Workman Pub.

Kid's Natural Foods Party & Picnic Color & Cookbook. Karen Whyte. (Illus.). 40p. (gr. 1-8). 1979. pap. 2.25 (ISBN 0-912300-13-2). Troubador Pr.

Kids of Mischief Island. D. W. Woody. 1981. 4.75 (ISBN 0-8062-1693-X). Carlton.

Kids on the Run: The Stories of Seven Teen-Age Runaways. James R. Berry. LC 77-15845. 112p. (gr. 7 up). 1978. 6.95 (ISBN 0-590-07507-1, Four Winds). Schol Bk Serv.

Kids' Stuff: Kindergarten - Nursery School. Collier et al. (ps-k). 1969. pap. 10.95 (ISBN 0-913916-00-5, IP005). Incentive Pubns.

Kids' Stuff: Reading & Writing Readiness. Cherrie Farnette et al. LC 75-5347. (Illus.). (gr. 1-2). 1975. 10.95 (ISBN 0-913916-13-7). Incentive Pubns.

Kidstories: Seasonal & Topical Sermons for Children. Betsy Larson. (Paperback Program Ser.). 128p. 1980. pap. 2.95 (ISBN 0-8010-5598-9). Baker Bk.

Kierkegaard: A Kind of Poet. Louis Mackey. LC 75-157050. (Orig.). 1971. 15.00x (ISBN 0-8122-7641-8); pap. 5.95x (ISBN 0-8122-1042-5). U of Pa Pr.

Kierkegaard & Christendom. John W. Elrod. LC 80-8547. 384p. 1981. 22.50x (ISBN 0-691-07261-2). Princeton U Pr.

Kierkegaard & the Existential Philosophy. Lev Shestov. Tr. by Elinor Hewitt. LC 68-29656. vii, 314p. 1969. 16.00 (ISBN 0-8214-0060-6). Ohio U Pr.

Kierkegaard As Educator. Ronald J. Manheimer. 1978. 15.75x (ISBN 0-520-03312-4). U of Cal Pr.

Kierkegaard Handbook. Frederick Sontag. LC 79-87741. 1980. pap. 6.95 (ISBN 0-8042-0654-6). John Knox.

Kierkegaard's Philosophy: Self-Deception & Cowardice in the Present Age. John D. Mullen. (Orig.). 1981. pap. 2.95 (ISBN 0-451-61945-5, ME1945, Ment). NAL.

Kierkegaard's Presence in Contemporary American Life: Essays from Various Disciplines. Ed. by Lewis A. Lawson. LC 76-142237. 1971. 10.00 (ISBN 0-8108-0358-5). Scarecrow.

Kierkegaard's Thought. Gregor Malantschuk. Tr. by Howard V. Hong & Edna H. Hong. LC 77-155000. 400p. (Eng.). 1974. 25.00x (ISBN 0-691-07166-7, 317); pap. 4.45 (ISBN 0-691-01982-7). Princeton U Pr.

Kierkegaard's Truth: The Disclosure of the Self. Ed. by Joseph H. Smith. LC 80-27055. (Psychiatry & the Humanities: Vol. 5). (Illus.). 456p. 1981. 36.50x (ISBN 0-300-02621-8). Yale U Pr.

Kiev Caves Paterikon: A Hagiography of the Kiev Caves Monastery. Lev Puhalo. 1980. pap. 7.50 (ISBN 0-913026-80-8). St Nectarios.

Kikuyu-English Dictionary. Ed. by T. G. Benson. 1964. 24.95x (ISBN 0-19-864405-1). Oxford U Pr.

Kildeer's Pride. Jed Cross. 192p. (Orig.). 1976. pap. 0.95 o.p. (ISBN 0-445-00687-0). Popular Lib.

Kilgallen. Lee Isreal. 1980. pap. 2.95 o.s.i. (ISBN 0-440-14565-1). Dell.

Kill. Emile Zola. 1957. 13.95 (ISBN 0-236-30899-8, Pub. by Paul Elek). Merrimack Bk Serv.

Kill Him, Again. William R. Garwood. LC 80-66355. 315p. 1980. 9.95 (ISBN 0-937618-00-4). Bath St Pr.

Kill Quick or Die. Stuart Jason. (Butcher Ser.: No. 1). 1979. pap. 1.75 (ISBN 0-523-40678-9). Pinnacle Bks.

Kill the Dead. Tanith Lee. (Science Fiction Ser.). 1980. pap. 1.75 (ISBN 0-87997-562-8, UE1562). Daw Bks.

Kill the Dutchman! Paul Sann. 352p. 1972. pap. 1.25 o.p. (ISBN 0-445-00138-0). Popular Lib.

Kill the Messenger Who Brings Bad News. Robert Kelly. 242p. 1979. signed 20.00 (ISBN 0-87685-433-1); pap. 7.50 (ISBN 0-87685-432-3). Black Sparrow.

Killer. Thomas E. Gaddis. 1970. 7.95 o.s.i. (ISBN 0-02-542100-X). Macmillan.

Killer. Steven Havill. LC 80-1987. (Double D Western Ser.). 192p. 1981. 9.95 (ISBN 0-385-17287-7). Doubleday.

Killer Bears. 1980. 12.50 o.p. (ISBN 0-679-51152-0). McKay.

Killer Bees. Melinda Blau. LC 77-10010. (Great Unsolved Mysteries of Our Time Ser.). (Illus.). (gr. 4-5). 1977. PLB 9.65 (ISBN 0-8172-1055-5). Raintree Pubs.

Killer Chromosomes. Warren Murphy. (Destroyer Ser.: No. 32). 1978. pap. 1.75 (ISBN 0-523-40908-7). Pinnacle Bks.

Killer Colt. James W. Smith. 1977. pap. 1.25 o.s.i. (ISBN 0-515-04376-1). Jove Pubns.

Killer Come to Shiloh. C. H. Hasseloff. 176p. (Orig.). 1981. pap. 1.95 (ISBN 0-553-14742-0). Bantam.

Killer Cops. Edwin D. Krell & Major J. Vasel. (Orig.). 1979. pap. 1.95 (ISBN 0-532-23265-8). Manor Bks.

Killer Dolphin. Ngaio Marsh. (Ngaio Marsh Mystery Ser.). 256p. 1980. pap. 1.95 (ISBN 0-515-05435-6). Jove Pubns.

Killer Genesis. Axel Kilgore. (Orig.). 1980. pap. 2.25 (ISBN 0-89083-678-7, Kable News Co). Zebra.

Killer Gray. Jason Manning. (Orig.). 1980. pap. 1.95 (ISBN 0-532-23212-7). Manor Bks.

Killer Insects. Don Causey. (Illus.). (gr. 4-6). 1979. PLB 6.90 s&l (ISBN 0-531-02924-7). Watts.

Killer Music. Lisa Eisenberg. LC 79-52657. (Laura Brewster Mysteries Ser.). (Illus.). 64p. (gr. 4 up). 1980. PLB 7.95 (ISBN 0-516-02209-1). Childrens.

Killer on the Heights. Michael Jahn. 1977. pap. 1.75 o.p. (ISBN 0-449-13906-9, GM). Fawcett.

Killer Silver. Charles R. Pike. LC 80-68163. (Jubal Cade Westerns Ser.). 144p. 1980. pap. 2.95 (ISBN 0-87754-233-3). Chelsea Hse.

Killer Spores. Richard Woodley. 1978. pap. 1.50 o.s.i. (ISBN 0-440-15926-1). Dell.

Killer Storms: Hurricanes, Typhoons, & Tornadoes. Gary Jennings. LC 78-101899. (Illus.). (gr. 7-9). 1970. 7.89 (ISBN 0-397-31128-1). Lippincott.

Killer Swan. Eth Clifford. (gr. 5-8). 1980. 6.95 (ISBN 0-395-29742-7). HM.

Killer with the Golden Touch. Alan Riefe. (Cage Ser.: No. 6). 176p. (Orig.). 1975. pap. 0.95 o.p. (ISBN 0-445-00672-2). Popular Lib.

Killer's Choice. Ed McBain. 192p. 1975. pap. 1.25 (ISBN 0-345-29288-X). Ballantine.

Killer's Choice - an 87th Precinct Mystery. Ed McBain. 1981. pap. 2.50 (ISBN 0-345-29288-X). Ballantine.

Killer's Corral. Merle Constiner. 1978. pap. 1.25 (ISBN 0-505-51237-8). Tower Bks.

Killers of Innocence. John Creasey. 1980. pap. 1.95 (ISBN 0-441-44275-7). Charter Bks.

Killers of Starfish. Jackson Gillis. LC 77-6231. 1977. 8.95 o.p. (ISBN 0-397-01201-2). Lippincott.

Killers of the Dream. rev. ed. Lillian Smith. 1961. 12.95 (ISBN 0-393-06332-1, Norton Lib); pap. 3.95 1978 (ISBN 0-393-00884-3). Norton.

Killers of the Seas. Edward R. Ricciuti. (Illus.). 208p. 1973. 10.00 o.s.i. (ISBN 0-8027-0415-8). Walker & Co.

Killing & Letting Die. B. Steinbock. 239p. 1980. pap. 9.00 (ISBN 0-13-515361-1). P-H.

Killing Defence at Bridge. H. W. Kelsey. 1978. 8.95 o.p. (ISBN 0-571-06869-3, Pub. by Faber & Faber). Merrimack Bk Serv.

Killing Effects of Calvinism. Bob L. Ross. 1980. pap. 1.25. Pilgrim Pubns.

Killing Ground. Charles R. Pike. LC 80-70090. (Jubal Cade Westerns Ser.). 144p. 1981. pap. 2.95 (ISBN 0-87754-239-2). Chelsea Hse.

Killing in Antiques. Bill Knox. LC 80-2967. 192p. 1981. 9.95 (ISBN 0-385-17625-2). Doubleday.

Killing in Defense of Private Property: The Development of a Roman Catholic Moral Teaching, Thirteenth to Eighteenth Centuries. Shaun J. Sullivan. LC 75-38843. (American Academy of Religion. Dissertation Ser.). (Illus.). 1976. pap. 7.50 (ISBN 0-89130-067-8, 010115). Scholars Pr Ca.

Killing in Gold. Joe L. Hensley. LC 76-56300. 1978. 7.95 o.p. (ISBN 0-385-12854-1). Doubleday.

Killing Kindness. Reginald Hill. 1981. 10.95 (ISBN 0-394-51910-8). Pantheon.

Killing Mr. Griffin. Lois Duncan. (YA) 1980. pap. 1.75 (ISBN 0-440-94515-1, LFL). Dell.

Killing No Murder. Harold Shaw. 192p. 1981. 8.95 (ISBN 0-684-16884-7, ScribT). Scribner.

Killing of Corporal Kunze. Wilma T. Parnell & Robert Taber. (Illus.). 224p. 1981. 10.00 (ISBN 0-8184-0313-6). Lyle Stuart.

Killing of Julia Wallace. Jonathan Goodman. LC 76-9918. 1977. 7.95 o.p. (ISBN 0-684-14793-9, ScribT). Scribner.

Killing of Karen Silkwood. Richard Rashke. 1981. 12.95 (ISBN 0-395-30233-1). HM.

Killing of Katie Steelstock. Michael Gilbert. LC 79-3409. (Harper Novel of Suspense Ser.). 304p. 1980. 12.95 (ISBN 0-06-011494-0, HarpT). Har-Row.

Killing Season. Barbara Brenner. LC 80-69993. 160p. (gr. 7 up). 1981. 8.95 (ISBN 0-590-07674-4, Four Winds). Schol Bk Serv.

Killing the King: Three Studies in Shakespeare's Tragic Structure. Maynard Mack, Jr. LC 72-91301. (Studies in English: No. 180). 240p. 1973. 15.00x o.p. (ISBN 0-300-01450-3). Yale U Pr.

Killing Time. Patricia Windsor. LC 80-7926. 196p. (YA) (gr. 7 up). 1980. 8.95 (ISBN 0-06-026549-3, HarpJ); PLB 8.79 (ISBN 0-06-026550-7). Har-Row.

Killing Time: A Play by Francis Warner. Francis Warner. (Oxford Theatre Texts Ser.: No. 3). (Illus.). 1976. text ed. 7.25x (ISBN 0-85635-198-9). Humanities.

Killing Time: Life in the Arkansas Penitentary. Bruce Jackson. 1977. 18.50 (ISBN 0-8014-1101-7); pap. 6.95 (ISBN 0-8014-9176-2). Cornell U Pr.

Killing Trail. Charles R. Pike. LC 80-68159. (Jubal Cade Westerns Ser.). 128p. 1980. pap. 2.95 (ISBN 0-87754-230-9). Chelsea Hse.

Killing Tree. Jay Bennett. LC 76-189567. 128p. (gr. 7-12). 1972. PLB 4.90 o.p. (ISBN 0-531-02559-4). Watts.

Kiln Book. 2nd ed. Frederick L. Olsen. LC 72-94254. 1978. pap. 9.50 o.p. (ISBN 0-935066-02-0). Keramos Bks.

Kiln Building with Space-Age Materials. Frank A. Colson. 127p. 1980. pap. 7.95 (ISBN 0-442-24423-1). Van Nos Reinhold.

Kilt Beneath My Cassock. R. H. Falconer. 1978. pap. 15.00x (ISBN 0-905312-02-3, Pub. by Scottish Academic Pr Scotland). Columbia U Pr.

Kimbangu. Marie Louise Martin. Tr. by D. M. Moore. 224p. 1976. 8.95 o.p. (ISBN 0-8028-3483-3). Eerdmans.

Kimberlites & Their Xenoliths. J. B. Dawson. (Minerals & Rocks: Vol. 15). (Illus.). 252p. 1980. 47.25 (ISBN 0-387-10208-6). Springer-Verlag.

Kime's International Law Directory for 1980. 88th ed. Ed. by James M. Matthews. 809p. 1981. 52.50x (ISBN 0-900503-12-2). Intl Pubns Serv.

Kin & Communities: Families in America. Allan J. Lichtman & Joan R. Challinor. LC 78-24246. (Illus.). 335p. 1979. text ed. 19.95x (ISBN 0-87474-608-6); pap. text ed. 8.95x (ISBN 0-87474-609-4). Smithsonian.

Kin, Clan, Raja, & Rule: State-Hinterland Relations in Preindustrial India. Richard G. Fox. LC 76-129614. (Center for South & Southeast Asia Studies, UC Berkeley). 1971. 17.50x (ISBN 0-520-01807-9). U of Cal Pr.

Kin-der-Kids: All Thirty-One Strips in Full Color. Lyonel Feininger. (Illus.). 32p. (Orig.). 1980. pap. 6.00 (ISBN 0-486-23918-7). Dover.

Kincaids. Matthew Braun. 1977. pap. 1.95 o.p. (ISBN 0-425-03442-9, Medallion). Berkley Pub.

Kind Are Her Answers. Mary Renault. 287p. 1976. Repr. of 1940 ed. lib. bdg. 13.95x (ISBN 0-89244-078-3). Queens Hse.

Kind of Prisoner. John Creasey. 1975. pap. 0.95 o.p. (ISBN 0-445-00675-7). Popular Lib.

Kind of Wild Justice. Bernard Ashley. LC 78-10899. (Illus.). (gr. 7 up). 1979. 9.95 (ISBN 0-87599-229-3). S G Phillips.

Kinder-Fun Insect Series. rev. ed. Patty J. Garber et al. Incl. Funny Little Ant; Ladybug, Ladybug; Fly, Fly; Little Yellow Butterfly; Little Mosquito; Bad Little Cricket. (Illus.). 16p. (For partially-sighted & partially-hearing children). (ps-2). 1973. Set. pap. text ed. 16.00x (ISBN 0-89039-055-X). Ann Arbor Pubs.

Kinder-Fun Sports Series. Patty J. Garber et al. Incl. Fun Balls; Jump, Jump, Jump; Home Run; Joey (Basketball; Football; Snow Fun. (Illus.). 16p. (For partially-sighted & partially-hearing children). (ps-2). 1973. Set. pap. text ed. 16.00 (ISBN 0-89039-056-8). Ann Arbor Pubs.

Kinderchirurgische Probleme in der paediatrische Praxis. Ed. by M. Bettex & A. Koch. (Paediatrische Fortbildungskurse fuer die Praxis: Vol. 49). (Illus.). 1980. soft cover 29.50 (ISBN 3-8055-0232-X). S Karger.

Kindergarten & Early Schooling. Dorothy H. Cohen & Marguerita Rudolph. (Illus.). 352p. 1977. text ed. 17.95 (ISBN 0-13-515239-9). P-H.

Kindergarten Cooks. Nellie Edge. LC 76-48558. (Illus.). (gr. k-6). 1976. pap. write for info. o.p. (ISBN 0-918146-00-3). Peninsula Pub WA.

Kindergarten Crusade: The Establishment of Preschool Education in the United States. Elizabeth D. Ross. LC 75-36986. ix, 119p. 1976. 9.00x (ISBN 0-8214-0206-4); pap. 4.25 o.s.i. (ISBN 0-8214-0228-5). Ohio U Pr.

Kindergarten: Its Encounter with Educational Thought in America. Evelyn Weber. LC 70-75202. 1969. pap. 8.25x (ISBN 0-8077-2315-0). Tchrs Coll.

Kindergarten Keys. rev. ed. Nell Nale et al. 1975. tchr's guidebk. 85.50 (ISBN 0-87892-655-0). Economy Co.

Kindergarten of the Movies: A History of the Fine Arts Company. Anthony Slide. LC 80-20391. 246p. 1980. 13.50 (ISBN 0-8108-1358-0). Scarecrow.

Kindergarten Pattern Book. Evelyn Grogg. Rev. by Sarah Eberle. (Illus.). 48p. (Orig.). 1981. pap. 3.95 (ISBN 0-87239-431-X, 2159). Standard Pub.

Kindergarten Program. Virginia H. Lucas et al. (Illus.). 1980. pupil bk. 2.97 (ISBN 0-88309-101-1); tchr's guide 4.97 (ISBN 0-88309-102-X). Zaner-Bloser.

Kindergarten: Program & Practices. Marjorie E. Ramsey & Kathleen Bayless. LC 80-11478. (Illus.). 1980. pap. text ed. 12.95 (ISBN 0-8016-4076-8). Mosby.

Kindergarten Screening. Shirley Zeitlin. (Illus.). 304p. 1976. 19.75 (ISBN 0-398-03574-1). C C Thomas.

Kindheit. Hans Carossa. Ed. by Jethro Bithell. 1965. Repr. of 1942 ed. pap. 4.50x o.p. (ISBN 0-631-01490-X, Pub. by Basil Blackwell). Biblio Dist.

Kindling. Cheli Duran. LC 78-23629. (gr. 7 up). 1979. 7.50 (ISBN 0-688-80199-4); PLB 7.20 (ISBN 0-688-84199-6). Greenwillow.

Kindling. Ed. by Juhn A. Wada. LC 76-5662. 1976. 20.50 (ISBN 0-89004-124-5). Raven.

Kindling of the Flame. Marguita Seavy & Susan Seary. (gr. 6 up). 1980. PLB 8.90 (ISBN 0-531-04161-1, E32). Watts.

Kindling Two. Ed. by Juhn A. Wada. 300p. 1981. 30.00 (ISBN 0-89004-630-1). Raven.

Kindly Bent to Ease Us. Klong-Chen Rab-'Byams-Pa. Tr. by Herbert V. Guenther. LC 75-29959. (Tibetan Translation Ser.: Vol. 5). 1975. 14.95 (ISBN 0-913546-39-9); pap. 7.95 (ISBN 0-913546-40-2). Dharma Pub.

Kindly Bent to Ease Us: Meditation, Pt. 2. Klong-Chen Rab-'Byams-Pa. LC 75-29959. (Tibetan Translation Ser.: Vol. 6). (Illus., Orig.). 1976. 12.95 (ISBN 0-913546-42-9); pap. 6.50 (ISBN 0-913546-43-7). Dharma Pub.

Kindly Bent to Ease Us: Wonderment, Part 3. Klong-Chen Rab-'Byams-Pa. Tr. by Herbert V. Guenther from Tibetan. LC 75-29959. (Tibetan Translation Ser: Vol. 7). (Illus.). 1976. 12.95 (ISBN 0-913546-44-5); pap. 6.50 (ISBN 0-913546-45-3). Dharma Pub.

Kindly Dig Your Grave & Other Wicked Stories. Stanley Ellin. Ed. by Ellery Queen. LC 78-82628. 1977. pap. 1.50 o.p. (ISBN 0-89559-008-5). Davis Pubns.

Kindly Ones. Anthony Powell. (A Dance to the Music of Time: No. 2). 1976. pap. 2.50 (ISBN 0-445-08446-4). Popular Lib.

Kindness. Jane Moncure. (What Does the Bible Say? Ser.). (Illus.). 32p. 4.95 (ISBN 0-89565-167-X, 4929). Standard Pub.

Kindness. rev. ed. Jane B. Moncure. LC 80-39535. (What Is It? Ser.). (Illus.). 32p. (gr. k-3). 1981. PLB 5.50 (ISBN 0-89565-204-8). Childs World.

Kindness to Pets. Virginia Parkinson. (Pointers for Little Persons Ser). (Illus.). (gr. k-3). 1961. PLB 5.99 (ISBN 0-8178-5032-5). Harvey.

Kindred. Octavia Butler. 1981. pap. write for info. (ISBN 0-671-83483-5). PB.

Kindred by Choice. Johann W. Von Goethe. Tr. by H. M. Waidson. 1980. pap. 4.95 (ISBN 0-7145-0324-X). Riverrun NY.

Kindred Spirit. Ginger Chambers. (Orig.). 1981. pap. 1.50 (ISBN 0-440-14395-0). Dell.

Kinds of Affection. Josephine Miles. LC 67-24108. (Wesleyan Poetry Program: Vol. 36). (Orig.). 1967. 10.00x (ISBN 0-8195-2036-5, Pub. by Wesleyan U Pr). Columbia U Pr.

Kinds of Mankind: An Introduction to Race & Racism. Morton Klass & Hal Hellman. 1971. text ed. write for info. scp (ISBN 0-397-31129-X, HarpC); pap. text ed. 4.50 o.p (ISBN 0-397-47267-6). Har-Row.

Kinematics. William J. Patton. (Illus.). 1979. text ed. 18.95 (ISBN 0-8359-3693-7); students manual avail. (ISBN 0-8359-3694-5). Reston.

Kinematics & Dynamics of Machines. 2nd ed. George H. Martin. (Illus.). 544p. 1982. text ed. 28.95x (ISBN 0-07-040657-X, C); write for info. solutions manual (ISBN 0-07-040658-8). McGraw.

Kinematics & Dynamics of Planar Machinery. Burton Paul. (Illus.). 1979. text ed. 32.95 (ISBN 0-13-516062-6). P-H.

Kinematics & Geometry of Planer & Spatial CAM Mechanisms. J. Chakraborty & S. G. Dhande. LC 76-50585. 1977. 14.95 (ISBN 0-470-15069-6). Halsted Pr.

Kinematics & Mechanisms Design. C. H. Suh & C. W. Radcliffe. LC 77-7102. 1978. 30.95 (ISBN 0-471-01461-3). Wiley.

Kinematics for Technology. Anthony Esposito. LC 72-96341. 1973. text ed. 19.95x (ISBN 0-675-09005-9); instructor's manual 3.95 (ISBN 0-686-66863-4). Merrill.

Kinematics of Machinery: Outlines of a Theory of Machines. Franz Reuleaux. Tr. by Alexander B. Kennedy. (Illus.). 1876. pap. text ed. 6.00 (ISBN 0-486-61124-8). Dover.

Kinematics of Mechanisms. N. Rosenauer & A. H. Willis. pap. text ed. 4.00 (ISBN 0-486-61796-3). Dover.

Kinesics & Context. Ray L. Whistell. 1975. pap. 1.95 o.p. (ISBN 0-345-24841-4). Ballantine.

Kinesics & Context: Essays on Body Motion Communication. Ray L. Birdwhistell. LC 77-122379. (Conduct & Communication Ser.: No. 2). 1970. 12.00x o.p. (ISBN 0-8122-7605-1); pap. 7.95x (ISBN 0-8122-1012-3, Pa Paperbks). U of Pa Pr.

Kinesics & Cross-Cultural Understanding. Genelle G. Morain. (Language in Education Ser.: No. 7). 1978. pap. 2.95 (ISBN 0-87281-089-5). Ctr Appl Ling.

Kinesiology. rev. 4th ed. John M. Cooper & Ruth B. Glassow. LC 75-33991. (Illus.). 1976. 13.95 (ISBN 0-8016-1048-6). Mosby.

Kinesiology. 2nd ed. Marilyn M. Hinson. 336p. 1981. text ed. write for info. (ISBN 0-697-07173-1). Wm C Brown.

Kinesiology: Of the Human Body Under Normal & Pathological Conditions. Arthur Steindler. (Illus.). 736p. 1977. 33.75 (ISBN 0-398-01846-4). C C Thomas.

Kinesiology: The Science of Movement. John Piscope. LC 80-21545. 650p. 1981. text ed. 18.95 (ISBN 0-471-03483-5). Wiley.

Kinesiology: Workbook & Laboratory Manual. Ruth Harris. (Illus.). 1977. 10.95 (ISBN 0-395-20668-5). HM.

Kinetic & Nonsteady-State Effects in Superconductors. B. T. Geilikman & V. Z. Kresin. Tr. by P. Shelnitz from Rus. LC 73-22089. 170p. 1974. 29.95 o.p. (ISBN 0-470-29513-9). Halsted*Pr.

Kinetic Methods of Analysis. K. B. Yatsimirskii. Tr. by P. J. Harvey. 1966. 25.00 (ISBN 0-08-011364-8); pap. 8.25 (ISBN 0-08-013827-6). Pergamon.

Kinetic Systems: Mathematical Description of Chemical Kinetics in Solution. Christos Capellos & Benon H. Bielski. LC 80-11940. 152p. 1980. pap. 7.75 (ISBN 0-89874-141-6). Krieger.

Kinetics & Dynamics of Elementary Gas Reactions. Ian W. Smith. LC 79-40533. (Illus.). 1980. 72.95 (ISBN 0-408-70790-9). Butterworths.

Kinetics & Mechanism: A Study of Homogeneous Reactions. 2nd ed. Arthur A. Frost & R. G. Pearson. LC 61-6773. 1961. 23.95 o.p. (ISBN 0-471-28347-9). Wiley.

Kinetics & Mechanism of Polyreactions: Symposium, 6 vols. International Symposium on Macro Molecular Chemistry. Ed. by F. Tuedoes. Vols. 1-5. pap. 64.00 o.p. (ISBN 0-685-27541-8); Vol. 6. pap. 35.00 o.p. (ISBN 0-685-27542-6). Adler.

Kinetics & Mechanisms of Polymerization Reactions: Applications of Physico-Chemical Principles. P. E. Allen & C. R. Patrick. LC 74-3476. 596p. 1974. 64.95 (ISBN 0-470-02320-1). Halsted Pr.

Kinetics & Noise Analysis of Zero-Power Reactors: An NPY-Project Report. (Technical Reports Ser.: No. 138). (Illus.). 110p. (Orig.). 1973. pap. 7.50 (ISBN 92-0-135072-4, IAEA). Unipub.

Kinetics of Coal Gasification. James L. Johnson. LC 79-10439. 1979. 27.50 (ISBN 0-471-05575-1, Pub. by Wiley-Interscience). Wiley.

Kinetics of Fast Enzyme Reactions: Theory & Practice. Keitaro Hiromi. LC 79-19391. 346p. 1980. 49.95x (ISBN 0-470-26866-2). Halsted Pr.

Kinetics of Inorganic Reactions. A. G. Sykes. 1966. 22.00 (ISBN 0-08-011441-5); pap. 10.75 (ISBN 0-08-011440-7). Pergamon.

Kinetics of Muscle Contraction. D. C. White & John Thorson. 1975. pap. text ed. 11.25 (ISBN 0-08-018149-X). Pergamon.

Kinflicks. Lisa Alther. 1976. 8.95 o.p. (ISBN 0-394-49836-4). Knopf.

King Alfred's Version of St. Augustine's Soliloquies. Ed. by Thomas A. Carnicelli. LC 69-12719. 1969. 7.50x (ISBN 0-674-50360-0). Harvard U Pr.

King & Joker. Peter Dickinson. 1977. pap. 1.50 (ISBN 0-380-01767-9, 35006). Avon.

King & Messiah. 2nd ed. Ed. by Aage Bentzen & G. W. Andelson. 1970. 12.50x o.p. (ISBN 0-631-12850-6, Pub. by Basil Blackwell). Biblio Dist.

King & No King. Francis Beaumont & John Fletcher. LC 77-171733. (English Experience Ser.: No. 290). 88p. Repr. of 1619 ed. 15.00 (ISBN 90-221-0290-4). Walter J Johnson.

King & the Cat. Thomas Starling. LC 74-82405. 1975. 6.95 (ISBN 0-914864-00-9). Spindrift.

King & the Quaker. Vincent Buranelli. LC 61-6620. 1962. 9.00x o.p. (ISBN 0-8122-7343-5). U of Pa Pr.

King & the Servant. G. A. Pottebaum. (Little People's Paperbacks Ser.). pap. 0.99 (ISBN 0-8164-2251-6). Crossroad NY.

King & the Whirlybird. Mabel Watts. LC 69-12605. (Illus.). (gr. k-3). 1969. 5.95 o.s.i. (ISBN 0-8193-0289-9, Four Winds); PLB 5.41 o.s.i. (ISBN 0-8193-0290-2). Schol Bk Serv.

King Arthur & His Knights of the Round Table. Roger L. Green. (Orig.). (gr. 5-7). 1974. pap. 2.95 (ISBN 0-14-030073-2, Puffin). Penguin.

King Arthur & the Knights of the Round Table. Roger L. Green. 1980. pap. 2.95 (ISBN 0-14-030073-2). Penguin.

King Arthur & the Magic Sword. Harold G. Shane. Ed. by William Clark. (Hero Legends Bk.). (Illus.). 16p. (gr. 3-5). 1980. pap. 22.00 ten bks & one cass. (ISBN 0-89290-079-2, BC15-2). Soc for Visual.

King Arthur: His Knights & Their Ladies. Johnston. (gr. 7-12). 1980. pap. 1.50 (ISBN 0-590-30007-5, Schol Pap). Schol Bk Serv.

King Arthur's Death: The Middle English 'stanzaic Morte Arthur' & 'alliterative Morte Arthur' Larry Benson. LC 73-13545. (Library of Literature Ser). 1974. pap. text ed. 8.35 o.p. (ISBN 0-672-61010-8). Bobbs.

King Arthur's Sword. Errol LeCain. (Illus.). (ps-5). 1968. 5.95 o.p. (ISBN 0-571-08637-3, Pub. by Faber & Faber). Merrimack Bk Serv.

King Basil's Birthday. Miriam Young. LC 73-182288. (gr. k-4). 1973. PLB 5.90 (ISBN 0-531-02594-2). Watts.

King Beetle-Tamer & Other Lighthearted Wonder Tales. Isabel Wyatt. LC 79-21245. (Illus.). 160p. (gr. 3-12). 1980. 9.95 (ISBN 0-89742-029-2); pap. 6.95 (ISBN 0-89742-028-4). Dawne-Leigh.

King Bird Rides. Max Brand. 1972. pap. 1.95 (ISBN 0-446-90305-1). Warner Bks.

King Carlo of Capri. Warren Miller & Edward Sorel. LC 58-1749. (Illus.). (gr. 1-4). 1958. 2.95 o.p. (ISBN 0-15-242744-9, HJ). HarBraceJ.

King Charles Spaniels. M. Joyce Birchall. Ed. by Christina Foyle. (Foyle's Handbks). (Illus.). 1973. 3.95 (ISBN 0-685-55788-X). Palmetto Pub.

King Coal: A Novel. Upton B. Sinclair. LC 74-22813. (Labor Movement Ser.). 408p. 1980. Repr. of 1921 ed. 24.00 (ISBN 0-404-58469-1). AMS Pr.

King-Crane Commission. Harry N. Howard. (Return to Zion Ser.). (Illus.). xiv, 369p. 1980. Repr. of 1963 ed. lib. bdg. 25.00x (ISBN 0-87991-121-2). Porcupine Pr.

King David's Spaceship. Jerry Pournelle. 1981. 11.95 (ISBN 0-671-25328-X). S&S.

King Fianchetto Defences. D. Marovic & I. Susic. 1977. 15.95 (ISBN 0-7134-0250-4); pap. 10.95 (ISBN 0-7134-0251-2). David & Charles.

King Fisher: His Life & Times. Ovie C. Fisher & J. C. Dykes. (Western Frontier Library: No. 32). 1967. Repr. of 1966 ed. 4.95 o.p. (ISBN 0-8061-0711-1). U of Okla Pr.

King George VI & Queen Elizabeth. Frances Donaldson. LC 77-5122. (Illus.). 1977. 12.95 o.p. (ISBN 0-397-01229-2). Lippincott.

King Grisly-Beard, 10 bks. & one cassette. Ed. by Alma Gilleo. LC 74-734822. (Fairy Tales of the Brothers Grimm Cassette Bks). (Illus.). 16p. (ps). 1976. 10 bks. & one cassette 21.00 (ISBN 0-89290-004-0). Soc for Visual.

King Harald & the Icelanders: Five Icelandic Stories. Tr. by Pardee Lowe, Jr. from Icelandic. (Illus.). 1979. 12.00 (ISBN 0-915778-21-1); deluxe ed. 40.00x deluxe ed (ISBN 0-915778-22-X). Penmaen Pr.

King Herla's Quest & Other Medieval Stories from Walter Map. Thomas B. Leekley. LC 56-12037. (Illus.). (gr. 6-9). 6.95 (ISBN 0-8149-0348-7). Vanguard.

King-Hunt in Chess. W. H. Cozens. (Illus.). (gr. 9 up). 1971. 6.95 o.p. (ISBN 0-8069-4916-3); PLB 6.69 o.p. (ISBN 0-8069-4917-1). Sterling.

King in Tudor Drama. Patricia S. Barry. (Salzburg Studies in English Literature: Elizabethan & Renaissance Studies: No. 58). (Orig.). 1977. pap. text ed. 25.00x (ISBN 0-391-01313-0). Humanities.

King James Version. Stanley Stewart. 1977. 8.95 o.p. (ISBN 0-394-40042-9). Random.

King James' Versions of the Games of Golfe. John R. De Monte. (Illus.). 82p. (Orig.). 1980. pap. 3.50 (ISBN 0-9605176-0-X). Raycol Prods.

King John. William Shakespeare. Ed. by Arthur Quiller-Couch et al. (New Shakespeare Ser). 1969. 23.95 (ISBN 0-521-07540-8); pap. 2.95x o.p. (ISBN 0-521-09483-6). Cambridge U Pr.

King John. rev. ed. W. L. Warren. (Campus Ser.: No. 209). 1978. o. p. 15.00x (ISBN 0-520-03610-7); pap. 6.50x (ISBN 0-520-03643-3). U of Cal Pr.

King John & Matilda: A Critical Edition. Robert Davenport. Ed. by Joyce O. Davis. LC 79-54334. (Renaissance Drama Ser.). 200p. 1980. lib. bdg. 22.00 (ISBN 0-8240-4452-5). Garland Pub.

King Kong Joke Book. Jim Simon. 1977. pap. 1.25 (ISBN 0-505-51124-X). Tower Bks.

King Krakus & the Dragon. Janina Domanska. LC 78-12934. (Illus.). (gr. k-3). 1979. 8.95 (ISBN 0-688-80189-7); PLB 8.59 (ISBN 0-688-84189-9). Greenwillow.

King Lazarus. Mongo Beti. 1971. pap. 1.50 o.s.i. (ISBN 0-02-048600-6, Collier). Macmillan.

King Lear. Ed. by E. A. Colman. (Challis Shakespeare Ser). 1981. pap. 3.50x (ISBN 0-686-68844-9, Pub. by Sydney U Pr Australia). Intl Schol Bk Serv.

King Lear. Helen Gardner. (John Cofin Memorial Lectures 1966). 1967. pap. text ed. 2.50x (ISBN 0-485-16205-9, Athlone Pr). Humanities.

King Lear. William Shakespeare. Ed. by Frank Kerrmode. LC 72-127580. (Casebook Ser). 1970. pap. text ed. 2.50 o.s.i. (ISBN 0-87695-050-0). Aurora Pubs.

King Lear. William Shakespeare. Ed. by Arthur Quiller-Couch et al. (New Shakespeare Ser). 1968. 23.95 (ISBN 0-521-07541-6); pap. 4.50x (ISBN 0-521-09484-4). Cambridge U Pr.

King Lear: An Annotated Bibliography. Larry S. Champion. LC 80-8489. (Garland Shakespeare Bibliographies). 900p. 1980. lib. bdg. 100.00 (ISBN 0-8240-9498-0). Garland Pub.

King Lear in Our Time. Maynard Mack. (California Library Reprint Series: No. 17). 1971. 12.00 o.p. (ISBN 0-520-01922-9); pap. 2.35 (ISBN 0-520-02157-6, CAL239). U of Cal Pr.

King Lear: Twentieth Century Interpretations. J. Adelman. 1978. 8.95 (ISBN 0-13-516195-9, Spec); pap. 2.95 (ISBN 0-13-516187-8). P-H.

King, Lords, & Peasants in Medieval England: The Common Law of Villeinage in the Twelfth & Thirteenth Centuries. Paul R. Hyams. (Oxford Historical Monograph). 350p. 1980. 49.50 (ISBN 0-19-821880-X). Oxford U Pr.

King Midas's Ears. (MacDonald Educational Ser.). (Illus., Arabic.). 3.50 (ISBN 0-686-53087-X). Intl Bk Ctr.

King of Kings: A Novel of the Life of David. Malachi Martin. 1981. 14.95 (ISBN 0-671-24707-7). S&S.

King of the Beggars, Bampfylde-Moore Carew. Bampfylde-Moore Carew. Ed. by C. H. Wilkinson. LC 80-2471. 1981. Repr. of 1931 ed. 39.50 (ISBN 0-404-19103-7). AMS Pr.

King of the B's: Working Within the Hollywood System: an Anthology of Film History & Criticism. Ed. by Charles Flynn & Todd McCarthy. LC 74-10478. 1975. pap. 6.95 o.p. (ISBN 0-525-47378-5). Dutton.

King of the Castle. Victoria Holt. 1978. pap. 2.25 (ISBN 0-449-23587-4, Crest). Fawcett.

King of the Dollhouse. Patricia Clapp. LC 74-21827. (Illus.). 96p. (gr. 1-5). 1974. 6.75 o.p. (ISBN 0-688-40982-2); PLB 6.96 (ISBN 0-688-50982-7). Lothrop.

King of the Dollhouse. Patricia Clapp. (gr. 2-3). 1976. pap. 1.25 o.p. (ISBN 0-590-02063-3, Schol Pap). Schol Bk Serv.

King of the Golden River. John Ruskin. LC 77-22976. (Illus.). (gr. 7-9). 1978. 9.50 (ISBN 0-688-80122-6); PLB 9.12 (ISBN 0-688-84122-8). Greenwillow.

King of the Golden River, Repr. Of 1851 Ed. John Ruskin. Bd. with Holiday Romance. Charles Dickens. (Illus.). Repr. of 1868 ed; Petsetilla's Posy. Tom Hood. (Illus.). Repr. of 1870 ed. LC 75-32165. (Classics of Children's Literature, 1621-1932: Vol. 29). (Illus.). 1977. PLB 38.00 (ISBN 0-8240-2278-5). Garland Pub.

King of the Grizzlies. Ernest T. Seton. Orig. Title: Biography of a Grizzly. (Illus.). (gr. 4-6). 1970. pap. 1.25 (ISBN 0-590-08786-X, Schol Pap); pap. 3.50 bk. & record (ISBN 0-590-20750-4). Schol Bk Serv.

King of the Hill. A. E. Hotchner. LC 72-77751. (YA) 1972. 10.00 o.p. (ISBN 0-06-011964-0, HarpT). Har-Row.

King of the Hill. Leslie A. Osborn. Date not set. 7.95 (ISBN 0-533-04592-4). Vantage.

King of the Jews. Leslie Epstein. 1979. pap. 2.50 (ISBN 0-380-48074-3, 48074). Avon.

King of the Mountains: A Treasury of Latin-American Folk Stories. Moritz A. Jagendorf & R. S. Boggs. LC 60-15073. (Illus.). (gr. 4-8). 1960. 8.95 (ISBN 0-8149-0338-X). Vanguard.

King of the Rainy Country. Nicolas Freeling. 160p. 1975. pap. 1.95 o.p. (ISBN 0-14-002853-6). Penguin.

King of the Road. Richard Petty. (Illus.). 1977. 9.95 o.s.i. (ISBN 0-02-596030-X, 59603). Macmillan.

King of the Sea. Derek Bickerton. 1981. pap. 2.50 (ISBN 0-425-04846-2). Berkley Pub.

King of the Stars. Leo P. Kelley. LC 78-68231. (Galaxy Five Ser.). (Illus.). 64p. (gr. 4 up). 1980. PLB 7.95 (ISBN 0-516-02253-9). Childrens.

King of the Sticks. Ivan Southall. LC 79-10473. (gr. 6 up). 1979. 6.95 (ISBN 0-688-80224-9); PLB 6.67 (ISBN 0-688-84224-0). Greenwillow.

King of the Wind. Marguerite Henry. LC 48-8773. (Illus.). (gr. 2-9). 1948. 5.95 (ISBN 0-528-82265-9); deluxe ed. 10.00 slipcased (ISBN 0-528-82267-5); PLB 5.97 o.p. (ISBN 0-528-80174-0); pap. 2.95 (ISBN 0-528-87686-4). Rand.

King on a Swing. Sesame Street. (Sesame Street Pop-up Ser: No. 6). (Illus.). (ps-2). 1972. 4.95 (ISBN 0-394-82461-X, BYR). Random.

King on the Court: Billie Jean King. Leila B. Gemme. LC 75-42488. (Sports Profiles Ser.). (Illus.). 48p. (gr. 4-11). 1976. PLB 8.50 (ISBN 0-8172-0128-9). Raintree Pubs.

King Over the Water. Michael Pye. (Illus.). 288p. 1981. 12.95 (ISBN 0-03-057551-6). HR&W.

King, Parliament, & Public Finance in Medieval England to 1369. G. L. Harriss. 576p. 1975. 49.50x (ISBN 0-19-822435-4). Oxford U Pr.

King Pawn Openings. D. Marovic & I. Susic. 1975. 19.95 (ISBN 0-7134-2920-8). David & Charles.

King Philip's War, 1675-76: The New England Indians Fight the Colonists. Louise D. Rich. LC 78-183577. (Focus Bks). (Illus.). 96p. (gr. 7 up). 1972. PLB 4.47 o.p. (ISBN 0-531-02453-9). Watts.

King Popiel & the Mice. Barbara Seidler. (Young Peoples Ser.). 1976. pap. text ed. 1.00x (ISBN 0-917004-07-8). Kosciuszko.

King, Queen, Knave. Vladimir Nabokov. 288p. 1980. pap. 5.95 (ISBN 0-07-045722-0, GB). McGraw.

King Silky! Leo Rosten. LC 79-3413. 352p. 1980. 11.95 (ISBN 0-06-013684-7, HarpT). Har-Row.

King Solomon's Ring. Konrad Z. Lorenz. LC 52-7373. (Apollo Eds.). (YA) (gr. 9-12). pap. 3.95 o.s.i. (ISBN 0-8152-0016-1, A16, TYC-T). T y Crowell.

King Solomon's Ring. Konrad Z. Lorenz. (Illus.). 1952. 6.95 o.s.i. (ISBN 0-690-47460-1, TYC-T). T Y Crowell.

King Stephen. R. H. C. Davis. LC 77-4291. (Illus.). 1977. pap. text ed. 8.95x (ISBN 0-582-48727-7). Longman.

King Stephen, 1135-1154. R. H. C. Davis. 1967. 17.50x (ISBN 0-520-00298-9). U of Cal Pr.

King Thrushbeard. Ed. & illus. by Felix Hoffman. LC 74-123890. (Illus.). (gr. k-3). 1970. 5.95 o.p. (ISBN 0-15-242940-9, HJ). HarBraceJ.

King Who Could Not Sleep. Benjamin Elkin. LC 74-12444. (Illus.). 40p. (gr. k-3). 1975. 5.95 o.s.i. (ISBN 0-8193-0775-0, Four Winds); PLB 5.41 o.s.i. (ISBN 0-8193-0776-9). Schol Bk Serv.

King Who Took Sunshine. James Reeves. pap. text ed. 2.50x o.p. (ISBN 0-435-21000-9). Heinemann Ed.

King William & the Scottish Politicans. P. W. Riley. 1979. text ed. 32.50x (ISBN 0-85976-040-5). Humanities.

King with Six Friends. Jay Williams. LC 68-21078. (Illus.). (gr. k-3). 1968. 5.95 o.s.i. (ISBN 0-8193-0341-0, Four Winds); PLB 5.41 o.s.i. (ISBN 0-8193-0342-9). Schol Bk Serv.

King Without a Crown: Albert, Prince Consort of England 1819-1861. Daphne Bennett. LC 77-22108. (Illus.). 1977. 12.95 o.p. (ISBN 0-397-01143-1). Lippincott.

Kingdom. Larry Christenson. (Trinity Bible Ser.). 1972. pap. 4.95 (ISBN 0-87123-548-X, 240548). Bethany Fell.

Kingdom. Ronald S. Joseph. 480p. (Orig.). 1978. pap. 2.75 (ISBN 0-446-85699-1). Warner Bks.

Kingdom & the Power. Gay Talese. LC 78-7770. 1978. pap. 6.95 (ISBN 0-385-14404-0, Anch). Doubleday.

Kingdom & the Power. Gay Talese. 1981. pap. 3.25 (ISBN 0-440-14397-7). Dell.

Kingdom Living Here & Now. John Macarthur, Jr. 1980. 8.95 (ISBN 0-8024-4564-0). Moody.

Kingdom Lost for a Drop of Honey. Maung Htin Aung & Helen G. Trager. LC 68-11653. (Illus.). 96p. (gr. 3-7). 1968. 5.95 o.s.i. (ISBN 0-8193-0219-8, Four Winds); PLB 5.41 o.s.i. (ISBN 0-8193-0220-1). Schol Bk Serv.

Kingdom of Childhood. Rudolf Steiner. 160p. 1974. 9.75 o.p. (ISBN 0-85440-058-3). Anthroposophic.

Kingdom of Evil: A Continuation of the Journal of Fantazius Mallare. Ben Hecht. LC 78-7288. (Illus.). 1978. pap. 3.95 o.p. (ISBN 0-15-647123-X, Harv). HarBraceJ.

Kingdom of God. John Bright. (Series A). 1957. pap. 2.95 o.p. (ISBN 0-687-20907-2, Apex). Abingdon.

Kingdom of God & the One Thousand Years Reign. H. M. Riggle. 160p. pap. 1.50. Faith Pub Hse.

Kingdom of Moltz. Irwin A. Schiff. LC 80-14628. 1980. pap. 3.95 (ISBN 0-930374-02-9). Freedom Bks.

Kingdom of Naples Under Alfonso the Magnanimous: The Making of a Modern State. Alan Ryder. 1976. 49.50x (ISBN 0-19-822535-0). Oxford U Pr.

Kingdom of Summer. Gillian Bradshaw. 1981. 12.95 (ISBN 0-671-25472-3). S&S.

Kingdom of the Crusaders. Dana C. Munro. LC 65-20472. 1966. Repr. of 1935 ed. 11.50 (ISBN 0-8046-0326-X). Kennikat.

Kingdom of the Cults. rev. ed. Walter R. Martin. LC 64-22840. 1968. 10.95 (ISBN 0-87123-300-2, 230300). Bethany Fell.

Kingdom of the Dwarfs. Robb Walsh. (Illus.). 144p. 1981. 14.95 (ISBN 0-87818-018-4); ltd. signed ed. 25.00 (ISBN 0-87818-019-2). Centaur.

Kingdom of the Dwarfs. David Wenzel. Robb Walsh. (Illus.). 144p. (Orig.). 1980. pap. 8.95 (ISBN 0-87818-017-6). Centaur.

Kingdom of the Heart. Lucy Walker. 1971. pap. 1.75 (ISBN 0-345-29276-6). Ballantine.

Kingdom of the Shining Ones. 5th ed. Flower A. Newhouse. 1955. 8.50 (ISBN 0-910378-03-7). Christward.

Kingdom of Valencia in the Seventeenth Century. J. Casey. LC 77-88669. (Cambridge Studies in Early Modern History). (Illus.). 1979. 38.50 (ISBN 0-521-21939-6). Cambridge U Pr.

Kingdom Within. John A. Sanford. LC 80-82087. 232p. 1980. pap. 5.95 (ISBN 0-8091-2329-0). Paulist Pr.

Kingdom Within: A Study of the Inner Meaning of Jesus' Sayings. John A. Sanford. LC 77-105548. 1970. 10.95 (ISBN 0-397-10101-5). Lippincott.

Kingdoms & Strongholds of the Crusaders. T. S. Boase. LC 73-157118. 1971. 15.00 o.p. (ISBN 0-672-51606-3). Bobbs.

Kingdoms of the Lord. David Payne. 304p. (Orig.). 1981. pap. 9.95 (ISBN 0-8028-1856-0). Eerdmans. Postponed.

Kingdoms of the Savanna. Jan Vansina. (Illus.). 1966. pap. 8.95x (ISBN 0-299-03664-2). U of Wis Pr.

Kingfisher. Gerald Seymour. 1979. pap. 2.25 (ISBN 0-380-40592-X, 40592). Avon.

Kingfisher Scream. Anthony Fox. LC 80-51769. 228p. 1981. 10.95 (ISBN 0-670-41352-6). Viking Pr.

Kings & Captains: Variations on a Heroic Theme. Charles Moorman. LC 78-147858. 208p. 1971. 10.00x (ISBN 0-8131-1248-6). U Pr of Ky.

Kings & Kingship in Early Scotland. Marjorie C. Anderson. 304p. 1981. 20.00x (ISBN 0-7073-0179-3, Pub. by Scottish Academic Pr Scotland). Columbia U Pr.

Kings & Kingsman: Early Mbundu States in Angola. Joseph C. Miller. (Oxford Studies in African Affairs Ser.). (Illus.). 1976. 45.00x (ISBN 0-19-822704-3). Oxford U Pr.

Kings & Queens of England & Scotland. David Piper. (Illus.). 1980. 17.95 (ISBN 0-571-11560-8, Pub. by Faber & Faber). Merrimack Bk Serv.

King's Ballet Master: A Biography of Denmark's August Bournonville. Walter Terry. LC 79-55736. (Illus.). 1979. 8.95 (ISBN 0-396-07722-6). Dodd.

King's Birthday Cake. John Cunliffe. (Illus.). (ps-2). 1979. PLB 8.95 (ISBN 0-233-96453-3). Andre Deutsch.

King's Book of Kings. Stuart C. Welch. 200p. 1981. 50.00 (ISBN 0-87099-028-4, 494208). NYGS.

King's Bride. E. T. Hoffmann. 1980. pap. 3.95 (ISBN 0-7145-0326-6). Riverrun NY.

King's Cannon. Jonathan Scofield. 1981. pap. 2.75 (ISBN 0-440-04292-5). Dell.

King's Choice. K. Shivkumar. LC 76-81195. (Illus.). (gr. k-3). 1971. 5.95 o.s.i. (ISBN 0-8193-0364-X, Four Winds); PLB 5.41 o.s.i. (ISBN 0-8193-0365-8). Schol Bk Serv.

King's Council in England During the Middle Ages. James F. Baldwin. 1913. 19.95x (ISBN 0-19-821394-8). Oxford U Pr.

King's Council in the Reign of Edward VI. D. E. Hoak. LC 75-9286. (Illus.). 394p. 1975. 51.50 (ISBN 0-521-20866-1). Cambridge U Pr.

King's Crusader. John Jakes. 1977. pap. 1.95 o.p. (ISBN 0-685-78258-1). Pinnacle Bks.

King's Curse. Warren Murphy. (Destroyer Ser.: No. 24). 1976. pap. 1.95 (ISBN 0-523-41239-8). Pinnacle Bks.

King's English. 3rd ed. Henry W. Fowler & F. G. Fowler. 1931. 12.95x (ISBN 0-19-869105-X). Oxford U Pr.

King's Falcon. Catharine Darby. (Falcon Ser.: No. 2). 1975. pap. 1.25 o.p. (ISBN 0-445-00321-9). Popular Lib.

King's Falcon. Paula Fox. LC 69-13322. (Illus.). (gr. 6-8). 1969. 6.95 (ISBN 0-87888-005-4). Bradbury Pr.

King's Fountain. Lloyd Alexander. (Illus.). (ps-3). 1971. PLB 7.95 o.p. (ISBN 0-525-33240-5). Dutton.

King's Friends: The Composition & Motives of the American Loyalist Claimants. Wallace Brown. LC 66-10179. (Illus.). 411p. 1965. 16.00 (ISBN 0-87057-092-7, Pub. by Brown U Pr). Univ Pr of New England.

King's Gambit. Viktor Korchnoi & Vladimir Zak. 1975. 14.95 (ISBN 0-7134-2914-3). David & Charles.

King's Highway. Charles H. Spurgeon. (Charles H. Spurgeon Library). 126p. 1975. pap. 2.50 o.p. (ISBN 0-8010-8040-1). Baker Bk.

Kings I & II. J. A. Montgomery & H. S. Gehman. LC 52-8522. (International Critical Commentary Ser.). 624p. Repr. of 1951 ed. 23.00x (ISBN 0-567-05006-8). Attic Pr.

King's Indian Defence. Leonard Barden et al. 1973. 22.50 (ISBN 0-7134-0367-5). David & Charles.

King's Indian Defence. Efim Geller. LC 79-56453. (Illus.). 288p. 1980. pap. 17.95 (ISBN 0-7134-2531-8, Pub. by Batsford England). David & Charles.

King's Music: An Anthology. Gerald R. Hayes. LC 78-66906. (Encore Music Editions Ser.). (Illus.). 1981. Repr. of 1937 ed. 14.00 (ISBN 0-88355-746-0). Hyperion Conn.

Kings of Love. P. L. Wilson & N. Pourjavady. LC 78-62008. 1979. 18.00 (ISBN 0-87773-733-9). Great Eastern.

Kings of the Rink. Stan Fischler. LC 78-7727. (Illus.). (gr. 5 up). 1978. 6.50 (ISBN 0-396-07609-2). Dodd.

Kings or People: Power & the Mandate to Rule. Reinhard Bendix. 1978. 25.00 (ISBN 0-520-02302-1); pap. 9.95 (ISBN 0-520-04090-2). U of Cal Pr.

King's Quair. James One of Scotland. (Clarendon Medieval & Tudor Ser.). 130p. 1971. 6.50x o.p. (ISBN 0-19-871022-4). Oxford U Pr.

King's Servants: The Civil Service of Charles I, 1625-1645. 2nd rev ed. G. E. Aylmer. 1974. 45.00x (ISBN 0-7100-1037-0). Routledge & Kegan.

King's State: Proprietary Dynasticism in Early Modern France. Herbert H. Rowen. 256p. 1980. 19.50 (ISBN 0-8135-0893-2). Rutgers U Pr.

Kings, the Court & Royal Power in France in the Eleventh Century. William M. Newman. LC 80-2030. 1981. Repr. of 1929 ed. 24.50 (ISBN 0-404-18582-7). AMS Pr.

King's Trial: Louis XVI Vs. the French Revolution. David P. Jordan. 1981. pap. 5.95 (ISBN 0-520-04399-5, CAL 497). U of Cal Pr.

King's Trousers. Robert Kraus. LC 79-14569. (Illus.). 40p. (gr. 1-4). 1981. 8.95 (ISBN 0-671-42259-6). Windmill Bks.

King's Two Bodies: A Study of Medieval Political Theology. Ernest H. Kantorowicz. 1957. 35.00x (ISBN 0-691-07120-9). Princeton U Pr.

King's White Elephant. Rosemary Harris. (Illus.). 1977. 6.95 (ISBN 0-571-10302-2, Pub. by Faber & Faber); pap. 2.95 (ISBN 0-571-11133-5). Merrimack Bk Serv.

Kingship & Common Profit in Gower's "Confessio Amantis". Russell A. Peck. LC 78-8984. (Literary Structures Ser.). 232p. 1978. 13.95x (ISBN 0-8093-0801-0). S Ill U Pr.

Kingsley Amis. Philip Gardner. (English Authors Ser.: No. 319). 1981. lib. bdg. 11.95 (ISBN 0-8057-6809-2). Twayne.

Kingston, Jamaica: Urban Growth & Social Change, 1692-1962. Colin G. Clarke. (Illus.). 1976. 40.00x (ISBN 0-520-02025-1). U of Cal Pr.

Kinins IIB: Systemic Proteases & Cellular Function. Ed. by Setsuro Fujii et al. LC 79-9079. (Advances in Experimental Medicine & Biology: Vol. 120B). 733p. 1979. 69.50 (ISBN 0-306-40197-5, Plenum Pr). Plenum Pub.

Kink & I: A Psychiatrist's Guide to Untwisted Living. James D. Mallory & Stanley C. Baldwin. 244p. 1973. pap. 3.50 (ISBN 0-88207-237-4). Victor Bks.

Kinnikinnick: The Mountain Flower Book. Millie Miller. Date not set. pap. 3.95 (ISBN 0-933472-09-9). Johnson Colo.

Kino: A History of the Russian & Soviet Film. Jay Leyda. (Illus.). 528p. 1973. pap. 4.95 o.s.i. (ISBN 0-02-012430-9, Collier). Macmillan.

Kino Alla Conquista Dell 'America. Annamaria Kelly. LC 80-53508. (Illus.). 148p. (Orig.). 1980. pap. 6.50 (ISBN 0-915076-05-5). SW Mission.

Kinsey, Photographer. Dave Bohn & Rodolfo Petschek. LC 78-1029. (Illus.). 1978. pap. 24.95 (ISBN 0-87701-107-9). Chronicle Bks.

Kinship & Casework. rev. ed. Hope J. Leichter & William E. Mitchell. LC 78-15482. 1978. pap. text ed. 11.75x (ISBN 0-8077-2530-7). Tchrs Coll.

Kinship & Economic Organization in Rural Japan. Chie Nakane. (Monographs on Social Anthropology: No. 32). 1967. text ed. 9.50x (ISBN 0-485-19532-1, Athlone Pr). Humanities.

Kinship & Marriage Among the Anlo Ewe. G. K. Nukunya. LC 68-18054. (Monographs on Social Anthropology Ser: No. 37). 1969. text ed. 23.50x (ISBN 0-485-19537-2, Athlone Pr). Humanities.

Kinship & Marriage Among the Nuer. Edward E. Evans-Pritchard. (Illus.). 1951. 24.00x (ISBN 0-19-823104-0). Oxford U Pr.

Kinship & Marriage in Burma: A Cultural & Psychodynamic Analysis. Melford E. Spiro. 1977. 21.50x (ISBN 0-520-03220-9). U of Cal Pr.

Kinship & Social Organization: Together with the Genealogical Method of Anthropological Enquiry. William H. Rivers. LC 67-17557. (Monographs on Social Anthropology). (Illus.). 1968. text ed. 10.75x (ISBN 0-485-19534-8, Athlone Pr). Humanities.

Kinship & the Social Order: The Legacy of Lewis Henry Morgan. Meyer Fortes. LC 80-67927. (Lewis Henry Morgan Lectures). 368p. Date not set. cancelled; pap. cancelled (ISBN 0-521-28211-X). Cambridge U Pr.

Kinship & Urbanization: White Collar Migrants in North India. Sylvia Vatuk. LC 75-161993. 1973. 20.00x (ISBN 0-520-02064-2). U of Cal Pr.

Kinship at the Core: An Anthropology of Elmdon, a Village in North-West Essex. Marilyn Strathern. LC 80-40550. (Illus.). 336p. Date not set. price not set (ISBN 0-521-23360-7). Cambridge U Pr.

Kinship, Descent & Alliance Among the Karo Batak. Masri Singarimbun. LC 73-93061. 1975. 22.75x (ISBN 0-520-02692-6). U of Cal Pr.

Kinship with All Life. J. Allen Boone. LC 54-6901. 160p. 1976. pap. 4.95 (ISBN 0-06-060912-5, RD128, HarpR). Har-Row.

Kinsman. Ben Bova. 1981. pap. 2.95 (ISBN 0-440-14527-9). Dell. Postponed.

Kintyre. Alasdair Carmichael. (Island Ser.). 1974. 16.95 (ISBN 0-7153-6317-4). David & Charles.

Kiowa Blood. Will C. Knott. 1980. pap. 1.75 o.p. (ISBN 0-425-04679-6). Berkley Pub.

Kiowa-Commanche Indians, 2 vols. Ed. by David A. Horr. (American Indian Ethnohistory Ser.: Plains Indians). 1974. Set. lib. bdg. 76.00 (ISBN 0-8240-0724-7); lib. bdg. 42.00 ea. Garland Pub.

Kiowa Flats Raiders. Patrick Andrews. (Orig.). 1980. pap. 1.75 (ISBN 0-532-23145-7). Manor Bks.

Kiowa Pass. Archie Joscelyn. 192p. (YA) 1976. 5.95 (ISBN 0-685-66480-5, Avalon). Bouregy.

Kiowa Trail. Louis L'Amour. 160p. (Orig.). 1980. pap. 1.95 (ISBN 0-553-13882-0). Bantam.

Kipling, Auden & Co. Essays & Reviews, 1935-1964. Randall Jarrell. 1980. 17.50 (ISBN 0-374-18153-5). FS&G.

Kipling Short Stories, 2 vols. Ed. by Andrew Rutherford. 1977. Vol. 1. pap. 2.95 (ISBN 0-14-003281-9); Vol. 2. pap. 3.95 (ISBN 0-14-003282-7). Penguin.

Kipling: The Glass, the Shadow & the Fire. Philip Mason. LC 74-29175. 336p. (YA) 1975. 10.00 o.s.i. (ISBN 0-06-012833-X, HarpT). Har-Row.

Kira Georgievna. V. Nekrasov. Ed. by M. Greene & H. Blair. (Rus). text ed. 17.50x (ISBN 0-521-05806-6). Cambridge U Pr.

Kirby Smith's Confederacy: The Trans-Mississippi South 1863-1865. Robert L. Kerby. LC 68-19752. 512p. 1972. 20.00x (ISBN 0-231-03585-3). Columbia U Pr.

Kirche Aethiopiens: Eine Bestandsaufnahme. Friedrich Heyer. (Theologische Bibliothek Toepelmann 22). 360p. 1971. 32.25 (ISBN 3-11-001850-0). De Gruyter.

Kirche und Staat in England und in Normandie Im XI. und XII. Jahrhundert: Eine Historische Studie. Heinrich Boehmer. LC 80-2234. 1981. Repr. of 1899 ed. 57.50 (ISBN 0-404-18755-2). AMS Pr.

Kirchenrecht der Morgenlandischen Kirche. 2nd ed. Nikodim Milash. LC 80-2360. 1981. Repr. of 1905 ed. 83.00 (ISBN 0-404-18910-5). AMS Pr.

Kirghiz & Wakhi of Afghanistan: Adaptation to Closed Frontiers. M. Nazif Mohib Shahrani. LC 79-11665. (Publications on Ethnicity & Nationality of the School of International Studies). (Illus.). 288p. 1979. 16.50 (ISBN 0-295-95669-0). U of Wash Pr.

Kirgiz Instrumental Music. Mark Slobin. LC 70-93475. (D (Monographs), No. 2). (Illus.). xiv, 158p. (Orig.). 1969. pap. text ed. 6.00x (ISBN 0-913360-01-5). Asian Music Pub.

Kirkland Revels. Victoria Holt. LC 62-7646. 1962. 10.95 (ISBN 0-385-00061-8). Doubleday.

Kirkland Revels. Victoria Holt. 1978. pap. 2.25 (ISBN 0-449-23920-9, Crest). Fawcett.

Kirk's Works. George Beahm. (Fantasy Artists Ser.: No. 2). (Illus., Orig.). 1980. pap. 10.00 (ISBN 0-9603276-1-4). Heresy Pr.

Kirlian Aura: The Galaxies of Life. Ed. by Stanley Krippner & Daniel Rubin. LC 73-10733. 224p. 1974. pap. 3.95 (ISBN 0-385-06574-4, Anch). Doubleday.

Kirsty at the Lodge. Eva Fitzpatrick & Joanna Stubbs. (Illus.). (ps-5). 1972. 6.95 (ISBN 0-571-09769-3, Pub. by Faber & Faber). Merrimack Bk Serv.

Kish Excavations 1923-1933: With a Microfiche Catalogue of the Objects of the Ashmolean Museum. P. R. Moorey. (Illus.). 1978. 49.50x (ISBN 0-19-813191-7). Oxford U Pr.

Kiso Nihongo Jo Jikan: Four Hours to Basic Japanese. George Ohsawa. Ed. by Herman Aihara. (Illus.). 1974. pap. 1.35 o.p. (ISBN 0-918860-06-7). G Ohsawa.

Kiss. Robert Duncan. 1978. pap. 1.95 (ISBN 0-445-04112-9). Popular Lib.

Kiss. Robert Lebeck. (Illus.). 176p. 1981. pap. 6.95 (ISBN 0-312-45687-5). St Martin.

Kiss & Its History. Christopher Nyrop. Tr. by William F. Harvey. LC 68-22040. 1968. Repr. of 1901 ed. 15.00 (ISBN 0-8103-3512-3). Gale.

Kiss & Kill. Martin Meyers. (Hardy Ser.: No. 1). 176p. 1975. pap. 1.25 o.p. (ISBN 0-445-08408-1). Popular Lib.

Kiss Before Dying. Ira Levin. 1975. pap. 1.95 (ISBN 0-515-05127-6). Jove Pubns.

Kiss for Christina. Blakely St. James. LC 80-83597. 256p. (Orig.). 1981. pap. 2.50 (ISBN 0-87216-793-3). Playboy Pbks.

Kiss Me Kill Me. Kate Cameron. 1979. pap. 1.50 (ISBN 0-505-51384-6). Tower Bks.

Kiss Mommy Goodbye. Joy Fielding. LC 80-1692. 312p. 1981. 11.95 (ISBN 0-385-17291-5). Doubleday.

Kiss of a Tyrant. Margaret Pargeter. (Harlequin Romances Ser.). 192p. 1980. pap. 1.25 (ISBN 0-373-02375-8, Pub. by Harlequin). PB.

Kiss of Life, No. 136. Barbara Cartland. 144p. 1981. pap. 1.75 (ISBN 0-553-14504-5). Bantam.

Kiss of Satan. H. A. Whyte. 1973. pap. 1.25 o.p. (ISBN 0-88368-030-0). Whitaker Hse.

Kiss of the Devil. Barbara Cartland. (Barbara Cartland Ser.: No. 18). 1981. pap. 1.75 (ISBN 0-515-05957-9). Jove Pubns.

Kiss on Each Cheek. Donald De Simone. 448p. (Orig.). 1981. pap. 2.95 (ISBN 0-523-40469-7). Pinnacle Bks.

Kiss Sacred & Profane: An Interpretative History of Kiss Symbolism & Related Religio-Erotic Themes. Nicolas J. Perella. LC 75-83292. (Illus.). 1969. 28.50x (ISBN 0-520-01392-1). U of Cal Pr.

Kiss the Girls & Make Them Die. Charles Runyon. 1977. pap. 1.50 o.s.i. (ISBN 0-515-03963-2). Jove Pubns.

Kissed by Moonlight. Dorothy Vernon. 192p. 1981. pap. 1.50 (ISBN 0-671-57059-5). S&S.

Kissimmee Kid. Vera Cleaver & Bill Cleaver. LC 80-29262. 160p. (gr. 5 up). 1981. 8.95 (ISBN 0-688-41992-5); PLB 8.59 (ISBN 0-688-51992-X). Morrow.

Kissing Games: A Study in Fokelore. David J. Gerrick. 1978. 3.00 o.p. (ISBN 0-685-30120-6). Dayton Labs.

Kissing Gate. Pamela Haines. LC 79-6581. 648p. 1981. 13.95 (ISBN 0-385-15309-0). Doubleday.

Kissing, Hugging, &... Wayne Judd. LC 79-20362. (Nugget Ser.). 1979. pap. 0.65 (ISBN 0-8127-0249-2). Southern Pub.

Kissing Kin. Elswyth Thane. (Williamsburg Ser.: No. 5). 1981. lib. bdg. 16.95 (ISBN 0-686-69444-9, Large Print Bks). G K Hall.

Kissinger & Detente. Ed. by Lester A. Sobel. 275p. 1975. lib. bdg. 17.50 (ISBN 0-87196-243-8). Facts on File.

Kissinger & the Meaning of History. P. Dickson. LC 78-5633. 1978. 19.95 (ISBN 0-521-22113-7). Cambridge U Pr.

Kissinger: Portrait of a Mind. new ed. Stephen R. Graubard. 288p. 1973. text ed. 9.95 (ISBN 0-393-05481-0); pap. text ed. 5.95x (ISBN 0-393-09278-X). Norton.

Kit Carson. Matthew G. Grant. LC 73-10063. 1974. PLB 5.95 (ISBN 0-87191-253-8). Creative Ed.

Kit Carson's Autobiography. Kit Carson. Ed. by Milo M. Quaife. LC 66-4130. (Illus.). 1966. pap. 3.95 (ISBN 0-8032-5031-2, BB 325, Bison). U of Nebr Pr.

Kit Carson's Long Walk & Other True Tales of Old San Diego. Henry Schwartz. LC 80-68570. 112p. (Orig.). 1980. pap. 3.95 (ISBN 0-933362-03-X). Assoc Creative Writers.

Kitab al-Ta Rifat (Book of Definitions) Arabic-Arabic Dictionary. A. Jurjani. 1969. 15.00x (ISBN 0-685-54029-4). Intl Bk Ctr.

Kitab-i-Iqan: The Book of Certitude. 2nd ed. Baha'u'llah. Tr. by Shoghi Efferdi from Persian. LC 51-22838. 9.00 (ISBN 0-87743-022-5, 7-03-08). Baha'i.

Kitchen Antiques. Jeffrey Weiss. LC 80-7831. (Illus.). 128p. (Orig.). 1980. pap. 8.95 (ISBN 0-06-090813-0, CN 813, CN). Har-Row.

Kitchen Communion. Cornelia M. Renfroe. LC 59-11220. (Illus.). 1959. 2.50 (ISBN 0-8042-2400-5). John Knox.

Kitchen Crafts. Linda Cross & John Cross. LC 73-8351. (Illus.). 224p. 1974. pap. 3.95 o.s.i. (ISBN 0-02-009430-2, Collier). Macmillan.

Kitchen Garden Book: Vegetables from Seed to Table. Stringfellow Barr & Stella Standard. (Handbooks Ser). 1977. pap. 2.95 o.p. (ISBN 0-14-046257-0). Penguin.

Kitchen Gardens. Mary M. Campbell. (Betty Crocker). 1974. pap. 4.95 (ISBN 0-307-09550-9, Golden Pr). Western Pub.

Kitchen Planning & Design. Peter Douglas. (Case Studies Ser.: Vol. 2). (Illus.). 128p. 1980. 19.95 (ISBN 0-7137-0982-0, Pub. by Blandford Pr England); pap. 14.95 (ISBN 0-7137-1034-9). Sterling.

Kitchen Sanitation. Ser-Vol-Tel Institute. (Foodservice Career Education Ser.). 1974. pap. 4.95 (ISBN 0-8436-2005-6). CBI Pub.

Kitchen Sense for Disabled People of All Ages. rev. ed. Sydney Foott et al. (Illus.). 218p. 1976. spiral bdg. 11.00x (ISBN 0-433-10665-4). Intl Ideas.

Kitchen Window. Dorothy P. Albaugh. 1978. pap. 2.00x o.p. (ISBN 0-915020-15-7). Bardic.

Kitchens & Bathrooms. Time-Life Books. LC 77-83171. (Home Repairs & Improvement Ser.). (Illus.). 1977. lib. bdg. 11.97 (ISBN 0-685-80981-1). Silver.

Kitchens & Bathrooms. Ed. by Time-Life Books. (Home Repair Ser.). (Illus.). 1977. 10.95 (ISBN 0-8094-2386-3). Time-Life.

Kite Mystery. Mary Adrian. LC 67-25609. (Illus.). (gr. 4-6). 1968. 5.95 (ISBN 0-8038-3937-5); PLB 3.33 (ISBN 0-8038-3938-3). Hastings.

Kites. Wyatt Brummitt. (Golden Guide Ser). (Illus.). 1971. PLB 9.15 (ISBN 0-307-64344-1, Golden Pr); pap. 1.95 (ISBN 0-307-64344-1). Western Pub.

Kites. Larry Kettelkamp. (Illus.). (gr. 3-7). 1959. PLB 7.44 (ISBN 0-688-31584-4). Morrow.

Kites for Kids. Burton Marks & Rita Marks. LC 79-22559. (Illus.). (gr. 3 up). 1980. 6.95 (ISBN 0-688-41930-5); PLB 6.67 (ISBN 0-688-51930-X). Lothrop.

Kites: How to Make & Fly Them. Marion Downer. LC 58-14497. (Illus.). (gr. 4-6). 1959. PLB 7.44 (ISBN 0-688-51227-5). Lothrop.

Kittelsen, Theodore: Drawings & Water Colors. C. Ostby. 1976. 60.00x (ISBN 0-686-68011-1, N-534). Vanous.

Kitten Book. Jan Pfloog. (Illus.). (gr. k-1). 1976. PLB 5.38 (ISBN 0-307-68947-6, Golden Pr). Western Pub.

Kitten Book & Other Stories. Helen Piers. (Illus.). (gr. k-3). 1970. PLB 4.90 o.p. (ISBN 0-531-01934-9). Watts.

Kitten for a Day. Ezra J. Keats. LC 73-23057. (Illus.). 32p. (ps-2). 1974. PLB 4.95 o.p. (ISBN 0-531-02714-7). Watts.

Kitten in the Pumpkin Patch. Richard Shaw. (Illus.). 40p. (gr. 2-5). 1973. 7.95 (ISBN 0-7232-6099-0). Warne.

Kittens. Zokeisha. (Puppet Story Board Bks.). (Illus.). 12p. (ps-k). Date not set. boards 2.95 (ISBN 0-686-69451-1, Little Simon). S&S.

Kittens & More Kittens. Marci Ridlon. (Beginning-to-Read Ser.). (Illus.). (gr. 2-4). 1967. pap. 1.50 o.p. (ISBN 0-695-34868-X). Follett.

Kitto's Comments & Applications, 2 vols. John Kitto. LC 80-8069. 1934p. 1981. Repr. of 1901 ed. Set. 49.95 (ISBN 0-8254-3025-9). Kregel.

Kitty. Warwick Deeping. 1976. lib. bdg. 16.75x (ISBN 0-89968-020-8). Lightyear.

Kitty: A Story of Triumph in a Soundless World. Kitty O'Neil & Bill Libby. (Illus.). 224p. 1981. 9.95 (ISBN 0-688-00355-9). Morrow.

Kitty O'Neil: Daredevil Woman. Karen Ireland. LC 80-80604. (Starpeople Ser.). (Illus.). 78p. (gr. 4 up). 1980. lib. bdg. 5.79 (ISBN 0-8178-0004-2). Harvey.

Kiva Art of the Anasazi at Pottery Mound, N.M. Frank C. Hibben. Ed. by Gweneth R. DenDooven. LC 75-19742. (Illus.). 1975. 35.00 (ISBN 0-916122-16-6); signed, limited ed. 100.00 (ISBN 0-685-60911-1). K C Pubns.

Kiziba: The Cultural Heritage of an Old African Kingdom. A. G. Ishumi. LC 80-19238. (African Ser.: Vol. 34). (Illus.). viii, 109p. (Orig.). 1980. pap. 7.00x (ISBN 0-915984-56-3). Syracuse U Foreign Comp.

Kjeld Abell. Frederick J. Marker. LC 76-6102. (World Authors Ser.: Denmark: No. 394). 1976. lib. bdg. 12.50 (ISBN 0-8057-6236-1). Twayne.

Klan. Patsy Sims. LC 77-2335. (Illus.). 384p. 1981. pap. 8.95 (ISBN 0-8128-6096-9). Stein & Day.

Klandestine. William H. Mc Ilhany. (Illus.). 1975. 8.95 o.p. (ISBN 0-87000-295-3). Arlington Hse.

Klaus Mann. Peter T. Hoffer. (World Authors Ser.: No. 435). 1978. lib. bdg. 12.50 (ISBN 0-8057-6309-0). Twayne.

Klaw & Erlanger: Famous Plays in Pictures. Kemp R. Niver. LC 75-44556. (Illus.). 1976. 15.00 (ISBN 0-913986-07-0). Locare.

Kleber's Convoy. Anthony Trew. 224p. 1975. pap. 1.50 o.p. (ISBN 0-445-03070-4). Popular Lib.

Klee, Paul. Christian Geelhaar. (Pocket Art Ser.). (Illus.). 112p. (gr. 9-12). 1981. pap. 3.50 (ISBN 0-8120-2186-X). Barron.

Kleinere Schriften 2. Band: Zur Classischen Philologie. Karl Lachmann. Ed. by J. Vahlen. viii, 274p. 1974. Repr. of 1876 ed. 38.25x (ISBN 3-11-002399-7). De Gruyter.

Kleist. Joachim Maass. Tr. by Ralph Manheim from Ger. 1981. 17.95 (ISBN 0-374-18162-4). FS&G.

Kline Guide to the Packaging Industry. Ed. by Susan Rich. (Illus.). 324p. 1980. pap. 100.00. Kline.

Kline Guide to the Paper Industry. 4th ed. Ed. by John E. Huber. (Illus.). 343p. 1980. pap. 110.00 (ISBN 0-685-99099-0). Kline.

Klingsor's Last Summer. Hermann Hesse. Tr. by Richard Winston & Clara Winston. 217p. 1970. 6.50 (ISBN 0-374-18166-7). FS&G.

Kluane: Pinnacle of the Yukon. John Theberge. LC 80-1078. (Illus.). 224p. 1981. 35.00 (ISBN 0-385-17122-6). Doubleday.

Klynt's Law. Elliott Baker. 1977. pap. 1.95 o.p. (ISBN 0-345-25720-0). Ballantine.

Klystrons & Microwave Triodes. Ed. by Donald R. Hamilton et al. (Illus.). 1966. pap. text ed. 4.50 (ISBN 0-486-61558-8). Dover.

Knapp Commission Report on Police Corruption. Frwd. by Michael Armstrong. LC 73-76969. 1973. 10.00 o.s.i.; pap. 5.95 (ISBN 0-8076-0689-8). Braziller.

Knapsack: A Pocket-Book of Prose & Verse. 7th ed. Ed. by Herbert E. Read. LC 79-51960. (Granger Poetry Library). 1981. Repr. of 1947 ed. 43.75x (ISBN 0-89609-193-7). Granger Bk.

Knave of Diamonds. Ethel Dell. (Barbara Cartland's Library of Love: Vol. 3). 280p. 1979. 12.95x (ISBN 0-7156-1379-0, Pub. by Duckworth England). Biblio Dist.

Knave of Diamonds. Ethel M. Dell. 1975. lib. bdg. 21.50x (ISBN 0-89966-069-X). Buccaneer Bks.

Knaves, Fools, Madmen & That Subtile Effluvium: A Study of the Opposition to the French Prophets in England, 1706-1710. Hillel Schwartz. LC 78-1692. (U of Fla. Social Science Monographs: No. 62). 1978. pap. 5.50 (ISBN 0-8130-0505-1). U Presses Fla.

Knee Deep in the Atlantic. Theodore Enslin et al. 1981. pap. 15.00 (ISBN 0-915316-89-7). Pentagram.

Knee in Sports. Karl K. Klein & Fred L. Allman, Jr. (Illus.). 6.95 o.p. (ISBN 0-8363-0061-0). Jenkins.

Knee-Knock Rise. Natalie Babbitt. (gr. 3-6). 1974. pap. 1.50 o.s.i. (ISBN 0-380-00849-1, 44875, Camelot). Avon.

Kneeling Christian. The Unknown Christian. 1979. pap. 2.50 (ISBN 0-310-33492-6); large print kivar 4.95 (ISBN 0-310-33497-7). Zondervan.

Knees. Karl K. Klein. 6.95 (ISBN 0-8363-0060-2). Jenkins.

Knife All Blade. Joao Cabral De Melo Neto. 1980. pap. 10.00 (ISBN 0-930502-01-9). Pine Pr.

Knife & Other Poems. Richard Tillinghast. (Wesleyan Poetry Program Ser.: No. 100). 26p. 1980. 8.00 (ISBN 0-8195-1100-5); pap. 3.95 (ISBN 0-8195-2100-0). Wesleyan U Pr.

Knife for All Seasons. Nancy Elmont. (Illus.). 160p. 1980. 8.95 (ISBN 0-916752-48-8). Dorison Hse.

Knifecraft. Sid Latham. LC 78-16825. (Illus.). 240p. 1978. 18.95 (ISBN 0-8117-0927-2). Stackpole.

Knifemakers Guild Directory. Beth Ingber-Irvin. (Illus.). 200p. 1981. pap. 12.95 (ISBN 0-917714-32-6). Beinfeld Pub.

Knight & Chivalry. 2nd ed. Richard Barber. (Illus.). 400p. 1975. 17.50x (ISBN 0-87471-653-5). Rowman.

Knight Endings. Yuri Averbakh & V. Chekhover. 1977. 18.95 (ISBN 0-7134-0552-X). David & Charles.

Knight Errant in Africa: A Journal. Austin L. Moore. 143p. 1966. 4.95 (ISBN 0-8040-0177-4). Swallow.

Knight of the Burning Pestle. Francis Beaumont. Ed. by John Doebler. LC 67-11462. (Regents Renaissance Drama Ser). 1967. 9.50x (ISBN 0-8032-0250-4); pap. text ed. 2.45x (ISBN 0-8032-5250-1, BB 223, Bison). U of Nebr Pr.

Knight of the Burning Pestle. Francis Beaumont & John Fletcher. LC 70-25848. (English Experience Ser.: No. 152). 76p. 1969. Repr. of 1613 ed. 8.00 (ISBN 90-221-0152-5). Walter J Johnson.

Knight of the Holy Spirit: A Study of William Lyon Mackenzie King. Joy E. Esbery. 336p. 1980. 20.00 (ISBN 0-8020-5502-8). U of Toronto Pr.

Knight of the Lion. Gerald McDermott. LC 78-54680. (Illus.). 96p. (gr. 3 up). 1979. 9.95 (ISBN 0-590-07504-7, Four Winds). Schol Bk Serv.

Knightly Tales of Sir Gawain. Louis B. Hall. LC 76-17866. (Illus.). 192p. 1976. 12.95 (ISBN 0-88229-350-8); pap. 7.95 (ISBN 0-88229-407-5). Nelson-Hall.

Knight's Acre. Norah Lofts. 320p. 1976. pap. 1.75 o.p. (ISBN 0-449-22685-9, X2685, Crest). Fawcett.

Knight's Gambit. William Faulkner. Ed. by Joseph Blotner. 256p. Date not set. pap. 1.95 (ISBN 0-394-72729-0, Vin). Random.

Knights of Glin. J. A. Gaughan. 1980. text ed. 19.50x (ISBN 0-391-01181-2). Humanities.

Knights of Labor in the South. Melton A. McLaurin. LC 77-87916. (Contributions in Labor History: No. 4). (Illus.). 1978. lib. bdg. 18.95 (ISBN 0-313-20033-5, MCK/). Greenwood.

Knights of Malta. Roger Peyrefitte. LC 59-12194. 1959. 12.95 (ISBN 0-87599-087-8). S G Phillips.

Knights of the Air. Ezra Bowen. Ed. by Time-Life Books. (Epic of Flight Ser.). (Illus.). 1980. 12.95 (ISBN 0-8094-3250-1). Time-Life.

Knights of the Broadax. LC 79-57239. (Illus.). 154p. (Orig.). 1981. pap. 6.95 (ISBN 0-87004-283-1). Caxton.

Knights of the Golden Rule: The Intellectual as Christian Social Reformer in the 1890s. Peter J. Frederick. LC 76-9497. 344p. 1976. 19.50x (ISBN 0-8131-1345-8). U Pr of Ky.

Knights of the Sky. Ed. by Eugene Valencia. 216p. 1980. 21.95 (ISBN 0-9604784-0-X); special numbered ed 100.00. Valencia.

Knight's Tale. Geoffrey Chaucer. Ed. by A. C. Spearing. (Selected Tales from Chaucer). 1966. text ed. 7.95x (ISBN 0-521-04633-5). Cambridge U Pr.

Knit & Crochet. Janet Dubane & Diane Friend. (Illus.). 64p. (Orig.). 1980. pap. 2.00 (ISBN 0-918178-21-5). Simplicity.

Knitted Cat. Antonella Bolliger-Savelli. LC 72-163240. (Illus.). 28p. (ps-2). 1972. 5.95 o.s.i. (ISBN 0-02-711700-6). Macmillan.

Knitting. Mary W. Phillips. (Illus.). (gr. 5 up). 1977. PLB 5.20 s&l o.p. (ISBN 0-531-00837-1). Watts.

Knitting. Sunset Editors. LC 76-7659. (Illus.). 80p. 1976. pap. 2.95 (ISBN 0-376-04432-2, Sunset Bks). Sunset-Lane.

Knitting & Crocheting Pattern Index. Robyne Halevy. LC 76-50550. 1977. 9.50 (ISBN 0-8108-0998-2). Scarecrow.

Knitting Nineteen Twenties & Nineteen Thirties Originals. Nancy Vale. (Illus.). 104p. 1980. pap. 8.95 (ISBN 0-686-61417-8, Pub. by Mills & Boon England). Hippocrene Bks.

Knitting Without Tears. Elizabeth Zimmerman. LC 70-140776. (Illus.). 1973. pap. 7.95 (ISBN 0-684-13505-1, SL466, ScribT). Scribner.

Knives & Knifemakers. Sid Latham. 1973. 17.50 (ISBN 0-87691-109-2). Winchester Pr.

Knives & Knifemakers. Sid Latham. (Illus.). 160p. 1974. pap. 7.95 (ISBN 0-02-011750-7, Collier). Macmillan.

Knives Eighty One. Ed. by Ken Warner. 192p. 1980. pap. 5.95 (ISBN 0-910676-15-1). DBI.

Knoche's Law. Keith Knoche. LC 73-85432. (Agape Ser.). 128p. (YA) 1973. pap. 2.50 o.p. (ISBN 0-8163-0011-9, 11380-3). Pacific Pr Pub Assn.

Knock. Jules Romains. Tr. by James B. Gidney from Fr. LC 61-18360. 1962. text ed. o.p. (ISBN 0-8120-5052-5); pap. text ed. 1.95 (ISBN 0-8120-0084-6). Barron.

Knock, Knock. Jules Feiffer. 1976. pap. 3.45 o.p. (ISBN 0-8090-1234-0, Mermaid). Hill & Wang.

Knock Knocks: The Most Ever. William Cole. LC 75-33205. (Illus.). 96p. (gr. 4 up). 1976. PLB 6.90 (ISBN 0-531-01142-9). Watts.

Knock Knocks You've Never Heard Before. William Cole. (Illus.). (gr. 4-6). 1977. PLB 6.90 s&l (ISBN 0-531-00385-X). Watts.

Knock Wood! Superstition Through the Ages. Daniel Deerforth. LC 79-164220. 200p. 1974. Repr. of 1928 ed. 20.00 (ISBN 0-8103-3964-1). Gale.

Knocknagow; or, the Cabins of Tipperary. Charles J. Kickham. (Nineteenth Century Fiction Ser.: Ireland: No. 68). 1979. lib. bdg. 46.00 (ISBN 0-8240-3517-8). Garland Pub.

Knocknagow or the Homes of Tipperary. abr. ed. Charles J. Kickham. 1978. pap. 3.50 (ISBN 0-85342-554-X). Irish Bk Ctr.

Knossos Tables: A Transliteration. 4th ed. John Chadwick et al. (Illus.). 1971. 53.00 (ISBN 0-521-08085-1). Cambridge U Pr.

Knot of Artifice: A Poetic of the French Lyric in the Early Seventeenth Century. 130p. 1981. 15.00 (ISBN 0-8142-0322-1). Ohio St U Pr.

Knot Tied: Marriage Ceremonies of All Nations. William Tegg. LC 75-99073. 1970. Repr. of 1877 ed. 26.00 (ISBN 0-8103-3585-9). Gale.

Knots & How to Tie Them. Boy Scouts of America. (Illus.). pap. text ed. 0.55x (ISBN 0-8395-3170-2). BSA.

Knots & Splices. Percy W. Blandford. LC 65-25270. (Illus.). 80p. 1965. lib. bdg. 4.50 o.p. (ISBN 0-668-01330-3). Arco.

Knots & Splices. Jeff Toghill. (Illus.). 64p. (Orig.). 1979. pap. 3.50 (ISBN 0-589-50079-1, Pub. by Reed Books Australia). C E Tuttle.

Knots, Groups, & 3-Manifolds. Ed. by L. P. Neuwirth. LC 75-5619. (Annals of Mathematics Studies: No. 84). 345p. 1975. 21.00 o.p. (ISBN 0-691-08170-0); pap. 7.50 (ISBN 0-691-08167-0). Princeton U Pr.

Knots, Ties & Splices: A Handbook for Seafarers, Travellers, & All Who Use Cordage. rev. ed. J. Irving & C. Searl. 1978. pap. 4.50 (ISBN 0-7100-8671-7). Routledge & Kegan.

Knotting Crafts. Glen Pownall. (New Crafts Books Ser.). 76p. 1980. 8.25 (ISBN 0-85467-020-3, Pub. by Viking Sevenseas New Zealand). Intl Schol Bk Serv.

Know About the Armada. Henry Garnett. (Illus.). (gr. 7 up). 1967. 7.95 (ISBN 0-8023-1121-0). Dufour.

Know About the Crusades. Henry Treece. (Illus.). (gr. 6-9). 1967. 7.50 (ISBN 0-8023-1112-1). Dufour.

Know & Grow Vegetables. Ed. by P. J. Salter & J. K. Bleasdale. (Illus.). 1979. 14.50x (ISBN 0-19-857563-7). Oxford U Pr.

Know First Aid for Dogs. Pet Library Ltd. (Know Your Pet Ser.: No. 584). (Illus.). pap. 1.50 o.p. (ISBN 0-385-09301-2). Doubleday.

Know How Book of Detection. Judy Hindley & Donald Rumbelow. LC 78-59661. (Know How Books). (gr. 4-5). 1978. text ed. 6.95 (ISBN 0-88436-532-8). EMC.

Know How Book of Experiments. Heather Amery. LC 78-17788. (Know How Books). (gr. 4-5). 1978. text ed. 6.95 (ISBN 0-88436-531-X). EMC.

Know How Book of Jokes & Tricks. Heather Amery & Ian Adair. LC 78-14807. (Know How Books). (gr. 4-5). 1978. text ed. 6.95 (ISBN 0-88436-530-1). EMC.

Know-How on the Job. Ken Kusterer. 1978. lib. bdg. 20.00 o.p. (ISBN 0-89158-260-6). Westview.

Know-How on the Job: The Important Working Knowledge of "Unskilled" Workers. Ken C. Kusterer. (Westview Replica Edition Ser.). 202p. 1980. pap. text ed. 9.50x (ISBN 0-89158-916-3). Westview.

Know How to Breed Egglayers. Pet Library Ltd. (Know Your Pet Ser.: No. 705). (Illus.). pap. 1.50 o.p. (ISBN 0-385-09343-8). Doubleday.

Know How to Breed Livebearers. Pet Library Ltd. (Know Your Pet Ser.: No. 706). (Illus.). pap. 1.50 o.p. (ISBN 0-385-09345-4). Doubleday.

Know How to Breed Tropical Fish. Pet Library Ltd. (Know Your Pet Ser.: No. 704). (Illus.). pap. 1.50 o.p. (ISBN 0-385-09340-3). Doubleday.

Know How to Choose Your Dog. Pet Library Ltd. (Know Your Pet Ser.: No. 581). (Illus.). pap. 1.50 o.p. (ISBN 0-385-09294-6). Doubleday.

Know How to Clip a Poodle. Pet Library Ltd. (Know Your Pet Ser.: No. 582). (Illus.). pap. 1.50 o.p. (ISBN 0-385-09295-4). Doubleday.

Know How to Groom Your Dog. Pet Library Ltd. (Know Your Pet Ser.: No. 583). (Illus.). pap. 1.50 o.p. (ISBN 0-385-09298-9). Doubleday.

Know How to Keep Salt Water Fishes. Pet Library Ltd. (Know Your Pet Ser.: No. 720). (Illus.). pap. 1.50 o.p. (ISBN 0-385-09363-2). Doubleday.

Know How to Raise Your Puppy. Pet Library Ltd. (Know Your Pet Ser.: No. 586). (Illus.). pap. 1.50 o.p. (ISBN 0-385-09304-7). Doubleday.

Know How to Train Your Dog. Pet Library Ltd. (Know Your Pet Ser.: No. 540). (Illus.). pap. 1.50 o.p. (ISBN 0-385-04480-1). Doubleday.

Know Jewish Living & Enjoy It. Morris Golomb. LC 78-54569. (gr. 3-7). 1981. 10.00 (ISBN 0-88400-054-0). Shengold.

Know Obedience & Show Training. Pet Library Ltd. (Know Your Pet Ser.: No. 539). (Illus.). pap. 1.50 o.p. (ISBN 0-385-09291-1). Doubleday.

Know the Marks of Cults. Dave Breese. LC 74-21907. 128p. 1975. pap. 2.95 (ISBN 0-88207-704-X). Victor Bks.

Know Thyself in Greek & Latin Literature. Eliza G. Wilkins. Ed. by Leonardo Taran. LC 78-66584. (Ancient Philosophy Ser.: Vol. 28). 111p. 1979. lib. bdg. 13.00 (ISBN 0-8240-9572-3). Garland Pub.

Know What You Believe. Paul E. Little. LC 76-105667. 192p. 1970. pap. 2.95 (ISBN 0-88207-024-X). Victor Bks.

Know Why You Believe. Paul E. Little. LC 67-12231. 1967. pap. 2.95 (ISBN 0-88207-022-3). Victor Bks.

Know Your Airedale. Pet Library Ltd. (Know Your Pet Ser.: No. 530). (Illus.). pap. 1.50 o.p. (ISBN 0-385-09277-6). Doubleday.

Know Your America, Vols. 1 & 2. Marion Patten & Mary Sherwin. 1981. 16.95 (ISBN 0-385-18503-0). Doubleday.

Know Your Aquarium. Pet Library Ltd. (Know Your Pet Ser.: No. 702). (Illus.). pap. 1.50 o.p. (ISBN 0-385-09338-1). Doubleday.

Know Your Aquarium Plants. Pet Library Ltd. (Know Your Pet Ser.: No. 717). (Illus.). 1971. pap. 1.50 o.p. (ISBN 0-385-05849-7). Doubleday.

Know Your Basset Hound. Pet Library Ltd. (Know Your Pet Ser.: No. 501). (Illus.). pap. 1.50 o.p. (ISBN 0-385-09195-8). Doubleday.

Know Your Beagle. Pet Library Ltd. (Know Your Pet Ser.: No. 502). (Illus.). pap. 1.50 o.p. (ISBN 0-385-09196-6). Doubleday.

Know Your Bettas. Pet Library Ltd. (Know Your Pet Ser.: No. 710). 64p. 1973. pap. 1.50 o.p. (ISBN 0-385-04533-6). Doubleday.

Know Your Bible. W. Graham Scroggie. 1965. 14.95 (ISBN 0-8007-0169-0). Revell.

Know Your Boston Terrier. Pet Library Ltd. (Know Your Pet Ser.: No. 503). (Illus.). pap. 1.50 o.p. (ISBN 0-385-09198-2). Doubleday.

Know Your Boxer. Pet Library Ltd. (Know Your Pet Ser.: No. 504). (Illus.). pap. 1.50 o.p. (ISBN 0-385-09199-0). Doubleday.

Know Your Bulldog. Pet Library Ltd. (Know Your Pet Ser.: No. 505). (Illus.). pap. 1.50 o.p. (ISBN 0-385-09201-6). Doubleday.

Know Your Cairn Terrier. Pet Library Ltd. (Know Your Pet Ser.: No. 532). (Illus.). pap. 1.50 o.p. (ISBN 0-385-09279-2). Doubleday.

Know Your Canary. Pet Library Ltd. (Know Your Pet Ser.: No. 652). (Illus.). pap. 1.50 o.p. (ISBN 0-385-09323-3). Doubleday.

Know Your Chihuahua. Pet Library Ltd. (Know Your Pet Ser.: No. 506). (Illus.). pap. 1.50 o.p. (ISBN 0-385-09203-2). Doubleday.

Know Your Cocker Spaniel. Pet Library Ltd. (Know Your Pet Ser.: No. 507). (Illus.). pap. 1.50 o.p. (ISBN 0-385-09211-3). Doubleday.

Know Your Collie. Pet Library Ltd. (Know Your Pet Ser.: No. 508). (Illus.). pap. 1.50 o.p. (ISBN 0-385-09217-2). Doubleday.

Know Your Dachshund. Pet Library Ltd. (Know Your Pet Ser.: No. 509). (Illus.). pap. 1.50 o.p. (ISBN 0-385-09218-0). Doubleday.

Know Your Dalmatian. Pet Library Ltd. (Know Your Pet Ser.: No. 510). (Illus.). pap. 1.50 o.p. (ISBN 0-385-09221-0). Doubleday.

Know Your Doberman Pinscher. Pet Library Ltd. (Know Your Pet Ser.: No. 511). (Illus.). pap. 1.50 o.p. (ISBN 0-385-09223-7). Doubleday.

Know Your Domestic & Exotic Cats. Pet Library Ltd. (Know Your Pet Ser.: No. 602). (Illus.). pap. 1.50 o.p. (ISBN 0-385-09305-5). Doubleday.

Know Your Eyes. Ira A. Abrahamson, Jr. LC 76-23195. 218p. (Orig.). 1977. 9.95 (ISBN 0-88275-928-0); pap. text ed. 6.95 (ISBN 0-88275-451-3). Krieger.

Know Your Feelings. Margaret Hyde & Elizabeth Forsyth. LC 74-12119. 128p. (gr. 7 up). 1975. PLB 5.90 o.p. (ISBN 0-531-02797-X). Watts.

Know Your Festivals & Enjoy Them. 2nd ed. Morris Golomb. LC 72-90771. (Illus.). 189p. (gr. 3-6). 1973. 7.95 (ISBN 0-88400-035-4). Shengold.

Know Your Fox Terrier. Pet Library Ltd. (Know Your Pet Ser.: No. 512). (Illus.). pap. 1.50 o.p. (ISBN 0-385-09226-1). Doubleday.

Know Your Genes. Aubrey Milunsky. 1978. pap. 1.95 (ISBN 0-380-40899-6, 40899). Avon.

Know Your Gerbils. Pet Library Ltd. (Know Your Pet Ser.: No. 757). 64p. 1973. pap. 1.50 o.p. (ISBN 0-385-04512-3). Doubleday.

Know Your German Shepherd. Pet Library Ltd. (Know Your Pet Ser.: No. 513). (Illus.). pap. 1.50 o.p. (ISBN 0-385-09228-8). Doubleday.

Know Your Goldfish. Pet Library Ltd. (Know Your Pet Ser.: No. 711). (Illus.). pap. 1.50 o.p. (ISBN 0-385-09346-2). Doubleday.

Know Your Great Dane. Pet Library Ltd. (Know Your Pet Ser.: No. 514). (Illus.). pap. 1.50 o.p. (ISBN 0-385-01515-1). Doubleday.

Know Your Guinea Pigs. Pet Library Ltd. (Know Your Pet Ser.: No. 753). 64p. 1973. pap. 1.50 o.p. (ISBN 0-385-04510-7). Doubleday.

Know Your Guppies. Pet Library Ltd. (Know Your Pet Ser.: No. 714). (Illus.). pap. 1.50 o.p. (ISBN 0-385-09362-4). Doubleday.

Know Your Hamster. Pet Library Ltd. (Know Your Pet Ser.: No. 754). (Illus.). pap. 1.50 o.p. (ISBN 0-385-09365-9). Doubleday.

Know Your Horse. W. S. Codrington. (Illus.). 14.75 (ISBN 0-85131-207-1, Dist. by Sporting Book Center); pap. 9.75 (ISBN 0-85131-208-X). J A Allen.

Know Your Irish Setter. Pet Library Ltd. (Know Your Pet Ser.: No. 515). (Illus.). pap. 1.50 o.p. (ISBN 0-385-01520-8). Doubleday.

Know Your Job Rights. Wesley M. Wilson. LC 75-28954. 180p. 1976. 8.95 o.p. (ISBN 0-87094-115-1). Dow Jones-Irwin.

Know Your Kerry Blue. Pet Library Ltd. (Know Your Pet Ser.: No. 534). (Illus.). pap. 1.50 o.p. (ISBN 0-385-09283-0). Doubleday.

Know Your Labrador Retriever. Pet Library Ltd. (Know Your Pet Ser.: No. 542). 64p. 1973. pap. 1.50 o.p. (ISBN 0-385-04507-7). Doubleday.

Know Your Lhasa Apso. Pet Library Ltd. (Know Your Pet Ser.: No. 529). (Illus.). pap. 1.50 o.p. (ISBN 0-385-09276-8). Doubleday.

Know Your Lovable Mutt. Pet Library Ltd. (Know Your Pet Ser.: No. 527). (Illus.). pap. 1.50 o.p. (ISBN 0-385-09268-7). Doubleday.

Know Your Maltese. Pet Library Ltd. (Know Your Pet Ser.: No. 516). (Illus.). pap. 1.50 o.p. (ISBN 0-385-09231-8). Doubleday.

Know Your Miniature Schnauzer. Pet Library Ltd. (Know Your Pet Ser.: No. 517). (Illus.). pap. 1.50 o.p. (ISBN 0-385-09232-6). Doubleday.

Know Your Model Aero Engine. R. H. Warring. (Illus., Orig.). 1979. pap. 8.50x (ISBN 0-85242-607-0). Intl Pubns Serv.

Know Your Monkey. Pet Library Ltd. (Know Your Pet Ser.: No. 755). (Illus.). pap. 1.50 o.p. (ISBN 0-385-09368-3). Doubleday.

Know Your Nutrition. rev. ed. Linda Clark. LC 80-84437. 275p. 1981. pap. 4.95 (ISBN 0-87983-247-9). Keats.

Know Your Ocelots & Margays. Pet Library Ltd. (Know Your Pet Ser.: No. 756). (Illus.). pap. 1.50 o.p. (ISBN 0-385-09369-1). Doubleday.

Know Your Old English Sheepdog. Pet Library Ltd. (Know Your Pet Ser.: No. 535). (Illus.). pap. 1.50 o.p. (ISBN 0-385-09284-9). Doubleday.

Know Your Oscilloscope. 4th ed. Robert G. Middleton. LC 80-52230. 1980. pap. 8.95. Sams.

Know Your Oscilloscope. 3rd ed. Paul C. Smith. Ed. by Robert G. Middleton. LC 74-15451. (Illus.). 1974. pap. 5.25 o.p. (ISBN 0-672-21102-5). Sams.

Know Your Own I.Q. Hans J. Eysenck. (Orig.). 1962. pap. 2.50 (ISBN 0-14-020516-0, Pelican). Penguin.

Know Your Own Mind. Harold Sherman. 1978. pap. 1.50 o.p. (ISBN 0-449-13932-8, GM). Fawcett.

Know Your Own Ship. T. Walton. Ed. by B. Baxter. 373p. 1970. 28.00x (ISBN 0-85264-151-6, Pub. by Griffin England). State Mutual Bk.

Know Your Parakeet. Pet Library Ltd. (Know Your Pet Ser.: No. 656). (Illus.). pap. 1.50 o.p. (ISBN 0-385-09327-6). Doubleday.

Know Your Parrot. Pet Library Ltd. (Know Your Pet Ser.: No. 657). (Illus.). pap. 1.50 o.p. (ISBN 0-385-09335-7). Doubleday.

Know Your Pekingese. Pet Library Ltd. (Know Your Pet Ser.: No. 518). (Illus.). pap. 1.50 o.p. (ISBN 0-385-09241-5). Doubleday.

Know Your Persian Cat. Pet Library Ltd. (Know Your Pet Ser.: No. 605). (Illus.). pap. 1.50 o.p. (ISBN 0-385-09310-1). Doubleday.

Know Your Poodle. Pet Library Ltd. (Know Your Pet Ser.: No. 520). (Illus.). pap. 1.50 o.p. (ISBN 0-385-09243-1). Doubleday.

Know Your Popular Cage Birds. Pet Library Ltd. (Know Your Pet Ser.: No. 651). (Illus.). pap. 1.50 o.p. (ISBN 0-385-09316-0). Doubleday.

Know Your Pug. Pet Library Ltd. (Know Your Pet Ser.: No. 521). (Illus.). pap. 1.50 o.p. (ISBN 0-385-09244-X). Doubleday.

Know Your Retriever. Pet Library Ltd. (Know Your Pet Ser.: No. 522). (Illus.). pap. 1.50 o.p. (ISBN 0-385-09250-4). Doubleday.

Know Your Saint Bernard. Pet Library Ltd. (Know Your Pet Ser.: No. 533). (Illus.). pap. 1.50 o.p. (ISBN 0-385-09282-2). Doubleday.

Know Your Scottish Terrier. Pet Library Ltd. (Know Your Pet Ser.: No. 423). (Illus.). pap. 1.50 o.p. (ISBN 0-385-09256-3). Doubleday.

Know Your Setters & Pointer. Pet Library Ltd. (Know Your Pet Ser.: No. 538). (Illus.). pap. 1.50 o.p. (ISBN 0-385-09287-3). Doubleday.

Know Your Shetland Sheepdog. Pet Library Ltd. (Know Your Pet Ser.: No. 524). (Illus.). pap. 1.50 o.p. (ISBN 0-385-09258-X). Doubleday.

Know Your Shih Tzu. Pet Library Ltd. (Know Your Pet Ser.: No. 528). (Illus.). pap. 1.50 o.p. (ISBN 0-385-09274-1). Doubleday.

Know Your Siamese Cat. Pet Library Ltd. (Know Your Pet Ser.: No. 605). (Illus.). pap. 1.50 o.p. (ISBN 0-385-09315-2). Doubleday.

Know Your Toy Fox Terrier. Pet Library Ltd. (Know Your Pet Ser.: No. 536). (Illus.). pap. 1.50 o.p. (ISBN 0-385-09285-7). Doubleday.

Know Your Weimaraner. Pet Library Ltd. (Know Your Pet Ser.: No. 525). (Illus.). pap. 1.50 o.p. (ISBN 0-385-09262-8). Doubleday.

Know Your Welsh Corgi. Pet Library Ltd. (Know Your Pet Ser.: No. 541). (Illus.). pap. 1.50 o.p. (ISBN 0-385-05470-X). Doubleday.

Know Your West Highland White Terrier. Pet Library Ltd. (Know Your Pet Ser.: No. 531). (Illus.). pap. 1.50 o.p. (ISBN 0-385-09278-4). Doubleday.

Know Your Wild Birds. Pet Library Ltd. (Know Your Pet Ser.: No. 659). (Illus.). pap. 1.50 o.p. (ISBN 0-385-09337-3). Doubleday.

Know Your Woods. Constantine & Hobbs. 1975. text ed. 19.80 (ISBN 0-87002-903-7). Bennett IL.

Know Your Woods. rev. ed. Albert Constantine. 1975. 17.50 (ISBN 0-684-14115-9, ScribT). Scribner.

Know Your Yorkshire Terrier. Pet Library Ltd. (Know Your Pet Ser.: No. 526). (Illus.). pap. 1.50 o.p. (ISBN 0-385-09266-0). Doubleday.

Know Yourself. Ernest Holmes & Willis Kinnear. (Orig.). 1970. pap. 3.50 (ISBN 0-911336-36-2). Sci of Mind.

Knowing & Enjoying Your Baby. Alan Sroufe. LC 77-21703. (Illus.). 1977. 10.95 (ISBN 0-13-516690-X, Spec); pap. 3.95 (ISBN 0-13-516682-9, Spec). P-H.

Knowing & Guessing: A Quantitative Study of Inference & Information. M. S. Watanabe. 1969. 39.95 (ISBN 0-471-92130-0, Pub. by Wiley-Interscience). Wiley.

Knowing & the Known. John Dewey & Arthur F. Bentley. LC 75-31432. 334p. 1976. Repr. of 1949 ed. lib. bdg. 25.00x (ISBN 0-8371-8498-3, DEKK). Greenwood.

Knowing Christ. S. Craig Glickman. 200p. 1980. pap. 4.95 (ISBN 0-8024-3502-5). Moody.

Knowing God: Religious Knowledge in the Theology of John Baillie. William P. Tuck. LC 78-52865. 1978. pap. text ed. 7.75x (ISBN 0-8191-0484-1). U Pr of Amer.

Knowing God: Study Guide. Pref. by James I. Packer. 1975. pap. 1.95 (ISBN 0-87784-413-5). Inter-Varsity.

Knowing God's Will. Steve B. Clark. (Living As a Christian Ser.). 1974. pap. 1.50 (ISBN 0-89283-005-0). Servant.

Knowing God's Will - & Doing It. J. Grant Howard. 128p. 1976. o. p. 4.95 (ISBN 0-310-26280-1); pap. 2.50 (ISBN 0-310-26282-8). Zondervan.

Knowing the Outdoors in the Dark. Vinson Brown. LC 71-179605. (Illus.). 192p. 1973. pap. 2.95 o.s.i. (ISBN 0-02-062260-0, Collier). Macmillan.

Knowing the Score: Notes on Film Music. Irwin Bazelon. LC 80-24925. (Illus.). 352p. 1981. pap. 6.95 (ISBN 0-668-05132-9, 5132). Arco.

Knowing Woman: Feminine Psychology. Irene Claremont De Castillejo. 192p. 1974. pap. 3.50 (ISBN 0-06-090349-X, CN349, CN). Har-Row.

Knowledge & Belief. Ed. by A. Philips Griffiths. 1967. pap. 4.95x (ISBN 0-19-500328-4). Oxford U Pr.

Knowledge & Concepts in Future Studies. S. Schwarz. LC 76-54238. (Westview Replica Edition Ser.). 1977. lib. bdg. 24.50x (ISBN 0-89158-123-5). Westview.

Knowledge & Cosmos: Development & Decline of the Medieval Perspective. Robert K. DeKosky. LC 79-66226. 1979. text ed. 18.50 (ISBN 0-8191-0814-6); pap. text ed. 12.00 (ISBN 0-8191-0815-4). U Pr of Amer.

Knowledge & Determination: The Transition from Hegel to Marx. Kyriakos M. Kontopoulos. 1980. text ed. 23.00x (ISBN 90-6032-125-1). Humanities.

Knowledge & Existence: An Introduction to Philosophical Problems. Joseph Margolis. 304p. 1973. text ed. 8.95x (ISBN 0-19-501589-4). Oxford U Pr.

Knowledge & Fallibilism: Essays on Improving Education. Ronald M. Swartz et al. LC 79-3068. 1980. 17.00x (ISBN 0-8147-7808-9). NYU Pr.

Knowledge & Ideology in the Sociology of Education. Gerald Bernbaum. (Studies in Sociology Ser.). 1977. pap. text ed. 4.00x (ISBN 0-333-15762-1). Humanities.

Knowledge & Passion. Michael Z. Rosaldo. LC 79-12632. (Cambridge Studies in Cultural Systems). (Illus.). 1980. 24.95 (ISBN 0-521-22582-5); pap. 6.95 (ISBN 0-521-29562-9). Cambridge U Pr.

Knowledge & Policy in Manpower: A Study of the Manpower, Research & Development Program in the Department of Labor. Assembly of Behavioral & Social Sciences, National Research Council. LC 75-37384. xi, 171p. 1975. pap. 6.25 (ISBN 0-309-02439-0). Natl Acad Pr.

Knowledge & Policy: The Uncertain Connection. Assembly of Behavioral & Social Sciences. 1978. pap. 8.25 (ISBN 0-309-02732-2). Natl Acad Pr.

Knowledge & Politics. Roberto M. Unger. LC 74-15369. 1976. pap. text ed. 5.95 (ISBN 0-02-932870-5). Free Pr.

Knowledge & Power. Ed. by Sanford A. Lakoff. LC 66-23079. 1966. 14.95 o.s.i. (ISBN 0-02-917760-X). Free Pr.

Knowledge & Reality in Plato's Philebus. Roger A. Shiner. 64p. 1974. pap. text ed. 10.00x (ISBN 90-232-1170-7). Humanities.

Knowledge & Social Structure: An Introduction to the Classical Argument in the Sociology of Knowledge. Peter Hamilton. (International Library of Sociology). 174p. 1974. 16.50x (ISBN 0-7100-7746-7); pap. 7.95 (ISBN 0-7100-7786-6). Routledge & Kegan.

Knowledge & Society: An Introduction to the Philosophy of the Social Sciences. Arnold B. Levison. LC 72-88122. 1974. pap. 7.50 (ISBN 0-672-63661-1). Pegasus.

Knowledge & Society: An Introduction to the Philosophy of the Social Sciences. Arnold B. Levison. LC 72-88122. 1974. 20.00x (ISBN 0-672-53661-7). Irvington.

Knowledge & the Curriculum: A Collection of Philosophical Papers. Paul H. Hirst. (International Library of the Philosophy of Education). 1975. 12.50x (ISBN 0-7100-7929-X); pap. 8.95 (ISBN 0-7100-7930-3). Routledge & Kegan.

Knowledge & the Flow of Information. Fred I. Dretske. LC 81-21633. (Illus.). 288p. 1981. text ed. 18.50 (ISBN 0-89706-009-1). Bradford Bks.

Knowledge Application: The Knowledge System in Society. Burkart Holzner & John H. Marx. 1978. text ed. 20.95 (ISBN 0-205-06516-3). Allyn.

Knowledge-Based Program Construction. D. R. Barstow. (Programming Language Ser.: Vol. 6). 1979. 16.95 (ISBN 0-444-00340-1, North Holland); pap. 9.95 (ISBN 0-444-00341-X). Elsevier.

Knowledge, Experience, & Action: An Essay on Education. Harold G. Cassidy. LC 70-81590. 1969. pap. 6.50x (ISBN 0-8077-1150-0). Tchrs Coll.

Knowledge Explosion: Liberation & Limitations. Ed. by Francis Sweeeney. 249p. 1969. 4.95 (ISBN 0-374-18204-3). FS&G.

Knowledge, Ideology & the Politics of Schooling: Towards a Marxist Analysis of Education. Rachel Sharp. 176p. 1980. 25.00 (ISBN 0-7100-0526-1); pap. 12.50 (ISBN 0-7100-0527-X). Routledge & Kegan.

Knowledge: Its Creation, Distribution, & Economic Significance, Vol. 1, Knowledge & Knowledge Production. Fritz Machlup. LC 80-7544. 264p. 1980. 17.50 (ISBN 0-691-04226-8). Princeton U Pr.

Knowledge, Mind & Nature. B. A. Aune. 1979. lib. bdg. 22.00 (ISBN 0-917930-27-4); pap. text ed. 7.50x (ISBN 0-917930-07-X). Ridgeview.

Knowledge of Actions. Betty Powell. 1967. text ed. 5.00x (ISBN 0-04-121004-2). Humanities.

Knowledge of Illness in a Sepik Society: A Study of the Gnau, New Guinea. Gilbert Lewis. (Monographs on Social Anthropology). (Illus.). 372p. 1975. text ed. 42.00x (ISBN 0-391-00389-5, Athlone Pr). Humanities.

Knowledge of Language. David E. Cooper. 196p. 1975. text ed. 15.50x (ISBN 0-391-00382-8); pap. text ed. 10.50x (ISBN 0-391-00383-6). Humanities.

Knowledge: Selected Interviews & Other Writings, 1972-1977. Michel Foucault. 1981. 12.95 (ISBN 0-394-51357-6); pap. 5.95 (ISBN 0-394-73954-X). Pantheon.

Knox County, Maine. Bernard H. Porter. (Illus.). 1969. 15.00 o.p. (ISBN 0-685-19456-6). Porter.

Knyght There Was: The Evolution of the Knight in Literature. Charles Moorman. LC 67-17846. 180p. 1967. 9.00x (ISBN 0-8131-1133-1). U Pr of Ky.

Knyha Mysttsiv I Diiachiv Ukrains'koi Kul'tury. LC 66-59166. (Ukra.) 1954. 15.00 (ISBN 0-918884-11-X). Slavia Lib.

Koalas. Patricia Hunt. LC 80-13717. (A Skylight Bk.). (Illus.). 48p. (gr. 2-5). 1980. PLB 4.95 (ISBN 0-396-07849-4). Dodd.

Koch: As Time Goes by, Memoirs of a Writer. Howard Koch. LC 78-22260. 1979. 10.95 (ISBN 0-15-109769-0). HarBraceJ.

Koda Rohan. Chieko Mulhern. (World Authors Ser.: No. 432). 1977. lib. bdg. 12.50 (ISBN 0-8057-6272-8). Twayne.

Kodak Black & White Darkroom Dataguide. rev. ed. Ed. by Eastman Kodak Company. 1979. pap. 9.95 (ISBN 0-87985-157-0, R-20). Eastman Kodak.

Kodak Color Darkroom Dataguide. rev. ed. Ed. by Eastman Kodak Company. (Illus.). 1980. pap. 9.95 (ISBN 0-87985-086-8, R-19). Eastman Kodak.

Kodak Guide to Thirty-Five MM Photography. Eastman Kodak Company. LC 79-54310. (Illus.). 288p. (Orig.). 1980. text ed. 16.50 (ISBN 0-87985-242-9, AC-95H); pap. text ed. 9.95 (ISBN 0-87985-236-4, AC-95S). Eastman Kodak.

Kodak Microelectronics Seminar - Interface '79, G-102: Proceedings. Eastman Kodak. (Illus.). 180p. 1980. pap. 4.50 (ISBN 0-87985-246-1). Eastman Kodak.

Kodak Sourcebook: Kodak Ektagraphic Slide Projectors. Ed. by Eastman Kodak Company. LC 77-90640. (Illus.). 1977. pap. 4.75 o.p. (ISBN 0-87985-201-1, S-74). Eastman Kodak.

Kodaly Approach, Method Book One. 2nd ed. Katinka S. Daniel. LC 79-53162. 204p. 1979. wire 20.00 (ISBN 0-916656-13-6); materials for transparencies 20.00 (ISBN 0-916656-14-4). Mark Foster Mus.

Kodaly Method: Comprehensive Music Education from Infant to Adult. Lois Choksy. LC 73-18316. (Illus.). 224p. 1974. 15.95 (ISBN 0-13-516765-5); pap. 11.50 (ISBN 0-13-516757-4). P-H.

Kodansha English-Japanese Dictionary. Ed. by Shigeo Kawamoto & Junzaburo Nishiwaki. Tr. by Shigehisa Narita & Mamoru Shimizu. 1557p. 1980. pap. 19.50 flexible soft-binding (ISBN 0-87011-420-4). Kodansha.

Kodansha Japanese-English Dictionary. Ed. by Shigeo Kawamoto et al. Tr. by Hamoru Shimizu & Shigehisa Harita. 1250p. 1980. flexible soft-binding 19.95 (ISBN 0-87011-421-2). Kodansha.

Kodiak & Afognak Life, 1868-1870. Eli L. Huggins. Ed. by Richard A. Pierce. (Materials for the Study of Alaska History Ser.: No. 20). (Illus.). 1981. 16.50x (ISBN 0-919642-96-9). Limestone Pr.

Kodiak: Island of Change, Vol. 4, No. 3. Ed. by Alaska Geographic Staff. LC 72-92087. (Alaska Geographic). (Illus.). 1977. pap. 7.95 o.p. (ISBN 0-88240-095-9). Alaska Northwest.

Kodokan Judo. Donn F. Draeger & Tadao Otaki. (Illus.). Date not set. cancelled (ISBN 0-8048-1187-3). C E Tuttle.

Kogoshui: Gleanings from Ancient Stories. Genchi Kato & H. Hoshino (Records of Asian History). (Illus.). 1972. text ed. 8.00x (ISBN 0-7007-0022-6). Humanities.

Kohelet und die fruehhellenistische Popularphilosphie. Rainer Braun. LC 72-76043. (Beiheft 130 Zur Zeitschrift Fuer Die Alttestamentliche Wissenschaft Ser.). 187p. 1973. text ed. 41.75x (ISBN 3-11-004050-6). De Gruyter.

Koi for Home & Garden. Glen Takeshita. 1969. 2.95 (ISBN 0-87666-754-X, PS659). TFH Pubns.

Kokutai No Hongi. Ed. by R. K. Hall. 1949. 12.50 (ISBN 0-89020-008-4). Brown Bk.

Kolmakovskiy Redoubt: The Ethnoarchaeology of a Russian Fort in Alaska. Wendell H. Oswalt. LC 80-53304. (Monumenta Archaeologica Ser.: No. 8). (Illus.). 212p. 1980. 10.50 (ISBN 0-917956-17-6). UCLA Arch.

Koman Riddles & Turkic Folklore. Andreas Tietze. (U. C. Publ. in Near Eastern Studies: Vol. 8). 1966. pap. 9.00x (ISBN 0-520-09301-1). U of Cal Pr.

Komantcia. Harold Keith. LC 65-14901. (gr. 7 up). 1965. 9.95 (ISBN 0-690-47744-9, TYC-J). T Y Crowell.

Kommissar Lasst Bitten. Herbert Reinecker. (Easy Readers, B). 1978. pap. text ed. 3.75 (ISBN 0-88436-291-4). EMC.

Kommunikationstheoretische Grundlagen des Sprachwandels. Ed. by Helmut Luedtke. (Grundlagen der Kommunikation). 280p. 1979. text ed. 58.00x (ISBN 3-11-007271-8). De Gruyter.

Kompendium der Schutzimpfungen. M. Schaer. (Illus.). 1979. pap. 11.50 (ISBN 3-8055-2994-5). S Karger.

Konds of Orissa. Krishan Sharma. 1979. text ed. 10.00x (ISBN 0-391-01816-7). Humanities.

Konds of Orissa: Anthropometric Study. Krishan Sharma. (Illus.). 112p. 1979. 11.25x (ISBN 0-8002-2298-9). Intl Pubns Serv.

Kone. Roger J. Cazziol. (Illus.). 1971. text ed. 2.25x (ISBN 0-521-07955-1). Cambridge U Pr.

Konfrontasi: The Indonesia-Malaysia Dispute 1963-1966. J. A. Mackie. (Illus.). 384p. 1974. 34.50x (ISBN 0-19-638247-5). Oxford U Pr.

Konfuzius und Sein Kult: Peking & Leipzig, 1928. Franz X. Biallas. LC 78-74282. (Oriental Religions Ser.: Vol. 13). 187p. 1981. lib. bdg. 22.00 (ISBN 0-8240-3915-7). Garland Pub.

Konica Guide. rev. ed. Lou Jacobs, Jr. (Illus.). 128p. 1980. 11.95 (ISBN 0-8174-4124-7); pap. 6.95 (ISBN 0-8174-4125-5). Amphoto.

Konigtum & Stamme in der Werdezeit Des Deutschen Reiches. Gerd Tellenbach. LC 80-2002. 1981. Repr. of 1939 ed. 18.50 (ISBN 0-404-18600-9). AMS Pr.

Konkordanz Zum Hebraeischen Alten Testaments. 2nd ed. Ed. by G. Lisowsky. 1958. 31.75 (ISBN 0-686-20117-5, 60910). United Bible.

Konrad. Christine Nostlinger. (Illus.). (gr. 4-6). 1977. lib. bdg. 7.90 s&l (ISBN 0-531-01341-3). Watts.

Konsonantensystem der deutschen Hochsprache. Hans U. Wuethrich. (Studia Linguistica Germanica, Vol. 11). 203p. 1974. 38.25x (ISBN 3-11-004735-7). De Gruyter.

Konstantin Batyushkov. Ilya Z. Serman. (World Authors Ser.: Russia: No. 287). 1974. lib. bdg. 12.50 (ISBN 0-8057-2118-5). Twayne.

Konstantin Paustovskii: Selected Stories. Ed. by P. Henry & P. Henry. 1967. pap. 6.25 (ISBN 0-08-011859-3). Pergamon.

Konstitution und Vorkommen der Organischen Pflanzenstoffe (Exklusive Alkaloide) Erganzungsband 2, 1. Teil. W. Karrer. (LMW-C 25). 1980. write for info. (ISBN 3-7643-1154-1). Birkhauser.

Kontexte. J. Alan Pfeffer. 1976. pap. 7.95x (ISBN 0-669-73940-5). Heath.

Kontinent Three. Ed. by Vladimir E. Maximov. LC 77-76282. 1978. pap. 3.95 o.p. (ISBN 0-385-12581-X, Anch). Doubleday.

Kontinuierliche Gruppen. Gerhard Kowalewski. LC 51-3003. (Ger). 14.95 (ISBN 0-8284-0070-9). Chelsea Pub.

Kontinuum und Andere Monographien, 4 vols. in 1. Hermann Weyl et al. Incl. Kantinuum; Mathematische Analyse Des Raumproblems; Neuere Funktionentheorie. Landau; Hypothesen. Reimann. LC 72-81808. 14.95 (ISBN 0-8284-0134-9). Chelsea Pub.

Kontorniat-Medaillons. Andreas Alfoeldi & Elisabeth Alfoeldi. (Antike Muenzen und Geschnittene Steine Ser., Vol. 6). 1976. 173.50x (ISBN 3-11-003484-0). De Gruyter.

Koobi Fora: Research Projects, Vol. 1. Ed. by Meave G. Leakey & Richard E. Leakey. (Illus.). 1978. text ed. 49.00x (ISBN 0-19-857392-8). Oxford U Pr.

Kookanoo & the Kangaroo. Mary Durack & Elizabeth Durack. LC 66-15844. (Foreign Lands Bks). (gr. 2-7). 1966. PLB 3.95 o.p. (ISBN 0-8225-0356-5). Lerner Pubns.

Koolah: The White Koala. Robert Hunt. LC 74-735895. (Wildlife Stories Book). (Illus.). (gr. 2-5). 1978. 10 bks. & one cassette 21.00 (ISBN 0-89290-036-9). Soc for Visual.

Koontz Child Developmental Program: Training Activities for the First 48 Months. Charles W. Koontz. LC 73-91239. 1974. pap. 17.50x (ISBN 0-87424-136-7). Western Psych.

Kopet: Chief Joseph's Last Years, a Documentary Narrative. Mick Gidley. LC 80-54428. (Illus.). 168p. 1981. 16.95 o.p. (ISBN 0-295-95794-8). U of Wash Pr.

Koran. Tr. by N. J. Dawood. (Classics Ser.). 1964. pap. 3.50 (ISBN 0-14-044052-6). Penguin.

Koran. Ed. & tr. by J. M. Rodwell. 1953. 10.50x (ISBN 0-460-00380-1, Evman); pap. 4.95 (ISBN 0-460-01380-7). Dutton.

Koran Interpreted. Arthur J. Arberry. 1964. pap. 11.95 (ISBN 0-02-083260-5). Macmillan.

Korea. C. T. Soh. (Geomedical Monographs: Vol. 6). (Illus.). 270p. 1980. 57.90 (ISBN 0-387-09128-9). Springer-Verlag.

Korea & the Limits of Limited War. E. Traverso. Ed. by Richard H. Brown & Van R. Halsey. (Amherst Ser.). (gr. 9-12). 1970. pap. text ed. 4.52 (ISBN 0-201-07582-2, Sch Div); tchrs' manual 1.92 (ISBN 0-201-07584-9). A-W.

Korea & the Politics of Imperialism, 1876-1910. C. I. Kim & Han-Kyo Kim. (Center for Japanese & Korean Studies, UC Berkeley). (Maps). 1968. 15.75x o.p. (ISBN 0-520-00646-1). U of Cal Pr.

Korea Annual 1980. 17th ed. LC 64-6162. (Illus.). 732p. 1980. pap. 30.00x (ISBN 0-8002-2733-6). Intl Pubns Serv.

Korea in Pictures. Sterling Publishing Company Editors. LC 68-8767. (Visual Geography Ser). (Illus., Orig.). (gr. 4-12). 1968. pap. 2.95 (ISBN 0-8069-1104-2). Sterling.

Korea in the World Today. Ed. by Roger Pearson. 1976. pap. 10.00 (ISBN 0-685-79962-X). Coun Am Affairs.

Korea Knot. rev. ed. Carl Berger. LC 57-7459. 1964. 9.00x o.p. (ISBN 0-8122-7471-7). U of Pa Pr.

Korean Criminal Code. (American Series of Foreign Penal Codes: Vol. 2). 1960. 15.00x (ISBN 0-8377-0022-1). Rothman.

Korean Karate: Free Fighting Techniques. Sihak H. Cho. LC 68-18608. (Illus.). 1968. 22.50 (ISBN 0-8048-0350-1). C E Tuttle.

Korean Karate: The Art of Tae Kwan Do. Duk S. Son & R. Clark. LC 68-17527. 1968. 11.95 (ISBN 0-13-516815-5). P-H.

Korean Minority in Japan. Richard H. Mitchell. (Center for Japanese & Korean Studies, UC Berkeley). 1967. 18.50x (ISBN 0-520-00870-7). U of Cal Pr.

Korean Pentecost & the Sufferings Which Followed. William Blair & Bruce Hunt. 1977. pap. 2.50 (ISBN 0-85151-244-5). Banner of Truth.

Korean Pottery & Porcelain of Yi Period. G. M. Gompertz. 1968. 33.00 (ISBN 0-571-08404-4, Pub. by Faber & Faber). Merrimack Bk Serv.

Korean Shamanistic Rituals. Jung Y. Lee. (Religion & Society Ser.). 1979. text ed. 44.50x (ISBN 90-279-3378-2). Mouton.

Korean Trade Directory, 1979 to 1980. 21st ed. Korean Traders Association. LC 60-45910. 579p. 1979. 35.00x (ISBN 0-8002-2520-1). Intl Pubns Serv.

Korean War. Dean Acheson. 1971. pap. text ed. 2.95x (ISBN 0-393-09978-4). Norton.

Koreans in America. Bong-Yong Choy. LC 79-9791. 1979. 18.95 (ISBN 0-88229-352-4). Nelson-Hall.

Koreans in Japan: Ethnic Conflict & Accommodation. Changsoo Lee & George DeVos. (Illus.). 448p. 1981. 30.00x (ISBN 0-520-04258-1). U of Cal Pr.

Koren. Tim Lukeman. LC 79-7692. (Science Fiction Ser.). 192p. 1981. 9.95 (ISBN 0-385-15239-6). Doubleday.

Koro: Economic Development & Social Change in Fiji. R. F. Watters. 1969. 16.50x o.p. (ISBN 0-19-821546-0). Oxford U Pr.

Korotka Istoriia Ukrains'koho Pys'mentsva. Serhii O. Iefremov. (Ukra.). 1972. 18.00 (ISBN 0-918884-22-5). Slavia Lib.

Koschitz's Manual of Useful Information. Koschitz. (Gambler's Book Shelf). 1976. pap. 2.95 (ISBN 0-89650-569-3). Gamblers.

Kosciusko Alpine Flora. Alec Costin et al. 408p. 1980. 35.00x (ISBN 0-643-02473-5, Pub. by CSIRO Australia). Intl Schol Bk Serv.

Kosciusko Alpine Flora. 408p. 1979. 37.50 (ISBN 0-643-02473-5, CO06, CSIRO). Unipub.

Kosher Cooking: The Natural Way. J. Kinderlehrer. 1980. 12.50 o.p. (ISBN 0-8246-0240-4). Jonathan David.

Kosher Gourmet Cookbook. Mildred Miller & Bascha Snyder. LC 74-80926. (Illus.). 1976. 10.00 (ISBN 0-8397-4830-2); pap. 7.50 (ISBN 0-8397-4831-0). Eriksson.

Kosmologie der Babylonier: Studien und Materialien. Mit einem mythologischen Anhang. Peter Jensen. 546p. 1974. Repr. of 1890 ed. 102.35x (ISBN 3-11-003425-5). De Gruyter.

Kossoh Town Boy. R. Wellesley Cole. (Illus.). 1960. 4.95 (ISBN 0-521-04686-6). Cambridge U Pr.

Kostas the Rooster. Traudl. LC 68-14071. (Illus.). (gr. k-3). PLB 5.28 o.p. (ISBN 0-688-51171-6). Lothrop.

Kostis Palamas. Thanasis Maskaleris. (World Authors Ser.: Greece: No. 197). lib. bdg. 10.95 (ISBN 0-8057-2666-7). Twayne.

Kotoku Shusui: Portrait of a Japanese Radical. F. G. Notehelfer. (Illus.). 1971. 42.50 (ISBN 0-521-07989-6). Cambridge U Pr.

Kounovsky's Instant Fitness: How to Stay Fit & Healthy in 6 Minutes a Day. Nicholas Kounovsky. 1978. 8.95 (ISBN 0-394-41316-4). Random.

Kourotropohos: Cults & Representations of the Greek Nursing Dieties. Theodora H. Price. 1978. text ed. 54.00x (ISBN 90-04052-51-8). Humanities.

Krafterzeugung Mit Sonnenenergie und Langzeit-Speicherund. (Ger.). 1975. pap. 15.00 o.p. (ISBN 0-89192-174-5). Interbk Inc.

Kraftwerke, Kernspaltwerke, 2 vols. (Illus.). 1975. Set. pap. 18.00 o.p. (ISBN 0-686-53146-9, Pub. by Gottlieb Duttweiler Inst). Interbk Inc.

Krag Rifle. William S. Brophy. 258p. 1978. 24.95 (ISBN 0-917714-21-0). Beinfeld Pub.

Krausist Movement & Ideological Change in Spain: Eighteen Fifty-Four to Eighteen Seventy-Four. J. Lopez-Morrillas. 180p. Date not set. price not set (ISBN 0-521-23256-2). Cambridge U Pr.

Kreativitaet des Unbewussten. Ed. by H. Dieckmann et al. (Journal: Analytische Psychologie: Vol. 11, No. 3). (Illus.). 216p. 1980. soft cover 17.50 (ISBN 3-8055-1543-X). S Karger.

Krebs. Wilhelm Reich. 461p. 1971. 40.00 (ISBN 0-374-13813-3). FS&G.

Kregel Reprint Library Series, 16 titles, 17 vols. Set. 216.00 (ISBN 0-8254-3034-8). Kregel.

Kreislauf des Jugendlichen bei Arbeit und Sport. 2nd ed. H. Mellerowicz. (Illus.). viii, 60p. 1980. pap. 11.50 (ISBN 3-8055-1140-X). S Karger.

Kremlin & Labor: A Study in National Security Policy. Roy Godson. LC 77-85317. 1977. 9.95x (ISBN 0-8448-1274-9); pap. 3.25x (ISBN 0-8448-1225-0). Crane-Russak Co.

Kremlin: Citadel of History. Mina C. Klein & H. Arthur Klein. (Illus.). 176p. (gr. 7 up). 1973. 8.95g (ISBN 0-02-750830-7). Macmillan.

Kress Library of Business & Economics. John M. Keynes et al. (Kress Library of Business & Economics: No. 1). 1939. pap. 5.00x (ISBN 0-678-09900-6, Baker Lib). Kelley.

Kriminalitaet: Straf-und Massnahmenvollzug. (Ger.). 1976. pap. 8.00 o.p. (ISBN 0-89192-129-X). Interbk Inc.

Kriminologie Im Strafprozess. Ed. by Herbert Jaeger. (Suhrkamp Taschenbuecher Wissenschaft: No. 300). 208p. pap. text ed. 7.15 (ISBN 3-518-07909-3, Pub. by Insel Verlag Germany). Suhrkamp.

Krishna Consciousness: The Topmost Yoga System. A. C. Bhaktivedanta. 96p. 1972. pap. 1.25 o.s.i. (ISBN 0-02-083570-1, Collier). Macmillan.

Krishna, Master of All Mystics. Retold by Joshua Greene. (Illus.). 16p. (gr. 1-4). 1981. pap. 2.95 (ISBN 0-89647-010-5). Bala Bks.

Krishna: Myths, Rites, & Attitudes. Ed. by Milton B. Singer. LC 80-29194. xvii, 277p. 1981. Repr. of 1966 ed. lib. bdg. 27.50x (ISBN 0-313-22822-1, SIKR). Greenwood.

Krishna Smiled: Assignment in Southeast Asia. Judith L. Laikin. LC 72-737. 268p. 1972. 9.95x (ISBN 0-8143-1473-2). Wayne St U Pr.

Krishnamurti: The Years of Awakening. Mary Lutyens. 1975. 8.95 o.p. (ISBN 0-374-18222-1). FS&G.

Krishnamurti: The Years of Awakening. Mary Lutyens. pap. 2.25 (ISBN 0-380-00734-7, 30072). Avon.

Kritische Darstellung der Metaphysik. Hans F. Fulda et al. (Suhrkamp Taschenbuecher Wissenschaft: Vol. 315). 152p. (Orig.). 1980. pap. text ed. 5.85 (ISBN 3-518-07915-8, Pub. by Insel Verlag Germany). Suhrkamp.

Krone Chronicles: A True Story. Sam Harrison. (Orig.). 1980. pap. 5.95 (ISBN 0-89865-030-5). Donning Co.

Krsna: The Supreme Personality of Godhead, 3 vols. Swami A. C. Bhaktivedanta. LC 74-118081. (Illus.). 1970. Set. pap. 6.95 (ISBN 0-912776-30-7); pap. 2.95 ea.; Vol. 1. pap. (ISBN 0-912776-31-5); Vol. 2. pap. (ISBN 0-912776-32-3); Vol. 3. pap. (ISBN 0-912776-33-1). Bhaktivedanta.

Krupskaia & Soviet Russian Librarianship: 1917-1939. Boris Raymond. LC 79-1041. 1979. 13.00 (ISBN 0-8108-1209-6). Scarecrow.

Kruse Professional Price Guide to Collector Cars. Kruse Classic Auction Co. LC 78-55416. (Collector Ser.). (Illus.). 1979. pap. 7.95 o.p. (ISBN 0-87637-337-6). Hse of Collectibles.

Krutch Omnibus: Forty Years of Social & Literary Criticism. Joseph W. Krutch. LC 80-14794. 342p. 1980. 6.95 (ISBN 0-688-00389-3, Quill). Morrow.

Kryptonite Kid. Joseph Torchia. LC 79-1078. 192p. 1980. pap. 2.95 (ISBN 0-03-057798-5). HR&W.

K'ton Ton in Israel. Sadie R. Weilerstein. (Illus.). (ps-3). 1964. 3.50 o.p. (ISBN 0-685-06932-X). Bloch.

Ku Chieh-kang & China's New History: Nationalism & the Quest for Alternative Traditions. Laurence A. Schneider. LC 73-129608. (Center for Chinese Studies, UC Berkeley). 1971. 22.75x (ISBN 0-520-01804-4). U of Cal Pr.

Ku Klux Klan. J. C. Lester & D. L. Wilson. LC 71-114758. (Civil Liberties in Amer. History Ser.). (Illus.). 208p. 1973. Repr. of 1905 ed. lib. bdg. 22.50 (ISBN 0-306-71927-4). Da Capo.

Ku Klux Klan: America's Recurring Nightmare. Fred J. Cooke. (Illus.). 160p. (YA) (gr. 7 up). 1980. PLB 8.29 (ISBN 0-671-34055-7). Messner.

Ku Klux Klan in the City, 1915-1930. Kenneth T. Jackson. (Urban Life in America Ser.). 1967. 17.95 (ISBN 0-19-500591-0); pap. text ed. 4.50x (ISBN 0-19-500918-5). Oxford U Pr.

Kubla Kahn & the Fall of Jerusalem. E. S. Shaffer. LC 74-79141. 320p. 1975. 54.00 (ISBN 0-521-20478-X). Cambridge U Pr.

KUBSIM: A Simulation in Collective Bargaining. Lawrence A. Klatt & Thomas F. Urban. (Management Ser.). 1975. pap. text ed. 5.95 o.p. (ISBN 0-88244-101-9). Grid Pub.

Kudrun: A Critical Appreciation. I. R. Campbell. LC 77-1721. (Anglica Germanica Ser.: No. 2). 1978. 55.00 (ISBN 0-521-21618-4). Cambridge U Pr.

Kudrun: Die Handschrift. Ed. by Franz H. Bauml. (Ger). 1969. 58.00x (ISBN 3-11-000376-7). De Gruyter.

Kudzu & Other Poems. Dorothy Donnelly. (Pourboire Ser.). 1979. pap. 3.50 (ISBN 0-930900-57-X). Burning Deck.

K'uei Yeh Chi. Ed. by Wu-chi Liu & Irving Y. Lo. LC 76-12366. 288p. (Chinese.). 1976. 19.50x (ISBN 0-253-33177-3); pap. text ed. 6.95x (ISBN 0-253-33178-1). Ind U Pr.

Kukai: Major Works, Translated with an Account of His Life & a Study of His Thought. Tr. by Yoshita S. Hakeda from Japanese. LC 72-3124. (Records of Civilization, Sources & Studies). 328p. 1972. 17.50x (ISBN 0-231-03627-2). Columbia U Pr.

Kukini 'aha 'ilono: Over a Century of Native Hawaiian Life & Thought from Hawaiian Newpapers, 1834-1948. Ed. by Rubellite K. Johnson. (Illus.). 1976. pap. text ed. 20.00 (ISBN 0-914916-27-0). Topgallant.

Kukulcan - Rainman: A Legend of the Maya. David Bolton. Ed. by Deborah Platt. (Illus.). 240p. 1980. 12.95 (ISBN 0-934506-02-7). Westminster Co.

Kultura Essays. Ed. by Leopold Tyrmand. LC 70-99732. 1970. 10.95 o.s.i. (ISBN 0-02-932820-9). Free Pr.

Kulturgeschicte der Oper. 2nd, rev. & enl. ed. Joseph Gregor. LC 80-2282. 1981. Repr. of 1950 ed. 57.50 (ISBN 0-404-18847-8). AMS Pr.

Kulu: The End of the Habitable World. Penelope Chetwode. (Illus.). 233p. 1972. 12.00 o.p. (ISBN 0-7195-2431-8). Transatlantic.

Kundalini. George S. Arundale. 1972. 3.50 (ISBN 0-8356-7102-X). Theos Pub Hse.

Kundalini, Evolution & Enlightenment. Ed. by John White. LC 78-1226. 1979. pap. 4.50 (ISBN 0-385-14095-9, Anch). Doubleday.

Kundalini-the Secret of Life. Swami Muktananda. (Illus., Orig.). 1979. pap. 3.25 (ISBN 0-914602-47-0). SYDA Found.

Kundalini Yoga for the West. Swami Sivananda Radha. LC 78-1857. (Illus.). 1978. 24.95 (ISBN 0-931454-01-8). Timeless Bks.

Kundu Drama. Ed. by Paul C. Harrison. Incl. A Beast Story. Adrienne Kennedy; Devil's Mask. Lennox Brown; Great Goodness of Life. Imanu Amiri; The Great MacDaddy. Paul C. Harrison; Kabnis. Jean Toomer; Mars. Clay Goss; The Owl Answers. Adrienne Kennedy; A Season in the Congo. Aime Cesaire. 10.00 (ISBN 0-394-48884-9, GP 717). Grove.

Kung Fu & Tai Chi: Chinese Karate & Classical Exercises. rev. ed. Bruce Tegner. LC 73-4315. (Orig.). 1973. pap. 2.95 o.p. (ISBN 0-87407-015-5). Thor.

Kung Fu for Young People: The Ving Tsun System. Russell Kozuki & Douglas Lee. LC 75-14504. (Illus.). 128p. 1975. 5.95 o.p. (ISBN 0-8069-4094-8); PLB 5.89 o.p. (ISBN 0-8069-4095-6). Sterling.

Kung Fu, History, Philosophy, & Techniques. David Chow & Richard Spangler. LC 73-14043. (Illus.). 220p. 1980. pap. 10.95 (ISBN 0-86568-011-6). Unique Pubns.

Kung Fu Meditations & Chinese Proverbial Wisdom. Adapted by Ellen K. Hua. LC 73-7731. (Illus.). 1973. 3.95 (ISBN 0-87407-511-4); pap. 2.50 (ISBN 0-87407-200-X, FPI). Thor.

Kung Fu No. 3: Superstition. Howard Lee. (Kung Fu Ser). 176p. (Orig.). 1973. pap. 1.25 o.s.i. (ISBN 0-446-76466-3). Warner Bks.

Kung-Fu: The Way of Life. Douglas L. Wong. LC 76-55617. (Illus.). 112p. 1975. pap. 4.95 (ISBN 0-86568-028-0). Unique Pubns.

Kung Fu Theory & Practice. Paul H. Crompton. (Illus.). 136p. 1976. 10.50 o.p. (ISBN 0-7207-0670-X). Transatlantic.

Kung San: Men, Women, & Work in a Foraging Society. Richard B. Lee. LC 78-29504. (Illus.). 1979. 42.50 (ISBN 0-521-22578-7); pap. 11.95x (ISBN 0-521-29561-0). Cambridge U Pr.

Kung Tzu-Chen. Shirleen S. Wong. (World Authors Ser.: China: No. 370). 1975. lib. bdg. 12.50 (ISBN 0-8057-6184-5). Twayne.

Kunjalis, Admirals of Calicut. O. K. Nambiar. 1963. 7.00x o.p. (ISBN 0-210-34057-6). Asia.

Kunst als Gesellschaftanalyse bei Heinrich Mann. Frithjof Trapp. (Quellen und Forschungen Zur Sprach und Kulturgeschichte der Germanischen Voelker NF 64-188). vi, 328p. 1975. text ed. 50.60x (ISBN 3-11-005968-1). De Gruyter.

Kunst der Islamischen Volker. E. Diez. (Handbuch der Kunstwissenschaft Ser.). (Illus.). xxii, 218p. (Ger.). 1981. Repr. of 1917 ed. lib. bdg. 150.00x (ISBN 0-89241-144-9). Caratzas Bros.

Kunst und Geschichte Nubiens in Christlicher Zeit: Ergebnisse und Probleme Auf Grund der Jungsten Ausgrabungen. Erich Dinkler. (Illus.). 379p. 1970. text ed. 92.00x (ISBN 0-685-23524-6). Humanities.

Kunst und Sehen: Eine Psychologie Des Schopferischen Auges. 2nd ed. Rudolf Arnheim. (Illus.). 1978. 24.70x (ISBN 3-11-006682-3). De Gruyter.

Kupper's Color Atlas. Harald Kuppers. (Pocket Art Ser.). (Illus.). 170p. (gr. 9-12). 1981. pap. 4.95 (ISBN 0-8120-2172-X). Barron.

Kura: Design & Tradition of the Japanese Storehouse. Teiji Itoh. LC 73-81112. (Illus.). 252p. 1973. 85.00 (ISBN 0-87011-217-1). Kodansha.

Kura: Design & Tradition of the Japanese Storehouse. abr. ed. Teiji Itoh. Tr. by Charles S. Terry from Japanese. LC 80-21087. (Illus.). 192p. 1980. pap. 15.00 (ISBN 0-914842-53-6). Madrona Pubs.

Kurdi I. V. Antibiotic Therapy Handbook. William J. Kurdi. Ed. by Kevin J. Kurdi. pap. 5.95. Med Educ.

Kurds. Martin Short & Anthony McDermott. (Minority Rights Group: No. 23). 1975. pap. 2.50 (ISBN 0-89192-109-5). Interbk Inc.

Kurds, Turks, & Arabs: Politics, Travel, & Research in North-Eastern Iraq, 1919-1925. Cecil J. Edmonds. LC 80-1930. 1981. Repr. of 1957 ed. 49.50 (ISBN 0-404-18960-1). AMS Pr.

Kuril Islands: Russo-Japanese Frontier in the Pacific. John J. Stephan. (Illus.). 256p. 1975. 29.95x (ISBN 0-19-821563-0). Oxford U Pr.

Kurs Istorii Ukrains'koho Iazyka: Vstup Fonetyka. Ievhen Tymchenko. LC 75-571931. (Shkil'na Biblioteka). (Ukra.). 1972. text ed. 10.00 (ISBN 0-918884-17-9). Slavia Lib.

Kurt Schwitters: A Portrait from Life. Kate T. Steinitz. 1968. 19.50x (ISBN 0-520-01219-4). U of Cal Pr.

Kurt Thomas: International Winner. Nancy Robison. LC 79-25572. (Sports Stars Ser.). (Illus.). 48p. (gr. 2-8). 1980. PLB 7.35 (ISBN 0-516-04307-2); pap. 1.95 (ISBN 0-516-44307-0). Childrens.

Kurt Tucholsky: The Ironic Sentimentalist. Peter Grenville. (German Literature & Society Ser.: Vol. 1). 1980. pap. text ed. write for info. (ISBN 0-85496-074-0). Humanities.

Kurt Vonnegut. James Lundquist. LC 76-15654. (Modern Literature Ser.). 1977. 10.95 (ISBN 0-8044-2564-7); pap. 3.45 (ISBN 0-8044-6458-8). Ungar.

Kurt Vonnegut, Jr. Peter J. Reed. (Writers for the Seventies Ser.). 214p. 1976. 9.95 (ISBN 0-690-01048-6, TYC-T); pap. 2.95 (ISBN 0-690-01049-4, TYC-T). T Y Crowell.

Kurt Vonnegut, Jr. Stanley Schatt. (U.S. Authors Ser.: No. 276). 1976. lib. bdg. 12.50 (ISBN 0-8057-7176-X). Twayne.

Kurt Vonnegut, Jr. Ed. by Stanley Schatt. LC 76-41754. (Twayne's U. S. Authors Ser.). 174p. 1976. pap. text ed. 4.95 (ISBN 0-672-61510-X). Bobbs.

Kuru: Early Letters & Field Notes from the Collection of D. Carleton Gajdusek. Ed. by Judith Farquhar & D. Carleton Gajdusek. 400p. 1980. text ed. 32.00 (ISBN 0-89004-359-0). Raven.

Kurventheorie. 2nd, rev. ed. Karl Menger. LC 63-11314. (Ger). 1968. 22.50 (ISBN 0-8284-0172-1). Chelsea Pub.

Kurze Vergleichende Grammatik der Indogermanischen Sprachen. Karl Brugmann. (Ger). 1969. Repr. of 1904 ed. 100.00x (ISBN 3-11-000179-9). De Gruyter.

Kut: Korean Shamanist Rituals. Halla Pai Huhm. 102p. 1980. 12.50 (ISBN 0-930878-18-3). Hollym Intl.

Kutani Ware. Sensaka Nakagawa. Tr. by John Bester. LC 77-86501. (Japanese Art Library: Vol. 7). 181p. 1979. 16.95 (ISBN 0-87011-322-4). Kodansha.

Kuwait & Her Neighbors. H. R. Dickson. 1956. 21.00 o.p. (ISBN 0-04-953002-X). Allen Unwin.

Kuwait & the Rim of Arabia: Kuwait, Bahrain, Quatar, United Arab Emirates, Yemen, Oman, People's Democratic Republic of Yemen. Gilda Berger. (First Bks). (Illus.). (gr. 4-6). 1978. PLB 6.45 s&l (ISBN 0-531-02235-8). Watts.

Kuwait Fund & the Political Economy of Arab Regional Development. Soliman Demir. LC 75-45305. (Special Studies). (Illus.). 160p. 1976. text ed. 24.95 (ISBN 0-275-22980-7). Praeger.

Kuwait: Trade & Investment. Ragaei El Mallakh. (Special Studies in International Economics & Business). 1979. lib. bdg. 32.50x (ISBN 0-89158-375-0). Westview.

Kwaidan: Stories & Studies of Strange Things. Lafcadio Hearn. LC 75-138067. (Illus.). 1971. pap. 4.95 (ISBN 0-8048-0954-2). C E Tuttle.

Kwakiutl Legends. James Wallas & Pamela Whitaker. 150p. 1981. text ed. price not set (ISBN 0-88839-094-7). Hancock Hse.

KWIC Index of Rock Mechanics Literature: Pt. 1, 1870-1968. E. Hoek & Imperial College of Science & Technology, Rock Mechanics Section. 1977. pap. text ed. 165.00 (ISBN 0-08-022063-0). Pergamon.

KWIC Index of Rock Mechanics Literature: Pt. 2, 1969-1976. Ed. by J. P. Jenkins & E. T. Brown. LC 79-40980. 742p. 1979. 142.00 (ISBN 0-08-022065-7). Pergamon.

Kwik-Sew Method for Easy Sewing. Kerstin Martensson. (Illus.). pap. 6.95 (ISBN 0-913212-09-1). Kwik Sew.

Kyokushin Way. Masutatsu Oyama. LC 79-1961. 1979. 8.95 (ISBN 0-87040-460-1). Japan Pubns.

Kyoto Ceramics. Masahiko Sato. Tr. by Anne V. Towle & Usher Coolidge. LC 72-92256. (Arts of Japan Ser: No. 2). (Illus.). 128p. (Orig.). 1973. 12.50 o.p. (ISBN 0-8348-2701-8). Weatherhill.

Kyoto in the Momoyama Period. Wendell Cole. (Centers of Civilization Ser.: Vol. 22). 166p. 1967. 5.95x (ISBN 0-8061-0748-0). U of Okla Pr.

Kyoto Rediscovered: A Portfolio of Woodblock Prints. Clifton Karhu. (Illus.). 216p. 1981. 125.00 (ISBN 0-8348-1521-4). Weatherhill.

Kyriakodromion (Sunday Sermonary) Apostolos Makrakis. Ed. by Orthodox Christian Educational Society. Tr. by D. Cummings from Hellenic. 637p. 1951. 8.00x (ISBN 0-938366-20-3). Orthodox Chr.

Kyrik & the Lost Queen. Gardner F. Fox. 1976. pap. 1.25 o.p. (ISBN 0-685-74571-6, LB420ZK, Leisure Bks). Nordon Pubns.

Kyrik & the Wizards Swords. Gardner F. Fox. (Orig.). 1976. pap. 1.25 o.p. (ISBN 0-685-64011-6, Leisure Bks). Nordon Pubns.

Kyrik Fights the Demon World. Gardner F. Fox. (Orig.). 1975. pap. 0.95 o.p. (ISBN 0-685-53902-4, LB284NK, Leisure Bks). Nordon Pubns.

Kyrik: Warlock Warrior. Gardner F. Fox. (Orig.). 1975. pap. 0.95 o.p. (ISBN 0-685-52180-X, LB252NK, Leisure Bks). Nordon Pubns.

L

L. A. Culture Quiz. David Peck & David Fine. (Illus.). 96p. (Orig.). 1981. 5.95 (ISBN 0-935232-07-9); pap. 3.95 (ISBN 0-935232-06-0). Deep River Pr.

L. C. Smith Shotguns. William S. Brophy. LC 77-84338. 244p. 1977. 24.95 (ISBN 0-917714-09-1). Beinfeld Pub.

L C to Dewey Conversion Tables. G. Swanson. 1974. 32.00 o.s.i. (ISBN 0-02-469550-5). Macmillan Info.

L. D. Landau. Livanova. Tr. by J. Sykes. 1980. 26.00 (ISBN 0-08-023076-8). Pergamon.

L. D. Landau, Vol. 2. D. Ter Haar. 1969. 16.50 (ISBN 0-08-006451-5); pap. 7.75 (ISBN 0-08-006450-7). Pergamon.

L D Program That Works. Edward G. Scagliotta. LC 75-13492. 1979. pap. 9.95 (ISBN 0-87804-319-5). Mafex.

L. D. S. Children's Comments, Vol. 1. Compiled by Arthur Wallace. 60p. 1978. pap. 1.95 (ISBN 0-937892-03-3). LL Co.

L-DOPA & Behavior. Ed. by S. Malitz. LC 75-181306. (Illus.). 1972. 13.50 (ISBN 0-911216-22-7). Raven.

L. Francis Hereshoff Reader. L. Francis Herreshoff. LC 77-85403. 1978. 17.50 (ISBN 0-87742-091-2). Intl Marine.

L. P. Hartley. P. Bloomfield. pap. 2.95 (ISBN 0-685-31890-7, WTW217, WTW217). British Bk Ctr.

L. P. Hartley. Edward T. Jones. (English Author Ser.: No. 232). 1978. 12.50 (ISBN 0-8057-6703-7). Twayne.

L S D Controversy: An Overview. Maurice S. Tarshis. (Illus.). 96p. 1972. 9.75 (ISBN 0-398-02523-1). C C Thomas.

La Fontaine & Cupid & Psyche Tradition. Thomas H. Brown. (Charles E. Merrill Monograph Series in the Humanities & Social Sciences: Vol. 1, No. 3). 105p. 1968. pap. 1.50 o.p. (ISBN 0-8425-0016-2). Brigham.

Lab Index 1980. Ed. by Richard Dauncey. (Annual Ser.). 1980. pap. text ed. 45.00 o.p. (ISBN 0-933916-03-5). Medical Busn.

Lab Manual for Criminalistics. R. James et al. 1980. 10.95 (ISBN 0-13-519819-4). P-H.

Lab Workbook for Introductory Cell Biology with Fundamentals of Biological Physics & Chemistry. John C. Jones. 1976. wire coil bdg. 5.95 o.p. (ISBN 0-88252-052-0). Paladin Hse.

Labanotation: The System of Analyzing & Recording Movement. rev. ed. Ann Hutchinson. LC 69-11446. 1970. pap. 8.95 (ISBN 0-87830-527-0, 18). Theatre Arts.

Labat's Regional Anesthesia: Techniques & Clinical Applications. 4th ed. John Adriani. (Modern Concepts of Medicine). (Illus.). 600p. 1981. 48.75x (ISBN 0-87527-187-1). Green.

Labelling of Deviance: Evaluating a Perspective. 2nd ed. Ed. by Walter R. Gove. LC 80-50397. (Illus.). 428p. 1980. 20.00x (ISBN 0-8039-1470-9); pap. 9.95x (ISBN 0-8039-1471-7). Sage.

Labor & Development in Latin America. Joseph R. Ramos. LC 74-108095. (Institute of Latin American Studies). (Illus.). 1970. 20.00x (ISBN 0-231-03250-1). Columbia U Pr.

Labor & Manpower Economics. 3rd ed. Abraham L. Gitlow. 1971. text ed. 14.95x o.p. (ISBN 0-256-00173-1). Irwin.

Labor & Socialism in America: The Gompers Era. William M. Dick. LC 71-189555. (National University Publications). 1972. 15.00 (ISBN 0-8046-9005-7). Kennikat.

Labor & the American Revolution. Phillip S. Foner. LC 76-18034. 1976. lib. bdg. 17.95 (ISBN 0-8371-9003-7, FLA/). Greenwood.

Labor & the Legal Process. Harry H. Wellington. LC 68-27769. 1968. 24.00x (ISBN 0-300-01038-9); pap. 5.95x o.p. 1969 (ISBN 0-300-01183-0, Y216). Yale U Pr.

Labor & the National Economy. rev. ed. Ed. by William G. Bowen & Orley Ashenfelter. (Problems of the Modern Economy Ser). 1975. 8.95x (ISBN 0-393-05456-X); pap. 4.95x (ISBN 0-393-09996-2). Norton.

Labor & the New Deal. Ed. by M. Derber & E. Young. LC 70-169656. (Fdr & the Era of the New Deal Ser.). 394p. 1972. Repr. of 1957 ed. lib. bdg. 29.50 (ISBN 0-306-70364-5). Da Capo.

Labor Argument in the American Protective Tariff Discussion. George B. Mangold. Bd. with Daniel Raymond: An Early Chapter in the History of Economic Theory in the United States. C. P. Neill. (Neglected American Economists Ser.). 1974. lib. bdg. 50.00 (ISBN 0-8240-1034-5). Garland Pub.

Labor, Class, & the International System. Alejandro Portes & John Walton. 1981. price not set (ISBN 0-12-562020-9). Acad Pr.

Labor: Clinical Evaluation & Management. 2nd ed. Emanuel A. Friedman. (Illus.). 1978. 32.00 (ISBN 0-8385-5580-2). ACC.

Labor Conditions in Communist Cuba. Cuban Economic Research Project, University of Miami. LC 63-21349. 1963. pap. 2.95x (ISBN 0-87024-303-9). U of Miami Pr.

Labor Courts & Grievance Settlement in Western Europe. Ed. by Benjamin Aaron. LC 72-123628. 1971. 28.50x (ISBN 0-520-01757-9). U of Cal Pr.

Labor Economics. 2nd ed. Roy B. Helfgott. 674p. 1981. text ed. 19.95 (ISBN 0-394-32325-4). Random.

Labor Economics: A Guide to Information Sources. Ross Azevedo. LC 73-17568. (Economics Information Guide Ser.: Vol. 8). 1978. 30.00 (ISBN 0-8103-1297-2). Gale.

Labor Economics: The Emerging Synthesis. Robert M. Fearn. 288p. 1981. text ed. 18.95 (ISBN 0-87626-473-9). Winthrop.

Labor Economics: Theory, Evidence & Policy. 2nd ed. Belton M. Fleisher & Thomas J. Kniesner. (Illus.). 1980. text ed. 21.00 (ISBN 0-13-517433-3). P-H.

Labor Economics: Wage, Employment, & Trade Unionism. 3rd ed. F. Ray Marshall et al. 1976. text ed. 16.95x o.p. (ISBN 0-256-01824-3). Irwin.

Labor Economics: Wages, Employment & Trade Unionism. 4th ed. F. Ray Marshall et al. 1980. 19.95 (ISBN 0-256-02334-4). Irwin.

Labor Education in the U. S. An Annotated Bibliography. Richard E. Dwyer. LC 77-21572. 1977. 14.50 (ISBN 0-8108-1058-1). Scarecrow.

Labor Guide to Labor Law. Bruce S. Feldacker. (Illus.). 1980. ref. ed. 24.95; text ed. 16.95 (ISBN 0-8359-3921-9). Reston.

Labor in America: A History. Foster R. Dulles. LC 66-19224. 1968. pap. 8.95x (ISBN 0-88295-729-5). AHM Pub.

Labor in the Public & Nonprofit Sectors. Ed. by Daniel S. Hamermesh. 250p. 1975. 16.00x (ISBN 0-691-04203-9). Princeton U Pr.

Labor in the United States. 5th ed. Sanford Cohen. (Economics Ser.). 1979. text ed. 18.95 (ISBN 0-675-08299-4). Merrill.

Labor Law Handbook. Wesley M. Wilson. 1963. with 1976 suppl. 22.50 (ISBN 0-672-82866-9, Bobbs-Merrill Law); 1976 suppl. 12.00 (ISBN 0-672-82776-X). Michie.

Labor Law in a Nutshell. Douglas L. Leslie. LC 79-158396. (Nutshell Ser.). 403p. 1979. pap. text ed. 6.95 (ISBN 0-8299-2053-6). West Pub.

Labor Leadership in Italy & Denmark. Joseph A. Raffaele. 1962. 35.00 (ISBN 0-299-02660-4). U of Wis Pr.

Labor Legislation in China. Augusta Wagner. LC 78-22780. (Modern Chinese Economy Ser.). 301p. 1980. lib. bdg. 33.00 (ISBN 0-8240-4283-2). Garland Pub.

Labor, Management, & Social Policy: Essays in the John R. Commons Tradition. Ed. by Gerald G. Somers. 1963. 27.50 (ISBN 0-299-02870-4). U of Wis Pr.

Labor-Management Relations & Public Agency Effectiveness: A Study of Urban Mass Transit. James L. Perry & Harold L. Angle. LC 80-10746. (Pergamon Policy Studies on Business). 208p. 1980. 24.00 (ISBN 0-08-025953-7). Pergamon.

Labor-Management Relations Handbook: For Hotels, Motels, Restaurants & Institutions. Herbert K. Witzky. LC 75-37532. 224p. 1976. 14.95 (ISBN 0-8436-2083-8). CBI Pub.

Labor Market for Humanities. Ann S. Bisconti et al. (Praeger Special Studies Ser.). (Illus.). 1979. 16.50 o.p. (ISBN 0-03-021981-7). Praeger.

Labor Market Segmentation. David Gordon. 350p. 1975. pap. text ed. 8.95x o.p. (ISBN 0-669-95547-7). Heath.

Labor Markets & Wage Determination: The Balkanization of Labor Markets & Other Essays. Clark Kerr. LC 75-17291. 1977. 15.75x (ISBN 0-520-03070-2). U of Cal Pr.

Labor Markets: Segments & Shelters. Marcia Freedman & Gretchen Maclachlan. LC 76-470. (Conservation of Human Resources Ser: No. 1). 224p. 1976. 18.50 (ISBN 0-916672-00-X). Allanheld.

Labor Migration Under Capitalism: The Puerto Rican Experience. History Task Force, Centro De Estudios Puertorriquenos. LC 78-13918. (Modern Reader Paperback Ser.). (Illus.). 287p. 1980. pap. 6.50 (ISBN 0-85345-494-9). Monthly Rev.

Labor Movement in China. Shih K. Tso. LC 79-2842. 230p. 1981. Repr. of 1928 ed. 19.75 (ISBN 0-8305-0018-9). Hyperion Conn.

Labor, Nationalism, & Politics in Argentina. Samuel L. Baily. 1967. 16.00 (ISBN 0-8135-0556-9). Rutgers U Pr.

Labor on the March: The Story of America's Unions. Joseph L. Gardner & Bernard A. Weisberger. LC 74-88864. (American Heritage Junior Library). (Illus.). 153p. (gr. 5 up). 1969. PLB 12.89 (ISBN 0-06-021938-6, J0210, Dist. by Har-Row); 9.95 (ISBN 0-8281-5015-X). Am Heritage.

Labor Organizations: A Macro & Micro Sociological Comparison. Mark Van De Vall. 1970. 32.50 (ISBN 0-521-07637-4). Cambridge U Pr.

Labor Party & the Struggle for Socialism. D. Coates. LC 74-19526. 272p. 1975. 36.00 (ISBN 0-521-20740-1); pap. 11.50x (ISBN 0-521-09939-0). Cambridge U Pr.

Labor Peacemaker: The Life & Works of Father Leo. C. Brown, S. J. Gladys W. Gruenberg. Ed. by George E. Ganss. (Original Studies Composed in English Ser.: No. 4). (Illus.). 176p. 1981. 7.50 (ISBN 0-912422-54-8); pap. 6.00 smythsewn paperbound (ISBN 0-912422-53-X); pap. 5.00 (ISBN 0-912422-52-1). Inst Jesuit. Postponed.

Labor Practices of U. S. Corporations in South Africa. Desaix Myers. LC 77-3020. (Special Studies). 1977. text ed. 21.95 (ISBN 0-275-24520-9). Praeger.

Labor Relations. 3rd ed. A. A. Sloane & F. Witney. 1977. text ed. 21.00 (ISBN 0-13-519595-0). P-H.

Labor Relations & Equal Opportunity in Higher Education. (Litigation & Administrative Course Handbook Ser. 1977-78: Vol. 111). 1977. pap. 20.00 o.p. (ISBN 0-685-05633-3, H4-3860). PLI.

Labor Relations & the Supervisor. M. Gene Newport. LC 68-19343. (Orig.). 1968. text ed. 8.95 (ISBN 0-201-05270-9). A-W.

Labor Relations: Development Structure Process. John A. Fossum. 1979. 19.50x (ISBN 0-256-02088-4). Business Pubns.

Labor Relations in a Public Service Industry: Unions, Management, & the Public Interest in Mass Transit. Kenneth M. Jennings, Jr. et al. LC 77-13717. (Praeger Special Studies). 1978. 32.95 (ISBN 0-03-040866-0). Praeger.

Labor Relations Law. 3rd ed. Benjamin Tyler & Fred Witney. 1979. text ed. 23.95 (ISBN 0-13-519645-0). P-H.

Labor Relations Process: Form & Content. William H. Holley, Jr. & Ken Jennings. 600p. 1980. text ed. 21.95 (ISBN 0-03-046556-7). Dryden Pr.

Labor Relations Yearbook--1979. BNA Editorial Staff of Labor Relations Reporter. 560p. 1980. 16.00 (ISBN 0-87179-334-2). BNA.

Labor Sector. 2nd ed. Neil W. Chamberlain & D. E. Cullen. Orig. Title: Firm: Microeconomic Planning & Action. 1972. 17.95 (ISBN 0-07-010428-X, C). McGraw.

Labor Spy Racket. Leo Huberman. LC 77-139201. (Civil Liberties in American History Ser). (Illus.). 1971. Repr. of 1937 ed. lib. bdg. 22.50 (ISBN 0-306-70080-8). Da Capo.

Labor Supply & Public Policy: A Critical Review. Michael C. Keeley. (Studies in Labor Economics Ser.). 1981. price not set (ISBN 0-12-403920-0). Acad Pr.

Labor Theory. Richard Perlman. LC 80-12286. 250p. 1981. Repr. of 1969 ed. lib. bdg. price not set (ISBN 0-89874-163-7). Krieger.

Labor Unions. Gary M. Fink. LC 76-8734. (Greenwood Encyclopedia of American Institutions). 544p. 1977. lib. bdg. 29.95 (ISBN 0-8371-8938-1, FLU/). Greenwood.

Labor Unions in the United States. Carolyn Sims. LC 72-172449. (First Bks). (Illus.). (gr. 4-6). 1971. PLB 4.90 o.p. (ISBN 0-531-00748-0). Watts.

Labor Viewpoint. Sol C. Chaikin. LC 80-12784. (Illus.). 250p. (Orig.). 1980. pap. 10.95 (ISBN 0-912526-26-2). Lib Res.

Laboratory Aide. 2nd ed. Arco Editorial Board. LC 73-100662. 224p. 1972. pap. 8.00 o.p. (ISBN 0-668-01121-1). Arco.

Laboratory & Engineering Notebook. lab man. 6.50x (ISBN 0-934786-05-4). G Davis.

Laboratory & Field Experiments in Motor Learning. R. N. Singer & C. Milne. (Illus.). 292p. 1975. 26.75 (ISBN 0-398-03262-9). C C Thomas.

Laboratory & Field Investigations in Marine Biology. James L. Sumich & Gordon H. Dudley. 1980. pap. write for info. (ISBN 0-697-04594-3). Wm C Brown.

Laboratory Animal Housing. Institute of Laboratory Animal Resources, National Research Council. 1979. pap. text ed. 12.00x (ISBN 0-309-02790-X). Natl Acad Pr.

Laboratory Animal Medical Subject Headings. Institute of Laboratory Animal Resources. LC 78-178256. 224p. 1972. pap. 8.00 (ISBN 0-309-01933-8). Natl Acad Pr.

Laboratory Animal: Principles & Practices. Ed. by W. Lane-Petter & A. E. Pearson. 1972. 40.50 (ISBN 0-12-435760-1). Acad Pr.

Laboratory Animal Technology. J. K. Inglis. 1980. 48.00 (ISBN 0-08-023772-X); pap. 23.00 (ISBN 0-08-023771-1). Pergamon.

Laboratory Animals in Gerontological Research. Institute Of Laboratory Animal Research. LC 68-60087. 1968. pap. 5.75 o.p. (ISBN 0-309-01591-X). Natl Acad Pr.

Laboratory Approach to Mathematics. Kenneth P. Kidd et al. 1970. pap. text ed. 11.14 (ISBN 0-574-34790-9, 3-4790). SRA.

Laboratory Assistant's Manual: A Guide for Medical Laboratory Assistants. Maurice G. Rogoff. (McGraw-Hill International Health Services Ser.). (Illus.). 1977. pap. text ed. 6.95 o.p. (ISBN 0-07-099552-4, C). McGraw.

Laboratory Diagnosis in Dermatology. Leon Goldman et al. LC 70-176170. 300p. 1981. 37.50 (ISBN 0-87527-194-4). Green.

Laboratory Diagnosis of Infectious Disease: A Guide for Clinicians. 1980 ed. Ed. by Cornelius J. O'Connell. LC 80-16360. 1980. pap. 12.50 (ISBN 0-87488-965-0). Med Exam.

Laboratory Diagnosis of Viral, Bedsonial & Rickettsial Diseases: A Handbook for Laboratory Workers. Abbas M. Behbehani. (Illus.). 244p. 1972. 27.50 (ISBN 0-398-02229-1). C C Thomas.

Laboratory Exercises for Biology. Ed. by San Francisco State College Staff. 1967. 4.25 (ISBN 0-917962-07-9). Peek Pubns.

Laboratory Exercises in Biology. Robert T. Kirkwood. 1981. pap. text ed. 5.95 (ISBN 0-8403-1754-9). Kendall-Hunt.

Laboratory Exercises in Comparative Biochemistry & Physiology. Ed. by G. A. Kerkut. Incl. Vol. 1. 1968. 56.00 (ISBN 0-12-404650-9); Vol. 2. 1969. write for info. (ISBN 0-12-404652-5); Vol. 3. 1970. 69.00 (ISBN 0-12-404653-3); Vol. 4. 1971. 53.50 (ISBN 0-12-404654-1); Vol. 5. 1972. 47.50 (ISBN 0-12-404655-X); Vol. 6. 1972. 46.50 (ISBN 0-12-404656-8). Acad Pr.

Laboratory Exercises in Earth Science. Claude J. Doiron. 1978. pap. text ed. 7.50 (ISBN 0-8403-1132-X). Kendall-Hunt.

Laboratory Exercises in Microbiology. Raymond B. Otero. 200p. 1973. 4.95 o.p. (ISBN 0-397-54147-3). Lippincott.

Laboratory Exercises in Microbiology. 2nd ed. Raymond B. Otero. 1977. pap. text ed. 6.50 (ISBN 0-8403-1743-3). Kendall-Hunt.

Laboratory Exercises in Oceanography. Bernard W. Pipkin et al. (Illus.). 1977. lab. manual 9.95x (ISBN 0-7167-0181-2); tchrs. manual avail. W H Freeman.

Laboratory Experience: A Principles of Biology Manual. 2nd ed. J. Alfred Chiscon et al. 1976. spiral ed. 7.95 o.p. (ISBN 0-8087-0362-5). Burgess.

Laboratory Experiences in Exercise Physiology. Ernest D. Michael et al. 1979. lab manual 4.95 (ISBN 0-932392-05-9). Mouvement Pubns.

Laboratory Experiments. pap. write for info. (ISBN 0-13-057679-4); student guide 7.95 (ISBN 0-13-057661-1). P-H.

Laboratory Experiments in College Physics. 5th ed. C. H. Bernard & C. D. Epp. 1981. 13.50 (ISBN 0-471-05441-0). Wiley.

Laboratory Experiments in College Physics. 4th ed. C. Henry Bernard. 1972. pap. text ed. 14.95 o.p. (ISBN 0-471-00029-9). Wiley.

Laboratory Experiments in Physiology. 9th ed. Alan Grinnell & Albert A. Barber. (Illus.). 208p. 1976. pap. 8.95 (ISBN 0-8016-2978-0). Mosby.

Laboratory Experiments to Chemistry: The Central Science. 2nd ed. Kenneth C. Kemp. 378p. 1981. wkbk. 10.95 (ISBN 0-13-128520-3). P-H.

Laboratory for General Botany. Alfieri et al. 1977. pap. text ed. 4.50 (ISBN 0-917962-00-1). Peek Pubns.

Laboratory for Liberty: The South Carolina Legislative Committee System, 1719-1776. George E. Frakes. LC 74-94066. (Illus.). 218p. 1970. 14.50x (ISBN 0-8131-1219-2). U Pr of Ky.

Laboratory Guide for Anatomy & Physiology. Irene Erskine. 176p. 1980. pap. text ed. 8.95 (ISBN 0-8403-2350-6). Kendall-Hunt.

Laboratory Guide for Elements of Physiology. 5th ed. W. S. Platner & D. K. Meyer. text ed. 3.95x spiral bdg. (ISBN 0-87543-039-2). Lucas.

Laboratory Guide for Freshman Biology. 2nd ed. George Stiles et al. 1980. pap. text ed. 12.95 (ISBN 0-8403-2227-5). Kendall-Hunt.

Laboratory Guide to Disordered Hemostasis. T. A. Harper. 1970. 14.95 (ISBN 0-407-74250-6). Butterworths.

Laboratory Guide to Frog Anatomy. Eli. C. Minkoff. LC 74-22206. 176p. 1975. pap. text ed. 7.75 (ISBN 0-08-018315-8). Pergamon.

Laboratory Guide to Human Physiology: A Concepts & Clinical Applications. 2nd ed. Stuart I. Fox. 285p. 1980. wire coil bdg. avail. (ISBN 0-697-04595-1); answers to questions available (ISBN 0-697-04596-X). Wm C Brown.

Laboratory Guide to Parasitology: With Introduction to Experimental Methods. Ralph W. Macy & Allen K. Berntzen. (Illus.). 316p. 1971. pap. 17.75 (ISBN 0-398-02154-6). C C Thomas.

Laboratory Handbook of Chromatigraphic & Allied Methods. O. Mikes. (Analytical Chemistry Ser.). 1979. 149.95x (ISBN 0-470-26399-7). Halsted Pr.

Laboratory Handbook of Paper & Thin-Layer Chromatography. Jiri Gasparic. Ed. by Jaroslov Churacek. LC 77-14168. 1978. 71.95 (ISBN 0-470-99298-0). Halsted Pr.

Laboratory Handbook of Petrographic Techniques. Charles S. Hutchison. LC 73-17336. 544p. 1974. 35.00 (ISBN 0-471-42550-8, Pub. by Wiley-Interscience). Wiley.

Laboratory Handbook of Photomacrography. Ed. by William White, Jr. 1981. write for info. Franklin Inst Pr.

Laboratory Indices of Nutritional Status in Pregnancy. Food & Nutrition Board. 1978. pap. 9.25 (ISBN 0-309-02729-2). Natl Acad Pr.

Laboratory Instructions in Microbiology. 2nd ed. Dean A. Anderson. LC 73-18202. 1974. text ed. 7.95 o.p. (ISBN 0-8016-0171-1). Mosby.

Laboratory Instrumentation. Ed. by M. Robert Hicks et al. (Illus.). 240p. 1980. pap. text ed. 17.50 (ISBN 0-06-141191-4). Har-Row.

Laboratory Introduction to Psychology. John W. Ost et al. 214p. 1969. 10.95 (ISBN 0-12-528856-5). Acad Pr.

Laboratory Investigations in General Biology, Vol. 2. Charles R. Wilson. 80p. 1978. pap. text ed. 6.95 o.p. (ISBN 0-8403-1816-2). Kendall-Hunt.

Laboratory Investigations in Human Physiology. George K. Russell. (Illus.). 1978. pap. text ed. 8.50 (ISBN 0-02-404680-9). Macmillan.

Laboratory Investigations in the Principles of Biology. 3rd ed. Thomas Mertens & Alice S. Bennett. 1973. spiral bdg. 8.95 (ISBN 0-8087-1360-4). Burgess.

Laboratory Investigations in Zoology. Jan Gault et al. 176p. 1980. pap. 8.95 (ISBN 0-8403-2261-5). Kendall-Hunt.

Laboratory Management. Jack E. Newell. LC 76-155040. (Series in Laboratory Medicine). 250p. 1972. 19.95 (ISBN 0-316-60451-8). Little.

Laboratory Manual & Workbook for Integrated Basic Science. 2nd rev. ed. Stewart M. Brooks. (Illus., Orig.). 1971. text ed. 8.95 (ISBN 0-8016-0811-2). Mosby.

Laboratory Manual for Basic Physiology & Anatomy. 4th ed. Ellen Chaffee et al. 222p. 1980. text ed. 8.95 (ISBN 0-397-54228-3). Lippincott.

Laboratory Manual for Basic Veterinary Microbiology. Olen R. Brown. (Lucas Text Ser). 1973. spiral bdg. 5.95x (ISBN 0-87543-087-2). Lucas.

Laboratory Manual for Biology of Animals. Margaret Hartman & Mercer P. Russell. 1980. coil binding 7.50 (ISBN 0-88252-108-X). Paladin Hse.

Laboratory Manual for Chemistry: A Lige Science Approach. Roger W. Armstrong. 1980. pap. write for info. (ISBN 0-02-303920-5). Macmillan.

Laboratory Manual for Entomology & Plant Pathology. Louis L. Pyenson & Harvey E. Barke. (Illus.). 1976. pap. text ed. 12.00 (ISBN 0-87055-200-7). AVI.

Laboratory Manual for Exercise Physiology. Ronald James Byrd & Freddie Melton Browning. (Illus.). 168p. 1972. 14.50 (ISBN 0-398-02459-6); pap. 9.75 (ISBN 0-398-02925-3). C C Thomas.

Laboratory Manual for Food Canners & Processors, Vol. 1 Microbiology & Processing. 3rd ed. Ed. by National Food Processors Association. (Illus.). 1968. 28.50 (ISBN 0-87055-027-6). AVI.

Laboratory Manual for Food Canners & Processors, Vol. 2. Analysis, Sanitation & Statistics. 3rd ed. Ed. by National Food Processors Association. (Illus.). 1968. 39.00 (ISBN 0-87055-028-4). AVI.

Laboratory Manual for General Botany. 4th ed. Charles DePoe et al. 1976. pap. text ed. 6.95 (ISBN 0-8403-1448-5). Kendall-Hunt.

Laboratory Manual for General Chemistry. J. A. Beran & J. E. Brady. 1978. pap. text ed. 10.95 (ISBN 0-471-03290-5). Wiley.

Laboratory Manual for General Zoology, Pt. 1. Henry R. Mushinsky. 1978. pap. text ed. 6.95 (ISBN 0-8403-1213-X). Kendall-Hunt.

Laboratory Manual for Human Anatomy & Physiology. Wittrup. 1981. cancelled; instr's guide cancelled. Burgess.

Laboratory Manual for Introductory Biology. Wendell Wall. coil binding 10.95 (ISBN 0-88252-101-2). Paladin Hse.

Laboratory Manual for Introductory Criminal Investigation. Jon Howington. pap. text ed. 8.50x (ISBN 0-8191-0070-6). U Pr of Amer.

Laboratory Manual for Mammalian Anatomy. Phoebe Rutherford. 1973. text ed. 7.95 spiral bdg. (ISBN 0-8087-1883-5). Burgess.

Laboratory Manual for Microbiology. new ed. Ellis Brockman. LC 74-28777. 1980. pap. 15.00 (ISBN 0-87812-085-8). Pendell Pub.

Laboratory Manual for Physiological Studies of Rice. 83p. 1976. pap. 4.00 (R020, IRRI). Unipub.

Laboratory Manual in Adapted Physical Education & Recreation: Experiments, Activities, & Assignments. Walter C. Crowe et al. (Illus.). 1977. pap. text ed. 9.50 (ISBN 0-8016-1099-0). Mosby.

Laboratory Manual in Chemistry. Walter Ahner. (gr. 11-12). 1964. pap. 5.42 (ISBN 0-87720-123-4). AMSCO Sch.

Laboratory Manual in Food Chemistry. A. E. Woods & L. W. Aurand. (Illus.). 1977. pap. text ed. 11.00 (ISBN 0-87055-220-1). AVI.

Laboratory Manual in Food Preservation. Marion L. Fields. 1977. 11.00 (ISBN 0-87055-241-4). AVI.

Laboratory Manual in General Biology. 9th ed. George B. Noland & William C. Beaver. 1975. pap. text ed. 8.95 (ISBN 0-8016-3685-X). Mosby.

Laboratory Manual in Physical Geography. 2nd ed. Neal G. Lineback. 1976. pap. text ed. 7.95 (ISBN 0-8403-1089-7). Kendall-Hunt.

Laboratory Manual in Physics. 2nd ed. Walter L. Ahner & Sheldon R. Diamond. (Orig.). (gr. 10-12). 1967. 5.50 (ISBN 0-87720-174-9); tchrs' ed. 3.45 (ISBN 0-87720-175-7). AMSCO Sch.

Laboratory Manual in Physiology & Anatomy. 3rd rev. ed. Ellen E. Chaffee. 250p. 1974. pap. text ed. 8.95 o.p. (ISBN 0-397-47313-3). Lippincott.

Laboratory Manual of Blood Coagulation. D. E. Austen & I. L. Rhymes. (Illus.). 160p. 1976. 17.00 (ISBN 0-8016-0376-5, Blackwell). Mosby.

Laboratory Manual of Cell Biology. David O. Hall & S. E. Hawkins. LC 74-21529. 1974. pap. 11.50x (ISBN 0-8448-0601-3). Crane-Russak Co.

Laboratory Manual of Elementary College Physics. 7th ed. Harry E. Hammond & L. V. Halbroyd. 1974. text ed. 4.50x spiral bdg. (ISBN 0-87543-101-1). Lucas.

Laboratory Manual of Physical Chemistry. 2nd ed. H. D. Crockford et al. 1976. text ed. 14.95 (ISBN 0-471-18844-1). Wiley.

Laboratory Manual of Qualitative Organic Analysis. 3rd ed. Harry T. Openshaw. 1955. 14.95x (ISBN 0-521-05865-1); pap. 9.95x (ISBN 0-521-29112-7). Cambridge U Pr.

Laboratory Manual on Crystal Growth. I. Tarjan & M. Matrai. (Illus.). 250p. 21.50 (ISBN 0-685-42284-4). Adler.

Laboratory Manual on the Use of Radiotracer Techniques in Industry & Environmental Pollution. (Technical Reports Ser.: No.161). (Illus.). 120p. 1976. pap. 10.25 (ISBN 92-0-165075-2, IAEA). Unipub.

Laboratory Manual to Accompany Basic Medical Microbiology. Robert R. Boyd & Bryan G. Hoerl. 1981. write for info. lab manual (ISBN 0-316-10434-5). Little.

Laboratory Manual to Introduction to the Microbial World. W. Segel & M. Wheelis. 1980. pap. 8.95 (ISBN 0-13-488031-5). P-H.

Laboratory Mathematics: Medical & Biological Applications. 2nd ed. June Campbell & Joe B. Campbell. LC 79-24996. (Illus.). 1980. pap. text ed. 12.95 (ISBN 0-8016-0702-7). Mosby.

Laboratory Medical Mycology. Yousef Al-Doory. LC 79-22500. (Illus.). 410p. 1980. text ed. 24.50 (ISBN 0-8121-0695-4). Lea & Febiger.

Laboratory Medicine, 4 vols. Loose Leaf References Services. Ed. by George J. Race. loose leaf bdg. 275.00 (ISBN 0-06-148009-6, Harper Medical); revision pages 50.00 (ISBN 0-685-57897-6). Har-Row.

Laboratory On-Line Computing: An Introduction for Engineers & Physics. J. Brignell & G. Rhodes. LC 75-6261. 1975. 28.95 (ISBN 0-470-10400-7). Halsted Pr.

Laboratory Operations for Rotating Electric Machinery & Transformer Technology. Richardson. 256p. 1980. pap. text ed. 7.95 (ISBN 0-8359-3925-1). Reston.

Laboratory Organization & Management. F Grover & P. Wallace. (Illus.). 1979. text ed. 19.95 (ISBN 0-408-70793-3). Butterworths.

Laboratory Outlines in Biology, II. Peter Abramoff & Robert G. Thomson. (Illus.). 1972. lab. manual 10.95x (ISBN 0-7167-0694-6); individual experiments 0.50 (ISBN 0-686-66666-6); instr's handbk avail. W H Freeman.

Laboratory Outlines in Zoology. Peter Abramoff & Robert G. Thomson. (Illus.). 1978. lab manual 10.95x (ISBN 0-7167-0017-4); individual experiments 0.50 (ISBN 0-686-68019-7); instr's handbk avail. (ISBN 0-685-93659-7). W H Freeman.

Laboratory Physics. H. F. Meiners et al. 1972. 14.95x (ISBN 0-471-59159-9). Wiley.

Laboratory Procedures for the Medical Assistant. Patricia Z. Boone. 1981. 15.00 (ISBN 0-8036-1003-3). Davis Co.

Laboratory Project in Modern Coordination Chemistry. Larry C. Nathan. LC 80-25233. 93p. (Orig.). 1981. pap. text ed. 8.95 (ISBN 0-8185-0433-1). Brooks-Cole.

Laboratory Regulation Manual. H. Robert Halper & Hope S. Foster. LC 76-56666. 1977. 270.00 (ISBN 0-912862-29-7). Aspen Systems.

Laboratory Safety: Theory & Practice. Ed. by Anthony A. Fuscaldo et al. LC 80-762. 1980. 39.50 (ISBN 0-12-269980-7). Acad Pr.

Laboratory Studies in General Biology. rev. ed. Robert W. Ball & K. W. Radford. 1981. pap. 8.95 (ISBN 0-917962-66-4). Peek Pubns.

Laboratory Studies in General Botany. William M. Carlton. (Illus., Orig.). 1961. pap. 12.95 (ISBN 0-8260-1805-X). Wiley.

Laboratory Studies in General Chemistry, 1001-1062, 62 studies. Harper W. Frantz & Lloyd E. Malm. 1966-68. loose-leaf 0.50 ea. o.p. W H Freeman.

Laboratory Studies in General, Organic, & Biological Chemistry. Harold L. Bird, Jr. (Illus.). 1972. lab manual 9.00x o.p. (ISBN 0-7167-0162-6). W H Freeman.

Laboratory Studies in Integrated Zoology. 5th ed. Frances M. Hickman. (Illus.). 1979. pap. text ed. 11.95 (ISBN 0-8016-2177-1). Mosby.

Laboratory Studies in Zoology. James F. Payne & Michael L. Kennedy. (Illus.). 165p. 1980. lab. manual 8.95 (ISBN 0-89459-073-1). Hunter NC.

Laboratory Techniques for High Schools: A Worktext of Biomedical Methods. rev. ed. Gabrielle I. Edwards & Marion Cimmino. LC 75-23111. (gr. 10-12). 1975. pap. text ed. 5.95 (ISBN 0-8120-0649-6). Barron.

Laboratory Techniques in Food Analysis. David Pearson. LC 72-14169. 315p. 1973. 28.95 (ISBN 0-470-67539-X). Halsted Pr.

Laboratory Techniques in Zoology. 2nd ed. R. Mahoney. LC 72-13645. 390p. 1973. 29.95 o.p. (ISBN 0-470-56375-3). Halsted Pr.

Laboratory Tests in the Diagnosis of Autoimmune Disorders. Robert M. Nakamura & Sharad Deodhar. LC 75-27329. (Illus.). 206p. 1975. pap. text ed. 22.00 (ISBN 0-89189-002-5, 45-A-003-00). Am Soc Clinical.

Laboratory Text for Organic Chemistry: A Source Book of Chemical & Physical Techniques. Daniel J. Pasto & Carol R. Johnson. 1979. pap. 17.95 (ISBN 0-13-521302-9). P-H.

Laboratory Text in Organic Chemistry. 3rd ed. James Cason & Henry Rapoport. (Chemistry Ser). 1970. pap. 16.95 ref. ed. (ISBN 0-13-521435-1). P-H.

Laboratory Topics in Biology. Ray Evert et al. 1979. text ed. 9.95x (ISBN 0-87901-103-3). Worth.

Laboratory Topics in Botany. Ray Evert & S. Eichhorn. 1976. 8.95 o.p. (ISBN 0-87901-060-6). Worth.

Laboratory Training Manual on the Use of Isotopes & Radiation in Entomology. (Technical Reports Ser.: No. 61). 1966. pap. 5.50 (ISBN 92-0-115366-X, IAEA). Unipub.

Laboratory Training Manual on the Use of Isotopes & Radiation in Soil-Plant Relations Research. (Technical Reports Ser.: No. 29). 1964. pap. 6.50 (ISBN 92-0-115064-4, IAEA). Unipub.

Laboratory Training Manual on the Use of Isotopes & Radiation in Entomology. 2nd ed. (Technical Reports Ser: No. 61). (Illus.). 1977. pap. 21.50 (ISBN 92-0-115177-2, IAEA). Unipub.

Laboratory Training Manual on the Use of Nuclear Techniques in Animal Parasitology: Immunology & Pathophysiology. (Illus.). 161p. (Orig.). 1975. pap. 10.75 (ISBN 92-0-115274-4, IAEA). Unipub.

Laboratory Training Manual on the Use of Nuclear Techniques in Animal Research. (Technical Reports Ser.: No. 193). 1979. pap. 35.50 (ISBN 92-0-115179-9, IDC 193, IAEA). Unipub.

Laboratory Training Manual on the Use of Radionuclides & Radiation in Animal Research. 3rd ed. (Technical Reports Ser.: No. 60). pap. 10.75 (ISBN 92-0-115072-5, IAEA). Unipub.

Laborer: Federal, State & City Jobs. 2nd ed. Arco Editorial Board. LC 62-18801. (Orig.). 1969. lib. bdg. 6.50 o. p. o.p. (ISBN 0-668-02147-0); pap. 4.00 o.p. (ISBN 0-668-00566-1). Arco.

Laboring Classes & Dangerous Classes in Paris During the First Half of the Nineteenth Century. Louis Chevalier. Tr. by Frank Jellinek from Fr. 544p. 1973. 27.50 (ISBN 0-86527-114-3). Fertig.

Laboring Classes & Dangerous Classes in Paris During the First Half of the Nineteenth Century. Luois Chevalier. Tr. by Frank Jellinek from Fr. LC 80-8678. 520p. (Orig.). 1981. pap. 8.95 (ISBN 0-691-00783-7). Princeton U Pr.

Laboring Classes in Renaissance Florence. Samuel K. Cohn, Jr. (Studies in Social Discontinuity). 1980. 29.50 (ISBN 0-12-179180-7). Acad Pr.

Labour Administration: A General Introduction. 88p. 1980. pap. 12.75 (ISBN 92-2-102350-8, ILO145, ILO). Unipub.

Labour & Racism. Annie Phizacklea & Bob Miles. 256p. 1980. 30.00 (ISBN 0-7100-0678-0); pap. 18.50 (ISBN 0-7100-0679-9). Routledge & Kegan.

Labour & War: The Theory of Labour Action to Prevent War. Bjarne Braatoy. LC 77-147508. (Library of War & Peace; Labor, Socialism & War). lib. bdg. 38.00 (ISBN 0-8240-0303-9). Garland Pub.

Labour Aristocracy in Victorian Edinburgh. Robert Q. Gray. (Illus.). 1976. text ed. 29.50x (ISBN 0-19-822442-7). Oxford U Pr.

Labour Economics. 2nd ed. J. D. Appleton. (Illus.). 240p. 1979. pap. text ed. 9.95 (ISBN 0-7121-1246-4, Pub. by Macdonald & Evans England). Intl Ideas.

Labour Governments Nineteen Forty-Five to Nineteen Fifty-One. Roger Eatwell. 1979. 40.00 (ISBN 0-7134-0262-8, Pub. by Batsford England); pap. 14.95 (ISBN 0-7134-0263-6). David & Charles.

Labour in Irish Politics: Eighteen Ninety to Nineteen Thirty. Arthur Mitchell. (Illus.). 317p. 1974. 20.00x (ISBN 0-686-28343-0, Pub. by Irish Academic Pr). Biblio Dist.

Labour in the South African Gold Mines 1936-1969. Francis Wilson. LC 77-161290. (African Studies: No. 6). 1972. 38.50 (ISBN 0-521-08303-6). Cambridge U Pr.

Labour into the Eighties. Ed. by David S. Bell. 168p. 1980. 25.00x (ISBN 0-7099-0443-6, Pub. by Croom Helm Ltd England). Biblio Dist.

Labour Law: Text & Materials. Paul Davies & Mark Freedland. (Law in Context Ser.). xliv, 766p. 1979. 50.00x (ISBN 0-297-77591-X, Pub. by Weidenfield & Nicolson); suppl., 1980 4.00 (ISBN 0-297-77888-9). Rothman.

Labour Market Adjustment. C. A. Pissarides. LC 75-21035. 1976. 44.50 (ISBN 0-521-21064-X). Cambridge U Pr.

Labour Market Economics. David Sapsford. (Illus.). 240p. 1981. text ed. 30.00x (ISBN 0-04-331082-6, 2621/2); pap. text ed. 14.95x3210-04-331083-4 (ISBN 0-04-331083-4). Allen Unwin.

Labour Market Information in Asia: Present Issues & Tasks for the Future. Report on Two Workshops Conducted with the Support of the Federal Republic of Germany. International Labour Office, Geneva. 116p. (Orig.). 1979. pap. 5.70 (ISBN 9-22-102168-8). Intl Labour Office.

Labour Market Information in Asia: Present Issues & Tasks for the Future. 116p. 1980. pap. 6.50 (ISBN 92-2-102168-8, ILO147, ILO). Unipub.

Labour Problems in Indian Industry. 3rd rev. ed. V. V. Giri. 564p. 1973. pap. text ed. 10.00x (ISBN 0-210-33692-7). Asia.

Labour Productivity Differentials Within International Companies. C. F. Pratten. LC 76-8294. (Department of Applied Economics. Occasional Papers: No. 50). (Illus.). 1976. pap. 15.95x (ISBN 0-521-29102-X). Cambridge U Pr.

Labour, Race & Colonial Rule: The Copperbelt from 1924 to Independence. Elena L. Berger. (Oxford Studies in African Affairs). 272p. 1974. 29.50x (ISBN 0-19-821690-4). Oxford U Pr.

Labour Shortage & Economic Analysis: A Study of Occupational Labour Markets. Barry Thomas & David Deaton. (Warwick Studies in Industrial Relations Ser.). 1977. 36.00x (ISBN 0-631-18310-8, Pub by Basil Blackwell England). Biblio Dist.

Labour Supply in Economic Development. Francis Knox. 1979. text ed. 20.50x (ISBN 0-566-00238-8, Pub. by Gower Pub Co England). Renouf.

Labour Turnover & Retention. Ed. by Barrie O. Pettman. LC 75-18452. 204p. 1976. 21.95 (ISBN 0-470-68448-8). Halsted Pr.

Labours of Hercules. Alice A. Bailey. 1977. pap. 3.25 (ISBN 0-85330-130-1). Lucis.

Labouryouse Journey & Serche of Johan Leylande for Englandes Antiquitees. John Leland. LC 74-28871. (English Experience Ser.: No. 750). 1975. Repr. of 1549 ed. 7.00 (ISBN 90-221-0750-7). Walter J Johnson.

Labrador. Robert Stewart. (World's Wild Places Ser.). (Illus.). 1977. lib. bdg. 11.97 (ISBN 0-686-51020-8). Silver.

Labrador. Robert Stewart. (World's Wild Places Ser.). (Illus.). 1977. 12.95 (ISBN 0-8094-2065-1). Time-Life.

Labrador Retriever: Its Care & Training. M. Satterthwaite. 100p. 1980. 3.95 (ISBN 0-903264-34-X, 4947-2, Pub. by K & R Bks England). Arco.

Labradors. Frank Warner Hill. LC 76-11026. (Illus.). 1976. bds. 2.25 o.p. (ISBN 0-668-03993-0). Arco.

Labyrinth. Aaron Fletcher. 1977. pap. 1.95 (ISBN 0-505-51121-5, BT51121). Tower Bks.

Labyrinth. Diane Stevens. 1977. pap. 1.50 o.p. (ISBN 0-445-04131-5). Popular Lib.

Labyrinth in the Mode of Production Controversy. Attila Agh. (Studies on Developing Countries: No. 105). 79p. (Orig.). 1980. pap. 8.50x (ISBN 963-301-062-4). Intl Pubns Serv.

Labyrinth: Some Uncollected Poems 1944-1972. James K. Baxter. 76p. 1974. 8.00x o.p. (ISBN 0-19-640018-X). Oxford U Pr.

Labyrinths: A Long Poem. Deb K. Das. (Bluebird Book). 26p. 1975. 8.00 (ISBN 0-88253-713-X); pap. text ed. 4.00 flexible bdg. (ISBN 0-89253-598-9). Ind-US Inc.

Labyrinths of Iron: A History of the Subways. Benson Bobrick. Ed. by Danielle Bobrick. LC 80-80046. (Illus.). 400p. 1981. 12.95 (ISBN 0-88225-299-2). Newsweek.

Labyrinths, Selected Stories & Other Writings. Jorge L. Borges. Ed. by Donald A. Yates & James E. Irby. LC 64-25440. (Fr). 1969. pap. 3.95 (ISBN 0-8112-0012-4, NDP186). New Directions.

L'academie Royale de Musique au 18 Siecle, 2 Vols. Emile Campardon. LC 73-141152. (Music Ser). 1971. Repr. of 1884 ed. lib. bdg. 95.00 (ISBN 0-306-70090-5). Da Capo.

Lace & Embroidery Collector. R. E. Head. LC 74-2031. 1971. Repr. of 1922 ed. 20.00 (ISBN 0-8103-3663-4). Gale.

Lace for Milady. Joan Smith. 201p. 1980. 11.95 (ISBN 0-8027-0659-2). Walker & Co.

Lace: Poetry from the Poor, the Homeless, the Aged, the Physically & Emotionally Disabled. Ed. by Arthur Dobrin. 96p. 15.00 (ISBN 0-89304-036-3); pap. 7.95 (ISBN 0-89304-037-1). Cross Cult.

Lacey. Lorinda Hagen. 1977. pap. 1.95 (ISBN 0-505-51209-2). Tower Bks.

Laches & Charmides. Plato. Ed. by Rosamond K. Sprague. LC 72-86556. (Liberal Arts Library Ser.). 112p. 1973. pap. text ed. 3.95 (ISBN 0-672-60379-9). Bobbs.
Lachlan's Woman. Alice Dwyer-Joyce. LC 78-19863. 1979. 7.95 o.p. (ISBN 0-312-46359-6). St Martin.
Lacquer Lady. F. Tennyson Jesse. (Virago Modern Classics Ser.). 1981. pap. 5.96. Dial.
Lacrosse for Beginners. Stuart James. (Illus.). 128p. (gr. 7 up). 1981. PLB price not set. Messner.
Lacrosse for Men & Women: Skills & Strategies for the Athlete & Coach. Mike Hanna et al. (Illus.). 160p. 1981. pap. 9.95 (ISBN 0-8015-4372-X, Hawthorn). Dutton.
Lactate: Physiologic, Methodologic & Pathologic Approach. Ed. by P. R. Moret et al. (Illus.). 270p. 1980. pap. 24.00 (ISBN 0-387-09829-1). Springer-Verlag.
Lactation: A Comprehensive Treatise. Ed. by Bruce L. Larson & Vearl R. Smith. Incl. Vol. 1, 1974. Development, Lactogenesis. 55.50 (ISBN 0-12-436701-1); subscription 47.50 (ISBN 0-686-67530-4); Vol. 2. 1974. 48.75, by subscription 41.75 (ISBN 0-12-436702-X); Vol. 3. Milk, Nutrition & Maintenance. 1974. 48.75, by subscription 41.75 (ISBN 0-12-436703-8); Vol. 4. 1978. 58.00, by subscription 50.00 (ISBN 0-12-436704-6). Acad Pr.
Lactation of the Dairy Cow. Colin T. Whittemore. LC 79-40442. (Longman Handbooks in Agriculture Ser.). (Illus.). 94p. 1980. pap. text ed. 9.95 (ISBN 0-582-45079-9). Longman.
Lacy Family in England & Normandy, 1066-1194. Wilfred E. Wightman. LC 80-2206. 1981. Repr. of 1966 ed. 37.50 (ISBN 0-404-18794-3). AMS Pr.
Lacy Makes a Match. Patricia Beatty. LC 79-9813. (gr. 7-9). 1979. 8.50 (ISBN 0-688-22200-5); PLB 8.16 (ISBN 0-688-32200-X). Morrow.
Lacy Techniques of Salesmanship. Paul Micali. 1973. pap. 5.50 (ISBN 0-8015-4368-1, Hawthorn). Dutton.
Ladder of Success in Imperial China. Ho Ping Ti. LC 76-6917. (China in the 20th Century Ser.). 1976. Repr. of 1962 ed. lib. bdg. 32.50 (ISBN 0-306-70759-4). Da Capo.
Ladders to Fire. Anais Nin. LC 61-66834. 152p. 1959. pap. 5.95 (ISBN 0-8040-0181-2, 79, 79). Swallow.
Lademanns Leksikon, 20 vols. (Danish.). 1970-1976. 850.00 (ISBN 0-8277-3066-7). Maxwell Sci Intl.
Ladies Advocate; or, Wit & Beauty a Match for Treachery & Inconstancy, 1749. Ed. by Michael F. Shugrue. (Novel in England 1700-1775 Ser.). 1974. lib. bdg. 50.00 (ISBN 0-8240-1126-0). Garland Pub.
Ladies & Gentlemen: A History of the School of Speech of North Western University. Lynn Rein. 1980. 15.95 (ISBN 0-8101-0538-1). Northwestern U Pr.
Ladies Home Journal Family Diet Book. E. Frances. 1973. 6.95 o.s.i. (ISBN 0-02-571700-6). Macmillan.
Ladies of Levittown. Gene Horowitz. 352p. 1981. pap. 2.95 (ISBN 0-449-24401-6, Crest). Fawcett.
Ladies of Saint Hedwig's. E. M. Almedingen. 1967. 7.95 o.s.i. (ISBN 0-8149-0015-1). Vanguard.
Ladies Who Lunch. Ann Reed & Marilyn Pfaltz. LC 72-1212. 1972. pap. 2.95 o.p. (ISBN 0-684-15059-X, SL723, ScribT). Scribner.
Lado English Series, Bk. 1. Robert Lado. (Illus.). (gr. 7-12). 1977. pap. text ed. 3.45 (ISBN 0-88345-328-2); wkbk 2.25 (ISBN 0-88345-334-7); cassettes 80.00 (ISBN 0-685-89607-2); teacher's manual 4.95 (ISBN 0-88345-340-1). Regents Pub.
Lado English Series, Bk. 2. Robert Lado. 1978. pap. text ed. 3.45 (ISBN 0-88345-329-0); tchr's manual 4.95 (ISBN 0-88345-341-X); wkbk. 2.25 (ISBN 0-88345-335-5); cassettes 80.00 (ISBN 0-686-59595-5); testbook 20.00 (ISBN 0-88345-382-7). Regents Pub.
Lado English Series, Bk. 3. Robert Lado. 1978. pap. text ed. 3.45 (ISBN 0-88345-330-4); tchr's manual 4.95 (ISBN 0-88345-342-8, 18759); wkbk. 2.25 (ISBN 0-88345-336-3); cassettes 80.00 (ISBN 0-685-92972-8). Regents Pub.
Lado English Series, Bk. 4. Robert Lado. 1978. pap. text ed. 3.45 (ISBN 0-88345-331-2); tchr's manual 4.95 (ISBN 0-88345-343-6, 18760); wkbk. 2.25 (ISBN 0-88345-337-1). Regents Pub.
Lado English Series, Bk. 5. Robert Lado. (Illus.). 198p. (gr. 7-12). 1980. pap. text ed. 3.75 (ISBN 0-88345-307-X, 18749); tchr's manual 4.95 (ISBN 0-88345-344-4); wkbk., 132 pp. 2.25 (ISBN 0-88345-338-X, 18755). Regents Pub.
Lado English Series, Bk. 6. Robert Lado. (Illus.). 1980. pap. text ed. 3.75 (ISBN 0-88345-333-9); tchr's manual 4.95 (ISBN 0-88345-345-2); wkbk. 2.25 (ISBN 0-88345-339-8). Regents Pub.
Lado English Series, Bk. 6. Robert Lado. (Illus.). 202p. (gr. 7-12). 1980. pap. text ed. 3.75 (ISBN 0-88345-333-9); wkbk 2.25 (ISBN 0-88345-339-8). Regents Pub.
Lads Before the Wind: Adventures in Porpoise Training. Karen Pryor. LC 74-15846. (Illus.). 288p. (YA) 1975. 9.95 o.p. (ISBN 0-06-013442-9, HarpT). Har-Row.
Lady. Anne Lambton. 352p. (Orig.). 1981. pap. 2.75 (ISBN 0-515-05532-8). Jove Pubns.
Lady & Her Tiger. Pat Derby & Peter S. Beagle. 1977. pap. 1.95 o.p. (ISBN 0-345-25711-1). Ballantine.
Lady & the President: The Letters of Dorothea Dix & Millard Fillmore. Charles M. Snyder. LC 75-3551. (Illus.). 400p. 1976. 15.50x (ISBN 0-8131-1332-6). U Pr of Ky.
Lady & the Rogue. Lisabet Norcross. 1978. pap. 1.50 o.s.i. (ISBN 0-515-04449-0). Jove Pubns.
Lady & the Tramp. Ed. by Derry Moffat. (Disney Classics Ser.). (Illus.). (gr. k-4). 1980. pap. 0.95 (ISBN 0-448-16109-5). G&D.
Lady Apprentices. Ruth Pomeranz. 144p. 1973. pap. text ed. 5.00x (ISBN 0-7135-1868-5, Pub. by Bedford England). Renouf.
Lady Barberina & Other Tales. Henry James. Ed. by Herbert Ruhm. LC 62-51791. 8.95 (ISBN 0-8149-0126-3). Vanguard.
Lady Bee's Bonnets. Jill Tomlinson. 1971. pap. 2.95 (ISBN 0-571-11133-5, Pub. by Faber &Faber). Merrimack Bk Serv.
Lady Blessington at Naples. Edith Clay. 1979. 25.00 (ISBN 0-241-89975-3, Pub. by Hamish Hamilton England). David & Charles.
Lady Cannoneer: A Biography of Angelina Belle Peyton Eberly, Heroine of Texas, Archives War. C. Richard King. (Illus.). 192p. 1981. 12.95 (ISBN 0-89015-280-2). Eakins.
Lady Chatterly's Lover. D. H. Lawrence. 384p. (Orig.). 1981. pap. 2.50 (ISBN 0-553-13530-9). Bantam.
Lady Dudley Challenge Cup. Jervis Foulds. (Illus.). 1978. 17.50 (ISBN 0-85131-294-2, Dist. by Sporting Book Center). J A Allen.
Lady Filmy Fern: Or the Voyage of the Window Box. Thomas Hennell. (Illus.). 1981. 12.95 (ISBN 0-241-10468-8, Pub. by Hamish Hamilton England). David & Charles.
Lady from Boston. Tom McHale. LC 76-42370. 1978. 8.95 o.p. (ISBN 0-385-01865-7). Doubleday.
Lady from Dubuque: A Play in Two Acts. Edward Albee. pap. 2.50 (ISBN 0-686-69575-5). Dramatists Play.
Lady from the Sea. Henrik Ibsen. 1979. 7.95x (ISBN 0-8464-0093-6). Beekman Pubs.
Lady Gregory: A Literary Portrait. rev. ed. Elizabeth Coxhead. 1976. Repr. of 1961 ed. text ed. 4.75x (ISBN 0-900675-74-8). Humanities.
Lady Isabella Persse Gregory. Edward J. Kopper, Jr. (English Authors Ser: No. 194). 1976. lib. bdg. 12.50 (ISBN 0-8057-6658-8). Twayne.
Lady Jane Gray: With Miscellaneous Poems in English & Latin. 1809. Francis Hodgson. Ed. by Donald H. Reiman. LC 75-31221. (Romantic Context Ser.: Poetry 1789-1830). 1978. lib. bdg. 47.00 (ISBN 0-8240-2171-1). Garland Pub.
Lady Killers. Alan Riefe. (Cage Ser.: No. 1). 176p. 1975. pap. 0.95 o.p. (ISBN 0-445-00649-8). Popular Lib.
Lady Laureates: Women Who Have Won the Nobel Prize. Olga S. Opfell. LC 78-15995. 1978. 14.00 (ISBN 0-8108-1161-8). Scarecrow.
Lady Luck Ain't No Lady. Ron Coleman. (Gambler's Book Shelf). 64p. 1975. pap. 2.95 (ISBN 0-89650-546-4). Gamblers.
Lady Miller & Batheaston Literary Circle. Ruth A. Hesselgrave. 1927. Limited Ed. 27.50x (ISBN 0-685-69826-2). Elliots Bks.
Lady Nijo's Own Story: The Candid Diary of a 13th Century Japanese Imperial Court Concubine. Tr. by Wilfrid Whitehouse & Eizo Yanagisawa. LC 73-93503. 1974. 10.00 o.p. (ISBN 0-8048-1117-2). C E Tuttle.
Lady of Mallow. Dorothy Eden. 1978. pap. 1.95 (ISBN 0-449-23167-4, Crest). Fawcett.
Lady of Pleasure. James Shirley. Ed. by Marilyn J. Thorensen & Stephen Orgel. LC 79-54328. (Renaissance Drama Second Ser.). 335p. 1980. lib. bdg. 37.50 (ISBN 0-8240-4478-9). Garland Pub.
Lady of Repute. Janice James. LC 78-20079. 264p. 1980. 10.95 (ISBN 0-385-13507-6). Doubleday.
Lady of the Haven. Graham Diamond. LC 78-55733. 384p. (Orig.). 1981. pap. 1.95 (ISBN 0-87216-477-2). Playboy Pbks.
Lady on the Run. Lucille Sherman. LC 80-83999. 1981. pap. 4.95 (ISBN 0-89081-278-0). Harvest Hse.
Lady Oracle. Margaret Atwood. 1977. pap. 1.95 (ISBN 0-380-01799-7, 35444). Avon.
Lady Pamela. Clare Darcy. LC 75-12192. 1975. 8.95 o.s.i. (ISBN 0-8027-0504-9). Walker & Co.
Lady Precious Stream: Retold by L. W. Taylor. S. I. Hsiung. (Oxford Progressive English Readers Ser.). (Illus.). (gr. k-6). 1971. pap. text ed. 2.95 (ISBN 0-19-638235-1). Oxford U Pr.
Lady Sackville: A Biography. Susan Mary Alsop. 1978. 10.00 o.p. (ISBN 0-385-11379-X). Doubleday.
Lady Sativa. Frank Lauria. 1979. pap. 1.95 o.p. (ISBN 0-345-27328-1). Ballantine.
Lady Sings the Blues. Billie Holiday & William Dufty. 1979. pap. 2.50 (ISBN 0-380-00491-7, 53173). Avon.
Lady Tennyson's Journal. Ed. by James O. Hoge & Hoge James O. LC 80-21387. 1981. price not set (ISBN 0-8139-0876-0). U Pr of Va.
Lady Thief. Kay Hooper. (Candlelight Romance Ser.). (Orig.). Date not set. pap. 1.50 (ISBN 0-440-14685-2). Dell.
Lady Vixen. Shirlee Busbee. 544p. 1979. pap. 2.75 (ISBN 0-380-75382-0, 75382). Avon.
Lady Was a Bishop: The Hidden History of Women with Clerical Ordination & the Jurisdiction of Bishops. Joan Morris. LC 72-89049. 192p. 1973. 6.95 o.s.i. (ISBN 0-02-587130-7). Macmillan.
Lady Who Got Me to Say So Long Mom. Peter Sears. LC 78-59482. 40p. 1979. pap. 3.00 (ISBN 0-932264-21-2). Trask Hse Bks.
Lady Who Loved New York. R. L. Gordon. LC 76-28359. 1977. 10.00 o.s.i. (ISBN 0-690-01213-6, TYC-T). T Y Crowell.
Lady Who Saw the Good Side of Everything. Pat D. Tapio. LC 75-4610. (Illus.). 32p. (ps-3). 1975. 6.95 (ISBN 0-395-28826-6, Clarion). HM.
Lady, Wilt Thou Love Me? Eighteen Love Poems for Ellen Terry. George B. Shaw. Ed. by Jack Werner. LC 80-20009. (Illus.). 64p. 1980. 8.95 (ISBN 0-8128-2758-9). Stein & Day.
Ladybug, Ladybug, Fly Away Home. Judy Hawes. LC 67-15399. (Let's-Read-&-Find-Out Science Bk). (Illus.). (gr. k-3). 1967. bds. 6.95 o.p. (ISBN 0-690-48383-X, TYC-J); PLB 7.89 (ISBN 0-690-48384-8); filmstrip with record 11.95 (ISBN 0-690-48385-6); filmstrip with cassette 14.95 (ISBN 0-690-48387-2). T Y Crowell.
Ladybug, Ladybug, Fly Away Home. Judy Hawes. LC 67-15399. (Crocodile Paperbacks Ser.). (Illus.). (ps-3). 1973. pap. 2.95 (ISBN 0-690-00200-9, TYC-J). T Y Crowell.
Ladycat. Nancy Greenwald. 1981. pap. 2.75 (ISBN 0-451-09762-9, E9762, Sig). NAL.
Lady's Drawing Room. Ed. by Michael F. Shugrue. (Novel in England 1700-1775). 1974. Repr. of 1744 ed. lib. bdg. 50.00 (ISBN 0-8240-1110-4). Garland Pub.
Lady's Girl. Evelyn Bolton. LC 74-9528. (Evelyn Bolton's Horse Stories Ser). (Illus.). 32p. (gr. 3-7). 1974. PLB 5.95 (ISBN 0-87191-372-0); pap. 2.95 (ISBN 0-89812-125-6). Creative Ed.
Lady's Not for Burning, a Phoenix Too Frequent, & an Essay, "an Experience of Critics". Christopher Fry. 1977. pap. 4.95 (ISBN 0-19-519916-2, 507, GB). Oxford U Pr.
Laetrile Control for Cancer. Glenn D. Kittler. 1963. 8.95 (ISBN 0-8392-1059-0). Astor-Honor.
Laetrile Phenomenon: Politics, Science, & Cancer. Ed. by Gerald E. Markle & James C. Petersen. LC 80-13466. 208p. 1980. 20.00 (ISBN 0-89158-854-X); pap. 9.75 (ISBN 0-86531-046-7). Westview.
Laetrile Poisoning & Cancer Politics. Bruce W. Halstead. LC 79-54034. (Illus.). 1981. pap. 8.95 (ISBN 0-933904-05-3). Gold Quill Pubs CA.
Lafayette. Matthew G. Grant. LC 73-18155. 1974. PLB 5.95 (ISBN 0-87191-301-1). Creative Ed.
Lafayette: A Historical Perspective. Orpha Valentine. Ed. by Doug Woolfolk. (Illus.). 120p. 1980. 12.50 (ISBN 0-86518-014-8). Moran Pub Corp.
Lafayette in the Age of the American Revolution: Selected Letters & Papers, 1776-1790 Vol. III: April 27, 1780-March 29, 1781. Ed. by Stanley J. Idzerda et al. LC 76-50268. (Lafayette Papers). (Illus.). 584p. 1981. 35.00x (ISBN 0-8014-1335-4). Cornell U Pr.
Lafayette in the Age of the American Revolution, Selected Letters & Papers, 1776-1790: April 1, 1781-December 23, 1781, Vol. IV. Ed. by Stanley J. Idzerda et al. LC 76-50268. (The Lafayette Papers Ser.). (Illus.). 1981. 38.50 (ISBN 0-8014-1335-4). Cornell U Pr.
Lafayette in the Age of the American Revolution, Vol. II, Selected Letters & Papers 1776-1790. Ed. by Stanley J. Idzerda et al. LC 76-50268. (Illus.). 1979. 22.50x (ISBN 0-8014-1246-3). Cornell U Pr.
Lafcadio Hearn's American Days. Edward L. Tinker. LC 71-99064. (Library of Lives & Letters). (Illus.). 1970. Repr. of 1924 ed. 20.00 (ISBN 0-8103-3366-X). Gale.
Lafcadio's Adventures. Andre Gide. Tr. by Dorothy Bussy from Fr. LC 79-24000. 1980. Repr. of 1925 ed. lib. bdg. 10.00x (ISBN 0-8376-0452-4). Bentley.
L'africaine, 2 vols. Giacomo Meyerbeer. Ed. by Philip Grossett & Charles Rosen. LC 76-49200. (Early Romantic Opera Ser.: Vol. 24). 944p. 1980. lib. bdg. 82.00 (ISBN 0-8240-2923-2). Garland Pub.
Lagging Productivity Growth. Schlomo Maital & Noah Meltz. 1980. 19.50 (ISBN 0-88410-689-6). Ballinger Pub.
Lago. John Lee. 1981. pap. 2.95 (ISBN 0-440-14788-3). Dell.
Lagonga: A History of the Marque. Arnold Davye et al. 1979. 42.00 (ISBN 0-7153-7695-0). David & Charles.
Lagos Consulate, 1851-1861. Robert S. Smith. 1979. 21.50x (ISBN 0-520-03746-4). U of Cal Pr.
Lagrangian Mechanics of Nonconservative Nonholding Systems. D. G. Edelen. (Mechanics: Dynamical Systems Ser.: No. 2). 250p. 1977. 30.00x (ISBN 90-286-0077-9). Sijthoff & Noordhoff.
Laico Examina el Padrenuestro. Tr. by Phillis Keller. (Spanish Bks.). (Span.). 1978. 1.80 (ISBN 0-8297-0770-0). Life Pubs Intl.
Laird of Abbotsford: A View of Sir Walter Scott. A. N. Wilson. 214p. 1980. text ed. 24.95x (ISBN 0-19-211756-4). Oxford U Pr.
Lais. Marie de France. Ed. by A. Ewert. (French Texts Ser). 1976. pap. text ed. 5.00x o.p. (ISBN 0-631-00470-X, Pub. by Basil Blackwell). Biblio Dist.
Lais of Marie De France. Marie De France. Tr. by Robert Hanning & Joan Ferrante. 1978. 14.95 o.p. (ISBN 0-525-14340-8). Dutton.
Laissez-Faire & State Intervention in Nineteenth-Century Britain. Arthur J. Taylor. (Studies in Economic & Social History). 64p. (Orig.). 1972. pap. text ed. 4.00x (ISBN 0-333-09925-7). Humanities.
Laity & Liturgy: A Handbook for the Parish Worship Committee. William S. Pregnall. 128p. (Orig.). 1975. pap. 3.95 (ISBN 0-8164-2593-0). Crossroad NY.
Lajos Kossuth: Hungary's Great Patriot. Emil Lengyel. LC 69-12097. (Biography Ser). (Illus.). (gr. 7 up). 1969. PLB 6.90 (ISBN 0-531-00892-4). Watts.
Lake. Yasunari Kawabata. Tr. by Reiko Tsukimura from Japanese. LC 73-89699. 160p. 1980. pap. 3.95 (ISBN 0-87011-365-8). Kodansha.
Lake Champlain: Key to Liberty. Ralph N. Hill. 296p. 1978. 14.95 (ISBN 0-936896-01-9). VT Life Mag.
Lake District (Cumberland, Lancashire, Westmoreland) Colourmaster. (Travel in England Ser.). (Illus.). 96p. 1975. Repr. 7.95 (ISBN 0-85933-006-0). Transatlantic.
Lake Is Always East. Ruth Caro et al. 128p. 1981. spiral bdg. 2.95 (ISBN 0-695-81566-0). Follett.
Lake Management. Ed. by S. E Jorgensen. (Water Development, Supply & Management). 1980. 42.00 (ISBN 0-08-022432-6). Pergamon.
Lake Mead-Hoover Dam: The Story Behind the Scenery. James C. Maxon. Ed. by Gweneth R. DenDooven. LC 79-87573. (Illus.). 1980. 7.95 (ISBN 0-916122-62-X); pap. 3.00 (ISBN 0-916122-61-1). K C Pubns.
Lake Mess Monster. Beverly Komoda. LC 80-17569. (Illus.). 48p. (ps-3). 1981. 4.95 (ISBN 0-8193-1033-6); PLB 5.95 (ISBN 0-8193-1034-4). Parents.
Lake Miwok Dictionary. Catherine A. Callaghan. (U. C. Publ. in Linguistics: Vol. 39). 1965. pap. 10.50x (ISBN 0-520-09233-3). U of Cal Pr.
Lake Placid: The Olympic Years, 1932-1980. George C. Ortloff & Stephen C. Ortloff. LC 76-45314. 1976. 19.95 (ISBN 0-9601170-1-6); pap. 9.95 o.p. (ISBN 0-9601170-2-4). Macromedia Inc.
Lake Superior. 2nd ed. Louis Agassiz. LC 73-89695. 476p. 1974. Repr. of 1850 ed. 24.50 (ISBN 0-88275-137-9). Krieger.
Lake Trout & Legend Society Cookbook. Membership of the Society. Ed. by Charlie Davis. (Illus.). 64p. 1980. softcover 2.00 (ISBN 0-930000-08-0). Mathom.
Lake Washington Story. Lucile McDonald. LC 79-20102. (Illus.). 1981. 19.95 (ISBN 0-87564-635-2). Superior Pub.
Lakeboat. David Mamet. LC 80-8919. 128p. 1981. 8.95 (ISBN 0-394-51952-3, Ever); pap. 3.95 (ISBN 0-394-17925-0). Grove.
Lakes. Delia Goetz. LC 72-7226. (Illus.). 64p. (gr. 3-7). 1973. 6.75 (ISBN 0-688-21866-0). Morrow.
Lakes & Ponds. Joachim Tourbier & Richard Westmacott. LC 76-19607. (Technical Bulletin Ser.: No. 72). (Illus.). 70p. 1976. pap. 14.50 (ISBN 0-87420-072-5). Urban Land.
Lakestown Rebellion. Kristin Hunter. LC 78-1085. 1978. 8.95 o.p. (ISBN 0-684-15572-9, ScribT). Scribner.

Lakota Belief & Ritual. James R. Walker. Ed. by Raymond J. DeMallie & Elaine A. Jahner. LC 79-19816. (Illus.). xxx, 329p. 1980. 21.50 (ISBN 0-8032-2551-2). U of Nebr Pr.

Lalique to Masks. Time-Life Books Editors. (Encyclopedia of Collectibles Ser.). (Illus.). 1979. lib. bdg. 10.98 (ISBN 0-686-50980-3). Silver.

Lama Knows: A Tibetan Legend Is Born. Robert B. Ekvall. (Illus.). 144p. 1981. pap. 5.95 (ISBN 0-88316-541-4). Chandler & Sharp.

Lamaar Ransom. David Galloway. 250p. 1981. 11.95 (ISBN 0-7145-3686-5). Riverrun NY.

Lamar Briggs: Paintings & Works on Paper. Intro. by Avis Berman. LC 80-69965. (Illus.). 108p. 1980. text ed. 260.00 (ISBN 0-938454-01-3); pap. text ed. 25.00 (ISBN 0-938454-00-5). Ai.

Lamarck & Modern Genetics. H. Graham Cannon. LC 75-10211. 152p. 1975. Repr. of 1959 ed. lib. bdg. 16.50x (ISBN 0-8371-8173-9, CALA). Greenwood.

Lamartine. Charles M. Lombard. (World Authors Ser.: France: No. 254). 1973. lib. bdg. 10.95 (ISBN 0-8057-2510-5). Twayne.

Lamb. MacLaverty. Date not set. 8.95 (ISBN 0-8076-0990-0). Braziller.

Lamb & the Elephant: Ideal Imitation & the Context of Renaissance Allegory. John M. Steadman. LC 73-93874. 1974. 18.50 (ISBN 0-87328-062-8). Huntington Lib.

Lamb As Critic. Charles Lamb. Ed. by Roy Park. LC 78-73572. xii, 367p. 1980. 21.50x (ISBN 0-8032-8700-3). U of Nebr Pr.

Lamb: Selected Essays. Charles Lamb. Ed. by John R. Nabholtz. LC 67-13464. (Crofts Classics Ser.). 1967. pap. text ed. 1.25x (ISBN 0-88295-052-5). AHM Pub.

Lambert Wickes: Sea Raider & Diplomat-the Story of a Naval Captain of the Revolution. William B. Clark. 1932. 42.50x (ISBN 0-685-69800-9). Elliots Bks.

Lambert's Birds of Garden & Woodland. Terence Lambert & Alan Mitchell. LC 76-21893. (Encore Edition). (Illus.). 1976. 4.95 o.p. (ISBN 0-684-15416-1, ScribT). Scribner.

Lambert's Birds of Shore & Estuary. Terence Lambert. (Encore Edition). (Illus.). 1979. 5.95 (ISBN 0-684-16906-1, ScribT). Scribner.

Lambs in the Meadow. Lee Reay. LC 79-66222. (Illus.). 1979. 8.95 (ISBN 0-934826-00-5); pap. 5.95 (ISBN 0-934826-01-3). Meadow Lane.

Lamb's Questions & Answers on the Marine Diesel Engine. 466p. 1978. 35.95x (ISBN 0-85264-248-2, Pub. by Griffin England). State Mutual Bk.

Lamb's Tales from the Great Operas. Donald Elliott & Clinton Arrowood. 1981. 9.95 (ISBN 0-87645-110-5). Gambit.

Lame, Mathieu Funktionen. Max J. Strutt. LC 66-23757. (Ger). 8.50 (ISBN 0-8284-0203-5). Chelsea Pub.

Lamia. Michael Gardine. (Orig.). 1981. pap. 2.25 o.s.i. (ISBN 0-440-14236-9). Dell.

L'amour Westerns: Part Two, 4 bks. Louis L'Amour. Incl. To Tame a Land; Heller with a Gun; Tall Stranger; Last Stand at Papago Wells. (Western Fiction Ser.). 1981. Set. lib. bdg. 40.00 (ISBN 0-8398-2661-3). Gregg.

Lamp & the Lampstand. K. P. Menon. 1967. pap. 2.65x o.p. (ISBN 0-19-635248-7). Oxford U Pr.

Lamp at Midnight. Barrie Stavis. (Illus.). 7.95 o.p. (ISBN 0-498-06488-3). A S Barnes.

Lamp in the Window. Wynder. 1970. pap. 1.25. Chr Lit.

Lamp Is Low. Robert Perlongo. 8.00 (ISBN 0-89253-714-0); flexible cloth 4.80 (ISBN 0-89253-715-9). Ind-US Inc.

Lamp of Fate. Margaret Pedler. 1976. lib. bdg. 15.25x (ISBN 0-89968-217-0). Lightyear.

Lampas: A New Approach to Greek. B. R. Rees & Margaret E. Jervis. 1972. pap. 4.95x o.p. (ISBN 0-631-12270-2, Pub. by Basil Blackwell). Biblio Dist.

Lamplight in the Sun. S. Santhi. 4.80 (ISBN 0-89253-766-3); flexible cloth 4.00 (ISBN 0-89253-767-1). Ind-US Inc.

Lampmaking. Bruce Murphy. LC 76-16360. (Illus.). 192p. 1976. 14.95 (ISBN 0-8069-5420-5); lib. bdg. 13.29 (ISBN 0-8069-5421-3). Sterling.

Lampmaking. rev. ed. Bruce Murphy & Ana Lopo. LC 76-16360. (Illus.). 192p. 1980. pap. 7.95 (ISBN 0-8069-8462-7). Sterling.

Lamps & Lighting. 2nd ed. Ed. by S. T. Henderson & A. M. Marsden. LC 72-83310. 600p. 1972. 42.50x (ISBN 0-8448-0063-5). Crane-Russak Co.

Lamps & Lights. Elizabeth Drury. 1979. 17.95x (ISBN 0-8464-0056-1). Beekman Pubs.

Lamps of Tiffany. Egon Neustadt. LC 78-142102. (Illus.). 224p. 1970. 165.00 (ISBN 0-913158-01-1); Museum Edition. 205.00 (ISBN 0-685-26779-2). Fairfield.

Lampshades, Simple & Advanced. Margaret Rourke. 1973. 2.95 o.p. (ISBN 0-263-51376-9). Transatlantic.

Lamy of Santa Fe: His Life & Times. Paul Horgan. 1980. 25.00 (ISBN 0-374-18301-5); Limited Ed. 150.00 (ISBN 0-374-18301-5); pap. 12.95 (ISBN 0-374-51588-3). FS&G.

Lancashire & Yorkshire Railway, Vol. 1. John Marshall. (Railway History Ser.). 1970. 14.95 (ISBN 0-7153-4352-1). David & Charles.

Lancashire & Yorkshire Railway, Vol. 2. John Marshall. (Railway History Ser.). (Illus.). 327p. 1970. 14.95 (ISBN 0-7153-4906-6). David & Charles.

Lancashire & Yorkshire Railway, Vol. 3. John Marshall. (Railway History Ser.). (Illus.). 288p. 1972. 14.95 (ISBN 0-7153-5320-9). David & Charles.

Lancashire & Yorkshire Railway in Pictures. John Marshall. 13.50 (ISBN 0-7153-7478-8). David & Charles.

Lancashire Gentry & the Great Rebellion 1640-60. B. G. Blackwood. (Illus.). 1978. text ed. 33.75x (ISBN 0-7190-1334-8). Humanities.

Lancashire Textile Industry in the Sixteenth Century. N. Lowe. 132p. 1972. 33.00x (ISBN 0-7190-1156-6, Pub. by Manchester U Pr England). State Mutual Bk.

Lancashire Watch Co., Prescott, Lancashire, England 1889-1910. 1973. 10.50 (ISBN 0-913602-08-6). K Roberts.

Lancaster - the Story of a Famous Bomber. Bruce Robertson. 18.95 o.p. (ISBN 0-900435-10-0). Aero.

Lancaster Course in Ophthalmic Histopathology. Ed. by William C. Frayer. (Illus.). 325p. 1980. Text, Slides & Fourteen Units With Lectures. 936.00 (ISBN 0-686-65874-4). Davis Co.

Lancaster Photo Album. Compiled by Neville Franklin. (Illus.). 96p. 1981. pap. 17.95 (ISBN 0-85059-477-4). Aztex.

Lancastrian Kings & Lollard Knights. K. B McFarlane. Ed. by J. R. Highfield & G. L. Harriss. 268p. 1972. 27.00x (ISBN 0-19-822344-7). Oxford U Pr.

Lancelot. Percy Walker. 1978. pap. 2.95 (ISBN 0-380-01861-6, 51920, Bard). Avon.

Lancelot Closes at Five. Marjorie W. Sharmat. LC 75-31945. (Illus.). 128p. (gr. 3-6). 1976. 8.95 (ISBN 0-02-782320-2, 78232). Macmillan.

Lancelot Du Lac: The Non-Cyclic Old French Prose Romance, 2 vols. Ed. by Elspeth Kennedy. 1152p. 1981. Set. 169.00 (ISBN 0-19-812064-8). Oxford U Pr.

Lancia: Seventy Years of Excellence. Wim O. Weernink. (Illus.). 1979. 49.95 (ISBN 0-900549-42-4). Motorbooks Intl.

Lancia: The Shield & the Flag. Nigel Trow. LC 79-56053. (Illus.). 272p. 1980. 38.00 (ISBN 0-7153-7882-1). David & Charles.

Land. Jaquetta Hawkes. LC 78-51961. 1978. 17.95 (ISBN 0-7153-7639-X). David & Charles.

Land Alone: Colorado's Western Slope. Duane Smith & Duane Vandenbusche. (Illus.). 300p. 1981. 16.95 (ISBN 0-87108-560-7). Pruett.

Land & Building Taxes: Their Effect on Economic Development: Proceedings. Committee on Taxation Resources and Economic Development Symposium, 4th. Ed. by Arthur P. Becker. (Illus.). 1969. 25.00 (ISBN 0-299-05460-8). U of Wis Pr.

Land & Family in Pisticci. J. Davis. (London School of Economics Monographs on Social Anthropology Ser: No. 48). 200p. 1973. text ed. 19.50x (ISBN 0-391-00288-0, Athlone Pr). Humanities.

Land & Its Rent. Francis A. Walker. LC 79-1595. 1981. Repr. of 1883 ed. 18.50 (ISBN 0-88355-900-5). Hyperion Conn.

Land & Labour in Latin America. Ed. by K. Duncan & I. Rutledge. LC 76-11076. (Cambridge Latin American Studies: No. 26). (Illus.). 1978. 49.95 (ISBN 0-521-21206-5). Cambridge U Pr.

Land & Liberty: The Mexican Revolution (1910-1919) Irving Werstein. (Illus.). 192p. (gr. 7 up). 1971. 5.95 o.p. (ISBN 0-8092-8692-0); PLB avail o.p. (ISBN 0-685-28674-6). Contemp Bks.

Land & Life: A Selection from the Writings of Carl Ortwin Sauer. Carl O. Sauer. Ed. by John Leighly. (California Library Reprint Ser.). 1974. 24.50x (ISBN 0-520-02633-0); pap. 3.95 (ISBN 0-520-01124-4, CAL 132). U of Cal Pr.

Land & Lineage in China. Hilary J. Beattie. LC 77-91080. (Cambridge Studies in Chinese History, Literature & Institutions). 1979. 34.95 (ISBN 0-521-21974-4). Cambridge U Pr.

Land & Nationalism: The Impact of Land Expropriation & Land Grievances Upon the Rise & Development of Nationalist Movements in Kenya, 1885-1939. Mwangi Wa-Githumo. LC 80-5589. 502p. 1981. lib. bdg. 24.50 (ISBN 0-8191-1491-X); pap. text ed. 15.50 (ISBN 0-8191-1492-8). U Pr of Amer.

Land & People: A Cultural Geography of Preindustrial New Jersey--Origins & Settlement Patterns, Vol. 1. Peter O. Wacker. 520p. 1975. 35.00 (ISBN 0-8135-0742-1). Rutgers U Pr.

Land & People in Nineteenth-Century Wales. David W. Howell. (Studies in Economic History). (Illus.). 1978. 22.00 (ISBN 0-7100-8673-3). Routledge & Kegan.

Land & People of Argentina. rev. ed. Elvajean Hall. LC 77-37251. (Portraits of the Nations Ser.). (Illus.). (gr. 6 up). 1972. 8.79 (ISBN 0-397-31257-1). Lippincott.

Land & People of Australia. G. O. Cairns. (gr. 5-9). 1954. 3.95g o.s.i. (ISBN 0-02-716410-1). Macmillan.

Land & People of Belgium. rev. ed. Dorothy Loder. LC 72-13301. (Portraits of the Nations Series). (Illus.). 1973. 8.79 (ISBN 0-397-31462-0). Lippincott.

Land & People of Burma. C. Maxwell-Lefroy. (gr. 5-9). 1965. 3.95g o.s.i. (ISBN 0-02-765330-7). Macmillan.

Land & People of Central America. rev. ed. Ruth Karen. LC 71-37744. (Portraits of the Nations Ser.). (Illus.). (gr. 7-9). 1972. 8.79 (ISBN 0-397-31553-8). Lippincott.

Land & People of Ceylon. rev. ed. Donald N. Wilber. LC 72-15668. (Portraits of the Nations Ser.). (Illus.). (gr. 6 up). 1972. 8.79 (ISBN 0-397-31399-3). Lippincott.

Land & People of Chile. J. David Bowen. LC 75-41364. (Portraits of the Nations). (gr. 7 up). 1976. 8.95 o.s.i. (ISBN 0-397-31557-0). Lippincott.

Land & People of Chile. George Pendle. (gr. 5-9). 1960. 3.95g o.s.i. (ISBN 0-02-770790-3). Macmillan.

Land & People of China. Derek Bryan. (gr. 7 up). 1965. 3.95g o.s.i. (ISBN 0-02-715110-7). Macmillan.

Land & People of France. rev. ed. Lillian J. Bragdon. LC 78-37605. (Portraits of the Nations Ser.). (Illus.). (gr. 6 up). 1972. 8.95 (ISBN 0-397-31297-0). Lippincott.

Land & People of Greece. rev. ed. Theodore Gianakoulis. LC 75-37745. (Portraits of the Nations Ser.). (Illus.). (gr. 6 up). 1972. 8.79 (ISBN 0-397-31523-6). Lippincott.

Land & People of Hungary. rev. ed. Emil Lengyel. LC 72-37763. (Portraits of the Nations Ser.). (Illus.). (gr. 6 up). 1972. 8.79 (ISBN 0-397-31545-7). Lippincott.

Land & People of Iran. rev. ed. Helen Hinckley. LC 70-37733. (Portraits of the Nations Series). (Illus.). 1973. 8.79 (ISBN 0-397-31202-4). Lippincott.

Land & People of Ireland. rev. ed. Elinor O'Brien. LC 76-38335. (Portraits of the Nations Ser.). (Illus.). (gr. 6 up). 1972. 8.79 (ISBN 0-397-31299-7). Lippincott.

Land & People of Nigeria. rev. ed. Brenda Lu Forman & Harrison Forman. LC 77-37925. (Portraits of the Nations Ser.). (Illus.). (gr. 6 up). 8.79 (ISBN 0-397-31205-9). Lippincott.

Land & People of Nineteenth-Century Cork. James S. Donnelly. 1975. 42.50 (ISBN 0-7100-7986-9). Routledge & Kegan.

Land & People of Pakistan. Herbert Feldman. (gr. 5-9). 1958. 3.95g o.s.i. (ISBN 0-02-734370-7). Macmillan.

Land & People of Peru. George Pendle. (gr. 5-9). 1968. 3.95 o.s.i. (ISBN 0-02-770890-X). Macmillan.

Land & People of Poland. Joan Charnock. (gr. 5-9). 1968. 3.95g o.s.i. (ISBN 0-02-718190-1). Macmillan.

Land & People of Poland. rev. ed. Eric P. Kelly. Rev. by Dragos D. Kostich. LC 73-37924. (Portraits of the Nations Ser.). (Illus.). (gr. 6 up). 1972. 8.79 (ISBN 0-397-31313-6). Lippincott.

Land & People of Russia. rev. ed. Alexander Nazaroff. LC 70-37860. (Portraits of the Nations Ser.). (Illus.). (gr. 6 up). 1972. 8.95 (ISBN 0-397-31514-7). Lippincott.

Land & People of Scotland. rev. ed. Freda M. Buchanan. LC 58-10146. (Portraits of the Nations Ser). (Illus.). (gr. 7-9). 1962. 7.95 o.p. (ISBN 0-397-31554-6). Lippincott.

Land & People of South Africa. rev. ed. Alan Paton. LC 79-3795. (Portraits of the Nations Ser.). (Illus.). (gr. 6 up). 1972. 8.79 (ISBN 0-397-31302-0). Lippincott.

Land & People of Spain. new rev. ed. Dorothy Loder. LC 72-1368. (Portrait of the Nation Series). (Illus.). (gr. 6 up). 1972. 8.79 (ISBN 0-397-31303-9). Lippincott.

Land & People of Thailand. Eunice S. Matthew. LC 64-13808. (Portraits of the Nations Ser.). (Illus.). (gr. 7-9). 1964. 8.95 (ISBN 0-397-30766-7). Lippincott.

Land & People of the Balkans. rev. ed. Dragos Kostich. LC 73-7709. (Portraits of the Nations Series). (Illus.). 1973. 8.95 (ISBN 0-397-31397-7). Lippincott.

Land & People of Venezuela. Raymond A. Wohlrabe & Werner E. Krusch. (Portraits of the Nations Ser). (Illus.). (gr. 7-9). 1963. PLB 8.79 o.p. (ISBN 0-397-30464-1). Lippincott.

Land & People of Yugoslavia. Angela Tillyard. (gr. 5-9). 1963. 3.95g o.s.i. (ISBN 0-02-789350-2). Macmillan.

Land & Poverty in the Middle East. Doreen Warriner. LC 79-1596. 1981. Repr. of 1948 ed. 16.00 (ISBN 0-88355-901-3). Hyperion Conn.

Land & Social Change in East Nepal: A Study of Hindu-Tribal Relations. Lionel Caplan. LC 73-81801. 1970. 17.50x (ISBN 0-520-01400-6). U of Cal Pr.

Land & Society in Colonial Mexico: The Great Hacienda. Francois Chevalier. Tr. by Alvin Eustis. Ed. & frwd. by Lesley B. Simpson. 1963. 19.50x o.p. (ISBN 0-520-00229-6); pap. 3.65 o.p. (ISBN 0-520-01665-3, CAL191). U of Cal Pr.

Land & the Environment: Planning in California Today. Sedway-Cooke. Ed. by Planning & Conservation Foundation. LC 75-19409. 160p. 1975. pap. 14.95 o.p. (ISBN 0-913232-21-1). W Kaufmann.

Land & Wildlife of Africa. rev. ed. Archie Carr. LC 64-23586. (Life Nature Library). (Illus.). (gr. 5 up). 1967. PLB 8.97 o.p. (ISBN 0-8094-0631-4, Pub. by Time-Life). Silver.

Land & Wildlife of Australia. rev. ed. David Bergamini. LC 64-16421. (Life Nature Library). (Illus.). (gr. 5 up). 1968. PLB 8.97 o.p. (ISBN 0-8094-0629-2, Pub. by Time-Life). Silver.

Land & Wildlife of Eurasia. rev. ed. Francois Bourliere. LC 63-21615. (Life Nature Library). (Illus.). 1967. PLB 8.97 o.p. (ISBN 0-8094-0628-4, Pub. by Time-Life). Silver.

Land & Wildlife of North America. Peter Farb. LC 64-8304. (Life Nature Library). (Illus.). (gr. 5 up). 1964. PLB 8.97 o.p. (ISBN 0-8094-0633-0, Pub. by Time-Life). Silver.

Land & Wildlife of South America. Marston Bates. LC 64-19009. (Life Nature Library). (Illus.). (gr. 5 up). 1964. PLB 8.97 o.p. (ISBN 0-8094-0630-6, Pub. by Time-Life). Silver.

Land & Wildlife of Tropical Asia. S. Dillon Ripley. LC 64-25408. (Life Nature Library). (Illus.). (gr. 5 up). 1964. PLB 8.97 o.p. (ISBN 0-8094-0632-2, Pub. by Time-Life). Silver.

Land Application of Residual Materials. Compiled by American Society of Civil Engineers. 192p. 1977. pap. text ed. 10.00 (ISBN 0-87262-081-6). Am Soc Civil Eng.

Land Aridization & Drought Control. Viktor Kovda. (Westview Special Studies in Natural Resources & Energy Management). 1980. lib. bdg. 27.50x (ISBN 0-89158-259-2). Westview.

Land Concentration & Rural Poverty. Keith Griffin. LC 75-34149. 300p. 1976. 29.50x o.p. (ISBN 0-8419-0246-1). Holmes & Meier.

Land Control & Social Structure in Indian History. Ed. by Robert E. Frykenberg. LC 69-16111. 1969. 21.50x (ISBN 0-299-05240-0). U of Wis Pr.

Land Endures. Mary Pearce. 252p. 1981. 10.95 (ISBN 0-312-46440-1). St Martin.

Land Evaluation for Rainfed Agriculture: Report of an Expert Consultation. (World Soil Resources Reports: No. 52). 122p. 1981. pap. 6.50 (ISBN 92-5-100994-5, F2104, FAO). Unipub.

Land Explorers. Simon Talbot. 1978. 16.95 (ISBN 0-7134-0990-8, Pub. by Batsford England). David & Charles.

Land Grabbers. D. B. Newton. (Johnny Logan Ser.: No. 3). 144p. 1975. pap. 0.95 o.p. (ISBN 0-445-00665-X). Popular Lib.

Land Grabbers. Lee D. Willoughby. 1981. pap. 2.75 (ISBN 0-440-04762-5). Dell.

Land Hermit Crabs. Paul J. Nash. (Illus., Orig.). 1976. text ed. 0.98 (ISBN 0-87666-907-0, A-325). TFH Pubns.

Land Improvement Investment & Agricultural Enterprises in Japan: As Seen in the Azusa River System. 36p. 1980. pap. 5.00 (ISBN 92-808-0088-4, TUNU-059, UNU). Unipub.

Land in America. Ed. by Richard N. Andrews. LC 77-14735. (Illus.). 1979. 21.00 (ISBN 0-669-01989-5). Lexington Bks.

Land Killer. Lee Hoffman. LC 78-406. 1978. 7.95 o.p. (ISBN 0-385-13379-0). Doubleday.

Land, Labour & Economic Discourse. Keith Tribe. 1978. 22.50 (ISBN 0-7100-0002-2); pap. 10.00 (ISBN 0-7100-0003-0). Routledge & Kegan.

Land, Labour Migration & Politics in Southern Africa: Botswana, Lesotho & Swaziland. Donald K. Kowet. 1978. pap. text ed. 18.00x (ISBN 0-8419-9734-9). Holmes & Meier.

Land, Landlords, & the British Raj: Northern India in the Nineteenth Century. Thomas R. Metcalf. (Center for South & Southeast Asia Studies, UC Berkeley). 1979. 25.00x (ISBN 0-520-03575-5). U of Cal Pr.

Land Law & Registration. S. R. Simpson. LC 74-16994. 700p. 1976. 90.00 (ISBN 0-521-20628-6); pap. 24.95 (ISBN 0-521-29419-3). Cambridge U Pr.

Land-Leaguers. Anthony Trollope. Ed. by Robert L. Wolff. (Ireland Nineteenth Century Fiction - Ser. Two: Vol. 57). 894p. 1979. lib. bdg. 32.00 (ISBN 0-8240-3506-2). Garland Pub.

Land Limitation & Agricultural Land Use Potential Map of Papua New Guinea. (Land Research Ser.: No. 36). (Illus.). 84p. 1975. 9.00 (ISBN 0-643-00164-6, CO16, CSIRO). Unipub.

Land Management Case Study: Westlake Village California. William Hansen & Bo Bigelow. LC 77-79282. (No. 73). 1976. 17.00 (ISBN 0-87420-073-3). Urban Land.

Land of Contrasts. Ed. by Neil Harris. LC 71-104962. (American Culture Ser). 1970. pap. 7.95 (ISBN 0-8076-0549-2). Braziller.

Land of Egypt. Jasper More. (Illus.). 192p. 1980. 24.00 (ISBN 0-7134-1635-1, Pub. by Batsford England). David & Charles.

Land of Enchantment: Memoirs of Marian Russell Along the Santa Fe Trail. Marian Russell. 176p. 1981. write for info. (ISBN 0-8263-0571-7). U of NM Pr.

Land of Lost Content. Robert Phillips. LC 70-134667. 1970. 7.95 (ISBN 0-8149-0674-5). Vanguard.

Land of Midian, 2 vols. Richard F. Burton. (Arabia Past & Present Ser.: No. 11). (Illus.). 1981. Set. 75.00 (ISBN 0-900891-55-6). Oleander Pr.

Land of Mist. Andrew Quiller. (Gladiator Ser.: No. 2). 1976. pap. 1.25 o.p. (ISBN 0-523-22896-1). Pinnacle Bks.

Land of Mist. Andrew Quiller. (Gladiators Ser.). 144p. 1981. pap. 2.95 (ISBN 0-87754-225-2). Chelsea Hse.

Land of Open Doors: Being Letters from Western Canada, 1911-1913. J. Burgon Bickersteth. LC 76-41611. 1976. pap. 5.50 (ISBN 0-8020-6266-0); pap. 5.50 (ISBN 0-8020-6266-0). U of Toronto Pr.

Land of Oz. L. Frank Baum. (Classics Ser). (Illus.). (gr. 4 up). 1968. pap. 1.25 (ISBN 0-8049-0181-3, CL-181). Airmont.

Land of Poco Tiempo. Charles F. Lummis. LC 66-22698. (Illus.). 1969. 8.95 o.p. (ISBN 0-8263-0070-7); pap. 5.95 (ISBN 0-8263-0071-5). U of NM Pr.

Land of Promise. Robert Thompson. pap. 3.95 (ISBN 0-89728-042-3, 670209). Omega Pubns OR.

Land of Saddle-Bags: A Study of the Mountain People of Appalachia. James W. Raine. LC 70-78223. (Illus.). 1969. Repr. of 1924 ed. 15.00 (ISBN 0-8103-0160-1). Gale.

Land of Seagull & Fox. Ed. by Ruth Q. Sun. LC 67-23010. (Illus.). 1967. 5.50 o.p. (ISBN 0-8048-0356-0). C E Tuttle.

Land of Strangers. Lillian Budd. 1979. pap. 2.25 (ISBN 0-380-48314-9, 48314). Avon.

Land of the Dacotahs. Bruce Nelson. LC 65-108129. (Illus.). 1964. pap. 3.95 (ISBN 0-8032-5145-9, BB 176, Bison). U of Nebr Pr.

Land of the Firebird. Suzanne Massie. 1980. 22.50 (ISBN 0-686-62882-9, 23051). S&S.

Land of the Giant Tortoise: The Story of the Galapagos. Millicent E. Selsam. LC 77-4897. (Illus.). 64p. (gr. 1-5). 1977. 7.95 (ISBN 0-590-07416-4, Four Winds). Schol Bk Serv.

Land of the Golden Mountain. C. Y. Lee. 1977. pap. 1.50 o.p. (ISBN 0-445-03213-8). Popular Lib.

Land of the Iron Dragon. Alida E. Young. LC 77-16892. (gr. 9 up). 1978. PLB 7.95 (ISBN 0-385-13568-8). Doubleday.

Land of the Long Night. Paul Du Chaillu. LC 75-159938. (Tower Bks). (Illus.). (gr. 5 up). 1971. Repr. of 1899 ed. 18.00 (ISBN 0-8103-3905-6). Gale.

Land of the Morning: Ten Stories from the Philippines. Alice G. Kelsey. (gr. 5-9). 1968. teachers' guide 0.85 (ISBN 0-685-11651-4); pap. 1.75 o.p. (ISBN 0-685-11651-4). Friend Pr.

Land of the North Umpquas: Peaceful Indians of the West. Lavolla J. Bakken. LC 73-84954. (Illus.). 1973. pap. 1.00 (ISBN 0-913508-03-9). Te Cum Tom.

Land of the Spotted Eagle. Luther Standing Bear. LC 77-14062. (Illus.). 1978. 12.95x (ISBN 0-8032-0964-9); pap. 4.50 (ISBN 0-8032-5890-9, BB 655, Bison). U of Nebr Pr.

Land Ownership & Use: Cases, Statutes & Other Materials. 2nd ed. Curtis J. Berger. 1975. 24.50 (ISBN 0-316-09152-9). Little.

Land Pirates. Jackson Cole. 128p. 1976. pap. 0.95 o.p. (ISBN 0-445-00686-2). Popular Lib.

Land Policy. Ed. by Otto Koenigsberger et al. 200p. 1980. 50.00 (ISBN 0-08-026078-0). Pergamon.

Land Policy & Urban Growth. H. Darin-Drabkin. LC 76-39912. 1977. text ed. 23.00 (ISBN 0-08-020401-5). Pergamon.

Land Policy in Planning. Nathaniel Lichfield & Haim Darin-Drabkin. (Urban & Regional Studies: No. 8). (Illus.). 334p. 1981. text ed. 39.95 (ISBN 0-04-333017-7, 2540). Allen Unwin.

Land Pooling by Local Government for Planned Urban Development in Perth. R. W. Archer. (Lincoln Institute Monograph: No. 80-4). (Illus.). 69p. 1980. pap. 5.00 (Australian Institute of Urban Studies). Lincoln Inst Land.

Land: Power & Wealth. Peter Wolf. (Illus.). 1981. 17.95 (ISBN 0-394-50437-2). Pantheon.

Land Preparation & Crop Establishment for Rainfed Lowland Rice. (IRRI Research Paper Ser.: No. 22). 24p. 1979. pap. 5.00 (R062, IRRI). Unipub.

Land Reclamation in Kerala. Velu R. Pillai & P. G. Panikar. 1965. 10.50x o.p. (ISBN 0-210-31242-4). Asia.

Land: Recreation & Leisure. Ed. by Robert E. Boley. LC 78-123466. (Special Report Ser). (Orig.). 1970. pap. 4.75 (ISBN 0-87420-554-9). Urban Land.

Land Reform: A World Survey. Russell King. LC 77-24633. (Advanced Economic Geography Ser.). (Illus.). 1978. lib. bdg. 37.50x (ISBN 0-89158-819-1). Westview.

Land Reform & Politics: A Comparative Analysis. Hung-chao Tai. 1974. 38.50x (ISBN 0-520-02337-4). U of Cal Pr.

Land Reform in Brazil: The Management of Social Change. Marta Cehelsky. (Westview Replica Edition Ser.). 1979. lib. bdg. 23.00 o.p. (ISBN 0-89158-075-1). Westview.

Land Reform: The Italian Experience. King. 34.95 (ISBN 0-408-70472-1). Butterworths.

Land Remembers. Gwyn Williams. 1977. 14.95 (ISBN 0-571-10323-5, Pub. by Faber & Faber). Merrimack Bk Serv.

Land Resource Economics: The Economics of Real Estate. 3rd ed. Raleigh Barlowe. (Illus.). 1978. ref. ed. 21.95 (ISBN 0-13-522532-9). P-H.

Land Revolution in China, 1930-34: A Study of Documents. Tso-liang Hsiao. LC 69-14205. (Publications on Asia of the School of International Studies: No. 18). 374p. 1969. 16.00 (ISBN 0-295-73857-X). U of Wash Pr.

Land Speed Recordbreakers. Richard L. Knudson. LC 80-12385. (Superwheels & Thrill Sports Bks.). (Illus.). (YA) (gr. 4 up). 1981. PLB 6.95g (ISBN 0-8225-0438-3). Lerner Pubns.

Land Survey Systems. John G. McEntyre. LC 78-8551. 1978. text ed. 25.95 (ISBN 0-471-02492-9). Wiley.

Land Surveying. Francis Hodgman. 1976. Repr. of 1913 ed. 15.00 (ISBN 0-686-18868-3, 609). CARBEN Survey.

Land Surveying. 2nd ed. Ramsay J. Wilson. (Illus.). 480p. 1977. pap. 14.95x (ISBN 0-7121-1242-1, Pub. by Macdonald & Evans England). Intl Ideas.

Land Tenure & Agrarian Reform in Asia: An Annotated Bibliography. Land Tenure Center. 1980. lib. bdg. 45.00 (ISBN 0-8161-8221-3). G K Hall.

Land That I Love. John N. Hamlet & W. Horace Carter. (Illus.). 295p. 1980. 6.95 (ISBN 0-937866-00-8). Atlantic Pub Co.

Land Travel from the Beginning. Alma Gilleo. LC 77-24068. (From the Beginning Ser.). (Illus.). (gr. 1-4). 1977. PLB 5.50 (ISBN 0-89565-000-2). Childs World.

Land Under England. Joseph O'Neill. LC 80-14273. 228p. 1980. pap. 10.95 (ISBN 0-87951-117-6). Overlook Pr.

Land Use: An Introduction to Proprietary Land Use Analysis. D. R. Denman & Sylvio Prodano. 1972. text ed. 25.00x (ISBN 0-04-333013-4). Allen Unwin.

Land Use & Environment Law Review: Annual. Frederic A. Strom. Incl. 1975 (ISBN 0-87632-116-3); 1976 (ISBN 0-87632-117-1); 1977 (ISBN 0-87632-118-X); 1978 (ISBN 0-87632-119-8); 1979 (ISBN 0-87632-120-1). LC 70-127585. 45.00 ea. Boardman.

Land Use & the Legislatures: The Politics of State Innovation. Nelson M. Rosenbaum. 93p. 1976. pap. 3.50 (ISBN 0-87766-174-X, 15400). Urban Inst.

Land Use & the Pipe: The Effect of Sewer Extension. Richard D. Tabors et al. 1976. 19.95x o.p. (ISBN 0-669-99275-5). Lexington Bks.

Land Use & Town & Country Planning. Ed. by W. F. Maunder & J. T. Coppock. 1978. text ed. 37.00 (ISBN 0-08-022451-2). Pergamon.

Land Use & Water Resources. H. C. Pereira. LC 72-85437. (Illus.). 180p. (Orig.). 1973. 39.00 (ISBN 0-521-08677-9); pap. 10.95x (ISBN 0-521-09750-9). Cambridge U Pr.

Land Use & Wildlife Resources. Committee On Agricultural Land Use And Wildlife Resources. LC 70-607553. (Orig.). 1970. pap. 9.25 (ISBN 0-309-01857-9). Natl Acad Pr.

Land Use Control: Interface of Law & Geography. Rutherford H. Platt. Ed. by Salvatore J. Natoli. LC 76-18389. (Resource Papers for College Geography Ser.). (Illus.). 1976. pap. text ed. 4.00 (ISBN 0-89291-109-3). Assn Am Geographers.

Land Use Controls. Robert C. Ellickson & A. Dan Tarlock. 1239p. 1981. price not set (ISBN 0-316-23299-8). Little.

Land Use, Environment, & Social Change: The Shaping of Island County, Washington. Richard White. LC 79-4845. (Illus.). 246p. 1980. 12.95 (ISBN 0-295-95691-7). U of Wash Pr.

Land Use in America. Richard H. Jackson. LC 80-20184. (Scripta Ser. in Geography). 224p. 1981. 29.95 (ISBN 0-470-27063-2). Halsted Pr.

Land Use in Big Cities: A Study of Delhi. C. S. Yadav. 1979. text ed. 21.25x (ISBN 0-391-01840-X). Humanities.

Land Use in the United States. Ed. by Grant S. McClellan. (Reference Shelf Ser: Vol. 43, No. 2). 1971. 6.25 (ISBN 0-8242-0447-6). Wilson.

Land-Use Planning: A Casebook on the Use, Misuse, & Re-Use of Urban Land. Charles M. Haar. 1980. pap. 5.95 suppl. (ISBN 0-316-33681-5). Little.

Land Use Policies & Agriculture. 1976. 4.50 o.p. (ISBN 92-64-11558-7). OECD.

Land Valuation Methods: Urban Land. Intro. by Charles C. Cook. (Lincoln Institute Monograph: No. 80-1). (Illus.). 200p. 1980. pap. text ed. 10.00. Lincoln Inst Land.

Land Without Evil: Tupi-Guarani Prophetism. Helene Clastres. Tr. by Jacqueline Grenez-Brovender. 160p. 1981. 18.50x (ISBN 0-8476-6271-3). Rowman.

Landau Strategy: How Working Women Win Top Jobs. Susanne Landau & Geoffrey Bailey. LC 80-83564. 224p. 1981. pap. 2.50 (ISBN 0-87216-806-9). Playboy Pbks.

Landau Strategy: How Working Women Win Top Jobs. Suzanne Landau & Geoffrey Bailey. 1981. pap. 4.95 (ISBN 0-686-68906-2). Bantam.

Landed Estates in the Colonial Philippines. Nicholas P. Cushner. (Monograph: No. 20). (Illus.). x, 146p. 1976. 10.50 o.p. (ISBN 0-686-63723-2). Yale U Pr.

Landed Gently. Alan Hunter. (Illus.). 1976. 6.95 o.s.i. (ISBN 0-02-557580-5). Macmillan.

Landed Interest & the Supply of Food. 4th ed. James Caird. LC 67-16346. Repr. of 1880 ed. 15.00x (ISBN 0-678-05034-1). Kelley.

Landfall. David Wagoner. 1981. 9.95 (ISBN 0-316-91706-0, Pub. by Atlantic Monthly Pr); pap. 5.95 (ISBN 0-316-91707-9). Little.

Landfalls of Paradise: The Guide to Pacific Islands. Earl R. Hinz. LC 79-17600. (Illus.). 384p. 1980. 29.95 (ISBN 0-930030-13-3). Western Marine Ent.

Landforms & Landscapes. 3rd ed. Sherwood D. Tuttle. 1980. pap. text ed. 4.95x (ISBN 0-697-05020-3). Wm C Brown.

Landing of the Pilgrims. James Daugherty. LC 80-21430. (Landmark Bks.). (Illus.). 160p. (gr. 5-9). 1981. pap. 2.95 (ISBN 0-394-84697-4). Random.

Landings. Dennis Hamley. (gr. 6 up). 1979. PLB 8.95 (ISBN 0-233-97110-6). Andre Deutsch.

Landlady. Constance Rauch. 256p. 1976. pap. 1.75 o.p. (ISBN 0-445-08468-5). Popular Lib.

Landlord & Tenant on the Cotton Plantation. T. J. Woofter, Jr. LC 77-165691. (FDR & the Era of the New Deal Ser.). 1971. Repr. of 1936 ed. lib. bdg. 27.50 (ISBN 0-306-70337-8). Da Capo.

Landlord & Tenant: Text & Materials on Housing & Law. 2nd ed. Martin Partington. (Law in Context Ser.). xxxviii, 554p. 1981. 54.00x (ISBN 0-297-77790-4, Pub. by Weidenfeld & Nicolson England). Rothman.

Landlord or Tenant? Magnus Magnusson. LC 79-305778. (Illus.). 1979. 10.50 (ISBN 0-370-30130-7, Pub. by Chatto Bodley Jonathan). Merrimack Bk Serv.

Landlording: A Handy Manual for Scrupulous Landlords & Landladies How Do It Themselves. 3rd ed. Leigh Robinson. 272p. 1980. pap. text ed. 15.00 (ISBN 0-932956-01-7); pap. text ed. 17.50 canadian edition. Express.

Landlords & Tenants in Imperial Rome. Bruce W. Frier. LC 79-3207. (Illus.). 248p. 1980. 17.50x (ISBN 0-691-05299-X). Princeton U Pr.

Landlords Are People Too. Suzanne Taylor-Moore. 48p. 1980. pap. 2.50 (ISBN 0-686-28086-5). MTM Pub Co.

Landmark Briefs & Arguments of the Supreme Court of the United States: Constitutional Law, 80 vols. Supreme Court of the United States & Philip B. Kurland. 1977. Set. 4640.00 (ISBN 0-89093-000-7). U Pubns Amer.

Landmark Experiments in 20th Century Physics. George L. Trigg. LC 74-21664. 1975. 24.50x (ISBN 0-8448-0602-1); pap. 9.50x (ISBN 0-8448-0603-X). Crane-Russak Co.

Landmarks in the History of Education. T. L. Jarman. 1973. pap. 8.95 (ISBN 0-7195-0710-3). Transatlantic.

Landmarks in the History of Physical Education. Ed. by P. C. McIntosh. 1957. 9.75 o.p. (ISBN 0-7100-1814-2). Routledge & Kegan.

Landmarks of Botanical History, 2 parts in 2 vols. E. L. Greene. Ed. by F. N. Egerton. 1981. Set. slipcased 65.00 (ISBN 0-686-65497-8). Hunt Inst Botanical.

Landmarks of Dutchess County, 1683-1867. (Architecture Worth Saving in New York State Ser.). (Illus.). 244p. 1969. pap. 4.95 smyth sewn (ISBN 0-89062-002-4, Pub. by NYSCA). Pub Ctr Cult Res.

Landmarks of Mapmaking. Charles Bricker. LC 76-23570. (Illus.). 1976. 40.00 o.s.i. (ISBN 0-690-01177-6, TYC-T). T Y Crowell.

Landmarks of Old Prince William. Fairfax Harrison. (Illus.). 724p. Repr. of 1924 ed. 25.00x o.p. (ISBN 0-685-65068-5). Va Bk.

Landmarks of the Western Heritage, 2 vols. 2nd ed. Ed. by C. Warren Hollister. Incl. Vol. 1. The Ancient Near East to 1789. 544p. pap. text ed. 14.95x (ISBN 0-471-40700-3); Vol. 2. 1715 to Present. 416p. pap. text ed. 14.95x (ISBN 0-471-40704-6). LC 72-7315. (Illus.). 1973. Wiley.

Landon Carter: An Inquiry into the Personal Values & Social Imperatives of the Eighteenth-Century Virginia Gentry. Jack P. Greene. LC 64-19201. 1976. pap. 3.95x (ISBN 0-8139-0111-1). U Pr of Va.

Landon Experiments. John P. Kennedy. 1976. pap. 1.75 o.p. (ISBN 0-8439-0371-6, Leisure Bks). Nordon Pubns.

Landownership in Nepal. Mahesh C. Regmi. LC 74-77734. 1976. 22.75x (ISBN 0-520-02750-7). U of Cal Pr.

Lands & Peoples, 6 vols. Ed. by William Shapiro. LC 80-84474. (Illus.). 1981. write for info. (ISBN 0-7172-8008-X). Grolier Ed Corp.

Lands & Peoples, 6 vols. Ed. by William E. Shapiro. LC 79-3290. (Illus.). 1980. write for info o.p. (ISBN 0-7172-8007-1). Grolier Ed Corp.

Lands Beyond the Forest. P. Sears. LC 68-8126. 1968. 7.95 o.p. (ISBN 0-13-522698-8). P-H.

Land's Industrial Machinery & Epuipment Pricing Guide. Charles Land. 1980. pap. text ed. 29.95 (ISBN 0-442-28820-4). Van Nos Reinhold.

Lands of Barbary. Geoffrey Furlonge. (Illus.). 1968. 9.95 (ISBN 0-7195-0470-8). Transatlantic.

Lands of St. Peter: The Papal State in the Middle Ages & the Early Renaissance. Peter Partner. LC 73-182793. (Illus.). 494p. 1972. 32.50x (ISBN 0-520-02181-9). U of Cal Pr.

Lands of the Alligator Rivers Area, Northern Territory. (Land Research Ser.: No. 38). 171p. 1976. pap. 13.50 (ISBN 0-643-00208-1, CO19, CSIRO). Unipub.

Lands of the Bible. Maureen Curley. (Children of the Kingdom Activities Ser.). (gr. 5-10). 1975. 7.95 (ISBN 0-686-13693-4). Pflaum Pr.

Lands of the Ramu-Mandang Area, Papua New Guinea. (Land Research Ser.: No. 37). (Illus.). 135p. 1976. pap. 13.50 (ISBN 0-643-00175-1, CO18, CSIRO). Unipub.

Landscape: An Introduction to Physical Geography. William Marsh & Jeffrey Dozier. LC 80-68120. (Geography Ser.). (Illus.). 656p. 1981. text ed. 20.95 (ISBN 0-201-04101-4). A-W.

Landscape & Poetry: A Study of Nature in Classical Tamil Poetry. S. X. Thani Nayagam. 1967. 6.00x (ISBN 0-210-22734-6). Asia.

Landscape Archaeology: An Introduction to Fieldwork Techniques on Post Roman Landscapes. Michael Astor & Trevor Rowley. 1975. 16.95 (ISBN 0-7153-6670-X). David & Charles.

Landscape Architecture. Boy Scouts Of America. LC 19-600. (Illus.). 48p. (gr. 6-12). 1969. pap. 0.70x (ISBN 0-8395-3355-1, 3355). BSA.

Landscape Artist in America: The Life & Work of Jens Jensen. Leonard K. Eaton. LC 64-23422. (Illus.). 1964. 15.00x o.s.i. (ISBN 0-226-18053-0). U of Chicago Pr.

Landscape Book, by American Artists & American Authors. Washington Irving et al. Ed. by H. Barbara Weinberg. LC 75-28865. (Art Experience in Late 19th Century America Ser.: Vol. 1). (Illus.). 1977. Repr. of 1868 ed. lib. bdg. 44.00 (ISBN 0-8240-2225-4). Garland Pub.

Landscape Contracting. Ronald C. Smith. LC 79-51504. 1979. pap. 15.00 (ISBN 0-918436-07-9). Environ Des VA.

Landscape Design: A Practical Approach. L. Hannenbaum. 1981. text ed. 16.95 (ISBN 0-8359-5577-X); instr's. manual free (ISBN 0-8359-5578-8). Reston.

Landscape Design That Saves Energy. Anne Moffat & Marc Schiller. (Illus.). 224p. 1981. 17.95 (ISBN 0-688-00031-2, Quill); pap. 9.95 (ISBN 0-688-00395-8). Morrow.

Landscape Design with Plants. Ed. by Brian Clouston. (Illus.). 1977. 50.00x (ISBN 0-434-36650-1). Intl Ideas.

Landscape from the Air. 2nd ed. F. J. Monkhouse. LC 70-134621. (Illus.). 1971. text ed. 5.75x (ISBN 0-521-08000-2). Cambridge U Pr.

Landscape Garden in Scotland. A. A. Tait. 300p. 1980. 25.00x (ISBN 0-85224-372-3, Pub. by Edinburgh U Pr Scotland). Columbia U Pr.

Landscape Gardening. James U. Crockett. (Encyclopedia of Gardening Ser). (Illus.). 1971. 11.95 (ISBN 0-8094-1089-3); lib. bdg. avail. (ISBN 0-685-04842-X). Time-Life.

Landscape Gardening. James U. Crockett. LC 64-140420. (Time-Life Encyclopedia of Gardening). (Illus.). (gr. 6 up). 1971. lib. bdg. 11.97 (ISBN 0-8094-1090-7, Pub. by Time-Life). Silver.

Landscape in Literature. Christopher Salter & William Lloyd. Ed. by Salvatore J. Natoli. LC 76-29268. (Resource Papers for College Geography Ser.). 1977. pap. text ed. 4.00 (ISBN 0-89291-118-2). Assn Am Geographers.

Landscape It Yourself. Harold Givens. LC 76-14436. (Illus.). 1977. pap. 8.95 (ISBN 0-15-147689-6, Harv). HarBraceJ.

Landscape, Landscape Architecture & Landscape Gardening: A Selective List of Books. Mary Vance. (Architecture Ser.: Bibliography A-197). 61p. 1980. pap. 6.50. Vance Biblios.

Landscape Literature of the Twentieth Century Books Reviewed in "Landscape Architecture" Magazine, 1910-1979. Bruce K. Ferguson. (Architecture Ser.: Bibliography A-259). 84p. 1980. pap. 9.00. Vance Biblios.

Landscape-Loftscape. new ed. Marcia Resnick. pap. cancelled o.p. (ISBN 0-89439-006-6). Printed Matter.

Landscape of American History: Essays in Memorium to Richard W. Griffin. Ed. by James T. Wall. LC 79-89255. 1979. pap. text ed. 9.00 (ISBN 0-8191-0811-1). U Pr of Amer.

Landscape of Industry. Robert L. Delevoy et al. (Archives d'Architecture Moderne Ser.). Orig. Title: Paysage de l'Industrie Region du Nord-Wallonie-Ruhr. (Illus.). 175p. (Orig., Eng. & Fr.). 1975. pap. 25.00x (ISBN 0-8150-0926-7). Wittenborn.

Landscape of Industry. Clifford Tandy. LC 75-28033. 314p. 1975. 55.95 (ISBN 0-470-84440-X). Halsted Pr.

Landscape of Nightmare: Studies in the Contemporary American Novel. Jonathan Baumbach. LC 65-11761. (The Gotham Library). (Orig.). 1965. 12.00x (ISBN 0-8147-0031-4); pap. 4.00x (ISBN 0-8147-0032-2). NYU Pr.

Landscape Operations: Management, Methods, & Materials. Leroy G. Hannebaum. (Illus.). 1980. text ed. 16.95 (ISBN 0-8359-3937-5); instrs' manual avail. Reston.

Landscape Painting with a Knife. Coulton Waugh. LC 74-11148. 192p. 1974. 21.95 o.p. (ISBN 0-8230-2632-9). Watson-Guptill.

Landscape Planning for Small Gardens. pap. 7.50x (ISBN 0-392-06854-0). Soccer.

Landscape Processes: An Introduction to Geomorphology. Darrell Weyman & Valerie Weyman. (Processes in Physical Geography Ser). (Illus.). 1977. pap. text ed. 6.95x (ISBN 0-04-551026-1). Allen Unwin.

Landscape Sumi-E in Three Weeks. Sadami Yamada. LC 65-27102. (Illus.). 32p. pap. 3.50 (ISBN 0-87040-075-4). Japan Pubns.

Landscape with Violence. John Wainwright. 1980. pap. 1.95 o.p. (ISBN 0-425-04464-5). Berkley Pub.

Landscape with Weeds. Graham Rose. (Illus.). 160p. 1980. 14.95 (ISBN 0-241-10353-3, Pub. by Hamish Hamilton England). David & Charles.

Landscape You Can Eat. Allan A. Swenson. (Illus.). 1977. 10.95 o.p. (ISBN 0-679-50647-0); pap. 5.95 o.p. (ISBN 0-679-50669-1). McKay.

Landscapes & Documents. Alan Rogers. 85p. 1974. pap. text ed. 3.75x (ISBN 0-7199-0883-3, Pub. by Bedford England). Renouf.

Landscapes for Living. Landscape Architecture Magazine. (Illus.). 1980. 19.95 (ISBN 0-07-036191-6). McGraw.

Landscapes of Britain. Roy Millward & Adrian Robinson. 1977. 14.95 (ISBN 0-7153-7181-9). David & Charles.

Landscapes of Fear. Yi-Fu Tuan. LC 79-1890. 272p. 1981. pap. 8.95 (ISBN 0-8166-1021-5). U of Minn Pr.

Landscapes of Learning. Maxine Greene. LC 78-6571. 1978. pap. text ed. 11.50x (ISBN 0-8077-2534-X). Tchrs Coll.

Landscapes of North Wales. Roy Millward & Adrian Robinson. LC 78-6690. (Illus.). 1978. 22.50 (ISBN 0-7153-7713-2). David & Charles.

Landscapes of Texas. Illus. by John Graves. LC 79-5274. (Louise Lindsey Merrick Texas Environment Ser.: No. 3). (Illus.). 162p. 1980. 24.95 (ISBN 0-89096-088-7). Tex A&M Univ Pr.

Landscapes 1975-1979, 2 vols. Michael A. Smith. (Illus.). 120p. 1981. Set. 275.00 (ISBN 0-9605646-0-8). Vol. I (ISBN 0-9605646-1-6). Vol. II (ISBN 0-9605646-2-4). Lodima.

Landscaping: Principles & Practices. Jack E. Ingels. LC 76-51686. 1978. pap. text ed. 11.24 (ISBN 0-8273-1634-8); instructor's guide 1.60 (ISBN 0-8273-1635-6). Delmar.

Landscaping with Native Plants in the Middle-Atlantic Region. Elizabeth N. DuPont. Ed. by Wick Williams. LC 78-21194. (Illus.). 1978. 6.95. Brandywine Conserv.

Landscaping Your Home. LC 73-91440. (Family Guide Book Ser). (Illus.). 1974. pap. 2.95 (ISBN 0-8487-0285-9). Oxmoor Hse.

Landseekers. Fred Grove. 1974. pap. 0.95 o.p. (ISBN 0-345-23798-6). Ballantine.

Landsmen. Peter Martin. 1979. pap. 2.50 o.p. (ISBN 0-445-04338-5). Popular Lib.

Lane Rebels: Evangelicalism & Antislavery in Antebellum America. Lawrence T. Lesick. LC 80-24123. (Studies in Evangelicalism: No. 2). 287p. 1980. 15.00 (ISBN 0-8108-1372-6). Scarecrow.

Lanfranc, a Study of His Life, Work & Writing. Allan J. Macdonald. LC 80-2223. 1981. Repr. of 1926 ed. 37.50 (ISBN 0-404-18768-4). AMS Pr.

Lanfranc of Bec. Margaret Gibson. 1978. 37.50x (ISBN 0-19-822462-1). Oxford U Pr.

Langauge of the Railroader. 9.95. Chatham Pub CA.

Langenscheidt's New Muret-Sanders English-German Dictionary, 2 vols, Part I. Ed. by Otto Springer. Incl. Vol. 1. A-M. 924p. 1962. 52.50x (ISBN 3-468-01120-2); Vol. 2. N-Z. 958p. 1963. 70.00x (ISBN 0-685-31317-4). (Eng. & Ger.). Hippocrene Bks.

Langenscheidt's New Muret-Sanders German-English Encyclopedic Dictionary: Part 2, Vol. 2, L-Z. Ed. by Otto Springer. 1975. 80.00x (ISBN 3-468-01126-1). Hippocrene Bks.

Langenscheidt's New Muret-Sanders German-English Encyclopedic Dictionary: Vol. 1 a-K, Pt. 2. Otto Springer. 1014p. 1974. 80.00x (ISBN 3-468-01124-5). Hippocrene Bks.

Langenscheidt's Standard French Dictionary: French-English, English-French. Kenneth Unwin. Orig. Title: Standard French Dictionary. 1216p. 1974. 11.95 (ISBN 0-88254-285-0). Hippocrene Bks.

Langenscheidt's Standard German Dictionary: German-English, English-German. Edmund Klatt et al. Orig. Title: Standard German Dictionary. 1264p. 1974. 11.95 (ISBN 0-685-39723-8). Hippocrene Bks.

Langenscheidt's Taschenworterbuch. 6th ed. Ed. by Edmund Klatt et al. 1264p. 1970. 10.95 (ISBN 3-468-11121-5). Hippocrene Bks.

Langenscheidt's Universal German-English, English-German Dictionary. 35th ed. (Universal Dictionaries Ser.). 512p. (Eng. & Ger.). 2.95 (ISBN 3-468-18121-3). Hippocrene Bks.

Langenscheidt's Universal Russian-English, English-Russian Dictionary. 415p. (Eng. & Rus.). 1972. 2.95 (ISBN 0-685-31341-7). Hippocrene Bks.

Langenscheidt's Universal Turkish-English, English-Turkish Dictionary. 9th ed. 408p. (Eng. & Turkish.). 1972. 2.95 (ISBN 0-685-31339-5). Hippocrene Bks.

Langer of North Dakota. Glenn H. Smith. Ed. by Frank Freidel. LC 78-62502. (Modern American History Ser.: Vol. 16). 1979. lib. bdg. 25.00 (ISBN 0-8240-3639-5). Garland Pub.

Lange's Commentary on the Holy Scriptures, 12 vols. John P. Lange. 1980. Repr. Set. 219.00 (ISBN 0-310-27198-3). Zondervan.

Langfristplanung in der Energiewirtschaft eine Computersimulation Fur Die BRD. Kurt Schmitz. (Interdisciplinary Systems Research Ser.: No. 65). 264p. (Ger.). 1979. pap. 24.00 (ISBN 3-7643-1068-5). Birkhauser.

Langrische Go Down. Aidan Higgins. 1980. 10.95 (ISBN 0-7145-0328-2); pap. 6.95 (ISBN 0-7145-0329-0). Riverrun NY.

Lang's Compendium of Culinary Nonsense & Trivia. George Lang. (Illus.). 1980. 10.00 (ISBN 0-517-54148-3). Potter.

Langston Hughes. James A. Emanuel. (U. S. Authors Ser.: No. 123). 1967. lib. bdg. 9.95 (ISBN 0-8057-0388-8). Twayne.

Langston Hughes. Elisabeth P. Myers. (gr. k-6). Date not set. pap. price not set (ISBN 0-440-44723-2, YB). Dell.

Langston Hughes, American Poet. Alice Walker. LC 73-9565. (Biography Ser). (Illus.). 40p. (gr. 2-5). 1974. PLB 7.89 (ISBN 0-690-00219-X, TYC-J). T Y Crowell.

Langston Hughes: An Introduction to Poetry. Onwuchekwa Jemie. LC 76-18219. (Columbia Introductions to Twentieth Century American Poetry Ser.). 1977. 15.00x (ISBN 0-231-03780-5). Columbia U Pr.

Langston Hughes, Poet of Harlem. Norita D. Larson. Ed. by Ann Redpath. (People to Remember Ser.). (Illus.). 32p. (gr. 5-9). 1981. PLB 5.95 (ISBN 0-87191-798-X). Creative Ed.

Langston Hughes Reader. Langston Hughes. LC 58-7871. 1958. 10.00 o.p. (ISBN 0-8076-0057-1). Braziller.

Language. Kenneth Cripwell. Ed. by Malcolm Yapp et al. (World History Ser.). (Illus.). (gr. 10). 1980. Repr. of 1977 ed. lib. bdg. 5.95 (ISBN 0-89908-146-0); pap. text ed. 1.95 (ISBN 0-89908-121-5). Greenhaven.

Language. Sapir. 1980. text ed. 10.50x (ISBN 0-246-11074-0). Humanities.

Language. 2nd ed. Edward Sapir. 1979. 11.95x (ISBN 0-8464-0059-6). Beekman Pubs.

Language. David Thomson. LC 75-24866. (Human Behavior). (Illus.). (gr. 5 up). 1975. lib. bdg. 9.99 o.p. (ISBN 0-685-72980-X, Pub. by Time-Life). Silver.

Language. David Thomson. (Human Behavior Ser.). 9.95 (ISBN 0-8094-1966-1). Time-Life.

Language: A Science of Human Behavior. Harry R. Warfel. LC 62-9619. 1962. 19.00x (ISBN 0-8201-1047-7). Schol Facsimiles.

Language Acquisition. Ed. by Paul Fletcher & Michael Garman. LC 78-67305. 1980. 59.50 (ISBN 0-521-22521-3); pap. 14.95x (ISBN 0-521-29536-X). Cambridge U Pr.

Language Acquisition & Linguistic Theory. Ed. by Susan Tavakolian. (Illus.). 336p. 1981. text ed. 19.95x (ISBN 0-262-20039-2). MIT Pr.

Language: Acquisition, Application, Appreciation. Ed. by Warren C. Born. Incl. Language Acquisition. Pierre F. Cintas; Language Application. Kenneth Elaster; Language Appreciation. Germaine Bure. 1977. pap. 7.95x (ISBN 0-915432-77-3). NE Conf Teach Foreign.

Language Across the Curriculum. Michael Marland. 1977. text ed. 21.95x (ISBN 0-435-80578-9); pap. text ed. 12.95x (ISBN 0-435-80631-9). Heinemann Ed.

Language: All About It. Irene B. McDonald. 112p. (Orig.). (gr. 10-12). 1980. pap. text ed. 3.25x (ISBN 0-88334-140-9). Ind Sch Pr.

Language & Being: Joseph Conrad & the Literature of Personality. Peter J. Glassman. LC 75-29092. 294p. 1976. 17.50x (ISBN 0-231-03999-9). Columbia U Pr.

Language & Communication. Helmut Esau et al. 1980. pap. 8.75. Hornbeam Pr.

Language & Communication in the Elderly: Clinical, Therapeutic, & Experimental Issues. Loraine K. Obler & Martin L. Albert. LC 80-5348. 1980. 22.95x (ISBN 0-669-03868-7). Lexington Bks.

Language & Communication: Student Booklet. American Psychological Association. (Human Behavior Curriculum Peoject Ser.). 64p. (Orig.). (gr. 9-12). 1981. pap. text ed. 3.95 (ISBN 0-8077-2625-7). Tchrs Coll.

Language & Communication: Teachers Handbook & Duplication Masters. American Psychological Association. (Human Behavir Curriculum Project Ser.). 48p. (Orig.). (gr. 9-12). 1981. pap. 9.95 (ISBN 0-8077-2626-5). Tchrs Coll.

Language & Cultural Description: Essays by Charles O. Frake. Charles O. Frake. Ed. by Anwar S. Dil. LC 79-67771. (Language Science & National Development Ser.). 360p. 1980. 17.50x (ISBN 0-8047-1074-0). Stanford U Pr.

Language & Cultural Diversity in American Education. Ed. by Roger D. Abraham & Rudolph D. Troike. 384p. 1972. pap. text ed. 9.95 (ISBN 0-13-522888-3). P-H.

Language & Culture: Heritage & Horizons. Ed. by Warren C. Born. 1976. pap. 7.95x (ISBN 0-915432-76-5). NE Conf Teach Foreign.

Language & Disadvantage. J. R. Edwards. (Studies in Language Disability & Remediation: Vol. 5). 172p. 1979. 22.50 (ISBN 0-444-19471-1); pap. 11.95 (ISBN 0-444-19470-3). Elsevier.

Language & Ethnic Relations: Language & Ethnic Interaction Section of the Sociolinguistics Program of the 9th World Congress of Sociology. Howard Giles & Bernard Saint-Jacques. LC 79-40709. (Illus.). 1979. 33.00 (ISBN 0-686-58671-9). Pergamon.

Language & History in Cornwall. Martyn F. Wakelin. (Illus.). 1975. text ed. 20.00x (ISBN 0-7185-1124-7, Leicester). Humanities.

Language & Imagery of the Bible. G. B. Caird. 1980. write for info. (ISBN 0-664-21378-2). Westminster.

Language & Knowledge in the Late Novels of Henry James. Ruth B. Yeazell. LC 75-46538. viii, 144p. 1980. lib. bdg. 6.00x (ISBN 0-226-95095-6). U of Chicago Pr.

Language & Language Disorders in Childhood. Ed. by L. A. Hersov et al. 1980. 21.00 (ISBN 0-08-025206-0); pap. 9.00 (ISBN 0-08-025205-2). Pergamon.

Language & Learning Disorders of the Pre-Academic Child. Tina E. Bangs. (Illus.). 1968. 18.95 (ISBN 0-13-522797-6). P-H.

Language & Learning: The Debate Between Jean Piaget & Noam Chomsky. Ed. by Massimo Piattelli-Palmarini. LC 80-10588. 1980. text ed. 20.00x (ISBN 0-674-50940-4). Harvard U Pr.

Language & Learning to Read: What Teachers Should Know About Language. R. E. Hodges & E. Hugh Rudorf. LC 70-175170. 1972. pap. text ed. 10.95 (ISBN 0-395-12639-8, 3-25626). HM.

Language & Life in the USA: Communicating in English, Vol. I. 4th ed. Gladys G. Doty & Janet Ross. (Illus.). 1981. pap. text ed. 9.50 scp (ISBN 0-06-041693-9, HarpC); avail. Har-Row.

Language & Life in the USA: Reading English, Vol. II. Gladys G. Doty & Janet Ross. (Illus.). 1981. pap. text ed. 8.50 scp (ISBN 0-06-041694-7, HarpC). Har-Row.

Language & Linguistics. J. F. Wallwork. 1969. pap. text ed. 6.95x (ISBN 0-435-10916-2); wkbk. 3.50x (ISBN 0-435-10917-0). Heinemann Ed.

Language & Linguistics: Bases for a Curriculum. Julia S. Falk. (Language in Education Ser.: No. 10). 1978. pap. text ed. 2.95 (ISBN 0-87281-088-7). Ctr Appl Ling.

Language & Logos in Boswell's Life of Johnson. William C. Dowling. LC 80-8545. (Essays in Literature Ser.). 232p. 1981. 15.00x (ISBN 0-691-06455-5). Princeton U Pr.

Language & Machines: Computers in Translation & Linguistics. 1966. pap. 5.00 (ISBN 0-309-01416-6). Natl Acad Pr.

Language & Man. Irving Adler & Joyce Adler. LC 78-109148. (Reason Why Ser). (Illus.). (gr. 3-6). 1970. lib. bdg. 7.89 (ISBN 0-381-99978-5, A42100, JD-J). John Day.

Language & Materialism: Developments in Semiology & the Theory of the Subject. Rosalind Coward & John Ellis. 1977. 15.00x (ISBN 0-7100-8620-2); pap. 7.95 (ISBN 0-7100-8627-X). Routledge & Kegan.

Language & Nationalism: The Philippine Experience Thus Far. Andrew B. Gonzalez. 179p. 1980. 18.25 (ISBN 0-686-28647-2); pap. 11.25x (ISBN 0-686-28648-0). Cellar.

Language & Negation: The Two-Level Structure That Prevents Paradox. Daniel A. Cowan. LC 76-21954. 112p. 1980. pap. 6.00 (ISBN 0-915878-03-8). Joseph Pub Co.

Language & Other Abstract Objects. Jerrold J. Katz. 1981. 25.00x (ISBN 0-8476-6912-2); pap. 9.95x (ISBN 0-8476-6913-0). Rowman.

Language & Perception: Essays in the Philosophy of Language. Frank B. Ebersole. LC 79-88305. 1979. pap. text ed. 11.00 (ISBN 0-8191-0776-X). U Pr of Amer.

Language & Psychology: Historical Aspects of Psycholinguistics. Arthur L. Blumenthal. LC 80-12611. 262p. 1980. Repr. of 1970 ed. lib. bdg. write for info. (ISBN 0-89874-167-X). Krieger.

Language & Reading Among Underachievers: A Practical Review. Caroline Moseley & David Moseley. (General Ser.). 1977. pap. text ed. 10.50x (ISBN 0-85633-136-8, NFER). Humanities.

Language & Reading Comprehension. Ed. by Stanley F. Wanat. LC 77-80380. (Linguistics & Reading Ser.: No. 2). 1977. pap. text ed. 5.50x (ISBN 0-87281-061-5). Ctr Appl Ling.

Language & Reality: A Rhetoric & Reader. Carol Boltz & Merle O. Thompson. LC 78-32080. (Illus.). 1979. pap. text ed. 9.95 (ISBN 0-88284-074-6). Alfred Pub.

Language & Situation: Language Varieties & Their Social Contexts. Michael Gregory & Susanne Carroll. (Language & Sociaty Ser). 1978. 12.50x (ISBN 0-7100-8756-X); pap. 6.25 (ISBN 0-7100-8773-X). Routledge & Kegan.

Language & Speech. George A. Miller. LC 80-27018. (Illus.). 1981. text ed. price not set (ISBN 0-7167-1297-0); pap. text ed. price not set (ISBN 0-7167-1298-9). W H Freeman.

Language & Speech: Introductory Perspectives. Frederick Williams. 1972. pap. text ed. 8.95 (ISBN 0-13-522789-5). P-H.

Language & Style of Anthony Trollope. J. W. Clark. (Andre Deutsch Language Library). 1977. lib. bdg. 19.00x (ISBN 0-233-96641-2). Westview.

Language & Symbolic Systems. Yuen-Ren Chao. (Orig.). 1968. 29.95 (ISBN 0-521-04616-5); pap. 10.95x (ISBN 0-521-09457-7, 457). Cambridge U Pr.

Language & Technique of the Film. Gianfranco Bettetini. (Approaches to Semiotics Ser: No. 28). 1973. text ed. 33.00x (ISBN 90-2792-412-0). Mouton.

Language & the Child. M. M. Lewis. 1969. pap. text ed. 3.00x (ISBN 0-901225-07-X, NFER). Humanities.

Language & the Existence of Freedom: A Study in Paul Ricoeur's Philosophy of Will. Stephen Skousgaard. LC 79-63257. 1979. pap. text ed. 7.50 (ISBN 0-8191-0725-5). U Pr of Amer.

Language & the Origins of Psychoanalysis. John Forrester. 304p. 1980. 22.50x (ISBN 0-231-05136-0). Columbia U Pr.

Language & the Pursuit of Truth. John Wilson. 1956. 22.95 (ISBN 0-521-06821-5); pap. 4.95x (ISBN 0-521-09421-6). Cambridge U Pr.

Language & Thinking in Human Developement. D. G. Boyle. 1971. text ed. 8.00x (ISBN 0-09-109590-5, Hutchinson U Lib). Humanities.

Language & Thought of the Child. 3rd ed. Jean Piaget. 1962. text ed. 15.50x (ISBN 0-7100-3041-X). Humanities.

Language & Woman's Place. Robin Lakoff. 160p. (Orig.). 1975. pap. 4.95 (ISBN 0-06-090389-9, CN389, CN). Har-Row.

Language Arts Activities for the Classroom. Tiedt. 1978. text ed. 16.95 (ISBN 0-205-05896-5); pap. text ed. 10.50 (ISBN 0-205-05912-0). Allyn.

Language Arts & Dialect Differences. Donna Christian. (Dialects & Educational Equity Ser.: No. 5). 1979. pap. 2.50 (ISBN 0-87281-124-7). Ctr Appl Ling.

Language Arts & the Young Child. Thomas D. Yawkey et al. LC 80-52447. 270p. 1981. pap. text ed. 7.50 (ISBN 0-87581-263-5). Peacock Pubs.

Language Arts for Today's Children. Ed. by Helen K. Mackintosh. LC 54-8794. 1954. 20.00x (ISBN 0-89197-264-1). Irvington.

Language Arts in the Elementary School. 3rd ed. Ruth G. Strickland. 1969. text ed. 12.95x (ISBN 0-669-20222-3). Heath.

Language Arts Library. (Classroom Libraries). (gr. 4-6). 111.45 o.p. (ISBN 0-531-00725-1). Watts.

Language As a Human Problem. Ed. by Einar Haugen & Morton Bloomfield. 1975 12.50x (ISBN 0-393-01112-7); pap. 7.95x (ISBN 0-393-09261-5). Norton.

Language, As a Music: Six Marginal Pretexts for Composition. Benjamin Boretz. LC 80-80807. (Illus.). 88p. 1980. lib. bdg. 15.75. Lingua Pr.

Language As a Social Resource: Essays by Allen D. Grimshaw. Allen D. Grimshaw. (Language Science & National Development). 400p. 1981. text ed. 18.75x (ISBN 0-8047-1108-9). Stanford U Pr.

Language As Gesture. R. P. Blackmur. LC 80-28610. (Morningside Book Ser.). 448p. 1981. pap. 8.50 (ISBN 0-231-05295-2). Columbia U Pr.

Language As Ideology. Gunther Kress. 1981. pap. price not set (ISBN 0-7100-0795-7). Routledge & Kegan.

Language As Ideology. Gunther Kress & Robert Hodge. 1979. 18.00x (ISBN 0-7100-0215-7). Routledge & Kegan.

Language As Symbolic Action: Essays on Life, Literature, & Method. Kenneth Burke. 1966. 20.00x (ISBN 0-520-00191-5); pap. 8.95 (ISBN 0-520-00192-3, CAL166). U of Cal Pr.

Language Assessment & Intervention for the Learning Disabled. Elisabeth H. Wiig & Eleanor M. Semel. (Special Education Ser.). 464p. 1980. text ed. 17.95 (ISBN 0-675-08180-7). Merrill.

Language Assessment Instruments: Infancy Through Adulthood. Arden R. Thorum. (Illus.). 320p. 1980. write for info. o.p. (ISBN 0-398-04107-5). C C Thomas.

Language Assessment Instruments: Infancy Through Adulthood. Arden R. Thorum. 320p. 1980. text ed. 19.75 (ISBN 0-398-04107-5). C C Thomas.

Language at Work. Peter Wright. 1968. pap. text ed. 6.95x o.p. (ISBN 0-435-10975-8). Heinemann Ed.

Language Behavior: A Book of Readings in Communication. Ed. by Johnnye Akin et al. LC 77-110948. (Janua Linguarum, Ser. Major: No. 41). 1970. text ed. 56.50x (ISBN 90-2791-244-0). Mouton.

Language, Children & Society: The Effect of Social Patterns on Children Learning to Communicate. new ed. Ed. by Olga K. Garnica & Martha L. King. (International Series in Psychobiology & Learning (Pal)). 1979. text ed. 60.00 (ISBN 0-08-023716-9). Pergamon.

Language Classroom. Ed. by William F. Bottiglia. Incl. Drop-Out of Students After the Second Year. Renee J. Fulton; Philosophy of the Language Laboratory. John B. Archer; Place of Grammar & the Use of English in the Teaching of Foreign Languages. James H. Grew; Spoken Language Tests. Nelson Brooks; Teaching Aids & Techniques. Jeanne V. Pleasants; Teaching Literature for Admission to College with Advanced Standing. Blanche A. Price. 84p. 1957. pap. 7.95x (ISBN 0-915432-57-9). NE Conf Teach Foreign.

Language, Cognitive Deficits, and Retardation. N. O'Connor. 376p. 1975. 33.95 (ISBN 0-407-00007-0). Butterworths.

Language: Concepts & Processes. Joseph A. De Vito. (Speech Communication Ser). (Illus.). 288p. 1973. pap. 10.95 ref. ed. o.p. (ISBN 0-13-522904-9). P-H.

Language Conflict & National Development: Group Politics & National Language Policy in India. Jyotirindra Das Gupta. LC 75-94992. (Center for South & Southeast Asia Studies, UC Berkeley). 1970. 16.50x (ISBN 0-520-01590-8). U of Cal Pr.

Language, Counter-Memory, Practice: Selected Essays & Interviews. Michel Foucault. Ed. by Donald F. Bouchard. Tr. by Sherry Simon from Fr. LC 77-4561. (Cornell Paperbacks Ser.). 240p. 1980. pap. 5.95 (ISBN 0-8014-9204-1). Cornell U Pr.

Language Curriculum & Materials for the Handicapped Learner. Frank B. Withrow & Carolyn J. Nygren. 1976. text ed. 17.95 (ISBN 0-675-08615-9). Merrill.

Language Death: A Case of Study at a Gaelic-Speaking Community. Nancy Dorian. 1980. text ed. 25.00x (ISBN 0-8122-7785-6); pap. text ed. 11.95x (ISBN 0-8122-1111-1). U of Pa Pr.

Language Developement & Assessment. Joan Reynell. (Studies in Developmental Pediatrics Ser.: Vol. 1). 178p. 1980. text ed. 16.50 (ISBN 0-88416-377-6). PSG Pub.

Language Development. Victor Lee. LC 78-9081. 1979. 21.95x (ISBN 0-470-26432-2). Halsted Pr.

Language Development & Language Disorders. Lois Bloom & Margaret Lahey. LC 77-21482. (Communication Disorders Ser.). 1978. text ed. 22.95 (ISBN 0-471-08220-1). Wiley.

Language Development, Grammer, & Semantics: The Contribution of Linguistics to Bilingual Education. Arnold M. Zwicky et al. LC 79-57530. (Bilingual Ed. Ser.: No. 7). 89p. 1980. text ed. 6.50x (ISBN 0-87281-111-5). Ctr Appl Ling.

Language Development in Deaf & Partially Hearing Children. D. M. Dale. (Illus.). 270p. 1975. 24.75 (ISBN 0-398-03164-9). C C Thomas.

Language Development of Exceptional Children. Harold D. Love et al. (Illus.). 244p. 1977. 17.50 (ISBN 0-398-03573-3). C C Thomas.

Language Development: The Key to Learning. Morris V. Jones. 336p. 1972. pap. 31.75 photocopy ed., spiral (ISBN 0-398-02324-7). C C Thomas.

Language Disabilities in Children & Adolescents. new ed. Elisabeth Wiig & Eleanor Semel. 1976. text ed. 18.50 (ISBN 0-675-08614-0). Merrill.

Language Disordered Child. G. M. Fraser & J. Blockley. Ed. by P. A. Berse. (General Ser.). 56p. 1973. pap. text ed. 6.75x (ISBN 0-85633-031-0, NFER). Humanities.

Language Disorders in Children. Frank R. Kleffner. LC 73-3116. (Studies in Communicative Disorders Ser). 60p. 1973. pap. text ed. 2.95 (ISBN 0-672-61292-5). Bobbs.

Language Disorders of Children: The Bases & Diagnoses. Mildred F. Berry. (Illus.). 1969. 18.95 (ISBN 0-13-522854-9). P-H.

Language Diversity & Language Contact: Essays by Stanley Lieberson. Stanley Lieberson. Ed. by Anwar S. Dil. (Language Science & National Development Ser.). 416p. 1981. 18.75x (ISBN 0-8047-1098-8). Stanford U Pr.

Language en Contexte: Etudes Philosophiques et Linguistiques de Pragmatique. Ed. by Herman Parret. (Linguisticae Investigationes Supplementa: No. 3). (Fr.). 1980. text ed. 85.50x (ISBN 90-272-3112-5). Humanities.

Language, Ethnicity, & Education in Wales. Bud B. Khleif. (Contributions to the Sociology of Language Ser.: No. 28). 1979. text ed. 50.00x (ISBN 90-279-7898-0). Mouton.

Language Experience Activities. Roach V. Allen. LC 75-31012. (Illus.). 384p. 1976. pap. text ed. 10.95 (ISBN 0-395-18626-9). HM.

Language-Experience Approach to Reading: A Handbook for Teachers of Reading. Denise D. Nessel & Margaret B. Jones. (Orig.). 1981. pap. 8.95. Tchrs Coll.

Language Experiences in Communication. Roach V. Allen. LC 75-31011. (Illus.). 512p. 1976. text ed. 17.95 (ISBN 0-395-18624-2); inst. manual 1.25 (ISBN 0-395-18798-2). HM.

Language Form & Linguistic Variation. Ed. by John Anderson. (Current Issue in Linguistic Theory: No. 15). 370p. 1980. text ed. 45.75x (ISBN 0-686-65680-6). Humanities.

Language Handbook: Concepts, Assessment, Intervention. John R. Muma. (Illus.). 1978. 19.95 (ISBN 0-13-522755-0). P-H.

Language Hermeneutic, & Word of God. Robert W. Funk. LC 66-20776. (Scholars Press Reprint Ser.: No. 1). 1966. pap. 9.00 (ISBN 0-89130-225-5, 000701). Scholars Pr Ca.

Language in America: A Report on Our Deteriorating Semantic Environment. Ed. by Neil Postman et al. LC 73-77137. 1969. pap. 5.50 (ISBN 0-672-63552-6). Pegasus.

Language in America: A Report on Our Deteriorating Semantic Environment. Ed. by Neil Postman et al. LC 73-77137. 1969. text ed. 22.50x (ISBN 0-672-53552-1). Irvington.

Language in Culture & Class. A. D. Edwards. 1976. 19.50x (ISBN 0-8448-1063-0). Crane-Russak Co.

Language in Early Childhood Education. rev. ed. Ed. by Courtney B. Cazden. (Illus.). 144p. 1980. pap. text ed. write for info. (ISBN 0-912674-74-1). Natl Assn Child Ed.

Language in Education: A Source Book. Ed. by A. Cashdan & E. Grugeon. 1972. 13.95x (ISBN 0-7100-7430-1); pap. 8.95 (ISBN 0-7100-7431-X). Routledge & Kegan.

Language in the Inner City: Studies in the Black English Vernacular. William Labov. LC 72-80376. (Conduct & Communication Ser). 438p. 1973. text ed. 18.00x (ISBN 0-8122-7658-2); pap. 7.95x (ISBN 0-685-29061-1, Pa Paperbks). U of Pa Pr.

Language in the U. S. A. Ed. by C. A. Ferguson et al. 650p. Date not set. price not set (ISBN 0-521-23140-X); pap. price not set (ISBN 0-521-29834-2). Cambridge U Pr.

Language in Thought & Action. Samuel I. Hayakawa. LC 78-53859. 1978. 10.95 (ISBN 0-15-148112-1). HarBraceJ.

Language in Uniform: A Reader on Propaganda. Ed. by Nick A. Ford. LC 67-18746. (Orig.). 1967. pap. 3.95 (ISBN 0-672-63054-0). Odyssey Pr.

Language Intervention Programs in the United States, 1960-1974: Theoretical Issues, Experimental Research & Practical Application. Walburga Von Raffler-Engel & Robert H. Hutcheson. 92p. (Orig.). 1975. pap. text ed. 12.00x (ISBN 90-232-1284-3). Humanities.

Language Intervention Strategies in Adult Aphasia. Roberta Chapey. (Illus.). 381p. 1981. 32.00 (ISBN 0-686-69565-8, 1511-7). Williams & Wilkins.

Language Laboratory & Modern Language Teaching. 3rd ed. Edward M. Stack. 1971. text ed. 8.95x (ISBN 0-19-501388-3). Oxford U Pr.

Language Learner. Ed. by Frederick D. Eddy. Incl. Definition of Language Competences Through Testing. Nelson Brooks; Elementary & Junior High School Curricula. Filomena C. Peloro; Modern Foreign Language Learning: Assumptions & Implications. Wilmarth H. Starr; Six-Year Sequence. Gordon R. Silber; Teaching Aids & Techniques: The Secondary School Language Laboratory. Frederick D. Eddy; Teaching of Classical & Modern Foreign Languages: Common Areas & Problems. Josephine P. Bree. 70p. 1959. pap. 7.95x (ISBN 0-915432-59-5). NE Conf Teach Foreign.

Language Learning & Communication Disorders in Children. G. Wyatt. LC 68-28371. (Illus.). 1969. 15.95 (ISBN 0-02-935550-8). Free Pr.

Language Learning: The Intermediate Phase. Ed. by William F. Bottiglia. Incl. Continuum: Listening & Speaking. Simon Belasco; Reading for Meaning. George Sherer; Writing an Expression. Marina Prochoroff. 85p. 1963. pap. 9.95 (ISBN 0-915432-63-3). NE Conf Teach Foreign.

Language, Literature & Meaning Two: Literary Theory & Criticism in Poland, Hungary & Czechoslovakia II: Current Trends in Literary Research. John Odmark. (Linguistic & Literary Studies in Eastern Europe: No. 2). 1980. text ed. 51.50x (ISBN 0-391-01281-9). Humanities.

Language, Logic, & God: With a New Preface. Frederick Ferre. viii, 184p. 1981. pap. text ed. 6.50x (ISBN 0-226-24456-3). U of Chicago Pr.

Language: Mirror, Tool & Weapon. George W. Kelling. LC 74-10511. 274p. 1974. 16.95 (ISBN 0-911012-85-0). Nelson-Hall.

Language Needs of Minority Group Children. June Derrick. (Orig.). 1977. pap. text ed. 6.25x (ISBN 0-85633-118-X, NFER). Humanities.

Language of Adam: On the Limits and Systems of Discourse. Russell Fraser. LC 77-3528. 1977. 17.50x (ISBN 0-231-04256-6). Columbia U Pr.

Language of Advertising & Merchandising in English. Hall. (English for Careers Ser.). (gr. 10 up). 1981. pap. text ed. 3.25 (ISBN 0-88345-352-5). Regents Pub.

Language of Agriculture in English. Murphy. (English for Careers Ser.). (gr. 10 up). 1981. pap. text ed. 3.25 o.p. (ISBN 0-88345-350-9, 18524). Regents Pub.

Language of American Popular Entertainment: A Glossary of Argot, Slang, & Terminology. Don B. Wilmeth. LC 80-14795. 296p. 1981. lib. bdg. 29.95 (ISBN 0-313-22497-8, WEN/). Greenwood.

Language of Argument. 3rd ed. Daniel McDonald. (Illus.). 1980. pap. text ed. 10.50 scp (ISBN 0-06-044358-8, HarpC). Har-Row.

Language of Autistic Children. Don W. Churchill. LC 78-18860. 1978. 14.95 (ISBN 0-470-26417-9). Halsted Pr.

Language of Canaan: Metaphor & Symbol in New England from the Puritans to the Transcendentalists. Mason I Lowance, Jr. LC 79-21179. 1980. 20.00x (ISBN 0-674-50949-8). Harvard U Pr.

Language of Dance. Mary Wigman. Tr. by Walter Sorell from Ger. LC 66-18118. (Illus.). 118p. (Orig.). 1975. pap. 9.95 (ISBN 0-8195-6037-5, Pub. by Wesleyan U Pr). Columbia U Pr.

Language of Education. Israel Scheffler. (American Lectures in Philosophy Ser.). 128p. 1978. 8.75 (ISBN 0-398-01656-9). C C Thomas.

Language of Electrical & Electronic Engineering in English. Hall. (English for Careers Ser.). (gr. 10 up). 1977. pap. text ed. 3.25 (ISBN 0-88345-301-0). Regents Pub.

Language of Fiction: Essays in Criticism & Verbal Analysis of the English Novel. David Lodge. LC 66-10731. 1967. 17.50x (ISBN 0-231-02854-7); pap. 6.00x (ISBN 0-231-08580-X, 80). Columbia U Pr.

Language of Form: The Isometric Theory. Richard L. Branham & David D. Stuhr. LC 80-82996. 496p. 1980. pap. text ed. 22.95 (ISBN 0-8403-2291-7). Kendall-Hunt.

Language of Gerard Manley Hopkins. James Milroy. 1978. lib. bdg. 28.50 o.p. (ISBN 0-233-96916-0). Westview.

Language of Goldfish. Zibby Oneal. 192p. 1981. pap. 1.95 (ISBN 0-449-70005-4, Juniper). Fawcett.

Language of Grammar. Robert DeMaria. LC 63-15677. 1973. 7.95 (ISBN 0-88427-008-4); pap. text ed. 5.95 (ISBN 0-88427-009-2, Dist. by Caroline House Pubs). North River.

Language of Images. Ed. by W. J. Mitchell. LC 80-5225. 1980. pap. 6.95 (ISBN 0-226-53215-1, P887, Phoen). U of Chicago Pr.

Language of Indrajit of Orcha. R. S. McGregor. LC 68-10472. (University of Cambridge Oriental Pubns.). 1968. 49.50 (ISBN 0-521-05630-6). Cambridge U Pr.

Language of Layout. Bud Donahue. LC 78-6949. (Art & Design Ser.). 1978. 19.95 (ISBN 0-13-522953-7, Spec); pap. 9.95 (ISBN 0-13-522961-8). P-H.

Language of Life. Elizabeth A. Gochnour & Theresa B. Smith. (Illus.). 1973. pap. 6.50x o.p. (ISBN 0-8134-1539-X, 1539). Interstate.

Language of Life. 2nd ed. Elizabeth A. Gochnour & Theresa B. Smith. (Illus.). 1981. pap. 6.50x (ISBN 0-8134-2162-4, 2162). Interstate.

Language of Logic. William E. Mann. LC 79-66151. 1979. pap. text ed. 9.50 (ISBN 0-8191-0795-6). U Pr of Amer.

Language of Mathematics. M. Evans Munroe. LC 63-14015. (Ann Arbor Science Library Ser). (Illus.). 1963. 4.00 o.p. (ISBN 0-472-00113-2). U of Mich Pr.

Language of Mathematics: An Individualized Introduction. N. E. Roueche & B. Washburn Mink. LC 78-13397. 1979. 17.95 (ISBN 0-13-522920-0). P-H.

Language of Medicine: A Guide for Stenotypists. E. S. Cooper. 1977. pap. 9.95 (ISBN 0-87489-045-4). Med Economics.

Language of Medicine: A Worktext Explaining Medical Terms. Davi-Ellen Chabner. LC 75-38150. (Illus.). 350p. 1976. pap. text ed. 14.95 o.p. (ISBN 0-7216-2480-4). Saunders.

Language of Medicine: A Write-in Text Explaining Medical Terms. 2nd ed. Davi-Ellen Chabner. (Illus.). 600p. 1981. text ed. 16.95 (ISBN 0-7216-2479-0). Saunders.

Language of Medicine in English. Bloom. (English for Careers Ser.). (gr. 10 up). 1981. pap. text ed. 3.25 (ISBN 0-88345-351-7). Regents Pub.

Language of Modern Poetry: Yeats, Elliot, Auden. A. C. Partridge. (Andre Deutsch Language Library). 1977. lib. bdg. 32.50x (ISBN 0-233-96642-0). Westview.

Language of Modern Politics. Kenneth Hudson. 1978. text ed. 20.75x (ISBN 0-333-21438-2). Humanities.

Language of Music. Deryck Cooke. 1959. pap. 8.95x (ISBN 0-19-284004-5, OPB). Oxford U Pr.

Language of Pattern: An Enquiry Inspired by Islamic Decoration. Keith Albarn et al. LC 73-20057. (Icon Editions). (Illus.). 112p. 1974. pap. 5.95x o.s.i. (ISBN 0-06-430050-1, IN-50, HarpT). Har-Row.

Language of Physics. Phyllis J. Fleming. LC 77-76110. (Physics Ser.). 1978. text ed. 18.95 (ISBN 0-201-02472-1); instr's man 1.00 (ISBN 0-201-02467-5); study guide 4.95 (ISBN 0-201-02474-8). A-W.

Language of Primary School Children. Connie Rosen & Harold Rosen. (Education Ser.). (Orig.). 1973. pap. 3.95 o.p. (ISBN 0-14-080340-8). Penguin.

Language of Real Estate. John W. Reilly. 1977. 35.95 o.p. (ISBN 0-88462-362-9). Real Estate Ed Co.

Language of Real Estate. John W. Reilly. 585p. (Orig.). 1977. pap. 19.95 (ISBN 0-88462-354-8). Real Estate Ed Co.

Language of Shakespeare. G. L. Brook. (Andre Deutsch Language Library). 1978. 25.00x (ISBN 0-233-96762-1). Westview.

Language of Show Dancing. Jacqueline Lowe & Charles Selber. LC 80-10751. (Illus.). (gr. 5 up). 1980. 9.95 (ISBN 0-684-16431-0). Scribner.

Language of Smell. Robert Burton. (Illus.). 1976. 12.95 (ISBN 0-7100-8429-3). Routledge & Kegan.

Language of Social Casework. Noel Timms. (Library of Social Work). 1968. pap. text ed. 3.75x (ISBN 0-7100-6214-1). Humanities.

Language of Social Research: A Reader in the Methodology of Social Research. P. F. Lazarsfeld & E. Katz. LC 55-7342. 1965. pap. text ed. 7.95 (ISBN 0-02-918270-0). Free Pr.

Language of Sociology. Charles W. Lachenmeyer. LC 72-164501. 125p. 1971. 15.00x (ISBN 0-231-03556-X); pap. 6.00x (ISBN 0-231-08338-6). Columbia U Pr.

Language of Stained Glass. Robert Sowers. (Illus.). 220p. 1981. 24.95 (ISBN 0-917304-61-6, Pub. by Timber Pr). Intl Schol Bk Serv.

Language of Tennyson's "In Memoriam". Alan Sinfield. 1971. pap. 24.50x (ISBN 0-631-12980-4, Pub. by Basil Blackwell). Biblio Dist.

Language of the Atharva-Veda. Yajan Veer. 1979. text ed. 16.50x (ISBN 0-391-01853-1). Humanities.

Language of the Christian Community. Sara Little. (Illus., Orig.). (gr. 11-12). 1965. pap. 3.45 (ISBN 0-8042-9240-X); tchrs' guide pap. 2.60. John Knox.

Language of the Earth. Rhodes & Stone. 350p. Date not set. text ed. 35.01 (ISBN 0-08-025981-2); pap. text ed. 17.51 (ISBN 0-08-025980-4). Pergamon.

Language of the Health Sciences: A Lexical Guide to Word Parts, Word Roots, & Their Meanings. Wallace F. White. LC 77-9310. 1977. pap. 12.95 (ISBN 0-471-02159-8, Pub. by Wiley Medical). Wiley.

Language of the New Testament. E. V. Goetchius. 1966. text ed. 9.95x (ISBN 0-684-41263-2, ScribC); wkbk. 8.95x (ISBN 0-684-41264-0). Scribner.

Language of the New Testament. W. H. Simcox. Date not set. 8.95 (ISBN 0-88469-140-3). BMH Bks.

Language of the Revenger's Tragedy. Daniel Jacobson. (Salzburg Studies in English Literature, Jacobean Drama Studies: No. 38). 246p. 1974. pap. text ed. 25.00x (ISBN 0-391-01433-1). Humanities.

Language of the Underworld. David W. Maurer. LC 79-57574. 1981. price not set (ISBN 0-8131-1405-5). U Pr of Ky.

Language of Time. Richard M. Gale. (International Library of Philosophy & Scientific Method). 1968. text ed. 14.50x (ISBN 0-7100-3637-X). Humanities.

Language of Tragedy. Moody E. Prior. LC 66-12753. (Midland Bks.: No. 86). 1966. pap. 2.95x o.p. (ISBN 0-253-20086-5). Ind U Pr.

Language of Twentieth-Century Music. Robert R. Fink & Robert Ricci. LC 74-13308. 1975. 12.95 (ISBN 0-02-870600-5). Schirmer Bks.

Language of Walter Scott. Graham Tulloch. (Andre Deutsch Language Library). 384p. 1980. lib. bdg. 35.00x (ISBN 0-86531-061-0, Pub. by Andre Deutsch). Westview.

Language Planning for Modernization: The Case of Indonesian & Malaysian. Takdir S. Alisjahbana. (Contributions to the Sociology of Language Ser.: No. 14). 1976. pap. text ed. 20.00x (ISBN 90-279-7712-7). Mouton.

Language Poets Use. Winifred Nowottny. 1962. pap. text ed. 8.25x (ISBN 0-485-12009-7, Athlone Pr). Humanities.

Language Proficiency in the Multiracial Junior School. E. C. McEwen et al. (Research Reports Ser). 113p. 1975. pap. text ed. 12.50x (ISBN 0-85633-067-1, NFER). Humanities.

Language Programs in the Public Schools. Ed. by Jewell A. Friend. LC 76-58879. 160p. 1977. pap. 4.95x (ISBN 0-8093-0811-8). S Ill U Pr.

Language, Schools, & Government in Cameroon. Hugh O. Vernon-Jackson. LC 67-21502. (Orig.). 1967. pap. text ed. 4.25x (ISBN 0-8077-2299-5). Tchrs Coll.

Language Services in Industry. Ian F. Finlay. 120p. 1973. 12.50x o.p. (ISBN 0-8464-0546-6). Beekman Pubs.

Language Shift: Social Determinants of Linguistic Change in Bilingual Austria. Susan Gal. (Language, Thought & Culture Ser.). 1979. 21.00 (ISBN 0-12-273750-4). Acad Pr.

Language Skills for Exceptional Learners. Margaret S. Webber. 275p. 1981. text ed. write for info. (ISBN 0-89443-343-1). Aspen Systems.

Language Skills for Journalists. R. Thomas Berner. LC 78-69584. 1978. pap. text ed. 10.50 (ISBN 0-395-26789-7); inst. manual 0.65 (ISBN 0-395-26790-0). HM.

Language: Social Psychological Perspectives: Selected Papers from the First International Conference on Social Psychology & Language Held at the University of Bristol, England, July 1979. Howard Giles & W. Peter Robinson. Ed. by Philip M. Smith. LC 80-40714. 450p. 1980. 60.00 (ISBN 0-08-024696-6). Pergamon.

Language Stimulus Program. Alec Allinson et al. Incl. Level 1. Magic Seasons; Level 3. Multiworlds; Level 4. Mediamind; Level 5. Manspace. (gr. 3-6). 1973. pap. 1.60 o.p. (ISBN 0-685-33454-6, Satellite Books); classroom module 96.00 ea. o.p. Bowmar-Noble.

Language Study for the Nineteen Eighties: Reports of the MLA-ACLS Language Task Forces. Ed. by Richard I. Brod. LC 79-87582. 106p. 1980. pap. 8.50x (ISBN 0-87352-088-2). Modern Lang.

Language Surveys in Developing Nations: Papers and Reports on Sociolinguistic Surveys. Ed. by Sirarpi Ohannessian et al. LC 75-7584. 1975. pap. text ed. 6.00 (ISBN 0-87281-037-2). Ctr Appl Ling.

Language Teacher. Ed. by Harold L. Levy. Incl. Foreign Language Program: Grades 3-12. Margaret E. Eaton; Ghosts in the Language Classroom. Donald D. Walsh; Means of Meeting the Shortage of Teachers. Carolyn E. Bock; Patterns As Grammar. Dorothy Brodin; Single vs. Multiple Languages in Secondary Schools; Teaching of Writing. Jeannette Atkins. 84p. 1958. pap. 7.95x (ISBN 0-915432-58-7). NE Conf Teach Foreign.

Language Teaching: Broader Contexts. Ed. by Robert G. Mead, Jr. Incl. Coordination of Foreign Language Teaching. Genevieve S. Blew; Research & Language Learning. Edward D. Sullivan; Wider Uses for Foreign Languages. Brownlee S. Corrin. 104p. 1966. pap. 7.95x (ISBN 0-915432-66-8). NE Conf Teach Foreign.

Language Teaching Games & Contests. 2nd ed. William R. Lee. 1979. pap. text ed. 5.95x (ISBN 0-19-432716-7). Oxford U Pr.

Language Teaching Techniques. Raymond C. Clark. LC 80-84109. (Pro Lingua Language Resource Handbook Ser.). (Illus.). 128p. (Orig.). 1980. pap. 5.50 (ISBN 0-86647-000-X). Pro Lingua.

Language Tests at School: A Pragmatic Approach. John W. Oller, Jr. (Applied Linguistics & Language Study). (Illus.). 1979. text ed. 18.75x (ISBN 0-582-55365-2); pap. text ed. 12.25x (ISBN 0-582-55294-X). Longman.

Language, the Learner & the School. Johanna S. DeStefano. LC 77-13511. 1978. pap. text ed. 10.95 (ISBN 0-471-02378-7). Wiley.

Language: The Loaded Wagon. Dwight Bolinger. (Illus.). 240p. (Orig.). 1980. text ed. 25.00 (ISBN 0-582-29107-0); pap. text ed. 11.95 (ISBN 0-582-29108-9). Longman.

Language Training for the Nonverbal-Language Delayed Child. Martha L. Cole & Jack T. Cole. 275p. 1981. text ed. price not set (ISBN 0-89443-344-X). Aspen Systems.

Language, Truth & Logic. 2nd ed. Alfred J. Ayer. 1936. pap. 2.00 (ISBN 0-486-20010-8). Dover.

Language Within Language: Immediacy, a Channel in Verbal Communication. Morton Wiener & Albert Mehrabian. LC 68-15231. (Century Psychology Ser.). 1968. 20.00x (ISBN 0-89197-267-6); pap. text ed. 8.95x (ISBN 0-89197-268-4). Irvington.

Languages & Linguistics. 2nd ed. Joe E. Pierce. 188p. 1980. pap. 11.95 (ISBN 0-913244-23-6). Hapi Pr.

Languages & Linguistics: An Introduction. 2nd ed. Joe E. Pierce. (Illus.). 190p. 1980. pap. 10.95 (ISBN 0-913244-23-6). Hapi Pr.

Languages & the Young School Child. Hans H. Stern. (Language & Language Learning Ser.). 1969. pap. 4.95x o.p. (ISBN 0-19-437035-6). Oxford U Pr.

Languages for Specific Purposes: Program Design & Evaluation. Ed. by Ronald Mackay & Joe Palmer. 144p. (Orig.). 1981. pap. text ed. 9.95 (ISBN 0-88377-184-5). Newbury Hse.

Languages in Conflict: Linguistic Acculturation on the Great Plains. Ed. by Paul Schach. LC 80-12710. xii, 186p. 1981. 17.50x (ISBN 0-8032-2106-1). U of Nebr Pr.

Languages of Australia. R. M. Dixon. LC 79-21353. (Cambridge Language Surveys Ser.). (Illus.). 400p. 1980. 69.50 (ISBN 0-521-22329-6); pap. 19.95 (ISBN 0-521-29450-9). Cambridge U Pr.

Languages of Love. Sara Maitland. LC 80-943. 288p. 1981. 10.95 (ISBN 0-385-17203-6). Doubleday.

Languages of the British Isles, Past & Present. W. B. Lockwood. (Andre Deutsch Language Library). 1977. lib. bdg. 29.50x (ISBN 0-233-96666-8). Westview.

Languages of the Soviet Union. B. Comrie. (Cambridge Language Surveys Ser.: No. 2). (Illus.). 320p. Date not set. price not set (ISBN 0-521-23230-9); pap. price not set (ISBN 0-521-29877-6). Cambridge U Pr.

Languages of the World. Kenneth Katzner. (Funk & W Bk.). 384p. 1974. 13.95 o.p. (ISBN 0-308-10120-0, TYC-T). T Y Crowell.

Languages of Theatre: Problems in the Translation & Transposition of Drama. O. Zuber. LC 79-41711. 178p. 1980. 32.50 (ISBN 0-08-025246-X). Pergamon.

Langue et Litterature: A Second Course in French. 2nd ed. Thomas H. Brown. (Illus.). 448p. 1974. text ed. 18.00x (ISBN 0-07-008400-9, C); instructor's manual 3.95 (ISBN 0-07-008401-7); 6.50x (ISBN 0-07-008402-5). McGraw.

Langue francaise, Vol. 2. Jean-Pol Caput. (Collection "L"). 287p. (Orig., Fr.). 1975. pap. 13.95 (ISBN 2-03-036009-0). Larousse.

Langue Francaise au Seizieme Siecle. Peter Rickard. (Illus., Fr.). 1968. 74.00 (ISBN 0-521-06921-1). Cambridge U Pr.

Langue francaise: Histoire d'une institution, 842-1715, Vol. 1. new ed. J. Caput. (Collection L). 320p. (Orig., Fr.). 1972. pap. 12.75 o.p. (ISBN 2-03-036004-X, 3384). Larousse.

Langue francaise, langue humaine. J. Duron. (Langue Vivante Ser). (Fr). pap. 8.25 (ISBN 0-685-13956-5, 3626). Larousse.

Langzeitstudie zum Ernaehrungs- und Gesundheitszustand einer Repraesentativen Stichprobe Heidelberger Frauen und Maenner. G. Schlierf. (Beitraege zu Infusionstherapie und Klinische Ernaehrung: Band 7). viii, 250p. 1981. pap. 18.00 (ISBN 3-8055-2384-X). S Karger.

Lankavatara Sutra: A Mahayana Text. Tr. by Daisetz T. Suzuki. (Illus.). 1972. Repr. of 1932 ed. 26.00 (ISBN 0-7100-2165-8). Routledge & Kegan.

Lanky Jones. Catherine Cookson. LC 80-22676. 192p. (gr. 6 up). 1981. 7.95 (ISBN 0-688-00430-X); PLB 7.63 (ISBN 0-688-00431-8). Morrow.

Lantern in the Night. Frances Barney. 192p. (YA) 1976. 4.95 o.p. (ISBN 0-685-64247-X, Avalon). Bouregy.

Lanthanide & Actinide Chemistry & Spectroscopy. Ed. by Norman Edelstein. LC 80-17468. (ACS Symposium Ser.: No. 131). 1980. 40.00 (ISBN 0-8412-0568-X). Am Chemical.

Lanza: His Tragic Life. Raymond Strait & Terry Robinson. LC 80-17281. 208p. 1980. 10.00 (ISBN 0-13-523407-7). P-H.

Lao Handbook of Maternal & Child Health. Aletha Robinson. 1980. pap. 0.50 (ISBN 0-9602790-1-6). The Garden.

Laocoon & Other Writings. Gotthold E. Lessing. 1959. 12.95x (ISBN 0-460-00843-9, Evman). Dutton.

Laparoscopy, Culdoscopy & Gynecography: Technique & Atlas. Melvin R. Cohen. LC 72-126452. (Major Problems in Obstetrics & Gynecology: Vol. 1). (Illus.). 1970. 15.00 (ISBN 0-7216-2650-5). Saunders.

Lapidary Carving for Creative Jewelry. Henry Hunt. LC 80-67509. (Illus.). 144p. (Orig.). 1981. 17.95 (ISBN 0-937764-01-9); pap. 12.95 (ISBN 0-937764-02-7). Desert Pr.

Laplace Transform Solution of Differential Equations. Robert D. Strum & John R. Ward. (Orig., Prog. Bk.). 1968. pap. 16.95 ref. ed. (ISBN 0-13-522805-0). P-H.

Laplace Transforms for Electronic Engineers. 2nd ed. J. G. Holbrook. 1966. 25.00 (ISBN 0-08-011411-3). Pergamon.

Laplace Transforms: Programmes & Problems. K. A. Stroud. LC 73-6317. 273p. 1973. pap. text ed. 12.95 (ISBN 0-470-83415-3). Halsted Pr.

Lapland. L. Crottel & M. Mendez. (Illus.). 1968. 17.50x (ISBN 0-686-66879-0, N503). Vanous.

Lapland. Walter Marsden. (World's Wild Places Ser.). (Illus.). 1976. 12.95 (ISBN 0-8094-2053-8). Time-Life.

Lapland. Walter Marsden. (World's Wild Places Ser.). (Illus.). 1979. lib. bdg. 11.97 (ISBN 0-686-51021-6). Silver.

Laplanders. R. Hoest. (Illus.). 20.00x o.p. (ISBN 0-686-17926-9, N385). Vanous.

Lapp Dictionary, 5 vols. Ed. by Konrad Nielsen & Asbjorn Nesheim. 3221p. 1980. 250.00x set (ISBN 82-00-14201-9). Universitet.

Lapps. Arthur Spencer. LC 77-88165. (This Changing World Ser.). 1978. 14.50x (ISBN 0-8448-1263-3). Crane-Russak Co.

Lapstrake Boatbuilding, Vol. 2. Walter J. Simmons. LC 78-55779. (Illus.). 1980. 17.50 (ISBN 0-87742-127-7). Intl Marine.

Lar Er Svenska. N. Hildeman et al. (gr. 9 up). 1971. pap. text ed. 16.00x (ISBN 9-1210-2141-4, SW158); exercise bk. (ISBN 0-686-66880-4, SW158E). key 3.00x 14.00x (ISBN 0-686-66880-4, SW158E). key to exercise bk 3.00x (ISBN 0-686-66881-2, SW158K); 7 45 rpm records 70.00x (ISBN 0-686-66882-0, SW158R); 3 tapes 95.00x (ISBN 0-686-66883-9, SW158T); 3 cassettes 100.00x (ISBN 0-686-66884-7, SW158C); wordlist 7.00 (ISBN 9-1200-0645-4, SW158W). Vanous.

Lara in London. Larissa Vassilyeva. Tr. by Olga Franklin. 1978. text ed. 15.00 (ISBN 0-08-023718-5); pap. text ed. 7.65 (ISBN 0-08-023717-7). Pergamon.

Larbi & Leila: A Tale of Two Mice. Harold Berson. LC 73-12378. (Illus.). (ps-3). 1974. 5.50 (ISBN 0-395-28766-9, Clarion). HM.

Lardin Gabas: A Land, a People, a Church. new ed. Ed. by Chalmer Faw. (Illus.). 128p. 1973. 2.50 (ISBN 0-87178-511-0). Brethren.

Laredo & the Rio Grande Frontier. J. B. Wilkinson. LC 75-27031. (Illus.). 476p. 1975. 14.95 o.p. (ISBN 0-8363-0134-X). Jenkins.

Large & Growly Bear. Gertrude Crampton. (Illus.). 24p. (ps-4). 1961. PLB 5.00 (ISBN 0-307-60510-8, Golden Pr). Western Pub.

Large & Small Holdings. Hermann Levy. LC 67-42. Repr. of 1911 ed. 25.00x (ISBN 0-678-05067-8). Kelley.

Large & Small Scale Ethyl Alcohol Manufacturing Processes from Agricultural Raw Materials. Ed. by J. K. Paul. LC 80-20219. (Chemical Tech. Rev. 169, Energy Tech. Rev. 58). (Illus.). 576p. 1981. 48.00 (ISBN 0-8155-0815-8). Noyes.

Large Bored Piles. Ed. by Institute of Civil Engineers. 160p. 1980. 40.00x (ISBN 0-901948-67-5, Pub. by Telford England). State Mutual Bk.

Large Catechism of Martin Luther. Martin Luther. Tr. by Robert H. Fischer from Ger. LC 61-3802. 112p. 1959. 4.95 (ISBN 0-8006-0885-2, 1-885). Fortress.

Large Corporation, the Perversion of the Democratic Order & the Corporate State. C. M. Flumiani. (Illus.). 1977. 39.50 (ISBN 0-89266-073-2). Am Classical Coll Pr.

Large Declaration Concerning the Late Tumults in Scotland: By the King. LC 72-181. (English Experience Ser.: No. 149). 1969. Repr. of 1639 ed. 69.00 (ISBN 90-221-0149-5). Walter J Johnson.

Large Engineering Systems, Two: Proceedings of the Second Symposium on Large Engineering Systems, University of Waterloo, Waterloo, Ontario, May 15, 1978. Ed. by G. J. Savage & P. H. Roe. (Illus.). 1979. 88.00 (ISBN 0-08-025090-4). Pergamon.

Large Families in London. Hilarly Land. 154p. 1969. pap. text ed. 6.25x (ISBN 0-7135-1577-5, Pub. by Bedford England). Renouf.

Large Ground Movements & Structures. James D. Geddes. LC 78-19092. 1978. 64.95 (ISBN 0-470-26460-8). Halsted Pr.

Large Industrial Enterprise: Some Spatial Perspectives. H. D. Watts. (Geography & Environment Ser.). (Illus.). 303p. 1980. 44.00x (ISBN 0-7099-0267-0, Pub. by Croom Helm Ltd England). Biblio Dist.

Large Mammals of West Africa. D. C. Happold. LC 74-169364. (West African Nature Handbooks). (Illus.). 105p. (Orig.). 1973. pap. 5.00 (ISBN 0-582-60428-1). Intl Pubns Serv.

Large Print Book & Its User. Ed. by L. J. Bell. 1980. pap. 33.00x (ISBN 0-85365-632-0, Pub. by Lib Assn England). Oryx Pr.

Large Print Book Catalog. LC 76-48929. 322p. 1976. 8.00 (ISBN 0-913578-13-4). Inglewood Ca.

Large Radiation Sources for Industrial Processes. (Illus., Orig.). 1970. pap. 36.50 (ISBN 92-0-060069-7, IAEA). Unipub.

Large Radiation Sources in Industry, 2 vols. 1960. 13.50 ea. (IAEA). Vol. 1 (ISBN 92-0-060060-3). Vol. 2 (ISBN 92-0-060160-X). Unipub.

Large Scale Development: Benefits, Constraints, & State & Local Policy Incentives. ULI Research Division. LC 77-74659. (Management & Control of Growth Ser.). (Illus.). 135p. 1977. pap. 11.00 (ISBN 0-87420-573-5). Urban Land.

Large Scale Flow Measurement of Hydrocarbon Fluids. Norwegian Petroleum Society. 173p. 1980. 75.00x (ISBN 82-7270-003-4, Pub. by Norwegian Info Norway). State Mutual Bk.

Large Scale Integration. Electronics Magazine. Ed. by Laurence Altman. LC 76-3298. (Illus.). 208p. 1976. pap. text ed. 9.95 (ISBN 0-07-099701-2, R-602). McGraw.

Large Scale Rorschach Techniques: A Manual for the Group Rorschach & Multiple Choice Tests. rev., 2nd ed. M. R Harrower & M. E. Steiner. (American Lectures in Psychology Ser.). (Illus.). 376p. 1973. 19.75 (ISBN 0-398-02739-0). C C Thomas.

Large Scale Systems: Theories & Applications: Proceedings of the 2nd IFAC Symposium on Large Scale Systems Theory & Applications, Toulouse, France 25-27 June 1980. A. Titli & M. G. Singh. LC 80-49946. (IFAC Proceedings Ser.). 550p. 1981. 105.00 (ISBN 0-08-024484-X). Pergamon.

Large Sutra on Perfect Wisdom, with the Divisions of the Abhisamayalankara. Ed. & tr. by Edward Conze. 1975. 35.00x (ISBN 0-520-02240-8). U of Cal Pr.

Large Synchronous Machines: Design, Manufacture & Operation. J. H. Walker. (Monographs in Electrical & Electronic Engineering). (Illus.). 250p. 1981. 59.00 (ISBN 0-19-859364-3). Oxford U Pr.

Large Type Books in Print, 1980. 4th ed. LC 74-102773. 1980. 19.95 (ISBN 0-8352-1296-3). Bowker.

Large Type Columbia-Viking Desk Encyclopedia. 50.00 o.p. (ISBN 0-531-00216-0). Watts.

Larger Bulbs. Brian Mathew. 1978. 30.00 (ISBN 0-7134-1246-1, Pub. by Batsford England). David & Charles.

Larger Life. Ernest Holmes & Willis H. Kinnear. 1969. pap. 4.50 (ISBN 0-911336-07-9). Sci of Mind.

Larger Meaning of Religion. James I. Wedgwood. 80p. 1981. pap. text ed. 3.70 (ISBN 0-918980-10-0). St Alban Pr.

Larger Species of Rhododendron. Peter Cox. (Illus.). 352p. 1980. 49.95 (ISBN 0-7134-1747-1, Pub. by Batsford England). David & Charles.

Larger Than Life: Joe Namath. Val Albrecht. LC 75-42313. (Sports Profiles Ser.). (gr. 4-11). 1976. PLB 8.50 (ISBN 0-8172-0112-2). Raintree Pubs.

Larger Units of Public Library Service in Canada. Violet L. Coughlin. LC 67-12066. 1968. 10.00 (ISBN 0-8108-0079-9). Scarecrow.

Lark Rise to Candleford: A Trilogy. Flora Thompson. (Illus.). 576p. 1979. Repr. of 1945 ed. text ed. 17.95x (ISBN 0-19-211759-9). Oxford U Pr.

Larosa International Pasta Cookbook. Joan Nathan. 7.95 (ISBN 0-916752-25-9). Green Hill.

Larousse Bi-Lingual French-English, English French Dictionary. (Apollo). 10.50 (ISBN 2-03-020903-1, 3767). Larousse.

Larousse citations francaises. 1978. pap. text ed. 12.75 (ISBN 2-03-029306-7). Larousse.

Larousse classique. Larousse And Co. (Illus., Fr.). 28.25 (ISBN 0-685-13957-3, 3747). Larousse.

Larousse de la Langue Francaise, 2 vols. (Fr.). 1977. 98.50 set. Pergamon.

Larousse de poche. Larousse And Co. (Fr.). pap. 6.95 (ISBN 2-03-020166-9, 1008). Larousse.

Larousse de poche, francais-allemand et allemand-francais. Larousse And Co. pap. 5.95 (ISBN 0-685-13959-X). Larousse.

Larousse de poche francais-espagnol, et espanol-frances. Larousse And Co. (Fr. & Span.). pap. 5.95 (ISBN 0-685-13961-1, 1010). Larousse.

Larousse de poche, francais-italien et italien-francais. Larousse And Co. (Fr. & It.). pap. 5.98 (ISBN 0-685-13960-3, 1012). Larousse.

Larousse de poche French-English & English-French. Larousse and Co. (Fr. & Eng.). pap. 5.95 (ISBN 2-03-029203-6, 1009). Larousse.

Larousse des citations: Francaises et etrangeres. new ed. Ed. by Robert Carlier et al. 895p. (Fr.). 1975. 32.00x (ISBN 2-03-021001-3, 3932). Larousse.

Larousse des debutants. Larousse And Co. (Illus., Fr.). 12.25 (ISBN 2-03-020151-0, 3752). Larousse.

Larousse des enfants. Simone Lamblin. (Illus., Fr.). (gr. 3 up). 1979. 33.75 (ISBN 2-03-051421-7). Larousse.

Larousse des fromages. new ed. Robert J. Courtine. (Illus.). 253p. (Fr.). 1973. 38.95x (ISBN 2-03-019012-8). Larousse.

Larousse des jeunes, 8 vols. new ed. Ed. by Michel Langrognet et al. (Illus.). 192p. (Fr.). (gr. 6-12). 1975. 23.25 ea. Vol. 1 (ISBN 2-03-051601-5, 3080). Vol. 2 (ISBN 2-03-051602-3, 3081). Vol. 3 (ISBN 2-03-051603-1, 3082). Vol. 4 (ISBN 2-03-051604-X, 3086). Vol. 5 (ISBN 2-03-051605-8, 3087). Vol. 6 (ISBN 2-03-051606-6, 3088). Vol. 7 (ISBN 2-03-051607-4, 3089). Vol. 8 (ISBN 2-03-051608-2, 3090). Larousse.

Larousse des plantes qui guerissent. new ed. Gerard Debuigne. (Illus.). 254p. (Fr.). 1974. 38.95x (ISBN 2-03-019013-6). Larousse.

Larousse des vins. new ed. Gerard Debuigne. (Illus.). 271p. (Fr.). 1970. 47.50x (ISBN 2-03-019010-1, 4095). Larousse.

Larousse du cheval. new ed. Ed. by Pierre Rousselet-Blanc. (Larousse des animaux familiers). (Illus.). 260p. (Fr.). 1975. 43.95x (ISBN 2-03-014855-5). Larousse.

Larousse du chien. Ed. by Pierre Rousselet-Blanc. (Decouvrir les animaux). (Illus.). 480p. (Fr.). 1975. 64.50x (ISBN 2-03-014850-4). Larousse.

Larousse Encyclopedia of the Animal World. Ed. by Pierre-Paul Grasse. LC 75-7569. Orig. Title: Vie Des Animaux. (Illus.). 1975. 50.00 o.p. (ISBN 0-88332-028-2). Larousse.

Larousse encyclopedique des debutants. new ed. 144p. (Fr.). 1975. 16.50 (ISBN 2-03-020145-6). Larousse.

Larousse Guide to Astronomy. David Baker. LC 78-54635. (Illus.). 1980. o.p. (ISBN 0-88332-095-9); pap. 8.95 (ISBN 0-88332-094-0). Larousse.

Larousse Guide to Shells of the World. A. P. Oliver. LC 79-91944. (Larousse Guide Books). (Illus.). 1980. 15.95 (ISBN 0-88332-107-6); pap. 8.95 (ISBN 0-88332-133-5). Larousse.

Larousse Guide to the Seashore & Shallow Seas of Britain & Europe. A. C. Campbell. LC 80-82755. (Larousse Nature Guides Ser.). (Illus.). 320p. (Orig.). 1981. 10.95 (ISBN 0-88332-251-X, 8068). Larousse.

Larousse Illustrated French-English, English-French Dictionary for Young Readers. Ed. by Fonteneau et al. 1974. 21.25 o.p. (ISBN 2-03-051431-4, 3794). Larousse.

Larousse medical illustre. Larousse And Co. (Illus., Fr.). 72.50x (ISBN 2-03-008500-6, 3912). Larousse.

Larousse pour tous. Larousse And Co. (Fr). 11.50 (ISBN 0-685-13965-4, 3751). Larousse.

Larry Bird: Cool Man on the Court. Bert Rosenthal. LC 80-27094. (Sport Stars Ser.). (Illus.). 48p. (gr. 2-8). 1981. PLB 7.35 (ISBN 0-516-04312-9). Childrens.

Larry Christenson's Financial Record System for Families & Individuals. Larry Christenson. 160p. (Orig.). 1980. spiral bdg. 4.95 (ISBN 0-87123-344-4, 210344). Bethany Fell.

Larry McMurtry. Charles D. Peavy. (United States Authors Ser.: No. 291). 1977. lib. bdg. 12.50 (ISBN 0-8057-7194-8). Twayne.

Larry Rivers. Sam Hunter. LC 69-12483. (Contemporary Art & Artists Ser). (Illus.). 1969. 65.00 o.p. (ISBN 0-8109-0451-9). Abrams.

Lars Ahlin. Torborg Lundell. LC 76-40314. (World Authors Ser.: No. 430). 1977. lib. bdg. 12.50 (ISBN 0-8057-6270-1). Twayne.

Lars Gyllensten. Hans Isaksson. (World Authors Ser.: No. 473). 1978. lib. bdg. 12.50 (ISBN 0-8057-6314-7). Twayne.

Larval Forms & Other Zoological Verses. Walter Garstang. 1966. Repr. of 1951 ed. 7.50x o.p. (ISBN 0-631-07090-7, Pub. by Basil Blackwell). Biblio Dist.

Laryngectomee Rehabilitation. Ed. by Robert L. Keith & Frederic L. Darley. LC 79-91246. (Illus.). 533p. 1980. text ed. 24.50 (ISBN 0-933014-56-2). College-Hill.

Laryngectomee Speech & Rehabilitation. Warren H. Gardner. (Illus.). 260p. 1978. 22.50 (ISBN 0-398-00643-1). C C Thomas.

Laryngl Disease in Children. Cotton & Seid. 1981. text ed. write for info. (ISBN 0-443-08054-2). Churchill.

Las Mil y una Noches: Relatos Ilustrados. (Span.). 9.00 (ISBN 84-241-5409-6). E Torres & Sons.

Las Vegas Calling. Frank Maggio. (Illus.). 1975. 6.50 (ISBN 0-913814-34-2). Nevada Pubns.

Las Vegas Guide for New Arrivals: How to Survive in the Fun Capital of the World. Eve Firestone & Jim Blackwell. (Illus.). 64p. (Orig.). 1980. pap. 2.95 (ISBN 0-89650-790-4). Gamblers.

Las Vegas Vengeance. Bruno Rossi. (Sharpshooter Ser: No. 14). (Orig.). 1975. pap. 1.25 o.p. (ISBN 0-685-52940-1, LB261ZK, Leisure Bks). Nordon Pubns.

Laser Advances & Applications Proceedings. National Quantum Electronics Conference, 4th, Heriot-Watt University Edinburgh, 1979. Ed. by B. S. Wherrett. LC 80-40119. 278p. 1980. 45.00 (ISBN 0-471-27792-4). Wiley.

Laser Applications: Video Disc, Vol. 4. Ed. by G. Goodman & M. Ross. 1980. 32.00 (ISBN 0-12-431904-1). Acad Pr.

Laser Beam Information Systems. Ed. by William C. House. 1978. text ed. 17.50 (ISBN 0-89433-049-7). Petrocelli.

Laser Doppler Technique. L. E. Drain. LC 79-40638. 1980. text ed. 50.25 (ISBN 0-471-27627-8, Pub. by Wiley-Interscience). Wiley.

Laser Electronics. Joseph T. Verdeyen. (Illus.). 480p. 1981. 32.50 (ISBN 0-13-485201-X). P-H.

Laser-Induced Chemical Processes. Ed. by Jeffrey I. Steinfeld. 255p. 1981. 32.50 (ISBN 0-306-40587-3, Plenum Pr). Plenum Pub.

Laser Interaction & Related Plasma Phenomena, Vol. 5. Ed. by H. J. Schwarz et al. 800p. 1981. 75.00 (ISBN 0-306-40545-8, Plenum Pr). Plenum Pub.

Laser Machinig and Welding. N. Rykalin et al. (Illus.). 1979. 48.00 (ISBN 0-08-022724-4). Pergamon.

Laser Physics. Murray Sargent, III et al. LC 74-5049. (Illus.). 1974. text ed. 30.50 (ISBN 0-201-06912-1, Adv Bk Prog); pap. text ed. 18.50 (ISBN 0-201-06913-X, Adv Bk Prog). A-W.

Laser Probes for Combustion Chemistry. Ed. by David R. Crosley. LC 80-17137. (ACS Symposium Ser.: No. 134). 1980. 44.50 (ISBN 0-8412-0570-1). Am Chemical.

Laser Raman Spectroscopy. Marvin C. Tobin. LC 80-11511. 184p. 1981. Repr. of 1971 ed. lib. bdg. write for info. (ISBN 0-89874-159-9). Krieger.

Laser Speckle & Related Phenomena. Ed. by J. C. Dainty. (Topics in Applied Physics: Vol. 9). (Illus.). 250p. 1976. 49.20 (ISBN 0-387-07498-8). Springer-Verlag.

Laser Spectrosopy: Basic Concepts & Instrumentation. W. Demtroeder. (Springer Series in Chemical Physics: Vol. 5). (Illus.). 700p. 1981. 35.00 (ISBN 0-387-10343-0). Springer-Verlag.

Laser Theory. F. S. Barnes. (IEEE Press Selected Reprint Ser.). 469p. 1972. 14.95 o.p. (ISBN 0-471-05190-X); pap. 11.45 o.p. (ISBN 0-471-05191-8, Pub. by Wiley-Interscience). Wiley.

Laser Velocimetry & Particle Sizing: Proceedings. new ed. Ed. by H. Doyle Thompson & Warren H. Stevenson. LC 79-59. (Illus.). 1979. text ed. 56.95 (ISBN 0-89116-150-3). Hemisphere Pub.

Lasers. William Burroughs. LC 77-88173. 1977. 9.95x (ISBN 0-8448-1088-6). Crane-Russak Co.

Lasers. George R. Harrison. LC 70-156888. (First Bks). (Illus.). (gr. 7 up). 1971. PLB 4.90 o.p. (ISBN 0-531-00749-9). Watts.

Lasers. O. S. Heavens. LC 72-2053. (Illus.). 168p. 1973. 9.95 o.p. (ISBN 0-684-13399-7, ScribT). Scribner.

Lasers. Jim Johnson. LC 80-17871. (Look Inside Ser.). (Illus.). 48p. (gr. 4-12). 1981. PLB 10.25 (ISBN 0-8172-1400-3). Raintree Child.

Lasers. 2nd ed. Bela A. Lengyel. LC 77-139279. (Ser. in Pure & Applied Optics). 1971. 36.50 (ISBN 0-471-52620-7, Pub. by Wiley-Interscience). Wiley.

Lasers & Holography: An Introduction to Coherent Optics. 2nd, rev. ed. Winston E. Kock. (Illus.). 128p. 1981. pap. price not set (ISBN 0-486-24041-X). Dover.

Lasers & Their Applications. 2nd ed. M. J. Beesley. 1976. 27.95 (ISBN 0-470-15166-8). Halsted Pr.

Lasers: Equipment & Applications. James R. Critser, Jr. (Ser. 6-78). Date not set. 300.00 (ISBN 0-914428-62-4). Lexington Data. Postponed.

Lasers in Biology & Medicine. Ed. by F. Hillenkamp et al. (NATO Advanced Study Institute Ser.-Series A-Life Sciences: Vol. 34). 450p. 1981. 49.50 (ISBN 0-306-40470-2, Plenum Pr). Plenum Pub.

Lasers in Chemical Analysis. Ed. by Gary Hieftje et al. LC 80-84082. (Contemporary Instrumentation & Analysis). (Illus.). 352p. 1981. price not set (ISBN 0-89603-027-X). Humana.

Lasers in Medicine, Vol. 1. Hans K. Koebner. LC 79-40525. 1980. 64.75 (ISBN 0-471-27602-2, Pub. by Wiley-Interscience). Wiley.

Lasers in Modern Industry. Ed. by John Ready. LC 79-66705. (Manufacturing Update Ser.). (Illus.). 1979. 29.00 (ISBN 0-87263-052-8). SME.

Lasers in Photomedicine & Photobiology: Proceedings. Ed. by R. Pratesi & C. A. Sacchi. (Springer Series in Optical Sciences: Vol. 22). (Illus.). 235p. 1980. 29.50 (ISBN 0-387-10178-0). Springer-Verlag.

Lasithi, A History of Settlement on a Highland Plain in Crete. Livingston V. Watrous. (Hesperia Ser.: Suppl. XVIII). 1981. price not set (ISBN 0-87661-518-3). Am Sch Athens.

Lasker's Manual of Chess. Emanuel Lasker. (YA) (gr. 7-12). pap. 5.00 (ISBN 0-486-20640-8). Dover.

Lasko Tangent. Richard N. Patterson. 208p. 1980. pap. 1.95 (ISBN 0-345-28705-3). Ballantine.

LASL Explosive Property Data. Ed. by Terry R. Gibbs & Alphonse Popolato. (Los Alamos Scientific Laboratory Series on Dynamic Material Properties). 1980. 40.00x (ISBN 0-520-04012-0). U of Cal Pr.

LASL Phermex Data, Vol. 1. Ed. by Charles L. Mader & Timothy R. Neal. (Los Alamos Scientific Laboratory Series on Dynamic Material Properties). 1980. 52.50 (ISBN 0-520-04009-0). U of Cal Pr.

LASL Phermex Data, Vol. 2. Ed. by Charles L. Mader. (Los Alamos Scientific Series on Dynamic Material Properties). 768p. 1980. 42.50x (ISBN 0-520-04010-4). U of Cal Pr.

LASL Shock Hugoniot Data. Stanley P. Marsh. (Los Alamos Scientific Laboratory Series on Dynamic Material Properties). 1980. 40.00 (ISBN 0-520-04008-2). U of Cal Pr.

Lassen Volcanic National Park. Jeffrey P. Schaffer. Ed. by Thomas Winnett. LC 80-53681. (Illus.). 224p. (Orig.). 1981. pap. 9.95 (ISBN 0-89997-004-4). Wilderness Pr.

Lassie & Her Friends. Cecily Hogan. (ps-1). PLB 5.38 (ISBN 0-307-68950-6, Golden Pr). Western Pub.

Lassie & the Secret Friend. Kennon Graham. (Illus.). 32p. (ps-1). 1972. PLB 7.62 (ISBN 0-307-60059-9, Golden Pr). Western Pub.

Lassie: Lost in the Snow. Steve Frazee. (gr. 3 up). 1979. pap. 1.25 (ISBN 0-307-21504-0, Golden Pr). Western Pub.

Lassie: The Mystery of Bristlecone Pine. Steve Frazee. (gr. 3 up). 1979. pap. 1.25 (ISBN 0-307-21505-9, Golden Pr). Western Pub.

Lassie: The Secret of the Smelter's Cave. Steve Frazee. (gr. 3 up). 1979. pap. 1.25 (ISBN 0-307-21514-8, Golden Pr). Western Pub.

Lassie: Trouble at Panter's Lake. Steve Frazee. (gr. 3 up). 1979. pap. 1.25 (ISBN 0-307-21515-6, Golden Pr). Western Pub.

Lassie's Big Clean-up Day. Kennon Graham. (Young Reader Ser.). 24p. (ps-3). 1980. PLB 5.00 (ISBN 0-307-60311-3, Golden Pr). Western Pub.

Lassiter: Lust for Gold. Jack Slade. 1977. pap. 1.25 (ISBN 0-505-51127-4). Tower Bks.

Last Act. Jane A. Hodge. 256p. 1981. pap. 2.50 (ISBN 0-449-24379-6, Crest). Fawcett.

Last Act: Being the Funeral Rites of Nations & Individuals. William Tegg. LC 72-10592. (Illus.). 404p. 1973. Repr. of 1876 ed. 20.00 (ISBN 0-8103-3172-1). Gale.

Last & Lost Poems of Delmore Schwartz. Robert Phillips. LC 78-63244. 1979. 8.95 (ISBN 0-8149-0808-X). Vanguard.

Last Angry Man. Gerald Green. 1980. pap. 3.50 (ISBN 0-425-04993-0). Berkley Pub.

Last Apaches. William Hopson. 256p. (YA) 1975. 5.95 (ISBN 0-685-50530-8, Avalon). Bouregy.

Last Barrier. Reshad Feild. LC 75-9345. 1977. pap. 5.95 (ISBN 0-06-062586-4, RD 202, HarpR). Har-Row.

Last Battle. C. S. Lewis. (Illus.). (gr. 4-6). 1956. 8.95 (ISBN 0-02-757890-9). Macmillan.

Last Byzantine Renaissance. Steven Runciman. (Wiles Lectures 1968-69). 1970. 15.50 (ISBN 0-521-07787-7). Cambridge U Pr.

Last Call. Warren Murphy. (Destroyer: No. 35). 1978. pap. 1.50 (ISBN 0-523-40157-4). Pinnacle Bks.

Last Captive. A. C. Greene. (Illus.). 185p. (gr. 6-9). 1972. 8.95 o.p. (ISBN 0-88426-004-6). Encino Pr.

Last Carnival. Alexandra Ellis. (Orig.). 1980. pap. 2.50 (ISBN 0-515-04816-X). Jove Pubns.

Last Catholic in America. John R. Powers. LC 79-24431. 1981. Repr. of 1973 ed. lib. bdg. 10.00x (ISBN 0-8376-0439-7). Bentley.

Last Cattle Drive. Robert Day. 1977. pap. 1.95 (ISBN 0-380-01832-2, 36228). Avon.

Last Centuries of Byzantium. Donald Nicol. 462p. 1980. text ed. 17.00x (ISBN 0-246-10559-3). Humanities.

Last Centuries of Byzantium. Donald M. Nicol. 1979. 19.95x (ISBN 0-8464-0103-7). Beekman Pubs.

Last Chance: Nuclear Proliferation & Arms Control. William Epstein. LC 75-22765. 1976. 17.95 (ISBN 0-02-909660-X). Free Pr.

Last Chance: Tombstone's Early Years. John M. Myers. LC 50-5638. (Illus.). 260p. 1973. pap. 2.45 (ISBN 0-8032-5780-5, BB 569, Bison). U of Nebr Pr.

Last Chapters: A Sociology of Aging & Dying. Victor W. Marshall. LC 79-26915. (Social Gerontology Ser.). (Orig.). 1980. pap. text ed. 8.95 (ISBN 0-8185-0399-8). Brooks-Cole.

Last Chopper: The Denouement of the American Role in Vietnam, 1964-1975. Weldon A. Brown. 1976. 17.50 (ISBN 0-8046-9121-5, Natl U). Kennikat.

Last Christian: A Biography of Francis Assisi. Adolf Holl & Peter Heinegg. LC 79-7868. 288p. 1980. 12.95 (ISBN 0-385-15499-2). Doubleday.

Last Colony: But Whose?; a Study of the Labour Movement, Labour Market & Labour Relations in Hong Kong. H. A. Turner. LC 80-41112. (Department of Applied Economics Papers in Industrial Relations & Labour: No. 5). (Illus.). 1981. 24.95 (ISBN 0-521-23701-7). Cambridge U Pr.

Last Communion. Nichol Yermokov. (Orig.). 1981. pap. price not set (ISBN 0-451-09822-6, Signet Bks). NAL.

Last Confucian: Liang Shu-Ming & the Chinese Dilemma of Modernity. Guy S. Alitto. LC 75-27920. (Center for Chinese Studies). 1979. 19.00x (ISBN 0-520-03123-7). U of Cal Pr.

Last Cowboy. Jane Kramer. LC 77-6150. 1978. 9.95 o.s.i. (ISBN 0-06-012454-7, HarpT). Har-Row.

Last Crime. John Domatilla. LC 80-20650. 1981. 8.95 (ISBN 0-689-11121-5). Atheneum.

Last Crossword Dictionary. Bruce Wetterau. (Orig.). 1981. pap. 3.50 (ISBN 0-451-09910-9, E9910). NAL.

Last Day of a Condemmed. Victor Hugo. Tr. by De B. Eugenia. LC 76-25870. 1977. Repr. of 1894 ed. 15.50 (ISBN 0-86527-269-7). Fertig.

Last Days of David & His Contemporaries. Gordon Lindsay. (Old Testament Ser.). 1.25 (ISBN 0-89985-144-4). Christ Nations.

Last Days of Freedom. Nika Stajka. 1981. 12.95 (ISBN 0-533-04637-8). Vantage.

Last Days of Imperial Russia: 1910-1917. Miriam L. Kochan. 1976. 5.98 o.s.i. (ISBN 0-02-564900-0). Macmillan.

Last Days of Maximilian Kolbe. Sergius C. Lorit. Tr. by Hugh Moran from Ital. LC 80-82418. Orig. Title: Kolbe: Cronaca Degli Ultimi Giorni. 144p. 1980. pap. 2.95 (ISBN 0-911782-35-4). New City.

Last Days of Patton. Ladislas Farago. 352p. 1981. 12.95 (ISBN 0-07-019940-X, GB). McGraw.

Last Days of Pompeii. Edward B. Lytton. Date not set. pap. 5.95 (ISBN 0-912800-74-7). Woodbridge Pr. Postponed.

Last Days of Socrates. Plato. Tr. by Hugh Tredennick. Incl. Euthyphro; Apology; Crito; Phaedo. (Classics Ser.). 1954. pap. 2.25 (ISBN 0-14-044037-2). Penguin.

Last Days of United Pakistan. G. W. Choudhury. LC 74-8977. 256p. 1975. 12.50x (ISBN 0-253-33260-5). Ind U Pr.

Last Decathlon. John Redgate. 1980. pap. 2.50 o.s.i. (ISBN 0-440-14643-7). Dell.

Last Door to Aiya: A Selection of the Best New Science Fiction from the Soviet Union. Tr. by Mirra Ginsburg. LC 68-16347. (YA) 1968. 9.95 (ISBN 0-87599-135-1). S G Phillips.

Last East Indian Voyage. Sir Henry Middleton. LC 74-25700. (English Experience Ser.: No. 307). 1971. Repr. of 1606 ed. 11.50 (ISBN 90-221-0307-2). Walter J Johnson.

Last Edwardian at Number Ten: An Impression of Harold Macmillian. George Hutchinson. (Illus.). 160p. 1980. 12.95 (ISBN 0-7043-2232-3, Pub. by Quartet England). Horizon.
Last Elizabethan Journal. Ed. by G. B. Harrison. 1974. 32.50x (ISBN 0-7100-7883-8). Routledge & Kegan.
Last Enemy. Berton Roueche. LC 75-6375. (Harper Novel of Suspense). 224p. 1975. 6.95 o.p. (ISBN 0-06-013687-1, HarpT). Har-Row.
Last Essays. Thomas R. Henn. 1978. text ed. 14.50x (ISBN 0-901072-03-6). Humanities.
Last Essays: Scott, Newman, Push Kiv, Hardy. G. M. Young. 288p. 1980. Repr. of 1950 ed. lib. bdg. 20.00 (ISBN 0-8495-6149-3). Arden Lib.
Last Exit. Fran P. Yariv. 256p. (Orig.). 1981. pap. 2.50 (ISBN 0-515-05416-X). Jove Pubns.
Last Exodus. Leonard Schroeter. LC 79-4922. 444p. (Orig.). 1979. pap. 7.95 (ISBN 0-295-95685-2). U of Wash Pr.
Last Finnish War. Waldemar Erfurth. 1979. 22.00 (ISBN 0-89093-205-0). U Pubns Amer.
Last Fix: Dan Russell & the World That Lost Him. Ellen Russell. LC 70-160409. 256p. 1971. 7.95 o.p. (ISBN 0-15-148480-5). HarBraceJ.
Last Flight from Iran. Martie Sterling & Robin Sterling. 272p. (Orig.). 1981. pap. 2.50 (ISBN 0-553-20005-4). Bantam.
Last Flower. Con Sellers. 1980. pap. write for info. PB.
Last Flower. James Thurber. (Illus.). 1971. pap. 3.50 o.p. (ISBN 0-06-090232-9, CN232, CN). Har-Row.
Last Flowers. Michael Barrett. 256p. 1957. 3.50 o.p. (ISBN 0-374-18344-9). FS&G.
Last Frontiers. Thayer Willis et al. 480p. 1973. 7.95 o.p. (ISBN 0-385-04286-8). Doubleday.
Last Gamble on Education: Dynamics of Adult Basic Education - New Dimensions in Program Analysis. Jack Mezirow et al. 206p. 1975. 11.00 (ISBN 0-685-63817-0). Adult Ed.
Last Gas Station & Other Stories. Tom Clark. 200p. 1980. 14.00 (ISBN 0-87685-457-9); signed ed. 20.00 (ISBN 0-87685-458-7); pap. 6.00 (ISBN 0-87685-456-0). Black Sparrow.
Last Generation of the Roman Republic. Erich S. Gruen. LC 72-89244. 1974. 33.75x (ISBN 0-520-02238-6). U of Cal Pr.
Last Good-Bye & Other Stories. Mack Jameson & Al Nist. Ed. by Winifred H. Roderman. (Read on - Write on Ser). (Illus.). 64p. (Orig.). (gr. 7-12). 1981. pap. text ed. 2.85 (ISBN 0-915510-55-3); tchrs. ed. free. Janus Bks.
Last Good Kiss. James Crumley. 1980. pap. write for info. (ISBN 0-671-82813-4). PB.
Last Gospel. Francis J. Ripley. 1962. 3.50 o.p. (ISBN 0-8362-0203-1, Pub. by Sheed). Guild Bks.
Last Great Cavalry Battles. Alexis Wrangel. (Illus.). 180p. 1981. 15.00 (ISBN 0-88254-518-3). Hippocrene Bks.
Last Great Ice Sheets. G. H. Denton & T. J. Hughes. LC 79-27808. 1980. write for info. (ISBN 0-471-06006-2, Pub. by Wiley-Interscience). Wiley.
Last Guru. Daniel M. Pinkwater. LC 78-14260. (gr. 5 up). 1978. 6.95 (ISBN 0-396-07636-X). Dodd.
Last Horizon. Raymond F. Dasmann. 1971. pap. 2.95 o.s.i. (ISBN 0-02-072790-9, Collier). Macmillan.
Last Immortal. J. O. Jeppson. 256p. 1981. pap. 2.25 (ISBN 0-449-24385-0, Crest). Fawcett.
Last Innocent Man. Phillip M. Margolin. 252p. 1981. 11.95 (ISBN 0-316-54617-8). Little.
Last Inspection & Other Stories. Alun Lewis. 1942. text ed. 3.95x (ISBN 0-04-823032-4). Allen Unwin.
Last Judgment in Sixteenth Century Northern Europe: a Study of the Relation Between Art & the Reformation. Craig Harbison. LC 75-23793. (Outstanding Dissertations in the Fine Arts - 16th Century). (Illus.). 1976. lib. bdg. 45.00 (ISBN 0-8240-1988-1). Garland Pub.
Last Laugh, Mr. Moto. John P. Marquand. (Mr. Moto Ser.). 1977. pap. 1.25 o.p. (ISBN 0-445-04078-5). Popular Lib.
Last Leaf. O. Henry. (Creative's Classics Ser.). (Illus.). 32p. (gr. 4-9). 1980. PLB 6.95 (ISBN 0-87191-774-2). Creative Ed.
Last Leaf. O'Henry. Ed. by Walter Pauk & Raymond Harris. (Jamestown Classics Ser.). (Illus.). 35p. (Orig.). (gr. 6-12). 1979. pap. text ed. 1.60x (ISBN 0-89061-195-5, 413); tchrs. ed. 3.00 (ISBN 0-89061-197-1, 415). Jamestown Pubs.
Last Letters of Aubrey Beardsley. Aubrey V. Beardsley. 158p. 1980. Repr. of 1904 ed. lib. bdg. 20.00 (ISBN 0-8482-4200-9). Norwood Edns.
Last Liberal Governments. P. Rowland. 1969. 8.95 o.s.i. (ISBN 0-02-605580-5). Macmillan.
Last Liberator. John Clive. 1981. pap. 2.75 (ISBN 0-440-15071-X). Dell.
Last Look at the Old Met. Judith Clancy. LC 79-103983. (Illus.). 1969. bds. 5.95 (ISBN 0-912184-02-7). Synergistic Pr.
Last Lunar Baedeker: The Poems of Mira Loy. Mira Loy. 1981. 25.00 (ISBN 0-912330-46-5, Dist by Gromon Press). Jargon Soc.
Last Mafioso: The Treacherous World of Jimmy Fratianno. Ovid DeMaris. 1981. 15.00 (ISBN 0-686-62159-X). Times Bks.
Last Man. Mary Shelley. Ed. by Hugh J. Luke, Jr. LC 65-19465. 1965. 10.95x (ISBN 0-8032-0173-7); pap. 1.95 (ISBN 0-8032-5182-3, BB 323, Bison). U of Nebr Pr.
Last Man Alive. Gordon D. Shirreffs. 1977. pap. 1.25 (ISBN 0-505-51167-3, BT51167). Tower Bks.
Last Meal on Earth. Owen Spann & Nancie Spann. Ed. by Jay Stewart. LC 78-75161. 1979. pap. 4.95 (ISBN 0-89395-022-X). Cal Living Bks.
Last Medici. rev. ed. Harold Acton. (Illus.). 416p. 1980. Repr. of 1958 ed. 22.50 (ISBN 0-500-25074-X). Thames Hudson.
Last Mission. Harry Mazer. (gr. 7 up). 1981. pap. 1.50 (ISBN 0-440-94797-9, LE). Dell.
Last Movement. Joan Aiken. LC 76-42055. 1977. 7.95 o.p. (ISBN 0-385-12620-4). Doubleday.
Last Mughal. G. D. Khosla. 376p. 1969. pap. 2.40 o.p. (ISBN 0-88253-050-X). Ind-US Inc.
Last Mystery of Edgar Allan Poe: The Troy Dossier. Manny Meyers. 1978. 8.95 o.p. (ISBN 0-397-01315-9). Lippincott.
Last Nazi. Max Lamb & Harry Sanford. (Orig.). 1980. pap. 2.25 (ISBN 0-505-51486-9). Tower Bks.
Last Night at the Ritz. Elizabeth Savage. 208p. 1974. pap. 1.25 o.p. (ISBN 0-445-00232-8). Popular Lib.
Last Nine Minutes: The Story of Flight 981. Moira Johnston. 1977. pap. 1.95 (ISBN 0-380-01808-X, 35642). Avon.
Last of Steam: Steam Locomotives Today. Colin Garratt. LC 76-43194. (Illus.). 128p. 1980. 24.95 (ISBN 0-8040-0754-3). Swallow.
Last of the Armageddon Wars. Ralph Dennis. (Hardman Ser.: No. 11). 1977. pap. 1.25 o.p. (ISBN 0-445-00450-9). Popular Lib.
Last of the Centaurs. Brian Robb. (Illus.). (gr. k-4). 1979. PLB 6.95 (ISBN 0-233-97000-2). Andre Deutsch.
Last of the Cherokee Warriors. 2nd ed. Phillip Steele. (Illus.). (gr. 6-12). 1978. pap. 3.95 (ISBN 0-88289-203-7); 5.95 (ISBN 0-911116-99-0). Pelican.
Last of the Country House Murders. Emma Tennant. LC 76-6976. 160p. (gr. 8 up). 1976. 7.95 o.p. (ISBN 0-525-66490-4). Elsevier-Nelson.
Last of the Dragons. E. Nesbit. LC 79-28584. (Illus.). 32p. (gr. k-4). 1980. 6.95 (ISBN 0-07-046285-2). McGraw.
Last of the Generations. B. J. Smith & James M. Ingley. 1981. 8.95 (ISBN 0-533-04609-2). Vantage.
Last of the Great Stations. Bill Bradley. Ed. by Jim Walker. LC 79-84387. (Special Ser.: No. 72). (Illus.). 1979. pap. 9.95 (ISBN 0-916374-36-X). Interurban.
Last of the Just. Andre Schwarz-Bart. Tr. by Stephen Becker from Fr. LC 79-24071. 1981. Repr. of 1960 ed. lib. bdg. 12.50x (ISBN 0-8376-0456-7). Bentley.
Last of the Mohicans. James F. Cooper. (Literature Ser). (gr. 7-12). 1970. pap. text ed. 3.58 (ISBN 0-87720-731-3). AMSCO Sch.
Last of the Mohicans: Abridged & Adapted to Grade 2 Reading Level. James F. Cooper. Ed. by John M. Hurdy. LC 67-25787. (Pacemaker Classics Ser.). (Illus., Orig.). 1967. pap. 3.80 (ISBN 0-8224-9215-6); tchr's manual free (ISBN 0-8224-5200-6). Pitman Learning.
Last of the Mohicans: Student Activity Book. Marcia Sohl & Gerald Dackerman. (Now Age Illustrated Ser.). (Illus.). (gr. 4-12). 1976. wkbk. 0.95 (ISBN 0-88301-291-X). Pendulum Pr.
Last of the Real Badmen: Henry Starr. Glenn Shirley. LC 75-38554. xiv, 208p. 1976. 11.95x (ISBN 0-8032-0871-5); pap. 2.95 (ISBN 0-8032-5837-2, BB 617, Bison). U of Nebr Pr.
Last of the Three-Foot Loggers. 14.95. Chatham Pub CA.
Last of the Zinja. Robert Shea. (Shike Ser.: Bk. 2). 460p. (Orig.). 1981. pap. 2.95 (ISBN 0-515-05944-7). Jove Pubns.
Last Official Jewish Joke Book. Larry Wilde. 192p. (Orig.). 1980. pap. 1.95 (ISBN 0-553-14349-2). Bantam.
Last Official Polish Joke Book. Larry Wilde. (Illus.). 1977. pap. 1.95 (ISBN 0-523-41468-4). Pinnacle Bks.
Last One Left. John D. MacDonald. 1978. pap. 2.50 (ISBN 0-449-13958-1, GM). Fawcett.
Last Operas & Plays. Gertrude Stein & Alice B. Toklas. 512p. Date not set. pap. 4.95 (ISBN 0-394-71695-7, Vin). Random.
Last Outlaw. Lawrence Cortesi. (Orig.). 1980. pap. write for info. (ISBN 0-505-51560-1). Tower Bks.
Last Phase of the East Asian World Order: Korea, Japan, & the Chinese Empire, 1860-1882. Key-Hiuk Kim. 1980. 22.75x (ISBN 0-520-03556-9). U of Cal Pr.
Last Place God Made. Jack Higgins. 1978. pap. 1.75 o.p. (ISBN 0-449-23468-1, Crest). Fawcett.
Last Place on Earth. Harold T. Hayes. LC 76-15562. (Illus.). 288p. 1980. pap. 8.95 (ISBN 0-8128-6087-X). Stein & Day.
Last Puppy. Frank Asch. (Illus.). (gr. 3-7). 8.95 (ISBN 0-13-524058-1). P-H.
Last Puritan: A Memoir in the Form of a Novel. George Santayana. 1936. 10.00 o.p. (ISBN 0-684-13132-3, ScribT). Scribner.
Last Raider. Douglas Reeman. pap. 2.25 (ISBN 0-515-05730-4). Jove Pubns.
Last Reformation. F. G. Smith. 256p. 5.00; pap. 3.50. Faith Pub Hse.
Last Resting Places, Being a Compendium of Fact Pertaining to the Mortal Remains of the Famous & Infamous. Ed. by E. H. Breisacher. LC 79-52704. (Illus.). 320p. 1981. 16.95 (ISBN 0-87850-032-4). Darwin Pr.
Last Reveille. David Morrell. 1978. pap. 1.95 o.p. (ISBN 0-449-23527-0, Crest). Fawcett.
Last Rights. H. H. Dooley. 224p. 1981. pap. 2.50 (ISBN 0-449-24392-3, Crest). Fawcett.
Last Rites. W. M. Ransom. 1978. 2.50 (ISBN 0-918116-13-9). Jawbone Pr.
Last Rodeo. Ernest Haycox. 165p. 1975. Repr. of 1956 ed. lib. bdg. 9.95 o.p. (ISBN 0-89190-976-1). Am Repr-Rivercity Pr.
Last Romantic. Dorothea Buske. LC 78-3966. 1979. 8.95 (ISBN 0-312-47135-1). St Martin.
Last Romantics. Graham Hough. 284p. 1961. pap. 5.75x (ISBN 0-686-63944-8). B&N.
Last Season of Weeb Ewbank. Paul Zimmerman. 1974. 10.00 o.p. (ISBN 0-374-18462-3). FS&G.
Last Shepherds. David Outerbridge & Julie Thayer. (Illus.). 1979. 15.95 o.p. (ISBN 0-670-41891-9, Studio). Viking Pr.
Last Shot. W. R. Raine. 1976. Repr. of 1926 ed. lib. bdg. 9.60 (ISBN 0-88411-553-4). Amereon Ltd.
Last Showdown. Max Brand. 192p. 1975. 5.95 o.p. (ISBN 0-396-07082-5). Dodd.
Last Special Issue: The Smith Special Issue 30. pap. 2.00 o.p. (ISBN 0-685-78401-0). The Smith.
Last Stage from Opal. Kelly P. Gast. LC 77-26525. 1978. 7.95 o.p. (ISBN 0-385-13473-8). Doubleday.
Last Stage to Gomorrah. Barry Cord. 1979. pap. 1.25 (ISBN 0-505-51339-0). Tower Bks.
Last Stage West. Frank Bonham. 1979. pap. 1.75 o.p. (ISBN 0-425-03884-X). Berkley Pub.
Last Stand at Papago Wells. Louis L'Amour. (Western Fiction Ser.). 1981. lib. bdg. 10.95 (ISBN 0-8398-2694-X). Gregg.
Last Stand at Saber River. Elmore Leonard. 176p. 1980. pap. 1.75 (ISBN 0-553-13696-8). Bantam.
Last Step: The American Ascent of K2. Rick Ridgeway. LC 80-19395. (Illus.). 400p. 1980. 25.00 (ISBN 0-89886-007-5). Mountaineers.
Last Supper & Lord's Supper. I. Howard Marshall. (Orig.). 1981. pap. price not set (ISBN 0-8028-1854-4). Eerdmans.
Last Surrender. new ed. Sallie L. Bell. 192p. (Orig.). 1974. pap. 2.25 (ISBN 0-310-21002-X). Zondervan.
Last Survival Manual: A Citizen's Guide to Nuclear Survival. Ray Allen & Geral Thackery. (Illus.). 288p. 1980. 24.95 (ISBN 0-937616-00-1). Am Res Pr.
Last Taboo--Sex & the Fear of Death. James L. Brain. LC 78-20060. (Illus.). 1979. 9.95 (ISBN 0-385-14581-0, Anchor Pr). Doubleday.
Last Things Now. David L. Edwards. LC 76-121056. (Orig.). 1970. pap. 1.95 o.p. (ISBN 0-8170-0493-9). Judson.
Last Titan, Percival Farquhar: American Entrepreneur in Latin America. Charles A. Gauld. 446p. 1972. 5.50 o.p. (ISBN 0-912098-04-X). Cal Inst Intl St.
Last Train from Canton. James L. Johnson. (Sebastian Suspense Ser.). 288p. (Orig.). 1981. pap. 6.95 (ISBN 0-310-26631-9). Zondervan.
Last Tribal War: A History of the Bondelswart Uprising Which Took Place in Southwest Africa in 1922. Richard Freislich. 117p. 1964. 19.50x (ISBN 0-686-28314-7, F Cass Co). Biblio Dist.
Last Trump. John Gardner. LC 80-16560. 256p. 1981. 11.95 (ISBN 0-07-022852-3, GB). McGraw.
Last Tudor King. Hester W. Chapman. (Illus.). 1959. 9.95 (ISBN 0-02-523790-X). Macmillan.
Last Twelve Verses of Mark. W. R. Farmer. LC 73-89003. (Society for New Testament Studies: Monograph Ser. No. Twenty-Five). 128p. 1974. 21.95 (ISBN 0-521-20414-3). Cambridge U Pr.
Last Two Elves in Denmark. Mary Calhoun. LC 68-11572. (Illus.). (gr. k-3). 1968. 5.75 o.p. (ISBN 0-688-21468-1); PLB 5.52 (ISBN 0-688-31468-6). Morrow.
Last Tycoon. F. Scott Fitzgerald. 1941. lib. rep. ed. 12.50 (ISBN 0-684-15311-4, ScribT); pap. 3.95 (ISBN 0-684-71764-6, SL242, ScribT). Scribner.
Last Unicorn. Peter Beagle. 1976. pap. 2.25 (ISBN 0-345-27505-5). Ballantine.
Last Valley. A. B. Guthrie, Jr. LC 75-17598. 304p. 1975. 8.95 o.s.i. (ISBN 0-395-21899-3). HM.
Last Voyage of Captain James Cook. Richard Hough. LC 79-63210. (Illus.). 1979. 10.95 (ISBN 0-688-03413-6). Morrow.
Last War Trail: The Utes & the Settlement of Colorado. Robert Emmitt. (Civilization of the American Indian Ser.: Vol. 40). (Illus.). 352p. 1954. 14.95 (ISBN 0-685-25209-4); pap. 5.95 (ISBN 0-8061-1043-0). U of Okla Pr.
Last Was Lloyd. Doris B. Smith. 144p. (gr. 3-7). 1981. 8.95 (ISBN 0-670-41921-4). Viking Pr.
Last White Class: A Play About Neighborhood Terror. Marge Piercy & Ira Wood. LC 79-18884. 160p. 1979. 10.95 (ISBN 0-89594-028-0); pap. 4.95 (ISBN 0-89594-027-2). Crossing Pr.
Last Wilderness. Murray Morgan. LC 76-41. 290p. 1976. pap. 5.95 (ISBN 0-295-95319-5). U of Wash Pr.
Last Word. Jamie Buckingham. 1978. pap. 3.95 (ISBN 0-88270-404-4). Logos.
Last Word: Exploring Careers in Contemporary Communication. Members & Friends of the Fashion Group Inc. Ed. by Regina Ovesy. 128p. (gr. 7-12). 1980. lib. bdg. 5.97 (ISBN 0-8239-0526-8). Rosen Pr.
Last Word in Make-up: A Practical Illustrated Handbook. rev. ed. Rudolph Liszt. (Illus.). 1980. 6.00 (ISBN 0-686-68849-X). Dramatists Play.
Last Word: Portraits of Fourteen Master Aphorists. Louis Kronenberger. LC 75-186440. 252p. 1972. 7.95 o.s.i. (ISBN 0-02-567100-6). Macmillan.
Last Words of Dutch Schultz. William S. Burroughs. LC 80-54557. (Illus.). 128p. 1981. pap. 4.95 (ISBN 0-394-17852-1). Seaver Bks.
Last Words of Dutch Schultz. William S. Burroughs. 128p. 1981. pap. 4.95 (ISBN 0-394-17852-1). Seaver Bks.
Last Words of Saints & Sinners. Herbert Lockyer. LC 78-85429. 1975. pap. 4.50 (ISBN 0-8254-3111-5). Kregel.
Last Words on Evolution. Ernst Haeckel. Tr. by Joseph McCabe from Ger. Bd. with Contributions to the Study of the Behavior of Lower Organisms. H. S. Jennings; Essay. Herbert Spencer. (Contributions to the History of Psychology Ser.: No. 3, Pt. D). 1978. Repr. of 1906 ed. 30.00 (ISBN 0-89093-172-0). U Pubns Amer.
Last Words (Real & Traditional) of Distinguished Men & Women. Frederic R. Marvin. LC 72-140424. 1971. Repr. of 1910 ed. 18.00 (ISBN 0-8103-3187-X). Gale.
Last World War & the End of Time. Emmett Culligan. (Illus.). 1975. pap. 4.50 o.p. (ISBN 0-89555-034-2, 301). TAN Bks Pubs.
Last Years of British Railways Steam: Reflections Ten Years After. O. S. Nock. 1978. 14.95 (ISBN 0-7153-7583-0). David & Charles.
Last Years of the English Slave Trade. Averil Mackenzie-Grieve. LC 68-21439. (Illus.). Repr. of 1941 ed. 25.00 (ISBN 0-678-05070-8). Kelley.
Lastborn of Elvinwood. Linda Haldeman. 1980. pap. 2.25 (ISBN 0-380-47985-0, 47985). Avon.
Lasting Honour: The Fall of Hong Kong Nineteen Forty-One. Oliver Lindsay. (Illus.). Date not set. cancelled (ISBN 0-241-89946-X). Hippocrene Bks.
Lasting Love. Antonia Blake. (Orig.). 1981. pap. 1.50 (ISBN 0-440-14968-1). Dell.
Lasting Relationships: How to Recognize the Man or Woman Who's Right for You. Myron Brenton. 224p. 1981. 10.95 (ISBN 0-89479-078-1). A & W Pubs.
Late Antique, Early Christian & Mediaeval Art: Selected Papers. Meyer Schapiro. Date not set. 25.00 (ISBN 0-686-68085-5). Braziller.
Late Antique-Early Christian Painting. Kurt Weitzmann. LC 76-16444. (Magnificent Paperback Art Ser.). 128p. 1977. 19.95 (ISBN 0-8076-0830-0); pap. 9.95 (ISBN 0-8076-0831-9). Braziller.
Late Baroque & Rococo Architecture. Christian Norberg-Schulz. LC 73-980. (History of World Architecture Ser.). (Illus.). 400p. 1975. 45.00 (ISBN 0-8109-1012-8). Abrams.
Late Baroque Churches of Venice. Douglas Lewis. LC 78-94704. (Outstanding Dissertations in the Fine Arts Ser.). 1979. lib. bdg. 52.00 (ISBN 0-8240-3236-5). Garland Pub.
Late Biblical Hebrew: Toward an Historical Typology of Biblical Hebrew Prose. Robert Polzin. LC 76-3559. (Harvard Semitic Monographs). (Illus.). 1976. 7.50 (ISBN 0-89130-101-1, 040012). Scholars Pr Ca.
Late Biological Effects of Ionizing Radiation, Vol. 1. 1979. pap. 51.50 (ISBN 0-685-94884-6, ISP489-1, IAEA). Unipub.
Late Biological Effects of Ionizing Radiation, Vol. 2. 1979. pap. 53.50 (ISBN 92-0-010778-8, ISP489-2, IAEA). Unipub.

Late Bloomer. David A. Kaufelt. pap. 2.50 (ISBN 0-440-15320-4). Dell.

Late Bloomer: Profiles of Women Who Found Their True Callings. Lois Rich-McCoy. LC 79-1679. (Illus.). 224p. 1980. 10.95 (ISBN 0-06-013593-X, HarpT). Har-Row.

Late Cuckoo. Louis Slobodkin. LC 62-19106. (Illus.). (ps-3). 5.95 (ISBN 0-8149-0400-9). Vanguard.

Late Effects of Head Injury. A. Earl Walker et al. 580p. 1969. pap. 31.50 spiral (ISBN 0-398-02005-1). C C Thomas.

Late Formative Irrigation Settlement Below Monte Alban: Survey & Excavation on the Xoxocotlan Piedmont, Oaxaca, Mexico. Michael J. O'Brien & Roger D. Mason. (Institute of Latin American Studies Special Publications). (Illus.). 266p. 1980. pap. 16.95x (ISBN 0-292-74628-8). U of Tex Pr.

Late Great Creature. Brock Brower. 288p. 1974. pap. 1.25 o.p. (ISBN 0-445-00187-9). Popular Lib.

Late Great Planet Earth. Hal Lindsey. 1976. pap. 2.50 mass market (ISBN 0-310-27772-8); pap. 4.95 (ISBN 0-310-27771-X); study guide 0.75 (ISBN 0-310-27773-6). Zondervan.

Late Great Planet Earth. Hal Lindsey & C. C. Carlson. 176p. 1980. pap. 2.50. Zondervan.

Late Great Planet Earth. Hal Lindsey & C. C. Carlson. 192p. 1980. pap. 2.50 (ISBN 0-553-14096-5). Bantam.

Late Harvest: Essays & Addresses in American Literature & Culture. Robert E. Spiller. LC 80-543. (Contributions to American Studies: No. 49). xi, 280p. 1981. lib. bdg. 25.00 (ISBN 0-313-22023-9, SLH/). Greenwood.

Late Israelite Prophecy. David L. Petersen. LC 76-26014. (Society of Biblical Literature. Monograph: Vol. 23). 1977. 9.00 (ISBN 0-89130-076-7, 060023); pap. 7.50 (ISBN 0-89130-146-1). Scholars Pr Ca.

Late Lancashire Witches. Thomas Heywood. Ed. by Laird H. Barber & Stephen Orgel. LC 78-66751. (Renaissance Drama Ser.). 1979. 41.00 (ISBN 0-8240-9752-1). Garland Pub.

Late Life: Communities & Environmental Policy. Jaber F. Gubrium. (Illus.). 304p. 1975. 19.75 (ISBN 0-398-03249-1); pap. 15.25 (ISBN 0-398-03248-3). C C Thomas.

Late Lord Byron. Doris L. Moore. LC 76-22934. (Illus.). 1977. Repr. of 1961 ed. 25.00 o.p. (ISBN 0-06-013013-X, HarpT). Har-Row.

Late-Medieval England, 1377-1485. J. Guth de Lloyd. LC 75-23845. (Conference on British Studies Bibliographical Handbooks Ser.). 164p. 1976. 17.95 (ISBN 0-521-20877-7). Cambridge U Pr.

Late Medieval Mysticism. Ed. by Ray C. Petry. (Library of Christian Classics Ichthus Edition). 1980. pap. 9.95 (ISBN 0-664-24163-8). Westminster.

Late Minoan I Destruction of Crete: Metal Groups & Stratigraphic Considerations. Hara Georgiou. (Monograph: IX). (Orig.). 1979. pap. text ed. 5.00 (ISBN 0-917956-06-0). UCLA Arch.

Late Modern: The Visual Arts Since 1945. Edward Lucie-Smith. (World of Art Ser.). (Illus.). 1975. pap. 9.95 (ISBN 0-19-519938-3). Oxford U Pr.

Late Nineteenth-Century American Liberalism: Representative Selections, 1880-1900. Ed. & intro. by Louis Filler. LC 61-18060. 250p. 1980. Repr. of 1962 ed. text ed. 21.50x o.p. (ISBN 0-8290-0180-8). Irvington.

Late Paleocene Mammals from the Cypress Hills, Alberta. Leonard Krishtalka. (Special Publications: No. 2). (Illus., Orig.). 1973. pap. 4.00 (ISBN 0-89672-027-6). Tex Tech Pr.

Late Phoenix. Catherine Aird. 176p. 1981. pap. 2.25 (ISBN 0-553-14517-7). Bantam.

Late Poems of Eliot Pound, Stevens & Williams. Kathleen Woodward. 193p. 1980. 14.50 (ISBN 0-8142-0306-X). Ohio St U Pr.

Late Precambrian Microfossils from the Visingso Beds in Southern Sweden. Gonzalo Vidal. (Fossils & Strata: No.9). 1976. pap. text ed. 18.00x (ISBN 8-200-09418-9, Dist. by Columbia U Pr). Universitet.

Late Roman Empire. Glanville Downey. LC 76-15145. (Berkshire Studies). 158p. 1976. pap. 5.50 (ISBN 0-88275-441-6). Krieger.

Late Seventeenth Century Scientists. Ed. by D. Hutchings. 1969. 19.50 (ISBN 0-08-013359-2); pap. 10.50 (ISBN 0-08-013358-4). Pergamon.

Late Winter Child. Vincent Buckley. (Orig.). 1980. pap. text ed. 6.50x (ISBN 0-85105-358-0, Dolmen Pr). Humanities.

Latency. Charles Sarnoff. LC 75-42548. 400p. 1981. Repr. of 1976 ed. 25.00 (ISBN 0-686-69588-7). Aronson.

Lateness. David Shapiro. LC 76-47073. 1980. pap. 5.95 (ISBN 0-87951-111-7). Overlook Pr.

Lateness: A Book of Poems. David Shapiro. LC 76-47073. 96p. 1978. 10.00 (ISBN 0-87951-058-7). Overlook Pr.

Later Auden: From "New Year Letter" to About the House. George W. Bahlke. LC 74-98179. 1970. 14.50 (ISBN 0-8135-0626-3). Rutgers U Pr.

Later Childhood & Adolescence: Parenthood in a Free Nation, Vol. 3. Ethel Kawin. (Illus.). 1969. pap. 3.00 (ISBN 0-931682-07-X). Purdue Univ Bks.

Later Chinese Porcelain. 4th ed. Soame Jenyns. (Illus.). 1971. 43.00 (ISBN 0-571-04761-0, Pub. by Faber & Faber). Merrimack Bk Serv.

Later Correspondence of George Third, 5 vols. George Third. Ed. by A. Aspinall. Incl. Vol. 1. 1783-1793 (ISBN 0-521-04066-3); Vol. 2. 1793-1797 (ISBN 0-521-04067-1); Vol. 3. 1798-1801 (ISBN 0-521-04068-X); Vol. 4. 1802-1807 (ISBN 0-521-06918-1); Vol. 5. 1807-1810, with Index to Vols. 1-5 (ISBN 0-521-07451-7). LC 61-52516. 700p. 120.00 ea. Cambridge U Pr.

Later English Broadside Ballads, Vol. 2. John Holloway & Joan Black. (Illus.). 1979. 40.00x (ISBN 0-7100-0282-3). Routledge & Kegan.

Later Ghaznavids: Splendor & Decay. Clifford E. Bosworth. LC 77-7879. 1977. text ed. 17.50x (ISBN 0-231-04428-3). Columbia U Pr.

Later History & Poetry. rev. ed. Harold S. Bender & Paul Erb. (Bible Survey Course No. 2). 1956. pap. 1.00 o.p. (ISBN 0-8361-1317-9). Herald Pr.

Later Islamic Pottery. 2nd ed. Arthur Lane. 1971. 24.95 o.p. (ISBN 0-571-04736-X, Pub. by Faber & Faber). Merrimack Bk Serv.

Later Life. Lewis R. Aiken. LC 77-11326. (Illus.). 1978. pap. text ed. 8.95 o.p. (ISBN 0-7216-1070-6). Saunders.

Later Medieval English Prose. Ed. by William Matthews. LC 63-9439. (Goldentree Books in English Literature). (Orig.). 1963. pap. text ed. 8.95x (ISBN 0-89197-270-6). Irvington.

Later Medieval Numismatics (11th-16th Centuries) Philip Grierson. 1980. 60.00x (ISBN 0-86078-043-0, Pub. by Variorum England). State Mutual Bk.

Later Middle Ages in England: 1216-1485. Bertie Wilkinson. LC 73-78343. (History of England Ser.). 1977. pap. text ed. 11.50x (ISBN 0-582-48032-9). Longman.

Later Parliaments of Henry VIII, 1536-1547. S. E. Lehmberg. LC 76-7804. 1977. 49.95 (ISBN 0-521-21256-1). Cambridge U Pr.

Later Poems of Rabindranath Tagore. Rabindranath Tagore. Tr. by Aurobindo Bose from Bengali. LC 75-34824. (Funk & W Bk.). 142p. 1976. 7.95 o.s.i. (ISBN 0-308-10239-8, TYC-T); pap. 3.95 (ISBN 0-308-10245-2, TYC-T). T Y Crowell.

Later Prehistory of Tangier, Morocco. Antonio Gilman. LC 75-20595. (American School of Prehistoric Research Bulletins Ser.: No. 29). (Illus.). 1976. pap. 17.00 (ISBN 0-87365-531-1). Peabody Harvard.

Later Renaissance in England: Nondramatic Verse & Prose, 1600-1660. Ed. by Herschel Baker. 1975. text ed. 21.50 (ISBN 0-395-16038-3). HM.

Later Roman Empire, Two Eighty-Four to Six Hundred Two: A Social, Economic, & Administrative Survey, 2 Vols. Arnold H. Jones. (Illus.). 1966. Repr. of 1964 ed. Set. 49.50 (ISBN 0-8061-0624-7). U of Okla Pr.

Later Shakespeare. Ed. by John R. Brown & Bernard Harris. (Stratford-Upon-Avon Studies: No. 8). 264p. 1966. pap. text ed. 9.95x (ISBN 0-8419-5815-7). Holmes & Meier.

Later Than We Thought: A Portrait of the Thirties. Rene Cutforth. LC 76-46679. 1977. 12.50x (ISBN 0-8448-1041-X). Crane-Russak Co.

Later Works of John Dewey, Nineteen Twenty-Five to Nineteen Fifty-Three: Volume 1, Nineteen Twenty-Five. John Dewey. Ed. by Jo Ann Boydston et al. 1981. price not set (ISBN 0-8093-0986-6). S Ill U Pr.

Later Years: 1938-1963. L. Thompson. Ed. by Robert Frost. pap. 17.95 o.p. (ISBN 0-686-67508-8). HR&W.

Lateral Awareness & Directionality Test. August Mauser & Joseph Lockavitch. 64p. 1980. pap. text ed. 7.50 manual (ISBN 0-87879-250-3). Acad Therapy.

Lateral Stresses in the Ground & Design of Earth Retaining Structures. Compiled by American Society of Civil Engineers. 336p. 1970. pap. text ed. 8.50 (ISBN 0-87262-023-9). Am Soc Civil Eng.

Lateral Thinking. E. De Bono. pap. 4.95 (ISBN 0-06-090325-2, CN325, CN). Har-Row.

Lateralisation of Language in the Child: Proceedings. International Symposium Held at St. Ode, Belgium, Oct. 1-3, 1979. Ed. by Yvan Lebrun & O. Zangwill. 1981. text ed. write for info. (ISBN 90-265-0337-7, Pub. by Swets Pub Serv Holland). Swets North Am.

Latest Rage the Big Drum: Dada & Surrealist Performance. Annabelle Melzer. (Studies in Fine Arts: The Avant-Garde, No. 7). 1980. 27.95 (ISBN 0-8357-1081-5). Univ Microfilms.

Latest Word on the Last Days. C. S. Lovett. (Illus., Orig.). 1980. pap. 5.95 (ISBN 0-938148-00-1). Personal Christianity.

Lathe of Heaven. Ursula LeGuin. 1973. pap. 1.95 (ISBN 0-380-01320-7, 43547). Avon.

Latin America. 4th ed. John F. Bannon & Robert R. Miller. 1977. text ed. 14.95 (ISBN 0-02-474350-X). Macmillan.

Latin America. 4th ed. H. Robinson. (Illus.). 544p. 1977. pap. text ed. 17.95x (Pub. by Macdonald & Evans England). Intl Ideas.

Latin America. Sam Summerlin. LC 72-4254. (Associated Press Bks). (Illus.). 192p. (gr. 7-12). 1972. PLB 5.95 o.p. (ISBN 0-531-02576-4). Watts.

Latin America, Vol. 7. 1979. lib. bdg. 17.50 o.p. (ISBN 0-87196-258-6). Facts on File.

Latin America: A Concise Interpretive History. 2nd ed. E. Bradford Burns. LC 76-21677. (Illus.). 1977. pap. text ed. 11.95 (ISBN 0-13-524314-9). P-H.

Latin America: A Guide to Economic History 1830-1930. Ed. by Roberto Cortes Conde & Stanley J. Stein. LC 74-30534. 1977. 46.50x (ISBN 0-520-02956-9). U of Cal Pr.

Latin America: A Regional Geography. 3rd ed. G. J. Butland. LC 72-5748. 1972. pap. 12.95 o.p. (ISBN 0-470-12658-2). Halsted Pr.

Latin America: A Sociocultural Interpretation. rev. ed. Julius Rivera. LC 77-27271. 268p. 1980. text ed. 18.95x (ISBN 0-8290-0129-8); pap. text ed. 8.95x (ISBN 0-8290-0444-0). Irvington.

Latin America & British Trade: 1806-1914. D. C. Platt. (Merchant Adventurers). (Illus.). 1972. text ed. 11.25x (ISBN 0-7136-1309-2). Humanities.

Latin America & the Law of the Sea, Release 1. A. Szekely. 1980. 32.50 (ISBN 0-379-10180-7). Oceana.

Latin America & the New International Economic Order. Ed. by Jorge Lozoya & Jaime Estevez. LC 79-27384. (Pergamon Policy Studies in the New International Economic Order). 112p. 1980. 16.50 (ISBN 0-08-025118-8). Pergamon.

Latin America & World Economy: A Changing International Order. Ed. by Joseph Grunwald. LC 77-17031. (Latin American International Affairs Ser.: Vol. 2). 1978. 20.00x (ISBN 0-8039-0864-4); pap. 9.95x (ISBN 0-8039-0966-7). Sage.

Latin America Annual Review. rev. ed. Ed. by Eduardo Crawley. (Annual Review Ser.). (Illus.). 1981. pap. 24.95 (ISBN 0-528-84518-7). Rand.

Latin America Annual Review. 1979. pap. 14.95 o.p. (ISBN 0-528-84207-2). Rand.

Latin America Business Travel Guide. Paddington Press. 448p. 1981. 19.95 (ISBN 0-87196-339-6); pap. 11.95 (ISBN 0-87196-345-0). Facts on File.

Latin America Comes of Age. Thomas J. Knight. LC 79-18702. 335p. 1979. 19.00 (ISBN 0-8108-1243-6). Scarecrow.

Latin America Fourteen Ninety-Two to Nineteen Forty-Two: A Guide to Historical & Cultural Development Before World War Two. A. Curtis Wilgus. 1973. Repr. of 1941 ed. 27.50 (ISBN 0-8108-0595-2). Scarecrow.

Latin America in Its Architecture. Ed. by Roberto Segre & Fernando K. Katz. Tr. by Edith Grossman from Span. LC 79-27695. (Latin America in Its Culture). Orig. Title: America Latina En Su Cultura. 300p. 1980. text ed. 25.00x (ISBN 0-8419-0532-0). Holmes & Meier.

Latin America in Its Literature. Ed. by Cesar F. Moreno & Ivan A. Schulman. Tr. by Mary G. Berg from Span. LC 79-26626. (Latin America in Its Culture). Orig. Title: America Latina En Su Cultura. 350p. 1980. text ed. 44.50x (ISBN 0-8419-0530-4). Holmes & Meier.

Latin America in the International Economy: Proceedings of a Conference Held by the International Economic Association at Mexico City. Ed. by V. L. Urguidi & R. Thorp. LC 72-13779. 1973. 26.50 o.p. (ISBN 0-470-89646-9). Halsted Pr.

Latin America in the International Political System. G. Pope Atkins. LC 76-20882. (Illus.). 1977. text ed. 16.95 (ISBN 0-02-901060-8). Free Pr.

Latin America in the Post-Import Substitution Era. Werner Baer & Larry Samuelson. 1977. pap. text ed. 21.00 (ISBN 0-08-021822-9). Pergamon.

Latin America in the United Nations. John A. Houston. LC 78-2805. (Carnegie Endowment for International Peace, United Nations Studies: No. 8). 1978. Repr. of 1956 ed. lib. bdg. 27.00x (ISBN 0-313-20335-0, HOLU). Greenwood.

Latin America in the Year Two-Thousand. Ed. by Joseph S. Tulchin. LC 74-19702. 408p. 1975. text ed. 14.95 (ISBN 0-201-07603-9). A-W.

Latin America: Its Peoples & Institutions. 2nd ed. Joseph A. Ellis. 1975. pap. text ed. 8.25x (ISBN 0-02-474200-7, 47420). Macmillan.

Latin America Nineteen Sixty-Seven to Nineteen Seventy-Eight: A Comprehensive Social Science Bibliography & Research Guide. Robert L. Delorme. 288p. 1981. text ed. 26.50 (ISBN 0-87436-292-X). ABC-Clio.

Latin America, Spain & Portugal: A Selected & Annotated Bibliographical Guide to Books Published 1954-1974. A. Curtis Wilgus. LC 76-58355. 1977. 40.00 (ISBN 0-8108-1018-2). Scarecrow.

Latin America: Struggle for Progress, Vol. 14. James D. Theberge et al. LC 75-44723. (Critical Choices for Americans Ser.). 1976. 16.95 (ISBN 0-669-00428-6). Lexington Bks.

Latin America: The Development of Its Civilization. 3rd ed. Helen M. Bailey & Abraham P. Nasatir. (Illus.). 896p. 1973. ref. ed. 20.95x (ISBN 0-13-524264-9). P-H.

Latin America: The Hegemonic Crisis & the Military Coup. Jose Nun. (Politics of Modernization Ser.: No. 7). 1969. pap. 2.00x o.p. (ISBN 0-87725-207-6). U of Cal Intl St.

Latin America: The Politics of Immobility. R. Adie & G. Poitras. 1974. pap. 10.50 (ISBN 0-13-524272-X). P-H.

Latin America, the United States, & the Inter-American System. John D. Martz & Lars Schoultz. (Westview Special Studies on Latin America & the Caribbean). 272p. 1980. lib. bdg. 26.00x (ISBN 0-89158-874-4). Westview.

Latin American Agriculture: A Bibliography. Martin H. Sable. LC 70-628991. (Center Special Study Ser.: No. 1). 1970. pap. 6.00 (ISBN 0-930450-02-7). Univ of Wis Latin Am.

Latin American & Cholesterol Conscious Cooking. Vilma J. Grace. (Illus.). 1979. pap. 5.95 (ISBN 0-87491-280-6). Acropolis.

Latin American Books: An Annotated Bibliography. Karna S. Wilgus. 80p. 1974. pap. 3.00 o.p. (ISBN 0-913456-84-5, Pub. by Ctr Inter-Am Rel). Interbk Inc.

Latin American Christian Democratic Parties. Edward J. Williams. LC 67-13159. 1967. 15.00x (ISBN 0-87049-073-7). U of Tenn Pr.

Latin American Civilization, 2 vols. 3rd ed. Ed. by Benjamin Keen. 1974. Vol. 1. pap. text ed. 11.50 (ISBN 0-395-17582-8); Vol. 2. pap. text ed. 11.50 (ISBN 0-395-17583-6). HM.

Latin American Cooking. Jonathan N. Leonard. LC 68-58451. (Foods of the World Ser). (Illus.). (gr. 6 up). 1968. PLB 14.94 (ISBN 0-8094-0063-4, Pub. by Time-Life). Silver.

Latin American Cooking. Jonathan N. Leonard. (Foods of the World Ser). (Illus.). 1968. 14.95 (ISBN 0-8094-0036-7). Time-Life.

Latin American Economic Integration & United States Policy. Joseph Grunwald et al. 1972. 10.95 (ISBN 0-8157-3300-3). Brookings.

Latin American Foreign Policies: An Analysis. Harold Eugene Davis et al. LC 74-24386. (Illus.). 488p. 1975. 25.00x o.p. (ISBN 0-8018-1694-7); pap. 5.95x (ISBN 0-8018-1695-5). Johns Hopkins.

Latin American Inflation. Susan Wachter. LC 75-3829. 1976. 17.95 (ISBN 0-669-99622-X). Lexington Bks.

Latin American Media: Guidance & Censorship. Marvin Alisky. 1981. 16.50 (ISBN 0-8138-1525-8). Iowa St U Pr.

Latin-American Mind. Leopoldo Zea. Tr. by James H. Abbott & Lowell Dunham. (Illus.). 1970. 14.95x o.p. (ISBN 0-8061-0563-1); pap. 6.95x o.p. (ISBN 0-8061-1278-6). U of Okla Pr.

Latin American Poetry. G. Brotherston. LC 75-2734. (Illus.). 256p. 1975. 36.00 (ISBN 0-521-20763-0); pap. 9.95x (ISBN 0-521-09944-7). Cambridge U Pr.

Latin American Policy of the U. S. Samuel F. Bemis. (Illus.). 1967. pap. 3.45 o.p. (ISBN 0-393-00412-0, Norton Lib). Norton.

Latin American Political Dictionary. Ernest E. Rossi & Jack C. Plano. 263p. 1980. 25.25 (ISBN 0-87436-302-0). ABC Clio.

Latin American Populism in Comparative Perspective. Ed. by Michael Conniff. (Illus.). 272p. 1981. 19.95 (ISBN 0-8263-0580-6); pap. 9.95 (ISBN 0-8263-0581-4). U of NM Pr.

Latin American Studies in the Non-Western World & Eastern Europe: A Bibliography on Latin America in the Languages of Africa, Asia, the Middle East, & Eastern Europe. Martin H. Sable. LC 73-13114. 1970. 21.00 (ISBN 0-8108-0344-5). Scarecrow.

Latin American Thought: A Historical Introduction. Harold E. Davis. LC 78-181564. 1974. pap. text ed. 5.95 (ISBN 0-02-907160-7). Free Pr.

Latin American Tradition: Essays on the Unity & the Diversity of Latin American Culture. Charles Wagley. LC 67-30968. 1968. 17.50x (ISBN 0-231-03006-1); pap. 6.00x (ISBN 0-231-08333-5). Columbia U Pr.

Latin American Urban Policies & the Social Sciences. Ed. by John Miller & Ralph A. Gakenheimer. LC 70-103481. 1971. 20.00x o.p. (ISBN 0-8039-0056-2). Sage.

Latin American Urban Research, Vol. 1. Ed. by Francine J. Rabinovitz & Felicity M. Trueblood. LC 78-103483. 1971. 20.00x (ISBN 0-8039-0062-7); pap. 9.95x (ISBN 0-8039-0619-6). Sage.

Latin American Urbanization. Douglas Butterworth & John K. Chance. LC 80-18486. (Urbanization in Developing Countries Ser.). (Illus.). 320p. 1981. text ed. 29.95 (ISBN 0-521-23713-0); pap. text ed. 8.95 (ISBN 0-521-28175-X). Cambridge U Pr.

Latin: An Intensive Course. Floyd L Moreland & Rita M. Fleischer. LC 75-36500. (Campus Ser.: No. 186). (gr. 10 up). 1977. 12.95x (ISBN 0-520-03183-0). U of Cal Pr.

Latin & American Dances. Doris Lavelle. (gr. 7 up). 1979. text ed. 17.95x (ISBN 0-273-41640-5, LTB). Soccer.

Latin Church in the Crusader States: The Secular Church. Bernard Hamilton. 402p. 1980. 40.00x (ISBN 0-86078-072-4, Pub. by Variorum England). State Mutual Bk.

Latin Church Music in England, Fourteen Sixty to Fifteen Seventy-Five. Hugh Benham. (Music Reprint Ser.: 1980). (Illus.). 1980. Repr. of 1977 ed. lib. bdg. 22.50 (ISBN 0-306-76025-8). Da Capo.

Latin Concise Dictionary. Cassells. 1977. 8.95 (ISBN 0-02-052263-0). Macmillan.

Latin Correspondence by Alberice Gentili & John Rainolds on Academic Drama. Leon Markowicz. (Salzburgh Studies in English Literature: Elizabethan & Renaissance Studies: No. 68). 1977. pap. text ed. 25.00x (ISBN 0-391-01473-0). Humanities.

Latin Dictionary. A. Wilson. (Teach Yourself Ser.). 1974. pap. 2.95 o.p. (ISBN 0-679-10204-3). McKay.

Latin-English Dictionary. Cassells. 1977. standard 14.95 (ISBN 0-686-63973-1); index 16.95 (ISBN 0-02-052258-4). Macmillan.

Latin for Local History: An Introduction. 2nd ed. Eileen A. Gooder. (Illus.). 1978. pap. text ed. 11.95x (ISBN 0-582-48728-5). Longman.

Latin for the Grades, 3 Bks. Charles I. Freundlich. (gr. 4-6). 1970. Bk. 1. pap. text ed. 3.75 (ISBN 0-87720-562-0); Bk. 2. pap. text ed. 3.75 (ISBN 0-87720-564-7); Bk. 3. pap. text ed. 3.75 (ISBN 0-87720-566-3). AMSCO Sch.

Latin Grammar: Grammar Vocabularies & Exercises in Preparation for the Reading of the Missal & Breviary. Cora C. Scanlon & Charles L. Scanlon. Ed. by Newton Thompson. LC 79-112494. 1976. pap. text ed. 6.00 (ISBN 0-89555-002-4, 168). TAN Bks Pubs.

Latin Hexametre Verse. Samuel E. Winbolt. Ed. by Steele Commager. LC 77-70818. (Latin Poetry Ser.). 1978. lib. bdg. 27.50 (ISBN 0-8240-2982-8). Garland Pub.

Latin Historians. Ed. by T. A. Dorey. (Studies in Latin Literature). 1966. 19.50x (ISBN 0-7100-1293-4). Routledge & Kegan.

Latin Image in American Film. Allen L. Woll. LC 77-620044. (Latin American Studies Ser: Vol. 39). 1978. pap. text ed. 4.75 o.p. (ISBN 0-87903-039-9). UCLA Lat Am Ctr.

Latin Image in American Film. rev. ed. Allen L. Woll. LC 80-620041. (Latin American Studies: Vol. 50). 1981. pap. price not set (ISBN 0-87903-050-X). UCLA Lat Am Ctr.

Latin-inus, -ina, -inus, & -ineus: From Proto-Indo-European to the Romance Languages. Jonathan L. Butler. (U. C. Publ. in Linguistics: Vol. 68). 1971. pap. 7.00x (ISBN 0-520-09360-7). U of Cal Pr.

Latin Is Alive & Well. B. C. Taylor. 1973. pap. text ed. 2.25x (ISBN 0-8077-8017-0). Tchrs Coll.

Latin Language. L. R. Palmer. (Great Languages Ser). 1961. text ed. 19.50x (ISBN 0-571-06813-8). Humanities.

Latin Legacy Versus Substratum Residue: The Unstressed Derivational Suffixes in the Romance Vernaculars of the Western Mediterranean. Jerry R. Craddock. (U. C. Publ. in Linguistics: Vol. 53). 1969. pap. 8.50x (ISBN 0-520-09248-1). U of Cal Pr.

Latin Love Poets from Catullus to Horace. R. O. Lyne. 320p. 1981. 37.50 (ISBN 0-19-814453-9); pap. 15.95 (ISBN 0-19-814454-7). Oxford U Pr.

Latin Made Simple. Rhoda A. Hendricks. LC 62-12101. pap. 3.50 (ISBN 0-385-01756-1, Made). Doubleday.

Latin Particle Quidem. Joseph B. Solodow. (American Philological Association, American Classical Studies). 1978. pap. 6.00 (ISBN 0-89130-252-2, 400404). Scholars Pr Ca.

Latin Poetry of English Poets. Ed. by J. W. Binns. 1974. 18.00x (ISBN 0-7100-7845-5). Routledge & Kegan.

Latin Poetry of George Herbert: A Bilingual Edition. Ed. by George Herbert. Tr. by Paul R. Murphy & Mark McCloskey. LC 64-22888. vii, 181p. 1965. 10.95x (ISBN 0-8214-0007-X). Ohio U Pr.

Latin Prose Composition. M. A. North & A. E. Hillard. 320p. (gr. 8-12). 1979. 20.00x (ISBN 0-7156-1321-9, Pub. by Duckworth England); pap. 10.95x (ISBN 0-7156-1322-7, Pub. by Duckworth England). Biblio Dist.

Latin Rhetorical Theory in Thirteenth & Fourteenth Century Castile. Charles Faulhaber. (U. C. Publ. in Modern Philology: Vol. 103). 1972. pap. 9.50x (ISBN 0-520-09403-4). U of Cal Pr.

Latin Tinge: The Impact of Latin American Music on the United States. John S. Roberts. LC 78-26534. (Illus.). 1979. 14.95 (ISBN 0-19-502564-4). Oxford U Pr.

Latin Word List. 1969. pap. 3.25 (ISBN 0-934338-20-5). NAIS.

Latin Word Lists. John K. Colby. 1978. pap. text ed. 1.50x (ISBN 0-88334-097-6). Ind Sch Pr.

Latin Works, 36 Vols. John Wycliffe. Ed. by Rudolf Buddensieg et al. Set. 1075.00 (ISBN 0-384-69800-X); 23.75 ea. Johnson Repr.

Latine Grammar of P. Ramus. Pierre De La Ramee. LC 78-26236. (English Experience Ser.: No. 289). 1971. Repr. of 1585 ed. 16.00 (ISBN 90-221-0289-0). Walter J Johnson.

Latino Language & Communicative Behavior, Vol. 6. Ed. by Richard P. Duran. 384p. 1981. 29.50 (ISBN 0-89391-038-4). Ablex Pub.

Latique Glass: The Complete Illustrated Catalogue for 1932. Rene Lalique. (Illus.). 160p. 1981. pap. price not set (ISBN 0-486-24122-X). Dover.

Latki & the Lightning Lizard. Betty Baker. LC 79-11197. (Illus.). (gr. 1-3). 1979. 8.95 (ISBN 0-02-708210-5). Macmillan.

Latrobe, Jefferson, & the National Capitol. Paul F. Norton. LC 76-23662. (Outstanding Dissertations in the Fine Arts Ser.). 1977. lib. bdg. 56.00x (ISBN 0-8240-2716-7). Garland Pub.

Latrogenic Diseases. 2nd ed. P. F. D'Arcy. (Illus.). 1980. text ed. 67.50x (ISBN 0-19-264179-4). Oxford U Pr.

Lattice Theory. T. Donnellan. LC 67-28661. 1968. 35.00 (ISBN 0-08-012563-8); pap. 9.75 (ISBN 0-08-012562-X). Pergamon.

Lattice Theory: First Concepts & Distributive Lattices. G. H. Gratzer. LC 75-151136. (Mathematics Ser). (Illus.). 1971. text ed. 25.95x (ISBN 0-7167-0442-0). W H Freeman.

Latvian Nation. Graham E. Smith. (Studies in Russian & East European History). (Illus.). 1981. 29.00x (ISBN 0-389-20025-5). B&N.

Laubmoose Fennoskansias. V. F. Brotherus. (Flora Fennica Ser.: Vol. 1). (Illus.). 635p. (Ger.). 1974. Repr. of 1923 ed. lib. bdg. 102.95x (ISBN 3-87429-078-6). Lubrecht & Cramer.

Laud Herbal Glossary. Ed. by J. Richard Stracke. LC 72-93569. 208p. (Orig.). 1976. pap. text ed. 34.25x (ISBN 90-6203-497-7). Humanities.

Lauda e i Primordi Della Melodia Italiana, 2 vols. Fernando Liuzzi. LC 80-2238. 1981. Repr. of 1935 ed. 185.00 (ISBN 0-404-19037-5). AMS Pr.

Lauds & Nightsounds. 2nd ed. Harvey Shapiro. LC 74-34539. 1978. 10.00 (ISBN 0-915342-07-3); pap. 4.00 (ISBN 0-915342-01-4). SUN.

Laugh & Learn Library, 4 bks. Richard Scarry. (Illus.). (ps-1). 1977. pap. 3.95 o.p. (ISBN 0-394-83336-8, BYR). Random.

Laugh, Clown, Cry: The Story of Charlie Chaplin. Walter Oleksy. LC 76-15001. (Focus Ser). (Illus.). (gr. 5 up). 1976. 6.60 o.p. (ISBN 0-8172-0427-X); PLB 6.60 o.p. (ISBN 0-8172-0426-1). Raintree Pubs.

Laugh It up. Marvin Townsend. Ed. by Patricia McCarthy. (Pal Paperbacks Ser., Kit A). (Illus., Orig.). (gr. 7-12). 1974. pap. text ed. 1.25 (ISBN 0-8374-3472-6). Xerox Ed Pubns.

Laugh with the Judge. Bruce Littlejohn. LC 74-22868. 1974. 6.95 o.p. (ISBN 0-87844-025-9). Sandlapper Store.

Laughable Limericks. Ed. by Sara Brewton & John E. Brewton. LC 65-16179. (Illus.). (gr. 2 up). 1965. 8.95 (ISBN 0-690-48667-7, TYC-J). T Y Crowell.

Laughable Loves. Milan Kundera. Tr. by Suzanne Rappaport from Czech. 266p. 1975. pap. 4.50 (ISBN 0-14-004044-7). Penguin.

Laughhter in the Court of Love: Comedy in Allegory, from Chaucer to Spencer. Frances M. Leonard. 192p. 1981. 18.95 (ISBN 0-937664-54-5). Pilgrim Bks OK.

Laughing All the Way. Barbara Howar. 1977. pap. 2.50 (ISBN 0-449-23145-3, Crest). Fawcett.

Laughing Cavalier. Emmuska Orczy. 1976. lib. bdg. 18.50x (ISBN 0-89968-076-3). Lightyear.

Laughing in the Hills. Bill Barich. 240p. 1981. pap. 3.95 (ISBN 0-14-005832-X). Penguin.

Laughing Orgasm & Other Perspectives for Erotic Love. Avodah Offit. LC 79-2589. 1980. cancelled o.p. (ISBN 0-397-01261-6). Lippincott.

Laughing Past History. Rhoda Gelfond. (Illus., Orig.). 1976. pap. 3.50 (ISBN 0-914278-09-6). Copper Beech.

Laughing Philosopher. Ed. by Alfred Crowquill. 329p. 1980. Repr. of 1899 ed. lib. bdg. 40.00 (ISBN 0-89760-123-8). Telegraph Bks.

Laughing Policeman. Maj Sjowall & Per Wahloo. 1977. pap. 1.65 (ISBN 0-394-72341-4, Vin). Random.

Laughing Time: Nonsense Poems. William J. Smith. LC 80-65839. (Illus.). 96p. (gr. 3 up). 1980. 9.95 (ISBN 0-440-05534-2). Delacorte.

Laughing Together: Giggles & Grins from Around the World. Compiled by Barbara K. Walker. LC 77-7789. (Illus., Paperback edition available only through the United Nations). (gr. 1 up). 1977. 8.95 (ISBN 0-590-07486-5, Four Winds). Schol Bk Serv.

Laughing Vaquero. William L. Hopson. 1978. pap. 1.25 (ISBN 0-505-51245-9). Tower Bks.

Laughing War. Martyn Burke. LC 77-16901. 312p. 1980. 10.95 (ISBN 0-385-13332-4). Doubleday.

Laughing Willows. Teresa Gerbers. (YA) 1977. 5.95 (ISBN 0-685-71793-3, Avalon). Bouregy.

Laughter & Despair: Readings in Ten Novels of the Victorian Era. U. C. Knoepflmacher. 1973. 17.50x (ISBN 0-520-01907-5); pap. 2.95x (ISBN 0-520-02352-8). U of Cal Pr.

Laughter & Tears of Children. Marilyn Bonham. 1967. 4.95 o.s.i. (ISBN 0-02-512890-6). Macmillan.

Laughter in the Background. N. B. Dorman. (gr. 9-12). 1980. 8.95 (ISBN 0-525-66714-8). Elsevier-Nelson.

Laughter on a Weekday. Louis Falstein. 1965. 8.95 (ISBN 0-8392-1147-3). Astor-Honor.

Launch. Edward Stewart. 1977. pap. 1.95 o.p. (ISBN 0-451-07743-1, J7743, Sig). NAL.

Launch: A Handbook of Classroom Ideas to Motivate the Teaching of Preschool & Kindergarten. (Spice Ser). 1972. 6.50 (ISBN 0-89273-111-7). Educ Serv.

Launch Duplicating Masters (Early Learning, 2 vols. (Spice Duplicating Masters Ser). (ps-k). 5.95 ea. Vol. 1 (ISBN 0-89273-512-0). Vol. 2 (ISBN 0-89273-513-9). Educ Serv.

Launching, Floating High & Landing--If Your Pilot Light Doesn't Go Out. Gary Paulsen. LC 78-26835. (Sports on the Light Side Ser.). (Illus.). (gr. 4-6). 1979. PLB 9.65 (ISBN 0-8172-0193-9). Raintree Pubs.

Launching of Sputnik, October 4, 1957. Gene Gurney & Clare Gurney. LC 75-5545. (World Focus Bks). 72p. (gr. 6-10). 1975. PLB 4.47 o.p. (ISBN 0-531-02175-0). Watts.

Launching Social Security: A Capture & Record Account, 1935-1937. Charles McKinley & Robert W. Frase. LC 70-121771. 1970. 35.00 (ISBN 0-299-05800-X). U of Wis Pr.

Launching Your Career. 1978. pap. 2.95 o.s.i. (ISBN 0-89584-016-2). Hippocrene Bks.

Laundry Worker. Jack Rudman. (Career Examination Ser.: C-435). (Cloth bdg. avail. on request). pap. 12.00 (ISBN 0-8373-0435-0). Natl Learning.

Laura. Vera Caspary. 224p. 1981. pap. 1.95 (ISBN 0-380-00043-1, 51565). Avon.

Laura Clay & the Woman's Rights Movement. Paul E. Fuller. LC 74-7875. (Illus.). 240p. 1975. 15.00x (ISBN 0-8131-1299-0). U Pr of Ky.

Laura Ingalls Wilder. Repr. 4.00 (ISBN 0-87675-102-8). Horn Bk.

Laura Riding's Pursuit of Truth. Joyce P. Wexler. LC 76-51688. xii, 169p. 1980. 14.00x (ISBN 0-8214-0364-8). Ohio U Pr.

Laura's Psalm. Gloria H. Hawley. 1981. pap. 4.95 (ISBN 0-86608-000-7, 14014P). Impact Tenn.

Laura's Story. Beatrice S. De Regniers. LC 78-12623. (Illus.). (ps-1). 1979. 8.95 (ISBN 0-689-30677-6). Atheneum.

Laurel & the Poppy. Margaret Gillett & Monika Kehoe. LC 66-10681. 1967. 7.95 (ISBN 0-8149-0106-9). Vanguard.

Laurel and Thorn: The Athlete in American Literature. Robert J. Higgs. LC 80-51014. 1981. price not set (ISBN 0-8131-1412-8). U Pr of Ky.

Lauren. Harriett Luger. (gr. 7-12). Date not set. pap. price not set (ISBN 0-440-94700-6, LE). Dell.

Lauren Bacall by Myself. Lauren Bacall. 1980. pap. 2.95 (ISBN 0-345-29216-2). Ballantine.

Laurence Olivier. Foster Hirsch. (Theatrical Arts Ser.). 1979. lib. bdg. 12.50 (ISBN 0-8057-9260-0). Twayne.

Laurence Stallings. Joan T. Brittain. LC 74-23831. (U. S. Authors Ser.: No. 250). 1975. lib. bdg. 10.95 (ISBN 0-8057-0686-0). Twayne.

Laurence Sterne & the Argument About Design. Mark Loveridge. 1981. 26.50x (ISBN 0-389-20106-5). B&N.

Lauren's Secret Ring. Monica DeBruyn. Ed. by Ann Fay. LC 79-27261. (Concept Bk.: Level 1). (Illus.). (gr. 1-3). 1980. 6.95g (ISBN 0-8075-4391-8). A Whitman.

Laurie Loves a Horse. LaVada Weir. LC 74-643. (Laurie Newman Adventures Ser). 32p. (gr. 7-9). 1974. 5.95 (ISBN 0-87191-352-6). Creative Ed.

Lauro Olmo: La Camisa. Ed. by A. K. Ariza & I. F. Ariza. 1968. 7.50 (ISBN 0-08-012616-2); pap. 3.50 (ISBN 0-08-012615-4). Pergamon.

Lausbubengeschichten. Thoma. Ed. by A. H. Dahlstrom. 1932. text ed. 7.95x o.p. (ISBN 0-669-29884-0). Heath.

Lautreamont. Wallace Fowlie. (World Authors Ser.: France: No. 284). 1974. lib. bdg. 10.95 (ISBN 0-8057-2511-3). Twayne.

Lautreamont: Du lieu commun a la parodie. new ed. Claude Bouche. (Collection themes et textes). 253p. (Orig.). 1974. pap. 6.75 (ISBN 2-03-035024-9, 2615). Larousse.

Lautreamont: The Violent Narcissus. Paul Zweig. LC 78-189562. 1972. 10.00 (ISBN 0-8046-9021-9, Natl U). Kennikat.

Lautreamont's Maldoror. Isidore Ducasse. Tr. by Alexis Lykiard from Fr. (Apollo Eds.). (Illus.). 218p. 1973. pap. 2.45 o.s.i. (ISBN 0-8152-0343-8, A343, TYC-T). T Y Crowell.

Lava, Hock & Soda-Water: Byron's Don Juan. Charles J. Clancy. (Salzburg Studies in English Literature, Romantic Reassessment: No. 41). 1974. pap. text ed. 25.00x (ISBN 0-391-01344-0). Humanities.

LaVarenne's Basic French Cookery. Anne Willan. 1980. 12.95 (ISBN 0-89586-086-4). H P Bks.

LaVarenne's Basic French Cookery. Anne Willan. (Orig.). 1980. 12.95 (ISBN 0-89586-086-4); pap. 7.95 (ISBN 0-89586-056-2). H P Bks.

Lavender & Old Lace. Myrtle Reed. 1976. lib. bdg. 13.50x (ISBN 0-89968-110-7). Lightyear.

Lavender Culture. Karla Jay & Allen Young. (Orig.). 1979. pap. 2.50 (ISBN 0-515-04462-8). Jove Pubns.

Lavender Shoes: Eight Tales of Disenchantment. Alison Uttley. (Illus.). (ps-5). 1970. 6.95 (ISBN 0-571-09361-2, Pub. by Faber & Faber). Merrimack Bk Serv.

Law. Diane Bell & Pam Ditton. (Illus.). 147p. 1980. pap. text ed. 9.95 (ISBN 0-908160-77-1). Bks Australia.

Law. Boy Scouts of America. LC 19-600. (Illus.). 64p. (gr. 6-12). 1975. pap. 0.70x (ISBN 0-8395-3389-6, 3389). BSA.

Law. James Read & Malcolm Yapp. Ed. by Margaret Killingray & Edmund O'Connor. (World History Ser.). (Illus.). (gr. 10). 1980. Repr. of 1977 ed. lib. bdg. 5.95 (ISBN 0-89908-144-4); pap. text ed. 1.95 (ISBN 0-89908-119-3). Greenhaven.

Law Above the Law. John W. Montgomery. LC 75-31395. 1975. pap. 2.25 (ISBN 0-87123-329-0, 200329). Bethany Fell.

Law: An Outline for the Intending Student. Ed. by R. H. Graveson. (Outlines Ser). 1967. cased 15.00x (ISBN 0-7100-2999-3); pap. 8.95 (ISBN 0-7100-6028-9). Routledge & Kegan.

Law & American History: Cases & Materials. Stephen B. Presser & Jamil S. Zainaldin. LC 80-15905. (American Casebook Ser.). 897p. 1980. text ed. 19.95 (ISBN 0-8299-2094-3). West Pub.

Law & Business of Licensing, 4 vols. Marcus B. Finnegan & Robert Goldscheider. LC 75-22337. 1977. Set. looseleaf with 1979 suppl. 210.00 (ISBN 0-87632-136-8). Boardman.

Law & Control in Society. Ronald L. Akers & Richard Hawkins. LC 74-22213. (Sociology Ser.). 384p. 1975. 17.95 (ISBN 0-13-526095-7). P-H.

Law & Development in Latin America. Kenneth L. Karst & Keith S. Rosen. LC 74-30525. 750p. 1976. 44.50x (ISBN 0-520-02955-0). U of Cal Pr.

Law & Diplomacy in Commodity Economics. Emiko Atimono. 200p. 1981. text ed. 57.95x (ISBN 0-8419-5080-6). Holmes & Meier.

Law & Dynamic Administration. Marshall E. Dimock. 176p. 1980. 19.95 (ISBN 0-03-057367-X); text ed. 8.95 (ISBN 0-03-057396-3). Praeger.

Law & Economic Policy in America: The Evolution of the Sherman Antitrust Act. William Letwin. LC 80-21868. xi, 304p. 1980. Repr. of 1965 ed. lib. bdg. 27.50x (ISBN 0-313-22651-2, LELE). Greenwood.

Law & Emergency Care. James E. George. LC 80-14606. 1980. 24.95 (ISBN 0-8016-1834-7). Mosby.

Law & Ethics in the Practice of Psychiatry. Ed. by Charles K. Hofling. LC 80-22091. 280p. 1980. 20.00 (ISBN 0-87630-250-9). Brunner-Mazel.

Law & Gospel. Werner Elert. Ed. by Franklin Sherman. Tr. by Edward H. Schroeder from Ger. LC 66-25263. (Facet Bks). 64p. (Orig.). 1967. pap. 1.50 (ISBN 0-8006-3035-1, 1-3035). Fortress.

Law & Grace. Alva J. McClain. pap. 1.75 (ISBN 0-88469-001-6). BMH Bks.

Law & Health Professionals: Fundamentals of the Law & Malpractice. John Adriani & J. D. Eaton. 144p. 1981. 10.50x (ISBN 0-87527-189-8). Green.

Law & Jurisprudence of England & America. J. F. Dillon. LC 75-99475. (American Constitutional & Legal History Ser). 1970. Repr. of 1894 ed. lib. bdg. 42.50 (ISBN 0-306-71854-5). Da Capo.

Law & Kingship in Thailand During the Reign of King Chulalongkorn. David M. Engel. LC 74-20343. (Michigan Papers on South & Southeast Asia: No. 9). 130p. 1975. pap. 4.50x (ISBN 0-89148-009-9). Ctr S&SE Asian.

Law & Legal Information Directory: A Guide to National & International Organizations, Bar Associations, Federal Court System, Federal Regulatory Agencies, Law Schools, Continuing Legal Education, Scholarships & Grants, Awards & Prizes, Special Libraries, Information Systems & Services, Research Centers, Etc. Ed. by Paul Wasserman & Marek Kaszubski. 800p. 1980. 110.00 (ISBN 0-8103-0169-5). Gale.

Law & Medical Men. R. Vashon Rogers, Jr. xiii, 214p. 1981. Repr. of 1884 ed. lib. bdg. 22.00x (ISBN 0-8377-1032-4). Rothman.

Law & Morality: A Reader. L. Blom-Cooper. Ed. by Gavin Dreway. 265p. 1976. 40.50x (ISBN 0-7156-0805-3, Pub. by Duckworth England); pap. 13.50x (ISBN 0-7156-0804-5). Biblio Dist.

Law & Offshore Oil Development: The North Sea Experience. David B. Keto. LC 78-19745. 1978. 20.95 (ISBN 0-03-046646-6). Praeger.

Law & Order. Brian Ashley. (Past into Present Ser.). (Illus.). 15.00x o.p. (ISBN 0-392-03663-0, LTB). Soccer.

Law & Philosophy: Readings in Legal Philosophy. Ed. by Edward A. Kent. 1970. text ed. 18.95 (ISBN 0-13-526459-6). P-H.

Law & Policy in China's Foreign Relations: A Study of Attitudes & Practices. James Chieh Hsiung. LC 75-180045. (East Asian Institute Ser.). 448p. 17.50x (ISBN 0-231-03552-7). Columbia U Pr.

Law & Policy of Toxic Substances Control: A Case Study of Vinyl Chloride. David D. Doniger. LC 78-24624. 1979. 12.50x (ISBN 0-8018-2234-3); pap. 4.95 (ISBN 0-8018-2235-1). Johns Hopkins.

Law & Politics in China's Foreign Trade. Ed. by Victor H. Li. LC 76-7790. (Asian Law Ser: No.4). 488p. 1977. 22.50 (ISBN 0-295-95512-0). U of Wash Pr.

Law & Politics in Jacobean England. L. A. Knafla. LC 76-4757. (Cambridge Studies in English Legal History). (Illus.). 1977. 59.00 (ISBN 0-521-21191-3). Cambridge U Pr.

Law & Politics in the International System: Case Studies in Conflict Resolution. Richard B. Finnegan et al. LC 79-66153. (Illus.). 1979. pap. text ed. 9.00 (ISBN 0-8191-0793-X). U Pr of Amer.

Law & Politics of Abortion. Ed. by Carl Schneider & Maris A. Vinovskis. LC 79-3134. 320p. 1980. 15.95x (ISBN 0-669-03386-3). Lexington Bks.

Law & Practice Relating to Pollution Control in the Member States of the European Communities. Commission of the European Communities. Ed. by Environmental Resources Ltd. Incl. Vol. 1 (ISBN 0-86010-040-5); Vol. 2a (ISBN 0-86010-041-3); Vol. 3 (ISBN 0-86010-029-4); Vol. 4 (ISBN 0-86010-033-2); Vol. 4a (ISBN 0-86010-035-9); Vol. 5 (ISBN 0-86010-032-4); Vol. 5a (ISBN 0-86010-034-0); Vol. 6 (ISBN 0-86010-031-6); Vol. 7 (ISBN 0-86010-039-1); Vol. 7a (ISBN 0-86010-042-1); Vol. 8 (ISBN 0-86010-030-8); Vol. 9 (ISBN 0-86010-037-5); Vol. 11 (ISBN 0-86010-038-3). 1976. 16.00x ea. (Pub. by Graham & Trotman England). State Mutual Bk.

Law & Procedure of International Tribunals. Jackson H. Ralston. LC 75-147738. (Library of War & Peace; International Law). lib. bdg. 38.00 (ISBN 0-8240-0496-5). Garland Pub.

Law & Psychiatry in the Canadian Context. Ed. by David N. Weisstub. 1980. 60.00 (ISBN 0-08-023134-9). Pergamon.

Law & Psychiatry: Proceedings of an International Symposium Held at Clarke Institute of Psychiatry, Toronto, Canada, Feb. 1977. Ed. by David N. Weisstub. LC 78-9436. 125p. 1978. 19.00 (ISBN 0-08-023133-0). Pergamon.

Law & Psychological Practice. Robert L. Schwitzgebel & R. Kirkland Schwitzgebel. LC 79-20112. 1980. text ed. 16.50 (ISBN 0-471-76694-1). Wiley.

Law & Public Education, Cases & Materials. Stephen R. Goldstein. (Contemporary Legal Education Ser). 944p. 1974. 22.00 (ISBN 0-672-81784-5, Bobbs-Merrill Law); 1978 suppl 5.50 (ISBN 0-672-83546-0). Michie.

Law & Social Action: Selected Essays of Alexander H. Pekelis. Alexander H. Pekelis. Ed. by Milton Konvitz. LC 77-87376. (American Constitutional & Legal History Ser). (Illus.). 1970. Repr. of 1950 ed. lib. bdg. 29.50 (ISBN 0-306-71600-3). Da Capo.

Law & Social Change. Stuart S. Nagel. LC 73-89941. (Contemporary Social Science Issues Ser.: No. 3). 1973. 4.95x o.p. (ISBN 0-8039-0334-0). Sage.

Law & Social Change in Mediterranean Europe & Latin America: A Handbook of Legal & Social Indicators for Comparative Study. J. H. Merryman. 1980. 47.50 (ISBN 0-379-20700-1). Oceana.

Law & Social Change in the USSR. John N. Hazard. LC 79-1608. 1980. Repr. of 1953 ed. 23.50 (ISBN 0-88355-911-0). Hyperion Conn.

Law & Social Process in United States History. James W. Hurst. LC 74-173669. (American Constitutional & Legal History Ser.). 359p. 1971. Repr. of 1960 ed. lib. bdg. 35.00 (ISBN 0-306-70409-9). Da Capo.

Law & Society. Adam Podgorecki. 1974. 23.50x (ISBN 0-7100-7983-4); pap. 10.00 (ISBN 0-7100-8035-2). Routledge & Kegan.

Law & Society. Steven Vago. (Ser. in Sociology). (Illus.). 352p. 1981. text ed. 16.95 (ISBN 0-13-526483-9). P-H.

Law & Society: An Interdisciplinary Introduction. Lee S. Weinberg & Judity W. Weinberg. LC 80-5229. 495p. 1980. pap. text ed. 21.50 (ISBN 0-8191-1055-8). U Pr of Amer.

Law & Society in the Visigothic Kingdom. P. D. King. LC 77-179163. (Cambridge Studies in Medieval Life & Thought: Third Ser., No. 5). 320p. 1972. 44.50 (ISBN 0-521-08421-0). Cambridge U Pr.

Law & Society in Traditional China. Ch'u Tung-Tsu. LC 79-1602. 1981. Repr. of 1961 ed. 22.50 (ISBN 0-88355-905-6). Hyperion Conn.

Law & Society in Transition. Phillippe Nonet & Philip Selznick. (Orig.). 1978. pap. 4.95x (ISBN 0-06-131954-6, TB 1954, Torch). Harrow.

Law & Sport. Gary Nygaard. (Brighton Ser. in Recreation & Leisure Studies). 1981. pap. text ed. 9.95x o.p. (ISBN 0-89832-013-5); 14.95. Brighton Pub Co.

Law & the Administration of Justice in the Old Testament & Ancient East. Hans J. Boecker. Tr. by Jeremy Moiser. LC 80-65556. 224p. 1980. pap. 12.50 (ISBN 0-8066-1801-9, 10-3761). Augsburg.

Law & the Administrative Process: Analytic Frameworks for Understanding Public Policy Making. David J. Gould. LC 79-63850. 1979. pap. text ed. 11.25 (ISBN 0-8191-0746-8). U Pr of Amer.

Law & the American Future: An American Assembly Book. Murray Schwartz. 1976. 9.95 (ISBN 0-13-526061-2, Spec); pap. 4.95 (ISBN 0-13-526053-1, Spec). P-H.

Law & the American Indian: Readings, Notes & Cases. Monroe E. Price. (Contemporary Legal Education Ser.). 1973. 22.00 (ISBN 0-672-81770-5, Bobbs-Merrill Law). Michie.

Law & the Arts: Arts & the Law. Jane S. Lynch et al. Ed. by Tem Horwitz. LC 79-54026. 240p. (Orig.). 1981. pap. 7.95x (ISBN 0-914090-71-2). Drama Bk.

Law & the Behavioral Sciences. Friedman & Macaulay. (Contemporary Legal Education Ser.). 1977. 25.00 (ISBN 0-672-82025-0, Bobbs-Merrill Law). Michie.

Law & the College Student: Justice in Evolution. William G. Millington. LC 79-14211. 629p. 1979. text ed. 15.95 (ISBN 0-8299-2047-1). West Pub.

Law & the Commonwealth. Richard T. Latham. Repr. of 1949 ed. lib. bdg. 16.75x (ISBN 0-8371-3974-0, LALC). Greenwood.

Law & the Computer: A Guide for Computer Professionals. Michael Gemignami. 320p. 1981. 18.95 (ISBN 0-8436-1604-0). CBI Pub.

Law & the Conditions of Freedom in the Nineteenth-Century United States. J. Willard Hurst. 1956. pap. 5.45 (ISBN 0-299-01363-4). U of Wis Pr.

Law & the Dangerous Criminal. Linda Sleffel. LC 77-287. (Dangerous Offender Project Ser.). 1977. 17.95 (ISBN 0-669-01481-8). Lexington Bks.

Law & the Life Insurance Contract. 4th ed. Janice E. Greider & William T. Beadles. 1979. text ed. 17.95 (ISBN 0-256-02158-9). Irwin.

Law & the New Woman. Mary McHugh. LC 75-15584. (Choosing Life Styles Ser). 128p. (gr. 7 up). 1975. PLB 5.90 o.p. (ISBN 0-531-01097-X). Watts.

Law & the Poor. Frank Parker. LC 72-97696. 256p. 1973. pap. 4.95x o.p. (ISBN 0-88344-276-0). Orbis Bks.

Law & the Poor: London, Nineteen Fourteen. Edward A. Parry. LC 79-56966. (English Working Class Ser.). 1980. lib. bdg. 30.00 (ISBN 0-8240-0117-6). Garland Pub.

Law & the Rise of Capitalism. Michael E. Tigar & Madeleine R. Levy. LC 77-70968. 1977. 16.00 o.p. (ISBN 0-85345-411-6, CL 411-6). Monthly Rev.

Law & the School Psychologist. Bartell Cardon et al. LC 68-52341. 105p. 1975. 12.95 (ISBN 0-87705-280-8). Human Sci Pr.

Law & the Underprivileged. Chris Smith & David C. Hoath. 280p. 1975. 20.00x (ISBN 0-7100-8259-2). Routledge & Kegan.

Law & Urban Growth: Civil Litigation in the Boston Trial Courts, 1880-1900. Robert Silverman. LC 80-7553. 224p. 1981. 16.50 (ISBN 0-691-04677-8). Princeton U Pr.

Law & Warfare: Studies in the Anthropology of Conflict. Ed. by Paul Bohannan. (Texas Press Sourcebooks: No. 1). (Illus.). 439p. 1976. pap. 7.95x (ISBN 0-292-74617-2). U of Tex Pr.

Law As Process: An Anthopological Approach. Sally F. Moore. 1978. 22.00x (ISBN 0-7100-8758-6). Routledge & Kegan.

Law Book Published, 1975-1977. Meura G. Pimsleur. 50.00 (ISBN 0-686-60607-8, 1971-1977); 85.00. ea. (1980-1981); 70.00 (ISBN 0-686-60608-6, 1980). Glanville.

Law Books Recommended for Libraries. Association Of American Law School. (Compilation of 46 subject lists complete in six binders). 1967-70. loose leaf 475.00x, with 1974-1976 suppl. (ISBN 0-8377-0201-1). Rothman.

Law Briefs on Litigation & the Rights of Exceptional Children, Youth, & Adults. Ernest E. Singletary et al. 1977. pap. text ed. 16.75x (ISBN 0-8191-0188-5). U Pr of Amer.

Law Clerks & the Judicial Process: Perceptions of the Qualities & Functions of Law Clerks in American Courts. John B. Oakley & Robert S. Thompson. 150p. 1981. 10.00x (ISBN 0-520-04046-5). U of Cal Pr.

Law Courts, Lawyers & Litigants. Frederick Payler. xiv, 242p. 1980. Repr. of 1926 ed. lib. bdg. 24.00x (ISBN 0-8377-1006-5). Rothman.

Law Courts of Medieval England. Alan Harding. (Historical Problems Studies & Documents). 1973. text ed. 17.95x (ISBN 0-04-942106-9). Allen Unwin.

Law Dictionary (Arabic-English) Harith Harugi. 1972. 25.00x (ISBN 0-685-72050-0). Intl Bk Ctr.

Law Dictionary: Criminal Justice Ed. Wesley Gilmer. LC 72-95860. pap. text ed. 6.00 (ISBN 0-87084-149-1). Anderson Pub Co.

Law Dictionary (English-Arabic) rev. ed. Harith Faruqi. 1972. 35.00x (ISBN 0-685-72049-7). Intl Bk Ctr.

Law Dictionary (English-Arabic) Ibrahim Wahab. 1972. 20.00x (ISBN 0-685-72048-9). Intl Bk Ctr.

Law Digest of New York. Gould Editorial Staff. (Supplemented annually). looseleaf 7.50 (ISBN 0-87526-252-X). Gould.

Law Enforcement: A Selected Bibliography. 2nd ed. George T. Felkenes & Harold K. Becker. LC 76-50010. 1977. 15.00 (ISBN 0-8108-0995-8). Scarecrow.

Law Enforcement: A Selective Bibliography. Emanuel T. Prostano & Martin L. Piccirillo. LC 73-86399. 1974. lib. bdg. 13.50 o.p. (ISBN 0-87287-077-4). Libs Unl.

Law Enforcement & Community Relations: A Selected Bibliography. Carol A. Martin. (Public Administration Ser.: Bibliography: P-634). 1980. pap. 7.50. Vance Biblios.

Law Enforcement & Correctional Rehabilitation. Ed. by John G. Cull & Richard E. Hardy. (American Lectures in Social & Rehabilitation Psychology Ser.). 280p. 1973. 18.75 (ISBN 0-398-02870-2). C C Thomas.

Law Enforcement & Criminal Justice: An Introduction. Georgette Bennett-Sandler et al. LC 78-69537. (Illus.). 1979. text ed. 15.75 (ISBN 0-395-27467-2); inst. manual 0.25 (ISBN 0-395-27466-4). HM.

Law Enforcement Guide to United States Supreme Court Decisions. Stanley Cohen. (Illus.). 232p. 1972. text ed. 19.75 (ISBN 0-398-02261-5). C C Thomas.

Law Enforcement Handgun Digest. 3rd ed. Jack Lewis. 288p. 1980. pap. 8.95 (ISBN 0-695-81413-3). Follett.

Law Enforcement Process. Alan Butler. LC 74-6878. (Illus.). 300p. 1976. text ed. 9.95x o.p. (ISBN 0-88284-015-0). Alfred Pub.

Law Enforcement Supervision: A Case Study Approach. Robert C. Wadman et al. (Criminal Justice Ser.). 1975. pap. text ed. 9.50 (ISBN 0-8299-0631-2). West Pub.

Law Every Nurse Should Know. 4th ed. Helen Creighton. 480p. 1981. text ed. 14.95 (ISBN 0-7216-2573-8). Saunders.

Law for Business. John D. Donnell et al. 18.95x (ISBN 0-256-02316-6). Irwin.

Law for Business Managers: The Regulatory Environment. Thomas Harron. 1977. text ed. 16.95 (ISBN 0-205-05743-8, 075743-8); instructor's manual free (075744-6). Allyn.

Law for Non-Lawyers. Brent E. Zepke. (Littlefield, Adams Quality Paperbacks: No. 355). 336p. (Orig.). 1981. pap. 4.95 (ISBN 0-8226-0355-1). Littlefield.

Law for the Elephant: Property & Social Behavior on the Overland Trail. John P. Reid. LC 79-26989. (Illus.). 1980. 18.50 (ISBN 0-87328-104-7). Huntington Lib.

Law for the Medical Practitioner. Charles W. Quimby, Jr. 1979. text ed. 17.50 (ISBN 0-914904-39-6). Health Admin Pr.

Law for the Reporter. 5th ed. Dale R. Spencer. 1980. text ed. 12.95x (ISBN 0-87543-137-2). Lucas.

Law for Tombstone. Chuck Martin. 1978. pap. 1.25 (ISBN 0-505-51268-8). Tower Bks.

Law in a Changing Society. 2nd ed. Wolfgang G. Friedmann. LC 67-26509. 550p. 1972. 27.50x (ISBN 0-231-03653-1). Columbia U Pr.

Law in America, 2 vols. Incl. Vol. 1. Stories of Great Crimes & Trials from American Heritage Magazine. American Heritage Editors. LC 74-4031. 382p; Vol. 2. American Heritage History of Law in America. Bernard Schwartz. LC 74-8264. (Illus.). 379p. 1974. Boxed Set. deluxe ed. 45.00 (ISBN 0-8281-0292-9, Dist. by Scribner). Am Heritage.

Law in Diplomacy. Percy E. Corbett. 9.50 (ISBN 0-8446-1125-5). Peter Smith.

Law in Imperial China. Clarence Morris & Derk Bodde. (Pennsylvania Paperbacks Ser). 620p. 1973. pap. 6.95x o.p. (ISBN 0-8122-1060-3). U of Pa Pr.

Law in Modern Society. Roberto M. Unger. LC 74-27853. 1977. pap. text ed. 6.95 (ISBN 0-02-932880-2). Free Pr.

Law in Philosophical Perspective: Selected Readings. Joel Feinberg & Hyman Gross. 1977. pap. text ed. 9.95x (ISBN 0-8221-0203-X). Dickenson.

Law in the Making. 7th ed. Carleton K. Allen. 1964. pap. 16.95x (ISBN 0-19-881029-6, OPB29). Oxford U Pr.

Law in the Middle East: Origin & Development of Islamic Law, Vol. 1. Ed. by Majid Khadduri & Herbert J. Liebesny. LC 80-1921. 1981. Repr. of 1955 ed. 41.50 (ISBN 0-404-18974-1). AMS Pr.

Law in the Modern State. Leon Duguit. LC 68-9647. 1970. Repr. 16.50 (ISBN 0-86527-115-1). Fertig.

Law in the Practice of Psychiatry: A Handbook for Clinicians. Seymour L. Halleck. (Critical Issues in Psychiatry Ser.). 310p. 1980. 21.50 (ISBN 0-306-40373-0, Plenum Pr). Plenum Pub.

Law in the School: A Guide for California Teachers, Parents & Students. 3rd ed. California Dept. of Justice & Deukmejian. LC 74-4146. 96p. 1980. pap. 3.95 (ISBN 0-87585-802-3). Patterson Smith.

Law in the Schools. William D. Valente. (Educational Administration Ser.: No. C21). 580p. 1980. text ed. 20.95 (ISBN 0-675-08165-3). Merrill.

Law in the Scientific Age. E. Patterson. LC 63-9872. 1963. 12.50x (ISBN 0-231-02617-X). Columbia U Pr.

Law in the Soviet Society. Ed. by Wayne R. LaFave. LC 65-19109. 297p. 1965. pap. 1.95 (ISBN 0-252-72524-7). U of Ill Pr.

Law, Its Nature, Functions & Limits. 2nd ed. Robert S. Summers & C. Howard. (Illus.). 1024p. 1972. text ed. 21.95 (ISBN 0-13-526400-6). P-H.

Law, Language & Communication. Walter Probert. (Amer. Lec. Behavioral Science & Law Ser.). 408p. 1972. 19.50 (ISBN 0-398-02477-4). C C Thomas.

Law: Law: Its Origin, Growth & Function. James Carter. LC 74-6413. (American Constitutional & Legal History Ser.). 1974. Repr. of 1907 ed. lib. bdg. 35.00 (ISBN 0-306-70631-8). Da Capo.

Law, Lawyers & Social Change. Horowitz & Karst. 1969. 16.50 (ISBN 0-672-81003-4, Bobbs-Merrill Law); 1978 suppl. by Warren S. Bracy 6.00 (ISBN 0-672-83545-2). Michie.

Law, Legislation, & Liberty: Rules & Order. F. A. Hayek. 15.00 (ISBN 0-226-32080-4). U of Chicago Pr.

Law, Legislation, & Liberty, Vol. 2. F. A. Hayek: The Mirage of Social Justice, Vol. 2. F. A. Hayek. LC 73-82488. (Multi-Volumed Set Ser.). 1977. lib. bdg. 15.00x (ISBN 0-226-32082-0); pap. 5.95 (ISBN 0-226-32083-9, P799). U of Chicago Pr.

Law, Legislation, & Liberty: The Political Order of a Free People. F. A. Hayek. pap. write for info. (ISBN 0-226-32090-1). U of Chicago Pr.

Law, Legislation, & Liberty: The Political Order of a Free People, Vol. 3. F. A. Hayek. LC 78-25905. 1979. 15.00x (ISBN 0-226-32087-1). U of Chicago Pr.

Law Library - a Living Trust. Institute For Law Librarians - 6th Biennial - 1963. (AALL Publications Ser: No. 7). 58p. (Orig.). 1964. pap. text ed. 8.50x (ISBN 0-8377-0105-8). Rothman.

Law Making in the Global Community. Ed. by Nicholas G Onuf. 600p. 1980. lib. bdg. write for info. (ISBN 0-89089-169-9). Carolina Acad Pr.

Law-Making Process. Michael Zander. (Law in Context Ser.). 332p. 1980. 40.00x (ISBN 0-297-77750-5, Pub. by Weidenfeld & Nicolson England). Rothman.

Law Man. Lee Leighton. 1977. pap. 1.75 (ISBN 0-441-47492-6). Ace Bks.

Law Manual. 9th ed. 15.00 (ISBN 0-932788-01-7). Bradley CPA.

Law, Medicine & Forensic Science. 2nd ed. William J. Curran & E. Donald Shapiro. 1046p. 1970. 24.25 (ISBN 0-316-16512-3). Little.

Law, Morality, & Society: Essays in Honour of H. L. A. Hart. Ed. by P. M. Hacker & J. Raz. 1977. 19.95x (ISBN 0-19-824557-2). Oxford U Pr.

Law of Armed Conflicts. Denise Bindschedler-Robert. 1971. pap. 2.25 (ISBN 0-87003-021-3). Carnegie Endow.
Law of Arrest & Search & Seizure. A. Markle. (Illus.). 320p. 1974. 19.75 (ISBN 0-398-03188-6). C C Thomas.
Law of Church-State Relations in a Nutshell. Leonard F. Manning. LC 80-22991. (Nutshell Ser.). 314p. 1980. pap. text ed. 6.95 (ISBN 0-8299-2113-3). West Pub.
Law of Citizenship & Aliens in India. Amarendro N. Sinha. 15.00x (ISBN 0-210-33895-4). Asia.
Law of Coal, Oil & Gas in Virginia & West Virginia. R. Tucker Donley. 1951. with 1972 suppl. 25.00 (ISBN 0-87215-084-4). Michie.
Law of Commons & Commoners; or a Treatise Shewing the Original & Nature of Common, & the Several Kinds Thereof. Ed. by David Berkowitz & Samuel Thorne. LC 77-89244. (Classics of English Legal History in the Modern Era Ser.: Vol. 138). 1979. Repr. of 1698 ed. lib. bdg. 55.00 (ISBN 0-8240-3175-X). Garland Pub.
Law of Constructive Contempt: The Shepherd Case Reviewed. John L. Thomas. 270p. 1980. Repr. of 1904 ed. lib. bdg. 24.00x (ISBN 0-8377-1203-3). Rothman.
Law of Copyright, Competition & Industrial Property. Konrad Zweigert & Jan Kropholler. Ed. by Gert Kolle & Hans P. Hallstein. (Sources of International Uniform Law Ser.: Vol. III-A First Supplement). 1340p. 1980. 175.00x (ISBN 9-0286-0099-X). Sijthoff & Noordhoff.
Law of Corporations in a Nutshell. Robert W. Hamilton. LC 80-21532. (Nutshell Ser.). 379p. 1980. pap. text ed. 6.95 (ISBN 0-8299-2108-7). West Pub.
Law of Corrections & Prisoners' Rights, 1977 Supplement: Cases & Materials. Sheldon Krantz. (American Casebook Ser.). 1973. pap. 5.95 o.p. (ISBN 0-685-80683-9). West Pub.
Law of Crimes in India, Vol. 1. R. C. Nigam. 1965. 25.00x (ISBN 0-210-27046-2). Asia.
Law of Criminal Procedure: An Analysis & Critique. David A. Jones. 600p. 1981. text ed. 17.95 (ISBN 0-316-47283-2); tchrs'. manual free (ISBN 0-316-47284-0). Little.
Law of Death & Disposal of the Dead. 2nd ed. H. Y. Bernard. 1979. 5.95 (ISBN 0-379-11000-8). Oceana.
Law of Deviation of Homeostasis & Diseases of Aging. Vladimir M. Dilman. LC 79-21456. (Illus.). 346p. 1981. 35.00 (ISBN 0-88416-250-8). PSG Pub.
Law of Evidence: A Compendium of the Law of Evidence, Vol. 35A & B. Sir Gefrey Gilbert & Thomas Peake. Ed. by David S. Berkowitz & Samuel E. Thorne. LC 77-86648. (Classics of English Legal History in the Modern Era Ser.: Vol. 97). 1979. lib. bdg. 55.00 (ISBN 0-8240-3084-2). Garland Pub.
Law of Evidence for Police. 2nd ed. Irving J. Klein. (Criminal Justice Ser.). 1978. text ed. 16.95 o.p. (ISBN 0-8299-0149-3); instrs.' manual avail. o.p. (ISBN 0-8299-0149-3). West Pub.
Law of Evidence in Virginia. Charles E. Friend. 1977. 40.00 (ISBN 0-87215-197-2); 1980 suppl. 10.00 (ISBN 0-87215-323-1). Michie.
Law of Franchising. Coleman R. Rosenfield. LC 78-118362. 1970. 45.00 o.p. (ISBN 0-686-14483-X). Lawyers Co-Op.
Law of Fraud & the Procedure Pertaining to the Redress Thereof. Melville M. Bigelow. lix, 696p. 1981. Repr. of 1877 ed. lib. bdg. 45.00x (ISBN 0-8377-0317-4). Rothman.
Law of Global Communications. Charles H. Alexandrowicz. LC 79-163081. (International Legal Studies Ser). 1971. 14.50 (ISBN 0-231-03529-2). Columbia U Pr.
Law of Gravity. Johanna Hurwitz. LC 77-13656. (Illus.). (gr. 3-7). 1978. 7.50 o.p. (ISBN 0-688-22142-4); PLB 7.63 (ISBN 0-688-32142-9). Morrow.
Law of Habeas Corpus. Robert J. Sharpe. 1976. 42.00x (ISBN 0-19-825332-X). Oxford U Pr.
Law of Hospital & Health Care Administration. Arthur F. Southwick. LC 78-4846. 1978. text ed. 29.50 (ISBN 0-914904-27-2). Health Admin Pr.
Law of Industrial Disputes in India. R. F. Rustamji. 1965. 25.00x (ISBN 0-210-27087-X). Asia.
Law of Infancy & Coverture. 2nd ed. Peregrine Bingham. viii, 396p. 1980. Repr. of 1849 ed. lib. bdg. 35.00x (ISBN 0-8377-0311-5). Rothman.
Law of Libel, in Which Is Contained a General History of This Law in the Ancient Codes, & of Its Introduction, & Successive Alterations in the Law of England, Comprehending a Digest of All the Leading Cases Upon Libels. Francis L. Holt. Ed. by David Berkowitz & Samuel Thorne. LC 77-89192. (Classics of English Legal History in the Modern Era Ser.: Vol. 115). 1979. Repr. of 1812 ed. lib. bdg. 55.00 (ISBN 0-8240-3152-0). Garland Pub.
Law of Life. Jack London. Ed. by Walter Pauk & Raymond Harris. (Classics Ser). (Illus.). (gr. 6-12). 1976. pap. text ed. 1.60x (ISBN 0-89061-040-1, 501); tchrs. ed. 3.00 (ISBN 0-89061-041-X, 503). Jamestown Pubs.
Law of Longer Life. C. Northcote Parkinson & Herman LeCompte. (Illus.). 1980. 10.95 (ISBN 0-916624-31-5). TSU Pr.
Law of Lotteries, Frauds & Obscenity in the Mails. John L. Thomas. xviii, 358p. 1980. Repr. of 1903 ed. lib. bdg. 32.50x (ISBN 0-8377-1202-5). Rothman.
Law of Maritime Personal Injuries, 2 vols. 3rd ed. Martin J. Norris. LC 75-4186. 1975. Set. 110.00 (ISBN 0-686-14495-3). Lawyers Co-Op.
Law of Modern Commercial Practices, 2vols. 2nd ed. Frederick A. Whitney. LC 65-4288. 1965. 85.00 (ISBN 0-686-14490-2). Lawyers Co-Op.
Law of Moses & Its Lesson. R. J. Reid. pap. 0.30 (ISBN 0-87213-693-0). Loizeaux.
Law of Municipal Tort Liability in Georgia. 3rd ed. Perry R. Sentell. LC 79-24276. 184p. 1980. pap. text ed. 15.00x (ISBN 0-89854-053-4). U of GA Inst Govt.
Law of Naturalization in the United States of America & of Other Countries. Prentiss Webster. xx, 403p. 1981. Repr. of 1895 ed. lib. bdg. 32.50x (ISBN 0-8377-1309-9). Rothman.
Law of Patents, 3 vols. William C. Robinson. 1971. Repr. of 1890 ed. Set. 125.00 (ISBN 0-87632-039-6). Boardman.
Law of Population: A Treatise in Six Books, 2 vols. M. T. Sadler. 138p. 1971. Repr. of 1830 ed. Set. 72.00x (ISBN 0-7165-1579-2, Pub. by Irish Academic Pr Ireland). Biblio Dist.
Law of Presidential Impeachment. Bar Association of the City of New York. 57p. 1974. pap. 1.00 o.p. (ISBN 0-06-087074-5, HW). Har-Row.
Law of Real Estate Brokers, N.Y. Ed. by Elliott L. Biskind & Clarence S. Barasch. LC 70-83769. 1969. with 1979 suppl. 45.00 (ISBN 0-87632-050-7). Boardman.
Law of Restitution, 4 vols. George E. Palmer. 1978. Set. 200.00 (ISBN 0-316-69005-8); pap. 25.00 supp. 1980 (ISBN 0-316-69006-6). Little.
Law of Retirement, Vol. 48. 2nd ed. L. F. Jessup. 1979. 5.95 (ISBN 0-379-11124-1). Oceana.
Law of Seamen, 3 vols. 3rd ed. Martin J. Norris. LC 74-112518. 1970. Set. 144.00 (ISBN 0-686-14494-5). Lawyers Co-Op.
Law of Sentencing, Vol.1. Arthur Campbell. LC 78-18626. 1978. 47.50. Lawyers Co-Op.
Law of Sports. John C. Weistart & Cym H. Lowell. 1979. 40.00 (ISBN 0-672-82337-3, Bobbs-Merrill Law). Michie.
Law of Subdivisions. E. C. Yokley. 1963. with 1980 suppl. 50.00 (ISBN 0-87215-061-5); 1980 suppl 25.00 (ISBN 0-87215-344-4). Michie.
Law of Support. 3rd ed. F. Kuchler. 1980. 5.95 (ISBN 0-379-11135-7). Oceana.
Law of Suretyship. Arthur A. Stearns. Ed. by James L. Elder. LC 74-170608. 720p. 1973. Repr. lib. bdg. 58.25x (ISBN 0-8371-6030-8, STLS). Greenwood.
Law of Tax-Exempt Organizations. 3rd ed. Bruce R. Hopkins. LC 80-81195. 1980. pap. 41.95 (ISBN 0-471-05122-5, Pub. by Wiley Interscience); pap. 19.50 1980 suppl. (ISBN 0-471-08171-X). Wiley.
Law of Tax-Exempt Organizations, 1981 Supplement. 3rd ed. Bruce R. Hopkins. 200p. 1981. pap. 15.95 (ISBN 0-471-09351-3, Pub. by Wiley Interscience). Wiley.
Law of the Commonwealth & Chief Justice Shaw. Leonard W. Levy. 1957. 7.50x o.p. (ISBN 0-8377-2401-5). Rothman.
Law of the Harvest. Sterling W. Sill. 392p. 1980. 8.50 (ISBN 0-88290-142-7). Horizon Utah.
Law of the Land. Arthur L. Goodhart. LC 66-16914. 1966. pap. 1.95x (ISBN 0-8139-0108-1). U Pr of Va.
Law of the Land: Debating National Land Use Legislation, 1970-75. Noreen Lyday. 53p. 1976. pap. 3.00 (ISBN 0-87766-175-8, 15200). Urban Inst.
Law of the New European Patent. Amedee Turner. 1979. lib. bdg. 50.00 (ISBN 0-8240-7126-3). Garland Pub.
Law of the Real Estate Business. 4th ed. William B. French & Harold F. Lusk. 1979. 18.95 (ISBN 0-256-02167-8). Irwin.
Law of the Rhythmic Breath. Ella A. Fletcher. LC 80-19750. 372p. 1980. Repr. of 1979 ed. lib. bdg. 11.95x (ISBN 0-89370-644-2). Borgo Pr.
Law of the Sea: Issues in Ocean Resource Management. Ed. by Don Walsh. LC 77-7823. (Praeger Special Studies). 1977. 29.95 (ISBN 0-03-022666-X). Praeger.
Law of Trade & Labor Combinations As Applicable to Boycotts, Strikes, Trade Conspiracies, Monopolies, Pools, Trusts, & Kindred Topics. Frederick H. Cooke. xxv, 214p. 1981. Repr. of 1898 ed. lib. bdg. 24.00x (ISBN 0-8377-0430-8). Rothman.
Law of Trusts, 6 Vols. 3rd ed. Austin W. Scott. 1980. Set. with 1980 supplement 275.00 (ISBN 0-316-77686-6). Little.
Law of Tug, Tow & Pilotage. 2nd, rev. ed. Alex L. Parks. 1981. text ed. 40.00 (ISBN 0-87033-263-5). Cornell Maritime.
Law of Tug, Tow & Pilotage. 2nd ed. Alex L. Parks. 1981. 60.00x (ISBN 0-87033-265-1). Cornell Maritime.
Law of Value & Historical Materialism. Samir Amin. 1978. 6.50 o.p. (ISBN 0-85345-470-1, CL-4701). Monthly Rev.
Law of War, 2 vols. Leon Friedman. 1972. Set. text ed. 65.00 o.p. (ISBN 0-394-47240-3). Random.
Law of War: A Documentary History, 2 vols. Compiled by Leon Friedan. LC 72-765. 1972. Set. lib. bdg. 85.00 (ISBN 0-313-20133-1). Greenwood.
Law of War & Peace in Islam: A Study of Moslem International Law. Majid Khadduri. LC 76-147599. (Library of War & Peace; International Law). lib. bdg. 38.00 (ISBN 0-8240-0360-8). Garland Pub.
Law of Zoning & Planning, with Forms, 4 vols. Charles A. Rathkopf & Arden H. Rathkopf. LC 56-2013. 1977. Set. looseleaf with 1979 suppl. 175.00 (ISBN 0-87632-020-5). Boardman.
Law Officer's Pocket Manual: 1980-81 Edition. John G. Miles, Jr. et al. 128p. 1980. 5.00 (ISBN 0-686-68899-6). BNA.
Law, or a Discourse Thereof Done into English. Sir Henry Finch. Ed. by David Berkowitz & Samuel Thorne. LC 77-86560. (Classics of English Legal History in the Modern Era Ser.: Vol. 65). 1979. Repr. of 1759 ed. lib. bdg. 55.00 (ISBN 0-8240-3052-4). Garland Pub.
Law or Grace. Martin R. De Haan. 1965. pap. 4.95 (ISBN 0-310-23401-8). Zondervan.
Law or War? Lucia A. Mead. LC 70-147601. (Library of War & Peace; International Law). lib. bdg. 38.00 (ISBN 0-8240-0362-4). Garland Pub.
Law, Order & Power. William J. Chambliss & Robert B. Seidman. 1971. text ed. 18.95 (ISBN 0-201-00957-9). A-W.
Law, Psychiatry & the Mentally Disordered Offender, Vol. 1. Ed. by Lynn M. Irvine, Jr. & Terry B. Brelje. 164p. 1972. 13.75 (ISBN 0-398-02530-4). C C Thomas.
Law, Psychiatry & the Mentally Disordered Offender, Vol. 2. Ed. by Lynn M. Irvine, Jr. & Terry B. Brelje. 148p. 1973. 13.75 (ISBN 0-398-02645-9). C C Thomas.
Law, Psychology, & the Courts: Rethinking Treatment of the Young & the Disturbed. Ellsworth A. Fersch, Jr. 184p. 1979. 17.50 (ISBN 0-398-03874-0). C C Thomas.
Law, Reason, & Justice: Essays in Legal Philosophy. Ed. by Graham Hughes. LC 69-19264. (Studies in Peaceful Change: Vol. 3). 269p. 1969. 15.00x (ISBN 0-8147-0212-0). NYU Pr.
Law Reference Handbook. 1980. pap. cancelled (ISBN 0-8120-0546-5). Barron.
Law Reform in the Muslim World. Norman Anderson. (Univ. of London Logical Ser.: No. 11). 1976. text ed. 27.25x (ISBN 0-485-13411-X, Athlone Pr). Humanities.
Law Relating to Friendly Societies. John T. Pratt. Ed. by David S. Berkowitz & Samuel E. Thorne. LC 77-86656. (Classics of English Legal History in the Modern Era Ser.: Vol. 40). 160p. 1979. lib. bdg. 40.00 (ISBN 0-8240-3089-3). Garland Pub.
Law Relating to the Mentally Defective. Herbert Davey. (Historical Foundations of Forensic Psychiatry & Psychology Ser.). 568p. 1980. Repr. of 1914 ed. lib. bdg. 49.50 (ISBN 0-306-76070-3). Da Capo.
Law Reporting in England Fourteen Eighty Five-Fifteen Eighty Five. L. W. Abbott. (University of London Legal Ser.: No. 10). (Illus.). 328p. 1973. text ed. 52.50x (ISBN 0-485-13410-1, Athlone Pr). Humanities.
Law School Admission Test. rev. ed. Alfred J. Candrilli et al. LC 80-22181. 448p. 1981. lib. bdg. 10.95 (ISBN 0-668-05146-9); pap. 6.95 (ISBN 0-686-69096-6). Arco.
Law, State & International Legal Order: Essays in Honor of Hans Kelsen. Ed. by Salo Engel & R. A. Metall. LC 64-16881. 1964. 19.50x (ISBN 0-87049-052-4). U of Tenn Pr.
Law, State & Society. Ed. by Bob Fryer et al. Alan Hunt & Doreen McBarret. 224p. 1981. 31.00x (ISBN 0-7099-1004-5, Pub. by Croom Helm LTD England). Biblio Dist.
Law West of Fort Smith: A History of Frontier Justice in the Indian Territory, 1834-1896. Glenn Shirley. LC 57-6193. (Illus.). 1968. pap. 4.25 (ISBN 0-8032-5183-1, BB 392, Bison). U of Nebr Pr.
Law Without Lawyers: A Comparative View of Law in the United States & China. Victor H. Li. LC 78-568. 1978. lib. bdg. 16.50x (ISBN 0-89158-160-X); pap. text ed. 7.50 (ISBN 0-89158-161-8). Westview.
Law Writers & the Courts. Clyde E. Jacobs. LC 73-251. (American Constitutional & Legal History Ser.). 234p. 1973. Repr. of 1954 ed. lib. bdg. 25.00 (ISBN 0-306-70570-2). Da Capo.
Lawes of the Market. LC 74-80198. (English Experience Ser.: No. 676). 22p. 1974. Repr. of 1595 ed. 3.50 (ISBN 90-221-0676-4). Walter J Johnson.
Lawes Resolutions of Women's Rights. Thomas Anstey et al. Ed. by Samuel E. Thorne. LC 77-89253. (Classics of English Legal History in the Modern Era Ser.: Vol. 82). 529p. 1979. lib. bdg. 40.00 (ISBN 0-8240-3181-4). Garland Pub.
Lawes Resolutions of Womens Rights: Or, the Lawes Provision for Women. LC 79-84103. (English Experience Ser.: No. 922). 424p. 1979. Repr. of 1632 ed. lib. bdg. 40.00 (ISBN 90-221-0922-4). Walter J Johnson.
Lawful Revolution. Istvan Deak. LC 78-22063. Orig. Title: Reluctant Rebels. (Illus.). 1979. 20.00 (ISBN 0-231-04602-2). Columbia U Pr.
Lawfull Magistrate Upon Colour of Religion. Henry Hammond. Ed. by David S. Berkowitz & Samuel E. Thorne. LC 77-89203. (Classics of English Legal History in the Modern Era Ser.: Vol. 58). 1979. lib. bdg. 40.00 (ISBN 0-8240-3157-1). Garland Pub.
Lawfullness of Deep Seabed Mining, Vols. 1 & 2. Ed. by Theodore G. Kronmiller. LC 79-23232. 1980. Set. lib. bdg. 80.00 (ISBN 0-686-61308-2). Vol. 1, 521p (ISBN 0-379-20461-4). Vol. 2, 460p (ISBN 0-379-20462-2). Oceana.
Lawless Judges. Louis P. Goldberg. LC 74-97451. Repr. of 1935 ed. 17.50x (ISBN 0-8371-2696-7). Negro U Pr.
Lawless Judges. Louis P. Goldberg & Eleanore Levenson. LC 73-138498. (Civil Liberties in American History Ser). 1970. Repr. of 1935 ed. lib. bdg. 29.50 (ISBN 0-306-70070-0). Da Capo.
Lawless: Kent Family Chronicle. John Jakes. 1978. pap. 2.95 (ISBN 0-515-05892-0). Jove Pubns.
Lawless Ones. Chuck Adams. 1979. pap. 1.75 (ISBN 0-505-51399-4). Tower Bks.
Lawless Range. Charles N. Heckelmann. 1977. pap. 1.25 o.p. (ISBN 0-445-00443-6). Popular Lib.
Lawley Road & Other Stories. R. K. Narayan. 159p. 1969. pap. 1.95 o.p. (ISBN 0-88253-062-3). Ind-US Inc.
Lawmaking. 2nd ed. Linda Riekes & Salley M. Ackerly. (Law in Action Ser.). (Illus.). (gr. 5-9). 1980. pap. 4.00 (ISBN 0-8299-1023-9); tchrs.' ed. 4.00 (ISBN 0-8299-1024-7). West Pub.
Lawns -- Basic Factors, Construction & Maintenance of Fine Turf Areas. rev. ed. Jonas Vengris. 10.00 (ISBN 0-913702-05-6). Thomson Pub CA.
Lawns & Ground Covers. James U. Crockett. (Encyclopedia of Gardening Ser). (Illus.). 1971. 11.95 (ISBN 0-8094-1093-1); lib. bdg. avail. (ISBN 0-685-00194-6). Time-Life.
Lawns & Ground Covers. James V. Crockett. LC 78-140420. (Time-Life Encyclopedia of Gardening). (Illus.). (gr. 6 up). 1971. lib. bdg. 11.97 (ISBN 0-8094-1094-X, Pub. by Time-Life). Silver.
Lawrence & the Nature Tradition: A Theme in English Fiction, 1859-1914. Roger Ebbatson. 1980. text ed. 40.00x (ISBN 0-391-01884-1). Humanities.
Lawrence & Women. Ed. by Anne Smith. LC 78-62592. (Critical Studies Ser.). 1978. 23.50x (ISBN 0-06-496377-2); pap. text ed. 8.95x (ISBN 0-389-20055-7). B&N.
Lawrence Bloomfield in Ireland: A Modern Poem. William Allingham. Ed. by Robert L. Wolff. (Ireland Nineteenth Century Fiction - Ser. Two: Vol. 61). 304p. 1979. lib. bdg. 32.00 (ISBN 0-8240-3510-0). Garland Pub.
Lawrence Durrell. John Unterecker. LC 64-22642. (Columbia Essays on Modern Writers Ser.: No. 6). (Orig.). 1964. pap. 2.00 (ISBN 0-231-02655-2, MW6). Columbia U Pr.
Lawrence Durrell. John A. Weigel. 1966. pap. 1.25 o.p. (ISBN 0-525-47185-5). Dutton.
Lawrence Durrell. John A. Weigel. (English Authors Ser.: No. 29). 1965. lib. bdg. 10.95 (ISBN 0-8057-1180-5). Twayne.
Lawrence Durrell: A Study. G. S. Fraser. 1973. pap. 4.95 (ISBN 0-571-04790-4, Pub. by Faber & Faber). Merrimack Bk Serv.
Lawrence of Arabia. Richard Ebert. LC 78-31450. (Raintree Great Adventures). (Illus.). (gr. 3-6). 1979. PLB 8.95 (ISBN 0-8393-0150-2). Raintree Child.
Lawrence of Arabia. Alistair MacLean. (World Landmark Ser: No. 52). (Illus.). (gr. 7-9). 1962. PLB 4.39 (ISBN 0-394-90552-0, BYR). Random.
Lawrence of Arabia & His World. Richard P. Graves. LC 76-7183. (Encore Edition). (Illus.). 128p. 1976. 3.95 (ISBN 0-684-16543-0, ScribT). Scribner.

Laws & Treaties of the World on the Protection of Performers, Producers of Phonograms, & Broadcasting Organizations. 78.25 (ISBN 92-3-100763-7, UM5, UNESCO). Unipub.

Laws for Liberated Living. Manley Beasley & Ras Robinson. 212p. 1980. pap. 4.95 (ISBN 0-937778-01-X); 3.00 (ISBN 0-937778-02-8). Fulness Hse.

Laws, Modalities, & Counterfactuals. Hans Reichenbach. LC 74-29798. Orig. Title: Nomological Statements & Admissible Operations. 1977. 16.50x (ISBN 0-520-02966-6). U of Cal Pr.

Laws of Armed Conflicts. rev. ed. D. Scindler & J. Toman. 904p. 1980. 105.00x (ISBN 90-286-0199-6). Sijthoff & Noordhoff.

Laws of History & the Caprice of Men. C. M. Flumiani. (Illus.). 1977. 49.75 (ISBN 0-89266-018-X). Am Classical Coll Pr.

Laws of Liberty & Property. Giles Jacob et al. Ed. by David. S. Berkowitz & Samuel E. Thorne. LC 77-89197. (Classics of English Legal History in the Modern Era Ser.: Vol. 56). 325p. 1979. lib. bdg. 40.00 (ISBN 0-8240-3156-3). Garland Pub.

Laws of Manu, Vol. 25. Ed. by F. Max Mueller. Tr. by Buhler. (Sacred Books of the East Ser.). 15.00x (ISBN 0-8426-1403-6). Verry.

Laws of Scientific Hand Reading. rev. ed. William G. Benham. (Illus.). 1946. 16.95 (ISBN 0-8015-4446-7, Hawthorn). Dutton.

Laws of Success. Napoleon Hill. 1977. 19.95 (ISBN 0-685-74304-7). Success Unltd.

Laws of Success. Sterling W. Sill. LC 75-18818. 219p. 1975. 6.95 (ISBN 0-87747-556-3). Deseret Bk.

Laws of the Game: How the Principles of Nature Govern Chance. Manfred Eigen & Ruthild Winkler. LC 79-3494. (Illus.). 384p. 1981. 17.95 (ISBN 0-394-41806-9). Knopf.

Laws of the Game: How the Principles of Nature Govern Chance. Manfred Eigen & Ruthild Winkler. LC 79-3494. (Illus.). 384p. 1981. cancelled o.p. (ISBN 0-394-41806-9). Knopf.

Laws of the Kings of England from Edmund to Henry I. Ed. by A. J. Robertson. LC 80-2210. 1981. Repr. of 1925 ed. 52.50 (ISBN 0-404-18784-6). AMS Pr.

Laws of the Turks & Caicos, Vol. 7. J. N. Glover. 1980. 47.50 (ISBN 0-379-12707-5). Oceana.

Laws of Virginia: Being a Supplement to Hening's the Statutes at Large. Ed. by Waverly K. Winfree. 486p. 1971. 15.00x o.p. (ISBN 0-88490-025-8, Virginia State Library). U Pr of Va.

Laws, Ordinances, Regulations, & Rules Relating to the Judicial Administration of the Republic of China. Republic of China. (Studies in Chinese Government & Law). 364p. 1977. Repr. of 1923 ed. 24.00 (ISBN 0-89093-062-7). U Pubns Amer.

Laws Respecting Women. 1973. 27.50 (ISBN 0-379-20200-X). Oceana.

Laws, Theories & Values. 2nd ed. Jorge A. Quintero. (Illus.). 144p. 1980. 10.50 (ISBN 0-87527-147-2). Green.

Lawsuit. Stuart M. Speiser. 600p. 1980. 40.00 (ISBN 0-8180-2200-0); pap. 9.95 (ISBN 0-8180-2201-9). Horizon.

Lawsuits & Litigants in Castile, 1500-1700. Richard L. Kagan. LC 80-17565. 304p. 1981. 23.00x (ISBN 0-8078-1457-1). U of NC Pr.

Lawton's & Foy's Textbook for Medical Assistants. 4th ed. M. Murray Lawton et al. LC 80-15524. (Illus.). 456p. 1980. text ed. 17.95 (ISBN 0-8016-2893-8). Mosby.

Lawyer in the Wilderness, Data Paper No. 114. K. H. Digby. 150p. 1980. 5.75 (ISBN 0-87727-114-3). Cornell SE Asia.

Lawyer Looks at the Constitution. Rex E. Lee. (Illus.). 256p. 1981. 19.95 (ISBN 0-8425-1904-1). Brigham.

Lawyer Looks at the Equal Rights Amendment. Rex E. Lee. LC 80-22202. (Illus.). 150p. 1980. pap. 7.95 (ISBN 0-8425-1883-5). Brigham.

Lawyers. T. Danielle. 1976. 17.50 (ISBN 0-379-00593-X). Oceana.

Lawyers: A Client's Manual. J. C. McGinn. 1979. 11.95 o.p. (ISBN 0-13-526814-1); pap. 5.95 o.p. (ISBN 0-13-526806-0); 14 sets tape 100.00 o.p. (ISBN 0-13-530444-X). P-H.

Lawyers & Politics in the Arab World, 1880-1960. Donald M. Reid. LC 80-71053. (Studies in Middle Eastern History: No. 5). 600p. 1981. 30.00 (ISBN 0-88297-028-3). Bibliotheca.

Lawyers & the Constitution. Benjamin Twiss. LC 73-10765. 271p. 1974. Repr. of 1942 ed. lib. bdg. 15.75x (ISBN 0-8371-7033-8, TWLC). Greenwood.

Lawyers & the Law in New York State: A Short History & Guide. Jack Henke. (Illus.). 187p. 1979. 11.95 (ISBN 0-89062-066-0, Pub. by Hughes Press); pap. 6.95 (ISBN 0-89062-065-2). Pub Ctr Cult Res.

Lawyers' Arbitration Letters, 1970 to 1979. American Arbitration Association. 1981. 15.95 (ISBN 0-02-900570-1). Free Pr.

Lawyers Desk Reference, 2 vols. 6th ed. Harry Philo et al. Date not set. 85.00 (ISBN 0-686-27087-8). Lawyers Co-Op.

Lawyer's Guide to International Business Transactions, Pt. IV. Ed. by Walter S. Surrey & Don Wallace, Jr. 471p. 1980. 55.00 (ISBN 0-686-28717-7, B96B4). ALI-ABA.

Lawyers in Early Modern Europe & America. Ed. by Wilfrid Prest. LC 80-22574. 224p. 1981. text ed. 27.50x (ISBN 0-8419-0679-3). Holmes & Meier.

Lawyer's Lawyer: The Life of John W. Davis. William H. Harbaugh. 550p. 1973. 25.00 (ISBN 0-19-501699-8). Oxford U Pr.

Lawyers of Hell. Ron Gorton. LC 78-27011. 1979. 9.95 (ISBN 0-8119-0319-2). Fell.

Lawyers on Their Own: A Study of Individual Practitioners in Chicago. Jerome E. Carlin. 1962. 15.00 (ISBN 0-8135-0412-0). Rutgers U Pr.

Lawyers, Psychiatrists & Criminal Law: Cooperation or Chaos? Harlow Huckabee. 220p. 1980. 16.75 (ISBN 0-398-04084-2). C C Thomas.

Lawyer's Robinson-Patman Act Sourcebook: Opinions of the FTC & the Courts, & Related Materials, 4 vols. Ed. by S. Chesterfield Oppenheim & Glen E. Weston. 2723p. 1971. 160.00 set (ISBN 0-316-65089-7). Little.

Lay Down Your Arms: The Autobiography of Martha von Trilling. Bertha Von Suttner. LC 79-147459. (Library of War & Peace; Peace Leaders: Biographies & Memoirs). lib. bdg. 38.00 (ISBN 0-8240-0318-7). Garland Pub.

Lay My Burden Down: A Folk History of Slavery. Federal Writers' Project. 285p. 1945. Repr. 39.00 (ISBN 0-403-02212-6). Somerset Pub.

Lay of the Last Minstrel: Vol. 1-2, Three Essays. J. H. Alexander. (Salzburg Studies in English Literature, Romantic Reassessment: No. 77). 1978. pap. text ed. 25.00x (ISBN 0-391-01290-8). Humanities.

Lay Preacher. Joseph Dennie. LC 43-9749. 1979. Repr. of 1796 ed. lib. bdg. 22.00x (ISBN 0-8201-1204-6). Schol Facsimiles.

Lay up Your Treasures in Heaven. Eleanor T. Mead. 1977. pap. 3.95 o.p. (ISBN 0-88270-257-2). Logos.

Layer Analysis: A Primer of Elementary Tonal Structures. Gerald Warfield. (Music Ser.). 1978. pap. text ed. 11.95x (ISBN 0-582-28069-9). Longman.

Layer Dictation: A New Approach to the Bach Chorales. Richard Brooks & Gerald Warfield. LC 77-17720. (Music Ser.). 1978. pap. text ed. 11.95x (ISBN 0-582-28046-X). Longman.

Layered Igneous Rocks. L. R. Wager & G. M. Brown. (Illus.). 1967. text ed. 41.95x (ISBN 0-7167-0236-3). W H Freeman.

Laying a Watercolour Wash. Leslie Worth. (Leisure Arts Painting Ser.). (Illus.). 32p. 1980. pap. 2.50 (ISBN 0-8008-4574-9, Pentalic). Taplinger.

Laying on of Hands. Kenneth E. Hagin. 1980. pap. 0.50 mini bk. (ISBN 0-89276-250-0). Hagin Ministries.

Laying on of Hands. Derek Prince. (Foundation Ser.: Bk. V). 1965-66. pap. 1.50 (ISBN 0-934920-04-4, B-14). Derek Prince.

Laying Waste: The Poisoning of America by Toxic Chemicals. Michael Brown. 1981. pap. 3.50. WSP.

Layle Jonathan, of Mountain Springs. Ruby A. Newman. 140p. (Orig.). 1981. pap. 3.50 (ISBN 0-932964-07-9). MN Pubs.

Layman Looks at the Lord's Prayer. W. Philip Keller. study ed 4.95 (ISBN 0-8024-4647-7). Moody.

Layman Looks at the Lord's Prayer: Leader's Guide. Welda Cockman. 1979. pap. 3.25 (ISBN 0-8024-4646-9). Moody.

Layman's Bible Book Commentary: Hebrews, James, 1 & 2 Peter, Vol.23. Foy Valentine. 1981. 4.75 (ISBN 0-8054-1193-3). Broadman.

Layman's Bible Book Commentary: Matthew, Vol. 15. Clair Crissey. 1981. 4.75 (ISBN 0-8054-1185-2). Broadman.

Layman's Bible Book Commentary: 1 & 2 Samuel & 1 Chronicles. Joe O. Lewis. LC 79-54796. 1981. 4.25 (ISBN 0-8054-1175-5). Broadman.

Layman's Guide to Acupuncture. Yoshio Manaka & Ian A. Urquhart. LC 72-78590. (Illus.). 144p. 1975. pap. 5.95 (ISBN 0-8348-0107-8). Weatherhill.

Layman's Guide to Construction Finishing Techniques. LC 77-88956. (Illus.). 1978. pap. 5.95 (ISBN 0-8069-8468-6, 022300). Sterling.

Layman's Guide to Copyright. William S. Strong. 192p. 1981. text ed. 12.50 (ISBN 0-262-19194-6). MIT Pr.

Layman's Guide to Interpreting the Bible. Walter A. Henrichsen. 1979. pap. 5.95 (ISBN 0-310-37701-3). Zondervan.

Layman's Guide to Psychiatry & Psychoanalysis. Eric Berne. 1976. pap. 2.50 (ISBN 0-345-28472-0). Ballantine.

Layman's Guide to the Inerrancy Debate. Richard Belcher. 1980. pap. 2.50 (ISBN 0-8024-2379-5). Moody.

Layman's Guide to the New Testament. William M. Ramsay. LC 79-87742. (Layman's Bible Commentary Ser.). 273p. (Orig.). 1980. pap. 10.00 (ISBN 0-8042-0322-9). John Knox.

Layman's Handbook of Interior Design. Ellen Angell. 1972. 5.00 o.p. (ISBN 0-682-47363-4, Banner). Exposition.

Layout & Graphic Design. Raymond A. Ballinger. 96p. 1980. pap. 8.95 (ISBN 0-442-20178-8). Van Nos Reinhold.

Laypersons Handbook of Radiation & How to Protect Yourself. Peter J. Peloquin. (Orig.). 1980. pap. 1.95 (ISBN 0-936448-01-6). Peloquin Pubn.

Laysan & Black Footed Albatrosses. Alfred M. Bailey. (Museum Pictorial: No. 6). 1952. pap. 1.10 o.p. (ISBN 0-916278-35-2). Denver Mus Natl Hist.

Lazaro Cardenas: Mexican Democrat. 2nd rev. enlarged ed. William C. Townsend. 1979. pap. 4.95 (ISBN 0-935340-00-9). Intl Friend.

Lazarus. Andre Malraux. Tr. by Terence Kilmartin. LC 76-58426. 1977. 7.95 o.p. (ISBN 0-03-015351-4). HR&W.

Lazarus, Come Out! The Story of My Life. Matthew Silvan. Ed. by Hugh Moran. Tr. by Vera Giannini from It. LC 80-82599. Orig. Title: Quella Violenza Di Dio. 224p. (Orig.). 1981. pap. 5.95 (ISBN 0-911782-36-2). New City.

Lazarus Guns. Paul Ledd. (Shelter Ser.: No. 5). 256p. (Orig.). 1980. pap. 1.95 (ISBN 0-89083-694-9). Zebra.

Lazarus Inheritance. Noel V. Carter. 1976. pap. 1.25 o.p. (ISBN 0-445-00432-0). Popular Lib.

Lazies: Tales of the Peoples of Russia. Ed. & tr. by Mirra Ginsburg. LC 72-92437. (Illus.). 80p. (gr. 3-6). 1973. 7.95 (ISBN 0-02-735840-2). Macmillan.

Lazlo Letters. Don Novello. LC 77-5811. (Illus.). 1977. 3.95 (ISBN 0-911104-96-8). Workman Pub.

Lazo Del Cazador. Tr. by Tom Taylor. (Spanish Bks.). (Span.). 1978. 1.75 (ISBN 0-8297-0776-X). Life Pubs Intl.

Lazy Bear. Brian Wildsmith. LC 73-8398. (Illus.). 32p. (gr. k-3). 1974. PLB 5.95 o.p. (ISBN 0-531-01559-9). Watts.

Lazy Indoor Gardener. Robert Pliner. 1976. pap. 3.95 (ISBN 0-394-73160-3). Random.

Lazy Investor's Way to Beat Inflation. Thurman L. Smith. (Illus.). 1979. pap. 5.95 (ISBN 0-934410-00-3). Explorer Pub Co.

Lazy South. David Bertelson. LC 80-24033. ix, 284p. 1980. Repr. of 1967 ed. lib. bdg. 25.00x (ISBN 0-313-22696-2, BELS). Greenwood.

Lazy Stories. Diane Wolkstein. LC 75-25781. (Illus.). 32p. (gr. 1-5). 1976. 6.95 o.p. (ISBN 0-8164-3135-3, Clarion). HM.

LBJ: Images of a Vibrant Life. (Illus.). 112p. 1973. 10.00 o.p. (ISBN 0-685-48120-4). Shoal Creek Pub.

LBJ: Thirty-Seven Years of Public Service. Joe B. Frantz. LC 73-91025. (Illus.). 120p. 1974. 3.95 o.p. (ISBN 0-88319-018-4). Shoal Creek Pub.

LBSC's Shop, Shed & Road. 2nd ed. Martin Evans. 192p. (Orig.). 1979. pap. 12.50x (ISBN 0-85242-708-5). Intl Pubns Serv.

Le Bossu & Voltaire on the Epic: Rene Le Bossu, Treatise of the Epick Poem, 1695 & Voltaire, Essay on Epick Poetry, 1727. Ed. by Stuart Curran. LC 73-133363. 1970. 37.00x (ISBN 0-8201-1086-8). Schol Facsimiles.

Le Corbusier. Maurice Besset. LC 76-11507. (Illus.). 1976. 50.00 o.p. (ISBN 0-8478-0048-2). Rizzoli Intl.

Le Corbusier. Francoise Choay. LC 60-6079. (Masters of World Architecture Ser). 1960. 7.95 o.p. (ISBN 0-8076-0104-7). Braziller.

Leabhar Na Feinne. J. F. Campbell. 272p. 1972. Repr. of 1872 ed. 36.00x (ISBN 0-7165-2060-5, Pub. by Irish Academic Pr Ireland). Biblio Dist.

Leaching & Recovering Copper from As-Mined Materials. Ed. by W. J. Schlitt. LC 79-57347. (Illus.). 124p. 1980. pap. 15.00x (ISBN 0-89520-272-7). Soc Mining Eng.

Lead Absorption in Children: Management, Clinical & Environmental Aspects. J. J. Chisolm & D. M. O'Hara. 1981. price not set. Urban & S.

Lead Acid Batteries. Hans Bode. LC 76-58418. (Electrochemical Society Ser). 1977. 41.50 (ISBN 0-471-08455-7, Pub. by Wiley-Interscience). Wiley.

Lead: Airborne Lead in Perspective. Committee on Biological Effects of Atmospheric Pollutants. LC 71-186214. (Biological Effects of Atmospheric Pollutants Ser.). (Illus.). 1972. pap. 9.50 (ISBN 0-309-01941-9). Natl Acad Pr.

Lead & the Human Organism. E. Kolisko. 1980. pap. 3.95x (ISBN 0-906492-31-9, Pub. by Kolisko Archives). St George Bk Serv.

Lead Hungry Lobos. Burt Arthur. 1978. pap. 1.25 (ISBN 0-505-51255-6). Tower Bks.

Lead in the Environment. Ed. by William R. Boggess. (Illus.). 272p. 1979. 45.00x (ISBN 0-7194-0024-4). Intl Pubns Serv.

Lead in the Environment. Ed. by P. Hepple. 1972. 18.60x (ISBN 0-85334-485-X). Intl Ideas.

Lead in the Human Environment. 1980. 16.75 (ISBN 0-309-03021-8). Natl Acad Pr.

Lead in the Marine Environment: Proceedings. International Experts Discussion on Lead Occurrence, Fate & Pollution in the Marine Environment, Rovinj, Yugoslavia, 18-22 October 1977. Ed. by Z. Konrad & M. Branica. LC 80-40023. (Illus.). 364p. 1980. pap. 69.00 (ISBN 0-08-022960-3). Pergamon.

Lead King: Moses Austin. James A. Gardner. 256p. 1980. 9.95 (ISBN 0-86629-004-4). Sunrise MO.

Lead Nineteen Sixty-Eight: Proceedings, International Conference on Lead - 3rd - Venice - 1968. Ed. by A. I. Hughes. LC 66-18688. 1970. 69.00 (ISBN 0-08-015644-4). Pergamon.

Lead Oxides: Chemistry, Technology, Battery Manufacturing Uses, History. Nels E. Hehner & Everett J. Ritchie. 1974. 15.00 (ISBN 0-685-56653-6). IBMA Pubns.

Lead the Way, Rangers - Fifth Ranger Bn. Henry S. Glassman. (Illus.). 104p. 1980. pap. 5.95 (ISBN 0-934588-03-1). Ranger Assocs.

Lead Tin Telluride, Silver Halides & Czochralski Growth. Wilcox. Date not set. price not set (ISBN 0-8247-1354-0). Dekker.

Lead Us into Temptation. Breandan O Heithir. 1978. 12.00 (ISBN 0-7100-0030-8). Routledge & Kegan.

Leader: A Political Biography of Gough Whitlam. James Walter. (Illus.). 295p. 1981. text ed. 18.00x (ISBN 0-7022-1557-0). U of Queensland Pr.

Leader at Large: The Long & Fighting Life of Norman Thomas. Charles Gorham. LC 72-119548. (Illus.). (gr. 7 up). 1970. 4.95 o.p. (ISBN 0-374-34372-1). FS&G.

Leader's Guide for Opening the Old Testament. Keith M. Bailey. 50p. (Orig.). 1980. pap. 1.25 (ISBN 0-87509-283-7). Chr Pubns.

Leader's Guide to Assertive Training Procedures for Women. Pearlman et al. 24p. 1973. pap. 3.75 (ISBN 0-686-11452-3). Am Personnel.

Leader's Guide to Back to School, Back to Work. Pearlman & Resnikoff. 24p. 1973. pap. 3.75 (ISBN 0-686-11451-5). Am Personnel.

Leaders in Anthropology: The Men & Women of the Science of Man. Jack F. Kinton. 1974. 8.95 (ISBN 0-685-79791-0); pap. 4.95 supplementary text (ISBN 0-685-79792-9). Soc Sci & Soc Res.

Leaders, Leading, & Leadership. Harold W. Boles. LC 80-65616. 170p. 1981. cancelled (ISBN 0-86548-023-0). Century Twenty One.

Leaders of Our People, 2 Bks. Joseph H. Gumbiner. (Illus.). (gr. 4-6). Bk. 1. 1963. text ed. 5.00 (ISBN 0-8074-0141-2, 122921); Bk. 2. 1965. text ed. 5.00 (ISBN 0-8074-0142-0, 123921); tchrs'. guide 3.25 (ISBN 0-8074-0143-9, 202922). UAHC.

Leaders of Public Opinion in Ireland, 2 vols. Wm. Edward Lecky. LC 76-159800. (Europe 1815-1945 Ser.). 720p. 1973. Repr. of 1903 ed. Set. lib. bdg. 59.50 (ISBN 0-306-70574-5). Da Capo.

Leaders of the French Revolution. J. M. Thompson. (Illus.). 272p. 1980. pap. 9.95x (ISBN 0-631-11931-0, Pub. by Basil Blackwell). Biblio Dist.

Leadership. James M. Burns. LC 76-5117. 1979. pap. 8.95 (ISBN 0-06-090697-9, CN 697, CN). Har-Row.

Leadership & Ambiguity: The American College President. Carnegie Commission on Higher Education. Ed. by Michael D. Cohen & James G. March. LC 73-7558. (Illus.). 304p. 1974. 13.50 o.p. (ISBN 0-07-010063-2, P&RB). McGraw.

Leadership & Change in Special Education. Leonard C. Burrello & Daniel D. Sage. (P-H Ser. in Special Education). 1979. 17.95 (ISBN 0-13-526921-0). P-H.

Leadership & Church Growth. J. J. Turner. pap. 2.50 (ISBN 0-89315-137-8). Lambert Bk.

Leadership & Effective Management. Fred E. Fiedler & Martin M. Chemers. 1974. pap. 8.95x o.p. (ISBN 0-673-07768-3). Scott F.

Leadership & Local Politics: A Study of Meerut District District in Uttar Pradesh (India) 1923-73. Shree Nagesh Jha. 175p. 1979. text ed. 14.50 (ISBN 0-8426-1640-3). Verry.

Leadership & Local Politics: Study of Meerut District in Uttar Pradesh, 1923 to 1973. 1979. 14.50 o.p. (ISBN 0-8426-1640-3). Verry.

Leadership & National Development in North Africa: A Comparative Study. Elbaki Hermassi. LC 70-182279. 250p. 1973. pap. 6.95x (ISBN 0-520-02894-5). U of Cal Pr.

Leadership Book. Charles J. Keating. LC 77-99300. 1978. pap. 2.95 (ISBN 0-8091-2090-9). Paulist Pr.

Leadership Dynamics: A Practical Guide to Effective Relationships. Edwin P. Hollander. LC 77-15884. 1978. 14.95 (ISBN 0-02-914820-0). Free Pr.
Leadership for Action in Rural Communities. Burton W. Kreitlow et al. LC 65-20644. (Illus.). 1965. 11.35 (ISBN 0-8134-0532-7); text ed. 8.50x (ISBN 0-685-12632-3, 532). Interstate.
Leadership for Change: A Guide for the Frustrated Nurse. Dorothy A. Brooten et al. LC 78-8661. pap. 7.50 (ISBN 0-397-54218-6). Lippincott.
Leadership, Goals & Power in Higher Education: A Contingency & Open-Systems Approach to Effective Management. Barry M. Richman & Richard N. Farmer. LC 74-9112. (Higher Education Ser.). 320p. 1974. 15.95x (ISBN 0-87589-235-3). Jossey-Bass.
Leadership Guide for Elementary School Improvement: Procedures for Assessment & Change. new ed. Carl D. Glickman & James P. Esposito. 1979. text ed. 17.75 (ISBN 0-205-06443-4). Allyn.
Leadership Ideology in Africa: Attitudes Toward Socioeconomic Development. Ukandi G. Damachi. LC 75-19772. (Illus.). 128p. 1976. text ed. 17.95 o.p. (ISBN 0-275-56760-5). Praeger.
Leadership in Administration of Vocational & Technical Education. Ralph C. Wenrich & William J. Wenrich. LC 73-86161. 1974. text ed. 20.95 (ISBN 0-675-08878-X). Merrill.
Leadership in Crisis: FDR & the Path to Intervention. Gloria J. Barron. LC 73-75576. 1973. 9.95 (ISBN 0-8046-9038-3, Natl U). Kennikat.
Leadership in Eastern Africa: Six Political Biographies. Ed. by Norman R. Bennett. LC 68-21921. (Pub. by Boston U Pr). 1968. 15.00x (ISBN 0-8419-8705-X, Africana). Holmes & Meier.
Leadership in Librarianship: A Futuristic View. Ed. by Donald E. Riggs. 1981. lib. bdg. 17.50x (ISBN 0-912700-64-5). Oryx Pr.
Leadership in Management. Barry Maude. 240p. 1978. text ed. 29.50x (ISBN 0-220-66361-0, Pub. by Busn Bks England). Renouf.
Leadership in Nineteenth Century Africa. Ed. by Obaro Ikime. (Illus.). 208p. (Orig.). 1974. pap. text ed. 7.00x (ISBN 0-391-00357-7). Humanities.
Leadership in Nursing. Charlotte Epstein. 225p. 1981. text ed. 14.95 (ISBN 0-8359-3970-7); pap. text ed. 12.95 (ISBN 0-8359-3969-3). Reston.
Leadership in Organizations. Gary Yukl. (Illus.). 336p. 1981. text ed. 16.95 (ISBN 0-13-527176-2). P-H.
Leadership in Soviet National Republics. Grey Hodnett. 409p. (Orig.). 1978. pap. text ed. 45.00 (ISBN 0-686-61282-5, Pub. by K G Saur). Gale.
Leadership in the Eighties: Essays on Higher Education. Chris Argyris & Richard M. Cyert. LC 80-80425. 100p. 1980. pap. text ed. 4.50 (ISBN 0-934222-01-0). Inst Ed Manage.
Leadership in the Secondary School. new ed. Frederick M. Raubinger et al. (Education-Administration Ser.). 464p. 1974. text ed. 20.95x (ISBN 0-675-08796-1). Merrill.
Leadership, Management & Role Delineation: Issues for the Dental Team. Irene R. Woodall. LC 77-8533. (Illus.). 1977. pap. 13.95 (ISBN 0-8016-5621-4). Mosby.
Leadership of Abraham Lincoln. Don E. Fehrenbacher. LC 77-114013. (Problems in American History Ser.). 194p. 1970. pap. text ed. 8.95 (ISBN 0-471-25689-7). Wiley.
Leadership: The Science & Art Today, Proceedings. Phi Delta Kappa Symposium on Educational Research, 12th. Ed. by William J. Gephart & Lavern Cunningham. LC 60-2874. 320p. 1973. 8.50 (ISBN 0-87581-155-8). Phi Delta Kappa.
Leadership: The Science & the Art Today. Ed. by Luvern L. Cunningham & William J. Gephart. LC 60-2874. 1973. text ed. 10.00 (ISBN 0-87581-155-8). Peacock Pubs.
Leadership Through Values: A Study in Personal & Organizational Development. Brian P. Hall. LC 80-81438. (Illus.). 112p. (Orig.). 1980. pap. 8.95 (ISBN 0-8091-2313-4). Paulist Pr.
Leading Constitutional Decisions. 15th ed. Robert F. Cushman. 1977. pap. text ed. 11.95 (ISBN 0-13-527358-7). P-H.
Leading Little Ones to God: A Child's Book of Bible Teaching. rev., 2nd ed. Marian M. Schoolland. (Illus.). 96p. 1981. 9.95 (ISBN 0-8028-4035-3). Eerdmans.
Leading the Family of God. Paul M. Miller. 216p. 1981. pap. 7.95 (ISBN 0-8361-1950-9). Herald Pr.
Leading the Lord's Singing. Jack Boyd. 1981. pap. write for info. (ISBN 0-89137-603-8). Quality Pubns.
Leading the Way: State Mandates for School Advisory Council in California, Florida, & South Carolina. Ross Zerchykov et al. 175p. (Orig.). 1980. pap. 6.00 (ISBN 0-917754-15-8). Inst Responsive.
Leaf & Bone: African Praise Poems. Judith Gleason. LC 79-56265. 228p. 1980. 14.95 (ISBN 0-670-42178-2). Viking Pr.
Leaf Magic. Margaret Mahy. LC 76-3538. (Illus.). (gr. k-4). 1977. 5.95 o.s.i. (ISBN 0-8193-0889-7, Four Winds); PLB 5.41 o.s.i. (ISBN 0-8193-0890-0). Schol Bk Serv.
Leaf Storm & Other Stories. Gabriel Garcia-Marquez. Tr. by Gregory Rabassa from Span. LC 76-138784. 192p. 1972. 10.95 o.s.i. (ISBN 0-06-012779-1, HarpT). Har-Row.
Leafy Salad Vegetables. Edward J. Ryder. (Illus.). 1979. text ed. 26.00 (ISBN 0-87055-323-2). AVI.
League for Industrial Democracy: A Documentary History, 3 vols. Compiled By Bernard K. Johnpoll. LC 80-537. (Documentary Reference Ser.). (Illus.). xiii, 2587p. 1980. Set. lib. bdg. 225.00 (ISBN 0-313-22084-0, YIN/). Greenwood.
League for Social Reconstruction: Intellectual Origins of the Democratic Left in Canada, 1930-1942. Michiel Horn. 1980. 20.00 (ISBN 0-8020-5487-0). U of Toronto Pr.
League of Dark Men. John Creasey. 176p. 1975. pap. 0.95 o.p. (ISBN 0-445-00655-2). Popular Lib.
League of Frightened Men. Rex Stout. 1979. pap. 1.75 o.s.i. (ISBN 0-515-05116-0). Jove Pubns.
League of the Iroquois. L. H. Morgan. (Illus.). 11.50 (ISBN 0-8446-2612-0). Peter Smith.
League of the Scarlet Pimpernel. Emmuska Orczy. 238p. 1981. Repr. lib. bdg. 12.95x (ISBN 0-89966-286-2). Buccaneer Bks.
Lean Machine: David Luna's Guide to Total Fitness & the Sensible Diet. David Luna. LC 79-89792. (Illus.). 131p. 1980. pap. 7.95 (ISBN 0-915238-34-9); 12.95 o.p. (ISBN 0-915238-36-5). Peace Pr.
Leandro Fernandez de Moratin. John Dowling. (World Authors Ser.: Spain: No. 149). lib. bdg. 10.95 (ISBN 0-8057-2630-6). Twayne.
Leaning Tower. Maria Talwick. 1977. pap. 1.95 o.p. (ISBN 0-345-25723-5). Ballantine.
Lean's Collectanea, 5 vols. Vincent S. Lean. LC 68-26583. 1969. Repr. of 1902 ed. Set. 130.00 (ISBN 0-8103-3203-5). Gale.
Leap to the Sun: Learning Through Dynamic Play. Judith Peck. (Illus.). 1979. 12.95 (ISBN 0-13-527275-0, Spec); pap. 5.95 (ISBN 0-13-527267-X). P-H.
Leaping Hare. David Thomson & George E. Evans. (Illus.). 1972. 9.95 (ISBN 0-571-09559-3, Pub. by Faber & Faber); pap. 4.95 (ISBN 0-571-10630-7). Merrimack Bk Serv.
Leaping into Language with Sound-a-Roo. Letty A. Lindley. 1981. pap. 9.95 (ISBN 0-8134-2165-9). Interstate.
Leaping Poetry: An Idea with Poems & Translations. Robert Bly. LC 73-6243. (A Seventies Press Bk). 112p. 1975. pap. 4,50 (ISBN 0-8070-6393-2, BP462). Beacon Pr.
Learn-a-Term. A. Brent Garber & Leroy Sparks. LC 77-82026. 1977. pap. text ed. 16.50 (ISBN 0-912862-48-3). Aspen Systems.
Learn Arabic Reading & Writing I. Mounir Ghandour. pap. 5.00; book & cassettes 30.00. Intl Bk Ctr.
Learn Burmese for English Speakers. pap. 7.00 (ISBN 0-685-90821-6). Saphrograph.
Learn Chess from the World Champions. Ed. by David N. L. Levy. 1978. text ed. 22.00 (ISBN 0-08-021387-1); pap. text ed. 9.50 (ISBN 0-08-021388-X). Pergamon.
Learn Dutch! A Dutch Grammar. F. G. Renier. 1960. pap. 3.95 o.p. (ISBN 0-7100-6818-2). Routledge & Kegan.
Learn English for Polish Speakers. pap. 7.00 (ISBN 0-685-77572-0, 061-5). Saphrograph.
Learn English for Science. A. R. Bolitho & P. L. Sandler. pap. text ed. 3.50x student bk. (ISBN 0-582-55247-8); pap. text ed. 2.50x tchr's bk. (ISBN 0-582-55482-9). Longman.
Learn French in Record Time. LC 58-8917. (Learn Language in Record Time Ser). 11.98, incl. 2 records o.p. (ISBN 0-385-00644-6). Doubleday.
Learn French the BBC Way: Book 1. (gr. 7-12). 1977. pap. text ed. 5.95 (ISBN 0-8120-0723-9); tape 5.20 (ISBN 0-8120-0743-3); tchr's manual 2.00 (ISBN 0-8120-0745-X). Barron.
Learn French the BBC Way: Book 2. (gr. 8-12). 1978. pap. text ed. 5.95 (ISBN 0-8120-0724-7); tape 5.20 (ISBN 0-8120-0744-1); tchr's manual 2.00 (ISBN 0-8120-0746-8). Barron.
Learn from the Grandmasters. R. D. Keene. 1975. pap. 9.95 (ISBN 0-7134-3043-5). David & Charles.
Learn German for English Speakers. P. F. Doring. pap. 7.00 (ISBN 0-87557-027-5). Saphrograph.
Learn German in Record Time. LC 58-8920. (Learn Language in Record Time Ser). 11.98, incl. 2 records o.p. (ISBN 0-385-00645-4). Doubleday.
Learn Gunsmithing: The Troubleshooting Method. John Traister. (Illus.). 288p. 1980. 12.95 (ISBN 0-87691-317-6). Winchester Pr.
Learn Hungarian. Zoltan Banhidi et al. 1965. text ed. 22.00x (ISBN 963-17-0971-X). Intl Learn Syst.
Learn Irish for English Speakers. pap. 7.00 (ISBN 0-685-90820-8). Saphrograph.
Learn Japanese in Record Time. LC 69-12578. (Learn Language in Record Time Ser). 10.98, incl. 2 records o.p. (ISBN 0-385-07866-8). Doubleday.
Learn Modern Greek in Record Time. LC 60-12824. (Learn Language in Record Time Ser). 10.98, incl. 2 records o.p. (ISBN 0-385-01042-7). Doubleday.
Learn Polish: For English Speakers. pap. 7.50 (ISBN 0-685-33021-4, 061-5). Saphrograph.
Learn Spanish in Record Time. LC 58-8918. (Learn Language in Record Time Ser). 11.98, incl. 2 records o.p. (ISBN 0-385-00643-8). Doubleday.
Learn to Count. Richard Scarry. (Golden Look-Look Bks.). (Illus.). (ps-1). 1976. PLB 5.38 (ISBN 0-307-61829-3, Golden Pr); pap. 0.95 (ISBN 0-307-11829-0). Western Pub.
Learn to Live. Ervin Seale. 1966. pap. 5.95 (ISBN 0-911336-08-7). Sci of Mind.
Learn to Read Arabic. Raja Nasr. 1977. pap. 5.00x (ISBN 0-917062-02-7); with cassette 20.00x (ISBN 0-685-77769-3). Intl Bk Ctr.
Learn to Relax. Willis A. Jewell. 1980. pap. 9.95. W a Jewell.
Learn to Relax: 13 Ways to Reduce Tension. C. Eugene Walker. 1975. 12.95 (ISBN 0-13-527564-4, Spec); pap. 3.45 (ISBN 0-13-527556-3, Spec). P-H.
Learn Touch Typing in Four Easy Lessons. Adolph Gerstenzang. (Secretarial Paperback Ser). (Illus.). 1968. pap. 1.50 o.p. (ISBN 0-8069-7404-4). Sterling.
Learned Societies & Printing Clubs of the United Kingdom. Abraham Hume. LC 66-16418. 1966. Repr. of 1853 ed. 18.00 (ISBN 0-8103-3081-4). Gale.
Learned Tico Brahe His Astronomicall Conjectur of the New & Much Admired Star Which Appeared in the Year 1572. Tycho Brahe. LC 74-6157. (English Experience Ser.: No. 86). 28p. 1969. Repr. of 1632 ed. 14.00 (ISBN 90-221-0086-3). Walter J Johnson.
Learner-Centered Reform: Current Issues in Higher Education 1975. Ed. by Dyckman W. Vermilye. LC 75-24001. (Higher Education Ser.). 252p. 1975. 12.95x o.p. (ISBN 0-87589-263-9). Jossey-Bass.
Learner Driver. Joseph Kells. LC 74-81073. (Illus.). 142p. 1975. 11.95 (ISBN 0-7153-6794-3). David & Charles.
Learners & Discerners: A Newer Criticism. Ed. by Robert Scholes. LC 64-13303. 1964. 10.95x (ISBN 0-8139-0213-4). U Pr of Va.
Learner's Chinese-English Dictionary. 1979. 12.50 (ISBN 0-8351-0641-1). China Bks.
Learning. A. Charles Catania. (Century Psychology Ser.). (Illus.). 1979. text ed. 18.95 (ISBN 0-13-527432-X). P-H.
Learning: A Conceptual Approach. K. P. Hillner. 1977. text ed. 33.00 (ISBN 0-08-017864-2); pap. text ed. 13.25 (ISBN 0-08-017865-0). Pergamon.
Learning a Foreign Language. Eugene A. Nida. (Orig.). 1957. pap. 4.50 o.p. (ISBN 0-377-29041-6). Friend Pr.
Learning About Jesus. rev. ed. Francis Schraff et al. 80p. (gr. 2-4). 1980. pap. 1.95 (ISBN 0-89243-129-6). Liguori Pubns.
Learning About Linguistics. F. C. Stork & J. D. Widdowson. 1980. pap. text ed. 8.50x (ISBN 0-09-118061-9, Hutchinson U Lib). Humanities.
Learning About Michigan's Government. rev., 2nd ed. Ferris E. Lewis & David B. McConnell. (Illus.). (gr. 7-10). 1973. text ed. 9.20x o.p. (ISBN 0-910726-30-2). Hillsdale Educ.
Learning About Rural Women. Ed. by Sondra Zeidenstein. (Studies in Family Planning Ser.: Vol. 10, Nos. 11-12). 118p. (Orig.). 1979. pap. 2.50. Population Coun.
Learning After College. Nevitt Sanford. 264p. 1980. 14.50 (ISBN 0-917430-04-2); pap. 9.95 (ISBN 0-917430-03-4). Montaigne.
Learning After College. new ed. R. Nevitt Sanford & Craig Comstock. 277p. (Orig.). 1980. 14.50 (ISBN 0-917430-04-2); pap. 9.95 (ISBN 0-917430-03-4). Montaigne.
Learning & Behavior Characteristics of Exceptional Children & Youth: A Humanistic Behavioral Approach. William I Gardner. 1977. text ed. 18.50x (ISBN 0-205-05586-9). Allyn.
Learning & Behaviour Difficulties in School. D. J. Leach & E. C. Raybould. (Psychology & Education Ser.). 1977. text ed. 11.75x (ISBN 0-7291-0076-6); pap. text ed. 5.25x (ISBN 0-7291-0071-5). Humanities.
Learning & Earning: Aspects of Day - Release in Further Education. Ed. by W. Van Der Eyken. S. M. Barry. (General Ser.). (Illus.). 111p. 1975. pap. text ed. 9.50x (ISBN 0-85633-079-5, NFER). Humanities.
Learning & Growing: A Guide to Child Development. Laurie Braga & Joseph Braga. 192p. 1975. 8.95 (ISBN 0-13-527614-4, Spec); pap. 3.95 (ISBN 0-13-527606-3, Spec). P-H.
Learning & Human Abilities: Educational Psychology. 4th ed. Herbert J. Klausmeier & William Goodwin. 576p. 1975. text ed. 20.95 scp (ISBN 0-06-043695-6, HarpC); avail instrs' manual (ISBN 0-06-363694-8). Har-Row.
Learning & Instruction. Ed. by Merlin C. Wittrock. LC 76-18038. (Readings in Educational Research Ser.). 1977. 25.00 (ISBN 0-8211-2255-X); text ed. 22.50 ten or more copies (ISBN 0-685-52960-6). McCutchan.
Learning & Instructional Improvement Digest. Ed. by G. Douglas Mayo & Burl E. Gilliland. LC 79-624710. (J. W. Brister Library Monographs: No. 8). 120p. (Orig.). 1979. pap. 6.95x (ISBN 0-87870-058-7). Memphis St Univ.
Learning & Memory. Wayne A. Wickelgren. (Experimental Psychology Ser.). 1977. 18.95 (ISBN 0-13-527663-2). P-H.
Learning & Memory: An Introduction. rev. ed. Jack Adams. 1980. 18.95x (ISBN 0-256-02314-X). Dorsey.
Learning & Memory: An Introduction. Jack A. Adams. 1980. text ed. 17.50 o.p. (ISBN 0-256-01783-2). Dorsey.
Learning & Performance of Physical Skills. 2nd ed. John D. Lawther. (Illus.). 1977. text ed. 12.95 (ISBN 0-13-527325-0). P-H.
Learning & Social Behavior. Barry McLaughlin. LC 74-143176. 1971. 12.95 (ISBN 0-02-920570-0). Free Pr.
Learning & Teaching Concepts: A Strategy for Testing Applications Theory. Herbert J. Klausmeier. Ed. by Thomas S. Sipple. LC 80-758. (Educational Psychology Ser.). 1980. 22.50 (ISBN 0-12-411450-4). Acad Pr.
Learning & Teaching Through Art & Crafts. Alan Cotton & Frank Haddon. 1979. 15.95 o.p. (ISBN 0-7134-2825-2, Pub. by Batsford England). David & Charles.
Learning & the Learner. Janet P. Moursund. LC 76-7717. 1976. pap. text ed. 11.95 (ISBN 0-8185-0197-9). Brooks-Cole.
Learning & the Professors. Ed. by Ohmer Milton & Edward J. Shoben, Jr. LC 67-22230. xvii, 216p. 1968. 12.00x (ISBN 0-8214-0036-3); pap. 5.95x (ISBN 0-8214-0105-X). Ohio U Pr.
Learning & the Simulation Game. John L. Taylor & Rex Walford. LC 78-21338. (Illus.). 228p. 1979. 17.50 (ISBN 0-8039-1207-2). Sage.
Learning & the Simulation Game. John L. Taylor & Rex Walford. LC 78-21338. (Illus.). 228p. 1979. pap. 8.50 (ISBN 0-8039-1208-0). Sage.
Learning & the Stimulation Game. John L. Taylor & Rex Walford. LC 78-21338. (Illus.). 228p. 1979. 17.50 (ISBN 0-8039-1207-2). Sage.
Learning & Working. 348p. 1980. pap. 17.00 (ISBN 92-3-101684-9, U958, UNESCO). Unipub.
Learning Arabic Thru Phrases, 4 vols. M. Karam. pap. text ed. 22.00x o.p. (ISBN 0-686-63575-2). Intl Bk Ctr.
Learning at Work: Human Resources & Organizational Development. Avice M. Saint. LC 73-81275. 1974. 19.95 (ISBN 0-911012-22-2); pap. 10.95x (ISBN 0-88229-575-6). Nelson-Hall.
Learning BASIC Fast. rev. ed. Claude J. De Rossi. LC 74-3355. (Illus.). 1979. pap. text ed. 12.95 (ISBN 0-8359-3977-4). Reston.
Learning Begins at Home: A Study of a Junior School & Its Parents. Michael Young & Patrick McGeeney. 1968. text ed. 10.00x (ISBN 0-7100-6529-9). Humanities.
Learning Business Mathematics with Electronic Calculators. 2nd ed. Richard R. McCready. 384p. 1979. pap. text ed. 13.95x (ISBN 0-534-00741-4). Wadsworth Pub.
Learning by Doing: Developing Teaching Skills. William A. Gray & Brian A. Gerrard. (Education Ser.). 1977. pap. text ed. 8.95 (ISBN 0-201-02547-7); instr's manual 2.75 (ISBN 0-201-02548-5). A-W.
Learning Can Be Fun. L. Smith. 4.00 o.p. (ISBN 0-8062-1184-9). Carlton.
Learning Center Ideabook: Activities for the Elementary & Middle Grades. new ed. Hiram Johnston et al. 1978. pap. text ed. 18.95 (ISBN 0-205-05894-9). Allyn.
Learning Center Ideas. June Crabtree. (Ideas Ser). (Illus.). 1977. pap. text ed. 1.75 (ISBN 0-87239-120-5, 7960). Standard Pub.
Learning Centers That Teach. Ed. by C. M. Charles. 1978. pap. 10.75 (ISBN 0-8191-0367-5). U Pr of Amer.
Learning Child. Dorothy H. Cohen. 384p. 1973. pap. 3.95 (ISBN 0-394-71877-1, Vin). Random.

Learning COBOL Fast: A Structured Approach. C. DeRossi. 1976. pap. text ed. 11.95 (ISBN 0-87909-447-8). Reston.

Learning Concepts, Inc. Jean P. Valette & Rebecca M. Valette. 1978. pap. text ed. 7.95x (ISBN 0-669-01162-2). Heath.

Learning Counseling & Problem-Solving Skills. Leslie E. Borck & Stephen B. Fawcett. 350p. (Orig.). 1981. text ed. 26.00 (ISBN 0-917724-30-5); pap. text ed. 13.95 (ISBN 0-917724-35-6). Haworth Pr.

Learning Difficulties: Causes & Psychological Implications - A Guide for Professionals. Kurt Glaser. (Illus.). 112p. 1974. 11.25 (ISBN 0-398-03157-6). C C Thomas.

Learning Disabiliies: Selected ACLD Papers. Samuel A. Kirk & Jeanne M. McCarthy. LC 74-20857. 1975. 15.75 (ISBN 0-395-20200-0). HM.

Learning Disabilities. 2nd ed. Johnson & Morasky. 450p. text ed. 17.95 (ISBN 0-205-06898-7, 2468980). Allyn.

Learning Disabilities: A Book of Readings. Ed. by Larry A. Faas. (Illus.). 272p. 1972. 13.75 (ISBN 0-398-02276-3). C C Thomas.

Learning Disabilities: A Competency Based Approach. Larry A Faas. LC 75-31010. (Illus.). 512p. 1976. pap. text ed. 15.25 (ISBN 0-395-20586-7); inst. resource guide 1.25 (ISBN 0-395-20585-9). HM.

Learning Disabilities: A Competency-Based Approach. 2nd ed. Larry A. Faas. (Illus.). 480p. 1981. pap. text ed. 15.95; instr's. manual 0.75 (ISBN 0-395-29700-1). HM.

Learning Disabilities: Activities for Remediation. 2nd ed. Joan M. Warner. 84p. 1980. pap. text ed. 3.95x (ISBN 0-8134-2118-7). Interstate.

Learning Disabilities: An Overflow of Theories, Approaches & Politics. Roa Lynn et al. LC 79-7477. (Illus.). 1979. text ed. 15.95 (ISBN 0-02-919490-3). Free Pr.

Learning Disabilities & Brain Function: A Neuropsychological Approach. W. H. Gaddes. (Illus.). 350p. 1980. 26.90 (ISBN 0-387-90486-7). Springer-Verlag.

Learning Disabilities & Games. Sophie L. Lovinger. LC 78-24619. (Illus.). 1979. text ed. 14.95x (ISBN 0-88229-353-2); pap. 7.95 (ISBN 0-88229-652-3). Nelson-Hall.

Learning Disabilities & Handicaps. Gilda Berger. (Impact Bks.). (Illus.). (gr. 7 up). 1978. PLB 6.90 s&l (ISBN 0-531-01457-6). Watts.

Learning Disabilities: Educational Strategies. 3rd ed. Bill Gearheart. (Illus.). 345p. 1981. text ed. 17.95 (ISBN 0-8016-1768-5). Mosby.

Learning Disabilities Handbook for Teachers. Ed. by Robert B. Blackwell & Robert R. Joynt. 208p. 1976. text ed. 16.50 (ISBN 0-398-02234-8). C C Thomas.

Learning Disabilities in Home, School, & Community. Ed. by William M. Cruickshank. 1979. pap. 7.95x (ISBN 0-8156-2208-2). Syracuse U Pr.

Learning Disabilities: Introduction to Educational & Medical Management. Lester Tarnopol. (Illus.). 412p. 1974. 18.75 (ISBN 0-398-01897-9); pap. 13.50 (ISBN 0-398-02894-X). C C Thomas.

Learning Disabilities Manual: Recommended Procedures & Practices. rev. ed. Margaret Van Dusen Pysh & James C. Chalfant. LC 79-90979. (Illus.). 100p. 1980. pap. 5.95 (ISBN 0-933922-00-0, P500). PEM Pr.

Learning Disabilities: Reference Book. Ed. by Special Learning Corp. (Special Education Ser.). (Illus., Orig.). 1980. pap. text ed. 64.00 (ISBN 0-89568-116-1). Spec Learn Corp.

Learning Disabilities: Revision. Ed. by Robert Piazza. (Special Education Ser.). (Illus., Orig.). 1980. pap. text ed. 9.95 (ISBN 0-89568-119-6). Spec Learn Corp.

Learning Disabilities: Systemizing Teaching & Service Delivery. David Sabatino et al. 350p. 1981. text ed. price not set (ISBN 0-89443-361-X). Aspen Systems.

Learning Disabilities: The Struggle from Adolescence Toward Adulthood. William M. Cruickshank et al. (Illus.). 304p. 1980. 18.00x (ISBN 0-8156-2220-1); pap. 8.95x (ISBN 0-8156-2221-X). Syracuse U Pr.

Learning Disabilities: Theories, Diagnosis, & Teaching Strategies. Janet W. Lerner. (Illus.). 560p. 1981. text ed. 17.95 (ISBN 0-395-29710-9); write for info. set study guide (ISBN 0-395-30371-0); write for info. instr's manual (ISBN 0-395-29711-7). HM.

Learning Disability-Minimal Brain Dysfunction Syndrome: Research Perspectives & Applications. Robert P. Anderson & Charles G. Halcomb. (Illus.). 296p. 1976. 24.50 (ISBN 0-398-03395-1). C C Thomas.

Learning Disability: The Unrealized Potential. Alan O. Ross. (McGraw-Hill Paperbacks). 228p. 1980. pap. 4.95 (ISBN 0-07-053878-6, P&RB). McGraw.

Learning Disabled Adolescent: Program Alternatives in the Secondary School. new ed. George E. Marsh et al. LC 77-18050. (Illus.). 1978. text ed. 16.95 (ISBN 0-8016-3118-1). Mosby.

Learning Disabled Child: A School & Family Concern. J. Jeffries McWhirter. LC 77-81300. (Illus.). 1977. text ed. 8.95 (ISBN 0-87822-147-6); pap. text ed. 8.95 (ISBN 0-87822-142-5). Res Press.

Learning Disc Basis & DOS. David A. Lien. Ed. by David Gunzel. (CompuSoft Learning Ser.). (Illus.). 300p. 1980. pap. 19.95 (ISBN 0-932760-02-3). CompuSoft.

Learning Disk Basic & Dos. David A. Lien. Ed. by David Gunzel. (CompuSoft Learning Ser.). (Illus.). 400p. (gr. 7 up). 1981. pap. 19.95 (ISBN 0-932760-02-3). CompuSoft.

Learning: Educational Applications. Walter B. Kolesnik. 240p. 1976. pap. text ed. 11.50 (ISBN 0-205-05443-9). Allyn.

Learning Electrocardiography: A Complete Course. 2nd ed. Jules Constant. (Illus.). 1981. text ed. write for info. (ISBN 0-316-15322-2). Little.

Learning Environments. Ed. by Thomas G. David & Benjamin D. Wright. 248p. 1975. 12.00x o.s.i. (ISBN 0-226-13724-4). U of Chicago Pr.

Learning Experience Guides for Nursing Students, 4 vols. 3rd ed. A. K. Roe & M. C. Sherwood. LC 78-8301. 1978. pap. 14.95 ea. Vol. 1 (ISBN 0-471-04186-6). Vol. 2 (ISBN 0-471-04614-0). Vol. 3 (ISBN 0-471-04187-4). Vol. 4 (ISBN 0-471-04613-2). Wiley.

Learning Experiences: An Approach to Teaching Physical Education. Dorothy Zakrajsek & Lois Carnes. 208p. 1981. write for info. (ISBN 0-697-07098-0). Wm C Brown.

Learning, Feeling, Doing: Designing Creative Learning Experiences for Elementary Health Education. Gwendolyn D. Scott & Mona Carlo. (Illus.). 1978. ref. ed. 14.95 (ISBN 0-13-527689-6). P-H.

Learning for Tomorrow: The Role of the Future in Education. Ed. by Alvin Toffler. 1974. 12.95 o.p. (ISBN 0-394-48313-8). Random.

Learning from Atlanta. Robert Brambilla. (Learningfrom the U. S. A. Ser.). 150p. (Orig.). 1981. pap. text ed. 6.95 (ISBN 0-87855-835-7). Transaction Bks.

Learning from Atlanta. Roberto Brambilla & Gianni Longo. (Learning from the USA Ser.). (Illus.). 150p. Date not set. pap. 6.95 (ISBN 0-936020-04-0). Inst for Environ Action. Postponed.

Learning from Changing: Organizational Diagnosis & Development. Clayton P. Alderfer & L. Dave Brown. LC 75-34081. (Sage Library of Social Research: Vol. 19). 1975. 18.00x (ISBN 0-8039-0554-8); pap. 8.95x (ISBN 0-8039-0555-6). Sage.

Learning from Clients: Interpersonal Helping As Viewed by Clients & Social Workers. Anthony N. Maluccio. LC 78-67753. 1979. 14.95 (ISBN 0-02-919820-8). Free Pr.

Learning from Conflict: A Handbook for Trainers & Group Leaders. Lois B. Hart. LC 80-17227. 224p. 1981. 8.95 (ISBN 0-201-03144-2). A-W.

Learning from Hebrews. Charles W. Ford. LC 80-67467. (Radiant Life Ser.). 128p. (Orig.). 1981. 1.95 (ISBN 0-88243-915-4, 02-0915); teacher's ed 2.50 (ISBN 0-88243-188-9, 32-0188). Gospel Pub.

Learning from Minneapolis, St. Paul. Roberto Brambilla & Gianni Longo. (Learning from the USA Ser.). (Illus.). 150p. (Orig.). Date not set. pap. 6.95 (ISBN 0-936020-03-2). Inst for Environ Action. Postponed.

Learning from Teaching: A Developmental Perspective. Jere E. Brophy & Carolyn M. Evertson. 228p. 1976. text ed. 10.95 o.p. (ISBN 0-685-57480-6); pap. text ed. 7.95x o.p. (ISBN 0-205-05488-9). Allyn.

Learning from Television: What the Research Says. Godwin C. Chu & Wilbur Schramm. 116p. 1979. pap. 6.00 (Pub Telecomm). NAEB.

Learning Functional Words & Phrases for Everyday Living. David J. Somers. Bk. 1, 1977. pap. 2.25x (ISBN 0-88323-135-2, 223); Bk. 2, 1980. pap. 2.25x (ISBN 0-88323-159-X, 249). Richards Pub.

Learning Games for the First Three Years. Joseph Sparling & Isabelle Lewis. 320p. 1981. pap. 2.95 (ISBN 0-425-04752-0). Berkley Pub.

Learning Genetics with Mice. Margaret E. Wallace. (Investigations in Biology Ser.). 1971. pap. text ed. 3.95x o.p. (ISBN 0-435-60284-5). Heinemann Ed.

Learning God's Word, 3 bks. Carroll. 1971. Bk. 1. pap. 1.65 (ISBN 0-87148-502-8); Bk. 2. pap. 1.25 (ISBN 0-87148-503-6); Bk. 3. pap. 1.25 (ISBN 0-87148-504-4). Pathway Pr.

Learning Home Economics, 4 bks. Beryl Ruth. Incl. Bk 1. About the Kitchen. 1972. pap. text ed. 2.95x o.p. (ISBN 0-435-42252-9); Bk 2. About the Home. 1973. pap. text ed. 2.95x o.p. (ISBN 0-435-42261-8); Bk 3. You & Your Family. 1971. pap. text ed. 2.95x o.p. (ISBN 0-435-42260-X); Bk 4. You & the Community. 1977. pap. text ed. 2.95x o.p. (ISBN 0-435-42249-9). Heinemann Ed.

Learning How to Learn: Psychology & Spirituality in the Sufi Way. Idries Shah. LC 80-8892. 304p. 1981. pap. 6.95 (ISBN 0-06-067255-2). Har-Row.

Learning in the Primary School. Kenneth R. Haslam. (Unwin Education Books). 1971. pap. text ed. 7.50x o.p. (ISBN 0-04-371018-2). Allen Unwin.

Learning Independently. 1st ed. Ed. by Paul Wasserman. LC 79-21025. 1979. 76.00 (ISBN 0-8103-0317-5). Gale.

Learning, Language, & Memory. John W. Donahoe & Michael G. Wessells. (Illus.). 1979. text ed. 18.95 scp (ISBN 0-06-041685-8, HarpC); instructors manual free (ISBN 0-06-361699-8). Har-Row.

Learning Later: Fresh Horizons in English Adult Education. Enid Hutchinson & Edward Hutchinson. 1978. 21.00x (ISBN 0-7100-8952-X). Routledge & Kegan.

Learning Level II. 2nd ed. David A. Lien. Ed. by David Gunzel. LC 79-91309. (CompuSoft Learning Ser.). (Illus.). 360p. 1980. pap. 15.95 (ISBN 0-932760-01-5). CompuSoft.

Learning Match: A Developmental Guide to Teaching Young Children. Betty Rowan et al. (Ser. in Early Childhood). (Illus.). 1980. text ed. 16.95 (ISBN 0-13-527044-8). P-H.

Learning Math Skills. Mary J. Carrell. 1978. pap. text ed. 2.25x (ISBN 0-88323-139-5, 228). Richards Pub.

Learning Mechanisms in Food Selection. Ed. by Lewis M. Barker et al. 632p. 1977. 19.00 (ISBN 0-918954-19-3). Baylor Univ Pr.

Learning Modules for the Basic Course in English, Vol. 1. Ed. by Providencia C. Monte. LC 79-22332. 304p. 1980. pap. 8.00 (ISBN 0-8477-3324-6). U of PR Pr.

Learning: Reinforcement Theory. 2nd ed. Fred S. Keller. (Psychology Studies). 1969. pap. text ed. 3.95x (ISBN 0-394-30898-0, RanC). Random.

Learning, Remembering & Knowing. P. Meredith. (Teach Yourself Ser.). 1974. pap. 2.95 o.p. (ISBN 0-679-10434-8). McKay.

Learning Science & Metric Through Cooking. Barbara Davis. LC 64-15112. (Illus.). (gr. 5 up). 1977. 7.95 (ISBN 0-8069-3090-X); PLB 7.49 (ISBN 0-8069-3091-8). Sterling.

Learning Skills Series: Arithmetic. W. F. Hunter & P. La Follette. 1969. 5.20 o.p. (ISBN 0-07-031314-8, W); 7.68x o.p. (ISBN 0-07-031315-6). McGraw.

Learning Soccer with Pele. Edson Arantes do Nascimento. LC 78-1334. (Illus.). 1978. 8.95 o.s.i. (ISBN 0-397-01280-2); pap. 4.95 o.s.i. (ISBN 0-397-01281-0). Lippincott.

Learning Theory of Piaget & Inhelder. Jeanette Gallagher & D. Kim Reid. LC 80-24410. (Orig.). 1981. pap. text ed. 7.95 (ISBN 0-8185-0343-2). Brooks-Cole.

Learning Through Feedback: A Systematic Approach for Improving Academic Performance. Ron Van Houten. LC 79-19379. 182p. (Orig.). 1980. text ed. 14.95x (ISBN 0-87705-424-X); pap. text ed. 5.95x (ISBN 0-87705-440-1). Human Sci Pr.

Learning Through Interaction. Gordon Wells et al. LC 80-41113. (Language at Home & at School Ser.: Vol. 1). (Illus.). 200p. Date not set. text ed. 39.50 (ISBN 0-521-23774-2); pap. text ed. 10.95 (ISBN 0-521-28219-5). Cambridge U Pr.

Learning Through Liturgy. John H. Westerhoff & Gwen K. Neville. 1978. 8.95 (ISBN 0-8164-0406-2). Crossroad NY.

Learning Through Movement: Teaching Cognitive Content Through Physical Activities. Peter H. Werner & Elsie Burton. LC 78-11895. (Illus.). 1979. pap. text ed. 10.95 (ISBN 0-8016-5415-7). Mosby.

Learning Through Noncompetitive Activities & Play. Dolores Michaelis & Bill Michaelis. LC 77-89123. (Learning Handbooks Ser.). 1977. pap. 3.95 (ISBN 0-8224-1906-8). Pitman Learning.

Learning Through Reading in the Content Areas. Richard Allington & Michael Strange. 1980. pap. text ed. 7.95 (ISBN 0-669-01375-7). Heath.

Learning Thru Discussion. rev., 2nd ed. Wm. F. Hill. LC 78-87064. 1977. 2.95x (ISBN 0-8039-0711-7). Sage.

Learning to Adjust. Alice Yardley. LC 73-81973. 144p. 1973. 3.25 o.p. (ISBN 0-590-07348-6, Citation). Schol Bk Serv.

Learning to Be Parents: Principles, Programs, & Methods. David Harman & Orville G. Brim, Jr. LC 80-24030. (Illus.). 276p. 1980. 14.95 (ISBN 0-8039-1272-2). Sage.

Learning to Be Rotuman: Enculturation in the South Pacific. Alan Howard. LC 77-122746. (Illus.). 1970. text ed. 11.00x (ISBN 0-8077-1520-4). Tchrs Coll.

Learning to Be: The Education of Human Potential. Ed. by John Mann. LC 73-143524. 1972. 8.95 (ISBN 0-02-919970-0); pap. text ed. 7.95 (ISBN 0-02-919910-7). Free Pr.

Learning to Believe: A Meditation on the Christian Creed. Carroll E. Simcox. LC 80-2372. 112p. 1981. pap. 5.95 (ISBN 0-8006-1497-6, 1-1497). Fortress.

Learning to Breathe Underwater. William Meissner. LC 79-18881. 66p. 1980. 8.95 (ISBN 0-8214-0418-0); pap. 5.95 (ISBN 0-8214-0426-1). Ohio U Pr.

Learning to Choose: Stories & Essays About Science, Technology, & Human Values. Lazer Goldberg. LC 76-13919. (Encore Edition). 224p. (gr. k-12). 1976. 3.95 o.p. (ISBN 0-684-15692-X, ScribT). Scribner.

Learning to Compute, 2 bks. Wilmer L. Jones. 1978. Bk. 1. pap. text ed. 3.31 (ISBN 0-15-550402-9, HC); Bk. 2. pap. text ed. 3.31 (ISBN 0-15-550403-7); tchr's. manual avail. (ISBN 0-15-550404-5). HarBraceJ.

Learning to Cook. Mary Foster. 1971. pap. text ed. 4.95x o.p. (ISBN 0-435-42501-3). Heinemann Ed.

Learning to Cook the Girl Way. Joy Law. pap. 4.50x o.p. (ISBN 0-392-06191-0, LTB). Soccer.

Learning to Feel: Feeling to Learn. Harold C. Lyon, Jr. LC 74-148507. 1971. pap. text ed. 7.95 (ISBN 0-675-09232-9). Merrill.

Learning to Labour: How Working Class Kids Get Working Class Jobs. Paul E. Willis. (Illus.). 1977. 21.00 (ISBN 0-566-00150-0, 00730-7, Pub. by Saxon Hse England). Lexington Bks.

Learning to Live. Orig. Title: Learning to Live from the Gospels & Learning to Live from the Acts. 1976. pap. 1.95 (ISBN 0-89129-193-8). Jove Pubns.

Learning to Live. Eugenia Price. (Orig.). pap. 1.95 (ISBN 0-89129-193-8). Jove Pubns.

Learning to Live Without Cigarettes. William A. Allen et al. 1968. pap. 1.95 (ISBN 0-385-06511-6, Dolp). Doubleday.

Learning to Look: A Handbook on Classroom Observation. Jane Stallings. 1977. pap. 11.95x (ISBN 0-534-00522-5). Wadsworth Pub.

Learning to Love, 3 vols. Richard Peace. Incl. Vol. 1. Learning to Love God. pap. 1.95 (ISBN 0-310-30751-1); Vol. 2. Learning to Love Ourselves. pap. 1.25 (ISBN 0-310-30761-9); Vol. 3. Learning to Love People. pap. 1.95 (ISBN 0-310-30771-6). Set. pap. 4.90 (ISBN 0-310-30788-0). Zondervan.

Learning to Love Again. Mel Krantzler. LC 77-6347. 1977. 7.95 o.s.i. (ISBN 0-690-01456-2, TYC-T). T Y Crowell.

Learning to Love: How to Make Bad Sex Good & Good Sex Better. Paul Brown & Carolyn Faulder. LC 78-52202. 188p. (Orig.). 1981. pap. 4.95 (ISBN 0-87663-559-1, Pica Pr). Universe.

Learning to Manage Our Fears. James W. Angell. 128p. 1981. 6.95 (ISBN 0-687-21329-0). Abingdon.

Learning to Program in Structured COBOL: Part 1. 2nd ed. Edward Yourdon et al. LC 78-63350. 252p. 1978. pap. 12.00 (ISBN 0-917072-12-X). Yourdon.

Learning to Program in Structured COBOL, Part 2. Timothy R. Lister & Edward Yourdon. LC 77-99232. 1977. pap. 12.00 (ISBN 0-917072-03-0). Yourdon.

Learning to Read: A Guide for Teachers & Parents. Brenda Thompson. 1970. 7.50x (ISBN 0-8464-0549-0). Beekman Pubs.

Learning to Read from the Bible, 4 vols. V. Gilbert Beers. Incl. Vol. 1. God Is My Helper (ISBN 0-310-20780-0). kivar (ISBN 0-310-20781-9); Vol. 2. God Is My Friend (ISBN 0-310-20790-8). kivar (ISBN 0-310-20791-6); Vol. 3. Jesus Is My Teacher (ISBN 0-310-20800-9). kivar (ISBN 0-310-20801-7); Vol. 4. Jesus Is My Guide (ISBN 0-310-20810-6). kivar (ISBN 0-310-20811-4). (Illus.). 96p. (Readers). (ps up). 1973. 6.95 ea.; kivar 3.95. Zondervan.

Learning to Read from the Bible Primers: Primers, 4bks. V. Gilbert Beers. Incl. May I Help You. pap. (ISBN 0-310-20821-1); Do You Know My Friend (ISBN 0-310-20830-0). pap. (ISBN 0-310-20831-9); Do You Love Me (ISBN 0-310-20840-8). pap. (ISBN 0-310-20841-6); Will You Come with Me (ISBN 0-310-20850-5). pap. (ISBN 0-310-20851-3). (ps-1). 1976. 6.95 ea.; pap. 3.95 ea. kivar. Zondervan.

Learning to Read Mechanical Drawings. rev. ed. Roy A. Bartholomew & Francis S. Orr. (gr. 9-12). 1970. pap. text ed. 5.20 (ISBN 0-87002-040-4); tchr. guide avail. (ISBN 0-685-03308-2). Bennett IL.

Learning to Read Music. Robert Lilienfeld. (Funk & W Bk.). 128p. 1976. pap. 4.95 o.s.i. (ISBN 0-308-10249-5, TYC-T). T Y Crowell.

Learning to Read: The Great Debate. Jeanne S. Chall. 1967. 12.50 (ISBN 0-07-010390-9, C); pap. 4.95 (ISBN 0-07-010391-7). McGraw.

Learning to Read Through Experience. 2nd ed. Dorris M. Lee & Richard V. Allen. (Illus.). (YA) (gr. 9-12). 1966. pap. text ed. 8.95 (ISBN 0-13-527523-7). P-H.

Learning to Rock Climb. Michael Loughman. (Outdoor Activities Guides). (Illus.). 192p. (Orig.). 1981. 14.95 (ISBN 0-87156-281-2); pap. 9.95 (ISBN 0-87156-279-0). Sierra.
Learning to Say Good-by: When a Parent Dies. Eda LeShan. LC 76-15155. (Illus.). (gr. 3 up). 7.95 (ISBN 0-02-756360-X, 75636). Macmillan.
Learning to Spell Correctly. Barbara Gregorvich & Mary H. Manoni. LC 78-730054. (Illus.). 1978. pap. text ed. 99.00 (ISBN 0-89290-127-6, 331-SATC). Soc for Visual.
Learning to Teach. Richard B. Dierenfield. LC 80-69119. 135p. 1981. perfect bdg. 10.95 (ISBN 0-86548-031-1). Century Twenty One.
Learning to Teach in Urban Schools. Dorothy M. McGeoch et al. LC 65-22440. 1965. pap. text ed. 4.75x (ISBN 0-8077-1737-1). Tchrs Coll.
Learning to Teach Practical Skills: A Self-Instruction Guide. Ian Winfield. 1979. 13.50 (ISBN 0-85038-198-3, Pub. by Kogan Pg.). Nichols Pub.
Learning to Teach: Teaching to Learn. Gwyneth Dow. (Education Bks.). 1979. 22.00x (ISBN 0-7100-0093-6). Routledge & Kegan.
Learning to Teach Through Playing: A Brass Method. Herbert C. Mueller. (Music Series). (Illus., Orig.). 1968. pap. 16.50 (ISBN 0-201-04890-6). A-W.
Learning to Teach Through Playing: A Woodwind Method. Lewis B. Hilton. (Music Ser). (Orig.). 1970. pap. text ed. 17.95 (ISBN 0-201-02850-6). A-W.
Learning to Teach Through Playing: String Techniques & Pedagogy. Robert H. Klotman & Ernest E. Harris. LC 77-116861. (Music Ser). 1971. pap. 17.95 (ISBN 0-201-03775-0). A-W.
Learning to Think--to Learn. M. Ann Dirkes. LC 80-65613. 145p. 1981. perfect bdg. 11.50 (ISBN 0-86548-032-X). Century Twenty One.
Learning to Think in a Math Lab. Manon P. Charbonneau. (Illus.). 1971. pap. 5.75 (ISBN 0-934338-12-4). NAIS.
Learning to Type in English As a Second Language. Alice C. Pack & Robert O. Joy. 1976. pap. text ed. 9.00x (ISBN 0-8191-0025-0). U Pr of Amer.
Learning to Use English, 2 Bks. Mary Finocchiaro. (Illus.). (gr. 7 up). 1966. Bk. 1. pap. text ed. 3.95 (ISBN 0-88345-089-5, 17400); Bk. 2. pap. text ed. 3.95 (ISBN 0-88345-090-9, 17401); tchr's manual 4.25 (ISBN 0-88345-091-7, 17402). Regents Pub.
Learning to Use Maps. Rogert E. Kranich & Jerry L. Messec. (Illus.). 1978. text ed. write for info. (ISBN 0-88323-150-6, 236); 2.25x (ISBN 0-686-67722-6); teacher's answer key free (239). Richards Pub.
Learning to Work. Ed. by Blanche Geer. LC 73-87855. (Sage Contemporary Social Science Issues: Vol. 4). 1974. 4.95x (ISBN 0-8039-0320-0). Sage.
Learning to Work in Groups. 2nd ed. Matthew B. Miles. 360p. 1981. pap. text ed. 12.95x (ISBN 0-8077-2586-2). Tchrs Coll.
Learning to Write, or Writing to Learn? Jeanette T. Williams. (General Ser.). (Illus.). 1977. pap. text ed. 7.75x (ISBN 0-85633-128-7, NFER). Humanities.
Learning Together. Ed. by Meyer Weinberg. LC 64-19114. 1964. pap. 3.75 (ISBN 0-912008-00-8). Integrated Ed Assoc.
Learning Together & Alone: Cooperation, Competition, & Individualization. David W. Johnson & Roger T. Johnson. (Illus.). 224p. 1975. pap. text ed. 10.95 (ISBN 0-13-527945-3). P-H.
Learning Together in the Christian Fellowship. Sara Little. LC 56-9220. (Orig.). 1956. pap. 3.95 (ISBN 0-8042-1320-8). John Knox.
Learning Tomorrows: Commentaries on the Future of Education. Ed. by Peter H. Wagschal. LC 78-19783. (Praeger Special Studies). 1979. 22.95 (ISBN 0-03-046716-0). Praeger.
Learning Traveler: Vacation Study Abroad, Vol. 2. rev. ed. Ed. by Gail A. Cohen. 186p. 1981. pap. text ed. 8.00 (ISBN 0-87206-107-8). Inst Intl Educ.
Learning Traveler: Vol. I, U. S. College-Sponsored Programs Abroad-Academic Year. rev. ed. Ed. by Gail A. Cohen. 186p. 1980. pap. text ed. 8.00 o.p. (ISBN 0-87206-102-7). Inst Intl Educ.
Learning Traveler: Vol. II, Vacation Study Abroad. rev. ed. Ed. by Gail A. Cohen. 185p. 1981. pap. text ed. 8.00 o.p. (ISBN 0-87206-107-8). Inst Intl Educ.
Learning Traveler Vol. 1: U. S. College-Sponsored Programs Abroad: Academic Year. rev. ed. Ed. by Gail A. Cohen. 186p. 1981. pap. text ed. 8.00 (ISBN 0-87206-108-6). Inst Intl Educ.
Learning Ways to Read Words, 4 bks. Shirley C. Feldman & Kathleen K. Merrill. Incl. Bk. 1. Ways to Read Words (ISBN 0-8077-2509-9); Bk. 2. More Ways to Read Words (ISBN 0-8077-2516-1); Bk. 3. Learning About Words (ISBN 0-8077-2517-X); Bk. 4. Learning More About Words (ISBN 0-8077-2518-8). 1978. pap. 12.50 set (ISBN 0-8077-2505-6); wkbk. 8.10. Tchrs Coll.
Learning with Computers. Alfred Bork. (Illus.). 250p. 1981. 24.00 (ISBN 0-932376-11-8). Digital Pr.
Learning with LDOCE. Janet Whitcut. (Illus.). 1979. pap. text ed. 2.75x (ISBN 0-582-55607-4); cassette 7.50x (ISBN 0-582-55629-5). Longman.
Learning with Puppets. David Currell. 208p. 1980. 15.95 (ISBN 0-8238-0250-7). Plays.
Learning with Simulations & Games. Ed. by Richard L. Dukes & Constance J. Seidner. LC 78-51496. (Sage Contemporary Social Science Anthologies: No. 2). 1978. pap. 5.50x (ISBN 0-8039-1036-3). Sage.
Learningames for the First Three Years. Joseph Sparling & Isabelle Lewis. 1981. pap. 2.95 (ISBN 0-425-04752-0). Berkley Pub.
Lease-Buy Decision: A Simplified Guide to Maximizing Financial & Tax Advantages in the 1980's. Pieter T. Elgers & John J. Clark. LC 80-66131. (Illus.). 1980. 16.95 (ISBN 0-02-909470-4). Free Pr.
Lease Financing: A Practical Guide. C. R. Baker & R. S. Hayes. 256p. 1981. 17.95 (ISBN 0-471-06040-2, Pub. by Wiley Interscience). Wiley.
Leasing: Experiences & Expectations, Report No. 791. Patrick J. Davey. (Illus.). v, 58p. (Orig.). 1980. pap. 15.00 (ISBN 0-8237-0222-7). Conference Bd.
Least Dangerous Branch: The Supreme Court at the Bar of Politics. Alexander M. Bickel. LC 62-20685. (Orig.). 1962. pap. 6.95 (ISBN 0-672-60757-3). Bobbs.
Least of My Sisters. Elizabeth A. Ellis. LC 79-66928. 229p. 8.95 (ISBN 0-533-04426-X). Vantage.
Least of These. Elizabeth Hamphill. (Illus.). 176p. 1981. 12.50 (ISBN 0-8348-0155-8). Weatherhill.
Least of These: Miki Sawada & Her Children. Elizabeth Hemphill. 176p. 1981. 12.50 (ISBN 0-8348-0155-8, Pub. by John Weatherhill Inc Japan). C E Tuttle.
Leather Braiding. Bruce Grant. (Illus.). 1950. 6.00 (ISBN 0-87033-039-X). Cornell Maritime.
Leather Guide 1979-80. (Benn Directories Ser). 1979. 52.50 (ISBN 0-686-60658-2, Pub by Benn Pubns). Nichols Pub.
Leather in Three Dimensions. Rex Lingwood. 144p. 1980. pap. 12.95 (ISBN 0-442-29733-5). Van Nos Reinhold.
Leathercraft. Chris Groneman. (gr. 9-12). 1963. pap. 7.96 (ISBN 0-87002-204-0). Bennett IL.
Leathercraft. Sid Latham. (Illus.). 1977. 13.95 (ISBN 0-87691-227-7). Winchester Pr.
Leathercraft. Sid Latham. (Illus.). 1978. pap. 6.95 o.p. (ISBN 0-695-80936-9). Follett.
Leathercraft. Glen Pownall. (Creative Leisure Ser.). (Illus.). 76p. 1974. 7.50x (ISBN 0-85467-019-X). Intl Pubns Serv.
Leathercraft. Glen Pownall. (New Crafts Books Ser.). 76p. 1980. 7.50 (ISBN 0-85467-019-X, Pub. by Viking Sevenseas New Zealand). Intl Schol Bk Serv.
Leathercraft. Fred W. Zimmerman. LC 77-8007. (Illus.). 1977. text ed. 4.80 (ISBN 0-87006-234-4). Goodheart.
Leathercrafting: Procedures & Projects. Raymond Cherry. LC 79-83885. (Illus.). 1979. pap. 5.00 (ISBN 0-87345-153-8, B81925). McKnight.
Leatherman. Dick Gackenbach. LC 77-2584. (Illus.). (gr. 2-5). 1977. 6.95 (ISBN 0-395-28855-X, Clarion). HM.
Leatherwood God. W. D. Howells. LC 74-189640. (Selected Edition of W. D. Howells: Center for Editions of American Authors: Vol. 27). 288p. 1976. 18.50x (ISBN 0-253-33285-0). Ind U Pr.
Leatherwork. Boy Scouts Of America. LC 19-600. (Illus.). 48p. (gr. 6-12). 1970. pap. 0.70x (ISBN 0-8395-3310-1, 3310). BSA.
Leatherwork. Ian Hamilton-Head. (Illus.). 1979. 14.95 (ISBN 0-7137-0928-6, Pub by Blandford Pr England). Sterling.
Leave a Touch of Glory. Helen Lowrie Marshall. LC 76-6203. 1976. 2.95 o.p. (ISBN 0-385-12306-X). Doubleday.
Leave of Absence: A Novel. Theodore Morrison. 1981. 12.95 (ISBN 0-393-01439-8). Norton.
Leave Well Enough Alone. Rosemary Wells. (gr. 7-10). 1980. pap. 1.95 (ISBN 0-686-42687-8). Archway.
Leaven & the Salt. Wendell Belew. (Home Mission Graded Ser.). 1977. pap. 1.50 (ISBN 0-937170-14-3). Home Mission.
Leaven of Democracy: The Growth of the Democratic Spirit in the Time of Jackson. Ed. by Clement Eaton. LC 63-17877. (American Epochs Ser). pap. 7.95 (ISBN 0-8076-0394-5). Braziller.
Leaven of Malice. Robertson Davies. 1980. pap. 3.50 (ISBN 0-14-005433-2). Penguin.
Leavenworth Case. Anna K. Green. 1976. lib. bdg. 12.95x (ISBN 0-89968-171-9). Lightyear.
Leavenworth Schools & the Old Army: Education, Professionalism, & the Officer Corps of the United States Army, 1881-1918. Timothy K. Nenninger. LC 77-91105. (Contributions in Military History: No. 15). 1978. lib. bdg. 17.95x (ISBN 0-313-20047-5, NFL/). Greenwood.
Leaves & Ashes. John Haines. 1974. pap. 2.00 o.p. (ISBN 0-87711-053-0). Kayak.
Leaves from Conjurors' Scrap Books, Or, Modern Magicians & Their Works. Hardin J. Burlingame. LC 74-148349. 1971. Repr. of 1891 ed. 18.00 (ISBN 0-8103-3371-6). Gale.
Leaves from Gerard's Herball. Marcus Woodward. (Illus.). 1969. pap. 4.50 (ISBN 0-486-22343-4). Dover.
Leaves from the Notebook of a Tamed Cynic: Prelude to Depression. Reinhold Niebuhr. LC 76-27833. (Prelude to Depression Ser.). 1976. Repr. of 1929 ed. lib. bdg. 19.50 (ISBN 0-306-70852-3). Da Capo.
Leaves of Fire, Flame of Love. Susan Chatfield. 1981. pap. 1.50 (ISBN 0-440-14937-1). Dell.
Leaves of Grass. Walt Whitman. 1971. pap. 1.95 (ISBN 0-451-51395-9, CJ1395, Sig Classics). NAL.
Leaves of Grass. Walt Whitman. Ed. by Sculley Bradley & Harold W. Blodgett. (Critical Editions Ser.). 500p. 1973. pap. text ed. 12.95x (ISBN 0-393-09388-3). Norton.
Leaves of Grass. Walt Whitman. Ed. by Malcolm Cowley. (Poets Ser). 1976. pap. 2.25 (ISBN 0-14-042199-8). Penguin.
Leaves of Grass: Comprehensive Reader's Edition. Walt Whitman. Ed. by Harold W. Blodgett & Sculley Bradley. LC 60-15980. (Illus.). 1965. 24.50x (ISBN 0-8147-0440-9). NYU Pr.
Leaves of Laurel. Incl. Childe Harold's Monitor. Repr. of 1818 ed; Friends. Francis Hodgson. Ed. by Donald H. Reiman. Repr. of 1818 ed. LC 75-31223. (Romantic Context Ser.: Poetry 1789-1830). 1978. Repr. of 1813 ed. lib. bdg. 47.00 (ISBN 0-8240-2173-8). Garland Pub.
Leaves of Morya's Garden: The Call. 3rd ed. 1978. Repr. of 1953 ed. softbound 9.00 (ISBN 0-933574-00-2). Agni Yoga Soc.
Leaves of Morya's Garden, Vol. II: Illumination. 1979. Repr. of 1952 ed. softcover 9.00 (ISBN 0-933574-01-0). Agni Yoga Soc.
Leaves on Grey. large print ed. Desmond Hogan. LC 80-25146. 213p. 1980. Repr. 8.95 (ISBN 0-89621-258-0). Thorndike Pr.
Leaves on Grey. Desmond Hogan. 8.95 (ISBN 0-8076-0948-X). Braziller.
Leaves on the Wind. Yvonne Norman. (YA) 1978. 5.95 (ISBN 0-685-85778-6, Avalon). Bouregy.
Leaving. Lynn Hall. LC 80-18636. 128p. (gr. 7 up). 1980. 7.95 (ISBN 0-684-16716-6). Scribner.
Leaving. Fran Pokras. 1978. pap. 1.75 o.s.i. (ISBN 0-515-04526-8). Jove Pubns.
Leaving Early: Perspectives & Problems in Current Retirement Practice & Policy. Jeanne P. Gordus. LC 80-39653. 88p. (Orig.). 1980. pap. text ed. 4.00 (ISBN 0-911558-78-0). Upjohn Inst.
Leaving Home. Arlene K. Richards & Irene Willis. LC 80-12721. 192p. (gr. 7 up). 1980. 8.95 (ISBN 0-689-30757-8). Atheneum.
Leaving School & Starting Work. E. Venables. 1968. 6.05 o.p. (ISBN 0-08-012954-4); pap. 3.30 o.p. (ISBN 0-08-012953-6). Pergamon.
Leaving Taos. Robert Peterson. LC 80-8693. (National Poetry Ser.). 96p. 1981. 9.95 (ISBN 0-06-014839-X, HarpT). Har-Row.
Leaving Taos. Robert Peterson. LC 80-8693. (National Poetry Ser.). 96p. 1981. pap. 5.95 (ISBN 0-06-090875-0, CN 875, CN). Har-Row.
Leaving Taos. Robert Peterson. LC 80-8693. (National Poetry Ser.). 1981. 9.95 (ISBN 0-06-014839-X, CN875, HarpT); pap. 5.95 (ISBN 0-06-090875-0). Har-Row.
Leaving the Hospital: Discharge Planning for Total Patient Care. Bascom W. Ratliff. 176p. 1981. 19.75 (ISBN 0-398-04146-6). C C Thomas.
Leaving the Sixth Form: A Selection of Opinions. K. R. Fogelman. 1972. pap. text ed. 4.50x (ISBN 0-85633-002-7, NFER). Humanities.
Lebanese Civil War. Marius Deeb. LC 79-19833. (Praeger Special Studies). 176p. 1980. 25.95 (ISBN 0-03-039701-4). Praeger.
Lebanese Cuisine. Madelain Farah. 1979. 8.00 (ISBN 0-89955-011-8, Pub. by Madelain Farah); pap. 6.50 (ISBN 0-89955-202-1). Intl Schol Bk Serv.
Lebanon. Shereen Khairallah. (World Bibliographical Ser.: No. 2). 154p. 1979. 25.25 (ISBN 0-903450-10-0). ABC-Clio.
Lebanon. Gerald Newman. (First Bks). (Illus.). (gr. 4-6). 1978. PLB 6.45 s&l (ISBN 0-531-02237-4). Watts.
Lebanon, Improbable Nation: A Study in Political Development. Leila Meo. LC 75-46621. 246p. 1976. Repr. of 1965 ed. lib. bdg. 20.25x (ISBN 0-8371-8727-3, MELE). Greenwood.
Lebanon in Turmoil: Syria & the Powers in 1860. Tr. by J. F. Scheltema. (Yale Oriental Researches Ser.: No. VII). 1920. 29.50x (ISBN 0-685-69861-0). Elliots Bks.
Lebanon, Land of the Cedars. Marie Khayat. 8.50x (ISBN 0-686-65475-7). Intl Bk Ctr.
Leben Des Galilei. Bertolt Brecht. Ed. by H. F. Brookes & C. E. Fraenkel. 1958. pap. text ed. 4.50x (ISBN 0-435-38110-5). Heinemann Ed.
Leben und Werke Des Trobadors Ponz De Capduoill. Max von Napolski. LC 80-2183. 1981. Repr. of 1879 ed. 26.50 (ISBN 0-404-19009-X). AMS Pr.
Lebendige Literatur: Deutsches Lesebuch Fur Anfanger. F. G. Ryder & E. A. McCormick. 1974. pap. text ed. 9.15 (ISBN 0-395-13826-4). HM.
Lebesgue Integral. John C. Burkill. (Cambridge Tracts in Mathematics & Mathematical Physics). 1951. 14.50 (ISBN 0-521-04382-4). Cambridge U Pr.
Lebesgue Integration & Measure. A. J. Weir. LC 72-83584. (Illus.). 220p. (Orig.). 1973. 37.95 (ISBN 0-521-08728-7); pap. 14.95x (ISBN 0-521-09751-7). Cambridge U Pr.
Lebesgue's Theory of Integration: Its Origins & Development. 3rd ed. Thomas Hawkins. LC 74-8402. xv, 227p. 1975. text ed. 11.95 (ISBN 0-8284-0282-5). Chelsea Pub.
Lebesque Integration. Chae. 352p. 1980. 35.00 (ISBN 0-8247-6983-X). Dekker.
Lecciones de teoria general del derecho. Emilio Menendez Menendez. LC 79-16559. (Sp.). 1980. pap. text ed. write for info. (ISBN 0-8477-3017-4). U of PR Pr.
Lecherous Limericks. Isaac Asimov. LC 75-7922. (Illus.). 96p. 1975. 6.95 o.p. (ISBN 0-8027-0515-4); pap. 3.95 (ISBN 0-8027-7096-7). Walker & Co.
L'echo De la Fabrique. Repr. of 1831 ed. 322.00 o.p. (ISBN 0-8287-0312-4). Clearwater Pub.
Leconte de Lisle. Robert T. Denomme. (World Authors Ser.: France: No. 278). 1973. lib. bdg. 10.95 (ISBN 0-8057-2518-0). Twayne.
Lectionary Preaching Workbook: Series A. John R. Brokhoff. 300p. (Orig.). 1980. pap. text ed. 17.25 (ISBN 0-89536-442-5). CSS Pub.
Lectura & Lengua. Laurel Briscoe. LC 77-83324. (Illus.). 1977. text ed. 16.05 (ISBN 0-395-25545-7); instructor's annotated edition 17.15 (ISBN 0-395-25539-2). HM.
Lecturas Modernas De Hispanoamerica: An Intermediate Spanish Reader. Miguel Navascues. (Illus.). 1980. pap. text ed. 8.95 (ISBN 0-13-527804-X). P-H.
Lecturas Para Hoy. Anthony Papalia & Jose A Mendoza. (Orig.). (gr. 9-12). 1972. pap. text ed. 4.58 (ISBN 0-87720-512-4). AMSCO Sch.
Lecturas Periodisticas. Milton M. Azevedo & Kathryn K. McMahon. 1978. pap. text ed. 7.95x o.p. (ISBN 0-669-00576-2). Heath.
Lecturas Periodisticas. 2nd ed. Milton M. Azevedo & Kathryn K. McMahon. 272p. 1981. pap. text ed. 8.95 (ISBN 0-669-04026-6). Heath.
Lecture Des Talismans Chinois: Shanghai, 1913. Henri Dore. LC 78-74290. (Oriental Religions Ser.: Vol. 17). 190p. 1981. lib. bdg. 20.00 postponed (ISBN 0-8240-3919-X). Garland Pub.
Lecture Notes in Queueing Systems. Brian Conolly. LC 75-7788. 176p. 1975. pap. 14.95 (ISBN 0-470-16857-9). Halsted Pr.
Lecture Notes on Community Medicine. R. D. Farmer & D. L. Miller. (Blackwell Scientific Pubns.). (Illus.). 1977. 12.25 (ISBN 0-632-00108-9). Mosby.
Lecture Notes on Medical Microbiology. 2nd ed. R. F. Gillies. (Illus.). 1978. softcover 13.00 (ISBN 0-632-00062-7, Blackwell). Mosby.
Lecture Notes on Urology. 2nd ed. John Blandy. (Illus.). 1978. softcover 17.50 o.p. (ISBN 0-397-60457-2). Lippincott.
Lecture Notes on Vertebrate Zoology. Ronald Pearson & John N. Ball. 225p. 1981. pap. 19.95 (ISBN 0-470-27143-4). Halsted Pr.
Lecture on Jung's Typology. Marie-Louise Von Franz & James Hillman. 150p. 1971. pap. text ed. 7.50 (ISBN 0-88214-104-X). Spring Pubns.
Lectures & Articles on Christian Science. Edward A. Kimball. (Illus.). 1976. 10.00 (ISBN 0-911588-01-9). N S Wait.
Lectures: Black Scholars on Black Issues. Ed. by Vivian V. Gordon. LC 79-63259. 1979. pap. text ed. 11.25 (ISBN 0-8191-0709-3). U Pr of Amer.
Lectures et Conversations. Ed. by Karl C. Sandberg. (Fr.). 1970. pap. text ed. 6.95x (ISBN 0-89197-272-2). Irvington.

Lectures in Abstract Algebra, Vol. 3: Theory of Fields & Galois Theory. N. Jacobson. LC 75-15564. (Graduate Texts in Ma Thematics: Vol. 32). 330p. 1976. 28.00 (ISBN 0-387-90168-X). Springer-Verlag.
Lectures in America. Gertrude Stein. LC 74-17454. 1975. pap. 2.45 o.p. (ISBN 0-394-71477-6, Vin). Random.
Lectures in America. Gertrude Stein. 246p. Date not set. pap. 2.45 o.p. (ISBN 0-394-71477-6, Vin). Random.
Lectures in Differentiable Dynamics. Lawrence Markus. LC 71-145637. (CBMS Regional Conference Series in Mathematics: No. 3). vi, 30p. 1971. 4.80 o.p. (ISBN 0-8218-1652-7, CBMS-3). Am Math.
Lectures in Electrical Engineering, Vol. 2, Electric Waves & Impulses. Charles P. Steinmetz. LC 70-137004. 1971. pap. text ed. 5.00 (ISBN 0-486-62515-X). Dover.
Lectures in Electrical Engineering, Vol. 3. Charles P. Steinmetz. LC 70-137004. 1971. pap. text ed. 5.00 (ISBN 0-486-62516-8). Dover.
Lectures in Homological Algebra. Peter Hilton. LC 70-152504. (CBMS Regional Conference Series in Mathematics: No. 8). 1971. pap. 5.20 o.p. (ISBN 0-8218-1657-8, CBMS-8). Am Math.
Lectures in Rings & Modules. 2nd ed. Joachim Lambek LC 75-41494. viii, 184p. 1976. 9.95 (ISBN 0-8284-1283-9). Chelsea Pub.
Lectures in Scattering Theory. A. G. Sitenko. Ed. & tr. by P. J. Shepherd. 280p. 1972. text ed. 34.00 (ISBN 0-08-016574-5). Pergamon.
Lectures in Systematic Theology. rev. ed. Henry C. Thiessen. Rev. by Vernon C. Doerksen. 1981. 13.95 (ISBN 0-8028-1815-3). Eerdmans.
Lectures in the Theory of Production. Luigi Pasinetti. LC 77-1541. Orig. Title: Lezioni Di Teoria Della Produzione. 1977. 17.50x (ISBN 0-231-04100-4). Columbia U Pr.
Lectures of Henry Fuseli- in "Lectures on Paintings by the Royal Academicians". Henry Fuseli. Ed. by Sydney J. Freedberg. LC 77-19376. (Connoisseurship Criticism & Art History Ser.: Vol. 10). 450p. 1979. lib. bdg. 40.00 (ISBN 0-8240-3268-3). Garland Pub.
Lectures on Algebraic Topology. A. Dold. (Grundlehren der Mathematischen Wissenschaften Ser.: Vol. 200). (Illus.). 377p. 1981. 38.00 (ISBN 0-387-10369-4). Springer-Verlag.
Lectures on Architecture & Painting: Delivered at Edinburgh in November 1853. John Ruskin. Ed. by Sydney J. Freedberg. LC 77-25766. (Connoisseurship Criticism & Art History Ser.: Vol. 21). (Illus.). 189p. 1979. lib. bdg. 22.00 (ISBN 0-8240-3279-9). Garland Pub.
Lectures on Art - Poems. Washington Allston. LC 75-171379. (Library of American Art Ser.). 1972. Repr. of 1892 ed. lib. bdg. 37.50 (ISBN 0-306-70414-5). Da Capo.
Lectures on Art, & Poems, 1850, & Monaldi, 1841. Washington Allston. LC 67-10124. 1967. 59.00x (ISBN 0-8201-1001-9). Schol Facsimiles.
Lectures on Art Delivered Before the University of Oxford in Hilary Term, 1870. John Ruskin. Ed. by Sydney J. Freedberg. LC 77-25767. (Connoisseurship Critism & Art History: Vol. 22). 155p. 1979. lib. bdg. 14.00. Garland Pub.
Lectures on Biostatistics: An Introduction to Statistics with Applications in Biology & Medicine. D. Colquhoon. 1971. pap. 16.95x (ISBN 0-19-854119-8). Oxford U Pr.
Lectures on Current Algebra & Its Applications. Sam B. Treiman & Roman Jackiw. LC 70-181519. (Princeton Series in Physics). 280p. 1972. 19.50x (ISBN 0-691-08118-2); pap. 6.95 o.p. (ISBN 0-691-08107-7). Princeton U Pr.
Lectures on Electrical Engineering, Vol. 1, Elements Of Electrical Engineering. Charles P. Steinmetz. LC 70-137004. 1971. pap. text ed. 5.00 (ISBN 0-486-62514-1). Dover.
Lectures on Electromagnetic Theory: A Short Course for Engineers. L. Solymar. (Illus.). 1976. text ed. 39.95x (ISBN 0-19-856126-1); pap. 17.95x (ISBN 0-19-856137-7). Oxford U Pr.
Lectures on Elementary Particles & Quantum Field Theory, 2 Vols. Ed. by Stanley Deser et al. 1971. Vol. 1. pap. 8.95x (ISBN 0-262-54013-4); Vol. 2. pap. 7.95x o.p. (ISBN 0-262-54015-0). MIT Pr.
Lectures on English Literature from Chaucer to Tennyson. Henry Reed. 411p. 1980. Repr. of 1876 ed. lib. bdg. 40.00 (ISBN 0-89984-430-8). Century Bookbindery.
Lectures on Equations Defining Space Curves. L. Szpiro. (Tata Institute Lectures on Mathematics). (Illus.). 81p. 1980. pap. 8.00 (ISBN 0-387-09544-6). Springer-Verlag.
Lectures on Ergodic Theory. Paul R. Halmos. LC 60-8964. 7.50 (ISBN 0-8284-0142-X). Chelsea Pub.
Lectures on Field Theory & the Many-Body Problem. Ed. by E. R. Caianiello. (Spring School Lectures, 1961). 1961. 40.50 o.p. (ISBN 0-12-154556-3). Acad Pr.
Lectures on Freshman Calculus. Allan Cruse & Millianne Granberg. LC 79-136118. (Mathematics Ser). 1971. text ed. 20.95 (ISBN 0-201-01301-0); instructor's manual 1.00 (ISBN 0-201-01302-9). A-W.
Lectures on Greek Poetry. J. W. Mackail. LC 66-23520. 1910. 10.50x (ISBN 0-8196-0180-2). Biblo.
Lectures on Hamiltonian Systems, & Rigorous & Formal Stability of Orbits About an Oblate Planet. Jurgen Moser & Walter T. Kyner. LC 52-42839. (Memoirs: No. 81). 1979. pap. 8.40 (ISBN 0-8218-1281-5, MEMO-81). Am Math.
Lectures on Housing, Manchester, 1914. B. Seebohm Rountree & A. C. Pigou. LC 79-56971. (English Working Class Ser.). 1980. lib. bdg. 12.00 (ISBN 0-8240-0122-2). Garland Pub.
Lectures on Human & Animal Psychology. Wilhelm M. Wundt. Tr. by J. Creighton from German. (Contributions to the History of Psychology D, I, Comparative Psychology Ser.). 1978. Repr. of 1894 ed. 30.00 (ISBN 0-89093-170-4). U Pubns Amer.
Lectures on Jurisprudence. Adam Smith. Ed. by R. L. Meek & D. D. Raphael. (Glasgow Edition of the Works & Correspondence of Adam Smith Ser.). 1978. 75.00x (ISBN 0-19-828188-9). Oxford U Pr.
Lectures on Language Performance. C. E. Osgood. (Springer Ser. in Language & Communication: Vol. 7). (Illus.). 368p. 1980. 22.00 (ISBN 0-387-09901-8). Springer-Verlag.
Lectures on Linear Least-Squares Estimation. T. Kailath. (CISM International Centre for Mechanical Sciences: Vol. 140). (Illus.). 1979. pap. 14.80 o.p. (ISBN 0-387-81386-1). Springer-Verlag.
Lectures on Linear Partial Differential Equations. Louis Nirenberg. LC 74-4400. (CBMS Regional Conference Series in Mathematics: No. 17). 1979. pap. 5.60 (ISBN 0-8218-1667-5, CBMS-17). Am Math.
Lectures on Mathematical Theory of Extremum Problems. I. V. Girsanov. Tr. by D. Louvish from Rus. LC 72-80360. (Lecture Notes in Economics & Mathematical Systems: Vol. 67). (Illus.). 139p. 1972. pap. 7.40 (ISBN 0-387-05857-5). Springer-Verlag.
Lectures on Nonlinear-Differential-Equation Models in Biology. J. D. Murray. (Illus.). 1978. 39.95x (ISBN 0-19-853350-0). Oxford U Pr.
Lectures on Partial & Pfaffian Differential Equations. W. Haack & W. Wendland. 1972. 86.00 (ISBN 0-08-016553-2); pap. 25.00 (ISBN 0-08-018997-0). Pergamon.
Lectures on Philosophical Theology. Immanuel Kant. Tr. by Allen W. Wood & Gertrude M. Clark. LC 78-58034. 1978. 15.00 (ISBN 0-8014-1199-8). Cornell U Pr.
Lectures on Philosophy. Simone Weil. Tr. by H. Price from Fr. LC 77-26735. 1978. 32.95 (ISBN 0-521-22005-X); pap. 7.50 (ISBN 0-521-29333-2). Cambridge U Pr.
Lectures on Psychical Research. C. D. Broad. (International Library of Philosophy & Scientific Method). 1962. text ed. 31.25x (ISBN 0-7100-3611-6). Humanities.
Lectures on Revivals. William B. Sprague. 1978. 12.95 (ISBN 0-85151-276-3). Banner of Truth.
Lectures on Rhetoric & Belles Lettres, 2 Vols. Hugh Blair. Ed. by Harold F. Harding. LC 65-13061. (Landmarks in Rhetoric & Public Address Ser). 1965. Set. 19.50x o.p. (ISBN 0-8093-0169-5). S Ill U Pr.
Lectures on Selected Topics in Equilibrium & Non-Equilibrium Statistical Mechanics. D. Ter-Haar & F. Henin. LC 77-8300. 1977. text ed. 25.00 (ISBN 0-08-017937-1). Pergamon.
Lectures on Solid State Physics. G. Busch & D. Schade. 1976. text ed. 64.00 (ISBN 0-08-016894-9); pap. text ed. 25.00 (ISBN 0-08-021653-6). Pergamon.
Lectures on Subgroups of Sylow Type in Finite Soluble Groups. W Gashutz. Tr. by U. Kuhn. (Notes on Pure Mathematics Ser.: No. 11). 100p. (Orig.). 1980. pap. text ed. 7.95 (ISBN 0-908160-22-4, 0571). Bks Australia.
Lectures on Symplectic Groups. O. T. O'Meara. LC 78-19101. (Mathematical Surveys: No. 16). 1978. 22.80 o.p. (ISBN 0-8218-1516-4, SURV 16). Am Math.
Lectures on Symplectic Manifolds. Alan Weinstein. LC 77-3399. (Conference Board of the Mathematical Sciences Ser.: No. 29). 1979. Repr. of 1977 ed. with corrections 6.80 (ISBN 0-8218-1679-9, CBMS29). Am Math.
Lectures on the Book of Philippians. Robert Johnstone. 1977. 16.50 (ISBN 0-686-12969-5). Klock & Klock.
Lectures on the Calculus of Variations. Gilbert A. Bliss. LC 46-5369. 304p. 1980. 9.00x (ISBN 0-226-05896-4, Phoen). U of Chicago Pr.
Lectures on the Calculus of Variations. 3rd ed. Oskar Bolza. LC 73-16324. 9.95 (ISBN 0-8284-0145-4). Chelsea Pub.
Lectures on the Constitution of the United States. Samuel F. Miller. xxi, 765p. 1981. Repr. of 1893 ed. lib. bdg. 45.00x (ISBN 0-8377-0836-2). Rothman.
Lectures on the Electrical Properties of Materials. 2nd ed. L. Solymar & D. Walsh. (Illus.). 1980. 36.50x (ISBN 0-19-851144-2); pap. 18.95x (ISBN 0-19-851145-0). Oxford U Pr.
Lectures on the English Comic Writers. William Hazlitt. 1963. 5.00x o.p. (ISBN 0-460-00411-5, Evman). Dutton.
Lectures on the Epistle of James. Robert Johnstone. 1977. 14.00 (ISBN 0-686-12968-7). Klock & Klock.
Lectures on the First & Second Epistles of Peter. John Lillie. 1978. 18.25 (ISBN 0-686-12954-7). Klock & Klock.
Lectures on the Interpretation of Pain in Orthopedic Practice. Arthur Steindler. (Illus.). 680p. 1959. pap. 34.75 spiral (ISBN 0-398-01847-2). C C Thomas.
Lectures on the Origin & Growth of Religion As Illustrated by Some Points in the History of Indian Buddhism. T. Rhys Davids. 267p. 1972. Repr. text ed. 12.50x o.p. (ISBN 0-8426-0402-2). Verry.
Lectures on the Phenomena of Life Common to Animals & Plants, Vol. 1. Claude Bernard. Tr. by Hebbel E. Hoff et al. (American Lectures in History of Medicine & Science Ser.). (Illus.). 336p. 1974. 34.75 (ISBN 0-398-02857-5). C C Thomas.
Lectures on the Philosophy of History. Georg W. Hegel. Tr. by J. Sibree. 1956. pap. text ed. 4.50 (ISBN 0-486-20112-0). Dover.
Lectures on the Philosophy of World History: Reason in History. Georg W. Hegel. Ed. by D. Forbes & H. B. Nisbet. (Cambridge Studies in the History & Theory of Politics). 290p. (Ger.). 1981. pap. 12.95 (ISBN 0-521-28145-8). Cambridge U Pr.
Lectures on the Theory of the Nucleus. A. G. Sitenko & V. K. Tartakovsky. LC 74-10827. 312p. 1975. text ed. 37.00 (ISBN 0-08-017876-6). Pergamon.
Lectures on the Whole of Anatomy. William Harvey. Tr. by C. D. O'Malley et al. 1961. 22.75x (ISBN 0-520-00540-6). U of Cal Pr.
Lectures on Theoretical Physics. Arnold Sommerfeld. Incl. Vol. 1. Mechanics. 1952. text ed. 19.95 (ISBN 0-12-654668-1); pap. 9.95 (ISBN 0-12-654670-3); Vol. 2. Mechanics of Deformable Bodies. 1950. text ed. 19.95 (ISBN 0-12-654650-9); pap. text ed. 9.95 (ISBN 0-12-654652-5); Vol. 3. Electrodynamics. 1952. text ed. 19.95 (ISBN 0-12-654662-2); pap. 9.95 (ISBN 0-12-654664-9); Vol. 4. Optics. 1954. text ed. 19.95 (ISBN 0-12-654674-6); pap. 9.95 (ISBN 0-12-654676-2); Vol. 5. Thermodynamics & Statistical Mechanics. 1956. text ed. 19.95 (ISBN 0-12-654680-0); pap. 9.95 (ISBN 0-12-654682-7); Vol. 6. Partial Differential Equations in Physics. 1949. 19.95 (ISBN 0-12-654656-8); pap. text ed. 9.95 (ISBN 0-12-654658-4). Acad Pr.
Lectures on Three-Manifold Topology. William Jaco. LC 79-28488. (CBMS Regional Conference Series in Mathematics: No. 43). 1980. 9.60 (ISBN 0-8218-1693-4). Am Math.
Lectures on Topics in Finite Element Solution of Elliptic Problems. B. Mercier. (Tata Institute Lectures on Mathematics). (Illus.). 191p. 1980. pap. 8.00 (ISBN 0-387-09543-8). Springer-Verlag.
Lectures to Relatives of Former Patients. Abraham A. Low. 1967. 6.95 (ISBN 0-8158-0139-4). Chris Mass.
Lecythidaceae - Part One the Actinomonophic-Flowered New World Lecythidaceae: Asteranthos, Gustavia, Grias, Allantoma & Cariniana. Ghillean T. Prance & Scott A. Mori. LC 79-4659. (Flora Neotropica Ser.: Vol. 21). 1979. pap. 28.00 (ISBN 0-89327-193-4). NY Botanical.
Ledermann Spricht Mit Hubert Fichte. Hans Eppendorfer. (Suhrkamp Taschenbuecher: No. 580). (Orig., Ger.). 1980. pap. text ed. 4.55 (ISBN 3-518-37080-4, Pub. by Insel Verlag Germany). Suhrkamp.
Ledge of Gold. Flora M. Hazard. LC 80-68079. (Illus.). (gr. 5-11). 1980. 5.95 (ISBN 0-8323-0371-2); pap. 3.95 (ISBN 0-8323-0372-0). Binford.
Ledger. Joan Hurling. 256p. 1981. 10.95 (ISBN 0-8149-0847-0). Vanguard.
Lee & Grant. Ken Jones & Peter Chamberlain. (Illus.). 1977. 13.85 o.p. (ISBN 0-85059-269-0). Aztex.
Lee Henry's Best Friend. Judy Delton. Ed. by Ann Fay. LC 79-16902. (Concept Bk.: Level I). (Illus.). (gr. k-3). 1980. 6.50g (ISBN 0-8075-4417-5). A Whitman.
Lee Strasberg: The Imperfect Genius of the Actors Studio. Cindy Adams. LC 79-7191. 1980. 13.95 (ISBN 0-385-12496-1). Doubleday.
Lee Trevino. Charles Morse & Ann Morse. LC 74-2420. (Creative's Superstars Ser). 32p. 1974. 5.95 (ISBN 0-87191-342-9). Creative Ed.
Leek & Manifold Railway. Keith Turner. LC 79-56057. (Illus.). 96p. 1980. 13.50 (ISBN 0-7153-7950-X). David & Charles.
Lee's Ferry: A Crossing on the Colorado. Evelyn B. Measeles. (Illus.). 150p. 1981. 12.95 (ISBN 0-87108-576-3). Pruett.
Lee's Lieutenants, 3 vols. Douglas S. Freeman. 1942-1944. Set. lib. rep. ed. 90.00x (ISBN 0-684-15630-X, ScribT). Scribner.
Left Against Zion: Communism, Israel & the Middle East. Ed. by Robert Wistrich. 309p. 1979. 24.00x (ISBN 0-85303-193-2, Pub by Vallentine Mitchell England); pap. 9.95x (ISBN 0-85303-199-1). Biblio Dist.
Left & Right: The Topography. J. A. Laponce. 284p. 1981. 27.50x (ISBN 0-8020-5533-8). U of Toronto Pr.
Left Brain, Right Brain. Sally P. Springer & Georg Deutsch. LC 80-25453. (Psychology Ser.). (Illus.). 1981. text ed. 11.95x (ISBN 0-7167-1269-5); pap. text ed. 6.95x (ISBN 0-7167-1270-9). W H Freeman.
Left Ear of the Machine. Bolon Dzacab & Fred Truck. 25.00 (ISBN 0-938236-00-8). Cookie Pr.
Left Hand of Darkness. Ursula K. LeGuin. 320p. (Orig.). 1976. pap. 2.25 (ISBN 0-441-47805-0). Ace Bks.
Left Hand, Right Hand. Osbert Sitwell. 7.00 (ISBN 0-8446-2949-9). Peter Smith.
Left-Handed Book. James T. Kay. LC 66-23271. (Illus.). 64p. 1966. pap. 2.95 (ISBN 0-87131-156-9). M Evans.
Left-Handed Book. Rae Lindsay. (gr. 4 up). 1980. PLB 6.45 (ISBN 0-531-02258-7). Watts.
Left-Handed Mariage & Adult Life. Walter Dyk & Ruth B. Dyk. (Illus.). 624p. 1980. 25.00 (ISBN 0-231-04946-3). Columbia U Pr.
Left Handed: Right Handed. Mark Brown. LC 80-66094. (Illus.). 160p. 1980. 14.95 (ISBN 0-7153-7510-5). David & Charles.
Left-Handed Shortstop. Patricia R. Giff. LC 80-65835. (Illus.). 128p. (gr. 5-8). 1980. 7.95 (ISBN 0-440-04553-3); PLB 7.45 (ISBN 0-440-04554-1). Delacorte.
Left of Africa. Hal Clement. (Lost Manuscripts Ser.). 160p. 1976. 12.95. Manuscript Pr.
Left on the Field to Die: Timothy Richardson, No. 1. Ira Rosenstein. 27p. (Orig.). 1980. pap. 2.00 (ISBN 0-9605438-0-5). Starlight Pr.
Left, Right, Left, Right. Muriel Stanek. LC 79-79548. (Concept Bks.). (Illus.). 40p. (gr. k-2). 1969. 6.95g (ISBN 0-8075-4421-3). A Whitman.
Left-Wing Communism. Vladimir I. Lenin. 1965. pap. 1.95 (ISBN 0-8351-0128-2). China Bks.
Leftist Movements in India, 1917-1947. Satyabrata R. Chowdhuri. LC 76-52206. 1976. 11.50x o.p. (ISBN 0-88386-803-2); pap. 8.50x o.p. (ISBN 0-685-71767-4). South Asia Bks.
Leg Art: Sixty Years of Hollywood Cheesecake. Madison S. Lacy & Don Morgan. (Illus.). 256p. 1981. 24.95 (ISBN 0-8065-0734-9). Citadel Pr.
Leg at Each Corner: Thelwell's Complete Guide to Equitation. Norman Thelwell. (Illus.). 1963. 4.50 o.p. (ISBN 0-525-14419-6). Dutton.
Lega Culture: Art, Initiation, & Moral Philosophy Among a Central African People. Daniel Biebuyck. LC 71-165226. 1973. 33.50x (ISBN 0-520-02085-5). U of Cal Pr.
Legacies in the Study of Behavior: The Wisdom & Experience of Many. Ed. by Joseph Cullen. (American Lectures in Objective Psychiatry Ser.). (Illus.). 288p. 1975. text ed. 24.50 (ISBN 0-398-03147-9). C C Thomas.
Legacy of a Lifetime: The Story of Baxter State Park in Maine. John W. Hakola. (Illus.). 448p. Date not set. 16.00 (ISBN 0-931474-18-3). TBW Bks.
Legacy of Beulah Land. Lonnie Coleman. 1981. pap. 2.95 (ISBN 0-440-15085-X). Dell.
Legacy of Egypt. 2nd ed. Ed. by J. R. Harris. (Legacy Ser.). (Illus.). 1971. 27.50x (ISBN 0-19-821912-1). Oxford U Pr.
Legacy of Greece: A New Appraisal. Ed. by M. I. Finley. (Illus.). 480p. 1981. 16.95 (ISBN 0-19-821915-6). Oxford U Pr.
Legacy of Holmes & Brandeis. Samuel J. Konefsky. LC 78-157828. (American Constitutional & Legal History, Ser.). 316p. 1974. Repr. of 1956 ed. lib. bdg. 29.50 (ISBN 0-306-70215-0). Da Capo.
Legacy of Islam. 2nd ed. Ed. by Joseph Schacht & C. E. Bosworth. (Legacy Ser). (Illus.). 583p. 1974. text ed. 29.50x (ISBN 0-19-821913-X). Oxford U Pr.
Legacy of Jesus. John MacArthur, Jr. 1981. text ed. 7.95 (ISBN 0-8024-8524-3). Moody.
Legacy of Leadership: Pictorial History of Trans World Airlines. Trans World Airlines. (Illus.). 1973. 15.00 o.p. (ISBN 0-911721-47-9). Aviation.
Legacy of Mark Rothko. Lee Seldes. 1978. 14.95 o.p. (ISBN 0-03-014751-4). HR&W.

Legacy of Merton Manor. Dorothy B. Francis. 192p. (YA) 1976. 4.95 o.p. (ISBN 0-685-61055-1, Avalon). Bouregy.

Legacy of Populism in Bolivia: From the MNR to Military Rule. Christopher Mitchell. LC 77-83461. (Praeger Special Studies). 1978. 23.95 (ISBN 0-03-039671-9). Praeger.

Legacy of Redfern. Jeanne Judson. (YA) 5.95 (ISBN 0-685-07441-2, Avalon). Bouregy.

Legacy of Rome. Ed. by Cyril Bailey. (Illus.). 524p. 1923. 22.50x (ISBN 0-19-821906-7). Oxford U Pr.

Legacy of Sacco & Vanzetti. Louis Joughin & Edmund M. Morgan. LC 77-92101. 596p. 30.00x (ISBN 0-691-04656-5); pap. 5.95 (ISBN 0-691-00588-5). Princeton U Pr.

Legacy of the Bloody Bride. Robert P. Richmond. (Orig.). 1979. pap. 1.95 (ISBN 0-532-23125-2). Manor Bks.

Legacy of the Blues: Art & Lives of Twelve Great Bluesmen. Samuel Charters. LC 76-51809. (Roots of Jazz Ser.). (Illus.). 1977. 21.50 (ISBN 0-306-70847-7); pap. 4.95 (ISBN 0-306-80054-3). Da Capo.

Legacy of the Bolshevik Revolution: A Critical History of the USSR. David Rousset. (Allison & Busby Motive Ser.). 416p. 1981. pap. 12.95 (ISBN 0-8052-8091-X, Pub. by Allison & Busby England). Schocken.

Legacy of the Great Wheel. Katy Turner. LC 80-83331. (Illus.). 128p. 1980. pap. 8.95 (ISBN 0-910458-15-4). Select Bks.

Legacy of the Lake. Michael A. Smith. 1980. pap. 2.25 (ISBN 0-686-69247-0, 75879). Avon.

Legacy of the Middle Ages. Ed. by C. G. Crump & E. F. Jacob. (Legacy Ser.). (Illus.). 1926. 29.50x (ISBN 0-19-821907-5). Oxford U Pr.

Legacy of Vietnam: The War, American Society, & the Future of American Foreign Policy. Ed. by Anthony Lake. LC 75-13571. 440p. 1976. 22.50x (ISBN 0-8147-4964-X); pap. 7.00x (ISBN 0-8147-4997-6). NYU Pr.

Legacy of Windhaven. Marie De Jourlet. (Windhaven Saga). 1978. pap. 2.75 (ISBN 0-523-41267-3). Pinnacle Bks.

Legal Abortion: The English Experience. A. Hordern. 1971. 30.00 (ISBN 0-08-016567-2). Pergamon.

Legal Accountability in the Nursing Process. Irene Murchison et al. 1978. pap. text ed. 10.50 (ISBN 0-8016-3603-5). Mosby.

Legal Administration, 3 pts. Incl. Pt. 1. General, 16 vols. Set. 1378.00x (ISBN 0-686-01177-5); Pt. 2. Criminal Law, 6 vols. Set. 423.00x (ISBN 0-686-01178-3); Pt. 3. Marriage - Divorce, 3 vols. Set. 198.00x (ISBN 0-686-01179-1). (British Parliamentary Papers Ser.). 1971 (Pub. by Irish Academic Pr Ireland). Biblio Dist.

Legal & Business Aspects of the Music Industry: Music, Videocassettes & Records, Course Handbook. Donald E. Biederman. LC 80-81531. (Patents, Copyrights, Trademarks & Literary Property 1979-80 Course Handbook Ser.). 736p. 1980. pap. text ed. 25.00 (ISBN 0-686-68825-2, G4-3676). PLI.

Legal & Business Problems of the Advertising Industry: 1980 Course Handbook. Felix H. Kent. LC 80-80906. (Patents, Copyrights, Trademarks, & Literary Property Course Handbook Ser.). (Illus.). 465p. 1980. pap. text ed. 25.00 (ISBN 0-686-68827-9, G4-3672). PLI.

Legal & Business Problems of the Advertising Industry 1978 Course Handbook. (Patents, Copyrights, Trademarks, & Literary Property Course Handbook Ser.,1977-78: Vol. 94). 1978. pap. 20.00 o.p. (ISBN 0-685-59698-2, G4-3640). PLI.

Legal & Business Problems of the Record Industry 1978 Course Handbook. (Patents, Copyrights, Trademarks, & Literary Property Course Handbook Ser., 1977-78: Vol. 98). 1978. pap. 20.00 o.p. (ISBN 0-685-59700-8, G4-3642). PLI.

Legal & Ethical Issues in Human Research & Treatment: Psychopharmacologic Considerations. Ed. by Donald M. Gallant & Robert Force. 1978. 15.00 (ISBN 0-470-26354-7). Halsted Pr.

Legal & Illicit Drug Use: Acute Reactions of Emergency Room Populations. James A. Inciardi et al. LC 78-19743. 1978. 25.95 (ISBN 0-03-046701-2). Praeger.

Legal & Legislative Information Processing. Beth K. Eres. LC 79-7063. (Illus.). xvi, 299p. 1980. lib. bdg. 29.95 (ISBN 0-313-21343-7, ERL/). Greenwood.

Legal Aspects of Business Administration. 3rd ed. Dow Votaw. 1969. text ed. 21.00 (ISBN 0-13-527531-8). P-H.

Legal Aspects of Business in Saudi Arabia. E. Kay. 160p. 1979. 40.00x (ISBN 0-86010-131-2, Pub. by Graham & Trotman England). State Mutual Bk.

Legal Aspects of Conscription & Exemption in North Carolina, 1861-1865. Memory F. Mitchell. (James Sprunt Study in History & Political Science: Vol. 47). (Orig.). 1965. pap. text ed. 3.50x (ISBN 0-8078-5047-0). U of NC Pr.

Legal Aspects of Health Care Administration. George D. Pozgar. LC 78-17276. 1979. text ed. 21.95 (ISBN 0-89443-044-0). Aspen Systems.

Legal Aspects of Health Policy: Issues & Trends. Ed. by Ruth Roemer & George McKray. LC 79-8583. (Illus.). x, 473p. 1980. lib. bdg. 45.00 (ISBN 0-313-21430-1, RIH/). Greenwood.

Legal Aspects of Hotel, Motel, & Restaurant Operation. 1st ed. Nathan Kalt. LC 78-142504. 1971. 19.95 (ISBN 0-672-96089-3); tchrs' manual 6.67 (ISBN 0-672-96091-5); wkbk. 9.95 (ISBN 0-672-96090-7). Bobbs.

Legal Aspects of International Business. C. Crosswell. 1980. 40.00 (ISBN 0-379-20683-8). Oceana.

Legal Aspects of International Investment. Stephen Gorove. (L. Q. C. Lamar Society of International Law, University of Mississippi Law Center, Monograph: No. 1). viii, 79p. (Orig.). 1977. pap. text ed. 10.00x (ISBN 0-8377-0607-6). Rothman.

Legal Aspects of International Terrorism. new ed. Ed. by Alona E. Evans & John F. Murphy. LC 78-404. 1978. 36.95 (ISBN 0-669-02185-7). Lexington Bks.

Legal Aspects of Life Insurance: Teaching, Pt. 3. Marlene Sorensen. (FLMI Insurance Education Program Ser.). 1978. instrs.' manual 8.00x (ISBN 0-915322-29-3). LOMA.

Legal Aspects of Marketing Behavior in Lebanon & Kuwait. Nimr Eid. 7.50x (ISBN 0-685-77095-8). Intl Bk Ctr.

Legal Aspects of Mental Retardation: A Search for Reliability. Robert H. Woody. 144p. 1974. 12.75 (ISBN 0-398-03243-2). C C Thomas.

Legal Aspects of Prisons & Jails. P. D. Clute. 248p. 1980. 21.75- (ISBN 0-398-04005-2); pap. 14.95 (ISBN 0-398-04006-0). C C Thomas.

Legal Aspects of Private Security. John C. Klotter et al. LC 79-55202. 368p. 1981. text ed. price not set (ISBN 0-87084-488-1). Anderson Pub Co.

Legal Aspects of the New International Economic Order. Ed. by Kamal Hossain. 300p. 1980. 32.50x (ISBN 0-89397-088-3). Nichols Pub.

Legal Aspects of the Transfer of Technology in Modern Society. 18p. 1980. pap. 5.00 (ISBN 92-808-0175-9, TUNU099, UNU). Unipub.

Legal Barriers to Solar Heating & Cooling of Buildings. Environmental Law Institute. 368p. 1980. 35.00 (ISBN 0-89499-006-3). Bks Business.

Legal Beagle. Legal Beagle. LC 79-56874. 1980. 8.95 (ISBN 0-533-04538-X). Vantage.

Legal Control of Government: Administrative Law in Britain & the United States. Bernard Schwartz & H. W. Wade. 1972. 45.00x (ISBN 0-19-825315-X). Oxford U Pr.

Legal Data Profiles for Selected Chemicals. (IRPTC Ser.: No. 2). 280p. 1981. pap. 28.00 (ISBN 0-686-69542-9, UNEP 40, UNEP). Unipub.

Legal Decisions & Information Systems. Jon Bing & Trygve Harvold. 1977. 25.00x (ISBN 82-00-05031-9, Dist. by Columbia U Pr). Universitet.

Legal Dimensions of Drug Abuse in the United States. Harvey R. Levine. (Criminal Law Education & Research Center Ser.). 208p. 1974. 13.75 (ISBN 0-398-02876-1). C C Thomas.

Legal-Economic History of Air Pollution Controls. Jan G. Laitos. LC 80-67046. (Scholarly Monograph Ser.). 350p. 1980. pap. 27.50 (ISBN 0-8408-0507-1). Carrollton Pr.

Legal Education in Colonial New York. Paul L. Hamlin. LC 70-129082. (American Constitutional and Legal History Ser.). (Illus.). 1970. Repr. of 1939 ed. lib. bdg. 25.00 (ISBN 0-306-70062-X). Da Capo.

Legal Effects of United Nations Resolutions. Jorge Castaneda. LC 75-94629. (International Organization Ser). 1970. 17.00x (ISBN 0-231-03318-4). Columbia U Pr.

Legal Effects of War. 4th ed. Arnold D. McNair & A. D. Watts. 69.00 (ISBN 0-521-05652-7). Cambridge U Pr.

Legal Environment of Business. 5th ed. Robert N. Corley et al. (Illus.). 608p. 1981. 19.95 (ISBN 0-07-013186-4, C); instr's manual 5.95 (ISBN 0-07-013187-2); test file 7.95 (ISBN 0-07-013189-9). McGraw.

Legal Environment of Business Study Guide. 2nd ed. Charles Latimer et al. 105p. 1980. pap. text ed. 7.50 (ISBN 0-88244-215-5). Grid Pub.

Legal Ethics & Legal Education. Michael J. Kelly. LC 80-10825. (Teaching of Ethics Ser.). 69p. 1980. pap. 4.00 (ISBN 0-916558-06-1). Hastings Ctr Inst Soc.

Legal Fictions. A. Laurence Polak. 127p. 1980. Repr. of 1945 ed. lib. bdg. 25.00 (ISBN 0-89987-699-4). Century Bookbindery.

Legal First Aid. Henry Shain. LC 75-12737. (Funk & W Bk.). (Illus.). 352p. 1975. 10.95 o.p. (ISBN 0-308-10201-0, TYC-T). T Y Crowell.

Legal Foundation of Public Administration. 407p. 1980. text ed. 17.95 (ISBN 0-8299-2120-6). West Pub.

Legal Foundations of Public Administration. Donald D. Barry & Howard R. Whitcomb. 407p. 1980. text ed. 17.95 (ISBN 0-8299-2120-6). West Pub.

Legal Framework for Oil Concessions in the Arab World. Simon G. Siksek. LC 79-2882. 140p. 1981. Repr. of 1960 ed. 15.00 (ISBN 0-8305-0050-2). Hyperion Conn.

Legal Framework of English Feudalism. S. F. Milsom. LC 75-23531. (Cambridge Studies in English Legal History). 1976. 33.95 (ISBN 0-521-20947-1). Cambridge U Pr.

Legal Guide for the Visual Artist. Tad Crawford. 1977. 10.95 o.p. (ISBN 0-8015-4471-8). Dutton.

Legal Guide for the Visual Artist. Tad Crawford. 1980. pap. 5.95 (ISBN 0-8015-4472-6, Hawthorn). Dutton.

Legal Handbook for Educators. Patricia A. Hollander. LC 77-26092. 1978. lib. bdg. 22.50x (ISBN 0-89158-420-X); pap. text ed. 13.75x (ISBN 0-86531-073-4). Westview.

Legal Impediments to International Intermodal Transportation. Maritime Transportation Research Board. LC 72-170156. 1971. pap. text ed. 5.50 (ISBN 0-309-01924-9). Natl Acad Pr.

Legal Imperialism: A Critical History of American Legal Assistance to the Third World. James A. Gardner. LC 79-5406. 259p. 1981. 20.00 (ISBN 0-299-08130-3). U of Wis Pr.

Legal Implications of Emergency Care. Neil L. Chayet. 1981. pap. 12.50 (ISBN 0-686-69605-0). ACC.

Legal Implications of Minimum Competency Testing. Joseph Beckham. LC 79-93114. (Fastback Ser.: No. 138). (Orig.). 1980. pap. 0.75 (ISBN 0-87367-138-4). Phi Delta Kappa.

Legal, Institutional, & Social Aspects of Irrigation & Drainage & Water Resources Planning & Management. Compiled by American Society of Civil Engineers. 912p. 1979. pap. text ed. 49.50 (ISBN 0-87262-140-5). Am Soc Civil Eng.

Legal Institutions in Manchu China: A Sociological Analysis. Sybille Van Der Sprenkel. (Monographs on Social Anthropology: No. 24). 1962. pap. text ed. 6.25x (ISBN 0-391-00755-6, Athlone Pr). Humanities.

Legal Isssues of European Integration 1979. 2nd ed. Ed. by D. J. Giljlstra et al. 130p. 1980. pap. 21.50 (ISBN 90-2681-178-0, Pub. by Kluwer Law & Taxation). Kluwer Boston.

Legal Issues in Pediatrics & Adolescent Medicine. Angela R. Holder. LC 76-41385. 1977. 35.95 (ISBN 0-471-40612-0, Pub. by Wiley-Medical). Wiley.

Legal Limits of Journalism. H. Lloyd. 1968. pap. 4.20 (ISBN 0-08-012914-5). Pergamon.

Legal Medicine Annual: 1975. Ed. by Cyril H. Wecht. (Illus.). 350p. 1975. text ed. 28.50 o.p. (ISBN 0-8385-5653-1). ACC.

Legal Medicine Annual 1978. Ed. by Cyril H. Wecht. (Illus.). 1978. 34.50 (ISBN 0-8385-5656-6). ACC.

Legal Medicine 1980. Cyril H. Wecht. (Illus.). 320p. 1980. text ed. 27.50 (ISBN 0-7216-9142-0). Saunders.

Legal Norms in a Confucian State. William Shaw. (Korea Research Monographs: No. 5). write for info. (ISBN 0-912966-32-7). IEAS Ctr Chinese Stud.

Legal Norms of Delinquency: A Comparative Study. (New York University Criminal Law Education & Research Center Monograph: No. 1). (Orig.). 1969. pap. text ed. 8.50x (ISBN 0-8377-0800-1). Rothman.

Legal Office Procedures. 2nd ed. Marjorie D. Bate & Mary C. Casey. (Illus.). 544p. 1980. pap. text ed. 15.25 (ISBN 0-07-004058-3, G); instructor's manual & key avail. (ISBN 0-07-004059-1). McGraw.

Legal Outlook: A Message to College & University People. Ulysses V. Spiva. LC 80-69232. 115p. 1981. perfect bdg. 9.95 (ISBN 0-86548-057-5). Century Twenty One.

Legal Overview of the New Student: As Educational Consumer, Citizen & Bargainer. Ed. by Robert A. Laudicina & Joseph L. Tramutola. (Illus.). 316p. 1976. 24.50 (ISBN 0-398-03575-X). C C Thomas.

Legal Periodicals Directory. Oxbridge Communications, Inc. 150p. 1981. lib. bdg. 35.00 (ISBN 0-87196-335-3). Facts on File.

Legal Perspective for Student Personnel Administrators. R. Laudicina & J. Tramutola. (Illus.). 152p. 1974. 14.75 (ISBN 0-398-03080-4). C C Thomas.

Legal Perspectives of American Business Associations. Arthur D. Wolfe & Frederick J. Naffziger. LC 76-5614. (Law Ser.). 1977. text ed. 20.95 o.p. (ISBN 0-88244-109-4). Grid Pub.

Legal Pluralism: An Introduction to Colonial & Neo - Colonial Laws. M. B. Hooker. 500p. 1975. 49.50x (ISBN 0-19-825329-X). Oxford U Pr.

Legal Policy Analysis. Stuart S. Nagel & Marian Neef. LC 76-14046. 1977. 23.95 (ISBN 0-669-00731-5). Lexington Bks.

Legal Problem Solving: Analysis Research & Writing. 3rd ed. Marjorie D. Rombauer. LC 78-3468. (American Casebook Ser). 352p. 1978. text ed. 13.95 (ISBN 0-8299-2002-1). West Pub.

Legal Problems & the Citizen. Brian Abel-Smith et al. 1973. text ed. 20.95x (ISBN 0-435-82865-7). Heinemann Ed.

Legal Process from a Behavorial Perspective. Stuart S. Nagel. 1969. text ed. 14.50 o.p. (ISBN 0-256-01151-6). Dorsey.

Legal P's & Q's in the Doctor's Office. Marjorie K. Heller. (Orig.). 1981. pap. 12.50 (ISBN 0-686-59766-4). Monarch Pr.

Legal P's & Q's in the Doctor's Office. 1978. write for info. o.p. (ISBN 0-915362-10-4). M K Heller.

Legal Psychology. M. Ralph Brown. (Historical Foundations of Forensic Psychiatry & Psychology Ser.). (Illus.). 346p. 1980. Repr. of 1926 ed. lib. bdg. 35.00 (ISBN 0-306-76065-7). Da Capo.

Legal Relations of Infants, Parent & Child, & Guardian & Ward: And a Particular Consideration of Guardianship in the State of New York. G. W. Field. xx, 376p. 1981. Repr. of 1888 ed. lib. bdg. 28.50x (ISBN 0-8377-0537-1). Rothman.

Legal Responsibility & Moral Responsibility. Walter Moberly. Ed. by Franklin Sherman. LC 65-21820. (Facet Bks). 64p. (Orig.). 1965. pap. 1.00 (ISBN 0-8006-3020-3, 1-3020). Fortress.

Legal Rights & Responsibilities of Indiana Teachers. 3rd ed. Fred Swalls. LC 75-36710. 1976. pap. text ed. 4.50x o.p. (ISBN 0-8134-1784-8, 1784). Interstate.

Legal Rights & Responsibilities of Indiana Teachers. 4th ed. Ed. by Fred Swalls et al. 1980. pap. text ed. 8.95x (ISBN 0-8134-2152-7, 2152). Interstate.

Legal Rights of Handicapped Persons: Cases, Materials, & Text. Ed. by Robert L. Burgdorf. 1178p. 1980. 24.50 (ISBN 0-933716-01-X). P H Brookes.

Legal Rights of Prisoners. Ed. by Geoffrey P. Alpert. LC 80-17241. (Sage Criminal Justice System Annuals: Vol. 14). (Illus.). 280p. 1980. 20.00 (ISBN 0-8039-1188-2). Sage.

Legal Rights of Prisoners. Ed. by Geoffrey P. Alpert. LC 80-17241. (Sage Criminal Justice System Annuals: Vol. 14). (Illus.). 280p. 1980. pap. 9.95 (ISBN 0-8039-1189-0). Sage.

Legal Rights of Prisoners: An Analysis of Legal Aid. Geoffrey P. Alpert. LC 78-4343. (Illus.). 1978. 18.95 (ISBN 0-669-02347-7). Lexington Bks.

Legal Rights of the Convicted. Hazel B. Kerper & Janeen Kerper. (Criminal Justice Ser.). 1974. text ed. 16.95 (ISBN 0-8299-0622-3); pap. text ed. write for info. (ISBN 0-8299-0622-3). West Pub.

Legal Rights Primer: In & Out of the Classroom. Joseph Roberts & Bonnie Hawk. 96p. (Orig.). 1980. pap. 5.00 (ISBN 0-87879-241-4). Acad Therapy.

Legal Secretary's Handbook. 11th ed. Ed. by Marian Freeman. LC 76-52065. 1980. incl. 1979 suppl. 45.00 (ISBN 0-911110-22-4). Parker & Son.

Legal Services & Community Mental Health Centers. Henry Weihofen. 74p. 1969. pap. 3.00 (ISBN 0-685-24859-3, P229-0). Am Psychiatric.

Legal Status of Rural Women: Limitations on the Economic Participation of Women in Rural Development. (FAO Economic & Social Development Paper Ser.: No. 9). 73p. 1980. pap. 7.50 (ISBN 92-5-100858-2, F1956, FAO). Unipub.

Legal Structure. M. D. Freeman. (Aspects of Modern Sociology Ser: Social Structure of Modern Britain). 1977. text ed. 8.50x (ISBN 0-582-48761-7); pap. text ed. 7.95x (ISBN 0-582-48762-5). Longman.

Legal Systems. Bernadine Meyer & Blair Kolasa. (Illus.). 1978. 18.95 (ISBN 0-13-529404-5). P-H.

Legal Theory. 5th ed. Wolfgang G. Friedmann. LC 67-26509. 1967. 27.50x (ISBN 0-231-03100-9). Columbia U Pr.

Legal Thesaurus. William C. Burton & Steven E. DeCosta. LC 80-83803. 1980. 35.00 (ISBN 0-02-691000-4). Free Pr.

Legal Writing Style. 2nd ed. Henry Weihofen. LC 79-23662. 332p. 1980. text ed. 11.95 (ISBN 0-8299-2066-8). West Pub.

Legality, Morality, & Ethics in Criminal Justice. Ed. by Nicholas N. Kittrie & Jackwell Susman. (Praeger Special Studies). 1978. 25.95 (ISBN 0-03-047521-X). Praeger.

Legality of Love. Jerry Sonenblick & Martha Sowerwine. 480p. (Orig.). 1981. pap. 3.95 (ISBN 0-515-05491-7). Jove Pubns.

Legend. Evelyn Anthony. 1976. pap. 1.50 o.p. (ISBN 0-345-25473-2). Ballantine.

Legend & Reality: Early Ceramics from South-East Asia. Roxanna M. Brown. (Oxford in Asia Studies in Ceramics). (Illus.). 246p. 1977. 43.00x (ISBN 0-19-580383-3). Oxford U Pr.

Legend in Green Velvet. Elizabeth Peters. LC 76-3617. 1976. 7.95 (ISBN 0-396-07283-6). Dodd.

Legend in His Time. Rochelle H. Dubois. (Illus., Orig.). (gr. 8-10). 1979. pap. 3.00 (ISBN 0-934536-01-5). Merging Media.

Legend, Myth & Magic in the Image of the Artists: A Historical Experiment. Ernst Kris & Otto Kurz. 1979. 17.50x (ISBN 0-300-02205-0). Yale U Pr.

Legend, Myth, & Magic in the Image of the Artist: A Historical Experiment. Ernst Kris & Otto Kurz. LC 78-24024. (Illus.). 175p. 1981. pap. 5.95 (ISBN 0-300-02669-2). Yale U Pr.

Legend of Duke Ernst. Tr. by J. W. Thomas & Carolyn Dussere. LC 79-19843. x, 126p. 1980. 11.50x (ISBN 0-8032-4406-1). U of Nebr Pr.

Legend of Grizzly Adams. Richard Dillon. 1977. pap. 1.50 o.p. (ISBN 0-425-03646-4, Medallion). Berkley Pub.

Legend of John Brown: Twenty-Two Gouaches by Jacob Lawrence. Detroit Institute of Arts. (Illus.). 1979. 6.00x (ISBN 0-8143-1633-6, Pub. by Detroit Inst Arts). Wayne St U Pr.

Legend of John Henry - the Steel Drivin' Man. David A. Bice. (Pringle Tree Ser.). (Illus.). 32p. (gr. 3-6). 1980. PLB 5.95 (ISBN 0-934750-05-X). Jalamap.

Legend of King Piast. Babara Seidler. Tr. by Jane Kedron. (Young People's Ser.). (Illus.). (gr. 2-8). 1977. pap. 1.00 (ISBN 0-917004-08-6). Kosciuszko.

Legend of Lost Earth. Hope Campbell. LC 76-48079. 160p. (YA) 1977. 6.95 (ISBN 0-590-07397-4, Four Winds). Schol Bk Serv.

Legend of New Amsterdam. Peter Spier. LC 78-6032. (Illus.). 32p. 1979. 7.95a (ISBN 0-385-13179-8); PLB (ISBN 0-385-13180-1). Doubleday.

Legend of Ogden Jenks. Robert Emmitt. 203p. 1980. pap. 5.95 (ISBN 0-8263-0559-8). U of NM Pr.

Legend of Old Befana. Tomie De Paola. LC 80-12293. (Illus.). 32p. (gr. k-3). 1980. pap. 3.95 (ISBN 0-15-243817-3, VoyB). HarBraceJ.

Legend of Old Befana. Tomie De Paola. LC 80-12293. (Illus.). 32p. (gr. k-3). 1980. 8.95 (ISBN 0-15-243816-5, HJ). HarBraceJ.

Legend of St. Urho. Aini Rajanen. LC 81-295. (Illus.). 48p. (ps up). 1981. 8.95 (ISBN 0-87518-215-1). Dillon.

Legend of Scarface: A Blackfeet Indian Tale. Robert San Souci. LC 77-15170. (gr. 1-3). 1978. 8.95a (ISBN 0-385-13247-6); PLB (ISBN 0-385-13248-4). Doubleday.

Legend of Semimaru: Blind Musician of Japan. Susan Matisoff. LC 77-24601. (Studies in Oriental Cultures Ser.: No. 14). 1978. 17.50x (ISBN 0-231-03947-6). Columbia U Pr.

Legend of Sleepy Hollow & Other Stories. Washington Irving. (Classics Ser). (gr. 6 up). 1964. pap. 1.25 (ISBN 0-8049-0050-7, CL-50). Airmont.

Legend of Sleepy Hollow, Rip Van Winkle, President Van Buren & Brown. E. R. Welles. 1973. pap. 2.00x (ISBN 0-913692-10-7). Learning Inc.

Legend of Tarik. Walter D. Myers. (Illus.). 192p. (gr. 7 up). 1981. 9.95 (ISBN 0-670-42312-2). Viking Pr.

Legend of the Damned. Gordon D. Shirreffs. 1979. pap. 1.75 o.p. (ISBN 0-449-14183-7, GM). Fawcett.

Legend of the Lone Ranger: A Novelization. Gary McCarthy. 160p. (Orig.). 1981. pap. 2.25 (ISBN 0-345-29438-6). Ballantine.

Legend of the Lone Ranger Storybook. Adapted by Larry Weinberg. LC 80-5751. (Movie Storybooks). (Illus.). 64p. (gr. 3-7). 1981. PLB 6.99 o.p. (ISBN 0-394-94683-9); pap. 5.95 boards o.p. (ISBN 0-394-84683-4). Random.

Legend of the Seventh Virgin. Victoria Holt. 1978. pap. 1.95 o.p. (ISBN 0-449-23281-6, Crest). Fawcett.

Legend of the Seventh Virgin. Victoria Holt. 288p. 1981. pap. 2.50 (ISBN 0-449-23281-6, Crest). Fawcett.

Legend of the Silver Bars. Neal Wakely. 112p. 1979. 5.95 (ISBN 0-8059-2592-9). Dorrance.

Legend of the Sons of God: A Fantasy? T. C. Lethbridge. (Illus.). 1972. 12.00 (ISBN 0-7100-7159-0). Routledge & Kegan.

Legend of the Wandering Jew. George K. Anderson. LC 65-14290. 489p. 1970. Repr. of 1965 ed. 20.00 (ISBN 0-87057-094-3, Pub. by Brown U Pr). Univ Pr of New England.

Legend of Witchwynd. Jeanne Hines. 256p. 1976. pap. 1.25 o.p. (ISBN 0-445-00420-7). Popular Lib.

Legendary Fictions of the Irish Celts. Patrick Kennedy. LC 68-25518. 1968. Repr. of 1866 ed. 18.00 (ISBN 0-8103-3467-4). Gale.

Legendary History of Britain in Lope Garcia De Salazar's Libro De las Bienandanzas e Fortunas. Harvey L. Sharrer. LC 78-53334. (Haney Foundation Ser). 1978. 15.00x (ISBN 0-8122-7749-X). U of Pa Pr.

Legendary Lore of the Holy Wells of England. Robert C. Hope. LC 68-21775. (Illus.). 1968. Repr. of 1893 ed. 15.00 (ISBN 0-8103-3445-3). Gale.

Legendary Women of the West. Brad Williams. (Illus.). (gr. 7 up). 1978. 7.95 o.p. (ISBN 0-679-20776-7). McKay.

Legendary Yachts. Bill Robinson. (Nautical Ser.). (Illus.). 1978. 7.98 o.p. (ISBN 0-679-51175-X). McKay.

Legende des Siecles. Victor Hugo. Ed. by H. J. Hunt. (French Texts Ser.). 1968. pap. text ed. 4.50x o.p. (ISBN 0-631-00490-4, Pub. by Basil Blackwell). Biblio Dist.

Legends & Myths of Hawaii: The Fables & Folk-Lore of a Strange People. Kalakaua. Ed. & illus. by R. M. Daggett. LC 72-77519. (Illus.). (gr. 9 up). 1972. pap. 7.75 (ISBN 0-8048-1032-X). C E Tuttle.

Legends & Superstitions of the Sea & of Sailors, in All Lands & at All Times. Fletcher S. Bassett. LC 70-119444. (Illus.). 1974. Repr. of 1885 ed. 28.00 (ISBN 0-8103-3375-9). Gale.

Legends for Geohydrochemical Maps. (Technical Papers in Hydrology Ser.). (Illus.). 61p. 1976. pap. 6.00 (ISBN 92-3-001207-6, U351, UNESCO). Unipub.

Legends from the Future. Ewald Bash. (Orig.). 1972. pap. 1.75 o.p. (ISBN 0-377-02101-6). Friend Pr.

Legends of Derbyshire. 2nd ed. John N. Merrill. (Illus.). 71p. (Orig.). (gr. 6 up). 1975. pap. 3.00 (ISBN 0-913714-15-1). Legacy Bks.

Legends of Florence, 2 Vols. Charles G. Leland. LC 68-27173. 1969. Repr. of 1895 ed. 15.00 ea. Vol. 1, First Ser (ISBN 0-8103-3843-2). Vol. 2, Second Ser. (ISBN 0-8103-3844-0); Set. write for info. (ISBN 0-8103-3899-8). Gale.

Legends of Flowers. Paolo Mantegazza. Tr. by Mrs. Alexander Kennedy. LC 73-180973. (Illus.). 190p. 1975. Repr. of 1927 ed. 15.00 (ISBN 0-8103-4051-8). Gale.

Legends of Highwaymen & Others. Richard Blakeborough. LC 75-154493. (Illus.). 1971. Repr. of 1924 ed. 18.00 (ISBN 0-8103-3373-2). Gale.

Legends of India. 2nd. ed. Muriel Wasi. (Illus.). 1973. pap. 2.25 (ISBN 0-88253-326-6). Ind-US Inc.

Legends of Lands End. Claude O. Lanciano, Jr. LC 72-18023. (Illus.). 1971. 4.30 (ISBN 0-9603558-1-2). Lands End Bks.

Legends of Le Detroit. Marie C. Hamlin. LC 68-26179. (Illus.). 1977. Repr. of 1884 ed. 18.00 (ISBN 0-8103-3330-9). Gale.

Legends of New York State. Catherine H. Ainsworth. LC 78-54873. (Folklore Bks.). vi, 96p. 1980. 4.00 (ISBN 0-933190-05-0). Clyde Pr.

Legends of the California Bandidos. Angus MacLean. 235p. 1977. 4.95 (ISBN 0-914330-09-8). Western Tanager.

Legends of the Earth. Dorothy B. Vitriano. 1976. pap. 4.95 (ISBN 0-8065-0534-6). Citadel Pr.

Legends of the Glasgow & South Western Railway: In LMS Days. David L. Smith. LC 80-66093. (Illus.). 176p. 1980. 17.95 (ISBN 0-7153-7981-X). David & Charles.

Legends of the Iroquois. William W. Canfield. LC 78-151808. (Empire State Historical Publications Ser., No. 93). 1971. Repr. of 1902 ed. 12.00 o.p. (ISBN 0-8046-8093-0). Kennikat.

Legends of the Madonna, As Represented in the Fine Arts. Anna B. Jameson. LC 70-89273. (Tower Bks). (Illus.). lxxvi, 344p. 1972. Repr. of 1890 ed. 24.00 (ISBN 0-8103-3114-4). Gale.

Legends of the Spanish Southwest. Cleve Hallenbeck. LC 71-164316. 1971. Repr. of 1938 ed. 20.00 (ISBN 0-8103-3799-1). Gale.

Leger. Werner Schmalenbach. LC 75-5520. (Library of Great Painters). (Illus.). 1976. 35.00 (ISBN 0-8109-0252-4). Abrams.

Leger & the Avant-Garde. Christopher Green. LC 75-11499. 1976. 40.00x (ISBN 0-300-01800-2). Yale U Pr.

Leges Henrici Primi. Ed. by L. J. Downer. 464p. 1972. 48.00x (ISBN 0-19-825301-X). Oxford U Pr.

Leggende E Racconti Italiani E Quindici Canzoni Popolari Tradizionali: An Easy Reader for Beginners. Luigi Borelli & Mary Borelli. 1979. pap. 3.95 (ISBN 0-913298-03-4). S F Vanni.

Leggere Con Piacere. Aristede B. Masella. (gr. 7 up). 1976. pap. text ed. 4.83 (ISBN 0-87720-591-4). AMSCO Sch.

Leggi Medioassire. Claudio Saporetti. Ed. by Giorgio Buccellati. (Illus.). 181p. (Orig., Ital.). 1979. pap. 9.50 (ISBN 0-89003-036-7). Undena Pubns.

Legibility in Children's Books: A Review of Research. L. Watts & J. Nisbet. (General Ser.). 100p. 1974. pap. text ed. 12.00x (ISBN 0-85633-034-5, NFER). Humanities.

Legion: Civic Choruses. William Harmon. LC 72-11053. (Wesleyan Poetry Program: Vol. 65). 1973. 10.00 (ISBN 0-8195-2065-9, Pub. by Wesleyan U Pr); pap. 4.95 (ISBN 0-8195-1065-3). Columbia U Pr.

Legionnaires. new ed. Per O. Enquist. 468p. 1973. 10.00 o.p. (ISBN 0-440-04725-0, Sey Lawr). Delacorte.

Legislacion de Aguas en los Paises del Grupo Andino. David R. Daines & Gonazalo Falconi. 200p. (Span.). 1974. pap. 10.00 (ISBN 0-87421-067-4). Utah St U Pr.

Legislation of Direct Elections to the European Parliament. Valentine Herman & Mark Hagger. 1979. text ed. 36.00 (ISBN 0-566-00247-7, Pub. by Gower Pub Co England). Renouf.

Legislation of Morality: Laws, Drugs & Moral Judgement. Troy Duster. LC 72-80469. (Illus.). 1972. pap. text ed. 7.95 (ISBN 0-02-908680-9). Free Pr.

Legislation on Wildlife, Hunting & Protected Areas in Some European Countries. (Legislative Study Ser.: No. 20). 49p. 1980. pap. 6.00 (ISBN 92-5-100878-7, F2042, FAO). Unipub.

Legislative & Judicial History of the Fifteenth Amendment. John M. Mathews. LC 77-129081. (American Constitutional & Legal History Ser). 1971. Repr. of 1909 ed. lib. bdg. 17.50 (ISBN 0-306-70063-8). Da Capo.

Legislative Assemblies. Robert Luce. LC 73-5617. (American Constitutional & Legal History Ser.). 692p. 1974. Repr. of 1924 ed. lib. bdg. 59.50 (ISBN 0-306-70583-4). Da Capo.

Legislative Influences on Corporate Pension Plans. Dennis E. Logue. 1979. pap. 5.25 (ISBN 0-8447-3337-7). Am Enterprise.

Legislative Origins of American Foreign Policy, 5 vols. Ed. by Richard D. Challener. Incl. Vol. 1. Proceedings, April 7, 1913 to March 7, 1923. 415p. lib. bdg. 40.00 (ISBN 0-8240-3030-3); Vol. 2. Proceedings, December 3, 1923 to March 3, 1933. 279p. lib. bdg. 28.00 (ISBN 0-8240-3031-1); Vol. 3. Legislative Origins of the Truman Doctrine, March to April, 1947. 235p. 23.00 (ISBN 0-8240-3032-X); Vol. 4. Foreign Relief Aid, 1947. 401p. lib. bdg. 36.00 (ISBN 0-8240-3033-8); Vol. 5. Foreign Relief Assistance Act of 1948. 809p. lib. bdg. 65.00 (ISBN 0-8240-3034-6). (Senate Foreign Relations Committee's Historical Ser.). 1979. Garland Pub.

Legislative Politics in New York State: A Comparative Analysis. Alan G. Hevesi. LC 74-6864. (Special Studies). 265p. 1975. text ed. 24.95 (ISBN 0-275-05520-5). Praeger.

Legislative Principles. Robert Luce. LC 77-148083. (American Constitutional & Legal History Ser). 1971. Repr. of 1930 ed. lib. bdg. 59.50 (ISBN 0-306-70144-8). Da Capo.

Legislative Problems. Robert Luce. LC 76-152834. (American Constitutional & Legal History Ser). 1971. Repr. of 1935 ed. lib. bdg. 59.50 (ISBN 0-306-70153-7). Da Capo.

Legislative Procedure. Robert Luce. LC 72-6113. (American Constitutional & Legal History Ser). 640p. 1972. Repr. of 1922 ed. lib. bdg. 59.50 (ISBN 0-306-70522-2). Da Capo.

Legislative Process. abr. ed. John M. Kernochan. 64p. 1980. pap. text ed. write for info. (ISBN 0-88277-023-3). Foundation Pr.

Legislative Process: A Comparative Approach. David M. Olson. (Illus.). 1980. text ed. 17.50 scp (ISBN 0-06-044919-5, HarpC). Har-Row.

Legislative Process in Canada: The Need for Reform. W. A. Neilson & J. C. MacPherson. 328p. 1978. pap. text ed. 12.95x (ISBN 0-920380-11-5, Pub. by Inst Res Pub Canada). Renouf.

Legislative Processes: National & State. Joseph P. Chamberlain. LC 73-95087. Repr. of 1936 ed. lib. bdg. 19.75x (ISBN 0-8371-2580-4, CHLP). Greenwood.

Legislative Reform. Leroy N. Rieselbach. LC 77-223. (Policy Studies Organization Ser.). (Illus.). 1978. 18.95 (ISBN 0-669-01436-2). Lexington Bks.

Legislative Reform & Public Policy. Ed. by Susan Welch & John G. Peters. LC 77-5046. (Special Studies). 1977. text ed. 21.95 o.p. (ISBN 0-275-24540-3). Praeger.

Legislative Review of Government Programs: Tools for Accountability. Edgar G. Crane, Jr. LC 76-12846. (Special Studies). 1977. text ed. 29.95 (ISBN 0-275-23720-6). Praeger.

Legislators & Party Loyalty: The Impact of Reapportionment in California. Bruce W. Robeck. LC 77-18634. 1978. pap. text ed. 7.50 (ISBN 0-8191-0424-8). U Pr of Amer.

Legitimacy in the Modern State. John H. Schaar. 341p. 1981. 15.95 (ISBN 0-87855-337-1). Transaction Bks.

Legitimacy through Liberalism: Vladimir Jovanovic & the Transformation of Serbian Politics. Gale Stokes. LC 75-1423. (Publications on Russia & Eastern Europe of the School of International Studies: No. 5). (Illus.). 296p. 1975. 13.50 (ISBN 0-295-95384-5). U of Wash Pr.

Legitimation of Belief. E. Gellner. LC 74-14337. 240p. 1975. 29.95 (ISBN 0-521-20467-4). Cambridge U Pr.

Legitimation of Belief. E. Gellner. LC 74-14337. 1979. pap. 9.95 (ISBN 0-521-29587-4). Cambridge U Pr.

Legitimation of Regimes: International Frameworks for Analysis. Ed. by Bogdan Denitch. LC 78-63117. (Sage Studies in International Sociology: Vol. 17). (Illus.). 305p. 1979. 18.00x (ISBN 0-8039-9898-8); pap. 9.95x (ISBN 0-8039-9899-6). Sage.

Legs. William Kennedy. 1976. pap. 1.75 o.s.i. (ISBN 0-446-84140-4). Warner Bks.

Legs, Hips, & Behind. Charles Bukowski. 40p. 1978. pap. 2.00 (ISBN 0-935390-03-0). Wormwood Rev.

Leguminosae: A Source Book of Characteristics, Uses & Nodulation. O. N. Allen & Ethel K. Allen. LC 80-5104. (Illus.). 806p. 1981. 60.00 (ISBN 0-299-08400-0). U of Wis Pr.

Leguminosae: A Source Book of Uses & Nodulation. Ethel K. Allen & O. N. Allen. 1152p. 1980. write for info. o.p. (ISBN 0-299-08400-0). U of Wis Pr.

Lehigh & New England. Kramer & Krause. (Carstens Hobby Bks.: No. C41). 1980. pap. 9.95 (ISBN 0-911868-41-0). Carstens Pubns.

Lehigh Valley Railroad. 25.00. Chatham Pub CA.

Lehrbuch der Algebra, Vols. 1, 2, & 3. 3rd ed. Heinrich Weber. LC 61-6890. 1979. Repr. of 1962 ed. Set. text ed. 85.00 (ISBN 0-8284-0144-6). Chelsea Pub.

Lehrbuch Der Topologie. Herbert Seifert & W. Threlfall. (Ger). 13.95 (ISBN 0-8284-0031-8). Chelsea Pub.

Leibniz: An Introduction. C. D. Broad & C. Lewy. LC 74-31784. 192p. 1975. 26.95 (ISBN 0-521-20691-X); pap. 7.95x (ISBN 0-521-09925-0). Cambridge U Pr.

Leibniz & Ludolf on Things Linguistic: Excerpts from Their Correspondence, (1688-1703) John T. Waterman. (Publications in Linguistics: No. 88). 1978. pap. 9.50x (ISBN 0-520-09586-3). U of Cal Pr.

Leibniz & the Seventeenth Century Revolution. R. W. Meyer. Tr. by J. P. Stern. 1952. text ed. 6.75x (ISBN 0-391-02000-5). Humanities.

Leibniz-Clarke Correspondence. Leibniz. Ed. by H. G. Alexander. 200p. 1977. 15.00x (ISBN 0-7190-0669-4, Pub. by Manchester U Pr England). State Mutual Bk.

Leibniz Clarke Correspondence: Together with Extracts from Newton's "Principia" & "Opticks". Ed. by H. G. Alexander. (Philosophical Classics Ser.). 1976. pap. 15.00x (ISBN 0-06-490150-5). B&N.

Leibniz in Paris, 1672-1676. J. E. Hofmann. LC 73-80469. (Illus.). 230p. 1974. 65.00 (ISBN 0-521-20258-2). Cambridge U Pr.

Leica & Leicaflex Lenses. G. Rogliatti. 1978. 25.95 (ISBN 0-906447-00-3, Pub. by Fountain). Morgan.

Leica CL. Theo Kisselbach. (Illus.). 1978. 15.00 (ISBN 3-77632-550-X, 4550). Hove Camera.

Leica Illustrated Guide, No. 2. James L. Lager. LC 78-54092. 1978. pap. 19.95 (ISBN 0-87100-138-1). Morgan.

Leica Illustrated Guide III. James L. Lager. LC 79-90513. (Orig.). 1979. pap. 14.95 (ISBN 0-87100-161-6). Morgan.

Leica Literature. James L. Lager. 512p. 1980. pap. 22.95 (ISBN 0-87100-174-8). Morgan.

Leica: The First Fifty Years. G. Rogliatti. 25.95 (ISBN 0-85242-594-5, Pub. by Fountain). Morgan.

Leicestershire: A Shell Guide. W. G. Hoskins. 1970. 9.95 (ISBN 0-571-09467-8, Pub. by Faber & Faber). Merrimack Bk Serv.

Leicestershire Plan. Ed. by A. N. Fairbairn. (Organization in Schools Ser.). 1980. text ed. 30.95x (ISBN 0-435-80298-4). Heinemann Ed.

Leiden. 88p. 1976. pap. 5.00 (ISBN 0-89192-036-6). Interbk Inc.

Leiden Des Jungen Werthers. 2nd ed. Johann W. Goethe. Ed. by E. L. Stahl. 1972. pap. 9.95x (ISBN 0-631-01900-6, Pub. by Basil Blackwell). Biblio Dist.

Leif Ericson. Matthew G. Grant. LC 73-14531. 1974. PLB 5.95 (ISBN 0-87191-278-3). Creative Ed.

Leif Erikson the Lucky. Malcolm C. Jensen. (Visual Biographies). (Illus.). (gr. 4 up). 1979. PLB 6.90 s&l (ISBN 0-531-02297-8). Watts.

Leigh Hunt. James R. Thompson. (English Authors Ser.: No. 210). 1977. lib. bdg. 10.95 (ISBN 0-8057-6679-0). Twayne.

Leisure. Kenneth Roberts. (Aspects of Modern Sociology, the Social Structure of Modern Britain Ser). 1970. pap. text ed. 9.75x (ISBN 0-582-48807-9). Humanities.

Leisure: An Introduction. 2nd ed. Ed. by Hilmi M. Ibrahim & Fred Martin. LC 77-89694. 1978. pap. text ed. 8.95x (ISBN 0-89260-085-3). Hwong Pub.

Leisure & Popular Culture in Transition. 2nd ed. Thomas M. Kando. LC 79-26032. (Illus.). 1980. text ed. 15.95 (ISBN 0-8016-2618-8). Mosby.

Leisure & Recreation: A Study of Leisure & Recreation in Their Sociological Aspects. 3rd ed. Martin H. Neumeyer & E. S. Neumeyer. 1958. 9.95 o.p. (ISBN 0-8260-6695-X). Wiley.

Leisure & the Family Life Cycle. Rhona Rapoport & Robert N. Rapoport. 1975. 32.00x (ISBN 0-7100-8134-0). Routledge & Kegan.

Leisure & the Family Life Cycle. Rhona Rapoport & Robert N. Rapoport. 1978. pap. 12.50 (ISBN 0-7100-8825-6). Routledge & Kegan.

Leisure Education: Theory & Practice. Jean Mundy & Linda Odum. LC 78-12434. 1979. text ed. 18.50 (ISBN 0-471-01347-1). Wiley.

Leisure Services Preparation: A Competency Based Approach. Edith L. Ball & Robert E. Cipriano. (Illus.). 1978. ref. ed. 16.95 (ISBN 0-13-528273-X). P-H.

Leisure Services: The Organized Recreation & Parks System. rev. 5th ed. H. Douglas Sessoms et al. (Illus.). 416p. 1975. text ed. 15.95 (ISBN 0-13-530105-X). P-H.

Lek Behavior in the Golden-Headed Manakin, Pipra erythrocephala in Trinidad (West Indies) A. Lill. (Advances in Ethology Ser.: Vol. 18). (Illus.). 84p. (Orig.). 1976. pap. text ed. 34.00 (ISBN 3-489-72536-0). Parey Sci Pubs.

Lekachmacher Family. Carol Richman. LC 76-23409. (Illus.). 1976. 7.95 (ISBN 0-914842-14-5). Madrona Pubs.

Lektsii Po Struktural'noi Poetike: Vvedenie, Teoriia Stikha. Iu. M. Lotman. LC 68-10643. (Slavic Reprint Ser.: No. 5). 191p. (Rus). 1968. pap. 4.00 (ISBN 0-87057-106-0, Pub. by Brown U Pr). Univ Pr of New England.

Lektuere Fuer Minuten. Reinhold Schneider. Ed. by Pirmin Meyer. 200p. 1980. pap. 6.50 quality paper (ISBN 3-458-04918-5, Pub. by Insel Verlag Germany). Suhrkamp.

Lelia: The Life of George Sand. Andre Maurois. Tr. by Gerard Hopkins. 1977. pap. 4.95 (ISBN 0-14-004354-3). Penguin.

Lemon-Aid. Phil Edmonston. 1977. 9.95 o.p. (ISBN 0-679-50764-7); pap. 4.95 o.p. (ISBN 0-679-50730-2). McKay.

Lemon Aid: Everything You Need to Know About American & Foreign Cars, Trucks, & Vans: Rating, Buying, Maintaining, Repairing, & Selling, & How to Turn a Bad Trip into a Good Buy. Phil Edmonston. LC 80-25807. (Illus.). 600p. 1981. pap. 8.95 (ISBN 0-8253-0014-2). Beaufort Bks NY.

Lemon Book. Ralph Nader et al. (Illus.). 300p. (Orig.). 1980. pap. 7.95 (ISBN 0-89803-039-0). Caroline Hse.

Lemon Meringue Dog. Walt Morey. LC 80-171. 176p. (gr. 4-7). 1980. 9.95 (ISBN 0-525-33455-6). Dutton.

Lemon Sole. B. Bennet Rae. (Illus.). 108p. 7.00 (ISBN 0-85238-013-5). Unipub.

Lemon Tree of Modern Sex. P. Lal. (Writers Workshop Greybird Ser.). 106p. 1975. 12.00 (ISBN 0-88253-572-2); pap. text ed. 6.75 (ISBN 0-88253-571-4). Ind-US Inc.

Lemonade Lady. Joan T. Weiss. LC 80-50703. (Illus.). 123p. (Orig.). (gr. 1-3). 1980. pap. 4.95 (ISBN 0-936822-00-7). Peppertree.

Lempriere's Classical Dictionary. new rev. ed. Ed. by F. A. Wright. 1969. Repr. of 1788 ed. 21.00 (ISBN 0-7100-1734-0). Routledge & Kegan.

Lenci Dolls. Dorothy Coleman. (Illus.). 1977. 13.95 (ISBN 0-686-68039-1); pap. 9.95 (ISBN 0-87588-119-X). Hobby Hse.

Lend-Lease, Loans, & the Coming of the Cold War: A Study of the Implementation of Foreign Policy. Leon C. Martel. (Special Studies in International Relations). 1979. lib. bdg. 28.50x (ISBN 0-89158-453-6). Westview.

Lend Me an Eye. Albert Vajda. 1974. 11.95 (ISBN 0-236-31058-5, Pub. by Paul Elek). Merrimack Bk Serv.

Lending Transactions & the Bankruptcy Reform Act of Nineteen Seventy-Eight. LC 79-83589. (Corporate Law & Practice Course Handbook Ser.: 1979-1980). 1980. pap. text ed. 25.00 (ISBN 0-686-59552-1, B4-6528). PLI.

Lengthening Shadow of Slavery: A Historical Justification for Affirmative Action for Blacks in Higher Education. John Fleming. LC 76-21656. 158p. 1976. pap. 5.95 (ISBN 0-88258-074-4). Howard U Pr.

Lengua Espanola: Gramatica y Cultura. 2nd ed. Matilde Castells & Harold E. Lionetti. LC 73-1315. (Illus.). 1978. 16.95x (ISBN 0-684-15333-5, ScribC); Teachers manual free (ISBN 0-684-15997-X); cuaderno de ejercicios workbook 6.95x (ISBN 0-684-15620-2); reel-reel tape 120.00 (ISBN 0-684-16053-6). Scribner.

Leni Riefenstahl: The Fallen Film Goddess. Glenn B. Infield. LC 76-7084. (Illus.). 1976. 9.95 o.s.i. (ISBN 0-690-01167-9, TYC-T). T Y Crowell.

Lenin. Michael Morgan. LC 74-158177. 226p. 1971. 9.50x o.p. (ISBN 0-8214-0094-0). Ohio U Pr.

Lenin. Michael Morgan. LC 74-158177. 1973. pap. 2.95 o.s.i. (ISBN 0-02-922040-8). Free Pr.

Lenin. Michael Morgan. 1972. 12.95 (ISBN 0-8214-0094-0). Lib Soc Sci.

Lenin & Leninism: State, Law & Society. Bernard W. Eissenstat. LC 71-145909. 1971. 29.50x (ISBN 0-89197-983-2). Irvington.

Lenin & the Cultural Revolution. Carmen Claudin-Urondo. Tr. by Brian Pearce from Fr. (Marxist Theory & Contemporary Capitalism Ser.). 1977. text ed. 13.00x (ISBN 0-391-00739-4). Humanities.

Lenin & the Russian Revolution. Christopher Hill. 1978. pap. 2.95 (ISBN 0-14-021297-3). Penguin.

Lenin & Trotsky. C. B. S. News Staff. Ed. by William E. Shapiro. LC 67-25100. (Illus.). (gr. 7 up). 1967. PLB 3.90 o.p. (ISBN 0-531-01134-8). Watts.

Lenin Chronology. Gerda Weber & Herman Weber. 226p. 1981. lib. bdg. 22.50 (ISBN 0-87196-515-1). Facts on File.

Lenin: Collected Works, 45 vols. Progress Publishers, Moscow. 1975. 299.00x set (ISBN 0-8464-0557-1). Beekman Pubs.

Lenin on Marx & Engels. 1975. pap. 1.50 (ISBN 0-8351-0183-5). China Bks.

Lenin on Politics & Revolution: Selected Writings. James E. Connor. LC 68-21041. 1968. pap. 7.50 (ISBN 0-672-63553-4). Pegasus.

Lenin on War & Peace. Vladimir I. Lenin. 1966. pap. 1.25 (ISBN 0-8351-0130-4). China Bks.

Leningrad Dutch. T. D. Harding. 1976. 18.95 (ISBN 0-7134-3129-6). David & Charles.

Leninism: A Sociological Interpretation. David Lane. (Themes in the Social Sciences Ser.). (Illus.). 176p. Date not set. price not set (ISBN 0-521-23855-2); pap. price not set (ISBN 0-521-28259-4). Cambridge U Pr.

Lenin's Government. T. H. Rigby. LC 78-18754. (Soviet & East European Studies). 1979. 44.50 (ISBN 0-521-22281-8). Cambridge U Pr.

Lenin's Legacy: The Story of the CPSU. Robert G. Wesson. Ed. by Richard F. Staar. LC 77-92341. (Publications Ser. No. 192: Histories of Ruling Communist Parties). 1978. pap. 7.50 (ISBN 0-8179-6922-5). Hoover Inst Pr.

Lennon Remembers. Jann Wenner. pap. 1.25 o.p. (ISBN 0-445-08191-0). Popular Lib.

Lennon-Yellow Elephant Called Trunk. Barbara Softly. LC 71-115818. (Illus.). 48p. (gr. k-2). PLB 5.29 (ISBN 0-8178-4772-3). Harvey.

Lenny. Valerie K. Smith. pap. 1.75 o.s.i. (ISBN 0-440-15672-6). Dell.

Lenny & Lola. Marc Brown. (ps-3). 1978. 6.95 o.p. (ISBN 0-525-33465-3). Dutton.

Lenora. Ann Gimbel. LC 77-71894. (Destiny Ser.). 1977. pap. 4.95 (ISBN 0-8163-0303-7, 12121-0). Pacific Pr Pub Assn.

LeNotre's Book of Desserts & Pastries. Gaston LeNotre. Tr. by Philip Hyman & Mary Hyman. LC 77-13231. 1977. 17.95 (ISBN 0-8120-5137-8). Barron.

Lens & All Its Jobs. Sidney F. Ray. (Media Manuals Ser.). Date not set. pap. 8.95 (ISBN 0-8038-4299-6). Hastings.

Lens Mechanism Technology. D. F. Horne. LC 75-21733. (Illus.). 150p. 1975. 79.50x (ISBN 0-8448-0770-2). Crane-Russak Co.

Lent. William Hordern & John Otwell. LC 74-24901. (Proclamation 1: Aids for Interpreting the Lessons of the Church Year Ser. B). 64p. 1974. pap. 1.95 (ISBN 0-8006-4073-X, 1-4073). Fortress.

Lent. Jack D. Kingsbury & Chester Pennington. Ed. by Elizabeth Achtemeier et al. LC 79-7377. (Proclamation 2: Aids for Interpreting the Lessons of the Church Year, Ser. A). 64p. (Orig.). 1980. pap. 2.50 (ISBN 0-8006-4093-4, 1-4093). Fortress.

Lent. Marianne H. Micks & Thomas E. Ridenhour. Ed. by Elizabeth Achtemeier et al. LC 79-7377. (Proclamation 2: Aids for Interpreting the Lessons of the Church Year Ser. C). 64p. 1979. pap. 2.50 (ISBN 0-8006-4082-9, 1-4082). Fortress.

Lent. Charles W. Smith & Helmut Koester. LC 74-76925. (Proclamation 1: Aids for Interpreting the Lessons of the Church Year, Ser. A). 64p. 1974. pap. 1.95 (ISBN 0-8006-4063-2, 1-4063). Fortress.

Lent. Herman G. Stuempfle, Jr. & Peter J. Kearney. LC 73-79350. (Proclmation 1: Aids for Interpreting the Lessons of the Church Year Ser. C). 64p. 1973. pap. 1.95 (ISBN 0-8006-4053-5, 1-4053). Fortress.

Lent...Easter...Pentecost. Marie Y. Lieser & Marjorie K. Hargreaves. (gr. k-4). 1978. with duplicating masters 9.95 (ISBN 0-686-13701-9). Pflaum Pr.

Lenten Psalms. John Adams. (Short Course Ser.). 124p. Repr. of 1912 ed. text ed. 2.95 (ISBN 0-567-08304-7). Attic Pr.

Lenticle: Two Radio Interviews with Fritz Faiss. Ed. by Fritz W. Faiss. (Illus.). 63p. 1972. deluxe ed. 50.00x ltd ed. signed (ISBN 0-916678-07-5); pap. 8.00x ltd ed., signed (ISBN 0-916678-08-3); pap. 5.00 single interview, ltd. ed., signed (ISBN 0-916678-09-1). Green Hut.

Lentil Soup. Joe Lasker. LC 77-7145. (Illus.). (gr. k-3). 1977. 6.50g o.p. (ISBN 0-8075-4438-8). A Whitman.

Leo. Julia Parker. (Pocket Guide to Astrology Ser.). (Orig.). 1980. pap. write for info. (ISBN 0-671-25553-3, Fireside). S&S.

Leo. Paula Taylor. (Sun Signs Ser.). (Illus.). (gr. 4-12). 1978. PLB 5.95 (ISBN 0-87191-645-2); pap. 2.95 (ISBN 0-89812-075-6). Creative Ed.

Leo & Emily. Franz Brandenberg. LC 80-19657. (Read-Alone Bk.). (Illus.). 56p. (gr. 1-3). 1981. 5.95 (ISBN 0-688-80292-3); PLB 5.71 (ISBN 0-688-84292-5). Greenwillow.

Leo & Theodore. Donald Newlove. LC 74-154265. 1973. 7.95 o.p. (ISBN 0-8415-0175-0). Dutton.

Leo Baeck: Teacher of Theresienstadt. Albert H. Friedlander. LC 68-11829. 1968. 8.95 o.p. (ISBN 0-03-068555-9). HR&W.

Leo Conversion. David N. Smith. LC 80-13316. (Illus.). 288p. 1980. 9.95 (ISBN 0-396-07854-0). Dodd.

Leo Frank Case. L. Dinnerstein. LC 68-99750. 16.00x (ISBN 0-231-03067-3). Columbia U Pr.

Leo Man. Rebecca Stratton. (Harlequin Romances Ser.). 1981. 192p. 1981. pap. 1.25 (ISBN 0-373-02405-3, Pub. by Harlequin). PB.

Leo Rosten's Treasury of Jewish Quotations. Leo Rosten. 672p. 1980. pap. 3.95 (ISBN 0-553-14331-X). Bantam.

Leo Szilard: His Version of the Facts. Selected Works & Correspondence. Ed. by Spencer Weart & Gertrude W. Szilard. (Illus.). 1978. 20.00x (ISBN 0-262-19168-7); pap. 7.95 (ISBN 0-262-69070-5). MIT Pr.

Leo the Late Bloomer. abr. ed. Robert Kraus. LC 80-51357. (Windmill Board Bks.). (Illus.). 16p. (ps). 1980. board book 3.50 (ISBN 0-671-41202-7, Pub. by Windmill). S&S.

Leo the Late Bloomer Takes a Bath. Robert Kraus. (Tubby Bks.). (Illus.). 10p. (ps). 1981. vinyl 2.95 (ISBN 0-671-42554-4). Windmill Bks.

Leo the Lop. Steve Cosgrove. (Serendipity Bks). (Illus.). (gr. k-4). 1978. PLB 6.95 (ISBN 0-87191-658-4). Creative Ed.

Leo the Lop. Tail Two. Steve Cosgrove. (Serendipity Bks). (Illus.). (gr. k-4). 1980. PLB 6.95 (ISBN 0-87191-779-3). Creative Ed.

Leo Tolstoy: An Annotated Bibliography of English-Language Sources to 1978. David R. Egan & Melinda A. Egan. LC 79-16536. (Scarecrow Author Bibliographies Ser.: No. 44). 303p. 1979. 16.50 (ISBN 0-8108-1232-0). Scarecrow.

Leon-Gontran, Damas, 1912-1978. Founder of Negritude: A Memorial Casebook. Daniel L. Racine. LC 79-64101. 1979. pap. text ed. 11.25 (ISBN 0-8191-0727-1). U Pr of Amer.

Leon, la Brula y el Guardarropa. C. S. Lewis. Tr. by Julio Orozco from Eng. LC 76-55492. (Cronicas de Narnia). 171p. (Orig., Span.). (gr. 4 up). 1977. pap. 2.95 (ISBN 0-89922-081-9). Edit Caribe.

Leon Trotsky. Robert D. Warth. (World Leaders Ser.: No. 72). 1977. lib. bdg. 12.50 (ISBN 0-8057-7720-2). Twayne.

Leonard Bacon: A Statesman in the Church. Theo. D. Bacon. 1931. 47.50x (ISBN 0-685-69788-6). Elliots Bks.

Leonard Cohen. Stephen Scobie. 294p. (Orig.). 1978. pap. 4.95 (ISBN 0-295-95686-0, Pub. by Douglas & McIntyre Canada). U of Wash Pr.

Leonard Everett Fisher's Liberty Book. Leonard Everett Fisher. LC 75-9672. 48p. (gr. 4 up). 1976. 5.95 o.p. (ISBN 0-385-04894-7). Doubleday.

Leonardo. Pedretti. 1980. pap. cancelled (ISBN 0-8120-2303-X). Barron.

Leonardo. Jack Wasserman. LC 80-645. (Illus.). 160p. 1980. 14.95 (ISBN 0-385-17167-6). Doubleday.

Leonardo Da Vinci. Peter Amey et al. Ed. by Malcolm Yapp et al. (World History Ser.). (Illus.). (gr. 10). 1980. lib. bdg. 5.95 (ISBN 0-89908-041-3); pap. text ed. 1.95 (ISBN 0-89908-016-2). Greenhaven.

Leonardo Da Vinci. Clifford Bax. 160p. 1980. Repr. of 1932 ed. lib. bdg. 27.50 (ISBN 0-8495-0464-3). Arden Lib.

Leonardo Da Vinci. (MacDonald Educational Ser.). (Illus., Arabic.). 3.50 (ISBN 0-686-53091-8). Intl Bk Ctr.

Leonardo Da Vinci. Bruno Santi. (Scala Art Book). (Illus.). 1978. pap. 7.95 o.p. (ISBN 0-8467-0454-4, Pub. by Two Continents). Hippocrene Bks.

Leonardo Da Vinci. John Thomas. LC 57-6244. (Illus.). (gr. 6-10). 1957. 9.95 (ISBN 0-87599-112-2). S G Phillips.

Leonardo Da Vinci. Jack Wasserman. LC 74-13112. (Library of Great Painters). (Illus.). 160p. 1975. 35.00 (ISBN 0-8109-0262-1). Abrams.

Leonardo Da Vinci. V. P. Zubov. Tr. by David Kraus. LC 67-27096. (Illus.). 1968. 16.50x (ISBN 0-674-52450-0). Harvard U Pr.

Leonardo da Vinci: Drawings of Textile Machines. Kenneth G. Ponting & M. Litt. (Illus.). 1979. text ed. 26.00x (ISBN 0-239-00193-1). Humanities.

Leonardo Da Vinci Nature Studies from the Royal Library at Windsor Castle. Carlo Pedretti. (Illus.). 95p. (Orig.). 1980. pap. 10.00 (ISBN 0-384-32298-0). J P Getty Mus.

Leonardo on the Eye: An English Translation & Critical Commentary of MS.D in the Bibliotheque Nationale, Paris, with Studies on Leonardo's Methodology & Theories on Optics. Donald S. Strong. LC 78-74382. (Fine Arts Dissertations, Fourth Ser.). (Illus.). 1980. lib. bdg. 44.00 (ISBN 0-8240-3968-8). Garland Pub.

Leonardo-Studien. Hans Ost. (Beitraege Zur Kunstgeschichte: Vol. 11). (Illus.). xii, 750p. (Ger.). 1975. 78.50x (ISBN 3-11-005727-1). De Gruyter.

Leonardo the Scientist. Carlo Zammattio et al. LC 80-18436. (Illus.). 192p. 1980. 9.95 (ISBN 0-07-007933-1). McGraw.

Leonardo Touch. Jeannette Eyerly. LC 76-18968. (gr. 5-12). 1976. 9.95 (ISBN 0-397-31684-4). Lippincott.

Leonardo Was Right. Roland Topor. Tr. by Barbara Wright. 1980. pap. 3.95 (ISBN 0-7145-3671-7). Riverrun NY.

Leonardo's Legacy: An International Symposium. Ed. by C. D. O'Malley. LC 68-14976. (UCLA Center for Medieval & Renaissance Studies). (Illus.). 1968. 36.75x (ISBN 0-520-00956-8). U of Cal Pr.

Leonce & Lena. Georg Buchner. Tr. & intro. by Michael Hamburger. Bd. with Lenz; Woyzeck. LC 78-184507. (German Literary Classics in Translation Ser). 120p. 1972. text ed. 9.00 (ISBN 0-226-07841-8). U of Chicago Pr.

Leonce & Lena. Georg Buchner. Tr. by Michael Hamburger from Ger. Incl. Lenz; Woyzeck. LC 78-184507. (German Literary Classics in Translation Ser). xiii, 99p. 1973. pap. 2.95 (ISBN 0-226-07842-6, P467, Phoen). U of Chicago Pr.

Leonid Andreyev. Josephine M. Newcombe. LC 72-79938. (Modern Literature Ser.). 1973. 10.95 (ISBN 0-8044-2657-0). Ungar.

Leopard's Prey. Leonard Wibberley. LC 78-149225. 192p. (gr. 7 up). 1971. 4.50 o.p. (ISBN 0-374-34378-0). FS&G.

Leopard's Tooth. William Kotzwinkle. LC 75-25504. (Illus.). 96p. (gr. 3-6). 1976. 6.95 (ISBN 0-395-28862-2, Clarion). HM.

Leopard's Tooth. William Kotzwinkle. 1978. pap. 1.25 (ISBN 0-686-68379-X, 37382, Camelot). Avon.

Leopold the First of Austria. John P. Spielman. 1977. 17.50 (ISBN 0-8135-0836-3). Rutgers U Pr.

Leopold Von Ranke: The Secret of World History; Selected Writings on the Art & Science of History. Ed. by Roger Wines. LC 80-65600. 160p. 1981. 17.50 (ISBN 0-8232-1050-2); pap. 7.50 (ISBN 0-8232-1051-0). Fordham.

Lepidoptera Genetics. Roy Robinson. 1971. 64.00 (ISBN 0-08-006659-3). Pergamon.

Leprechaun Tales. Kathleen Green. LC 68-10771. (Illus.). (gr. 4-7). 1968. 4.50 o.p. (ISBN 0-397-31025-0). Lippincott.

Leprechauns Never Lie. Lorna Balian. LC 79-25950. (Illus.). 32p. (gr. k-3). 1980. PLB 7.95g (ISBN 0-687-21371-1). Abingdon.

Leprechaun's Story. Richard Kennedy. LC 79-11410. (Illus.). (ps-3). 1979. PLB 8.95 (ISBN 0-525-33472-6, Unicorn Bk.). Dutton.

Leprosy: Diagnosis & Management. 2nd ed. Harry L. Arnold, Jr. & Paul Fasal. (American Lecture Dermatology Ser.). (Illus.). 108p. 1973. 18.75 (ISBN 0-398-02681-5). C C Thomas.

Lermontov. Janko Lavrin. 1959. pap. text ed. 3.25x (ISBN 0-391-02003-X). Humanities.

Lermontov: An Essay in Literary Historical Evaluation. Boris Eikhenbaum. Tr. by Ray Parrott & Harry Weber. 1981. 16.50. Ardis Pubs.

Leroy & the Old Man. W. E. Butterworth. LC 79-6553. 160p. (gr. 7 up). 1980. 7.95 (ISBN 0-590-07638-8, Four Winds). Schol Bk Serv.

Leroy Anderson: Twenty-Five Melodies for Piano Solo. Leroy Anderson. Orig. Title: Leroy Anderson (Almost Complete) (Illus.). 1980. pap. 6.95. Dover.

LeRoy Neiman Posters. Leroy Neiman. (Illus.). 64p. 1980. pap. 12.95 (ISBN 0-686-62713-X, 84911-3); signed, lim. ed. o.p. 150.00 (ISBN 0-686-62714-8, 2237-1). Abrams.

Leroy the Lobster & Crabby Crab. Harriman. 1967. pap. 3.00 (ISBN 0-89272-000-X). Down East.

Les. Arkady Strugatskii & Boris Strugatskii. (Rus.). 1981. 10.00 (ISBN 0-88233-656-8); pap. 4.50 (ISBN 0-88233-657-6). Ardis Pubs.

Lesbian: A Celebration of Difference. Bernice Goodman. 1977. pap. 3.50 (ISBN 0-918314-04-6). Out & Out.

Lesbian Body. Monique Wittig. LC 75-7738. 1975. 5.95 o.p. (ISBN 0-688-02900-0). Morrow.

Lesbian Community. Deborah G. Wolf. LC 77-93478. 1979. 10.95 (ISBN 0-520-03657-3); pap. 4.95 (ISBN 0-520-04248-4, CAL 484). U of Cal Pr.

Lesbian Couple. Donna M. Tanner. LC 77-16720. 1978. 15.95x (ISBN 0-669-02078-8). Lexington Bks.

Lesbian Crossroads: Personal Stories of Lesbian Struggles & Triumphs. Ruth Baetz. LC 80-12440. 288p. 1980. 10.95 (ISBN 0-688-03712-7). Morrow.

Lesbian Estate: Poems, 1970-1974. Lynn Lonidier. 1977. pap. 4.00 o.p. (ISBN 0-686-19040-8). Man-Root.

Lesbian-Feminism in Turn-of-the-Century Germany. Ed. by Lillian Faderman & Brigitte Eriksson. LC 79-92799. 125p. (Orig.). 1980. pap. 5.95 (ISBN 0-930044-13-4). Naiad Pr.

Lesbian Poetry: An Anthology. Ed. by Elly Bulkin & Joan Larkin. (Orig.). 1981. pap. price not set (ISBN 0-930436-08-3). Persephone.

Lesbian Reader. Ed. by Gina Covina & Laurel Galana. 1975. pap. 5.95 (ISBN 0-686-22379-9). Amazon Pr.

Lesbianism: A Study of Female Homosexuality. David H. Rosen. (Illus.). 140p. 1974. 11.75 (ISBN 0-398-02924-5); pap. 7.50 (ISBN 0-398-03116-9). C C Thomas.

Lesbians Speak Out. Ed. by Judy Grahn. (Illus.). 1974. pap. 5.00 (ISBN 0-88447-028-8). Diana Pr.

Lesions of the Brachial Plexus. Robert Leffert. (Illus.). Date not set. text ed. price not set (ISBN 0-443-08026-7). Churchill. Postponed.

Lesions of the Nervous System in Cancer Patients. Ed. by J. Hildebrand. LC 78-3000. (European Organization for Research on Treatment of Cancer Monograph: Vol. 5). 1978. 20.00 (ISBN 0-89004-269-1). Raven.

Leslie. Zoa Sherburne. 192p. (gr. 7 up). 1972. 6.25 o.p. (ISBN 0-688-21814-8); PLB 6.96 (ISBN 0-688-31814-2). Morrow.

Leslie Charteris Count on the Saint: The Pastor's Problem & the Unsaintly Santa. Leslie Charteris. LC 80-939. (Crime Club Ser.). 192p. 1980. 8.95 (ISBN 0-385-17191-9). Doubleday.

Leslie Charteris' Send for the Saint: The Midas Double & the Pawn Gambit. Leslie Charteris. LC 77-92210. 1978. 7.95 o.p. (ISBN 0-385-14138-6). Doubleday.

Leslie Charteris' The Saint in Trouble: The Imprudent Professor & the Red Sabbath. Leslie Charteris. LC 78-18551. 1978. 7.95 o.p. (ISBN 0-385-14612-4). Doubleday.

Leslie Stephen. David D. Zink. (English Authors Ser.: No. 142). lib. bdg. 10.95 (ISBN 0-8057-1512-6). Twayne.

Lesotho. Coleen Schwager & Dirk Schwager. 1975. text ed. 20.00x o.p. (ISBN 0-620-01444-X). Verry.

Lesotho. Shelagh M. Willet & David Ambrose. (World Bibliographical Ser.: No. 3). 600p. 1980. write for info. (ISBN 0-903450-11-9). Abc-Clio.

Less Than a Score, but a Point: Poems. T. J. Reddy. LC 74-7173. 1974. pap. 2.95 o.p. (ISBN 0-394-71080-0, V-80, Vin). Random.

Less Than Nothing Is Really Something. Robert Froman. LC 72-7546. (Young Math Ser). (Illus.). (gr. 1-5). 1973. 7.95 (ISBN 0-690-48862-9, TYC-J). T Y Crowell.

Less Time, More Options: Education Beyond the High School. Carnegie Commission On Higher Education. 1971. 2.95 o.p. (ISBN 0-07-010026-8, P&RB). McGraw.

Lesser Festivals, Vols. 1 & 2. Philip Pfatteicher. LC 74-24917. (Proclamation 1: Aids for Interpretig the Lessons of the Church Year Ser.). 64p. 1975. pap. 1.95 ea. (1-1309); Vol. 1. pap. (ISBN 0-8006-1309-0, 1-1310); Vol. 2. pap. (ISBN 0-8006-1310-4). Fortress.

Lesser Festivals 1: Saints' Days & Special Occasions. Richard L. Thulin. Ed. by Elizabeth Achtemeier et al. LC 79-7377. (Proclamation 2: Aids for Interpreting the Lessons of the Church Year). 64p. (Orig.). 1980. pap. 2.50 (ISBN 0-8006-1393-7, 1-1393). Fortress.

Lesser Festivals 2: Saints' Days & Special Occasions. John B. Trotti. Ed. by Elizabeth Achtemeier et al. (Proclamation 2: Aids for Interpreting Thee Lessons of the Church Year). 64p. (Orig.). 1980. pap. 2.50 (ISBN 0-8006-1394-5, 1-1394). Fortress.

Lesser Festivals 3: Saints' Days & Special Occasions. Richard Reid & Milton Crum, Jr. Ed. by Elizabeth Achtemeier et al. LC 79-7377. (Proclamation 2: Aids for Interpreting the Lessons of the Church Year). 64p. (Orig.). 1981. pap. 2.50 (ISBN 0-8006-1395-3, 1-1395). Fortress.

Lesser Festivals 4: Saints' Days & Special Occasions. Lorenz Nieting. Ed. by Elizabeth Achtemeier et al. LC 79-7377. (Proclamation Two Ser.: Aids for Interpreting the Lessons of the Church Year). 64p. (Orig.). 1981. pap. 2.50 (ISBN 0-8006-1396-1, 1-1396). Fortress.

Lesser Love. Cecile Gilmore. (YA) 1971. 5.95 (ISBN 0-685-23396-0, Avalon). Bouregy.

Lesser Parables of Our Lord. William Arnot. LC 80-8066. 464p. 1981. Repr. of 1884 ed. 10.95 (ISBN 0-8254-2121-7). Kregel.

Lessico Universale Italiano Di Lingua, Lettere, Arti, Scienze Techniche, 25 vols. (Ital.). 1968. 1975.00 (ISBN 0-8277-3059-4). Maxwell Sci Intl.

Lesson in Love. Marie T. Baird. 1975. pap. 1.25 o.p. (ISBN 0-445-00246-8). Popular Lib.

Lesson of the Scaffold: The Public Execution Controversy in Victorian England. David D. Cooper. LC 73-92901. (Illus.). xi, 212p. 1974. 12.95x (ISBN 0-8214-0148-3). Ohio U Pr.

Lesson Planning for Meaningful Variety in Teaching. Richard M. Henak. 110p. 1980. 6.25 (ISBN 0-8106-1515-0). NEA.

Lesson Plans for Using the Outdoors in Teaching. Mary D. Houts. LC 75-22544. 1976. pap. text ed. 2.95x o.p. (ISBN 0-685-73368-8, 1760). Interstate.

Lessons from America: An Exploration. Richard Rose. LC 74-925. 308p. 1974. 19.95 (ISBN 0-470-73350-0). Halsted Pr.

Lessons from Dam Incidents. Compiled by American Society of Civil Engineers. 392p. 1975. pap. text ed. 18.00 (ISBN 0-87262-104-9). Am Soc Civil Eng.

Lessons from Great Lives. Sterling W. Sill. LC 80-84567. 300p. 1981. 7.95 (ISBN 0-88290-172-9, 2049). Horizon Utah.

Lessons from Our Living Past. Jules Harlow. LC 72-2055. (Illus.). 128p. (gr. 4-6). 1972. text ed. 6.95x (ISBN 0-87441-085-1). Behrman.

Lessons from the Parables. Neil R. Lightfoot. (Minister's Paperback Library). 184p. 1976. pap. 3.95 (ISBN 0-8010-5564-4). Baker Bk.

Lessons in Chess Strategy. W. H. Cozens. 1970. 2.95 o.p. (ISBN 0-87749-052-X). Sterling.

Lessons in Holiness. T. K. Doty. pap. 2.00 o.p. (ISBN 0-686-12889-3). Schmul Pub Co.

Lessons Learned: South Vietnam Conflict. Stanley A. Janet. 1981. 6.95 (ISBN 0-533-03712-3). Vantage.

Lessons of the Past: The Use & Misuse of History in American Foreign Policy. Ernest R. May. 224p. 1973. 12.95 (ISBN 0-19-501698-X). Oxford U Pr.

Lessons of the Road. Michael Schiffer. 1980. 10.95 (ISBN 0-686-68922-4, Kenan Pr). S&S.

Lessons of the Vietnam War: Philosophical Considerations on the Vietnam Revolution. Shingo Shibata. (Philosophical Currents Ser: No. 6). 229p. 1973. pap. text ed. 24.00x (ISBN 90-6032-016-6). Humanities.

Lessons of Vietnam. Ed. by W. Scott Thompson & D. D. Frizzell. LC 76-20821. 1977. 19.50x (ISBN 0-8448-0973-X). Crane-Russak Co.

Lessons on New Testament Evidences. Wallace Wartick. 250p. 1980. pap. 4.95 (ISBN 0-89900-141-6). College Pr Pub.

Lessons on Rings, Modules & Multiplicities. Douglas G. Northcott. LC 68-21397. 1968. 48.00 (ISBN 0-521-07151-8). Cambridge U Pr.

Lest We Forget. Margaret Eck. 72p. pap. 0.75; pap. 2.00 3 copies. Faith Pub Hse.

Lester Frank Ward. Clifford H. Scott. LC 76-16539. (U.S. Authors Ser.: No. 275). 1976. lib. bdg. 12.50 (ISBN 0-8057-7175-1). Twayne.

Lester's Turn. Jan Slepian. LC 80-29467. 144p. (gr. 6 up). 1981. PLB 8.95 (ISBN 0-02-782940-5). Macmillan.

Let Freedom Ring. Arthur Garfield Hays. LC 71-166329. (Civil Liberties in American History Ser). (Illus.). 1972. Repr. of 1937 ed. lib. bdg. 47.50 (ISBN 0-306-70227-4). Da Capo.

Let Go! Fenelon. 1973. pap. 2.25 (ISBN 0-88368-010-6). Whitaker Hse.

Let Go & Let God. A. E. Cliffe. 1951. pap. 2.95 o.p. (ISBN 0-13-531509-3). P-H.

Let It Come Down. Paul Bowles. 300p. 1980. 14.00 (ISBN 0-87685-480-3); signed ed. o.p. 20.00 (ISBN 0-87685-481-1); pap. 7.50 (ISBN 0-87685-479-X). Black Sparrow.

Let Justice Roll Down. John M. Perkins. LC 74-30172. 1976. pap. 4.95 (ISBN 0-8307-0345-4, 54-040-02). Regal.

Let Loose on Mother Goose. Terry Graham. (Illus.). 96p. (ps-k). 1981. pap. text ed. 6.95 (ISBN 0-86530-030-5, IP 305). Incentive Pubns.

Let Love Come Last. Taylor Caldwell. 1977. pap. 2.75 (ISBN 0-515-05440-2). Jove Pubns.

Let Me Count the Ways. Peter De Vries. 1977. pap. 1.50 o.p. (ISBN 0-445-08531-2). Popular Lib.

Let Me Hear the Music. Carol Barford. LC 78-23966. (gr. 6 up). 1979. 7.95 (ISBN 0-395-28959-9, Clarion). HM.

Let Me Introduce You to the Bible. William MacDonald. 1981. pap. 1.95 (ISBN 0-937396-22-2). Walterick Pubs.

Let Me Take You on a Trail. John Hawkinson. LC 71-188428. (Activity Bks.). (Illus.). 48p. (gr. 5 up). 1972. 6.50g (ISBN 0-8075-4452-3). A Whitman.

Let My Children Work. John P. Blessington. LC 72-79377. 200p. 1975. pap. 2.95 (ISBN 0-385-00875-9, Anch). Doubleday.

Let My People Know: American Indian Journalism, 1828-1978. James E. Murphy & Sharon M. Murphy. LC 80-5941. 300p. 1981. 14.95 (ISBN 0-8061-1623-4). U of Okla Pr.

Let None Deal Treacherously. Paige Cothren. 224p. (Orig.). 1981. pap. 4.95 (ISBN 0-937778-03-6). Fulness Hse.

Let Not Your Hart. James Seay. LC 71-105509. (Wesleyan Poetry Program: Vol. 50). 1970. 10.00x (ISBN 0-8195-2050-0, Pub. by Wesleyan U Pr); pap. 4.95x (ISBN 0-8195-1050-5). Columbia U Pr.

Let Our Children Go. Ted Patrick & Tom Dulack. 1977. pap. 2.25 (ISBN 0-345-25663-8). Ballantine.

Let Out the Sunshine. Regina R. Barnett. 144p. (Orig.). 1981. pap. text ed. 12.00 (ISBN 0-697-01762-1). Wm C Brown.

Let Sleeping Dogs Die. Tim Heald. 192p. 1981. pap. 2.25 (ISBN 0-345-28903-X). Ballantine.

Let the Children Paint. Kathryn S. Wright. 4.50 (ISBN 0-8164-0162-4); film strip 4.50 (ISBN 0-685-20292-5). Crossroad NY.

Let the Children Sing: Music in Religious Education. Kathryn S. Wright. LC 73-17915. 1974. 7.95 (ISBN 0-8164-0256-6). Crossroad NY.

Let the Children Speak. Patricia K. Light. LC 74-313. 1975. 14.95 (ISBN 0-669-92676-0). Lexington Bks.

Let the Crags Comb Out Her Dainty Hair. Jacqueline Marten. 256p. 1975. pap. 1.25 o.p. (ISBN 0-445-00302-2). Popular Lib.

Let the Earth Hear. Paul Freed. 1980. 8.95 (ISBN 0-8407-5188-5). Nelson.

Let the Evidence Speak. Buryl Eads. Ed. by Amy Reynolds. LC 79-17377. (Illus., Orig.). 1979. pap. 4.95 (ISBN 0-931948-02-9). Peachtree Pubs.

Let the Guns Roar. Charles N. Heckelmann. 1977. pap. 1.25 o.p. (ISBN 0-445-08609-2). Popular Lib.

Let the People Cry Amen! An Inquiry into the Oral History of the Old Testament. John F. Sheehan. LC 76-45676. 1977. pap. 5.95 (ISBN 0-8091-2003-8). Paulist Pr.

Let the People Sing. Harold E. Hannum. Ed. by Tom Davis. 112p. 1981. pap. write for info. (ISBN 0-8280-0029-8). Review & Herald.

Let the Seals Live. Sue Flint. 192p. 1980. 14.95 (ISBN 0-906191-35-1, Pub. by Thule Pr England). Intl Schol Bk Serv.

Let the Sunshine in: Learning Activities for Multiply Handicapped Deaf Children, Pt. 1. Foster et al. 1973. pap. 4.50 (ISBN 0-913072-15-X). Natl Assn Deaf.

Let Them Be Judged: The Judicial Integration of the Deep South. Frank T. Read & Lucy S. McGough. LC 78-876. 1978. 27.50 (ISBN 0-8108-1118-9). Scarecrow.

Let Them Live. Dorothy P. Lathrop. (Illus.). (gr. 4-6). 1966. 6.95g (ISBN 0-02-753800-1). Macmillan.

Let Them Live: A Worldwide Survey of Animals Threatened with Extinction. Kai Curry-Lindahl. (Illus.). 416p. 1972. 9.95 (ISBN 0-688-00046-0); pap. 3.95 o.p. (ISBN 0-688-05046-8). Morrow.

Let There Be Music. new ed. Samuel L. Forcucci. (gr. 9-12). 1973. text ed. 14.40 (ISBN 0-205-03768-2, 5837685); tchrs'. guide 2.40 (ISBN 0-205-03794-1, 5837944). Allyn.

Let This Cup Pass. Jane McWhorter. 1979. pap. 3.75 (ISBN 0-89137-414-0). Quality Pubns.

Let Us Be Holy. Judson Cornwall. 1979. pap. 4.95 (ISBN 0-88270-278-5). Logos.

Let Us Die Fighting: Nambia Under the Germans. Horst Drescher. 1981. 18.95 (ISBN 0-905762-77-0); pap. 8.95 (ISBN 0-905762-37-1). Lawrence Hill.

Let Us Draw Near. Judson Cornwall. 1977. pap. 4.95 (ISBN 0-88270-226-2). Logos.

Let Us Praise: A Prominent Charismatic Leader Tells How & Why to Praise God. Judson Cornwall. LC 73-75957. 1973. pap. 4.95 (ISBN 0-88270-039-1). Logos.

Let Us See Jesus. Judson Conrwall. 1981. pap. 4.95 (ISBN 0-8007-5052-7). Revell.

Let'er Buck. Douglas K. Hall. LC 73-76497. 1973. 10.00 o.p. (ISBN 0-8415-0274-9). Dutton.

Let'er Buck: A Story of the Passing of the Old West. Charles W. Furlong. LC 77-159961. 280p. 1971. Repr. of 1921 ed. 18.00 (ISBN 0-8103-3405-4). Gale.

Let'er Rip Tumbleweeds. Tom K. Ryan. (Illus.). 128p. 1977. pap. 1.50 (ISBN 0-449-13894-1, GM). Fawcett.

Lethal Aspects of Urban Violence. Harold M. Rose. LC 77-18680. (Illus.). 1979. 14.95 (ISBN 0-669-02117-2). Lexington Bks.

Letitia. Lorinda Hagen. 1978. pap. 1.95 (ISBN 0-505-51242-4). Tower Bks.

L'etranger. A. Camus. Ed. by G. Bree & C. Lynes. 1955. pap. 7.95 (ISBN 0-13-530790-2). P-H.

Let's Be Friends Again. Judith A. Enderle. LC 78-73536. (Illus.). (gr. k-3). Date not set. price not set (ISBN 0-89799-156-7); pap. price not set (ISBN 0-89799-074-9). Dandelion Pr. Postponed.

Let's Be Nature's Friend! Jack Stokes. LC 76-15087. (Illus.). (gr. k-3). 1977. 6.95 o.p. (ISBN 0-679-20355-9). McKay.

Let's Boogie! James Stevenson. LC 78-17558. (Illus.). 1978. 8.95 (ISBN 0-396-07633-5). Dodd.

Let's Celebrate. Pasadena Art Alliance. (Orig.). 1980. pap. 4.50. Pasadena Art.

Let's Celebrate Christmas: Parties, Plays, Legends, Carols, Poetry, Stories. Horace J. Gardner. (Illus.). (gr. 6-12). 1940. 9.50 o.p. (ISBN 0-8260-3320-2). Ronald Pr.

Let's Communicate: A Self-Help Program on Writing Letters & Memos. George W. Martin. LC 71-109516. (Supervisory Management Ser). 1970. pap. text ed. 8.95 (ISBN 0-201-04500-1). A-W.

Let's Communicate: Using Grammar Effectively. Paul E. Herman & Sheila H. Ihde. 235p. (Orig.). (gr. 4-6). 1979. pap. text ed. 5.25x (ISBN 0-88334-123-9). Ind Sch Pr.

Let's Cook It & Edith. Edith Melberg. (Illus.). 196p. Date not set. pap. 7.95 o.s.i. (ISBN 0-89716-054-1). Peanut Butter.

Let's Cook It Right. Adelle Davis. 1970. pap. 2.95 (ISBN 0-451-09427-1, E9427, Sig). NAL.

Let's Cook Today. Ed. by Eleanor Dunn. (gr. k-3). 1974. 3.95x (ISBN 0-933892-03-9). Child Focus Co.

Let's Count All the Animals. Jim Kulas. (Tell-a-Tale Reader Ser.). (Illus.). (gr. k-3). 1979. PLB 4.77 (ISBN 0-307-68407-5, Golden Pr). Western Pub.

Let's Cure the Court Crunch. Peoria Tennis Association Facilities Committee. 1977. pap. text ed. 2.00 (ISBN 0-938822-05-5). USTA.

Let's Dance-Country Style. Ronald Smedley & John Tether. 1975. 6.95 (ISBN 0-236-31061-5, Pub. by Paul Elek). Merrimack Bk Serv.

Let's Dance: Social, Ballroom & Folk Dancing. Peter Buckman. (Illus.). 1979. pap. 8.95 o.p. (ISBN 0-14-005325-5). Penguin.

Let's Discover Series, 16 vols. Ed. by Patricia Daniels. Incl. Vol. 1. Warm-blooded Animlas. LC 80-22951; Vol. 2. Prehistoric World. LC 80-22949; Vol. 3. People & Customs. LC 80-22960; Vol. 4. Cold-blooded Animals. LC 80-24150; Vol. 5. Earth. LC 80-22952; Vol. 6. Sea. LC 80-22953; Vol. 7. People of Long Ago. LC 80-22955; Vol. 8. What People Do. LC 80-22965; Vol. 9. You & Your Body. LC 80-22970; Vol. 10. Sport & Entertainment. LC 80-22975; Vol. 11. World of Machines. LC 80-22980; Vol. 12. Land Travel. LC 80-22954; Vol. 13. Ships & Boats. LC 80-22959; Vol. 14. Flying. LC 80-22964; Vol. 15. Outer Space. LC 80-22974; Vol. 16. Index. LC 80-22978. (Illus.). (gr. k-3). 1981. Set, 80 Pages Ea. PLB 239.79 (ISBN 0-8172-1782-7). Raintree Pubs.

Let's Do Yoga. Ruth Richards & Joy Abrams. LC 74-22199. (Illus.). 48p. (gr. 2-5). 1975. reinforced bdg. 5.95 o.p. (ISBN 0-03-014006-4). HR&W.

Let's Eat Right to Keep Fit. Adelle Davis. 1970. pap. 2.95 (ISBN 0-451-09644-4, E9644, Sig). NAL.

Let's Fall in Love. Carol Hill. 256p. 1975. pap. 1.95 o.p. (ISBN 0-345-24425-7). Ballantine.

Let's Find Out About a Book. Mildred L. Nickel. LC 79-131146. (Let's Find Out Bks). (Illus.). (gr. 3 up). 1971. PLB 4.47 o.p. (ISBN 0-531-00066-4). Watts.

Let's Find Out About Animal Homes. Charles Shapp & Martha Shapp. LC 68-10132. (Let's Find Out Bks). (Illus.). (gr. k-3). 1962. PLB 4.47 o.p. (ISBN 0-531-00003-6). Watts.

Let's Find Out About Animals of Long Ago. Charles Shapp & Martha Shapp. LC 68-10132. (Let's Find Out Bks). (Illus.). (gr. k-3). 1968. PLB 5.90 (ISBN 0-531-00004-4). Watts.

Let's Find Out About Babies. Martha Shapp & Charles Shapp. LC 74-3503. (Let's Find Out Bks). (Illus.). 48p. (gr. k-3). 1975. PLB 6.45 (ISBN 0-531-00109-1). Watts.

Let's Find Out About Bees. Cathleen Fitzgerald. LC 78-186938. (Let's Find Out Bks). (Illus.). 48p. (gr. 3-4). 1973. PLB 4.47 o.p. (ISBN 0-531-00079-6). Watts.

Let's Find Out About Birds. Charles Shapp & Martha Shapp. LC 67-13731. (Let's Find Out Bks). (Illus.). (gr. k-3). 1967. PLB 4.47 o.p. (ISBN 0-531-00006-0). Watts.

Let's Find Out About Boats. Ann R. Campbell. LC 67-16966. (Let's Find Out Bks). (Illus.). (gr. k-3). 1967. PLB 4.47 o.p. (ISBN 0-531-00007-9). Watts.

Let's Find Out About Butterflies. Roz Abisch. LC 73-182899. (Let's Find Out Books). (Illus.). 48p. (gr. k-3). 1972. PLB 4.47 o.p. (ISBN 0-531-00077-X). Watts.

Let's Find Out About Cavemen. Charles Shapp & Martha Shapp. LC 76-175800. (Let's Find Out Bks). (Illus.). 48p. (gr. k-3). 1972. PLB 4.47 o.p. (ISBN 0-531-00078-8). Watts.

Let's Find Out About Christmas. Franklin Watts. (Let's Find Out Bks). (Illus.). (gr. k-3). 1967. PLB 4.47 o.p. (ISBN 0-531-00010-9). Watts.

Let's Find Out About Color. Ann Campbell. LC 74-3302. (Let's Find Out Bks). (Illus.). 48p. (gr. k-3). 1975. PLB 4.90 o.p. (ISBN 0-531-00110-5). Watts.

Let's Find Out About Communications. Valerie Pitt. LC 72-7084. (Let's Find Out Bks). (Illus.). 48p. (gr. 3-4). 1973. PLB 4.47 o.p. (ISBN 0-531-00083-4). Watts.

Let's Find Out About Daniel Boone. Charles Shapp & Martha Shapp. LC 67-15732. (Let's Find Out Bks). (Illus.). (gr. k-3). 1967. PLB 4.47 o.p. (ISBN 0-531-00008-7). Watts.

Let's Find Out About Earth. David C. Knight. LC 74-3501. (Let's Find Out Bks). (Illus.). 48p. (gr. k-3). 1975. PLB 4.90 o.p. (ISBN 0-531-00111-3). Watts.

Let's Find Out About Easter. Franklin Watts. LC 69-12595. (Let's Find Out Bks). (Illus.). (gr. k-3). 1969. PLB 4.47 o.p. (ISBN 0-531-00018-4). Watts.

Let's Find Out About Eskimos. Eleanor Wiesenthal & Ted Wiesenthal. LC 70-87929. (Let's Find Out Bks). (Illus.). (gr. k-3). 1969. PLB 4.47 o.p. (ISBN 0-531-00061-3). Watts.

Let's Find Out About Firemen. Charles Shapp & Martha Shapp. LC 65-24104. (Let's Find Out Bks). (Illus.). (gr. k-3). 1962. PLB 4.47 o.p. (ISBN 0-531-00023-0). Watts.

Let's Find Out About Frogs. Corinne J. Naden. LC 79-189120. (Let's Find Out Bks). (Illus.). 48p. (gr. 3-4). 1972. PLB 4.47 o.p. (ISBN 0-531-00081-8). Watts.

Let's Find Out About Halloween. Paulette Cooper. LC 70-182290. (Let's Find Out Bks). (Illus.). 48p. (gr. k-2). 1972. PLB 4.47 o.p. (ISBN 0-531-00075-3). Watts.

Let's Find Out About Hospitals. Eleanor Kay. LC 75-131145. (Let's Find Out Bks). 48p. (gr. k-3). 1971. PLB 4.47 o.p. (ISBN 0-531-00072-9). Watts.

Let's Find Out About Houses. Martha Shapp & Charles Shapp. LC 74-3000. (Let's Find Out Bks). (Illus.). 48p. (gr. k-3). 1975. PLB 6.45 (ISBN 0-531-00100-8). Watts.

Let's Find Out About Indians. Charles Shapp & Martha Shapp. (Let's Find Out Bks). (Illus.). (gr. k-3). 1962. PLB 4.47 o.p. (ISBN 0-531-00027-3). Watts.

Let's Find Out About Manners. Valerie Pitt. LC 70-183898. (Let's Find Out Bks). (Illus.). 48p. (gr. 3-4). 1972. PLB 4.47 o.p. (ISBN 0-531-00082-6). Watts.

Let's Find Out About Mars. David C. Knight. LC 66-10159. (Let's Find Out Bks). (Illus.). (gr. k-3). 1966. PLB 4.47 o.p. (ISBN 0-531-00032-X). Watts.

Let's Find Out About Milk. David C. Whitney. LC 67-14832. (Let's Find Out Bks). (Illus.). (gr. k-3). 1967. PLB 4.47 o.p. (ISBN 0-531-00033-8). Watts.

Let's Find Out About Mosquitoes. David Webster. LC 74-4154. (Let's Find Out Bks). (Illus.). 48p. (gr. k-3). 1974. PLB 4.47 o.p. (ISBN 0-531-02740-6). Watts.

Let's Find Out About Names. Valerie Pitt. LC 76-131156. (Let's Find Out Bks). (Illus.). (gr. k-3). 1971. PLB 4.47 o.p. (ISBN 0-531-00069-9). Watts.

Let's Find Out About Neighbors. Valerie Pitt. LC 78-101750. (Let's Find Out Bks). (Illus.). (gr. k-3). 1970. PLB 4.47 o.p. (ISBN 0-531-00058-3). Watts.

Let's Find Out About Policemen. Charles Shapp & Martha Shapp. (Let's Find Out Bks). (Illus.). (gr. k-3). 1962. PLB 4.47 o.p. (ISBN 0-531-00036-2). Watts.

Let's Find Out About Rivers. Eleanor Wiesenthal & Ted Wiesenthal. LC 79-150732. (Let's Find Out Bks). (Illus.). (gr. k-3). 1971. PLB 4.47 o.p. (ISBN 0-531-00074-5). Watts.

Let's Find Out About Safety. Martha Shapp & Charles Shapp. LC 74-2998. (Let's Find Out Bks). (Illus.). 48p. (Color ed.). (gr. k-3). 1975. PLB 4.90 o.p. (ISBN 0-531-00102-4). Watts.

Let's Find Out About Snakes. Charles Shapp & Martha Shapp. LC 68-19238. (Let's Find Out Bks). (Illus.). (gr. k-3). 1968. PLB 4.47 o.p. (ISBN 0-531-00043-5). Watts.

Let's Find Out About Sound. David Knight. LC 74-2997. (Let's Find Out Bks). (gr. k-2). 1975. PLB 6.45 (ISBN 0-531-00103-2). Watts.

Let's Find Out About Space Travel. Charles Shapp & Martha Shapp. LC 70-131141. (Let's Find Out Bks). (Illus.). (gr. k-3). 1971. PLB 4.47 o.p. (ISBN 0-531-00068-0). Watts.

Let's Find Out About Spring. Charles Shapp & Martha Shapp. (Let's Find Out Bks). (Illus.). (gr. k-3). 1963. PLB 4.47 o.p. (ISBN 0-531-00044-3). Watts.

Let's Find Out About Streets. Valerie Pitt. LC 72-87932. (Let's Find Out Bks). (Illus.). (gr. k-3). 1969. PLB 4.47 o.p. (ISBN 0-531-00063-X). Watts.

Let's Find Out About Subtraction. David C. Whitney. LC 68-11890. (Let's Find Out Bks). (Illus.). (gr. k-3). 1968. PLB 4.47 o.p. (ISBN 0-531-00045-1). Watts.

Let's Find Out About Telephones. David C. Knight. LC 67-10006. (Let's Find Out Bks). (Illus.). (gr. k-3). 1967. PLB 4.47 o.p. (ISBN 0-531-00048-6). Watts.

Let's Find Out About Thanksgiving. Charles Shapp & Martha Shapp. LC 64-18887. (Let's Find Out Bks). (Illus.). (gr. k-3). 1964. PLB 4.47 o.p. (ISBN 0-531-00049-4). Watts.

Let's Find Out About the City. Valerie Pitt. LC 68-10507. (Let's Find Out Bks). (Illus.). (gr. k-3). 1968. PLB 4.47 o.p. (ISBN 0-531-00012-5). Watts.

Let's Find Out About the Community. Valerie Pitt. LC 79-185688. (Let's Find Out Bks). (Illus.). 48p. (gr. 3-4). 1972. PLB 4.47 o.p. (ISBN 0-531-00080-X). Watts.

Let's Find Out About the Family. Valerie Pitt. LC 78-117180. (Let's Find Out Bks). (gr. k-3). 1970. PLB 4.90 o.p. (ISBN 0-531-00065-6). Watts.

Let's Find Out About the Moon. rev. ed. Martha Shapp & Charles Shapp. LC 72-4414. (Let's Find Out Bks). (Illus.). (gr. k-3). 1975. PLB 4.90 o.p. (ISBN 0-531-00101-6). Watts.

Let's Find Out About the Ocean. David C. Knight. LC 77-100095. (Let's Find Out Bks). (Illus.). (gr. k-3). 1970. PLB 4.47 o.p. (ISBN 0-531-00056-7). Watts.

Let's Find Out About the Sun. Charles Shapp & Martha Shapp. LC 74-2996. (Let's Find Out Bks). (Illus.). 48p. (gr. k-3). 1975. PLB 6.45 (ISBN 0-531-00104-0). Watts.

Let's Find Out About Trees, Arbor Day. Martha Shapp & Charles Shapp. LC 74-100097. (Let's Find Out Bks). (Illus.). (gr. k-3). 1970. PLB 4.47 o.p. (ISBN 0-531-00057-5). Watts.

Let's Find Out About Water. Martha Shapp & Charles Shapp. LC 74-2995. (Let's Find Out Bks). (Illus.). 48p. (gr. k-3). 1975. PLB 6.45 (ISBN 0-531-00108-3). Watts.

Let's Find Out About Weather. David C. Knight. LC 67-10010. (Let's Find Out Bks). (Illus.). (gr. k-3). 1967. PLB 4.47 o.p. (ISBN 0-531-00053-2). Watts.

Let's Find Out About What Electricity Does. Martha Shapp & Charles Shapp. LC 74-2993. (Let's Find Out Bks). (Illus.). 48p. (gr. k-3). 1975. PLB 6.45 (ISBN 0-531-00105-9). Watts.

Let's Find Out About What's Big & What's Small. Martha Shapp & Charles Shapp. LC 74-2992. (Let's Find Out Bks). (Illus.). 48p. (gr. k-3). 1975. PLB 6.45 (ISBN 0-531-00106-7). Watts.

Let's Find Out About What's Light & What's Heavy. Martha Shapp & Charles Shapp. LC 74-2991. (Let's Find Out Bks). (Illus.). 48p. (gr. k-3). 1975. PLB 6.45 (ISBN 0-531-00107-5). Watts.

Let's Find Out About Winter. Charles Shapp & Martha Shapp. (Let's Find Out Bks). (Illus.). (gr. k-3). 1963. PLB 4.47 o.p. (ISBN 0-531-00055-9). Watts.

Let's Find Out About Words. Cathleen FitzGerald. LC 78-134370. (Let's Find Out Bks). (Illus.). (gr. k-3). 1971. PLB 4.47 o.p. (ISBN 0-531-00070-2). Watts.

Let's Folk Dance. Herbert Rothgarber. 1980. pap. 3.00 (ISBN 0-918812-10-0). Magnamusic.

Let's Get Down to Cases, 2 pts. 1976. 4.50 set (ISBN 0-686-68031-6); Pt. 1 (ISBN 0-8144-6953-1); pt. 2 o.p. (ISBN 0-8144-6954-X). Am Mgmt.

Let's Get Moving. D. Stuart Briscoe. LC 77-91773. 1978. pap. 2.50 (ISBN 0-8307-0538-4, S322-1-02). Regal.

Let's Go, Britain & Ireland: The Budget Guide 1981 to 1982 Edition. Harvard Student Agencies. (Illus.). 550p. 1981. pap. 5.50 (ISBN 0-525-93143-0). Dutton.

Let's Go, Britain & Ireland: The Budget Guide 1980 to 1981 Edition. Harvard Student Agencies. (Illus.). 1980. pap. 5.50 (ISBN 0-525-93090-6). Dutton.

Let's Go, Europe Nineteen Seventy-Nine to Nineteen Eighty. Harvard Student Agencies. 1979. pap. 5.95 o.p. (ISBN 0-87690-301-4). Dutton.

Let's Go, Europe: The Budget Guide 1980 to 1981 Edition. Harvard Student Agencies. 1980. pap. 5.95 (ISBN 0-525-93091-4). Dutton.

Let's Go, Europe 1981-82. Harvard Student Agencies. (Illus.). 736p. 1981. pap. 6.95 (ISBN 0-525-93142-2). Dutton.

Let's Go Flying: An Introduction to Aviation Coloring & Activity Book. Ed. by Linda Hooker & Jo McCarrell. (Illus.). 1975. wkbk 2.50 (ISBN 0-911721-88-6, Pub. by Ninety-Nines); tchr's guide avail. Aviation.

Let's Go, France Nineteen Seventy-Nine to Nineteen Eighty. Harvard Student Agencies. 1979. pap. 3.95 o.p. (ISBN 0-87690-303-0). Dutton.

Let's Go, France: The Budget Guide 1980 to 1981 Edition. Harvard Student Agencies. (Illus.). 1980. pap. 4.95 (ISBN 0-525-93088-4). Dutton.

Let's Go, France: The Budget Guide 1981 to 1982 Edition. Harvard Student Agencies. (Illus.). 352p. 1981. pap. 4.95 (ISBN 0-525-93144-9). Dutton.

Let's Go, Greece, Israel & Europe: The Budget Guide 1981 to 1982 Edition. Harvard Student Agencies. (Illus.). 352p. 1981. pap. 4.95 (ISBN 0-525-93146-5). Dutton.

Let's Go, Italy Nineteen Seventy-Nine to Nineteen Eighty. Harvard Student Agencies. 1979. pap. 3.95 o.p. (ISBN 0-87690-304-9). Dutton.

Let's Go, Italy: The Budget Guide 1980 to 1981 Edition. Harvard Student Agencies. (Illus.). 1980. pap. 5.50 (ISBN 0-525-93089-2). Dutton.

Let's Go, Italy: The Budget Guide 1981 to 1982 Edition. Harvard Student Agencies. (Illus.). 412p. 1981. pap. 5.50 (ISBN 0-525-93145-7). Dutton.

Let's Go, Italy 1980-81. (Illus.). 1981. pap. 5.95 (ISBN 0-525-93145-7). Dutton.

Let's Go Play at the Adams. Mendal W. Johnson. 288p. 1980. pap. 2.50 (ISBN 0-553-14139-2). Bantam.

Let's Go to Meherabad. Bhau Kalchuri. 100p. 1981. price not set. Meher Baba Info.

Let's Go, Trucks! David Harrison. (Illus.). 24p. (gr. k-2). 1976. PLB 5.00 (ISBN 0-307-60185-4, Golden Pr). Western Pub.

Let's Go, USA: The Budget Guide 1981 to 1982 Edition. Harvard Student Agencies. (Illus.). 556p. 1981. pap. 7.95 (ISBN 0-525-93141-4). Dutton.

Let's Grow Things. Deborah Manley. LC 78-26879. (Ready, Set, Look Ser.). (Illus.). (gr. k-3). 1979. PLB 9.65 (ISBN 0-8172-1308-2). Raintree Pubs.

Let's Grow Tomatoes. Jacob R. Mittleider. LC 80-84563. (Illus.). 150p. 1981. pap. 4.95 (ISBN 0-88290-176-1, 4027). Horizon Utah.

Let's Halt Awhile in Great Britain (Including Ireland) 1979. Ashley Courtenay. (Illus.). 1979. pap. 12.95 o.p. (ISBN 0-8038-4310-0). Hastings.

Lets Halt Awhile in Great Britain 1981. Ashley Courtenay. (Illus.). 600p. (Orig.). 1981. pap. 13.95 (ISBN 0-8038-4338-0). Hastings.

Let's Have a Banquet. Joyce Landorf. 1968. pap. 3.95 (ISBN 0-310-27131-2). Zondervan.

Let's Have a Party. Maureen Roffey. (Illus.). 1978. 6.95 (ISBN 0-370-01278-X, Pub. by Chatto Bodley Jonathan). Merrimack Bk Serv.

Let's Have a Play. Margaret Hillert. (Just Beginning-to-Read Ser.). (Illus.). 32p. (gr. 1-6). 1981. PLB 4.39 (ISBN 0-695-41544-1); pap. 1.50 (ISBN 0-695-31544-7). Follett.

Let's Have Fun with English. Ruth Rackmill. LC 80-68407. 120p. 1981. perfect bdg. 6.95 (ISBN 0-86548-061-3). Century Twenty One.

Let's Kill Uncle Lionel. John Creasy. 1976. 6.95 o.p. (ISBN 0-679-50589-X). McKay.

Let's Kiss the Pussy-Cats. Virginia Fallon. 28p. 1980. pap. 2.00 (ISBN 0-934616-19-1). Valkyrie Pr.

Let's Learn About Aging: A Book of Readings. Ed. by John R. Barry & C. Ray Wingrove. LC 76-45168. 1977. text ed. 18.50 (ISBN 0-470-98965-3); pap. text ed. 12.95 (ISBN 0-470-98967-X). Halsted Pr.

Let's Learn About Jesus: A Child's Coloring Book of the Life of Christ. Bessie Dean. (Children's Inspirational Coloring Bk.). (Illus.). (ps-6). 1979. pap. 3.95 (ISBN 0-88290-131-1). Horizon Utah.

Let's Learn About Jewish Symbols. Joyce Fischman. LC 68-9347. (Illus.). (ps-k). 1969. pap. text ed. 3.50 (ISBN 0-8074-0144-7, 101035); tchrs'. guide o.p. 3.00. UAHC.

Let's Live! Curtis C. Mitchell. 160p. 1975. 6.95 (ISBN 0-8007-0716-8). Revell.

Let's Look at Castles. Alan R. Warwick. LC 67-17416. (Let's Look Ser). (Illus.). (gr. 4-8). 1965. 4.95g o.p. (ISBN 0-8075-4464-7). A Whitman.

Let's Look at Costume. Edmund Cooper. LC 67-17421. (Let's Look Ser). (Illus.). (gr. 4-8). 1965. 4.95g o.p. (ISBN 0-8075-4470-1). A Whitman.

Let's Look at Houses & Homes. Joan Morey. LC 78-85228. (Let's Look Ser). (Illus.). (gr. 4-8). 1969. 4.95g o.p. (ISBN 0-8075-4477-9). A Whitman.

Let's Look at Indonesia. David Ellis. 1973. pap. 1.00 (ISBN 0-85363-077-1). OMF Bks.

Let's Look at Insects. Walter Shepherd. Date not set. price not set (ISBN 0-392-08023-0, SpS). Soccer.

Let's Look at Korea. Kathleen Wallis. 1977. pap. 1.25 (ISBN 0-85363-118-2). OMF Bks.

Let's Look at Malaysia. Miriam Dunn. pap. 1.25 (ISBN 0-85363-096-8). OMF Bks.

Let's Look at Musical Instruments & the Orchestra. C. O. Rhodes. LC 71-85229. (Let's Look Ser). (Illus.). (gr. 4-8). 1969. 4.95g o.p. (ISBN 0-8075-4483-3). A Whitman.

Let's Look at Prehistoric Animals. Alan R. Warwick. LC 67-26522. (Let's Look Ser). (Illus.). (gr. 4-8). 1966. 4.95g o.p. (ISBN 0-8075-4489-2). A Whitman.

Let's Look at Puppets. A. R. Philpott. LC 67-26517. (Let's Look Ser). (Illus.). (gr. 4-8). 1966. 4.95g o.p. (ISBN 0-8075-4494-9). A Whitman.

Let's Look at Ships. Gerald Bowman. LC 68-22910. (Let's Look Series). (Illus.). (gr. 4-8). 1965. 4.95g o.p. (ISBN 0-8075-4501-5). A Whitman.

Let's Look at Thailand. Mary Gurtler. 1974. pap. 1.25 (ISBN 0-85363-104-2). OMF Bks.

Let's Look at the Phillipines. Rosemary Dowsett. 1974. pap. 0.90 (ISBN 0-85363-103-4). OMF Bks.

Let's Look at Trains. Ernest Carter. 17.50x (ISBN 0-392-08037-0, SpS). Soccer.

Let's Look at Trains. Ernest F. Carter. LC 68-22191. (Let's Look Ser). (Illus.). (gr. 4-8). 1964. 4.95g o.p. (ISBN 0-8075-4507-4). A Whitman.

Let's Make a Mobile. Victoria S. Morris. (Mobiles Ser.: Vol. 1). (gr. 1-8). 1972. pap. 2.00 o.p. (ISBN 0-914318-02-0). V S Morris.

Let's Make It Happen. Girl Scouts of the U.S.A. Program Dept. (GS Catalogue: No. 20-815). (gr. 9-12). 2.50 (ISBN 0-88441-322-5). GS.

Let's Make Magic. Edward F. Dolan. LC 79-8014. (Illus.). 96p. (gr. 2-6). 1981. 7.95a (ISBN 0-385-15192-6); PLB (ISBN 0-385-15193-4). Doubleday.

Let's Make More Presents: Easy & Inexpensive Gifts for Every Occasion. Esther Hautzig. LC 72-92445. (How-to Bk.). (Illus.). 160p. (gr. 5 up). 1973. 8.95 (ISBN 0-02-743490-7). Macmillan.

Let's Make Presents: One Hundred Gifts for Less Than One Dollar. Esther Hautzig. LC 61-14532. (Illus.). (gr. 4 up). 1962. 10.95 (ISBN 0-690-48951-X, TYC-J). T Y Crowell.

Let's Plan: A Guide to the Planning Process for Voluntary Organizations. John C. DeBoer. LC 72-124329. (Illus., Orig.). 1970. pap. 3.95 (ISBN 0-8298-0177-4). Pilgrim NY.

Let's Play Cards. John Belton & Joella Cramblit. LC 75-9606. (Games & Activities Ser.). (Illus.). 48p. (gr. k-3). 1975. PLB 9.30 (ISBN 0-8172-0025-8). Raintree Pubs.

Let's Play Chess: A Step-by-Step Guide for Beginners. Bruce Pandolfini. LC 80-11410. (Illus.). 160p. (gr. 7-12). 1980. PLB 7.79 (ISBN 0-671-34054-9). Messner.

Let's Play Make Believe. Paul Ricchiuti. 1975. pap. 1.65 (ISBN 0-8163-0187-5, 12150-9). Pacific Pr Pub Assn.

Let's Play Tennis! Fred Stolle & Martin Appel. (Illus.). Date not set. pap. cancelled (ISBN 0-671-33068-3). Wanderer Bks.

Let's Pray Together: Eight Studies on Prayer. Margaret Fromer & Sharrel Keyes. LC 74-76160. (Fisherman Bible Study Guide). 1974. pap. 1.95 (ISBN 0-87788-801-9). Shaw Pubs.

Let's Pretend. Pat Schories. (Peggy Cloth Bks.). (Illus.). (ps-1). 1980. pap. 3.50 (ISBN 0-448-40026-X). G&D.

Let's Pretend It Happened to You. Bernice W. Carlson. LC 73-1488. (Illus.). 112p. (ps-3). 1973. 5.95 o.p. (ISBN 0-687-21503-X). Abingdon.

Let's Pretend: Mae Dee & Her Family Ten Years Later. Ada D. Simond. LC 78-62431. (National History Ser.). (Illus.). (gr. 5 up). Date not set. 8.95 (ISBN 0-89482-012-5); softcover 5.95 (ISBN 0-89482-013-3). Stevenson Pr.

Let's Reach for the Sun. George Reynoldson. (Illus.). 144p. 1978. pap. 9.95 o.p. (ISBN 0-9603570-0-9). Space-Time.

Let's Reach for the Sun: Thirty Original Solar & Earth Sheltered Home Designs. rev. ed. (Illus.). 144p. 1981. pap. 9.95 (ISBN 0-9603570-1-7). Space-Time.

Let's Reach for the Sun: 30 Original Solar & Earth Sheltered Home Designs. rev. ed. George Reynoldson. Ed. by Jeanne Erdahl. (Illus.). 144p. 1981. pap. 9.95 (ISBN 0-9603570-1-7). Space-Time.

Let's Read Hebrew. rev. ed. Anna P. Koch. 1974. pap. 2.95x (ISBN 0-8197-0029-0). Bloch.

Let's Speak French, Bks. 1-3. Josee Okin & Conrad J. Schmitt. 1966. Bks. 1-2. text ed. 5.28x ea. (W). Bk. 1 (ISBN 0-07-047642-X). Bk. 2 (ISBN 0-07-047644-6). Bk. 3. text ed. 11.72x (ISBN 0-07-047638-1); tchrs. guide bks. 1 & 2 8.08x (ISBN 0-07-047645-4). Bk. 3. tchrs. guide 9.32x (ISBN 0-07-047639-X). McGraw.

Let's Speak Rusyn: Transcarpathian Edition. Paul R. Magocsi. LC 79-18393. (Illus.). 106p. 1979. pap. 6.95 (ISBN 0-917242-01-7). Carpatho-Rusyn Res Ctr.

Let's Start Praying Again. Basset, Bernard, S.J. 120p. 1973. pap. 1.95 o.p. (ISBN 0-385-05091-7, Im). Doubleday.

Let's Stay Lovers. Eve R. Mayer. 1981. 7.95 (ISBN 0-533-04917-2). Vantage.

Let's Talk. Mary Finocchiaro. (gr. 9 up). 1970. pap. text ed. 3.50 (ISBN 0-88345-094-1, 17743). Regents Pub.

Let's Talk About God. Margaret Anderson. LC 75-6055. (Illus.). 192p. (Orig.). (YA) 1975. 3.50 (ISBN 0-87123-340-1, 210340). Bethany Fell.

Let's Talk About the Jewish Holidays. Dorothy K. Kripke. LC 75-104328. (Illus.). (gr. k-4). 1970. 5.95 (ISBN 0-8246-0106-8). Jonathan David.

Let's Talk: An Introduction to Interpersonal Communication. 3rd ed. Sathre-Eldon et al. 1980. pap. text ed. 7.95x (ISBN 0-673-15376-2). Scott F.

Let's Talk Cats. Susie Page. LC 80-12852. (Illus.). 1980. 12.95 (ISBN 0-8289-0392-1). Greene.

Let's Talk Hebrew. Ben A Benjamin. 1961. 4.00 (ISBN 0-914080-01-6). Shulsinger Sales.

Let's Talk 'Iipay Aa: An Introduction to the Mesa Grande Diegueno Language. Ted Couro & Margaret Langdon. 1975. pap. 7.50 (ISBN 0-686-22652-6). Malki Mus Pr.

Let's Talk in Korean. K. Lee Pong & Sik R. Chi. LC 78-72953. 1978. 3.50 (ISBN 0-930878-10-8). Hollym Intl.

Let's Think About You. Gerald P. Cosgrave. 1978. pap. text ed. 4.25x (ISBN 0-8077-8064-2, Pub. by Guid Ctr U of Toronto). Tchrs Coll.

Let's Tune Up. John W. Travis. Ed. by R. Annabel Rathman. LC 68-14025. (Illus.). 1968. 20.00x (ISBN 0-9600394-2-2); pap. 17.50x (ISBN 0-9600394-3-0). Travis.

Let's Visit Japan. rev ed. John C. Caldwell. LC 59-7658. (Let's Visit Ser). (Illus.). (gr. 3-7). 1966. PLB 7.89 o.p. (ISBN 0-381-99889-4, A43010, JD-J). John Day.

Let's Write a Feature, 1969 Edition. Thomas Duffy. (Lucas Text Ser). text ed. 4.00x perfect bdg. (ISBN 0-87543-056-2). Lucas.

Let's Write English. rev. ed. George E. Wishon & Julia M. Burks. 430p. (gr. 9-12). 1980. pap. text ed. 5.20 (ISBN 0-278-47520-5); tchrs. ed. 1.20 (ISBN 0-278-47522-1). Litton Educ Pub.

Letter Assembly in Printing. D. Wooldridge. (Library of Printing Technology). Date not set. 18.95 (ISBN 0-8038-4274-0). Hastings.

Letter Concerning Toleration. 2nd ed. John Locke. 1955. pap. 2.50 (ISBN 0-672-60183-4, LLA22). Bobbs.

Letter Forms: 110 Complete Alphabets. Frederick Lambert. 128p. 1972. pap. 3.50 (ISBN 0-486-22872-X). Dover.

Letter from an Outlying Province. Patricia Cumming. LC 76-19884. 80p. 1976. pap. 4.95 (ISBN 0-914086-14-6). Alicejamesbooks.

Letter from the Dead. Anna Clarke. LC 80-2043. (Crime Club Ser.). 192p. 1981. 9.95 (ISBN 0-385-17330-X). Doubleday.

Letter Names of the Latin Alphabet. Arthur E. Gordon. (U. C. Publ. in Classical Studies: Vol. 9). 1973. pap. 9.00x (ISBN 0-520-09422-0). U of Cal Pr.

Letter of Joy. Arnold Bittlinger. Tr. by Susan Wiesmann from Ger. LC 75-2265. 128p. 1975. pap. 3.50 (ISBN 0-87123-338-X, 210338). Bethany Fell.

Letter of Meric Casaubon to Peter du Moulin Concerning Natural Experimental Philosophie. Meric Casaubon. LC 76-47045. 1976. Repr. of 1669 ed. 60.00x (ISBN 0-8201-1284-4). Schol Facsimiles.

Letter of Paul to the Galatians. Robert L. Johnson. Ed. by Everett Ferguson et al. LC 76-95018. (Living Word New Testament Commentary Ser: Vol. 10). 1969. 7.95 (ISBN 0-8344-0013-8). Sweet.

Letter of Paul to the Philippians. Pat E. Harrell. Ed. by Everett Ferguson et al. LC 71-79956. (Living Word New Testament Commentary Ser.: Vol. 12). 1969. 7.95 (ISBN 0-8344-0004-9). Sweet.

Letter of Paul to the Romans. Richard Batey. Ed. by Everett Ferguson et al. LC 68-58865. (Living Word New Testament Commentary Ser.: Vol. 7). 1969. 7.95 (ISBN 0-8344-0002-2). Sweet.

Letter to a King: A Picture History of the Inca Civilization. Huaman Poma. Tr. by Christopher Dilke. 1978. 10.00 o.p. (ISBN 0-525-14480-3). Dutton.

Letter to a Teacher. Schoolboys Of Barbiana. 1971. Repr. of 1970 ed. 5.95 o.p. (ISBN 0-394-43294-0, Vin). Random.

Letter to an Imaginary Friend, Pt. 1 & 2. Thomas McGrath. LC 77-81967. 214p. 1969. 11.95 (ISBN 0-8040-0185-5); pap. 5.95 (ISBN 0-8040-0186-3). Swallow.

Letter to Einstein Beginning Dear Albert. Paul Hoover. LC 79-12329. 1979. 3.00 (ISBN 0-916328-12-0, Pub. by Yellow Pr). SBD.

Letter to Philemon. Winthrop Neilson & Frances Neilson. 1973. pap. 1.25 o.s.i. (ISBN 0-515-03216-6). Jove Pubns.

Letter to Pilgrims. Robert Jewett. 244p. (Orig.). 1981. pap. 7.95 (ISBN 0-8298-0425-0). Pilgrim NY.

Letter to the Hebrews. James Thompson. Ed. by Everett Ferguson. LC 70-163750. (Living Word New Testament Commentary Ser.: Vol. 15). 1971. 7.95 (ISBN 0-8344-0071-5). Sweet.

Letter to the World. Emily Dickinson. Ed. by Rumer Godden. LC 78-78083. (Illus.). (gr. 7 up). 1969. 3.95 o.p. (ISBN 0-02-730550-3). Macmillan.

Letter to Titus. William MacDonald. 54p. pap. 1.50. Walterick Pubs.

Letter Tracking: Reusable Edition. Ed. by W. Edwards & S. Edwards. (Large Type Tracking Ser.). (gr. k-1). 1973. wkbk. 4.00 (ISBN 0-89039-019-3). Ann Arbor Pubs.

Letter Tracking: Reusable Edition. Ed. by W. Edwards & S. Edwards. (Ann Arbor Tracking Program Ser.). (gr. 3-8). 1975. wkbk. 5.00 (ISBN 0-89039-153-X). Ann Arbor Pubs.

Letter Writer. G. S. Humphreys. (Teach Yourself Ser.). 1975. pap. 3.50 (ISBN 0-679-10475-5). McKay.

Letter Writing for the Office: Syllabus. 2nd ed. Carl W. Salser. 1975. pap. text ed. 7.65 (ISBN 0-89420-026-7, 216720); cassette recordings 193.70 (ISBN 0-89420-160-3, 110800). Natl Book.

Letter Written to the Governours of the East Indian Merchants. LC 72-5978. (English Experience Ser.: No. 506). 16p. Repr. of 1603 ed. 5.00 (ISBN 90-221-0506-7). Walter J Johnson.

Lettera 1. Armin Haab et al. (Visual Communication Bks.). 1960. pap. 24.00 o.p. (ISBN 0-8038-4233-3). Hastings.

Lettera 2. Ed. by Armin Haab et al. (Visual Communication Bks.). (Illus., Eng.,). 1961. pap. 24.00 o.p. (ISBN 0-8038-4232-5). Hastings.

Lettera 3. Armin Haab & Walter Haettenschweiler. LC 60-50012. (Visual Communication Bks.). 1968. pap. 24.00 o.p. (ISBN 0-8038-4231-7). Hastings.

Lettera 4. Armin Haab & Walter Hattenschweiler. (Visual Communication Bks.). 1972. pap. 25.00 o.p. (ISBN 0-8038-4282-1). Hastings.

Letterbox: The Art & History of Letters. Jan Adkins. (Illus.). (gr. 3 up). 1981. 10.95 (ISBN 0-8027-6385-5); PLB 11.85 (ISBN 0-8027-6386-3). Walker & Co.

Lettering. Graily Hewitt. (Illus.). 336p. 1981. 10.00 (ISBN 0-8008-4726-1, Pentalic); pap. 9.95 (ISBN 0-8008-4728-8). Taplinger.

Lettering. Graily Hewitt. (Illus.). 336p. 1981. pap. 9.95 (ISBN 0-8008-4728-8, 76-26844). Taplinger.

Lettering & Alphabets. J. Albert Cavanaugh. (Illus.). 8.50 (ISBN 0-8446-0541-7). Peter Smith.

Lettering Techniques. John Lancaster. LC 79-56448. (Illus.). 120p. 1980. 24.00 (ISBN 0-7134-0220-2, Pub. by Batsford England). David & Charles.

Letters. Wittter Bynner. Ed. by James Kraft. 1981. 30.00 (ISBN 0-374-18504-2). FS&G.

Letters. St. Bernard de Clairvaux. Tr. by Bruno S. James. LC 78-63344. (Crusades Ser.). 552p. 1980. Repr. of 1953 ed. 47.50 (ISBN 0-404-17004-8). AMS Pr.

Letters. Laurence Sterne. Ed. by L. P. Curtis. 1935. 33.00x o.p. (ISBN 0-19-811453-2). Oxford U Pr.

Letters Addressed to the Daughter of a Nobleman on the Formation of the Religious & the Moral Principle, 2 vols. Elizabeth Hamilton. Ed. by Gina Luria. (Feminist Controversy in England, 1788-1810 Ser.). 1974. Set. lib. bdg. 90.00 (ISBN 0-8240-0865-0); lib. bdg. 50.00 ea. Garland Pub.

Letters & Diaries of John Henry Newman: Liberalism in Oxford, January 1835 to December 1836, Vol. 5. Thomas Gornall. 464p. 1981. 65.00 (ISBN 0-19-920117-X). Oxford U Pr.

Letters & Diaries of John Henry Newman. John H. Newman. Ed. by Charles S. Dessain & Charles S. Dessain. Incl. Vol. 11. Littemore to Rome, October 1845 to December 1846. 1961. o.p. (ISBN 0-19-920044-0); Vol. 19. Consulting the Laity, January 1859 to June 1861. 1969. 34.95x (ISBN 0-19-920051-3); Vol. 20. Standing Firm Amid Trials, July 1861 to December 1863. 1970. 34.95x (ISBN 0-19-920052-1); Vol. 21. The/Apologia, January 1864 to June 1865. Ed. by Edward E. Kelly. 1971. 36.00x (ISBN 0-19-920053-X); Vol. 22. Between Pussey & the Extremists, July 1865 to December 1866. 1972. 34.95x (ISBN 0-19-920054-8). Oxford U Pr.

Letters & Diaries of Oskar Schlemmer. Oskar Schlemmer. Ed. by Tut Schlemmer. Tr. by Krishna Winston from Ger. LC 77-184362. Orig. Title: Briefe und Tagebucher. (Illus.). 368p. 1972. 30.00x (ISBN 0-8195-4047-1, Pub. by Wesleyan U Pr). Columbia U Pr.

Letters & Documents in the Enoch Pratt Free Library. Edgar Allan Poe. Bd. with Merun & Recollections of Edgar A. Poe. Lambert A. Wilmer. LC 41-10640. 30.00x (ISBN 0-8201-1199-6). Schol Facsimiles.

Letters & Essays, Moral & Miscellaneous. Mary Hays. Ed. by Gina Luria. (Feminist Controversy in England, 1788-1810 Ser.). 1974. lib. bdg. 50.00 (ISBN 0-8240-0869-3). Garland Pub.

Letters & Journals of Fanny Burney: 1812-1814, Letters 632-834, Vol. VII. Fanny Burney. Ed. by Edward A. Bloom & Lillian D. Bloom. 1979. 69.00x (ISBN 0-19-812468-6). Oxford U Pr.

Letters & Journals of Paula Modersohn-Becker. Tr. by J. Diane Radycki. LC 80-18993. 370p. 1980. 17.50 (ISBN 0-8108-1344-0). Scarecrow.

Letters & Journals of Thomas Wentworth Higginson, 1846-1906. Thomas W. Higginson. Ed. by Mary T. Higginson. LC 73-87489. (American Public Figures Ser). 1969. Repr. of 1921 ed. lib. bdg. 37.50 (ISBN 0-306-71495-7). Da Capo.

Letters & Memoir of Joseph Charles Philpot. Joseph C. Philpot. (Giant Summit Ser.). 568p. 1981. pap. 9.95 (ISBN 0-8010-7060-0). Baker Bk.

Letters & Notes on the Manners, Customs & Conditions of the North American Indians, Vol. 1. George Catlin. LC 64-18844. (Illus.). 264p. 1973. pap. 5.50 (ISBN 0-486-22118-0). Dover.

Letters & Notes on the Manners, Customs & Conditions of the North American Indians, Vol. 2. George Catlin. LC 64-18844. (Illus.). 266p. 1973. pap. 5.50 (ISBN 0-486-22119-9). Dover.

Letters & Papers from Prison. enl. ed. Dietrich Bonhoeffer. 448p. 1972. 12.95 (ISBN 0-02-513110-9). Macmillan.

Letters & Papers of John Singleton Copley & Henry Pelham, 1739-1776. John S. Copley. LC 78-100615. (Library of American Art Ser.). (Illus.). 1970. Repr. of 1914 ed. lib. bdg. 39.50 (ISBN 0-306-71406-X). Da Capo.

Letters & Papers of Major-General John Sullivan, Continental Army, Vol.3,1779-1795. John Sullivan. Ed. by Otis G. Hammond. LC 32-27568. (Illus.). 677p. 1939. 17.50x (ISBN 0-915916-01-0). U Pr of New Eng.

Letters & People of the Spanish Indies. J. Lockhart & E. Otte. LC 75-6007. (Cambridge Latin American Studies: No. 22). 322p. 1976. 29.95 (ISBN 0-521-20883-1); pap. 8.95x (ISBN 0-521-20990-0). Cambridge U Pr.

Letters & Prose Writings of William Cowper, Volume II: Letters 1782-1786. Ed. by James King & Charles Ryskamp. (Illus.). 586p. 1981. 98.00 (ISBN 0-19-812607-7). Oxford U Pr.

Letters & Times of the Tylers, 3 Vols. Lyon G. Tyler. LC 71-75267. (American Public Figures Ser). 1970. Repr. of 1884 ed. lib. bdg. 125.00 (ISBN 0-306-71316-0). Da Capo.

Letters Concerning Mythology. Thomas Blackwell. LC 75-27887. (Renaissance & the Gods Ser.: Vol. 42). (Illus.). 1976. Repr. of 1748 ed. lib. bdg. 73.00 (ISBN 0-8240-2091-X). Garland Pub.

Letters for All Occasions. Alfred S. Myers. (Orig.). 1952. pap. 2.95 (ISBN 0-06-463237-7, EH 237, EH). Har-Row.

Letters for Everyday Use. Angelica W. Cass. Date not set. pap. cancelled (ISBN 0-671-09224-3). Monarch Pr. Postponed.

Letters for Literary Ladies. Maria Edgeworth. (Feminist Controversy in England, 1788-1810 Ser.). 1974. lib. bdg. 50.00 (ISBN 0-8240-0855-3). Garland Pub.

Letters for the International Exchange of Publications, Vol. 13. Alex Allardyce & Peter Genzel. (IFLA Publications Ser.). 148p. 1978. 17.25 (ISBN 0-89664-113-9, Pub. by K G Saur). Shoe String.

Letters from A. E. Alan Denson. (Collected Edition of the Writings of G. W. Russell VII). 1980. text ed. write for info. (ISBN 0-391-01139-1). Humanities.

Letters from a "Modernist" The Letters from George Tyrrell to Wilfrid Ward, 1893-1908. Ed. by Mary J. Weaver. LC 80-28372. 230p. 1981. 30.00 (ISBN 0-915762-12-9). Patmos Pr.

Letters from a Roman Catholic. Carolynne Simms. 1976. pap. 3.00. Am Atheist.

Letters from Africa, 1914 to 1931. Isak Dinesen. Ed. by Frans Lasson. Tr. by Anne Born. LC 80-25856. 1981. 25.00 (ISBN 0-226-15309-6). U of Chicago Pr.

Letters from Alabama, 1817-1822. Anne N. Royall. Ed. by Lucille Griffith. LC 70-76584. (Southern Historical Ser: Vol. 14). 233p. 1969. 11.50 o.p. (ISBN 0-8173-5219-8). U of Ala Pr.

Letters from an American Farmer. J. Hector De Crevecoeur. Repr. of 1782 ed. 8.00 (ISBN 0-8446-1139-5). Peter Smith.

Letters from Bedford Park: A Selection from the Correspondence of John Butler Yeats, 1890-1901. J. B. Yeats. Ed. by William M. Murphy. 77p. (Hand printed limited ed). 1972. text ed. 13.00x (ISBN 0-391-01593-1). Humanities.

Letters from California, 1846-1847. William R. Garner. Ed. by Donald M. Craig. LC 71-124736. (Illus.). 1970. 17.50 (ISBN 0-520-01565-7). U of Cal Pr.

Letters from Carrie. Janet Harder. (Illus.). 152p. (gr. 6 up). 1980. 10.95 (ISBN 0-932052-23-1). North Country.

Letters from England. Karel Capek. Tr. by Paul Selver. 192p. 1980. Repr. of 1926 ed. lib. bdg. 25.00 (ISBN 0-8495-0952-1). Arden Lib.

Letters from Erik Benzelius the Younger from Learned Foreigners, 2 vols. Ed. by Alvar Erikson. Orig. Title: Acta Regiae Societatis Scientarium et Literarum. (Orig.). 1980. 31.00. Vol. 1, 1697-1722. Vol. 2, 1723-1743 (ISBN 91-85252-22-0). Humanities.

Letters from Illinois. Morris Birkbeck. LC 68-8685. (American Scene Ser). 1970. Repr. of 1818 ed. lib. bdg. 19.50 (ISBN 0-306-71170-2). Da Capo.

Letters from India, Describing a Journey in the British Dominions of India, Tibet, Lahore & Cashmere, During the Years 1828-31, 2 vols. Victor Jacquemont. (Oxford in Asia Historical Reprints). (Illus.). 1976. 39.95x (ISBN 0-19-577216-4). Oxford U Pr.

Letters from Ring. Ring Lardner. Ed. by Clifford M. Caruthers. 1979. 10.95 (ISBN 0-911938-08-7); pap. 6.95 (ISBN 0-911938-09-5). Walden Pr.

Letters from Rome on the Council, by Quirinus, 2 vols in 1. Johann J. Von Dollinger. LC 78-127193. (Europe 1815-1945 Ser). 856p. 1973. Repr. of 1870 ed. lib. bdg. 75.00 (ISBN 0-306-70040-9). Da Capo.

Letters from Russia, 1919. P. D. Ouspensky. 1978. pap. 5.06 (ISBN 0-7100-0077-4). Routledge & Kegan.

Letters from Siberia & Other Poems. Roger Mitchell. LC 79-151102. (Illus.). 80p. 1970. 5.00 (ISBN 0-685-23806-7, Pub. by New Rivers Pr); signed ed. 10.00 (ISBN 0-685-23807-5); pap. 2.50 (ISBN 0-685-23808-3). SBD.

Letters from Spain. Karel Capek. 192p. 1980. Repr. of 1931 ed. lib. bdg. 25.00 (ISBN 0-8495-0999-8). Arden Lib.

Letters from Sunnyside & Spain. Washington Irving. Ed. by S. T. Williams. 1928. 13.50x (ISBN 0-685-89761-3). Elliots Bks.

Letters from the Country. Carol Bly. LC 80-8194. 192p. 1981. 9.95 (ISBN 0-06-010357-4, HarpT). Har-Row.

Letters from the Desert. Carlo Carretto. 1976. pap. 1.50 (ISBN 0-89129-061-3). Jove Pubns.

Letters from the Field: Nineteen Twenty-Five to Nineteen Seventy-Five. Margaret Mead. Ed. by Ruth N. Anshen. LC 73-4110. (World Perspectives Ser.). (Illus.). 1978. 13.95 o.s.i. (ISBN 0-06-012961-1, HarpT). Har-Row.

Letters from the Frontiers Written During a Period of Thirty Years Service in the Army of the United States. George A. McCall. LC 74-22038. (Bicentennial Floridiana Facsimile & Reprint Ser.). 1974. Reprint of 1868 ed. 13.50 (ISBN 0-8130-0374-1). U Presses Fla.

Letters from the Great Blasket. Eibhlis Ni Shuilleabhain. (Illus.). 1978. pap. 3.95 (ISBN 0-85342-526-4). Irish Bk Ctr.

Letters from the Great Turke. I. Ahmad. LC 72-164. (English Experience Ser.: No. 292). 16p. Repr. of 1606 ed. 7.00 (ISBN 90-221-0292-0). Walter J Johnson.

Letters from the Living to the Living, Vol. 7. LC 78-170511. (Novel in England, 1700-1775). lib. bdg. 50.00 (ISBN 0-8240-0519-8). Garland Pub.

Letters from the Marchioness De M to the Count De R, Vol. 60. Claude P. Crebillon. LC 72-170590. (Novel in England, 1700-1775). lib. bdg. 50.00 (ISBN 0-8240-0572-4). Garland Pub.

Letters from the Underworld: The Gentle Maiden & the Landlady. Fyodor M. Dostoyevsky. 1979. pap. 2.95 (Evman). Dutton.

Letters from the West. James Hall. LC 67-10123. 1967. Repr. of 1828 ed. 41.00x (ISBN 0-8201-1024-8). Schol Facsimiles.

Letters Home & Further Indiscretions. Francis Colburn. 96p. 1978. 10.00 (ISBN 0-933050-00-3); pap. 6.95 (ISBN 0-933050-01-1). New Eng Pr VT.

Letters in Primitive Christianity. William G. Doty. Ed. by Dan O. Via, Jr. LC 72-87058. (Guides to Biblical Scholarship: New Testament Ser.). 96p. 1973. pap. 3.25 (ISBN 0-8006-0170-X, 1-170). Fortress.

Letters of A. E. Housman. Henry Maas. 488p. 1980. text ed. 14.50x (ISBN 0-246-64007-3). Humanities.

Letters of A. E. Housman. Henry Maas. 1979. 15.95x (ISBN 0-8464-0090-1). Beekman Pubs.

Letters of A. W. Pink. A. W. Pink. 1978. pap. 2.50 (ISBN 0-85151-262-3). Banner of Truth.

Letters of a Westchester Farmer, 1774-1775. Samuel Seabury. Ed. by Clarence H. Vance. LC 70-103943. (Era of the American Revolution Ser). 1970. Repr. of 1930 ed. lib. bdg. 22.50 (ISBN 0-306-71868-5). Da Capo.

Letters of a Woman Homesteader. Elinore P. Stewart. LC 61-16191. 1961. pap. 3.50 (ISBN 0-8032-5193-9, BB 115, Bison). U of Nebr Pr.

Letters of Aldous Huxley. Aldous Huxley. Ed. by Grover Smith. LC 69-15263. 1970. 15.00 o.s.i. (ISBN 0-06-013937-4, HarpT). Har-Row.

Letters of Anton Chekhov. Ed. by Simon Karlinsky. Tr. by Michael H. Heim from Rus. (Illus.). 512p. 1973. 20.00 o.s.i. (ISBN 0-06-012263-3, HarpT). Har-Row.

Letters of Apollonius of Tyana: A Critical Text with Prolegomena, Translation & Commentary. Robert J. Penella. 146p. 1980. text ed. 25.25x (ISBN 90-04-05972-5). Humanities.

Letters of Bliss Carman. Ed. by H. Pearson Gundy. (Illus.). 500p. 1981. 55.00 (ISBN 0-7735-0364-1). McGill-Queens U Pr.

Letters of Brigham Young to His Sons. Dean C. Jessee. LC 74-80041. (Mormon Heritage Ser., Vol. 1). 1974. 10.95 o.p. (ISBN 0-87747-522-9). Deseret Bk.

Letters of Brunswick & Hessian Officers During the American Revolution. Ed. by William L. Stone. LC 76-112706. (Era of the American Revolution). 1970. Repr. of 1891 ed. lib. bdg. 32.50 (ISBN 0-306-71919-3). Da Capo.

Letters of Charles & Mary Lamb, 3 vols. Ed. by Edwin W. Marns, Jr. 40.00 ea. Vol. I, 1975 (ISBN 0-8014-0930-6). Vol. II-1976 (ISBN 0-8014-0977-2). Vol. III-1978 (ISBN 0-8014-1129-7). Cornell U Pr.

Letters of Charles Dickens: The Pilgrim Edition, Vol. 3, 1842-1843. Charles Dickens. Ed. by Madeline House et al. 657p. 1974. text ed. 55.00x (ISBN 0-19-812474-0). Oxford U Pr.

Letters of Charles O'connor of Belanagare, Seventeen Seventy-Two to Seventeen Ninety, Vol. II. Robert E. Ward & Catherine C. Ward. LC 80-11602. (Sponsor Ser.). 341p. 1980. 24.75 (ISBN 0-8357-0535-8, SS-00145, Pub. by Monograph). Univ Microfilms.

Letters of Cicero: A Selection in Translations. Ed. & tr. by L. P. Wilkinson. 1966. text ed. 4.50x (ISBN 0-09-078690-4, Hutchinson U Lib). Humanities.

Letters of Claudio Monteverdi. Denis Stevens. LC 80-66219. 432p. 1980. 45.00 (ISBN 0-521-23591-X). Cambridge U Pr.

Letters of D. H. Lawrence, Vol. 1. Ed. by J. T. Boulton. LC 78-7531. (Illus.). 1979. 39.50 (ISBN 0-521-22147-1). Cambridge U Pr.

Letters of Dante Gabriel Rossetti. Dante G. Rossetti. Ed. by O. Doughty & J. R. Wahl. 1965-67. Vols. 3 & 4. 75.00x (ISBN 0-19-811462-1). Oxford U Pr.

Letters of E.B. White. E.B. White. Incl. Essays of E.B. White. 1979. Box Set. pap. 12.95 o.p. (ISBN 0-06-090736-3, CN 736, CN). Har-Row.

Letters of Edward Fitzgerald. Edward Fitzgerald. Ed. by J. M. Cohen. LC 60-9249. (Centaur Classics Ser.). 1960. 7.95x o.p. (ISBN 0-8093-0028-1). S Ill U Pr.

Letters of Evelyn Waugh. Evelyn Waugh. Ed. by Mark Amory. LC 80-17818. 684p. 1980. 25.00 (ISBN 0-89919-021-9). Ticknor & Fields.

Letters of F. Scott Fitzgerald. F. Scott Fitzgerald. 1975. 12.50 o.p. (ISBN 0-684-10157-2, ScribT). Scribner.

Letters of F. Scott Fitzgerald. F. Scott Fitzgerald. (Hudson River Edition Ser.). 1981. write for info. (ISBN 0-684-16476-0, ScribT). Scribner.

Letters of Four Seasons. Daisaku Ikeda & Yasushi Inoue. Tr. by Richard L. Gage. LC 79-91521. 112p. 1980. 10.95 (ISBN 0-87011-413-1). Kodansha.

Letters of George Catlin & His Family: A Chronicle of the American West. Ed. by Marjorie C. Roehm. 1966. 27.50x (ISBN 0-520-01078-7). U of Cal Pr.

Letters of George Gissing to Eduard Bertz: 1887-1903. George R. Gissing. Ed. by Arthur C. Young. LC 80-12936. xl, 337p. 1980. Repr. of 1961 ed. lib. bdg. 28.25x (ISBN 0-313-22454-4, GILE). Greenwood.

Letters of George Meredith, 3 Vols. George Meredith. Ed. by C. L. Cline. 1970. 98.00x (ISBN 0-19-811473-7). Oxford U Pr.

Letters of George Moore (Eighteen Fifty-Two to Nineteen Thirty-Three) to His Brother Col. M. Moore National Library of Ireland Mss 2646-7. George Moore. 1980. text ed. write for info. (ISBN 0-391-01200-2). Humanities.

Letters of Grover Cleveland. Ed. by Allan Nevins. LC 70-123752. (American Public Figures Ser). 1970. Repr. of 1933 ed. lib. bdg. 59.50 (ISBN 0-306-71982-7). Da Capo.

Letters of H. L. Mencken. Ed. by Guy J. Forgue. 506p. Date not set. price not set (ISBN 0-930350-17-0); pap. price not set (ISBN 0-930350-18-9). NE U Pr.

Letters of Hart Crane & His Family. Thomas S. Lewis. LC 73-21675. 704p. 1974. 30.00 (ISBN 0-231-03740-6). Columbia U Pr.

Letters of Helena Roerich, Vol. I. 1979. Repr. of 1954 ed. flexible cover 12.00 (ISBN 0-933574-14-2). Agni Yoga Soc.

Letters of Helena Roerich, Vol. II. 1940. flexible cover 12.00 (ISBN 0-933574-15-0). Agni Yoga Soc.

Letters of Horatio Greenough. Ed. by Frances Greenough. LC 70-96437. (Library of American Art Ser.). 1970. Repr. of 1887 ed. lib. bdg. 29.50 (ISBN 0-306-71828-6). Da Capo.

Letters of Horatio Greenough, American Sculptor. Ed. by Nathalia Wright. LC 77-176417. (Illus.). 516p. 1972. 37.50x (ISBN 0-299-06070-5). U of Wis Pr.

Letters of Jan Swammerdam to Melchisedec Thevenot, with English Translation & a Biographical Sketch. G. A. Lindeboom. 202p. 1975. text ed. 47.50 (ISBN 90-265-0222-2, Pub. by Swets Pub Serv Holland). Swets North Am.

Letters of John. J. W. Roberts. Ed. by Everett Ferguson. (Living Word New Testament Commentary Ser.: Vol. 18). 1968. 7.95 (ISBN 0-8344-0033-2). Sweet.

Letters of John & Jude. W. Donald Reeder. (Teach Yourself the Bible Ser). 1965. pap. 1.75 (ISBN 0-8024-4674-4). Moody.

Letters of John Calvin. John Calvin. 261p. 1980. pap. 4.95 (ISBN 0-85151-323-9). Banner of Truth.

Letters of John Davenport, Puritan Divine. John Davenport. Ed. by Isabel M. Calder. 1937. 47.50x (ISBN 0-685-69794-0). Elliots Bks.

Letters of John Hay & Extracts from His Diary, 3 Vols. John Hay. LC 71-93245. 1969. Repr. of 1908 ed. Set. text ed. 50.00 (ISBN 0-87752-051-8). Gordian.

Letters of John Newton. John Newton. 1976. pap. 2.45 (ISBN 0-85151-120-1). Banner of Truth.

Letters of John Randolph & John Brockenbrough. Ed. by Kenneth P. Shorey. (Illus.). 1978. write for info o.p. (ISBN 0-916624-25-0). Troy State Univ.

Letters of John Ruskin to Bernard Quaritch. John Ruskin. 125p. 1980. Repr. of 1938 ed. lib. bdg. 25.00 (ISBN 0-8495-4637-0). Arden Lib.

Letters of John Wilmot, Earl of Rochester. John Wilmot. Ed. by Jeremy Treglown. LC 80-20592. 1980. lib. bdg. 26.00x (ISBN 0-226-81181-6). U of Chicago Pr.

Letters of Katherine Mansfield, 2 vols. in 1. Katherine Mansfield. Ed. by John M. Murry. LC 74-16016. 528p. 1975. Repr. of 1929 ed. 27.50 (ISBN 0-86527-271-9). Fertig.

Letters of Lanfranc, Archbishop of Canterbury. Lanfranc. Ed. by Helen Clover & Margaret Gibson. (Oxford Medieval Texts Ser.). (Illus.). 218p. 1979. text ed. 47.00x (ISBN 0-19-822235-1). Oxford U Pr.

Letters of Lewis Carroll, 2 vols. Lewis Carroll. Ed. by Morton H. Cohen & Roger L. Green. (Illus.). 1979. Set. 65.00 (ISBN 0-19-520090-X). Oxford U Pr.

Letters of Long Ago. Agnes J. Reid. (Utah, the Mormons & the West Ser.: No. 2). 93p. 1973. 9.50 (ISBN 0-87480-158-3, Tanner). U of Utah Pr.

Letters of Marsilio Ficino, Vol. 3, Bk. 4. Marsilio Ficino. 160p. 1980. 39.00x (ISBN 0-85683-045-3, Pub. by Shepheard-Walwyn England). State Mutual Bk.

Letters of P. H. Pearse. P. H. Pearse. Ed. by Seamas O'Buachalla. 528p. 1980. text ed. 31.25x (ISBN 0-391-01678-4). Humanities.

Letters of Pacificus & Helvidius. Alexander Hamilton. LC 76-41676. 1976. Repr. of 1845 ed. 20.00x (ISBN 0-8201-1279-8). Schol Facsimiles.

Letters of Paul, Hebrews & Psalms. Arthur S. Way. 468p. 1981. text ed. 12.95 (ISBN 0-8254-4016-5). Kregel.

Letters of Paul to the Ephesians, Colossians, & Philemon. Michael Weed. Ed. by Everett Ferguson. LC 79-134688. (The Living Word Commentary Ser.: Vol. 11). 1971. 7.95 (ISBN 0-8344-0055-3). Sweet.

Letters of Paul to the Thessalonians. Raymond C. Kelcy. Ed. by Everett Ferguson et al. LC 68-55947. (Living Word New Testament Commentary Ser.: Vol. 13). 1968. 7.95 (ISBN 0-8344-0017-0). Sweet.

Letters of Paul to Timothy & Titus. Carl Spain. Ed. by Everett Ferguson. LC 75-133509. (Living Word New Testament Commentary Ser.: Vol. 14). 1970. 7.95 (ISBN 0-8344-0006-5). Sweet.

Letters of Peter & Jude. Raymond C. Kelcy. Ed. by Everett Ferguson. LC 78-179612. (The Living Word New Testament Commentary Ser.: Vol. 17). 1972. 7.95 (ISBN 0-8344-0073-1). Sweet.

Letters of Randolph Bourne: A Comprehensive Edition. Eric J. Sandeen. 466p. 1981. 30.00 (ISBN 0-87875-190-4). Whitston Pub.

Letters of Richard Brinsley Sheridan, 3 Vols. Richard B. Sheridan. Ed. by Cecil Price. 1966. 79.00x (ISBN 0-19-811438-9). Oxford U Pr.

Letters of Richard Henry Lee, 2 Vols. Ed. by James C. Ballagh. LC 79-107678. (Era of the American Revolution Ser). 1970. Repr. of 1914 ed. 85.00 (ISBN 0-306-71894-4). Da Capo.

Letters of Rosa Luxemburg. Ed. by Stephen Bronner. 1979. lib. bdg. 24.00x (ISBN 0-89158-186-3); pap. text ed. 9.50 (ISBN 0-89158-188-X). Westview.

Letters of St. Isidore of Seville: Isidore of Seville. 2nd ed. Ed. by Gordon B. Ford, Jr. LC 71-498089. 1970. 15.00 o.p. (ISBN 0-916760-03-0). Medieval Latin.

Letters of Saint Oliver Plunkett, Sixteen Twenty-Five to Sixteen Eighty-One: Archbishop of Armagh & Primate of All Ireland. Ed. by John Hanly. 1979. text ed. 75.00x (ISBN 0-391-01120-0, Dolmen Pr). Humanities.

Letters of Samuel Rutherford. Frank Gaebelein. 480p. 1980. pap. 8.95 (ISBN 0-8024-4673-6). Moody.

Letters of Samuel Rutherford. Samuel Rutherford. 1973. pap. 2.45 (ISBN 0-85151-163-5). Banner of Truth.

Letters of Sean O'Casey: 1910-1941, Vol. 1. Ed. by David Krause. (Illus.). 800p. 1975. 60.00 (ISBN 0-02-566660-6). Macmillan.

Letters of Shahcoolen: A Hindu Residing in Philadelphia. Benjamin Silliman. LC 62-7013. 1962. Repr. of 1802 ed. 20.00x (ISBN 0-8201-1041-8). Schol Facsimiles.

Letters of Sidney & Beatrice Webb. Ed. by M. MacKenzie. Incl. Vol. 1.; Vol. 2. (ISBN 0-685-85982-7); Vol. 3.. LC 77-1665. 1978. 69.95 ea.; Set. 185.00 (ISBN 0-521-22015-7). Cambridge U Pr.

Letters of Swami Vivekananda. 2nd ed. Swami Vivekananda. 7.50 o.s.i. (ISBN 0-87481-093-0); pap. 6.95 o.s.i. (ISBN 0-87481-192-9). Vedanta Pr.

Letters of the Third Viscount Palmerston to Laurence & Elizabeth Sulivan: 1804-1863. Ed. by Kenneth Bourne. (Royal Historical Society: Camden Society Fourth Ser.: Vol. 23). 350p. 1979. 20.00x (ISBN 0-8476-3306-3). Rowman.

Letters of Theodore Dwight Weld, Angelina Grimke Weld, & Sarah Grimke. Ed. by Gilbert H. Barnes & Dwight L. Dumond. LC 77-121103. (American Public Figures Ser). 1970. Repr. of 1934 ed. lib. bdg. 75.00 (ISBN 0-306-71981-9). Da Capo.

Letters of Thomas Arnold the Younger: Eighteen Fifty to Nineteen Hundred. Thomas Arnold. Ed. by James Bertram. 336p. 1980. 38.00x (ISBN 0-19-647980-0). Oxford U Pr.

Letters of Thomas Babington Macaulay, Vol. 5. Ed. by T. Pinney. LC 73-75860. (Illus.). 425p. Date not set. 85.00 (ISBN 0-521-22749-6). Cambridge U Pr.

Letters of Thomas Babington Macaulay, Vol. 6. Ed. by T. Pinney. LC 73-75860. (Illus.). 350p. Date not set. price not set (ISBN 0-521-22750-X). Cambridge U Pr.

Letters of Vincent Van Gogh. Ed. by Mark Roskill. LC 63-13089. 1963. pap. 4.95 (ISBN 0-689-70167-5). Atheneum.

Letters of Virginia Woolf: Nineteen Thirty-Six to Nineteen Forty-One, Vol. VI. Woolf. Ed. by Nigel Nicholson & Joanne Trautmann. LC 75-25538. 576p. 1980. 19.95 (ISBN 0-15-150929-8). HarBraceJ.

Letters of Warren Akin, Confederate Congressman. Warren Akin. Ed. by Bell I. Wiley. LC 59-15538. 151p. 1959. 10.00 (ISBN 0-8203-0116-7). U of Ga Pr.

Letters of William Blake with Related Documents. 3rd ed. Ed. by Geoffrey Keynes & William Blake. (Illus.). 272p. 1980. 55.00x (ISBN 0-19-812654-9). Oxford U Pr.

Letters of William Cullen Bryant: Vol. III. Ed. by William C. Bryant, II & Thomas G. Voss. LC 74-27169. (Illus.). 500p. 1981. 35.00 (ISBN 0-8232-0993-8). Fordham.

Letters of William Hazlitt. Ed. by Herschel M. Sikes et al. LC 78-54079. 1978. cOBE 22.50x (ISBN 0-8147-4986-0); pap. 9.00x cobe (ISBN 0-8147-4987-9). NYU Pr.

Letters on an Elk Hunt by a Woman Homesteader. Elinore P. Stewart. LC 79-13840. (Illus.). 1978. 10.95x (ISBN 0-8032-4112-7); pap. 3.75 (ISBN 0-8032-9112-4, BB 703, Bison). U of Nebr Pr.

Letters on Education, with Observations on Religious & Metaphysical Subjects. Catharine Macaulay. (Feminist Controversy in England, 1788-1810 Ser.). 1974. lib. bdg. 50.00 (ISBN 0-8240-0872-3). Garland Pub.

Letters on Probability. Laszlo Vekerdi. Tr. by Alfred Renyi from Hung. LC 74-179559. (Waynebooks Ser: No. 33). 112p. (Eng.). 1973. pap. 3.95x (ISBN 0-8143-1465-1). Wayne St U Pr.

Letters on the Intellectual & Moral Character of Women. William Duff. (Feminist Controversy in England, 1788-1810 Ser.). 1974. lib. bdg. 50.00 (ISBN 0-8240-0854-5). Garland Pub.

Letters, Principal Doctrines & Vatican Sayings. Epicurus. Tr. by Russell Geer. LC 61-18059. (Orig.). 5.50 o.p. (ISBN 0-672-51060-X); pap. 3.95 (ISBN 0-672-60353-5, LLA141). Bobbs.

Letters (Selwyn Image Letters) Ed. by A. H. Mackmurdo. LC 76-17780. (Aesthetic Movement & the Arts & Crafts Movement Ser.: Vol. 37). 1977. Repr. of 1932 ed. lib. bdg. 44.00 (ISBN 0-8240-2486-9). Garland Pub.

Letters Slate Cut. David Kindersley & Lida L. Cardozo. (Illus.). 96p. 1981. pap. 9.95 (ISBN 0-8008-4741-5, Pentalic). Taplinger.

Letters That Have Helped Me. new ed. William Q. Judge. Ed. & intro. by Jasper Niemand. (Illus.). x, 300p. 1946. 6.00 (ISBN 0-938998-08-0). Theosophy.

Letters to a New Elder: The Melchizedek Priesthood, Its Duty Fulfillment. Robb Russon. pap. 2.95 (ISBN 0-89036-144-4). Hawkes Pub Inc.

Letters to a Young Lady, in Which the Duties & Character of Women Are Considered, 3 vols. Jane West. Ed. by Gina Luria. (Feminist Controversy in England, 1788-1810 Ser.). 1974. lib. bdg. 50.00 ea. (ISBN 0-8240-0885-5). Garland Pub.

Letters to an Actress: The Story of Turgenev & Savina. Ed. by Nora Gottlieb & Raymond Chapman. LC 73-92898. 155p. 1973. 8.95 (ISBN 0-8214-0146-7). Ohio U Pr.

Letters to & from Caesar Rodney. George H. Ryden. LC 75-107417. (Era of the American Revolution Ser). 1970. Repr. of 1933 ed. lib. bdg. 49.50 (ISBN 0-306-71881-2). Da Capo.

Letters to Chris. Joan Tate. pap. text ed. 1.95x o.p. (ISBN 0-435-11887-0). Heinemann Ed.

Letters to Christopher: Stephen Spender's Letters to Christopher Isherwood 1929-1939, with "The Line of the Branch--Two Thirties Journals ". Stephen Spender. Ed. by Lee Bartlett. (Illus.). 230p. (Orig.). 1980. 14.00 (ISBN 0-87685-470-6); pap. 7.50 (ISBN 0-87685-476-5). Black Sparrow.

Letters to Elderly Alcoholics. Cecil Carle. 1980. pap. 3.95. Hazelden.

Letters to Emilia: Record of a Friendship. Helena Modjeska. Ed. by Marion M. Coleman. Tr. by Michael Kwapiszewski. (Illus.). 1967. pap. 2.00 (ISBN 0-910366-05-5). Alliance Coll.

Letters to Friend & Foe. Baruch Spinoza. LC 66-22242. 1967. 2.75 o.p. (ISBN 0-8022-1620-X). Philos Lib.

Letters to His Family: An Autobiography. Piotr I. Tchaikovsky. Ed. by Percy M. Young. Tr. by Galina Von Meck. LC 80-6162. 576p. 1981. 25.00 (ISBN 0-8128-2802-X). Stein & Day.

Letters to His Son & Others. Chesterfield. 1957. 12.95x (ISBN 0-460-00823-4, Evman). Dutton.

Letters to His Wife. Ferruccio Busoni. Tr. by Rosamond Ley. LC 74-34378. (Music Reprint Ser). (Illus.). 319p. 1975. Repr. of 1938 ed. lib. bdg. 25.00 (ISBN 0-306-70732-2). Da Capo.

Letters to John Theobald. Ezra Pound. Ed. by Donald Pearce & Herbert Schneidau. (Illus.). 196p. 1981. 20.00 (ISBN 0-933806-02-7). Black Swan CT.

Letters to Karen: On Keeping Love in Marriage. Charlie W. Shedd. (YA) (gr. 9 up). 1965. 7.95 (ISBN 0-687-21568-4). Abingdon.

Letters to Karen: On Keeping Love in Marriage. Charlie W. Shedd. 1968. pap. 1.25 (ISBN 0-380-00207-8, 30148). Avon.

Letters to Malcolm: Chiefly on Prayer. C. S. Lewis. LC 64-11536. 124p. 1973. pap. 2.50 (ISBN 0-15-650880-X, HB250, Harv). HarBraceJ.

Letters to My Daughters. Judith Minty. 24p. (Orig.). 1981. pap. 4.00 (ISBN 0-932412-03-3). Mayapple Pr.

Letters to Philip. Charlie W. Shedd. 1976. pap. 1.50 (ISBN 0-89129-117-2). Jove Pubns.

Letters to Philip. Charlie W. Shedd. (Orig.). pap. 1.95 (ISBN 0-515-05827-0). Jove Pubns.

Letters to Serena. John Toland. Ed. by Rene Wellek. LC 75-11259. (British Philosophers & Theologians of the 17th & 18th Centuries: Vol. 58). 1977. Repr. of 1704 ed. lib. bdg. 42.00 (ISBN 0-8240-1809-5). Garland Pub.

Letters to Teresa. Samuel Fisk. 91p. 1973. pap. 1.95 (ISBN 0-87398-516-8, Pub. by Bibl Evang Pr). Sword of Lord.

Letters to the Happy Hooker. Ed. by Xaviera Hollander. (Orig.). 1973. pap. 2.50 (ISBN 0-446-91491-6). Warner Bks.

Letters to the Modern Church. Wayne Hoffman. LC 79-88401. 1979. pap. 2.75 (ISBN 0-933350-23-6). Morse Pr.

Letters to the Pope. Mary E. Twyman. 158p. 1981. 6.95 (ISBN 0-934400-15-6). Landmark Bks.

Letters to the Thessalonians. Margaret Fromer & Sharrel Keyes. LC 75-33441. (Fisherman Bible Studyguides). 1975. pap. 1.25 saddle-stich (ISBN 0-87788-489-7). Shaw Pubs.

Letters to Thomas & Adele Seltzer. D. H. Lawrence. Ed. by Gerald M. Lacy. (Illus.). 290p. (Orig.). 1976. 14.00 (ISBN 0-87685-225-8); pap. 6.00 (ISBN 0-87685-224-X). Black Sparrow.

Letters to Timothy. Gary Leggett. LC 80-82830. (Radiant Life Ser.). 128p. 1981. 1.95 (ISBN 0-88243-877-8, 02-0877). Gospel Pub.

Letters to W. B. Yeats, 2 vols. Ed. by Richard J. Finneran et al. LC 77-5645. 1977. 50.00x set (ISBN 0-685-81542-0). Vol. 1 (ISBN 0-231-04424-0). Vol. 2 (ISBN 0-231-04425-9). Columbia U Pr.

Letters to Yesenin. Jim Harrison. (Orig.). pap. 2.45 o.s.i. (ISBN 0-912090-32-4). Sumac Mich.

Letters Upon the Poetry & Music of the Italian Opera: Addressed to a Friend. John Brown. LC 80-2261. 1981. Repr. of 1789 ed. 22.50 (ISBN 0-404-18814-1). AMS Pr.

Letters, Vols. XV-XVI, Vols. Xv-xvi. 1980. 50.00 (ISBN 0-686-65204-5). Ohio St U Pr.

Letters Written by a Peruvian Princess, 1748. Francoise Graffigny. Ed. by Michael F. Shugrue. LC 74-16070. (Novel in England, 1700-1775 Ser.). 1974. lib. bdg. 50.00 (ISBN 0-8240-1121-X). Garland Pub.

Letters Written During a Short Residence in Sweden, Norway, & Denmark. Mary Wollstonecraft. Ed. by Carol H. Poston. LC 75-38056. (Illus.). xxiv, 202p. 1976. 11.50x (ISBN 0-8032-0862-6); pap. 4.95 (ISBN 0-8032-5832-1, BB 613, Bison). U of Nebr Pr.

Letters: 165-203. St. Augustine. (Fathers of the Church Ser.: Vol. 30). 21.00 (ISBN 0-8132-0030-X). Cath U Pr.

Letters: 204-272. St. Augustine. (Fathers of the Church Ser.: Vol. 32). 16.00 (ISBN 0-8132-0032-6). Cath U Pr.

Letting Love in. James Scroggs. LC 77-27268. 1978. 10.95 (ISBN 0-13-531566-2, Spec); pap. 5.95 (ISBN 0-13-531558-1, Spec). P-H.

Lettres Inedites a Henry Ceard. Emile Zola. Ed. by Albert J. Salvan. LC 59-10016. (Brown University Studies: No. 22). 174p. (Orig., Fr.). 1959. pap. 4.00x (ISBN 0-87057-060-9). Univ Pr of New England.

Lettres Philosophiques. rev. ed. Francois Voltaire. Ed. by F. A. Taylor. (French Texts Ser.). 1976. pap. text ed. 9.95x (ISBN 0-631-00450-5, Pub. by Basil Blackwell). Biblio Dist.

Letty. Clare Darcy. 1981. pap. price not set (ISBN 0-451-09810-2, Signet Bks). NAL.

Letty. Clare Darcy. (Large Print Bks.). 1980. lib. bdg. 12.95 (ISBN 0-8161-3127-9). G K Hall.

Letzte Sommer. Ricarda Huch. Ed. by Dieter Cunz. (Ger). 1963. pap. 2.95x (ISBN 0-393-09603-3, NortonC). Norton.

Leukemia & Lymphoma in the Nervous System. Carl Pochedly. (Illus.). 248p. 1977. 30.00 (ISBN 0-685-73596-6). C C Thomas.

Leukemia in Childhood. Andre D. Lascari. (Illus.). 504p. 1973. 22.75 (ISBN 0-398-02810-9). C C Thomas.

Leukemic Cell. Daniel Catovsky. (Methods in Haematology). (Illus.). 230p. 1981. lib. bdg. 35.00 (ISBN 0-443-01911-8). Churchill.

Leukocyte Chemotaxis: Methods, Physiology, & Clinical Implications. Ed. by John I. Gallin & Paul G. Quie. LC 76-58053. 1978. 42.50 (ISBN 0-89004-198-9). Raven.

Leukocyte Function. Ed. by Martin Cline. (Methods in Hematology). (Illus.). 224p. 1981. lib. bdg. 25.00 (ISBN 0-686-28872-6). Churchill.

Leukozytenseparation und Transfusion. V. Kretschmer. (Beitraege Zu Infusionstherapie und Klinische Ernaehrung Ser.: Vol. 6). (Illus.). viii, 200p. 1981. 18.00 (ISBN 3-8055-1946-X). S Karger.

Level One Mathematics: For the College Boards. Barnett Rich. (gr. 11-12). 1970. pap. text ed. 7.75 (ISBN 0-87720-231-1). AMSCO Sch.

Level Three: A Black Philosophy Reader. Ed. by Charles A. Frye. LC 80-5801. 217p. 1980. lib. bdg. 18.00 (ISBN 0-8191-1241-0); pap. text ed. 9.75 (ISBN 0-8191-1242-9). U Pr of Amer.

Levellers & the English Revolution. Henry Holorenshaw. LC 73-80559. 1971. Repr. 12.50 (ISBN 0-86527-116-X). Fertig.

Levels of Knowing & Existence: Studies in General Semantics. Harry L. Weinberg. LC 73-80740. 1973. pap. 5.50x (ISBN 0-910780-07-2). Inst Gen Semantics.

Levels of Schizophrenia. Albert E. Scheflen. LC 80-21030. 200p. 1981. 17.50 (ISBN 0-87630-252-5). Brunner-Mazel.

Lever. rev. ed. Harlan Wade. LC 78-21175. (Book About Ser.). (Illus.). (gr. k-3). 1979. PLB 6.60 o.p. (ISBN 0-8172-1538-7). Raintree Pubs.

Leveraged & Single-Investor Leasing Nineteen Eighty Course Handbook. (Commercial Law & Practice Course Handbook Ser., 1979-80: Vol. 231). 1980. pap. 25.00 (ISBN 0-685-59691-5, A4-3074). PLI.

Leviathan. John G. Davis. 1977. pap. 1.95 o.p. (ISBN 0-449-23339-1, Crest). Fawcett.

Leviathan. Hugh Fox. 1981. pap. 5.00 (ISBN 0-914140-10-8). Carpenter Pr.

Leviathan, 2 Pts. Thomas Hobbes. Ed. by Herbert W. Schneider. LC 58-9957. 1958. Set. pap. 6.50 (ISBN 0-672-60246-6, LLA69). Bobbs.

Leviathan. Thomas Hobbes. 1953. 6.00x (ISBN 0-460-00691-6, Evman); pap. 5.95 (ISBN 0-460-01691-1). Dutton.

Leviathan. Robert J. Shea & Anton R. Wilson. (Illuminatus 3). 256p. 1975. pap. 1.95 o.s.i. (ISBN 0-440-14742-5). Dell.

Levier. Harlan Wade. Tr. by Claude Potvin & Rose-Ella Potvin. (Book About Ser.). Orig. Title: Lever. (Illus., Fr.). (gr. k-3). 1979. PLB 7.30 (ISBN 0-8172-1464-X). Raintree Pubs.

Levi's Denim Art Contest: Catalogue of Winners. Richard Owens & Baron Wolman. (Illus.). 1974. pap. 3.00 o.p. (ISBN 0-916290-00-X). Squarebooks.

Levitation: Five Fictions. Cynthia Ozick. LC 80-7997. 256p. 1981. cancelled (ISBN 0-394-94563-8). Knopf.

Leviticus. Andrew Bonar. (Banner of Truth Geneva Series Commentaries). 1978. 14.95 (ISBN 0-85151-086-8). Banner of Truth.

Leviticus. Irving L. Jensen. (Bible Self Study Ser.). 1970. pap. 2.25 (ISBN 0-8024-1003-0). Moody.

Leviticus: An Introduction & Commentary. R. K. Harrison & D. J. Wiseman. LC 80-7985. (Tyndale Old Testament Commentaries Ser.). 180p. 1980. 8.95 (ISBN 0-87784-890-4). Inter-Varsity.

Levkas Man. Hammond Innes. (YA) 1971. 6.95 o.p. (ISBN 0-394-44240-7). Knopf.

Levy Caper. David Shaw. LC 74-10897. 324p. 1974. 6.95 o.s.i. (ISBN 0-02-610010-X). Macmillan.

Lew Wallace: Militant Romantic. Robert E. Morsberger & Katherine M. Morsberger. (Illus.). 384p. 1980. 17.95 (ISBN 0-07-043305-4). McGraw.

Lewis & Clark. Matthew G. Grant. LC 73-14582. 1974. PLB 5.95 (ISBN 0-87191-277-5). Creative Ed.

Lewis & Clark Country. Archie Satterfield. LC 78-8324. (Illus.). 144p. 1978. 27.50 (ISBN 0-915796-12-0). Beautiful Am.

Lewis & Clark Expedition: 1804-1806. Dan Lacy. LC 73-12088. (Focus Bks). (Illus.). 72p. (gr. 7 up). 1974. PLB 4.47 o.p. (ISBN 0-531-01048-1). Watts.

Lewis Carroll. Richard Kelly. (English Authors Ser.: No. 212). 1977. lib. bdg. 10.95 (ISBN 0-8057-6681-2). Twayne.

Lewis Carroll: An Annotated International Bibliography, 1960-1977. Edward Guillano. LC 80-13975. 1981. 15.00x (ISBN 0-8139-0862-0). U Pr of Va.

Lewis Carroll & the Kitchins. Lewis Carroll, pseud. Tr. by Morton N. Cohen. LC 79-92406. (Carroll Studies: No. 4). (Illus.). 80p. (Orig.). pap. 15.00 (ISBN 0-930326-04-0). Lewis Carroll Soc.

Lewis Carroll: Fragments of a Looking Glass. Jean Gattegno. Tr. by Rosemary Sheed from Fr. LC 75-23388. (Illus.). 320p. 1976. 8.95 o.s.i. (ISBN 0-690-01028-1, TYC-T). T Y Crowell.

Lewis Carroll Picture Book: A Selection from the Unpublished Writings & Drawings of Lewis Carroll, Together with Reprints from Scare & Unacknowledged Work. Charles L. Dodgson. LC 70-159931. (Tower Bks). (Illus.). 1971. Repr. of 1899 ed. 18.00 (ISBN 0-8103-3915-3). Gale.

Lewis Cass. Andrew C. McLaughlin. LC 80-24025. (American Statesmen Ser.). 390p. 1981. pap. 5.95 (ISBN 0-87754-192-2). Chelsea Hse.

Lewis Namier & Zionism. Norman Rose. 192p. 1980. 29.50x (ISBN 0-19-822621-7). Oxford U Pr.

Lewis's Pharmacology. 5th ed. James Crossland. 960p. 1981. lib. bdg. price not set; pap. text ed. 49.50 (ISBN 0-443-01173-7). Churchill.

Lex Parliamentaria; or, a Treatise of Law & Custom of the Parliaments of England. George Petyt. Ed. by David Berkowitz & Samuel Thorne. LC 77-89215. (Classics of English Legal History in the Modern Era Ser.: Vol. 126). 1979. Repr. of 1690 ed. lib. bdg. 55.00 (ISBN 0-8240-3163-6). Garland Pub.

Lex Spuriorum; or the Law Relating to Bastardy, Collected from the Common, Civil & Ecclesiastical Laws. John Brydall. LC 77-86581. (Classics of English Legal History in the Modern Era Ser.: Vol. 17). 1978. Repr. of 1703 ed. lib. bdg. 55.00 (ISBN 0-8240-3064-8). Garland Pub.

Lex Terrae. David Jenkins et al. Ed. by David S. Berkowitz & Samuel E. Thorne. LC 77-89226. (Classics of English Legal History in the Modern Era Ser.: Vol. 70). 313p. 1979. lib. bdg. 40.00 (ISBN 0-8240-3169-5). Garland Pub.

Lex Testamentaria. William Nelson. Ed. by David S. Berkowitz & Samuel E. Thorne. LC 77-89254. (Classics of English Legal History in the Modern Era Ser.: Vol. 81). 552p. 1979. lib. bdg. 40.00 (ISBN 0-8240-3180-6). Garland Pub.

Lexeconics: The Interaction of Law & Economics. Ed. by Gerald Sirkin. (Social Dimensions of Economics, CCNY Ser.: Vol. 2). 272p. 1981. lib. bdg. 17.50 (ISBN 0-89838-053-7, Pub. by Martinus Nijhoff). Kluwer Boston.

Lexical Aids for Students of New Testament Greek. 3rd ed. Bruce M. Metzger. 1969. pap. 4.95x (ISBN 0-8401-1618-7). Allenson.

Lexical Reconstruction. D. Dyen & D. F. Aberle. LC 73-92780. (Illus.). 484p. 1974. 59.50 (ISBN 0-521-20369-4). Cambridge U Pr.

Lexical Semantics. Yuri D. Apresjan. Tr. by Alexander Lehrman from Rus. (Linguistica Extranea: Studia: No. 13). 450p. 1981. 35.00 (ISBN 0-89720-039-X); pap. 22.50 (ISBN 0-89720-040-3). Karoma.

Lexico-Concordancia Del Nuevo Testamento En Griego y Espanol. George Parker. Orig. Title: Lexicon-Concordance of the New Testament in Greek & Spanish. 1000p. (Span.). Date not set. pap. price not set (ISBN 0-311-42066-4). Casa Bautista.

Lexicon Arabico-Latinum. George W. Freytag. 70.00x. Intl Bk Ctr.

Lexicon of Black English. J. L. Dillard. LC 76-30389. 1977. pap. 6.95 (ISBN 0-8164-9320-0); 12.95 o.p. (ISBN 0-8164-9309-X, Continuum). Continuum.

Lexicon of Jewish Cooking. rev. ed. Patti Shosteck. 1981. pap. 6.95 (ISBN 0-8092-5995-8). Contemp Bks.

Lexicon of Musical Invective: Critical Assaults on Composers Since Beethoven's Time. 2nd ed. Nicolas Slonimsky. LC 65-26270. 331p. 1969. pap. 7.95 (ISBN 0-295-78579-9, WP52). U of Wash Pr

Lexicon of Succulent Plants. Hermann Jacobsen. (Illus.). 1974. 37.50 (ISBN 0-7137-0652-X, Pub by Blandford Pr England). Sterling.

Lexicon to Achilles Tatius. Ed. by James N. O'Sullivan. (Unter Suchungen Zur Antiken Literatur und Gesschichte: No. 18). 442p. 1980. text ed. 124.00x (ISBN 3-11-007844-9). De Gruyter.

Lexikits. Ed. by Eleanor Dunn. (gr. k-3). 1973. 6.95x (ISBN 0-933892-04-7). Child Focus Co.

Lexikon Allergologicum. K. Wilken-Jensen. 1965. 15.00 (ISBN 0-08-011838-0). Pergamon.

Lexikon der Deutschen Konzertliteratur, 2 Vols. Theodor Muller-Reuter. LC 70-171079. (Music Ser). 1972. Repr. of 1921 ed. lib. bdg. 95.00 (ISBN 0-306-70274-6). Da Capo.

Lexikothek Bertelsmann, 25 vols. (Ger.). 1972. 1875.00 (ISBN 0-8277-3031-4). Maxwell Sci Intl.

Lexilogs. Ed. by Eleanor Dunn. (gr. k-3). 1973. 6.95x (ISBN 0-933892-05-5). Child Focus Co.

Lexington & Concord. Arthur B. Tourtellot. (Illus.). 1963. pap. 5.95 (ISBN 0-393-00194-6, Norton Lib). Norton.

Lexington, Concord & Bunker Hill. Francis Russell. LC 63-10834. (American Heritage Junior Library). (Illus.). 153p. 1963. 6.95 (ISBN 0-06-024976-5, Dist. by Har-Row). Am Heritage.

Lexique de l'anglais des affaires. new ed. Ivan De Renty. 320p. 1973. pap. 7.95 (ISBN 0-88332-247-1, 4100). Larousse.

Lexis-Dictionnaire de la Largue francaise. Ed. by Jean Dubois. 1979. 56.25 (ISBN 0-686-60644-2, 2427). Larousse.

Ley e Historia del Antiguo Testamento. Samuel Schultz. Tr. by Fernando P. Villalobos from Eng. (Curso Para Meastros Cristianos Ser.: No. 1). Orig. Title: Old Testament Survey - Law & History. (Illus.). 122p. (Span.). 1972. pap. 2.50 (ISBN 0-89922-008-8); instructor's manual 1.50 (ISBN 0-89922-009-6). Edit Caribe.

Leyendas De Guatemala. Miguel A. Asturias. (Easy Readers, C). 1978. pap. text ed. 3.75 (ISBN 0-88436-290-6). EMC.

Leyes De Movimiento De Newton. Derick Unwin. (Sp.). 1970. pap. 2.00 (ISBN 0-06-317011-6, IntlDept). Har-Row.

Leysin Version of James Elroy Flecker's Hassan. James Hogg. (Salzburg Studies in English Literature: Poetic Drama & Poetic Theory: No. 30). 142p. 1976. pap. text ed. 25.00x (ISBN 0-391-01417-X). Humanities.

LH - Releasing Hormone. Ed. by Carl Beling. (Illus.). 368p. 1979. text ed. 39.50 (ISBN 0-89352-045-4). Masson Pub.

Lhasa Apsos. Diane McCarty. (Illus.). 125p. 1979. 2.95 (ISBN 0-87666-681-0, KW-076). TFH Pubns.

Li Ho. Kuo-Ching Tu. (World Authors Ser.: No. 537). 1979. lib. bdg. 14.95 (ISBN 0-8057-6379-1). Twayne.

Li-Hung-Chang. Robert K. Douglas. (Studies in Chinese History & Civilization). 1977. Repr. of 1895 ed. 19.75 (ISBN 0-89093-110-0). U Pubns Amer.

Li Yu. Nathan K. Mao & Liu Ts'Un-Yan. (World Authors Ser.: No. 448). 1977. lib. bdg. 12.50 (ISBN 0-8057-6283-3). Twayne.

Liability Issues in Community-Based Programs: Legal Principles, Problem Areas, & Recommendations. Alan Vanbiervliet & Jan Sheldon-Wildgen. 136p. 1981. pap. text ed. 10.95 (ISBN 0-933716-08-7). P H Brookes.

Liability Issues in Community-Based Programs: Legal Principles, Problem Areas & Rdcommendations. Alan Van Bieryliet & Jan Sheldon-Wildgen. 136p. 1980. pap. 10.95 (ISBN 0-933716-08-7). P H Brookes.

Liability Risk Management for Local Governments. Ramon A. Perez. 1981. spiral bdg. 25.00 (ISBN 0-88406-148-5). GA St U Busn Pub.

Liable to Floods: Village Landscape on the Edge of Fens. J. R. Ravensdale. LC 73-80473. (Illus.). 254p. 1974. 31.95 (ISBN 0-521-20285-X). Cambridge U Pr.

Liaisons Dangereuses. Choderlos de Laclos. Tr. by P. W. Stone. (Classics Ser). 1977. pap. 2.95 (ISBN 0-14-044116-6). Penguin.

Liam O'Flaherty. Paul A. Doyle. (English Authors Ser.: No. 108). lib. bdg. 10.95 (ISBN 0-8057-1424-3). Twayne.

Liang Chien-Wen Ti. John Marney. LC 75-22198. (World Authors Ser.: China: No. 374). 1976. lib. bdg. 12.50 (ISBN 0-8057-6221-3). Twayne.

Liassic Therapsid Oligokyphus. Walter G. Kuhne. (Illus.). iii, 150p. 1956. 16.50x (ISBN 0-565-00115-9, Pub. by British Mus Nat Hist England). Sabbot-Natural Hist Bks.

Libby. Milt Machlin. (Orig.). 1980. pap. 2.75 (ISBN 0-505-51533-4). Tower Bks.

Libby Shadows a Lady. Catherine Woolley. LC 74-2029. (Illus.). 192p. (gr. 3-7). 1974. PLB 7.92 (ISBN 0-688-31787-1). Morrow.

Libby's Uninvited Guest. Catherine Woolley. LC 70-108722. (Illus.). (gr. 3-7). 1970. 8.25 (ISBN 0-688-21809-1). Morrow.

Libel, Slander, & Related Problems. Robert D. Sack. 700p. 1980. text ed. 50.00 (ISBN 0-686-68826-0, G1-0658). PLI.

Liber Amicorum Weijnen: A Collection on Essays Presented to Professor Dr. A. Weijnen on the Occasion of His Seventieth Birthday. Ed. by Joep Kruijsen. 396p. 1980. pap. text ed. 42.75 (ISBN 90-232-1749-7). Humanities.

Liber Amoris: Or, the New Pygmalion. William Hazlitt. Ed. by Gerald Lahey. LC 79-47996. 256p. 1980. 17.50x (ISBN 0-8147-4999-2); pap. 7.95x (ISBN 0-8147-5000-1). NYU Pr.

Liberacion: El Evangelo de Dios. James E. Adams. 1980. pap. 2.45. Banner of Truth.

Liberacion Nacional En Costa Rica: The Development of a Political Party in a Transitional Society. Burt H. English. LC 73-107880. (Latin American Monographs: Ser. 2, No. 8). (Illus.). 1971. 8.25 (ISBN 0-8130-0296-6). U Presses Fla.

Liberal & Conservative National Economic Policies & Their Consequences, 1919-79. Leon H. Keyserling. (Illus.). 1979. 3.00. Conf Econ Prog.

Liberal Arts Physics: Invariance & Change. John M. Bailey. LC 73-21531. (Illus.). 1974. text ed. 22.95x (ISBN 0-7167-0343-2); tchr's manual avail. W H Freeman.

Liberal Europe: The Age of Bourgeois Realism 1848-1875. W. E. Mosse. (Library of European Civilization). (Illus.). 180p. 1974. 10.00 (ISBN 0-500-32032-2). Transatlantic.

Liberal Hour. John K. Galbraith. pap. 0.95 o.p. (ISBN 0-451-60873-9, MQ873, Ment). NAL.

Liberal Imagination: Essays on Literature & Society. Lionel Trilling. LC 76-13426. 320p. 1976. 10.00 o.p. (ISBN 0-684-14731-9, ScribT); pap. 3.95 o.p. (ISBN 0-684-14732-7, SL673, ScribT). Scribner.

Liberal Imperialists: The Ideas & Politics of a Post-Gladstonian Elite. H. C. Matthew. (Oxford Historical Monographs). 1973. 36.00x (ISBN 0-19-821842-7). Oxford U Pr.

Liberal Judaism at Home: The Practices of Modern Reform Judaism. rev. ed. Morrison D. Bial. 1971. pap. 5.00 (ISBN 0-8074-0075-0, 383110); tchrs'. guide 1.50 (ISBN 0-8074-0225-7, 203110). UAHC.

Liberal Kentucky, 1780-1828. Niels H. Sonne. LC 39-20412. 300p. 1968. pap. 5.00x (ISBN 0-8131-0119-0). U Pr of Ky.

Liberal Mind 1914-1929. M. Bentley. LC 76-11072. (Cambridge Studies in the History & Theory of Politics). 1977. 36.00 (ISBN 0-521-21243-X). Cambridge U Pr.

Liberal Studies: An Outline Course, 2 Vols. N. C. Dexter & E. G. Rayner. 1963. Vol. 1. pap. 7.00 (ISBN 0-08-010451-7); Vol. 2. pap. 6.25 (ISBN 0-08-010453-3). Pergamon.

Liberal Studies in Further Education: An Informal Survey. James Watson. (General Ser.). 72p. 1973. pap. text ed. 12.00x (ISBN 0-85633-023-X, NFER). Humanities.

Liberal Theory of Justice: A Critical Examination of the Principal Doctrines in - A Theory of Justice by John Rawls. Brian Barry. (Illus.). 180p. 1973. text ed. 15.95 o.p. (ISBN 0-19-824509-2); pap. text ed. 4.95x (ISBN 0-19-875032-3). Oxford U Pr.

Liberal Tradition. Lewis W. Douglas. LC 77-171382. (FDR & the Era of the New Deal Ser). 136p. 1972. Repr. of 1935 ed. lib. bdg. 15.00 (ISBN 0-306-70376-9). Da Capo.

Liberal Verse & Prose from the South: London, 4 vols. Byron & Leigh Hunt. (Salzburger Studien zur Anglistik und Amerikanistik: No. 7). (Orig.). 1979. pap. text ed. 35.75x ea.; Bk. 1, 1822. pap. text ed. (ISBN 0-391-01334-3); Bk. 2, 1823. pap. text ed. (ISBN 0-391-01335-1); Bk. 3, 1823. pap. text ed. (ISBN 0-391-01336-X); Bk. 4, 1823. pap. text ed. (ISBN 0-391-01337-8). Humanities.

Liberalism, a Socio-Economic Exposition. Ludwig Von Mises. Tr. by Ralph Raico from Ger. LC 78-8457. (Studies in Economic Theory). 207p. 1979. 15.00; pap. 4.95. NYU Pr.

Liberalism & Sociology: Lt. Hobhouse & Political Argument in English 1880-1914. Stefan Collini. LC 78-23779. 1979. 32.95 (ISBN 0-521-22304-0). Cambridge U Pr.

Liberalism & the Retreat from Politics. William J. Newman. LC 64-10787. 1964. 5.00 o.s.i. (ISBN 0-8076-0252-3). Braziller.

Liberalism & Tradition. B. Reardon. LC 75-7214. 320p. 1975. 42.00 (ISBN 0-521-20776-2). Cambridge U Pr.

Liberals & Conservatives: A Debate on the Welfare State. rev. ed. Ed. by David L. Bender. (Opposing Viewpoints Ser.: Vol. 2). (Illus.). (gr. 9 up). 1973. lib. bdg. 8.95 (ISBN 0-912616-26-1); pap. 3.95 (ISBN 0-912616-08-3). Greenhaven.

Liberals & Social Democrats. P. Clarke. LC 78-6970. 1978. 36.00 (ISBN 0-521-22171-4). Cambridge U Pr.

Liberated Female: Life, Work & Sex in Socialist Hungary. Ivan Volgyes & Nancy Volgyes. LC 77-82813. (Special Studies on the Soviet Union & Eastern Europe). 1977. lib. bdg. 18.50x (ISBN 0-89158-815-9). Westview.

Liberated for Life: Galatians - a Bible Commentary for Laymen. John F. MacArthur, Jr. LC 75-23511. (Orig.). 1976. pap. 2.25 (ISBN 0-8307-0363-2, S301-1-05). Regal.

Liberated People. Douglas Simpson. 1981. pap. 3.95 (ISBN 0-89265-064-8). Randall Hse.

Liberated Sex. K. Magner & J. Magner. (Orig.). 1977. pap. 1.50 o.p. (ISBN 0-425-03407-0). Berkley Pub.

Liberated Woman's Songbook. Jerry Silverman. Ed. by Robert Markel. (Illus.). 1971. 7.95 o.s.i. (ISBN 0-02-610780-5). Macmillan.

Liberating Education. Farnum Gray & George C. Mager. LC 73-7240. 1973. 15.50x (ISBN 0-8211-0609-0); text ed. 14.00x (ISBN 0-685-42638-6). McCutchan.

Liberation. Martin Blumenson. (World War Two Ser.). (Illus.). 1979. 12.95 (ISBN 0-8094-2510-6). Time-Life.

Liberation. Martin Blumenson. (World War II Ser.). (Illus.). 1979. lib. bdg. 14.94 (ISBN 0-686-51051-8). Silver.

Liberation & Exploitation: The Struggle for Ethiopia. Christian P. Potholm. 1977. pap. text ed. 7.00x (ISBN 0-8191-0040-4). U Pr of Amer.

Liberation Ethics. John M. Swomley, Jr. 248p. 1972. 6.95 o.s.i. (ISBN 0-02-615800-0); pap. 1.95 o.s.i. (ISBN 0-02-089620-4). Macmillan.

Liberation Manifesto. E. K. Liberatore. 1981. softbound 9.95 (ISBN 0-87100-177-2). Morgan.

Liberation of Lily. Talitha D. Fair. (Orig.). 1981. pap. 4.95 (ISBN 0-89636-059-8). Accent Bks.

Liberation of Planet Earth. Hal Lindsey. 244p. 1974. pap. 5.95 (ISBN 0-310-27721-3, 18193P); pap. 3.95 mass market (ISBN 0-310-27722-1); study guide 0.75 (ISBN 0-310-27723-X). Zondervan.

Liberation of Women: A Study of Patriarchy & Capitalism. Roberta Hamilton. (Controversies in Sociology Ser.). 1978. text ed. 17.95x (ISBN 0-04-301085-7); pap. text ed. 7.95x (ISBN 0-04-301086-5). Allen Unwin.

Liberation, Revolution & Freedom. Ed. by Thomas McFadden. 224p. 1975. 8.95 (ISBN 0-8164-0271-X). Crossroad NY.

Liberations: New Essays on the Humanities in Revolution. Ed. by Ihab Hassan. LC 77-142729. 1971. 12.50 o.p. (ISBN 0-8195-4034-X, Pub. by Wesleyan U Pr); pap. 5.95 (ISBN 0-8195-6025-1). Columbia U Pr.

Liberian Bureaucracy: An Analysis & Evaluation of the Environment, Structures & Functions. Anthony J. Nimley. LC 79-63561. 1979. pap. text ed. 11.25 (ISBN 0-8191-0732-8). U Pr of Amer.

Liberlaism: A Socio-Economic Exposition. Ludwig Von Mises. 1978. write for info. NYU Pr.

Libertarian Alternative: Essays in Social & Political Philosophy. Ed. by Tibor R. Machan. LC 73-80501. 1974. 18.95 (ISBN 0-911012-72-9); pap. 11.95 (ISBN 0-88229-511-X). Nelson-Hall.

Libertas As a Political Idea at Rome. Chaim Wirszubski. (Cambridge Classical Studies). 1950. 17.95 (ISBN 0-521-06848-7). Cambridge U Pr.

Liberties of an American: The Supreme Court Speaks. 2nd ed. Leo Pfeffer. 5.25 o.p. (ISBN 0-8446-2739-9). Peter Smith.

Libertine in Love. Caroline Courtney. 1980. pap. 1.75 (ISBN 0-446-94295-2). Warner Bks.

Liberty. Everett D. Martin. 307p. 1981. Repr. of 1930 ed. lib. bdg. 20.00. Arden Lib.

Liberty & Language. Geoffrey Sampson. 1979. 17.95 (ISBN 0-19-215951-8). Oxford U Pr.

Liberty & Law: The Nature of Individual Rights. Dayle A. Casey. Ed. by Richard H. Brown & Van R. Halsey. (Amherst Ser). (gr. 9-12). 1972. pap. text ed. 4.52 (ISBN 0-201-00906-4, Sch Div). A-W.

Liberty & Reformation in the Puritan Revolution. William Haller. LC 54-6482. 1955. pap. 7.50x (ISBN 0-231-08547-8, 47). Columbia U Pr.

Liberty & the Rule of Law. Ed. by Robert L. Cunningham. LC 78-6372. (Illus.). 496p. 1979. 25.00 (ISBN 0-89096-056-9). Tex A&M Univ Pr.

Liberty & the Struggle for the Franchise. Ed. by D. Story. (Themes in Modern History Ser.: Documentary Research Folder: No. 1). 1972. 4.25x (ISBN 0-7022-0788-8). U of Queensland Pr.

Liberty Bell U. S. Album. Larry Grossman. (Illus.). 1980. 2.95 (ISBN 0-685-99702-2). Grossman Stamp.

Liberty, Equality, Fraternity. James F. Stephen. Ed. by R. J. White. (Cambridge Studies in the History & Theory of Politics). 1968. 36.00 (ISBN 0-521-06550-X). Cambridge U Pr.

Liberty in the Balance. 5th, rev. ed. H. Frank Way. (Foundations of American Government & Political Science Ser.). 144p. 1981. pap. text ed. 6.95 (ISBN 0-07-068661-0, C). McGraw.

Liberty Lane: A Ballad Play of Dublin in Two Acts with a Prologue by Austin Clarke. Austin Clarke. (Dolmen Editions: No. XXVII). 1978. text ed. 22.25x (ISBN 0-85105-324-6, Dolmen Pr). Humanities.

Liberty Line: The Legend of the Underground Railroad. Larry Gara. LC 61-6552. 216p. 1967. pap. 5.50x (ISBN 0-8131-0115-8). U Pr of Ky.

Liberty of Obedience. Elisabeth Elliot. (Festival Bks). 1981. pap. 1.50 (ISBN 0-687-21730-X). Abingdon.

Liberty: Selected Readings. Joel Feinberg & Hyman Gross. 1977. pap. text ed. 9.95x (ISBN 0-8221-0202-1). Dickenson.

Liberty Ships. 2nd ed. L. A. Sawyer & W. H. Mitchell. LC 70-124469. (Illus.). 1973. 12.75 (ISBN 0-87033-152-3). Cornell Maritime.

Liberty Sword. Gardner F. Fox. 1976. pap. 1.25 o.p. (ISBN 0-685-69145-4, LB358ZK, Leisure Bks). Nordon Pubns.

Liberty Tavern. Thomas Fleming. 480p. 1977. pap. 2.50 (ISBN 0-446-91220-4). Warner Bks.

Liberty's Daughters: The Revolutionary Experience of American Women. Mary B. Norton. 1980. 15.00 (ISBN 0-316-61251-0); pap. 7.95 (ISBN 0-316-61252-9). Little.

Liberty's Women. Ed. by Merriam Company. 1980. 15.00 (ISBN 0-87779-064-7). Merriam.

Libra. James A. Lely. (Sun Signs Ser.). (Illus.). (gr. 4-12). 1978. PLB 5.95 (ISBN 0-87191-647-9); pap. 2.95 (ISBN 0-685-86522-3). Creative Ed.

Libra. Julia Parker. (Pocket Guide to Astrology Ser.). (Orig.). 1980. pap. write for info. (ISBN 0-671-25554-1, Fireside). S&S.

Librarian. 4th ed. Arco Editorial Board. LC 75-37087. (Orig.). 1975. lib. bdg. 14.00 o. p. (ISBN 0-668-01403-2); pap. 10.00 (ISBN 0-668-00060-0). Arco.

Librarian & the Handicapped Child. Margaret Marshall. LC 80-51349. (Grafton Books on Library & Information Science). 160p. 1981. lib. bdg. 25.00x (ISBN 0-86531-056-4, Pub. by Andre Deutsch). Westview.

Librarian at Play. 2nd ed. Edmund L. Pearson. LC 79-53354. (Short Story Index in Reprint Ser.). Date not set. Repr. of 1912 ed. 22.50x (ISBN 0-8486-5010-7). Core Collection. Postponed.

Librarian Authors. Rudolf Engelbarts. LC 80-28035. 123p. 1981. lib. bdg. write for info. (ISBN 0-89950-007-2). McFarland & Co.

Librarian Phone Book 1980: 1980. 445p. 1979. 17.95 o.p. (ISBN 0-8352-1254-8). Bowker.

Librarian: Selections from the Column of That Name by Edmund L. Pearson. Ed. by Jane B. Durnell & Norman D. Stevens. LC 75-35725. 1976. 27.50 (ISBN 0-8108-0851-X). Scarecrow.

Librarians & Labor Relations: Employment Under Union Contracts. Robert C. O'Reilly & Marjorie I. O'Reilly. LC 80-1049. (Contributions in Librarianship & Information Science Ser.: No. 35). 208p. 1981. lib. bdg. 25.00 (ISBN 0-313-22485-4, OLL/). Greenwood.

Librarian's Glossary & Reference Book. L. M. Harrod. LC 76-52489. 1977. lib. bdg. 45.00x (ISBN 0-89158-727-6). Westview.

Librarians Guide to Personal Development: An Annotated Bibliography. Compiled by Valerie Noble. (Bibliography Ser.: No. 7). 1980. pap. 4.50 (ISBN 0-87111-272-8). SLA.

Librarian's Handbook, Vol. 1. Ed. by L. J. Taylor. 1977. pap. 33.00x (ISBN 0-85365-079-9, Pub. by Lib Assn England). Oryx Pr.

Librarian's Handbook, Vol. 2. Ed. by L. J. Taylor. 1980. pap. 49.50x (ISBN 0-85365-651-7, Pub. by Lib Assn England). Oryx Pr.

Librarian's Manual: A Treatise on Bibliography, Comprising a Select & Descriptive List of Bibliographical Works; to Which Are Added, Sketches of Public Libraries. Reuben A. Guild. LC 70-174942. (Illus.). x, 304p. 1972. Repr. of 1858 ed. 22.00 (ISBN 0-8103-3811-4). Gale.

Librarians Phone Book 1981. 2nd ed. Ed. by Jaques Cattell Press. 445p. 1980. pap. 9.95 (ISBN 0-8352-1321-8). Bowker.

Librarianship. William R. Maidment. LC 75-17. (Profession Ser). 144p. 1975. 11.95 o.p. (ISBN 0-7153-6897-4). David & Charles.

Librarianship & Information, Nineteen Seventy-One to Nineteen Seventy-Five. Ed. by H. A. Whatley. 1977. 32.50x (ISBN 0-85365-099-3, Pub. by Lib Assn England). Oryx Pr.

Librarianship & Literature. Ed. by A. T. Milne. 1970. text ed. 17.00x (ISBN 0-485-11117-9, Athlone Pr). Humanities.

Librarianship in Australia, New Zealand & Oceania. D. H. Borchardt & J. Horacek. 1976. 10.25 (ISBN 0-08-019920-8); pap. text ed. write for info. (ISBN 0-08-019752-3). Pergamon.

Librarianship in Developing Societies. Antonio A. Briquet de Limos. (Occasional Papers: No. 148). 1981. pap. 3.00 (ISBN 0-686-69073-7). U of Ill Lib Sci.

Libraries & How to Use Them. Jeanne B. Hardendorff. LC 78-12992. (First Bks.). (Illus.). (gr. 4 up). 1979. PLB 6.45 s&l (ISBN 0-531-02259-5). Watts.

Libraries & Information Technology: A System Challenge. Computer Science and Engineering Board. 96p. (Orig.). 1972. pap. text ed. 3.50 (ISBN 0-309-01938-9). Natl Acad Pr.

Libraries & Librarians of the Pacific Northwest. Ed. by Morton Kroll. LC 60-9873. (PNLA Library Development Project Reports, Ser.: Vol. 4). 281p. 1960. 10.50 (ISBN 0-295-73827-8). U of Wash Pr.

Libraries & Library Services in the Southeast: A Report of the Southeastern States Cooperative Library Survey, 1972-1974. Mary E. Anders. LC 75-44140. (Illus.). 272p. 1976. 18.50 (ISBN 0-8173-9705-1). U of Ala Pr.

Libraries & Young Adults: Media, Services, & Librarianship. JoAnn V. Rogers. LC 79-15. 1979. 17.50x (ISBN 0-87287-195-9). Libs Unl.

Libraries As Communication Systems. J. M. Orr. LC 76-8739. (Contributions in Librarianship & Information Science: No. 17). 240p. 1977. lib. bdg. 16.95 (ISBN 0-8371-8936-5, ORL/). Greenwood.

Libraries Designed for Users: A Planning Handbook. Nolan Lushington & Willis N. Mills, Jr. (Illus.). 1980. 24.50 (ISBN 0-208-01888-3, Lib Prof Pubns). Shoe String.

Libraries for the Handicapped. M. J. Lewis. 1969. pap. 3.30x (ISBN 0-85365-281-3, Pub. by Lib Assn England). Oryx Pr.

Libraries in Colleges of Education. 2nd ed. P. Platt. 1972. 19.50x (ISBN 0-85365-335-6, Pub. by Lib Assn England). Oryx Pr.

Libraries in Scandinavia. K. C. Harrison. (Grafton Books in Library Science). 1977. lib. bdg. 12.00 o.p. (ISBN 0-233-95968-8). Westview.

Libraries in Society: A Reader. Ed. by David E. Gerard. 1979. 16.00 (ISBN 0-89664-402-2, Pub. by K G Saur). Shoe String.

Libraries in the Political Process. Ed. by E. J. Josey. (Neal-Schuman Professional Books Ser.). 1980. lib. bdg. 18.95x (ISBN 0-912700-25-4). Oryx Pr.

Libraries in the Political Scene: Georg Leyh & German Librarianship, 1933-53. Tr. by Marta L. Dosa. LC 72-5218. (Contributions in Librarianship & Information Science: No. 7). 256p. 1973. lib. bdg. 16.95 (ISBN 0-8371-6443-5, DGL/). Greenwood.

Libraries in the United Kingdom & the Republic of Ireland. Ed. by F. J. Hamilton. 1979. pap. 7.95x (ISBN 0-85365-741-6, Pub. by Lib Assn England). Oryx Pr.

Libraries of University Departments of Adult Education & Extra-Mural Studies. R. K. Fisher. 1974. pap. 8.75x (ISBN 0-85365-377-1, Pub. by Lib Assn England). Oryx Pr.

Library & Information Manager's Guide to Online Services. Ed. by Ryan Hoover. (Communications Library Ser.). (Illus.). 269p. 1980. 29.50x (ISBN 0-914236-60-1); pap. text ed. 24.50x (ISBN 0-914236-52-0). Knowledge Indus.

Library & Information Services for Handicapped Individuals. Kieth C. Wright. LC 78-26472. 1979. lib. bdg. 17.50x (ISBN 0-87287-129-0). Libs Unl.

Library & Information Services to Local Government. L. Grayson. 1979. pap. 12.50x (ISBN 0-85365-810-2, Pub. by Lib Assn England). Oryx Pr.

Library & Library Related Publications: A Directory of Publishing Opportunities in Journals, Serials & Annuals. Peter Hernon et al. LC 73-84183. 180p. 1973. lib. bdg. 10.00 o.p. (ISBN 0-87287-068-5). Libs Unl.

Library & the Community. K. C. Harrison. (Grafton Books on Library Service). 1977. lib. bdg. 15.00x (ISBN 0-233-96875-X). Westview.

Library Assistance to Readers. Robert L. Collison. 1963. 4.75 o.p. (ISBN 0-8022-0284-5). Philos Lib.

Library Association Yearbooks, Nineteen Seventy-Eight. 1978. pap. 19.75x (ISBN 0-85365-880-3, Pub. by Lib Assn England). Oryx Pr.

Library Association Yearbooks, Nineteen Seventy-Nine. 1979. pap. 19.75x (ISBN 0-85365-751-3, Pub. by Lib Assn England). Oryx Pr.

Library Association Yearbooks, Nineteen Seventy-Six. 1976. pap. 19.75x (ISBN 0-85365-398-4, Pub. by Lib Assn England). Oryx Pr.

Library Association Yearbooks, Nineteen Seventy-Seven. 1977. pap. 19.75x (ISBN 0-85365-309-7, Pub. by Lib Assn England). Oryx Pr.

Library Association Yearbooks, 1975. 1975. pap. 19.75x (ISBN 0-85365-487-5, Pub. by Lib Assn England). Oryx Pr.

Library Association Yearbooks, 1980. 1980. pap. 21.00x (ISBN 0-85365-971-0, Pub. by Lib Assn England). Oryx Pr.

Library Catalog of the Conservation Center of the Institute of Fine Arts. New York University. 1980. lib. bdg. 95.00 (ISBN 0-8161-0303-8). G K Hall.

Library Catalog of the Metropolitan Museum of Art. 2nd ed. Metropolitan Museum of Art (New York) 1980. lib. bdg. 4650.00 (ISBN 0-8161-0295-3). G K Hall.

Library Cataloging: A Guide for a Basic Course. J. Philip Immroth & Jay E. Daily. LC 72-147066. 1971. 10.00 (ISBN 0-8108-0396-8). Scarecrow.

Library Catalogue of the Martin P. Catherwood Library of the New York State School of Industrial & Labor Relations: Fourth Supplement. Martin P. Catherwood Library-Cornell University. (Library Catalogs & Supplements Ser.). 1980. lib. bdg. 260.00 (ISBN 0-8161-0333-X). G K Hall.

Library Catalogue of the Radzinowicz Library, 6 vols. Institute of Criminology, University of Cambridge, England. Ed. by R. Perry. (Bib.Guides). 1979. Set. lib. bdg. 475.00 (ISBN 0-8161-0242-2). G K Hall.

Library Catalogue of the School of Oriental & African Studies: Third Supplement, 19 vols. School of Oriental & African Studies, University of London. 1979. Set. lib. bdg. 1990.00 (ISBN 0-8161-0261-9). G K Hall.

Library Collections: Their Origin, Selection, & Development. Richard K. Gardner. (Library Education Ser.). 384p. 1981. text ed. 17.95 (ISBN 0-07-022850-7, C). McGraw.

Library Community Services. LC 77-28184. 98p. 1977. 6.00 (ISBN 0-913578-18-5). Inglewood Ca.

Library Display Ideas. Linda C. Franklin. LC 80-17036. (Illus.). 243p. 1980. lib. bdg. 11.95x (ISBN 0-89950-008-0); pap. 7.95x (ISBN 0-89950-009-9). McFarland & Co.

Library Displays. Mona Garvey. LC 79-86918. 1969. 10.00 (ISBN 0-8242-0395-X). Wilson.

Library Education. Louis Shores. LC 74-187784. 178p. 1972. lib. bdg. 11.50x o.p. (ISBN 0-87287-043-X). Libs Unl.

Library Fiscal Controls. Jennifer S. Cargill & Brian Alley. 1981. price not set (ISBN 0-912700-79-3). Oryx Pr.

Library History. James G. Olle. (Outlines of Modern Librarianship Ser.). 114p. 1979. text ed. 12.00 (ISBN 0-89664-414-6, Pub. by K G Saur). Shoe String.

Library Humor: A Bibliothecal Miscellany to 1970. Norman D. Stevens. LC 76-149995. 1971. 13.50 (ISBN 0-8108-0379-8). Scarecrow.

Library in the Independent School. Pauline H. Anderson. 42p. 1980. pap. 6.50 (ISBN 0-934338-43-4). NAIS.

Library Instruction & Faculty Development. Ed. by Nyal Z. Williams & Jack T. Tsukamoto. (Library Orientation Ser.: No. 11). 1980. 10.00 (ISBN 0-87650-125-0). Pierian.

Library Instruction in the Elementary School. Melvyn K. Bowers. LC 72-155283. 1971. 10.00 (ISBN 0-8108-0391-7). Scarecrow.

Library Journal Book Review, 1979. Ed. by Jaques Cattell Press. LC 68-59515. 769p. 1980. 28.95 (ISBN 0-8352-1272-6). Bowker.

Library Journal Book Review 1980. Ed. by Jacques Cattell Press. LC 68-59515. 760p. 32.50 (ISBN 0-8352-1344-7). Bowker.

Library Life - American Style: A Journalist's Field Report. Arthur Plotnik. LC 75-16280. (Illus.). 226p. 1975. 10.00 (ISBN 0-8108-0852-8). Scarecrow.

Library Literature, 7 vols. Incl. Vols. 1970 to Date. on a service basis avail.; Seven Vols. 1921-51. 40.00 ea.; Six Vols. 1952-69. 80.00 ea.; 1979 Annual. 1980. Wilson.

Library Literature Eight: The Best of 1977. Ed. by William A. Katz. LC 78-154842. 1978. lib. bdg. 13.00 (ISBN 0-8108-1125-1). Scarecrow.

Library Literature Five: The Best of 1974. Ed. by William A. Katz & Robert Burgess. LC 78-154842. 443p. 1975. 13.00 (ISBN 0-8108-0808-0). Scarecrow.

Library Literature Four: The Best of 1973. Ed. by William A. Katz & Sherry Gaherty. 1974. 13.00 (ISBN 0-8108-0702-5). Scarecrow.

Library Literature Nine: The Best of 1978. Ed. by William A. Katz. LC 78-154842. 1979. 13.00 (ISBN 0-8108-1213-4). Scarecrow.

Library Literature Seven: The Best of 1976. Ed. by William A. Katz. LC 78-154842. 1977. 13.00 (ISBN 0-8108-1017-4). Scarecrow.

Library Literature Six: The Best of 1975. Ed. by William A. Katz. LC 78-154842. 1976. 13.00 (ISBN 0-8108-0923-0). Scarecrow.

Library Literature Ten: The Best of 1979. Ed. by Bill Katz. LC 78-154842. 512p. 1980. 13.00 (ISBN 0-686-65869-8). Scarecrow.

Library Literature: The Best of 1970. Ed. by William A Katz & Joel J. Schwartz. LC 78-154842. 1971. 13.00 (ISBN 0-8108-0418-2). Scarecrow.

Library Literature Three: The Best of 1972. Ed. by William A. Katz & Janet Klaessig. LC 78-15482. 1973. 13.00 (ISBN 0-8108-0613-4). Scarecrow.

Library Literature Two: The Best of 1971. Ed. by William A. Katz. LC 78-154842. 1972. 13.00 (ISBN 0-8108-0519-7). Scarecrow.

Library Management. Robert D. Stueart & John T. Eastlick. LC 76-49568. (Library Science Text Ser.). 1977. lib. bdg. 15.00x (ISBN 0-87287-127-4). Libs Unl.

Library Management. 2nd ed. Robert D. Stueart & John T. Eastlick. LC 80-22895. (Library Science Text Ser.). 292p. 1980. text ed. 22.50x (ISBN 0-87287-241-6); pap. text ed. 14.50x (ISBN 0-87287-243-2). Libs Unl.

Library Management Cases. Mildred H. Lowell. LC 75-23077. 1975. 10.00 (ISBN 0-8108-0845-5). Scarecrow.

Library Management 1979. Ed. by Janette S. Closurdo. 1980. pap. 8.50. SLA.

Library Media Programs & the Special Learner. D. Phillip Baker & David R. Bender. 400p. 1981. 18.50 (ISBN 0-208-01852-2, Lib Prof Pubns); pap. text ed. 14.50x (ISBN 0-208-01846-8, Lib Prof Pubns). Shoe String.

Library Networks: 1980-1981. 4th ed. Susan K. Martin. LC 78-10666. (Professional Librarian Ser.). 176p. 1980. text ed. 29.50x (ISBN 0-914236-55-5); pap. text ed. 24.50x (ISBN 0-914236-66-0). Knowledge Indus.

Library Objectives, Goals, & Activities. LC 73-22178. 105p. 1973. 5.00 (ISBN 0-913578-05-3). Inglewood Ca.

Library of Congress & National Union Catalogue Author Lists, 1942-1962: A Master Cummulation, 152 vols. Gale Research Co. LC 73-82135. 1969. fiche only 1390.00 (ISBN 0-8103-0950-5); fiche only 125.00 (ISBN 0-8103-0951-3). Gale.

Library of Congress Classification Adapted for Children's Materials. 3rd ed. LC 76-48893. 131p. 1976. 5.00 (ISBN 0-913578-14-2). Inglewood Ca.

Library of Congress Classification Schedules: A Cumulation of Additions & Changes Through 1978, 32 bound cumulations. Ed. by Helen Savage. 1979. Set. pap. 1350.00 (ISBN 0-8103-1150-X). Gale.

Library of Congress Subject Headings: Principles & Application. Lois M. Chan. LC 78-9497. (Research Studies in Library Science: No. 15). 1978. lib. bdg. 22.50x (ISBN 0-87287-187-8). Libs Unl.

Library of Golf 1743-1966: A Bibliography of Golf Books. Ed. by Joseph Murdoch. LC 67-29083. (Illus.). 1968. 30.00 (ISBN 0-8103-0961-0). Gale.

Library of Literary Criticism of English & American Authors, 8 vols. Charles W. Moulton. Set. 108.00 (ISBN 0-8446-1318-5); 13.50 ea. Peter Smith.

Library of Shopping Center Management Forms. 1977. 69.30 (ISBN 0-685-81741-5). Intl Coun Shop.

Library Orientation: Syllabus. Janet Bohlool. 1970. pap. text ed. 5.45 (ISBN 0-89420-080-1, 216720); cassette recordings 101.35 (ISBN 0-89420-161-1, 140800). Natl Book.

Library Programs: How to Select, Plan & Produce Them. John S. Robotham & Lydia LaFleur. LC 76-2033. 307p. 1976. 14.50 (ISBN 0-8108-0911-7). Scarecrow.

Library Public Relations. Mona Garvey. 1980. 14.00 (ISBN 0-8242-0651-7). Wilson.

Library Research for the Analysis of Public Policy. Renee S. Captor. (Learning Packages in the Policy Sciences Ser.: No. 19). 36p. 1979. pap. text ed. 3.00 (ISBN 0-936826-08-8). Pol Stud Assocs.

Library Research Guide to History. Elizabeth Frick. (Library Research Guides Ser.: No. 4). 1980. 9.95 (ISBN 0-87650-119-6); pap. 5.95 (ISBN 0-87650-123-4). Pierian.

Library Resource Provision in Schools: Guidelines & Recommendations. 1977. pap. 4.25x (ISBN 0-85365-700-9, Pub. by Lib Assn England). Oryx Pr.

Library School Review, Vol. 18. Ed. by Marylouise D. Meder. 1979. pap. 2.00. Sch Lib Sci.

Library Science Dissertations 1925-1972: An Annotated Bibliography. Gail Schlachter & Dennis Thomison. LC 73-90497. (Research Studies in Library Science Ser.: No. 12). 293p. 1974. lib. bdg. 12.50 o.p. (ISBN 0-87287-074-X). Libs Unl.

Library Science Research Reader & Bibliographic Guide. Ed. by Charles H. Busha. 210p. 1981. lib. bdg. 18.50 (ISBN 0-87287-237-8). Libs Unl.

Library Science Today. Ed. by P. N. Kaula. (Ranganathan Festschrift, Vol. 1). 1964. 30.00x (ISBN 0-210-34099-1). Asia.

Library Searching: Resources & Strategies with Examples from the Environmental Sciences. Jacquelyn M. Morris & Elizabeth A. Elkins. (Library Resources Ser.). 1978. text ed. 8.95x o.p. (ISBN 0-88432-004-9); pap. text ed. 5.95x (ISBN 0-88432-005-7). J Norton Pubs.

Library Service for Genealogists. Ed. by J. Carlyle Parker. LC 80-26032. (Gale Genealogy & Local History Ser.: Vol. 15). 285p. 1981. 30.00 (ISBN 0-8103-1489-4). Gale.

Library Service to Children: An International Survey, Vol. 12. Ed. by Colin Ray. (IFLA Publications Ser.). 1978. 24.50 (ISBN 0-89664-004-3, Pub. by K G Saur). Shoe String.

Library Service to the Disadvantaged. Eleanor F. Brown. LC 78-162668. (Illus.). 1971. 18.50 (ISBN 0-8108-0437-9). Scarecrow.

Library Service to the Spanish Speaking. LC 77-22847. 51p. 1977. 5.00 (ISBN 0-913578-16-9). Inglewood Ca.

Library Services for Children in New Zealand Schools & Public Libraries: Statistical Appendix to the Report. Ed. by S. A. Fenwick. (New Zealand Council for Educational Research, Studies in Education: No. 24, Pt. 2). 1977. pap. text ed. 6.00x o.p. (ISBN 0-8426-1052-9). Verry.

Library Services for Young People in England & Wales, 1830-1970. Alec Ellis. 1971. 26.00 (ISBN 0-08-016586-9). Pergamon.

Library Services to the Blind & Physically Handicapped. Maryalls G. Strom. LC 77-24686. 1977. 14.50 (ISBN 0-8108-1068-9). Scarecrow.

Library Skills. Peter W. Preksto, Jr. (Basic Skills Library). (Illus.). (gr. 4 up). 1979. PLB 5.95 (ISBN 0-87191-714-9). Creative Ed.

Library Staff Development & Continuing Education: Principles & Practices. Barbara Conroy. LC 78-18887. 1978. 23.50x (ISBN 0-87287-177-0). Libs Unl.

Library Structures & Staffing Systems. M. Tunley. Ed. by A. Wilson. (Management Pamphlet Ser.). 1979. pap. 8.95x (ISBN 0-85365-771-8, Pub. by Lib Assn England). Oryx Pr.

Library Studies Duplicating Masters, 2 vols. 1976. 5.95 ea. Vol. 1 (ISBN 0-89273-537-6). Vol. 2 (ISBN 0-89273-538-4). Educ Serv.

Library Surveys. Ed. by Maurice F. Tauber & Irlene R. Stephens. LC 67-25304. (Columbia Library Service Studies: No. 16). 1967. 22.50x (ISBN 0-231-03056-8). Columbia U Pr.

Library Technical Services Management: Alternatives for Technical Services Librarians. Jennifer S. Cargill & Brian Alley. 1981. price not set postponed (ISBN 0-912700-55-6). Oryx Pr.

Library Work with Children. L. M. Harrod. (Grafton Books in Library Science). 1977. lib. bdg. 17.00x (ISBN 0-233-95994-7). Westview.

Library's Public: A Report of the Public Library Inquiry. Bernard Berelson & Lester Ansheim. LC 75-31430. 174p. 1976. Repr. of 1949 ed. lib. bdg. 21.50x (ISBN 0-8371-8499-1, BELP). Greenwood.

Libretto for the Republic of Liberia. Melvin Tolson. 1970. pap. 1.50 o.s.i. (ISBN 0-02-070900-5, Collier). Macmillan.

Libro de Buen Amor. Arcipreste de Hita. (Span.). 7.95 (ISBN 84-241-5640-4). E Torres & Sons.

Libro de los Estados. Don J. Manuel. Ed. by R. B. Tate & Ian MacPherson. 420p. (Sp.). 1974. 49.50x (ISBN 0-19-815713-4). Oxford U Pr.

Libro De Medicion. Marvin L. Sohns & Audrey V. Buffington. (Illus.). 212p. (Span.). 1980. pap. 9.95 (ISBN 0-86582-029-5). Enrich.

Libro De Poemas, Poema Del Cante Jondo, Romancero Gitano, Poeta En Nueva York, Odas, Llanto Por Sanchez Mejias, Bodas De Sangre, Yerma. Garcia Lorca. Date not set. 4.50x o.s.i. (ISBN 0-686-09290-2). Colton Bk.

Libro De Repaso De la Cosmetologia: Spanish. 1978. 5.72 (ISBN 0-912126-44-2, 1267-02). Keystone Pubns.

Libros en Venta Supplement 1976-77. Ed. by Mary C. Turner. 1978. 59.00 o.p. (ISBN 0-8352-1027-8). Bowker.

Libros En Venta Supplement 1978. Ed. by Mary C. Turner. 1980. 42.50 (ISBN 0-8352-1278-5). Bowker.

Libya: The Elusive Revolution. Ruth First. LC 75-9944. 294p. 1975. text ed. 23.50x (ISBN 0-8419-0211-9, Africana). Holmes & Meier.

Libyan Mammals. Ernst Hufnagl. (Illus.). 16.00 (ISBN 0-902675-08-7). Oleander Pr.

Libyan Oil Industry. Frank C. Waddams. LC 80-13939. (Illus.). 352p. 1980. text ed. 30.00x (ISBN 0-8018-2431-1). Johns Hopkins.

Lice. Blaise Cendrars. Tr. by Nina Rootes from Fr. 1979. 18.00x (ISBN 0-8464-0045-6). Beekman Pubs.

Lice. Blaise Cendrars. LC 80-9058. 189p. 1981. 12.95 (ISBN 0-8128-2815-1). Stein & Day.

Licensing - Certification of Appraisers, with a Suggested Model Bill. LC 72-76987. (ASA Monograph: No. 5). 1972. 5.00 (ISBN 0-937828-14-9). Am Soc Appraisers.

Licensing & Certification of Psychologists & Counselors: A Guide to Current Policies, Procedures, & Legislation. Bruce R. Fretz & David H. Mills. LC 80-8011. (Social & Behavioral Science Ser.). 1980. text ed. 13.95x (ISBN 0-87589-470-4). Jossey-Bass.

Licensing & Regulatory Control of Nuclear Installations. (Legal Ser.: No. 10). (Illus.). 313p. 1976. pap. 29.00 (ISBN 92-0-176175-9, ISP 421, IAEA). Unipub.

Licensing Check Lists. D. Edmunds Brazell. 49p. (Orig.). 1981. pap. 12.50x (ISBN 0-911378-36-7). Sheridan.

Licensing in Foreign & Domestic Operations, 4 vols. rev. ed. Lawrence J. Eckstrom & Robert Goldscheider. 1979. looseleaf in post binders pages 210.00 (ISBN 0-87632-075-2). Boardman.

Licht's International Sugar Economic Yearbook & Directory 1979. Ed. by Helmut Ahlfeld. LC 51-36145. (Illus.). 522p. (Eng. & Ger.). 1979. 85.00x (ISBN 0-8002-2348-9). Intl Pubns Serv.

Lichtstreifen. P. Willig. 141p. 1973. pap. 5.75 (ISBN 0-08-016281-9); pap. text ed. 3.30 (ISBN 0-08-017826-X). Pergamon.

Licking Hitler. David Hare. 1979. pap. 5.95 (ISBN 0-571-11326-5, Pub. by Faber & Faber). Merrimack Bk Serv.

L'Idalma Overo Chi la Dura la Vince. Bernardo Pasquini. Ed. by Howard M. Brown. LC 76-20996. (Italian Opera 1640-1770 Ser.). 1978. lib. bdg. 70.00 (ISBN 0-8240-2610-1). Garland Pub.

Liddell Hart: A Study of His Military Thought. Brian Bond. (Illus.). 1977. 20.00 (ISBN 0-8135-0846-0). Rutgers U Pr.

Lie. Ann Helena. LC 77-23395. (Moods & Emotions Ser.). (Illus.). (gr. k-3). 1977. PLB 8.95 (ISBN 0-8172-0958-1). Raintree Pubs.

Lie Algebras. Wan-Z-Xian. LC 74-13832. 244p. 1976. text ed. 37.00 (ISBN 0-08-017952-5). Pergamon.

Lie Detector in Employment. Mary A. Coghill. (Key Issues Ser.: No. 2). 1973. pap. 2.00 (ISBN 0-87546-208-1). NY Sch Indus Rel.

Lie Groups & Compact Groups. John F. Price. LC 76-14034. (London Mathematical Society Lecture Notes Ser.: No. 25). 1977. pap. 16.95x (ISBN 0-521-21340-1). Cambridge U Pr.

Lie Groups, Lie Algebras, & Their Representations. V. S. Varadarajian. (Modern Analysis Ser.). 496p. 1974. ref. ed. 26.95 (ISBN 0-13-535732-2). P-H.

Liebelei, Leutnant Gustl, Die Letzten Masken. Arthur Schnitzler. Ed. by J. P. Stern. 1966. text ed. 7.50x (ISBN 0-521-06201-2). Cambridge U Pr.

Liebesspiele. Ed. by Eli Sobel & Hans Wagener. (Orig.). 1970. pap. text ed. 3.95x (ISBN 0-19-501056-6). Oxford U Pr.

Lied: The Unfolding of Its Style. Anneliese Landau. LC 79-6725. 1980. text ed. 15.00 (ISBN 0-8191-0935-5); pap. text ed. 7.50 (ISBN 0-8191-0936-3). U Pr of Amer.

Lieder Des Blondel De Nesle. Blondel De Nesle. LC 80-2157. 1981. Repr. of 1904 ed. 35.50 (ISBN 0-404-19023-5). AMS Pr.

Lieder Des Trobadors Guiraut d'Espanha: Inaugural-Dissertation. Guiraut D'Espanha. Ed. by Otto Hoby. LC 80-2178. 1981. Repr. of 1915 ed. 24.50 (ISBN 0-404-19008-1). AMS Pr.

Lieder und Romanzen Des Audefroi le Bastard. Audefroi Le Bastard. LC 80-2159. 1981. Repr. of 1914 ed. 26.50 (ISBN 0-404-19021-9). AMS Pr.

Liefer in Anomyman Englischen Drama, 1580-1603. Hans-Joachim Hermes. (Salzburg Studies in English Literature, Elizabethan & Renaissance Studies: No. 40). (Illus.). 323p. 1974. pap. text ed. 25.00x (ISBN 0-391-01407-2). Humanities.

Lies. Richard Neely. 1979. pap. 1.75 o.s.i. (ISBN 0-515-04879-8). Jove Pubns.

Lieutenant Lookest & Other Stories. Masuji Ibuse. Tr. by John Bester from Jap. LC 71-135143. 308p. 1971. 8.95 (ISBN 0-87011-147-7). Kodansha.

Life: A Question of Survival. Dorothy M. Schlitt et al. (Illus., Orig.). (gr. 7-11). 1972. pap. text ed. 6.64x (ISBN 0-913688-03-7); teacher's guide 5.32x (ISBN 0-913688-04-5). Pawnee Pub.

Life, Adventures, & Pyracies of the Famous Captain Singleton... Being Set on Shore in the Island of Madagascar. Daniel Defoe. LC 70-170544. (Foundations of the Novel Ser.: Vol. 33). lib. bdg. 50.00 (ISBN 0-8240-0545-7). Garland Pub.

Life, Adventures, Intrigues & Amours of the Celebrated Jemmy Twitcher, 1770. Ed. by Michael F. Shugrue. Bd. with Life, Adventures, & Amours of Sir Richard Perrot, 1770. LC 74-31492. (Novel in England, 1700-1775 Ser). 1974. lib. bdg. 50.00 (ISBN 0-8240-1191-0). Garland Pub.

Life After Birth: Spirituality for College Students. William Toohey. 112p. 1980. pap. 3.95 (ISBN 0-8164-2290-7). Seabury.

Life After Death? Dennis M. Battle. (Illus.). 52p. 1981. pap. 2.00 (ISBN 0-933464-13-4). D M Battle Pubns.

Life After Doomsday: A Survivalist Guide to Nuclear War & Other Disasters. Bruce D. Clayton. (Illus.). 192p. 1981. pap. 8.95 (ISBN 0-8037-4752-7). Dial.

Life After Eighty: Environmental Choices We Can Live with. Ed. by Kathleen Courrier & Richard Munson. LC 80-11783. 304p. 1980. pap. 6.95 (ISBN 0-931790-13-1). Brick Hse Pub.

Life After Life. Raymond A. Moody, Jr. LC 75-37963. 1976. 5.95 o.p. (ISBN 0-8117-0946-9). Stackpole.

Life After Youth. Ed. by Luella Slover. 1981. pap. write for info. (ISBN 0-8309-0303-8). Herald Hse.

Life Against Death: The Psychoanalytical Meaning of History. Norman O. Brown. LC 59-5369. 1959. 20.00x (ISBN 0-8195-3005-0, Pub. by Wesleyan U Pr); pap. 8.95 (ISBN 0-8195-6010-3). Columbia U Pr.

Life Among the Indians: Being an Interesting Narrative of the Captivity of the Oatman Girls, Among the Apache & Mohave Indians. Royal Stratton. LC 75-7096. (Indian Captivities Ser.: Vol. 71). (Bnd. with 2nd ed., changed 1857). 1977. Repr. of 1857 ed. lib. bdg. 44.00 (ISBN 0-8240-1695-5). Garland Pub.

Life Among the Moonies: Three Years in the Unification Church. Deanna Durham. (Orig.). 1981. pap. 2.95 (ISBN 0-88270-496-6). Logos.

Life Among the Paiutes: Their Wrongs & Claims. Hopkins. LC 71-102992. 11.95 (ISBN 0-912494-18-2); pap. 6.95 (ISBN 0-912494-06-9). Chalfant Pr.

Life & Activities of Sir John Hawkins: Musician, Magistrate & Friend of Johnson. Percy A. Scholes. LC 77-26652. (Music Reprint Ser., 1978). (Illus.). 1978. Repr. of 1953 ed. lib. bdg. 27.50 (ISBN 0-306-77571-9). Da Capo.

Life & Adventures of Alonso, the Chattering Lay Brother & Servant of Many Masters. Geronimo A. Rivera. LC 80-2468. 1981. Repr. of 1845 ed. 57.50 (ISBN 0-404-19100-2). AMS Pr.

Life & Adventures of Common Sense, 1769, 2 vols. in 1. Herbert Lawrence. LC 74-23918. (Novel in England, 1700-1775 Ser). 1974. lib. bdg. 50.00 (ISBN 0-8240-1187-2). Garland Pub.

Life & Adventures of Joe Thompson, 1750, 2 vols. in 1. Edward Kimber. LC 74-17302. (Novel in England, 1700-1775 Ser). 1974. lib. bdg. 50.00 (ISBN 0-8240-1130-9). Garland Pub.

Life & Adventures of John Muir. James M. Clarke. LC 79-64178. (Sierra Club Paperback Library Ser.). (Illus.). 326p. 1980. pap. 7.95 (ISBN 0-87156-241-3). Sierra.

Life & Adventures of L. D. Lafferty: Being a True Biography of One of the Most Remarkable Men of the Great Southwest. A. H. Abney. LC 75-7116. (Indian Captivities Ser.: Vol. 89). 1976. Repr. of 1875 ed. lib. bdg. 44.00 (ISBN 0-8240-1713-7). Garland Pub.

Life & Adventures of Mr. Francis Clive, 1764, 2 vols. in 1. Phoebe Gibbes. LC 75-1172. (Novel in England, 1700-1775 Ser). 1974. lib. bdg. 50.00 (ISBN 0-8240-1168-6). Garland Pub.

Life & Adventures of Peter Wilkins, a Cornish Man, 1751, 2 vols. in 1. Robert Paltock. LC 74-16040. (Novel in England, 1700-1775 Ser). 1974. lib. bdg. 50.00 (ISBN 0-8240-1134-1). Garland Pub.

Life & Adventures of Sir Bartholomew Sapskull Baronet, 1768, 2 vols. in 1. William Donaldson. LC 74-26834. (Novel in England, 1700-1775 Ser). 1974. lib. bdg. 44.00 (ISBN 0-8240-1183-X). Garland Pub.

Life & Adventures of William Buckley. John Morgan. 1979. Repr. of 1852 ed. text ed. 19.50x (ISBN 0-904573-12-5). Humanities.

Life & Agony of the Elephant Man. Fred Shannon. (Orig.). 1979. pap. 2.25 (ISBN 0-532-23280-1). Manor Bks.

Life & Art of Jerome Tiger: War to Peace, Death to Life. Peggy Tiger & Molly Babcock. LC 80-5245. (Illus.). 300p. 1980. 39.95 (ISBN 0-8061-1656-0). U of Okla Pr.

Life & Confession of the Noted Outlaw James Copeland. facsimile ed. J. R. Pitts. LC 80-20865. (Illus.). 256p. 1980. Repr. of 1909 ed. 12.50 (ISBN 0-87805-125-2). U Pr of Miss.

Life & Correspondence of Rufus King, 6 vols. Rufus King. Ed. by Charles R. King. LC 69-16653. (American Public Figures Ser.). 1971. Repr. of 1894 ed. Set. lib. bdg. 245.00 (ISBN 0-306-71125-7). Da Capo.

Life & Correspondence of Theodore Parker, 2 Vols. John Weiss. LC 76-106987. (American Public Figures Ser). 1864. Set. lib. bdg. 85.00 (ISBN 0-306-71874-X). Da Capo.

Life & Death. George Ohsawa. 30p. 1971. pap. 1.00 o.p. (ISBN 0-918860-03-2). G Ohsawa.

Life & Death Decisions. Arthur Winter. 88p. 1980. text ed. 11.50 (ISBN 0-398-03957-7). C C Thomas.

Life & Death in a Coral Sea. Jacques-Yves Cousteau & Philippe Diole. 1971. 12.95 o.p. (ISBN 0-385-06893-X). Doubleday.

Life & Death in a Coral Sea. Jacques-Yves Cousteau & Philippe Diole. LC 69-13003. (Undersea Discoveries of Jacques-Yves Cousteau). (Illus.). 1978. pap. 8.95 (ISBN 0-89104-089-7). A & W Pubs.

Life & Death of an Oilman. J. J. Mathews. 1974. pap. 5.95 (ISBN 0-8061-1238-7). U of Okla Pr.

Life & Death of Benjamin Robert Haydon, Historical Painter, 1786-1846. 2nd ed. Eric George. 1967. 16.95x (ISBN 0-19-817156-0). Oxford U Pr.

Life & Death of Planet Earth. Tom Valentine. (Illus.). 176p. 1980. pap. 1.95 o.p. (ISBN 0-523-40960-5). Pinnacle Bks.

Life & Death of Rochester Sneath. Humphry Berkeley. (Illus.). 96p. 1981. 11.95 (ISBN 0-241-10416-5, Pub. by Hamish Hamilton England). David & Charles.

Life & Death of Sacco & Vanzetti. Eugene Lyons. LC 74-107414. (Civil Liberties in American History Ser). 1970. Repr. of 1927 ed. lib. bdg. 20.00 (ISBN 0-306-71888-X). Da Capo.

Life and Death of the Cold War: Selected Studies in Postwar Statecraft. Morton A. Kaplan. LC 76-20539. 1976. 19.95 (ISBN 0-88229-335-4); pap. 10.95 (ISBN 0-88229-500-4). Nelson-Hall.

Life & Death of the SLA. Les Payne et al. 1976. pap. 1.95 o.p. (ISBN 0-345-25449-X). Ballantine.

Life & Death with Liberty & Justice: A Contribution to the Euthanasia Debate. Germain Grisez & Joseph M. Boyle, Jr. LC 78-31249. 544p. 1980. pap. text ed. 9.95 (ISBN 0-268-01263-6). U of Notre Dame Pr.

Life & Diary of David Brainerd. Jonathan Edwards. 384p. 1980. pap. 7.95 (ISBN 0-8024-4772-4). Moody.

Life & Glories of St. Joseph. LC 80-53744. 1980. pap. write for info. (ISBN 0-89555-161-6). Tan Bks Pubs.

Life & Growth of Language. William D. Whitney. LC 79-53017. 1980. pap. text ed. 5.00 (ISBN 0-486-23866-0). Dover.

Life & Health: Insurance Law. William F, Meyer. LC 72-76891. (Insurance Law Library). 1972. 47.50 (ISBN 0-686-14516-X). Lawyers Co-Op.

Life & Holiness. Thomas Merton. pap. 1.95 (ISBN 0-385-06277-X, D183, Im). Doubleday.

Life & Labor in Ancient Mexico: The Brief & Summary Relation of the Lords of New Spain. Alonso De Zorita. Tr. by Benjamin Keen. 1964. 20.00 (ISBN 0-8135-0442-2). Rutgers U Pr.

Life & Labours of Asahel Nettleton. Bennet Tyler & Andrew Bonar. 1975. 8.95 (ISBN 0-85151-208-9). Banner of Truth.

Life & Legend of Gene Fowler. H. Allen Smith. 1977. 10.00 o.p. (ISBN 0-688-03188-9). Morrow.

Life & Letters of Emily Dickinson. Martha D. Bianchi. LC 70-162296. 386p. 1972. Repr. of 1924 ed. 15.00x (ISBN 0-8196-0276-0). Biblo.

Life & Letters of George Bancroft, 2 Vols. in 1. George Bancroft. Ed. by Mark D. Howe. LC 78-106990. (American Public Figures Ser). 1970. Repr. of 1908 ed. lib. bdg. 65.00 (ISBN 0-306-71877-4). Da Capo.

Life & Letters of George Cabot. George Cabot. Ed. by Henry C. Lodge. LC 71-124902. (American Public Figures Ser). xi, 617p. 1974. Repr. of 1877 ed. lib. bdg. 69.50 (ISBN 0-306-71001-3). Da Capo.

Life & Letters of Harriet Beecher Stowe. Annie Fields. LC 77-102057. (Library of Lives & Letters). (Illus.). 1970. Repr. of 1897 ed. 20.00 (ISBN 0-8103-3602-2). Gale.

Life & Letters of J. Alden Weir. Dorothy W. Young. LC 76-146157. (Library of American Art Ser.). 1971. Repr. of 1960 ed. lib. bdg. 29.50 (ISBN 0-306-70097-2). Da Capo.

Life & Letters of J. H. Thornwell. B. M. Palmer. 1974. 13.95 (ISBN 0-85151-195-3). Banner of Truth.

Life & Letters of Joel Barlow: Poet, Statesman, Philosopher. Charles B. Todd. LC 70-106988. (American Public Figures Ser). 1970. Repr. of 1886 ed. lib. bdg. 32.50 (ISBN 0-306-71875-8). Da Capo.

Life & Letters of John Winthrop, 2 Vols. John Winthrop. Ed. by Robert C. Winthrop. LC 72-152833. (American Public Figures Ser). 1971. Repr. of 1864 ed. Set. lib. bdg. 75.00 (ISBN 0-306-70147-2). Da Capo.

Life & Letters of Leslie Stephen. Frederick W. Maitland. LC 67-23873. 1968. Repr. of 1906 ed. 15.00 (ISBN 0-8103-3058-X). Gale.

Life & Letters of Lewis Carroll. Stuart D. Collingwood. LC 67-23871. 1967. Repr. of 1899 ed. 18.00 (ISBN 0-8103-3061-X). Gale.

Life & Letters of Lord Macaulay. George O. Trevelyan. 1978. pap. 14.95 (ISBN 0-19-822487-7). Oxford U Pr.

Life & Letters of Paul. Irene Johnson. (Find-a-Word Puzzles Ser.). 48p. (Orig.). (gr. 6 up). 1981. pap. 1.25 (ISBN 0-87239-448-4, 2838). Standard Pub.

Life & Letters of Thomas Cromwell, 2 vols. Roger B. Merriman. Incl. Vol. 1. Life, Letters of 1535; Vol. 2- Letters from 1536, Notes, Index. 1902. 59.00x (ISBN 0-19-822305-6). Oxford U Pr.

Life & Letters of Washington Allston. Jared B. Flagg. LC 68-27719. (Library of American Art Ser). 1969. Repr. of 1892 ed. lib. bdg. 42.50 (ISBN 0-306-71168-0). Da Capo.

Life & Letters of Washington Irving, 4 vols. Pierre M. Irving. LC 67-23893. 1967. Repr. of 1863 ed. 50.00 set (ISBN 0-8103-3044-X). Gale.

Life & Liberation of Padmasambhava, 2 vols. Yeshe Tsogyal. Tr. by G. C. Toussaint & Kenneth Douglas. (Tibetan Translation Ser.). (Illus.). 1978. 55.00 set (ISBN 0-685-80849-1). Vol. I (ISBN 0-913546-18-6). Vol. II (ISBN 0-913546-20-8). Dharma Pub.

Life & Love: A Christian View of Sex. Clyde M. Narramore. (gr. 6 up). pap. 2.25 (ISBN 0-310-29922-5). Zondervan.

Life & Loves of Mr. Jiveass Nigger. Cecil Brown. 1978. pap. 1.25 o.p. (ISBN 0-449-22975-0, Crest). Fawcett.

Life & Memoirs of Ephraim Tristram Bates, 1756. (Novel in England, 1700-1775 Ser). 1974. lib. bdg. 50.00 (ISBN 0-8240-1146-5). Garland Pub.

Life & Mind of John Dewey. George Dykhuizen. LC 73-4602. (Illus.). 472p. 1973. 19.95x (ISBN 0-8093-0616-6). S Ill U Pr.

Life & Miracles of Saint Benedict: Book Two of Dialogues. Gregorius I. Tr. by Odo J. Zimmermann & Benedict R. Avery. LC 80-19624. xv, 87p. 1980. Repr. of 1949 ed. lib. bdg. 13.75x (ISBN 0-313-22766-7, GRLI). Greenwood.

Life & Music of John Field, 1782-1837: Creator of the Nocturne. Patrick Piggott. (Illus.). 1974. 37.50x (ISBN 0-520-02412-5). U of Cal Pr.

Life & Poems of Brookes More. Wilmon Brewer. (Illus.). 1980. 3.00. M Jones.

Life & Professional Career of Emma Abbott. Sadie E. Martin. LC 80-2290. 1981. Repr. of 1891 ed. 28.50 (ISBN 0-404-18858-3). AMS Pr.

Life & Public Services, Addresses & Letters of Elias Boudinot, President of the Continental Congress, 2 Vols. Elias Boudinot. Ed. by Jane J. Boudinot. LC 72-119059. (Era of the American Revolution Ser). 1971. Repr. of 1896 ed. 75.00 (ISBN 0-306-71946-0). Da Capo.

Life & Public Services of Justin Smith Morrill. William B. Parker. LC 79-87371. (American Scene Ser). (Illus.). 1971. Repr. of 1924 ed. lib. bdg. 42.50 (ISBN 0-306-71595-3). Da Capo.

Life & Public Services of Salmon Portland Chase. J. W. Schuckers. LC 76-118202. (American Constitutional & Legal History Ser). 1970. Repr. of 1874 ed. lib. bdg. 59.50 (ISBN 0-306-71934-7). Da Capo.

Life & Public Services of William Pitt Fessenden, 2 Vols. William P. Fessenden. Ed. by Francis Fessenden. LC 70-87532. (American Public Figures Ser). (Illus.). 1970. Repr. of 1907 ed. lib. bdg. 69.50 (ISBN 0-306-71446-9). Da Capo.

Life & Remarkable Adventures of Israel R. Potter. Israel R. Potter. 4.50 o.p. (ISBN 0-8446-2752-6). Peter Smith.

Life & Science in the Twentieth Century. G. E. Allen. LC 77-83985. (History of Science Ser.). (Illus.). 1978. 23.95 (ISBN 0-521-21864-0); pap. 8.50x (ISBN 0-521-29296-4). Cambridge U Pr.

Life & Speeches of Daniel O'Connell, M.P. 264p. 1980. Repr. of 1878 ed. lib. bdg. 65.00 (ISBN 0-89984-365-4). Century Bookbindery.

Life & Speeches of Thomas E. Watson. Thomas E. Watson. (Studies in Populism). 1980. lib. bdg. 75.00 (ISBN 0-686-68880-5). Revisionist Pr.

Life & Teaching of Jesus Christ. E. R. Lewis. (London Divinity Ser.). pap. 3.95 (ISBN 0-227-67519-3). Attic Pr.

Life & Teaching of Lucius Annaeus Seneca. George G. Strem. LC 79-67526. 175p. 1981. 10.00 (ISBN 0-533-04463-4). Vantage.

Life & Teaching of the Masters of the Far East, 5 vols. Spalding. 25.00 set (ISBN 0-87516-088-3); pap. 15.00 set (ISBN 0-686-67590-8). R Collier.

Life & Teachings of Christ, Vol. 1. Gordon Lindsay. (Life of Christ & Parable Ser.). pap. 4.00 (ISBN 0-89985-967-4). Christ Nations.

Life & Teachings of Christ, Vol. 2. Gordon Lindsay. (Life of Christ & Parable Ser.). pap. 4.00 (ISBN 0-89985-968-2). Christ Nations.

Life & Teachings of Christ, Vol. 3. Gordon Lindsay. (Life of Christ & Parable Ser.). pap. 4.00 (ISBN 0-89985-969-0). Christ Nations.

Life & the Scientific & Medical Career of Benjamin Waterhouse: With Some Account of the Introduction of Vaccination in America. an Original Anthology, 2 vols. Ed. by I. Bernard Cohen. LC 79-8004. (Three Centuries of Science in America Ser.). (Illus.). 1980. Set. lib. bdg. 60.00x (ISBN 0-405-12591-7). Arno.

Life & Thought of A. D. Gordon. Herbert H. Rose. 1964. 3.50x (ISBN 0-8197-0176-9). Bloch.

Life & Thought of Isaiah Bowman. Geoffrey Martin. (Illus.). 272p. 1980. 22.50 (ISBN 0-208-01844-1, Archon). Shoe String.

Life & Times in Shoe City: The Shoe Workers of Lynn. Pamela Guren et al. Ed. by Anne Farnam. (Illus.). 1979. pap. 4.00 (ISBN 0-88389-100-X). Essex Inst.

Life & Times in Shoe City: The Shoe Workers of Lynn, An Exhibition at the Essex Institute, Salem. Keith Melder. (Illus.). 56p. 1979. pap. 2.00 (ISBN 0-88389-101-8). Essex Inst.

Life & Times of a Maine Clam. Dethier. 1981. 5.95 (ISBN 0-89272-085-9). Down East.

Life & Times of Akhnaton, Pharaoh of Egypt. Arthur Weigall. LC 79-115209. 1971. Repr. of 1922 ed. 14.50 o.p. (ISBN 0-8046-1102-5). Kennikat.

Life & Times of an Involuntary Genius. Andrei Codrescu. LC 74-24906. 192p. 1976. pap. 3.95 o.p. (ISBN 0-8076-0773-8). Persea Bks.

Life & Times of Asher Brown Durand. John Durand. LC 68-8688. (Library of American Art Ser). 1970. Repr. of 1894 ed. lib. bdg. 27.50 (ISBN 0-306-71167-2). Da Capo.

Life & Times of Benjamin Franklin, 2 vols. James Parton. LC 72-126603. (American Scene Ser). (Illus.). 1971. Repr. of 1864 ed. Set. lib. bdg. 95.00 (ISBN 0-306-70048-4). Da Capo.

Life & Times of Cavour, 2 Vols. William R. Thayer. LC 68-9634. (Illus.). 1971. Repr. of 1911 ed. Set. 38.50 (ISBN 0-86527-117-8). Fertig.

Life & Times of Charles Follen McKim. Charles Moore. LC 70-99857. (Architecture & Decorative Art Ser). (Illus.). 1969. Repr. of 1929 ed. lib. bdg. 32.50 (ISBN 0-306-71324-1). Da Capo.

Life & Times of Confederation, 1864-1867: Politics, Newspapers, & the Union of British North America. Peter B. Waite. LC 63-796. 1962. pap. 8.50 (ISBN 0-8020-6014-5). U of Toronto Pr.

Life & Times of Eamon De Valera. Constantine Fitzgibbon & George Morrison. LC 73-7353. (Illus.). 156p. 1974. 8.95 o.s.i. (ISBN 0-02-538500-3). Macmillan.

Life & Times of Emile Zola. F. W. Hemmings. LC 77-73899. (Illus.). 1977. encore ed. 4.95 o.p. (ISBN 0-684-16356-X, ScribT). Scribner.

Life & Times of Francie Nichol of South Shields. Joe Robinson. 1975. 8.95 o.p (ISBN 0-04-920042-9). Allen Unwin.

Life & Times of Frederick Douglass. Frederick Douglass. Ed. by Barbara Ritchie. LC 66-10063. (gr. 7 up). 1966. 7.95 (ISBN 0-690-50088-2, TYC-J). T Y Crowell.

Life & Times of Hannibal Hamlin, 2 Vols. Charles E. Hamlin. LC 70-137914. (American History & Culture in the Nineteenth Century Ser). 1971. Repr. of 1899 ed. Set. 35.00x (ISBN 0-8046-1482-2). Kennikat.

Life & Times of Henry Clay, 2 vols. Calvin Colton. (Neglected American Economists Ser.). 1974. Set. lib. bdg. 90.00 (ISBN 0-8240-1008-6); lib. bdg. 50.00 ea. Garland Pub.

Life & Times of James Catnach, Late of Seven Dials, Ballad Monger. Charles Hindley. LC 68-20122. 1968. Repr. of 1878 ed. 24.00 (ISBN 0-8103-3412-7). Gale.

Life & Times of John Barrymore. John Barrymore. 1978. Repr. of 1943 ed. 15.85x (ISBN 0-89966-250-1). Buccaneer Bks.

Life & Times of Joseph Warren. R. Frothingham. LC 72-146148. (Era of the American Revolution Ser). 1971. Repr. of 1865 ed. lib. bdg. 49.50 (ISBN 0-306-70133-2). Da Capo.

Life & Times of Liberal Democracy. C. B. Macpherson. 1977. text ed. 6.95x (ISBN 0-19-219120-9); pap. text ed. 4.50x (ISBN 0-19-289106-5). Oxford U Pr.

Life & Times of Maharaja Chhatrasal Bundela. Bhagwan Das Gupta. 178p. 1980. text ed. 10.00x (ISBN 0-391-01771-3). Humanities.

Life & Times of Martin Luther. J. H. D'Aubigne. pap. 9.95 (ISBN 0-8024-4899-2). Moody.

Life & Times of Menelik II: Ethiopia 1844-1913. Harold G. Marcus. (Oxford Studies in African Affairs). (Illus.). 1975. 29.95x (ISBN 0-19-821674-2). Oxford U Pr.

Life & Times of Philip Schuyler, 2 vols. Benson J. Lossing. LC 78-167944. (Era of the American Revolution Ser). 1052p. 1973. Repr. of 1873 ed. Set. lib. bdg. 75.00 (ISBN 0-306-70533-8). Da Capo.

Life & Times of Po Chu-I. Arthur D. Waley. 1949. 9.50 o.p. (ISBN 0-04-951011-8). Allen Unwin.

Life & Times of Samuel Bowles, 2 Vols. Samuel Bowles. Ed. by George S. Merriam. LC 75-87417. (American Scene Ser). 1970. Repr. of 1885 ed. lib. bdg. 75.00 (ISBN 0-306-71562-7). Da Capo.

Life & Times of William Lowndes Yancey, 2 vols. J. W. Du Bose. Set. 18.00 (ISBN 0-8446-1161-1). Peter Smith.

Life & Travels of Josiah Mooso: A Life on the Frontier Among Indians & Spaniards, Not Seeing the Face of a White Woman for 15 Years. LC 75-7124. (Indian Captivities Ser.: Vol. 97). 1976. Repr. of 1888 ed. lib. bdg. 44.00 (ISBN 0-8240-1721-8). Garland Pub.

Life & Work. Lethaby et al. Ed. by Peter Stansky & Rodney Shewan. LC 76-17779. (Aesthetic Movement & the Arts & Crafts Movement Ser.). (Illus.). 1978. Repr. of 1926 ed. lib. bdg. 44.00x (ISBN 0-8240-2485-0). Garland Pub.

Life & Work of Albert Carrier-Belleuse. June E. Hargrove. LC 76-23625. (Outstanding Dissertations in the Fine Arts - 19th Century). (Illus.). 1977. Repr. lib. bdg. 70.00 (ISBN 0-8240-2695-0). Garland Pub.

Life & Work of Alexander Thomson. Ronald McFadzean. (Illus.). 1979. 48.00 (ISBN 0-7100-8858-2). Routledge & Kegan.

Life & Work of C. R. Cockerell. David Watkin. (Studies in Architecture). (Illus.). 1975. 37.50 o.p. (ISBN 0-8390-0152-5). Allanheld & Schram.

Life & Work of Edward Lamson Henry N. A. Elizabeth McCausland. LC 74-100614. (Library of American Art Ser.). (Illus.). 1970. Repr. of 1945 ed. lib. bdg. 39.50 (ISBN 0-306-71866-9). Da Capo.

Life & Work of Evgenij Zamjatin. Alex M. Shane. LC 68-19643. 1968. 23.75x (ISBN 0-520-01164-3). U of Cal Pr.

Life & Work of George Inness. Nicolai Cikovsky, Jr. LC 76-23605. (Outstanding Dissertations in the Fine Arts - American). (Illus.). 1977. Repr. of 1965 ed. lib. bdg. 70.00 (ISBN 0-8240-2679-9). Garland Pub.

Life & Work of Gerardus Joannes Vossius (1577-1659) C. S. Rademaker. (Respublica Literaria Neerlandica). 472p. 1980. text ed. 48.50x (ISBN 90-232-1785-3). Humanities.

Life & Work of John Nash, Architect. John Summerson. (Illus.). 288p. 1980. text ed. 35.00x (ISBN 0-262-19190-3). MIT Pr.
Life & Work of Roger Bacon. John H. Bridges. Ed. by H. Gordon Jones. LC 79-8597. Repr. of 1914 ed. 21.50 (ISBN 0-404-18450-2). AMS Pr.
Life & Work of St. Paul. F. W. Farrar. Date not set. 2 vol. set 43.95 (ISBN 0-86524-055-8). Klock & Klock.
Life & Work of the Seventh Earl of Shaftesbury, 3 vols. E. Hodder. 2150p. 1971. Repr. of 1886 ed. 110.00x (ISBN 0-686-20140-X, Pub. by Irish Academic Pr Ireland). Biblio Dist.
Life & Work of Walt Whitman: A Soviet View. Maurice Mendelson. Tr. by Andrew Bromfield from Rus. 1976. 10.00x o.p. (ISBN 0-8464-0569-5). Beekman Pubs.
Life & Works of Jahiz. Charles Pellat. Tr. by D. M Hawke. (Islamic World Series). 1969. 18.50x (ISBN 0-520-01498-7). U of Cal Pr.
Life & Works of John Hay, 1838-1905: A Commemorative Catalogue. Brown University Library. (Illus.). 51p. 1961. 5.00x (ISBN 0-87057-063-3, Pub. by Brown U Pr). Univ Pr of New England.
Life & Works of John Knowles Paine. John C. Schmidt. Ed. by George Euelow. (Studies in Musicology). 597p. 1981. 49.95 (ISBN 0-8357-1126-9, Pub. by UMI Res Pr). Univ Microfilms.
Life & Works of the Troubadour Raimbaut D'Orange. W. T. Pattison. LC 80-2182. 1981. Repr. of 1952 ed. 35.00 (ISBN 0-404-19015-4). AMS Pr.
Life & Works of William Hodges. Isabel C. Stuebe. LC 78-74383. (Outstanding Dissertations in the Fine Arts, Fourth Ser.). (Illus.). 1979. lib. bdg. 50.00 (ISBN 0-8240-3969-6). Garland Pub.
Life & Writings of Ernest Hemingway. Robert B. Pearsall. LC 72-93573. 282p. (Orig.). 1973. pap. text ed. 20.00x (ISBN 0-391-02005-6). Humanities.
Life Apart. E. J. Miller & G. V. Gwynne. LC 72-304977. xii, 240p. 1972. 9.75 o.p. (ISBN 0-422-73910-3). Lippincott.
Life, Art, & Letters of George Inness. George Inness, Jr. LC 76-87444. (Library of American Art Ser). 1969. Repr. of 1917 ed. lib. bdg. 32.50 (ISBN 0-306-71515-5). Da Capo.
Life As It Was Meant to Be: The Authentic Life from I & II Thessalonians. Lloyd J. Oglivie. LC 80-50541. 160p. 1980 text ed. 8.95 (ISBN 0-8307-0740-9, 5108705). Regal.
Life As Theater: A Dramaturgical Sourcebook. Dennis Brissett & Charles Edgley. LC 74-82604. 392p. 1975. 21.95x (ISBN 0-202-30277-6). Aldine Pub.
Life As Yoga. Tr. by Vimala Thakar & Devendra Singh. 1977. 12.50 (ISBN 0-89684-241-X, Pub. by Motilal Banarsidass India); pap. 8.50 (ISBN 0-686-68508-3). Orient Bk Dist.
Life at Its Best. Meher Baba. 1976. pap. 2.50 o.p. (ISBN 0-525-47434-X). Dutton.
Life at the Dakota: New York's Most Unusual Address. Stephen Birmingham. LC 79-4800. (Illus.). 1979. 12.95 (ISBN 0-394-41079-3). Random.
Life Before Birth. British Museum, Natural History. LC 78-60029. (Illus.). 1979. 7.95 (ISBN 0-521-22382-2); pap. 3.95 (ISBN 0-521-29464-9). Cambridge U Pr.
Life Before Death. Ann Cartwright et al. (Social Studies in Medical Care). 310p. 1973. 22.50x (ISBN 0-7100-7540-5). Routledge & Kegan.
Life Before Man. Margaret Atwood. 304p. 1981. pap. 2.95 (ISBN 0-445-04636-8). Popular Lib.
Life Before Man. Ed. by Time Life Books. LC 72-86602. (Emergence of Man Ser). (Illus.). (gr. 6 up). 1972. lib. bdg. 9.63 o.p. (ISBN 0-8094-1252-7, Pub. by Time-Life). Silver.
Life Before Man: The Story of Fossils. 2nd ed. Duncan Forbes. (Illus.). 64p. (gr. 4-9). 1974. 6.95 (ISBN 0-7136-1300-9). Transatlantic.
Life Begins at One Thousand Five Hundred. Russell Myers. 128p. 1981. pap. 1.50 (ISBN 0-449-14378-3, GM). Fawcett.
Life Below Stairs: Domestic Servants in England from Victorian Times. Frank E. Huggett. LC 77-83231. (Illus.). 1978. 12.00 o.p. (ISBN 0-684-15513-3, ScribT). Scribner.
Life Beyond Earth: The Intelligent Earthling's Guide to Extraterrestrial Life. Gerald Feinberg & Robert Schapiro. LC 80-14009. (Illus.). 480p. 1980. 14.95 (ISBN 0-688-03642-2, Quill); pap. 9.95 (ISBN 0-688-08642-X, Quill). Morrow.
Life Can Be Beautiful. Lois S. Bogart. 1981. 4.95 (ISBN 0-8062-1589-5). Carlton.
Life Changes: Approaches to Social & Political Theory. Ralf Dahrendorf. LC 79-18685. x, 182p. 1981. pap. 5.95 (ISBN 0-226-13443-1). U of Chicago Pr.
Life Choices. Gordon Miller. 176p. 1981. pap. 2.50 (ISBN 0-553-14154-5). Bantam.
Life Comes from Life. Swami A. C. Bhaktivedanta. LC 75-39756. (Illus.). 1979. 5.95 (ISBN 0-912776-84-5); text ed. 5.95 (ISBN 0-685-70923-X). Bhaktivedanta.
Life Course: Integrative Theories & Exemplary Populations. Ed. by Kurt W. Back. (AAAS Selected Symposium: No. 41). 160p. 1980. lib. bdg. 18.50x (ISBN 0-89158-777-2). Westview.
Life, Crime, & Capture of John Wilkes Booth. George A. Townsend. LC 80-129018. (Illus.). 65p. pap. text ed. 10.00 (ISBN 0-686-28746-0). J L Barbour.
Life Cycle & Behavior of Cercoleipus Coelontous (Acarina: Mesostigmata). Including a Survey of Phoretic Mite Associates of California Scolytidae. Donald N. Kinn. (U. C. Publ. in Entomology: Vol. 65). 1971. pap. 6.50x (ISBN 0-520-09379-8). U of Cal Pr.
Life Cycle Costing: A Better Method for Government Procurement. Robert Seldon. (Westview Special Studies in Public Policy & Public Management). 1979. lib. bdg. 32.00x (ISBN 0-89158-277-0). Westview.
Life Cycle of a Fox. Julian May. LC 73-1224. (Illus.). (gr. 2-4). 1973. PLB 4.95 o.p. (ISBN 0-87191-238-4). Creative Ed.
Life Cycle of a Moth. Julian May. LC 73-1059. (Illus.). (gr. 2-4). 1973. PLB 4.95 o.p. (ISBN 0-87191-236-8). Creative Ed.
Life Cycle of a Rabbit. Julian May. LC 73-1185. (Illus.). (gr. 2-4). 1973. PLB 4.95 o.p. (ISBN 0-87191-237-6). Creative Ed.
Life Cycle of a Raccoon. Julian May. LC 73-1187. (Illus.). (gr. 2-4). 1973. PLB 4.95 o.p. (ISBN 0-87191-234-1). Creative Ed.
Life Cycle of a Turtle. Julian May. LC 73-1061. (Illus.). (gr. 2-4). 1973. PLB 4.95 o.p. (ISBN 0-87191-239-2). Creative Ed.
Life Cycle of an Opossum. Julian May. LC 73-1225. (Illus.). (gr. 2-4). 1973. PLB 4.95 o.p. (ISBN 0-87191-235-X). Creative Ed.
Life Cycle of Groups: Group Developmental Stage Theory. Roy LaCoursiere. LC 79-27112. 320p. 1980. text ed. 24.95 (ISBN 0-87705-469-X). Human Sci Pr.
Life Cycle of Magazines: A Historical Study of the Decline & Fall of the General Interest Mass Audience Magazines in the United States, During the Period 1946-1972. A. J. Zuilen. 1977. pap. text ed. 28.50x (ISBN 90-6296-041-3). Humanities.
Life, Death & Beyond. J. J. Turner. pap. 1.95 (ISBN 0-89315-138-6). Lambert Bk.
Life, Death & Medicine: A Scientific American Book. Scientific American Editors. LC 73-16097. (Illus.). 1973. pap. text ed. 7.95x (ISBN 0-7167-0891-4). W H Freeman.
Life, Death & the Government Regulating America's Health. Maidens. 192p. 1981. lib. bdg. 19.95 (ISBN 0-87196-336-1). Facts on File.
Life Designs: Individuals, Marriages, & Families. John H. Gagnon & Cathy S. Greenblat. 1978. 16.95x (ISBN 0-673-07911-2). Scott F.
Life Divine, 2 vols. Sri Aurobindo. 1977. 12.50 o.p. (ISBN 0-89071-269-7); pap. 10.00 o.p. (ISBN 0-89071-270-0). Matagiri.
Life Divine. Sri Aurobindo. 1112p. 1980. 18.75 (ISBN 0-89071-290-5, Pub. by Sri Aurobindo Ashram India); pap. 14.00 (ISBN 0-89071-289-1). Matagiri.
Life Drawings of Michelangelo. Michelangelo. (Dover Art Library). (Illus.). 1980. pap. 2.00 (ISBN 0-486-23876-8). Dover.
Life (Elevator) Servicing & Maintenance. Ed. by L. B. Chiles et al. (Engineering Craftsmen: No. J25). (Illus.). 1974. spiral bdg. 16.50x (ISBN 0-85083-236-5). Intl Ideas.
Life-Extending Technologies: A Technology Assessment. Theodore J. Gordon. 1980. 33.00 (ISBN 0-08-023132-2). Pergamon.
Life Extension: Adding Years to Your Life & Life to Your Years, a Practical Approach. Durk Pearson. (Orig.). 1981. 12.95 (ISBN 0-446-51229-X). Warner Bks.
Life-Extension, Purposeful Relaxation, Differential (Multiple) "Feeling" (Psychophysiological) Awareness & Communication, Set-t-a. Russell E. Mason. 1975. hardback, paper, & tape 50.00x (ISBN 0-89533-018-0); tape-1a, t-3, t-4, t-16, t-17, notes, H.E.S.T-a, set incl., positive personalities: joy, significance, & sexual feelings & values. F I Comm.
Life Financial Reports, Nineteen Eighty Edition. Ed. by Price Gaines. LC 76-6785. 816p. 1980. pap. 24.00 (ISBN 0-87218-011-5). Natl Underwriter.
Life for a Wanderer: A New Look at Christian Spirituality. Andrew M. Greeley. LC 70-78701. 1971. pap. 1.45 (ISBN 0-385-02961-6, Im). Doubleday.
Life for Africa: The Story of Bram Fischer. Naomi Mitchison. 1973. 8.95 (ISBN 0-85036-170-2). Dufour.
Life for Dance. Rudolf Laban. LC 74-32538. (Illus.). 1975. 10.45 (ISBN 0-87830-073-2). Theatre Arts.
Life for Sound Money: Per Jacobsson-His Biography. Erin E. Jacobsson. LC 78-41135. (Illus.). 1979. 49.50x (ISBN 0-19-828411-X). Oxford U Pr.
Life Forces: A Contemporary Guide to the Cult & Occult. Louis Stewart. (Illus.). 1980. 20.00 o.p. (ISBN 0-8362-7903-4); pap. 9.95 o.p. (ISBN 0-8362-7906-9). Andrews & McMeel.
Life-God's Way. Nancy Murdoch & Linda Fassett. 1976. pap. 1.95 (ISBN 0-87123-327-4, 210327). Bethany Fell.
Life Goes to the Movies. Editors of Time-Life Books. LC 75-13606. (Illus.). 1975. kivar 19.92 o.p. (ISBN 0-8094-1645-X, Pub. by Time-Life). Silver.
Life Goes to the Movies. 300p. 1975. 24.95 (ISBN 0-8094-1643-3). Time-Life.
Life Histories of North American Birds of Prey, 2 vols. Arthur C. Bent. (Illus.). Set. 22.00 (ISBN 0-8446-1630-3). Peter Smith.
Life Histories of North American Flycatchers, Larks, Swallows & Their Allies. Arthur C. Bent. (Illus.). 12.00 (ISBN 0-8446-1634-6). Peter Smith.
Life Histories of North American Jays, Crows & Titmice, 2 vols. Arthur C. Bent. (Illus.). Set. 18.00 (ISBN 0-8446-1638-9). Peter Smith.
Life Histories of North American Marsh Birds. Arthur C. Bent. (Illus.). 1927. pap. 6.50 (ISBN 0-486-21082-0). Dover.
Life Histories of North American Nuthatches, Wrens, Thrashers & Their Allies. Arthur C. Bent. (Illus.). 111.50 (ISBN 0-8446-1640-0). Peter Smith.
Life Hungers to Abound: Poems of the Family. Ed. by Helen Plotz. LC 78-5829. (gr. 5-9). 1978. 8.95 (ISBN 0-688-80176-5); PLB 8.59 (ISBN 0-688-84176-7). Greenwillow.
Life I Chose. Giorgio Amendola. Tr. by William Packer from Ital. 1980. text ed. write for info. cancelled (ISBN 0-918294-06-1). Karz Pub.
Life in a Castle. Althea Braithwaite. (Dinosaur Ser.). (Illus.). (gr. 5 up). 1978. pap. 8.75 pack of 5 o.p. (ISBN 0-85933-009-5, Pub. by Paul Elek). Merrimack Bk Serv.
Life in a Castle. Althea Braithwaite. (Illus.). 32p. 1980. 3.50 o.p. (ISBN 0-85122-172-6, Pub. by Dinosaur Pubns). pap. 1.75 o.p. (ISBN 0-85122-172-6, Pub. by Dinosaur Pubns); pap. in 5 pk. avail. o.p. Merrimack Bk Serv.
Life in a Fishbowl. Tom S. Coke. 1978. pap. 2.50 (ISBN 0-88207-764-3). Victor Bks.
Life in a Gothic Novel. Barbara Drake. (WEP Poetry Ser: No. 4). 24p. (Orig.). 1981. pap. 2.50 (ISBN 0-917976-09-6). White Ewe.
Life in a Medieval Castle. Joseph Gies & Frances Gies. LC 74-13058. (Medieval Life Ser). (Illus.). 320p. (Bibl., index). 1974. 9.95 o.s.i. (ISBN 0-690-00561-X, TYC-T). T Y Crowell.
Life in a Medieval City. Joseph Gies & Frances Gies. LC 74-13058. (Apollo Eds.). 274p. 1973. pap. 3.95 o.s.i. (ISBN 0-8152-0345-4, A345, TYC-T). T Y Crowell.
Life in a Medieval Village. G. Morgan. LC 74-12981. (Introduction to the History of Mankind Ser). 48p. (gr. 6-11). 1975. text ed. 3.95 (ISBN 0-521-20404-6). Cambridge U Pr.
Life in a Mexican Village: Tepoztlan Restudied. Oscar Lewis. 8.50 (ISBN 0-8446-2469-1). Peter Smith.
Life in a New Dimension. Don Double. 1979. pap. 1.95 o.p. (ISBN 0-88368-083-1). Whitaker Hse.
Life in a Railway Factory: London Nineteen Fifteen. Alfred Williams. LC 79-56941. 1980. lib. bdg. 28.00 (ISBN 0-8240-0126-5). Garland Pub.
Life in America One Hundred Years Ago. Gaillard Hunt. LC 74-6223. (Illus.). xiv, 298p. 1976. Repr. of 1914 ed. 15.00 (ISBN 0-8103-4017-8). Gale.
Life in & Around the Salt Marshes. Michael Ursin. LC 72-78275. (Illus.). 1972. 6.95 o.s.i. (ISBN 0-690-48982-X, TYC-T). T Y Crowell.
Life in & Around the Salt Marshes. Michael J. Ursin. (Apollo Eds.). (Illus.). 144p. 1972. pap. 2.95 o.s.i. (ISBN 0-8152-0329-2, A329, TYC-T). T Y Crowell.
Life in Anglo-Saxon England. R. I. Page. 1972. 19.95 (ISBN 0-7134-1461-8, Pub. by Batsford England). David & Charles.
Life in California Before the Conquest. Alfred Robinson. LC 68-30553. (American Scene Ser). (Illus.). 1968. Repr. of 1846 ed. lib. bdg. 35.00 (ISBN 0-306-71142-7). Da Capo.
Life in Classical Athens. T. B. Webster. 1978. 19.95 (ISBN 0-7134-1279-8, Pub. by Batsford England). David & Charles.
Life in England: A Pictorial History, 2 vols. Amabel Williams-Ellis & William Stobbs. Incl. Pt. 2. Tudor England. o.p. (ISBN 0-685-32717-5); Pt. 3. Seventh Century England (ISBN 0-216-87195-6); Pt. 4. Hanoverian England. o.p. (ISBN 0-685-32718-3); Pt. 5. Waterloo to 1914. o.p. (ISBN 0-685-32719-1); Pt. 6. Modern Times (ISBN 0-216-87198-0). (Illus.). 1970. 5.00 ea. o.p. Dufour.
Life in Ireland. L. M. Cullen. 1979. pap. 14.95 (ISBN 0-7134-1449-9, Pub. by Batsford England). David & Charles.
Life in New Testament Times. R. Gower. (Ladybird Ser). 1969. lib. bdg. 1.49 (ISBN 0-87508-844-9). Chr Lit.
Life in Our Times. John K. Galbraith. 576p. 1981. 15.95 (ISBN 0-686-69050-8). HM.
Life in Photography. Edward Steichen. LC 63-11119. 1968. 19.95 (ISBN 0-385-05571-4). Doubleday.
Life in Roman Britain. Anthony Birley. 1976. pap. 13.50 (ISBN 0-7134-3161-X, Pub. by Batsford England). David & Charles.
Life in Scotland. Rosalind Mitcheson. 1978. 25.00 (ISBN 0-7134-1559-2, Pub. by Batsford England). David & Charles.
Life in Stuart England. Maurice Ashley. 1967. 19.95 (ISBN 0-7134-1457-X, Pub. by Batsford England). David & Charles.
Life in the Coral Reef. LC 77-79255. (Wild, Wild World of Animals Ser.). (Illus.). 1978. lib. bdg. 11.977 (ISBN 0-686-51174-3). Silver.
Life in the Coral Reef. Time Life Books Editors. (Wild, Wild World of Animals Ser.). (Illus.). 1977. 10.95 (ISBN 0-913948-15-2). Time-Life.
Life in the Dark: How Animals Survive at Night. Seymour Simon. LC 74-934. (Animal Environment Ser.). (Illus.). 72p. (gr. 4-6). 1974. PLB 4.90 o.p. (ISBN 0-531-02719-8). Watts.
Life in the Far West. George F. Ruxton. Ed. by LeRoy R. Hafen. (Illus.). 1951. 9.95 (ISBN 0-8061-0221-7); pap. 4.95 (ISBN 0-8061-1534-3). U of Okla Pr.
Life in the Far West, 1846-47: Among the Indians & the Mountain Men. G. F. Ruxton. LC 72-11539. (Beautiful Rio Grande Classics Ser). lib. bdg. 12.00 o.p. (ISBN 0-87380-098-2). Rio Grande.
Life in the Fiction of Ford Madox Ford. Thomas C. Moser. LC 80-7548. 360p. 1981. 22.50 (ISBN 0-691-06445-8); pap. 8.95 (ISBN 0-691-10102-7). Princeton U Pr.
Life in the Forest. Denise Levertov. LC 78-9356. 1978. 8.00 (ISBN 0-8112-0692-0); pap. 3.95 (ISBN 0-8112-0693-9). New Directions.
Life in the Homeric Age. Thomas D. Seymour. LC 63-12451. (Illus.). 1907. 15.00x (ISBN 0-8196-0125-X). Biblo.
Life in the Leatherwoods. John Q. Wolf. Ed. by John Q. Wolf, Jr. LC 74-3412. 1974. 9.95 (ISBN 0-87870-020-X); pap. 3.95 o.p. (ISBN 0-87870-021-8). Memphis St Univ.
Life in the Living Word. Robert E. Coleman. (Spire Bks). 1975. pap. 1.50 (ISBN 0-8007-8193-7). Revell.
Life in the Middle Ages. George G. Coulton. 71.95 (ISBN 0-521-06947-5); pap. 18.50x (ISBN 0-521-09400-3). Cambridge U Pr.
Life in the Old Stone Age. 2nd ed. Charles Higham. (Introduction to the History of Mankind Ser). (Illus.). (gr. 4-9). 1971. 3.95 (ISBN 0-521-21869-1). Cambridge U Pr.
Life in the Peace Zone: An American Company Town. M. Wilkerson & J. Van Der Zee. 1971. pap. 3.95 o.s.i. (ISBN 0-02-096850-7, Collier). Macmillan.
Life in the Renaissance. Marzieh Gail. (gr. 6-10). 1969. PLB 7.99 o.p. (ISBN 0-394-90298-X, BYR). Random.
Life in the Sea. Creative Editors. LC 70-140638. (Our Changing Environment Ser). (Illus.). (gr. 4-8). 1971. PLB 6.95 o.p. (ISBN 0-87191-073-X). Creative Ed.
Life in the South, from the Commencement of the War: Being a Social History of Those Who Took Part in the Battles, from a Personal Acquaintance with Them in Their Own Homes, 2 vols. Catherine C. Hopley. LC 68-16240. (American Scene Ser.). 831p. 1974. Repr. of 1863 ed. Set. lib. bdg. 65.00 (ISBN 0-306-71015-3). Da Capo.
Life in the Studio. Nancy Hale. 1980. pap. 2.75 (ISBN 0-380-75721-4, 75721, Discus). Avon.
Life in the Theatre. David Mamet. LC 77-91884. 8.95 (ISBN 0-394-50158-6, GP806). Grove.
Life in the Tomb. Stratis Myrivilis. Tr. by Peter Bien from Greek. LC 76-50678. (Illus.). 345p. 1977. text ed. 17.50x (ISBN 0-87451-134-8). U Pr of New Eng.
Life in the Universe. Ed. by John Billingham et al. 400p. 1981. text ed. 20.00x (ISBN 0-262-02155-2); pap. text ed. 12.50x (ISBN 0-262-52062-1). MIT Pr.
Life in the Universe: The Ultimate Limits to Growth. Ed. by W. A. Gale. (AAAS Selected Symposium: No. 31). 1979. lib. bdg. 14.50x (ISBN 0-89158-378-5). Westview.
Life in the Villa in Roman Britain. John Burke. 1978. 19.95 (ISBN 0-7134-1013-2, Pub. by Batsford England). David & Charles.
Life in the Ward. Rose L. Coser. 1962. 7.50 o.p. (ISBN 0-87013-068-4). Mich St U Pr.
Life in These United States. Terry Stokes. LC 78-13018. (Raccoon Book). 1979. signed 4.95 (ISBN 0-918518-14-8); pap. 3.95 (ISBN 0-918518-11-3). St Luke TN.
Life in Upper Canada. Wesley B. Turner. (gr. 6-10). 1980. PLB 6.90 (ISBN 0-531-00447-3). Watts.
Life in Victorian London. L. C. Seaman. 1973. 19.95 (ISBN 0-7134-1465-0, Pub. by Batsford England). David & Charles.

Life in Wales. A. H. Dodd. 1972. 19.95 (ISBN 0-7134-1463-4, Pub. by Batsford England). David & Charles.

Life in Wellington's Army. Antony Brett-James. 1972. text ed. 13.50x (ISBN 0-04-940042-8). Allen Unwin.

Life in Zoos & Preserves. LC 78-56897. (Wild, Wild World of Animals Ser.). (Illus.). 1978. lib. bdg. 11.97 (ISBN 0-686-51173-5). Silver.

Life in Zoos & Preserves. new ed. Time-Life Television Editors. (Wild, Wild World of Animals Ser). (Illus.). 1978. 10.95 (ISBN 0-913948-21-7). Time-Life.

Life Insurance. 10th ed. A. Huebner & K. Black. 1981. 22.95 (ISBN 0-13-535799-3). P-H.

Life Insurance. 9th ed. S. S. Huebner & K. Black. (Illus.). 608p. 1976. 20.95 (ISBN 0-13-535781-0). P-H.

Life Insurance. 2nd ed. David R. Turner. LC 70-92372. 1970. pap. 6.00 o.p. (ISBN 0-668-02343-0). Arco.

Life Insurance Desk Book. 4th ed. Ibp Research & Editorial Staff. 1976. 32.50 o.p. (ISBN 0-685-73750-0). P-H.

Life Insurance in Estate Planning. Munch. 1981. text ed. price not set (ISBN 0-316-58930-6). Little.

Life Insurance: The Great National Consumer Dilemma. Venita VanCaspel. 1980. pap. 1.50 (ISBN 0-8359-4022-5). Reston.

Life Insurance: Theory & Practice. rev. ed. Robert I. Mehr. 1977. 19.95x (ISBN 0-256-01938-X). Business Pubns.

Life Is a Dream. Pedro Calderon. Tr. by William E. Colford from Span. 1958. pap. text ed. 2.25 (ISBN 0-8120-0127-3). Barron.

Life Is a Weaver. Ada B. Stough. 1979. pap. 4.95 (ISBN 0-910286-59-0). Boxwood.

Life Is Just a Bunch of Ziggys. Tom Wilson. LC 73-9101. (Alligator Bks.). (Illus.). 96p. (Orig.). 1973. pap. 2.50 (ISBN 0-8362-0551-0). Andrews & McMeel.

Life Is No Yuk for the Yak. Don Lessem. 1977. 5.95 o.p. (ISBN 0-686-58576-3). Scribner.

Life Is Real Only Then, When "I Am". G. I. Gurdjieff. 1981. 12.95 (ISBN 0-525-14547-8); pap. 6.95 o.p. (ISBN 0-525-47661-X). Dutton.

Life Is the Healer. Eileen J. Garrett. LC 57-13489. 3.75 o.p. (ISBN 0-685-57230-7). Garrett-Helix.

Life Is Tremendous. Charlie Jones. 1981. pap. 2.25 (ISBN 0-8423-2184-5). Tyndale.

Life Is with People: Household Organization of the Contemporary Paiute Indians. Martha C. Knack. (Anthropological Papers Ser.: No. 19). 106p. (Orig.). 1981. pap. 6.95 (ISBN 0-87919-091-4). Ballena Pr.

Life Is Worth Living. Fulton J. Sheen. 1978. pap. 3.95 (ISBN 0-385-14510-1, Im). Doubleday.

Life: Jesus-Style. James Long. 1978. pap. 2.50 (ISBN 0-88207-575-6). Victor Bks.

Life, Liberty, & Property: The Economics & Politics of Land-Use Planning & Environmental Controls. Gordon C. Bjork. LC 80-8038. 160p. 1980. 16.50x (ISBN 0-669-03952-7). Lexington Bks.

Life Line to a Promised Land. Ira A. Hirschmann. (Return to Zion Ser.). (Illus.). xvi, 214p. 1980. Repr. of 1946 ed. lib. bdg. 15.00x (ISBN 0-87991-120-4). Porcupine Pr.

Life, Love & God. Rita Dodson. Date not set. 4.95 (ISBN 0-533-04647-5). Vantage.

Life Machine. A. J. Budrys. 1979. 9.95 o.p. (ISBN 0-399-12257-5). Berkley Pub.

Life Manipulation. David G. Lygre. 177p. 1980. pap. 7.95 (ISBN 0-8027-7162-9). Walker & Co.

Life, Marriage & Death in a Medieval Parish. Zvi Razi. LC 79-8491. (Past & Present Publications). (Illus.). 1980. 27.50 (ISBN 0-521-23252-X). Cambridge U Pr.

Life More Abundant. Charles L. Allen. 1976. pap. 1.50 (ISBN 0-89129-212-8). Jove Pubns.

Life of a Prig. Thomas de Longueville. Ed. by Robert L. Wolff. (Victorian Fiction Ser.). 1975. Repr. of 1885 ed. lib. bdg. 66.00 (ISBN 0-8240-1538-X). Garland Pub.

Life of a Public Man: Edward, First Baron Montego of Boughton. Esther Cope. LC 79-54279. (Memoirs Ser.: Vol. 142). 1980. 9.50 (ISBN 0-87169-142-6). Am Philos.

Life of a Sheriff. Virginia L. Tompkins. Date not set. 5.95 (ISBN 0-533-04768-4). Vantage.

Life of Adam. Giovanni Loredano. LC 67-26617. 1967. Repr. of 1659 ed. 20.00x (ISBN 0-8201-1031-0). Schol Facsimiles.

Life of an Ordinary Woman. Anne Ellis. LC 80-138. (Illus.). xxiv, 301p. 1980. pap. 6.25 (ISBN 0-8032-6704-5, BB 736, Bison). U of Nebr Pr.

Life of Animals with Hooves. W. R. Hamilton. LC 78-56566. (Easy Reading Edition of Introduction to Nature Ser.). (Illus.). 1979. lib. bdg. 7.98 (ISBN 0-686-51137-9). Silver.

Life of Anne Catherine Emmerich, 2 vols. Carl E. Schmoger. 1976. Vol.1. pap. 9.00 o.p. (ISBN 0-89555-059-8, 338-I); Vol.2. pap. 9.00 o.p. (ISBN 0-89555-060-1, 338-I*I); Set. pap. 18.00 o.p. (ISBN 0-89555-062-8). TAN Bks Pubs.

Life of Beetles. M. E. Evans. 1977. pap. text ed. 9.95x (ISBN 0-04-595012-1). Allen Unwin.

Life of Benvenuto Cellini. Benvenuto Cellini. 1979. 5.00x o.p. (ISBN 0-460-00051-9, Evman). Dutton.

Life of Billy Yank. Bell I. Wiley. LC 75-162619. 1978. pap. 8.95 (ISBN 0-8071-0476-0). La State U Pr.

Life of Birds. Maurice Burton. LC 77-88440. (Easy Reading Edition of Introduction to Nature Ser.). (Illus.). 1978. lib. bdg. 7.95 (ISBN 0-686-51139-5). Silver.

Life of Birds, 2 vols. Jean Dorst. (Illus.). 700p. 1974. 50.00x (ISBN 0-231-03909-3). Columbia U Pr.

Life of Bret Harte, with Some Account of the California Pioneers. Henry C. Merwin. LC 67-23887. 1967. Repr. of 1911 ed. 20.00 (ISBN 0-8103-3042-3). Gale.

Life of Buddha: According to the Legend of Ancient India. A. Ferdinand Herold. LC 55-12748. 1954. pap. 5.95 (ISBN 0-8048-0382-X). C E Tuttle.

Life of Buddha: As Legend & History. Edward J. Thomas. (History of Civilization Ser). 1969. Repr. of 1949 ed. 24.00 (ISBN 0-7100-4972-2). Routledge & Kegan.

Life of Buddha: As Legend & History. Edward J. Thomas. (History of Civilization Ser). 1975. pap. 11.95 (ISBN 0-7100-8162-6). Routledge & Kegan.

Life of Cardinal Mannings, Archbishop of Westminster, 2 vols. Edmund S. Purcell. LC 70-126605. (Europe 1815-1945 Ser.). 1534p. 1974. Repr. of 1896 ed. Set. lib. bdg. 85.00 (ISBN 0-306-70050-6). Da Capo.

Life of Charles Dickens. Thomas Wright. 392p. 1980. Repr. of 1935 ed. lib. bdg. 45.00 (ISBN 0-8492-2999-5). R West.

Life of Charles Jared Ingersoll. William M. Meigs. LC 71-127194. (American Scene Ser). 1970. Repr. of 1897 ed. lib. bdg. 35.00 (ISBN 0-306-70041-7). Da Capo.

Life of Charlotte Bronte. Elizabeth Gaskell. 1958. 12.95x (ISBN 0-460-00318-6, Evman); pap. 2.95 (ISBN 0-460-01318-1). Dutton.

Life of Charlotte Bronte. Elizabeth C. Gaskell. (World's Classics Ser: No. 214). 1975. 14.95 (ISBN 0-19-250214-X). Oxford U Pr.

Life of Christ. William Barclay. LC 76-9989. (Harper Jubilee Giant). (Illus.). 96p. 1977. pap. 3.95 o.p. (ISBN 0-06-060403-4, HJG O1, HarpR). Har-Row.

Life of Christ. Irving R. Jensen. (Bible Self Study Ser.). pap. 2.25 (ISBN 0-8024-1067-7). Moody.

Life of Christ. Armin J. Panning. 1971. pap. 2.50 (ISBN 0-8100-0018-0, 09-0932). Northwest Pub.

Life of Christ in Stained Glass. LC 78-59793. (Illus.). 1978. 25.00 o.s.i. (ISBN 0-8027-0618-5). Walker & Co.

Life of Christ in the Paintings by Tissot. Virgil Beauchamp. 1979. deluxe ed. 29.75 (ISBN 0-930582-29-2). Gloucester Art.

Life of Christ Story-N-Puzzle Book. Ruby Maschke. 48p. (Orig.). (gr. 4 up). 1981. pap. 1.25 (ISBN 0-87239-449-2, 2839). Standard Pub.

Life of Christina Rossetti. Mary F. Sandars. LC 74-141488. (Illus.). 291p. 1980. Repr. of 1930 ed. lib. bdg. 27.50x (ISBN 0-8371-5874-5). Greenwood.

Life of David, 2 vols. in one. Arthur W. Pink. (Giant Summit Ser.). 768p. 1981. pap. 10.95 (ISBN 0-8010-7061-9). Baker Bk.

Life of David Haggart, Alias John Wilson, Alias John Morison, Alias Barney M'Coul, Alias John M'Colgan, Alias Daniel O'Brien, Alias the Switcher: Written by Himself, While Under Sentence of Death. David Haggart. LC 80-2482. 1981. Repr. of 1821 ed. 37.50 (ISBN 0-404-19116-9). AMS Pr.

Life of Dr. William F. Carver of California, Champion Rifle-Shot of the World: Truthful Story of His Capture by the Indians When a Child. LC 75-7527. (Indian Captivities Ser.: Vol. 92). 1977. Repr. of 1878 ed. lib. bdg. 44.00 (ISBN 0-8240-1716-1). Garland Pub.

Life of Elbridge Gerry, 2 Vols. James T. Austin. LC 77-99470. (American Public Figures Ser). 1970. Repr. of 1828 ed. lib. bdg. 69.50 (ISBN 0-306-71841-3). Da Capo.

Life of Elijah. A. W. Pink. 1976. pap. 4.95 (ISBN 0-85151-041-8). Banner of Truth.

Life of Emerson. Van Wyck Brooks. LC 80-2528. 1981. Repr. of 1932 ed. 37.00 (ISBN 0-404-19252-1). AMS Pr.

Life of Emma Thursby. R. McCandless Gipson. (Music Reprint Ser.). 1980. Repr. of 1940 ed. lib. bdg. 32.50 (ISBN 0-306-76016-9). Da Capo.

Life of Ernest Renan. Francis Espinasse. 242p. 1980. Repr. of 1895 ed. lib. bdg. 15.00 (ISBN 0-89760-205-6). Telegraph Bks.

Life of Faith. William Romaine. (Summit Bks.). 178p. 1981. pap. 1.95 (ISBN 0-8010-7704-4). Baker Bk.

Life of Fishes. Maurice Burton. LC 77-88434. (Easy Reading Edition of Introduction to Nature Ser.). (Illus.). 1978. lib. bdg. 7.95 (ISBN 0-686-51140-9). Silver.

Life of Friedrich Engels, 2 vols. W. O. Henderson. Incl. Vol. 1. Young Revolutionary; Vol. 2. Marx's Alter Ego. (Illus.). 1974. 65.00x set (ISBN 0-7146-3065-9, F Cass Co). Biblio Dist.

Life of General Custer. Milton Ronsheim. (Custer Monograph: No. 1). (Illus.). 67p. 1978. pap. 8.00x limited ed. (ISBN 0-686-28492-5). Monroe County Lib.

Life of George Bent: Written from His Letters. George E. Hyde. Ed. by Savoie Lottinville. (Illus.). 1968. 14.50 o.p. (ISBN 0-8061-0769-3). U of Okla Pr.

Life of George Bent: Written from His Letters. Ed. by George E. Hyde. (Illus.). 1979. pap. 6.95 o.p. (ISBN 0-8061-1577-7). U of Okla Pr.

Life of George Cabot Lodge. Henry Adams. LC 78-16619. 1978. Repr. of 1911 ed. 24.00x (ISBN 0-8201-1316-6). Schol Facsimiles.

Life of George Gershwin. Robert Rushmore. (Illus.). (gr. 9 up). 1968. 6.95 (ISBN 0-02-777890-8, CCPr). Macmillan.

Life of Gerald Griffin by His Brother. Daniel Griffin. (Nineteenth Century Fiction Ser.: Ireland: Vol. 32). 422p. 1979. lib. bdg. 46.00 (ISBN 0-8240-3481-3). Garland Pub.

Life of Goethe. George H. Lewes. LC 65-21308. (Illus.). 604p. 1980. 15.00 (ISBN 0-8044-2521-3). Ungar.

Life of Guido Reni. Carlo C. Melvasia. Tr. by Catherine Enggass & Robert Enggass. LC 80-11650. (Illus.). 150p. 1981. 11.95x (ISBN 0-271-00264-6). Pa St U Pr.

Life of Gustave Dore. Blanchard Jerrold. LC 69-17492. (Illus.). 1969. Repr. of 1891 ed. 24.00 (ISBN 0-8103-3532-8). Gale.

Life of Handel. Victor Schoelcher. (Music Reprint Ser.). 1979. Repr. of 1857 ed. lib. bdg. 35.00 (ISBN 0-306-79572-8). Da Capo.

Life of Harriet Beecher Stowe. Charles E. Stowe. LC 67-23881. 1967. Repr. of 1889 ed. 20.00 (ISBN 0-8103-3046-6). Gale.

Life of Henry David Thoreau, Including Many Essays Hitherto Unpublished & Some Accounts of His Family & Friends. Ed. by Franklin B. Sanborn. LC 67-23890. 1968. Repr. of 1917 ed. 20.00 (ISBN 0-8103-3047-4). Gale.

Life of Henry Laurens Mitchell: Florida's 16th Governor. George B. Church, Jr. 1978. 7.50 o.p. (ISBN 0-533-03070-6). Vantage.

Life of Hon. William F. Cody: Known As Buffalo Bill, the Famous Hunter, Scout, & Guide. William F. Cody. LC 78-18732. (Illus.). 1978. 15.00x (ISBN 0-8032-1406-5); pap. 4.95 (ISBN 0-8032-6303-1, BB 686, Bison). U of Nebr Pr.

Life of Horace Greeley: Founder of the N. Y. Tribune. Lurton D. Ingersoll. (American Newspapermen 1790-1933 Ser.). (Illus.). 688p. 1974. Repr. 26.50x (ISBN 0-8464-0018-9). Beekman Pubs.

Life of Hydrotransport Pipelines. rev. ed. S. P. Turchaninov. Ed. by W. C. Cooley. Tr. by Albert L. Peabody from Rus. LC 79-66406. Orig. Title: Dolgovechnost' Gidrotransportnykh Truboprovodov. (Illus.). 50.00x o.p. (ISBN 0-918990-04-1). Terraspace.

Life of Insects. Maurice Burton. LC 78-56576. (Easy Reading Edition of Introduction to Nature Ser.). (Illus.). 1979. lib. bdg. 7.95 (ISBN 0-686-51141-7). Silver.

Life of Invertebrates. S. N. Prasad. 800p. 1980. text ed. 50.00 (ISBN 0-7069-1042-7, Pub. by Vikas India). Advent Bk.

Life of James Allan, the Celebrated Northumberland Piper: Containing His Travels, Adventures, & Wonderful Escapes, Etc. James Allan. LC 80-2469. 1981. Repr. of 1817 ed. 62.50 (ISBN 0-404-19101-0). AMS Pr.

Life of James Otis of Massachusetts. William Tudor. LC 70-118203. (Era of the American Revolution Ser). Repr. of 1823 ed. lib. bdg. 49.50 (ISBN 0-306-71936-3). Da Capo.

Life of Jesus. Shusaku Endo. Tr. by Richard Schuchert from Japanese. LC 78-61721. 192p. 1980. pap. 2.95 (ISBN 0-8091-2319-3). Paulist Pr.

Life of Jesus. new ed. Friedrich Schleiermacher. Ed. by Jack C. Verheyden & Leander E. Keck. Tr. by Gilmour MacLean from Ger. LC 72-87056. (Lives of Jesus Ser.). 542p. 1975. pap. 14.95 (ISBN 0-8006-1272-8, 1-1073). Fortress.

Life of Jesus Christ. 2nd ed. J. Stalker. (Handbooks for Bible Classes). 157p. 1891. text ed. 8.95 (ISBN 0-567-28130-2). Attic Pr.

Life of Jesus for Everyman. William Barclay. LC 75-12282. 96p. 1975. pap. 3.95 (ISBN 0-06-060404-2, RD 319, HarpR). Har-Row.

Life of John Banim, the Irish Novelist. John Banim & Michael Banim. Ed. by Robert L. Wolff. (Ireland, Nineteenth Century Fiction - Ser. Two: Vol. 25). 350p. 1979. lib. bdg. 32.00 (ISBN 0-8240-3474-0). Garland Pub.

Life of John Buncle, Esq., 1756-1766, 2 vols. in 1. Thomas Amory. LC 74-31048. (Novel in England, 1700-1775 Ser). 1974. lib. bdg. 50.00 (ISBN 0-8240-1144-9). Garland Pub.

Life of John Bunyan. John Bunyan. (Summit Bks). 1977. pap. 1.95 (ISBN 0-8010-0717-8). Baker Bk.

Life of John Caldwell Calhoun, Vol 1. William M. Meigs. LC 75-127195. (American Scene Ser). 1970. Repr. of 1917 ed. lib. bdg. 69.50 (ISBN 0-306-70042-5). Da Capo.

Life of John Dryden. Sir Walter Scott. Ed. by Bernard Kreissman. LC 63-8121. 1963. pap. 2.95x (ISBN 0-8032-5177-7, BB 157, Bison). U of Nebr Pr.

Life of John J. Crittenden, 2 Vols. Mrs. Chapman Coleman. LC 72-99469. (American Public Figures Ser). 1970. Repr. of 1871 ed. lib. bdg. 69.50 (ISBN 0-306-71843-X). Da Capo.

Life of John McLean. Francis P. Weisenburger. LC 76-150296. (American Constitutional & Legal History Ser.). 1971. Repr. of 1937 ed. lib. bdg. 29.50 (ISBN 0-306-70106-5). Da Capo.

Life of John O'Hara. Frank MacShane. (Illus.). 300p. 1981. 14.95 (ISBN 0-525-13720-3). Dutton.

Life of John Pendleton Kennedy. Henry T. Tuckerman. 490p. 1980. lib. bdg. 65.00 (ISBN 0-89987-813-X). Darby Bks.

Life of John Wesley Hardin As Written by Himself. John W. Hardin. (Western Frontier Library: No. 16). (Illus.). 1977. pap. 3.95 (ISBN 0-8061-1051-1). U of Okla Pr.

Life of John William Strutt, Third Baron Rayleigh, O.M., F.R.S. Robert J. Strutt. (Illus.). 1968. 35.00x (ISBN 0-299-04690-7). U of Wis Pr.

Life of Johnson. James Boswell. (English Library Ser.). 1979. pap. 2.95 (ISBN 0-14-043116-0). Penguin.

Life of Johnson, 2 vols. in 1. James Boswell. 1976. 23.00x (ISBN 0-460-00001-2, Evman). Dutton.

Life of Kakuzo. Yasuko Horioka. 1963. 5.50 o.p. (ISBN 0-89346-074-5, Pub. by Hokuseido Pr). Heian Intl.

Life of King Edward Who Rests at Westminster: Attributed to a Monk of St. Bertin. Ed. by Frank Barlow. Tr. by Frank Barlow. LC 80-2170. 1981. Repr. of 1962 ed. 34.50 (ISBN 0-404-18751-X). AMS Pr.

Life of Lady Mary Wortley Montagu. Robert Halsband. 1956. 23.50x (ISBN 0-19-811548-2). Oxford U Pr.

Life of Laurence Oliphant: Traveller, Diplomat & Mystic. Philip Henderson. 281p. 1981. Repr. of 1956 ed. lib. bdg. 30.00 (ISBN 0-8495-2364-8). Arden Lib.

Life of Lazarillo De Tormes. Tr. by Harriet De Onis from Span. (gr. 11 up). 1959. pap. text ed. 2.95 (ISBN 0-8120-0128-1). Barron.

Life of Lazarillo De Tormes. Tr. by J. Gerald Markley. LC 55-34585. 1954. pap. 2.50 (ISBN 0-672-60203-2, LLA37). Bobbs.

Life of Lidian Jackson Emerson by Ellen Tucker Emerson. Ed. by Delores B. Carpenter. (American Literary Manuscripts Ser.). 1980. lib. bdg. 25.00 (ISBN 0-8057-9651-7). Twayne.

Life of Liszt. Louis Nohl. LC 70-140402. 1970. Repr. of 1889 ed. 18.00 (ISBN 0-8103-3610-3). Gale.

Life of Liza Lehmann. Liza Lehmann. (Music Reprint Ser.: 1980). (Illus.). 1980. Repr. of 1918 ed. lib. bdg. 22.50 (ISBN 0-306-76010-X). Da Capo.

Life of Madam De Beaumont, a French Lady. Penelope Aubin. Bd. with Strange Adventures of the Count De Vinevil & His Family. LC 75-170548. (Foundations of the Novel 1700-1739). lib. bdg. 50.00 (ISBN 0-8240-0548-1). Garland Pub.

Life of Madam Guyon. T. C. Upham. 1961. 10.50 (ISBN 0-227-67521-5). Attic Pr.

Life of Mahatma Gandhi. Louis Fischer. 1962. pap. 1.95 o.s.i. (ISBN 0-02-002830-X, Collier). Macmillan.

Life of Mammals: Their Anatomy & Physiology. 2nd ed. John Z. Young & M. J. Hobbs. (Illus.). 528p. 1975. text ed. 39.00x (ISBN 0-19-857156-9). Oxford U Pr.

Life of Mary Magdalene in the Paintings of the Great Masters, 2 vols. Ralph De Jong. (Illus.). 1979. deluxe ed. 69.75 (ISBN 0-930582-30-6). Gloucester Art.

Life of Maxwell Anderson. Alfred S. Shivers. LC 80-5721. 356p. 1981. 16.95 (ISBN 0-8128-2789-9). Stein & Day.

Life of Meat Eaters. Maurice Burton & Robert Burton. LC 77-88439. (Easy Reading Edition of Introduction to Nature Ser.). (Illus.). 1978. lib. bdg. 7.95 (ISBN 0-686-51142-5). Silver.

Life of Miguel De Cervantes. Henry E. Watts. LC 79-141743. 1971. Repr. of 1891 ed. 15.00 (ISBN 0-8103-3631-6). Gale.

Life of Milton. William Hayley. LC 78-122485. 1970. Repr. of 1796 ed. 37.00x (ISBN 0-8201-1081-7). Schol Facsimiles.

Life of Mr. Jonathan Wild. Henry Fielding. LC 74-17291. (Novel in England, 1700-1775 Ser). 1974. Repr. of 1754 ed. lib. bdg. 50.00 (ISBN 0-8240-1108-2). Garland Pub.

Life of Monkeys & Apes. Michael Boorer. LC 78-56603. (Easy Reading Edition of Introduction to Nature Ser.). (Illus.). 1978. lib. bdg. 7.95 (ISBN 0-686-51143-3). Silver.

Life of Mozart. Edward Holmes. (Music Reprint Ser.). 1979. Repr. of 1845 ed. lib. bdg. 29.50 (ISBN 0-306-79560-4). Da Capo.

Life of Music in North India: The Organization of an Artistic Tradition. Daniel M. Neuman. LC 79-16889. (Illus.). 1979. 16.95x (ISBN 0-8143-1632-8). Wayne St U Pr.

Life of Napoleon. Stendhal, pseud. LC 76-13154. 1977. Repr. of 1956 ed. 15.00 (ISBN 0-86527-272-7). Fertig.

Life of Napoleon Bonaparte, 4 vols. William M. Sloane. 1980. Repr. of 1910 ed. Set. lib. bdg. 125.00 (ISBN 0-8492-8128-8). R West.

Life of O. O. McIntyre. Charles B. Driscoll. (American Newspapermen 1790-1933 Ser.). (Illus.). 344p. 1974. Repr. of 1938 ed. 17.50x (ISBN 0-8464-0022-7). Beekman Pubs.

Life of Oliver Ellsworth. William G. Brown. LC 76-118028. (American Constitutional & Legal History Ser). 1970. Repr. of 1905 ed. lib. bdg. 37.50 (ISBN 0-306-71940-1). Da Capo.

Life of Orator Henley. Graham Midgley. (Illus.). 1973. text ed. 19.25x o.p. (ISBN 0-19-812032-X). Oxford U Pr.

Life of Oscar Wilde. Hesketh Pearson. 389p. 1980. Repr. of 1947 ed. lib. bdg. 35.00 (ISBN 0-89987-658-7). Century Bookbindery.

Life of Our Lord. Charles Dickens. LC 80-22131. (Illus.). 1981. Repr. of 1934 ed. price not set (ISBN 0-664-21382-0). Westminster.

Life of Our Lord in Art: With Some Account of the Artistic Treatment of the Life of St. John the Baptist. Estelle M. Hurll. LC 76-89272. 1969. Repr. of 1898 ed. 18.00 (ISBN 0-8103-3137-3). Gale.

Life of Pachomius. Apostolos N. Athanassakis. LC 75-37766. (Society of Biblical Literature. Texts & Translation-Early Christian Literature Ser.). 1976. pap. 9.00 (ISBN 0-89130-065-1, 060207). Scholars Pr Ca.

Life of Pierre Charles l'Enfant. H. Paul Caemmerer. LC 71-87546. (Architecture & Decorative Art Ser.: Vol. 33). 1970. Repr. of 1950 ed. lib. bdg. 45.00 (ISBN 0-306-71381-0). Da Capo.

Life of Plants. John Simmons. LC 77-88438. (Easy Reading Edition of Introduction to Nature Ser.). (Illus.). 1978. lib. bdg. 7.95 (ISBN 0-686-51144-1). Silver.

Life of Prayer. A. B. Simpson. 122p. 1975. pap. 2.00 (ISBN 0-87509-164-4). Chr Pubns.

Life of Prehistoric Animals. Roger Hamilton. LC 77-88446. (Easy Reading Edition of Introduction to Nature Ser.). (Illus.). 1978. lib. bdg. 7.95 (ISBN 0-686-50007-5). Silver.

Life of R. M. M'Cheyne. Andrew Bonar. 1978. pap. 2.50 (ISBN 0-85151-085-X). Banner of Truth.

Life of Rabindranath Tagore. Prabhat K. Mukherjee. 1976. lib. bdg. 10.00 (ISBN 0-89253-024-3). Ind-US Inc.

Life of Ramakrishna. Romain Rolland. 3.95 (ISBN 0-87481-080-9). Vedanta Pr.

Life of Reason: Volume One, Reason in Common Sense. George Santayana. 1980. pap. text ed. 4.00 (ISBN 0-486-23919-5). Dover.

Life of Reason: Volume Two, Reason in Society. George Santayana. 224p. 1980. pap. 3.50 (ISBN 0-486-24003-7). Dover.

Life of Reptiles, 2 Vols. Angus Bellairs. LC 70-99976. (Natural History Ser.). (Illus.). 1970. Set. 27.50x o.s.i. (ISBN 0-87663-113-8). Universe.

Life of Reptiles & Amphibians. Maurice Burton. LC 77-88437. (Easy Reading Edition of Introduction to Nature Ser.). (Illus.). 1978. lib. bdg. 7.95 (ISBN 0-686-51145-X). Silver.

Life of Richard Wagner, 4 vols. E. Newman. 1976. pap. 14.50 ea.; Vol. 1. pap. (ISBN 0-521-08786-4); Vol. 2. pap. (ISBN 0-521-29095-3); Vol. 3. pap. (ISBN 0-521-29096-1); Vol. 4. pap. (ISBN 0-521-29097-X); pap. 44.50 set (ISBN 0-521-29149-6). Cambridge U Pr.

Life of Richard Wagner: Being an Authorized English Version of das Leben Richard Wagner, Vol. 1. William A. Ellis & C. F. Glassenapp. (Music Reprint Ser.: 1977). 1977. Repr. of 1902 ed. lib. bdg. 37.50 (ISBN 0-306-70881-7). Da Capo.

Life of Richard Wagner: Being an Authorized English Version of Das Leben Richard Wagner, Vol. 2. William A. Ellis & C. F. Glasenapp. LC 77-2022. (Music Reprint Ser., 1977). 1977. Repr. of 1902 ed. lib. bdg. 37.50 (ISBN 0-306-70882-5). Da Capo.

Life of Richard Wagner: Being an Authorized English Version of Das Leben Richard Wagner, Vol. 3. William A. Ellis & C. F. Glasenapp. LC 77-2022. (Music Reprint Ser., 1977). 1977. Repr. of 1903 ed. lib. bdg. 37.50 (ISBN 0-306-70883-3). Da Capo.

Life of Richard Wagner: Being an Authorized English Version of Das Leben Richard Wagner, Vol. 5. William A. Ellis & C. F. Glasenapp. LC 77-2022. (Music Reprint Ser., 1977). 1977. Repr. of 1906 ed. lib. bdg. 37.50 (ISBN 0-306-70885-X). Da Capo.

Life of Richard Wagner: Being an Authorized English Version of Das Leben Richard Wagner, Vol. 6. William A. Ellis & C. F. Glasenapp. LC 77-2022. (Music Reprint Ser). Repr. of 1908 ed. lib. bdg. 37.50 (ISBN 0-306-70886-8). Da Capo.

Life of Robert Burns. Catherine Carswell. LC 78-164157. (Illus.). 1971. Repr. of 1931 ed. 24.00 (ISBN 0-8103-3788-6). Gale.

Life of Robert Lewis Dabney. Thomas C. Johnson. 1977. 13.95 (ISBN 0-85151-253-4). Banner of Truth.

Life of Rossini. rev. ed. Stendhal. Ed. by Richard N. Coe. LC 71-121698. 592p. 1972. Repr. of 1824 ed. pap. 3.95 (ISBN 0-295-95189-3). U of Wash Pr.

Life of Rutherford Birchard Hayes, 2 Vols. Charles R. Williams. LC 79-87678. (American Scene Ser). 1970. Repr. of 1914 ed. lib. bdg. 85.00 (ISBN 0-306-71714-X). Da Capo.

Life of St. Anselm, Archbishop of Canterbury. Eadmer. Ed. & tr. by R. W. Southern. (Oxford Medieval Texts Ser.). 386p. 1972. 31.00x (ISBN 0-19-822225-4). Oxford U Pr.

Life of Saint Benedict: Book II of the Dialogues of Gregory the Great. Gregory The Great. Tr. by Myra L. Uhlfelder. LC 66-30611. (Orig.). 1967. pap. 2.50 (ISBN 0-672-60468-X, LLA216). Bobbs.

Life of Saint Paul. J. Stalker. (Handbooks for Bible Classes). 150p. 1967. pap. text ed. 3.50 (ISBN 0-567-28131-0). Attic Pr.

Life of Sea Mammals. Ray Gambell. LC 78-56582. (Easy Reading Edition of Introduction to Nature Ser.). (Illus.). 1978. lib. bdg. 7.95 (ISBN 0-686-51146-8). Silver.

Life of Sharks. Paul Budker. Tr. by Peter Whitehead. LC 71-148462. (Illus.). 1971. 17.50x (ISBN 0-231-03551-9); pap. 5.95 (ISBN 0-231-08314-9). Columbia U Pr.

Life of Sir James Fitzjames Stephen, a Judge of the High Court of Justice. Leslie Stephen. LC 75-190291. (Illus.). x, 504p. 1972. Repr. of 1895 ed. lib. bdg. 27.50x (ISBN 0-8377-2606-9). Rothman.

Life of Stephen F. Austin, Founder of Texas, 1793-1836. Eugene C. Barker. LC 68-27723. (American Scene Ser). (Illus.). 1968. Repr. of 1925 ed. 49.50 (ISBN 0-306-71153-2). Da Capo.

Life of Strange Mammals. Michael Boorer. LC 78-56571. (Easy Reading Edition of Introduction to Nature Ser.). (Illus.). 1978. lib. bdg. 7.95 (ISBN 0-686-51147-6). Silver.

Life of Swami Vivekananda, Vol. 1. rev. ed. Eastern & Western Disciples of Vivekananda. 629p. 1980. 16.00x (ISBN 0-87481-196-1). Vedanta Pr.

Life of Swami Vivekananda, Pt. 2. rev. ed. 1980. 16.00x (ISBN 0-87481-496-0). Vedanta Pr.

Life of the Blessed Virgin Mary. Anne C. Emmerich. Tr. by Michael Palairet from Ger. 1970. pap. 6.00 (ISBN 0-89555-048-2, 107). TAN Bks Pubs.

Life of the Green Plant. 3rd ed. A. Galston et al. 1980. 17.95 (ISBN 0-13-536326-8); pap. 13.95 (ISBN 0-13-536318-7). P-H.

Life of the Humber. Harry Fletcher. (Illus.). 1975. 10.95 o.p. (ISBN 0-571-10723-0, Pub. by Faber & Faber). Merrimack Bk Serv.

Life of the Hummingbird. Alexander F. Skutch. 1973. 9.95 o.p. (ISBN 0-517-50572-X). Crown.

Life of the Hummingbird. Alexander F. Skutch. (Illus.). 96p. 1980. 15.95 (ISBN 0-517-50572-X). Crown.

Life of the Marquis of Dalhousie, 2 vols. William Lee-Warner. (Illus.). 896p. 1972. Repr. of 1904 ed. Set. 70.00x (ISBN 0-686-28321-X, Pub. by Irish Academic Pr). Biblio Dist.

Life of the Mind in Representational Charts. Georg W. Hegel. Ed. by Charles E. Gary. (Illus.). 1979. 37.75 (ISBN 0-89266-202-6). Am Classical Coll Pr.

Life of the Past. N. Gary Lane. 1978. pap. text ed. 13.95 (ISBN 0-675-08411-3). Merrill.

Life of the Right Honourable Richard Brinsley Sheridan. G. G. Sigmond. 206p. 1980. Repr. of 1848 ed. lib. bdg. 30.00 (ISBN 0-8414-8049-4). Folcroft.

Life of the Unborn: Nurturing Your Child Before Birth. Leni Schwartz. 312p. 1981. 12.95 (ISBN 0-399-90090-X). Marek.

Life of Thomas Cooper. Thomas Cooper. (Victorian Library). 408p. 1971. Repr. of 1872 ed. text ed. 13.00x (ISBN 0-391-00159-0, Leicester). Humanities.

Life of Thomas Hart Benton. William M. Meigs. LC 71-126599. (American Scene Ser). 1970. Repr. of 1904 ed. lib. bdg. 49.50 (ISBN 0-306-70043-3). Da Capo.

Life of Thomas Hutchinson: Royal Governor of the Province of Massachusetts Bay. James K. Hosmer. LC 70-124926. (American Scene Ser). (Illus.). 454p. 1972. Repr. of 1896 ed. lib. bdg. 42.50 (ISBN 0-306-71038-2). Da Capo.

Life of Thomas Jefferson. James Parton. LC 76-126604. (American Scene Ser). (Illus.). 1971. Repr. of 1874 ed. lib. bdg. 59.50 (ISBN 0-306-70049-2). Da Capo.

Life of Tom Horn, Government Scout & Interpreter, Written by Himself, Together with His Letters & Statements by His Friends: A Vindication. Tom Horn. (Western Frontier Library: No. 26). 1964. pap. 4.95 (ISBN 0-8061-1044-9). U of Okla Pr.

Life of Torah: Readings in the Jewish Religious Experience. Jacob Neusner. 1974. pap. text ed. 7.95x (ISBN 0-8221-0124-6). Dickenson.

Life of Tukaram. Justin E. Abbot. 346p. 1980. text ed. 13.50 (ISBN 0-8426-1644-6); pap. text ed. 9.00 (ISBN 0-8426-1654-3). Verry.

Life of Vertebrates. 2nd ed. John Z. Young. 1962. 14.95x (ISBN 0-19-501109-0). Oxford U Pr.

Life of Vivekananda. Romain Rolland. 7.95 (ISBN 0-87481-090-6). Vedanta Pr.

Life of Walter Scott. William Baxter. 8.00 (ISBN 0-89225-114-X). Gospel Advocate.

Life of Washington the Great, Repr. Of 1806 Ed. 5th, rev. ed. Mason L. Weems. Bd. with Eclectic First Reader. William H. McGuffey. Repr. of 1836 ed. LC 75-32156. (Classics of Children's Literature, 1621-1932: Vol. 21). 1976. PLB 38.00 (ISBN 0-8240-2270-X). Garland Pub.

Life of William Blake: With Selections from His Poems & Other Writings, 2 vols. enl. ed. Alexander Gilchrist. (Illus.). 993p. 1969. Set. 35.00. Phaeton.

Life of William Carleton. William Carleton. Ed. by Robert L. Wolff. (Ireland Nineteenth Century Fiction - Ser. Two: Vol. 44). 728p. 1979. lib. bdg. 32.00 (ISBN 0-8240-3493-7). Garland Pub.

Life of William Pinkney. William Pinkney, Jr. LC 75-75276. (American History, Politics & Law Ser). 1969. Repr. of 1853 ed. lib. bdg. 39.50 (ISBN 0-306-71307-1). Da Capo.

Life of William Plumer. William Plumer, Jr. LC 77-87384. (American History, Politics & Law Ser). 1969. Repr. of 1857 ed. lib. bdg. 55.00 (ISBN 0-306-71608-9). Da Capo.

Life on Earth. 2nd ed. E. O. Wilson & T. Eisner. LC 78-4656. (Illus.). 1978. text ed. 18.95x (ISBN 0-87893-936-9); student study guide 6.95x (ISBN 0-87893-679-3). Sinauer Assoc.

Life on Ice. Seymour Simon. LC 75-37512. (How Animals Survive in Their Environment Ser.). (Illus.). 96p. (gr. 4-6). 1976. PLB 4.90 o.p. (ISBN 0-531-01133-X). Watts.

Life on Television: Content Analysis of U.S. TV Drama. Bradley S. Greenberg. LC 80-14478. (Communication & Information Science Ser.). 224p. 1980. text ed. 22.50 (ISBN 0-89391-039-2); pap. text ed. 12.95 (ISBN 0-89391-062-7). Ablex Pub.

Life on the C & O Canal: Eighteen Fifty-Nine. Ed. by Hahn & Clark. 1977. 2.50 (ISBN 0-933788-54-1). Am Canal & Transport.

Life on the English Manor. Henry S. Bennett. (Cambridge Studies in Medieval Life & Thought). 1960. 32.95 (ISBN 0-521-04154-6); pap. 8.95x (ISBN 0-521-09105-5). Cambridge U Pr.

Life on the Mississippi. Mark Twain. (Literature Ser). (gr. 7-12). 1969. pap. text ed. 3.58 (ISBN 0-87720-707-0). AMSCO Sch.

Life on the Mississippi. holiday ed. Mark Twain. 10.95 o.s.i. (ISBN 0-06-014455-6, HarpT). Har-Row.

Life on the Mississippi. Mark Twain. (Illus., TV tie-in edition). 1980. pap. 1.75 (ISBN 0-451-51448-3, CE1448, Sig Classics). NAL.

Life on the Planet Earth. new ed. Harold J. Morowitz & Lucille S. Morowitz. (Illus.). 400p. 1974. text ed. 14.95x (ISBN 0-393-09269-0). Norton.

Life on the Seashore. Heather Angel. LC 78-64656. (Fact Finders Ser.). (Illus.). 1979. lib. bdg. 3.96 (ISBN 0-686-51128-X). Silver.

Life on the Texas Range. Erwin E. Smith & J. E. Haley. LC 52-13181. (Illus.). 1973. 19.95 (ISBN 0-292-74605-9); pap. 9.95 (ISBN 0-292-74623-7). U of Tex Pr.

Life on Ye Ol' Homestead: Tucson Mountains. Bob Riddell. (Illus.). 100p. (Orig.). 1980. pap. 3.95 (ISBN 0-9604184-0-7). Roberts Ent.

Life, Oneself & the Conquest of the Universe. Victor De Maestri. (Intimate Life of Man Library). (Illus.). 1979. 29.75 (ISBN 0-89266-185-2). Am Classical Coll Pr.

Life: Origin & Evolution: Readings from Scientific American. Intro. by Clair E. Folsome. LC 78-15129. (Illus.). 1979. text ed. 16.95x (ISBN 0-7167-1033-1); pap. text ed. 8.95x (ISBN 0-7167-1032-3). W H Freeman.

Life Outdoors: A Curmudgeon Looks at the Natural World. Wayne Hanley. (Illus.). 144p. 1980. cancelled (ISBN 0-8289-0417-0); pap. 5.95 (ISBN 0-8289-0403-0). Greene.

Life Planning. Kirk E. Farnsworth & Wendell H. Lawhead. 96p. (Orig.). 1981. pap. 6.95 (ISBN 0-87784-840-8). Inter-Varsity.

Life-Read All About It. B. Milbauer & K. K. Jacobson. (Getting in Touch Ser: Bk. 3). (gr. 5-8). 0.95 o.p. (ISBN 0-531-02089-4, P43). Watts.

Life Reinsurance. Eli A. Grossman. 79p. (Orig.). 1980. pap. text ed. 4.50 (ISBN 0-915322-38-2). Loma.

Life Science: Intermediate Level. Milton S. Lesser. (gr. 7-10). 1967. pap. text ed. 5.42 (ISBN 0-87720-005-X); tchr's ed. 4.00 (ISBN 0-87720-004-1); wkbk ed. plus free unit tests 6.42 (ISBN 0-87720-003-3). AMSCO Sch.

Life Science Monograph, No. 2. Ed. by G. Raspe. Tr. by J. Long et al. 221p. 1972. text ed. 36.00 (ISBN 0-08-017596-1). Pergamon.

Life Sciences. Committee On Research In The Life Sciences. LC 71-606918. (Illus., Orig.). 1970. pap. 11.50 (ISBN 0-309-01770-X). Natl Acad Pr.

Life Sciences & Space Research. Ed. by R. Holmquist. LC 63-6132. 1977. text ed. 53.00 (ISBN 0-08-021635-8). Pergamon.

Life Sciences & Space Research XVIII: Committee on Space Research. Ed. by Holmquist. 1980. 53.00 (ISBN 0-08-024436-X). Pergamon.

Life Sciences & Space Research XVII. Ed. by R. Holmquist. (Illus.). 1979. text ed. 53.00 (ISBN 0-08-023416-X). Pergamon.

Life Sciences Jobs Handbook. R. B Uleck Associates. (Illus., Orig.). 1979. pap. 9.95 (ISBN 0-937562-01-7). Ulecк Assoc.

Life Scripts from Loving Free. Paula McDonald & Dick McDonald. 1977. pap. 2.25 o.p. (ISBN 0-345-25766-9). Ballantine.

Life Sentences: Aspects of the Social Role of Language. Rom Harre. LC 75-40021. 1976. text ed. 25.50 (ISBN 0-471-35245-4); pap. 12.75 (ISBN 0-471-35244-6, Pub. by Wiley-Interscience). Wiley.

Life Situations: Essays Written & Spoken by Jean-Paul Sartre. Jean-Paul Sartre. 1977. 8.95 o.p. (ISBN 0-394-40845-4). Pantheon.

Life-Span Development & Behavior, Vol. 3. Ed. by P. B. Baltes & O. C. Brim Jr. 1980. 35.00 (ISBN 0-12-431803-7). Acad Pr.

Life-Span Developmental Psychology. James E. Birren et al. (Illus.). 640p. 1981. text ed. 18.95 o.p. (ISBN 0-395-29717-6); price not set instr's. manual o.p. (ISBN 0-395-29718-4). HM.

Life-Span Human Development. Dorothy Rogers. LC 80-25158. 512p. 1981. text ed. 17.95 (ISBN 0-8185-0389-0). Brooks-Cole.

Life Spent for Ireland. W. J. Daunt. 440p. 1972. Repr. of 1896 ed. 17.00x (ISBN 0-7165-0025-6, Pub. by Irish Academic Pr Ireland). Biblio Dist.

Life-Stories. Nonna Osipova. (Illus.). 60p. (Orig.). 1980. pap. 4.00 o.s.i. (ISBN 0-935500-02-2, TX198-101). Am Samizdat.

Life Story of an Old Rebel. John Denvir. 306p. 1972. Repr. of 1910 ed. 15.00x (ISBN 0-7165-0012-4, Pub. by Irish Academic Pr Ireland). Biblio Dist.

Life Story of the Fish. 2nd ed. Brian Curtis. 1949. pap. 4.00 (ISBN 0-486-20929-6). Dover.

Life Stress. Rosalind Forbes. LC 78-55848. 1979. pap. 3.95 (ISBN 0-385-14441-5, Dolp). Doubleday.

Life Stress & Coronary Heart Disease. Ulf De Faire & Tores Theorell. 250p. 1981. 18.50 (ISBN 0-87527-201-0). Green.

Life Stress & Illness. Ed. by E. K. Gunderson & Richard H. Rahe. (Illus.). 274p. 1979. 17.50 (ISBN 0-398-03003-0). C C Thomas.

Life Stress & Mental Health. T. S. Langner & S. T. Michael. LC 63-16587. 1963. 14.95 o.s.i. (ISBN 0-02-917900-9). Free Pr.

Life Studies & For the Union Dead. Robert Lowell. 72p. 1967. pap. 3.95 (ISBN 0-374-50628-0, N329). FS&G.

Life-Style Evangelisim: Crossing Traditional Boundaries to Reach the Unbelieving World. Joseph C. Aldrich. (Critical Concern Bks.). 1981. 8.95 (ISBN 0-930014-46-4). Multnomah.

Life-Style Violent Juvenile. Andrew H. Vachss & Yitzhak Bakal. LC 77-2520. 1979. 25.95 (ISBN 0-669-01515-6). Lexington Bks.

Life Styles. Ulick O'Connor. 1973. pap. text ed. 3.00x (ISBN 0-85105-250-9, Dolmen Pr). Humanities.

Life Styles: An Introduction to Cultural Anthropology. Arthur S. Gregor. LC 78-3416. (Illus.). 1978. 9.95 (ISBN 0-684-15599-0, ScribT). Scribner.

Life Techniques in Gestalt Therapy. Ed. by Joen Fagan & Irma L. Shepherd. 224p. 1973. pap. 1.50 o.p. (ISBN 0-06-080281-2, P281, PL). Har-Row.

Life Testing & Reliability Estimation. S. K. Sinha & B. K. Kale. 1980. 16.95x (ISBN 0-470-26911-1). Halsted Pr.

Life That I've Lived. Shepard B. Clough. LC 80-5503. 297p. 1981. lib. bdg. 19.75 (ISBN 0-8191-1116-3); pap. text ed. 10.75 (ISBN 0-8191-1117-1). U Pr of Amer.

Life: The First Decade Nineteen Thirty-Six to Nineteen Forty-Five. Ed. by Doris C. O'Neil. LC 79-88091. (Illus.). 1980. 22.50 (ISBN 0-8212-0682-6, 528854); pap. 9.95 (ISBN 0-8212-0760-1, 524298PB). NYGS.
Life, the Individual, the Species. Theodore Lane. LC 75-43551. (Illus.). 720p. 1976. text ed. 15.95 o.p. (ISBN 0-8016-2814-8). Mosby.
Life: The Lore & Folk Poetry of the Black Hustler. Dennis Wepman et al. LC 76-12047. 1976. 15.00 (ISBN 0-8122-7710-4); pap. 5.95x (ISBN 0-8122-1089-1). U of Pa Pr.
Life: The Unfinished Experiment. encore ed. S. E. Luria. LC 72-1179. (Encore Edition). 192p. 1973. pap. 0.95 (ISBN 0-684-16374-8, ScribT). Scribner.
Life-Threatening Emergencies in the Dental Practice. Milan Schijatscky. (Illus.). 163p. 1975. 24.50. Quint Pub Co.
Life Through Time. 2nd ed. Harold L. Levin & Robert J. Wallace. Date not set. pap. text ed. cancelled (ISBN 0-697-05036-X). Wm C Brown.
Life Time Encyclopedia of Real Estate Classified Advertising. Turner. 1977. 24.95 o.p. (ISBN 0-13-536458-2). P-H.
Life, Times, & Adventures of George Barrington, the Celebrated Thief & Pickpocket. George Barrington. Bd. with Memoirs of George Barrington, Containing Every Emarkable Circumstance, from His Birth to the Present Time. LC 80-2470. 1981. 29.50 (ISBN 0-404-19102-9). AMS Pr.
Life, Times & Treacherous Death of Jesse James. Frank Triplett. Ed. by Joseph Snell. LC 70-75734. (Illus.). 344p. 1970. 16.95 (ISBN 0-8040-0187-1, SB); limited ed. 30.00 (ISBN 0-8040-0188-X). Swallow.
Life to Live - a Way to Pray. John Coburn. 160p. (Orig.). 1973. pap. 3.95 (ISBN 0-8164-2079-3, SP80). Crossroad NY.
Life to Live: A Novel. Yvonne Burgess. LC 80-17914. 183p. 1981. 8.95 (ISBN 0-8008-4816-0). Taplinger.
Life-Tree Leaves. Sri Chinmoy. 63p. 1974. pap. 2.00 o.p. (ISBN 0-88497-166-X). Aum Pubns.
Life, Trial & Execution of Captain John Brown, Known As "Old Brown of Ossawatomie". John Brown. LC 69-18827. (Law, Politics & History Ser). 1969. Repr. of 1859 ed. lib. bdg. 17.50 (ISBN 0-306-71250-4). Da Capo.
Life with God. Herman C. Theiss. pap. 4.85 (ISBN 0-933350-05-8); tchrs. manual 1.65 (ISBN 0-933350-55-4). Morse Pr.
Life with Grandma. Doreen Tovey. 1964. 7.95 o.p. (ISBN 0-236-31146-8, Pub. by Paul Elek). Merrimack Bk Serv.
Life with the Mentally Sick Child. P. R. Lacey. LC 71-97950. 1970. 11.25 (ISBN 0-08-006978-9); pap. 5.75 (ISBN 0-08-006977-0). Pergamon.
Life with the Painters of la Ruche. Marevna. LC 73-10564. (Illus.). 240p. 1974. 6.95 o.s.i. (ISBN 0-02-579450-7). Macmillan.
Life with Wings. Marge Green. 1966. 6.45 (ISBN 0-89137-403-5); pap. 3.75 (ISBN 0-89137-402-7). Quality Pubns.
Life with Working Parents: Practical Hints for Everyday Situations. Esther Hautzig. LC 76-15223. (Illus.). (gr. 5 up). 1976. 8.25 (ISBN 0-02-743500-8, 74350). Macmillan.
Life Without Death. Nils O. Jacobson. 320p. 1974. 10.00 o.s.i. (ISBN 0-440-04801-X, Sey Lawr). Delacorte.
Life Without End. Bob Hendren. LC 80-54164. (Journey Bks.). 144p. (Orig.). 1981. pap. 2.35 (ISBN 0-8344-0118-5). Sweet.
Life Worth Living. G. Raymond Carlson. (Radiant Life Ser). 1975. pap. 1.95 (ISBN 0-88243-876-X, 02-0876); teacher's ed. 2.50 (ISBN 0-88243-160-9, 32-0160). Gospel Pub.
Life Worth Living. Phyllis Karas. 392p. 1981. 12.95 (ISBN 0-312-48503-4). St Martin.
Life-Writing: A Glossary of Terms in Biography, Autobiography, & Related Forms. Donald J. Winslow. (Biography Monographs Ser.). 64p. (Orig.). pap. 4.50x (ISBN 0-8248-0748-0). U Pr of Hawaii.
Life, Writings & Correspondence of George Borrow, 2 Vols. William I. Knapp. LC 67-23870. 1967. Repr. of 1899 ed. Set. 28.00 (ISBN 0-8103-3051-2). Gale.
Lifeboat Earth. Stanley Schmidt. 1978. pap. 1.75 o.p. (ISBN 0-425-03820-3, Dist. by Putnam). Berkley Pub.
Lifeboat: The Story of Coxwain Dick Evans & His Many Rescues. Ian Skidmore. LC 78-66965. 1979. 14.95 (ISBN 0-7153-7691-8). David & Charles.
Lifeboats to the Rescue. John Beattie. LC 80-70704. (Illus.). 160p. 1981. 17.95 (ISBN 0-7153-8103-2). David & Charles.
Lifeclass. Jean Medawar. (Illus.). 80p. (gr. 3-6). 1981. 13.50 (ISBN 0-686-69427-9, Pub. by Hamish Hamilton England). David & Charles.
Lifeforce. Jean Houston. 1980. 12.95 (ISBN 0-440-05011-1). Delacorte.
Lifegain: The Exciting New Program That Will Change Your Health - & Your Life. Robert Allen & Shirley Linde. (Appleton Consumerhealth Guides). 288p. 1981. 12.95 (ISBN 0-8385-5671-X). ACC.
Lifeline Earthquake Engineering. Compiled by American Society of Civil Engineers. 496p. 1977. pap. text ed. 23.00 (ISBN 0-87262-086-7). Am Soc Civil Eng.
Lifeline of Texas. Roe Richmond. (Lashtrow Ser.: No. 6). 1981. pap. 1.95 (ISBN 0-8439-0892-0, Leisure Bks). Nordon Pubns.
Lifelong Education: A Psychological Analysis. A. J. Cropley. LC 77-5702. 1977. text ed. 23.00 (ISBN 0-08-021814-8); pap. 8.50 o.p. (ISBN 0-08-021815-6). Pergamon.
Lifelong Education & School Curriculum: Interim Findings of an Exploratory Study on School Curriculum, Structures & Teacher Education in the Perspective of Lifelong Education. (Unesco Institute for Education Monographs, No. 1). 90p. (Orig.). 1974. pap. 2.50 (ISBN 92-820-1004-X, U354, UNESCO). Unipub.
Lifelong Education & the Training of Teachers. Ed. by A. J. Cropley & H Ravindra. 1978. text ed. 37.00 (ISBN 0-08-022987-5); pap. text ed. 15.00 (ISBN 0-08-023008-3). Pergamon.
Lifelong Education, Schools & Curricula in Developing Countries. (UIE Monographs Ser.: No. 4). 146p. 1976. pap. 2.50 (ISBN 92-820-1007-4, U356, UNESCO). Unipub.
Lifelong Learners-A New Clientele for Higher Education: Current Issues in Higher Education 1974. Ed. by Dyckman W. Vermilye. LC 74-6738. (Higher Education Ser.). 195p. 1974. 12.95x o.p. (ISBN 0-87589-240-X). Jossey-Bass.
Lifelong Learning During Adulthood: An Agenda for Research. 1978. pap. 4.50 o.p. (ISBN 0-87447-055-2, 237407). College Bd.
Lifelong Learning in the Visual Arts: A Book of Readings. Ed. by Donald Hoffman et al. 160p. 1980. 9.25 (ISBN 0-686-27494-6). Natl Art Ed.
Life's a Dream. Pedro Calderon De La Barca. Tr. by Kathleen Raine & R. M. Nadal. LC 69-17967. 1.95x (ISBN 0-87830-072-4). Theatre Arts.
Life's All a Fragment: Tennyson. Charles Tennyson. 264p. 1980. Repr. of 1953 ed. lib. bdg. 30.00 (ISBN 0-89760-881-X). Telegraph Bks.
Life's Basis: Biomolecules. Gary E. Parker & Thomas R. Mertens. LC 72-10744. (Self-Teaching Guides Ser.). 1973. pap. text ed. 2.95 o.p. (ISBN 0-471-65919-3). Wiley.
Life's Career--Aging: Cultural Variations on Growing Old. Ed. by Barbara G. Myerhoff & Andrei Simic. LC 77-14268. (Sage Series Cross Cultural Research & Methodology: Vol. 4). 1978. 20.00x (ISBN 0-8039-0867-9); pap. 9.95 (ISBN 0-8039-1346-X). Sage.
Life's Christ Places. Joseph Agnew. 206p. 1911. text ed. 2.95 (ISBN 0-567-02008-8). Attic Pr.
Life's Deeper Aspects. N. Sri Ram. 1968. 2.00 o.p. (ISBN 0-8356-7172-0). Theos Pub Hse.
Life's Detours. C. L. Paddock. (Uplook Ser.). 32p. 1952. pap. 0.75 (ISBN 0-8163-0074-7, 12225-9). Pacific Pr Pub Assn.
Life's Golden Gleanings. Ruby E. Stover. 94p. pap. 1.00. Faith Pub Hse.
Life's Joys. Mable L. Everette. 1981. 4.50 (ISBN 0-8062-1667-0). Carlton.
Life's Morning Hour. E. H. Visiak. 1969. text ed. 6.25x (ISBN 0-212-99826-9). Humanities.
Life's Progress Through the Passions; or, the Adventures of Natura, 1748. Eliza Haywood. LC 74-16053. (Novel in England, 1700-1775 Ser). 1974. lib. bdg. 50.00 (ISBN 0-8240-1123-6). Garland Pub.
Life's Story & Healings. Nellie Poulos. 160p. pap. 1.50. Faith Pub Hse.
Life's Thundering Melodies. Marguerite Stanley. 66p. (Orig.). 1980. pap. text ed. 5.50 (ISBN 0-932218-12-1). Hall Pr.
Life's Way. Fredrick W. Allen. 1981. 5.95 (ISBN 0-533-04847-8). Vantage.
Lifesavers: A Guide to First Free Aid, Health & Safety Information. Paul Hartunian. 50p. (Orig.). 1981. pap. 3.95. Tri-Med.
Lifesaving. Boy Scouts Of America. LC 19-600. (Illus.). 56p. (gr. 6-12). 1965. pap. 0.55x o.p. (ISBN 0-8395-3278-4, 3278). BSA.
Lifesaving. 64p. (gr. 6-12). 1980. pap. 0.70x. BSA.
Lifesaving & Marine Safety. U. S. U. L. A. 1981. price not set (Assn Pr). Follett.
Lifeship. Gordon R. Dickson & Harry Harrison. LC 75-25079. 192p. (YA) 1976. 9.95 o.s.i. (ISBN 0-06-011764-8, HarpT). Har-Row.
Lifespan - & Factors Affecting It: Aging Theories in Gerontology. Daniel Hershey. (Illus.). 165p. 1974. pap. 11.25 o.p. (ISBN 0-398-03041-3). C C Thomas.
Lifespan Human Development. Sueann R. Ambron & David M. Brodzinsky. 644p. 1979. text ed. 17.95 (ISBN 0-03-042406-2, HoltC); wkbk. 6.95 (ISBN 0-03-046046-8); instructor's manual avail. (ISBN 0-03-044991-X). HR&W.
Lifestyle: The Autobiography of Robb. Robb. (Illus.). 1979. 19.95 (ISBN 0-241-10169-7, Pub. by Hamish Hamilton England). David & Charles.
Lifestyles & Consumer Behavior of Older Americans. Howard Schutz et al. LC 79-13212. 276p. 1979. 23.95 (ISBN 0-03-049821-X). Praeger.
Lifestyles for the Aging. Edna W. Chandler. 160p. 1980. 9.95 (ISBN 0-525-66685-0). Elsevier-Nelson.
Lifetime Guarantee. Alice Bloch. (Orig.). 1981. pap. price not set (ISBN 0-930436-09-1). Persephone.
Lifetime of a Jew: Throughout the Ages of Jewish History. rev. ed. Hayyim Schauss. (Illus.). (YA) (gr. 9 up). 1976. pap. 5.50 (ISBN 0-8074-0096-3, 383473). UAHC.
Lift (Elevator) Erection. Ed. by L. B. Chiles et al. (Engineering Craftsmen: No. J26). (Illus.). 1978. spiral bdg. 21.50x (ISBN 0-85083-414-7). Intl Ideas.
Lift (Elevator) Practice. Ed. by L. B. Chiles et al. (Engineering Craftsmen Ser.: No. J5). (Illus.). 203p. 1979. spiral bdg. 28.95x (ISBN 0-85083-458-9). Intl Ideas.
Lift Trucks: A Practical Guide for Buyers & Users. Daniel Bowman. LC 72-83304. (Illus.). 1973. 19.95 (ISBN 0-8436-1007-7). CBI Pub.
Lift up Your Heart. Fulton J. Sheen. 280p. 1975. pap. 2.45 (ISBN 0-385-09001-3, Im). Doubleday.
Lifting, Handling & Helping Patients. Patricia A. Downie & Pat Kennedy. (Illus.). 160p. 1981. 19.95 (ISBN 0-571-11630-2, Pub. by Faber & Faber); pap. 8.95 (ISBN 0-571-11631-0). Merrimack Bk Serv.
Lifting, Moving & Transferring Patients: A Manual. Marilyn Rantz & Donald C. Courtial. (Illus.). 219p. 1981. pap. text ed. 9.95 (ISBN 0-8016-4087-3). Mosby.
Lifting Tackle Manual. D. E. Dickie & Douglas Short. 1981. text ed. price not set (ISBN 0-408-00446-0, Fnewnes-Butterworth). Butterworth.
Lifting the Curse. Beryl Kingston. 1980. 17.50x (ISBN 0-85223-176-8, Pub. by Telford England). State Mutual Bk.
Lifting up for the Downcast. William Bridge. 1979. pap. 3.95 (ISBN 0-85151-298-4). Banner of Truth.
Ligand Assay: Analysis of International Developments on Isotopic & Nonisotopic Immunoassay. Ed. by John Langan & Jeremy Clapp. (Illus.). 304p. 1980. 37.50 (ISBN 0-89352-094-2). Masson Pub.
Ligand-Field Parameters. M. Gerloch & R. C. Slade. LC 72-93139. (Illus.). 250p. 1973. 42.50 (ISBN 0-521-20137-3). Cambridge U Pr.
Light. Donald Crews. LC 80-20273. (Illus.). 32p. (ps-1). 1981. 7.95 (ISBN 0-688-00303-6); lib. bdg. 7.63 (ISBN 0-688-00310-9). Greenwillow.
Light. Ernest Holmes et al. Ed. by Willis Kinnear. 93p. 1971. pap. 4.50 (ISBN 0-911336-09-5). Sci of Mind.
Light. Saint-Marcoux. LC 58-8068. (gr. 9 up). 6.95 (ISBN 0-8149-0382-7). Vanguard.
Light a Single Candle. Beverly Butler. (YA) (gr. 7-9). 1970. pap. 1.75 (ISBN 0-671-41133-0). PB.
Light Absorption of Organic Colorants: Theoretical Treatment & Empirical Rules. J. Fabian & H. Hartmann. (Reactivity & Structure Ser.: Vol. 12). (Illus.). 280p. 1980. 79.00 (ISBN 0-387-09914-X). Springer-Verlag.
Light Abstractions. (Illus.). 85p. 1980. 10.00 (ISBN 0-686-66028-5). U Mo-St Louis.
Light & Color. L. W. Anderson. LC 77-27460. (Read About Science Ser.). (Illus.). (gr. k-3). 1978. PLB 9.95 (ISBN 0-8393-0077-8). Raintree Child.
Light & Color: Images from New Mexico. (Illus.). 1980. pap. 12.95 (ISBN 0-89013-134-1). Museum NM Pr.
Light & Dark. Barbara Howes. LC 59-12478. (Wesleyan Poetry Program: Vol. 1). (Orig.). 1959. 10.00x (ISBN 0-8195-2001-2, Pub. by Wesleyan U Pr); pap. 4.95 (ISBN 0-8195-1001-7). Columbia U Pr.
Light & Electron Microscopic Studies of Ascobolus Stercorarius: Aseus & Ascosporeontogeny. Kenneth Wells. (U. C. Publ. in Botany: Vol. 62). 1972. pap. 8.50x (ISBN 0-520-09420-4). U of Cal Pr.
Light & Film. LC 77-116582. (Life Library of Photography). (Illus.). 1970. 14.95 (ISBN 0-8094-1011-7). Time-Life.
Light & Its Uses: Making & Using Lasers, Holograms, Interferometers, & Spectroscopes-C. L. Stong's: "the Amateur Scientist" Readings from Scientific American. Intro. by Jearl Walker. LC 79-27551. (Illus.). 1980. text ed. 17.95x (ISBN 0-7167-1184-2); pap. text ed. 8.95x (ISBN 0-7167-1185-0). W H Freeman.
Light & Lens: Methods of Photography. Ed. by Donald L. Werner. LC 73-84659. (Illus.). 80p. 1973. pap. 8.00 (ISBN 0-87100-043-1, Pub. by Hudson River Mus). Pub Ctr Cult Res.
Light & Life. L. O. Bjorn. LC 76-27618. 1976. pap. 7.95x (ISBN 0-8448-1006-1). Crane-Russak Co.
Light & Other Poems. Ruth Weiss. LC 76-23153. (Illus.). 1976. 10.00 o.p. (ISBN 0-914024-23-X); pap. 3.00 (ISBN 0-914024-25-6). SF Arts & Letters.
Light & Peace. R. P. Quadrupani. LC 79-67860. 193p. 1980. pap. 3.00 (ISBN 0-89555-133-0). Tan Bks Pubs.
Light & Shadow. Carol Schwalbery. LC 74-174587. (Finding-Out Book). 64p. (gr. 2-4). 1972. PLB 6.95 (ISBN 0-8193-0538-3). Enslow Pubs.
Light & Shadows: A History of Motion Pictures. 2nd ed. Thomas W. Bohn et al. LC 77-25909. 1978. pap. text ed. 11.50x (ISBN 0-88284-057-6). Alfred Pub.
Light & the Dark. C. P. Snow. LC 76-29285. 1961. lib. rep. ed. 17.50x (ISBN 0-684-14841-2, ScribT). Scribner.
Light Around the Body. Robert Bly. 1967. 8.95 (ISBN 0-06-010388-4, HarpT); pap. 3.95 (ISBN 0-06-010389-2, CN-786, HarpT). Har-Row.
Light As an Ecological Factor 2: Proceedings. Ed. by G. C. Evans et al. LC 76-921. 1976. 54.95 (ISBN 0-470-15043-2). Halsted Pr.
Light at the Center: Context & Pretext of Modern Mysticism. Agehananda Bharati. 1976. lib. bdg. 11.95 (ISBN 0-915520-03-6); pap. 6.95 (ISBN 0-915520-04-4). Ross-Erikson.
Light at the End of the Tunnel. Harry Hone. (Illus.). 1980. pap. text ed. 10.00 (ISBN 0-9601168-4-2). Am Biog Ctr.
Light at the Top of the Stairs. Dorothy Martin. 256p. 1974. pap. 2.50 (ISBN 0-8024-4748-1). Moody.
Light-Bearer. Sam Nicholson. 1980. pap. 1.95 (ISBN 0-425-04587-0). Berkley Pub.
Light Beyond the Forest. Rosemary Sutcliff. LC 79-23396. 144p. (gr. 4-7). 1980. 8.95 (ISBN 0-525-33665-6). Dutton.
Light Construction Techniques: From Foundation to Finish. Ball. (Illus.). 416p. 1980. ref. ed. 24.95; text ed. 17.95 (ISBN 0-8359-4035-7). Reston.
Light Continent: A Study of East African Society. U. R. Ehrenfels. 7.50x (ISBN 0-210-33696-X). Asia.
Light-Emitting Diodes. Arpad A. Bergh & Paul J. Dean. (Monographs in Electrical & Electronic Engineering). (Illus.). 1976. text ed. 89.00x (ISBN 0-19-859317-1). Oxford U Pr.
Light Entertainment. Richard Dyer. (BFI Television Monographs: No. 2). (Orig.). 1977. pap. 3.25 o.p. (ISBN 0-85170-036-5). NY Zoetrope.
Light for My Life. Desmond B. Hills. Ed. by Bobbie J. Van Dolson. 384p. (gr. 3-8). 1981. price not set (ISBN 0-8280-0041-7). Review & Herald.
Light for Them That Sit in Darkness. John Bunyan. pap. 3.50 (ISBN 0-685-19838-3). Reiner.
Light from Many Lamps. Ed. by Lillian E. Watson. 1980. pap. write for info. (ISBN 0-671-83507-6). PB.
Light from the Ancient East. Adolf Deissman. (Twin Brooks Ser). 1978. pap. 10.95 (ISBN 0-8010-2886-8). Baker Bk.
Light from the Ancient Past, 2 vols. 2nd ed. Jack Finegan. (Illus.). 1959. Vol. 1 2nd Ed. 25.00 (ISBN 0-691-03550-4); Vol. 1 2nd Edition. pap. 8.95 (ISBN 0-691-00207-X); 25.00 (ISBN 0-691-03551-2); Vol. 2. pap. 8.95 (ISBN 0-691-00208-8). Princeton U Pr.
Light from the West: The Irish Mission & the Emergence of Modern Europe. Willism H. Marnell. 1978. 11.95 (ISBN 0-8164-0389-9). Crossroad NY.
Light Heart. 10.00 (ISBN 0-8015-4543-9, Hawthorn). Dutton.
Light Heart. Elswyth Thane. (Williamsburg Ser.: No. 4). 1981. lib. bdg. 17.95 (ISBN 0-8161-3163-5, Large Print Bks). G K Hall.
Light-Horse Harry Lee: The Legacy of the American Revolution. Charles Royster. LC 80-2706. (Illus.). 320p. 1981. 15.00 (ISBN 0-394-51337-1). Knopf.
Light Horsekeeping. Helen Mather. 1970. 7.95 o.p. (ISBN 0-525-14620-2). Dutton.
Light in Britain. Grace Cooke & Ivan Cooke. (Illus.). 1971. 5.50 (ISBN 0-85487-006-7). De Vorss.
Light in the Aquarium. Rolf Kubler. Tr. by Christa Ahrens from Ger. 1973. pap. 2.95 (ISBN 0-87666-096-0, PS-301). TFH Pubns.
Light in the Darkness: Studies in the Gospel of John. Homer A. Kent, Jr. (Illus.). pap. 4.95 (ISBN 0-88469-055-5). BMH Bks.
Light in the Far East: Archbishop Harold Henry's Forty-Two Years in Korea. Edward Fischer. 1976. 8.95 (ISBN 0-8164-0307-4). Crossroad NY.
Light in the Forest. Conrad Richter. (Literature Ser.). (gr. 9-12). 1970. pap. text ed. 3.58 (ISBN 0-87720-755-0). AMSCO Sch.

Light in the Valley: No. 1. Mary Mackie. (Starlight Romances Ser.). 144p. 1981. pap. 1.75 (ISBN 0-553-14366-2). Bantam.
Light: Its Interaction with Art & Antiquities. Thomas B. Brill. (Illus.). 300p. 1980. 29.50 (ISBN 0-306-40416-8, Plenum Pr). Plenum Pub.
Light Metres: Poems. Felicia Lamport. (Illus.). 120p. 1981. 9.95 (ISBN 0-89696-090-0). Everest Hse.
Light Motorcycle Repair. Ross R. Olney. LC 75-8901. (Career Concise Guides Ser.). (Illus.). 72p. (gr. 5 up). 1975. PLB 4.90 o.p. (ISBN 0-531-02832-1). Watts.
Light My Candle. Anita Bryant & Bob Green. (Illus.). 160p. 1974. 5.95 o.p. (ISBN 0-8007-0690-0). Revell.
Light of Asia & the Indian Song of Songs: Gita Govinda. Tr. by Edwin Arnold. 1949. pap. 2.00 (ISBN 0-88253-115-8). Ind-US Inc.
Light of Dark. Themba Hlongwane. 1978. 4.00 o.p. (ISBN 0-682-49074-1). Exposition.
Light of Egypt, 2 vol. Burgoyne. (Illus.). 1980. pap. 15.00 (ISBN 0-89540-064-2). Sun Pub.
Light of Exploration. R. P. Kaushik. LC 76-39622. 1977. 7.95 (ISBN 0-918038-01-4); pap. 3.95 (ISBN 0-918038-00-6). Journey Pubns.
Light of Kirpal. Kirpal Singh. LC 80-52537. 496p. 1980. pap. 12.00 (ISBN 0-89142-033-9). Sant Bani Ash.
Light of Love: Lines to Live by, Day by Day. Barbara Cartland. (Orig.). 1981. pap. 2.50 (ISBN 0-440-15402-2). Dell.
Light of Nature Pursued, 7 vols. Abraham Tucker. Ed. by Rene Wellek. LC 75-11262. (British Philosophers & Theologians of the 17th & 18th Centuries: Vol. 60). 1977. Repr. of 1805 ed. Set. lib. bdg. 231.00 (ISBN 0-8240-1811-7); lib. bdg. 42.00 ea. Garland Pub.
Light of Reason. M. Hollis. 1973. pap. 2.95 o.p. (ISBN 0-531-06046-2, Fontana Pap). Watts.
Light of the Beyond. Sri Chinmoy. (Teachings of an Illumined Master). 221p. (Orig.). 1980. pap. 4.95 (ISBN 0-88497-481-2). Aum Pubns.
Light of the Law. Saul J. Kassin. LC 80-51979. 288p. 1981. 12.95 (ISBN 0-88400-069-9). Shengold.
Light of the Mind: St. Augustine's Theory of Knowledge. Ronald H. Nash. LC 69-19765. 1969. 11.00 o.p. (ISBN 0-8131-1175-7). U Pr of Ky.
Light of Western Stars. Zane Grey. 1980. pap. write for info. (ISBN 0-671-83498-3). PB.
Light on a Mountain. Helena E. Ruhnau. (Illus.). 1975. 7.95 (ISBN 0-686-14460-0); pap. 4.50 (ISBN 0-686-28553-0). Colleasius Pr.
Light on Life's Pathway. John Hash. 1977. pap. 3.95 o.p. (ISBN 0-8407-9502-5, Pub. by Action Press). Nelson.
Light on Lucrezia. Jean Plaidy. 240p. 1977. pap. 1.75 o.p. (ISBN 0-449-23108-9, Crest). Fawcett.
Light on Pranayama: The Yogic Art of Breathing. B. K. Iyengar. 320p. 1981. 12.95 (ISBN 0-8245-0048-2). Crossroad NY.
Light on the Epistles: A Reader's Guide. John L. McKenzie. 204p. 1975. 12.95 (ISBN 0-88347-057-8). Thomas More.
Light on the Gospels. John L. McKenzie. 216p. 1976. 12.95 (ISBN 0-88347-065-9). Thomas More.
Light on the Heavy. Jerry Jenkins. 1978. pap. 2.50 (ISBN 0-88207-769-4). Victor Bks.
Light on the Horizon: The Quaker Pilgrimage of Tom Jones. Thomas E. Jones. LC 74-14286. 200p. 1973. 3.95 (ISBN 0-913408-13-1). Friends United.
Light on the Path. Swami Muktananda. 1972. 2.95 (ISBN 0-914602-54-3). SYDA Found.
Light Princess. George Macdonald. LC 62-12814. (Illus.). (gr. 1-5). 1962. PLB 7.89 o.p. (ISBN 0-690-49308-8, TYC-J). T Y Crowell.
Light Princess & Other Fantasy Stories. George MacDonald. Ed. by George G. Sadler. (Fantasy Stories of George MacDonald Ser.). 176p. 1980. pap. 2.95 (ISBN 0-8028-1861-7). Eerdmans.
Light Scattering by Irregularly Shaped Particles. Ed. by D. W. Schuerman. 345p. 1980. 39.50 (ISBN 0-306-40421-4, Plenum Pr). Plenum Pub.
Light Scattering by Phonon Polaritons. R. Claus et al. (Springer Tracts in Modern Physics Ser.: Vol. 75). (Illus.). 240p. 1975. 34.20 o.p. (ISBN 0-387-07423-6). Springer-Verlag.
Light Scattering in Liquids & Macromolecular Solutions. Ed. by V. Degiorgio et al. 290p. 1980. pap. 35.00 (ISBN 0-306-40558-X, Plenum Pr). Plenum Pub.
Light Scattering in Planetary Atmospheres. V. V. Sobolev. Tr. by W. M. Irvine. 1974. text ed. 46.00 (ISBN 0-08-017934-7). Pergamon.
Light Scattering in Solids. Ed. by Birman et al. 535p. 1979. 55.00 (ISBN 0-306-40313-7, Plenum Pr). Plenum Pub.
Light Scattering in Solids. Ed. by M. Cardona. LC 75-20237. (Topics in Applied Physics Ser.: Vol. 8). (Illus.). 250p. 1975. 45.90 (ISBN 0-387-07354-X). Springer-Verlag.
Light Shadows. Francis Warner. (Oxford Theatre Texts: No. 6). 1980. text ed. 8.50x (ISBN 0-86140-040-2). Humanities.
Light Shines on Mystery Babylon the Great. Walter A. Dawes. (Orig.). 1981. pap. price not set (ISBN 0-938792-10-5). New Capernaum.
Light Shineth in Darkness: Five Studies in Revelation After Christ. Udo Schaefer. Tr. by Helene M. Neri & Oliver Coburn. LC 78-320332. 1977. pap. 4.95 (ISBN 0-85398-072-1, 7-32-28, Pub. by G Ronald England). Baha'i.
Light Sources. W. Elenbaas. LC 72-79283. (Philips Technical Library). 320p. 1972. 32.50x (ISBN 0-8448-0057-0). Crane-Russak Co.
Light to Live by (Wedding Edition) Herbert Lockyer. 384p. 1981. 7.95 (ISBN 0-310-28260-8). Zondervan.
Light Touching Silver: Photographs by Joseph Jachna. Joseph Jachna. Ed. by Steven Klindt. (Illus.). 48p. (Orig.). 1980. pap. 5.00 (ISBN 0-932026-05-2). Chicago Contemp Photo.
Light Upon the Word. Compiled by H. L. Steveson. 1980. pap. 6.95 (ISBN 0-8007-1105-X). Revell.
Light Water Lattices. (Technical Reports Ser.: No. 12). 1962. pap. 13.00 (ISBN 92-0-055062-2, IAEA). Unipub.
Light Water Reactor Nuclear Fuel Cycle. Ed. by Raymond G. Wymer & Benedict L. Vondra, Jr. 256p. 1981. 64.95 (ISBN 0-8493-5687-3). CRC Pr.
Light Within Us. Albert Schweitzer. LC 75-139151. 1971. Repr. of 1959 ed. lib. bdg. 11.75x (ISBN 0-8371-5767-6, SCLW). Greenwood.
Lighten Our Darkness: Toward an Indigenous Theology of the Cross. Douglas J. Hall. LC 75-38963. pap. 9.95 (ISBN 0-664-24359-2). Westminster.
Lightening Round. Dennis St. Sauver. (Tromp It Ser.). (gr. 4-8). 1973. PLB 4.95 (ISBN 0-912022-40-X); pap. 2.95 (ISBN 0-685-93058-0). EMC.
Lighter Verses. Mirza Ghalib. (Translated from Urdu). 8.00 (ISBN 0-89253-756-6); flexible cloth 4.80 (ISBN 0-89253-757-4). Ind-US Inc.
Lighthorsemen. Bill Burchardt. LC 80-1986. (Double D Western Ser.). 192p. 1981. 9.95 (ISBN 0-385-17148-X). Doubleday.
Lighthouse. Eugenia Price. LC 79-163223. 1971. 8.95 o.s.i. (ISBN 0-685-00291-8). Lippincott.
Lighthouse Boy. Clark. 1976. pap. 3.75 (ISBN 0-89272-043-3). Down East.
Lighthouse Keeper's Lunch. Ronda Armitage. (Illus.). (ps-2). 1979. PLB 8.95 (ISBN 0-233-96868-7). Andre Deutsch.
Lighthouse Mystery. Gertrude C. Warner. LC 63-20354. (Boxcar Children Mysteries-Pilot Bk.). (Illus.). 128p. (gr. 3-7). 1963. 6.95g (ISBN 0-8075-4545-7). A Whitman.
Lighthouse of Langdon: Presenting Twentieth Century Jeharah to Doomsday Man. Rohen Langdon. 64p. 1980. 9.00 (ISBN 0-682-49637-5). Exposition.
Lighting. 2nd ed. D. C. Pritchard. (Environmental Physics Ser.). (Illus.). 1978. pap. text ed. 11.95x (ISBN 0-582-41083-5). Longman.
Lighting Craft. Glen Pownall. (New Crafts Ser.). 84p. 1980. 8.25 (ISBN 0-85467-022-X, Pub. by Viking Sevenseas New Zealand). Intl Schol Bk Serv.
Lighting Crafts. Glen Pownall. (Creative Leisure Ser.). (Illus.). 84p. 1974. 7.50x (ISBN 0-85467-022-X). Intl Pubns Serv.
Lighting Fittings, Performance & Design. A. R. Bean & R. H. Simons. (International Series in Electrical Engineering: Vol. 1). 1968. 23.10 o.p. (ISBN 0-08-012594-8). Pergamon.
Lighting for Location Motion Pictures. Alan J. Ritsko. 224p. 1980. pap. 8.95 (ISBN 0-442-23136-9). Van Nos Reinhold.
Lighting Meets the West Wind: The Malaita Massacre. Roger M. Kessing & Peter Corris. (Illus.). 236p. 1980. text ed. 28.00x (ISBN 0-19-554223-1). Oxford U Pr.
Lighting of Building. R. G. Hopkinson & J. D. Kay. 1972. 16.95 (ISBN 0-571-04770-X, Pub. by Faber & Faber); pap. 7.95 (ISBN 0-571-09933-5). Merrimack Bk Serv.
Lighting the Stage: Art & Practices. 2nd ed. W. F. Bellman. 1974. text ed. 24.50 scp (ISBN 0-7002-2421-1, HarpC). Har-Row.
Lightning & Its Spectrum: An Atlas of Photographs. Leon E. Salanave. LC 80-18882. (Illus.). 1980. 25.00x (ISBN 0-8165-0374-5). U of Ariz Pr.
Lightning & the Sun. Savitrix Devi. (Illus.). 440p. (Orig.). 1960. pap. 12.00 (ISBN 0-911038-84-1, Samisdat). Noontide.
Lightning & Thunder. Martin L. Keen. LC 69-12115. (Illus.). (gr. 4 up). 1969. PLB 4.29 o.p. (ISBN 0-671-32116-1). Messner.
Lightning Forward: A History of the 25th Infantry Division (Tropic Lightning) 1941-1978. Melvin Walthall. 1979. 10.00 o.p. (ISBN 0-686-67704-8). Exposition.
Lightning in the Bottle. Charles Beamer. 320p. 1981. pap. 8.95 (ISBN 0-8407-5233-4). Nelson.
Lightning on Ice. Maurice Phillips. LC 63-8733. (gr. 6-9). 1963. 5.95 o.p. (ISBN 0-385-05139-5). Doubleday.
Lightning Southpaw. Robert S. Bowen. (gr. 7-12). 1967. 7.25 o.p. (ISBN 0-688-40992-X). Lothrop.
Lightning: The Poetry of Rene Char. Nancy K. Piore. LC 80-22001. (Illus.). 150p. 1981. 17.95x (ISBN 0-930350-08-1). NE U Pr.
Lightplane Since Nineteen Hundred & Nine. 3rd ed. John W. Underwood. (Illus.). 1981. pap. 10.00 (ISBN 0-911721-56-8). Aviation.
Lights! Action! Camera! Learn! William H. Blazier. LC 74-80347. 1974. 10.00 (ISBN 0-686-10561-3). Allison Pubs.
Lights! Action! Murder! Glen Chase. (Cherry Delight Ser.). (Orig.). 1975. pap. 1.25 o.p. (ISBN 0-685-53127-9, LB274ZK, Leisure Bks). Nordon Pubns.
Lights Along the Delaware. K. H. Bidde & M. W. Rivinus. 1965. 4.95 (ISBN 0-8059-0245-7). Dorrance.
Lights & Pigments: Color Principles for Artists. Roy Osborne. LC 80-8790. (Icon Editions). (Illus.). 176p. (Orig.). 1981. pap. 5.95 (ISBN 0-06-430113-3, HarpT). Har-Row.
Lights & Shadows of Irish Life, 3 vols. Anna Maria Hall. Ed. by Robert L. Wolff. (Ireland Nineteenth Century Fiction, Ser. Two: Vol. 47). 1979. lib. bdg. 46.00 ea. (ISBN 0-8240-3496-1). Garland Pub.
Lights, Camera...Murder. David Snell. LC 79-16542. 1979. 10.95 (ISBN 0-312-48605-7). St Martin.
Light's Manual: Intertidal Invertebrates of the Central California Coast. 3rd ed. Ed. by Ralph I. Smith & James T. Carlton. 1975. 26.50x (ISBN 0-520-02113-4). U of Cal Pr.
Lights of Love, No. 46. Barbara Cartland. 1978. pap. 1.50 o.p. (ISBN 0-685-86779-X). Jove Pubns.
Lights on the Lake. Gregory Maguire. 262p. (gr. 5 up). 1981. 9.95 (ISBN 0-374-34463-9). FS&G.
Lights on Yoga. Sri Aurobindo. 1979. pap. 2.00 (ISBN 0-89744-916-9). Auromere.
Lightweight Aggregate Concrete: Design & Technology. Ed. by Andrew Short. (Euro-International Concrete Committee). (Illus.). 1978. text ed. 38.00x (ISBN 0-904406-24-5). Longman.
Lightweight Bikes. Mick Woollett. (Illus.). 64p. 1981. pap. 5.95 (Pub. by Batsford England). David & Charles.
Lightweight Building Construction. Gyula Sebestyen. LC 77-21902. 1978. 47.95 (ISBN 0-470-99166-6). Halsted Pr.
Lightweight Concrete. 3rd ed. Andrew Short & William Kinnibugh. (Illus.). 1978. text ed. 71.30x (ISBN 0-85334-734-4). Intl Ideas.
Lightweight Equipment for Hiking, Camping & Mountaineering. 13th ed. Don Schaefer. 1972. pap. 1.00 o.p. (ISBN 0-915746-04-2). Potomac Appalach.
Lignin Biodegradation & Transformation. Ronald L. Crawford. 192p. 1981. 22.50 (ISBN 0-471-05743-6, Pub. by Wiley-Interscience). Wiley.
Lignin Biodegradation: Microbiology, Chemistry & Potential Applications, 2 vols. T. Kent Kirk et al. 1980. 64.95 ea.; Vol. 2, 272p. (ISBN 0-8493-5459-5); Vol. 2. (ISBN 0-8493-5460-9). CRC Pr.
Lignite Technology. Ed. by Perry Nowacki. LC 79-26051. (Energy Technology Review Ser. No. 53; Chemical Technology Review Ser.: No. 146). (Illus.). 1980. 42.00 (ISBN 0-8155-0783-6). Noyes.
Like a Brother, Like a Lover: Male Homosexuality in the American Novel & Theatre from Herman Melville to James Baldwin. Georges-Michel Sarotte. LC 77-80912. 1978. 10.00 o.p. (ISBN 0-385-12765-0, Anchor Pr). Doubleday.
Like a Mantle, the Sea. Stella Shepherd. LC 73-85450. (Illus.). 184p. 1971. 9.50x (ISBN 0-8214-0133-5). Ohio U Pr.
Like a Mighty River. David Manuel. LC 77-90948. (Illus.). 220p. 1977. 5.95 (ISBN 0-932260-02-0). Rock Harbor.
Like a Red, Red Rose. Florence Musgrave. (Illus.). (gr. 6-9). 1958. 4.95 o.p. (ISBN 0-8038-4236-8). Hastings.
Like a Shock of Wheat. Marvin Hein. LC 80-22224. 192p. 1981. pap. 7.95 (ISBN 0-8361-1938-X). Herald Pr.
Like & Unlike: Stages 1, 2, & 3. Albert James. LC 77-83007. (Science 5-13 Ser.). (Illus.). 1977. pap. text ed. 8.25 (ISBN 0-356-04350-9). Raintree Child.
Like Chocolate Chip Cookies. Gary Trudeau. 1980. pap. 1.50 o.p. (ISBN 0-445-00622-6). Popular Lib.
Like Christ. Andrew Murray. 240p. 1974. pap. 2.25 (ISBN 0-87123-337-1, 200337). Bethany Fell.
Like Christ. Andrew Murray. 240p. 1981. pap. 2.50 (ISBN 0-88368-099-8). Whitaker Hse.
Like Everybody Else. Barbara Girion. LC 80-21850. 192p. (gr. 6-8). 1980. 8.95 (ISBN 0-684-16715-8). Scribner.
Like Father. David Black. LC 78-6841. 1978. 8.95 (ISBN 0-396-07587-8, Dist. by W.W. Noryon). Dembner Bks.
Like Fathers, Like Sons: Portraits of Intimacy & Strain. Thomas J. Cottle. 300p. 1981. price not set (ISBN 0-89391-054-6). Ablex Pub.
Like It Is: Arthur E. Thomas Interviews Leaders on Black America. Ed. by Emily Rovetch. 1981. text ed. 9.95 (ISBN 0-525-93193-7); pap. 5.95 (ISBN 0-525-93194-5); tchr's. guide 3.95 (ISBN 0-525-93195-3). Dutton.
Like It Is: From Voices of Today's Youth. Tamara De Ford. Ed. by Mary Faville & Ray Otero. (Illus.). 185p. 1980. pap. text ed. 9.95 (ISBN 0-931908-06-X). Sag Scriptory.
Like, Love, Lust: A View of Sex & Sexuality. John Langone. 144p. 1981. pap. 2.25 (ISBN 0-380-54189-0, 54189). Avon.
Like, Love, Lust: A View of Sex & Sexuality. John Langone. 204p. (gr. 7 up). 1980. 7.95 (ISBN 0-316-51429-2). Little.
Like Mad. Mad Magazine Editors. (Mad Ser.). (Illus.). 1973. pap. 1.75 (ISBN 0-446-94371-1). Warner Bks.
Like Nothing at All. Aileen Fisher. LC 60-9159. (Illus.). (ps-3). 1979. PLB 8.79 (ISBN 0-690-49379-7, TYC-J). T Y Crowell.
Like the Lion's Tooth. Marjorie Kellogg. (YA) (RL 10). 1973. pap. 1.25 (ISBN 0-451-05655-8, Y5655, Sig). NAL.
Like You & Me. Eric P. Hamp & Jean Greenlaw. (Design for Reading Ser). (Illus.). (preprimer 2). 1972. pap. text ed. 2.92 (ISBN 0-06-516001-0, SchDept). Har-Row.
Like Yourself: And Others Will Too. Abraham Twerski. LC 78-16816. 1978. 10.95 (ISBN 0-13-536474-4, Spec); pap. 5.95 (ISBN 0-13-536466-3). P-H.
Likeness: A Conceptual History of Ancient Portraiture. James D. Breckenridge. LC 68-29325. (Illus.). 1969. 18.25x o.s.i. (ISBN 0-8101-0024-X). Northwestern U Pr.
Lilac Fairy Book. Andrew Lang. (Illus.). 7.50 (ISBN 0-8446-2425-X). Peter Smith.
Lilac Fairy: Prologue from the Sleeping Beauty. Valerie J. Sutton. (Illus.). 1973. pap. text ed. 1.25x o.p. (ISBN 0-914336-11-8). Move Short Soc.
Liliana's Journal: Warsaw 1939-1945. Liliana Zuker-Bujanowska. (Illus.). 176p. 1980. 9.95 (ISBN 0-8037-4997-X). Dial.
Liliane. Annabel Erwin. 400p. (Orig.). 1976. pap. 2.50 o.s.i. (ISBN 0-446-91219-0). Warner Bks.
Lilia's Yoga & Your Life. Lilias M. Folan. 1981. 8.95 (ISBN 0-02-080060-6, Collier). Macmillan.
Lilies, Rabbits, & Painted Eggs: The Story of the Easter Symbols. Edna Barth. LC 74-79033. (Illus.). (gr. 2-5). 1970. 8.95 (ISBN 0-395-28844-4, Clarion). HM.
Lilies, Rabbits, & Painted Eggs: The Story of the Easter Symbols. Edna Barth. (Illus.). 64p. (gr. 3-6). 1981. pap. 3.95 (ISBN 0-686-69042-7, Clarion). HM.
Lilith: The Roundtree Women. Margaret Lewerth. (Orig.). 1981. pap. 3.25 (ISBN 0-440-14630-5). Dell.
Lillian Hellman. Doris V. Falk. LC 78-4299. (Modern Literature Ser.). 1978. 10.95 (ISBN 0-8044-2194-3); pap. 3.45 (ISBN 0-8044-6144-9). Ungar.
Lillian Hellman. Katherine Lederer. (United States Authors Ser.: No. 338). 1979. 9.95 (ISBN 0-8057-7275-8). Twayne.
Lillian Hellman: A Bibliography, 1926-1978. Mary M. Riordan. LC 80-16147. (Author Bibliographies Ser.: No. 50). 244p. 1980. 13.50 (ISBN 0-8108-1320-3). Scarecrow.
Lillibooks, 3 bks. Louise Louis. Incl. Marriage Idyll. 8p; Persistent Pilgrim. 16p; Sheltered Hours. 16p. (Illus.). 1979. Set. pap. 3.99. Pen-Art.
Lillibooks & Consulate of One, 4 bks. Louise Louis. 1977. Set. pap. 3.99. Pen-Art.
Lillie. David Butler. (Orig.). 1979. pap. 2.75 (ISBN 0-446-95818-2). Warner Bks.
Lillie May Nicholson: 1884-1964 an Artist Rediscovered. Walter A. Nelson-Rees. LC 80-53867. (Illus.). 88p. 1981. 38.50 (ISBN 0-938842-00-5). WIM Oakland.
Lilly on Dolphins-Humans of the Sea. Lilly, John C., M.D. LC 75-2854. 520p. 1975. pap. 4.50 (ISBN 0-385-11037-5, Anch). Doubleday.
Lily at the Table. Linda Heller. LC 79-11415. (Illus.). (ps-2). 1979. 8.95 (ISBN 0-02-743530-X). Macmillan.
Limb-Deficient Child. Ed. by Berton Blakeslee. (Illus.). 1963. 32.50x (ISBN 0-520-00125-7). U of Cal Pr.
Limb to Limb. John Russo. (Orig.). 1981. pap. price not set (ISBN 0-671-41690-1). PB.
Limba Stories & Story-Telling. Ruth H. Finnegan. LC 80-25904. (Oxford Library of African Literature). xii, 352p. 1981. Repr. of 1967 ed. lib. bdg. 28.75x (ISBN 0-313-22723-3, FILS). Greenwood.
Limbo. Carobeth Laird. LC 79-10937. 190p. 1979. pap. 5.95 (ISBN 0-88316-536-8). Chandler & Sharp.

Lime Pit. Jonathan Valin. LC 79-28205. 256p. 1980. 8.95 (ISBN 0-396-07818-4). Dodd.

Limericks for Children. Veronica Potz & Lawrence J. Babin. (See-Hear-Color Me Book Ser.). 1981. 6.95 (ISBN 0-912492-15-5). Pyquag.

Limericks Historical & Hysterical: Plagiarized, Arranged, Annotated & Some Written by Ray Allen Billington. Ray A. Billington. 1981. 9.95 (ISBN 0-393-01453-3). Norton.

Limericks Lewd & Lusty. Compiled by Harold H. Hart. 352p. 1981. pap. 3.95 (ISBN 0-89104-196-6). A & W Pubs.

Limericks: Too Gross. Issac Asimov & John Ciardi. 1978. 8.95 (ISBN 0-393-04522-6); pap. write for info. (ISBN 0-393-04530-7). Norton.

Limestone & Dolomite Resources: Lower Cretaceous Rocks, Texas. P. U. Rodda et al. (Illus.). 286p. 1966. 4.50 (RI 56). Bur Econ Geology.

Limestones & Caves of North-West England. Ed. by A. C. Waltham. (Illus.). 1974. 22.50 (ISBN 0-7153-6181-3). David & Charles.

Limestones & Caves of the Mendip Hills. Ed. by D. I. Smith & D. P. Drew. LC 74-76186. 1975. 22.50 (ISBN 0-7153-6572-X). David & Charles.

Limit Analysis of Structures at Thermal Cycling. D. A. Gokhfeld & O. F. Cherniavsky. (Mechanics of Plastic Solids Ser.: No. 4). 576p. 1980. 110.00x (ISBN 90-286-0455-3). Sijthoff & Noordhoff.

Limit Design for Reinforced Concrete Structures. M. Z. Cohn. (Bibliography: No. 8). 1970. pap. 26.25 (ISBN 0-685-85146-X, B-8) (ISBN 0-685-85147-8). ACI.

Limit-State Design of Prestressed Concrete, Vol. 2: The Design of the Member. Y. Guyon. Tr. by F. H. Turner from Fr. LC 72-2655. 469p. 1974. 52.95 (ISBN 0-470-33791-5). Halsted Pr.

Limit State Design of Reinforced Concrete Structures. Derrick Beckett. LC 74-20975. 134p. 1975. 19.95 (ISBN 0-470-06128-6). Halsted Pr.

Limit State Theory for Reinforced Concrete Design. 2nd ed. B. P. Hughes. (Illus.). 1977. 24.95x (ISBN 0-8464-0572-5); pap. text ed. 17.50x (ISBN 0-8464-0573-3). Beekman Pubs.

Limitation of Activity & Mobility Due to Chronic Conditions, U. S., 1972. Charles S. Wilder. LC 74-12431. (Data from the Health Interview Survey Ser. 10: No. 96). 54p. 1975. pap. text ed. 1.15 (ISBN 0-8406-0024-0). Natl Ctr Health Stats.

Limited Entry as a Fishery Management Tool. Ed. by R. Bruce Rettig & Jay J. Ginter. (Washington Sea Grant Ser.). 584p. 1980. pap. 15.00 (ISBN 0-295-95741-7). U of Wash Pr.

Limited Entry into the Commercial Fisheries. Ed. by J. Carl Mundt. Institute for Marine Studies. 154p. 1976. pap. 5.50 (ISBN 0-295-95496-5). U of Wash Pr.

Limited Government: A Comparison. Carl J. Friedrich. LC 74-802. (Contemporary Comparative Politics Ser.). 176p. 1974. ref. ed. 7.95 (ISBN 0-13-537167-8); pap. 6.95 (ISBN 0-13-537159-7). P-H.

Limited War Revisited. Robert E. Osgood. (Westview Special Study). 1979. lib. bdg. 16.50x (ISBN 0-89158-465-X). Westview.

Limiting Dilution Analysis of Cells in the Immune System. Ivan Lefkovitz & Hermann Waldmann. LC 77-82502. (Illus.). 1980. 43.50 (ISBN 0-521-22771-2). Cambridge U Pr.

Limiting God. John Hunter. 160p. 1972. pap. 2.95 (ISBN 0-310-26462-6). Zondervan.

Limiting Steps in Ion Uptake by Plants from Soil. (Technical Reports Ser: No. 65). 1966. pap. 7.50 (ISBN 92-0-115566-2, IAEA). Unipub.

Limits. Robie Liscomb. 1980. pap. 3.00. Pentagram.

Limits. Maxine Schall. Ed. by Carol Southern. 320p. 1981. 11.95 (ISBN 0-517-54143-2). Potter.

Limits: A Transition to Calculus. O. Lexton Buchanan, Jr. Ed. by Albert E. Meder, Jr. (Modern Mathematics Ser). (gr. 9 up). 1974. pap. 6.08 (ISBN 0-395-17941-6); instr's. guide & solution key 3.12 (ISBN 0-395-17942-4). HM.

Limits & Possibilities of Schooling: An Introduction to the Sociology of Education. Christopher J. Hurn. 1978. text ed. 15.95 (ISBN 0-205-05969-4). Allyn.

Limits of a Modern World. Robert McCutcheon. (Science in a Social Context Ser.). 1979. pap. text ed. 3.95 (ISBN 0-408-71310-0). Butterworths.

Limits of Administration. Christopher C. Hood. LC 75-37850. 208p. 1976. 29.95 (ISBN 0-471-01652-7, Pub. by Wiley-Interscience). Wiley.

Limits of Altruism: An Ecologist's View of Survival. Garrett Hardin. LC 77-74451. 160p. 1977. 10.00x (ISBN 0-253-33435-7). Ind U Pr.

Limits of Corporate Power: Existing Constraints on the Exercise of Corporate Discretion. Ira M. Millstein & Salem M. Katsh. LC 80-69280. (Studies of the Modern Corporation). (Illus.). 1981. 15.95 (ISBN 0-02-921490-4). Free Pr.

Limits of Defiance: Strikes, Rights, & Government. Jean M. Morman & Norman Laliberte. LC 73-149012. (Illus.). (gr. 10-12). 1971. PLB 6.90 (ISBN 0-531-01980-2). Watts.

Limits of Development Research. Paul Streeten. 75p. 1975. pap. text ed. 5.75 (ISBN 0-08-019796-5). Pergamon.

Limits of Dissent: Clement L. Vallandigham & the Civil War. Frank L. Klement. LC 71-111512. (Illus.). 367p. 1970. 16.00x (ISBN 0-8131-1218-4). U Pr of Ky.

Limits of Human Nature: Essays Based on a Course of Lectures Given at the Institute of Contemporary Arts, London. Jonathan Benthall. 1974. pap. 3.95 o.p. (ISBN 0-525-47359-9). Dutton.

Limits of Indeterminacy in Measure of T-Means of Subseries of a Trigonometric Series. D. E. Men'sov. (Trudy Steklov Ser.: No. 149). Date not set. cancelled (ISBN 0-8218-3044-9). Am Math.

Limits of Intervention: An Inside Account of How the Johnson Policy of Escalation Was Reversed in Vietnam. rev. ed. Townsend Hoopes. LC 78-94505. 1973. pap. 8.95 (ISBN 0-582-28082-6, Pub. by MacKay). Longman.

Limits of Legitimacy: Political Contradictions of Contemporary Capitalism. Alan Wolfe. LC 76-51567. 1980. pap. text ed. 9.95 (ISBN 0-02-934860-9). Free Pr.

Limits of Life. Ed. by Cyril Ponnamperuma & Lynn Margulis. 200p. 1980. PLB 26.50 (ISBN 90-277-1155-0, Pub. by D. Reidel). Kluwer Boston.

Limits of Planning. (Analysis Ser.). 1980. pap. 14.95 (ISBN 0-938526-02-2). Inst Analysis.

Limits of Power: The Politics of Local Planning Policy. Andrew Blowers. (Urban & Regional Planning Ser.: Vol. 21). (Illus.). 23.00 (ISBN 0-08-023016-4). Pergamon.

Limits of Professional Power: National Health Care in the Federal Republic of Germany. Deborah A. Stone. LC 80-16864. (Illus.). 244p. 1981. lib. bdg. 18.50x (ISBN 0-226-77553-4). U of Chicago Pr.

Limits of Progressive School Reform in the Nineteen Seventies: A Case Study. Frederick P. Sperounis. LC 80-5063. 286p. 1980. pap. text ed. 10.25 (ISBN 0-8191-1031-0). U Pr of Amer.

Limits of Reason: The German Democratic Press & the Collapse of Weimar Democracy. Modris Eksteins. (Oxford Historical Monographs). 362p. 1975. 42.00x (ISBN 0-19-821862-1). Oxford U Pr.

Limits of Reform in the Enlightenment: Attitudes Toward the Education of the Lower Classes in Eighteenth Century France. Harvey Chisick. LC 80-7512. 296p. 1981. 22.50 (ISBN 0-691-05305-7). Princeton U Pr.

Limits of the Welfare State. John Fry. 240p. 1979. text ed. 24.00x (ISBN 0-566-00235-3, Pub. by Gower Pub Co England). Renouf.

Limits of Trade Union Militancy: The Lancashire Textile Workers, 1910-1914. Joseph L. White. LC 77-87965. (Contributions in Labor History: No. 5). (Illus.). 1978. lib. bdg. 17.95 (ISBN 0-313-20029-7, WLT/). Greenwood.

Limits to Action: The Allocation of Individual Behavior. John E. Staddon. LC 79-6794. 1980. 24.00 (ISBN 0-12-662650-2). Acad Pr.

Limits to Citizen Participation: The Decline of Community Organizations. Marilyn Gittell et al. LC 80-15950. (Sage Library of Social Research: Vol. 109). (Illus.). 280p. 1980. 18.00 (ISBN 0-8039-1478-4); pap. 8.95 (ISBN 0-8039-1479-2). Sage.

Limits to Growth. D. L. Meadows & D. H. Meadows. pap. 1.95 (ISBN 0-451-08985-5, J8985, Sig). NAL.

Limits to Pain. Nils Christie. 96p. 1981. pap. 10.00x (ISBN 82-00-05528-0). Universitet.

Limnofauna Europaea: A Checklist of the Animals Inhabiting European Inland Waters, with Accounts of Their Distribution & Ecology (Except Protozoa) Ed. by Joachim Illies. 532p. 1978. text ed. 120.00 (ISBN 90-265-0275-3, Pub. by Swets Pub Serv Holland). Swets North Am.

Limnology. 2nd ed. Paul S. Welch. (Illus.). 1952. text ed. 25.00 o.p. (ISBN 0-07-069179-7, C). McGraw.

Linacre Studies: Essays on the Life & Work of Thomas Linacre. Ed. by Francis Maddison & Margaret Pelling. (Illus.). 1977. 49.00x (ISBN 0-19-858150-5). Oxford U Pr.

Linc the Lucky Lincoln. LC 80-50626. (Orig.). 1980. pap. 3.00 (ISBN 0-935248-01-3). Simplex Comm.

Linclon Motorcar: Sixty Years of Excellence. Thomas E. Bonsall. 325p. 1981. 32.95 (ISBN 0-934780-05-6). Bookman Dan.

Lincoln: A Big Man. Helen Kay. (Illus.). (gr. 2-4). 1958. PLB 3.84 o.s.i. (ISBN 0-8038-4237-6). Hastings.

Lincoln & Continental: The Postwar Years. Paul Woudenberg. LC 80-12242. (Marques of America Ser.). (Illus.). 152p. 1980. 18.95 (ISBN 0-87938-063-2). Motorbooks Intl.

Lincoln & Kennedy: Medical & Ballistic Comparisons of Their Assassinations. John K. Lattimer. 1980. 19.95 (ISBN 0-15-152281-2). HarBraceJ.

Lincoln & the Emancipation Proclamation, January 1, 1863: The Document That Turned the Civil War into a Fight for Freedom. Frank B. Latham. LC 69-13759. (Focus Bks). (Illus.). (gr. 7 up). 1969. PLB 4.90 o.p. (ISBN 0-531-01002-3); pap. 1.25 o.p. (ISBN 0-531-02331-1). Watts.

Lincoln & the Radicals. T. Harry Williams. (Illus.). 1941. pap. 8.95x (ISBN 0-299-00274-8). U of Wis Pr.

Lincoln & the South. James G. Randall. LC 80-22084. (Walter Lynwood Fleming Lectures in Southern History, L. S. U.). (Illus.). viii, 161p. 1980. Repr. of 1946 ed. lib. bdg. 18.75x (ISBN 0-313-22843-4, RALS). Greenwood.

Lincoln Center: The Building of an Institution. Edgar B. Young. 320p. 1980. 24.95 (ISBN 0-8147-9656-7). NYU Pr.

Lincoln Country-In Pictures. Carl Frazier & Rosalie Frazier. (Illus.). (gr. 4-6). 1963. 5.95 (ISBN 0-8038-4238-4). Hastings.

Lincoln Finds a General, 4 vols. Kenneth P. Williams. 1949. 8.50 ea. o.s.i. Vol. 1. Vol. 2. Vol. 3. Vol. 4. Macmillan.

Lincoln Institute of Land Policy. Laura Geringer. (Illus.). (gr. 2-5). 1978. 6.95 (ISBN 0-8038-6747-6). Hastings.

Lincoln Library of Language Arts, 2 vols. 5th ed. Frontier Press Company. LC 80-54173. 1981. Set. 54.95 (ISBN 0-912168-06-4). Frontier Pr Co.

Lincoln Library of Sports Champions, 20 vols. 3rd ed. LC 80-54174. 1981. Set. 249.95 (ISBN 0-912168-07-2). Frontier Pr Co.

Lincoln Library of the Arts, 2 vols. 3rd ed. LC 73-78393. (Illus.). (gr. 6 up). 1980. Set. 59.95 (ISBN 0-912168-05-6). Frontier Pr Co.

Lincoln Motorcar: Sixty Years of Excellence. Thomas E. Bonsall. (Illus.). 1981. 32.95 (ISBN 0-934780-05-6). Bookman Dan.

Lincoln Nobody Knows. Richard N. Current. 314p. 1963. pap. 5.25 (ISBN 0-8090-0059-8, AmCen). Hill & Wang.

Lincoln Nobody Knows. Richard N. Current. LC 80-16138. x, 314p. 1980. Repr. of 1958 ed. lib. bdg. 25.00x (ISBN 0-313-22450-1, CULN). Greenwood.

Lincoln Reader. Ed. by Paul M. Angle. LC 80-25663. (Illus.). xii, 564p. 1981. Repr. of 1947 ed. lib. bdg. 49.50x (ISBN 0-313-22757-8, ANLR). Greenwood.

Lincoln Reconsidered: Essays on the Civil War Era. David H. Donald. LC 80-22804. (Illus.). xiii, 200p. 1981. Repr. of 1956 ed. lib. bdg. 23.50x (ISBN 0-313-22575-3, DOLR). Greenwood.

Lincoln Steffens. Russell M. Horton. LC 74-3089. (World Leaders Ser: No. 35). 168p. 1974. lib. bdg. 9.95 (ISBN 0-8057-3721-9). Twayne.

Lincoln Steffens. Patrick F. Palermo. (United States Authors Ser.: No. 320). 1978. 12.50 (ISBN 0-8057-7253-7). Twayne.

Lincoln Steffens. Robert Stinson. LC 79-4831. (Modern Literature Ser.). 1980. 10.95 (ISBN 0-8044-2829-8). Ungar.

Lincoln the Atheist. Joseph Lewis. 1979. pap. 3.00. Am Atheist.

Lincoln: The Growth of a Medieval City. Dulcie Duke. LC 73-80476. (Introduction to the History of Mankind Ser). (Illus.). 48p. (gr. 9-12). 1974. pap. text ed. 3.95 (ISBN 0-521-08712-0). Cambridge U Pr.

Lincoln's Asssassination, April 14, 1865: Investigation of a President's Murder Uncovers a Web of Conspiracy. Theodore Roscoe. LC 73-152852. (Focus Bks). (Illus.). (gr. 7 up). 1971. PLB 4.47 o.p. (ISBN 0-531-00993-9). Watts.

Lincoln's Favorite Poets. David J. Harkness & R. Gerald McMurtry. LC 59-9718. 1959. 7.50x (ISBN 0-87049-026-5). U of Tenn Pr.

Lincoln's Mothers. Dorothy C. Wilson. LC 80-950. 432p. 1981. 13.95 (ISBN 0-385-15146-2, Galilee). Doubleday.

Lincolnshire: A Shell Guide. Jack Yates & Henry Thorold. (Shell Guide Ser.). (Illus.). 1968. 14.95 (ISBN 0-571-06297-0, Pub. by Faber & Faber). Merrimack Bk Serv.

Lincolnshire Village: The Parish of Corby Glen in Its Historical Context. Daniel I. Steel. (Illus.). 242p. 1979. lib. bdg. 22.00 (ISBN 0-582-50285-3). Longman.

Linda Craig: The Clue on the Desert Trail. Ann Sheldon. Ed. by Wendy Barish. (Linda Craig Ser.). 192p. (gr. 3-7). 1981. 7.95 (ISBN 0-671-42651-6, Wanderer); pap. 1.95 (ISBN 0-671-42652-4). S&S.

Linda Craig: The Mystery in Mexico. Ann Sheldon. Ed. by Wendy Barish. (Linda Craig Ser.). 192p. (gr. 3-7). Date not set. Repr. of 1964 ed. 7.95 (ISBN 0-671-42649-4). Wanderer Bks.

Linda Craig: The Mystery or Horseshoe Canyon. Ann Sheldon. Ed. by Wendy Barish. (Linda Craig Ser.). 192p. (gr. 3-7). 1981. 7.95 (ISBN 0-671-42653-2, Wanderer); pap. 1.95 (ISBN 0-671-42654-0). S&S.

Linda Craig: The Secret of Rancho Del Sol. Ann Sheldon. Ed. by Wendy Barish. (Linda Craig Ser.). 192p. (gr. 3-7). 1981. 7.95 (ISBN 0-671-42647-8, Wanderer); pap. 1.95 (ISBN 0-671-42648-6). S&S.

Linda Goodman's Love Signs: A New Approach to the Human Heart. Linda Goodman. (Illus.). 1980. pap. 7.95 (ISBN 0-449-90043-6, Columbine). Fawcett.

Linda Goodman's Sun Signs for Aries to Pisces, 12 bks. Linda Goodman. 96p. 1979. pap. 1.25 o.s.i. (ISBN 0-686-65662-8). Bantam.

Linda Ronstadt: A Photo-Bio. Vivian Claire. 1979. pap. 2.25 (ISBN 0-515-05159-4). Jove Pubns.

Lindlahr Vitamin Cookbook. Victor H. Lindlahr. LC 80-19202. 319p. 1980. Repr. of 1972 ed. lib. bdg. 9.95x (ISBN 0-89370-611-6). Borgo Pr.

Lindsay's Promise. Woody Klein. (Illus.). 1970. 6.95 o.s.i. (ISBN 0-02-563910-2). Macmillan.

Lindy. Jean C. Higgins. LC 70-91245. 1970. pap. 1.50 o.p. (ISBN 0-8170-0461-0). Judson.

Line by Line. Amy Schor. 256p. 1981. 11.95 (ISBN 0-399-90083-7). Marek.

Line Coincidence Tables for Inductively Coupled Plasma Atomic Emission Spectrometry, 2 vols. P. W. Boumans. LC 80-41344. (Illus.). 941p. 1980. 250.00 set (ISBN 0-08-026243-0). Pergamon.

Line Drive. Terry Bledsoe & Peter Sanders. LC 75-22007. (Venture Ser, a Reading Incentive Program). (Illus.). 76p. (gr. 7-12,RL 4.5-6.5). 1975. text ed. 23.25 ea. pack of 5 (ISBN 0-8172-0241-2). Follett.

Line Driver & Line Receiver Data Book for Design Engineers Nineteen Eighty One. rev. ed. Texas Instruments, Inc. Engineering Staff. LC 80-54794. 296p. 1981. pap. write for info. (ISBN 0-89512-106-9, LCCJ290A). Tex Instr Inc.

Line in the Water. Amrita Pritam. Tr. by Krishna Gorowara from Punjabi. (Mayfair Paperbacks). 141p. 1975. 5.95 (ISBN 0-89253-012-X); pap. 2.50 (ISBN 0-89253-023-5). Ind-US Inc.

Line of Chance. Thomas Caplan. 1981. pap. 2.95 (ISBN 0-671-83137-2). PB.

Line of Succession. Brian Garfield. 1972. 7.95 o.s.i. (ISBN 0-440-04847-8). Delacorte.

Line on Texas. Norman Baxter. LC 80-15870. (Illus.). 1980. pap. 6.95 (ISBN 0-88415-429-7). Pacesetter Pr.

Lineage Organization in Southeastern China. rev. ed. Maurice Freedman. (Monographs on Social Anthropology: No. 18). 1965. pap. text ed. 9.50x (ISBN 0-485-19618-2, Athlone Pr). Humanities.

Lineaments of Mind. John Cohen. LC 79-21794. (Illus.). 1980. text ed. 19.95x (ISBN 0-7167-1175-3). W H Freeman.

Lineamientos Para Alcanzar el Mayor Empleo y Crecimiento En America Latina. (Span.). 1972. 3.00 o.p. (ISBN 0-8270-3535-7). OAS.

Linear Active Networks. Robert Spence. LC 73-88242. 1970. 32.95 (ISBN 0-471-81525-X, Pub. by Wiley-Interscience). Wiley.

Linear Algebra. George Hadley. (Illus.). 1961. 17.95 (ISBN 0-201-02655-4). A-W.

Linear Algebra. 2nd ed. Kenneth Hoffman & Ray Kunze. LC 75-142120. (Illus.). 1971. ref. ed. 20.95 (ISBN 0-13-536797-2). P-H.

Linear Algebra. Burton W. Jones. LC 72-83244. 1973. text ed. 19.95x (ISBN 0-8162-4544-4). Holden-Day.

Linear Algebra. 2nd ed. Serge A. Lang. LC 70-129520. (Mathematics Ser). 1971. text ed. 16.95 (ISBN 0-201-04211-8). A-W.

Linear Algebra. David C. Murdoch. LC 72-121911. 1970. text ed. 21.95x o.p. (ISBN 0-471-62500-0). Wiley.

Linear Algebra. Robert R. Stoll & Edward T. Wong. 1968. text ed. 19.95 (ISBN 0-12-672150-5); answer bklt. 2.00 (ISBN 0-12-672152-1). Acad Pr.

Linear Algebra: An Introductory Approach. 3rd ed. Charles W. Curtis. 522p. 1974. text ed. 20.95 (ISBN 0-205-04008-X, 5640083). Allyn.

Linear Algebra & Analytic Geometry. H. W. Brinkmann & E. A. Klotz. LC 79-132056. (Mathematics Ser). 1971. text ed. 17.95 o.p. (ISBN 0-201-00648-0). A-W.

Linear Algebra & Geometry. D. M. Bloom. LC 77-26666. 1979. 41.50 (ISBN 0-521-21959-0); pap. 21.95x (ISBN 0-521-29324-3). Cambridge U Pr.

Linear Algebra & Geometry: A Second Course. Irving Kaplansky. LC 74-2393. xiv, 143p. 1974. Repr. of 1969 ed. text ed. 9.50 (ISBN 0-8284-0279-5). Chelsea Pub.

Linear Algebra & Its Applications. Gilbert Strang. 1976. 17.50 o.p. (ISBN 0-12-673650-2). Acad Pr.

Linear Algebra & Its Applications. 2nd ed. W. Gilbert Strang. LC 79-53993. 1980. 18.95 (ISBN 0-12-673660-X). Acad Pr.

Linear Algebra Problem Solver: A Supplement to Any Class Text. Research & Education Association Staff. LC 79-92402. (Illus.). 1024p. 1980. pap. text ed. 22.85x (ISBN 0-87891-518-4). Res & Educ.

Linear Algebra with Applications. 2nd ed. Hugh Campbell. (Illus.). 1980. text ed. 18.95 (ISBN 0-13-536979-7). P-H.

Linear Algebra with Applications. Hugh G. Campbell. LC 76-133903. (A-C Mathematics Ser). (Illus., Orig.). 1971. text ed. 17.95 (ISBN 0-13-536953-3). P-H.

Linear Algebra with Applications: Including Linear Programming. Hugh G. Campbell. LC 72-133902. (Mathematics Ser). (Illus., Orig.). 1971. text ed. 18.95 (ISBN 0-13-536946-0). P-H.

Linear & Combinatorial Programming. Katta G. Murty. LC 76-7047. 560p. 1976. 30.95 (ISBN 0-471-57370-1). Wiley.

Linear & Integer Programming. Stanley Zionts. (Illus.). 528p. 1974. text ed. 21.95 (ISBN 0-13-536763-8). P-H.

Linear & Tensor Algebra. Robert Hermann. (Interdisciplinary Mathematics Ser: No. 2). 163p. 1973. 9.00 (ISBN 0-915692-01-5). Math Sci Pr.

Linear Associative Algebras. Alexander Abian. 1971. text ed. 21.00 (ISBN 0-08-016564-8). Pergamon.

Linear Circuits, Complete. Ronald E. Scott. Incl. Pt. 2. Frequency-Domain Analysis. 1961. Set. 25.95 (ISBN 0-201-06820-6). A-W.

Linear Circuits for Electronics Technology. Gary Miller. (Illus.). 368p. 1974. ref. ed. 19.95 (ISBN 0-13-536698-4). P-H.

Linear Control System Analysis & Design. 2nd ed. John D'Azzo & Constantine Houpis. (Electrical Engineering Ser.). (Illus.). 864p. 1981. text ed. write for info (ISBN 0-07-016183-6, C); write for info solutions manual (ISBN 0-07-016184-4). McGraw.

Linear Electric Field Effect in Paramagnetic Resonance. W. B. Mims. (Illus.). 1976. 24.95x (ISBN 0-19-851944-3). Oxford U Pr.

Linear Engineering Systems: Tools & Techniques. Michael P. Smyth. 386p. 1972. text ed. 28.00 (ISBN 0-08-016324-6). Pergamon.

Linear Equations. P. M. Cohn. (Library of Mathematics). 1971. pap. 3.50 (ISBN 0-7100-6181-1). Routledge & Kegan.

Linear Hypothesis: A General Theory. 2nd ed. G. A. Seber. LC 79-67711. (Griffin's Statistical Monographs & Courses: No. 19). 1981. 21.50 (ISBN 0-02-852000-9). Macmillan.

Linear IC Applications Handbook. George B. Clayton. LC 77-71. 1977. 9.95 o.p. (ISBN 0-8306-7938-3); pap. 6.95 o.p. (ISBN 0-8306-6938-8, 938). TAB Bks.

Linear Integrated Circuits. Thomas Young. (Kosow Electrical Ser.). 464p. 1981. text ed. 18.95 (ISBN 0-471-97941-4). Wiley.

Linear Network Theory: Analysis, Properties, Design & Synthesis. Norman Balabanian & Theodore Bickert. 450p. 1981. text ed. 32.95 (ISBN 0-916460-10-X). Matrix Pubns.

Linear Operators, 3 pts. Nelson Dunford & Jacob T. Schwartz. Incl. Pt. 1. General Theory. 1958. 54.50 (ISBN 0-470-22605-6); Pt. 2. Spectral Theory, Self Adjoint Operators in Hilbert Space. 69.95 (ISBN 0-470-22638-2); Pt. 3. Spectral Operators. 1971. 59.50 (ISBN 0-471-22639-4). LC 57-10545. (Pure & Applied Mathematics Ser, Pub. by Wiley-Interscience). Wiley.

Linear Optimal Control Systems. Huibert Kwakernaak & Raphael Sivan. LC 72-3576. 544p. 1972. 44.00 (ISBN 0-471-51110-2, Pub. by Wiley-Interscience). Wiley.

Linear Order & Generative Theory. Ed. by Jurgen Meisel & Martin Pam. (Current Issues in Linguistic Theory: No. 7). 1978. text ed. 57.00x (ISBN 90-272-0908-1). Humanities.

Linear Orderings. Joseph G. Rosenstein. LC 80-2341. (Pure & Applied Mathematics Ser.). 1981. write for info. (ISBN 0-12-597680-1). Acad Pr.

Linear Panel Analysis: Quantitative Models of Change. Ronald Kessler & David Greenberg. (Quantitative Studies in Social Relations). 1981. price not set (ISBN 0-12-405750-0). Acad Pr.

Linear Prediction of Speech. J. E. Markel & A. H. Gray. (Communications & Cybernetics Ser.: Vol. 12). (Illus.). 305p. 1976. 43.10 (ISBN 0-387-07563-1). Springer-Verlag.

Linear Problems in P-th Order & Stable Processes. S. Cambanis & Grady Miller. 49p. 1980. pap. 1.60 (1272). U of NC Pr.

Linear Programming. George Hadley. (Illus.). 1962. 18.95 (ISBN 0-201-02660-0). A-W.

Linear Programming. Ronald I. Rothnberg. 1979. 22.95 (North Holland). Elsevier.

Linear Programming. Kathleen Trustrum. (Library of Mathematics). 1971. pap. 5.00 (ISBN 0-7100-6779-8). Routledge & Kegan.

Linear Programming: An Emphasis on Decision Making. Ann J. Hughes & Dennis E. Grawoig. LC 72-1938. 1973. text ed. 19.95 (ISBN 0-201-03024-1). A-W.

Linear Programming & Extensions. Nesa Wu & Richard Coppins. (Industrial Engineering & Management Science Ser.). (Illus.). 480p. 1981. 25.95 (ISBN 0-07-072117-3, C); solutions manual 8.95 (ISBN 0-07-072118-1). McGraw.

Linear Programming & Network Flows. Mokhtar S. Bazaraa & John J. Jarvis. LC 76-42241. 1977. text ed. 29.95 (ISBN 0-471-06015-1). Wiley.

Linear Programming Applications to Agriculture. Raymond R. Beneke & Ronald D. Winterboer. LC 72-2298. (Illus.). 251p. 1973. text ed. 12.95 (ISBN 0-8138-1035-3). Iowa St U Pr.

Linear Programming: Basic Theory & Applications. Leonard W. Swanson. LC 79-10092. (Quantitative Methods for Management Ser.). (Illus.). 1979. 22.00 (ISBN 0-07-062580-8, C); instructor's manual 4.95 (ISBN 0-07-062581-6). McGraw.

Linear Programming for Operations Research. Donald M. Simmons. LC 70-188129. 1972. text ed. 23.95x (ISBN 0-8162-7986-1). Holden-Day.

Linear Programming Models: With Illustrations Using LINDO. Linus Schrage. (Illus.). 288p. (Orig.). 1981. pap. text ed. 16.00x (ISBN 0-89426-031-6); tchrs'. ed. 16.00x (ISBN 0-89426-033-2). Scientific Pr.

Linear Statistical Inference & Its Applications. 2nd ed. C. Radhakrishna Rao. LC 72-13093. (Ser. in Probability & Mathematical Statistics). 608p. 1973. 36.95 (ISBN 0-471-70823-2). Wiley.

Linear Systems. Thomas Kailath. (Information & Systems Sciences Ser.). (Illus.). 1980. text ed. 28.95 (ISBN 0-13-536961-4). P-H.

Linear Systems & Operators in Hilbert Space. Paul A. Fuhrmann. 336p. 1981. text ed. 44.95 (ISBN 0-07-022589-3). McGraw.

Linear Systems in Communication & Control. Dean K. Frederick & A. Bruce Carlson. LC 71-155118. 1971. 33.50 (ISBN 0-471-27721-5). Wiley.

Linear Systems Theory and Introductory Algebraic Geometry. Robert Hermann. (Interdisciplinary Mathematics Ser: No. 8). 282p. 1974. 24.00 (ISBN 0-915692-07-4). Math Sci Pr.

Linear Transformations in Hilbert Space & Their Applications to Analysis. M. H. Stone. LC 33-2746. (Colloquium Pbns. Ser: Vol. 15). 1979. Repr. of 1974 ed. 36.90 (ISBN 0-8218-1015-4, COLL-15). Am Math.

Linebackers. Sam Masegawa. LC 74-23365. (Stars of the NFL Ser.). (gr. 4-12). 1975. PLB 7.95 (ISBN 0-87191-419-0). Creative Ed.

Lineman's & Cableman's Handbook. 6th ed. Edwin B. Kurtz & Thomas M. Shoemaker. 768p. Date not set. 32.50 (ISBN 0-07-035678-5, P&RB). McGraw. Postponed.

Liner Conferences in the Container Age: U. S. Policy at Sea. Gunnar K. Sletmo & Ernest W. Williams, Jr. LC 80-70838. (Studies of the Modern Corporation). (Illus.). 1981. 29.95 (ISBN 0-02-929200-X). Free Pr.

Lines & Fragments. Helen B. Stevens. 68p. 1980. 4.50 (ISBN 0-8059-2756-5). Dorrance.

Lines Are Coming: A Book About Drawing. Hans-Georg Rauch. LC 78-12861. (Illus.). (gr. 2 up). 1978. reinforced bdg 8.95 (ISBN 0-684-15989-9, ScribJ). Scribner.

Lines of Inquiry. N. Rudd. LC 75-12467. 280p. 1976. 36.00 (ISBN 0-521-20993-5). Cambridge U Pr.

Lines of Pacific Electric, Northern & Eastern Districts. Ed. by Jim Walker. (Illus.). 112p. 1976. pap. 7.00 (ISBN 0-916374-21-1). Interurban.

Lines of Pacific Electric, Western & Southern Districts. 2nd rev. ed. Ira Swett & Jim Walker. (Special Ser.: No. 60). 1975. pap. 10.00 o.p. (ISBN 0-916374-02-5). Interurban.

Linescapes. rev. ed. Theodore L. Harris et al. (Keys to Reading Ser.). (Illus.). 192p. (gr. 7). 1975. pap. text ed. 3.99 (ISBN 0-87892-458-2); resource bk. 9.90 (ISBN 0-87892-461-2); 3.26 (ISBN 0-87892-462-0); Thoughtvault tchr's ed. 3.96 (ISBN 0-87892-462-0); dupl. masters 19.53 (ISBN 0-87892-498-1). Economy Co.

Lingapurana: A Study. N. Gangadharan. 1980. 22.50x (ISBN 0-8364-0618-4, Pub. by Ajanta). South Asia Bks.

Lingerie Parisienne. Juliette Morel. LC 76-44581. (Illus.). 1977. pap. 3.95 o.p. (ISBN 0-312-48702-9). St Martin.

Lingering Shadow of Nazism. Max E. Riedlsperger. (Eastern European Monographs: No. 42). 1978. 14.00x (ISBN 0-914710-35-4, Dist. by Columbia U Pr). East Eur Quarterly.

Lingering Shadows. Mohan Rakesh. Tr. by Jai Ratan. 214p. 1970. pap. 2.50 (ISBN 0-88253-075-5). Ind-US Inc.

Lingua Press Collection Three Catalogue, Vol. 3. Lingua Press. Ed. by Kenneth Gaburo. (Illus.). 150p. 1981. softcover 8.50. Lingua Pr.

Lingua Press Collection Two Catalogue, Vol. 2. Lingua Press. Ed. by Kenneth Gaburo. 132p. 1978. soft cover 3.95. Lingua Pr.

Linguisitcs in the Netherlands 1977-1979. Ed. by W. Zonneveld & F. Weerman. (Publications in Language Sciences: No. 1). 483p. 1980. pap. text ed. write for info. (ISBN 90-70176-09-2). Humanities.

Linguist in Speech Pathology. Walt Wolfram. (Language in Education Ser.: No. 2). 1978. pap. 2.95 (ISBN 0-87281-078-X). Ctr Appl Ling.

Linguistic Affairs of India. Ram Gopal. 1967. 8.50x (ISBN 0-210-27158-2). Asia.

Linguistic & Literary Studies in Honor of Archibald A. Hill: General & Theoretical Linguistics, 4 vols, Vol. 1. Ed. by Mohammad A. Jazayery et al. (Illus., Orig.). 1976. pap. text ed. 45.75x (ISBN 90-3160-108-X). Humanities.

Linguistic Basis of Logic Translation. Herbert R. Otto. LC 78-63261. 1978. pap. text ed. 9.25 (ISBN 0-8191-0617-8). U Pr of Amer.

Linguistic Behavior. J. Bennett. LC 75-44575. 260p. 1976. 31.95 (ISBN 0-521-21168-9). Cambridge U Pr.

Linguistic Behaviour. J. Bennett. LC 75-44575. 1979. pap. 11.50x (ISBN 0-521-29751-6). Cambridge U Pr.

Linguistic Change. E. H. Sturtevant. 183p. 1980. Repr. of 1942 ed. lib. bdg. 30.00 (ISBN 0-89987-765-6). Darby Bks.

Linguistic Description of Opaque Contexts. Janet D. Fodor. Ed. by Jorge Hankamer. LC 78-66537. (Outstanding Dissertations in Linguistics Ser.). 1979. lib. bdg. 42.00 (ISBN 0-685-94397-6). Garland Pub.

Linguistic Diversity & Language Belief in Kenya: The Special Position of Swahili. John Rhoades. LC 77-20016. (Foreign & Comparative Studies-African Ser.: No. 26). 1977. pap. text ed. 6.00x (ISBN 0-915984-23-7). Syracuse U Foreign Comp.

Linguistic Evidence in Dating Early Hebrew Poetry. David A. Robertson. LC 72-87886. (Society of Biblical Literature. Dissertation Ser.: No. 3). 1973. pap. 7.50 (ISBN 0-89130-159-3, 060103). Scholars Pr Ca.

Linguistic Evolution with Special Reference to English. M. L. Samuels. LC 72-176255. (Cambridge Studies in Linguistics: No. 5). (Illus.). 256p. 1973. 32.50 (ISBN 0-521-08385-0); pap. 9.95x (ISBN 0-521-09913-7). Cambridge U Pr.

Linguistic Foundations for Reading. Mary A. Hall & Christopher J. Ramig. 1978. pap. text ed. 6.95 (ISBN 0-675-08448-2). Merrill.

Linguistic Grammar of English. M. W. Sullivan. (gr. 10-12). 1972. pap. text ed. 5.00 (ISBN 0-8449-2720-1). Learning Line.

Linguistic Guide to English Proficiency Testing in Schools. Thomas G. Dieterich & Cecilia Freeman. (Language in Education Ser.: No. 23). 53p. 1979. pap. text ed. 5.95 (ISBN 0-87281-110-7). Ctr Appl Ling.

Linguistic Key to the Greek New Testament, 2 vols. Fritz Bienecker. Vol. 1. 14.95 (ISBN 0-310-32020-8); Vol. 2. 17.95; Set. 31.90 (ISBN 0-310-32048-8). Zondervan.

Linguistic Method of Teaching Second Languages. Joe E. Pierce. 145p. 1973. pap. 6.95 (ISBN 0-913244-05-8). Hapi Pr.

Linguistic Ramifications of the Essence-Existence Debate. Germain Kopaczynski. LC 79-5373. 1979. pap. text ed. 9.50 (ISBN 0-8191-0865-0). U Pr of Amer.

Linguistic Shaping of Thought: A Study in the Impact of Language on Thinking in China & the West. Alfred H. Bloom. 128p. 1981. prof. & reference 16.50 (ISBN 0-89859-089-2). L Erlbaum Assocs.

Linguistic Structures & Linguistic Laws. Ferenc Kovacs. Tr. by Sandor Simon from Hungarian. 1971. text ed. 42.75x (ISBN 90-6032-492-7). Humanities.

Linguistic Studies in Memory of Richard Slade Harrell. Ed. by Don G. Stuart. LC 67-31586. 1967. pap. 2.95 o.p. (ISBN 0-87840-156-3). Georgetown U Pr.

Linguistic Survey of India, 1903-28, 11 Vols. in 19. Ed. by George A. Grierson. 1967. 600.00x set (ISBN 0-8426-1284-X). Verry.

Linguistic Symposium on Romance Languages, No. 9. Ed. by William W. Cressey & Donna J. Napoli. (Orig.). 1981. pap. text ed. 8.95x (ISBN 0-87840-081-8). Georgetown U Pr.

Linguistic Theory & Structural Stylistics. Talbot J. Taylor. (Language & Communication Library: Vol. 2). 140p. Date not set. 17.00 (ISBN 0-08-025821-2). Pergamon.

Linguistic Theory, Linguistic Description & Language Teaching. E. Roulet. LC 75-326964. 112p. 1975. pap. text ed. 9.00x (ISBN 0-582-55075-0). Longman.

Linguistic Theory of Numerals. J. R. Hurford. LC 74-25652. (Studies in Linguistics: No. 16). 260p. 1975. 42.50 (ISBN 0-521-20735-5). Cambridge U Pr.

Linguistics. Peter H. Salus. LC 69-13632. (Speech Communication Ser). 1969. pap. 8.95 (ISBN 0-672-61084-1, SC14). Bobbs.

Linguistics: A Relational Grammar of Kinyarwanda. Alexandre Kimenyi. (UC Publications in Linguistics: Vol. 91). 1980. 13.00x (ISBN 0-520-09598-7). U of Cal Pr.

Linguistics Across Cultures: Applied Linguistics for Language Teachers. Robert Lado. 1957. pap. 4.95x (ISBN 0-472-08542-5). U of Mich Pr.

Linguistics & Applied Linguistics: Aims & Methods. Robert L. Politzer. 1972. 5.95. Heinle & Heinle.

Linguistics & English Linguistics. 2nd ed. Harold B. Allen. LC 75-42974. (Goldentree Bibliographies in Language & Literature Ser.). 1977. pap. text ed. 12.95x (ISBN 0-88295-558-6). AHM Pub.

Linguistics & Evolutionary Theory. J. Peter Maher. (Amsterdam Classics in Linguistics Ser.: No. 6). 165p. 1980. text ed. 25.75x (ISBN 90-272-0877-8). Humanities.

Linguistics & Language: A Survey of Basic Concepts & Implications. 2nd ed. Julia S. Falk. LC 77-22927. 1978. pap. text ed. 13.95x (ISBN 0-471-02529-1). Wiley.

Linguistics & Literary Criticism. Giacimo Devoto. Tr. by M. F. Edgerton, Jr. 1963. 6.00 (ISBN 0-913298-08-5). S F Vanni.

Linguistics & Literary Theory. new ed. Karl D. Uitti. 264p. 1974. pap. text ed. 5.95x (ISBN 0-393-09293-3). Norton.

Linguistics & Theology: The Significance of Noam Chomsky for Theological Construction. Irene Lawrence. LC 80-24210. (ATLA Monograph: No. 16). 214p. 1980. 12.50 (ISBN 0-8108-1347-5). Scarecrow.

Linguistics, English & the Language Arts. Carl A. Lefevre. LC 73-15655. 371p. 1974. Repr. of 1970 ed. text ed. 8.00x (ISBN 0-8077-2428-9). Tchrs Coll.

Linguistics in Language Teaching. D. A. Wilkins. 250p. 1972. 12.50x o.p. (ISBN 0-262-23060-7). MIT Pr.

Linguistics in the Netherlands. A. Kraak. 280p. 1974. text ed. 13.75x (ISBN 90-232-1251-7). Humanities.

Linguistics Speculations. Fred W. Householder. LC 78-145601. (Illus.). 1971. 39.95 (ISBN 0-521-07986-1). Cambridge U Pr.

Linguistique et discours litteraire. new ed. Jean-Michel Adam. (Collection L). (Orig., Fr.). 1976. pap. text ed. 19.95 (ISBN 0-685-66283-7). Larousse.

Linguistique et enseignement du francais. Genouvrier. 13.95 (ISBN 2-03-042171-5, 4539). Larousse.

Linguistique generale. Ed. by John Lyons. (Langue et langage). (Fr). 1970. pap. 20.25 (ISBN 0-685-13970-0, 3635). Larousse.

Linguostylistics: Theory & Method. Olga Akhmanova. (Janua Linguarum, Ser. Minor: No. 181). 1976. pap. text ed. 22.35x (ISBN 9-0279-3175-5). Mouton.

Link. Matthew Manning. (Illus.). 192p. 1976. pap. 1.75 o.p. (ISBN 0-345-25050-8). Ballantine.

Link Between Science & Applications of Automatic Control: Proceedings, 4 vols. International Federation of Automatic Control, 7th Triennial World Congress, Helsinki, Finland, June 1978. Ed. by A. Niemi et al. (International Federation of Automatic Control Ser.). 1979. Set. 680.00 (ISBN 0-08-022414-8). Pergamon.

Link of Three. Mildred Davidson. 192p. (gr. 3-7). 1981. 9.95 (ISBN 0-7011-2486-5, Pub. by Chatto-Bodley-Jonathan). Merrimack Bk Serv.

Link Sixty-Eight: An M6800 Linking Loader. Robert D. Grappel & Jack E. Hemenway. LC 78-17819. 1979. pap. 8.00 (ISBN 0-931718-09-0, BYTE Bks). McGraw.

Link the Dots. 2nd ed. Isobel R. Beard. (Activity Fun Books). (Illus.). (ps-3). 1969. 0.99 o.p. (ISBN 0-695-90456-6). Follett.

Linked Lives. Gertrude Douglas. Ed. by Robert L. Wolff. (Victorian Fiction Ser.). 1975. Repr. of 1876 ed. lib. bdg. 66.00 (ISBN 0-8240-1537-1). Garland Pub.

Linking Objects and Linking Phenomena. Vamik D. Volken. 330p. 1981. text ed. 20.00 (ISBN 0-8236-3030-7, 00-3030). Intl Univs Pr.

Linking Research to Crop Production. Ed. by R. C. Staples & R. J. Kuhr. LC 79-25737. 250p. 1980. 29.50 (ISBN 0-306-40331-5, Plenum Pr). Plenum Pub.

Linking Science Education to Real Life. 90p. 1981. pap. 7.00 (UB90, UNESCO Regional Office). Unipub.

Linking Social Structure & Personality. Ed. by Glen H. Elder, Jr. LC 73-94131. (Sage Contemporary Social Science Issues: Vol. 12). 1974. 4.95x (ISBN 0-8039-0396-0). Sage.

Links. Charles Panati. 1979. pap. 2.25 o.p. (ISBN 0-425-04048-8). Berkley Pub.

Linotte: The Early Diary of Anais Nin 1914-1920, Vol. 1. Anais Nin. Tr. by Jean Sherman. LC 77-20314. (Illus.). 1978. 14.95 o.p. (ISBN 0-15-152488-2). HarBraceJ.

Linscotts Catalog of Immunological & Biological Reagents. William D. Linscott. 112p. (Orig.). 1979. 20.00 (ISBN 0-9604920-0-3). W D Linscott.

L'integration Des Juifs Nord-Africains En France. Doris Bensimon-Donath. (Publications De L'institut D'etudes et De Recherches Interethniques et Interculturelles: No. 1). 1971. pap. 20.50x (ISBN 90-2796-930-2). Mouton.

Linton Park, Number One: Charlotte. Hilary Desmond. 176p. (Orig.). 1981. pap. 1.75 (ISBN 0-523-41062-X). Pinnacle Bks.

Linus Pauling: Scientist & Crusader. Florence W. White. (Illus.). 96p. (gr. 5-9). 1980. 8.95 (ISBN 0-8027-6389-8); PLB 9.85 (ISBN 0-8027-6390-1). Walker & Co.

Linz Cafe. Christopher Alexander. (Illus.). 96p. 1981. 19.95 (ISBN 0-19-520263-5). Oxford U Pr.

Lion. William Pene Du Bois. (Viking Seafarer Ser). (Illus.). (gr. 1-3). 1974. pap. 1.50 o.p. (ISBN 0-670-05093-8, Puffin). Penguin.

Lion & Kangaroo. Gavin Souter. 344p. 1980. 8.95x (ISBN 0-00-634512-3, Pub. by W Collins Australia). Intl Schol Bk Serv.

Lion & the Cross. Joan L. Hamilton. 1981. pap. 2.75 (ISBN 0-345-28632-4). Ballantine.

Lion Hound. Jim Kjelgaard. (gr. 4-8). 1980. pap. 1.75 (ISBN 0-686-57992-5). Bantam.

Lion House Recipes. Compiled by Helen Thackeray. LC 80-19719. (Illus.). 122p. 1980. 8.95 (ISBN 0-87747-831-7). Deseret Bk.

Lion in a Paper Tent. Betty Siegel. 42p. 1980. pap. 3.25 (ISBN 0-937308-03-X). Hearthstone.

Lion in the Box. Marguerite De Angeli. LC 74-33676. 80p. (gr. 3-7). 1975. 5.95 (ISBN 0-385-03317-6). Doubleday.

Lion in the Garden: Interviews with William Faulkner, 1926-1962. Ed. by James B. Meriwether & Michael Millgate. LC 80-17080. xvi, 299p. 1980. 17.50x (ISBN 0-8032-3068-0); pap. 5.95 (ISBN 0-8032-8108-0, BB 749, Bison). U of Nebr Pr.

Lion in the Meadow. Margaret Mahy. (Illus.). (gr. k-3). 1969. PLB 4.90 o.p. (ISBN 0-531-00130-X). Watts.

Lion of Ireland. Morgan Llywelyn. LC 80-84371. 560p. 1981. pap. 3.50 (ISBN 0-87216-825-5). Playboy Pbks.

Lion of Judah Hath Prevailed: Being the Biography of His Imperial Majesty Haile Selassie I. Christine Sandford. LC 73-135611. (Illus.). 192p. 1972. Repr. of 1955 ed. lib. bdg. 20.25x (ISBN 0-8371-5198-8, SLJ&). Greenwood.

Lion of the Kalahari. Sam B. Hobson & George Hobson. Tr. by Esther Linfield from Afrikaans. LC 76-3432. (Eng.). (gr. 5-9). 1976. 7.75 o.p. (ISBN 0-688-80049-1); PLB 7.44 o.p. (ISBN 0-688-84049-3). Greenwillow.

Lion of the Lavabeds. Walker A. Tompkins. 144p. (Orig.). 1976. pap. 0.95 o.p. (ISBN 0-445-00706-0). Popular Lib.

Lion of White Hall: The Life of Cassius M. Clay (1810-1903) David Smiley. 7.50 (ISBN 0-685-25623-5). Peter Smith.

Lion on the Run. Marian Rumsey. LC 72-7880. (Illus.). 160p. (gr. 3-7). 1973. 7.75 (ISBN 0-688-21770-2); PLB 7.44 (ISBN 0-688-31770-7). Morrow.

Lion Outwitted by Hare & Other African Tales. Phyllis Savory. LC 74-126432. (Folklore Ser). (Illus.). (gr. 3 up). 1971. 5.95g o.p. (ISBN 0-8075-4556-2). A Whitman.

Lion, the Witch & the Wardrobe. C. S. Lewis. (Illus.). (gr. 4-6). 1951. 8.95 (ISBN 0-02-758110-1). Macmillan.

Lion Triumphant. Philippa Carr. 384p. 1977. pap. 2.50 (ISBN 0-449-23233-6, Crest). Fawcett.

Lion Without Claws. Philippa Wiat. LC 77-73019. 1978. 7.95 o.p. (ISBN 0-312-48736-3). St Martin.

Lionardo Salvati: A Critical Biography. Peter M. Brown. (Oxford Modern Language & Literature Monographs). 297p. 1974. text ed. 37.50x (ISBN 0-19-815523-9). Oxford U Pr.

Lionel: A Collectors Guide & History, Vol. IV:1970-1980. Tom McComas & James Tuohy. 138p. 1980. 24.95 (ISBN 0-937522-00-7). TM Prods.

Lionel Nineteen Thirty-Eight Catalogue. Ed. by Bruce C. Greenberg. (Illus.). 1975. pap. 6.00 o.p. (ISBN 0-89778-313-1). Greenberg Pub Co.

Lionel 1932 Catalogue. Ed. by Bruce C. Greenberg. (Illus.). 1975. pap. 6.00 o.p. (ISBN 0-89778-317-4). Greenberg Pub Co.

Lionel 1933 Catalogue. Ed. by Bruce C. Greenberg. (Illus.). 1975. pap. 6.00 o.p. (ISBN 0-89778-309-3). Greenberg Pub Co.

Lioness & the Lily, No. 135. Barbara Cartland. 144p. 1981. pap. 1.75 (ISBN 0-553-14503-7). Bantam.

Lions. Mary Chipperfield. LC 77-13039. (Animals of the World Ser.). (Illus.). (gr. 4-8). 1977. PLB 10.65 (ISBN 0-8172-1075-X). Raintree Pubs.

Lions. Cynthia Overbeck. (Lerner Natural Science Bks.). (Illus.). (gr. 4-10). 1981. PLB 7.95 (ISBN 0-8225-1463-X). Lerner Pubns.

Lions & the Lambs. Thomas Fensch. 1977. 7.95 o.p. (ISBN 0-498-07388-2). A S Barnes.

Lion's Cavalcade. Alan Aldridge & Ted Walker. (Illus.). (gr. 3 up). 1981. 10.95 (ISBN 0-224-01701-2, Pub. by Chatto-Bodley-Jonathan). Merrimack Bk Serv.

Lion's Roar of Queen Srimala. Tr. by Alex Wayman & Hideko Wayman. 160p. 1974. 17.50x (ISBN 0-231-03726-0). Columbia U Pr.

Lion's Shadow. Elizabeth Hunter. 192p. (Orig.). 1980. pap. 1.50 (ISBN 0-671-57018-8). S&S.

Lion's Shadow. Elizabeth Hunter. (Silhouette Ser.: No. 18). pap. 1.50 (ISBN 0-686-68327-7). PB.

Lion's Share: A Short History of British Imperialism, 1850-1970. Bernard Porter. LC 75-16224. 400p. 1976. text ed. 22.00x (ISBN 0-582-48103-1); pap. text ed. 11.95x (ISBN 0-582-48104-X). Longman.

Lion's Way. Lewis Orde. LC 80-66493. 1981. 12.95 (ISBN 0-87795-268-X). Arbor Hse.

Liosta Focal As Ros Muc. T. O'Maille. 270p. 1974. 20.00x (ISBN 0-7165-2238-1, Pub. by Irish Academic Pr Ireland). Biblio Dist.

Lipics & Bioprotein. Ed. by M. Fondu. (Journal: Nutrition & Metabolism: Vol. 24, Supplement 1). (Illus.). iv, 212p. 1980. 29.50 (ISBN 3-8055-1266-X). S Karger.

Lipid Analysis. W. W. Christie. 1973. text ed. 42.00 (ISBN 0-08-017753-0). Pergamon.

Lipid Biochemistry of Fungi & Other Organisms. John D. Weete & Darrell J. Weber. 400p. 1980. 45.00 (ISBN 0-306-40570-9, Plenum Pr). Plenum Pub.

Lipid Metabolism in Ruminant Animals. Ed. by W. W. Christie. (Illus.). 464p. 1981. 70.00 (ISBN 0-08-023789-4). Pergamon.

Lipids: Proceedings, 2 vols. Ed. by R. Paoletti et al. Incl. Vol. 1. Biochemistry. LC 75-21982. 298p. 37.50 (ISBN 0-89004-028-1); Vol. 2. Technology. LC 75-26387. 286p. 37.50 (ISBN 0-89004-029-X). 1975. Set. 68.00 (ISBN 0-685-61106-X). Raven.

Lipika. Rabindranath Tagore. Tr. by Indu Dutt. 127p. 1969. pap. 3.00 (ISBN 0-88253-094-1). Ind-US Inc.

Lipoprotein Structure. Ed. by Angelo M. Scanu & Frank R. Landsberger. (N.Y. Academy of Sciences Annals: Vol. 348). 436p. 1980. 76.00x (ISBN 0-89766-082-X). NY Acad Sci.

Liposomes in Biological Systems. G. Gregoriadis & A. C. Allison. LC 79-40507. 1980. 68.50 (ISBN 0-471-27608-1, Pub. by Wiley-Interscience). Wiley.

Lippincott Manual of Nursing Practice. 2nd ed. Lillian S. Brunner. LC 78-6987. 1978. text ed. 29.95 (ISBN 0-397-54212-7). Lippincott.

Lippincott's State Board Examination Review for Nurses. Luverne W. Lewis. LC 77-27368. 1978. pap. text ed. 13.95 (ISBN 0-397-54214-3). Lippincott.

Lipreading: For the Oral Deaf & Hard-Of-Hearing Person. Elizabeth Hazard. 228p. 1971. 14.75 (ISBN 0-398-02161-9). C C Thomas.

Liptako Speaks: History from Oral Tradition in Africa. Paul Irwin. LC 80-7531. (Illus.). 250p. 1981. 16.00 (ISBN 0-691-05309-X). Princeton U Pr.

Liquid & Amorphous Metals: Mechanics of Plastic Solids. Ed. by E. Luscher & H. Coufal. (NATO-Advanced Study Institute Ser.). 672p. 1980. 75.00x (ISBN 9-0286-0680-7). Sijthoff & Noordhoff.

Liquid Chromotography in Clinical Analysis. Ed. by Pokar Kabra & Laurence J. Marton. LC 80-84083. (Biological Methods Ser.). 352p. 1981. 49.50 (ISBN 0-89603-026-1). Humana.

Liquid Crystals. S. Chandrasekhar. LC 75-32913. (Cambridge Monographs in Physics). (Illus.). 1977. 71.50 (ISBN 0-521-21149-2). Cambridge U Pr.

Liquid Crystals. S. Chandrasenkhar. (Cambridge Monographs in Physics). (Illus.). 352p. 1980. pap. 22.95 (ISBN 0-521-29841-5). Cambridge U Pr.

Liquid Crystals & Plastic Crystals, Vol. 1: Preparation, Constitution & Applications. Ed. by G. W. Gray & P. A. Winsor. LC 73-11504. (Illus.). 383p. 1974. 59.95 (ISBN 0-470-32339-6). Halsted Pr.

Liquid Crystals & Plastic Crystals, Vol. 2: Physico-Chemical Properties & Methods of Investigation. Ed. by G. W. Gray & P. A. Winsor. LC 73-11505. (Illus.). 314p. 1974. 59.95 (ISBN 0-470-32340-X). Halsted Pr.

Liquid Crystals of One- & Two-Dimensional Order: Proceedings. W. Helfreich & G. Heppke. (Springer Series in Chemical Physics: Vol. 11). (Illus.). 416p. 1981. 39.50 (ISBN 0-387-10399-6). Springer-Verlag.

Liquid Dawn & Crystal Fire. Phillip A. Harrell. 40p. (Orig.). 1980. pap. 2.00 (ISBN 0-934852-51-0). Lorien Hse.

Liquid Fuels. D. A. Williams & G. Jones. 1963. pap. 9.75 (ISBN 0-08-010385-5). Pergamon.

Liquid Gas Carrier Register 1977. LC 75-644549. 124p. 1977. 35.00x o.p. (ISBN 0-900291-21-4). Intl Pubns Serv.

Liquid Metals. Norman H. March. 1968. 25.00 (ISBN 0-08-012331-7). Pergamon.

Liquid or Solid? That's a Good Question! Tobi Tobias. LC 77-4845. (Illus.). 1977. PLB 7.95 o.p. (ISBN 0-516-03537-1). Childrens.

Liquid Phase. D. H. Trevena & R. J. Cooke. LC 75-19034. (Wykeham Science Ser.: No. 37). 1975. 9.95x (ISBN 0-8448-1164-5). Crane-Russak Co.

Liquid Phase High Pressure Chemistry. Neil S. Isaacs. 384p. 1981. 100.00 (ISBN 0-471-27849-1, Pub. by Wiley-Interscience). Wiley.

Liquid Scintillation Counting. K. D. Neame & C. A. Homewood. LC 74-11613. 180p. 1974. 17.95 o.p. (ISBN 0-470-63085-X). Halsted Pr.

Liquid State Physics. C. A. Croxton. LC 72-89803. (Physics Monographs). (Illus.). 400p. 1974. 57.50 (ISBN 0-521-20117-9). Cambridge U Pr.

Liquidator. (Nick Carter Ser.). 1978. pap. 1.75 (ISBN 0-441-48455-7). Charter Bks.

Liquidity Creation & Distribution in the Eurocurrency Markets. John Hewson. LC 75-2804. 208p. 1975. 19.50 (ISBN 0-669-99556-8). Lexington Bks.

Liquids & Their Properties: A Molecular & Microscopic Treatise. H. N. Temperley & D. H. Trevena. LC 77-8177. 1978. 59.95 (ISBN 0-470-99203-4). Halsted Pr.

Liquified Petroleum Gases: A Guide to Properties, Applications & Usage of Propane & Butane. A. F. Williams & W. L. Lom. LC 73-15141. (Illus.). 403p. 1973. 65.95 (ISBN 0-470-94850-7). Halsted Pr.

Liriche Di Rigaut De Berbezilh, a Cura Di Alberto Varvaro. Rigaut De Barbezieux. LC 80-2187. 1981. Repr. of 1960 ed. 39.50 (ISBN 0-404-19018-9). AMS Pr.

Lisa, Bright & Dark. John Neufeld. (gr. 7 up). 1969. 9.95 (ISBN 0-87599-153-X). S G Phillips.

Lisle Letters, 6 vols. Ed. by Muriel S. Byrne. LC 80-12019. 1981. Set. 250.00x (ISBN 0-226-08801-4). U of Chicago Pr.

Lisp. Patrick H. Winston & Berthold K. Horn. (Illus.). 300p. 1981. pap. text ed. 13.95 (ISBN 0-201-08329-9). A-W.

LISP One-Point-Five Primer. Clark Weissman. (Orig.). 1967. pap. 16.95x (ISBN 0-8221-1050-4). Dickenson.

LISP 1.5 Programmer's Manual. John McCarthy. 1962. 6.00x (ISBN 0-262-13011-4). MIT Pr.

Lisrel Four: Analysis of Linear Structural Relationships by the Method of Maximum Likelihood. Karl G. Joreskog & Dag Sorbom. pap. 10.00 (ISBN 0-89498-004-1). Natl Ed Res.

Lissa. Mira Stables. (Regency Romance Ser.). 1979. pap. 1.75 o.p. (ISBN 0-449-24138-6, Crest). Fawcett.

List of Architectural Books Available in America Before the Revolution. rev. ed. Helen Park. LC 76-189461. (Art & Architecture Bibliographies Ser: No. 1). (Illus.). 80p. 1973. 12.95x (ISBN 0-912158-21-2). Hennessey.

List of Books. Frederic Raphael et al. 1981. 10.95 (ISBN 0-517-54017-7, Harmony). Crown.

List of Books on the History of Industry & the Industrial Arts. John Crerar Library. LC 67-14030. 1966. Repr. of 1915 ed. 22.00 (ISBN 0-8103-3104-7). Gale.

List of Doctoral Dissertations by Chinese Students in the United States: 1961-1964. Tze-Chung Li. LC 67-30284. 1967. pap. 3.50 (ISBN 0-686-24155-X). CHCUS Inc.

List of Editions of the Holy Scriptures & Parts Thereof Printed in American Previous to 1860. Edmund B. O'Callaghan. LC 66-25690. 1966. Repr. of 1861 ed. 20.00 (ISBN 0-8103-3313-9). Gale.

List of Emigrants from England to America 1682-1692. Ed. by Michael Ghirelli. LC 68-15793. 1968. 10.00 (ISBN 0-685-32673-X). C E Tuttle.

List of Industry Analysts in the Federal Government. 1981. pap. 10.00 (ISBN 0-686-26067-8). Wash Res.

List of Newspapers in Library of Yale. Yale Univ. Library. (Yale Historical Pubs., Miscellany Ser.: No. II). 1916. 42.50x (ISBN 0-685-69889-0). Elliots Bks.

List of Shipping: Nomenclature 1979. 1979. pap. 18.75 (ISBN 0-660-50173-2, SSC 132, SSC). Unipub.

List of the Books, Periodicals & Pamphlets in the Library of the Royal Aeronautical Society: With Which Is Incorporated the Institution of Aeronautical Engineers. Royal Aeronautical Society. Ed. by James Gilbert. LC 79-7295. (Flight: Its First Seventy-Five Years Ser.). 1979. Repr. of 1941 ed. lib. bdg. 21.00x (ISBN 0-405-12202-0). Arno.

List of Trading Vessels in the Maritime Fur Trade, 1785-1825. Frederic William Howay. (Materials for the Study of Alaska History Ser.: No. 2). 1973. pap. 8.50x (ISBN 0-919642-51-9). Limestone Pr.

List of Translations of Foreign Literature on Hydraulics. Compiled by American Society of Civil Engineers. (ASCE Manual & Report on Energy Practice Ser.: No. 35). 144p. 1968. pap. text ed. 6.00 (ISBN 0-87262-212-6). Am Soc Civil Eng.

Lista De Encabezamientos De Materia Para Bibliotecas, 3 Vols. y Suplementos-1967. (Manuales Del Bibliotecario Ser: No. 6). (Span.). 1977. Set. 25.00 (ISBN 0-8270-3105-X). Vol. I (ISBN 0-8270-3105-X). Vol. II (ISBN 0-8270-3115-7). Supl. 1 (ISBN 0-8270-3125-4). Supl. 2 (ISBN 0-8270-3130-0). OAS.

Listen. 3rd ed. Joseph Kerman. 1980. 14.95x (ISBN 0-87901-127-0); single record 3.95; 10 record set 25.95. Worth.

Listen: A Guide to the Pleasures of Music. 3rd ed. Roland Nadeau & William Tesson. 544p. 1980. pap. text ed. 14.95 (ISBN 0-8403-2332-8). Kendall-Hunt.

Listen America. Jerry Falwell. LC 79-6279. 288p. 1980. 8.95 (ISBN 0-385-15897-1, Galilee). Doubleday.

Listen & Help Tell the Story. Bernice W. Carlson. (Illus.). (gr. k-2). 1965. 8.95 o.p. (ISBN 0-687-22096-3). Abingdon.

Listen, Beloved. Martha Smock. LC 80-50624. 177p. 1980. 3.95 (ISBN 0-87159-101-4). Unity Bks.

Listen for the Whisperer. Phyllis A. Whitney. LC 76-168682. 1972. 5.95 o.p. (ISBN 0-385-03354-0). Doubleday.

Listen Listen Listen. Louis Gittner. Ed. by Starr Farish. 320p. (Orig.). 1980. pap. 7.95 (ISBN 0-9605492-0-X). Louis Found.

Listen to Danger. Dorothy Eden. 208p. 1976. pap. 1.95 (ISBN 0-441-48481-6). Ace Bks.

Listen to Light: Haiku. Raymond Roseliep. (Illus.). 128p. 1980. 10.00 (ISBN 0-934184-05-4); pap. 5.00 (ISBN 0-934184-06-2). Alembic Pr.

Listen to That! (Golden Photo Board Bks.). (Illus.). 12p. (ps). 1980. 1.50 (ISBN 0-307-06073-X, Golden Pr). Western Pub.

Listen to the Animals. William L. Coleman. LC 79-11312. (ps-6). 1979. pap. 3.95 (ISBN 0-87123-341-X, 210341). Bethany Fell.

Listen to the Blues. Bruce Cook. LC 72-11126. (Encore Edition). 1975. pap. 0.95 o.p. (ISBN 0-684-15762-4, SL 533, ScribT). Scribner.

Listen to the Children: A Study of the Impact on the Mental Health of Children of a Parent's Catastrophic Illness. Cancer Care, Inc. & The National Cancer Foundation, Inc. LC 77-94376. 1977. 2.50 (ISBN 0-686-26199-2). Cancer Care.

Listen to the King: Meditations Just from the Scriptures. Compiled By Walter E McAlister. (Direction Bks.). 96p. (Orig.). 1980. pap. 2.95 (ISBN 0-8010-6104-0). Baker Bk.

Listen to the Land. Editors of Farm Journal & Kathryn Larson. LC 76-56946. (Illus.). 1977. 8.95 o.p. (ISBN 0-13-537084-1). P-H.

Listen to the Light. John S. Niendorff. 96p. 1980. pap. 2.50 (ISBN 0-911336-84-2). Sci of Mind.

Listen to the Skylark. Jane McCarthy. 192p. (YA) 1975. 5.95 (ISBN 0-685-52912-6, Avalon). Bouregy.

Listen to the Warm. Rod McKuen. (Pocket ed.). 1969. 5.95 (ISBN 0-394-40378-9); deluxe ed. 5.00 pocket ed. (ISBN 0-394-40380-0). Random.

Listener. John Gill. 1977. pap. 1.95 o.p. (ISBN 0-445-08555-X). Popular Lib.

Listener's Guide to Music: With a Concert-Goer's Glossary. 10th ed. Percy A. Scholes. (Illus.). (YA) (gr. 9 up). 1961. pap. 4.95x (ISBN 0-19-284002-9). Oxford U Pr.

Listener's Handbook: A Guide to Music Appreciation. 3rd ed. Ira Schroeder. (Illus.). (gr. 9-12). 1966. text ed. 3.95x o.p. (ISBN 0-8138-1010-8). Iowa St U Pr.

Listening. Norman Wakefield. 1981. pap. 4.95 (ISBN 0-8499-2920-2). Word Bks.

Listening. Jack Winder. Ed. by Alton Jordan. (Elephant Ser.). (Illus.). (gr. k-3). 1975. PLB 3.50 (ISBN 0-89868-021-2, Read Res); text ed. 1.75 soft bd. (ISBN 0-89868-054-9). ARO Pub.

Listening Across the Border. Gladys St. John. 1981. 8.95 (ISBN 0-533-04797-8). Vantage.

Listening Aids Through the Grades: Two Hundred Thirty-Two Listening Activities. rev ed. David H. Russell & Elizabeth F. Russell. Ed. by Dorothy G. Hennings. LC 79-607. 1979. pap. text ed. 5.95x (ISBN 0-8077-2558-7). Tchrs Coll.

Listening for the Visually Impaired: A Teaching Manual. Claudell S. Stocker. 192p. 1974. pap. 11.75 (ISBN 0-398-02936-9). C C Thomas.

Listening Links. M. Geddes & G. Sturtridge. 1979. pap. text ed. 3.95x (ISBN 0-435-28051-1); tchrs. ed. 7.95x (ISBN 0-435-28052-X); of three tapes 60.00 set (ISBN 0-435-28053-8); of three cassettes 54.00 set (ISBN 0-435-28054-6). Heinemann Ed.

Listening to Billie. Alice Adams. 1977. 7.95 (ISBN 0-394-41069-6). Knopf.

Listening to Spoken English. G. Brown. (Applied Linguistics & Language Study Ser.). 1978. pap. text ed. 8.50x (ISBN 0-582-55077-7). Longman.

Listening to the Giants. Warren W. Wiersbe. 1979. 11.95 (ISBN 0-8010-9618-9). Baker Bk.

Listening Walk. Paul Showers. LC 61-10495. (Let's-Read & Find-Out Science Bk). (Illus.). (gr. k-3). 1961. 7.89 (ISBN 0-690-49663-X, TYC-J). T Y Crowell.

Listening with the Third Ear. Theodor Reik. 1977. pap. 2.25 o.p. (ISBN 0-685-86426-X). Jove Pubns.

Lister Legacy. Jan Drabek. 384p. 1980. 13.95 (ISBN 0-8253-0015-0). Beaufort Bks NY.

Listeriosis. 2nd ed. Heinz P. Seeliger. 1961. 15.50 (ISBN 0-02-852020-3). Hafner.

Lists of Words Occurring Frequently in the Hebrew Bible. John D. Watts. (Heb, & Eng). 1960. pap. 1.95 (ISBN 0-8028-1214-7). Eerdmans.

Literacy. Elizabeth H. Grundin. 1979. text ed. 14.25 (ISBN 0-06-318128-2, IntlDept); pap. text ed. 9.25 (ISBN 0-06-318140-1). Har-Row.

Literacy & the Social Order. David Cressy. (Illus.). 250p. 1980. 32.95 (ISBN 0-521-22514-0). Cambridge U Pr.

Literacy, Bible Reading & Church Growth Through the Ages. Morris Watkins. LC 78-15315. (Illus.). 1978. pap. 5.95 (ISBN 0-87808-325-1). William Carey Lib.

Literacy Education for Adolescents & Adults: A Teacher's Resource Book. Edwin Smith. LC 74-101315. 1970. text ed. 6.00x o.p. (ISBN 0-87835-001-2). Boyd & Fraser.

Literacy for Working: Functional Literacy in Rural Tanzania. Margo Viscusi. (Educational Studies & Documents, No. 5). (Illus.). 57p. (Orig.). 1972. pap. 2.50 (ISBN 92-3-100905-2, U360, UNESCO). Unipub.

Literacy in Colonial New England: An Inquiry into the Social Context of Literacy in the Early Modern West. Kenneth A. Lockridge. (Illus.). 1974. 6.95x (ISBN 0-393-05522-1); pap. 3.95x (ISBN 0-393-09263-1). Norton.

Literacy in Traditional Societies. Ed. by Jack R. Goody. LC 69-10427. 1969. 29.95 (ISBN 0-521-07345-6); pap. 11.95x (ISBN 0-521-29005-8). Cambridge U Pr.

Literarische Mord. Fritz Woelcken. Ed. by E. F. Bleiler. LC 78-60827. (Fiction of Popular Culture Ser.: Vol. 19). 1979. lib. bdg. 38.00 (ISBN 0-8240-9649-5). Garland Pub.

Literary Agents: A Complete Guide. LC 78-23329. (Illus.). 1978. pap. 3.95 (ISBN 0-913734-08-X). Poets & Writers.

Literary & Art Anthology, Vol. 2. Ed. by Jim Villani. 88p. 1976. pap. 4.95 (ISBN 0-917530-02-0). Pig Iron Pr.

Literary & Art Anthology, Vol. 3. Ed. by Jim Villani. 104p. 1977. pap. 4.95 (ISBN 0-917530-06-3). Pig Iron Pr.

Literary & Art Anthology, Vol. 4. Ed. by Jim Villani. 104p. 1978. pap. 4.95 (ISBN 0-917530-09-8). Pig Iron Pr.

Literary & Art Anthology, Vol. 5. Ed. by Jim Villani. 96p. 1979. pap. 4.95 (ISBN 0-917530-10-1). Pig Iron Pr.

Literary & Art Anthology, Vol. 6. Ed. by Jim Villani. 96p. 1979. pap. 4.95 (ISBN 0-917530-11-X). Pig Iron Pr.

Literary & Lexical Texts & the Earliest Administrative Documents from Nippur. Aage Westenholz. (Bibliotheca Mesopotamica Ser.: Vol. 1). (Illus.). 200p. 1975. 18.50 (ISBN 0-89003-008-1); pap. 12.00 (ISBN 0-686-68506-7). Undena Pubns.

Literary Approach to the New Testament. John P. Pritchard. LC 72-1793. (Illus.). 355p. 1981. pap. 7.95 (ISBN 0-8061-1710-9). U of Okla Pr.

Literary Art & the Unconscious. David J. Gordon. LC 75-27662. 1976. 12.50 (ISBN 0-8071-0197-4). La State U Pr.

Literary Background of Bach's Cantatas. James Day. (Student's Music Library-Historical & Critical Studies Ser). (Illus.). 1961. 10.95 (ISBN 0-234-77522-X). Dufour.

Literary Ballad in Early Nineteenth-Century Russian Literature. Michael Katz. (Oxford Modern Languages & Literature Monographs). 1976. 37.50x (ISBN 0-19-815528-X). Oxford U Pr.

Literary Blunders. Henry B. Wheatley. LC 68-30616. 1969. Repr. of 1893 ed. 18.00 (ISBN 0-8103-3317-1). Gale.

Literary Britain: A Reader's Guide to Its Writers & Landmarks. Frank Morley. LC 78-2147. (Illus.). 482p. 1980. 19.95 (ISBN 0-06-013056-3, HarpT). Har-Row.

Literary Career of Sir Joshua Reynolds. Frederick W. Hilles. 1967. Repr. of 1936 ed. 15.00 o.p. (ISBN 0-208-00418-1, Archon). Shoe String.

Literary Cat. Walter Chandoha. (Illus.). 1977. 10.00 o.p. (ISBN 0-397-01213-6). Lippincott.

Literary Cat. J. C. Suares & Seymour Chwast. LC 77-23583. (Illus.). (YA) 1977. 12.95 o.p. (ISBN 0-399-12034-3, Dist. by Putnam). Berkley Pub.

Literary Concordances: A Complete Handbook for the Preparation of Manual & Computer Concordances. T. H. Howard-Hill. 1979. text ed. 15.00 (ISBN 0-08-023021-0). Pergamon.

Literary Context of Chaucer's Fabliaux: Texts & Translations. Geoffrey Chaucer. Ed. by Larry Benson & Theodore Andersson. LC 70-138663. 1971. 13.85 o.p. (ISBN 0-672-51120-7); pap. 8.50 (ISBN 0-672-61008-6, LL28). Bobbs.

Literary Criticism. John Ruskin. Ed. by Harold Bloom. 8.50 (ISBN 0-8446-1691-5). Peter Smith.

Literary Criticism: A Glossary of Major Terms. Patrick Murray. 208p. 1978. pap. text ed. 7.95 (ISBN 0-582-35247-9). Longman.

Literary Criticism & Authors' Biographies: An Annotated Index. Compiled by Alison P. Seidel. LC 78-11857. 1978. 11.00 (ISBN 0-8108-1172-3). Scarecrow.

Literary Criticism & Historical Understanding. Ed. by Phillip Damon. LC 67-24335. 1967. 12.50x (ISBN 0-231-03086-X). Columbia U Pr.

Literary Criticism, Idea & Act: The English Institute, 1939-1972. Ed. by W. K. Wimsatt. 1974. 30.00x (ISBN 0-520-02585-7). U of Cal Pr.

Literary Criticism in Antiquity, 2 vols. John W. Atkins. Incl. Vol. 1. Greek. 6.00; Vol. 2. Graeco-Roman. 6.75 (ISBN 0-8446-1033-X). Peter Smith.

Literary Criticism of Alexander Pope. Alexander Pope. Ed. by Bertrand A. Goldgar. LC 64-17231. (Landmark Edns.). 1979. 15.00x (ISBN 0-8032-0459-0). U of Nebr Pr.

Literary Criticism of Dante Alighieri. Dante Alighieri. Ed. & tr. by Robert S. Haller. LC 72-85402. (Regents Critics Ser). xlix, 190p. 1974. 11.00x (ISBN 0-8032-0467-1); pap. 2.75x (ISBN 0-8032-5469-5, BB 417, Bison). U of Nebr Pr.

Literary Criticism of F. R. Leavis. R. P. Bilan. LC 78-18089. 1979. 32.50 (ISBN 0-521-22324-5). Cambridge U Pr.

Literary Criticism of George Henry Lewes. George H. Lewes. Ed. by Alice R. Kaminsky. LC 64-17230. (Regents Critics Ser). 1965. 9.95x (ISBN 0-8032-0456-6); pap. 2.75x (ISBN 0-8032-5455-5, BB 402, Bison). U of Nebr Pr.

Literary Criticism of Henry James. Sarah B. Daugherty. LC 80-36753. xiv, 232p. 1981. 15.95x (ISBN 0-8214-0440-7). Ohio U Pr.

Literary Criticism of John Dryden. John Dryden. Ed. by Arthur C. Kirsch. LC 66-23019. (Regents Critics Ser). 1967. 9.95x o.p. (ISBN 0-8032-0453-1). U of Nebr Pr.

Literary Criticism of T. S. Eliot: New Essays. Ed. by David Newton-De Molina. 1977. text ed. 26.00x (ISBN 0-485-11167-5, Athlone Pr). Humanities.

Literary Criticism of the New Testament. William A. Beardslee. Ed. by Dan O. Via, Jr. LC 77-94817. (Guides to Biblical Scholarship: New Testament Ser.). 96p. (Orig.). 1970. pap. 2.50 (ISBN 0-8006-0185-8, 1-185). Fortress.

Literary Criticism: Plato to Dryden. Ed. by Allan H. Gilbert. LC 61-12266. (Waynebooks Ser: No. 1). 1962. pap. 6.50x (ISBN 0-8143-1160-1). Wayne St U Pr.

Literary Criticism: Pope to Croce. Ed. by Gay W. Allen & Harry H. Clark. LC 61-12267. (Waynebooks Ser: No. 2). 1962. 9.95x (ISBN 0-8143-1157-1); pap. 6.50x (ISBN 0-8143-1158-X). Wayne St U Pr.

Literary Criticisms: Plato Through Johnson. Compiled by Vernon Hall. LC 76-123515. (Goldentree Bibliographies in Language & Literature Ser). (Orig.). 1970. pap. 6.95x (ISBN 0-88295-516-0). AHM Pub.

Literary Democracy: The Declaration of Cultural Independence in America 1837-1861. Larzer Ziff. 1981. 17.95 (ISBN 0-670-43026-9). Viking Pr.

Literary Disruptions: The Making of a Post-Contemporary American Fiction. 2nd ed. Jerome Klinkowitz. LC 80-1592. 280p. 1980. 15.95 (ISBN 0-252-00809-X); pap. 6.50 (ISBN 0-252-00810-3). U of Ill Pr.

Literary Dog. J. C. Suares. 1978. pap. 7.95 o.p. (ISBN 0-425-03961-7). Berkley Pub.

Literary Engagement Calendar. William Bramhall. (Illus.). 112p. 1981. spiral 6.95 (ISBN 0-525-93196-1). Dutton.

Literary Essays: Contributed by the Edinburgh Review. Lord Maculay. 706p. 1980. Repr. of 1923 ed. lib. bdg. 30.00 (ISBN 0-89760-544-6). Telegraph Bks.

Literary Forgeries. James A. Farrer. LC 68-23156. 1969. Repr. of 1907 ed. 15.00 (ISBN 0-8103-3305-8). Gale.

Literary Function of Possession in Luke-Acts. Luke T. Johnson. LC 77-21055. (Society of Biblical Literature. Dissertation Ser.: No. 39). 1977. pap. 7.50 (ISBN 0-89130-200-X, 060139). Scholars Pr Ca.

Literary Guide to Ireland. Susan Cahill & Thomas Cahill. LC 72-1181. 1979. pap. 4.95 o.p. (ISBN 0-684-15892-2, ScribT). Scribner.

Literary Hearthstones: William Cowper. Marion Harland. 237p. 1980. Repr. of 1899 ed. lib. bdg. 30.00 (ISBN 0-89984-286-0). Century Bookbindery.

Literary Herbal. Avril Rodway. (Leprechaun Library). (Illus.). 64p. 1980. 3.95 (ISBN 0-399-12545-0). Putnam.

Literary Heritage of Southeast Asia. Himansu B. Sarkar. 1980. 11.50x (ISBN 0-8364-0606-0, Pub. by Mukhopadhyay India). South Asia Bks.

Literary History of America. Barrett Wendell. LC 68-30589. 1968. Repr. of 1900 ed. 26.00 (ISBN 0-8103-3226-4). Gale.

Literary History of England. 2nd student ed. Ed. by A. Baugh et al. 1967. 34.95 (ISBN 0-13-537605-X). P-H.

Literary History of England: The Restoration & Eighteenth Century 1660-1789. 2nd ed. George Sherburn & Donald F. Bond. LC 66-26100. 1967. pap. text ed. 14.95x (ISBN 0-89197-277-3). Irvington.

Literary History of Persia, 4 Vols. Edward G. Browne. 1928. 62.00 ea. Vol. 1 (ISBN 0-521-04344-1). Vol. 2 (ISBN 0-521-04345-X). Vol. 3 (ISBN 0-521-04346-8). Vol. 4. Cambridge U Pr.

Literary History of Philadelphia. Ellis P. Oberholtzer. LC 72-81510. 1969. Repr. of 1906 ed. 24.00 (ISBN 0-8103-3563-8). Gale.

Literary History of the Arabs. 2nd ed. Reynold A. Nicholson. 1969. 78.00 (ISBN 0-521-05823-6); pap. 21.50x (ISBN 0-521-09572-7). Cambridge U Pr.

Literary Impact of the Authorized Version. C S. Lewis. Ed. by John Reumann. LC 63-17883. (Facet Bks). 48p. (Orig.). 1963. pap. 1.00 (ISBN 0-8006-3003-3, 1-3003). Fortress.

Literary Impressionism, James & Chekhov. H. Peter Stowell. LC 78-23737. 286p. 1980. 17.00x (ISBN 0-8203-0468-9). U of Ga Pr.

Literary Industries. Hubert H. Bancroft. LC 67-29422. (Works of Hubert Howe Bancroft Ser.). 1967. Repr. of 1888 ed. 25.00x (ISBN 0-914888-43-9). Bancroft Pr.

Literary Irony & the Literary Audience: Studies in the Victimization of the Reader in Augustan Fiction. John G. McKee. LC 74-7611. (Orig.). 1976. pap. text ed. 9.25x (ISBN 90-6203-051-3). Humanities.

Literary Journal in America to 1900: A Guide to Information Sources. Ed. by Edward E. Chielens. LC 74-11533. (American Literature, English Literature & World Literatures in English Information Guide Ser.: Vol. 3). 228p. 1975. 30.00 (ISBN 0-8103-1239-5). Gale.

Literary Journal in America, 1900-1950: A Guide to Information Sources. Edward E Chielens. LC 74-11534. (American Literature, English Literature, & World Literature in English Information Guide Ser.: Vol. 16). 1977. 30.00 (ISBN 0-8103-1240-9). Gale.

Literary L. A. Lionel Rolfe. (Illus.). 96p. (Orig.). 1981. pap. 5.95 (ISBN 0-87701-177-X). Chronicle Bks.

Literary Landmarks: Essays on the Theory & Practice of Literature. Francis Fergusson. 1975. 11.00 (ISBN 0-8135-0815-0). Rutgers U Pr.

Literary Landscape of the British Isles: A Narrative Atlas. David Daiches & John Flower. 288p. 1981. pap. 7.95 (ISBN 0-14-005735-8). Penguin.

Literary Language & Its Public in Late Latin Antiquity & in the Middle Ages. Erich Auerbach. Tr. by R. Manheim. (Bollingen Ser.: No. 74). 1965. 21.00 o.p. (ISBN 0-691-09782-8). Princeton U Pr.

Literary Legacy of C. S. Lewis. Chad Walsh. 1979. 10.95 o.p. (ISBN 0-15-152725-3). HarBraceJ.

Literary Lifelines: The Richard Aldington-Larence Durrell Correspondence. Ed. by Ian S. MacNiven & Harry T. Moore. 288p. 1981. 17.50 (ISBN 0-670-42817-5). Viking Pr.

Literary Magazine: Or, Universal Review. Nos. 1-27. 1756-1758, 3 vols. Samuel Johnson. Ed. by Donald D. Eddy. (Samuel Johnson & Periodical Literature Ser.: Vol. 5). 1979. lib. bdg. 58.50 (ISBN 0-8240-3430-9). Garland Pub.

Literary Masters of Norway. Intro. by Carl H. Grondahl. LC 79-309381. (Tokens of Norway Ser.). (Illus.). 89p. (Orig.). 1978. pap. 12.50x (ISBN 82-518-0727-1). Intl Pubns Serv.

Literary Meaning & Augustan Values. Irvin Ehrenpreis. LC 73-94275. 120p. 1974. 7.95x (ISBN 0-8139-0564-8). U Pr of Va.

Literary Memoranda of William Hickling Prescott, 2 vols. William H. Prescott. Ed. by C. Harvey Gardiner. LC 61-9004. (Illus.). 1961. boxed 22.50x (ISBN 0-8061-0495-3); pap. 8.95x (ISBN 0-8061-1161-5). U of Okla Pr.

Literary Microcosm: Theories of Interpretation of the Later Neoplatonists. James Coulter. (Columbia Studies in the Classical Tradition: No. II). 1976. text ed. 27.50x (ISBN 90-04-04489-2). Humanities.

Literary North Carolina: A Brief Historical Survey. Richard Walser. (Illus.). 1970. 5.00; pap. 2.00 (ISBN 0-86526-048-6). NC Archives.

Literary Origins of Surrealism: A New Mysticism in French Poetry. Anna Balakian. 1966. 10.00x (ISBN 0-8147-0024-1); pap. 4.00x (ISBN 0-8147-0025-X). NYU Pr.

Literary Patterns, Theological Themes & the Genre of Luke-Acts. Charles H. Talbert. LC 74-78620. (Society of Biblical Literature. Monograph). 159p. 1974. 9.00 (ISBN 0-89130-059-7, 060020); pap. 7.50 (ISBN 0-89130-058-9). Scholars Pr Ca.

Literary Pilgrim in England. Edward Thomas. 318p. 1980. pap. 9.95 (ISBN 0-19-281291-2). Oxford U Pr.

Literary Places: A Guided Pilgrimage; New York & New England. John Deedy. (Illus.). 1978. 12.95 o.p. (ISBN 0-8362-7102-5); pap. 5.95 o.p. (ISBN 0-8362-7101-7). Andrews & McMeel.

Literary Politicians. Mitchell S. Ross. LC 76-52222. 1978. 10.00 o.p. (ISBN 0-385-13077-5). Doubleday.

Literary Presentations of Divided Germany. Peter Hutchinson. LC 76-51414. (Anglica Germanica Ser.: No. 2). 1977. 28.50 (ISBN 0-521-21609-5). Cambridge U Pr.

Literary Publishing in America, 1790-1850. William Charvat. LC 59-12190. (Rosenbach Publication Ser). 1959. 7.50x o.p. (ISBN 0-8122-7214-5). U of Pa Pr.

Literary Research Guide. Ed. by Margaret C. Patterson. LC 75-13925. 1976. 28.00 (ISBN 0-8103-1102-X). Gale.

Literary Romanticism in America. William L. Andrews. LC 80-24365. 168p. 1981. 14.95x (ISBN 0-8071-0760-3). La State U Pr.

Literary San Francisco: A Pictorial History from the Beginnings to the Present. Lawrence Ferlinghetti & Nancy J. Peters. LC 79-3598. (Illus.). 224p. 1980. 15.95 (ISBN 0-06-250325-1, HarpR). Har-Row.

Literary Sources of Secular Music in Italy: 1500. Walter H. Rubsamen. LC 72-4482. (Music Ser.). 82p. 1972. Repr. of 1943 ed. lib. bdg. 15.00 (ISBN 0-306-70496-X). Da Capo.

Literary South. Louis D. Rubin, Jr. LC 78-24221. 1979. text ed. 19.95x (ISBN 0-471-04659-0). Wiley.

Literary Structure of Psalm Two. Pierre Auffret. (JSOT Supplement Ser.: No. 3). 43p. 1977. pap. text ed. 3.00x o.p. (ISBN 0-905774-02-7, Pub by JSOT Pr England). Eisenbrauns.

Literary Survey of the Bible. Joyce Vedral. LC 72-94184. 280p. (gr. 10-12). 1973. text ed. 5.95 o.p. (ISBN 0-88270-024-3); pap. text ed. 3.50 o.p. (ISBN 0-88270-025-1); tchrs. manual 2.50 o.p. (ISBN 0-88270-026-X). Logos.

Literary Text: An Examination of Critical Methods. P. M. Wetherill. 1974. 20.00x (ISBN 0-520-02709-4). U of Cal Pr.

Literary Transcendentalism: Style & Vision in the American Rennaisance. Lawrence Buell. LC 73-8409. 336p. (Orig.). 1975. pap. 4.95 (ISBN 0-8014-9152-5). Cornell U Pr.

Literary Translation As an Art Form. J. Levy. Tr. by S. Flatauer. (Approaches to Translation Studies: No. 6). 1980. pap. text ed. write for info. (ISBN 0-391-01196-0). Humanities.

Literary Use of the Psychoanalytic Process. Meredith A. Skura. LC 80-23390. 288p. 1981. 19.50x (ISBN 0-300-02380-4). Yale U Pr.

Literary Women. Ellen Moers. LC 74-33686. 336p. 1976. 10.00 o.p. (ISBN 0-385-07427-1). Doubleday.

Literary Works of Leonardo Da Vinci: A Commentary of Jean Paul Richter's Edition, 2 vols. Carlo Pedretti. 1977. Set. 88.50x (ISBN 0-520-03329-9). U of Cal Pr.

Literary World of Ana Maria Mantute. Margaret E. Janes. LC 77-119813. (Studies in Romance Languages: No. 3). 160p. 1970. 10.00x (ISBN 0-8131-1228-1). U Pr of Ky.

Literatur Wissenschaft und Geschichtsphilosophie: Festschrift Fuer Wilhelm Emrich. Ed. by Helmnt Arntzen et al. 602p. 1975. 115.00x (ISBN 3-11-005726-3). De Gruyter.

Literatura Afro-Hispano Americana: Poesia y prosa de ficcion. Ed. by Enrique Noble. LC 77-189125. 216p. 1973. pap. text ed. 8.95x (ISBN 0-471-00757-9). Wiley.

Literatura Chicana: Texto & Contexto. A. Castenada Shular et al. 1972. ref. ed. 12.95 (ISBN 0-13-537563-0); pap. text ed. 10.50 (ISBN 0-13-537555-X). P-H.

Literatura Del Siglo XX: Nueva Edicion, Revisada y Aumentada. Ed. by E. G. DaCal & M. Ucelay. (Spanish.). 1968. 28.50x o.p. (ISBN 0-03-055170-6); pap. text ed. 16.50x o.p. (ISBN 0-686-57886-4). Irvington.

Literature. Joseph K. Davis et al. 1977. 13.95x (ISBN 0-673-15009-7). Scott F.

Literature. 2nd ed. Hans P. Guth. (Orig.). 1968. pap. 12.95x (ISBN 0-534-00667-1). Wadsworth Pub.

Literature. Jack Rudman. (Undergraduate Program Field Test Ser.: UPFT-14). (Cloth bdg. avail. on request). pap. 9.95 (ISBN 0-8373-6014-5). Natl Learning.

Literature: A College Anthology. Patick W. Shaw. LC 76-19905. (Illus.). 1976. text ed. 15.50 (ISBN 0-395-24841-8); instructors' manual 1.25 (ISBN 0-395-24842-6). HM.

Literature Against Itself: Literary Ideas in Modern Society. Gerald Graff. LC 78-9879. x, 250p. 1981. pap. 5.95 (ISBN 0-226-30598-8). U of Chicago Pr.

Literature Among the Primitives. John Greenway. LC 64-13289. xviii, 346p. 1964. Repr. of 1964 ed. 15.00 (ISBN 0-8103-5001-7). Gale.

Literature & Aesthetics. Monroe C. Beardsley. LC 68-57656. 1968. pap. 2.50 (ISBN 0-672-60903-7). Bobbs.

Literature & Evil. Georges Bataille. Tr. by Alastair Hamilton. 1981. 12.95 (ISBN 0-89396-013-6); pap. 6.95 (ISBN 0-89396-014-4). Urizen Bks.

Literature & Existentialism. Jean-Paul Sartre. 1980. pap. 3.95 (ISBN 0-8065-0685-7). Lyle Stuart.

Literature & Ideas in America: Essays in Memory of Harry Hayden Clark. Ed. by Robert Falk. LC 74-27708. xi, 243p. 1975. 13.95x (ISBN 0-8214-0180-7). Ohio U Pr.

Literature & Ideology in Haiti: 1915-1961. J. Michael Dash. 1981. 26.50x (ISBN 0-389-20092-1). B&N.

Literature & Insurgency. John C. Underwood. 1914. 17.50x (ISBN 0-8196-0160-8). Biblo.

Literature & Its Interpretation. Ed. by L. Nyiroe. (De Proprietatibus Litteraruum, Series Minor: No. 24). 1979. pap. text ed. 41.25x (ISBN 90-279-3387-1). Mouton.

Literature & Liberalism: An Anthology of Sixty Years of the New Republic. Ed. by Edward Zwick. LC 76-2448. 1976. 15.00 o.p. (ISBN 0-915220-06-7, 23097); pap. 5.95 o.p. (ISBN 0-915220-31-8). New Republic.

Literature & Meaning of Scripture. Ed. by Morris A. Inch & C. Hassell Bullock. 360p. 1981. 14.95 (ISBN 0-8010-5032-4). Baker Bk.

Literature & Negation. Maire J. Kurrik. LC 79-15949. (Illus.). 1979. 25.00x (ISBN 0-231-04342-2). Columbia U Pr.

Literature & Philosophy: An Analysis of the Philosophical Novel. Stephen D. Ross. LC 69-11284. (Century Philosophy Ser.). (Orig.). 1969. pap. text ed. 5.95x (ISBN 0-89197-278-1). Irvington.

Literature & Politics. Murray Sperber. (Humanities Ser.). (gr. 12 up). 1978. pap. text ed. 7.45x (ISBN 0-8104-5878-0). Hayden.

Literature & Revolution. Leon Trotsky. 1960. pap. 6.95 (ISBN 0-472-06043-0, 43, AA). U of Mich Pr.

Literature & Society. Ed. by Peter Davison et al. LC 77-90613. (Literary Taste, Culture & Mass Communication Ser.: Vol. 5). 1978. lib. bdg. 32.00x (ISBN 0-914146-48-3). Somerset Hse.

Literature & Society in Germany, 1918-1945. Ronald Taylor. (Studies in Contemporary Literature & Culture). 363p. 1980. 28.50x (ISBN 0-389-20036-0). B&N.

Literature & the Christian Life. Sallie M. TeSelle. (Publications in Religion Ser.: No. 12). 1966. 17.50x o.p. (ISBN 0-300-00989-5). Yale U Pr.

Literature & the Inner Exile: Authoritarian Spain, 1939-1975. Paul Ilie. LC 80-18281. 208p. 1981. text ed. 14.50x (ISBN 0-8018-2424-9). Johns Hopkins.

Literature & the Left in France. John E. Flower. LC 76-2895. 1980. text ed. 28.50x (ISBN 0-06-492135-2). B&N.

Literature & the Social Worker: A Selected Reading List for Use in Bibliotherapy. Ed. by C. Morris. (Library Association Book Ser.). 1975. 3.30x (ISBN 0-85365-078-0, Pub. by Lib Assn England). Oryx Pr.

Literature at Nurse. George Moore. Ed. by Ian Fletcher & John Stokes. Bd. with Mere Accident. LC 76-20110. (Decadent Consciousness Ser.). 1978. lib. bdg. 38.00 (ISBN 0-8240-2769-8). Garland Pub.

Literature at Nurse, or, Circulating Morals: A Polemic on Victorian Censorship. George Moore. (Society & the Victorians). 96p. 1976. Repr. of 1885 ed. text ed. 5.25x (ISBN 0-391-00588-X). Humanities.

Literature Education in Ten Countries. Ed. by A. C. Purves et al. LC 73-8044. (International Studies in Evaluation Ser.: Vol. 2). 428p. 1973. pap. 14.95 (ISBN 0-470-70229-X). Halsted Pr.

Literature Eins. 2nd ed. Ed. by Robert Spaethling & Eugene Weber. 1979. pap. 5.95x (ISBN 0-393-95041-7). Norton.

Literature: Fiction. James B. Hogins. LC 73-90125. (Illus.). 368p. 1974. pap. text ed. 5.25 (ISBN 0-574-19130-5, 13-2130). SRA.

Literature for Adolescents: Teaching Poems, Stories, Novels, & Plays. Stephen Dunning & Alan B. Howes. 491p. 1975. 9.95x (ISBN 0-673-05841-7). Scott F.

Literature for Early Childhood. Joan I. Glazer. (Illus.). 240p. 1981. pap. text ed. 8.95 (ISBN 0-686-69494-5). Merrill.

Literature Guide to the Identification of Mushrooms. Ed. by Roy Watling. 120p. (Orig.). 1980. pap. 6.75. Mad River.

Literature in America: A Century of Expansion. D. Hausdorf. LC 73-139984. 1971. pap. text ed. 8.95 (ISBN 0-02-914240-7). Free Pr.

Literature in America: Founding of a Nation. K. Silverman. LC 73-139984. 1971. pap. text ed. 7.95 (ISBN 0-02-928760-X). Free Pr.

Literature in Celtic Countries. J. E. Williams. (Taliesin Congress Lectures). 218p. 1979. pap. text ed. 10.00x o.p. (ISBN 0-686-64124-8). Verry.

Literature in Four Aspects. Ed. by Ray Frazer & Harold D. Kelling. 1965. pap. text ed. 13.95x (ISBN 0-669-20628-8). Heath.

Literature, Obscenity, & Law. Felice F. Lewis. LC 75-42094. 310p. 1978. pap. 8.95 (ISBN 0-8093-0870-3). S Ill U Pr.

Literature of American Jews. Theodore L. Gross. LC 72-93311. 1973. 12.95 (ISBN 0-02-913190-1). Free Pr.

Literature of American Music in Books & Folk Mmusic Collections: A Fully Annotated Bibliography. David Horn. LC 76-13160. 1977. 24.00 (ISBN 0-8108-0996-6). Scarecrow.

Literature of Change: Studies in the Nineteenth Century Provincial Novel. 2nd ed. John Lucas. 217p. 1980. 20.00x (ISBN 0-389-20020-4); pap. 11.50x (ISBN 0-389-20021-2). B&N.

Literature of England: Single Volume Edition. rev. ed. George K. Anderson & William E. Buckler. 1967. 17.95x (ISBN 0-673-05656-2). Scott F.

Literature of Fact: Literary Nonfiction in American Writing. Ronald Weber. LC 80-16323. viii, 181p. 1980. 15.00x (ISBN 0-8214-0558-6). Ohio U Pr.

Literature of Fact: Selected Papers from the English Institute. Ed. by Angus Fletcher. 1976. 12.50x (ISBN 0-231-04144-6). Columbia U Pr.

Literature of Horror & the Supernatural. J. Olander & M. Greenberg. 1978. 8.95 (ISBN 0-13-537761-7); pap. 2.95 (ISBN 0-13-537753-6). P-H.

Literature of Java: Supplement Catalogue Raisonne of Javanese Manuscripts in the Library of the University of Leiden & Other Public Collections in the Netherlands. Theodore G. Pigeaud. (Codices Manuscript Ser.: No. XX). (Illus.). 390p. 1980. pap. 64.10 (ISBN 90-6021-453-6, Pub. by Leiden University Press). Kluwer Boston.

Literature of Music. James E. Matthew. LC 69-12688. (Music Ser). 1969. Repr. of 1896 ed. lib. bdg. 27.50 (ISBN 0-306-71227-X). Da Capo.

Literature of Slang. William J. Burke. LC 67-982. 1965. Repr. of 1939 ed. 15.00 (ISBN 0-8103-3243-4). Gale.

Literature of Sports. Tom Dodge. 1980. pap. text ed. 9.95 (ISBN 0-669-02744-8). Heath.

Literature of Terror: A History of Gothic Fiction from 1765 to the Present Day. David Punter. (Illus.). 256p. 1980. lib. bdg. 30.00 (ISBN 0-582-48920-2); pap. text ed. 14.95 (ISBN 0-582-48921-0). Longman.

Literature of Terrorism: A Selectively Annotated Bibliography. Compiled by Edward F. Mickolus. LC 80-541. xi, 553p. 1980. lib. bdg. 55.00 (ISBN 0-313-22265-7, MLT/). Greenwood.

Literature of the American Indian. Thomas E. Sanders & Walter W. Peek. LC 72-89050. 480p. 1973. text ed. 15.95x (ISBN 0-02-477640-8). Macmillan.

Literature of the American Indian. abridged ed. Thomas E. Sanders & Walter W. Peek. 1976. pap. 7.95x (ISBN 0-02-477650-5). Macmillan.

Literature of the American Nation: From Independence to the Gilded Age. Robert D. Mead. 1976. pap. 1.95 o.p. (ISBN 0-451-61470-4, MJ1470, Ment). NAL.

Literature of the American People. Ed. by Arthur H. Quinn. 1172p. 1951. 59.50x (ISBN 0-89197-279-X). Irvington.

Literature of the American West. Ed. by J. Golden Taylor. LC 71-132448. 1971. pap. text ed. 12.25 (ISBN 0-395-05458-3). HM.

Literature of the English Renaissance, Vol. 2. rev. ed. Ed. by Hardin Craig. (Orig.). 1962. pap. 0.95 o.s.i. (ISBN 0-02-050000-9, Collier). Macmillan.

Literature of the Fantastic. J. Olander & M. Greenberg. 1978. 8.95 (ISBN 0-13-537662-9); pap. 2.95 (ISBN 0-13-537654-8). P-H.

Literature of the Hundred Flowers, 2 vols. Hualing Nieh. LC 80-36748. 1981. Vol. 1, 288p. 27.50 (ISBN 0-231-05074-7); Vol. 2, 560p. 42.50 (ISBN 0-231-05076-3). Columbia U Pr.

Literature of the Low Countries: A Short History of Dutch Literature in the Netherlands & Belgium. Reinder P. Meijer. 1971. text ed. 34.50x (ISBN 0-8057-3431-7); pap. text ed. 18.50x (ISBN 0-89197-825-9). Irvington.

Literature of the Middle Ages. William T. Jackson. LC 60-13153. 1960. 20.00x (ISBN 0-231-02429-0). Columbia U Pr.

Literature of the Occult: A Collection of Critical Essays. Ed. by Peter B. Messent. (Twentieth Century Views Ser.). 224p. 1981. text ed. 12.95 (ISBN 0-13-537712-9, Spec); pap. text ed. 4.95 (ISBN 0-13-537704-8, Spec). P-H.

Literature of the Old Testament. 3rd ed. Julius A. Bewer. Ed. by Emil G. Kraeling. LC 62-17061. 1962. 27.50x (ISBN 0-231-02478-9). Columbia U Pr.

Literature of the People's Republic of China. Ed. by Kai-Yu Hsu. LC 78-24807. (Chinese Literature in Translation Ser.). 1000p. 1980. 37.50x (ISBN 0-253-16015-4). Ind U Pr.

Literature of the Restoration & Eighteenth Century, Vol. 3. rev. ed. Ed. by Louis I. Bredvold. (Orig.). 1962. pap. 0.95 o.s.i. (ISBN 0-02-048800-9, Collier). Macmillan.

Literature of the South. rev. ed. T. D. Young et al. 1968. 17.95x (ISBN 0-673-05660-0). Scott F.

Literature of the Spanish People. 2nd ed. Gerald Brenan. 1953. 52.00 (ISBN 0-521-04313-1); pap. 12.95 (ISBN 0-521-29043-0). Cambridge U Pr.

Literature of the United States. 3rd ed. Walter Blair et al. (Single volume edition). 1970. 17.95x (ISBN 0-673-05928-6). Scott F.

Literature of the Woodwind Quintet. Harry B. Peters. LC 70-149999. 1971. 10.00 (ISBN 0-8108-0368-2). Scarecrow.

Literature of Vermont: A Sampler. Ed. by Arthur W. Biddle & Paul A. Eschholz. LC 73-76017. (Illus.). 390p. 1973. 17.50 (ISBN 0-87451-074-0); pap. 6.50 o.p. (ISBN 0-87451-078-3). U Pr of New Eng.

Literature of Western Australia. Ed. by Bruce Bennett. 1980. 17.95x (ISBN 0-85564-152-5, Pub by U of W Austral Pr). Intl Schol Bk Serv.

Literature on Judicial Selection. Nancy Chian & Larry Berkson. LC 80-69415. 112p. (Orig.). 1980. pap. 4.00 (8564). Am Judicature.

Literature on the General History of Physics in the First Half of the 20th Century. J. L. Heilbron & B. R. Wheaton. LC 80-51580. (Berkeley Papers in the History of Science: No. V). (Orig.). 1981. pap. write for info. (ISBN 0-918102-05-7). U Cal Hist Sci Tech.

Literature One: Supplementary Readings with Exercises. Ed. by Robert Spaethling & Eugene Weber. (Ger). 1972. pap. text ed. 4.95 (ISBN 0-19-501550-9); tapes set 29.95 (ISBN 0-19-501703-X). Oxford U Pr.

Literature, Religion & Society in Wales, 1660-1730. Geraint H. Jenkins. (Studies in Welsh History Ser.: Vol. 2). 1978. text ed. 40.00x (ISBN 0-7083-0669-1). Verry.

Literature Through Performance: "Shakespeare's Mirror" & "a Canterbury Caper". Katherine H. Burkman. LC 76-25615. (Illus.). xxvii, 104p. 1978. 10.00x (ISBN 0-8214-0365-6); pap. 3.50x (ISBN 0-8214-0384-2). Ohio U Pr.

Literature Without Qualities: American Writing Since 1945. Werner Berthoff. (Quantum Bks.). 1980. 11.95 (ISBN 0-520-03696-4). U of Cal Pr.

Lithic Industries in India: A Study of South Western Orissa. K. C. Tripathy. 190p. 1980. text ed. 12.50x (ISBN 0-391-02139-7). Humanities.

Lithium & Animal Behavior, Vol. I. Donald F. Smith. (Lithium Research Review Ser.). 66p. 1980. Repr. of 1977 ed. 11.95x (ISBN 0-87705-961-6). Human Sci Pr.

Lithium Carbonate in Psychiatry. 15p. 1970. pap. 1.00 (ISBN 0-685-24850-X, P245-0). Am Psychiatric.

Lithium-Drifted Germanium Detectors. 1966. pap. 10.75 (ISBN 92-0-031066-4, IAEA). Unipub.

Lithium Effects of Granulopiesis & Immune Function. Ed. by Arthur H. Rossof & William A. Robinson. (Advances in Experimental Medicine & Biology Ser.: Vol. 127). 470p. 1980. 47.50 (ISBN 0-306-40359-5). Plenum Pub.

Lithium for Medea. Kate Braverman. 288p. 1981. pap. 2.75 (ISBN 0-523-41185-5). Pinnacle Bks.

Lithium Research & Therapy. F. N. Johnson. 1975. 77.50 (ISBN 0-12-386550-6). Acad Pr.

Lithium Treatment of Manic-Depressive Illness. M. Schou. (Illus.). viii, 72p. 1980. pap. 14.50 (ISBN 3-8055-0392-X). S Karger.

Lithographic Technology. Ervin A. Dennis. LC 79-16756. 1980. 19.95 (ISBN 0-672-97164-X); tchr's manual 6.67 (ISBN 0-672-97165-8); student manual 7.95 (ISBN 0-672-97166-6). Bobbs.

Lithography Eighteen Hundred to Eighteen Fifty: The Techniques of Drawing on Stone in England & France & Their Application in Works of Topography. Michael Twyman. 1970. 26.00x (ISBN 0-19-215168-1). Oxford U Pr.

Lithoko: Sotho Praise Poems. Ed. by M. Damane & P. B. Sanders. Tr. by M. Damane & P. B. Sanders. (Oxford Library of African Literature). 297p. 1974. 21.00x o.p. (ISBN 0-19-815143-8). Oxford U Pr.

Lithuanian Cemetery. Ed. by A. Kezys. LC 75-21496. 1977. 19.95 (ISBN 0-8294-0279-9). Loyola.

Lithuanian Village. Leon Kobrin. Tr. by Isaac Goldberg from Yiddish. LC 79-53454. (Short Story Index in Reprint Ser.). Date not set. Repr. of 1920 ed. 18.75x (ISBN 0-8486-5007-7). Core Collection. Postponed.

Lithuanians in Multi-Ethnic Chicago Until World War II. David Fainhaus. LC 76-5693. 1977. 20.00 (ISBN 0-8294-0370-1). Loyola.

Litigation on Behalf of Women: A Review for the Ford Foundation. Ford Foundation. Ed. by Margaret A. Berger. LC 80-66052. 1980. pap. 4.50 (ISBN 0-916584-15-1). Ford Found.

Litigation Under the Federal Freedom of Information Act & Privacy Act: 1981 Edition. Christine M. Marwick. LC 80-683. 400p. 1980. pap. 25.00 (ISBN 0-86566-019-0). Ctr Natl Security.

Litigious Society. Jethro Lieberman. LC 80-68181. 256p. 1980. 13.95 (ISBN 0-465-04134-5). Basic.

Lito the Shoeshine Boy. David Mangurian. LC 74-26826. (Illus.). 64p. (gr. 3 up). 1975. 7.95 (ISBN 0-590-07382-6, Four Winds). Schol Bk Serv.

Litterature et signification. Tzvetan Todorov. (Fr). pap. 12.25 (ISBN 0-685-13971-9, 3636). Larousse.

Litterature francaise, 2 Vols. A. Adams et al. (Illus., Fr.). 76.50 ea. Larousse.

Litterbugs Come in Every Size. Norah Smaridge. (Illus.). (ps-4). 1972. PLB 7.62 (ISBN 0-307-60455-1, Golden Pr). Western Pub.

Little ABC Book of Rudolf Koch. Rudolf Koch. LC 76-14224. (Illus.). 1980. pap. 6.95 (ISBN 0-87923-295-1). Godine.

Little Alphabet. Trina S. Hyman. (Illus.). 32p. 1980. 4.95 (ISBN 0-316-38705-3). Little.

Little America: Town at the End of the World. Paul A. Carter. LC 79-13727. (Illus.). 1979. 16.95 (ISBN 0-231-04682-0). Columbia U Pr.

Little Appaloosa. Berta Hader & Elmer Hader. (gr. 7 up). 1949. 8.95 (ISBN 0-02-739020-9). Macmillan.

Little Arthur's History of England. (gr. 4-6). 1972. pap. 6.95 (ISBN 0-7195-3242-6). Transatlantic.

Little Athletes. 1979. pap. 1.00 (ISBN 0-8351-0731-0). China Bks.

Little Bear Learns to Read the Cookbook. Janice. LC 69-14315. (Illus.). (gr. k-3). 1969. 7.25 (ISBN 0-688-41072-3); PLB 6.96 (ISBN 0-688-51072-8). Lothrop.

Little Beard Book. Daniel Walter. (Illus.). 1975. pap. 2.00 (ISBN 0-686-22349-7). Oll Korrect.

Little Bedtime Book. Richard Scarry. LC 78-55298. (Richard Scarry's Best Little Books Ever). (Illus.). (ps-2). 1978. pap. 0.95 (ISBN 0-394-83967-6, BYR). Random.

Little Bible: Selections for School & Home. (Illus.). 492p. 1931. 2.75x (ISBN 0-19-234101-4). Oxford U Pr.

Little Big Man. Thomas Berger. 448p. 1978. pap. 2.95 (ISBN 0-449-23854-7, Crest). Fawcett.

Little Bird. Donna L. Pape. LC 78-73535. (First Reader Ser.). (Illus.). (gr. k-3). Date not set. price not set (ISBN 0-89799-157-5); pap. price not set (ISBN 0-89799-075-7). Dandelion Pr. Postponed.

Little Bit India-Little Bit U. S. A. Poems from East & West. Soma Vira. 1981. 7.95 (ISBN 0-533-04911-3). Vantage.

Little Black Boy, I Saw Your Face. Joanna Tisdale. 1981. 7.95 (ISBN 0-533-04828-1). Vantage.

Little Black Chaing. Dorothy K. L'Hommedieu. (Illus.). (ps-4). 1958. 2.75 o.p. (ISBN 0-374-34587-2). FS&G.

Little Black Pony Races. Walter Farley. (Illus.). (ps-1). 1968. 2.95 (ISBN 0-394-81349-9, BYR); PLB 3.69 (ISBN 0-394-91349-3). Random.

Little Black Puppy. Charlotte Zolotow. (Eager Readers Ser.). (gr. k-3). 1975. PLB 5.00 (ISBN 0-307-60804-2, Golden Pr). Western Pub.

Little Blue & Rusty: Red Kangaroos. Sally Glendinning. LC 80-13935. (Young Animal Adventures Ser.). 40p. (gr. 2). 1980. PLB 5.88 (ISBN 0-8116-7502-5). Garrard.

Little Book. Illus. by Eloise Wilkin. (Baby's First Golden Bks.). (Illus.). 8p. (ps). Date not set. 1.25 (ISBN 0-307-10755-8, Golden Pr). Western Pub.

Little Book on Religion: For People Who Are Not Religious. Samuel Sandmel. LC 75-1831. 1975. pap. 3.95 (ISBN 0-89012-002-1). Anima Pubns.

Little Box. Vasko Popa. Tr. by Charles Simic. LC 78-134539. 1973. 7.50 (ISBN 0-685-31528-2). Charioteer.
Little Boy & the Birthdays. Helen E. Buckley. (Illus.). (gr. k-3). 1965. PLB 6.96 o.p. (ISBN 0-688-51202-X). Lothrop.
Little Boy & the Giant. David Harrison. (Young Reader Ser.). (Illus.). (gr. k-3). 1979. PLB 5.00 (ISBN 0-307-60536-1, Golden Pr). Western Pub.
Little Boy Blue. Edward Bunker. LC 80-16924. 324p. 1981. 13.95 (ISBN 0-670-43107-9). Viking Pr.
Little Boy Lost. Jerry Ludwig. 1977. 7.95 o.p. (ISBN 0-440-04796-X). Delacorte.
Little Boy Samuel. Jane B. Moncure. LC 79-12174. (Bible Story Bks.). (Illus.). (ps-3). PLB 5.50 (ISBN 0-89565-084-3). Childs World.
Little Boy Who Lives Up High. John Hawkinson & Lucy Hawkinson. LC 67-26515. (Self Starter Bks.). (Illus.). (ps-2). 1967. 6.50g (ISBN 0-8075-4580-5). A Whitman.
Little Boy Who Loved Dirt & Almost Became a Superslob. Judith Vigna. LC 74-14519. (Illus.). 32p. (ps-1). 1975. 6.95g (ISBN 0-8075-0865-9). A Whitman.
Little Broomstick. Mary Stewart. (Illus.). 192p. (gr. 3-7). 1972. PLB 7.44 (ISBN 0-688-31507-0). Morrow.
Little Brother Fate. Mary-Carter Roberts. 1957. 3.75 o.p. (ISBN 0-374-18848-3). FS&G.
Little Brown Baby: Paul Laurence Dunbar Poems for Young People. Paul L. Dunbar. LC 40-4721. (Illus.). (gr. 4-6). 1940. 4.95 (ISBN 0-396-01993-5). Dodd.
Little Brown Bear. 2nd ed. Elizabeth U. McWebb. (Illus.). 55p. 1978. Repr. of 1962 ed. 8.00x (ISBN 0-686-28491-7). Monroe County Lib.
Little Brown Reader. 2nd ed. Marcia Stubbs & Sylvan Barnet. 1980. pap. text ed. 8.95 (ISBN 0-316-82002-4); instr's manual free (ISBN 0-316-82003-2). Little.
Little Brute Family. Russell Hoban. (Illus.). (gr. k-2). 1966. 6.95 (ISBN 0-02-744110-5). Macmillan.
Little Brute Family. Russell Hoban. (Illus.). (gr. k-2). 1972. pap. 1.95 o.s.i. (ISBN 0-02-043650-5, Collier). Macmillan.
Little Brute Family. Russell Hoban. (Snuggle & Read Ser.). (Illus.). 32p. (ps-2). 1980. pap. 1.95 (ISBN 0-380-51151-7, 51151, Camelot). Avon.
Little Bug. Dick Gackenbach. (Illus.). 32p. (ps-2). 1981. 7.95 (ISBN 0-395-30080-0, Clarion). HM.
Little C. Lions. Margaret Waddington. (Illus.). 65p. 1980. pap. 3.95 (ISBN 0-914960-29-6). Academy Bks.
Little Camels of the Sky. Elena Guro. Tr. by Kevin O'Brien from Rus. 1981. 11.00 (ISBN 0-88233-437-9). Ardis Pubs.
Little Cat Lost. Compton Mackenzie. (Illus.). (gr. 2-5). 1966. 4.95g o.s.i. (ISBN 0-02-761990-7). Macmillan.
Little Cats. Herbert S. Zim. LC 77-20257. (Illus.). (gr. 3-7). 1978. 6.95 (ISBN 0-688-22149-1); PLB 6.67 (ISBN 0-688-32149-6). Morrow.
Little Chen & the Dragon Brothers. 1980. pap. 1.50 (ISBN 0-8351-0731-0). China Bks.
Little Chick's Big Day. Mary Kwitz. LC 80-7905. (Early I Can Read Bks.). (Illus.). 32p. (ps-3). 1981. 6.95 (ISBN 0-06-023667-1, HarpJ); PLB 7.89g (ISBN 0-06-023668-X). Har-Row.
Little Colonel. new ed. Annie F. Johnston. (Illus.). 1974. 5.95 (ISBN 0-88289-050-6). Pelican.
Little Commonwealth: Family Life in Plymouth Colony. John Demos. (Illus.). 1971. pap. 4.95 (ISBN 0-19-501355-7, 344, GB). Oxford U Pr.
Little Critic: Essays, Satires & Sketches on China. (First Series: 1930-1932) Yu-T'Ang Lin. LC 79-2831. 299p. 1981. Repr. of 1936 ed. 22.50 (ISBN 0-8305-0009-X). Hyperion Conn.
Little Critic: Essays, Satires & Sketches on China (Second Series: 1933-1935. Yu-T'Ang Lin. LC 79-2832. 258p. 1981. Repr. of 1939 ed. 19.50 (ISBN 0-8305-0010-3). Hyperion Conn.
Little Crumb. Joan Pizzo. (Illus.). 29p. (Orig.). (gr. k-6). 1980. PLB 10.95; pap. 7.95. Back Bay.
Little Dab of Color. Bruce W. Bell. (gr. 5 up). 1980. 7.95 (ISBN 0-688-51956-3); lib. bdg. 7.63 (ISBN 0-688-51956-3). Morrow.
Little Dab of Color. W. Bruce Bell. LC 80-11986. 192p. (gr. 5 up). 1980. 7.95 (ISBN 0-688-41956-9); PLB 7.63 (ISBN 0-688-51956-3). Lothrop.
Little Dictators. Antony Polonsky. 1975. 22.00 (ISBN 0-7100-8095-6). Routledge & Kegan.
Little Dinosaur. Bob Reese. Ed. by Dan Wasserman. (Ten Word Bks.). (Illus.). (gr. k-1). 1979. PLB 4.50 (ISBN 0-89868-070-0); pap. 1.95 (ISBN 0-89868-081-6). ARO Pub.
Little Dinosaurs & Early Birds. John Kaufmann. LC 75-37575. (Let's Read & Find Out Science Book Ser.). (Illus.). (gr. k-3). 1977. PLB 7.89 (ISBN 0-690-01110-5, TYC-J). T Y Crowell.
Little Doctor. Georges Simenon. Tr. by Jean Stewart from Fr. (Helen & Kurt Wolff Bk.). 1981. 10.95 (ISBN 0-15-152768-7). HarBraceJ.
Little Dog of Fo. Rosemary Harris. (Illus.). (ps-5). 1976. 6.95 (ISBN 0-571-10897-0, Pub. by Faber & Faber). Merrimack Bk Serv.
Little Dorrit. Charles Dickens. Ed. by John Holloway. (English Library Ser.). 1968. pap. 3.95 (ISBN 0-14-043025-3). Penguin.
Little Dorrit. Charles Dickens. Ed. by Harvey P. Sucksmith. (Claredon Dickens Ser.). (Illus.). 1979. 74.00x (ISBN 0-19-812513-5). Oxford U Pr.
Little Drummer Boy. Ezra J. Keats. LC 68-25714. (Illus.). (gr. k-3). 1968. 8.95 (ISBN 0-02-749530-2). Macmillan.
Little Drummer Boy. Ezra J. Keats. LC 68-25714. (gr. k-3). 1972. pap. 2.50 (ISBN 0-02-044090-1, Collier); pre-pack 30.00 (ISBN 0-02-044080-4). Macmillan.
Little Duster. Bill Charmatz. (gr. k-2). 1967. 5.95g o.s.i. (ISBN 0-02-718180-4). Macmillan.
Little Ed Book. Guy Claxton. 1978. pap. 6.00 (ISBN 0-7100-8868-X). Routledge & Kegan.
Little Eddie. Carolyn Haywood. (Illus.). (gr. 1-5). 1947. PLB 7.92 (ISBN 0-688-31682-4). Morrow.
Little English Handbook: Choices & Conventions. 3rd ed. Edward P. Corbett. 300p. 1981. pap. text ed. 5.95 (ISBN 0-471-07856-5). Wiley.
Little Eva, Baby Doll, & Blondy Ryan. Vic Maestri. (Orig.). pap. 4.50 (ISBN 0-682-49710-X). Exposition.
Little Faith. John Skoyles. LC 80-70564. (Poetry Ser.). 1980. 9.95 (ISBN 0-915604-43-4); pap. 4.95 (ISBN 0-915604-44-2). Carnegie-Mellon.
Little Fire Engine. Graham Greene. 48p. (gr. 1-3). 1973. PLB 5.95 o.p. (ISBN 0-385-08908-2). Doubleday.
Little Fish That Got Away. Cook. (ps-3). pap. 1.25 (ISBN 0-590-01503-6, Schol Pap). Schol Bk Serv.
Little Fox in the Middle. Pearl S. Buck. (Illus.). (gr. 1-3). 1968. 3.95g o.s.i. (ISBN 0-02-715140-9, CCPr). Macmillan.
Little Foxes & Another Part of the Forest. Lillian Hellman. (Plays Ser). 1976. pap. 2.95 o.p. (ISBN 0-14-048132-X). Penguin.
Little Fuzzy. H. Beam Piper. 160p. (Orig.). 1976. pap. 1.95 (ISBN 0-441-48492-1). Ace Bks.
Little Ghost Godfrey. Inger Sandberg. Tr. by Nancy S. Leupold. LC 69-16928. (Illus.). (ps-3). 1968. 4.95 o.s.i. (ISBN 0-440-04864-8, Sey Lawr). Delacorte.
Little Giant James. Denis Wrigley. (Dinosaur Ser.). (Illus.). (gr. k-3). 1978. pap. 7.25 pack of 5 o.p. (ISBN 0-85122-076-2, Pub. by Dino Pub); pap. 1.45 ea. o.p. Merrimack Bk Serv.
Little Girl & Her Mother. Beatrice De Regniers & Esther Gilman. LC 63-13794. (gr. 4 up). 6.95 (ISBN 0-8149-0295-2). Vanguard.
Little Gloria: Happy at Last. Barbara Goldsmith. Date not set. pap. 3.50 (ISBN 0-440-15109-0). Dell.
Little Goat. Judy Dunn. LC 77-91658. (Picturebacks Ser.). (Illus.). (ps-1). 1979. PLB 4.99 (ISBN 0-394-93872-0, BYR); pap. 1.25 (ISBN 0-394-83872-6). Random.
Little Golden Picture Dictionary. Nancy Hulick. (gr. k-1). 1959. PLB 5.00 (ISBN 0-307-60369-5, Golden Pr). Western Pub.
Little Gorilla. Bornstein. (ps-3). pap. 1.50 (ISBN 0-590-11869-2, Schol Pap). Schol Bk Serv.
Little Gorilla. Ruth Bornstein. LC 75-25508. (Illus.). 32p. (ps-2). 1976. 6.95 (ISBN 0-395-28773-1, Clarion). HM.
Little Grain of Wheat. G. A. Pottebaum. (Little People's Paperbacks Ser.). 1979. pap. 0.99 (ISBN 0-8164-2243-5). Crossroad NY.
Little Green Book: A Guide to Self-Reliant Living in the '80s. John Lobell. LC 80-53445. (Illus.). 224p. (Orig.). 1981. pap. 5.95 (ISBN 0-394-74924-3). Shambhala Pubn.
Little Green Frog. Beth C. Harris. (gr. 4-6). pap. 1.50 (ISBN 0-8024-1480-X). Moody.
Little Green Man. Mischa Damjan. LC 76-166286. (gr. k-3). 1972. 5.95 o.s.i. (ISBN 0-8193-0535-9, Four Winds); PLB 5.41 o.s.i. (ISBN 0-8193-0536-7). Schol Bk Serv.
Little Grey Rabbit. Joan C. Bowden. (Tell-a-Tale Readers). (Illus.). (gr. k-3). 1979. PLB 4.77 (ISBN 0-307-68651-5, Whitman). Western Pub.
Little Group of Willful Men. Thomas W. Ryley. 1975. 13.95 (ISBN 0-8046-9088-X, Natl U). Kennikat.
Little Groups of Neighbors: The Selective Service System. James W. Davis, Jr. & Kenneth M. Dolbeare. LC 80-25861. xv, 276p. 1981. Repr. of 1968 ed. lib. bdg. 35.00x (ISBN 0-313-22777-2, DALN). Greenwood.
Little Hands with First Drawing Practice. Henry J. Filson. (Draw-Sketch Practice Ser.). (Illus.). 28p. (gr. 5 up). 1978. bdg. 2.75plastic (ISBN 0-918554-01-2). Old Violin.
Little "Harmless" Manifesto: An Essay on the Spirituality of the Focolare Movement Based Upon Its Experiences. Chiara Lubich. LC 72-97595. 1973. pap. 0.95 o.p. (ISBN 0-911782-17-6). New City.
Little Harry. Achim Broger. Tr. by Elizabeth D. Crawford from Ger. LC 78-26028. (Illus.). (gr. 4-6). 1979. 7.50 (ISBN 0-688-22185-8); PLB 7.20 (ISBN 0-688-32185-2). Morrow.
Little Heroes. Arthur Dobrin. (Ethical Humanist Society Monograph: No. 1). (Illus.). 1977. pap. 2.50x (ISBN 0-89304-200-5, CCC111). Cross Cult.
Little History of Ireland. Seamus Maccall. LC 80-21515. 59p. (Orig.). 1980. pap. 3.50 (ISBN 0-937702-00-5). Irish Bks Media.
Little History of the Horn-Book. Beulah Folmsbee. LC 42-36336. (Illus.). 1942. 7.50 (ISBN 0-87675-085-4). Horn Bk.
Little Horses of Tarquinia. Marguerite Duras. Tr. by Peter Den Beeg. 1980. pap. 4.95 (ISBN 0-7145-0348-7). Riverrun NY.
Little House on the Prairie. Laura I. Wilder. (YA) 1975. pap. 1.50 (ISBN 0-06-080357-6, P357, PL). Har-Row.
Little John Bear in the Big City. pap. 3.50 incl. record (ISBN 0-590-20613-3, Schol Pap). Schol Bk Serv.
Little John Bear in the Big City. Bernice Myers. LC 78-15595. (Illus.). 32p. (gr. k-3). 1979. 5.95 (ISBN 0-590-07601-9, Four Winds). Schol Bk Serv.
Little Johnny's Confession. Brian Patten. 62p. (Orig.). 1968. 3.95 (ISBN 0-8090-6580-0); pap. 1.50 o.p. (ISBN 0-8090-1340-1). Hill & Wang.
Little Karoo. Pauline Smith. 1978. 7.95 (ISBN 0-224-60699-9, Pub. by Chatto Bodley Jonathan). Merrimack Bk Serv.
Little Kingdoms: The Counties of Kentucky, 1850-1891. Robert M. Ireland. LC 76-24341. (Illus.). 200p. 1977. 13.00x (ISBN 0-8131-1351-2). U Pr of Ky.
Little Knowledge. Michael Bishop. (YA) 1977. 8.95 o.p. (ISBN 0-399-11943-4). Berkley Pub.
Little Knowledge. Michael Bishop. 1978. pap. 1.75 o.p. (ISBN 0-425-04305-3, Medallion). Berkley Pub.
Little Known Business Secrets & Shortcuts for Entrepreneurs & Managers. International Business & Management Institute. (Illus.). 110p. (Orig.). pap. 25.00 (ISBN 0-935402-03-9). Intl Comm Serv.
Little Lamb. Judy Dunn. LC 76-24167. (Picturebacks Ser). (Illus.). (ps-1). 1977. pap. 1.25 (ISBN 0-394-83455-0, BYR). Random.
Little Laughter. Ed. by Kathleen Love. LC 57-10283. (Illus.). (gr. 1 up). 1957. 6.95 (ISBN 0-690-49804-7, TYC-J). T Y Crowell.
Little League Little Brother. Curtis Bishop. LC 68-10778. (gr. 4-6). 1968. PLB 4.69 o.p. (ISBN 0-397-31030-7). Lippincott.
Little League Stepson. Curtis Bishop. LC 65-13432. (gr. 4-6). 1965. PLB 4.69 o.p. (ISBN 0-397-30814-0). Lippincott.
Little League to Big League. Jim Brosnan. (Major League Baseball Library: No. 10). (Illus.). 1968. PLB 3.69 (ISBN 0-394-90190-8, BYR). Random.
Little League Victory. Curtis Bishop. LC 67-10343. (gr. 4-6). 1967. 5.50 o.p. (ISBN 0-397-30962-7). Lippincott.
Little Leftover Witch. Florence Laughlin. (Illus.). (gr. 4-5). 1960. 7.95 (ISBN 0-02-754560-1). Macmillan.
Little Less Than Kind. large type ed. Charlotte Armstrong. pap. 1.25 o.p. (ISBN 0-425-03018-0). Berkley Pub.
Little Lion of the Southwest: A Life of Manuel Antonio Chaves. Marc Simmons. Tr. by Jose Cisneros. LC 73-1500. 263p. 1974. 10.95 (ISBN 0-8040-0632-6, SB). Swallow.
Little Lion That Couldn't Roar. Betty Barath. 1980. 4.00 (ISBN 0-8062-1299-3). Carlton.
Little Little. M. E. Kerr. LC 80-8454. 160p. (YA) (gr. 7 up). 1981. 8.95 (ISBN 0-06-023184-X, HarpJ); PLB 8.79g (ISBN 0-06-023185-8). Har-Row.
Little Lives. John H. Spyker. 1980. pap. 2.25 (ISBN 0-380-48322-X, 48322). Avon.
Little Lord Fauntleroy. Frances Burnett. 1977. 10.95x (ISBN 0-89967-002-4). Harmony & Co.
Little Lord Fauntleroy. Frances H. Burnett. LC 75-32191. (Classics of Children's Literature, 1621-1932: Vol. 53). (Illus.). 1976. Repr. of 1886 ed. PLB 38.00 (ISBN 0-8240-2302-1). Garland Pub.
Little Lord Jesus. Lucy Diamond. (Ladybird Ser). (Illus.). 1954. bds. 1.49 (ISBN 0-87508-846-5). Chr Lit.
Little Lost Lamb. Ruth S. Odor. LC 79-13155. (Bible Story Books). (Illus.). (ps-3). 1979. 5.50 (ISBN 0-89565-088-6). Childs World.
Little Love & Good Company. Cathleen Nesbitt. LC 76-43369. (Illus.). 1977. 8.95 (ISBN 0-916144-10-0). Stemmer Hse.
Little Major Leaguer. C. Paul Jackson. (Illus.). (gr. 3-6). 1963. 4.95 o.s.i. (ISBN 0-8038-4242-2). Hastings.
Little Malcolm & His Struggle Against the Eunuchs. David Halliwell. 1961. pap. 5.95 (ISBN 0-571-08167-3, Pub. by Faber & Faber). Merrimack Bk Serv.
Little Man. Erich Kastner. (Illus.). (gr. 5 up). 1980. pap. 1.95 (ISBN 0-380-51185-1, 51185, Camelot). Avon.
Little Man & the Big Thief. Erich Kastner. (Illus.). 176p. (gr. 5 up). 1981. pap. 1.95 (ISBN 0-380-53728-1, 53728, Camelot). Avon.
Little Man with Three Legs. Jim Stickter. LC 80-8771. (Illus.). 224p. (Orig.). 1980. 10.00 (ISBN 0-930770-17-X). Hemisphere Hse.
Little Marcy & Her Friends. Marcy Tigner. LC 80-80092. (Orig.). 1980. pap. 1.25 (ISBN 0-89081-229-2). Harvest Hse.
Little Marcy Loves Jesus. Marcy Tigner. (Orig.). 1980. pap. 1.25 (ISBN 0-89081-227-6). Harvest Hse.
Little Match Girl. Hans C. Andersen. LC 68-28050. (Illus.). (gr. k-3). 1968. reinforced bdg 7.95 (ISBN 0-395-21625-7); pap. 1.95 (ISBN 0-395-13712-8). HM.
Little Men. Louisa M. Alcott. (gr. 7 up). 1871. 9.95 (ISBN 0-316-03094-5). Little.
Little Men. Louisa M. Alcott. (gr. 6-8). 1963. 4.95g o.s.i. (ISBN 0-02-700150-4). Macmillan.
Little Mermaid. 3rd ed. Hans C. Andersen. pap. 5.00x (ISBN 8-7142-7783-2, D714). Vanous.
Little Missionary Truck That Could Do Anything. Miriam Wood. (Penguin Ser.). 1980. 4.50 (ISBN 0-8280-0050-6, 12450-3). Review & Herald.
Little Monasteries. Frank O'Connor. 48p. 1976. pap. text ed. 2.75x (ISBN 0-85105-296-7, Dolmen Pr). Humanities.
Little Monster at Home. (Golden Look-Look Bks.). (ps-3). 1978. PLB 5.38 (ISBN 0-307-61846-3, Golden Pr); pap. 0.95 (ISBN 0-307-11846-0). Western Pub.
Little Monster at School. (Golden Look-Look Bks.). (ps-3). 1978. PLB 5.38 (ISBN 0-307-61845-5, Golden Pr); pap. 0.95 (ISBN 0-307-11845-2). Western Pub.
Little Monster's Alphabet Book. (Golden Look-Look Bks.). (ps-3). 1978. PLB 5.38 (ISBN 0-307-61847-1, Golden Pr); pap. 0.95 (ISBN 0-307-11847-9). Western Pub.
Little Monster's Bedtime Book. Mercer Mayer. (Golden Look-Look Bks.). (ps-3). 1978. PLB 5.38 (ISBN 0-307-61848-X, Golden Pr); pap. 0.95 (ISBN 0-307-11848-7). Western Pub.
Little Monster's Counting Book. Mercer Mayer. (Golden Look-Look Bks.). (ps-3). 1978. PLB 5.38 (ISBN 0-307-61844-7, Golden Pr); pap. 0.95 (ISBN 0-307-11844-4). Western Pub.
Little Monster's Neighborhood. Mercer Mayer. (Golden Look-Look Bks.). (ps-3). 1978. PLB 5.38 (ISBN 0-307-61849-8, Golden Pr); pap. 0.95 (ISBN 0-307-11849-5). Western Pub.
Little Monster's Scratch & Sniff Mystery. Mercer Mayer. 32p. 1980. 4.95 (ISBN 0-307-13546-2). Western Pub.
Little Monster's Scratch & Sniff Mystery. Mercer Mayer. 32p. 1980. lib. bdg. 9.92 (ISBN 0-307-64546-0). Western Pub.
Little Moscows: Communism & Working-Class Militancy in Inter-War Britain. Stuart Macintyre. 213p. 1980. 30.00x (ISBN 0-7099-0083-X, Pub. by Croom Helm Ltd England). Biblio Dist.
Little Mouse. Alana Willoughby. Ed. by Alton Jordan. (I Can Read Underwater Bks). (Illus.). (gr. k-3). 1974. PLB 3.50 (ISBN 0-89868-007-7, Read Res); text ed. 1.75 softbd. (ISBN 0-89868-040-9). ARO Pub.
Little Mouse on the Prairie. Stephen Cosgrove. (Creative Fantasies Ser.). (Illus.). (gr. k-4). 1979. PLB 6.95 (ISBN 0-87191-690-8). Creative Ed.
Little Mouse Was a Grouch. Glenna C. Smith. Ed. by Alton Jordan. (Buppet Series). (Illus.). (gr. k-3). 1981. PLB 4.50 (ISBN 0-89868-095-6, Read Res); pap. text ed. 1.95 (ISBN 0-89868-106-5). ARO Pub.
Little Mouse Who Tarried. Hirosuke Hamada. Tr. by Alvin Tresselt from Jap. LC 72-153794. Orig. Title: Konezumi Chorochoro. (Illus.). (gr. k-4). 1971. 5.95 o.s.i. (ISBN 0-8193-0504-9, Four Winds); PLB 5.41 o.s.i. (ISBN 0-8193-0505-7). Schol Bk Serv.
Little Mysteries. Ken Mikolowski. LC 79-15299. (Illus., Orig.). 1979. pap. 3.00 (ISBN 0-915124-31-9, Bookslinger). Toothpaste.
Little Nature Books. Bill Martin, Jr. Incl. Poppies Afield; Frogs in a Pond; Butterflies Becoming; Germanation; Ants Underground; A Mushroom Is Growing; A Hydro Goes Walking; Moon Cycle; Messenger Bee; June Bugs. (Illus.). (gr. 1-6). 1975. 111.00 (ISBN 0-87827-196-1); tchr's guide incl. (ISBN 0-685-55948-3); recordings incl. Ency Brit Ed.
Little Nemo in the Palace of Ice, & Further Adventures. Winsor McCay. LC 75-19834. (Illus.). 32p. (Orig.). 1976. pap. 4.50 (ISBN 0-486-23234-4). Dover.
Little New Kangaroo. Bernard Wiseman. LC 72-92444. (Ready-to-Read Ser.). (Illus.). 40p. (gr. k-3). 1973. 7.95 (ISBN 0-02-793220-6). Macmillan.
Little Nursery Rhymes. Zokeisha. (Puppet Story Board Bks.). (Illus.). 12p. (ps-k). Date not set. boards 2.95 (ISBN 0-671-42642-7, Little Simon). S&S.
Little Old Man Who Could Not Read. Black. (gr. 2-3). 1980. pap. 3.50 incl. record (ISBN 0-590-24004-8, Schol Pap). Schol Bk Serv.

Little Order: A Selection from His Journalism. Auberon Waugh. 240p. 1980. 11.95 (ISBN 0-316-92632-9). Little.

Little Order: A Selection from His Journalism. Evelyn Waugh. Ed. by Donat Gallagher. 224p. 1981. 12.95 (ISBN 0-316-92633-7). Little.

Little Organ Lexicon. Ch. W. Lindow & Homer D. Blanchard. (The Little Organ Book Ser.: No. 2). 44p. 1981. pap. write for info. Praestant.

Little Orphan Annie & Little Orphan Annie in Cosmic City. Harold Gray. (Illus.). 1974. pap. 2.75 (ISBN 0-486-23107-0). Dover.

Little Park. Dale Fife. LC 73-7322. (Self Starter Ser.). (Illus.). 32p. (gr. k-2). 1973. 6.50g (ISBN 0-8075-4634-8). A Whitman.

Little Pear & His Friends. Eleanor F. Lattimore. LC 34-27286. (Illus.). (gr. k-3). 5.95 o.p. (ISBN 0-15-246861-7, HJ). HarBraceJ.

Little Pear & the Rabbits. Eleanor F. Lattimore. (Illus.). (gr. 2-5). 1956. 6.25 o.p. (ISBN 0-688-21715-X). Morrow.

Little People. David Wilkerson. (gr. 8-12). 1969. pap. 1.25 o.p. (ISBN 0-685-19670-4). Jove Pubns.

Little Peoples' Beginning on Michigan. Lois Parker & David McConnell. (Illus.). 32p. (Orig.). (gr. 1-2). 1981. pap. 2.75 (ISBN 0-910726-06-X). Hillsdale Educ.

Little Pieces of the West Wind. Christian Garrison. LC 75-887. (Illus.). 32p. (ps-3). 1975. 8.95 (ISBN 0-87888-105-0). Bradbury Pr.

Little Pilgrimages Among Old New England Inns: Being an Account of Little Journeys to Various Quaint Inns & Hostelries of Colonial New England. Mary C. Crawford. LC 76-107629. (Illus.). 1970. Repr. of 1907 ed. 18.00 (ISBN 0-8103-3536-0). Gale.

Little Pilgrim's Progress. Helen L. Taylor. (gr. 2-6). pap. 2.50 (ISBN 0-8024-0003-5). Moody.

Little Prince. Antoine De Saint-Exupery. Tr. by Katherine Woods. LC 67-1144. (Illus.). (gr. 3-7). 1968. pap. 1.95 (ISBN 0-15-652820-7, HPL30, HPL). HarBraceJ.

Little Prince. Antoine de Saint-Exupery. Tr. by Katherine Woods. LC 67-1144. (Illus.). (gr. 3-7). 1943. 5.95 (ISBN 0-15-246503-0, HJ). HarBraceJ.

Little Prince. Antoine De Saint-Exupery. Tr. by Katherine Woods from Fr. LC 67-1144. (Illus.). 95p. (gr. 4-6). 1943. pap. 1.95 (ISBN 0-15-246507-3, VoyB). HarBraceJ.

Little Princess, Sara Crewe. Nancy Seale. (Orig.). 1981. playscript 2.00 (ISBN 0-87602-231-X). Anchorage.

Little Quiet Dreaming, a Little Time to Think. Lillian P. Selber. LC 73-85884. (Illus.). 63p. 1973. 2.95 (ISBN 0-88415-450-5). Pacesetter Pr.

Little Rabbit. Judy Dunn. LC 79-5241. (Picturebacks Ser.). (Illus.). 32p. (ps). 1980. PLB 4.99 o.p. (ISBN 0-394-94377-5, BYR); pap. 1.25 (ISBN 0-394-84377-0). Random.

Little Rabbit's Loose Tooth. Lucy Bate. (gr. k-3). 1978. pap. 1.95 (ISBN 0-590-11870-6, Schol Pap); pap. 3.50 bk. & record (ISBN 0-590-20621-4). Schol Bk Serv.

Little Red Box. Ernest L. Norman. 1968. 3.95 (ISBN 0-932642-47-0); pap. 2.95 (ISBN 0-685-62826-4). Unarius.

Little Red Darts Book. Gyles Brandreth. (Illus.). 1979. 6.50 (ISBN 0-370-30136-6, Pub. by Chatto Bodley Jonathan). Merrimack Bk Serv.

Little Red Engine & the Rocket. Diana Ross. (gr. k-2). 12.50 (ISBN 0-571-05256-8). Transatlantic.

Little Red Engine & the Taddlecombe Outing. Diana Ross. (gr. 1-3). 1969. 7.95 (ISBN 0-571-08697-7). Transatlantic.

Little Red Engine Goes Carolling. Diana Ross. (gr. 1-3). 1971. 7.95 (ISBN 0-571-09775-8). Transatlantic.

Little Red Engine Goes to Market. Diana Ross. (Illus.). (gr. k-2). 7.95 (ISBN 0-571-06330-6). Transatlantic.

Little Red Engine Goes to Town. Diana Ross. (Illus.). (gr. k-2). 7.95 (ISBN 0-571-06420-5). Transatlantic.

Little Red Hen. Adapted by & illus. by Janina Domanska. LC 72-92436. (Illus.). 32p. (ps-2). 1973. 8.95 (ISBN 0-02-732820-1). Macmillan.

Little Red Hen. Paul Galdone. LC 72-97770. (Illus.). (ps-2). 1973. 6.95 (ISBN 0-395-28803-7, Clarion). HM.

Little Red Hen. Illus. by T. Izawa & S. Hijkata. (Puppet Storybooks). (Illus.). 18p. (gr. k-2). 1981. 3.50 (ISBN 0-448-09756-7). G&D.

Little Red Hen. (Illus.). Arabic 2.50x (ISBN 0-685-82839-5). Intl Bk Ctr.

Little Red Hen: La Pequena Gallina Roja. Letty Williams. LC 78-75684. (Illus., Eng. & Span.). (ps-3). 1969. 6.95 o.p.; pap. 1.25 (ISBN 0-13-537894-X). P-H.

Little Red Riding Hood. Margaret Hillert. (Just Beginning-to-Read Ser.). (Illus.). 32p. (gr. 1-6). 1981. PLB 4.39 (ISBN 0-695-41543-3); pap. 1.50 (ISBN 0-695-31543-9). Follett.

Little Red Riding Hood. (Illus.). Arabic 2.50x (ISBN 0-685-82840-9). Intl Bk Ctr.

Little Red Riding Hood. Ed. by Matt H. Newman. (Children's Stories Bk). (Illus.). 18p. (ps). 1980. pap. 22.00 ten bks & one cass. (ISBN 0-89290-084-9, BC13-1). Soc for Visual.

Little Red Riding Hood. Harriet Pincus. LC 68-11505. (Illus.). 32p. (ps-3). 1973. pap. 1.25 (ISBN 0-15-652850-9, AVB75, VoyB). HarBraceJ.

Little Red Riding Hood. Ed. & illus. by Harriet Pincus. LC 68-11505. (Illus.). (gr. k-3). 1968. 6.95 (ISBN 0-15-247132-4, HJ). HarBraceJ.

Little Red Riding Hood. Mabel Watts. (Illus.). 24p. (ps-3). 1977. Repr. of 1972 ed. PLB 5.00 (ISBN 0-307-60232-X, Golden Pr). Western Pub.

Little Rhetoric. Edward P. Corbett. LC 76-45081. 1977. pap. text ed. 8.50 (ISBN 0-471-17231-6). Wiley.

Little Rhetoric & Handbook. Edward P. Corbett. LC 76-45189. 1977. text ed. 10.95 (ISBN 0-471-17232-4); instructors manual avail. (ISBN 0-471-03048-1). Wiley.

Little Rock Handbook. James W. Bell. (Illus.). iv, 88p. (Orig.). 1980. pap. 7.95 (ISBN 0-939130-00-9). J W Bell.

Little Rystu. Mirra Ginsburg. LC 76-30485. (Illus.). (gr. k-3). 1978. 7.95 (ISBN 0-688-80097-1); PLB 7.63 (ISBN 0-688-84097-3). Greenwillow.

Little Science, Big Science. Derek J. Price. LC 63-10524. (George B. Pegram Lecture Ser). (Illus.). 1963. pap. 5.00x (ISBN 0-231-08562-1). Columbia U Pr.

Little Secrets. Frank Bonville. (Gambler's Book Shelf). 1976. pap. 2.95 (ISBN 0-89650-570-7). Gamblers.

Little Seed... David Maryland Webb. LC 79-67086. (Illus.). 39p. (Orig.). (gr. 3-8). 1979. pap. 4.95 (ISBN 0-935054-00-6). Webb-Newcomb.

Little Shepherd of Kingdom Come. John Fox. 1976. lib. bdg. 17.75x (ISBN 0-89968-039-9). Lightyear.

Little Ship Astro-Navigation. M. J. Rantzen. 1978. 10.95 o.p. (ISBN 0-214-20373-5, 8039, Dist. by Arco). Barrie & Jenkins.

Little Ship Handling. M. J. Rantzen. 1978. 8.50 o.p. (ISBN 0-214-20040-X, 8041, Dist. by Arco). Barrie & Jenkins.

Little Ship Meteorology. M. J. Rantzen. 1978. 9.95 o.p. (ISBN 0-214-20006-X, 8042, Dist. by Arco). Barrie & Jenkins.

Little Ship Navigation. M. J. Rantzen. 1978. 11.95 o.p. (ISBN 0-214-20374-3, 8043, Dist. by Arco). Barrie & Jenkins.

Little Sleepyheads. rev. ed. Illus. by Frances Hook. (Illus.). 32p. (ps). pap. 1.95 (ISBN 0-89542-932-2). Ideals.

Little Spotted Fish. Jane Yolen. LC 74-14819. 32p. (ps-4). 1975. 7.95 (ISBN 0-395-28835-5, Clarion). HM.

Little Stone House. Berta Hader & Elmer Hader. (gr. k-3). 1944. 4.95g o.s.i. (ISBN 0-02-739380-1). Macmillan.

Little Store on the Corner. Alice P. Miller. (Illus.). (gr. k-3). 1974. pap. 1.25 (ISBN 0-590-04839-2, Schol Pap); pap. 3.50 bk. & record (ISBN 0-590-20740-7). Schol Bk Serv.

Little Stories for Big People. Sol Gonshack. (Illus.). (gr. 7 up). 1976. pap. 2.95 (ISBN 0-88345-263-4). Regents Pub.

Little Stripe. Jocelyn Arundel. (gr. 2-4). 1967. 4.95g o.s.i. (ISBN 0-8038-4245-7). Hastings.

Little Swineherd & Other Tales. Paula Fox. (gr. k-6). 1981. pap. 1.75 (ISBN 0-440-45302-X, YB). Dell.

Little Threads & Other Object Lessons for Children. Harvey D. Moore. LC 73-21959. 80p. 1974. 3.95 o.p. (ISBN 0-687-22169-2). Abingdon.

Little Tiger. William Stobbs. 1975. 3.95 (ISBN 0-7207-0769-2, Pub. by Michael Joseph). Merrimack Bk Serv.

Little Touch of Drama. Valerian Pidmohylny. Tr. by George S. Luckyj from Ukrainian. LC 72-86407. (Ukrainian Classics in Translation Ser: No. 1). 1972. lib. bdg. 11.50x (ISBN 0-87287-051-0). Ukrainian Acad.

Little Treasury of Familiar Prose. Raymond Lister. (Little Treasury Ser.). 1964. 2.50 (ISBN 0-212-35942-8). Dufour.

Little Treasury of Familiar Verse. Raymond Lister. (Little Treasury Ser). 2.50 (ISBN 0-212-35912-6). Dufour.

Little Treasury of Love Lyrics. Raymond Lister. (Little Treasury Ser.). 1963. 2.50 (ISBN 0-685-09180-5). Dufour.

Little Treasury of Religious Verse. Raymond Lister. (Little Treasury Ser.). 1964. 2.50 (ISBN 0-212-35941-X). Dufour.

Little Treatise on Baile & Maineprize. Edward Coke & Anthony Highmore, Jr. Ed. by David S. Berkowitz & Samuel E. Thorne. LC 77-86576. (Classics of English Legal History in the Modern Era Ser.: Vol. 13). 352p. 1979. lib. bdg. 40.00 (ISBN 0-8240-3062-1). Garland Pub.

Little Trolley Books. Karen K. Welch & Joan W. Cole. (Crossties Ser.). (gr. k-2). 1977. Set. pap. text ed. 119.85 54 bks. (ISBN 0-8332-1126-9); dupl. masters 30.99 (ISBN 0-8332-1129-3); tchrs'. guide 0.78 (ISBN 0-8332-1127-7). Economy Co.

Little Tuppen. Paul Galdone. LC 67-10364. (Illus.). (ps-1). 1967. 6.95 (ISBN 0-395-28805-3, Clarion). HM.

Little Turtle's Big Adventure. David Harrison. (ps-2). 1969. PLB 4.99 (ISBN 0-394-90837-6, BYR). Random.

Little Tyke. Georges Westbeau. LC 56-13322. 115p. pap. 4.95 (ISBN 0-8163-0048-8, 12480-0). Pacific Pr Pub Assn.

Little Valley. Raymond Otis. LC 79-56813. (Zia Bks.). 285p. 1980. pap. 5.95 (ISBN 0-8263-0534-2). U of NM Pr.

Little Victories, Big Defeats: War As the Ultimate Pollution. Compiled by Georgess McHargue. LC 74-5749. 192p. (gr. 7 up). 1974. 6.95 o.s.i. (ISBN 0-440-04899-0). Delacorte.

Little Wax Doll. Norah Lofts. 1975. pap. 1.25 o.p. (ISBN 0-449-22270-5, P2270, Crest). Fawcett.

Little Way. Bernard Bro. pap. 5.95 (ISBN 0-87061-052-X). Chr Classics.

Little Wheels, Big Wheels. (Illus.). 24p. (ps). 1980. 1.50 (ISBN 0-307-11983-1, Golden Pr); PLB 6.08 (ISBN 0-307-61983-4). Western Pub.

Little Wild Chimpanzee. Michel. (gr. 3). 1980. pap. 1.25 (ISBN 0-590-30151-9, Schol Pap). Schol Bk Serv.

Little Wild Chimpanzee. Anna Michel. LC 77-20986. (I AM READING Bk.). (Illus.). (gr. 1-4). 1978. 3.95 (ISBN 0-394-83716-9); PLB 5.99 (ISBN 0-394-93716-3). Pantheon.

Little Wild Elephant. Anna Michel. LC 78-18407. (I Am Reading Bk.). (Illus.). (gr. 1-4). 1979. 4.95 (ISBN 0-394-83884-X); PLB 5.99 (ISBN 0-394-93884-4). Pantheon.

Little Wild Lion Club. Anna Michel. LC 79-17509. (I Am Reading Book Ser.). (Illus.). 48p. (gr. 1-4). 1980. 4.95 (ISBN 0-394-84352-5); PLB 5.99 (ISBN 0-394-94352-X). Pantheon.

Little Witch. Anna E. Bennett. (Illus., Orig.). (gr. 3-5). pap. 1.25 o.p. (ISBN 0-590-08066-0, Schol Pap). Schol Bk Serv.

Little Witch. Anna E. Bennett. (Illus.). 128p. (gr. 2-5). 1981. pap. 1.95 (ISBN 0-06-440119-7, Trophy). Har-Row.

Little Witch's Black Magic Book of Disguises. Linda Glovach. (gr. k-6). 1973. 5.95 (ISBN 0-13-537910-5); pap. 1.95 (ISBN 0-13-537944-X). P-H.

Little Witch's Halloween Book. Linda Glovach. LC 75-11713. (Illus.). (gr. 1-4). 1975. 7.95 (ISBN 0-13-537985-7). P-H.

Little Women. Louisa M. Alcott. LC 68-21171. (gr. 7 up). 1868. 10.95 (ISBN 0-316-03095-3). Little.

Little Women. Louisa M. Alcott. (Illus.). (gr. 6-8). 1962. 6.95g o.s.i. (ISBN 0-02-700180-6). Macmillan.

Little Women. Louisa M. Alcott. 1963. 8.50 (ISBN 0-685-20188-0). Saphrograph.

Little Women. Louisa M. Alcott. LC 78-2919. (Raintree's Illustrated Classics). (Illus.). (gr. 5-8). 1978. PLB 9.65 (ISBN 0-8393-6210-2). Raintree Child.

Little Women. (Illustrated Junior Library). (Illus.). 560p. 1981. pap. 5.95 (ISBN 0-448-11019-9). G&D.

Little Wood Duck. Brian Wildsmith. LC 72-3828. (Illus.). 32p. (gr. k-3). 1973. PLB 5.95 o.p. (ISBN 0-531-02593-4). Watts.

Little Wooden Doll. Margery Bianco. (Illus.). (gr. 3-4). 1967. 6.95 (ISBN 0-02-710110-X). Macmillan.

Little Wooden Farmer. Alice Dalgliesh. LC 68-12081. (Illus.). (gr. k-1). 1971. pap. 0.95 o.s.i. (ISBN 0-02-042790-5, Collier). Macmillan.

Little Wooden Farmer. Alice Dalgliesh. LC 68-12081. (Illus.). (ps-1). 1968. 4.95g o.s.i. (ISBN 0-02-725920-X). Macmillan.

Little Woodland Books. Tr. by Bill Maiten. (10 books & 10 cassettes). 111.00 (ISBN 0-87827-322-0). Ency Brit Ed.

Little Workers in the Kitchen. Georgina Elarson. 1979. pap. 5.95 (ISBN 0-8163-0240-5). Pacific Pr Pub Assn.

Littlefield Lands: Colonization on the Texas Plains, 1912-1920. David B. Gracy, 2nd. (M. K. Brown Range Life Ser.: No. 8). (Illus.). 1968. 9.95 (ISBN 0-292-78359-0). U of Tex Pr.

Littlest Angel. Charles Tazewell. 32p. (gr. k-6). 1980. pap. cancelled o.s.i. (ISBN 0-89542-922-5); pap. 2.25 o.s.i. (ISBN 0-89542-923-3). Ideals.

Littlest Helper. Naida Dickson. (Early Childhood Bk.). (Illus.). (ps-2). PLB 4.95 o.p. (ISBN 0-513-00511-0). Denison.

Littlest House. Elizabeth Coatsworth. (Illus.). (gr. 3-5). 1967. 4.25g o.s.i. (ISBN 0-02-721050-2). Macmillan.

Littlest League. Syd Hoff. LC 75-25782. (Illus.). 48p. (ps-2). 1981. pap. 1.95 (ISBN 0-671-42580-3, Pub. by Windmill). S&S.

Littlest Reindeer. Johanna De Witt. (Pacesetters). (Illus.). 32p. (gr. k-3). 1979. PLB 7.95 (ISBN 0-516-03534-7). Childrens.

Littleton: A Pictorial History. Nancy Clark. Ed. by Donna R. Friedman. (Illus.). 208p. 1981. pap. price not set (ISBN 0-89865-112-3). Donning Co.

Liturature & Film: An Annotated Bibliography, 1900 to 1977. Jeffrey Welch. LC 80-8509. 350p. 1981. lib. bdg. 40.00 (ISBN 0-8240-9478-6). Garland Pub.

Liturgical Change: How Much Do We Need. Leonel Mitchell. 96p. 1975. pap. 3.50 (ISBN 0-8164-2113-7). Crossroad NY.

Liturgical Experience of Faith. Ed. by Herman Schmidt & David Power. (Concilium Ser.: Religion in the Seventies: Vol. 82). 156p. 1973. pap. 4.95 (ISBN 0-8164-2538-8). Crossroad NY.

Liturgical Revolution, Vol. One: Cranmer's Godly Order. Michael Davies. 1977. 7.95 o.p. (ISBN 0-87000-395-X). Arlington Hse.

Liturgical Revolution: Vol. Three: Pope Paul's New Mass. Michael Davies. 1979. 9.95 o.p. (ISBN 0-87000-413-1). Arlington Hse.

Liturgical Revolution: Vol. Two, Pope John's Council. Michael Davies. 1977. 9.95 o.p. (ISBN 0-87000-396-8). Arlington Hse.

Liturgy & Cultural Religious Tradition. Herman Schmidt & David Power. (Concilium Ser.: Vol. 102). 1977. pap. 4.95 (ISBN 0-8164-2146-3). Crossroad NY.

Liturgy & Learning Through the Life Cycle. John H. Westerhoff & William H. Willimon. 176p. 1980. 9.95 (ISBN 0-8164-0471-2). Seabury.

Liturgy & Social Justice. Ed. by Mark Searle. 1980. pap. write for info (ISBN 0-8146-1209-1). Liturgical Pr.

Liturgy in Transition. Ed. by Herman Schmidt. LC 70-129761. (Concilium Ser.: Religion in the Seventies: Vol. 62). 1971. pap. 4.95 (ISBN 0-8164-2518-3). Crossroad NY.

Liturgy of St. John Chrysostom. (Eng. & Arab.). 1978. pap. 3.00 (ISBN 0-911726-39-X). Alleluia Pr.

Liturgy, Self-Expression of the Church. Herman Schmidt. LC 77-168650. (Concilium Ser.: Religion in the Seventies: Vol. 72). 1972. pap. 4.95 (ISBN 0-8164-2528-0). Crossroad NY.

Liu Shao-Ch'i & the Chinese Cultural Revolution: The Politics of Mass Criticism. Lowell Dittmer. (Center for Chinese Studies). 1975. 20.00x (ISBN 0-520-02574-1); pap. 4.95 (ISBN 0-520-02957-7). U of Cal Pr.

Liu Tsung-Yuan. William H. Nienhauser, Jr. et al. (World Authors Ser.: China: No. 255). 1971. lib. bdg. 10.95 (ISBN 0-8057-2538-5). Twayne.

Liv Ullman & Ingmar Bergman. Bernie Garfinkel. 1978. pap. 1.75 o.p. (ISBN 0-425-03653-7). Berkley Pub.

Live Alone & Be Happier Than Anybody. Harriet Labarre. 1977. pap. 1.75 o.p. (ISBN 0-445-08613-0). Popular Lib.

Live & Be Free Through Psychocybernetics. rev. ed. Maxwell Maltz. 1978. pap. 2.25 (ISBN 0-446-92670-1). Warner Bks.

Live & Let Die. Ian Fleming. 224p. 1980. pap. 2.25 (ISBN 0-515-05889-0). Jove Pubns.

Live & Remember. Valentin Rasputin. Tr. by Antonina W. Bouis from Rus. 1978. 11.95 (ISBN 0-02-601130-1). Macmillan.

Live by the Spirit: How to Grow in Your Relationship with God. Michael Harper. 154p. 1980. pap. 2.25 (ISBN 0-89283-094-8). Servant.

Live Foods for Aquarium & Terrarium Animals. Willy Jocher. Tr. by Gwynne Vevers. (Illus.). 1973. pap. 5.95 (ISBN 0-87666-097-9, PS-309). TFH Pubns.

Live Happily with Yourself. Don W. Hillis. 1978. pap. 1.75 (ISBN 0-88207-507-1). Victor Bks.

Live High on Low Fat. new rev. enlarged ed. Sylvia Rosenthal. LC 75-8938. 1975. 9.95 o.s.i. (ISBN 0-397-01060-5). Lippincott.

Live Like a King: Leader's Guide. N. Cockman. 1979. pap. 3.25 (ISBN 0-8024-4906-9). Moody.

Live Longer. Max L. Feinman & Josleen Wilson. 1978. pap. 2.50 (ISBN 0-515-05722-3). Jove Pubns.

Live Longer & Love It. Gordon R. Heath. LC 80-81595. (Illus.). 78p. (Orig.). 1980. pap. 5.95 (ISBN 0-937092-00-2). Methuselah Bks.

Live-Longer Diet for Dogs & Cats. Howard Padwee. (Illus.). 128p. 1980. 8.95 (ISBN 0-312-48885-8). St Martin.

Live Longer Now. Jon N. Leonard et al. 236p. 1981. pap. 2.50 (ISBN 0-441-48516-2). Charter Bks.

Live Longer Now Cookbook. Jon N. Leonard & Elaine A. Taylor. 384p. 1981. pap. 2.50 (ISBN 0-441-48521-9). Charter Bks.

Live: Poetry for Students, Awakening Students to Their Potential for Self-Expression. Irene Payan. 1980. 2.95 (ISBN 0-932212-20-4). Avery Color.

Live Steam: Locomotives & Lines Today. David Eatwell & John H. Cooper-Smith. (Illus.). 120p. 1980. 19.95 (ISBN 0-7134-2079-0, Pub. by Batsford England). David & Charles.
Live to Ninety & Stay Young. Andrew Stewart. 184p. 1968. 5.25x (ISBN 0-8464-1029-X). Beekman Pubs.
Live to One Hundred. F. A. Farr. 200p. 1981. 28.50 o.p. (ISBN 0-686-68305-6). Porter.
Liveable Streets. Donald Appleyard. 336p. 1981. 27.50 (ISBN 0-520-03689-1). U of Cal Pr.
Livebearers. Wilfred L. Whitern. (Illus.). 93p. 1979. 2.95 (ISBN 0-87666-518-0, KW-049). TFH Pubns.
Liveliest Art: A Panoramic History of the Movies. rev. ed. Arthur Knight. (Illus.). 1978. 19.95 (ISBN 0-02-564210-3). Macmillan.
Livelihood & Poverty: A Study in the Economic Conditions of Working-Class Households in Northampton, Warrington, Stanley, & Reading, London, 1915. A. L. Bowley & A. R. Burnett-Hurst. LC 79-59651. (English Working Class Ser.). 1980. lib. bdg. 22.00 (ISBN 0-8240-0105-2). Garland Pub.
Lively Art of Writing. Lucille V. Payne. pap. 1.95 (ISBN 0-451-61896-3, MJ1896, Ment). NAL.
Lively Experiment: The Shaping of Christianity in America. Sidney E. Mead. 1963. pap. 4.95x (ISBN 0-06-065545-3, RD-194, HarpR). Har-Row.
Lively Lady. Kenneth Roberts. 1976. pap. 1.95 o.p. (ISBN 0-449-30784-0, Prem). Fawcett.
Lively Lady. Kenneth Roberts. 12.95 (ISBN 0-385-04261-2). Doubleday.
Lively Latin. John K. Colby. (gr. 8-10). 1971. pap. text ed. 2.95x (ISBN 0-88334-035-6). Ind Sch Pr.
Lively Way to Modeling Sculpture: A Book for Beginners. Arthur Zaidenberg. LC 74-134676. (Illus.). (gr. 9 up). Date not set. 4.95 (ISBN 0-8149-0446-7). Vanguard. Postponed.
Liver. 2nd ed. Ed. by Edward A. Gall & F. K. Mostofi. LC 79-28745. (I.A.P. Ser.). 540p. 1980. Repr. lib. bdg. cancelled (ISBN 0-89874-122-X). Krieger.
Liver: An Atlas of Scanning Electron Microscopy. Pietro Motta et al. LC 77-95454. (Illus.). 1978. 46.00 (ISBN 0-89640-026-3). Igaku-Shoin.
Liver & Anasthesia. Leo Struin. LC 72-97914. (Major Problem in Anaesthesia: Vol. 3). (Illus.). 1976. text ed. 26.00 (ISBN 0-7216-8625-7). Saunders.
Liver & Billiary Tract Disease in Children. Daniel Alagille & Michel Odievre. LC 79-12254. 1979. 43.95 (ISBN 0-471-05256-6, Pub. by Wiley-Medical). Wiley.
Liver Biopsy Interpretation. 3rd ed. P. Scheuer. 1980. text ed. 65.00 (ISBN 0-02-859180-1). Macmillan.
Liver Carcinogenesis. Ed. by Karoly Lapis & Jan V. Johannessen. LC 79-134. (Illus.). 1979. text ed. 40.00 (ISBN 0-89116-149-X, Co-Pub. by McGraw Intl). Hemisphere Pub.
Liver Disease in Primary Care Medicine. Raymond S. Koff. 256p. 1980. 19.95x (ISBN 0-8385-5678-7). ACC.
Liver Pathophysiology: Its Relevance to Human Disease. Charles S. Davidson. 296p. 1970. pap. 11.50 o.p. (ISBN 0-316-17429-7). Little.
Liver: Proceedings. South African International Liver Conference, 1973. Ed. by S. J. Saunders & John Terblanche. (Illus.). 432p. 1973. pap. text ed. 20.00x (ISBN 0-8464-0575-X). Beekman Pubs.
Liver Regeneration in Man. Carroll M. Leevy. (Amer. Lec. in Living Chemistry Ser.). (Illus.). 128p. 1973. 13.75 (ISBN 0-398-02776-5). C C Thomas.
Liverpool & Manchester Railway. R. H. Thomas. LC 79-57313. (Illus.). 264p. 1980. 45.00 (ISBN 0-7134-0537-6, Pub. by Batsford England). David & Charles.
Liverpool & the Mersey: An Economic History of a Port 1700-1970. Francis E. Hyde. (Illus.). 256p. 1971. 13.50x o.p. (ISBN 0-87471-337-4). Rowman.
Liverpool Registry of Merchant Ships. R. C. Jarvis & R. Craig. 278p. 1967. 33.00x (ISBN 0-686-63740-2, Pub. by Manchester U Pr England). State Mutual Bk.
Liverworts Pallavicinia & Symphyogyna & Their Conducting System. James L. Smith. (U. C. Publ. in Botany: Vol. 39). 1966. pap. 6.50x (ISBN 0-520-09012-8). U of Cal Pr.
Lives. Derek Mahon. 1972. pap. 3.50x o.p. (ISBN 0-19-211816-1). Oxford U Pr.
Lives: An Anthropological Approach to Biography. L. L. Langness & Gelya F. Frank. Ed. by R. N. Edgerton. (Chandler & Sharp Publications in Anthropology Ser.). 224p. (Orig.). 1981. pap. 5.95 (ISBN 0-88316-542-2). Chandler & Sharp.
Lives at Stake: The Science & Politics of Environmental Health. Laurence Pringle. LC 80-14272. (Illus.). 144p. (gr. 6 up). 1980. PLB 8.95 (ISBN 0-02-775410-3). Macmillan.
Lives He Touched: The Relationships of Jesus. David A. Redding. LC 77-20443. 1978. 5.95 o.p. (ISBN 0-06-066815-6, HarpR). Har-Row.
Lives of Animals. Sydney Anderson. LC 65-28581. (Lives of Animals Ser). (Illus.). (gr. 6 up). 1966. PLB 7.95 (ISBN 0-87191-007-1). Creative Ed.
Lives of Cleopatra & Octavia, 1757. Sarah Fielding. LC 74-17294. (Novel in England, 1700-1775 Ser). 1974. lib. bdg. 50.00 (ISBN 0-8240-1147-3). Garland Pub.
Lives of English Poets. Samuel Johnson. 1977. 8.00x (ISBN 0-460-00770-X, Evman); pap. 5.95 (ISBN 0-460-01770-5). Dutton.
Lives of Henry Fielding & Samuel Johnson, with Essays from Gray's Inn Journal, 1752-1792. Arthur Murphy. LC 68-24212. 1968. 49.00x (ISBN 0-8201-1035-3). Schol Facsimiles.
Lives of Irish Saints, 2 Vols. Ed. by Charles Plummer. 1922. 44.00x set (ISBN 0-19-821389-1). Oxford U Pr.
Lives of Labor-Lives of Love: Fragments of Friendly Autobiographies. Sheldon Glueck. LC 76-24259. (Illus.). 1977. 8.50 o.p. (ISBN 0-682-48632-9, Banner). Exposition.
Lives of Pearl Buck: A Tale of China & America. Irvin Block. Ed. by Milton Meltzer. LC 73-8891. (Women of America Ser.). (gr. 5-9). 1973. 8.95 o.p. (ISBN 0-690-00165-7, TYC-J). T Y Crowell.
Lives of Philip & Matthew Henry. J. B. Williams. 1974. 14.95 (ISBN 0-85151-178-3). Banner of Truth.
Lives of St. Thomas More. William Roper & Nicholas Harpsfield. Ed. by E. E. Reynolds. 1963. 12.95x (ISBN 0-460-00019-5, Evman); pap. 1.95 o.p. (ISBN 0-460-01019-0). Dutton.
Lives of Saints for Young People, Vol. 1. Lev Puhalo. 1975. pap. 2.50 (ISBN 0-913026-11-5). St Nectarios.
Lives of Saints for Young People, Vol. 4. Lev Puhalo. 1977. pap. 2.50 (ISBN 0-913026-91-3). St Nectarios.
Lives of the Desert Fathers: The Historia Monachorum in Aegypto. Tr. by Benedicta Ward & Norman Russell. (Cistercian Studies: No. 34). 1981. price not set (ISBN 0-87907-834-0); pap. price not set (ISBN 0-87907-934-7). Cistercian Pubns.
Lives of the English Poets, 2 Vols. Samuel Johnson. (World's Classics Ser.). Vol. 1. 11.95 (ISBN 0-19-250083-X); Vol. 2. 8.95 (ISBN 0-19-250084-8). Oxford U Pr.
Lives of the Italian Americans: Fifty Illustrated Biographies. Adolph Caso. (Illus.). 175p. 1980. 12.50 (ISBN 0-937832-00-6). Dante Univ Bkshlf.
Lives of the Lord Chancellors & Keepers of the Great Seal of Ireland, 2 Vols. J. Roderick O'Flanagan. 1971. Repr. of 1870 ed. 60.00x (ISBN 0-8377-2500-3). Rothman.
Lives of the Prophets. Charles C. Torrey. (Society of Biblical Literature. Monographs: No. 1). 1946. pap. 6.00 (ISBN 0-89130-171-2, 060001). Scholars Pr Ca.
Lives of the Saints, 4 vols. A. Butler. Ed. by Attwater Thurston. 1962. Set. 78.50 (ISBN 0-87061-045-7). Vol. 1 (ISBN 0-87061-046-5). Vol. 2 (ISBN 0-87061-047-3). Vol. 3 (ISBN 0-87061-048-1). Vol. 4 (ISBN 0-87061-049-X). Chr Classics.
Lives of the Saints, Vols. 2 & 3. L. Puhalo. 1977. pap. 2.50 ea.; Vol. 2. (ISBN 0-913026-75-1); Vol. 3. (ISBN 0-913026-77-8). St Nectarios.
Lives of the Tudor Age, 1485 to 1603. Ann Hoffmann. LC 76-15685. (Lives of the...Age Ser.). (Illus.). 1977. text ed. 25.00x (ISBN 0-06-494331-3). B&N.
Lives You Live As Revealed in the Heavens. Ted George. LC 77-73594. 1977. 12.00 (ISBN 0-932782-00-0). Arthur Pubns.
Livestock & Meat Marketing. 2nd ed. John H. McCoy. (Illus.). 1979. text ed. 26.50 (ISBN 0-87055-321-6). AVI.
Livestock Feeds & Feeding. D. C. Church et al. 1977. 17.00 (ISBN 0-686-26680-3). Dairy Goat.
Livestock Health & Housing. 2nd ed. David Sainsbury & Peter Sainsbury. 388p. 1979. pap. 27.50 (ISBN 0-8121-0751-9). Lea & Febiger.
Livestock of China. George E. Taylor. LC 78-74304. (Modern Chinese Economy Ser.). 174p. 1980. lib. bdg. 22.00 (ISBN 0-8240-4286-7). Garland Pub.
Living, Vol. 3. David A. Clemens. LC 79-55503. (Steps to Maturity Ser.). 1980. tchrs' manual 14.95 (ISBN 0-86508-006-2); students' manual 12.50 (ISBN 0-86508-005-4). BCM Inc.
Living - When a Loved One Has Died. Earl A. Grollman. LC 76-48508. (Illus.). 1977. 7.95 (ISBN 0-8070-2740-5); pap. 4.95 (ISBN 0-8070-2741-3, BP560). Beacon Pr.
Living After the Holocaust: Reflections by the Post-War Generation in America. Lucy Y. Steinitz. Ed. by David M. Szonyi. LC 76-8322. (Illus.). 1976. 6.95x; pap. 4.95 (ISBN 0-8197-0016-9). Bloch.
Living Alone. John Givens. LC 80-69366. 1981. 9.95 (ISBN 0-689-11147-9). Atheneum.
Living American House: The 350-Year Story of a Home - an Ecological History. George Ordish. (Illus.). 1981. 11.95 (ISBN 0-686-69231-4). Morrow.
Living Anatomy. R. D. Lockhart. 1970. pap. 6.95 (ISBN 0-571-09177-6, Pub. by Faber & Faber). Merrimack Bk Serv.
Living & Active Word: A Way to Preach from the Bible Today. O. C. Edwards. 166p. 1975. 7.95 (ISBN 0-8164-0265-5). Crossroad NY.
Living & Dying Gracefully. Herbert N. Conley. LC 79-65569. 70p. 1979. 4.95 (ISBN 0-8091-0298-6). Paulist Pr.
Living & Fossil Brachiopods. M. J. Rudwick. 1970. pap. text ed. 7.50x (ISBN 0-09-103081-1, Hutchinson U Lib). Humanities.
Living & Growing Together: The Christian Family Today. Ed. by Gary R. Collins. LC 76-19525. 1976. pap. 4.25 o.p. (ISBN 0-87680-844-5, 98087). Word Bks.
Living & Learning. Sadie O. Engen et al. 1980. 6.95 (ISBN 0-8280-0051-4, 12510-4). Review & Herald.
Living Architecture: Indian. Andreas Volwahsen. (Illus.). 1969. 15.00 (ISBN 0-912158-36-0). Hennessey.
Living Art of Nigeria. William Fagg & Michael Foreman. LC 72-77278. (Illus.). 160p. 1972. 12.95 o.s.i. (ISBN 0-02-536950-4). Macmillan.
Living at Summerhill. Herb Snitzer. LC 64-17368. Orig. Title: Summerhill: A Loving World. (Illus.). 1968. pap. 1.95 o.s.i. (ISBN 0-02-015750-9, Collier). Macmillan.
Living at Your Best with Multiple Sclerosis. rev. ed. George H. Hess. (Illus.). 128p. 1972. pap. 11.75 photocopy ed., spiral (ISBN 0-398-02621-1). C C Thomas.
Living Barns: How to Find & Restore a Barn of Your Own. Ed. by Ernest Burden. 1979. pap. 9.95 o.p. (ISBN 0-316-52886-2). NYGS.
Living Better: Recipes for a Healthy Heart. Joyce D. Margie et al. LC 80-66979. 320p. Date not set. 14.95 (ISBN 0-8019-7018-0). Chilton.
Living Beyond Crisis: Essays on Discovery & Being in the World. Ed. by Stephen Rowe. LC 80-18135. 261p. 1980. pap. 8.95 (ISBN 0-8298-0402-1). Pilgrim NY.
Living Beyond Depression. Matilda Nordtvedt. LC 78-58082. 1978. pap. 2.25 (ISBN 0-87123-339-8, 200339). Bethany Fell.
Living Bible: A Topical Approach to the Jewish Scriptures. Sylvan D. Schwartzman & Jack D. Spiro. (Illus.). (gr. 8-10). 1962. text ed. 5.00 (ISBN 0-8074-0097-1, 161751); tchrs'. guide o.p. 2.75. UAHC.
Living Bibles International. Kenneth N. Taylor. 1979. pap. 6.20. Liv Bibles Intl.
Living Black American Authors: A Biographical Directory. Ed. by Ann A. Shockley & Sue P. Chandler. LC 73-17005. 220p. 1973. 15.95 o.p. (ISBN 0-8352-0662-9). Bowker.
Living Bread. Thomas Merton. 157p. 1956. 12.95 (ISBN 0-374-14613-6); pap. 5.95 (ISBN 0-374-51520-4). FS&G.
Living by the Word. O. W. Polen. LC 77-79942. 1977. pap. 1.25 (ISBN 0-87148-509-5). Pathway Pr.
Living Canoeing. 3rd ed. Alan Byde. (Illus.). 266p. 1979. 18.00 (ISBN 0-7136-1912-0). Transatlantic.
Living Chemistry. David Ucko. 1977. text ed. 18.50 (ISBN 0-12-705950-4); lab manual 6.50 (ISBN 0-12-705956-3); transparency masters avail. (ISBN 0-12-705956-3). Acad Pr.
Living Church: A Guide for Revitalization. Donald J. MacNair. (Illus.). 167p. (Orig.). 1980. pap. 4.50 (ISBN 0-934688-00-1). Great Comm Pubns.
Living Cinema: New Directions in Contemporary Film-Making. Louis Marcorelles. Tr. by Isabel Quigley. (Illus.). 1973. pap. 5.50 (ISBN 0-04-791026-7). Allen Unwin.
Living Commandments. John S. Spong. LC 77-8344. 1977. 6.95 (ISBN 0-8164-0356-2). Crossroad NY.
Living Communication. Abne M. Eisenberg. (Speech Communications Ser.). (Illus.). 336p. 1975. pap. text ed. 13.95 (ISBN 0-13-538900-3). P-H.
Living Control Systems. Leonard E. Bayliss. (Illus.). 1966. 13.95x (ISBN 0-7167-0651-2). W H Freeman.
Living Country Blues. Harry Oster. (Funk & W Bk.). (Illus.). 464p. 1976. pap. 5.95 o.s.i. (ISBN 0-308-10236-3, TYC-T). T Y Crowell.
Living Country Characters: Step-by-Step Instructions for Eighteen Projects. Bill Higgingbotham. (Illus., Orig.). 1981. pap. price not set (ISBN 0-486-24135-1). Dover.
Living Dead: A Study of the Vampire in Romantic Literature. James B. Twitchell. LC 79-54290. 1981. 14.95 (ISBN 0-8223-0438-4). Duke.
Living Embryos. 2nd ed. J. Cohen. 1967. 16.50 (ISBN 0-08-012317-1); pap. 7.75 (ISBN 0-08-012316-3). Pergamon.
Living English Structure. rev. ed. W. Stannard Allen. 1974. pap. text ed. 5.50x (ISBN 0-582-52506-3); key 1.75 (ISBN 0-582-55204-4). Longman.
Living Faith. Helen Roseveare. (Orig.). 1981. pap. 3.95 (ISBN 0-8024-4941-7). Moody.
Living Fellowship: A Dynamic Witness. Richard C. Halverson. 1977. pap. 1.50 o.p. (ISBN 0-310-25782-4). Zondervan.
Living Female Writers of the South. Ed. by Mary T. Tardy. LC 75-44070. 1979. Repr. of 1872 ed. 50.00 (ISBN 0-8103-4286-3). Gale.
Living Fishes of the World. Earl Herold. LC 61-6384. 1975. 19.95 o.p. (ISBN 0-385-00988-7). Doubleday.
Living Forest. Jack McCormick. LC 57-11791. (Illus.). 1959. lib. bdg. 8.79 o.p. (ISBN 0-06-071021-7, HarpT). Har-Row.
Living Free. Neva Coyle. 160p. 1981. pap. 3.95 (ISBN 0-87123-346-0, 210346). Bethany Fell.
Living from Lobsters. 2nd ed. Robert Stewart. (Illus.). 70p. 9.75 (ISBN 0-85238-099-2, FN). Unipub.
Living Function of Sleep, Life & Aging. Betty Y. Ho. LC 79-13810. (Illus., Orig.). 1967. pap. 3.50 (ISBN 0-9600148-0-2). Juvenescent.
Living God. Robert Culver. 1978. pap. 3.95 (ISBN 0-88207-765-1). Victor Bks.
Living God: Readings in Christian Theology. Ed. by Millard J. Erickson. 1973. pap. 9.95 (ISBN 0-8010-3305-5). Baker Bk.
Living God's Joy. Douglas Cooper. LC 78-71158. (Redwood Ser.). 1979. pap. 3.95 (ISBN 0-8163-0241-3). Pacific Pr Pub Assn.
Living God's Love. Douglas Cooper. LC 74-27171. (Redwood Ser.). 1975. pap. 3.95 (ISBN 0-8163-0176-X, 12523-7). Pacific Pr Pub Assn.
Living God's Way. F. E. Marsh. LC 80-8073. 224p. 1981. pap. 4.95 (ISBN 0-8254-3233-2). Kregel.
Living Groups: Group Psychotherapy & General Systems Theory. Ed. by James E. Durkin. 400p. 1981. 25.00 (ISBN 0-87630-253-3). Brunner-Mazel.
Living Happily Ever After. Bob Mumford. 64p. 1973. 2.95 o.p. (ISBN 0-8007-0596-3). Revell.
Living Hard: Southern Americans in the Great Depression. John L. Robinson. LC 80-5817. 272p. 1981. lib. bdg. 19.75 (ISBN 0-8191-1379-4); pap. text ed. 10.75 (ISBN 0-8191-1380-8). U Pr of Amer.
Living High. rev. ed. June Burn. (Illus.). 1962. 6.95 o.p. (ISBN 0-686-00955-X). Wellington.
Living Hymn Stories. Wilbur Konkel. 1971. pap. 2.50 (ISBN 0-87123-334-7, 210334). Bethany Fell.
Living Image. Gladys S. Gallant. LC 77-15178. 1978. 7.95 o.p. (ISBN 0-385-13651-X). Doubleday.
Living Images: Film Comment & Criticism. Stanley Kauffmann. LC 74-1822. 416p. (YA) 1975. 11.95 o.p. (ISBN 0-06-012269-2, HarpT); pap. 5.95 o.s.i. (ISBN 0-06-012268-4, TD 206, HarpT). Har-Row.
Living in a Medieval Village. R. J. Unstead. LC 73-1667. (Living in Medieval Times Ser.). (Illus.). 44p. (gr. 4 up). 1973. PLB 5.95 o.p. (ISBN 0-201-08493-7, A-W Childrens). A-W.
Living in Hope. Boros, Ladislaus, S.J. 120p. 1973. pap. 1.45 (ISBN 0-385-00133-9, Im). Doubleday.
Living in Sin: The Victorian Sexual Revolution. Wendell S. Johnson. LC 78-26845. 1979. 14.95 (ISBN 0-88229-445-8); pap. 7.95 (ISBN 0-88229-649-3). Nelson-Hall.
Living in Sonshine! James Long. 1980. pap. 2.50 (ISBN 0-88207-576-4). Victor Bks.
Living in Step. Ruth Roosevelt. (Paperbacks Ser.). 1977. Repr. of 1976 ed. pap. 4.95 (ISBN 0-07-053596-5, SP). McGraw.
Living in the Classroom: The Currency-Based Token Economy. James S. Payne et al. LC 75-19004. 1976. text ed. 19.95 (ISBN 0-87705-276-X); pap. text ed. 8.95 (ISBN 0-87705-283-2). Human Sci Pr.
Living in the Environment. 2nd ed. G. Tyler Miller, Jr. 1979. text ed. 19.95x (ISBN 0-534-00684-1). Wadsworth Pub.
Living in the Shadow of the Second Coming: American Premillennialism 1875-1925. Timothy P. Weber. 1979. 15.95 (ISBN 0-19-502494-X). Oxford U Pr.
Living in the U. S. A. rev. ed. Alison R. Lanier. LC 72-2212. 1978. pap. text ed. 6.75x (ISBN 0-933662-10-6, Pub. by Overseas Brief). Intercult Pr.
Living in Troubled Lands. Patrick Collins. 190p. 1980. 12.95 (ISBN 0-87364-205-8). Paladin Ent.
Living Insects of the World. Klots, Alexander B., Dr. & Elsie B. Klots. LC 59-9100. 1975. 19.95 o.p. (ISBN 0-385-06873-5). Doubleday.
Living It Up. George Burns. 1978. pap. 2.50 (ISBN 0-425-04811-X, Medallion). Berkley Pub.
Living Jesus. Harold Cooper. (Illus.). 106p. pap. text ed. 1.50 (ISBN 0-89114-077-8); tchrs. ed. 1.00 (ISBN 0-89114-078-6). Baptist Pub Hse.
Living Land: An Outdoor Guide to North Carolina. Marguerite Schumann. (Illus.). 200p. Date not set. pap. 7.50 (ISBN 0-914788-29-9). East Woods.

Living Life to the Fullest. Maxine Kipp. LC 79-52997. (Radiant Life Ser). 1980. pap. 2.95 (ISBN 0-88243-896-4, 02-0896); teacher's ed 2.95 (ISBN 0-88243-187-0, 32-0187). Gospel Pub.

Living Light. Sam Hamill. 1977. 2.50 (ISBN 0-918116-12-0). Jawbone Pr.

Living Logos: A Philosophico-Religious Essay in Free Verse. Bruce B. Wavell. LC 77-18478. 1978. pap. text ed. 8.75x (ISBN 0-8191-0324-1). U Pr of Amer.

Living Memories. Rochelle H. Dubois. 1979. 2.50 o.p. (ISBN 0-686-23747-1). Merging Media.

Living Messages of the Books of the New Testament. Ed. by Thomas B. Warren & Garland Elkins. 1976. 10.95 (ISBN 0-934916-35-7). Natl Christian Pr.

Living Monsters. Ann M. Drozd. Ed. by Patricia McCarthy. (Pal Paperbacks Kit A Ser.). (Illus., Orig.). (gr. 7-12). 1974. pap. text ed. 1.25 (ISBN 0-8374-3471-8). Xerox Ed Pubns.

Living Monument. M. C. Bradbrook. LC 76-7142. (Illus.). 1976. 38.00 (ISBN 0-521-21255-3); pap. 10.95 (ISBN 0-521-29530-0). Cambridge U Pr.

Living More Simply. Ed. by Ronald J. Sider. LC 79-3634. (Orig.). 1980. pap. 4.95 (ISBN 0-87784-808-4). Inter-Varsity.

Living More with Less. Doris Longacre. LC 80-15461. 296p. 1980. pap. 6.95 (ISBN 0-8361-1930-4). Herald Pr.

Living My Life, 2 Vols. Emma Goldman. LC 73-109546. (Civil Liberties in American History Ser.). Repr. of 1931 ed. lib. bdg. 75.00 (ISBN 0-306-71900-2). Da Capo.

Living New England Artists: Biographical Sketches. Frank T. Robinson. Ed. by H. Barbara Weinberg. LC 75-28880. (Art Experience in Late 19th Century America Ser.: Vol. 14). (Illus.). 1976. Repr. of 1888 ed. lib. bdg. 44.00 (ISBN 0-8240-2238-6). Garland Pub.

Living New Testament Paraphrased. pap. 2.95 o.p. (ISBN 0-452-00359-8, FM359, Mer). NAL.

Living Nutrition. 3rd ed. Frederick J. State & Margaret McWilliams. 470p. 1981. text ed. 16.95 (ISBN 0-471-04940-9). Wiley.

Living Obediently: Jonah. J. Allen Blair. LC 63-18265. 1963. pap. 2.25 (ISBN 0-87213-050-9). Loizeaux.

Living Ocean. E. J. Wood. 250p. 1980. 29.00x (ISBN 0-85664-026-3, Pub. by Croom Helm England). State Mutual Bk.

Living on a Shoestring. Mike Edelhart. LC 79-6535. (Illus.). 216p. 1980. pap. 5.95 (ISBN 0-385-15580-8, Anch). Doubleday.

Living on: How Consciousness Continues & Evolves After Death. Paul Beard. 212p. 1981. 12.95 (ISBN 0-8264-0036-1); pap. 5.95 (ISBN 0-8264-0037-X). Continuum.

Living on the Moon. Raymond Mungo. 1979. pap. cancelled (ISBN 0-9601428-7-8). Entwhistle Bks.

Living on the Sun: Harnessing Renewable Energy for an Equitable Society. Godfrey Boyle. (Ideas in Progress Ser.). (Illus.). 1978. 11.95 (ISBN 0-7145-1094-7, Pub. by M Boyars); pap. 5.95 (ISBN 0-7145-0862-4). Merrimack Bk Serv.

Living on the Third Planet. Hannes Alfven & Kerstin Alfven. Tr. by Eric Johnson from Swedish. LC 70-179799. 1972. text ed. 10.95x (ISBN 0-7167-0340-8). W H Freeman.

Living on Wheels: The Secrets of a Safe, Happy, & Comfortable Living in a Motor Home. Richard A. Wolters. 1973. 8.95 (ISBN 0-87690-100-3). Dutton.

Living on Your Own. Greta Walker. 1977. s&l 6.90 o.p. (ISBN 0-531-00126-1). Watts.

Living or Dying: Adaptation to Hemodialysis. Norman Levy. 164p. 1974. pap. 16.75 photocopy ed., spiral (ISBN 0-398-02987-3). C C Thomas.

Living Out God's Love. Jan Lin. 128p. 1981. pap. 4.95 (ISBN 0-8170-0897-7). Judson.

Living Past: Fifteen Historic Places in Minnesota. rev. ed. Nancy Eubank. (Minnesota Historic Sites Pamphlet Ser.: No. 7). (Illus.). 1978. pap. 2.75 (ISBN 0-87351-077-1). Minn Hist.

Living Past of Greece. A. R. Burn & Mary Burn. (Illus.). 282p. 1980. 17.50 (ISBN 0-316-11710-2). Little.

Living Peacefully: First Peter. J. Allen Blair. 1959. pap. 3.50 (ISBN 0-87213-052-5). Loizeaux.

Living Plants of the World. Lorus Milne & Margery Milne. 1967. 20.00 o.p. (ISBN 0-394-43343-2). Random.

Living Poets. Compiled by Michael Morpurgo & Clifford Simmons. (Orig.). 1975. pap. 6.50 (ISBN 0-7195-3000-8). Transatlantic.

Living Prayer. Anthony Bloom. 1975. pap. 4.95 (ISBN 0-87243-054-5). Templegate.

Living Prayer. Glenn Clark. 1980. pap. 0.50 (ISBN 0-910924-88-0). Macalester.

Living Prehistory: An Introduction to Physical Anthropology & Archaeology. Sharon S. McKern & Thomas W. McKern. LC 73-90645. 1974. pap. 10.95 (ISBN 0-8465-3753-2). Benjamin-Cummings.

Living Quarters. Vincent Canby. 1975. 6.95 o.p. (ISBN 0-394-49513-6). Knopf.

Living Quarters. Vincent Canby. 224p. 1976. pap. 1.75 o.p. (ISBN 0-345-25205-5). Ballantine.

Living Reminder: Service & Prayer in Memory of Jesus Christ. Henri J. Nouwen. 1977. 5.95 (ISBN 0-8164-1219-7). Crossroad NY.

Living Rich. Martin S. Ackerman & Diane L. Ackerman. LC 80-80978. 224p. 1980. pap. 2.50 (ISBN 0-87216-697-X). Playboy Pbks.

Living Salt Free and Easy! Anna H. Thorburn & Phyllis Turner. LC 74-16983. (Illus.). 210p. 1975. 8.95 (ISBN 0-913264-19-9). Douglas-West.

Living Sea. Jacques-Yves Cousteau & James Dugan. (Illus.). 320p. 1975. pap. 1.95 (ISBN 0-685-52455-8, 24504-0-195). Ballantine.

Living Soul. E. E. Cleveland. LC 73-91286. 219p. 1974. pap. text ed. 1.95 (ISBN 0-8127-0078-3). Southern Pub.

Living Stage: A History of the World Theatre. Kenneth MacGowan & W. Melnitz. 1955. text ed. 19.95 (ISBN 0-13-538942-9). P-H.

Living Stone. Howell Roland, Jr. (Orig.). 1979. pap. 1.95 (ISBN 0-532-23138-4). Manor Bks.

Living Temple: George Herbert & Catechizing. Stanley E. Fish. LC 73-90664. (Quantum Bks.). 1978. 16.50x (ISBN 0-520-02657-8). U of Cal Pr.

Living That Counts. William J. Krutza & Philip P. DiCicco. (Contemporary Discussion Ser.). 1972. pap. 2.50 (ISBN 0-8010-5318-8). Baker Bk.

Living: The Adult Centering Book. C. Hendricks & C. Leavenworth. 1978. 8.95 (ISBN 0-13-538512-1); pap. 3.95 (ISBN 0-13-538504-0). P-H.

Living the Bible with Children. Dorothy J. Furnish. LC 79-12297. 1979. pap. 4.95 (ISBN 0-687-22368-7). Abingdon.

Living the Faith: A Call to the Church. Ed. by Kathleen Jones. 192p. 1980. text ed. 16.95x (ISBN 0-19-213233-4). Oxford U Pr.

Living the Liturgy. S. Harakas. 1974. pap. 3.50 (ISBN 0-937032-17-4). Light&Life Pub Co MN.

Living the Lords Prayer. Everett L. Fullam & Bob Slosser. 120p. 1980. pap. 4.95 (ISBN 0-912376-62-7). Chosen Bks Pub.

Living Theater of Medieval Art. Henry Kraus. LC 67-24004. (Illus.). 272p. 1972. pap. 7.50x (ISBN 0-8122-1056-5, Pa Paperbks). U of Pa Pr.

Living Things. Jeanne Bendick. LC 69-12869. (Science Experiences Ser). (Illus.). (gr. 4-6). 1969. PLB 4.90 o.p. (ISBN 0-531-01432-0); pap. 1.25 o.p. (ISBN 0-531-02324-9). Watts.

Living Things-Environmental Sciences: Curriculum Enrichment Units for the Gifted & Academically Talented. Eric Olgilvie & David George. (Special Education Ser.). (Illus.). 1980. 59.00 (ISBN 0-89568-231-1). Spec Learn Corp.

Living Thinwork: Where Do Labor Processes Come from? Mike Hales. (Illus.). 192p. 1980. text ed. 26.00x (ISBN 0-906336-14-7); pap. text ed. 9.25x (ISBN 0-906336-15-5). Humanities.

Living Time. M. Nicoll. 5.95 o.p. (ISBN 0-685-01077-5). Weiser.

Living Today. Oppenheim. (gr. 9-12). 1981. text ed. price not set (ISBN 0-87002-343-8). Bennett Co.

Living Today: Decorating Your Home. Margaret Cullen. 1971. pap. text ed. 3.95x o.p. (ISBN 0-435-42205-7). Heinemann Ed.

Living Today: Feeding the Family. Margaret Cullen. 1971. pap. text ed. 3.95x o.p. (ISBN 0-435-42200-6). Heinemann Ed.

Living Today: Good Grooming & Clothes Care. Margaret Cullen. 1971. pap. text ed. 3.95x o.p. (ISBN 0-435-42202-2). Heinemann Ed.

Living Today: Health & Care of the Family. Margaret Cullen. 1971. pap. text ed. 3.95x o.p. (ISBN 0-435-42201-4). Heinemann Ed.

Living Today: Homemaking. Margaret Cullen. 1972. pap. text ed. 3.95x o.p. (ISBN 0-435-42204-9). Heinemann Ed.

Living Today: Housing the Family. Margaret Cullen. 1972. pap. text ed. 3.95x o.p. (ISBN 0-435-42203-0). Heinemann Ed.

Living Today: Managing Your Money. Margaret Cullen. 1974. pap. text ed. 3.95x o.p. (ISBN 0-435-42208-1). Heinemann Ed.

Living Today: The Family & the Social Services. Margaret Cullen. 1973. pap. text ed. 3.95x o.p. (ISBN 0-435-42206-5). Heinemann Ed.

Living Today: The Kitchen. Margaret Cullen. 1974. pap. text ed. 3.95x o.p. (ISBN 0-435-42207-3). Heinemann Ed.

Living Today: Topics & Questions in Home Economics. Margaret Cullen. 1975. pap. text ed. 3.95x o.p. (ISBN 0-435-42209-X). Heinemann Ed.

Living Together. John Gunstone. LC 76-57794. 1977. pap. 1.95 (ISBN 0-87123-325-8, 200325). Bethany Fell.

Living Together. Marvin Mitchelson. 1981. 10.95 (ISBN 0-671-24981-9). S&S.

Living Together. Carole Mortimer. (Harlequin Presents Ser.). 192p. 1981. pap. 1.50 (ISBN 0-373-10423-5, Pub. by Harlequin). PB.

Living Together: A Daily Workbook for Strengthening Relationships. Mort Katz. (Illus.). 1981. pap. 5.95 (ISBN 0-87863-002-3). Farnswth Pub.

Living Together Book. Kas Schwan et al. LC 79-67611. (Illus.). 64p. (Orig.). 1980. pap. 4.95 (ISBN 0-87223-601-3, Dist. by Har-Row). Wideview Bks.

Living Together: Communication in the Unmarried Relationship. Joseph Simons. LC 78-972. 1978. 12.95 (ISBN 0-88229-274-9); pap. 6.95 (ISBN 0-88229-599-3). Nelson-Hall.

Living Together in the Sea. Leon P. Zann. (Illus.). 416p. 1980. 20.00 (ISBN 0-87666-500-8, H-990). TFH Pubns.

Living Toward a Vision: Biblical Reflections on Shalom. Walter Brueggemann. LC 76-22172. (Shalom Resource Ser.). 1976. pap. 5.95 (ISBN 0-8298-0322-X). Pilgrim NY.

Living Tradition of Iran's Crafts. Jasleen Dhamija. 1979. 40.00x (ISBN 0-7069-0728-0, Pub. by Croom Helm Ltd England). Biblio Dist.

Living Treasures of Japan. Barbara Adachi. LC 73-80959. (Illus.). 164p. 1973. 22.50 (ISBN 0-87011-204-X). Kodansha.

Living Trophies: A Shocking Look at the Conditions in America's Zoos. Peter Batten & Deborah Stancil. LC 75-40211. (Illus.). 272p. 1976. 9.95 o.s.i. (ISBN 0-690-01096-6, TYC-T). T y Crowell.

Living Victoriously: Philippians. J. Allen Blair. LC 62-290. 1962. pap. 2.75 (ISBN 0-87213-056-8). Loizeaux.

Living Way Commentary, 2 vols. Clyde M. Woods. Incl. Vol. 1. Geh-Exodus. pap. 6.95 (ISBN 0-89315-139-4); Vol. 2. Lev., Num., Devt. pap. 6.95 (ISBN 0-89315-140-8). vols. 1 & 2 combined 12.95 (ISBN 0-89315-141-6). Lambert Bk.

Living Wild: The Secrets of Animal Survival. David F. Robinson. Ed. by Alma D. MacConomy. LC 80-80702. (Illus.). 208p. 1980. 14.95 (ISBN 0-912186-37-2). Natl Wildlife.

Living with a Car. Alexander Spearl. 12.50x (ISBN 0-392-05915-0, SpS). Soccer.

Living with a Mentally Retarded Child: A Primer for Parents. Beatrice Buckler. 1971. 7.95 o.p. (ISBN 0-8015-4614-1). Dutton.

Living with a Parent Who Drinks Too Much. Judith S. Seixas. LC 78-11108. (gr. 3-6). 1979. 7.50 (ISBN 0-688-80196-X); PLB 7.20 (ISBN 0-688-84196-1). Greenwillow.

Living with Angels. Dorie D'Angelo. 1980. pap. 7.50 (ISBN 0-912216-22-0). Angel Pr.

Living with Anxiety & Depression. encore ed. Herbert Krauss & Beatrice Krauss. 1980. Encore Ed. pap. 4.95 (ISBN 0-88347-035-7). Thomas More.

Living with Books: The Art of Book Selection. 2nd ed. Helen E. Haines. LC 50-4478. 1950. 22.50x (ISBN 0-231-01803-7). Columbia U Pr.

Living with Capitalism: Class Relations & the Modern Factory. Theo Nichols & Huw Beynon. 1977. 18.00x (ISBN 0-7100-8594-X); pap. 10.00 (ISBN 0-7100-8595-8). Routledge & Kegan.

Living with Cerebral Palsy. T. T. Ingram et al. (Clinics in Developmental Medicine Ser. No. 14). 105p. 1964. 5.00 o.p. (ISBN 0-685-24717-1). Lippincott.

Living with Children: New Methods for Parents & Teachers. rev. ed. Gerald R. Patterson. LC 76-23974. 1976. pap. text ed. 5.95 (ISBN 0-87822-130-1). Res Press.

Living with Contradictions: A Married Feminist. Angela B. McBride. 1977. pap. 4.95 (ISBN 0-06-090556-5, CN 556, CN). Har-Row.

Living with Differences. Shirley Schwarzrock & C. Gilbert Wrenn. (Coping with Ser.). (gr. 7-12). 1973. pap. text ed. 1.30 (ISBN 0-913476-19-6). Am Guidance.

Living with Energy. Ron Alves & Charles Milligan. (Illus.). 1978. 14.95 o.p. (ISBN 0-670-43584-8, Studio). Viking Pr.

Living with Energy: Alternative Sources in Your Home. Ronald Alves & C. Milligan. (Large Format Ser). (Illus.). 1978. pap. 5.95 o.p. (ISBN 0-14-004681-X). Penguin.

Living with Epileptic Seizures. Samuel Livingston. (Illus.). 368p. 1963. 9.75 (ISBN 0-398-01135-4). C C Thomas.

Living with Loneliness. Shirley Schwarzrock & C. Gilbert Wrenn. (Coping with Ser.). (Illus.). 31p. (gr. 7-12). 1970. pap. text ed. 1.30 (ISBN 0-913476-32-3). Am Guidance.

Living with Multiple Sclerosis: A Social Psychological Analysis. Marcella Z. Davis. 80p. 1973. 9.50 (ISBN 0-398-02850-8). C C Thomas.

Living with Myasthenia Gravis: A Bright New Tomorrow. Jean W. Kempton. (Illus.). 112p. 1972. 9.75 (ISBN 0-398-02329-8). C C Thomas.

Living with Mysterious Epilepsy: My 48-Year Victory Over Fear. Ruth C. Adam. Ed. by Walter C. Alvarez. LC 73-92057. 1974. 6.00 o.p. (ISBN 0-682-47906-3, Banner). Exposition.

Living with Nature in Hawaii. rev. ed. Jan Moon. 136p. 1979. pap. 5.50 (ISBN 0-912180-06-4). Petroglyph.

Living with Our Hyperactive Children: Parents' Own Stories. Ed. by Marvin L. Bittinger. (Illus.). 1977. 8.95 (ISBN 0-8467-0275-4, Pub. by Two Continents). Hippocrene Bks.

Living with Pets. Ernest Hart. LC 76-39727. 1977. 15.00 (ISBN 0-8149-0778-4). Vanguard.

Living with Plants: A Guide to the Practical Application of Botany. Donna N. Schumann. (Illus.). 328p. (Orig.). 1980. pap. 14.20 (ISBN 0-916422-20-8). Mad River.

Living with Sex: The Students' Dilemma. Richard F. Hettlinger. 1966. pap. 3.95 (ISBN 0-8164-2043-2, SP32). Crossroad NY.

Living with Sorrow. Dennis Geaney. 1977. pap. 4.95 (ISBN 0-88347-074-8). Thomas More.

Living with Stress & Promoting Well Being: A Handbook for Nurses. Karen E. Claus & June T. Bailey. LC 80-14605. (Illus.). 1980. pap. text ed. 9.95 (ISBN 0-8016-1148-2). Mosby.

Living with Surgery: Before & After. rev. ed. Paul J. Melluzzo & Eleanor Nealon. LC 80-53188. 304p. 1980. pap. 6.95 (ISBN 0-7216-6261-7). Saunders.

Living with Surgery: Before & After. Paul J. Melluzzo & Eleanor Nealon. LC 80-51388. 320p. (Orig.). 1981. pap. 6.95 (ISBN 0-03-059081-7). HR&W.

Living with Technology: Issues at Mid-Career. Lotte Bailyn. 160p. 1980. text ed. 15.00x (ISBN 0-262-02153-6). MIT Pr.

Living with the Lama. T. Lobsang Rampa. pap. 2.50 (ISBN 0-685-01080-5). Weiser.

Living with the Neighbours: The Role of Economic History. Peter Mathias. (Inaugural Lectures Ser). 24p. 1971. pap. 1.00x o.p. (ISBN 0-19-951286-8). Oxford U Pr.

Living with Unfulfilled Desires. Walter Trobisch. LC 79-2718. (Orig.). 1979. pap. 3.50 (ISBN 0-87784-736-3). Inter-Varsity.

Living with Your Digestive System: This Book Can Save Your Life. Salvatore Bernace & Janet L. Walters. (Illus.). 224p. 1981. 10.95 (ISBN 0-525-93133-3). Dutton.

Living with Your Eye Operation. Theodore Berland & Richard A. Perritt. 1974. 5.95 o.p. (ISBN 0-312-49175-1). St Martin.

Living Without Fear. Wilma Burton. 1981. pap. 3.95 (ISBN 0-89107-184-9). Good News.

Living Without Fear. Ernest Holmes. 1962. pap. 3.50 (ISBN 0-911336-28-1). Sci of Mind.

Living Without Gasoline. Robert A. Hopkins. LC 76-19477. 1979. 10.95 (ISBN 0-917240-06-5). Am Metric.

Living Word: How the Gospels Work, Vol. 2. William J. O'Malley. LC 80-80534. (Orig.). (gr. 9-12). 1980. pap. 4.95 (ISBN 0-8091-9559-3). Paulist Pr.

Living Word of St. John. new ed. White Eagle. 208p. 1979. 13.95 (ISBN 0-85487-044-X). De Vorss.

Living Word: Scripture & Myth, Vol. 1. William J. O'Malley. LC 80-80534. (Orig.). (gr. 9-12). 1980. pap. text ed. 4.95 (ISBN 0-8091-9558-5). Paulist Pr.

Living World. Ed. by Jane Olliver. (Visual World Ser.). (Illus.). 1977. PLB 7.90 (ISBN 0-531-09085-X). Watts.

Living World, 2 bks. David Stanbury. Ed. by Joseph Elder. LC 76-126509. (Illus.). 224p. (gr. 7 up). 1973. pap. text ed. 2.50 ea. o.s.i. (CCPr). Bk. 1 (78672). Bk. 2 (78673). Macmillan.

Living World of Audubon. Roland C. Clement. (Illus.). 1980. 9.95 (ISBN 0-686-68770-1, Fireside). S&S.

Living World of Nature. 1980. pap. 2.50 (ISBN 0-425-04720-2). Berkley Pub.

Livingstone's Missionary Correspondence, 1841-1856. David Livingstone. Ed. & intro. by I. Schapera. (Illus.). 1961. 20.00x (ISBN 0-520-00761-1). U of Cal Pr.

Livingstone's Pocket Medical Dictionary. Nancy Roper. 1976. pap. 4.95 o.p. (ISBN 0-443-01603-8, SL674, ScribT). Scribner.

Living...Without Milk. 3rd ed. Jacqueline Hostage. LC 78-72504. (Illus.). 128p. (Orig.). 1981. text ed. 7.95 (ISBN 0-932620-06-X); pap. 3.95 (ISBN 0-932620-05-1). Betterway Pubns.

Livre Blanc. Jean Cocteau. 10.95x (ISBN 0-8464-0576-8). Beekman Pubs.

Livre De Mon Ami. Anatole France. Ed. by J. Heywood Thomas. (French Texts Ser.). 1957. pap. text ed. 9.95x (ISBN 0-631-00380-0, Pub. by Basil Blackwell). Biblio Dist.

Livre Para Perdoar. Tr. by Augsberger. (Portuguese Bks.). 1979. 1.30 (ISBN 0-8297-0735-2). Life Pubs Intl.

Livre Rouge De la Justice Rurale. Documents Pour Servir L'histoire D'une Republique Sans Republicains. Jules Guesde. (Fr.). 1977. lib. bdg. 17.50x o.p. (ISBN 0-8287-0404-X); pap. text ed. 7.50x o.p. (ISBN 0-685-77013-3). Clearwater Pub.

Livy: His Historical Aims & Methods. P. G. Walsh. 1961. 39.00 (ISBN 0-521-06729-4). Cambridge U Pr.

Liza Hunt, Pediatric Nurse. Virginia Smiley. 192p. (YA) 1976. 5.95 (ISBN 0-685-64248-8, Avalon). Bouregy.

Liza Lou & the Yeller Belly Swamp. Mercer Mayer. LC 80-16605. (Illus.). 48p. (gr. k-5). 1980. Repr. of 1976 ed. 8.95 (ISBN 0-590-07771-6, Four Winds). Schol Bk Serv.

Liza Minnelli. David Paige. (Stars of Stage & Screen Ser.). (Illus.). (gr. 4-12). 1977. PLB 5.95 (ISBN 0-87191-558-8). Creative Ed.

Lizard. Date not set. 4.95 (ISBN 0-8120-5379-6). Barron. Postponed.

Lizard & Other Distractions: Stories. Philip Ward. 1970. 4.00 (ISBN 0-902675-52-4). Oleander Pr.

Llamados a Ensenar. Lois Lebar & Miguel Berg. Tr. by Jose M. Blanch from Eng. LC 77-5183. Orig. Title: Called to Teach. (Illus.). 160p. (Orig., Span.). 1970. pap. 2.50 o.s.i. (ISBN 0-89922-006-1). Edit Caribe.

Llana of Gathol. Edgar R. Burroughs. 1973. pap. 1.95 o.p. (ISBN 0-345-25829-0). Ballantine.

Llandoverian & Wenlockian Graptolites from Bornholm. Merete Bjerreskov. (Fossils & Strata: No.8). 1975. pap. text ed. 25.00x (ISBN 8-200-09392-1, Dist. by Columbia U Pr). Universitet.

Llave De Oro. Ed. by Esteban Marosi & Angela Whidden. Tr. by Karen Ballin. 168p. (Span.). 1980. pap. 1.75 (ISBN 0-8297-0546-5). Vida Pubs.

Llegando Al Alcoholico. Adrian Gonzalez Quiroz. 1979. pap. 0.85 (ISBN 0-311-46077-1). Casa Bautista.

Llevando los Pequenitos a Dios, 2 vols, Vols. 2 & 3. M. Schoolland. Vol. 2. 1.40 o.p. (ISBN 0-686-12555-X); Vol. 3. 1.30 o.p. (ISBN 0-686-12556-8). Banner of Truth.

Llewellyn's Personal Guide & Astrological Almanac for 1981, 12 bks. 64p. 1980. pap. 1.50. Bantam.

Lloyd George: The People's Champion, 1902-1911. John Grigg. 1979. 29.50x (ISBN 0-520-03634-4). U of Cal Pr.

Lluvia De Cuentos. Elsie G. Correa. (Illus.). 3.10 o.p. (ISBN 0-8477-3115-4). U of PR Pr.

LMS Wagon. R. J. Essery & K. Morgan. 1977. 14.95 (ISBN 0-7153-7357-9). David & Charles.

Lo Paso Bien En los Estados Inidos. Heywood Wald. (gr. 9-12). 1981. pap. 0.95 (ISBN 0-8120-2318-8). Barron.

Lo Que Dices Recibes. Tr. by Henrrieta Mears. (Spanish Bks.). (Span.). 1978. 1.90 (ISBN 0-8297-0808-1). Life Pubs Intl.

Lo Que los Jovenes Deben Saber Acerca De las Drogas. Guillermo H. Perez. 1978. pap. 0.85 (ISBN 0-311-46070-4). Casa Bautista.

Lo Que los Padres y Maestros Deben Saber Acerca De las Drogas. Guillermo H. Vasquez. 1978. pap. 0.95 (ISBN 0-311-46080-1). Casa Bautista.

Lo Que Nos Dice la Biblia. 1980. pap. 6.95 (ISBN 0-686-69351-5). Vida Pubs.

Lo, the Poor Indian: A Saga of the Suisun Indians of California. Ethel M. Read. LC 80-82306. 580p. (Orig.). 1980. 18.00 (ISBN 0-914330-34-9); pap. 10.00 (ISBN 0-914330-37-3). Panorama West.

Load-Bearing Composite Materials. Michael R. Piggott. 1980. 39.00 (ISBN 0-08-024230-8); pap. 15.00 (ISBN 0-08-024231-6). Pergamon.

Loaded & Rollin' Trucks & Their Drivers. rev. ed. John Lynott. (Encore Edition). (Illus.). 1979. pap. 2.95 (ISBN 0-684-16911-8, SL856, ScribT). Scribner.

Loan Compounds in Bulgarian Reflecting the Turkish Indefinite Izafet-Construction. Alf Grannes. 70p. 1980. pap. 16.00x (ISBN 82-00-01951-9). Universitet.

Loan Package. Emmett Ramey & Alex Wong. 180p. 1981. 3 ring binder 29.95 (ISBN 0-916378-12-8). Oasis Pr.

Loanshark. Peter McCurtin. 1979. pap. 1.75 (ISBN 0-505-51437-0). Tower Bks.

Lob-Lie-by-the-Fire, Repr. Of 1874 Ed. Juliana H. Ewing. Bd. with Jackanapes. Repr. of 1884 ed; Daddy Darwin's Dovecot. Repr. of 1884 ed. LC 75-32178. (Classics of Children's Literature, 1621-1932: Vol. 41). (Illus.). 1976. PLB 38.00 (ISBN 0-8240-2290-4). Garland Pub.

Lobbies & Lobbyists: In Whose Best Interest? Alvin Wolf. Ed. by Jack Fraenkel. (Crucial Issues in American Government Ser.). (gr. 9-12). 1976. pap. text ed. 4.96 (ISBN 0-205-04909-5, 7649096). Allyn.

Lobbying. Karen Sagstetter. (American Government Ser.). (Illus.). (gr. 7 up). 1978. PLB 6.90 s&l (ISBN 0-531-01413-4). Watts.

Lobbying in American Politics. Fred J. Cook. LC 75-34286. 160p. (gr. 6 up). 1976. PLB 5.90 o.p. (ISBN 0-531-01143-7). Watts.

Lobbyists & Legislators: A Theory of Political Markets. Michael J. Hayes. 256p. 1981. 18.00 (ISBN 0-8135-0910-6). Rutgers U Pr.

Lobengula of Zimbabwe. A. H. Bhebe. (Illus.). 48p. 1977. pap. text ed. 2.75x (ISBN 0-435-94476-2). Heinemann Ed.

Lobo. Gladys Y. Cretan. (Illus.). (gr. k-3). 1969. PLB 6.96 o.p. (ISBN 0-688-50035-8). Lothrop.

Lobo & Brewster. Gladys Y. Cretan. LC 73-135295. (Illus.). (gr. k-3). 1971. 7.25 o.p. (ISBN 0-688-41149-5); PLB 6.48 o.p. (ISBN 0-688-51149-X). Lothrop.

Lobo & Spanish Gold: A Texas Maverick in Mexico. Carl E. Ricketts. LC 74-77508. (Illus.). 210p. 1974. 8.50 (ISBN 0-89052-006-2). Madrona Pr.

Lobo Brand. Oscar Friend. 256p. (YA) 1973. 5.95 (ISBN 0-685-32414-1, Avalon). Bouregy.

Lobsterman. Ipcar. 1980. Repr. 2.95 (ISBN 0-89272-032-8). Down East.

Local & Central Impulses for Change & Development. Jan Lundqvist. 1975. pap. text ed. 15.50x (ISBN 8-200-01457-6, Dist. by Columbia U Pr). Universitet.

Local Anesthetics. P. Lechat. 1971. 55.00 (ISBN 0-08-015836-6). Pergamon.

Local Church Looks to the Future. Lyle E. Schaller. (Orig.). 1968. pap. 4.50 (ISBN 0-687-22524-8). Abingdon.

Local Community Fact Book of Chicago. Ed. by Louis Wirth & Eleanor H. Bernet. LC 50-5597. (Illus.). 1950. pap. 7.00x o.s.i. (ISBN 0-226-90243-9). U of Chicago Pr.

Local Differences & Time Differences in Nasca Pottery. Donald A. Proulx. (U. C. Publ. in Anthropology: Vol. 5). 1968. pap. 8.00x (ISBN 0-520-09004-7). U of Cal Pr.

Local Economic Development. Curtis H. Martin & Robert Leone. LC 76-55537. (Illus.). 1977. 16.95 (ISBN 0-669-01319-6). Lexington Bks.

Local Education Authority Advisers & the Mechanisms of Innovation. R. Bolam & G. Smith. (NFER General). (Orig.). 1979. pap. text ed. 22.00x (ISBN 0-85633-175-9, NFER). Humanities.

Local Energy Centres. Ed. by N. J. Lucas. (Illus.). 1978. text ed. 42.60x (ISBN 0-85334-782-4). Intl Ideas.

Local Finance in Perspective. K. Venkataraman. 4.50x o.p. (ISBN 0-210-27146-9). Asia.

Local Fiscal Crisis in Western Europe: Myths & Realities. Ed. by L. J. Sharpe. (Sage Research Ser. in European Politics: Vol. 3). 300p. 1981. 20.00 (ISBN 0-8039-9813-9). Sage.

Local Government & Education. 2nd ed. D. E. Regan. (New Local Government Ser.). 1979. pap. text ed. 11.95x (ISBN 0-04-352065-0). Allen Unwin.

Local Government & Politics in New Zealand. Graham Bush. 200p. 1980. text ed. 22.95x (ISBN 0-86861-074-7, 2500); pap. text ed. 14.95x (ISBN 0-86861-082-8, 2501). Allen Unwin.

Local Government at Work: A Case Study of a County Borough. Herbert V. Wiseman. (Library of Political Science). 1967. text ed. 5.75x (ISBN 0-7100-5128-X); pap. 2.75x (ISBN 0-7100-5117-4). Humanities.

Local Government Auditing: A Manual for Public Officials. Ed. by Peter F. Rousmaniere et al. Arnold Olenick & Vincent Pirnicory. 90p. 1979. pap. 14.95 (ISBN 0-916450-27-9). Coun on Municipal.

Local Government Finance: Capital Facilities Planning & Debt Administration in Local Government. Alan W. Steiss. 288p. 1975. 21.95 (ISBN 0-669-00126-0). Lexington Bks.

Local Government Finance in a Unitary State. C. D. Foster et al. (Illus.). 640p. 1980. text ed. 60.00x (ISBN 0-04-336066-1, 2473). Allen Unwin.

Local Government: How to Get into It, How to Administer It Effectively. Byron S. Matthews. LC 78-110451. 1970. 14.95 (ISBN 0-911012-04-4). Nelson-Hall.

Local Government in Peninsular Malaysia. M. W. Norris. 121p. 1980. text ed. 27.00x (ISBN 0-566-00283-3, Pub. by Gower Pr England). Renouf.

Local Government: Is Is Manageable? Gordon Bayley. 1979. 15.00 (ISBN 0-08-024279-0). Pergamon.

Local Government: Its Role in Development Administration. V. G. Nandedkar. 1979. text ed. 12.50x (ISBN 0-686-61444-5). Humanities.

Local Government Law, Cases & Materials. 2nd ed. William D. Valente. LC 80-10272. (American Casebook Ser.). 1048p. 1980. text ed. 21.95 (ISBN 0-8299-2087-0). West Pub.

Local Government Police Management. Ed. by Bernard L. Garmire. LC 77-3926. (Municipal Management Ser). (Illus.). 1977. text ed. 28.00 (ISBN 0-87326-016-3). Intl City Mgt.

Local Government Program Budgeting Theory & Practice: With Special Reference to Los Angeles. Werner Z. Hirsch et al. LC 74-5746. 236p. 1974. text ed. 19.50 o.p. (ISBN 0-275-28859-5). Praeger.

Local Government Reform & Reorganization: An International Perspective. Ed. by Arthur B. Gunlicks. (National University Publications, Political Science Ser.). 1981. 17.50 (ISBN 0-8046-9272-6). Kennikat.

Local Government Service: In England & Wales. K. P. Poole. (New Local Government Ser.). (Illus.). 1978. text ed. 25.00x (ISBN 0-04-352073-1); pap. text ed. 10.95x (ISBN 0-04-352074-X). Allen Unwin.

Local Grazetteers of Southwest China: A Handbook. Jae-Hyon Byon. (Parerga Ser.: No. 5). 154p. 1979. pap. 5.50 (ISBN 0-295-95702-6). U of Wash Pr.

Local Habituation. Norman Nicholson. 1973. pap. 8.95 (ISBN 0-571-10425-8, Pub. by Faber & Faber). Merrimack Bk Serv.

Local Habituation. Norman Nicholson. 1972. pap. 3.95 (ISBN 0-571-09982-3, Pub. by Faber & Faber). Merrimack Bk Serv.

Local Institutions of Virginia. E. Ingle. 1973. Repr. of 1885 ed. pap. 11.00 (ISBN 0-384-25741-0). Johnson Repr.

Local Level Planning & Rural Development: Alternative Strategies. Ed. by United Nations Asian & Pacific Development Inst. 409p. 1980. text ed. 20.50x (ISBN 0-391-02171-0, Pub. by Concept India). Humanities.

Local Operator & Markow Processes. L. Stoica. (Lecture Notes in Mathematics: Vol. 816). 104p. 1980. pap. 9.80 (ISBN 0-387-10028-8). Springer-Verlag.

Local Politics & Development in the Middle East. Ed. by Louis J. Cantori & Iliya Harik. (Special Studies on the Middle East). 350p. 1981. lib. bdg. 24.50x (ISBN 0-86531-169-2). Westview.

Local Politics & Nation-States: Case Studies in Politics & Policy. Ann T. Schulz. LC 79-11416. (Studies in International & Comparative Politics: No. 12). 234p. 1980. text ed. 21.50 (ISBN 0-87436-289-X). ABC-Clio.

Local Politics & the Rise of the Party. Ken Young. 256p. 1975. text ed. 19.50x (ISBN 0-7185-1140-9, Leicester). Humanities.

Local Politics in Communist Countries. Ed. by Daniel N. Nelson. LC 78-58121. 240p. 1981. 17.50 (ISBN 0-8131-1398-9). U Pr of Ky.

Local Politics of Rural Development: Peasant & Party-State in Zambia. Michael Bratton. LC 79-56775. (Illus.). 350p. 1980. text ed. 17.50x (ISBN 0-87451-178-X). U Pr of New Eng.

Local Religion in Sixteenth-Century Spain. William A. Christian, Jr. LC 80-7513. 296p. 1981. 18.50x (ISBN 0-691-05306-5). Princeton U Pr.

Local Service Airline Experiment. George C. Eads. (Studies in the Regulation of Economic Activity: No. 6). 225p. 1972. 11.95 (ISBN 0-8157-2022-X). Brookings.

Local Stresses in Pressure Vessels. 2nd ed. B. Fred Forman. 1979. 60.00 (ISBN 0-914458-05-1). Pressure.

Locality Principles in Syntax. Jan Koster et al. (Studies in Generative Grammar: No. 5). (Orig.). 1979. pap. text ed. 20.00x (ISBN 90-70176-06-8). Humanities.

Locating & Correcting Reading Difficulties. 2nd ed. Eldon Ekwall. (Elementary Education Ser.). 1977. pap. text ed. 7.95 (ISBN 0-675-08560-8). Merrill.

Locating & Correcting Reading Difficulties. 3rd ed. Eldon E. Ekwall. (Illus.). 192p. 1981. pap. text ed. 6.95 (ISBN 0-675-08062-2). Merrill.

Locating Language in Time & Space, Vol. I. Ed. by William Labov. LC 80-757. (Quantitative Analysis of Linguistic Structure Ser.). 1980. 24.50 (ISBN 0-12-432101-1). Acad Pr.

Locating, Recruiting, & Hiring the Disabled. Rami Rabby. 1981. pap. 3.95 (ISBN 0-87576-095-3). Pilot Bks.

Location & Land Use: Toward a General Theory of Land Rent. William Alonso. LC 63-17193. (Joint Center for Urban Studies Publications Ser). (Illus.). 1964. 10.00x (ISBN 0-674-53700-9). Harvard U Pr.

Location & Space in Social Administration. Bryan Massam. LC 74-26536. 192p. 1975. 24.95 (ISBN 0-470-57600-6). Halsted Pr.

Location in Space. 2nd ed. Peter Lloyd & Peter Dicken. 1977. text ed. 19.80 (ISBN 0-06-318058-8, IntlDept); pap. text ed. 16.75 (ISBN 0-06-318059-6). Har-Row.

Location of Immigrant Industry Within a U. K. Assisted Area: The Scottish Experience. R. A. Henderson. (Progress in Planning Ser.: Vol. 14, Part 2). (Illus.). 121p. 1980. pap. 13.50 (ISBN 0-08-026807-2). Pergamon.

Location of Industry & International Competitiveness. Seev Hirsch. 1967. 22.00x (ISBN 0-19-828236-2). Oxford U Pr.

Locational Analysis in Human Geography, 2 vols. 2nd ed. Peter Haggett et al. LC 77-8967. 1977. Set. 54.95 (ISBN 0-470-99207-7); Vol. 1, Locational Models. pap. 14.95 (ISBN 0-470-99208-5); Vol. 2, Locational Methods. pap. 19.95 (ISBN 0-470-99209-3). Halsted Pr.

Locations. Jim Harrison. LC 68-21703. 1968. 4.95 o.p. (ISBN 0-393-04257-X). Norton.

Loch Ness Monster. Elwood Baumann. LC 72-182896. (Illus.). 160p. (gr. 6 up). 1972. PLB 7.45 (ISBN 0-531-02031-2). Watts.

Loch Ness Monster. 3rd ed. Tim Dinsdale. (Illus.). 1976. pap. 7.95 (ISBN 0-7100-8394-7). Routledge & Kegan.

Loch Ness Monster. Ellen Rabinowich. (Easy-Read Fact Bks.). (Illus.). (gr. 2-4). 1979. PLB 6.45 s&l (ISBN 0-531-02274-9). Watts.

Locke & the Compass of Human Understanding. John W. Yolton. LC 76-112477. 1970. 29.95 (ISBN 0-521-07838-5). Cambridge U Pr.

Locke on Human Understanding: Selected Essays. Ed. by I. C. Tipton. 1977. pap. text ed. 5.95x (ISBN 0-19-875039-0). Oxford U Pr.

Locke Reader. Ed. by J. W. Yolton. LC 76-9181. 1977. 29.95 (ISBN 0-521-21282-0); pap. 9.95x (ISBN 0-521-29084-8). Cambridge U Pr.

Locke, Rousseau, & the Idea of Consent: An Inquiry into the Liberal-Democratic Theory of Political Obligation. Jules Steinberg. LC 77-91094. (Contributions in Political Science: No. 6). 1978. lib. bdg. 16.50 (ISBN 0-313-20052-1, SLR/). Greenwood.

Locke: Symposium Wolfenbuttel, Nineteen Hundred Seventy-Nine. Ed. by Reinhard Brand. 288p. 1980. text ed. 48.75x (ISBN 3-11-008266-7). De Gruyter.

Locked in. Gerald Locklin. 1980. 3.00 (ISBN 0-917554-18-3). Maelstrom.

Locked in a Room with Open Doors. Ernest T. Campbell. LC 73-91554. 1976. pap. 3.95 o.p. (ISBN 0-87680-852-6, 98082). Word Bks.

Locke's Essay Concerning Human Understanding, Bks. II & IV. Ed. & intro. by Mary W. Calkins. 1962. Repr. of 1905 ed. 19.95 (ISBN 0-87548-033-0). Open Court.

Locke's Second Treatise of Civil Government. Ed. by Lester Dekoster. 1978. pap. 2.95 o.p. (ISBN 0-8028-1732-7). Eerdmans.

Locke's Theory of Sensitive Knowledge. Kathleen M. Squadrito. LC 78-62265. 1978. pap. text ed. 9.25 (ISBN 0-8191-0571-6). U Pr of Amer.

Lockhart Collection of Chinese Copper Coins. J. Stewart Lockhart. LC 74-27610. (Illus.). 240p. 1975. Repr. 35.00x (ISBN 0-88000-056-2). Quarterman.

Locking up Children: Secure Provision Within the Child-Care System. Spencer Millham et al. (Illus.). 1978. 21.95 (ISBN 0-566-00170-5, 01320-X, Pub. by Saxon Hse). Lexington Bks.

Locking up the Range: Federal Land Controls & Grazing. Gary Libecap. (Pacific Institute for Public Policy Research Ser.). 1981. price not set professional reference (ISBN 0-88410-382-X). Ballinger Pub.

Lockley Files. Fred Lockley. Ed. by Mike Helm. (Illus.). 300p. (Orig.). 1981. pap. 9.95 (ISBN 0-931742-08-0). Rainy Day Oreg.

Lockout. LC 79-57121. (Feminist Novels Ser.). 100p. 1980. pap. 4.95 (ISBN 0-935772-02-2). Diotima Bks.

Locks & Keys. Gail Gibbons. LC 79-7825. (Illus.). 32p. (gr. 1-4). 1980. 7.95 (ISBN 0-690-04058-X, TYC-J); PLB 7.89 (ISBN 0-690-04059-8). T Y Crowell.

Locks Catalog. Wilson Bohannon C0., (Illus.). Repr. of 1911 ed. 15.00 (ISBN 0-87556-350-3). Saifer.

Locks, Safes, & Security: A Handbook for Law Enforcement Personnel. Marc W. Tobias. 352p. 1971. pap. 18.00 spiral (ISBN 0-398-02155-4). C C Thomas.

Lockwood Concern. John O'Hara. 1977. pap. 1.95 o.p. (ISBN 0-445-08564-9). Popular Lib.

Locomotion: A World Survey of Railway Traction. O. S. Nock. LC 75-27489. (Encore Edition). (Illus.). 1976. 6.95 o.p. (ISBN 0-684-15431-5, ScribT). Scribner.

Locomotion from Pre-to Post-natal Life. Andre Thomas & S. Autgaerden. (Clinics in Developmental Medicine Ser. No. 24). 90p. 1966. 11.00 (ISBN 0-685-24723-6). Lippincott.

Locomotive Adventure, Vol. 2. H. Halcroft. 17.75x (ISBN 0-392-08040-0, SpS). Soccer.

Locomotive at the Grouping, London, Midland, & Scottish. 14.95x (ISBN 0-392-08071-0, SpS). Soccer.

Locomotive Engineer Album. George Abdill. (Encore Ed.). (Illus.). 9.95 (ISBN 0-87564-534-8). Superior Pub.

Locomotive of the North Eastern Railway. 14.95x (ISBN 0-392-08071-0, SpS). Soccer.

Locomotives at the Grouping, Great Western Railway. Johnston Casserly. 14.95x (ISBN 0-392-08054-0, SpS). Soccer.

Locomotives of the Glasgow & Southwestern Railway. David L. Smith. 1976. 13.95 (ISBN 0-7153-6960-1, Pub. by Batsford England). David & Charles.

Locust. Robert Barrass. (Illus.). 73p. (gr. 10 up). 1975. 8.95x (ISBN 0-903330-11-3). Transatlantic.

Lodestar: Rocket Ship to Mars. Franklyn M. Branley. LC 51-764. (gr. 5-9). 1951. 7.95 o.p. (ISBN 0-690-50443-8, TYC-J). T Y Crowell.

Lodestars for the Journey of Life. Margaret Isherwood. 91p. 1980. pap. text ed. 6.50 (ISBN 0-227-67840-0). Attic Pr.

Lodoiska. Maria L. Cherubini. Ed. by Philip Gossett & Charles Rosen. LC 76-49217. (Early Romantic Opera Ser.: Vol. 33). 1979. lib. bdg. 82.00 (ISBN 0-8240-2932-1). Garland Pub.

L'Oeuvre de Jean Prevost. Marc Bertrand. (U. C. Publ. in Modern Philology: Vol. 90). 1968. pap. 8.00x (ISBN 0-520-09285-6). U of Cal Pr.

Loffelchen: Eine Erzahlung. Albrecht Goes. Ed. by Christoph E. Schweitzer. LC 68-13150. (Orig., Ger.). 1968. pap. text ed. 1.95x (ISBN 0-89197-280-3). Irvington.

Loftier Flight: The Life & Accomplishments of Charles Louis Didelot, Balletmaster. Mary G. Swift. LC 73-15007. (De la Torre Bueno Prize Book, 1973). (Illus.). 336p. 1974. 17.50x (ISBN 0-8195-4070-6, Pub. by Wesleyan U Pr). Columbia U Pr.

Lofting. Allan Vaitses. LC 78-75110. 1980. pap. 15.00 (ISBN 0-87742-113-7). Intl Marine.

Log Book. Barbara T. Smith. LC 81-65196. (Illus.). 100p. (Orig.). 1981. 15.00 (ISBN 0-937122-03-3). Astro Artz.

Log Cabin in America: From Pioneer Days to the Present. C. A. Weslager. (Illus.). 1969. 23.00 (ISBN 0-8135-0596-8). Rutgers U Pr.

Log-Cabin Myth: A Study of the Early Dwellings of the English Colonists in North America. Harold R. Shurtleff. (Illus.). 1967. 8.50 (ISBN 0-8446-1404-1). Peter Smith.

Log Cabin Village: A History & Guide. Terry G. Jordan et al. (Illus.). 1980. 15.00; pap. 6.95 (ISBN 0-87611-050-2). Tex St Hist Assn.

Log College. Archibald Alexander. 1968. 9.95 (ISBN 0-686-12475-8). Banner of Truth.

Log-Linear Models. David Knoke & Peter J. Burke. LC 80-17031. (Quantitative Applications in the Social Sciences Ser.: No. 20). (Illus.). 80p. 1980. pap. 3.50 (ISBN 0-8039-1492-X). Sage.

Log of a Cowboy. Andy Adams. Orig. Title: Public Domain. 1976. pap. 1.25 o.p. (ISBN 0-685-64012-4, LB344ZK, Leisure Bks). Nordon Pubns.

Log of the Centurion. Ed. by Leo Heaps. LC 73-10831. (Illus.). 304p. 1974. 8.95 o.p. (ISBN 0-02-549750-2). Macmillan.

Log of the Mahina. John Neal. (Illus.). 288p. 4.95 o.p. (ISBN 0-918074-00-2). Western Marine Ent.

Log of the Mayflower. Philip J. Simon. LC 56-9513. 208p. 1980. Repr. of 1958 ed. 7.95 (ISBN 0-911180-02-8, Pub. by Priam Pr). Chicago Review.

Log of the Mayflower. Phillip J. Simon. LC 56-9513. 208p. 1980. pap. 7.95 (ISBN 0-911180-02-8). Priam Pr.

Log of the Union: John Boit's Remarkable Voyage, 1794-1796. John Boit. Intro. by Edmund Hayes, Sr. LC 80-83181. (North Pacific Studies: No. 6). (Illus.). 250p. 1981. 14.95 (ISBN 0-87595-068-X); pap. 9.95 (ISBN 0-87595-089-2). Oreg Hist Soc.

Log Structures, Preservation & Problem-Solving. Harrison Goodall & Renee Friedman. 120p. 1980. pap. 10.95 (ISBN 0-910050-46-5). AASLH.

Logarithmic & Trigonometric Tables to Five Places. rev. ed. Kaj L. Nielsen. (Orig.). 1971. pap. 2.95 (ISBN 0-06-460044-0, CO 44, COS). Har-Row.

Logarithmic Potential, 2 vols. in 1. 2nd ed. Griffith C. Evans. Incl. Fundamental Existence Theorems. Gilbert A. Bliss. Repr. of 1927 ed. write for info. o.p. (ISBN 0-685-22943-2). Chelsea Pub.

Loggers. Richard Williams. (Old West). (Illus.). (gr. 5 up). 1976. kivar 12.96 (ISBN 0-8094-1527-5, Pub. by Time-Life). Silver.

Loggers. Richard L. Williams. (Old West Ser.). (Illus.). 1976. 12.95 (ISBN 0-8094-1525-9). Time-Life.

Logging & Lumbering. Kathleen Abrams & Lawrence Abrams. LC 80-19473. (Illus.). 96p. (gr. 4 up). 1980. PLB 7.79 (ISBN 0-671-34007-7). Messner.

Logging & Pulpwood Production. J. Kenneth Pearce & George Stenzel. 400p. 1972. 24.95 (ISBN 0-471-06839-X, Pub. by Wiley-Interscience). Wiley.

Logging Railroads of the White Mountains. C. Francis Belcher. (Illus.). 250p. (Orig.). 1980. pap. 6.95 (ISBN 0-910146-32-2). Appalach Mtn.

Logic. Wilfrid Hodges. 1980. 3.95 (ISBN 0-14-021985-4). Penguin.

Logic. Immanuel Kant. Tr. by Robert S. Hartman & Wolfgang Schwarz. LC 72-10560. (LLA Ser). 279p. 1974. 5.50 o.p. (ISBN 0-672-61228-3). Bobbs.

Logic, 2 vols. Hermann Lotze. Ed. by Maurice Natanson. LC 78-66738. (Phenomenology Background, Foreground & Influences Ser.: Vol. 8). 1980. Set. lib. bdg. 77.00 (ISBN 0-8240-9562-6). Garland Pub.

Logic. A. A. Luce. (Teach Yourself Ser.). 1975. pap. 2.95 o.p. (ISBN 0-679-10435-6). McKay.

Logic. 2nd ed. Wesley C. Salmon. (Foundations of Philosophy Ser). (Illus.). 160p. 1973. pap. 7.95 ref. ed. (ISBN 0-13-540104-6). P-H.

Logic: A First Course. Albert Blumberg. 1976. text ed. 14.95 (ISBN 0-394-31442-5); tchr's manual free (ISBN 0-394-31178-7). Knopf.

Logic: A Philosophical Introduction. J. Kaminsky & A. R. Kaminsky. 1974. 14.95 (ISBN 0-201-03576-6). A-W.

Logic: An Orthodox Christian Approach. Apostolos Makrakis. Ed. by Orthodox Christian Educational Society. Tr. by Denver Cummings from Hellenic. (Logos & Holy Spirit in the Unity of Christian Thought Ser.: Vol. 3). 200p. 1977. pap. 3.50x (ISBN 0-938366-04-1). Orthodox Chr.

Logic & Arithmetic: Natural Numbers. David Bostock. 229p. 1974. 29.95x (ISBN 0-19-824366-9). Oxford U Pr.

Logic & Art: Essays in Honor of Nelson Goodman. Ed. by Richard S. Rudner & Israel Scheffler. LC 76-140799. 1971. 13.95 (ISBN 0-672-51639-X). Bobbs.

Logic & Contemporary Rhetoric. 3rd ed. Howard Kahane. 288p. 1980. pap. text ed. 9.95x (ISBN 0-534-00850-X). Wadsworth Pub.

Logic & Contemporary Rhetoric: The Use of Reason in Everyday Life. 2nd ed. Howard Kahane. 1976. pap. 7.95x o.p. (ISBN 0-534-00449-0). Wadsworth Pub.

Logic & Language. Ed. by A. G. Flew. (First Ser.). 1968. pap. 12.50x (ISBN 0-631-03420-X, Pub. by Basil Blackwell). Biblio Dist.

Logic & Language. Ed. by A. G. Flew. (Second Ser.). 1973. Repr. of 1953 ed. 12.50x (ISBN 0-631-03430-7, Pub. by Basil Blackwell England). Biblio Dist.

Logic & Language: An Introduction to Elementary Logic & the Theory of Linguistic Descriptions. John Heil. 1978. pap. text ed. 16.75x (ISBN 0-8191-0396-9). U Pr of Amer.

Logic & Memory Experiments: Using TTL Integrated Circuits. Peter R. Rony. Incl. Bk. 1. pap. 10.95 (ISBN 0-672-21542-X); Bk. 2. pap. 10.95 (ISBN 0-672-21543-8). LC 78-57209. 1978. Bks 1 & 2. pap. 19.95 (ISBN 0-672-21544-6). Sams.

Logic & Ontology. Ed. by Milton K. Munitz. LC 72-96480. (Studies in Contemporary Philosophy). 320p. 1973. 17.50x (ISBN 0-8147-5363-9); pap. 7.00x (ISBN 0-8147-5377-9). NYU Pr.

Logic & Philosophy. 3rd ed. Howard Kahane. 1978. text ed. 17.95x (ISBN 0-534-00555-1). Wadsworth Pub.

Logic & Philosophy: Selected Readings. Ed. by Gary Iseminger. (Century Philosophy Ser). 1980. text ed. 18.95x o. p. (ISBN 0-89197-829-1); pap. text ed. 8.95x (ISBN 0-89197-830-5). Irvington.

Logic & Proof. M. S. Bittinger. 1970. pap. 5.95 (ISBN 0-201-00597-2). A-W.

Logic & Scientific Methods: An Introductory Course. 3rd ed. Herbert L. Searles. LC 68-13474. (Illus.). 1968. 13.95x o.p. (ISBN 0-8260-7970-9). Wiley.

Logic & Virtue of Atheism. Joseph McCabe. 1980. pap. 3.29. Am Atheist.

Logic As a Positive Science. Galvano D. Volpe. 288p. 1981. 19.95 (ISBN 0-8052-7096-5, Pub. by NLB England). Schocken.

Logic Book. Merrie Bergmann et al. 608p. 1980. text ed. 17.95 (ISBN 0-394-32323-8). Knopf.

Logic, Computers & Sets. Hao Wang. LC 70-113155. Orig. Title: Survey of Mathematical Logic. 1970. Repr. of 1962 ed. text ed. 19.95 (ISBN 0-8284-0245-0). Chelsea Pub.

Logic Design & Switching Theory. Saburo Muroga. LC 78-12407. 1979. 35.00 (ISBN 0-471-04418-0, Pub. by Wiley-Interscience). Wiley.

Logic Design for Behavioral Scientists. Roy Udolf. LC 73-75522. 1973. 16.95 (ISBN 0-911012-54-0). Nelson-Hall.

Logic Design of Digital Systems. 2nd ed. Dietmeyer. 1978. text ed. 28.95 (ISBN 0-205-05960-0). Allyn.

Logic for Mathematicians. A. G. Hamilton. LC 77-84802. (Illus.). 1978. 57.50 (ISBN 0-521-21838-1); pap. 14.95x (ISBN 0-521-29291-3). Cambridge U Pr.

Logic in Linguistics. Ed. by J. Allwood et al. LC 76-46855. (Cambridge Textbooks in Linguistics Ser.). (Illus.). 1977. 29.95 (ISBN 0-521-21496-3); pap. 9.50 (ISBN 0-521-29174-7). Cambridge U Pr.

Logic, Induction & Ontology, Vol. 2. Pranab K. Sen. (Jadavpur Studies in Philosophy). 1980. text ed. write for info. (ISBN 0-391-01765-9). Humanities.

Logic Matters. P. T. Geach. 1972. 17.50x (ISBN 0-520-01851-6, CAMPUS 222); pap. 5.95 (ISBN 0-686-66341-1). U of Cal Pr.

Logic of Chance. 4th ed. John Venn. LC 62-11698. (YA) (gr. 7-12). 12.95 (ISBN 0-8284-0173-X); pap. 4.95 o.p. (ISBN 0-8284-0169-1). Chelsea Pub.

Logic of Comparative Social Inquiry. Adam Przeworski & Henry Teune. (Comparative Studies in Behavioral Science Ser). 1970. 20.50 (ISBN 0-471-70142-4, Pub. by Wiley-Interscience). Wiley.

Logic of Culture: Advances in Structural Theory & Methods. Ed. by Ino Rossi. 320p. 1981. text ed. 24.95x (ISBN 0-89789-015-9). J F Bergin.

Logic of God: Theology & Verification. Malcolm L. Diamond & Thomas V. Litzenburg, Jr. LC 74-32235. 562p. 1975. 17.95 (ISBN 0-672-60792-1). Bobbs.

Logic of Inconsistency: A Study in Nonstandard Possible-World Semantics & Ontology. Nicholas Rescher & Robert Brandom. (American Philosophical Quarterly Library of Philosophy). 174p. 1979. 22.50x (ISBN 0-8476-6248-9). Rowman.

Logic of Liberty: Reflections & Rejoinders. Michael Polanyi. LC 51-8809. (Midway Reprint Ser.). 1981. 9.00x (ISBN 0-226-67296-4). U of Chicago Pr.

Logic of "Maoism" Critiques & Explication. Ed. by James C. Hsiung. LC 74-3515. 300p. 1974. text ed. 32.50 (ISBN 0-275-09070-1). Praeger.

Logic of Marx. Jindrich Zeleny. Ed. by Terrell Carver. 251p. 1980. 27.50x (ISBN 0-8476-6767-7). Rowman.

Logic of "Normalization". Fred Eidlin. (East European Monograph: No. 74). 256p. 1980. 20.00x (ISBN 0-914710-68-0). East Eur Quarterly.

Logic of Passion: The Literary Criticism of William Hazlitt. John L. Mahoney. (Salzburg Studies in English Literature Romantic Reassessment Ser.: No. 75). 1978. pap. text ed. 25.00x (ISBN 0-391-01468-4). Humanities.

Logic of Poverty: The Case of the Brazilian Northeast. Simon Mitchell. (Direct Edition Ser.). 200p. (Orig.). 1981. pap. 18.95 (ISBN 0-7100-0637-3). Routledge & Kegan.

Logic of Power. Ingmar Porn. 1970. pap. 6.50x o.p. (ISBN 0-631-12510-8, Pub. by Basil Blackwell). Biblio Dist.

Logic of Science in Sociology. Walter L. Wallace. LC 71-149845. 1971. 15.95x (ISBN 0-202-30193-1); pap. 6.95x (ISBN 0-202-30194-X). Aldine Pub.

Logic of Scientific Discovery. rev. ed. Karl R. Popper. pap. 6.95x (ISBN 0-06-130576-6, TB576, Torch). Har-Row.

Logic of Scientific Inference: An Introduction. Jennifer Trusted. (Modern Introductions to Philosophy Ser.). 144p. 1980. text ed. 20.00x (ISBN 0-333-26669-2); pap. text ed. 10.00x (ISBN 0-333-26670-6). Humanities.

Logic of Significance & Context, Vol. 1. L. Goddard & R. Routley. LC 73-8025. 641p. 1973. 44.95 (ISBN 0-470-30865-6). Halsted Pr.

Logic of Statistical Inference. Ian M. Hacking. 1966. 35.50 (ISBN 0-521-05165-7); pap. 11.50x (ISBN 0-521-29059-7). Cambridge U Pr.

Logic of Theism: An Analysis of the Thought of Austin Farrer. Jeffrey C. Eaton. LC 80-67260. 288p. 1980. lib. bdg. 19.25 (ISBN 0-8191-1337-9); pap. text ed. 10.50 (ISBN 0-8191-1338-7). U Pr of Amer.

Logic of Unity. 3rd ed. Geoffrey Parker. (Illus.). 224p. 1981. pap. text ed. 14.95 (ISBN 0-582-30031-2). Longman.

Logic of Welfare Reform. Frank Levy. (Welfare Reform Policy Analysis Ser.: No. 6). 81p. 1981. pap. 6.00 (ISBN 0-87766-282-7, 29700). Urban Inst.

Logic of World Power: An Inquiry into the Origins, Currents & Contradictions of World Politics. Franz Schurmann. LC 73-18732. 1974. 15.00 o.s.i. (ISBN 0-394-48481-9). Pantheon.

Logic, Ontology & Action, Vol. 1. Ed. by H. D. Lewis. (Jadavpur Studies in Philosophy). 1980. text ed. write for info. (ISBN 0-391-01764-0). Humanities.

Logic, Semantics, Metamathematics. Alfred Tarski. Ed. by John Corcoran. Tr. by J. H. Woodger from Polish. 1981. lib. bdg. 35.00 (ISBN 0-915144-75-1); pap. text ed. 17.50 (ISBN 0-915144-76-X). Hackett Pub. Postponed.

Logic, Sets, & Numbers: A Positive Approach to Math. 2nd ed. Louis Roethel & Abraham Weinstein. 1976. 19.95x (ISBN 0-534-00491-1). Wadsworth Pub.

Logic, Style, & Arrangement: Literature for Composition. Harvey M. Craft. 1971. pap. text ed. 7.95x (ISBN 0-02-474010-1, 47401). Macmillan.

Logic: Techniques of Formal Reasoning. 2nd ed. Donald Kalish et al. 520p. 1980. text ed. 7.95 (ISBN 0-686-64982-6, HC). HarBraceJ.

Logic: Theory of Inquiry. John Dewey. 1981. Repr. of 1938 ed. 24.50x (ISBN 0-89197-831-3). Irvington.

Logic Workbook. James W. Miller. 1958. 4.95x (ISBN 0-19-500988-6); pap. 3.95x teacher's key (ISBN 0-19-500989-4). Oxford U Pr.

Logica Modernorum, Vol. 2. Lambertus M. De Rijk. (Philos. Texts & Studies: Vol. 16). 1967. text ed. 116.50x (ISBN 90-232-0440-9). Humanities.

Logical Abilities in Children, 4 vols. Daniel N. Osherson. Incl. Vol. 1. Organization of Length & Class: Empirical Consequences of a Piagetion Formulism. 11.95 (ISBN 0-470-65723-5); Vol. 2. Logical Inference. 11.95 (ISBN 0-470-65724-3); Vol. 3. Reasoning in Adolesence-Deductive Inference. LC 75-25623. 1975. 14.95 (ISBN 0-470-65730-8); Vol. 4. Reasoning & Concepts. 14.95 (ISBN 0-470-99009-0). LC 74-2298. 1974-77. Halsted Pr.

Logical Analysis of Quantum Mechanics. E. Scheibe. 1973. 46.00 (ISBN 0-08-017158-3). Pergamon.

Logical & Conceptual Analytic Techniques for Educational Researchers. Elizabeth Steiner. LC 77-18575. 1978. pap. text ed. 5.75x (ISBN 0-8191-0406-X). U Pr of Amer.

Logical Bridge Play. H. W. Kelsey. 1976. 11.95 (ISBN 0-686-24615-2, Pub. by Faber & Faber). Merrimack Bk Serv.

Logical Consequences: A New Approach to Discipline. Rudolf Dreikurs & Loren Grey. LC 68-28720. 1968. 9.95 (ISBN 0-8015-4638-9, Hawthorn); pap. 4.50 (ISBN 0-8015-4632-X, Hawthorn). Dutton.

Logical Design of Computers. S. H. Lavington. 50p. 1972. 18.00x (ISBN 0-7190-0480-2, Pub. by Manchester U Pr England). State Mutual Bk.

Logical Design of Multiple Microprocessor Systems. Bowen & Behr. (Illus.). 272p. 1980. text ed. 21.50 (ISBN 0-13-539908-4). P-H.

Logical Design of Operating Systems. Alan C. Shaw. (Illus.). 304p. 1974. 25.95 (ISBN 0-13-540112-7). P-H.

Logical Design Using Integrated Circuits. William D. Becher. 1977. text ed. 21.50x (ISBN 0-8104-5859-4). Hayden.

Logical Foundations of Mathematics. William S. Hatcher. LC 80-41253. (Foundations & Philosophy of Science & Technology Ser.). 400p. 1981. 48.00 (ISBN 0-08-025800-X). Pergamon.

Logical Investigations, 2 vols. Edmund Husserl. Tr. by J. N. Findlay. (International Library of Philosophy & Scientific Method). 1970. Set. 52.00x (ISBN 0-391-00053-5). Humanities.

Logical Papers: A Selection. Gottfried Leibniz. Tr. by G. H. Parkinson. 1966. 24.00x (ISBN 0-19-824306-5). Oxford U Pr.

Logical Positivism. Ed. by Alfred J. Ayer. LC 58-6467. 1966. pap. text ed. 9.95 (ISBN 0-02-900130-7). Free Pr.

Logical Principles of Proclus' As Systematic Ground of the Cosmos. James Lowry. (Elementa Ser.: No. 13). 118p. 1980. text ed. 17.25x (ISBN 90-6203-781-X). Humanities.

Logical Programming with System 360. Don Stabley. LC 75-96047. 1970. 29.95 (ISBN 0-471-81945-X). Wiley.

Logical Structure of the World & Pseudoproblems in Philosophy. Rudolf Carnap. Tr. by Rolf A. George. Orig. Title: Logische Aufbau der Welt. 1967. pap. 8.95x (ISBN 0-520-01417-0, CAL184). U of Cal Pr.

Logical Way of Doing Things. Ed. by Karel Lambert. LC 69-15450. 1969. 20.00x o.p. (ISBN 0-300-01133-4). Yale U Pr.

Logical Works, 2 vols. George Boole. Incl. Vol. 1. Studies in Logic & Probability. 500p. 22.50 (ISBN 0-87548-038-1); Vol. 2. Laws of Thought. xvi, 448p. 22.50 (ISBN 0-87548-039-X). 1952. Open Court.

Logier's Comprehensive Course in Music: Harmony & Practical Composition. Johann B. Logier. LC 76-15186. (Music Reprint Ser.). 1976. Repr. of 1888 ed. lib. bdg. 32.50 (ISBN 0-306-70794-2). Da Capo.

Logike of the Most Excellent Philosopher P. Ramus, Martyr. Pierre de La Ramee. Tr. by Rolandus Makilmenaeus. LC 77-26225. (English Experience Ser.: No. 107). 101p. 1969. Repr. of 1555 ed. 11.50 (ISBN 90-221-0107-X). Walter J Johnson.

Lognormal: De Wijsian Geostatistics for Ore Evaluation. D. G. Krige. 50p. 1980. 18.50x (ISBN 0-620-03006-2, Pub. by Mining Journal England). State Mutual Bk.

Lognormal Distribution. John Aitchison & J. A. Brown. (Cambridge Department of Applied Economic Monographs). 1957. 29.50 (ISBN 0-521-04011-6). Cambridge U Pr.

Logos International Bible Commentary, Vo. 1. Stephen D. Swihart. 1981. write for info. (ISBN 0-88270-500-8). Logos.

Logos of the Soul. Evangelos Christou. Ed. by James Hillman. (Dunquin Ser.). 1963. pap. text ed. 6.50 (ISBN 0-88214-202-X). Spring Pubns.

Logotherapy: New Help for Problem Drinkers. James C. Crumbaugh et al. LC 79-18635. 176p. 1981. 10.95 (ISBN 0-88229-421-0). Nelson-Hall.

Lois Mailou Jones, Reflective Moments. Edmund B. Gaither. (Illus.). 1973. pap. 3.50 o.p. (ISBN 0-87846-172-8). Mus Fine Arts Boston.

Lojor's Letters: A Space-Age Story About a Boy & a Gnome & Learning Italic Handwriting. Jacqueline Svaren. (Illus.). 72p. (Orig.). (gr. 1 up). 1980. pap. 12.50 (ISBN 0-931474-04-3). TBW Bks.

Lokmanya Tilak. Ram Gopal. 9.75x o.p. (ISBN 0-210-22661-7). Asia.

Loligo Pealei. J. M. Arnold. LC 74-77352. 1974. 7.00 (ISBN 0-685-52859-6). Marine Bio.

Lollipops. Incl. People; Birds; Weather; Animals. (Illus.). 1976. pap. text ed. 13.50 set of 16 bks, 4 of ea title (ISBN 0-8372-2161-7). Bowmar-Noble.

Lolly. Judy Romberger. LC 80-2062. 256p. 1981. 12.95 (ISBN 0-385-15860-2). Doubleday.

Lombard Architecture, 4 Vols. A. Kingsley Porter. LC 67-8936. (Illus.). 1967. 150.00 o.p. (ISBN 0-87817-018-9). Hacker.

Lombard Laws. Katherine F. Drew. (Middle Ages Ser). 240p. 1973. 15.00x (ISBN 0-8122-7661-2); pap. 5.95x (ISBN 0-8122-1055-7, Pa Paperbacks). U of Pa Pr.

Lombardi: Winning Is the Only Thing. Jerry Kramer. LC 76-3503. (Illus.). 1976. 14.95 o.p. (ISBN 0-690-01131-8, TYC-T). T Y Crowell.

Lomi-Lomi Hawaiian Massage. Paul A. Lawrence. LC 80-83756. (Positive Health Ser.). (Illus.). 80p. 1981. 12.95 (ISBN 0-938034-01-4); pap. 5.95 (ISBN 0-938034-02-2). PAL Pr.

Lomokome Papers. Herman Wouk. (Illus.). 113p. 1976. Repr. of 1968 ed. lib. bdg. 12.95x (ISBN 0-89244-086-4). Queens Hse.

London. Aubrey Menen. (Great Cities Ser.). (Illus.). 1976. 14.95 (ISBN 0-8094-2254-9). Time-Life.

London. Aubrey Menen. (The Great Cities Ser.). (Illus.). (gr. 6 up). 1976. PLB 14.94 (ISBN 0-8094-2255-7, Pub by Time-Life). Silver.

London: A Poem... 1738 & 48. Samuel Johnson. Incl. The Vanity of Human Wishes - 1749 & 55. 1976. 17.95x o.p. (ISBN 0-8277-3876-5); pap. 9.50x o.p. (ISBN 0-685-62021-2). British Bk Ctr.

London A to Z. Robert S. Kane. LC 73-9035. pap. 3.95 (ISBN 0-385-08649-0, Dolp). Doubleday.

London Affair. Anthony Stuart. LC 80-66500. 1981. 9.95 (ISBN 0-87795-275-2). Arbor Hse.

London Bibliography of the Social Sciences, Eleventh Supplement, 1976, Vol. 34. Terry Chisholm. LC 31-9970. 1977. lib. bdg. 40.00 (ISBN 0-7201-0721-0, Pub. by Mansell England). Merrimack Bk Serv.

London Blitz: The City Ablaze, December 29, 1940. David Johnson. LC 80-6199. 224p. 1981. 13.95 (ISBN 0-8128-2799-6). Stein & Day.

London Bridge Is Falling Down. LC 67-17695. (Illus.). (gr. k-3). 1967. pap. 1.49 (ISBN 0-385-08025-5, Zephyr). Doubleday.

London Brighton & South Coast Railway, Vol I: Origins & Formation. John H. Turner. (Illus.). 1977. 12.95 o.s.i. (ISBN 0-7134-0275-X). Hippocrene Bks.

London, Brighton & South Coast Railway, Vol. 1. John H. Turner. 1977. 30.00 (ISBN 0-7134-0275-X, Pub. by Batsford England). David & Charles.

London, Brighton & South Coast Railway, Vol. 2. John H. Turner. 1978. 30.00 (ISBN 0-7134-1198-8, Pub. by Batsford England). David & Charles.

London, Brighton & South Coast Railway, Vol. 3. John H. Turner. 1979. 30.00 (ISBN 0-7134-1389-1, Pub. by Batsford England). David & Charles.

London Child of the 1870's. M. Vivian Hughes. (Oxford Paperbacks Ser.: No. 383). 146p. 1977. pap. text ed. 3.95x (ISBN 0-19-281216-5); pap. 3.95 o.p. (ISBN 0-686-68023-5). Oxford U Pr.

London Clearing Banks. Edward Nevin & E. W. Davis. 1970. 24.95 (ISBN 0-236-17654-4, Pub. by Paul Elek). Merrimack Bk Serv.

London Clearing Banks' Evidence to the Wilson Committee. Committee of London Clearing Banks. (Illus.). 1978. text ed. 25.00x (ISBN 0-582-03029-3). Longman.

London Deal. N. J. Crisp. 208p. 1981. pap. 1.95 (ISBN 0-380-50740-4, 50740). Avon.

London, Eight Hundred to Twelve Sixteen: The Shaping of a City. Christopher Brooke. LC 73-92620. (History of London Ser). (Illus.). 1975. 32.50x (ISBN 0-520-02686-1). U of Cal Pr.

London, Eighteen Eight Eighteen Seventy: The Infernal Wen. Francis Sheppard. (History of London Series). (Illus.). 1971. 24.50x (ISBN 0-520-01847-8). U of Cal Pr.

London Girl of the Eighteen Eighties. M. Vivian Hughes. 254p. (Orig.). 1978. pap. 4.95x (ISBN 0-19-281243-2). Oxford U Pr.

London Goldsmiths, 1697-1837. Arthur Grimwade. 1976. 108.00 (ISBN 0-571-10550-5, Pub. by Faber & Faber). Merrimack Bk Serv.

London: Hotels & Restaurants. rev. ed. 106p. 1980. pap. 2.50 o.p. (ISBN 0-7095-0167-6, Pub. by B T A). Merrimack Bk Serv.

London: Hotels & Restaurants Incl. Budget Accom. rev. ed. Automobile Association & British Tourist Authority. (Illus.). 146p. 1981. pap. write for info. (ISBN 0-7095-0576-0, Pub. by Auto Assn-British Tourist Authority England). Merrimack Bk Serv.

London in Color. Richard Church. (Illus.). 160p. 1980. 24.00 (ISBN 0-7134-0020-X, Pub. by Batsford England). David & Charles.

London in the Age of Reform. Ed. by John Stevenson. 1977. 30.50x (ISBN 0-631-17820-1, Pub. by Basil Blackwell). Biblio Dist.

London Labour & the London Poor: A Cyclopedia of the Conditions & Earnings of Those That Will Work, Those That Cannot Work & Those That Will Not Work, 4 vols. Henry Mayhew. LC 67-16357. 1981. Repr. of 1862 ed. 85.00x (ISBN 0-678-05073-2). Kelley.

London Magazine Poems, Nineteen Sixty-One-Sixty-Six. Ed. by London Magazine. 1966. pap. 3.50 (ISBN 0-85105-003-4). Dufour.

London Map. 1979. pap. 1.75 o.p. (ISBN 0-900568-89-5, ADON 8105-8, Pub. by Nicholson). Barrie & Jenkins.

London Merchant. George Lillo. Ed. by William McBurney. LC 65-11521. (Regents Restoration Drama Ser). 1965. 7.50x (ISBN 0-8032-0365-9); pap. 2.50x (ISBN 0-8032-5365-6, BB 252, Bison). U of Nebr Pr.

London Money Market. 1st ed. E. R. Shaw. 1975. 17.95x (ISBN 0-434-91830-X). Intl Ideas.

London Money Market. 2nd ed. E. R. Shaw. 1978. pap. text ed. 14.95x (ISBN 0-434-91832-6). Intl Ideas.

London Night Life. 1979. pap. 2.50 o.p. (ISBN 0-900568-82-8, ADON 8103-6, Pub. by Nicholson). Barrie & Jenkins.

London Nineteen Eighty: Phillips & Drew Kings Chess Tournament. W. R. Hartston & S. Reuben. (Pergamon Chess Ser.). (Illus.). 230p. 1981. 21.60 (ISBN 0-08-024141-7); pap. 21.60 (ISBN 0-08-024140-9). Pergamon.

London on Five Hundred Dollars a Day. Ferne Kadish & Katheleen Kirtland. (Illus.). 190p. 1975. 7.95 o.s.i. (ISBN 0-02-560510-0). Macmillan.

London Particulars. C. H. Rolph. 192p. 1980. 19.50x (ISBN 0-19-211755-6). Oxford U Pr.

London, Past & Present: A Dictionary of Its History Associations & Traditions, 3 Vols. Henry B. Wheatley. LC 68-17956. 1968. Repr. of 1891 ed. Set. 78.00 (ISBN 0-8103-3499-2). Gale.

London Perceived. Victor S. Pritchett. LC 62-14471. 1966. pap. 2.25 o.p. (ISBN 0-15-652970-X, HB103, Harv). HarBraceJ.

London Police in the Nineteenth Century. J. Wilkes. LC 76-57247. (Cambridge Introduction to the History of Mankind Ser.). (Illus.). 1977. 3.95 (ISBN 0-521-21406-8). Cambridge U Pr.

London School of Economics & Its Problems, 1919-1937. William H. Beveridge & P. Bew. 1960. text ed. 6.50x (ISBN 0-391-02007-2). Humanities.

London Season. Joan Wolf. (Orig.). 1981. pap. 1.95 (ISBN 0-451-09570-7, J9570, Sig). NAL.

London Signs: A Reference Book of London Signs from Earliest Times to About Mid-Nineteenth Century. Bryant Lillywhite. 1972. 25.00 o.p. (ISBN 0-04-942101-8). Allen Unwin.

London Signs & Inscriptions. Philip Norman. LC 68-22039. (Camden Library Ser). (Illus.). 1968. Repr. of 1893 ed. 15.00 (ISBN 0-8103-3496-8). Gale.

London Stage, Nineteen Hundred to Nineteen Nine: A Calendar of Plays & Players, 2 vols. J. P. Wearing. LC 80-28353. 1202p. 1981. Set. 50.00 (ISBN 0-8108-1403-X). Scarecrow.

London Stage, Seventeen Hundred to Seventeen Twenty-Nine: A Critical Introduction, Pt. 2. Emmett L. Avery. LC 60-6539. (Arcturus Books Paperbacks). (Illus.). 199p. 1968. pap. 5.95 (ISBN 0-8093-0337-X). S Ill U Pr.

London Stage, Sixteen Sixty to Seventeen-Hundred: A Critical Introduction, Pt. 1. Emmett L. Avery & Arthur H. Scouten. LC 60-6539. (Arcturus Books Paperbacks Ser.). (Illus.). 203p. 1968. pap. 5.95 (ISBN 0-8093-0336-1). S Ill U Pr.

London Stage, 1729-1747: A Critical Introduction. Arthur H. Scouten. LC 60-6539. (Arcturus Books Paperbacks). (Illus.). 206p. 1968. pap. 6.95 (ISBN 0-8093-0338-8). S Ill U Pr.

London Stage, 1776-1800: A Critical Introduction. Charles B. Hogan. LC 60-6539. (Arcturus Books Paperbacks). (Illus.). 230p. 1968. pap. 6.95 (ISBN 0-8093-0340-X). S Ill U Pr.

London Stage 1890-1899: A Calendar of Plays & Players, 2 vols. J. P. Wearing. LC 76-1825. 1242p. 1976. Set. 47.50 (ISBN 0-8108-0910-9). Scarecrow.

London Street Finder. 1978. 1.95 o.p. (ISBN 0-900568-98-4, 8016, Pub. by R. Nickelson). Barrie & Jenkins.

London Street Games. 2nd ed. Norman Douglas. LC 68-31089. 1968. Repr. of 1931 ed. 15.000 (ISBN 0-8103-3477-1). Gale.

London: The Unique City. 2nd ed. Steen E. Rasmussen. (Illus.). Date not set. pap. 9.95 (ISBN 0-262-68027-0). MIT Pr.

London Theatre Today: A Guide for Travelers. Mildred Fischer. (Illus.). 144p. (Orig.). 1981. pap. 4.50 (ISBN 0-914846-09-4). Golden West Pub.

London Theatre World, Sixteen Sixty to Eighteen Hundred. Ed. by Robert D. Hume. LC 79-20410. (Illus.). 416p. 1980. 24.95x (ISBN 0-8093-0926-2). S Ill U Pr.

London Two Thousand. Peter Hall. (Illus., Orig.). 1971. pap. 5.95 (ISBN 0-571-09705-7, Pub. by Faber & Faber). Merrimack Bk Serv.

London: Urban Patterns, Problems, & Policies. Ed. by David Donnison & David Eversley. LC 73-80440. (Centre for Environmental Studies Ser.: Vol. 2). 1973. 32.50x (ISBN 0-8039-0270-0). Sage.

London Venture. Michael Arlen. Ed. by Herbert Van Thal. 1920-1968. pap. 2.50 (ISBN 0-304-92614-0). Dufour.

London Yankees: Portraits of American Writers & Artists in England, 1894-1914. Stanley Weintraub. Tr. by Eileen Ellenboger. LC 78-22276. 1979. 14.95 (ISBN 0-15-152978-7). HarBraceJ.

London, Your Sightseeing Guide. rev. ed. (Illus.). 92p. 1980. pap. 2.95 (ISBN 0-7095-0147-1, Pub. by B T A). Merrimack Bk Serv.

London Zoo. Sally Holloway. (Folio Miniature Ser.). 1976. 4.95 (ISBN 0-7181-1475-2, Pub. by Michael Joseph). Merrimack Bk Serv.

Londonderrys: Portrait of a Noble Family. H. Montgomery Hyde. (Illus.). 1979. 30.00 (ISBN 0-241-10153-0, Pub. by Hamish Hamilton England). David & Charles.

Londoners: An Absurdity. Robert S. Hichens. Ed. by Ian Fletcher & John Stokes. LC 76-24388. (Decadent Consciousness Ser.: Vol. 16). 1977. Repr. of 1898 ed. lib. bdg. 38.00 (ISBN 0-8240-2764-7). Garland Pub.

London's First Railway. R. H. Thomas. 1972. 27.00 (ISBN 0-7134-0468-X, Pub. by Batsford England). David & Charles.

London's Historic Railway Stations. John Betjeman. (Illus.). 1978. pap. 10.95 (ISBN 0-7195-3426-7). Transatlantic.

London's Homeless. John Greve. 76p. 1964. pap. text ed. 3.75x (Pub. by Bedford England). Renouf.

London's Local Railways. Alan Jackson. LC 77-85017. 1978. 38.00 (ISBN 0-7153-7479-6). David & Charles.

London's Lost Route to the Sea: An Historical Account of the Inland Navigations Which Linked the Thames to the English Channel. 3rd ed. P. A. Vine. (Inland Waterways Histories Ser.). 1973. 14.95 (ISBN 0-7153-6203-8). David & Charles.

London's Pageantry. Colourmaster. (Travel in England Ser.). (Illus.). 64p. 1975. 7.95 (ISBN 0-85933-110-5). Transatlantic.

London's Railways Today. John Glover. LC 80-70293. (Illus.). 96p. 1981. 17.95 (ISBN 0-7153-8070-2). David & Charles.

London's Restaurants. 1978. pap. 2.95 o.p. (ISBN 0-686-01035-3, 8077, Dist. by Arco). Barrie & Jenkins.

London's River: The Story of a City. Eric De Mare. (Illus.). 1978. 7.95 (ISBN 0-370-00846-4, Pub. by Chatto Bodley Jonathan). Merrimack Bk Serv.

London's Waterways. Martyn Denney. (Illus.). 1978. 11.50 o.s.i. (ISBN 0-7134-0558-9). Hippocrene Bks.

London's Zoo. Gwynne Vevers. LC 76-363958. (Illus.). 1979. 12.50 (ISBN 0-370-10440-4, Pub. by Chatto Bodley Jonathan). Merrimack Bk Serv.

Lone Bull's Horse Raid. Paul Goble & Dorothy Goble. LC 73-76546. (Illus.). 64p. (gr. 4-6). 1973. 9.95 (ISBN 0-87888-059-3). Bradbury Pr.

L'one Dictionaire Encyclopedique. (Illus.). 1520p. (Fr.). 1980. 99.95 (ISBN 2-03-020127-8). Larousse.

Lone Fox Dancing. Ruskin Bond. 8.00 (ISBN 0-89253-497-4); flexible cloth 4.00 (ISBN 0-89253-498-2). Ind-US Inc.

Lone Gun. Howard Rigsby. 144p. 1978. pap. 1.25 o.p. (ISBN 0-449-14005-9, GM). Fawcett.

Lone Pilgrim. Laurie Colwin. LC 80-24572. 224p. 1981. 9.95 (ISBN 0-394-51453-X). Knopf.

Lone Ranger. Illus. by Tom Beecham. LC 80-52867. (Rocking Bks.). (Illus.). 24p. (ps-3). 1981. pap. 2.95 saddle stitched (ISBN 0-394-84690-7). Random.

Lone Ranger. Frank Striker. (Western Fiction Ser.). 1980. lib. bdg. 9.95 (ISBN 0-8398-2676-1). Gregg.

Lone Ranger: A Pop-up Book. Ib Penick. LC 80-52868. (Pop-up Bks.: No. 43). (Illus.). 16p. (ps-3). 1981. pap. 4.95 boards o.p. (ISBN 0-394-84691-5). Random.

Lone Ranger & the Gold Robbery. Fran Striker. (Lone Ranger Ser.: No. 3). 1978. pap. 1.75 (ISBN 0-523-40876-5, Dist. by Independent News Co.). Pinnacle Bks.

Lone Star Man: The Life of Ira Aten. Harold Preece. 1960. 6.95 (ISBN 0-8038-4255-4). Hastings.

Lone Wolf Howling: The Thematic Content of Ronald Duncan's Plays. William B. Wahl. (Salzburg Studies in English Literature, Poetic Drama, & Poetic Theory: No. 19). 320p. 1973. pap. text ed. 25.00x (ISBN 0-391-01552-4). Humanities.

Lone Woman & Others. Constance Urdang. LC 80-5261. (Pitt Poetry Ser.). 1980. 9.95 (ISBN 0-8229-3430-2); pap. 4.50 (ISBN 0-8229-5320-X). U of Pittsburgh Pr.

Loneliness. Craig W. Ellison. LC 79-55681. 1980. 8.95 (ISBN 0-915684-57-8). Christian Herald.

Loneliness. Ed. by Paul A. Wellington. 1980. pap. 2.50 (ISBN 0-8309-0287-2). Herald Hse.

Loneliness & Communion: A Study of Wordsworth's Thought & Experience. Kenneth Eisold. (Salzburg Studies in English Literature, Romantic Reassessment: No. 13). 1973. pap. text ed. 25.00x (ISBN 0-391-01371-8). Humanities.

Loneliness & Existential Freedom. James Park. (Existential Freedom Ser.: No. 4). 1974. pap. 2.00x (ISBN 0-89231-004-9). Existential Bks.

Loneliness Is Not a Disease. Tim Timmons. LC 80-83845. 1981. pap. 4.95 (ISBN 0-89081-264-0). Harvest Hse.

Loneliness Is Rotting on a Bookrack. Johnny Hart. (B.C. Ser.). (Illus.). 1978. pap. 1.50 (ISBN 0-449-13942-5, GM). Fawcett.

Loneliness: Living Between the Times. Nancy Potts. 1978. pap. 3.95 (ISBN 0-88207-630-2). Victor Bks.

Loneliness of Children. John Killinger. LC 79-56378. 320p. 1980. 12.95 (ISBN 0-8149-0830-6). Vanguard.

Loneliness: Understanding & Dealing with It. Harvey H. Potthoff. LC 76-13900. 128p. 1976. 5.95 o.p. (ISBN 0-687-22579-5). Abingdon.

Lonely & Afraid: Counseling the Hard to Reach. Alice H. Collins. LC 78-76614. 1969. pap. 8.50 (ISBN 0-672-63055-9). Odyssey Pr.

Lonely, but Never Alone. Nicky Cruz & Madalene Harris. 192p. (Orig.). 1981. pap. 5.95 (ISBN 0-310-43361-4). Zondervan.

Lonely Eagles. Robert C. Rose. (Illus.). 1976. pap. 6.00 (ISBN 0-911720-68-5, Pub. by Tuskegee). Aviation.

Lonely Gun. Gordon D. Shirreffs. 1977. pap. 1.50 (ISBN 0-505-51175-4). Tower Bks.

Lonely Hunter: A Biography of Carson McCullers. Virginia Spencer Carr. LC 74-9478. 1976. pap. 5.95 (ISBN 0-385-12289-6, Anch). Doubleday.

Lonely Lady of San Clemente: The Story of Pat Nixon. Lester David. LC 78-3299. (Illus.). 1978. 9.95 o.s.i. (ISBN 0-690-01688-3, TYC-T). T Y Crowell.

Lonely Law. Matt Stuart. 1977. pap. 1.25 o.p. (ISBN 0-445-00434-7). Popular Lib.

Lonely Londoners. Samuel Selvon. 126p. (Orig.). 1979. 9.00 (ISBN 0-89410-113-7); pap. 5.00 (ISBN 0-89410-112-9). Three Continents.

Lonely Man. Faith Baldwin. 1980. pap. write for info. (ISBN 0-671-83095-3). PB.

Lonely Place. Ruth M. Sears. (Orig.). 1976. pap. 1.25 o.p. (ISBN 0-685-64013-2, LB343ZK, Leisure Bks). Nordon Pubns.

Lonely Rose. Penni Shubin. LC 78-10136. Date not set. 11.95 (ISBN 0-87949-153-1). Ashley Bks.

Lonely Scoundrel: A Supplement to the Perishing Republic. Jerome Bahr. LC 73-80240. 89p. 1974. 7.00 o.p. (ISBN 0-686-63592-2). Trempealeau.

Lonely Sky. William Bridgeman & Jacqueline Hazard. Ed. by James Gilbert. LC 79-7232. (Flight: Its First Seventy-Five Years Ser.). (Illus.). 1979. Repr. of 1955 ed. lib. bdg. 24.00x (ISBN 0-405-12148-2). Arno.

Lonely the Autumn Bird: Two Novels. Richard McBride. LC 63-21868. 93p. (Orig.). 1963. pap. 3.25 (ISBN 0-8040-0189-8). Swallow.

Lonely Toys. Miriam Lynch. 1978. pap. 1.50 o.p. (ISBN 0-523-40168-X). Pinnacle Bks.

Lonely Warrior: Kamehameha the Great of Hawaii. Kathleen D. Mellen. (Kathleene Dickenson Mellen's Epic Saga of the Hawaiian Kingdom Ser.). (Illus.). 177p. 1980. pap. 6.95 o.p. (ISBN 0-8038-4334-8). Hastings.

Lonely Wayfaring Man: Emerson & Some Englishmen. Townshend Scudder. LC 80-2545. 1981. Repr. of 1936 ed. 32.50 (ISBN 0-404-19270-X). AMS Pr.

Loner. James W. Smith. 1977. pap. 1.25 o.s.i. (ISBN 0-515-04377-X). Jove Pubns.

Loner. Ester Wier. (Illus.). (gr. 7-9). 1963. 5.95 o.p. (ISBN 0-679-20097-5). McKay.

Lonergan Enterprise. Frederick E. Crowe. LC 80-51569. 120p. (Orig.). 1980. pap. 5.00 (ISBN 0-936384-02-6). Cowley Pubns.

Loners, Losers, & Lovers: Elderly Tenants in a Slum Hotel. Joyce Stephens. LC 75-40874. 138p. 1976. pap. 6.95 (ISBN 0-295-95762-X). U of Wash Pr.

Loners: Short Stories About the Young & Alienated. Ed. by L. M. Schulman. (gr. 7 up). 1970. 5.95g o.s.i. (ISBN 0-02-781390-8). Macmillan.

Lonesome Coyote. Gordon Allred. (gr. 6-11). 1969. 4.25 o.p. (ISBN 0-8313-0003-5); PLB 6.19 o.p. (ISBN 0-685-13775-9). Lantern.

Lonesome End. Curtis Bishop. LC 63-18501. (gr. 7-9). 1963. PLB 4.69 o.p. (ISBN 0-397-30695-4). Lippincott.

Lonesome Little Colt. Clarence W. Anderson. (gr. k-3). 1961. 4.95g o.s.i. (ISBN 0-02-704840-3). Macmillan.

Lonesome River. Frank Gruber. 1979. pap. 1.75 o.p. (ISBN 0-451-08844-1, E8856, Sig). NAL.

Long African Day. Norman Myers. LC 71-182022. (Illus.). 400p. 1972. 25.00 o.s.i. (ISBN 0-02-588200-7). Macmillan.

Long Afternoon. John Kollock. 8.95 (ISBN 0-932298-01-X). Green Hill.

Long Ago in Florence: The Story of Della Robbia Sculpture. Marion Downer. LC 68-27707. (Illus.). (gr. 3-6). 1968. 6.50 o.p. (ISBN 0-688-41205-X); PLB 6.24 (ISBN 0-688-51205-4). Lothrop.

Long & Short of Measurement. Vicki Cobb. LC 72-4903. (Finding-Out Books for Science & Social Studies, Grades 1-4). (Illus.). 64p. (gr. 2-4). 1973. PLB 6.95 (ISBN 0-8193-0628-2, Pub. by Parents). Enslow Pubs.

Long & the Short & the Tall. Willis Hall. pap. 1.35x o.s.i. (ISBN 0-87830-532-7). Theatre Arts.

Long Arm of Gil Hamilton. Larry Niven. 1976. pap. 1.95 (ISBN 0-345-28922-6). Ballantine.

Long Black Song: Essays in Black American Literature & Culture. Houston A. Baker, Jr. LC 72-77261. 1972. 10.95x (ISBN 0-8139-0403-X). U Pr of Va.

Long Chance. Peter Kyne. 1976. lib. bdg. 14.85x (ISBN 0-89968-054-2). Lightyear.

Long Christmas Dinner & Other Plays in One Act. Thornton Wilder. 1980. pap. 2.50 (ISBN 0-380-50245-3, 50245, Bard). Avon.

Long Day at Shiloh. Don Bannister. LC 80-24112. 288p. 1981. 11.95 (ISBN 0-394-50680-4). Knopf.

Long Default: New York City & the Urban Fiscal Crisis. William K. Tabb. LC 80-8933. 1981. 16.00 (ISBN 0-85345-571-6). Monthly Rev.

Long Distance. LaVada Weir. LC 74-971. (Laurie Newman Adventures Ser). 32p. (gr. 3-9). 1974. 5.95 (ISBN 0-87191-333-X). Creative Ed.

Long Divorce. Edmund Crispin. (Penguin Crime Monthly Ser.). 256p. 1981. pap. 2.95 (ISBN 0-14-001304-0). Penguin.

Long Fellow: Story of the Great Irish Patriot, Eamon De Vallera. Jack Steffan. (gr. 7 up). 1966. 4.95 o.s.i. (ISBN 0-02-786930-X). Macmillan.

Long Goodbye. Raymond Chandler. 1977. pap. 2.25 (ISBN 0-345-28859-9). Ballantine.

Long Goodbye: A Trilogy. Yury V. Trifonov. Tr. by Helen Burlingame & Ellendea Proffer. LC 77-17658. (Ardis Bk.). 1978. 15.00 o.s.i. (ISBN 0-06-014371-1, HarpT). Har-Row.

Long Haul: A Social History of the British Commercial Vehicle Industry. Michael Seth-Smith. (Illus.). 1975. text ed. 15.00x (ISBN 0-09-124440-4). Humanities.

Long Haul: Truckers, Truck Stops, & Trucking. James H. Thomas. (Illus.). 12.95 (ISBN 0-87870-055-2); pap. 6.95 (ISBN 0-87870-057-9). Memphis St Univ.

Long Island Light. William Heyen. LC 78-68733. 1979. 10.00 (ISBN 0-8149-0811-X); pap. 7.95 (ISBN 0-8149-0817-9); ltd. ed. 20.00 (ISBN 0-8149-0818-7). Vanguard.

Long Island Seafood Cookbook. J. George Frederick. Ed. by Jean Joyce. 1971. pap. 4.00 (ISBN 0-486-22677-8). Dover.

Long John Nebel: Biography of Charlatan. Donald Bain. (Illus.). 1974. 8.95 o.s.i. (ISBN 0-02-505950-5). Macmillan.

Long Lavender Look. John D. MacDonald. LC 78-37010. 1972. 5.50 o.s.i. (ISBN 0-397-00739-6). Lippincott.

Long Life to You: Modern Medicine at Work. Leo Schneider. LC 68-25195. (Illus.). (gr. 7 up). 1968. 4.95 o.p. (ISBN 0-15-248632-1, HJ). HarBraceJ.

Long Look at Man: Who Is He? What Is He? Where Is He Going? Elva B. Smith. 1981. 3.50 (ISBN 0-8059-2693-3). Dorrance.

Long Lost Coelacanth & Other Living Fossils. Aliki. LC 72-83773. (Let's-Read-&-Find-Out Science Bk.). (Illus.). 40p. (gr. k-3). 1973. 7.95 (ISBN 0-690-50478-0, TYC-J); PLB 6.89 o.p. (ISBN 0-690-50479-9). T Y Crowell.

Long Lost Love. Julia Alcott. Date not set. pap. 1.25 o.p. (ISBN 0-451-07190-5, Y7190, Sig). NAL.

Long March, Nineteen Thirty-Four to Thirty-Five: A Red Army Survives to Bring Communism to China. Robert Goldston. LC 74-157748. (World Focus Bks). (Illus.). (gr. 7 up). 1971. PLB 4.47 o.p. (ISBN 0-531-02153-X). Watts.

Long Old Road: An Autobiography. Horace R. Cayton. LC 64-24280. (Paperbacks Ser.: No. 53). 412p. 1970. pap. 3.95 (ISBN 0-295-95069-2, WP53). U of Wash Pr.

Long-Range Environmental Outlook. Environmental Studies Board. x, 198p. 1980. pap. text ed. 10.50 (ISBN 0-309-03038-2). Natl Acad Pr.

Long-Range Environmental Outlook. 1980. 11.25. Natl Acad Pr.

Long-Range Forecasting: From Crystal Ball to Computer. J. Scott Armstrong. LC 77-25176. 1978. 33.50 (ISBN 0-471-03002-3, Pub by Wiley-Interscience). Wiley.

Long Range Planning: Executive Viewpoint. E. Kirby Warren. 1966. ref. ed. 15.95 (ISBN 0-13-540187-9). P-H.

Long-Range Planning for Urban Research & Development: Technological Considerations. Committee On Urban Technology - Division Of Engineering. (Illus., Orig.). 1969. pap. 4.75 (ISBN 0-309-01729-7). Natl Acad Pr.

Long Range Planning for Your Business: An Operating Manual. Merritt L. Kastens. (Illus.). 1976. 13.95 (ISBN 0-8144-5413-5). Am Mgmt.

Long Revenge. June Tompson. 160p. 1981. pap. 2.25 (ISBN 0-553-14723-4). Bantam.

Long Road to Freedom. Hall. LC 78-60562. 1978. pap. 6.50 (ISBN 0-913408-41-7). Friends United.

Long Road to Peace. Srinibas Bhattacharya. 1977. 5.00 o.p. (ISBN 0-533-02008-5). Vantage.

Long Run. Joe Henderson. LC 75-20958. (Illus.). 1976. pap. 3.95 (ISBN 0-89037-101-6); handbk. 5.95 (ISBN 0-89037-102-4). Anderson World.

Long Shadow. Denise Robins. 1979. pap. 1.75 (ISBN 0-380-47167-1, 47167). Avon.

Long Ships Passing. Walter Havighurst. 1961. 12.95 (ISBN 0-02-549090-7); pap. 1.65 (ISBN 0-02-033100-2). Macmillan.

Long Ships Passing: The Story of the Great Lakes. rev. ed. Walter Havinghurst. LC 75-16406. (Illus.). 368p. (gr. 9-12). 1975. 12.95 (ISBN 0-02-549100-8, 54910). Macmillan.

Long Shot. Paul Monette. pap. 5.95. Avon.

Long Shots. Edwin Corley. LC 80-1089. 408p. 1981. 12.95 (ISBN 0-385-15922-6). Doubleday.

Long Steel Rail: The Railroad in American Folksong. Norm Cohen. LC 80-14874. (Music in American Life Ser.). (Illus.). 738p. 1981. 49.95 (ISBN 0-252-00343-8). U of Ill Pr.

Long Term Care: Experience & a Framework for Analysis. William Scanlow et al. (Health Policy & the Elderly Ser.). 162p. 1979. pap. 7.00 (ISBN 0-87766-246-0, 25300). Urban Inst.

Long Term Care in Transition: Nursing Homes on the Cutting Edge. David B. Smith. (Illus.). 350p. 1981. text ed. price not set (ISBN 0-914904-65-5). Health Admin Pr.

Long-Term Environmental Radiation Standards. Committee on Radioactive Waste Management. 1979. pap. 5.50 (ISBN 0-309-02879-5). Natl Acad Pr.

Long-Term Hazards from Environmental Chemicals. Royal Society of London. Ed. by Richard Doll & A. E. McClean. 1979. 25.00x (ISBN 0-85403-110-3, Pub. by Royal Soc London). Scholium Intl.

Long Term Marriage. Floyd Thatcher & Harriett Thatcher. 1980. 8.95 (ISBN 0-8499-0096-4). Word Bks.

Long Term Results in Plastic & Reconstruction Surgery. Robert M. Goldwyn. 1980. text ed. 95.00 (ISBN 0-316-31972-4, Little Med Div). Little.

Long-Term Worldwide Effects of Multiple Nuclear - Weapons Detonations. Assembly of Mathematical & Physical Sciences, National Research Council. LC 75-29733. xvi, 213p. 1975. pap. 8.50 (ISBN 0-309-02418-8). Natl Acad Pr.

Long Time Coming. Phyllis A. Whitney. (RL 7). 1976. pap. 1.50 (ISBN 0-451-09310-0, W9310, Sig). NAL.

Long Time Coming: The Struggle to Unionize America's Farm Workers. Richard Meister & Anne Loftis. LC 76-54510. 1977. 17.95 (ISBN 0-02-583920-9, 58392). Macmillan.

Long Tomorrow. Leigh Brackett. 256p. 1975. pap. 1.50 o.p. (ISBN 0-345-24833-3). Ballantine.

Long Vendetta. Jonathan Gant. (YA) 4.95 o.p. (ISBN 0-685-07442-0, Avalon). Bouregy.

Long View: The Final Volume in the Saga of Rissa. F. M. Busby. LC 76-28472. 1976. 7.95 o.p. (ISBN 0-399-11875-6, Dist. by Putnam). Berkley Pub.

Long Vowels. Virginia Polish. (Starting off with Phonics Ser.: Bk. 6). (gr. k). 1980. pap. text ed. 2.21 (ISBN 0-87895-056-7); tchrs. manual 2.00 (ISBN 0-87895-066-4). Modern Curr.

Long Walk. Lynn R. Bailey. 1979. 8.95 (ISBN 0-87026-047-2). Westernlore.

Long Waves of Capitalist Development. Ernest Mandell. LC 80-16244. (Studies in Moderm Capitalism). 112p. 1980. 14.95 (ISBN 0-521-23000-4). Cambridge U Pr.

Long Way. Bernard Moitessier. 1979. 17.95x (ISBN 0-8464-0075-8). Beekman Pubs.

Long Way, Baby: Behind-the-Scenes in Women's Pro Tennis. Grace Lichtenstein. LC 74-1166. 1974. 6.95 o.p. (ISBN 0-688-00263-3). Morrow.

Long Way Down. Robb White. LC 77-79561. (gr. 7-12). 1977. PLB 5.95 (ISBN 0-385-13149-6); PLB (ISBN 0-385-13149-6). Doubleday.

Long Way Down. Collin Wilcox. 1979. pap. 1.75 (ISBN 0-515-05195-0). Jove Pubns.

Long Way from Home. Maureen C. Wartski. LC 80-19247. (gr. 6 up). 1980. PLB 9.95 (ISBN 0-664-32674-9). Westminster.

Long Way from Verona. Jane Gardam. LC 76-171923. 192p. (YA) (gr. 7-12). 1972. 4.95 o.s.i. (ISBN 0-02-735780-5). Macmillan.

Long Way from Verona. Jane Gardam. LC 76-171923. 256p. (gr. 7 up). 1974. pap. 1.25 o.s.i. (ISBN 0-02-043220-8, 04322, Collier). Macmillan.

Long Way Home. Margot Benary-Isbert. LC 59-7519. (gr. 7-9). 1959. 5.95 o.p. (ISBN 0-15-248830-8, HJ). HarBraceJ.

Long Way to Texas. Lee McElroy. LC 76-2786. 192p. 1976. 5.95 o.p. (ISBN 0-385-12128-8). Doubleday.

Long Way to Whiskey Creek. Patricia Beatty. LC 75-134486. (Illus.). (gr. 5-9). 1971. pap. 7.20 o.p. (ISBN 0-688-31427-9). Morrow.

Long Winters Night. Sandra Stanford. 192p. 1981. pap. 1.50 (ISBN 0-671-57058-7). S&S.

Long Wire. Barry Cord. 1978. pap. 1.25 (ISBN 0-505-51238-6). Tower Bks.

Long Year A.D. 69. Kenneth Wellesley. LC 76-5390. 1977. 24.50 o.p. (ISBN 0-89158-609-1). Westview.

Longarm. Tabor Evans. (Orig.). 1978. pap. 1.95 (ISBN 0-515-05983-8). Jove Pubns.

Longarm & the Avenging Angels, No. 3. Tabor Evans. 1978. pap. 1.95 (ISBN 0-515-05899-8, 04791-0). Jove Pubns.

Longarm & the Bandit Queen. Tabor Evans. (Longarm Ser.: No. 17). 256p. (Orig.). 1981. pap. 1.75 (ISBN 0-515-05309-0). Jove Pubns.

Longarm & the Boot Hillers. Tabor Evans. (Longarm Ser.: No. 34). (Orig.). 1981. pap. 1.95 (ISBN 0-515-05590-5). Jove Pubns.

Longarm & the Dragon Hunters. Tabor Evans. (Longarm Ser.: No. 26). 255p. (Orig.). 1980. pap. 1.75 (ISBN 0-515-05582-4). Jove Pubns.

Longarm & the Ghost Dancers. Tabor Evans. (Longarm Ser.: No. 22). 223p. (Orig.). 1980. pap. 1.75 (ISBN 0-515-05314-7). Jove Pubns.

Longarm & the Golden Lady. Tabor Evans. (Longarm Ser.: No. 32). (Orig.). 1981. pap. 1.95 (ISBN 0-515-05588-3). Jove Pubns.

Longarm & the Hatchet Men, No. 9. Tabor Evans. 1979. pap. 1.95 (ISBN 0-515-05973-0). Jove Pubns.

Longarm & the Highgraders: No. 7. Tabor Evans. (Orig.). 1979. pap. 1.95 (ISBN 0-515-05901-3). Jove Pubns.

Longarm & the Laredo Loop. Tabor Evans. (Longarm Ser.: No. 33). (Orig.). 1981. pap. 1.95 (ISBN 0-515-05589-1). Jove Pubns.

Longarm & the Loggers, No. 6. Tabor Evans. (Orig.). 1979. pap. 1.95 (ISBN 0-515-05900-5). Jove Pubns.

Longarm & the Molly Maguires. Tabor Evans. (Longarm Ser.: No. 10). 1979. pap. 1.75 (ISBN 0-515-04753-8). Jove Pubns.

Longarm & the Mounties. Tabor Evans. (Longarm Ser.: No. 16). 252p. (Orig.). 1980. pap. 1.75 (ISBN 0-515-05308-2). Jove Pubns.

Longarm & the Nesters: No. 8. Tabor Evans. (Orig.). 1979. pap. 1.95 (ISBN 0-515-05985-4). Jove Pubns.

Longarm & the Railroaders. Tabor Evans. (Longarm Ser.: No. 24). 252p. (Orig.). 1980. pap. 1.75 (ISBN 0-515-05316-3). Jove Pubns.

Longarm & the Rurales. Tabor Evans. (Longarm Ser.: No. 27). (Orig.). pap. 1.75 (ISBN 0-515-05583-2). Jove Pubns.

Longarm & the Sheepherders. Tabor Evans. (Longarm Ser.: No. 21). 256p. (Orig.). 1980. pap. 1.95 (ISBN 0-515-05906-4). Jove Pubns.

Longarm & the Texas Rangers. Tabor Evans. (Longarm Ser.: No. 11). (Orig.). 1979. pap. 1.95 (ISBN 0-515-05902-1). Jove Pubns.

Longarm & the Town Tamer. Tabor Evans. (Longarm Ser.: No. 23). 269p. (Orig.). 1980. pap. 1.75 (ISBN 0-515-05315-5). Jove Pubns.

Longarm & the Wendigo. Tabor Evans. (Longarm Ser.: No. 4). 256p. (Orig.). 1979. pap. 1.95 (ISBN 0-515-05972-2). Jove Pubns.

Longarm at Robber's Roost. Tabor Evans. (Longarm Ser.: No. 20). 256p. (Orig.). 1980. pap. 1.95 (ISBN 0-515-05931-5). Jove Pubns.

Longarm in Leadville. Tabor Evans. (Longarm Ser.: No. 14). (Orig.). 1979. pap. 1.75 (ISBN 0-515-05306-6). Jove Pubns.

Longarm in Lincoln County. Tabor Evans. (Longarm Ser.: No. 12). 254p. (Orig.). 1979. pap. 1.95 (ISBN 0-515-05903-X). Jove Pubns.

Longarm in Northfield. Tabor Evans. (Longarm Ser.: No. 31). (Orig.). 1981. pap. 1.95 (ISBN 0-515-05586-7). Jove Pubns.

Longarm in the Four Corners. Tabor Evans. (Longarm Ser.: No. 19). 224p. (Orig.). 1980. pap. 1.95 (ISBN 0-515-05905-6). Jove Pubns.

Longarm in the Indian Nation. Tabor Evans. (Longarm Ser.: N0. 5). 272p. (Orig.). 1979. pap. 1.75 (ISBN 0-515-04796-1). Jove Pubns.

Longarm in the Sand Hills. Tabor Evans. (Longarm Ser.: No. 13). (Orig.). 1979. pap. 1.75 (ISBN 0-515-05305-8). Jove Pubns.

Longarm on the Big Muddy. Tabor Evans. (Longarm Ser.: No. 29). 224p. (Orig.). 1981. pap. 1.95 (ISBN 0-515-05585-9). Jove Pubns.

Longarm on the Border: No. 2. Tabor Evans. (Orig.). 1978. pap. 1.95 (ISBN 0-515-05378-3). Jove Pubns.

Longarm on the Devil's Trail. Tabor Evans. (Longarm Ser.: No. 15). 224p. (Orig.). 1979. pap. 1.95 (ISBN 0-515-05904-8). Jove Pubns.

Longarm on the Humboldt. Tabor Evans. (Longarm Ser.: No. 28). 256p. (Orig.). 1981. pap. 1.95 (ISBN 0-515-05584-0). Jove Pubns.

Longarm on the Old Mission Trail. Tabor Evans. (Longarm Ser.: No. 25). 253p. (Orig.). 1980. pap. 1.95 (ISBN 0-515-05974-9). Jove Pubns.

Longarm on the Yellowstone. Tabor Evans. (Longarm Ser.: No. 18). 256p. (Orig.). 1980. pap. 1.75 (ISBN 0-515-05310-4). Jove Pubns.

Longarm South of the Gila. Tabor Evans. (Longarm Ser.; Men's Western Ser.: No. 30). 256p. (Orig.). 1981. pap. 1.95 (ISBN 0-515-05587-5). Jove Pubns.

Longboat to Hawaii. Alexander C. Brown. LC 74-22317. (Illus.). 254p. 1974. 12.50 (ISBN 0-87033-201-5). Cornell Maritime.

Longden Legend. B. K. Beckwith. LC 72-5185. (Illus.). 256p. 1973. 9.95 o.p. (ISBN 0-498-01242-5); pap. 2.95 o.p. (ISBN 0-498-01950-0). A S Barnes.

Longer Thou Livest. W. Wager. Ed. by R. Mark Benbow. Bd. with Enough Is As Good As a Feast. LC 67-15815. (Regents Renaissance Drama Ser). 1967. 9.75x (ISBN 0-8032-0284-9); pap. 1.65x (ISBN 0-8032-5285-4, BB 225, Bison). U of Nebr Pr.

Longest Day. Cornelius Ryan. 352p. 1975. pap. 2.75 (ISBN 0-445-08380-8). Popular Lib.

Longest Highway. Hilary Milton. LC 78-74526. 1979. pap. 2.50 (ISBN 0-89191-138-3). Cook.

Longest Street: A History of Lafourche Parish & GrandIsle. Tanya Ditto. Ed. by Doug Woolfolk. (Illus.). 136p. 1980. 13.00 (ISBN 0-86518-013-X). Moran Pub Corp.

Longevity Factor. Walter McQuade & Ann Aikman. 1981. pap. 2.95 (ISBN 0-671-81611-X). PB.

Longevity of Athletes. Anthony P. Polednak. (Illus.). 284p. 1979. text ed. 13.75 (ISBN 0-398-03867-8). C C Thomas.

Longhorn Brand. Wade Hamilton. 1978. pap. 1.25 (ISBN 0-505-51248-3). Tower Bks.

Longhorns. J. Frank Dobie. LC 79-67706. (Illus.). 405p. 1980. pap. 7.95 (ISBN 0-292-74627-X). U of Tex Pr.

Longing for Darkness: Kamante's Tales from Out of Africa. Ed. by Peter Beard. LC 74-19092. (Illus.). 242p. 1975. 19.95 o.p. (ISBN 0-15-153080-7). HarBraceJ.

Longings. Sylvia W. Greene. 352p. (Orig.). 1981. pap. 2.50 (ISBN 0-89083-706-6). Zebra.

Longinus on the Sublime: The Peri Hupsous in Translations by Nicolas Boileau-Despreaux (1674) & William Smith (1739) Cassius Longinus. LC 75-8892. 390p. 1975. lib. bdg. 40.00x (ISBN 0-8201-1153-8). Schol Facsimiles.

Longitudinal Data Analysis. James S. Coleman. LC 80-66309. Date not set. text ed. 15.00x (ISBN 0-465-04224-4). Basic. Postponed.

Longitudinal Research in Drug Use: Empirical Findings & Methodological Issues. Ed. by Denise B. Kandel. 1978. 22.50 (ISBN 0-470-26287-7). Halsted Pr.

Longman Anthology of American Drama. Lee Jacobus. (Illus.). 512p. 1981. pap. text ed. 14.95 (ISBN 0-582-28242-X). Longman.

Longman Atlas of Modern British History: A Visual Guide to British Society & Politics, 1700-1970. Christopher Cook & John Stevenson. (Illus.). 1978. text ed. 17.95x (ISBN 0-582-36485-X); pap. text ed. 10.95x (ISBN 0-582-36486-8). Longman.

Longman Dictionary of Contemporary English. Ed. by Paul Proctor. (Illus.). 1979. text ed. 12.95x (ISBN 0-582-52571-3). Longman.

Longman Dictionary of English Idioms. Laurence Urdang Associates. (Illus.). 1979. 15.95x (ISBN 0-582-55524-8). Longman.

Longman Dictionary of Scientific Usage. A. Godman & E. M. F. Payne. (Illus.). 1979. pap. text ed. 13.50x (ISBN 0-582-52587-X). Longman.

Longman Structural Readers: Handbook. W. Stannard Allen. 1976. pap. text ed. 1.75x (ISBN 0-582-53699-5). Longman.

Longmoor Military Railway. D. W. Ronald & R. J. Carter. 1974. 17.95 (ISBN 0-7153-6357-3). David & Charles.

Longs Peak: Its Story & a Climbing Guide. 8th rev. ed. Paul W. Nesbit. LC 72-86007. (Illus.). 1972. pap. 2.50x o.p. (ISBN 0-911746-02-1). Nesbit.

Longsword, Earl of Salisbury. Thomas Leland. Ed. by Michael F. Shugrue. (Flowering of the Novel Ser.: 1740-1775). lib. bdg. 50.00 (ISBN 0-8240-1159-7). Garland Pub.

Longton Hall Porcelain. Bernard Watney. 1957. 22.00 (ISBN 0-571-06580-5, Pub. by Faber & Faber). Merrimack Bk Serv.

Lontime Californ' A Documentary Study of an American Chinatown. Victor G. Nee & Brett De B. Nee. (Pantheon Village Ser.). 1981. pap. 6.95 (ISBN 0-394-73846-2). Pantheon.

Look Again. Tana Hoban. LC 72-127469. (Illus.). (gr. k-2). 1971. 8.95 (ISBN 0-02-744050-8). Macmillan.

Look-Alike Girl. Carol B. York. LC 80-22102. 96p. (gr. 4 up). 1980. 7.95 (ISBN 0-8253-0016-9). Beaufort Bks NY.

Look Alive, Libby. Catherine Woolley. (Illus.). (gr. 3-7). 1962. 8.25 (ISBN 0-688-21754-0). Morrow.

Look at a Flower. Ann O. Dowden. LC 63-12650. (Illus.). (gr. 5 up). 1963. 10.95 (ISBN 0-690-50656-2, TYC-J). T Y Crowell.

Look at a Gull. Dare Wright. (Illus.). (gr. k-3). 1967. PLB 4.99 (ISBN 0-394-91628-X, BYR). Random.

Look at Flowers. Rena K. Kirkpatrick. LC 77-27433. (Look at Science Ser.). (Illus.). (gr. k-3). 1978. PLB 9.95 (ISBN 0-8393-0061-1). Raintree Child.

Look at Insects. Rena K. Kirkpatrick. LC 77-27130. (Look at Science Ser.). (Illus.). (gr. k-3). 1978. PLB 9.95 (ISBN 0-8393-0062-X). Raintree Child.

Look at Leaves. Rena K. Kirkpatrick. LC 77-26662. (Look at Science Ser.). (Illus.). (gr. k-3). 1978. PLB 9.95 (ISBN 0-8393-0060-3). Raintree Child.

Look at Magnets. Rena K. Kirkpatrick. LC 77-26665. (Look at Science Ser.). (Illus.). (gr. k-3). 1978. PLB 9.95 (ISBN 0-8393-0063-8). Raintree Child.

Look at Mormonism. Gary J. Coleman. pap. 3.95 (ISBN 0-89036-142-8). Hawkes Pub Inc.

Look at Pond Life. Rena K. Kirkpatrick. LC 77-27243. (Look at Science Ser.). (Illus.). (gr. k-3). 1978. PLB 9.95 (ISBN 0-8393-0059-X). Raintree Child.

Look at Rainbow Colors. Rena K. Kirkpatrick. LC 77-27593. (Look at Science Ser.). (Illus.). (gr. k-3). 1978. PLB 9.95 (ISBN 0-8393-0064-6). Raintree Child.

Look at Seeds & Weeds. Rena K. Kirkpatrick. LC 77-27459. (Look at Science Ser.). (Illus.). (gr. k-3). 1978. PLB 9.95 (ISBN 0-8393-0065-4). Raintree Child.

Look at Shore Life. Rena K. Kirkpatrick. LC 77-27589. (Look at Science Ser.). (Illus.). (gr. k-3). 1978. PLB 9.95 (ISBN 0-8393-0067-0). Raintree Child.

Look at the Child. Aline D. Wolf. LC 78-58153. (Illus.). 1978. 4.95 (ISBN 0-9601016-2-4). Parent-Child Pr.

Look at the Harlequins! Vladimir Nabokov. 264p. 1981. pap. 5.95 (ISBN 0-07-045717-4). McGraw.

Look at the Vice Presidency. 2ed ed. Robert I. Alotta. 1981. write for info. Messner.

Look at This. Harlow Rockwell. LC 77-12716. (Ready-to-Read Ser.). (Illus.). (gr. 1-4). 1978. 7.95 (ISBN 0-02-777590-9, 77759). Macmillan.

Look at Trees. Rena K. Kirkpatrick. LC 77-27242. (Look at Science Ser.). (Illus.). (gr. k-3). 1978. PLB 9.95 (ISBN 0-8393-0066-2). Raintree Child.

Look at Weather. Rena K. Kirkpatrick. LC 78-6815. (Look at Science Ser.). (Illus.). (gr. k-3). 1978. PLB 9.95 (ISBN 0-8393-0069-7). Raintree Child.

Look at Your Eyes. Paul Showers. LC 62-12821. (Let's-Read-&-Find-Out Science Bk). (Illus.). (gr. k-3). 1962. bds. 6.95 (ISBN 0-690-50727-5, TYC-J); PLB 7.89 (ISBN 0-690-50728-3); filmstrip with record 11.95 (ISBN 0-690-50731-3); film with cassette 14.95 (ISBN 0-690-50733-X). T Y Crowell.

Look Back, a Look Ahead. Ed. by George B. Hafer. LC 80-10370. (Proceedings Ser.). (Illus.). 207p. (Orig.). pap. text ed. 10.00 (ISBN 0-87757-134-1). Am Mktg.

Look Back in Anger. John Osborne. Ed. by John R. Taylor. LC 76-127573. (Casebook Ser). 1970. pap. text ed. 2.50 o.s.i. (ISBN 0-87695-044-6). Aurora Pubs.

Look Back in Joy: Celebration of Gay Lovers. Malcolm Boyd. 128p. (Orig.). 1981. 20.00 (ISBN 0-917342-85-2, Pub. by Gay Sunshine); pap. 6.95 (ISBN 0-917342-77-1). Bookpeople.

Look Back on Death. Lesley Egan. LC 77-27725. 1978. 7.95 o.p. (ISBN 0-385-14303-6). Doubleday.

Look Back on Death. new large print ed. Lesley Egan. LC 80-28019. 1981. Repr. of 1978 ed. 9.95 (ISBN 0-89621-267-X). Thorndike Pr.

Look Back with Love: A Recollection of the Blue Ridge. Alberta P. Hannum. LC 70-89659. (Illus.). 1969. 10.00 (ISBN 0-8149-0007-0). Vanguard.

Look Better, Feel Better. Bess M. Mensendieck. (Illus.). 1954. 8.95 o.s.i. (ISBN 0-06-111140-6, HarpT). Har-Row.

Look Closely at Om. M. K. Kaw. 9.00 (ISBN 0-89253-768-X); flexible cloth 4.80 (ISBN 0-89253-769-8). Ind-US Inc.

Look for the Woman. Jay R. Nash. Ed. by George C. De Kay. (Illus.). 320p. 1981. 14.95 (ISBN 0-87131-336-7). M Evans.

Look High, Grow Tall. Elsa Turner. 4.50 o.p. (ISBN 0-685-48833-0). Nortex Pr.

Look Homeward Angel. Thomas Wolfe. 1929. pap. 5.95 (ISBN 0-684-71941-X, ScribT). Scribner.

Look How the Fish Live. J. F. Powers. 1976. pap. 1.95 o.p. (ISBN 0-345-25225-X). Ballantine.

Look! I Can Cook! A Simplified Guide to Cooking & Household Skills. Kay Bryan. LC 79-89358. 1979. pap. 7.95 (ISBN 0-88290-130-3). Horizon Utah.

Look-It-Up Book of Presidents. Wyatt Blassingame. LC 68-23656. (Look-It-up Book No. 5). (Illus.). (gr. 3-5). 1968. PLB 5.99 o.p. (ISBN 0-394-90748-5, BYR). Random.

Look-It-up Book of Space. Ira M. Freeman. LC 71-84840. (Look-It-up Books Ser.: No. 7). (Illus.). (gr. 3-5). 1969. PLB 5.99 (ISBN 0-394-90840-6, BYR). Random.

Look-It-Up Book of Stars and Planets. Patricia Lauber. (Look-It-up Books Ser.). (Illus.). (gr. 1-6). 1967. 4.95 o.p. (ISBN 0-394-81683-8, BYR); PLB 5.99 (ISBN 0-394-91683-2). Random.

Look Like Yourself & Love It! The 4-T Guide to Personal Style. Jane Segerstrom. LC 80-50836. (Illus.). 168p. (Orig.). 1980. pap. 14.95 (ISBN 0-936740-06-X). Triad Pr TX.

Look! No Doomsday. G. E. Vandeman. LC 71-141942. 1972. pap. 0.95 o.p. (ISBN 0-8163-0099-2, 12558-3). Pacific Pr Pub Assn.

Look No Further. Richard T. Hougen. 1958. 8.95 (ISBN 0-687-22622-8). Abingdon.

Look, Now Hear This: Combined Auditory Training & Speechreading Instruction. Janet Jeffers & Margaret Barley. (Illus.). 230p. 1979. text ed. 17.75 (ISBN 0-398-03830-9). C C Thomas.

Look Now, Pay Later: The Rise of Network Broadcasting. Laurence Bergreen. 1981. pap. 3.95 (ISBN 0-451-61966-8, ME1966, Ment). NAL.

Look of Music: Rare Musical Instruments, 1500-1900. Phillip Young. (Illus.). 240p. 1980. 35.00 (ISBN 0-295-95784-0); pap. 16.95 (ISBN 0-295-95785-9). U of Wash Pr.

Look of the Land. John F. Hart. LC 74-20995. (Foundations of Cultural Geography Ser.). (Illus.). 224p. 1975. text ed. 10.95 ref. ed. (ISBN 0-13-540534-3); pap. text ed. 5.95 (ISBN 0-13-540526-2). P-H.

Look of the West, 1860. Sir Richard Burton. LC 63-17030. (Illus.). 1963. pap. 3.75 (ISBN 0-8032-5029-0, BB 148, Bison). U of Nebr Pr.

Look Pride. Erwin A. Decker. 1981. 7.95 (ISBN 0-8062-1642-5). Carlton.

Look What I Wrote. Bonnie N. Miller. LC 79-67864. 1980. 8.95 (ISBN 0-934588-01-5). Ranger Assocs.

Look Who's Beautiful. Julia First. (gr. 5 up). 1980. PLB 7.90 (ISBN 0-531-04109-3, B21). Watts.

Look Who's Cooking. John Carafoli & Marci Carafoli. LC 73-93550. (Beginning-to-Read Bks). (Illus.). 32p. (gr. 2-4). 1974. 2.50 o.p. (ISBN 0-695-80475-8); lib. bdg. 3.39 o.p. (ISBN 0-695-40475-X); pap. 1.50 o.p. (ISBN 0-685-50751-3). Follett.

Look Who's Here. Bil Keane. (Family Circus Ser.). (Illus.). (gr. 4 up). 1978. pap. 1.50 (ISBN 0-449-14207-8, GM). Fawcett.

Look Within. Silo. 1980. pap. 3.95 (ISBN 0-87728-494-6). Weiser.

Look Younger, Live Longer. Gayelord Hauser. 1977. pap. 1.95 o.p. (ISBN 0-449-22931-9, Crest). Fawcett.

Looking Ahead: A Woman's Guide to the Problems & Joys of Growing Older. Troll et al. 1977. 10.95 (ISBN 0-13-540310-3, Spec); pap. 4.95 (ISBN 0-13-540302-2). P-H.

Looking at... Important Topics in the Social Studies. Ed. by Ann M. Williams. LC 80-22709. 90p. (Orig.). 1980. pap. 6.95 (ISBN 0-89994-250-4). Soc Sci Ed.

Looking at Ancient History. R. J. Unstead. (Illus.). (gr. 4-6). 1960. 9.95 (ISBN 0-02-790650-7). Macmillan.

Looking at Art. Alice E. Chase. LC 66-11947. (Illus.). (gr. 7-9). 1966. 8.95 o.p. (ISBN 0-690-50869-7, TYC-J). T Y Crowell.

Looking at Astrology. Liz Greene. LC 77-83149. (Illus.). 30p. (gr. 2-7). 1981. pap. 4.95 (ISBN 0-916360-13-X). CRCS Pubns WA.

Looking at Brazil. Sarita Kendall. LC 73-19605. (gr. 4-6). 1974. 8.95 (ISBN 0-397-31527-9). Lippincott.

Looking at Cows-Field Archaeology in the Nineteen-Eighties. Christopher Taylor. 1980. pap. 1.25x (ISBN 0-686-64696-7, Pub. by Coun Brit Arch England). Intl Schol Bk Serv.

Looking at English: An ESL Text-Workbook for Beginners, Bk. 1. Fred Malkemes & Deborah S. Pires. (English As a Second Language Ser.). (Illus.). 256p. 1981. pap. text ed. 7.95 (ISBN 0-13-540401-0). P-H.

Looking at English: An ESL Text-Workbook for Beginners, Bk. 2. Fred Malkemes & Deborah S. Pires. (Illus.). 288p. 1981. pap. text ed. 8.95 (ISBN 0-13-540427-4). P-H.

Looking at Faces & Remembering Them. Jacques Penry. 1971. pap. 9.95 (ISBN 0-236-17664-1, Pub. by Paul Elek). Merrimack Bk Serv.

Looking at Germany. George Kirby. LC 77-37629. (Looking at Other Countries Ser.). (Illus.). (gr. 4-6). 1972. 8.95 (ISBN 0-397-31337-3). Lippincott.

Looking at Guinea-Bissau: A New Nation's Development Strategy. Denis Goulet. LC 78-55460. (Occasional Papers: No. 9). 72p. 1978. 2.50 (ISBN 0-686-28695-2). Overseas Dev Council.

Looking at Innovation - Two Approaches to Educational Research. Peter Sheldrake & Stewart Berry. (General Ser.). 152p. 1975. pap. text ed. 13.25x (ISBN 0-85633-055-8, NFER). Humanities.

Looking at Italy. Rupert Martin. LC 67-10032. (Looking at Other Countries Ser). (Illus.). (gr. 4-6). 1967. 8.95 o.p. (ISBN 0-397-30966-X). Lippincott.

Looking at Life, Bk. 1. Daniel Castro. LC 77-99081. (Orig.). 1978. pap. 2.00 o.p. (ISBN 0-918038-06-5). Journey Pubns.

Looking at Lizards. Jane E. Hartman. LC 78-5357. (Illus.). (gr. 5-9). 1978. 7.95 (ISBN 0-8234-0330-0). Holiday.

Looking at Mammals. Peter Stanbury. 1972. 14.95x o.p. (ISBN 0-435-60800-2). Heinemann Ed.

Looking at Ourselves. Vincent Barry. 1977. 15.95x o.p. (ISBN 0-534-00464-4). Wadsworth Pub.

Looking at Sails. Bruce Banks & Dick Kenny. (Illus.). 1980. 12.95 (ISBN 0-393-03251-5). Norton.

Looking at School Achievement. Ray Sumner. (Exploring Education Ser). 95p. 1974. pap. text ed. 5.75x (ISBN 0-85633-038-8, NFER). Humanities.

Looking at Schools: Good, Bad, & Indifferent. Edward A. Wynne. LC 79-2798. 272p. 1980. 23.95 (ISBN 0-669-03292-1). Lexington Bks.

Looking at Spain. Rupert Martin. LC 73-78938. (Looking at Other Countries Ser). (Illus.). (gr. 4-6). 1970. 8.95 (ISBN 0-397-31137-0). Lippincott.

Looking at the American Government: Past & Present. Charles LaCerra, Jr. LC 78-61390. 1978. pap. text ed. 9.00 (ISBN 0-8191-0602-X). U Pr of Amer.

Looking at the Dance. Edwin Denby. 1978. pap. 2.50 o.p. (ISBN 0-445-04270-2). Popular Lib.

Looking at UFOs. (gr. 2-4). 1980. PLB 6.45 (ISBN 0-531-04098-4). Watts.

Looking Backward. Edward Bellamy. (Literature Ser). (gr. 9-12). 1970. pap. text ed. 3.50 (ISBN 0-87720-733-X). AMSCO Sch.

Looking Beyond. Frank W. Lemons. 78p. 1969. 2.95 (ISBN 0-87148-506-0); pap. 2.25 (ISBN 0-87148-507-9). Pathway Pr.

Looking Down Dark Holes & Climbing Mountains. Thomas Weinberg. (Illus.). 150p. (Orig.). 1979. pap. 6.95 (ISBN 0-9603484-0-9, Dist. by Bookpeople). Gordons & Weinberg.

Looking for a Bluebird. Joseph Wechsberg. LC 73-16801. (Illus.). 210p. 1974. Repr. of 1945 ed. lib. bdg. 19.75x (ISBN 0-8371-7234-9, WELO). Greenwood.

Looking for Fred Schmidt. Seymour Epstein. 320p. 1976. pap. 1.75 o.p. (ISBN 0-445-08423-5). Popular Lib.

Looking for Gold. Bradford Angier. (Illus.). 224p. 1981. pap. 8.95 (ISBN 0-8117-2034-9). Stackpole.

Looking for Ideas: A Display Manual for Libraries & Bookstores. Clair H. Wallick. LC 74-13003. (Illus.). 1970. 10.00 (ISBN 0-8108-0342-9). Scarecrow.

Looking for Rachel Wallace. Robert B. Parker. 1981. pap. 2.50 (ISBN 0-440-15316-6). Dell.

Looking for Susie. Bernadine Cook. (ps-3). 1959. PLB 4.95 o.p. (ISBN 0-201-09267-0, A-W Childrens). A-W.

Looking for Work. Susan Cheever. 256p. 1981. pap. 2.50 (ISBN 0-449-24389-3, Crest). Fawcett.

Looking for Zoe. Daniel B. Dodson. LC 80-16930. 340p. 1981. 12.95 (ISBN 0-396-07878-8). Dodd.

Looking Forward. Franklin D. Roosevelt. LC 72-2382. (FDR & the Era of the New Deal Ser). 284p. 1973. Repr. of 1933 ed. lib. bdg. 27.50 (ISBN 0-306-70477-3). Da Capo.

Looking Glasse for London & England by Thomas Lodge & Robert Greene: A Critical Edition. George A. Clugston. Ed. by Stephen Orgel. LC 79-3098. (Renaissance Drama Second Ser.). 300p. 1980. lib. bdg. 33.00 (ISBN 0-8240-4482-7). Garland Pub.

Looking Glasse for London & England by Thomas Lodge & Robert Greene: An Elizabethan Text. Ed. by Tetsumaro Hayashi. LC 76-15212. 1970. 10.00 (ISBN 0-8108-0348-8). Scarecrow.

Looking-Glasse for Married Folkes. Robert Snawsel. LC 74-28886. (English Experience Ser.: No. 763). 1975. Repr. of 1631 ed. 7.00 (ISBN 90-221-0763-9). Walter J Johnson.

Looking Good, Feeling Beautiful. Avon Products. 14.95 (ISBN 0-671-25224-0). S&S.

Looking in: Exploring One's Personal Health Values. Donald A. Read. (Health Education Ser.). (Illus.). 1977. pap. text ed. 8.95 (ISBN 0-13-540484-3). P-H.

Looking in Looking Out. Siddharth Kak. (Redbird Bk.). 1976. lib. bdg. 8.00 (ISBN 0-89253-116-9); flexible bdg. 4.80 (ISBN 0-89253-134-7). Ind-US Inc.

Looking Inside the Wonders of Nature. David Sharp. LC 76-9914. (Illus.). 64p. (gr. 10 up). 1977. 4.95 o.p. (ISBN 0-528-82213-6). Rand.

Looking Inward: Studies in James Joyce, E.M. Forster, & the Twentieth Century Novel. Laura K. Devlin. 1980. lib. bdg. 59.95 (ISBN 0-87700-269-X). Revisionist Pr.

Looking on Darkness. Andre Brink. LC 75-4515. 408p. 1975. 8.95 o.p. (ISBN 0-688-02924-8). Morrow.

Looking Out of the Window. Hazel S. Gamec. (Illus.). 12p. 1980. write for info. (ISBN 0-938042-01-7). Printek.

Looking Outward: Years of Crisis at the United Nations. Adlai Stevenson. Ed. by Robert L. Schiffer & Selma Schiffer. 1963. 10.95 o.s.i. (ISBN 0-06-014115-8, HarpT). Har-Row.

Looking South: Latin American Art in New York Collections. Intro. by Monroe Wheeler. (Illus.). 60p. 1972. pap. 2.00 o.p. (ISBN 0-913456-14-4). Interbk Inc.

Looking....Seeing. Harry Chapin. LC 77-11564. (Illus.). 1978. pap. 4.95 o.p. (ISBN 0-690-01657-3, TYC-T). T Y Crowell.

Looming Shadow. Legsons Kayira. 1970. pap. 1.25 o.s.i. (ISBN 0-02-034010-9, Collier). Macmillan.

Loon Feather. Iola Fuller. LC 40-27210. (gr. 10 up). 1940. 9.50 o.p. (ISBN 0-15-153201-X). HarBraceJ.

Loon in My Bathtub. Ronald Rood. LC 64-23363. (Illus.). 192p. 1974. 7.95 o.p. (ISBN 0-8289-0228-3); pap. 3.95 (ISBN 0-8289-0229-1). Greene.

Loon Lake. E. L. Doctorow. LC 79-5526. 1980. 12.95 (ISBN 0-394-50691-X); limited ed. 35.00 (ISBN 0-394-51176-X). Random.

Loony Laws: You Never Knew You Were Breaking. Robert W. Pelton. LC 80-54814. (Illus.). 160p. 1981. 9.95 (ISBN 0-8027-0687-8); pap. 4.95 (ISBN 0-8027-7174-2). Walker & Co.

Loony Limericks: From Alabama to Wyoming. Jack Stokes. LC 77-10304. (gr. 3-7). 1978. PLB 4.95 (ISBN 0-385-12917-3). Doubleday.

Loops. Gene Frumkin. (Orig.). 1980. pap. 3.00x (ISBN 0-88235-039-0). San Marcos.

Loose Boundary Hydraulics. 2nd ed. A. J. Raudkivi. Ed. by J. D. Francis. 326p. 1976. text ed. 37.00 (ISBN 0-08-018772-2); pap. text ed. 23.00 (ISBN 0-08-018771-4). Pergamon.

Loose Change. Sara Davidson. 1981. pap. price not set (ISBN 0-671-43119-6). PB.

Loose Chippings. Thomas G. Wheeler. LC 69-11990. (Illus.). (YA) 1969. 9.95 (ISBN 0-87599-152-1). S G Phillips.

Loose Ends: Primary Papers in Archetypal Psychology. James Hillman. 212p. 1975. pap. 8.50 (ISBN 0-88214-308-5). Spring Pubns.

Loose Leaves from a Busy Life. Morris Hillquit. LC 78-146160. (Civil Liberties in American History Ser). 1971. Repr. of 1934 ed. lib. bdg. 35.00 (ISBN 0-306-70102-2). Da Capo.

Loosening the Grip: A Handbook of Alcohol Information. Jean Kinney & Gwen Leaton. LC 78-2219. (Illus.). 1978. pap. text ed. 11.95 (ISBN 0-8016-2673-0). Mosby.

Looters of the Public Domain. S. A. Puter. LC 70-38833. (Illus.). 495p. 1972. Repr. of 1908 ed. lib. bdg. 55.00 (ISBN 0-306-70449-8). Da Capo.

Lope de Vega: El Castigo sin Venganza. Ed. by C. A. Jones. 1966. 6.10 (ISBN 0-08-011775-9); pap. 4.80 (ISBN 0-08-011774-0). Pergamon.

Lopez of Newport: Colonial American Merchant Prince. Stanley F. Chyet. LC 78-93898. 1970. 11.95x (ISBN 0-8143-1407-4). Wayne St U Pr.

Lopsided World. Barbara Ward. 1968. 3.95 (ISBN 0-393-05360-1, NortonC); pap. 2.95x (ISBN 0-393-09805-2). Norton.

Lorca En la Lirica Puertorriquena. Juan A. Pagan. LC 80-17628. (Mente y Palabra Ser.). (Illus.). 486p. 1980. 6.25 (ISBN 0-8477-0574-9); pap. 5.00 (ISBN 0-8477-0575-7). U of PR Pr.

Lorca: The Theatre Beneath the Sand. Gwynne Edwards. LC 79-56839. 320p. 1980. 20.00 (ISBN 0-7145-2698-3, Pub. by M Boyars). Merrimack Bk Serv.

Lorca's "Poet in New York" The Fall into Consciousness. Betty Jean Craige. LC 76-4339. (Studies in Romance Languages: No. 15). 112p. 1977. 10.50x (ISBN 0-8131-1349-0). U Pr of Ky.

Lord & Peasant in Nineteenth Century Britain. Dennis R. Mills. (Illus.). 232p. 1980. 31.50x (ISBN 0-8476-6806-1). Rowman.

Lord & Savior: Friend & Brother, Spirit Masters for The Jesus Book. Religious Education Staff. (To Live Is Christ Ser.). 1979. 10.95 (ISBN 0-697-01692-7). Wm C Brown.

Lord Apache. Robert J. Steelman. LC 76-53416. 1977. 6.95 o.p. (ISBN 0-385-12430-9). Doubleday.

Lord Bentinck & Indian Education, Crime, & Status of Women. Isaiah Azariah. LC 78-64822. 1978. pap. text ed. 9.00 (ISBN 0-8191-0641-0). U Pr of Amer.

Lord Byron. 2nd ed. Paul G. Trueblood. (English Authors Ser.: No. 78). 1977. lib. bdg. 10.95 (ISBN 0-8057-6694-4). Twayne.

Lord Byron: A Study of the Development of His Philosophy, with Special Emphasis Upon the Dramas. Frank Rainwater. 50p. 1980. Repr. of 1949 ed. lib. bdg. 8.50 (ISBN 0-8492-7731-0). R West.

Lord Byron: The Complete Poetical Works, Vol. I. Ed. by Jerome J. McGann. 516p. 1980. 98.00x (ISBN 0-19-811890-2); pap. 59.00 (ISBN 0-19-812763-4). Oxford U Pr.

Lord Byron's Wife. Malcolm Elwin. (Illus.). 1974. Repr. of 1962 ed. text ed. 20.75x (ISBN 0-7195-3010-5). Humanities.

Lord, Change Me. Evelyn Christenson. 1977. pap. 3.50 (ISBN 0-88207-756-2). Victor Bks.

Lord Chesterfield & His World. Samuel Shellabarger. LC 72-156737. 1971. Repr. of 1951 ed. 15.00x (ISBN 0-8196-0271-X). Biblo.

Lord Dragonfly: Five Sequences. William Heyen. 64p. (Orig.). 1981. 30.00 (ISBN 0-8149-0853-5); pap. 8.95 (ISBN 0-8149-0839-X). Vanguard.

Lord Emsworth & Others. P. G. Wodehouse. 224p. 1975. pap. 2.95 (ISBN 0-14-002568-5). Penguin.

Lord, Give Me Patience. Keith Knoche. LC 77-93362. (Agape Ser.). 1978. pap. 3.50 (ISBN 0-8163-0205-7, 12611-0). Pacific Pr Pub Assn.

Lord God Made Them All. James Herriot. 320p. 1981. 12.95 (ISBN 0-312-49834-9). St Martin.

Lord Gore. Jack Roberts. (Illus.). 220p. 27.00 (ISBN 0-913582-07-7). Sundance.

Lord Haldane: Scapegoat for Liberalism. Stephen E. Koss. LC 69-19460. (Illus.). 1969. 17.50x (ISBN 0-231-03201-3). Columbia U Pr.

Lord Harry's Folly. Catherine Coulter. 1980. pap. 1.75 (ISBN 0-451-09531-6, E9531, Sig). NAL.

Lord Hervey, Eighteenth Century Courtier. Robert Halsband. (Illus.). 400p. 1974. 19.95 (ISBN 0-19-501731-5). Oxford U Pr.

Lord How Different. Carolyn Pomonis. Ed. by Gerald Hausman. LC 80-299. 128p. (Orig.). 1980. pap. 6.95 (ISBN 0-913270-85-7, Sundial Bks). Sunstone Pr.

Lord, I Want to Have a Quiet Time. Carolyn Nystrom. LC 80-69305. 224p. (gr. 7-12). 1981. pap. 5.95 (ISBN 0-915684-77-2). Christian Herald.

Lord, I'm Listening. Donna Leonard. 1979. pap. 2.95 (ISBN 0-88207-745-7). Victor Bks.

Lord Is... Edwin H. Young. LC 80-68750. 1981. pap. 3.25 (ISBN 0-8054-1526-2). Broadman.

Lord Is My Strength. Joan Rosenthal. 1976. pap. 1.25 (ISBN 0-89129-086-9). Jove Pubns.

Lord Is My Strength. Joan Rosenthal. (Orig.). pap. 1.25 (ISBN 0-89129-086-9). Jove Pubns.

Lord Jim. Joseph Conrad. Ed. by Thomas Moser. (Critical Editions Ser). (Annotated). (gr. 9-12). 1968. pap. text ed. 5.95x (ISBN 0-393-09656-4). Norton.

Lord Jim. Joseph Conrad. (Literature Ser). (gr. 7-12). 1969. pap. text ed. 3.75 (ISBN 0-87720-708-9). AMSCO Sch.

Lord Jim. Joseph Conrad. LC 44-22843. 1927. 12.95 (ISBN 0-385-04265-5). Doubleday.

Lord Jim. Joseph Conrad. lib. bdg. 11.95x (ISBN 0-89966-057-6). Buccaneer Bks.

Lord Jim. Joseph Conrad. pap. 1.95. Bantam.

Lord Jim, with Reader's Guide. Joseph Conrad. (Literature Program Ser.). (Orig.). (gr. 9-12). 1973. pap. text ed. 4.42 (ISBN 0-87720-820-4); tchr's ed. 2.85 (ISBN 0-87720-920-0). AMSCO Sch.

Lord Kames & the Scotland of His Day. Ian S. Ross. (Illus.). 420p. 1972. 39.95x (ISBN 0-19-822361-7). Oxford U Pr.

Lord Kelvin & the Age of the Earth. Joe D. Burchfield. 274p. 1975. pap. 8.95 o.p. (ISBN 0-88202-013-7, Sci Hist). N Watson.

Lord Leighton. Leonee Ormond & Richard Ormond. LC 75-2773. (Studies in British Art Ser.). 192p. 1976. 60.00x (ISBN 0-300-01896-7). Yale U Pr.

Lord, Let Me Love. Marjorie Holmes. 288p. 1981. pap. 2.75 (ISBN 0-553-14915-6). Bantam.

Lord, Let Me Love: A Marjorie Holmes Treasury. Marjorie Holmes. LC 77-26516. 1978. 8.95 (ISBN 0-385-14093-2, Galilee). Doubleday.

Lord Libertine. Anthony Esler. 1977. pap. 1.75 o.p. (ISBN 0-449-23170-4, Crest). Fawcett.

Lord Loves His People. 1980. 6.00 (ISBN 0-8198-4400-4). Dghtrs St Paul.

Lord McNair: Selected Papers & Bibliography. Ed. by C. Parry. 1974. 32.00 (ISBN 0-379-00228-0). Oceana.

Lord, Make My Life a Miracle. Raymond C. Ortlund. LC 73-89714. (Orig.). 1974. pap. 2.50 (ISBN 0-8307-0284-9, 50-117-01); study guide 1.59 (ISBN 0-8307-0626-7, 6101305). Regal.

Lord Marques Idlenes: Conteining Mainfold Matters of Acceptable Devise. William Paulet. LC 79-84131. (English Experience Ser.: No. 949). 112p. 1979. Repr. of 1586 ed. lib. bdg. 11.50 (ISBN 90-221-0949-6). Walter J Johnson.

Lord Mayor's Court of London: Depositions Relating to Americans Sixteen Forty-One to Seventeen Thirty-Six. Peter W. Coldham. Ed. by George E. Russell. LC 80-80349. 119p. Date not set. lib. bdg. price not set (ISBN 0-915156-23-7, SP 44); pap. price not set (ISBN 0-686-27217-X). Natl Genealogical.

Lord Mountbatten: His Butler's Story. Charles Smith. LC 80-51787. (Illus.). 224p. 1980. 12.95 (ISBN 0-8128-2751-1). Stein & Day.

Lord North, 2 Vols. Alan Valentine. (Illus.). 1967. Set. 27.50 (ISBN 0-8061-0752-9); Set. pap. 12.50x (ISBN 0-8061-1344-8). U of Okla Pr.

Lord of Beasts: The Saga of Buffalo Jones. Robert Easton & MacKenzie Brown. LC 61-14501. (Illus.). 1970. pap. 2.95 (ISBN 0-8032-5727-9, BB 522, Bison). U of Nebr Pr.

Lord of Creation. Rosalind Cowdray. (Harlequin Romances Ser.). 192p. (Orig.). 1981. pap. 1.25 (ISBN 0-373-02381-2, Pub. by Harlequin). PB.

Lord of Holderness, Ten Eighty-Six to Twelve Sixty: A Study in Feudal Society. Barbara English. (Illus.). 288p. 1979. 49.50x (ISBN 0-19-713437-8). Oxford U Pr.

Lord of Light. Roger Zelazny. 1976. pap. 2.25 (ISBN 0-380-01403-3, 44834). Avon.

Lord of My Rocking Boat. Carole Mayhall. (Orig.). 1981. price not set. NavPress.

Lord of Nardos. R. Winterbotham. 5.95 (ISBN 0-685-07443-9, Avalon). Bouregy.

Lord of Rushie River. Cicely M. Barker. (Cicely Mary Barker Storybooks). (Illus.). (gr. k-4). 1977. 2.95 (ISBN 0-8467-0258-4, Pub. by Two Continents). Hippocrene Bks.

Lord of the Far Island. Victoria Holt. 320p. 1978. pap. 2.25 (ISBN 0-449-22874-6, Crest). Fawcett.

Lord of the Four Quarters: Myths of the Royal Father. J. W. Perry. (Patterns of Myth). (Illus.). 1970. pap. 1.50 o.s.i. (ISBN 0-02-066810-4, Collier). Macmillan.

Lord of the Four Quarters: Myths of the Royal Father. John W. Perry. Ed. by Alan W. Watts. LC 65-19324. (Patterns of Myth Ser). 1965. 6.95 o.p. (ISBN 0-8076-0321-X). Braziller.

Lord of the High Valley. Margaret Way. (Harlequin Romances Ser.). 192p. (Orig.). 1981. pap. 1.25 (ISBN 0-373-02387-1, Pub. by Harlequin). PB.

Lord of the Rings. 1980. 2.50 o.p. (ISBN 0-686-62912-4). Ballantine.

Lord of the Rings: Anniversary Edition, 3 vols. J. R. Tolkien. 1981. Set. 50.00 (ISBN 0-686-69051-6). HM.

Lord of Tranerica. Stanton Coblentz. (YA) 5.95 (ISBN 0-685-07444-7, Avalon). Bouregy.

Lord, Open the Heavens! A Heartcry for Revival. Stephen Olford. LC 80-52053. 144p. 1980. pap. 3.95x (ISBN 0-87788-335-1). Shaw Pubs.

Lord Orlando's Protegee. Margaret Sebastian. 224p. 1981. pap. 1.95 (ISBN 0-515-05810-6). Jove Pubns.

Lord Peter. Dorothy Sayers. 1972. pap. 5.95 o.p. (ISBN 0-380-01694-X, 42606). Avon.

Lord Peter. Dorothy Sayers. 1980. pap. 6.95 (ISBN 0-380-51672-1, 51672). Avon.

Lord Ravan of Lanka. P. S. Vasudev. (Bluebird Bk.). 118p. 1975. 14.00 (ISBN 0-88253-829-2); pap. 8.00 (ISBN 0-88253-830-6). Ind-US Inc.

Lord Rayleigh, the Man & His Work. R. B. Lindsay. LC 79-94934. (Men of Physics Ser.). 1970. 23.00 (ISBN 0-08-006821-9); pap. 11.25 (ISBN 0-08-006820-0). Pergamon.

Lord Rivington's Lady. Eileen Jackson. 1977. pap. 1.75 (ISBN 0-451-09408-5, E9408, Sig). NAL.

Lord Rivington's Lady: A Regency Romance. Eileen Jackson. LC 75-40762. 1976. 7.95 o.s.i. (ISBN 0-8027-0533-2). Walker & Co.

Lord Satan's Bride. Anne Stuart. (Orig.). 1981. pap. 1.50 (ISBN 0-440-14787-5). Dell.

Lord Sin. Constance Gluyas. 1980. pap. 2.75 (ISBN 0-451-09521-9, E9521, Sig). NAL.

Lord Somers: A Political Portrait. William L. Sachse. LC 75-885. 336p. 1975. 30.00x (ISBN 0-299-06890-0). U of Wis Pr.

Lord, the People Have Driven Me on. Benjamin E. Mays. 1981. 7.95 (ISBN 0-533-04503-7). Vantage.

Lord Valentine's Castle. Robert Silverberg. 480p. 1981. pap. 2.95 (ISBN 0-553-14428-6). Bantam.

Lord, What Are You Doing Next Tuesday? Ona B. Dukes & Beverly Johnston. 1978. pap. 2.95 (ISBN 0-8272-2114-2). Bethany Pr.

Lord Won't Mind. Gordon Merrick. 1971. pap. 2.25 (ISBN 0-380-01404-1, 36772). Avon.

Lord, You Love to Say Yes. Ruth H. Calkin. LC 75-18923. (Illus.). 160p. 1976. pap. 2.50 (ISBN 0-912692-81-2). Cook.

Lords & Peasants in a Changing Society: The Estates of the Bishopric of Worcester, 680-1540. Christopher Dyer. LC 79-51225. (Past & Present Publications Ser.). (Illus.). 466p. 1980. 49.50 (ISBN 0-521-22618-X). Cambridge U Pr.

Lords Locator for Fine Restaurants: Midwestern Edition. 208p. (Orig.). 1980. pap. 5.95 vinyl covered (ISBN 0-936002-02-6). C Kerr Ent.

Lords Locator for Fine Restaurants: Northeastern Edition. 2nd ed. 1981. pap. 5.95 vinyl covered (ISBN 0-686-69473-2). C Kerr Ent.

Lords Locator for Fine Restaurants: Southern Edition. 240p. (Orig.). 1980. pap. 5.95 vinyl covered (ISBN 0-936002-03-4). C Kerr Ent.

Lords Locator for Fine Restaurants: Western Edition. 208p. (Orig.). 1980. pap. 5.95 vinyl covered (ISBN 0-936002-04-2). C Kerr Ent.

Lords of Castle Weirwyck. Elaine F. Wells. 256p. (Orig.). 1980. pap. 1.95 (ISBN 0-89083-668-X). Zebra.

Lords of the Earth. Don Richardson. LC 77-74534. 1977. pap. 5.95 (ISBN 0-8307-0529-5, 54-057-18). Regal.

Lords of the Earth: The History of the Navajo Indians. Jules Loh. LC 76-150671. (Illus.). (gr. 7-12). 1971. 5.95 o.s.i. (ISBN 0-02-759290-1, CCPr). Macmillan.

Lord's Oysters. Gilbert Byron. LC 74-9246. xiv, 330p. 1967. Repr. of 1957 ed. 15.00 (ISBN 0-8103-5032-7). Gale.

Lord's Prayer. Thomas Watson. 1978. 9.95 (ISBN 0-85151-145-7). Banner of Truth.

Lord's Prayer & Jewish Liturgy. Jakob L. Petuchowski & Michael Brocke. 1978. 14.50 (ISBN 0-8164-0381-3). Crossroad NY.

Lord's Prayer & Other Prayers. Hilda L. Rostron. (Ladybird Ser.). (Illus.). (gr. 1-2). 1961. bds. 1.49 (ISBN 0-87508-848-1). Chr Lit.

Lord's Prayer for Children. Reda Lucy, pseud. (Illus.). 24p. (Orig.). (ps-3). 1981. pap. 1.95 (ISBN 0-87516-437-4). De Vorss.

Lord's Prayer: The Prayer of Jesus. F. Sheed. (Illus., Orig.). 1976. pap. 4.95 (ISBN 0-8164-2597-3). Crossroad NY.

Lord's Sermons. Jakob Lorber. Tr. by Violet Ozols & Hildegard Von Koerber. LC 80-50280. (Jakob Lorber Ser.). 278p. 1981. 12.95 (ISBN 0-934616-06-X). Valkyrie Pr.

Lord's Table: Eucharist & Passover in Early Christianity. Gillian Feeley-Harnick. 1980. text ed. 19.95x (ISBN 0-8122-7786-4). U of Pa Pr.

Lords Temporal & Lords Spiritual. Boden Clarke. LC 80-10979. (Stokvis Studies in Historical Chronology & Thought: No. 1). 64p. 1981. lib. bdg. 8.95x (ISBN 0-89370-800-3); pap. 2.95x (ISBN 0-89370-900-X). Borgo Pr.

Lore of the Great Turtle: Indian Legends of Mackinac Retold. Dirk Gringhuis. LC 73-636148. (Illus.). 96p. (Orig.). 1970. pap. 2.50 (ISBN 0-911872-11-6). Mackinac Island.

Lore of the Lakes. Dana T. Bowen. 1940. 9.50 (ISBN 0-685-11634-4). Freshwater.

Lore of the Unicorn. Odell Shepard. 1967. 12.95 o.p. (ISBN 0-04-291004-8). Allen Unwin.

Lore of the Witch World. Andre Norton. (Science Fiction Ser.). 1980. pap. 1.95 (ISBN 0-87997-560-1, UE1560). Daw Bks.

Lorentzian Distance Function & Global Lorentzian Geometry. Beem. Date not set. price not set (ISBN 0-8247-1369-9). Dekker.

Lorenzo: D. H. Lawrence & the Women Who Loved Him. Emily Hahn. LC 75-11865. 368p. 1975. 12.95 o.p. (ISBN 0-397-00772-8). Lippincott.

Lorenzo de' Medici. Sara Sturm. (World Authors Ser.: Italy: No. 288). 1974. lib. bdg. 12.50 (ISBN 0-8057-2609-8). Twayne.

Lorenzo De'Medici & the Renaissance. Charles L. Mee, Jr. & John Walker. (Horizon Caravel Bks). (Illus.). 153p. (gr. 6 up). 1969. 9.95 (ISBN 0-8281-0000-4, J036-0, Dist. by Har-Row); PLB 12.89 (ISBN 0-06-024173-X, Dist. by Har-Row). Am Heritage.

Lori. John Benton. (Spire Bks.). 160p. 1980. pap. 2.50 (ISBN 0-8007-8385-9). Revell.

Lorielle. Marilyn Granbeck. (Historical Romance Ser.). 1980. pap. 2.75 (ISBN 0-515-04627-2). Jove Pubns.

Lories & Lorikeets. Rosemary Low. (Illus.). 1979. pap. 6.95 (ISBN 0-87666-980-1, PS-773). TFH Pubns.

Lorrain. (Selected Artists Art Ser). (Illus.). 1977. pap. 5.95 (ISBN 0-8120-0818-9). Barron.

Los Angeles: A Guide to the City & Its Environs. Federal Writers' Project. 1941. Repr. 39.00 (ISBN 0-403-02202-9). Somerset Pub.

Los Angeles: An Illustrated History. Bruce Henstell. LC 80-7642. (Illus.). 224p. 1980. 25.00 (ISBN 0-394-50941-2). Knopf.

Los Angeles Barrio, Eighteen Fifty to Eighteen Ninety: A Social History. Richard Griswold del Castillo. 1980. 18.50x (ISBN 0-520-03816-9). U of Cal Pr.

Los Angeles: Commemorating Two Hundred Years. Brian Berger. Ed. by Robert D. Shangle. LC 80-16824. 1980. 27.50 (ISBN 0-89802-176-6). Beautiful Am.

Los Angeles County Museum of Art Bulletin, 1979, Vol. 25. Ebria Feinblatt et al. LC 58-35949. (Illus.). 80p. (Orig.). 1980. pap. 6.00 (ISBN 0-87587-092-9). La Co Art Mus.

Los Angeles County Museum of Art Report, July 1, 1977-June 30, 1978. Museum Staff. Ed. by Jeanne D'Andrea & Alison Hirsch. LC 80-641019. (Illus.). 84p. (Orig.). 1980. pap. 2.00 (ISBN 0-87587-093-7). La Co Art Mus.

Los Angeles Job Bank: A Comprehensive Guide to Major Employers Throughout Greater Los Angeles. Ed. by Robert Lang Adams & Associates. (Job Bank Ser.). 300p. (Orig.). 1981. pap. 9.95 (ISBN 0-937860-04-2). Adams Inc MA.

Los Angeles Municipal Code, 5 vols. 4th rev. ed. City of Los Angeles, City Attorney's Office. Ed. by City Clerk's Office. 3300p. 1972. looseleaf 275.00 (ISBN 0-911110-33-X); with current 1980 changes avail. (ISBN 0-685-26720-2). Parker & Son.

Los Angeles on Five Hundred Dollars a Day: Tax & Gratuities Not Included. Ferne Kadish & Kathleen Kirtland. 256p. 1976. pap. 4.95 (ISBN 0-02-097770-0, Collier). Macmillan.

Los Angeles on Five Hundred Dollars a Day: Tax & Gratuities Not Included. Ferne Kadish & Kathleen Kirtland. 256p. 1976. 8.95 o.s.i. (ISBN 0-02-560520-8). Macmillan.

Los Angeles Prints: Eighteen Eighty-Three to Nineteen Eighty. Ebria Feinblatt & Bruce Davis. (Illus.). 112p. (Orig.). 1980. pap. 10.00 (ISBN 0-87587-097-X). La Co Art Mus.

Los Angeles Rams. Julian May. (NFL Today). (Illus.). (gr. 3-6). 1977. PLB 6.45 (ISBN 0-87191-596-0); pap. 2.95 (ISBN 0-686-67473-1). Creative Ed.

Los Angeles Runners Guide. Lee Shear & Ed Reiners. LC 80-52538. 252p. (Orig.). 1980. pap. 6.95 (ISBN 0-87477-162-5). J P Tarcher.

Los Angeles: The Architecture of Four Ecologies. Reyner Banham. LC 72-148430. (Icon Editions). (Illus.). 1971. 8.95x o.s.i. (ISBN 0-06-430370-5, HarpT). Har-Row.

Los Angeles: The Centrifugal City. Rodney Steiner. 224p. 1981. pap. text ed. 12.95 (ISBN 0-8403-2333-6). Kendall-Hunt.

Los Angeles: The Enormous Village. 2nd ed. John Weaver. Orig. Title: El Pueblo Grande. (Illus.). 240p. 1980. 15.00 (ISBN 0-88496-158-3); pap. 8.95 (ISBN 0-88496-153-2). Capra Pr.

Los Angeles Times Stylebook: A Manual for Writers, Editors, Journalists & Students. Ed. by Frederick S. Holley. 1981. pap. 6.95 (ISBN 0-452-00552-3, F552, Mer). NAL.

Los Angeles: Two Hundred. David Lavender. Ed. by Ellen S. Blakey & Larry P. Silvey. LC 80-66342. (American Portrait Ser.). (Illus.). 240p. 1980. 24.95 (ISBN 0-932986-08-0). Continent Herit.

Los Angeles Two Hundred: A Bicentennial Celebration. Art Seidenbaum. (Illus.). 320p. 1980. 30.00 (ISBN 0-686-62686-9, 1257-0). Abrams.

Lose Ten Years in Ten Days. Alexandra York. (Illus.). 192p. 1981. 10.95 (ISBN 0-02-633270-1). Macmillan.

Lose Weight, Feel Great. John Yudkin. (Illus.). 219p. 1974. pap. 1.75 (ISBN 0-915962-02-0). Larchmont Bks.

Loser Takes All. Graham Greene. 1977. pap. 2.95 (ISBN 0-14-003277-0). Penguin.

Losers Keepers. Alexander Mason. (Orig.). 1980. pap. 2.25 (ISBN 0-505-51505-9). Tower Bks.

Losing Battles. Eudora Welty. LC 78-58857. 416p. 1978. pap. 2.45 (ISBN 0-394-72668-5, Vin). Random.

Losing Ground: Environmental Stress & World Food Prospects. E. P. Eckholm. 1978. text ed. 27.00 (ISBN 0-08-021496-7); pap. text ed. 11.25 (ISBN 0-08-021495-9). Pergamon.

Losing It: The Economic Fall of the Middle Class. Robert C. Yeager. 224p. 1980. 10.95 (ISBN 0-07-072256-0, GB). McGraw.

Losing Willy. Kenneth Mahood. LC 77-6267. (Illus.). (ps-2). 1978. PLB 6.95 (ISBN 0-13-540583-1); pap. 2.95 (ISBN 0-13-540591-2). P-H.

Losing Your Best Friend. Corinne Bergstrom. LC 79-20622. 32p. 1980. 8.95 (ISBN 0-87705-471-1). Human Sci Pr.

Loss & Discovery. Wayne C. Cheatle. 1981. 4.95 (ISBN 0-8062-1653-1). Carlton.

Loss & Gain: The Story of a Convert, 1848. John H. Newman. Ed. by Robert L. Wolff. Bd. with Callista: A Sketch of the Third Century, 1856. (Victorian Fiction Ser.). 1975. lib. bdg. 66.00 (ISBN 0-8240-1530-4). Garland Pub.

Loss & Grief: Psychological Management in Medical Practice. Ed. by Bernard Schoenberg et al. LC 75-118356. 398p. 1973. 22.50x (ISBN 0-231-03329-X, CP165); pap. 10.00x (ISBN 0-231-08331-9). Columbia U Pr.

Loss & How to Cope with It. Joanna Bernstein. 160p. (gr. 6 up). 1981. pap. 3.95 (ISBN 0-395-30012-6, Clarion). HM.

Loss & How to Cope with It. Joanne BerNstein. LC 76-50027. (gr. 5 up). 7.95 (ISBN 0-395-28891-6, Clarion). HM.

Loss of Loved Ones. David M. Moriarty. 288p. 1981. 18.50 (ISBN 0-87527-198-7). Green.

Loss of Mastery: Puritan Historians in Colonial America. Peter Gay. (Jefferson Memorial Lectures). 1966. 14.00x (ISBN 0-520-00456-6). U of Cal Pr.

Loss of the Bismarck. B. B. Schofield. LC 75-187003. (Sea Battles in Close-up Ser: No. 3). (Illus.). 1972. 6.75 o.s.i. (ISBN 0-87021-840-9). Naval Inst Pr.

Loss Prevention: A Management Guide to Improving Retail Security. Ed. by Leonard Daykin. 1981. 19.50 (ISBN 0-911790-51-9). Prog Grocer.

Loss Prevention: Controls & Concepts. Saul D. Astor. LC 77-28164. 1978. 15.95 (ISBN 0-913708-29-1). Butterworths.

Loss Prevention in the Process Industry, 2 vols. new ed. Frank P. Lees. 1980. 195.00 set (ISBN 0-408-10604-2); Vol. 1. 99.00 (ISBN 0-408-10697-2); Vol. 2. 99.00 (ISBN 0-408-10698-0). Butterworths.

Loss Prevention of Rotating Machinery. LC 71-187881. 52p. 1972. pap. 7.50 o.p. (ISBN 0-685-25543-3, G00017). ASME.

Loss Rate Concept in Safety Engineering. Browning. 176p. 1980. 27.50 (ISBN 0-8247-1249-8). Dekker.

Lost Americans. Frank C. Hibben. (Apollo Eds.). pap. 2.95 (ISBN 0-8152-0003-X, A3, TYC-T). T Y Crowell.

Lost & Found: A Hidden Animal Book. Dahlov Ipcar. (gr. k-3). 1981. 8.95a (ISBN 0-385-15170-5); PLB (ISBN 0-385-15171-3). Doubleday.

Lost Art of Handfinishing Furniture. Pat Scattergood & Terry Scattergood. 1980. 4.00 (ISBN 0-8062-1324-8). Carlton.

Lost Atlantis. James Bramwell. LC 80-19561. 288p. 1980. Repr. of 1974 ed. lib. bdg. 10.95x (ISBN 0-89370-623-X). Borgo Pr.

Lost Bear, Found Bear. Patrick Mayers. LC 72-13353. (Self Starter Ser.). (Illus.). 32p. (ps-1). 1973. 6.50g (ISBN 0-8075-4760-3). A Whitman.

Lost Bellybutton. Margaret M. Gullette. LC 76-26377. (Illus.). 31p. (ps-2). 1976. pap. 2.50 (ISBN 0-914996-11-8). Lollipop Power.

Lost but Not Forever. Gary Bell & Davin R. Seay. LC 80-81472. 1981. pap. 4.95 (ISBN 0-89081-253-5). Harvest Hse.

Lost Colony. Dan Lacy. LC 70-182898. (First Bks). (Illus.). 72p. (gr. 4 up). 1972. PLB 4.90 o.p. (ISBN 0-531-00761-8). Watts.

Lost Continents: The Atlantis Theme. L. Sprague De Camp. 384p. 1975. pap. 1.95 (ISBN 0-345-27089-4). Ballantine.

Lost Copper. Wendy Rose. 1980. 8.95 (ISBN 0-686-27943-3). Malki Mus Pr.

Lost Country. Kathleen Raine. 1971. text ed. 5.00x (ISBN 0-85105-194-4, Dolmen Pr). Humanities.

Lost Country Life. Dorothy Hartley. (Illus.). 1981. pap. 6.95 (ISBN 0-394-74838-7). Pantheon.

Lost Crucifix of Our Lady of Guadalupe. Fisher Alsup. Ed. by Polly Koch. 230p. 1977. 4.95 o.p. (ISBN 0-88319-028-1). Shoal Creek Pub.

Lost Domain. Henri Alain-Fournier. Tr. by Frank Davison. (World's Classics Ser.). 1959. 4.95 o.p. (ISBN 0-19-250569-6). Oxford U Pr.

Lost Enchantment. Barbara Cartland. (Barbara Cartland Ser.: No. 15). 256p. 1981. pap. 1.75 (ISBN 0-515-05942-0). Jove Pubns.

Lost Frontier. Knut Peterson. 1981. 10.95 (ISBN 0-87949-172-8). Ashley Bks.

Lost Goddesses of Early Greece: A Collection of Pre-Hellenic Mythology. Charlene Spretnak. LC 80-68169. (Illus.). 132p. 1981. pap. 5.95 (ISBN 0-8070-3239-5, BP 617). Beacon Pr.

Lost Grove: Autobiography of a Spanish Poet in Exile. Rafael Alberti. LC 74-79760. 1977. 12.95 (ISBN 0-520-02786-8); pap. 5.95 (ISBN 0-520-04265-4). U of Cal Pr.

Lost Grove: The Autobiography of a Spanish Poet in Exile. Rafael Alberti. Ed. by Gabriel Berns. (Illus.). 331p. 1981. pap. 5.95 (CAL 464). U of Cal Pr.

Lost Half-Hour: A Collection of Stories. Ed. by Eulalie S. Ross. LC 65-23537. (Illus.). (gr. 4-6). 1963. 5.95 o.p. (ISBN 0-15-249360-3, HJ). HarBraceJ.

Lost Herd. Archie Joscelyn. (YA) 1978. 5.95 (ISBN 0-685-86409-X, Avalon). Bouregy.

Lost Hill. Ruth L. Anderson. (Illus.). (gr. 4-6). 1976. pap. 2.25x (ISBN 0-933892-06-3). Child Focus Co.

Lost Horizon. James Hilton. (Illus.). 1936. Repr. of 1922 ed. 10.95 (ISBN 0-688-02007-0). Morrow.

Lost Horizon. Adapted by Catherine Wichterman. (Contemporary Motivators Ser.). (Illus.). 32p. (Orig.). 1979. pap. text ed. 1.25 (ISBN 0-88301-309-6). Pendulum Pr.

Lost in America. Isaac B. Singer. LC 79-6037. 1981. 17.95 (ISBN 0-686-69069-9). Doubleday.

Lost in the Annals: The Story of the New Madrid Earthquake, Eighteen Eleven to Eighteen Twelve. Myrl R. Mueller. (Orig.). 1980. pap. 4.95 (ISBN 0-917200-29-2). ESPress.

Lost in the Cave. Linda P. Silbert & Alvin J. Silbert. (Little Twirps, TM Understanding People Books). (Illus.). (gr. k-4). 1978. pap. 2.25 (ISBN 0-89544-057-1). Silbert Bress.

Lost in the Great Atlantic Valley. Ed. by E. F. Bleiler. (Frank Reade Library: Vol. 6). 1980. lib. bdg. 44.00 (ISBN 0-8240-3545-3). Garland Pub.

Lost in the Jungle. Paul Du Chaillu. LC 79-159939. 1971. Repr. of 1872 ed. 18.00 (ISBN 0-8103-3766-5). Gale.

Lost in the Museum. Miriam Cohen. LC 78-16765. (Illus.). (gr. k-3). 1979. 7.75 (ISBN 0-688-80187-0); PLB 7.44 (ISBN 0-688-84187-2). Greenwillow.

Lost in the Storm. Carol Carrick. LC 74-1051. (Illus.). 32p. (ps-3). 1974. 6.95 (ISBN 0-395-28776-6, Clarion). HM.

Lost in the Zoo. Berta Hader & Elmer Hader. (gr. k-3). 1951. 5.50g o.s.i. (ISBN 0-02-739680-0). Macmillan.

Lost Island. Phyllis A. Whitney. 1978. pap. 2.25 (ISBN 0-449-23886-5, Crest). Fawcett.

Lost Jews: Last of the Ethiopian Falashas. Louis Rapoport. LC 79-92340. (Illus.). 264p. 1980. 13.95 (ISBN 0-8128-2720-1). Stein & Day.

Lost Key to Prediction: The Arabic Parts in Astrology. Robert Zoller. 350p. 1980. pap. 8.95 (ISBN 0-89281-013-0). Inner Tradit.

Lost Lady. Willa Cather. 192p. 1972. pap. 2.45 o.p. (ISBN 0-394-71705-8, V705, Vin). Random.

Lost Lands & Forgotten People. James C. Cornell, Jr. LC 78-57795. (Illus.). (gr. 5 up). 1978. 8.95 (ISBN 0-8069-3926-5); PLB 8.29 (ISBN 0-8069-3927-3). Sterling.

Lost Laughter. Barbara Cartland. 1980. 9.95 (ISBN 0-525-14891-4). Dutton.

Lost Laughter, No. 131. Barbara Cartland. 176p. 1980. pap. 1.75 (ISBN 0-553-13985-1). Bantam.

Lost Love. Gauri Deshpande. 8.00 (ISBN 0-89253-685-3). Ind-US Inc.

Lost Love, Last Love. Rosemary Rogers. 1980. pap. 2.95 (ISBN 0-380-75515-7, 75515). Avon.

Lost New Orleans. Mary Cable. 256p. 1980. 21.95 (ISBN 0-395-27623-3). HM.

Lost Nickel. Walter Richardson & Roberta Kerr. 1981. 4.50 (ISBN 0-533-03282-2). Vantage.

Lost on Both Sides, Dante Gabriel Rossetti: Critic & Poet. Robert M. Cooper. LC 71-91957. 268p. 1970. 14.00x (ISBN 0-8214-0069-X). Ohio U Pr.

Lost Peace: America's Search for a Negotiated Settlement of the Vietnam War. Allan E. Goodman. LC 77-77566. (Publication Ser: No. 173). (Illus.). 1978. 22.50 (ISBN 0-8179-6731-1). Hoover Inst Pr.

Lost Pharaohs: The Romance of Egyptian Archaeology. Leonard Cottrell. LC 72-90140. Repr. of 1951 ed. lib. bdg. 21.75x (ISBN 0-8371-2260-0, COLP). Greenwood.

Lost Plays of the Irish Renaissance, Vol. 2. Ed. by William Feeney. 10.00 (ISBN 0-912262-70-2). Proscenium.

Lost Pony Tracks. Ross Santee. LC 53-12239. (Illus.). vi, 303p. 1972. pap. 5.95 (ISBN 0-8032-5740-6, BB 521, Bison). U of Nebr Pr.

Lost Princess: A Double Story. George MacDonald. (Childrens Illustrated Classics Ser). (Illus.). 1976. Repr. of 1967 ed. 9.00x o.p. (ISBN 0-460-05069-9, Pub. by J. M. Dent England). Biblio Dist.

Lost Profile. Francois Sagan. 192p. 1976. 6.95 o.s.i. (ISBN 0-440-05017-0). Delacorte.

Lost Queen. Norah Lofts. 288p. 1975. pap. 1.50 o.p. (ISBN 0-449-22154-7, Q2154, Crest). Fawcett.

Lost Reform: The Campaign for Compulsory Health Insurance in the United States from 1932 to 1943. Daniel S. Hirshfield. LC 71-115187. (Commonwealth Fund Publications Ser). 1970. 11.00x (ISBN 0-674-53917-6). Harvard U Pr.

Lost River Canyon. Archie Joscelyn. 192p. (YA) 1976. 5.95 (ISBN 0-685-62024-7, Avalon). Bouregy.

Lost River Loot. Jackson Cole. 144p. 1975. pap. 0.95 o.p. (ISBN 0-445-00633-1). Popular Lib.

Lost Science of Man. Ernest Becker. LC 75-142076. 1971. 6.95 o.s.i.; pap. 2.95 (ISBN 0-8076-0599-9). Braziller.

Lost Sheep. (Tell-a-Bible Story Ser.). (Illus.). 28p. bds. 0.69 (ISBN 0-686-68646-2, 3690). Standard Pub.

Lost Sheep. Mandeville. (Ladybird Ser.). 1979. pap. 1.49 (ISBN 0-87508-849-X). Chr Lit.

Lost Sheep. Regine Schindler. LC 80-68546. Orig. Title: Das Verlorene Shaf. 32p. (gr. k-3). 1981. Repr. 5.95 (ISBN 0-687-22780-1). Abingdon.

Lost Songs: Political & Other Poems. Philip Ward. (Oleander Modern Poets Ser.: Vol. II). (Illus.). 48p. 1981. pap. 4.95 (ISBN 0-902675-51-6). Oleander Pr.

Lost Splendor. Donna C. Zide. 464p. (Orig.). 1980. pap. 2.50 (ISBN 0-446-91274-3). Warner Bks.

Lost Stage Valley. Frank Bonham. 1978. pap. 1.50 o.p. (ISBN 0-425-03752-5, Medallion). Berkley Pub.

Lost Stage Valley. Frank Bonham. 1981. pap. 1.75 (ISBN 0-425-04813-6). Berkley Pub.

Lost Star. H. M. Hoover. 160p. 1979. pap. 1.75 (ISBN 0-380-49635-6, 49635). Avon.

Lost Star & Other Tales. Anna B. Kolath. 4.50 (ISBN 0-8062-1655-7). Carlton.

Lost String Quartet. N. M. Bodecker. LC 80-1106. (Illus.). 32p. (gr. 1 up). 1981. 9.95 (ISBN 0-689-50200-1, McElderry Bk). Atheneum.

Lost Summer. Oppenheimer. (gr. 7-12). pap. 1.25 (ISBN 0-686-68468-0, Schol Pap). Schol Bk Serv.

Lost Survivors of the Deluge. Gerd Von Hassler. Ed. by Martin Ebon. (Illus., Orig.). 1978. pap. 1.75 o.p. (ISBN 0-451-08365-2, E8365, Sig). NAL.

Lost Threshold. Thomas G. Wheeler. LC 68-16349. (Illus.). (gr. 7 up). 1968. 9.95 (ISBN 0-87599-140-8). S G Phillips.

Lost Trails of the Cimarron. Harry E. Chrisman. LC 61-14370. (Illus.). 313p. 1964. pap. 6.95 (ISBN 0-8040-0615-6, SB). Swallow.

Lost Traveller. Antonia White. (Virago Modern Classic). 314p. 1980. pap. 5.95 (ISBN 0-8037-4935-X). Dial.

Lost Tribes: History, Doctrine, Prophecies & Theories About Israel's Lost Ten Tribes. R. Clayton Brough. LC 79-89351. 1979. 5.95 (ISBN 0-88290-123-0). Horizon Utah.

Lost Wild Worlds, the Story of Extinct & Vanishing Wildlife of the Eastern Hemisphere. Robert M. McClung. (Illus.). 256p. (gr. 7 up). 1976. 9.50 (ISBN 0-688-22090-8). Morrow.

Lost Wine: Seven Centuries of French into English Lyrical Poetry. John Theobald. (Illus.). 1981. 25.00 (ISBN 0-914676-36-9, Star & Elephants Bks). Green Tiger.

Lost World. Arthur Conan Doyle. (Looking Glass Library: No. 10). 1959. PLB 4.39 o.p. (ISBN 0-394-90460-5, BYR). Random.

Lost World. Arthur Conan Doyle. (gr. 10 up). pap. 0.95 o.p. (ISBN 0-425-03514-X, Medallion). Berkley Pub.

Lost World. Arthur C. Doyle. lib. bdg. 13.95x (ISBN 0-89966-233-1). Buccaneer Bks.

Lost World. Randall Jarrell. 1965. 3.95 o.s.i. (ISBN 0-02-558980-6). Macmillan.

Lost World Does It Exist? Robert Johnstone. 1978. text ed. 13.00x (ISBN 0-901072-75-3). Humanities.

Lost World of the Aegean. Maitland Edey. LC 74-21774. (Emergence of Man Ser.). (Illus.). 160p. (gr. 6 up). 1975. PLB 9.63 o.p. (ISBN 0-8094-1289-6). Silver.

Lost World of Thomas Jefferson. Daniel J. Boorstin. LC 80-26835. 320p. 1981. pap. 6.95 (ISBN 0-226-06496-4). U of Chicago Pr.

Lost Years of Jesus Revealed. C. F. Potter. 1979. pap. 1.75 o.p. (ISBN 0-449-14194-2, GM). Fawcett.

Lot & Lots Wife. Gordon Lindsay. (Old Testament Ser.: Vol. 4). pap. 1.25 (ISBN 0-89985-958-5). Christ Nations.

Lothair. Benjamin Disraeli. Ed. by Vernon Bogdanor. (Oxford English Novels Ser). 414p. 1975. 16.95x (ISBN 0-19-255356-9). Oxford U Pr.

Lothair, Repr. Of 1870 Ed. Benjamin Disraeli. Ed. by Robert L. Wolff. Bd. with Lothaw; or, the Adventures of a Young Gentleman in Search of a Religion. Bret Harte. (Victorian Fiction Ser). 1975. lib. bdg. 66.00 (ISBN 0-8240-1556-8). Garland Pub.

Lots More Tell & Draw Stories. lib. bdg. 6.75 (ISBN 0-934876-07-X); pap. 4.25 (ISBN 0-934876-03-7). Creative Storytime.

Lots of Things, 2 Vols. Yvette Dogin. (Illus.). (gr. 4 up). Set. wkbk 4.50 (ISBN 0-912486-04-X); Bk. 1, 1978. wkbk 2.25 (ISBN 0-912486-37-6); Bk. 2, 1972. wkbk. 2.25 (ISBN 0-912486-06-6). Finney Co.

Lotta on Troublemaker Street. Astrid Lindgren. (gr. k-2). 1963. 4.25 o.s.i. (ISBN 0-02-759030-5). Macmillan.

Lotte soll nicht sterben. Lenz. (Easy Reader, A). pap. 3.75 (ISBN 0-88436-039-3, GEA110052). EMC.

Lotteries. Daoma Winston. 1981. pap. 2.75 (ISBN 0-671-41277-9). PB.

Lottery. Shirley Jackson. 224p. 1975. pap. 2.50 (ISBN 0-445-00300-6). Popular Lib.

Lottery. Shirley Jackson. LC 79-24173. 1980. Repr. of 1949 ed. 12.50x (ISBN 0-8376-0455-9). Bentley.

Lottery or, The Adventures of James Harris. Shirley Jackson. LC 79-24173. 1980. Repr. of 1949 ed. lib. bdg. 12.50x (ISBN 0-8376-0455-9). Bentley.

Lotte's Locket. Virginia Sorensen. LC 64-17087. (Illus.). (gr. 4-6). 1964. 5.95 o.p. (ISBN 0-15-249457-X, HJ). HarBraceJ.

Lotto-Keno Supersystems: Winning Combinations & Systems for Lotto 6/40 & Keno Players. Zdenek V. Pavlik. (Illus.). 80p. 1980. 6.00 (ISBN 0-682-49616-2). Exposition.

Lotus Caves. John Christopher. LC 74-78074. (gr. 6-9). 1969. 7.95g o.s.i. (ISBN 0-02-718390-4). Macmillan.

Lotus Eaters. Gerald Green. 1980. pap. 2.95 (ISBN 0-425-04571-4). Berkley Pub.

Lotus Elan & Europa: A Collector's Guide. John Bolster. (Collector's Guide Ser.). (Illus.). 138p. 1980. 18.95 (ISBN 0-900549-48-3, Pub. by Motor Racing England). Motorbooks Intl.

Lotus Elan Nineteen Sixty-Two to Nineteen Seventy-Three. Ed. by R. M. Clarke. (Brooklands Bks.). (Illus.). 100p. (Orig.). 1980. pap. 11.95. Motorbooks Intl.

Lotus Leaves. Jai Nimbark. 12.00 (ISBN 0-89253-628-4); flexible cloth 4.80 (ISBN 0-89253-629-2). Ind-US Inc.

Loud & Clear: A Guide to Effective Communication. Sy Lazarus. LC 75-4925. 152p. 1975. 10.95 (ISBN 0-8144-5375-9). Am Mgmt.

Loud-Noisy, Dirty-Grimy, Bad & Naughty Twins: A Book of Synonyms. Sylvia R. Tester. LC 77-9483. (Using Words Ser.). (Illus.). (gr. k-3). 1977. PLB 5.50 (ISBN 0-913778-89-3). Childs World.

Loud, Resounding Sea. Frank Bonham. LC 63-15082. (gr. 6 up). 1963. 6.95 o.p. (ISBN 0-690-51082-9, TYC-J). T Y Crowell.

Louder & Louder: The Dangers of Noise Pollution. Thomas Perera & Gretchen Perera. LC 72-10868. (Illus.). 64p. (gr. 4-6). 1973. PLB 4.90 o.p. (ISBN 0-531-02618-3). Watts.

Louie. Ezra J. Keats. LC 75-6766. (Illus.). 32p. (ps-3). 1975. 8.25 (ISBN 0-688-80002-5); PLB 7.92 (ISBN 0-688-84002-7). Greenwillow.

Louie's Search. Ezra J. Keats. LC 80-10176. (Illus.). 32p. (gr. k-3). 1980. 9.95 (ISBN 0-590-07743-0, Four Winds). Schol Bk Serv.

Louis. Jane Morgan. 1979. pap. 1.95 o.p. (ISBN 0-425-04151-4). Berkley Pub.

Louis Armstrong. Genie Iverson. LC 76-4975. (Biography Ser.). (Illus.). 40p. (gr. 1-4). 1976. PLB 7.89 (ISBN 0-690-01127-X, TYC-J). T Y Crowell.

Louis Armstrong. Hugues Panassie. (Illus.). 148p. 1980. lib. bdg. 19.50 (ISBN 0-306-79611-2); pap. 5.95 (ISBN 0-306-80116-7). Da Capo.

Louis Armstrong - a Self Portrait. Richard Meryman. LC 70-152507. 1971. 6.95x o.s.i. (ISBN 0-87130-026-5); pap. 3.95 (ISBN 0-87130-027-3). Eakins.

Louis B. Brandeis & the Progressive Tradition. Melvin Urofsky. 208p. 1981. 11.95 (ISBN 0-316-88787-0). Little.

Louis Blanc: His Life & His Contribution to the Rise of French Jacobin-Socialism. Leo A. Loubere. LC 80-23424. (Northwestern University Studies in History: No.1). xii, 256p. 1980. Repr. of 1961 ed. lib. bdg. 27.50x (ISBN 0-313-22690-3, LOBL). Greenwood.

Louis Botha or John X. Merriman: The Choice of South Africa's First Prime Minister. N. G. Garson. (Commonwealth Papers: No. 12). 1969. pap. text ed. 2.25x (ISBN 0-485-17612-2, Athlone Pr). Humanities.

Louis Braille & His Magic Dots. Yvonne Davy. LC 75-36533. (Panda Ser.). 1976. pap. 4.95 (ISBN 0-8163-0226-X, 12680-5). Pacific Pr Pub Assn.

Louis D. Brandeis, Felix Frankfurter & the New Deal. Nelson L. Dawson. 280p. 1980. 19.50 (ISBN 0-208-01817-4, Archon). Shoe String.

Louis Ferdinand Celine. David Hayman. LC 65-26339. (Columbia Ser.: No. 13). (Orig.). 1965. pap. 2.00 (ISBN 0-231-02701-X, MW13). Columbia U Pr.

Louis-Ferdinand Celine. David O'Connell. LC 76-26059. (World Author Ser: France: No. 416). 1976. lib. bdg. 12.50 (ISBN 0-8057-6256-6). Twayne.

Louis I. Kahn. Vincent Scully, Jr. LC 62-16265. (Makers of Contemporary Architecture Ser). (Illus., Orig.). 1962. 4.95 o.p. (ISBN 0-8076-0198-5); pap. 3.95 o.p. (ISBN 0-8076-0390-2). Braziller.

Louis McLane: Federalist & Jacksonian. John A. Munroe. (Illus.). 768p. 1974. 45.00 (ISBN 0-8135-0757-X). Rutgers U Pr.

Louis MacNeice. Elton E. Smith. (English Authors Ser.: No. 99). lib. bdg. 10.95 (ISBN 0-8057-1364-6). Twayne.

Louis Moreau Gottschalk. J. G. Doyle. (Bibliographies in American Music). 1981. write for info. (ISBN 0-911772-66-9). Info Coord.

Louis Pasteur: Free Lance of Science. Rene Dubos. LC 75-21919. (Encore Edition). (Illus.). 1976. Repr. of 1950 ed. 4.95 o.p. (ISBN 0-684-15691-1, ScribT). Scribner.

Louis Sullivan. Albert Bush-Brown. LC 60-13306. (Masters of World Architecture Ser). 1960. 7.95 o.p. (ISBN 0-8076-0129-2); pap. 3.95 o.p. (ISBN 0-8076-0227-2). Braziller.

Louis the Fish. Arthur Yorinks. LC 80-16855. (Illus.). 32p. (ps-3). 1980. 9.95 (ISBN 0-374-34658-5). FS&G.

Louis the Fourteenth & the Greatness of France. Maurice Ashley. 1965. pap. 5.95 (ISBN 0-02-901080-2). Free Pr.

Louis the Fourteenth in Historical Thought. William F. Church. (Historical Controversies Ser.). 128p. 1976. pap. text ed. 2.95x (ISBN 0-393-09211-9). Norton.

Louis the Fourteenth: Memoires for the Instruction of the Dauphin. Tr. by Paul Sonnino. 1970. 12.95 (ISBN 0-02-930130-0). Free Pr.

Louis the Fourteenth of France: 2nd ed. David Ogg. (Oxford Paperbacks University Ser). pap. 4.95x (ISBN 0-19-888021-9). Oxford U Pr.

Louis the Fourteenth of France: Pattern of Majesty. Monroe Stearns. LC 77-137152. (Biography Ser). (Illus.). (gr. 7 up). 1971. PLB 5.90 o.p. (ISBN 0-531-00962-9). Watts.

Louis the Ninth: The Challenge of the Crusade. William C. Jordan. LC 79-83996. (Illus.). 1979. 17.50 (ISBN 0-691-05285-9). Princeton U Pr.

Louisa Calder's Creative Crochet. Louisa Calder & Mary Konior. (Illus.). 144p. 1979. 12.95 o.p. (ISBN 0-670-44203-8, Studio). Viking Pr.

Louisa May. Martha Saxton. 1978. pap. 3.50 (ISBN 0-380-48868-X, 48868, Discus). Avon.

Louisa May Alcott. Ednah D. Cheney. LC 80-24025. (American Men & Women of Letters Ser.). 410p. 1981. pap. 5.95 (ISBN 0-87754-162-0). Chelsea Hse.

Louise Farrenc, Eighteen Hundred Four to Eighteen Seventy-Five: Composer, Performer, Scholar. Bea Friedland. Ed. by George Buelow. (Studies in Musicology). 270p. 1981. 34.95 (ISBN 0-8357-1111-0, Pub. by UMI Res Pr). Univ Microfilms.

Louise Imogen Guiney. Henry G. Fairbanks. (U. S. Authors Ser.: No. 224). 1973. lib. bdg. 10.95 (ISBN 0-8057-0342-X). Twayne.

Louise Nevelson. Arnold Glimcher. 1976. pap. 13.95 o.p. (ISBN 0-525-47439-0). Dutton.

Louisiana. 28.00 (ISBN 0-89770-094-5). Curriculum Info Ctr.

Louisiana: A Bicentennial History. Joe G. Taylor. (States & the Nation Ser.). (Illus.). 1976. 12.95 (ISBN 0-393-05602-3, Co-Pub by AASLH). Norton.

Louisiana: A Guide to the State. Federal Writers' Project. 711p. 1941. Repr. 69.00 (ISBN 0-403-02169-3). Somerset Pub.

Louisiana Almanac, 1969. Ed. by Hodding Carter. 1969. pap. 7.95 (ISBN 0-911116-49-4). Pelican.

Louisiana Athletes: The Top Twenty. Marty Mule & Bob Remy. (Illus.). (gr. 6 up). 1981. 8.95 (ISBN 0-88289-282-7). Pelican.

Louisiana Chronology & Factbook, Vol. 18. R. I. Vexler. 1978. 8.50 (ISBN 0-379-16143-5). Oceana.

Louisiana: In Words & Pictures. Dennis Fradin. (Young People's Stories of Our States Ser.). (Illus.). 48p. (gr. 2-5). 1981. PLB 8.65g (ISBN 0-516-03918-0, Time Line). Childrens.

Louisiana Lady. Cynthia Van Hazinga. 320p. (Orig.). 1981. pap. 2.75 (ISBN 0-515-05152-7). Jove Pubns.

Louisiana Life & Health. 1980. 16.00 (ISBN 0-930868-14-5). Merritt Co.

Louisiana Lil. Donald McGregor. (Orig.). 1980. pap. 1.75 (ISBN 0-8439-0737-1, Leisure Bks). Nordon Pubns.

Louisiana Property & Casualty. 1979. 16.00 (ISBN 0-930868-15-3). Merritt Co.

Louisiana Purchase, April 1803: Thomas Jefferson Doubles the Area of the United States. James P. Barry. LC 72-6836. (Focus Bks.). (Illus.). 96p. (gr. 7-12). 1973. PLB 4.90 o.p. (ISBN 0-531-02460-1). Watts.

Louisiana Sports Encyclopedia. Bob Remy. 1977. pap. 8.95 (ISBN 0-88289-120-0). Pelican.

Louisiana Sports Record Book. Ed. by James Calhoun. 104p. 1971. pap. 1.95 (ISBN 0-911116-55-9). Pelican.

Louisiana State Industrial Directory, Nineteen Eighty-One. State Industrial Directories Corp. Date not set. pap. price not set (ISBN 0-89910-047-3). State Indus D.

Louisiana's Fabulous Foods & How to Cook Them. Helen H. Hardy & Raymond J. Martinez. 80p. pap. 2.95 (ISBN 0-911116-82-6). Pelican.

Louly. Carol R. Brink. LC 73-21885. (Illus.). 208p. (gr. 4-7). 1974. 5.95g o.s.i. (ISBN 0-02-713680-9). Macmillan.

Loundoun County, Virginia: Marriage Records to 1891. Aurelia M. Jewell. 100p. 1975. 12.50 (ISBN 0-685-65071-5). Va Bk.

Louvor Em Acao. Tr. by Merlin Carothers. (Portugese Bks.). (Port.). 1979. 1.25 (ISBN 0-8297-0638-0). Life Pubs Intl.

Louvre. Michel LaClotte. LC 79-57409. (Abbeville Library of Art: No. 3). (Illus.). 112p. 1980. pap. 4.95 (ISBN 0-89659-097-6). Abbeville Pr.

Love. Leo Buscaglia. 1978. pap. 2.50 o.p. (ISBN 0-449-23452-5, Crest). Fawcett.

Love. Loe Buscaglia. 208p. 1981. pap. 2.50 (ISBN 0-449-23452-5, Crest). Fawcett.

Love. Ernesto Cardenal. 160p. (Span.). 1981. pap. 4.95 (ISBN 0-8245-0043-1). Crossroad NY.

Love. Jane B. Moncure. Ed. by Jane Buerger. (Illus.). 1980. 4.95 (ISBN 0-89565-165-3, 4927). Standard Pub.

Love. rev. ed. Jane B. Moncure. LC 80-27479. (What Is It? Ser.). (Illus.). 32p. (gr. k-3). 1981. PLB 5.50 (ISBN 0-89565-205-6). Childs World.

Love, Vol. VI. Denise Robins. 592p. 1980. pap. 2.75 (ISBN 0-345-28520-4). Ballantine.

Love, Vol. VII. Denise Robins. 720p. 1980. pap. 2.75 (ISBN 0-345-28521-2). Ballantine.

Love a Hostage. Grace Lang. (YA) 1970. 5.95 (ISBN 0-685-07445-5, Avalon). Bouregy.

Love, Acceptance & Forgiveness. Jerry Cook & Stanley C. Baldwin. LC 79-63763. 128p. 1979. pap. 3.95 (ISBN 0-8307-0654-2, 5411106). Regal.

Love Affair. Emile Zola. 1957. 13.95 (ISBN 0-236-30905-6, Pub. by Paul Elek). Merrimack Bk Serv.

Love After Hours. Barbara Brett. 352p. 1981. pap. 2.50 (ISBN 0-380-76257-9, 76257). Avon.

Love Against Hate. Karl A. Menninger. LC 42-50183. 1959. pap. 3.50 (ISBN 0-15-653892-X, HB28, Harv). HarBraceJ.

Love Against Hate. Karl A. Menninger & Jeanetta L. Menninger. LC 42-50183. 1959. 10.75 o.p. (ISBN 0-15-153891-3). HarBraceJ.

Love, Altruism, & World Crisis: The Challenge of Pitirim Sorokin. Joseph A. Matter. LC 73-84209. 1974. 17.95 (ISBN 0-88229-114-9). Nelson-Hall.

Love Among the Butterflies: The Secret Life of a Victorian Lady. Margaret Fontaine. 256p. 1981. 19.95 (ISBN 0-316-28942-6). Little.

Love Among the Cannibals. Wright Morris. LC 76-16574. 1977. 12.50x (ISBN 0-8032-0880-4); pap. 3.25 (ISBN 0-8032-5842-9, BB 620, Bison). U of Nebr Pr.

Love Among the Mashed Potatoes. Gregory McDonald. 1978. 8.95 o.p. (ISBN 0-525-14905-8). Dutton.

Love & Attraction: An International Conference. Ed. by Mark Cook & Glenn Wilson. LC 78-40286. 1979. text ed. 72.00 (ISBN 0-08-022234-X); pap. text ed. 22.00 o.p. (ISBN 0-08-022235-8). Pergamon.

Love & Being: An Investigation into the Metaphysics of St. Thomas Aquinas. Bernard J. Diggs. 180p. 1947. 6.75 (ISBN 0-913298-45-X). S F Vanni.

Love & Commitment. Gary Schwartz et al. LC 79-25460. (Sociological Observations: Vol. 9). (Illus.). 271p. 1980. 18.95 (ISBN 0-8039-1419-9); pap. 8.95 (ISBN 0-8039-1420-2). Sage.

Love & Commitment: You Don't Have to Settle for Less. Carol Leavenworth. (Illus.). 192p. 1981. 10.95t (ISBN 0-13-540971-3, Spec); pap. 5.95b (ISBN 0-13-540963-2). P-H.

Love & Death. Woody Allen. 1978. 7.95 o.p. (ISBN 0-394-50070-9). Random.

Love & Death in the Philosophy of Gabriel Marcel. Barbara E. Wall. 1977. pap. text ed. 6.50x o.p. (ISBN 0-8191-0190-7). U Pr of Amer.

Love & Ethics in the Lais of Marie De France: No. 4. 1976. 10.50 o.p. (ISBN 0-686-23381-6). Classical Folia.

Love & Friendship & Other Early Works. Jane Austen. Ed. by Harriet Bell. (Illus.). 128p. 1981. 8.95 (ISBN 0-517-54459-8, Harmony); pap. 3.95 (ISBN 0-517-54372-9). Crown.

Love & Gifts. Jim McNair. LC 76-6555. 1976. 3.50 (ISBN 0-87123-328-2, 210328). Bethany Fell.

Love & Hate on the Tennis Court. Stanley H. Cath et al. LC 77-476. (Encore Edition). 1977. 3.50 o.p. (ISBN 0-684-15938-4, ScribT). Scribner.

Love & Honor. Leslie Arlen. 384p. 1980. pap. 2.95 (ISBN 0-515-05868-8, Jove). Jove Pubns.

Love & Its Derangements & Other Poems. Joyce C. Oates. 192p. 1977. pap. 1.75 o.p. (ISBN 0-449-30811-1, Prem). Fawcett.

Love & Knishes: An Irrepressible Guide to Jewish Cooking. Sara Kasdan. LC 56-12031. (Illus.). 1956. 8.95 (ISBN 0-8149-0132-8). Vanguard.

Love & Lifestyles. Mary T. Judd. LC 80-54285. (Illus.). 200p. (Orig.). (gr. 12). 1981. pap. text ed. 5.25 (ISBN 0-88489-132-1). St Mary's.

Love & Living. Thomas Merton. Ed. by Naomi B. Stone & Bro. Paterick Hart. 240p. 1979. 10.00 (ISBN 0-374-19237-5). FS&G.

Love & Love Sickness: The Science of Sex; Gender. Difference & Pair Bonding. John Money. LC 79-3679. 1980. 16.95x (ISBN 0-8018-2317-X); pap. text ed. 5.95 (ISBN 0-8018-2318-8). Johns Hopkins.

Love & Loving. Eugene Raudsepp. (Best Thoughts Ser.). (Illus.). 80p. 1981. pap. 2.50 (ISBN 0-8431-0389-2). Price Stern.

Love & No Marriage. Rachel Lindsay. (Harlequin Presents Ser.). 192p. 1980. pap. 1.50 (ISBN 0-373-10381-6, Pub. by Harlequin). PB.

Love & Other Deaths. D. M. Thomas. 1975. 10.95 (ISBN 0-236-31016-X, Pub. by Paul Elek). Merrimack Bk Serv.

Love & Play. Andrew M. Greeley. LC 77-5798. (Orig.). 1977. pap. 3.95 (ISBN 0-8164-1222-7). Crossroad NY.

Love & Religion: A Study of Sexual Delusion. Albert L. Schutz. Ed. by Anne N. Lowenkopf. (Illus., Orig.). 1981. 14.50 (ISBN 0-936596-02-3); pap. 9.95 (ISBN 0-936596-02-3). Quantal.

Love & Responsibility. Pope John Paul II. Tr. by H. T. Willetts. 1981. 11.95 (ISBN 0-374-19247-2). FS&G.

Love & Sex & Growing up. Corinne B. Johnson & Eric W. Johnson. LC 77-22462. 1977. 6.95 o.p. (ISBN 0-397-31768-9). Lippincott.

Love & Sex in Plain Language. 3rd ed. Eric W. Johnson. LC 77-5705. (Illus.). (YA) 1977. 8.95 (ISBN 0-397-01231-4). Lippincott.

Love & Sexuality. Eugene Raudsepp. (Best Thoughts Ser.). (Illus.). 80p. 1981. pap. 2.50 (ISBN 0-8431-0387-6). Price Stern.

Love & Success. Karl Stern. 1975. 8.95 o.p. (ISBN 0-374-19258-8); pap. 4.95 o.p. (ISBN 0-374-51386-4). FS&G.

Love & Sympathy in Theravada Buddhism. Harvey B. Aronson. 1980. 11.00x (ISBN 0-8364-0627-3, Pub. by Motilal Banarsidass). South Asia Bks.

Love & Terror. William Herrick. LC 80-25140. 256p. 1981. 12.95 (ISBN 0-8112-0791-9). New Directions.

Love & the Quest for Identity in the Fiction of Henry James. Philip Sicker. LC 79-17311. 1980. 16.00x (ISBN 0-691-06417-2); pap. 8.50 (ISBN 0-691-10092-6), Princeton U Pr.

Love & the Urban Ghetto. Paul H. Furfey. LC 77-16700. 1978. pap. 3.95x o.p. (ISBN 0-88344-292-2). Orbis Bks.

Love Around the House. Elizabeth Baker. 1979. pap. 2.50 (ISBN 0-88207-603-5). Victor Bks.

Love at Leisure. Daisy Thomson. (Orig.). 1978. pap. 1.50 o.s.i. (ISBN 0-515-04558-6). Jove Pubns.

Love Beyond Reason. Karen Van Der Zee. (Harlequin Romances Ser.). 192p. 1981. pap. 1.25 (ISBN 0-373-02406-1, Pub. by Harlequin). PB.

Love Bites. Freda Garmaise. 11.95 (ISBN 0-671-42036-4). S&S.

Love Bug. Walt Disney Productions. LC 78-13896. (Walt Disney's Wonderful World of Reading Ser.). (Illus.). (gr. k-3). 1979. 3.95 o.p. (ISBN 0-394-84139-5, BYR); PLB 4.39 o.p. (ISBN 0-394-94139-X). Random.

Love Child. Fiona Hill. 1979. pap. 1.95 o.p. (ISBN 0-425-04102-6). Berkley Pub.

Love Child. Fiona Hill. LC 77-82863. (YA) 1977. 8.95 o.p. (ISBN 0-399-12061-0, Dist. by Putnam). Berkley Pub.

Love Child. Eve Shelnutt. 1979. pap. 4.50 (ISBN 0-87685-384-X); pap. 4.50 (ISBN 0-87685-384-X). Black Sparrow.

Love Comes Softly. Janette Oke. 192p. (Orig.). 1979. pap. 3.50 (ISBN 0-87123-342-8, 210342). Bethany Fell.

Love Comes to Anne. Warner. (gr. 7-12). 1980. pap. 1.50 (ISBN 0-590-30027-X, Schol Pap). Schol Bk Serv.

Love Crisis: Hit & Run Lovers, Sexual Stingies, Unreliables, Kinkies, & Other Typical Men of Today. Carol Botwin & Jerome Fine. 256p. 1980. pap. 2.50 (ISBN 0-553-13814-6). Bantam.

Love, Death & the Universe. Nigel Rees. (Illus.). 128p. 1981. pap. 6.95 (ISBN 0-02-029340-2). Macmillan.

Love Etc. Bel Kaufman. 1981. pap. 2.75 (ISBN 0-380-53629-3, 53629). Avon.

Love Explosion. Robert H. Rimmer. 1980. pap. 2.75 (ISBN 0-451-09519-7, E9519, Sig). NAL.

Love: Familystyle: How to Have a Happy Home. Clarence W. Kerr. pap. 1.95 (ISBN 0-89107-142-3). Good News.

Love Finds a Way. Felicia Bryce. (YA) 1977. 4.95 o.p. (ISBN 0-685-73808-6, Avalon). Bouregy.

Love for Cooking. Uta Hagen. LC 76-12538. (Illus.). 1976. 10.95 o.s.i. (ISBN 0-02-547380-8, 54738). Macmillan.

Love for Love. William Congreve. Ed. by Emmett L. Avery. LC 66-20827. (Regents Restoration Drama Ser). 1966. 9.25x (ISBN 0-8032-0353-5); pap. 3.95x (ISBN 0-8032-5353-2, BB 259, Bison). U of Nebr Pr.

Love for Sale. Barbara Cartland. (Barbara Cartland Ser.: No. 129). (Orig.). 1980. pap. 1.75 (ISBN 0-553-13984-3). Bantam.

Love for Sale. Barbara Cartland. 1980. 9.95 (ISBN 0-525-14906-6). Dutton.

Love Forever More. Patricia Matthews. 1977. pap. 2.75 (ISBN 0-523-41203-7). Pinnacle Bks.

Love Forty. Robert Barker. LC 75-2241. 216p. 1975. 7.95 o.p. (ISBN 0-397-01069-9). Lippincott.

Love-from Black Men to Black Women. Ed. by Frances Johnson Barnes. 1976. 5.00 o.p. (ISBN 0-682-48569-1). Exposition.

Love from Trieste. Kirsten Thorup. Tr. by Nadia Christensen & Alexander Taylor. 64p. (Orig.). 1980. pap. 5.00 (ISBN 0-915306-20-4). Curbstone.

Love from Uncle Clyde. Nancy W. Parker. LC 76-54957. (gr. k-3). 1977. 5.95 (ISBN 0-396-07426-X). Dodd.

Love Genie. Joanne Webster. (gr. 9-12). 1980. 8.95 (ISBN 0-525-66699-0). Elsevier-Nelson.

Love Goddess. David Hanna. 1977. pap. 1.75 (ISBN 0-505-51130-4). Tower Bks.

Love, Guilt & Reparation. Melanie Klein. 1975. 20.00 o.p. (ISBN 0-440-05021-9, Sey Lawr). Delacorte.

Love Has a Price Tag. Elisabeth Elliot. LC 79-50944. 148p. 1981. pap. 5.95 (ISBN 0-915684-87-X). Christian Herald.

Love Has His Way. Barbara Cartland. LC 80-108. 1979. 6.95 (ISBN 0-87272-085-3, Duron Bks). Brodart.

Love, Hate, Fear, Anger, & the Other Lively Emotions. June Callwood. LC 80-19320. 168p. 1980. Repr. of 1971 ed. lib. bdg. 9.95x (ISBN 0-89370-602-7). Borgo Pr.

Love, Honor & Be Free. Maxine Hancock. study ed. 5.95 (ISBN 0-8024-5015-6). Moody.

Love, Honor & Be Free: Leader's Guide. Maxine Hancock. 1979. pap. 3.25 (ISBN 0-8024-5016-4). Moody.

Love Hunter. Jon Hassler. 320p. 1981. 12.95 (ISBN 0-688-00483-0). Morrow.

Love in a Cold Climate. Nancy Mitford. Bd. with Pursuit of Love. 1975. pap. 1.95 o.p. (ISBN 0-445-08405-7). Popular Lib.

Love in Amsterdam. Nicolas Freeling. 192p. 1975. pap. 1.95 o.p. (ISBN 0-14-002281-3). Penguin.

Love in Being. Tom Armstrong. (Illus.). 64p. 1981. 5.95 (ISBN 0-9604246-1-X). Jemta Pr.

Love in Deed. rev. ed. Judith Tate-O'Brien. (Illus.). 68p. 1980. pap. 2.95 (ISBN 0-936098-07-4). Natl Marriage.

Love in Exile. Blanche Chenier. (Regency Love Story Ser.). (Orig.). 1980. pap. 1.75 (ISBN 0-449-50046-2, Coventry). Fawcett.

Love in Paris. Murray Kalis. 224p. 1981. pap. 1.95 (ISBN 0-449-14382-1, GM). Fawcett.

Love in the Later Years: The Emotional, Physical, Sexual & Social Potential of the Elderly. James A. Peterson & Barbara Payne. 192p. 1975. 7.95 o.p. (ISBN 0-8096-1898-2, Assn Pr). Follett.

Love in the Moon, No. 138. Barbara Cartland. 160p. (Orig.). 1981. pap. 1.95 (ISBN 0-553-14585-1). Bantam.

Love in the Mortar Joints: The Story of Habitat for Humanity. Millard Fuller & Diane Scott. 150p. 1980. pap. 4.95 (ISBN 0-695-81444-3, Assn Pr). Follett.

Love in the Rain. Nagib Mahfouz. pap. 5.50 arabic (ISBN 0-685-82841-7). Intl Bk Ctr.

Love in the Ruins. Walker Percy. LC 71-143301. 416p. 1971. 15.95 (ISBN 0-374-19302-9). FS&G.

Love in the Ruins. Walker Percy. 384p. 1981. pap. 2.95 (ISBN 0-380-38984-3, 53843). Avon.

Love in the Skies. Virginia Jordan. 80p. 1981. 5.50 (ISBN 0-682-49684-7). Exposition.

Love in Twelfth Century France. John C. Moore. LC 75-170268. (Orig.). 1972. 10.00x (ISBN 0-8122-7648-5); pap. 4.95x (ISBN 0-8122-1027-1, Pa Paperbks). U of Pa Pr.

Love in Winter. Storm Jameson. pap. 1.95 o.p. (ISBN 0-425-03207-8). Berkley Pub.

Love Is. Dottie Rambo. (Creek Bank Kids Ser.: Vol. 9). (ps-8). 1980. 3.95 (ISBN 0-914850-92-X). Impact Tenn.

Love Is a Couple. Gallagher, Chuck, Fr., S.J. 1978. pap. 2.95 (ISBN 0-385-13595-5, Im). Doubleday.

Love Is a Dog from Hell: Poems 1974-1977. Charles Bukowski. 260p. (Orig.). 1980. 14.00 (ISBN 0-87685-363-7); pap. 6.00 (ISBN 0-87685-362-9). Black Sparrow.

Love Is a Sad Song. Ruskin Bond. 104p. 1976. pap. 1.80 (ISBN 0-89253-027-8). Ind-US Inc.

Love Is an Attitude. Walter Rinder. LC 74-147246. (Illus., Orig.). 1970. 5.95 o.p. (ISBN 0-912310-04-9); pap. 4.95 (ISBN 0-912310-03-0). Celestial Arts.
Love Is an Everyday Thing. Colleen T. Evans. (Orig.). pap. 1.50 (ISBN 0-89129-243-8). Jove Pubns.
Love Is for Living. Carlo Carretto. Tr. by Jeremy Moiser from Ital. LC 76-49878. Orig. Title: Cio Che Conta E Amare. 1977. Repr. 6.95x (ISBN 0-88344-291-4); pap. 4.95 (ISBN 0-88344-293-0). Orbis Bks.
Love Is for Tomorrow. Hope Traver. 271p. 1978. pap. 4.95 (ISBN 0-930756-37-1, 4230-TR1). Women's Aglow.
Love Is Forever. Margaret E. Bell. (gr. 7 up). 1954. PLB 8.40 (ISBN 0-688-31449-X). Morrow.
Love Is Just a Word. Johannes M. Simmel. 448p. 1980. pap. 2.95 (ISBN 0-445-04622-8). Popular Lib.
Love Is Letting Go of Fear. Gerald Jampolsky. 144p. 1981. pap. 2.50 (ISBN 0-553-14651-3). Bantam.
Love Is Like Peanuts. Betty Bates. 1981. pap. 1.75 (ISBN 0-671-56109-X). PB.
Love Is Not a Special Way of Feeling. Charles G. Finney. Orig. Title: Attributes of Love. 1963. pap. 1.95 (ISBN 0-87123-005-4, 200005). Bethany Fell.
Love Is Not Enough. Bruno Bettelheim. 1950. 17.95 (ISBN 0-02-903280-6). Free Pr.
Love Is Not Enough. Bruno Bettelheim. 1971. pap. 2.95 (ISBN 0-380-01405-X, 47498, Discus). Avon.
Love Is Not for Cowards: The Autobiography of Shirley Dyckes Kelley. Shirley D. Kelley. LC 77-26211. 1978. 9.95 o.p. (ISBN 0-13-541029-0). P-H.
Love Is of the Valley. Jean Stubbs. 378p. 1981. 12.95 (ISBN 0-312-49942-6). St Martin.
Love Is Prayer - Prayer Is Love. St. Alphonsus Liguori. LC 72-97592. 1973. pap. 2.50 (ISBN 0-89243-047-8, 41500). Liguori Pubns.
Love Is the Answer. 96p. 1978. pap. 3.50 (ISBN 0-911336-74-5). Sci of Mind.
Love Is the Enemy, No. 9. Barbara Cartland. 1978. pap. 1.50 o.s.i. (ISBN 0-515-04565-9). Jove Pubns.
Love Is the Motive. Carol Amen. LC 77-12655. (Better Living Ser.). 1977. pap. 0.95 (ISBN 0-8127-0153-4). Southern Pub.
Love Island. Justine Valenti. (Orig.). 1981. pap. 1.50 (ISBN 0-440-14709-3). Dell.
Love Killers. Jackie Collins. Orig. Title: Lovehead. 192p. 1975. pap. 2.25 (ISBN 0-446-92842-9). Warner Bks.
Love Kindling Fire: A Study Christopher Marlowe's the Tragedy of Dido Queen of Carthage. Mary E. Smith. (Salzburg Studies in English Literature: Elizabethan & Renaissance: No.63). 1977. pap. text ed. 25.00x (ISBN 0-391-01529-X). Humanities.
Love Knows No Barriers. Margaret Hess. 1979. pap. 2.50 (ISBN 0-88207-780-5). Victor Bks.
Love, Labour & Liberty: The Eighteenth-Century Scottish Lyric. Ed. by Thomas Crawford. (Essays, Prose, & Scottish Literature Ser.). 1979. 9.95 (ISBN 0-85635-182-2, Pub. by Carcanet New Pr England); pap. 5.95 (ISBN 0-85635-195-4). Persea Bks.
Love, Laughter & Tears. Adela Rogers St. Johns. LC 76-50786. 1978. 10.00 o.p. (ISBN 0-385-12054-0). Doubleday.
Love Letters. Madeleine L'Engle. 365p. 1966. 7.95 (ISBN 0-374-19325-8). FS&G.
Love Lies Bleeding. Edmund Crispin. 9.95 (ISBN 0-8027-5444-9). Walker & Co.
Love Lies North. Glenna Finley. Date not set. pap. 1.75 o.p. (ISBN 0-451-08740-2, E8740, Sig). NAL.
Love Life. Donald G. Barnhouse. LC 72-94754. 1977. pap. 2.95 (ISBN 0-8307-0451-5, S270-1-29). Regal.
Love Life for Every Married Couple. E. Wheat. 288p. 1980. pap. 5.95 (ISBN 0-310-42511-5). Zondervan.
Love Like Ours. Denise Robins. 1976. pap. 1.25 o.p. (ISBN 0-345-25494-5). Ballantine.
Love Listens. Don Hall. 288p. (Orig.). 1981. pap. 2.50 (ISBN 0-523-41034-4). Pinnacle Bks.
Love, Love at the End. D. Berrigan. 1971. pap. 1.45 o.s.i. (ISBN 0-02-083750-X, Collier). Macmillan.
Love Makes the World Go Round. Keith Huttenlocker. 1976. pap. 1.50 (ISBN 0-89129-181-4). Jove Pubns.
Love, Marriage & Romance in Old London. C. J. Thompson. LC 70-76076. (Illus.). 1971. Repr. of 1936 ed. 18.50 (ISBN 0-8103-3211-6). Gale.
Love, Mary. Mary Gwynn. LC 80-24996. 224p. 1981. price not set (ISBN 0-688-00429-6). Morrow.
Love Me, Love My Doggerel. Louise F. Kerr. LC 70-107863. 1969. 3.00 (ISBN 0-937684-02-3). Tradd St Pr.
Love Me with Tough Love. Anne Ortlund. 1979. 7.95 (ISBN 0-8499-0145-6). Word Bks.
Love, Mystery & Misery: Feeling in Gothic Fiction. Coral A. Howells. 1978. text ed. 28.50x (ISBN 0-485-11181-0, Athlone Pr). Humanities.
Love Never Ends. Joyce G. Rice. pap. 3.95 (ISBN 0-89036-147-9). Hawkes Pub Inc.
Love Notes to Jeanette. Harold Myra. 1979. pap. 3.95 (ISBN 0-88207-638-8). Victor Bks.
Love of a Good Man. Howard Barker. 1981. pap. 9.95 (ISBN 0-7145-3767-5). Riverrun NY.
Love of Eternal Wisdom. St. Louis De Montfort. pap. 4.95 (ISBN 0-910984-05-0) (ISBN 0-910984-51-4). Montfort Pubns.
Love of God According to Saiva Siddhanta: A Study in the Mysticism & Theology of Saivism. Mariasusai Dhavamony. 1971. 23.00x o.p. (ISBN 0-19-826523-9). Oxford U Pr.
Love of Gold. Emily Hahn. LC 80-7877. 224p. 1980. 10.95 (ISBN 0-690-01832-0). Lippincott & Crowell.
Love of Krishna: The Krsnakarnamrta of Lilasuka Bilvamangala. Ed. & tr. by Frances Wilson. LC 74-153426. (Haney Foundation Ser.). 448p. 1975. 15.00x (ISBN 0-8122-7655-8). U of Pa Pr.
Love of the Land. Darrell Sifford. (Illus.). 288p. 1980. 11.95 (ISBN 0-89795-010-0). Farm Journal.
Love of the Lion. Angela Gray. 1980. pap. 2.50 (ISBN 0-671-41464-X). PB.
Love on the Run. Barbara Cartland. (Barbara Cartland Ser.: No. 17). 256p. (Orig.). 1981. pap. 1.75 (ISBN 0-515-05956-0). Jove Pubns.
Love Poem for a Bank Robber. Jane Teller. (Illus., Orig.). 1981. pap. 2.50 (ISBN 0-914140-09-4). Carpenter Pr.
Love Poem to an African Violet. Agadem L. Diara. 1981. pap. 2.50 (ISBN 0-913358-13-4). Shabazz Pr. Postponed.
Love Poems. Mirza Ghalib. (Translated from Urdu). 6.75 (ISBN 0-89253-758-2); flexible cloth 4.80 (ISBN 0-89253-759-0). Ind-US Inc.
Love Poems & Sonnets of William Shakespeare. William Shakespeare. LC 57-11411. 6.95 (ISBN 0-385-01733-2). Doubleday.
Love: Poems by Danielle Steel. Danielle Steel. (Orig.). 1981. pap. 2.50 (ISBN 0-440-15377-8). Dell.
Love Poems of a Marriage. Evelyn Barkins. LC 74-20656. 1970. pap. 2.95 (ISBN 0-8119-0387-7). Fell.
Love Poems of Karl Marx. Ed. by Reinhard Lettau & Lawrence Ferlinghetti. LC 76-8200. 1977. pap. 2.00 o.p. (ISBN 0-87286-087-6). City Lights.
Love Poems of Tagore. Rabindranath Tagore. Tr. by Rabindra N. Chowdhury from Benjali. 189p. 1976. pap. 2.50 o.p. (ISBN 0-89253-062-6). InterCulture.
Love Potion. Carol Zezza. 1978. pap. 1.95 o.s.i. (ISBN 0-515-04629-9). Jove Pubns.
Love Power: New Dimensions for Building Strong Families. Alan Stine. LC 78-70360. 1978. 5.95 (ISBN 0-88290-105-2). Horizon Utah.
Love Project Way. Arleen Lorrance & Diane K. Pike. 216p. (Orig.). 1980. pap. 6.95 (ISBN 0-916192-15-6). L P Pubns.
Love Reaches Out. Ulrich Schaffer. LC 75-70810. (Jubilee Bk). 96p. (Orig.). 1976. pap. 1.95 (ISBN 0-06-067080-0, HJ24, HarpR). Har-Row.
Love Run. Jay Parini. 1980. 10.95 (ISBN 0-316-69065-1, Pub. by Atlantic-Little Brown). Little.
Love Scene. Jesse L. Lasky, Jr. & Pat Silver. 1981. pap. 2.75 (ISBN 0-425-05022-X). Berkley Pub.
Love Scene: The Story of Laurence Olivier & Vivien Leigh. Jesse Lasky, Jr. & Pat Silver. LC 78-4765. (Illus.). 1978. 10.95 o.p. (ISBN 0-690-01413-9, TYC-T). T Y Crowell.
Love, Sex & Marriage: A Jewish View. Roland B. Gittelsohn. (Illus.). (gr. 6-10). 1980. pap. 7.95x (ISBN 0-8074-0046-7, 142683). UAHC.
Love, Sex & Sex Roles. Constantina Safilios-Rothschild. LC 76-44439. 1977. 9.95 (ISBN 0-13-540948-9, Spec); pap. 5.95 (ISBN 0-13-540930-6). P-H.
Love, Sex & the Teenager. Rhoda L. Lorand. 1965. 6.95 o.s.i. (ISBN 0-685-15488-2). Macmillan.
Love, Sex, Death, & the Meaning of Life: Woody Allen's Comedy. Foster Hirsh. (McGraw-Hill Paperbacks Ser.). (Illus.). 192p. (Orig.). 1981. pap. 5.95 (ISBN 0-07-029054-7, GB). McGraw.
Love, Sex, Feminism. John Wilson. LC 79-24902. 1980. 18.95 (ISBN 0-03-056103-5). Praeger.
Love Slaves. Samuel L. Brengle. 1960. Repr. of 1923 ed. 3.25 (ISBN 0-86544-004-2). Salvation Army.
Love So Bold. Annelise Kamada. (Orig.). 1978. pap. 2.50 o.s.i. (ISBN 0-446-81638-8). Warner Bks.
Love So Freely Given. Ada L. Roberts. 1981. 8.95 (ISBN 0-533-04814-1). Vantage.
Love So Wild. Deborah Chester. 1981. pap. 2.50 (ISBN 0-345-28773-8). Ballantine.
Love Song. Leslie Tonner. 1981. pap. 2.50 (ISBN 0-425-04832-2). Berkley Pub.
Love Song to the Plains. Mari Sandoz. LC 61-6441. (Illus.). 1966. pap. 3.50 (ISBN 0-8032-5172-6, BB 349, Bison). U of Nebr Pr.
Love Songs. Sara Teasdale. LC 75-19068. (Illus.). 96p. 1975. 9.95 (ISBN 0-02-616880-4, 61688). Macmillan.
Love Songs for an Age of Anxiety. Bradley R. Strahan. (Black Buzzard Chapbook Ser.). (Illus.). 20p. (Orig.). 1981. pap. 1.50 (ISBN 0-938872-00-1). Black Buzzard.
Love Songs for Marisa. John Nist. 1978. 10.95 (ISBN 0-89002-116-3); pap. 3.50 (ISBN 0-89002-115-5). Northwoods Pr.
Love Story. Eric Segal. (Arabic.). pap. 6.95x (ISBN 0-686-63552-3). Intl Bk Ctr.
Love Story. Erich Segal. 1977. pap. 1.75 (ISBN 0-380-01760-1, 34934). Avon.
Love Story of a Jewish Cat. Max Stein. (Illus.). 1979. pap. 3.95 (ISBN 0-8467-0582-6, Pub. by Two Continents). Hippocrene Bks.
Love Talker. Elizabeth Peters. LC 79-22104. 256p. 1980. 8.95 (ISBN 0-396-07780-3). Dodd.
Love Talker. Elizabeth Peters. (Large Print Bks.). 1980. lib. bdg. 13.95 (ISBN 0-8161-3135-X). G K Hall.
Love the Unknown. Dallas Kenmare. 8.95 (ISBN 0-85307-067-9). Transatlantic.
Love Thy Teen-Ager. Mary A. Schatz. (Uplook Ser.). 32p. 1973. pap. 0.75 (ISBN 0-8163-0014-3, 12693-8). Pacific Pr Pub Assn.
Love Triumphant. Caroline Courtney. 1980. pap. 1.75 (ISBN 0-446-94293-6). Warner Bks.
Love Unveiled. Ruth Watt. 192p. (YA) 1976. 5.95 (ISBN 0-685-62025-5, Avalon). Bouregy.
Love View. Bernard Gunther. 1971. pap. 2.95 o.s.i. (ISBN 0-02-076830-3, Collier). Macmillan.
Love Waits at Penrhyn. Pat Phillips. 192p. (YA) 1975. 5.95 (ISBN 0-685-53495-2, Avalon). Bouregy.
Love with No Strings: The Human Touch in Christian Social Ministries. Elaine Furlow. Ed. by Everett Hullum. (Human Touch Photo-Text Ser.: Volume Iv). (Illus.). 1977. 6.95 (ISBN 0-937170-15-1). Home Mission.
Love Within & Outside the Cloister. Leland De Saint-Pierre. (Intimate Life of Man Library Bk). (Illus.). 1979. 29.45 (ISBN 0-89266-168-2). Am Classical Coll Pr.
Love Without Boundaries: Mother Teresa of Calcutta. Georges Gorree & Jean Barbier. LC 75-37364. 1976. pap. 3.95 (ISBN 0-87973-679-8). Our Sunday Visitor.
Love Wounds & Multiple Fractures: Poems. Carolanne Ely. 1975. pap. 3.00 (ISBN 0-915342-02-2). SUN.
Love Your Neighbor. Louis Evely. 120p. 1975. pap. 1.45 (ISBN 0-385-06256-7, Im). Doubleday.
Lovebirds: Their Care & Breeding. 142p. 1980. 5.95 (ISBN 0-903264-39-0, 4902-2, Pub. by K & R Bks England). Arco.
Lovechild. Mary Hanes. Date not set. pap. 1.50 o.p. (ISBN 0-451-07260-X, W7260, Sig). NAL.
Lovecraft: A Biography. L. Sprague De Camp. 480p. 1976. pap. 1.95 o.p. (ISBN 0-345-25115-6). Ballantine.
Lovecraft: A Look Behind the Cthulhu Mythos. Lin Carter. 1976. pap. 1.50 o.p. (ISBN 0-345-25295-0). Ballantine.
Lovecraft's Follies: A Play. James Schevill. LC 77-150761. 90p. 1971. 5.00 (ISBN 0-8040-0501-X); pap. 2.95 (ISBN 0-8040-0502-8). Swallow.
Loved & Forgiven. Lloyd J. Ogilvie. LC 76-29889. 1977. pap. 2.50 (ISBN 0-8307-0442-6, S313-1-03). Regal.
Lovefire. Julia Grice. 1977. pap. 2.25 (ISBN 0-380-01741-5, 42499). Avon.
Lovely Lord of the Lord's Day. Glenn Coon & Ethel Coon. LC 75-464238. 1976. pap. 4.95 (ISBN 0-8163-0225-1, 12740-7). Pacific Pr Pub Assn.
Lovely Paper Flowers. Ondori Publishing Co. Staff. (Ondori Handicrafts Ser). (Illus., Orig.). 1977. pap. 6.50 (ISBN 0-87040-413-X). Japan Pubns.
Lovely Vassilisa. Retold by Barbara Cohen. LC 80-12494. (Illus.). 48p. (ps-4). 1980. 9.95 (ISBN 0-689-30773-X). Atheneum.
Lovely Wanton. Constance Fecher. 1977. pap. 1.75 o.s.i. (ISBN 0-440-16982-8). Dell.
Lovely World of Richi-San. Allan R. Bosworth. (Illus.). 1960. 6.95 o.p. (ISBN 0-06-010400-7, HarpT). Har-Row.
Lovepoems. Penny Harter. 56p. (Orig.). 1981. pap. 3.95 (ISBN 0-89120-016-9, Old Plate). From Here.
Lovequest. Louise Vaughan. 1979. pap. 2.25 o.s.i. (ISBN 0-515-04696-5). Jove Pubns.
Lovers. Richard Posner. 1978. pap. 1.95 o.p. (ISBN 0-449-13989-1, GM). Fawcett.
Lovers. Rosemarie Santini. (Book III of Agnes Nixon's All My Children Ser.). 240p. (Orig.). 1981. pap. 2.50 (ISBN 0-515-04896-8). Jove Pubns.
Lovers All Untrue. Norah Lofts. 1977. pap. 1.50 o.p. (ISBN 0-449-22792-8, Q2792, Crest). Fawcett.
Lovers & Liars. Doris Bingham. 1981. pap. 2.25 (ISBN 0-8439-0905-6, Leisure Bks). Nordon Pubns.
Lovers & Not People. Timeri Murari. 1979. pap. 2.25 o.s.i. (ISBN 0-515-04763-5). Jove Pubns.
Lovers & Other Stories. Pearl S. Buck. LC 76-56819. (John Day Bk.). 1977. 9.95 (ISBN 0-381-97109-0, TYC-T). T Y Crowell.
Lovers Book: Your Secret Source of Love. Bruce Davis & Genny W. Davis. (Illus.). 1980. pap. 3.95 (ISBN 0-02-529860-7); write for info. prepack (ISBN 0-02-529890-9). Macmillan.
Lovers for Life: The Key to a Loving & Lasting Marriage. Roberta DeVille & Jard DeVille. LC 80-10652. 224p. 1980. 8.95 (ISBN 0-688-03618-X). Morrow.
Lovers in a Winter Circle. Jonathan Kirsch. (Orig.). 1978. pap. 1.75 o.p. (ISBN 0-451-08119-6, E8119, Sig). NAL.
Lover's Knot. Janet Templeton. LC 80-2083. 192p. 1981. 9.95 (ISBN 0-385-17209-5). Doubleday.
Lovers Meeting. Mollie Hardwick. (gr. 7-12). 1980. lib. bdg. 15.95 (ISBN 0-8161-3064-7, Large Print Bks). G K Hall.
Lover's Point. C. Y. Lee. 1958. 3.75 o.p. (ISBN 0-374-19380-0). FS&G.
Loves & Tragedies. James M. Bryant. (Illus.). 1968. 22.00 (ISBN 0-686-27960-3). J M Bryant.
Love's Answer from Eternity. Guy Chester Belt. 1973. 4.00 o.p. (ISBN 0-682-47696-X). Exposition.
Love's Architecture: Devotional Modes in Seventeenth-Century English Poetry. Anthony Low. LC 77-94391. 1978. 17.50x (ISBN 0-8147-4984-4); pap. 8.00x (ISBN 0-8147-4985-2). NYU Pr.
Love's Bold Embrace. Brynn Gilbert. 1979. pap. 2.25 (ISBN 0-505-51402-8). Tower Bks.
Love's Burning Flame. Iris Bancroft. 1980. pap. cancelled (ISBN 0-686-68083-9). Bantam.
Love's Claimant. Jillian Kearney. 160p. (Orig.). 1981. pap. 1.75 (ISBN 0-446-94671-0). Warner Bks.
Love's Cruelty: Edited from the Quarto of 1640 with Introduction & Notes. James Shirley. Ed. by Stephen Orgel. LC 79-54354. (Renaissance Drama Second Ser.). 220p. 1980. lib. bdg. 24.00 (ISBN 0-8240-4471-1). Garland Pub.
Love's Dark Conquest. Ralph Hayes. 1978. pap. 1.95 (ISBN 0-505-51260-2). Tower Bks.
Love's Defiant Prisoner. Patricia Phillips. 1978. pap. 1.95 o.s.i. (ISBN 0-515-04375-3). Jove Pubns.
Love's Enduring Promise. Janette Oke. 206p. (Orig.). 1980. pap. 3.50 (ISBN 0-87123-345-2, 210345). Bethany Fell.
Love's Escapade. Rachel C. Payes. LC 80-85108. (Seven Sisters Regency Romance Ser.: No. 5). 192p. (Orig.). 1981. pap. 1.95 (ISBN 0-87216-834-4). Playboy Pbks.
Love's Fatal Glance: A Study of Eye Imagery in the Poets of the Ecole lyonnaise. Lancelot K. Donaldson-Evans. LC 80-10415. (Romance Monographs: No. 39). 155p. 1980. 14.50 (ISBN 84-499-3694-2). Romance.
Love's Intrigues. Jane Barker. Bd. with Lovers Week. Mary Hearne; Female Deserters. Mary Hearne. LC 70-170528. (Foundations of the Novel 1700-1739). lib. bdg. 50.00 (ISBN 0-8240-0531-7). Garland Pub.
Love's Journey. Wendy Martin. 192p. (YA) 1976. 5.95 (ISBN 0-685-66479-1, Avalon). Bouregy.
Love's Kingdom: With a Short Treatise of the English Stage. Richard Flecknoe. LC 74-170431. (English Stage Ser.: Vol. 17). lib. bdg. 50.00 (ISBN 0-8240-0600-3). Garland Pub.
Love's Labor Lost. Ron Chaddick. LC 80-82093. (Understand Ye Shakespeare Ser.). 1980. pap. 8.95 deluxe ed. (ISBN 0-933350-35-X). Morse Pr.
Love's Labor's Lost. William Shakespeare. Ed. by Alfred Harbage. 1963. pap. 2.95 (ISBN 0-14-071427-8, Pelican). Penguin.
Love's Labour's Lost. William Shakespeare. Ed. by Arthur Quiller-Couch et al. (New Shakespeare Ser). (Illus.). 1969. 23.95 (ISBN 0-521-07542-4); pap. 4.50x (ISBN 0-521-09485-2). Cambridge U Pr.
Love's Long Journey. Ana Leigh. 1981. pap. 2.250 (ISBN 0-8439-0884-X, Leisure Bks). Nordon Pubns.
Love's Magic Moment. Patricia Matthews. 1979. pap. 2.75 (ISBN 0-523-41200-2). Pinnacle Bks.
Love's Masquerade. Caroline Courtney. 1980. pap. 1.75 (ISBN 0-446-94292-8). Warner Bks.
Loves of Othniel & Achsah, Translated from the Chaldee, 1769, 2 vols. William Tooke. LC 74-14953. (Novel in England, 1700-1775 Ser). 1974. lib. bdg. 50.00 ea. (ISBN 0-8240-1188-0). Garland Pub.
Love's Pilgrimage. Kristin Michaels. (Orig.). 1981. pap. 1.75 (ISBN 0-451-09681-9, E9681, Sig). NAL.

Love's Promenade. Rachel C. Payes. LC 80-83568. (Seven Sisters Regency Romance Ser.: No. 3). 192p. (Orig.). 1981. pap. 1.95 (ISBN 0-87216-805-0). Playboy Pbks.

Love's Raging Torment. Alma Ashley. 1978. pap. 2.25 (ISBN 0-505-51250-5). Tower Bks.

Love's Rebellious Pleasure. Violet Ashton. 1978. pap. 1.95 o.p. (ISBN 0-449-13979-4, GM). Fawcett.

Love's Renegade. Rachel C. Payes. LC 80-83594. (Seven Sisters Regency Romance Ser.: No. 2). 192p. (Orig.). 1981. pap. text ed. 1.95 (ISBN 0-87216-809-3). Playboy Pbks.

Love's Savage Embrace. Charlotte Prentiss. 304p. (Orig.). 1981. pap. 2.75 (ISBN 0-515-05272-8). Jove Pubns.

Love's Scarlet Banner. Fiona Harrowe. (Orig.). 1977. pap. 1.95 o.p. (ISBN 0-449-13904-2, GM). Fawcett.

Love's Secret Storm. Leonora Pruner. (Orig.). 1981. pap. 3.95 (ISBN 0-87123-347-9, 210347). Bethany Fell.

Love's Serenade. Rachel C. Payes. LC 80-84374. (Seven Sisters Regency Romance Ser.). 192p. 1981. pap. 1.95 (ISBN 0-87216-817-4). Playboy Pbks.

Love's Tempest. Elinor Larkin. (Orig.). 1981. pap. 1.50 (ISBN 0-440-14948-7). Dell.

Love's Tender Fury. Jennifer Wilde. 512p. (Orig.). 1976. pap. 2.95 (ISBN 0-446-93904-8). Warner Bks.

Love's the First. P. Lal. 32p. 1973. 5.00 (ISBN 0-88253-263-4); flexible bdg. 4.00 (ISBN 0-89253-602-0). Ind-US Inc.

Love's Triumphant Heart. Violet Ashton. 1977. pap. 1.75 o.p. (ISBN 0-449-13771-6, 0-449-13771-6, GM). Fawcett.

Love's Way. Joan C. Prime. (YA) 1978. 5.95 (ISBN 0-685-85779-4, Avalon). Bouregy.

Lovestorm. Susan M. Johnson. LC 80-85106. 352p. (Orig.). 1981. pap. 2.95 (ISBN 0-87216-833-6). Playboy Pbks.

Lovey - a Very Special Child. Mary MacCracken. LC 76-15389. 1976. 10.95 (ISBN 0-397-01129-6). Lippincott.

Loving: A Psychological Approach. Howard L. Miller & Paul S. Siegel. LC 72-3770. 224p. 1972. pap. 9.95x (ISBN 0-471-60390-2). Wiley.

Loving Father. G. A. Pottebaum. (Little People's Paperbacks Ser.). 1979. pap. 0.99 (ISBN 0-8164-2250-8). Crossroad NY.

Loving Gentleman. Meta C. Wilde & Orin Borsten. 1977. pap. 1.95 o.s.i. (ISBN 0-515-04421-0). Jove Pubns.

Loving Lucy. Bart Andrews & Thomas Watson. (Illus.). 224p. 1980. 10.95 (ISBN 0-312-49974-4). St Martin.

Loving One Another. Gene Getz. 1979. pap. 3.50 (ISBN 0-88207-786-4). Victor Bks.

Loving, Parenting, & Dying: The Family Cycle in England & America, Past & Present. Martin Quitt & Vivian Fox. 200p. 1980. 27.00 (ISBN 0-914434-14-4); pap. 10.95 (ISBN 0-914434-15-2). Psychohistory Pr.

Loving Partnership. Jean Marsh. (Aston Hall Romances Ser.). 192p. (Orig.). 1981. pap. 1.75 (ISBN 0-523-41132-4). Pinnacle Bks.

Loving Sands, Deadly Sands. Charlotte Keppel. 1975. 7.95 o.p. (ISBN 0-440-05085-5). Delacorte.

Loving Season. Rebecca Burton. 1979. pap. 2.25 (ISBN 0-505-51413-3). Tower Bks.

Loving Sex for Both Sexes: Straight Talk for Teen-Agers. Dale Carlson. (gr. 9 up). 1979. PLB 9.90 s&l (ISBN 0-531-02872-0); pap. 5.95 (ISBN 0-531-02497-0). Watts.

Loving Spirit. Daphne Du Maurier. LC 71-184733. 384p. 1971. Repr. lib. bdg. 12.50x (ISBN 0-8376-0415-X). Bentley.

Loving Strangers. Jack Mayfield. 1978. pap. 1.95 o.p. (ISBN 0-451-08216-8, J8216, Sig). NAL.

Loving Styles: A Guide for Increasing Intimacy. Martin F. Rosenman. 1979. 10.95 (ISBN 0-13-541052-5, Spec); pap. 4.95 (ISBN 0-13-541045-2). P-H.

Loving the Days. John C. Witte. LC 78-7629. (Wesleyan Poetry Program: Vol. 93). 1978. pap. 10.00x (ISBN 0-8195-2093-4, Pub. by Wesleyan U Pr); pap. 4.95 (ISBN 0-8195-1093-9). Columbia U Pr.

Loving Warriors: Selected Letters of Lucy Stone & Henry B. Blackwell, 1853-1893. Ed. by Leslie Wheeler. (Illus.). 1981. 19.95. Dial.

Lovozero Alkali Massif. K. A. Vlasov et al. Ed. by S. I. Tomkeieff & M. H. Battey. (Illus.). 1966. 49.25 o.s.i. (ISBN 0-02-854230-4). Hafner.

Low Back & Leg Pain from Herniated Cervical Disk. Herman Kabat. 164p. 1980. 14.50 (ISBN 0-87527-246-0). Green.

Low Back & Neck Pain: Causes & Conservative Treatment. P. C. Williams. (Illus.). 96p. 1980. pap. 6.95 (ISBN 0-398-03193-2). C C Thomas.

Low Back Pain. 2nd ed. Bernard E. Finneson. (Illus.). 640p. 1981. text ed. 42.00 (ISBN 0-397-50493-4). Lippincott.

Low Back Pain, Vol. 2. R. Grahame & J. A. Anderson. (Annual Research Reviews). 83p. 1981. 14.00 (ISBN 0-88831-095-1). Eden Med Res.

Low Back Patient. Joan G. LaFreniere. (Illus.). 208p. 1979. 20.50 (ISBN 0-89352-033-0). Masson Pub.

Low-Back Patient & Therapeutic Exercise Handouts 1979. Date not set. Set Of 25. 25.00. Masson Pub.

Low-Background High-Efficiency Geiger-Muller Counter. (Technical Reports Ser.: No. 33). 1964. pap. 2.75 (ISBN 92-0-135064-3, IAEA). Unipub.

Low Blood Sugar Cookbook. Margo Blevin & Geri Ginder. LC 72-79378. 384p. 1973. 10.95 (ISBN 0-385-05174-3). Doubleday.

Low Blood Sugar Gourmet Cookbook. Sylvia G. Dannett & Maureen McCabe. 176p. 1975. pap. 3.50 (ISBN 0-06-463428-0, EH 428, EH). Har-Row.

Low Calorie Way. Barbara Kyte & Kathy Greenberg. LC 80-84335. (Illus.). 1981. pap. 2.50 (ISBN 0-915942-17-8). Owlswood Prods.

Low Carbohydrate Dieter's Cookbook. William Thorne. 1978. pap. 1.50 o.p. (ISBN 0-523-40194-9). Pinnacle Bks.

Low-Carbohydrate Gourmet: A Cookbook for Hungry Dieters. Harriet Brownlee. LC 74-14657. 320p. 1975. 8.95 o.p. (ISBN 0-688-02874-8). Morrow.

Low Cholesterol Cookbook. Mabel Cavaiani. 272p. 1974. pap. 2.95 (ISBN 0-06-463408-6, EH 408, EH). Har-Row.

Low-Cost Car Repairs. John Mills. (Illus.). 1967. 7.95 (ISBN 0-571-08052-9, Pub. by Faber & Faber); pap. 4.95 (ISBN 0-571-08982-8). Merrimack Bk Serv.

Low-Cost Educational Materials - Inventory, Vol. 1. 158p. 1981. pap. 13.75 (UB89, UNESCO Regional Office). Unipub.

Low-Cost, Energy-Efficient Shelter for the Owner & Builder. Ed. by Eugene Eccli. LC 75-38886. 1976. 12.95 (ISBN 0-87857-116-7); pap. 8.95 (ISBN 0-87857-114-0). Rodale Pr Inc.

Low-Cost Housing Technology: An East-West Perspective. Ed. by L. J. Goodman et al. (Illus.). 500p. 1980. 69.00 (ISBN 0-08-023250-7). Pergamon.

Low Countries 1780-1940. E. H. Kossman. (History of Modern Europe Ser.). 1978. 49.50x (ISBN 0-19-822108-8). Oxford U Pr.

Low Country Commonwealth. Jean Francois Le Petit. Tr. by E. Grimeston. LC 72-25634. (English Experience Ser.: No. 208). 1969. Repr. of 1609 ed. 30.00 (ISBN 90-221-0208-4). Walter J Johnson.

Low East. Davd Henderson. 80p. 1980. 30.00 (ISBN 0-913028-73-8); pap. 4.95 (ISBN 0-913028-72-X). North Atlantic.

Low Energy & Radiation Cures, C-026. Ed. by Business Communications. 1981. 800.00 (ISBN 0-89336-213-1, C-026). BCC. Postponed.

Low Energy Electron Diffraction. Ed. by Templeton & Somorjai. pap. 5.00 (ISBN 0-686-60375-3). Polycrystal Bk Serv.

Low-Energy Ion Beams Nineteen Eighty. Ed. by I. H. Wilson. (Institute of Physics Conference Ser.: No. 54). 1981. 85.00 (ISBN 0-9960033-4-7, Pub. by a Hilger England). Heyden.

Low-Fat Cookery. Evelyn S. Stead & Gloria K. Warren. LC 72-3329. 284p. 1972. pap. 1.45 o.p. (ISBN 0-668-02672-3). Arc Bks.

Low-Fat Gourmet. Elizabeth Forsythe. 156p. 1981. 14.95 (ISBN 0-7207-1226-2). Merrimack Bk Serv.

Low Fat, Low Cholesterol Diet. rev. ed. Clara-Beth Young Bond et al. LC 76-103741. 1971. 9.95 (ISBN 0-385-03905-0). Doubleday.

Low Income Housing Policies in South Africa. David Dewar & George Ellis. (Illus.). 256p. 1980. pap. 15.00x (ISBN 0-8476-3285-7). Rowman.

Low Latitude Aeronomical Processes: Proceedings. COSPAR, Twenty-Second Plenary Meeting, Bangalore, India, 1979. Ed. by A. P. Mitra. LC 79-41341. 1980. 69.00 (ISBN 0-08-024439-4). Pergamon.

Low Level Lead Exposure: The Clinical Implications of Current Research. Ed. by Herbert L. Needleman. 336p. 1980. text ed. 36.50 (ISBN 0-89004-455-4). Raven.

Low Reynolds Number Hydrodynamics. Ed. by J. Happel & H. Brenner. 556p. 1977. Repr. of 1975 ed. 45.00x (ISBN 90-01-37115-9). Sijthoff & Noordhoff.

Low, Slow, Delicious: Recipes for Casseroles & Electric Slow-Cooking Pots. Martha Lomask. (Illus.). 160p. 1981. 19.95 (ISBN 0-571-11384-2, Pub. by Faber & Faber). Merrimack Bk Serv.

Low Speed Marine Diesel. John B. Woodward. (Ocean Engineering: a Wiley Ser.). 368p. 1981. 33.50 (ISBN 0-471-06335-5, Pub.by Wiley-Interscience). Wiley.

Low-Speed Wind Tunnel Testing. Alan Pope & J. J. Harper. LC 66-17619. 1966. 37.50 (ISBN 0-471-69392-8, Pub. by Wiley-Interscience). Wiley.

Low Temperature Biology of Foodstuffs. Ed. by J. Hawthorne & E. J. Rolfe. 1969. 55.00 (ISBN 0-08-013294-4). Pergamon.

Low-Temperature Plasma Technology Applications. Robert P. Ouellette et al. LC 80-65514. (Electrotechnology Ser.: Vol. 5). (Illus.). 148p. 1980. 29.95 (ISBN 0-250-40375-7). Ann Arbor Science.

Low-Temperature Properties of Polymers. I. I. Perepechko. 272p. 1981. 40.00 (ISBN 0-08-025301-6). Pergamon.

Low Temperatures & Electric Power. International Institute of Refrigeration. Ed. by A. Van Iherbeek. 1971. 67.00 (ISBN 0-08-016370-X). Pergamon.

Low Vision: A Symposium Marking the 20th Anniversary of the Lighthouse Low Vision Service. Eleanor E. Faye & Clare M. Hood. (Illus.). 320p. 1975. 27.50 (ISBN 0-398-03372-2). C C Thomas.

Low-Wage Workers in an Affluent Society. Charles T. Stewart, Jr. LC 73-78912. 1974. 15.95 (ISBN 0-88229-101-7). Nelson-Hall.

Lowell: A Study of Industrial Development. Margaret T. Parker. LC 73-118421. 1970. Repr. of 1940 ed. 15.00 o.p. (ISBN 0-8046-1373-7). Kennikat.

Lowell Offering: Writings by New England Mill Women 1840-1845. Ed. by Benita Eisler. LC 77-24986. (Illus.). 1978. 12.50 o.p. (ISBN 0-397-01225-X). Lippincott.

Lowell Offering: Writings by New England Mill Women, 1840-1845. Ed. by Benita Eisler. LC 77-24986. 223p. 1980. pap. 4.95 (ISBN 0-06-090796-7, CN 796, CN). Har-Row.

Lowenfeld World Technique: Studies in Personality. R. Bowyer. 1970. 27.00 (ISBN 0-08-013029-1); pap. 15.00 (ISBN 0-08-013028-3). Pergamon.

Lower & Middle Paleolithic Periods in Britain. Derek A. Roe. (Archaeology in Britain Ser.). (Illus.). 384p. 1981. 95.00 (ISBN 0-7100-0600-4). Routledge & Kegan.

Lower Cretaceous Sands of Texas: Stratigraphy & Resources. W. L. Fisher & P. U. Rodda. (Illus.). 116p. 1967. 1.75 (RI 59). Bur Econ Geology.

Lower East Side: A Portrait in Time. Diana Cavallo. LC 75-127459. (gr. 5-9). 1971. 6.95 o.s.i. (ISBN 0-02-717880-3, CCPr). Macmillan.

Lower Illinois Valley, Greene County 1821, Containment: Morgan to 1823, Scott to 1823, Macoupin to 1829, Jersey to 1839. Eileen S. Cunningham. 1980. 98.40 (AU00128); pap. 88.40. E S Cunningham.

Lower Illinois Valley Limestone Houses. Eileen S. Cunningham. 1976. 17.00 (AU00127); pap. 12.00. E S Cunningham.

Lower Illinois Valley Local Sketches of Long Ago. Mary H. Catherwood. 55p. 1980. Repr. 3.00 (ISBN 0-686-27587-X). E S Cunningham.

Lower Palaeolithic Archaeology in Britain: As Represented by the Thames Valley. John Wymer. LC 67-30791. (Illus.). 1969. text ed. 25.50x (ISBN 0-212-35964-9). Humanities.

Lower Tertiary Nannoplankton from the California Coast Ranges, Pt. 2: Eocene. F. R. Sullivan. (U. C. Publ. in Geological Sciences: Vol. 53). 1965. pap. 7.50x (ISBN 0-520-09153-1). U of Cal Pr.

Lowland Maya Settlement Patterns. Ed. by Wendy Ashmore. (School of American Research Advanced Seminar Ser.). 464p. 1980. 30.00x (ISBN 0-8263-0556-3). U of NM Pr.

Lows D. Brandeis & the Progressive Tradition. Melvin I. Urofsky. (Library of American Biography). 1980. pap. text ed. 4.95 (ISBN 0-316-88788-9). Little.

Loyal Servant. John Griffiths. 352p. 1981. 11.95 (ISBN 0-87223-659-5). Seaview Bks.

Loyal Subjects Looking-Glasse. William Willymat. LC 73-38231. (English Experience Ser.: No. 495). 76p. 1972. Repr. of 1604 ed. 6.00 (ISBN 90-221-0495-8). Walter J Johnson.

Loyalty & Security: Employment Tests in the United States. Ralph S. Brown, Jr. LC 79-151417. (Civil Liberties in American History Ser). 522p. 1972. Repr. of 1958 ed. lib. bdg. 47.50 (ISBN 0-306-70218-5). Da Capo.

Loyalty in the Spirituality of St. Thomas More. Brian Byron. (Bibliotheca Humanistica & Reformatorica: No. 4). 1972. text ed. 34.25x (ISBN 90-6004-293-X). Humanities.

LSAT Law School Admission Test: A Practical Guide. R. Z. Volkell. 1977. 6.95 (ISBN 0-471-02138-5). Wiley.

LSD, Marijuana, Yoga, & Hypnosis. Theodore X. Barber. LC 73-115935. 1970. 18.95x (ISBN 0-202-25004-0). Aldine Pub.

L.S.E Essays on Cost. Ed. by James M. Buchanan & G. F. Thirlby. (Institute for Humane Studies Ser. in Economic Theory). 1981. text ed. 20.00x (ISBN 0-8147-1034-4); pap. text ed. 7.00x (ISBN 0-8147-1035-2). NYU Pr.

Lu Hsun & His Predecessors. V. I. Semanov. Tr. by Charles A. Alber from Rus. LC 80-50885. 1980. 25.00 (ISBN 0-87332-153-7). M E Sharpe.

Lu Hsun's Vision of Reality. William A. Lyell, Jr. LC 74-30527. 1976. 22.75x (ISBN 0-520-02940-2). U of Cal Pr.

Lu Xun: Selected Works, 4 vols. 1980. Set. 24.95 (ISBN 0-8351-0747-7). China Bks.

Lu You. Michael S. Duke. (World Author Ser.: No. 427). 1977. lib. bdg. 12.50 (ISBN 0-8057-6267-1). Twayne.

Luapula Peoples of Northern Rhodesia. Ian G. Cunnison. 1959. text ed. 18.25 (ISBN 0-7190-1015-2). Humanities.

Lubbock: A Pictorial History. Nancy Bronwell. Ed. by Donna R. Friedman. (Illus.). 208p. 1980. pap. write for info. (ISBN 0-89865-076-3). Donning Co.

Lubitsch Touch: A Critical Study. 2nd ed. Herman Weinberg. LC 76-44119. (Illus.). 1977. pap. 4.00 o.p. (ISBN 0-486-23483-5). Dover.

Lubricant Additives-Recent Developments. M. William Ranney. LC 77-94235. (Chemical Technology Review Ser.: No. 104). (Illus.). 1978. 39.00 o.p. (ISBN 0-8155-0693-7). Noyes.

Lubricants,Cutting Fluids & Coolants. W. J. Olds. LC 72-83305. 1973. 17.95 (ISBN 0-8436-0812-9). CBI Pub.

Lubrication - Successes & Failures. Institute of Marine Engineers, Ministry of Defense. (Illus.). 70p. 1973. limp bdg. 10.55 (ISBN 0-900976-12-8, Pub. by Inst Marine Eng). Intl Schol Bk Serv.

Luca della Robbia. John Pope-Hennessy. LC 79-13566. (Illus.). 1980. 95.00x (ISBN 0-8014-1256-0). Cornell U Pr.

Lucas, Vol. 2. Harold Nockolds. 1978. 35.00 (ISBN 0-7153-7316-1). David & Charles.

Lucas Fernandez. John Lihani. (World Authors Ser.: Spain: No. 251). 1971. lib. bdg. 10.95 (ISBN 0-8057-2290-4). Twayne.

Lucas: The First Hundred Years, Vol. 1. Harold Nockolds. 1976. 35.00 (ISBN 0-7153-7306-4). David & Charles.

Lucasta. Sheila Bishop. 1978. pap. 1.50 o.p. (ISBN 0-449-23458-4, Crest). Fawcett.

Lucca, Thirteen Sixty-Nine to Fourteen Hundred: Politics & Society in an Early Renaissance City-State. Christine Meek. (Oxford Historical Monographs). 438p. 1978. text ed. 45.00x (ISBN 0-19-821866-4). Oxford U Pr.

Luces Bajo el Almud. Justo L. Gonzalez. LC 77-11753. 76p. (Orig., Span.). 1977. pap. 1.95 (ISBN 0-89922-102-5). Edit Caribe.

Luces Encendidas Para Cada Dia. Miguel Limardo. 1978. 2.95 (ISBN 0-311-40038-8). Casa Bautista.

Lucia Speaks: Memoirs & Letters of Sister Lucia. Sr. Lucia. 272p. 1977. pap. 3.00 o.p. (ISBN 0-911988-04-1). AMI Pr.

Lucian. W. Lucas Collisn. 180p. 1981. Repr. lib. bdg. 30.00 (ISBN 0-89987-113-5). Darby Bks.

Luciana Avedon's Body Book. Luciana Avedon & Jeanne Molli. LC 76-15189. (Illus.). 208p. 1976. 12.95 (ISBN 0-87131-211-5). M Evans.

Lucid Exposition of the Middle Way: The Essential Chapters from the Prasannapada of Candrakirti. Tr. by Mervyn Sprung et al from Sanskrit. LC 79-13033. 1980. 17.50 (ISBN 0-87773-711-8, Prajna). Great Eastern.

Lucie: A Tale of a Donkey. Phillipe Dumas. (Illus.). (ps-2). 1979. 7.95 (ISBN 0-13-541169-6). P-H.

Lucifer Comet. Ian Wallace. (Science Fiction Ser.). 1980. pap. 2.25 (ISBN 0-87997-581-4, UE1584). DAW Bks.

Lucifer Key. Malcolm MacPherson. 1981. 12.95 (ISBN 0-525-14985-6). Dutton.

Lucifer Mask. Kathleen Rich. 1977. pap. 1.50 (ISBN 0-505-51186-X). Tower Bks.

Lucifer Wine. Irma Walker. 1979. pap. 1.95 o.p. (ISBN 0-345-27324-9). Ballantine.

Lucilius und Kallimachos. Mario P. Piwonka. Ed. by Steele Commager. LC 77-70830. (Latin Poetry Ser.). 1978. lib. bdg. 41.00 (ISBN 0-8240-2976-3). Garland Pub.

Lucille Ball. David Paige. (Stars of Stage & Screen Ser.). (Illus.). (gr. 4-12). 1977. PLB 5.95 (ISBN 0-87191-557-X). Creative Ed.

Lucinda Brayford. Martin Boyd. 14.95 (ISBN 0-392-08085-0, SpS). Soccer.

Lucius, Adventures of a Roman Boy. Alfred J. Church. LC 60-16706. (gr. 7-11). 8.50x (ISBN 0-8196-0108-X). Biblo.

Lucius Junius Brutus. Nathaniel Lee. Ed. by John Loftis. LC 67-12644. (Regents Restoration Drama Ser). 1967. 7.25x (ISBN 0-8032-0363-2); pap. 1.65x (ISBN 0-8032-5362-1, BB 266, Bison). U of Nebr Pr.

Luck of Brin's Five. Cherry Wilder. 224p. 1980. pap. 2.25 (ISBN 0-671-41637-5). PB.

Luck of Nineveh. Arnold C. Brackman. 352p. 1981. pap. 8.95 (ISBN 0-442-28260-5). Van Nos Reinhold.

Luck of Pokey Bloom. Ellen Confod. (gr. 4-6). 1977. pap. 1.25 (ISBN 0-671-29841-0). PB.

Luck of Pokey Bloom. Ellen Conford. (Illus.). 144p. (gr. 4-6). 1975. 7.95 (ISBN 0-316-15305-2). Little.
Luck of Pokey Bloom. Ellen Conford. (gr. 4-6). 1977. 1.75 (ISBN 0-671-41895-5). Archway.
Luck of Roaring Camp. Bret Harte. Ed. by Walter Pauk & Raymond Harris. (Classics Ser). (Illus.). (gr. 6-12). 1976. pap. text ed. 1.60x (ISBN 0-89061-054-1, 529); tchrs. ed. 3.00 (ISBN 0-89061-055-X, 531). Jamestown Pubs.
Luck Runs Out. Charlotte MacLeod. 192p. 1981. pap. 2.25 (ISBN 0-380-54171-8, 54171). Avon.
Luckie Star. Ann Waldron. (gr. 4-7). 1977. PLB 7.50 o.p. (ISBN 0-525-34270-2). Dutton.
Luckiest Girl. Beverly Cleary. (gr. 7 up). 1958. PLB 9.55 (ISBN 0-688-31741-3). Morrow.
Luckiest Girl. Beverly Cleary. (gr. 7-12). 1980. pap. 1.75 (ISBN 0-440-94899-1, LFL). Dell.
Lucknow: The Last Phase of an Oriental Culture. Abdul H. Sharar. Tr. by E. S. Harcourt & Fakhir Hussain. (Illus.). 1977. lib. bdg. 29.50 o.p. (ISBN 0-89158-640-7). Westview.
Lucks & Talismans: A Chapter of Popular Superstition. Charles R. Beard. LC 74-174903. xxii, 258p. Repr. of 1934 ed. 22.00 (ISBN 0-8103-3871-8). Gale.
Lucky. Suzanne Taylor-Moore. 1977. 6.95 (ISBN 0-686-10585-0). MTM Pub Co.
Lucky Devil. Arthur Maling. LC 77-11782. (Harper Novel of Suspense). 1978. 8.95 o.s.i. (ISBN 0-06-012854-2, HarpT). Har-Row.
Lucky Dream & Number Book. Robert Andrew. 1966. pap. 1.95 (ISBN 0-446-84939-1). Warner Bks.
Lucky Hans. Gerald Rose & Elizabeth Rose. (Illus.). (ps-5). 1976. 8.95 (ISBN 0-571-10905-5, Pub. by Faber & Faber). Merrimack Bk Serv.
Lucky Jim. Kingsley Amis. 256p. 1976. Repr. of 1954 ed. lib. bdg. 12.95x (ISBN 0-89244-069-4). Queens Hse.
Lucky Ladybugs. Gladys Conklin. (Illus.). (gr. k-3). 1968. reinforced bdg. 7.95 (ISBN 0-8234-0072-7). Holiday.
Lucky Larribee. Max Brand. 1975. pap. 1.75 (ISBN 0-686-58223-3). Warner Bks.
Lucky Man. Mary B. Christian. LC 79-11024. (Ready-to-Read Ser.). (Illus.). (gr. 1-4). 1979. 7.95 (ISBN 0-02-718270-3, 71827). Macmillan.
Lucky Poet: A Self-Study in Literature & Political Ideas Being the Autobiography of Hugh Macdiarmid. Hugh MacDiarmid. LC 76-138287. 1972. 20.00x (ISBN 0-520-01852-4). U of Cal Pr.
Lucky Porcupine! Miriam Schlein. LC 79-19673. (Illus.). 48p. (gr. 2-6). 1980. 7.95 (ISBN 0-590-07543-8, Four Winds). Schol Bk Serv.
Lucky Starr & the Big Sun of Mercury. Isaac Asimov. pap. 0.95 (ISBN 0-451-06772-X, Q6772, Sig). NAL.
Lucky Starr & the Moons of Jupiter. Isaac Asimov. 144p. (RL 5). 1972. pap. 0.95 (ISBN 0-451-07048-8, Q7048, Sig). NAL.
Lucky Starr & the Moons of Jupiter. Isaac Asimov. (Lucky Star Ser.). 1978. pap. 1.50 o.p. (ISBN 0-449-23422-3, Crest). Fawcett.
Lucky Starr & the Pirates of the Asteroids. Isaac Asimov. (David Starr Ser). (RL 5). 1971. pap. 0.95 o.p. (ISBN 0-451-07047-X, Q7047, Sig). NAL.
Lucky Starr & the Pirates of the Asteroids. Isaac Asimov. (Lucky Star Ser.). 1979. pap. 1.50 o.p. (ISBN 0-449-23421-5, Crest). Fawcett.
Lucky to Be Alive? Alice Cromie. 1979. pap. 1.95 (ISBN 0-345-28432-1). Ballantine.
Lucky You! John Burstein. LC 80-14641. (Illus.). 32p. (ps-3). 1980. 4.95 (ISBN 0-07-009243-5). McGraw.
Lucretia Borgia: A Biography. Rachel Erlanger. LC 75-39117. (Illus.). 1978. 13.95 (ISBN 0-8015-4725-3, Hawthorn); pap. 7.95 (ISBN 0-8015-4724-5, Hawthorn). Dutton.
Lucretius & His Influence. George D. Hadzsits. LC 63-10292. (Our Debt to Greece & Rome Ser). Repr. of 1930 ed. 27.50x (ISBN 0-8154-0106-X). Cooper Sq.
Lucy. Joan Tate. pap. text ed. 1.95x o.p. (ISBN 0-435-11875-7). Heinemann Ed.
Lucy & Ricky & Fred & Ethel: The Story of "I Love Lucy". Bart Andrews. 1977. pap. 2.50 (ISBN 0-445-04028-9). Popular Lib.
Lucy Larcom: Life, Letters & Diary. Daniel D. Addison. LC 75-99065. (Library of Lives & Letters). 1970. Repr. of 1894 ed. 18.00 (ISBN 0-8103-3611-1). Gale.
Lucy Stone: Pioneer of Woman's Rights. Alice S. Blackwell. LC 77-164111. (Illus.). viii, 301p. 1971. Repr. of 1930 ed. 18.00 (ISBN 0-8103-3824-6). Gale.
Lucy: The Beginnings of Human Evolution. Donald C. Johanson & Maitland A. Edey. (Illus.). 1981. 13.95 (ISBN 0-671-25036-1). S&S.
Lucy Winchester. Christmas C. Kauffman. 540p. 1974. pap. 5.50 (ISBN 0-8024-5040-7). Moody.
Lud-in-the-Mist. Hope Mirrlees. (Del Rey Bks). 1977. pap. 1.95 o.p. (ISBN 0-345-25848-7). Ballantine.
Luddites: Machine-Breakers of the Early Nineteenth Century. Douglas Liversidge. (World Focus Bks.). (Illus.). 96p. (gr. 7-12). 1972. PLB 5.90 (ISBN 0-531-02162-9). Watts.
Ludi Jr. William Kloefkorn. LC 76-2268. (Orig.). 1976. limited signed 10.00x (ISBN 0-915316-24-2); pap. 5.00x (ISBN 0-915316-23-4). Pentagram.
Ludi Victor. James Leigh. 320p. Date not set. 11.95 (ISBN 0-698-11038-2). Coward.
Ludo & the Star Horse. Mary Stewart. LC 74-26662. (Illus.). 192p. (gr. 3-7). 1975. 7.75 (ISBN 0-688-22017-7); PLB 7.44 (ISBN 0-688-32017-1). Morrow.
Ludovico Ariosto. Robert Griffin. (World Authors Ser.: Italy: No. 301). 1974. lib. bdg. 10.95 (ISBN 0-8057-2063-4). Twayne.
Ludus Patronymicus: Or, the Etymology of Curious Surnames. Richard S. Charnock. LC 68-23141. 1968. Repr. of 1868 ed. 15.00 (ISBN 0-8103-3122-5). Gale.
Ludvig Holberg. F. J. Jansen. LC 74-2171. (World Authors Ser.: Denmark: No. 321). 136p. 1974. lib. bdg. 10.95 (ISBN 0-8057-2431-1). Twayne.
Ludwig Becker: Artist & Naturalist with the Burke & Wills Expedition. Ed. by Marjorie Tipping. LC 79-67093. 1979. text ed. 70.00x (ISBN 0-522-84189-9, Pub. by Melbourne U Pr). Intl Schol Bk Serv.
Ludwig Feuerbach. Frederick Engels. 1976. 3.50 (ISBN 0-8351-0141-X); pap. 1.95 (ISBN 0-8351-0142-8). China Bks.
Ludwig Mies Van Der Rohe. Arthur Drexler. LC 60-6077. (Masters of World Architecture Ser). 1960. 7.95 o.s.i. (ISBN 0-8076-0108-X); pap. 3.95 o.s.i. (ISBN 0-8076-0222-1). Braziller.
Ludwig Thoma. Bruno F. Steinbruckner. (World Authors Ser.: No. 494). 1978. lib. bdg. 14.95 (ISBN 0-8057-6335-X). Twayne.
Ludwig Van Beethoven. Hans C. Fischer & Eric Kock. LC 78-145443. (Illus.). 1971. 12.50 o.p. (ISBN 0-312-50015-7, L77200). St Martin.
Ludwig Wittgenstein: Letters to Russell, Keynes, & Moore. Ed. by G. H. Von Wright. LC 73-18518. 194p. 1974. 16.50x o.p. (ISBN 0-8014-0822-9). Cornell U Pr.
Ludwig Wittgenstein: Personal Recollections. Ed. by Rush Rhees. 256p. 1981. 22.50x (ISBN 0-8476-6253-5). Rowman.
Ludwig Wittgenstein: Philosophy & Language. Ed. by Alice Ambrose & Morris Lazerowitz. (Muirhead Library of Philosophy). 1972. text ed. 26.00x (ISBN 0-391-00190-6). Humanities.
Ludwig Wittgenstein's Tractatus Logico-Philosophicus: A Transcendental Critique of Ethics. Robert J. Cavalier. LC 79-3724. 1980. text ed. 15.50 (ISBN 0-8191-0915-0); pap. text ed. 9.25 (ISBN 0-8191-0916-9). U Pr of Amer.
Luftverunreinigung und Herz-Kreislauf-System. L. Laszt & R. Schaad. (Illus.). viii, 140p. 1980. pap. 28.75 (ISBN 3-8055-3067-6). S Karger.
Luftwaffe Aircraft & Aces. Edward T. Maloney. (Illus.). 1969. pap. 5.95 (ISBN 0-911721-74-6, Pub. by WW). Aviation.
Luftwaffe Camouflage of World War Two. Bryan Philpott. (Illus.). 64p. 1975. 4.95 o.p. (ISBN 0-85059-213-5). Aztex.
Luftwaffe Handbook. Alfred Price. (Encore Edition). (Illus.). 1977. 3.95 (ISBN 0-684-16691-7, ScribT). Scribner.
Luftwaffe War Diaries. Cajus Bekker. Tr. by Frank Ziegler. 608p. 1975. pap. 3.95 (ISBN 0-345-28799-1). Ballantine.
Lugard & the Abeokuta Uprising: The Demise of Egba Independence. Harry A. Gailey. 1981. 27.50x (ISBN 0-7146-3114-0, F Cass Co). Biblio Dist.
Luge. Piotr Rogowski & Mario Wala. (Illus.). 1979. pap. 15.00 (ISBN 0-8467-0586-9, Pub. by Two Continents). Hippocrene Bks.
Luigi Cherubini: The Middle Years, Seventeen Ninety-Five to Eighteen Fifteen. Stephen C. Willis. Ed. by George Buelow. (Studies in Musicology). 303p. 1981. 29.95 (ISBN 0-8357-1118-8, Pub. by UMI Res Pr). Univ Microfilms.
Luigi Jazz Dance Technique. Luigi Wydro & Kenneth Wydro. LC 80-1091. (Illus.). 192p. Date not set. pap. 12.95 (ISBN 0-385-15588-3, Dolph). Doubleday.
Luigi Pirandello. Olga Ragusa. LC 68-54457. (Columbia Essays on Modern Writers Ser.: No. 37). (Orig.). 1968. pap. 2.00 (ISBN 0-231-02952-7, MW37). Columbia U Pr.
Luis Armed Story. Tom Veitch. LC 78-9676. 1978. 14.95 (ISBN 0-916190-06-4); pap. 6.00 (ISBN 0-916190-07-2). Full Court NY.
Luis Bunuel. Virginia Higginbotham. (Theatrical Arts Ser.). 1979. lib. bdg. 12.50 (ISBN 0-8057-9261-9). Twayne.
Luis Bunuel: A Critical Biography. Francisco Aranda. Ed. by David Robinson. LC 76-7621. 1976. lib. bdg. 22.50 (ISBN 0-306-70754-3); pap. 4.95 (ISBN 0-306-80028-4). Da Capo.
Luis Cernuda. Salvador Jimenez-Fajardo. (World Authors Ser.: No. 455). 1978. lib. bdg. 11.95 (ISBN 0-8057-6292-2). Twayne.
Luis de Gongora. David W. Foster & Virginia R. Foster. (World Authors Ser.: Spain: No. 226). 1973. lib. bdg. 10.95 (ISBN 0-8057-2386-2). Twayne.
Luis Llorens Torres En Su Centenario. Seminario De Estudios Hispanicos & Federico de Onis. LC 80-21479. (Coleccion UPREX, 57 Ser.: Estudios Literarios). 1981. pap. write for info. (ISBN 0-8477-0057-7). U of PR Pr.
Luis Palau Story. Luis Palau. (Illus.). 160p. 1980. 8.95 (ISBN 0-8007-1134-3). Revell.
Luis Quinones de Benavente. Hannah E. Bergman. (World Authors Ser.: Spain: No. 216). lib. bdg. 10.95 (ISBN 0-8057-2140-1). Twayne.
Luis Romero. Bradley Shaw & Gonzalez Del-Valle. (World Authors Ser.: No. 520). 1979. lib. bdg. 13.50 (ISBN 0-8057-6361-9). Twayne.
Luisa's American Dream. Claudia Mills. LC 80-69997. 160p. (gr. 7 up). 1981. 8.95 (ISBN 0-590-07684-1, Four Winds). Schol Bk Serv.
Luise. Dawn S. Field. 1978. pap. 1.95 o.p. (ISBN 0-425-03767-3, Medallion). Berkley Pub.
Lukacs & Heidegger: Towards a New Philosophy. Lucien Goldmann. Tr. by William Q. Boelhower. 15.00x (ISBN 0-7100-8625-3). Routledge & Kegan.
Lukacs & Heidegger: Towards a New Philosophy. Lucien Goldmann. Tr. by William Q. Boelhower. 1979. pap. 7.95 (ISBN 0-7100-8794-2). Routledge & Kegan.
Lukacs' Concept of Dialect. Istvan Meszaros. (Illus.). pap. 4.95 (ISBN 0-686-23497-9, Merlin Pr). Carrier Pigeon.
Lukacs' Concept of Dialectic: With Biography, Bibliography & Documents. I. Meszaros. (Illus.). 211p. 1972. text ed. 8.25x (ISBN 0-85036-159-1). Humanities.
Lukacs, Marx & the Sources of Critical Theory. Andrew Feenberg. (Philosophy & Society Ser.). 1981. 22.50x (ISBN 0-8476-6272-1). Rowman.
Luke. Frederick W. Danker. Ed. by Gerhard Krodel. LC 76-5954. (Proclamation Commentaries: the New Testament Witnesses for Preaching). 128p. 1976. pap. 2.95 (ISBN 0-8006-0583-7, 1-583). Fortress.
Luke. Irving L. Jensen. (Bible Self Study Ser.). 1970. pap. 2.25 (ISBN 0-8024-1042-1). Moody.
Luke. Eugene LaVerdiere. (New Testament Message Ser.). 10.95 (ISBN 0-89453-128-X); pap. 5.95 (ISBN 0-89453-193-X). M Glazier.
Luke & Angela. Christine Nostlinger. Tr. by Anthea Bell. LC 80-8804. 144p. (gr. 7 up). 1981. 8.95 (ISBN 0-15-249902-4, HJ). HarBraceJ.
Luke Four-Eighteen: Sermons to Touch the Heart & Grip the Soul. Clifford R. Coonfare. 96p. 1980. pap. 5.95 (ISBN 0-8059-2747-6). Dorrance.
Luke Street Series, 8 bks. Incl. Cheat's House: Luke 19: 1-10 (ISBN 0-310-40882-2, 11525); Country House: Luke 24: 13-49 (ISBN 0-310-40902-0, 11527); Crowded House: Luke 5: 18-26 (ISBN 0-310-40842-3, 11521); Guest House: Luke 10: 38-42 (ISBN 0-310-40872-5, 11524); Leader's House: Luke 8: 40-56 (ISBN 0-310-40862-8, 11523); Secret House: Luke 22: 7-54 (ISBN 0-310-40892-X, 11526); Sick House: Luke 4: 38-40 (ISBN 0-310-40832-6, 11520). (Illus.). (gr. k-2). 1980. pap. 0.95 ea. Zondervan.
Luke Sutton Outlaw. Leo P. Kelly. LC 80-2322. 192p. 1981. 9.95 (ISBN 0-385-17254-0). Doubleday.
Luke, the Gospel of God's Man. Keith L. Brooks. (Teach Yourself the Bible Ser). 1964. pap. 1.75 (ISBN 0-8024-5047-4). Moody.
Luke the Historian in the Light of Research. A. T. Robertson. (A. T. Robertson Library). 1977. pap. 3.95 o.p. (ISBN 0-8010-7646-3). Baker Bk.
Luke Was There. Clymer. (gr. 3-5). pap. 0.95 o.s.i. (ISBN 0-686-68477-X, 29790). Archway.
Luke's Garden. Joan Tate. pap. text ed. 1.95x o.p. (ISBN 0-435-11889-7). Heinemann Ed.
Lulu. Lulu Roman. (Illus.). 1978. 7.95 (ISBN 0-8007-0956-X). Revell.
Lulu Plays. Frank Wedekind. Tr. by Stephen Spender from Ger. (Illus.). 1977. pap. 5.95 (ISBN 0-7145-0868-3). Riverrun NY.
Lulu Plays & Other Sex Tragedies. Frank Wedekind. Tr. by Stephen Spender. 1979. pap. 5.95 (ISBN 0-7145-0868-3). Riverrun NY.
Lum Fu & the Golden Mountain. Hisako Kimishima. Tr. by Alvin Tresselt from Japanese. LC 77-136991. Orig. Title: Yama Ippai No Kinka. (Illus.). (gr. k-3). 1971. 5.95 o.s.i. (ISBN 0-8193-0469-7, Four Winds); PLB 5.41 o.s.i. (ISBN 0-8193-0470-0). Schol Bk Serv.
Lumbering in the Last of the White-Pine States. Marx Swanholm. LC 78-14221. (Minnesota Historic Sites Pamphlet Ser.: No. 17). (Illus.). 1978. 2.00 (ISBN 0-87351-131-X). Minn Hist.
Lumberjack. Stephen W. Meader. LC 34-31292. (Illus.). (gr. 7-9). 1934. 4.95 o.p. (ISBN 0-15-249904-0, HJ). HarBraceJ.
Luminescence & Energy Transfer. Ed. by J. D. Dunitz et al. (Structure & Bonding Ser.: Vol. 42). (Illus.). 133p. 1981. 40.00 (ISBN 0-387-10395-3). Springer-Verlag.
Luminous Sanity: Literary Criticism of John G. Neihardt. John T. Richards. 1973. pap. 4.20 (ISBN 0-686-27393-1). Neihardt Found.
Lumoischialgie. Ed. by W. Mueller & F. J. Wagenhaeuser. (Fortibildungskurse Fuer Rhermatologie Ser.: Vol. 6). (Illus.). viii, 240p. 1981. pap. 54.00 (ISBN 3-8055-2207-X). S Karger.
Lumps, Bumps & Rashes: A Look at Kid's Diseases. Alan E. Nourse. LC 75-34276. (First Bks. Ser.). (Illus.). 72p. (gr. 4 up). 1976. PLB 6.45 (ISBN 0-531-00845-2). Watts.
Lumumba. Heinz & Donnay. pap. 1.45 (ISBN 0-394-17185-3, B272, BC). Grove.
Lunar Mineralogy. Judith W. Frondel. LC 75-9786. 323p. 1975. 33.00 (ISBN 0-471-28289-8, Pub. by Wiley-Interscience). Wiley.
Lunar Science - a Post-Apollo View. Stuart R. Taylor. LC 74-17227. 372p. 1975. text ed. 31.00 (ISBN 0-08-018274-7); pap. text ed. 16.00 (ISBN 0-08-018273-9). Pergamon.
Lunatics & Other Lovers. Stan Hager. 1979. 10.00 o.p. (ISBN 0-912950-14-5); pap. 4.50 o.p. (ISBN 0-912950-13-7). Blue Oak.
Lunation Cycle. rev. ed. Dane Rudhyar. 1971. pap. 5.95 (ISBN 0-394-73020-8). Shambhala Pubns.
Lunchbox Cookbook. Beverly Nemiro & Marie Von Allman. LC 65-25794. 127p. 1965. 4.95 (ISBN 0-8040-0192-8, SB). Swallow.
Luncheon & Supper Dishes for Foodservice Menu Planning. Eulalia C. Blair. LC 72-92379. (Foodservice Menu Planning Ser.). 1973. 16.50 (ISBN 0-8436-0559-6). CBI Pub.
Luncheon Cooking. Ser-Vol-Tel Institute. (Foodservice Career Education Ser.). 1974. pap. 4.95 (ISBN 0-8436-2031-5). CBI Pub.
Lunchroom Waste: A Study of "How Much & How Come". Clista Dow & Linda H. Smith. 1978. pap. 3.95 (ISBN 0-936386-04-5). Creative Learning.
Lune. C. Pavese. Ed. by A. D. Thompson. 208p. 1980. 15.00x (ISBN 0-7190-0771-2, Pub. by Manchester U Pr England). State Mutual Bk.
Lung & Its Disorders in the Newborn Infant. 4th ed. Mary E. Avery et al. (Major Problems in Clinical Pediatrics: Vol. 1). (Illus.). 560p. 1981. text ed. price not set (ISBN 0-7216-1462-0). Saunders.
Lung Cancer. Ed. by Robert B. Livingston. (Cancer Treatment & Research Ser.: No. 1). (Illus.). 320p. 1981. PLB 47.50 (ISBN 90-247-2394-9, Pub. by Martinus Nijhoff). Kluwer Boston.
Lung Cancer: Progress in Therapeutic Research. Ed. by Franco Muggia & Marcel Rozencweig. LC 77-84552. (Progress in Cancer Research & Therapy Ser.: Vol. 11). 1978. 52.00 (ISBN 0-89004-223-3). Raven.
Lung Connective Tissue. Ed. by John A. Pickrell. 240p. 1981. 59.95 (ISBN 0-8493-5749-7). CRC Pr.
Lung Metabolism: Proteolysis & Antiproteolysis, Biochemical Pharmacology, Handling of Bioactive Substances. Ed. by Alain F. Junod & Rodolphe DeHaller. 1976. 40.00 (ISBN 0-12-392250-X). Acad Pr.
Lungeing the Horse & Rider. Sheila Inderwick. LC 77-76095. 1977. 15.95 (ISBN 0-7153-7370-6). David & Charles.
Lungs in Systemic Diseases. Eli H. Rubin & Stanley S. Siegelman. (Illus.). 334p. 1969. 28.50 (ISBN 0-398-01626-7). C C Thomas.
L'Universelle Bordas, 10 vols. (Fr.). 1976. 495.00 set. Pergamon.
Luo Religion & Folklore. Hans-Egil Hauge. (Scandinavian University Books). 154p. 1974. pap. 18.00x (ISBN 8-200-02327-3, Dist. by Columbia U Pr). Universitet.
Lupercal. Ted Hughes. 1960. 4.95 o.p. (ISBN 0-571-07035-3, Pub. by Faber & Faber). Merrimack Bk Serv.
Lupercal. Ted Hughes. 1970. pap. 4.95 (ISBN 0-571-09246-2, Pub. by Faber & Faber). Merrimack Bk Serv.
Lupita Manana. Patricia Beatty. LC 81-505. 192p. (gr. 7-9). 1981. 8.95 (ISBN 0-688-00358-3); 8.59 (ISBN 0-688-00359-1). Morrow.
Lupus-The Body Against Itself. Blau, Sheldon Paul, M.D. & Dodi Schultz. LC 76-40881. 1977. 7.95 (ISBN 0-385-04562-X). Doubleday.
Lurcher. Frank Walker. 1978. 8.95 o.s.i. (ISBN 0-440-05083-9). Delacorte.
Lure & Romance of Alchemy. C. J. Thompson. LC 76-167224. (Illus.). vi, 249p. 1975. Repr. of 1932 ed. 18.00 (ISBN 0-8103-4000-3). Gale.
Lure of Kentucky: A Historical Guide Book. Maude W. Lafferty. LC 71-153018. (Illus.). 1971. Repr. of 1939 ed. 18.00 (ISBN 0-8103-3344-9). Gale.

Lure of Lust. (Illus.). 4.95 (ISBN 0-910550-42-5). Centurion Pr.

Lure of Politics. Krishan K. Channan. 64p. 1980. 6.00 (ISBN 0-682-49641-3). Exposition.

Lure of the Heavens: A History of Astrology. Donald Papon. (Illus.). 320p. 1980. pap. 7.95 (ISBN 0-87728-502-0). Weiser.

Lurie's Worlds 1970-1980. Ranan R. Lurie. LC 80-15526. (Illus.). 452p. 1980. 45.00 (ISBN 0-8248-0731-6); pap. 14.95 (ISBN 0-8248-0723-5). U Pr of Hawaii.

Lurking Fear & Other Stories. H. P. Lovecraft. 1975. pap. 1.50 o.p. (ISBN 0-345-24690-X). Ballantine.

Luscher Color Test. Max Luscher. 1980. pap. write for info. (ISBN 0-671-83170-4). PB.

Luscious Low Calorie with Poundation Conversation by Maxine. Maxine T. Vaneven. LC 75-34770. (Illus.). 1975. pap. 3.95 (ISBN 0-916774-01-5). Tolvan Co.

Lusiad; or the Discovery of India. Luis De Camoens. Ed. by Burton Feldman & Robert Richardson. LC 78-60914. (Myth & Romanticism Ser.: Vol. 6). 1980. lib. bdg. 66.00 (ISBN 0-8240-3555-0). Garland Pub.

Lusitania & Mauretania. (Ocean Liners of the Past: No. 2). 35.75 o.p. (ISBN 0-85059-054-X). Aztex.

Lusitania Disaster: An Episode in Modern Warfare & Diplomacy. Thomas A. Bailey & Paul B. Ryan. LC 75-2806. (Illus.). 1975. 12.95 (ISBN 0-02-901240-6). Free Pr.

Lust for Life. Irving Stone. 1981. pap. 3.50 (ISBN 0-451-09898-6, E9898, Sig). NAL.

Lust Motif in the Plays of Thomas Middleton. Barbara J. Baines. (Salzburg Studies in English Literature, Jacobean Drama Studies: No. 29). 160p. 1973. pap. text ed. 25.00x (ISBN 0-391-01306-8). Humanities.

Lust: The Other Side of Love. Mel White. 1978. 7.95 (ISBN 0-8007-0932-2). Revell.

Lustful Maidens & Ascetic Kings: Buddhist & Hindu Stories of Life. Roy C. Amore & Larry D. Shinn. (Illus.). 150p. 1981. 14.95 (ISBN 0-19-502838-4); pap. 5.95 (ISBN 0-19-502839-2). Oxford U Pr.

Lusty Wind for California. Inglis Fletcher. 576p. 1980. pap. 2.95 (ISBN 0-553-13393-4). Bantam.

Lute Player. Norah Lofts. 1976. pap. 1.95 o.p. (ISBN 0-449-22948-3, Crest). Fawcett.

Luther: An Experiment in Biography. H. G. Haile. LC 79-6282. (Illus.). 456p. 1980. 14.95 (ISBN 0-385-15960-9). Doubleday.

Luther & His Mother. Ian Siggins. LC 80-2386. 96p. (Orig.). 1981. pap. 4.95 (ISBN 0-8006-1498-4, 1-1498). Fortress.

Luther & Staupitz: An Essay in the Intellectual Origins of the Protestant Reformation. David C. Steinmetz. LC 80-23007. (Duke Monographs in Medieval & Renaissance Studies: No. 4). 1981. 16.75 (ISBN 0-8223-0447-3). Duke.

Luther & the Papacy: Stages in a Reformation Conflict. Scott H. Hendrix. LC 80-2393. 224p. 1981. 14.95 (ISBN 0-8006-0658-2, 1-658). Fortress.

Luther: Early Theological Works. Ed. by James Atkinson. (Library of Christian Classics Ichthus Edition). 1980. pap. 9.95 (ISBN 0-664-24166-2). Westminster.

Luther, Erasmus & Loyola. Peter Amey et al. Ed. by Malcolm Yapp et al. (World History Ser.). (Illus.). (gr. 10). 1980. lib. bdg. 5.95 (ISBN 0-89908-043-X); pap. text ed. 1.95 (ISBN 0-89908-018-9). Greenhaven.

Luther, Erasmus, & the Reformation: A Catholic-Protestant Reappraisal. Ed. by John C. Olin et al. LC 68-8749. x, 150p. 1969. 12.50 o.p. (ISBN 0-8232-0830-3). Fordham.

Lutheran Church in North American Life: 1776-1976, 1580-1980. Ed. by John E. Groh & Robert H. Smith. LC 78-71233. 1979. 5.95 (ISBN 0-915644-17-7, Clayton). Luth Acad.

Lutheranism: The Theological Movement & Its Confessional Writings. Eric W. Gritsch & Robert W. Jenson. LC 76-7869. 228p. 1976. pap. 7.50 (ISBN 0-8006-1246-9, 1-1246). Fortress.

Lutherans & Catholics in Dialogue: Personal Notes for a Study. Paul C. Empie. LC 80-69754. (Orig.). 1981. pap. 3.95 (ISBN 0-8006-1449-6, 1-1449). Fortress.

Lutherans in North America. rev. ed. Ed. by E. Clifford Nelson. LC 74-26337. (Illus.). 576p. 1980. o. p. 22.50x (ISBN 0-8006-0409-1); pap. 14.95 (ISBN 0-8006-1409-7, 1-1409). Fortress.

Luther's English Connection. J. E. McGoldrick. 1979. pap. 7.50 (ISBN 0-8100-0070-9, 15-0368). Northwest Pub.

Luther's Ninety-Five Theses. Martin Luther. Tr. by C. M. Jacobs. 1957. pap. 0.95 (ISBN 0-8006-1265-5, 1-1265). Fortress.

Luther's View of Church History. John M. Headley. 1963. pap. 37.50x (ISBN 0-686-51413-0). Elliots Bks.

Luther's Works: Career of the Reformer I, Vol. 31. Ed. by Harold J. Grimm & Helmut T. Lehmann. LC 55-9893. 1957. 14.95 (ISBN 0-8006-0331-1, 1-331). Fortress.

Luther's Works: Career of the Reformer II, Vol. 32. Ed. by George W. Forell & Helmut T. Lehmann. LC 55-9893. 1958. 10.00 (ISBN 0-8006-0332-X, 1-332). Fortress.

Luther's Works: Career of the Reformer IV, Vol. 34. Ed. by Lewis W. Spitz & Helmut T. Lehmann. LC 55-9893. 1960. 10.00 (ISBN 0-8006-0334-6, 1-334). Fortress.

Luther's Works: Church & Ministry I, Vol. 39. Ed. by Eric W. Gritsch & Helmut T. Lehmann. LC 55-9893. 1970. 15.95 (ISBN 0-8006-0339-7, 1-339). Fortress.

Luther's Works: Church & Ministry II, Vol. 40. Ed. by Conrad Bergendoff & Helmut H. Lehman. LC 55-9893. 1958. 10.95 (ISBN 0-8006-0340-0, 1-340). Fortress.

Luther's Works: Church & Ministry III, Vol. 41. Ed. by Helmut T. Lehmann & Eric W. Gritsch. LC 55-9893. 1966. 16.95x (ISBN 0-8006-0341-9, 1-341). Fortress.

Luther's Works: Devotional Writing II, Vol. 43. Ed. by Gustav K. Wiencke & Helmut T. Lehman. LC 55-9893. 1968. 15.95 (ISBN 0-8006-0343-5, 1-343). Fortress.

Luther's Works: Devotional Writings I, Vol. 42. Ed. by Martin O. Dietrich & Helmut T. Lehmann. LC 55-9893. (Prog. Bk.). 1969. 15.95 (ISBN 0-8006-0342-7, 1-342). Fortress.

Luther's Works: Letters I, Vol. 48. Ed. by Gottfried G. Krodel & Helmut T. Lehman. LC 55-9893. 1963. 15.95 (ISBN 0-8006-0348-6, 1-348). Fortress.

Luther's Works: Letters III, Vol. 50. Ed. by Gottfried G. Krodel & Helmut T. Lehmann. LC 74-76934. 416p. 1975. 16.95 (ISBN 0-8006-0350-8, 1-350). Fortress.

Luther's Works: Liturgy & Hymns, Vol. 53. Ed. by Ulrich S. Leupold & Helmut T. Lehmann. LC 55-9893. 1965. 12.95 (ISBN 0-8006-0353-2, 1-353). Fortress.

Luther's Works: Sermons I, Vol. 51. Ed. by Helmut T. Lehmann & John W. Doberstein. Tr. by John W. Doberstein. LC 55-9893. 1959. 16.95 (ISBN 0-8006-0351-6, 1-353). Fortress.

Luther's Works: Sermons II, Vol. 52. Ed. by Hans J. Hillerbrand & Helmut T. Lehmann. LC 55-9893. 416p. 1974. 15.95 (ISBN 0-8006-0352-4, 1-352). Fortress.

Luther's Works: Table Talk, Vol. 54. Ed. by Theodore G. Tappert & Helmut T. Lehmann. Tr. by Theodore G. Tappert. LC 55-9893. 1967. 12.95 (ISBN 0-8006-0354-0, 1-354). Fortress.

Luther's Works: The Christian in Society I, Vol. 44. Ed. by Helmut T. Lehmann & James Atkinson. LC 55-9893. 1966. 16.95 (ISBN 0-8006-0344-3, 1-344). Fortress.

Luther's Works: The Christian in Society II, Vol. 45. Ed. by Walter I. Brandt & Helmut T. Lehmann. LC 55-9893. 1962. 15.95 (ISBN 0-8006-0345-1, 1-345). Fortress.

Luther's Works: The Christian in Society III, Vol. 46. Ed. by Robert C. Schultz & Helmut T. Lehmann. LC 55-9893. 1967. 15.95 (ISBN 0-8006-0346-X, 1-346). Fortress.

Luther's Works: The Christian in Society IV, Vol. 47. Ed. by Franklin Sherman & Helmut T. Lehman. LC 55-9893. 1971. 8.00 (ISBN 0-8006-0347-8, 1-347). Fortress.

Luther's Works, Vol. 33: Career of the Reformer III. new ed. Ed. by Philip S. Watson & Helmut T. Lehmann. LC 55-9893. 1972. 10.95 (ISBN 0-8006-0333-8, 1-333). Fortress.

Luther's Works, Vol. 35: Word & Sacrament I. Ed. by Theodore Bachmann & Helmut T. Lehmann. LC 55-9893. 426p. 1960. 14.50 (ISBN 0-8006-0335-4, 1-335). Fortress.

Luther's Works, Vol. 36: Word & Sacrament II. Ed. by Abdel R. Wentz & Lehmann. LC 55-9893. 400p. 1959. 16.95 (ISBN 0-8006-0336-2, 1-336). Fortress.

Luther's Works, Vol. 37: Word & Sacrament III. Ed. by Robert H. Fischer & Helmut T. Lehmann. LC 55-9893. 1961. 12.95x (ISBN 0-8006-0337-0, 1-337). Fortress.

Luther's Works, Vol. 49: Letters II. Ed. & tr. by Krodel. LC 55-9893. 480p. 1972. 9.50 (ISBN 0-8006-0349-4, 1-349). Fortress.

Luther's Works: Word & Sacrament IV, Vol. 38. Ed. by Martin E. Lehman & Helmut T. Lehman. LC 55-9893. 1971. 16.95 (ISBN 0-8006-0338-9, 1-338). Fortress.

Lutoslawski & His Music. Steven Stucky. (Illus.). 300p. Date not set. price not set (ISBN 0-521-22799-2). Cambridge U Pr.

Lutyens: Country Houses. Paul D. O'Neill. 168p. 1981. 19.95 (ISBN 0-8230-7361-0, Whitney Lib). Watson-Guptill.

Luxury Cruise. Joseph Bennett. LC 62-11667. 1962. 4.50 o.s.i. (ISBN 0-8076-0170-5). Braziller.

Luxury Designs for Apartment Living. Barbara T. Bradford. LC 77-16899. (Illus.). 352p. 1981. 29.95 (ISBN 0-385-12769-3). Doubleday.

Luxury Home Plans. Heritage Home Plans, Inc. LC 79-2769. (Illus.). 1980. pap. 7.95 (ISBN 0-15-654309-5, Harv). HarBraceJ.

Luzumiyyat. Abu 'Ala Al Ma 'arri, pseud. Tr. by Arthur Wormhoudt from Arabic. (Arab Translation Ser.: No. 39). 1978. pap. 6.50 (ISBN 0-916358-89-5). Wormhoudt.

LYAPAS: A Programming Language for Logic & Coding Algorithms. Ed. by M. A. Gavrilov & A. D. Zakrevsky. (ACM Monograph Ser). 1969. 55.25 (ISBN 0-12-277850-2). Acad Pr.

Lyautey in Morocco: Protectorate Administration, 1912-1925. Alan Scham. LC 74-92680. 1970. 21.75x (ISBN 0-520-01602-5). U of Cal Pr.

Lycanthia. Tanith Lee. 1981. pap. 2.25 (ISBN 0-87997-610-1, UE1610). DAW Bks.

Lyceens et Collegiens Sous le Second Empire. Patrick Harrigan. LC 79-15711. (Illus.). 240p. (Orig., Fr.). 1979. pap. 21.00 (ISBN 2-901725-06-6, IS-00083, Pub. by Maison Science France). Univ Microfilms.

Lydia: A Novel. Lois T. Henderson. LC 79-50946. 1981. pap. 5.95 (ISBN 0-915684-88-8). Christian Herald.

Lydia Bailey. Kenneth Roberts. 1976. pap. 1.75 o.p. (ISBN 0-449-30693-3, X693, Prem). Fawcett.

Lydia Bailey. Kenneth Roberts. 12.95 (ISBN 0-385-04271-X). Doubleday.

Lydia Maria Child. William S. Osborne. (United States Authors Ser.: No. 380). 1980. lib. bdg. 12.95 (ISBN 0-8057-7315-0). Twayne.

Lydia; or, Filial Piety, Seventeen Fifty-Five, 4 vols. in 2. John Shebbeare. LC 74-17448. (Novel in England, 1700-1775 Ser). 1974. Set. lib. bdg. 90.00 (ISBN 0-8240-1143-0); lib. bdg. 50.00 ea. Garland Pub.

Lyfe of Soule: An Edition with Commentary. Helen M. Moon. (Salzburg Studies in English Literature, Elizabethan & Renaissance Studies: No. 75). pap. text ed. 25.00x (ISBN 0-391-01484-6). Humanities.

Lying: Moral Choice in Public & Private Life. Sissela Bok. LC 78-21949. 1979. pap. 3.95 (ISBN 0-394-72804-1, Vin). Random.

Lying Stones of Johann Bartholomew Adam Beringer Being His Lithographiae Wirceburgensis. Johann B. Beringer. Tr. by Melvin E. Jahn & Daniel J. Woolf. 1963. 26.75x (ISBN 0-520-00110-9). U of Cal Pr.

Lying Three. Ralph McInerny. LC 79-68734. (Father Dowling Mystery Ser.). 1979. 8.95 (ISBN 0-8149-0819-5). Vanguard.

Lyle. G. K. Hunter. Incl. Peele. G. K. Hunter. pap. 2.95 (ISBN 0-8277-6206-2, WTW206). British Bk Ctr.

Lyle, Lyle, Crocodile. Bernard Waber. LC 65-19305. (Illus.). 48p. (gr. k-3). 1973. pap. 2.95 (ISBN 0-395-13720-9, Sandpiper). HM.

Lyle Official Antiques Review 1973 to 74. Compiled by Tony Curtis. 1973. text ed. 25.00 (ISBN 0-8277-2219-2). British Bk Ctr.

Lyme Miscellany, 1776-1976. Ed. by George J. Willauer, Jr. LC 76-41483. 1977. 20.00x (ISBN 0-8195-5009-4, Pub. by Wesleyan U Pr). Columbia U Pr.

Lymphatic System. M. Battezzati & I. Donini. Tr. by U. Cameron-Curry from It. LC 73-9924. 496p. 1974. 52.95 (ISBN 0-470-05706-8). Halsted Pr.

Lymphatic System Metastasis. Leonard Weiss et al. (Medical Publications Ser.). 1980. lib. bdg. 55.00 (ISBN 0-8161-2142-7). G K Hall.

Lymphatic System of the Female Genitalia. Albert A. Plentl & Emanuel A. Friedman. LC 70-158402. (Major Problems in Obstetrics & Gynecology Ser.: Vol. 2). (Illus.). 1971. 17.50 (ISBN 0-7216-7266-3). Saunders.

Lymphatics, Lymph & the Lymphomyelard Complex. J. M. Yoffey & F. C. Coortice. 1971. 98.00 (ISBN 0-12-772050-2). Acad Pr.

Lymphocyte Circulation: Experimental & Clinical Aspects. Maria De Sousa. 316p. 1981. 57.00 (ISBN 0-471-27854-8, Pub. by Wiley-Interscience). Wiley.

Lymphocyte Hybridomas: Second Workshop. Ed. by F. Melchers et al. (Illus.). 1979. 16.40 (ISBN 0-387-09670-1). Springer-Verlag.

Lymphokines. Ed. by William E. Stewart & John Hadden. LC 80-85521. (Contemporary Immunology Ser.). (Illus.). 1981. 59.50 (ISBN 0-89603-012-1). Humana.

Lympholsines. Ed. by William E. Stewart & John Hadden. (Illus.). 500p. 1981. cancellrd (ISBN 0-89603-012-1). Humana.

Lymphomas Other Than Hodgkin's Disease. Ed. by A. E. Stuart et al. (Illus.). 75p. 1981. text ed. 30.00x (ISBN 0-19-261296-4). Oxford U Pr.

Lymphoproliferative Diseases. Ed. by David W. Molander. (Illus.). 592p. 1975. text ed. 52.75 (ISBN 0-398-03025-1). C C Thomas.

Lymphoreticular Disease: An Introduction for the Pathologist & Oncologist. Ian Carr et al. 1978. soft cover 26.00 (ISBN 0-397-60436-X, Pub. by Blackwell Scientific). Mosby.

Lynch Law: An Investigation into the History of Lynching in the United States. James E. Cutler. LC 77-88428. Repr. of 1905 ed. 17.50x (ISBN 0-8371-1821-2). Negro U Pr.

Lynching & Rape: An Exchange of Views. Jane Addams & Ida B. Wells. Ed. by Bettina Aptheker. 1977. 1.25 (ISBN 0-89977-023-1). Am Inst Marxist.

Lynchtree County. Robert H. Robinson. (Orig.). 1980. pap. 2.50 (ISBN 0-505-51553-9). Tower Bks.

Lyndon: An Oral Biography. Merle Miller. 1980. 17.95 (ISBN 0-399-12357-1). Putnam.

Lyndon B. Johnson: The Exercise of Power. Evans & Novak. pap. 1.95 o.p. (ISBN 0-451-07250-2, J7250, Sig). NAL.

Lynmara Legacy. Catherine Gaskin. 1977. pap. 1.95 o.p. (ISBN 0-449-23060-0, Crest). Fawcett.

Lynton & Barnstable Railway Album. J. D. Prideaux. 1974. 17.95 (ISBN 0-7153-6809-5). David & Charles.

Lyonel Feininger: A Definitive Catalogue of His Graphic Work: Etchings, Lithographs, Woodcuts. Leona E. Prasse. LC 74-108899. (Illus.). 304p. 1972. 35.00x (ISBN 0-910386-18-8, Pub. by Cleveland Mus Art). Ind U Pr.

Lyposomes in Applied Biology & Therapeutics. Ed. by J. T. Dingle et al. (Lyposomes in Biology & Pathology Ser.: Vol. 6). 714p. 1979. 109.50 (ISBN 0-686-63105-6, North Holland). Elsevier.

Lyra Graeca, 3 Vols. Tr. by J. M. Edmonds. (Loeb Classical Library: No. 142-144). 9.50x ea. Vol. 1 (ISBN 0-674-99157-5). Vol. 2 (ISBN 0-674-99158-3). Vol. 3 (ISBN 0-674-99159-1). Harvard U Pr.

Lyric & Dramatic Milton: Selected Papers from the English Institute. Ed. by Joseph H. Summers. LC 65-22231. 1965. 12.50x (ISBN 0-231-02863-6). Columbia U Pr.

Lyric & Dramatic Poems. John G. Neihardt. LC 65-22374. 1965. pap. 3.50 (ISBN 0-8032-5143-2, BB 322, Bison). U of Nebr Pr.

Lyric Forms in the Sonnet Sequences of Barnabe Barnes. Ed. by Phillip E. Blank, Jr. LC 72-94447. (De Proprietatubus Litterarum, Series Practica, No. 18). 162p. (Orig.). 1974. pap. text ed. 27.05x (ISBN 90-2793-062-7). Mouton.

Lyric Verse. Ed. by Edwin Rakow. LC 63-12620. 1962. pap. 3.95 (ISBN 0-672-73225-4). Odyssey Pr.

Lyrical & the Epic: Studies of Modern Chinese Literature. Jaroslav Prusek. Ed. by Leo Ou-fan Lee. LC 80-7491. (Studies in Chinese Literature & Society). 320p. 1980. 22.50x (ISBN 0-253-10283-9). Ind U Pr.

Lyrical Drama, 2 vols. Henry S. Edwards. LC 80-2274. 1981. Repr. of 1881 ed. 67.50 (ISBN 0-404-18840-0). AMS Pr.

Lyricism in the Poetry of T. S. Eliot. Ann P. Brady. LC 77-788. (National Univ. Publications Literary Criticism Ser.). 1977. 9.95 o.p. (ISBN 0-8046-9183-5). Kennikat.

Lyrics to a Lassie & Other Verse. Paul Terry. 64p. (Orig.). 1980. pap. 4.95 (ISBN 0-937768-01-4). Expressions TX.

Lyrics: You Touched My Heart. Curtiss L. Young. 1979. 4.00 o.p. (ISBN 0-8062-1228-4). Carlton.

LyricTime: Dickinson & the Limits of Genre. Sharon Cameron. LC 78-9983. 1979. text ed. 15.00x (ISBN 0-8018-2171-1). Johns Hopkins.

Lyrische und Satirische Elemente in Roy Campbell's Dichtung, 2 vols. Maria E. Eisl. (Salzburg Studies in England Literature, Poetic Drama & Poetic Theory: No. 46). (Illus.). 1979. Set. pap. text ed. 50.25x (ISBN 0-391-01165-0). Humanities.

Lysias & the Corpus Lysiacum. K. J. Dover. LC 68-63337. (Sather Classical Lectures: No. 39). 1968. 19.50x (ISBN 0-520-00351-9). U of Cal Pr.

Lysistrata. Aristophanes. Tr. by Robert H. Webb. 106p. 1963. 4.95 (ISBN 0-8139-0010-7). U Pr of Va.

Lysosomes & Cell Function. Dennis Pitt. LC 75-308385. (Integrated Themes in Biology Ser). (Illus.). 160p. 1975. pap. text ed. 11.50x (ISBN 0-582-44344-X). Longman.

Lysosomes & Lysosomal Storage Diseases. Ed. by John W. Callahan & J. Alexander Lowden. 455p. 1980. text ed. 42.00 (ISBN 0-89004-476-7). Raven.

Lytell Treatise for to Lerne Englisshe & Frensshe. LC 73-6167. (English Experience Ser.: No. 630). 27p. 1973. Repr. of 1497 ed. 6.00 (ISBN 90-221-0630-6). Walter J Johnson.

Lytle Treatise Composyd by Johan Stadysshe...Against the Protestacion of Robert Barnes at the Tyme of His Death. John Standish. LC 79-85138. (English Experience Ser.: No. 955). 100p. 1979. Repr. of 1540 ed. lib. bdg. 8.00 (ISBN 90-221-0955-0). Walter J Johnson.

Lyttleton: His Treatise of Tenures. Thomas Littlton. Ed. by David S. Berkowitz & Samuel E. Thorne. LC 77-89237. (Classics of English Legal History in the Modern Era Ser.: Vol. 73). 727p. 1979. lib. bdg. 40.00 (ISBN 0-8240-3172-5). Garland Pub.

M

M & M & the Haunted House Game. Pat Ross. (I Am Reading Bk.). (Illus.). (gr. 1-4). 1980. 4.95 (ISBN 0-394-84185-9); PLB 5.99 (ISBN 0-394-94185-3). Pantheon.

M. & M. Karolik Collection of American Watercolors & Drawings, 1800-1875, 2 vols. Henry P. Rossiter. (Illus.). 1962. Set. boxed 30.00 (ISBN 0-87846-173-6). Mus Fine Arts Boston.

M & M Mobiles: More & More Mobiles. (Mobiles Ser.: Vol. 3). (gr. 1-8). 1975. pap. 3.00 o.p. (ISBN 0-914318-04-7). V S Morris.

M. C. Higgins, the Great. Virginia Hamilton. LC 72-92439. 288p. (gr. 7 up). 1974. 8.95 (ISBN 0-02-742480-4). Macmillan.

M. G. Lewis. Joseph J. Irwin. LC 76-26062. (English Author Ser.: No. 198). 1976. lib. bdg. 10.95 (ISBN 0-8057-6670-7). Twayne.

M. I. N. D Over Weight: "How to Stay Slim the Rest of Your Life". William M. Macleod & Gael S. Macleod. LC 80-21001. 1981. 7.95 (ISBN 0-13-583385-X). P-H.

M Is for Move. Vicky Shiefman. LC 80-23526. (Illus.). (ps-2). 1981. PLB 7.95 (ISBN 0-525-35905-2). Dutton.

M. M. Warburg & Co., 1798-1938 Merchant Bankers of Hamburg. E. Rosenbaum & A. J. Sherman. LC 79-511. (Illus.). 1979. text ed. 24.50x o.p. (ISBN 0-8419-0477-4). Holmes & Meier.

M O S Integrated Circuit Design. Ed. by E. Wolfendale et al. LC 72-1927. 120p. 1973. 24.95 (ISBN 0-470-95947-9). Halsted Pr.

M O S Memory Data Book for Design Engineers, 1980. Engineering Staff of Texas Instruments. LC 79-93268. 192p. pap. 3.75 (ISBN 0-89512-105-0, LCC4782). Tex Instr Inc.

M R Cumulative Index. Date not set. cancelled (ISBN 0-8218-0035-3). Am Math.

M. W. Sullivan Stories, 60 bks. Sullivan Assoc. pap. text ed. 1.50 ea. (ISBN 0-8449-1908-X). Learning Line.

M: Writings '67-'72. John Cage. LC 72-11051. (Illus.). 224p. 1973. pap. 7.95 (ISBN 0-8195-6035-9, Pub. by Wesleyan U Pr). Columbia U Pr.

Ma & Pa. 2nd rev. ed. George W. Hilton. LC 80-19531. (Illus.). 210p. 1980. 12.95 (ISBN 0-8310-7127-3). Howell-North.

Ma & Son. Lao She. Tr. by Jean M. James from Chinese. Orig. Title: Erh Ma. 1980. 21.60 (ISBN 0-89644-634-4). Chinese Materials.

Ma Lien & the Magic Brush. Hisako Kimishima. LC 68-21077. Orig. Title: Ma Lien to Haho No Fude. (Illus.). (gr. k-3). 1968. 5.95 o.s.i. (ISBN 0-8193-0343-7, Four Winds); PLB 5.41 o.s.i. (ISBN 0-8193-0344-5). Schol Bk Serv.

Ma Premiere Encyclopedie. Larousse And Co. (Illus., Fr.). 12.95x (ISBN 0-685-13974-3, 3797). Larousse.

Ma'am Jones of the Pecos. Eve Ball. LC 68-9336. (Illus.). 1969. pap. 7.50 (ISBN 0-8165-0404-0). U of Ariz Pr.

Ma'asir-I-Jahanjiri: A Contemporary Account of Jahangir. Khwaza K. Husaini. Ed. & tr. by Azra Nizami. 537p. (Persian & Eng.). 1978. lib. bdg. 35.00x (ISBN 0-210-40566-X). Asia.

Mabel Clements. Repr. 7.00 (ISBN 0-686-12393-X). Church History.

Mabinogi & Other Medieval Welsh Tales. Ed. by Patrick K. Ford. 1977. 16.50x (ISBN 0-520-03205-5); pap. 3.95 (ISBN 0-520-03414-7). U of Cal Pr.

Mac Perry's Florida Lawn & Garden Care. Mac Perry. 1980. pap. 7.95 (ISBN 0-916224-57-0). Banyan Bks.

Macaca Mulatta: Management of a Laboratory Breeding Colony. D. A. Valerio et al. 21.50 o.p. (ISBN 0-12-710050-4); pap. 15.50 o.p. (ISBN 0-12-710056-3). Acad Pr.

Macaulay. Jane Millgate. (Routledge Author Guides Ser.). 1973. cased 14.50 (ISBN 0-7100-7663-0); pap. 6.95 (ISBN 0-7100-7685-1). Routledge & Kegan.

Macaws: Taming & Training. Risa Teitler. (Illus.). 1979. 2.95 (ISBN 0-87666-884-8, KW-054). TFH Pubns.

Macbeth. Ed. by A. P. Riemer. 1980. pap. 3.50x (ISBN 0-424-00081-4, Pub. by Sydney U Pr Australia). Intl Schol Bk Serv.

Macbeth. William Shakespeare. Ed. by John Wain. LC 78-127579. (Casebook Ser). 1970. pap. text ed. 2.50 o.s.i. (ISBN 0-87695-051-9). Aurora Pubs.

Macbeth. William Shakespeare. Ed. by Arthur Quiller-Couch et al. (New Shakespeare Ser). 23.95 (ISBN 0-521-07543-2); pap. 4.50x (ISBN 0-521-09486-0). Cambridge U Pr.

Macbeth. William Shakespeare. Ed. by Maynard Mack & Robert W. Boynton. (Shakespeare Ser). (gr. 10-12). 1972. pap. text ed. 0.75 o.p. (ISBN 0-8104-6015-7). Hayden.

Macbeth. William Shakespeare. Ed. by Louis B. Wright & Virginia LaMar. pap. 2.25 (ISBN 0-671-43294-X). PB.

Macbeth & the Players. Dennis Bartholomeusz. LC 69-10270. (Illus.). 1969. 48.00 (ISBN 0-521-06925-4, 4); pap. 10.95 (ISBN 0-521-29322-7). Cambridge U Pr.

Macbeth, with Reader's Guide. William Shakespeare. (Literature Program). 1972. pap. text ed. 4.25 (ISBN 0-87720-803-4); tchr's ed. 2.75 (ISBN 0-87720-903-0). AMSCO Sch.

McBroom & the Great Race: The McBroom Ser. Sid Fleischman. (Illus.). 64p. (gr. 3-7). 1980. 7.95 (ISBN 0-316-28568-4, Atlantic-Little Brown). Little.

Maccabees. Moshe Pearlman. (Illus.). 272p. 1973. 12.95 o.s.i. (ISBN 0-02-595300-1). Macmillan.

McCall-Crabbs Standard Test Lessons in Reading, Books A-f. 4th ed. William A. McCall & Lelah Crabbs Schroeder. 1979. Kit & Manual. pap. text ed. 12.00 (ISBN 0-8077-5554-0). Tchrs Coll.

McCall's Book of Handcrafts. McCall's Editors. (Illus.). 1972. 10.00 (ISBN 0-394-48300-6). Random.

McCall's Superb Dessert Cookbook. Ed. by Mary Eckley. 1978. 9.95 (ISBN 0-394-41279-6). Random.

McCarthy Era-Beginning of the End: Audio Cassette. Ed. by G. D. Days. LC 80-740530. cassette 9.00 (ISBN 0-918628-08-3). Congeros Pubns.

McCartys. E. Richard Churchill. 1978. 2.00 (ISBN 0-913488-02-X). Timberline Bks.

McCollough Effect. C. D. Shute. LC 78-15609. (Illus.). 1979. 32.95 (ISBN 0-521-22395-4). Cambridge U Pr.

McConnell's Manual for Baptist Churches. F. M. McConnell. 1975. 5.00 (ISBN 0-8170-0100-X). Judson.

McCracken's Removable Partial Prosthodontics. 6th ed. Davis Henderson & Victor L. Steffel. (Illus.). 516p. 1981. text ed. 28.75 (ISBN 0-8016-2146-1). Mosby.

McDade. Wayne C. Ulsh. 1981. pap. 1.95 (ISBN 0-8439-0875-0, Leisure Bks). Nordon Pubns.

Macdermots of Ballycloran. Anthony Trollope. Ed. by Robert L. Wolff. (Ireland Nineteenth Century Fiction - Ser. Two: Vol. 53). 1372p. 1979. lib. bdg. 32.00 (ISBN 0-8240-3502-X). Garland Pub.

MacDonald Countries, 8 bks. Incl. Canada. Jeanette Harris. LC 77-70185 (ISBN 0-382-06110-1); Egypt. Michael Von Haag. LC 77-70186 (ISBN 0-382-06112-8); India. Natasha Taalyarkhan. LC 77-70187 (ISBN 0-382-06113-6); Mexico. John Howard. LC 77-70189 (ISBN 0-382-06114-4); Nigeria. Richard Synge. LC 77-70190 (ISBN 0-382-06115-2); Turkey. David Hotham. LC 77-70192 (ISBN 0-382-06116-0); Netherlands. Frank E. Huggett. LC 77-70193 (ISBN 0-382-06117-9); Belgium & Luxembourg. Jean Marey & George Marey. LC 77-70194 (ISBN 0-382-06118-7). (gr. 6 up). 1977. lib. bdg. 7.95 (ISBN 0-686-57952-6). Silver.

McDonnell Douglas F-15 "Eagle". James P. Stevenson. LC 78-17244. (Aero Ser.: Vol. 28). 1978. pap. 7.95 (ISBN 0-8168-0604-7). Aero.

McDonnell Douglas Story. Douglas J. Ingells. LC 79-54064. 1979. 17.95 (ISBN 0-8168-4995-1). Aero.

MacDoodle Street. Mark Alan Stamaty. 96p. 1981. pap. 6.95 (ISBN 0-312-92519-0). St Martin.

McDowell Series of Plastic Surgery Indexes: Nineteen Forty-Six to Nineteen Seventy-One the Great Index, Vol. Iv. American Society of Plastic & Reconstructive Surgeons & Frank McDowell. (Illus.). 1168p. 1981. 225.00 (ISBN 0-686-69564-X, 5767-7). Williams & Wilkins.

McDuff in the Daffodils. Victoria Hamilton. (Illus.). 44p. (Orig.). (gr. 4-12). 1974. pap. 2.95 (ISBN 0-939198-00-2). Blue Heron.

McEckr'n. J. F. Hopkins. 1980. 9.95 (ISBN 0-312-52365-3). St Martin.

Macedonian-English, English-Macedonian Dictionary, 2 vols. 1978. Set. 20.00. Macedonian-English 476pp. English-Macedonian 422pp. Heinman.

McGarr at the Dublin Horse Show. Bartholomew Gill. 1981. pap. 2.25 (ISBN 0-440-15379-4). Dell.

McGarr on the Cliffs of Moher. Bartholomew Gill. LC 78-2645. 1978. 7.95 o.p. (ISBN 0-684-15570-2, ScribT). Scribner.

McGoogan Moves the Mighty Rock. Dick Gackenbach. LC 80-8455. (Illus.). 48p. (gr. 1-4). 1981. 8.95 (ISBN 0-06-021967-X, HarpJ); PLB 8.79g (ISBN 0-06-021968-8). Har-Row.

McGraw-Hill Encyclopedia of Energy. 2nd ed. McGraw-Hill Book Co. Ed. by Sybil P. Parker. LC 80-18078. (Illus.). 856p. 1980. 34.50 (ISBN 0-07-045268-7). McGraw.

McGraw-Hill Encyclopedia of Ocean & Atmospheric Sciences. McGraw-Hill Encyclopedia of Science & Technology Staff. Ed. by Sybil P. Parker. (Illus.). 1979. write for info. (ISBN 0-07-045267-9). McGraw.

McGraw-Hill Vocabulary, Bk 1. 2nd ed. Gene Stanford. Ed. by Hester E. Weeden. (Illus.). 128p. (gr. 7-12). 1981. pap. text ed. 3.84 (ISBN 0-07-060771-0). McGraw.

McGraw-Hill Vocabulary: Book 2. 2nd ed. Gene Stanford. (McGraw-Hill Vocabulary Ser.). Orig. Title: Vocab 2. (Illus.). 128p. 1981. pap. text ed. 4.24 (ISBN 0-07-060772-9). McGraw.

McGraw-Hill's National Electrical Code Handbook. 16th ed. Joseph F. McPartland. (Illus.). 1979. 19.95 (ISBN 0-07-045690-9). McGraw.

McGregor School. Gerald E. Clarke. 1980. 5.50 (ISBN 0-8233-0310-1). Golden Quill.

McGuffey's Illustrated Address Book. McGuffey Editions. 160p. 1980. 6.95 (ISBN 0-442-21257-7). Van Nos Reinhold.

McGuffey's Pictorial Eclectic Primer. William Holmes McGuffey. (Illus.). 60p. (gr. k-3). 1965. pap. 3.50 (ISBN 0-917420-02-0). Buck Hill.

Machado de Assis: The Brazilian Master & His Novels. Helen Caldwell. LC 76-89891. 1970. 16.50x (ISBN 0-520-01608-4). U of Cal Pr.

Machiavelli & the Art of Renaissance History. Peter E. Bondanella. LC 73-9729. 200p. 1973. text ed. 12.95x (ISBN 0-8143-1499-6). Wayne St U Pr.

Machiavelli & the United States, 6 vols. in 1. Anthony J. Pansini. LC 70-108252. 1371p. (500th anniv. ed). 1969. 20.00 (ISBN 0-685-23384-7, 911876-02). Greenvale.

Machiavelli Rethought: A Critique of Strauss' Machiavelli. Angelo Caranfa. LC 77-94393. 1978. pap. text ed. 7.00x (ISBN 0-8191-0421-3). U Pr of Amer.

Machiavelli to Marx: Modern Western Political Thought. Dante Germino. LC 77-181415. 1979. 8.50x (ISBN 0-226-28850-1, Midway). U of Chicago Pr.

Machiavelli's New Modes & Orders: A Study of the "Discourses on Livy". Harvey C. Mansfield, Jr. LC 79-12380. 1979. 27.50x (ISBN 0-8014-1182-3). Cornell U Pr.

Machiavelli's Thoughts on the Management of Men. Niccolo Machiavelli. (Illus.). 1978. deluxe bdg. 47.45 (ISBN 0-918968-08-9). Inst Econ Finan.

Machina Carnis: The Biochemistry of Muscular Contraction in Its Historical Development. Dorothy M. Needham. (Illus.). 1972. 99.50 (ISBN 0-521-07974-8). Cambridge U Pr.

Machine Age Maya: The Industrialization of a Guatemalan Community. Manning Nash. LC 67-20810. 1967. pap. 3.95x (ISBN 0-226-56863-6, P262, Phoen). U of Chicago Pr.

Machine & Assembly Language Programming of the PDP-Eleven. Arthur Gill. LC 78-9690. (Illus.). 1978. 19.95 (ISBN 0-13-541870-4). P-H.

Machine Calculation for Business & Personal Use. 2nd ed. Gilbert J. Ribera. LC 79-83523. 1979. pap. text ed. 13.95x (ISBN 0-8162-7180-1); solutions manual 2.50x (ISBN 0-686-67449-9). Holden-Day.

Machine Computation: An Algorithmic Approach. Richard F. Gonzalez & Claude McMillan, Jr. (Irwin-Dorsey Information Processing Ser). 1971. text ed. 16.95x (ISBN 0-256-00234-7). Irwin.

Machine Design. 2nd ed. Robert H. Creamer. LC 75-12093. (Engineering Technology Ser.). (Illus.). 544p. 1976. text ed. 21.95 (ISBN 0-201-01178-6); instr's guide 1.50 (ISBN 0-201-01179-4). A-W.

Machine Design. Albert Leyer. 1974. 19.95x (ISBN 0-216-87457-2). Intl Ideas.

Machine Devices & Instrumentation: Mechanical; Electromechanical; Hydraulic; Thermal; Pneumatic; Photoelectric; Optical. Ed. by Nicholas P. Chironis. 1966. 33.50 o.p. (ISBN 0-07-010785-8, P&RB). McGraw.

Machine Embroidery with Style. D. Bennett. LC 80-13914. (Connecting Threads Ser.). (Illus.). 100p. 1980. pap. 8.95 (ISBN 0-914842-45-5). Madrona Pubs.

Machine Guarding: A Historical Perspective. Verne L. Roberts. LC 80-84798. (Illus.). 282p. 1980. text ed. 59.95 (ISBN 0-938830-00-7). Inst Product.

Machine Gunners. Robert Westall. LC 76-13630. (gr. 5-9). 1976. 8.25 (ISBN 0-688-80055-6); PLB 7.92 (ISBN 0-688-84055-8). Greenwillow.

Machine in the Garden: Technology & the Pastoral Ideal in America. Leo Marx. (Illus.). 1967. pap. 6.95 (ISBN 0-19-500738-7, GB). Oxford U Pr.

Machine Intelligence, 2 vols. Ed. by N. L. Collins & D. Michie. (Machine Intelligence Ser.). 1975. Set. 45.95 (ISBN 0-470-59332-6). Halsted Pr.

Machine Intelligence, Vols. 4-7. B. Meltzer & D. Michie. Vol. 4, 1969. 18.95x o.p. (ISBN 0-470-59336-9); Vol. 5, 1970. 27.95x o.p. (ISBN 0-470-59337-7); Vol. 6, 1971. 41.95x (ISBN 0-470-59339-3); Vol. 7. 1973 o.p. 41.00x (ISBN 0-470-60110-8). Halsted Pr.

Machine Intelligence: Machine Expertise & the Human Interface. J. E. Hayes et al. LC 79-40785. (Machine Intelligence Ser.: Vol. 9). 1979. 92.95x (ISBN 0-470-26714-3). Halsted Pr.

Machine Intelligence 8: Machine Representations of Knowledge. Ed. by E. W. Elcock & D. Michie. 1977. 95.95 (ISBN 0-470-99059-7). Halsted Pr.

Machine Interpretations of Patterson Functions & Alternative Direct Approaches & the Austin Symposium on Gas Phase Molecular Structure. Ed. by Bradley & Hanson. pap. 5.00 (ISBN 0-686-60373-7). Polycrystal Bk Serv.

Machine Patchwork: Technique & Design. Dorothy Osler. LC 79-57311. (Illus.). 120p. 1980. 19.95 (ISBN 0-7134-3295-0, Pub. by Batsford England). David & Charles.

Machine Printing. W. R. Durrant et al. (Library of Printing Technology). Date not set. 17.95 (ISBN 0-8038-4671-1). Hastings.

Machine Shop Practice, 2 vols. K. H. Meltrecht. (Illus.). 1971. 14.00ea. o.p. (ISBN 0-686-57944-5); Vol. 1. (ISBN 0-8311-1069-4); Vol. 2. (ISBN 0-8311-1070-8). Indus Pr.

Machine Shop Practice. 2nd ed. K. H. Moltrecht. (Illus.). 1981. Vol. 1, 512 Pp. 19.95 (ISBN 0-8311-1126-7); Vol. 2, 528 Pp. 19.95 (ISBN 0-8311-1132-1). Indus Pr.

Machine Shop Training Course, 2 Vols. 5th ed. Franklin D. Jones. (Illus.). (gr. 11-12). 1964. 14.00 ea. Vol. 1 (ISBN 0-8311-1039-2). Vol. 2 (ISBN 0-8311-1040-6). Indus Pr.

Machine Stitchery. Gay Swift. LC 74-23867. (Illus.). 96p. 1975. 10.50 o.p. (ISBN 0-8231-5046-1). Branford.

Machine Stitches. Anne Butler. 1976. 17.95 (ISBN 0-7134-3150-4). David & Charles.

Machine Support Design Based on Vibration Calculus. Mihaly Makhult. Tr. by Seebestyen Meszner from Ger. & Hungarian. (Illus.). 136p. 1977. text ed. 32.50x (ISBN 0-569-08228-5, Pub. by Collets England). Scholium Intl.

Machine That Oils Itself: A Critical Look at the Mental Health Establishment. Robert C. Reinehr. LC 75-23326. 264p. 1975. 14.95 (ISBN 0-88229-248-X). Nelson Hall.

Machine Tool Practices. Richard R. Kibbe et al. LC 78-18533. 1979. text ed. 25.95x (ISBN 0-471-04331-1); tchrs. manual avail. (ISBN 0-471-05120-9). Wiley.

Machine Tool Structures, Vol. 1. F. Koenigsberger & J. Tlusty. LC 79-84073. 1970. 94.00 (ISBN 0-08-013405-X). Pergamon.

Machine Tool Technology. Willard J. McCarthy & Victor Repp. (Illus.). (gr. 11-12). 1979. text ed. 18.60 (ISBN 0-87345-143-0); Study Guide 1. 3.68 (ISBN 0-87345-144-9); Study Guide 2. 3.68 (ISBN 0-87345-145-7); ans. key avail. McKnight.

Machine Tool Value Guide, Vol. 1. Compiled By National Research & Appraisal Co. 1980. pap. 50.00 (ISBN 0-89692-102-6). Equipment Guide.

Machine Tool Value Guide: Grinding Machines, Vol. III. Equipment Guide-Book Co. Ed. by Jiri Husek. 600p. 1981. pap. 50.00 (ISBN 0-89692-104-2). Equipment Guide.

Machine Tools. Herbert S. Zim & James R. Skelly. LC 69-10403. (How Things Work Ser., No. 1). (Illus.). (gr. 3-7). 1960. PLB 6.48 (ISBN 0-688-31555-0); pap. 1.25 (ISBN 0-688-26555-3). Morrow.

Machine Tools & Machining Practices, 2 vols. Warren T. White et al. LC 76-27863. 1977. Vol. 1. text ed. 25.95 (ISBN 0-471-94035-6); Vol. 2. text ed. 25.95 (ISBN 0-471-94036-4). Wiley.

Machine Trades Projects & Procedures: Standard & Metric. Frank Accurso. LC 77-8691. 1978. pap. text ed. 9.50 (ISBN 0-672-97101-1); tchr's manual 3.33 (ISBN 0-672-97155-0). Bobbs.

Machine Transcription & Dictation. Joyce Kupsh et al. LC 77-15790. (Wiley Word Processing Ser.). 1978. 13.95 (ISBN 0-471-02734-0); tchrs. manual 2.00 (ISBN 0-471-04211-0). Wiley.

Machine Transcription in Modern Business. Lois Meyer & Ruth Moyer. LC 77-25874. 1978. pap. text ed. 14.95 (ISBN 0-471-02735-9); scripts 3.75 (ISBN 0-471-03800-8). Wiley.

Machine Translation. Bozena Henisz-Dostert et al. (Trends in Linguistics, Studies, & Monographs: No. 16). 1979. text ed. 44.25x (ISBN 90-279-7836-0). Mouton.

Machine Woodworking. rev. ed. Robert E. Smith. (Illus.). (gr. 9-10). 1958. text ed. 13.28 (ISBN 0-87345-010-8). McKnight.

Machine Woodworking Technology for Hand Woodworkers. F. E. Sherlock. (Illus.). 222p. 1975. pap. 16.50x (ISBN 0-408-00113-5). Transatlantic.

Machinery. Boy Scouts Of America. LC 19-600. (Illus.). 64p. (gr. 6-12). 1962. pap. 0.70x (ISBN 0-8395-3337-3, 3337). BSA.

Machinery Buyers Guide 1980. Ed. by Fred Browne. 1499p. (Orig.). 1980. pap. 47.50x (ISBN 0-8002-2472-8). Intl Pubns Serv.

Machinery of Change in Local Government: 1888-1974. Clifford Pearce. (Institute of Local Government Studies). 240p. 1980. text ed. 37.50x (ISBN 0-04-352091-X, 2541). Allen Unwin.

Machinery of Justice in England. 7th ed. Richard M. Jackson. LC 77-4401. 1978. 74.50 (ISBN 0-521-21688-5); pap. 24.95 (ISBN 0-521-29231-X). Cambridge U Pr.

Machinery of the Mind. Dion Fortune. 1980. pap. 4.95 (ISBN 0-87728-505-5). Weiser.

Machinery Question & the Making of Political Economy: 1815-1848. Maxine Berg. LC 79-51223. (Illus.). 1980. 39.50 (ISBN 0-521-22782-8). Cambridge U Pr.

Machinery's Handbook. 21st rev. ed. Erik Oberg et al. Ed. by Paul B. Schubert. (Illus.). 2482p. 1979. 34.00 (ISBN 0-8311-1129-1); text ed. 19.00 o.p. (ISBN 0-8311-1108-9). Indus Pr.

Machines. Anne Rockwell. (Illus.). (ps-2). 1972. 7.95 (ISBN 0-02-777520-8). Macmillan.

Machines & Liberty 1789-1914. Martin Roberts. (Portrait of Europe Ser.). (Illus.). 360p. 1973. pap. write for info. Oxford U Pr.

Machines & the Man: A Sourcebook on Automation. Ed. by Robert P. Weeks. LC 61-6338. (Illus., Orig.). 1961. pap. text ed. 5.95x (ISBN 0-89197-282-X). Irvington.

Machines, Languages & Computation. Peter J. Denning et al. (Automatic Computation Ser.). (Illus.). 1978. ref. ed. 25.95 (ISBN 0-13-542258-2). P-H.

Machines on a Farm. Althea. (Illus.). 24p. 1980. pap. 1.45 ea. (ISBN 0-85122-167-X, Pub. by Dinosaur Pubns); pap. in 5 pk. avail. Merrimack Bk Serv.

Machines Who Think. Pamela McCorduck. LC 79-13809. (Illus.). 1979. text ed. 15.95x (ISBN 0-7167-1072-2). W H Freeman.

Machining Data Handbook, 2 vols. 3rd ed. Ed. by The Technical Staff of the Machinability Data Center. LC 80-81480. (Illus.). 1980. Set. 150.00x (ISBN 0-936974-00-1). Metcut Res Assocs.

Machining for Toolmaking & Experimental Work, 3 vols. 2nd ed. Ed. by P. Heritage et al. (Engineering Craftsmen: No. H1). (Illus.). 1977. Set. spiral bdg. 36.50x (ISBN 0-85083-024-9). Intl Ideas.

Machining Fundamentals. Daniel Follette. Ed. by Roy Williams & E. J. Weller. LC 80-51218. (Illus.). 400p. 1980. 27.50 (ISBN 0-87263-054-4). SME.

Machining of Plastics. Akira Kobayashi. LC 79-20877. 270p. 1980. Repr. of 1967 ed. lib. bdg. 24.50 (ISBN 0-89874-007-X). Krieger.

Machining Science & Applications. M. Kronenberg. 1966. text ed. 60.00 (ISBN 0-08-011627-2). Pergamon.

Machinist--Machinist's Helper. 3rd ed. Arco Editorial Board. LC 79-28693. 256p. 1980. pap. 8.00 (ISBN 0-668-04933-2). Arco.

Machinist: Basic Skill Development. George Lehrling. (Illus.). 1978. pap. text ed. 10.65 o.p. (ISBN 0-8269-1950-2). Am Technical.

Machinists Library, 3 vols. Rex Miller. Incl. Vol. 1. Basic Machine Shop (ISBN 0-672-23301-0); Vol. 2. Machine Shop (ISBN 0-672-23302-9); Vol. 3. Toolmakers Handy Book (ISBN 0-672-23303-7). LC 78-57172. 1978. 10.95 ea. (ISBN 0-672-23300-2); 29.95 set (ISBN 0-685-92871-3). Audel.

Machisma: Women & Daring. Grace Lichtenstein. LC 79-7114. 360p. 1981. 14.95 (ISBN 0-385-15109-8). Doubleday.

Macho Camacho's Beat. Luis R. Sanchez. Tr. by Gregory Rabassa. 1981. 10.95 (ISBN 0-394-50976-5). Pantheon.

Mach's Philosophy of Science. J. Bradley. (Illus.). 240p. 1971. text ed. 17.25x (ISBN 0-485-11124-1, Athlone Pr). Humanities.

Machu Picchu. John Hemming. Ed. by Edwin Bayrd. LC 80-82066. (Illus.). 1981. 16.95 (ISBN 0-88225-302-6). Newsweek.

McInnis-Hammondsport Plan: A Manual. Philip J. McInnis. LC 77-78982. 72p. 1977. tchrs. ed. 6.50 o.s.i. (ISBN 0-8027-9047-X). Walker Educ.

McKay & Patera Tables of Dimensions. McKay & Patera. 336p. Date not set. 39.75 (ISBN 0-8247-1227-7). Dekker.

McKay's Bees. Thomas McMahon. 176p. 1981. pap. 2.75 (ISBN 0-380-53579-3, 53579, Bard). Avon.

McKay's Big Book of Cowboys & Cowgirls. Ed. by Alex Whitney. (gr. 4 up). Date not set. cancelled (ISBN 0-679-20540-3). McKay.

McKay's Big Book of Dinosaurs. Ed. by Alex Whitney. (gr. 4 up). Date not set. cancelled (ISBN 0-679-20536-5). McKay.

McKay's Big Book of Magic. Ed. by Chet Fish. (gr. 4-12). Date not set. cancelled (ISBN 0-679-20542-X). McKay.

McKay's Big Book of Model Trains. Ed. by Alex Whitney. (gr. 4 up). Date not set. cancelled (ISBN 0-679-20539-X). McKay.

McKay's Big Book of Police Work. Ed. by Chet Fish. (gr. 4 up). Date not set. cancelled (ISBN 0-679-20537-3). McKay.

McKay's Big Book of Space Travel. Ed. by Chet Fish. (gr. 4 up). Date not set. cancelled (ISBN 0-679-20541-1). McKay.

McKay's Big Book of the Army. Ed. by Alan Tucker. (gr. 4 up). 1980. cancelled (ISBN 0-679-20538-1). McKay.

McKay's Big Book of Villains. Ed. by Alex Whitney. (gr. 4 up). 7.95 o.p. (ISBN 0-679-20535-7). McKay.

M'kee & Bros. Victorian Glass: Five Complete Glass Catalogues from 1859 - 60, 71. Intro. by Lowell Iness. (Illus.). 160p. 1981. pap. price not set (ISBN 0-486-24121-1). Dover.

McKee Glass. Sandra Stout. (Illus.). 19.50 (ISBN 0-686-51456-4). Wallace-Homestead.

McKee of Centre Street. Helen Reilly. 299p. 1980. Repr. of 1933 ed. lib. bdg. 14.25x (ISBN 0-89968-214-6). Lightyear.

Mackenzie Today. Alfred P. Aquilina. Ed. by Margaret Campbell. (Illus.). 50p. (Orig.). 1981. pap. 4.00 (ISBN 0-88839-082-3). Hancock Hse.

Mackenzie: Yesterday & Beyond. Alfred P. Aquilina. (Illus.). pap. 6.95 (ISBN 0-88839-083-1). Hancock Hse.

Mackenzie's Rock. Alexander Mackenzie. 31p. Repr. of 1905 ed. pap. 2.50 (ISBN 0-8466-0048-X, SJS48). Shorey.

McKinley's Bulldog: The Battleship Oregon. Stanford Sternlicht. LC 77-8603. 1977. text ed. 13.95 (ISBN 0-88229-263-3); pap. 6.95 (ISBN 0-88229-516-0). Nelson-Hall.

Mackintosh Watercolours. Roger Billcliffe. LC 78-53795. (Illus.). 144p. 1979. pap. 12.50 (ISBN 0-8008-5043-2). Taplinger.

M'lady Gets a Beastie. Gwendolyn Dieterle. 32p. (gr. 3-5). 1981. 5.95 (ISBN 0-89962-203-8). Todd & Honeywell.

Maclaren's Men. Robert W. Marsh. 1979. pap. 1.75 (ISBN 0-505-51435-4). Tower Bks.

MacLyon. Lolah Burford. LC 73-21292. 384p. 1974. 8.95 o.s.i. (ISBN 0-02-518190-4, 51819). Macmillan.

McMahon's American Gardener. Bernard McMahon. LC 75-29506. (Funk & W Bk.). (Illus.). 640p. 1976. 10.00 o.s.i. (ISBN 0-308-10223-1, TYC-T); pap. 5.95 o.s.i. (ISBN 0-308-10224-X, TYC-T). T Y Crowell.

McMaster University, Vol. 2: The Early Years in Hamilton, 1930-1957. Charles M. Johnston. 329p. 1981. 25.00x (ISBN 0-8020-3372-5). U of Toronto Pr.

Macmillan Atlas History of Christianity. Franklin H. Littell. LC 75-22113. (Illus.). 163p. 1976. 21.95 (ISBN 0-02-573140-8, 57314). Macmillan.

Macmillan Baseball Calendar, 1981. Reichler. 108p. Date not set. 7.95 (ISBN 0-02-926130-9). Macmillan.

Macmillan Bible Atlas. rev. ed. Yohanon Aharoni & Michael Avi-Yonah. LC 77-4313. (Illus.). 1977. 24.95 (ISBN 0-02-500590-1). Macmillan.

Macmillan Children's Calendar, 1981. Jean Doty & Roy Doty. Ed. by Phyllis Larkin. 15p. (gr. 3 up). 1980. spiral bdg 4.95 (ISBN 0-02-732980-1). Macmillan.

Macmillan Dictionary of Historical Slang. Eric Partridge. Ed. by Jacqueline Simpson. 1072p. 1975. 29.95 (ISBN 0-02-594950-0). Macmillan.

Macmillan Handbook of Chess. I. A. Horowitz & Fred Reinfeld. (Illus.). 1956. 10.95 (ISBN 0-02-554140-4). Macmillan.

Macorvan Curse. Florence Bowes. LC 79-48086. (Romantic Suspense Ser). 192p. 1980. 8.95 (ISBN 0-385-15844-0). Doubleday.

Macrame. Imelda M. Pesch. LC 76-126848. (Little Craft Book Ser.). (gr. 6 up). 1970. 5.95 (ISBN 0-8069-5158-3); PLB 6.69 (ISBN 0-8069-5159-1). Sterling.

Macrame. Mary A. Pilcher. 1972. 5.50 o.p. (ISBN 0-8231-5038-0). Branford.

Macrame. 2nd ed. Sunset Editors. LC 75-6225. (Illus.). 80p. 1975. pap. 3.95 (ISBN 0-376-04544-2, Sunset Bks.). Sunset-Lane.

Macrame: A Comprehensive Study. Heidy Willsmore. (Illus.). 1979. 23.00 (ISBN 0-571-11310-9, Pub. by Faber & Faber). Merrimack Bk Serv.

Macrame: Advanced Technique & Design. Norman Rack & Lillian Rack. LC 72-175416. 144p. 1972. pap. 3.95 o.p. (ISBN 0-385-08749-7). Doubleday.

Macrame, Step by Step. Mary W. Phillips. (Step by Step Craft Ser). 1974. pap. 2.95 (ISBN 0-307-42005-1, Golden Pr). Western Pub.

Macro & Semi-Micro Chemical Analysis Without H2S. 2nd rev. ed. K. N. Johri. pap. 3.00x o.p. (ISBN 0-210-31239-4). Asia.

Macro Economics. Helmut A. Merklein. 1972. 14.95x (ISBN 0-534-00175-0). Wadsworth Pub.

Macro Implementation of SNOBOL4: A Case Study of Machine-Independent Software Development. Ralph E. Griswold. LC 72-184097. 1972. text ed. 30.95x (ISBN 0-7167-0447-1). W H Freeman.

Macro Marketing: A Social Perspective. 2nd ed. Reed Moyer & Michael D. Hutt. LC 77-26816. (Wiley Ser. in Marketing). 1978. text ed. 10.50 (ISBN 0-471-02699-9); teacher's manual (ISBN 0-471-02768-5). Wiley.

Macro Philosophy for the Aquarian Age. rev. 2nd ed. Thea Alexander. 160p. 1971. pap. 4.00 (ISBN 0-913080-01-2). Macro Bks.

Macro Processors. A. J. Cole. (Cambridge Computer Science Texts Ser.: No. 4). (Illus.). 200p. 1976. 12.95x (ISBN 0-521-29024-4). Cambridge U Pr.

Macro Study Series. Incl. How to Develop Your Marco Awareness (ISBN 0-913080-05-5); How to Live a Macro Lifestyle (ISBN 0-913080-06-3); How to Interpret Your Dreams from a Macro View (ISBN 0-913080-07-1); Prophetess: Conversations with Rana (ISBN 0-913080-08-X); Simultaneous Time: Your Parallel Lives, Twin Souls, & Soul Mates (ISBN 0-685-99310-8); How to Do Personal Evolution Tutoring (ISBN 0-913080-10-1); Macro Study Guide & Workbook (ISBN 0-913080-11-X). ISBN 0-686-53130-2). 4.00 ea. Macro Bks.

Macrobiotic Cooking for Everyone. Edward Esko & Wendy Esko. LC 79-89344. (Illus., Orig.). 1980. pap. 12.95 (ISBN 0-87040-469-5). Japan Pubns.

Macrobiotics: An Invitation to Health & Happiness. George Ohsawa. 77p. 1971. pap. 3.95 (ISBN 0-918860-02-4). G Ohsawa.

Macroecomomics. 2nd ed. Robert J. Gordon. 1981. text ed. 16.95 (ISBN 0-316-32125-7); wkbk. 6.95 (ISBN 0-316-32127-3). Little.

Macroeconometric Model of a Developing Economy: Ghana (Simulations & Policy Analysis) Jacob K. Atta. LC 80-67178. 346p. (Orig.). 1981. pap. text ed. 12.50 (ISBN 0-8191-1504-5). U Pr of Amer.

Macroeconomic Alternatives. Martin Bronfenbrenner. LC 79-50880. (Illus.). 1979. text ed. 16.50x (ISBN 0-88295-404-0). AHM Pub.

Macroeconomic Analysis & Stabilization Policy. S. J. Turnovsky. LC 76-46862. (Illus.). 1977. 44.50 (ISBN 0-521-21520-X); pap. 15.95x (ISBN 0-521-29187-9). Cambridge U Pr.

Macroeconomic, Models & Policy. Y. P. Venieris & F. D. Sebold. 1977. 23.95 (ISBN 0-471-90560-7). Wiley.

Macroeconomic Policy: New Cambridge, Keynesian and Monetarist Controversies. K. Cuthbertson. LC 79-12195. (New Studies in Economic Ser.). 209p. 1979. 27.95x (ISBN 0-470-26740-2). Halsted Pr.

Macroeconomic Principles. W. Albrecht, Jr. 1979. pap. 10.95 (ISBN 0-13-542738-X); study guide & wkbk. 8.95 (ISBN 0-13-227553-8). P-H.

Macroeconomic Readings. John Lindauer. LC 68-9816. (Orig.). 1968. pap. text ed. 9.95 (ISBN 0-02-919110-6). Free Pr.

Macroeconomic Themes: Edited Readings in Macroeconomics. Ed. by M. J. C. Surrey. (Illus.). 1976. text ed. 37.50x (ISBN 0-19-877059-6); pap. text ed. 14.50x (ISBN 0-19-877060-X). Oxford U Pr.

Macroeconomic Theory. Robert H. Burton & Gordon Brunhild. (Illus.). 544p. 1973. ref. ed. 18.95x (ISBN 0-13-542639-1). P-H.

Macroeconomic Theory. William R. Hosek. 1975. text ed. 17.50x (ISBN 0-256-01669-0). Irwin.

Macroeconomic Theory & Policy. Frank Zahn. (Illus.). 320p. 1975. 17.95 (ISBN 0-13-542555-7). P-H.

Macroeconomics. 2nd ed. Charles W. Baird & Alexander E. Cassuto. 336p. 1980. text ed. 16.95 (ISBN 0-574-19400-2, 13-2400); instr's. guide avail. (ISBN 0-574-19401-0, 13-2401). SRA.

Macroeconomics. Michael E. Bradley. 1980. pap. text ed. 11.95x (ISBN 0-673-15336-3); study guide 5.95x (ISBN 0-673-15423-8). Scott F.

Macroeconomics. Robert D. Cherry. LC 79-3130. (Economics Ser.). 1980. text ed. 16.95 (ISBN 0-201-00911-0). A-W.

Macroeconomics. 2nd ed. Rudiger Dornbusch & Stanley Fischer. (Illus.). 736p. 1980. text ed. 18.95 (ISBN 0-07-017754-6, C); instructor's manual 6.95 (ISBN 0-07-017755-4); study guide 6.95 (ISBN 0-07-017756-2). McGraw.

Macroeconomics. William A. Kelly, Jr. (Illus.). 496p. 1981. text ed. 17.95 (ISBN 0-13-542761-4). P-H.

Macroeconomics. Peter E. Kennedy. 448p. 1975. 14.95x o.p. (ISBN 0-205-04282-1, 0942820). Allyn.

Macroeconomics. 5th ed. Maurice W. Lee. 1971. text ed. 18.95x (ISBN 0-256-00296-7). Irwin.

Macroeconomics. Duncan McDougall & James P. Quirk. 1981. pap. text ed. 11.95 (ISBN 0-574-19415-0, 13-2415); instr's guide avail. (ISBN 0-574-19416-9, 13-2416). SRA.

Macroeconomics. Poindexter. 1976. 18.95 (ISBN 0-03-089419-0). Dryden Pr.

Macroeconomics. 2nd ed. J. Carl Poindexter, Jr. LC 79-51107. 560p. 1981. text ed. 17.95 (ISBN 0-03-050271-3). Dryden Pr.

Macroeconomics. 3rd ed. Lewis C. Solmon. LC 79-25516. 480p. 1980. pap. text ed. 12.95 (ISBN 0-201-07217-3); student guide avail. (ISBN 0-201-07220-3). A-W.

Macroeconomics. Jack Vernon. 464p. 1980. text ed. 19.95 (ISBN 0-03-042336-8). Dryden Pr.

Macroeconomics. rev. ed. Paul Wonnacott. 1978. text ed. 18.95 (ISBN 0-256-02032-9). Irwin.

Macroeconomics: A Neoclassical Introduction. Merton H. Miller & Charles W. Upton. 1974. text ed. 16.00x o.p. (ISBN 0-256-01550-3). Irwin.

Macroeconomics: A Programmed Book. 3rd ed. Richard E. Attiyeh et al. (Illus.). 272p. (Prog. Bk.). 1974. pap. 9.95 ref. ed. (ISBN 0-13-542662-6). P-H.

Macroeconomics: An Introduction to Theory & Policy. Frederick Brooman & Henry D. Jacoby. LC 73-75979. 1970. 22.95x (ISBN 0-202-06026-8). Aldine Pub.

Macroeconomics: Analysis & Policy. 3rd. ed. Lloyd G. Reynolds. 1979. pap. text ed. 11.50 (ISBN 0-256-02173-2); review guide & wkbk. 5.95 (ISBN 0-256-02170-8). Irwin.

Macroeconomics & Monetary Theory. Harry G. Johnson. 214p. 1972. 14.95x (ISBN 0-202-06053-5). Aldine Pub.

Macroeconomics for Management. Mary L. Hatten. (Illus.). 384p. 1981. text ed. 18.95 (ISBN 0-13-542498-4). P-H.

Macroeconomics for Managers. W. Duncan Reekie. 160p. 1980. 18.00x (ISBN 0-86003-510-7, Pub. by Allan Pubs England); pap. 9.00x (ISBN 0-86003-610-3). State Mutual Bk.

Macroeconomics: Measurement, Theory, & Policy. M. Lovell. LC 75-2001. 541p. 1975. 23.50 (ISBN 0-471-54850-2). Wiley.

Macroeconomics: Private & Public Choice. James D. Gwartney. 1977. text ed. 10.50 o.p. (ISBN 0-12-311060-2). Acad Pr.

Macroeconomics: Private & Public Choice. 2nd ed. James D. Gwartney & Richard Stroup. 1980. pap. text ed. 12.95 (ISBN 0-12-311070-X). Acad Pr.

Macroeconomics: Theory, Evidence & Policy. Frank C. Wykoff. (Illus.). 1976. 18.95 (ISBN 0-13-543959-0). P-H.

Macroeconomics: Theory, Evidence & Policy. 2nd ed. Frank C. Wykoff. (Illus.). 640p. 1981. 19.95 (ISBN 0-13-543967-1). P-H.

Macroeconomics 1979: Readings on Contemporary Issues. Ed. by Peter D. McClelland. LC 77-6193. (Continuation Ser.). (Orig.). 1979. text ed. 7.95x soft cover o.p. (ISBN 0-8014-9870-8). Cornell U Pr.

Macroengineering & the Infra-Structure of Tomorrow. Frank P. Davidson et al. 1979. lib. bdg. 27.50x (ISBN 0-89158-294-0). Westview.

Macroevolution: Pattern & Process. Steven M. Stanley. LC 79-15464. (Illus.). 1979. text ed. 22.95x (ISBN 0-7167-1092-7). W H Freeman.

Macrolichens of Denmark, Finland, Norway, & Sweden. Eilif Dahl & Hildur Krog. (Scandinavian University Books). (Illus.). 180p. 1973. 17.00x (ISBN 8-200-02262-5, Dist. by Columbia U Pr). Universitet.

Macromarketing, Vol. II: Distributive Processes from a Societal Perspective, an Elaboration of Issues. Ed. by Charles C. Slater & Phillip D. White. 477p. 1978. 10.00 (ISBN 0-686-69388-4). U CO Busn Res Div.

Macromarketing, Vol. III: New Steps on the Learning Curve. Ed. by George Fisk & Robert W. Nason. 421p. 1979. 12.00 (ISBN 0-686-69387-6). U CO Busn Res Div.

Macromolecular Physics: Crystals, Structure, Morphology & Defects. Bernard Wunderlich. 1973. Vol. 1, 1973. 52.75 (ISBN 0-12-765601-4); Vol. 2, 1976. 62.75 (ISBN 0-12-765602-2). Acad Pr.

Macromolecular Science. Colleen M. Koruza. (IRS Physical Chemistry Ser. Two: Vol. 8). 1975. 29.95 (ISBN 0-408-70607-4). Butterworths.

Macromoleculas. (Serie De Quimica: No. 3). (Illus., Span.). 1968. pap. 1.50 o.p. (ISBN 0-685-19219-9). OAS.

Macronyssidae & Laelepidae (Acarina: Mesostigmata) Parasitic on Bats. F. J. Radovsky. (U. C. Publ. in Entomology: Vol. 46). 1967. pap. 10.00x (ISBN 0-520-09118-3). U of Cal Pr.

Macropedius. Thomas W. Best. (World Authors Ser.: Netherlands: No. 218). lib. bdg. 10.95 (ISBN 0-8057-2560-1). Twayne.

Macrophage Regulation of Immunity. Ed. by Emil R. Unanue & Alan S. Rosenthal. LC 79-24609. 1980. 27.50 (ISBN 0-12-708550-5). Acad Pr.

Macrophages & Lymphocytes: Nature, Functions, & Interaction, Pt. A. Ed. by M. R. Escobar & H. Friedman. LC 79-9566. (Advances in Experimental Medicine & Biology Ser.: Vol. 121A). 660p. 1980. 59.50 (ISBN 0-306-40285-8, Plenum Pr). Plenum Pub.

Macrophages & Lymphocytes: Nature, Functions & Interaction, Pt. B. Ed. by M. R. Escobar & H. Friedman. (Advances in Experimental Medicine & Biology: Vol. 121B). 625p. 1980. 59.50 (ISBN 0-306-40286-6, Plenum Pr). Plenum Pub.

Macropolitics: Essays on the Philosophy & Science of Politics. Morton Kaplan. LC 68-8153. 1968. 20.00x (ISBN 0-89197-833-X). Irvington.

Macroscopic Electromagnetism. F. M. Robinson. LC 73-4280. 256p. 1973. 37.00 (ISBN 0-08-017647-X). Pergamon.

Macrostructures: An Interdisciplinary Study of Global Structures in Discourse, Interaction & Cognition. Teun A. Van Dijk. LC 79-27844. 336p. 1980. text ed. 24.95 (ISBN 0-89859-039-6). L Erlbaum Assocs.

Mac's Giant Book of Quips & Quotes. E. C. McKenzie. 1980. 14.95 (ISBN 0-8010-6075-3). Baker Bk.

McTeague. Frank Norris. 1977. pap. 2.25 (ISBN 0-449-30810-3, Prem). Fawcett.

McTeague. Frank Norris. Ed. by Donald Pizer. LC 77-479. (Norton Critical Editions). 1977 12.95 (ISBN 0-393-04460-2); pap. text ed. 6.95x 1978 (ISBN 0-393-09136-8). Norton.

McTeague. Frank Norris. 1976. lib. bdg. 18.95x (ISBN 0-89968-071-2). Lightyear.

McTeague: A Story of California. Frank Norris. LC 72-184736. 1971. lib. bdg. 12.50x (ISBN 0-8376-0406-0). Bentley.

McTeague: A Story of San Francisco. Frank Norris. 9.00 (ISBN 0-8446-2663-5). Peter Smith.

Mad About Mad. Sergio Aragones. (Mad Ser.). (Illus.). 1977. pap. 1.75 (ISBN 0-446-94394-0). Warner Bks.

Mad About the Buoy. (Mad Ser.: No. 53). (Illus.). 1980. pap. 1.75 (ISBN 0-446-94449-1). Warner Bks.

Mad Adventures of Captain Klutz. Don Martin. (Mad Ser.). (Illus., Orig.). 1974. pap. 1.75 (ISBN 0-446-94417-3). Warner Bks.

Mad Anne Bailey. David A. Bice. (Pringle Tree Ser.). (Illus.). 36p. (gr. 3-6). 1980. 5.95 (ISBN 0-934750-06-8). Jalamap.

Mad Around the World. Jacobs Frank & Peter P. Porges. (Mad Ser.). (Illus.). 1979. pap. 1.50 (ISBN 0-446-88390-5). Warner Bks.

Mad As a Hatter. Sergio Aragones. (Mad Ser.). (Illus., Orig.). 1981. pap. 1.75 (ISBN 0-446-94116-6). Warner Bks.

Mad As the Devil. Sergio Aragones. (Mad Ser.). (Illus.). 1975. pap. 1.75 (ISBN 0-446-94395-9). Warner Bks.

Mad at You! Mad Magazine Editors. (Mad Ser.: No. 40). (Illus.). 1975. pap. 1.75 (ISBN 0-446-94590-0). Warner Bks.

Mad Book of Mysteries. Lou Silverstone & Jack Rickard. (Mad Ser.). (Illus., Orig.). 1980. pap. 1.75 (ISBN 0-446-84843-3). Warner Bks.

Mad Book of Revenge. Stan Hart & Paul Coker. (Mad Ser.). (Illus.). 192p. (Orig.). 1976. pap. 1.50 (ISBN 0-446-88732-3). Warner Bks.

Mad Couple Well Match'd. Richard Brome. Ed. by Steen H. Spove & Stephen Orgel. LC 78-13873. (Renaissance Drama Ser.). 1979. lib. bdg. 31.00 (ISBN 0-8240-9730-0). Garland Pub.

Mad Dog Black Lady. Wanda Coleman. 138p. (Orig.). 1979. pap. 4.50 (ISBN 0-87685-411-0). Black Sparrow.

Mad for Kicks. Mad Magazine Editors. (Mad Ser.: No. 54). (Illus., Orig.). 1980. pap. 1.50 (ISBN 0-446-98461-2). Warner Bks.

Mad Frontier. Mad Magazine Editors. (Mad Ser.). (Illus.). 1975. pap. 1.75 (ISBN 0-446-94373-8). Warner Bks.

Mad Goes Wild. Frank Jacobs & Bob Clarke. (Mad Ser.). (Illus., Orig.). 1981. pap. 1.75 (ISBN 0-446-94283-9). Warner Bks.

Mad Guide to Careers. Stan Hart & Paul Coker. (Mad Ser.). (Illus., Orig.). 1978. pap. 1.50 (ISBN 0-446-88302-6). Warner Bks.

Mad Guide to Fraud & Deception. Dick De Bartolo & Henry North. 192p. (Orig.). 1981. pap. 1.75 (ISBN 0-446-94154-9). Warner Bks.

Mad Guide to Leisure Time. Dick DeBartolo & George Woodbridge. (Mad Ser.). (Illus.). 192p. (Orig.). 1976. pap. 1.75 (ISBN 0-446-94431-9). Warner Bks.

Mad Hatter's Holiday. Peter Lovesey. 1981. pap. 2.95 (ISBN 0-14-005804-4). Penguin.

Mad in Orbit. Mad Magazine Editors. (Mad Ser.). (Illus.). 1975. pap. 1.50 (ISBN 0-446-88762-5). Warner Bks.

Mad in Pursuit. Violette Leduc. Tr. by Derek Coltman from Fr. 351p. 1971. 8.95 o.p. (ISBN 0-374-19508-0). FS&G.

Mad King. Edgar R. Burroughs. 256p. 1976. pap. 1.95 (ISBN 0-441-51404-9). Ace Bks.

Mad Libs, No. 11. Roger Price & Leonard Stern. 48p. 1980. pap. 1.75 (ISBN 0-8431-0248-9). Price Stern.

Mad Libs, No. 12. Roger Price & Leonard Stern. 48p. 1980. pap. 1.75 (ISBN 0-8431-0249-7). Price Stern.

Mad Libs No. 2. Roger Price & Leonard Stern. 1959. pap. 1.75 (ISBN 0-8431-0056-7). Price Stern.

Mad Look at the Future. Lou Siverstone & Jack Rickard. (Mad Ser.). (Illus., Orig.). 1978. pap. 1.50 (ISBN 0-446-88174-0). Warner Bks.

Mad Look at TV. Dick DeBartolo & Angelo Torres. (Mad Ser). (Illus.). 192p. (Orig.). 1974. pap. 1.75 (ISBN 0-446-94436-X). Warner Bks.

Mad-ly Yours. Sergio Aragones. (Mad Ser.). (Illus.). 192p. 1972. pap. 1.75 (ISBN 0-446-94396-7). Warner Bks.

Mad Make-Out Book. Larry Siegel & Angelo Torres. 1979. pap. 1.50 (ISBN 0-446-88947-4). Warner Bks.

Mad Marginals. Sergio Aragones. (Mad Ser.). (Illus.). 1974. pap. 1.75 (ISBN 0-446-94284-7). Warner Bks.

Mad Monk. Lewis Lancaster. (Lancaster - Miller Art Ser.). (Illus.). 1980. 7.95 (ISBN 0-89581-017-4). Lancaster-Miller.

Mad Power. Mad Magazine Editors. (Mad Ser.: No. 29). (Illus.). 1977. pap. 1.75 (ISBN 0-446-94375-4). Warner Bks.

Mad Scientists in Fact & Fiction. Melvin Berger. (gr. 5 up). 1980. PLB 7.90 (ISBN 0-531-04153-0). Watts.

Mad Scramble. Mad Magazine Editors. (Mad Ser.: No. 45). (Illus.). 192p. 1977. pap. 1.75 (ISBN 0-446-94437-8). Warner Bks.

Mad Stew. Nick Meglin. (Mad Ser.). (Illus., Orig.). 1978. pap. 1.75 (ISBN 0-446-94437-8). Warner Bks.

Mad-Vertising. DeBartolo Dick & Bob Clarke. (Mad Ser.). (Illus., Orig.). 1979. pap. 1.50 (ISBN 0-446-98100-1). Warner Bks.

Mad World, My Masters. Thomas Middleton. Ed. by Standish Henning. LC 65-10544. (Regents Renaissance Drama Ser.). 1965. 7.50x (ISBN 0-8032-0279-2); pap. 1.85x (ISBN 0-8032-5278-1, BB 211, Bison). U of Nebr Pr.

Mad Worry Book. Tom Koch & Bob Clarke. (Mad Ser.). (Illus.). 1980. pap. 1.75 (ISBN 0-446-94448-3). Warner Bks.

Madagascar & the Protestant Impact. Bonar A. Gow. LC 78-11216. (Dalhousie African Studies). 1979. text ed. 37.50x (ISBN 0-8419-0463-4, Africana). Holmes & Meier.

Madak Alley. Nagib Mahfouz. pap. 5.50 arabic (ISBN 0-685-82842-5); pap. 3.95 English (ISBN 0-686-67892-3). Intl Bk Ctr.

Madam Kitty. Peter Norden. 1977. pap. 1.50 (ISBN 0-345-24228-9). Ballantine.

Madam Says Keep the Lorry off the Grass. Jackie Matte. 138p. 1980. 7.95 (ISBN 0-533-04740-4). Vantage.

Madame Benoit's World of Food. Jehane Benoit. (Illus.). 304p. 1980. 16.95 (ISBN 0-07-082974-8, GB). McGraw.

Madame Bovary. Gustave Flaubert. Ed. by Paul De Man. (Critical Editions). (gr. 9-12). 1965. pap. text ed. 5.95x (ISBN 0-393-09608-4, NortonC). Norton.

Madame Bovary. Gustave Flaubert. (Classics Ser). (gr. 11 up). pap. 1.50 (ISBN 0-8049-0089-2, CL-89). Airmont.

Madame Bovary. Gustave Flaubert. (Literature Ser). (gr. 10-12). 1970. pap. text ed. 3.58 (ISBN 0-87720-744-5). AMSCO Sch.

Madame Bovary. Gustave Flaubert. Tr. by Mildred Marmur. (Orig.). 1964. pap. 2.25 (ISBN 0-451-51365-7, CE1365, Sig Classics). NAL.

Madame Bovary. Gustave Flaubert. pap. 1.75. Bantam.

Madame Campan: Educator of Women, Confidante of Queens. Millicent S Mali. LC 78-65428. 1978. pap. text ed. 9.75 (ISBN 0-8191-0662-3). U Pr of Amer.

Madame Castel's Lodger. Frances P. Keyes. 1977. pap. 1.95 o.p. (ISBN 0-449-23288-3, Crest). Fawcett.

Madame Curie. Eileen Bigland. LC 57-5540. (Illus.). (gr. 7-9). 1957. 9.95 (ISBN 0-87599-013-4). S G Phillips.

Madame Curie - Albert Einstein. Naunerle Farr. (Pendulum Illustrated Biography Ser.). (Illus.). (gr. 4-12). 1979. text ed. 4.50 (ISBN 0-88301-368-1); pap. text ed. 1.45 (ISBN 0-88301-356-8); wkbk. 0.95 (ISBN 0-88301-380-0). Pendulum Pr.

Madame Guyon. new ed. Madame Guyon. 382p. 1974. pap. 6.95 (ISBN 0-8024-5135-7). Moody.

Madame Prime Minister: The Story of Indira Gandhi. Emmeline Garnett. LC 67-15005. (Illus.). (gr. 7 up). 1967. 4.50 o.p. (ISBN 0-374-34686-0). FS&G.

Madame Rolland & the Age of Revolution. Gita May. LC 70-108418. (Illus.). 1970. 20.00x (ISBN 0-231-03379-6). Columbia U Pr.

Madame Vestris & the London Stage. William W. Appleton. LC 73-10106. (Illus.). 240p. 1974. text ed. 17.50x (ISBN 0-231-03794-5). Columbia U Pr.

Maddocks & the Wonder of Wales. Elizabeth Beazley. (Illus.). 1967. 9.50 (ISBN 0-571-08023-5, Pub. by Faber & Faber). Merrimack Bk Serv.

Made in America. Peter Maas. 304p. 1980. pap. 2.50 (ISBN 0-553-13743-3). Bantam.

Made in America. Susan Smith. LC 71-145708. 1971. Repr. of 1929 ed. 15.00 (ISBN 0-8103-3396-1). Gale.

Made in Austria. 312p. (Orig.). 1978. pap. 27.50x (ISBN 0-8002-2234-2). Intl Pubns Serv.

Made in Britain: A Unique Contribution to World Industrial Archaeology, Vol. 1. Peter English. Ed. by I. C. Faulds. 1980. text ed. 15.50x (ISBN 0-904980-28-6). Humanities.

Made in Japan. Glen Chase. (Cherry Delight Ser.). 1976. pap. 1.25 o.p. (ISBN 0-685-74574-0, LB423ZK, Leisure Bks). Nordon Pubns.

Made in West Africa. Christine Price. LC 74-4202. 160p. (gr. 5 up). 1975. PLB 9.95 o.p. (ISBN 0-525-34400-4). Dutton.

Made, Not Born: New Perspectives on Christian Initiation & the Catechumenate. Ed. by The Murphy Center for Liturgical Research. 200p. 1976. 9.95x o.p. (ISBN 0-268-00708-X). U of Notre Dame Pr.

Made of Gold: The Life of Angela Burdett Coutts. Diana Orton. (Illus.). 1980. 45.00 (ISBN 0-241-89656-8, Pub. by Hamish Hamilton England). David & Charles.

Made of Mud: Stoneware Potteries in Central Pennsylvania, 1831-1929. Jeannette Lasansky. LC 79-2708. (Illus.). 1979. pap. 7.95 (ISBN 0-271-00228-X, Keystone Bks). Pa St U Pr.

Made Simple Self Teaching Encyclopedia. Date not set. pap. price not set o.p. (ISBN 0-685-48902-7). Cadillac.

Made to Measure: Children's Books in Developing Countries. 129p. 1981. pap. 8.25 (ISBN 92-3-101783-7, U1047, UNESCO). Unipub.

Made with Oak. Herbert H. Wise & Jeffrey Weiss. (Illus.). 96p. 1975. pap. 6.95 (ISBN 0-8256-3052-5, Quick Fox). Music Sales.

Madeleine & Andre Gide. Jean Schlumberger. Tr. by Richard H. Akeroyd. (Illus.). 1980. 12.00 (ISBN 0-916620-45-X). Portals Pr.

Madeleine Ferat. Emile Zola. 1957. 13.95 (ISBN 0-236-30907-2, Pub. by Paul Elek). Merrimack Bk Serv.

Madeline. Ludwig Bemelmans. LC 39-21791. (gr. k-3). 1977. pap. 2.75 (ISBN 0-14-050198-3, Puffin). Penguin.

Mademoiselle. Rose Lewis. 192p. (Orig.). 1981. pap. 1.95 (ISBN 0-523-40962-1). Pinnacle Bks.

Mademoiselle De Maupin. Theophile Gautier. Tr. & intro. by Joanna Richardson. 304p. 1981. pap. 4.95 (ISBN 0-14-044398-3). Penguin.

Mademoiselle De Scudery. Nicole Aronson. (World Authors Ser.: No. 441 France). 1978. 12.50 (ISBN 0-8057-6278-7). Twayne.

Mademoiselle Miss & Other Stories. Henry Harland. LC 76-24385. (Decadent Consciousness Ser.: Vol. 12). 1977. Repr. of 1893 ed. lib. bdg. 38.00 (ISBN 0-8240-2760-4). Garland Pub.

Madera. Harlan Wade. Tr. by Mamie M. Contreras from Eng. LC 78-26849. (Book About Ser.). Orig. Title: Wood. (Illus., Sp.). (gr. k-3). 1979. PLB 7.30 (ISBN 0-8172-1483-6). Raintree Pubs.

Madge's Magic Show. Mike Thaler. (Easy-Read Story Books Ser.). (Illus.). (gr. k-3). 1978. PLB 6.45 s&l (ISBN 0-531-01450-9). Watts.

Madhusudan Saraswati on the Bhagavaddita. S. K. Gupta. 1977. 25.00 (ISBN 0-89684-246-0, Pub. by Motilal Banarsidass India). Orient Bk Dist.

Madison Avenue Handbook 1980. 1980. spiral bdg. 13.95 o.p. (ISBN 0-87314-010-9). Peter Glenn.

Madison Avenue Handbook 1981. Ed. by Peter Glenn et al. 1981. price not set (ISBN 0-87314-011-7). Peter Glenn.

Madison Connection: Voices of the '60s. Miriam Hall et al. (Harvest Bk. Ser.: Nos. 17-20). (Illus.). 180p. 1980. write for info. (0146-5414). Harvest Pubns.

Madison, God's Beautiful Farm. Ira M. Gish & H. K. Christman. LC 78-70891. (Redwood Ser.). 1979. pap. 3.95 (ISBN 0-8163-0243-X). Pacific Pr Pub Assn.

Madison Poems & Collages. D. A. Levy. 1980. 12.00. Quixote.

Madly Singing in the Mountains: An Appreciation & Anthology of Arthur Waley. Ed. by Ivan Morris. 400p. 1981. pap. 7.95 (ISBN 0-916870-35-9). Creative Arts Bk.

Madman at My Door. Hillary Waugh. 1979. pap. 2.25 (ISBN 0-380-47159-0, 47159). Avon.

Madness & Modern Society. Klaus Doerner. Tr. by Jean Steinberg. 1981. 17.50 (ISBN 0-916354-42-3); pap. 8.95 (ISBN 0-916354-54-7). Urizen Bks.

Madness & Morals: Ideas on Insanity in the Nineteenth Century. Vieda Skultans. 1975. 20.00x (ISBN 0-7100-8022-0). Routledge & Kegan.

Madness & Sexual Politics in the Feminist Novel: Studies in Bronte, Woolf, Lessing & Atwood. Barbara H. Rigney. LC 78-53291. 1978. 15.00 (ISBN 0-299-07710-1); pap. 5.95 (ISBN 0-299-07714-4). U of Wis Pr.

Madness Beyond Belief. S. Diane Bogus. 300p. (Orig.). Date not set. price not set (ISBN 0-934172-05-6); pap. price not set. WIM Pubns.

Madness in Society: Chapters in the Historical Sociology of Mental Illness. George Rosen. LC 68-13112. 352p. 1980. pap. 7.50 (ISBN 0-226-72642-8, P913). U of Chicago Pr.

Madonna in the Paintings of the Great Masters. Marcel Belvianes. (Illus.). 1980. Repr. 37.50 (ISBN 0-89901-010-5). Found Class Reprints.

Madonna of the Cello. Robert Bagg. LC 61-6972. (Wesleyan Poetry Program: Vol. 9). (Orig.). 1961. 7.50x (ISBN 0-8195-2009-8); pap. 4.00 (ISBN 0-8195-1009-2). Columbia U Pr.

Madonna of the Seven Hills. Jean Plaidy. 288p. 1976. pap. 1.75 o.p. (ISBN 0-449-23026-0, Crest). Fawcett.

Madre y Hogar. J. Espada Marrero. 50p. (Span.). 1980. pap. 1.05 (ISBN 0-311-07302-6). Casa Bautista.

Madrid & Southern Spain. Andre Launay & Maureen Pendered. 19.95 (ISBN 0-7134-3081-8). David & Charles.

Madrigali a Quattr Cinque e Sei Vodi, Libro Primo 1588: Luca Marenzio, the Secular Works, No. 7. Luca Marenzio. Ed. by Steven Ledbetter. xxvi, 167p. 1977. lib. bdg. 25.00 (ISBN 0-8450-7107-6). Broude.

Mad's Bizarre Bazaar. Don Edwing. 192p. (Orig.). 1980. pap. 1.75 (ISBN 0-446-94285-5). Warner Bks.

Mad's Cradle to Grave Primer. Larry Siegel & George Woodbridge. (Mad Ser.). (Illus.). 192p. (Orig.). 1973. pap. 1.75 (ISBN 0-446-94438-6). Warner Bks.

Mad's Dave Berg Looks, Listens & Laughs. Dave Berg. (Mad Ser.). (Illus.). 1979. pap. 1.50 (ISBN 0-446-88667-X). Warner Bks.

Mad's Don Martin Carries on. Don Martin. (Mad Ser.). (Illus.). 1973. pap. 1.75 (ISBN 0-446-94419-X). Warner Bks.

Mad's Don Martin Digs Deeper. Don Martin. (Mad Ser.). (Illus., Orig.). 1979. pap. 1.75 (ISBN 0-446-94420-3). Warner Bks.

Mad's Maddest Artist Don Martin Bounces Back. Don Martin. (Mad Ser.). (Illus.). 1976. pap. 1.75 (ISBN 0-446-94420-3). Warner Bks.

Mad's Snappy Answers to Stupid Questions. Al Jaffee. (Mad Ser.). (Illus.). 1975. pap. 1.75 (ISBN 0-446-94409-2). Warner Bks.

Mad's Talking Stamps. Frank Jacobs. (Mad Ser.). (Illus.). 192p. (Orig.). 1974. pap. 1.50 (ISBN 0-446-88752-8). Warner Bks.

Madstones & Twisters. Ed. by Mody C. Boatwright et al. LC 58-9269. (Texas Folklore Society Publication Ser.: No. 28). 180p. 1980. Repr. of 1958 ed. 5.95 (ISBN 0-87074-017-2). SMU Press.

Maelcho: A Sixteenth-Century Narrative. Emily Lawless. Ed. by Robert L. Wolff. (Ireland Nineteenth Century Fiction - Ser. Two: Vol. 74). 672p. 1979. lib. bdg. 32.00 (ISBN 0-8240-3523-2). Garland Pub.

Maerchen Vom Herrlichen Falken. Bilibin. (Insel Taschenbucher Fur Kinder: It 487). 64p. (Ger.). 1980. pap. text ed. 4.55 (ISBN 3-458-32187-X, Pub. by Insel Verlag Germany). Suhrkamp.

Maestro de Dolores. Robert Lazear. (Illus.). 342p. (Orig., Span.). 1979. pap. 4.50 (ISBN 0-89922-138-6). Edit Caribe.

Maestro Eficiente. Doak S. Campbell. Tr. by Jose M. Rodriguez from Eng. Orig. Title: When Do Teachers Teach. 160p. (Span.). 1980. pap. 1.95 (ISBN 0-311-11029-0). Casa Bautista.

Mafia Death Watch. Bruno Rossi. (Sharpshooter Ser). (Orig.). 1975. pap. 1.25 o.p. (ISBN 0-685-53903-2, LB286ZK, Leisure Bks). Nordon Pubns.

Mafia-Syndicate: Organized Crime - the Government Within the Government. A. Yards. LC 76-23355. 202p. 1977. pap. 4.95 (ISBN 0-686-22703-4). A Yards.

Mafia: Two Hundred Years of Terror. David Hanna. (Orig.). 1980. pap. 2.25 (ISBN 0-532-23131-7). Manor Bks.

Magazine Article Writing. Mary T. Dillon. 1977. 9.95 (ISBN 0-87116-107-9). Writer.

Magazine: Everything You Need to Know to Make It in the Magazine Business. Leonard Mogel. (Illus.). 1979. text ed. 16.95 (ISBN 0-13-543710-5, Spec); pap. 7.95 (ISBN 0-13-543702-4). P-H.

Magazine Industry Market Place 1981. 2nd ed. LC 79-6964. 608p. 1980. pap. 35.00 (ISBN 0-8352-1292-0). Bowker.

Magazine Maze: A Prejudiced Perspective. Herbert R. Mayes. LC 79-8028. 384p. 1980. 14.95 (ISBN 0-385-15322-8). Doubleday.

Magazine Picture Library. Janet McAlpin. (Practical Language Teaching Ser.). (Illus.). 96p. 1980. pap. text ed. 6.95x (ISBN 0-04-371061-1, 2366). Allen Unwin.

Magazine Publishing Management. Ed. by Folio Magazine Editors. 1977. loose leaf ed. 49.95 o.p. (ISBN 0-918110-01-7). Folio.

Magazine Reviews of Keats's Lamia Volume (1820) Tsokan Huang. (Salzburg Studies in English Literature, Romantic Reassessment: No. 26). 123p. 1973. pap. text ed. 25.00x (ISBN 0-391-01424-2). Humanities.

Magda Goebbels: The First Lady of the Third Reich. Hans-Oho Meissner. (Illus.). 288p. 1981. 14.95 (ISBN 0-686-69087-7). Dial.

Magellan. (gr. 1). 1974. pap. text ed. 2.80 (ISBN 0-205-03877-8, 8038775); tchrs'. ed. 12.00 (ISBN 0-205-03866-2, 803866X). Allyn.

Magellanic Clouds. Diane Wakoski. 154p. (Orig.). 1978. 10.00 (ISBN 0-87685-078-6); pap. 5.00 (ISBN 0-87685-077-8). Black Sparrow.

Maggie, a Girl of the Streets: A Story of New York. Stephen Crane. LC 66-20867. 1978. Repr. of 1893 ed. 22.00 (ISBN 0-8201-1268-2). Schol Facsimiles.

Maggie Adams, Dancer. Karen S. Dean. 1980. pap. 1.75 (ISBN 0-380-75366-9, 75366, Camelot). Avon.

Maggie Flying Bird. Maron Lawson. LC 74-6551. (Illus.). 160p. (gr. 7 up). 1974. 6.75 o.p. (ISBN 0-688-21825-3); PLB 6.96 (ISBN 0-688-31825-8). Morrow.

Maggie Lane's Needlepoint Pillows. Maggie Lane. LC 76-24824. (Illus.). 96p. 1976. encore ed. 4.95 o.p. (ISBN 0-684-16199-0, ScribT); pap. 6.95 o.p. (ISBN 0-684-14724-6, SL672, ScribT). Scribner.

Maggie Lane's Oriental Patchwork: Elegant Designs for Easy Living. Maggie Lane. LC 78-7957. (Encore Edition). (Illus.). 1978. 6.95 (ISBN 0-684-16907-X, ScribT). Scribner.

Maggie the Freak. Eve Bunting. (Young Romance Ser.). (Illus.). (gr. 3-9). 1978. PLB 5.95 (ISBN 0-87191-633-9); pap. 2.95 (ISBN 0-685-59452-1). Creative Ed.

Maggie's Way. Martha B. Barrett. (Orig.). 1981. pap. 2.75 (ISBN 0-451-09601-0, E9601, Sig). NAL.

Maggot. Robert Flanagan. 1971. pap. 2.50 (ISBN 0-446-91830-X). Warner Bks.

Maggot. Mary A. Walker. LC 80-12238. 156p. (gr. 5-9). 1980. 8.95 (ISBN 0-689-30789-6). Atheneum.

Maggot Pie: Country Dances. 2nd ed. Marjorie Heffer & William Porter. 55p. (Orig.). (gr. 6 up). 1979. pap. 3.00 (ISBN 0-913714-51-8). Legacy Bks.

Magic. William Goldman. 1976. 7.95 o.s.i. (ISBN 0-440-05159-2). Delacorte.

Magic: A Biography of Earvin Johnson. James Haskins. (Illus.). (gr. 4-12). 1981. PLB 7.95 (ISBN 0-89490-044-7). Enslow Pubs.

Magic: A Pictorial History of Conjuring in the Theater. David Price. LC 78-75326. (Illus.). Date not set. cancelled (ISBN 0-498-02359-1). A S Barnes. Postponed.

Magic: An Introduction. Betty Kobs & Douglas Kobs. LC 75-42496. (Games & Activities Ser.). (Illus.). (gr. k-3). 1976. PLB 9.30 (ISBN 0-8172-0058-4). Raintree Pubs.

Magic: An Occult Primer. David Conway. 1972. 11.95 o.p. (ISBN 0-525-15010-2). Dutton.

Magic & English Romanticism. Anya Taylor. LC 78-5590. 288p. 1979. 16.00x (ISBN 0-8203-0453-0). U of Ga Pr.

Magic & Healing. C. J. Thompson. LC 73-2850. (Illus.). 176p. 1973. Repr. of 1947 ed. 18.00 (ISBN 0-8103-3275-2). Gale.

Magic & Meaning of Voodoo. Barbara Christesen. LC 77-12781. (Myth, Magic & Superstition Ser.). (Illus.). (gr. 4-5). 1977. PLB 9.65 (ISBN 0-8172-1030-X). Raintree Pubs.

Magic & Religion: Their Origins & Consequences. George B. Vetter. LC 73-82103. 1958. 6.00 (ISBN 0-8022-1776-1). Philos Lib.

Magic As a Hobby. Bill Severn. (Illus.). 1979. 14.95 o.p. (ISBN 0-679-51201-2); pap. 9.95 (ISBN 0-679-51202-0). McKay.

Magic Barrel. Bernard Malamud. 214p. 1958. 14.95 (ISBN 0-374-19576-5); pap. 4.95 (ISBN 0-374-50412-1). FS&G.

Magic Barrel. Bernard Malamud. 1980. pap. 2.50 (ISBN 0-380-49973-8, 49973). Avon.

Magic Boat & Other Chinese Folk Stories. M. A. Jagendorf & Virginia Weng. LC 79-67814. (Illus.). (gr. 4-9). 1980. 8.95 (ISBN 0-8149-0823-3). Vanguard.

Magic Bottle. Ed. by Mary Verdick. (Pal Paperbacks - Pal Skills Ser.). (Illus., Orig.). (gr. 7-12). 1978. pap. text ed. 1.25 (ISBN 0-8374-6712-8). Xerox Ed Pubns.

Magic Box. Geraldine Marie. (Illus.). 32p. (ps-3). 1981. 5.95 (ISBN 0-525-66721-0). Elsevier-Nelson.

Magic Bubble. Pat Hurley. 1978. pap. 3.50 (ISBN 0-88207-181-5). Victor Bks.

Magic Bullet; A Novel of Presidential Assassination. J. David Andrews. 185p. (Orig.). 1980. pap. 7.50 (ISBN 0-938330-00-4). Planetary Pr.

Magic Catalogue: A Guide to the World of Magic. William Doerflinger. 1977. 19.95 (ISBN 0-87690-272-7); pap. 9.95 o.p. Dutton.

Magic Cauldron: Witchcraft for Good & Evil. Margaret O'Connell. LC 75-26757. (Illus.). 256p. (gr. 9-12). 1975. 10.95 (ISBN 0-87599-187-4). S G Phillips.

Magic Circle: An Overview of the Human Development Program. Geraldine Ball. 1974. 4.95 (ISBN 0-86584-007-5). Human Dev Train.

Magic Circus. Wayne Anderson & Christopher Logue. (Illus.). 1979. 7.95 o.p. (ISBN 0-670-44809-5, Studio). Viking Pr.

Magic, Divination & Witchcraft Among the Barotse of Northern Rhodesia. Barrie Reynolds. (Illus.). 1963. 17.95x (ISBN 0-520-01063-9). U of Cal Pr.

Magic Door. Howard Fast. (Illus.). (gr. 3-7). 1980. pap. 1.95 (ISBN 0-380-51193-2, 51193, Camelot). Avon.

Magic Dwells: A Poetic & Psychological Study of the Navaho Emergence Myth. Sheila Moon. LC 72-105501. 1970. 12.50x (ISBN 0-8195-4018-8, Pub. by Wesleyan U Pr); pap. 5.95 (ISBN 0-8195-6036-7). Columbia U Pr.

Magic Eye for Ida. Kay Chorao. LC 72-85337. (Illus.). 48p. (gr. 1-3). 1973. 6.95 (ISBN 0-395-28783-9, Clarion). HM.

Magic Fishbone. Charles Dickens. LC 53-10806. (Illus.). (gr. 3 up). 1953. 5.95 (ISBN 0-8149-0296-0). Vanguard.

Magic Flute. Carl L. Gieseke & Emanuel Schikaneder. Tr. by Edward J. Dent. 1937. 1.50 o.p. (ISBN 0-19-313310-5). Oxford U Pr.

Magic Flute: Mozart. John Milnes et al. Tr. by Anthony Beasch & Anthony Besch. 1980. pap. 4.95 (ISBN 0-7145-3768-3). Riverrun NY.

Magic for Every Occasion. Graham Reed. (Illus.). 128p. (gr. 5 up). 1981. 9.95 (ISBN 0-525-66733-4). Elsevier-Nelson.

Magic Forest. Stewart E. White. 1976. lib. bdg. 9.95x (ISBN 0-89968-126-3). Lightyear.

Magic Friend-Maker. Gladys Bond. (Illus.). 24p. (ps-4). 1966. PLB 5.00 (ISBN 0-307-60137-4, Golden Pr). Western Pub.

Magic from Your Pocket. Bill Severn. (Illus.). 1965. 5.50 (ISBN 0-571-06357-8, Pub. by Faber & Faber). Merrimack Bk Serv.

Magic Grandfather. Jay Williams. LC 78-22285. (Illus.). 160p. (gr. 3-7). 1979. 8.95 (ISBN 0-590-07588-8, Four Winds). Schol Bk Serv.

Magic Ground. Joseph Csida. 1981. pap. 3.50 (ISBN 0-671-83135-6). PB.

Magic Growing Powder. Janet Quin-Harkin. LC 80-18019. (Illus.). 48p. (ps-3). 1981. 4.95 (ISBN 0-8193-1037-9); PLB 5.95 (ISBN 0-8193-1038-7). Parents.

Magic Hat. 2nd ed. Kim W. Chapman. LC 76-20842. (Illus.). 47p. (gr. k-4). 1976. pap. 3.00 (ISBN 0-914996-10-X). Lollipop Power.

Magic House of Numbers. Irving Adler. LC 73-19471. (Illus.). 144p. (gr. 5-9). 1974. PLB 8.79 (ISBN 0-381-99986-6, JD-J). John Day.

Magic in Frosting. John McNamara. LC 72-79676. 1972. 10.95 o.p. (ISBN 0-686-60806-2). Exposition.

Magic in Herbs. Leonie De Sounin. 1972. pap. 1.25 (ISBN 0-515-02855-X, N2855). Jove Pubns.

Magic in Names, & in Other Things. Edward Clodd. LC 67-23906. 1968. Repr. of 1920 ed. 15.00 (ISBN 0-8103-3024-5). Gale.

Magic in the Web: Action and Language in Othello. Robert B. Heilman. LC 56-6993. 304p. 1969. pap. 4.50 o.p. (ISBN 0-8131-0122-0). U Pr of Ky.

Magic Is Fragile. Elsie Mack. 256p. (YA) 1973. 5.95 (ISBN 0-685-27366-0, Avalon). Bouregy.

Magic Jim. Diane R. Massie. LC 67-18462. (Illus.). (gr. 1-3). 1967. 5.95 o.s.i. (ISBN 0-8193-0177-9, Four Winds); PLB 5.41 o.s.i. (ISBN 0-8193-0178-7). Schol Bk Serv.

Magic Johnson: Court Magician. Rich Levin. LC 80-25814. (Sports Stars Ser.). (Illus.). 48p. (gr. 2-8). 1981. PLB 7.35 (ISBN 0-516-04313-7). Childrens.

Magic Labyrinth. Philip J. Farmer. 1981. pap. 2.75 (ISBN 0-425-04854-3). Berkley Pub.

Magic Lights & Streets of Shining Jet. Ed. by Dennis Saunders. LC 76-20519. (Illus.). (gr. 3-7). 1978. 8.95 (ISBN 0-688-80065-3); PLB 8.59 (ISBN 0-688-84065-5). Greenwillow.

Magic Little Ones. Beverly Bedell. LC 75-2964. (Beginning-to-Read Bks). (Illus.). 32p. (gr. 1-3). 1975. PLB 3.39 o.s.i. (ISBN 0-695-80588-6); pap. 1.50 o.s.i. (ISBN 0-695-30588-3). Follett.

Magic Machine. Theodore J. Cohen & Jacqueline H. Bray. (Illus.). (ps-3). 1979. 2.00 (ISBN 0-931718-17-1, BYTE Bks). McGraw.

Magic Made Easy. Larry Kettelkamp. (Illus.). (gr. 3-7). 1954. PLB 6.67 (ISBN 0-688-31579-8). Morrow.

Magic Made Easy. rev. ed. Larry Kettelkamp. LC 80-22947. (Illus.). 96p. (gr. 4-6). 1981. pap. 6.95 (ISBN 0-688-00377-X); PLB 6.67 (ISBN 0-688-00458-X). Morrow.

Magic, Magic. Betty Kobs & Douglas Kobs. LC 76-53540. (Games & Activities Ser.). (Illus.). (gr. k-5). 1977. PLB 9.30 (ISBN 0-8172-0070-3). Raintree Pubs.

Magic Merry-Go-Round. V. Gilbert Beers. 32p. (gr. 2-4). 1973. 4.95 (ISBN 0-8024-5138-1). Moody.

Magic Michael. Louis Slobodkin. (gr. k-3). 1944. 7.95 (ISBN 0-02-784680-6). Macmillan.

Magic Mirror of M. C. Escher. Bruno Ernst. (Illus.). 1976. 15.00 o.p. (ISBN 0-394-49217-X). Random.

Magic Mirror of M. C. Escher. Bruno Ernst. (Illus.). 1977. pap. 10.95 (ISBN 0-345-24243-2). Ballantine.

Magic Moment. Pamela D'Arcy. 192p. (Orig.). 1980. pap. 1.75 (ISBN 0-515-05200-0). Jove Pubns.

Magic Moscow. Daniel Pinkwater. LC 80-12785. (Illus.). 64p. (gr. 5 up). 1980. 7.95 (ISBN 0-590-07583-7, Four Winds). Schol Bk Serv.

Magic Moth. Virginia Lee. LC 73-171862. (Illus.). 64p. (gr. 3 up). 1972. 6.95 (ISBN 0-395-28863-0, Clarion). HM.

Magic Moth. Virginia Lee. (Illus.). 64p. (gr. 3-6). 1981. pap. 2.95 (ISBN 0-395-30008-8, Clarion). HM.

Magic Moving Alphabet. Frank Moore. (Illus.). 1978. pap. 2.50 (ISBN 0-486-23593-9). Dover.

Magic Moving Picture Book. Bliss, Sands & Co. Orig. Title: Motograph Moving Picture Book. 32p. (gr. 4 up). 1975. Repr. of 1898 ed. pap. 2.50 (ISBN 0-486-23224-7). Dover.

Magic Mushroom Cultivation. Steven H. Pollock. (Illus.). 1981. pap. 6.00 (ISBN 0-930074-01-7). Herbal Med.

Magic, Mysticism, & Modern Medicine. Irving Oyle. LC 75-28763. 1976. pap. 4.95 o.p. (ISBN 0-89087-121-3). Celestial Arts.

Magic, Myths & Medicine. Richard Hunderfund. (Illus.). 1980. write for info. (ISBN 0-89863-036-3). Star Pub CA.

Magic Names of Fashion. Ernestine Carter. LC 80-82524. 1980. 12.95 (ISBN 0-13-545426-3). P-H.

Magic Nutcracker. Margaret Hillert. (Just-Beginning-to-Read Ser.). 1980. PLB 4.39 (ISBN 0-695-41456-9); pap. 1.50 (ISBN 0-695-31456-4). Follett.

Magic of a Powerful Memory. rev. & abr. ed. Chester V. Young. LC 80-70955. 254p. 1981. Repr. of 1971 ed. 10.95 (ISBN 0-8119-0416-4). Fell.

Magic of ESOT: The Fabulous New Instrument of Corporate Finance. rev. ed. Robert A. Frisch. LC 75-13780. (Illus.). 200p. 1976. 14.95 o.p. (ISBN 0-87863-108-9). Farnswth Pub.

Magic of His Kiss. Jessica Steele. (Harlequin Romances). 192p. 1981. pap. 1.25 (ISBN 0-373-02394-4, Pub. by Harlequin). PB.

Magic of Honey. Dorothy Perlman. 1978. pap. 1.95 (ISBN 0-380-00029-6, 39099). Avon.

Magic of Light. Jean Rosenthal & Lael Wertenbaker. LC 72-6465. (Illus.). 1973. 15.00 (ISBN 0-87830-075-9, Co-Pub by Little). Theatre Arts.

Magic of Origami. Alice Gray & Kunihiko Kasahara. LC 77-74654. (Illus.). 1977. 12.50 (ISBN 0-87040-390-7). Japan Pubns.

Magic of Oz. L. Frank Baum. 256p. 1981. pap. 2.25 (ISBN 0-345-28235-3, Del Rey). Ballantine.

Magic of the Glits. C. S. Adler. LC 78-12149. (Illus.). (gr. 5-8). 1979. 8.95 (ISBN 0-02-700120-2). Macmillan.

Magic of the Mind. Ernest Holmes & Willis Kinnear. 1960. pap. 3.50 (ISBN 0-911336-26-5). Sci of Mind.

Magic of the Minimum Dose. Dorothy Sheperd. 214p. 1964. text ed. 15.50x (ISBN 0-8464-1030-3). Beekman Pubs.

Magic of the Swatchways. Maurice Griffiths. 236p. 1980. 18.95x (ISBN 0-85177-045-2, Xpub. by Cornell England). State Mutual Bk.

Magic of Thinking Big. David J. Schwartz. 1962. pap. 3.95 (ISBN 0-346-12292-9). Cornerstone.

Magic of Thinking Rich. Ralph Charrell. 11.95 (ISBN 0-671-42376-2). S&S.

Magic of Your Radial Arm Saw. R. J. DeCristoforo. 1980. text ed. 12.95 (ISBN 0-8359-4183-3). Reston.

Magic Pencil Counting Book. Hazel S. Gamec. (Illus.). 12p. 1980. write for info. (ISBN 0-938042-00-9). Printek.

Magic Picture Book. A. DuGuay Pine. 125p. 1980. 6.95 (ISBN 0-8059-2738-7). Dorrance.

Magic Porridge Pot. Paul Galdone. LC 76-3531. (Illus.). (ps-3). 1976. 7.95 (ISBN 0-395-28805-3, Clarion). HM.

Magic Porridge Pot. (Illus.). Arabic 2.50x (ISBN 0-685-82843-3). Intl Bk Ctr.

Magic Power of Positive Ideas. Uriah J. Fields. 100p. 1981. pap. 4.50 (ISBN 0-938844-00-8). Am Mutuality.

Magic Realism in Cervantes: Don Quixote As Seen Through Tom Sawyer and The Idiot. Arturo Serrano-Plaja. Tr. by Robert S. Rudder. LC 71-94991. 1970. 15.75x (ISBN 0-520-01591-6). U of Cal Pr.

Magic, Reason & Experience: Studies in the Origin & Development of Greek Science. G. R. Lloyd. LC 78-25710. (Illus.). 1979. 59.50 (ISBN 0-521-22373-3); pap. 19.95 (ISBN 0-521-29641-2). Cambridge U Pr.

Magic, Science, & Civilization. Jacob Bronowski. (Bampton Lectures in America: No. 20). 1978. 10.00 (ISBN 0-231-04484-4). Columbia U Pr.

Magic, Science & Civilization. Jacob Bronowski. (Bamptom Lectures in America Ser.: No. 20). 104p. 1981. pap. 4.95 (ISBN 0-231-04485-2). Columbia U Pr.

Magic, Science & Religion & Other Essays. Bronislaw Malinowski. LC 54-4389. 1954. pap. 2.95 o.p. (ISBN 0-385-09246-6, A23, Anch). Doubleday.

Magic: Science of the Future. Joseph Goodavage. (Orig.). 1976. pap. 1.50 o.p. (ISBN 0-451-07081-X, W7081, Sig). NAL.

Magic Show in a Book. Shari Lewis. LC 79-23941. (Kids-Only Club Bks.). (Illus.). 96p. (Orig.). (gr. 3-6). 1980. pap. 3.95 (ISBN 0-03-049746-9). HR&W.

Magic Squares. Paul Calter. LC 77-1213. (Illus.). (gr. 7 up). 1977. 7.95 o.p. (ISBN 0-525-66433-5). Elsevier-Nelson.

Magic: Stage Illusions, Special Effects & Trick Photography. Albert A. Hopkins. (Illus.). 576p. 1976. pap. 6.95 (ISBN 0-486-23344-8). Dover.

Magic Stone. Leonie Kooiker. Tr. by Richard Winston & Clara Winston. (Illus.). (gr. 3-7). 1978. 7.95 (ISBN 0-688-22143-2); PLB 7.63 (ISBN 0-688-32143-7). Morrow.

Magic Story: Message of a Master. J. McDonald. pap. 1.50 (ISBN 0-910140-23-5). R Collier.

Magic Tales & Magic Tricks. William Wiesner. LC 73-19269. (Encore Ser.). (Illus.). 64p. (gr. 2-6). 1974. 4.95 (ISBN 0-684-16587-2, ScribJ). Scribner.

Magic Through Science. Robert Gardner. LC 77-76239. (gr. 3-5). 1978. 6.95 (ISBN 0-385-12437-6); PLB (ISBN 0-385-12438-4). Doubleday.

Magic Time. Kit Reed. 240p. 1981. pap. 2.25 (ISBN 0-425-04745-8). Berkley Pub.

Magic Tools for Stock Market Success. Gordon W. Overland. (Illus.). 149p. 1980. deluxe ed. 67.85 (ISBN 0-918968-77-1). Inst Econ Pol.

Magic Tricks. Paul Glickman. (gr. 1-3). 1980. PLB 7.90 (ISBN 0-531-04141-7). Watts.

Magic Tricks. Walt Disney Productions. (Winnie-the-Pooh Hunny Pot Bk.). 24p. (ps-3). 1980. PLB 5.38 (ISBN 0-307-68870-4, Golden Pr). Western Pub.

Magic Tricks You Can Do! Robyn Supraner. LC 80-19780. (Illus.). 48p. (gr. 2-5). 1980. PLB 6.92 (ISBN 0-89375-418-8); pap. 1.75 (ISBN 0-89375-419-6). Troll Assocs.

Magic Variety Show: Novelty Acts for the Amateur Entertainer. Eric Hawkesworth. 96p. 1973. 7.95 (ISBN 0-571-10186-0). Transatlantic.

Magic Walking Stick. John Buchan. LC 75-32205. (Classics of Children's Literature, 1621-1932: Vol. 66). (Illus.). 1976. Repr. of 1932 ed. PLB 38.00 (ISBN 0-8240-2315-3). Garland Pub.

Magic White & Black; or, the Science of Finite & Infinite Life. Franz Hartmann. LC 80-19323. 298p. 1980. Repr. of 1971 ed. lib. bdg. 11.95x (ISBN 0-89370-603-5). Borgo Pr.

Magic Windows. new ed. William D. Sheldon et al. (gr. 3). 1973. text ed. 9.20 (ISBN 0-205-03542-6, 5235421); tchrs'. guide 9.20 (ISBN 0-205-03543-4, 523543X); tchrs'. activity bk. 3.92 (ISBN 0-205-03544-2, 5235448); tchr's activity bk. 3.92 (ISBN 0-205-03545-0, 5235456); activities masters 28.00 (ISBN 0-205-03546-9, 5235464). Allyn.

Magic Windows: An Antique Revolving Picture Book. Ernest Nister. (Illus.). 14p. (ps up). 1981. 6.95 (ISBN 0-399-20773-2). Philomel.

Magic with Everyday Objects. George Schindler. (Illus.). 1980. pap. 4.95 (ISBN 0-8128-6030-6). Stein & Day.

Magic with Rope, Ribbon & String. 1980. 8.95 (ISBN 0-679-20813-5). McKay.

Magic Without Magic: John Archibald Wheeler, a Collection of Essays in Honor of His 60th Birthday. Ed. by John R. Klauder. LC 75-183745. (Illus.). 1972. text ed. 28.95x (ISBN 0-7167-0337-8). W H Freeman.

Magic World of Xhosa. Aubrey Elliot. (Encore Edition). 1970. 2.95 o.p. (ISBN 0-684-15241-X, ScribT). Scribner.

Magic Years. Selma Fraiberg. LC 59-6073. 1968. 12.95 (ISBN 0-684-10166-1, ScribT); pap. 4.95 (ISBN 0-684-71768-9, SL161, ScribT). Scribner.

Magical & Mystical Sites: Europe & the British Isles. Elizabeth Pepper & John Wilcock. LC 76-5533. (Illus.). (YA) 1977. 10.95 o.s.i. (ISBN 0-06-014614-1, HarpT). Har-Row.

Magical Friday. Ted Simmons. LC 74-24635. (Illus.). 76p. 1975. text ed. 7.00 o.p. (ISBN 0-685-51344-0); pap. 1.95 o.p. (ISBN 0-912662-07-7). Fur Line Pr.

Magical Jewels of the Middle Ages & the Renaissance. Joan Evans. 7.50 (ISBN 0-8446-5572-4). Peter Smith.

Magical Language. Paul F. Case. 320p. pap. 9.95 (ISBN 0-87728-526-8). Weiser.

Magical Maze. Violet F. Collins. 100p. (Orig.). (gr. 1-8). 1981. write for info. (ISBN 0-9604578-0-1); write for info. tchr's ed. (ISBN 0-9604578-1-X). Baraka Bk.

Magical Medicine: A Nigerian Case Study. Una Maclean. 1974. pap. 1.95 o.p. (ISBN 0-14-021220-5, Pelican). Penguin.

Magical Medicine: The Folkloric Component of Folk Medicine in the Folk Belief, Custom, & Ritual of Non-Primitive Peoples. Wayland D. Hand. 296p. 1981. 22.50 (ISBN 0-520-04129-1). U of Cal Pr.

Magical Melons. Carol R. Brink. (Illus.). (gr. 5-7). 1963. 8.95 (ISBN 0-02-714210-8). Macmillan.

Magical Realm of Sallie Middleton. Sallie Middleton & Celestine Sibley. LC 80-80974. 112p. 1980. 19.95 (ISBN 0-8487-0503-3). Oxmoor Hse.

Magical Record of the Beast 666 by Symonds & Grant. Aleister Crowley. 16.00 o.p. (ISBN 0-685-47276-0). Weiser.

Magical Ritual Methods. William G. Gray. pap. 6.95 (ISBN 0-87728-498-9). Weiser.

Magician. Uri Shulevitz. LC 72-85186. (Illus.). 32p. (gr. k-3). 1973. 8.95 (ISBN 0-02-782510-8). Macmillan.

Magician & the Cinema. Erik Barnouw. (Illus.). 112p. 1981. 12.95 (ISBN 0-19-502918-6). Oxford U Pr.

Magician & the Sorcerer. David McKee. LC 73-22280. (Illus.). 32p. (ps-3). 1974. 5.95 o.s.i. (ISBN 0-8193-0772-6, Four Winds); PLB 5.41 o.s.i. (ISBN 0-8193-0773-4). Schol Bk Serv.

Magician of Cracow. Krystyna Turska. LC 75-8846. (Illus.). 32p. (gr. k-4). 1975. 9.25 (ISBN 0-688-80010-6). Greenwillow.

Magician of Sunset Boulevard. Frederick Kohner. Ed. by C. N. Anderson. LC 78-175270. 10.00 (ISBN 0-89430-004-0). Morgan-Pacific.

Magician, the Witch & the Law. Edward Peters. LC 78-51341. (Middle Ages Ser.). 1978. 16.95x (ISBN 0-8122-7746-5). U of Pa Pr.

Magicians. Geoffrey F. Lamb. LC 79-366524. (Pegasus Books: No. 15). (Illus.). 1968. 7.50x (ISBN 0-234-77022-8). Intl Pubns Serv.

Magician's Sleeve. J. C. Conaway. 1979. pap. 1.75 o.p. (ISBN 0-449-14120-9, GM). Fawcett.

Magick, in Theory & Practice. Aleister Crowley. 10.00 (ISBN 0-8446-5476-0). Peter Smith.

Magick of Camelot. Arthur H. Landis. 1981. pap. 2.25 (ISBN 0-87997-623-3, UE1623, Daw Bks). NAL.

Magie dans L'Inde Antique: Paris, 1904. Victor Henry. LC 78-74261. (Oriental Religions Ser.: Vol. 5). 325p. 1980. lib. bdg. 33.00 (ISBN 0-8240-3903-3). Garland Pub.

Magill Books Index. Ed. by Frank N. Magill. LC 80-53597. 800p. 1980. 35.00 (ISBN 0-89356-200-9). Salem Pr.

Magills Quotations in Context, First Series. Ed. by Frank N. Magill. 1966. 20.00 o.s.i. (ISBN 0-06-003657-5, HarpT); lib. bdg. 16.29 o.s.i. (ISBN 0-06-003658-3). Har-Row.

Magill's World Philosophy, 2 vols. 40.00 set o.p. (ISBN 0-89356-144-4). Salem Pr.

Maginot Line: Myth & Reality. Anthony Kemp. LC 80-6260. 128p. 1981. 11.95 (ISBN 0-8128-2811-9). Stein & Day.

Magistrate's Justice. Pat Carlen. 134p. 1976. 30.50x (ISBN 0-85520-121-5, Pub. by Martin Robertson England). Biblio Dist.

Magna Carta in the Seventeenth Century. Maurice Ashley. LC 65-23456. (Illus., Orig.). 1965. pap. 1.95x (ISBN 0-8139-0014-X). U Pr of Va.

Magna Carta Latina: The Privilege of Singing, Articulating & Reading a Language & Keeping It Alive. 2nd ed. Eugen Rosenstock-Huessy & Ford L. Battles. LC 75-23378. (Pittsburgh Reprint Ser.: No. 1). 1975. pap. text ed. 5.25 (ISBN 0-915138-07-7). Pickwick.

Magna Carta: The Heritage of Liberty. Anne Pallister. 144p. 1971. 22.50x (ISBN 0-19-827181-6). Oxford U Pr.

Magna Charta of Woman. Jessie Penn-Lewis. LC 75-28655. 1975. pap. 2.50 (ISBN 0-87123-377-0, 200377). Bethany Fell.

Magnavox Color TV Service Manual, Vol. 2. Stan Prentiss. LC 70-117189. (Schematic Servicing Manual Ser). (Illus.). 1972. pap. 7.95 (ISBN 0-8306-1589-X, 589). TAB Bks.

Magnesium Deficiency in the Pathogenesis of Disease. Ed. by Mildred S. Seelig. (Topics in Bone & Mineral Disorders Ser.). 500p. 1980. 39.50 (ISBN 0-306-40202-5, Plenum Pr). Plenum Pub.

Magnesium: Series in Cations of Biologic Significance. Jerry K. Aikawa. 144p. 1981. 49.95 (ISBN 0-8493-5871-X). CRC Pr.

Magnet Schools: An Approach to Voluntary Desegregation. Charles B. McMillan. LC 79-93118. (Fastback Ser.: No. 141). 50p. (Orig.). 1980. pap. 0.75 (ISBN 0-87367-141-4). Phi Delta Kappa.

Magnetic & Other Properties of Oxides & Related Compounds: Part B: Spinels, Fe Oxides & Fe- Me- O-Compounds. (Landolt-Boernstein Ser. Group III: Vol. 12). (Illus.). 770p. (Suppl & extension to vol. 4). 1980. 439.00 (ISBN 0-387-09421-0). Springer-Verlag.

Magnetic Bubbles. T. H. O'Dell. LC 74-12048. 159p. 1974. 34.95 (ISBN 0-470-65259-4). Halsted Pr.

Magnetic Garnets. Winkler. 1980. write for info. (ISBN 0-9940013-3-9, Pub. by Vieweg & Sohn Germany). Heyden.

Magnetic Ions in Metals: A Review of Thier Study by Electron Spin Resonance. R. H. Taylor. LC 76-53798. 1977. 19.95 (ISBN 0-470-99024-4). Halsted Pr.

Magnetic Light. LC 79-54136. 1980. 5.00 (ISBN 0-935490-01-9). Euclid Pub.

Magnetic Materials & Their Applications. Carl Heck. LC 73-77001. 1974. 65.00x o.p. (ISBN 0-8448-0206-9). Crane-Russak Co.

Magnetic Properties of Coordination & Organometallic Transition Metal Compounds: Supplement Three, (1971, 1972) E. G. Koenig. (Landolt-Boernstein-Numerical Data & Functional Relationships in Science & Technology: Group II, Vol. 11 (Supplement to Vol. 2)). (Illus.). 800p. 1980. 702.10 (ISBN 0-387-09908-5). Springer-Verlag.

Magnetic Properties of Free Radicals: Organic Cation Radicals & Polyradicals. Ed. by H. Fischer & K. H. Hellwege. (Landolt-Bernstein Ser. Group II: Vol. 9, Pt. 2). 380p. 1980. 270.30 (ISBN 0-387-09666-3). Springer-Verlag.

Magnetic Resonance. K. A. McLauchlan. (Oxford Chemical Ser). 108p. 1972. pap. text ed. 7.95x (ISBN 0-19-855403-6). Oxford U Pr.

Magnetic Resonance in Colloid & Interface Science. Ed. by Jacques P. Fraissard & Henry A. Resing. (NATO Advanced Study Institutes C. Mathematical & Physical Sciences Ser.: No. 61). 710p. 1980. lib. bdg. 76.00 (ISBN 90-277-1153-4, Pub. by D. Reidel). Kluwer Boston.

Magnetic Therapy: Healing in Your Hands. Abbot G. Burke. LC 80-22941. (Illus.). 86p. (Orig.). 1980. pap. text ed. 4.95 (ISBN 0-932104-04-5). St George Pr.

Magneticall Advertisements. William Barlow. LC 68-54616. (English Experience Ser.: No. 47). Repr. of 1616 ed. 14.00 (ISBN 90-221-0047-2). Walter J Johnson.

Magnetism, 2 vols. S. V. Vonsovskii. Tr. by R. Hardin from Rus. LC 73-16426. 1974. Set. 134.95 (ISBN 0-470-91193-X). Halsted Pr.

Magnetism: A Treatise on Modern Theory & Materials, 5 vols. Ed. by George T. Rado & H. Suhl. 1963-1973. Vol. 1. 55.25 (ISBN 0-12-575301-2); Vol. 2A. 48.50 (ISBN 0-12-575302-0); Vol. 2B. 48.50 (ISBN 0-12-575342-X); Vol. 3. 48.75 (ISBN 0-12-575303-9); Vol. 4. 45.50 (ISBN 0-12-575304-7); Vol. 5. 52.50 (ISBN 0-12-575305-5). Acad Pr.

Magnetism & Magnetic Materials Digest. Incl. 1965. Ed. by R. L. White & K. A. Wickersheim. 1965. 29.50 (ISBN 0-12-747150-2); 1966. Ed. by Warren C. Haas & H. S. Jarrett. 1968. 43.50 (ISBN 0-12-312750-5); 1967. Ed. by W. D. Doyle & A. B. Harris. 1967. 41.00 (ISBN 0-12-221550-8); 1968. Ed. by H. Chang & T. R. McGuire. 1968. 43.50 (ISBN 0-12-170450-5). Acad Pr.

Magnetism & Metallurgy, 2 Vols. Ed. by A. E. Berkowitz & E. Kneller. Vol. 1 1970. 61.00 (ISBN 0-12-091701-7); Vol. 2 1969. 52.50 (ISBN 0-12-091702-5); 92.50 set (ISBN 0-685-05134-X). Acad Pr.

Magnetism in Crystalline Materials (Applications of the Groups of Cambiant Symmetry) A. P. Cracknell. 1975. text ed. 37.00 (ISBN 0-08-017935-5). Pergamon.

Magnetohydrodynamic & Magnetohydrostatic Methods of Mineral Separation. U. Andres. 1976. 39.95 (ISBN 0-470-15014-9). Halsted Pr.

Magnetohydrodynamic Energy for Electric Power Generation. R. F. Grundy. LC 77-15220. (Energy Technology Review Ser.: No. 20). (Illus.). 1978. 36.00 (ISBN 0-8155-0689-9). Noyes.

Magnetohydrodynamic Flow in Ducts. Herman Branover. LC 78-67721. 1979. 54.95x (ISBN 0-470-26539-6). Halsted Pr.

Magnetohydrodynamics. T. G. Cowling. LC 76-38002. (Monographs on Astronomical Subjects). 1977. 39.50x (ISBN 0-8448-1060-6). Crane-Russak Co.

Magnets, Bulbs, Batteries. (Illus.). Arabic 2.50x (ISBN 0-685-82844-1). Intl Bk Ctr.

Magnificat. Bruce Angrave. 1978. pap. 2.25 o.p. (ISBN 0-425-03823-8, Medallion). Berkley Pub.

Magnificat: The Prayer of Mary. S. Callahan. (Orig.). 1976. pap. 4.95 (ISBN 0-8164-2594-9). Crossroad NY.

Magnificent Builders & Their Dream Houses. Joseph J. Thorndike, Jr. LC 78-18371. (Illus.). 352p. 1978. 12.95 (ISBN 0-8281-3064-7, Dist. by Scribner); deluxe ed. 39.95 slipcased (ISBN 0-8281-3072-8). Am Heritage.

Magnificent Challenge. Sue Alden. (YA) 1976. 4.95 o.p. (ISBN 0-685-69053-9, Avalon). Bouregy.

Magnificent Defeat. Frederick Buechner. (YA) (gr. 9-12). 1968. pap. 1.65 (ISBN 0-8164-2045-9, SP44). Crossroad NY.

Magnificent Duchess. Sarah Stamford. 1975. 6.95 o.p. (ISBN 0-440-05252-1). Delacorte.

Magnificent Foragers: Smithsonian Explorations in the Natural Sciences. Smithsonian Institution. 1978. 16.95 (ISBN 0-89599-001-6). Smithsonian Expo Bks.

Magnificent Macrame: 50 Projects You Can Create. Marie-Janine Solvit. LC 78-66295. (Illus.). 1979. 19.95 (ISBN 0-8069-5390-X); lib. bdg. 16.79 (ISBN 0-8069-5391-8). Sterling.

Magnificent Matriarch: Kaahumanu, Queen of Hawaii, 1772-1838. new ed. Kathleen D. Mellen. (Illus.). 302p. 1980. pap. 7.95 o.p. (ISBN 0-8038-4732-7). Hastings.

Magnificent Muslims. Marguerite Brown. 1981. write for info. (ISBN 0-911026-10-X). New World Press NY.

Magnificos Tres. Tr. by Dean Merrill. (Spanish Bks.). (Span.). 1979. 1.50 (ISBN 0-8297-0733-6). Life Pubs Intl.

Magnolias. Julie Ellis. 272p. 1977. pap. 1.75 o.p. (ISBN 0-449-23131-3, Crest). Fawcett.

Magnum Bonum; or, Mother Carey's Brood, 1879. Charlotte M. Yonge. Ed. by Robert L. Wolff. (Victorian Fiction Ser). 1975. lib. bdg. 66.00 (ISBN 0-8240-1598-3). Garland Pub.

Magnus Machina: The Great Machine. Jan Cox. 1970. 7.95 (ISBN 0-87707-092-X); pap. 5.95 (ISBN 0-686-65960-0). Chan Shal Imi.

Magnus Machina: The Great Machine, (Work Maps of the Inner Terrain of Modern Man) rev., enl. ed. Jan. 216p. 1980. 6.00 (ISBN 0-936380-05-5). Chan Shal Imi.

Magoumaz: Pays Mafa (Nord Cameroun) (Etude D'un Terroir De Montagne) Jean Boulet. (Atlas des Structures Agraires au Sud de Shara: No. 11). (Illus.). 92p. (Fr.). 1975. pap. text ed. 34.10x (ISBN 90-279-7575-2). Mouton.

Magritte. Andre Breton. (Illus.). 1964. pap. 3.50 o.p. (ISBN 0-913456-87-X). Interbk Inc.

Magritte. Andre Breton. (Illus.). 1964. pap. 3.50 (ISBN 0-914412-24-8). Inst for the Arts.

Magritte. Jacques Dopagne. (Masters of Art Ser.). (Illus.). 1979. pap. 3.95 (ISBN 0-8120-2154-1). Barron.

Magritte. Ed. by David Larkin. 1976. pap. 6.95 (ISBN 0-345-25593-3). Ballantine.

Magritte: Ideas & Images. Harry Torczyner. LC 77-79323. (Contemporary Artists Ser.). (Illus.). 1977. 55.00 o.p. (ISBN 0-8109-1300-3). Abrams.

Magruder's American Government Nineteen Eighty. William A. McClenaghan. (gr. 9-12). 1980. text ed. 17.60 (ISBN 0-205-06891-X, 7668910); tchrs'. guide 6.12 (ISBN 0-205-06892-8, 7668929). Allyn.

Magruder's American Government: 1976. rev. ed. William A. McClenaghan. (gr. 9-12). 1976. text ed. 17.60 (ISBN 0-205-05651-2, 7656513); tchrs'. guide 6.12 (ISBN 0-205-05652-0, 7656521); dup. mast 42.00 (ISBN 0-205-05653-9, 765653X); tests 42.00 (ISBN 0-205-05654-7, 7656548). Allyn.

Magruder's American Government, 1978. rev. ed. William A. McClenaghan. (gr. 9-12). 1978. text ed. 17.60 (ISBN 0-205-05862-0, 7658621); tchr's guide 6.12 (ISBN 0-205-05863-9, 765863X). Allyn.

Magruder's American Government, 1979. annual rev. ed. William A. McClenaghan. (gr. 7-12). 1979. text ed. 17.60 (ISBN 0-205-06430-2, 7664303). Allyn.

Magus. rev. ed. John Fowles. 1979. pap. 3.50 (ISBN 0-440-15162-7). Dell.

Mah Jong: The Rules to Play the Chinese Game. Tze-Chung Li. 1981. write for info. (ISBN 0-937256-02-1). Chinese Culture.

Mahabharata, 114 vols. Tr. by P. Lal. 1973. 6.00 ea. Ind-US Inc.

Mahabharata. Tr. by Chakravarthi V. Narasimhan. LC 64-10347. 254p. (English version based on selected verses). 1973. pap. 6.00 (ISBN 0-231-08321-1). Columbia U Pr.

Mahabharata. C. Rajagopalachari. 1979. pap. 3.50 (ISBN 0-89744-929-0). Auromere.

Mahabharata. 2nd ed. Tr. by S. Rameshwar Rao. Orig. Title: Children's Mahabharata. 219p. 1976. pap. text ed. 2.85 (ISBN 0-89253-041-3). Ind-US Inc.

Mahabharata. Barend A. Van Nooten. (World Authors Ser.: India: No. 131). lib. bdg. 10.95 (ISBN 0-8057-2564-4). Twayne.

Mahabharata: Bhagvat-Geeta. LC 59-6527. 174p. (English.). 1972. Repr. of 1785 ed. 20.00x (ISBN 0-8201-1109-0). Schol Facsimiles.

Mahadev Govind Ranade. T. V. Parvate. 1964. 10.75x o.p. (ISBN 0-210-26898-0). Asia.

Mahalia Jackson Cooks Soul. Mahalia Jackson. LC 74-114780. cancelled o.s.i. (ISBN 0-87695-014-4). Aurora Pubs.

Mahalo Nui Translations. Carol Roes. 1980. pap. 3.00 (ISBN 0-930932-20-X). M. Loke.

Mahan on Sea Power. rev. ed. William E. Livezey. LC 79-6720. (Illus.). 389p. 1981. 15.95 (ISBN 0-8061-1569-6). U of Okla Pr.

Mahanarayana Upanisasd. Upanisads. Tr. by P. Lal. 1973. 11.00 (ISBN 0-88253-302-9); flexible cloth 6.75 (ISBN 0-89253-522-9). Ind-US Inc.

Maharajas & Men. Debesh Das. 1981. 11.00x o.p. (ISBN 0-685-59379-7). South Asia Bks.

Mahatma Gandhi. Haridas Chaudhuri & Leonard R. Frank. (Orig.). 1969. pap. 1.00 (ISBN 0-89744-993-2, Pub. by Cultural Integration). Auromere.

Mahatma Gandhi. H. S. Polak et al. 1966. pap. 3.00 (ISBN 0-88253-170-0). Ind-US Inc.

Mahatma Gandhi & Comparative Religion. K. L. Rao. 1979. 15.00x (ISBN 0-89684-034-4). South Asia Bks.

Mahatma Gandhi, Bibliography. 2nd ed. Jagdish Sharma. (National Bibliographies Ser No. 1). 1968. 12.50x o.p. (ISBN 0-8426-1521-0). Verry.

Mahatma Letters to A. P. Sinnett. 2nd, facsimile of 1926 ed. Compiled by A. Trevor Barker. LC 75-10574. 1975. 10.00 (ISBN 0-911500-20-0); pap. 5.95 softcover (ISBN 0-911500-21-9). Theos U Pr.

Mahayana Buddhist Sculpture of Ceylon. Diran D. Dohanian. LC 76-23613. (Outstanding Dissertations in the Fine Arts). (Illus.). 1977. Repr. of 1964 ed. lib. bdg. 48.00 (ISBN 0-8240-2685-3). Garland Pub.

Mahayana Way to Buddhahood. Susumu Yamaguchi. Tr. by Buddhist Books International. 1981. 9.95 (ISBN 0-914910-11-6); pap. 6.95 (ISBN 0-914910-12-4). Buddhist Bks.

Mahdi of Alah: The Story of the Dervish, Mohammed Ahmed. Richard A. Bermann. Tr. by Robin John. LC 80-1935. 1981. Repr. of 1932 ed. 36.00 (ISBN 0-404-18955-5). AMS Pr.

Mahican-Language Hymns, Biblical Prose, & Vocabularies from Moravian Sources: With 11 Mohawk Hymns (Transcription & Translation) Carl Masthay. LC 80-82410. 1980. write for info. Cresset Pubs.

Mahogany Tree: A Very Informal History of "Punch". Arthur Prager. LC 77-81360. 1979. 15.00 (ISBN 0-8015-4780-6, Hawthorn). Dutton.

Mahogany Trinrose. Jacqueline Lichtenberg. LC 79-8563. (Double D Science Fiction Ser.). 256p. 1981. 10.95 (ISBN 0-385-15476-3). Doubleday.

Maico Service-Repair Handbook: 250-501cc Singles, 1968-1975. Mike Bishop. Ed. by Jeff Robinson. (Illus.). 120p. 1975. pap. text ed. 9.95 (ISBN 0-89287-019-2, M357). Clymer Pubns.

Maid & the Mouse & the Odd-Shaped House. Paul O. Zelinsky. LC 80-2774. (Illus.). 32p. (ps-2). 1981. PLB 9.95 (ISBN 0-396-07938-5). Dodd.

Maid of the North & Other Folk Tales Heroines. Ethel J. Phelps. LC 80-21500. (Illus.). 192p. (gr. 2-6). 1981. 10.95 (ISBN 0-03-056893-5). HR&W.

Maiden Voyage. Denton Welch. 1981. Repr. of 1943 ed. 12.95 (ISBN 0-8290-0358-4). Irvington.

Maidens, Meal & Money. Ed. by C. Meillassoux. Tr. by Felicity Edholm from French. LC 79-52834. (Themes in the Social Sciences Ser.). 200p. write for info. (ISBN 0-521-22902-2); pap. write for info. (ISBN 0-521-29708-7). Cambridge U Pr.

Maides Tragedy. Francis Beaumont & John Fletcher. LC 70-38151. (English Experience Ser.: No. 431). 82p. 1972. Repr. of 1619 ed. 13.00 (ISBN 90-221-0431-1). Walter J Johnson.

Maid's Revenge: Edited from the Quarto of 1639 with Introduction and Notes. James Shirley. Ed. by Stephen Orgel. LC 79-3100. (Renaissance Drama Second Ser.). 185p. 1980. lib. bdg. 22.00 (ISBN 0-8240-4485-1). Garland Pub.

Maid's Tragedy. Francis Beaumont & John Fletcher. Ed. by Howard B. Norland. LC 67-21895. (Regents Renaissance Drama Ser). 1968. pap. 1.85x (ISBN 0-8032-5253-6, BB 224, Bison). U of Nebr Pr.

Maigret & the Apparition. Georges Simenon. LC 80-14212. 1980. pap. 2.95 (ISBN 0-15-655127-6, Harv). HarBraceJ.

Maigret et le Clochard. Simenon. (Easy Reader, B). pap. 3.75 (ISBN 0-88436-047-4, FRA201052). EMC.

Maigret et le Fantome. Georges Simenon. (Easy Readers, B). (Illus.). 1977. pap. text ed. 3.75 (ISBN 0-88436-287-6). EMC.

Maigret Loses His Temper. Georges Simenon. Tr. by Rbt Eglesfield. LC 80-14212. (Helen & Kurt Wolff Bk.). 1980. pap. 2.95. HarBraceJ.

Mail & Telephone Surveys: The Total Design Method. Don. A. Dillman. LC 78-581. 1978. 29.50 (ISBN 0-471-21555-4, Pub. by Wiley-Interscience). Wiley.

Mail Order Moonlighting. Cecil C. Hoge, Sr. LC 78-61866. 1978. 10.95 (ISBN 0-913668-95-8); pap. 7.95 (ISBN 0-913668-94-X). Ten Speed Pr.

Mail Order Riches Success Kit. 2nd ed. Tyler G. Hicks. 927p. 1981. pap. 99.50 (ISBN 0-914306-41-3). Intl Wealth.

Mail Order U. S. A. A Consumer's Guide to Over 2,000 Top Mail Order Catalogs in the United States & Canada. 3rd ed. Dorothy O'Callaghan. LC 78-51830. 1981. pap. 7.00 (ISBN 0-914694-03-0). Mail Order.

Mail Order....Starting up, Making It Pay. J. Frank Brumbaugh. LC 78-14623. 1979. 13.95 o.p. (ISBN 0-8019-6804-6); pap. 7.95 (ISBN 0-8019-6805-4). Chilton.

Maillard Reactions in Food: Proceedings of the International Symposium, Uddevalla, Sweden, September 1979. C. Ericksson. (Progress in Food & Nutrition Science Ser.: Vol. 5). (Illus.). 500p. 1981. 156.00 (ISBN 0-08-025496-9). Pergamon.

Maillol Nudes: Thirty-Five Lithographs by Aristide Maillol. Illus. by Aristide Maillol. (Dover Art Library). Orig. Title: Dialogues of the Courtesans. (Illus.). 1980. pap. 2.00 (ISBN 0-486-24000-2). Dover.

Main Currents in Early Christian Thought. Robert R. Barr. (Guide to the Fathers of the Church Ser). (Orig.). 1966. pap. 3.95 (ISBN 0-8091-1625-1). Paulist Pr.

Main Currents in Modern American History. Gabriel Kolko. LC 76-5138. 416p. 1976. 17.50 o.s.i. (ISBN 0-06-012451-2, HarpT). Har-Row.

Main Currents in Sociological Thought: Durkhelm, Pareto & Weber, Vol. 2. Raymond Aron. LC 68-14142. 1970. pap. 3.95 (ISBN 0-385-01976-9, A600B, Anch). Doubleday.

Main Currents in Sociological Thought: Montesquieu, Comte, Marx, Tocqueville, the Sociologists, & the Revolution of 1848, Vol. 1. Raymond Aron. LC 68-14142. 1968. pap. 3.95 (ISBN 0-385-08804-3, A600A, Anch). Doubleday.

Main Currents in the History of American Journalism. Willard G. Bleyer. LC 70-77720. (American Scene Ser). (Illus.). v, 464p. 1973. Repr. of 1927 ed. lib. bdg. 45.00 (ISBN 0-306-71358-6). Da Capo.

Main Currents of Marxism, 3 vols. Leszek Kolakowski. 1980. Vol. 1. 26.50x (ISBN 0-19-824547-5); Vol. 2. 26.50x (ISBN 0-19-824569-6); Vol. 3. 26.50x (ISBN 0-19-824570-X). Oxford U Pr.

Main Currents of Spanish Literature. Jeremiah D. Ford. LC 68-13689. 1968. Repr. of 1919 ed. 12.00x (ISBN 0-8196-0213-2). Biblo.

Main Economic Indicators, Historical Statistics 1960 to 1979. (Illus.). 637p. (Orig., Fr. & Eng.). 1980. pap. text ed. 27.50x (ISBN 92-64-02110-8). OECD.

Main Hurdman & Cranston Guide to Preparing Financial Reports, 1981. Morton B. Solomon et al. 272p. 1981. 75.00 (ISBN 0-471-09104-9, Pub. by Wiley-Interscience). Wiley.

Main Ingredients: Positive Thinking, Exercise & Diet. Susan S. Jones. 1978. 12.50 o.s.i. (ISBN 0-89557-029-7). Bi World Indus.

Main Issues in Bioethics: The Main Issues. Andrew C. Varga. 208p. (Orig.). 1980. pap. 8.95 (ISBN 0-8091-2327-4). Paulist Pr.

Main Line to Oblivion: The Disintegration of the New York Railroads in the Twentieth Century. Robert B. Carson. LC 75-139352. (American Studies Ser). 1971. 15.00 (ISBN 0-8046-9003-0). Kennikat.

Main Problems in American History, 2 Vols. 4th ed. Ed. by Howard H. Quint et al. 1978. text ed. 11.25x ea. (ISBN 0-686-66399-3); Vol. 1. (ISBN 0-256-02051-5); Vol. 2. (ISBN 0-256-02052-3). Dorsey.

Main Report. Internaional Associaion of Logopedics & Phoniatrics, 18th Congress, Washington, D.C., August 1980. Ed. by B. Fritzell et al. (Journal: Folia Phoniatricia: Vol. 32, No. 2). (Illus.). 72p. 1980. soft cover 19.75 (ISBN 3-8055-1235-X). S Karger.

Main St. to Malibu: Yesterday & Today. Fred E. Basten. LC 80-83608. (Illus.). 128p. (Orig.). 1980. pap. 9.95 (ISBN 0-937536-00-8). Graphics Calif.

Main Street & the Mind of God. William F. Keucher. LC 74-2891. 128p. (Orig.). 1974. pap. 2.65 o.p. (ISBN 0-8170-0639-7). Judson.

Main Street & Wall Street. William Ripley. LC 72-93640. 1973. Repr. of 1927 ed. text ed. 13.00 (ISBN 0-914348-07-8). Scholars Bk.

Main Street Militants: An Anthology from "Grassroots Editor". Ed. by Howard R. Long. LC 78-16336. (Arcturus Books Paperbacks Ser.). 178p. 1979. pap. 5.95 (ISBN 0-8093-0894-0). S Ill U Pr.

Main-Travelled Roads. Hamlin Garland. 1962. pap. 1.95 (ISBN 0-451-51378-9, CJ1378, Sig Classics). NAL.

Main Trends in Interdisciplinary Research. Jean Piaget. 1973. pap. 1.95x o.p. (ISBN 0-06-131755-1, TB1755, Torch). Har-Row.

Main Trends in the Science of Language. Roman Jakobson. 1973. pap. 1.95x o.p. (ISBN 0-06-131809-4, TB1809, Torch). Har-Row.

Main Trends in World Power: Political Impact of Strategic Weapons. Ray S. Cline et al. 1978. pap. text ed. 2.95 o.p. (ISBN 0-89206-004-2). CSI Studies.

Main Trends in World Power: Political Impact of Strategic Weapons. 60p. 1978. pap. 7.50 (ISBN 0-89206-004-2, CSIS001, CSIS). Unipub.

Main Trends of Research in the Social & Human Sciences: Social Sciences, Part 1. Pref. by R. Maheu. LC 70-114641. 1970. 65.25 (ISBN 92-3-100828-5, U363, UNESCO); Part 2, (vols. 1 & 2) 137.50 (ISBN 92-3-101013-1). Unipub.

Maine. 23.00 (ISBN 0-89770-095-3). Curriculum Info Ctr.

Maine: A Guide Down East. Federal Writers' Project. 476p. 1936. Repr. 49.00 (ISBN 0-403-02170-7). Somerset Pub.

Maine: A History. Charles E. Clark. (State & the Nation Ser.). (Illus.). 1977. 12.95 (ISBN 0-393-05653-8, Co-Pub by AASLH). Norton.

Maine Animals. Ed. by Thorndike Press. LC 78-9725. (Maine Nature Ser.). (Illus.). lib. bdg. 8.50 o.p. (ISBN 0-89621-013-8); pap. 2.95x (ISBN 0-89621-012-X). Thorndike Pr.

Maine Atlas & Gazetteer. 2nd ed. Ed. by David DeLorme. (Illus.). 96p. 1978. pap. 6.95 (ISBN 0-89933-003-7). DeLorme Pub.

Maine Bar Directory, 1981. 1981. price not set (ISBN 0-89442-022-4). Tower Pub Co.

Maine Birds. Ed. by Thorndike Press. LC 78-9702. (Maine Nature Ser.). (Illus.). 1978. 8.50x o.p. (ISBN 0-89621-011-1); pap. 2.95x o.p. (ISBN 0-89621-010-3). Thorndike Pr.

Maine Chronology & Factbook. R. I. Vexler. 1978. 8.50 (ISBN 0-379-16144-3). Oceana.

Maine Coast: A Nature Lover's Guide. Dorcas S. Miller. LC 79-10290. (Illus.). 192p. 1978. lib. bdg. 10.25 o.p. (ISBN 0-914788-12-4). East Woods.

Maine Dirigo: I Lead. Ed. by Dean B. Bennett & Barbara E. Young. LC 80-68242. (Maine Studies Curriculum Project). (Illus.). 300p. 1980. text ed. 13.50 (ISBN 0-89272-103-0). Down East.

Maine Doings. Robert P. Coffin. LC 78-26413. 1978. lib. bdg. 11.50 o.p. (ISBN 0-89621-025-1); pap. 4.95 (ISBN 0-89621-024-3). Thorndike Pr.

Maine Fish. Ed. by Thorndike Press. LC 78-17234. (Maine Nature Ser.). (Illus.). 1978. 8.50x o.p. (ISBN 0-89621-015-4); pap. 2.95x o.p. (ISBN 0-89621-014-6). Thorndike Pr.

Maine Massacre. Jan Van de Wetering. (Orig.). 1980. pap. write for info. (ISBN 0-671-82865-7). PB.

Maine One Hundred Years Ago. Nichols & Pachard. (Sun Historical Ser.). (Illus.). pap. 3.50 (ISBN 0-89540-049-9). Sun Pub.

Maine Register: Nineteen Eighty to Nineteen Eighty-One. 1980. 65.00 (ISBN 0-89442-013-5). Tower Pub Co.

Maine Rivers. Ed. by Thorndike Press. LC 79-12996. (Maine Nature Ser.). (Illus., Orig.). 1979. lib. bdg. 8.50x o.p. (ISBN 0-89621-039-1); pap. 2.95x (ISBN 0-89621-038-3). Thorndike Pr.

Maine State Industrial Directory, 1981. State Industrial Directories Corp. 1980. pap. write for info. (ISBN 0-89910-045-7). State Indus Dir.

Maine Way -- a Collection of Maine Fish & Game Recipes: A Collection of Marine Fish & Game Recipes. Ed. by Judy Marsh & Carole Dyer. (Illus.). 96p. (Orig.). 1978. pap. 3.95 (ISBN 0-686-69324-8). DeLorme Pub.

Maine Woods. Henry D. Thoreau. (Apollo Eds.). (YA) (gr. 9-12). pap. 4.95 (ISBN 0-8152-0117-6, A117, TYC-T). T Y Crowell.

Mainland. Chris Searle. LC 76-365792. 1979. 9.95 (ISBN 0-7145-1069-6, Pub. by M Boyars); pap. 5.95 (ISBN 0-7145-0480-7). Merrimack Bk Serv.

Mainline: New Concept English. L. G. Alexander et al. write for info. (ISBN 0-686-10913-9). Longman.

Mainstream of Algebra & Trigonometry. A. W. Goodman. LC 72-5241. 475p. 1973. text ed. 17.95 o.p. (ISBN 0-395-16004-9, 3-19075); solutions manual. pap. 4.75 o.p. (ISBN 0-395-16005-7, 3-19076). HM.

Mainstream of Algebra & Trigonometry. 2nd ed. A. W. Goodman et al. LC 79-90059. (Illus.). 1980. text ed. 18.95 (ISBN 0-395-26765-X); solutions manual 2.25 (ISBN 0-395-26761-7). HM.

Mainstream of Civilization: One-Vol. Edition. 3rd ed. Joseph R. Strayer & Hans W. Gatzke. 840p. 1979. text ed. 18.95 (ISBN 0-15-551562-4, HC); test manual avail. (ISBN 0-15-551563-2). HarBraceJ.

Mainstream of Physics. Arthur Beiser. 1962. 15.95 (ISBN 0-201-00495-X). A-W.

Mainstream of Western Political Thought. Judith Best. 144p. 1980. text ed. 17.95x (ISBN 0-87705-271-9); pap. text ed. 8.95x (ISBN 0-87705-243-3). Human Sci Pr.

Mainstreaming. Ed. by Sara Lake. (Special Interest Resource Guides in Education). 1980. pap. text ed. 7.50x (ISBN 0-912700-73-4). Oryx Pr.

Mainstreaming Handicapped Students: A Guide for the Classroom Teacher. Ann P. Turnbull & Jane B. Schulz. 1979. text ed. 18.95 (ISBN 0-205-06107-9). Allyn.

Mainstreaming of Children with a Hearing Loss: Practical Guidelines & Implications. Verna V. Yater. (Illus.). 304p. 1977. 28.50 (ISBN 0-398-03586-5); pap. 19.25 (ISBN 0-398-03589-X). C C Thomas.

Mainstreaming: Practical Ideas for Educating Hearing-Impaired Students. Milo E. Bishop. 1979. 10.00 (ISBN 0-88200-126-4). Bell Assn Deaf.

Mainstreaming the Learning Disabled Adolescent: A Manual of Strategies & Materials. Dolores M. Woodward. 200p. 1981. text ed. write for info. (ISBN 0-89443-299-0). Aspen Systems.

Mainstreaming the Learning Disabled Adolescent: A Staff Development Guide. William E. Chaiken & Mary J. Harper. (Illus.). 162p. 1979. text ed. 14.75 (ISBN 0-398-03871-6). C C Thomas.

Mainstreaming the Non-English Speaking Student. Raymond J. Rodrigues & Robert H. White. (Theory & Research into Practice Ser.). (Orig.). 1981. write for info. (ISBN 0-8141-3036-4, 30364). NCTE.

Mainstreaming: What to Expect...What to Do. Robert B. Blackwell & Robert R. Joynt. 1980. 15.95 (ISBN 0-87804-416-7). Mafex.

Mainstreaming with Learning Sequences. Jo Ellen Fleming & Dena Goplerud. 1980. pap. 9.50 (ISBN 0-8224-4260-4). Pitman Learning.

Mainstreams of Finite Mathematics with Applications. Chris P. Tsokos. (Mathematics Ser.). 1978. text ed. 18.95 (ISBN 0-675-08436-9); instructor's manual 3.95 (ISBN 0-685-86838-9). Merrill.

Mainstreams of Music, 4 vols. D. Ewan. (gr. 7-12). 1975. Set. 43.80 o.p. (ISBN 0-531-01102-X). Watts.

Maintaining & Troubleshooting HPLC Systems: A Users Guide. Dennis J. Runser. 208p. 1981. 22.50 (ISBN 0-471-06479-3, Pub. by Wiley Interscience). Wiley.

Maintaining Effective Token Economies. Roger L. Patterson. (Illus.). 192p. 1976. 19.50 (ISBN 0-398-03435-4). C C Thomas.

Maintaining Fishes for Experimental & Instructional Purposes. William M. Lewis. LC 62-15001. (Arcturus Books Paperbacks Ser.). 109p. 1963. pap. 3.95 (ISBN 0-8093-0078-8). S Ill U Pr.

Maintaining Interior Plantscapes. George H. Manaker. (Illus.). 336p. 1981. text ed. 17.95 o.p. (ISBN 0-13-545459-X). P-H.

Maintaining Sanity in the Classroom: Illustrated Teaching Techniques. Rudolf Dreikurs et al. 1971. pap. 14.95 scp (ISBN 0-06-041758-7, HarpC). Har-Row.

Maintaining Unity. Churches Alive Inc. (Love One Another Bible Study). 1979. wkbk. 1.50 (ISBN 0-934396-07-8). Churches Alive.

Maintenance. (Library of Boating Ser.). (Illus.). 1976. 14.95 (ISBN 0-8094-2116-X). Time-Life.

Maintenance. Ed. by Time Life Books. LC 75-18911. (Library of Boating Ser.). (Illus.). (gr. 6 up). 1975. PLB 13.95 (ISBN 0-8094-2117-8, Pub. by Time-Life). Silver.

Maintenance & Repair of Small Engines. J. Howard Turner. 9.95 (ISBN 0-914452-45-2). Green Hill.

Maintenance Management. Lawrence Mann. 1976. 24.95 (ISBN 0-669-00143-0). Lexington Bks.

Maintenance Mechanics Qualification Program. Clinton C. Bell. (Illus.). 56p. 1981. pap. write for info. (ISBN 0-89852-389-3). TAPPI.

Maintenance Methods for the Pulp & Paper Industry. Miller Freeman Publications, Inc. Ed. by Matthew Coleman. LC 80-82934. (Pulp & Paper Focus Bk.). (Illus.). 192p. 1980. pap. 29.50 (ISBN 0-87930-088-4). Miller Freeman.

Maintenance of Factory Services: Part Two, 2 vols. Ed. by J. Vaughan et al. (Engineering Craftsmen: No. J23). (Illus.). 1969. Set. spiral bdg. 33.95x (ISBN 0-685-90156-4). Intl Ideas.

Maintenance of Factory Services: Part One. Ed. by J. Vaughan et al. (Engineering Craftsmen: No. J3). (Illus.). 1968. spiral bdg. 24.00x (ISBN 0-85083-028-1). Intl Ideas.

Maintenance of Maritime Structures. Thomas Telford Ltd, Editorial Staff. 252p. 1980. 40.00x (ISBN 0-7277-0050-2, Pub. by Telford England). State Mutual Bk.

Maintenance of Numerically Controlled Machine Tools, 2 vols. 2nd ed. Ed. by C. Brothwell et al. (Engineering Craftsmen: No. J27). (Illus.). 1973. Set. spiral bdg. 52.00x (ISBN 0-85083-155-5). Intl Ideas.

Maintenance Planning, Control & Documentation. E. N. White. 1979. text ed. 35.25x (ISBN 0-566-02144-7, Pub. by Gower Pub Co England). Renouf.

Maintenance Turns to the Computer. James K. Hildebrand. LC 75-109095. 1972. 11.95 (ISBN 0-8436-0808-0). CBI Pub.

Maiolica: A Historical Treatise on the Glazed & Enamelled Earthenwares of Italy. Charles D. Fortnum. Ed. by Wolfgang M. Freitag. LC 78-50321. (Ceramics & Glass Ser.: Vol. 7). (Illus.). 1979. lib. bdg. 55.00 (ISBN 0-8240-3393-0). Garland Pub.

Mais Puro Que O Diamante. Tr. by J. C. De Ferriere. (Portugese Bks.). (Port.). 1979. 1.10 (ISBN 0-686-28816-5). Life Pubs Intl.

Mais Que Passarinhos. Tr. by Mary Welch. (Portugese Bks.). (Port.). 1979. 1.25 (ISBN 0-8297-0801-4). Life Pubs Intl.

Maitreys Six: Order. Ed. by Vincent G. Stuart. 1977. pap. 4.50 o.p. (ISBN 0-394-73350-9). Random.

Maize. Gil Ott. (Illus.). 1980. ltd. signed ed. 20.00x (ISBN 0-915316-70-6); pap. 5.00x (ISBN 0-915316-69-2). Pentagram.

Maize Breeding & Genetics. Ed. by David B. Walden. LC 78-6779. 1978. 62.50 (ISBN 0-471-91805-9, Pub. by Wiley-Interscience). Wiley.

Maize in Tropical Africa. Marvin P. Miracle. (Illus.). 1966. 25.00 (ISBN 0-299-03850-5). U of Wis Pr.

Majestic. Ray Hubbard. 432p. (Orig.). 1981. pap. 2.75 (ISBN 0-553-13218-0). Bantam.

Majestic Lights. Robert Eather. 1980. write for info (ISBN 0-87590-215-4). Am Geophysical.

Majesty & Mystery. Robert B. Ruddell et al. (Pathfinder - Allyn & Bacon Reading Program: Level 17). (gr. 5). 1978. text ed. 8.80 (ISBN 0-205-05208-8, 5452082); tchr's guide 14.60 (ISBN 0-205-05210-X, 5452104); 3.88. Allyn.

Majesty's Rancho. Zane Grez. 1980. pap. write for info. (ISBN 0-671-83506-8). PB.

Majken. Carl Lawrence. 192p. 1981. pap. 4.95 (ISBN 0-8407-5762-X). Nelson.

Major. Ralph Connor. 1976. lib. bdg. 16.75x (ISBN 0-89968-014-3). Lightyear.

Major Amputations for Vascular Disease. J. Miles Little. LC 74-84692. (Illus.). 128p. 1975. text ed. 21.00 (ISBN 0-443-01250-4). Churchill.

Major Appliance Repair Guide. Wayne Lemons & Billy Price. LC 70-162406. (Illus.). 1971. 8.95 o.p. (ISBN 0-8306-1555-5); pap. 5.95 o.p. (ISBN 0-8306-0555-X, 555). TAB Bks.

Major Appliances & Electric Housewares. Fairchild Market Research Division. (Fairchild Fact File Ser.). 1979. pap. 10.00 (ISBN 0-87005-324-8). Fairchild.

Major Barbara. George B. Shaw. Ed. by Elizabeth T. Forter. LC 77-145842. (Crofts Classics Ser.). 1971. text ed. 5.95x (ISBN 0-88295-087-8); pap. text ed. 2.95x (ISBN 0-88295-088-6). AHM Pub.

Major Barbara. George B. Shaw. Ed. by Bernard Dukore. LC 79-56708. (Bernard Shaw Early Texts: Play Manuscripts in Facsimile). 1981. lib. bdg. 70.00 (ISBN 0-8240-4583-1). Garland Pub.

Major Bible Themes. rev. ed. Lewis S. Chafer & John F. Walvoord. 10.95 (ISBN 0-310-22390-3). Zondervan.

Major Bible Truths. F. E. Marsh. LC 79-2533. 1980. 9.95 (ISBN 0-8254-3232-4). Kregel.

Major Characters of Lord Byron's Plays. Allen P. Whitmore. (Salzburg Studies in English Literature, Poetic Drama & Poetic Theory: No. 6). 145p. 1974. pap. text ed. 25.00x (ISBN 0-391-01566-4). Humanities.

Major Companies of Europe 1975. (Jane's U.S.A.). (gr. 5-8). 60.00 o.p. (ISBN 0-531-02751-1). Watts.

Major European Governments. 5th ed. Alex N. Dragnich & Jorgen S. Rasmussen. 1978. text ed. 18.50x (ISBN 0-256-02054-X). Dorsey.

Major Features of Evolution. George G. Simpson. LC 53-10263. (Columbia Biological Ser.: No. 17). 1953. 27.50 (ISBN 0-231-01821-5). Columbia U Pr.

Major Film Theories: An Introduction. J. Dudley Andrew. (Illus.). 275p. (Orig.). 1976. pap. 5.95 (ISBN 0-19-501991-1, 450, GB). Oxford U Pr.

Major General George H. Thomas: A Summary in Perspective. Hans Juergensen. (Illus.). 50p. (Orig.). 1980. pap. 3.00 (ISBN 0-934996-08-3). Am Stud Pr.

Major Governments of Asia. 2nd ed. George M. Kahin. LC 63-15940. (Illus.). 1963. 24.50x o.p. (ISBN 0-8014-0218-2). Cornell U Pr.

Major Indian Novels: The Pattern of Meaning. B. M. Bhalla. 204p. 1980. text ed. price not set o.p. (ISBN 0-391-02075-7). Humanities.

Major Interpretations of the American Past. Ed. by Richard L. Rapson. LC 72-149210. (Literature of History Ser). (Orig.). 1971. 18.95x (ISBN 0-89197-284-6); pap. text ed. 7.95x (ISBN 0-89197-285-4). Irvington.

Major Job-Providing Organizations & Systems of Cities. A. R. Pred. LC 74-79830. (CCG Resource Papers Ser.: No. 27). (Illus.). 1974. pap. text ed. 4.00 (ISBN 0-89291-074-7). Assn Am Geographers.

Major League Baseball, 1976. Ed. by Barry Larit. 1976. pap. 1.75 o.p. (ISBN 0-345-25441-4). Ballantine.

Major League Baseball 1977. 1977. pap. 1.95 o.p. (ISBN 0-345-25769-3). Ballantine.

Major Legal Systems in the World Today: An Introduction to the Comparative Study of Law. 2nd ed. Rene David & John E. Brierly. LC 78-67751. 1978. 25.00 (ISBN 0-02-907590-4); pap. text ed. 10.95 (ISBN 0-02-907610-2). Free Pr.

Major Modern Dramatists, 2 vols. Ed. by Rita Stein et al. LC 78-4310. (Library of Literary Criticism). 1100p. 1980. 65.00 (ISBN 0-8044-3270-8). Ungar.

Major Neurological Syndromes. Mircea A. Morariu. (Illus.). 368p. 1979. text ed. 25.75 (ISBN 0-398-03831-7). C C Thomas.

Major Operation. James White. 192p. 1981. pap. 2.25 (ISBN 0-345-29381-9). Ballantine.

Major Papers on Early Primate, Compiled from the Publications of the American Museum of Natural History: 1902 to 1940. LC 78-72712. 1980. 55.50 (ISBN 0-404-18282-8). AMS Pr.

Major Peace Treaties of Modern History, 1967-1979. Ed. by Fred L. Israel. LC 67-27855. (Major Peace Treaties of Modern History, 1648-1979, Ser.: Vol. 5). 490p. 1981. pap. 19.95 (ISBN 0-87754-126-4). Chelsea Hse.

Major Poems: 5 Vols. in 1. Timothy Dwight. LC 68-24207. 1969. 52.00x (ISBN 0-8201-1059-0). Schol Facsimiles.

Major Poets of the Earlier Seventeenth Century. Ed. by Barbara K. Lewalski & Andrew J. Sabol. LC 70-789379. 1973. 28.90 o.p. (ISBN 0-672-53184-4); pap. 17.50 o.p. (ISBN 0-672-63184-9). Odyssey Pr.

Major Presidential Decisions. Ed. by Fred L. Israel. LC 80-22040. 850p. 1980. pap. 11.95 (ISBN 0-87754-218-X). Chelsea Hse.

Major Problems in American Foreign Policy. Thomas G. Paterson. 1978. Vol. 1. pap. text ed. 8.95x (ISBN 0-669-00475-8); Vol. 2. pap. text ed. 9.95x (ISBN 0-669-00476-6). Heath.

Major Problems in State Constitutional Revision. Pi Sigma Alpha Committee on Publications. Ed. by W. Brooke Graves. LC 78-779. xiv, 306p. 1978. Repr. of 1960 ed. lib. bdg. 24.50x (ISBN 0-313-20266-4, PSAM). Greenwood.

Major Problems of the World at the End of the 20th Century & Possible Solutions to Avoid an Epochal Catastrophe. Christopher Baldwin. (Illus.). 106p. 1980. 49.75 (ISBN 0-930008-65-0). Inst Econ Pol.

Major Research in Upland Rice. 255p. 1975. pap. 11.00 (R021, IRRI). Unipub.

Major Rock Paintings of Southern Africa. Ed. by Tim Maggs. LC 80-7664. (Illus.). 96p. 1980. 50.00x (ISBN 0-253-19226-9). Ind U Pr.

Major Shakespearean Tragedies: A Critical Bibliography. Edward Quinn et al. LC 72-77284. 1973. 12.95 (ISBN 0-02-925590-2). Free Pr.

Major Socialist Parties of India: A Study in Leftist Fragmentation. Lewis P. Fickett, Jr. LC 76-20536. (Foreign & Comparative Studies-South Asian Ser.: No. 2). 1976. pap. text ed. 4.50x (ISBN 0-915984-76-8). Syracuse U Foreign Comp.

Major Stepton's War. Matthew Vaughan. LC 77-11369. 1978. 7.95 o.p. (ISBN 0-385-13607-2). Doubleday.

Major Symptoms of Hysteria. Pierre Janet. 345p. 1980. Repr. of 1920 ed. lib. bdg. 40.00 (ISBN 0-8492-1367-3). R West.

Major Themes from the Minor Prophets. Gerald H. Twombly. (Adult Study Guide). 144p. (Orig.). 1981. pap. 3.95 (ISBN 0-88469-132-2). BMH Bks.

Major Themes in Modern Arabic Thought: An Anthology. Trevor J. LeGassick. 1979. text ed. 12.50 (ISBN 0-472-08561-1). U of Mich Pr.

Major Themes in Northern Black Religious Thought, 1800-1860. Monroe Fordham. LC 75-10618. 1975. 8.50 o.p. (ISBN 0-682-48256-0, University). Exposition.

Major Themes in Prize-Winning American Drama. Jane F. Bonin. LC 74-34492. 205p. 1975. 10.00 (ISBN 0-8108-0799-8). Scarecrow.

Major Themes in Sociological Theory. 2nd ed. Calvin J. Larson. LC 77-77775. 1977. pap. 9.95x (ISBN 0-679-30348-0, Pub. by MacKay). Longman.

Major Transitions in the Human Life Cycle. Howard Spierer. 60p. 1977. pap. 5.00 (ISBN 0-89192-240-7). Interbk Inc.

Major Trends in Mexican Philosophy. Tr. by A. Robert Caponigri. 1966. 10.95x o.p. (ISBN 0-268-00163-4). U of Notre Dame Pr.

Major Variety & Oddity Guide of U. S. Coins. 8th ed. Frank G. Spadone. LC 80-84159. (Collector Ser.). (Illus.). 128p. 1981. pap. 4.95 (ISBN 0-87637-162-4, 162-04). Hse of Collectibles.

Major Wine Grape Varieties of Australia. A. J. Antcliff. 1980. 15.00x (ISBN 0-643-02517-0, Pub. by CSJRO Australia). State Mutual Bk.

Major Wine Grape Varieties of Australia. 61p. 1979. pap. 6.50 (ISBN 0-643-02517-0, CO12, CSIRO). Unipub.

Major Writers of Early American Literature: Introductions to Nine Major Writers. Ed. by Everett H. Emerson. LC 72-1378. 312p. 1972. 25.00x (ISBN 0-299-06190-6); pap. 8.50 (ISBN 0-299-06194-9). U of Wis Pr.

Majorca. Ann Hoffman. (Island Ser.). 1978. 14.95 (ISBN 0-7153-7492-3). David & Charles.

Majority & Minority: The Dynamics of Ethnic & Racial Relations. 2nd ed. Norman R. Yetman & C. Hoy Steele. 660p. 1975. text ed. 13.60 (ISBN 0-205-04815-3, 8148155). Allyn.

Majority Finds Its Past: Placing Women in History. Gerda Lerner. 1979. 14.95 (ISBN 0-19-502597-0). Oxford U Pr.

Majority Finds Its Past: Placing Women in History. Gerda Lerner. (Galaxy Book: No. 624). 250p. 1981. pap. 5.95 (ISBN 0-19-502899-6). Oxford U Pr.

Majority Finds Its Past: Placing Women in History. Gerda Lerner. 250p. 1981. pap. 5.95 (ISBN 0-19-502899-6, GB 624, OPB). Oxford U Pr.

Majority Rule & the Judiciary. William L. Ransom. LC 78-166099. (American Constitutional & Legal History Ser). 1971. Repr. of 1912 ed. pap. 19.50 (ISBN 0-306-70205-3). Da Capo.

Major's Lady. Roseleen Milne. 1980. pap. write for info. (ISBN 0-671-83652-8). PB.

Major's Physical Diagnosis: An Introduction to the Clinical Process. 9th ed. Mahlon H. Delp & Robert T. Manning. (Illus.). 650p. 1981. text ed. write for info. (ISBN 0-7216-3002-2). Saunders.

Makaha: The Legend of the Broken Promise. Philipo Springer. Ed. by Ruth Tabrah. LC 74-80511. (Illus.). (gr. 1-7). 1974. 5.95 (ISBN 0-89610-008-1). Island Her.

Makam: Modal Practice in Turkish Art Music. Karl Signell. LC 74-76787. (D Monographs: No. 4). 1976. pap. text ed. 9.00x (ISBN 0-913360-07-4). Asian Music Pub.

Makarios: Pragmatism V. Idealism. P. N. Vanezis. (Illus.). 203p. 1975. 9.95 (ISBN 0-200-72207-7). Transatlantic.

Make a Chair from a Tree: An Introduction to Working Green Wood. John D. Alexander, Jr. LC 78-58222. (Illus., Orig.). 1978. pap. 7.95 (ISBN 0-918804-01-9, Dist. by Van Nostrand Reinhold). Taunton.

Make a Joyful Noise Unto the Lord: Hymns As a Reflection of Victorian Social Attitudes. Susan S. Tamke. LC 76-51693. 209p. 1978. 12.00x (ISBN 0-8214-0371-0); pap. text ed. 5.00x (ISBN 0-8214-0382-6). Ohio U Pr.

Make-A-Mix Cookery. Karine Eliason et al. LC 78-50687. (Illus.). 1978. pap. 5.95 (ISBN 0-89586-008-2). H P Bks.

Make a Mobile. Kate Pountney. LC 74-9824. (Illus.). 64p. (gr. 3 up). 1974. 9.95 (ISBN 0-87599-206-4). S G Phillips.

Make a Wish Come True. Robert T. Smith. LC 72-89459. 32p. (gr. 5-12). 1973. PLB 4.95 (ISBN 0-87191-224-4). Creative Ed.

Make a Witch, Make a Goblin: A Book of Halloween Crafts. Arnold Dobrin. LC 77-177. (Illus.). 128p. (gr. 2-5). 1977. 7.95 (ISBN 0-590-07450-4, Four Winds). Schol Bk Serv.

Make & Furnish Your Own Miniature Rooms. Marian M. O'Brien. 1976. 16.95 o.p. (Hawthorn); pap. 9.95 (ISBN 0-8015-4811-X, Hawthorn). Dutton.

Make & Tell: Christmas Holiday Book of Family Fun & Crafts. Meg Braga. (Illus.). 1978. Repr. of 1974 ed. saddlestitched 1.95 (ISBN 0-87788-535-4). Shaw Pubs.

Make-Believe. Gyo Fujikawa. (Gyo Fujikawa Tiny Board Books). (Illus.). 14p. (ps-k). 1981. 1.95 (ISBN 0-448-15127-8). G&D.

Make Every Word Count. Gary Provost. LC 80-23699. 256p. 1980. 10.95 (ISBN 0-89879-020-4). Writers Digest.

Make Hay While the Sun Shines. Alison M. Abel. (Illus.). 1977. 7.95 (ISBN 0-571-11006-1, Pub. by Faber & Faber). Merrimack Bk Serv.

Make It Again, Sam. Michael B. Druxman. LC 74-19810. (Illus.). 320p. 1975. 17.50 o.p. (ISBN 0-498-01470-3). A S Barnes.

Make It: An Index to Projects & Materials. Joyce F. Shields. LC 74-17114. 1975. 18.50 (ISBN 0-8108-0772-6). Scarecrow.

Make It & Wear It. Ruth Katz. LC 80-54707. (Illus.). 48p. (gr. 5-9). 1981. 7.95 (ISBN 0-8027-6418-5); PLB 8.95 (ISBN 0-8027-6419-3). Walker & Co.

Make It in Cheesecloth. Hazel Todhunter. 1979. 14.95 (ISBN 0-7134-1264-X, Pub. by Batsford England). David & Charles.

Make It Plain! Paul Heubach. LC 80-13864. (Orion Ser.). 128p. 1980. pap. 2.50 (ISBN 0-8127-0295-6). Southern Pub.

Make-It, Play-It Game Book. Roz Abisch. LC 74-78855. (Illus.). 96p. (gr. 1-5). 1974. 5.95 o.s.i. (ISBN 0-8027-6198-4). Walker & Co.

Make Learning a Joy. Ed. by Jim Larson. (Illus.). 80p. (Orig.). 1975. pap. 1.65 o.p. (ISBN 0-8307-0362-4, 54-023-01). Regal.

Make Love Your Aim. Eugenia Price. 192p. 1972. pap. 2.95 (ISBN 0-310-31312-0). Zondervan.

Make Me a Hero. Jerome Brooks. LC 79-20269. 176p. (gr. 5-9). 1980. PLB 8.95 (ISBN 0-525-34475-6). Dutton.

Make Mine Music: How to Make & Play Instruments & Why They Work. Tom Walther. (Brown Paper School Ser.). (Illus.). 128p. (Orig.). (gr. 3 up). 1981. 9.95 (ISBN 0-316-92111-4); pap. 5.95 (ISBN 0-316-92112-2). Little.

Make Straight the Way of the Lord. Lanza Del Vasto. 1974. 7.95 o.p. (ISBN 0-394-49387-7). Knopf.

Make That Story Live! Ruth S. Ensign. (Orig.). (gr. 7-9). 1965. pap. 1.50 (ISBN 0-8042-9317-1). John Knox.

Make up, Costumes & Masks for the Stage. Ole Bruun-Rasmussen & Grete Petersen. LC 76-19803. (Illus.). (gr. 5 up). 1976. 10.95 (ISBN 0-8069-7024-3); PLB 9.97 (ISBN 0-8069-7025-1). Sterling.

Make-up, Costumes & Masks for the Stage. Ole Bruun-Rasmussen & Grete Petersen. LC 76-19803. (Illus.). 96p. (gr. 4-12). 1981. pap. 6.95 (ISBN 0-8069-8992-0). Sterling.

Make-up for School Plays. Eric Jones. 1969. 16.95 (ISBN 0-7134-2063-4, Pub. by Batsford England). David & Charles.

Make-Up: The Dramatic Student's Approach. 2nd ed. Charles Thomas. 1968. pap. 3.25 (ISBN 0-87830-560-2). Theatre Arts.

Make up Your Mind. Charles R. Swindoll. (Illus.). 100p. 1981. pap. 8.95 (ISBN 0-930014-61-8). Multnomah.

Make Way for Lucia: The Complete Lucia, Including Queen Lucia, Miss Mapp, Mapp & Lucia, Lucia in London, Trouble for Lucia & the Worshipful Lucia & the Male Impersonator. E. F. Benson. LC 76-783. 576p. 1977. 14.95 o.p. (ISBN 0-690-01105-9, TYC-T). T Y Crowell.

Make Your Juicer Your Drug Store. Laura Newman. LC 66-125414. (Illus.). 192p. 1978. pap. 2.50 (ISBN 0-87904-001-7). Lust.

Make Your Own Baby Furniture. Florence Adams. LC 80-10495. (Illus.). 224p. 1980. pap. 9.95 (ISBN 0-87131-320-0). M Evans.

Make Your Own Backpack & Other Wilderness Camp Gear. Hugh Nelson. (Illus.). 131p. (Orig.). 1981. pap. 12.95 (ISBN 0-8040-0355-6). Swallow.

Make Your Own Booklet. John Dumpleton. LC 79-3815. 1980. pap. 2.95 (ISBN 0-8008-5058-0, Pentalic). Taplinger.

Make Your Own Comics for Fun & Profit. Richard Cummings. (gr. 7 up). 1975. 9.95 (ISBN 0-8098-3929-6). Walck.

Make Your Own Dollhouse. Richard Cummings. (Illus.). 1978. 8.95 o.p. (ISBN 0-679-20439-3). McKay.

Make Your Own Dollhouses & Dollhouse Miniatures. Marian M. O'Brien. 224p. 1977. 16.95 o.p. (Hawthorn); pap. 9.95 (ISBN 0-8015-4799-7, Hawthorn). Dutton.

Make Your Own Dress Patterns. Brenda Redmile. 1978. 17.95 (ISBN 0-7134-0389-6, Pub. by Batsford England). David & Charles.

Make Your Own Electricity. Terence McLaughlin. LC 76-54075. 1977. 10.50 (ISBN 0-7153-7418-4). David & Charles.

Make Your Own Groceries. Daphne M. Hartwig. LC 79-2453. (Illus.). 1979. pap. 12.95 (ISBN 0-672-52279-9). Bobbs.

Make Your Own Musical Instruments. rev. ed. Muriel Mandell & Robert E. Wood. LC 57-11535. (Illus.). (gr. 3-8). 1959. 6.95 (ISBN 0-8069-5022-6); PLB 7.49 (ISBN 0-8069-5023-4). Sterling.

Make Your Own Professional Movies. Nancy Goodwin & James Manilla. LC 70-152286. 1971. 9.95 (ISBN 0-02-544700-9). Macmillan.

Make Your Own Rugs. Dietrich Kirsch & Jutta Kirsch-Korn. 1970. 11.95 (ISBN 0-7134-2461-3, Pub. by Batsford England). David & Charles.

Make Your Own Sea-Angling Tackle. Leonard F. Burrell. (Illus.). 108p. 1976. 12.00 (ISBN 0-7207-0894-X). Transatlantic.

Make Your Own Silk Flowers. Dee Entrekin. LC 74-31705. (Illus.). 80p. 1975. 12.95 (ISBN 0-8069-5318-7); PLB 11.69 (ISBN 0-8069-5319-5). Sterling.

Make Your Own Silk Flowers. Dee Entrekin. LC 74-31705. (Illus.). 80p. 1981. pap. 6.95 (ISBN 0-8069-8994-7). Sterling.

Make Your Own Soap Plain & Fancy. Dorothy Richter. LC 73-83663. 160p. 1974. pap. 1.95 (ISBN 0-385-01776-6, Dolp). Doubleday.

Make Your Own World. Gordon Collier. 9.95 (ISBN 0-912576-04-9). R Collier.

Make Your Sunday School Grow Through Evaluation. Harold J. Westing. 120p. 1976. pap. 1.95 o.p. (ISBN 0-88207-464-4). Victor Bks.

Make Your Tomorrow Better: A Psychological Resource for Singles, Parents & the Entire Family. Michael E. Cavanagh. LC 80-80638. 320p. (Orig.). 1980. pap. 8.95 (ISBN 0-8091-2293-6). Paulist Pr.

Maker of Modern Japan: The Life of Shogun Tokugawa Ieyasu. A. L. Sadler. LC 78-54935. (Illus.). 1978. pap. 8.50 (ISBN 0-8048-1297-7). C E Tuttle.

Maker of Universes. Philip J. Farmer. 1977. pap. 2.25 (ISBN 0-441-51624-6). Ace Bks.

Maker of Universes. rev. ed. Philip J. Farmer. (World of Tiers Ser.). 224p. 1980. Repr. of 1962 ed. 15.00 (ISBN 0-932096-07-7). Phantasia Pr.

Makers of America, 10 Vols. Ed. by Wayne Moquin. (Illus.). (gr. 7-12). 1971. Set. 129.00 (ISBN 0-87827-000-0). Ency Brit Ed.

Makers of American Diplomacy. Frank J. Merli & Theodore A. Wilson. LC 73-1321. (Illus.). 672p. (Paper text edition in two vols.). 1974. Vol. 1. pap. 9.95x o.p. (ISBN 0-684-13797-6, ScribC); Vol. 2. pap. 9.95x o.p. (ISBN 0-684-13798-4, ScribC). Scribner.

Makers of American History. rev. ed. Orrel Baldwin. (Illus.). 480p. (gr. 4-6). 1979. text ed. 8.19 (ISBN 0-8372-3692-4); tchrs' guide 2.40 (ISBN 0-686-60060-6). Bowmar-Noble.

Makers of British Canada. Tina Van Tuyl. 1978. 1.95 (ISBN 0-87463-338-9). Chr Sch Intl.

Makers of History, Charles I. Jacob Abbott. 285p. 1980. Repr. of 1903 ed. lib. bdg. 20.00 (ISBN 0-89984-002-7). Century Bookbindery.

Makers of History, Joseph Bonaparte. John S. Abbott. 391p. 1980. Repr. of 1903 ed. lib. bdg. 20.00 (ISBN 0-89984-049-3). Century Bookbindery.

Makers of Literary Criticism, Vol. 1. Ed. by B. Rajan & A. G. George. 10.00x (ISBN 0-210-26992-8). Asia.

Makers of Literary Criticism, Vol. 2. Ed. by B. Rajan & A. G. George. 10.00x (ISBN 0-210-26991-X). Asia.

Makers of Modern Culture. Justin Wintle. 704p. 1981. 34.95 (ISBN 0-87196-493-7). Facts on File.

Makers of Modern Strategy: Military Thought from Machiavelli to Hitler. Ed. by Edward M. Earle. 1943. 35.00 (ISBN 0-691-06907-7); pap. 6.95 (ISBN 0-691-01853-7). Princeton U Pr.

Makers of Naval Policy Seventeen Ninety-Eight to Nineteen Forty-Seven. Robert G. Albion. Ed. by Rowena Reed. LC 79-90772. 752p. 1980. 22.95x (ISBN 0-87021-360-1). Naval Inst Pr.

Makers of Puritan History. Marcus L. Loane. (Canterbury Bks). Orig. Title: Pioneers of Religious Freedom. 240p. 1980. pap. 6.95 (ISBN 0-8010-5593-8). Baker Bk.

Makers of Rome. Plutarch. Tr. by Ian Scott-Kilvert. (Classics Ser.). 368p. 1965. pap. 3.25 (ISBN 0-14-044158-1). Penguin.

Makeshift Mistress. Amanda Mack. (Orig.). 1981. pap. 1.50 o.s.i. (ISBN 0-440-15874-5). Dell.

Makeup for Theatre, Film & Television: A Step by Step Photographic Guide. Lee Baygan. (Illus.). 206p. 1981. 22.50x (ISBN 0-89676-023-5). Drama Bk.

Makin' Free: African - Americans in the Northwest Territory. Reginald R. Larrie. (Illus.). 1981. 6.95 (ISBN 0-87917-072-7). Blaine Ethridge.

Making a Ballet. Mary Clarke & Clement Crisp. (Illus.). 192p. 1975. 14.95 (ISBN 0-02-525790-0). Macmillan.

Making a Comprehensive Work: The Road from Bomb Alley. Peter Dawson. 160p. 1981. 25.00x (ISBN 0-631-12534-5, Pub. by Basil Blackwell England); pap. 12.50x. Biblio Dist.

Making a Judgment: Advanced Level. James A. Giroux & James E. Twining. Ed. by Edward Spargo. (Comprehension Skills Ser). (Illus.). (gr. 9-12). 1974. pap. text ed. 2.40x (ISBN 0-89061-013-4). Jamestown Pubs.

Making a Judgment: Middle Level. Glenn R. Williston. (Comprehension Skills Ser.). (Illus.). 64p. (gr. 6-8). 1976. pap. text ed. 2.40x (ISBN 0-89061-065-7, CB2M). Jamestown Pubs.

Making a Shadowgraph Show. Eric Hawkesworth. 1969. 5.95 o.p. (ISBN 0-571-08900-3, Pub. by Faber & Faber). Merrimack Bk Serv.

Making a Start on Child Study. Lesley Webb. (Blackwell's Practical Guides Ser.). (Illus.). 1975. pap. 6.25x (ISBN 0-631-16480-4, Pub. by Basil Blackwell). Biblio Dist.

Making Accounting Decisions. George Staubus. LC 77-73906. 1978. text ed. 20.00 (ISBN 0-914348-19-1). Scholars Bk.

Making All Things New: An Invitation to Life in the Spirit. Henri J. Nouwen. LC 80-8897. 96p. 1981. 6.95 (ISBN 0-06-066326-X). Har-Row.

Making America Work: Productivity & Responsibility. James O'Toole. 244p. 1981. 14.95 (ISBN 0-8264-0045-0). Continuum.

Making an Inference: Advanced Level. James A. Giroux & Glenn R. Williston. Ed. by Edward Spargo. (Comprehension Skills Ser). (Illus.). (gr. 9-12). 1974. pap. text ed. 2.40x (ISBN 0-89061-016-9). Jamestown Pubs.

Making an Inference: Middle Level. Glenn R. Williston. (Comprehension Skills Ser.). (Illus.). 64p. (gr. 6-8). 1976. pap. text ed. 2.40x (ISBN 0-89061-068-1, CB5M). Jamestown Pubs.

Making & Decorating Pottery Tiles. B. C. Southwell. 1972. 9.95 (ISBN 0-571-09603-4, Pub. by Faber & Faber). Merrimack Bk Serv.

Making & Designing Clothes. Cecile Miles. (Illus.). 160p. 1975. 9.95x o.p. (ISBN 0-8464-0584-9). Beekman Pubs.

Making & Managing a Pub. W. C. Stevenson. LC 79-51101. (Making & Managing Ser.). (Illus.). 1980. 17.95 (ISBN 0-7153-7801-5). David & Charles.

Making & Managing a Small Holding. Michael Allaby. LC 79-51103. (Making & Managing Ser.). (Illus.). 1980. 17.95 (ISBN 0-7153-7803-1). David & Charles.

Making & Managing an Antique Shop. Ronald Rawlings. LC 79-51100. (Making & Managing Ser.). (Illus.). 1980. 17.95 (ISBN 0-7153-7800-7). David & Charles.

Making & Managing an Art & Craft Shop. Ralph Lewis. LC 80-68685. (Making & Managing Ser.). (Illus.). 128p. 1981. 16.95 (ISBN 0-7153-8065-6). David & Charles.

Making & Meaning of an American Classic: James Fenimore Cooper's 'the Prairie' Orm Overland. 1973. text ed. 21.00x (ISBN 8-200-04613-3, Dist. by Columbia U Pr). Universitet.

Making & Printing Color Negatives. John Vickers. 1974. 15.95 o.p. (ISBN 0-85242-280-6, Pub. by Fountain). Morgan.

Making & Thinking: A Study of Intelligent Activities. Andrew Harrison. LC 78-56369. 1978. text ed. 19.50 (ISBN 0-915144-55-7). Hackett Pub.

Making & Using Inexpensive Classroom Media. Betty J. Wagner & E. Arthur Stunard. LC 76-29236. (Learning Handbooks Ser.). 1976. pap. 3.95 (ISBN 0-8224-1907-6). Pitman Learning.

Making BASIC Work for You: Reward Edition. Claude DeRossi. (Illus.). 224p. 1980. pap. text ed. 6.95 (ISBN 0-8359-4185-X). Reston.

Making Bureaucracies Work. Ed. by Carol H. Weiss & Allen H. Barton. LC 80-12774. (Sage Focus Editions: Vol. 22). (Illus.). 309p. 1980. 18.95x (ISBN 0-8039-1413-X); pap. 9.95x (ISBN 0-8039-1414-8). Sage.

Making Camping & Outdoor Gear. David Platten. LC 80-68902. (Illus.). 160p. 1981. 16.95 (ISBN 0-7153-8023-0). David & Charles.

Making Canadian Indian Policy: The Hidden Agenda 1968-1970. Sally M. Weaver. (Studies in the Structure of Power). 352p. 1980. 25.00x (ISBN 0-8020-5504-4); pap. 10.00 (ISBN 0-8020-6403-5). U of Toronto Pr.

Making Change Happen? Ed. by Dale Mann. LC 78-21849. (Orig.). 1978. pap. text ed. 14.95x (ISBN 0-8077-2548-X). Tchrs Coll.

Making Changes: A Guide to Future Oriented Education. John W. Thomas. (Education Futures: No. 6). (Illus.). (gr. 6-12). 1981. pap. text ed. 8.95 (ISBN 0-88280-081-7); tchrs' ed. 19.95 (ISBN 0-88280-082-5). ETC Pubns.

Making Children's Costumes. Priscilla Lobley. LC 77-185256. 7.95 (ISBN 0-8008-5077-7, K872). Taplinger.

Making Cities Work: The Dynamics of Urban Innovation. Ed. by David Morley et al. LC 79-5489. 288p. 1980. lib. bdg. 30.00x (ISBN 0-89158-656-3, Pub. by Croom Helm England). Westview.

Making Costume Dolls. Jean Greenhowe. 1974. 14.95 (ISBN 0-7134-2313-7, Pub. by Batsford England). David & Charles.

Making Costumes for Parties, Plays & Holidays. Alice Gilbreath. LC 73-13996. (Illus.). 96p. (gr. 3-7). 1974. PLB 6.96 (ISBN 0-688-30103-7). Morrow.

Making Decisions. Lynn Blinn. LC 79-54910. 1981. pap. 5.28 (ISBN 0-8273-1712-3); instr's manual 1.50 (ISBN 0-8273-1711-5). Delmar.

Making Decisions: A Multi-Disciplinary Introduction. 2nd. ed. Percy H. Hill et al. 1980. pap. text ed. 14.50 (ISBN 0-201-03103-5). A-W.

Making Do: How Women Survived the Thirties. Jeane Westin. LC 75-170. 360p. 1976. 9.95 o.p. (ISBN 0-695-80593-2). Follett.

Making Dolls' Clothes. Diana Walker. LC 79-56449. (Illus.). 72p. 1980. 14.95 (ISBN 0-7134-3319-1, Pub. by Batsford England). David & Charles.

Making Ends Meet: How Families Cope with Inflation & Recession. David Caplovitz. LC 79-14438. (Sage Library of Social Research: No. 86). 1979. 18.00x (ISBN 0-8039-1292-7); pap. 8.95x (ISBN 0-8039-1293-5). Sage.

Making Energy Work. Herbert L. Beierle. 1980. 5.00 (ISBN 0-686-23895-8). God Unltd U of Healing.

Making Every Moment Count. Carolyn Davis. (Illus.). 1980. 7.95 (ISBN 0-87707-225-6). CSA Pr.

Making Eyes with Madeleine Mono. Madeleine Mono. LC 80-7892. (Illus.). 128p. 1981. 10.95 (ISBN 0-690-01945-9, HarpT). Har-Row.

Making Fabric Wall Hangings. Alice Timmins. LC 71-119561. (Illus.). 1970. 9.25 (ISBN 0-8231-5024-0). Branford.

Making Federalism Work: A Study of Program Coordination at the Community Level. James L. Sundquist. 1969. 14.95 (ISBN 0-8157-8218-7); pap. 5.95 (ISBN 0-8157-8217-9). Brookings.

Making Felt Toys. Suzy Ives. (Illus.). 1971. 7.25 o.p. (ISBN 0-8231-5029-1). Branford.

Making for the Falcon: Studies in Recent Film. Jerry Holt. 1976. pap. text ed. 7.25x (ISBN 0-8191-0017-X). U Pr of Amer.

Making Foreign Economic Policy. I. M. Destler. LC 79-5119. 256p. 1980. 14.95 (ISBN 0-8157-1822-5); pap. 5.95 (ISBN 0-8157-1821-7). Brookings.

Making Furry Toys. Marianne Forster. 1972. pap. 4.95 (ISBN 0-236-15424-9, Pub. by Paul Elek). Merrimack Bk Serv.

Making Games in Wood. Katharina Zechlin. LC 80-54353. (Illus.). 80p. 1981. pap. 6.95 (ISBN 0-8069-8996-3). Sterling.

Making Gifts. Anne Hulbert. 1975. 14.95 (ISBN 0-7134-2948-8, Pub. by Batsford England). David & Charles.

Making God Real in the Orthodox Christian Home. A. M. Coniaris. 1977. pap. 4.95 (ISBN 0-937032-07-7). Light & Life Pub Co MN.

Making Good Marriages Better. Philip J. Guerin. 1973. pap. 0.95 o.p. (ISBN 0-89570-083-2). Claretian Pubns.

Making Government Work: Essays in Honor of Conley H. Dillon. Ed. by James C. Strouse et al. LC 80-8308. 478p. 1981. lib. bdg. 23.75 (ISBN 0-8191-1306-9); pap. text ed. 15.75 (ISBN 0-8191-1307-7). U Pr of Amer.

Making Hats. Peter Morgan. 1978. 11.95 (ISBN 0-7134-1078-7, Pub. by Batsford England). David & Charles.

Making Historical Costume Dolls. Jack Cassin-Scott. LC 74-26667. (Illus.). 96p. 1975. 10.00 (ISBN 0-8231-3031-2). Branford.

Making Home Furnishings. Editors of Time-Life Books. LC 75-15877. (Art of Sewing). (Illus.). (gr. 6 up). 1975. PLB 11.97 (ISBN 0-8094-1755-3, Pub. by Time-Life). Silver.

Making Ice-Cream & Other Cold Sweets. Bee Nilson. 1973. 7.95 (ISBN 0-7207-0612-2, Pub. by Michael Joseph). Merrimack Bk Serv.

Making Inequality: The Hidden Curriculum of High School Tracking. James E. Rosenbaum. LC 76-2008. 225p. 1976. 17.95 o.p. (ISBN 0-471-73605-8, Pub. by Wiley-Interscience). Wiley.

Making Inflation Pay: Jonathon's Guide to Financial Success in the 1980's. Jonathon Hefferlin. 224p. 1981. 10.95 (ISBN 0-936602-09-0). Harbor Pub CA.

Making Institutions Work. Geoffrey Vickers. LC 73-11543. 1973. 19.95 (ISBN 0-470-90689-8). Halsted Pr.

Making It. Barbara Corcoran. 176p. (YA) (gr. 7 up). 1981. 8.95 (ISBN 0-316-15731-7, Pub. by Atlantic). Little.

Making It Big: A Guide to Beauty, Health & Style for the Large Woman. Jean DuCoffe & Sherry S. Cohen. 1980. 14.95 (ISBN 0-671-25097-3). S&S.

Making It Crazy: An Ethnography of Psychiatric Clients in an American Community. Sue E. Estroff. 338p. 1981. 19.95 (ISBN 0-520-03963-7). U of Cal Pr.

Making It: Forty & Beyond, Surviving the Mid-Life Crisis. Joel Davitz & Lois Davitz. 1979. pap. 6.95 (ISBN 0-03-051561-0). Winston Pr.

Making It in Hollywood: An Actor's Guide. Fred Owens. 96p. (Orig.). 1980. pap. 5.00 (ISBN 0-936182-01-6). Diamond Heights.

Making It in Management. Raymond Dreyfack. 156p. 1980. cancelled (ISBN 0-87863-006-6). Farnswth Pub.

Making It in Management: A Behavioral Approach for Women Executives. Margaret Fenn. LC 78-17005. (Illus.). 1978. 10.95 (ISBN 0-13-547638-0, Spec); pap. 5.95 (ISBN 0-13-547620-8). P-H.

Making It in Music. Victor Rappaport. 1979. 12.95 (ISBN 0-13-547612-7, Spec); pap. 5.95 (ISBN 0-13-547604-6, Spec). P-H.

Making It on a Pastor's Pay. Manfred Holck, Jr. LC 73-18105. 1974. 4.95 o.p. (ISBN 0-687-23034-9). Abingdon.

Making It on Your First Job: When You're Young, Inexperienced & Ambitious. Peggy J. Schmidt. 288p. 1981. pap. 2.95 (ISBN 0-380-77354-6). Avon.

Making It to Number One. Jim Benagh. LC 75-42497. 1976. 10.00 (ISBN 0-396-07210-0). Dodd.

Making It Together: A Survival Manual for the Executive Family. Ronya Kozmetsky & George Kozmetsky. LC 80-69284. 1981. 12.95 (ISBN 0-02-917910-6). Free Pr.

Making Jewellery. K. J. Hartwell. LC 75-512157. 80p. 1975. 7.50 (ISBN 0-7175-0466-2). Dufour.

Making Jewelry. Eileen Deacon. LC 77-7942. (Beginning Crafts Ser.). (Illus.). (gr. k-3). 1977. PLB 9.30 (ISBN 0-8393-0116-2). Raintree Child.

Making Lampshades. Angela Fishburn. LC 77-7729. (Illus.). 1977. pap. 5.95 (ISBN 0-8069-8494-5). Sterling.

Making Large Toys & Play Equipment. S. F. King. (Illus.). 128p. 1980. 10.95 (ISBN 0-263-06399-2, Pub. by Mills & Boon England). Hippocrene Bks.

Making "Legend of the Werewolf". Edward Buscombe. (BFI Ser.). (Orig.). 1977. pap. 4.50 o.p. (ISBN 0-85170-057-8). NY Zoetrope.

Making Life Meaningful. Joseph Stein. LC 78-15347. 1979. 12.95 (ISBN 0-88229-375-3); pap. 6.95 (ISBN 0-88229-651-5). Nelson-Hall.

Making Loose Covers. Donald Porter. 1975. 17.95 (ISBN 0-7134-2911-9, Pub. by Batsford England). David & Charles.

Making MBO-R Work. Arthur C. Beck & Ellis D. Hillmar. LC 75-18151. 239p. 1975. text ed. 8.95 (ISBN 0-201-00469-0). A-W.

Making Mediterranean Furniture. Jay W. Hedden & Monte Burch. LC 72-3336. (Illus.). 1978. pap. 3.95 o.p. (ISBN 0-668-04432-2). Arco.

Making Meetings Work: A Guide for Leaders & Group Members. Leland P. Bradford. LC 76-16886. 122p. 1976. pap. 12.50 (ISBN 0-88390-122-6). Univ Assocs.

Making Miniature Toys & Dolls. Jean Greenhouse. 1980. 19.95 (ISBN 0-7134-3271-3). David & Charles.

Making Model Buildings. Stuart Dalby. (Illus.). 96p. 12.95 (ISBN 0-7137-0976-6, Pub. by Blandford Pr England). Sterling.

Making Money. Ian Andersen. LC 77-93232. 1978. 10.00 (ISBN 0-8149-0797-0). Vanguard.

Making Money with Words. Clement D. Hellyer. (Illus.). 256p. 1981. 10.95 (ISBN 0-13-547414-0, Spec); pap. 5.95 (ISBN 0-13-547406-X). P-H.

Making Moral Decisions. Richard Reichert. LC 79-63483. (Illus.). (gr. 11-12). 1979. pap. text ed. 3.30x (ISBN 0-88489-109-7); tchrs. guide 1.40x (ISBN 0-88489-118-6). St Marys.

Making Music for Money. James L. Collier. LC 75-31843. (Career Concise Guides Ser.). (Illus.). 72p. (gr. 7 up). 1976. PLB 6.45 (ISBN 0-531-02903-4). Watts.

Making Musical Miniatures. Jean Greenhowe. (Illus.). 120p. 1980. 17.95 (ISBN 0-7134-1631-9, Pub. by Batsford England). David & Charles.

Making Musical Things. Ann Wiseman. (Illus.). 64p. (gr. 2 up). 1979. 8.95 (ISBN 0-684-16114-1). Scribner.

Making New Testament Toys. Margaret Hutchings. 1975. pap. 3.95 o.p. (ISBN 0-8015-4802-0). Dutton.

Making News: A Study in the Construction of Reality. Gaye Tuchman. LC 78-53075. (Illus.). 1980. pap. text ed. 8.95 (ISBN 0-02-932960-4). Free Pr.

Making Nursery Toys. Nancy Catford. 1969. 6.95 (ISBN 0-236-17610-2, Pub. by Paul Elek). Merrimack Bk Serv.

Making Ocean Policy: The Politics of Government Organization. Ed. by Francis W. Hoole et al. (Westview Special Studies in Natural Resources & Energy Management). 300p. 1981. lib. bdg. 22.50x (ISBN 0-89158-966-X). Westview.

Making of a Code: The Issues Underlying AACR2. Ed. by Doris H. Clack. LC 80-17496. 264p. 1980. pap. 15.00 (ISBN 0-8389-0309-6). ALA.

Making of a Cook. Madeleine Kamman. LC 75-162974. 1978. pap. 8.95 (ISBN 0-689-70559-X, 238). Atheneum.

Making of a Counter Culture. Theodore Roszak. LC 69-15215. pap. 2.50 (ISBN 0-385-07329-1, A697, Anch). Doubleday.

Making of a Detective. Robert H. Millimaki. LC 76-8519. (gr. 4-6). 1976. 10.95 (ISBN 0-397-31694-1). Lippincott.

Making of a Disciple. Keith Phillips. 1981. 7.95 (ISBN 0-8007-1181-5). Revell.

Making of a Don. Frederick Notarianni. 176p. 1981. 9.00 (ISBN 0-682-49685-5). Exposition.

Making of a Library: The Academic Library in Transition. Robert S. Taylor. LC 71-180245. (Information Sciences Ser). 1972. 22.95 o.p. (ISBN 0-471-84831-X, Pub. by Wiley-Interscience). Wiley.

Making of a Missionary. J. Herbert Kane. 160p. 1975. pap. 4.45 (ISBN 0-8010-5358-7). Baker Bk.

Making of a Nation, 1775-1789. Richard B. Morris. LC 63-8572. (Life History of the United States). (Illus.). (gr. 5 up). 1974. PLB 9.96 (ISBN 0-8094-0551-2, Pub. by Time-Life). Silver.

Making of a New Eastern Question: British Palestine Policy & the Origins of Israel, 1917-1925. D. E. Knox. 1981. 17.95 (ISBN 0-8132-0555-7). Cath U Pr.

Making of a New Europe: R. W. Seton-Watson & the Last Years of Austria-Hungary. Hugh Seton-Watson & Christopher Seton-Watson. 528p. 1981. 50.00 (ISBN 0-295-95792-1). U of Wash Pr.

Making of a Pastoral Person. Gerald R. Niklas. 159p. (Orig.). 1981. pap. 5.95 (ISBN 0-8189-0409-7). Alba.

Making of a Southerner. Katharine D. Lumpkin. LC 80-24622. (Brown Thrasher Ser.). 264p. 1981. pap. 6.95 (ISBN 0-8203-0545-6). U of Ga Pr.

Making of a State. Thomas G. Masaryk. 1970. Repr. of 1927 ed. 16.50 (ISBN 0-86527-119-4). Fertig.

Making of a Television Commercial. H. Ted Busch & Terry Landeck. LC 80-23192. (Illus.). 228p. 1981. 10.95 (ISBN 0-02-518830-5). Macmillan.

Making of a Television Series: A Case Study in the Sociology of Culture. Philip Elliott. LC 79-89075. (Communication & Society: Vol. 2). (Illus.). 1979. 18.50x (ISBN 0-8039-1355-9); pap. 8.95x (ISBN 0-8039-1356-7). Sage.

Making of a Tory Humanist. Michael H. Friedman. LC 79-10968. 1979. 22.50x (ISBN 0-231-04668-5). Columbia U Pr.

Making of Adolph Hitler. Eugene Davidson. (Illus.). 1977. 22.95 o.s.i. (ISBN 0-02-529700-7). Macmillan.

Making of American Politics. Michael J. Heale. LC 77-24250. 1978. text ed. 21.00x (ISBN 0-582-48735-8); pap. text ed. 12.95x (ISBN 0-582-48736-6). Longman.

Making of an Entrepreneur: Keys to Your Success. George C. Ballas & Dave Hollas. (Illus.). 1980. 12.95 (ISBN 0-13-546788-8, Spec); pap. 6.95 (ISBN 0-13-546770-5). P-H.

Making of Black Revolutionaries: A Memoir. J. Forman. 1972. 12.50 o.s.i. (ISBN 0-02-539700-1). Macmillan.

Making of Blind Men. Robert A. Scott. 160p. 1981. pap. 4.95 (ISBN 0-87855-687-7). Transaction Bks.

Making of Books. 5th ed. Sean Jennett. 1974. 24.00 o.p. (ISBN 0-571-04786-6, Pub. by Faber & Faber). Merrimack Bk Serv.

Making of Child & Family Policy. Harold C. Wallach. Ed. by Lyn Chambers. (AAAS Selected Symposium Ser.: No. 56). 160p. 1980. lib. bdg. 20.00x (ISBN 0-89158-956-2). Westview.

Making of China: Main Themes in Premodern Chinese History. Chun-shu Chang. (Illus.). 352p. 1975. Repr. 17.95 (ISBN 0-13-545640-1). P-H.

Making of Christian Doctrine. Maurice F. Wiles. 1967. 23.95 (ISBN 0-521-06803-7); pap. 7.95x (ISBN 0-521-09962-5). Cambridge U Pr.

Making of Christianity & the Greek Spirit. Evelyn Capel. 1980. pap. 10.75 (ISBN 0-903540-41-X, Pub. by Floris Books). St George Bk Serv.

Making of Cities. Walter Bor. (Illus.). 1972. 24.00x (ISBN 0-249-44071-7). Intl Ideas.

Making of Contemporary Europe. R. Ben Jones. 225p. 1981. text ed. 38.50x (ISBN 0-8419-0668-8); pap. text ed. 19.50x (ISBN 0-8419-0669-6). Holmes & Meier.

Making of Decisions. William J. Gore & James Dyson. LC 64-23084. 1964. 15.95 (ISBN 0-02-912590-1). Free Pr.

Making of Domesday Book. Vivian H. Galbraith. LC 80-2224. 1981. Repr. of 1961 ed. 36.50 (ISBN 0-404-18761-7). AMS Pr.

Making of Economic Society. 6th ed. Robert L. Heilbroner. (Illus.). 1980. pap. text ed. 11.95 (ISBN 0-13-545830-7). P-H.

Making of Elizabethan Foreign Policy, 1558-1603. R. B. Wernham. (Illus.). 120p. 1981. 15.50x (ISBN 0-520-03966-1); pap. 3.95x (ISBN 0-520-03974-2, CAMPUS 244). U of Cal Pr.

Making of Geology: Earth Science in Britain, 1660-1815. Roy Porter. LC 76-56220. 1977. 35.50 (ISBN 0-521-21521-8). Cambridge U Pr.

Making of George Washington. 2nd ed. William H. Wilbur. LC 73-85936. 1974. pap. 1.95 (ISBN 0-912530-02-2). Patriotic Educ.

Making of Golden Gate Park: The Early Years, 1865-1906. Raymond Clary. LC 79-51159. (Illus.). 224p. 1980. 25.00 (ISBN 0-89395-024-6); pap. 10.95 (ISBN 0-89395-025-4). Cal Living Bks.

Making of Israel's Army. Yigal Allon. LC 73-133424. (Illus.). 1970. 10.00x o.s.i. (ISBN 0-87663-137-5). Universe.

Making of James Clavell's Shogun. Frwd. by James Clavell. (Illus.). 1980. pap. 8.95 (ISBN 0-440-55709-7, Delta). Dell.

Making of Kew. Madeleine Bringham. (Folio Miniature Ser.). 1975. 4.95 (ISBN 0-7181-1304-7, Pub. by Michael Joseph). Merrimack Bk Serv.

Making of Mankind. Richard E. Leakey. (Illus.). 256p. 1981. 25.00 (ISBN 0-525-15055-2). Dutton.

Making of Men. Paul Weiss. LC 67-10046. 167p. 1967. 10.95x (ISBN 0-8093-0264-0). S Ill U Pr.

Making of Men. Paul Weiss. LC 67-10046. (Arcturus Books Paperbacks). 167p. 1969. pap. 7.95 (ISBN 0-8093-0405-8). S Ill U Pr.

Making of Menander's Comedy. Sander M. Goldberg. 1980. 17.50 (ISBN 0-520-04250-6). U of Cal Pr.

Making of Modern Africa, Vol. 2: The Late 19th Century to the Present Day. E. A. Ayandele et al. (Growth of African Civilization Ser). (Orig.). 1971. pap. text ed. 7.75x (ISBN 0-391-00149-3). Humanities.

Making of Modern Belize. C. H. Grant. LC 75-36022. (Cambridge Commonwealth Ser.). (Illus.). 400p. 1976. 49.50 (ISBN 0-521-20731-2). Cambridge U Pr.

Making of Modern Drama. Richard Gilman. LC 74-1171. 292p. 1974. 10.00 o.p. (ISBN 0-374-20018-1); pap. 4.50 (ISBN 0-374-51148-9). FS&G.

Making of Modern Greece: From Byzantium to Independence. D. A. Zakythinos. Tr. by K. R. Johnstone from Greek. 235p. 1976. 21.50x o.p. (ISBN 0-87471-796-5). Rowman.

Making of Modern Japan: An Introduction. Kenneth B. Pyle. (Civilization & Society Ser.). 1978. pap. text ed. 6.95x (ISBN 0-669-84657-0). Heath.

Making of Our America. (gr. 3). 1974. pap. text ed. 7.20 (ISBN 0-205-03891-3, 8038910); tchrs'. guide 11.40 (ISBN 0-205-03892-1, 8038929). Allyn.

Making of Political Women: A Study of Socialization & Role Conflict. Rita M. Kelly & Mary A. Boutilier. LC 77-17081. 1978. text ed. 18.95 (ISBN 0-88229-290-0). Nelson-Hall.

Making of Politicians: Studies from Africa & Asia. Ed. by W. H. Morris-Jones. (Commonwealth Papers: No. 20). 272p. 1976. pap. text ed. 26.00x (ISBN 0-485-17620-3, Athlone Pr). Humanities.

Making of Post-Christian Britain. Alan D. Gilbert. 192p. 1980. text ed. 23.00 cased (ISBN 0-582-48563-0). Longman.

Making of Psychological Anthropology. Ed. by George D. Spindler. LC 76-24597. 1978. 35.00x (ISBN 0-520-03320-5); pap. 10.75x (ISBN 0-520-03957-2). U of Cal Pr.

Making of Psychology. Richard Evans. 1976. text ed. 6.95x o.p. (ISBN 0-394-31153-1). Random.

Making of Shakespeare's Dramatic Poetry. G. R. Hibbard. 184p. 1981. 17.50x (ISBN 0-8020-2400-9); pap. 7.50 (ISBN 0-8020-6424-8). U of Toronto Pr.

Making of South-East Asia: Vol. 2, The Western Impact--Economic & Social Change. D. J. Tate. (Illus.). 632p. 1979. text ed. 49.50x (ISBN 0-19-580332-9). Oxford U Pr.

Making of Southeast Asia. G. Coedes. Tr. by H. M. Wright. (gr. 9-12). 1969. 15.00x (ISBN 0-520-00248-2); pap. 3.95x (ISBN 0-520-01420-0, CAMPUS20). U of Cal Pr.

Making of Space 1999. Tim Heald. 1976. pap. 1.95 o.p. (ISBN 0-345-25265-9). Ballantine.

Making of the American Mistress. Melissa Sands. (Orig.). 1981. pap. 2.50 (ISBN 0-425-04751-2). Berkley Pub.

Making of the British Countryside. Ron Freethy. LC 80-68688. (Illus.). 192p. 1981. 24.00 (ISBN 0-7153-8012-5). David & Charles.

Making of the Central Pennines. J. Porter. 160p. 1980. 20.85x (ISBN 0-903485-80-X, Pub. by Allan Pubs England). State Mutual Bk.

Making of the Diplomatic Mind: The Training Outlook & Style of United States Foreign Service Officers 1908-31. Robert D. Schulzinger. LC 75-15790. 260p. 1975. 20.00x (ISBN 0-8195-4086-2, Pub. by Wesleyan U Pr). Columbia U Pr.

Making of the Habsburg Monarchy: Fifteen Fifty to Seventeen Hundred. R. J. Evans. 1979. 59.00x (ISBN 0-19-822560-1). Oxford U Pr.

Making of the Modern Homosexual. Ed. by Kenneth Plummer. 1980. 22.50x (ISBN 0-389-20159-6). B&N.

Making of the Modern World: Eighteen Fifteen to Nineteen Fourteen. Ed. by Norman F. Cantor & Michael S. Werthman. LC 67-16644. (AHM Structure of European History Ser.: Vol. 5). 240p. 1967. pap. text ed. 5.95x (ISBN 0-88295-714-7). AHM Pub.

Making of the Movie "Jaws". Edith Blake. 1975. pap. 1.50 o.p. (ISBN 0-345-24882-1). Ballantine.

Making of the New Poor Law: The Politics of Inquiry, Enactment, & Implementation, 1832-1839. Anthony Brundage. 1978. 15.00 (ISBN 0-8135-0855-X). Rutgers U Pr.

Making of the President Nineteen Sixty. Theodore H. White. LC 79-25849. (gr. 10 up). 1961. 10.00 o.p. (ISBN 0-689-10291-7). Atheneum.

Making of the President Nineteen Sixty. Theodore H. White. 1967. pap. 2.00 (ISBN 0-451-61874-2, ME1874, Ment). NAL.

Making of the President, Nineteen Sixty. Theodore H. White. LC 79-25849. 1980. pap. 8.95 (ISBN 0-689-70600-6, 259). Atheneum.

Making of the President Nineteen Sixty-Four. Theodore H. White. 1966. pap. 1.75 o.p. (ISBN 0-451-61255-8, ME1255, Ment). NAL.

Making of the Reparation & Economic Sections of the Treaty. Bernard M. Baruch. LC 68-9615. 1970. Repr. 17.50 (ISBN 0-86527-120-8). Fertig.

Making of the Soviet State Apparatus. Olga A. Narkiewicz. 1970. text ed. 11.00x (ISBN 0-7190-0401-2). Humanities.

Making of the Third Party System: Voters & Parties in Illinois, Eighteen Fifty to Eighteen Seventy-Six. Stephen L. Hansen. Ed. by Robert Berkhofer. (Studies in American History & Culture). 277p. 1980. 27.95 (ISBN 0-8357-1096-3, Pub. by UMI Res Pr). Univ Microfilms.

Making of the Vedanta. T. G. Mainkar. 1980. 14.00x (ISBN 0-8364-0623-0, Pub. by Ajanta). South Asia Bks.

Making of Theatre: From Drama to Performance. Robert W. Corrigan. 1980. pap. text ed. 8.95x (ISBN 0-673-15403-3). Scott F.

Making of Tomorrow (1940-Present) The Educational Research Council. (American Adventure Concepts & Inquiry Ser). (gr. 8). 1977. pap. text ed. 9.40 (ISBN 0-205-04627-4, 8046271). Allyn.

Making of United States International Economic Policy: Principles, Problems, & Proposals for Reform. Stephen D. Cohen. LC 77-7469. (Praeger Special Studies). 1977. text ed. 24.95 (ISBN 0-03-021926-4); pap. 10.95 (ISBN 0-03-021921-3). Praeger.

Making Old Testament Toys. Margaret Hutchings. 1975. pap. 3.95 o.p. (ISBN 0-8015-4804-7). Dutton.

Making Paper Flowers. Susanne Strose. LC 69-19490. (Little Craft Book Ser). (Illus.). (gr. 6 up). 1969. 4.95 o.p. (ISBN 0-8069-5130-3); PLB 5.89 o.p. (ISBN 0-8069-5131-1). Sterling.

Making Patterns for Children's Clothes. Brenda Redmile. (Illus.). 120p. 1980. 17.95 (ISBN 0-7134-2141-X, Pub. by Batsford England). David & Charles.

Making Peace in the Global Village. Robert M. Brown. LC 80-27213. (Orig.). 1981. pap. 5.95 (ISBN 0-664-24343-6). Westminster.

Making People Laugh. Anton Brooks. (Illus.). 1980. pap. 12.95 o.p. (ISBN 0-930490-18-5). Future Shop.

Making People Pay. Paul Rock. (International Library of Sociology). 1973. 25.00x (ISBN 0-7100-7684-3). Routledge & Kegan.

Making Photograms. Verna Haffer. Date not set. 12.50 o.p. (ISBN 0-8038-4650-9). Hastings.

Making Photographs. Ross Harris. 194p. 1979. pap. 9.95 (ISBN 0-442-25177-7). Van Nos Reinhold.

Making Play. John Jacob. (Orig.). 1975. pap. 2.50x (ISBN 0-915316-21-8); pap. 3.00 ltd. signed ed. (ISBN 0-915316-22-6). Pentagram.

Making Pop-up Greeting Cards. Eric Kenneway. (gr. 9-12). 8.95 (ISBN 0-263-05065-3). Transatlantic.

Making Pottery Figures. Marjorie Drawbell. (gr. 9 up). 6.95 (ISBN 0-85458-080-8); pap. 7.50 (ISBN 0-85458-081-6). Transatlantic.

Making Puppets & Puppet Theatres. Joan Moloney. LC 74-78175. (Illus.). 1974. 9.95 (ISBN 0-8119-0242-0). Fell.

Making Puppets Come Alive: A Method of Learning & Teaching Hand Puppetry. Larry Engler & Carol Fijan. LC 72-6623. (Illus.). 192p. 1980. pap. 7.95 (ISBN 0-8008-5073-4). Taplinger.

Making Reality: Coping with Limitations Successfully. James P. Meade, Jr. 1981. 7.50 (ISBN 0-8062-1652-2). Carlton.

Making Robots. Dave Ross. (gr. 1-3). 1980. PLB 7.90 (ISBN 0-531-04142-5). Watts.

Making Rugs for Pleasure & Profit. Marion Koenig & Gill Speirs. LC 80-17110. (Illus.). 80p. 1980. 10.95 (ISBN 0-668-05079-9, 5079-9). Arco.

Making Schools More Effective: New Directions from Follow Through. Ed. by W. Ray Rhine. (Educational Psychology Ser.). 1981. price not set (ISBN 0-12-587060-4). Acad Pr.

Making Schools Work: A Reporter's Journey Through Some of America's Most Remarkable Schools. Robert Benjamin. 208p. 1981. 12.95 (ISBN 0-8264-0040-X). Continuum.

Making Sense. Geoffrey Sampson. 224p. 1980. text ed. 16.95x (ISBN 0-19-215950-X). Oxford U Pr.

Making Sense of Grammer. Jordan & LeMaster. LC 79-24986. 1980. pap. 6.95x (ISBN 0-8077-2577-3). Tchrs Coll.

Making Sense of History. Peter Skagestad. 1975. pap. text ed. 10.50 (ISBN 8-200-01460-6, Dist. by Columbia U Pr). Universitet.

Making Sense of It: Patterns in English Grammar. Steven Zemelman. 1980. pap. text ed. 6.95 (ISBN 0-13-547570-8). P-H.

Making Sense of Money. Vicki Cobb. LC 74-131256. (Finding-Out Books for Science & Social Studies, Grades 1-4). (Illus.). (gr. 2-4). 1971. PLB 6.95 (ISBN 0-8193-0439-5, Pub. by Parents). Enslow Pubs.

Making Sneakers. Bruce McMillan. (gr. k-3). 1980. pap. 6.95 (ISBN 0-395-29161-5). HM.

Making Soft Dinos. Linda Bourke. LC 79-56337. (Illus.). 76p. (gr. 5 up). 1980. lib. bdg. 6.99 (ISBN 0-8178-0012-3). Harvey.

Making Soft Furnishings. Caroline Sullivan. LC 78-74080. (Penny Pincher Ser.). 1979. 2.95 (ISBN 0-7153-7752-3). David & Charles.

Making Soft Toys. Freya Jaffke. Tr. by Rosemary Gebert from Ger. LC 80-66665. Orig. Title: Spielzeug Von Eltern Selbstgemacht. (Illus.). 1981. pap. 6.95 (ISBN 0-89742-044-6). Dawne-Leigh.

Making Space Puppets. Dave Ross. (gr. 1-3). 1980. PLB 7.90 (ISBN 0-531-04143-3). Watts.

Making Systems Work: The Psychology of Business Systems. William C. Ramsgard. LC 77-5933. (Business Data Processing Ser.). 1977. 29.50 (ISBN 0-471-01522-9, Pub. by Wiley-Interscience). Wiley.

Making Television: A Video Guide for Teachers. John Lebaron. (Orig.). 1981. pap. 12.50 (ISBN 0-8077-2636-2). Tchrs Coll.

Making the Fascist State. Herbert W. Schneider. LC 67-24597. 1968. Repr. 16.50 (ISBN 0-86527-121-6). Fertig.

Making the Grade: Careers in E. E. Teaching. Judy Bradley & Jane Silverleaf. 1979. text ed. 20.75x (ISBN 0-85633-179-1, NFER); pap. text ed. 15.25x (ISBN 0-85633-177-5, NFER). Humanities.

Making the House Fall Down. Beatrice Hawley. LC 77-82222. 64p. 1977. pap. 4.95 (ISBN 0-914086-19-7). Alicejamesbooks.

Making the Media Revolution: A Handbook of Video-Tape Production. Peter Weiner. LC 72-92867. (Illus.). 224p. 1973. 12.95 (ISBN 0-02-625690-8). Macmillan.

Making the Most of Family Living. Edlen Chalmers. LC 79-84303. 1979. pap. 5.95 (ISBN 0-8163-0244-8). Pacific Pr Pub Assn.

Making the Most of Fruit on Foodservice Menus. Ed. by Jule Wilkinson. LC 76-51342. (Foodservice Menu Planning Ser.). (Illus.). 1977. 15.95 (ISBN 0-8436-2150-8). CBI Pub.

Making the Most of Management Consulting Services. Jerome H. Fuchs. LC 74-6808. 224p. 1975. 15.95 (ISBN 0-8144-5371-6). Am Mgmt.

Making the Most of Marin. Patricia Arrigoni. (Illus., Orig.). 1981. pap. 7.95 (ISBN 0-89141-108-9). Presidio Pr.

Making the Most of Marriage. 5th ed. Paul H. Landis. 624p. 1975. text ed. 17.95 (ISBN 0-13-547968-1). P-H.

Making the Most of the Least: Alternative Development for Poor Nations. Ed. by Leonard Berry & Robert W. Kates. LC 79-11619. 1980. text ed. 35.00x (ISBN 0-8419-0434-0). Holmes & Meier.

Making the Most of Your First Job. Catalyst Staff. 288p. 1981. 11.95 (ISBN 0-399-12609-0). Putnam.

Making the News. Elliot Golding. (Illus.). 241p. 1979. text ed. 35.00x (ISBN 0-582-50460-0). Longman.

Making the Scene. William Sheldon & Nina C. Woessner. (Orig.). (RL 6). 1972. pap. text ed. 4.96 (ISBN 0-205-03100-5, 5231000); tchrs'. guide 2.40 (ISBN 0-205-03098-X, 5230985); dup. masters 20.00 (ISBN 0-205-03099-8, 5230993). Allyn.

Making the Training Process Work. Donald F. Michalak & Edwin G. Yager. LC 78-17907. (Continuing Management Education Ser.). 1979. text ed. 13.95 scp (ISBN 0-06-044429-0, HarpC). Har-Row.

Making Things Better by Making Them Worse. Allen Fay. LC 77-81960. 1978. 7.95 o.p. (ISBN 0-8015-4807-1). Dutton.

Making Thoughts Become: A Handbook for Teachers & Adults. Betty B. Taylor. (Illus.). 1978. pap. 4.25x (ISBN 0-933198-00-0, Pub. by Childs Art Carnival). Pub Ctr Cult Res.

Making Three-Dimensional Pictures. Robin Capon. 1976. 16.95 o.p. (ISBN 0-7134-3109-1, Pub. by Batsford England). David & Charles.

Making Touch. Gary Elder. (Illus.). 40p. 1981. pap. 4.00 (ISBN 0-914974-28-9). Holmgangers.

Making Toys in Wood. Charles H. Hayward. LC 74-6435. (Illus.). 158p. 1974. 8.95 o.p. (ISBN 0-8069-8498-8); pap. 4.95 o.p. (ISBN 0-8069-8496-1). Sterling.

Making Toys in Wood. rev. ed. Charles H. Hayward. LC 80-52501. (Illus.). 168p. 1980. pap. 5.95. Sterling.

Making Tracks. Rob Phillips. 1981. pap. 2.25 (ISBN 0-8439-0888-2, Leisure Bks). Nordon Pubns.

Making UFOs. Dave Ross. (gr. 1-3). 1980. PLB 7.90 (ISBN 0-531-04144-1). Watts.

Making Vocational Choices: A Theory of Careers. John L. Holland. LC 73-4847. (Counseling & Human Development Ser). (Illus.). 192p. 1973. pap. text ed. 10.95 (ISBN 0-13-547810-3). P-H.

Making Wage Incentives Work. H. K. Von Kaas. LC 75-138572. 1971. 17.50 o.p. (ISBN 0-8144-5251-5). Am Mgmt.

Making Waves with Creative Problem-Solving. Vaune Ainsworth-Land & Norma Fletcher. (Illus.). 52p. (Orig.). 1979. pap. text ed. 3.95 (ISBN 0-914634-66-6, 7913). DOK Pubs.

Making Wood Signs. Patrick Spielman. LC 80-54342. (Illus.). 144p. 1981. 10.95 (ISBN 0-8069-5434-5); lib. bdg. 9.89 (ISBN 0-8069-5435-3); pap. 6.95. Sterling.

Making Wooden Toys. Roger Polley. 1978. 17.95 (ISBN 0-7134-0823-5, Pub. by Batsford England). David & Charles.

Making Your Children's Clothes. Gail Fox. (Penny Pinchers Ser.). 1978. 2.95 (ISBN 0-7153-7549-0). David & Charles.

Making Your Lawn & Garden Grow. Elvin McDonald. 7.95 (ISBN 0-916752-07-0). Green Hill.

Making Your News Service More Effective. Ed. by Joel S. Berger. 1978. looseleaf bdg. 16.50 (ISBN 0-89964-029-X). CASE.

Making Your Own Telescope. rev. ed. Allyn J. Thompson. (Illus.). 1980. Repr. of 1947 ed. 8.95 (ISBN 0-933346-12-3). Sky Pub.

Making Your Practice More Malpractice-Proof. 1975. pap. 3.50 (ISBN 0-87489-059-4). Med Economics.

Makioka Sisters. Junichiro Tanizaki. Tr. by Edward T. Seidensticker from Jap. (Perigee Japanese Library). 538p. 1981. pap. 6.95 (ISBN 0-399-50520-2, Perigee). Putnam.

Makko-Ho: Five Minutes' Physical Fitness. Haruka Nagai. LC 72-84812. (Illus.). 80p. 1972. pap. 4.95 o.p. (ISBN 0-87040-170-X). Japan Pubns.

Maksim Gorki. Gerhard Habermann. Tr. by Ernestine Schlant. LC 75-129114. (Modern Literature Ser.). 1971. 10.95 (ISBN 0-8044-2326-1); pap. 3.45 (ISBN 0-8044-6239-9). Ungar.

Maky a Slip. Colin Mackenzie. 9.50 (ISBN 0-392-07132-0, SpS). Soccer.

Malacca, Singapore & Indonesia. M. Leifer. (International Straits of the World: No. 2). 288p. 1978. 35.00x (ISBN 90-286-0778-1). Sijthoff & Noordhoff.

Maladies of Marcel Proust. Bernard Straus. LC 80-11204. 175p. 1980. text ed. 24.50x (ISBN 0-8419-0546-0). Holmes & Meier.

Malagasy & the Europeans. Phares M. Mutibwa. (Ibadan History Ser). (Illus.). 395p. 1974. text ed. 18.00x (ISBN 0-391-00348-8). Humanities.

Malagasy Republic. Anthony D. Marshall. LC 72-4337. (First Bks). (Illus.). 96p. (gr. 5-9). 1972. PLB 4.90 o.p. (ISBN 0-531-00780-4). Watts.

Malago's Visit. Craig Salcido. (Orig.). 1980. pap. 1.75 (ISBN 0-505-51488-5). Tower Bks.

Malamud Reader. Bernard Malamud. 528p. 1967. pap. 9.95 (ISBN 0-374-51513-1). FS&G.

Malaria: Epidemiology, Chemotherapy, Morphology & Metabolism, Vol. 1. Ed. by Julius P. Kreier. LC 80-530. 1980. 49.00 (ISBN 0-12-426101-9). Acad Pr.

Malaria: Pathology, Vecter Studies & Culture, Vol. 2. Ed. by Julius P. Kreier. LC 80-530. 1980. 38.50 (ISBN 0-12-426102-7). Acad Pr.

Malatesta of Rimini & the Papal State. P. J. Jones. LC 72-87178. (Illus.). 360p. 1974. 49.95 (ISBN 0-521-20042-3). Cambridge U Pr.

Malawi. Robert B. Boeder. (World Bibliographical Ser.). 165p. 1980. 28.50 (ISBN 0-903450-22-4). ABC Clio.

Malawi in Pictures. Sterling Publishing Company Editors. LC 72-95206. (Visual Geography Ser.). (Illus.). 64p. (gr. 6 up). 1973. pap. 2.95 (ISBN 0-8069-1166-2). Sterling.

Malay Archipelago. A. R. Wallace. Date not set. 12.50 (ISBN 0-8446-3129-9). Peter Smith.

Malay Kinship & Marriage in Singapore. Judith Djamour. (Monographs on Social Anthropology: No. 21). (Orig.). 1959. pap. text ed. 10.50x (ISBN 0-485-19621-2, Athlone Pr). Humanities.

Malayan Forest Primates: Ten Years' Study in a Tropical Rain Forest. Ed. by David J. Chivers. 375p. 1980. 42.50. Plenum Pub.

Malayan Lower Carboniferous Fossils & Their Bearing on the Visean Palaeogeography of Asia. Helen M. Muir-Wood. (Illus.). 118p. 1948. 11.50x (ISBN 0-565-00374-7, Pub. by Brit Mus Nat Hist England). Sabbot-Natural Hist Bks.

Malaysia. Phillip Purcell. (Nations & Peoples Library). (Illus.). 1965. 8.50x o.s.i. (ISBN 0-8027-2112-5); pap. 3.50 o.s.i. (ISBN 0-8027-7059-2). Walker & Co.

Malaysia. Lim H. Tee. (World Bibliographical Ser.: No. 12). 1981. write for info. (ISBN 0-903450-23-2). Abc-Clio.

Malaysia & Singapore. Gladys Nichol. (Batsford Travel Ser.). (Illus.). 1978. 12.95 o.s.i. (ISBN 0-7134-0839-1). Hippocrene Bks.

Malaysia & Singapore. Frederick K. Poole. LC 74-13439. (Illus.). 92p. (gr. 5-8). 1975. PLB 3.90 o.p. (ISBN 0-531-02778-3). Watts.

Malaysia: Development Patterns & Policy, 1947 to 1971. V. V. Bhanoji Rae. 270p. 1981. 17.50 (ISBN 0-8214-0512-8). Swallow.

Malaysia: Economic Expansion & National Unity. John Gullick. (Illus.). 272p. 1980. lib. bdg. 25.00x (ISBN 0-86531-089-0). Westview.

Malaysia: Growth & Equity in a Multiracial Society. Kevin Young et al. LC 79-3677. (World Bank Country Economic Report Ser.). (Illus.). 368p. 1980. text ed. 25.00 (ISBN 0-8018-2384-6); pap. text ed. 7.95 (ISBN 0-8018-2385-4). Johns Hopkins.

Malaysia-Indonesia Conflict. Ed. by Avrahm G. Mezerik. 1965. pap. 15.00 (ISBN 0-685-13205-6, 86). Intl Review.

Malaysia's Parliamentary System: Representative Politics & Policymaking in a Divided Society. Lloyd D. Musolf & J. Frederick Springer. (Westview Relica Edition). 1979. lib. bdg. 20.00x (ISBN 0-89158-460-9). Westview.

Malcolm. James Purdy. 1980. pap. 3.95 (ISBN 0-14-005595-9). Penguin.

Malcolm Forbes: Peripatetic Millionaire. Arthur Jones. LC 77-6885. (Illus.). 1977. 10.00 o.s.i. (ISBN 0-06-012204-8, HarpT). Har-Row.

Malcolm Lowry. Richard H. Costa. LC 75-185451. (World Authors Ser.: Canada: No. 217). lib. bdg. 10.95 (ISBN 0-8057-2548-2). Twayne.

Malcolm Lowry. Daniel B. Dodson. LC 70-126542. (Columbia Essays on Modern Writers Ser.: No. 51). (Orig.). 1970. pap. 2.00 (ISBN 0-231-03244-7, MW51). Columbia U Pr.

Malcolm Lowry: His Art & Early Life. Muriel C. Bradbrook. (Illus.). 170p. 1975. 28.50 (ISBN 0-521-20473-9); pap. 7.95x (ISBN 0-521-09985-4). Cambridge U Pr.

Malcolm Muggeridge: A Life. Ian Hunter. 1980. 13.95 (ISBN 0-8407-4084-0). Nelson.

Malcolm X. John H. Clarke. 1969. 7.95 o.s.i. (ISBN 0-02-525850-8). Macmillan.

Malcontent. John Marston. Ed. by M. L. Wine. LC 64-17228. (Regents Renaissance Drama Ser). 1964. 8.50x (ISBN 0-8032-0277-6); pap. 3.95x (ISBN 0-8032-5276-5, BB 206, Bison). U of Nebr Pr.

Male - Female. William Steig. LC 79-171491. (Illus.). 128p. 1972. 6.95 (ISBN 0-374-20092-0); pap. 3.95 (ISBN 0-374-51011-3, N430). FS&G.

Male Accessory Sex Organs: Structure & Function in Mammals. Ed. by David Brandes. 1974. 60.00 (ISBN 0-12-125650-2). Acad Pr.

Male & Female: Christian Approaches to Sexuality. Ruth T. Barnhouse & Urban T. Holmes. (Orig.). 1976. pap. 4.95 (ISBN 0-8164-2118-8). Crossroad NY.

Male & Female Graduate Students: The Question of Equal Opportunity. Lewis C. Solmon. LC 75-43725. (Special Studies). 1976. text ed. 25.95 (ISBN 0-275-22870-3). Praeger.

Male & Female Under 18. Compiled by Nancy Larrick & Eve Merriam. (YA) 1973. pap. 1.50 (ISBN 0-380-00711-8, 76448, Discus). Avon.

Male-Female Language: With a Comprehensive Bibliography. Mary R. Key. LC 74-19105. (Illus.). 1975. 10.00 (ISBN 0-8108-0748-3). Scarecrow.

Male Fertility & Sterility. R. E. Mancini & L. Martini. 1975. 74.00 (ISBN 0-12-467250-7). Acad Pr.

Male Homosexual in Literature: A Bibliography. Ian Young. LC 75-25611. 1975. 11.00 (ISBN 0-8108-0861-7). Scarecrow.

Male Mid-Life Crisis. Nancy Mayer. LC 73-79637. 1978. 8.95 o.p. (ISBN 0-385-01529-1). Doubleday.

Male Model. Charles Hix & Michael Taylor. (Illus.). 192p. 1980. pap. 7.95 (ISBN 0-312-50938-3). St Martin.

Male Novelists & Their Female Voices: Literary Masquerades. Anne R. Taylor. LC 80-50841. 238p. 1981. 15.00x (ISBN 0-87875-195-5). Whitston Pub.

Male Nurse. R. G. Brown. 139p. 1973. pap. text ed. 5.00x (ISBN 0-7135-1878-2, Pub. by Bedford England). Renouf.

Male Ordeal: Role Crisis in a Changing World. Eric Skjei & Richard Rabkin. 320p. 1981. 13.95 (ISBN 0-399-12575-2, Perigee). Putnam.

Male Practice: How Doctors Manipulate Women. Robert S. Mendelson. 1981. 10.95 (ISBN 0-8092-5974-5). Contemp Bks.

Male Reproductive System: Fine Structure Analysis by Scanning & Transmission Electron Microscopy. Robert Yates & Mildred Gordon. LC 77-71435. (Illus.). 214p. 1977. 47.75 (ISBN 0-89352-004-7). Masson Pub.

Male Sexual Fantasies: The Destruction of the Feminine Personality; The Christian Mandate Against Pornography. J. R. Braun. 48p. (Orig.). 1980. pap. 1.95 (ISBN 0-933656-05-X). Trinity Pub Hse.

Male Trouble. Gilbert Cant. 1977. pap. 1.75 o.s.i. (ISBN 0-515-04378-8). Jove Pubns.

Maledicta Yearbook, 1979. Ed. by Reinhold Aman. LC 77-649633. (Maledicta: International Journal of Verbal Aggression Ser.: Vol. 3, Nos. 1-2). (Illus.). 320p. (Orig.). 1980. pap. 20.00 (ISBN 0-916500-54-3). Maledicta.

Malformations of the External Genitalia. Ed. by M. Westenfelder. (Monographs in Paediatrics: Vol. 12). (Illus.). 200p. 1981. soft cover 60.00 (ISBN 3-8055-1509-X). S Karger.

Malibu Tiles Coloring Book. Ed. by David Greenberg. (Illus.). 128p. 1980. lib. bdg. cancelled (ISBN 0-89471-118-0); pap. cancelled (ISBN 0-89471-144-X). Running Pr.

Malice in Blunderland. Thomas L. Martin, Jr. (McGraw-Hill Paperbacks Ser.). 156p. 1980. pap. 3.95 (ISBN 0-07-040634-0). McGraw.

Malice of Empire. Yao Hsin-Nung. Tr. & intro. by Jeremy Ingalls. LC 69-19942. 1970. 15.75x (ISBN 0-520-01560-6). U of Cal Pr.

Malignancy & the Hemostatic System. Ed. by Maria B. Donati et al. (Monographs of the Mario Negri Institute for Pharmacological Research). 148p. 1981. text ed. 17.00 (ISBN 0-89004-463-5). Raven.

Malignant Melanoma. Irving M. Ariel. 544p. 1981. 42.50 (ISBN 0-8385-6114-4). ACC.

Malignant Melanoma. Alfred W. Kopf et al. LC 78-71687. (Illus.). 256p. 1979. 57.25 (ISBN 0-89352-040-3). Masson Pub.

Malignant Melanoma: Clinical & Histological Diagnosis. Vincent J. McGovern. LC 76-3793. 1976. 36.95 (ISBN 0-471-58417-7, Pub. by Wiley Medical). Wiley.

Malignant Neglect. Environmental Defense Fund & Robert H. Boyle. LC 79-22826. (Illus.). 1980. pap. 3.95 (ISBN 0-686-59861-X, Vin). Random.

Malinki of Malawi. Josephine C. Edwards. LC 78-55903. (Destiny Ser.). 1978. pap. 4.95 (ISBN 0-8163-0089-5, 13054-2). Pacific Pr Pub Assn.

Malka - A Total Celebration (a survival manual) Malka Golden-Wolfe. LC 80-53000. (Illus., Orig.). 1980. pap. 5.85 (ISBN 0-937946-00-1). Univ Goddess.

Mallarme & the Art of Being Difficult. M. Bowie. LC 77-82488. 1978. 29.95 (ISBN 0-521-21813-6). Cambridge U Pr.

Mallen Girl. Catherine Cookson. 288p. 1981. pap. 2.50 (ISBN 0-553-13933-9). Bantam.

Mallen Streak. Catherine Cookson. 288p. 1981. pap. 2.50 (ISBN 0-553-13932-0). Bantam.

Mallory of Everest. Showell Styles. LC 68-20610. (Illus.). (gr. 7 up). 1968. 4.95 o.s.i. (ISBN 0-02-788540-2). Macmillan.

Mallos, Megarsos, Antioche du Pyramos. F. Imhoof-Blumer. 37p. (Fr.). 1979. pap. 5.00 (ISBN 0-916710-58-0). Obol Intl.

Mally. Sandra Heath. 224p. (Orig.). 1980. pap. 1.75 (ISBN 0-451-09342-9, E9342, Sig). NAL.

Malnourished Mind. Elie A. Shneour. LC 73-9175. 216p. 1974. 6.95 o.p. (ISBN 0-385-03909-3, Anchor Pr); pap. 2.95 o.p. (ISBN 0-385-00835-X, Anch). Doubleday.

Malnutrition & Retarded Human Development. Sohan L. Manocha. (Illus.). 400p. 1972. 39.50 (ISBN 0-398-02548-7). C C Thomas.

Malnutrition & the Eye. Donald S. McLaren. 1963. 49.00 o.p. (ISBN 0-12-484250-X). Acad Pr.

Malnutrition & the Immune Response. Ed. by Robert M. Suskind. LC 75-14589. 1977. 43.50 (ISBN 0-89004-060-5). Raven.

Malnutrition, Behavior & Social Organization. Ed. by Lawrence S. Greene. 1977. 29.50 (ISBN 0-12-298050-6). Acad Pr.

Malory: Style & Vision in "le Morte d'Arthur". Mark Lambert. LC 74-29727. (Studies in English Ser.: No. 186). 224p. 1975. 15.00x o.p. (ISBN 0-300-01835-5). Yale U Pr.

Malory: Works. Thomas Malory. Ed. by Eugene Vinaver. 1977. pap. 7.95 (ISBN 0-19-281217-3). Oxford U Pr.

Malpractice in Psychotherapy. Barry R. Furrow. LC 79-3253. 192p. 1980. 18.95x (ISBN 0-669-03399-5). Lexington Bks.

Malpractice of Psychiatrists: Malpractice in Psychoanalysis, Psychotherapy & Psychiatry. Donald J. Dawidoff. (American Lecture in Behavioral Science & Law Ser.). 184p. 1973. 16.75 (ISBN 0-398-02711-0). C C Thomas.

Malpractitioners. John Guinther. LC 77-92215. 1978. 10.00 o.p. (ISBN 0-385-12898-3, Anchor Pr). Doubleday.

Malraux. Axel Madsen. LC 76-7558. 1976. 11.95 o.p. (ISBN 0-688-03075-0). Morrow.

Malsum. Gerald J. O'Hara. 320p. 1981. pap. 2.50 (ISBN 0-380-77289-2, 77289). Avon.

Malta. Nigel Dennis. LC 73-83041. (Illus.). 64p. 1974. 6.95 (ISBN 0-8149-0732-6). Vanguard.

Malta. Nina Nelson. 1978. 22.50 (ISBN 0-7134-0941-X). David & Charles.

Maltaverne. Francois Mauriac. Tr. by Jean Stewart from Fr. 1970. 5.95 o.p. (ISBN 0-374-20112-9). FS&G.

Malthus & His Work. 2nd ed. James Bonar. LC 66-9610. Repr. of 1924 ed. 24.00x (ISBN 0-678-05029-5). Kelley.

Maltreated Child: The Maltreatment Syndrome in Children - A Medical, Legal & Social Guide. 4th ed. Vincent J. Fontana. (Illus.). 192p. 1979. 17.50 (ISBN 0-398-03904-6). C C Thomas.

Maltreatment of the School-Aged Child. Ed. by Richard Volpe et al. LC 79-3581. 224p. 1980. 18.95x (ISBN 0-669-03463-0). Lexington Bks.

Mama. Gregorio M. Sierra. 1937. pap. 2.95x (ISBN 0-393-09456-1, NortonC). Norton.

Mama Hattie's Girl. Lois Lenski. (Regional Stories Ser). (Illus.). (gr. 4-6). 1953. 5.95 o.p. (ISBN 0-397-30243-6). Lippincott.

Mama Mia Italian Cookbook. Angela Catanzaro. 1955. 5.95 o.p. (ISBN 0-87140-969-0). Liveright.

Mama Was a Preacher. Marvin Jackson. 5.95 (ISBN 0-686-05781-3). Prod Hse.

Mamalian Cell Membranes, 5 vols. Ed. by G. A. Jamieson & D. M. Robinson. (Illus.). 1977. text ed. 159.95 set (ISBN 0-686-25573-9). Butterworths.

Mama's Bank Account. Kathryn Forbes. (gr. 10 up). 1968. pap. 2.50 (ISBN 0-15-656377-0, HPL27, HPL). HarBraceJ.

Mamluk Military Society. David Ayalon. 364p. 1980. 69.00x (Pub. by Variorum England). State Mutual Bk.

Mammakarzinom: Neue Aspekte Fuer Die Praxis, 1981. Ed. by A. Goldhirsch. (Journal: Gynaekologische Rundschau: Vol. 21, No. 1). (Illus.). 68p. 1981. pap. write for info. (ISBN 3-8055-2188-X). S Karger.

Mammal Remains from Archaeological Sites, Part I: Southeastern & Southwestern United States. Stanley J. Olsen. LC 65-689. (Peabody Museum Papers: Vol. 56, No. 1). 1964. pap. 15.00 (ISBN 0-87365-162-6). Peabody Harvard.

Mammalian Alimentary System: A Functional Approach. David S. Madge. LC 75-34543. (Special Topics in Biology Ser). 200p. 1976. pap. 14.50x (ISBN 0-8448-0850-4). Crane-Russak Co.

Mammalian Cell Mutagenesis: The Maturation of Test Systems. Ed. by Abraham W. Hsie et al. LC 79-21186. (Banbury Report Ser.: No. 2). (Illus.). 504p. 1979. 45.00x (ISBN 0-87969-201-4). Cold Spring Harbor.

Mammalian Chimaeras. Anne McLaren. LC 75-40988. (Developmental and Cell Biology Ser.: No. 4). (Illus.). 160p. 1976. 35.50 (ISBN 0-521-21183-2). Cambridge U Pr.

Mammalian Communication: A Behavioral Analysis of Meaning. Roger Peters. LC 80-15229. (Orig.). 1980. pap. text ed. 9.95 (ISBN 0-8185-0388-2). Brooks-Cole.

Mammalian Genetics & Cancer: Proceedings. Symposium in Honor of the Jackson Laboratory's Fiftieth Anniversary, Bar Harbor, Maine, July 1979. Ed. by Elizabeth S. Russell. 1981. 42.00x (ISBN 0-8451-0045-9). A R Liss.

Mammalian Kidney. D. B. Moffat. LC 74-82590. (Biological Structure & Function Ser.: No. 5). (Illus.). 272p. 1975. 53.50 (ISBN 0-521-20599-9). Cambridge U Pr.

Mammalian Olfaction: Reproducive Processes, & Behavior. Ed. by Richard L. Doty. 1976. 38.50 (ISBN 0-12-221250-9). Acad Pr.

Mammalian Population Genetics. Ed. by Michael H. Smith & James Joule. 1981. 25.00 (ISBN 0-8203-0547-2). U of Ga Pr.

Mammalian Skull. W. J. Moore. (Biological Structure & Function Ser.: No. 8). (Illus.). 400p. Date not set. 85.00 (ISBN 0-521-23318-6). Cambridge U Pr.

Mammals. Boy Scouts of America. LC 19-600. (Illus.). 48p. (gr. 6-12). 1972. pap. 0.70x (ISBN 0-8395-3271-7, 3271). BSA.

Mammals. Richard Carrington. LC 63-20048. (Life Nature Library). (Illus.). (gr. 5 up). 1963. PLB 8.97 o.p. (ISBN 0-8094-0625-X, Pub. by Time-Life). Silver.

Mammals. Richard Carrington. (Young Readers Library). (Illus.). 1977. lib. bdg. 7.95 (ISBN 0-686-51091-7). Silver.

Mammals. Barbara Lowery. (Easy-Read Fact Book Ser.). (Illus.). 48p. (gr. 2-4). 1976. PLB 4.47 o.p. (ISBN 0-531-01215-8). Watts.

Mammals & Waterbirds of Puget Sound. Tony Angell & Kenneth Balcomb. 1981. write for info. U of Wash Pr.

Mammals around the Pacific. George G. Simpson. (Thomas Burke Memorial Lecture Ser.: No. 2). 1966. pap. 4.00 (ISBN 0-295-74056-6). U of Wash Pr.

Mammals in Color. Leif Lyneborg. (European Ecology Ser.). (Illus.). 1971. 9.95 (ISBN 0-7137-0548-5, Pub by Blandford Pr England). Sterling.

Mammals in the Seas, Vol. II: Pinniped Species Summaries & Report on Sirenians. (FAO Fisheries Ser.: No. 5, Vol. II). 151p. 1979. 20.25 (ISBN 92-5-100512-5, F2102, FAO). Unipub.

Mammals of Great Smoky Mountains National Park. Alicia V. Linzey & Donald W. Linzey. LC 74-111048. (Illus.). 1971. pap. 4.95 (ISBN 0-87049-114-8). U of Tenn Pr.

Mammals of Idaho. Earl J. Larrison & Donald R. Johnson. LC 80-51876. (GEM Bks-Natural History Ser.). (Illus.). 200p. 1981. pap. 6.95 (ISBN 0-89301-070-7). U Pr of Idaho.

Mammals of North America, 2 vols. 2nd. ed. E. Raymond Hall. LC 79-4109. 1981. Set. 70.00 (ISBN 0-471-05595-6, Pub. by Wiley-Interscience); Vol. 1. 40.00 (ISBN 0-471-05443-7); Vol. 2. 40.00 (ISBN 0-471-05444-5). Wiley.

Mammals of the Eastern United States. 2nd ed. William J. Hamilton, Jr. & John O. Whitaker, Jr. LC 79-12920. (HANH Ser.). (Illus.). 368p. 1979. 19.95x (ISBN 0-8014-1254-4). Comstock.

Mammals of the Pacific States: California, Oregon, Washington. Lloyd G. Ingles. (Illus.). 1965. 14.95 (ISBN 0-8047-0297-7); text ed. 11.20 (ISBN 0-8047-0298-5). Stanford U Pr.

Mammals of the San Francisco Bay Region. William D. Berry & Elizabeth Berry. (California Natural History Guides: No. 2). 1959. 12.95x (ISBN 0-520-03088-5); pap. 3.95 (ISBN 0-520-00116-8). U of Cal Pr.

Mammals of the Southwestern United States: With Special Reference to New Mexico. Vernon Bailey. (Illus.). 8.00 (ISBN 0-8446-0016-4). Peter Smith.

Mammals of Wisconsin. Hartley H. Jackson. (Illus.). 1961. 22.50x (ISBN 0-299-02150-5). U of Wis Pr.

Mammals: Their Latin Names Explained. A. F. Gotch. (Illus.). 1979. 18.95 (ISBN 0-7137-0939-1, Pub. by Blandford Pr England). Sterling.

Mammography. 2nd ed. Robert L. Egan. (Amer. Lec. Roentgen Diagnosis Ser.). (Illus.). 526p. 1972. text ed. 52.50 (ISBN 0-398-02195-3). C C Thomas.

Mammography. John N. Wolfe. (Illus.). 168p. 1967. 17.50 (ISBN 0-398-02107-4). C C Thomas.

Mammoth Book of Crossword Puzzles. Compiled by Harold H. Hart. 512p. 1981. pap. 8.95 (ISBN 0-89104-204-0). A & W Pubs.

Mammoth Corridors. Earle Birney. 1980. pap. 5.00 (ISBN 0-936892-07-2). Stone Pr MI.

Mammoth, the Owl, & the Crab. Claudia Fregosi. LC 74-13836. (Illus.). 32p. (ps-2). 1975. 8.95 (ISBN 0-02-735690-6). Macmillan.

Mammoth Vehicles of the World: Land-Sea-Air. John H. Brandner. (Illus.). Date not set. pap. 16.95 (ISBN 0-89404-009-X). Aztex. Postponed.

Mammy Tittleback & Her Family. Helen H. Jackson. 1976. lib. bdg. 8.50x (ISBN 0-89968-052-6). Lightyear.

M.A.N. Pat Kennett. (World Trucks: No. 4). (Illus.). 1979. 15.95 (ISBN 0-89404-015-4). Aztex.

Man: A Novel. Oriana Fallaci. 1980. 15.95 (ISBN 0-671-25241-0). S&S.

Man Across the Sea: Problems of Pre-Columbian Contacts. Ed. by Carroll L. Riley et al. 1971. 25.00x (ISBN 0-292-70117-9). U of Tex Pr.

Man Adapting. enl. ed. Rene Dubos. LC 80-16492. (Silliman Lectures Ser.). (Illus.). 527p. 1980. pap. 7.95x (ISBN 0-300-02581-5). Yale U Pr.

Man Among the Stars. Wolfgang D. Mueller. (Illus.). 1956. 10.95 (ISBN 0-87599-079-7). S G Phillips.

Man & Animals: One Hundred Centuries of Man's Relationship with Animals. J. J. Barloy. LC 77-30501. (Illus.). 1978. 9.95 o.p. (ISBN 0-86033-012-5). Gordon-Cremonesi.

Man & Beast. R. A. Marchant. LC 68-21304. (Illus.). (gr. 7 up). 1968. 4.95g o.s.i. (ISBN 0-02-762390-4). Macmillan.

Man & Biologically Active Substances: Introduction to the Pharmacology of Health. 2nd ed. I. I. Brekhman. 90p. 1980. 18.25 (ISBN 0-08-023169-1); pap. 5.95 (ISBN 0-08-025524-8). Pergamon.

Man & Birds: Evolution & Behavior. Andrew J. Meyerriecks. LC 79-175222. (Topics in Biological Science Ser). 1972. pap. 4.95 (ISBN 0-672-63558-5). Pegasus.

Man & Boy. Wright Morris. LC 51-2263. viii, 212p. 1974. pap. 2.25 (ISBN 0-8032-5787-2, BB 575, Bison). U of Nebr Pr.

Man & Citizen: Thomas Hobbes De Homine. Ed. by Bernard Gert. Tr. by Charles T. Wood. 1972. pap. text ed. 5.95x (ISBN 0-391-00849-8). Humanities.

Man & Culture: An Evaluation of the Work of Bronislaw Malinowski. Ed. by Raymond Firth. 1957. pap. 20.00 o.p. (ISBN 0-7100-6892-1). Routledge & Kegan.

Man & Culture: An Evaluation of the Work of Bronislaw Malinouski. Ed. by Raymond Firth. 292p. 1980. 27.50x (ISBN 0-7100-1376-0, Pub. by Routledge England). Humanities.

Man & Development - Binadamu Na Maendeleo. Julius K. Nyerere. 128p. 1974. pap. text ed. 4.95x (ISBN 0-19-519785-2). Oxford U Pr.

Man & Earth: Their Changing Relationship. Gail W. Finsterbusch. LC 76-26914. (Studies in Sociology). (gr. 12). 1976. pap. 3.50 (ISBN 0-672-61325-5). Bobbs.

Man & Economics. Robert A. Mundell. LC 68-13522. (Illus.). 1968. pap. 2.95 o.p. (ISBN 0-07-044038-7, SP). McGraw.

Man & Environment. K. Hewitt & F. K. Hare. LC 72-90876. (CCG Resource Papers Ser.: No. 20). (Illus.). 1973. pap. text ed. 4.00 (ISBN 0-89291-067-4). Assn Am Geographers.

Man & Environment: Symposium containing contribution of 30 international scientists. Ed. by Research Institute of Geography, Hungarian Academy of Sciences, Budapest. 1974. 18.75 o.p. (ISBN 0-685-42266-6). Adler.

Man & Environmental Processes. Ed. by K. J. Gregory & D. E. Walling. (Studies in Physical Geography Ser.). 224p. 1980. lib. bdg. 27.50x (ISBN 0-89158-696-2, Pub. by Dawson England); pap. text ed. 13.50x (ISBN 0-89158-865-5). Westview.

Man & His Environment. Ed. by Indera P. Singh & S. C. Tiwari. (International Conference of Anthropological & Ethnological Sciences Ser.: No. 10). 299p. 1980. text ed. 18.00x (ISBN 0-391-02140-0). Humanities.

Man & His Environment, Vol. 2: Proceedings of the Second Banff Conference. Ed. by M. F. Mohtadi. 216p. 1975. text ed. 37.00 (ISBN 0-08-019922-4). Pergamon.

Man & His Habitat: Essays Presented to Emyr Estyn Evans. R. H. Buchanan et al. 1971. 26.50 (ISBN 0-7100-6908-1). Routledge & Kegan.

Man & His Mission: Cardinal Leger in Africa. Ken Bell & Henriette Major. Tr. by Jane Springer. 1976. 35.00 o.p. (ISBN 0-13-548115-5). P-H.

Man & His Music: The Story of Musical Experience in the West. Alec Harman et al. 1978. 29.95 o.p. (ISBN 0-214-15665-6, 8022, Dist. by Arco). Barrie & Jenkins.

Man & His Place in History. Walter Johannes & Stein. 1980. pap. 4.25x (ISBN 0-906492-35-1, Pub. by Kolisko Archives). St George Bk Serv.

Man & His Resources. Charles W. Mattison & Joseph Alvarez. LC 66-25119. (In Todays World Ser). (Illus.). (gr. 4-8). 1967. PLB 7.95 (ISBN 0-87191-001-2). Creative Ed.

Man & His Symbols. Carl G. Jung. LC 64-18631. 1969. Repr. of 1964 ed. 10.95 (ISBN 0-385-05221-9). Doubleday.

Man & His Urban Environment: A Sociological Approach. rev. ed. William H. Michelson. 1976. 8.95 (ISBN 0-201-04726-8). A-W.

Man & His Whole Earth. Gary Null. LC 75-29260. 160p. 1976. 6.95 o.p. (ISBN 0-8117-0969-8). Stackpole.

Man & His Whole Earth. Gary Null & Steven Null. 1977. pap. 1.50 o.s.i. (ISBN 0-515-03620-X). Jove Pubns.

Man & Machines. R. Page. pap. text ed. 3.35 (ISBN 0-08-016889-2). Pergamon.

Man & Maid. Elinor Glyn. (Barbara Cartland's Library of Love: Vol. 10). 182p. 1979. 12.95x (ISBN 0-7156-1386-3, Pub. by Duckworth England). Biblio Dist.

Man & Mankind: Conflict & Communication Between Cultures. Edmund S. Glenn. 300p. 1981. price not set (ISBN 0-89391-068-6). Ablex Pub.

Man & Metaphysics. Donald H. Yott. 1980. pap. 5.95 (ISBN 0-87728-488-1). Weiser.

Man & Modern Society: Philosophical Essays. Homer T. Rosenberger. LC 72-85861. (Horizons of the Humanities Ser.: Vol. 1). 272p. 1972. lib. bdg. 8.00 (ISBN 0-917264-05-3). Rose Hill.

Man & Natural Resources: An Agricultural Perspective. C. S. Hicks. 250p. 1980. 29.00x (Pub. by Croom Helm England). State Mutual Bk.

Man & Nature. Ed. by George McLean. 1979. 9.95 (ISBN 0-19-561093-8). Oxford U Pr.

Man & Nature. Yi-Fu Tuan. LC 71-182310. (CCG Resource Papers Ser.: No. 10). (Illus.). 1971. pap. text ed. 4.00 (ISBN 0-89291-057-7). Assn Am Geographers.

Man & Nature in the Renaissance. A. G. Debus. LC 77-91085. (Cambridge History of Science Ser.). (Illus.). 1978. 22.95 (ISBN 0-521-21972-8); pap. 7.95x (ISBN 0-521-29328-6). Cambridge U Pr.

Man & Nature: Principles of Human & Environmental Biology. John W. Kimball. LC 74-19694. 480p. 1975. text ed. 18.95 (ISBN 0-201-03688-6). A-W.

Man & Nature: The Ecological Crisis & Social Progress. Evgenii K. Fedorov. (Orig.). 1981. 8.00 (ISBN 0-7178-0573-5); pap. 2.75 (ISBN 0-7178-0567-0). Intl Pub Co.

Man & Organization. Ed. by J. Child. LC 73-8645. 261p. 1974. 16.95 (ISBN 0-470-15580-9). Halsted Pr.

Man & Society: A Critical Examination of Some Important Social & Political Theories from Machiavelli to Marx, Vol. 2. John Plamenatz. 1975. pap. text ed. 14.95 (ISBN 0-582-48046-9). Longman.

Man & Society in an Age of Reconstruction. Karl Mannheim. Tr. by Edward Shils from Ger. (Studies in Modern Social Structure). 490p. 40.00 (ISBN 0-7100-1788-X). Routledge & Kegan.

Man & Society in Calamity, the Effects of War, Revolution, Famine, Pestilence Upon Human Mind, Behavior, Social Organization & Cultural Life. Pitirim A. Sorokin. LC 69-10157. (Illus.). 1968. Repr. of 1942 ed. lib. bdg. 25.50x (ISBN 0-8371-0236-7, SOMS). Greenwood.

Man & Space. Arthur C. Clarke. LC 64-25368. (Life Science Library). (Illus.). (gr. 5 up). 1969. PLB 8.97 o.p. (ISBN 0-8094-0464-8, Pub. by Time-Life). Silver.

Man & System: Foundations for the Study of Human Relations. Harry H. Turney-High. LC 68-16216. (Illus.). 1968. 28.50x (ISBN 0-89197-547-0). Irvington.

Man & the Biology of Arid Zones. J. L. Cloudesley-Thompson. LC 77-20663. (Contemporary Biology Ser). 1978. pap. 17.95 (ISBN 0-8391-1192-4). Univ Park.

Man & the Biosphere. Paul G. Risser & Kathy D. Cornelison. LC 79-4953. (Illus.). 109p. 1979. pap. 6.95 (ISBN 0-8061-1610-2). U of Okla Pr.

Man & the Chemical Elements. J. N. Friend. 354p. 1961. 19.50x (ISBN 0-85264-053-6, Pub. by Griffin England). State Mutual Bk.

Man & the Movies. Ed. by William R. Robinson. LC 67-24549. (Illus.). 1967. 22.50 (ISBN 0-8071-0718-2). La State U Pr.

Man & the Organization. Rafael Steinberg. (Human Behavior Ser). 176p. 1975. 9.95 (ISBN 0-8094-1912-2); lib. bdg. avail. (ISBN 0-685-52490-6). Time-Life.

Man & the Organization. Raphael Steinberg. LC 74-23044. (Human Behavior Ser.). (Illus.). 176p. (gr. 5 up). 1975. PLB 9.99 o.p. (ISBN 0-8094-1913-0). Silver.

Man and the Physical Universe. Ernest E. Snyder. LC 75-30446. (Physical Science Ser.). 373p. 1976. text ed. 19.95 (ISBN 0-675-08631-0). Merrill.

Man & the Zodiac. David Anrais. pap. 5.95 (ISBN 0-87728-014-2). Weiser.

Man & Transformation: Papers from the Eranosyears, Vol. 5. Ed. by Joseph Campbell. Tr. by Ralph Manheim from Fr. LC 72-1982. (Bollingen Ser.: Xxx). (Illus.). 452p. 1980. 20.00x (ISBN 0-691-09733-X); pap. 5.95 (ISBN 0-691-01834-0). Princeton U Pr.

Man & Water: A History of Hydro-Technology. Norman Smith. LC 75-24865. 1976. 12.95 o.p. (ISBN 0-684-14522-7, ScribT). Scribner.

Man & Woman. D. Von Hildebrand. 1981. pap. 3.95 (ISBN 0-89526-883-3). Regnery-Gateway.

Man & Woman in Christ: An Examination of the Roles of Men & Women in the Light of Scripture & the Social Sciences. Stephen B. Clark. 754p. (Orig.). 1980. 15.95 (ISBN 0-89283-084-0). Servant.

Man & Woman Spirit Masters. Religious Education Staff. (To Live Is Christ Ser.). 1980. 10.95 (ISBN 0-697-01752-4). Wm C Brown.

Man & Woman Teacher Manual. rev. ed. Daniel J. Pierson. (To Live in Christ Ser.). 264p. 1980. pap. 4.75 (ISBN 0-697-01751-6). Wm C Brown.

Man As He Is, 4 vols. Robert Bage & Ronald Paulson. LC 78-60853. (Novel 1720-1805 Ser.: Vol. 12). 1979. Set. 124.00 (ISBN 0-8240-3661-1); lib. bdg. 31.00 ea. Garland Pub.

Man at Leisure. Alexander Trocchi. LC 74-195409. 1979. 9.95 (ISBN 0-7145-0357-6, Pub. by M Boyars); pap. 5.95 (ISBN 0-7145-0358-4). Merrimack Bk Serv.

Man at Play. Hugo Rahner. 1972. pap. 1.95 (ISBN 0-8164-2556-6). Crossroad NY.

Man Becoming: God in Secular Experience. Gregory Baum. (Library of Contemporary Theology). 1979. pap. 8.95 (ISBN 0-8164-2203-6). Crossroad NY.

Man Beneath the Gift: The Story of My Life. Ralph A. DiOrio & Donald Gropman. LC 80-17619. (Illus.). 224p. 1980. 9.95 (ISBN 0-688-03740-2). Morrow.

Man Beneath the Sea: A Review of Underwater Ocean Engineering. Walter Penzias & M. W. Goodman. LC 70-148506. 1973. 59.95 (ISBN 0-471-68018-4). Wiley.

Man Builds Tomorrow. Etta S. Ress & Gina Liebow. LC 66-25120. (Illus.). (gr. 4-8). 1966. PLB 7.95 (ISBN 0-87191-000-4). Creative Ed.

Man Called Intrepid. William Stevenson. (Illus.). 1979. pap. 3.50 (ISBN 0-345-28124-1). Ballantine.

Man Called Intrepid: The Secret War. William Stevenson. Tr. by John Moore. LC 75-29051. (Illus.). 512p. 1976. 15.95 (ISBN 0-15-156795-6). HarBraceJ.

Man Called Masters. Lucy Walker. 1976. pap. 1.25 o.p. (ISBN 0-345-25232-2). Ballantine.

Man Called Pedro. Barbara Westphal. LC 75-25227. (Destiny Ser.). 1975. pap. 4.95 (ISBN 0-8163-0214-6, 13075-7). Pacific Pr Pub Assn.

Man Called Peter. Catherine Marshall. (Spire Bk). pap. 1.95 o.p. (ISBN 0-8007-8027-2). Revell.

Man, Climate & Architecture. 2nd ed. B. Givoni. (Illus.). 1976. 74.50x (ISBN 0-85334-678-X). Intl Ideas.

Man-Computer Interaction: Human Factors of Computers & People. Ed. by B. Shackel. (NATO Advanced Study Institute Ser.: Applied Sciences, No. 44). 550p. 1980. 60.00x (ISBN 90-286-0910-5). Sijthoff & Noordhoff.

Man Condemned. Peter Alding. 1981. 9.95 (ISBN 0-8027-5443-0). Walker & Co.

Man Could Get Killed. x ed. Luke Short. 192p. 1980. pap. 1.95 o.s.i. (ISBN 0-515-05558-1). Jove Pubns.

Man Does Survive Death. D. Scott Rogo. 1977. pap. 3.95 (ISBN 0-8065-0582-6). Citadel Pr.

Man East & West: Essays in East-West Philosophy. Howard L. Parsons. (Philosophical Currents Ser: No. 8). 211p. 1975. pap. text ed. 20.50x (ISBN 90-6032-020-4). Humanities.

Man-Eater. Ted Willis. LC 76-25009. 1977. 7.95 o.p. (ISBN 0-688-03124-2). Morrow.

Man Eater of Manjari. Ruskin Bond. 112p. 1975. pap. 2.15 (ISBN 0-88253-734-2). Ind-US Inc.

Man-Eating Myth: Anthropology & Anthropophagy. W. Arens. (Illus.). 220p. 1980. pap. 4.95 (ISBN 0-19-502793-0, GB 615). Oxford U Pr.

Man, Economy & State: A Treatise on Economic Principles, 2 vols. 2nd ed. Murray N. Rothbard. LC 76-167504. (Studies in Economic Theory). 1979. 30.00; pap. 10.00. NYU Pr.

Man, Economy, & State: A Treatise on Economic Principles. Murray N. Rothbard. 1978. write for info. NYU Pr.

Man, Energy, Society. Earl Cook. LC 75-33774. (Illus.). 1976. text ed. 21.95x (ISBN 0-7167-0725-X); pap. text ed. 11.95x (ISBN 0-7167-0724-1). W H Freeman.

Man, Fishes, & the Amazon. Nigel J. Smith. 176p. 1981. 20.00x (ISBN 0-231-05156-5). Columbia U Pr.

Man Flies on. Althea Braithwaite. (Dinosaur Ser.). (Illus.). (gr. 5 up). 1978. pap. 1.75 ea. (ISBN 0-85933-155-5, Pub. by Paul Elek); pap. 8.75 pack of 5. Merrimack Bk Serv.

Man for All Seasons. Robert Bolt. 1962. 8.95 (ISBN 0-394-40623-0). Random.

Man from Amazibu Bay. Yvonne Whittal. (Harlequin Romances Ser.). 192p. 1980. pap. 1.25 o.p. (ISBN 0-373-02358-8, Pub. by Harlequin). PB.

Man from Atlantis: No. 1. Richard Woodley. 1977. pap. 1.50 o.s.i. (ISBN 0-440-15368-9). Dell.

Man from Atlantis: No. 2. Richard Woodley. pap. 1.50 o.s.i. (ISBN 0-440-15369-7). Dell.

Man from Cannae. John Jakes. 1977. pap. 1.95 o.p. (ISBN 0-523-40161-2). Pinnacle Bks.

Man from Cape Clear. Conchur O'Siochain. Tr. by Riobard P. Breatnach. 1975. pap. 6.25 (ISBN 0-686-28551-4). Irish Bk Ctr.

Man from Glengarry. Ralph Connor. 1976. lib. bdg. 19.50x (ISBN 0-89968-017-8). Lightyear.

Man from Ida Grove. Harold Hughes & Dick Schneider. 346p. 1979. 10.95 (ISBN 0-912376-38-4). Chosen Bks Pub.

Man from Kabul. Gerard De Villiers. (Malko Ser., No. 3). 192p. 1973. pap. 0.95 o.p. (ISBN 0-523-00253-X). Pinnacle Bks.

Man from Krypton: The Gospel According to Superman. John Wesley White. LC 78-73455. 1978. pap. 2.25 (ISBN 0-87123-384-3, 200384). Bethany Fell.

Man from Lordsburg. Jack Slade. (Lassiter Ser.). 1978. pap. 1.25 (ISBN 0-505-51296-3). Tower Bks.

Man from Mars. W. C. Chalk. pap. text ed. 2.75x o.p. (ISBN 0-435-11220-1). Heinemann Ed.

Man from O.R.G.Y. Thy Neighbor's Orgy. Ted Mark. 272p. (Orig.). 1981. pap. 2.25 (ISBN 0-89083-701-5). Zebra.

Man from Out Back, No. 8. Lucy Walker. 192p. (Orig.). Date not set. pap. 1.75 (ISBN 0-345-29500-5). Ballantine.

Man from Outback. Lucy Walker. 1974. 220p. 1.75 (ISBN 0-345-29500-5). Ballantine.

Man from Savage Creek. Max Brand. 208p. 1980. pap. 1.95 (ISBN 0-446-90815-0). Warner Bks.

Man from the Beginning. Stanley A. Freed & Ruth Freed. LC 65-28357. (Creative Science Ser). (Illus., Orig.). (gr. 6 up). 1967. PLB 7.95 (ISBN 0-87191-008-X). Creative Ed.

Man from the Cave. Colin Fletcher. LC 80-22548. (Illus.). 352p. 1981. 16.95 (ISBN 0-394-40695-8). Knopf.

Man from the Past. 2nd ed. Roy C. Higby. (Illus.). (gr. 5-12). Date not set. pap. 4.25 (ISBN 0-914692-02-X). Big Moose.

Man from Tombstone & Gunfight at Ringo Junction. Jack Slade. (Lassiter Ser.). 1978. pap. 2.25 (ISBN 0-505-51285-8). Tower Bks.

Man Have I Got Problems. David Wilkerson. 1973. pap. 1.25 o.s.i. (ISBN 0-515-04668-X). Jove Pubns.

Man, His First Two Million Years: A Brief Introduction to Anthropology. Ashley Montagu. LC 80-15749. (Illus.). vi, 262p. 1980. Repr. of 1969 ed. lib. bdg. 23.50x (ISBN 0-313-22600-8, MOMH). Greenwood.

Man Hunt. Giles Lutz. 1981. pap. 1.75 (ISBN 0-345-29218-9). Ballantine.

Man I Pretend to Be: The Colloquies & Selected Poems of Guido Gozzano. Ed. by Michael Palma. LC 80-8551. (Lockert Library of Poetry in Translation). 264p. 1981. 16.00x (ISBN 0-691-06467-9); pap. 5.95x (ISBN 0-691-01378-0). Princeton U Pr.

Man in a Million. Rowena Wilson. (Candlelight Romance Ser.). (Orig.). Date not set. pap. 1.50 (ISBN 0-440-15528-2). Dell.

Man in a New Society. Ed. by Franz Bockle. (Concilium Ser.: Religion in the Seventies: Vol. 75). 1972. pap. 4.95 (ISBN 0-8164-2531-0). Crossroad NY.

Man in Adaptation. Ed. by Yehudi A. Cohen. Incl. Biosocial Background. 2nd ed. LC 74-169511. 1974. Vol. 1. lib. bdg. 24.95x (ISBN 0-202-01111-9); pap. 12.95x (ISBN 0-202-01112-7); Cultural Present. 2nd ed. 1974. Vol. 2. lib. bdg. 24.95x (ISBN 0-202-01109-7); pap. 12.95x (ISBN 0-202-01110-0); Institutional Framework. 1971. Vol. 3. 24.95x (ISBN 0-202-01095-3); pap. 9.95x (ISBN 0-202-01096-1). Aldine Pub.

Man in Africa. Colin M. Turnbull. LC 75-32015. 280p. 1977. pap. 2.95 o.p. (ISBN 0-385-05674-5, Anch). Doubleday.

Man in Aspic. Constantine Fitzgibbon. 1979. 14.95x (ISBN 0-8464-0084-7). Beekman Pubs.

Man in Black: His Own Story in His Own Words. Johnny Cash. (Large Print Ser.). 1976. kivar 4.95 (ISBN 0-310-22327-X); pap. 2.95 (ISBN 0-310-22322-9). Zondervan.

Man in Charge. John Weitz & Everett Mahlin. 192p. 1974. 6.95 o.s.i. (ISBN 0-02-625770-X). Macmillan.

Man in Christ. James S. Stewart. (James S. Stewart Library). 1975. pap. 5.95 (ISBN 0-8010-8045-2). Baker Bk.

Man in Communication. P. Schouls. 1968. pap. 1.50 o.p. (ISBN 0-686-11991-6). Wedge Pub.

Man in Conflict. Louis Katzher. 1975. pap. text ed. 7.95x (ISBN 0-8221-0165-3). Dickenson.

Man in Contemporary Society. student ed. Columbia College - Contemporary Civilization Staff. LC 62-17503. (gr. 12 up). 1962. 22.50x (ISBN 0-231-02587-4). Columbia U Pr.

Man in Evolution. 2nd rev. ed. G. De Purucker. Ed. by Grace F. Knoche. LC 76-45503. 1977. softcover 5.00 (ISBN 0-911500-55-3). Theos U Pr.

Man in Evolutionary Perspective. Ed. by C. Loring Brace & James F. Metress. LC 72-14184. 496p. 1973. pap. text ed. 15.50 (ISBN 0-471-09420-X). Wiley.

Man in Extreme Environments. A. W. Sloan. (Environmental Studies Ser.). (Illus.). 144p. 1979. text ed. 13.75 (ISBN 0-398-03941-0). C C Thomas.

Man in Flight: Biomedical Achievements in Aerospace. Eloise Engle & Arnold Lott. LC 79-63780. (Supplement to the American Astronautical Society History Ser.). (Illus.). 414p. 1979. 20.00x (ISBN 0-915268-24-8). Univelt Inc.

Man in Focus: New Approaches to Commercial Communications. Goren Tamm et al. (Communication Arts Bks.). 160p. (gr. 11-12). 1980. 14.50 o.p. (ISBN 0-8038-4734-3); pap. cancelled o.p. (ISBN 0-8038-4735-1). Hastings.

Man in His Working Environment. International Labour Office. (Workers' Education Manual). (Illus.). 142p. 1979. pap. 7.15 (ISBN 92-2-102060-6). Intl Labour Office.

Man in His World. Calvin Wells. (Illus.). 1971. text ed. 9.00x (ISBN 0-212-98383-0). Humanities.

Man in Lower Ten. Mary R. Rinehart. 1976. lib. bdg. 12.95x (ISBN 0-89968-180-8). Lightyear.

Man in Marxist Theory & the Psychology of Personality. Lucien Seve. (Marxist Theory & Contemporary Capitalism Ser.). 1978. text ed. 42.00x (ISBN 0-391-00743-2); pap. text ed. 17.00x, 1980 (ISBN 0-391-01913-9). Humanities.

Man in Motion. Michael Mewshaw. 1970. 5.95 o.p. (ISBN 0-394-43481-1). Random.

Man in Nature: America Before the Days of the Whiteman. Carl O. Sauer. (New World Writing Ser.). (Illus.). 1975. 17.50 (ISBN 0-913666-28-9); pap. 9.95 (ISBN 0-913666-01-7). Turtle Isl Foun.

Man in Orbit: And Down to Earth. Douglas O. Pitches. LC 80-50670. 81p. 1981. 5.95 (ISBN 0-533-04649-1). Vantage.

Man in Society. Margaret E. Hogg. (Biology of Man Ser.). 1968. pap. text ed. 7.95x o.p. (ISBN 0-435-60427-9). Heinemann Ed.

Man in Space. Henry Brinton. (Junior Ref. Ser). (Illus.). (gr. 7 up). 1969. 7.95 (ISBN 0-7136-1504-4). Dufour.

Man in Space. Tim Furniss. (Today's World Ser.). (Illus.). 72p. (gr. 7-9). 1981. 15.95 (ISBN 0-7134-3582-8, Pub. by Batsford England). David & Charles.

Man in Space: Chelovek V Kosmose. Ed. by O. G. Gazenko. Tr. by H. A. Bjurstedt. (Illus., Eng., Fr., Rus.). 1974. 20.00 o.p. (ISBN 0-87703-122-3). Univelt Inc.

Man in the Andes: A Multidisciplinary Approach of High Altitude Quechua. Ed. by P. T. Baker & Michael A. Little. LC 76-17025. 1976. 37.50 (ISBN 0-12-786115-7). Acad Pr.

Man in the Black Square. Taiko Walker & Ashley Walker. Bd. with Hotels Aren't for Sleeping. 1980. 7.95 (ISBN 0-533-04549-5). Vantage.

Man in the Brown Suit. Agatha Christie. 1981. pap. 2.25 (ISBN 0-440-15230-5). Dell.

Man in the Cold. Jacques LeBlanc. (American Lectures in Environmental Studies Ser.). (Illus.). 208p. 1975. 21.75 (ISBN 0-398-03429-X). C C Thomas.

Man in the Dark Suit. Dennis Caro. 1980. pap. write for info. (ISBN 0-671-83153-4). PB.

Man in the Iron Mask. Alexandre Dumas. (Classics Ser.). (gr. 9 up). 1967. pap. 1.95 (ISBN 0-8049-0150-3, CL-150). Airmont.

Man in the Iron Mask. Alexandre Dumas. 1976. lib. bdg. 11.95x (ISBN 0-89968-146-8). Lightyear.

Man in the Marxist Theory & the Psychology of Personality. Lucien Seve. (Marxist Theory & Contemporary Capitalism Ser.). 508p. 1980. text ed. 42.00x o.p. (ISBN 0-391-00743-2); pap. text ed. 15.50x o.p. (ISBN 0-391-01913-9). Humanities.

Man in the Maze. Robert Silverberg. 1978. pap. 1.50 (ISBN 0-380-00198-5, 38539). Avon.

Man in the Middle. Heal. 9.95 (ISBN 0-686-69285-3). Scribner.

Man in the New World. K. G. Saiyidain. 1964. 3.75x o.p. (ISBN 0-210-31216-5). Asia.

Man in the Queue. Josephine Tey. LC 79-28589. 1981. Repr. of 1929 ed. lib. bdg. 10.00x (ISBN 0-8376-0450-8). Bentley.

Man in the Shadows. Rosemary Carter. (Harlequin Romances Ser.). 192p. (Orig.). 1981. pap. 1.25 (ISBN 0-373-02380-4, Pub. by Harlequin). PB.

Man in the Sky. Althea Braithwaite. (Dinosaur Ser.). (Illus.). (gr. 5 up). 1978. pap. 1.75 ea. (ISBN 0-85933-011-7, Pub. by Paul Elek); pap. 8.75 pack of 5. Merrimack Bk Serv.

Man in the Sycamore Tree: The Good Times & Hard Life of Thomas Merton. Edward Rice. LC 76-121809. 1972. pap. 2.45 (ISBN 0-385-02730-3, Im). Doubleday.

Man in the Universe. Fred Hoyle. LC 66-17067. 1966. 12.00x (ISBN 0-231-02941-1). Columbia U Pr.

Man in the Universe: Some Cultural Continuities in Indian Thought. W. Norman Brown. (Rabindranath Tagore Memorial Lectures). 1966. 14.00x (ISBN 0-520-00185-0). U of Cal Pr.

Man in the Web of Life. John H. Storer. (Orig.). (RL 8). 1968. pap. 0.95 o.p. (ISBN 0-451-03664-6, Q3664, Sig). NAL.

Man in the World: The Political Theology of Johannes Baptist Metz. Roger D. Johns. LC 76-26491. (American Academy of Religion. Dissertation Ser.). 1976. pap. 7.50 (ISBN 0-89130-079-1, 010116). Scholars Pr Ca.

Man in Tropical Africa: Human Ecology in Tropical Africa. D. F. Owen. 220p. 1973. 12.95x (ISBN 0-19-519746-1). Oxford U Pr.

Man into Wolf: An Anthropological Study of Sadism, Masochism, & Lycanthropy. Robert Eisler. LC 77-2497. 264p. 1978. text ed. 11.95 (ISBN 0-915520-16-8); pap. text ed. 5.95 (ISBN 0-915520-06-0). Ross-Erikson.

Man Is the Measure: A Cordial Invitation to the Central Problems of Philosophy. Reuben Abel. LC 75-16646. (Illus.). 1976. 12.95 (ISBN 0-02-900140-4); pap. text ed. 8.95 (ISBN 0-02-900110-2). Free Pr.

Man-Killer. Joanne M. Arnold. Ed. by Patricia McCarthy. (Pal Paperbacks Ser., Kit A). (Illus., Orig.). 1974. pap. text ed. 1.25 (ISBN 0-8374-3474-2). Xerox Ed Pubns.

Man, Land & the Forest Environment. Marion Clawson. LC 76-45999. (Geo. S. Long Publication Ser.). (Illus.). 86p. 1977. 8.95 (ISBN 0-295-95540-6). U of Wash Pr.

Man Lay Dead. Ngaio Marsh. 1976. Repr. of 1934 ed. lib. bdg. 9.70 (ISBN 0-88411-488-0). Amereon Ltd.

Man-Living-Health: A Theory of Nursing. Parse. 192p. 1981. pap. 11.95 (ISBN 0-471-04443-1, Pub. by Wiley Med). Wiley.

Man-Machine Engineering. Alphonse Chapanis. LC 65-15099. (Behavioral Science in Industry Ser). (Orig.). 1966. pap. text ed. 6.95x (ISBN 0-8185-0306-8). Brooks-Cole.

Man-Made America: Chaos or Control. Christopher Tunnard & Boris Pushkarev. Ed. by Harriet Bell. 1981. 12.95 (ISBN 0-517-54379-6, Harmony). Crown.

Man-Made Fibers. H. F. Mark et al. LC 67-13954. (Polymer Engineering & Technology Ser.). 1967-68. Vol. 1. 40.00 (ISBN 0-470-56985-9, Pub. by Wiley-Interscience); Vol. 2. 42.50 (ISBN 0-470-56986-7); 62.50 (ISBN 0-470-56987-5). Wiley.

Man-Made Gemstones. D. Elwell. LC 78-41291. 1979. 49.95 (ISBN 0-470-26606-6). Halsted Pr.

Man-Made Landscape. (Museums & Monuments Ser.: Vol. XVI). 1978. pap. 15.75 (ISBN 92-3-101455-2, U815, UNESCO). Unipub.

Man-Made Landscape. F. J. Monkhouse & A. V. Hardy. (Illus.). 96p. 1974. text ed. 5.75x (ISBN 0-521-20365-1). Cambridge U Pr.

Man-Made World. Engineering Concepts Curriculum Project. 1971. text ed. 15.52 o.p. (ISBN 0-07-019502-1, W); teachers' set 29.88 o.p. (ISBN 0-07-019503-X); teachers' manual 10.08 o.p. (ISBN 0-685-14421-6); transparency masters 19.80 o.p. (ISBN 0-07-019504-8). McGraw.

Man, Magic & Fantasy. Marc E. Jones. LC 78-63049. 1979. 13.50 o.p. (ISBN 0-87878-016-5, Sabian). Great Eastern.

Man-making Words: Selected Poems of Nicolas Guillen. Nicolas Guillen. Ed. by Robert Marquez & David McMurray. LC 78-181363. 248p. (Span. & Eng.). 1972. pap. 5.95x (ISBN 0-87023-101-4). U of Mass Pr.

Man, Medicine & Morality. A. Kennedy Clark. (Illus.). 1969. 5.95 o.p. (ISBN 0-571-09052-4, Pub. by Faber & Faber). Merrimack Bk Serv.

Man, Mind, & the Universe. Gustaf Stromberg. 1966. pap. 4.00 (ISBN 0-911336-10-9). Sci of Mind.

Man, Minerals, & Masters. Charles W. Littlefield. (Illus.). 140p. 1980. pap. 5.50 (ISBN 0-89540-059-6). Sun Pub.

Man, Nature & Art. R. Wheeler. 1968. 18.75 (ISBN 0-08-012690-1); pap. 9.25 (ISBN 0-08-012689-8). Pergamon.

Man Nobody Knows. Bruce Barton. 1925. pap. 4.85 (ISBN 0-672-50743-9). Bobbs.

Man of Affairs. John D. MacDonald. 176p. 1978. pap. 1.75 o.p. (ISBN 0-449-14051-2, GM). Fawcett.

Man of Destiny & Caesar & Cleopatra: Play Manuscripts in Facsimile. George B. Shaw. LC 79-56707. (Bernard Shaw Early Ser.). 1981. lib. bdg. 70.00 (ISBN 0-8240-4582-3). Garland Pub.

Man of Dharma & the Rasa of Silence. P. Lal. (Redbird Book). 61p. 1975. 8.00 (ISBN 0-88253-831-4); pap. 4.80 (ISBN 0-88253-832-2). Ind-US Inc.

Man of Feeling. Henry Mackenzie. LC 74-18367. (Novel in England, 1700-1775 Ser). 1974. Repr. of 1771 ed. lib. bdg. 50.00 (ISBN 0-8240-1196-1). Garland Pub.

Man of Geneva. Elsie M. Johnson. 1977. pap. 3.45 (ISBN 0-85151-254-2). Banner of Truth.

Man of His Counsel. Effie Williams. 112p. pap. 1.00. Faith Pub Hse.

Man of Honour. Jane Ashford. 2400p. (Orig.). 1981. pap. 1.75 (ISBN 0-446-94797-0). Warner Bks.

Man of Last Resort. Melville D. Post. 284p. 1980. Repr. of 1897 ed. lib. bdg. 14.25x (ISBN 0-89968-198-0). Lightyear.

Man of Law. John Wainwright. 224p. 1981. 9.95 (ISBN 0-312-51088-3). St Martin.

Man of Mode. George Etherege. Ed. by W. B. Carnochan. LC 66-17766. (Regents Restoration Drama Ser). xxii, 158p. 1966. 9.75x (ISBN 0-8032-0357-8); pap. 3.75x (ISBN 0-8032-5356-7, BB 256, Bison). U of Nebr Pr.

Man of Power. Mary Wibberley. (Harlequin Romances Ser.). 192p. (Orig.). 1981. pap. 1.25 (ISBN 0-373-02388-X, Pub. by Harlequin). PB.

Man of Steel. Terry Bradshaw & David Diles. 1980. pap. 4.95 (ISBN 0-310-39461-9). Zondervan.

Man of the High Country. Mary Moore. (Harlequin Romances Ser.). 192p. 1980. pap. 1.25 o.p. (ISBN 0-373-02349-9, Pub. by Harlequin). PB.

Man of the Outback. Anne Hampson. 192p. (Orig.). 1980. pap. 1.50 (ISBN 0-671-57028-5). S&S.

Man of the People. Chinua Achebe. LC 66-22929. pap. 1.95 (ISBN 0-385-08616-4, A594, Anch). Doubleday.

Man of the Southern. Jim Evans. (Steam Past Ser.). (Illus.). 96p. 1980. 17.50 (ISBN 0-04-385078-2, 2406). Allen Unwin.

Man of the World, 2 vols. in 1. Henry Mackenzie. LC 74-17142. (Novel in England, 1700-1775 Ser). 1974. Repr. of 1773 ed. lib. bdg. 50.00 (ISBN 0-8240-1202-X). Garland Pub.

Man on a Donkey. H. F. Prescott. 640p. 1981. pap. 8.95 (ISBN 0-02-023830-4). Macmillan.

Man on Earth: A Preliminary Evaluation of the Ecology of Man. SPR Charter. LC 78-75232. 1979. text ed. 8.00 (ISBN 0-89615-007-0); pap. 10.95 (ISBN 0-89615-051-8). Guild of Tutors.

Man on His Nature. Charles S. Sherrington. 1951. 39.95 (ISBN 0-521-06436-8); pap. 11.95x (ISBN 0-521-09203-5). Cambridge U Pr.

Man on His Past. Herbert Butterfield. 32.95 (ISBN 0-521-07265-4); pap. 8.50x (ISBN 0-521-09567-0). Cambridge U Pr.

Man on Horseback: The Story of the Mounted Man from the Scythians to the American Cowboy. Glenn R. Vernam. LC 64-20544. (Illus.). xii, 436p. 1972. pap. 4.95 (ISBN 0-8032-5770-8, BB 561, Bison). U of Nebr Pr.

Man on the Bridge. Ian S. Black. 1977. pap. 1.95 o.s.i. (ISBN 0-515-04416-4). Jove Pubns.

Man on the Spot. Pericynthion. 1981. 12.95 (ISBN 0-936278-02-1). Green Hill.

Man Over Money: The Southern Populist Critique of American Capitalism. Bruce Palmer. LC 79-24698. (Fred W. Morrison Ser. in Southern Studies). xviii, 311p. 1980. 19.50x (ISBN 0-8078-1427-X). U of NC Pr.

Man, Play, & Games. Roger Caillois. LC 61-14109. 1961. 12.95 (ISBN 0-02-905200-9). Free Pr.

Man Ray. Janus. (Illus.). 160p. 1981. 19.95 (ISBN 0-8120-5374-5). Barron.

Man, Reality & Values. R. A. Siddiqi. 1964. 5.00x o.p. (ISBN 0-210-27048-9). Asia.

Man, Religion & Science. Oscar Zaglits. Date not set. 10.95 (ISBN 0-533-04808-7). Vantage.

Man, Religion, & Science: A Functional View. William Bailey. LC 80-65860. (Illus.). 242p. (Orig.). 1981. pap. 9.95 (ISBN 0-9604196-0-8). W Bailey Pub.

Man: Ruined & Restored. Leslie B. Flynn. 1978. pap. 3.95 (ISBN 0-88207-762-7). Victor Bks.

Man, Space & Environment: Concepts in Contemporary Human Geography. Ed. by Paul W. English & Robert C. Mayfield. (Orig.). 1972. text ed. 9.95x (ISBN 0-19-501441-3). Oxford U Pr.

Man Spoke, a World Listened. Paul L. Maier. 1980. pap. 8.95 (ISBN 0-570-03822-7, 12-2762). Concordia.

Man Studies Himself. Wilbert J. Levy. (gr. 10-12). 1973. pap. text ed. 3.83 (ISBN 0-87720-370-9). AMSCO Sch.

Man Studies His Past. Wilbert J. Levy. (gr. 10-12). 1973. pap. text ed. 3.83 (ISBN 0-87720-371-7). AMSCO Sch.

Man Studies the World Around Him. Wilbert J. Levy. (gr. 10-12). 1973. pap. text ed. 3.83 (ISBN 0-87720-372-5). AMSCO Sch.

Man the Animal. Margaret E. Hogg. (Biology of Man Ser.). 1966. pap. text ed. 11.50x o.p. (ISBN 0-435-60426-0). Heinemann Ed.

Man the Artist. J. Slater. 1976. 3.35 (ISBN 0-08-006899-5). Pergamon.

Man: The Bridge Between Two Worlds. Franz E. Winkler. LC 80-82064. 268p. 1980. pap. 4.95 (ISBN 0-913098-32-9). Myrin Institute.

Man the Builder. G. E. Sandstrom. 1970. 19.50 o.p. (ISBN 0-07-054663-0, P&RB). McGraw.

Man the Hunter. Ed. by Richard B. Lee & Irven De Vore. LC 67-17603. 1968. pap. 11.50x (ISBN 0-202-33032-X). Aldine Pub.

Man, the State & War: A Theoretical Analysis. Kenneth N. Waltz. LC 59-11482. (Institute of War & Peace Studies Ser). 1959. 17.50x (ISBN 0-231-02292-1); pap. 6.00x (ISBN 0-231-08564-8). Columbia U Pr.

Man to Man: Gay Couples in America. Charles Silverstein. LC 80-23566. 384p. 1981. 12.95 (ISBN 0-688-00041-X). Morrow.

Man to Watch. Jane Donnelly. (Harlequin Romance Ser.). (Orig.). 1980. pap. 1.25 o.p. (ISBN 0-373-02325-1, Pub. by Harlequin). PB.

Man-Transportation Interface. Compiled by American Society of Civil Engineers. 384p. 1972. pap. text ed. 12.50 (ISBN 0-87262-041-7). Am Soc Civil Eng.

Man: Twelve Thousand Years Under the Sea. Robert F. Burgess. LC 80-186. (Illus.). 448p. 1980. 12.95 (ISBN 0-396-07801-X). Dodd.

Man Under Stress. Ed. by A. T. Welford. LC 74-5440. 140p. 1974. 15.95 (ISBN 0-470-93315-1). Halsted Pr.

Man up a Tree (Zacchaeus) Scripture Union. 1978. pap. 0.49 (ISBN 0-87508-932-1). Chr Lit.

Man v. Machine. Mohandas K. Gandhi. Ed. by A. T. Hingorani. 113p. (Orig.). 1980. pap. 2.00 (ISBN 0-934676-18-6). Greenlf Bks.

Man Versus Society in Eighteenth Century Britain. Ed. by James L. Clifford. LC 68-12057. 1968. 22.95 (ISBN 0-521-04675-0). Cambridge U Pr.

Man Visible & Invisible. rev. ed. Charles W. Leadbeater. (Illus.). 1969. pap. 6.50 (ISBN 0-8356-0311-3, Quest). Theos Pub Hse.

Man Was Not Born to Cry. Joel S. Goldsmith. 1977. pap. 4.95 (ISBN 0-8065-0569-9). Citadel Pr.

Man Who Awoke. Laurence Manning. 1979. pap. 1.75 (ISBN 0-345-27969-7, Del Rey Bks). Ballantine.

Man Who Beat Clout City. Robert McClory. LC 77-88692. (Illus.). 224p. 1977. 11.95 (ISBN 0-8040-0777-2). Swallow.

Man Who Bought Himself: The Story of Peter Still. Peggy Mann & Vivian Siegal. LC 75-15514. 224p. (gr. 5 up). 1975. 8.95 (ISBN 0-02-762220-7, 76222). Macmillan.

Man Who Brought the Dodgers Back to Brooklyn. David Ritz. 1981. price not set (ISBN 0-671-25356-5). S&S.

Man Who Built London Transport: A Biography of Frank Pick. Christian Barman. 1979. 24.00 (ISBN 0-7153-7753-1). David & Charles.

Man Who Called Himself Devlin. William M. Green. (Orig.). pap. 1.95 (ISBN 0-515-05245-0). Jove Pubns.

Man Who Changed China: The Story of Sun Yat-Sen. Pearl S. Buck. (World Landmark Ser.: No. 9). (Illus.). (gr. 7-9). 1953. PLB 5.99 (ISBN 0-394-90509-1). Random.

Man Who Could Read Cards. R. L. Broyles. (Orig.). 1980. pap. 1.95 (ISBN 0-532-23310-7). Manor Bks.

Man Who Didn't Wash His Dishes. Phyllis Krasilovsky. (Illus.). (gr. k-3). 1950. pap. 1.95 (ISBN 0-385-13343-X, Zephyr). Doubleday.

Man Who Dreamed of Tomorrow: A Conceptual Biography of Wilhelm Reich. W. Edward Mann & Edward Hoffman. LC 80-50405. 304p. 1980. 12.95 (ISBN 0-87477-143-9). J P Tarcher.

Man Who Fell in Love with a Chicken. David B. Axelrod. Ed. by Stanley H. Barkan. (Cross-Cultural Review Chapbook 2). 16p. 1980. pap. 2.00 (ISBN 0-89304-801-1). Cross Cult.

Man Who Fell to Earth. Walter Tevis. 192p. (Orig.). 1981. pap. 2.25 (ISBN 0-553-14274-7). Bantam.

Man Who Fell to Earth. Walter Tevis. (Alpha Books). 94p. (Orig.). 1979. pap. 2.25x (ISBN 0-19-424231-5). Oxford U Pr.

Man Who Founded Georgia: The Story of James Edward Oglethorpe. J. Gordon Vaeth. LC 68-19026. (America in the Making Ser). (Illus.). (gr. 7 up). 1968. 3.50g o.s.i. (ISBN 0-02-791090-3, CCPr). Macmillan.

Man Who Freed the Slaves: The Story of William Wilberforce. Audrey Lawson & Herbert Lawson. (gr. 7 up). 4.95 (ISBN 0-571-05061-1). Transatlantic.

Man Who Gave the Beatles Away. Allan Williams & William Marshall. (Illus.). 1975. 9.95 o.s.i. (ISBN 0-02-629050-2). Macmillan.

Man Who Keeps Going to Jail. Dell Erwin & John Erwin. (Illus.). 1980. pap. 1.95 (ISBN 0-89191-200-2). Cook.

Man Who Kept Cigars in His Cap. James Heynen. LC 77-95332. Orig. Title: Boys. (Illus.). 1978. 10.00 (ISBN 0-915308-18-5); pap. text ed. 5.00 (ISBN 0-915308-17-7). Graywolf.

Man Who Kept House. Kathleen Hague & Michael Hague. LC 80-26258. (Illus.). 32p. (ps-3). 1981. 11.95 (ISBN 0-15-251698-0, HJ). HarBraceJ.

Man Who Kept the Secrets: Richard Helms & the CIA. Thomas Powers. 1981. pap. 3.50 (ISBN 0-671-83654-4). PB.

Man Who Killed Boys. Clifford L. Linedecker. 1980. 10.00 (ISBN 0-312-51157-4). St Martin.

Man Who Killed Fortescue. Dorothy S. Tillet. LC 80-8413. 320p. 1981. pap. 2.25 (ISBN 0-06-080536-6, P 536, PL). Har-Row.

Man Who Killed Hitler. R. Page Jones. 256p. (Orig.). 1980. pap. 2.25 (ISBN 0-515-04855-0). Jove Pubns.

Man Who Killed the Deer. Frank Waters. LC 73-149327. 266p. 1942. 9.95 o.p. (ISBN 0-8040-0193-6, SB); pap. 5.95 (ISBN 0-8040-0194-4, 12). Swallow.

Man Who Killed the Deer. Frank Waters. pap. 2.50 (ISBN 0-671-43295-8). PB.

Man Who Lived Two Lives. John W. Stokes. LC 79-57548. 1981. 6.75 (ISBN 0-533-04561-4). Vantage.

Man Who Lost China. Brian Crozier. LC 76-10246. (Encore Edition). (Illus.). 480p. 1976. 5.95 o.p. (ISBN 0-684-15940-6, ScribT). Scribner.

Man Who Lost Everything. Paul Kuttner. LC 76-17142. 352p. 1976. 8.95 (ISBN 0-8069-0152-7); lib. bdg. 7.49 (ISBN 0-8069-0153-5). Sterling.

Man Who Lost His Shadow. Fathy Ghanem. Tr. by Desmond Stewart from Arabic. 352p. (Orig.). 1980. 12.00x (ISBN 0-89410-206-0); pap. 6.00x (ISBN 0-89410-207-9). Three Continents.

Man Who Lost the War. W. T. Tyler. 384p. 1981. pap. 2.95 (ISBN 0-425-04852-7). Berkley Pub.

Man Who Loved Books. Jean Fritz. (Illus.). 48p. (gr. 7-11). 1981. 8.95 (ISBN 0-399-20715-5). Putnam.

Man Who Loved Children. Christina Stead. LC 65-10128. 576p. 1980. 12.95 o.p. (ISBN 0-03-047265-2); pap. 7.95 (ISBN 0-03-057642-3). HR&W.

Man Who Met Jesus at Bethesda. Neal A. Boehlke. (Arch Bk.). (gr. k-4). 1981. pap. 0.79 (ISBN 0-570-06143-1, 59-1260). Concordia.

Man Who Moved a Mountain. Richard C. Davids. LC 75-99609. (Illus.). 270p. 1972. pap. 4.25 (ISBN 0-8006-1237-X, 1-1237). Fortress.

Man Who Moved the World. Sheldon A. Jacobson. LC 80-83024. (Illus.). 298p. 1980. 10.95 (ISBN 0-9604800-0-5). Galley OR.

Man Who Needed Action. Michael Geller. 1979. pap. 1.75 (ISBN 0-505-51436-2). Tower Bks.

Man Who Never Died: A Play About Joe Hill. Barrie Stavis. LC 70-88295. (Illus.). 128p. 1972. 7.95 o.p. (ISBN 0-498-07538-9). A S Barnes.

Man Who Owned New York. John J. Osborn, Jr. 256p. 1981. 10.95 (ISBN 0-686-69052-4). HM.

Man Who Photographed the World: Burton Holmes (Travelogues 1892-1938) Ed. by Genoa Caldwell. LC 77-8075. (Illus.). 1977. 30.00 o.p. (ISBN -08109-1059-4). Abrams.

Man Who Robbed the Pierre. Ira Berkow. 288p. 1981. 11.95 (ISBN 0-87460-381-1). Lion.

Man Who Rode Sharks. William R. Royal & Robert F. Burgess. LC 78-1854. (Illus.). 1978. 8.95 (ISBN 0-396-07537-1). Dodd.

Man Who Sang the Sillies. John Ciardi. LC 61-11734. (Illus.). (gr. 4-6). 1961. 8.95 (ISBN 0-397-30568-0). Lippincott.

Man Who Shook Hands. Diane Wakoski. LC 77-80917. 1978. 6.95 o.p. (ISBN 0-385-13407-X); pap. 4.95 o.p. (ISBN 0-385-13408-8). Doubleday.

Man Who Shook Hands. Diane Wakoski. 118p. 1978. 5.50 (ISBN 0-87685-467-6). Black Sparrow.

Man Who Sold Death. (Nick Carter Ser.). 1978. pap. 1.75 (ISBN 0-441-51921-0). Charter Bks.

Man Who Stole the Atlantic Ocean. Louis Phillips. 1979. pap. 1.25 (ISBN 0-380-48173-1, 48173, Camelot). Avon.

Man Who Stopped Time. Judith A. Green. (Adult Learner Ser.). (Illus.). 189p. (Orig.). 1979. pap. text ed. 3.60x (ISBN 0-89061-173-4, 201). Jamestown Pubs.

Man Who Took the Next Train. Ed. by Jack L. Stoll. 365p. (Orig.). 1980. text ed. 14.95 (ISBN 0-918258-15-4); pap. text ed. 7.95 (ISBN 0-686-69212-8). New Earth.

Man Who Walked in His Head. Patrick Segal. Tr. by John Stephens from Fr. LC 79-21426. 1980. Repr. 10.95 (ISBN 0-688-03529-9). Morrow.

Man Who Wanted Tomorrow. Brian Freemantle. 1978. pap. 1.75 o.s.i. (ISBN 0-515-04437-7). Jove Pubns.

Man Who Was There. Wright Morris. LC 76-16590. 1977. 11.95x (ISBN 0-8032-0881-2); pap. 3.25 (ISBN 0-8032-5813-5, BB 598, Bison). U of Nebr Pr.

Man Who Wasn't There. Roderick MacLeish. 1976. 7.95 o.p. (ISBN 0-394-49361-3). Random.

Man Who Would Be Perfect: John Humphrey Noyes & the Utopian Impulse. Robert D. Thomas. LC 76-53198. 1977. 13.95x (ISBN 0-8122-7724-4). U of Pa Pr.

Man Who Wrestled with God. John A. Sanford. 144p. 1981. pap. 6.95 (ISBN 0-8091-2367-3). Paulist Pr.

Man Whose Name Was Not Thomas. M. J. Graig. (Illus.). 32p. (gr. k-3). 1981. 7.95a (ISBN 0-385-15064-4); PLB (ISBN 0-385-15065-2). Doubleday.

Man with a Maid. Anonymous. LC 8-27284. 1968. pap. 2.95 (ISBN 0-394-17479-8, B181, BC). Grove.

Man with a Maid. 1974. pap. 1.95 (ISBN 0-345-23709-9). Ballantine.

Man with a Maid, Bk. 2. Anonymous. LC 79-15758. 1979. pap. 2.95 (ISBN 0-394-17091-1, B434, BC). Grove.

Man with a Mission: Pele. Larry Adler. LC 76-11007. (Sports Profiles Ser.). (Illus.). 48p. (gr. 4-11). 1976. PLB 8.50 (ISBN 0-8172-0142-4). Raintree Pubs.

Man with Bogart's Face. Andrew J. Feneday. 184p. 1979. pap. 1.95 (ISBN 0-380-01849-7, 49015). Avon.

Man with the Golden Arm. Nelson Algren. LC 78-72524. 1979. Repr. of 1949 ed. lib. bdg. 12.50x (ISBN 0-8376-0425-7). Bentley.

Man with the Scar. Judith A. Green. (Adult Learner Ser.). (Illus.). 203p. (Orig.). 1979. pap. text ed. 3.60x (ISBN 0-89061-153-X, 202). Jamestown Pubs.

Man with Three Eyes. E. L. Arch. (YA) 5.95 (ISBN 0-685-07446-3, Avalon). Bouregy.

Man with Two Memories. J. B. Haldane. 1976. 12.95 (ISBN 0-85036-209-1). Dufour.

Man with Two Shadows. Kevin Desmond. (Illus.). 160p. 1981. 10.95 (ISBN 0-906071-09-7). Proteus Pub NY.

Man Without a Country. Edward E. Hale. 1976. lib. bdg. 12.95x (ISBN 0-89968-152-2). Lightyear.

Man Without a Face. Isabelle Holland. LC 71-37736. (gr. 7 up). 1972. 9.95 (ISBN 0-397-31211-3, LSC-9). Lippincott.

Man Without a Face. Isabelle Holland. (gr. 6-12). 1980. pap. 1.50 (ISBN 0-440-96097-5, LFL). Dell.

Man Without a Heart. Anne Hampson. 192p. 1981. pap. 1.50 (ISBN 0-671-57052-8). S&S.

Man, Woman & Child. Erich Segal. 192p. 1981. pap. 2.95 (ISBN 0-345-29318-5). Ballantine.

Man, Woman & Child. Erich Segal. (Large Print Bks.). 1980. lib. bdg. 10.95 (ISBN 0-8161-3124-4). G K Hall.

Manage Your Plant for Profit & Your Promotion. Richard W. Ogden. 1978. 14.95 (ISBN 0-8144-5466-6). Am Mgmt.

Managed Casualty: The Japanese-American Family in World War II. Leonard Broom & John L. Kitsuse. (Library Reprint Ser.: No. 40). 1974. Repr. 20.00x (ISBN 0-520-02523-7). U of Cal Pr.

Managed Integration: Dilemmas of Doing Good in the City. Harvey L. Molotch. LC 74-142049. 280p. 1973. 18.50x (ISBN 0-520-01889-3). U of Cal Pr.

Managemant Today. 2nd ed. James A. Belasco & David R. Hampton. 550p. 1981. text ed. 18.95 (ISBN 0-471-08579-0); write for info. tchr's. ed. (ISBN 0-471-08934-6). Wiley.

Management. 2nd ed. William G. Glueck. 640p. 1980. text ed. 20.95 (ISBN 0-03-050906-8). Dryden Pr.

Management. 7th, rev. ed. Harold Koontz et al. (Illus.). 1980. text ed. 18.95 (ISBN 0-07-035377-8); instructor's manual 9.95 (ISBN 0-07-035378-6); study guide 6.95 (ISBN 0-07-035379-4). McGraw.

Management. 5th ed. Justin G. Longenecker & Charles D. Pringle. (Illus.). 544p. 1981. text ed. 19.95 (ISBN 0-675-08061-4); tchr's. manual avail.; study guide 6.95 (ISBN 0-675-09995-1). Merrill.

Management. J. A. Stoner. (Illus.). 1978. text ed. 21.00 (ISBN 0-13-549303-X); study guide & wkbk 7.95 (ISBN 0-13-549329-3). P-H.

Management: A Book of Readings. 5th ed. Harold K. O'Donnell & Heinz Weihrich. (Illus.). 736p. text ed. 18.95x (ISBN 0-07-035418-9); pap. 14.95x (ISBN 0-07-035417-0). McGraw.

Management: A Humanist Art. David E. Lilienthal. LC 67-20667. (B. F. Fairless Memorial Lectures). 1967. 9.00x (ISBN 0-231-03064-9). Columbia U Pr.

Management: A Life Cycle Approach. David A. Tansik et al. 1980. 18.95x (ISBN 0-256-02278-X). Irwin.

Management: A Problem-Solving Process. Robert Kreitner. LC 79-88719. (Illus.). 1980. text ed. 18.75 (ISBN 0-395-28490-2); inst. manual 1.75 (ISBN 0-395-28491-0). HM.

Management Accounting. Donald L. Madden. LC 80-17277. (Teaching Guides Ser.). 326p. 1980. 8.95 (ISBN 0-471-03135-6, Pub. by Wiley-Interscience). Wiley.

Management Accounting. Norman Thornton. 1978. pap. text ed. 21.00x (ISBN 0-434-91960-8). Intl Ideas.

Management Accounting & Behavioral Science. 2nd ed. E. H. Caplan. 1981. pap. 6.50 (ISBN 0-201-00952-8). A-W.

Management Accounting: Concepts & Applications. Ronald J. Thacker & Loudell Ellis. (Illus.). 587p. 1980. text ed. 17.95 (ISBN 0-8359-4194-9); student guide 8.95 (ISBN 0-8359-4196-5); test bank free (ISBN 0-8359-4197-3); instr's. manual free (ISBN 0-8359-4195-7). Reston.

Management Accounting for Hotels & Restaurants. Richard Kotas & L. Kreul. (gr. 10 up). 1979. text ed. 15.50x (ISBN 0-8104-9472-8). Hayden.

Management Accounting in Practice. 4th ed. F. Clive De Paula. 1972. 13.95x (ISBN 0-8464-0587-3); pap. 9.50x. Beekman Pubs.

Management Accounting: Techniques for Non-Financial Mangers. L. Simpson. 246p. 1979. pap. 12.25x (ISBN 0-220-67023-4, Pub. by Busn Bks England). Renouf.

Management: An Integrated Approach. Irwin T. Weinstock & Paul E. Torgerson. LC 71-162354. (Illus.). 1972. text ed. 18.95 (ISBN 0-13-548396-4). P-H.

Management: Analysis, Concepts, Cases. 3rd ed. Joseph L. Massie et al. (Illus.). 800p. 1975. ref. ed. 21.00 (ISBN 0-13-548412-X). P-H.

Management & Administration. Andrew F. Sikula. LC 72-95954. 1973. text ed. 15.95x (ISBN 0-675-09000-8). Merrill.

Management & Administration of Pharmacy-I. 1978. pap. 15.00 (ISBN 0-930530-09-8). Am Soc Hosp Pharm.

Management & Administration of the School Library Media Program. Dorothy T. Taggart. 261p. 1980. 17.50 (ISBN 0-208-01853-0, Lib Prof Pubns); text ed. 13.50x (ISBN 0-208-01848-4, Lib Prof Pubns). Shoe String.

Management & Business Studies. 2nd ed. C. S. Leeds et al. 448p. 1978. pap. text ed. 16.95x (ISBN 0-7121-1298-7, Pub. by Macdonald & Evans England). Intl Ideas.

Management & Control in Public Enterprise. Sucha S. Khera. 1972. pap. 4.95 o.p. (ISBN 0-210-27109-4). Asia.

Management & Control of Growth: Issues, Techniques, Problems, Trends, 3 vols. Ed. by Randall W. Scott. LC 74-83560. 1800p. 1975. Set. pap. text ed. 36.50 (ISBN 0-87420-565-4). Urban Land.

Management & Control of Growth: Techniques in Application. Frank Schnidman et al. LC 78-73139. (Management & Control of Growth Ser.: Vol. 4). 352p. 1978. pap. text ed. 19.50 (ISBN 0-87420-578-6). Urban Land.

Management & Control of Growth: Updating the Law. Ed. by Frank Schnidman & Jane A. Silveman. LC 80-50920. (Management & Control of Growth Ser.: Vol. V). 352p. 1980. pap. text ed. 19.50 (ISBN 0-87420-592-1, M12). Urban Land.

Management & Diseases of Sheep. 469p. 1981. 85.00 (ISBN 0-85198-451-7, CAB 9, Cab). Unipub.

Management & Economics Journals: An International Selection. Ed. by Vasile G. Tega. LC 76-4578. (Management Information Guide Ser.: No. 33). 1977. 30.00 (ISBN 0-8103-0833-9). Gale.

Management & Feeding of Buffaloes. S. K. Ranjhan & N. N. Pathak. Date not set. text ed. 15.00x (ISBN 0-7069-0778-7, Pub. by Vikas India). Advent Bk.

Management & Ideology: The Legacy of the International Scientific Management Movement. Judith A. Merkle. 300p. 1980. 18.50x (ISBN 0-520-03737-5). U of Cal Pr.

Management & Improvement of Guidance. 2nd ed. George E. Hill. 1974. text ed. 20.95 (ISBN 0-13-548453-7). P-H.

Management & Industrial Structure in Japan. Naoto Sasaki. (Illus.). 160p. 1981. 24.00 (ISBN 0-08-024056-9); pap. 13.00 (ISBN 0-08-024057-7). Pergamon.

Management & Motivation: An Introduction to Supervision. Jay L. Todes et al. 1977. text ed. 16.95 scp (ISBN 0-06-046636-7, HarpC); instructor's manual avail. (ISBN 0-685-74059-5). Har-Row.

Management & Organization. Robert M. Fulmer. LC 78-15830. 1980. pap. 4.95 (ISBN 0-06-460176-5, CO 176, COS). Har-Row.

Management & Organizational Behavior. Burt Scanlan & J. Bernard Keys. LC 78-15477. (Management Ser.). 1979. text ed. 21.95 (ISBN 0-471-02484-8); tchrs. manual (ISBN 0-471-04774-0); study guide (ISBN 0-471-04773-2). Wiley.

Management & Organizations. E. Frank Harrison. LC 77-75476. (Illus.). 1977. text ed. 18.95 (ISBN 0-395-25481-7); inst. manual 0.50 (ISBN 0-395-25482-5). HM.

Management & Supervision of Small Jails. Frances O. Jansen & Ruth Johns. (Illus.). 360p. 1978. 23.75 (ISBN 0-398-03680-2). C C Thomas.

Management & Technology: An Anglo-American Exchange of Views. Ed. by A. G. Mencher. 96p. 1972. 23.00 (ISBN 0-08-018748-X). Pergamon.

Management & the Local Independent Union. Leo Troy. 1966. pap. 2.50 (ISBN 0-87330-003-3). Indus Rel.

Management & the Use of Grasslands, Democratic Republic of the Congo. 152p. 1966. pap. 8.00 (F1918, FAO). Unipub.

Management & Unions. Allan Flanders. (Orig.). 1975. pap. 4.95 (ISBN 0-571-10711-7, Pub. by Faber & Faber). Merrimack Bk Serv.

Management & Utilization of Pastures, East Africa: Kenya, Tanzania, Uganda. (Pasture & Fodder Crop Studies: No. 3). 124p. 1969. pap. 7.75 (ISBN 92-5-100420-X, F1970, FAO). Unipub.

Management & Worker: The Japanese Solution. James C. Abegglen. LC 72-96130. 200p. 1973. 14.50x (ISBN 0-87011-199-X). Kodansha.

Management Applications of System Theory. Constantin Negoita. (Interdisciplinary Systems Research: No. 57). 1979. 19.50 (ISBN 3-7643-1032-4). Birkhauser.

Management Assistance for the Arts: A Survey of Programs. Ellen Thurston. Ed. by Stephen Benedict. LC 80-440. 54p. (Orig.). 1980. pap. 4.00 (ISBN 0-89062-046-6, Pub. by Ctr for Arts Info). Pub Ctr Cult Res.

Management Auditing: Concepts & Practice. John A. Edds. 432p. 1980. text ed. 20.95 (ISBN 0-8403-2209-7). Kendall-Hunt.

Management Audits of Subordinate Claims Offices of National Insurance Companies. John H. Roush, Jr. LC 74-31546. 197p. 17.00. J H Roush.

Management: Basic Elements of Managing Organizations. rev ed. Ross A. Webber. 1979. text ed. 19.50 (ISBN 0-256-02234-8). Irwin.

Management by Exception: Systematizing & Simplifying the Manager's Job. Lester R. Bittel. 1964. 18.50 o.p. (ISBN 0-07-005484-3, P&RB). McGraw.

Management by Motivation. Saul W. Gellerman. LC 68-12699. (Illus.). 1968. 16.95 (ISBN 0-8144-5157-8). Am Mgmt.

Management by Multiple Objective. Sang M. Lee. (Illus.). 240p. 1981. 20.00 (ISBN 0-89433-083-7). Petrocelli.

Management by Objectives. S. K. Chakraborty. LC 76-901892. 1976. 12.00x o.p. (ISBN 0-333-90112-6). South Asia Bks.

Management by Objectives. Glenn Varney. 1979. 59.50 (ISBN 0-85013-106-5). Dartnell Corp.

Management by Objectives & Results for Business & Industry. 2nd ed. George L. Morrisey. (Illus.). 260p. 1977. pap. text ed. 8.95 (ISBN 0-201-04906-6); inst. guide 1.00 (ISBN 0-201-04907-4). A-W.

Management by Objectives & Results in the Public Sector. George L. Morrisey. LC 76-1746. (Illus.). 204p. 1976. pap. text ed. 8.95 (ISBN 0-201-04825-6); instr's guide 1.00 (ISBN 0-201-04813-2). A-W.

Management by Objectives for Hospitals. Arthur X. Deegan, 2nd. LC 76-45523. 1977. 24.95 (ISBN 0-912862-33-5). Aspen Systems.

Management by Objectives Workbook. rev. ed. Glenn H. Varney. 1972. 4.95 (ISBN 0-686-05624-8). Mgmt Advisory.

Management by Responsibility. Gary M. Durst. (Illus.). 100p. 1980. pap. write for info. (ISBN 0-9602552-1-4). Ctr Art Living.

Management Career Progress in a Japanese Organization. Mitsuru Wakabayashi. Ed. by Gunter Dufey. (Research for Business Decisions). 550p. 1980. 29.95 (ISBN 0-8357-1108-0, Pub. by UMI Res Pr). Univ Microfilms.

Management Characteristics & Labour. H. A. Turner et al. LC 77-76076. (DAE Papers in Industrial Relations Ser.: No. 3). (Illus.). 1977. 14.50 (ISBN 0-521-21734-2); pap. 7.95x (ISBN 0-521-29245-X). Cambridge U Pr.

Management Classics. 2nd ed. Michael Matteson & John Ivancevich. 1981. pap. text ed. write for info. (ISBN 0-8302-5469-2). Goodyear.

Management: Competencies & Incompetencies. William P. Anthony. LC 79-25171. 604p. 1981. text ed. price not set (ISBN 0-201-00085-7). A-W.

Management: Concepts & Controversies. Joseph A. Litterer. LC 77-20031. 1978. pap. text ed. 11.50 (ISBN 0-471-03611-0). Wiley.

Management: Concepts & Practices. Mondy et al. 704p. 1980. text ed. 18.95 (ISBN 0-205-06859-6, 0868590); study guide 6.95 (ISBN 0-205-06861-8, 0868612). Allyn.

Management: Concepts & Situations. Howard M. Carlisle. LC 75-29382. (Illus.). 608p. 1976. text ed. 18.95 (ISBN 0-574-19230-1, 13-2230); instr's guide avail. (ISBN 0-574-19231-X, 13-2231). SRA.

Management Consultant. Alfred Hunt. LC 76-49741. 1977. 14.95 (ISBN 0-8260-4557-X). Ronald Pr.

Management: Contingencies, Structure & Process. Henry L. Tosi & Stephen J. Carroll. LC 75-43280. (Series in Critical Sociologies). (Illus.). 608p. 1976. text ed. 21.95 (ISBN 0-914292-04-8). Wiley.

Management: Contingency Approaches. 2nd ed. Don Hellriegel & John W. Slocum, Jr. LC 77-76177. 1978. text ed. 17.95 (ISBN 0-201-02854-9). A-W.

Management Control. 2nd ed. Samuel Eilon. 1979. text ed. 19.00 (ISBN 0-08-022482-2); pap. text ed. 9.75 (ISBN 0-08-022481-4). Pergamon.

Management Control & Decision Systems: Text, Cases, & Readings. Alan L. Patz & A. J. Rowe. (Ser. on Management, Accounting & Information Systems). 1977. 24.50 (ISBN 0-471-67195-9). Wiley.

Management Control in Airframe Subcontracting. N. E. Harlan. 1970. 19.75 (ISBN 0-08-018741-2). Pergamon.

Management Control in Nonprofit Organizations. rev. ed. Robert Anthony & Regina E. Herzlinger. 1980. 20.50x (ISBN 0-256-02326-3). Irwin.

Management Control in Nonprofit Organizations. Robert N. Anthony & Regina E. Herzlinger. 1975. text ed. 16.95x o.p. (ISBN 0-256-01748-4). Irwin.

Management Control Systems. 3rd ed. Robert N. Anthony & John Dearden. 1976. 18.50x o.p. (ISBN 0-256-01816-2). Irwin.

Management Control Systems. 4th ed. Robert N. Anthony & John Dearden. 1980. 20.95x (ISBN 0-256-02325-5). Irwin.

Management Controls & Marketing Planning. R. M. Wilson. 224p. 1979. 21.95x (ISBN 0-470-26673-2); pap. 21.95 (ISBN 0-470-27053-5). Halsted Pr.

Management Data Bases. R. Clay Sprowls. LC 76-6100. 1976. text ed. 24.95 (ISBN 0-471-81865-8, Pub. by Wiley Hamilton). Wiley.

Management Decision Sciences: Cases & Readings. William L. Berry et al. 1980. 19.95x (ISBN 0-256-02219-4). Irwin.

Management Decision Support Systems. Andrew M. McCosh & Michael S. Scott-Morton. LC 77-13305. 1978. 21.95 (ISBN 0-470-99326-X). Halsted Pr.

Management: Decisions & Behavior. rev. ed. Max D. Richards & Paul S. Greenlaw. 1972. text ed. 18.95 (ISBN 0-256-00474-9). Irwin.

Management Decisions & Organizational Policy. 3rd ed. Olm et al. 560p. 1981. text ed. 21.95 (ISBN 0-205-07215-1, 0872156); free tchr's ed. (ISBN 0-205-07216-X). Allyn.

Management Decisions & Organizational Policy: Text, Cases & Readings. 2nd ed. F. Bridges et al. 1977. text ed. 20.95 (ISBN 0-205-05793-4, 0857939); instructor's manual o.p. incl. (ISBN 0-205-05794-2). Allyn.

Management Development: Context & Strategies. Ed. by J. Burgoyne & R. Stuart. text ed. 24.00x (ISBN 0-566-02101-3, Pub. by Gower Pub England). Renouf.

Management Development: Context & Struggles. J. Burgoyne & R. Stuart. 160p. text ed. 24.00x (ISBN 0-566-02101-3, Pub. by Gower Pub Co England). Renouf.

Management Development in Population Programs. Ed. by Sagar C. Jain. 200p. (Orig.). 1981. pap. 15.00 (ISBN 0-89055-307-6). U of NC Pr.

Management Dictionary. 5th rev. enl. ed. Werner Sommer & Hanns-Martin Schoenfeld. 621p. 1979. text ed. 34.25x. De Gruyter.

Management Education: Implications for Libraries & Library Schools. Ed. by Herman H. Fussler & John E. Jenck. LC 73-92600. vi, 116p. 1974. 10.00x (ISBN 0-226-27560-4). U of Chicago Pr.

Management Essentials: Concepts & Applications. Howard M. Carlisle. LC 78-16303. 1979. text ed. 16.95 (ISBN 0-574-19370-7, 13-2370); instr's guide avail. (ISBN 0-574-19371-5, 13-2371); study guide 5.95 (ISBN 0-574-19372-3, 13-2372); lecture suppl. 2.95 (ISBN 0-574-19373-1, 13-2373). SRA.

Management Essentials in Nursing. Claire Keane. 1980. text ed. 15.95 (ISBN 0-8359-4220-1); pap. text ed. 12.95 (ISBN 0-8359-4202-3). Reston.

Management Fin. Inst. 2nd ed. Rolichek. 1976. 22.95 (ISBN 0-03-089912-5). Dryden Pr.

Management for Business & Industry. Claude S. George, Jr. Orig. Title: Management in Industry. 1970. text ed. 20.95 (ISBN 0-13-548578-9). P-H.

Management for Engineers. John M. Amos & Bernard R. Sarchet. (P-H Ser. in Industrial Systems Engineering). (Illus.). 384p. 1981. text ed. 18.95 (ISBN 0-686-68606-3). P-H.

Management for Librarians: Fundamentals & Issues. John R. Rizzo. LC 79-8950. (Contributions in Librarianship & Information Science: No. 33). (Illus.). xvii, 339p. 1980. lib. bdg. 35.00 (ISBN 0-313-21990-7, RML/). Greenwood.

Management for Modern Families. 4th ed. Irman H. Gross et al. (Illus.). 1980. text ed. 16.95 (ISBN 0-13-549477-X). P-H.

Management for Nurses: A Multidisciplinary Approach. 2nd ed. Berger et al. LC 79-19965. 1980. pap. 11.50 (ISBN 0-8016-4815-7). Mosby.

Management for Nurses: A Multidisciplinary Approach. Ed. by Sandra Stone et al. LC 75-15561. 1976. pap. 9.95 (ISBN 0-8016-4812-2). Mosby.

Management for Productivity. Byron N. McClenney. 126p. (Orig.). 1980. pap. 5.00 (ISBN 0-87117-103-1). Am Assn Comm Jr Coll.

Management for Proprietors & Partnerships. Luanna C. Blagrove. (Illus.). 165p. 1981. text ed. 24.95 (ISBN 0-9604466-7-2). Blagrove Pubns.

Management for the Nineteen Eighties. W. Christopher. 1979. pap. 6.95 (ISBN 0-13-549154-1, Spec). P-H.

Management for Your Church: How to Realize Your Church Potential Through Systems Approach. Alvin J. Lindgren & Norman L. Shawchuck. LC 77-425. 1977. 8.95 (ISBN 0-687-23062-4). Abingdon.

Management Forum. Theodore F. Gautschi. (Illus.). 271p. 1979. pap. 16.00 (ISBN 0-536-03096-0). Herman Pub.

Management: Functions & Behavior. rev. ed. Robert L. Trewatha & M. Gene Newport. 1979. text ed. 17.50x (ISBN 0-256-02214-3). Business Pubns.

Management Fundamentals. Richard M. Hodgetts. LC 80-65800. 464p. 1981. text ed. 17.95 (ISBN 0-03-058104-4). Dryden Pr.

Management Game. Richard M. Greene, Jr. 1973. pap. 4.95 (ISBN 0-8015-4866-7, Hawthorn). Dutton.

Management Glossary: (English-Arabic) H. Johannsen. 15.00 (ISBN 0-685-89878-4). Intl Bk Ctr.

Management Guide to Casualty & Property Insurance. Edward W. Siver. 1981. write for info. (ISBN 0-87251-049-2). Crain Bks.

Management Guide to Computer Security & Control. William E. Perry. (Business Data Processing: a Wiley Ser.). 275p. 1981. 20.95 (ISBN 0-471-05235-3, Pub. by Wiley-Interscience). Wiley.

Management Handbook for the Hydrocarbon Processing Industries. Ed. by Charles H. Vervalin. 242p. 1981. pap. text ed. 16.95 (ISBN 0-87201-480-0). Gulf Pub.

Management Handbook Operating Guidelines & Techniques. Paul Mali. LC 80-20514. 1440p. 1981. 37.50 (ISBN 0-471-05263-9). Wiley.

Management in a Knowledge Society. Dale Zand. Ed. by William R. Newton. (Illus.). 224p. Date not set. 12.95 (ISBN 0-07-072743-0, P&RB). McGraw.

Management in Institutions of Higher Learning. Ed. by Edwin Rausch. LC 79-650. 1980. 26.95 (ISBN 0-669-02856-8). Lexington Bks.

Management in International Perspective. Ed. by S. Benjamin Prasad. LC 67-10930. (Orig.). 1967. pap. text ed. 6.95x (ISBN 0-89197-289-7). Irvington.

Management in Japan & India: With Reference to the United States. William A. Long & K. K. Seo. LC 77-7824. (Praeger Special Studies). 1977. text ed. 34.50 (ISBN 0-03-022651-1). Praeger.

Management in the Education Service: Challenge & Response. Society of Education Officers. (Open University Set Bk.). 128p. 1975. pap. 5.25 (ISBN 0-7100-8292-4). Routledge & Kegan.

Management in the Professions: Guidelines to Improved Professional Performance. Michael Allsopp. 201p. 1979. text ed. 29.50x (ISBN 0-220-67011-0, Pub. by Busn Bks England). Renouf.

Management in the World Today: A Book of Readings. Don Hellriegel & John W. Slocum, Jr. 400p. 1975. pap. text ed. 8.95 (ISBN 0-201-02833-6). A-W.

Management Information Systems. George K. Chacko. (Illus.). 454p. text ed. 27.00 (ISBN 0-89433-095-0). Petrocelli.

Management Information Systems. Raymond McLeod. LC 78-14983. 1979. text ed. 18.95 (ISBN 0-574-21245-0, 13-4245); instr's guide avail. (ISBN 0-574-21246-9, 13-4246); casebook 4.95 (ISBN 0-574-21247-7, 13-4247). SRA.

Management Information Systems: A Framework for Planning & Development. Sherman S. Blumenthal. 1969. ref. ed. 17.95 (ISBN 0-13-548636-X). P-H.

Management Information Systems & Organizational Behavior. Pat A. Federico et al. Ed. by Kim Brun & Douglas B. McCalla. LC 80-15174. 204p. 1980. 20.95 (ISBN 0-03-057021-2). Praeger.

Management Information Systems Handbook. 2nd ed. W. Hartman et al. 1970. 48.50 o.p. (ISBN 0-07-026957-2, P&RB). McGraw.

Management Information Systems: Selected Readings. 2nd ed. Ed. by M. J. Riley. 400p. 1981. pap. text ed. 14.50 (ISBN 0-8162-7190-9). Holden-Day.

Management: Its Nature & Significance. E. F. Brech. 1967. 15.00x o.p. (ISBN 0-8464-0590-3). Beekman Pubs.

Management, Machines & Methods in Civil Engineering. John Christian. 375p. 1981. 34.95 (ISBN 0-471-06334-7, Pub. by Wiley-Interscience). Wiley.

Management Model for Competency-Based Hper Programs. Jack Netcher. LC 76-57884. (Illus.). 1977. pap. 7.95 o.p. (ISBN 0-8016-3630-2). Mosby.

Management Motivation in the Smaller Business. M. J. Stanworth & J. Curran. 1973. 17.95x o.p. (ISBN 0-8464-0591-1). Beekman Pubs.

Management of Acute Hand Injuries: A Biological Approach. 2nd ed. Paul M. Weeks & R. Christie Wray. LC 78-5718. 1978. text ed. 48.50 (ISBN 0-8016-5371-1). Mosby.

Management of Aphasia. Ed. by Yvan Lebrun & Richard Hoops. (Neurolinguistics Ser.: Vol. 8). 124p. 1978. text ed. 26.00 (ISBN 90-265-0280-X, Pub. by Swets Pub Serv Holland). Swets North Am.

Management of Archives. Theodore R. Schellenberg. LC 65-14409. (Studies in Library Service: No. 14). 1965. 25.00x (ISBN 0-231-02812-1). Columbia U Pr.

Management of Archives & Manuscript Collections for Librarians. Ed. by Richard H. Lytle. LC 79-92650. 124p. 1980. Repr. of 1975 ed. 7.00 (ISBN 0-931828-27-9). Soc Am Archivists.

Management of Bank Portfolios. Stephen P. Bradley & Dwight B. Crane. LC 75-23030. 299p. 1975. 29.95 (ISBN 0-471-09522-2, Pub. by Wiley-Interscience). Wiley.

Management of Behavior in the Classroom: A Handbook of Psychological Strategies. Ed. by Betty W. Phillips. LC 79-66965. 232p. 1980. pap. text ed. 9.80x (ISBN 0-87424-162-6). Western Psych.

Management of Big Cities: Interest Groups & Social Change Strategies. David Rogers. LC 77-151671. 1971. 12.50 (ISBN 0-8039-0092-9); pap. 8.95x. Sage.

Management of Brain Damaged Children: A Parents' & Teachers' Guide. Frances G. Berko et al. 84p. 1970. 12.75 (ISBN 0-398-00141-3). C C Thomas.

Management of Business Logistics. 2nd ed. John J. Coyle & Edward Bardi. 500p. 1980. text ed. 17.95 (ISBN 0-8299-0325-9); instrs.' manual avail. (ISBN 0-8299-0472-7). West Pub.

Management of Compensation. Allan N. Nash & Stephen J. Carroll. LC 74-18922. (Behavioral Science in Industry Ser.). (Illus.). 1975. text ed. 11.95x (ISBN 0-8185-0135-9); pap. text ed. 8.95 (ISBN 0-8185-0135-9). Brooks-Cole.

Management of Development Projects: An International Case Study Approach. Ed. by Louis J. Goodman & Ralph N. Love. LC 78-26673. (Pergamon Policy Studies: No. 11). 272p. 1979. 29.50 (ISBN 0-08-022493-8). Pergamon.

Management of Diabetes Mellitus. Ed. by Rubin Bressler. LC 80-10866. 325p. 1981. 29.50 (ISBN 0-88416-259-1, 259). PSG Pub.

Management of Difficult Surgical Problems. Ed. by Stanley J. Dudrick & Thomas A. Miller. (Seminars in Surgery Ser.: No. 1). (Illus.). Date not set. text ed. 35.00x (ISBN 0-292-75049-8). U of Tex Pr.

Management of Educational Reforms in Sri-Lanka. (International Bureau of Education Ser: Experiments & Innovations in Education, No. 25). 41p. 1977. pap. 2.50 (ISBN 92-3-101372-6, U365, UNESCO). Unipub.

Management of Endocrine Disorders. Ed. by Jerome M. Hershman. LC 80-10850. (Illus.). 259p. 1980. pap. 13.50 (ISBN 0-8121-0715-2). Lea & Febiger.

Management of Engineering of Control Systems for Water Pipelines. Compiled by American Society of Civil Engineers. 208p. 1978. pap. text ed. 16.25 (ISBN 0-87262-132-4). Am Soc Civil Eng.

Management of Engineering Projects. M. Snowden. 1977. 19.95 (ISBN 0-408-00273-5). Butterworths.

Management of Epilepsy. Robert B. Aird & Dixon M. Woodbury. (American Lectures in Living Chemistry). (Illus.). 468p. 1974. 29.75 (ISBN 0-398-02881-8). C C Thomas.

Management of Expanding Enterprise. W. H. Newman. LC 55-7927. 1955. 20.00x (ISBN 0-231-02102-X). Columbia U Pr.

Management of Foreign Exchange Risk. Laurent L. Jacque. LC 77-12281. (Illus.). 1978. 24.95 (ISBN 0-669-01954-2). Lexington Bks.

Management of Fungus Diseases of the Lungs. Ed. by Howard A. Buechner. (Illus.). 248p. 1971. 22.50 (ISBN 0-398-00247-9). C C Thomas.

Management of Genetic Disorders: Proceedings. Ed. by Christos S. Bartsocas & Constantine J. Papadatos. LC 79-5298. (Progress in Clinical & Biological Research Ser.: Vol. 34). 1979. 32.00x (ISBN 0-8451-0034-3). A R Liss.

Management of Head Injuries. Bryan Jennett & Graham Teasdale. LC 80-16785. (Contemporary Neurology Ser.: Vol. 20). (Illus.). 361p. 1980. text ed. 35.00 (ISBN 0-8036-5017-5). Davis Co.

Management of Head Injuries. Ed. by H. Krayenbuehl et al. (Progress in Neurological Surgery: Vol. 10). (Illus.). 1981. 75.00 (ISBN 3-8055-0134-X). S Karger.

Management of Human Resources. Gellerman. 1976. 10.95 (ISBN 0-03-080485-X). Dryden Pr.

Management of Human Resources: Newer Approaches. Edwin Miller et al. (Illus.). 1980. pap. text ed. 13.95 (ISBN 0-13-549410-9). P-H.

Management of Infections of the Oral & Maxillofacial Regions. Richard G. Topazian & Morton H. Goldberg. (Illus.). 500p. 1981. text ed. price not set (ISBN 0-7216-8879-9). Saunders.

Management of Information Systems. Kenneth L. Kraemer et al. 416p. 1980. 25.00 (ISBN 0-231-04886-6). Columbia U Pr.

Management of Juvenile Diabetes Mellitus. 3rd ed. Howard S. Traisman. LC 79-24675. (Illus.). 1980. text ed. 42.50 (ISBN 0-8016-5020-8). Mosby.

Management of Large Capital Projects. 246p. 1980. 60.00x (ISBN 0-7277-0066-9, Pub. by Telford England). State Mutual Bk.

Management of Libraries & Information Centers, 3 vols. Mildred H. Lowell. Incl. Vol. 1. Case Method in Teaching Library Management. 10.00 (ISBN 0-8108-0089-6); Vol. 2. Process of Managing: Syllabus & Cases. 12.00 (ISBN 0-8108-0090-X); Vol. 4. Role Playing & Other Management Cases. 1971. 16.50 (ISBN 0-8108-0424-7). LC 68-12642. (Illus.). 1968. Scarecrow.

Management of Library Networks: Policy Analysis, Implementation, & Control. William B. Rouse & Sandra H. Rouse. LC 80-12644. (Information Sciences Ser.). 288p. 1980. 25.95 (ISBN 0-471-05534-4, Pub. by Wiley Interscience). Wiley.

Management of Low & Intermediate Level Radioactive Wastes. (Illus., Orig.). 1971. pap. 46.25 (ISBN 92-0-020170-9, IAEA). Unipub.

Management of Low-Level Radioactive Waste, 2 vols. Ed. by Melvin W. Carter et al. 1979. 155.00 (ISBN 0-08-023907-2). Pergamon.

Management of Maintenance & Engineering Systems in Hospitality Industries. Frank D. Borsenik. LC 78-13677. (Service Management Ser.). 1979. text ed. 22.95 (ISBN 0-471-03213-1); solutions manual avail. (ISBN 0-471-05185-3); tchrs. manual (ISBN 0-471-05374-0). Wiley.

Management of Marketing. M. T. Wilson. LC 80-23617. 141p. 1981. 29.95 (ISBN 0-470-27074-8). Halsted Pr.

Management of Medical Problems in Surgical Patients. Mark E. Molitch. 1981. 30.00 (ISBN 0-8036-6286-6). Davis Co.

Management of Migratory Shore & Upland Game Birds in North America. Ed. by Glen C. Sanderson. LC 79-23802. (Illus.). 1980. pap. 10.95 (ISBN 0-8032-9117-5, BB725, Bison). U of Nebr Pr.

Management of Motivation & Renumeration. D. A. Whitmore & J. Ibbetson. 230p. 1977. text ed. 29.50x (ISBN 0-220-66319-X, Pub. by Busn Bks England). Renouf.

Management of National & Regional Water Resources. Institute of Civil Engineers, UK. 98p. 1980. 60.00x (ISBN 0-901948-65-9, Pub. by Telford England). State Mutual Bk.

Management of Natural Resources in Africa: Traditional Strategies & Modern Decision Making. (MAB Technical Note Ser.: No. 9). 1979. pap. 10.00 (ISBN 92-3-101587-7, U867, UNESCO). Unipub.

Management of Office Operations. C. L. Littlefield et al. (Illus.). 1978. ref. 18.95 (ISBN 0-13-548834-6). P-H.

Management of Oil & Gas Exploration Risk. John M. Cozzolino. LC 77-84169. (Business Risk Analysis Ser.). 1977. 47.50 (ISBN 0-9601408-1-6). Cozzolino Assocs.

Management of Organizational Behavior: Utilizing Human Resources. 3rd ed. Paul Hersey & Ken Blanchard. LC 76-28443. (Illus.). 1977. ref. ed. 15.95x (ISBN 0-13-548875-3); pap. 10.95x (ISBN 0-13-548867-2). P-H.

Management of Organizations. 4th ed. Herbert G. Hicks & C. Ray Gullett. (Illus.). 656p. 1981. text ed. 16.95 (ISBN 0-07-028773-2, C); instr's manual 5.95 (ISBN 0-07-028774-0); study guide 5.95 (ISBN 0-07-028777-5). McGraw.

Management of Owner-Operator Fleets. David H. Maister. LC 79-5112. 256p. 1980. 23.95 (ISBN 0-669-03197-6). Lexington Bks.

Management of Patient Care: Putting Leadership Skill to Work. 4th ed. Thora Kron. LC 75-38153. (Illus.). 1976. pap. text ed. 9.95 (ISBN 0-7216-5528-9). Saunders.

Management of Patient Care: Putting Leadership Skills to Work. Thora Kron. (Illus.). 247p. 1981. pap. text ed. 9.95 (ISBN 0-7216-5529-7). Saunders.

Management of Physical Distribution and Transportation. 6th ed. Charles A. Taff. 1978. text ed. 19.50 (ISBN 0-256-02016-7). Irwin.

Management of Public Enterprise: A Bibliography. Compiled by Nelson R. Maurice. (Miscellaneous Publications Ser.). (Orig.). 1975. pap. 7.50 (ISBN 0-86603-009-3). Bureau Busn Res U Wis.

Management of Public Relations: Analysis & Planning External Relations. Robert D. Ross. LC 77-9288. (Marketing Management Ser.). 1977. 23.95 (ISBN 0-471-03109-7). Ronald Pr.

Management of Radioactive Wastes from the Nuclear Fuel Cycle, 2 vols. (STI-PUB-433). (Illus.). 1977. Vol. 1. pap. 39.75 (ISBN 92-0-020276-4, ISP 433-1, IAEA); Vol. 2. pap. 32.00 (ISBN 92-0-020376-0, ISP 433-2). Unipub.

Management of Retirement Homes & Long Term Care Facilities. John H. Coggeshall. LC 73-4450. 1973. 13.95 o.p. (ISBN 0-8016-1008-7). Mosby.

Management of Sales Forecasting. Frank H. Eby & William J. O'Neill. 1977. 23.95 (ISBN 0-669-00046-9). Lexington Bks.

Management of Scientific Research in India: Administrative Staff College of India Occasional Papers. Jitendra Singh. (Illus.). 311p. 1974. 15.00 o.p. (ISBN 0-88253-485-8). InterCulture.

Management of Self-Esteem: How People Can Feel Good About Themselves & Better About Their Organizations. Pete Bradshaw. (Illus.). 368p. 1981. 10.95 (ISBN 0-13-549535-0, Spec); pap. 4.95 (ISBN 0-13-549527-X). P-H.

Management of Sensorineural Deafness. A. Morisson. 1975. 48.95 (ISBN 0-407-00024-0). Butterworths.

Management of Service Operations. W. Earl Sasser et al. 1978. text ed. 23.95 (ISBN 0-205-06104-4, 0861049); instr's man. avail. (ISBN 0-205-06105-2, 0861057). Allyn.

Management of Shipboard Maintenance. B. E. Thomas. (Illus.). 143p. 1981. 18.50x (ISBN 0-540-07354-7). Sheridan.

Management of Small Business. new ed. Victor A. Grieco. (Business Ser). 1975. text ed. 18.95 (ISBN 0-675-08731-7); instructors manual 3.95 (ISBN 0-685-50983-4). Merrill.

Management of Small Offset Print Departments. 2nd ed. Harry T. Chambers. 217p. 1979. text ed. 22.00x (ISBN 0-220-67007-2, Pub. by Busn Bks England). Renouf.

Management of Squatter Upgrading. D. Pasteur. 1979. text ed. 30.75x (ISBN 0-566-00266-3, Pub. by Gower Pub Co England). Renouf.

Management of Stress: Using TM at Work. David R. Frew. LC 76-18164. 1977. 15.95 (ISBN 0-88229-254-4). Nelson-Hall.

Management of Surgical Infections. Ed. by Morris D. Kerstein. LC 80-16740. (Illus.). 224p. 1980. monograph 23.00 (ISBN 0-87993-067-5). Futura Pub.

Management of Sustainable Growth. Ed. by Harlan Cleveland. LC 80-24162. (Pergamon Policy Studies on International Development). 386p. 1981. 40.00 (ISBN 0-08-027171-5). Pergamon.

Management of Technology: Change in a Society of Organized Advocacies. rev. ed. Joseph A. Raffaele. LC 79-63752. 1979. pap. text ed. 11.75 (ISBN 0-8191-0739-5). U Pr of Amer.

Management of Textile Production. A. Ormerod. (Illus.). 1979. text ed. 44.95 (ISBN 0-408-00381-2). Butterworths.

Management of the Australian Economy. Joseph Martin. (Illus.). 1979. 20.50x (ISBN 0-7022-1358-6); pap. 9.75x (ISBN 0-7022-1359-4). U of Queensland Pr.

Management of the British Economy, Nineteen Forty- Five-Sixty. J. C. Dow. LC 64-21542. (National Institute of Economic & Social Research Economic & Social Studies: No. 22). 1970. pap. 14.95x (ISBN 0-521-09467-4). Cambridge U Pr.

Management of the Burned Child. P. P. Rickham & W. C. Hecker. (Progress in Pediatric Surgery Ser.: Vol. 14). 1981. write for info. (ISBN 0-8067-1514-6). Urban & S.

Management of the Cardiac Patient with Renal Failure. William Likoff et al. 1981. 25.00 (ISBN 0-8036-5643-2). Davis Co.

Management of the Family Company. 19p. 1973. 2.75 (APO43, APO). Unipub.

Management of the Firm. David Coleman. 13.95; pap. 9.95 (ISBN 0-930726-02-2). Green Hill.

Management of the Geriatric Dental Patient. Kenneth Freedman. (Illus.). 148p. 1980. 42.00 (ISBN 0-931386-05-5). Quint Pub Co.

Management of the Infertile Couple. Maxwell Roland. (Illus.). 256p. 1968. 14.75 (ISBN 0-398-01603-8). C C Thomas.

Management of the Information Department. Denis V. Arnold. LC 76-43375. 1978. lib. bdg. 18.50x (ISBN 0-89158-716-0). Westview.

Management of the Multinationals: Policies, Operations, & Research. Ed. by S. Prakash Sethi & Richard H. Holton. LC 73-17644. (Illus.). 1974. 19.95 (ISBN 0-02-928410-4). Free Pr.

Management of the Patient-Ventilator System: A Team Approach. Kathren V. Martz et al. LC 78-31819. (Illus.). 1979. pap. text ed. 12.95 (ISBN 0-8016-3139-4). Mosby.

Management of the Sales Force. 5th ed. William J. Stanton & Richard H. Buskirk. 1978. text ed. 19.95x (ISBN 0-256-02046-9). Irwin.

Management of the Total Enterprise: Cases & Concepts in Business Policy. Robert L. Katz. 1970. ref. ed. 20.95 (ISBN 0-13-548933-4). P-H.

Management of the Unconscious Patient. 1st ed. Edward Hitchcock & Alastair Massan. (Illus.). 96p. 1970. 3.50 (ISBN 0-632-07860-X, Blackwell Scientific). Mosby.

Management of Thoracic Emergencies. 3rd ed. John Borrie. (Illus.). 500p. 1979. 39.50x (ISBN 0-8385-6124-1). ACC.

Management of Thoracic Trauma Victims. J. Kent Trinkle. (Illus.). 139p. 1980. pap. text ed. 11.75 (ISBN 0-397-50415-2). Lippincott.

Management of Training: A Handbook for Training Directors. C. P. Otto & R. O. Glaser. 1970. 20.95 (ISBN 0-201-05510-4). A-W.

Management of Transportation Carriers. Grant M. Davis et al. LC 73-21465. (Special Studies). (Illus.). 308p. 1975. text ed. 32.95 (ISBN 0-275-08680-1). Praeger.

Management of Turfgrass Disease. Joseph M. Vargas, Jr. (Orig.). 1981. write for info. (ISBN 0-8087-2214-X). Burgess.

Management of Vehicle Production. John R. Hartley. (Illus.). 216p. 1980. text ed. 32.00 (ISBN 0-408-00396-0). Butterworths.

Management of Wastes & Milling of Uranium & Thorium Ores: A Code of Practice & Guide to the Code. (Safety Ser: No. 44). (Illus.). 1977. pap. 6.50 (ISBN 92-0-123276-4, ISP 457, IAEA). Unipub.

Management of Water Quality & the Environment: Proceedings of a Conference Held by the International Economic Assoc. at Lyngby. Ed. by J. G. Rothenberg & I. G. Heggie. LC 74-7584. (International Economic Association Ser.). 1974. 36.95 (ISBN 0-470-73960-6). Halsted Pr.

Management of Word Processing Operations. Paula B. Cecil. 1980. 18.95 (ISBN 0-8053-1759-7). Benjamin-Cummings.

Management of Work: A Socio-Technical Systems Approach. Thomas G. Cummings & Suresh Srivastva. LC 76-47659. 1977. 15.00x o.p. (ISBN 0-87338-188-2, Pub. by Comp. Adm. Research Inst.). Kent St U Pr.

Management of Work: A Workbook. William E. Broadwell, Jr. (Business Ser). (Illus.). 1971. 8.95 (ISBN 0-201-00672-3). A-W.

Management Operations in Education. Guilbert C. Hentschke. LC 75-9168. (Illus.). 280p. 1976. 20.00x (ISBN 0-8211-0757-7); text ed. 18.00x (ISBN 0-685-61057-8). McCutchan.

Management Option. Sudhalter. LC 80-12992. 256p. 1980. 16.95 (ISBN 0-87705-084-8). Human Sci Pr.

Management or Control? The Organizational Challenge. Russell Stout, Jr. LC 79-3302. 224p. 1980. 12.95x (ISBN 0-253-12082-9). Ind U Pr.

Management Performance Appraisal: A National Study. Ferdinand F. Fournies. 1977. 12.00 (ISBN 0-917472-03-9). F Fournies.

Management: Perspectives from the Social Sciences. G. William Bullock, Jr. & Clifton F. Conrad. LC 80-6097. 343p. 1981. lib. bdg. 19.75 (ISBN 0-8191-1466-9); pap. text ed. 11.00 (ISBN 0-8191-1467-7). U Pr of Amer.

Management Planning & Control Systems: Advanced Concepts & Cases. Jerry Dermer. 1977. 18.95x (ISBN 0-256-01874-X). Irwin.

Management Policies for Commercial Banks. 3rd ed. Howard Crosse & Goerge Hempel. (Illus.). 1980. text ed. 18.95 (ISBN 0-13-549030-8). P-H.

Management Policies in Local Government Finance. Ed. by J. Richard Aronson & Eli Schwartz. LC 75-9500. (Municipal Management Ser.). 1975. 20.00 o.p. (ISBN 0-87326-000-7). Intl City Mgt.

Management Policy. Melvin J. Stanford. (Illus.). 1979. ref. 21.00 (ISBN 0-13-548974-1). P-H.

Management Policy: Strategies & Plans. Milton Leontiades. 680p. 1981. text ed. 18.95 (ISBN 0-316-52104-3); tchrs'. manual free (ISBN 0-316-52105-1). Little.

Management Practices for the Health Professional. 2nd ed. Beafort B. Longest, Jr. (Illus.). 1980. text ed. 15.95 (ISBN 0-8359-4224-4). Reston.

Management Primer. Karl E. Ettinger. Ed. by Ralph C. Hook, Jr. & John R. Overton. LC 72-86485. 353p. 1973. 18.25 (ISBN 92-833-1023-3, APO48, APO). Unipub.

Management Primer on Water Pollution Control. Frank L. Cross, Jr. LC 74-76523. 150p. 1974. pap. 25.00 (ISBN 0-87762-136-5). Technomic.

Management Principles & Practice: A Guide to Information Sources. Ed. by K. G. Bakewell. LC 76-16127. (Management Information Guide Series: No. 32). 1977. 30.00 (ISBN 0-8103-0832-0). Gale.

Management Principles & Practices: A Contingency & Questionnaire Approach. Robert J. Thierauf et al. LC 77-23297. (Management & Administration Ser.). 1977. text ed. 23.95x (ISBN 0-471-29504-3); tchr's manual avail. (ISBN 0-471-03728-1). Wiley.

Management Problems & Solution: A Guide to Problem Solving. Stanley E. Carnarius. LC 76-1741. 128p. 1976. pap. 8.95 (ISBN 0-201-00881-5). A-W.

Management Procedures. Leslie Lee & Robert Comte. LC 74-18677. (Allied Health Ser). 1975. pap. 6.35 (ISBN 0-672-61397-2). Bobbs.

Management Procedures for Institutions. Ray M. Powell. LC 78-51525. (Studies in the Management of Not-for-Profit Institutions: No. 2). (Illus.). 1980. text ed. 12.95x (ISBN 0-268-01344-6). U of Notre Dame Pr.

Management Properties of Ferralsols. (Soils Bulletin: No. 23). 120p. 1980. pap. 6.75 (ISBN 0-686-62996-5, F-1165, FAO). Unipub.

Management Reports on Financial Statements. (Financial Report Survey Ser.: No. 19). 1980. pap. 9.00. Am Inst CPA.

Management Science. Sang M. Lee et al. 1050p. 1981. write for info. (ISBN 0-697-08046-3); instr's manual avail. Wm C Brown.

Management Science - Operations Research: Model Formulation & Solution Methods. Elwood S. Buffa & James S. Dyer. LC 76-25058. (Management & Administration Ser.). 1977. 25.50 (ISBN 0-471-11915-6); instructor's manual avail. (ISBN 0-471-02200-4). Wiley.

Management Science: A Self-Correcting Approach. Barry Render & Ralph M. Stair, Jr. 1978. pap. text ed. 12.95 (ISBN 0-205-06079-X, 1060791). Allyn.

Management Science: An Introduction. David D. Dannebring & Martin K. Starr. (Quantitative Methods in Management Ser.). 1981. text ed. 22.00 (ISBN 0-07-015352-3, C); write for info study guide (ISBN 0-07-015353-1); write for info instrs.' manual (ISBN 0-07-015354-X). McGraw.

Management Science: An Introduction. Fadil H. Zuwaylif et al. LC 78-5827. (Management & Administration Ser.). 1979. text ed. 24.95 (ISBN 0-471-98675-5); sol. manual avail. (ISBN 0-471-03222-0). Wiley.

Management Science & Environmental Problems. J. C. Papageorgiou. (Illus.). 160p. 1980. 16.75 (ISBN 0-398-03995-X). C C Thomas.

Management Science & the Manager: A Casebook. E. F. Newson. (Illus.). 1980. pap. text ed. 11.95 (ISBN 0-13-549444-3). P-H.

Management Science for Management Decisions. Ulysses S. Knotts & Ernest W. Swift. 1978. text ed. 19.95 (ISBN 0-205-06039-0, 1060392); instr's man. avail. (ISBN 0-205-06040-4, 1060406); sol. man. avail. (ISBN 0-205-06041-2, 1060414). Allyn.

Management Science: Introduction to Modern Quantitative Analysis & Decision Making. Gerald E. Thompson. 1976. text ed. 19.95 (ISBN 0-07-064360-1, C); instructor's manual 4.95 (ISBN 0-07-064361-X). McGraw.

Management Science-Operations Research: Formulation & Solution Methods. 2nd ed. Elwood S. Buffa & James S. Dyer. LC 80-18082. 725p. 1981. text ed. 25.95 (ISBN 0-471-05851-3). Wiley.

Management Science: Quantitative Methods in Context. Ed. by Lee J. Krajewski & Howard E. Thompson. LC 80-17103. (Management Ser.). 560p. 1981. text ed. write for info. (ISBN 0-471-06109-3). Wiley.

Management Science: Text & Applications. John J. Dinkel et al. 1978. text ed. 20.95x (ISBN 0-256-02037-X). Irwin.

Management Services Technical Studies, 9 vols. American Institute Of Certified Public Accountants. Set. post binder 47.50 o.p. (ISBN 0-685-05615-5). Am Inst CPA.

Management Standards for Developing Information Systems. Norman Enger. 1980. pap. 5.95 (ISBN 0-8144-7527-2). Am Mgmt.

Management Standards for Developing Information Systems. new ed. Norman L. Enger. LC 76-41827. (Illus.). 1977. 13.95 (ISBN 0-8144-5425-9). Am Mgmt.

Management Strategies for Women: Or, Now That I'm Boss, How Do I Run This Place? Ann M. Thompson & Marcia D. Wood. 1981. 10.95 (ISBN 0-671-25476-6). S&S.

Management Stress. Leonard Moss. (Occupational Stress Ser.). 224p. 1981. pap. text ed. 6.50 (ISBN 0-201-05050-1). A-W.

Management: Structures, Functions, & Practices. A. Elkins. 1980. 17.95 (ISBN 0-201-01517-X). A-W.

Management Style of the Chief Accountant: A Situational Perspective. Eugene F. McKenna. 1978. 24.95 (ISBN 0-566-00216-7, 02176-8, Pub. by Saxon Hse England). Lexington Bks.

Management Sucession: From Owner-Founder to Professional Resident. Maryam Tashakori. (Praeger Special Studies). 140p. 1980. 19.95 (ISBN 0-03-047076-5). Praeger.

Management System for the Seventies. John Argenti. 1972. text ed. 16.50x (ISBN 0-04-658044-1). Allen Unwin.

Management System: Systems Are for People. Leslie H. Matthies. LC 76-4572. (Wiley Series on Systems & Controls for Financial Management). 240p. 1976. 26.50 (ISBN 0-471-57697-2, Pub. by Wiley-Interscience). Wiley.

Management Systems. 2nd ed. Burton Grad et al. 504p. 1979. text ed. 21.95 (ISBN 0-03-047541-4). Dryden Pr.

Management Systems. Adrian M. McDonough & Leonard J. Garrett. 1965. text ed. 17.95 (ISBN 0-256-00321-1). Irwin.

Management Systems: Conceptual Considerations. rev. ed. Peter P. Schoderbek et al. 1980. pap. 11.95x (ISBN 0-256-02275-5). Business Pubns.

Management Systems in the Human Services: An Introduction to New Technologies. Ed. by Murray L. Gruber. 325p. 1981. 19.50x (ISBN 0-87722-207-X). Temple U Pr.

Management Techniques Applied to the Construction Industry. 2nd ed. R. Oxley & J. Poskitt. 1971. pap. 14.95x (ISBN 0-8464-0593-8). Beekman Pubs.

Management Techniques for Librarians. G. E. Evans. (Library & Information Science Ser.). 276p. 1976. 17.00 (ISBN 0-12-243850-7). Acad Pr.

Management: The Art of Working with & Through People. Donald C. Mosley & Paul H. Pietri, Jr. 1974. pap. 12.95x o.p. (ISBN 0-8221-0137-8). Dickenson.

Management: The Basic Concepts. Henry H. Albers. LC 73-172949. 1979. text ed. 18.95 (ISBN 0-471-01925-9); text ed. 14.95 Arabic ed. (ISBN 0-471-06348-7); pap. 8.95 (ISBN 0-471-05142-X). Wiley.

Management: The Basic Concepts. Henry H. Albers. 336p. 1981. Repr. of 1972 ed. lib. bdg. price not set (ISBN 0-89874-312-5). Krieger.

Management: The Managerial Ethos & the Future of Planet Earth. Thomas Berry. 1980. pap. 2.00 (ISBN 0-89012-016-1). Anima Pubns.

Management: Theory & Application. Leslie W. Rue & Lloyd L. Byars. 1977. 15.95x o.p. (ISBN 0-256-01885-5). Irwin.

Management: Theory & Application. rev. ed. Leslie W. Rue & Lloyd L. Byars. 1980. 18.95x (ISBN 0-256-02346-8). Irwin.

Management Today. James A. Belasco et al. LC 74-28245. 528p. 1975. text ed. 19.95 (ISBN 0-471-06365-7); instructor's manual avail. (ISBN 0-471-06366-5). Wiley.

Management Tools for Everyone. Steve M. Erickson. (Illus.). 160p. 1981. 17.50 (ISBN 0-89433-131-0). Petrocelli.

Management: Toward Accountability for Performance. rev. ed. Robert Albanese. 1978. text ed. 19.50x (ISBN 0-256-02039-6). Irwin.

Managements Complete Guide to Employee Benefits. J. W. Lawson & Ballard Smith. 259p. 1980. 69.50 (ISBN 0-85013-119-7). Dartnell Corp.

Management's Guide to Effective Employment Interviewing. Roland T. Ramsay. 1980. 59.50 (ISBN 0-85013-089-1). Dartnell Corp.

Management's Guide to Word Processing. Walter Kleinschrod. 1980. 59.50 (ISBN 0-85013-070-0). Dartnell Corp.

Manager & Industrial Relations. Trevor Owen. 1979. 35.00 (ISBN 0-08-022471-7); pap. 12.75 (ISBN 0-08-022472-5). Pergamon.

Manager & Subordinates. Gellerman. 1976. 13.95 (ISBN 0-03-089928-1). Dryden Pr.

Manager & the Environment: General Theory & Practice of Environmental Management. Jack G. Beale. LC 79-40712. (Illus.). 192p. 1980. 33.00 (ISBN 0-08-024043-7); pap. 16.75 (ISBN 0-08-024044-5). Pergamon.

Manager & Training. Alan Mumford. (Times Management Library). 1971. 12.00x o.p. (ISBN 0-8464-0594-6, 0-273-3155-2). Beekman Pubs.

Manager As an Editor: Reviewing Memos, Letters & Reports. Louis J. Visco. 172p. 1981. pap. 8.95 (ISBN 0-8436-0852-8). CBI Pub.

Manager As Communicator. Sandra E. O'Connell. 1980. text ed. 13.95 (ISBN 0-06-044881-4, HarpC). Har-Row.

Manager Beyond the Organization. Ray Arabinda. 1980. 9.50x (ISBN 0-8364-0636-2, Pub. by Macmillan India). South Asia Bks.

Manager in the International Economy. 4th ed. Louis T. Wells & Raymond Vernon. (Illus.). 1981. text ed. 18.95 (ISBN 0-13-549550-4). P-H.

Managerial Accounting. Davidson et al. 1978. 20.95 (ISBN 0-03-017416-3). Dryden Pr.

Managerial Accounting. 3rd ed. Drebin. 1978. 20.95 (ISBN 0-7216-3188-6). Dryden Pr.

Managerial Accounting. 3rd ed. Arthur J. Francia & Robert H. Strawser. (Illus.). 565p. 1980. pap. text ed. 18.95 (ISBN 0-931920-20-5); practice problems 4.95x; study guide 5.95x; work papers 6.95x. Dame Pubns.

Managerial Accounting. Lester E. Heitger & Serge Matulich. 1980. text ed. 18.95 (ISBN 0-07-027941-1); study guide 6.95 (ISBN 0-07-027942-X); job costing packet (ISBN 0-07-027943-8); profit planning packet (ISBN 0-07-027946-2); solutions manual 25.00 (ISBN 0-07-027944-6); examination questions 15.00 (ISBN 0-07-027945-4); overhead transparencies 325.00 (ISBN 0-07-074792-X). McGraw.

Managerial Accounting: An Introduction to Planning, Information Processing & Control. 2nd ed. Ronald M. Copeland & Paul E. Dascher. LC 74-5147. 658p. 1978. text ed. 21.95 (ISBN 0-471-17171-9); study guide 7.95 (ISBN 0-471-02346-9). Wiley.

Managerial Accounting: Concepts & Uses. 2nd ed. Rudolph W. Schattke et al. 656p. 1981. text ed. 19.95 (ISBN 0-205-07319-0, 0543268); avail. tchrs guide (ISBN 0-205-06073-0); avail. study guide (ISBN 0-205-07322-0). Allyn.

Managerial Accounting: Concepts for Planning, Control, Decision Making. rev. ed. Ray H. Garrison. 1979. 18.95x (ISBN 0-256-02209-7); study guide 5.95x (ISBN 0-256-02249-6). Business Pubns.

Managerial Accounting Information: An Introduction to Its Content & Usefulness. A. Thompson Montgomery. LC 78-67943. 1979. text ed. 18.95 (ISBN 0-201-04927-9). A-W.

Managerial Accounting: The Behavioral Foundations. J. L. Livingstone. LC 74-23018. (Accounting Ser.). 1975. pap. text ed. 8.95 o.p. (ISBN 0-88244-079-9). Grid Pub.

Managerial & Professional Staff Grading. Joan Doulton & David Hay. (Studies in Management). 1962. pap. text ed. 4.95x (ISBN 0-04-658028-X). Allen Unwin.

Managerial & Supervisory Practice. 7th ed. William M. Berliner. 1979. 17.95x (ISBN 0-256-02040-X). Irwin.

Managerial Choice: To Be Efficient & to Be Human. Frederick Herzberg. 1976. pap. 11.95 (ISBN 0-256-01882-0). Irwin.

Managerial Communication. Michael Lillico. LC 77-188641. 168p. 1972. text ed. 18.00 (ISBN 0-08-016633-4). Pergamon.

Managerial Communication: A Finger on the Pulse. Paul R. Timm. (Illus.). 1980. text ed. 15.95 (ISBN 0-13-549824-4). P-H.

Managerial Control & Organizational Democracy. Ed. by Bert King et al. LC 77-13200. (Scripta Ser. in Personality & Social Psychology). 1978. 22.95 (ISBN 0-470-99323-5). Halsted Pr.

Managerial Cost Accounting: Analysis & Control. 4th ed. Gordon Shillinglaw. 1977. text ed. 20.50 (ISBN 0-256-01905-3). Irwin.
Managerial Cost Accounting for Hospitals. American Hospital Association. LC 79-29708. (Financial Management Ser.). (Illus.). 144p. 1980. manual 20.00 (ISBN 0-87258-296-5, 1333). Am Hospital.
Managerial Decision Making. J. Bridge & J. C. Dodds. LC 75-18977. 309p. 1975. 15.95 (ISBN 0-470-10365-5). Halsted Pr.
Managerial Decision Making. K. J. Radford. (Illus.). 256p. 1975. 14.95 (ISBN 0-87909-473-7). Reston.
Managerial Dilemmas & Executive Growth. Frank V. Manning. 1981. text ed. 17.95 (ISBN 0-8359-4231-7). Reston.
Managerial Economics. Joel Dean. 1951. ref. ed. 19.95 (ISBN 0-13-549972-0). P-H.
Managerial Economics. D. N. Dwivedi. 1980. text ed. 20.00x (ISBN 0-7069-0794-9, Pub. by Vikas India). Advent Bk.
Managerial Economics. 2nd ed. James R. McGuigan & R. Charles Moyer. 1979. text ed. 19.50 (ISBN 0-8299-0176-0); solutions manual avail. (ISBN 0-8299-0558-8); study guide 6.95 (ISBN 0-8299-0287-2); study guide 6.95 (ISBN 0-8299-0559-6). West Pub.
Managerial Economics. 3rd ed. Papper. 1979. 21.95 (ISBN 0-03-045126-4). Dryden Pr.
Managerial Economics. W. Duncan Reekie. 440p. 1975. 45.00x (ISBN 0-86003-007-5, Pub. by Allan Pubs England); pap. 22.50x (ISBN 0-86003-108-X). State Mutual Bk.
Managerial Economics. 5th ed. K. K. Seo & Bernard J. Winger. 1979. 19.00 (ISBN 0-256-02177-5). Irwin.
Managerial Economics. Samuel C. Webb. LC 75-31039. (Illus.). 608p. 1976. text ed. 20.95 (ISBN 0-395-20589-1); solutions manual 2.75 (ISBN 0-395-20590-5). HM.
Managerial Economics: Analysis and Cases. 4th ed. William R. Henry & Warren W. Haynes. 1978. 19.95x (ISBN 0-256-02079-5). Business Pubns.
Managerial Economics: Readings, Cases & Exercises. R. Charles Moyer et al. 1979. pap. text ed. 11.95 (ISBN 0-8299-0157-4); pap. text ed. solutions manual avail. (ISBN 0-8299-0632-0). West Pub.
Managerial Economics: Text & Cases. rev ed. Charles J. Christenson et al. 1973. text ed. 18.95x (ISBN 0-256-00089-1). Irwin.
Managerial Economics: Theory, Practice & Problems. Evan J. Douglas. (Illus.). 1979. ref. 20.95 (ISBN 0-13-550236-5). P-H.
Managerial Finance. 7th ed. J. Fred Weston & Eugene F. Brigham. LC 80-65811. 1088p. 1981. text ed. 20.95 (ISBN 0-03-058186-9). Dryden Pr.
Managerial Finance: Essentials. 2nd ed. Charles Kroncke et al. (Illus.). 1978. text ed. 19.50 (ISBN 0-8299-0159-0); study guide 6.95 (ISBN 0-8299-0161-2); instrs.' manual avail. (ISBN 0-8299-0550-2). West Pub.
Managerial Finance: Principles & Practice. Steven E. Bolten. LC 75-31036. (Illus.). 896p. 1976. text ed. 20.95 (ISBN 0-395-20462-3); instr's. manual 2.00 (ISBN 0-395-20461-5). HM.
Managerial Finance: Theory & Techniques. Dennis J. O'Connor & Alberto T. Bueso. (Illus.). 528p. 1981. text ed. 21.00 (ISBN 0-13-550269-1); pap. 8.95 study guide (ISBN 0-13-550293-4). P-H.
Managerial Innovation & Change in the Metropolitan Hospital. Dalton E. McFarland. LC 79-14557. (Praeger Special Studies Ser.). 336p. 1979. 28.95 (ISBN 0-03-051341-3). Praeger.
Managerial Insights: Analysis, Decisions, & Implementation. Robert H. Doktor & Michael A. Moses. (Illus.). 432p. 1973. pap. text ed. 11.95 (ISBN 0-13-550103-2). P-H.
Managerial Introduction to Marketing. 3rd ed. Thomas A. Staudt & Donald Taylor. (Illus.). 576p. 1976. 18.95x (ISBN 0-13-550186-5). P-H.
Managerial Mind. David W. Ewing. LC 64-16957. 1968. pap. text ed. 2.95 (ISBN 0-02-910050-X). Free Pr.
Managerial Mind: Science & Theory in Policy Decisions. 4th ed. Charles E. Summer, Jr. et al. 1977. text ed. 20.50x (ISBN 0-256-01922-3). Irwin.
Managerial Odyssey: Problems in Business & Its Enviroment. Arthur Elkins & Dennis W. Callaghan. 600p. 1981. text ed. 17.50 (ISBN 0-201-03962-1). A-W.
Managerial Planning with Linear Programming: In Process Industry Operations. Julius S. Aronofsky et al. LC 78-2848. 1978. 41.95 (ISBN 0-471-03360-X). Ronald Pr.
Managerial Process & Organizational Behavior. 2nd ed. Alan C. Filley et al. 1976. text ed. 18.95x (ISBN 0-673-07857-4). Scott F.
Managerial Process in Human Service Agencies. David W. Young. LC 78-19767. (Praeger Special Studies). 1979. 27.95 (ISBN 0-03-047081-1). Praeger.
Managerial Roles in Industrial Relations: Towards a Definitive Survey of Research & Formulation of Models. Michael Poole & Roger Mansfield. 1980. text ed. 27.75x (ISBN 0-566-00377-5, Pub. by Gower Pub Co England). Renouf.
Managerial Stress. Ed. by Dan Gowler & Karen Legge. LC 74-20107. 236p. 1975. 14.95 (ISBN 0-470-31985-2). Halsted Pr.
Managerial Woman. Margaret Hennig & Anne Jardim. 221p. 1981. pap. 5.95 (ISBN 0-385-02291-3, Anch). Doubleday.
Managers. Jay H. Smith. LC 76-8905. (Stars of the Nl & Al Ser.). (Illus.). (gr. 4-12). 1976. PLB 7.95 (ISBN 0-87191-516-2). Creative Ed.
Managers & Their Careers. Jay W. Lorsch & Louis B. Barnes. 1972. pap. text ed. 8.95 (ISBN 0-256-01296-2). Irwin.
Managers & Work Reform: A Limited Engagement. Ivar Berg et al. LC 77-83165. (Illus.). 1978. 15.95 (ISBN 0-02-902900-7). Free Pr.
Managers & Workers: Origins of the New Factory System in the United States, 1880-1920. Daniel Nelson. 1979. pap. 6.95 (ISBN 0-299-06904-4). U of Wis Pr.
Managers: Corporate Life in America. Diane R. Margolis. 312p. 1981. pap. 5.95 (ISBN 0-688-00351-6, Quill). Morrow.
Manager's Desk Guide to Communication. Thomas E. Anastasi, Jr. 300p. 1981. 15.95 (ISBN 0-8436-0855-2). CBI Pub.
Managers for the Year Two Thousand. William H. Newman. (Illus.). 1978. ref. ed. 15.95 (ISBN 0-13-549378-1); pap. 8.95 o.p. P-H.
Manager's Guide to Computer Timesharing. Timothy P. Haidinger & Dana R. Richardson. LC 74-18413. (Manager's Guide Ser.). 192p. 1975. 18.95 (ISBN 0-471-33925-3, Pub. by Wiley-Interscience). Wiley.
Manager's Guide to Industrial Relations. L. F. Neal & Andrew Robertson. (Studies in Management). 1977. write for info o.p. (ISBN 0-04-658023-9). Allen Unwin.
Manager's Guide to Interpersonal Relations. Donald Sanzotta. (Illus.). 1979. 12.95 (ISBN 0-8144-5508-5). Am Mgmt.
Manager's Guide to Operations Research. R. L. Ackoff & Patrick Rivett. LC 63-14115. (Managers Guide Ser.). 1963. 15.95 (ISBN 0-471-00335-2, Pub by Wiley-Interscience). Wiley.
Manager's Guide to Speaking & Listening. J. Campbell Connelly. LC 67-29357. 1967. 7.95 o.p. (ISBN 0-8144-5156-X). AM Mgmt.
Manager's Guide to the Tutor-Notetaker. Russel T. Osguthorpe. 122p. 1980. pap. text ed. 6.00 (ISBN 0-88200-129-9, N6796). Alexander Graham.
Manager's Personal Problem Solver: A Handbook of Creative Solutions to Human Relations Problems in Your Organization. John F. Lorentzen. 1980. 15.95 (ISBN 0-13-549915-1, Spec); pap. 6.95 (ISBN 0-13-549907-0, Spec). P-H.
Manager's Standard Manual. Thomas A. Rullo. LC 77-10033. (Illus.). 1977. text ed. 12.00 (ISBN 0-89433-000-4); pap. text ed. 10.00 (ISBN 0-89433-018-7). Petrocelli.
Managing: A Contemporary Introduction. 2nd ed. J. L. Massie & John Douglas. LC 76-22521. (Illus.). 1977. text ed. 19.95 (ISBN 0-13-548545-2); student resource manual 6.95 (ISBN 0-13-548149-X). P-H.
Managing: A Contemporary Introduction. 3rd ed. Joseph L. Massie & John Douglas. (Illus.). 544p. 1981. text ed. 17.95 (ISBN 0-13-550327-2); pap. 7.95 student manual (ISBN 0-13-550368-X). P-H.
Managing a Programming Project. 2nd ed. Philip Metzger. (Illus.). 288p. 1981. text ed. 21.50 (ISBN 0-13-550772-3). P-H.
Managing a Real Estate Team. Hire. 1980. 18.95 (ISBN 0-03-056788-2). Dryden Pr.
Managing a Successful Community Association. 2nd ed. LC 76-22827. (Illus.). 1976. pap. 9.75 (ISBN 0-87420-571-9). Urban Land.
Managing Advancing Technology, 2 vols. Ed. by Staff of Innovation. LC 79-182225. 1972. Set. 27.50 o.p. (ISBN 0-8144-5283-3). AM Mgmt.
Managing an Appraisal Office. Harry Lewman. 1971. 3.00 o.s.i. (ISBN 0-911780-27-0). Am Inst Real Estate Appraisers.
Managing & Accounting for Inventories: Control, Income Recognition, & Tax Strategy. 3rd ed. C. Paul Jannis et al. 1979. 34.50 (ISBN 0-471-05016-4, Pub by Ronald Pr). Wiley.
Managing & Being Managed: Preparation for Professional Nursing Practice. Teddy Langford. (Illus.). 304p. 1981. text ed. 15.95 (ISBN 0-13-550525-9); pap. text ed. 10.95 (ISBN 0-13-550517-8). P-H.
Managing Architectural & Engineering Practice. Weld Coxe. LC 80-17196. 192p. 1980. 18.95 (ISBN 0-471-08203-1, Pub. by Wiley-Interscience). Wiley.
Managing Behavioral Processes: Applications of Theory & Research. Richard E. Simmons. Ed. by Kenneth D. Mackenzie. LC 77-86007. (Organizational Behavior Ser.). (Illus.). 1978. pap. text ed. 9.95x (ISBN 0-88295-454-7). AHM Pub.
Managing by Design. Rollin Glaser & Christine Glaser. LC 80-22455. 192p. 1981. text ed. 9.95 (ISBN 0-201-02717-8). A-W.
Managing by Objectives: An Operating Guide to Faster & More Profitable Results. Paul Mali. LC 72-1803. (Illus.). 314p. 1972. 24.95 (ISBN 0-471-56575-X, Pub. by Wiley-Interscience). Wiley.
Managing Change in Educational Organizations: Sociological Perspectives Stragegies & Case Studies. Ed. by J. Victor Baldridge et al. LC 74-24479. 500p. 1975. 20.50 (ISBN 0-8211-0128-5); text ed. 18.50 (ISBN 0-685-51463-3). McCutchan.
Managing Change: Today's Challenge to Management. John E. Flaherty. 12.50 (ISBN 0-8424-0115-6). Green Hill.
Managing Commercial Banks. Emmanuel N. Roussakkis. LC 77-4380. (Special Studies). 1977. text ed. 24.95 (ISBN 0-03-021966-3). Praeger.
Managing Community Development & the New Federalism. Donald F. Kettl. LC 79-23504. 19.95 (ISBN 0-03-053311-2). Praeger.
Managing Contraceptive Pill Patients. 2nd rev. ed. Richard P. Dickey. (Illus.). 116p. 1980. vinyl 7.95 (ISBN 0-917634-08-X). Creative Infomatics.
Managing Corporate Contributions, Report No. 792. Kathryn Troy. (Illus.). vii, 95p. (Orig.). 1980. pap. 30.00 (ISBN 0-8237-0228-6). Conference Bd.
Managing Corporate Meetings: A Legal & Procedural Guide. G. S. Hills. LC 75-35288. 1976. 42.95 (ISBN 0-8260-4121-3). Ronald Pr.
Managing Creatively: A Very Practical Guide, 2 vols. Ted Pollock. Incl. Vol. 1. Managing Yourself Creatively. LC 75-145863. 9.95 (ISBN 0-8436-0714-9); Vol. 2. Managing Others Creatively. LC 70-161280. 9.95 (ISBN 0-8436-0715-7). 1971. 16.95 set (ISBN 0-8436-0717-3). CBI Pub.
Managing Creatively: Action Learning in Action. Richard C. Stapleton. 1976. pap. text ed. 9.45 (ISBN 0-8191-0035-8). U Pr of Amer.
Managing Development: The Political Dimension. Marc Lindenberg & Benjamin Crosby. LC 80-83345. (Library of Management for Development). 228p. (Orig.). 1981. 19.50x (ISBN 0-931816-49-1); pap. 9.95x (ISBN 0-931816-49-1). Kumarian Pr.
Managing Educational Costs. Philip H. Coombs & Jacques Hallak. (Illus.). 200p. 1972. pap. text ed. 5.95x (ISBN 0-19-501557-6). Oxford U Pr.
Managing Employee Honesty. Charles R. Carson. LC 76-51836. (Illus.). 1977. 16.95 (ISBN 0-913708-27-5). Butterworths.
Managing Employee Turnover: A Postive Approach. Edward Roseman. 241p. 1981. 17.95 (ISBN 0-8144-5585-9). Am Mgmt.
Managing Engineering & Research. 3rd ed. Delmar W. Karger & Robert G. Murdick. (Illus.). 1980. 29.50 (ISBN 0-8311-1125-9). Indus Pr.
Managing Engineering & Research. 2nd ed. Delmar W. Karger & Robert G. Murdick. (Illus.). 1969. 20.00 o.p. (ISBN 0-8311-1063-5). Indus Pr.
Managing Environmental Change: A Legal & Behavioral Perspective. Joseph F. Dimento. LC 75-19776. (Special Studies). (Illus.). 1976. text ed. 19.95 o.p. (ISBN 0-275-56640-4). Praeger.
Managing Essentials. Glueck. 1979. 13.95 (ISBN 0-03-045416-6). Dryden Pr.
Managing Executive Stress: A Systems Approach. James W. Greenwood, III & James W. Greenwood, Jr. LC 79-4100. 1979. 19.95 (ISBN 0-471-04084-3, Pub. by Wiley-Interscience). Wiley.
Managing Farm Business. Larry J. Connor et al. (Illus.). 384p. 1981. text ed. 17.95 (ISBN 0-13-550376-0). P-H.
Managing Fire Services. Ed. by John L. Bryan & Raymond C. Picard. LC 79-10067. (Municipal Management Ser.). (Illus.). 1979. text ed. 34.00 (ISBN 0-87326-018-X). Intl City Mgt.
Managing Fiscal Stress: The Crisis in the Public Sector. Ed. by Charles H. Levine. LC 79-27266. (Chatham House Series on Change in American Politics). 1980. pap. text ed. 11.95x (ISBN 0-934540-02-0). Chatham Hse Pubs.
Managing for Perfomance. John M. Ivancevich et al. 1980. 18.95x (ISBN 0-256-02274-7); wkbk. 5.50x (ISBN 0-256-02356-5). Business Pubns.
Managing for Productivity in Data Processing. James R. Johnson. 1980. pap. text ed. 21.50 (ISBN 0-89435-041-2). QED Info Sci.
Managing for Productivity: Motivating Employees. Robert F. Guder. Ed. by Harry Reilly. 100p. 1980. binder 110.00 (ISBN 0-89290-090-3, SUB 111); participant 45.00 (ISBN 0-89290-089-X). Soc for Visual.
Managing for Responsive Research & Development. Stewart P. Blake. LC 77-26120. (Illus.). 1978. text ed. 21.95x (ISBN 0-7167-0036-0). W H Freeman.
Managing for Results: How to Effectively Get Things Done. Charles E. Watson. LC 80-24047. 208p. 1981. pap. text ed. price not set. A-W.
Managing Government Organizations: An Intro to Public Administration. Pursley & Snortland. (Illus.). 1980. text ed. 16.95 (ISBN 0-87872-245-9). Duxbury Pr.
Managing Group & Intergroup Relations. Jay W. Lorsch & Paul R. Lawrence. 1972. pap. text ed. 10.95 (ISBN 0-256-00264-9). Irwin.
Managing Growth in the Nineteen Eighties: Toward a New Economics. Robert D. Hamrin. LC 79-19459. (Praeger Special Studies). (Illus.). 318p. 1980. 24.95 (ISBN 0-03-054061-5); pap. 10.95 (ISBN 0-03-054056-9). Praeger.
Managing Health & Human Service Programs: A Guide for Managers. Stephen L. White. LC 80-1057. (Illus.). 1981. 17.95 (ISBN 0-02-934550-2). Free Pr.
Managing Health Care Org. Rakech. 1977. 18.95 (ISBN 0-7216-7451-8). Dryden Pr.
Managing Health Records: Administrative Principles. Joan G. Liebler. 306p. 1979. text ed. 26.50 (ISBN 0-89443-168-4, 79-22455). Aspen Systems.
Managing High-Technology Programs & Projects. Russell D. Archibald. LC 76-3789. 288p. 1976. 29.95 (ISBN 0-471-03308-1, Pub. by Wiley-Interscience). Wiley.
Managing Hospital Architecture, Health Facilities Programming & Design. David Porter. (Illus.). 450p. text ed. write for info. (ISBN 0-914904-53-1); pap. text ed. write for info. Health Admin Pr.
Managing Hospital Costs Effectively As a System: A Primer for Hospital Administration. Addison C. Bennett. (Illus.). 72p. (Orig.). 1980. pap. 18.75 (ISBN 0-87258-327-9, 1404). Am Hospital.
Managing Human Resources. Inbucon Consultants. LC 76-39984. 1976. 14.95 (ISBN 0-470-98954-8). Halsted Pr.
Managing Human Resources: A Challenge to Urban Governments. Ed. by Charles H. Levine. LC 77-79869. (Urban Affairs Annual Reviews Ser.: Vol. 13). (Illus.). 1977. 20.00x (ISBN 0-8039-0741-9); pap. 9.95x (ISBN 0-8039-0938-1). Sage.
Managing Human Services. Ed. by Wayne F. Anderson et al. LC 77-2464. (Municipal Management Ser.). (Illus.). 1977. text ed. 22.00 (ISBN 0-87326-017-1). Intl City Mgt.
Managing Inappropriate Behaviors in the Classroom. Thomas C. Lovitt. LC 78-54144. 1978. pap. text ed. 5.00 (ISBN 0-86586-055-6). Coun Exc Child.
Managing Induced Rural Development. Jon R. Moris. 1981. pap. 8.00 (ISBN 0-89249-033-0). Intl Development.
Managing Industrial & Agricultural Wastes: Some Experiences. 137p. 1980. pap. 13.25 (ISBN 92-833-1460-3, APO 89, APO). Unipub.
Managing Information for Rural Development Projects. Nicolas Imboden & OECD. (Illus.). 87p. (Orig.). 1980. pap. 6.50 (ISBN 92-64-12039-4, 41-80-03-1). OECD.
Managing Innovation. Edwin A. Gee & Chaplin Tyler. LC 76-7056. (Systems & Controls for Financial Management Ser). 1976. 31.50 (ISBN 0-471-29503-5). Ronald Pr.
Managing Institutional Planning: Health Facilities & PL93-641. Martin S. Perlin. LC 76-29788. 1976. 24.75 (ISBN 0-912862-31-9). Aspen Systems.
Managing International Economic Interdependence: Selected Papers of C. Fred Bergsten. C. Fred Bergsten. LC 77-2517. 1977. 23.95 (ISBN 0-669-01516-4). Lexington Bks.
Managing Job Stress. Brief et al. (Orig.). 1981. pap. text ed. 8.95 (ISBN 0-316-10799-9). Little.
Managing Livestock Wastes. James A. Merkel. (Illus.). 1981. text ed. 22.50 (ISBN 0-87055-373-9). AVI.
Managing Local Government for Improved Performance: A Practical Approach. B. Rapp & F. Patitucci. LC 76-25240. 1977. lib. bdg. 35.00x (ISBN 0-89158-121-9); pap. 14.50x (ISBN 0-89158-412-9). Westview.
Managing Local Government Under Union Pressure. David T. Stanley. (Studies of Unionism in Government). 1972. pap. 5.95 (ISBN 0-8157-8101-6). Brookings.
Managing Low & Moderate Income Housing. Edwin D Abrams & Edward B Blackman. LC 72-14209. (Special Studies in U.S. Economic, Social & Political Issues). 1973. 28.50x (ISBN 0-275-28816-1). Irvington.
Managing Management Climate. George G. Gordon & Walter Cummins. (Illus.). 1979. 19.95 (ISBN 0-669-02545-3). Lexington Bks.

Managing Metrication in Business & Industry. 203p. 1976. 37.00 (ISBN 0-8247-6469-2). Am Natl.

Managing Multinational Corporations. Arvind V. Phatak. LC 73-18134. (Special Studies). 364p. 1974. text ed. 19.95 o.p. (ISBN 0-275-08600-3); pap. text ed. 10.95 o.p. (ISBN 0-275-88940-8). Praeger.

Managing Multiple Activities in Industrial Education. new ed. George H. Silvius & Estell H. Curry. 1971. text ed. 16.09 (ISBN 0-87345-456-1). McKnight.

Managing Municipal Leisure Services. Ed. by Sidney G. Lutzin. LC 80-17378. (Municipal Management). 1980. pap. text ed. 12.95 (ISBN 0-87326-023-6). Intl City Mgt.

Managing Non-Profit Organizations. Ed. by Patrick H. Montana & Diane Borst. 1979. pap. 6.95 (ISBN 0-8144-7512-4). Am Mgmt.

Managing Ocean Resources: A Primer. Ed. by Robert L. Freidheim. LC 79-53772. (Westview Special Studies in Natural Resources & Energy Management). 1979. lib. bdg. 22.00x (ISBN 0-89158-572-9). Westview.

Managing of Police Organizations. 2nd ed. Paul M. Whisenand & R. Fred Ferguson. (Illus.). 1978. text ed. 18.95 (ISBN 0-13-550731-6). P-H.

Managing Opportunity. R. W. Ferrell. LC 77-168772. 1972. 14.50 o.p. (ISBN 0-8144-5281-7, 49189). Am Mgmt.

Managing Organizational Behavior. Ramon Aldag & Arthur Brief. (Illus.). 500p. 1981. text ed. 15.95 (ISBN 0-8299-0306-2). West Pub.

Managing Organizational Behavior. Cyrus F. Gibson. 1980. 18.50 (ISBN 0-256-02237-2). Irwin.

Managing Organizations. William D. Brinckloe & Mary T. Coughlin. 1977. text ed. 14.95x (ISBN 0-02-471200-0). Macmillan.

Managing Organizations: Structure, Functions & Practices. Arthur Elkins. LC 79-5371. 1980. text ed. cancelled (ISBN 0-201-01517-X). A-W.

Managing Others Creatively. Ted Pollock. 1974. pap. 4.50 (ISBN 0-8015-4854-3, Hawthorn). Dutton.

Managing Our Work. rev. ed. John W. Alexander. LC 72-186572. (Illus.). 104p. 1975. pap. 3.50 (ISBN 0-87784-352-X). Inter-Varsity.

Managing Paperwork: The Key to Productivity. Frank M. Knox. LC 80-19685. 1980. 16.95 (ISBN 0-444-00452-1, Thomond Pr). Elsevier.

Managing Pastures & Cattle Under Coconuts. Donald A. Plucknett. (Tropical Agriculture Ser.). 1979. lib. bdg. 27.50x (ISBN 0-89158-299-1). Westview.

Managing People: Influencing Behavior. David W. Thompson. LC 77-15993. 1978. pap. text ed. 9.95 (ISBN 0-8016-4933-1). Mosby.

Managing Personal Finance. Holley H. Ulbrich & Bruce Yandle. 1979. 15.50x (ISBN 0-256-02208-9). Business Pubns.

Managing Personnel & Human Resources: Strategies & Programs. Herbert G. Heneman, III et al. 350p. 1981. 15.95 (ISBN 0-87094-234-4). Dow Jones-Irwin.

Managing Police Organizations. Tansik & Elliot. (Illus.). 250p. 1981. pap. text ed. 9.95 (ISBN 0-87872-275-0). Duxbury Pr.

Managing Presidential Objectives. Richard Rose. LC 76-4424. 1976. 17.95 (ISBN 0-02-926840-0). Free Pr.

Managing Productivity. Joel E. Ross. (Illus.). 192p. 1977. text ed. 16.95 (ISBN 0-87909-459-1). Reston.

Managing Public Systems. Ross Clayton et al. 1980. text ed. 15.95 (ISBN 0-87872-249-1). Duxbury Pr.

Managing Research Development. Jack E. Gibson. 450p. 1981. 35.00 (ISBN 0-471-08799-8, Pub. by Wiley-Interscience). Wiley.

Managing Residential Facilities for the Developmentally Disabled. R. C. Scheerenberger. (Illus.). 320p. 1975. 22.75 (ISBN 0-398-03199-1). C C Thomas.

Managing Rural Development: Peasant Participation in Rural Development. Coralie Bryant & Louise G. White. LC 80-80681. (Kumarian Press Development Monographs). 62p. (Orig.). 1980. pap. 5.95x (ISBN 0-931816-50-5). Kumarian Pr.

Managing Sales Force. M. T. Wilson. (Illus.). 184p. 1970. 19.50 (ISBN 0-7161-0048-7). Herman Pub.

Managing Social Service Systems. John W. Sutherland. LC 77-21806. (Illus.). 1977. text ed. 17.50 (ISBN 0-89433-004-7). Petrocelli.

Managing Software Development & Maintenance. Carma McClure. 224p. 1981. text ed. 16.95 (ISBN 0-442-22569-5). Van Nos Reinhold.

Managing Special Programs in Higher Education. Ronald Simmons. 160p. 1980. text ed. 16.50x (ISBN 0-87073-064-9). Schenkman.

Managing Student Behavior Problems. Daniel Duke. LC 80-10443. 1980. pap. 11.95x (ISBN 0-8077-2583-8). Tchrs Coll.

Managing Systems Development. Jeffrey S. Keen. (Information Processing). 320p. 1981. 27.50 (ISBN 0-471-27839-4, Pub. by Wiley-Interscience). Wiley.

Managing Technological Innovation. B. C. Twiss. (Illus.). 272p. 1974. text ed. 18.95x o.p. (ISBN 0-582-45040-3). Longman.

Managing Technological Innovation. 2nd. ed. Brian C. Twiss. 272p. 1980. text ed. 25.00 (ISBN 0-582-49708-6). Longman.

Managing the Advertising Process. Sherrie H. Kennedy & David R. Corkindale. LC 75-28612. (Illus.). 296p. 1976. 24.95 (ISBN 0-347-01109-8, 00205-4, Pub. by Saxon Hse). Lexington Bks.

Managing the Catalog Department. Donald Foster. LC 75-19081. 1975. 10.00 (ISBN 0-8108-0836-6). Scarecrow.

Managing the Commons. Ed. by Garrett Hardin & John Baden. LC 76-40055. (Illus.). 1977. pap. text ed. 9.95x (ISBN 0-7167-0476-5). W H Freeman.

Managing the Company Tax Function. Arnold Olenick. 1976. 29.95 o.p. (ISBN 0-13-550723-5). P-H.

Managing the Computer. G. W. Radley. 1975. text ed. 21.00x (ISBN 0-7002-0256-0). Intl Ideas.

Managing the Corporate Media Center. Eugene Marlow. (Video Bookshelf Ser.). (Illus.). 175p. 1981. text ed. 19.95 (ISBN 0-914236-68-7). Knowledge Indus.

Managing the Courts. Friesen et al. 1971. text ed. 14.00 (ISBN 0-672-81533-8, Bobbs-Merrill Law). Michie.

Managing the Finances of Health Care Organizations. Ed. by Gerald E. Bisbee, Jr. & Robert A. Vraciu. (Illus.). 1980. text ed. 28.95 (ISBN 0-914904-50-7); pap. text ed. 15.95 (ISBN 0-914904-51-5). Health Admin Pr.

Managing the Flow of Technology. Thomas J. Allen. 1977. text ed. 24.00x (ISBN 0-262-01048-8). MIT Pr.

Managing the Health Service. S. C. Haywood. (Illus.). 1974. text ed. 18.95x (ISBN 0-04-350046-3); pap. text ed. 8.95x o.p. (ISBN 0-04-350047-1). Allen Unwin.

Managing the Human Service Organization: From Survival to Achievement. Richard Steiner. LC 77-2150. (Sourcebooks for Improving Human Services: Vol. 1). (Illus.). 1977. 18.00x (ISBN 0-8039-0850-4); pap. 8.95x (ISBN 0-8039-8050-7). Sage.

Managing the Information Systems Audit: A Case Study-Policies, Procedures, & Guidelines. Billy E. Smith. (Illus.). 65p. 1980. pap. text ed. 22.50 (ISBN 0-89413-086-2); avail. wkbk. (ISBN 0-89413-087-0). Inst Inter Aud.

Managing the Interview. Richard F. Olson. LC 80-17112. (Self-Teaching Guide Ser.). 183p. 1980. 7.95 (ISBN 0-471-04859-3, Pub. by Wiley-Interscience). Wiley.

Managing the Large Law Firm 1978. (Commercial Law & Practice Course Handbook Series: Vol. 187). 1978. 20.00 o.p. (ISBN 0-685-63702-6, A4-3016). PLI.

Managing the Learning Process in Business Education. Calfrey C. Calhoun. 624p. 1980. text ed. 17.95x (ISBN 0-534-00834-8). Wadsworth Pub.

Managing the Managers. Edward McSweeney. LC 77-3761. 1978. 9.95 o.s.i. (ISBN 0-06-012959-X, HarpT). Har-Row.

Managing the Manager's Growth. Valerie Stewart & Andrew Stewart. 1979. 22.95 (ISBN 0-470-26561-2). Halsted Pr.

Managing the Manufacture of Complex Products. C. C. New. 379p. 1977. text ed. 29.50x (ISBN 0-220-66318-1, Pub. by Busn Bks England). Renouf.

Managing the Modern City. Ed. by James M. Banovetz. LC 58-9090. (Muncipal Management Ser.). 1971. text ed. 22.00 (ISBN 0-87326-004-X). Intl City Mgt.

Managing the Modern Organization. 3rd ed. Theo Haimann et al. LC 77-75879. (Illus.). 1977. text ed. 18.95 (ISBN 0-395-25512-0); inst. manual 0.95 (ISBN 0-395-25513-9); study guide 6.95 (ISBN 0-395-25514-7). HM.

Managing the Money Supply. Richard Coghland & Carolyn Sykes. 224p. 1980. 21.00x (ISBN 0-85941-164-8, Pub. by Woodhead-Faulkner England). State Mutual Bk.

Managing the Office Building. Ed. by Nancye J. Kirk. (Illus.). 400p. 1980. text ed. 21.95 (ISBN 0-912104-45-7). Inst Real Estate.

Managing the Organizational Decision Process. John B. Benton. LC 72-12933. (Illus.). 288p. 1973. 19.95 (ISBN 0-669-85589-8). Lexington Bks.

Managing the Paperwork Pipeline: Achieving Cost-Effective Paperwork & Information Processing. Monroe S. Kuttner. LC 77-15041. 1978. 27.95 (ISBN 0-471-03154-2, Pub. by Wiley-Interscience). Wiley.

Managing the People's Money. Joseph E. Goodbar. 1935. 47.50x (ISBN 0-685-89765-6). Elliots Bks.

Managing the Public Sector. Grover Starling. 1977. 17.95x (ISBN 0-256-01936-3). Dorsey.

Managing the Public's Business: The Job of the Government Executive. Laurence E. Lynn, Jr. LC 80-68176. 416p. 1981. 17.50 (ISBN 0-465-04378-X). Basic.

Managing the Resource Allocation Process. Joseph L. Bower. 1972. pap. text ed. 5.95x o.p. (ISBN 0-256-00457-9). Irwin.

Managing the Sea's Living Resources. H. Gary Knight. LC 76-20042. (Lexington Books Studies in Marine Affairs). 1977. 17.95 (ISBN 0-669-00874-5). Lexington Bks.

Managing the Severely Retarded: A Sampler. David Gibson & Roy I. Brown. (Illus.). 500p. 1976. 32.75 (ISBN 0-398-03513-X). C C Thomas.

Managing the Small Business. rev ed. Donald P. Stegall et al. 1976. text ed. 18.50 (ISBN 0-256-01784-0). Irwin.

Managing the Socially Responsible Corporation. Ed. by Melvin Anshen. LC 73-13364. (Studies of the Modern Corporation). (Illus.). 288p. 1974. 15.95 (ISBN 0-02-900680-5). Macmillan.

Managing the State. Martha Weinberg. 1977. text ed. 16.00x (ISBN 0-262-23077-1); pap. text ed. 5.95x (ISBN 0-262-73048-0). MIT Pr.

Managing the Survival of Smaller Companies. 2nd ed. A. C. Hazel & A. S. Reid. 159p. 1977. text ed. 18.50x (ISBN 0-220-66328-9, Pub. by Busn Bks England). Renouf.

Managing the Training Function. Christopher Gane. (Professional Management Library). (Illus.). 183p. 1972. text ed. 11.25x o.p. (ISBN 0-04-658045-X). Allen Unwin.

Managing the Transport Services Function. F. Woodward. 336p. 1978. text ed. 25.25x (ISBN 0-566-02032-7, Pub. by Gower Pub Co England). Renouf.

Managing Time. Norman Kobert. LC 80-13891. 140p. 1980. flexible cover 50.00 (ISBN 0-932648-11-8). Boardroom.

Managing to Reduce Delay. National Center for State Courts. (Orig.). 1980. pap. 5.50 (ISBN 0-89656-041-4, R0049). Natl Ctr St Courts.

Managing Today & Tomorrow. Thomas W. Johnson & John E. Stinson. LC 77-76123. (Illus.). 1978. text ed. 15.95 (ISBN 0-201-03487-5); instr's man. 3.95 (ISBN 0-201-03488-3). A-W.

Managing Transnationalism in Northern Europe. Bengt Sundelius. LC 78-59862. (Westview Replica Edition). 1978. lib. bdg. 19.00x (ISBN 0-89158-282-7). Westview.

Managing Transport: Managing the Transport System to Improve the Urban Environment. 312p. 1979. 16.00 (ISBN 92-64-11895-0). OECD.

Managing Water Rates & Finances Handbook. American Water Works Association. (AWWA Handbooks-General Ser.). (Illus.). 208p. 1980. pap. text ed. 17.00 (ISBN 0-89867-228-7). Am Water Wks Assn.

Managing with Arthritis: Aids & Advice for Coping with the Activities of Daily Living. Occupational Therapy Dept. Christchurch Hospital. 55p. 1980. 12.00x (ISBN 0-7233-0598-6, Pub. by Whitcoulls New Zealand). State Mutual Bk.

Managing with Less. Ed. by Elizabeth K. Kellar. LC 79-26163. 1979. pap. 10.00 (ISBN 0-87326-995-0). Intl City Mgt.

Managing with People. Raymond J. Burby. 1968. pap. text ed. 8.95 (ISBN 0-201-00723-1). A-W.

Managing with People: A Manager's Handbook of Organization Development. 2nd ed. Jack K. Fordyce & Raymond Weil. 1979. pap. text ed. 8.95 (ISBN 0-201-02031-9). A-W.

Managing Work in Process. Kivenko. Date not set. price not set (ISBN 0-8247-1268-4). Dekker.

Managing Your Coronary. 4th ed. William A. Brams. LC 73-13869. 1975. 6.95 o.p. (ISBN 0-397-01010-9). Lippincott.

Managing Your Emotions. Erwin Lutzer. LC 80-69311. 128p. 1981. 7.95 (ISBN 0-915684-81-0). Christian Herald.

Managing Your Export Office. Eric Swift. 150p. 1977. text ed. 22.00x (ISBN 0-220-66310-6, Pub. by Busn Bks England). Renouf.

Managing Your Money. Elizabeth James & Carol Barkin. LC 76-48287. (Money Ser.). (Illus.). (gr. 4-6). 1977. PLB 8.65 (ISBN 0-8172-0279-X). Raintree Pubs.

Managing Your Money in Retirement. Kenneth Lysons. LC 79-56045. (Illus.). 1980. 17.95 (ISBN 0-7153-7736-1). David & Charles.

Managing Your Sales Office. Peter J. Youdale. 1975. 18.00x o.p. (ISBN 0-8464-0601-2). Beekman Pubs.

Managing Your Sales Team. Albert H. Dunn & Eugene M. Johnson. (Illus.). 224p. 1980. 13.95 (ISBN 0-13-550905-X, Spec); pap. 6.95 (ISBN 0-13-550897-5). P-H.

Managing Your Schools: What's Ahead. Robert Olds. 1979. pap. 11.95 (ISBN 0-87545-016-4). Natl Sch PR.

Managing Your Small Business. Robert T. Justis. (Illus.). 288p. 1981. text ed. 18.95 (ISBN 0-686-68607-1). P-H.

Managing Your Time. Ted W. Engstrom & Alex MacKenzie. LC 67-17239. (Orig.). (YA) 1968. pap. 2.95 (ISBN 0-310-24262-2). Zondervan.

Managing Yourself Creatively. Ted Pollock. 1974. pap. 3.95 (ISBN 0-8015-4860-8, Hawthorn). Dutton.

Managing Yourself Leaders Guide. Steve Douglass. 150p. (Orig.). 1980. pap. 2.95 (ISBN 0-918956-69-2). Campus Crusade.

Manantiales En el Desierto. Charles E. Cowman & Antonio Serrano. 1980. pap. 3.50 (ISBN 0-311-40028-0, Edit Mundo). Casa Bautista.

Manbirds: Hang Gliders & Hang Gliding. Maralys Wills. 320p. 1981. 17.95 (ISBN 0-13-551101-1). P-H.

Manchester Fourteen Miles. Margaret Penn. 244p. Date not set. pap. 8.95 (ISBN 0-521-28065-6). Cambridge U Pr.

Manchester "Union Leader" in New Hampshire Elections. Eric P. Veblen. LC 74-15446. (Illus.). 218p. 1975. 12.50 (ISBN 0-87451-106-2). U Pr of New Eng.

Manchild in the Promised Land. Claude Brown. (RL 7). 1971. pap. 2.25 (ISBN 0-451-08206-0, E9282, Sig). NAL.

Manchild in the Promised Land. Claude Brown. (gr. 8 up). 1965. 12.95 (ISBN 0-02-517320-0). Macmillan.

Manchu. Robert Elegant. 592p. 1980. 12.95 (ISBN 0-07-019163-8, GB). McGraw.

Manchu Monarch: An Interpretation of Chia Ch'ing. Alexandra E. Grantham. (Studies in Chinese History & Civilization). 1977. Repr. of 1934 ed. 19.00 (ISBN 0-89093-076-7). U Pubns Amer.

Manchu Palace Memorials from the Palace Museum in Taipei. Ch'en Chieh-Hsien. (Indiana University Uralic & Altaic Ser.: Vol. 139). 350p. write for info. Ind U Res Inst.

Manchuria: A Survey of Its Economic Development. Baron Y. Sakatani. LC 78-74315. (Modern Chinese Economy Ser.). 305p. 1980. lib. bdg. 33.00 (ISBN 0-8240-4279-4). Garland Pub.

Manchuria: Its People, Resources & Recent History, London, 1904. Alexander Hosie. LC 78-74311. (Modern Chinese Economy Ser.: Vol. 24). 326p. 1980. lib. bdg. 38.00 (ISBN 0-8240-4272-7). Garland Pub.

Mandala Two to the Fifth Power. Mary Erulkar, pseud. (Writers Workshop Redbird Ser.). 48p. 1975. 12.00 (ISBN 0-88253-574-9); pap. text ed. 4.80 (ISBN 0-88253-573-0). Ind-US Inc.

Mandalas: The Dynamics of Vedic Symbolism. James N. Powell. Ed. by S. K. Ghai. 127p. 1980. 9.95 (ISBN 0-914794-36-1). Wisdom Garden.

Mandan & Hidatsa Music. Frances Densmore. LC 72-1886. (Music Ser.). (Illus.). 236p. 1972. Repr. of 1923 ed. lib. bdg. 19.50 (ISBN 0-306-70514-1). Da Capo.

Mandarin & Other Stories. Eca de Queiroz. Tr. by R. F. Goldman from Port. LC 65-13907. 176p. 1965. 10.95x (ISBN 0-8214-0008-8). Ohio U Pr.

Mandarin-Capitalists from Nanyang: Overseas Chinese Enterprise in the Modernisation of China 1893-1911. Michael R. Godley. (Cambridge Studies in Chinese History, Literature & Institutions Ser.). (Illus.). 288p. Date not set. price not set (ISBN 0-521-23626-6). Cambridge U Pr.

Mandarin Chinese: A Functional Reference Grammar. Charles N. Li & Sandra A. Thompson. 1981. price not set (ISBN 0-520-04286-7). U of Cal Pr.

Mandarin Ducks & Butterflies: Popular Fiction in the Early Twentieth-Century Chinese Cities. Perry Link. (Illus.). 352p. 1981. 20.00x (ISBN 0-520-04111-9). U of Cal Pr.

Mandarin Orange Sunday. Angelique Durand. 384p. (Orig.). 1981. pap. 2.75 (ISBN 0-553-14709-9). Bantam.

Mandarin Way. rev. & expanded ed. Cecilia Sun Yun Chiang & Allan Carr. Ed. by Sharon Silva. LC 80-66580. (Illus.). 288p. 1980. 11.95 (ISBN 0-89395-062-9); pap. 7.95 (ISBN 0-89395-059-9). Cal Living Bks.

Mandarins & Merchants: A China Agency of the Early Nineteenth Century. W. E. Cheong. (Scandinavian Inst. of Asian Studies, Monographs: No. 26). (Illus.). 1977. pap. text ed. 13.00x (ISBN 0-7007-0094-3). Humanities.

Mandatory Housing Finance Programs: A Comparative International Analysis. Morris L. Sweet & S. George Walters. LC 75-19826. (Special Studies). (Illus.). 276p. 1976. text ed. 19.50 o.p. (ISBN 0-275-09290-9). Praeger.

Mandelstam. Clarence Brown. LC 72-90491. (Illus.). 400p. 1973. 38.50 (ISBN 0-521-20142-X); pap. 9.95 (ISBN 0-521-29347-2). Cambridge U Pr.

Mandelstam: The Later Poetry. Jennifer Baines. LC 76-8515. 1977. 36.00 (ISBN 0-521-21273-1). Cambridge U Pr.

Mandelstamm I Tjutcev. E. Toddes. (Pdr Press Publications on Osip Mandel'shtam Ser.: No. 1). (Orig.). 1974. pap. text ed. 3.50x (ISBN 90-3160-033-4). Humanities.
M&O Master's Handbook. Ed. by Richard A. Block & Charles B. Collins. (Illus.). 271p. (Orig.). 1979. pap. text ed. 18.00 (ISBN 0-934114-16-1). Marine Educ.
Mandragola. Niccolo Machiavelli. Tr. by Anne Paolucci & Henry Paolucci. LC 57-14629. 1957. pap. 2.50 (ISBN 0-672-60231-8, LLA58). Bobbs.
Mandragola. Niccolo Machiavelli. Tr. by Mera J. Flaumenhaft from It. 64p. pap. text ed. 2.50x (ISBN 0-917974-57-3). Waveland Pr.
Mandragon. R. M. Koster. 346p. 1981. pap. 5.95 (ISBN 0-688-00348-6, Quill). Morrow.
Mandrivka U Viky. Wasyl Luciw. (Shkil'na Biblioteka). (Ukra.). 1970. pap. text ed. 6.00 (ISBN 0-685-89030-9). Slavia Lib.
Mandukya Upanishad. Tr. by Swami Gambhirananda from Sanskrit. (Upanishads with Shankara's Commentary Ser.). 240p. 1980. pap. 3.50 (ISBN 0-87481-202-X). Vedanta Pr.
Mandy. Paul B. Ricchiuti. (Uplook Ser.). 1978. pap. 0.75 (ISBN 0-8163-0206-5, 13105-2). Pacific Pr Pub Assn.
Mandy's Favorite Louisiana Recipes. Natalie Scott. 64p. 1978. pap. 2.25 (ISBN 0-88289-142-1). Pelican.
Maneras De Narrar: Contraste De Lino Novas Calvo y Alfonso Hernandez Cata. A. Gutierrez De La Solana. 1972. 10.95 (ISBN 0-88303-017-9); pap. 8.95 (ISBN 0-685-73219-3). E Torres & Sons.
Manet. Pierre Courthion. (Library of Great Painters Ser). (Illus.). 1963. 35.00 (ISBN 0-8109-0260-5). Abrams.
Manfac. Martin Caidin. (Orig.). Date not set. pap. 2.95 (ISBN 0-440-15587-8). Dell.
Mangan Inheritance. Brian Moore. 1980. pap. 2.95 (ISBN 0-14-005671-8). Penguin.
Manganese. Medical Sciences Division. LC 73-18174. (Medical & Biologic Effects of Environmental Pollutants Ser.). 192p. 1973. pap. 9.00 (ISBN 0-309-02143-X). Natl Acad Pr.
Mangement Pragmatics. Ross Webber. 1979. pap. 10.50x (ISBN 0-256-02232-1). Irwin.
Mangled Medicine. M. J. Teitelbaum & D. Johnson. (Illus.). 1972. 6.95 (ISBN 0-87489-038-1). Med Economics.
Mango & Tamarind Tree. Leslie De Noronha. 12.00 (ISBN 0-89253-632-2); flexible cloth 6.75 (ISBN 0-89253-633-0). Ind-US Inc.
Mango Tooth. Charlotte Pomerantz. LC 76-22664. (Illus.). (gr. k-3). 1977. PLB 7.92 (ISBN 0-688-84070-1). Greenwillow.
Manhattan Carnival. Frederick Feirstein. 60p. 1981. 9.95 (ISBN 0-914378-68-6); pap. 5.95 (ISBN 0-914378-69-4). Countryman.
Manhattan Is Missing. E. W. Hildick. (gr. 3). 1973. pap. 1.95 (ISBN 0-380-01488-2, 55012, Camelot). Avon.
Manhattan Island to My Self. Mariana R. Cook. (Illus.). 1978. 10.00 o.p. (ISBN 0-89396-005-5). Urizen Bks.
Manhattan Transfer. John Dos Passos. LC 79-10459. 1980. Repr. of 1953 ed. lib. bdg. 15.00x (ISBN 0-8376-0433-8). Bentley.
Manhattanville Music Curriculum Project Interaction: Early Childhood Music Curriculum. 2nd ed. Americole Biasini et al. 119p. (Orig.). 1972. pap. text ed. 5.50 o.p. (ISBN 0-686-63974-X). Media Materials.
Manhattanville Music Curriculum Synthesis: A Structure for Music Education. Ronald B. Thomas. 165p. (Orig.). 1971. pap. 5.50 o.p. (ISBN 0-686-63975-8). Media Materials.
Manhood of Humanity. 2nd ed. Alfred Korzybski. 326p. 1950. 9.00x (ISBN 0-937298-00-X). Inst Gen Semantics.
Manhunter. Gordon D. Shirreffs. 160p. 1981. pap. 1.75 (ISBN 0-449-13728-7, GM). Fawcett.
Maniac in the Cellar: Sensation Novels of the Eighteen Sixties. Winifred Hughes. LC 80-7530. 232p. 1980. 15.00x (ISBN 0-691-06441-5). Princeton U Pr.
Manic: Anatomy of a Mental Illness. Charles F. Hellmuth. 1977. 7.95 o.p. (ISBN 0-8059-2417-5). Dorrance.
Manic Illness. Ed. by Baron Shopsin. LC 78-66347. 1979. text ed. 21.00 (ISBN 0-89004-211-X). Raven.
Manifest Destiny & the Coming of the Civil War, 1840-1861. Don E. Fehrenbacher. LC 72-118950. (Goldentree Bibliographies in American History Ser). (Orig.). 1970. pap. 6.95x (ISBN 0-88295-512-8). AHM Pub.
Manifesto Addressed to the President of the United States from the Youth of America. Ed. by Alan Rinzler. 1970. pap. 1.50 o.s.i. (ISBN 0-02-074640-7, Collier). Macmillan.
Manifesto for a Nonviolent Revolution. George Lakey. 1980. staple back bdg. 1.75 (ISBN 0-86571-004-X). Movement New Soc.
Manifesto of the Communist Party. Karl Marx & Frederick Engels. 1965. 2.95 (ISBN 0-8351-0561-X); pap. 1.25 (ISBN 0-8351-0146-0). China Bks.
Manifesto to the Mexican Republic. Jose Figueroa. Tr. by C. Alan Hutchinson. 1978. 19.95 (ISBN 0-520-03347-7). U of Cal Pr.
Manifolds All of Whose Geodesics Are Closed. A. L. Besse. (Ergebnisse der Mathmatik und Ihrer Grenzbebiete: Vol. 93). (Illus.). 1978. 41.00 (ISBN 0-387-08158-5). Springer-Verlag.
Manin & the Venetian Revolution of 1848. George M. Trevelyan. LC 75-80597. xvi, 284p. 1974. Repr. of 1923 ed. 16.00 (ISBN 0-86527-122-4). Fertig.
Manipulated Man. Ed. by Franz Bockle. (Concilium Ser.: Religion in the Seventies: Vol. 65). 1971. pap. 4.95 (ISBN 0-8164-2521-3). Crossroad NY.
Manipulation of Air-Sensitive Compounds. D. F. Shriver. LC 81-60. 320p. 1981. Repr. of 1969 ed. lib. bdg. price not set (ISBN 0-89874-323-0). Krieger.
Manipulation: Past & Present. Eiler H. Schiotz & James Cyriax. (Illus.). 1975. 18.95x (ISBN 0-433-07010-2). Intl Ideas.
Manipulation People Like. Cabot J. Jaffee & Wayne A. Burroughs. LC 78-15278. 1978. 10.95 (ISBN 0-88229-347-8). Nelson-Hall.
Manipulation, Traction & Massage. 2nd ed. Joseph K. Rogoff. (Rehabilitation Medicine Library Ser.). (Illus.). 250p. 1980. lib. bdg. 25.50 (ISBN 0-683-07324-9). Williams & Wilkins.
Manipulative Books. Beth Clure & Helen Rumsey. (I Can Do It Ser.). (ps-2). 1969. set & tchrs. guide avail. o.p. (ISBN 0-685-28637-1); resource bk. & tchrs. guide 6.00 o.p. (ISBN 0-8372-0703-7). Bowmar-Noble.
Manitou. Graham Masterson. 1977. pap. 1.95 o.p. (ISBN 0-523-40233-3). Pinnacle Bks.
Mankind at the Turning Point: The Second Report to the Club of Rome. Mihajlo Mesarovic & Eduard Pestel. 224p. 1974. 12.95 o.p. (ISBN 0-525-15230-X); pap. 4.95 o.p. (ISBN 0-525-03945-7). Dutton.
Mankind in Barbary: The Individual & Society in the Novels of Norman Mailer. Stanley T. Gutman. LC 75-18290. 238p. 1975. text ed. 15.00x (ISBN 0-87451-118-6). U Pr of New Eng.
Mankind Two Thousand. 2nd ed. Ed. by Robert Jungk & Johan Galtung. (Future Research Monographs from Institute for Fredsforskning: No. 1). 1969. pap. 22.00x (ISBN 8-200-04584-6, Dist. by Columbia U Pr). Universitet.
Mankind's Quest for Identity. Hugo Gerstner. 1981. 22.50 (ISBN 0-930376-23-4). Pathotox Pubs.
Manna: A Book of Table Devotions. Ed. by Floyd D. Carey & James F. Byrd. 1973. pap. 3.25 (ISBN 0-87148-564-8). Pathway Pr.
Manna: An Historical Geography. R. A. Donkin. (Biogeographica Ser.: No. 17). (Illus.). vii, 160p. 1980. lib. bdg. 47.40 (ISBN 90-6193-218-1, Dr W Junk Pub). Kluwer Boston.
Manna: True Stories of U. S. A. Life, 1900 to 1940 & the Utopia of Manna. John H. Vassos. 64p. 1981. 8.00x (ISBN 0-682-49655-3). Exposition.
Manned Kiting: The Basic Handbook of Tow Launched Hang Gliding. 2nd ed. Dan Poynter. LC 74-20186. (Illus.). 1975. pap. 3.95 (ISBN 0-915516-04-7). Para Pub.
Manned Spacecraft. Kenneth Gatland. (YA) (gr. 9 up). 1967. 3.50 o.s.i. (ISBN 0-02-542890-X). Macmillan.
Mannerism - Style & Mood. Daniel B. Rowland. 1964. 29.50x (ISBN 0-685-69860-2). Elliots Bks.
Mannerism & Imagination: A Reexamination of Sixteenth Century Italian Aesthetic. Milton Kirchman. (Elizabethan Studies: No. 88). 1980. pap. text ed. 25.00x (ISBN 0-391-02162-1). Humanities.
Mannerism on Space Communication. Anthony L. Coundakis. 256p. 1981. 12.50 (ISBN 0-682-49734-7). Exposition.
Manners & Customs of Bible Lands. Fred H. Wight. 1953. 9.95 (ISBN 0-8024-5175-6). Moody.
Manners & Customs of Several Indian Tribes Located West of the Mississippi... to Which Is Prefixed the History of the Author's Life During a Residence of Several Years Among Them. John D. Hunter. LC 75-7061. (Indian Captivities Ser.: Vol. 39). 1976. Repr. of 1823 ed. lib. bdg. 44.00 (ISBN 0-8240-1663-7). Garland Pub.
Manners & Customs of the Police. Donald Black. 1980. 28.00 (ISBN 0-12-102880-1); pap. 9.50 (ISBN 0-12-102885-2). Acad Pr.
Manners Can Be Fun. rev. ed. Munro Leaf. LC 58-5611. (Illus.). (gr. k-3). 1958. 7.95 (ISBN 0-397-31603-8). Lippincott.
Manners, Customs & Observances. Leopold Wagner. LC 68-22059. 1968. Repr. of 1894 ed. 15.00 (ISBN 0-8103-3097-0). Gale.
Manners in God's House: Ethel Uhrich. (Illus.). 1972. pap. 2.95 (ISBN 0-87239-272-4, 2586). Standard Pub.
Manners to Grow On. Tina Lee. LC 54-9846. (gr. 4-7). 1955. 4.95 o.p. (ISBN 0-385-07398-4); PLB (ISBN 0-385-07664-9). Doubleday.
Manning on Decoupage. Hiram Manning. (Illus.). 256p. 1980. pap. 6.00 (ISBN 0-486-24028-2). Dover.
Manohar Malgonkar. G. S. Amur. (Indian Writers Ser.). 1976. 8.50 (ISBN 0-89253-506-7). Ind-US Inc.
Manohar Malgonkar. James Y. Dayananda. (World Authors Ser.: India: No. 340). 1975. lib. bdg. 12.50 (ISBN 0-8057-2566-0). Twayne.
Manon & the Prince. Peggy Caudle. 1979. 4.00 (ISBN 0-8062-1370-1). Carlton.
Manor & the Estate. Isaac B. Singer. 818p. 1979. 15.00 (ISBN 0-374-20225-7). FS&G.
Manpower & Oil in Arab Countries. Albirt Y. Badr & Simon G. Siksek. LC 79-2850. (Illus.). 270p. 1981. Repr. of 1959 ed. 22.50 (ISBN 0-8305-0026-X). Hyperion Conn.
Manpower & the Growth of Producer Services. Harry I. Greenfield. LC 66-28265. 1967. 20.00x (ISBN 0-231-03028-2). Columbia U Pr.
Manpower Aspects of Educational Planning: Problems for the Future. 1968. pap. 9.25 (ISBN 92-803-1026-7, U366, UNESCO). Unipub.
Manpower Assessment & Planning Projects in the Arab Region - Current Issues & Perspectives. 31p. 1980. pap. 6.50 (ISBN 92-2-102173-4, ILO146, ILO). Unipub.
Manpower Development for Nuclear Power: A Guidebook. (Technical Reports Ser.: No. 200). 492p. 1980. pap. 58.50 (ISBN 92-0-155080-4, IOC200, IAEA). Unipub.
Manpower Economics. Edward B. Jakubauskas & Neil A. Palomba. LC 79-186208. 1973. text ed. 15.95 (ISBN 0-201-03284-8). A-W.
Manpower for Environmental Pollution Control. Committee for Study of Environmental Manpower. 1977. 11.25 (ISBN 0-309-02634-2). Natl Acad Pr.
Manpower Information for Effective Management, 2 pts. Felician F. Foltman. Incl. Pt. 1. Collecting & Managing Employee Information (ISBN 0-87546-217-0); Pt. 2. Skills Inventories & Manpower Planning (ISBN 0-87546-218-9). (Key Issues Ser.: Nos. 10 & 14). 1973. pap. 2.00 ea. NY Sch Indus Rel.
Manpower Planning & Control. Gordon McBeath. 218p. 1978. text ed. 24.50x (ISBN 0-220-66348-3, Pub. by Busn Bks England). Renouf.
Manpower Planning & the Development of Human Resources. Thomas H. Patten, Jr. LC 76-137109. 1971. 45.95 (ISBN 0-471-66944-X, Pub. by Wiley-Interscience). Wiley.
Manpower Planning in Libraries. N. Moore. Ed. by A. Wilson. (Library Association Management Pamphlet Ser.). 1980. pap. 8.95x (ISBN 0-85365-532-4, Lib Assn England). Oryx Pr.
Manpower Policies for the Use of Science & Technology in Development. Charles V. Kidd. (Policy Studies). 1980. 22.00 (ISBN 0-08-025124-2). Pergamon.
Manpower Policy for Primary Health Care. Institute of Medicine. LC 78-56907. 1978. 6.25 (ISBN 0-309-02764-0). Natl Acad Pr.
Manpower Problems in the Hotel & Catering Industry. G. Mars et al. 180p. 1979. text ed. 23.00x (ISBN 0-566-00214-0, Pub. by Gower Pub Co England). Renouf.
Manpower Requirements & Developement for Nuclear Power Programmes. 628p. 1980. pap. 78.50 (ISBN 92-0-050080-3, ISP523, IAEA). Unipub.
Manpower Strategy for the Metropolis. Eli Ginzberg & Conservation of Human Resources Staff. LC 68-27290. 1968. 18.50x (ISBN 0-231-03161-0). Columbia U Pr.
Man's Ancestors: An Introduction to Primate & Human Evolution. Ian Tattersall. (Illus.). 1971. pap. 7.50 (ISBN 0-7195-2188-2). Transatlantic.
Man's Calling. Alonzo Gibbs. (gr. 7-12). 1966. 6.00 o.p. (ISBN 0-688-41236-X); PLB 6.24 (ISBN 0-688-51236-4). Lothrop.
Man's Conquest of the Pacific: The Prehistory of Southeast Asia & Oceania. Peter Bellwood. 1979. 35.00x (ISBN 0-19-520103-5). Oxford U Pr.
Man's Estate: Masculine Identity in Shakespeare. Coppelia Kahn. 200p. 1981. 16.00x (ISBN 0-520-03899-1). U of Cal Pr.
Man's Freedom. Paul Weiss. LC 67-23318. (Arcturus Books Paperbacks). 335p. 1967. pap. 8.95 (ISBN 0-8093-0277-2). S Ill U Pr.
Man's Guide to Business & Social Success. Barry James. 1969. 13.65 (ISBN 0-87350-151-9); instructor's manual 14.95 (ISBN 0-685-16768-2). Milady.
Man's Impact on Environment. T. R. Detwyler. 1970. text ed. 13.95 o.p. (ISBN 0-07-016592-0, C). McGraw.
Man's Mathematical Models: Fundamental Concepts for the Nonmathematician. Bill R. Williams & Gwen Crotts. LC 73-93104. 1975. 15.95 (ISBN 0-88229-110-6). Nelson-Hall.
Man's Need & God's Action. Reuel L. Howe. 1953. pap. 4.95 (ISBN 0-8164-2046-7, SP7). Crossroad NY.
Man's New Shapes: French Avant-Garde Drama's Metamorphoses. Kenneth S. White. LC 79-62911. 1979. pap. text ed. 6.50 (ISBN 0-8191-0717-4). U Pr of Amer.
Man's Origin, Man's Destiny. A. W. Wilder-Smith. LC 74-28508. 320p. 1975. pap. 5.95 (ISBN 0-87123-356-8, 210356). Bethany Fell.
Man's Past & Present: A Global History. 2nd ed. Leften Stavrianos. LC 74-28215. (Illus.). 576p. 1975. pap. text ed. 16.95 (ISBN 0-13-552091-6). P-H.
Man's Physical Environment. A. Faniran. (Orig.). 1980. pap. text ed. 22.50x (ISBN 0-435-95042-8). Heinemann Ed.
Man's Place in Evolution. British Museum. (Natural History Ser.). (Illus.). 120p. 1981. 22.50 (ISBN 0-521-23177-9); pap. 7.95 (ISBN 0-521-29849-0). Cambridge U Pr.
Man's Place in Nature. Charles F. Hockett. (Illus.). 736p. 1973. text ed. 17.95 o.p. (ISBN 0-07-029120-9, C); instructor's manual 3.95 o.p. (ISBN 0-07-029133-0). McGraw.
Man's Place: Masculinity in Transition. Joe L. Dubbert. 1979. text ed. 11.95 (ISBN 0-13-552059-2, Spec); pap. text ed. 5.95 (ISBN 0-13-552042-8). P-H.
Man's Presumptuous Brain: An Evolutionary Interpretation of Psychosomatic Diseases. Albert T. Simeons. 1962. pap. 4.50 o.p. (ISBN 0-525-47109-X). Dutton.
Man's Quest for God: Studies in Prayer & Symbolism. Abraham J. Heschel. LC 54-10371. 1954. 5.95 o.p. (ISBN 0-684-13582-5, ScribT). Scribner.
Man's Quest for God: Studies in Prayer & Symbolism. Abraham J. Heschel. LC 54-10371. (Hudson River Edition Ser.). 1981. 15.00x (ISBN 0-684-16829-4, ScribT). Scribner.
Man's Rough Road. Albert G. Keller. 1932. 37.50x (ISBN 0-685-69831-9). Elliots Bks.
Man's Search for Certainty. Don E. Stevens. LC 80-15743. 288p. 1980. 9.95 (ISBN 0-396-07860-5). Dodd.
Man's Self-Discovery in the Order of the Universe. Vernon De Castille. 1979. 37.50 (ISBN 0-89266-147-X). Am Classical Coll Pr.
Man's Touch. Charles F. Stanley. 1977. pap. 2.95 (ISBN 0-88207-753-8). Victor Bks.
Man's Ultimate Commitment. Henry N. Wieman. LC 58-5488. (Arcturus Books Paperbacks). 1963. pap. 3.25 o.p. (ISBN 0-8093-0084-2). S Ill U Pr.
Man's Unconquerable Mind. Gilbert Highet. LC 54-6133. 1954. 11.00x (ISBN 0-231-02016-3); pap. 3.95 (ISBN 0-231-08501-X). Columbia U Pr.
Man's Unfinished Journey: A World History. Marvin Perry et al. 1978. text ed. 19.04 (ISBN 0-395-25382-9); instructor's guide & key pap. 8.96 (ISBN 0-395-18017-1); workguide 5.48 (ISBN 0-395-18284-0). HM.
Man's Useful Plants. Michael Weiner. LC 74-18469. (Illus.). 160p. (gr. 7 up). 1976. 9.95 (ISBN 0-02-792600-1, 79260). Macmillan.
Man's World. Charlotte Lamb. (Harlequin Presents Ser.). 192p. (Orig.). 1981. pap. 1.50 (ISBN 0-373-10412-X, Pub. by Harlequin). PB.
Mansfield on the Condition of the Western Forts, 1853-54. Joseph K. Mansfield. Ed. by Robert W. Frazer. (American Exploration & Travel Ser.: No. 41). (Illus.). 1963. pap. 5.95 (ISBN 0-8061-1083-X). U of Okla Pr.
Mansfield Park. Jane Austen. Ed. by John Lucas. (Oxford English Novels Ser.). 1970. 11.95x o.p. (ISBN 0-19-255336-4). Oxford U Pr.
Mansfield Park. Jane Austen. (Illus.). 1955. 10.50x (ISBN 0-460-00023-3, Evman); pap. 2.95 (ISBN 0-460-01023-9, EP1023). Dutton.
Mansfield Park. Jane Austen. (Zodiac Press Ser.). 1978. 9.95 (ISBN 0-7011-1233-6, Pub. by Chatto Bodley Jonathan). Merrimack Bk Serv.
Mansfield Park. Jane Austen. lib. bdg. 15.95x (ISBN 0-89966-244-7). Buccaneer Bks.
Mansfield Park. Jane Austen. Ed. by James Kinsley & John Lucas. (World's Classics Ser.). 256p. 1981. pap. 2.95 (ISBN 0-19-281526-1). Oxford U Pr.
Mansfield: The Story of Vermont's Loftiest Mountain. Robert L. Hagerman. LC 75-21700. (Illus.). 128p. 1975. 9.95 (ISBN 0-914016-21-0); pap. 6.95 (ISBN 0-914016-22-9). Phoenix Pub.
Mansion. William Faulkner. 436p. Date not set. pap. 3.95 (ISBN 0-394-70282-4, Vin). Random.
Mansion of Magnanimitie: Wherein Is Shewed the Acts of Sundrie English Kings. Richard Crompton. LC 74-28841. (No. 722). 1975. Repr. of 1599 ed. 9.50 (ISBN 90-221-0722-1). Walter J Johnson.

Mansion of Secrets. Frances K. Judd. (Skylark Ser.). 176p. (gr. 4-9). 1980. pap. 1.75 (ISBN 0-553-15070-7). Bantam.
Mansions in Miniature: Four Centuries of Dolls' Houses. Leonie Von Wilckens. Orig. Title: Das Puppenhaus. (Illus.). 252p. 1980. 50.00 (ISBN 0-670-45410-9, Studio). Viking Pr.
Mansville Brand. W. G. Schreiber. (YA) 1978. 5.95 (ISBN 0-685-84749-7, Avalon). Bouregy.
Manticore. Robertson Davies. 1977. pap. 2.95 (ISBN 0-14-004388-8). Penguin.
Mantouche Factor. Michael Bradley. (Orig.). 1981. pap. 2.50 (ISBN 0-446-91546-7). Warner Bks.
Mantramanjari: The Vedic Experience. Raimundo Panikkar. 1977. 33.75x (ISBN 0-520-02854-6). U of Cal Pr.
Mantras for the Morning: An Introduction to Holistic Prayer. Robert F. Morneau. (Illus.). 120p. 1981. pap. 4.25 (ISBN 0-8146-1210-5). Liturgical Pr.
Mantras: Sacred Words of Power. John Blofeld. 1977. pap. 4.50 o.p. (ISBN 0-525-47451-X). Dutton.
Mantras: Words of Power. Swami Sivananda Radha. LC 80-10293. (Illus.). 150p. 1980. pap. 5.95 (ISBN 0-931454-05-0). Timeless Bks.
Manual & Code of Rules for Simple Cataloging. 2nd ed. Anthony Croghan. 1974. pap. 6.95x plus 24 audio cassettes (ISBN 0-9501212-6-6). J Norton Pubs.
Manual & Identification Guide to the United States Regular Issues 1847 Through 1934. Charles N. Micarelli. (Illus., Orig.). 1979. pap. text ed. write for info. o.p. (ISBN 0-9603474-0-2). Adriatic Stamp.
Manual Art: A Practical Guide to Drawing & Painting. Frank Rosenow. (Illus.). 1980. 9.95 (ISBN 0-393-01398-7). Norton.
Manual Biblico Llustrado. David Alexander. Tr. by Pedro Vega et al from Eng. (Illus.). 680p. (Span.). 1976. 26.95 (ISBN 0-89922-077-0). Edit Caribe.
Manual Bibliografico De Estudios Espanoles (Handbook of Hispanic Bibliography) Fernando Gonzalez Olle. (Sp.). 1978. 61.50 (ISBN 84-313-0464-2, Dist. by Ediciones Universidad de Navarra, S.A.). Bowker.
Manual De Ejercicios Espanol e Ingles. Guillermo Rojas. LC 77-84424. 1977. pap. 3.00 (ISBN 0-915808-25-0). Editorial Justa.
Manual De Espanol. rev. ed. Maria Arsuaga De Vila. LC 80-36752. 253p. 1980. Set. write for info. (ISBN 0-8477-3177-4). Vol. 1,pt. 1 (ISBN 0-8477-3195-2). Vol. 1,pt. 2 (ISBN 0-8477-3196-0). U of PR Pr.
Manual De Espanol, 2 pts, Vol. 1. new ed. Maria Arsuaga De Vila. 1980. Pt. 1. pap. 5.60 (ISBN 0-8477-3178-2); Pt. 2. pap. 5.60. U of PR Pr.
Manual De Finanzas Para Iglesias. F. W. Patterson. (Illus.). 118p. 1980. pap. 1.95 (ISBN 0-311-17005-6). Casa Bautista.
Manual De Gramatica Historica. M. Pidal. 12.50x (ISBN 0-686-00874-X). Colton Bk.
Manual De Modismos Americanos Mas Comunes. Solomon Wiener. (gr. 9 up). 1958. pap. text ed. 1.95 (ISBN 0-88345-097-6, 17403). Regents Pub.
Manual De Normas Vigentes En Materia De Direitos Humanos: Actualizado Em Julho De 1980. OAS General Secretariat. (Human Rights Ser.). 149p. (Port.). 1980. pap. text ed. 4.00 (ISBN 0-8270-1203-9). OAS.
Manual De Normas Wicentes En Materia De Derechos Humanos. OAS General Secretariat Inter-American Commission of Human Rights. (Human Rights Ser.). 153p. 1980. text ed. 6.00 (ISBN 0-8270-1153-9). OAS.
Manual De Practicas Orcamentaries Modernas. Alexander Hamilton Institute, Inc. Ed. by James M. Jenks. (Illus.). 84p. (Orig., Portuguese.). 1978. pap. 58.25x (ISBN 0-86604-002-1, TX-15-336). Hamilton Inst.
Manual De Practicia Presupuestaria Moderna. Alexander Hamilton Institute, Inc. Ed. by James M. Jenks. (Illus.). 90p. (Orig., Span.). 1976. pap. 52.75x (ISBN 0-86604-001-3, A783161). Hamilton Inst.
Manual De Tecnicas De Investigacion Social. Ronald J. Duncan et al. LC 80-23411. (Illus.). 78p. 1980. 5.00 (ISBN 0-913480-46-0). Inter Am U Pr.
Manual Del Esposo. Tr. by Dean Merrill. (Spanish Bks.). (Span.). 1979. 1.90 (ISBN 0-8297-0891-X). Life Pubs Intl.
Manual Del Ministro. (Spanish Bks.). 1979. 2.50 (ISBN 0-8297-0581-3). Life Pubs Intl.
Manual Do Ministro. (Portugese Bks.). (Port.). 1979. 2.85 (ISBN 0-8297-0672-0). Life Pubs Intl.
Manual for Authors of Mathematical Papers. 1979. Repr. of 1973 ed. 1.00 (ISBN 0-8218-0022-1, MFA). Am Math.
Manual for Authors: Reviews in Graph Theory, 4 vols. Ed. by William G. Brown. Set. write for info. o.p. (ISBN 0-8218-0214-3); Vol. 1. write for info. o.p. (ISBN 0-8218-0210-0); Vol. 2. write for info. o.p. (ISBN 0-8218-0211-9); Vol. 3. write for info. o.p. (ISBN 0-8218-0212-7); Vol. 4. write for info. o.p. (ISBN 0-8218-0213-5). Am Math.
Manual for Basic DIALOG Searching. Tze-Chung Li. LC 80-67847. 1980. 3.00 (ISBN 0-937256-01-3). CHCUS Inc.
Manual for Behavior Rating Scale. Veralee Hardin & Robert L. Busch. 1975. saddle stitched 19.75. Lucas.
Manual for Clinical Psychology Practicums. James Choca. LC 80-18731. 172p. 1980. 15.00 (ISBN 0-87630-258-4); pap. 9.95 (ISBN 0-87630-240-1). Brunner-Mazel.
Manual for Corporation Officers: The Law, Procedures, & Forms. William J. Grange et al. (Illus.). 1967. 30.50 (ISBN 0-8260-3485-3). Ronald Pr.
Manual for Determining Small Dosage Calculations of Pesticides & Conversion Tables. J. W. Neal, Jr. 1976. 6.25 (ISBN 0-686-18863-2). Entomol Soc.
Manual for Environmental Impact Evaluation. Sherman J. Rosen. (Illus.). 1976. 18.95x (ISBN 0-13-553453-4). P-H.
Manual for Field Collectors of Rice. 32p. 1975. pap. 5.00 (R110, IRRI). Unipub.
Manual for Group Leaders & Participants: Parenthood in a Free Nation, Vol. 4. Ethel Kawin. 1970. pap. 1.75 (ISBN 0-931682-08-8). Purdue Univ Bks.
Manual for Integrated Circuit Users. J. Lenk. LC 72-96757. 1973. 19.95 (ISBN 0-87909-482-6). Reston.
Manual for M. O. S. Users. J. Lenk. 1975. 18.95 (ISBN 0-87909-478-8). Reston.
Manual for Maintenance Inspection of Bridges. 1978. 2.50. AASHTO.
Manual for News Writing. Robert Knight. (Lucas Text Ser). 1970. text ed. 2.00x spiral bdg. (ISBN 0-87543-070-8). Lucas.
Manual for Pharmacy Technicians. 2nd ed. Jane M. Durgin et al. LC 77-20007. (Illus.). 1978. pap. 15.50 (ISBN 0-8016-1479-1). Mosby.
Manual for Prison Law Libraries. O. James Werner. (A. A. L. L. Publication Ser.: No. 12). 117p. 1976. text ed. 12.50x (ISBN 0-8377-0110-4). Rothman.
Manual for Reducing Transportation Costs. National Retail Merchants Assn. 1981. pap. text ed. 25.25 (ISBN 0-685-74622-4, T90576). Natl Ret Merch.
Manual for Repertory Grid Technique. F. Fransella & D. Bannister. 1977. 27.00 (ISBN 0-12-265450-1); pap. 12.00 (ISBN 0-12-265456-0). Acad Pr.
Manual for Residential & Day Treatment of Children. Miltiades G. Evangelakis. (Illus.). 392p. 1974. text ed. 22.75 (ISBN 0-398-03118-5). C C Thomas.
Manual for Stepfamilies. Emily B. Visher & John S. Visher. 150p. 1981. 10.00 (ISBN 0-87630-268-1). Brunner-Mazel.
Manual for Surgical Pathologists. Eugene Fazzini et al. (Illus.). 112p. 1972. pap. 12.75 photocopy ed., spiral bdg. (ISBN 0-398-02277-1). C C Thomas.
Manual for the Adult Neuropsychological Evaluation. Dennis Swiercinsky. (Illus.). 208p. 1978. spiral vinyl 19.75 (ISBN 0-398-03751-5). C C Thomas.
Manual for the Basic Course in English: Structure. 6th ed. Ester Torrado & Rhenna L Adams. pap. 3.75 o.p. (ISBN 0-8477-3314-9). U of PR Pr.
Manual for the Biology of the Vertebrates. James A. Organ. (Illus.). 1977. lab manual 7.95 (ISBN 0-89529-009-X). Avery Pub.
Manual for the Care of Wild Birds. Billie C. Sheaffer. (Illus.). 64p. 1980. 5.00 (ISBN 0-682-49617-0). Exposition.
Manual for the Course Evaluation Instrument. Donald P. Schwab. (Wisconsin Business Monographs: No. 10). (Orig.). 1976. pap. 4.50 (ISBN 0-86603-002-6). Bureau Busn Res U Wis.
Manual for the Home & Farm Production of Alcohol Fuel. Stephen W. Mathewson. 1980. 12.95 (ISBN 0-89815-030-2); pap. 7.95 (ISBN 0-89815-029-9). Ten Speed Pr.
Manual for the Operation of Research Reactors. (Technical Reports Ser.: No. 37). 1964. pap. 8.25 (ISBN 92-0-155364-1, IAEA). Unipub.
Manual for Theory & Practice of Group Counseling. Gerald Corey. 150p. 1980. pap. text ed. 5.95 (ISBN 0-8185-0432-3). Brooks-Cole.
Manual for Translaters of Mathematical Russian. S. H. Gould. 1980. Repr. of 1973 ed. 4.00 (ISBN 0-8218-0028-0, MTR). Am Math.
Manual for Travel Counsellors. 12th, rev. ed. Kenneth N. Carlson. LC 73-92320. (Illus.). 260p. 1981. 11.75x (ISBN 0-938428-00-4). Res Pubns WA.
Manual for Users of Standardized Tests. Jonell H. Kirby et al. 8.75 (ISBN 0-936224-01-0). Schol Test.
Manual Greek Lexicon of the New Testament. 3rd ed. G. Abbott-Smith. 528p. 1977. text ed. 20.00 (ISBN 0-567-01001-5). Attic Pr.
Manual in Clinical Dietetics. 2nd ed. Pauline Schatz. 1978. spiral bdg. 6.95x (ISBN 0-916434-31-1). Plycon Pr.
Manual Metal-Arc Welding. Ed. by N. C. Balchin. (Engineering Craftsmen: No. F24). (Illus.). 1977. spiral bdg. 16.50x (ISBN 0-85083-395-7). Intl Ideas.
Manual of AACR for Cartographic Materials. Barbara N. Moore. Ed. by Marilyn J. McClaskey & Edward Swanson. 50p. 1980. pap. 6.00 (ISBN 0-936996-07-2). Soldier Creek.
Manual of AACR 2 Advanced Examples. Ed. by Edward Swanson & Marilyn J. McClaskey. 50p. 1980. pap. 6.00 (ISBN 0-936996-02-1). Soldier Creek.
Manual of AACR 2 Examples. 2nd ed. Ed. by Edward Swanson & Marilyn H. Jones. 87p. (Orig.). 1980. pap. 7.50 (ISBN 0-936996-01-3). Soldier Creek.
Manual of AACR 2 Examples for Early Printed Books. Mary D. Hanley. Ed. by Edward Swanson & Marilyn J McClaskey. 1980. pap. 6.00 (ISBN 0-936996-10-2). Soldier Creek.
Manual of AACR 2 Examples for Legal Materials. Phyllis Marion. Ed. by Marilyn J. McClaskey & Edward Swanson. 50p. 1980. pap. 6.00 (ISBN 0-936996-08-0). Soldier Creek.
Manual of AACR 2 Examples for Liturgical Works & Sacred Scripture. Irene A. Schilling. Ed. by Edward Swanson & Marilyn J. McClaskey. 50p. 1980. pap. 6.00 (ISBN 0-936996-06-4). Soldier Creek.
Manual of AACR 2 Examples for Manuscripts. Edward Swanson. 50p. 1980. pap. 6.00 (ISBN 0-936996-12-9). Soldier Creek.
Manual of AACR 2 Examples for Motion Pictures & Videorecordings. Jean Aichele & Nancy B. Olson. Ed. by Marilyn J. McClasky & Edward Swanson. 50p. 1980. pap. 6.00 (ISBN 0-936996-11-0). Soldier Creek.
Manual of AACR 2 Examples for Musical Scores & Musical Sound Recordings. Wesley Simonton & Phillip Mannie. Ed. by Edward Swanson & Marilyn J. McClasky. 1980. pap. 6.00 (ISBN 0-936996-05-6). Soldier Creek.
Manual of AACR 2 Examples for Serials. Julia C. Blixrud. Ed. by Janet E. Snesrud & Marilyn J. McClaskey. 50p. 1980. pap. 6.00 (ISBN 0-936996-04-8). Soldier Creek.
Manual of AACR 2 Level 1 Examples. Ed. by Marilyn J. McClaskey & Edward Swanson. 50p. 1980. pap. 6.00 (ISBN 0-936996-03-X). Soldier Creek.
Manual of Above Knee Wood Socket Prosthetics. rev. ed. Miles H. Anderson et al. (Illus.). 296p. 1980. pap. 21.50 spiral bdg. (ISBN 0-398-04071-0). C C Thomas.
Manual of Advanced Lithography. Richard Vicary. LC 76-56890. (Illus.). 1977. 12.50 o.p. (ISBN 0-684-14937-0, ScribT). Scribner.
Manual of Akkadian. David Marcus. LC 78-63068. 1978. pap. text ed. 9.00 (ISBN 0-8191-0608-9). U Pr of Amer.
Manual of Ambulatory Pediatrics. Stephen H. Sheldon. 275p. 1981. 9.50 (ISBN 0-89004-632-8). Raven.
Manual of Anatomy & Physiology. fetal pig ed. Anne B. Donnersberger et al. 1978. pap. text ed. 10.95x (ISBN 0-669-01490-7); instr's manual (ISBN 0-669-01632-2). Heath.
Manual of Anatomy & Physiology: Lab Animal: the Cat. 2nd ed. Anne Donnersberger et al. 1979. pap. text ed. 11.95 (ISBN 0-669-02481-3); answer key (ISBN 0-669-03168-2). Heath.
Manual of Ancient Sex & Sun Worship Rituals. James R. Baldisan. 1979. Repr. of 1857 ed. deluxe ed. 51.75 (ISBN 0-930582-26-8). Gloucester Art.
Manual of Antibiotics & Infectious Diseases. 4th ed. John E. Conte, Jr. & Steven L. Barriere. (Illus.). 275p. 1981. text ed. price not set (ISBN 0-8121-0768-3). Lea & Febiger.
Manual of Applied Geology for Engineers. 414p. 1980. pap. 75.00x (ISBN 0-7277-0038-3, Pub. by Telford England). State Mutual Bk.
Manual of Aquatic Plants. rev. ed. Norman C. Fassett. 1957. 15.00x (ISBN 0-299-01450-9). U of Wis Pr.
Manual of Archival Techniques. Ed. by Roland M. Baumann. (Illus.). 127p. 1979. pap. 4.00 (ISBN 0-89271-000-4). Pa Hist & Mus.
Manual of Arms, a Practical Guide to the Heraldic Art. W. Elmer Hinton, Jr. LC 79-55379. (Illus., Orig.). Date not set. pap. 4.99 (ISBN 0-935426-00-0). Gamesmasters.
Manual of Articulatory Phonetics. William A. Smalley. LC 73-14763. (Applied Cultural Anthropology Ser.). (Illus.). 522p. 1973. pap. text ed. 7.95x (ISBN 0-87808-139-9). William Carey Lib.
Manual of Astrology. Sepharial. 263p. 1981. pap. 10.00 (ISBN 0-89540-065-0). Sun Pub.
Manual of Babylonian Jewish Aramaic. David Marcus. LC 80-6073. 104p. (Orig.). 1981. pap. text ed. 7.75 (ISBN 0-8191-1363-8). U Pr of Amer.
Manual of Basic Neuropathology. 2nd ed. Raymond Escourolle & Jacques Poirier. Tr. by Lucien J. Rubinstein. LC 77-80748. (Illus.). 1978. pap. text ed. 13.50 (ISBN 0-7216-3406-0). Saunders.
Manual of Bible History. rev. ed. W. G. Blaikie & C. D. Matthews. 432p. 1940. 13.95 (ISBN 0-471-07008-4). Wiley.
Manual of Bookbinding. Arthur Johnson. (Illus.). 1978. 15.95 o.p. (ISBN 0-684-15332-7, ScribT). Scribner.
Manual of Brands & Marks. Manfred R. Wolfenstine. Ed. by Ramon F. Adams. LC 68-31379. (Illus.). 355p. 1981. 24.95 (ISBN 0-8061-0867-3). U of Okla Pr.
Manual of Cardiac Surgery, Vol. I. B. J. Harlan et al. (Comprehensive Manuals of Surgical Specialities Ser.). (Illus.). 204p. 1980. 140.00 (ISBN 0-387-90393-3). Springer-Verlag.
Manual of Cardiovascular Assessment. Sara J. Wells et al. 1981. pap. text ed. 14.95 (ISBN 0-8359-4233-3). Reston.
Manual of Cardiovascular Diagnosis & Therapy. Joseph S. Alpert & James M. Rippe. 1980. 12.95 (ISBN 0-316-03502-5). Little.
Manual of Cataloguing Practice. K. G. Bakewell. LC 73-171838. 312p. 1972. text ed. 50.00 (ISBN 0-08-016697-0). Pergamon.
Manual of Christian Beliefs. Edwin Lewis. 162p. 1927. text ed. 2.95 (ISBN 0-567-02170-X). Attic Pr.
Manual of Christian Reformed Church Government: 1980 Edition. rev. ed. William P. Brink & Richard R. DeRidder. LC 80-24129. 1980. pap. text ed. 4.45 (ISBN 0-933140-19-3). Bd of Pubns CRC.
Manual of Church History, 2 vols. Albert H. Newman. 7.50 ea. o.p.; Vol. 1. (ISBN 0-8170-0097-6); Vol. 2. (ISBN 0-8170-0098-4). Judson.
Manual of Civil Engineering Plant & Equipment. 2nd ed. Ed. by J. M. Paxton. (Illus.). 1971. 123.00x (ISBN 0-85334-500-7). Intl Ideas.
Manual of Clinical Dietetics. The Chicago Dietetic Association & The South Suburban Dietetic Association. 1981. text ed. price not set (ISBN 0-7216-2537-1). Saunders.
Manual of Clinical Immunology. 2nd ed. Ed. by N. R. Rose & H. Friedman. (Illus.). 1980. 25.00 (ISBN 0-914826-25-5); flexible binding 21.00 (ISBN 0-914826-27-1). Am Soc Microbio.
Manual of Clinical Laboratory Methods. 4th ed. Opal Hepler. (Illus.). 416p. 1977. pap. 22.50 spiral (ISBN 0-398-03057-X). C C Thomas.
Manual of Clinical Microbiology. 3rd ed. Ed. by E. H. Lennette et al. (Illus.). 1980. 25.00 (ISBN 0-914826-24-7). Am Soc Microbio.
Manual of Clinical Microbiology. Ed. by Edwin H. Lennette et al. LC 74-81968. (Illus.). 1974. text ed. 20.00 o.p. (ISBN 0-914826-00-X); pap. text ed. 16.00 o.p. (ISBN 0-914826-01-8). Am Soc Microbio.
Manual of Clinical Nephrology of the Rogosin Kidney Center. Ed. by Jhoong S. Cheigh et al. (Developments in Nephrology: No. 1). (Illus.). 470p. 1981. PLB 65.00 (ISBN 90-247-2397-3, Pub. by Martinus Nijhoff). Kluwer Boston.
Manual of Clinical Periodontics. 2nd ed. Howard L. Ward & Marvin R. Simring. LC 77-26934. 1978. text ed. 16.95 (ISBN 0-8016-5343-6). Mosby.
Manual of Clinical Pharmacology. David H. Robertson & Craig R. Smith. (Illus.). 290p. 1981. price not set softcover (ISBN 0-683-07300-1). Williams & Wilkins.
Manual of Clinical Problems in Cardiology: With Annotated Key References. David Hillis et al. 1980. 12.95 (ISBN 0-316-36400-2). Little.
Manual of Clinical Problems in Oncology. Carol S. Portlock & Donald R. Goffinet. (Little, Brown Spiral Manual Series). 1980. pap. 12.95 (ISBN 0-316-71424-0). Little.
Manual of Common Beetles of Eastern North America, 2 vols. Elizabeth Dillon & Lawrence Dillon. (Illus.). 1972. pap. 7.00 ea. Vol. 1 (ISBN 0-486-61180-9). Vol. 2 (ISBN 0-486-61190-6). Dover.
Manual of Comparative Anatomy: A General Laboratory Guide. rev. ed. 3rd ed. Bruce M. Harrison. 1970. 9.50 (ISBN 0-8016-2078-3). Mosby.
Manual of Comparative Anatomy: A Laboratory Guide & Brief Text. Bruce E. Holmes. 416p. 1980. pap. text ed. 12.95 (ISBN 0-8403-2254-2). Kendall-Hunt.
Manual of Coronary Care. Joseph S. Alpert & Gary S. Francis. 1977. spiral bdg. 10.95 o.p. (ISBN 0-316-03499-1). Little.
Manual of Coronary Care. 2nd ed. Joseph S. Alpert & Gary S. Francis. 1980. pap. 11.95 (ISBN 0-316-03503-3). Little.
Manual of Cultivated Plants. rev. ed. Liberty H. Bailey. 1949. 29.95 (ISBN 0-02-505520-8). Macmillan.

Manual of Cultivated Trees & Shrubs. 2nd ed. A. Rehder. 1940. 14.95 o.s.i. (ISBN 0-02-601920-5). Macmillan.

Manual of Cytotechnology. 5th rev ed. Ed. by Catherine M. Keebler & James W. Reagan. LC 77-9249. (Illus.). 1977. binder 45.00 (ISBN 0-89189-034-3, 45-3-001-00). Am Soc Clinical.

Manual of Death Education & Simple Burial. 8th ed. Ernest Morgan. 1977. pap. 2.00 o.p. (ISBN 0-914064-05-3). Celo Pr.

Manual of Dermatology. 2nd ed. Donald M. Pillsbury & Charles L. Heaton. LC 79-3927. (Illus.). 360p. 1980. text ed. 25.00 (ISBN 0-7216-7242-6). Saunders.

Manual of Developmental Diagnosis: The Administration & Interpretation of the Revised Gesell & Amtruda Developmental & Neurologic Examination. Hilda Knobloch et al. (Illus.). 286p. 1980. text ed. write for info. (ISBN 0-06-141437-9, Harper Medical). Har-Row.

Manual of Dosimetry in Radiotherapy. John B. Massey. (Technical Reports Ser.: No. 110). (Illus., Orig.). 1970. pap. 9.75 (ISBN 92-0-115370-8, IDC 110, IAEA). Unipub.

Manual of Dragonflies of North America (Anisoptera) Including the Greater Antilles & the Provinces of the Mexican Border. James G. Needham & Minter J. Westfall. (Lbrary Reprint Ser.: No. 65). 1981. Repr. of 1975 ed. 42.50x (ISBN 0-520-02913-5). U of Cal Pr.

Manual of Economic Analysis of Chemical Processes. Institut Francais De Pertrole. Tr. by Ryle Miller & Ethel B. Miller. (Illus.). 1980. 37.95 (ISBN 0-07-031745-3). McGraw.

Manual of Electronystagmography. Hugh O. Barber. LC 80-17349. (Illus.). 232p. 1980. text ed. 32.50 (ISBN 0-8016-0449-4). Mosby.

Manual of Elocution for the Ministry. D. Frank Philip. 122p. Repr. of 1948 ed. text ed. 3.50 (ISBN 0-567-02207-2). Attic Pr.

Manual of Emergency Medical Therapeutics. new ed. Mickey S. Eisenberg & Michael Copass. (Illus.). 1978. pap. text ed. 12.95 (ISBN 0-7216-5048-1). Saunders.

Manual of English Grammar. Ester Torrado. Handbook Unit 2. pap. 3.75 o.p. (ISBN 0-8477-3308-4); Set. (ISBN 0-8477-3306-8). U of PR Pr.

Manual of English Grammar for Spanish Speakers: Workbooks, 4 units. Doris Torregrosa de Torres. pap. 12.50 set (ISBN 0-8477-3317-3); Unit 1-2. (ISBN 0-8477-3318-1). Unit 3-4. (ISBN 0-8477-3319-X). Set. (ISBN 0-8477-3317-3). U of PR Pr.

Manual of European Bird Keeping. Frank Meaden. (Illus.). 1979. 17.95 (ISBN 0-7137-0935-9, Pub by Blandford Pr England). Sterling.

Manual of Fisheries Science, Pt. 2: Methods of Resource Investigation & Their Application. (FAO Fisheries Technical Paper Ser.: No. 115, Rev. 1). 224p. Date not set. pap. 14.50 (ISBN 92-5-100842-6, F854, FAO). Unipub.

Manual of Food Irradiation Dosimetry. (Illus.). 1978. pap. 14.50 (ISBN 92-0-115277-9, IDC 178, IAEA). Unipub.

Manual of Foreign Languages. 4th ed. Georg F. Von Ostermann. 1952. Repr. of 1970 ed. 30.00 (ISBN 0-87632-165-1). Boardman.

Manual of Forensic Quotations. Leon Mead & Gilbert F. Newell. LC 68-26591. 1968. Repr. of 1903 ed. 15.00 (ISBN 0-8103-3188-8). Gale.

Manual of Four-Handed Dentistry. J. Ellis Paul. (Illus.). 155p. 1980. 42.00 (ISBN 0-931386-09-8). Quint Pub Co.

Manual of Freshwater Algae. L. A. Whitford & George Schumacher. 15.00 (ISBN 0-916822-01-X). Sparks Pr.

Manual of Good Practice for Radiation Protection of the Patient: Diagnostic Radiology. Ed. by W. A. Langmead. 1980. Part 1. 15.00x (Pub. by Brit Inst Radiology). State Mutual Bk.

Manual of Graphic Techniques. Tom Porter & Robert Greenstreet. (Illus.). 1980. pap. 9.95 (ISBN 0-684-16504-X, ScribT). Scribner.

Manual of Gynecologic Oncology. Hugh R. Barber. 356p. 1980. pap. text ed. 17.75 (ISBN 0-397-50474-8). Lippincott.

Manual of Hadith: Arabic Text & English Translation. 2nd, 1944 ed. Maulana M. Ali. 1978. text ed. 13.00x (ISBN 0-391-00548-0). Humanities.

Manual of Heraldry. Francis J. Grant. LC 75-23365. (Illus.). 1976. Repr. of 1929 ed. 15.00 (ISBN 0-8103-4252-9). Gale.

Manual of Historic Ornament: Treating Upon the Evolution, Tradition & Development of Architecture & the Applied Arts. 5th ed. Richard Glazier. LC 70-163174. (Tower Bks). (Illus.). vi, 183p. 1972. Repr. of 1933 ed. 24.00 (ISBN 0-8103-3937-4). Gale.

Manual of Hydrotherapy & Massage. Fred B. Moor et al. LC 64-23214. 169p. 1964. 4.95 (ISBN 0-8163-0023-2, 13160-7). Pacific Pr Pub Assn.

Manual of Instructions for Using the Gottschalk-Gleser Content Analysis Scales: Anxiety, Hostility, Social Alienation-Personal Disorganization. Louis A. Gottschalk et al. 1969. 8.50 o.p. (ISBN 0-520-01483-9). U of Cal Pr.

Manual of Instructions for Using the Gottschalk-Gleser Content Analysis Scales: Anxiety, Hostility, Social Alienation - Personal Disorganization. Louis A. Gottschalk et al. 1979. Repr. of 1969 ed. 12.00x (ISBN 0-520-03814-2). U of Cal Pr.

Manual of Internal Fixation: Technique Recommended by the AO-Group. M. E. Mueller et al. Tr. by J. Schatzker et al from Ger. LC 76-138812. (Illus.). 1970. 95.00 o.p. (ISBN 0-387-05219-4); slides 210.70 o.p. (ISBN 0-387-92101-X). Springer-Verlag.

Manual of Karate. E. J. Harrison. LC 66-16205. (Illus.). 160p. (gr. 7 up). 1975. 6.95 (ISBN 0-8069-4092-1); PLB 6.69 (ISBN 0-8069-4093-X). Sterling.

Manual of Laboratory Immunology. Julia E. Peacock & Russell H. Tomar. LC 80-16716. (Illus.). 228p. 1980. pap. 17.00 (ISBN 0-8121-0719-5). Lea & Febiger.

Manual of Lake Morphometry. Lars Hakanson. (Illus.). 100p. 1981. pap. 13.90 (ISBN 0-387-10480-1). Springer-Verlag.

Manual of Laparoscopy & Culdoscopy. Logan & Edwards. 1981. text ed. price not set. Butterworth.

Manual of Law Librarianship: The Use & Organization of Legal Literature. Ed. by Elizabeth Moyes. LC 76-25099. 1976. lib. bdg. 50.00x (ISBN 0-89158-637-7). Westview.

Manual of Linear Integrated Circuits. 2nd ed. Sol Prensky & Arthur Seidman. (Illus.). 1981. text ed. 19.95 (ISBN 0-8359-4241-4). Reston.

Manual of Lower Extremities Orthotics. Ed. by Miles H. Anderson. (Illus.). 552p. 1978. 40.50 (ISBN 0-398-02217-8). C C Thomas.

Manual of Manuscript Transcription for the Dictionary of the Old Spanish Language. 2nd ed. Ed. by David Mackenzie. (Illus.). 122p. 1981. pap. 15.00. Hispanic Seminary.

Manual of Mechanical Orthopaedics. Z. Alfonso Tohen. (Illus.). 340p. 1973. 18.75 (ISBN 0-398-02614-9). C C Thomas.

Manual of Medical Therapeutics. 23rd ed. Washington University Dept. of Medicine. Ed. by Jeffrey J. Freitag & Leslie W. Miller. (Little Brown Spiral Manual Ser.). 1980. 12.95 (ISBN 0-316-92403-2). Little.

Manual of Methods for Fish Stock Assessment, Pt. II: Tables of Yield Functions. rev. ed. (FAO Fisheries Technical Paper Ser.: No. 38, Rev. 1). 1980. pap. 6.00 (ISBN 92-5-000840-6, F848, FAO). Unipub.

Manual of Methods for General Bacteriology. Ed. by Philipp Gerhardt. (Illus.). 1981. pap. 25.00 (ISBN 0-914826-29-8); flexible bdg. 21.00 (ISBN 0-914826-30-1). Am Soc Microbio.

Manual of Mineralogy After J. D. Dana. 19th ed. Cornelius S. Hurlbut, Jr. & Cornelis Klein. LC 77-1131. 1977. 27.95 (ISBN 0-471-42226-6). Wiley.

Manual of Modern Budgetary Practices. Alexander Hamilton Institute, Inc. Ed. by James M. Jenks. (Illus.). 85p. (Orig.). 1976. pap. 57.25x (ISBN 0-86604-000-5, A783160). Hamilton Inst.

Manual of Neonatal Care. Ed. by John P. Cloherty & Ann B. Stark. (Spiral Manual Ser.). 1980. 12.95 (ISBN 0-316-14749-4). Little.

Manual of Nuer Law: Being an Account of Customary Law, Its Evolution & Development in the Courts Established by the Sudan Government. Paul P. Howell. LC 73-106840. (Illus.). Repr. of 1954 ed. 15.00x (ISBN 0-8371-3462-5). Negro U Pr.

Manual of Nursing Arts & Procedures. Lily P. Ram. 1978. 10.00 (ISBN 0-7069-0686-1, Pub. by Vikas India). Advent Bk.

Manual of Nursing Procedures. Ed. by Massachusetts General Hospital Department of Nursing et al. 1980. text ed. write for info. (ISBN 0-316-54958-4); pap. text ed. price not set (ISBN 0-316-54958-4). Little.

Manual of Occular Diagnosis & Therapy. Deborah Pavan-Langston. 1980. 12.95 (ISBN 0-316-69537-8). Little.

Manual of Occultism. Sepharial. LC 80-53345. 356p. 1980. Repr. of 1979 ed. lib. bdg. 11.95x (ISBN 0-89370-646-9). Borgo Pr.

Manual of Oncology Therapeutics. Kay See-Lasley & Robert Ignoffo. 300p. 1981. pap. text ed. 19.95 (ISBN 0-8016-4448-8). Mosby.

Manual of Operating Room Technology. Frances Ginsberg et al. LC 66-17293. (Illus., Orig.). pap. 5.75 o.p. (ISBN 0-397-54052-3). Lippincott.

Manual of Operative Dentistry. 4th ed. H. M. Pickard. (Illus.). 1976. pap. 15.50x (ISBN 0-19-267004-2). Oxford U Pr.

Manual of Orthopedics. Nancy E. Hilt & Shirley B. Cogburn. LC 79-31732. (Illus.). 1979. text ed. 36.50 (ISBN 0-8016-2198-4). Mosby.

Manual of Osteopathic Technique. 2nd ed. Alan Stoddard. 1979. text ed. 32.50x (ISBN 0-09-051120-4, Hutchinson U Lib). Humanities.

Manual of Patient Education for Cardiopulmonary Dysfunction. Barara S. Czerwinski. LC 79-21435. (Illus.). 1980. pap. text ed. 13.95 (ISBN 0-8016-1197-0). Mosby.

Manual of Pediatric Nursing Practice. Massachusetts General Hospital Pediatric Nursing Service. Ed. by Barbara H. Pikl. (Little, Brown Spiral Manual Series). 1980. pap. write for info. (ISBN 0-316-54958-4). Little.

Manual of Pediatric Therapeutics. 2nd ed. Children's Hospital Medical Center, Boston. Ed. by John W. Graef & Thomas E. Cone, Jr. 450p. 1980. 13.95 (ISBN 0-316-13911-4). Little.

Manual of Petroleum Measurement Standards. American Petroleum Institute. LC 80-67080. (Chapter 11.1 -- Volume Correction Factors: Vol. VI). (Illus.). 563p. 1980. write for info. (ISBN 0-89364-027-1). Am Petroleum.

Manual of Petroleum Measurement Standards. American Petroleum Institute. LC 80-67080. (Chapter 11.1 -- Volume Correction Factors Ser.: Vol. I). (Illus.). 678p. 1980. write for info. (ISBN 0-89364-022-0). Am Petroleum.

Manual of Petroleum Measurement Standards. American Petroleum Institute. LC 80-67080. (Chapter 11.1 -- Volume Correction Factors: Vol. II). (Illus.). 592p. 1980. write for info. (ISBN 0-89364-023-9). Am Petroleum.

Manual of Petroleum Measurement Standards. American Petroleum Institute. LC 80-67080. (Chapter 11.1 -- Volume Correction Factors: Vol. III). (Illus.). 563p. 1980. write for info. (ISBN 0-89364-024-7). Am Petroleum.

Manual of Petroleum Measurement Standards. American Petroleum Institute. LC 80-67080. (Chapter 11.1 -- Volume Correction Factors: Vol. IV). (Illus.). 878p. 1980. write for info. (ISBN 0-89364-025-5). Am Petroleum.

Manual of Petroleum Measurement Standard. American Petroleum Institute. LC 80-67080. (Chapter 11.1 --Volume Corrections Factors: Vol. V). (Illus.). 812p. 1980. write for info. (ISBN 0-89364-026-3). Am Petroleum.

Manual of Petroleum Measurement Standards. American Petroleum Institute. (Chapter 11.1 -- Volume Corrections Factors: Vol. VIII). (Illus.). 881p. 1980. write for info. (ISBN 0-89364-030-1). Am Petroleum.

Manual of Petroleum Measurement Standards. American Petroleum Institute. LC 80-67080. (Chapter 11.1 -- Volume Correction Factors: Vol. IX). (Illus.). 587p. 1980. write for info. (ISBN 0-89364-032-8). Am Petroleum.

Manual of Petroleum Measurement Standard. American Petroleum Institute. LC 80-67080. (Chapter 11.1 -- Volume Correction Factors: Vol. X). (Illus.). 420p. 1980. write for info. (ISBN 0-89364-033-6). Am Petroleum.

Manual of Petroleum Measurement Standards. American Petroleum Institute. (Chapter 11.1 -- Vol. Correction Factors). (Illus.). 1980. write for info. (ISBN 0-89364-021-2). Am Petroleum.

Manual of Petroleum Measurement Standards. American Petroleum Institute. LC 80-67080. (Chapter 11.1 -- Volume Correction Factors). 1980. write for info. (ISBN 0-89364-035-2). Am Petroleum.

Manual of Petroleum Measurements Standards. American Petroleum Institute. LC 80-67080. (Chapter 11.1 -- Volume Correction Factors: Vol. VII). (Illus.). 958p. 1980. write for info. (ISBN 0-89364-029-8). Am Petroleum.

Manual of Political Economy. E. Peshine Smith. (Neglected American Economists Ser.). 1974. lib. bdg. 50.00 (ISBN 0-8240-1010-8). Garland Pub.

Manual of Printing Office Practice. Theodore L. De Vinne. Ed. by Irving Lew. (Bibliographical Reprint Ser.). 1980. Repr. of 1926 ed. text ed. 25.00 ltd. ed. (ISBN 0-89782-003-7). Battery Pk.

Manual of Procedure for Town & Village Courts (N.Y., 2 vols. Eugene W. Salisbury. (Both volumes supplemented annually). 1978. Vol. 1. looseleaf 12.50 (ISBN 0-87526-180-9); Vol. 2. looseleaf 12.50 (ISBN 0-87526-181-7). Gould.

Manual of Psychiatric Peer Review. Ed. by Peer Review Committee of the American Psychiatric Assn. et al. 160p. 1981. spiral bdg. 11.00 (ISBN 0-685-76788-4, P168-0). Am Psychiatric.

Manual of Psychology. George F. Stout. (Contributions to the History of Psychology Ser.: Orientations). 1978. Repr. of 1899 ed. write for info. U Pubns Amer.

Manual of Pulmonary Function Testing. 2nd ed. Gregg Ruppel. LC 78-21100. (Illus.). 1979. pap. text ed. 12.50 (ISBN 0-8016-4209-4). Mosby.

Manual of Pulmonary Procedures. Stephen J. Jay & Robert B. Stonehill. (Blue Book Ser.). (Illus.). 224p. 1980. 19.95 (ISBN 0-7216-8607-9). Saunders.

Manual of Radiographic Techniques of the Skull. Korach. 1981. write for info (ISBN 0-89352-098-5). Masson Pub.

Manual of Radioisotope Production. (Technical Reports Ser.: No. 63). 1966. pap. 20.00 (ISBN 92-0-145366-3, IAEA). Unipub.

Manual of Real Estate: Law, Procedures, & Forms. 2nd ed. William J. Grange & Thomas C. Woodbury. (Illus.). 461p. 1968. 26.50 (ISBN 0-8260-3500-0, 39381). Ronald Pr.

Manual of Respiratory Therapy. 2nd ed. Joan P. Taylor. LC 77-22882. (Illus.). 1978. pap. text ed. 13.95 (ISBN 0-8016-0836-8). Mosby.

Manual of Sailboat Racing. Thomas J. McDermott. 1964. 10.95 (ISBN 0-02-583070-8). Macmillan.

Manual of Sampling Techniques. Ranjan K. Som. 390p. 1973. 27.50x o.p. (ISBN 0-8448-0785-0). Crane-Russak Co.

Manual of Seamanship for the Officer of the Deck, Ship Under Sail Alone: The 1903 Edition. Patrick W. Hourigan. LC 79-93029. 148p. 1980. 7.50 (ISBN 0-87021-361-X). Naval Inst Pr.

Manual of Singlehanded Sailing. Tony Meisel. LC 80-22856. (Illus.). 224p. 1981. lib. bdg. 12.95 (ISBN 0-668-04998-7, 4998). Arco.

Manual of Socialpsychologic Assessment. Francis. 1976. pap. 11.95 (ISBN 0-8385-6127-6). ACC.

Manual of Soil Laboratory Testing: Vol. I, Soil Classification & Compaction Testing. K. H. Head. (Manual of Sail Laboratory Testing Ser.). 339p. 1980. 44.95x (ISBN 0-470-26973-1). Halsted Pr.

Manual of Spinal Surgery. D. A. Jenkins et al. 1981. text ed. price not set. Butterworth.

Manual of Standard Practice for Detailing Reinforced Concrete Structures: ACI 315-74. 6th ed. ACI Committee 315. 1974. loose-leaf 40.85 (ISBN 0-685-85073-0, 315-74) (ISBN 0-685-85074-9). ACI.

Manual of Standardized Methods for Veterinary Microbiology. Ed. by George E. Cottral. LC 77-90900. (Illus.). 720p. 1978. 40.00 (ISBN 0-8014-1119-X). Comstock.

Manual of Steam Locomotive Restoration & Preservation. D. W. Harvey. LC 79-56051. (Illus.). 96p. 1980. 14.95x (ISBN 0-7153-7770-1). David & Charles.

Manual of Stress Management. Clorinda Margolis & Linda Shrier. 1981. write for info. Franklin Inst Pr.

Manual of Structured Experiences for Cross-Cultural Learning. Ed. by William W. Weeks et al. LC 79-100422. 1977. pap. text ed. 5.95 (ISBN 0-933934-05-X). Intercult Pr.

Manual of Style. rev. 12th ed. University of Chicago Press. LC 68-40582. 1969. 17.50 (ISBN 0-226-77008-7). U of Chicago Pr.

Manual of Surgical Intensive Care. Committee on Pre & Postoperative Care American College of Surgeons. Ed. by John M. Kinney. LC 76-51009. (Illus.). 1977. text ed. 14.50 o.p. (ISBN 0-7216-1180-X). Saunders.

Manual of Surgical Pathology Gross Room Procedures. Juan Rosai. (Illus.). 128p. 1981. 17.95x (ISBN 0-8166-1027-4). U of Minn Pr.

Manual of Swedish Handweaving. new ed. Ulla Cyrus-Zetterstroem. (Illus.). 184p. 1977. 15.75 (ISBN 0-8231-5019-4). Branford.

Manual of Symbols & Terminology for Physiochemical Quantities & Units. Ed. by D. H. Whiffen. 1979. pap. text ed. 10.25 (ISBN 0-08-022386-9). Pergamon.

Manual of the Art of Bookbinding Containing Full Instructions in the Different Branches of Forwarding, Gilding & Finishing. James B. Nicholson. Ed. by John Bidwell. LC 78-74391. (Nineteenth-Century Book Arts & Printing History Ser.: Vol. 6). (Illus.). 1980. lib. bdg. 33.00 (ISBN 0-8240-3880-0). Garland Pub.

Manual of the Flowering Plants of California. Willis L. Jepson. (Illus.). 1925. 40.00x (ISBN 0-520-00606-2). U of Cal Pr.

Manual of the Guild of Handicraft. C. R. Ashbee. Ed. by Peter Stansky & Rodney Shewan. LC 76-17776. (Aesthetic Movement & the Arts & Crafts Movement Ser.: Vol. 32). 1978. Repr. of 1892 ed. lib. bdg. 44.00 (ISBN 0-8240-2481-8). Garland Pub.

Manual of the Plants of Colorado. rev. ed. H. D. Harrington. LC 73-5952. 1964. 41.00 o.p. (ISBN 0-8040-0195-2, SB); microfilm 81.90 o.p. (ISBN 0-686-66544-9). Swallow.

Manual of the Trees of North America, 2 Vols. 2nd ed. Charles S. Sargent. (Illus.). 1922. pap. text ed. 5.00 ea.; Vol. 1. pap. text ed. (ISBN 0-486-20277-1); Vol. 2. pap. text ed. (ISBN 0-486-20278-X). Dover.

Manual of Therapeutic Exercise. Patricia Sullivan et al. 1981. text ed. 15.95 (ISBN 0-8359-4245-7). Reston.

Manual of Thoracic Surgery. Arndt Von Hippel. (Illus.). 264p. 1978. 18.75 (ISBN 0-398-03689-6); pap. 11.50 (ISBN 0-398-03690-X). C C Thomas.

Manual of Time Study for Supervisors. Thomas. 4.00 o.p. (ISBN 0-686-00164-8). Columbia Graphs.

Manual of Tropical Housing & Building Design: Climatic Design, Pt. 1. O. H. Koenigsberger et al. (Illus.). 344p. 1974. pap. text ed. 14.95x (ISBN 0-582-44546-9). Longman.

Manual of United States Surveying. J. H. Hawes. 1977. Repr. of 1882 ed. 12.50 (ISBN 0-686-18921-3, 612). CARBEN Survey.

Manual of Weighttraining. 3rd ed. Ed. by George Kirkley & John Goodbody. (Illus.). 1979. pap. text ed. 12.50x o.p. (ISBN 0-392-07003-0, SpS). Soccer.

Manual of Wildlife Conservation. The Wildlife Society, Inc. Ed. by Richard D. Teague. LC 72-143895. (Illus.). 206p. (Orig.). 1971. pap. text ed. 4.25 (ISBN 0-933564-01-5). Wildlife Soc.

Manual of Worship. John E. Skoglund. LC 68-20431. 1968. bds. 5.95 o.p. (ISBN 0-8170-0395-9). Judson.

Manual of Writings in Middle English, 1050-1500, 6 vols. Ed. by Albert E. Hartung & Burke Severs. Incl. Vol. 1. 338p. 1967. 17.50 (ISBN 0-208-00893-4); pap. 10.50; Vol. 2. 329p. 1970. 17.50 (ISBN 0-208-00894-2); Vol. 3. 960p. 1972. 17.50 (ISBN 0-208-01220-6); Vol. 4. 1313p. 1973. 17.50 (ISBN 0-208-01342-3); Vol. 5. 440p. 1976. 25.00 (ISBN 0-208-01459-4); Vol. 6. 500p. 1980. 25.00 (ISBN 0-208-01715-1). Shoe String.

Manual on Bookselling: How to Open & Run Your Own Bookstore. Ed. by American Bookseller's Association. (Illus.). 146p. 1980. 11.95 (ISBN 0-517-53705-2, Harmony); pap. 6.95 (ISBN 0-517-53706-0, Harmony). Crown.

Manual on Control of Infection in Surgical Patients. Ed. by William A Altemeier et al. LC 76-15400. 1976. 21.75 (ISBN 0-397-50355-5). Lippincott.

Manual on Decontamination of Surfaces: Procedures & Data. (Safety Ser.: No. 48). 1979. pap. 7.00 (ISBN 92-0-123079-6, ISP483, IAEA). Unipub.

Manual on Environmental Legislation. 116p. 1981. pap. 13.00 (UNEP46, UNEP). Unipub.

Manual on Environmental Monitoring in Normal Operation. (Safety Ser.: No. 16). 1966. pap. 5.00 (ISBN 92-0-123066-4, ISP 98, IAEA). Unipub.

Manual on Hospital Chaplaincy. American Hospital Association. 96p. 1970. pap. 8.75 (ISBN 0-87258-060-1, 1515). Am Hospital.

Manual on How to Establish a Trust & Reduce Taxation. Martin Larson. 195.00 (ISBN 0-935036-01-6). Liberty Lobby.

Manual on How to Play the Five String Banjo for the Complete Ignoramus. Wayne Erbsen. (Illus.). 52p. 1973. pap. 4.95 (ISBN 0-686-64083-7, PCB 103). Fischer Inc NY.

Manual on K F: The Library of Congress Classification Schedule for Law of the United States. Patricia L. Piper et al. LC 72-86471. (AALL Publications Ser.: No. 11). 135p. 1972. text ed. 22.50x (ISBN 0-8377-0109-0). Rothman.

Manual on Management of Group Feeding Programmes. (FAO Food & Nutrition Paper Ser.). 124p. 1980. pap. 7.00 (ISBN 92-5-100931-7, F2041, FAO). Unipub.

Manual on Mass Media in Population & Development. (Illus.). 1978. pap. 7.00 (ISBN 92-3-101439-0, U820, UNESCO). Unipub.

Manual on Mutation Breeding. 2nd ed. (Illus.). 1977. pap. 21.50 (ISBN 92-0-115077-6, IAEA). Unipub.

Manual on Nonviolence & Children. Ed. by Stephanie Judson. (Illus.). 115p. (Orig.). 1977. pap. 5.00 (ISBN 0-9605062-1-7). Friends Peace Comm.

Manual on Oil Pollution, 3 pts. Incl. Pt. I. Prevention. 1976. pap. 8.25 (ISBN 0-686-64934-6, IMCO 23); Pt. II. Contingency Planning. 1978. pap. 11.00 (ISBN 0-686-64935-4, IMCO 24); Pt. IV. Practical Information on Means of Dealing with Oil Spillages. 1977. Repr. of 1972 ed. pap. 12.00 (ISBN 0-686-64936-2, IMCO 25). IMCO). Unipub.

Manual on Peace Walks. Paul Salstrom. 27p. 1967. pap. 1.00 (ISBN 0-934676-11-9). Greenlf Bks.

Manual on Plant Layout & Materials Handling. LC 72-186284. 80p. 1972. 7.25 (ISBN 92-833-1011-X, APO45, APO). Unipub.

Manual on Radiation Haematology. (Technical Reports Ser.: No. 123). (Illus., Orig.). 1971. pap. 25.75 (ISBN 92-0-115071-7, IAEA). Unipub.

Manual on Radiation Sterilization of Medical & Biological Materials. (Technical Reports Ser.: No. 149). (Illus.). 327p. (Orig.). 1974. pap. 24.25 (ISBN 92-0-115073-3, IAEA). Unipub.

Manual on Retinal Detachment. Donald M. Shafer. 150p. 1981. write for info. (1550-8). Williams & Wilkins.

Manual on the Global Data-Processinng System, Vol. II: Regional Aspects. 74p. 1981. pap. 7.00 (W475, WMO). Unipub.

Manual Para la Preparacion De Informes y Tesis. Irma G. Deserrano. LC 76-11003. 1980. 6.25 (ISBN 0-8477-2311-9); pap. 5.00 (ISBN 0-8477-2312-7). U of PR Pr.

Manuals of Food Quality Control, 3 vols. Incl. Vol. 1. Food Control Laboratory. 75p. pap. 7.50 (ISBN 92-5-100839-6, F1960); Vol. 2. Additives, Contaminants, Techniques. 317p. pap. 20.75 (ISBN 92-5-100867-1, F1961); Vol. 3. Commodities. 420p. pap. 26.75 (ISBN 92-5-100844-2, F1962). (FAO Food & Nutrition Papers: No. 14). 1980 (FAO). Unipub.

Manuals of Food Quality Control: Microbiological Analysis. (FAO Food & Nutrition Paper: No. 14-4). 119p. 1981. pap. 7.75 (ISBN 92-5-100849-3, F2070, FAO). Unipub.

Manuel Breton De los Herreros. Gerard Flynn. (World Authors Ser.: No. 487). 1978. lib. bdg. 11.95 (ISBN 0-8057-6328-7). Twayne.

Manuel D'archeologie Chretienne: Depuis les origines jusqu'au VIII siecle, 2 vols. H. Leclercq. (Illus., Fr.). 1981. Repr. of 1907 ed. lib. bdg. 160.00x (ISBN 0-89241-148-1). Vol. 1, 592p. Vol. 2, 682p. Caratzas Bros.

Manuel D'archeologie Romaine, 2 vols. R. Cagnat & V. Chapot. (Illus., Fr.). 1981. Repr. of 1920 ed. lib. bdg. 150.00x (ISBN 0-89241-139-2). Vol. 1. 735p. Vol. 2, 574p. Caratzas Bros.

Manuel d'Art Musulman, 2 vols. H. Saladin & G. Migeon. Incl. Vol. I. Architecture. xxii, 596p; Vol. II. Les Arts Plastiques. iii, 477p. (Illus., Fr.). 1981. Repr. of 1907 ed. Set. lib. bdg. 160.00x (ISBN 0-89241-155-4). Caratzas Bros.

Manuel De Pratiques Budgetaires Modernes. Alexander Hamilton Institute, Inc. Ed. by Jjames M. Jenks. (Illus.). 87p. (Orig., Fr.). 1978. pap. 49.50 (ISBN 0-86604-003-X, TX-30-652). Hamilton Inst.

Manuel Galvez. Myron I. Lichtblau. (World Authors Ser.: Argentina: No. 203). lib. bdg. 10.95 (ISBN 0-8057-2340-4). Twayne.

Manuel Ii Palaeologus, 1391-1425: A Study in Late Byzantine Statesmanship. John W. Barker. 1969. 40.00 (ISBN 0-8135-0582-8). Rutgers U Pr.

Manuel Machado: A Revaluation. J. Gordon Brotherston. LC 68-11281. (Illus.). 1968. 32.00 (ISBN 0-521-04334-4). Cambridge U Pr.

Manuel Tamayo y Baus. Gerard Flynn. (World Authors Ser.: Spain: No. 263). 1973. lib. bdg. 10.95 (ISBN 0-8057-2880-5). Twayne.

Manuel, Young Mexican-American. Carla Greene. (Illus.). (gr. 3-6). 1969. 4.25 o.p. (ISBN 0-8313-0069-8, 8313); PLB 6.19 (ISBN 0-685-13776-7). Lantern.

Manuela (La Caballeresa Del Sol) A Novel. Demetrio Aguilera Malta. Tr. by Willis K. Jones from Span. LC 67-11700. (Contemporary Latin American Classic). 320p. 1967. 9.95x (ISBN 0-8093-0256-X). S Ill U Pr.

Manuever's Manual. 4th ed. (Pilot Training Ser.). (Illus.). 210p. 1980. pap. text ed. 6.95 (ISBN 0-88487-065-0, JS314302). Jeppesen Sanderson.

Manufacture of Knowledge: An Essay on the Constructivist & Contextual Nature of Science. Karin D. Knorr. 200p. Date not set. 39.01 (ISBN 0-08-025777-1); pap. 19.21 (ISBN 0-08-025778-X). Pergamon.

Manufacture of Liquers, Wines, & Cordials Without the Aid of Distillation. Pierre LaCour. (Illus.). 1980. Repr. of 1853 ed. lib. bdg. 25.00 (ISBN 0-915262-52-5). S J Durst.

Manufacture of News: Social Problems, Deviance & the Mass Media. Ed. by Stanley Cohen & Jock Young. LC 73-87747. (Communication & Society: Vol. 3). 1973. 20.00x (ISBN 0-8039-0325-1); pap. 9.95x (ISBN 0-8039-1174-2). Sage.

Manufacture of Soda: With Special Reference to the Ammonia Process. 2nd ed. 1969. 27.50 o.s.i. (ISBN 0-02-846100-2). Hafner.

Manufactured Carbon. H. W. Davidson et al. 1968. 15.00 (ISBN 0-08-012667-7); pap. 7.00 (ISBN 0-08-012666-9). Pergamon.

Manufactured Exports from Developing Countries. Thomas K. Morrison. LC 76-25353. (Illus.). 1976. text ed. 17.95 o.p. (ISBN 0-275-56880-6). Praeger.

Manufacturer's Representative. Frank Lebell. 192p. 1981. 19.95 (ISBN 0-89047-037-5). Herman Pub.

Manufacturing. R. T. Wright & T. R. Jensen. LC 76-5892. (Illus.). 1976. Set. text ed. 10.64 (ISBN 0-87006-203-4); lab manual 4.00 (ISBN 0-87006-281-6). Goodheart.

Manufacturing: A Basic Text for Industrial Arts. James Fales et al. (Illus.). 1980. 15.96 (ISBN 0-87345-586-X, B82088); instr's guide 5.28 (ISBN 0-87345-587-8). McKnight.

Manufacturing Analysis. N. H. Cook. 1966. 19.95 (ISBN 0-201-01211-1). A-W.

Manufacturing Control: The Last Frontier for Profits. George Plossl. LC 73-8965. 1973. 16.95 (ISBN 0-87909-483-4). Reston.

Manufacturing Engineering Transactions: 1974, Vol. 3. Daniel B. Dallas. 1975. 25.00 o.p. (ISBN 0-87263-104-4). SME.

Manufacturing in the Corporate Strategy. Wickham Skinner. LC 78-602. (Manufacturing Management Ser.). 1978. 27.95 (ISBN 0-471-01612-8, Pub. by Wiley-Interscience). Wiley.

Manufacturing Laboratory Manual. R. Thomas Wright & Thomas R. Jensen. 192p. 1980. 4.00 (ISBN 0-87006-292-1). Goodheart.

Manufacturing Management & Control. Dean S. Ammer. (Illus.). 1968. pap. 8.95 (ISBN 0-13-555839-5). P-H.

Manufacturing Organization & Management. 3rd ed. John A. Ritchey & O. S. Hulley. (Int'l. Series in Industrial & Systems Engineering). (Illus.). 608p. 1975. 19.95 (ISBN 0-13-555854-9). P-H.

Manufacturing Process. Johnson. 1979. text ed. 23.72 (ISBN 0-87002-299-7); study guide 5.28 (ISBN 0-87002-044-7). Bennett IL.

Manufacturing Processes. 7th ed. B. H. Amstead et al. LC 76-26542. 1977. 26.95x (ISBN 0-471-06245-6). Wiley.

Manufacturing Processes. 7th ed. B. H. Amstead et al. LC 78-16185. 1979. text ed. 27.95 (ISBN 0-471-03575-0); solutions manual avail. (ISBN 0-471-03679-X). Wiley.

Manufacturing Processes, Herbert W. Yankee. LC 78-13059. (Illus.). 1979. 26.95 (ISBN 0-13-555557-4). P-H.

Manufacturing Processes & Materials for Engineers. 2nd ed. L. E. Doyle et al. 1969. text ed. 26.95 (ISBN 0-13-555862-X). P-H.

Manufacturing Productivity Solutions II. Intro. by Don Burnham. LC 80-54415. (Illus.). 161p. 1980. pap. text ed. 20.00 (ISBN 0-87263-106-0). SME.

Manufacturing Technology, Vol. 1. G. Kenlay & K. W. Harris. (Illus.). 155p. 1979. pap. 12.95x (ISBN 0-7131-3401-1). Intl Ideas.

Manufacturing Technology, Vol. 1. H. C. Town & H. Moore. 1979. 27.00 (ISBN 0-7134-1094-9, Pub. by Batsford England); pap. 14.95 (ISBN 0-7134-1095-7). David & Charles.

Manufacturing Technology, No. 3. Harris. 1981. text ed. price not set (ISBN 0-408-00493-2). Butterworth.

Manufacturing Technology: Advanced Machines & Processes. H. C. Town & H. Moore. (Illus.). 352p. 1980. 39.00 (ISBN 0-7134-1096-5, Pub. by Batsford England); pap. 17.95 (ISBN 0-7134-1097-3). David & Charles.

Manuscript Books of Emily Dickinson: 1883-1895. Emily Dickinson. Ed. by Ralph W. Franklin. LC 80-17861. 1980. pre-Apr. 85.00x (ISBN 0-674-54828-0, Belknap Pr); text ed. 100.00 (ISBN 0-686-63335-0). Harvard U Pr.

Manuscript Collection of the American Antiquarian Society. William L. Joyce. 30p. 1980. pap. 3.00x (ISBN 0-912296-43-7, Dist. by U Pr of Va). Am Antiquarian.

Manuscript Collections of the Maryland Historical Society. A. J. Pedley. LC 68-23074. 1968. 15.00 (ISBN 0-938420-08-9). Md Hist.

Manuscript Illustrations of the Uttaradhyayana Sutra. W. Norman Brown. (American Oriental Ser.: Vol. 21). (Illus.). 1941. 8.00x o.p. (ISBN 0-686-00010-2). Am Orient Soc.

Manuscript of Shakespeare's Hamlet, 2 Vols. John D. Wilson. 1934. Set. 60.00 (ISBN 0-521-06833-9). Cambridge U Pr.

Manuscript Painting in Paris During the Reign of St. Louis. Robert Branner. LC 73-78514. (Studies in the History of Art). (Illus.). 1977. 65.00x (ISBN 0-520-02462-1). U of Cal Pr.

Manuscript, Society & Belief in Early Christian Egypt. Colin H. Roberts. (Schweich Lectures Ser.). 1979. 23.50x (ISBN 0-19-725982-0). Oxford U Pr.

Manuscript Solicitation for Libraries, Special Collections, Museums & Archives. Edward C. Kemp. LC 77-29015. 1978. lib. bdg. 20.00x (ISBN 0-87287-183-5). Libs Unl.

Manuscript Tracking: Reusable Edition. Ed. by W. Edwards & S. Edwards. (Large Type Tracking Ser.). (gr. k-1). 1975. 4.00 (ISBN 0-89039-017-7). Ann Arbor Pubs.

Manuscript Tradition of Polybius. J. M. Moore. (Cambridge Classical Studies). 1966. 17.95 (ISBN 0-521-05755-8). Cambridge U Pr.

Manuscripts & Documents: Their Deterioration & Restoration. rev. ed. W. J. Barrow. LC 72-89855. (Illus.). 86p. 1972. 8.95x (ISBN 0-8139-0408-0). U Pr of Va.

Manuscripts Collections of the Minnesota Historical Society, Guide No. 2. Compiled by Lucile M. Kane & Kathryn A. Johnson. LC 35-27911. 212p. 1955. pap. 3.75 (ISBN 0-87351-011-9). Minn Hist.

Manuscripts Collections of the Minnesota Historical Society Guide, No. 3. Compiled by Lydia A. Lucas. LC 35-27911. 189p. 1977. pap. 7.00 (ISBN 0-87351-120-4). Minn Hist.

Manuscripts Collections of the Minnesota Regional Research Centers: Guide No. 2. Compiled by James E. Fogerty. 92p. 1980. pap. 4.50 (ISBN 0-87351-150-6). Minn Hist.

Manuscripts of Captain H. V. Knox (from Vol. VI) Great Britain Historical Manuscripts Commission. Report on Manuscripts in Various Collections. Ed. by George Billias. LC 72-8832. (American Revolutionary Ser.). Repr. of 1901 ed. lib. bdg. 18.00x (ISBN 0-8398-0804-6). Irvington.

Manuscripts of the Earl of Dartmouth, 3 vols. Great Britain Historical Manuscripts Commission. Ed. by George Billias. LC 72-8795. (American Revolutionary Ser.). Repr. of 1896 ed. Set. lib. bdg. 85.00x (ISBN 0-8398-0802-X). Irvington.

Manuskript. Ed. by S Karger AG. (Illus.). 1980. pap. 9.00 (ISBN 3-8055-0182-X). S Karger.

Manwolf. Gloria Skurzynski. 192p. (gr. 6 up). 1981. 9.95 (ISBN 0-395-30079-7, Clarion). HM.

Manx National Songbook, Vol. 1. Deemster Gill et al. 1979. text ed. 14.50x (ISBN 0-904980-30-8). Humanities.

Manx National Songbook, Vol. 2. Charles Guard. 1980. text ed. 22.25x (ISBN 0-904980-32-4). Humanities.

Many a Secret Place: The Story Ofthe Master Spy Sidney George Reilly. Edward Van Der Rhoer. 288p. 1981. 12.50 (ISBN 0-684-16870-7, ScribT). Scribner.

Many Americans-One Nation. rev. ed. Illus. by Mac Conner et al. (Bowmar-Noble Social Studies Program). (Illus.). 469p. (gr. 5). 1979. text ed. 9.99 (ISBN 0-8372-3688-6); tchrs. ed. 12.75 (ISBN 0-8372-3689-4); tests 9.30 (ISBN 0-8372-3729-7). Bowmar-Noble.

Many-Body Problem in Quantum Mechanics. Norman H. March et al. (Cambridge Monographs on Physics). 1968. 47.95 (ISBN 0-521-05671-3). Cambridge U Pr.

Many-Colored Land. Julian May. (Saga of Pliocene Exile Ser.). 432p. 1981. 12.95 (ISBN 0-686-69053-2). HM.

Many-Colored Toga: The Diary of Henry Fountain Ashurst. Henry F. Ashurst. Ed. by George Sparks. LC 62-10625. (Illus.). 1962. 2.00 (ISBN 0-8165-0056-8). U of Ariz Pr.

Many-Coloured Mantle. Thomas Ansell. 10.00 (ISBN 0-89253-452-4); flexible cloth 4.80 (ISBN 0-89253-453-2). Ind-US Inc.

Many Deadly Returns. Patricia Moyes. 1981. pap. 2.25 o.s.i. (ISBN 0-440-16172-X). Dell.

Many Dimensional Man: Decentralizing Self, Society & the Sacred. James A. Ogilvy. LC 76-57273. 1977. 17.95x (ISBN 0-19-502231-9). Oxford U Pr.

Many Electron Problem. K. S. Vishwanathan. 10.00x (ISBN 0-310-26904-0). Asia.

Many-Faced Argument: Recent Studies in the Ontological Argument for the Existence of God. Ed. by John H. Hick & Arthur C. McGill. (Orig.). 1967. 8.95 (ISBN 0-02-551360-5); pap. 11.95 (ISBN 0-02-085440-4). Macmillan.

Many Faces of Communism. Ed. by Morton A. Kaplan. LC 77-99096. 1978. 19.95 (ISBN 0-02-917230-6). Free Pr.

Many Faces of Educational Consumerism. Joan S. Stark et al. LC 77-8722. 1977. 19.95 (ISBN 0-669-01631-4). Lexington Bks.

Many Faces of Ernie. Judy Freudberg. (Young Reader Ser.). (Illus.). (gr. k-3). 1979. PLB 5.00 (ISBN 0-307-60108-0, Golden Pr). Western Pub.

Many Faces of Information Science. Ed. by Edward C. Weiss. LC 77-12103. (AAAS Selected Symposium Ser.: No. 3). (Illus.). 1978. lib. bdg. 16.00x (ISBN 0-89158-430-7). Westview.

Many Faces of Jane Fonda: An A-Z Miscellany. Ed. by Mike Lavelle. (Illus.). 260p. (Orig.). 1980. pap. 7.95 (ISBN 0-89803-037-4). Caroline Hse.

Many Faces of Slavery. I. E. Levine. LC 74-28162. 192p. (gr. 9 up). 1975. PLB 5.29 o.p. (ISBN 0-671-32713-5). Messner.

Many Faces of the Civil War. Irving Werstein. LC 61-14461. (Illus.). (gr. 7 up). 1961. PLB 4.79 o.p. (ISBN 0-671-32484-5). Messner.

Many-Faceted Jacksonian Era: New Interpretations. Edward Pessen. (Contributions in American History: No. 67). (Illus.). 1977. lib. bdg. 22.50 (ISBN 0-8371-9720-1, PJE/). Greenwood.

Many Facets of Human Settlement: Science & Society. Ed. by Irene Tinker & Mayra Buvinic. LC 77-6307. 1977. text ed. 125.00 (ISBN 0-08-021994-2). Pergamon.

Many Facets of Rational-Emotive Therapy: Proceedings. National Conference on Rational Psychotherapy, 2nd, June 1977. Ed. by Raymond Di Giuseppe. LC 78-71033. Date not set. pap. cancelled (ISBN 0-917476-17-4). Rational Living.

Many Friends Cookbook: An International Cookbook for Boys & Girls. Terry Cooper & Marilyn Ratner. LC 79-24832. (Illus.). 64p. (gr. 3-6). 1980. pap. 6.95 (ISBN 0-399-20755-4). Philomel.

Many Friends Cooking. Terry Touff Cooper & Marilyn Ratner. LC 79-24832. (gr. 3 up). spiral bdg. 6.00 (ISBN 0-935738-00-2, 5065). US Comm UNICEF.

Many Furs: A Grimm's Fairy Tale. Grimm & Jacquelyn Sage. Tr. by Jacquelyn Sage from Ger. (Illus.). 32p. (gr. 1-4). 1981. 12.95 (ISBN 0-89742-041-1). Dawne-Leigh.

Many Heroes. 2nd ed. Alan Levy. LC 80-65002. 384p. 1980. Repr. of 1972 ed. 12.50 (ISBN 0-933256-12-4, Pub. by Second Chance Pr). Watts.

Many Junipers, Heartbeats. Jane Miller. (Illus., Orig.). 1980. pap. 4.50 (ISBN 0-914278-29-0). Copper Beech.

Many Lines to Thee: Letters to G. K. A. Bell from the Martello Tower at Sandycove, Rutland Square & Trinity College, Dublin, 1904-7. Oliver S. Gogarty. Ed. & intro. by James F. Carens. (Illus.). 168p. 1971. text ed. 13.75x (ISBN 0-85105-198-7, Dolmen Pr). Humanities.

Many Loves & Other Plays. William C. Williams. Incl. Many Loves; A Dream of Love; Tituba's Children; The First President; The Cure. LC 61-9334. 1961. pap. 9.95 (ISBN 0-8112-0232-1, NDP191). New Directions.

Many Marriages by Sherwood Anderson. Ed. by Douglas G. Rogers. LC 78-2353. 1978. 12.00 (ISBN 0-8108-1122-7). Scarecrow.

Many Mexicos, Silver Anniversary Edition. Lesley B. Simpson. (YA) (gr. 9 up). 1966. 16.95x (ISBN 0-520-01179-1); pap. 4.65 (ISBN 0-520-01180-5, CAL29). U of Cal Pr.

Many-Particle Physics. Gerald D. Mahan. (Physics of Solids & Liquids Ser.). 980p. 1981. 85.00 (ISBN 0-306-40411-7, Plenum Pr). Plenum Pub.

Many People Come, Looking, Looking. Galen Rowell. LC 80-19394. (Illus.). 182p. 1980. 30.00 (ISBN 0-916890-86-4). Mountaineers.

Many People, Many Faiths: An Introduction to the Religious Life of Mankind. Robert S. Ellwood, Jr. (Illus.). 400p. 1976. ref. ed. 16.95x (ISBN 0-13-555995-2). P-H.

Many Rivers to Cross. Steve Frazee. 176p. 1981. pap. 1.75 (ISBN 0-449-14012-1, GM). Fawcett.

Many Sisters: Women in Cross-Cultural Perspectives. Ed. by Carolyn J. Matthiasson. LC 74-2654. (Illus.). 1979. pap. text ed. 9.95 (ISBN 0-02-920320-1). Free Pr.

Many Splendored Fishes of the Atlantic Coast. Gar Goodson. LC 76-3231. 1976. pap. 4.95 (ISBN 0-916240-01-0). Marquest Colorguide.

Many Thing Begin for Change. A. L. Ulasi. 1975. pap. 1.75 o.p. (ISBN 0-531-06064-0, Fontana Pap). Watts.

Many Voices, One World. 312p. 1980. pap. 13.50 (ISBN 92-3-101802-7, U1034, UNESCO). Unipub.

Many Waters Cannot Quench Love. Violet Bibby. LC 75-14446. 160p. (gr. 7 up). 1975. 7.25 (ISBN 0-688-22042-8); PLB 6.96 (ISBN 0-688-32042-2). Morrow.

Many-Windowed House: Collected Essays on American Writers & American Writing. Malcolm Cowley. Ed. by Henry D. Piper. LC 74-112384. 297p. 1970. 14.95x (ISBN 0-8093-0444-9). S Ill U Pr.

Many-Windowed House: Collected Essays on American Writers & American Writing. Malcolm Cowley. Ed. by Henry D. Piper. LC 72-11923. (Arcturus Books Paperbacks). 297p. 1973. pap. 6.95 (ISBN 0-8093-0626-3). S Ill U Pr.

Many Winters. Nancy Wood. LC 74-3554. 80p. (gr. 6 up). 1974. 7.95 (ISBN 0-385-02226-3); limited edition 25.00 (ISBN 0-385-07107-8). Doubleday.

Many Worlds: A Russian Life. Sophie Koulomzin. LC 80-19332. 368p. 1980. pap. 8.95. St Vladimirs.

Many Worlds: A Russian Life. Sophie Koulomzin. LC 80-19332. 368p. 1980. pap. 8.95 (ISBN 0-913836-72-9, BS597 K64A35). St Martin.

Many Worlds of Benjamin Franklin. Frank R. Donovan & Whitfield J. Bell. LC 63-21834. (American Heritage Junior Library). (Illus.). 153p. (gr. 5 up). 1963. 9.95 (ISBN 0-8281-0390-9, J013-0). Am Heritage.

Many Worlds, One God. Kenneth J. Delano. 1977. 7.00 o.p. (ISBN 0-682-48644-2). Exposition.

Manyoshu: A New & Complete Translation. H. H. Honda. 45.00 o.p. (ISBN 0-89346-075-3, Pub. by Hokuseido Pr). Heian Intl.

Manyoshu: The Nippon Gakujutsu Shinkokai Translation of One Thousand Poems. Manyoshu. LC 65-15376. (Records of Civilization Ser.: No. 70). 1969. pap. 10.00x (ISBN 0-231-08620-2). Columbia U Pr.

Mao & the Chinese Revolution. Jerome Ch'En. (Illus.). 1967. pap. 6.95 (ISBN 0-19-500270-9, GB). Oxford U Pr.

Mao Tse-Tung. Alan Dures & Katherine Dures. (Leaders Ser.). (Illus.). 96p. (gr. 9-12). 1980. 16.95 (ISBN 0-7134-1923-7, Pub. by Batsford England). David & Charles.

Mao Tse-Tung. Desmond Painter. Ed. by Malcolm Yapp & Margaret Killingray. (World History Ser.). (Illus.). (gr. 10). 1980. lib. bdg. 5.95 (ISBN 0-89908-127-4); pap. write for info. (ISBN 0-89908-102-9). Greenhaven.

Mao Tse-Tung & I Were Beggars. Siao-Yu. LC 59-15411. (Illus.). 320p. 1973. pap. 1.95 o.s.i. (ISBN 0-02-037000-8, Collier). Macmillan.

Mao Tse-Tung in the Scales of History. Ed. by D. Wilson. LC 76-57100. (Contemporary China Institute Publications Ser.). 1977. 36.50 (ISBN 0-521-21583-8); pap. 8.95 (ISBN 0-521-29190-9). Cambridge U Pr.

Mao Tse Tung on Literature & Art. 1967. 2.95 (ISBN 0-8351-0456-7). China Bks.

Mao Tse-Tung: The Man & the Myth. Eric Chou. LC 80-22758. 304p. 1981. 16.95 (ISBN 0-8128-2769-4). Stein & Day.

Mao Tsetung Poems. Mao Tsetung. 1976. red silk 4.95 (ISBN 0-8351-0257-2). pap. 2.95 (ISBN 0-8351-0258-0). China Bks.

Mao Zedong & the Political Economy of the Border Region. Ed. by Andrew Watson. LC 78-67434. (Publications of the Contemporary China Institute). (Illus.). 1980. 29.95 (ISBN 0-521-22551-5); pap. 11.95 (ISBN 0-521-29547-5). Cambridge U Pr.

Mao Zedong's "Talks at the Yan'an Conference on Literature & Art" A Translation of the 1943 Text with Commentary. Bonnie S. McDougall. LC 80-18443. (Michigan Papers in Chinese Studies: No. 39). 128p. 1980. pap. 5.00 (ISBN 0-89264-039-1). U of Mich Ctr Chinese.

Maori Land Tenure: Studies of a Changing Institution. Ian H. Kawharu. 1977. 49.50x (ISBN 0-19-823177-6). Oxford U Pr.

Maori People in the Nineteen-Sixties: A Symposium. Ed. by Erik Schwimmer. (Illus.). 1968. text ed. 11.00x (ISBN 0-900966-00-9). Humanities.

Maori Storehouses & Kindred Structures: Houses, Platforms, Racks & Pits Used for Storing Food, Etc. Elsdon Best. (New Zealand Dominion Museum Bulletin: No. 5). (Illus.). 1977. text ed. 9.50x o.p. (ISBN 0-8426-1041-3). Verry.

Maoris of New Zealand. Joan Metge. 1976. 26.00x (ISBN 0-7100-8352-1); pap. 12.50 (ISBN 0-7100-8381-5). Routledge & Kegan.

Mao's China: A History of the People's Republic. Maurice Meisner. LC 76-51566. (The Transformation of Modern China Ser.). 1979. pap. text ed. 8.95 (ISBN 0-02-920810-6). Free Pr.

Mao's First Heir-Apparent. Tien-Min Li. LC 72-152427. (Special Project). 223p. 1975. 10.00 (ISBN 0-8179-4141-X). Hoover Inst Pr.

Mao's Revolution & the Chinese Political Culture. Richard H. Solomon. (Center for Chinese Studies, Univ. of Michigan). 1971. 28.50x (ISBN 0-520-01806-0); pap. 5.95 (ISBN 0-520-02250-5, CAL246). U of Cal Pr.

Mao's Way. Edward E. Rice. LC 70-186116. (Center for Chinese Studies, Uc Berkeley). 600p. 1972. 25.00x (ISBN 0-520-02199-1); pap. 4.95 (ISBN 0-520-02623-3). U of Cal Pr.

MAP: A Market Anti-Inflation Plan. Abba Lerner & David Colander. 128p. 1980. pap. text ed. write for info. (HC). HarBraceJ.

Map & Compass. rev. ed. Terry Brown & Rob Hunter. (Venture Guides Ser.). (Illus.). 1978. pap. 2.95 o.p. (ISBN 0-902875-99-X). Hippocrene Bks.

Map Data Processing. Ed. by Herbert Freeman & Goffredo G. Pieroni. 1980. 26.00 (ISBN 0-12-267180-5). Acad Pr.

MAP for Fractions. Charles T. Gatje & John F. Gatje. Tr. by Rafael Marcos. (Orig., Span.). (gr. 5 up). 1981. pap. text ed. 1.75 (ISBN 0-937534-07-2). G & G Pubs.

Map History of the British People Since 1700. Brian Catchpole. 1975. pap. text ed. 8.95x (ISBN 0-435-31160-3). Heinemann Ed.

Map Interpretation. G. H. Dury. 19.50x (SpS). Soccer.

Map Is a Picture. Barbara Rinkoff. LC 65-11648. (Let's-Read-&-Find-Out Science Bk). (Illus.). (gr. k-3). 1965. bds. 7.89 (ISBN 0-690-51793-9, TYC-J). T Y Crowell.

Map Librarian in Modern World. Ed. by H. Wallis. L. Zogner. 295p. (Orig.). 1979. pap. text ed. 32.00 (ISBN 0-89664-131-7, Pub. by K G Saur). Gale.

Map Librarianship: An Introduction. Mary Larsgaard. LC 77-28821. (Library Science Text Ser.). 1978. 22.50x (ISBN 0-87287-182-7). Libs Unl.

Map Librarianship: Readings. Roman Drazniowsky. LC 74-19244. (Illus.). 1975. 22.00 (ISBN 0-8108-0739-4). Scarecrow.

Map of Educational Research. Robert H. Thouless. 1969. text ed. 20.00x (ISBN 0-901225-06-1, NFER). Humanities.

Map of Misreading. Harold Bloom. 218p. 1980. pap. 4.95 (ISBN 0-19-502809-0, GB 623). Oxford U Pr.

Map of the World Distribution of Arid Regions. 54p. 1979. pap. 18.75 (ISBN 92-3-101484-6, U933, UNESCO). Unipub.

Map Reading & Interpretation. P. Speak & A. H. Carter. (Illus., New Edition with Metric Examples). 1974. pap. text ed. 6.50x (ISBN 0-582-31010-5). Longman.

Map Reading Skills. Peter W. Preksto, Jr. (Basic Skills Library). (Illus.). (gr. 4 up). 1979. PLB 5.95 (ISBN 0-87191-715-7). Creative Ed.

Map Skills. Educational Challenges, Inc. Ed. by Heidi Hayes. Incl. Book C (ISBN 0-8372-3505-7). tchr's ed.; Book D (ISBN 0-8372-3506-5). tchr's ed. (ISBN 0-8372-9196-8); Book E (ISBN 0-8372-3507-3). tchr's ed (ISBN 0-8372-9197-6); Book F (ISBN 0-8372-3508-1). tchr's ed (ISBN 0-8372-9198-4). (Elementary Skills Ser). 1977. 1.35 ea. Bowmar-Noble.

Map Use: Reading, Analysis & Interpretation. rev. ed. Phillip C. Muehrcke. LC 78-70573. (Illus.). xi, 469p. 1980. pap. text ed. 16.25 (ISBN 0-9602978-1-2). JP Pubns WI.

Maphaeus Vegius & His Thirteenth Book of the "Aeneid". Anna C. Brinton. Ed. by Steele Commager. LC 77-70765. (Latin Poetry Ser.). 1978. lib. bdg. 22.00 (ISBN 0-8240-2963-1). Garland Pub.

Maple Leaf & the White Eagle: Canadian-Polish Relations, 1918-1978. Aloysius Balawyder. (East European Monographs: No. 66). 1980. 20.00x (ISBN 0-914710-59-1, Dist. by Columbia U Pr). East Eur Quarterly.

Maple Leaf Rag: An Anthology of New Orleans Poetry. Ed. by Maxine Cassin et al. (Illus.). 116p. (Orig.). 1980. pap. 4.95x (ISBN 0-938498-01-0). New Orleans Poetry.

Maple Street. Nan H. Agle. LC 78-97034. (gr. 3-7). 1970. 6.95 (ISBN 0-395-28838-X, Clarion). HM.

Maple Tree. Millicent E. Selsam. LC 68-25933. (Illus.). (gr. 2-5). 1968. PLB 7.92 (ISBN 0-688-31496-1). Morrow.

Mapmakers. John N. Wilford. LC 80-2716. (Illus.). 448p. 1981. 20.00 (ISBN 0-394-46194-0). Knopf.

Mapping from Aerial Photographs. C. D. Burnside. LC 79-11497. 304p. 1979. 45.50 (ISBN 0-470-26690-2). Halsted Pr.

Mapping of America. Seymour I. Schwartz & Ralph E. Ehrenberg. (Illus.). 360p. 1980. 60.00 (ISBN 0-686-62687-7, 1307-0). Abrams.

Maps & Air Photographs: Images of Earth. 2nd ed. G. C. Dickinson. LC 78-31287. 348p. 1979. 39.95x o.p. (ISBN 0-470-26640-6); pap. 17.95 o.p. (ISBN 0-470-26641-4). Halsted Pr.

Maps & Man: An Examination of Cartography in Relation to Culture & Civilization. N. Thrower. 1972. pap. 7.95 (ISBN 0-13-555953-7). P-H.

Maps & Windows. Jane Cooper. 1974. pap. 2.95 o.s.i. (ISBN 0-02-069300-1, Collier). Macmillan.

Maps, Distortion, & Meaning. Mark S. Monmonier. Ed. by Salvatore Natoli. LC 76-44640. (Resource Papers for College Geography Ser). 48p. 1977. pap. text ed. 4.00 (ISBN 0-89291-120-4). Assn Am Geographers.

Maps for the Local Historian- a Guide to the British Sources. J. B. Harley. 86p. 1972. pap. text ed. 4.90x (ISBN 0-7199-0834-5, Pub. by Bedford England). Renouf.

Maps of Canada: A Guide to Official Canadian Maps, Charts, Atlases & Gazetteers. N. L. Nicholson & L. M. Sebert. (Illus.). 200p. 1981. 32.50 (ISBN 0-208-01782-8, Archon). Shoe String.

Maps of Famous Cartographers Depicting North America: An Historical Atlas of the Great Lakes & Michigan, with Bibliography of the Printed Maps of Michigan to 1880. 2nd ed. L. C. Karpinski. (Illus.). 1977. text ed. 82.75x (ISBN 90-6041-109-9). Humanities.

Maps, Tracks, & the Bridges of Konigsberg: A Book About Networks. Michael Holt. LC 74-31176. (Young Math Ser.). (Illus.). 40p. (gr. k-3). 1975. 7.95 (ISBN 0-690-00746-9, TYC-J); PLB 7.89 (ISBN 0-690-00753-1). T Y Crowell.

Mar de Puerto Rico: Una Introduccion a las Pesquerias de la Isla. Jose A. Suarez-Caabro. (Illus., Sp.). 1979. 20.00 (ISBN 0-8477-2323-2). U of PR Pr.

Marathon Groups: Reality & Symbol. Elizabeth E. Mintz. LC 73-157796. (Century Psychology Ser.). 1971. 24.00x (ISBN 0-89197-293-5); pap. text ed. 6.95x (ISBN 0-89197-294-3). Irvington.

Marathon Running. Jerolyn Nentl. Ed. by Howard Schroeder. LC 79-27799. (Funseekers Ser.). (Illus.). (gr. 3-5). 1980. lib. bdg. 5.95 (ISBN 0-89686-074-4); pap. 2.95 (ISBN 0-89686-078-7). Crestwood Hse.

Marathon: The Longest Race. George Sullivan. LC 80-6776. (Illus.). (gr. 5-8). 1980. PLB 9.95 (ISBN 0-664-32671-4). Westminster.

Marathon: The World of Long Distance Athletes. Gail Campbell. LC 76-58625. (Illus.). (gr. 7). 1977. 9.95 (ISBN 0-8069-4114-6); PLB 9.29 (ISBN 0-8069-4115-4). Sterling.

Marathon: What It Takes to Go the Distance. Marc Bloom. LC 80-18859. (Illus.). 304p. 1981. 15.95 (ISBN 0-03-052476-8); pap. 8.95 (ISBN 0-686-69124-5). HR&W.

Marathons. Tree Communications. (Illus.). 1979. pap. 7.95 o.p. (ISBN 0-385-15227-2, Dolp). Doubleday.

Marauders. Peter McCurtin. (Sundance Ser.: No. 31). 1980. pap. 1.75 (ISBN 0-8439-0740-1, Leisure Bks). Nordon Pubns.

Maravillas De la Creacion. Orig. Title: Wonders of Creation. 1979. 14.95 (ISBN 0-311-09092-3, Edit Mundo). Casa Bautista.

Marbacka. Selma Lagerlof. Tr. by Velma S. Howard. LC 70-167024. (Illus.). viii, 288p. 1974. Repr. of 1926 ed. 18.00 (ISBN 0-8103-4031-3). Gale.

Marble Jungle. Clay Richards. 1961. 7.95 (ISBN 0-8392-1064-7). Astor-Honor.

Marbleface. Max Brand. 240p. 1981. pap. 1.95 (ISBN 0-446-90307-8). Warner Bks.

Marbles, Knives & Axes. Konrad F. Schreier, Jr. LC 78-15942. 70p. 1978. pap. 4.50 (ISBN 0-917714-19-9). Beinfeld Pub.

Marc-Antoine Charpentier's Pestis Mediolanensis: (the Plague of Milan) H. Wiley Hitchcock. LC 79-320. (Early Musical Masterworks-Critical Editions & Commentaries Ser.). 1979. 19.00x (ISBN 0-8078-1365-6). U of NC Pr.

Marc Chagall: An Introduction. Howard Greenfeld. LC 80-14277. 192p. 1980. Repr. of 1967 ed. 13.95 (ISBN 0-87951-115-X). Overlook Pr.

Marc Connelly. Paul T. Nolan. (U. S. Authors Ser.: No. 149). 1969. lib. bdg. 10.95 (ISBN 0-8057-0152-4). Twayne.

Marc Gold: "Did I Say That?" Articles & Commentary on the Try Another Way System. Marc Gold. LC 80-51793. (Illus.). 347p. 1980. pap. text ed. 15.95 (ISBN 0-87822-219-7, 2197). Res Press.

Marcel Ayme. Dorothy Brodin. LC 68-54455. (Columbia Essays on Modern Writers Ser.: No. 38). (Orig.). 1968. pap. 2.00 (ISBN 0-231-03128-9). Columbia U Pr.

Marcel Duchamp: Eros, C'est la Vie. Alice G. Marquis. 429p. 1980. lib. bdg. 28.50 (ISBN 0-87875-187-4). Whitston Pub.

Marcel Pagnol. C. E. Caldicott. (World Author Ser.: No. 391). 1977. lib. bdg. 12.50 (ISBN 0-8057-6233-7). Twayne.

Marcel Proust. Patrick Brady. (World Authors Ser.: France: No. 404). 1977. lib. bdg. 12.50 (ISBN 0-8057-6307-4). Twayne.

Marcel Proust. James R. Hewitt. LC 74-76127. (Modern Literature Ser.). 136p. 1975. 10.95 (ISBN 0-8044-2382-2). Ungar.

Marcel Proust & the Strategy of Reading. Walter Kasell. (Purdue Univ. Monographs in Romance Languages: No. 4). 130p. 1980. text ed. 23.00x (ISBN 90-272-1714-9). Humanities.

March Nineteen Thirty-Nine: A Study in the Continuity of British Foreign Policy. Simon K. Newman. 1976. 36.00x (ISBN 0-19-822532-6). Oxford U Pr.

March of Australian Women. Bessie S. Rischbrith. 15.00x (ISBN 0-392-08104-0, SpS). Soccer.

March of Faith: Samuel Morris. Lindley Baldwin. 1969. pap. 1.95 (ISBN 0-87123-360-6, 200360). Bethany Fell.

March of the Lemmings. James R. Newton. LC 75-42491. (Lets-Read-&-Find-Out Bk). (Illus.). 40p. (gr. k-3). 1976. PLB 7.89 (ISBN 0-690-01085-0, TYC-J). T Y Crowell.

Marchand Woman. John Ives. 1981. pap. 2.75 (ISBN 0-425-04731-8). Berkley Pub.

Marchants Aviso, 1589. John Browne. Ed. by Patrick McGrath. (Kress Library of Business & Economics: No. 13). 1957. pap. 5.00x (ISBN 0-678-09906-5, Baker Lib). Kelley.

Marchesi & Music: Passages from the Life of a Famous Singing-Teacher. Mathilde Marchesi. LC 77-27354. (Music Reprint Ser., 1978). 1978. Repr. of 1898 ed. lib. bdg. 27.50 (ISBN 0-306-77577-8). Da Capo.

Marching Drummer's Companion. 2nd ed. George Kusel. 52p. 1981. pap. 4.95 (ISBN 0-9604476-0-1). Kusel.

March's Thesaurus & Dictionary. 2nd ed. Francis March et al. LC 79-92443. 1360p. 1980. 19.95 (ISBN 0-89659-107-7); pap. 10.95 (ISBN 0-89659-161-1). Abbeville Pr.

Marco Moonlight. Clyde R. Bulla. LC 75-33203. (Illus.). (gr. 3-7). 1976. 7.95 (ISBN 0-690-01011-7, TYC-J). T Y Crowell.

Marco Polo. (gr. 1). 1974. pap. text ed. 2.80 (ISBN 0-205-03869-7, 8038694); tchrs'. guide 12.00 (ISBN 0-205-03866-2, 803866X). Allyn.

Marco Polo. (MacDonald Educational Ser.). (Illus., Arabic.). 3.50 (ISBN 0-686-53098-5). Intl Bk Ctr.

Marco Polo. Marilyn Sharp. 338p. 1981. 12.95 (ISBN 0-399-90106-X). Marek.

Marco Polo's Asia: An Introduction to His "Description of the World" Called "Il Milione". Leonardo Olschki. Tr. by John A. Scott. 1960. 27.50x (ISBN 0-520-00975-4). U of Cal Pr.

Marco Polo's Travels in Xanadu with Kublai Khan. R. P. Lister. (Illus.). 1976. 13.95 o.p. (ISBN 0-86033-008-7). Gordon-Cremonesi.

Marconi's International Register: 81st Annual Edition. 81th, rev. ed. 1980. lib. bdg. 60.00 (ISBN 0-916446-06-9). Tele Cable.
Marcos Presenta Al Salvador. Raymond B. Brown. Tr. by Olivia Y Alfredo Lerin. Orig. Title: Mark - the Saviour for Sinners. 1978. pap. 1.95 (ISBN 0-311-04346-1). Casa Bautista.
Marcus Aurelius, His Life & His World. Arthur Farquharson. Ed. & pref. by D. A. Rees. LC 75-11854. (Illus.). 154p. 1975. Repr. of 1951 ed. lib. bdg. 13.75x (ISBN 0-8371-8139-9, FAMAU). Greenwood.
Marcus Garvey. Daniel S. Davis. LC 72-3992. (Illus.). 192p. (gr. 7-12). 1972. PLB 5.88 o.p. (ISBN 0-531-02577-2). Watts.
Marcus Garvey: An Annotated Bibliography. Compiled By Lenwood G. Davis. LC 80-653. 200p. 1980. lib. bdg. 22.50 (ISBN 0-313-22131-6, DMG/). Greenwood.
Marcy Tarrant. Edith Engren. 1978. pap. 1.95 o.p. (ISBN 0-449-13974-3, GM). Fawcett.
Mare Crisium: The View from Luna Twenty-Four. Ed. by Lunar & Planetary Institute, Houston, Texas. 733p. 1979. 49.00 (ISBN 0-08-022965-4). Pergamon.
Mares, Foals & Foaling. Friedrich Andrist. Tr. by A. Dent. pap. 3.35 (ISBN 0-85131-053-2, Dist. by Sporting Book Center). J A Allen.
Margaret Ayer Barnes. Lloyd C. Taylor, Jr. (U. S. Authors Ser.: No. 231). 1974. lib. bdg. 10.95 (ISBN 0-8057-0037-4). Twayne.
Margaret Bourke-White. Genie Iverson. (People to Remember Ser.). 32p. (gr. 4-12). 1980. PLB 5.95 (ISBN 0-87191-743-2). Creative Ed.
Margaret Fuller Ossoli. Thomas W. Higginson. LC 80-24233. (American Men & Women of Letters Ser.). 324p. 1981. pap. 4.95 (ISBN 0-87754-159-0). Chelsea Hse.
Margaret Fuller's Woman in the Nineteenth Century: A Literary Study of Form & Content, of Sources & Influence. Brian C. Decker. LC 79-7475. (Contributions in Women's Studies: No. 13). 1980. lib. bdg. 17.95 (ISBN 0-313-21475-1, UMF/) (ISBN 0-86577). Greenwood.
Margaret Mead. Ann Morse & Charles Morse. LC 75-1343. (People to Remember Ser.). (Illus.). 32p. (gr. 3-6). 1975. PLB 5.95 (ISBN 0-87191-425-5). Creative Ed.
Margaret Mead Herself. Patricia D. Frevert. Ed. by Ann Redpath. (People to Remember Ser.). (Illus.). 32p. (gr. 5-9). 1981. PLB 5.95 (ISBN 0-87191-799-8). Creative Ed.
Margaret Mead: Student of the Global Village. Carol B. Church. Ed. by David L. Bender & Gary E. McCuen. (Focus on Famous Women Ser). (Illus.). (gr. 3-9). 1976. 6.95 (ISBN 0-912616-46-6); read-along cassette 9.95 (ISBN 0-89908-245-9). Greenhaven.
Margaret Mitchell's "Gone with the Wind" Letters: 1936-1949. Ed. by Richard B. Harwell. (Illus.). 1976. 12.95 o.s.i. (ISBN 0-02-548650-0). Macmillan.
Margaret Percival, 1847. Elizabeth M. Sewell. Bd. with Experience of Life; or, Aunt Sarah, 1852. (Victorian Fiction Ser). 1975. lib. bdg. 66.00 (ISBN 0-8240-1550-9). Garland Pub.
Margaret Rudkin Pepperidge Farm Cookbook. Margaret Rudkin. (Illus.). 1963. 17.95 (ISBN 0-689-00027-8). Atheneum.
Margaret Rutherford: A Blithe Spirit. Dawne L. Simmons. (Illus., Orig.). 1981. pap. 7.95 (ISBN 0-89407-032-0). Strawberry Hill.
Margary Affair & the Chefoo Agreement. Shen-Tsu Wang. LC 79-2844. (Illus.). 138p. 1981. Repr. of 1940 ed. 14.50 (ISBN 0-8305-0020-0). Hyperion Conn.
Margate & Its Theatres. Malcolm Morley. 8.95 (ISBN 0-392-08118-0, SpS). Soccer.
Margin of a Stream. P. S. Sastri. (Redbird Book). 59p. 1975. 14.00 (ISBN 0-88253-712-1); pap. 4.80 (ISBN 0-88253-844-6). Ind-US Inc.
Marginal Fields-Criteria for Development. Norwegian Petroleum Society. 197p. 1980. 60.00x (ISBN 82-7270-006-9, Pub. by Norwegian Info Norway). State Mutual Bk.
Marginal Notes for the New Testament. Ed. by R. G. Bratcher. 1980. softcover 2.30 (ISBN 0-8267-0026-8, 08558). United Bible.
Marginal Notes for the Old Testament. Ed. by R. G. Bratcher. 1980. softcover 2.50 (ISBN 0-8267-0025-X, 08557). United Bible.
Marginal Workers, Marginal Jobs: The Underutilization of American Workers. Teresa A. Sullivan. (Illus.). 1978. 17.95x o.p. (ISBN 0-292-75038-2). U of Tex Pr.
Marginalia. Edgar A. Poe. LC 80-22585. 1980. write for info. (ISBN 0-8139-0812-4). U Pr of Va.
Marginality & Identity. Noel P. Gist & Roy D. Wright. (Monographs & Studies in Sociology & Anthropology in Honour of Nels Anderson Ser: Vol. 3). (Illus.). 161p. 1973. text ed. 31.00x (ISBN 90-040-3638-5). Humanities.
Margins for Survival: Overcoming Political Limits in Steering Technology. Edward Wenk, Jr. LC 78-40932. (Illus.). 1979. 30.00 (ISBN 0-08-023373-2); pap. 13.25 (ISBN 0-08-023372-4). Pergamon.
Margit Kovacs. I. Brestyanszky. (Illus.). 1977. 25.00 (ISBN 0-912728-22-1). Newbury Bks Inc.
Margot Fonteyn: Autobiography. Margot Fonteyn. (Illus.). 1977. pap. 2.50 o.s.i. (ISBN 0-446-81380-X). Warner Bks.
Marguerite De Angeli's Book of Nursery & Mother Goose Rhymes. Marguerite De Angeli. (Illus.). (gr. 1-3). 1979. pap. 4.95 (ISBN 0-385-15291-4, Zephyr). Doubleday.
Marguerite Duras. Alfred Cismaru. (World Authors Ser.: France: No. 147). lib. bdg. 10.95 (ISBN 0-8057-2280-7). Twayne.
Marguerite Henry's All About Horses. Marguerite Henry. (gr. 4-8). 1967. deluxe ed. 4.95 (ISBN 0-394-81699-4, BYR); PLB 6.99 (ISBN 0-394-91699-9). Random.
Maria. Eugenia Price. LC 77-1707. 1977. 10.00 o.s.i. (ISBN 0-397-01058-3). Lippincott.
Maria. Richard L. Spivey. LC 78-71373. (Illus.). 1979. 37.50 (ISBN 0-87358-181-4). Northland.
Maria Callas: The Woman Behind the Legend. Arianna Stassinopoulos. 1981. 13.95 (ISBN 0-671-25583-5). S&S.
Maria Canossa. Sandra Paretti. 294p. 1981. 11.95 (ISBN 0-312-51449-2). St Martin.
Maria, Daughter of Shadow. Winnie Zerne. LC 73-89474. (Desting Ser.). 1976. pap. 4.95 (ISBN 0-8163-0224-3, 13211-8). Pacific Pr Pub Assn.
Maria Edgeworth & the Public Scene. Michael C. Hurst. LC 70-88024. 1969. 10.95x o.p. (ISBN 0-87024-135-4). U of Miami Pr.
Maria Gisborne & Edward E. Williams, Shelley's Friends: Their Journals & Letters. Maria Gisborne & Edward E. Williams. Ed. by Frederick L. Jones. (Illus.). 1951. 11.95 o.p. (ISBN 0-8061-0232-2). U of Okla Pr.
Maria Looney & the Cosmic Circus. Jerome Beatty, Jr. 1978. pap. 1.95 (ISBN 0-380-40311-0, 40311, Camelot). Avon.
Maria Luisa. Winifred Madison. LC 79-159825. 192p. (gr. 4-9). 1971. PLB 8.79 (ISBN 0-397-31280-6). Lippincott.
Maria Magdalena. 5th ed. Friedrich Hebbel. Ed. by G. Brychan Rees. 1968. pap. 4.50x o.p. (ISBN 0-631-01350-4, Pub. by Basil Blackwell). Biblio Dist.
Maria Montessori: Knight of the Child. Bruno Leone. Ed. by David L. Bender & Gary E. McCuen. (Focus on Famous Women Ser.). (Illus.). (gr. 3 up). 1978. 6.95 (ISBN 0-912616-47-4); read along cassette 9.95 (ISBN 0-89908-246-7). Greenhaven.
Maria Nephele. Odysseus Elytis. Tr. by Athan Anagnostopoulos from Greek. 64p. 1981. 10.00 (ISBN 0-395-29465-7). HM.
Maria Sabina: Her Life & Chants. Alvaro Estrada. Ed. by Jerome Rothenberg. Tr. by Henry Munn from Span. LC 80-20866. (New Wilderness Ser.). 220p. 1981. 16.95 (ISBN 0-915520-33-8); pap. 8.95 (ISBN 0-915520-32-X). Ross-Erikson.
Maria Sklodowska-Curie: Centenary Lectures. 1968. pap. 10.25 (ISBN 92-0-030168-1, IAEA). Unipub.
Maria Tallchief. Tobi Tobias. LC 77-87159. (Biography Ser). (Illus.). (gr. 2-5). 1970. PLB 7.89 (ISBN 0-690-51829-3, TYC-J). T Y Crowell.
Maria Teresa. Mary Atkinson. LC 79-90393. (Illus.). 40p. (gr. k-3). 1979. pap. 3.00 (ISBN 0-914996-21-5). Lollipop Power.
Maria: The Genuine Memoirs of a Young Lady of Rank & Fortune, 1765, 2 vols. in 1. Edward Kimber. LC 74-16057. (Novel in England, 1700-1775 Ser). 1974. lib. bdg. 50.00 (ISBN 0-8240-1171-6). Garland Pub.
Mariage De Figaro. Pierre Beaumarchais. Ed. by E. J. Arnould. (French Texts Ser.). 1976. pap. text ed. 10.00x (ISBN 0-631-00540-4, Pub. by Basil Blackwell). Biblio Dist.
Mariage En Droit Canonique Oriental. Jean Dauvillier. LC 80-2357. 1981. Repr. of 1936 ed. 35.00 (ISBN 0-404-18905-9). AMS Pr.
Mariamme. Glen Petrie. 1978. pap. 1.95 o.s.i. (ISBN 0-515-04561-6). Jove Pubns.
Marian Anderson. Tobi Tobias. LC 79-139101. (Biograohy Ser.). (Illus.). (gr. 1-5). 1972. PLB 7.89 (ISBN 0-690-51847-1, TYC-J). T Y Crowell.
Marian Anderson: An Annotated Bibliography & Discography. Compiled by Janet L. Sims. LC 80-1787. (Illus.). viii, 243p. 1981. lib. bdg. 29.95 (ISBN 0-313-22559-1, SIM/). Greenwood.
Mariana Mesa. Charles R. McGimsey, 3rd. (Peabody Museum Papers Ser.: Vol. 72). pap. 25.00 (ISBN 0-87365-198-7). Peabody Harvard.
Mariana Pineda, la Zapatera, la Casa De Romancero Gitano, Poeta En Nueva York, Odas, Llanto Por Sanchez Mejias, Bodas De Sangre, Yerma (in Spanish) Garcia Lorca. 4.50x o.s.i. (ISBN 0-686-12053-1). Colton Bk.
Marianne into Battle: Republican Imagery & Symbolism in France, 1789-1880. Maurice Agulhon. Tr. by Janet Lloyd. (Co-Publication with the Maison Des Sciences De L'homme). (Illus.). 224p. Date not set. price not set (ISBN 0-521-23577-4); pap. price not set (ISBN 0-521-28224-1). Cambridge U Pr.
Marianne Moore: A Collection of Critical Essays. Ed. by Charles Tomlinson. 1969. pap. 1.95 o.p. (ISBN 0-13-556035-7, Spec). P-H.
Marianne Moore: An Introduction to the Poetry. George W. Nitchie. LC 79-96998. 1969. 15.00x (ISBN 0-231-03119-X); pap. 5.00 (ISBN 0-231-08312-2, CP148). Columbia U Pr.
Marianne Moore: The Cage & the Animal. Donald Hall. LC 71-114171. (American Authors Ser). 1970. 8.95 (ISBN 0-672-53560-2). Pegasus.
Mariano De Larra & Spanish Political Rhetoric. Pierre L. Ullman. 1971. 35.00 (ISBN 0-299-05750-X). U of Wis Pr.
Mariano Picon Salas. Thomas D. Morin. (World Authors Ser.: No. 545). 1979. lib. bdg. 14.50 (ISBN 0-8057-6388-0). Twayne.
Marie & Bruce. Wallace Shawn. LC 80-991. 160p. 1980. pap. 4.95 (ISBN 0-394-17661-8, E-757, Ever). Grove.
Marie Curie: Discoverer of Radium. Joanne L. Henry. (gr. 4-6). 1968. 8.95 (ISBN 0-02-743680-2). Macmillan.
Marie Laveau. Francine Prose. 1977. 8.95 o.p. (ISBN 0-399-11873-X). Berkley Pub.
Marie Laveau. Francine Prose. 1977. pap. 2.25 o.p. (ISBN 0-425-03727-4). Berkley Pub.
Marie Laveau Voodoo Queen & Folk Tales Along the Mississippi. Raymond J. Martinez. 96p. pap. 3.50 (ISBN 0-911116-83-4). Pelican.
Marie Louise & Christophe. Natalie S. Carlson. LC 73-19365. (Illus.). 32p. (ps-3). 1974. 5.95 (ISBN 0-684-13736-4). Scribner.
Marie Louise's Heyday. Natalie S. Carlson. LC 75-8345. (Illus.). 32p. (ps-3). 1975. 6.95 (ISBN 0-684-14360-7). Scribner.
Marigold Garden. K. Greenway. LC 72-3992. (Peter Possum Paperbacks Ser). 1967. pap. 0.95 o.p. (ISBN 0-531-05120-X). Watts.
Marihuana - Biological Effects, Analysis, Metabolism, Cellular Responses, Reproduction & Brain: Proceedings. International Congress of Pharmacology, 7th, Reims, 1978. Satellite Symposium. Ed. by Gabriel G. Nahas & William D. Paton. (Illus.). 1979. text ed. 80.00 (ISBN 0-08-023759-2). Pergamon.
Marihuana Conviction: A History of Marihuana Prohibition in the United States. Richard J. Bonnie & Charles H. Whitebread. LC 73-89907. 395p. 1974. 17.50x (ISBN 0-8139-0417-X). U Pr of Va.
Marihuana Today: A Compilation of Medical Findings for the Layman. 3rd, rev. ed. G. K. Russell. LC 77-79477. (Illus.). 80p. 1979. pap. 3.45 (ISBN 0-08-025509-4). Pergamon.
Marijuana. 1971. Repr. pap. 0.50 o.p. (ISBN 0-685-77453-8, 181). Am Psychiatric.
Marijuana. Eve Stwertka & Albert Stwertka. (First Bks.). (Illus.). (gr. 4 up). 1979. PLB 6.45 s&l (ISBN 0-531-02944-1). Watts.
Marijuana--Friend or Foe? Bernard Lall & Geeta Lall. LC 78-23656. (Better Living Ser.). 1979. pap. 0.95 (ISBN 0-8127-0222-0). Southern Pub.
Marijuana Botany. Robert C. Clarke. (Illus.). 224p. 1981. pap. 7.95 (ISBN 0-915904-45-4). And-or Pr.
Marijuana-the Deceptive Weed. rev. ed. Gabriel G. Nahas. LC 72-76743. 1975. 19.00 (ISBN 0-911216-39-1). Raven.
Marijuana: The New Prohibition. John Kaplan. LC 75-7614. (Apollo Eds.). 400p. 1975. pap. 3.95 o.s.i. (ISBN 0-8152-0381-0, A-381, TYC-T). T Y Crowell.
Marijuana Use & Criminal Sanctions: Essays on the Theory & Practice of Law Reform. Richard J. Bonnie. 264p. 1980. 20.00 (ISBN 0-87215-244-8). Michie.
Marika. Darwin Porter. 1979. pap. 2.50 o.p. (ISBN 0-425-04262-6). Berkley Pub.
Marilka. Janina Domanska. (Illus.). (gr. k-3). 1970. 4.95g o.s.i. (ISBN 0-02-732880-5). Macmillan.
Marilyn. Norman Mailer. (Illus.). 384p. 1975. pap. 3.50 (ISBN 0-446-96747-5). Warner Bks.
Marilyn: An Untold Story. Norman Rosten. pap. 1.50 (ISBN 0-451-08880-8, W8880, Sig). NAL.
Marilyn Chambers: My Story. Marilyn Chambers. (Illus., Orig.). 1975. pap. 1.95 o.s.i. (ISBN 0-446-79827-4). Warner Bks.
Marin County Speaks Out: "Quips-Quotes-Opinions of the 'real' People" 1980. Gary Wilding. LC 79-93227. 300p. (Orig.). 1980. pap. 5.95 (ISBN 0-936092-02-5, 103). Harbinger Pr.
Marin Flora: Manual of the Flowering Plants & Ferns of Marin County, California. 2nd ed. John T. Howell. LC 71-100608. (Supplement). 1970. 16.75 (ISBN 0-520-00578-3). U of Cal Pr.
Marina. Laura Blackman. 1981. pap. 2.95 (ISBN 0-451-09721-1, E9721, Sig). NAL.
Marina. Harry Essex. LC 81-80082. 288p. (Orig.). 1981. pap. 2.95 (ISBN 0-87216-850-6). Playboy Pbks.
Marina & Ruby. Patricia S. Fusco & Marina Fusco. (Illus.). 1977. 17.50 o.p. (ISBN 0-688-03229-X). Morrow.
Marina Cvetaeva: Her Life & Art. Simon Karlinsky. 1966. 20.00x (ISBN 0-520-00632-1). U of Cal Pr.
Marina Maher's Terrific Tips. Marina Maher. (Orig.). Date not set. pap. 4.95 (ISBN 0-440-58369-1, Dell Trade Pbks). Dell.
Marina Mystery. Constance Leonard. LC 80-2781. 160p. (gr. 8 up). 1981. PLB 7.95 (ISBN 0-396-07930-X). Dodd.
Marina Tsvetaeva: A Pictorial Biography, Eighteen Ninety-Two to Nineteen Forty-One. Ed. by Ellendea C. Proffer. (Illus.). 1980. 20.00 (ISBN 0-88233-358-5); pap. 11.00 (ISBN 0-88233-359-3). Ardis Pubs.
Marinas: A Working Guide to Their Development and Design. 2nd ed. Donald W. Adie. LC 77-136. (Illus.). 1977. 52.50 (ISBN 0-8436-0151-5, Architectural Pr). CBI Pub.
Marine Algae of New England & Adjacent Coast. W. C. Farlow. (Illus.). 1969. Repr. of 1881 ed. 50.00 (ISBN 3-7682-0582-7). Lubrecht & Cramer.
Marine Aquaria. Warren E. Burgess. (Illus.). 96p. text ed. 2.95 (ISBN 0-87666-533-4, KW-088). TFH Pubns.
Marine Aquarium. Robert F. O'Connell. 1973. 4.95 o.p. (ISBN 0-8200-0110-4, SL488, ScribT). Scribner.
Marine Aquarium Fish Identifier. Wilbert Neugebauer. LC 74-82341. (Identifier Ser). (Illus.). 256p. 1975. 6.95 (ISBN 0-8069-3724-6); PLB 6.69 (ISBN 0-8069-3725-4). Sterling.
Marine Aquarium Guide. Peter Chlupaty. (Orig.). pap. 1.79 o.p. (ISBN 0-87666-100-2, M519). TFH Pubns.
Marine Aquarium Guide. de Grass Vander Nieuwenhuizen. 240p. 1974. 6.98 o.p. (ISBN 0-385-03518-7). Doubleday.
Marine Aquarium Keeping: The Science, Animals & Art. Stephen Spotte. LC 73-4425. (Illus.). 176p. 1973. 15.00 (ISBN 0-471-81759-7, Pub. by Wiley-Interscience). Wiley.
Marine Art Clipbook. Peter H. Spectre & George Putz. 160p. 1980. pap. 8.95 (ISBN 0-442-25190-4). Van Nos Reinhold.
Marine Atlas of the Pacific Coastal Waters of South America. Merritt R. Stevenson et al. LC 79-85448. (Illus.). 1970. 75.00x (ISBN 0-520-01616-5). U of Cal Pr.
Marine Benthic Dynamics. Ed. by Kenneth R. Tenore & Bruce C. Coull. LC 80-15941. (Belle Baruch Lib. in Marine Science: No. 11). 474p. 1980. text ed. 27.50 (ISBN 0-87249-401-2). U of SC Pr.
Marine Biology. John Reseck, Jr. (Illus.). 1979. text ed. 16.95 (ISBN 0-8359-4276-7); instrs'. manual avail. Reston.
Marine Cargo Operations. Charles L. Sauerbier. 1956. 39.50 (ISBN 0-471-75504-4, Pub. by Wiley-Interscience). Wiley.
Marine Carving Handbook. Jay Hanna. LC 74-33147. (Illus.). 96p. 1975. 9.95 (ISBN 0-87742-052-1). Intl Marine.
Marine Chemistry. National Academy Of Sciences. LC 71-177418. 1971. pap. 2.75 (ISBN 0-309-01928-1). Natl Acad Pr.
Marine Conversions: Car Engine Conversions for Boats. Nigel Warren. 1979. 14.95x (ISBN 0-8464-0074-X). Beekman Pubs.
Marine Corrosion. T. Howard Rogers. 1968. text ed. 34.95 (ISBN 0-600-41190-7). Butterworths.
Marine Corrosion: Causes & Prevention. Francis L. LaQue. LC 75-16307. (Corrosion Monograph Ser). 332p. 1975. 32.50 (ISBN 0-471-51745-3, Pub. by Wiley-Interscience). Wiley.
Marine Ecology: A Comprehensive Integrated Treatise on Life in Oceans & Coastal Waters, Vols. 1-4. O. Kinne. Incl. Vol. 1, 3 pts. 1970. Pt. 1. 69.95 (ISBN 0-471-48001-0); Pt. 2. 64.50 (ISBN 0-471-48002-9); Pt. 3. 69.95 (ISBN 0-471-48003-7); Vol. 2, 2 pts. 1975. Pt. 1. 68.25 (ISBN 0-471-48004-5); Pt. 2. 83.95 (ISBN 0-471-48006-1); Vol. 3, 3 pts. 1976. Pt. 1. 87.25 (ISBN 0-471-48005-3); Pt. 2. 113.50 (ISBN 0-471-01577-6); Pt. 3. 52.50 (ISBN 0-471-48007-X); Vol. 4. 1978. Pt. 1. 111.00 (ISBN 0-471-48008-8). LC 79-221779 (Pub. by Wiley-Interscience). Wiley.
Marine Ecology & Fisheries. D. H. Cushing. LC 74-82218. (Illus.). 228p. 1975. 52.50 (ISBN 0-521-20501-8); pap. 17.50x (ISBN 0-521-09911-0). Cambridge U Pr.
Marine Electrical Practice. 5th ed. Watson. 1981. text ed. price not set (ISBN 0-408-00498-3). Butterworth.
Marine Engine Room Blue Book. William B. Paterson. LC 65-25382. (Illus.). 1966. pap. 8.50x (ISBN 0-87033-044-6). Cornell Maritime.

Marine Engineering Systems: An Introduction for Merchant Navy Officers. A. J. Weddle. (Illus.). 1976. text ed. 16.50x (ISBN 0-434-92233-1). Sheridan.

Marine Engineer's Guide to Fluid Flow. Peter G. Robinson. LC 75-25933. (Illus.). 1975. 5.00x (ISBN 0-87033-215-5). Cornell Maritime.

Marine Environment & Oil Facilities. Thomas Telford Ltd. Editorial Staff. 168p. 1980. 69.00x (ISBN 0-7277-0075-8, Pub. by Telford England). State Mutual Bk.

Marine Environmental Studies in Boca de Quadra & Smeaton Bay: Physical & Chemical, Nineteen Seventy-Nine. D. C. Burrell et al. (Science Technical Report Ser.: No. R80-1). (Illus.). 144p. pap. 10.50 (ISBN 0-914500-10-4). U of AK Inst Marine.

Marine Fire Prevention, Fire Fighting & Fire Safety. Joseph Connor. (Illus.). 404p. 1979. pap. text ed. 9.95 (ISBN 0-87618-994-X). R J Brady.

Marine Fishes of the Pacific Coast from Alaska to the Equator. Lionel A. Walford. LC 74-80976. 205p. 1975. Repr. of 1937 ed. 15.00x (ISBN 0-87474-153-X). Smithsonian.

Marine Geotechnology: Marine Slope Stability Conference, Vol. 2. Ed. by Adrian Richards. 1978. 45.00x (ISBN 0-8448-1352-4). Crane-Russak Co.

Marine Insurance & General Average in the United States. 2nd ed. Leslie J. Buglass. 1981. 22.50x (ISBN 0-87033-274-0). Cornell Maritime.

Marine Insurance Claims: American Law & Practice. 2nd ed. Leslie J. Buglass. LC 63-20544. 1972. 7.00x (ISBN 0-87033-045-4). Cornell Maritime.

Marine Insurance Digest. 2nd ed. Hugh A. Mullins & Leslie J. Buglass. LC 59-15426. 1959. 7.00x (ISBN 0-87033-046-2). Cornell Maritime.

Marine Invertebrates: Comparative Physiology. Carl S. Hammen. LC 80-51505. (Illus.). 180p. 1980. text ed. 12.00x (ISBN 0-87451-188-7). U Pr of New Eng.

Marine Life: An Illustrated Encyclopedia of Invertebrates in the Sea. J. David George & Jennifer George. LC 79-10976. 1979. 45.95 (ISBN 0-471-05675-8, Pub. by Wiley-Interscience). Wiley.

Marine Mammals. Richard J. Harrison & Judith E. King. (Repr. of 1965 ed.). 1968. pap. text ed. 10.50x (ISBN 0-09-074342-3, Hutchinson U Lib). Humanities.

Marine Mammals. Alura M. Sale. LC 78-16859. (Illus.). 272p. 1979. 26.50 (ISBN 0-914718-35-5); pap. text ed. 16.95 (ISBN 0-914718-48-7). Pacific Search.

Marine Mammals of California. Robert T. Orr. LC 78-165233. (California Natural History Guides Ser.: No. 29). 88p. 1972. pap. 5.95 (ISBN 0-520-02077-4). U of Cal Pr.

Marine Mammals of the World, 2 vols. Stephen Leatherwood & Bruce R. Mate. 1980. 90.00 set (ISBN 0-525-10474-7). Dutton.

Marine Mussels. Ed. by B. L. Bayne. LC 75-25426. (International Biological Programme Ser.: No. 10). (Illus.). 400p. 1976. 99.00 (ISBN 0-521-21058-5). Cambridge U Pr.

Marine Mysteries & Dramatic Disasters of New England. Edward R. Snow. LC 76-28985. 1976. 8.95 (ISBN 0-396-07378-6). Dodd.

Marine Natural Products: Chemical & Biological Perspectives, Vol. 4. Ed. by Paul J. Scheuer. 1981. price not set (ISBN 0-12-624004-3). Acad Pr.

Marine Navigation Instruments. Jean Randier. (Illus.). 219p. 1980. text ed. 47.50x (ISBN 0-7195-3733-9). Humanities.

Marine Outfall Systems: Planning, Design, & Construction. Robert A. Grace. LC 77-20980. (P-H Environmental Engineering Ser.). 1978. ref. 38.50 (ISBN 0-13-556951-6). P-H.

Marine Plankton: Practical Guide. G. E. Newell & R. C. Newell. 1966. pap. text ed. 10.00x (ISBN 0-09-110541-2, Hutchinson U Lib). Humanities.

Marine Policy for America: The United States at Sea. Gerard J. Mangone. LC 77-243. 1977. 26.95 (ISBN 0-669-01432-X). Lexington Bks.

Marine Pollutant Transfer. H. L. Windom & R. A. Duce. (Illus.). 1976. 25.95 (ISBN 0-669-00855-9). Lexington Bks.

Marine Pollution by Oil. Institute of Petroleum Oil Pollution Analysis Committee, London. (Illus.). 1974. 40.90x (ISBN 0-85334-452-3). Intl Ideas.

Marine Production Mechanisms. Ed. by M. J. Dunbar. LC 77-88675. (International Biological Programme Ser: No. 20). (Illus.). 1979. 72.00 (ISBN 0-521-21937-X). Cambridge U Pr.

Marine Recreational Fisheries, Vol. 3. Richard H. Stroud. Ed. by Henry Clepper. LC 76-22389. 1978. 15.00 (ISBN 0-686-65030-1). Sport Fishing.

Marine Recreational Fisheries, Vol. 4. Richard H. Stroud. Ed. by Henry Clepper. LC 76-22389. 1979. 15.00 (ISBN 0-686-65031-X). Sport Fishing.

Marine Recreational Fisheries, Vol. 5. Ed. by Henry Clepper. LC 76-22389. 1980. 15.00. Sport Fishing.

Marine Refrigeration & Fish Preservation. John T. Mead. LC 73-78044. (Illus.). 256p. 1973. 21.00 o.p. (ISBN 0-912524-08-1). Busn News.

Marine Refrigeration & Fish Preservation. rev. ed. John T. Mead. LC 80-25359. (Illus.). 1980. 25.00 (ISBN 0-912524-19-7). Busn News.

Marine Shells of the Western Coast of Florida. rev. ed. Louise M. Perry & Jeanne S. Schwengel. 1955. 10.00 (ISBN 0-87710-370-4); pap. 8.00 (ISBN 0-87710-369-0). Paleo Res.

Marine Sources of Energy. Jacques A. Constans. (Pergamon Policy Studies). (Illus.). 1980. 28.00 (ISBN 0-08-023897-1). Pergamon.

Marine Steam Boilers. 4th ed. J. H. Milton & R. M. Leach. (Illus.). 700p. 1980. text ed. 33.75 (ISBN 0-408-00416-9). Butterworths.

Marine Steam Engines & Turbines. 4th ed. S. C. McBirnie & W. J. Fox. (Illus.). 672p. 1980. text ed. 39.95 (ISBN 0-408-00387-1). Butterworths.

Marine Transportation of LNG (Liquefied Natural Gas) & Related Products. Richard G. Wooler. LC 75-23457. (Illus.). 348p. 1975. 18.00x (ISBN 0-87033-193-0). Cornell Maritime.

Mariner's Catalog. National Fisherman International Marine Publishing Company. (Funk & W Bk.). 192p. 1974. pap. 4.95 o.s.i. (ISBN 0-308-10134-0, F110, TYC-T). T Y Crowell.

Mariner's Catalog, Vol. 7. Ed. by Geo Putz & Peter Spectre. LC 73-88647. (Illus.). 1979. pap. 8.95 (ISBN 0-87742-115-3). Intl Marine.

Mariner's Pocket Companion, Nineteen Eighty. Wallace E. Tobin. LC 75-21689. 1979. pap. 5.95 o.p. (ISBN 0-87021-380-6). Naval Inst Pr.

Mariners, Renegades & Castaways. 2nd ed. C. L. James. xvi, 154p. 1978. pap. 3.00 (ISBN 0-935590-10-2). Bewick Edns.

Marinetti: Selected Writings. Filippo Marinetti. Tr. by R. W. Flint. 1973. 12.95 (ISBN 0-374-20290-7); pap. 4.95 (ISBN 0-686-66758-1). FS&G.

Mario Vargas Llosa: A Collection of Critical Essays. Ed. by Charles Rossman & Alan W. Friedman. 1978. 10.95 (ISBN 0-292-75039-0). U of Tex Pr.

Marion. Cliff Green. (Australian Theatre Workshop Ser.). 1974. pap. text ed. 6.95x (ISBN 0-686-65322-X, 00526). Heinemann Ed.

Marion Bentley. Helena Benjamin. LC 79-66926. 93p. 1980. 6.95 (ISBN 0-533-04428-6). Vantage.

Marion Brown's Southern Cook Book. rev. ed. Marion Brown. 489p. 1968. 12.95 (ISBN 0-8078-1065-7); pap. 8.50 (ISBN 0-8078-4078-5). U of NC Pr.

Marion Harland's Autobiography. Mary V. Terhune. Ed. by Annette K. Baxter. LC 79-8816. (Signal Lives Ser.). 1980. Repr. of 1910 ed. lib. bdg. 45.00x (ISBN 0-405-12860-6). Arno.

Marionettes. Susan Hestenes. 1975. 3.50x (ISBN 0-686-17212-4). Sandollar Pr.

Marionettes: How to Make & Work Them. Helen Fling. (Illus.). 192p. 1973. pap. 3.50 (ISBN 0-486-22909-2). Dover.

Marionettes: How to Make & Work Them. Helen Fling. (Illus.). 7.25 (ISBN 0-8446-4736-5). Peter Smith.

Marionettes, Onstage! Leonard Suib & Muriel Broadman. LC 75-6363. (Illus.). 256p. 1975. 16.95 o.s.i. (ISBN 0-06-014166-2, HarpT). Har-Row.

Mariposa Gold. Albert Butler. (YA) 1977. 4.95 o.p. (ISBN 0-685-71790-9, Avalon). Bouregy.

Marisol Poems. Millie Mae Wicklund. 1981. pap. 1.50. Ghost Dance.

Marital Choices: Forecasting, Assesing & Improving a Relationship. William J. Lederer. 1981. 12.95 (ISBN 0-393-01412-6). Norton.

Marital Counseling: A Biblical Behavioral Cognitive Approach. H. Norman Wright. 370p. 1981. 16.95 (ISBN 0-938786-00-8). Chr Marriage.

Marital Deduction & the Use of Formula Provisions. 2nd ed. Richard B. Covey. 1978. with 1980 suppl. 17.50 (ISBN 0-672-83719-6, Bobbs-Merrill Law); 1980 suppl. 7.50 (ISBN 0-672-83718-8). Michie.

Marital Expectations: What to Do When They Go Unmet. Andrew S. Miller. 125p. (Orig.). 1980. pap. 3.50 (ISBN 0-937442-00-3). Bibl Based Develop.

Marital Game: Personal Growth & Fulfillment. 2nd ed. Cathy S. Greenblat et al. 1977. pap. text ed. 6.95x (ISBN 0-685-86656-4). Random.

Marital Intimacy. Mary G. Durkin & Joan M. Anzia. 92p. 1980. pap. 6.95 (ISBN 0-8362-3601-7). Andrews & McMeel.

Marital Love & Hate. I. Charney. 1972. 5.95 o.s.i. (ISBN 0-02-523990-2). Macmillan.

Marital Property. Ian F. Baxter. LC 72-97627. (American Family Law Library). 640p. 1973. 47.50 (ISBN 0-686-05456-3). Lawyers Co-Op.

Marital Therapy: Moral, Sociological, & Psychological Factors. Ed. by Hirsch L. Silverman. (Illus.). 576p. 1972. 32.75 (ISBN 0-398-02415-4); pap. 19.75 (ISBN 0-398-03065-0). C C Thomas.

Maritime Adaptations: Essays on Contemporary Fishing Communities. Ed. by Alexander Spoehr. LC 79-22486. 1980. 12.95x (ISBN 0-8229-1139-6). U of Pittsburgh Pr.

Maritime Antiques. Alan Major. 1981. 12.95 (ISBN 0-498-02496-2). A S Barnes.

Maritime Archaeology. K. Muckelroy. LC 78-5693. (New Studies in Archaeology). 1979. 49.50 (ISBN 0-521-22079-3); pap. 14.50x (ISBN 0-521-29348-0). Cambridge U Pr.

Maritime Arts by William Gilkerson. William Gilkerson. (Illus.). 100p. (Orig.). 1981. pap. write for info. (ISBN 0-87577-061-4). Peabody Mus Salem.

Maritime Careers. John F. Waters. (Career Concise Guides Ser.). (Illus.). 1977. 6.45 (ISBN 0-531-01283-2). Watts.

Maritime Carriage of Nuclear Materials. (Illus.). 418p. 1973. pap. 31.25 (ISBN 92-0-070073-X, ISP 312, IAEA). Unipub.

Maritime Dictionary: Covering Shipbuilding, Shipping, Marine Engineering & Related Fields, 2 vols. 3rd enl. ed. Robert Dluhy. Incl. Vol. 1. (Ger. -Eng.). 1967. 60.00x (ISBN 0-8002-1299-1); Vol. 2. (Eng. -Ger.). 1968. LC 74-357050. 60.00x (ISBN 0-8002-1300-9). Intl Pubns Serv.

Maritime Foundations of Andean Civilization. M. E. Moseley. LC 74-84816. 138p. 1975. text ed. 5.50 o.p. (ISBN 0-8465-4800-3, 54800). Benjamin-Cummings.

Maritime Metrication: A Recommended Metric Conversion Plan for the U.S. Maritime Industry. Maritime Transportation Research Board, National Research Council. LC 76-1348. 121p. 1976. pap. 5.25 (ISBN 0-309-02447-1). Natl Acad Pr.

Maritime New York in Nineteenth Century Photographs. Harry Johnson & Frederick Lightfoot. (Illus.). 160p. (Orig.). 1980. pap. 7.95 (ISBN 0-486-23963-2). Dover.

Maritime Poems of World War II. Elmer B. Fulton. 1981. 5.75 (ISBN 0-8062-1665-4). Carlton.

Maritime Transport Nineteen Seventy-Nine. OECD. (Illus.). 151p. (Orig.). 1980. pap. text ed. 10.50x (ISBN 92-64-12122-6). OECD.

Maritime Transport: The Evolution of International Marine Policy & Shipping Law. Edgar Gold. LC 80-8641. (Illus.). 1981. write for info. (ISBN 0-669-04338-9). Lexington Bks.

Marius on the Elements. Richard C. Dales. 200p. 1977. 13.50x (ISBN 0-520-02856-2). U of Cal Pr.

Marius the Epicurean. Walter Pater. Ed. by Robert L. Wolff. (Victorian Fiction Ser.). 1975. Repr. of 1885 ed. lib. bdg. 66.00 (ISBN 0-8240-1558-4). Garland Pub.

Marivaux. Oscar A. Haac. (World Authors Ser.: France: No. 294). 1974. lib. bdg. 10.95 (ISBN 0-8057-2593-8). Twayne.

Marjabelle Stewart's Book of Modern Table Manners. Marjabelle Y. Stewart. (Illus.). 192p. 1981. 14.95 (ISBN 0-312-51525-1); pap. 7.95 (ISBN 0-312-51526-X). St Martin.

Marjorie Kinnan Rawlings. Samuel I. Bellman. (U. S. Authors Ser.: No. 241). 1974. lib. bdg. 10.95 (ISBN 0-8057-0610-0). Twayne.

Mark. Joseph A. Alexander. (Thornapple Commentaries Ser.). 1980. pap. 8.95 (ISBN 0-8010-0150-1). Baker Bk.

Mark. Keith L. Brooks. (Teach Yourself the Bible Ser). 64p. 1961. pap. 1.75 (ISBN 0-8024-5183-7). Moody.

Mark. Wilfrid Harrington. Ed. by Donald Senior. (New Testament Message Ser.: Vol. 4). 270p. 1979. 10.95 (ISBN 0-89453-127-1); pap. 6.95 (ISBN 0-89453-192-1). M Glazier.

Mark. Irving L. Jensen. (Bible Self-Study Ser). (Illus.). 1972. pap. 2.25 (ISBN 0-8024-1041-3). Moody.

Mark Coffin, U. S. S. Allen Drury. 1980. pap. 2.75 (ISBN 0-441-51965-2). Ace Bks.

Mark Ethridge: The Life & Times of a Great Newspaperman. Willie S. Ethridge. (Illus.). 484p. 1981. 20.00 (ISBN 0-8149-0852-7). Vanguard.

Mark: Good News for Hard Times: A Popular Commentary on the the Earliest Gospel. George T. Montague. 200p. (Orig.). 1981. pap. 5.95 (ISBN 0-89283-096-4). Servant.

Mark Harris. Norman Lavers. (United States Authors Ser.: No. 304). 1978. lib. bdg. 12.50 (ISBN 0-8057-7209-X). Twayne.

Mark: Meditations. August Van Ryn. 1957. pap. 2.25 (ISBN 0-87213-892-5). Loizeaux.

Mark, Neighborhood Bible Study. Marilyn Kunz & Catherine Schell. pap. 1.75 (ISBN 0-8423-4101-3). Tyndale.

Mark of a Man. Elisabeth Elliot. 1981. 7.95 (ISBN 0-8007-1178-5). Revell.

Mark of Cain. Ruth Mellinkoff. (Quantum Bk.). 128p. 1981. 12.50x (ISBN 0-520-03969-6). U of Cal Pr.

Mark of Cain. Dan O'Neill. 1979. pap. 2.95 (ISBN 0-89728-016-4, 546726). Omega Pubns OR.

Mark of the Sword: A Narrative History of the Cutler's Company, 1189 - 1975. Tom Girtin. (Illus.). 1975. text ed. 15.75x (ISBN 0-09-124790-X). Humanities.

Mark One-New Directions in Creativity. Joseph S. Renzulli. 23.84 (ISBN 0-06-539000-8, SchDept). Har-Row.

Mark Rothko, Nineteen Three-Nineteen Seventy: A Retrospective. new ed. Diane Waldman. LC 78-58411. (Illus.). 30.00 (ISBN 0-89207-014-5); softcover 14.85 (ISBN 0-89207-014-5). S R Guggenheim.

Mark Rutherford (William H. White) Stephen Merton. (English Authors Ser.: No. 53). lib. bdg. 10.95 (ISBN 0-8057-1468-5). Twayne.

Mark Skousen's Guide to Financial Privacy. Mark Skousen. 1979. 14.95 o.p. (ISBN 0-932496-02-4). Alexandria Hse.

Mark Spitz. James Olsen. LC 76-5815. (Creative Superstars Ser.). 1974. o. p. 5.95 (ISBN 0-87191-263-5); pap. 2.95 (ISBN 0-686-66998-3). Creative Ed.

Mark Spitz Complete Book of Swimming. Mark Spitz & Alan LeMond. LC 75-42490. (Illus.). 192p. 1976. 10.00 o.s.i. (ISBN 0-690-00690-X, TYC-T). T Y Crowell.

Mark Strong's Napa Valley-1886-1924. new ed. David Kernberger & Kathleen Kernberger. (Illus.). 1978. spiral bd. leatherette 8.40 (ISBN 0-933206-00-3). Historic Photos.

Mark Three-New Directions in Creativity. Joseph S. Renzulli. 23.84 (ISBN 0-06-539002-4, SchDept). Har-Row.

Mark Traynor's Beauty Book. Mark Traynor & Diane Seide. LC 79-7881. (Illus.). 256p. 1980. 11.95 (ISBN 0-385-14775-9). Doubleday.

Mark Traynor's Guide to Professional Make-up Techniques. Mark Traynor. 5.71 (ISBN 0-685-92164-6, 1579-00). Keystone Pubns.

Mark Twain. Ginny Benson. LC 74-2105. (People to Remember Ser.). 40p. 1974. 5.95 (ISBN 0-87191-325-9). Creative Ed.

Mark Twain, 3 vols. Albert B. Paine. LC 80-18842. (American Men & Women of Letters Ser.). 1730p. 1980. Set. pap. 19.95 (ISBN 0-87754-170-1). Chelsea Hse.

Mark Twain. Monroe Stearns. LC 65-13679. (Biography Ser). (gr. 7 up). 1965. PLB 5.90 o.p. (ISBN 0-531-00927-0). Watts.

Mark Twain: A Portrait. Edgar L. Masters. LC 66-15216. 1938. 10.50x (ISBN 0-8196-0171-3). Biblo.

Mark Twain, an American Voice. Patricia D. Frevert. Ed. by Ann Redpath. (People to Remember Ser.). (Illus.). 32p. (gr. 5-9). 1981. PLB 5.95 (ISBN 0-87191-802-1). Creative Ed.

Mark Twain & Bret Harte. Margaret Duckett. (Illus.). 1964. 17.50 o.p. (ISBN 0-8061-0634-4). U of Okla Pr.

Mark Twain & Huck Finn: 1855-1873. Walter Blair. Ed. by Michael B. Frank & Kenneth M Sanderson. (California Library Reprint). 1974. 24.50x (ISBN 0-520-02521-0). U of Cal Pr.

Mark Twain & the Bible. Allison Ensor. LC 76-80092. 144p. 1969. 7.50x (ISBN 0-8131-1181-1). U Pr of Ky.

Mark Twain & the South. Arthur G. Pettit. LC 73-86405. 240p. 1974. 13.00x (ISBN 0-8131-1310-5). U Pr of Ky.

Mark Twain: God's Fool. Hamlin Hill. 320p. 1975. pap. 3.95 o.p. (ISBN 0-06-090391-0, CN391, CN). Har-Row.

Mark Twain in England. Dennis Welland. 1978. text ed. 21.00x (ISBN 0-391-00553-7). Humanities.

Mark Twain in Hawaii. Mark Twain, pseud. Ed. by William R. Jones. (Illus.). 96p. 1981. pap. 4.95 (ISBN 0-89646-070-3). Outbooks.

Mark Twain in Love. Albert G. Miller. LC 73-5243. (gr. 7-9). 1973. 5.95 o.p. (ISBN 0-15-230295-6, HJ). HarBraceJ.

Mark Twain: The Critical Heritage. Ed. by Fredrick Anderson. (Critical Heritage Ser.). 1971. 30.00 (ISBN 0-7100-7084-5). Routledge & Kegan.

Mark Twain: The Man & His Work. 3rd ed. Edward C. Wagenknecht. 1967. 14.95 (ISBN 0-8061-0737-5). U of Okla Pr.

Mark Twain's Correspondence with Henry Huttleston Rogers, 1893-1909. Mark Twain. Ed. by Lewis Leary. LC 68-23900. (Mark Twain Papers). 1969. 32.50x (ISBN 0-520-01467-7). U of Cal Pr.

Mark Twain's Hannibal, Huck & Tom. Mark Twain. Ed. by Walter Blair. LC 69-10575. (Mark Twain Papers). 1969. 24.50x (ISBN 0-520-01501-0). U of Cal Pr.

Mark Twain's Huckleberry Finn: Race, Class & Society. Michael Egan. (Text & Context Ser.). 1977. text ed. 9.25x (ISBN 0-391-00930-3); pap. text ed. 4.75x (ISBN 0-85621-061-7). Humanities.

Mark Twain's Letters to His Publishers, 1867-1894. Mark Twain. Ed. by Hamlin Hill. (Mark Twain Papers). 1967. 24.50x (ISBN 0-520-00560-0). U of Cal Pr.
Mark Twain's Letters to Mary. Samuel L. Clemens. Ed. by Lewis Leary. 1961. pap. 5.00x (ISBN 0-231-08545-1). Columbia U Pr.
Mark Twain's Mysterious Stranger Manuscripts. Mark Twain. Ed. by William M. Gibson. LC 69-10576. (Mark Twain Papers). 1969. 24.50 (ISBN 0-520-01473-1). U of Cal Pr.
Mark Twain's Notebooks & Journals: Vol. 3, 1883-1891. Mark Twain. Ed. by Frederick Anderson et al. (Mark Twain Papers Ser.). 1980. 42.50x (ISBN 0-520-03383-3). U of Cal Pr.
Mark Twain's Notebooks & Journals, 1855-1873, Vol. 1. Mark Twain. Ed. by Frederick Anderson et al. 700p. 1976. 30.00x (ISBN 0-520-02326-9). U of Cal Pr.
Mark Twain's Notebooks & Journals, 1877-1883, Vol. 2. Mark Twain. Ed. by Frederick Anderson et al. 700p. 1976. 30.00x (ISBN 0-520-02542-3). U of Cal Pr.
Mark Twain's Vocabulary. Frances G. Emberson. 53p. 1980. Repr. of 1935 ed. lib. bdg. 12.50 (ISBN 0-89987-206-9). Darby Bks.
Mark Two-New Directions in Creativity. Joseph S. Renzulli. 23.84 (ISBN 0-06-539001-6, SchDept). Har-Row.
Mark Will Ward - a Black Family in the City. Bob Fitch & Lynne Fitch. LC 74-190185. (gr. 5-9). 1970. PLB 6.95 (ISBN 0-87191-051-9). Creative Ed.
Mark Wilton: The Merchant's Clerk, Repr. Of 1848. Charles B. Tayler. Bd. with Eric; or, Little by Little, 1858. Frederick W. Farrar. (Victorian Fiction Ser.). 1975. lib. bdg. 66.00 (ISBN 0-8240-1566-5). Garland Pub.
Markan Public Debate: Literary Technique, Concentric Structure & Theology in Mark 2: 1-3: 6. Joanna Dewey. LC 79-17443. (Society of Biblical Literature Ser.: No. 48). 12.00x (ISBN 0-89130-337-5); pap. 7.50x (ISBN 0-89130-338-3). Scholars Pr CA.
Market & the State: Essays in Honour of Adam Smith. Ed. by Thomas Wilson & Andrew S. Skinner. 1977. 37.50x (ISBN 0-19-828406-3). Oxford U Pr.
Market Assistant. Thomas F. De Voe. LC 72-174033. (Illus.). 455p. 1975. Repr. of 1867 ed. 32.00 (ISBN 0-8103-4117-4). Gale.
Market Economy. J. D. Farquhar & K. Heidensohn. 160p. 18.00x (ISBN 0-86003-004-0, Pub. by Allan Pubs England); pap. 9.00x (ISBN 0-86003-103-9). State Mutual Bk.
Market for Government Data Bases Sold Through Commercial Firms. 1980. 950.00 (ISBN 0-686-28893-9, A829). Frost & Sullivan.
Market for Human Blood. Douglas E. Hough. LC 77-3856. 1978. 17.95 (ISBN 0-669-01729-9). Lexington Bks.
Market for Owned Houses in England & Wales Since Nineteen Forty-Five. A. J. Cornford. 1979. text ed. 28.25x (ISBN 0-566-00195-0, Pub. by Gower Pub Co England). Renouf.
Market in a Socialist Economy. Wlodzimierz Brus. 1972. 19.00x (ISBN 0-7100-7276-7). Routledge & Kegan.
Market Power of Multinationals: A Quantitative Analysis of U. S. Corporations in Brazil & Mexico. John M. Connor. LC 77-14302. (Praeger Special Studies). 1977. 28.95 (ISBN 0-03-023036-5). Praeger.
Market Research Handbook. 813p. 1980. pap. 46.50 (ISBN 0-686-68837-6, SSC146, SSC). Unipub.
Market Sketchbook. Victor Steinbrueck. LC 68-8513. (Illus.). 192p. 1968. limited ed. 100.00 (ISBN 0-295-95665-8); pap. 7.95 (ISBN 0-295-95631-3). U of Wash Pr.
Market Structure, Bargaining Power, & Resource Price Formation. Walter C. Labys. LC 78-19541. 256p. 1980. 23.95 (ISBN 0-669-02511-9). Lexington Bks.
Market System: An Introduction to Microeconomics. 4th ed. Robert H. Havemen. LC 80-21972. (Introduction to Economics Ser.). 304p. 1981. text ed. 11.95 (ISBN 0-471-08530-8). Wiley.
Marketing. 9th ed. Theodore N. Beckman et al. 642p. 1973. 19.95 o.p. (ISBN 0-8260-0831-3); instructors' manual avail. o.p. (ISBN 0-471-07435-7). Wiley.
Marketing. Ronald W. Hasty & R. Ted Will. LC 74-23166. 400p. 1975. text ed. 20.50 scp (ISBN 0-06-389407-6, HarpC); scp study guide 6.50 (ISBN 0-06-389408-4). Har-Row.
Marketing. 3rd ed. Myron S. Heidingsfield & Albert B. Blankenship. 1974. pap. 3.95 (ISBN 0-06-460157-9, CO 157, COS). Har-Row.
Marketing. David L. Kurtz & Louis E. Boone. LC 80-65788. 736p. 1981. text ed. 18.95 (ISBN 0-03-057431-5). Dryden Pr.
Marketing. 2nd ed. M. Mandell & L. Rosenberg. 1981. 21.00 (ISBN 0-13-556225-2); pap. 7.95 study guide (ISBN 0-13-556233-3). P-H.
Marketing. 2nd ed. Maurice Mandell & Larry J. Rosenberg. (Illus.). 608p. 1981. text ed. 21.00 (ISBN 0-13-556225-2). P-H.
Marketing. Rom J. Markin. LC 78-11242. (Wiley Series in Marketing). 1979. text ed. 21.95 (ISBN 0-471-01999-2); tchrs. manual avail. (ISBN 0-471-02001-X); study guide avail. (ISBN 0-471-02000-1); tests avail. (ISBN 0-471-04828-3). Wiley.
Marketing. L. Rosenberg. (Illus.). 1977. 19.95 (ISBN 0-13-556100-0); wkbk. & study guide 4.95 (ISBN 0-13-556118-3). P-H.
Marketing. Walter B. Wentz. (Illus.). 1979. text ed. 18.50 (ISBN 0-8299-0227-9); study guide 6.95 (ISBN 0-8299-0263-5); instr.' manual avail. (ISBN 0-8299-0581-2). West Pub.
Marketing: A Contemporary Introduction. Robin Peterson. LC 76-25215. (Marketing Ser.). 1977. pap. text ed. 21.95 (ISBN 0-471-68331-0); instructor's manual avail. (ISBN 0-471-01859-7); study guide avail. (ISBN 0-471-01551-2). Wiley.
Marketing a New Product: Its Planning, Development & Control. Michael P. Peters & Robert D. Hisrich. LC 77-84070. 1978. 17.95 (ISBN 0-8053-4102-1). Benjamin-Cummings.
Marketing: An Environmental Approach. John R. Kerr & James E. Littlefield. (Illus.). 672p. 1974. ref. ed. 18.95 (ISBN 0-13-557330-0). P-H.
Marketing: An Environmental Perspective. Robert F. Gwinner et al. (Illus.). 1977. text ed. 18.50 (ISBN 0-8299-0119-1); instrs.' manual avail. (ISBN 0-8299-0484-0). West Pub.
Marketing: An Integrated Approach. Carl McDaniel, Jr. 1979. text ed. 20.50 scp (ISBN 0-06-044355-3, HarpC); inst. manual avail. (ISBN 0-06-364106-2); scp study guide 6.50 (ISBN 0-06-044356-1); test bank avail. (ISBN 0-06-364236-0); tapes o.p. 30.00 (ISBN 0-686-67347-6). Har-Row.
Marketing & Advertising Careers. Solomon Wiener et al. (Career Concise Guides Ser). (Illus.). (gr. 7 up). 1977. PLB 6.45 (ISBN 0-531-01307-3). Watts.
Marketing & Distribution. R. E. Mason & P. M. Rath. 1968. text ed. 12.96 o.p. (ISBN 0-07-040675-8, G); tchr's manual & key 4.00 o.p. (ISBN 0-07-040678-2); tests 2.24 o.p. (ISBN 0-07-040677-4). McGraw.
Marketing & Distribution. 2nd ed. Ralph E. Mason et al. LC 73-2826. (Illus.). 576p. (gr. 11-12). 1974. text ed. 12.96 (ISBN 0-07-040690-1, G); teachers manual & key 4.00 (ISBN 0-07-040692-8); project activity guide 5.96 (ISBN 0-07-040691-X). McGraw.
Marketing & Distribution Systems in Eastern Europe. A. Coskun Samli. LC 78-19754. 1978. 22.95 (ISBN 0-03-046486-2). Praeger.
Marketing & Economics. R. R. Whitelaw. 1969. 23.00 (ISBN 0-08-006583-X); pap. 11.25 (ISBN 0-08-006582-1). Pergamon.
Marketing & Financial Control. A. S. Johnson. 1967. 23.00 (ISBN 0-08-012614-6); pap. text ed. 11.25 (ISBN 0-08-012613-8). Pergamon.
Marketing & PR Media Planning. F. W. Jefkins. LC 74-618347. 1974. text ed. 28.00 (ISBN 0-08-018086-8); pap. text ed. 13.25 (ISBN 0-08-018085-X). Pergamon.
Marketing & Sales Forecasting. F. Keay. 132p. 1972. text ed. 25.00 (ISBN 0-08-016737-3); pap. text ed. 12.75 (ISBN 0-08-016738-1). Pergamon.
Marketing & Society: Cases & Commentaries. Roy D. Adler. (Illus.). 528p. 1981. text ed. 14.95 (ISBN 0-13-557074-3). P-H.
Marketing & the Brand Manager. G. Medcalf. 1967. 23.00 (ISBN 0-08-012602-2); pap. 11.25 (ISBN 0-08-012601-4). Pergamon.
Marketing & the Computer. I. S. Hugo. 1967. 25.00 (ISBN 0-08-012606-5); pap. 13.25 (ISBN 0-08-012605-7). Pergamon.
Marketing & the Sales Manager. F. H. Elsby. 1969. 25.00 (ISBN 0-08-006537-6); pap. 13.25 (ISBN 0-08-006536-8). Pergamon.
Marketing & Work Study. R. Dow. 1969. 27.00 (ISBN 0-08-006430-2); pap. 14.00 (ISBN 0-08-006429-9). Pergamon.
Marketing: Application & Cases. Douglas W. Mellott, Jr. (Illus.). 1978. 8.95 (ISBN 0-8359-4253-8). Reston.
Marketing Approach to Student Recruitment. Ed. by Virginia L. Carter & Catherine Garigan. 1979. pap. 10.50 (ISBN 0-89964-031-1). CASE.
Marketing: Basic Concepts & Decisions. William M. Pride & O. C. Ferrell. LC 76-10892. (Illus.). 1976. text ed. 17.50 o.p. (ISBN 0-395-24529-X); inst. manual 4.00 o.p. (ISBN 0-395-24530-3); study guide 6.95 o.p. (ISBN 0-395-24756-X). HM.
Marketing: Basic Concepts & Decisions. 2nd ed. William M. Pride & O. C. Perrell. LC 79-88040. 1980. text ed. 18.50 (ISBN 0-395-28059-1); study guide pap. 7.25 (ISBN 0-395-28163-6); instr's manual 3.25 (ISBN 0-395-28161-X). HM.
Marketing Boards & Ministries: A Study of Agricultural Marketing Boards As Political & Administrative Instruments. P. J. Giddings. 1974. 19.50 (ISBN 0-347-01033-4, 93484-4, Pub. by Saxon Hse England). Lexington Bks.
Marketing by Objectives for Hospitals. Robin S. MacStravic. LC 80-10903. 280p. 1980. text ed. 26.95 (ISBN 0-89443-174-9). Aspen Systems.
Marketing Cases. F. H. Elsby. LC 70-122006. 1970. 25.00 (ISBN 0-08-015784-X); pap. text ed. 13.25 (ISBN 0-08-015783-1). Pergamon.
Marketing Channels. 2nd ed. Boone & Johnson. 1977. 14.95 (ISBN 0-87814-026-3). Pennwell Pub.
Marketing Channels. Ronald Michman. LC 75-11303. (Marketing Ser.). 1974. pap. text ed. 9.95 o.p. (ISBN 0-88244-058-6). Grid Pub.
Marketing Channels. Rosenbloom. 1978. 20.95 (ISBN 0-03-017831-2). Dryden Pr.
Marketing Channels. Louis W. Stern & Adel I. El-Ansary. 1977. ref. ed. 20.95x (ISBN 0-13-557124-3). P-H.
Marketing Channels & Institutions: Selected Reading. 2nd ed. Bruce J. Walker & Joel B. Haynes. LC 76-50175. (Marketing Ser.). 1978. pap. text ed. 10.50 (ISBN 0-88244-149-3). Grid Pub.
Marketing Channels & Strategies. 2nd ed. Ronald D. Michman & Stanley D. Sibley. LC 78-4987. (Marketing Ser.). 1980. text ed. 20.95 (ISBN 0-88244-176-0). Grid Pub.
Marketing Classics. 3rd ed. Ed. by Ben M. Enis & Keith K. Cox. 1977. pap. text ed. 13.95 (ISBN 0-205-05715-2, 0857157). Allyn.
Marketing Classics: A Selection of Influential Articles. 4th ed. Ben M. Enis & Keith M. Cox. 528p. 1981. text ed. 13.95 (ISBN 0-205-05715-2); free (ISBN 0-205-07326-3). Allyn.
Marketing Communication: Modern Promotional Strategy. Frederick E. Webster, Jr. 694p. 1971. 24.95 (ISBN 0-8260-9230-6). Wiley.
Marketing Communications. 2nd ed. Edgar Crane. LC 72-4505. (Marketing Ser). 1972. 20.95 o.p. (ISBN 0-471-18401-2). Wiley.
Marketing Communications & Promotion. 2nd ed. William G. Nickels. LC 79-17114. (Grid Ser. in Marketing). 1980. text ed. 20.50 (ISBN 0-88244-197-3). Grid Pub.
Marketing Concepts & Strategies in the Next Decade. L. W. Rodger. LC 73-1797. 248p. 1973. 18.95 (ISBN 0-470-72932-5). Halsted Pr.
Marketing: Concepts & Strategy. 3rd ed. Martin L. Bell. LC 78-69572. (Illus.). 1979. text ed. 19.95 (ISBN 0-395-26503-7); inst. manual 1.50 (ISBN 0-395-26504-5). HM.
Marketing: Contemporary Dimensions. 2nd ed. Robert A. Robicheaux & William M. Pride. LC 79-89125. 1980. pap. text ed. 9.50 (ISBN 0-395-28500-3). HM.
Marketing Decision Making. rev. ed. David W. Cravens & Gerald E. Hills. 1980. 20.95x (ISBN 0-256-02348-4). Irwin.
Marketing Decision Making: Concepts & Strategy. David W. Cravens et al. 1976. text ed. 16.95x o.p. (ISBN 0-256-01799-9). Irwin.
Marketing Doctoral Dissertation Abstracts, 1979. Ed. by John K. Ryans, Jr. (Bibliography Ser.: No. 38). 142p. 1980. 15.00 (ISBN 0-87757-146-5). Am Mktg.
Marketing Doctoral Dissertation Abstracts, 1974-75. Ed. by Donald L. Shawver. LC 76-21300. (Bibliography Ser.: No. 24). 1977. pap. 12.00 o.p. (ISBN 0-87757-079-5). Am Mktg.
Marketing Doctoral Dissertation Abstracts 1976. Ed. by Donald L. Shawver. LC 77-9426. 1978. 10.00 o.p. (ISBN 0-87757-099-X). Am Mktg.
Marketing Doctoral Dissertations Abstracts, 1977. Ed. by Edward W. Cundiff. LC 78-13138. (Bibliography Ser.: No. 32). 1979. 10.00 o.p. (ISBN 0-87757-114-7). Am Mktg.
Marketing Economics Guide Nineteen Seventy-Nine to Nineteen Eighty: Current Market Dimensions for 1500 Cities, All 3100 Counties All Metro Areas. Ed. by Alfred Hong. LC 73-647896. (Illus.). 1979. 20.00 (ISBN 0-914078-33-X). Marketing Econs.
Marketing Economics Guide 1973-74: Current Market Dimensions for 1500 Cities, All 3100 Counties, All Metro Areas. new ed. Ed. by Alfred Hong. (Illus.). 264p. 1973. 20.00 (ISBN 0-914078-09-7). Marketing Econs.
Marketing Economics Guide 1974-75: Current Market Dimensions for 1500 Cities, All 3100 Counties, All Metro Areas. Ed. by Alfred Hong. (Illus.). 280p. 1974. 20.00 (ISBN 0-914078-10-0). Marketing Econs.
Marketing Economics Guide 1975-76: Current Market Dimensions for 1500 Cities, All 3100 Counties, All Metro Areas. Ed. by Alfred Hong. LC 73-647896. (Illus.). 280p. 1975. 20.00 (ISBN 0-914078-11-9). Marketing Econs.
Marketing Economics Guide 1976-77: Current Market Dimensions for 1500 Cities, All 3100 Countie S, All Metro Areas. new ed. Alfred Hong. LC 76-647896. (Illus.). 280p. 1976. 20.00 (ISBN 0-914078-21-6). Marketing Econs.
Marketing Economics Guide 1977-78: Current Market Dimensions for 1500 Cities, All 3100 Counties, All Metro Areas. Ed. by Alfred Hong. LC 73-647896. (Illus.). 1977. 20.00 (ISBN 0-914078-22-4). Marketing Econs.
Marketing Economics Guide 1978-79: Current Market Dimensions for 1500 Cities, All 3100 Counties All Metro Areas. Ed. by Alfred Hong. LC 73-647896. (Illus.). 1978. 20.00 (ISBN 0-914078-32-1). Marketing Econs.
Marketing Economics Key Plants, 1973: The Guide to Industrial Purchasing Power (National Edition) new ed. Ed. by Alfred Hong. LC 73-642154. 600p. 1973. 90.00 (ISBN 0-914078-00-3). Marketing Econ.
Marketing Economics Key Plants, 1977-78: Guide to Industrial Purchasing Power. National Edition. Ed. by Alfred Hong. LC 73-642154. 1977. 90.00 (ISBN 0-914078-23-2). Marketing Econs.
Marketing: Executive & Buyer Behavior. John A. Howard. LC 63-10525. 1963. 20.00x (ISBN 0-231-01979-3). Columbia U Pr.
Marketing for Hospitals in Hard Times. Ed. by Lee F. Block. 200p. 1981. text ed. 17.95 (ISBN 0-931028-16-7); pap. 13.95 (ISBN 0-931028-15-9). Teach'em.
Marketing for Non-Profit Organizations. Phillip Kotler. (Illus.). 448p. 1975. ref. ed. 19.95 (ISBN 0-13-556084-5). P-H.
Marketing for Non-Profit Organizations. David L. Rados. LC 80-25948. (Illus.). 512p. 1981. 24.95 (ISBN 0-86569-055-3). Auburn Hse.
Marketing Fundamentals for Responsive Management. 2nd ed. R. F. Hartley. 1976. text ed. 20.50 scp (ISBN 0-912212-05-5, HarpC). Har-Row.
Marketing Fundamentals: Texts & Cases. Harry A. Lipson & John R. Darling. LC 80-12441. 590p. 1980. Repr. of 1974 ed. lib. bdg. 22.00 (ISBN 0-89874-166-1). Krieger.
Marketing Health Care. Robin E. MacStravic. LC 76-58967. 1977. 25.75 (ISBN 0-912862-41-6). Aspen Systems.
Marketing Human Services. Bob Rubright & Dan MacDonald. 300p. 1981. text ed. price not set (ISBN 0-89443-338-5). Aspen Systems.
Marketing in a Competitive Economy. 3rd ed. L. W. Rodger. LC 73-3342. 253p. 1965. pap. 18.95 (ISBN 0-470-72928-7). Halsted Pr.
Marketing in a Regulated Environment. George S. Dominguez. LC 77-22099. (Marketing Management Ser.). 1978. 26.95 (ISBN 0-471-02402-3). Ronald Pr.
Marketing in Action: A Decision Game Student's Manual. 4th ed. Thomas E. Ness. Tr. by Ralph L. Day. 1978. pap. text ed. 8.95x (ISBN 0-256-01924-X). Irwin.
Marketing in Action: An Experiential Approach. Robin Peterson et al. (Illus.). 1978. pap. text ed. 9.95 (ISBN 0-8299-0204-X); instrs.' manual avail. (ISBN 0-8299-0565-0). West Pub.
Marketing in an Age of Change. Jon G. Udell & Gene R. Laczniak. (Marketing Ser.). 650p. 1981. text ed. 19.95 (ISBN 0-471-08169-8); tchrs.' ed. avail. (ISBN 0-471-08184-1); test file avail. (ISBN 0-471-08187-6). Wiley.
Marketing in College Admissions: A Broadening of Perspectives. 160p. (Orig.). 1980. pap. 9.95 (ISBN 0-87447-133-8, 001338). College Bd.
Marketing in Europe. Richard L. Bickers. 1971. 21.50 (ISBN 0-7161-0058-4). CBI Pub.
Marketing in Japan. Ed. by Robert J. Ballon. LC 73-79771. (Illus.). 200p. 1973. 14.50x (ISBN 0-87011-200-7). Kodansha.
Marketing in Regulated Environment. G. S. Dominguez. (Marketing Management Ser.). 341p. 1978. 26.95 (ISBN 0-471-02402-3). Wiley.
Marketing in the Construction Industry. Ed. by Institute of Marketing. 1974. pap. 12.95x (ISBN 0-434-90845-2). Intl Ideas.
Marketing in the Developing World. S. P. Padolecchia. 190p. 1979. 14.00x (ISBN 0-7069-0667-5, Pub. by Croom Helm Ltd England). Biblio Dist.
Marketing in the Eighties, Changes & Challenges: Proceedings. Annual Educators Conference Chicago, Illinois, August, 1980. Ed. by Richard P. Bagozzi et al. LC 80-15934. (No. 46). (Illus., Orig.). 1980. pap. text ed. 30.00 (ISBN 0-87757-141-4). Am Mktg.
Marketing Industrial Buildings & Sites. H. McKinley Conway. LC 78-74933. 358p. 1980. 35.00 (ISBN 0-910436-15-0). Conway Pubns.
Marketing Information: A Professional Reference Guide. Ed. by Jac L. Goldstucker. 1981. 29.95 (ISBN 0-88406-132-9). Ga St U Busn Pub.
Marketing Interaction. Keiser & Lupul. (Orig.). 1977. pap. 10.95 (ISBN 0-87814-029-8). Pennwell Pub.
Marketing Looks Outward: 1976 International Marketing Conference Proceedings. Ed. by William B. Locander. LC 76-30865. 1977. 10.00 o.p. (ISBN 0-87757-087-6). Am Mktg.

Marketing Management. 3rd ed. Kenneth R. Davis. 1972. pap. text ed. instr's. manual o.p. avail. o.p. (ISBN 0-8260-2510-2); instructors' manual avail. o.p. (ISBN 0-471-07455-1). Wiley.

Marketing Management. 4th ed. Kenneth R. Davis. (Marketing Ser.). 800p. 1981. text ed. 20.95 (ISBN 0-471-05948-X). Wiley.

Marketing Management: A Planning Approach. G. David Hughes. LC 77-83036. 1978. text ed. 17.95 (ISBN 0-201-03057-8); instr's resource manual o. p. 6.95 (ISBN 0-201-03056-X). A-W.

Marketing Management: Analysis & Planning. 3rd ed. John A. Howard. 1973. text ed. 15.50x o.p. (ISBN 0-256-00227-4). Irwin.

Marketing Management: Analysis, Planning & Control. 4th ed. Philip Kotler. 1980. text ed. 21.00 (ISBN 0-13-557975-9). P-H.

Marketing Management: Analysis, Planning & Control. 3rd ed. Phillip Kotler. 1976. 17.95 o.p. (ISBN 0-13-557959-7). P-H.

Marketing Management & Strategy: A Reader. rev. ed. Philip Kotler & Keith Cox. (Illus.). 1980. pap. text ed. 12.95 (ISBN 0-13-558122-2). P-H.

Marketing Management Casebook. rev. ed. Harper W. Boyd, Jr. et al. 1976. 17.50x o.p. (ISBN 0-256-01837-5). Irwin.

Marketing Management Casebook. 3rd ed. Robert T. Davis et al. 1980. 20.95x (ISBN 0-256-02347-6). Irwin.

Marketing Management in Multinational Firms: The Consumer Packaged Goods Industry. Ulrich E. Wiechmann. LC 75-19831. (Special Studies). 1976. text ed. 22.95 (ISBN 0-275-55850-9). Praeger.

Marketing Management Perspectives & Applications. Ed. by Robert B. Woodruff et al. 1976. pap. text ed. 9.95x o.p. (ISBN 0-256-01843-X). Irwin.

Marketing Management: Strategies & Cases. M. Wayne DeLozier & Arch G. Woodside. (Marketing & Management Ser.). 1978. text ed. 19.95 (ISBN 0-675-08417-2); instructors manual 3.95 (ISBN 0-686-67981-4). Merrill.

Marketing Mangement: Text & Cases. 2nd ed. Douglas J. Dalrymple & Leonard J. Parsons. LC 79-24833. (Wiley Ser. in Marketing). 1980. text ed. 23.95 (ISBN 0-471-03606-4); tchrs' manual avail. (ISBN 0-471-07767-4). Wiley.

Marketing Mass Transit. Ben Morris. Ed. by Helen Mischa. 150p. (Orig.). 1980. pap. 11.00x (ISBN 0-89894-034-6); pap. text ed. 11.50x (ISBN 0-686-64262-7). Advocate Pub Group.

Marketing Mistakes. 2nd ed. Robert F. Hartley. LC 80-13236. (Marketing Ser.). 220p. 1980. pap. text ed. 8.95 (ISBN 0-88244-225-2). Grid Pub.

Marketing of Professional Accounting Services. James J. Mahon. LC 78-18221. 1978. 23.95 (ISBN 0-471-04480-6, Pub. by Wiley-Interscience). Wiley.

Marketing of Shellfish. W. S. Nowak. (Illus.). 280p. 15.25 (ISBN 0-85238-010-0, FN). Unipub.

Marketing One & Two. Richard G. Fraser. 1977. No. 1, 224p. text ed. 13.27 (ISBN 0-7715-0870-0); No. 2, 208p. text ed. 13.27 (ISBN 0-7715-0872-7); tchr's. guide 6.60 (ISBN 0-7715-0871-9). Forkner.

Marketing Overseas. H. Deschampsneufs. 1967. 25.00 (ISBN 0-08-012523-9); pap. 13.25 (ISBN 0-08-012522-0). Pergamon.

Marketing Planning & Competitive Strategy. Eugene J. Kelley. (Foundations of Marketing Ser). 1972. pap. 6.95 ref. ed. (ISBN 0-13-558304-7). P-H.

Marketing Principles: A Broadened Concept of Marketing. Williams G. Nickels. LC 77-24308. 1978. text ed. 18.95 (ISBN 0-13-558205-9); study guide 5.95 (ISBN 0-13-558213-X). P-H.

Marketing: Principles & Practices. Douglas W. Mellott, Jr. (Illus.). 1978. ref. ed. 15.95 (ISBN 0-87909-455-9); instrs'. manual avail. Reston.

Marketing Problems: Cases for Analysis. Norman A. Govoni et al. LC 76-19946. (Marketing Ser.). 1977. pap. text ed. 9.50 (ISBN 0-88244-128-0). Grid Pub.

Marketing Real Estate. William M. Shenkel. (Illus.). 1980. text ed. 19.95 (ISBN 0-13-557488-9). P-H.

Marketing Research. George J. Kress. (Illus.). 1979. text ed. 18.95 (ISBN 0-8359-4271-6); instrs'. manual avail. (ISBN 0-8359-4272-4). Reston.

Marketing Research. Tony Proctor & Marilyn A. Stone. (Illus.). 192p. 1978. pap. text ed. 9.95x (ISBN 0-7121-1291-X, Pub. by Macdonald & Evans England). Intl Ideas.

Marketing Research: A Management Information Approach. Danny N. Bellenger & Barnett A. Greenberg. 1978. text ed. 18.95x (ISBN 0-256-01990-8). Irwin.

Marketing Research: A Short Course for Professionals. Bertram Schoner & Kenneth P. Uhl. (Wiley Professional Development Programs). 1976. 23.95 (ISBN 0-471-01701-9). Wiley.

Marketing Research: A Structure for Decision Making. F. E. Brown. LC 79-25541. 1980. text ed. 18.95 (ISBN 0-201-00205-1). A-W.

Marketing Research & Knowledge Development: An Assessment for Marketing Management. John G. Myers et al. (Illus.). 1980. text ed. 19.95 (ISBN 0-13-557686-5). P-H.

Marketing Research: Information for Decision Making. Eli P. Cox, 3rd. 1979. text ed. 20.50 scp (ISBN 0-912212-14-4, HarpC); free instr. manual (ISBN 0-06-361361-1). Har-Row.

Marketing Research: Private & Public Sector Decisions. David A. Aaker & George S. Day. LC 79-18532. (Wiley Series in Marketing). 1980. text ed. 21.95 (ISBN 0-471-00059-0); tchrs'. manual avail. (ISBN 0-471-07766-6). Wiley.

Marketing Research: Text & Cases. 4th ed. Harper W. Boyd, Jr. et al. 1977. text ed. 19.95x (ISBN 0-256-01838-3). Irwin.

Marketing Scientific & Technical Information. Ed. by William R. King & Gerald Zaltman. (Special Studies in Science & Technology). 1979. lib. bdg. 24.50x (ISBN 0-89158-397-1). Westview.

Marketing, Society, & Conflict. Sidney J. Levy & Gerald Zaltman. (Economic Institutions & Social Systems Ser). (Illus.). 176p. 1975. text ed. 12.95 ref. ed. (ISBN 0-13-557819-1); pap. text ed. 9.95 (ISBN 0-13-557801-9). P-H.

Marketing Strategy: A Marketing Decision Game. 2nd ed. Louis E. Boone & Edwin C. Hackleman. LC 74-27870. (Illus.). 224p. 1975. pap. text ed. 11.95 (ISBN 0-675-08713-9); manual 3.95 (ISBN 0-686-67124-4); card deck 3.95 (ISBN 0-686-67125-2). Merrill.

Marketing Strategy & Plans. David J. Luck & O. C. Ferrell. (Illus.). 1979. ref. ed. 19.95 (ISBN 0-13-558254-7). P-H.

Marketing Strategy & Structure. David Rachman. LC 73-17352. (Illus.). 448p. 1974. text ed. 17.95 (ISBN 0-13-558338-1). P-H.

Marketing Systems for Developing Countries: Proceedings, Vol. 1. International Conference on Marketing Systems for Developing Countries. Ed. by D. N. Izraeli & F. Messner. LC 76-8243. 1977. 34.95 (ISBN 0-470-15094-7). Halsted Pr.

Marketing: Text, Techniques, & Cases. 4th ed. Harry L. Hansen. 1977. text ed. 19.95 (ISBN 0-256-01642-9). Irwin.

Marketing the Arts: Praeger Series in Public & Nonprofit Sector Marketing. Michael P. Mokwa & William M. Dawson. Ed. by S. Permut. LC 79-26603. (Praeger Special Studies Ser.). 304p. 1980. 22.95 (ISBN 0-03-052141-6). Praeger.

Marketing the Library Service. D. A. Yorke. Ed. by A. Wilson. (Management Pamphlet Ser.). 1977. 3.95x (ISBN 0-85365-590-1, Pub. by Lib Assn England). Oryx Pr.

Marketing: The Management of Distribution Channels. M. Guirdham. 222p. 1972. text ed. 32.00 (ISBN 0-08-016964-3); pap. text ed. 18.00 (ISBN 0-08-016965-1). Pergamon.

Marketing: The Uses of Advertising. D. Lowndes. LC 72-97953. 1970. 19.50 (ISBN 0-08-006935-5); pap. 9.75 (ISBN 0-08-006934-7). Pergamon.

Marketing Theory: Conceptual Foundations of Research in Marketing. Shelby D. Hunt. LC 75-26013. (Marketing Ser.). 1976. text ed. 16.95 o.p. (ISBN 0-88244-097-7). Grid Pub.

Marketing Through Measurement. F. Keay & G. F. Wensley. 1970. text ed. 27.00 (ISBN 0-08-015765-3); pap. 14.00 (ISBN 0-08-015764-5). Pergamon.

Marketing Through Research. G. Wills. 1967. 28.00 (ISBN 0-08-012620-0); pap. 14.50 (ISBN 0-08-012619-7). Pergamon.

Marketing to Middle East Consumers. Middle East Market Research Bureau Ltd. 226p. 1980. 55.00x (ISBN 0-86010-198-3, Pub. by Graham & Trotman England). State Mutual Bk.

Marketing Today. 2nd ed. R. W. Chapman. 1973. 17.50x (ISBN 0-7002-0202-1). Intl Ideas.

Marketing Today's Fashion. H. DePaula & C. Mueller. 1980. 15.95 (ISBN 0-13-558155-9). P-H.

Marketing Your Skills After Retirement. 86p. 1974. looseleaf 7.95 o.p. (ISBN 0-8360-0009-9). World Trade.

Marketplace Guide to Oak Furniture Styles & Values. Peter S. Blundell. (Illus.). 1980. 17.95 (ISBN 0-89145-141-2). Collector Bks.

Markets & Hierarchies - Analysis & Antitrust Implications: A Study in the Economics of Internal Organization. Oliver E. Williamson. LC 74-27597. (Illus.). 1975. 17.95 (ISBN 0-02-935360-2). Free Pr.

Markets for Small Scale Electrical Generation Systems: E-043. 1981. 875.00 (ISBN 0-89336-284-0). BCC.

Markets for Valves & Their Materials. 1980. 850.00 (ISBN 0-89336-266-2, GB-059). BCC.

Markets of Bawdrie: The Dramatic Criticism of Stephen Gossor. F. Kinney. (Salzburg Studies in English Literature, Elizabethan & Renaissance Studies: No. 4). 291p. 1974. pap. text ed. 25.00x (ISBN 0-391-01445-5). Humanities.

Marking-Out Practice for Engineers. Ian Bradley. LC 78-670183. (Illus.). 1977. pap. 7.50x (ISBN 0-85242-595-3). Intl Pubns Serv.

Markings. 9th ed. Dag Hammarskjold. 1965. 8.95 (ISBN 0-571-06015-3, Pub. by Faber & Faber); pap. 4.95 (ISBN 0-571-06591-0). Merrimack Bk Serv.

Marko the Rich & Vasily the Unlucky. Tr. by Thomas P. Whitney from Rus. LC 73-6043. (Illus.). 32p. (gr. 1-4). 1974. 5.95g o.s.i. (ISBN 0-02-792710-5). Macmillan.

Markov Chains: Theory & Applications. Dean L. Isaacson & Richard W. Madsen. LC 75-30646. (Probability & Mathematical Statistics Ser.). 1976. 28.95 (ISBN 0-471-42862-0, Pub. by Wiley-Interscience). Wiley.

Markov Random Fields & Their Applications. Ross Kindermann & J. Laurie Snell. (Contemporary Mathematics Ser.: Vol. 1). 1980. 8.80 (ISBN 0-8218-5001-6). Am Math.

Marks on German Bohemian & Austrian Porcelain, Seventeen Ten to the Present. Robert E. Rontgen. Tr. by Robert E. Rontgen. (Illus.). 704p. 1981. 75.00 (ISBN 0-916838-38-2). Schiffer.

Mark's Sketch Book of Christ. Helen Tenney. 1975. spiral bound 4.95 (ISBN 0-85151-075-2). Banner of Truth.

Mark's Story of Jesus. Werner H. Kelber. LC 78-14668. 96p. 1979. pap. 2.95 (ISBN 0-8006-1355-4, 1-1355). Fortress.

Markus-Stoff Bei Lukas. Tim Schramm. LC 79-96099. (New Testament Studies Monographs: No. 14). (Ger). 1971. 32.50 (ISBN 0-521-07743-5). Cambridge U Pr.

Marlbouough As Military Commander. David Chandler. 1979. 30.00 (ISBN 0-7134-2075-8, Pub. by Batsford England). David & Charles.

Marlin History: Collectors Edition. William S. Frost. 5.95 (ISBN 0-685-48801-2). Nortex Pr.

Marlinspike Sailor. rev. ed. Hervey G. Smith. LC 77-143856. (Illus.). 1969. 10.00 (ISBN 0-8286-0044-9). De Graff.

Marlon Brando. David Paige. (Stars of Stage & Screen Ser.). (Illus.). (gr. 4-12). 1977. PLB 5.95 (ISBN 0-87191-552-9). Creative Ed.

Marlow Chronicles. Lawrence Sanders. 1979. pap. text ed. 2.50 (ISBN 0-425-04390-8). Berkley Pub.

Marlowe: A Critical Study. J. B. Steane. 1964. 54.00 (ISBN 0-521-06545-3); pap. 13.95x (ISBN 0-521-09624-3). Cambridge U Pr.

Marlowe: Five Plays. Christopher Marlowe. Ed. by Havelock Ellis. Incl. Pts. 1-2. Tamburlaine the Great; Doctor Faustus; The Jew of Malta; Edward the Second. 344p. (Orig.). 1956. pap. 5.95 (ISBN 0-8090-0701-0, Mermaid). Hill & Wang.

Marlowe, Tamburlaine, & Magic. James R. Howe. LC 75-36978. x, 220p. 1976. 12.95x (ISBN 0-8214-0200-5). Ohio U Pr.

Marlowe: The Critical Heritage, Fifteen Eighty-Eight to Eighteen Ninety-Six. Ed. by Millar MacLure. 1979. 24.00x (ISBN 0-7100-0245-9). Routledge & Kegan.

Marlows & the Traitor. Antonia Forest. (Illus.). (gr. 5 up). 1953. 6.50 (ISBN 0-571-06769-7, Pub. by Faber & Faber); pap. 2.95 (ISBN 0-571-05911-2). Merrimack Bk Serv.

Marlwych Mystery; or, Parson Thring's Secret. Arthur W. Marchmont. 1976. lib. bdg. 15.80x (ISBN 0-89968-066-6). Lightyear.

Marmalade Man. Charlotte V. Allen. 1981. 13.95 (ISBN 0-525-15294-6). Dutton.

Maroc. new ed. Ed. by Daniel Moreau. (Collection monde et voyages). (Illus.). 159p. (Fr.). 1973. 21.00x (ISBN 2-03-053111-1). Larousse.

Maroni De Chypre. Jane Johnson. (Studies in Mediterranean Archaeology Ser.: LIX). 1980. text ed. 42.00x (ISBN 91-85058-94-7). Humanities.

Maroni River Caribs of Surinam. Peter Kloos. (Studies of Developing Countries). 1971. pap. text ed. 26.50x (ISBN 90-232-0903-6). Humanities.

Marquard Von Lindau: Die Zehe Gebot. Jacobus W. Van Maren. (Dutch.). 1980. pap. 52.50 (ISBN 90-6203-771-2). Humanities.

Marquette Shipwrecks. 4th ed. (Illus.). 3.95 o.s.i. (ISBN 0-932212-07-7). Avery Color.

Marquette's Explorations: The Narratives Reexamined. Raphael Hamilton. (Illus.). 1970. 19.50 (ISBN 0-299-05570-1). U of Wis Pr.

Marquis De Lafayette: Bright Sword for Freedom. Hodding Carter. (World Landmark Ser. No. 34). (Illus.). (gr. 7-9). 1958. 4.39 o.p. (ISBN 0-394-90534-2). Random.

Marquis De Lafayette in the American Revolution with Some Account of the Attitude of France Toward the War of Independence, 2 Vols. Charlemagne Tower. LC 79-112310. (Era of the American Revolution Ser). 1970. Repr. of 1901 ed. lib. bdg. 75.00 (ISBN 0-306-71914-2). Da Capo.

Marquis De Mores: Emperor of the Badlands. Donald Dresden. LC 69-16720. (Illus.). 1970. 13.95 (ISBN 0-8061-0869-X); pap. 6.95 o.p. (ISBN 0-8061-1196-8). U of Okla Pr.

Marquis De Sade: A Bibliography. E. Pierre Chanover. LC 72-10288. (Author Bibliographies Ser.: No. 12). 1973. 8.00 o.p. (ISBN 0-8108-0561-8). Scarecrow.

Marquis Who's Who Publications Index to All Books 1974. 1st ed. LC 74-17540. 488p. 1974. 19.50 (ISBN 0-8379-1401-9). Marquis.

Marquis Who's Who Publications Index to All Books 1975. 2nd ed. LC 75-25185. 500p. 1975. 24.95 (ISBN 0-8379-1402-7). Marquis.

Marquis Who's Who Publications Index to All Books 1978. LC 74-17540. 1979. 14.50 (ISBN 0-8379-1404-3). Marquis.

Marquise & the Novice. Victoria Ramstetter. LC 80-83118. (Illus.). 100p. (Orig.). 1981. pap. 4.95 (ISBN 0-930044-16-9). Naiad Pr.

Marquise Went Out at Five. Claude Mauriac. Tr. by Richard Howard. 1981. pap. 4.95 (ISBN 0-7145-0367-3). Riverrun NY.

Marra's World. Elizabeth Coatsworth. LC 75-9520. (Illus.). 80p. (gr. 3-5). 1975. 7.25 (ISBN 0-688-80007-6); PLB 6.96 (ISBN 0-688-84007-8). Greenwillow.

Marriage. 3rd ed. Bob Blood & Margaret Blood. LC 77-3847. 1978. text ed. 15.95 (ISBN 0-02-904180-5). Free Pr.

Marriage - Dead or Alive? A. Guggenbuhl-Craig. 1977. pap. 6.00 (ISBN 0-88214-309-3). Spring Pubns.

Marriage Act, 2 vols. in 1. John Shebbeare. LC 74-17449. (Novel in England, 1700-1775 Ser). 1974. Repr. of 1754 ed. lib. bdg. 50.00 (ISBN 0-8240-1139-2). Garland Pub.

Marriage & Adoption in China, 1845-1945. Arthur P. Wolf & Chieh-Shan Huang. LC 78-66182. 1980. 18.95x (ISBN 0-8047-1027-9). Stanford U Pr.

Marriage & Alternatives: Exploring Intimate Relationships. Roger W. Libby & Robert N. Whitehurst. 1977. pap. 9.95x (ISBN 0-673-15050-X). Scott F.

Marriage & Families: Enrichment Through Communication. Ed. by Sherod Miller. LC 75-27012. (Sage Contemporary Social Science Issues Ser.: Vol. 20). 1975. 4.95x (ISBN 0-8039-0569-6). Sage.

Marriage & Family Development. 5th ed. Evelyn M. Duvall. LC 76-30744. 1977. scp 19.50 (ISBN 0-397-47362-1, HarpC). Har-Row.

Marriage & Family Enrichment: New Perspectives & Programs. Ed. by Herbert A. Otto. LC 75-30743. 1976. 14.95 (ISBN 0-687-23621-5); pap. 8.95 (ISBN 0-687-23620-7). Abingdon.

Marriage & Family Experience: A Text with Readings. F. Bryan Strong et al. (Illus.). 1979. pap. text ed. 16.50 (ISBN 0-8299-0278-3); instrs.' manual avail. (ISBN 0-8299-0577-4). West Pub.

Marriage & Family in a Decade of Change: A Humanistic Reader. Ed. by Gwen B. Carr. 1972. pap. text ed. 6.50 (ISBN 0-201-00899-8). A-W.

Marriage & Family Interaction. 5th ed. Robert R. Bell. 1979. text ed. 18.50x (ISBN 0-256-02110-4); pap. study guide 5.95 (ISBN 0-256-02243-7). Dorsey.

Marriage & Family Relations. 2nd ed. Robert C. Williamson. LC 70-37027. 1972. text ed. 18.95 (ISBN 0-471-94905-1). Wiley.

Marriage & Family Today. Keith Melville. 1977. text ed. 14.95x o.p. (ISBN 0-394-31072-1). Random.

Marriage & Parenthood. F. Philip Rice. 1979. text ed. 18.95 (ISBN 0-205-06517-1, 8165173); instr's man. avail. (ISBN 0-205-06539-2, 8165394). Allyn.

Marriage & Personal Development. Rubin Blanck & Gertrude Blanck. LC 68-9577. 1968. 17.50x (ISBN 0-231-03150-5). Columbia U Pr.

Marriage & Rank in Bengali Culture: A History of Caste & Clan in Middle-Period Bengal. Ronald B. Inden. LC 73-85789. 176p. 1976. 17.50x (ISBN 0-520-02569-5). U of Cal Pr.

Marriage & the Family. Carlfred B. Broderick. (Illus.). 1979. text ed. 17.95 (ISBN 0-13-559112-0). P-H.

Marriage & the Family. Gilbert D. Nass. (Illus.). 1978. text ed. 16.95 (ISBN 0-201-02500-0); instr's man 3.00 (ISBN 0-201-02502-7); study guide 4.95 (ISBN 0-201-02501-9); tests 2.00 (ISBN 0-201-02503-5). A-W.

Marriage & the Family & Child-Rearing Practices. Sheila Corwin. Ed. by Therese A. Zak. (Lifeworks Ser.). (Illus.). 160p. 1981. text ed. 4.56 (ISBN 0-07-013198-8). McGraw.

Marriage As a Trade. Cicely M. Hamilton. LC 71-149782. 1971. Repr. of 1909 ed. 15.00 (ISBN 0-8103-3394-5). Gale.

Marriage As Equal Partnership. Dwight H. Small. 1980. pap. 2.95 (ISBN 0-8010-8177-7). Baker Bk.

Marriage Bargain. Joanna Scott. 192p. 1981. pap. 1.50 (ISBN 0-671-57068-4). S&S.

Marriage Bed. (Illus.). 4.95 (ISBN 0-910550-43-3). Centurion Pr.

Marriage: Bibliotheca Neerlandica Ser. Gerald Walschap. Incl. Ordeal. 1963. 10.00 (ISBN 0-8277-0261-2). British Bk Ctr.

Marriage Chest. Dorothy Eden. 160p. 1978. pap. 1.50 o.p. (ISBN 0-449-23032-5, Crest). Fawcett.

Marriage, Class & Colour in Nineteenth Century Cuba. Verena Martinez-Alier. LC 73-82463. 224p. 1974. 30.95 (ISBN 0-521-20412-7); pap. 10.95x (ISBN 0-521-09846-7). Cambridge U Pr.

Marriage Contract: Couples, Lovers & the Law. Lenore J. Weitzman. 1980. 14.95 (ISBN 0-13-558403-5, Spec); pap. 5.95 (ISBN 0-13-558395-0). P-H.

Marriage Counseling: Fact or Fallacy? Jerold R. Kuhn. LC 80-22269. 146p. 1980. Repr. of 1973 ed. lib. bdg. 9.95x (ISBN 0-89370-622-1). Borgo Pr.

Marriage Counselling. Booker Wallis. 17.95x (ISBN 0-392-08121-0, SpS). Soccer.

Marriage Counselling in the Community. W. L. Herbert & F. J. Jarvis. 1970. 8.25 (ISBN 0-08-006911-8); pap. 5.25 o.p. (ISBN 0-08-006910-X). Pergamon.

Marriage Covenant. John C. Reid. LC 67-11305. (Orig.). 1967. pap. 1.00 (ISBN 0-8042-1710-6). John Knox.

Marriage Customs in Many Lands. Henry N. Hutchinson. LC 73-5520. (Illus.). xii, 348p. 1975. Repr. of 1897 ed. 28.00 (ISBN 0-8103-3971-4). Gale.

Marriage Dialogue. Lynn A. Scorseby. LC 76-45150. 1977. text ed. 6.95 (ISBN 0-201-06789-7). A-W.

Marriage, Divorce & Adoption: New York. Eugene R. Canudo. 1979. pap. 5.50x (ISBN 0-87526-222-8). Gould.

Marriage, Divorce & Remarriage. Jay E. Adams. 1980. pap. 3.50 (ISBN 0-87552-068-5). Presby & Reformed.

Marriage, Divorce & Remarriage. Jay E. Adams. 120p. 1981. pap. 3.50 (ISBN 0-8010-0168-4). Baker Bk.

Marriage, Duty, & Desire in Victorian Poetry & Drama. Richard D. McGhee. LC 80-11962. 336p. 1980. 22.50x (ISBN 0-7006-0203-8). Regents Pr KS.

Marriage Enrichment Manual. Ed. by Jean M. Hiesberger. (Paths of Life Ser.). 1980. cancelled (ISBN 0-8091-9187-3). Paulist Pr.

Marriage Enrichment: Philosophy Process & Program. Larry Hof & William Miller. (Illus.). 192p. 1980. text ed. 14.95 (ISBN 0-87619-717-9). R J Brady.

Marriage Feast. Par Lagerkvist. Tr. by Alan Blair & Carl E. Lindin. 1973. 6.95 o.p. (ISBN 0-8090-6786-2); pap. 2.95 (ISBN 0-8090-1372-X). Hill & Wang.

Marriage: For Better or for Worse? Robert H. Loeb, Jr. (gr. 9 up). 1980. PLB 8.90 (ISBN 0-686-65254-1, G25). Watts.

Marriage in a Changing World. 2nd ed. Gerald R. Leslie & Elizabeth M. Leslie. LC 79-16195. 1980. text ed. 16.95x (ISBN 0-471-05593-X); tchrs'. manual avail. (ISBN 0-471-06271-5); study guide avail. (ISBN 0-471-06104-2). Wiley.

Marriage in Today's World: Student Activity Book. John Lederach & Naomi Lederach. 56p. 1980. pap. 2.50 (ISBN 0-8361-1946-0). Herald Pr.

Marriage in Trouble: A Time of Decision. Eleanor C. Haspel. LC 76-4780. 308p. 1976. 12.95 (ISBN 0-88229-222-6); pap. 6.95 (ISBN 0-88229-428-8). Nelson-Hall.

Marriage Insurance. Betty Doty. 8.95 (ISBN 0-930822-01-3). Green Hill.

Marriage Is a Family Affair. G. P. Sholerar. Date not set. text ed. price not set (ISBN 0-89335-120-2). Spectrum Pub.

Marriage Is for Grownups. Joseph W. Bird & Lois F. Bird. LC 79-78725. 1971. pap. 2.95 (ISBN 0-385-04256-6, Im). Doubleday.

Marriage Is for Those Who Love God & One Another. Thomas B. Warren. 1976. 4.95 (ISBN 0-934916-37-3). Natl Christian Pr.

Marriage Litigation in Medieval England. R. H. Helmholz. LC 73-93395. (Studies in English Legal History). 272p. 1975. 36.00 (ISBN 0-521-20411-9). Cambridge U Pr.

Marriage of Convenience. Tim Jeal. 1981. pap. price not set. PB.

Marriage of Heaven & Hell. William Blake. (Illus.). 82p. 1975. 19.95 (ISBN 0-19-212588-5). Oxford U Pr.

Marriage of Lit-Lit. Jack London. Ed. by Walter Pauk & Raymond Harris. (Classics Ser). (Illus.). (gr. 6-12). 1976. pap. text ed. 1.60x (ISBN 0-89061-044-4, 509); tchrs. ed. 3.00 (ISBN 0-89061-045-2, 511). Jamestown Pubs.

Marriage of Wisdom & Other Tales. Wilton Sankawulo. (Secondary Readers Ser.). 1974. pap. text ed. 2.50x (ISBN 0-435-92820-1). Heinemann Ed.

Marriage, Religion, & Society: Tradition & Change in an Indian Village. G. R. Gupta. LC 73-5903. 180p. 1974. 12.95 (ISBN 0-470-33648-X). Halsted Pr.

Marriage Season. Sally Dubois. (Candlelight Romance Ser.). (Orig.). 1981. pap. 1.50 (ISBN 0-440-16058-8). Dell.

Marriage Secret. Bill Marshall & Christina M. Marshall. 1980. 8.95 (ISBN 0-8437-3349-7). Hammond Inc.

Marriage, Sexuality & Celibacy: A Greek Orthodox Perspective. D. J. Constantelos. 1975. pap. 3.95 (ISBN 0-937032-15-8). Light&Life Pub Co MN.

Marriage Survival Kit. Mort Katz. LC 75-536. 1974. 5.95 o.p. (ISBN 0-87863-080-5). Farnswth Pub.

Marriage Takes More Than Love. Jack Mayhall & Carole Mayhall. LC 77-85736. 1978. pap. 4.50 (ISBN 0-89109-426-1, 14266). NavPress.

Marriage, the Family & Personal Fulfillment. 2nd ed. David A. Schulz & Stanley F. Rogers. (P-H Ser. in Sociology). (Illus.). 1980. text ed. 17.95 (ISBN 0-13-559385-9). P-H.

Marriage: The Mystery of Christ & the Church. David Engelsma. LC 74-31902. 1975. pap. 2.95 (ISBN 0-8254-2520-4). Kregel.

Marriage Today: A Commentary on the Code of Canon Law. 3rd ed. Bernard Siegle. LC 79-18786. 1979. pap. 10.95 (ISBN 0-8189-0384-8). Alba.

Marriage Voices: A Novel. Benjamin Barber. LC 80-18831. 256p. 1981. 10.95 (ISBN 0-671-44808-0). Summit Bks.

Marriage: Who, When & Why? D. Knox. 1974. pap. 9.95 (ISBN 0-13-559336-0). P-H.

Marriageable Asset. Ruth Gerber. (Orig.). 1981. pap. 1.50 o.s.i. (ISBN 0-440-14974-6). Dell.

Marriages & Deaths from the New Yorker: Double Quatro Edition 1836-1841. Kenneth Scott. LC 80-80958. 308p. Date not set. price not set (ISBN 0-915156-46-6, SP46). Natl Genealogical.

Marriages & Infidelities. Joyce C. Oates. LC 72-83348. 416p. 1972. 10.95 (ISBN 0-8149-0718-0). Vanguard.

Marriages & Infidelities. Joyce C. Oates. 416p. 1978. pap. 2.50 o.p. (ISBN 0-449-23724-9, Crest). Fawcett.

Married Feminist. Angela B. McBride. LC 74-15839. 224p. 1976. 8.95 o.s.i. (ISBN 0-06-012881-X, HarpT). Har-Row.

Married Life. rev. ed. Audrey Riker et al. (gr. 10-12). 1976. text ed. 14.20 (ISBN 0-87002-071-4); student guide 2.60 (ISBN 0-87002-208-3). tchr's guide avail. Bennett IL.

Married Love & Other Poems. Srinivas Rayaprol. (Writers Workshop Redbird Ser.). 1976. 8.00 (ISBN 0-89253-724-8); pap. text ed. 4.00 (ISBN 0-89253-725-6). Ind-US Inc.

Married Single. Helen Sommers. 1981. 4.95 (ISBN 0-8062-1548-8). Carlton.

Married to Medicine. Carla Fine. LC 80-69372. 1981. 11.95 (ISBN 0-689-11128-2). Atheneum.

Married to the Enemy. Philip B. Knoche. (Uplook Ser.). 1976. pap. 0.75 (ISBN 0-8163-0262-6, 13263-9). Pacific Pr Pub Assn.

Married Women & Work: Nineteen Fifty-Seven & Nineteen Seventy-Six. Alfreda P. Iglehart. LC 78-75320. (Illus.). 128p. 1979. 13.95 (ISBN 0-669-02838-X). Lexington Bks.

Married Women's Work: Being the Report of an Inquiry Undertaken by the Women's Industrial Council, London Nineteen Fifteen. Clementina Black. LC 79-56947. (Englishworking Class Ser.). 1980. lib. bdg. 25.00 (ISBN 0-8240-0102-8). Garland Pub.

Marrow of Tradition. Charles W. Chesnutt. 1969. pap. 4.95 (ISBN 0-472-06147-X, 147, AA). U of Mich Pr.

Marrow of Tradition. Charles W. Chesnutt. 1969. 6.95 (ISBN 0-472-09147-6). U of Mich Pr.

Marry in Haste. Jane A. Hodge. 1976. pap. 1.50 o.p. (ISBN 0-449-23068-6, Crest). Fawcett.

Mars. Dinah Moche. LC 78-2762. (Easy-Read-Fact Bks.). (Illus.). (gr. 2-4). 1978. PLB 6.45 s&l (ISBN 0-531-01374-X). Watts.

Marsanne. Virginia Coffman. 1977. pap. 1.75 o.p. (ISBN 0-449-23373-1, Crest). Fawcett.

Marse Henry: An Autobiography, 2 vols. Henry Watterson. (American Newspapermen 1790-1933 Ser.). (Illus.). 629p. 1974. Repr. of 1919 ed. Set. 37.00x (ISBN 0-8464-0002-2). Beekman Pubs.

Marsh: A Century of Cranberries. Lela P. Winn. 144p. 1981. 7.50 (ISBN 0-682-49697-9). Exposition.

Marsha. Margaret M. Craig. (gr. 7-10). pap. 0.95 o.p. (ISBN 0-425-03512-3, Highland). Berkley Pub.

Marshal from Texas. Owen G. Irons. 192p. (YA) 1975. 5.95 (ISBN 0-685-53496-0, Avalon). Bouregy.

Marshal of Packersville. Cy Martin. (YA) 1976. 5.95 (ISBN 0-685-68914-X, Avalon). Bouregy.

Marshall Attack. R. G. Wade & T. D. Harding. (Batsford Chess Ser.). (Illus.). 1976. 13.95 o.p. (ISBN 0-7134-2847-3). Hippocrene Bks.

Marshall Attack. Robert Wade & T. D. Harding. 1974. 21.50 (ISBN 0-7134-2847-3). David & Charles.

Marshall Plan: Nineteen Forty Seven-Nineteen Fifty One. Theodore A. Wilson. LC 77-89364. (Headline Ser.: 236). (Illus., Orig.). 1977. pap. 2.00 (ISBN 0-87124-042-4). Foreign Policy.

Marshall's Mission to China: The Report & Appended Documents. George C. Marshall. 1976. Set. 60.00 (ISBN 0-89093-115-1). U Pubns Amer.

Marshal's Lady. Sarah Stamford. 1981. 11.95 (ISBN 0-525-15320-9). Dutton.

Marshland Mystery. (Trixie Belden Mystery Stories Ser.). (gr. 4 up). 1977. PLB 5.52 (ISBN 0-307-61578-2 Golden Pr); pap. 1.25 (ISBN 0-307-21578-4). Western Pub.

Marsilio Ficino: The Philebus Commentary. Ed. by Michael J. Allen. 1981. 32.50x (ISBN 0-520-03977-7). U of Cal Pr.

Marta. Rodolfo Celletti. LC 62-9936. 1962. 4.95 o.s.i. (ISBN 0-3076-0177-2). Braziller.

Martereau. Nathalie Sarraute. 1959. 4.50 o.s.i. (ISBN 0-8076-0071-7). Braziller.

Martha Berry. Mary K. Phelan. LC 77-158699. (Biography Ser.). (Illus.). (gr. 2-5). 1972. PLB 7.89 (ISBN 0-690-52113-8, TYC-J). T Y Crowell.

Martha Graham: Sixteen Dances in Photographs. rev. ed. Barbara Morgan. LC 80-81766. (Illus.). 168p. 1980. Repr. of 1941 ed. 35.00 (ISBN 0-87100-176-4). Morgan.

Martha Helps the Rebel. Carole Charles. LC 75-33126. (Stories of the Revolution). (Illus.). (gr. 2-6). 1975. PLB 5.50 (ISBN 0-913778-22-2). Childs World.

Martha, Martha! Marge Green. 1964. 6.45 (ISBN 0-89137-401-9); pap. 3.75 (ISBN 0-89137-400-0). Quality Pubns.

Martha Washington's Book of Cookery. Ed. by Karen Hess. LC 80-18257. 464p. 1981. 19.95 (ISBN 0-231-04930-7). Columbia U Pr.

Martha's Vineyard. Henry B. Hough. (Large Format Ser.). (Illus.). 1979. pap. 5.95 o.s.i. (ISBN 0-14-005165-1). Penguin.

Martha's Vineyard Cook Book. Louise T. King & Jean S. Wexler. LC 70-144180. (Illus.). 1971. 12.50 o.p. (ISBN 0-06-012398-2, HarpT). Har-Row.

Martial Arts. Ken Reisberg. (First Bks.). (Illus.). (gr. 4 up). 1979. s&l 6.45 (ISBN 0-531-04077-1). Watts.

Martial Arts Film. Marilyn D. Mintz. 9.95 o.p. (ISBN 0-498-01775-3). A S Barnes.

Martial Arts in Actor Training. Ed. by Phillip B. Zarrilli. 1981. 13.95x (ISBN 0-89676-052-9); pap. 10.00x (ISBN 0-89676-053-7). Drama Bk.

Martial Musician's Mentor: A Complete Course of Instruction for the Fife, Pt. 1. rev., 2nd ed. George Kusel. (Illus.). 52p. (gr. 6 up). 1979. pap. 4.95 (ISBN 0-9604476-1-X). Kusel.

Martial Spirit: An Introduction to the Origin, Philosophy & Psychology of the Martial Arts. Herman Kauz. LC 77-77808. (Illus.). 1978. 11.95 (ISBN 0-87951-067-6). Overlook Pr.

Martial, the Twelve Books Epigrams. Tr. by J. A. Pott & F. A. Wright. 402p. 1981. Repr. lib. bdg. 65.00 (ISBN 0-89987-566-1). Darby Bks.

Martian Chronicles. Ray Bradbury. LC 72-94171. 288p. 1973. 8.95 o.p. (ISBN 0-385-03862-3). Doubleday.

Martian Odyssey. Ronald J. Ebner. 1981. 4.95 (ISBN 0-8062-1624-7). Carlton.

Martian Time-Slip. 4th ed. Philip K. Dick. 224p. 1981. pap. 2.25 (ISBN 0-345-29560-9). Ballantine.

Martian Way & Other Stories. Isaac Asimov. 1978. pap. 1.95 (ISBN 0-449-23783-4, Crest). Fawcett.

Martianus Capella & the Seven Liberal Arts: The Marriage of Philology & Mercury, Vol. 2. Ed. by William H. Stahl & Richard C. Johnson. LC 76-121876. 1977. 27.50x (ISBN 0-231-03719-8). Columbia U Pr.

Martianus Capella & the Seven Liberal Arts, Vol. 1. William H. Stahl. LC 76-121876. (Records of Civilization, Sources & Studies). 1971. 17.50x (ISBN 0-231-03254-4). Columbia U Pr.

Martin. Helene Frederic & Martine Malinsky. Tr. by John McGreal & Susan Lipshitz. Orig. Title: Martin: un Enfant Battait Sa Mere. 108p. 1981. price not set (ISBN 0-7100-0814-7). Routledge & Kegan.

Martin A. Hansen. Faith Ingwersen & Neils Ingwersen. (World Authors Ser.: No. 419). 1976. lib. bdg. 11.95 (ISBN 0-8057-6259-0). Twayne.

Martin Bormann: Nazi in Exile. Paul Manning. (Illus.). 320p. 1981. 14.95 (ISBN 0-686-69395-7). Lyle Stuart.

Martin Buber. Werner Manheim. (World Authors Ser.: Germany: No. 269). 1974. lib. bdg. 10.95 (ISBN 0-8057-2182-7). Twayne.

Martin Buber. Ronald G. Smith. LC 67-10206. (Makers of Contemporary Theology Ser). 1967. pap. 3.45 (ISBN 0-8042-0697-X). John Knox.

Martin Buber: A Bibliography of His Writings, 1897-1978. Compiled by Margot Cohn & Rafael Buber. 164p. 1980. 35.00 (ISBN 3-598-10146-5, Dist by Gale Research Co.). K G Saur.

Martin Buber: A Living Memory. Shalom ben-Chorin. Tr. by Judith M. Herman from Ger. LC 79-89933. Orig. Title: Zwiesprache mit Martin Buber. (Orig.). 1980. pap. cancelled (ISBN 0-89793-010-X). Hunter Hse.

Martin Buber: The Life of Dialogue. 3rd, rev. ed. Maurice Friedman. 1976. pap. 9.00 (ISBN 0-226-26356-8). U of Chicago Pr.

Martin Dies. William Gellermann. LC 77-151620. (Civil Liberties in American History Ser.). 1972. Repr. of 1944 ed. lib. bdg. 29.50 (ISBN 0-306-70200-2). Da Capo.

Martin Eden. Jack London. (Literature Ser). (gr. 7-12). 1969. pap. text ed. 3.67 (ISBN 0-87720-709-7). AMSCO Sch.

Martin Eden. Jack London. 1957. 12.95 (ISBN 0-02-574510-7). Macmillan.

Martin Eden with Reader's Guide. Jack London. (AMSCO Literature Program Ser). (gr. 10-12). 1971. pap. text ed. 4.33 (ISBN 0-87720-812-3); tchr's ed. 2.80 (ISBN 0-87720-912-X). AMSCO Sch.

Martin Fierro, un Siglo. limited ed. Ed. by Jose E. Clemente. (Illus., Span., Special centennial vol., vols. no. 500-1000 only, for sale). 1972. 50.00 (ISBN 0-935738-03-7). US Comm UNICEF.

Martin Heidegger. John Macquarrie. LC 68-11970. (Makers of Contemporary Theology Ser). 1968. pap. 3.45 (ISBN 0-8042-0659-7). John Knox.

Martin Luther. Judith O'Neill. LC 74-12959. (Introduction to the History of Mankind). (Illus.). 48p. (gr. 6-11). 1975. pap. text ed. 3.95 (ISBN 0-521-20403-8). Cambridge U Pr.

Martin Luther--Reformer or Revolutionary? 3rd ed. Ed. by Brian Tierney et al. (Historical Pamphlets). 1977. pap. text ed. 1.50x (ISBN 0-394-32055-7). Random.

Martin Luther & the Drama. Thomas I. Bacon. (Amsterdamer Pulkationen Zur Sprache und Literature: No. 25). 1976. text ed. 14.25x (ISBN 90-6203-359-8). Humanities.

Martin Luther Christmas Book with Celebrated Woodcuts by His Contemporaries. Tr. by Roland H. Bainton. LC 59-2930. 80p. 1948. pap. 3.25 (ISBN 0-8006-1843-2, 1-1843). Fortress.

Martin Luther King: The Man Who Climbed the Mountain. Gary Paulsen & Dan Theis. LC 76-13483. (Illus.). 64p. (gr. 4-6). 1976. 6.60 o.p. (ISBN 0-8172-0415-6); PLB 6.60 o.p. (ISBN 0-8172-0414-8). Raintree Pubs.

Martin Luther King: The Peaceful Warrior. Ed Clayton. (gr. 4-6). 1969. pap. 1.75 (ISBN 0-671-75986-8). Archway.

Martin Luther King: The Peaceful Warrior. Ed Clayton. (gr. 4-6). 1969. pap. 1.50 (ISBN 0-671-29932-8). PB.

Martin Luther Treasury. Ed. by Erwin P. Rudolph. 1979. pap. 1.95 (ISBN 0-88207-518-7). Victor Bks.

Martin Marprelate, Gentleman. Leland H. Carlson. (Illus.). 400p. 1981. price not set (ISBN 0-87328-112-8). Huntington Lib.

Martin Salander. Gottfried Keller. 1981. pap. 4.95 (ISBN 0-7145-0371-1). Riverrun NY.

Martin Scorsese: The First Decade. Mary P. Kelly. (Illus., Orig.). 1980. pap. 9.90 (ISBN 0-913178-67-5). Redgrave Pub Co.

Martin Van Buren. Edward M. Shepard. LC 80-25465. (American Statesmen Ser.). 1981. pap. 6.95 (ISBN 0-87754-189-2). Chelsea Hse.

Martingale Limit Theory & Its Application. P. G. Hall & C. C. Hayde. LC 80-536. (Probability & Mathematical Statistics Ser.). 1980. 36.00 (ISBN 0-12-319350-8). Acad Pr.

Martinis & Whipped Cream. Sidney Petrie & Robert B. Stone. 272p. 1968. pap. 2.25 o.s.i. (ISBN 0-446-82506-9). Warner Bks.

Martin's Father. 2nd ed. Margrit Eichler. LC 77-81779. 31p. (ps-1). 1977. pap. 2.75 (ISBN 0-914996-16-9); 6.50 o.p. (ISBN 0-914996-17-7). Lollipop Power.

Martin's Magic Formula for Getting the Right Job. Phyllis Martin. 160p. 1981. 10.95 (ISBN 0-312-51702-5). St Martin.

Marty Mann Answers Your Questions About Drinking & Alcoholism. Marty Mann. 128p. 1981. 8.95 (ISBN 0-03-081857-5); pap. 3.95 (ISBN 0-686-69289-6). HR&W.

Marty Mann's New Primer on Alcoholism. Marty Mann. 256p. 1981. 10.95 (ISBN 0-03-029595-5); pap. 5.95 (ISBN 0-686-69290-X). HR&W.

Martydom & Persecution in the Early Church. W. H. Frend. (Twin Brooks Ser.). 645p. 1981. pap. 12.95 (ISBN 0-8010-3502-3). Baker Bk.

Martyr of Antioch: A Dramatic Poem, Repr. Of 1822 Ed. Henry H. Milman. Bd. with Anne Boleyn: A Dramatic Poem. Repr. of 1826 ed. LC 75-31234. (Romantic Context: Poetry 1789-1830 Ser.: Vol. 85). 1976. lib. bdg. 47.00 (ISBN 0-8240-2184-3). Garland Pub.

Martyrology Pronouncing Dictionary. Anthony I. Russo-Alesi. LC 79-167151. 1973. Repr. of 1939 ed. 15.00 (ISBN 0-8103-3272-8). Gale.

Martyrs. Francois R. De Chateaubriand. Ed. & tr. by O. W. Wight. LC 76-15294. 451p. 1976. Repr. of 1859 ed. 22.50 (ISBN 0-86527-275-1). Fertig.

Martyr's Message of Hope: Six Homilies of Oscar Romero. Oscar Romero. 125p. (Orig.). 1981. pap. 4.95 (ISBN 0-934134-09-X). Natl Cath Reporter.

Maru. Bessie Head. (African Writers Ser.). 1972. pap. text ed. 3.75x (ISBN 0-435-90101-X). Heinemann Ed.

Marune: Alastor Nine Hundred Thirty-Three. Jack Vance. 1981. pap. 2.25 (ISBN 0-87997-591-1, UE1591). Daw Bks.

Marune: Alastor 933. Jack Vance. 160p. (Orig.). 1975. pap. 1.50 o.p. (ISBN 0-345-24518-0). Ballantine.

Marvellous in Fielding's Novels. Mitchell Kalpakgian. LC 80-1411. 243p. 1981. lib. bdg. 18.75 (ISBN 0-8191-1505-3); pap. text ed. 9.75 (ISBN 0-8191-1506-1). U Pr of Amer.

Marvellous Matches. Friedrich Feld. LC 66-10787. (Illus.). (gr. 4-7). 1961. 3.95 o.p. (ISBN 0-8075-4978-9). A Whitman.

Marvelous Misadventures of Sebastian. Lloyd Alexander. LC 70-166879. (gr. 4 up). 1970. PLB 10.95 (ISBN 0-525-34739-9); pap. 1.95 o.p. (ISBN 0-525-45009-2). Dutton.

Marvelous Palace & Other Stories. Pierre Boulle. LC 77-77035. 1978. 8.95 (ISBN 0-8149-0788-1). Vanguard.

Marvelous Work & a Wonder. Le Grand Richards. 424p. 14.00 (ISBN 0-87747-686-1); pap. 1.50 (ISBN 0-87747-614-4). Deseret Bk.

Marvels of Professor Pettingruel. Opal L. Nations. (Illus.). 1978. sewn in wrappers 5.00 (ISBN 0-685-50395-X). Black Stone.

Marvin Jones: The Public Life of an Agrarian Advocate. Irvin M. May, Jr. LC 79-5282. (The Centennial Series of the Association of Former Students: No. 8). (Illus.). 312p. 1980. 22.95x (ISBN 0-89096-093-3). Tex A&M Univ Pr.

Marx. Peter Singer. 1980. 7.95 (ISBN 0-8090-7550-4); pap. 2.95 (ISBN 0-8090-1412-2). Hill & Wang.

Marx & Engels on Ecology. Ed. by Howard L. Parsons. LC 77-71866. (Contributions in Philosophy: No.8). 1977. lib. bdg. 18.95 (ISBN 0-8371-9538-1, PME/). Greenwood.

Marx & Engels: On Ireland - an Annotated Checklist. Ellen Hazelkorn. (Bibliographical Ser.: No. 15). 1981. 2.00 (ISBN 0-89977-031-2). Am Inst Marxist.

Marx & Engels on Law & Laws. Paul Phillips. 238p. 1981. 27.50x (ISBN 0-389-20120-0). B&N.

Marx & Engels on Literature & Art: A Selection of Writings. Ed. by Lee Baxandall & Stefan Morawski. LC 73-93501. 150p. 1973. 9.50 (ISBN 0-914386-01-8); pap. 3.95 (ISBN 0-914386-02-6). Telos Pr.

Marx & Engels on the Means of Communication. Karl Marx & Engels Frederick. Ed. by Yves De La Haye. 176p. (Orig.). 1980. pap. 5.00 (ISBN 0-88477-013-3). Intl General.

Marx & Keynes: The Limits of the Mixed Economy. Paul Mattick. LC 69-15526. (Extending Horizons Ser.). 1973. pap. 3.45 (ISBN 0-87558-069-6). Porter Sargent.

Marx & Philosophy of Culture. Robert D'Amico. LC 80-24405. (University of Florida Humanities Monograph: No. 50). viii, 108p. (Orig.). 1981. pap. 7.00 (ISBN 0-8130-0689-9). U Presses Fla.

Marx & the Authentic Man: A First Introduction to the Philosophy of Karl Marx. Henry J. Koren. 1973. Repr. of 1967 ed. text ed. 5.00x o.p. (ISBN 0-391-00315-1, J26202). Humanities.

Marx & the Proletariat: A Study in Social Theory. Timothy McCarthy. LC 78-4025. (Contributions in Political Science: No. 18). 1978. lib. bdg. 15.00 (ISBN 0-313-20412-8, MPL/). Greenwood.

Marx & Wittgenstein. David Rubenstein. 240p. 1981. write for info. (ISBN 0-7100-0688-8). Routledge & Kegan.

Marx Beyond Marx: Notebooks on the Grundrisse. Antonio Negri. Orig. Title: Marx Oltre Marx. 232p. 1981. 21.95x (ISBN 0-89789-018-3). J F Bergin.

Marx Chronology. Macmillan Rubel. 226p. 1981. lib. bdg. 22.50 (ISBN 0-87196-516-X). Facts on File.

Marx, Engels & the Workers of the World. Edward Rice. LC 76-56183. (Illus.). 192p. (gr. 7 up). 1977. 8.95 (ISBN 0-590-07407-5, Four Winds). Schol Bk Serv.

Marx-Engels Dictionary. James Russell. LC 80-786. (Illus.). xxv, 140p. 1981. lib. bdg. 19.95 (ISBN 0-313-22035-2, RME/). Greenwood.

Marx, Engels, Marxism. V. I. Lenin. 1978. 7.95 (ISBN 0-8351-0553-9); pap. 4.95 (ISBN 0-8351-0545-8). China Bks.

Marx: His Theory & Its Context. Angus Walker. (Illus.). 1978. pap. text ed. 9.95x (ISBN 0-582-44196-X). Longman.

Marx Vs. Russia. J. A. Doerig. LC 62-12958. 1962. pap. 1.95 (ISBN 0-8044-6123-6). Ungar.

Marxian Dilemma: Transformation of Values to Prices. Ed. by A. J. Fonseca. 1980. 10.00x (ISBN 0-8364-0654-0, Pub. by Manohar India). South Asia Bks.

Marxian Economic Theory. Meghnad Desai. 1974. 13.50x o.p. (ISBN 0-85641-012-8, Pub. by Basil Blackwell England). Biblio Dist.

Marxian Economics. Meghnad Desai. 265p. 1979. 27.50x (ISBN 0-8476-6204-7). Rowman.

Marxian Political Economy. J. Becker. LC 76-9172. (Illus.). 1977. 26.50x (ISBN 0-521-21349-5). Cambridge U Pr.

Marxism & "Anthropology" The Concept of Human Essence in the Philosophy of Marx. George Markus. (Dialectic & Society Ser.: No. 4). 1978. pap. text ed. 10.00x (ISBN 90-232-1615-6). Humanities.

Marxism & Buddhism. P. K. Bhattacharya. 1976. 3.50x o.p. (ISBN 0-686-59641-2). South Asia Bks.

Marxism & Christianity. Guilio Girardi. 1968. 5.95 o.s.i. (ISBN 0-02-543940-5). Macmillan.

Marxism & Class Theory: A Bourgeois Critique. Frank Parkin. LC 79-14222. 1979. 17.50x (ISBN 0-231-04880-7). Columbia U Pr.

Marxism & Democracy. Alan Hunt. 1980. text ed. 20.75x (ISBN 0-391-01879-5). Humanities.

Marxism & Education: A Study of Phenomenological & Marxist Approaches to Education. Madan Sarup. (Education Bks). 1978. 18.50x (ISBN 0-7100-8944-9); pap. 7.95 (ISBN 0-7100-8945-7). Routledge & Kegan.

Marxism & Literary Criticism. Terry Eagleton. 1976. 10.95x (ISBN 0-520-03237-3); pap. 2.65 (ISBN 0-520-03243-8, CAL 337). U of Cal Pr.

Marxism & Literature. Raymond Williams. (Marxist Introductions Ser.). 1977. 12.95x (ISBN 0-19-876056-6). Oxford U Pr.

Marxism & Materialism. rev. ed. David Ruben. (Marxist Theory & Contemporary Capitalism Ser.). 1978. text ed. 27.50x (ISBN 0-391-00966-4); pap. text ed. 11.00x (ISBN 0-391-00965-6). Humanities.

Marxism & Philosophy. Karl Korsch. Tr. by Fred Halliday from Ger. LC 71-158921. 1971. 7.50 o.p. (ISBN 0-85345-153-2, CL-1532); pap. 3.45 (ISBN 0-85345-189-3, PB-1893). Monthly Rev.

Marxism & the Good Society. Ed. by John P. Burke et al. 224p. Date not set. price not set (ISBN 0-521-23392-5). Cambridge U Pr.

Marxism & the Mass Media: Towards a Basic Bibliography, Nos. 1-2-3. rev. ed. Ed. by Intl. Mass Media Research Ctr. International Mass Media Research Center. (Illus.). 106p. (Orig.). 1978. pap. 6.00 (ISBN 0-88477-009-5). Intl General.

Marxism & the Mass Media: Towards a Basic Bibliography, No. 4-5. International Mass Media Research Center. (Illus.). 96p. (Orig.). 1976. pap. 6.00 (ISBN 0-88477-007-9). Intl General.

Marxism & the Muslim World. Maxime Rodinson. 1979. text ed. 24.50 o.p. (ISBN 0-685-63693-3, 0-911156-33-2). Porter.

Marxism & the Problems of Linguistics. Joseph Stalin. pap. 1.00 (ISBN 0-8351-0150-9). China Bks.

Marxism & the Science of War. Ed. by Bernard Semmel. 288p. 1981. 37.50 (ISBN 0-19-876112-0); pap. 17.95 (ISBN 0-19-876113-9). Oxford U Pr.

Marxism, Feminism & Free Love: The Story of the Ruskin Commonwealth. Francelia Butler & Jan Bakker. (Illus.). 140p. 1980. Repr. lib. bdg. 12.95x (ISBN 0-87991-034-8). Porcupine Pr.

Marxism Ideology & Literature. C. Slaughter. 1979. text ed. 20.00x (ISBN 0-391-01190-1); pap. text ed. 10.25x (ISBN 0-333-23217-8). Humanities.

Marxism in Modern France. George Lichtheim. LC 66-14788. 1966. 20.00x (ISBN 0-231-02908-X); pap. 6.00x (ISBN 0-231-08584-2). Columbia U Pr.

Marxism in the Modern World. Ed. by Milorad M. Drachkovitch. 1965. 12.50x (ISBN 0-8047-0254-3); pap. 3.25 o.p. (ISBN 0-8047-0255-1). Stanford U Pr.

Marxism of Marx. John Lewis. 266p. 1972. pap. text ed. 8.95x o.p. (ISBN 0-8464-0614-4). Beekman Pubs.

Marxism, Science & the Movement of History. Burger et al. (Philosophical Currents Ser.: No. 27). 1981. pap. text ed. 34.25x. Humanities.

Marxist Analysis & Social Anthropology. Ed. by Maurice Bloch. LC 75-4109. (Association of Social Anthropologists Studies: No. 3). 240p. 1975. 19.95 (ISBN 0-470-08205-4). Halsted Pr.

Marxist Conception of Ideology. M. Seliger. LC 76-11092. (International Studies). 1977. 29.50 (ISBN 0-521-21229-4); pap. 10.50x (ISBN 0-521-29625-0). Cambridge U Pr.

Marxist Model of Social Change. R. R. Sharma. 256p. 1980. text ed. 14.50x (ISBN 0-391-01766-7). Humanities.

Marxist Models of Literary Realism. George Bisztray. LC 77-23833. 1978. 14.00x (ISBN 0-231-04310-4). Columbia U Pr.

Marxist Perspectives in the Sociology of Education. Maurice Levitas. 216p. 1974. 21.00x (ISBN 0-7100-7896-X); pap. 8.95 (ISBN 0-7100-7897-8). Routledge & Kegan.

Marxist Philosophy of Ernest Bloch. C. Wayne Hudson. Date not set. price not set (ISBN 0-312-51860-9). St Martin.

Marxist Social Thought. Ed. by Robert Freedman. LC 68-13362. (Orig.). 1968. pap. 4.95 o.p. (ISBN 0-15-657650-3, HB137, Harv). HarBraceJ.

Marxist Theories of Imperialism. Anthony Brewer. 304p. 1980. 35.00 (ISBN 0-7100-0531-8); pap. 16.50 (ISBN 0-7100-0621-7). Routledge & Kegan.

Marxist Theory of Schooling: A Study in Epistemology & Education. Michael Matthews. 1981. text ed. 30.00x (ISBN 0-391-01801-9). Humanities.

Marx's Capital & Capitalism Today, Vol. 1. Antony Cutler et al. 1977. 22.00x (ISBN 0-7100-8745-4); pap. 10.50 (ISBN 0-7100-8746-2). Routledge & Kegan.

Marx's Capital & Capitalism Today, Vol. 2. Antony Cutler et al. 1978. 22.00x (ISBN 0-7100-8855-8); pap. 10.50 (ISBN 0-7100-8856-6). Routledge & Kegan.

Marx's Economics: A Dual Theory of Value & Growth. M. Morishima. LC 72-83591. (Illus.). 224p. 1973. 32.95 (ISBN 0-521-08747-3); pap. 14.95x (ISBN 0-521-29303-0). Cambridge U Pr.

Marx's Interpretation of History. Melvin Rader. 1979. 14.95x (ISBN 0-19-502474-5); pap. text ed. 5.95x (ISBN 0-19-502475-3). Oxford U Pr.

Marx's Politics: Communists & Citizens. Alan Gilbert. 320p. 1981. 19.00 (ISBN 0-8135-0903-3). Rutgers U Pr.

Marx's Social Ontology. Carol C. Gould. 1978. 15.00x (ISBN 0-262-07071-5); pap. 5.95 (ISBN 0-262-57056-4). MIT Pr.

Marx's Theory of Alienation. I. Meszaros. 356p. 1973. text ed. 13.00x (ISBN 0-85036-144-3). Humanities.

Marx's Theory of Alienation. Istvan Meszaros. 1970. pap. 10.95 (ISBN 0-686-23498-7, Merlin Pr). Carrier Pigeon.

Marx's Theory of Politics. J. M. Maguire. LC 77-90214. 1979. 29.95 (ISBN 0-521-21955-8). Cambridge U Pr.

Mary. Richard J. Cushing. 1960. 3.50 o.s.i. (ISBN 0-8198-0087-2); pap. 2.25 o.s.i. (ISBN 0-8198-0088-0). Dghtrs St Paul.

Mary, a Fiction. Mary Wollstonecraft. Ed. by Gina Luria. (Feminist Controversy in England, 1788-1810 Ser.). 1974. lib. bdg. 50.00 (ISBN 0-8240-0888-X). Garland Pub.

Mary: A History of Doctrine & Devotion, 2 Vols. Hilda C. Graef. (Illus.). 1963-66. Vol. 1. 5.95 o.p. (ISBN 0-8362-0118-3, Pub. by Sheed); Vol. 2. 4.00 o.p. (ISBN 0-8362-0072-1, Pub. by Sheed). Guild Bks.

Mary Alice, Operator Number Nine. Jeffrey Allen. (Illus.). 32p. (gr. 1-3). 1976. 6.95 (ISBN 0-316-03425-8). Little.

Mary: An Autobiography. Mary E. Mebane. LC 80-51999. 256p. 1981. 12.95 (ISBN 0-670-45938-0). Viking Pr.

Mary & the Fathers of the Church. Date not set. cancelled (ISBN 0-8198-0626-9). Dghtrs St Paul.

Mary Anne. Daphne Du Maurier. LC 76-184729. 352p. 1971. Repr. of 1954 ed. lib. bdg. 12.50x (ISBN 0-8376-0411-7). Bentley.

Mary Baker Eddy, Vol. 1: The Years of Discovery, 1821-1875. Robert Peel. 1972. 7.50 o.p. (ISBN 0-03-057555-9); pap. 3.95 (ISBN 0-03-086648-0). HR&W.

Mary Barnes: Two Accounts of a Journey Through Madness. Mary Barnes & Joe Berke. 1978. pap. 2.50 o.p. (ISBN 0-345-27527-6). Ballantine.

Mary Barnes: Two Accounts of Journey Through Madness. Mary Barnes & Joseph Berke. 1973. pap. 1.95 o.p. (ISBN 0-345-23221-6). Ballantine.

Mary Barton. Elizabeth Gaskell. 1961. 7.50x (ISBN 0-460-00598-7, Evman); pap. 4.50 (ISBN 0-460-01598-2). Dutton.

Mary Brown: From Harper's Ferry to California. Daniel Rosenberg. (Occasional Papers: No. 17). 1976. pap. 1.50 (ISBN 0-89977-024-X). Am Inst Marxist.

Mary Cassatt: Paintings & Prints. Frank Getlein. LC 80-66523. (Illus.). 160p. 1980. 22.50 (ISBN 0-89659-181-6); pap. 14.95 (ISBN 0-89659-155-7). Abbeville Pr.

Mary Catherine & the Little Pig's Tail. Dorothy V. Coke. (Illus.). 1981. 4.95 (ISBN 0-533-04761-7). Vantage.

Mary Celeste. Stanley Miller. 182p. 1981. 9.95 (ISBN 0-312-51862-5). St Martin.

Mary Chesnut's Civil War. Ed. by C. Vann Woodward. LC 80-36661. (Illus.). 960p. 1981. 29.95x (ISBN 0-300-02459-2). Yale U Pr.

Mary Colter: Builder Upon the Red Earth. Virginia L. Grattan. LC 79-52507. (Illus.). 1980. 15.50 (ISBN 0-87358-197-0); pap. 9.95 (ISBN 0-87358-198-9). Northland.

Mary Ellen's Best of Helpful Hints. Mary E. Pinkham & Pearl Higgenbotham. (Illus.). 144p. 1979. deluxe ed. 7.95 (ISBN 0-446-51211-7); pap. 4.50 (ISBN 0-446-97752-7). Warner Bks.

Mary Ellen's Best of Helpful Kitchen Hints. Mary E. Pinkham. (Illus., Orig.). 1980. pap. 4.50 (ISBN 0-446-97212-6). Warner Bks.

Mary, Hope of the World. James Alberione. 1958. 4.00 o.s.i. (ISBN 0-8198-0089-9); pap. 3.00 o.s.i. (ISBN 0-8198-0090-2). Dghtrs St Paul.

Mary I: The History of an Unhappy Tudor Queen. Winifred Roll. (Illus.). 1979. 9.95g (ISBN 0-13-559096-5). P-H.

Mary in the New Testament: A Collaborative Assessment by Protestant & Roman Catholic Scholars. Ed. by Raymond E. Brown et al. LC 78-8797. 336p. 1978. pap. 3.95 (ISBN 0-8006-1345-7, 1-1345). Fortress.

Mary Jo's Grandmother. Janice M. Udry. LC 78-126433. (Mary Jo Stories Ser). (Illus.). 32p. (gr. k-3). 1970. 6.95g (ISBN 0-8075-4984-3). A Whitman.

Mary Lacey. Maureen Connell. LC 80-7893. 288p. 1981. 10.95 (ISBN 0-690-01950-5, HarpT). Har-Row.

Mary Lavin. Richard Peterson. (English Author Ser.: No. 239). 1978. 12.50 (ISBN 0-8057-6707-X). Twayne.

Mary Lyons of Putnam Hill. Evelyn I. Banning. LC 66-10683. (gr. 4 up). 1965. 6.95 (ISBN 0-8149-0269-3). Vanguard.

Mary McLeod Bethune. Eloise Greenfield. LC 76-11522. (Biography Ser.). (Illus.). (gr. 2-5). 1977. PLB 7.89 (ISBN 0-690-01129-6, TYC-J). T Y Crowell.

Mary Magdalene & the Theory of Sin, 2 vols. Felix De Simoni. LC 72-84832. (Illus.). 35p. 1972. 77.50 (ISBN 0-913314-04-8). Am Classical Coll Pr.

Mary-Marie. Eleanor H. Porter. 1976. lib. bdg. 14.25x (ISBN 0-89968-102-6). Lightyear.

Mary Martin's Needlepoint. Mary Martin. LC 70-79725. (Illus.). 1969. 15.95 o.p. (ISBN 0-688-02060-7); pap. 5.95 o.p. (ISBN 0-688-05207-X). Morrow.

Mary Musgrove: Georgia Indian Princess. Helen Todd. LC 80-54424. 147p. (gr. 6-12). 1981. pap. 4.49 (ISBN 0-9605514-0-9). Seven Oaks.

Mary Myth: On the Femininity of God. Andrew M. Greeley. 1977. 12.95 (ISBN 0-8164-0333-3). Crossroad NY.

Mary Peters. Mary E. Chase. 1944. 4.95 o.s.i. (ISBN 0-02-524330-6). Macmillan.

Mary Pickford: Comedienne. LC 72-103050. (Illus.). 1969. 10.00 (ISBN 0-913986-02-X). Locare.

Mary Plain Goes to America. Gwynedd Rae. 1957. 6.25 (ISBN 0-7100-1997-1). Routledge & Kegan.

Mary Plain's 'whodunit' Gwynedd Rae. 1965. 7.25 (ISBN 0-7100-1999-8). Routledge & Kegan.

Mary Powell & Deborah's Diary. Anne Manning et al. Ed. by Ernest Rhys. 228p. 1980. Repr. lib. bdg. 20.00 (ISBN 0-8495-3796-7). Arden Lib.

Mary Shelley. William A. Walling. (English Authors Ser.: No. 128). lib. bdg. 10.95 (ISBN 0-8057-1484-7). Twayne.

Mary Sidney, Countess of Pembroke: A Critical Study of Her Writings & Literary Milieu. G. F. Waller. (Elizabethan Studies: No. 87). 1980. pap. text ed. 25.00x (ISBN 0-391-02161-3). Humanities.

Mary, the Spirit & the Church. Vincent Branick. LC 80-82856. 128p. (Orig.). 1981. pap. 4.95 (ISBN 0-8091-2343-6). Paulist Pr.

Mary Thomas's Book of Knitting Patterns. Mary Thomas. (Illus.). 340p. 1972. pap. 4.50 (ISBN 0-486-22818-5). Dover.

Mary Tudor, the White Queen. Walter C. Richardson. LC 68-11050. (Illus.). 1969. 10.00 o.p. (ISBN 0-295-95006-4). U of Wash Pr.

Mary Tyler Moore. David Paige. (Stars of Stage & Screen Ser.). (Illus.). (gr. 4-12). 1977. PLB 5.50 o.p. (ISBN 0-87191-559-6). Creative Ed.

Mary Wakefield. Mazo De La Roche. 1977. pap. 1.50 o.p. (ISBN 0-449-23057-0, Crest). Fawcett.

Mary Wollstonecraft: A Critical Biography. Ralph M. Wardle. LC 51-12250. 1966. pap. 3.75x (ISBN 0-8032-5211-0, BB 340, Bison). U of Nebr Pr.

Maryland. Carl Bode. (States & the Nation Ser.). (Illus.). 1978. 12.95 (ISBN 0-393-05672-4, Co-Pub by AASLH). Norton.

Maryland. 28.00 (ISBN 0-89770-096-1). Curriculum Info Ctr.

Maryland: A Guide to the Old Line State. Federal Writers' Project. 1940. Repr. 49.00 (ISBN 0-403-02171-5). Somerset Pub.
Maryland: A History, 1632-1974. Richard Walsh & William L. Fox. LC 74-11875. (Illus.). 1974. 12.50 (ISBN 0-938420-09-7). Md Hist.
Maryland Chronology & Factbook, Vol. 20. R. I. Vexler. 1978. 8.50 (ISBN 0-379-16145-1). Oceana.
Maryland Colony. F. Van Wyck Mason. LC 69-10782. (Forge of Freedom Ser). (Illus.). (gr. 5 up). 1969. 8.95 (ISBN 0-02-762870-1, CCPr). Macmillan.
Maryland Folk Legends & Folk Songs. George C. Carey. LC 75-180857. 1971. pap. 4.00 (ISBN 0-87033-158-2, Pub. by Tidewater). Cornell Maritime.
Maryland Folklore & Folklife. George G. Carey. LC 71-142189. (Illus.). 1971. pap. 5.00 (ISBN 0-87033-154-X, Pub. by Tidewater). Cornell Maritime.
Maryland Heritage: Five Baltimore Institutions Celebrate the Bicentennial. Ed. by John B. Boles. LC 76-10079. (Illus.). 1976. 16.00 (ISBN 0-938420-10-0); pap. 7.50 (ISBN 0-686-16684-1). Md Hist.
Maryland Main & the Eastern Shore. Hulbert Footner. LC 67-1719. 1967. Repr. of 1942 ed. 15.00 (ISBN 0-8103-5034-3). Gale.
Maryland Manual of Oral History. Betty M. Key. 1979. 2.00 (ISBN 0-938420-11-9). Md Hist.
Maryland Manual: 1979-1980. Ed. by Edward C. Papenfuse & Gregory A. Stiverson, Jr. (Illus.). 1979. 8.00 (ISBN 0-686-21209-6). MD Hall Records.
Maryland Pattern Jury Instructions: Civil. Committee on Pattern Jury Instructions of the Maryland Bar Association, Inc. LC 77-72007. 1977. 47.50 (ISBN 0-686-21281-9). Lawyers Co-Op.
Maryland Rules of Procedure Annotated (Red Book) 1979. Ed. by Michie Editorial Staff. 1352p. pap. 30.00 o.p. (ISBN 0-87215-242-1). Michie.
Maryland State Industrial Directory 1980. State Industrial Directories Corp. 1980. pap. 35.00 (ISBN 0-89910-040-6). State Indus Dir.
Maryland Supplement for Modern Real Estate Practice. rev. 2nd ed. H. Warren Crawford & John F. Rodgers. 176p. (Orig.). 1978. pap. 9.25 (ISBN 0-88462-303-3). Real Estate Ed Co.
Maryland Supplement for Modern Real Estate Practice. 3rd ed. H. Warren Crawford & John F. Rodgers. 140p. (Orig.). 1981. pap. 7.95 (ISBN 0-88462-267-3). Real Estate Ed Co.
Mary's Baby. Lyle J. Randegart. 1981. 6.75 (ISBN 0-8062-1656-5). Carlton.
Mary's Little Donkey. Gunhild Sehlin. (Illus.). 1979. 7.95 (ISBN 0-903540-29-0, Pub. by Floris Books). St George Bk Serv.
Marzipan Moon. Nancy Willard. LC 80-24221. (Illus.). 48p. (ps-3). 1981. pap. 4.95 (ISBN 0-15-252963-2, VoyB). HarBraceJ.
Marzipan Moon. Nancy Willard. LC 80-24221. (Illus.). 48p. (ps-3). 1981. 9.95 (ISBN 0-15-252962-4, HJ). HarBraceJ.
Mas Cuentos Picantes de Rosendo Rosell. Rosendo Rosell. LC 79-5001. (Coleccion Caniqui). (Illus.). 138p. 1980. pap. 5.95 (ISBN 0-89729-219-7). Ediciones.
Mas Oyama's Essential Karate. Mas Oyama. LC 77-79509. (Illus.). 1978. 14.95 (ISBN 0-8069-4120-0); lib. bdg. 14.99 (ISBN 0-8069-4121-9). Sterling.
Mas Que Pajarillos. Tr. by Mary Welch. (Spanish Bks.). (Span.). 1977. 1.60 (ISBN 0-8297-0749-2). Life Pubs Intl.
Mas Vale Creerlo. 1980. pap. 1.60 (ISBN 0-686-69361-2). Vida Pubs.
Masacio. Christopher Lloyd. (Oresko-Jupiter Art Bks). (Illus.). 96p. 1981. 17.95 (ISBN 0-933516-86-X, Pub. by Oresko-Jupiter England). Hippocrene Bks.
Masada. Gann. pap. 2.75 (ISBN 0-515-05443-7). BJ Pub Group.
Masada. Ernest K. Gann. Orig. Title: Antagonists. 320p. 1981. pap. 2.95 (ISBN 0-515-05443-7). Jove Pubns.
Masada Plan. Leonard Harris. 1981. pap. 2.75 (ISBN 0-445-04189-7). Popular Lib.
Masai: Herders of East Africa. Sonia Bleeker. (Illus.). (gr. 3-6). 1963. PLB 6.67 (ISBN 0-688-31460-0). Morrow.
Masamune Hakucho. Robert Rolf. (World Authors Ser.: No. 533). 1979. lib. bdg. 14.95 (ISBN 0-8057-6375-9). Twayne.
Masaryks: The Making of Czechoslovakia. Zbynek Zeman. LC 76-2316. (Illus.). 230p. 1976. text ed. 19.50x (ISBN 0-06-497968-7). B&N.
Masarykuv Slovnik Naucny, 7 vols. (Bohemian.). 1925-1933. Set. 435.00 (ISBN 0-8277-3050-0). Maxwell Sci Intl.
Masculine-Feminine or Human. 2nd ed. Janet S. Chafetz. LC 77-83425. 1978. pap. text ed. 7.50 (ISBN 0-87581-231-7). Peacock Pubs.
Masculine Focus in Home Economics. B. Greenwood & J. Dowell. LC 75-10815. 1975. pap. 2.50 (ISBN 0-686-14990-4, 261-08422). Home Econ Educ.
Masculinity & Femininity: Their Psychological Dimensions, Correlates & Antecedents. Janet T. Spence & Robert L. Helmreich. LC 77-10693. (Illus.). 1978. 14.95x o.p. (ISBN 0-292-76443-X). U of Tex Pr.
MASH: A Computer System for Microanalytic Simulation for Policy Exploration. George Sadowsky. 158p. 1977. pap. 9.00 (ISBN 0-87766-190-1, 17600). Urban Inst.
MASH: The Exclusive Inside Story of TV's Most Popular Show. David Reiss. LC 80-685. (Illus.). 160p. pap. 8.95 (ISBN 0-672-52656-5). Bobbs.
Mashenka. Vladimir Nabokov. (Rus.). 1979. 15.00 (ISBN 0-88233-092-6); pap. 6.00 (ISBN 0-88233-093-4). Ardis Pubs.
Mask. Eve Bunting. (Science Fiction Ser.). (Illus.). (gr. 3-9). 1978. PLB 5.95 (ISBN 0-87191-625-8); pap. 2.95 (ISBN 0-89812-056-X). Creative Ed.
Mask-Making. Chester J. Alkema. LC 80-54343. (Illus.). 96p. 8.95 (ISBN 0-8069-7038-3); lib. bdg. 8.29 (ISBN 0-8069-7039-1). Sterling.
Mask Making. rev ed. Matthew Baranski. LC 54-12542. (Illus.). (gr. 3-9). 1966. 7.75 o.p. (ISBN 0-87192-016-6). Davis Mass.
Mask of Cthulhu. August Derleth. 1976. pap. 1.50 o.p. (ISBN 0-345-25095-8). Ballantine.
Mask of Dust. W. C. Chalk. pap. text ed. 2.75x o.p. (ISBN 0-435-11227-9). Heinemann Ed.
Mask of Love. Julia Thatcher. (Orig.). 1980. pap. 1.95 (ISBN 0-445-04553-1). Popular Lib.
Mask of Religion. G. Peter Fleck. LC 79-9644. (Library of Liberal Religion). 204p. 1980. 7.95 (ISBN 0-87975-125-8). Prometheus Bks.
Mask of Sanity. 5th ed. Hervey M. Cleckley. LC 75-31875. 544p. 1976. 23.50 (ISBN 0-8016-0985-2). Mosby.
Mask of the Enchantress. Victoria Holt. 1980. lib. bdg. 16.95 (ISBN 0-8161-3142-2, Large Print Bks). G K Hall.
Mask of the Jaguar. Jessica North. 288p. 1981. 10.95 (ISBN 0-698-11050-1). Coward.
Mask, the Unicorn & the Messiah: A Study in Solar-Eclipse Symbolism. Elmer G. Suhr. (Illus.). 1970. 7.95 (ISBN 0-87037-025-1). Helios.
Maske: Thaery. Jack Vance. 1976. 7.95 o.p. (ISBN 0-399-11797-0). Berkley Pub.
Masked Gods: Navaho & Pueblo Ceremonialism. Frank Waters. LC 73-1799. 438p. 1950. 15.00 (ISBN 0-8040-0196-0, SB); pap. 7.95 (ISBN 0-8040-0641-5, SB). Swallow.
Masks. Chester J. Alkema. (Little Craft Book Ser). (Illus.). (gr. 5 up). 1971. 4.95 o.p. (ISBN 0-8069-5166-4); PLB 5.89 o.p. (ISBN 0-8069-5167-2). Sterling.
Masks. Krystyna Baker. Date not set. price not set (ISBN 0-89672-086-1); price not set ltd. signed ed. (ISBN 0-89672-092-6); pap. price not set (ISBN 0-89672-085-3). Tex Tech Pr.
Masks & Mask Makers. Kari Hunt & Bernice W. Carlson. (Illus.). (gr. 4 up). 1961. 5.95 (ISBN 0-687-23705-X). Abingdon.
Masks, Modes, & Morals: The Art of Evelyn Waugh. William J. Cook, Jr. LC 73-118125. 1971. 18.00 (ISBN 0-8386-7707-X). Fairleigh Dickinson.
Masks of Black Africa. Ladislas Segy. 11.50 (ISBN 0-8446-5455-8). Peter Smith.
Masks of Hate: The Problem of False Solutions in the Culture of an Acquisitive Society. David Holbrook. 276p. 1976. Repr. of 1972 ed. 26.00 (ISBN 0-08-015799-8). Pergamon.
Masks of King Lear. Marvin Rosenberg. LC 74-115492. 448p. 1972. 22.75x (ISBN 0-520-01718-8). U of Cal Pr.
Masks of Loneliness: Alfred Adler in Perspective. Manes Sperber. LC 73-13167. 250p. 1974. 7.95 o.s.i. (ISBN 0-02-612950-7). Macmillan.
Masks of Macbeth. Marvin Rosenberg. 1978. 35.00x (ISBN 0-520-03262-4). U of Cal Pr.
Masks of the Dreamer. Mike Lowery. LC 79-65336. (Wesleyan Poetry Program: Vol. 96). 1979. 10.00x (ISBN 0-8195-2096-9, Pub. by Wesleyan U Pr); pap. 4.95 (ISBN 0-8195-1096-3). Columbia U Pr.
Masks of the Illuminati. Robert A. Wilson. (Orig.). 1981. pap. 2.95 (ISBN 0-671-82585-2). PB.
Masks of the Soul. Jolande Jacobi. 1976. pap. text ed. 2.95 o.p. (ISBN 0-8028-1656-8). Eerdmans.
Masks of Time. Robert Silverberg. 1973. pap. 1.25 o.p. (ISBN 0-345-23446-4). Ballantine.
Masks Tents Vessels Talismans. Janet Kardon. LC 79-92164. (Illus.). 1979. pap. 5.00 (ISBN 0-88454-053-7). U of Pa Contemp Art.
Masochism, an Interpretation of Coldness & Cruelty. Gilles Deleuze. LC 78-148733. Orig. Title: Sacher-Masoch: Une Interpretation. 1971. 6.95 o.p. (ISBN 0-8076-0561-1). Braziller.
Mason Oaks: An Online Case Study in Business Systems Design. Alan L. Eliason. 128p. 1981. pap. text ed. 5.95 (ISBN 0-574-21310-4, 13-4310); instr's guide avail. (ISBN 0-574-21311-2, 13-4311). SRA.
Mason Porcelain & Ironstone, 1796-1853. Reginald Haggar & Elizabeth Adams. (Illus.). 1977. 42.00 (ISBN 0-571-10945-4, Pub. by Faber & Faber). Merrimack Bk Serv.
Masonic Thread in Mozart. Katharine Thomson. (Illus.). 1977. text ed. 13.50x (ISBN 0-85315-381-7). Humanities.
Masonry. Boy Scouts Of America. LC 19-600. (Illus.). 64p. (gr. 6-12). 1952. pap. 0.55x o.p. (ISBN 0-8395-3339-X, 3339). BSA.
Masonry. (Home Repair & Improvement Ser.). (Illus.). 1976. 10.95 (ISBN 0-8094-2362-6). Time-Life.
Masonry. (Illus.). 64p. (gr. 6-12). 1980. pap. 0.70x. BSA.
Masonry. Ed. by Time Life Books. LC 76-25711. (Home Repair & Improvement). (Illus.). (gr. 7 up). 1976. PLB 11.97 (ISBN 0-8094-2363-4, Pub. by Time-Life). Silver.
Masonry & Concrete. Monte Burch. Ed. by Shirley Horowitz & Gail Kummings. (Illus.). 144p. (Orig.). 1981. pap. 6.95 (ISBN 0-932944-30-2). Creative Homeowner.
Masonry & Concrete. Byron W. Maguire. (Illus.). 1978. ref. ed. 18.95 (ISBN 0-87909-521-0). Reston.
Masonry Contractors Handbook. Kenneth Nolan. 256p. (Orig.). 1981. pap. 13.50 (ISBN 0-910460-81-7). Craftsman.
Masonry Skills. Richard T. Kreh. LC 75-27994. 1976. pap. 10.80 (ISBN 0-8273-1090-0); instructor's guide 1.60 (ISBN 0-8273-1091-9). Delmar.
Masons & Builders Library, 2 vols. 2nd ed. Louis M. Dezettel. LC 78-186134. (Illus.). 1972. 9.95 ea. Vol. 1 (ISBN 0-672-23182-4, 23182). Vol. 2 (ISBN 0-672-23183-2, 23183). Set. 17.95 (ISBN 0-672-23185-9, 23185). Audel.
Masquerade. Susan Shreve. LC 79-20073. 224p. 1980. 7.95 (ISBN 0-394-84142-5); PLB 7.99 (ISBN 0-394-94142-X). Knopf.
Masquerade. Cecilia Sternberg. 1981. pap. 2.75 (ISBN 0-451-09603-7, E9603, Sig). NAL.
Masquerade. Kit Williams. LC 80-14127. (Illus.). 32p. 1980. 9.95 (ISBN 0-8052-3747-X). Schocken.
Masquerade: Amazing Deception & Camouflage Strategies of World War II. Seymour Reit. LC 77-70122. (Illus.). 1978. 11.95 o.p. (ISBN 0-8015-4931-0). Dutton.
Masqueraders. Georgette Heyer. 1979. pap. 2.25 (ISBN 0-449-23253-0, Crest). Fawcett.
Masques. Bill Pronzini. LC 80-70219. 288p. 1981. 11.95 (ISBN 0-87795-308-2). Arbor Hse.
Mass Advertising As Social Forecast: A Method for Futures Research. Robert B. Fowles. LC 75-35344. (Illus.). 160p. 1976. lib. bdg. 13.95 (ISBN 0-8371-8595-5, FMA/). Greenwood.
Mass Appeal. Bill C. Davis. 80p. 1981. pap. 2.50 (ISBN 0-380-77396-1, Bard). Avon.
Mass Communication. 2nd ed. John R. Bittner. (Ser. in Speech Communication). (Illus.). 1980. pap. text ed. 14.95 (ISBN 0-13-559278-X). P-H.
Mass Communication: An Introduction Theory & Practice of Mass Media in Society. J. Bittner. (Speech Communication Ser.). 1977. text ed. 14.95 o.p. (ISBN 0-13-559310-7); pap. text ed. 11.95 o.p. (ISBN 0-13-559302-6); teaching mass communication o.p. avail. o.p. (ISBN 0-685-78781-8). P-H.
Mass Communication & Everyday Life: A Perspective on Theory & Effects. Dennis K. Davis & Stanley J. Baran. 240p. 1980. pap. text ed. 7.95x (ISBN 0-534-00883-6). Wadsworth Pub.
Mass Communication & Journalism in India. D. S. Mehta. 1979. 15.00x o.p. (ISBN 0-8364-0450-5). South Asia Bks.
Mass Communication & Society. Ed. by James Curran et al. LC 78-68700. 1979. pap. 9.95x (ISBN 0-8039-1193-9). Sage.
Mass Communication Research: Major Issues & Future Directions. Ed. by W. Phillips Davison & Frederick T. C. Yu. LC 74-5576. (Special Studies). 215p. 1974. 20.95 o.p. (ISBN 0-275-09320-4); pap. 9.95 student ed. o.p. (ISBN 0-275-88870-3). Praeger.
Mass Communication Review Yearbook, Vol. 1. Ed. by G. Cleveland Wilhoit & Harold De Bock. (Illus.). 751p. 1980. 35.00x (ISBN 0-8039-1186-6). Sage.
Mass Communication: Teaching & Studies at University. May Katzen. 278p. 1975. pap. text ed. 17.00 (ISBN 92-3-101158-8, U369, UNESCO). Unipub.
Mass Communications. James D. Halloran. 90p. 1980. text ed. write for info. (ISBN 0-7185-1128-X, Leicester). Humanities.
Mass Communications. Ed. by William P. Lineberry. (Reference Shelf Ser: Vol. 41, No. 3). 1969. 6.25 (ISBN 0-8242-0108-6). Wilson.
Mass Communications. R. A. Vogel & M. Krabbe. LC 76-44136. (Ser. in Speech Communication). 1977. pap. text ed. 5.95 (ISBN 0-8465-7601-5); instr's. guide 3.95 (ISBN 0-8465-7607-4). Benjamin-Cummings.
Mass Communications & Youth: Some Current Perspectives. Ed. by F. Gerald Kline & Peter Clarke. LC 73-89939. (Sage Contemporary Social Science Issues: No. 5). 1974. 4.95x (ISBN 0-8039-0335-9). Sage.
Mass Communications Dictionary: A Reference Work of Common Terminologies for Press, Print, Broadcast, Film, Advertising & Communications Research. Ed. by Howard B. Jacobson. Repr. of 1961 ed. lib. bdg. 25.00x (ISBN 0-8371-2124-8, JAMC). Greenwood.
Mass Communications Law, Cases & Comment. 3rd ed. Donald M. Gillmor & Jerome A. Barron. LC 79-15306. (American Casebook Ser.). 1008p. 1979. text ed. 19.95 (ISBN 0-8299-2050-1). West Pub.
Mass. Gen. Hosp. Handbook of General Hospital Psychiatry. Thomas P. Hackett & Ned H. Cassem. LC 78-15146. (Illus.). 1978. pap. 19.95 (ISBN 0-8016-0931-3). Mosby.
Mass Media. Stuart Hood. (Studies in Contemporary Europe). (Orig.). 1973. pap. text ed. 3.00x (ISBN 0-333-12704-8). Humanities.
Mass Media: An Introduction to Modern Communication. 2nd ed. Hiebert Bohn & Ungurait. LC 77-17721. (Illus.). 1979. pap. text ed. 12.95x (ISBN 0-582-28070-2). Longman.
Mass Media & Communication. 2nd rev. & enl. ed. Ed. by Charles S. Steinberg. (Studies in Public Communication). 650p. 1972. 14.00 o.s.i. (ISBN 0-8038-4664-9); pap. text ed. 8.50x (ISBN 0-8038-4663-0). Hastings.
Mass Media & Cultural Relationships. Anthony Piepe et al. 184p. 1977. text ed. 23.00x (ISBN 0-566-00161-6, Pub. by Gower Pub Co England). Renouf.
Mass Media & the First Amendment: An Introduction to the Issues, Problems, & Practices. Maurice R. Cullen, Jr. 1981. pap. text ed. write for info. (ISBN 0-697-04344-4); write for info. instr's. manual (ISBN 0-697-04346-0). Wm C Brown.
Mass Media & the Law in Illinois. Harry W. Stonecipher & Robert Trager. LC 76-25463. (New Horizons in Journalism Ser.). 256p. 1976. 14.95x (ISBN 0-8093-0788-X). S Ill U Pr.
Mass Media & the Popular Arts. F. Rissover & D. Birch. 12.95x (ISBN 0-07-052950-7, C); pap. 8.95 (ISBN 0-07-052944-2); instructor's manual 5.50 (ISBN 0-07-052944-2). McGraw.
Mass Media & the School Newspaper. De Witt C. Reddick. 1976. text ed. 13.95x (ISBN 0-534-00436-9). Wadsworth Pub.
Mass Media: Aspen Guide to Communication Industry Trends. Christopher H. Sterling & Timothy Haight. LC 76-24370. (Special Studies). 1978. text ed. 34.95 (ISBN 0-275-24020-7). Praeger.
Mass Media Book. Rod Holmgren & William Norton. 416p. 1972. pap. text ed. 10.95 (ISBN 0-13-559781-1). P-H.
Mass Media College Catalog. rev. ed. Ed. by Michael C. Helmantoler. 132p. 1980. pap. 15.00 (ISBN 0-87117-048-5). Am Assn Comm Jr Coll.
Mass Media, Education, & a Better Society. Jay W. Stein. LC 79-11517. 1979. 16.95 (ISBN 0-88229-310-9). Nelson-Hall.
Mass Media: How Americans Choose Their President. Thomas E. Patterson. 220p. 1980. 21.95 (ISBN 0-03-057728-4); pap. 8.95 (ISBN 0-03-057729-2). Praeger.
Mass Media, Ideologies & the Revolutionary Movement. Armand Mattelart. (Marxist Theory & Contemporary Capitalism Ser.: No. 30). 288p. 1980. text ed. 32.50x (ISBN 0-391-01777-2). Humanities.
Mass Media in America. 2nd ed. Don Pember. LC 76-50018. (Illus.). 1977. pap. text ed. 11.95 (ISBN 0-574-22705-9, 13-5705); instr's guide avail. (ISBN 0-574-22706-7, 13-5706). SRA.
Mass Media in America. 3rd ed. Don Pember. 416p. 1981. pap. text ed. 11.95 (ISBN 0-574-22715-6, 13-5715); instr's. guide avail. (ISBN 0-574-22716-4, 13-5716). SRA.
Mass Media in an African Context: An Evaluation of Senegal's Pilot Project. (Reports & Papers on Mass Communication, No. 69). 53p. (Orig.). 1974. pap. 2.50 (ISBN 92-3-101138-3, U370, UNESCO). Unipub.
Mass Media in Black Africa: Philosophy & Control. Dennis J. Wilcox. LC 74-30713. (Illus.). 188p. 1975. text ed. 18.95 o.p. (ISBN 0-275-05990-1). Praeger.
Mass Media in Society: The Need of Research. (Reports & Papers on Mass Communication Ser). (Orig.). 1970. pap. 2.50 (ISBN 92-3-100953-2, U372, UNESCO). Unipub.
Mass Media Issues: Analysis & Debate. George Rodman. 320p. 1981. pap. text ed. 10.95 (ISBN 0-574-22570-6, 13-5570). SRA.

Mass Media Issues: Articles & Commentaries. Leonard Sellers & William R. Rivers. (Illus.). 432p. 1977. pap. text ed. 12.95 (ISBN 0-13-559500-2). P-H.

Mass Media Law. 2nd ed. Don R. Pember. 500p. 1981. text ed. write for info. (ISBN 0-697-04347-9). Wm C Brown.

Mass Media Law & Regulation. 2nd ed. William E. Francois. LC 77-92582. (Law Ser.). 1978. 20.50 (ISBN 0-88244-168-X). Grid Pub.

Mass Media Policies in Changing Cultures. Ed. by George Gerbner. LC 77-2399. 1977. 27.50 (ISBN 0-471-01514-8, Pub. by Wiley-Interscience). Wiley.

Mass Media: Systems & Effects. W. Phillips Davison & James Boylan. LC 74-31000. 245p. 1976. pap. text ed. 10.95x (ISBN 0-03-038896-1). Praeger.

Mass Media Vs. the Italian Americans. Adolph Caso. 262p. 1980. 12.00 (ISBN 0-8283-1737-2). Dante U Am.

Mass Merchandising of Automobile Insurance. Bernard L. Webb. 309p. 1969. pap. 10.00 o.p. (ISBN 0-88245-007-7). Merritt Co.

Mass of the Roman Rite. Joseph Junemann. 25.00 (ISBN 0-87061-054-6). Chr Classics.

Mass Persuasion in History: An Historical Analysis of the Development of Propaganda Techniques. Oliver Thomson. 1977. 14.50 (ISBN 0-8448-1076-2). Crane-Russak Co.

Mass Persuasion: The Social Psychology of a War Bond Drive. Robert K. Merton. LC 77-136076. 1971. Repr. of 1946 ed. lib. bdg. 19.75x (ISBN 0-8371-5226-7, MEMP). Greenwood.

Mass Psychology of Fascism. Wilhelm Reich. Tr. by Vincent R. Carfagno. 1980. pap. write for info. (ISBN 0-374-50884-4). FS&G.

Mass Spectrometer. J. R. Majer & M. Berry. LC 77-15307. (Wykeham Science Ser.: No. 44). 1977. 16.95x (ISBN 0-8448-1171-8). Crane-Russak Co.

Mass Spectrometer Respiratory Monitoring Systems. American Society for Hospital Engineering. LC 79-26957. (Illus., Orig.). 1980. pap. 9.75 (ISBN 0-87258-279-5, 1167). Am Hospital.

Mass Spectrometry & Ion-Molecule Reactions. P. F. Knewstubb. LC 69-16282. (Cambridge Chemistry Textbooks Ser). (Illus.). 1969. 27.50 (ISBN 0-521-07489-4); pap. 11.50x (ISBN 0-521-09563-8). Cambridge U Pr.

Mass Spectrometry & NMR Spectroscopy in Pesticide Chemistry. Ed. by Rizwanel Haque & Francis J. Biros. LC 73-20005. (Environmental Science Research Ser.: Vol. 4). 348p. 1974. 35.00 (ISBN 0-306-36304-6, Plenum Pr). Plenum Pub.

Mass Spectrometry for Organic Chemists. R. A. Johnstone. (Illus.). 1972. 32.50 (ISBN 0-521-08381-8); pap. 11.95x (ISBN 0-521-09685-5). Cambridge U Pr.

Mass Spectrometry in Biochemistry & Medicine. Ed. by A. Frigerio & N. Castagnoli, Jr. LC 73-91164. (Monographs of the Mario Negri Institute for Pharmacological Research). 379p. 1974. 48.00 (ISBN 0-911216-53-7). Raven.

Mass Spectrometry in Drug Metabolism. Alberto Frigerio & Emilio L. Ghisalberti. LC 76-53013. 532p. 1977. 49.50 (ISBN 0-306-31018-X, Plenum Pr). Plenum Pub.

Mass Spectrometry of Steroids. Ze'Ev V. Zaretskei. LC 75-38916. 1976. 30.95 (ISBN 0-470-15225-7). Halsted Pr.

Mass Spectronomy, Pt. B. Merritt & McEwen. 416p. 1980. 49.75 (ISBN 0-8247-6947-3). Dekker.

Mass Transfer in Heterogeneous Catalysis. Charles N. Satterfield. LC 80-23432. 286p. 1981. Repr. of 1970 ed. text ed. write for info. (ISBN 0-89874-198-X). Krieger.

Mass Transfer Operations. 2nd ed. Robert E. Treybal. (Chemical Engineering Ser.). 1968. text ed. 26.50 (ISBN 0-07-065176-0, C); solutions manual 9.95 (ISBN 0-07-065177-9). McGraw.

Mass Transfer Operations. Robert E. Treybal. (Chemical Engineering Ser.). (Illus.). 1979. text ed. 29.00x (ISBN 0-07-065176-0, C). McGraw.

Massachusetts. 33.00 (ISBN 0-89770-097-X). Curriculum Info Ctr.

Massachusetts: A Guide to Its Places & People. Federal Writers' Project. 675p. 1937. Repr. 49.00 (ISBN 0-403-02150-2). Somerset Pub.

Massachusetts Bay: The Crucial Decade, 1640-1650. Robert E. Wall, Jr. LC 72-75210. 296p. 1972. 20.00x o.p. (ISBN 0-300-01484-8). Yale U Pr.

Massachusetts Colony. Robert Smith. LC 69-19575. (Forge of Freedom Ser). (Illus.). (gr. 5-8). 1969. 8.95 (ISBN 0-02-785880-4, CCPr). Macmillan.

Massachusetts Constitution: A Citizen's Edition. 2nd ed. Elwyn E Mariner. LC 72-166478. 1977. pap. 3.75 (ISBN 0-685-58338-4). Mariner.

Massachusetts General Hospital Department of Nursing Operating Room Procedure Manual. Massachusetts General Hospital. 1981. text ed. 13.95 (ISBN 0-8359-4252-X). Reston.

Massachusetts Help to Ireland During the Great Famine. Crosby Forbes & Henry Lee. LC 67-24085. (Illus.). 1967. 6.00x (ISBN 0-686-10827-2). Mus Am China.

Massachusetts: In Words & Pictures. Dennis Fradin. LC 80-26161. (Young People's Stories of Our States Ser.). (Illus.). 48p. (gr. 2-5). 1981. PLB 8.65g (ISBN 0-516-03921-0, Time Line). Childrens.

Massachusetts Retirement Plan. 9th ed. Elwyn E. Mariner. 1977. pap. 2.50. Mariner.

Massachusetts Supplement for Modern Real Estate Practice. 2nd ed. David L. Kent. 112p. (Orig.). 1979. pap. 7.95 (ISBN 0-88462-255-X). Real Estate Ed Co.

Massacre. Robert Payne. (Illus.). 192p. 1973. 5.95 o.s.i. (ISBN 0-02-595240-4). Macmillan.

Massacre: A Survey of Today's American Indian. Robert Gessner. LC 72-38831. (Civil Liberties in American History Ser). 418p. 1972. Repr. of 1931 ed. lib. bdg. 35.00 (ISBN 0-306-70445-5). Da Capo.

Massacre at Fall Creek. Jessamyn West. 320p. 1976. pap. 1.95 o.p. (ISBN 0-449-22771-5, C2771, Crest). Fawcett.

Massacre at Fort Caid. W. G. Schreiber. (YA) 1977. 5.95 (ISBN 0-685-74265-2, Avalon). Bouregy.

Massacre at Mountain Meadows: An American Legend & a Monumental Crime. William Wise. LC 76-16014. 1976. 11.95 o.s.i. (ISBN 0-690-01174-1, TYC-T). T Y Crowell.

Massacre at Paris: With the Death of the Duke of Guise. Christopher Marlowe. LC 73-25759. (English Experience Ser.: No. 335). 1971. Repr. of 1600 ed. 8.00 (ISBN 90-221-0335-8). Walter J Johnson.

Massacre at Salt Creek. Blaine M. Yorgason. LC 78-22744. 1979. 8.95 (ISBN 0-385-15200-0). Doubleday.

Massage & Bodywork Resource Guide. John Watson. (Illus.). 360p. (Orig.). 1981. pap. 6.95 (ISBN 0-913300-13-6). Unity Pr.

Massage & Meditation. George Downing. 1974. 7.95 o.p. (ISBN 0-394-49237-4); pap. 1.65 (ISBN 0-394-70648-X). Random.

Massage: The Loving Touch. Stephen Lewis. 1974. pap. 1.95 o.p. (ISBN 0-523-25135-1). Pinnacle Bks.

Massage: The Oriental Method. Katsusuke Seriwaza. LC 73-188762. (Illus.). 80p. 1972. 6.95 o.p. (ISBN 0-87040-080-0); pap. 6.95 (ISBN 0-87040-168-8). Japan Pubns.

Massee's Wine Almanac. William E. Massee. LC 80-13391. 240p. 1980. 12.95 (ISBN 0-13-559658-0); pap. 6.95 (ISBN 0-13-559641-6). P-H.

Masses & Man: Nationalist & Fascist Perceptions of Reality. George L. Mosse. LC 80-15399. xi, 362p. 1980. 25.00 (ISBN 0-86527-334-0). Fertig.

Masses in Latin America. Ed. by Irving L. Horowitz. LC 73-83045. 1970. 19.95 (ISBN 0-19-500586-4). Oxford U Pr.

Masses in Latin America. Ed. by Irving L. Horowitz. LC 73-83045. 1970. pap. 7.95 (ISBN 0-19-500795-6, 297, GB). Oxford U Pr.

Massimo Scolari. Ed. by Francesco Moschini. LC 80-50657. (Illus.). 240p. 1980. pap. 17.50 (ISBN 0-8478-0317-1). Rizzoli Intl.

Massine on Choreography: Theory & Exercises in Composition. Leonide Massine. (Illus.). 1977. 45.00 (ISBN 0-571-09302-7, Pub. by Faber & Faber). Merrimack Bk Serv.

Massinger & Field's "the Fatal Dowry" A Critical Edition. Carol Bishop. (Salzburg Studies in English Literature, Jacobean Drama Studies: No. 63). 267p. 1976. pap. text ed. 25.00x (ISBN 0-391-01326-2). Humanities.

Massinger's Imagery. Francis D. Evenhuis. (Salzburg Studies in English Literature, Jacobean Drama Studies: No. 14). 176p. 1973. pap. text ed. 25.00x (ISBN 0-391-01373-4). Humanities.

Massism Vs. Natural Religion. Gerald Tholen. 1980. pap. 3.00. Am Atheist.

Mastaba of Queen Mersyankh III, Vol. 1. Dows Dunham et al. (Illus.). 1974. 35.00 (ISBN 0-87846-174-4). Mus Fine Arts Boston.

Master. Tom Clark. 1979. 17.50x (ISBN 0-915316-65-X); pap. 4.50x (ISBN 0-915316-66-8). Pentagram.

Master & Man. Leo Tolstoy. Ed. by Eleanor Aitken. LC 70-77293. 1969. text ed. 14.50x (ISBN 0-521-07466-5). Cambridge U Pr.

Master & Margarita. M. Bulgakov. pap. 0.95 o.p. (ISBN 0-451-50699-5, CQ699, Sig Classics). NAL.

Master & Margarita. Mikhail Bulgakov. Tr. by Mirra Ginsburg from Russian. 1967. pap. 4.95 (ISBN 0-394-17439-9, B147, BC). Grove.

Master As I Saw Him. Sr. Nivedita. 6.50 (ISBN 0-87481-088-4). Vedanta Pr.

Master-at-Arms. Rafael Sabatini. 1977. pap. 1.95 o.p. (ISBN 0-685-75020-5, 345-25302-7-195). Ballantine.

Master Blender: Sound-Symbol Skillsbook. (Part of McInnis-Hammondsport Plan Ser.). (gr. k-6). 1981. 16.50 (ISBN 0-8027-9123-9). Walker & Co.

Master Book of Escapes. Donald McCormick. LC 74-10347. (Illus.). 192p. (gr. 5 up). 1975. PLB 4.95 o.p. (ISBN 0-531-02801-1). Watts.

Master Book of Mathematical Puzzles & Recreations. Fred Schuh. Ed. by T. H. O'Beirne. Tr. by F. Gobel. LC 68-28064. Orig. Title: Wonderlijke Problemen Leerzaam Tijoverdrijf Door Puzzle En Spel. (Illus.). 430p. 1969. pap. 4.95 (ISBN 0-486-22134-2). Dover.

Master Builder. Henrik Ibsen. 1979. 7.95x (ISBN 0-8464-0095-2). Beekman Pubs.

Master Builders: A History of Structural & Environmental Design from Ancient Egypt to the Nineteenth Century. Henry J. Cowan. LC 77-5125. 1977. 26.50 (ISBN 0-471-02740-5, Pub. by Wiley-Interscience). Wiley.

Master Crossword Puzzle Dictionary. Herbert M. Baus. (Thumb Indexed). 1981. 27.50 (ISBN 0-385-15118-7). Doubleday.

Master Fly Weaver (the Art of Weaving Hair Hackles) George Grant. 150p. 1980. 50.00x (ISBN 0-918400-03-1, Pub. by Champoeg Pr). Intl Schol Bk Serv.

Master Game. Robert S. De Ropp. 1968. 5.95 o.s.i. (ISBN 0-440-05481-8, Sey Lawr). Delacorte.

Master Guide to Electronic Circuits. Thomas M. Adams. (Illus.). 616p. 1980. 19.95 o.p. (ISBN 0-8306-9971-6); pap. 15.95 (ISBN 0-8306-1184-3, 1184). TAB Bks.

Master H. LC 61-17664. 1976. 5.00 (ISBN 0-935490-05-1). Euclid Pub.

Master Handbook of Digital Logic Applications. William Hunter. LC 76-24788. (Illus.). 1976. 12.95 o.p. (ISBN 0-8306-6874-8); pap. 7.95 (ISBN 0-8306-5874-2). TAB Bks.

Master Handbook of Electrical Wiring. Art Margolis. (Illus.). 1978. pap. 9.95 (ISBN 0-8306-1019-7, 1019). TAB Bks.

Master Handbook of One Thousand and One Practical Electronic Circuits. Ed. by Ken Sessions. LC 75-31458. 602p. 1975. pap. 13.95 (ISBN 0-8306-4800-3, 800). TAB Bks.

Master Hi-Fi Loudspeakers & Enclosures. D. Berriman. 1979. pap. 5.95 (ISBN 0-8104-0845-7, Co-Pub. by Newnes Butterworth England). Hayden.

Master Index to the J. F. K. Assassination Investigation: The Reports & Supporting Volumes of the House Select Committee on Assassinations & the Warren Commission. Sylvia Meagher & Gary Owens. LC 80-17494. xii, 435p. 1980. 20.00 (ISBN 0-8108-1331-9). Scarecrow.

Master Key Systems & Run up. (Gambler's Book Shelf). 1977. pap. 2.95 (ISBN 0-89650-583-9). Gamblers.

Master-Key to Riches. Napoleon Hill. 1978. pap. 2.25 (ISBN 0-449-23953-5, Crest). Fawcett.

Master Lawnmower Repair Book. Harold Fichter. (Illus.). 1978. pap. 7.95 (ISBN 0-8306-1067-7, 1067). TAB Bks.

Master Manager. R. G. Siu. LC 80-13390. 341p. 1980. 17.50 (ISBN 0-471-07961-8). Wiley.

Master Mariner: Darken Ship. Nicholas Monsarrat. LC 80-20222. (Illus.). 192p. 1981. 9.95 (ISBN 0-688-00017-7). Morrow.

Master Minds: Portraits of Contemporary American Artists & Intellectuals. Richard Kostelanetz. 1969. 7.95 o.s.i. (ISBN 0-02-566510-3). Macmillan.

Master of Ballantrae. Robert L. Stevenson. Incl. Weir of Hermiston. 1956. 11.50x (ISBN 0-460-00764-5, Evman); pap. 3.25 (ISBN 0-460-01764-0). Dutton.

Master of Boranga. Mike Sirota. (Ro-Lan Ser.: No. 1). 320p. (Orig.). 1980. pap. 1.95 (ISBN 0-89083-616-7). Zebra.

Master of Craighill. Shelia Strutt. (Harlequin Romance Ser.). (Orig.). 1980. pap. 1.25 o.p. (ISBN 0-373-02333-2, Pub. by Harlequin). PB.

Master of Desolation: The Reminiscences of Capt. Joseph J. Fuller, Vol. 9. Ed. by Briton C. Busch. (American Maritime Library). 349p. 1980. 24.00 (ISBN 0-913372-21-8). Mystic Seaport.

Master of Go. Yasunari Kawabata. Tr. by Edward G. Seidensticker from Jap. (Perigee Japanese Library). 196p. 1981. pap. 4.95 (ISBN 0-399-50528-8, Perigee). Putnam.

Master of Greystone. Glenda Carrington. 1977. pap. 1.50 o.p. (ISBN 0-425-03443-7, Medallion). Berkley Pub.

Master of Oakwindsor. Douglas K. Hall. 1976. 8.95 o.s.i. (ISBN 0-690-01171-7, TYC-T). T Y Crowell.

Master of Rosewood. Karl Tunberg & Terence Tunberg. (Orig.). 1980. pap. 2.50 (ISBN 0-446-91134-8). Warner Bks.

Master of the Dead, & Other Strange Unsolved Mysteries. Ronan. (gr. 7-12). 1980. pap. 1.25 (ISBN 0-590-30005-9, Schol Pap). Schol Bk Serv.

Master of the Inn. Robert Herrick. 274p. 1980. Repr. of 1908 ed. lib. bdg. 12.95x (ISBN 0-89968-188-3). Lightyear.

Master of Urulu. Helen Bianchin. (Harlequin Romances Ser.). 192p. (Orig.). 1981. pap. 1.25 (ISBN 0-373-02378-2, Pub. by Harlequin). PB.

Master Optical Techniques. A. S. DeVany. LC 80-24442. (Pure & Applied Optics Ser.). 625p. 1981. 45.00 (ISBN 0-471-07720-8, Pub. by Wiley-Interscience). Wiley.

Master Photography. Michael Busselle. LC 78-50818. 1978. 14.95 o.s.i. (ISBN 0-528-81079-0). Rand.

Master Plan of Evangelism. Robert E. Coleman. 1978. pap. 2.95 (ISBN 0-8007-5007-1, Power Bks); pap. 1.75 o.p. (ISBN 0-8007-8303-4, Spire Bks). Revell.

Master Problem. James Marchant. Ed. by Charles Winick. LC 78-60869. (Prostitution Ser.: Vol. 12). 371p. 1979. lib. bdg. 36.00 (ISBN 0-8240-9716-5). Garland Pub.

Master Puppeteer. Katherine Paterson. (Illus.). 192p. (gr. 5 up). 1981. pap. 1.95 (ISBN 0-380-53322-7, 53322, Camelot). Avon.

Master Rosalind. John Beatty & Patricia Beatty. LC 74-5050. 224p. (gr. 7 up). 1974. 8.25 (ISBN 0-688-21819-9); PLB 7.92 (ISBN 0-688-31819-3). Morrow.

Master Sales Control Atlas. rev. ed. American Map Company. 1979. 251.85 (ISBN 0-8416-9560-1). Am Map.

Master Snickup's Cloak. Alexander Theroux. LC 79-1799. (Illus.). 1979. 7.95 o.p. (ISBN 0-06-014283-9, HarpT); lib. bdg. 7.89 o.p. (ISBN 0-06-014284-7). Har-Row.

Master Sniper. Stephen Hunter. 304p. 1981. pap. 2.95 (ISBN 0-425-04800-4). Berkley Pub.

Master Standard Data. R. M. Crossan & W. Harold. LC 80-11165. 268p. 1980. Repr. of 1962 ed. lib. bdg. 14.50 (ISBN 0-89874-133-5). Krieger.

Master Tables for Electromagnetic Depth Sounding Interpretation. Rajni K. Verma. (IFI Data Base Library Ser.). 480p. 1980. 75.00 (ISBN 0-306-65188-2, IFI). Plenum Pub.

Master Tung's Western Chamber Romance: A Chinese Chantefable. Li-Li Ch'En. LC 75-12469. (Studies in Chinese History, Literature, & Institutions Ser.). 268p. 1976. 42.50 (ISBN 0-521-20871-8). Cambridge U Pr.

Mastering Adolescence in a Dangerous World. I. Newton Kugelmass. LC 77-81795. 264p. 1981. 22.50 (ISBN 0-87527-167-7). Green.

Mastering Baseball. Dick Groch. LC 77-91156. 1978. 9.95 o.p. (ISBN 0-8092-7816-2); pap. 6.95 (ISBN 0-8092-7815-4). Contemp Bks.

Mastering Bowling. Dawson Taylor. (Mastering Ser.). (Illus.). 1981. 12.95 (ISBN 0-8092-7049-8); pap. 6.95 (ISBN 0-8092-7047-1). Contemp Bks.

Mastering Color & Design in Watercolor. Christopher Schink. 144p. 1981. 22.50 (ISBN 0-8230-3015-6). Watson-Guptill.

Mastering Competitive Debate. Dana Hensley & Diana Prentice. 1977. lib. bdg. 6.000 (ISBN 0-931054-05-2). Clark Pub.

Mastering English. Betty H. Pryce. LC 75-2090. (High School Equivalency Prog. Ser.). 161p. (Orig.). (gr. 9-12). 1975. pap. text ed. 5.00 (ISBN 0-913310-39-5). Par Inc.

Mastering Fundamental Mathematics. David H. Galerstein. (Orig.). (gr. 7). 1976. pap. text ed. 5.83 (ISBN 0-87720-226-5). AMSCO Sch.

Mastering Magic: Secrets of the Great Magicians Revealed. Walter B. Gibson. LC 77-1535. 1977. pap. 4.95 (ISBN 0-8119-0277-3). Fell.

Mastering Management. A. Leslie Derbyshire. LC 80-83028. 300p. 1981. 9.95 (ISBN 0-88290-159-1, 2046). Horizon Utah.

Mastering Mathematics. Louise Del Santo. LC 75-2049. (High School Equivalency Prog. Ser.). 205p. (Orig.). (gr. 9-12). 1975. pap. text ed. 5.00 (ISBN 0-913310-38-7). Par Inc.

Mastering Medical Language. Anthony L. Spatola. (Illus.). 464p. 1981. pap. text ed. 15.95 (ISBN 0-13-560151-7). P-H.

Mastering Medicine: Professional Socialization in Medical School. Robert H. Coombs. LC 77-85351. 1978. 17.95 (ISBN 0-02-906640-9). Free Pr.

Mastering Old Testament Facts, 3 bks. Madeline H. Beck & Lamar Williamson, Jr. Incl. Bk. 1. Introduction on-Deut. 1979 (ISBN 0-8042-0134-X); Bk. 2. Joshua-Esther. 1979 (ISBN 0-8042-0135-8); Bk. 3. Job, Psalms, Proverbs, Ecclesiastes, Song of Solomon. 106p. (gr. 9-12). 1980 (ISBN 0-8042-0136-6). (Illus., Orig.). pap. text ed. 4.95 ea. John Knox.

Mastering Softball. Ed Zolna & Mike Conklin. (Mastering Ser.). (Illus.). 1981. 12.95 (ISBN 0-8092-7184-2); pap. 5.95 (ISBN 0-8092-7183-4). Contemp Bks.

Mastering Spanish Verbs. Julio I. Andujar. (Orig.). (gr. 9 up). 1968. pap. text ed. 3.95 (ISBN 0-88345-100-X, 17452). Regents Pub.

Mastering Stress in Child Rearing: Parental Coping Versus Spontaneous Remission. James E. Teele. LC 79-48006. 1981. price not set (ISBN 0-669-03622-6). Lexington Bks.

Mastering the Chopin Etudes & Other Essays. Abby Whiteside. LC 79-85263. 1969. 12.50 (ISBN 0-684-10654-X, ScribT). Scribner.

Mastering the Decisive Power of Logical Thinking. Charles M. Rhodes. (Illus.). 1980. deluxe ed. 39.75 (ISBN 0-89266-223-9). Am Classical Coll Pr.

Mastering the Essentials of Psychology & Life. 10th ed. Karl A. Minke & John G. Carlson. 1980. pap. text ed. 5.95x (ISBN 0-673-15170-0). Scott F.

Mastering the International Phonetic Alphabet. Donald M. Decker. (gr. 9 up). 1970. pap. text ed. 1.95 (ISBN 0-88345-099-2, 17757). Regents Pub.

Mastering the Intimate Life of Man. Wendall L. Monroe. (Illus.). 153p. 1980. deluxe ed. 37.85 (ISBN 0-89266-243-3). Am Classical Coll Pr.

Mastering the Twenty Basic Coefficients for Success in Commodity Futures Trading. Clyde E. Warrick. (Illus.). 1980. deluxe ed. 37.45 (ISBN 0-918968-54-2). Inst Econ Pol.

Mastering Women's Gymnastics. Robert Ito & Pam C. Dolney. LC 77-23696. 1978. 9.95 (ISBN 0-8092-7744-1); pap. 6.95 (ISBN 0-8092-7743-3). Contemp Bks.

Mastering Your Migraine. Peter Evans. 1979. 8.95 (ISBN 0-87690-331-6); pap. 3.95 (ISBN 0-87690-332-4). Dutton.

Mastering Your Tennis Strokes. Arthur Ashe et al. Ed. by Larry Sheehan. LC 75-41854. 1976. 12.95 (ISBN 0-689-10718-8); pap. 8.95 (ISBN 0-689-70562-X). Atheneum.

Masterman Ready, 3 vols. Frederick Marryat. LC 75-32160. (Classics of Children's Literature, 1621-1932: Vol. 25). 1976. Repr. of 1842 ed. Set. lib. bdg. 105.00 (ISBN 0-8240-2274-2); PLB 38.00 ea. Garland Pub.

Masterpiece. Emile Zola. 1968. pap. 5.95 (ISBN 0-472-06145-3, 145, AA). U of Mich Pr.

Masterpiece Affair. Kenneth Royce. 1974. pap. 1.25 o.p. (ISBN 0-380-00106-3, 20420). Avon.

Masterpiece Furniture Making. Franklin H. Gottshall. LC 79-12. (Illus.). 224p. 1979. 24.95 (ISBN 0-8117-0974-4). Stackpole.

Masterpieces from the Collection of the Princes of Liechtenstein. Reinhold Baumstark. Tr. by Robert E. Wolf from Ger. LC 80-18070. (Illus.). 298p. 1981. 100.00 (ISBN 0-933920-09-1). Hudson Hills. Postponed.

Masterpieces from the Robert Von Hirsch Sale at Sotheby's. (Illus.). 160p. 1978. 12.50 (ISBN 0-85667-060-X, Pub by Sotheby Parke Bernet England); pap. 8.75 (ISBN 0-85667-061-8). Biblio Dist.

Masterpieces of American Furniture. Lester Margon. 1965. 15.00 o.s.i. (ISBN 0-8038-0150-5). Architectural.

Masterpieces of Black African Art. 1969. pap. 2.50 (ISBN 0-87365-999-6). Peabody Harvard.

Masterpieces of Calligraphy: Two Hundred & Sixty-One Examples, 1500-1800. Peter Jessen. (Illus.). 1981. pap. price not set (ISBN 0-486-24100-9). Dover.

Masterpieces of European Furniture Thirteen Hundred to Eighteen Forty. Lester Margon. Date not set. 16.50 (ISBN 0-8038-0151-3). Hastings.

Masterpieces of Furniture in Photographs & Measured Drawings. rev. ed. Verna C. Salomonsky. (Illus.). 1953. pap. 5.00 (ISBN 0-486-21381-1). Dover.

Masterpieces of Greek Coinage. Charles Seltman. (Illus.). 128p. 1980. 20.00 (ISBN 0-916710-72-6). Obol Intl.

Masterpieces of Religious Verse. James D. Morrison. 1977. pap. 9.95 (ISBN 0-8010-6038-9). Baker Bk.

Masterpieces of the Centennial International Exhibition. Illustrated, 3 vols. Ed. by H. Barbara Weinberg. Incl. Vol. 1. Fine Art. Edward Strahan; Vol. 2. Industrial Art. Walter Smith; Vol. 3. History, Mechanics, Science. Joseph M. Wilson. LC 75-28867. (Art Experience in Late 19th Century America Ser.: Vol. 3). (Illus.). 1976. Repr. of 1876 ed. Set. lib. bdg. 172.00 (ISBN 0-8240-2227-0). Garland Pub.

Masterpieces of the Orient. Ed. by G. L Anderson. pap. 8.95x (ISBN 0-393-09542-8, NortonC); expanded pap. 1976 15.95x (ISBN 0-393-09196-1). Norton.

Masterpieces of the People's Republic of the Congo. (Illus.). 57p. (Orig.). 1980. pap. text ed. 9.95 (ISBN 0-89192-314-4). Interbk Inc.

Masterpieces of the Vatican. Mario Fellucci. (Science of Man Library Bk). (Illus.). 40p. 1975. 60.00 (ISBN 0-913314-54-4). Am Classical Coll Pr.

Masterpieces of World Literature in Digest Form, 4 vols. Ed. by Frank N. Magill. Incl. Series 1. 1952. o.p. (ISBN 0-06-003870-5); Series 2. 1956. o.p. (ISBN 0-06-003690-7); lib. bdg. 19.79 (ISBN 0-06-003900-0); Series 3. 1960. 22.50 (ISBN 0-06-003750-4); Series 4. 1969. 22.50 (ISBN 0-06-003751-2); lib. bdg. 19.79 (ISBN 0-06-003752-0). HarpT). Har-Row.

Masters. C. P. Snow. 1960. lib. rep. ed. 17.50x (ISBN 0-684-14744-0, ScribT, SL886, ScribT). Scribner.

Masters & Johnson Explained. rev. ed. Nat Lehrman. LC 76-19839. 272p. 1981. pap. 2.75 (ISBN 0-87216-808-5). Playboy Pbks.

Master's Comfort & Hope. A. E. Garvie. (Scholar As Preacher Ser.). 253p. 1917. text ed. 7.75 (ISBN 0-567-04416-5). Attic Pr.

Master's Immortal Sermon. Ellen G. White. 96p. 1971. pap. 0.95 o.p. (ISBN 0-8163-0056-9, 13325-6). Pacific Pr Pub Assn.

Master's Indwelling. Andrew Murray. LC 76-23363. 1977. pap. 2.25 (ISBN 0-87123-355-X, 200355). Bethany Fell.

Master's Men. William Barclay. (Festival Books). 1976. pap. 1.75 (ISBN 0-687-23732-7). Abingdon.

Master's Men. William Barclay. (Orig.). pap. 1.50 (ISBN 0-89129-132-6). Jove Pubns.

Masters of Ancient Comedy: Selections from Aristophanes, Menander, Plautus & Terence. Ed. & tr. by Lionel Casson. (Funk & W Bk.). 433p. 1967. pap. 2.95 o.s.i. (ISBN 0-308-60016-9, TYC-T). T Y Crowell.

Masters of Equitation. W. Sidney Felton. (Illus.). 7.35 (ISBN 0-85131-091-5, Dist. by Sporting Book Center). J A Allen.

Masters of Menace: Greenstreet & Lorre. Ted Sennett. 1979. pap. 8.95 o.p. (ISBN 0-525-47533-8). Dutton.

Masters of Modern Drama. Ed. by Haskell Block & Robert Shedd. 1962. 29.95 (ISBN 0-394-40625-7); text ed. 27.95 (ISBN 0-394-30084-X). Random.

Masters of Science-Fiction, No. 1: Essays on Science-Fiction Authors. Brian M. Stableford. LC 80-24116. (Milford Series: Popular Writers of Today: Vol. 32). 64p. (Orig.). 1981. lib. bdg. 8.95x (ISBN 0-89370-147-5); pap. text ed. 2.95x (ISBN 0-89370-247-1). Borgo Pr.

Masters of Shades & Shadows. Ed. by Seon Manley & Gogo Lewis. LC 77-76255. (gr. k up). 1978. PLB 7.95 (ISBN 0-385-12744-8). Doubleday.

Masters of Space. E. E. Smith. (Family D'Alembert Ser.). (Orig.). 1979. pap. 1.75 (ISBN 0-515-04335-4). Jove Pubns.

Masters of the Drama. 3rd ed. John Gassner. (Illus.). 1953. 10.00 o.p. (ISBN 0-486-20100-7). Dover.

Masters of the Heart. Andrew Canale. LC 78-58953. 1978. 9.95 (ISBN 0-8091-0271-4). Paulist Pr.

Masters of the Macabre. Ed. by Seon Manley & Gogo Lewis. LC 69-11002. 336p. (gr. 9 up). 1975. 6.95 o.p. (ISBN 0-385-03270-6). Doubleday.

Masters of the Reformation: Rival Roads to a New Ideology. H. A. Oberman. Tr. by D. Martin from German. 432p. Date not set. price not set (ISBN 0-521-23098-5). Cambridge U Pr.

Masters of the Vortex. E. E. Smith. (Lensman Ser.). pap. 1.75 (ISBN 0-515-05328-7). Jove Pubns.

Masters of Wisdom. J. G. Bennett. 1980. pap. 5.95 (ISBN 0-87728-466-0). Weiser.

Masters of 20th Century Art. Sam Hunter. LC 79-56348. (Illus.). 106p. 1980. pap. 14.95 (ISBN 0-89659-088-7). Abbeville Pr.

Masters on the Dry Fly. Ed. by J. Michael Migel. (Illus.). 1977. 12.00 o.p. (ISBN 0-397-01188-1). Lippincott.

Masters on the Nymph. Michael J. Migel & Leonard M. Wright, Jr. LC 78-20638. (Illus.). 1979. 14.95 (ISBN 0-385-15151-9, NLB). Doubleday.

Masters or Servants? A Study of Selected English Painters & Their Patrons of the Late 18th & Early 19th Centuries. Josephine Gear. LC 76-23619. (Outstanding Dissertations in the Fine Arts - 18th Century). (Illus.). 1977. Repr. lib. bdg. 56.00 (ISBN 0-8240-2690-X). Garland Pub.

Masters: Portraits of Great Teachers. Ed. by Joseph Epstein. LC 80-68180. 224p. 1981. 14.95 (ISBN 0-465-04420-4). Basic.

Masters: Portraits of Sixteen Great Teachers. Ed. by Joseph Epstein. LC 80-68180. 224p. 1980. 13.95 (ISBN 0-465-04420-4). Basic.

Masters: Profiles of a Tournament. 3rd rev. ed. Ed. by Dawson Tyalor. (Illus.). 192p. 1981. 19.95 (ISBN 0-498-01661-7). A S Barnes.

Master's Secrets of Putting. 2nd rev. ed. Dawson Taylor & Horton Smith. (Illus.). 200p. 1982. price not set (ISBN 0-498-02513-6). A S Barnes.

Masters, Unions & Men. R. Price. LC 79-21229. (Illus.). 1980. 39.95 (ISBN 0-521-22882-4). Cambridge U Pr.

Masterworks of Children's Literature, Fifteen Fifty to Nineteen Hundred, 7 vols. Ed. by Jonathan Cott. LC 78-56257. (Illus.). Date not set. Set. 225.00 (ISBN 0-87754-089-6). Chelsea Hse.

Masterworks of English Children's Literature, 1550-1900, 5 vols. Ed. by Jonathan Cott. 3100p. 1979. Set. 150.00 (ISBN 0-88373-134-7). Stonehill Pub Co.

Masterworks of Philosophy, Vol. 3. S. E. Frost. (Masterworks Ser.). 192p. 1972. Pts. 1-2. pap. 1.95 (ISBN 0-07-040803-3, SP). McGraw.

Masterworks of the British Cinema. Intro. by John R. Taylor. Incl. Brief Encounter. David Lean; The Third Man. Carol Reed; Kind Hearts & Coronets. Robert Hamer; Saturday Night & Sunday Morning. Karel Reisz. LC 74-11709. (Icon Editions). (Illus.). 352p. 1975. pap. 4.95 o.s.i. (ISBN 0-06-430060-9, IN-60, HarpT). Har-Row.

Masterworks of the French Cinema. Intro. by John Weightman. Incl. Italian Straw Hat. Rene Claire; Grand Illusion. Jean Renoir; Ronde. Max Ophuls; Wages of Fear. Henri-Georges Clouzot. LC 73-21853. (Icon Editions: Masterworks Film Ser). (Illus.). 312p. 1974. pap. 4.95 o.s.i. (ISBN 0-06-430051-X, IN-51, HarpT). Har-Row.

Masterworks of the German Cinema: The Golem, Nosferatu M, the Threepenny Opera. Intro. by Roger Manvell. LC 73-13005. (Icon Editions). (Illus.). 300p. 1974. pap. 4.95 o.s.i. (ISBN 0-06-430047-1, IN-47, HarpT). Har-Row.

Mastery of the Metropolis. Webb S. Fiser. LC 80-23244. x, 168p. 1981. Repr. of 1962 ed. lib. bdg. 17.50x (ISBN 0-313-22732-2, FIMAM). Greenwood.

Mastery Through Accomplishment. Hazrat I. Khan. LC 79-101639. (Collected Works of Hazrat Inayat Khan Ser.). 320p. 1978. 8.95 (ISBN 0-930872-06-1); pap. 5.95 (ISBN 0-930872-07-X). Sufi Order Pubns.

Mastiff. Marie A. Moore. LC 77-87765. (Other Dog Bk.). (Illus.). 112p. 1978. 14.95 (ISBN 0-87714-059-6). Denlingers.

Masting & Rigging of English Ships of War 1625-1860. James Lees. LC 76-45985. (Illus.). 1979. 36.95 (ISBN 0-87021-847-6). Naval Inst Pr.

Mastro-Don Gesuald. Giovanni Verga. 1979. 15.75x (ISBN 0-520-03598-4). U of Cal Pr.

Masugi Nephritis & Its Immunopathologic Implications. Atsushi Okabayashi & Yoichiro Kondo. LC 79-91335. (Illus.). 1980. 41.00 (ISBN 0-89640-039-5). Igaku-Shoin.

Matadora. Barbara Faith. (Orig.). 1981. pap. write for info. (ISBN 0-671-41784-3). PB.

Matagorda. Louis L'Amour. 176p. (Orig.). 1981. pap. 2.25 (ISBN 0-553-14743-9). Bantam.

Match at Midnight (1633) Ed. by Stephen B. Young & Stephen Orgel. LC 79-54324. (Renaissance Drama Second Ser.). 270p. 1980. lib. bdg. 30.00 (ISBN 0-8240-4481-9). Garland Pub.

Match Fishing Our Way. Ken Giles & Clive Smith. 1978. 13.50 (ISBN 0-7153-7692-6). David & Charles.

Match Point. Maureen Reardon & Peter Sanders. LC 75-22012. (Venture Ser, a Reading Incentive Program). (Illus.). 76p. (gr. 7-12,RL 4.5-6.5). 1975. text ed. 23.25 ea. pack of 5 (ISBN 0-8172-0235-8). Follett.

Match Point. Owenita Sanderlin. (gr. 3 up). 1979. pap. 1.25 (ISBN 0-307-21518-0, Golden Pr). Western Pub.

Match-Point Bridge. H. W. Kelsey. 1970. 6.95 o.p. (ISBN 0-571-09436-8, Pub. by Faber & Faber). Merrimack Bk Serv.

Match-Winning Tennis: Tactics, Temperament & Training. C. M. Jones. (Illus.). 1971. 9.95 (ISBN 0-571-09289-6). Transatlantic.

Matches, Flames & Rails: The Diamond Match Co. in the High Sierra. rev., 2nd ed. Kent Stephens. LC 80-51156. 1980. 17.95 (ISBN 0-87046-056-0). Trans-Anglo.

Matches, Flumes & Rails. 17.95. Chatham Pub CA.

Matching the Hatch. Ernest G. Schweibert, Jr. (Illus.). 1978. pap. 6.95 o.p. (ISBN 0-695-80924-5). Follett.

Matchless Rogue: A Brief Account of the Life of Don Thomazo, the Unfortunate Son. Elizabeth Cellier. LC 80-2473. 1981. Repr. of 1680 ed. 23.50 (ISBN 0-404-19105-3). AMS Pr.

Matchlock Gun. Walter D. Edmonds. LC 41-17547. (Illus.). (gr. 4-6). 1941. PLB 5.95 (ISBN 0-396-06369-1). Dodd.

Matchsafes to Nursing Bottles. Time-Life Books Editors. (Encyclopedia of Collectibles Ser.). (Illus.). 1979. lib. bdg. 10.98 (ISBN 0-8094-2787-7); kivar bdg. 8.95 (ISBN 0-8094-2788-5). Silver.

Matchstick Modelling. Roy Ashley. (Illus.). 80p. 1980. 10.95 (ISBN 0-7207-1150-9, Pub. by Michael Joseph). Merrimack Bk Ser V.

Matchstick Puzzles, Tricks & Games. Gilbert Obermair. LC 77-79510. (Illus.). (gr. 4 up). 1977. 5.95 (ISBN 0-8069-4564-8); PLB 5.89 (ISBN 0-8069-4565-6). Sterling.

Matchstick Puzzles, Tricks & Games. Gilbert Obermair. LC 77-79510. (Illus.). 128p. (gr. 4 up). 1980. pap. 3.50 (ISBN 0-8069-8934-3). Sterling.

Mate & Stalemate: Working with Marital Problems in a Social Services Dept. Janet Mattinson & Ian Sinclair. (Practice of Social Work: Vol. 1). 1979. 21.95x (ISBN 0-631-11821-7, Pub. by Basil Blackwell England). Biblio Dist.

Mate in Two Moves: The Two-Move Chess Problem Made Easy. Brian Harley. 1970. pap. 3.50 (ISBN 0-486-22434-1). Dover.

Mate Selection: A Study of Complementary Needs. Robert F. Winch. (Reprints in Sociology Ser). lib. bdg. 26.50x (ISBN 0-697-00215-2); pap. text ed. 8.95x (ISBN 0-89197-842-9). Irvington.

Matematicas: Repaso Para el Examen De Equivalencia De la Escuela Superior En Espanol. rev. ed. Antonio A. Acosta & Joraida Calvo. LC 80-25182. 256p. (Orig.). 1981. pap. 5.00 (ISBN 0-668-04821-2, 4821-2). Arco.

Materia Medica of Ayurveda. Ed. by V. Dash & L. Kashyap. 1980. text ed. 38.00x (ISBN 0-391-01813-2). Humanities.

Materia Medica of New Homoeopathic Remedies. O. A. Julian. 637p. 1980. 60.00x (Pub. by Beaconsfield England). State Mutual Bk.

Material & Process Applications: Land, Sea, Air, Space. Eugene R. Crilly. (Science of Advanced Materials & Process Engineering Ser.). 1981. price not set. Soc Adv Material.

Material Culture & the Study of American Life. Ian M. Quimby. (Winterthur Bk.). (Illus.). 1978. 12.95x (ISBN 0-393-05661-9); pap. 5.95x (ISBN 0-393-09037-X). Norton.

Material-Environment Interactions in Structural & Pressure Containment Service. Ed. by George V. Smith. (MPC: No. 15). 160p. 1980. 30.00 (G00188). ASME.

Material for Thought, No. 8. Far West Press Editors. LC 79-56899. 88p. 1979. pap. 2.95 (ISBN 0-914480-05-7). Far West Pr.

Material Goods. Janet Burroway. LC 80-12381. 77p. 1981. 7.95 (ISBN 0-8130-0670-8). U Presses Fla.

Material Handling Systems Design. James M. Apple. (Illus.). 600p. 1972. 33.00 (ISBN 0-8260-0485-7, Pub. by Wiley-Interscience). Wiley.

Material Plane. Thomas Farber. 1980. 9.95 o.p. (ISBN 0-525-15424-8). Dutton.

Material Relics of Music in Ancient Palestine and Its Environs. Bathyah Boyer. LC 64-251. 1963. pap. 9.00 (ISBN 0-913932-33-7). Boosey & Hawkes.

Material Science & Metallurgy. 3rd ed. Pollack. (Illus.). 416p. 1980. text ed. 21.95 (ISBN 0-8359-4280-5). Reston.

Material Specifications: Ferrous Materials, 3 pts, Pt. A. (Boiler & Pressure Vessel Code Ser.: Sec II). 1980. 125.00 (P0002A); loose-leaf 172.00 (V0002A). ASME.

Material Specifications: Nonferrous Materials, 3 pts, Pt. B. (Boiler & Pressure Vessel Code Ser.: Sec. II). 1980. 110.00 (P0002B); loose-leaf 150.00 (V0002B). ASME.

Material Specifications: Welding Rods, Electrodes & Filler Metals, 3 pts, Pt. C. (Boiler & Pressure Vessel Code Ser.: Sec. II). 1977. 35.00 o.p. (ISBN 0-685-76796-5, R0002C); pap. 50.00 loose-leaf o.p. (ISBN 0-685-76797-3, W0002C). ASME.

Material Specifications: Welding Rods, Electrodes & Filler Metals. (Boiler & Pressure Vessel Code Ser.: Sec II). 1980. 55.00 (P0002C); pap. 70.00 loose-leaf (V0002C). ASME.

Material Specifications: Welding Rods, Electrodes & Filler Metals, 3 pts, Pt. C. (Boiler & Pressure Vessel Code Ser.: Sec. II). 1980. loose leaf 70.00 (P0002C); pap. 70.00 loose leaf (V0002C). ASME.

Material Testing Laboratories. L. F. Gillemot. 1970. pap. 2.50 (ISBN 92-3-100826-9, U373, UNESCO). Unipub.

Materialien Zur Ästhetischen Theorie Adornos. Ed. by Burkhardt Lindner & Martin Luedke. (Suhrkamp Taschenbuecher Wissenschaft). 560p. (Orig.). pap. text ed. 11.70 (ISBN 3-518-07722-8). Suhrkamp.

Materialism & Empirio-Criticism. Vladimir I. Lenin. pap. 3.25 (ISBN 0-8351-0151-7). China Bks.

Materialism & the Mind-Body Problem. David Rosenthal. LC 77-157186. (Central Issues in Philosophy Ser). (Illus.). 1971. pap. 9.00 ref. ed. (ISBN 0-13-560177-0). P-H.

Materialist Reading of the Gospel of Mark. Fernando Belo. Tr. by Matthew O'Connell. LC 80-24756. 384p. (Orig.). 1981. pap. 12.95 (ISBN 0-88344-323-6). Orbis Bks.

Materials. Alan Everett. (Mitchell's Building Construction Ser.). 1978. pap. 14.95 (ISBN 0-470-26353-9). Halsted Pr.

Materials & Building Research, Vol. 1. UTI. 1979. 50.00 (ISBN 0-86095-825-6). Longman.

Materials & Coatings to Resist High Temperature Corrosion. Ed. by D. R. Holmes & A. Rahmel. (Illus.). 1978. text ed. 91.10x (ISBN 0-85334-784-0). Intl Ideas.

Materials & Man's Needs. Science & Public Policy Comm., Comm. on the Survey of Materials Science & Engineering. LC 74-2118. (Illus.). 246p. 1974. pap. 8.00 (ISBN 0-309-02220-7). Natl Acad Pr.

Materials & Manufacturing Technology. Roy A. Lindberg. (Illus.). 1968. text ed. 23.95x (ISBN 0-205-01947-1, 321947X). Allyn.

Materials & Methods for Business Research. John C. Tyson & Linda J. Piele. LC 80-20332. (Bibliographic Instruction Ser.). 1980. lib. bdg. 14.95x (ISBN 0-918212-15-4); wkbk. 5 or more 4.95 (ISBN 0-918212-14-6). Neal-Schuman.

Materials & Methods for Sociology Research. James Gruber & Judith Pryor. LC 79-14814. (Bibliographic Instruction Ser.). 1980. lib. bdg. 14.95x (ISBN 0-918212-13-8); wkbk. 5 or more 4.95x (ISBN 0-918212-12-X). Neal-Schuman.

Materials & Methods of Architectural Construction. 3rd ed. Harry Parker et al. LC 58-8213. 1958. 34.00 (ISBN 0-471-66297-6, Pub. by Wiley-Interscience). Wiley.

Materials & Methods Used in Marking Experiments in Fishery Research. (Fisheries Technical Paper: No. 190). 1979. pap. 7.75 (ISBN 92-5-100773-X, F1636, FAO). Unipub.

Materials & Procedures for Residential Construction. Alonzo Wass & Gordon Sanders. (Illus.). text ed. 19.95 (ISBN 0-8359-4284-8). Reston.

Materials & Process Selection in Engineering. M. M. Farag. (Illus.). 1979. 57.00x (ISBN 0-85334-824-3). Intl Ideas.

Materials & Process Specifications & Standards. Committee on Materials Specifications, Testing Methods & Standards, National Research Council. LC 77-92433. (Illus.). 1977. pap. text ed. 8.50 (ISBN 0-309-02731-4). Natl Acad Pr.

Materials & Processes for Electron Devices. National Materials Advisory Board. LC 72-84753. (Illus.). 240p. 1972. pap. 9.75 (ISBN 0-309-02040-9). Natl Acad Pr.

Materials & Structure of Music, Vol. 2. 3rd ed. William B. Christ et al. 480p. 1981. text ed. 14.95 (ISBN 0-13-560433-8); pap. text ed. 10.95 wkbk. P-H.

Materials & Structures. 2nd ed. M. J. Smith. (Illus.). 180p. 1980. pap. text ed. 13.95x (ISBN 0-7114-5639-9). Intl Ideas.

Materials & Structures of Music, Vol. 1. 3rd ed. William Christ et al. 1980. text ed. 16.95 (ISBN 0-13-540417-7); wkbk. 7.95 (ISBN 0-13-560425-7). P-H.

Materials & Techniques of 20th Century Artists. Dee Driscole & Dorothy Ross. LC 76-29167. (Illus.). 48p. 1976. pap. 4.95x (ISBN 0-910386-37-4, Pub. by Cleveland Mus Art). Ind U Pr.

Materials Aspects of World Energy Needs. 1980. 14.00 (ISBN 0-686-65116-2). Natl Acad Pr.

Materials Availability for the Automotive Industries. Society of Automotive Engineers. 1980. 15.00 (ISBN 0-89883-233-0). Soc Auto Engineers.

Materials Availability Handbook. Eugene Wiemers. (Occasional Papers Ser.: No. 149). 1981. pap. 3.00 (ISBN 0-686-69450-3). U of Ill Lib Sci.

Materials Deterioration & Mechanisms of Deterioration. Ed. by Applied Science Publishers Ltd London. (Illus.). 1976. 50.40x (ISBN 0-85334-705-0). Intl Ideas.

Materials, Energies & Environmental Design. Arnold J. Aho. 1981. lib. bdg. 28.50 (ISBN 0-8240-7178-6). Garland Pub.

Materials for a Basic Course in Property. Edward R. Cohen. LC 78-17714. (American Casebook Ser.). 526p. 1978. text ed. 17.95 (ISBN 0-8299-2008-0). West Pub.

Materials for Advanced Batteries. Ed. by D. W. Murphy et al. (NATO Conference Ser. (Series VI--Materials Science): Vol. 2). 355p. 1981. 39.50 (ISBN 0-306-40564-4, Plenum Pr). Plenum Pub.

Materials for Classroom Management. Terrence Piper. LC 73-91796. 1974. duplicatable materials 4.95 (ISBN 0-8224-4412-7). Pitman Learning.

Materials for Listening Comprehension & Note Taking in English. Michael Berman. pap. 3.95 (ISBN 0-08-025316-4). Pergamon.

Materials for Occupational Education: An Annotated Source Guide. 2nd ed. Patricia G. Schuman. (Neal-Schuman Sourcebook Ser.). 1980. 24.95x (ISBN 0-918212-17-0). Neal-Schuman.

Materials for West African History in the Archives of Belgium & Holland. Patricia Carson. (Guides to Materials for West African History in European Archives: Vol. 1). 1962. 3.50x (ISBN 0-485-17201-1, Athlone Pr). Humanities.

Materials for West African History in the Archives of the United Kingdom. Noel Matthews. (Guides to Materials for West African History in European Archives Ser: No. 5). 225p. 1973. pap. text ed. 12.00x (ISBN 0-485-17205-4, Athlone Pr). Humanities.

Materials for West African History in French Archives: Guides to Materials for West African History in European Archives. Patricia Carson. (Vol. 4). 1968. text ed. 7.00x (ISBN 0-485-17204-6, Athlone Pr). Humanities.

Materials Handling Handbook. Ed. by Harold A. Bolz et al. LC 57-11291. 1958. 60.00 (ISBN 0-8260-1175-6, Pub. by Wiley-Interscience). Wiley.

Materials Handling in Farm Production: A Guide to the Control of Handling Costs on the Farm. Bill Butterworth. LC 78-21166. 1979. pap. 12.95x (ISBN 0-470-26589-2). Halsted Pr.

Materials in the Biological Environment. Black. 320p. 1981. 32.50 (ISBN 0-8247-1267-6). Dekker.

Materials Management. 3rd ed. Dean S. Ammer. 1974. text ed. 17.95x o.p. (ISBN 0-256-01556-2). Irwin.

Materials Management & Purchasing. 4th ed. Dean S. Ammer. 1980. 20.95x (ISBN 0-256-02146-5). Irwin.

Materials Management for Health Services. Arnold Reisman. LC 79-3524. 1981. 35.95 (ISBN 0-669-03458-4). Lexington Bks.

Materials Management Systems: A Modular Library. Robert G. Brown. LC 77-8281. 436p. 1977. 31.50 (ISBN 0-471-11182-1). Ronald Pr.

Materials of Construction. Frank Dagostino. 1981. text ed. 18.95 (ISBN 0-8359-4286-4). Reston.

Materials of Construction. 6th ed. Adelbert P. Mills et al. LC 55-7368. 1955. text ed. 31.95x (ISBN 0-471-60654-5). Wiley.

Materials of Construction for Shipboard Waste Incinerators. National Materials Advisory Board, National Research Council. 1977. pap. 8.75 (ISBN 0-309-02606-7). Natl Acad Pr.

Materials of Construction for Steam Power Plant. L. M. Wyatt. (Illus.). 1976. 63.30x (ISBN 0-85334-661-5). Intl Ideas.

Materials of Dance As a Creative Art Activity. 4th ed. Ed. by Barbara Mettler & June Warner. 1974. 15.00x o.p. (ISBN 0-912536-02-0). Mettler Studio.

Materials of Interior Design. Dennis G. Murphy. Ed. by Gladys N. Murphy. (Interior Furnishings & Products Ser.). (Illus.). 208p. (Orig.). 1978. 10.50 (ISBN 0-938614-00-2, 211-196). Stratford Hse.

Materials of Music Composition Book 1: Fundamentals. H. Owen Reed & Robert G. Sidnell. LC 76-55643. 1978. pap. text ed. 14.95 (ISBN 0-201-06125-2). A-W.

Materials of Music Composition Through Jazz, Rock, Pop, Folk, & Art Music, Book II: Exploring The Parameters. H. O. Reed & R. G. Sidnell. 1980. 14.95 (ISBN 0-201-06126-0); write for info. (ISBN 0-201-06122-8). A-W.

Materials on Accounting for Lawyers. David R. Herwitz. LC 80-18163. (University Casebook Ser.). 636p. 1980. text ed. write for info. (ISBN 0-88277-014-4). Foundation Pr.

Materials on Japanese Social & Economic History: Tokugawa, Japan. Neil S. Smith. (Studies in Japanese History & Civilization). 176p. 1979. Repr. of 1937 ed. 19.50 (ISBN 0-89093-262-X). U Pubns Amer.

Materials on Legal Drafting. F. Reed Dickerson. (American Casebook Ser.). 407p. 1981. text ed. 14.95. West Pub.

Materials Science. 2nd ed. J. C. Anderson et al. LC 74-9620. 1975. 21.95 (ISBN 0-470-02830-0). Halsted Pr.

Materials Science & Technology for Design Engineers. Ed. by Alex E. Javitz. (Materials for Electrical & Electronics Design Ser.). (Illus.). 560p. 1972. 27.55 o.p. (ISBN 0-8104-5640-0). Hayden.

Materials Science for Engineers. Lawrence H. Van Vlack. LC 74-91151. (Metallurgy & Materials Ser). 1970. text ed. 24.95 (ISBN 0-201-08074-5). A-W.

Materials Science in Engineering. 3rd ed. Keyser. (Engineering Ser.). 488p. 1980. text ed. 20.95 (ISBN 0-675-08182-3). Merrill.

Materials Science Research Series, Vol. 2. Ed. by H. M. Otte & S. R. Locke. LC 63-17645. 319p. 1965. 39.50 (ISBN 0-306-38502-3, Plenum Pr). Plenum Pub.

Materials Technology - An Interamerican Approach. Frwd. by R. D. Wylie. 1968. pap. 27.00 o.p. (ISBN 0-685-06528-6, H00034). ASME.

Materials Technology in the Near-Term Energy Program. National Research Council, Commission on Sociotechnical Systems. xiii, 122p. 1974. pap. 7.00 (ISBN 0-309-02322-X). Natl Acad Pr.

Maternal & Child Health Nursing. 3rd ed. Joanne K. Griffin et al. (Nursing Examination Review Books: Vol. 3). 1972. pap. 6.00 spiral bdg. (ISBN 0-87488-503-5). Med Exam.

Maternal & Child Health Nursing. 4th ed. A. Joy Ingalls & M. Constance Salerno. LC 78-32131. (Illus.). 1979. text ed. 17.95 (ISBN 0-8016-2326-X). Mosby.

Maternal & Child Health Practices: Problems, Resources & Methods of Delivery. Ed. by Helen M. Wallace et al. (Illus.). 1400p. 1973. 52.75 (ISBN 0-398-02617-3). C C Thomas.

Maternal & Newborn Care: Nursing Interventions. Ed. by Mary H. Browning & Ruth P. Lewis. 258p. 1973. 6.50 o.p. (ISBN 0-686-11198-2, C07). Am Journal Nurse.

Maternal & Parental Benefits & Leaves: An International Review. Sheila B. Kamerman. LC 80-69763. (Impact on Policy Monograph Ser.: No. 1). (Illus.). 80p. (Orig.). 1980. pap. text ed. 5.00 (ISBN 0-938436-00-7). Columbia U Ctr Soc Sci.

Maternal-Child Nursing. Violet Broadribb & Charlotte Corliss. 600p. 1973. text ed. 12.50 o.p. (ISBN 0-397-54140-6). Lippincott.

Maternal Deprivation Reassessed. rev. ed. Michael Rutter. 1981. pap. 3.95 (ISBN 0-14-080561-3). Penguin.

Maternal Effects in Development. Ed. by D. R. Newth & M. Balls. LC 78-73812. (British Society for Developmental Biology Symposium: No. 4). (Illus.). 1980. 92.00 (ISBN 0-521-22685-6). Cambridge U Pr.

Maternal-Fetal Endocrinology. Dan Tulchinsky & Kenneth J. Ryan. LC 79-66046. (Illus.). 418p. 1980. text ed. 42.00 (ISBN 0-7216-8911-6). Saunders.

Maternal-Infant Bonding: The Impact of Early Separation or Loss on Family Development. Klaus & Kennell. LC 76-5397. Orig. Title: Care of the Family of the Normal or Sick Newborn. (Illus.). 224p. 1976. text ed. 14.95 (ISBN 0-8016-2631-5); pap. 11.95 (ISBN 0-8016-2630-7). Mosby.

Maternal Influences & Early Behavior. new ed. Ed. by Robert W. Bell & William F. Smotherman. LC 78-17074. (Illus.). 465p. 1980. text ed. 45.00 (ISBN 0-89335-059-1). Spectrum Pub.

Maternal-Newborn Nursing: Care of the Growing Family. 2nd ed. Adele Pillitteri. 1981. text ed. write for info. (ISBN 0-316-70792-9). Little.

Maternal-Newborn Nursing: Poetest Self-Assessment & Review. Ed. by Joellen Watson & Beverly Gorvine. LC 78-50597. (Nursing: Pretest Self-Assessment & Review Ser.). 1978. pap. 6.95 (ISBN 0-07-051570-0). McGraw-Pretest.

Maternal Nutrition. Barbara Luke. 1980. text ed. 9.95 (ISBN 0-316-53610-5). Little.

Maternal Nutrition & the Course of Pregnancy. Food and Nutrition Board - Division of Biology and Agriculture. LC 72-605179. (Illus., Orig.). 1970. pap. text ed. 8.25 (ISBN 0-309-01761-0). Natl Acad Pr.

Maternity Care: The Nurse & the Family. 2nd ed. Margaret D. Jensen et al. LC 80-20723. (Illus.). 966p. 1981. text ed. 24.95 (ISBN 0-8016-2492-4). Mosby.

Maternity: Letters from Working-Women, Collected by the Women's Co-Operative Guild with a Preface by the Right Hon. Herbert Samuel, M.P., London 1915. Women's Co-Operative Guild. LC 79-56940. (English Working Class Ser.). 1980. lib. bdg. 20.00 (ISBN 0-8240-0127-3). Garland Pub.

Maternity Nursing. 2nd ed. Arlyne Friesner. Ed. by Beverly Raff. LC 77-80106. (Nursing Outline Ser.). 1977. pap. 8.50 (ISBN 0-87488-377-6). Med Exam.

Maternity Nursing. 3rd ed. Constance Lerch & Virginia Bliss. LC 77-13983. (Illus.). 1978. text ed. 18.95 (ISBN 0-8016-2961-6). Mosby.

Maternity Nursing. Sharon Reeder et al. LC 79-22993. 775p. 1980. text ed. 22.95x (ISBN 0-397-54253-4). Lippincott.

Maternity Nursing: A Self Study Guide. 4th ed. Constance Lerch & Jane Bliss. (Illus.). 1978. pap. text ed. 9.50 (ISBN 0-8016-2959-4). Mosby.

Maternity Nursing Case Studies. Mildred A. Disbrow et al. 1976. spiral bdg. 9.50 (ISBN 0-87488-036-X). Med Exam.

Materno Foetal Transmission of Immunoglobulins. Ed. by W. A. Hemmings. LC 75-2721. (Clinical & Experimental Immunoreproduction: No. 2). (Illus.). 400p. 1975. 57.50 (ISBN 0-521-20747-9). Cambridge U Pr.

Math, No. 1. Carolyn A. Maher et al. Ed. by Leo Gafney. (General Math Ser.). (Illus.). (gr. 7-9). 1981. text ed. write for info pupil's ed. (ISBN 0-07-039591-8, W); tchr's ed., 448 p. 13.20 (ISBN 0-07-039592-6); wkbk. to pupils ed. 4.80 (ISBN 0-07-039593-4); wkbk. to tchrs. ed. 5.20 (ISBN 0-07-039594-2). McGraw.

Math-a-Dot Series, Math Learning Games. Judith N. Parsons. Incl. Level I. Addition & Subtraction. (gr. 1-2). 1975 (ISBN 0-8224-4415-1); Level II. Addition & Subtraction. (gr. 1-3). 1975 (ISBN 0-8224-4416-X); Level III. Addition & Subtraction. (gr. 2-4). 1974 (ISBN 0-8224-4417-8); Level IV. Multiplication. (gr. 3-4). 1979 (ISBN 0-8224-4418-6); Level V. Division. (gr. 4-5). 1979 (ISBN 0-8224-4419-4). (Makemaster Bk.). pap. 5.50 ea. Pitman Learning.

Math-a-Riddle Secret-Message Challenges to Build Basic Skills. Judith N. Parsons. Incl. Bk. I. Subtraction. (gr. 2-4) (ISBN 0-8224-4433-X); Bk. II. Multiplication. (gr. 3-5) (ISBN 0-8224-4434-8). (Makemaster Bk.). 1979. pap. 5.50 ea. Pitman Learning.

Math Activities for Child Involvement. 3rd ed. Enoch Dumas & C. W. Schminke. 1977. pap. 17.95 (ISBN 0-685-71779-8); pap. text ed. 10.95 (ISBN 0-205-05577-X). Allyn.

Math Activities for Children: A Diagnostic Approach. Richard W. Copeland. (Elementary Curriculum Ser.). 1979. pap. text ed. 8.95 (ISBN 0-675-08316-8). Merrill.

Math Activity Packet for Fractions. Charles T. Gatje & John F. Gatje. (Orig.). 1976. pap. text ed. 1.50 (ISBN 0-937534-01-3). G&G Pubs.

Math Can Be Easy. Mary G. Santos. 90p. (Orig.). 1980. pap. 6.00 (ISBN 0-914562-10-X). Merriam-Eddy.

Math Exercises (in Addition) Larry D. Andrew & Patricia Andrew. 1980. pap. 1.95 (ISBN 0-931992-36-2). Penns Valley.

Math Exercises (in Division) Larry D. Andrew & Patricia Andrew. 1980. pap. 1.95 (ISBN 0-931992-39-7). Penns Valley.

Math Exercises (in Multiplication) Larry D. Andrew & Patricia Andrew. 1980. pap. 1.95 (ISBN 0-931992-38-9). Penns Valley.

Math Exercises (in Subtraction) Larry D. Andrew & Patricia Andrew. 1980. pap. 1.95 (ISBN 0-931992-37-0). Penns Valley.

Math for Medical Techs. Joanne R. Bobek. 1973. 8.00 o.p. (ISBN 0-87488-964-2). Med Exam.

Math for Meds: A Programmmed Text. 3rd ed. Anna M. Curren. LC 76-43259. 1979. pap. text ed. 6.95 (ISBN 0-918082-01-3). Wallcur Inc.

Math House Proficiency Review Tapes: Applications Involving Measurement, Unit C. (YA) (gr. 7 up). 1980. manual & cassettes 159.95 (ISBN 0-917792-05-X). Math Hse.

Math House Proficiency Review Tapes: Applications Involving Money, Unit D. Lionel J. Soracco, Jr. (YA) (gr. 7 up). 1980. manual & cassettes 159.95 (ISBN 0-917792-06-8). Math Hse.

Math House Proficiency Review Tapes: Operations with Decimals & Percent, Unit B. Lionel J. Soracco, Jr. (YA) (gr. 7 up). 1980. manual & cassettes 159.95 (ISBN 0-917792-04-1). Math Hse.

Math House Proficiency Review Tapes: Operations with Whole Numbers & Fractions, Unit A. Lionel J. Sorracco, Jr. (YA) (gr. 7 up). 1980. manual & cassettes 159.95 (ISBN 0-917792-03-3). Math Hse.

Math in & Out of the Mainstream. Lorraine D. Lyon & Elizabeth Karplus. 112p. (Orig.). 1980. pap. text ed. 7.00 (ISBN 0-87879-245-7). Acad Therapy.

Math in Stride, Bk. 1. Clara E. Clark & Betty J. Sternberg. (Illus.). 166p. (Orig.). (gr. k-2). 1980. pap. 5.65 (ISBN 0-934734-06-2). Construct Educ.

Math in Stride, Bk. 2. Clara E. Clark & Betty J. Sternberg. (Illus.). 203p. (Orig.). (gr. 1-3). 1980. pap. 5.80 (ISBN 0-934734-07-0). Construct Educ.

Math in Stride, Bk. 3. Clara E. Clark & Betty J. Sternberg. (Illus.). 219p. (Orig.). (gr. 2-4). 1980. pap. 5.95 (ISBN 0-934734-08-9). Construct Educ.

Math Mat Activities. Wallace P. Judd. (Illus.). 80p. (Orig.). (gr. k-12). 1974. wkbk. 3.50 o.p. (ISBN 0-88488-011-7). Creative Pubns.

Math Poetry & Stuff. Norman E. Dodson. 1981. 5.95 (ISBN 0-8062-1618-2). Carlton.

Math Primer for Students in Radiologic Technology. rev. ed. The Catholic Hospital Association. Ed. by Sr. Francita Barringhaus. LC 73-86652. 44p. 1973. pap. text ed. 2.50 o.p. (ISBN 0-87125-009-8). Cath Health.

Math Principles for Food Service Occupations. Robert G. Haines. LC 77-88118. 1979. pap. text ed. 7.00 (ISBN 0-8273-1680-1); instructor's guide 1.60 (ISBN 0-685-91755-X). Delmar.

Math Puzzles. Peggy Adler & Irving Adler. LC 78-2833. (Illus.). (gr. 4-6). 1978. PLB 6.90 s&l (ISBN 0-531-02216-1). Watts.

Math Review. pocket ed. 150p. (gr. 7-12). 1981. pap. text ed. 2.50 (ISBN 0-8120-2198-3). Barron. Postponed.

Math Skills for Science. R. W. Bibeau. (gr. 10-12). 1973. 4.00 o.p. (ISBN 0-201-00437-2, Sch Div); tchr's guide 2.22 o.p. (ISBN 0-201-05753-0); dupl. masters 36.12 o.p. (ISBN 0-685-64744-7, 0438). A-W.

Math Skills for the Sciences. John G. Pearson et al. LC 75-40065. (Wiley Self-Teaching Guides Ser). 1976. text ed. 5.95 (ISBN 0-471-67541-5). Wiley.

Math Squared: Graph Paper Activities for Fun & Fundamentals. David P. Stern. LC 80-15932. 115p. 1981. pap. text ed. 5.50x (ISBN 0-8077-2585-4). Tchrs Coll.

Math Without Fear. Carol G. Crawford. (New Viewpoints Vision Bks.). 288p. 1980. 11.95 (ISBN 0-531-06377-1). Watts.

Math Word Problems. Susan Mahoney & Barbara Gregorvich. LC 79-730247. (Illus.). 1979. pap. text ed. 99.00 (ISBN 0-89290-130-6, A515-SATC). Soc for Visual.

Math Word Problems, 3 vols. Sullivan Associates. (gr. 2-6). 1972. pap. text ed. 2.50 each ans. key 1, 2, 3 (ISBN 0-686-57755-8). Learning Line.

Math Workbook for Foodservice-Lodging. H. W. Crawford & Milton C. McDowell. 1971. pap. 11.95 (ISBN 0-8436-0519-7); pap. text ed. 11.95 (ISBN 0-8436-0534-0); answer bk. 1.95 (ISBN 0-8436-0538-3). CBI Pub.

Mathamatics As a Cultural System. Raymond I. Wilder. (Foundations & Philosophy of Science & Technology Ser.). 170p. 1981. 25.00 (ISBN 0-08-025796-8). Pergamon.

Mathematical Actives: Essays on Mathematics & Its Historical Development. Ed. by Joseph W. Dauben. LC 80-1781. 1981. write for info. (ISBN 0-12-204050-3). Acad Pr.

Mathematical Analysis. K. G. Binmore. LC 76-28006. (Illus.). 1977. 47.00 (ISBN 0-521-21480-7); pap. 13.95x (ISBN 0-521-29167-4). Cambridge U Pr.

Mathematical Analysis: A Modern Approach to Advanced Calculus. 2nd ed. Tom M. Apostol. LC 72-11473. 1974. text ed. 21.95 (ISBN 0-201-00288-4). A-W.

Mathematical Analysis: A Special Course. G. Y. Shilov. 1965. 37.00 (ISBN 0-08-010796-6); pap. 21.00 (ISBN 0-08-013616-8). Pergamon.

Mathematical Analysis & Applications. Ed. by Leopoldo Nachbin. (Advances in Mathematics Supplementary Studies: Vol. 7). 1981. Pt. A. write for info. (ISBN 0-12-512801-0); Pt. B. write for info. (ISBN 0-12-512802-9). Acad Pr.

Mathematical Analysis for Business & Economics. Jagdish C. Arya & Robin W. Lardner. (Illus.). 768p. 1981. text ed. 19.95 (ISBN 0-13-561019-2). P-H.

Mathematical Analysis for Business Decisions. rev. ed. James E. Howell & Daniel Teichroew. 1971. text ed. 14.95x o.p. (ISBN 0-256-00197-9). Irwin.

Mathematical Analysis of Bluffing in Poker. R. Christensen. 60p. 1981. 9.50 (ISBN 0-686-28920-X). Entropy Ltd.

Mathematical Applications for Management, Life & Social Studies. Ronald J. Harshbarger & James J. Reynoldds. 604p. 1981. text ed. 17.95 (ISBN 0-669-03209-3); solutions guide avail. (ISBN 0-669-03211-5). Heath.

Mathematical Applications in Political Science, Vol. 3. Ed. by Joseph L. Bernd & Archer Jones. LC 67-28023. 1967. 7.50x (ISBN 0-8139-0027-1). U Pr of Va.

Mathematical Applications in Political Science, Vol. 4. Ed. by Joseph L. Bernd. LC 67-28023. (Illus.). 122p. 1969. 7.50x (ISBN 0-8139-0262-2). U Pr of Va.

Mathematical Applications in Political Science, Vol. 5. Ed. by Joseph L. Bernd & James F. Herndon. LC 67-28023. (Illus.). 100p. 1971. 7.50x (ISBN 0-8139-0313-0). U Pr of Va.

Mathematical Applications in Political Science, Vol. 6. Ed. by Joseph L. Bernd & James F. Herndon. LC 67-28023. (Illus.). 1972. 10.00x (ISBN 0-8139-0386-6). U Pr of Va.

Mathematical Applications in Political Science, Vol. 7. Ed. by Joseph L. Bernd & James F. Herndon. LC 67-28023. (Illus.). 90p. 1974. 10.00x (ISBN 0-8139-0506-0). U Pr of Va.

Mathematical Approach to Evaluating Systems. Barbara F. Medina. 250p. 1981. price not set (ISBN 0-677-05570-6). Gordon.

Mathematical Aspects of Computer Science: Proceedings of a Symposium, New York City, Apr. 1966. Ed. by J. T. Schwartz. LC 67-16554. 1978. Repr. of 1967 ed. 12.80 (ISBN 0-8218-1319-6, PSAPM-19). Am Math.

Mathematical Aspects of Computerized Tomography: Proceedings. Ed. by G. T. Herman & F. Natterer. (Lecture Notes in Medical Information Ser.: Vol. 8). 309p. 1981. pap. 28.10 (ISBN 0-387-10277-9). Springer-Verlag.

Mathematical Aspects of Production & Distribution of Energy. Ed. by Peter D. Lax. LC 77-7174. (Proceedings of Symposia in Applied Mathematics: No. 21). 1979. Repr. of 1977 ed. with corrections 12.80 (ISBN 0-8218-0121-X, PSAPM-21). Am Math.

Mathematical Astronomy with a Pocket Calculator. Aubrey Jones. LC 78-12075. 1979. 16.95 (ISBN 0-470-26552-3). Halsted Pr.

Mathematical Basis of Statistics. Jean-Rene Barra & L. Herbach. LC 80-519. (Probability & Mathematical Statistical Ser.). 1981. write for info. (ISBN 0-12-079240-0). Acad Pr.

Mathematical Bioeconomics: The Optimal Management of Renewable Resources. Colin W. Clark. LC 76-16473. (Pure & Applied Mathematics Ser.). 1976. 26.95 (ISBN 0-471-15856-9, Pub. by Wiiley-Interscience). Wiley.

Mathematical Biology-a Conference on Theoretical Aspects of Molecular Science: Proceedings of a Conference Held at Southern Illinois University at Carbondale, May 27-28, 1980. Ed. by T. A. Burton. (Illus.). 241p. 1981. 30.00 (ISBN 0-08-026348-8). Pergamon.

Mathematical Carnival: A New Round-up of Tantalizers & Puzzles from "Scientific American". Martin Gardner. 1977. pap. 3.95 o.p. (ISBN 0-394-72349-X, Vin). Random.

Mathematical Concepts for Nursing: A Workbook. Helen Readey & William Readey. LC 79-20751. 1980. 7.95 (ISBN 0-201-06166-X). A-W.

Mathematical Concepts in Pharmacology. Margaret L. Franks & Joy D. Graves. (Skills Work Book for the Health Sciences). 1973. 3.95x (ISBN 0-88236-600-9). Anaheim Pub Co.

Mathematical Cosmology. P. R. Landsberg & D. A. Evans. 1980. pap. 14.95x (ISBN 0-19-851147-7). Oxford U Pr.

Mathematical Cosmology: An Introduction. Peter T. Landsberg & David Evans. (Illus.). 1978. pap. 18.95x o.p. (ISBN 0-19-851136-1). Oxford U Pr.

Mathematical Cosmology & Extragalactic Astronomy. E. Segal. (Pure & Applied Mathematics Ser.: Vol. 68). 1976. 32.00 (ISBN 0-12-635250-X). Acad Pr.

Mathematical Criminology. David F. Greenberg. (Illus.). 1979. text ed. 22.50x (ISBN 0-8135-0873-8). Rutgers U Pr.

Mathematical Cuneiform Texts. O. Neugebauer & A. Sachs. (American Oriental Ser.: Vol. 29). 1945. 10.00x (ISBN 0-686-00013-7). Am Orient Soc.

Mathematical Developments Arising from the Hilbert Problems: Proceedings, 2 pts, Vol. 28. Symposia in Pure Mathematics-Northern Illinois Univ., May 1974. Ed. by F. E. Browder. LC 76-20437. 1976. softcover 16.60 (ISBN 0-8218-1428-1, PSPUM-28). Am Math.

Mathematical Dictionary for Economics & Business Administration. Wayne A. Skrapek et al. 1978. text ed. 29.95 o.p. (ISBN 0-205-05011-5). Allyn.

Mathematical Discovery on Understanding, Learning & Teaching Problem Solving, 2 Vols. Gyorgy Polya. LC 62-8784. 1962. Vol. 1. 18.95 (ISBN 0-471-69333-2); Vol. 2. 16.95 o.p. (ISBN 0-471-69335-9). Wiley.

Mathematical Economics & Operations Research: A Guide to Information Sources. Ed. by Joseph Zaremba. LC 73-17586. (Economics Information Guide Ser.: Vol. 10). 1978. 30.00 (ISBN 0-8103-1298-0). Gale.

Mathematical Economics: Topics in Multi-Sectoral Economics. J. E. Woods. (Modern Economics Ser.). (Illus.). 1978. pap. text ed. 19.95 (ISBN 0-582-44675-9). Longman.

Mathematical Enterprises for Schools. A. J. Cameron. 1966. 7.50 (ISBN 0-08-011833-X). Pergamon.

Mathematical Foundation of Computer Science: Proceedings. Ed. by P. Dembrinski. (Lecture Notes in Computer Science: Vol. 88). 723p. 1980. pap. 37.20 (ISBN 0-387-10027-X). Springer-Verlag.

Mathematical Foundations for Management Science & Systems Analysis. J. William Schmidt. (Operations Research & Industrial Engineering Ser.). 1974. text ed. 22.95 (ISBN 0-12-627050-3). Acad Pr.

Mathematical Foundations in Engineering & Science: Algebra & Analysis. A. Michel & C. Herget. 1981. 27.95 (ISBN 0-13-561035-4). P-H.

Mathematical Foundations of Computer Science 1979: Proceedings, 8th Symposium, Olomouc, Czechoslovakia, September 3-7, 1979. Ed. by J. Becvar. (Lecture Notes in Computer Science: Vol. 74). 1979. pap. 26.40 (ISBN 0-387-09526-8). Springer-Verlag.

Mathematical Foundations of Information Theory. Alexander I. Khinchin. 1957. pap. text ed. 2.50 (ISBN 0-486-60434-9). Dover.

Mathematical Foundations of Programming. Frank S. Beckman. LC 79-1453. 1980. text ed. 20.95 (ISBN 0-201-14462-X). A-W.

Mathematical Foundations of Statistical Mechanics. Alexander I. Khinchin. Tr. by George Gamow. 1949. pap. text ed. 3.00 (ISBN 0-486-60147-1). Dover.

Mathematical Frontiers of the Social & Policy Sciences. Ed. by Loren Cobb & Robert M. Thrall. (AAAS Selected Symposium Ser.: No. 54). 186p. 1980. lib. bdg. 22.00x (ISBN 0-89158-953-8). Westview.

Mathematical Games for One or Two. Mannis Charosh. LC 74-187934. (Young Math Ser.). (Illus.). (gr. 1-5). 1972. 7.95 (ISBN 0-690-52324-6, TYC-J); PLB 7.89 (ISBN 0-690-52325-4). T Y Crowell.

Mathematical Gardiner. Ed. by David A. Klarner. 382p. 1980. 19.95x (ISBN 0-534-98015-5). Wadsworth Pub.

Mathematical Ideas. Mary O. Miklos. LC 80-5871. 344p. 1980. pap. text ed. 11.50 (ISBN 0-8191-1099-X). U Pr of Amer.

Mathematical Ideas. 3rd ed. Charles D. Miller & Vern E. Heeren. 1978. 16.59x (ISBN 0-673-15090-9). Scott F.

Mathematical Ideas in Biology. J. Maynard Smith. LC 68-25088. (Illus.). 1968. 21.50 (ISBN 0-521-07335-9); pap. 7.95x (ISBN 0-521-09550-6). Cambridge U Pr.

Mathematical Introduction to Logic. Herbert B. Enderton. 1972. 20.95 (ISBN 0-12-238450-4). Acad Pr.

Mathematical Land Use Theory. George J. Papageorgiou. LC 75-21303. (Illus.). 1976. 32.95 (ISBN 0-669-00164-3). Lexington Bks.

Mathematical Learning. L. Feldman. 224p. 1969. 23.00 (ISBN 0-677-13250-6). Gordon.

Mathematical Logic. 2nd ed. R. L. Goodstein. 1965. text ed. 6.50x (ISBN 0-7185-1010-0, Leicester). Humanities.

Mathematical Logic. J. R. Shoenfield. 1967. text ed. 19.95 (ISBN 0-201-07028-6). A-W.

Mathematical Methods & Applications of Scattering Theory: Proceedings. Ed. by J. A. DaSanto. (Lecture Notes in Physics: Vol. 130). 331p. 1980. pap. 22.00 (ISBN 0-387-10023-7). Springer-Verlag.

Mathematical Methods for Chemists. R. K. Mackie et al. LC 72-4758. (Illus.). 154p. 1972. text ed. 13.95 (ISBN 0-470-56295-1). Halsted Pr.

Mathematical Methods for Digital Computers, 2 Vols. Ed. by Anthony Ralston & H. S. Wilf. LC 60-6509. 1960. Vol. 1. 29.95 (ISBN 0-471-70686-8); Vol. 2. 31.95 (ISBN 0-471-70689-2, Pub by Wiley-Interscience). Wiley.

Mathematical Methods for Economists. rev. ed. Stephen Glaister. 1978. pap. 14.50x (ISBN 0-631-19050-3, Pub. by Basil Blackwell England). Biblio Dist.

Mathematical Methods for Geographers & Planners. A. G. Wilson & M. J. Kirkby. (Illus.). 344p. 1975. text ed. 19.00x o.p. (ISBN 0-19-874022-0); pap. text ed. 7.50x o.p. (ISBN 0-19-874023-9). Oxford U Pr.

Mathematical Methods for Physicists. 2nd ed. George Arfken. 1970. text ed. 25.95 (ISBN 0-12-059851-5). Acad Pr.

Mathematical Methods for Social & Management Scientists. T. Marll McDonald. 544p. 1974. text ed. 19.95 (ISBN 0-395-17089-3); instructor's manual pap. 2.25 (ISBN 0-395-17858-4). HM.

Mathematical Methods for Texture Analysis. 2nd ed. Hans Bunge. Tr. by Peter Morris from Ger. LC 79-40054. 1981. text ed. 79.00 (ISBN 0-408-10642-5). Butterworths.

Mathematical Methods for the Physical Sciences. K. F. Riley. LC 73-89765. 512p. (Orig.). 1974. 57.50 (ISBN 0-521-20390-2); pap. 22.95x (ISBN 0-521-09839-4). Cambridge U Pr.

Mathematical Methods in Chemical Engineering. 2nd ed. Ed. by V. G. Jenson & G. V. Jeffreys. 1978. text ed. 32.00 (ISBN 0-12-384456-8). Acad Pr.

Mathematical Methods in Chemical Engineering: Matrices & Their Application. Neal R. Amundson. 1966. ref. ed. 25.95 (ISBN 0-13-561084-2). P-H.

Mathematical Methods in Clinical Practice. Ed. by G. I. Marchuk & N. I. Nisevich. (Illus.). 150p. 1981. 60.00 (ISBN 0-08-025493-4). Pergamon.

Mathematical Methods in the Physical Sciences. Merle C. Potter. (Illus.). 1978. ref. ed. 24.95 (ISBN 0-13-561134-2). P-H.

Mathematical Methods in the Social & Managerial Sciences. Patrick Hayes. LC 74-22361. 448p. 1975. 35.50 (ISBN 0-471-36490-8, Pub. by Wiley-Interscience). Wiley.

Mathematical Methods of Physics. 2nd ed. Jon Mathews & Robert L. Walker. 1970. text ed. 24.95 (ISBN 0-8053-7002-1). Benjamin-Cummings.

Mathematical Model for Handling in a Warehouse. E. Kay. LC 68-21104. 1968. 22.00 (ISBN 0-08-012832-7); pap. 10.75 (ISBN 0-08-012831-9). Pergamon.

Mathematical Model of Aggregate Plant Production. Compiled by American Society of Civil Engineers. 120p. 1974. pap. text ed. 6.50 (ISBN 0-87262-071-9). Am Soc Civil Eng.

Mathematical Model Techniques for Learning Theories. Gustav Levine & C. Burke. 1972. text ed. 17.95 (ISBN 0-12-445250-7). Acad Pr.

Mathematical Modeling & Digital Simulation for Engineers & Scientists. J. M. Smith. LC 76-52419. 1977. 29.00 (ISBN 0-471-80344-8, Pub. by Wiley-Interscience). Wiley.

Mathematical Modeling for Industrial Processes. L. P. Hyvaerinen. LC 70-111899. (Lecture Notes in Operations Research & Mathematical Systems: Vol. 19). (Illus.). 1970. pap. 10.70 o.p. (ISBN 0-387-04943-6). Springer-Verlag.

Mathematical Modeling in Epidemiology. J. C. Frauenthal. (Universitexts Ser.). 118p. 1980. pap. 16.80 (ISBN 0-387-10328-7). Springer-Verlag.

Mathematical Modeling of Biological Systems: An Introductory Guidebook. Harvey J. Gold. LC 77-8193. 1977. 27.95 (ISBN 0-471-02092-3, Pub. by Wiley-Interscience). Wiley.

Mathematical Modeling of Energy Systems. Ed. by Ibbrahim Kavrakoglu. (NATO Advanced Study Institute Ser.: Applied Science, No. 37). 490p. 1980. 55.00x (ISBN 90-286-0690-4). Sijthoff & Noordhoff.

Mathematical Modeling of Hydrologic Processes. G. G. Svanidze. LC 79-57578. 1980. 25.00 (ISBN 0-686-64298-8). WRP.

Mathematical Modeling with Computers. Samuel L. Jacoby & Janusz S. Kowalik. (Illus.). 1980. text ed. 23.95 (ISBN 0-13-561555-0). P-H.

Mathematical Modelling in Water & Wastewater Treatment. D. A. Morley. (Illus.). 1979. 62.10x (ISBN 0-85334-842-1). Intl Ideas.

Mathematical Models & Applications: With Emphasis on the Social,Life, & Management Sciences. Daniel Maki & Maynard Thompson. (Illus.). 464p. 1973. ref. ed. 23.95 (ISBN 0-13-561670-0). P-H.

Mathematical Models for Environmental Problems: Proceedings of the University of Southampton, England, 8-12 September, 1975. Ed. by C. A. Brebbia. LC 75-41453. 1976. 49.95 (ISBN 0-470-15206-0). Halsted Pr.

Mathematical Models for the Growth of Human Populations. J. H. Pollard. LC 72-91957. 204p. 1973. 29.50 (ISBN 0-521-20111-X); pap. 9.95x (ISBN 0-521-29442-8). Cambridge U Pr.

Mathematical Models in International Relations. Ed. by Dina A. Zinnes & John V. Gillespie. LC 75-25000. (Special Studies). (Illus.). 1976. text ed. 45.00 (ISBN 0-275-55870-3). Praeger.

Mathematical Models in Molecular & Cellular Biology. Ed. by L. A. Segel. LC 79-52854. (Illus.). 600p. Date not set. 100.00 (ISBN 0-521-22925-1). Cambridge U Pr.

Mathematical Models in the Earth Sciences: Proceedings of the 7th Geochautauqua, Syracuse University, Oct. 1978. Ed. by J. M. Cubitt. 90p. pap. 41.25 (ISBN 0-08-025305-9). Pergamon.

Mathematical Models in the Social, Management & Life Sciences. D. N. Burghes. LC 79-40989. 287p. 1980. pap. 19.95 (ISBN 0-470-27073-X). Halsted Pr.

Mathematical Models in the Social, Management & Life Sciences. D. N. Burghes & A. D. Wood. LC 79-40989. (Mathematics & Its Applications Ser.). 287p. 1980. 39.95x (ISBN 0-470-26862-X); pap. text ed. 19.95 (ISBN 0-470-27073-X). Halsted Pr.

Mathematical Models in Water Pollution Control. Ed. by A. James. LC 77-7214. 1978. 55.50 (ISBN 0-471-99471-5, Pub. by Wiley-Interscience). Wiley.

Mathematical Models: Mechanical Vibrations, Population, Dynamics & Traffic Flow, An Introduction to Applied Mathematics. R. Haberman. 1977. 23.95 (ISBN 0-13-561738-3). P-H.

Mathematical Models of Metabolic Regulation. Keleti. 1976. 17.00 (ISBN 0-9960001-2-7, Pub. by Kaido Hungary). Heyden.

Mathematical Models of Sociology. Ed. by P. Krishnan. (Sociological Review Monograph: No. 24). 229p. 1979. pap. 22.50x (ISBN 0-8476-2297-5). Rowman.

Mathematical Models of the Chemical, Physical & Mathematical Properties of Engineering Alloys. John Zotos. LC 76-22228. 1977. 28.95 (ISBN 0-669-00884-2). Lexington Bks.

Mathematical Models of the Dynamics of the Human Eye. R. Collins & T. J. Van Der Werff. (Lecture Notes in Biomathematics: Vol. 34). 99p. 1980. pap. 9.80 (ISBN 0-387-09751-1). Springer-Verlag.

Mathematical Optimization & Economic Theory. Michael D. Intriligator. (Mathematical Economics Ser.). 1971. text ed. 22.95 (ISBN 0-13-561753-7). P-H.

Mathematical Panorama: Topics for the Liberal Arts. William P. Berlinghoff et al. 1980. text ed. 15.95 (ISBN 0-669-02423-6). Heath.

Mathematical Papers. William K. Clifford. LC 67-28488. 1968. Repr. 29.50 (ISBN 0-8284-0210-8). Chelsea Pub.

Mathematical Papers. George Green. LC 70-92316. 15.00 o.p. (ISBN 0-8284-0229-9). Chelsea Pub.

Mathematical Papers of Isaac Newton, Vol. 5. Isaac Newton. Ed. by D. T. Whiteside et al. LC 65-11203. (Illus.). 600p. 1972. 150.00 (ISBN 0-521-08262-5). Cambridge U Pr.

Mathematical Papers of Isaac Newton, Vol. 1, 1664-1666. Isaac Newton. Ed. by D. T. Whiteside & M. A. Hoskin. 150.00 (ISBN 0-521-05817-1). Cambridge U Pr.

Mathematical Papers of Isaac Newton, Vol. 3, 1670-1673. Isaac Newton. Ed. by D. T. Whiteside & M. A. Hoskin. LC 65-11203. (Illus.). 150.00 (ISBN 0-521-07119-4). Cambridge U Pr.

Mathematical Papers of Isaac Newton, Vol. 6: 1684-1691. Isaac Newton. Ed. by D. T. Whiteside & M. A. Hoskin. LC 73-86046. (Illus.). 6000p. 1975. 150.00 (ISBN 0-521-08719-8). Cambridge U Pr.

Mathematical Papers of Isaac Newton: Vol. 8, 1697-1722. Isaac Newton. Ed. by D. T. Whiteside. LC 65-11203. (Illus.). 750p. Date not set. price not set (ISBN 0-521-20103-9). Cambridge U Pr.

Mathematical Papers of Sir William Rowan Hamilton, Vol. 3. William R. Hamilton. Ed. by H. Halberstam & R. E. Ingram. 1967. 130.00 (ISBN 0-521-05183-5). Cambridge U Pr.

Mathematical Physics. E. Butkov. 1968. 27.95 (ISBN 0-201-00727-4). A-W.

Mathematical Physics. B. D. Gupta. 1977. 35.00 (ISBN 0-7069-0514-8, Pub. by Vikas India). Advent Bk.

Mathematical Physics. Donald H. Menzel. Orig. Title: Theoretical Physics. 1953. pap. text ed. 6.00 (ISBN 0-486-60056-4). Dover.

Mathematical Physics Review, Vol.i. Ed. by S. O. Novikov. (Soviet Scietific Reviews Ser.). 218p. 1980. 44.50 (ISBN 3-7186-0019-6). Harwood Academic.

Mathematical Plums. Ed. by Ross Honsberger. LC 79-65513. (Dolciani Mathematical Expositions: Vol. IV). 14.00 (ISBN 0-88385-304-3). Math Assn.

Mathematical Principles of Natural Philosophy and His System of the World. (Principia) Sir Isaac Newton. Rev. by Florian Cajori. Tr. by Andrew Motte. Incl. Vol. I. Motions of Bodies. pap. 5.95x (ISBN 0-520-00928-2, CAMPUS70); Vol. II. System of the World. pap. 5.95 (ISBN 0-520-00929-0, CAMPUS71). 1962. Set. pap. 5.95x (ISBN 0-520-00927-4). U of Cal Pr.

Mathematical Problems in the Theory of Phase Transitions. Ya G. Sinai. 128p. 1981. 27.00 (ISBN 0-08-026469-7). Pergamon.

Mathematical Programming. 2nd ed. Claude McMillan. LC 74-23273. (Management & Administration Ser.). 650p. 1975. text ed. 27.95 (ISBN 0-471-58572-6); solutions manual avail. (ISBN 0-471-58573-4). Wiley.

Mathematical Programming for Management & Business. G. Hayhurst. 1976. pap. 13.50x (ISBN 0-7131-3355-4). Intl Ideas.

Mathematical Programming in Statistics. Subramanvam Arthanari & Yadolah Dodge. LC 80-21637. (Probability & Math Statistics Ser.: Applied Probability & Statistics). 375p. 1981. 25.00 (ISBN 0-471-08073-X, Pub. by Wiley-Interscience). Wiley.

Mathematical Programming: Structures & Algorithms. Jeremy F. Shapiro. LC 79-4478. 1979. 26.95 (ISBN 0-471-77886-9, Pub by Wiley-Interscience). Wiley.

Mathematical Programming with Business Applications. N. K. Kwak. (Illus.). 384p. 1972. text ed. 21.50 (ISBN 0-07-035717-X, C); instructor's manual 4.95 (ISBN 0-07-035718-8). McGraw.

Mathematical Psychology: An Elementary Introduction. Clyde Coombs et al. 1969. text ed. 21.95 (ISBN 0-13-562157-7). P-H.

Mathematical Puzzles. Martin Gardner. LC 61-6142. (Illus.). (gr. 7 up). 1961. 7.95 (ISBN 0-690-52360-2, TYC-J). T Y Crowell.

Mathematical Recreations & Essays. rev. ed. W. Rouse Ball. 1960. 12.95 (ISBN 0-02-506430-4); pap. 1.95 (ISBN 0-02-091480-6). Macmillan.

Mathematical Recreations & Essays. 12th ed. Walter W. Ball & H. S. Coxeter. LC 72-186276. 446p. 1974. pap. 6.00 (ISBN 0-8020-6138-9). U of Toronto Pr.

Mathematical Reviews Cumulative Author Indexes. American Mathematical Society. Incl. Twenty Volume Author Index of Mathematical Reviews, 1940-59, 2 pts. 1977. 140.00 set (ISBN 0-685-22496-1, MREVIN 40-59); Author Index of Mathematical Reviews, 1960-64, 2 pts. 1966. 90.00 set (ISBN 0-8218-0026-4, MREVIN 60-64); Author Index of Mathematical Reviews, 1965-72. 1974. 200.00 (ISBN 0-8218-0027-2, MREVIN 65-72). Repr. Am Math.

Mathematical Reviews Cumulative Index: 1973-1979. Date not set. cancelled (ISBN 0-8218-0035-3). Am Math.

Mathematical Sciences: A Report. Division of Mathematics - Committee on Support of Research in Mathematical Sciences. 1968. pap. 7.25 (ISBN 0-309-01681-9). Natl Acad Pr.

Mathematical Sciences Administrative Directory. 170p. (Published annually). 6.00 o.p. (ISBN 0-8218-0002-7, ADMDIR). Am Math.

Mathematical Sciences: Undergraduate Education. National Academy Of Sciences - Division Of Mathematics Committee On Support Of Research In Mathematical Sciences. 1968. pap. 5.50 (ISBN 0-309-01682-7). Natl Acad Pr.

Mathematical Snapshots. 3rd ed. Hugo Steinhaus. (Illus.). 1969. 15.95 (ISBN 0-19-500117-6). Oxford U Pr.

Mathematical Sociology. Robert K. Leik & Barbara F. Meeker. LC 74-22271. (Methods of Social Science Ser.). (Illus.). 272p. 1975. 19.95 (ISBN 0-13-562108-9). P-H.

Mathematical Sociology: A Selective Annotated Bibliography. Janet Holland & M. D. Steuer. LC 72-97255. 1970. 8.50x (ISBN 0-8052-3336-9). Schocken.

Mathematical Statistical Mechanics. Colin J. Thompson. LC 78-70319. 1979. 15.00x (ISBN 0-691-08219-7); pap. 5.95 (ISBN 0-691-08220-0). Princeton U Pr.

Mathematical Statistics. 3rd ed. John E. Freund & Ronald E. Walpole. 1980. text ed. 20.95 (ISBN 0-13-562066-X). P-H.

Mathematical Statistics: A Decision Theoretic Approach. Thomas S. Ferguson. (Probability and Mathematical Statistics: Vol. 1). 1967. text ed. 22.95 (ISBN 0-12-253750-5). Acad Pr.

Mathematical Statistics: Basic Ideas & Selected Topics. P. J. Bickel & K. A. Doksum. LC 76-8724. 1977. 28.95x (ISBN 0-8162-0784-4). Holden-Day.

Mathematical Statistics with Applications. 2nd ed. William Mendenhall & Richard L. Schaeffer. 500p. 1981. text ed. 22.95 (ISBN 0-87872-279-3). Duxbury Pr.

Mathematical Systems in International Relations Research. Ed. by John V. Gillispie & Dina A. Zinnes. LC 75-23964. 1977. text ed. 45.95 (ISBN 0-275-55620-4). Praeger.

Mathematical Taxonomy. N. Jardine & R. Sibson. LC 70-149578. 1971. 38.50 (ISBN 0-471-44050-7, Pub. by Wiley-Interscience). Wiley.

Mathematical Teasers. Julio A. Mira. LC 74-101122. (Orig.). 1970. pap. 2.95 (ISBN 0-06-463230-X, EH 230, EH). Har-Row.

Mathematical Techniques & Physical Applications. J. Killingbeck & G. H. Cole. (Pure & Applied Physics Ser). 1971. text ed. 22.95 (ISBN 0-12-406850-2); solutions manual 3.00 (ISBN 0-12-406856-1). Acad Pr.

Mathematical Techniques in Chemistry. Joseph B. Dence. LC 75-16337. 442p. 1975. text ed. 22.95 (ISBN 0-471-20319-X, Pub. by Wiley-Interscience). Wiley.

Mathematical Theory of Communication. Claude E. Shannon & Warren Weaver. LC 49-11922. 1949. 6.00 o.p. (ISBN 0-252-72548-4); pap. 2.95 (ISBN 0-252-72548-4). U of Ill Pr.

Mathematical Theory of Diffusion & Reaction in Permeable Catalysts, 2 vols. Rutherford Aris. Incl. Vol. 1. Theory of the Steady State. 470p. 55.00x (ISBN 0-19-851931-1); Vol. 2. Questions of Uniqueness, Stability, & Transient Behaviour. 232p. 34.95x (ISBN 0-19-851942-7). (Illus.). 1975. 75.00x set (ISBN 0-19-519829-8). Oxford U Pr.

Mathematical Theory of Expanding & Contracting Economies. Oskar Morgenstern & G. L. Thompson. LC 75-18399. 288p. 1976. 22.95 (ISBN 0-669-00089-2). Lexington Bks.

Mathematical Theory of Insurance. Karl Borch. LC 73-11670. 352p. 1974. 24.95 (ISBN 0-669-86942-2). Lexington Bks.

Mathematical Theory of Non-Uniform Gases. 3rd ed. S. Chapman & T. G. Cowling. LC 70-77285. (Illus.). 1970. 47.95 (ISBN 0-521-07577-7). Cambridge U Pr.

Mathematical Theory of Program Correctness. M. De Bakker. 1980. 28.00 (ISBN 0-13-562132-1). P-H.

Mathematical Theory of Quantitative Genetics. M. G. Bulmer. (Illus.). 220p. 1980. 74.00 (ISBN 0-19-857530-0). Oxford U Pr.

Mathematical Theory of Relativity. 3rd ed. Arthur S. Eddington. LC 74-1458. ix, 270p. 1975. text ed. 11.95 (ISBN 0-8284-0278-7). Chelsea Pub.

Mathematical Theory of Switching Circuits & Automata. Sze-Tsen Hu. LC 68-18370. (Illus.). 1968. 24.50x (ISBN 0-520-00581-3). U of Cal Pr.

Mathematical Theory of Symmetry in Solids: Representation Theory for Point Groups & Space Groups. C. J. Bradley & A. P. Cracknell. (Illus.). 762p. 1971. 125.00x (ISBN 0-19-851920-6). Oxford U Pr.

Mathematical Thought from Ancient to Modern Times. Morris Kline. 1300p. 1972. 60.00 (ISBN 0-19-501496-0). Oxford U Pr.

Mathematical Understanding of Chemical Engineering Systems: Selected Papers of Neal R. Amundson. Ed. by Rutherford Aris & Arvind Varma. LC 79-40686. (Illus.). 1980. 130.00 (ISBN 0-08-023836-X). Pergamon.

Mathematical Work of Charles Babbage. J. M. Dubbey. LC 77-71409. (Illus.). 1978. 47.50 (ISBN 0-521-21649-4). Cambridge U Pr.

Mathematically Speaking. Morton Davis. 484p. 1980. text ed. 16.95 (ISBN 0-686-68334-X, HC); instr's guide avail. HarBraceJ.

Mathematician's Apology. rev. ed. Godfrey H. Hardy. LC 67-21958. 1969. 18.95 (ISBN 0-521-05207-6); pap. 5.50x (ISBN 0-521-09577-8). Cambridge U Pr.

Mathematics. Stanley H. Kaplan & Max Peters. Incl. Ninth Year (Elementary Algebra) LC 58-33441. 1977. pap. 3.50 (ISBN 0-8120-0196-6); Tenth Year. pap. 3.95 (ISBN 0-8120-0204-0); Eleventh Year. LC 57-58722. 1977. pap. 3.95 (ISBN 0-8120-0112-5). (Regents Exams & Answers Ser.). (gr. 9-12). 1977. Barron.

Mathematics. Jack Rudman. (Undergraduate Program Field Test Ser.: UPFT-15). (Cloth bdg. avail. on request). pap. 9.95 (ISBN 0-8373-6015-3). Natl Learning.

Mathematics: A Cultural Approach. Morris Kline. 1962. text ed. 19.95 (ISBN 0-201-03770-X). A-W.

Mathematics: A Foundation for Decisions. Dennis E. Grawoig et al. LC 75-12097. (Illus.). 542p. 1976. text ed. 18.95 (ISBN 0-201-02598-1); instr's guide 4.50 (ISBN 0-201-02595-7). A-W.

Mathematics, a Human Endeavor: A Textbook for Those Who Think They Don't Like the Subject. Harold R. Jacobs. LC 70-116898. (Illus.). 1970. text ed. 11.95x (ISBN 0-7167-0439-0); tchr's guide 6.95x (ISBN 0-7167-0446-3). W H Freeman.

Mathematics: A Modeling Approach. Marvin L. Bittinger & J. Conrad Crown. 1981. write for info. (ISBN 0-201-03116-7). A-W.

Mathematics: A Practical Approach. Kenneth Kalmanson & Patricia C. Kenschaft. LC 77-81755. (Illus.). 1978. text ed. 18.95x (ISBN 0-87901-085-1). Worth.

Mathematics: A Way of Thinking. new ed. Mary Baratta-Lorton. (gr. 1-8). 1977. tchr's. ed. 19.75 (ISBN 0-201-04322-X, Sch Div). A-W.

Mathematics Activities Handbook for Grades 5-12. 1976. 11.95 o.p. (ISBN 0-13-562280-8). P-H.

Mathematics: An Activity Approach. Albert B. Bennett & Leonard T. Nelson. 1979. text ed. 11.50 (ISBN 0-205-06518-X, 5665183); avail. instr's man. 3.95 (ISBN 0-205-06540-6, 566540X). Allyn.

Mathematics: An Everyday Experience. 2nd ed. Charles D. Miller & Vern E. Heeren. 1980. text ed. 16.95x (ISBN 0-673-15279-0). Scott F.

Mathematics: An Everyday Language. R. E. Wheeler & E. R. Wheeler. LC 78-13072. 1979. text ed. 19.95x (ISBN 0-471-03423-1); student supplement 7.50 (ISBN 0-471-04924-7); tchrs. manual 2.85 (ISBN 0-471-05409-7). Wiley.

Mathematics: An Informal Approach. Albert B. Bennett & Leonard T. Nelson. 1979. text ed. 17.80 (ISBN 0-205-06519-8, 5665191); avail. instr's man. 4.50 (ISBN 0-205-06541-4, 5665418). Allyn.

Mathematics: An Introduction to Its Spirit & Use: Readings from Scientific American. Intro. by Morris Kline. LC 78-7878. (Illus.). 1979. text ed. 19.95x (ISBN 0-7167-0370-X); pap. text ed. 9.95x (ISBN 0-7167-0369-6). W H Freeman.

Mathematics & Computing: With FORTRAN Programming. William S. Dorn & Herbert J. Greenberg. LC 67-19940. 1967. 24.95x o.p. (ISBN 0-471-21915-0). Wiley.

Mathematics & Humor. John A. Paulos. LC 80-12742. 1980. 12.95 (ISBN 0-226-65024-3). U of Chicago Pr.

Mathematics & Shop Series, 6 bks. Incl. Automotive Shop Math Book, 2 bks. Bk. 1 (ISBN 0-8273-0534-6). Bk. 2 (ISBN 0-8273-0535-4); Basic Algebra, Geometry & Trigonometry (ISBN 0-8273-0533-8); Basic Measurement; Business Math (ISBN 0-8273-0532-X); Electronics Shop Math (ISBN 0-8273-0536-2). 1970. Set. pap. 10.00 o.p. (ISBN 0-686-65024-7); pap. 1.80 ea. o.p.; ans. key 0.35 o.p. (ISBN 0-8273-0530-3). Delmar.

Mathematics & Statistics for Economics. 3rd ed. G. S. Monga. 1979. 18.95 (ISBN 0-7069-0588-1, Pub. by Vikas India). Advent Bk.

Mathematics & Statistics for the Bio-Sciences. G. Eason et al. LC 79-41815. (Ellis Horwood Series: Mathematics & Its Applications). 578p. 1980. 78.95x (ISBN 0-470-26963-4). Halsted Pr.

Mathematics & the Conditions of Learning: A Study of Arithmetic in the Primary School. J. B. Biggs. (General Ser.). 1970. Repr. of 1967 ed. text ed. 22.50x (ISBN 0-901225-24-X, NFER). Humanities.

Mathematics & the Liberal Arts. Jack C. Gill. LC 72-95501. 1973. pap. text ed. 15.95 (ISBN 0-675-08981-6); media: audiocassettes 89.50, 2-4 sets, 65.00 ea., 5 or more sets, 49.50 ea. (ISBN 0-675-08973-5); instructor's manual 3.95 (ISBN 0-686-66864-2). Merrill.

Mathematics & the Physical World. Morris Kline. (Illus.). 496p. 1981. pap. price not set (ISBN 0-486-24104-1). Dover.

Mathematics & the Primary School Curriculum. E. Choat. 128p. 1980. pap. text ed. 18.75x (ISBN 0-85633-206-2, NFER). Humanities.

Mathematics & the Real World. Bernhelm Booss & Mogens Niss. (Interdisciplinary Systems Research: No. 68). 1979. pap. 22.00 (ISBN 3-7643-1079-0). Birkhauser.

Mathematics & the Study of Social Relations. Patrick- Doreian. LC 75-163328. (Illus.). 1971. 8.00x (ISBN 0-8052-3415-2). Schocken.

Mathematics & Your Career. Alvin E. Geier & Nathaniel Lamm. (gr. 10-12). 1978. pap. text ed. 6.58 (ISBN 0-87720-241-9). AMSCO Sch.

Mathematics Applicable: Introductory Probability. Schools Council Sixth Form Mathematics Project. 1975. pap. text ed. 3.95x (ISBN 0-435-51698-1). Heinemann Ed.

Mathematics Applied to Business & the Social Sciences. Robert F. Brown & Brenda W. Brown. 640p. 1980. text ed. 19.95x (ISBN 0-534-00754-6). Wadsworth Pub.

Mathematics Applied to Electronics. James Harter & Wallace Beitzel. (Illus.). 1980. text ed. 18.95 (ISBN 0-8359-4288-0); instrs'. manual avail. Reston.

Mathematics As a Second Language. 2nd ed. Frances Lake & Joseph Neiomark. LC 76-14659. (Illus.). 1977. text ed. 17.95 (ISBN 0-201-04099-9). A-W.

Mathematics at the Farm. Vincent F. O'Connor. LC 77-19169. (Raintree Mathematics Ser.). (Illus.). (gr. k-3). 1978. PLB 8.95 (ISBN 0-8393-0055-7). Raintree Child.

Mathematics at Work. 2nd ed. Holbrook L. Horton. (Illus.). 1957. 16.00 (ISBN 0-8311-1047-3). Indus Pr.

Mathematics at Work: Algebra. Bertrand B. Singer. (Illus.). (gr. 9-12). 1977. pap. text ed. 12.95x (ISBN 0-07-057491-X, G); ans. key 1.95x (ISBN 0-07-057492-8); instructor's manual 5.95x (ISBN 0-07-057486-3). McGraw.

Mathematics: Contemporary Topics & Applications. Howard A. Silver. (Illus.). 1979. text ed. 17.95 (ISBN 0-13-563304-4). P-H.

Mathematics Encyclopedia: A Made Simple Book. Max Shapiro & Cadillac Publishing Company. LC 76-23817. 1977. pap. 5.95 (ISBN 0-385-12427-9, Made). Doubleday.

Mathematics for a Liberal Education. M. M. Ohmer. LC 79-119669. (Mathematics Ser). (Illus.). 1971. text ed. 13.95x (ISBN 0-201-05435-3); instructor's manual 2.75 (ISBN 0-201-05436-1). A-W.

Mathematics for Auto Mechanics. T. G. Hendrix & C. S. LaFevor. LC 77-72431. 1978. pap. text ed. 9.04 (ISBN 0-8273-1630-5); instructor's guide 1.60 (ISBN 0-8273-1631-3). Delmar.

Mathematics for Biomedical Applications. Stanton A. Glantz. LC 77-20320. 1979. 32.50x (ISBN 0-520-03599-2). U of Cal Pr.

Mathematics for Business & Consumers. rev. ed. Robert D. Mason et al. 1980. pap. text ed. 13.95x (ISBN 0-256-02433-2). Business Pubns.

Mathematics for Business Applications. new ed. Harold D. Shane. (Mathematics Ser.). 432p. 1976. text ed. 19.95x (ISBN 0-675-08668-X). Merrill.

Mathematics for Business Careers. Jack Cain & Robert A. Carman. LC 79-21747. 1981. pap. text ed. 16.95 (ISBN 0-471-03163-1). Wiley.

Mathematics for Business: In a Consumer Age. Stanley A. Salzman & Charles D. Miller. 1978. 14.95x (ISBN 0-673-15092-5). Scott F.

Mathematics for Business with Machine Applications. Wallace & Pitz. 448p. 1977. text ed. 17.27 (ISBN 0-7715-0901-4); tchr's. manual with text solutions 11.93 (ISBN 0-7715-0902-2); tchr's. ed., wkbk. 1 9.27 (ISBN 0-7715-0904-9); tchr's. ed., wkbk. 2 9.93 (ISBN 0-7715-0906-5); wkbk. 1, units 1-9 4.60 (ISBN 0-7715-0903-0); wkbk. 2, units 10-22 5.27 (ISBN 0-7715-0905-7). Forkner.

Mathematics for Careers: Measurement & Geometry. St. Paul Technical Vocational Institute Curriculum Commitee. LC 80-67549. (General Mathematics Ser.). 176p. 1981. pap. text ed. 7.40 (ISBN 0-8273-2058-2); price not set instr's. guide (ISBN 0-8273-2059-0). Delmar.

Mathematics for Carpenters. Robert Bradford. LC 75-19525. 1975. pap. 9.40 (ISBN 0-8273-1116-8); instructor's guide 1.60 (ISBN 0-8273-1117-6). Delmar.

Mathematics for Computer Graphics. Roy A. Liming. LC 79-65814. 1979. 35.00 (ISBN 0-8168-6751-8). Aero.

Mathematics for Construction Students. 3rd ed. C. W. Schofield. (Illus.). 1975. pap. text ed. 11.00x (ISBN 0-7131-3333-3). Intl Ideas.

Mathematics for Consumer Survival. Marvin L. Bittinger et al. (Illus.). 640p. text ed. 10.00 (ISBN 0-87150-501-0); tchr's manual 5.00 (ISBN 0-686-64028-4); wkbk 4.00 (ISBN 0-686-64029-2). Prindle.

Mathematics for Data Processing. Frank J. Clark. LC 73-8868. (Illus.). 432p. 1974. 17.95 (ISBN 0-87909-470-2); students manual avail. Reston.

Mathematics for Decision Making: A Programmed Basic Text, 2 vols. E. W. Martin, Jr. 1969. text ed. 18.95x ea. Vol. 1 (ISBN 0-256-00354-8). Vol. 2 (ISBN 0-256-00371-8). Irwin.

Mathematics for Electronic-Electricity. National Radio Institute Staff. (Illus.). 1963. 8.25 (ISBN 0-8104-0465-6). Hayden.

Mathematics for Electronic Technology. D. P. Howson. 280p. 1976. text ed. 29.00 (ISBN 0-08-018219-4); pap. text ed. 17.00 (ISBN 0-08-018218-6). Pergamon.

Mathematics for Elemenatry School Teachers. James E. Schultz. (Mathematics Ser.). 1977. text ed. 17.50 (ISBN 0-675-08509-8); instructor's manual 3.95 (ISBN 0-685-74286-5). Merrill.

Mathematics for Elementary Education. Donald F. Devine & Jerome E. Kaufman. LC 73-14692. 609p. 1973. 19.95 (ISBN 0-471-20969-4). Wiley.

Mathematics for Elementary Teachers. Jack E. Forbes & Robert E. Eicholz. LC 75-137839. (Mathematics Ser). 1971. text ed. 16.95 (ISBN 0-201-01853-5); instr's manual 2.50 (ISBN 0-201-01854-3). A-W.

Mathematics for Elementary Teachers. Eugene F. Krause. (Illus.). 1978. text ed. 17.95 (ISBN 0-13-562702-8). P-H.

Mathematics for Elementary Teachers: A Content Approach. Ruth Heintz. LC 79-18727. (Illus.). 512p. 1980. text ed. 17.95 (ISBN 0-201-03227-9); instructor's manual 2.50 (ISBN 0-201-03228-7). A-W.

Mathematics for Engineering Technology & Computing. H. G. Martin. 1970. 19.50 (ISBN 0-08-013961-2); pap. 9.75 (ISBN 0-08-013960-4). Pergamon.

Mathematics for Engineers & Applied Scientists. Stanley C. Lennox & Mary Chadwick. LC 79-670196. 1977. pap. text ed. 15.50x o.p. (ISBN 0-435-71282-9). Heinemann Ed.

Mathematics for Financial Analysis. Michael Gartenberg & Barry Shaw. 240p. 1976. text ed. 23.00 (ISBN 0-08-019599-7). Pergamon.

Mathematics for Geographers & Planners. 2nd ed. A. G. Wilson & M. J. Kirby. (Contemporary Problems in Geography Ser.). (Illus.). 424p. 1980. text ed. 36.00x (ISBN 0-19-874114-6); pap. text ed. 19.95x (ISBN 0-19-874115-4). Oxford U Pr.

Mathematics for Health Careers. Jerome D. Hayden & Howard T. Davis. LC 78-59567. (Health Occupations Ser.). (gr. 10). 1980. pap. text ed. 14.40 (ISBN 0-686-59748-6); instructor's guide 1.75 (ISBN 0-8273-1717-4). Delmar.

Mathematics for Health Practitioners: Basic Concepts & Clinical Applications. Lawrence Verner. LC 78-12176. 1978. pap. 8.75 (ISBN 0-397-54223-2). Lippincott.

Mathematics for Introductory Statistics: A Programmed Review. Andrew R. Baggaley. 1969. pap. 11.95 (ISBN 0-471-04008-8). Wiley.

Mathematics for Liberal Arts. Morris Kline. 1967. text ed. 18.95 (ISBN 0-201-03771-8); instr's manual 2.50 (ISBN 0-201-03772-6). A-W.

Mathematics for Management. Richard C. Lucking. LC 80-40127. 1980. 52.00 (ISBN 0-471-27779-7, Pub. by Wiley-Interscience); pap. write for info. (ISBN 0-471-27781-9). Wiley.

Mathematics for Managerial Decisions. Robert L. Childress. LC 73-17352. (Illus.). 656p. 1974. ref. ed. 19.95 (ISBN 0-13-562231-X). P-H.

Mathematics for Nurses with Clinical Applications. Mary K. Miller. LC 80-26040. 385p. (Orig.). 1981. pap. text ed. 14.95 (ISBN 0-8185-0429-3). Brooks-Cole.

Mathematics for Nursing Science: A Programmed Text. 2nd ed. Sally I. Lipsey. LC 76-44843. 1977. text ed. 10.95 (ISBN 0-471-01798-1, Pub. by Wiley-Medical). Wiley.

Mathematics for Operations Research. W. H. Marlow. LC 78-534. 1978. 29.95 (ISBN 0-471-57233-0, Pub. by Wiley-Interscience). Wiley.

Mathematics for Physical Geographers. Graham N. Sumner. LC 78-12156. 1979. 17.95x (ISBN 0-470-26557-4). Halsted Pr.

Mathematics for Plumbers & Pipefitters. D'Arcangelo et al. LC 73-2166. 199p. 1973. 6.80 (ISBN 0-8273-0291-6); instr's manual 1.60 (ISBN 0-8273-0292-4). Delmar.

Mathematics for Plumbers & Pipefitters. 3rd rev. ed. B. F. D'Arcangelo et al. (Applied Mathematics Ser.). (Illus.). 210p. 1981. pap. text ed. price not set (ISBN 0-8273-1291-1); price not set instr's. guide. Delmar.

Mathematics for Practical Use. Kaj L. Nielsen. (Orig.). 1962. pap. 2.95 (ISBN 0-06-463212-1, EH 212, EH). Har-Row.

Mathematics for Retail Buying. 2nd ed. Bette Tepper & Newton E. Godnick. (Illus.). 224p. 1973. pap. 10.00 (ISBN 0-87005-215-2); answer manual 3.00 (ISBN 0-87005-216-0). Fairchild.

Mathematics for Sheet Metal Fabrication. LC 79-118846. 1970. pap. text ed. 8.80 (ISBN 0-8273-0295-9); instr's manual 1.60 (ISBN 0-8273-0296-7). Delmar.

Mathematics for Statistics. W. L. Bashaw. LC 69-16123. 1969. pap. 13.95 (ISBN 0-471-05531-X). Wiley.

Mathematics for Technical & Vocational Schools. 6th ed. John C. Boyce et al. LC 74-10539. 572p. 1975. text ed. 18.95 (ISBN 0-471-09340-8); solutions manual avail. (ISBN 0-471-09341-6). Wiley.

Mathematics for Technical Careers. new ed. Ralph H. Hannon. (Mathematics Ser.). 304p. 1976. text ed. 17.95 (ISBN 0-675-08656-6); instructor's manual 3.95 (ISBN 0-686-67254-2). Merrill.

Mathematics for Technical Education. Dale Ewen & Michael A. Topper. (Technical Mathematics Ser.). (Illus.). 384p. 1976. 17.95x (ISBN 0-13-565150-6); study guide 2.95 (ISBN 0-13-565143-3). P-H.

Mathematics for Technologists in Radiology, Nuclear Medicine & Radiation Therapy. S. Stefani & Lincoln B. Hubbard. LC 78-32110. (Illus.). 1979. pap. text ed. 13.95 (ISBN 0-8016-4762-2). Mosby.

Mathematics for the Biological Sciences. J. C. Arya & R. W. Lardner. (Illus.). 1979. 22.95 (ISBN 0-13-562439-8). P-H.

Mathematics for the Biological Sciences: From Graph Through Calculus to Differential Equations. J. C. Newby. (Illus.). 250p. 1980. 59.00 (ISBN 0-19-859623-5); pap. 27.00 (ISBN 0-19-859624-3). Oxford U Pr.

Mathematics for the College Boards: PSAT, SAT. Barnett Rich. (Illus., Orig.). (gr. 10-12). 1967. wkbk. 7.75 (ISBN 0-87720-201-X). AMSCO Sch.

Mathematics for the College Student: Elementary Concepts. 2nd ed. A. William Gray & Otis M. Ulm. LC 73-7359. 1975. text ed. 9.95x (ISBN 0-02-474700-9, 47470). Macmillan.

Mathematics for the Health Sciences. Sandra Murrell & Paul Olsen. (Developmental & Precalculus Math Ser.). (Illus.). 432p. 1981. pap. text ed. 13.95 (ISBN 0-201-04647-4). A-W.

Mathematics for the Manager. J. Tennant-Smith. 1971. 17.95x (ISBN 0-17-761010-7). Intl Ideas.

Mathematics for the Physical Sciences. Herbert S. Wilf. 1978. pap. text ed. 4.50 (ISBN 0-486-63635-6). Dover.

Mathematics for the Technologies. Lawrence M. Clar & James A. Hart. (Illus.). 1978. text ed. 18.95 (ISBN 0-13-565200-6). P-H.

Mathematics for the Technologies with Calculus. Lawrence Clar & James Hart. (P-H Ser. in Technical Mathematics). (Illus.). 1978. ref. ed. 21.95 (ISBN 0-13-562553-X). P-H.

Mathematics: Friend or Foe? Dorothy Evans. (Classroom Close-Ups Ser.). 1977. text ed. 14.95x o.p. (ISBN 0-04-372022-6); pap. text ed. 8.95x (ISBN 0-04-372023-4). Allen Unwin.

Mathematics I & II: Grade 8 Mathematics, 2 bks. Charles Brumfiel & Eugene Krause. 1975. Bk. 1. text ed. 11.20 (ISBN 0-201-00603-0, Sch Div); Bk. 2. text ed. 11.20 (ISBN 0-201-00605-7); Bk. 1. tchr's. ed. 14.52 (ISBN 0-201-00604-9); Bk. 2. tchr's. ed. 14.52 (ISBN 0-201-00606-5). A-W.

Mathematics: Ideas & Applications. Daniel D. Benice. 1978. 14.95 (ISBN 0-12-088250-7); instrs'. ed. 3.00 (ISBN 0-12-088252-3). Acad Pr.

Mathematics in Aristotle. Thomas Heath. LC 78-66593. (Ancient Philosophy Ser.). 305p. 1980. lib. bdg. 30.00 (ISBN 0-8240-9595-2). Garland Pub.

Mathematics in Buildings. Vincent F. O'Connor. LC 77-19158. (Raintree Mathematics Ser.). (Illus.). (gr. k-3). 1978. PLB 8.95 (ISBN 0-8393-0053-0). Raintree Child.

Mathematics in Civilization. H. L. Resnikoff & R. O. Wells. LC 72-83805. (Illus.). 24.50x (ISBN 0-03-085035-5); pap. text ed. 8.95x (ISBN 0-89197-843-7). Irvington.

Mathematics in Everyday Things. William C. Vergara. (Illus.). 1959. 10.95 o.s.i. (ISBN 0-06-006990-2, HarpT). Har-Row.

Mathematics in Our World. Robert E. Eicholz et al. **Incl. Bk. 1. (gr. 1). text ed. 3.92 kindergarten (ISBN 0-201-09800-8); text ed. 6.08 (ISBN 0-201-09810-5); tchr's. ed. 14.12 (ISBN 0-201-09811-3); wkbk. 2.76 (ISBN 0-201-09813-X); wkbk. tchr's. ed. 3.00 (ISBN 0-201-09814-8); duplicator masters 38.88 (ISBN 0-201-09812-1); enrichment wkbk. 2.76 (ISBN 0-201-09815-6); tchr's. enrichment wkbk. 3.00 (ISBN 0-201-09816-4); Bk. 2. (gr. 2). text ed. 6.08 (ISBN 0-201-09820-2); tchr's ed. 14.12 (ISBN 0-201-09821-0); wkbk. 2.76 (ISBN 0-201-09823-7); wkbk. tchr's ed. 3.00 (ISBN 0-201-09824-5); duplicator masters 38.88 (ISBN 0-201-09822-9); enrichment wkbk. 2.76 (ISBN 0-201-09825-3); tchr's enrichment wkbk 3.00 (ISBN 0-201-09826-1); Bk. 3. (gr. 3). text ed. 10.24 (ISBN 0-201-09830-X); tchr's ed. 16.00 (ISBN 0-201-09831-8); duplicator masters 38.88 (ISBN 0-201-09832-6); wkbk 3.52 (ISBN 0-201-09833-4); wkbk 3.68 (ISBN 0-201-09835-0); wkbk tchr's ed. 3.80 (ISBN 0-201-09836-9); Bk. 4. (gr. 4). text ed. 10.24 (ISBN 0-201-09840-7); tchr's ed. 16.00 (ISBN 0-201-09841-5); duplicator masters 38.88 (ISBN 0-201-09842-3); wkbk 3.52 (ISBN 0-201-09843-1); wkbk tchr's ed. 4.16 (ISBN 0-201-09844-X); Bk. 5. (gr. 5). text ed. 10.24 (ISBN 0-201-09850-4); tchr's ed. 16.00 (ISBN 0-201-09851-2); duplicator masters 38.88 (ISBN 0-201-09852-0); wkbk 3.52 (ISBN 0-201-09853-9); wkbk tchr's ed. 4.16 (ISBN 0-201-09854-7); Bk. 6. (gr. 6). text ed. 10.24 (ISBN 0-201-09860-1); tchr's ed. 16.00 (ISBN 0-201-09861-X); duplicator masters 38.88 (ISBN 0-201-09862-8); wkbk 3.52 (ISBN 0-201-09863-6); wkbk. tchr's ed. 4.16 (ISBN 0-201-09864-4); Bk. 7. (gr. 7). 1980. text ed. 12.32 (ISBN 0-201-09870-9); tchr's ed. 16.00 (ISBN 0-201-09871-7); Bk. 8. (gr. 8). 1978. text ed. 12.32 (ISBN 0-201-09880-6); tchr's ed. 16.00 (ISBN 0-201-09881-4); wkbk 3.52 (ISBN 0-201-09883-0); tchr's ed. wkbk 3.52 (ISBN 0-201-09884-9). (gr. 1-6). 1978. duplicator masters 43.40 ea. (ISBN 0-201-09882-2, Sch Div). A-W.**

Mathematics in Our World. 2nd ed. Robert E. Eicholz et al. **Incl. Bk. 1. (gr. k). student ed. 3.92 (ISBN 0-201-16000-5); tchr's ed. 11.76 (ISBN 0-201-16001-3); (gr. 1). pap. 6.08 student ed. (ISBN 0-201-16010-2); tchr's ed. 16.00 (ISBN 0-201-16011-0); wkbk. 2.76 (ISBN 0-201-16013-7); tchr's ed. wkbk. 3.00 (ISBN 0-201-16014-5); (gr. 2). student ed. 6.08 (ISBN 0-201-16020-X); tchr's ed. 16.00 (ISBN 0-201-16021-8); wkbk. 2.76 (ISBN 0-201-16023-4); tchr's ed. wkbk. 3.00 (ISBN 0-201-16024-2); (gr. 3). student ed. 10.24 (ISBN 0-201-16030-7); tchr's ed. 16.00 (ISBN 0-201-16031-5); wkbk. 3.52 (ISBN 0-201-16033-1); tchr's ed. wkbk. 4.16 (ISBN 0-201-16034-X); consumable ed. 7.20 (ISBN 0-201-16009-9); (gr. 4). student ed. 10.24 (ISBN 0-201-16040-4); tchr's ed. 16.00 (ISBN 0-201-16041-2); wkbk. 3.52 (ISBN 0-201-16043-9); tchr's ed. wkbk. 4.16 (ISBN 0-201-16044-7); (gr. 5). student ed. 10.24 (ISBN 0-201-16050-1); tchr's ed. 16.00 (ISBN 0-201-16051-X); wkbk. 3.52 (ISBN 0-201-16053-6); tchr's ed. wkbk. 4.16 (ISBN 0-201-16054-4); (gr. 6). student ed. 10.24 (ISBN 0-201-16060-9); tchr's ed. 16.00 (ISBN 0-201-16064-1); wkbk. 3.52 (ISBN 0-201-16063-3); tchr's ed. wkbk. 4.16 (ISBN 0-201-16064-1); (gr. 7). student ed. 12.32 (ISBN 0-201-16070-6); tchr's ed. 16.00 (ISBN 0-201-16071-4); wkbk. 3.52 (ISBN 0-201-16073-0); tchr's ed. wkbk. 4.16 (ISBN 0-201-16074-9); (gr. 8). student ed. 12.32 (ISBN 0-201-16080-3); tchr's ed. 16.00 (ISBN 0-201-16081-1); wkbk. 3.52 (ISBN 0-201-16083-8); tchr's ed. wkbk. 4.16 (ISBN 0-201-16084-6). (gr. 1-8). 1981 (Sch Div). A-W.**

Mathematics in Our World. Robert E. Eicholz et al. **Incl. Enrichment Workbook Grade 3. 1979. tchr's ed 3.40 o.p. (ISBN 0-201-09836-9); wkbk 3.12 o.p. (ISBN 0-201-09835-0); Enrichment Workbook Grade 4. 1979. tchrs' ed 3.40 o.p. (ISBN 0-201-09846-6); wkbk 3.12 o.p. (ISBN 0-201-09845-8); Enrichment Workbook Grade 5. 1979. tchrs' ed 3.40 o.p. (ISBN 0-201-09856-3); wkbk 3.12 o.p. (ISBN 0-201-09855-5); Enrichment Workbook Grade 6. 1979. tchrs' ed 3.40 o.p. (ISBN 0-201-09866-0); wkbk 3.12 o.p. (ISBN 0-686-60616-7); Enrichment Workbook Grade 7. 1979. tchrs' ed 3.40 o.p. (ISBN 0-201-09874-1); wkbk 3.04 o.p. (ISBN 0-686-60617-5); Enrichment Workbook Grade 8. 1979. tchrs' ed 3.40 o.p. (ISBN 0-686-68528-8); wkbk 3.04 o.p. (ISBN 0-686-60618-3). (gr. 3-8). A-W.**

Mathematics in Our World Primer. Robert Eicholz et al. (Mathematics in Our World Ser.). 1978. pap. text ed. 3.92 (ISBN 0-201-09800-8, Sch Div); tchr's ed. 11.76 (ISBN 0-201-09801-6). A-W.

Mathematics in Our World: Spanish Edition. Robert E. Eicholz et al. (gr. 1-6). 1981. Bk. 1. text ed. 6.08 (ISBN 0-201-09700-1, Sch Div); Bk. 2. text ed. 6.08 (ISBN 0-201-09701-X); Bk. 3. text ed. 6.76 (ISBN 0-201-09702-8). A-W.

Mathematics in Our World: Test Duplicator Masters. Robert E. Eicholz et al. (Mathematics in Our World Ser.). (gr. 7-8). 1979. Gr. 7. 34.48 (ISBN 0-201-09875-X, Sch Div); Gr. 8. 43.40 (ISBN 0-201-09882-2). A-W.

Mathematics in Secondary Schools. P. G. Scopes. LC 72-78894. (Illus.). 128p. 1973. pap. text ed. 6.95x (ISBN 0-521-09728-2). Cambridge U Pr.

Mathematics in the Archeological & Historical Sciences. P. G. Kendall et al. 1972. 31.50 (ISBN 0-85224-213-1, Pub. by Edinburgh U Pr Scotland). Columbia U Pr.

Mathematics in the Circus Ring. Vincent F. O'Connor. LC 77-19168. (Raintree Mathematics Ser.). (Illus.). (gr. k-3). 1978. PLB 8.95 (ISBN 0-8393-0056-5). Raintree Child.

Mathematics in the Kitchen. Vincent F. O'Connor. LC 77-19160. (Raintree Mathematics Ser.). (Illus.). (gr. k-3). 1978. PLB 8.95 (ISBN 0-8393-0054-9). Raintree Child.

Mathematics in the Toy Store. Vincent F. O'Connor. LC 77-19155. (Raintree Mathematics Ser.). (Illus.). (gr. k-3). 1978. PLB 8.95 (ISBN 0-8393-0052-2). Raintree Child.

Mathematics in Western Culture. Morris Kline. 1953. 19.95 (ISBN 0-19-500603-8). Oxford U Pr.

Mathematics in Western Culture. Morris Kline. (Illus.). 1964. pap. 8.95 (ISBN 0-19-500714-X, GB). Oxford U Pr.

Mathematics Laboratory in the Elementary School: What?, Why? & How. Frank Swetz. Ed. by S. W. Valenza, Jr. LC 80-81349. (Illus., Orig.). 1980. 6.95 (ISBN 0-936918-03-9); pap. text ed. 6.95 (ISBN 0-686-61581-6). Intergalactic NJ.

Mathematics: Level Two Achievement Test. Morris Bramson. LC 66-18139. (College Board Achievement Tests Ser). (Orig.). 1966. pap. 0.95 o.p. (ISBN 0-668-01456-3). Arc Bks.

Mathematics Made Simple. rev. ed. A. P. Sperling & Monroe Stuart. LC 62-16025. pap. 3.50 (ISBN 0-385-02088-0, Made). Doubleday.

Mathematics Makes Sense. William D. Lewis. LC 66-21185. 1969. pap. 1.45 o.p. (ISBN 0-668-01854-2). Arc Bks.

Mathematics-Methods Program: Addition & Subtraction. John F. LeBlanc et al. (Mathematics Ser). 176p. 1976. pap. text ed. 4.25 (ISBN 0-201-14608-8); instr's man. 1.50 (ISBN 0-201-14609-6). A-W.

Mathematics-Methods Program: Analysis of Shapes. John F. LeBlanc et al. (Mathematics Ser.). (Illus.). 112p. 1976. pap. text ed. 3.25 (ISBN 0-201-14618-5); instr's man. 1.50 (ISBN 0-201-14619-3). A-W.

Mathematics Methods Program: Awareness Geometry. John F. Leblanc et al. 40p. 1976. pap. text ed. 2.95 (ISBN 0-201-14614-2); instructor's manual 1.50 (ISBN 0-201-14615-0). A-W.

Mathematics-Methods Program: Experiences in Problem Solving. John F. LeBlanc et al. (Mathematics Ser). 64p. 1976. pap. text ed. 2.95 (ISBN 0-201-14628-2); instr's man. 1.50 (ISBN 0-201-14629-0). A-W.

Mathematics-Methods Program: Graphs, the Picturing of Information. John F. Leblanc et al, (Mathematics Ser.). (Illus.). 160p. 1976. pap. text ed. 3.95 (ISBN 0-201-14622-3); instr's man. 1.50 (ISBN 0-201-14623-1). A-W.

Mathematics-Methods Program: Measurement. John F. Leblanc et al. (Mathematics Ser.). (Illus.). 144p. 1976. pap. text ed. 3.50 (ISBN 0-201-14620-7); instr's man. 1.50 (ISBN 0-201-14621-5). A-W.

Mathematics-Methods Program: Multiplication & Division. John F. LeBlanc et al. (Mathematics Ser.). (Illus.). 1976. 3.95 (ISBN 0-201-14610-X); instr's man. 1.50 (ISBN 0-201-14611-8). A-W.

Mathematics-Methods Program: Number Theory. John F. Leblanc et al. (Mathematics Ser.). (Illus.). 128p. 1976. pap. text ed. 3.50 (ISBN 0-201-14624-X); instr's manual 1.50 (ISBN 0-201-14625-8). A-W.

Mathematics-Methods Program: Numeration. John F. LeBlanc et al. (Mathematics Ser.). 128p. 1976. pap. 3.95 (ISBN 0-201-14606-1); instr's man. 1.50 (ISBN 0-201-14607-X). A-W.

Mathematics-Methods Program: Probability & Statistics. John F. LeBlanc et al. (Mathematics Ser). 128p. 1976. pap. text ed. 3.25 (ISBN 0-201-14626-6); instr's man. 1.50 (ISBN 0-201-14627-4). A-W.

Mathematics Methods Program: Rational Numbers with Integers & Reals. John F. LeBlanc et al. (Mathematics Ser). (Illus.). 240p. 1976. pap. text ed. 4.50 (ISBN 0-201-14612-6); instructor's manual 1.50 (ISBN 0-201-14613-4). A-W.

Mathematics-Methods Program: Transformational Geometry. John F. Leblanc et al. (Mathematics Ser.). (Illus.). 132p. 1976. pap. text ed. 3.50 (ISBN 0-201-14616-9); instr's manual 1.50 (ISBN 0-201-14617-7). A-W.

Mathematics: Models & Applications. Lawrence C. Eggan & Charles Vanden Eynden. 1979. text ed. 16.95x (ISBN 0-669-01051-0); inst. manual free (ISBN 0-669-01052-9). Heath.

Mathematics of Accounting. 4th ed. A. Curtis & J. Cooper. 1961. 21.95 (ISBN 0-13-563908-5); text ed. 25.95 (ISBN 0-686-66514-7). P-H.

Mathematics of Business. Grace Bush & John Young. LC 73-93624. (Illus.). 384p. 1974. pap. text ed. 11.95 (ISBN 0-574-19105-4, 13-2105); instr's guide avail. (ISBN 0-574-19106-2, 13-2106). SRA.

Mathematics of Business Affairs. rev. ed. Harold Feldman & John H. Hindle. LC 73-94292. 378p. 1980. pap. text ed. 11.25 (ISBN 0-913310-09-3). PAR Inc.

Mathematics of Cell Electrophysiology. Cronin. 144p. 1981. 19.75 (ISBN 0-8247-1157-2). Dekker.

Mathematics of Classical & Quantum Physics, 2 pts. F. W. Byron & R. W. Fuller. (Physics Ser.). 1969. 16.95; Pt. 1. (ISBN 0-201-00745-2); Pt. 2. (ISBN 0-201-00746-0). A-W.

Mathematics of Diffusion. 2nd ed. J. Crank. (Illus.). 424p. 1975. 45.00x o.p. (ISBN 0-19-853344-6). Oxford U Pr.

Mathematics of Drugs & Solutions with Clinical Applications. Lloyd I. Richardson & Judith K. Richardson. 1976. 7.95 o.p. (ISBN 0-07-052309-6, HP); instructor's manual 2.95 o.p. (ISBN 0-07-052310-X). McGraw.

Mathematics of Engineering Systems. Francis H. Raven. 1966. text ed. 29.95x (ISBN 0-07-051230-2, C). McGraw.

Mathematics of Environmental Processes. Thomas D. Waite & Neil J. Freeman. LC 76-25770. 1977. 21.00x (ISBN 0-669-00979-2). Lexington Bks.

Mathematics of Finance. 5th ed. Robert Cissell et al. LC 77-73993. (Illus.). 1977. text ed. 18.95 (ISBN 0-395-25807-3); inst. manual 1.00 (ISBN 0-395-25806-5). HM.

Mathematics of Finance. 3rd ed. Hummel & Seebeck. 1970. text ed. 16.50 (ISBN 0-07-031161-7, C). McGraw.

Mathematics of Finance. 4th ed. John Riner et al. 1969. ref. ed. 19.95 (ISBN 0-13-565036-4). P-H.

Mathematics of Heredity. Gustave Malecot. Tr. by D. M. Yermanos from Fr. LC 69-12603. (Illus.). 1969. text ed. 15.95x (ISBN 0-7167-0678-4). W H Freeman.

Mathematics of Investment. Roger Osborn. (Illus.). 9.50 (ISBN 0-8363-0066-1). Jenkins.

Mathematics of Merchandising. 2nd ed. A. P. Kneider. (Illus.). 320p. 1981. pap. text ed. 15.95 (ISBN 0-686-63445-4). P-H.

Mathematics of Microcirculation Phenomena. Ed. by Joseph F. Gross. 189p. 1980. text ed. 24.00 (ISBN 0-89004-449-X). Raven.

Mathematics of Retail Merchandising. 2nd ed. B. P. Corbman & M. Krieger. 411p. 1972. 19.95 (ISBN 0-471-06587-0). Wiley.

Mathematics of Retail Merchandising. 2nd ed. Bernard P. Corbman & Murray Krieger. 450p. 1972. 19.95 (ISBN 0-8260-2150-6). Ronald Pr.

Mathematics of the Decision Sciences, 2 vols. Incl. Pt. 1. with corrections 22.40 (ISBN 0-8218-1111-8, LAM-11); Pt. 2. with corrections 23.60 (ISBN 0-8218-1112-6, LAM-12). LC 62-21481. 1970. Repr. of 1968 ed. Am Math.

Mathematics of the Energy Crises. Ed. by R. Gagliardi & S. W. Valenza, Jr. LC 78-53592. 96p. (gr. 7-12). 1978. 6.96 (ISBN 0-936918-01-2). Intergalactic NJ.

Mathematics of the Shop. 4th ed. McMackin et al. LC 76-6726. 1978. 13.60 (ISBN 0-8273-1297-0); tchr's ed. 1.60 (ISBN 0-8273-1298-9). Delmar.

Mathematics of Time. S. Smale. (Illus.). 151p. 1981. pap. 16.00 (ISBN 0-387-90519-7). Springer-Verlag.

Mathematics on the Playground. Vincent F. O'Connor. LC 77-19180. (Raintree Mathematics Ser.). (Illus.). (gr. k-3). 1978. PLB 8.95 (ISBN 0-8393-0051-4). Raintree Child.

Mathematics Para Administration y Economia. new ed. Jean Draper. 1976. text ed. 12.00x (ISBN 0-06-310100-9, IntlDept). Har-Row.

Mathematics: Problem Solving Through Recreational Mathematics. Bonnie Averbach & Orin Chein. LC 80-11989. (Mathematical Sciences Ser.). (Illus.). 1980. text ed. 16.95x (ISBN 0-7167-1124-9); instrs'. guide avail. W H Freeman.

Mathematics Project Series, 24 bks. Nuffield Foundation. Incl. Beginnings. LC 68-21009. 1968. pap. 7.50 (ISBN 0-471-65169-9); Checking Up One. LC 77-39607. 1970. pap. 3.95 (ISBN 0-471-65181-8); Checking Up Two. 1972. pap. 5.50 (ISBN 0-471-65205-9); Computation & Structure. LC 68-21012. 1968. Cir. 2. pap. 5.95 (ISBN 0-471-65175-3); Cir. 3. pap. 5.95 (ISBN 0-471-65214-8); Cir. 4. pap. 5.95 (ISBN 0-471-65217-2); Cir. 5. pap. 4.95 (ISBN 0-471-65218-0); Computers & Young Children. LC 75-39285. 1972. pap. 6.95 (ISBN 0-471-65179-6); Graphs Heading to Algebra: Square Two. LC 70-88358. 1969. pap. 5.95 (ISBN 0-471-65213-X); Guides to the Guides. 1975. pap. 3.50 (ISBN 0-471-65207-5); How to Build a Pond. pap. 4.50 (ISBN 0-471-65177-X); I Do & I Understand. LC 67-25008. 1967. pap. 3.95 (ISBN 0-471-65171-0); Into Secondary School. LC 72-126926. 1970. pap. 3.95 (ISBN 0-471-65182-6); Later Primary Years. LC 70-39605. 1972. pap. 9.50 (ISBN 0-686-65751-9); Logic. LC 73-39606. 1972. pap. 7.50 (ISBN 0-471-65199-0); Mathematics: The First Three Years. LC 73-168554. 1970. pap. 7.50 (ISBN 0-471-65189-3); Maths with Everything. 1971. pap. 3.95 (ISBN 0-471-65187-7); Module on Angles, Courses & Bearings. 1973. pap. 6.50 (ISBN 0-471-65194-X); Module on Decimals One. 1973. pap. 6.50 (ISBN 0-471-65201-6); Module on Number Patterns One. 1973. pap. 6.50 (ISBN 0-471-65202-4); Module on Speed & Gradient One. 1973. pap. 5.95 (ISBN 0-471-65193-1); Module on Symmetry. 1973. pap. 6.50 (ISBN 0-471-65195-8); Primary Years. 1972. pap. 9.50 (ISBN 0-686-65752-7); Probability & Statistics. 1969. pap. 5.95 (ISBN 0-471-65219-9); Shape & Size, 3 pts. LC 68-21011. 1968-1971. Tri. 2. pap. 5.95 (ISBN 0-471-65178-8); Tri. 3. pap. 4.50 (ISBN 0-471-65212-1); Tri. 4. pap. 4.50 (ISBN 0-471-65186-9); Story So Far. LC 69-88360. 1969. pap. 4.95 (ISBN 0-471-65220-2); Your Child & Mathematics. 1968. pap. 3.95 (ISBN 0-471-65210-5). Wiley.

Mathematics Readiness Program. Sara Throop & Barbara H. Wick. (gr. k). 1975. pap. text ed. 3.84 (ISBN 0-87895-024-9); tchrs' ed. 2.00 (ISBN 0-87895-025-7). Modern Curr.

Mathematics Revealed. Elizabeth Berman. 546p. 1979. 12.95 (ISBN 0-12-092450-1); instrs'. manual 3.00 (ISBN 0-12-092452-8). Acad Pr.

Mathematics, Science & Epistomology: Philosophical Papers, Vol. 2. I. Lakatos. Ed. by J. Worrall & G. Currie. LC 77-71415. 1978. 32.50 (ISBN 0-521-21769-5). Cambridge U Pr.

Mathematics, Simplified & Self Taught. 5th ed. Arco Editorial Board. LC 65-21203. (Orig.). 1968. pap. 5.00 (ISBN 0-668-00567-X); lib. bdg. 10.00 (ISBN 0-668-01399-0). Arco.

Mathematics: Society & Curricula. H. B. Griffiths & A. G. Howson. (Illus.). 400p. 1974. 49.50 (ISBN 0-521-20287-6); pap. 17.50x (ISBN 0-521-09892-0). Cambridge U Pr.

Mathematics Study Material: High School Equivalency-GED. William E. Lockhart. (Michigan Prescriptive Program Ser.). (gr. 10). 1975. pap. text ed. 8.00 (ISBN 0-89039-120-3). Ann Arbor Pubs.

Mathematics Teaching. T. H. F. Brissenden. 1980. text ed. 21.00 (ISBN 0-06-318159-2, IntlDept); pap. text ed. 11.90 (ISBN 0-06-318160-6). Har-Row.

Mathematics Textbooks, 7 bks. Incl. Bk. 1. Study of Numbers up to 20. 102p. pap. text ed. 1.65 (ISBN 0-87825-011-5); Bk. 2. Study of Numbers up to 1,000. 147p. pap. text ed. 2.50 (ISBN 0-87825-012-3); Bk. 3. Applied Arithmetic. 53p. pap. text ed. 1.65 (ISBN 0-87825-013-1); Bk. 4. Fractions, Decimals, Percentages. 65p. pap. text ed. 1.65 (ISBN 0-87825-014-X); Bk. 5. Study of Numbers. 83p. pap. text ed. 1.65 (ISBN 0-87825-015-8); Bk. 6. Applied Mathematics. 104p. pap. text ed. o.s.i. (ISBN 0-87825-016-6); Bk. 7. Algebra & Geometry. 92p. pap. text ed. O.S.I (ISBN 0-87825-017-4). Ed Solutions.

Mathematics: The Alphabet of Science. 3rd ed. Margaret F. Willerding & H. S. Engelsohn. LC 76-48913. 376p. 1977. 21.95 (ISBN 0-471-94653-2); instructors' manual avail. (ISBN 0-471-02388-4). Wiley.

Mathematics: The Formal Tools of Engineering. Michael P. Smyth. (Advances in Modern Engineering Ser.). (Illus.). 160p. 1974. pap. text ed. 8.95 (ISBN 0-201-07078-2). A-W.

Mathematics: The Loss of Certainty. Morris Kline. (Illus,). 400p. 1980. 19.95 (ISBN 0-19-502754-X). Oxford U Pr.

Mathematics, the Man-Made Universe: An Introduction to the Spirit of Mathematics. 3rd ed. Sherman K. Stein. LC 75-25950. (Mathematics Ser.). (Illus.). 1976. text ed. 19.95x (ISBN 0-7167-0465-X); tchrs manual avail. W H Freeman.

Mathematics Through the Senses: Games, Dance & Art. Z. P. Dienes. (General Ser). 160p. (Orig.). 1973. pap. text ed. 13.75x (ISBN 0-901225-87-8, NFER). Humanities.

Mathematics Today. Lynn A. Steen. LC 80-10888. (Illus.). 384p. 1980. pap. 4.95 (ISBN 0-394-74503-5, Vin). Random.

Mathematics: Tools & Models. Dalton R. Hunkins & Thomas L. Pirnot. LC 76-15462. (Illus.). 1977. text ed. 17.95 (ISBN 0-201-03046-2); instr's man 2.00 (ISBN 0-201-03047-0). A-W.

Mathematics Two: Checkbook. Bird & May. 1981. text ed. price not set (ISBN 0-408-00610-2). Butterworths.

Mathematics Two Checkbook. May Bird. 1981. text ed. price not set (ISBN 0-408-00633-1); pap. text ed. price not set (ISBN 0-408-00609-9). Butterworths.

Mathematics: With Applications. William C. Stewart. 1979. 16.95x (ISBN 0-256-02114-7). Business Pubns.

Mathematics: With Applications in Management & Economics. 4th ed. Earl K. Bowen. 1976. text ed. 16.95x o.p. (ISBN 0-256-01839-1). Irwin.

Mathematics: With Applications in Management & Economics. 5th ed. Earl K. Bowen. 1980. 19.95x (ISBN 0-256-02349-2). Irwin.

Mathematics: With Applications in the Management, Natural, & Social Sciences. 2nd ed. Margaret L. Lial & Charles D. Miller. 1979. text ed. 18.95x (ISBN 0-673-15185-9); study guide 5.95x (ISBN 0-673-15187-5). Scott F.

Mathematics with Applications in the Management, Natural, & Social Sciences. Gareth Williams. 656p. 1981. text ed. 22.00 (ISBN 0-205-07188-0, 567188-4); tchrs'. ed. avail. (ISBN 0-205-07189-9). Allyn.

Mathematics with Understanding. H. Fletcher & A. A. Howell. Vol. 1. 19.50 (ISBN 0-08-015657-6); Vol. 2. 16.25 (ISBN 0-08-016745-4); Vol. 1. pap. 9.75 (ISBN 0-08-015656-8). Pergamon.

Mathematics Workbook for College Entrance Examinations. rev. ed. Brownstein. (gr. 10-12). 1976. pap. text ed. 5.95 (ISBN 0-8120-0654-2). Barron.

Mathematics Workbook for the SAT (College Entrance Examinations) Brigitte Saunders. 1980. pap. 5.00 (ISBN 0-668-04820-4). Arco.

Mathematische Abhandlungen, 3 vols. Helmut Hasse. Ed. by Heinrich W. Leopoldt & Peter Roquette. xxxvi, 1592p. 1975. 300.00x (ISBN 3-11-005931-2). De Gruyter.

Mathematische Werke, 2 vols. Gotthold F. Eisenstein. LC 75-17855. 926p. 1975. 60.00 set o.p. (ISBN 0-8284-0280-9). Chelsea Pub.

Mather Mine, Negaunee & Ishpeming Michigan. Ed. by Burton H. Boyum. 87p. 1980. 18.95. Longyear Res.

Mather Mine, Negaunee & Ishpeming Michigan. Ed. by Burton H. Boyum. LC 79-89638. 1979. 18.95 (ISBN 0-938746-04-9). Marquette Cnty.

Mathew G. Lewis, Charles Robert Maturin & the Germans: An Interpretive Study of the Influence of German Literature on Two Gothic Novels. Syndy M Conger. (Salzburg Studies in English Literature, Romantic Reassessment: No. 67). 1977. pap. text ed. 25.00x (ISBN 0-391-01349-1). Humanities.

Mathew's Ear. Honor Prime. (Illus.). (ps-5). 1964. 5.95 (ISBN 0-571-06063-3, Pub. by Faber & Faber). Merrimack Bk Serv.

Mathews: Masterpieces of the California Decorative Style. Harvey L. Jones. (Illus.). 116p. 1980. 24.95 (ISBN 0-87905-075-6). Peregrine Smith.

Mathpower U. S. A. Thirty Subject Volume. Heinz-Guenther Pink. 1980. write for info. (ISBN 0-915946-08-4). Pink Hse Pub.

Matias de los Reyes & the Craft of Fiction. Carroll B. Johnson. (U. C. Publ. in Modern Philology: Vol. 101). 1973. pap. 13.75x (ISBN 0-520-09386-0). U of Cal Pr.

Matilda. Paul Gallico. 1978. pap. 1.95 o.p. (ISBN 0-425-03556-5, Medallion). Berkley Pub.

Matilda & Her Family. Miriam E. Mason. (gr. 2-4). 1967. 3.50g o.s.i. (ISBN 0-02-764390-5). Macmillan.

Matilda Hippo Has a Big Mouth. Dennis Panek. LC 80-13260. (Illus.). (ps-2). 1980. 8.95 (ISBN 0-87888-161-1). Bradbury Pr.

Matilda: Or the Indian Captive. a Canadian Tale Founded on Fact. James Russell. LC 75-7073. (Indian Captivities Ser.: Vol. 51). 1976. Repr. of 1833 ed. lib. bdg. 44.00 (ISBN 0-8240-1675-0). Garland Pub.

Matinee. Donna Schuman & Judy Roche. 1980. pap. 2.75 (ISBN 0-440-15223-2). Dell.

Mating Dance. Rona Randall. 1980. pap. 2.75 (ISBN 0-686-69245-4, 50591). Avon.

Mating Reflex. Jim Hall. LC 80-70563. (Poetry Ser.). 1980. 9.95 (ISBN 0-915604-41-8); pap. 4.95 (ISBN 0-915604-42-6). Carnegie-Mellon.

Matisse. Lawrence Gowing. (World of Art Ser.). (Illus.). 1979. 17.95 (ISBN 0-19-520157-4); pap. 9.95 (ISBN 0-19-520158-2). Oxford U Pr.

Matisse. John Jacobus. LC 72-6633. (Library of Great Painters). (Illus.). 160p. 1973. 35.00 (ISBN 0-8109-0277-X). Abrams.

Matisse, No. 46-47. (Maeght Gallery: Derriere le Miroir Ser.). (Fr.). 1977. pap. 19.95 (ISBN 0-8120-0911-8). Barron.

Matisse & the Fauves. Renata Negri. (Illus.). 1975. Repr. 5.95 o.p. (ISBN 0-88308-013-3). Lamplight Pub.

Matisse: Fifty Years of His Graphic Art. William S. Lieberman. 12.50 o.s.i. (ISBN 0-8076-0037-7). Braziller.

Matisse Line Drawings & Prints. Herni Matisse. (Illus.). 1980. pap. 2.00 (ISBN 0-486-23877-6). Dover.

Matisse: The Artist & His Time. Guiseppe Marchiori. (Illus.). 1967. 12.50 o.p. (ISBN 0-688-61064-1). Reynal.

Mato, Come Heal Me. Craig Volk. (Outlaws Ser.: Vol. 4). 1980. 8.95x (ISBN 0-917624-17-3); pap. 5.95x (ISBN 0-917624-15-7). Lame Johnny.

Matriarch. Charles MacKinnon. 312p. 1975. 8.95 o.p. (ISBN 0-440-05459-1). Delacorte.

Matrices & Linear Programming with Business Applications. Toshinori Munakata. 1979. text ed. 18.95x (ISBN 0-8162-6166-0); solutions manual 5.95x (ISBN 0-8162-6167-9). Holden-Day.

Matrices & Linear Transformations. 2nd ed. Charles G. Cullen. LC 70-174334. 1972. text ed. 16.95 (ISBN 0-201-01209-X). A-W.

Matrices & Mathematical Prgramming: An Introduction for Economists. Nicholas Rau. 1980. 18.50 (ISBN 0-312-52299-1). St Martin.

Matrices & Tensors in Physics. A. W. Joshi. LC 75-26772. 251p. 1976. 8.95 (ISBN 0-470-45086-X). Halsted Pr.

Matrices & Transformations. Anthony J. Pettofrezzo. 1978. pap. text ed. 3.00 (ISBN 0-486-63634-8). Dover.

Matrices for Scientists. I. P. Williams. 1972. text ed. 8.00x (ISBN 0-09-110250-2, Hutchinson U Lib); pap. text ed. 3.25x (ISBN 0-09-110251-0). Humanities.

Matrics: Reusable Edition. Frances F. Loose. (gr. 9-12). 1975. wkbk. 3.00 (ISBN 0-89039-128-9). Ann Arbor Pubs.

Matrilineal Kinship. Ed. by David M. Schneider & Kathleen Gough. (California Library Reprint Ser.). 1974. 35.00x (ISBN 0-520-02587-3); pap. 9.95x (ISBN 0-520-02529-6, CAMPUS 103). U of Cal Pr.

Matrimonial Trials of Henry VIII. Henry A. Kelly. LC 75-7483. xiv, 314p. 1976. 15.00x (ISBN 0-8047-0895-9). Stanford U Pr.

Matrix. Stanley M. Davis et al. LC 77-81192. (Organization Development Ser.). 1977. pap. text ed. 7.95 (ISBN 0-201-01115-8). A-W.

Matrix Algebra: A Programmed Introduction. Richard C. Dorf. 1969. pap. 14.95 (ISBN 0-471-21909-6). Wiley.

Matrix Algebra for Business & Economics. S. R. Searle & W. H. Hausman. LC 66-11528. 1970. 31.95 (ISBN 0-471-76941-X, Pub. by Wiley-Interscience). Wiley.

Matrix Algebra for the Biological Sciences: Including Applications in Statistics. S. R. Searle. LC 66-11528. (Quantitative Methods for Biologists & Medical Statistics Ser.). 1966. 25.95 (ISBN 0-471-76930-4, Pub. by Wiley-Interscience). Wiley.

Matrix Analysis of Electrical Machinery. 2nd ed. Norman N. Hancock. LC 74-3286. 1974. text ed. 25.00 (ISBN 0-08-017898-7); pap. text ed. 12.50 (ISBN 0-08-017899-5). Pergamon.

Matrix Analysis of Interregional Population Growth & Distribution. Andrei Rogers. 1968. 18.50x (ISBN 0-520-01083-3). U of Cal Pr.

Matrix Analysis of Vibration. R. E. Bishop et al. (Illus.). 1979. 83.50 (ISBN 0-521-04257-7). Cambridge U Pr.

Matrix Computation & Mathematical Software. John R. Rice. Ed. by Charles E. Stewart. (Computer Science Ser.). (Illus.). 288p. Date not set. text ed. 23.95 (ISBN 0-07-052145-X); solutions manual 5.95 (ISBN 0-07-052146-8). McGraw.

Matrix Computation for Engineers & Scientists. Alan Jennings. LC 76-21079. 1977. 41.25 (ISBN 0-471-99421-9, Pub. by Wiley-Interscience). Wiley.

Matrix Computation for Engineers & Scientists. Alan Jennings. LC 76-21079. 330p. 1980. pap. 16.50 (ISBN 0-471-27832-7, Pub. by Wiley Interscience). Wiley.

Matrix Computer Analysis of Structures. Moshe F. Rubinstein. (Illus.). 1966. 26.95 (ISBN 0-13-565481-5). P-H.

Matrix Computer Methods of Vibration Analysis. D. J. Hatter. LC 73-10064. 206p. 1974. 22.95 o.p. (ISBN 0-470-35995-1). Halsted Pr.

Matrix Derivatives. Rogers. 224p. 1980. 27.50 (ISBN 0-8247-1176-9). Dekker.

Matrix Isolation. S. Cradock & A. J. Hinchcliffe. LC 74-31786. (Illus.). 140p. 1975. 29.95 (ISBN 0-521-20759-2). Cambridge U Pr.

Matrix Management. Kenneth Knight. LC 78-1516. 1978. text ed. 20.00 (ISBN 0-89433-082-9). Petrocelli.

Matrix Methods: An Introduction. R. Bronson. 1970. text ed. 19.95 (ISBN 0-12-135250-1). Acad Pr.

Matrix Methods Applied to Engineering Rigid Body Mechanics. T. Crouch. LC 80-41186. 385p. 1980. 45.00 (ISBN 0-08-024245-6); pap. 18.00 (ISBN 0-08-024246-4). Pergamon.

Matrix Methods in Accounting: An Introduction. J. K. Shank. 1972. pap. text ed. 6.50 (ISBN 0-201-07053-7). A-W.

Matrix Methods in Economics. Clopper Almon. 1967. 14.95 (ISBN 0-201-00224-8). A-W.

Matrix Methods of Structural Analysis. M. B. Kanchi. LC 80-18442. 432p. 1981. 17.95 (ISBN 0-470-26945-6). Halsted Pr.

Matrix Methods of Structural Analysis. 2nd ed. R. K. Livesley. 208p. 1975. text ed. 28.00 (ISBN 0-08-018888-5); pap. text ed. 15.00 (ISBN 0-08-018887-7). Pergamon.

Matrix Methods of Structural Analysis. C. K. Wang. (Illus.). 1977. Repr. of 1966 ed. text ed. 18.50x (ISBN 0-89534-000-3). Am Pub Co WI.

Matrix Organization & Project Management: Theory & Practice. Ed. by Ray Hill & B. Joseph White. (Michigan Business Papers Ser.: No. 64). (Illus.). 1979. pap. 12.95 (ISBN 0-87712-196-6). U Mich Busn Div Res.

Matrix Structural Analysis. J. J. Azar. 1972. text ed. 28.00 (ISBN 0-08-016781-0). Pergamon.

Matrix Structural Analysis. William McGuire & Richard H. Gallagher. LC 78-8471. 1979. text ed. 31.95 (ISBN 0-471-03059-7); solution manual avail. (ISBN 0-471-05535-2). Wiley.

Matrix Theory & Applications for Engineers & Mathematicians. Alexander Graham. LC 79-40988. (Mathematics & Its Applications Ser.). 295p. 1979. 49.95x (ISBN 0-470-26713-5). Halsted Pr.

Matrix Theory & Applications for Engineers & Mathematicians. Alexander Graham. LC 79-40988. (Mathematics & Its Applications). 295p. 1980. pap. 24.95 (ISBN 0-470-27072-1). Halsted Pr.

Matt Gargan's Boy. Alfred Slote. LC 74-26669. (gr. 3-5). 1975. 8.79 (ISBN 0-397-31617-8). Lippincott.

Matt Gargan's Boy. Alfred Slote. (gr. 3-7). 1977. pap. 1.95 (ISBN 0-380-01730-X, 34199, Camelot). Avon.

Matter. Ralph E. Lapp. LC 63-21668. (Life Science Library). (Illus.). (gr. 5 up). 1969. PLB 8.97 o.p. (ISBN 0-8094-0459-1, Pub. by Time-Life). Silver.

Matter & Method. R. Harre. 1979. Repr. of 1964 ed. lib. bdg. 20.00 (ISBN 0-917930-28-2); pap. text ed. 5.00x (ISBN 0-917930-08-8). Ridgeview.

Matter & Spirit. William R. Clayton. LC 80-81694. 1981. 8.75 (ISBN 0-8022-2368-0). Philos Lib.

Matter, Energy & Life: An Introduction for Biology Students. 3rd ed. Jeffrey W. Baker & Garland E. Allen. 1975. pap. text ed. 8.50 o.p. (ISBN 0-201-00389-9). A-W.

Matter, Energy, & Life: An Introduction to Chemical Concepts, 4-E. Jeffrey J. W. Baker & Garland E. Allen. LC 80-17946. (Life Sciences Ser.). 256p. 1981. 8.95 (ISBN 0-201-00169-1). A-W.

Matter in Motion: The Spirit & Evolution of Physics. Ernest S. Abers & Charles F. Kennel. 1977. pap. 15.95 o.p. (ISBN 0-205-05790-X, 7357907); tchr's. manual free o.p. (ISBN 0-205-05791-8, 7357915). Allyn.

Matter, Life & Generation: Eighteenth Century Embryology & the Haller-Wolff Debate. Shirley A. Roe. LC 80-19611. (Illus.). 216p. Date not set. price not set (ISBN 0-521-23540-5). Cambridge U Pr.

Matter of Chance. David H. Mellor. LC 70-152629. (Illus.). 1971. 29.95 (ISBN 0-521-08194-7). Cambridge U Pr.

Matter of Choice: A Study of Guidance & Subject Options. Margaret I. Reid et al. (Research Reports Ser.). (Illus.). 260p. (Orig.). 1974. pap. text ed. 18.25x (ISBN 0-85633-046-9, NFER). Humanities.

Matter of Degree, a Directory of Geography Courses 1979-1980. 1980. pap. 2.95x (ISBN 0-686-27384-2, Pub. by GEO Abstracts England). State Mutual Bk.

Matter of Degree: Heat Life & Death. Lucy Kavaler. LC 80-8789. 224p. 1981. 14.95 (ISBN 0-06-014854-3, HarpT). Har-Row.

Matter of Feeling. Janine Boissard. 256p. 1981. pap. 2.25 (ISBN 0-449-70001-1, Juniper). Fawcett.

Matter of Intelligence. George Wittman. LC 75-11669. 252p. 1975. 7.95 o.s.i. (ISBN 0-02-630850-9). Macmillan.

Matter of Life. Robert Edwards & Patrick Steptoe. LC 80-17293. (Illus.). 208p. 1980. Repr. 9.95 (ISBN 0-688-03698-8). Morrow.

Matter of Life & Death. M. Basilea Schlink. LC 73-10827. 96p. 1973. pap. 1.25 (ISBN 0-87123-359-2, 200359). Bethany Fell.

Matter of My Book: Montaigne's "Essais" As the Book of the Self. Richard Regosin. 1977. 14.95x (ISBN 0-520-03476-7). U of Cal Pr.

Matter of Paradise. Brown Meggs. 1975. 6.95 o.p. (ISBN 0-394-49627-2). Random.

Matter of Taste. Sylvia W. Humphrey. 1965. 6.95 o.s.i. (ISBN 0-02-557120-6). Macmillan.

Matter of Taste. Terrence Ingram. 152p. 1980. 20.95x (ISBN 0-00-211444-5, Pub. by W Collins Australia). Intl Schol Bk Serv.

Matter of Taste-Doctors Discovery for Permanent Weight Loss. John Piscano & Henry Lichter. LC 78-26573. 1979. 9.95 (ISBN 0-8119-0318-4). Fell.

Matter of Time. rev. ed. Robert H. Firth. LC 80-68365. 143p. 1981. pap. write for info. (ISBN 0-9605060-0-4). Firth.

Matters of Fact: A Sociological Inquiry. Stanley Raffel. 1979. 18.00 (ISBN 0-7100-0034-0). Routledge & Kegan.

Matters of the Heart. W. D. Ehrhart. (Orig.). pap. write for info. (ISBN 0-938566-04-0). Adasta Pr.

Matthean Redaction of a Primitive Apostolic Commissioning: An Exegesis of Matthew 28: 16-20. Benjamin J. Hubbard. LC 74-16566. (Society of Biblical Literature. Dissertation Ser.). 1974. pap. 7.50 (ISBN 0-89130-219-0, 060119). Scholars Pr Ca.

Matthew. Joseph A. Alexander. (Thornapple Commentaries Ser.). 1980. pap. 8.95 (ISBN 0-8010-0146-3). Baker Bk.

Matthew. Gerald Dye. (Double Trouble Puzzles Ser.). (Illus.). 1977. pap. 1.25 (ISBN 0-87239-149-3, 2820). Standard Pub.

Matthew. Irving L. Jensen. (Bible Self Study Ser). 1974. pap. 2.25 (ISBN 0-8024-1040-5). Moody.

Matthew. John P. Meier. (New Testament Message Ser.). 12.95 (ISBN 0-89453-126-3); pap. 7.95 (ISBN 0-89453-191-3). M Glazier.

Matthew Arnold. Douglas Bush. (Masters of World Literature Ser.). 1971. 10.95 (ISBN 0-02-519630-8). Macmillan.

Matthew Arnold. Douglas Bush. 1971. pap. 2.95 o.s.i. (ISBN 0-02-049280-4, Collier). Macmillan.

Matthew Arnold. Fraser Neiman. LC 68-24283. (English Authors Ser.: No. 69). 1969. lib. bdg. 10.95 (ISBN 0-8057-1012-4). Twayne.

Matthew Arnold & His Critics: A Study of Arnold's Controversies. Sidney Coulling. LC 74-82498. xiv, 351p. 1974. 16.00x (ISBN 0-8214-0161-0). Ohio U Pr.

Matthew Arnold & John Stuart Mill. Edward Alexander. LC 65-14321. 1965. 16.00x (ISBN 0-231-02786-9). Columbia U Pr.

Matthew Arnold & the Education of the New Order. Ed. by Peter Smith & Geoffrey Summerfield. LC 69-10433. (Cambridge Texts & Studies in Education: No. 3). 1969. 24.50 (ISBN 0-521-07341-3). Cambridge U Pr.

Matthew Arnold & the Three Classes. Patrick J. McCarthy. LC 64-14237. 1964. 20.00x (ISBN 0-231-02693-5). Columbia U Pr.

Matthew Arnold: Poetry & Prose. Ed. by John Bryson. 1979. 14.95 o.p. (ISBN 0-8464-0083-9). Beekman Pubs.

Matthew Arnold: Prose Writings. Ed. by Carl Dawson & John Pfordresher. (Critical Heritage Ser.). 1979. 15.00x (ISBN 0-7100-0244-0). Routledge & Kegan.

Matthew Arnold: Selected Poems & Prose. Ed. by Denys Thompson. (Poetry Bookshelf Ser.). 1971. pap. text ed. 5.95 (ISBN 0-435-15063-4). Heinemann Ed.

Matthew Brady. Harrison et al. (Illus.). 35p. (gr. 1-9). 1981. 2.95 (ISBN 0-86575-190-0). Dormac.

Matthew Brady & His World. Ed. by Time-Life Books. 1977. 29.95 (ISBN 0-8094-2575-0). Time-Life.

Matthew Fontaine Maury. Charles L. Lewis. LC 79-6116. (Navies & Men Ser.). (Illus.). 1980. Repr. of 1927 ed. lib. bdg. 25.00x (ISBN 0-405-13045-7). Arno.

Matthew Fontaine Maury, Scientist of the Sea. Frances L. Williams. (Illus.). 1963. 32.50 (ISBN 0-8135-0433-3). Rutgers U Pr.

Matthew G. Lewis, Charles Robert Maturin & the Germans: An Interpretative Study of the Influence of German Literature on Two Gothic Novels. Syndy M. Conger. Ed. by Devendra P. Varma. LC 79-8448. (Gothic Studies & Dissertations Ser.). 1980. Repr. of 1977 ed. lib. bdg. 28.00x (ISBN 0-405-12652-2). Arno.

Matthew Henry's Commentary on the Whole Bible. Matthew Henry. Ed. by Leslie F. Church. 1966. 24.95 (ISBN 0-310-26010-8). Zondervan.

Matthew Henry's Sermon Outlines. Ed. by Sheldon B. Quincer. 1955. pap. 3.95 (ISBN 0-8028-1155-8). Eerdmans.

Matthew Henson: Co-Discoverer of the North Pole. Julian May. LC 72-85038. 40p. (gr. 4-8). 1972. PLB 5.95 o.p. (ISBN 0-87191-218-X). Creative Ed.

Matthew-John. Matthew Henry. (Commentary on the Whole Bible Ser: Vol. 5). 12.00 (ISBN 0-8007-0201-8). Revell.

Matthew Josephson, Bourgeois Bohemiam. David Shi. LC 80-24493. (Illus.). 328p. 1981. 19.95 (ISBN 0-300-02563-7). Yale U Pr.

Matthew Looney, 4 vols. Jerome Beatty, Jr. Incl. Matthew Looney & the Space Pirates. 1975. Vol. 1. pap. 1.25 (ISBN 0-380-00848-3, 24315); Matthew Looney in the Outback. 1973. Vol. 2. pap. 1.50 (ISBN 0-380-00847-5, 31575); Matthew Looney's Invasion of the Earth. 1973. Vol. 3. pap. 1.25 (ISBN 0-380-01493-9, 23069); Matthew Looney's Voyage to the Earth. Vol. 4. pap. 1.50 (ISBN 0-380-01494-7, 47423). (gr. 8 up). 1978. pap. 5.25 boxed set (ISBN 0-380-39693-9, 39693, Camelot). Avon.

Matthew Looney & the Space Pirates. Jerome Beatty, Jr. (gr. 4-8). 1974. pap. 1.50 (ISBN 0-380-00848-3, 50484, Camelot). Avon.

Matthew Looney's Voyage to the Earth. Jerome Beatty, Jr. (Illus.). 176p. (gr. 3-7). 1972. pap. 1.50 (ISBN 0-380-01494-7, 53660, Camelot). Avon.

Matthew-Luke Commentary of Philoxenus. Douglas J. Fox. LC 78-12852. 1979. 13.50 (ISBN 0-89130-350-2); pap. 9.00 (ISBN 0-89130-266-2, 060143). Scholars Pr Ca.

Matthew Lyon: "New Man" of the Democratic Revolution, 1749-1822. Aleine Austin. LC 80-281. (Illus.). 208p. 1980. 16.50x (ISBN 0-271-00262-X). Pa St U Pr.

Matthew, the Gospel of God's King. Keith L. Brooks. (Teach Yourself the Bible Ser). 1963. pap. 1.75 (ISBN 0-8024-5212-4). Moody.

Matthias Erzberger & the Dilemma of German Democracy. Klaus Epstein. LC 75-80546. 1971. Repr. of 1959 ed. 25.00 (ISBN 0-86527-123-2). Fertig.

Mattie: The Letters of Martha Mitchell Whitman. Ed. by Randall H. Waldron. LC 77-81906. (Illus.). 1978. 12.00x (ISBN 0-8147-9178-6). NYU Pr.

Matupit: Land, Politics & Change Among the Tolai of New Britain. A. L. Epstein. LC 70-92679. 1969. 20.00x (ISBN 0-520-01556-8). U of Cal Pr.

Mature Advertising: A Handbook of Effective Advertising Copy. Robert B. Parker. 176p. 1981. 19.95 (ISBN 0-201-05714-X). A-W.

Mature Man's Guide to Style. Bill Gale. LC 80-13843. (Illus.). 320p. 1980. 12.95 (ISBN 0-688-03688-0). Morrow.

Mature Metropolis. Ed. by Charles L. Leven. LC 77-10363. 1978. 24.95 (ISBN 0-669-01844-9). Lexington Bks.

Mature Mind. H. A. Overstreet. (Keith Jennison Large Type Bks). (gr. 9 up). 1965. PLB 8.95 o.p. (ISBN 0-531-00234-9). Watts.

Mature Student's Guide to Reading & Composition, Bk. 1. Delores H. Lipscomb et al. 280p. pap. text ed. 9.27 (ISBN 0-574-26000-5, 3-46000); tchr's manual avail. (ISBN 0-574-26002-1, 3-46002); Set Of 150. flash cards 10.30 (ISBN 0-574-26004-8, 3-46004); phono record avail. (3-46003). SRA.

Mature Student's Guide to Reading & Composition: A Guide to Composition & Reading, Bk. 2. Delores H. Lipscomb et al. pap. text ed. 9.27 (ISBN 0-574-26005-6, 3-46005); intr's. guide 3.47 (ISBN 0-574-26008-0). SRA.

Maturing in a Changing World. E. Shipton et al. 1971. text ed. 5.60 o.p. (ISBN 0-13-566166-8). P-H.

Maturity. Bruno Ugolotti. 1978. 6.95 o.p. (ISBN 0-533-02968-6). Vantage.

Maud Flies Solo. Gibbs Davis. 176p. (gr. 5-7). 1981. 8.95 (ISBN 0-87888-173-5). Bradbury Pr.

Maude & Claude Go Abroad. Susan Meddaugh. (Illus.). (gr. k-3). 1980. reinforced bdg. 7.95 (ISBN 0-395-29162-3). HM.

Maugham. Ted Morgan. 1981. pap. 9.95 (ISBN 0-671-42811-X, Touchstone). S&S.

Maui-Maui. Steve Cosgrove. (Serendipity Bks). (Illus.). (gr. k-4). 1980. PLB 6.95 (ISBN 0-87191-778-5). Creative Ed.

Maulever Hall. Jane A. Hodge. 1977. pap. 1.50 o.s.i. (ISBN 0-515-04332-X). Jove Pubns.

Mauleverer. A. C. Fox-Davies. 1976. lib. bdg. 14.95x (ISBN 0-89968-163-8). Lightyear.

Maunsell's Nelsons. D. W. Winkworth. (Steam Past Ser.). (Illus.). 128p. 1980. 17.50 (ISBN 0-04-385079-0, 2407). Allen Unwin.

Maura's Dream. Joel Gross. LC 80-52416. 416p. 1981. 12.95 (ISBN 0-87223-654-4). Seaview Bks.

Maurice. E. M. Forster. 256p. 1981. pap. 4.95 (ISBN 0-393-00026-5). Norton.

Maurice Barres. A. A. Greaves. (World Authors Ser.: No. 454). 1978. lib. bdg. 12.50 (ISBN 0-8057-6291-4). Twayne.

Maurice Bowra: A Celebration. Ed. by Hugh Lloyd-Jones. (Illus.). 156p. 1974. 10.50x (ISBN 0-7156-0789-8, Pub. by Duckworth England). Biblio Dist.

Maurice Burton's Daily Telegraph Nature Book. Maurice Burton. LC 75-10701. (Illus.). 128p. 1975. 5.95 (ISBN 0-7153-7078-2). David & Charles.

Maurice Falcolm Tauber: A Biobibliography 1934-1973. Marion Szigethy. LC 74-7401. 1974. 10.00 (ISBN 0-8108-0725-4). Scarecrow.

Maurice Maeterlinck. Bettina L. Knapp. (World Authors Ser.: France: No. 342). 1975. lib. bdg. 10.95 (ISBN 0-8057-2562-8). Twayne.

Maurice Messegue's Way to Natural Health & Beauty. Maurice Messegue. Tr. by Clara Winston from Fr. LC 74-8944. 324p. 1974. 6.95 o.s.i. (ISBN 0-02-584370-2). Macmillan.

Maurice Sceve. Ruth E. Mulhauser. LC 76-28722. (World Authors Ser: France: No. 424). 1977. lib. bdg. 12.50 (ISBN 0-8057-6264-7). Twayne.

Maurice Sceve: Poet of Love. Coleman. LC 74-31794. 212p. 1975. 44.50 (ISBN 0-521-20745-2). Cambridge U Pr.

Maurice the Snake & Gaston the Near-Sighted Turtle. Timothy Edler. (Tim Edler's Tales from the Atchafalaya). (Illus.). (gr. k-8). 1977. lea. 5.00 (ISBN 0-931108-00-4). Little Cajun.

Maurice's Room. Paula Fox. (Illus.). (gr. 3-5). 1966. 4.95g o.s.i. (ISBN 0-02-735730-9). Macmillan.

Maurice's Room. Paula Fox. LC 66-10167. (gr. 3-5). 1972. pap. 1.50 o.s.i. (ISBN 0-02-043200-3, Collier). Macmillan.

Maury Maverick: A Political Biography. Richard B. Henderson. (Illus.). 1970. 17.95 (ISBN 0-292-70090-3). U of Tex Pr.

Mauthner's Critique of Language. Gershon Weiler. LC 76-114605. 1971. 42.00 (ISBN 0-521-07861-X). Cambridge U Pr.

Maverick: A Director's Personal Experience in Opera & Theatre. Frank Corsaro. LC 77-77036. (Illus.). 1978. 12.95 (ISBN 0-8149-0790-3). Vanguard.

Maverick Guide to Australia. rev. ed. Robert W. Bone. (Maverick Guide Ser.). (Illus.). 324p. (Orig.). 1981. pap. 9.95 (ISBN 0-88289-278-9). Pelican.

Maverick Guide to Hawaii: 1981 Edition. Robert W. Bone. LC 80-25076. (Illus.). 437p. (Orig.). 1981. pap. 8.95 (ISBN 0-88289-277-0). Pelican.

Maverick Guide to New Zealand: 1981 Edition. Richard W. Bone. LC 80-25250. (Illus., Orig.). 1981. pap. 9.95 (ISBN 0-88289-269-X). Pelican.

Maverick Guns. J. E. Grinstead. 1978. pap. 1.25 (ISBN 0-505-51269-6). Tower Bks.

Maverick Showdown. W. F. Bragg. 1981. pap. 1.75 (ISBN 0-8439-0910-2, Leisure Bks). Nordon Pubns.

Maverick Town: The Story of Old Tascosa. rev. ed. John L. McCarty. (Illus.). 1946. 13.95 (ISBN 0-8061-0157-1). U of Okla Pr.

Mawson's Will. Lennard Bickel. 1978. pap. 2.95 (ISBN 0-380-39131-7, 52076, Discus). Avon.

Max. Rachel Isadora. LC 76-9088. (Illus.). 32p. (gr. k-3). 1976. 8.95 (ISBN 0-02-747450-X). Macmillan.

Max Beerbohm in Perspective. Bohun Lynch. LC 74-13999. (Illus.). xx, 185p. 1975. Repr. of 1922 ed. 18.00 (ISBN 0-8103-4065-8). Gale.

Max Brand the Big "Westerner". Robert Easton. LC 68-16732. (Illus.). 1970. 17.90 (ISBN 0-8061-0870-3); pap. 8.95 (ISBN 0-8061-1233-6). U of Okla Pr.

Max Ernst. Sarane Alexander. (Filipacchi Art Bks). (Illus.). 72p. 1980. cancelled (ISBN 2-85018-100-5); pap. cancelled (ISBN 2-85018-101-3). Hippocrene Bks.

Max Ernst. Uwe M. Schneede. Tr. by R. W. Last from Ger. (World of Art Ser.). (Illus.). 1972. pap. 9.95 (ISBN 0-19-520004-7). Oxford U Pr.

Max Ernst-Exhibition Catalog: Inside the Sight. Intro. by Werner Hofmann. (Illus.). 164p. 1973. pap. 6.00 (ISBN 0-914412-06-X). Interbk Inc.

Max Ernst: Inside the Sight. Werner Hofmann et al. LC 77-125283. (Illus.). 1973. pap. 6.00 (ISBN 0-914412-06-X). Inst for the Arts.

Max Frisch. Carol Petersen. Tr. by Charlotte LaRue. LC 72-153124. (Modern Literature Ser.). 10.95 (ISBN 0-8044-2692-9). Ungar.

Max of Skamania. Suzanne Taylor-Moore. 1980. pap. 14.95 (ISBN 0-686-28087-3). MTM Pub Co.

Max St. Peter McBride & Theodora. Barbara Fisher. (Illus.). 58p. (Orig.). (gr. k-3). 1981. pap. 2.00 (ISBN 0-934830-20-7). Ten Penny.

Max Scheler. Eugene Kelly. (Modern Masters Ser.: No. 55). 1977. lib. bdg. 12.50 (ISBN 0-8057-7707-5). Twayne.

Max Weber. Donald G. Macrae. LC 72-181978. (Modern Masters Ser). 1974. pap. 2.25 o.p. (ISBN 0-670-01976-3). Penguin.

Max Weber: A Biography. Marianne Weber. Ed. & tr. by Harry Zohn. LC 74-23904. 719p. 1975. 31.50 (ISBN 0-471-92333-8, Pub. by Wiley-Interscience). Wiley.

Max Weber: A Catalogue Raisonne of His Graphic Work. Daryl R. Rubenstein. LC 80-13883. (Illus.). 200p. 1980. incl. fiche 38.50x (ISBN 0-226-69598-0). U of Chicago Pr.

Max Weber: An Intellectual Portrait. Reinhard Bendix. 1978. 25.00x (ISBN 0-520-03503-8, CAMPUS 187); pap. 6.95x (ISBN 0-520-03194-6). U of Cal Pr.

Max Weber & the Destiny of Reason. Franco Ferrarotti. Tr. by Mario DiSanto from Ital. LC 80-5457. Orig. Title: Max Weber e il destino ragione. 150p. 1981. 17.50 (ISBN 0-87332-170-7). M E Sharpe.
Max Weber & the Theory of Modern Politics. David Beetham. 1974. text ed. 17.95x o.p. (ISBN 0-04-329018-3). Allen Unwin.
Max Weber on Methodology of the Social Sciences. Max Weber. 1949. text ed. 10.95 (ISBN 0-02-934360-7). Free Pr.
Max Weber: Selections in Translation. Ed. by W. G. Runciman. Tr. by E. Matthews. LC 77-80846. 1978. 39.00 (ISBN 0-521-21757-1); pap. 9.95x (ISBN 0-521-29268-9). Cambridge U Pr.
Max Weber's Ideal Type Theory. Rolf E. Rogers. LC 68-54974. 1969. 4.50 o.p. (ISBN 0-8022-2260-9). Philos Lib.
Max Weber's Vision of History: Ethics & Methods. Guenther Roth & Wolfgang Schluchter. LC 77-20328. 1979. 17.50x (ISBN 0-520-03604-2). U of Cal Pr.
Maxcy-Rosenau Preventive Medicine & Public Health Medicine. 10th ed. Sartwell. 1973. 45.00 o.p. (ISBN 0-8385-6186-1). ACC.
Maxcy-Rosenau Public Health & Preventive Medicine. 11th ed. Ed. by John M. Last. 1492p. 1980. text ed. 64.50x (ISBN 0-8385-6186-1). ACC.
Maxie. Mildred Kantrowitz. LC 80-15289. (Illus.). 36p. (ps-3). 1980. Repr. of 1970 ed. 8.95 (ISBN 0-590-07776-7, Four Winds). Schol Bk Serv.
Maximal Problems of Philosophy. Maximilian Kruger. (Illus.). 137p. 1981. 39.45 (ISBN 0-89266-274-3). Am Classical Coll Pr.
Maximes. Francois La Rochefoucauld. (Documentation thematique). (Illus., Fr.). pap. 2.95 (ISBN 0-685-13985-9, 123). Larousse.
Maximillian, You're the Greatest. Joseph Rosenbloom. (gr. 4 up). 1980. 8.95 (ISBN 0-525-66705-9). Elsevier-Nelson.
Maximizing Hospital Cash Resources. C. W. Frank. LC 78-14271. (Illus.). 1978. text ed. 25.95 (ISBN 0-89443-076-9). Aspen Systems.
Maximizing Minicourses: A Practical Guide to a Curriculum Alternative. Albert I. Oliver. LC 77-13942. 1978. pap. text ed. 6.50x (ISBN 0-8077-2520-X). Tchrs Coll.
Maximizing Revenue: Minimizing Expenditure. Charles K. Coe. 76p. (Orig.). 1981. pap. 7.50 (ISBN 0-89854-070-4). U of GA Inst Govt.
Maxims & Reflections. Francesco Guicciardini. LC 64-23752. 1972. pap. 4.95x (ISBN 0-8122-1037-9, Pa. Paperbacks). U of Pa Pr.
Maxims of Chess. John W. Collins. 1978. 10.95 o.p. (ISBN 0-679-13066-7). McKay.
Maxims of Chess. 1981. pap. 5.95 (ISBN 0-679-14403-X). McKay.
Maxims of George Washington. LC 76-55672. 64p. 1978. 8.00 (ISBN 0-913720-07-0). Sandstone.
Maxims of the Civil Law: Essays in the Evolution of Law. Walter S. Johnson. LC 74-26294. 252p. 1973. Repr. of 1929 ed. lib. bdg. 22.50x (ISBN 0-912004-10-X). W W Gaunt.
Maximum Feasible Misunderstanding. Daniel P. Moynihan. LC 69-18005. 1970. 5.95 o.s.i. (ISBN 0-02-922000-9); pap. text ed. 5.95 (ISBN 0-02-922010-6). Free Pr.
Maximum Principles & Their Applications. Rene Sperb. (Mathematics in Science & Engineering). 1981. price not set (ISBN 0-12-656880-4). Acad Pr.
Maximum Security Ward. Ramon Guthrie. 1970. 7.50 o.p. (ISBN 0-374-20468-3). FS&G.
Max's Dream. William Mayne. LC 77-12728. (Illus.). (gr. 5-9). 1978. 7.95 (ISBN 0-688-80131-5); PLB 7.63 (ISBN 0-688-84131-7). Greenwillow.
Maxwell Anderson. Alfred S. Shivers. (U.S. Authors Ser: No. 279). 1976. lib. bdg. 10.95 (ISBN 0-8057-7179-4). Twayne.
Maxwell Drewitt. Charlotte Riddell. (Nineteenth Century Fiction Ser.: Ireland: Vol. 62). 888p. 1979. lib. bdg. 46.00 (ISBN 0-8240-3511-9). Garland Pub.
May Day. James Scully. LC 80-80653. 72p. (Orig.). 1980. pap. 3.00 (ISBN 0-936484-00-4). Minn Rev Pr.
May I Bring a Friend. Beatrice S. De Regniers. LC 64-19562. (Illus.). (ps-2). 1964. PLB 8.95 (ISBN 0-689-20615-1). Atheneum.
May I Hate God. Pierre Wolff. LC 78-70815. 1979. pap. 2.45 (ISBN 0-8091-2180-8). Paulist Pr.
May I Join You? Beverly Gaw & James E. Sayer. LC 78-23300. (Illus.). 1979. pap. text ed. 9.95x (ISBN 0-88284-069-X). Alfred Pub.
May Movement: Revolt & Reform. Alain Touraine. Tr. by Leonard F. Mayhew. LC 76-103977. 1979. 24.50x (ISBN 0-394-46256-4); pap. text ed. 9.95x (ISBN 0-89197-626-4). Irvington.
May My Words Feed Others: An Anthology of Verse & Fiction from the Reconstructionist Magazine. Ed. by Chayym Zeldis. LC 72-6377. 284p. 1973. 12.95 o.p. (ISBN 0-498-01249-2). A S Barnes.
May Sarton. Agnes Sibley. (U. S. Authors Ser.: No. 213). lib. bdg. 10.95 (ISBN 0-8057-0656-9). Twayne.
May Sarton: A Bibliography. Lenora P. Blouin. (Author Bibliography Ser.: No. 34). 1978. 12.00 (ISBN 0-8108-1054-9). Scarecrow.
May Sinclair. Hrisey D. Zegger. (English Authors Ser: No. 192). 1976. lib. bdg. 12.50 (ISBN 0-8057-6666-9). Twayne.
May Sixty-Eight & Film Culture. Sylvia Harvey. (BFI Ser.). (Orig.). 1978. pap. 5.00 o.p. (ISBN 0-85170-081-0). NY Zoetrope.
May the Wind Be at Your Back: The Prayer of St. Patrick. A. M. Greeley. (Orig.). 1976. pap. 4.95 (ISBN 0-8164-2595-7). Crossroad NY.
Maya. rev. ed. Michael D. Coe. (Ancient People & Places Ser.). (Illus.). 180p. 1980. 19.95 (ISBN 0-500-02097-3); pap. 9.95 (ISBN 0-500-27195-X). Thames Hudson.
Maya Chontal Indians of Acalan-Tixchel: A Contribution to the History & Ethnography of the Yucatan Peninsula. France V. Scholes et al. LC 68-15677. (Civilization of the American Indian Ser.: Vol. 91). (Illus.). 1968. 22.50x (ISBN 0-8061-0813-4). U of Okla Pr.
Maya Design Coloring Book. Wilson G. Turner. (Illus.). 48p. (Orig.). (gr. 1-6). 1980. pap. 2.00 (ISBN 0-486-24047-9). Dover.
Maya Hieroglyphic Writing: An Introduction. J. Eric Thompson. (Civilization of the American Indian Ser.: No. 56). (Illus.). 1975. 29.95 o.p. (ISBN 0-8061-0447-3); pap. 17.95 (ISBN 0-8061-0958-0). U of Okla Pr.
Maya in Sankara: Measuring the Immeasurable. L. Thomas O'Neal. 1980. 16.00x (ISBN 0-8364-0611-7). South Asia Bks.
Maya: Indians of Central America. Sonia Bleeker. (Illus.). (gr. 3-6). 1961. PLB 6.67 (ISBN 0-688-31461-9). Morrow.
Maya Land in Color. Walter R. Aguiar. (Profiles of America Ser.). (Illus.). 1978. 6.95 (ISBN 0-8038-4703-3). Hastings.
Maya World. rev. ed. Elizabeth P. Benson. LC 77-4955. (Illus.). 1977. 11.95 (ISBN 0-690-01673-5, TYC-T). T Y Crowell.
Mayan Poems. James Schevill. (Illus., Orig.). 1978. pap. 4.50 (ISBN 0-914278-16-9). Copper Beech.
Mayan Texts III. Ed. by Louanna Furbee. LC 76-15159. (International Journal of American Linguistics Native American Texts Ser.: No. 5). 122p. (Orig.). 1980. pap. 10.75 (ISBN 0-8357-0567-6, IS-00115, Pub. by U of Chicago Pr). Univ Microfilms.
Maybe Next Summer. Don Schellie. LC 79-6338. 256p. (gr. 7-12). 1980. 8.95 (ISBN 0-590-07585-3, Four Winds). Schol Bk Serv.
Mayday. Thomas H. Block. 1980. pap. 2.95 (ISBN 0-425-04729-6). Berkley Pub.
Mayday! Mayday! Hilary Milton. (gr. 5 up). 1979. PLB 7.90 s&l (ISBN 0-531-02890-9). Watts.
Mayday: The History of a Village Holocaust. Grant Parker. LC 80-83408. 260p. (Orig.). 1980. pap. 5.95 (ISBN 0-9604958-0-0). Libty Pr MI.
Mayenne. E. C. Tubb. Bd. with Jondelle. (Science Fiction Ser.). 1981. pap. 2.50 (ISBN 0-87997-614-4, UE1614). NAL.
Mayer & Thalberg: The Make-Believe Saints. Samuel Marx. (Illus.). 336p. 1980. pap. 2.95 (ISBN 0-446-83987-6). Warner Bks.
Mayflower. Vernon Heaton. (Illus.). 200p. 1980. 19.95 (ISBN 0-8317-5745-0). Mayflower Bks.
Mayflower Compact November Eleventh, Sixteen Twenty: The First Democratic Document in America. John E. Walsh. LC 73-134369. (Focus Bks). (Illus.). (gr. 7 up). 1971. PLB 4.47 o.p. (ISBN 0-531-01019-8); pap. 1.25 o.p. (ISBN 0-531-02327-3). Watts.
Mayhem on the Coney Beat. Michael Geller. (Bud Dugan Ser.: No. 1). 1979. pap. 1.75 (ISBN 0-505-51353-6). Tower Bks.
Mayo Brothers. Jane Goodsell. LC 70-139104. (Biography Ser). (Illus.). (gr. 2-5). 1972. PLB 6.49 o.p. (ISBN 0-690-52751-9, TYC-J). T Y Crowell.
Mayor of Casterbridge. Thomas Hardy. (Literature Ser). (gr. 10-12). 1970. pap. text ed. 3.58 (ISBN 0-87720-745-3). AMSCO Sch.
Mayor of Casterbridge. Thomas Hardy. pap. 1.95 (ISBN 0-451-51230-8, CJ1230, Sig Classics). NAL.
Mayor of Casterbridge. Thomas Hardy. Ed. by James K. Robinson. LC 76-57983. (Norton Critical Editions). 1977. pap. text ed. 6.95x (ISBN 0-393-09174-0). Norton.
Mayor of Casterbridge. Thomas Hardy. pap. 1.95. Bantam.
Mayor of Wind-Gap & Canvassing, 3 vols. John Banim & Michael Banim. Ed. by Robert L. Wolff. (Ireland Nineteenth Century Fiction - Ser. Two). 1066p. 1979. lib. bdg. 96.00 (ISBN 0-8240-3472-4). Garland Pub.
Mazarinades: A Checklist of Copies in Major Collections in the United States. Robert O. Lindsay & John Neu. LC 74-150720. 1972. 20.50 (ISBN 0-8108-0369-0). Scarecrow.
Mazda GLC Shop Manual: 1977-1979. Jim Combs. Ed. by Eric Jorgensen. (Illus.). 1978. pap. 10.95 (ISBN 0-89287-288-8, A262). Clymer Pubns.
Mazda RX-7 Nineteen Seventy-Eight to Eighty-One. LC 80-70342. (Illus.). 208p. 1980. pap. 8.95. Chilton.
Mazda Service Repair Handbook. Alan Ahlstrand. Ed. by Eric Jorgensen. (RX-2 & RX-3, 1971-1977). (Illus.). 1978. pap. 10.95 (ISBN 0-89287-236-5, A164). Clymer Pubns.
Maze Book. Paul McCreary. (Educational Ser.). (Illus.). (gr. 2-4). 1979. pap. 4.50 (ISBN 0-89039-218-8). Ann Arbor FL.
Mazel Tov, Y'all: A Bake Book for Happy Occasions. Sara Kasdan. LC 68-8082. (Illus.). 1968. 8.95 (ISBN 0-8149-0131-X). Vanguard.
Mazepyntsi Po Poltavi. Mykola Bytyns'Kyi. LC 75-561602. (Ukrainian.). 1974. 6.00 (ISBN 0-918884-19-5). Slavia Lib.
Mazes & Labyrinths. W. H. Matthews. LC 70-75946. 1969. Repr. of 1922 ed. 18.00 (ISBN 0-8103-3839-4). Gale.
Mazes: 60 Beautiful & Beastly Labyrinths with Solutions. Rolf Myller. (Illus.). 160p. (gr. 1 up). 1976. pap. 3.95 (ISBN 0-394-83254-X). Pantheon.
Mazungumzo: Interviews with East African Writers, Publishers, Editors & Scholars. Bernth Lindfors. LC 80-25684. (Africa Ser., Ohio University Papers in International Studies). 179p. 1981. pap. 13.00 (ISBN 0-89680-108-X). Ohio U Ctr Intl.
Mazzini: Prophet of Modern Europe. Gwilym O. Griffith. LC 78-80552. 1970. Repr. 19.50 (ISBN 0-86527-124-0). Fertig.
MBO II: A System of Managerial Leadership for the 80's. George S. Odiorne. LC 78-72336. 1979. 16.95 (ISBN 0-8224-0977-1). Pitman Learning.
Mbunas, Malawi Cichlids. P. B. Jackson & Tony Ribbinck. (Illus.). 128p. (Orig.). 1975. pap. 5.95 (ISBN 0-87666-454-0, PS-740). TFH Pubns.
Me. Barbara J. Crane. (Crane Reading System-English Ser.). (gr. k-2). 1977. pap. text ed. 2.80 (ISBN 0-89075-092-0). Crane Pub Co.
Me. 288p. (Orig.). 1981. pap. 2.95 (ISBN 0-553-13646-1). Bantam.
Me: A Book of Poems. Ed. by Lee B. Hopkins. LC 72-115782. (Illus.). (gr. k-3). 1970. 7.95 (ISBN 0-395-28815-0, Clarion). HM.
Me & Clara & Baldwin the Pony. Dimiter Inkiow. Tr. by Paul McGuire from Ger. LC 79-21820. (Me-&-Clara Storybook). (Illus.). 96p. (gr. k-4). 1980. 3.95 (ISBN 0-394-84434-3); PLB 4.99 (ISBN 0-394-94434-8). Pantheon.
Me & Fat Glenda. Lila Perl. LC 71-179439. 192p. (gr. 3-6). 1972. 8.95 (ISBN 0-395-28871-1, Clarion). HM.
Me & Fat Glenda. Lila Perl. (gr. 4-6). 1973. pap. 1.75 (ISBN 0-671-42190-5). Archway.
Me & My Family Tree. Paul Showers. LC 77-26595. (Let's-Read-&-Find-Out Science Bk). (Illus.). (gr. k-3). 1978. 7.95 (ISBN 0-690-03886-0, TYC-J); PLB 7.89 (ISBN 0-690-03887-9). T Y Crowell.
Me & My Little Brain. John D. Fitzgerald. (gr. 4-7). 1972. pap. 1.50 (ISBN 0-440-45533-2, YB). Dell.
Me & My Mona Lisa Smile. Sheila Hayes. 128p. (gr. 7 up). 1981. 9.95 (ISBN 0-525-66731-8). Elsevier-Nelson.
Me & Neesie. Eloise Greenfield. LC 74-23078. (Illus.). 40p. (gr. 1-4). 1975. PLB 7.89 (ISBN 0-690-00715-9, TYC-J). T Y Crowell.
Me & the Bad Guys. Shirley Gordon. LC 79-9611. (Illus.). 80p. (gr. 3-6). 1980. 7.95 (ISBN 0-06-022116-X, HarpJ); PLB 7.89 (ISBN 0-06-022117-8). Har-Row.
Me & the Spitter. Gaylord Perry. 1974. pap. 1.25 o.p. (ISBN 0-451-05927-1, Y5927, Sig). NAL.
Me & the Terrible Two. Ellen Conford. (gr. 4-6). 1977. pap. 1.75 (ISBN 0-671-41769-X). Archway.
Me & the Weirdos. Jane Sutton. (gr. 2-5). 1981. 6.95 (ISBN 0-395-30447-4). HM.
Me Bandy, You Cissie: The Journals of Bartholomew Bandy. Donald Jack. 1979. 8.95 o.p. (ISBN 0-385-14396-6). Doubleday.
Me Either, and Other One-Act Plays. Ed. by Jerry O'Malley. 1976. pap. 0.60 (ISBN 0-8272-2311-0). Bethany Pr.
Me Grandad Had an Elephant & Other Stories. Varkom Muhammed Basheer. Tr. by R. E. Asher from Malayam. 150p. 1980. 12.00x (ISBN 0-85224-386-3, Pub. by Edinburgh U Pr Scotland); pap. 6.00x (ISBN 0-85224-387-1, Pub. by Edinburgh U Pr Scotland). Columbia U Pr.
Me, Julie Mountain. Mary Hanagan. 74p. 1979. 4.95 (ISBN 0-8059-2645-3). Dorrance.
Me, Molly Midnight, the Artist's Cat. Nadja Maril. (Illus.). (gr. k up). 1977. 7.95 (ISBN 0-916144-15-1); pap. 3.95 (ISBN 0-916144-16-X). Stemmer Hse.
Me, Myself & I: Every Woman's Journey to Her Self. Ann Schoonmaker. LC 76-62958. 1977. 7.95 o.p. (ISBN 0-06-067120-3, HarpR). Har-Row.
Me 'n' Steve. Roy O. Brotherton. (Illus.). (gr. 4-7). 1965. 4.75g o.s.i. (ISBN 0-02-715050-X). Macmillan.
Me Nobody Knows: Children's Voices from the Ghetto. Ed. by Stephen M. Joseph. 1969. pap. 1.75 (ISBN 0-380-01339-8, 48934, Discus). Avon.
Me Tanner, You Jane. Lawrence Block. LC 79-93176. (Cock Robin Mystery Ser). 1970. 4.50 o.s.i. (ISBN 0-02-511610-X). Macmillan.
Me the Flunkie. Ed. by Andrew Summers. 1974. pap. 1.25 o.p. (ISBN 0-449-30649-6, P649, Prem). Fawcett.
Me: Understanding Myself & Others. Audrey Riker. 1977. 9.68 (ISBN 0-87002-182-6); student guide 2.92 (ISBN 0-87002-190-7); tchr's guide 3.40 (ISBN 0-87002-188-5). Bennett IL.
Mea Culpa: A Woman's World. Henry Harland. Ed. by Ian Fletcher & John Stokes. LC 76-24386. (Decadent Consciousness Ser.). 1977. lib. bdg. 38.00 (ISBN 0-8240-2761-2). Garland Pub.
Meadow Lake: Gold Town. Paul Fatout. LC 69-15995. (Illus.). xiv, 178p. 1974. pap. 1.95 (ISBN 0-8032-5788-0, BB 576, Bison). U of Nebr Pr.
Meah Shaerim Centennial: A Study of the Neturei Karta. 1980. lib. bdg. 59.95 (ISBN 0-686-68746-9). Revisionist Pr.
Meal Management. University of Missouri - Home Economics Resource Unit. text ed. 2.50x spiral bdg. o.p. (ISBN 0-87543-026-0). Lucas.
Meal Planning & Service. rev. ed. Beth B. McLean. (Illus.). (gr. 9-12). 1964. text ed. 12.60 (ISBN 0-87002-218-0). Bennett IL.
Meals in Minutes. Monica Hockney. 3.95 (ISBN 0-685-44121-0). Transatlantic.
Mealybugs of California: With Taxonomy, Biology, & Control of North American Species. Howard L. McKenzie. (Illus.). 1968. 57.50x (ISBN 0-520-00844-8). U of Cal Pr.
Mean-Field Magnetohydrodynamics & Dynamo Theory. F. Krause & K-H. Radler. (Illus.). 270p. Date not set. 36.00 (ISBN 0-08-025041-6). Pergamon.
Mean Max. pap. 3.50 incl. record (ISBN 0-590-20610-9, Schol Pap). Schol Bk Serv.
Mean Old Mean Hyena. Jack Prelutsky. LC 78-2300. (Illus.). (gr. k-3). 1978. 7.95 (ISBN 0-688-80163-3); PLB 7.63 (ISBN 0-688-84163-5). Greenwillow.
Mean Things Happening in This Land: The Life & Times of H. L. Mitchell. H. L. Mitchell. LC 78-65660. 372p. 1979. text ed. 10.95 (ISBN 0-916672-25-5). Allanheld.
Meaning & Action: A Critical History of Pragmatism. H. Standish Thayer. 592p. 1981. 25.00 (ISBN 0-915144-73-5); pap. text ed. 12.50 (ISBN 0-915144-74-3). Hackett Pub.
Meaning & Behaviour in the Built Environment. Ed. by Geoffrey Broadbent et al. LC 79-41490. 336p. 1980. 55.00 (ISBN 0-471-27708-8, Pub. by Wiley-Interscience). Wiley.
Meaning & Existence. Gustav Bergmann. (Orig.). 1960. pap. 7.95x (ISBN 0-299-01984-5). U of Wis Pr.
Meaning & Form. Dwight Bolinger. (English Language Ser.). (Illus.). 1979. pap. text ed. 10.50x (ISBN 0-582-29104-6). Longman.
Meaning & Form. Dwight Bolinger. LC 76-44857. (English Language Ser.). (Illus.). 1977. text ed. 18.95x (ISBN 0-582-55103-X). Longman.
Meaning & Modality. C. Lewy. LC 76-11084. 1977. 23.50 (ISBN 0-521-21314-2). Cambridge U Pr.
Meaning & Order in Moroccan Society. C. Geertz et al. LC 78-54327. (Illus.). 1979. 49.50 (ISBN 0-521-22175-7). Cambridge U Pr.
Meaning & Reference. Ed. by S. Blackburn. 192p. 1975. 29.50x (ISBN 0-521-20720-7). Cambridge U Pr.
Meaning & Saying: Essays in the Philosophy of Language. Frank B. Ebersole. LC 79-88304. 1979. pap. text ed. 10.00 (ISBN 0-8191-0775-1). U Pr of Amer.
Meaning & Significance of Christian Hope. H. Roy White. 1981. 5.95 (ISBN 0-533-04536-3). Vantage.
Meaning & the English Verb. Geoffrey N. Leech. 1971. pap. text ed. 4.25x (ISBN 0-582-52214-5). Longman.
Meaning & the Moral Sciences. Hilary Putnam. (International Library of Philosophy & Scientific Method). 1978. 16.00 (ISBN 0-7100-8754-3). Routledge & Kegan.
Meaning & the Moral Sciences. Hilary Putnam. (International Library of Philosophy). 1979. pap. 6.95 (ISBN 0-7100-0437-0). Routledge & Kegan.
Meaning & the Objective of History. Theodore J Norvell. (Illus.). 123p. 1980. deluxe ed. 37.65 (ISBN 0-89266-238-7). Am Classical Coll Pr.

Meaning & Understanding International Conference, June 1979. Ed. by H. H. Parret. (Foundation of Communication Ser.). 288p. 1980. text ed. 61.50x (ISBN 3-11-008116-4). De Gruyter.

Meaning & Value in Western Thought: A History of Ideas in Western Culture. J. William Angell & Robert M. Helm. LC 80-67174. (Ancient Foundations Ser.: Vol. I). 434p. 1981. lib. bdg. 22.75 (ISBN 0-8191-1368-9); pap. text ed. 13.95 (ISBN 0-8191-1369-7). U Pr of Amer.

Meaning & Value of the Sacraments. Flower A. Newhouse. LC 77-186123. 123p. 1971. 5.50 (ISBN 0-910378-07-X). Christward.

Meaning in Children's Art. E. Mattel & B. Mayan. 1981. 15.95 (ISBN 0-13-567115-9); pap. 12.95 (ISBN 0-13-567107-8). P-H.

Meaning in Crafts. 3rd ed. Edward L. Mattil. LC 73-123087. 1971. ref. ed. 16.50 (ISBN 0-13-567156-6). P-H.

Meaning in Culture. F. Allan Hanson. 1975. 16.50x (ISBN 0-7100-8132-4). Routledge & Kegan.

Meaning in Life As Experienced by Persons Labeled Retarded in a Group Home: Their Quest to Be. Lous Heshusius. (Illus.). 176p. 1980. 19.50 (ISBN 0-398-04064-8); pap. 15.75 (ISBN 0-398-04079-6). C C Thomas.

Meaning in Star Trek. Karin Blair. LC 77-7438. (Illus.). 1978. 9.95 (ISBN 0-89012-010-2). Anima Pubns.

Meaning in the Arts. Louis A. Reid. (Muirhead Library of Philosophy). 1969. text ed. 11.50x o.p. (ISBN 0-04-701004-5). Humanities.

Meaning in the Visual Arts. Erwin Panofsky. LC 55-9754. 1955. pap. 3.50 o.p. (ISBN 0-385-09248-2, A59, Anch). Doubleday.

Meaning of Bama in the Old Testament. P. H. Vaughan. LC 73-89004. (Society for Old Testament Study Monographs: No. 3). (Illus.). 96p. 1974. 23.95 (ISBN 0-521-20425-9). Cambridge U Pr.

Meaning of Blindness: Attitudes Toward Blindness & Blind People. Michael E. Monbeck. LC 73-77853. 224p. 1973. 8.50x (ISBN 0-253-33727-5). Ind U Pr.

Meaning of Children: Attitudes & Opinions of a Selected Group of U.S. University Graduates. Eulah C. Laucks. (Special Studies in Contemporary Social Issues). 225p. 1981. lib. bdg. 20.00x (ISBN 0-89158-881-7). Westview.

Meaning of Conservatism. Roger Scruton. 205p. 1980. 26.50x (ISBN 0-389-20082-4). B&N.

Meaning of Criminal Insanity. Herbert Fingarette. LC 70-165223. 300p. 1972. 21.50x (ISBN 0-520-02082-0); pap. 4.25x (ISBN 0-520-02631-4). U of Cal Pr.

Meaning of Deepening: Gaining a Clearer Apprehension of the Purpose of God for Man. Daniel C. Jordan. LC 72-84824. (Comprehensive Deepening Program Ser.). 1973. pap. text ed. 4.00 (ISBN 0-87743-046-2, 7-64-01). Baha'i.

Meaning of Evolution: A Study of the History of Life & of Its Significance for Man. rev. ed. George G. Simpson. (Terry Lectures Ser.). (Illus.). 1967. pap. 5.45x (ISBN 0-300-00229-7, Y23). Yale U Pr.

Meaning of Fiction. Albert Cook. LC 60-9591. 1960. 8.95x o.p. (ISBN 0-8143-1136-9). Wayne St U Pr.

Meaning of Gifts. Paul Tournier. LC 63-19172. 1963. 4.25 (ISBN 0-8042-2124-3). John Knox.

Meaning of Gifts. Paul Tournier. LC 63-19122. 1976. pap. 1.25 (ISBN 0-8042-3604-6). John Knox.

Meaning of Hope: A Biblical Exposition with Concordance. C. F. Moule. Ed. by John Reumann. LC 63-17881. (Facet Bks). 80p. (Orig.). 1963. pap. 1.00 (ISBN 0-8006-3001-7, 1-3001). Fortress.

Meaning of Human Nutrition. M. W. Lamb & M. L. Harden. 1973. text ed. 18.50 (ISBN 0-08-017078-1); pap. text ed. 9.50 (ISBN 0-08-017079-X). Pergamon.

Meaning of Jesus Christ. William M. Ramsay. (Orig.). (gr. 9-10). 1964. pap. 3.45 (ISBN 0-8042-9220-5); tchrs' guide pap. 2.60. John Knox.

Meaning of Life. Ed. by E. D. Klemke. 288p. 1981. pap. text ed. 6.95x (ISBN 0-19-502871-6). Oxford U Pr.

Meaning of Life. Gene Liberty. (Orig.). (gr. 7-10). 1975. pap. text ed. 5.50 (ISBN 0-87720-010-6). AMSCO Sch.

Meaning of Life: Questions, Answers & Analysis. Steven Sanders & David Cheny. 1980. pap. text ed. 7.95 (ISBN 0-13-567438-7). P-H.

Meaning of Man. Sidi Ali Al-Jamal Of Fez. Ed. by Abd Al-Kabir Al Munawarra. Tr. by Aisha Abd Ar-Rahman At-Tarjumana from Arabic. Orig. Title: Foundations of the Science of Knowledge. (Illus.). 455p. (Orig.). 1977. 20.00 (ISBN 0-9504446-6-9); pap. 12.00 (ISBN 0-9504446-5-0). Iqra.

Meaning of Nationalism. Louis L. Snyder. LC 68-8338. (Illus.). 1968. Repr. of 1954 ed. lib. bdg. 19.25x (ISBN 0-8371-0233-2, SNMN). Greenwood.

Meaning of Persons. Paul Tournier. 1957. 7.95 (ISBN 0-06-068370-8, HarpR); pap. 1.95 (ISBN 0-685-11826-6, P-304, HarpR). Har-Row.

Meaning of Relativity. 5th ed. Albert Einstein. 1956. 11.00 (ISBN 0-691-08007-0); pap. 3.95 (ISBN 0-691-02352-2). Princeton U Pr.

Meaning of Sociology. Joel M. Charon. LC 79-24396. 1980. pap. 7.95 (ISBN 0-88284-097-5). Alfred Pub.

Meaning of the Cross. Gordon Watt. 1970. pap. 1.25. Chr Lit.

Meaning of the Finite Verb Forms in the Old Church Slavonic Codex Suprasliensis: A Synchronic Study. Tine H. Amse-De Jong. (Slavistic Printings & Reprintings Ser.: No. 319). 228p. (Orig.). 1974. pap. text ed. 52.95x (ISBN 90-2793-012-0). Mouton.

Meaning of the Renaissance & Reformation. Richard L. Demolen et al. 440p. 1974. pap. text ed. 9.75 (ISBN 0-395-12632-0). HM.

Meaning of Transcendence. Robert P. Orr. Ed. by Wendell Dietrich. LC 80-12872. (American Academy of Religion Dissertation Ser.). 1981. 13.50 (ISBN 0-89130-407-X); pap. 9.00. Scholars Pr CA.

Meaning of Truth: A Sequel to Pragmatism. William James. 1970. pap. 3.45 o.p. (ISBN 0-472-06162-3, 162, AA). U of Mich Pr.

Meaning Well. Sheila Cole. LC 73-12225. (Illus.). 72p. (gr. 4-7). 1974. PLB 5.90 (ISBN 0-531-02665-5). Watts.

Meaningful to Behold. Geshe Gyatso. Ed. by Jonathan Landaw. Tr. by Tenzin Norbu from Tibetan. 365p. (Orig.). 1981. pap. 12.95 (ISBN 0-86171-003-7). Great Eastern.

Meanings & Situations. Arthur Brittan. (International Library of Sociology). 222p. 1973. 18.50 (ISBN 0-7100-7509-X); pap. 6.00 (ISBN 0-7100-7551-0). Routledge & Kegan.

Meanings of Modern Art. John Russell. LC 80-8217. (Illus.). 384p. 1981. 29.95 (ISBN 0-06-013701-0, HarpT). Har-Row.

Means for Increasing the Effectiveness of Hydrotransport. Vera N. Pokrovskaya. Ed. by W. C. Cooley & R. R. Faddick. Tr. by Albert Peabody from Rus. LC 77-77841. (Illus., Eng.). 1977. 40.00x o.p. (ISBN 0-918990-02-5). Terraspace.

Means of Evil. Ruth Rendell. 160p. 1981. pap. 2.25 (ISBN 0-553-14153-8). Bantam.

Meanwhile Back at the Henhouse. Thomas Bledsoe. LC 66-25670. 185p. 1966. 4.95 (ISBN 0-8040-0197-9). Swallow.

Measure Algebras. Joseph L. Taylor. LC 73-5930. (CBMS Regional Conference Series in Mathematics: No. 16). 1979. pap. 7.20 (ISBN 0-8218-1666-7, CBMS-16). Am Math.

Measure & Category. 2nd ed. J. C. Oxtoby. (Graduate Texts in Mathematics: Vol. 2). 106p. 1980. 19.80 (ISBN 0-387-90508-1). Springer-Verlag.

Measure & Category: A Survey of the Analogies Between Topological & Measure Spaces. J. C. Oxtoby. LC 73-149248. (Graduate Texts in Mathematics: Vol. 2). 1971. 14.50 o.p. (ISBN 0-387-90025-X); pap. text ed. 7.50 o.p. (ISBN 0-387-05349-2). Springer-Verlag.

Measure & Design in American Painting, 1760-1860. Lisa F. Andrus. LC 76-23601. (Outstanding Dissertations in the Fine Arts - American). (Illus.). 1977. Repr. lib. bdg. 56.00 (ISBN 0-8240-2675-6). Garland Pub.

Measure & Integration. Sterling K. Berberian. LC 74-128871. 1970. Repr. of 1965 ed. text ed. 11.95 (ISBN 0-8284-0241-8). Chelsea Pub.

Measure for Measure. William Shakespeare. Ed. by Arthur Quiller-Couch et al. (New Shakespeare Ser). 1969. 23.95 (ISBN 0-521-07544-0); pap. 4.50x (ISBN 0-521-09488-7). Cambridge U Pr.

Measure for Measure. William Shakespeare. Ed. by Robert C. Bald. 1956. pap. 2.50 (ISBN 0-14-071403-0, Pelican). Penguin.

Measure for Measure As Royal Entertainment. Josephine W. Bennett. LC 66-15764. 1966. 20.00x (ISBN 0-231-02921-7). Columbia U Pr.

Measure for Measure: Calorie & Carbohydrate Recipes. Ed. by Elizabeth O'Reilly. (Illus.). 1974. wire bound 11.95x (ISBN 0-433-24220-5). Intl Ideas.

Measure, Integration, & Functional Analysis. Robert Ash. 284p. 1971. 22.95 (ISBN 0-12-065260-9). Acad Pr.

Measure of a Family. Gene A. Getz. LC 76-46872. (Orig.). 1977. pap. 2.95 (ISBN 0-8307-0445-0, 50-150-06). Regal.

Measure of a Man: A Practical Guide to Christian Maturity. Gene A. Getz. LC 74-175983. (Orig.). 1974. pap. 2.95 (ISBN 0-8307-0291-1, 50-121-04). Regal.

Measure of a Marriage Workbook. Gene A. Getz. 96p. 1980. lab manual 5.95 (ISBN 0-8307-0756-5). Regal.

Measure of a Woman. Gene A. Getz. LC 77-7433. (Orig.). 1977. pap. 2.50 (ISBN 0-8307-0537-6, 50-161-18). Regal.

Measure of Days. Christa Wakefield. (Orig.). 1979. pap. 1.95 (ISBN 0-686-68908-9). Manor Bks.

Measure of Greatness. Parton Keese. LC 80-17027. (Illus.). 200p. 1981. 9.95 (ISBN 0-13-567800-5). P-H.

Measure of Poe. Louis Broussard. LC 69-16715. 1969. 5.95 o.p. (ISBN 0-8061-0859-2). U of Okla Pr.

Measure-Theoretic Probability. Henry A. Krieger. LC 80-1431. 394p. 1980. lib. bdg. 20.50 (ISBN 0-8191-1228-3); pap. text ed. 12.50 (ISBN 0-8191-1229-1). U Pr of Amer.

Measure Up. Charles H. Kahn et al. LC 67-31749. (Illus., Special Education Ser. for slow learners). (gr. 4-12). 1968. pap. 2.72 (ISBN 0-8224-4460-7); tchrs' manual free (ISBN 0-8224-4461-5). Pitman Learning.

Measure with Metric. Franklyn M. Branley. LC 74-4056. (Young Math Ser.). (Illus.). 40p. (gr. k-3). 1975. PLB 7.89 (ISBN 0-690-01117-2, TYC-J); pap. 2.95 (ISBN 0-690-01265-9, TYC-J); filmstrip with record 11.95 (ISBN 0-690-00996-8); filmstrip with cassette 14.95 (ISBN 0-690-00997-6). T Y Crowell.

Measured Drawings of Early American Furniture. Burl N. Osburn & Bernice B. Osburn. LC 74-79956. (Illus.). 96p. 1975. pap. 3.50 (ISBN 0-486-23057-0). Dover.

Measurement, Accounting, & Organizational Information. Theodore J. Mock & Hugh D. Grove. LC 78-10536. (Accounting & Information Systems Ser.). 1979. text ed. 21.95x (ISBN 0-471-61202-2). Wiley.

Measurement & Classification of Psychiatric Symptoms. J. K. Wing et al. LC 73-89008. (Illus.). 224p. 1974. 27.50 (ISBN 0-521-20382-1). Cambridge U Pr.

Measurement & Control of Cardiovascular Risk Factors. Ed. by Ruth J. Hegyeli. (Atherosclerosis Reviews: Vol. 7). 1979. 36.50 (ISBN 0-89004-396-5). Raven.

Measurement & Control of Diesel Particulate Emissions. Society of Automotive Engineers. 1979. 22.95 (ISBN 0-89883-105-9). Soc Auto Engineers.

Measurement & Control of Respirable Dust in Mining. 1980. 11.00 (ISBN 0-309-03047-1). Natl Acad Pr.

Measurement & Evaluation. 2nd ed. John R. Hills. (Illus.). 480p. 1981. pap. text ed. 14.95 (ISBN 0-675-08044-4); instr's. manual 3.95 (ISBN 0-686-69495-3). Merrill.

Measurement & Evaluation in Schools. John R. Hills. (Illus.). 352p. 1976. pap. text ed. 13.95x (ISBN 0-675-08632-9); instructor's manual 3.95 (ISBN 0-686-67250-X). Merrill.

Measurement & Evaluation in the Schools. Donald L. Beggs & Ernest L. Lewis. 1975. 15.75 (ISBN 0-395-18609-9); insturctor's manual 1.50 (ISBN 0-395-18795-8). HM.

Measurement & Evaluation of Learning. 4th ed. Arnold J. Lien & Harriet S. Lien. 1980. text ed. 13.95x (ISBN 0-697-06128-0) (ISBN 0-697-06124-8). instructor's manual available. Wm C Brown.

Measurement & Interpretation of Productivity. 1980. 18.00 (ISBN 0-309-02898-1). Natl Acad Pr.

Measurement Book. Marvin L. Sohns & Audrey V. Buffington. (Illus.). 1977. pap. 9.95 (ISBN 0-933358-00-8). Enrich.

Measurement Comparisons. Judith A. Magarian. (Illus.). 24p. (gr. k-3). 1980. pap. 3.95 (ISBN 0-933358-64-4). Enrich.

Measurement Concepts in Physical Education: An Introduction. Frank M. Verducci. LC 79-27528. (Illus.). 374p. 1980. pap. 15.95 (ISBN 0-8016-5225-1). Mosby.

Measurement, Detection & Control of Environmental Pollutants. (Proceedings Ser). (Illus.). 1976. pap. 62.25 (ISBN 0-685-77310-8, ISP 432, IAEA). Unipub.

Measurement for Evaluation in Physical Education. 2nd ed. Ted A. Baumgartner & Andrew S. Jackson. (Illus.). 576p. 1981. text ed. write for info. (ISBN 0-395-29623-4); write for info. instr's manual (ISBN 0-395-29637-4). HM.

Measurement for Management Decision. Richard H. Mason & E. Burton Swanson. (Computer Science: Decision Support). (Illus.). 448p. 1981. text ed. 15.95 (ISBN 0-201-04646-6). A-W.

Measurement in Physical Education. 2nd ed. Carlton R. Meyers. (Illus.). 642p. 1974. 21.50 (ISBN 0-8260-6051-X). Wiley.

Measurement in the Social Sciences: Theories & Strategies. Ed. by H. M. Blalock, Jr. LC 73-89514. 512p. 1974. pap. text ed. 13.95x (ISBN 0-202-30272-5). Aldine Pub.

Measurement of Airborne Particles. Richard D. Cadle. LC 75-22121. (Environmental Science & Technology Ser.). 352p. 1975. 37.50 (ISBN 0-471-12910-0, Pub. by Wiley-Interscience). Wiley.

Measurement of Aircraft Speed & Altitude. William Gracey. 300p. 1980. 30.00 (ISBN 0-471-08511-1, Pub. by Wiley-Interscience). Wiley.

Measurement of Airway Resistance with the Body Plethysmograph. Allan Hemingway. (Illus.). 116p. 1973. 13.50 (ISBN 0-398-02633-5). C C Thomas.

Measurement of Appearance. Richard S. Hunter. LC 75-20429. 348p. 1975. 31.50 (ISBN 0-471-42141-3, Pub. by Wiley-Interscience). Wiley.

Measurement of Behavior. R. Vance Hall. (Managing Behavior Ser.: Part 1). 1974. 3.25 (ISBN 0-89079-001-9). H & H Ent.

Measurement of Blood Flow: Applications to the Splanchnic Circulation. Neil Granger & Gregory B. Bulkley. (Illus.). 496p. 1981. write for info. (3730-7). Williams & Wilkins.

Measurement of Children's Civic Attitudes in Different Nations. A. N. Oppenheim & J. Torney. LC 74-10468. (I E A Studies in Evaluation: No. 2). 84p. (Orig.). 1974. pap. 10.95 (ISBN 0-470-65480-5). Halsted Pr.

Measurement of Dissolved Oxygen. Michael L. Hitchman. LC 77-26710. (Monographs on Analytical Chemistry & Its Applications: Vol. 49). 1978. 28.00 (ISBN 0-471-03885-7, Pub. by Wiley-Interscience). Wiley.

Measurement of Facies. (Clinics in Developmental Medicine Ser., Research Monographs: Vol. 3A). 115p. 1970. 12.50 o.p. (ISBN 0-685-59046-1). Lippincott.

Measurement of Human Aggressiveness. G. Edmunds & D. G. Kendrick. LC 79-40970. 223p. 1980. 29.95x (ISBN 0-470-26871-9). Halsted Pr.

Measurement of Interpersonal Values. Leonard V. Gordon. LC 74-22623. 122p. (Orig.). 1975. text ed. 12.00 (ISBN 0-574-72770-1); pap. text ed. 8.20 (ISBN 0-574-72764-7). SRA.

Measurement of Man at Work. Ed. by W. T. Singleton et al. 1971. 24.00x (ISBN 0-85066-041-6); pap. 16.95x (ISBN 0-85066-071-8). Intl Ideas.

Measurement of Mechanical Properties. Ed. by R. F. Bunshah. LC 67-20260. 1971. 45.00 (ISBN 0-685-55315-9). Krieger.

Measurement of Output of Research & Experimental Development. Christopher Freeman. 1970. pap. 2.50 (ISBN 92-3-100760-2, U376, UNESCO). Unipub.

Measurement of Readability. facsimile ed. George R. Klare. 1963. pap. 6.90x o.p. (ISBN 0-8138-2385-4). Iowa St U Pr.

Measurement of Responsibility: A Study of Work, Payment & Individual Capacity. E. Jaques. LC 72-5856. 144p. 1972. 12.95 (ISBN 0-470-44020-1). Halsted Pr.

Measurement of Sensation: A Critique of Perceptual Psychophysics. C. Wade Savage. LC 69-15941. 1970. 29.50x (ISBN 0-520-01527-4). U of Cal Pr.

Measurement of Short-Range Radiations. (Technical Reports Ser.: No. 150). (Illus.). 114p. (Orig.). 1974. pap. 11.25 (ISBN 92-0-125173-4, IAEA). Unipub.

Measurement of Social Competence. Edgar A. Doll. (Illus.). 1953. 15.00 (ISBN 0-913476-09-9). Am Guidance.

Measurement of Unemployment: Methods & Sources in Great Britain. W. R. Garside. 300p. 1981. 37.50x (ISBN 0-631-12643-0). Biblio Dist.

Measurement of Unsteady Fluid Dynamic Phenomena. Ed. by B. Richards. LC 76-11843. (Thermal & Fluids Engineering Series). (Illus.). 450p. 1977. text ed. 44.50 (ISBN 0-89116-012-4, Co-Pub. by McGraw Intl). Hemisphere Pub.

Measurement Theory for the Behavioral Sciences. Edwin E. Ghiselli et al. LC 80-27069. (Psychology Ser.). (Illus.). 1981. text ed. 21.95x (ISBN 0-7167-1048-X); pap. text ed. 13.95 (ISBN 0-7167-1252-0). W H Freeman.

Measurements in High-Voltage Test Circuits. G. W. Bowdler. LC 72-86488. 192p. 1973. text ed. 30.00 (ISBN 0-08-016838-8). Pergamon.

Measurements, Instrumentation & Data Transmission. B. F. Gray. LC 76-49922. (Illus.). 1977. text ed. 13.50x (ISBN 0-582-41065-7); pap. text ed. 9.50x (ISBN 0-582-41066-5). Longman.

Measurements of Production & Productivity in Indian Industry. G. C. Beri. 5.25x o.p. (ISBN 0-210-33666-8). Asia.

Measurements of Time Reversal in Objective Quantum Theory. F. J. Belinfante. 1975. text ed. 18.75 (ISBN 0-08-018152-X). Pergamon.

Measures of Man: Methodologies in Biological Anthropology. Ed. by Eugene Giles & Jonathan S. Friedlaender. LC 76-28638. (Peabody Museum Press Ser.). (Illus.). 1976. 32.00 (ISBN 0-87365-782-9); pap. 25.00 (ISBN 0-685-84631-8). Peabody Harvard.

Measures of Noncompactness in Banach Spaces. Banas & Goebel. 112p. 1980. 59.75 (ISBN 0-8247-6981-3). Dekker.

Measuring. Jeanne Bendick. LC 76-150734. (Science Experiences Ser). (Illus.). (gr. 3-5). 1971. PLB 4.90 o.p. (ISBN 0-531-01435-5). Watts.

Measuring. Roy S. Hinrichs. LC 80-67036. (Industrial Arts Ser.). 96p. 1981. pap. 4.60 (ISBN 0-8273-1916-9). Delmar.

Measuring Accuracy of Parameters Used in Formation Evaluation in the North Sea. Norwegian Petroleum Society. 193p. 1980. 75.00x (ISBN 82-7270-002-6, Pub. by Norwegian Info Norway). State Mutual Bk.

Measuring & Assessing Organizations. Andrew H. Van de Ven & Diane L. Ferry. LC 79-20003. (Organizational Assessment & Change Ser.). 1980. 34.95 (ISBN 0-471-04832-1, Pub. by Wiley-Interscience). Wiley.

Measuring & Enhancing the Productivity of Service & Government Organizations. (Illus.). 296p. 1975. 21.75 (ISBN 92-833-1029-2, APO49, APO). Unipub.

Measuring & Evaluating Educational Achievement. 2nd ed. J. Stanley Ahmann & Marvin D. Glock. 324p. 1975. pap. text ed. 12.95 o.p. (ISBN 0-205-04776-9, 2247763). Allyn.

Measuring & Forecasting Engineering Personnel Requirements. Date not set. 50.00 (126-79). AAES.

Measuring Behavior. 2nd ed. John O. Cooper. (Special Education Ser.). (Illus.). 224p. 1981. pap. text ed. 7.95 (ISBN 0-675-08078-9). Merrill.

Measuring Benefits of Government Investments. Ed. by Robert Dorfman et al. (Studies of Government Finance). 429p. 1965. pap. 6.95 (ISBN 0-8157-1901-9). Brookings.

Measuring COM Recording Speeds: MS21-1979. National Micrographics Assn. 1979. 3.50 (ISBN 0-89258-058-5). Natl Micrograph.

Measuring Disability. Sally Sainsbury. 125p. 1973. pap. text ed. 6.25x (ISBN 0-7135-1899-5, Pub. by Bedford England). Renouf.

Measuring Executive Effectiveness. Ed. by Frederic R. Wickert & Dalton E. McFarland. LC 67-18987. (Illus.). 1967. 24.50x (ISBN 0-89197-298-6). Irvington.

Measuring Human Behavior: Tools for the Assessment of Social Functioning. Ed. by Dale G. Lake et al. LC 72-82083. 1973. pap. text ed. 11.75x (ISBN 0-8077-1648-0). Tchrs Coll.

Measuring Inequality: Techniques for the Social Sciences. F. A. Cowell. LC 77-20851. 1978. 11.95 (ISBN 0-470-99349-9). Halsted Pr.

Measuring Instructional Intent, or Got a Match? Robert F. Mager. LC 73-80970. 1973. pap. 4.95 (ISBN 0-8224-4462-3). Pitman Learning.

Measuring Morale: Key to Increased Productivity. Alexander Hamilton Unstitute, Inc. (Illus.). 53p. (Orig.). 1976. pap. 53.25x (ISBN 0-86604-010-2, A806007). Hamilton Inst.

Measuring Purchasing Performance. John Stevens. 254p. 1978. text ed. 23.50x (ISBN 0-220-66331-9, Pub. by Busn Bks England). Renouf.

Measuring Spoken Language Proficiency. Ed. by James R. Frith. 69p. (Orig.). 1980. pap. text ed. 3.95 (ISBN 0-87840-188-1). Georgetown U Pr.

Measuring the Condition of the World's Poor: The Physical Quality of Life Index. Morris D. Morris. LC 79-16613. 190p. 1979. pap. 5.95 (ISBN 0-08-023889-0). Overseas Dev Council.

Measuring the Economic Benefits of New Technologies to Small Rice Farmers. (IRRI Research Paper Ser.: No. 28). 21p. 1979. pap. 5.00 (R068, IRRI). Unipub.

Measuring the Effect of Advertising. David R. Corkindale & Sherrel H. Kennedy. LC 75-35021. (Illus.). 1976. 26.95 (ISBN 0-347-01110-1, 00207-0). Lexington Bks.

Measuring the Effectiveness of Local Government Services: Recreation. Harry P. Hatry & Diana R. Dunn. 47p. 1971. pap. 1.75 o.p. (ISBN 0-87766-012-3, 70002). Urban Inst.

Measuring the Quality of Library Service: A Handbook. M. Fancher Beeler et al. LC 74-12107. (Illus.). 1974. 10.00 (ISBN 0-8108-0732-7). Scarecrow.

Measuring the Skills of Composition. 1981. pap. 11.95 (ISBN 0-932166-04-0). Instruct Object.

Measuring Work Quality for Social Reporting. Ed. by A. D. Biderman & T. F. Drury. 1976. 22.95 (ISBN 0-470-15218-4). Halsted Pr.

Meat & Fish Management for Food Service. Stephen A. Mutkoski & Marcia L. Schurer. 1981. text ed. 17.95 (ISBN 0-534-00907-7, Breton Pubs). Wadsworth Pub.

Meat & Poultry Entrees for Foodservice Menu Planning. Eulalia C. Blair. LC 78-9126. (Foodservice Menu Planning Ser.). (Illus.). 1978. 16.50 (ISBN 0-8436-2152-4). CBI Pub.

Meat Animals: Growth & Productivity. Ed. by D. Lister et al. LC 76-985. (NATO Advanced Study Institutes Ser., Series A: Life Sciences: Vol. 8). 541p. 1976. 42.50 (ISBN 0-306-35608-2, Plenum Pr). Plenum Pub.

Meat at Any Price. Ninette Lyon. (Illus., Orig.). 1969. pap. 4.95 (ISBN 0-571-09078-8, Pub. by Faber & Faber). Merrimack Bk Serv.

Meat Balances in OECD Member Countries: 1973 to 1978. Organization for Economic Cooperation & Development. (Illus.). 85p. (Orig.). 1980. pap. text ed. 7.50x (ISBN 92-64-02090-X, 5180053). OECD.

Meat: Cherry's Market Diary. limited ed. 1980. 2.00 o.p. (ISBN 0-686-64497-2). Maelstrom.

Meat Eaters Are Threatened. Jon McClure. (Health Ser.). (Orig.). 1973. pap. 1.25 o.s.i. (ISBN 0-515-02984-X, V2984). Jove Pubns.

Meat for Men. Leonard Ravenhill. LC 51-418. 1979. pap. 3.50 (ISBN 0-87123-362-2, 210362). Bethany Fell.

Meat for Your Freezer. Michael E. Richards. 1974. 6.95 (ISBN 0-571-10223-9, Pub. by Faber & Faber). Merrimack Bk Serv.

Meat, from Ranch to Table. Walter Buehr. (Illus.). (gr. 5-9). 1956. PLB 6.96 (ISBN 0-688-31557-7). Morrow.

Meat Handbook. 4th ed. Albert Levie. (Illus.). 1979. text ed. 21.00 (ISBN 0-87055-315-1). AVI.

Meat: How Men Look, Act, Talk, Walk, Dress, Undress, Taste & Smell: True Homosexual Experiences from S.T.H. Compiled by Gay Sunshine Press. (Illus.). 192p. (Orig.). 1981. pap. 10.00 (ISBN 0-917342-78-X, Pub by Gay Sunshine). Bookpeople.

Meat Makes the Meal. Margaret Murphy. (Berkley-Dorison House Bks). (Illus.). (YA) 1978. 7.95 o.p. (ISBN 0-916752-11-9, Dist. by Putnam). Berkley Pub.

Meat Makes the Meal. Margaret D. Murphy. 7.95 (ISBN 0-916752-11-9). Green Hill.

Meat Meals in Minutes. write for info. (ISBN 0-87502-085-2). Benjamin Co.

Meat, Poultry & Seafood Technology. Robert L. Henrickson. LC 77-25350. (Illus.). 1978. ref. ed. 17.95 (ISBN 0-13-568600-8). P-H.

Meat Science. 2nd ed. R. A. Lawrie. 1974. text ed. 38.00 o.p. (ISBN 0-08-017133-8); pap. text ed. 17.05 o.p. (ISBN 0-08-017811-1). Pergamon.

Meat Technology: Practical Textbook for Student & Butcher. 5th ed. Frank Gerrard. (Illus.). 1977. 27.50x (ISBN 0-7198-2607-1). Intl Ideas.

Meat We Eat. 11th ed. John R. Romans & P. Thomas Ziegler. LC 77-70869. 1977. 23.35 (ISBN 0-8134-1945-X); pap. text ed. 17.50x (ISBN 0-685-86006-X). Interstate.

Meatballs. Claro. (gr. 7-12). 1980. pap. 1.50 (ISBN 0-590-30920-X, Schol Pap). Schol Bk Serv.

Meatless Main Dishes. Ed. by Better Homes & Gardens Books Editors. (Illus.). 96p. 1981. 4.95 (ISBN 0-696-00645-6). Meredith Corp.

Mecanica Para Ingenieros, Tomo Primero: Estatica. Ferdinand L. Singer. 1976. text ed. 10.00x (ISBN 0-06-316997-5, IntlDept). Har-Row.

Mecanografia Al Dia. rev. ed. Maria D. Andujar & Jose L. Iglesias. (gr. 10 up). 1977. pap. text ed. 2.45 (ISBN 0-88345-306-1). Regents Pub.

Mecanografia Cien, Libro 1. Wenceslao Ortega & Alberto Sampere. (Span.). 1971. pap. text ed. 6.80 (ISBN 0-06-316640-2, IntlDept). Har-Row.

Mecanografia Cien: Practicas Secretariales. Wenceslao Ortega & Alberto Sampere. 180p. (Span.). 1972. pap. text ed. 4.00 (ISBN 0-06-316641-0, IntlDept). Har-Row.

Mecca the Blessed, Madinah the Radiant. Emel Esin. 1963. 21.95 (ISBN 0-236-31090-9, Pub. by Paul Elek). Merrimack Bk Serv.

Mecca Today. Jean Hureau. (J. A. Editions: Today Ser.). (Illus.). 240p. 1980. cancelled (ISBN 0-88254-538-8, Pub. by J. A. Editions France). Hippocrene Bks.

Mechanical & Electrical Cost Data, 1980. 3rd ed. Robert S. Godfrey. 360p. 1980. pap. 27.50 (ISBN 0-911950-23-0). Means.

Mechanical & Electrical Cost Data, 1981. 4th ed. Robert S. Godfrey. LC 79-643328. 400p. 1981. pap. 29.50 (ISBN 0-911950-31-1). Means.

Mechanical & Thermal Properties of Materials. A. Collieu & Derek J. Powney. LC 72-85498. 240p. 1973. 19.50x (ISBN 0-8448-0074-0). Crane-Russak Co.

Mechanical Artificial Ventilation: A Manual for Students & Practitioners. 3rd ed. Terring W. Heironimus, 3rd & Robert A. Bageant (Amer. Lec. in Anesthesiology Ser.). (Illus.). 560p. 1977. 33.50 (ISBN 0-398-03541-5). C C Thomas.

Mechanical Behavior of Materials. F. A. McClintock & A. S. Argon. 1966. 27.95 (ISBN 0-201-04545-1). A-W.

Mechanical Behaviour of Ceramics. R. W. Davidge. LC 77-90206. (Solid State Science Ser.). (Illus.). 1979. 47.50 (ISBN 0-521-21915-9). Cambridge U Pr.

Mechanical Behaviour of Materials Under Pressure. Ed. by H. L. Pugh. (Illus.). 1970. 104.40x (ISBN 0-444-20043-6). Intl Ideas.

Mechanical Design in Organisms. S. A. Wainwright et al. LC 75-11890. 433p. 1976. 24.95 (ISBN 0-470-91660-5). Halsted Pr.

Mechanical Engineering. A. E. Peatfield. Incl. Vol. 1. Hand Tools. 1973; Vol. 2. Engineering Components. 1974 (ISBN 0-679-10480-1); Vol. 3. Workshop Practice. 1973. o.p. (ISBN 0-679-10481-X). (Teach Yourself Ser.). pap. 2.95 ea. o.p. McKay.

Mechanical Engineering Craft Studies, Vol. I. Bourbousson & Ashworth. 1974. 5.95 (ISBN 0-408-00120-8). Butterworths.

Mechanical Engineering Craft Studies, Vol. 2. Bourbousson & Ashworth. 1974. text ed. 9.95 (ISBN 0-408-00112-7). Butterworths.

Mechanical Engineering for Public Cleansing. Douglas M. Hamilton & William Robb. (Illus.). 1969. 18.60x (ISBN 0-85334-121-4). Intl Ideas.

Mechanical Engineering Review Manual. 5th ed. Michael R. Lindeburg. LC 80-83176. (Engineering Review Manual Ser.). (Illus.). 704p. 1980. pap. 26.50 (ISBN 0-932276-21-0); wkbk. 7.00 (ISBN 0-932276-23-7). Prof Engine.

Mechanical Engineers' Handbook, 2 pts. 12th ed. R. T. Kent. Incl. Pt. 1. Design & Production. Ed. by C. Carmichael. 1611p (ISBN 0-471-46959-9); Pt. 2. Power. Ed. by J. K. Salisbury. 1409p (ISBN 0-471-46992-0). 1950. 39.95 ea. (Pub. by Wiley-Interscience). Wiley.

Mechanical Engineers in America Born Prior to 1861: A Biographical Dictionary. 350p. 1980. 20.00 (H00176). ASME.

Mechanical Estimating of Water & Waste Treatment Plants. Frederick J. Zikorus. LC 80-65512. (Illus.). 300p. Date not set. 75.00 (ISBN 0-250-40370-6). Ann Arbor Science. Postponed.

Mechanical Fasteners for Industrial Curtain Walls. National Academy Of Sciences. 1961. 3.00 o.p. (ISBN 0-309-00916-2). Natl Acad Pr.

Mechanical Fitting, Vol. 1. Ed. by T. Briggs et al. (Engineering Craftsmen: No. H3). 1968. spiral bdg. 13.50x (ISBN 0-85083-012-5). Intl Ideas.

Mechanical Fitting, Vol. 2. 2nd ed. Ed. by G. Barnet et al. (Engineering Craftsmen: No. H25). (Illus.). 1973. spiral bdg. 17.95x (ISBN 0-85083-186-5). Intl Ideas.

Mechanical Fixing Devices in the Building Industry. Paul Marsh & Derrick Beckett. 1978. text ed. 30.00x (ISBN 0-904406-12-1). Longman.

Mechanical Foundations of Human Motion: A Programmed Text. J. V. Krause & Jerry N. Barham. (Illus.). 1975. pap. text ed. 13.95 (ISBN 0-8016-0474-5). Mosby.

Mechanical Kinesiology. Jerry N. Barham. LC 77-23969. (Illus.). 1978. 18.95 (ISBN 0-8016-0476-1). Mosby.

Mechanical Maintenance (and Installation) II, 2 vols. Ed. by J. Vaughan et al. (Engineering Craftsmen Ser.: No. J21). (Illus.). 342p. 1970. Set. 28.95x (ISBN 0-85083-080-X). Intl Ideas.

Mechanical Maintenance & Installation: Supplementary Training Manual. Ed. by A. T. Gamlin et al. (Engineering Craftsmen: No. J21S). (Illus.). 1976. pap. 21.50x (ISBN 0-85083-332-9). Intl Ideas.

Mechanical Maintenance: Part One. Ed. by A. Baugh et al. (Engineering Craftsmen: No. J1). (Illus.). 1978. spiral bdg. 21.00x (ISBN 0-85083-016-8). Intl Ideas.

Mechanical Measurement & Instrumentation. Edgar E. Ambrosius et al. (Illus.). 1966. 16.95 o.p. (ISBN 0-8260-0380-X). Wiley.

Mechanical Measurements. 2nd ed. Thomas G. Beckwith & N. Lewis Buck. (Mechanical Engineering Ser). 1969. text ed. 24.95 (ISBN 0-201-00454-2). A-W.

Mechanical Measurements. R. S. Sirohi. LC 80-27233. 210p. 1981. 13.95 (ISBN 0-470-27107-8). Halsted Pr.

Mechanical People: Perceptions of the Industrial Order in Massachusetts, 1815-1880. Carl Siracusa. LC 78-26715. 1979. 22.50x (ISBN 0-8195-5029-9, Pub. by Wesleyan U Pr). Columbia U Pr.

Mechanical Plant in Construction. Ed. by Leslie Gardener. (Illus.). 138p. 1979. 55.00 (ISBN 0-7114-4306-8). Transatlantic.

Mechanical Press Handbook. 3rd ed. Ed. by Harold R. Daniels. LC 71-79187. (Illus.). 1969. 27.50 (ISBN 0-89047-036-7). Herman Pub.

Mechanical Properties of Biological Materials. Ed. by J. F. Vincent & J. D. Currey. LC 80-40111. (Society of Experimental Biology Symposia Ser.: No. 34). (Illus.). 400p. 1981. 69.50 (ISBN 0-521-23478-6). Cambridge U Pr.

Mechanical Properties of Biomaterials. G. W. Hastings & D. F. Williams. LC 79-41776. (Advances in Biomaterials Ser.). 536p. 1980. 105.95 (ISBN 0-471-27761-4, Pub. by Wiley-Interscience). Wiley.

Mechanical Properties of Matter. A. H. Cottrell. LC 80-12439. 340p. 1981. Repr. of 1964 ed. lib. bdg. write for info. (ISBN 0-89874-168-8). Krieger.

Mechanical Science for Higher Technicians, Nos. 4-5. Bacon & Stephens. 1981. text ed. price not set (ISBN 0-408-00570-X). Butterworth.

Mechanical Science for Technicians. Ian McDonagh. (Illus.). 121p. 1979. pap. 11.95x (ISBN 0-7131-3411-9). Intl Ideas.

Mechanical Science for Technicians, No. 3. W. Bolton. (Technician Ser.). (Illus.). 128p. 1980. pap. text ed. 12.50. Butterworths.

Mechanical Support of the Failing Heart & Lungs. Bregman. (Illus.). 1977. 19.50 (ISBN 0-8385-6196-9). ACC.

Mechanical Systems for the Recovery of Oil Spilled on Water. Institute of Petroleum. (Illus.). 1975. 29.90x (ISBN 0-85334-451-5). Intl Ideas.

Mechanical Trades Pocket Manual. Carl A. Nelson. LC 73-91639. 208p. (Orig.). 1974. pap. 8.95 (ISBN 0-672-23215-4). Audel.

Mechanical Ventilation of the Lungs. Kirby & Smith. 1981. text ed. write for info. (ISBN 0-443-08063-1). Churchill.

Mechanical Vibrations. 2nd ed. Austin H. Church. LC 63-14755. 1963. text ed. 34.95 (ISBN 0-471-15678-7). Wiley.

Mechanical Vibrations: Theory & Applications. 2nd ed. Francis S. Tse et al. 1978. text ed. 27.95 (ISBN 0-205-05940-6, 3259404); sol. man. avail. (ISBN 0-205-05941-4, 3259412). Allyn.

Mechanics. P. Abbott. (Teach Yourself Ser.). 1974. pap. 3.95 o.p. (ISBN 0-679-10403-8). McKay.

Mechanics. D. S. Mathur. 1978. 20.00 (ISBN 0-7069-0623-3, Pub. by Vikas India). Advent Bk.

Mechanics. 3rd ed. Keith R. Symon. LC 75-128910. (Physics & Physical Science Ser). 1971. text ed. 24.95 (ISBN 0-201-07392-7). A-W.

Mechanics & Motion. L. MacKinnon. (Oxford Physics Ser.). (Illus.). 1978. 23.50x (ISBN 0-19-851825-0); pap. 9.95x (ISBN 0-19-851843-9). Oxford U Pr.

Mechanics & Properties of Matter. M. Nelkon. 1969. text ed. 7.95 o.p. (ISBN 0-435-68633-X). Heinemann Ed.

Mechanics & Thermodynamics of Propulsion. Philip G. Hill & C. R. Peterson. 1965. 28.95 (ISBN 0-201-02838-7). A-W.

Mechanics Applied to the Transport of Bulk Materials, Bk. No. G00146. Ed. by S. C. Cowin. LC 87-3754. (Applied Mechanics Division Ser.: Vol. 31). 140p. 1979. 20.00 o.p. (ISBN 0-686-62960-4). ASME.

Mechanics: Classical & Quantum. Thomas T. Taylor. 1976. text ed. 42.00 (ISBN 0-08-018063-9); pap. text ed. 24.00 (ISBN 0-08-020522-4). Pergamon.

Mechanics for Technology. Charles D. Bruch. LC 75-31719. 400p. 1976. text ed. 20.95 (ISBN 0-471-11369-7); instructor's manual avail. (ISBN 0-471-11373-5). Wiley.

Mechanics, Heat, & Sound. Issac Maleh. (Merrill Physical Science Library). pap. text ed. 3.75x (ISBN 0-675-09638-3). Merrill.

Mechanics, Heat, & Sound. 2nd ed. Francis W. Sears. (Illus.). 1950. 17.95 (ISBN 0-201-06905-9). A-W.

Mechanics in Agriculture. 2nd ed. Lloyd J. Phipps. LC 76-24049. 1977. 19.65 (ISBN 0-685-80737-1); text ed. 14.75x (ISBN 0-8134-1841-0). Interstate.

Mechanics Lien Laws & Federal Tax Lien Law. Ed. by NACM. 1981. pap. 4.50 (ISBN 0-686-69391-4). NACM.

Mechanic's Lien Laws & Federal Tax Lien Law. NACM Publications Editors. 1980. pap. 4.25 o.p. (ISBN 0-934914-35-4). NACM.

Mechanics of Bimodulus Materials, Bk. No. G00150. Ed. by C. W. Bert. LC 90-75422. (Applied Mechanics Division Ser.: Vol. 33). 96p. 1979. 18.00 (ISBN 0-686-62957-4). ASME.

Mechanics of Composite Materials. R. M. Christensen. LC 79-14093. 1979. 33.50 (ISBN 0-471-05167-5, Pub. by Wiley-Interscience). Wiley.

Mechanics of Composite Materials: International Conference on the Mechanics & Chemistry & Solid Propellants. Ed. by F. W. Wendt et al. 1970. 105.00 (ISBN 0-08-006421-3). Pergamon.

Mechanics of Continua. 2nd ed. A. Cemal Eringen. LC 78-2334. 520p. 1981. Repr. of 1967 ed. lib. bdg. 39.50 (ISBN 0-88275-663-X). Krieger.

Mechanics of Continuous Media. S. C. Hunter. LC 76-7923. (Mathematics & Its Applications Ser.). 567p. 1977. text ed. 66.95 (ISBN 0-470-15092-0). Halsted Pr.

Mechanics of Continuous Media Paper. S. C. Hunter. 567p. 1980. pap. 34.00 (ISBN 0-470-27015-2, Pub. by Halsted Pr). Wiley.

Mechanics of Fibre Composites. V. K. Tewary. LC 77-29117. 1978. 14.95x (ISBN 0-470-99240-9). Halsted Pr.

Mechanics of Flexible Fiber Assemblies. Ed. by J. W. Hearle. (NATO-Advanced Study Institute Ser.). 700p. 1980. 72.50x (ISBN 9-0286-0720-X). Sijthoff & Noordhoff.

Mechanics of Fluids. 3rd. ed. Walshaw & Jobson. 1979. pap. 22.00 (ISBN 0-582-44495-0). Longman.

Mechanics of Inheritance. 2nd ed. Franklin W. Stahl. Ed. by Sigmund Suskind & Philip Hartman. LC 69-19870. (Foundations of Modern Genetics Ser). 1969. pap. 10.95 ref. ed. (ISBN 0-13-571042-1). P-H.

Mechanics of Machines: Advanced Theory & Examples. 2nd ed. John Hannah & R. C. Stephens. (Illus.). 456p. 1972. pap. 18.95x (ISBN 0-7131-3254-X). Intl Ideas.

Mechanics of Machines: Elementary Theory & Examples. 3rd ed. John Hannah & R. C. Stephens. (Illus.). 1970. 18.95x (ISBN 0-7131-3231-0); pap. text ed. 11.95x (ISBN 0-7131-3232-9). Intl Ideas.

Mechanics of Materials. Ferdinand P. Beer & E. Russell Johnston, Jr. (Illus.). 672p. 1981. text ed. 26.95x (ISBN 0-07-004284-5, C); write for info solutions manual (ISBN 0-07-004291-8). McGraw.

Mechanics of Materials. 3rd ed. Archie Higdon et al. LC 75-28453. 1976. text ed. 24.95x (ISBN 0-471-38812-2); instr's manual avail. (ISBN 0-471-01679-9). Wiley.

Mechanics of Materials. 2nd ed. Irving J. Levinson. 1970. text ed. 19.95 (ISBN 0-13-571380-3). P-H.

Mechanics of Materials. 2nd ed. Howard P. Popov. 1976. 24.95 (ISBN 0-13-571356-0). P-H.

Mechanics of Materials: An Individualized Approach. Hornsey et al. LC 76-18470. (Illus.). 1977. pap. 18.95 incl. ref. manual & study guide (ISBN 0-395-24993-7); solutions manual 2.15 (ISBN 0-395-24994-5). HM.

Mechanics of Materials: SI Version. 3rd ed. Archie Higdon et al. LC 77-7069. 1978. text ed. 26.95 (ISBN 0-471-02379-5); solutions manual 10.00 (ISBN 0-471-03683-8). Wiley.

Mechanics of Materials: SI Version. 2nd ed. Egor O. Popov. (Illus.). 1978. 24.95 (ISBN 0-13-571299-8). P-H.

Mechanics of Non-Newtonian Fluids. William R. Schowalter. LC 76-51440. 1977. text ed. 52.00 (ISBN 0-08-021778-8). Pergamon.

Mechanics of Nondestructive Testing. Ed. by W. W. Stinchcomb et al. 415p. 1980. 47.50 (ISBN 0-306-40567-9). Plenum Pub.

Mechanics of Polymers. R. G. Arridge. (Illus.). 276p. 1975. 28.00x (ISBN 0-19-859136-5). Oxford U Pr.

Mechanics of Sediment Transportation & Alluvial Stream Problems. R. J. Garde & K. Ranga Raju. LC 77-13628. 1978. 22.95 (ISBN 0-470-99329-4). Halsted Pr.

Mechanics of Solids: The Rodney Hill 60th Anniversary Volume. Ed. by H. G. Hopkins & M. J. Sewell. (Illus.). 720p. Date not set. 101.00 (ISBN 0-08-025443-8). Pergamon.

Mechanics of Solids with Application to Thin Bodies. Gerald Wempner. (Mechanics of Elastics & Viscoelastic Solids). 620p. 1980. 35.00x (ISBN 90-286-0880-X). Sijthoff & Noordhoff.

Mechanics of Superconducting Structures. Ed. by F. C. Moon. (AMD: No. 41). 148p. 1980. 24.00 (G00174). ASME.

Mechanics of Swimming & Flying. Stephen Childress. LC 80-23364. (Cambridge Studies in Mathematical Biology: No. 2). (Illus.). 170p. Date not set. price not set (ISBN 0-521-23613-4); pap. price not set (ISBN 0-521-28071-0). Cambridge U Pr.

Mechanics of the Horse. James R. Rooney. 1980. lib. bdg. 12.50 (ISBN 0-88275-693-1). Krieger.

Mechanics of the Mind. Colin Blakemore. LC 76-53515. (BBC Reith Lectures: 1976). 1977. 34.95 (ISBN 0-521-21559-5); pap. 8.95x (ISBN 0-521-29185-2). Cambridge U Pr.

Mechanics of Vehicle Collisions. Haim Reizes. (Illus.). 152p. 1973. 16.75 (ISBN 0-398-02639-4). C C Thomas.

Mechanics of Vibration. R. E. Bishop & D. C. Johnson. (Illus.). 1979. 97.50 (ISBN 0-521-04258-5). Cambridge U Pr.

Mechanics of Vibrations. K. Marguerre. Ed. by H. Wolfel. (Mechanics of Structural Systems Ser.: No. 2). 282p. 1979. 30.00x (ISBN 90-286-0086-8). Sijthoff & Noordhoff.

Mechanics Problem Solver: A Supplement to Any Class Text. Research & Education Association Staff. LC 79-92403. (Illus.). 1088p. 1980. pap. text ed. 22.85x (ISBN 0-87891-519-2). Res & Educ.

Mechanics Today, Vol. 6. Ed. by S. Nemat-Nasser. LC 80-41699. (Illus.). 225p. 1981. 50.00 (ISBN 0-08-024749-0); pap. 40.00 (ISBN 0-08-027318-1). Pergamon.

Mechanics' Vest Pocket Reference Book. John H. Wolfe & E. R. Phelps. 1945. 6.95 (ISBN 0-13-572024-9). P-H.

Mechanisation in Building. 2nd ed. H. G. Vallings. (Illus.). 1976. text ed. 33.60x (ISBN 0-85334-651-8). Intl Ideas.

Mechanism & Control of Pain. Ed. by Louis I. Grossman. LC 79-84476. (Masson Monographs in Dentistry: Vol. 1). 256p. 1979. 26.00 (ISBN 0-89352-048-9). Masson Pub.

Mechanism Drafting & Design: A Workbook. John G. Nee. LC 80-80861. (Illus.). 1980. pap. text ed. 14.95x (ISBN 0-911168-45-1). Prakken.

Mechanism of Action of Benzodiazepines. Ed. by E. Costa & P. Greengard. LC 75-10978. (Advances in Biochemical Psychopharmacology Ser.: Vol. 14). 190p. 1975. 23.00 (ISBN 0-89004-039-7). Raven.

Mechanism of Action of Dehydrogenases: A Symposium in Honor of Hugo Theorell. Ed. by George W. Schwert & Alfred D. Winer. LC 73-80094. (Illus.). 272p. 1970. 11.00x (ISBN 0-8131-1188-9). U Pr of Ky.

Mechanism of Consolidated Accounts: Accounting for Holding Companies. R. E. Ellmer. 1974. 17.95x (ISBN 0-434-90530-5). Intl Ideas.

Mechanism of Nervous Action. rev ed. Edgar D. Adrian. LC 33-4029. 1959. 12.50x (ISBN 0-8122-7118-1). U of Pa Pr.

Mechanism of Neuronal & Extraneuronal Transport of Catecholamines. Ed. by David M. Paton. LC 74-14477. 405p. 1976. 37.50 (ISBN 0-89004-014-1). Raven.

Mechanism of the Linotype. John S. Thompson. Ed. by John Bidwell. Bd. with History of Composing Machines. LC 78-74413. (Nineteenth Century Book Arts & Printing History Ser.: Vol. 23). (Illus.). 1980. lib. bdg. 38.00 (ISBN 0-8240-3897-5). Garland Pub.

Mechanisms & Dynamics of Machinery, SI Version. 3rd ed. Hamilton H. Mabie & Fred W. Ocvirk. LC 78-1382. 1978. text ed. 28.95 (ISBN 0-471-02380-9); solutions manual avail. (ISBN 0-471-04134-3). Wiley.

Mechanisms in Bacterial Toxinology. Alan W. Bernheimer. LC 76-8274. (Developments in Medical Microbiology & Infectious Disease Ser). 288p. 1976. 40.50 o.p. (ISBN 0-471-07105-6, Pub by Wiley Medical). Wiley.

Mechanisms in Radiobiology, 2 vols. Ed. by Maurice Errera & Arne Forssberg. Incl. Vol. 1. General Principles. 1961. 48.50 (ISBN 0-12-241101-3); Vol. 2. Multicellular Organisms. 1960. 48.00 (ISBN 0-12-241102-1). Acad Pr.

Mechanisms of Cardiac Morphogenesis & Teratogenesis. Ed. by Tomas Pexieder. (Perspectives in Cardiovascular Research Ser.: Vol. 5). (Illus.). 525p. 1980. text ed. 48.00 (ISBN 0-89004-460-0). Raven.

Mechanisms of Cell Change. J. D. Ebert & T. S. Okada. LC 78-24040. 343p. 1979. 46.50 (ISBN 0-471-03097-X). Wiley.

Mechanisms of Conditioned Behavior: A Critical Look at the Phenomena of Conditioning. Wanda Wyrwicka. (Illus.). 192p. 1972. 15.50 (ISBN 0-398-02444-8). C C Thomas.

Mechanisms of Deformation & Fracture: Proceedings of the Interdisciplinary Conference, Held at the University of Lulea-Sweden, 20-22, September 1978. Ed. by K. Easterling. (Strength & Fracture of Materials & Structures). 1979. 89.00 (ISBN 0-08-024258-8). Pergamon.

Mechanisms of Development. Richard G. Ham & Marilyn J. Veomett. LC 79-9236. (Illus.). 1979. text ed. 25.95 (ISBN 0-8016-2022-8). Mosby.

Mechanisms of Drug Action on the Nervous System. R. W. Ryall. LC 78-5965. (Cambridge Texts in the Physiological Sciences Ser.: No. 1). (Illus.). 1979. 24.95 (ISBN 0-521-22125-0); pap. 7.95x (ISBN 0-521-29364-2). Cambridge U Pr.

Mechanisms of Evolution. W. H. Dowdeswell. (Scholarship Series in Biology). 1975. text ed. 11.95x o.p. (ISBN 0-435-61251-4). Heinemann Ed.

Mechanisms of Growth Control. Robert O. Becker. (Illus.). 377p. write for info. (ISBN 0-398-04469-4). C C Thomas.

Mechanisms of Immunity to Virus-Induced Tumors. Blasecki. 376p. 1981. 49.50. Dekker.

Mechanisms of Immunopathology. S. Cohen et al. LC 78-18290. (Basic & Clinical Immunologies Ser.). 1979. 32.95 (ISBN 0-471-16429-1, Pub. by Wiley Medical). Wiley.

Mechanisms of Localized Bone Loss. Ed. by John E. Horton et al. (Illus.). 1978. pap. 18.00 (ISBN 0-917000-03-X). Info Retrieval.

Mechanisms of Memory. E. Roy John. 1967. text ed. 21.95 (ISBN 0-12-385850-X). Acad Pr.

Mechanisms of Neurological Disease. Anthony J. Lewis. 1976. 27.95 (ISBN 0-316-52336-4). Little.

Mechanisms of Neurotoxic Substances. Ed. by Kedar N. Prasad & Antonia Vernadakis. 1981. text ed. price not set (ISBN 0-89004-638-7). Raven.

Mechanisms of Pain & Analgesic Compounds. Ed. by Roland F. Beers & Edward G. Bassett. LC 78-52524. (Miles Symposium Ser.: No. 11). 1979. text ed. 52.50 (ISBN 0-89004-304-3). Raven.

Mechanisms of Release of Biogenic Amines. Ed. by U. S. Von Euler et al. 1966. 60.00 (ISBN 0-08-011698-1). Pergamon.

Mechanisms of Saccharide Polymerization & Depolymerization. Ed. by J. John Marshall. LC 80-16155. 1980. 32.00 (ISBN 0-12-474150-9). Acad Pr.

Mechanisms of Speech Recognitions. W. A. Ainsworth. 1976. text ed. 30.00 (ISBN 0-08-020395-7); pap. text ed. 17.25 (ISBN 0-08-020394-9). Pergamon.

Mechanisms of Syntactic Change. Ed. by Charles N. Li. 1977. 20.00x (ISBN 0-292-75035-8). U of Tex Pr.

Mechanisms of Tumor Immunity. Ed. by Ira Green et al. LC 76-48047. (Basic & Clinical Immunology Ser.). 1977. 45.00 (ISBN 0-471-32481-7, Pub. by Wiley Medical). Wiley.

Mechanisms of Tumor Promotion & Cocarcinogenesis. Ed. by Thomas J. Slaga et al. LC 77-17752. (Carcinogenesis: a Comprehensive Survey: Vol. 2). 1978. 56.00 (ISBN 0-89004-208-X). Raven.

Mechanistic Studies of DNA Replication & Genetic Recombination. Ed. by Bruce Alberts & C. Fred Fox. (ICN-UCLA Symposia on Molecular & Cellular Biology Ser.: Vol. XIX). 1980. 48.00 (ISBN 0-12-048850-7). Acad Pr.

Mechanix Illustrated Fix-It Home Repairs Handbook. rev. ed. Mechanix Illustrated Editors. LC 72-95382. (Illus.). 112p. 1973. Repr. of 1970 ed. lib. bdg. 3.95 o.p. (ISBN 0-668-02937-4). Arco.

Mechanization for Road & Bridge Construction. Institute of Civil Engineers, UK. 54p. 1980. 55.00x (ISBN 0-901948-58-6, Pub. by Telford England). State Mutual Bk.

Mechanization in Agriculture. J. L. Meij. 1960. 47.50x (ISBN 0-686-50048-2). Elliots Bks.

Mechanized In-House Information Systems. Jennifer E. Rowley. 1979. 19.50 (ISBN 0-89664-404-9, Pub. by K G Saur). Shoe String.

Mechanized Infantry. Brigadier R. Simpkin. (Illus.). 144p. 1980. 26.00 (ISBN 0-08-027030-1). Pergamon.

Mechanizing Microbiology. Anthony N. Sharpe & David S. Clark. (Amer. Lec. in Clinical Microbiology Ser.). (Illus.). 352p. 1978. 33.75 (ISBN 0-398-03658-6). C C Thomas.

Mechta I Mysl I. S. Turgeneva. M. O. Gershenzon. LC 74-19760. (Slavic Reprint Ser.: No. 8). 169p. (Rus.). 1970. pap. 4.00 (ISBN 0-87057-124-9, Pub. by Brown U Pr). Univ Pr of New England.

Mecklenburg Collection: Part I. Ed. by Hugh Hencken. LC 68-22588. (ASPR Bulletin: No. 25). 1968. pap. text ed. 12.00 (ISBN 0-87365-526-5). Peabody Harvard.

Mecklenburg Collection, Pt. II: The Iron Age Cemetary of Magdalenska gora in Slovenia. Hugh Hencken. Ed. by Lorna Condon. LC 78-52401. (American School of Prehistoric Research Bulletin Ser.: No. 32). 1978. pap. text ed. 30.00 (ISBN 0-87365-539-7). Peabody Harvard.

Mecklenburg Declaration of Independence. William Henry Hoyt. LC 76-166330. (Era of the American Revolution Ser). 284p. 1972. Repr. of 1907 ed. lib. bdg. 32.50 (ISBN 0-306-70248-7). Da Capo.

Medal of Honor Heroes. Red Reeder. (gr. 4-8). 1965. 2.95 o.p. (ISBN 0-394-80411-2). Random.

Medallas De Proclamaciones y Juras De los Reyes De Espana En America. Jose T. Medina. LC 72-85123. (Illus.). 356p. (Span.). 1973. Repr. of 1917 ed. 35.00x (ISBN 0-88000-017-1). Quarterman.

Medea. Euripides. Tr. by Gilbert Murray. 1910. pap. text ed. 3.95x (ISBN 0-04-882038-5). Allen Unwin.

Medea. Euripides. Ed. by Denys Page. (Plays of Euripides Ser.). 1976. pap. text ed. 12.95 (ISBN 0-19-872092-0). Oxford U Pr.

Medea. Seneca. Tr. by Moses Hadas. LC 56-1501. 1956. pap. 1.45 o.p. (ISBN 0-672-60228-8, LLA55). Bobbs.

Medea. Seneca. Ed. by C. D. Costa. 179p. 1973. 17.95x (ISBN 0-19-814451-2). Oxford U Pr.

Medecin de campagne. new ed. Honore De Balzac. (Documentation thematique). (Illus.). 167p. (Orig., Fr.). 1975. pap. 2.95 (ISBN 0-685-54485-0, 116). Larousse.

Media About Media: An Annotated Listing of Media Software. James E. Duane. LC 80-21339. (Instructional Media Library: Vol. 6). 232p. 1981. 18.95 (ISBN 0-87778-166-4). Educ Tech Pubns.

Media: An Introductory Analysis of American Mass Communication. 2nd ed. Peter M. Sandman et al. 1976. 16.95x (ISBN 0-13-572586-0); pap. text ed. 12.95x (ISBN 0-13-572578-X). P-H.

Media & Catechetics Today: Towards the Year 2000. Pref. by Francis D. Kelley. 3.00. Natl Cath Educ.

Media & Kids: Real-World Learning in the Schools. James Morrow & Murray Suid. 1977. pap. text ed. 10.75x (ISBN 0-8104-5798-9). Hayden.

Media & the Law. Ed. by Howard Simons & Joseph A. Califano. LC 75-19822. (Special Studies). 1976. text ed. 26.95 (ISBN 0-275-55820-7); pap. 11.95 (ISBN 0-275-89530-0). Praeger.

Media & the Russian Public. Ellen Mickiewicz. 170p. 1981. 19.95 (ISBN 0-03-057681-4); pap. 8.95 (ISBN 0-03-057679-2). Praeger.

Media Are American. Jeremy Tunstall. 1979. pap. 8.00x (ISBN 0-231-04293-0). Columbia U Pr.

Media Are American. Jeremy Tunstall. LC 77-2581. 1977. 17.50x (ISBN 0-231-04292-2). Columbia U Pr.

Media Awards Handbook. Milton L. Levy. LC 68-24272. 190p. 1980. pap. 20.00 (ISBN 0-910744-03-3). Media Awards.

Media Canada: Guidelines for Educators. 2nd rev. ed. Ed. by James D. Miller. 1970. 4.50 (ISBN 0-08-016508-7). Pergamon.

Media Controversies. Ed. by Lester A. Sobel. 1980. 17.50 (ISBN 0-87196-242-X, Checkmark). Facts on File.

Media Equipment: A Guide & Dictionary. Kenyon C. Rosenberg & John S. Doskey. LC 76-25554. (Illus.). 150p. 1976. lib. bdg. 17.50x (ISBN 0-87287-155-X). Libs Unl.

Media Guide International. Set. 280.00 (ISBN 0-686-62227-8). Directories Intl.

Media Guide International: Airline Inflight-Travel Publications Edition. 1981. 25.00 (ISBN 0-685-76911-9). Directories Intl.

Media Guide International: Business Publications Edition, 4 vols. LC 71-31661. (Issued annnually 1 vol. ea. for Latin America, Mid East/Africa, Europe, Asia/Australia). Set. 220.00 (ISBN 0-685-41698-4). Directories Intl.

Media Guide International: Listing Advertising Rates & Data for Business Professional Publications Worldwide (Except in North America, 6 vols. Set. 252.00 o.p. (ISBN 0-686-62724-5). Directories Intl.

Media Guide International: Newspaper-News Magazine Edition. LC 72-90023. 1981. 65.00 (ISBN 0-685-77712-X). Directories Intl.

Media Handbook: A Guide to Selecting, Producing & Using Media for Patient Education Programs. American Hospital Association. LC 78-13341. (Illus.). 136p. (Orig.). 1978. pap. 17.50 (ISBN 0-87258-230-2, 1258). Am Hospital.

Media Imperialism Reconsidered: The Homogenizing of Television Culture. Chin-Chuan Lee. LC 80-16763. (People & Communication Ser.: Vol. 10). (Illus.). 276p. 1980. 20.00 (ISBN 0-8039-1495-4). Sage.

Media Imperialism Reconsidered: The Homogenizing of Television Culture. Chin-Chuan Lee. LC 80-16763. (People & Communication Ser.: Vol. 10). (Illus.). 276p. 1980. pap. 9.95 (ISBN 0-8039-1496-2). Sage.

Media in America: A Social & Political History. John Tebbel. LC 74-9891. 384p. 1975. 11.95 (ISBN 0-690-00500-8, TYC-T). T Y Crowell.

Media in Instruction: Sixty Years of Research. Gene L. Wilkinson. 52p. (Orig.). 1980. pap. 5.95 (ISBN 0-89240-041-2, 0-89240-041-2). Assn Ed Comm Tech.

Media Law Dictionary. John Murray. LC 78-63257. 1978. pap. text ed. 7.50 (ISBN 0-8191-0616-X). U Pr of Amer.

Media-Made Dixie: The South in the American Imagination. Jack T. Kirby. LC 77-14551. 1978. 11.95 (ISBN 0-8071-0375-6). La State U Pr.

Media Made in California: Hollywood, Politics, & the News. Jeremy Tunstall & David Walker. (Illus.). 224p. 1981. 15.95 (ISBN 0-19-502922-4). Oxford U Pr.

Media Manipulation: A Study of the Press & Bismarck in Imperial Germany. Robert H. Keyserlingk. 1977. pap. text ed. 8.00x o.p. (ISBN 0-685-87413-3). Renouf.

Media Men. John Morrison. 52p. (Today's World Ser.). 1978. 16.95 (ISBN 0-7134-0047-1, Pub. by Batsford England). David & Charles.

Media, Messages & Men. 2nd ed. John C. Merrill & Ralph L. Lowenstein. 1979. pap. text ed. 9.95 (ISBN 0-582-29008-2). Longman.

Media Personnel Directory. Ed. by Alan E. Abrams. LC 79-12885. 1979. 40.00 (ISBN 0-8103-0421-X). Gale.

Media Personnel in Education: A Competency Approach. M. Chisolm & D. P. Ely. (Illus.). 1976. 18.95x (ISBN 0-13-572461-9). P-H.

Media Planning. 2nd ed. James R. Adams. 232p. 1977. pap. 12.25x (ISBN 0-220-66337-8, Pub. by Busn Bks England). Renouf.

Media Planning: Quick & Easy Guide. Jim Surmanek. LC 80-67810. 1980. pap. text ed. 8.95 (ISBN 0-87251-046-8). Crain Bks.

Media, Politics, & Culture: A Socialist View. Ed. by Carl Gardner. (Communications & Culture). 1979. text ed. 23.00x (ISBN 0-333-23588-6); pap. text ed. 10.50x (ISBN 0-333-23589-4). Humanities.

Media Power Politics. David L. Paletz & Robert M. Entman. LC 80-1642. 1981. 15.95 (ISBN 0-02-923650-9). Free Pr.

Media Review Digest, Vol. 5. Ed. by C. Edward Wall et al. 1974-75. 120.00 set (ISBN 0-685-57150-5). Vol. 1 (ISBN 0-87650-065-3). Vol. 2 (ISBN 0-87650-066-1). Pierian.

Media Review Digest, Vol. 6. C. Edward Wall. 1975-76. 120.00 set (ISBN 0-685-70577-3). Vol. 1 (ISBN 0-87650-076-9). Vol. 2 (ISBN 0-87650-079-3). Pierian.

Media Review Digest, Vol. 9. 1979. Ed. by C. Edward Wall et al. 1980. 120.00 (ISBN 0-87650-101-3). Pierian.

Media Review Digest, Vol. 9. Ed. by Edward C. Wall et al. 1979. 120.00 (ISBN 0-87650-101-3). Pierian.

Media Review Digest, Vol. 10, 1980. Ed. by C. Edward Wall et al. 1980. 120.00 (ISBN 0-87650-129-3). Pierian.

Mediaeval Craftsmen. John Harvey. 1975. 33.00 (ISBN 0-7134-2934-8, Pub. by Batsford England). David & Charles.

Mediaeval Greece. Nicholas Cheetham. LC 80-13559. 352p. 1981. 27.50x (ISBN 0-300-02421-5). Yale U Pr.

Median Line. William Haggard. LC 80-54394. 1981. 9.95 (ISBN 0-8027-5433-3). Walker & Co.

Mediating Structures & Education. David Seeley. 300p. Date not set. 16.50 (ISBN 0-88410-825-2). Ballinger Pub. Postponed.

Mediating Structures & Welfare. Nathan Glazer. 250p. Date not set. price not set (ISBN 0-88410-823-6). Ballinger Pub. Postponed.

Mediator. Boyd K. Packer. 1978. 3.95 (ISBN 0-87747-738-8); pap. text ed. 1.95 (ISBN 0-87747-736-1). Deseret Bk.

Medicaid Decisions: Systematic Analysis of the Cost Problem. Stephen M. Davidson. LC 80-10998. 1980. 23.50 (ISBN 0-88410-142-8). Ballinger Pub.

Medicaid Eligibility: Problems & Solutions. Marilyn P. Rymer et al. (Westview Replica Edition: an Urban Systems Research Report). 1979. lib. bdg. 28.50x (ISBN 0-89158-478-1). Westview.

Medicaid Experience. Allen D. Spiegel. LC 78-27669. (Illus.). 1979. text ed. 35.75 (ISBN 0-89443-088-2). Aspen Systems.

Medical & Clinical Aspects of Aging, Proceedings, Vol. 4. International Association Of Gerontology - 5th Congress. Ed. by H. T. Blumenthal. (Aging Around the World Ser.). 1962. 30.00x (ISBN 0-231-08952-X). Columbia U Pr.

Medical & Dental Hypnosis & Its Clinical Application. 2nd ed. J. Hartland. 1971. 25.00 o.s.i. (ISBN 0-02-858000-1); pap. text ed. 26.95 (ISBN 0-02-858010-9). Macmillan.

Medical & Health Information Directory: A Guide to Professional & Nonprofit Organizations, Government Agencies, Educational Institutons, Grant Award Sources, Health Care Insurers, Journals, Newsletters, Review Serials, Etc. 2nd ed. Ed. by Anthony T. Kruzas. LC 77-82802. 1980. 92.00 (ISBN 0-8103-0267-5). Gale.

Medical & Legal Professions. Ed. by Walter H. Rubsamen. (Ballad Opera Ser.). 1974. lib. bdg. 50.00 (ISBN 0-8240-0903-7). Garland Pub.

Medical & Psychological Aspects of Disability. A. Beatrix Cobb. (Amer. Lec. Social & Rehabilitation Psychology Ser.). (Illus.). 384p. 1977. 19.75 (ISBN 0-398-02653-X). C C Thomas.

Medical & Surgical Cardiology. William Cleland et al. (Illus.). 1168p. 1969. 38.50 (ISBN 0-397-60130-1, Blackwell). Mosby.

Medical & Surgical Management of Heart Disease: A Concise Guide for Non-Cardiologists. Lawrence I. Bonchek & Harold L. Brooks. 1981. text ed. price not set. Little.

Medical & Veterinary Protozoology. rev. ed. K. M. Adam et al. 1980. 50.00 (ISBN 0-443-00764-0). Churchill.

Medical Anthropology in African Newspapers: An Annotated Facsimile Edition from the Third World. Vincent Van Amelsvoort. 116p. 1976. pap. text ed. 9.25x (ISBN 90-6234-105-5). Humanities.

Medical Aspects of the Imported Fire Ant. Robert B. Rhoades. LC 77-1736. (Illus.). 1977. 4.75 o.p. (ISBN 0-8130-0559-0). U Presses Fla.

Medical Assistant: Clinical Practice. Betty J. Atkinson. LC 76-5301. 1976. pap. 8.00 (ISBN 0-8273-0351-3); instructor's guide 1.60 (ISBN 0-8273-0352-1). Delmar.

Medical Assistant's Examination Review Book, Vol. 1. 2nd. ed. LaVerne Dreizen & Thelma Audet. 1979. 9.50 (ISBN 0-87488-490-X). Med Exam.

Medical Astrology. Boris Paque. Tr. by John Broglio from Fr. Date not set. 20.00 (ISBN 0-88231-051-8). ASI Pubs Inc. Postponed.

Medical Audiology: Disorders of Hearing. Ed. by Frederick N. Martin. (Illus.). 512p. 1981. text ed. 32.00 (ISBN 0-13-572677-8). P-H.

Medical Behavioral Science. Ed. by Theodore Millon. LC 74-4581. (Illus.). 545p. 1975. text ed. 19.95 o.p. (ISBN 0-7216-6387-7). Saunders.

Medical Bibliography in an Age of Discontinuity. Scott Adams. 256p. 1981. 21.50 (ISBN 0-912176-09-1). Med Lib Assn.

Medical Books & Serials in Print, 1981. 10th ed. 1650p. 1981. 52.00 (ISBN 0-8352-1356-0). Bowker.

Medical Books for the Layperson: An Annotated Bibliography, Supplement. Compiled by Marilyn M. Philbrook. 1978. pap. 2.00 (ISBN 0-89073-060-1). Boston Public Lib.

Medical Care Chartbook. 7th ed. Avedis Donabedian et al. (Illus.). 420p. 1980. text ed. 42.50 (ISBN 0-914904-61-2); pap. 22.50 (ISBN 0-914904-62-0). Health Admin Pr.

Medical Care for Mountain Climbers. Peter Steele. 1976. pap. 11.00x (ISBN 0-433-31560-1). Intl Ideas.

Medical Care for the Aged. Henry P. Brehm & Rodney M. Coe. LC 78-19786. 1980. 19.95 (ISBN 0-03-046306-8). Praeger.

Medical Care in the United States. Ed. by Eric F. Oatman. (Reference Shelf Ser.: Vol. 50, No. 1). 1978. 6.25 (ISBN 0-8242-0622-3). Wilson.

Medical Care of Newborn Babies, Vol. 44-45. Pamela A. Davies et al. (Clinics in Developmental Medicine Ser.). 1972. 32.00 (ISBN 0-685-34616-1). Lippincott.

Medical Care of the Adolescent. 3rd ed. Gallagher. (Illus.). 1975. 38.50 o.p. (ISBN 0-8385-6199-3). ACC.

Medical Center Lab. Melvin Berger. LC 76-12964. (Scientists at Work Seires). (Illus.). (gr. 3 up). 1976. PLB 9.89 (ISBN 0-381-99602-6, JD-J). John Day.

Medical Choice in a Mexican Village. James C. Young. 200p. 1981. 19.50 (ISBN 0-8135-0895-9). Rutgers U Pr.

Medical Choices, Medical Chances: Decision Making for Patients, Families, & Physicians. Harold Bursztajn et al. 1981. 14.95 (ISBN 0-440-05750-7, Sey Lawr). Delacorte.

Medical College Admission Test. David R. Turner. 1977. pap. 6.00 o.p. (ISBN 0-668-04289-3). Arco.

Medical Complications in Cancer Patients. Ed. by Jean Klastersky & Maurice J. Staquet. (European Organization for Research on Treatment of Cancer (EORTC), Monograph: Vol. 7). Orig. Title: Medical Disorders in Cancer Patients. 323p. 1980. text ed. 31.50 (ISBN 0-89004-519-4). Raven.

Medical Conditions & Terms Made Simple. Ronald S. Biviano. LC 80-68397. 100p. (Orig.). 1981. pap. 10.00 (ISBN 0-9605476-0-6). Biviano.

Medical Consequences of Alcohol Abuse. P. M. Clark & L. J. Kricka. LC 80-41993. (Chemical Science Ser.). 282p. 1980. 97.95 (ISBN 0-470-27076-4). Halsted Pr.

Medical Correspondence Workbook. M. Tratsart. 1974. wire bound wkbk. 14.95x (ISBN 0-433-32645-X). Intl Ideas.

Medical Data Transmission by Public Telephone Systems. Ed. by V. Mengden & Just. 1979. pap. text ed. 24.00 (ISBN 0-8067-0961-8). Urban & S.

Medical-Dental Terminology: Syllabus. 2nd ed. LeGrand H. Woolley. 1974. pap. text ed. 6.10 (ISBN 0-89420-003-8, 217705); cassette recordings 177.70 (ISBN 0-89420-162-X, 196700). Natl Book.

Medical Diagnostic Apparatus-Systems. James R. Critser, Jr. (Serie 10DAS-79). 142p. 1980. 80.00 (ISBN 0-914428-66-7). Lexington Data.

Medical Dictation & Transcription. 2nd ed. P. Davis. 400p. 1981. pap. 12.95 (ISBN 0-471-06023-2, Pub. by Wiley Med). Wiley.

Medical Dictionary for the Lay Person. Chapman. 1981. pap. 2.95 (ISBN 0-8120-2247-5). Barron.

Medical Diseases of the Kidney. Robert T. McCluskey & Conrad L. Pirani. (Anatomic Pathology Slide Seminar Ser.). (Illus.). 1972. atlas 63.50 o.p. (ISBN 0-89189-055-6, 15-1-012-00); slides 22.50 o.p. (ISBN 0-685-78075-9, 01-1-072-00). Am Soc Clinical.

Medical Disorders in Obstetric Practice. 4th ed. Cyril G. Barnes. (Illus.). 1974. text ed. 42.50 (ISBN 0-632-09810-4, Blackwell). Mosby.

Medical Divination. H. Tomlinson. 1980. 15.75x (ISBN 0-85032-133-6, Pub. by Daniel Co England). State Mutual Bk.

Medical Divination. H. Tomlinson. 88p. 1966. 5.50x (ISBN 0-8464-1031-1). Beekman Pubs.

Medical Education Financing: Policy Analyses & Options for the Nineteen Eighties. Ed. by Jack Hadley. (Illus.). 1980. 25.00 (ISBN 0-88202-129-X). N Watson.

Medical Education in Arkansas, Eighteen Seventy Nine-Nineteen Seventy Eight. W. David Baird. LC 79-126280. (Illus.). 1979. 21.95x (ISBN 0-87870-052-8). Memphis St Univ.

Medical Education in the United States: A Guide to Information Sources. Ed. by Francesco Cordasco & David N. Alloway. LC 79-24030. (Education Information Guide Ser.: Vol. 8). 1980. 30.00 (ISBN 0-8103-1458-4). Gale.

Medical Electroencephalography. Frederic A. Gibbs & Erna L. Gibbs. 1967. 18.95 (ISBN 0-201-02365-2). A-W.

Medical Embryology. 4th ed. Jan Langman. 328p. 1981. write for info. (4858-9). Williams & Wilkins.

Medical English, Arabic Dictionary. Jusuf Hitti. (Illus.). 1973. 35.00x (ISBN 0-685-72051-9). Intl Bk Ctr.

Medical Equipment Management in Hospitals. American Hospital Association. American Society for Hospital Engineering. LC 78-1041. (Illus.). 528p. (Orig.). 1978. pap. 45.00 (ISBN 0-87258-241-8, 1272). Am Hospital.

Medical Equipment Service Manual: Theory & Maintenance Procedures. F. Biloon. LC 77-513. 1978. 23.95 (ISBN 0-13-572644-1). P-H.

Medical Establishment & Social Responsibility. Duane F. Stroman. 1976. 15.00 (ISBN 0-8046-9136-3, Natl U). Kennikat.

Medical Ethics: A Clinical Textbook & Reference for the Health Care Professions. Natalie Abrams & Michael Buckner. 1981. text ed. write for info. (ISBN 0-89706-012-1); pap. text ed. write for info. (ISBN 0-89706-013-X). Bradford Bks.

Medical Ethics & the Law. Marc D. Hiller. Date not set. write for info. (ISBN 0-88410-707-8). Ballinger Pub. Postponed.

Medical Ethics in Imperial China: A Study in Historical Anthropology. Paul Unschuld. LC 78-80479. (Comparative Studies of Health Systems & Medical Care). 1979. 15.75x (ISBN 0-520-03543-7). U of Cal Pr.

Medical First Aid Guide for Use in Accidents Involving Dangerous Goods. (Illus.). 147p. 1973. 16.50 (IMCO). Unipub.

Medical Formulary or Agrabadhin. Al-Kindi. Tr. by Martin Levey. (Medieval Science Pubns., No. 7). 1966. 32.50x (ISBN 0-299-03600-6). U of Wis Pr.

Medical Greek & Latin Workbook. James A. McCulloch. 174p. 1977. pap. 8.50 (ISBN 0-398-01249-0). C C Thomas.

Medical Holocausts I: Exterminative Medicine in Nazi Germany & Contemporary America. William Brennan. LC 80-82305. (Nordland Series in Contemporary American Social Problems). 375p. 1980. pap. 12.95 (ISBN 0-913124-39-7). Nordland Pub.

Medical Holocausts II: The Language of Exterminative Medicine in Nazi Germany & Contemporary America. William Brennan. LC 80-82305. (Nordland Series in Contemporary American Social Problems). 320p. 1980. pap. 12.95 (ISBN 0-913124-40-0). Nordland Pub.

Medical Hubris: A Reply to Ivan Illich. David Horrobin. LC 80-66836. 146p. 1980. 9.95 (ISBN 0-88831-080-3); pap. 6.95 (ISBN 0-88831-086-2). Eden Med Res.

Medical Hubris: A Reply to Ivan Illich. David F. Horrobin. 1977. 9.00 o.p. (ISBN 0-88831-001-3). Eden Med Res.

Medical Illustration: A Guide for the Doctor-Author & Exhibitor. William E. Loechel. (Illus.). 360p. 1964. pap. 34.75 photocopy ed., spiral (ISBN 0-398-01139-7). C C Thomas.

Medical Immunology. Ed. by W. James Irvine. (Illus.). 506p. 1980. pap. text ed. 25.00x (ISBN 0-07-032049-7, HP). McGraw.

Medical Impairment to Driving. Julian A. Waller. (Illus.). 104p. 1974. 10.75 (ISBN 0-398-02891-5); pap. 7.50 (ISBN 0-398-02895-8). C C Thomas.

Medical Information Systems: A New Resource for Hospitals. Melville H. Hodge. LC 77-12739. 1977. 25.75 (ISBN 0-912862-47-5). Aspen Systems.

Medical Instrumentation & Electrical Safety: The View from the Nursing Station. Stuart A. Hoenig & Daphne H. Scott. LC 77-5878. 1977. 15.95 (ISBN 0-471-40566-3, Pub. by Wiley Medical). Wiley.

Medical Instrumentation: Application & Design. John G. Webster. LC 77-76419. (Illus.). 1978. text ed. 29.95 (ISBN 0-395-25411-6); sol. manual 2.00 (ISBN 0-395-25412-4). HM.

Medical Itch. Claude Benjamin. (Illus.). 1964. 7.95 (ISBN 0-8392-1067-1). Astor-Honor.

Medical Jurisprudence, As It Relates to Insanity, According to the Law of England. John Haslam. Ed. by David S. Berkowitz & Samuel E. Thorne. LC 77-86661. (Classics of English Legal History in the Modern Era Ser.: Vol. 109). 1979. lib. bdg. 55.00 (ISBN 0-8240-3096-6). Garland Pub.

Medical Laboratory for Developing Countries. Maurice King. (Illus.). 1973. pap. text ed. 22.50x (ISBN 0-19-264910-8). Oxford U Pr.

Medical Language. Jim Richey. (Survival Vocabulary Ser.). (Illus.). 48p. (gr. 7 up). 1980. pap. text ed. 2.45 (ISBN 0-915510-48-0). Janus Bks.

Medical Librarian Examination Review Book, Vol. 1. 2nd ed. Ed. by Jane M. Fulcher. 1972. spiral bdg. 8.50 o.s.i. (ISBN 0-87488-495-0). Med Exam.

Medical Malpractice: ALR 20 Cases & Annotations, 3 vols. Lawyers Co-Op Editorial Staff. LC 70-1405. 1966. 105.00 (ISBN 0-686-14517-8). Lawyers Co-Op.

Medical Malpractice Insurance: A Legislator's View. Tarky Lombardi, Jr. & Gerald N. Hoffman. 1978. 11.95x (ISBN 0-8156-0128-X). Syracuse U Pr.

Medical Malpractice Law. 2nd ed. Angela R. Holder. LC 77-27288. 1978. 36.50 (ISBN 0-471-03882-2, Pub. by Wiley Medical). Wiley.

Medical Men & Their Work: A Sociological Reader. Ed. by Eliot Freidson & Judith Lorber. LC 70-140627. 1972. 22.95x (ISBN 0-202-30231-8); pap. text ed. 12.95x (ISBN 0-202-30230-X). Aldine Pub.

Medical Merry-Go-Round: A Plea for Reasonable Medicine. Morton Glasser & Gretel H. Pelto. 1980. pap. 6.90 (ISBN 0-913178-54-3). Redgrave Pub Co.

Medical Messiahs: A Social History of Health Quackery in Twentieth-Century America. James H. Young. 1967. 20.00x (ISBN 0-691-04526-7); pap. 6.95 (ISBN 0-691-00579-6). Princeton U Pr.

Medical Microbiological Techniques. Baker & Breach. LC 80-40010. 1980. 49.00 (ISBN 0-407-00099-2). Butterworths.

Medical Microbiology. Robert F. Boyd & J. Joseph Marr. 1980. text ed. 24.95 (ISBN 0-316-10432-9). Little.

Medical Microbiology, Vol. 1. 13th ed. Ed. by J. P. Duguid et al. (Illus.). 1979. text ed. 35.00 (ISBN 0-443-01787-5); pap. text ed. 25.00 (ISBN 0-443-01788-3). Churchill.

Medical Microbiology: Quality Cost & Clinical Relevance. Raymond C. Bartlett. LC 73-18482. (Quality Control Methods in the Clinical Laboratory Ser.). 272p. 1974. 32.50 (ISBN 0-471-05475-5, Pub. by Wiley Medical). Wiley.

Medical Ministry. Ellen G. White. 1963. pap. 6.50 (ISBN 0-8163-0157-3, 13371-0); pap. 5.95 deluxe ed. (ISBN 0-8163-0158-1, 13370-2). Pacific Pr Pub Assn.

Medical, Moral & Legal Implications of Recent Medical Advances: A Symposium. Ed. by D. W. Dowd et al. LC 71-152124. (Symposia on Law & Society Ser). 1971. Repr. of 1968 ed. lib. bdg. 14.50 (ISBN 0-306-70128-6). Da Capo.

Medical Mycology Handbook. Mary C. Campbell & Joyce L. Stewart. LC 80-11935. 436p. 1980. 25.00 (ISBN 0-471-04728-7, Pub. by Wiley Med). Wiley.

Medical Mycology Manual with Human Mycoses Monograph. 4th ed. E. S. Beneke & A. L. Rogers. 76p. 1980. pap. 19.95 (ISBN 0-8087-4042-3). Burgess.

Medical Neurobiology. William D. Willis, Jr. & Robert G. Grossman. (Illus.). 611p. 1981. text ed. 29.50 (ISBN 0-8016-5584-6). Mosby.

Medical Office Design, Territory & Conflict. Henry P. Doble, Jr. 320p. 1981. 36.50 (ISBN 0-87527-243-6). Green.

Medical Paediatrics. William B. Doig & Alison Montford. (Modern Practical Nursing Ser: No. 1). (Illus.). 1972. pap. text ed. 9.95x (ISBN 0-433-07694-1). Intl Ideas.

Medical Parasitology. 3rd ed. J. Walter Beck & John E. Davies. LC 80-25201. (Illus.). 300p. 1981. text ed. 21.95 (ISBN 0-8016-0552-0). Mosby.

Medical Parasitology. 5th ed. Edward K. Markell & Marietta Voge. (Illus.). 400p. 1981. text ed. price not set (ISBN 0-7216-6082-7). Saunders.

Medical Pharmacology: Principles & Concepts. 9th ed. Andres Goth. LC 78-4107. 1978. text ed. 26.50 (ISBN 0-8016-1948-3). Mosby.

Medical Phrase Index. Jean Lorenzini. 1978. 28.50 (ISBN 0-87489-149-3); pap. 21.50 (ISBN 0-87489-198-1). Med Economics.

Medical Physics: External Senses, Vol. 2. Arthur Damask. 1981. write for info. (ISBN 0-12-201202-X). Acad Pr.

Medical Physiology, 2 vols. 14th ed. Vernon B. Mountcastle. LC 79-25943. (Illus.). 1980. Set. 54.50 (ISBN 0-8016-3560-8); Vol. 1. 42.50 (ISBN 0-8016-3562-4); Vol. 2. 37.00 (ISBN 0-8016-3566-7). Mosby.

Medical Physiology Textbook Study Guide. 2nd ed. James L. Poland. LC 79-51989. 1979. pap. 8.50 (ISBN 0-87488-155-2). Med Exam.

Medical Practice & Psychiatry: The Impact of Changing Demands, Vol. 5. GAP Committee on Public Education. (Report No. 58). 1964. pap. 2.00 (ISBN 0-87318-077-1). Adv Psychiatry.

Medical Practice Management. rev. ed. H. Cotton. 1977. 23.95 (ISBN 0-87489-098-5). Med Economics.

Medical Problems in the Classroom: An Educator's Guide. Raymond M. Peterson & James O. Cleveland. (Illus.). 328p. 1976. 24.75 (ISBN 0-398-03287-4). C C Thomas.

Medical Products Liability: A Comprehensive Guide & Sourcebook. Ed. by Research Group & Duane Gingerich. (Health Care Economics & Technology Ser.). 500p. 1981. 59.50x (ISBN 0-86621-001-6). F&S Pr.

Medical Profession in Mid-Victorian London. M. Jeanne Peterson. 1978. 22.75x (ISBN 0-520-03343-4). U of Cal Pr.

Medical Psychiatry Journal Articles. Ed. by F. Gordon Foster & Richert E. Goyette. 1974. spiral bdg. 15.50 (ISBN 0-87488-530-2). Med Exam.

Medical Psychology: Contributions to Behavioral Medicine. Ed. by Charles Prokop & L. A. Bradley. LC 80-1676. 1981. price not set (ISBN 0-12-565960-1). Acad Pr.

Medical Radiesthesia & Radionics: An Introduction. Vernon D. Wethered. 1980. 30.00x (ISBN 0-85207-109-4, Pub. by Daniel Co England). State Mutual Bk.

Medical Radiesthesia & Radionics: An Introduction. Vernon D. Wethered. 196p. 1957. 11.95x (ISBN 0-8464-1032-X). Beekman Pubs.

Medical Radiographic Techniques. Robert Zimmerman. LC 74-18672. (Allied Health Ser). 1975. pap. 8.35 (ISBN 0-672-61392-1). Bobbs.

Medical Radioisotope Scanning-1959. 1959. pap. 7.50 (ISBN 92-0-010059-7, IAEA). Unipub.

Medical Radioisotope Scanning-1964, 2 vols. 1964. Vol. 1. pap. 22.50 (ISBN 92-0-010264-6, IAEA); Vol. 2. pap. 18.75 (ISBN 92-0-010364-2). Unipub.

Medical Radioisotope Scintigraphy, 2 Vols. 1968. Vol. 1. pap. 47.25 (ISBN 92-0-010069-4, IAEA); Vol. 2. pap. 50.50 (ISBN 92-0-010169-0). Unipub.

Medical Radioisotope Scintigraphy-1972, 2 vols. (Illus.). 745p. 1973. pap. 49.25 ea. (IAEA); Vol. 1. pap. (ISBN 92-0-010173-9); Vol. 2. pap. (ISBN 92-0-010273-5). Unipub.

Medical Radionuclide Imaging, Vol. II. (Proceedings Ser). (Illus.). 1977. pap. 48.25 (ISBN 92-0-110177-5, ISP 440-2, IAEA). Unipub.

Medical Radionuclide Imaging: Vol. 1, Proceedings of a Symposium, los Angeles 25-29 Oct, 1976. (Illus.). 1977. pap. 62.75 (ISBN 92-0-110077-9, ISP 440-1, IAEA). Unipub.

Medical Readings on Drug Abuse. O. Byrd. (gr. 10-12). 1970. pap. text ed. 7.95 (ISBN 0-201-00749-5); pap. text ed. 7.25 (ISBN 0-201-00748-7). A-W.

Medical Record Departments in Hospitals: Guide to Organization. American Hospital Association. 100p. 1972. pap. 10.00 (ISBN 0-87258-089-X, 2345). Am Hospital.

Medical Record Library Science Examination Review Book, Vol. 1. 3rd ed. Ed. by M. Pauline Gregorio. 1976. spiral bdg. 10.00 (ISBN 0-87488-496-9). Med Exam.

Medical Records. Bernard Benjamin. 1977. 24.60x (ISBN 0-433-02450-X). Intl Ideas.

Medical Records Administration Continuing Education Review. Elaine O. Patrikas et al. 1975. spiral bdg. 14.00 (ISBN 0-87488-369-5). Med Exam.

Medical Records in Health Information. Kathleen Waters & Gretchen Murphy. LC 79-18793. 1979. text ed. 32.95 (ISBN 0-89443-157-9). Aspen Systems.

Medical Records Technology. Alice Mosier & Frank J. Pace. LC 74-18676. (Allied Health Ser). 1975. pap. 8.35 (ISBN 0-672-61396-4). Bobbs.

Medical Report & Testimony. G. H. Pearce. (Illus.). 1979. text ed. 17.95x (ISBN 0-04-610012-1). Allen Unwin.

Medical Report & Testimony. G. H. Pearce. 104p. 1980. 35.00x (Pub. by Beaconsfield England). State Mutual Bk.

Medical Research Index, 2 vols. 2nd ed. Francis Hodgson. 1360p. 1980. text ed. 150.00x (ISBN 0-582-90005-0). Churchill.

Medical Research Index, 2 vols. 5th ed. LC 45-718. 1200p. 1979. Set. 175.00x (ISBN 0-8002-2386-1). Intl Pubns Serv.

Medical Risks: Patterns of Mortality & Survival. Ed. by Richard B. Singer & Louis Levinson. LC 74-31609. 1976. 37.95 (ISBN 0-669-98228-8). Lexington Bks.

Medical School Admission Adviser. Marvin Fogel & Mort Walker. 1976. pap. 5.95 o.p. (ISBN 0-8015-1628-5). Dutton.

Medical School Game. David Simmons. pap. 4.95 o.p. (ISBN 0-8473-1109-0). Sterling.

Medical School: The Interview & the Applicant. rev ed. Marguerite Lerner. 175p. 1980. pap. 3.95 (ISBN 0-8120-0752-2). Barron.

Medical Sciences Knowledge Profile Examination (MSKP) Jack Rudman. (Admission Test Ser.: AT-86). (Cloth bdg. avail. on request). pap. 17.95 (ISBN 0-686-68260-2). Natl Learning.

Medical Secretary Medi-Speller: A Transcription Aid. Harriette L. Carlin. 260p. 1973. pap. 11.50 (ISBN 0-398-02579-7). C C Thomas.

Medical Self-Care: Access to Health Tools. Tom Ferguson. LC 80-14678. 320p. 1980. 19.95 (ISBN 0-671-40033-9); pap. 8.95 (ISBN 0-671-44816-1). Summit Bks.

Medical Shorthand. 2nd ed. Phyllis Davis. 275p. 1981. pap. 11.95 (ISBN 0-471-06024-0). Wiley.

Medical Side of Benjamin Franklin. William Pepper. (Illus.). 137p. 1970. Repr. of 1910 ed. 15.00 (ISBN 0-87266-039-7). Argosy.

Medical Social Work in Action. Zofia Butrym. 128p. 1968. pap. text ed. 5.00x (Pub. by Bedford England). Renouf.

Medical Social Work: The Pre-Professional Paradox. Toba S. Kerson. 320p. 1980. text ed. 19.50x (ISBN 0-8290-0237-5). Irvington.

Medical Sociology. William C. Cockerham. LC 77-13162. (P-H Ser. in Sociology). (Illus.). 1978. ref. 17.95x (ISBN 0-13-573402-9). P-H.

Medical Sociology. John A. Denton. LC 77-94098. (Illus.). 1978. text ed. 19.25 (ISBN 0-395-25805-7). HM.

Medical Sociology. 2nd ed. David Mechanic. LC 77-3850. 1978. text ed. 16.95 (ISBN 0-02-920720-7). Free Pr.

Medical Sociology: A General Systems Approach. Leon Robertson & Margaret Heagerty. LC 75-9779. 220p. 1975. 17.95 (ISBN 0-88229-127-0); pap. 9.95x (ISBN 0-88229-578-0). Nelson-Hall.

Medical Spelling Guide: A Reference Aid. Carrie E. Johnson. 560p. 1966. 14.75 (ISBN 0-398-00931-7). C C Thomas.

Medical Staff Cost Containment: Digest of Hospital Projects & Selected Bibliography. American Hospital Association. 72p. 1980. pap. 8.75 (ISBN 0-87258-314-7, 1538). Am Hospital.

Medical State Board Examination Review Book, 2 pts. 6th ed. Ed. by Leopold Gilbert & Sol Daniel. Incl. Vol. 1. Basic Sciences. 287p; Vol. 2. Clinical Sciences. 239p. 1976. spiral bdg. 12.00 ea. o.p. Med Exam.

Medical Supervision of Radiation Workers. (Safety Ser.: No. 25). (Illus., Orig.). 1968. pap. 8.25 (ISBN 92-0-123068-0, IAEA). Unipub.

Medical Surgical Nursing. 3rd ed. Ed. by Marguerite C. Holmes & Harriet Levine. (Nursing Examination Review Books Vol. 1). 1972. spiral bdg. 6.00 (ISBN 0-87488-501-9). Med Exam.

Medical-Surgical Nursing & Related Physiology. 2nd ed. Jeannette E. Watson. LC 78-64732. (Illus.). 1043p. 1979. text ed. 22.00 (ISBN 0-7216-9136-6). Saunders.

Medical-Surgical Nursing: Concepts & Clinical Practice. Wilma J. Phipps et al. LC 78-27863. (Illus.). 1979. text ed. 30.95 (ISBN 0-8016-3932-8). Mosby.

Medical-Surgical Nursing: Pretest Self-Assessment & Review. Ed. by Helen Chuan. Margaret Allman. LC 78-50598. (PreTest Self-Assessment & Review). (Illus.). 1978. pap. 6.95 (ISBN 0-07-051567-0). McGraw-Pretest.

Medical-Surgical Nursing Procedures. Lucile Broadwell & Barbara Milutnovic. LC 76-4305. 1977. pap. text ed. 12.40 (ISBN 0-8273-0353-X); instructor's guide 1.60 (ISBN 0-8273-0354-8). Delmar.

Medical-Surgical Nursing: Workbook for Nurses. 5th ed. Gail H. Hood & Judy Dincher. LC 79-24346. (Illus.). 1980. pap. text ed. 8.95 (ISBN 0-8016-2567-X). Mosby.

Medical-Surgical Tips-Techniques. Medical Economics Company. (Illus.). 1975. pap. 12.50 (ISBN 0-87489-089-6). Med Economics.

Medical Technology: Advanced Medical Apparatus-Systems. James R. Critser, Jr. (Ser. 10 AMA-78). 1980. 300.00 (ISBN 0-914428-59-4). Lexington Data.

Medical Technology: Advanced Medical Apparatus-Systems. James R. Critser, Jr. (Ser 10AMA-77). 1978. 300.00 (ISBN 0-914428-46-2). Lexington Data.

Medical Technology & the Health Care System: A Study of the Diffusion of Equipment-Embodied Technology. Assembly of Engineering, Institute of Medicine, National Research Council. 1979. pap. text ed. 10.75 (ISBN 0-309-02865-5). Natl Acad Pr.

Medical Technology: Electrical-Electronic Apparatus 1976. James R. Critser, Jr. (Ser. 10 - 76). 1977. 200.00 (ISBN 0-914428-41-1). Lexington Data.

Medical Technology Examination Review Book, Vol. 1. 4th ed. Aaron A. Alter et al. 1977. spiral bdg. 9.50 (ISBN 0-87488-451-9). Med Exam.

Medical Technology Examination Review Book, Vol. 2. 4th ed. Aaron A. Alter et al. 1978. spiral bdg. 9.50 (ISBN 0-87488-452-7). Med Exam.

Medical Technology, Health Care & the Consumer. Allen Spiegel. LC 79-25539. 352p. 1980. 29.95x (ISBN 0-87705-498-3). Human Sci Pr.

Medical Terminology. 4th ed. G. L. Smith & P. E. Davis. 300p. 1980. pap. 11.95 (ISBN 0-471-05827-0, Pub. by Wiley Med). Wiley.

Medical Terminology: A Programmed Orientation to. R. J. Brady. (Illus.). 1970. pap. 9.95 (ISBN 0-87618-074-8). R J Brady.

Medical Terminology: A Self-Learning Module. Jacqueline J. Birmingham. (Illus.). 448p. 1981. pap. text ed. 11.95 (ISBN 0-07-005386-3, HP). McGraw.

Medical Terminology: A Text-Workbook. Alice Prendergast. LC 76-62907. 1977. pap. text ed. 10.95 (ISBN 0-201-05966-5, M&N Div); instr's man. 9.95 (ISBN 0-201-05967-3). A-W.

Medical Terminology in Hospital Practice. 3rd ed. P. M. Davies. 1979. pap. 15.95x (ISBN 0-433-07183-4). Intl Ideas.

Medical Therapeutic Apparatus-Systems: Series No. 10tas-79. James R. Critser, Jr. 1981. 60.00 (ISBN 0-914428-69-1). Lexington Data.

Medical Transcriptionist Handbook. Charles T. McConnico. 256p. 1972. text ed. 12.75 (ISBN 0-398-02367-0). C C Thomas.

Medical Typist's Guide for Histories & Physicals. 2nd ed. Carol C. Alcazar. 1974. spiral bdg. 7.00 (ISBN 0-87488-976-6). Med Exam.

Medical Uses of Ca-47 (Technical Reports Ser.: No. 10). 1962. pap. 5.00 (ISBN 92-0-115162-4, IDC 10, IAEA). Unipub.

Medical Uses of Ca-47 Second Panel Report. (Technical Reports Ser.: No. 32). 1964. pap. 8.25 (ISBN 92-0-115264-7, IAEA). Unipub.

Medical Word Building. Park-Davis & Company. 1970. pap. 7.95 (ISBN 0-87489-043-8). Med Economics.

Medical Work in Education. Eugen Kolisko. 1980. pap. 1.95x (ISBN 0-906492-38-6, Pub. by Kolisko Archives). St. George Bk Serv.

Medical Writing. Ed. by Felix Marti-Ibanez. 1956. 3.00 o.p. (ISBN 0-910922-03-9). MD Pubns.

Medical Writing: The Technic & the Art. 4th ed. Morris Fishbein. (Illus.). 216p. 1978. 13.75 (ISBN 0-398-02279 8). C C Thomas.

Medical X-Ray Techniques in Diagnostic Radiology. G. J. Van Der Plaats. 1979. lib. bdg. 79.50 (ISBN 90-247-2155-5, Martinus Nijhoff Pubs). Kluwer Boston.

Medicare: The Politics of Federal Hospital Insurance. Judith Feder. LC 77-4611. (Illus.). 1977. 19.95- (ISBN 0-669-01447-8). Lexington Bks.

Medication Guide for Patient Counseling. Dorothy L. Smith. LC 76-54361. (Illus.). 1977. pap. 12.00 o.p. (ISBN 0-8121-0586-9). Lea & Febiger.

Medications & Mathematics for the Nurse. 288p. 1981. text ed. 13.95 (ISBN 0-442-21882-6). Van Nos Reinhold.

Medications & Mathematics for the Nurse. Esther G. Skelley. LC 76-5302. 1976. pap. 7.40 (ISBN 0-8273-1343-8); instructor's guide 1.60 (ISBN 0-8273-1344-6). Delmar.

Medici. Marcel Brion. 1969. 25.00 (ISBN 0-236-17727-3, Pub. by Paul Elek). Merrimack Bk Serv.

Medici Ring. Nicole St. John. 1975. 6.95 o.p. (ISBN 0-394-49342 7). Random.

Medicinal Botany II: From the Shepard's Purse. Max G. Barlow. 1981. 25.95x (ISBN 0-9602812-1-5). Spice West.

Medicinal Chemistry Advances: Proceedings of the Seventh International Symposium on Medicinal Chemistry, Torremolinos, 2-5 September 1980. F. G. De las Heras & S. Vega. (Illus.). 500p. 1981. 80.00 (ISBN 0-08-025297-4); pap. 25.00 (ISBN 0-08-026198-1). Pergamon.

Medicinal Herbs in the Bible. M. De Waal. Ed. by Jane Meijlink. 96p. 1981. pap. 4.95 (ISBN 0-87728-527-6). Weiser.

Medicinal Plants of the West Indies. Edward S. Ayensu. Ed. by Keith Irvine. LC 79-48009. (Medicinal Plants of the World Ser.). (Illus.). 1981. 29.95 (ISBN 0-917256-12-3). Ref Pubns.

Medicine. 7th ed. Ed. by Michael A. Baker. (Medical Examination Review Ser.: Vol. 2). 1980. pap. 8.50 (ISBN 0-87488-102-1). Med Exam.

Medicine. Jane Gray. LC 74-76181. (Professions Ser.). (Illus.). 168p. 1974. 11.95 (ISBN 0-7153-6623-8). David & Charles.

Medicine. 6th ed. Ed. by Nathaniel Wisch et al. (Medical Examination Review Books: Vol. 2). 1980. pap. 8.50 o.p. (ISBN 0-87488-102-1). Med Exam.

Medicine. Herbert S. Zim. LC 74-4299. (Illus.). 64p. (gr. 3-7). 1974. 6.25 o.p. (ISBN 0-688-21786-9); PLB 6.48 (ISBN 0-688-31786-3). Morrow.

Medicine Among the American Indians. E. Stone. (Illus.). 1962. Repr. of 1932 ed. pap. 7.50 o.s.i. (ISBN 0-02-853000 4). Hafner.

Medicine Among the American Indians: CIBA Symposia, 1939, Vol. 1, No. 1. William Krogman et al. 198 . pap. 4.95 (ISBN 0-686-69101-6). Acoma Bks.

Medicine: An Outline for the Intending Student. Ed. by E. D. Acheson. (Outlines Ser). 1970. cased 14.00 (ISBN 0-7100-6866-2); pap. 7.95x (ISBN 0-7100-6867-0). Routledge & Kegan.

Medicine & Clinical Engineering. Bertil Jacobson & John G. Webster. LC 76-13842. (Illus.). 1977. text ed. 28.95 (ISBN 0-13-572966-1). P-H.

Medicine & Literature. Ed. by Enid R. Peschel. 1980. 15.00 (ISBN 0-88202-127-3); text ed. 12.95. N Watson.

Medicine & Religion: Strategies of Care. Ed. by Donald W. Shriver, Jr. LC 79-23420. (Contemporary Community Health Ser.). 1980. pap. 10.95 (ISBN 0-8229-3412-4). U of Pittsburgh Pr.

Medicine & Slavery: The Health Care of Blacks in Antebellum Virginia. Todd L. Savitt. LC 78-8520. (Blacks in the New World Ser.). (Illus.). 321p. 1981. pap. 7.50 (ISBN 0-252-00874-X). U of Ill Pr.

Medicine & Society. Henry Miller. (Science & Engineering Policy Ser). 100p. 1973. text ed. 8.95x o.p. (ISBN 0-19-858321-4); pap. text ed. 3.00x o.p. (ISBN 0-19-858322-2). Oxford U Pr.

Medicine & Stamps, 2 vols. R. A. Kyle & M. A. Shampo. LC 79-26733. 528p. 1980. Vol. 1. lib. bdg. 11.50 (ISBN 0-89874-085-1); Vol. 2. lib. bdg. 13.50 (ISBN 0-89874-072-X); Set. lib. bdg. 20.00 (ISBN 0-89874-234-X). Krieger.

Medicine & the Reign of Technology. S. J. Reiser. LC 77-87389. (Illus.). 1978. 21.50 (ISBN 0-521-21907-8). Cambridge U Pr.

Medicine & the Reign of Technology. Stanley J. Reiser. LC 77-87389. (Illus.). 317p. (Orig.). 1981. pap. 8.95 (ISBN 0-521-28223-3). Cambridge U Pr.

Medicine Calf. Bill Hotchkiss. 1981. 13.95 (ISBN 0-393-01389-8). Norton.

Medicine in Canadian Society: Historical Perspectives. Ed. by S. E. Shortt. 400p. 1981. 23.95x (ISBN 0-7735-0356-0); pap. 11.95 (ISBN 0-7735-0369-2). McGill-Queens U Pr.

Medicine in Literature: An Anthology for Reading & Writing. Ed. by Joseph F. Ceccio. LC 77-17721. (English & Humanities Ser.). 1978. pap. text ed. 9.95x (ISBN 0-582-28051-6). Longman.

Medicine Lodge: The Story of a Kansas Frontier Town. Nellie S. Yost. LC 79-132588. (Illus.). 237p. 1970. 8.95 o.p. (ISBN 0-8040-0198-7, SB); pap. 4.95 (ISBN 0-8040-0199-5). Swallow.

Medicine Man of the Apache. John G. Bourke. 1979. 10.00 (ISBN 0-87026-049-9). Westernlore.

Medicine Man Who Went to School. Biloine W. Young & Mary Wilson. (Illus.). 28p. (gr. 1-4). 1972. 1.50 o.p. (ISBN 0-8309-0086-1). Independence Pr.

Medicine Men of Hooper Bay. Charles E. Gillham. (Illus.). (gr. 4-6). 1966. 3.95g o.s.i. (ISBN 0-02-735990-5). Macmillan.

Medicine, Mind, & Man: An Introduction to Psychology for Students of Medicine & Allied Professions. John Cohen & John H. Clark. LC 78-27201. (Illus.). 1979. text ed. 21.95x (ISBN 0-7167-1089-7); pap. text ed. 11.95x (ISBN 0-7167-1090-0). W H Freeman.

Medicine Nineteen Seventy-Eight. David J. Weatherall. LC 78-58440. 1978. 24.50 (ISBN 0-471-04888-7, Pub. by Wiley Medical). Wiley.

Medicine: PreTest Self-Assessment & Review. Ed. by John Dwyer. LC 77-86707. (Clinical Sciences: PreTest Self-Assessment & Review Ser.). (Illus.). 1978. pap. 9.95 (ISBN 0-07-051601-4). McGraw-Pretest.

Medicine Show. rev. & updated ed. Consumer Reports Editors. 384p. 1980. 10.00 (ISBN 0-394-51106-9); pap. 5.95 (ISBN 0-394-73887-X). Pantheon.

Medicine Talk: A Guide to Walking in Balance & Surviving on the Earth Mother. Brad Steiger. LC 74-1774. 216p. 1976. pap. 2.95 o.p. (ISBN 0-385-09734-4). Doubleday.

Medicine's Metaphors: Messages & Menaces. S. Vaisrub. 1977. 9.95 (ISBN 0-87489-011-X). Med Economics.

Medicion De la Moral: Clave Para Aumentar la Productividad. Alexander Hamilton Institute, Nc. Ed. by James M. Jenks. (Illus.). 50p. (Orig., Span.). 1976. pap. 48.75x (ISBN 0-86604-011-0, A811102). Hamilton Inst.

Medicolegal Investigation of Death. 2nd ed. W. U. Spitz & R. S. Fisher. 1980. 45.00 o.p. (ISBN 0-398-03973-9). C C Thomas.

Medicolegal Investigation of Death: Guidelines for the Application of Pathology to Crime Investigation. 2nd ed. Ed. by Werner U. Spitz & Russell S. Fisher. (Illus.). 600p. 1980. 47.75 (ISBN 0-398-03973-9). C C Thomas.

Medicolegal Investigation of the President John F. Kennedy Murder. Charles G. Wilber. (Illus.). 336p. 1978. 19.50 (ISBN 0-398-03679-9). C C Thomas.

Medidas Principales En la Planificacion De la Iglesia Local: Key Steps in Local Church Planning. Richard E. Rusbuldt et al. Tr. by Oscar E. Rodriguez from Eng. 134p. (Span.). 1981. pap. 5.95 (ISBN 0-8170-0933-7). Judson.

Medieval & Modern Greek. Robert Browning. (Illus.). 1969. pap. text ed. 6.00x (ISBN 0-09-099601-1, Hutchinson U Lib). Humanities.

Medieval & Modern: Including Ancient & Classical, 6th Ed. & Medieval & Modern, 11th Ed. Ancient, Medieval & Modern. 10th ed. Ramsey Muir. Ed. by Harold Fullard & R. E. Treharne. (Illus.). 1964. Repr. of 1911 ed. 19.50x (ISBN 0-06-495016-6). B&N.

Medieval & Renaissance Music on Long-Playing Records: Supplement 1962-1971. James Coover & Richard Colvig. (Detroit Studies in Music Bibliography: No. 26). 1973. 8.50 (ISBN 0-685-30212-1); pap. 7.00 (ISBN 0-685-30212-1). Info Coord.

Medieval & Renaissance Spirituality. Paul M. Clogan. LC 70-99227. (Medievalia et Humanistica: Studies in Medieval & Renaissance Culture Ser.: No. 4). 1973. 24.95 (ISBN 0-913904-00-7). Medieval.

Medieval Art. LC 76-14067. (Garland Library of the History of Art: Vol. V). 1977. lib. bdg. 50.00 (ISBN 0-8240-2415-X). Garland Pub.

Medieval Celtic Literature: A Select Bibliography. Rachel Bromwich. LC 74-82287. 1974. 10.00x o.p. (ISBN 0-8020-2170-0); pap. 5.00x (ISBN 0-8020-6252-0). U of Toronto Pr.

Medieval Chinese Oligarchy. D. G. Johnson. LC 76-44875. (Westview Special Studies on China & East Asia & Studies of the East Asian Institute, Columbia University). 1977. lib. bdg. 25.00x (ISBN 0-89158-140-5). Westview.

Medieval Chronicles & the Rotation of the Earth. Robert R. Newton. LC 78-39780. 848p. 1972. 30.00x o.p. (ISBN 0-8018-1402-2). Johns Hopkins.

Medieval Church Music-Dramas: A Repertory of Complete Plays. Ed. by Fletcher Collins, Jr. LC 75-33896. 1976. 15.00x o.p. (ISBN 0-8139-0644-X). U Pr of Va.

Medieval Cities. Howard Saalman. LC 68-24702. (Planning & Cities Ser). (Illus., Orig.). 1968. pap. 5.95 o.s.i. (ISBN 0-8076-0471-2). Braziller.

Medieval Civilization. The Educational Research Council. (Human Adventure, Concepts & Inquiry Ser). (gr. 5). 1975. pap. text ed. 6.20 (ISBN 0-205-04448-4, 8044481); tchrs'. guide 5.20 (ISBN 0-205-04449-2, 804449X). Allyn.

Medieval Contribution to Political Thought: Thomas Aquinas, Marsilius of Padua, Richard Hooker. Alexander P. D'Entreves. 1959. Repr. of 1939 ed. text ed. 8.50x (ISBN 0-391-00513-8). Humanities.

Medieval Councils, Decretals & Collections of Canon Law: Selected Essays. Stephan Kuttner. 338p. 1980. 75.00x (ISBN 0-86078-071-6, Pub. by Variorum England). State Mutual Bk.

Medieval Culture & Society. Ed. by David Herlihy. LC 68-13326. (Documentary History of Western Civilization Ser). 1968. 15.00x o.s.i. (ISBN 0-8027-2013-7). Walker & Co.

Medieval Days & Ways. Gertrude Hartman. (Illus.). (gr. 8-9). 1937. 11.95 (ISBN 0-02-743090-1). Macmillan.

Medieval Drama. David Bevington. 1975. text ed. 21.95 (ISBN 0-395-13915-5). HM.

Medieval Drama. Ed. by Neville Denny. (Stratford-Upon-Avon Studies: No. 16). 254p. 1973. text ed. 27.50x (ISBN 0-8419-5824-6); pap. text ed. 19.50 (ISBN 0-8419-5823-8). Holmes & Meier.

Medieval Dream-Poetry. A. C. Spearing. LC 75-46114. 1976. 42.00 (ISBN 0-521-21194-8); pap. 10.95x (ISBN 0-521-29069-4). Cambridge U Pr.

Medieval Economy & Society: An Economic History of Britain, 1100-1500. M. M. Postan. LC 72-87202. 1973. 18.50x (ISBN 0-520-02325-0). U of Cal Pr.

Medieval Education & the Reformation. John Lawson. LC 67-18836. (Students Library of Education). 1967. pap. text ed. 3.00x (ISBN 0-7100-4209-4). Humanities.

Medieval Eloquence: Studies in the Theory & Practice of Medieval Rhetoric. James J. Murphy. 1978. 22.75x (ISBN 0-520-03345-0). U of Cal Pr.

Medieval England: An Aerial Survey. 2nd ed. M. W. Beresford & J. K. St. Joseph. LC 77-90200. (Cambridge Air Surveys). 1979. 29.95 (ISBN 0-521-21961-2). Cambridge U Pr.

Medieval England: Rural Society & Economic Change 1086-1348. Edward Miller & John Hatcher. LC 77-21445. (Social & Economic History of England Ser.). 1979. text ed. 26.00x (ISBN 0-582-48218-6); pap. text ed. 13.95 (ISBN 0-582-48547-9). Longman.

Medieval English Gardens. Theresa MacLean. LC 79-56277. (Illus.). 288p. 1981. 25.00 (ISBN 0-670-46482-1). Viking Pr.

Medieval English Lyrics. Ed. by R. T. Davies. 1966. 17.95 (ISBN 0-571-05522-2, Pub. by Faber & Faber); pap. 7.95 (ISBN 0-571-06571-6). Merrimack Bk Serv.

Medieval English Poetry. John Speirs. 1957. 9.95 (ISBN 0-571-06738-7, Pub. by Faber & Faber). Merrimack Bk Serv.

Medieval Erotic Alba: Structure As Meaning. Jonathan Saville. LC 77-190191. 320p. 1972. text ed. 22.50x (ISBN 0-231-03569-1). Columbia U Pr.

Medieval Experience: Foundations of Western Culture Singularity. Francis Oakley. LC 73-19356. 250p. 1974. pap. text ed. 6.95x o.p. (ISBN 0-684-13737-2, ScribC). Scribner.

Medieval Finance: A Comparison of Financial Institutions in Northwestern Europe. Bryce Lyon & A. E. Verhulst. LC 67-19657. 100p. 1968. Repr. of 1967 ed. 5.00x (ISBN 0-87057-102-8, Pub. by Brown U Pr). Univ Pr of New England.

Medieval Foundation of England. Arthur Bryant. LC 67-12856. 1968. pap. 1.95 o.s.i. (ISBN 0-02-030710-1, Collier). Macmillan.

Medieval Foundations of Renaissance Humanism. Walter Ullman. LC 77-278. 1977. 19.50x (ISBN 0-8014-1110-6). Cornell U Pr.

Medieval French Drama. Grace Frank. 1954. 29.50x (ISBN 0-19-815317-1). Oxford U Pr.

Medieval French Literature & Law. R. Howard Bloch. LC 76-7754. 1977. 19.50x (ISBN 0-520-03230-6). U of Cal Pr.

Medieval Greek Texts: Being a Collection of the Earliest Composition in Vulgar Greek, Prior to the Year 1500. Ed. by Wilhelm Wagner. 190p. 1970. Repr. of 1870 ed. text ed. 28.50x (ISBN 90-6032-432-3). Humanities.

Medieval History of Iran, Afghanistan & Central Asia. C. E. Bosworth. 374p. 1980. 75.00x (ISBN 0-86078-000-7, Pub. by Variorum England). State Mutual Bk.

Medieval Imagination: Rhetoric & the Poetry of Courtly Love. Douglas Kelly. LC 78-3522. 1978. 32.50 (ISBN 0-299-07610-5). U of Wis Pr.

Medieval India. Romila Thapar. (Illus.). 1970. pap. 2.00 (ISBN 0-88253-276-6). Ind-US Inc.

Medieval Inquisition. Jean Guiraud. Tr. by E. C. Messenger. LC 78-63181. (Hereseis 2 Ser.). 216p. 1980. Repr. of 1929 ed. 19.00 (ISBN 0-404-16222-3). AMS Pr.

Medieval Inquisition: Foundations of Medieval History. Bernard Hamilton. LC 80-27997. 110p. (Orig.). 1981. pap. text ed. 13.00x (ISBN 0-8419-0695-5). Holmes & Meier.

Medieval Irish Lyrics. James Carney. 1967. 14.50x (ISBN 0-520-00210-5). U of Cal Pr.

Medieval Latin & the Rise of the European Love Lyric, 2 Vols. 2nd ed. Peter Dronke. (Latin). 1969. Set. 59.00x (ISBN 0-19-814346-X). Oxford U Pr.

Medieval Learning & Literature: Essays Presented to Richard William Hunt. Ed. by J. J. G. Alexander & M. T. Gibson. (Illus.). 500p. 1976. 67.00x (ISBN 0-19-822402-8). Oxford U Pr.

Medieval Library, 28 vols. Ed. by Israel Gollancz. Repr. of 1926 ed. write for info. Cooper Sq.

Medieval Literature & Folklore Studies. Ed. by Jerome Mandel & Bruce A. Rosenberg. LC 70-127053. 1971. 27.50 (ISBN 0-8135-0676-X). Rutgers U Pr.

Medieval Logic & Metaphysics: A Modern Introduction. D. P. Henry. (Orig.). 1972. text ed. 7.50x (ISBN 0-09-110830-6, Hutchinson U Lib); pap. text ed. 6.75x (ISBN 0-09-110831-4, Hutchinson U Lib). Humanities.

Medieval Lore. Anglicus Bartholomaeus. Ed. by R. Steele. LC 66-23970. (Medieval Library). Repr. of 1926 ed. 8.50x (ISBN 0-8154-0016-0). Cooper Sq.

Medieval Lyric. P. Dronke. 1978. 28.50 (ISBN 0-521-21944-2); pap. 8.95x (ISBN 0-521-29319-7). Cambridge U Pr.

Medieval Machine: The Industrial Revolution of the Middle Ages. Jean Gimpel. 1977. pap. 3.95 (ISBN 0-14-004514-7). Penguin.

Medieval Man: His Understanding of Himself, His Society, & the World: Illustrated from His Own Literature. Urban Holmes. (Studies in the Romance Languages & Literatures). 1980. pap. 16.00x o.p. (ISBN 0-8078-9212-2). U of NC Pr.

Medieval Manuscripts for Mass & Office: A Guide to Their Organization & Terminology. Andrew Hughes. 496p. 1981. 45.00x (ISBN 0-8020-5467-6). U of Toronto Pr.

Medieval Manuscripts of Keble College, Oxford: A Descriptive Catalogue with Summary Descriptions of the Greek & Oriental Manuscripts. Compiled by M. B. Parkes. (Illus.). 365p. 1979. 175.00x (ISBN 0-85967-504-1, Pub. by Scolar Pr England). Biblio Dist.

Medieval Medicus: A Social History of Anglo-Norman Medicine. Edward J. Kealey. LC 80-21870. (Illus.). 208p. 1981. text ed. 16.95x (ISBN 0-8018-2533-4). Johns Hopkins.

Medieval Music. Richard H. Hoppin. (Introduction to Music History Ser.). (Illus.). 1978. 14.95x (ISBN 0-393-09090-6). Norton.

Medieval Music: The Sixth Liberal Art. 2nd ed. Andrew Hughes. (Toronto Medieval Bibliographies Ser.). 1980. 25.00x (ISBN 0-8020-2358-4). U of Toronto Pr.

Medieval Mysteries, Moralities & Interludes. Ed. by Vincent F. Hopper & Gerald B. Lahey. LC 61-18362. (gr. 10 up). 1962. pap. text ed. 3.95 (ISBN 0-8120-0135-4). Barron.

Medieval Mystical Tradition in England. Ed. by Marion Glasscoe. 249p. 1981. pap. 12.00x (Pub. by U Exeter, England). Humanities.

Medieval Number Symbolism: Its Sources, Meaning & Influence on Thought & Expression. Vincent F. Hopper. LC 70-85372. 241p. 1969. Repr. of 1938 ed. 22.50x (ISBN 0-8154-0305-4). Cooper Sq.

Medieval Papalism: The Political Theories of the Medieval Canonists. Walter Ullman. LC 79-1644. 1981. Repr. of 1949 ed. 19.50 (ISBN 0-88355-946-3). Hyperion Conn.

Medieval People. J. J. Bagley. (People in Period Ser.). 1978. 16.95 (ISBN 0-7134-1046-9, Pub. by Batsford England). David & Charles.

Medieval People. 10th rev. & enl. ed. Eileen Power. 1963. pap. 3.95 (ISBN 0-06-463253-9, EH 253, EH). Har-Row.

Medieval People. 10th rev. & enl. ed. Eileen Power. 210p. 1963. 13.50x (ISBN 0-686-63945-6). B&N.

Medieval Philosophy: From St. Augustine to Nicholas of Cusa. Ed. by John F. Wippel & Allen B. Wolter. LC 69-10043. 1969. pap. text ed. 7.95 (ISBN 0-02-935650-4). Free Pr.

Medieval Province of Armagh, Fourteen Seventy-Fifteen Forty-Five. Aubrey Gwynn. 1949. 8.50 (ISBN 0-85221-022-1). Dufour.

Medieval Religion & Technology: Collected Essays. Lynn White, Jr. LC 77-83113. (Center for Medieval & Renaissance Studies, UCLA: No. 13). 1978. 26.50x (ISBN 0-520-03566-6). U of Cal Pr.

Medieval Rhetoric & Poetic to 1400. C. S. Baldwin. 1959. 7.50 (ISBN 0-8446-1043-7). Peter Smith.

Medieval Romance: Themes & Approaches. J. E. Stevens. 1973. text ed. 15.00x (ISBN 0-09-114000-5, Hutchinson U Lib). Humanities.

Medieval Scribes, Manuscripts & Libraries: Essays Presented to N. R. Ker. Ed. by M. B. Parkes & Andrew G. Watson. (Illus.). 408p. 1978. 80.00x (ISBN 0-85967-450-9, Pub. by Scolar Pr England). Biblio Dist.

Medieval Secular Literature: Four Essays. Ed. by William Matthews. (UCLA Center for Medieval & Renaissance Studies). 1965. 16.50x (ISBN 0-520-00832-4). U of Cal Pr.

Medieval Settlement: Continuity & Change. Ed. by P. H. Sawyer. LC 77-71251. 1977. 47.50x o.p. (ISBN 0-8448-1092-4). Crane-Russak Co.

Medieval Society: 400-1450. 2nd ed. Ed. by Norman F. Cantor & Michael S. Werthman. LC 72-76355. (AHM Structure of European History Ser.: Vol. 2). 303p. 1972. pap. text ed. 5.95x (ISBN 0-88295-711-2). AHM Pub.

Medieval Song: An Anthology of Hymns & Lyrics. Ed. by James J. Wilhelm. 1971. pap. 3.95 o.p. (ISBN 0-525-47297-5). Dutton.

Medieval Southampton: The Port & Trading Community A. D. 1000-1600. Colin Platt. (Illus.). 300p. 1973. 27.50x (ISBN 0-7100-7653-3). Routledge & Kegan.

Medieval Technology & Social Change. Lynn White, Jr. 1966. pap. 4.95 (ISBN 0-19-500266-0, GB). Oxford U Pr.

Medieval Texts & Studies. C. R. Cheney. 382p. 1973. 33.00x (ISBN 0-19-822399-4). Oxford U Pr.

Medieval Texts & Their First Appearance in Print. E. P. Goldschmidt. LC 68-54232. 1969. Repr. of 1943 ed. 9.50x (ISBN 0-8196-0226-4). Biblo.

Medieval Theatre Costume. Iris Brooke. LC 67-25699. (Illus.). 1967. 8.95 (ISBN 0-87830-081-3). Theatre Arts.

Medieval Times. (Picture Panorama of British History Ser.). 1977. pap. 4.95 (ISBN 0-263-06240-6). Transatlantic.

Medieval Town. Fritz Rorig. Tr. by D. J. Matthew. 1967. 20.00x (ISBN 0-520-01088-4); pap. 5.75x (ISBN 0-520-01579-7, CAMPUS23). U of Cal Pr.

Medieval Trade & Finance. M. M. Postan. (Illus.). 350p. 1973. 41.95 (ISBN 0-521-08745-7). Cambridge U Pr.

Medieval Village. M. E. Reeves. (Then & There Ser.). (Illus.). 1972. pap. text ed. 2.65x (ISBN 0-582-20375-9). Longman.

Medieval Vision: Essays in History & Perception. Carolly Erickson. LC 75-10179. 256p. 1976. text ed. 14.95 (ISBN 0-19-501964-4); pap. text ed. 5.95x (ISBN 0-19-501963-6). Oxford U Pr.

Medieval Woman's Guide to Health: The First English Gynecological Handbook. Beryl Rowland. Tr. by Beryl Rowland. Rossell H. Robbins. LC 80-82201. (Illus.). 194p. 1981. 17.50x (ISBN 0-87338-243-9). Kent St U Pr.

Medieval Women. Derek Baker. (Illus.). 412p. 1981. pap. 16.95x (ISBN 0-631-12539-6, Pub. by Basil Blackwell England). Biblio Dist.

Medieval Women. Ed. by Derek Baker. (Illus.). 1978. 35.50x (ISBN 0-631-19260-3, Pub. by Basil Blackwell England). Biblio Dist.

Medieval Women. Eileen Power & M. Poston. LC 75-7212. (Illus.). 144p. 1976. pap. 21.50 (ISBN 0-521-20769-X); pap. 5.50x (ISBN 0-521-09946-3). Cambridge U Pr.

Medievalia et Humanistica, Vols. 1-3 & 6-9. Ed. by P. M. Clogan. Incl. Vol. 1. LC 75-32451. 251p. 1976 (ISBN 0-521-21032-1); Vol. 2. Medieval & Renaissance Studies in Review. LC 75-32452. 223p (ISBN 0-521-21033-X); Vol. 3. Social Dimension in Medieval & Renaissance Studies. LC 75-32453. 328p (ISBN 0-521-21034-8); Vol. 6. LC 75-16872. 1979 (ISBN 0-521-20999-4); Vol. 7. Studies in Medieval & Renaissance Culture: Medieval Poetics. LC 76-12914. 1977 (ISBN 0-521-21331-2); Vol. 8. Studies in Medieval & Renaissance Culture Transformation & Continuity. LC 75-32451. 1978 (ISBN 0-521-21783-0); Vol. 9. LC 75-32451. 1979 (ISBN 0-521-22446-2). 36.00 ea. Cambridge U Pr.

Medievalia et Humanistica: Studies in Medieval & Renaissance Culture. Paul M. Clogan. (New Ser.: No. 10). 1981. 25.00x (ISBN 0-8476-6944-0). Rowman.

Meditaciones Del Quijote. Jose Ortega Y Gasset. Ed. by Revista De Occidente. 1957. pap. 3.65 o.p. (ISBN 0-8477-0721-0). U of PR Pr.

Meditaciones Para la Nueva Madre. H. G. Brenneman. 1978. 2.20 (ISBN 0-311-40032-9). Casa Bautista.

Meditacoes De Um Leigo. Tr. by Phillip Keller. (Portugese Bks.). (Port.). 1979. write for info. (ISBN 0-8297-0788-3). Life Pubs Intl.

Meditate. Swami Muktananda. (Transpersonal & Humanistic Psychology Ser.). 9.95 (ISBN 0-87395-497-1). State U NY Pr.

Meditate the Tantric Yoga Way. Swami Jyotirmayananda. 1973. 5.50 o.p. (ISBN 0-04-149022-3). Allen Unwin.

Meditating Person: Bridges Between Cultures. Ed. by Stephen Bochner. 380p. 1981. text ed. 22.50x (ISBN 0-686-64398-4); pap. text ed. 11.25x (ISBN 0-87073-893-3). Schenkman.

Meditation. Grace Cooke. 1955. 6.50 (ISBN 0-85487-011-3). De Vorss.

Meditation. Alan Watts. 1976. pap. 2.95 (ISBN 0-515-05842-4). Jove Pubns.

Meditation - Gateway to Light. rev. ed. Elsie Sechrist. 53p. 1972. pap. 1.95 (ISBN 0-87604-062-8). ARE Pr.

Meditation & Spiritual Life. Swami Yatiswarananda. 700p. 1980. 18.95 (ISBN 0-87481-403-0). Vedanta Pr.

Meditation & the Fulness of Life: An Exposition of Romans 9-11. Jim Wilson. 1974. pap. 4.75 (ISBN 0-227-67810-9). Attic Pr.

Meditation & the Mind of Man. rev. ed. Herbert B. Puryear & Mark Thurston. 1975. pap. 4.95 (ISBN 0-87604-105-5). ARE Pr.

Meditation: Der Weg Zum Licht. Elsie Sechrist. Tr. by Helge F. Kronberger from Eng. (Illus.). 53p. (Ger.). 1980. pap. 6.00 (ISBN 0-87604-131-4). ARE Pr.

Meditation Gut Enlightenment: The Way of Hara. Haruo Yamaoka. 1976. pap. 2.50 o.p. (ISBN 0-89346-001-X). Heian Intl.

Meditation Made Easy. W. P. Petersen & Terry Fehr. (Concise Guides Ser.). (Illus.). (gr. 6 up). 1979. s&l 6.45 (ISBN 0-531-02894-1). Watts.

Meditation Notes on Paul the Apostle. James Alberione. 1973. 2.00 o.s.i. (ISBN 0-8198-0252-2). Dghtrs St Paul.

Meditation on the Signs of the Zodiac. John Jocelyn. LC 79-3594. (Harper Library of Spiritual Wisdom). 288p. 1980. pap. 5.95 (ISBN 0-06-064140-1, RD 403). Har-Row.

Meditation: Self-Regulation Strategy & Altered States of Consciousness. Deane Shapiro, Jr. 1980. 19.95 (ISBN 0-202-25132-2). Aldine Pub.

Meditation: The Art of Ecstasy. Bhagwan S. Rajneesh. (Orig.). 1976. pap. 5.95 (ISBN 0-06-090529-8, CN529, CN). Har-Row.

Meditation: The Art of Ecstasy. Bhagwan S. Rajneesh. Ed. by Ma S. Bharti. 1978. pap. 2.95 (ISBN 0-06-080394-0, P394, PL). Har-Row.

Meditation: The Inward Art. Bradford Smith. LC 63-14633. 1968. pap. 3.95 o.s.i. (ISBN 0-397-10062-0, LP6). Lippincott.

Meditation Yoga. Masahiro Oki. Tr. by David N. Bradshaw from Japanese. LC 77-93244. 1978. 12.00 (ISBN 0-87040-435-0). Japan Pubns.

Meditations. Marcus Aurelius. Tr. by G. M. Grube. LC 63-12205. (Orig.). 1963. pap. 3.95 (ISBN 0-672-60402-7). Bobbs.

Meditations. Marcus Aurelius. Tr. by Maxwell Staniforth. (Classics Ser.). (Orig.). (YA) (gr. 9 up). 1964. pap. 2.75 (ISBN 0-14-044140-9). Penguin.

Meditations. Bernard Gunther et al. (Essence Books Ser.). (Illus.). (YA) 1973. pap. 0.50 o.s.i. (ISBN 0-02-080240-4, Collier). Macmillan.

Meditations. Chiara Lubich. LC 74-79452. 1974. pap. 1.95 (ISBN 0-911782-20-6). New City.

Meditations & Devotions. John H. Newman. 10.50 o.p. (ISBN 0-87061-037-6). Chr Classics.

Meditations & Devotions for Adults. Alec J. Langford. LC 76-223. 1976. 4.95 o.p. (ISBN 0-687-24090-5). Abingdon.

Meditations for the Later Years. Josephine Robertson. LC 73-19935. 80p. 1974. 5.95 o.p. (ISBN 0-687-24099-9). Abingdon.

Meditations on First Philosophy. Rene Descartes. Tr. by Laurence J. Lafleur. 1960. pap. 2.95 (ISBN 0-672-60191-5, LLA29). Bobbs.

Meditations on Freedom & the Spirit. Karl Rahner. 1978. pap. 3.95 (ISBN 0-8164-2162-5). Crossroad NY.

Meditations on Hope & Love. Karl Rahner. LC 77-76614. 1977. pap. 3.95 (ISBN 0-8164-2155-2). Crossroad NY.

Meditations on Saint Luke. Arturo Paoli. Tr. by Bernard McWilliams from Spanish. LC 76-58539. 1977. 8.95x o.p. (ISBN 0-88344-314-7); pap. 4.95x o.p. (ISBN 0-88344-315-5). Orbis Bks.

Meditations on the Sacraments. Karl Rahner. 1977. 5.95 (ISBN 0-8164-0344-9). Crossroad NY.

Meditations Through the Quran. Ernest G. McClain. (Illus.). 1980. write for info. N Hays.

Meditators. Douglas Shah. 1975. 5.95 o.p. (ISBN 0-88270-125-8); pap. 3.50 o.p. (ISBN 0-88270-126-6). Logos.

Mediterranean. A. B. Whipple & Time-Life Books Editors. (World War II Ser). (Illus.). 208p. 1981. 13.95 (ISBN 0-8094-3383-4). Time-Life.

Mediterranean & the Mediterranean World in the Age of Philip Second, 2 vols. rev. 2nd ed. Fernand Braudel. Tr. by Sian Reynolds from Fr. (Illus.). 1418p. 1976. Vol. 1. pap. 8.95 (ISBN 0-06-090566-2, CN566, CN); Vol. 2. pap. 9.95 (ISBN 0-06-090567-0, CN567, CN). Har-Row.

Mediterranean & the Mediterranean World in the Age of Philip II, Vol. 1. Fernand Braudel. Tr. by Sian Reynolds from Fr. LC 72-138708. (Illus.). 640p. 1972. 20.00 o.s.i. (ISBN 0-06-010452-X, HarpT). Har-Row.

Mediterranean & the Mediterranean World in the Age of Philip II, Vol. 2. Fernand Braudel. Tr. by Sian Reynolds from Fr. LC 72-138708. (Illus.). 656p. 1974. 20.00 o.s.i. (ISBN 0-06-010456-2, HarpT). Har-Row.

Mediterranean Caper. J. L. Bouma. 1981. pap. 2.25 (ISBN 0-8439-0873-4, Leisure Bks). Nordon Pubns.

Mediterranean Fascism, 1919-1949. Ed. by Charles F. Delzell. (Documentary History of Western Civilization Ser). 1971. 15.00x o.p. (ISBN 0-8027-2051-X). Walker & Co.

Mediterranean: Its Role in American Foreign Policy. William Reitzel. LC 71-79310. 1969. Repr. of 1948 ed. 12.50 (ISBN 0-8046-0531-9). Kennikat.

Mediterranean Monk Seal: Proceedings. International Conference on the Mediterranean Monk Seal, 1st, Rhodes, Greece, 1978. Ed. by K. Ronald & R. Duguy. LC 79-41227. (UNEP Technical Ser.: Vol. 1). (Illus.). 250p. 1979. 23.00 (ISBN 0-08-025654-6); pap. 17.25 (ISBN 0-08-025655-4). Pergamon.

Mediterranean Pollution: Proceedings of a Conference Held in Palma, Mallorca, Sept. 1979. S. H. Jenkins. (Progress in Water Technology Ser.: Vol. 12, Nos. 1 & 4). 850p. 1980. 100.00 (ISBN 0-08-026058-6). Pergamon.

Mediterranean Society: The Jewish Communities of the Arab World As Portrayed in the Documents of the Cairo Geniza. S. D. Goitein. Incl. Vol. I. Economic Foundations. 1968. 21.50x (ISBN 0-520-00484-1); Vol. 2. The Community. 1971. 30.00x (ISBN 0-520-01867-2); Vol. 3. The Family. 1978. 27.50x (ISBN 0-520-03265-9). (Near Eastern Center, UCLA). U of Cal Pr.

Mediterranean Valleys: Geological Change in Historical Times. Claudio Vita-Finzi. LC 69-10341. (Illus.). 1969. 32.50 (ISBN 0-521-07355-3). Cambridge U Pr.

Medium Rare. Bill Plympton. 1978. 2.95 o.p. (ISBN 0-03-021466-1). HR&W.

Medium, the Mystic & the Physicist. Lawrence LeShan. 304p. 1975. pap. 1.95 o.p. (ISBN 0-685-50990-7, 24408-7-195). Ballantine.

Mediums, Mystics & the Occult. Milbourne Christopher. LC 74-26812. (Illus.). 288p. 1975. 9.95 (ISBN 0-690-00476-1, TYC-T). T Y Crowell.

Medley of Statistical Techniques for Researchers. Gordon C. Ashton & Ian McMillan. 64p. 1981. pap. 6.25 (ISBN 0-686-69139-3). Kendall-Hunt.

Medley on the Music Question. G. C. Brewer. 1976. 2.50 (ISBN 0-89225-121-2). Gospel Advocate.

Medullary Aplasia. Ed. by Yves Najean. LC 80-80966. (Illus.). 312p. 1980. 39.50 (ISBN 0-89352-064-0). Masson Pub.

Medusa & the Snail. Lewis Thomas. 1980. pap. 7.95 (ISBN 0-8161-3102-3, Large Print Bks). G K Hall.

Medusa Conspiracy. Ethan I. Shedley. LC 79-56261. 372p. 1980. 13.95 (ISBN 0-670-46571-2). Viking Pr.

Medusae of the British Isles II. Frederick S. Russell. 1970. 75.00 (ISBN 0-521-07293-X). Cambridge U Pr.

Meeres und der Liebe Wellen. Franz Grillparzer. Ed. by Douglas Yates. (German Text Ser.). 1947. pap. 9.95x (ISBN 0-631-01400-4, Pub. by Basil Blackwell). Biblio Dist.

Meet Andrew Jackson. Ormonde De Kay, Jr. (Step-up Books Ser.). (Illus.). (gr. 2-6). 1967. PLB 4.99 (ISBN 0-394-90066-9, BYR). Random.

Meet Cree: A Guide to the Cree Language. H. Christoph Wolfart & Janet F. Carroll. 160p. 1981. 12.50x (ISBN 0-8032-4716-8). U of Nebr Pr.

Meet Dr. Franklin. 2nd ed. Ed. by Roy N. Lokken. 295p. 1981. 20.00 (ISBN 0-89168-035-7). Franklin Inst Pr.

Meet Elvis Presley. Friedman. (gr. 7-12). pap. 1.25 (ISBN 0-590-11875-7, Schol Pap). Schol Bk Serv.

Meet Jesus. Knofel Staton. LC 80-53674. 192p. (Orig.). 1981. pap. 3.50 (ISBN 0-87239-426-3, 40092). Standard Pub.

Meet Me in Time. Charlotte V. Allen. (Orig.). 1978. pap. 2.25 o.s.i. (ISBN 0-446-82530-1). Warner Bks.

Meet Me on the Mountain. William J. Petersen. 1979. pap. 2.95 (ISBN 0-88207-784-8). Victor Bks.

Meet Miss Liberty. Lillie Patterson. (gr. 4-6). 1962. 7.95g (ISBN 0-02-770570-6). Macmillan.

Meet Our Sages. Jacob Neusner. LC 80-12771. (Illus.). 128p. (gr. 5-8). 1980. pap. text ed. 4.95x (ISBN 0-87441-327-3). Behrman.

Meet the Austins. Madeleine L'Engle. (YA) (gr. 7-12). 1981. pap. 1.95 (ISBN 0-440-95777-X, LE). Dell.

Meet the Austins. Madelene L'Engle. LC 60-9726. (gr. 3-8). 1960. 6.95 (ISBN 0-8149-0352-5). Vanguard.

Meet the Bible. David Brown. 1980. 1.25 (ISBN 0-686-28784-3). Forward Movement.

Meet the Centers. Sean O'Reilly. (Meet the Players: Basketball). (Illus.). (gr. 2-4). 1977. PLB 5.95 (ISBN 0-87191-601-0); pap. 2.95 (ISBN 0-89812-203-1). Creative Ed.

Meet the Coaches. Sean O'Reilly. LC 76-54899. (Meet the Players: Basketball). (Illus.). (gr. 2-4). 1977. PLB 5.95 (ISBN 0-87191-600-2); pap. 2.95 (ISBN 0-89812-206-6). Creative Ed.

Meet the Computer. Bruce Lewis. LC 77-2856. (gr. 4-5). 1977. 5.95 (ISBN 0-396-07456-1). Dodd.

Meet the Defensive Linemen. Ian Thorne. (Meet the Players: Football). (Illus.). (gr. 2-4). 1975. PLB 5.45 o.p. (ISBN 0-87191-467-0). Creative Ed.

Meet the Forwards. Sean O'Reilly. LC 76-52952. (Meet the Players: Basketball). (Illus.). (gr. 2-4). 1977. PLB 5.95 (ISBN 0-87191-603-7); pap. 2.95 (ISBN 0-89812-205-8). Creative Ed.

Meet the Giant Snakes. Seymour Simon. LC 78-74162. (gr. 1-4). 7.95 o.s.i. (ISBN 0-8027-6356-1); PLB 7.85 (ISBN 0-8027-6357-X). Walker & Co.

Meet the Goalies. Linda Thomas. (Meet the Players: Hockey). (Illus.). (gr. 2-4). 1976. PLB 5.95 o.p. (ISBN 0-87191-533-2). Creative Ed.

Meet the Guards. Sean O'Reilly. LC 76-51833. (Meet the Players: Basketball). (Illus.). (gr. 2-4). 1977. PLB 5.95 (ISBN 0-87191-602-9); pap. 2.95 (ISBN 0-89812-204-X). Creative Ed.

Meet the Hitters. Thomas Braun. (Meet the Players: Baseball). (Illus.). (gr. 2-4). 1977. PLB 5.95 o.p. (ISBN 0-87191-579-0). Creative Ed.

Meet the Infielders. Jay H. Smith. (Meet the Players: Baseball). (Illus.). (gr. 2-4). 1977. PLB 5.95 o.p. (ISBN 0-87191-578-2). Creative Ed.

Meet the Linebackers. Ian Thorne. (Meet the Players: Football). (Illus.). (gr. 2-4). 1975. PLB 5.45 o.p. (ISBN 0-87191-471-9). Creative Ed.

Meet the Malones. Lenora M. Weber. LC 43-12453. (gr. 5 up). 1943. 10.95 (ISBN 0-690-52999-6, TYC-J). T Y Crowell.

Meet the Managers. Jay H. Smith. (Meet the Players: Baseball). (Illus.). (gr. 2-4). 1977. PLB 5.95 (ISBN 0-87191-577-4). Creative Ed.

Meet the Men Who Sailed the Seven Seas. John Dyment. (Step-up Bk). (gr. 2-6). 1966. PLB 4.69 (ISBN 0-394-90064-2, BYR). Random.

Meet the Meters. Glenn F. Leslie & Marvin Gold. 1976. pap. 2.95 o.p. (ISBN 0-345-25246-2). Ballantine.

Meet the Orchestra. William W. Suggs. (gr. 4-6). 1966. 4.95 o.s.i. (ISBN 0-02-788610-7). Macmillan.

Meet the Pitchers. Jay H. Smith. (Meet the Players: Baseball). (Illus.). (gr. 2-4). 1977. PLB 4.95 o.p. (ISBN 0-87191-576-6). Creative Ed.

Meet the Quarterbacks. Ian Thorne. (Meet the Players: Football). (Illus.). (gr. 2-4). 1975. PLB 5.45 o.p. (ISBN 0-87191-469-7). Creative Ed.

Meet the Real Pilgrims: Everyday Life on Plimouth Plantation in 1627. Robert H. Loeb, Jr. LC 78-1208. 1979. 7.95a (ISBN 0-385-14152-1); PLB (ISBN 0-385-14153-X). Doubleday.

Meet the Receivers. Ian Thorne. (Meet the Players: Football). (Illus.). (gr. 2-4). 1975. PLB 5.45 o.p. (ISBN 0-87191-468-9). Creative Ed.

Meet the Running Backs. Ian Thorne. (Meet the Players: Football). (Illus.). (gr. 2-4). 1977. PLB 5.45 o.p. (ISBN 0-87191-470-0). Creative Ed.

Meet the Stars of Country Music, Vol. 1. Carolyn Holloran. 1977. 4.95 o.s.i. (ISBN 0-87695-204-X). Aurora Pubs.

Meet the Stars of Country Music, Vol. 2. Carolyn Hollaran. 1978. 4.95 o.s.i. (ISBN 0-87695-212-0). Aurora Pubs.

Meet the Vampire. Georgess McHargue. LC 78-20393. (Eerie Ser.). (Illus.). (gr. 2-4). 1979. 7.95 (ISBN 0-397-31833-2); pap. 7.89 (ISBN 0-397-31851-0). Lippincott.

Meet Theodore Roosevelt. Ormonde De Kay, Jr. (Step-up Books Ser.). (Illus.). (gr. 2-6). 1967. PLB 4.99 (ISBN 0-394-90065-0, BYR). Random.

Meet Yourself in the Parables. Warren W. Wiersbe. 1979. pap. [illegible].95 (ISBN 0-88207-790-2). Victor Bks.

Meeting: A One-Act Play. Peggy A. Orsborn. LC 67-31721. (Illus.). (gr. 6-12). 1968. tchr's ed & spirit master reader [illegible].95 (ISBN 0-910030-06-5). Afro Am.

Meeting at Telgte. Gunter Grass. Tr. by Ralph Manheim from Ger. (Helen & Kurt Wolff Bk.). 1981. 9.95 (ISBN 0-15-162138-1). HarBraceJ.

Meeting Basic Competencies in Communications. Eileen Corcoran. 1979. pap. 2.25x (ISBN 0-88323-152-2, 242); tchr's answer key 1.00x (ISBN 0-88323-156-[illegible], 246). Richards Pub.

Meeting Basic Competencies in Math. Eileen Corcoran. 1978. pap. text ed. 2.25x (ISBN 0-88323-138-7, 227); tchrs answer key free (ISBN 0-88323-141-[illegible], 230). Richards Pub.

Meeting Basic Competencies in Practical Science & Health: A Workstudy Book to Improve Daily Living Skills. Eileen L. Corcoran. (Illus.). 1979. 2.25x (ISBN 0-88323-146-8, 237); tchrs answer key free (ISBN 0-88323-154-9, 245). Richards Pub.

Meeting Basic Competencies in Reading. Eileen L. Corcoran. 1977. pap. text ed. 1.95 (ISBN 0-88323-134-4, 221); tchrs answer key 1.00 (ISBN 0-88323-144-[illegible], 232). Richards Pub.

Meeting by the River. Christopher Isherwood. 1978. pap. 1.95 (ISBN 0-380-01945-0, 37945, Bard). Avon.

Meeting Ends: A Play by Francis Warner. Francis Warner. (Oxford Theatre Texts Ser.: No. 4). (Illus.). 1974 text ed. 5.25x (ISBN 0-85635-105-9). Humanities.

Meeting God at Every Turn. Catherine Marshall. (Illus.). 250p. 1981. [illegible].95 (ISBN 0-912376-61-9). Chosen Bks Pub.

Meeting God in Man. Boros, Ladislaus, S.J. 1971. pap. 1.45 (ISBN 0-385-05377-0, Im). Doubleday.

Meeting Human Needs: An Overview of Nine Countries. Ed. by Daniel Thursz & Joseph L. Vigilante. LC 73-86705. (Social Service Delivery Systems: Vol. 1). 1975. 20.00x (ISBN 0-8039-0314-6); pap. 9.95x (ISBN 0-8039-0589-0). Sage.

Meeting Human Needs Two: Additional Perspectives from Thirteen Countries. Ed. by Daniel Thursz & Joseph L. Vigilante. LC 76-6314. (Social Service Delivery Systems: Vol. 2). (Illus.). 286p. 1976. 20.00x (ISBN 0-8039-0590-4); pap. 9.95x (ISBN 0-8039-0591-2). Sage.

Meeting Post: A Story of Lapland. Lee Kingman. LC 73-139105. (Stories from Many Lands Ser). (Illus.). (gr. 2-5). 1972. 3.95 o.p. (ISBN 0-690-52975-9, TYC-J); PLB 7.89 (ISBN 0-690-52976-7). T Y Crowell.

Meeting the Basic Needs of the Rural Poor: The Integrated, Community-Based Approach. Ed. by Philip H. Coombs. LC 80-19838. (Pergamon Policy Studies on International Development). 828p 1980. 49.50 (ISBN 0-08-026306-2). Pergamon.

Meeting the Challenge of Supervision. Merle C. Nutt. LC 70-179468. 1972. text ed. 10.00 o.p. (ISBN 0-682-47408-[illegible], University). Exposition.

Meeting the Needs of Learning Disabled Children in the Regular Class. Wineva Grzynkowicz. 208p. 1975. pap. 16.50 photocopy ed. spiral (ISBN 0-398-03159-2). C C Thomas.

Meeting the Needs of the Handicapped. Ed. by Carol H. Thomas & James L. Thomas. 1980. lib. bdg. 18.50x (ISBN 0-912700-54-8). Oryx Pr.

Meeting with David B. Axelrod & Gnazino Russo. David B. Axelrod. Ed. & tr. by Nat Scammacca. LC 79-90012. (Sicilian Antigruppo Ser.: No. 3). (Illus.). 1979. signed ltd. o. s. i. 10.00 (ISBN 0-89304-505-5); pap. 3.00x (ISBN 0-89304-507-1); signed ltd. ed. 6.00x (ISBN 0-89304-506-3). Cross Cult.

Meeting with Nicolo D'Alessandro & Nat Scammacca. Ed. by Nat Scammacca. (Sicilian Antigruppo Ser.: No. 1). (Illus.). 4.00 o.p. (ISBN 0-89304-501-2); signed ltd. ed. o.p. 6.00 (ISBN 0-89304-502-0); pap. 3.00 (ISBN 0-89304-500-4); pap. 6.00 signed ltd. ed. (ISBN 0-89304-503-9). Cross Cult.

Meg Miller. large type ed. Margaret SeBastian. pap. 1.50 o.p. (ISBN 0-425-03191-8). Berkley Pub.

Meg Miller. Margaret Sebastian. 208p. 1981. pap. 1.95 (ISBN 0-515-05811-4). Jove Pubns.

Meg of Heron's Neck. Ladd. 1977. pap. 3.50 (ISBN 0-89272-035-2). Down East.

Mega, Vol. 1, Pt.10. K. Marx & F. Engels. 1390p. 60.00 (Pub. by Dietz Germany). Imported Pubns.

Mega, Vol. 1, Pt. 22. K. Marx & F. Engels. 1790p. 60.00 (Pub. by Dietz Germany). Imported Pubns.

Mega, Vol. 2, Pt. 1.1. K. Marx & F. Engels. 464p. 60.00 (Pub. by Dietz Germany). Imported Pubns.

Mega, Vol. 2,pt. 3.1. K. Marx & F. Engels. 499p. 60.00 (Pub. by Dietz Germany). Imported Pubns.

Mega, Vol. 2,pt. 3.2. K. Marx & F. Engels. 800p. 60.00 (Pub. by Dietz Germany). Imported Pubns.

Mega, Vol. 2,pt. 3.3. K. Marx & F. Engels. 930p. 60.00 (Pub. by Dietz Germany). Imported Pubns.

Mega, Vol. 2,pt. 3.4. K. Marx & F. Engels. 479p. 60.00 (Pub. by Dietz Germany). Imported Pubns.

Mega, Vol. 3,pt. 1. K. Marx & F. Engels. 479p. 60.00 (Pub. by Dietz Germany). Imported Pubns.

Mega, Vol. 4,pt. 1. K. Marx & F. Engels. 1047p. 60.00 (Pub. by Dietz Germany). Imported Pubns.

Mega-Nutrition: The New Prescription for Maximum Health,Energy & Longevity. Richard A. Kunin. 1981. pap. 6.95 (ISBN 0-452-25271-7, Z5271, Plume Bks). NAL.

Megacorp. Jonathan Black. (Orig.). 1981. pap. 3.95 (ISBN 0-451-09889-7, E9889, Sig). NAL.

Megacorp & Oligopoly. A. S. Eichner. LC 75-17115. (Illus.). 450p. 1976. 35.50 (ISBN 0-521-20885-8). Cambridge U Pr.

Megacorporation in American Society: The Scope of Corporate Power. Phillip I. Blumberg. LC 75-6667. 1975. pap. text ed. 9.95 (ISBN 0-13-574053-3). P-H.

Megagauss Physics & Technology. Ed. by Peter J. Turchi. 678p. 1980. 69.50 (ISBN 0-306-40461-3, Plenum Pr). Plenum Pub.

Megalithic Art of the Maltese Islands. Michael Ridley. (Illus.). 1978. 9.95 o.p. (ISBN 0-85642-056-5, Pub. by Blanford Pr England); pap. 3.50 o.p. (ISBN 0-85642-057-3). Sterling.

Megalithic Art of Western Europe. Elizabeth S. Twohig. (Illus.). 432p. 1980. 89.00 (ISBN 0-19-813193-3). Oxford U Pr.

Megalithic Lunar Observatories. Alexander Thom. 1971. 21.00x (ISBN 0-19-858132-7). Oxford U Pr.

Megalithic Remains in Britain & Brittany. A. Thom. (Illus.). 1979. 28.00x (ISBN 0-19-858156-4). Oxford U Pr.

Megalithic Science: Ancient Mathematics & Science in Northwest Europe. Douglas C. Heggie. (Illus.). 256p. 1981. 27.50 (ISBN 0-500-05036-8). Thames Hudson.

Megalithic Sites in Britain. Alexander Thom. (Illus.). 1967. 28.00x (ISBN 0-19-813148-8). Oxford U Pr.

Megaliths & Masterminds. Peter L. Brown. (Illus.). 1979. 14.95 o.p. (ISBN 0-684-15908-2, ScribT). Scribner.

Megalomania & Mediocrity in the Leadership of Nations: The Meaning for the World. Kenneth G. Rockwell. (Major Currents in Contemporary World History Library). (Illus.). 117p. 1981. 39.95 (ISBN 0-89266-292-1). Am Classical Coll Pr.

Megara: The Political History of a Greek City-State to 336 B. C. Ronald P. Legon. LC 80-69828. (Illus.). 344p. 1981. 25.00x (ISBN 0-8014-1370-2). Cornell U Pr.

Megasthenes & Indian Religion. Allan Dahlquist. 1977. 10.00 (ISBN 0-89684-277-0, Pub. by Motilal Banarsidass India). Orient Bk Dist.

Megastructure: Urban Futures of the Recent Past. Reyner Banham. LC 76-12061. (Icon Editions Ser.). (Illus.). 240p. 1977. 25.00 o.s.i. (ISBN 0-06-430371-3, HarpT). Har-Row.

Megatectonics of Continents & Oceans. Ed. by Helgi Johnson & Bennett L. Smith. LC 69-13555. 1970. 20.00x (ISBN 0-8135-0625-5). Rutgers U Pr.

Megavitamin & Orthomolecular Therapy in Psychiatry. (Task Force Report: No. 7). 54p. 1973. 5.00 (ISBN 0-685-38358-X, P193-0). Am Psychiatric.

Megavitamin Therapy. Ruth Adams & Frank Murray. 277p. (Orig.). 1973. pap. 1.95. Larchmont Bks.

Megavitamins: A New Key to Health. Lynn Lilliston. 224p. 1976. pap. 1.50 o.p. (ISBN 0-449-13736-8, GM). Fawcett.

Megillah: Book of Esther. Arthur Szyk. 1974. 14.95x (ISBN 0-685-84454-4). Bloch.

Meg's Eggs. Helen Nicoll & Jan Pienkowski. (Picture Puffin Bks.). (Illus.). (ps-2). 1976. pap. 1.95 (ISBN 0-14-050118-5, Puffin). Penguin.

Meg's Mysterious Island. Ladd. 1977. pap. 3.50 (ISBN 0-89272-034-4). Down East.

Meg's World. John Kollock. 4.95 (ISBN 0-932298-15-X). Green Hill.

Meh'Am Lo'ez Haggadah. Tr. & intro. by Aryeh Kaplan. 216p. pap. 4.95 Ashkenazic (ISBN 0-686-27546-2). Maznaim.

Mehdi: Nothing Is Impossible. Roy Alexander. LC 77-95190. 1978. 8.95 (ISBN 0-87863-157-7). Farnswth Pub.

Mei Yao-Ch'en & the Development of Early Sung Poetry. Jonathan Chaves. (Studies in Oriental Culture Ser.). 240p. 1976. 15.00x (ISBN 0-231-03965-4). Columbia U Pr.

Meiji Japan. H. Bolitho. LC 76-54130. (History of Mankind Ser.). (Illus.). 1977. 3.95 (ISBN 0-521-20922-6). Cambridge U Pr.

Meilluer: Mobility of Employment International for Librarians in Europe. A. Thompson. (Research Publication Ser.: No. 20). 1977. pap. 15.50x (ISBN 0-85365-660-6, Pub. by Lib Assn England). Oryx Pr.

Mein Onkel Franz. Kaestner. (Easy Reader, A). pap. 2.90 (ISBN 0-88436-037-7, GEA10051). EMC.

Meinong. Reinhardt Grossman. (Arguments of the Philosophers Ser.). 1974. 19.00 (ISBN 0-7100-7831-5). Routledge & Kegan.

Meiotic System. B. John & K. R. Lewis. (Protoplasmatologia: Vol. 6, Pt. F1). (Illus.). 1965. pap. 93.30 o.p. (ISBN 0-387-80733-0). Springer-Verlag.

Meir Goldschmidt. Kenneth H. Ober. (World Author Ser: Denmark: No. 414). 1976 lib. bdg. 12.50 (ISBN 0-8057-6253-1). Twayne.

Meistererzahlungen. Ed. by Anna Otten. (Orig., Ger.). 1969. pap. text ed. 8.50 (ISBN 0-13-574251-X). P-H.

Mel Ramos: Watercolors. Mel Ramos. (Lancaster-Miller Art Ser.). (Illus.). 1980. 8.95 (ISBN 0-89581-009-3). Lancaster-Miller.

Melancholy Man: A Study of Dickens' Novels. 2nd ed. John Lucas. (Illus.). 375p. 1980. 20.00x (ISBN 0-389-20033-6). B&N.

Melancholy Marriage: Depression in Marriage & Psychosocial Approaches to Therapy. Mary K. Hinchcliffe et al. LC 78-4526. 1978. 23.95 (ISBN 0-471-99650-5, Pub. by Wiley-Interscience). Wiley.

Melanchton & Bucer. Ed. by Wilhelm Pauck. (Library of Christian Classics Ichthus Edition). 1980. pap. 9.95 (ISBN 0-664-24164-6). Westminster.

Melange. Shyree A. Latham. (Contemporary American Poets Ser.). 51p. (Orig.). 1981. 10.95 (ISBN 0-86663-702-8); pap. 8.95 (ISBN 0-86663-703-6); delux ed. 20.95 (ISBN 0-86663-704-4). Ide Hse.

Melanges De Linguistics et De Litterature Offerts a Lein Geschiere Par Ses Amis, Collegues et Elves. 297p. (Fr.). 1975. pap. text ed. 40.00x (ISBN 90-6203-209-5). Humanities.

Melanie Brown & the Jar of Sweets. Pamela Oldfield. (Illus.). (ps-5). 1974. 8.50 (ISBN 0-571-10619-6, Pub. by Faber & Faber). Merrimack Bk Serv.

Melanie Brown Goes to School. Pamela Oldfield. (Illus.). (ps-5). 1970. 5.95 o.p. (ISBN 0-571-09421-X, Pub. by Faber & Faber). Merrimack Bk Serv.

Melanocytic Nevi & Related Tumors of the Skin. Richard J. Reed. (Atlas Ser.). 1975. 58.00 (ISBN 0-89189-100-5, 15-1-013-00). Am Soc Clinical.

Melatonin - Current Status & Perspectives: Proceedings of an International Symposium on Melatonin, Held in Bremen, F. R. Germany, September 18-30, 1980. Ed. by N. Birau & W. Schlott. (Advances in the Biosciences Ser.: Vol. 29). (Illus.). 420p. 1981. 65.00 (ISBN 0-08-026400-X). Pergamon.

Melba. John Hetherington. (Illus.). 1968. 7.50 o.p. (ISBN 0-374-20560-4). FS&G.

Melba. John Hetherington. (Illus., Orig.). 1973. pap. 5.95 (ISBN 0-571-10286-7, Pub. by Faber & Faber). Merrimack Bk Serv.

Melba: A Biography. Agnes Murphy. LC 77-8029. (Music Reprint Ser.). (Illus.). 1977. Repr. of 1909 ed. lib. bdg. 32.50 (ISBN 0-306-77428-3). Da Capo.

Melchizedek Tradition. F. L. Horton. LC 75-32479. (Society for New Testament Studies Monographs: No. 30). 220p. 1976. 36.00 (ISBN 0-521-21014-3). Cambridge U Pr.

Melinda. Carla Lambert. (Orig.). 1979. pap. 1.95 (ISBN 0-532-23285-2). Manor Bks.

Melinda. Gaia Servadio. Tr. by L. K. Conrad from It. LC 68-14913. 1968. 6.95 (ISBN 0-374-20588-4). FS&G.

Melinda. Sylvia R. Tester. LC 76-30615. (Illus.). (ps-3). 1977. 5.50 (ISBN 0-913778-73-7). Childs World.

Melindy's Medal. Georgene Faulkner & John Becker. (Illus.). (gr. 3-6). 1945. 3.50 o.p. (ISBN 0-671-32327-X); PLB 4.79 o.p. (ISBN 0-671-32057-2). Messner.

Melissa. Diane Baumgartner. (Orig.). 1980. pap. 4.95 (ISBN 0-89191-233-9). Cook.

Melissa. Taylor Caldwell. 1979. pap. 2.95 (ISBN 0-515-05845-9). Jove Pubns.

Melissa's Friend Fabrizzio. Lisl Weil. (gr. k-2). 1967. 3.95g o.s.i. (ISBN 0-02-792450-5). Macmillan.

Mellona. Kathalyn Krause. 1979. pap. 2.25 (ISBN 0-505-51360-9). Tower Bks.

Mellons: The Chronicle of America's Richest Family. David E. Koskoff. LC 77-25947. (Illus.). 1978. 14.50 o.s.i. (ISBN 0-690-01190-3, TYC-T). T Y Crowell.

Mellor's Comprehensive Treatise on Inorganic & Theoretical Chemistry: Pt. 5 Boron. Mellor. (Illus.). 825p. 1980. lib. bdg. 170.00 (ISBN 0-582-46277-0). Longman.

Mellowed by Time. 3rd ed. Elizabeth O. Verner. LC 70-127297. 1978. 12.00 (ISBN 0-937684-03-1). Tradd St Pr.

Melmoth the Wanderer: A Tale. Charles R. Maturin. LC 61-5561. 1961. pap. 4.50x (ISBN 0-8032-5127-0, BB 114, Bison). U of Nebr Pr.

Melnikov: Solo Architect in a Mass Society. S. Fredrick Starr. LC 77-85566. (Illus.). 295p. 1981. pap. 9.95 (ISBN 0-691-00331-9). Princeton U Pr.

Melodia: The Dutch Street-Organ. Antonia Ridge & Mies Bouhuys. (Illus.). (ps-5). 1969. 6.95 (ISBN 0-571-08721-3, Pub. by Faber & Faber). Merrimack Bk Serv.

Melodie De Tur-Di-Di. Lavater. Date not set. 12.95 (ISBN 0-8120-5312-5). Barron. Postponed.

Melodies to Harmonize with. Frank Mainous. (Illus.). 1978. pap. 11.95 ref. ed. (ISBN 0-13-574277-3). P-H.

Melodrama. Ed. by Daniel Gerould. LC 79-52615. (New York Literary Forum Ser.). (Illus.). 296p. (Orig.). 1980. pap. 12.50x (ISBN 0-931196-06-X). NY Lit Forum.

Melody Jones. David Galloway. 1981. 9.95 (ISBN 0-7145-3807-8); pap. 4.95 (ISBN 0-7145-3733-0). Riverrun NY.

Melody of Prayer. S. Harakas. 1979. pap. 1.45 (ISBN 0-686-27068-1). Light&Life Pub Co MN.

Melody of Words. Antonia B. Laird. 1978. 5.00 o.p. (ISBN 0-8233-0286-5). Golden Quill.

Melting Pot: Ethnic Cuisine in Texas. Research Staff of Inst. of Texan Cultures. (Illus.). 230p. 1977. 10.95 (ISBN 0-933164-18-1). U of Tex Inst Tex Culture.

Melvil Dewey: His Enduring Presence in Librarianship. Sarah K. Vann. LC 77-21852. (Heritage of Librarianship Ser.: No. 4). 1978. lib. bdg. 20.00x (ISBN 0-87287-134-7). Libs Unl.

Melville. Edward H. Rosenberry. (Illus.). 1979. 17.00x (ISBN 0-7100-8989-9). Routledge & Kegan.

Melville & the Art of Burlesque. Joseph Flibbert. LC 74-80748. (Melville Studies in American Culture: No. 3). 163p. (Orig.). 1976. pap. text ed. 17.25x (ISBN 90-6203-268-0). Humanities.

Melville J. Herskovitz. George E. Simpson. (Leaders of Modern Anthropology Ser.). 200p. 1973. 15.00x (ISBN 0-231-03385-0); pap. 6.00x (ISBN 0-231-03396-6). Columbia U Pr.

Melville: The Critical Heritage. Ed. by Watson G. Branch. (Critical Heritage Ser.). 1974. 38.00x (ISBN 0-7100-7774-2). Routledge & Kegan.

Melville's Israel Potter: A Pilgrimage & Progress. Arnold Rampersad. 133p. 1969. 4.95 (ISBN 0-87972-000-X); pap. 1.95x (ISBN 0-87972-001-8). Bowling Green Univ.

Melville's Moby-Dick: A Jungian Commentary. Edward F. Edinger. LC 78-6146. 1978. pap. 3.95 (ISBN 0-8112-0691-2). New Directions.

Melville's Short Fiction, 1853-1856. William B Dillingham. LC 76-28922. 390p. 1977. 20.00x (ISBN 0-8203-0411-5). U of Ga Pr.

Melville's Use of Classical Mythology. Gerard M. Sweeney. (Melville Studies in American Culture: Vol. 5). 169p. (Orig.). 1976. pap. text ed. 11.50x (ISBN 90-6203-258-3). Humanities.

Melvin & Howard. George Gipe & Alice Winokur. 224p. 1980. pap. 2.25 (ISBN 0-515-05442-9). Jove Pubns.

Melvin B. Tolson. Joy Flasch. (U. S. Authors Ser.: No. 215). lib. bdg. 10.95 (ISBN 0-8057-0736-0). Twayne.

Melymbrosia: Being a Scholar's Edition of the Earliest Extant Version of "the Voyage Out". Virginia Woolf. Ed. by Louise A. DeSalvo. 432p. 1981. 20.00 (ISBN 0-87104-277-0). NY Pub Lib.

Member of the Wedding. Carson McCullers. (Literature Ser). (gr. 10-12). 1970. pap. text ed. 3.58 (ISBN 0-87720-756-9). AMSCO Sch.

Members Only. Patricia Welles. 1981. 12.95 (ISBN 0-87795-270-1). Arbor Hse.

Membrane & Ultrafiltration Technology: Recent Advances. Ed. by Jeanette Scott. LC 79-24503. (Chemical Tecnology Review Ser.: No. 147). (Illus.). 1980. 48.00 (ISBN 0-8155-0784-4). Noyes.

Membrane Antigens. Alena Lengerova. (Illus.). 1977. 38.80 (ISBN 0-685-85899-5). Adler.

Membrane Glycoproteins. R. C. Hughes. 1976. 64.95 (ISBN 0-408-70705-4). Butterworths.

Membrane-Membrane Interactions. Ed. by Norton B. Gilula. (Society of General Physiologists Ser.: Vol. 34). 1980. text ed. 29.00 (ISBN 0-89004-377-9). Raven.

Membrane Physiology & Cell Excitation. Bruce Hendy. 160p. 1980. 30.00x (Pub. by Croom Helm England). State Mutual Bk.

Membrane Separation Processes. James R. Critser, Jr. (Ser. 5-79). 1980. 110.00 (ISBN 0-914428-72-1). Lexington Data.

Membrane Spectroscopy. Ed. by E. Grell. (Molecular Biology, Biochemistry, & Biophysics Ser.: Vol. 31). (Illus.). 512p. 1981. 87.40 (ISBN 0-387-10332-5). Springer-Verlag.

Membrane Structure. D. Branton & D. W. Deamer. Ed. by M. Alfert et al. (Protoplasmatologia: Vol. 2, Pt. E1, 2, 3). (Illus.). 70p. 1972. 24.80 o.p. (ISBN 0-387-81031-5). Springer-Verlag.

Membrane Structure & Function, 3 vols. E. Edward Bittar. LC 79-14969. (Membrane Structure & Function Ser.). 1980. Vol. 1. 24.00 (ISBN 0-471-03816-4, Pub. by Wiley-Interscience); Vol. 2. 42.50 (ISBN 0-471-03817-2); Vol. 3. 22.50 (ISBN 0-471-03818-0). Wiley.

Membrane Structure & Function, Vol. 4. E. Edward Bittar. (Membrane Structure & Function Ser.). 200p. 1980. 24.50 (ISBN 0-471-08774-2, Pub. by Wiley-Interscience). Wiley.

Membrane Transduction Mechanisms. Ed. by Richard A. Cone & John E. Dowling. LC 78-65280. (Society of General Physiologists Ser.). 1979. text ed. 29.00 (ISBN 0-89004-236-5). Raven.

Membrane Transport Processes, Vol. 1. Ed. by Joseph F. Hoffman. LC 76-19934. 1978. 43.50 (ISBN 0-89004-170-9). Raven.

Membrane Transport Processes, Vol. 2. Ed. by D. C. Tosteson & Yu. A. Ovchinnikov. LC 76-19934. 1977. 43.50 (ISBN 0-89004-174-1). Raven.

Membrane Transport Processes, Vol. 3. Ed. by Charles F. Stevens & Richard W. Tsien. LC 76-19934. 1979. text ed. 16.00 (ISBN 0-89004-224-1). Raven.

Membranes & Disease. Ed. by Liana Bolis et al. LC 75-30235. 1976. 39.00 (ISBN 0-89004-082-6). Raven.

Membranes & Their Cellular Functions. 2nd ed. J. B. Finean et al. LC 78-9016. 1978. pap. text ed. 12.95 (ISBN 0-470-26389-X). Halsted Pr.

Membranes, Dissipative Structures & Evolution. Ed. by G. Nicolis & R. Lefever. LC 74-23611. (Advances in Chemical Physics Ser: Vol. 29). 390p. 1975. 43.50 (ISBN 0-471-63792-0, Pub. by Wiley-Interscience). Wiley.

Membranes in Ground Engineering. P. R. Rankilor. LC 80-40504. 432p. 1981. 49.50 (ISBN 0-471-27808-4, Pub. by Wiley-Interscience). Wiley.

Membranes, Ions & Impulses: A Chapter of Classical Biophysics. Kenneth S. Cole. (Biophysics Series: No. 1). (Illus.). 1968. 30.00x (ISBN 0-520-00251-2). U of Cal Pr.

Membranes, Molecules, Toxins, & Cells. Ed. by Konrad E. Bloch et al. LC 80-16595. 292p. 1981. 33.50 (ISBN 0-88416-309-1, 309). PSG Pub.

Membranes of Mitochondria & Chloroplasts. Ed. by Efraim Racker. LC 72-97168. (ACS Monograph: No. 165). 1970. 28.50 (ISBN 0-8412-0287-7). Am Chemical.

Membranes, Receptors, & the Immune Response: Eighty Years After Ehrich's Side Chain Theory. Ed. by Edward P. Cohen & Heinz Kohler. LC 80-7811. (Progress in Clinical & Biological Research Ser.: Vol. 42). 404p. 1980. 34.00 (ISBN 0-8451-0042-4). A R Liss.

Membranous Elements & Movement of Molecules. Ed. by Eric Reid. LC 77-77378. (Methodological Surveys Ser: Vol. 6). 1977. 53.95 (ISBN 0-470-99186-0). Halsted Pr.

Memo from Mercury: Information Technology Is Different. Gordon B. Thompson. 62p. 1979. pap. text ed. 3.00x (ISBN 0-920380-29-8, Pub. by Inst Res Pub Canada). Renouf.

Memo to Ambulatory Health Care Planners. 70p. (Orig.). 1976. pap. text ed. 2.00 (ISBN 0-89192-310-1). Interbk Inc.

Memoir. 4th ed. Sappho. Tr. by H. T. Wharton. 217p. 1974. Repr. of 1898 ed. text ed. 21.75x (ISBN 90-6090-002-2). Humanities.

Memoir of Abijah Hutchinson: A Soldier of the Revolution, Repr. Of 1843 Ed. K. M. Hutchinson. Bd. with Narrative of the Massacre at Chicago, August 15, 1812, & of Some Preceding Events. Juliette A. Kinzie. Repr. of 1844 ed; History of the Cooper Mines & Newgate Prison... Also, of the Captivity of Daniel Hayes... by the Indians in 1707. Noah A. Phelps. Repr. of 1845 ed; Long Journey. the Story of Daniel Hayes. Repr. of 1876 ed; Bible Boy Taken Captive by the Indians. Herman Cope. Repr. of 1845 ed. LC 75-7082. (Indian Captivities Ser.: Vol. 59). 1977. lib. bdg. 44.00 (ISBN 0-8240-1683-1). Garland Pub.

Memoir of Benjamin Robbins Curtis, 2 Vols. Benjamin R. Curtis. LC 77-75298. (The American Scene Ser). 1970. Repr. of 1879 ed. 95.00 (ISBN 0-306-71267-9). Da Capo.

Memoir of Central India, Including Malwa, & Adjoining Provinces: With the History, & Copious Illustrations, of the Past & Present Condition of That Country, 2 vols. 3rd ed. John Malcolm. 1127p. 1980. Repr. 84.00x (ISBN 0-7165-2129-6, Pub. by Irish Academic Pr). Biblio Dist.

Memoir of Michael William Balfe. Charles L. Kenney. LC 77-13360. (Music Reprint Ser., 1978). (Illus.). 1978. Repr. of 1875 ed. lib. bdg. 25.00 (ISBN 0-306-77528-X). Da Capo.

Memoir of the Life & Times of General John Lamb. I. Q. Leake. LC 72-152230. (Era of the American Revolution Ser). 1971. Repr. of 1850 ed. lib. bdg. 49.50 (ISBN 0-306-70122-7). Da Capo.

Memoir of the Life & Times of the Reverend Isaac Backus. Alvah Hovey. LC 73-148598. (Era of the American Revolution Ser.). 367p. 1972. Repr. of 1858 ed. lib. bdg. 37.50 (ISBN 0-306-70415-3). Da Capo.

Memoir of the Life of Josiah Quincy. Josiah Quincy. LC 78-146274. (Era of American Revolution Ser.). 1971. Repr. of 1825 ed. lib. bdg. 49.50 (ISBN 0-306-70098-0). Da Capo.

Memoir of the Nature of the Church of Christ. Apostolos Makrakis. Ed. by Orthodox Christian Educational Society. Tr. by Denver Cummings from Hellenic. 175p. 1947. 3.00x (ISBN 0-938366-21-1). Orthodox Chr.

Memoir of the Warsaw Uprising. Miron Bialoszewski. Tr. by Madeline Levine from Polish. 1977. 15.00 (ISBN 0-88233-275-9). Ardis Pubs.

Memoir of Theophilus Parsons. Theophilus Parsons. LC 71-118032. (American Constitutional & Legal History Ser). 1970. Repr. of 1859 ed. lib. bdg. 45.00 (ISBN 0-306-71939-8). Da Capo.

Memoir on the Origin of Printing. Ralph Willett. Ed. by Irving Lew. (Bibliographical Reprint Ser.). 1980. Repr. of 1820 ed. ltd. ed. 25.00 (ISBN 0-89782-032-0). Battery Pk.

Memoire Sur la Population. Chevalier De Cerfvol. (Principal French Demographic Works of the 18th Century Ser.). (Fr.). 1976. lib. bdg. 25.00x o.p. (ISBN 0-8287-0175-X); pap. text ed. 15.00x o.p. (ISBN 0-685-71505-1). Clearwater Pub.

Memoires d'outre-tombe, 2 vols. Francois-Rene De Chateaubriand. (Documentation thematique). (Fr). pap. 2.95 ea. Larousse.

Memoires Interieurs. Francois Mauriac. Tr. by Gerard Hopkins from Fr. 1961. 4.75 o.p. (ISBN 0-374-20644-9). FS&G.

Memoirs. Charles G. Leland. LC 68-22036. 1968. Repr. of 1893 ed. 20.00 (ISBN 0-8103-3533-6). Gale.

Memoirs & Letters of James Kent. James Kent. Ed. by William Kent. LC 78-99481. (American Public Figures Ser). 1970. Repr. of 1898 ed. lib. bdg. 32.50 (ISBN 0-306-71847-2). Da Capo.

Memoirs & Opinions: Nineteen-Twenty-Six to Nineteen-Seventy-Four. Allen Tate. LC 75-10757. 225p. 1975. 10.95 (ISBN 0-8040-0662-8). Swallow.

Memoirs & Remains of R. M. M'Cheyne. Andrew A. Bonar. 1978. 14.95 (ISBN 0-85151-084-1). Banner of Truth.

Memoirs of a Castrato. Henry L. Young. 1981. 7.95 (ISBN 0-533-04707-2). Vantage.

Memoirs of a Cavalier. Daniel Defoe. LC 74-170545. (Novel in England, 1700-1775 Ser). lib. bdg. 50.00 (ISBN 0-8240-0546-5). Garland Pub.

Memoirs of a Certain Island Adjacent to the Kingdom of Utopia, Vol. 45. Eliza Haywood. LC 75-170564. (Novel in England, 1700-1775 Ser). lib. bdg. 50.00 (ISBN 0-8240-0557-0). Garland Pub.

Memoirs of a Conservative. R. Rhodes-James. 1970. 9.95 o.s.i. (ISBN 0-02-602490-X). Macmillan.

Memoirs of a Coquet, or the History of Miss Harriet Airy, 1765. Ed. by Michael F. Shugrue. (Flowering of the Novel, 1740-1775 Ser: Vol. 70). 1974. lib. bdg. 50.00 (ISBN 0-8240-1169-4). Garland Pub.

Memoirs of a Coxcomb. John Cleland. LC 74-14913. (Novel in England, 1700-1775 Ser). 1974. Repr. of 1751 ed. lib. bdg. 50.00 (ISBN 0-8240-1132-5). Garland Pub.

Memoirs of a Dutiful Daughter. Simone De Beauvoir. 1974. pap. 4.95 (ISBN 0-06-090351-1, CN351, CN). Har-Row.

Memoirs of a Fox-Hunting Man. Siegfried Sassoon. 313p. 1980. pap. 6.95 (ISBN 0-571-06454-X, Pub. by Faber & Faber). Merrimack Bk Serv.

Memoirs of a Ghillie. Gregor Mackenzie. LC 78-52176. 1978. 16.95 (ISBN 0-7153-7584-9). David & Charles.

Memoirs of a Lawman. Ed. by Wilson Rockwell. LC 62-19354. 378p. 1962. 12.95 (ISBN 0-8040-0200-2, SB). Swallow.

Memoirs of a London Doll. new ed. Richard H. Horne. Ed. by Margery Fisher. LC 68-18475. (Illus.). (gr. 3-5). 1968. 4.50g o.s.i. (ISBN 0-02-744540-2). Macmillan.

Memoirs of a Lost World: Special Project. Lascelle De Basily. LC 75-29793. 308p. 1975. 8.00 (ISBN 0-8179-4151-7, Pub.by Laselle de Basily). Hoover Inst Pr.

Memoirs of a Magdalen, or, the History of Louisa Mildmay, 1767, 2 vols. in 1. Hugh Kelly. LC 74-16055. (Novel in England, 1700-1775 Ser). 1974. lib. bdg. 50.00 (ISBN 0-8240-1175-9). Garland Pub.

Memoirs of a Mathematician Manque. Jagjit Singh. 176p. 1980. text ed. 15.00x (ISBN 0-7069-1128-8, Pub. by Vikas India). Advent Bk.

Memoirs of a Modern Scotland. Ed. by Karl Miller. (Illus.). 1970. 7.95 (ISBN 0-571-08750-7, Pub. by Faber & Faber). Merrimack Bk Serv.

Memoirs of a Natural-Born Expatriate. Richard McBride. LC 66-25960. 115p. 1966. 5.95 (ISBN 0-8040-0201-0); pap. 2.75 (ISBN 0-8040-0202-9). Swallow.

Memoirs of a Naturalist. Herbert L. Stoddard. LC 69-16713. (Illus.). 303p. (Orig.). 1969. 15.95 (ISBN 0-8061-0857-6); pap. 6.95 (ISBN 0-8061-1167-4). U of Okla Pr.

Memoirs of a Peg-Top. Mary J. Kilner. Ed. by Alison Lurie & Justin G. Schiller. LC 75-32145. (Classics of Children's Literature Ser.: 1621-1932). PLB 38.00 (ISBN 0-8240-2268-8). Garland Pub.

Memoirs of a Revolutionary, 1901-1944. Victor Serge. Tr. by Peter Sedgwick. (Oxford Paperbacks Ser). (Orig.). 1967. pap. 8.95x (ISBN 0-19-281037-5). Oxford U Pr.

Memoirs of a White Crow Indian. Thomas H. Leforge. Narrated by Thomas B. Marquis. LC 74-6222. xxiv, 356p. 1974. 14.95x (ISBN 0-8032-0885-5); pap. 6.50 (ISBN 0-8032-5800-3, BB 584, Bison). U of Nebr Pr.

Memoirs of Aaron Burr, 2 Vols. Ed. by M. L. Davis. LC 73-152836. (Era of the American Revolution Ser). 1971. Repr. of 1836 ed. Set. lib. bdg. 65.00 (ISBN 0-306-70139-1). Da Capo.

Memoirs of American Prisons: An Annotated Bibliography. Daniel Suvak. LC 78-11107. 1979. lib. bdg. 11.00 (ISBN 0-8108-1180-4). Scarecrow.

Memoirs of an Alaskan Farmer. Ray Rebarchek. LC 79-56330. 1981. 8.95 (ISBN 0-533-04526-6). Vantage.

Memoirs of an American Prima Donna. Clara L. Kellogg. LC 77-16534. (Music Reprint Ser., 1978). (Illus.). 1978. Repr. of 1913 ed. lib. bdg. 32.50 (ISBN 0-306-77527-1). Da Capo.

Memoirs of an Anti-Semite. Gregor Von Rezzori. 1981. 13.95 (ISBN 0-670-46783-9). Viking Pr.

Memoirs of an Anti-Zionist Jew. Elmer Berger. 159p. (Orig.). 1978. pap. 5.00x (ISBN 0-911038-87-6, Inst Hist Rev). Noontide.

Memoirs of an Oxford Scholar, Containing His Amour with the Beautiful Miss L., of Essex. LC 74-31077. (Novel in England, 1700-1775 Ser). 1974. Repr. of 1756 ed. lib. bdg. 50.00 (ISBN 0-8240-1145-7). Garland Pub.

Memoirs of an Unfortunate Young Nobleman, Returned from a Thirteen Years' Slavery in America, 1743. James Annesley. LC 75-16366. (Novel in England, 1700-1775 Ser). 1974. lib. bdg. 50.00 (ISBN 0-8240-1107-4). Garland Pub.

Memoirs of Arthur Hamilton B.A. A. C. Benson. LC 76-20043. (Decadent Consciousness Ser.: Vol. 4). 1977. Repr. of 1886 ed. lib. bdg. 38.00 (ISBN 0-8240-2753-1). Garland Pub.

Memoirs of Bartholomew Fair. Henry Morley. LC 67-24348. 1968. Repr. of 1880 ed. 20.00 (ISBN 0-8103-3495-X). Gale.

Memoirs of Bryan Perdue, 3 vols. Thomas Holcroft. Ed. by Ronald Paulson. LC 78-60851. (Novel 1720-1805 Ser.: Vol. 15). 1979. Set. lib. bdg. 93.00 (ISBN 0-8240-3664-6); lib. bdg. 31.00 ea. Garland Pub.

Memoirs of Carl Flesch. Carl Flesch. (Music Reprint Ser.). 1979. Repr. of 1957 ed. lib. bdg. 29.50 (ISBN 0-306-77574-3). Da Capo.

Memoirs of Charles Dennis Rusoe d'Eres, a Native of Canada, Who Was with the Scanyawtauragahrooote Indians Eleven Years, Repr. Of 1800 Ed. Bd. with Life & Travels of James Tudor Owen. Repr. of 1801 ed; Connecticut, Rhode Island, Massachusetts, New Hampshire & Vermont Farmers Almanac for 1803... Also Containing an Affecting Account of the Death of Miss Polly & Hannah Watts... Taken Prisoners & Murdered by the Indians. Repr. of 1802 ed. LC 75-7047. (Indian Captivities Ser.: Vol. 25). 1977. lib. bdg. 44.00 (ISBN 0-8240-1649-1). Garland Pub.

Memoirs of Emma Courtney, 2 vols. Mary Hays. (Feminist Controversy in England, 1788-1810 Ser.). 1974. Set. lib. bdg. 76.00 (ISBN 0-8240-0870-7); lib. bdg. 50.00 ea. Garland Pub.

Memoirs of George E. Harmon. (Illus.). 56p. 0.60; 2 copies 1.00. Faith Pub Hse.

Memoirs of Heinrich Schliemann. Ed. by Leo Deuel. LC 74-15820. (Illus.). 320p. 1977. 25.00 o.s.i. (ISBN 0-06-011106-2, HarpT). Har-Row.

Memoirs of Henry Villard, 2 Vols. Henry Villard. Ed. by Fanny G. Villard. LC 72-87695. (American Public Figures Ser). 1969. Repr. of 1904 ed. lib. bdg. 75.00 (ISBN 0-306-71696-8). Da Capo.

Memoirs of Jesus Christ. Marcus Harrison. 1977. pap. 1.95 o.p. (ISBN 0-345-25466-X). Ballantine.

Memoirs of John H. Reagan, Postmaster General of the Confederacy & Early Texas Statesman. John H. Reagan. 12.50 o.p. (ISBN 0-8363-0068-8). Jenkins.

Memoirs of Li Tsung-Jen. Ed. by T. K. Tong & Li Tsung-Jen. 1979. lib. bdg. 33.00x (ISBN 0-89158-343-2). Westview.

Memoirs of Madame Desbordes-Valmore: With a Selection from Her Poems. Charles A. Sainte-Beuve. Tr. by Harriet W. Preston from Fr. LC 77-11483. (Symbolists Ser.). 240p. 1980. Repr. of 1873 ed. 27.50 (ISBN 0-404-16344-0). AMS Pr.

Memoirs of Madame Malibran De Beriot. Isaac Nathan. LC 80-2291. 1981. Repr. of 1836 ed. 18.50 (ISBN 0-404-18860-5). AMS Pr.

Memoirs of Marshal G. Zhukov. Marshal G. Zhukov. 1971. 15.00 o.p. (ISBN 0-440-05571-7, Sey Lawr). Delacorte.

Memoirs of Miles Byrne, 3 vols. in one. Miles Byrne. Repr. of 1863 ed. 36.00x (ISBN 0-686-28340-6, Pub. by Irish Academic Pr). Biblio Dist.

Memoirs of Modern Philosophers: A Novel, 3 vols. Elizabeth Hamilton. Ed. by Gina Luria. (Feminist Controversy in England, 1788-1810). 1974. lib. bdg. 50.00 ea. (ISBN 0-8240-0866-9). Garland Pub.

Memoirs of Peter Henry Bruce: A Military Officer in the Services of Prussia, Russia, & Great Britian. Peter H. Bruce. (Russia Through European Eyes Ser). 1970. Repr. of 1782 ed. 49.50 (ISBN 0-306-77029-6). Da Capo.

Memoirs of Philippe De Commynes, Vol. 1, Bks 1-5 & Vol. 2, Bks. 6-8. Philippe De Commynes. Ed. by Samuel Kinser. Tr. by Isabelle Cazeaux from Fr. LC 68-9363. (Illus.). 1969. Vol. 1. 19.50x (ISBN 0-87249-224-9); Vol. 2. 19.50x (ISBN 0-87249-224-9); Set. 37.50x (ISBN 0-87249-199-4). U of SC Pr.

Memoirs of Prince Metternich, 1773-1835, 5 Vols. Clemens V. Metternich. LC 68-9611. 1970. Repr. of 1881 ed. Set. 85.00 (ISBN 0-86527-128-3). Fertig.

Memoirs of Prota Matija Nenadovic. Proto M. Nenadovic. Ed. by Lovett F. Edwards. 1969. 10.25x o.p. (ISBN 0-19-821476-6). Oxford U Pr.

Memoirs of Rear-Admiral Paul Jones. John Paul Jones. LC 77-166333. (Era of the American Revolution Ser.). (Illus.). 1972. Repr. of 1830 ed. lib. bdg. 45.00 (ISBN 0-306-70247-9). Da Capo.

Memoirs of Richard Nixon, Vol. 1. Richard Nixon. 736p. 1981. pap. 2.95 (ISBN 0-446-93259-0). Warner Bks.

Memoirs of Richard Nixon, Vol. 2. Richard Nixon. 728p. 1981. pap. 2.95 (ISBN 0-446-93260-4). Warner Bks.

Memoirs of Sherlock Holmes. Arthur Conan Doyle. (gr. 10 up). pap. 1.95 (ISBN 0-425-04821-7, Medallion). Berkley Pub.

Memoirs of Signior Guadentio Di Lucca. Simon Berington. LC 74-170596. (Novel in England, 1700-1775 Ser.). lib. bdg. 50.00 (ISBN 0-8240-0578-3). Garland Pub.

Memoirs of the Author of a Vindication of the Rights of Woman. William Godwin. (Feminist Controversy in England, 1788-1810 Ser.). 1974. lib. bdg. 50.00 (ISBN 0-8240-0861-8). Garland Pub.

Memoirs of the Baron Du Tan, to Which Is Added the Calabrian or, the History of Charles Brachy, & the Hermit, 1744. Madeleine Angelique Poisson De Gomez. LC 74-16060. (Novel in England, 1700-1775 Ser). 1974. lib. bdg. 50.00 (ISBN 0-8240-1111-2). Garland Pub.

Memoirs of the Celebrated & Beautiful Mrs. Ann Carson, Daughter of an Officer of the U. S. Navy & Wife of Another, Whose Life Terminated in the Philadelphia Prison, 2 vols. in 1. Ann Carson. Ed. by Annette K. Baxter. LC 79-8780. (Signal Lives Ser.). 1980. Repr. of 1838 ed. lib. bdg. 37.00x (ISBN 0-405-12829-0). Arno.

Memoirs of the Four-Foot Colonel, Data Paper No. 113. Smith Dun. 125p. 1980. 6.00 (ISBN 0-87727-113-5). Cornell SE Asia.

Memoirs of the Life & Adventures of Tsonnonthouan, a King of the Indian Nation Called Roundheads, 1763, 2 vols. in 1. (Novel in England, 1700-1775 Ser). 1974. lib. bdg. 50.00 (ISBN 0-8240-1164-3). Garland Pub.

Memoirs of the Life & Times of the Famous Jonathan Wilde. Alexander Smith. LC 76-170567. (Foundations of the Novel Ser.: Vol. 48). lib. bdg. 50.00 (ISBN 0-8240-0560-0). Garland Pub.

Memoirs of the Life & Writings of the Abate Metastasio, 3 Vols. Charles Burney. LC 76-162295. (Music Ser) 1971. Repr. of 1796 ed. lib. bdg. 95.00 (ISBN 0-306-71110-9). Da Capo.

Memoirs of the Opera, 2 vols. G. Hogarth. LC 71-166101. (Music Ser.). 1972. Repr. of 1851 ed. Set. lib. bdg. 49.50 (ISBN 0-306-70256-8). Da Capo.

Memoirs of the Peace Conference, 2 vols. David Lloyd George. 1939. Set. 75.00x (ISBN 0-686-51415-7). Elliots Bks.

Memoirs of the Polish Baroque: The Writings of Jan Chryzostom Pasek, a Squire of the Commonwealth of Poland & Lithuania. Jan C. Pasek. Ed. by Catherine S. Leach. LC 74-77731. 1977. 32.50 (ISBN 0-520-02752-3, CAL 447); pap. 5.95 (ISBN 0-520-04089-9). U of Cal Pr.

Memoirs of the Remarkable Life & Surprizing Adventures of Miss Jenny Cameron: Philamours & Philamena; or, Genuine Memoirs of a Late Affecting Transaction, 1746. Archibald Arbuthnot. LC 74-26901. (Novel in England, 1700-1775 Ser). 1974. lib. bdg. 50.00 (ISBN 0-8240-1117-1). Garland Pub.

Memoirs of the Twentieth Century: Being Original Letters of State Under George the Sixth. Samuel Madden. LC 74-170588. (Foundations of the Novel Ser.: Vol. 58). lib. bdg. 50.00 (ISBN 0-8240-0570-8). Garland Pub.

Memoirs of the Verney Family, 1465-1696, 4 vols. Frances P. Verney. Incl. Vol. I. During the Civil War. 362p. Vol. II. During the Civil War. 454p; Vol. III During the Commonwealth, 1650-1660. 494p; Vol. IV. From the Restoration to the Revolution, 1660-1692. 510p. (Illus.). 1971. Repr. of 1892 ed. Set. 145.00x (ISBN 0-7130-0021-X, Pub. by Woburn Pr England). Biblio Dist.

Memoirs of the Year Two Thousand Five Hundred, 1772, 2 vols. in 1. Sebastien Mercier. LC 74-16201. (Novel in England, 1700-1775 Ser). 1974. lib. bdg. 50.00 (ISBN 0-8240-1199-6). Garland Pub.

Memoirs of War, Nineteen Fourteen to Nineteen Fifteen. Marc Bloch. Tr. by Carole Fink from Fr. LC 79-6849. Orig. Title: Souvenirs De Guerre. (Illus.). 184p. 1980. 15.00 (ISBN 0-8014-1220-X). Cornell U Pr.

Memoirs of William Hickey. Ed. by Peter Quennell. (Illus.). 470p. 1975. 25.00 (ISBN 0-7100-8129-4). Routledge & Kegan.

Memoirs, Official & Personal. Thomas L. McKenney. LC 72-94789. xxvii, 340p. 1973. pap. 3.95 (ISBN 0-8032-5776-7, BB 565, Bison). U of Nebr Pr.

Memoirs, 1870-1873. Louis A. Thiers. LC 79-80598. 834p. 1973. Repr. of 1915 ed. 19.50 (ISBN 0-86527-329-4). Fertig.

Memoirs, 1942-1943. Benito Mussolini. Ed. by Raymond Klibansky. Tr. by Frances Lobb from It. xxviii, 320p. 1975. Repr. of 1949 ed. 20.00 (ISBN 0-86527-126-7). Fertig.

Memoirs...of Captain Mackheath, Repr. Of 1728. Ed. by Michael F. Shugrue. Bd. with Trip to the Moon. Repr. of 1728 ed; Adventures of Abdalla. Jean P. Bignon. Repr. of 1729 ed. LC 79-170573. (Foundations of a Novel Ser.). lib. bdg. 50.00 (ISBN 0-8240-0564-3). Garland Pub.

Memorable Quotations of John F. Kennedy. Maxwell Meyersohn. LC 65-21411. 1965. 6.95 o.s.i. (ISBN 0-690-53070-6, TYC-T). T Y Crowell.

Memorandum. Vaclav Havel. Tr. by Vera Blackwell from Czech. LC 80-485. 160p. 1980. pap. 5.95 (ISBN 0-394-17653-7, E446, Ever). Grove.

Memorandum on Unfair Competition at the Common Law. U. S. Federal Trade Commission. 305p. 1980. Repr. of 1916 ed. lib. bdg. 28.50x (ISBN 0-8377-1228-9). Rothman.

Memorial. Christopher Isherwood. LC 72-106718. Repr. of 1946 ed. lib. bdg. 22.50x (ISBN 0-8371-3544-3). Irvington.

Memorial Feast for Kokotoy-Khan: A Kirghiz Epic Poem. Ed. by A. T. Hatto. (London Oriental Ser.). 1977. 89.00x (ISBN 0-19-713593-5). Oxford U Pr.

Memorial Hall Murder. Jane Langton. 1981. pap. 2.95 (ISBN 0-14-005704-8). Penguin.

Memorials for Children of Change: The Art of Early New England Stonecarving. Dickran Tashjian & Ann Tashjian. LC 73-6006. (Illus.). 336p. 1974. 27.95x (ISBN 0-8195-4061-7, Pub. by Wesleyan U Pr). Columbia U Pr.

Memorials: Nineteen Seventy-Eight Descendents, Vol. 10. LC 73-76887. (Illus.). 1980. pap. 10.00 (ISBN 0-8137-8078-0). Geol Soc.

Memorials: Nineteen Seventy-Seven Decedents. Ed. by Geological Society of America. LC 73-76887. (Vol. 9). (Illus.). 1979. pap. 9.00 (ISBN 0-8137-8077-2). Geol Soc.

Memorials of a Half-Century in Michigan & the Lake Region. Bela Hubbard. LC 75-23322. (Illus.). 1978. Repr. of 1888 ed. 22.00 (ISBN 0-8103-4268-5). Gale.

Memorials of a Southern Planter. Susan D. Smedes. Ed. by Fletcher M. Green. 408p. pap. 8.95 (ISBN 0-87805-132-5). U Pr of Miss.

Memorials of Ancient Wrongs. Peter Everett. 1980. 10.95 (ISBN 0-316-25837-7). Little.

Memorials of Sarah Childress Polk: Wife of the Eleventh President of the United States. Anson Nelson & Fanny Nelson. LC 73-22435. (Illus.). 322p. 1974. Repr. of 1892 ed. 16.75 (ISBN 0-87152-163-6). Reprint.

Memorials of the Faithful. Abdu'l-Baha. Tr. by Marzieh Gail. LC 77-15797. 1971. 9.00 (ISBN 0-87743-041-1, 7-06-12). Baha'i.

Memorials of the Quick & the Dead. Maureen Duffy. 1979. 14.95 (ISBN 0-241-10316-9, Pub. by Hamish Hamilton England). David & Charles.

Memories & Adventures. Louise Heritte-Viardot. LC 77-22220. (Music Reprint Ser.). (Illus.). 1977. Repr. of 1913 ed. lib. bdg. 25.00 (ISBN 0-306-77515-8). Da Capo.

Memories & Commentaries. Igor Stravinsky & Robert Craft. (Orig.). 1981. pap. 4.95 (ISBN 0-520-04402-9, CAL 502). U of Cal Pr.

Memories Are Like Dying Embers. Diana Levy. 40p. 1980. 4.95 (ISBN 0-533-04286-0). Vantage.

Memories, Dreams, Reflections. rev. ed. C. G. Jung. Ed. by Aniela Jaffe. Tr. by Richard Winston & Clara Winston. LC 62-14264. 1963. 17.50 (ISBN 0-394-43580-X). Pantheon.

Memories of a Catholic Girlhood. Mary McCarthy. LC 57-8842. (Illus.). 1957. 4.75 o.p. (ISBN 0-15-158859-7). HarBraceJ.

Memories of a Catholic Girlhood. Mary McCarthy. LC 57-8842. 1972. pap. 3.95 (ISBN 0-15-658650-9, HB231, Harv). HarBraceJ.

Memories of Abdu'l-Baha: Recollections of the Early Days of the Baha'i Faith in California. Ramona A. Brown. LC 79-16412. (Illus.). 1980. 10.00 (ISBN 0-87743-128-0, 7-32-10); pap. 5.00 (ISBN 0-87743-139-6, 7-32-11). Baha'i.

Memories of Afghanistan. M. H. Anwar. 1981. 8.95 (ISBN 0-8062-1696-4). Carlton.

Memories of an American Impressionist. Abel G. Warshawsky. Ed. by Ben L. Bassham. LC 80-82203. (Illus.). 259p. 1980. 17.50 (ISBN 0-87338-249-8). Kent St U Pr.

Memories of Another Day. Harold Robbins. 1980. pap. 3.50. PB.

Memories of Evil Days. Julien Green. Ed. by Jean-Pierre J. Piriou. LC 75-44037. 200p. 1976. 13.95x (ISBN 0-8139-0553-2). U Pr of Va.

Memories of Gurdjieff. A. L. Staveley. 1978. 6.95 (ISBN 0-89756-025-6). Two Rivers.

Memories of My Father. Kermit Roosevelt. (Illus.). 98p. Date not set. Repr. of 1920 ed. 44.85 (ISBN 0-89901-026-1). Found Class Reprints.

Memories of the Future. Paul Horgan. 216p. 1966. 4.95 (ISBN 0-374-20756-9). FS&G.

Memories of the Industrial Workers of the World (IWW) Elizabeth G. Flynn. (Occasional Papers: No. 24). 1977. 1.00 (ISBN 0-89977-025-8). Am Inst Marxist.

Memories of the Lakes. Dana T. Bowen. 1946. 9.50 (ISBN 0-685-11635-2). Freshwater.

Memories of the Moderns. Harry Levin. LC 80-36827. 256p. 1980. 15.95 (ISBN 0-8112-0733-1). New Directions.

Memories of the Opera. Guilio Gatti-Casazza. 1980. 19.95 (ISBN 0-7145-3518-4); pap. 9.95 (ISBN 0-7145-3665-2). Riverrun NY.

Memory & Cognition. W. Kintsch. LC 76-49031. 1977. 22.95x (ISBN 0-471-48072-X). Wiley.

Memory & Dreams: A Modern Physics Approach. C. Torda. (Illus.). 453p. 1980. 24.95. Walters.
Memory & Storage Technolgy, Vol II. Ed. by Stephen W. Miller. (Information Technology Ser.). (Illus.). 182p. 1977. pap. 20.00 (ISBN 0-88283-015-5). AFIPS Pr.
Memory Book. Jerry Lucas & Harry Lorayne. 224p. 1975. pap. 1.95 (ISBN 0-345-27808-9). Ballantine.
Memory Design: Microcomputers to Mainframes. Electronics Magazine. Ed. by Laurence Altman. LC 77-26332. (Illus.). 180p. 1978. pap. text ed. 12.95 (ISBN 0-07-099718-7, R-732). McGraw.
Memory Dynamics: A Complete Memory System. William Fauver & Robert L. Birch. 1981. 49.95; spiral binding 39.95. Knowledge Bank.
Memory: How It Works & How to Improve It. Roy A. Gallant. LC 79-6342. (Illus.). 128p. (gr. 7 up). 1980. 8.95 (ISBN 0-590-07613-2, Four Winds). Schol Bk Serv.
Memory in a House. Lucy M. Boston. LC 73-10690. (Illus.). 152p. 1974. 6.95 o.s.i. (ISBN 0-02-513730-1, 51373). Macmillan.
Memory Made Easy: The Complete Book of Memory Training. Robert L. Montgomery. (Illus.). 1979. 10.95 (ISBN 0-8144-5523-9). Am Mgmt.
Memory Matters. Mark Brown. LC 77-71252. (Illus.). 1977. 14.50x (ISBN 0-8448-1091-6). Crane-Russak Co.
Memory of a Large Christmas. Lillian Smith. (Illus.). 96p. 1980. pap. 2.95 (ISBN 0-393-00038-9). Norton.
Memory of Eva Ryker. Donald Stanwood. 1979. pap. 2.50 o.s.i. (ISBN 0-440-15550-9). Dell.
Memory of Old Jack. Wendell Berry. LC 73-15432. 1974. 6.95 o.p. (ISBN 0-15-158865-1). HarBraceJ.
Memory of Old Jack. Wendell Berry. LC 75-6530. 223p. 1975. pap. 3.50 (ISBN 0-15-658670-3, HPL64, HPL). HarBraceJ.
Memory, Related Functions & Age. Jack Botwinick & Martha Storandt. (Illus.). 208p. 1974. 18.75 (ISBN 0-398-03143-6). C C Thomas.
Memory: Surprising New Insights into How We Remember & Why We Forget. Elizbeth Loftus. (Illus.). 224p. 1980. (ISBN 0-201-04473-0); pap. 5.95 (ISBN 0-201-04474-9). A-W.
Memory Systems Design & Applications. Dave Bursky. 240p. pap. 11.95 (ISBN 0-8104-0980-1). Hayden.
Memos from Egypt: Joint U.S. Egyptian Study Group on Building Materials & Building Technology. William Caudill. LC 75-13629. 260p. 1975. pap. 9.95 (ISBN 0-8436-0157-4). CBI Pub.
Memos from Purgatory. Harlan Ellison. 1975. pap. 1.50 o.s.i. (ISBN 0-515-03706-0, V3706). Jove Pubns.
Memphis Blues. Bengt Olsson. (Paul Oliver Blues Ser.). pap. 2.95 (ISBN 0-913714-48-8). Legacy Bks.
Memphis Commercial Appeal: The History of a Southern Newspaper. Thomas H. Baker. LC 74-165066. 1971. 20.00 (ISBN 0-8071-0944-4). La State U Pr.
Memphis During the Progressive Era, 1900-1917. William D. Miller. (Illus.). 242p. 1957. 10.00 (ISBN 0-87057-043-9, Pub. by Brown U Pr). Univ Pr of New England.
Memphis Memoirs. Paul R. Coppock. LC 80-24019. (Illus.). 265p. 1980. 14.95 (ISBN 0-87870-110-9). Memphis St Univ.
Men! LaVada Weir. LC 74-974. (Laurie Newman Adventures Ser). 32p. (gr. 3-9). 1974. 5.95 (ISBN 0-87191-336-4). Creative Ed.
Men: A Book for Women. Ed. by James Wagenvoord. 1978. pap. 7.95 (ISBN 0-380-40212-2, 45708). Avon.
Men Against McCarthy. Richard M. Fried. 376p. 1976. 22.50x (ISBN 0-231-03872-0); pap. 10.00x (ISBN 0-231-08360-2). Columbia U Pr.
Men Against the Clouds. Richard L. Burdsall & Arthur B. Emmons, 3rd. LC 79-25369. (Illus.). 1980. pap. 9.95 (ISBN 0-916890-93-7). Mountaineers.
Men & Beasts. Rhodri Jones. (Themes Ser.). pap. text ed. 1.95x o.p. (ISBN 0-435-14480-4); tchr's ed. 2.95x o.p. (ISBN 0-435-14484-7). Heinemann Ed.
Men & Books Famous in the Law. Frederick C. Hicks. LC 72-81454. (Illus.). vi, 259p. 1972. Repr. of 1921 ed. 20.00x (ISBN 0-8377-2230-6). Rothman.
Men & Brethren. James G. Cozzens. LC 36-755. (Illus.). 1958. 4.00 o.p. (ISBN 0-15-159135-0). HarBraceJ.
Men & Discoveries in Chemistry. B. Morgan. (Illus.). (gr. 9 up). 1962. 7.50 (ISBN 0-7195-0944-0). Transatlantic.
Men & Discoveries in Electricity. B. Morgan. (Illus.). (gr. 9 up). 6.95 (ISBN 0-7195-0943-2). Transatlantic.
Men & Discoveries in Mathematics. Bryan Morgan. 1972. 10.95 (ISBN 0-7195-2587-X). Transatlantic.
Men & Discoveries in Mathematics. Bryan Morgan. 235p. 1980. 15.00x (ISBN 0-7195-2587-X, Pub. by Murray Pubs England). State Mutual Bk.
Men & Family Planning. Bruce Stokes. (Worldwatch Papers Ser.). 1980. pap. 2.00 (ISBN 0-916468-40-2). Worldwatch Inst.
Men & Horses. Ross Santee. LC 76-57158. (Illus.). 1977. 11.95x (ISBN 0-8032-0919-3); pap. 3.50 (ISBN 0-8032-5859-3, BB 639, Bison). U of Nebr Pr.
Men & Ideas in Economics: A Dictionary of World Economists Past & Present. Ludwig H. Mai. (Quality Paperbacks Ser.: No. 284). 270p. (Orig.). 1977. pap. 4.95 (ISBN 0-8226-0284-9). Littlefield.
Men & Institutions in American Mathematics. J. Dalton Tarwater et al. (Graduate Studies: No. 13). (Orig.). 1976. pap. 6.00 (ISBN 0-89672-023-3). Tex Tech Pr.
Men & Machines of American Journalism: A Pictorial Essay. Peter C. Marzio. LC 73-5371. (Illus.). 144p. 1973. pap. 4.95 (ISBN 0-87474-629-9). Smithsonian.
Men & Measures of Half a Century. Hugh McCulloch. LC 77-87404. (American Scene Ser.). 1969. Repr. of 1888 ed. lib. bdg. 55.00 (ISBN 0-306-71548-1). Da Capo.
Men & Milestones of the Middle Ages. Gordon P. Stillman. (gr. 9-11). 1970. pap. text ed. 4.50x (ISBN 0-88334-029-1). Ind Sch Pr.
Men & Mules on a Mission of Democracy. P. Sharma. 5.50x o.p. (ISBN 0-210-33704-4). Asia.
Men & Music in Western Culture. D. Walter. 1969. pap. 8.95 o.p. (ISBN 0-13-574871-2). P-H.
Men & Nations. Louis J. Halle. 1962. 15.00x o.p. (ISBN 0-691-07123-3); pap. 5.95 o.p. (ISBN 0-691-01954-1). Princeton U Pr.
Men & Societies: Experimental Courses in the Humanities & Social Sciences. Robert I. Smith. 1968. text ed. 6.50 o.p. (ISBN 0-435-80835-4). Heinemann Ed.
Men & Their Sex. Robert L. Rowan. (Illus.). 159p. 1979. 12.50 (ISBN 0-934200-01-7); pap. 6.95. Irvington.
Men & Their Work. Everett C. Hughes. LC 80-29143. 184p. 1981. Repr. of 1958 ed. lib. bdg. 17.50x (ISBN 0-313-22791-8, HUMW). Greenwood.
Men & Women. Robert Browning. Ed. by Paul Turner. 1972. pap. 6.95x (ISBN 0-19-911019-0). Oxford U Pr.
Men & Women. Peter Swerdloff. (Human Behavior Ser.). 176p. 1975. 9.95 (ISBN 0-8094-1924-6); lib. bdg. avail. (ISBN 0-685-53585-1). Time-Life.
Men & Women. Peter Swerdloff. LC 75-10885. (Human Behavior). (Illus.). (gr. 5 up). 1975. PLB 9.99 o.p. (ISBN 0-8094-1925-4, Pub. by Time-Life). Silver.
Men & Women Use... Menus. Tina Wold & John Frost. LC 80-68806. 120p. (Orig.). 1980. pap. 5.95 (ISBN 0-9604802-0-X). Frost Art.
Men at War: The Best War Stories of All Time. Hemmingway. Date not set. 5.98 (ISBN 0-517-02084-X). Bonanza.
Men at Work. C. R. Bell. (Advances in Psychology). (Illus.). 1974. pap. text ed. 5.95x (ISBN 0-04-150046-6). Allen Unwin.
Men at Work. Rhodri Jons. (Themes Ser.). pap. text ed. 2.95x o.p. (ISBN 0-435-14490-1); tchr's ed. 0.95x o.p. (ISBN 0-435-14491-X). Heinemann Ed.
Men at Work: Applications of Ergonomics to Performance & Design. Roy J. Shephard. (Illus.). 408p. 1974. 32.75 (ISBN 0-398-02965-2). C C Thomas.
Men for the Mountains. Sid Marty. LC 78-71651. 1979. 12.95 (ISBN 0-8149-0812-8). Vanguard.
Men for the Mountains. Sid Marty. (Illus.). 272p. 1981. Repr. of 1978 ed. pap. 6.95 (ISBN 0-89886-027-X). Mountaineers.
Men from P.I.G. & R.O.B.O.T. Harry Harrison. LC 77-22875. (gr. 5 up). 1978. 7.95 (ISBN 0-689-30634-2). Atheneum.
Men from the Village Deep in the Mountains, & Other Japanese Folk Tales. Tr. & illus. by Garrett Bang. LC 72-92431. (Illus.). 96p. (gr. 3-6). 1973. 7.95 (ISBN 0-02-708350-0). Macmillan.
Men Homeward. A. A. Cleary. 54p. 1980. pap. 5.95x (ISBN 0-904461-35-1, Pub. by Ceolfrith Pr England). Intl Schol Bk Serv.
Men in a Developing Society: Geographic & Social Mobility in Monterrey, Mexico. Jorge Balan et al. LC 72-6282. (Latin American Monographs Ser.: No. 30). 432p. 1973. 15.00x (ISBN 0-292-75004-8). U of Tex Pr.
Men in Arms: A History of Warfare & Its Interrelationships with Western Society. rev. ed. 2nd ed. Richard A. Preston & Sidney Wise. LC 76-101676. (Illus.). 440p. (Orig.). 1970. pap. text ed. 11.95 (ISBN 0-03-045681-9). Praeger.
Men in Cages. H. U. Triston. LC 70-174122. (Illus.). 1971. Repr. of 1938 ed. 20.00 (ISBN 0-8103-3801-7). Gale.
Men in Difficult Times: Masculinity Today & Tomorrow. Ed. by Robert A. Lewis. (Illus.). 352p. 1981. 14.95 (ISBN 0-13-574418-0, Spectrum); pap. 7.95 (ISBN 0-13-574400-8). P-H.
Men in Her Death. Anne Morice. 224p. 1981. 9.95 (ISBN 0-312-52939-2). St Martin.
Men in Love, Male Sexual Fantasies: The Triump of Love Over Rage. Nancy Friday. 1981. pap. 3.50 (ISBN 0-440-15404-9). Dell.
Men in Mid-Career: A Study of British Managers & Technical Specialists. Cyril Sofer. (Studies in Sociology: No. 4). 1970. 29.95 (ISBN 0-521-07788-5); pap. 14.95x (ISBN 0-521-09606-5). Cambridge U Pr.
Men in Rebellion: Higher Governmental Leaders & the Coming of the American Revolution. James K. Martin. 1973. 16.00 (ISBN 0-8135-0750-2). Rutgers U Pr.
Men in Space. Thomas D. Segal. LC 75-28519. (Illus.). 225p. 1975. 19.95 (ISBN 0-87364-033-0). Paladin Ent.
Men in the Middle: Leadership & Role Conflict in a Nigerian Society. Alvin Magid. LC 75-42145. 1976. text ed. 29.50x o.p. (ISBN 0-8419-0254-2, Africana). Holmes & Meier.
Men in the Sun. Ghassan Kanafani. Tr. by Hilary Kilpatrik from Arabic. 1978. 8.00 (ISBN 0-89410-021-1); pap. 5.00 (ISBN 0-89410-022-X). Three Continents.
Men in White. Wallace Rayburn. 1975. 8.95 o.p. (ISBN 0-7207-0831-1, Pub. by Michael Joseph). Merrimack Bk Serv.
Men Loving Men: A Gay Sex Guide & Consciousness Book. Mitchell Walker. 1977. pap. 8.95 o.p. (ISBN 0-917342-52-6, Pub. by Gay Sunshine). Bookpeople.
Men, Money & Medicine. Eli Ginzberg & Miriam Ostow. LC 79-101134. 1970. 17.50x (ISBN 0-231-03366-4). Columbia U Pr.
Men of Action: A History of the U. S. Life Saving Service on the Pacific Coast. Ernest L. Osborne & Victor West. LC 80-69563. (Illus.). 150p. (Orig.). 1981. pap. 10.00 (ISBN 0-932368-05-0). Bandon Hist.
Men of Albemarle. Inglis Fletcher. 512p. 1980. pap. 2.75 (ISBN 0-553-13394-2). Bantam.
Men of Bastogne. Fred MacKenzie. 1978. pap. 1.95 (ISBN 0-441-52442-7). Charter Bks.
Men of Cajamarca: A Social & Biographical Study of the First Conquerors of Peru. James Lockhart. LC 72-185236. (Latin American Monographs: No. 27). 490p. 1972. 17.95 (ISBN 0-292-75001-3). U of Tex Pr.
Men of Conscience. Brian Inglis. LC 76-116780. (Illus.). 1971. 10.00 o.s.i. (ISBN 0-02-558190-2). Macmillan.
Men of Denwich: The Story of a Vanished Town. Rowland Parker. LC 78-14167. (Illus.). 1979. 11.95 o.p. (ISBN 0-03-046801-9). HR&W.
Men of Letters in Colonial Maryland. J. Leo Lemay. LC 79-177357. (Illus.). 428p. 1972. 18.50x (ISBN 0-87049-137-7). U of Tenn Pr.
Men of Maize. Miguel A. Asturius. 400p. 1975. 10.00 o.p. (ISBN 0-440-05583-0, Sey Lawr). Delacorte.
Men of Metals. Samuel L. Hoyt. 1979. 18.00 (ISBN 0-87170-059-X). ASM.
Men of the Blue Ghost (USS Lexington CV-16) Historic Events of World War II in the Pacific As Told by the Men Who Lived Them, 1943-6. Lee F. Reese. (Illus.). 980p. 1980. 50.00 (ISBN 0-686-64547-2). Lex Bk Co CA.
Men of the Burma Road. Chiang Yee. (Illus.). (gr. 4-6). 4.50 (ISBN 0-685-20604-1). Transatlantic.
Men of the Covenant. Alexander Smellie. 1975. 13.95 (ISBN 0-85151-212-7). Banner of Truth.
Men of the Hills. Henry Treece. LC 58-5448. (Illus.). (gr. 6-9). 1958. 9.95 (ISBN 0-87599-115-7). S G Phillips.
Men of the Mirage. Kelman Frost. LC 69-14323. (gr. 7-12). 1969. 5.25 o.p. (ISBN 0-688-41602-0); PLB 6.00 (ISBN 0-688-51602-5). Lothrop.
Men-of-War. D. Howarth. Ed. by Time-Life Books. (Seafarers). (Illus.). 1979. 13.95 (ISBN 0-8094-2666-8). Time-Life.
Men of War. David P. Howarth. (Seafarers Ser.). (Illus.). 1978. lib. bdg. 11.97 (ISBN 0-686-50987-0). Silver.
Men on the Move. Nels Anderson. LC 74-7427. (FDR & the Era of the New Deal Ser.). xii, 357p. 1974. Repr. of 1940 ed. lib. bdg. 37.50 (ISBN 0-306-70588-5). Da Capo.
Men Released from Prison. J. Irvin Waller. LC 73-85690. 1974. pap. 7.50 (ISBN 0-8020-6372-1). U of Toronto Pr.
Men to Match My Mountains: The Story of the Opening of the Far West 1840-1900. Irving Stone. LC 56-9405. 1956. 11.95 (ISBN 0-385-04662-6). Doubleday.
Men Under Stress. Roy R. Grinker, Sr. & John Speigel. 1979. Repr. of 1945 ed. 28.50x (ISBN 0-89197-645-0). Irvington.
Men Who Dared the Sea: The Ocean Adventures of the Ancient Mariners. Gardner Soule. LC 75-34451. 1976. 9.95 o.s.i. (ISBN 0-690-01095-8, TYC-T). T Y Crowell.
Men Who Govern: A Biographical Profile of Federal Political Executives. David T. Stanley et al. 1967. 10.95 (ISBN 0-8157-8108-3). Brookings.
Men Who Knew Christ. William S. LaSor. LC 70-135026. (Orig.). 1971. pap. 1.95 o.p. (ISBN 0-8307-0086-2, S252-1-04). Regal.
Men Who Knew God. William S. LaSor. LC 72-109369. pap. 1.65 o.p. (ISBN 0-8307-0064-1, S251108). Regal.
Men Who Rape: The Psychology of the Offender. A. N. Groth. LC 79-18624. 245p. 1979. 15.00 (ISBN 0-306-40268-8, Plenum Pr). Plenum Pub.
Men with the Pink Triangle. Heinz Heger. Tr. by David Fernbach. LC 80-69205. (Illus.). 120p. (Orig.). 1980. pap. 4.95 (ISBN 0-932870-06-6). Carrier Pigeon.
Men Without Mercy. Alfred Doblin. Tr. by Trevor Blewitt & Phyllis Blewitt. LC 75-31978. 446p. 1976. Repr. of 1937 ed. 19.75 (ISBN 0-86527-277-8). Fertig.
Men, Women & Bridge: Startling Tales of the Bridge Table. Richard Crawford. LC 77-93316. (Illus.). 1978. 8.95 (ISBN 0-8069-4934-1); lib. bdg. 8.29 (ISBN 0-8069-4935-X). Sterling.
Men, Women, & Change. Letha D. Scanzoni & John Scanzoni. (Illus.). 576p. 1981. 18.95 (ISBN 0-07-055054-9); instr's manual 5.95 (ISBN 0-07-055055-7). McGraw.
Men, Women & Issues in American History, 2 vols. rev. ed. Ed. by Howard H. Quint & Milton Cantor. 1980. pap. text ed. 9.50x ea. Vol. 1 (ISBN 0-256-02311-5). Vol. 2 (ISBN 0-256-02312-3). Dorsey.
Men, Women & Manners in Colonial Times, 2 Vols. Sydney G. Fisher. LC 70-95776. 1969. Repr. of 1897 ed. Set. 26.00 (ISBN 0-8103-3567-0). Gale.
Menace. Thom Gunn. 1980. signed ed. 15.00 (ISBN 0-686-28715-0). Man-Root.
Menace of Narcotics. Robert L. Sumner. 72p. 1971. pap. 1.95 (ISBN 0-87398-558-3, Pub. by Bibl Evang Pr). Sword of Lord.
Menaechmi. Plautus. Tr. by Frank O. Copley. LC 50-5706. 1956. pap. 3.75 (ISBN 0-672-60178-8, LLA17). Bobbs.
Menagier De Paris: A Critical Edition. Ed. by Georgine E. Brereton & Janet M. Ferrier. 600p. 1981. 99.00 (ISBN 0-19-815748-7). Oxford U Pr.
Menahem Begin: The Legend & the Man. Eitan Haber. 1978. 9.95 o.p. (ISBN 0-440-05553-9). Delacorte.
Menander: A Commentary. A. W. Gomme & F. H. Sandbach. 1973. 56.00x (ISBN 0-19-814197-1). Oxford U Pr.
Mencius on the Mind: Experiments in Multiple Definition. Ivor A. Richards. LC 79-2838. (Illus.). 1981. Repr. of 1932 ed. 16.50 (ISBN 0-8305-0015-4). Hyperion Conn.
Mencken. Carl Bode. LC 72-11997. (Arcturus Books Paperbacks). (Illus.). 1973. pap. 8.95 (ISBN 0-8093-0627-1). S Ill U Pr.
Mend Your Own China & Glass. Susan Wells. (Illus.). 80p. 1976. 9.50 (ISBN 0-7135-1875-8); pap. 8.95 (ISBN 0-7135-1883-9). Transatlantic.
Mendacity Without Scruples. Frank B. Carter, Jr. Ed. by Sylvia Ashton. LC 77-78384. 1978. 8.95 (ISBN 0-87949-093-4). Ashley Bks.
Mende Government & Politics Under Colonial Rule: A Historical Study of Political Change in Sierra Leone 1890-1937. Arthur Abraham. (Illus.). 1979. 29.50x (ISBN 0-19-711638-8). Oxford U Pr.
Mendele Mocher Seforim. Theodore L. Steinberg. (World Authors Ser.: Yiddish: No. 405). 1977. lib. bdg. 12.50 (ISBN 0-8057-6308-2). Twayne.
Mendelssohn: His Life & Times. Mozelle Moshansky. LC 78-53224. (Life & Times of the Composer Ser.). (Illus.). 1981. 16.95 (ISBN 0-8467-0488-9, Pub by Midas Bks); pap. 7.95 (ISBN 0-8467-0461-7). Hippocrene Bks.
Mendelssohn in Scotland. David Jenkins & Mark Visocchi. 1979. 17.95 (ISBN 0-903443-18-X, Pub. by Hamish Hamilton England). David & Charles.
Mendes I. R. K. Holz et al. Ed. by E. S. Hall & B. V. Bothmer. (Illus.). 83p. 45.00 (ISBN 0-936770-02-3). Am Res Ctr Egypt.
Mending Our Nets. Diocese of Cleveland & Rosemary Torrence. 160p. (Orig.). 1980. pap. 7.95 (ISBN 0-697-01757-5). Wm C Brown.
Mending Our Nets. Rosemary Torrence. 176p. 1980. wire coil bdg. 7.95 (ISBN 0-697-01757-5); pap. 7.95. Wm C Brown.
Mendip: A New Study. Robin Atthill. LC 76-45509. (Illus.). 1977. 28.00 (ISBN 0-7153-7297-1). David & Charles.
Mendoza Family in the Spanish Renaissance, 1350-1550. Helen Nader. 1979. 21.00 (ISBN 0-8135-0876-2). Rutgers U Pr.

Meng Ch'iu: Famous Episodes from Chinese History & Legend. Li Han & Hsu Tzu-Kuang. Tr. by Burton Watson from Chinese. LC 79-89264. 184p. 1980. 15.00 (ISBN 0-87011-278-3). Kodansha.

Menippean Satire: An Annotated Catalogue of Texts & Criticism. Eugene P. Kirk. LC 79-7921. (Garland Reference Library of the Humanities). 1980. lib. bdg. 40.00 (ISBN 0-8240-9533-2). Garland Pub.

Menj! Nicki Weiss. LC 80-15955. (Read-Alone Bk.). (Illus.). 48p. (gr. 1-3). 1981. 5.95 (ISBN 0-688-80306-7); PLB 5.71 (ISBN 0-688-84306-9). Greenwillow.

Mennonite Cookbook. LC 80-28579. (Illus.). 294p. 1981. spiral bdg. 9.95 (ISBN 0-8253-0041-X). Beaufort Bks NY.

Mennonite Hymnal. Ed. by Lester Hostetler & Walter E. Yoder. LC 69-18131. 1969. 6.95x (ISBN 0-87303-515-1). Faith & Life.

Mennonite Maid Cookbook. Lydia A. Beery. 1971. pap. 5.00 (ISBN 0-87813-205-8). Park View.

Meno. Plato. Tr. by Benjamin Jowett. LC 51-7881. 1949. pap. 2.50 (ISBN 0-672-60173-7, LLA12). Bobbs.

Meno. Plato. Ed. by R. S. Bluck. (Gr). 1961. text ed. 63.00 (ISBN 0-521-05961-5). Cambridge U Pr.

Menominee Music. Frances Densmore. LC 72-1882. (Music Ser.). (Illus.). 286p. 1972. Repr. of 1932 ed. lib. bdg. 19.50 (ISBN 0-306-70510-9). Da Capo.

Menominio Language. Leonard Bloomfield. 1962. 47.50x (ISBN 0-686-50049-0). Elliots Bks.

Menopause: A Positive Approach. Rosetta Reitz. 1979. pap. 3.50 (ISBN 0-14-005120-1). Penguin.

Menopause Book. Ed. by Louisa Rose et al. Elizabeth Cornell & Nancy Kemeny. 272p. 1980. pap. 5.95 (ISBN 0-686-62823-3, Hawthorn). Dutton.

Menopause: Comprehensive Management. Ed. by Bernard A. Eskin. LC 80-80302. (Illus.). 224p. 1980. 27.50 (ISBN 0-89352-085-3). Masson Pub.

Menopause Myth. Sheldon H. Cherry. (Orig.). 1976. pap. 1.95 o.p. (ISBN 0-685-57525-X, 0-25355-8-150). Ballantine.

Menopause: Vitamins & You. Muriel C. Clausen. 105p. (Orig.). 1980. pap. 4.75 (ISBN 0-9603664-1-5). M C Clausen.

Menotti: A Biography. John Gruen. LC 77-9304. (Illus.). 1978. 16.95 (ISBN 0-02-546320-9). Macmillan.

Men's & Women's Hosiery & Legwear. Fairchild Market Research Division. (Fact File Ser). 1978. pap. 10.00 (ISBN 0-87005-223-3). Fairchild.

Men's Clothing, Tailored Sportswear, Rainwear. Fairchild Market Research Division. (Fairchild Fact File Ser.). 1979. pap. 10.00 (ISBN 0-87005-325-6). Fairchild.

Men's Club. Leonard Michaels. 1981. 9.95 (ISBN 0-374-20782-8). FS&G.

Men's Cottage. Moses Goldberg. (Orig.). 1980. playscript 2.00 (ISBN 0-87602-229-8). Anchorage.

Men's Fashions: 1860-1970. Susan B. Sirkis. (Wish Booklets Ser: Vol. 21). (Illus.). 52p. 1978. pap. 5.50x (ISBN 0-913786-21-7). Wish Bklets.

Men's Furnishings, Career - Work Wear. Fairchild Market Research Division. (Fairchilds Fact File Ser.). 1979. pap. 10.00 (ISBN 0-87005-318-3). Fairchild.

Men's Gymanastics. Eddie Arnold & Broan Stocks. (EP Sport Ser.). (Illus.). 1979. 12.95 (ISBN 0-8069-9128-3, Pub. by EP Publishing England); pap. 6.95 (ISBN 0-8069-9130-5). Sterling.

Men's Gymnastics. Sho Fukushima & Wrio Russell. (Illus.). 1980. 25.00 (ISBN 0-571-11478-4, Pub. by Faber & Faber). Merrimack Bk Serv.

Men's Liberation: A New Definition of Masculinity. Jack Nichols. (Orig.). 1975. pap. 3.95 (ISBN 0-14-004036-6). Penguin.

Men's Outerwear Design. Masaaki Kawashima. LC 77-79658. (Illus.). 1978. text ed. 14.50 (ISBN 0-87005-196-2). Fairchild.

Men's Rights: A Handbook for the 80's. Bill Wishard & Laurie Wishard. LC 80-20194. 264p. 1980. 12.95 (ISBN 0-89666-011-7); pap. 6.95 (ISBN 0-89666-012-5). Cragmont Pubns.

Men's Sportswear & Casual Wear. Fairchild Market Research Division. (Fact File Ser). 1978. pap. 10.00 (ISBN 0-87005-251-9). Fairchild.

Men's Sportswear, Casual Wear, Jeans & Active Wear. Fairchild Market Research Division. (Fact File Ser.). (Illus.). 100p. 1980. pap. 10.00 (ISBN 0-87005-351-5). Fairchild.

Men's Studies Modified: The Impact of Feminism on the Academic Disciplines. Ed. by Dale Spender. (Athene Ser.: Vol. 1). 350p. 1981. 40.00 (ISBN 0-08-026770-X); pap. 18.90 (ISBN 0-08-026117-5). Pergamon.

Men's, Women's & Children's Bodywear, Legwear-Hosiery. Fairchild Market Research Division. (Fact File Ser.). (Illus.). 100p. 1980. pap. 10.00 (ISBN 0-87005-348-5). Fairchild.

Men's, Women's & Children's Footwear. Fairchild Market Research Division. (Fairchild Fact File Ser.). 1979. pap. 10.00 (ISBN 0-87005-322-1). Fairchild.

Men's, Women's & Children's Footwear, 1980. Fairchild Market Research Division. (Fact File Ser.). (Illus.). 100p. 1980. pap. 10.00 (ISBN 0-87005-349-3). Fairchild.

Mensaje a la Conciencia. Dardo Bruchez. 128p. (Orig., Span.). 1979. pap. 2.50 (ISBN 0-89922-143-2). Edit Caribe.

Mensaje De la Biblia: Unger's Bible Handbook. Merrill F. Unger. 960p. 1975. 9.95 (ISBN 0-8024-5244-2). Moody.

Mensaje De los Salmos, Tomo III. Rolando C. Gutierrez. 160p. 1981. pap. write for info. (ISBN 0-311-04028-4). Casa Bautista.

Mensaje De los Salmos En Nuestro Contexto, Tomo II. Rolando Gutierrez. 1980. pap. 4.45 (ISBN 0-311-04025-X). Casa Bautista.

Mensaje de los Salmos en Nuestro Contexto Tomo I. Rolando C. Gutierrez. 1979. 4.45 (ISBN 0-311-04023-3). Casa Bautista.

Mensajes al Pueblo Puertorriqueno: Pronunciados Ante las Camaras Legislativas, 1949-1964. Luis Munoz Martin. Ed. by Gerard P. Marin & Louis J. Rios. 358p. 1980. 15.00 (ISBN 0-913480-47-9); pap. 6.95 (ISBN 0-913480-48-7); Rack Size. 4.95 (ISBN 0-913480-49-5). Inter Am U Pr.

Mensch und Zeit: An Anthology of German Radio Plays. Ed. by Anna Otten. Incl. Knopfe. Ilse Aichinger; Schildkrotenspiel. Georg Von Der Vring; Verschlossene Tur. Fred Von Hoerschelmann; Zinngeschrei. Gunter Eich; Begegnung in Balkanexpress. Wolfgang Hildesheimer; Nachtliches Gesprach Mit Einem Verachteten Menschen. Friedrich Durrenmatt. LC 66-19203. (Illus., Orig., Ger.). 1966. pap. text ed. 5.95x (ISBN 0-89197-300-1); script 1.00x (ISBN 0-89197-301-X). Irvington.

Menstrual Cycle: A Synthesis of Interdisciplinary Research, Vol. 1. Alice Dan et al. LC 80-18837. (Illus.). 1980. text ed. 28.00 (ISBN 0-8261-2630-8). Springer Pub.

Menstrual Cycle, Vol. 2: Research & Implications for Women's Health. Ed. by Pauline Komnenich et al. 256p. 1981. text ed. 25.50 (ISBN 0-8261-2980-3). Springer Pub.

Menstruation. Hilary C. Maddux. 1981. pap. 2.50 (ISBN 0-440-05582-2). Dell.

Menstruation: Just Plain Talk. Alan Nourse. (gr. 4 up). PLB 6.45 (ISBN 0-686-65171-5). Watts.

Mental Development Evaluation of the Pediatric Patient. Lawrence C. Hartlage & David G. Lucas. (Illus.). 92p. 1973. 9.75 (ISBN 0-398-02522-3). C C Thomas.

Mental Disabilities & Criminal Responsibilities. Herbert Fingarette & Ann F. Hasse. LC 77-91756. 1979. 21.50x (ISBN 0-520-03630-1). U of Cal Pr.

Mental Disorder: An Introductory Textbook for Nurses. H. Snell. (Illus.). 1977. pap. text ed. 8.95x (ISBN 0-04-610005-9). Allen Unwin.

Mental Disorder in Earlier Britain. Basil Clarke. 1975. 50.00 (ISBN 0-7083-0562-8). Verry.

Mental Evaluation of the Disability Claimant. Frank O. Volle. 132p. 1975. 14.75 (ISBN 0-398-03338-2). C C Thomas.

Mental Examiner's Source Book. Julian C. Davis & John P. Foreyt. (Illus.). 248p. 1975. 19.75 (ISBN 0-398-03410-9). C C Thomas.

Mental Growth of Children from Two to Fourteen Years: Study of the Predictive Value of the Minnesota Pre-School Scales. Florence Goodenough & Katharine Maurer. LC 70-141548. (Univ. of Minnesota Institute of Child Welfare Monographs: No. 20). (Illus.). 130p. 1975. Repr. of 1942 ed. lib. bdg. 15.75x (ISBN 0-8371-5895-8, CWGM). Greenwood.

Mental Handicap. D. J. Eden. 128p. 1976. pap. 11.25x (ISBN 0-04-371042-5). Intl Pubns Serv.

Mental Handicap: A Select Annotated Bibliography. Compiled by S. S. Segal. (Bibliographic Ser.). (Orig.). 1972. pap. text ed. 3.75x (ISBN 0-901225-90-8, NFER). Humanities.

Mental Handicap: An Introduction. D. J. Eden. (Unwin Education Bks.). 1976. pap. text ed. 7.95x (ISBN 0-04-371042-5). Allen Unwin.

Mental Handicap: An Introduction. David Eden. LC 75-34375. 128p. 1976. 13.95 (ISBN 0-470-01373-7). Halsted Pr.

Mental Handicap & Community Care: A Study of Mentally Handicapped People in Sheffield. Michael Bayley. (Int'l. Library of Social Policy). (Illus.). 420p. 1973. 32.50x (ISBN 0-7100-7662-2). Routledge & Kegan.

Mental Health & Industry. Kieffer. LC 80-18057. 1980. 18.95 (ISBN 0-87705-085-6). Human Sci Pr.

Mental Health & Mental Illness. Nesta Roberts. (Library of Social Policy & Administration). (Orig.). 1967. text ed. 4.50x (ISBN 0-7100-4022-9); pap. text ed. 3.25x (ISBN 0-7100-4025-3). Humanities.

Mental Health & Primary Medical Care, Vol. 10. Gap Committee on Preventive Psychiatry. LC 80-19016. (Publication Ser.: No. 105). pap. 4.00 (105, Mental Health Materials Center). Adv Psychiatry.

Mental Health & Retardation Politics: The Mind Lobbies in Congress. Daniel A. Felicetti. LC 74-14042. (Illus.). 218p. 1975. text ed. 22.95 (ISBN 0-275-09930-X). Praeger.

Mental Health & Social Policy. 2nd ed. David Mechanic. (Ser. in Social Policy). 1980. pap. text ed. 10.95 (ISBN 0-13-576025-9). P-H.

Mental Health Concepts Applied to Nursing. L. C. Dunlap. 256p. 1978. 15.95 (ISBN 0-471-04360-5). Wiley.

Mental Health Concepts in Medical-Surgical Nursing: A Workbook. 2nd ed. Carol R. Kneisl & Sue Ann Ames. LC 78-16371. (Illus.). 1979. pap. 9.50 (ISBN 0-8016-0161-4). Mosby.

Mental Health Counsellors at Work. T. M. Magoon et al. 1971. 32.00 (ISBN 0-08-006422-1). Pergamon.

Mental Health Education in the New Medical Schools. Ed. by Donald G. Langsley et al. LC 73-48. (Social & Behavioral Science Ser.). 1973. 13.95x o.p. (ISBN 0-87589-167-5). Jossey-Bass.

Mental Health Expenditures & Funding Through 1985. Donald E. Yett & Daniel Levine. LC 74-15534. (Human Resources Research Center Monographs). Date not set. cancelled o.p. (ISBN 0-669-94250-2). Lexington Bks.

Mental Health for the Nonprofessional. A. W. Wiener. 88p. 1980. 9.75 (ISBN 0-398-04010-9); pap. 5.95 (ISBN 0-398-04011-7). C C Thomas.

Mental Health from Infancy Through Adolescence. Joint Commission on Mental Health of Children. LC 78-123939. (Illus.). 512p. 1973. 15.00x o.s.i. (ISBN 0-06-012228-5, HarpT). Har-Row.

Mental Health in America, 1957-1976. Joseph Veroff et al. LC 80-68959. 1981. 37.50x (ISBN 0-465-04479-4). Basic.

Mental Health in Classroom & Corridor. Alicerose S. Barman. LC 68-25763. 1968. 9.20 o.p. (ISBN 0-672-75107-0). Bobbs.

Mental Health in Organizations: Personal Adjustment & Constructive Intervention. Erich P. Prien et al. LC 78-16757. 1978. 15.95 (ISBN 0-88229-175-0). Nelson-Hall.

Mental Health in the Classroom. 1968. 2.50 (ISBN 0-917160-05-3). Am Sch Health.

Mental Health in the Developing World: A Case Study in Latin America. Mario Argandona & Ari Kiev. LC 72-78606. 1972. 9.95 o.s.i. (ISBN 0-02-900850-6). Free Pr.

Mental Health in the Twenty-First Century. Thomas A. Williams & James H. Johnson. LC 78-20270. 208p. 1979. 21.95x (ISBN 0-669-02718-9). Lexington Bks.

Mental Health Industry: A Cultural Phenomenon. Peter A. Magaro et al. LC 77-14434. (Series on Personality Processes). 1978. 23.95 (ISBN 0-471-02406-6, Pub. by Wiley-Interscience). Wiley

Mental Health Issues & the Urban Poor. Ed. by Dorothy Evans & William Claiborn. LC 73-19708. 1974. text ed. 21.00 (ISBN 0-08-017831-6); pap. text ed. 10.75 (ISBN 0-08-017830-8). Pergamon.

Mental Health Law in Mississippi. David A. Pritchard. LC 78-62247. 1978. pap. text ed. 11.25 (ISBN 0-8191-0568-6). U Pr of Amer.

Mental Health Law: Major Issues. David B. Wexler. 265p. 1981. 25.00 (ISBN 0-306-40538-5, Plenum Pr). Plenum Pub.

Mental Health Nursing: A Bio-Psycho-Cultural Approach. Elaine A. Pasquali et al. (Illus.). 635p. 1981. text ed. 19.95 (ISBN 0-8016-3758-9). Mosby.

Mental Health Nursing: A Socio-Psychological Approach. 2nd ed. Helen K. Grace & Dorothy Camilleri. 592p. 1981. text ed. write for info. (ISBN 0-697-05517-5); instrs.' manual avail. (ISBN 0-697-05518-3). Wm C Brown.

Mental Health on the Campus: A Field Study. R. M. Glasscote & M. E. Fishman. 216p. 1973. 8.50 (ISBN 0-685-77454-6, P202-0). Am Psychiatric.

Mental Health on the Community College Campus. Gerald Amada. 157p. 1977. pap. text ed. 8.50 (ISBN 0-8191-0357-8). U Pr of Amer.

Mental Health or Mental Illness. William Glasser. LC 60-15216. (Illus.). 1961. 7.95 o.s.i. (ISBN 0-06-002010-5, HarpT). Har-Row.

Mental Health Programs for Preschool Children: A Field Study. Raymond M. Glasscote & M. E. Fishman. 182p. 1974. pap. 8.50 (ISBN 0-685-65571-7, P208-3). Am Psychiatric.

Mental Health Services for the Mentally Retarded. Ed. by Elias Katz et al. (Illus.). 292p. 1972. 17.50 (ISBN 0-398-02516-9). C C Thomas.

Mental Health Skills for Clergy. Dana Charry. 160p. 1981. 10.95 (ISBN 0-8170-0886-1). Judson.

Mental Health Worker. Jane Henry Stolten. 1981. pap. text ed. price not set (ISBN 0-316-81744-9). Little.

Mental Hygiene: Dynamics of Adjustment. 5th ed. Herbert A. Carroll. 1969. text ed. 16.95x (ISBN 0-13-576314-2). P-H.

Mental Hygiene in the Nursery School. 1953. pap. 2.50 (ISBN 92-3-100418-2, U381, UNESCO). Unipub.

Mental Illness & Civil Liberty. Cyril Greenland. 126p. 1970. pap. text ed. 5.00x (ISBN 0-7135-1826-X, Pub. by Bedford England). Renouf.

Mental Illness & Psychology. Michel Foucault. Tr. by A. M. Smith. 1976. pap. 3.95x (ISBN 0-06-131801-9, TB 1801, CN). Har-Row.

Mental Illness & Psychotropic Medications, 2 vols. Jonathan O. Cole. (Illus.). 131p. 1977. Set. 43.00 (ISBN 0-685-62203-7); Bk. 1. 18.50 (ISBN 0-89147-036-0); Bk. 2. 24.50 (ISBN 0-89147-037-9). CAS.

Mental Illness in Later Life. Ewald W. Busse & Eric Pfeiffer. 301p. 1973. casebound 12.00 (ISBN 0-685-38355-5, P188-1); pap. 9.00 (ISBN 0-685-38356-3, 188). Am Psychiatric.

Mental Illness in Pregnancy & the Puerperium. Ed. by Merton Sandler. (Illus.). 1979. text ed. 21.95x (ISBN 0-19-261150-X). Oxford U Pr.

Mental Illness: Law & Public Policy. Baruch A. Brody & H. Tristram Englehardt. (Philosophy & Medicine Ser.: No. 5). 276p. 1980. lib. bdg. 28.95 (ISBN 0-686-27528-4). Kluwer Boston.

Mental Illness Programs for Employees. W. B. Goldbeck. (Springer Ser. in Industry & Health Care: Vol. 9). 250p. 1980. pap. 12.00 (ISBN 0-387-90479-4). Springer-Verlag.

Mental Illness: Progress & Prospects. Robert H. Felix. LC 67-20278. 1967. 12.50x (ISBN 0-231-03055-X). Columbia U Pr.

Mental Images & Their Transformations. Roger N. Shepard & Lynn A. Cooper. (Illus.). 1981. text ed. write for info. (ISBN 0-89706-008-3). Bradford Bks.

Mental Institutions in America: Social Policy to 1875. Gerald N. Grob. LC 72-92868. 1973. 15.95 (ISBN 0-02-913040-9). Free Pr.

Mental Life of Monkeys & Apes. Robert M. Yerkes. LC 79-22241. (History of Psychology Ser.). 1979. 30.00x (ISBN 0-8201-1341-7). Schol Facsimiles.

Mental Power Thru Sleep Suggestion. Melvin Powers. pap. 3.00 (ISBN 0-87980-097-6). Wilshire.

Mental Radio. rev. 2nd ed. Upton Sinclair. (Illus.). 256p. 1962. 11.75 (ISBN 0-398-01766-2). C C Thomas.

Mental Representation of Grammatical Relations. Ed. by Joan Bresnan. (Cognitive Theory & Mental Representation Ser.: Vol. 1). 700p. 1981. text ed. 35.00x (ISBN 0-262-02158-7). MIT Pr.

Mental Retardation. Robert E. Dunbar. (First Bks). (Illus.). (gr. 4-6). 1978. PLB 6.45 (ISBN 0-531-01491-6). Watts.

Mental Retardation. B. H. Kirman. 1968. 675.00 (ISBN 0-08-013371-1). Pergamon.

Mental Retardation. James S. Payne & James R. Patton. (Special Education Ser.). (Illus.). 480p. 1981. text ed. 24.95 (ISBN 0-675-08027-4); write for info. Merrill.

Mental Retardation. Bernard Schlanger. LC 73-9613. (Studies in Communicative Disorders Ser.). 1973. 2.50 (ISBN 0-672-61289-5). Bobbs.

Mental Retardation. rev. ed. Ed. by Special Learning Corp. (Special Education Ser.). (Illus., Orig.). 1980. pap. text ed. write for info. (ISBN 0-89568-195-1). Spec Learn Corp.

Mental Retardation: A Developmental Approach. Charles Cleland. (Spec. Educ. Ser.). 1978. ref. ed. 18.95x (ISBN 0-13-576504-8). P-H.

Mental Retardation: A Family Crisis; the Therapeutic Role of the Physician, Vol. 5. GAP Committee on Mental Retardation. (Report No. 56). 1963. pap. 1.00 o.p. (ISBN 0-87318-075-5). Adv Psychiatry.

Mental Retardation: A Life Cycle Approach. 2nd ed. Philip C. Chinn et al. LC 78-31835. 1979. text ed. 18.95 (ISBN 0-8016-0968-2). Mosby.

Mental Retardation: A Phenomenological Approach. Jerry Jacobs. (Illus.). 244p. 1980. 24.50 (ISBN 0-398-04062-1); pap. 16.75 (ISBN 0-398-04063-X). C C Thomas.

Mental Retardation: A Programmed Manual for Volunteer Workers. Alden S. Gilmore & Thomas A. Rich. (Illus.). 152p. 1973. 9.75 (ISBN 0-398-00681-4). C C Thomas.

Mental Retardation & Developmental Disabilities, Vol. XII. Ed. by Joseph Wortis. LC 73-647002. 200p. 1981. 20.00 (ISBN 0-87630-263-0). Brunner-Mazel.

Mental Retardation & Developmental Disabilities: An Annual Review. Ed. by Joseph Wortis. Incl. Vol. 5. 1973. o.p. (ISBN 0-87630-068-9); Vol. 6. 1974 (ISBN 0-685-57356-7); Vol. 7. 1975 (ISBN 0-685-57357-5); Vol. 8. 1976 (ISBN 0-685-57358-3); Vol. 9. 1977; Vol. 10. 1978; Vol. 11. LC 73-647002. 1979 (ISBN 0-87630-214-2). LC 75-86629. Vols. 6-11. 20.00 ea. Brunner-Mazel.

Mental Retardation & Modern Society. Michael P. Maloney & Michael P. Ward. (Illus.). 1979. text ed. 12.95x (ISBN 0-19-502473-7). Oxford U Pr.

Mental Retardation & Physical Disability: A Book of Readings. Ed. by Richard E. Hardy & John G. Cull. (American Lectures in Social & Rehabilitation Psychology Ser.). (Illus.). 264p. 1974. 14.75 (ISBN 0-398-02879-6). C C Thomas.

Mental Retardation Dictionary. Alexander J. Tymchuk. LC 73-80058. 149p. 1980. pap. 7.00x (ISBN 0-87424-125-1). Western Psych.

Mental Retardation for Special Educators. J. P. Das & David Baine. (Illus.). 332p. 1978. 27.50 (ISBN 0-398-03665-9); pap. 18.50 (ISBN 0-398-03666-7). C C Thomas.

Mental Retardation: Introduction & Personal Perspectives. new ed. Ed. by James M. Kauffman & James S. Payne. (Special Education Ser). 456p. 1975. text ed. 18.50x (ISBN 0-675-08728-7). Merrill.

Mental Retardation, Its Nature & Incidence: A Population Survey of the State of Delaware. Joseph F. Jastak & Halsey M. MacPhee. LC 62-19658. 184p. 10.00 (ISBN 0-87413-103-0). U Delaware Pr.

Mental Retardation: Nature, Needs, & Advocacy. Donald F. Sellin. 1979. text ed. 19.95 (ISBN 0-205-05989-9, 2459892); tests avail. (ISBN 0-205-05990-2, 2459906). Allyn.

Mental Retardation: Nursing Approaches to Care. Ed. by Judith B. Curry & Kathryn K. Peppe. LC 77-26307. 1978. pap. text ed. 11.50 (ISBN 0-8016-1196-2). Mosby.

Mental Retardation: Rehabilitation & Counseling. Philip L. Browning. (Illus.). 464p. 1974. 24.75 (ISBN 0-398-03006-5). C C Thomas.

Mental Retardation: Social & Education Perspectives. Clifford J. Drew & Michael L. Hardman. LC 73-26680. (Illus.). 1977. pap. 12.00 (ISBN 0-8016-1462-7). Mosby.

Mental Retardation: The Changing Outlook. Robert P. Ingalls. LC 77-23359. 1978. text ed. 21.95x (ISBN 0-471-42716-0). Wiley.

Mental-Spiritual Health Models: An Analysis of the Models of Boisen, Hiltner & Clinebell. Hugh W. Sanborn. LC 79-65295. 1979. pap. text ed. 8.75 (ISBN 0-8191-0784-0). U Pr of Amer.

Mental State of Hystericals. Pierre Janet. (Contributions to the History of Psychology Ser.: Pt. 2, Medical Psychology). 1978. Repr. of 1901 ed. 30.00 (ISBN 0-89093-166-6). U Pubns Amer.

Mental Subnormality. H. Kekstadt & D. A. Primrose. (Modern Practical Nursing Ser: N0. 15). (Illus.). 1975. pap. text ed. 9.95x (ISBN 0-685-83644-4). Intl Ideas.

Mental Walk Through Life in Poetry. Joseph V. Bologna. 1977. 5.50 o.p. (ISBN 0-533-02399-8). Vantage.

Mentality of Apes. rev. 2nd ed. Wolfgang Kohler. Tr. by Ella Winter from Ger. (International Library of Psychology). (Illus.). 344p. 1973. 32.00 (ISBN 0-7100-7525-1). Routledge & Kegan.

Mentally Abnormal Offender & the Law. H. Rollin. 1969. 15.00 (ISBN 0-08-013385-1); pap. 7.00 (ISBN 0-08-013384-3). Pergamon.

Mentally Handicapped Adolescent: The Slough Project of the National Society for Mentally Handicapped Children. E. P. Baranyay. 1971. text ed. 22.00 (ISBN 0-08-016271-1). Pergamon.

Mentally Ill in America. Albert Deutsch. LC 49-7527. 1949. 23.50x (ISBN 0-231-01656-5). Columbia U Pr.

Mentally Ill in Community-Based Sheltered Care: A Study of Community Care & Social Integration. Steven P. Segal & Uri Aviram. (Health, Medicine & Society Ser.). 26.50 (ISBN 0-471-77400-6, Pub. by Wiley-Interscience). Wiley.

Mentally Ill Offender: A Survey of Treatment Programs. Charles Kanno & Patricia L. Scheidemandel. 76p. 1969. pap. 3.00 (ISBN 0-685-24860-7, P244-0). Am Psychiatric.

Mentally Ill Offenders & the Criminal Justice System: Issues in Forensic Services. Ed. by Nancy J. Beran & Beverly G. Toomey. LC 78-19782. (Praeger Special Studies). 1979. 24.95 (ISBN 0-03-046426-9). Praeger.

Mentally Retarded: An Educational Psychology. Kathryn Blake. (Special Education Ser.). (Illus.). 416p. 1976. 18.95x (ISBN 0-13-576280-4). P-H.

Mentally Retarded Child & His Family. Harold D. Love. (Illus.). 216p. 1973. text ed. 11.25 (ISBN 0-398-02728-5); pap. text ed. 7.95 (ISBN 0-398-02760-9). C C Thomas.

Mentally Retarded Child & His Motor Behavior: Practical Diagnosis & Movement Experiences. Thais R. Beter & Wesley E. Cragin. (Illus.). 208p. 1972. 19.75 (ISBN 0-398-02230-5). C C Thomas.

Mentally Retarded Citizen & the Law: The President's Committee on Mental Retardation. Michael Kindred et al. LC 74-21489. 1976. 25.00 (ISBN 0-02-916860-0). Free Pr.

Mentally Retarded in Society. 2nd ed. Stanley P. Davies & E. G. Ecob. LC 58-59911. 1959. 17.50x (ISBN 0-231-02220-4). Columbia U Pr.

Mente y lo Desconocido. J. Stafford Wright. Tr. by James S. Gilchrist from Eng. LC 76-9906. 228p. (Orig., Span.). 1976. pap. 3.50 (ISBN 0-89922-070-3). Edit Caribe.

Menten Affair. Hans Knoop. 1979. 12.95 (ISBN 0-02-564500-5). Macmillan.

Mentor Book of Major American Poets. Ed. by Oscar Williams & Honig. pap. 2.50 (ISBN 0-451-61773-8, ME1773, Ment). NAL.

Mentor Book of Major British Poets. Ed. by Oscar Williams. pap. 2.95 (ISBN 0-451-61876-9, ME1876, Ment). NAL.

Mentor: Secrets Ot the Ages. Art Fettig. (Illus.). 112p. 1981. 9.95 (ISBN 0-8119-0333-8). Fell.

Menu Design, Merchandising & Marketing. 2nd ed. Albin G. Seaberg. LC 72-149403. 1973. 22.95 (ISBN 0-8436-0572-3). CBI Pub.

Menu French. David Atkinson. (International Ser. in Hospitality Management). (Illus.). 96p. 1980. 15.00 (ISBN 0-08-024309-6); pap. 6.75 (ISBN 0-08-024308-8). Pergamon.

Menu Planning. 2nd ed. Eleanor Eckstein. (Illus.). text ed. 21.50 (ISBN 0-87055-260-0). AVI.

Menu Planning & Foods Merchandising. 1st ed. Restaurant Business Inc. LC 73-163322. 1971. 14.50 (ISBN 0-672-96092-3); tchrs' manual 5.90 (ISBN 0-672-96094-X); wkbk. 6.50 (ISBN 0-672-96093-1). Bobbs.

Menu Pricing & Strategy. Jack E. Miller. LC 79-25932. (Illus.). 1980. pap. 13.95 (ISBN 0-8436-2144-3). CBI Pub.

Menu Terminology. H. C. Clarke. 1969. pap. 5.25 (ISBN 0-08-006525-2). Pergamon.

Menus: Analysis & Planning. Lothar A. Kreck. LC 74-28068. (Illus.). 200p. 1975. 16.95 (ISBN 0-8436-2050-1). CBI Pub.

Menus for Entertaining. Juliette Elkon & Elaine Ross. 1960. 8.95 (ISBN 0-8038-4617-7). Hastings.

Menus for Romance. Diana Haven. (Candlelight Romance Cookbook Ser.). (Orig.). pap. 1.50 (ISBN 0-440-16169-X). Dell.

Menus of the Valley's Finest Restaurants: Nineteen Eighhty-One Edition. Ed. by John Long et al. 176p. 1980. pap. 5.95 (ISBN 0-930380-12-6, 0148-4133). Quail Run.

Menzel Symposium on High Pressure Steam Curing. 1972. pap. 20.75 (ISBN 0-685-85106-0, SP-32) (ISBN 0-685-85107-9). ACI.

Mephisto. Klaus Mann. 1979. pap. 2.25 o.p. (ISBN 0-345-25393-0). Ballantine.

Meran & Other Semi-Slav Systems. T. D. Harding. 1980. cancelled (ISBN 0-7134-2447-8); pap. cancelled (ISBN 0-686-63372-5). David & Charles.

Merc: American Soldiers of Fortune. Jay Mallin & Robert K. Brown. 1980. pap. 2.50 (ISBN 0-451-09529-4, E9529, Sig). NAL.

Mercantile Law. M. C. Kuchhal. (Illus.). 1979. text ed. 20.00x (ISBN 0-7069-0641-1, Pub. by Vikas India). Advent Bk.

Merce Cunningham. James Klosty. 1975. 15.95 o.p. (ISBN 0-8415-0359-1); pap. 8.95 (ISBN 0-8415-0372-9). Dutton.

Mercedes-Benz Racing Cars. Karl Ludvigsen. (Illus.). 1971. 35.00 (ISBN 0-87880-009-3). Norton.

Mercedes-Benz Roadsters. Leonard Setright. (AutoHistory Ser.). (Illus.). 1979. 12.95 (ISBN 0-85045-325-9, Pub. by Osprey England). Motorbooks Intl.

Mercedes-Benz Tune-up Maintenance: Gas & Diesel, 1958-1978. Mike Bishop. Ed. by Eric Jorgensen. (Illus.). 1977. pap. 10.95 (ISBN 0-89287-175-X, A180). Clymer Pubns.

Mercenary. Joseph Freytag. (Orig.). 1977. pap. 1.25 o.p. (ISBN 0-685-77273-X). Pinnacle Bks.

Mercenary-Green Hell. Leon DaSilva. 1976. pap. 1.50 o.p. (ISBN 0-685-73458-7, LB388, Leisure Bks). Nordon Pubns.

Merchandise Buyers' Game. Katherine Fulkerson. 1981. pap. text ed. 2.95 (ISBN 0-933836-13-9). Simtek.

Merchandising & Operating Results of Department & Specialty Stores (MOR) 200p. 1980. pap. text ed. 45.00 (ISBN 0-686-60192-0, C139). Natl Ret Merch.

Merchandising Mathematics. Leslie R. Peltz. LC 79-494. 1979. pap. 9.50 (ISBN 0-672-97273-5); tchr's manual 3.33 (ISBN 0-672-97274-3). Bobbs.

Merchandising Mathmatics. Carlo & Murphy. 136p. 1981. pap. 6.60 (ISBN 0-8273-1416-7); instructor's guide 1.60 (ISBN 0-8273-1417-5). Delmar.

Merchant Campbell, 1769-1846. Margaret Steven. 1965. 11.25x o.p. (ISBN 0-19-550275-2). Oxford U Pr.

Merchant Class of Medieval London. Sylvia L. Thrupp. 1962. pap. 5.95 (ISBN 0-472-06072-4, 72, AA). U of Mich Pr.

Merchant Fleets in Profile 4: The Ships of the Hamburg-American, Adler & Carr Lines. Duncan Haws. 248p. 1980. 37.95 (ISBN 0-85059-397-2). Aztex.

Merchant of Menace. John Stevenson. (Orig.). 1980. pap. 1.75 (ISBN 0-505-51507-5). Tower Bks.

Merchant of Venice. William Shakespeare. Ed. by Arthur Quiller-Couch et al. (New Shakespeare Ser). 23.95 (ISBN 0-521-07545-9); pap. 4.50x (ISBN 0-521-09488-7). Cambridge U Pr.

Merchant of Venice. William Shakespeare. Ed. by Louis B. Wright & Virginia A. LaMar. (Folger Library). (Illus.). (gr. 9 up). 1957. 2.25 o.p. (ISBN 0-671-43296-6). PB.

Merchant of Venice Notes. Cliff's Notes Editors. (Orig.). pap. 1.95 (ISBN 0-8220-0052-0). Cliffs.

Merchant Princes. Leon Harris. 1980. pap. 3.25 (ISBN 0-425-04700-8). Berkley Pub.

Merchant Ship Construction. D. A. Taylor. (Illus.). 240p. 1980. text ed. 39.95 (ISBN 0-408-00408-8). Butterworths.

Merchant Ship Search & Rescue Manual (MERSAR) (Illus.). 53p. 1977. 8.25 (IMCO). Unipub.

Merchant Ships of the World in Color, 1910-1929. Laurence Dunn. LC 74-23925. (Illus.). 215p. 1975. 6.95 o.s.i. (ISBN 0-02-533920-6). Macmillan.

Merchants & Rulers in Gujarat: The Response to the Portuguese in the Sixteenth Century. M. N. Pearson. 1976. 18.50x (ISBN 0-520-02809-0). U of Cal Pr.

Merchants Avizo. LC 70-7710. (English Experience Ser.: No. 98). 1969. Repr. of 1607 ed. 9.50 (ISBN 90-221-0098-7). Walter J Johnson.

Merchants of Buenos Aires, Seventeen Seventy-Eight to Eighteen Hundred & Ten. Susan M. Socolow. LC 77-85216. (Cambridge Latin American Studies: No. 30). (Illus.). 1979. 35.50 (ISBN 0-521-21812-8). Cambridge U Pr.

Merchants of Moscow, Fifteen Eighty to Sixteen Fifty. Paul Bushkovitch. LC 79-14491. (Illus.). 1980. 21.00 (ISBN 0-521-22589-2). Cambridge U Pr.

Merchant's Prologue & Tale. Geoffrey Chaucer. Ed. by M. Hussey. (Selected Tales from Chaucer). 1966. text ed. 4.95x (ISBN 0-521-04631-9). Cambridge U Pr.

Mercian Studies. Ed. by Ann Dornier. 250p. 1977. pap. text ed. 18.25x (ISBN 0-7185-1148-4, Leicester). Humanities.

Merck Manual of Diagnosis and Therapy. 13th ed. Ed. by Robert Berkow. LC 1-31760. (Illus.). 1980p. 1977. 14.50 (ISBN 0-911910-02-6). Merck.

Mercury Contamination in Man & His Environment. (Technical Reports Ser.: No. 137). (Illus.). 181p. (Orig.). 1973. pap. 14.50 (ISBN 92-0-115172-1, IDC 137, IAEA). Unipub.

Mercury, Mercurials & Mercaptans. Morton W. Miller & Thomas W. Clarkson. (Illus.). 404p. 1973. 27.50 (ISBN 0-398-02600-9). C C Thomas.

Mercury Outboards, Fifty to One Hundred Seventy-Five Hp: 1964-1977. (Illus.). 192p. 8.00 o.p. (ISBN 0-89287-150-4, B653). Western Marine Ent.

Mercury Outboards, Four to Forty HP: 1964-1978. (Illus.). 168p. 8.00 o.p. (ISBN 0-89287-222-5, B650). Western Marine Pub.

Mercy. Joyce MacIver. 1976. pap. 1.95 (ISBN 0-380-00843-2, 31096). Avon.

Mercy Drop & Other Plays. Robert Patrick. LC 79-53945. (Illus.). 1980. pap. 5.00 (ISBN 0-930762-03-7). Calamus Bks.

Mercy, Lord! My Husband's in the Kitchen & Other Equal Opportunity Conversations with God. Toby D. Schwartz. LC 80-715. (Illus.). 96p. 1981. 6.95 (ISBN 0-385-17058-0). Doubleday.

Mercy with Love. Francis X. Markley. (Illus.). 128p. 1980. 7.95 (ISBN 0-89962-025-6). Todd & Honeywell.

Mere Christianity. C. S. Lewis. 1964. 8.95 (ISBN 0-02-570610-1); pap. 2.95 (ISBN 0-02-086810-3). Macmillan.

Meredith: A Change of Masks, a Study of the Novels. Gillian Beer. 1970. text ed. 23.25x (ISBN 0-485-11122-5, Athlone Pr). Humanities.

Mereford Tapestry. Charles MacKinnon. 480p. 1974. 8.95 o.p. (ISBN 0-440-05589-X). Delacorte.

Merely Players: An Anthology of Life Poems. Ed. by Lee B. Hopkins. LC 79-12474. 1979. 7.95 (ISBN 0-525-66645-1). Elsevier-Nelson.

Mergenthaler VIP Typeface Catalogs, 2 vols. Volk & Huxley. 1152p. 1980. Set. pap. 40.00 (ISBN 0-442-23999-8); pap. 24.95 ea. Vol. 1 (ISBN 0-442-24001-5). Vol. 2 (ISBN 0-442-24000-7). Van Nos Reinhold.

Merger Yearbook Nineteen Eighty. Andrew D. Clapp. 1981. 68.00 (ISBN 0-939008-03-3). Cambridge Corp.

Mergers & Concentration in British Industry. P. E. Hart et al. (National Institute of Economic & Social Research, Occasional Papers: No. 26). (Illus.). 176p. 1973. 20.95 (ISBN 0-521-20238-8). Cambridge U Pr.

Meristems, Growth & Development in Woody Plants. J. A. Romberger. (Landmark Reprints in Plant Science Ser.). 1963. text ed. 15.00 (ISBN 0-86598-005-5). Allanheld.

Merkabah in Rabbinic Literature. David Halperin. (American Oriental Ser.: Vol. 62). 1980. 14.00x. Am Orient Soc.

Merkwuerdige und Interessante Lebensgeschichte der Frau Von Wallwille, Welche Vier Jahre Lang an Eien Irokesen Verheyrathet War. Maria Wallwille. LC 75-7054. (Indian Captivities Ser.: Vol. 32). 1976. Repr. of 1809 ed. lib. bdg. 44.00 (ISBN 0-8240-1656-4). Garland Pub.

Merleau-Ponty & Marxism: From Terror to Reform. Barry Cooper. LC 78-16829. 1979. 20.00x (ISBN 0-8020-5435-8). U of Toronto Pr.

Merlin's Catalog of Magic. Charles B. Townsend. (Puzzler Ser.). 128p. (Orig.). (gr. 9 up). 1981. pap. 4.95 (ISBN 0-8437-2099-9). Hammond Inc.

Merlin's Godson. H. Warner Munn. 320p. 1976. pap. 2.25 (ISBN 0-345-28982-X). Ballantine.

Merlins of the Welsh Marches. D. A. Orton. LC 80-66090. 192p. 1980. 19.95 (ISBN 0-7153-7992-5). David & Charles.

Merlin's Tale of King Arthur's Magic Sword. Keith Engar. (Orig.). 1981. playscript 2.00 (ISBN 0-87602-228-X). Anchorage.

MERMAC Manual: Test & Questionnaire Analysis Programs Written for the IBM System-360. Ed. by Richard E. Spencer et al. LC 71-131006. 1971. pap. 4.95 (ISBN 0-252-00131-1); 3,500.00 (ISBN 0-252-00227-X); supplement to manual 4.95 (ISBN 0-252-00651-8). U of Ill Pr.

Mermaid & the Minotaur: Sexual Arrangements & Human Malaise. Dorothy Dinnerstein. LC 75-23879. 352p. 1976. 10.95 o.s.i. (ISBN 0-06-011047-3, HarpT). Har-Row.

Mermaid in Nikoli. William Woods. 1967. 4.95 o.p. (ISBN 0-8090-6895-8). Hill & Wang.

Mermaid's Cape. Margaret K. Wetterer. LC 80-20338. (Illus.). 32p. (gr. 1-4). 1981. 8.95 (ISBN 0-689-50197-8, McElderry Bk). Atheneum.

Merman's Children. Poul Anderson. 1980. pap. 2.50 (ISBN 0-425-04643-5). Berkley Pub.

Meromorphic Functions. Walter K. Hayman. (Oxford Mathematical Monographs Ser). 1964. 34.95x o.p. (ISBN 0-19-853510-4). Oxford U Pr.

Merrie Melodies & Looney Tunes. Barry Putterman. LC 78-69637. (Illus.). 1979. 17.50 o.p. (ISBN 0-498-02211-0). A S Barnes.

Merrill Studies in The Bridge. David R. Clark. 1970. pap. text ed. 2.95 (ISBN 0-675-09292-2). Merrill.

Merrill's Guide to Computer Performance Evaluation: Analysis of Smf-Rmf Data with SAS. H. W. Merrill. (Illus.). 352p. 1980. 395.00 (ISBN 0-686-65590-7). SAS Inst.

Merry Christmas! A History of the Holiday. Patricia B. Stevens. LC 79-13762. (Illus.). (gr. 6 up). 1979. 9.95 (ISBN 0-02-788210-1). Macmillan.

Merry Christmas from Betsy. Carolyn Haywood. (Illus.). (gr. 4-6). 1970. PLB 7.92 (ISBN 0-688-31695-6). Morrow.

Merry Christmas: Things to Make & Do. Robyn Supraner. LC 80-23884. (Illus.). 48p. (gr. 2-5). 1980. PLB 6.92 (ISBN 0-89375-422-6); pap. 1.75 (ISBN 0-89375-423-4). Troll Assocs.

Merry Christmas to You. rev. ed. Ed. by Wilhelmina Harper. (Illus.). (gr. 2 up). 1965. PLB 7.95 o.p. (ISBN 0-525-34852-2). Dutton.

Merry-Go-Riddle. Ann Bishop. LC 73-7321. (Riddle Bk.). (Illus.). 40p. (gr. 1-3). 1973. 5.75g (ISBN 0-8075-5072-8). A Whitman.

Merry-Go-Round. Leonard Bischel. (Illus.). 72p. (Orig.). (gr. 1-5). 1980. pap. 4.95 (ISBN 0-935110-01-1, 28711-TXU). Blackjack Ent.

Merry-Go-Round. Helme Heine. 26p. (gr. 1-6). 1980. 4.95 (ISBN 0-8120-5393-1). Barron.

Merry, Merry FIBruary. Doris Orgel. LC 77-650. (Illus.). 40p. (ps-4). 1977. 7.95 (ISBN 0-590-17708-7, Four Winds); 7.95 (ISBN 0-590-07708-2). Schol Bk Serv.

Merry Missionary: A Story About Philip Neri. Kenneth Christopher. (Stories About Christian Heroes Ser.). (Illus.). 32p. (gr. 6-9). pap. 1.95 (ISBN 0-686-63634-1). Winston Pr.

Merry-Mouse Book of Nursery Rhymes. Priscilla Hillman. LC 80-2053. (Illus.). 32p. (gr. k-1). 1981. 4.95a (ISBN 0-385-17102-1); PLB (ISBN 0-385-17103-X). Doubleday.

Merry Passages & Jeasts: A Manuscript Jestbook of Sir Nicholas le Strange, 1603-1655. Nicholas Le Strange. Ed. by H. F. Lippincott. (Salzburg Studies in English Literature, Elizabethan & Renaissance Studies: No. 29). (Illus.). 266p. 1974. pap. text ed. 25.00x (ISBN 0-391-01460-9). Humanities.

Merry Songs & Ballads: Musa Pedestris, 6 vols. John S. Farmer. Set. 61.50x (ISBN 0-8154-0066-7). Cooper Sq.

Merry Wives of Windsor. William Shakespeare. Ed. by Arthur Quiller-Couch et al. (New Shakespeare Ser). 1969. 23.95 (ISBN 0-521-07546-7); pap. 4.50x (ISBN 0-521-09489-5). Cambridge U Pr.

Merry Wives of Windsor. rev. ed. William Shakespeare. Ed. by George L. Kittredge & Irving Ribner. LC 69-15381. 1969. pap. 3.95x o.p. (ISBN 0-471-00533-9). Wiley.

Merry's Treasure. Patty Brisco. (YA). 1970. 5.95 (ISBN 0-685-07447-1, Avalon). Bouregy.

Mert the Blurt. Robert Kraus & Jose Aruego. LC 80-14508. (Illus.). 32p. (ps-2). 1980. 8.95 (ISBN 0-671-96265-5, Pub. by Windmill). S&S.

Merv. Merv Griffin & Peter Barsocchini. 1980. 11.95 (ISBN 0-671-22764-5). S&S.

Mervyn Peake. John Watney. LC 76-17422. (Illus.). 1977. 10.95 o.p. (ISBN 0-312-53025-0). St Martin.

Merwan: Stories of Meher Baba for Children. Anne E. Giles. LC 80-53858. (Illus.). 96p. (Orig.). (gr. 3-7). 1980. pap. 4.95 (ISBN 0-913078-41-7). Sheriar Pr.

Mesajero y Su Mensaje. Tr. by Alice Luce. (Spanish Bks.). 1980. 1.25 (ISBN 0-8297-0582-1). Life Pubs Intl.

MESBIC: An Exciting New Financial Concept with Great Growth Potential for Business. David D. Seltz. 1981. 15.00 (ISBN 0-87863-197-6). Farnswth Pub.

Mesmerism: A Translation of the Original Medical & Scientific Writings of F. A. Mesmer, M.D. Franz A. Mesmer. Tr. by George Bloch from Lat., Fr. & Ger. LC 80-14736. 180p. 1980. 11.50 (ISBN 0-913232-88-2). W Kaufmann.

Mesmerism in India. James Esdaile. Bd. with Numerous Cases of Surgical Operations; Philosophy of Sleep. (Contributions to the History of Psychology Ser., Vol. X, Pt. A: Orientations). 1978. Repr. of 1846 ed. 30.00 (ISBN 0-89093-159-3). U Pubns Amer.

Mesolabium Architectionicum That Is a Most Rare Instrument of Measuring. William Bedwell. LC 72-172. (English Experience Ser.: No. 224). 24p. Repr. of 1631 ed. 7.00 (ISBN 90-221-0224-6). Walter J Johnson.

Mesolithic Cultures of Britain. Susann Palmer. (Illus.). 1978. 9.95 o.p. (ISBN 0-85642-062-X, Pub. by Blandford Pr England). Sterling.

Mesolithic Prelude: The Paleolithic-Neolithic Transition in Europe & the Near East. J. G. Clark. 100p. 1980. 15.00x (ISBN 0-85224-365-0, Pub. by Edinburgh U Pr Scotland). Columbia U Pr.

Mesopotamia. Stephen Tapscott. LC 75-11617. (Wesleyan Poetry Program: Vol. 78). 72p. (Orig.). 1975. pap. 4.95x (ISBN 0-8195-1078-5, Pub. by Wesleyan U Pr). Columbia U Pr.

Mesozoic & Cenozoic Paleocontinental Maps. A. G. Smith & J. C. Briden. LC 76-114025. (Cambridge Earth Science Ser.). (Illus.). 1977. 7.95x (ISBN 0-521-29117-8). Cambridge U Pr.

Mesozoic Mammals: The First Two-Thirds of Mammalian History. Ed. by Jason A. Lillegraven et al. 1980. 37.50x (ISBN 0-520-03582-8); pap. 10.75x (ISBN 0-520-03951-3, CAMPUS NO. 234). U of Cal Pr.

Mesozoic Palynology of Svalbard. Tor Bjaerke & Svein B. Manum. (Norsk Polarinstitutt Skrifter: No. 165). (Illus.). 1978. pap. 8.00x (ISBN 82-00-29719-5, Dist. by Columbia U Pr). Universitet.

Mesquite Collector Series. Incl. No. 1. Life of Texas Jack. Glenn Shirley; No. 2. Pink Higgins, the Reluctant Gunfighter: And Other Tales of the Panhandle. Jerry Sinise; No. 3. Murder in the Palo Duro: And Other Mysteries of the Panhandle. George Turner; No. 4. David Lipscomb: A Journalist in Texas, 1872. John L. Robinson. 6.95 ea. Nortex Pr.

Message & Existence: An Introduction to Christian Theology. Langdon Gilkey. 272p. 1980. pap. 4.95 (ISBN 0-8164-2023-8). Crossroad NY.

Message-Attitude-Behavior Relationship: Theory, Methodology & Application. Ed. by Donald P. Cushman & Robert D. McPhee. LC 80-529. (Human Communications Research Ser.). 1980. 27.00 (ISBN 0-12-199760-X). Acad Pr.

Message Dimensions of Television News. Frank. LC 73-8791. (Illus.). 1973. 14.95 (ISBN 0-669-90274-8). Lexington Bks.

Message for the Youth of America. Zee Raf. LC 79-64406. 1980. 7.95 (ISBN 0-533-04302-6). Vantage.

Message from Angola. William Leslie. Date not set. 4.95 (ISBN 0-8062-1654-9). Carlton.

Message from Malaga. Helen MacInnes. 1979. pap. 2.25 (ISBN 0-449-23795-8, Crest). Fawcett.

Message from the President of the United States, Transmitting a Report of the Secretary of War, Relative to Murders Committed by the Indians in the State of Tennessee. Jan. 11, 1813, Repr. Of 1812 Ed. Incl. Travels of James Dolphin, with an Account of His Being Taken by the Indian Savages, & Redeemed by a Spanish Lady in the City of Old Mexico. Repr. of 1812 ed; Journal: Containing an Accurate & Interesting Account of the Hardships, Sufferings, Battles. Defeat & Captivity of Those Heroic Kentucky Volunteers & Regulars, Commanded by General Winchester... Also Two Narratives by Men... Taken Captive by the Indians. Elias Darnell. Repr. of 1813 ed; Murder of the Whole Family of Samuel Wells, Consisting of His Wife & Sister & Eleven Children, by the Indians. Repr. of 1813 ed; Affecting Narrative of the Captivity & Sufferings of Mrs. Mary Smith, Who with Her Husband & Three Daughters Were Taken Prisoners by the Indians. Repr. of 1815 ed; Affecting Account of the Tragical Death of Major Swan, & of the Captivity of Mrs. Swan & Infant Child, by the Savages. Eliza Swan. Repr. of 1815 ed; Narrative of Henry Bird, Who Was Carried Away by the Indians, After the Murder of His Whole Family. Henry Bird. Repr. of 1815 ed; Narrative of the Life & Death of Lieut. Joseph Morgan Wilcox, Who Was Massacred by the Creek Indians on the Alabama River. Repr. of 1816 ed. LC 75-7055. (Indian Captivities Ser.: Vol. 33). 1976. lib. bdg. 44.00 (ISBN 0-8240-1657-2). Garland Pub.

Message Measurement Inventory: A Profile for Communication Analysis. Raymond G. Smith. LC 77-17677. 224p. 1978. 12.50x (ISBN 0-253-33750-X). Ind U Pr.

Message of Aquaria. H. A. Curtiss & F. H. Curtiss. 487p. 1981. pap. 17.50 (ISBN 0-89540-065-0). Sun Pub.

Message of Pope John Paul I. 1978. 3.95 o.s.i. (ISBN 0-8198-0540-8); pap. 2.95 o.s.i. (ISBN 0-8198-0541-6). Dghtrs St Paul.

Message of St. John: The Spiritual Teachings of the Beloved Disciple. Thomas E. Crane. LC 80-11779. 184p. (Orig.). 1980. pap. 5.95 (ISBN 0-8189-0402-X). Alba.

Message of the Bible: A Concise Introduction to the Old & New Testament. William Neil. LC 79-3602. 224p. (Orig.). 1980. pap. 3.95 (ISBN 0-06-066092-9, RD 322, HarpR, HarpR). Harrow.

Message of the Grail. K. O. Schmidt. Tr. by Leone Muller from Ger. LC 75-1994. 1975. 4.95 o.p. (ISBN 0-87707-153-5); text ed. 4.95 o.p. (ISBN 0-685-53509-6). CSA Pr.

Message of Thomas Merton. Ed. by Patrick Hart. (Cistercian Studies: No. 42). 1981. price not set (ISBN 0-87907-842-1). Cistercian Pub.

Message to a Priest Who Has Abandoned the Catholic Church. Samuel H. Markwest. (Illus.). 1980. 29.75 (ISBN 0-89266-227-1). Am Classical Coll Pr.

Message to an Aborted Baby Killed by the Cowardice of His Mother & the Venal Complicity of the Attending Physician. Charles Visentin. (Illus.). 1976. 29.50 (ISBN 0-89266-015-5). Am Classical Coll Pr.

Message to the Charismatic Movement. Larry Christenson. 1972. pap. 1.75 (ISBN 0-87123-372-X, 200372). Bethany Fell.

Messages. Sidney Goldfarb. LC 74-143298. 96p. 1971. 6.95 (ISBN 0-374-20861-1); pap. 2.95 o.p. (ISBN 0-374-50933-6). FS&G.

Messages: A Reader in Human Communication. 2nd ed. Jean Civikly. 1977. pap. text ed. 8.95x o.p. (ISBN 0-394-31268-6). Random.

Messages & Myths: Understanding Interpersonal Communication. Dan Millar & Frank Millar. LC 75-33811. 250p. 1976. pap. text ed. 7.95x (ISBN 0-88284-022-3). Alfred Pub.

Messages & Papers of Jefferson Davis & the Confederacy, 1861-65, 2 vols. Compiled by James D. Richardson. LC 66-29296. 1400p. 1981. Set. pap. 29.95 (ISBN 0-87754-206-6). Chelsea Hse.

Messages from Michael. Chelsea Q. Yarbro. LC 80-82567. 288p. 1980. pap. 2.50 (ISBN 0-87216-766-6). Playboy Pbks.

Messages from the Universal House of Justice: 1968-1973. The Universal House of Justice. LC 75-11795. 1976. 9.00 (ISBN 0-87743-076-4, 7-25-05); pap. 5.00 (ISBN 0-87743-096-9, 7-25-06). Baha'i.

Messages of Freedom. Ed. by Aligarh Muslim University. 1964. 4.50x o.p. (ISBN 0-210-26962-6). Asia.

Messages Without Words. Barbara Sundene Wood. LC 77-27848. (Read About Sciences Ser.). (Illus.). (gr. k-3). 1978. PLB 9.95 (ISBN 0-8393-0084-0). Raintree Child.

Messe: Etudes Archeologiques sur ses Monuments, 8 vols. C. Rohault Fleury. (Illus.). 1722p. (Fr.). 1981. Repr. of 1889 ed. lib. bdg. 600.00x (ISBN 0-89241-153-8). Caratzas Bros.

Messenger of the Cross. Watchman Nee. Tr. by Stephen Kaung. (Orig.). 1980. pap. text ed. write for info. (ISBN 0-935008-50-0); pap. 2.95 (ISBN 0-935008-50-0). Christian Fellow Pubs.

Messenger's Motive: Ethical Problems of the News Media. Hung L. Hulteng. 250p. 1976. pap. 8.95 (ISBN 0-13-577460-8). P-H.

Messengers of Grace: Evangelical Missionaries in the South Seas 1797-1860. Niel Gunson. (Illus.). 1978. 41.00x (ISBN 0-19-550517-4). Oxford U Pr.

Messerschmitt BF 109 at War. encore ed. Andre Van Ishoven. (Illus.). 1978. 4.95 o.p. (ISBN 0-684-16367-5). Scribner.

Messerschmitt BF 109, Versions B-E. R. Cross et al. (No. 2). (Illus.). 1_2p. 1976. 21.95 (ISBN 0-85059-106-6). Aztex.

Messerschmitt Me-262. Edward T. Maloney. (Illus.). 56p. 1980. pap. 6.95 (ISBN 0-9600248-5-9, Pub. by WW Two). Aviation.

Messerschmitt Me 262: Arrow to the Future. Walter J. Boyne. (Illus.). 192p. (Orig.). 1980. 19.95 (ISBN 0-87474-276-5); pap. 9.95 (ISBN 0-87474-275-7). Smithsonian.

Messerschmitt 109, a Famous German Fighter. Heinz J. Nowarra. LC 63-14331. (Harleyford Ser). (Illus.). 1963. 1_.95 (ISBN 0-8168-6375-X). Aero.

Messiah; a Poem. Joseph Cottle. LC 75-31187. (Romantic Context Ser.: Poetry 1789-1830: Vol. 39). 1978. Repr. of 1815 ed. lib. bdg. 47.00 (ISBN 0-8240-2138-X). Garland Pub.

Messiah, a Study in Interpretation. Percy M. Young. 1961. 6.95 (ISBN 0-234-77215-8). Dufour.

Messiah & Temple: The Trial of Jesus in the Gospel of Mark. Donald Juel. LC 76-46397. (Society of Biblical Literature. Dissertation Ser.). 1977. pap. 7.50 (ISBN 0-89130-120-8, 060131). Scholars Pr Ca.

Messiah Texts. Raphael Patai. 1979. pap. 7.95 (ISBN 0-686-68433-_, 46482). Avon.

Messiahship of Jesus. Arthur W. Kac. 350p. 1980. pap. 9.95 (ISBN 0-8024-5421-6). Moody.

Messianic Expectation in the Old Testament. Joachim Becker. Tr. by David E. Green from Ger. LC 79-8891. 96p. 1980. 7.95 (ISBN 0-8006-0545-4, 1-545). Fortress.

Messianic Secret. William Wrede. Tr. by J. C. Greig. 1972. 20.00 (ISBN 0-227-67717-X). Attic Pr.

Messier Catalogue. Charles Messier. Ed. by P. H. Niles. LC 80-70586. 52p. (Orig.). 1981. pap. 1.50 (ISBN 0-96027_8-2-4). Auriga.

Messy Mark. Sharon Peters. (Illus.). 32p. (gr. k-2). 1980. PLB 2.96 (ISBN 0-89375-381-5); pap. 0.95 (ISBN 0-89375-281-9). Troll Assocs.

Mesure Des Gestes: Prolegomenes a la Semiotique Gestuelle. Paul Bouissac. (Approaches to Semiotics, Paperback Ser.: No. 3). 1973. pap. 42.35x (ISBN 90-279-2377-9). Mouton.

Meta Phenomenon. Robert A. Samek. LC 80-81699. 1981. 15.00 (ISBN 0-8022-2372-9). Philos Lib.

Metabolic Activation of Polynuclear Aromatic Hydrocarbons. Wing-Sum Tsang & Gary W. Griffin. (Illus.). 1979. 37.00 (ISBN 0-08-023835-1). Pergamon.

Metabolic & Endocrine Physiology. 4th ed. Jay Tepperman. (Illus.). 1980. write for info. (ISBN 0-8151-8755-5); pap. write for info. (ISBN 0-8151-8756-4). Year Bk Med.

Metabolic Basis of Surgical Care. William F. Walker & Ivan A. Johnston. (Illus.). 1971. 17.95x (ISBN 0-433 34580-2). Intl Ideas.

Metabolic Compartmentation in the Brain. Ed. by R. Balazs & J. E. Cremer. LC 72-11227. 383p. 1973. 37.95 (ISBN 0-470-04582-5). Halsted Pr.

Metabolic Diseases of Bone. Jenifer Jowsey. LC 76-50149. (Monographs in Clinical Orthopaedics Ser.: Vol. 1). (Illus.). 1977. text ed. 29.00 (ISBN 0-7216-5224-7). Saunders.

Metabolic Disorders, Methods of Examination. Tr. by Straub W. (Developments in Ophthalmology: Vol 4). (Illus.). 1981. 78.00 (ISBN 3-8055-2014-X). S Karger.

Metabolic Risk Factors in Ischemic Cardiovascular Disease. Ed. by Lars A. Carlson & Bengt Pernow. 1981. text ed. price not set (ISBN 0-89004-614-X). Raven.

Metabolism & Mitochondria. M. A. Tribe et al. LC 75-25427. (Basic Biology Course Ser.: Bk. 8). (Illus.). 160p. 1976. 35.50 (ISBN 0-521-20952-8); pap. 11.95x (ISBN 0-521-20953-6). Cambridge U Pr.

Metabolism in Architecture. Kisho Kurokawa. (Illus.). 1977. 35.00 o.p. (ISBN 0-89158-734-9). Westview.

Metabolism of Hydrocarbons, Oils, Fuels & Lubricants. Ed. by Applied Science Publishers Ltd London. (Illus.) 1976. 50.40x (ISBN 0-85334-703-4). Intl Ideas.

Metachromatic Reaction. J. W. Kelly. (Protoplasmatologia: Vol. 2, Pt. D2). (Illus.). 1956. pap. 32.50 o.p. (ISBN 0-387-80422-6). Springer-Verlag.

Metacritique. Garbis Kortian. Tr. by J. Habermas from Fr. LC 79-7652. 140p. 1980. 24.95 (ISBN 0-521-22374-1); pap. 8.95 (ISBN 0-521-29618-8). Cambridge U Pr.

Metadrama in Shakespeare's Henriad: Richard II to Henry V. James L. Calderwood. LC 77-93467. 1979. 15.75x (ISBN 0-520-03652-2). U of Cal Pr.

Metaesthetics & Other Essays. Sisirkumar Ghose. 67p. 1975. 8.00 (ISBN 0-88253-719-9); pap. 4.00 (ISBN 0-88253-843-8). Ind-US Inc.

Metafictional Characters in Modern Drama. June Schlueter. LC 79-4207. 1979. 17.50x (ISBN 0-231-04752-5). Columbia U Pr.

Metahistory: The Historical Imagination in Nineteenth-Century Europe. Hayden White. LC 73-8110. 462p. 1974. 22.50x (ISBN 0-8018-1469-3); pap. 6.95 (ISBN 0-8018-1761-7). Johns Hopkins.

Metal & Inorganic Waste Reclaiming Encyclopedia. Ed. by Marshall Sittig. LC 80-21669. (Pollution Tech. Rev. 70; Chem. Tech. Rev. 175). (Illus.). 591p. (Orig.). 1981. 54.00 (ISBN 0-8155-0823-9). Noyes.

Metal & Machines. Byron J. Alpers & Mitchell L. Afrow. (Shoptalk - Vocational Reading Skills). (gr. 9-12). 1978. pap. text ed. 5.12 (ISBN 0-205-05823-X, 4958233); tchr's guide 5.40 (ISBN 0-205-05824-8, 4958241). Allyn.

Metal & Wire Sculpture. Elmar Gruber. LC 69-19489. (Little Craft Book Ser). (Illus.). (gr. 8 up). 1969. 4.95 o.p. (ISBN 0-8069-5128-1); PLB 5.89 o.p. (ISBN 0-8069-5129-X). Sterling.

Metal-Arc Gas Shielded Welding. Ed. by N. C. Balchin et al. (Engineering Craftsmen: No. F23). (Illus.). 1977. spiral bdg. 17.50x (ISBN 0-85083-385-X). Intl Ideas.

Metal-Benders. John Hasted. (Illus.). 272p. 1980. 25.00 (ISBN 0-7100-0597-0). Routledge & Kegan.

Metal Bridges. Compiled by American Society of Civil Engineers. 448p. 1974. pap. text ed. 49.00 (ISBN 0-87262-101-4). Am Soc Civil Eng.

Metal Bulletin Handbook 1978. LC 70-2106. (Illus.). 1977. 45.00x o.p. (ISBN 0-900542-19-5). Intl Pubns Serv.

Metal Casting of Sculpture & Ornament. 2nd ed. Carl D. Clarke. (Illus.). 250p. 1980. 18.00 (ISBN 0-685-50214-7). Standard Arts.

Metal Complexes in Organic Chemistry. R. P. Houghton. LC 78-51685. (Cambridge Texts in Chemistry & Biochemistry). 1979. 59.50 (ISBN 0-521-21992-2); pap. 18.50x (ISBN 0-521-29331-6). Cambridge U Pr.

Metal Contamination of Food. Conor Reilly. xvi, 231p. 1980. 42.50x (ISBN 0-85334-905-3). Burgess-Intl Ideas.

Metal-Crafting Encyclopedia. Sterling Editors. LC 75-14518. (Illus.). 200p. 1975. 17.95 o.p. (ISBN 0-8069-5336-5); lib. bdg. 15.99 o.p. (ISBN 0-8069-5337-3). Sterling.

Metal Craftsman Handbook. William T. Squires. 1981. 7.95 (ISBN 0-89606-050-0). Green Hill.

Metal Cutting. E. M. Trent. 1977. 34.95 (ISBN 0-408-10603-4). Butterworths.

Metal Deformation Processes: Friction & Lubrication. John A. Schey. (Illus.). 824p. 110.00 (ISBN 0-08-024658-3); soft cover 95.00 (ISBN 0-08-024657-5); microfiche x 58.00 (ISBN 0-08-024656-7); microfilm xx 35.00 (ISBN 0-08-024655-9). Pergamon.

Metal: Design & Technique. Wilhelm B. Feldweg. 1975. 70.95 o.p. (ISBN 0-7134-3070-2, Pub. by Batsford England). David & Charles.

Metal Fatigue. N. E. Frost et al. (Oxford Engineering Science Ser). 1975. 55.00x (ISBN 0-19-856114-8). Oxford U Pr.

Metal Fatigue: Theory & Design. A. G. Madayag. 1969. 36.50 (ISBN 0-471-56315-3, Pub. by Wiley-Interscience). Wiley.

Metal Forming: Tool Profiles & Flow. T. Z. Blazynski. LC 75-42156. 1976. 47.95 (ISBN 0-470-15003-3). Halsted Pr.

Metal Hydrides. Ed. by W. M. Mueller et al. 1969. 55.75 o.p. (ISBN 0-12-509550-3). Acad Pr.

Metal Ion Activation of Dioxygen. Ed. by Thomas G. Spiro. LC 79-13808. (Metal Ions in Biology Ser.: Vol. 2). 1980. 29.50 (ISBN 0-471-04398-2, Pub. by Wiley-Interscience). Wiley.

Metal Ions in Biological Systems, Vol. II. Sigel. 448p. 1980. 55.00 (ISBN 0-8247-1004-5). Dekker.

Metal Ions in Solution. John Burgess. 1978. 65.95 o.p. (ISBN 0-470-26293-1). Halsted Pr.

Metal Ions in Solutions. John Burgess. (Chemical Science). 481p. 1980. pap. 29.95x (ISBN 0-470-26987-1). Halsted Pr.

Metal Lathe. David J. Gingery. LC 80-66142. (Build Your Own Metal Working Shop from Scrap Ser.: Bk. 2). (Illus.). 128p. (Orig.). 1980. pap. 7.95 (ISBN 0-9604330-1-5). D J Gingery.

Metal Manufacturing Technology. Jack W. Chaplin. (gr. 10 up). 1976. text ed. 15.72 (ISBN 0-87345-132-5). McKnight.

Metal Monster. A. Merritt. (Orig.). 1976. pap. 1.50 o.p. (ISBN 0-380-00862-9, 31294). Avon.

Metal Shaper. David J. Gingery. LC 80-66142. (Build Your Own Metal Working Shop from Scrap: Bk. 3). (Illus.). 84p. (Orig.). 1980. pap. 6.95 (ISBN 0-9604330-2-3). D J Gingery.

Metal Techniques for Craftsmen. Oppi Untracht. LC 65-16397. 1968. 22.95 (ISBN 0-385-03027-4). Doubleday.

Metal Technology. Rex Miller & Thomas J. Morrisey. LC 74-77817. 1976. 16.50 (ISBN 0-672-21079-7); tchr's guide 3.33 (ISBN 0-672-21107-6); lab bk. 3.95 (ISBN 0-672-21106-8). Bobbs.

Metal Toxicity in Mammals. T. D. Luckey & B. Venugopal. Incl. Vol. 1. Physiologic & Chemical Basis for Metal Toxicity. 238p. 29.50 (ISBN 0-306-37176-6); Vol. 2. Chemical Toxicity of Metals & Metalloids. 419p. 35.00 (ISBN 0-306-37177-4). (Illus.). 1977 (Plenum Pr). Plenum Pub.

Metal Working. Oscar Almeida. (Drake Home Craftsman Ser.). (Illus.). 1976. pap. 5.95 (ISBN 0-8069-8506-2). Sterling.

Metal Working. T. Gardner Boyd. LC 77-89986. (Illus.). 1978. text ed. 4.80 (ISBN 0-87006-258-1). Goodheart.

Metalcraft Today. L. Armstrong & P. K. Guy. 1975. pap. text ed. 3.95x (ISBN 0-435-75700-8). Heinemann Ed.

Metallic Coatings for Corrosion Control. Carter. 1977. text ed. 31.95 (ISBN 0-408-00270-0). Butterworths.

Metallic Elements. R. V. Parish. 1977. pap. text ed. 21.00x (ISBN 0-582-44278-8). Longman.

Metallic Glasses. Ed. by J. J. Gilman. (TN 693.m4m37). 1977. 58.00 (ISBN 0-87170-051-4). ASM.

Metallic Materials Specification Handbook. 3rd ed. Robert B. Ross. LC 79-40761. 1980. cancelled o.p. (ISBN 0-470-26757-7). Halsted Pr.

Metallica: Or, the Treatise of New Metallicall Inventions. Simon Sturtevant. LC 74-28887. (English Experience Ser.: No. 764). 1975. Repr. of 1612 ed. 9.50 (ISBN 90-221-0764-7). Walter J Johnson.

Metallographic Etching. Gunter Petzow. 1978. 24.00 (ISBN 0-87170-002-6). ASM.

Metallography As a Quality Control Tool. Ed. by J. L. McCall & P. M. French. 345p. 1980. 39.50 (ISBN 0-306-40423-0, Plenum Pr). Plenum Pub.

Metallurgical Engineering Vol. 1. Engineering Principles. R. Schuhmann. (Illus.). 1952. 22.95 (ISBN 0-201-06770-6). A-W.

Metallurgical Evolution of Stainless Steels. Ed. by F. B. Pickering. 1979. 38.00 (ISBN 0-87170-077-8). ASM.

Metallurgical Thermodynamics. 2nd ed. David R. Gaskell. (Materials Engineering Ser.). 560p. 1981. text ed. 29.95 (ISBN 0-07-022946-5). McGraw.

Metallurgy & Plastics for Engineers. Merle C. Nutt. LC 76-19249. 1977. text ed. 35.00 (ISBN 0-08-021684-6). Pergamon.

Metallurgy for Engineers. 4th ed. E. C. Rollason. (Illus.). 1973. pap. 18.95x (ISBN 0-7131-3282-5). Intl Ideas.

Metallurgy of Nuclear Fuels. V. S. Yemel'yan ov & A. I. Yevstyukin. 1969. 94.00 (ISBN 0-08-012073-3). Pergamon.

Metallurgy of Zirconium. D. L. Douglass. (Illus.). 470p. (Orig.). 1972. pap. 26.75 (ISBN 92-0-159071-7, IAEA). Unipub.

Metalogic: An Introduction to the Metatheory of Standard First Order Logic. Geoffrey Hunter. LC 71-131195. 1971. 18.50x (ISBN 0-520-01822-2); pap. 6.95x (ISBN 0-520-02356-0). U of Cal Pr.

Metalogicon of John of Salisbury. John Of Salisbury. Tr. by Daniel McGarry. 8.50 (ISBN 0-8446-0159-4). Peter Smith.

Metals & Metabolism, No. 26. D. A. Phipps. (Oxford Chemistry Ser). (Illus.). 1976. pap. 12.50x (ISBN 0-19-855413-3). Oxford U Pr.

Metals: Background Information. Don Radford. LC 77-83004. (Science 5-13 Ser.). (Illus.). 1977. pap. text ed. 8.25 (ISBN 0-356-04104-2). Raintree Child.

Metals, Ceramics & Polymers. Oliver H. Wyatt & D. Dew-Hughes. LC 70-178286. (Illus.). 500p. 1974. 86.50 (ISBN 0-521-08238-2); pap. 24.50x (ISBN 0-521-09834-3). Cambridge U Pr.

Metals Engineering. Boy Scouts of America. LC 19-600. (Illus.). 64p. (gr. 6-12). 1972. pap. 0.70x (ISBN 0-8395-3269-5, 3269). BSA.

Metals in Biochemistry. P. M. Harrison & R. J. Hoare. LC 79-41813. 80p. 1980. pap. 5.95 (ISBN 0-412-13160-9, 6361). Methuen Inc.

Metals Reference Book. 5th ed. Ed. by C. J. Smithells. 1976. 160.00 (ISBN 0-408-70627-9). Butterworths.

Metals: Stages 1 & 2. Don Radford. LC 77-83004. (Science 5-13). (Illus.). 1977. pap. text ed. 8.25 (ISBN 0-356-04103-4). Raintree Child.

Metals: Thermal & Mechanical Data. S. Allard. 1969. text ed. 105.00 (ISBN 0-08-006588-0). Pergamon.

Metalsmith Papers. Society of North American Goldsmiths. 96p. (Orig.). 1980. pap. text ed. 12.00 (ISBN 0-9604446-0-2). SNAG.

Metalsmiths. Percy Knauth. (Emergence of Man Ser.). (Illus.). 1974. 9.95 (ISBN 0-8094-1308-6); lib. bdg. avail. (ISBN 0-685-48124-7). Time-Life.

Metalsmiths. Percy Knauth. LC 73-89680. (Emergence of Man Ser.). (gr. 6 up). 1973. PLB 9.63 o.p. (ISBN 0-8094-1309-4, Pub. by Time-Life). Silver.

Metalwork. Boy Scouts Of America. LC 19-600. (Illus.). 36p. (gr. 6-12). 1969. pap. 0.70x (ISBN 0-8395-3312-8, 3312). BSA.

Metalwork. rev. ed. John L. Feirer & John R. Lindbeck. (gr. 7-9). 1970. 10.60 (ISBN 0-87002-017-X); student guide 3.00 (ISBN 0-87002-048-X). Bennett IL.

Metalwork: A Course for Schools & Colleges. M. J. Holdanowicz. 1971. pap. text ed. 3.95x o.p. (ISBN 0-435-75395-9). Heinemann Ed.

Metalwork: S.I. Metric Edition. Feirer & Lindbeck. 1979. text ed. 13.28 (ISBN 0-87002-292-X); student guide 5.28 (ISBN 0-87002-316-0). Bennett IL.

Metalwork Technology. G. H. Thomas. (gr. 9 up). 1970. 10.95x (ISBN 0-7195-2654-X). Transatlantic.

Metalwork Technology & Practice. rev. & 5th ed. Oswald A. Ludwig & Willard J. McCarthy. (Illus.). (gr. 11-12). 1975. text ed. 17.28 (ISBN 0-87345-117-1); study guide 5.00 (ISBN 0-87345-118-X); ans key avail. (ISBN 0-685-04228-6). McKnight.

Metalworking. Los Angeles Unified School District. Ed. by Richard A. Vorndran. LC 77-73297. 96p. (gr. 7-9). 1978. pap. text ed. 4.40 (ISBN 0-02-820420-4). Glencoe.

Metalworking. McKnight Staff Members & Wilbur R. Miller. LC 78-53387. (Basic Industrial Arts Ser.). (Illus.). 1978. 6.00 (ISBN 0-87345-792-7); softbound 4.48 (ISBN 0-87345-784-6). McKnight.

Metalworking: An Introduction. Gregory S. Graham. 1980. text ed. write for info. (ISBN 0-534-00843-7, Breton Pubs). Wadsworth Pub.

Metalworking Industry. Glynnis Trainer. 200p. 1981. cancelled (ISBN 0-86569-062-6). Auburn Hse.

Metalworking Lubrication. Ed. by S. Kalpakjian & S. C. Jain. 259p. 1980. 40.00 (H00159). ASME.

Metamorphasis of Tobacco. John Beaumont. LC 70-171734. (English Experience Ser.: No. 360). 44p. Repr. of 1602 ed. 7.00 (ISBN 90-221-0360-9). Walter J Johnson.

Metamorphic Petrology. 2nd ed. Francis J. Turner. LC 79-27496. (International Earth & Planetary Sciences Ser.). (Illus.). 512p. 1980. text ed. 29.95 (ISBN 0-07-065501-4, C). McGraw.

Metamorphic Processes: Reactions & Microstructure Development. R. H. Vernon. LC 75-9139. 1976. 24.95 (ISBN 0-470-90655-3). Halsted Pr.

Metamorphic Textures. A. Spry. 1969. 42.00 (ISBN 0-08-013316-9); pap. 19.25 (ISBN 0-08-013315-0). Pergamon.

Metamorphism & Metamorphic Belts. A. Miyashiro. LC 72-13983. 1978. pap. 29.95 (ISBN 0-470-99390-1). Halsted Pr.

Metamorphoseon. Ovid. Ed. by Jacobus Pontanus. LC 75-27868. (Renaissance & the Gods Ser.: Vol. 24). (Illus.). 1977. Repr. of 1618 ed. lib. bdg. 73.00 (ISBN 0-8240-2073-1). Garland Pub.

Metamorphoseon Ovidianarum. Crispin Van de Pusse. LC 78-68195. (Philosophy of Images Ser.). (Illus.). 1980. lib. bdg. 66.00 (ISBN 0-8240-3682-4). Garland Pub.

Metamorphoseon...Ovidianarum. Antonio Tempesta. LC 75-27861. (Renaissance & the Gods Ser.: Vol. 19). (Illus.). 1976. Repr. of 1606 ed. lib. bdg. 73.00 (ISBN 0-8240-2067-7). Garland Pub.

Metamorphoseos. Ovid. LC 75-278944. (Renaissance & the Gods Ser.: Vol. 3). (Illus.). 1977. Repr. of 1518 ed. lib. bdg. 73.00 (ISBN 0-8240-2052-9). Garland Pub.

Metamorphoses. Ovid. Tr. by Garth et al. LC 75-27884. (Renaissance & the Gods Ser.: Vol. 39). (Illus.). 1976. Repr. of 1732 ed. lib. bdg. 73.00 (ISBN 0-8240-2088-X). Garland Pub.

Metamorphoses, Bk. 1. Ovid. Ed. by A. G. Lee. 1953. pap. text ed. 7.50 (ISBN 0-521-05870-8). Cambridge U Pr.

Metamorphoses, Bk. 8. Ovid. Ed. by A. S. Hollis. (Illus.). 1970. 17.95x (ISBN 0-19-814440-7). Oxford U Pr.

Metamorphoses of the Self: The Mystic, the Sensualist, & the Artist in the Works of Julien Green. John M. Dunaway. LC 78-88007. (Studies in Romance Languages: No. 19). 128p. 1978. 11.50x (ISBN 0-8131-1364-4). U Pr of Ky.

Metamorphosis. Ovid. Tr. by A. E. Watts from Latin. (Illus.). 440p. 1980. pap. 9.50 (ISBN 0-86547-019-7). N Point Pr.

Metamorphosis. Anthony J. Summers. 1979. 2.75 (ISBN 0-918476-06-2). Cornerstone Pr.

Metamorphosis: A Problem in Developmental Biology. Ed. by William Etkin & Lawrence I. Gilbert. LC 67-29170. 459p. 1968. 32.50 (ISBN 0-306-50019-1, Plenum Pr). Plenum Pub.

Metamorphosis in Keats. Barry Gradman. LC 79-3756. 160p. 1980. 13.95x (ISBN 0-8147-2977-0); pap. 5.95x (ISBN 0-8147-2978-9). NYU Pr.

Metamorphosis in the Arts. Richard Kostelanetz. LC 80-68968. 328p. 1981. 18.00 (ISBN 0-686-69406-6); pap. 8.00 (ISBN 0-686-69407-4). Assembling Pr.

Metamorphosis of a Death Symbol: The Changing Meaning of the Transi Tomb in the Late Middle Ages & the Renaissance. Kathleen R. Cohen. (California Studies in the History of Art: Vol. 15). 1974. 50.00x (ISBN 0-520-01844-3). U of Cal Pr.

Metamorphosis of a Poet. George S. Holton. 1981. 7.95 (ISBN 0-533-04886-9). Vantage.

Metamorphosis of the Cassowaries: Umeda Society, Language & Ritual. Alfred Gell. (London School of Economics Monographs on Social Anthropology Ser). (Illus.). 385p. 1975. text ed. 25.25x (ISBN 0-391-00388-7, Athlone Pr). Humanities.

Metamorphosis Ovidiana Moraliter... Explanata Libellus. Thomas Waleys. Ed. by Stephen Orgel. LC 78-68208. (Philosophy of Images: Vol. 1). 1979. lib. bdg. 66.00 (ISBN 0-8240-3675-1). Garland Pub.

Metamorphosis, Seu Fabulae Poeticae. Georg Sabinus. LC 75-27857. (Renaissance & the Gods Ser.: Vol. 14). (Illus.). 1976. Repr. of 1589 ed. lib. bdg. 73.00 (ISBN 0-8240-2063-4). Garland Pub.

Metaphor. H. W. Fowler et al. Ed. by Steele Commager. Incl. English Idioms; English Influence on the French Vocabulary; Briton, British, Britisher; Split Infinitive; Logic & Grammar; Four Words; Subjunctives; Medium Aevum & the Middle Age; Index to Tracts I-XIX. (Society for Pure English Ser.: Vol. 2). 1979. lib. bdg. 42.00 (ISBN 0-8240-3666-2). Garland Pub.

Metaphor: A Psychoanalytic View. Robert Rogers. LC 77-80477. 1978. 11.95x (ISBN 0-520-03548-8). U of Cal Pr.

Metaphor & Thought. Ed. by Andrew Ortony. LC 78-32011. (Illus.). 1979. 45.00 (ISBN 0-521-22727-5); pap. 13.95x (ISBN 0-521-29626-9). Cambridge U Pr.

Metaphor in the Works of Isaac Babel. Danuta Mendelson. 1981. 17.50 (ISBN 0-88233-702-5). Ardis Pubs.

Metaphor of Chance: Vision & Technique in the Works of Thomas Hardy. Bert G. Hornback. LC 77-122099. viii, 177p. 1971. 12.00x (ISBN 0-8214-0077-0). Ohio U Pr.

Metaphor of Painting: Essays on Baudelaire, Ruskin, Proust & Pater. Lee M. Johnson. Ed. by Donald B. Kuspit. (Studies in Fine Arts: Criticism). 249p. 1980. 24.95 (ISBN 0-8357-1092-0, Pub. by UMI Res Pr). Univ Microfilms.

Metaphorical Brain: An Introduction to Cybernetics As Artificial Intelligence & Brains Theory. Michael Arbib. LC 72-2490. (Illus.). 243p. 1972. 24.95 (ISBN 0-471-03249-2, Pub by Wiley-Interscience). Wiley.

Metaphors of Consciousness. Ed. by Ronald S. Valle & Rolf Von Eckartsberg. 500p. 1981. 25.00 (ISBN 0-306-40520-2, Plenum Pr). Plenum Pub.

Metaphors of Masculinity: Sex & Status in Andalusian Folklore. Stanley Brandes. LC 79-5258. (American Folklore Society Ser.). 224p. 1980. 19.95x (ISBN 0-8122-7776-7); pap. 9.95. U of Pa Pr.

Metaphysic of Experience, 4 vols. Shadworth H. Hodgson & Maurice Nathanson. LC 78-66730. (Phenomenology Ser.). 858p. 1980. lib. bdg. 193.00 (ISBN 0-8240-9564-2). Garland Pub.

Metaphysica. Aristotle. Ed. by Werner Jaeger. (Oxford Classical Texts Ser). 1957. 24.00x (ISBN 0-19-814513-6). Oxford U Pr.

Metaphysical Art. Massimo Carra et al. Tr. by Caroline Tisdall. (World of Art Ser.). (Illus.). 1971. text ed. 9.95 (ISBN 0-19-520008-X). Oxford U Pr.

Metaphysical Elements of Justice: Part I of the Metaphysics of Morals. Immanuel Kant. Tr. by John Ladd. (Orig.). 1965. pap. 4.95 (ISBN 0-672-60250-4, LLA72). Bobbs.

Metaphysical Foundations of Modern Physical Science. 2nd ed. Edwin A. Burtt. (International Library of Psychology, Philosophy & Scientific Method). 1967. Repr. of 1932 ed. text ed. 27.50x (ISBN 0-7100-3032-0); pap. text ed. 5.95x (ISBN 0-391-01633-4). Humanities.

Metaphysical Novel in England & America: Dickens, Bulwer, Hawthorne, Melville. Edwin M. Eigner. LC 76-50246. 1978. 16.50x (ISBN 0-520-03382-5). U of Cal Pr.

Metaphysical Novel in England: The Romantic Phase. Robert L. Platzner. Ed. by Devendra P. Varma. LC 79-8468. (Gothic Studies & Dissertations Ser.). 1980. lib. bdg. 29.00x (ISBN 0-405-12656-5). Arno.

Metaphysical Poetry. Ed. by Malcolm Bradbury & David Palmer. (Stratford-Upon-Avon Studies: No. 11). 280p. 1970. text ed. 19.50x (ISBN 0-8419-5823-8). Holmes & Meier.

Metaphysical Tales: Short Fiction by Eugene K. Garber. Eugene K. Garber. 128p. 1981. text ed. 10.00x (ISBN 0-8262-0325-6). U of Mo Pr.

Metaphysical Thinking. Elmer Sprague. 1978. pap. 5.95x (ISBN 0-19-502263-7). Oxford U Pr.

Metaphysical Thought of Godfrey of Fontaines: A Study in Late Thirteenth Century Philosophy. John F. Wippel. 1980. text ed. write for info. (ISBN 0-8132-0556-5, Dist. by Isbs). Intl Schol Bk Serv.

Metaphysics. 2nd ed. Richard Taylor. LC 73-5748. (Foundations of Philosophy Ser). 133p. 1974. pap. 7.95 ref. ed. (ISBN 0-13-578468-9). P-H.

Metaphysics. Ed. by Julius R. Weinberg & Keith E. Yandell. LC 73-148058. 1971. pap. text ed. 9.75x (ISBN 0-03-085668-X). Irvington.

Metaphysics, Bks. 4-6. Aristotle. Tr. by Christopher Kirwan. (Clarendon Aristotle Ser.). 214p. 1971. 16.95x (ISBN 0-19-872027-0). Oxford U Pr.

Metaphysics: An Introduction. Keith Campbell. 1976. pap. text ed. 10.95x (ISBN 0-8221-0175-0). Dickenson.

Metaphysics: Books M & N. Aristotle. Ed. by Julia Annas. (Clarendon Aristotle Ser.). 1976. 24.95x (ISBN 0-19-872085-8). Oxford U Pr.

Metaphysics, Materialism, & the Evolution of the Mind: Early Writings of Charles Darwin. Charles Darwin. LC 80-15763. 1980. pap. 6.95 (ISBN 0-226-13659-0, P906, Phoen). U of Chicago Pr.

Metaphysics of Absurdity. H. Gene Blocker. LC 78-78399. 1979. pap. text ed. 9.00 (ISBN 0-8191-0712-3). U Pr of Amer.

Metaphysics of American Civilization. Charles R. Saindower. (American Culture Library Book). (Illus.). 1979. 37.75 (ISBN 0-89266-201-8). Am Classical Coll Pr.

Metaphysics of History at the End of the Twentieth Century. William Dellaquila. (Illus.). 1977. 49.45 (ISBN 0-89266-028-7). Am Classical Coll Pr.

Metaphysics of Naturalism. Sterling P. Lamprecht. LC 67-18049. (Century Philosophy Ser.). 1967. 24.00x (ISBN 0-89197-302-8). Irvington.

Metaphysics of Sex. Julius Evola. Tr. by J. A. Ormrod from Ital. (Illus.). 1981. pap. 8.95 (ISBN 0-89281-025-4). Inner Tradit.

Metaphysics of the Jewish, the Aegyptian & the Assyrian Spirit. Georg W. Hegel. (Illus.). 109p. 1981. 41.75 (ISBN 0-89266-280-8). Am Classical Coll Pr.

Metaphysics of the Womb. Henry D. Thornton. (Illus.). 141p. 1981. 49.85 (ISBN 0-89266-271-9). Am Classical Coll Pr.

Metaphysische und transzendentale Dynamik in Kant opus postumum. Burkhard Tuschling. (Quellen und Studien Zur Philosophie, 3). 224p. 1971. 33.50x (ISBN 3-11-001889-6). De Gruyter.

Metapoetic of the Passage: Architextures in Surrealiam & After. Mary A. Cawa. LC 80-54468. 192p. 1981. 12.00x (ISBN 0-87451-194-1). U Pr of New Eng.

Metasex, Mirth & Madness. Marco Vassi. LC 75-165. 1975. 7.95 o.p. (ISBN 0-89110-002-4). Penthouse Pr.

Metasphere: The Altered State of Word. James Guy. LC 80-83463. (Illus.). 137p. (Orig.). 1980. pap. 7.00 (ISBN 0-9604918-7-2). Lampkin Pub.

Metastatic Bone Disease. Association of Bone & Joint Surgeons. Ed. by Marshall R. Urist. (Clinical Orthopaedics Ser., Vol. 73). 1970. 15.00 (ISBN 0-685-22889-4). Lippincott.

Meteorites. Fritz Heide. Ed. by Edward Anders & Eugene DuFresne. (Illus.). 1964. 6.50x o.s.i. (ISBN 0-226-32338-2). U of Chicago Pr.

Meteorites. C. B. Moore. (Earth Science Curriculum Project Pamphlet Ser). 1971. pap. 3.20 (ISBN 0-395-02624-5, 2-14610). HM.

Meteorites & Their Origins. G. J. McCall. LC 72-7640. 352p. 1973. 19.95 (ISBN 0-470-58115-8). Halsted Pr.

Meteorological Factors Affecting the Epidemology of the Cotton Leaf Worm & the Pink Boolworm. (Technical Note Ser.: No. 167). 46p. 1980. pap. 10.00 (ISBN 92-63-10532-4, W473, WMO). Unipub.

Meteorology. E. D. Fickett. Repr. of 1900 ed. pap. 1.50 (ISBN 0-8466-0029-3, SJS29). Shorey.

Meteorology: An Introductory Course, 2 vols. Arnt Eliassen. 1977. Vol. I. pap. 22.00x (ISBN 82-00-02392-3, Dist. by Columbia U Pr); Vol. II. pap. 15.00 (ISBN 82-00-02411-3). Universitet.

Meteorology for Glider Pilots. 3rd ed. C. E. Wallington. (Illus.). 331p. 1980. 24.00 (ISBN 0-7195-3303-1). Transatlantic.

Meteorology: Forecasting the Weather. Heinz Wachter. LC 73-3786. (International Library). (gr. 7 up). 1973. PLB 6.90 o.p. (ISBN 0-531-02115-7). Watts.

Meteorology: The Earth & Its Weather. Joseph S. Weisberg. LC 75-26094. (Illus.). 320p. 1976. text ed. 17.95 (ISBN 0-395-20673-1); inst. manual 1.50 (ISBN 0-395-20674-X); slides 11.25 (ISBN 0-395-24686-5). HM.

Meteorology: The Earth & Its Weather. 2nd ed. Joseph S. Weisberg. (Illus.). 432p. 1981. text ed. 18.95 (ISBN 0-395-29516-5); instr's manual avail. (ISBN 0-395-29517-3). HM.

Meter: A Handbook of Activities to Motivate the Teaching of the Metric System. (The Spice Ser.). 1975. 6.50 (ISBN 0-89273-118-4). Educ Serv.

Meter Duplicating Masters: Metric System, 3 vols. (Spice Ser.). 1976. 5.95 ea. Vol. 1, Grades K-3 (ISBN 0-89273-541-4). Vol. 2, Grades 3-6 (ISBN 0-89273-542-2). Vol. 3, Grades 6-8 (ISBN 0-89273-543-0). Educ Serv.

Meters of Greek & Latin Poetry. rev. ed. James Halporn et al. LC 79-6718. 138p. 1980. pap. 4.95x (ISBN 0-8061-1558-0). U of Okla Pr.

Methadone Maintenance: A Technological Fix. Dorothy Nelkin. LC 72-96071. (Science, Technology & Society Ser). 192p. 1973. 6.95 o.s.i. (ISBN 0-8076-0681-2); pap. 1.95 (ISBN 0-8076-0680-4). Braziller.

Methadone Treatment in Narcotic Addiction: Program Management,Findings, & Prospects for the Future. R. G. Newman. 1977. 29.00 (ISBN 0-12-517050-5). Acad Pr.

Methane Digesters for Fuel Gas & Fertilizer. (Illus.). 1973. pap. text ed. 4.00 (ISBN 0-9600984-2-9). L J Fry.

Methane Generation & Recovery from Landfills. Emcon Associates. LC 80-67725. 139p. 1980. 14.95 (ISBN 0-250-40360-9). Ann Arbor Science.

Method & Appraisal in Economics. Ed. by S. J. Latsis. LC 75-44581. 220p. 1976. 38.50 (ISBN 0-521-21076-3). Cambridge U Pr.

Method & Appraisal in the Physical Sciences. Ed. by C. Howson. LC 75-44580. 280p. 1976. 44.50 (ISBN 0-521-21110-7). Cambridge U Pr.

Method & Madness. Eva Hesse. Date not set. 20.00 (ISBN 0-89396-024-1). Urizen Bks. Postponed.

Method & Means of Public Speaking. William S. Smith & Donald J. Canty. (Orig.). 1962. pap. 5.95 (ISBN 0-672-60859-6). Bobbs.

Method & Measurement in Sociology. Aaron V. Cicourel. LC 64-16970. 1964. 14.95 (ISBN 0-02-905480-X). Free Pr.

Method & Techniques for Understanding Music Notation. Adela Bay. LC 80-10292. (Illus.). 143p. 1980. pap. 11.95 (ISBN 0-89116-190-2). Hemisphere Pub.

Method & Theory in Experimental Psychology. Charles E. Osgood. 1953. text ed. 17.95x (ISBN 0-19-501008-6). Oxford U Pr.

Method for Easy Comprehension of History. Jean Bodin. Tr. by Beatrice Reynolds. (Columbia University Records of Civilization Ser). 1969. pap. 5.95x (ISBN 0-393-09863-X, NortonC). Norton.

Method for Priority Determination in Science & Technology. (Science Policy Studies & Documents: No. 40). 1978. pap. 4.75 (ISBN 92-3-101485-4, U841, UNESCO). Unipub.

Method for Studying-Model Hamiltonians. N. N. Bogolyubov. 180p. 1972. text ed. 37.00 (ISBN 0-08-016742-X). Pergamon.

Method for the Spanish Guitar. F. Sor. LC 77-158960. (Music Ser). 1971. Repr. lib. bdg. 17.50 (ISBN 0-306-70188-X). Da Capo.

Method in Ministry: Theological Reflection and Christian Ministry. James D. Whitehead & Evelyn E. Whitehead. 240p. 1980. 12.95 (ISBN 0-8164-0455-0). Seabury.

Method in Orchestration. Ian Parrott. (Student's Music Library Ser). 1956. 6.95 (ISBN 0-234-77310-3). Dufour.

Method in Theology. Bernard Lonergan. (Library of Contemporary Theology). 1979. pap. 9.95 (ISBN 0-8164-2204-4). Crossroad NY.

Method Modeling. Valerie Cragin. LC 80-81778. (Illus.). 160p. (Orig.). 1980. pap. 13.95 (ISBN 0-8227-4045-1). Petersen Pub.

Method of Averaging Functional Corrections: Theory & Applications. Anton Y. Luchka. (Orig.). 1965. 22.00 o.p. (ISBN 0-12-458150-1). Acad Pr.

Method of Averaging in the Theory of Orthogonal Series, & Some Questions in the Theory of Bases. S. V. Bockarev. (Trudy Steklov: No. 146). 1980. 26.00 (ISBN 0-8218-3045-7). Am Math.

Method of Coordinates, Vol. 1. J. M. Gelfand Library of School Mathematics. 1967. 7.50x (ISBN 0-262-07028-6). MIT Pr.

Method of Holding the Three Ones. Tr. by Poul Anderson. (Studies on Asian Topics: No. 1). (Orig.). 1980. pap. text ed. 6.50x (ISBN 0-7007-0113-3). Humanities.

Method of Lighting the Stage. 4th ed. Stanley McCandless. LC 56-10331. 1958. 7.45 (ISBN 0-87830-082-1). Theatre Arts.

Method of Psychiatry. Ed. by Stanley E. Greben et al. LC 80-10348. (Illus.). 375p. 1980. text ed. 20.00 (ISBN 0-8121-0710-1). Lea & Febiger.

Method of Science. R. Harre & D. G. Eastwood. LC 76-116973. (Wykeham Science Ser.: No. 8). 1970. 9.95x (ISBN 0-8448-1110-6). Crane-Russak Co.

Method Study & the Furniture Industry. R. H. Glossop. LC 75-112711. 1970. 21.00 (ISBN 0-08-015653-3). Pergamon.

Methode Orange, Bk 1. (Methode Orange Ser.). (Illus.). (gr. 7-12). 1979. text ed. 5.25 (ISBN 0-88345-407-6). Regents Pub.

Methode Orange, Bk 1. Reboullet et al. (Methode Orange Ser.). (Illus., Fr.). (gr. 7-12). 1979. pap. text ed. 4.25 (ISBN 0-88345-406-8). Regents Pub.

Methode Orange - Workbook 1. Reboullet et al. (Methode Orange Ser.). (Illus., Fr.). (gr. 7-12). 1979. pap. text ed. 4.25 (ISBN 0-686-67708-0); tchrs' manual 5.95 (ISBN 0-88345-411-4); cassettes 70.00 (ISBN 0-686-60844-5); slides 120.00 (ISBN 0-686-60845-3). Regents Pub.

Methodism in American History. rev. ed. William W. Sweet. 1954. 6.50 (ISBN 0-687-25081-1). Abingdon.

Methodist Publishing House: A History, Vol. 1. James P. Pilkington. (Illus.). 1968. 7.50 (ISBN 0-687-26700-5). Abingdon.

Methodist Union Catalog Pre-1976 Imprints, 20 vols, Vol. I, A-bj. Ed. by Kenneth E. Rowe. LC 75-33190. 1975. 25.00 (ISBN 0-8108-0880-3). Scarecrow.

Methodist Union Catalog: Pre-1976 Imprints, Vol. II: Bl-cha. Ed. by Kenneth E. Rowe. LC 75-33190. 1976. 25.00 (ISBN 0-8108-0920-6). Scarecrow.

Methodist Union Catalog: Pre-1976 Imprints, Che-Dix, Vol. 3. Ed. by Kenneth E. Rowe. LC 75-33190. 1978. 25.00 (ISBN 0-8108-1067-0). Scarecrow.

Methodist Union Catalog: Pre-1976 Imprints: Volume IV, Do-Fy. Ed. by Kenneth E. Rowe. LC 75-33190. 436p. 1979. 25.00 (ISBN 0-8108-1225-8). Scarecrow.

Methodo Scientifica pertractatum: Mos geometricus und Kalkuelbegriff in der Philosophischen Theorienbildung des 17. und 18. Hans W. Arndt. (Quellen und Studien Zur Philosophie Ser.: Vol. 4). 1971. 42.35x (ISBN 3-11-003942-7). De Gruyter.

Methodological Aspects of Transformational Generative Phonology. Rudolph P. Botha. (Janua Linguarum, Ser. Minor: No. 112). 266p. 1971. pap. text ed. 24.70x (ISBN 90-2791-761-2). Mouton.

Methodological Issues in Religious Studies. Ed. by Robert D. Baird. LC 75-44170. (Orig.). 1976. lib. bdg. 14.95x (ISBN 0-914914-08-1); pap. text ed. 5.95x (ISBN 0-914914-07-3). New Horizons.

Methodological Problems in Minority Research. Ed. by William T. Liu. (Orig.). 1981. pap. write for info. (ISBN 0-934584-09-5). Pacific-Asian.

Methodological Status of Grammatical Argumentation. Rudolf B. Botha. LC 79-126050. (Janua Linguarum Ser.Maior: No. 105). (Orig.). 1970. pap. text ed. 12.95x (ISBN 90-2790-714-5). Mouton.

Methodologies for Analyzing Public Policies. Frank P. Scioli & Thomas J. Cook. LC 75-8152. (Policy Studies Organization Policy Study Ser.). 160p. 1975. 17.95 (ISBN 0-669-00596-7). Lexington Bks.

Methodology for Assessing Impacts of Radioactivity on Aquatic Ecosystems. (Technical Reports Ser.: No. 190). 1979. pap. 47.25 (ISBN 92-0-125379-6, IDC190, IAEA). Unipub.

Methodology for Determining Insect Control Recommendations. (IRRI Research Paper Ser.: No. 46). 31p. 1980. pap. 5.00 (R086, IRRI). Unipub.

Methodology in Computer Graphics: Proceedings. IFIP Workshop on Methodology in Computer Graphics, France, May 1976. Ed. by R. A. Guedj & H. Tucker. 1979. 29.50 (ISBN 0-444-85301-4, North Holland). Elsevier.

Methodology in Economic Research. Ed. by A. K. Dasgupta. 6.50x (ISBN 0-210-27183-3). Asia.

Methodology in Systems Modelling & Simulation: Proceedings. Symposium on Modelling & Simulation Methodology, Israel, August 1978. Ed. by B. P. Zeigler et al. 1979. 66.00 (ISBN 0-444-85340-5, North Holland). Elsevier.

Methodology of Comparative Political Research. Ed. by Robert T. Holt & John E. Turner. LC 70-80471. 1972. 10.95 (ISBN 0-02-914850-2); pap. text ed. 5.95 (ISBN 0-02-914840-5). Free Pr.

Methodology of Economics: Or How Economists Explain. Mark Blaug. LC 80-13802. (Cambridge Surveys of Economic Literature). 325p. 1980. 29.50 (ISBN 0-521-22288-5); pap. 9.95 (ISBN 0-521-29437-1). Cambridge U Pr.

Methodology of Scientific Research Programmes: Philosophical Papers, Vol. 1. I. Lakatos. Ed. by J. Worrall & G. Currie. LC 77-71415. 1978. 32.50 (ISBN 0-521-21644-3). Cambridge U Pr.

Methodology of the Social Sciences. Felix Kaufman. 1978. Repr. of 1944 ed. text ed. 13.50x (ISBN 0-391-00931-1). Humanities.

Methods & Evaluation in Clinical & Counseling Psychology. T. C. Kahn et al. 375p. 1975. text ed. 23.00 (ISBN 0-08-017862-6); pap. text ed. 16.00 (ISBN 0-08-017863-4). Pergamon.

Methods & Goals in Human Behavior Genetics. Ed. by Steven G. Vandenberg. 1965. 38.00 o.p. (ISBN 0-12-710650-2). Acad Pr.

Methods & Issues in Social Research. James A. Black & Dean J. Champion. LC 75-26659. 445p. 1976. 18.95 (ISBN 0-471-07705-4). Wiley.

Methods & Materials of Commercial Construction. Frank R. Dagostino. LC 73-196221. 304p. 1974. text ed. 13.50 (ISBN 0-87909-486-9); ref. ed. 18.00 (ISBN 0-686-66910-X). Reston.

Methods & Materials of Demography. Henry Shyrock & Jacob Siegel. (Studies in Population Ser.). 577p. 1976. text ed. 19.75 (ISBN 0-12-641150-6). Acad Pr.

Methods & Materials of Residential Construction. Laurence E. Reiner. (Illus.). 336p. 1981. text ed. 24.95 (ISBN 0-13-578864-1). P-H.

Methods & Models for Assessing Energy Resources: First IIASA Conference on Energy Resources, 20-21 May, 1975, Laxenburg, Austria. Ed. by M. Grenon. (IIASA Proceedings: Vol. 5). (Illus.). 1979. 89.00 (ISBN 0-08-024443-2). Pergamon.

Methods & Models for Education in Parapsychology. D. Scott Rogo. LC 73-75209. (Parapsychological Monograph No. 14). 1973. pap. 2.50 (ISBN 0-912328-22-3). Parapsych Foun.

Methods & Perspectives in Geography. J. Beaujeu-Garnier. Tr. by Jennifer Bray from French. LC 75-23484. (Illus.). 144p. 1976. text ed. 11.95x (ISBN 0-582-48069-8). Longman.

Methods & Techniques in Clinical Chemistry. Paul L. Wolf et al. LC 78-39685. 400p. 1972. 29.95 (ISBN 0-471-95900-6, Pub. by Wiley Medical). Wiley.

Methods & Techniques in Post-Secondary Education. (Educational Studies & Documents Ser.: No. 31). 138p. 1980. pap. 7.00 (ISBN 92-3-101575-3, U1045, UNESCO). Unipub.

Methods Engineering. Edward V. Krick. LC 62-8775. (Illus.). 1962. text ed. 28.95x (ISBN 0-471-50754-7). Wiley.

Methods for Assessing Age Discrimination in Federal Programs. Michael Gutowski & Jeffrey Koshel. (Institute Paper). 69p. 1977. pap. 3.50 (ISBN 0-87766-209-6, 20400). Urban Inst.

Methods for Chemical Analysis of Fresh Waters. 2nd ed. H. Golterman. (Blackwell Scientific Pubns.: IBP Handbk. No. 8). (Illus.). 1978. pap. 16.25 (ISBN 0-632-00459-2). Mosby.

Methods for Evaluating Biological Nitrogen Fixation. Ed. by F. J. Bergersen. LC 79-41785. 640p. 1980. 114.00 (ISBN 0-471-27759-2, Pub. by Wiley-Interscience). Wiley.

Methods for Land Economics Research. Ed. by W. L. Gibson, Jr. et al. LC 66-19269. 1967. pap. 3.95x (ISBN 0-8032-5225-0, BB 352, Bison). U of Nebr Pr.

Methods for Learning Disorders. 2nd ed. Patricia L. Myers & Donald D. Hammill. LC 75-37504. 1976. text ed. 21.95 (ISBN 0-471-62751-8). Wiley.

Methods for Obtaining & Handling Marine Eggs & Embryos. D. P. Costello & Catherine Henley. LC 76-171320. 1971. 10.00 (ISBN 0-685-52860-X). Marine Bio.

Methods for Research on the Ecology of Soil-Borne Plant Pathogens. Leander F. Johnson & Elroy Curl. LC 77-176196. 1972. text ed. 24.95 (ISBN 0-8087-1016-8). Burgess.

Methods for Statistical Data Analysis of Multivariate Observations. Ramanathan Gnanadesikan. LC 76-14994. (Probability & Mathematical Statics Ser.). 1977. 29.95 (ISBN 0-471-30845-5, Pub. by Wiley-Interscience). Wiley.

Methods for Teaching: A Skills Approach. David Jacobsen et al. (Illus.). 304p. 1981. pap. text ed. 11.95 (ISBN 0-675-08079-7). Merrill.

Methods for Teaching the Mildly Handicapped Adolescent. George E. Marsh. LC 80-13396. (Illus.). 1980. pap. text ed. 13.95 (ISBN 0-8016-3115-7). Mosby.

Methods for the Statistical Analysis of Reliability & Life Data. Nancy R. Mann et al. LC 73-20461. (Ser. in Probability & Mathematical Statistics). 576p. 1974. 35.50 (ISBN 0-471-56737-X, Pub. by Wiley-Interscience). Wiley.

Methods in Adaptive Control: Proceedings. Ed. by H. Unbehauen. (Lecture Notes in Control & Information Sciences: Vol. 24). (Illus.). 309p. 1980. pap. 21.60 (ISBN 0-387-10226-4). Springer-Verlag.

Methods in Behavioral Research. 2nd ed. Paul C. Cozby. (Illus.). 300p. 1981. pap. text ed. price not set (ISBN 0-87484-521-1). Mayfield Pub.

Methods in Brain Research. Ed. by P. B. Bradley. LC 74-404. 557p. 1975. 84.25 (ISBN 0-471-09514-1, Pub. by Wiley-Interscience). Wiley.

Methods in Cancer Research. Ed. by Harris Busch et al. Incl. Vol. 1. 1967. 65.00, by subscription 53.00 (ISBN 0-12-147661-8); Vol. 2. 1967. 69.00, by subscription 56.00 (ISBN 0-12-147662-6); Vol. 3. 1967. 69.00, by subscription 56.00 (ISBN 0-12-147663-4); Vol. 4. 1968. 69.00, by subscription 56.00 (ISBN 0-12-147664-2); Vol. 5. 1970. 55.50, by subscription 45.00 (ISBN 0-12-147665-0); Vol. 6. 1971. 55.50, by subscription 45.00 (ISBN 0-12-147666-9); Vol. 7. 1973. 49.00, by subscription 40.00 (ISBN 0-12-147667-7); Vol. 8. 1973. 49.00, by subscription 40.00 (ISBN 0-12-147668-5); Vol. 9. 1973. 49.00, by subscription 40.00 (ISBN 0-12-147669-3); Vol. 10. 1974. 49.00, by subscription 40.00 (ISBN 0-12-147670-7); Vol. 11. 1975. 49.00, by subscription 40.00 (ISBN 0-12-147671-5); Vol. 12. 1976. 49.00, by subscription 40.00 (ISBN 0-12-147672-3); Vol. 13. 1976. 47.00, by subscription 39.00 (ISBN 0-12-147673-1). Acad Pr.

Methods in Carbohydrate Chemistry, 8 vols. Ed. by Roy L. Whistler & Melville L. Wolfrom. Incl. Vol. 1. Analysis & Preparation of Sugars. 1962. 55.25 (ISBN 0-12-746201-5); Vol. 2. Reactions of Carbohydrates. 1963. 55.25 (ISBN 0-12-746202-3); Vol. 3. Cellulose. 1963. 52.50 (ISBN 0-12-746203-1); Vol. 4. Starch. 1964. 52.50 (ISBN 0-12-746204-X); Vol. 5. General Polysaccharides. 1965. 52.50 (ISBN 0-12-746205-8); Vol. 6. 1971. 55.25 (ISBN 0-12-746206-6); Vol. 7. 46.50 (ISBN 0-12-746207-4); Vol. 8. 1980. 38.50 (ISBN 0-12-746208-2). Acad Pr.

Methods in Cell Biology: Three-Dimensioal Ultrastructure in Biology, Vol. 22. Ed. by David Prescott & James Turner. 1981. write for info. (ISBN 0-12-564122-2). Acad Pr.

Methods in Cell Biology: Vol. 21, Methods to Culture Normal Human Tissues & Cells, Pt. A: Respiratory, Cardiovascular, & Intgumentary Systems. Ed. by David M. Prescott & Curtis Harris. (Serial Publication Ser.). 1980. 39.50 (ISBN 0-12-564121-4). Acad Pr.

Methods in Cell Biology: Vol. 21, Methods to Culture Normal Human Tissues & Cells, Pt. B: Endocrine, Urogenital, & Gastro-Intestinal Systems. Ed. by David M. Prescott & Curtis Harris. (Serial Publication Ser.). 1980. 49.50 (ISBN 0-12-564140-0). Acad Pr.

Methods in Cell Physiology. Ed. by David M. Prescott. Incl. Vol. 1. 1964. 47.50 (ISBN 0-12-564101-X); Vol. 2. 1966. 47.50 (ISBN 0-12-564102-8); Vol. 3. 1969. 47.50 (ISBN 0-12-564103-6); Vol. 4. 1970. 47.50 (ISBN 0-12-564104-4); Vol. 5. 1972. 47.50 (ISBN 0-12-564105-2); Vol. 6. 1973. 47.50 (ISBN 0-12-564106-0); Vol. 7. 1974. 47.50 (ISBN 0-12-564107-9); Vol. 8. 1974. 49.00 (ISBN 0-12-564108-7); Vol. 9. 1975. 47.50 (ISBN 0-12-564109-5); Vol. 10. 1975. 47.50 (ISBN 0-12-564110-9); Vol. 11. Yeast Cells. 1975. 47.50 (ISBN 0-12-564111-7); Vol. 12. 1975. 47.50 (ISBN 0-12-564112-5); Vol. 13. 1976. 47.50 (ISBN 0-12-564113-3); Vol. 14. 1976. 48.00 (ISBN 0-12-564114-1); Vol. 15. 1977. 47.00 (ISBN 0-12-564115-X); Vol. 16. Chromatin & Chromosomal Protein Research I. Ed. by Gary Stein & Janet Stein. 1977. 48.50 (ISBN 0-12-564116-8). Acad Pr.

Methods in Clinical Bacteriology: A Manual of Tests & Procedures. Dorothy Branson. (American Lectures in Clinical Microbiology Ser.). 240p. 1972. pap. 14.75 (ISBN 0-398-02241-0). C C Thomas.

Methods in Electromagnetic Wave Propagation. D. S. Jones. (Engineering Science Ser.). (Illus.). 1979. 74.00x (ISBN 0-19-856131-8). Oxford U Pr.

Methods in Enzymology, Vols. 47-62. Incl. Vol. 47. Enzyme Structure, Pt. E. Ed. by C. H. Hirs & S. N. Timasheff. 1977. 59.50 (ISBN 0-12-181947-7); Vol. 48. Enzyme Structures, Pt. F. Ed. by C. H. Hirs. 1978. 57.00 (ISBN 0-12-181948-5); Vol. 49. Enzyme Structure, Pt. G. Ed. by C. H. Hirs & S. N. Timasheff. 1978. 57.00 (ISBN 0-12-181949-3); Vol. 50. Complex Carbohydrates, Pt. C. Ed. by Sidney P. Colowick & Nathan O. Kaplan. 1978. 51.00 (ISBN 0-12-181950-7); Vol. 51. Purine & Pyrimidine Nucleotide Metabolism. Ed. by Sidney P. Colowick et al. 1978. 47.50 (ISBN 0-12-181951-5); Vol. 52. Biomembranes, Pt. C, Biological Oxidations; Microsomal Electron Transport & Cytochrome P-450 Systems. Ed. by Sidney P. Colowick & Nathan O. Kaplan. 1978. 48.00 (ISBN 0-12-181952-3); Vol. 53. Pt. D Biological Oxidations; Mitochondrial & Microbial Systems. Ed. by Sidney Fleischer & Lester Packer. 1978. 48.00 (ISBN 0-12-181953-1); Vol. 54. Pt. E Biological Oxidations; Specialized Techniques. Ed. by Sidney Fleischer & Lester Packer. 1978. 47.00 (ISBN 0-12-181954-X); Vol. 55. Pt. F, Bioenergetics Oxidative Phosphorylation. Ed. by Sidney P. Colowick & Sidney Fleischer. 1979. 58.00 (ISBN 0-12-181955-8); Vol. 56. Biomembranes, Pt. G; Bioenergetics, Biogenesis of Mitochondria, Organization & Transport. Ed. by Sidney P. Colowick et al. 1979. 52.00 (ISBN 0-686-62056-9); Vol. 57. Bioluminescence & Chemiluminescence. Ed. by Marlene Deluca. 1978. 48.00 (ISBN 0-12-181957-4); Vol. 58. Cell Culture. Ed. by Sidney Colowick & William Jacoby. 1979. 50.00 (ISBN 0-12-181958-2); Vol. 59. Nucleic Acids & Proteins Synthesis, Pt. G, Moldave. Ed. by Sidney Colowick. 1979. 52.50 (ISBN 0-12-181959-0); Vol. 60. Pt. H, Moldave. Ed. by Sidney Colowick. 1979. 52.50 (ISBN 0-12-181960-4); Vol. 61. Enzyme Structure, Pt. H. Ed. by Sidney Colowick & C. H. Hirs. 1979. 48.00 (ISBN 0-12-181961-2); Vol. 62. Vitamins & Coenzymes, Pt. D. Ed. by Sidney Colowick et al. 1979. 50.00 (ISBN 0-12-181962-0). Acad Pr.

Methods in Enzymology, Vol. 71: Lipids, Part C. Ed. by S. P. Colowick et al. 1981. write for info. (ISBN 0-12-181971-X). Acad Pr.

Methods in Experimental Psychology. Richard Marken. LC 80-20320. 375p. (Orig.). 1981. pap. text ed. 12.95 (ISBN 0-8185-0431-5). Brooks-Cole.

Methods in Human Development: Activity Guide for Pre-School & Kindergarten. rev. ed. Harold Bessell & Geraldine Ball. 1972. 9.95 (ISBN 0-86584-000-8). Human Dev Train.

Methods in Human Development: Theory Manual. rev. ed. Harold Bessell. 1973. 7.95 o.p. (ISBN 0-686-05865-8). Human Dev Train.

Methods in Immunodiagnosis. 2nd ed. Noel Rose & Pierluigi E. Bigazzi. LC 80-15273. 256p. 1980. 18.50 (ISBN 0-471-02208-X, Pub. by Wiley Med). Wiley.

Methods in Immunology & Immunochemistry, 5 vols. Ed. by Curtis A. Williams & Merrill W. Chase. Vol. 1. 1968. 49.25, subscription 39.25 (ISBN 0-12-754401-1); Vol. 2. 1968. 42.25, subscription 39.25 (ISBN 0-12-754402-X); Vol. 3. 1971. 49.25, by subscription 42.25 (ISBN 0-12-754403-8); Vol. 4 1977. 49.25, subscription 42.25 (ISBN 0-12-754404-6); Vol. 5 1976. 49.25, subscription 42.25 (ISBN 0-12-754405-4). Acad Pr.

Methods in Mammalian Embryology. Ed. by Joseph C. Daniel, Jr. LC 76-116894. (Animal Science Ser.). (Illus.). 1971. text ed. 39.95x (ISBN 0-7167-0819-1). W H Freeman.

Methods in Microbiology, Vols. 10 & 11. Ed. by J. R. Norris & T. Bergen. 1978-79. Vol. 10. 52.00 (ISBN 0-12-521510-X); Vol. 11. 40.50 (ISBN 0-12-521511-8). Acad Pr.

Methods in Neurobiology. Ed. by Robert Lahue. 1981. 50.00 ea.; Set. 89.50 (ISBN 0-686-69459-7); Vol. 1, 640 Pp. for two vol. set 89.50 (ISBN 0-306-40517-2). Vol. Ii, 700 Pp (ISBN 0-306-40518-0). Plenum Pub.

Methods in Nonlinear Plasma Theory. R. J. Davidson. (Pure & Applied Physics Ser.). 1972. 48.00 o.s.i. (ISBN 0-12-205450-4). Acad Pr.

Methods in Pharmacology: Vols. 4A & 4B: Renal Pharmacology. Ed. by M. Martinez-Maldonado. Incl. Vol. 4A. 387p. 1976. 45.00 (ISBN 0-306-35264-8); Vol. 4B. 413p. 1978. 39.50 (ISBN 0-306-35265-6). Plenum Pr). Plenum Pub.

Methods in Plant Ecology. Ed. by S. B. Chapman. LC 75-37570. 1977. pap. 19.95 o.p. (ISBN 0-470-99201-8). Halsted Pr.

Methods in Prostaglandin Research. Ed. by J. C. Frolich. LC 78-66346. (Advances in Prostaglandin & Thromboxane Research: Vol. 5). 1978. 29.00 (ISBN 0-89004-204-7). Raven.

Methods in Pulmonary Physiology. H. Bartels. Tr. by M. Workman. (Illus.). 1963. 45.75 o.s.i. (ISBN 0-02-840980-9). Hafner.

Methods in Special Education. Norris G. Haring & R. L. Schiefelbusch. 1967. text ed. 16.00 o.p. (ISBN 0-07-026421-X, C). McGraw.

Methods in Teaching Basic Business Subjects. 4th ed. Vernon A. Musselman & Donald L. Musselman. 332p. 1980. pap. text ed. 6.95x (ISBN 0-8134-2107-1). Interstate.

Methods in Teaching Developmental Reading. 2nd ed. Edward C. Kennedy. LC 80-52445. 368p. 1981. pap. text ed. 9.95 (ISBN 0-87581-258-9). Peacock Pubs.

Methods, Logic, & Research of Sociology. Robert K. Leik. LC 72-85667. (Studies in Sociology Ser). 1972. 2.95 (ISBN 0-672-61242-9). Bobbs.

Methods of Analysis & Evaluation of Information Needs. Werner Kunz et al. 84p. 1976. text ed. 18.00 (ISBN 3-7940-3450-3, Pub. by K G Saur). Shoe String.

Methods of Applied Mathematics. 2nd ed. Francis B. Hildebrand. 1965. ref. ed. 24.95 (ISBN 0-13-579201-0). P-H.

Methods of Biochemical Analysis. Ed. by David Glick. LC 54-7273. Vol. 23, 1976. 35.00 (ISBN 0-471-01413-3, Pub. by Wiley Interscience); Vol. 25, 1979. 33.95 (ISBN 0-471-04397-4); Vol. 26, 1980. 32.50 (ISBN 0-471-04798-8). Wiley.

Methods of Biochemical Analysis, Vol. 21. Ed. by David Glick. 582p. 1981. Repr. of 1973 ed. lib. bdg. write for info. (ISBN 0-89874-130-0). Krieger.

Methods of Biochemical Analysis, Vol. 27. David Glick. 464p. 1981. 29.50 (ISBN 0-471-06503-X, Pub. by Wiley-Interscience). Wiley.

Methods of Caries Prediction. 326p. 1977. 15.00 (ISBN 0-917000-05-6). Info Retrieval.

Methods of Cell Separation, 3 vols. Ed. by Nicholas Catsimpoolas. LC 77-11018. (Biological Separations Ser.). (Illus.). 32.50 (ISBN 0-306-34604-4, Plenum Pr); Vol. 2, 315p, 1979. 32.50 (ISBN 0-306-40094-4); Vol. 3, 215p, 1980. 27.50 (ISBN 0-306-40377-3). Plenum Pub.

Methods of Clinical Experimentation to Improve Patient Care. P. J. Wooldridge & R. C. Leonard. LC 77-11072. (Illus.). 1978. pap. text ed. 10.00 (ISBN 0-8016-5622-2). Mosby.

Methods of Construction of Celtic Art. George Bain. (Illus.). 9.50 (ISBN 0-8446-4706-3). Peter Smith.

Methods of Correlation & Regression Analysis: Linear & Curvilinear. 3rd ed. Mordecai Ezekiel & Karl A. Fox. LC 59-11993. (Illus.). 1959. 36.95 (ISBN 0-471-25014-7, Pub. by Wiley-Interscience). Wiley.

Methods of Digital Holography. L. P. Yaroslavskii & N. S. Merzlyakov. 250p. 1980. 45.00 (ISBN 0-306-10963-8, Consultants). Plenum Pub.

Methods of Electronic Audio Surveillance. 2nd pt. ed. David A. Pollock. (Illus.). 418p. 1979. pap. text ed. 16.50 (ISBN 0-398-02382-4). C C Thomas.

Methods of Estimating the Demand for Specialists & of Planning Specialized Training Within the U. S. S. R. K. G. Nozhko. 1964. pap. 2.50 (ISBN 92-3-100559-6, U382, UNESCO). Unipub.

Methods of Experimental Physics. Ed. by L. Marton. Incl. Vol. 1. Classical Methods. Ed. by Immanuel Estermann. 1959. 47.50 (ISBN 0-12-475901-7); Vol. 3. Molecular Physics. Ed. by Dudley Williams. 1961. write for info. (ISBN 0-12-475903-3); Vol. 4. Atomic & Electron Physics, Pts. A-B. Ed. by Vernon W. Hughes & Howard L. Schultz. 1967. Pt. A. 58.50 (ISBN 0-12-475904-1); Pt. B. 48.50 (ISBN 0-12-475944-0); Vol. 6. Solid State Physics. Ed. by K. Lark-Horovitz & Vivian A. Johnson. 1959. Pt. A. 43.50 (ISBN 0-12-475906-8); Pt. B. 43.50 (ISBN 0-12-475946-7); Vol. 7. Atomic & Electron Physics: Atomic Interactions. Ed. by B. Bederson & W. Fite. 1968. Pt. A. 61.75 (ISBN 0-12-475907-6); Pt. B. 53.00 (ISBN 0-12-475947-5); Vol. 8. Problems & Solutions for Students. Ed. by L. Marton & W. F. Hornyak. 1969. 41.00 (ISBN 0-12-475908-4); Vol. 9. Plasma Physics. Ed. by Hans R. Griem & Ralph H. Lovberg. 1970-71. Pt. A. 52.50 (ISBN 0-12-475909-2); Pt. B. 45.00 (ISBN 0-12-475949-1); Vol. 10. Physical Principles of Far-Infrared Radiation. L. C. Robinson. 1973. 52.50 (ISBN 0-12-475910-6). Acad Pr.

Methods of Experimental Physics: Fluid Dynamics, Vol. 18A. Ed. by Claire Marton. LC 79-26343. 1981. write for info. (ISBN 0-12-475960-2). Acad Pr.

Methods of Experimental Physics: Fluid Dynamics, Vol. 18B. Ed. by Claire Marton. 1981. write for info. (ISBN 0-12-475956-4). Acad Pr.

Methods of Experimental Physics: Vol. 17, Atomic Physics Accelerators. Ed. by L. Marton & Patrick Richard. (Serial Pub.). 1980. 70.00 (ISBN 0-12-475959-9). Acad Pr.

Methods of Experimental Psychology. Mukul K. Dey. LC 79-66485. 1979. pap. text ed. 8.25 (ISBN 0-8191-0818-9). U Pr of Amer.

Methods of Forceful Indoctrination; Observations & Interviews, Vol. 3. Group for the Advancement of Psychiatry. (Symposium No. 4). 1957. pap. 1.00 o.p. (ISBN 0-87318-046-1). Adv Psychiatry.

Methods of Group Psychotherapy & Encounter: A Tradition of Innovation. Jerrold L. Shapiro. LC 77-83390. 1978. text ed. 14.50 (ISBN 0-87581-229-5). Peacock Pubs.

Methods of Instruction for Severely Handicapped Students. Ed. by Wayne Sailor. LC 80-16668. (Illus.). 352p. (Orig.). 1980. pap. text ed. 16.95 (ISBN 0-933716-06-0). P H Brookes.

Methods of Instruction in Social Studies Education. James L. Barth. LC 79-66224. 1979. pap. text ed. 11.25 (ISBN 0-8191-0817-0). U Pr of Amer.

Methods of Learning Communication Skills. Peter R. Day. 324p. 1977. text ed. 35.00 (ISBN 0-08-018954-7); pap. text ed. 19.50 (ISBN 0-08-018953-9). Pergamon.

Methods of Long Term Planning & Forecasting. Ed. by T. S. Khachaturov. (International Economic Association Ser). 1976. 69.95 (ISBN 0-470-47368-1). Halsted Pr.

Methods of Mathematical Physics, 2 Vols. R. Courant & D. Hilbert. Set. 60.50 (ISBN 0-471-17990-6, Pub. by Wiley-Interscience); Vol. 1, 1953. 31.95 (ISBN 0-470-17952-X); Vol. 2, 1962. 43.50 (ISBN 0-470-17985-6). Wiley.

Methods of Mathematical Physics. 3rd ed. Harold Jeffreys & Bertha S. Jeffreys. (Illus.). 1956. pap. 22.95x (ISBN 0-521-09723-1). Cambridge U Pr.

Methods of Media Preparation for the Biological Sciences. Joyce A. Stewart. (Illus.). 108p. 1974. text ed. 10.75 (ISBN 0-398-02990-3). C C Thomas.

Methods of Modern Mathematical Physics, 4 vols. Michael Reed & Barry Simon. Incl. Vol. 1. Functional Analysis. 1972. 24.95 (ISBN 0-12-585001-8); Vol. 2. Fourier Analysis Self-Adjointness. 1975. 34.50 (ISBN 0-12-585002-6); Vol. 3. Scattering Theory. 1979. 42.00 (ISBN 0-12-585003-4); Vol. 4. 1978. 34.00 (ISBN 0-12-585004-2). Acad Pr.

Methods of Modern Mathematical Physics: Functional Analysis, Vol. 1. rev. & enl. ed. Ed. by Michael Reed & Barry Simon. 1980. 24.00 (ISBN 0-12-585050-6). Acad Pr.

Methods of Modifying Speech Behaviors: Learning Theory in Speech Pathology. Donald E. Mowrer. (Special Education Ser.). 1978. text ed. 16.95 (ISBN 0-675-08438-5). Merrill.

Methods of Molecular Quantum Mechanics. R. McWeeny & B. T. Sutcliffe. (Theoretical Chemistry Ser). 1970. 39.00 (ISBN 0-12-486550-X). Acad Pr.

Methods of Operations Research. Philip M. Morse & George E. Kimball. (Illus.). 179p. 1980. pap. 14.95 (ISBN 0-932146-03-1). Peninsula.

Methods of Organ Playing. 6th ed. Harole Gleason. 1979. 18.95 (ISBN 0-13-579466-8). P-H.

Methods of Real Analysis. 2nd ed. Richard R. Goldberg. LC 75-30615. 1976. text ed. 25.95 (ISBN 0-471-31065-4). Wiley.

Methods of Research in Communication. Philip Emmert & William D. Brooks. 517p. 1970. text ed. 14.95 (ISBN 0-395-04396-4). HM.

Methods of Research in Social Psychology. J. Merrill Carlsmith et al. 352p. 1976. text ed. 18.95 (ISBN 0-201-00346-5). A-W.

Methods of Rhetorical Criticism: A Twentieth-Century Perspective. rev. 2nd ed. Ed. by Bernard L. Brock & Robert L. Scott. 520p. 1980. 16.95 (ISBN 0-8143-1648-4). Wayne St U Pr.

Methods of Screening Rices for Varietal Resistance to Cercospora Leaf Spot. (IRRI Research Paper Ser.: No. 19). 9p. 1979. pap. 5.00 (R059, IRRI). Unipub.

Methods of Seduction. (Illus.). pap. 5.00 (ISBN 0-910550-44-1). Centurion Pr.

Methods of Self-Change: An ABC Primer. Kjell Rudestam. LC 79-25306. 1980. text ed. 10.95 (ISBN 0-8185-0362-9). Brooks-Cole.

Methods of Social Research. Kenneth D. Bailey. LC 77-6938. (Illus.). 1978. text ed. 16.95 (ISBN 0-02-901250-3). Free Pr.

Methods of Social Research. M. Stacey. 1969. 13.75 (ISBN 0-08-013355-X); pap. 6.25 (ISBN 0-08-013354-1). Pergamon.

Methods of Structural Analysis. Compiled by American Society of Civil Engineers. 1120p. 1976. pap. text ed. 39.50 (ISBN 0-87262-163-4). Am Soc Civil Eng.

Methods of Surveying & Monitoring Marine Radioactivity. (Safety Ser., No. 11). 1962. pap. 3.75 (ISBN 92-0-123165-2, IAEA). Unipub.

Methods of Teaching Elementary School Mathematics. new ed. Robert J. Underhill. (Elementary Education Ser). 224p. 1975. pap. text ed. 7.95x (ISBN 0-675-08780-5); media: audiocassettes & filmstrips 495.00 (ISBN 0-675-08781-3); 2-3 sets 395.00; 4 or more set 315.00. Merrill.

Methods of Teaching Librarianship. Ricardo Nassif. 1969. pap. 6.00 (ISBN 92-3-100758-0, U384, UNESCO). Unipub.

Methods of Teaching Shop & Technical Subjects. D. M. Kidd & G. B. Leighbody. LC 66-26821. 1968. pap. text ed. 6.60 (ISBN 0-8273-0360-2). Delmar.

Methods of Topology in Euclidean Spaces. Gregory L. Naber. LC 79-7225. (Illus.). 1980. 23.95x (ISBN 0-521-22746-1). Cambridge U Pr.

Methods of Uncle Abner. Melville D. Post. Ed. by Tom Schantz & Enid Schantz. (Illus.). 96p. 1974. 6.95 (ISBN 0-915230-03-8). Rue Morgue.

Methos in Enzymology: Lipids, Pt. D, Vol. 72. Ed. by S. P. Colowick et al. (Serial Publications). 1981. price not set (ISBN 0-12-181972-8). Acad Pr.

Methuens & Portugal. A. D. Francis. 1966. 53.50 (ISBN 0-521-05028-6). Cambridge U Pr.

Methuselah Factors: Living Long & Living Well. Dan Georgakas. 1981. 14.95 (ISBN 0-671-24064-1). S&S.

Methuselah's Gang. Poochoo. Tr. by Nelly Segal from Hebrew. LC 80-1010. (Illus.). 192p. (gr. 3-6). 1980. 7.95g (ISBN 0-396-07886-9). Dodd.

Metier De Sociologue: Prealables Epistemologiques. 2nd ed. Ed. by Pierre J. Bourdieu et al. (Textes De Sciences Sociales: No. 1). 1973. pap. 20.50x (ISBN 0-686-20919-2). Mouton.

Metodo Directo De Conversacion En Espanol, 2 Bks. Juvenal L. Angel & Robert J. Dixson. (gr. 9 up). 1969. Bk. 1. pap. text ed. 2.75 (ISBN 0-88345-102-6, 17761); Bk. 2. pap. text ed. 2.75 (ISBN 0-88345-103-4, 17762). Regents Pub.

Metodos De Ensenanza. Luisa Walker. (Spanish Bks.). 1979. 1.50 (ISBN 0-8297-0583-X). Life Pubs Intl.

Metodos Estadisticos Aplicados. N. M. Downie & Robert W. Heath. (Sp.). 1971. pap. 8.00 (ISBN 0-06-310074-6, IntlDept). Har-Row.

Metric Affine Geometry. Ernst Snapper & Robert J. Troyer. 435p. 1971. text ed. 20.95 (ISBN 0-12-653650-3). Acad Pr.

Metric Architectural Drawing: A Manual for Designers & Draftsmen. Bernard L. Frishman & Lionel Loshak. 160p. 1981. 20.00 (ISBN 0-471-07724-0, Pub. by Wiley-Interscience). Wiley.

Metric Can Be Fun. Munro Leaf. LC 75-29223. (gr. 1-3). 1976. 6.79 (ISBN 0-397-31679-8); pap. 1.95 (ISBN 0-397-31680-1). Lippincott.

Metric Conversion in the Construction Industries: Planning, Coordination & Timing. 62p. 1980. 15.00. Am Natl.

Metric Conversion Scale. 1973. lot of 10 8.00 (ISBN 0-686-65406-4). Bennett IL.

Metric Drafting. Paul Wallach. Ed. by Richard A. Vorndran. 1979. text ed. 18.95 (ISBN 0-02-829690-7); instrs'. manual 6.20 (ISBN 0-02-829700-8); problems book 6.95 (ISBN 0-02-829710-5). Glencoe.

Metric Edition of Learning to Read Mechanical Drawings. (Illus.). pap. 3.96 o.p. (ISBN 0-686-51651-6, 040-4). Bennett IL.

Metric Editorial Guide. 3rd rev. ed. Ed. by Len Boselovic. 1979. pap. text ed. 3.00 (ISBN 0-916148-13-0). Am Natl.

Metric-English Ruler. lot of 10 4.80 (ISBN 0-686-65407-2). Bennett IL.

Metric Guide for Educational Materials: A Handbook for Teachers, Writers & Publishers. Educational Materials Sector Committee of the American National Metric Council. 1977. pap. text ed. 3.00 (ISBN 0-916148-09-2). Am Natl.

Metric Guide to Mechanical Design & Drafting. F. Gutmann. (Illus.). 1978. 12.00 (ISBN 0-8311-1122-4). Indus Pr.

Metric Is Coming. National Science Teachers Association. 1973. pap. 0.75 o.p. (ISBN 0-685-42400-6, 471-14662). Natl Sci Tchrs.

Metric Made Easy. Mary A. McAllister. (Illus.). 1975. pap. 1.98x o.p. (ISBN 0-685-56032-5). Nature Bks Pubs.

Metric Madness: One Hundred Fifty Reasons for Not Converting to the Metric System. J. W. Batchelder. (Illus.). 250p. 1981. 12.95 (ISBN 0-8159-6220-7); pap. 5.95 (ISBN 0-8159-6219-3). Devin.

Metric Manual. rev. ed. Lawrence D. Pedde et al. (Illus.). 1979. 24.00 (ISBN 0-8103-1020-1). Gale.

Metric Math Book. Rita Sheperak & Jerry DeBruin. (gr. k-8). 1976. 11.95 (ISBN 0-916456-08-0, GA63). Good Apple.

Metric Math: The Modernized Metric System. James R. Smart. LC 73-93954. (Contemporary Undergrad Math Ser). 1974. pap. text ed. 4.95x o.p. (ISBN 0-8185-0126-X). Brooks-Cole.

Metric Measure. Herbert S. Zim & James R. Skelly. LC 74-702. (Illus.). 64p. (gr. 3-7). 1974. PLB 6.48 (ISBN 0-688-30118-5). Morrow.

Metric Measurement. Susan Mahoney & Richard G. Mills. LC 76-731369. (Illus.). 1976. pap. text ed. 60.00 (ISBN 0-89290-128-4, 507-SAR-SATC). Soc for Visual.

Metric Measurement in Food Preparation & Service. Lynne N. Ross. (Illus.). 1978. pap. 3.95 (ISBN 0-8138-0985-1). Iowa St U Pr.

Metric Pattern Cutting. Winifred Aldrich. (Illus.). 1977. pap. 18.95 (ISBN 0-263-06119-1). Transatlantic.

Metric Planes & Metric Vector Spaces. Rolf Lingenberg. LC 78-21906. (Pure & Applied Mathematics: Texts, Monographs & Tracts). 1979. 25.50 (ISBN 0-471-04901-8, Pub. by Wiley-Interscience). Wiley.

Metric Practices in Drafting. Lindbeck. 1979. pap. 2.64 (ISBN 0-87002-298-9). Bennett IL.

Metric Puzzles. Peggy Adler & Irving Adler. LC 77-1948. (gr. 4-6). 1977. PLB 6.90 s&l (ISBN 0-531-01295-6). Watts.

Metric Puzzles, Tricks & Games. Steve Morgenstern. (gr. 3 up). 1978. 6.95 (ISBN 0-8069-4588-5); PLB 6.69 (ISBN 0-8069-4589-3). Sterling.

Metric Reference for Consumers. Consumer Liaison Committee of the American National Metric Council. 1976. pap. text ed. 2.50 (ISBN 0-916148-10-6). Am Natl.

Metric Spaces. Edward T. Copson. (Cambridge Tracts in Mathematics & Mathematical Physics). 1968. 23.95 (ISBN 0-521-04722-6). Cambridge U Pr.

Metric System. James Hahn & Lynn Hahn. LC 74-31386. (First Bks.). (Illus.). (gr. 3-7). 1975. PLB 4.90 o.p. (ISBN 0-531-00834-7). Watts.

Metric System: A Critical Study of Its Principles & Practice. M. Danloux-Dumesnils. 1969. pap. text ed. 4.50x (ISBN 0-485-12013-5, Athlone Pr). Humanities.

Metric System: A Laboratory Approach for Teachers. Nancy C. Whitman & Frederick G. Braun. LC 77-22793. 1978. pap. text ed. 11.50 (ISBN 0-471-02763-4). Wiley.

Metric System: Content & Methods. 2nd ed. Paul F. Ploutz. (Elementary Education Ser.). 1977. pap. text ed. 8.95 (ISBN 0-675-08538-1). Merrill.

Metric System Made Simple. Albert F. Kempf & Thomas J. Richards. LC 75-36631. 144p. 1977. 3.50 (ISBN 0-385-11032-4, Made). Doubleday.

Metric System: Measures for All Mankind. Frank Ross, Jr. LC 74-14503. (Illus.). 128p. (gr. 7-10). 1974. 10.95 (ISBN 0-87599-198-X). S G Phillips.

Metric System Simplified. Gerard W. Kelly. LC 77-93317. 96p. (gr. 4 up). 1974. 5.95 (ISBN 0-8069-3058-6); PLB 5.89 (ISBN 0-8069-3059-4). Sterling.

Metric System: Syllabus. Don H. Parker et al. 1974. pap. text ed. 16.50 units of 10 (ISBN 0-89420-052-6, 280222); cassette recordings 18.15 (ISBN 0-89420-163-8, 280000). Natl Book.

Metric Workbook for Food Service & Lodging. Hollie Crawford & Milton C. McDowell LC 76-22181. 224p. 1976. pap. 11.95 (ISBN 0-8436-2103-6); pap. text ed. 8.95 o.p. (ISBN 0-8436-2104-4); answer book 1.95 (ISBN 0-8436-2168-0). CBI Pub.

Metric World: A Survival Guide. Susan Ostergard et al. LC 75-6919. (Illus.). 176p. 1975. pap. text ed. 9.50 (ISBN 0-8299-0059-4); instrs.' manual avail. (ISBN 0-8299-0605-3). West Pub.

Metrical Visions. George Cavendish. Ed. by Anthony S. Edwards. (Renaissance English Text Society Ser.: Vol. 9). 1980. 15.00. Newberry.

Metrical Visions. Renaissance English Text Society & George Cavendish. Ed. by A. S. Edwards. LC 80-12390. 260p. 1980. text ed. 19.50 (ISBN 0-87249-391-1). U of SC Pr.

Metrication: The Australian Experience. 210p. 1975. 4.00. Am Natl.

Metrics for Elementary & Middle Schools. V. Ray Kurtz. 120p. 1978. pap. 4.50 (ISBN 0-686-63709-7, 1714-5-06). NEA.

Metrics for Everyday Use. new ed. Jane Reid. LC 74-24660. 24p. (gr. 7-12). 1975. pap. text ed. 2.60 (ISBN 0-87002-216-4). Bennett IL.

Metrics in Career Education. John R. Lindbeck. 120p. (gr. 7-12). 1975. pap. text ed. 3.60 (ISBN 0-87002-082-X). Bennett IL.

Metrology Needs in the Measurement of Environmental Radioactivity: Seminar Sponsored by the International Committee for Radionuclide Metrology. Ed. by J. M. Hutchinson & W. B. Mann. (Illus.). 1980. pap. 35.00 (ISBN 0-08-022943-3). Pergamon.

Metrology of Radionuclides. 1960. 13.50 (ISBN 92-0-030060-X, IAEA). Unipub.

Metronidazole. Ed. by I. Phillips & J. Collier. (Royal Society of Medicine International Congress & Symposium Ser.: No. 18). 1980. 29.50 (ISBN 0-8089-1236-4). Grune.

Metropolis...& Beyond: Selected Essays. Hans Blumenfeld. LC 78-17955. 1979. 28.50 (ISBN 0-471-04281-1, Pub. by Wiley-Interscience). Wiley.

Metropolitan America. A. K. Campbell & S. Sacks. LC 67-14373. 1967. 12.95 (ISBN 0-02-905230-0). Free Pr.

Metropolitan America in Contemporary Perspective. Ed. by Amos H. Hawley & V. P. Rock. LC 75-8613. 450p. 1975. 25.00 o.p. (ISBN 0-470-36305-3). Halsted Pr.

Metropolitan City Expenditures: A Comparative Analysis. Roy W. Bahl. LC 68-12965. (Illus.). 152p. 1969. 10.00x (ISBN 0-8131-1173-0). U Pr of Ky.

Metropolitan Community. (gr. 3). 1974. pap. text ed. 5.80 (ISBN 0-205-03893-X, 8038937); tchrs'. guide 11.40 (ISBN 0-205-03894-8, 8038945). Allyn.

Metropolitan Community: Its People & Government. Amos H. Hawley & Basil G. Zimmer. LC 77-92358. 1970. 12.50x (ISBN 0-8039-0066-X); pap. 3.50x (ISBN 0-8039-0067-8). Sage.

Metropolitan Development & Change: The West Midlands: a Policy Review. F. E. Joyce. (Illus.). 1977. 27.95 (ISBN 0-566-00193-4, 01793-0, Pub. by Saxon Hse England). Lexington Bks.

Metropolitan Economy. Thomas M. Stanback & Richard V. Knight. LC 77-133492. 1970. 20.00x (ISBN 0-231-03426-1). Columbia U Pr.

Metropolitan Financing: Principles & Practice. Ed. by George F. Break. LC 77-77437. 1978. 25.00 (ISBN 0-299-07280-0). U of Wis Pr.

Metropolitan Financing: The Milwaukee Experience, 1920-1970. Donald J. Curran. LC 72-7984. 192p. 1973. 20.00x (ISBN 0-299-06290-2). U of Wis Pr.

Metropolitan Kano, 2 vols. B. A. Trevallion. 1967. Set. 75.00 (ISBN 0-08-012635-9). Pergamon.

Metropolitan Latin American: The Challenge & the Response. Ed. by Wayne A. Cornelius & Robert V. Kemper. LC 77-79867. (Latin American Urban Research: Vol. 6). (Illus.). 1978. 20.00x (ISBN 0-8039-0661-7); pap. 9.95x (ISBN 0-8039-0662-5). Sage.

Metropolitan Museum of Art. Howard Hibbard. (Illus.). 600p. 1980. 50.00 (ISBN 0-06-011887-3, HarpT). Har-Row.

Metropolitan Museum of Art: Notable Acquisitions, 1965-1975. Curatorial Staff, Metropolitan Museum of Art. LC 75-31761. (Illus.). 304p. 1975. pap. 15.95 (ISBN 0-87099-141-8). Metro Mus Art.

Metropolitan Neighborhoods: Participation & Conflict Over Change. J. Wolpert et al. LC 72-75260. (CCG Resource Papers Ser.: No. 16). (Illus.). 1972. pap. text ed. 4.00 (ISBN 0-89291-063-1). Assn Am Geographers.

Metropolitan Opera. rev. ed. Irving Kolodin. (Illus.). 1966. 17.50 o.p. (ISBN 0-394-40837-3). Knopf.

Metropolitan Opera House. Helen L. Wright. 1980. pap. 14.95. Greylock Pubs.

Metropolitan Opera House. Helen L. Wright. 1979. write for info. Immediate Pr.

Metropolitan Schools: Administrative Decentralization vs. Community Control. Allan C. Ornstein. LC 73-20487. 1974. 10.00 (ISBN 0-8108-0653-3). Scarecrow.

Metropolitan Tabernacle Pulpit, 12 vols, Vols. 28-31, 34-37. Charles H. Spurgeon. 1971. 11.95 ea. Banner of Truth.

Metropolitan Tabernacle Pulpit, 1861-1917, Vols. 7-63. C. H. Spurgeon. (C. H. Spurgeon's Sermon Ser.). Repr. black or gold bdgs. (vols. 7-61) 11.95 ea.; (vols. 62-63 combined) 15.95. Pilgrim Pubns.

Metropolitan Transportation Politics & the New York Region. Jameson W. Doig. LC 66-16768. (Metropolitan Politics Ser.). (Illus.). 1966. 22.50x (ISBN 0-231-02791-5). Columbia U Pr.

Metropolitan Transportation Problem. rev. ed. Wilfred Owen. 1966. 11.95 (ISBN 0-8157-6772-2). Brookings.

Metropolitee. Alexandre Le Maitre. (Principal French Demographic Works of the 18th Century Ser.). (Fr.). 1976. lib. bdg. 35.00x o.p. (ISBN 0-8287-0530-5); pap. text ed. 25.00x o.p. (ISBN 0-685-71515-9). Clearwater Pub.

Metternich. Andrew Milne. 189p. 1975. 12.00x o.p. (ISBN 0-87471-591-1). Rowman.

Metternich & His Times. Guillaume De Sauvigny. 1962. text ed. 12.50x (ISBN 0-232-48202-0). Humanities.

Metternich's Europe. Ed. by Mack Walker. LC 68-27383. (Documentary History of Western Civilization Ser). 15.00x o.s.i. (ISBN 0-8027-2014-5). Walker & Co.

Meu Livro De Jesus. (Portugese Bks.). (Port.). 1979. 3.00 (ISBN 0-8297-0758-1). Life Pubs Intl.

Meu Livro De Jesus. (Portugese Bks.). (Port.). 1979. 3.00 (ISBN 0-8297-0757-3). Life Pubs Intl.

Mexican Agriculture: Fifteen Twenty-One to Sixteen Thirty. A. G. Frank. LC 78-6201. (Studies in Modern Capitalism Ser.). 1979. 16.95 (ISBN 0-521-22209-5). Cambridge U Pr.

Mexican American Coloring Book. Ludwig & Santibanez. (Illus.). 32p. (gr. 4 up). pap. 2.50 (ISBN 0-930504-00-3). Polaris Pr.

Mexican American People: The Nation's Second Largest Minority. Leo Grebler et al. LC 73-81931. 1970. 30.00 (ISBN 0-02-912800-5). Free Pr.

Mexican-American War: An Annotated Bibliography. Compiled by Norman E. Tutorow. LC 80-1789. (Illus.). 456p. 1981. lib. bdg. 39.95 (ISBN 0-313-22181-2, TMA/). Greenwood.

Mexican Americans. 2nd ed. Manuel P. Servin. LC 73-8357. Orig. Title: Awakened Minority. 320p. 1974. pap. text ed. 7.95x (ISBN 0-02-477940-7, 47794). Macmillan.

Mexican Americans: Political Power, Influence, or Resource. Ed. by Frank L. Baird. (Graduate Studies: No. 14). (Illus., Orig.). 1977. pap. 7.00 (ISBN 0-89672-024-1). Tex Tech Pr.

Mexican Architecture. Ed. by Society of Mexican Architects. (Illus.). 1956. 60.00 (ISBN 0-685-39858-7). Heinman.

Mexican Democracy: A Critical View. rev ed. Kenneth Johnson. LC 77-83473. (Praeger Special Studies). 1978. 25.95 (ISBN 0-03-027711-6); pap. 10.95 (ISBN 0-03-028151-2). Praeger.

Mexican Financial Development. Dwight S. Brothers & M. Leopoldo Solis. 1965. 12.95x (ISBN 0-292-73304-6). U of Tex Pr.

Mexican Gunhawk. Byron Highfill. 176p. (Orig.). 1980. pap. 1.95 (ISBN 0-89083-650-7). Zebra.

Mexican Homes of Today. V. C. Shipway & W. Shipway. Date not set. 18.95 (ISBN 0-8038-0157-2). Hastings.

Mexican House: Old & New. V. C. Shipway & W. Shipway. Date not set. 18.95 (ISBN 0-8038-0158-0). Hastings.

Mexican Interiors. Verna C. Shipway & Warren Shipway. Date not set. 18.95 (ISBN 0-8038-0159-9). Hastings.

Mexican Majolica in Northern New Spain. Mark Barnes & Ron May. 1980. Repr. 4.95 (ISBN 0-686-62076-3). Acoma Bks.

Mexican Militarism: The Political Rise & Fall of the Revolutionary Army, 1910-1940. Edwin Lieuwen. LC 80-28937. (Illus.). xiii, 194p. 1981. Repr. of 1968 ed. lib. bdg. 23.50x (ISBN 0-313-22911-2, LIMM). Greenwood.

Mexican National Petroleum Industry. Antonio J. Bermudez. 268p. 1963. pap. 4.00 o.p. (ISBN 0-912098-00-7). Cal Inst Intl St.

Mexican Native Costumes: Oaxaca, Nayarit, San Luis Potosi. R. Valdiosera. 12.50 (ISBN 0-911268-17-0). Rogers Bk.

Mexican Nights. Jeanne Stephens. 192p. (Orig.). 1980. pap. 1.50 (ISBN 0-671-57022-6). S&S.

Mexican Nobility at Independence, 1780-1826. Doris M. Ladd. LC 75-720106. (Latin American Monographs: No. 40). 1976. 15.95x (ISBN 0-292-75026-9); pap. 7.95 (ISBN 0-292-75027-7). U of Tex Pr.

Mexican Oil & Natural Gas: Political, Strategic & Economic Implications. Richard B. Mancke. LC 78-65353. 1979. 22.95 (ISBN 0-03-048451-0). Praeger.

Mexican Political System. 2nd ed. Vincent L. Padgett. LC 75-27497. (Illus.). 352p. 1976. pap. text ed. 9.75 (ISBN 0-395-20364-3). HM.

Mexican Profit-Sharing Decision. Susan K. Purcell. LC 74-84148. 224p. 1976. 24.50x (ISBN 0-520-02843-0). U of Cal Pr.

Mexican Revolution. Charles C. Cumberland. Incl. Genesis Under Madero. ix, 298p. 1952. 15.00x (ISBN 0-292-75018-8); pap. 7.95 (ISBN 0-292-75017-X); The Constitutionalist Years. LC 74-38506. (Illus.). xx, 450p. 1972. 17.50x (ISBN 0-292-75000-5); pap. 9.95 (ISBN 0-292-75016-1). U of Tex Pr.

Mexican Revolution & the Catholic Church, 1910-1929. Robert E. Quirk. LC 73-75399. 288p. 1973. 10.00x (ISBN 0-253-33800-X). Ind U Pr.

Mexican Revolution: Federal Expenditure & Social Change Since 1910. 2nd rev ed. James W. Wilkie. LC 74-103072. 1970. 21.50x (ISBN 0-520-01919-9); pap. 5.50x (ISBN 0-520-01869-9, CAMPUS36). U of Cal Pr.

Mexican Revolution, Nineteen Fourteen to Nineteen Fifteen: The Convention of Aguascalientes. Robert E. Quirk. LC 80-28130. 325p. 1981. Repr. of 1960 ed. lib. bdg. 27.50x (ISBN 0-313-22894-9, QUMR). Greenwood.

Mexican Revolution Nineteen Ten - Nineteen Fourteen: The Diplomacy of Anglo-American Conflict. Peter Calvert. (Cambridge Latin American Studies: No. 3). (Illus.). 1968. 39.95 (ISBN 0-521-04423-5). Cambridge U Pr.

Mexican Society During Revolution. John Rutherford. 352p. 1971. 29.95x (ISBN 0-19-827183-2). Oxford U Pr.

Mexican Standoff. Glen Chase. (Cherry Delight Ser: No. 21). (Orig.). 1975. pap. 1.25 o.p. (ISBN 0-685-52941-X, LB260ZK, Leisure Bks). Nordon Pubns.

Mexican Tapestry Weaving. Joanne Hall. LC 77-351132. (Illus.). 1976. wrap-around spiral bdg., leatherette 9.95 (ISBN 0-9602098-0-8). J Arvidson.

Mexican Village: Life in a Zapotec Community. Paul Deegan. LC 76-140642. (World's People Ser.). (Illus.). (gr. 4-8). 1971. PLB 6.95 (ISBN 0-87191-047-0). Creative Ed.

Mexican War. David Nevin. LC 77-95212. (Old West Ser.). (Illus.). 1978. lib. bdg. 12.96 (ISBN 0-686-51079-8). Silver.

Mexican War. David Nevin. Ed. by Time-Life Books. (Old West). (Illus.). 1978. 12.95 (ISBN 0-8094-2300-6). Time-Life.

Mexican War: A Lithographic Record. Ronnie C. Tyler. LC 93-88280. (Illus.). 108p. 1974. 10.00 (ISBN 0-87611-031-6); collector's ed. 45.00 (ISBN 0-87611-032-4); portfolio of 16 prints 7.50 (ISBN 0-87611-034-0). Tex St Hist Assn.

Mexican War: Changing Interpretations. Ed. by Odie B. Faulk & Joseph A. Stout, Jr. LC 72-94389. 243p. 1973. 10.95x (ISBN 0-8040-0642-3, SB); pap. 4.95x (ISBN 0-8040-0643-1). Swallow.

Mexican War Diary of General George B. McClellan. William S. Myers. LC 71-87641. (American Scene Ser). 98p. 1972. Repr. of 1917 ed. lib. bdg. 17.50 (ISBN 0-306-71789-1). Da Capo.

Mexican War (1846-1848) K. Jack Bauer. LC 74-3489. (Illus.). 480p. 1974. 14.95 o.s.i. (ISBN 0-02-507890-9). Macmillan.

Mexican Women in the United States: Struggles Past & Present. Ed. by Magdalena Mora & Adelaida Del Castillo. LC 80-10682. (Occasional Papers Ser.: No. 2). (Illus.). 214p. (Orig.). 1980. pap. 12.95 (ISBN 0-89551-022-7). UCLA Chicano Stud.

Mexicano-Chicano Concerns & School Desegregation in Los Angeles. Carlos M. Haro. (Monograph Ser.: No. 9). (Illus.). 98p. (Orig.). 1979. pap. 4.95 (ISBN 0-89551-012-X). Ucla Chicano Stud.

Mexicano Resistance in the Southwest: The Sacred Right of Self-Preservation. Robert J. Rosenbaum. (Illus.). 245p. 1981. text ed. 14.95x (ISBN 0-292-77562-8). U of Tex Pr.

Mexicans: How They Live & Work. Peter Calvert. LC 74-17467. 168p. 1975. text ed. 8.95 (ISBN 0-03-029696-X, HoltC). HR&W.

Mexicans in America. Jane Pinchot. LC 72-3587. (In America Bks.). (Illus.). 104p. (gr. 5-11). 1973. PLB 5.95 o.p. (ISBN 0-8225-0222-4). Lerner Pubns.

Mexicans in America. rev. ed. Jane Pinchot. (In America Bks.). (Illus.). 104p. (gr. 5-11). PLB 5.95. Lerner Pubns.

Mexicans: The Making of a Nation. Victor Alba. LC 67-20469. 1970. pap. 5.95 (ISBN 0-672-63564-X). Pegasus.

Mexico. Peter Calvert. (Nations of the Modern World Ser.). 1977. 17.25x (ISBN 0-510-37905-2). Westview.

Mexico. Ralph Hancock. (gr. 7 up). 1964. 5.95 o.s.i. (ISBN 0-02-742600-9). Macmillan.

Mexico. rev. ed. Patricia F. Ross. LC 73-90742. (American Neighbors Ser.). (Illus.). 208p. (gr. 5 up). 1975. text ed. 9.95, 5 or more copies 7.96 o.p. (ISBN 0-88296-096-2); tchrs'. guide 6.96 o.p. (ISBN 0-686-67148-1). Fideler.

Mexico: Activities & Projects in Color. Claude Soleillant. LC 77-81955. (Activities & Projects Ser.). (Illus.). 96p. (English.). (gr. 3 up). 1978. 9.95 (ISBN 0-8069-4552-4); PLB 9.29 (ISBN 0-8069-4553-2). Sterling.

Mexico & Central America. Frank Bellamy. LC 76-55108. 1977. 10.00 (ISBN 0-8467-0272-X, Pub. by Two Continents); pap. 6.95 (ISBN 0-8467-0336-X). Hippocrene Bks.

Mexico & Guatemala on Fifteen & Twenty Dollars a Day: 1981-82. 512p. 1981. pap. 6.95 (ISBN 0-671-41422-4). Frommer-Pasmantier.

Mexico & the Old Southwest: People, Palaver, & Places. Haldeen Braddy. LC 71-141307. 1971. 12.50 (ISBN 0-8046-9001-4, Natl U); pap. 4.95 (ISBN 0-8046-9046-4). Kennikat.

Mexico & the Spanish Civil War. T. G. Powell. 240p. 1981. 17.50x (ISBN 0-8263-0546-6). U of NM Pr.

Mexico & the Spanish Cortes, 1810-1822: Eight Essays. Ed. by Nettie L. Benson. (Latin American Monograph Ser.: No. 5). 1966. 10.95x (ISBN 0-292-73606-1). U of Tex Pr.

Mexico City. John Cottrell. (Great Cities Ser.). (Illus.). 1979. lib. bdg. 14.94 (ISBN 0-8094-3105-X); kivar bdg. 9.93 (ISBN 0-8094-3106-8). Silver.

Mexico City Blues. Jack Kerouac. 1959. pap. 3.95 (ISBN 0-394-17287-6, E552, Ever). Grove.

Mexico: Civilizaciones y Culturas. rev. ed. Luis Leal. (Illus.). 1971. pap. text ed. 7.50 (ISBN 0-395-12744-0, 3-32161). HM.

Mexico, Crucible of the Americas. Lila Perl. LC 77-20203. (Illus.). (gr. 5-9). 1978. 8.95 (ISBN 0-688-22148-3); PLB 8.59 (ISBN 0-688-32148-8). Morrow.

Mexico in American & British Letters: A Bibliography of Fiction & Travel Books Citing Original Editions. Drewey W. Gunn. LC 73-20354. 1974. 10.00 (ISBN 0-8108-0692-4). Scarecrow.

Mexico in Pictures. (Illus.). 12.50 (ISBN 0-911268-04-9). Rogers Bk.

Mexico in Pictures. rev. ed. Sterling Publishing Company Editors. LC 60-14339. (Visual Geography Ser). (Illus., Orig.). (gr. 4-12). 1961. PLB 4.99 (ISBN 0-8069-1013-5); pap. 2.95 o.p. (ISBN 0-8069-1012-7). Sterling.

Mexico: Places & Pleasures. rev ed. Kate Simon. LC 78-3317. (Illus.). 1979. 14.95 (ISBN 0-690-01653-0, TYC-T); pap. 5.95 (ISBN 0-690-01778-2, TYC-T). T Y Crowell.

Mexico State Papers: 1744-1843. Michael P. Costeloe. (Institute of Latin American Studies Monograph Ser.: No. 6). 144p. 1976. text ed. 19.50x (ISBN 0-485-17706-4, Athlone Pr). Humanities.

Mexico: The Macmillan Concise Illustrated Encyclopedia. Unibook Staff. Ed. by Pascal O. Rubio, 3rd. (Illus.). 416p. 1981. 21.95 (ISBN 0-02-620910-1). Macmillan.

Mexico Today. rev. ed. John A. Crow. LC 71-156517. (Illus.). 1972. 13.95 o.p. (ISBN 0-06-010923-8, HarpT). Har-Row.

Mexico: Travel Guide. 6th ed. Sunset Editors. LC 76-46655. (Illus.). 144p. 1977. pap. 5.95 (ISBN 0-376-06457-9, Sunset Bks). Sunset-Lane.

Mexico's Economy: A Policy Analysis with Forecasts to 1990. Robert E. Looney. LC 78-3132. (Westview Special Studies on Latin America Ser.). 1978. lib. bdg. 28.50x (ISBN 0-89158-093-X). Westview.

Mexico's Volcanoes: A Climbing Guide. R. J. Secor. (Illus.). 96p. (Orig.). 1981. pap. 6.95 (ISBN 0-89886-016-4). Mountaineers.

Mexique. new ed. Ed. by Daniel Moreau. (Collection monde et voyages). (Illus.). 159p. (Fr.). 1973. 21.00x (ISBN 2-03-053108-1, 3900). Larousse.

Meydan-Larousse, 13 vols. (Turkish.). 1970. 1050.00 (ISBN 0-8277-3069-1). Maxwell Sci Intl.

Meyerbeer et Son Temps. Ange H. Blaze De Bury. LC 80-2257. 1981. Repr. of 1865 ed. 40.50 (ISBN 0-404-18813-3). AMS Pr.

Meyerhold at Work. Ed. by Paul Schmidt. Tr. by Ilya Levin & Vern McGee. LC 80-15265. (Slavic Ser.: No. 2). 263p. Date not set. text ed. 19.95x (ISBN 0-292-75058-7). U of Tex Pr.

Meyerhold at Work, Vol2. Ed. by Paul Schmidt. (University of Texas Press Slavic Ser: Vol. 2). 340p. Date not set. 19.95x (ISBN 0-292-75058-7). U of Tex Pr.

Meyerhold: The Director. Konstantin Rudnitsky. Tr. by George Petrov from Rus. (Illus.). 1981. 42.50 (ISBN 0-88233-313-5). Ardis Pubs.

Meyers Enzyklopaedisches Lexikon, 25 vols. Incl. Atlas; Supplement. (Ger., 17 vols. avail.). 1971-1979. Set. 2050.00 (ISBN 0-685-40124-3). Maxwell Sci Intl.

Mezzo Cammin. Winston Weathers. (Orig.). 1981. pap. 4.50x (ISBN 0-912484-20-9). Joseph Nichols.

MG Experience. Dick Jacobs. (Illus.). 1976. 15.95 (ISBN 0-85184-013-2, Pub. by Transport Bookman Ltd. England). Motorbooks Intl.

MG Sports Cars. Autocar Editors. LC 78-65889. 1979. 14.95 (ISBN 0-312-50156-0). St Martin.

MG: The A B & C. Chris Harvey. (Illus.). 1980. 36.50 (ISBN 0-902280-69-4, Pub. by Oxford Ill England). Motorbooks Intl.

MGA: A History, & Restoration Guide. Robert P. Vitrikas. (Illus.). 208p. 1980. pap. 19.95 (ISBN 0-89404-031-6). Aztex.

MGA-MGB All Models: 1956-1979 Service, Repair Handbook. 3rd ed. Alan Ahlstrand. Ed. by Jeff Robinson. (Illus.). 1978. pap. 10.95 (ISBN 0-89287-279-9, A165). Clymer Pubns.

MGM. Ed. & intro. by Ed Buscombe. (BFI Dossiers Ser.: No. 1). (Orig.). 1980. pap. 6.00 (ISBN 0-918432-33-2). NY Zoetrope.

MGM Ziegfeld Trilogy: A Literary & Pictorial Treasury. Fredrick Santon. LC 78-75335. (Illus.). cancelled (ISBN 0-498-02330-3). A S Barnes.

MHD Flows & Turbulence: Proceedings. H. Branover. 1977. 39.95 (ISBN 0-470-99061-9). Halsted Pr.

Mhudi. new ed. Illus. by Sol T. Plaatje. 1978. pap. 5.00 (ISBN 0-89410-031-9, Co-Pub by Heinemann Educ. Bks). Three Continents.

Mhudi. Solomon T. Plaatje. Ed. by Tim Couzens. (Illus.). 165p. 1975. Repr. 22.00x (ISBN 0-909078-01-7, Pub. by Quagga Press). Three Continents.

Mi Desarrollo Sexual. Paul D. Simmons & Kenneth Crawford. Tr. by Dafne Sabanes De Plou from Eng. (El Sexo En la Vida Cristiana). 96p. (Span.). (gr. 10-12). Date not set. Repr. pap. price not set (ISBN 0-311-46253-7, Edit Mundo). Casa Bautista.

Mi Guia Telefonica. M. Imbo. Ed. by Philip Mann. Tr. by Georgian Kreps from Eng. (Shape Board Play Book). Orig. Title: My Telephone Book. (Illus.). 14p. (Span.). (ps-3). 1981. bds. 3.50 plastic come bdg. (5009SP). Tuffy Bks.

Mi Libro De Jesus. (Spanish Bks.). 1977. 3.50 (ISBN 0-8297-0754-9). Life Pubs Intl.

Mi Libro De Relatos Biblicos. (Spanish Bks.). 1977. 3.50 (ISBN 0-8297-0755-7). Life Pubs Intl.

Mi Paraguas Rojo. Robert Bright. Tr. by Marion H. Redfield. LC 68-20836. Orig. Title: My Red Umbrella. (Illus., Span.). (ps-1). 1968. PLB 6.00 (ISBN 0-688-31788-X). Morrow.

Mi Primer Diccionario Illustrado De Ingles. rev. ed. Dixson & Fox. 67p. (gr. 3-6). 1974. 5.75 (ISBN 0-88345-253-7); pap. 3.75 (ISBN 0-88345-232-4). Regents Pub.

Mi Primer Gran Libro Fabulas. Richard Scary. 12.95 o.p. (ISBN 0-686-65647-4). Larousse.

Mi Primer Libro de Teatro. (Span.). 9.00 (ISBN 84-241-5624-2). E Torres & Sons.

Mi Querido Reloj. M. Imbo. Ed. by Philip Mann. Tr. by Georgian Kreps from Eng. (Shape Board Lay Book). Orig. Title: Happy Clock Book. (Illus.). 14p. (Span.). (ps-3). 1981. bds. 3.50 plastic comb bdg (ISBN 0-89828-204-7, 5008SP). Tuffy Bks.

Mi Segundo Libro de Teatro. (Span.). 9.00 (ISBN 84-241-5633-1). E Torres & Sons.

M.I.A. (Missing in Action) H. Phillip Causer. LC 77-88747. (Illus.). 1977. 9.95 (ISBN 0-918442-00-1). Phipps Pub.

Miami Alive. Ethel Blum. 1981. pap. 5.95 (ISBN 0-935572-09-0). Alive Pubns.

Miami Alive. Ethel Blum. (Span.). 1981. pap. 5.95 (ISBN 0-935572-06-6). Alive Pubns.

Miami Dolphins. Julian May. (NFL Today Ser.). (gr. 4-8). 1980. lib. bdg. 6.45 (ISBN 0-87191-725-4); pap. 2.95 (ISBN 0-89812-228-7). Creative Ed.

Miami Dolphins. Julian May. LC 74-4139. (Superbowl Champions Ser). 48p. 1974. PLB 6.45 (ISBN 0-87191-328-3); pap. 2.95 (ISBN 0-89812-088-8). Creative Ed.

Miami Millions. John Maccabee. 416p. (Orig.). 1980. pap. 2.50 (ISBN 0-553-13313-6). Bantam.

Miami, Wea, & El-River Indians of Southern Indian. Erminie Wheeler-Voegelin. Ed. by David A. Horr. (American Indian Ethnohistory Ser.). 1974. lib. bdg. 42.00 (ISBN 0-8240-0806-5). Garland Pub.

Mic Dictionar Enciclopedic, 1 vol. (Romanian.). 1972. 95.00 (ISBN 0-8277-3060-8). Maxwell Sci Intl.

Micah, Zephaniah, Nahum, Habakkuk, Obadiah & Joel. J. M. Smith et al. (International Critical Commentary Ser.). 560p. 1911. text ed. 23.00x (ISBN 0-567-05019-X). Attic Pr.

Mice. Eileen Everett. 1976. pap. 1.00 o.p. (ISBN 0-08-016241-X). Pergamon.

Mice: All About Them. Alvin Silverstein & Virginia Silverstein. LC 79-9621. (Illus.). 160p. (gr. 4up). 1980. 9.95 (ISBN 0-397-31922-3); PLB 9.79 (ISBN 0-397-31923-1). Lippincott.

Mice Are Rather Nice. Vardine Moore. LC 80-23121. 112p. (gr. 3-7). 1981. PLB 7.95 (ISBN 0-689-30819-1). Atheneum.

Mice Came in Early This Year. Eleanor Lapp. Ed. by Caroline Rubin. LC 76-45629. (Self-Starter Bks). (Illus.). (ps-2). 1976. 6.50g (ISBN 0-8075-5111-2). A Whitman.

Mice, Men & Elephants. Herbert S. Zim. LC 42-36123. (Illus.). (gr. 7-9). 5.95 o.p. (ISBN 0-15-253305-2, HJ). HarBraceJ.

Mice, Moose & Men: How Their Populations Rise & Fall. Robert M. McClung. LC 73-4926. (Illus.). 64p. (gr. 3-7). 1973. 7.25 (ISBN 0-688-20087-7); PLB 6.96 (ISBN 0-688-30087-1). Morrow.

Mice Twice. Joseph Low. LC 79-23274. (Illus.). 32p. (ps-3). 1980. 9.95 (ISBN 0-689-50157-9, McElderry Bk). Atheneum.

Micellization, Solubilization, & Microemulsions, 2 vols. Ed. by K. L. Mittal. 1977. Vol. 1. 487p. 45.00 (ISBN 0-306-31023-6, Plenum Pr); Vol. 2. 945p. 45.00 (ISBN 0-306-31024-4). Plenum Pub.

Michael. (Illus.). 1979. pap. 12.95 (ISBN 0-8032-6305-8, Buffalo Bill Hist. Ctr.). U of Nebr Pr.

Michael & the Dentist. Bernard Wolf. LC 80-12343. (Illus.). 48p. (ps-3). 1980. 7.95 (ISBN 0-590-07637-X, Four Winds). Schol Bk Serv.

Michael Arlen. Harry Keyishian. (English Author Ser.: No. 174). 1975. lib. bdg. 9.95 (ISBN 0-8057-1011-6). Twayne.

Michael Bird-Boy. Tomie De Paola. (Illus.). (ps-2). 1975. 5.95 (ISBN 0-13-580803-0); pap. 2.50 (ISBN 0-13-580811-1). P-H.

Michael Collins. Leon O'Broin. (Gill's Irish Lives Ser.). 156p. 1980. 20.00 (ISBN 0-7171-1076-1, Pub. by Gill & Macmillan Ireland); pap. 6.50 (ISBN 0-7171-0968-2). Irish Bk Ctr.

Michael Drayton & Samuel Daniel: A Reference Guide. James L. Harner. (Reference Bks.). 1980. lib. bdg. 30.00 (ISBN 0-8161-8322-8). G K Hall.

Michael Faraday: A List of His Lectures & Published Writings. Alan E. Jeffreys. 1961. 25.00 (ISBN 0-12-383050-8). Acad Pr.

Michael Faraday: His Life & Work. 2nd ed. Silvanus P. Thompson. Date not set. 12.95 (ISBN 0-8284-0311-2). Chelsea Pub.

Michael Hendee. Cynthia Butler. (N. H.-Vermont Historiettes). (Illus.). 56p. (gr. 2-3). 1976. 4.95x (ISBN 0-915892-05-7); pap. text ed. 1.95x (ISBN 0-915892-14-6). Regional Ctr Educ.

Michael of Wales. Paul Conklin. LC 76-53431. (gr. 4-7). 1977. 5.95 (ISBN 0-396-07415-4). Dodd.

Michael Sadleir Eighteen Eighty-Eight to Nineteen Fifty-Seven. Roy Stokes. LC 80-11419. (Great Bibliographers Ser.: No. 5). 162p. 1980. 10.00 (ISBN 0-8108-1292-4). Scarecrow.

Michael Snow. (Illus.). 1972. pap. 2.00 (ISBN 0-913456-23-3). Interbk Inc.

Michael Speransky: Statesman of Imperial Russia, 1772 to 1839. Marc Raeff. LC 78-59037. 1980. Repr. of 1957 ed. 27.50 (ISBN 0-88355-709-6). Hyperion Conn.

Michael Steiner. Kenworth Moffett. (Illus.). 1974. pap. 1.50 (ISBN 0-87846-079-9). Mus Fine Arts Boston.

Michael Strogoff. Jules Verne. (Illustrated Classic). (Illus.). (gr. 7-11). 1927. 10.00 o.p. (ISBN 0-684-20972-1, ScribT). Scribner.

Michaelmas. A. J. Budrys. LC 76-56214. (YA) 1977. 7.95 o.p. (ISBN 0-399-11653-2, Dist. by Putnam). Berkley Pub.

Michaelmas. Algis Budrys. 1978. pap. 1.95 o.p. (ISBN 0-425-03812-2, Medallion). Berkley Pub.

Michaelmas Term. Thomas Middleton. Ed. by Richard Levin. LC 66-17765. (Regents Renaissance Drama Ser). 1967. 9.25x (ISBN 0-8032-0280-6); pap. 1.65x (ISBN 0-8032-5280-3, BB 220, Bison). U of Nebr Pr.

Michael's Wife. Marlys Millhiser. 1976. pap. 1.50 o.p. (ISBN 0-449-22903-3, Crest). Fawcett.

Michel de Montaigne: Essais. Ed. by Carol J. Chapman & Francois J. Mouret. (Athlone Renaissance Library). 1978. text ed. 26.50x (ISBN 0-485-13810-7, Athlone Pr); pap. text ed. 12.50x (ISBN 0-485-12810-1). Humanities.

Michel Erhart: Ein Beitrag zur schwaebischen Plastik der Spaetgotik. Anja Broschek. LC 72-81548. (Beitraege Zur Kunstgeschichte: Vol. 8). 1973. 91.20x (ISBN 3-11-001765-2). De Gruyter.

Michel Fokine & His Ballets. Cyril W. Beaumont. LC 80-69956. (Illus.). 1981. pap. 8.95 (ISBN 0-87127-120-6). Dance Horiz.

Michelangelo, 6 vols. Charles Q. De Tolnay. Incl. Vol. 1. The Youth of Michelangelo. 1969. 55.00 (ISBN 0-691-03858-9); Vol. 2. The Sistine Ceiling. 1969. 55.00 (ISBN 0-691-03856-2); Vol. 3. The Medeci Chapel. 1970. 55.00 (ISBN 0-691-03854-6); Vol. 4. The Tomb of Julius Two. 1970. 55.00 (ISBN 0-691-03857-0); Vol. 5. The Final Period. 1970. 55.00 (ISBN 0-691-03855-4); Vol. 6. Michelangelo, Architect. 40.00 (ISBN 0-691-03853-8); Michelangelo: Sculpter-Painter-Architect. (One vol. condensation). 27.50 (ISBN 0-691-03876-7). Princeton U. Pr.

Michelangelo. Howard Hibbard. LC 74-6576. (Icon Editions). (Illus.). 348p. 1975. 16.95 (ISBN 0-06-433323-X, HarpT); pap. 6.95 (ISBN 0-06-430056-0, IN-56, HarpT). Har-Row.

Michelangelo. Michelangelo. Ed. by Frederick Hartt. (Library of Great Painters Ser). 1965. 35.00 (ISBN 0-8109-0299-0). Abrams.

Michelangelo. Ernest Raboff. LC 71-139055. (gr. 3-7). 6.95 (ISBN 0-385-07517-0). Doubleday.

Michelangelo. Monroe Stearns. (Art Biography Ser). (Illus.). (gr. 7 up). 1970. PLB 5.88 o.p. (ISBN 0-531-00944-0). Watts.

Michelangelo & the Language of Art. David Summers. LC 80-7556. (Illus.). 532p. 1981. 47.50x (ISBN 0-691-03957-7); pap. 16.50 (ISBN 0-691-10097-7). Princeton U Pr.

Michelangelo Pistoletto. Ed. by Dave Hickey et al. (Illus.). 1980. pap. 5.00. Inst for the Arts.

Michelangelo: Six Lectures by Johannes Wilde. Johannes Wilde. Ed. by John Shearman & Michael Hirst. (Oxford Studies in the History of Art & Architecture). (Illus.). 1979. pap. 12.95x (ISBN 0-19-817346-6). Oxford U Pr.

Michelangelo: The Complete Works. Lutz Heusinger. (Illus., Orig.). 1978. pap. 7.95 o.p. (ISBN 0-8467-0469-2, Pub. by Two Continents). Hippocrene Bks.

Michelangelo: The Sistine Chapel Ceiling. Ed. & intro. by Charles Seymour, Jr. (Critical Studies in Art History). (Illus.). 243p. 1972. pap. 6.95x (ISBN 0-393-09889-3). Norton.

Michelangelo's Life & His Magnetic Art. Pierce A. Fairfield. (Illus.). 1979. deluxe ed. 39.75 (ISBN 0-930582-43-8). Gloucester Art.

Michelin Green Guide Belgique et Grand Duche du Luxembourg. Michelin Guides & Maps. 1978. pap. 7.95 (ISBN 2-06-005100-2). Michelin.

Michelin Green Guide London. 2nd ed. Michelin. 1980. pap. 7.95 (ISBN 2-06-015431-6). Michelin.

Michelin Green Guide Rome. 2nd ed. Michelin. (Fr.). 1979. pap. 7.95 (ISBN 2-06-005580-6). Michelin.

Michelin Green Guide to Alpes. Michelin Guides & Maps. (Green Guide Ser.). (Fr.). pap. 7.95 (ISBN 2-06-003000-5). Michelin.

Michelin Green Guide to Austria. 5th ed. Michelin Guides & Maps Division. (Green Guide Ser.). (Avail. in Ger., Fr.). pap. 7.95 (ISBN 2-06-015120-1). Michelin.

Michelin Green Guide to Auvergne. 1st ed. Michelin Guides & Maps. (Green Guide Ser.). (Fr.). 1978. pap. 7.95 (ISBN 2-06-003030-7). Michelin.

Michelin Green Guide to Bourgogne. 16th ed. Michelin Guides & Maps. (Fr.). 1980. pap. 7.95 (ISBN 2-06-003060-9). Michelin.

Michelin Green Guide to Brittany. 16th ed. Michelin Guides & Maps. (Green Guide Ser.). (Avail. in Fr). 1980. pap. 7.95 (ISBN 2-06-013120-0). Michelin.

Michelin Green Guide to Causses-Cevennes. 2nd ed. Michelin Guides & Maps. (Green Guide Ser.). (Fr.). 1979. pap. 7.95 (ISBN 2-06-003150-8). Michelin.

Michelin Green Guide to Chateaux Loire. 6th ed. Michelin Guides & Maps Division. (Green Guide Ser.). (Avail. in Fr., Ger.). pap. 7.95 (ISBN 2-06-013210-X). Michelin.

Michelin Green Guide to Corse. 3rd ed. Michelin Guides & Maps. (Green Guide Ser.). (Fr.). 1979. pap. 7.95 (ISBN 2-06-003251-2). Michelin.

Michelin Green Guide to Cote De L'atlantique. 9th ed. Michelin Guides & Maps. (Green Guide Ser.). (Fr.). 1978. pap. 7.95 (ISBN 2-06-003330-6). Michelin.

Michelin Green Guide to Environs De Paris. 19th ed. Michelin Guides & Maps. (Green Guide Ser.). (Fr.). 1979. pap. 7.95 (ISBN 2-06-100351-6). Michelin.

Michelin Green Guide to French Riviera. 7th ed. Michelin Guides & Maps Dept. (Green Guide Ser.). (Avail. in Fr.). pap. 7.95 (ISBN 2-06-013300-9). Michelin.

Michelin Green Guide to Germany. 4th ed. Michelin Guides & Maps Dept. (Green Guide Ser.). (Avail. in Fr., Ger.). pap. 7.95 (ISBN 2-06-015030-2). Michelin.

Michelin Green Guide to Hollande. Michelin. 1979. pap. 7.95 (ISBN 2-06-005530-X). Michelin.

Michelin Green Guide to Italy. 8th ed. Michelin Guides & Maps Dept. (Green Guide Ser.). (Avail. in Fr., Ger., Ital.). pap. 7.95 (ISBN 2-06-121401-0). Michelin.

Michelin Green Guide to Jura. 2nd ed. Michelin Guides & Maps. (Green Guide Ser.). (Fr.). 1979. pap. 7.95 (ISBN 2-06-003391-8). Michelin.

Michelin Green Guide to Londres. 2nd ed. Michelin Guides & Maps. (Green Guide Ser.). (Fr.). 1976. pap. 7.95 (ISBN 2-06-005420-6). Michelin.

Michelin Green Guide to Maroc. 3rd ed. Michelin Guides & Maps. (Green Guide Ser.). (Fr.). 1979. pap. 7.95 (ISBN 2-06-005450-8). Michelin.

Michelin Green Guide to New York City. 5th ed. Michelin Guides & Maps. (Green Guide Ser.). (Avail. in fr.). 1979. pap. 7.95 (ISBN 2-06-015510-X). Michelin.

Michelin Green Guide to Nord De La France. 4th ed. Michelin Guides & Maps. (Green Guide Ser.). (Fr.). 1977. pap. 7.95 (ISBN 2-06-003420-5). Michelin.

Michelin Green Guide to Normandy. 5th ed. Michelin Guides & Maps Dept. (Green Guide Ser.). (Avail. in Fr.). pap. 7.95 (ISBN 2-06-013480-3). Michelin.

Michelin Green Guide to Paris. 3rd ed. Michelin Guides & Maps Dept. (Green Guide Ser.). (Avail. in Fr., Ger.). pap. 7.95 (ISBN 2-06-013540-0). Michelin.

Michelin Green Guide to Portugal. 2nd ed. Michelin Guides & Maps Dept. (Green Guide Ser.). (Avail. in Fr.). pap. 7.95 (ISBN 2-06-015570-3). Michelin.

Michelin Green Guide to Provence. Michelin Guides & Maps. (Green Guide Ser.). (Fr.). 1979. pap. 6.95 o.p. (ISBN 2-06-003630-5). Michelin.

Michelin Green Guide to Provence Eng. Michelin. (Avail. Fr. & Ger.). 1980. pap. 7.95 (ISBN 2-06-013640-7). Michelin.

Michelin Green Guide to Pyrenees. Michelin Guides & Maps. (Green Guide Ser.). (Fr.). 1978. pap. 7.95 (ISBN 2-06-003660-7). Michelin.

Michelin Green Guide to Spain. rev. 1st ed. Michelin Guides & Maps. (Green Guide Ser.). (Avail. in Fr. & Span.). pap. 7.95 (ISBN 2-06-121900-4). Michelin.

Michelin Green Guide to Switzerland. 6th ed. Michelin Guides & Maps. (Green Guide Ser.). (Avail. in Fr., Ger.). pap. 7.95 (ISBN 2-06-121801-6). Michelin.

Michelin Green Guide to Vallee Du Rhone. 4th ed. Michelin Guides & Maps. (Green Guide Ser.). (Fr.). 1979. pap. 7.95 (ISBN 2-06-003690-9). Michelin.

Michelin Green Guide to Vosges. 2nd ed. Michelin Guides & Maps. (Green Guide Ser.). 1980. pap. 7.95 (ISBN 2-06-003720-4). Michelin.

Michelin Red Guide to Benelux: Belgium, Luxembourg, Netherlands. Michelin Guides & Maps. (Red Guide Ser.). 1980. 12.95 (ISBN 2-06-006001-X). Michelin.

Michelin Red Guide to France. (Red Guide Ser.). 1981. pap. 14.95 (ISBN 2-06-006401-5). Michelin.

Michelin Red Guide to Germany. Michelin Guides & Maps. (Red Guide Ser.). 1981. 14.95 (ISBN 3-92-107801-6). Michelin.

Michelin Red Guide to Great Britain & Ireland. Michelin Guides & Maps. (Red Guide Ser.). 1981. 12.95 (ISBN 2-06-006501-1). Michelin.

Michelin Red Guide to Italy. Michelin Guides & Maps. (Red Guide Ser.). 1981. 14.95 (ISBN 2-06-006701-4). Michelin.

Michelin Red Guide to London. Michelin Guides & Maps. (Red Guide Ser.). 1981. pap. 3.95 (ISBN 2-06-006601-8). Michelin.

Michelin Red Guide to Paris: Paris Hotels & Restaurants. Michelin Guides & Maps. (Red Guide Ser.). 1981. Avail. In Fr. & Eng. pap. 3.25 (ISBN 2-06-006901-7). Michelin.

Michelin Red Guide to Spain & Portugal. Michelin Guides & Maps. (Red Guide Ser.). 1981. 12.95 (ISBN 2-06-006301-9). Michelin.

Michelle. Carolyn E. Phillips. LC 80-52202. (Illus.). 176p. 1980. text ed. 7.95 (ISBN 0-8307-0757-3, 5109000). Regal.

Michelozzo. Harriet M. Caplow. LC 76-23604. (Outstanding Dissertations in the Fine Arts - 2nd Series - 15th Century). (Illus.). 1977. Repr. of 1970 ed. lib. bdg. 115.50 (ISBN 0-8240-2678-0). Garland Pub.

Michener Miscellany, 1950-1970. James Michener. 384p. 1975. pap. 1.95 o.p. (ISBN 0-449-22526-7, C2526, Crest). Fawcett.

Michie on Banks & Banking, 11 vols. with 1980 cum. suppl. Michie Editorial Staff. Set. with 1980 cum. suppl. 400.00 (ISBN 0-87215-034-8); 1980 cum. suppl. 97.50 (ISBN 0-87215-345-2). Michie.

Michie's Jurisprudence of Virginia & West Virginia, 40 vols., with 1979 cum. suppl. rev. ed. Michie Editorial Staff. 1948. 975.00 set (ISBN 0-87215-128-X); 1979 cum. suppl. only 145.00 (ISBN 0-87215-350-9). Michie.

Michigan. Bruce Catton. (States & the Nation Ser.). (Illus.). 224p. 1976. 12.95 (ISBN 0-393-05572-8, Co-Pub by AASLH). Norton.

Michigan. 33.00 (ISBN 0-89770-098-8). Curriculum Info Ctr.

Michigan Arithmetic Program,Multiplication, Level 2: Consuable Edition. Kitty Wehrli. (gr. 3). 1975. 7.00 (ISBN 0-89039-132-7). Ann Arbor Pubs.

Michigan County Maps & Outdoor Guide. Michigan United Conservation Clubs. 1977. pap. 8.00 (ISBN 0-933112-04-1). Mich United Conserv.

Michigan Criminal Justice Law Manual. George T. Flekenes. (Criminal Justice Ser.). 300p. 1981. pap. text ed. 18.95 (ISBN 0-8299-0369-0). West Pub.

Michigan Cross Country Skiing Atlas. 3rd ed. Dennis R Hansen. (Illus.). 240p. Date not set. pap. 5.95 (ISBN 0-686-65601-6). Hansen Pub MI. Postponed.

Michigan Labor: A Brief History from 1818 to the Present. Doris B. McLaughlin. LC 73-633304. (Orig.). 1970. 9.50x (ISBN 0-87736-312-9); pap. 4.50x (ISBN 0-87736-333-1). U of Mich Inst Labor.

Michigan Manuscript 18 of the Gospels. William M. Read. LC 44-13750. (Publications in Language & Literature: No. 11). (Illus.). 75p. 1942. pap. 5.00 (ISBN 0-295-95219-9). U of Wash Pr.

Michigan Map Skills & Information Workbook. Paul McCreary. (Illus.). 32p. (Orig.). (gr. 6-10). 1978. wkbk. 4.50 (ISBN 0-910726-92-2). Hillsdale Educ.

Michigan One Hundred Years Ago. Kirke et al. (Sun Historical Ser.-). (Illus.). pap. 3.50 (ISBN 0-89540-053-7). Sun Pub.

Michigan Papyri XIV. Vincent P. McCarren. (American Studies in Papyrology: No. 22). 15.00x (ISBN 0-89130-295-6). Scholars Pr CA.

Michigan Programmed Spelling Series, Basic Word List Level 1: Reusable Edition. Enid L. Huelsberg. (gr. 1). 1974. wkbk. 7.00 (ISBN 0-89039-085-1). Ann Arbor Pubs.

Michigan Programmed Spelling Series, Basic Word List, Level 3: Reusable Edition. Enid L. Huelsberg. (gr. 3). 1974. wkbk. 7.00 (ISBN 0-89039-089-4). Ann Arbor Pubs.

Michigan Programmed Spelling Series, High School & College, Level 7: Reusable Edition. Enid L. Huelsberg. (gr. 7-9). 1975. wkbk. 7.00 (ISBN 0-89039-137-8). Ann Arbor Pubs.

Michigan Programmed Spelling Series,Basic Work List,Level 2: Reusable Edition. Enid L. Huelsberg. (gr. 2). 1974. 7.00 (ISBN 0-89039-087-8). Ann Arbor Pubs.

Michigan Programmed Spelling Series,High School & College, Level 8: Reusable Edition. Enid L. Huelsberg. (gr. 10-12). 1975. wkbk. 7.00 (ISBN 0-89039-138-6). Ann Arbor Pubs.

Michigan Programmed Spelling Series,Use Frequency Based Words, Level 4: Reusable Edition. Enid L. Huelsberg. (gr. 4). 1975. wkbk. 7.00 (ISBN 0-89039-091-6). Ann Arbor Pubs.

Michigan Programmed Spelling Series,Use Frequency Based Words,Level 5: Reusable Edition. Enid L. Huelsberg. (gr. 5). 1975. wkbk. 7.00 (ISBN 0-89039-093-2). Ann Arbor Pubs.

Michigan Programmed Spelling Series,Use Frequency Based Words,Level 6: Reusable Edition. Enid L. Huelsberg. (gr. 6). 1975. wkbk. 7.00 (ISBN 0-89039-095-9). Ann Arbor Pubs.

Michigan Property Tax: A Crumbling Cornerstone. F. L. Van Voorhees. 35p. 1972. 2.00 (ISBN 0-932826-07-5). New Issues MI.

Michigan State Industrial Directory, Nineteen Eighty-One. State Industrial Directories Corp. Date not set. pap. price not set (ISBN 0-89910-048-1). State Indus D.

Michigan: State Legislators & Their Work. Gerald H. Stollman. LC 77-18633. 1978. text ed. 12.50x o.p. (ISBN 0-8191-0425-6). U Pr of Amer.

Michigan Statistical Abstract: 1980. 15th ed. LC 56-62855. (MSU Business Studies). 1980. pap. 10.95. Mich St U Busn.

Michigan Supplement for Modern Real Estate Practice. 2nd ed. Daniel Page & Hugo Braun. 150p. (Orig.). 1980. pap. 7.95 (ISBN 0-88462-257-6). Real Estate Ed Co.

Michigan Trees: A Guide to the Trees of Michigan & the Great Lakes. Burton V. Barnes & Warren H. Wagner, Jr. (Biological Science). (Illus.). 360p. 1981. text ed. 10.95 (ISBN 0-472-08017-2); pap. text ed. 5.95 (ISBN 0-472-08018-0). U. of Mich Pr.

Michigan Trees Worth Knowing. rev., 5th ed. Norman F. Smith. LC 78-61161. (Illus.). 1978. 9.95 (ISBN 0-910726-69-8); pap. 6.50 (ISBN 0-910726-72-8). Hillsdale Educ.

Michigan Wildlife Sketches. rev., 6th ed. G. W. Bradt. (Illus.). 1971. pap. 2.75 (ISBN 0-910726-71-X). Hillsdale Educ.

Michigan Yesterday & Today. rev., 8th ed. Ferris E. Lewis. (Illus.). (gr. 10-12). 1975. text ed. 12.20x o.p. (ISBN 0-910726-50-7); tchrs'. guide 3.00x o.p. (ISBN 0-910726-51-5). Hillsdale Educ.

Michigan's Heartland. Forrest B. Meek. Date not set. 14.50 (ISBN 0-9602472-0-3). Edgewood.

Michigan's Timber Battleground. 2nd ed. Forrest B. Meek. 483p. lib. bdg. 9.95 softcover sewn binding (ISBN 0-9602472-1-1). Edgewood.

Michilimackinac: A Handbook to the Site. 1st ed. David A. Armour & Keith R. Widder. (Illus.). 48p. (Orig.). 1980. pap. 1.50 (ISBN 0-911872-39-6). Mackinac Island.

Michio Ito: The Dancer & His Dances. Helen Caldwell. (Illus.). 1977. 19.50 (ISBN 0-520-03219-5). U. of Cal Pr.

Mickey Mantle: Slugs It Out. Julian May. LC 72-77303. (Sports Close-up Ser.). (gr. 3-9). 1972. PLB 5.95 o.p. (ISBN 0-87191-202-3); pap. 2.95 o.p. (ISBN 0-686-67382-4). Crestwood Hse.

Mickey Mouse & Goofy: The Big Bear Scare. Walt Disney. (Young Reader Ser.). (gr. k-3). 1979. PLB 5.00 (ISBN 0-307-60318-0, Golden Pr). Western Pub.

Mickey Mouse & the Great Lot Plot. Walt Disney Studios. (Illus.). 24p. (gr. k-3). 1976. PLB 5.00 (ISBN 0-307-60129-3, Golden Pr). Western Pub.

Mickey Mouse & the Marvelous Smell Machine. Walt Disney Studio. (Golden Fragrance Book Ser.). (Illus.). (gr. k-3). 1979. PLB 9.92 (ISBN 0-307-64544-4, Golden Pr); pap. 4.95 (ISBN 0-307-13544-6). Western Pub.

Mickey Mouse & the Mouseketeers: Ghost Town Adventures. Walt Disney. (Illus.). (gr. k-3). 1977. PLB 5.00 (ISBN 0-307-60135-8, Golden Pr). Western Pub.

Mickey Mouse & the Second Wish. Walt Disney. (Tell-a-Tale Readers). (Illus.). (gr. k-3). 1973. PLB 4.77 (ISBN 0-307-68418-0, Whitman). Western Pub.

Mickey Mouse & the World's Friendliest Monster. Walt Disney. (Tell-a-Tale Readers). (Illus.). (gr. k-3). 1976. PLB 4.77 (ISBN 0-307-68605-1, Whitman). Western Pub.

Mickey Mouse: Best Neighbor Contest. Walt Disney. (Illus.). (gr. k-3). 1977. PLB 5.00 (ISBN 0-307-60134-X, Golden Pr). Western Pub.

Mickey Mouse Book. Al White. (ps-1). 1965. PLB 5.38 (ISBN 0-307-68914-X, Golden Pr). Western Pub.

Mickey Mouse Club. Walt Disney. (Illus.). 24p. (ps-2). 1977. Repr. of 1975 ed. PLB 5.38 (ISBN 0-307-68997-2, Golden Pr). Western Pub.

Mickey Mouse, Hideaway Island. Walt Disney Studios. (Big Picture Bks.). 24p. (gr. k-3). 1979. PLB 7.62 (ISBN 0-307-60829-8, Golden Pr); pap. 1.95 (ISBN 0-307-10829-5). Western Pub.

Mickey Mouse in Space. (Wipe off Bks.). 9p. (ps). Date not set. 2.39 (ISBN 0-307-01848-2, Golden Pr). Western Pub.

Mickey Mouse Joins the Foreign Legion. (Illus.). 42p. 1981. 3.95 (ISBN 0-89659-175-1). Abbeville Pr.

Mickey Mouse Meets Robin Hood. (Illus.). 36p. 1981. 3.95 (ISBN 0-89659-176-X). Abbeville Pr.

Mickey Mouse: Missing Mouseketeers. Walt Disney. (Illus.). (gr. k-3). 1977. PLB 5.00 (ISBN 0-307-60057-2, Golden Pr). Western Pub.

Mickey Mouse: The Kitten Sitters. Walt Disney. (Young Reader Ser.). (Illus.). (gr. k-3). 1976. PLB 5.00 (ISBN 0-307-60133-1, Golden Pr); pap. 1.95 (ISBN 0-307-10823-6). Western Pub.

Micro Aspects of Development. Ed. by Eliezer B. Ayal. LC 72-89641. (Special Studies in International Economics & Development). 1973. 28.75x (ISBN 0-275-28685-1); pap. text ed. 10.95x (ISBN 0-89197-846-1). Irvington.

Micro-Economic Theory. M. L. Jhingan. 1979. text ed. 25.00x (ISBN 0-7069-0569-5, Pub. by Vikas India). Advent Bk.

Micro-Economics of Demographic Change: Family Planning & Economic Wellbeing. Theodore K. Ruprecht & Frank I. Jewett. LC 75-57. (Illus.). 176p. 1975. text ed. 25.00 (ISBN 0-275-05530-2). Praeger.

Micro Systems in Business. A. Osborne et al. (Micro Monograph Ser.: No. 1). 122p. 1980. pap. text ed. 27.00x (ISBN 0-903796-63-5, Pub. by Online Conferences England). Renouf.

Micro-Theory & Economic Choices. R. Stephen Polkinghorn. 1979. 17.95x (ISBN 0-256-02143-0). Irwin.

Microaggragates: Experimental & Clinical Aspects. Kozloff & Solis. 1981. write for info. (ISBN 0-87527-177-4). Green.

Microanalysis by the Ring Oven Technique. 2nd ed. H. Weisz. 1970. 25.00 (ISBN 0-08-015702-5). Pergamon.

Microanalytic Simulation Models for Analysis of Public Welfare Policies. Robert Harris. (Institute Paper). 50p. 1977. pap. 3.50 (ISBN 0-87766-223-1, 22800). Urban Inst.

Microbeam Analysis: Proceedings. Annual Conference of Microbeam Analysis Society, 9th, 1974. 20.00 (ISBN 0-686-50179-9); 1975 (10th conf.) 20.00 (ISBN 0-686-50180-2); 1976 (11th conf.) 20.00 (ISBN 0-686-50181-0); 1978 (13th conf.) o. 20.00 (ISBN 0-686-50183-7); 1979 (14th conf.) 25.00 (ISBN 0-686-67766-8); 1980 (15th conf.) 25.00 (ISBN 0-686-67767-6). San Francisco Pr.

Microbes & Biological Productivity. Ed. by D. E. Hughes & Rose. (Illus.). 1971. 42.50 (ISBN 0-521-08112-2). Cambridge U Pr.

Microbes & Man: A Laboratory Manual for Students in the Health Sciences. Isabel J. Barnes et al. (Illus.). 1974. lab. man 10.95x (ISBN 0-7167-0585-0); tchr's manual avail. W H Freeman.

Microbes & Men. Robert Reid. 1975. 8.95 o.p. (ISBN 0-8415-0348-6). Dutton.

Microbes & Morals. Theodor Rosebury. 352p. 1976. pap. 1.95 o.p. (ISBN 0-345-24893-7). Ballantine.

Microbes at Work. Millicent E. Selsam. (Illus.). (gr. 5-9). 1953. PLB 7.92 (ISBN 0-688-31497-X). Morrow.

Microbes in Action: A Laboratory Manual of Microbiology. 2nd ed. Harry W. Seeley, Jr. & Paul J. Van Demark. (Illus.). 1972. lab manual 9.95x (ISBN 0-7167-0689-X); tchr's manual avail. W H Freeman.

Microbes in Action: A Laboratory Manual of Microbiology. 3rd ed. Harry W. Seeley, Jr. & Paul J. VanDemark. (Illus.). 1981. write for info. (ISBN 0-7167-1259-8); instrs'. manual avail. W H Freeman.

Microbes in Your Life. Leo Schneider. LC 66-13796. (Illus.). (gr. 7 up). 1966. 6.50 o.p. (ISBN 0-15-253574-8, HJ). HarBraceJ.

Microbial Adhesion to Surfaces. R. C. Berkeley et al. LC 80-41358. 600p. 1981. 110.00 (ISBN 0-470-27083-7). Halsted Pr.

Microbial & Molecular Genetics. 2nd ed. J. R. Fincham. LC 75-21729. 155p. 1976. pap. 9.95x (ISBN 0-8448-0769-9). Crane-Russak Co.

Microbial Aspects of Dental Caries, 3 vols. 1976. Set. 40.00 (ISBN 0-917000-01-3). Info Retrieval.

Microbial Differentiation. Ed. by J. M. Ashworth & J. E. Smith. (Society for General Microbiology Ser.: No. 23). (Illus.). 500p. 1973. 49.50 (ISBN 0-521-20104-7). Cambridge U Pr.

Microbial Ecology. Martin Alexander. LC 71-137105. (Illus.). 1971. 26.95 (ISBN 0-471-02054-0). Wiley.

Microbial Ecology: A Conceptual Approach. J. M. Lynch & N. J. Poole. 1979. 49.50 o.p. (ISBN 0-470-26532-9); pap. 21.95 (ISBN 0-470-26533-7). Halsted Pr.

Microbial Energetics. Ed. by B. A. Haddock & W. A. Hamilton. LC 76-54367. (Society for General Microbiology: Symposium 27). (Illus.). 1977. 65.00 (ISBN 0-521-21494-7). Cambridge U Pr.

Microbial Energy Conversion. H. G. Schlegel. LC 76-56894. 1977. pap. text ed. 81.00 (ISBN 0-08-021791-5). Pergamon.

Microbial Growth. Ed. by P. S. Dawson. LC 74-26644. (Benchmark Papers in Microbiology Ser: Vol. 8). 400p. 1975. 43.00 (ISBN 0-12-786330-3). Acad Pr.

Microbial Pathogenicity in Man & Animals: Proceedings. Ed. by H. Smith & J. H. Pearce. LC 75-177940. (Illus.). 1972. 50.50 (ISBN 0-521-08430-X). Cambridge U Pr.

Microbial Physiology. I. W. Dawes & I. W. Sutherland. (Basic Microbiology Ser.: Vol. 4). 1976. pap. text ed. 14.95 (ISBN 0-470-15159-5). Halsted Pr.

Microbial Physiology. G. Sojka. LC 77-11223. 1981. text ed. write for info. (ISBN 0-12-655250-9). Acad Pr.

Microbial Technology: Society for General Microbiology Symposium 29. A. T. Bull et al. LC 78-12206. (Illus.). 1979. 59.50 (ISBN 0-521-22500-0). Cambridge U Pr.

Microbial Ultrastructure. Ed. by R. Fuller. 1977. 47.00 (ISBN 0-12-269450-3). Acad Pr.

Microbiological Applications of Gas Chromatography. D. B. Drucker. LC 80-40447. 300p. Date not set. price not set (ISBN 0-521-22365-2). Cambridge U Pr.

Microbiological Problems in Food Preservation by Irradiation. 1967. pap. 6.50 (ISBN 92-0-111067-7, IAEA). Unipub.

Microbiological Safety of Foods. Ed. by Betty C. Hobbs & J. H. Christian. 1974. 67.00 (ISBN 0-12-350750-2). Acad Pr.

Microbiological Specifications & Testing Methods for Irradiated Food. (Technical Reports Ser.: No. 104). (Illus., Orig.). 1970. pap. 7.50 (ISBN 92-0-115170-5, IAEA). Unipub.

Microbiology. Neal D. Buffaloe & Dale V. Ferguson. LC 75-19538. (Illus.). 448p. 1976. text ed. 19.50 (ISBN 0-395-18712-5); inst. manual 1.25 (ISBN 0-395-18918-7). HM.

Microbiology. 2nd ed. Neal D. Buffaloe & Dale V. Ferguson. (Illus.). 752p. 1981. text ed. 20.95 (ISBN 0-395-29649-8); write for info. lab manual (ISBN 0-395-29652-8); write for info. instr's manual (ISBN 0-395-29650-1); write for info. set study guide (ISBN 0-395-29651-X). HM.

Microbiology. Bernard D. Davis. (Illus.). 1274p. 1980. 39.50 (ISBN 0-06-140691-0, Harper Medical). Har-Row.

Microbiology. 2nd ed. Bernard D. Davis et al. (Illus.). 1973. text ed. 34.95x o.p. (ISBN 0-06-140683-X, Harper Medical). Har-Row.

Microbiology. 5th ed. Louis P. Gebhardt & Paul S. Nicholes. LC 74-10691. 1975. text ed. 15.95 (ISBN 0-8016-1784-7); lab manual 8.50 (ISBN 0-8016-1773-1). Mosby.

Microbiology. 3rd ed. Daniel Kaminsky et al. (Nursing Examination Review Book: Vol. 7). 1974. spiral bdg. 6.00 (ISBN 0-87488-507-8). Med Exam.

Microbiology. Cynthia F. Norton. LC 80-23350. (Life Sciences Ser.). (Illus.). 850p. 1981. text ed. 19.95 (ISBN 0-201-05304-7). A-W.

Microbiology. 2nd ed. Ed. by Richard C. Tilton. LC 79-8372. (Basic Sciences PreTest Self-Assessment & Review Ser.). (Illus.). 1979. 9.95 (ISBN 0-07-050966-2). McGraw-Pretest.

Microbiology. G. D. Wasley & R. W. Warner. (Teach Yourself Ser.). 1974. pap. 3.95 o.p. (ISBN 0-679-10404-6). McKay.

Microbiology: A Programmed Introduction to. R. J. Brady. (Illus.). 1969. pap. 9.95 (ISBN 0-87618-075-6). R J Brady.

Microbiology & Human Disease. 3rd ed. George A. Wistreich & Max D. Lechtman. 1981. text ed. 21.95x (ISBN 0-02-470910-7). Macmillan.

Microbiology & Immunology: A Positive Statement Manual. Hugh H. Fudenberg & Charles D. Graber. 1977. spiral bddg. 9.75 (ISBN 0-87488-242-7). Med Exam.

Microbiology & Pathology. 12th ed. Alice L Smith. LC 79-27338. (Illus.). 756p. 1980. text ed. 19.95 (ISBN 0-8016-4673-1). Mosby.

Microbiology Applied to Technology: Proceedings XIIth International Congress of Microbiology. Ed. by DECHMA, Deutsche Gesellschaft Fuer Chemisches Apparatewesen E. V. (DECHEMA Monographs: Vol. 83). 230p. (Orig.). 1979. pap. text ed. 25.80 (ISBN 3-527-10766-5). Verlag Chemie.

Microbiology for Dental Students. 2nd ed. T. H. Melville & Conrad Russell. (Illus.). 1975. pap. text ed. 18.95x (ISBN 0-433-21149-0). Intl Ideas.

Microbiology for Environment Science Engineers. Anthony Gaudy & Elizabeth Gaudy. (Water Resources & Environmental Engineering Ser.). (Illus.). 704p. 1980. 25.95 (ISBN 0-07-023035-8); solutions manual 16.50 (ISBN 0-07-023036-6). McGraw.

Microbiology for Health Careers. E. B. Ferris. (Illus.). 147p. 1974. pap. 7.00 (ISBN 0-8273-1326-8); instructor's guide 1.60 (ISBN 0-8273-1327-6). Delmar.

Microbiology for Health Students. C. Thomas Settlemire & William Hughes. (Illus.). 1978. text ed. 15.95 case (ISBN 0-8359-4360-7); instrs'. manual avail. Reston.

Microbiology for Medical Technologists: PreTest Self-Assessment & Review. Ed. by Sheila R. Berg. LC 78-51703. (PreTest Self-Assessment & Review Ser.). (Illus.). 1979. pap. 9.95 (ISBN 0-07-051572-7). McGraw-Pretest.

Microbiology for Nursing & Allied Health Students. Mary L. Christensen. (Illus.). 624p. write for info. (ISBN 0-398-04176-8). C C Thomas.

Microbiology Hazards. C. H. Collins. 1981. text ed. price not set (ISBN 0-408-10650-6). Butterworth.

Microbiology in Clinical Dentistry. Frank J. Orland. (Illus.). 250p. 1981. 23.50 (ISBN 0-88416-171-4). PSG Pub.

Microbiology Laboratory Manual & Workbook. 4th ed. Alice L. Smith. LC 76-30332. (Illus.). 1977. pap. 8.95 (ISBN 0-8016-4706-1). Mosby.

Microbiology Laboratory Manual & Workbook. 5th ed. Alice L. Smith. (Illus.). 179p. 1981. paper perfect 9.95 (ISBN 0-8016-4707-X). Mosby.

Microbiology Nineteen Eighty. Ed. by David Schlessinger. (Illus.). 1980. text ed. 22.00 (ISBN 0-914826-23-9). Am Soc Microbio.

Microbiology, Nineteen Eighty-One. Ed. by David Schlessinger. (Illus.). 1981. 22.00 (ISBN 0-914826-31-X). Am Soc Microbio.

Microbiology Nineteen Seventy-Nine. Ed. by David Schlessinger. (Illus.). 1979. text ed. 22.00 (ISBN 0-914826-20-4). Am Soc Microbio.

Microbiology of Food Fermentations. 2nd ed. Carl S. Pederson. (Illus.). 1979. text ed. 27.50 (ISBN 0-87055-277-5). AVI.

Microbiology of Foods. John C. Ayres et al. LC 79-16335. (Food & Nutrition Ser.). (Illus.). 1980. text ed. 21.95x (ISBN 0-7167-1049-8). W H Freeman.

Microbiology Review. 7th ed. Ed. by Charles W. Kim. LC 80-20088. 1980. pap. 8.50 spiral bdg. (ISBN 0-87488-203-6). Med Exam.

Microbiology 1974. Ed. by David Schlessinger. LC 74-33538. (Annual Microbiology Ser.). 1975. 22.00 (ISBN 0-914826-02-6). Am Soc Microbio.

Microbiology 1975. Ed. by David Schlessinger. LC 74-33538. (Annual Microbiology Ser.). 1975. 22.00 (ISBN 0-914826-05-0). Am Soc Microbio.

Microbiology 1976. Ed. by David Schlessinger. LC 74-33538. (Annual Microbiology Ser.). 1976. 22.00 (ISBN 0-914826-11-5). Am Soc Microbio.

Microbiology 1977. Ed. by David Schlessinger. LC 74-33538. (Annual Microbiology Ser.). 1977. 22.00 (ISBN 0-914826-13-1). Am Soc Microbio.

Microbiology 1978. Ed. by David Schlessinger. LC 74-33538. (Illus.). 1978. text ed. 22.00 (ISBN 0-914826-15-8). Am Soc Microbio.

Microcapsules & Other Capsules: Advances Since 1975. M. H. Gutcho. LC 79-15917. (Chemical Technology Review Ser.: No. 135). (Illus.). 1980. 40.00 (ISBN 0-8155-0776-3). Noyes.

Microchemical Analysis of Nervous Tissue. Neville N. Osborne. 1974. text ed. 37.00 (ISBN 0-08-018100-7). Pergamon.

Microcirculation, 3 vols. G. Kaley & B. M. Altura. (Illus.). 1978. Vol. I. 52.50 (ISBN 0-8391-0966-0); Vol. II. 52.50 (ISBN 0-8391-0980-6); Vol. III. 65.00 (ISBN 0-8391-1592-X). Univ Park.

Microcirculation: Current Concepts. Ed. by Richard Effros et al. 1981. write for info. (ISBN 0-12-232560-5). Acad Pr.

Microcomputer-Analog Converter Software & Hardware Interfacing. Jonathan A. Titus et al. LC 78-57201. 1978. pap. 10.50 (ISBN 0-672-21540-3). Sams.

Microcomputer & the School Library Media Specialist. Pierre P. Barrette. 200p. 1981. lib. bdg. 13.50x (ISBN 0-87287-226-2). Libs Unl.

Microcomputer Architecture & Programming. John F. Wakerly. 600p. 1981. text ed. 23.95 (ISBN 0-471-05232-9). Wiley.

Microcomputer Design. 14.95 o.p. (ISBN 0-686-16100-9). Qwint Systems.

Microcomputer Design. Carol A. Ogdin. (Illus.). 1978. ref. 16.95 (ISBN 0-13-580977-0); pap. 12.95 (ISBN 0-13-580985-1). P-H.

Microcomputer Experimentation with Intel SDK-85. Lance A. Leventhal & Colin Walsh. 1980. text ed. 15.95 (ISBN 0-13-580860-X). P-H.

Microcomputer for External Control Devices. James A. Gupton. LC 80-67640. 1980. pap. 13.95 (ISBN 0-918398-28-2). Dilithium Pr.

Microcomputer Fundamentals. Roy W. Goody. 300p. 1979. pap. text ed. 13.95 (ISBN 0-574-21540-9, 13-4540); instr's. guide avail. (ISBN 0-574-21541-7, 13-4541). SRA.

Microcomputer Interfacing. B. Artwick. 1980. 21.95 (ISBN 0-13-580902-9). P-H.

Microcomputer Management & Programming. Carol A. Ogdin. (Illus.). 1980. text ed. 21.95 (ISBN 0-13-580936-3). P-H.

Microcomputer: Problem Solving Using Pascal. K. L. Bowles. LC 77-11959. 1977. pap. 9.80 (ISBN 0-387-90286-4). Springer-Verlag.

Microcomputer Systems & Applied BASIC. James L. Poirot. (Illus.). 150p. (Orig.). (gr. 6-12). 1980. pap. 8.95 (ISBN 0-88408-136-2). Sterling Swift.

Microcomputer Workbook: Apple II Ed. 2nd ed. James L. Poirot & Don A. Retzlaff. 137p. (gr. 11-12). 1981. pap. text ed. 5.95 (ISBN 0-88408-139-7). Sterling Swift.

Microcomputer Workbook: Apple II Edition. James L. Poirot & Donald A. Retzlaff. 144p. (Orig.). (gr. 11-12). 1979. wkbk 4.95 (ISBN 0-88408-120-6). Sterling Swift.

Microcomputer Workbook: TRS-80ed. James L. Poirot & Danold A. Retzlaff. 128p. 1979. pap. 4.95 wkbk. (ISBN 0-88408-121-4). Sterling Swift.

Microcomputers - Microprocessors: Hardware, Software & Applications. J. L. Hilburn & P. Julich. 1976. text ed. 24.95 (ISBN 0-13-580969-X). P-H.

Microcomputers & the Three R's. Carol Doerr. 1979. pap. 8.85x (ISBN 0-8104-5113-1). Hayden.

Microcomputers for Engineers & Scientists. Glenn A. Gibson & Yu-Cheng Liu. (Illus.). 1980. text ed. 28.95 (ISBN 0-13-580886-3). P-H.

Microcosm & Mediator: The Theological Anthropology of Maximus the Confessor. Lars Thunberg. Rev. by A. L. Allchin. LC 80-2368. 1981. Repr. of 1965 ed. 58.00 (ISBN 0-404-18917-2). AMS Pr.

Microcosmographia Academia. F. M. Cornford. 1980. pap. 2.95 (ISBN 0-370-00145-1, Pub. by Chatto, Bodley Head & Jonathan). Merrimack Bk Serv.

Microcosmus, or a Little Description of the Great World. Peter Heylyn. LC 74-28863. (English Experience Ser.: No. 743). 1975. Repr. of 1621 ed. 31.00 (ISBN 90-221-0743-4). Walter J Johnson.

Microecology: Social Situations & Intimate Space. Donald W. Ball. LC 72-10541. (Studies in Sociology Ser). 40p. 1973. pap. text ed. 2.50 (ISBN 0-672-61209-7). Bobbs.

Microeconomic Foundations of Macroeconomics. Ed. by G. C. Harcourt. 1978. lib. bdg. 50.00 o.p. (ISBN 0-89158-730-6). Westview.

Microeconomic Issues Today. Robert B. Carson. 182p. (Orig.). 1980. text ed. 12.95 (ISBN 0-312-53175-3); write for info instrs'. manual (ISBN 0-312-53176-1); write for info. instructor's manual (ISBN 0-312-53177-X). St Martin.

Microeconomic Models. K. C. Kogiku. LC 78-11695. 320p. 1981. Repr. of 1971 ed. lib. bdg. write for info. (ISBN 0-88275-781-4). Krieger.

Microeconomic Principles. William P Albrecht, Jr. (Illus.). 1979. pap. text ed. 10.95 (ISBN 0-13-581314-X); study guide & wkbk. 8.95 (ISBN 0-13-227553-8). P-H.

Microeconomic Theory. 4th ed. Charles E. Ferguson & John P. Gould. (Economics Ser.). (Illus.). 450p. 1975. text ed. 16.50x o.p. (ISBN 0-256-01637-2). Irwin.

Microeconomic Theory. 5th ed. J. P. Gould & C. E. Ferguson. 1980. 18.95x (ISBN 0-256-02157-0). Irwin.

Microeconomic Theory. 2nd ed. Nicholson. 1978. 21.95 (ISBN 0-03-020831-9). Dryden Pr.

Microeconomics. Michael E. Bradley. 1980. pap. text ed. 11.95x (ISBN 0-673-15335-5); study guide 5.95x (ISBN 0-673-15286-3). Scott F.

Microeconomics. Steven T. Call & William L. Holahan. 544p. 1980. text ed. 19.95x (ISBN 0-534-00804-6). Wadsworth Pub.

Microeconomics. Robert W. Clower & John F. Due. 1972. text ed. 12.95x o.p. (ISBN 0-256-00453-6). Irwin.

Microeconomics. 2nd ed. H. Gravelle & R. Rees. (Modern Economic Series). (Illus.). 1981. pap. text ed. 25.00 (ISBN 0-582-44075-0). Longman.

Microeconomics. James P. Quirk & Duncan McDougall. 1981. pap. text ed. 11.95 (ISBN 0-574-19410-X, 13-2410); instr's guide avail. (ISBN 0-574-19411-8, 13-2411). SRA.

Microeconomics. 2nd ed. R. Rees & H. F. E. Gravelle. (Modern Economics Ser.). (Illus.). 620p. 1981. pap. text ed. 8.50 (ISBN 0-582-44075-0). Longman.

Microeconomics. 3rd ed. Lewis C. Solmon. LC 79-25515. 528p. 1980. pap. text ed. 12.95 (ISBN 0-201-07218-1); student guide avail. (ISBN 0-201-07221-1). A-W.

Microeconomics: A Programmed Book. 3rd ed. Richard E. Attiyeh et al. (Illus.). 256p. pap. 9.95 ref. ed. (ISBN 0-13-581421-9). P-H.

Microeconomics: A Synthesis of Modern & Neoclassical Theory. R. R. Russell & M. Wilkinson. (Economics Ser.). 1979. text ed. 26.95 (ISBN 0-471-94652-4). Wiley.

Microeconomics: Analysis & Applications. G. Bach. 1977. pap. 10.95 (ISBN 0-13-581306-9). P-H.

Microeconomics: Analysis & Policy. 3rd. ed. Lloyd G. Reynolds. 1979. pap. text ed. 11.50 (ISBN 0-256-02172-4); review guide & wkbk 5.95 (ISBN 0-256-02169-4). Irwin.

Microeconomics for Business Decisions: Theory & Application. J. Heineke. 1976. text ed. 16.95 (ISBN 0-13-581389-1). P-H.

Microeconomics: Private & Public Choice. James D. Gwartney. 1977. 10.50 o.p. (ISBN 0-12-311065-3). Acad Pr.

Microeconomics: Public & Private Sector Choice. 2nd ed. James D. Gwartney. 1980. 12.95 (ISBN 0-12-311070-X). Acad Pr.

Microeconomics: Resource Allocation & Price Theory. John C. Redman & Barbara J. Redman. (Illus.). 1981. text ed. 17.50 (ISBN 0-87055-367-4). AVI.

Microeconomics: Theory & Applications. Robert Y. Awh. LC 75-38643. 1976. text ed. 22.95 (ISBN 0-471-03849-0); instructors manual (ISBN 0-471-03854-7); wkbk 6.50 (ISBN 0-471-03853-9). Wiley.

Microeconomics: Theory & Applications. 3rd ed. Edwin Mansfield. (Illus.). 1979. text ed. 16.95x (ISBN 0-393-95002-6); text ed. 16.50x shorter ed. (ISBN 0-393-95010-7); instrs'. manual 3.95x (ISBN 0-393-95044-1). Norton.

Microelectronics: A Scientific American Book. Scientific American Editors. LC 77-13955. (Illus.). 1977. pap. text ed. 8.95x (ISBN 0-7167-0066-2). W H Freeman.

Microelectronics at Work: Productivity & Jobs in the World Economy. Colin Norman. LC 80-53425. (Worldwatch Papers). 1980. pap. 2.00 (ISBN 0-916468-38-0). Worldwatch Inst.

Microelectronics: Capitalist Technology & the Working Class. Ed. by Conference of Socialist Economists. (Illus.). 152p. 1981. text ed. write for info. (ISBN 0-906336-16-3); pap. text ed. write for info. (ISBN 0-906336-17-1). Humanities.

Microelectronics Interconnection & Packaging. Electronics Magazine. Ed. by Jerry Lyman. LC 79-21990. (Illus.). 320p. 1979. pap. 12.95 (ISBN 0-07-606600-2, R-927). McGraw.

Microelectronics Interconnection & Packaging. Electronics Magazine. (Electronics Book Ser.). (Illus.). 1980. 19.95 (ISBN 0-07-019184-0). McGraw.

Microelectronics of the Engineering Industry. N. Swords-Isherwood. 300p. 1980. 32.50x (ISBN 0-89397-094-8). Nichols Pub.

Microelectronics Systems One: Checkbook. Vears. 1981. text ed. price not set (ISBN 0-408-00552-1). Butterworth.

Microevolution of Human Populations. Francis E. Johnston. (Illus.). 160p. 1973. pap. 9.95 ref. ed. (ISBN 0-13-581512-6). P-H.

MicroFilm: A History, 1839 to 1900. Frederic Luther. 1981. Repr. of 1959 ed. 25.00 (ISBN 0-913672-34-3). Microform Rev.

Microfilm in Business. Joseph L. Kish, Jr. & J. Morris. (Illus.). 1966. 16.50 (ISBN 0-8260-5060-3). Ronald Pr.

Microfilm of Marriage & Death. Abstracts from Washington Intelligence (Washington, D.C.) 1800-1850. George A. Martin. 1976. of 3 rolls 61.00 set (ISBN 0-915156-02-4). Natl Genealogical.

Microfilm Readers: ANSI-NMA MS20-1979. National Micrographics Assn. 1980. 4.50 (ISBN 0-89258-061-5). Natl Micrograph.

Microfilming Newspapers: ANSI-NMA MS111-1977. National Micrographics Assn. 1978. 4.50 (ISBN 0-89258-050-X). Natl Micrograph.

Microform Market Place Nineteen Eighty to Nineteen Eighty-One. 4th ed. Ed. by Ardis V. Carleton. 250p. 1980. pap. text ed. 20.95 (ISBN 0-913672-37-8). Microform Rev.

Microforms. E. Dale Cluff. Ed. by James E. Duane. LC 80-21457. (Instructional Media Library: Vol. 7). (Illus.). 104p. 1981. 13.95 (ISBN 0-87778-167-2). Educ Tech Pubns.

Microforms: The Librarians' View, 1980-1981. 3rd ed. Alice H. Bahr. (Professional Librarian Ser.). (Illus.). 135p. 1981. pap. text ed. 24.50 (ISBN 0-914236-70-9). Knowledge Indus.

Microfossils. M. D. Brasier. (Illus., Orig.). 1980. text ed. 27.50x (ISBN 0-04-562001-6); pap. text ed. 14.95x (ISBN 0-04-562002-4). Allen Unwin.

Microfoundations. E. R. Weintraub. LC 78-16551. (Cambridge Surveys of Economic Literature Ser.). 1979. 26.50 (ISBN 0-521-22305-9); pap. 7.95x (ISBN 0-521-29445-2). Cambridge U Pr.

Micrographics. William Saffady. LC 78-1309. (Library Science Text Ser.). 1978. 22.50x (ISBN 0-87287-175-4). Libs Unl.

Micromanipulators & Micromanipulation. Hamed M. El-Badry. (Illus.). 1963. 34.90 o.p. (ISBN 0-387-80648-2). Springer-Verlag.

Micromechanisms in Particle-Hardened Alloys. J. W. Martin. LC 78-70411. (Cambridge Solid State Science Ser.). (Illus.). 1980. 57.50 (ISBN 0-521-22623-6); pap. 17.50 (ISBN 0-521-29580-7). Cambridge U Pr.

Microneurosurgery. 2nd ed. Robert W. Rand. LC 78-7230. 1978. text ed. 74.50 (ISBN 0-8016-4077-6). Mosby.

Microorganisms & Man. Orville Wyss & C. E. Eklund. LC 70-146674. 1971. text ed. 19.95x (ISBN 0-471-96900-1). Wiley.

Microorganisms & Nitrogen Sources Transport & Utilization of Amino Acids Peptides, Proteins & Related Subjects. J. W. Payne. LC 79-42900. 800p. 1980. 135.00 (ISBN 0-471-27697-9). Wiley.

Micropalaeontology of Oceans. B. M. Funnell & W. R. Riedel. 1971. 145.00 (ISBN 0-521-07642-0). Cambridge U Pr.

Micropezidae of California (Diptera) Richard W. Merritt & Maurice T. James. (Bulletin of the California Insect Survey: Vol. 14). 1973. 8.00x (ISBN 0-520-09435-2). U of Cal Pr.

Microphone Handbook. John Eargle. 1980. write for info. Elar Pub Co.

Microprobe Analysis. Ed. by Christian A. Andersen. LC 72-8837. 656p. 1973. 43.00 (ISBN 0-471-02835-5, Pub. by Wiley-Interscience). Wiley.

Microprocessor & Digital Computer Technology. George B. Rutkowski & Jerome E. Olesky. (Illus.). 416p. 1981. text ed. 22.95 (ISBN 0-13-581116-3). P-H.

Microprocessor & Its Application. Ed. by D. Aspinall. LC 78-54572. (Illus.). 1978. 47.50 (ISBN 0-521-22241-9). Cambridge U Pr.

Microprocessor & Microcomputer Basics. Jefferson Boyce. (Illus.). 1979. text ed. 18.95 (ISBN 0-13-581249-6). P-H.

Microprocessor Background for Management Personnel. J. Cooper. 208p. 1981. 14.95 (ISBN 0-13-580829-4). P-H.

Microprocessor Interfacing. Peter Gise. 288p. 1982. text ed. 19.95 (ISBN 0-8359-4364-X). Reston.

Microprocessor Principles, Programming & Interfacing. Kenneth Muchow & Bill Deem. 1982. text ed. 18.95 (ISBN 0-8359-4383-6); instrs.' manual avail. (ISBN 0-8359-4384-4). Reston.

Microprocessor Programming & Software Development. F. Duncan. 1979. 29.95 (ISBN 0-13-581405-7). P-H.

Microprocessor Software Design. Max Schindler. 304p. 1980. pap. 13.25 (ISBN 0-8104-5190-5). Hayden.

Microprocessor Software: Programming Concepts & Techniques. Gene Streitmatter. (Illus.). 400p. 1981. text ed. 17.95 (ISBN 0-8359-4375-5). Reston.

Microprocessor System Debugging. Noordin Ghani & Edward Farrell. (Computer Engineering Ser.). 160p. 1981. 28.00 (ISBN 0-471-27860-2, Pub. by Wiley-Interscience). Wiley.

Microprocessor Systems Design. Ed Klingman. LC 76-45190. (Illus.). 1977. 26.95 (ISBN 0-13-581413-8). P-H.

Microprocessor Systems Design & Applications. Dave Bursky. 192p. pap. 9.95 (ISBN 0-8104-0976-3). Hayden.

Microprocessor Technology. John D. Kershaw. 1980. text ed. 18.95 (ISBN 0-534-00748-1, Breton Pubs). Wadsworth Pub.

Microprocessors. Electronics Magazine. Ed. by L. Aitman. 1975. 23.50x (ISBN 0-07-019171-9, P&RB). McGraw.

Microprocessors. Electronics Magazine. Ed. by Laurence Altman. (Illus.). 1975. pap. text ed. 8.95 (ISBN 0-07-019171-9, R-520). McGraw.

Microprocessors - Microcomputers: An Introduction. Donald D. Givone & Robert P. Roesser. (Illus.). 1979. text ed. 22.95 (ISBN 0-07-023326-8); solns. manual 4.95 (ISBN 0-07-023327-6). McGraw.

Microprocessors: An Introduction to the Principles & Applications. Michael J. Debenham. 1979. 21.00 (ISBN 0-08-024206-5); pap. 8.75 (ISBN 0-08-024207-3). Pergamon.

Microprocessors & Digital Computer Technology. J. Olesky & G. Rutkowski. 1981. 22.95 (ISBN 0-13-581116-3). P-H.

Microprocessors & Microcomputer Systems. Dwight H. Sawin. 1977. 21.95 (ISBN 0-669-00564-9). Lexington Bks.

Microprocessors & Microcomputers. Branko Soucek. LC 75-33123. 1976. 30.00 (ISBN 0-471-81391-5, Pub. by Wiley-Interscience). Wiley.

Microprocessors & Microcomputers: One-Chip Controllers to High-End Systems. Electronics Magazine. Ed. by Raymond P. Capece & John G. Posa. LC 80-11816. (Illus.). 484p. 1980. 24.50 (ISBN 0-07-019141-7, R-011); pap. text ed. 14.95 (ISBN 0-07-606670-3). McGraw.

Microprocessors & Programmed Logic. K. Short. 1980. 28.95 (ISBN 0-13-581173-2). P-H.

Microprocessors for Measurement & Control. David Auslander & Paul Sagues. 300p. (Orig.). 1981. pap. 15.99 (ISBN 0-931988-57-8). Osborne-McGraw.

Microprocessors-Microcomputers-System Design. Texas Instruments, Inc. (Texas Instruments Bk. Ser.). (Illus.). 1980. 24.50 (ISBN 0-07-063758-X, P&RB). McGraw.

Microprocessors: Theory & Application. Streitmatter & Fiore. (Illus.). 1979. text ed. 18.95 (ISBN 0-8359-4371-2); students manual avail. (ISBN 0-8359-4372-0). Reston.

Microprocessors: Theory & Practice. K. G. Nichols. (Computer Systems Engineering Ser.). 1981. text ed. price not set (ISBN 0-8448-1384-2). Crane-Russak Co.

Microprogrammed Control & Reliable Design of Small Computers. George D. Kraft & Wing N. Toy. (Illus.). 248p. 1981. text ed. 21.95 (ISBN 0-13-581140-6). P-H.

Micropublishers' Trade List Annual, 1980. Ed. by Deborah O'Hara. 14000p. 1980. 98.50 (ISBN 0-913672-38-6). Microform Rev.

Micros--A Pervasive Force: A Study of the Impact of Microelectronics on Business & Society 1946-1990. Michael Orme. LC 79-23839. 214p. 1978. 31.95x (ISBN 0-470-26891-3). Halsted Pr.

Microscale Manipulations in Chemistry. T. S. Ma & V. Horak. LC 75-20093. (Chemical Analysis Ser: Vol. 44). 480p. 1976. 42.50 (ISBN 0-471-55799-4, Pub. by Wiley-Interscience). Wiley.

Microscope Past & Present. S. Bradbury. 1969. 15.00 (ISBN 0-08-012848-3); pap. text ed. 7.75 (ISBN 0-08-013249-9). Pergamon.

Microscope Techniques: A Comprehensive Handbook for General & Applied Microscopy. W. Burrells. LC 77-26687. 1978. 34.95 (ISBN 0-470-99376-6). Halsted Pr.

Microscopes & Their Uses. Claude Marmasse. 329p. 1980. 20.00 (ISBN 0-677-05510-2). Gordon.

Microscopic Analysis of the Anastomoses between the Cranial Nerves. Ernst P. Bischoff. Tr. by Ernest Sachs, Jr. & Eva W. Valtin. LC 77-72520. (Illus.). 148p. 1977. text ed. 13.50x (ISBN 0-87451-143-7). U Pr of New Eng.

Microscopic Anatomy of the Dog: A Photographic Atlas. William S. Adam et al. 304p. 1970. pap. 32.50 photocopy ed. spiral (ISBN 0-398-00006-9). C C Thomas.

Microscopic & Endoscopic Surgery with the Carbon Dioxide Laser. Ed. by Albert H. Andrews. 1981. write for info. (ISBN 0-88416-211-7). PSG Pub.

Microscopic Diagnosis in Forensic Pathology. Joshua A. Perper & Cyril H. Wecht. (Illus.). 472p. 1980. 54.75 (ISBN 0-398-03969-0). C C Thomas.

Microscopic Identification of Crystals. Richard E. Stoiber & Stearns A. Morse. 286p. 1981. Repr. of 1972 ed. lib. bdg. 16.50 (ISBN 0-89874-276-5). Krieger.

Microscopic Innervation of the Heart & Blood Vessels in Vertebrates Including Man. A. Abraham. 1969. 64.00 (ISBN 0-08-012342-2). Pergamon.

Microscopy Handbook. Loquin & Langeron. 1981. text ed. price not set. Butterworth.

Microsets: Putting Economic Theory to Work. Patrick O'Donoghue & Tanya Roberts. 1980. text ed. 6.95x (ISBN 0-393-95141-3). Norton.

Microsoft Basic. Ken Knecht. LC 79-53476. 225p. 1979. pap. 10.95 (ISBN 0-918398-23-1). Dilithium Pr.

Microsoft Fortran. Paul M. Chirlian. 325p. 1981. pap. 14.95 (ISBN 0-918398-46-0). Dilithium Pr.

Microsomes & Drug Oxidations. Ed. by Volker Ullrich et al. 1977. text ed. 90.00 (ISBN 0-08-021523-8). Pergamon.

Microsomes, Drug Oxidations & Chemical Carcinogenesis, Vol. I. Ed. by Minor J. Coon. LC 80-11363. 1980. 39.50 (ISBN 0-12-187701-9). Acad Pr.

Microstructure Science & Engineering, 2 vols. Ed. by Norman G. Einspruch. 1981. Vol. 1. write for info. (ISBN 0-12-234101-5); Vol. 2. write info. (ISBN 0-12-234102-3). Acad Pr.

Microsurgery for Cerebral Ischemia. Ed. by S. Peerless & C. W. McCormick. (Illus.). 362p. 1981. 89.80 (ISBN 0-387-90495-6). Springer-Verlag.

Microsurgery of Glaucoma. Mikhail M. Krasnov. LC 78-26221. (Illus.). 1979. text ed. 35.00 (ISBN 0-8016-2743-5). Mosby.

Microsurgery of Retinal Detachment. Mireille Bonnet. (Illus.). 1980. text ed. 27.00 (ISBN 0-89352-067-5). Masson Pub.

Microsurgery of the Anterior Segment of the Eye: The Cornea, Vol. 2. Richard C. Troutman. LC 74-12453. (Illus.). 1977. 56.50 (ISBN 0-8016-5106-9). Mosby.

Microsurgery of the Brain, 2 vols. W. Seeger. (Illus.). 750p. 1980. Set. 215.00 (ISBN 0-387-81573-2). Springer-Verlag.

Microsurgery Practice Manual. Robert D. Acland. LC 79-17533. (Illus.). 1979. pap. text ed. 14.95 (ISBN 0-8016-0076-6). Mosby.

Microsurgery: Proceedings. International Microsurgical Society, 5th, Germany, Oct. 1978. Ed. by T. S. Lie. (International Congress Ser.: No. 465). 1979. 78.00 (ISBN 0-444-90077-2, Excerpta Medica). Elsevier.

Microsurgical Composite Tissue Transplantation. Donald Serafin & Harry Buncke. LC 78-12279. (Illus.). 1978. text ed. 55.50 (ISBN 0-8016-0882-1). Mosby.

Microteaching: Planning & Implementing a Competency-Based Training Program. Richard N. Jensen. (Illus.). 92p. 1974. text ed. 9.75 (ISBN 0-398-02930-X). C C Thomas.

Microtechniques for the Clinical Laboratory: Concepts & Applications. Ed. by Mario Werner. LC 75-34373. 1976. 51.50 (ISBN 0-471-93370-8, Pub. by Wiley Medical). Wiley.

Microtron. S. P. Kapitza & V. N. Melekhin. Ed. by Ednor Rowe. Tr. by I. N. Sviatoslavsky. (Accelerators & Storage Rings: Vol. 1). 222p. 1979. lib. bdg. 24.50 (ISBN 0-906346-01-0). Harwood Academic.

Microvascular Anastomoses for Cerebral Ischemia. Ed. by J. M. Fein & O. H. Reichman. (Illus.). 1978. 44.60 (ISBN 0-387-90240-6). Springer-Verlag.

Microwave Auditory Effects & Applications. James C. Lin. (Illus.). 232p. 1978. 29.75 (ISBN 0-398-03704-3). C C Thomas.

Microwave Baking. Val Collins. (Illus.). 128p. 1980. 17.95 (ISBN 0-7153-8018-4). David & Charles.

Microwave Cook Book. 2nd ed. Sunset Editors. LC 80-53481. (Illus.). 1981. pap. 3.95 (ISBN 0-376-02504-2, Sunset Books). Sunset-Lane.

Microwave Cooking: Everyday Dinners in Half an Hour. Litton. 1980. 10.95 (ISBN 0-442-24851-2). Van Nos Reinhold.

Microwave Cooking in Multiple Speeds. Frigidaire. 256p. 1980. 12.95 (ISBN 0-385-13233-6). Doubleday.

Microwave Cooking My Way. new ed. Grace Wheeler. LC 80-53591. 240p. 1980. 7.95 (ISBN 0-914488-25-2). Rand-Tofua.

Microwave Cooking My Way: It's a Matter of Time. Grace Wheeler. Ed. by Elizabeth Rand. LC 80-53591. (Illus.). 240p. 1981. plastic comb bound 7.95 (ISBN 0-914488-25-2). Rand-Tofua.

Microwave Cooking on a Diet. Litton. 160p. 1981. 10.95 (ISBN 0-442-24526-2). Van Nos Reinhold.

Microwave Design Engineering & Applications. Gandhi. 400p. Date not set. text ed. price not set (ISBN 0-08-025589-2); pap. text ed. price not set (ISBN 0-08-025588-4). Pergamon.

Microwave Devices & Circuits. S. Liao. 1980. 29.95 (ISBN 0-13-581207-0). P-H.

Microwave Devices: Device Circuit Interaction. Ed. by M. J. Howes & D. V. Morgan. LC 75-15887. (Solid State Devices & Circuits Ser.). 426p. 1976. 55.00 (ISBN 0-471-41729-7, Pub. by Wiley-Interscience). Wiley.

Microwave Electronics. Ronald F. Soohoo. LC 75-127893. (Engineering Ser). 1971. text ed. 19.95 (ISBN 0-201-07086-3). A-W.

Microwave Engineering & Applications. Om P. Gandhi. (Illus.). 543p. 1981. 60.00 (ISBN 0-08-025589-2); pap. 24.50 (ISBN 0-08-025588-4). Pergamon.

Microwave Factor. Nicholas Brady. 1977. pap. 1.75 (ISBN 0-505-51170-3). Tower Bks.

Microwave Heating. 2nd ed. David A. Copson. (Illus.). 1975. lib. bdg. 49.00 (ISBN 0-87055-182-5). AVI.

Microwave Industry, G-020: Trends, Developments. Business Communications Co. 1981. 825.00 (ISBN 0-89336-275-1). BCC.

Microwave Integrated Circuits. Ed. by K. C. Gupta & A. Singh. LC 74-8772. 380p. 1974. 18.95 (ISBN 0-470-33640-4). Halsted Pr.

Microwave Oven Service & Repair. Clayton Hallmark. (Illus.). 1977. pap. 12.95 (ISBN 0-8306-6962-0, 962). TAB Bks.

Microwave Radar Transmitters: Systems, Modulators & Devices. George W. Ewell. (Illus.). 300p. 1981. 21.50 (ISBN 0-07-019843-8, P&RB). McGraw.

Microwave Receivers. Ed. by Stanley N. Van Voorhis. (Illus.). 1948. pap. text ed. 5.00 (ISBN 0-486-61561-8). Dover.

Microwave Research Institute Symposia. Ed. by J. Fox. Incl. Vol. 1. Modern Network Synthesis. 1952. 19.95 (ISBN 0-470-27093-4); Vol. 4. Modern Advances in Microwave Techniques. LC 55-12897. 1955. o.p. (ISBN 0-470-27192-2); Vol. 5. Modern Network Synthesis. LC 56-2590. 1956. o.p. (ISBN 0-470-27225-2); Vol. 6. Nonlinear Circuit Analysis. LC 55-3575. 1956. o.p. (ISBN 0-470-27258-9); Vol. 9. Millimeter Waves. LC 60-10073. 1960. o.p. (ISBN 0-470-27357-7); Vol. 11. Electromagnetics & Fluid Dynamics of Gaseous Plasma. LC 62-13174. 1962. 25.95 (ISBN 0-470-27423-9); Vol. 13. Optical Lasers. LC 63-22084. o.p. (ISBN 0-470-27428-X); Vol. 15. System Theory. LC 65-28522. 1965. 26.50 (ISBN 0-470-27430-1); Vol. 17. Modern Optics. LC 67-31757. 1967. o.p. (ISBN 0-470-27433-6); Vol. 19. Computer Processing in Communications. LC 77-122632. 1970. o.p. (ISBN 0-471-27436-4); Vol. 20. Submillimeter Waves. 1971. o.p. (ISBN 0-471-27437-2); Vol. 21. Computers & Automata. 1972. 33.95 (ISBN 0-471-27438-0); Vol. 22. Computer Communications. 1972. 37.95 (ISBN 0-471-27439-9); Vol. 24. Computer Software Engineering. 1977. 44.95 (ISBN 0-470-98948-3). Pub. by Wiley-Interscience). Wiley.

Microwave Research Institute Symposia: Computer Communications, Vol. 22. Jerome Fox. LC 72-92508. 1972. 37.95 (ISBN 0-470-27439-5). Halsted Pr.

Microwaves. K. C. Gupta. LC 80-11904. 256p. 1980. 14.95x (ISBN 0-470-26966-9). Halsted Pr.

Microwaves: An Introduction to Microwave Theory & Techniques. A. J. Baden-Fuller. 1979. 41.00 (ISBN 0-08-024228-6); pap. 16.25 (ISBN 0-08-024227-8). Pergamon.

Mid-Century Child & Her Books. Caroline M. Hewins. LC 69-16070. 1969. Repr. of 1926 ed. 15.00 (ISBN 0-8103-3857-2). Gale.

Mid-Century Drama. Laurence Kitchin. 1969. pap. 4.95 (ISBN 0-571-09077-X, Pub. by Faber & Faber). Merrimack Bk Serv.

Mid-Tudor Polity, c. Fifteen Forty to Fifteen Sixty. Ed. by Robert Tittler & Jennifer Loach. 227p. 1980. 20.00x (ISBN 0-8476-6257-8). Rowman.

Mid-Twentieth Century American Philosophy: Personal Statements. Ed. by Peter A. Bertocci. LC 73-18467. 251p. 1974. text ed. 12.50x (ISBN 0-391-00340-2). Humanities.

Mid-Wales. Automobile Association - British Tourist Authority. (Regional Guide Ser.). (Illus.). 1979. pap. 2.95 o.p. (ISBN 0-900784-51-2, Pub. by B T a). Merrimack Bk Serv.

Mid Wales: A Tourist Guide. Wales Tourist Board. (Illus.). 84p. Date not set. pap. price not set (ISBN 0-900784-72-5, Pub. by Auto Assn-British Tourist Authority England). Merrimack Bk Serv.

Midaq Alley. Naguib Mahfouz. Tr. by Trevor Le Gassick. 9.00 (ISBN 0-914478-53-2, Co-Pub. by Heinemann Educ. Bks); pap. 5.00 (ISBN 0-914478-54-0). Three Continents.

Midas Manual. Deek Gladson. 1981. pap. 4.00 (ISBN 0-89316-623-5); plastic bdg. 6.00 (ISBN 0-89316-624-3). Exanimo Pr.

Midas of the Rockies: The Story of Stratton & Cripple Creek. Frank Waters. LC 73-163716. 347p. 1972. pap. 5.95 (ISBN 0-8040-0591-5). Swallow.

Middle-Age Crisis. Barbara Fried. LC 75-36729. 160p. 1976. pap. 3.95 o.p. (ISBN 0-06-063016-7, RD137, HarpR). Har-Row.

Middle Age of African History. Ed. by Roland Oliver. (Orig.). (gr. 9-12). 1967. pap. 3.95x (ISBN 0-19-500356-X). Oxford U Pr.

Middle Age: The Prime of Life. Marjorie Fiske. (Life Cycle Ser.). 1980. pap. text ed. write for info. (ISBN 0-06-384749-3, HarpC). Har-Row.

Middle Ages. Alan Clifford. Ed. by Malcolm Yapp et al. (World History Ser.). (Illus.). (gr. 10). 1980. Repr. of 1977 ed. lib. bdg. 5.95 (ISBN 0-89908-028-6); pap. text ed. 1.95 (ISBN 0-89908-003-0). Greenhaven.

Middle Ages. Peter Lane. 96p. 1980. 14.95 (ISBN 0-7134-0033-1, Pub. by Batsford England). David & Charles.

Middle Ages. Paul Titley. (Let's Make History). (Orig.). 1980. pap. 3.50 (ISBN 0-263-06338-0). Transatlantic.

Middle Ages in French Literature 1851-1900. new ed. Jannie R. Dakyns. (Oxford Modern Languages & Literature Monographs). 364p. 1973. 29.95x (ISBN 0-19-815522-0). Oxford U Pr.

Middle Ages Ser. Richard C. Dales. (Sources of Medieval History Ser.). (Illus.). 1973. text ed. 14.00x (ISBN 0-8122-7673-6); pap. text ed. 5.95x (ISBN 0-8122-1057-3). U of Pa Pr.

Middle America: Its Lands & Peoples. 2nd ed. John P. Augelli & Robert C. West. (Anthropology Ser.). (Illus.). 576p. 1976. text ed. 22.95 (ISBN 0-13-581546-0). P-H.

Middle Atmosphere As Observed from Baloons, Rockets & Satellites. Royal Society et al. (Royal Society Ser.). (Illus.). 268p. 1980. lib. bdg. 71.00x (ISBN 0-85403-137-5, Pub. by Royal Soc London). Scholium Intl.

Middle-Class Blacks in a White Society. William A. Muraskin. 1975. 22.75x (ISBN 0-520-02705-1). U of Cal Pr.

Middle Class Couples: A Study of Segregation, Domination & Inequality in Marriage. Stephen Edgell. 160p. 1980. text ed. 18.50x (ISBN 0-04-301109-8, 2381). Allen Unwin.

Middle Class in Politics. Ed. by J. Garrard et al. 380p. 1978. text ed. 24.00x (ISBN 0-566-00225-6, Pub. by Gower Pub Co England). Renouf.

Middle Class in Politics. Ed. by J. Garrard et al. 1978. text ed. 24.00x (ISBN 0-566-00225-6, Pub. by Gower Pub Co England). Renouf.

Middle-Class Negro in the White Man's World. Eli Ginzberg et al. LC 67-26364. 1969. 15.00x (ISBN 0-231-03096-7); pap. 5.00x (ISBN 0-231-08596-6). Columbia U Pr.

Middle Class Support: A Route to Socioeconomic Security. Ed. by Robert Theobald. LC 72-91921. 199p. 1972. pap. 4.95x (ISBN 0-8040-0612-1). Swallow.

Middle Classic Mesoamerica: 400-700 A. D. Ed. by Esther Pasztory. (Illus.). 1978. 25.00x (ISBN 0-231-04270-1). Columbia U Pr.

Middle Colonies & the Coming of the American Revolution. John A. Neuenschwander. LC 73-83267. (National University Pubns.). 288p. 1974. 17.50 (ISBN 0-8046-9054-5). Kennikat.

Middle Commentary on Aristotle Topics. Averroes. Ed. by Charles E. Butterworth & Ahmad Abd al-Magid Haridi. (Corpvs Commentariorvm Averrois in Aristotelem). 317p. (Orig., Arabic.). 1979. pap. 10.00 (ISBN 0-936770-03-1). Am Res Ctr Egypt.

Middle Distance. J. McCormick. LC 76-139233. 1971. 9.25 o.s.i. (ISBN 0-02-920520-4). Free Pr.

Middle Distances: Contemporary Theory, Technique, & Training. Ed. by Jess Jarver. (Illus., Orig.). 1979. pap. text ed. 7.50 (ISBN 0-911520-87-2). Tafnews.

Middle East. 2nd ed. Stephen H. Longrigg. LC 75-91722. 1970. lib. bdg. 17.95x (ISBN 0-202-10008-1). Aldine Pub.

Middle East: A Political & Economic Survey. Peter Mansfield. (Illus.). 1980. 29.95 (ISBN 0-19-215851-1). Oxford U Pr.

Middle East & Beyond. Nikki Keddie. 1980. 29.50x (ISBN 0-7146-3151-5, F Cass Co). Biblio Dist.

Middle East & North Africa: Definition & Analysis of Regional Balances of Power. Enver M. Koury. LC 74-84755. 132p. 1974. pap. 6.00 (ISBN 0-934484-06-6). Inst Mid East & North Africa.

Middle East & North Africa 1980-81. 985p. 1981. 80.00 (ISBN 0-905118-50-2, EUR 23, Europa). Unipub.

Middle East & North Africa 1980-81. 27th ed. LC 48-3250. (Illus.). 1005p. 1980. 80.00x (ISBN 0-905118-50-2). Intl Pubns Serv.

Middle East & the European Common Market. Rouhollah K. Ramazani. LC 64-13718. 1964. 7.50x o.p. (ISBN 0-8139-0201-0). U Pr of Va.

Middle East & Why. Clarke Newlon. LC 76-53443. (gr. 7 up). 1977. 6.95 (ISBN 0-396-07425-1). Dodd.

Middle East Annual Review, 1979. 1979. pap. 16.95 o.p. (ISBN 0-528-84230-7). Rand.

Middle East Annual Review, 1981. 7th ed. Ed. by Michael Field. Date not set. pap. 24.95 (ISBN 0-528-84519-5). Rand.

Middle East Business Travel Guide. Paddington Press. 288p. 1981. 19.95 (ISBN 0-87196-343-4); pap. 11.95 (ISBN 0-87196-323-X). Facts on File.

Middle East Contemporary Survey, Vol. 1. (Illus.). 1978. text ed. 77.50x (ISBN 0-8419-0323-9). Holmes & Meier.

Middle East Contemporary Survey, Vol. 2. Ed. by Colin Legum & Haim Shaked. LC 78-648245. (Illus.). 1979. text ed. 77.50x (ISBN 0-8419-0398-0). Holmes & Meier.

Middle East Contemporary Survey: 1978-1979, Vol. 3. Ed. by Colin Legum & Haim Shaked. LC 78-648245. (Illus.). 1980. text ed. 97.50x (ISBN 0-8419-0609-2). Holmes & Meier.

Middle East Economies in the 1970's: A Comparative Approach. Hossein Askari & John T. Cummings. (Illus.). 1976. text ed. 46.95 (ISBN 0-275-23130-5). Praeger.

Middle East in China's Foreign Policy: 1949-1977. Y. Shichor. LC 78-58801. (International Studies). (Illus.). 1979. 29.95 (ISBN 0-521-22214-1). Cambridge U Pr.

Middle East in the Twentieth Century. Richard Lawless. (Illus.). 96p. 1980. 16.95 (ISBN 0-7134-2494-X, Pub. by Batsford England). David & Charles.

Middle East in World Affairs. 4th ed. George Lenczowski. LC 79-17059. (Illus.). 1980. 29.50 (ISBN 0-8014-0255-7); pap. 14.95 (ISBN 0-8014-9872-4). Cornell U Pr.

Middle East Industrialisation: A Study of Saudi & Iranian Downstream Investment. Louis Turner & James Bedore. LC 79-89599. (Praeger Special Studies). (Illus.). 230p. 1980. 29.95 (ISBN 0-03-053381-3). Praeger.

Middle East: Issues & Events of 1979. Ed. by Janet Byrne. LC 80-1718. (News in Print Ser.). (Illus.). 1980. lib. bdg. 24.95x (ISBN 0-405-12878-9). Arno.

Middle East: Its Oil, Economics, & Investment Policies: A Guide to Sources of Financial Information. David Nicholas. LC 80-28555. xxiv, 201p. 1981. lib. bdg. 40.00 (ISBN 0-313-22986-4, NME/). Greenwood.

Middle East: Life & Work for the Civil Engineer. 85p. 1980. 29.00x (ISBN 0-7277-0064-2, Pub. by Telford England). State Mutual Bk.

Middle East Negotiations: A Conversation with Joseph Sisco. 1980. pap. 3.25 (ISBN 0-8447-3394-6). Am Enterprise.

Middle East: Oil, Conflict & Hope, Vol. 10. A. L. Udovitch. LC 75-44728. (Critical Choices for Americans Ser.). 1976. 25.95 (ISBN 0-669-00424-3). Lexington Bks.

Middle East: Regional Study. rev. ed. Hyman Kublin et al. (World Regional Studies). (gr. 9-12). 1973. pap. text ed. 6.60 (ISBN 0-395-13931-7). HM.

Middle East: Selected Readings. rev ed. Hyman Kublin. LC 72-12182. (World Regional Studies). (Illus.). 246p. (gr. 9-12). 1973. pap. text ed. 6.60 (ISBN 0-395-13932-5, 2-31076). HM.

Middle East: U. S. Policy, Israel, Oil & the Arabs. 4th ed. Congressional Quarterly. 1979. pap. text ed. 7.95 (ISBN 0-87187-176-9). Congr Quarterly.

Middle East: 1914-1979. T. G. Fraser. 1980. 19.95 (ISBN 0-312-53181-8). St Martin.

Middle Eastern Cooking. Harry G. Nickles. LC 70-85530. (Foods of the World Ser). (Illus.). (gr. 6 up). 1969. PLB 14.94 (ISBN 0-8094-0068-5, Pub. by Time-Life). Silver.

Middle Eastern Cooking. Harry G. Nickles. (Foods of the World Ser). (Illus.). 1969. 14.95 (ISBN 0-8094-0041-3). Time-Life.

Middle Eastern Muslim Women Speak. Ed. by Elizabeth W. Fernea & Basima Q. Bezirgan. (Illus.). 1977. 16.95x (ISBN 0-292-75033-1); pap. 8.95x (ISBN 0-292-75041-2). U of Tex Pr.

Middle English Bible: Prefatory Epistles of Saint Jerome. Ed. by Conrad Lindberg. 1979. pap. 19.50x (ISBN 82-00-01773-7, Dist. by Columbia U Pr.). Universitet.

Middle-English Dictionary: Containing Words Used by English Writers from the Twelfth to the Fifteenth Century. Francis H. Stratmann. Ed. by Henry Bradley. 1891. 39.00x (ISBN 0-19-863106-5). Oxford U Pr.

Middle English Humorous Tales in Verse. George H. McKnight. LC 78-128190. 1971. Repr. of 1913 ed. text ed. 7.50 (ISBN 0-87752-131-X). Gordian.

Middle English Letter of Alexander to Aristotle. Vincent Dimarco & Leslie Perelman. (Costerus New Ser.: No. XIII). 1978. pap. text ed. 17.75x (ISBN 90-6203-662-7). Humanities.

Middle English Mystics. Wolfgang Riehle. 256p. 1981. 32.50 (ISBN 0-7100-0612-8). Routledge & Kegan.

Middle English Poetry: An Anthology. Ed. by Lewis J. Owen & Nancy H. Owen. LC 76-138662. (Library of Literature Ser). 1971. pap. 7.50 (ISBN 0-672-60984-3, LL-12). Bobbs.

Middle English Prose: Essays on Bibliographical Problems. Ed. by A. S. Edwards & Derek Pearsall. LC 80-8595. 150p. 1981. lib. bdg. 25.00 (ISBN 0-8240-9453-0). Garland Pub.

Middle English Romances of the Thirteenth & Fourteenth Centuries. Dieter Mehl. 1969. 28.00x (ISBN 0-7100-6240-0). Routledge & Kegan.

Middle English Treatise on the Playing of Miracles. Ed. by Clifford Davidson. LC 81-40028. 93p. 1981. lib. bdg. 14.75 (ISBN 0-8191-1514-2); pap. text ed. 6.75 (ISBN 0-8191-1515-0). U Pr of Amer.

Middle Fork & the Sheepeater War. Cort Conley & John Carrey. LC 80-17367. 1977. pap. 9.95 (ISBN 0-9603566-1-4). Backeddy Bks.

Middle High German Reader: With Grammar, Notes & Glossary. M. O. Walshe. 232p. 1974. pap. text ed. 11.95x (ISBN 0-19-872082-3); pap. text ed. 8.95x (ISBN 0-19-872082-3). Oxford U Pr.

Middle Kingdom: The Faerie World of Ireland. D. A. MacManus. 1973. pap. text ed. 6.75x (ISBN 0-900675-82-9). Humanities.

Middle Mist. Mary Renault. 288p. 1976. Repr. of 1945 ed. lib. bdg. 13.95x (ISBN 0-89244-080-5). Queens Hse.

Middle of the Journey. Lionel Trilling. LC 76-626. 320p. 1976. 8.95 o.p. (ISBN 0-684-14619-3, ScribT). Scribner.

Middle of the Sandwich. Time Kennemore. 112p. (gr. 3-7). 1981. 12.95 (ISBN 0-571-11678-7, Pub. by Faber & Faber). Merrimack Bk Serv.

Middle School. Les Tickle & Andy Hargreaves. 1980. text ed. 21.00 (ISBN 0-06-318134-7, IntlDept); pap. text ed. 13.10 (ISBN 0-06-318135-5). Har-Row.

Middle School: Selected Readings on an Emerging School Program. Ed. by Louis G. Romano et al. LC 72-97847. 1973. 20.95 (ISBN 0-911012-82-6); pap. 11.95 (ISBN 0-88229-572-1). Nelson-Hall.

Middle Scots Poets. Ed. by A. M. Kinghorn. (York Medieval Texts). 1970. pap. 8.95 (ISBN 0-8101-0329-X). Northwestern U Pr.

Middle Sister. Miriam E. Mason. (Illus.). (gr. 4-6). 1947. 3.95 o.s.i. (ISBN 0-02-764500-2). Macmillan.

Middle Way: Puritanism & Ideology in American Romantic Fiction. Michael T. Gilmore. 1977. 16.00 (ISBN 0-8135-0837-1). Rutgers U Pr.

Middle Western Farm Novel in the Twentieth Century. Roy W. Meyer. LC 64-17221. viii, 265p. 1974. pap. 3.45x (ISBN 0-8032-5798-8, BB 587, Bison). U of Nebr Pr.

Middle Works of John Dewey, 1899-1924, Vols. 1-8, Vols. 1-8. MLA-CEAA textual ed. John Dewey. Ed. by Jo Ann Boydston. Incl. Vol. 1 (1899-1901): Collected Articles & "The School & Society" & "The Educational Situation". Intro. by Joe R. Burnett. 1976. 19.95x (ISBN 0-8093-0753-7); Vol. 2 (1902-1903): Collected Articles & "Studies in Logical Theory" & "The Child & the Curiculum". Intro. by Sidney Hook. 1976. 19.95x (ISBN 0-8093-0754-5); Vol. 3 (1903-1906): Collected Articles. Ed. by Patricia R. Baysinger. 1977. 19.95x (ISBN 0-8093-0775-8); Vol. 4 (1907-1909): Collected Articles & "The Pragmatic Movement of Contemporary Thought" & "Moral Principles in Education". Ed. by Barbara Levine. 1977. 19.95x (ISBN 0-8093-0775-8); Vol. 5 (1908): "Ethics". Charles L. Stevenson. 1978. 18.95x (ISBN 0-8093-0834-7); Vol. 6 (1910-1911): Collected Essays & "The Problem of Truth". H. S. Thayer. 1978. 24.95x (ISBN 0-8093-0835-5); Vol. 9 (1916) Ed. by Jo Ann Boydston. 480p. 1980. 19.95x (ISBN 0-8093-0933-5); Vol. 10 (1916-7) Ed. by Jo Ann Boydston. 564p. 22.50x (ISBN 0-686-66317-9); Vol. 7. Ed. by Jo Ann Boydston. 1979. 24.95x (ISBN 0-8093-0881-9); Vol. 8. Ed. by Jo Ann Boydston. 1979. 24.95x (ISBN 0-8093-0882-7). LC 76-7231. S Ill U Pr.

Middle Years. Paul E. Johnson. LC 70-154489. (Pocket Counsel Bks). (Orig.). 1971. pap. 1.75x o.p. (ISBN 0-8006-1105-5, 1-1105). Fortress.

Middlearth. Ted Simmons. LC 74-24634. (Illus.). 74p. 1975. 4.95 o.p. (ISBN 0-912662-06-9); pap. 3.95 o.p. (ISBN 0-912662-35-2). Fur Line Pr.

Middleman. David Chandler. LC 80-66504. 1981. 12.95 (ISBN 0-87795-279-5). Arbor Hse.

Middleman. Mark Smith. 1977. pap. 1.95 (ISBN 0-380-01766-0, 34991). Avon.

Middleman in Higher Education: Improving Articulation Among High School, Community College, & Senior Institutions. Frederick C. Kintzer. LC 72-11969. (Higher Education Ser.). 1973. 12.95x o.p. (ISBN 0-87589-160-8). Jossey-Bass.

Middlemarch. George Eliot. (Zodiac Press Ser.). 1979. 15.95 (ISBN 0-7011-1245-X, Pub. by Chatto Bodley Jonathan). Merrimack Bk Serv.

Middleton's Cynics. Charles A. Hallett. (Salzburg Studies in English Literature, Jacobean Drama Studies Ser.: No. 47). 308p. 1975. pap. text ed. 25.00x (ISBN 0-391-01396-3). Humanities.

Midget Motoring & Karting. Kenton McFarland & James C. Sparks, Jr. (Illus.). (gr. 7 up). 1961. PLB 10.95 (ISBN 0-525-34880-8). Dutton.

Midi-Pyreneen. (Beautes de la France). (Illus.). 1978. 18.25x (ISBN 2-03-013924-6, 3155). Larousse.

Midland & South Western Junction Railway. Colin G. Maggs. LC 79-56254. (Illus.). 184p. 1980. 17.95 (ISBN 0-7153-7978-X). David & Charles.

Midland Route: A Colorado Midland Guide & Data Book. Edward M. Mc Farland. (Illus.). 300p. 1980. 44.95 (ISBN 0-87108-569-0). Pruett.

Midlothian Speeches, 1879. W. E. Gladstone. (Victorian Library). 1971. Repr. of 1879 ed. text ed. 9.00x (ISBN 0-391-00110-8, Leicester). Humanities.

Midnight. Mao Dun. 1980. 100.95 (ISBN 0-8351-0614-4). China Bks.

Midnight. John Russo. 1980. pap. 2.25. PB.

Midnight Adventures of Kelly, Dot, & Esmeralda. Illus. by John S. Goodall. LC 75-190555. (ps-12). 1973. 4.95 (ISBN 0-689-30505-2, McElderry Bk). Atheneum.

Midnight Alarm: The Story of Paul Revere's Ride. Mary K. Phelan. LC 68-17080. (Illus.). (gr. 4-7). 1968. 8.95 (ISBN 0-690-53638-0, TYC-J). T Y Crowell.

Midnight Baby: An Autobiography. Dory Previn. 1976. 8.95 o.s.i. (ISBN 0-02-599000-4). Macmillan.

Midnight Court. 3rd ed. Brian Merriman. Tr. by David Marcus. 1975. pap. text ed. 1.75x (ISBN 0-85105-273-8, Dolmen Pr). Humanities.

Midnight Economist I. William R. Allen. 1980. pap. 1.45 (ISBN 0-89803-028-5). Caroline Hse.

Midnight Encounter. Glenna Finley. (Orig.). 1981. pap. 1.75 (ISBN 0-451-09680-0, E9680, Sig). NAL.

Midnight Fox. Betsy Byars. (gr. 3-7). 1975. pap. 1.50 o.s.i. (ISBN 0-380-00197-7, 46987, Camelot). Avon.

Midnight Fury. Susan E. Gross. 320p. 1981. pap. 2.75 (ISBN 0-449-14392-9, GM). Fawcett.

Midnight in the Century. Maurice English. LC 64-20847. 69p. 1964. 4.00 (ISBN 0-8040-0204-5). Swallow.

Midnight Mass. Paul Bowles. 120p. 1981. 14.00 (ISBN 0-87685-477-3); signed ed. 20.00 (ISBN 0-87685-478-1); pap. 5.00 (ISBN 0-87685-476-5). Black Sparrow.

Midnight Movies. David A. Kaufelt. 1981. pap. 2.75 (ISBN 0-440-15728-5). Dell.

Midnight Son. Steven B. Miller. LC 79-10759. (Illus.). 128p. (gr. 5 up). 1981. 14.95 (ISBN 0-590-07582-9, Four Winds); pap. 9.95 (ISBN 0-590-07811-9, Four Winds). Schol Bk Serv.

Midnight's Children. Salman Rushdie. LC 80-2712. 448p. 1981. 13.95 (ISBN 0-394-51470-X). Knopf.

Midnignt Son. Steven B. Miller. LC 79-10759. (Illus.). 128p. 1981. 14.95 (ISBN 0-590-07582-9, Four Winds); pap. 9.95 (ISBN 0-686-69196-2). Schol Bk Serv.

Midrash Pesher of Habakkuk. William H. Brownlee. LC 76-30560. (Society of Biblical Literature Monograph Ser.). 1979. 10.50 (ISBN 0-89130-096-1, 060024); pap. 9.00 (ISBN 0-89130-147-X). Scholars Pr Ca.

Midrash Rabbah, 5 vols. Set. 135.00x (ISBN 0-685-01047-3). Bloch.

Midshipman's Journal on Board H.M.S. Seringapatam During the Year, 1830. John Orlebar. LC 76-11241. 1976. pap. 3.95 (ISBN 0-914488-10-4). Rand-Tofua.

Midsummer Bride. Mary Lewis. 192p. (Orig.). 1980. pap. 1.50 (ISBN 0-671-57007-2). S&S.

Midsummer Night's Dream. William Shakespeare. Ed. by Arthur Quiller-Couch et al. (New Shakespeare Ser). 23.95 (ISBN 0-521-07547-5); pap. 4.50x (ISBN 0-521-09490-9). Cambridge U Pr.

Midsummer Night's Dream. William Shakespeare. Ed. by Louis B. Wright & Virginia LaMar. (gr. 10 up). pap. 2.25 (ISBN 0-671-43297-4). PB.

Midsummer Nights' Dream. William Shakespeare. LC 77-512. (Illus.). 1977. 32.50 (ISBN 0-913870-41-2). Abaris Bks.

Midtown North. Myer Kutz. 1976. pap. 1.25 o.p. (ISBN 0-685-69154-3, LB351ZK, Leisure Bks). Nordon Pubns.

Midwest Plan Service Structures & Environment Handbook. 9th ed. Midwest Plan Service. LC 77-24236. 1977. spiral bdg. 8.00 o.p. (ISBN 0-89373-030-0, MWPS-1). Midwest Plan Serv.

Midwestern Junior League Cookbook. Ed. by Ann Seranne. 1978. 12.95 (ISBN 0-679-51204-7). McKay.

Midwestern Progressive Politics: 1870-1958. rev. ed. Russel B. Nye. 1963. 6.50 o.p. (ISBN 0-87013-042-0). Mich St U Pr.

Midwestern Village. Richard A. Coffey. Ed. by Paul Deegan. LC 70-156065. (World's People Ser.). (Illus.). (gr. 5-9). 1971. text ed. 6.95 (ISBN 0-87191-077-2). Creative Ed.

Midwife. Gay Courter. 512p. 1981. 13.95 (ISBN 0-395-29463-0). HM.

Midwifery Revision. Sara E. Roch. (Illus.). 352p. 1980. text ed. 10.00 (ISBN 0-443-01964-9). Churchill.

Midworld. Alan D. Foster. 1976. pap. 1.50 o.p. (ISBN 0-345-25364-7). Ballantine.

MIG Master: The Story of the F-8 Crusader. Barrett Tillman. LC 80-83019. (Illus.). 260p. 1980. 17.95 (ISBN 0-933852-17-7). Nautical & Aviation.

MIG Pilot: The Final Escape of Lieutenant Belenko. John Barron. 232p. 1981. pap. 2.95 (ISBN 0-380-53868-7). Avon.

MIG Pilot: The Story of Viktor Belenko. John Barron. 1980. 10.95 (ISBN 0-07-003850-3). McGraw.

Might As Well Be Dead. Rex Stout. 160p. 1980. pap. 1.95 (ISBN 0-553-14447-2). Bantam.

Mightiest Lover of All. Lawrence Maxwell. (Uplook Ser.). 1978. pap. 0.75 (ISBN 0-8163-0090-9, 13494-0). Pacific Pr Pub Assn.

Mighty Cortez Fish Trap. Jerry Klink. LC 72-6388. (Illus.). 256p. 1973. 8.95 o.p. (ISBN 0-498-01172-0). A S Barnes.

Mighty Faith. J. Oswald Sanders. 1980. pap. 0.90 (ISBN 0-85363-030-5). OMF Bks.

Mighty Ferment: Britain in the Age of Revolution, 1750-1850. David Snodin. LC 77-16482. (Illus.). (gr. 6 up). 1978. 8.95 (ISBN 0-395-28925-4, Clarion). HM.

Mighty Human Cell. Patricia M. Kelly. LC 67-10823. (Illus.). (gr. 4-8). 1967. PLB 7.89 (ISBN 0-381-99768-5, A49000, JD-J). John Day.

Mighty Opposites: Shakespeare & Renaissance Contrariety. Robert Grudin. 1979. 15.75x (ISBN 0-520-03666-2). U of Cal Pr.

Mighty Voices: Studies in T. S. Eliot. M. N. Naik. 128p. 1980. text ed. 9.50x (ISBN 0-391-01788-8). Humanities.

Migraine. Frederic Speer. LC 76-25172. (Illus.). 1977. 12.95 (ISBN 0-88229-301-X); pap. 6.95 (ISBN 0-88229-467-9). Nelson-Hall.

Migraine: Classification, Diagnosis & Treatment. Joel R. Saper. 1981. write for info. (ISBN 0-88416-282-6, 282). PSG Pub.

Migraine: The Facts. Clifford F. Rose & M. Gawel. (Illus.). 150p. 1980. text ed. 11.95x (ISBN 0-19-261161-5). Oxford U Pr.

Migrant Birds in the Neotropics: Ecology, Behavior, Distribution & Conservation. Ed. by Allen Keast & Eugene S. Morton. LC 80-607031. (Symposia of the National Zoological Park: No. 5). 576p. (Orig.). 1980. text ed. 35.00x (ISBN 0-87474-660-4); pap. text ed. 17.50x (ISBN 0-87474-661-2). Smithsonian.

Migrant Cocoa Farmers of Southern Ghana. Polly Hill. 42.95 (ISBN 0-521-05264-5). Cambridge U Pr.

Migrant Education: Teaching the Wandering Ones. Joyce B. King-Stoops. LC 80-82678. (Fastback Ser.: No. 145). (Orig.). 1980. pap. 0.75 (ISBN 0-87367-145-7). Phi Delta Kappa.

Migrant Farm Workers: A Culture of Despair. Ronald L. Goldfarb. 232p. 1981. text ed. 16.00 (ISBN 0-8138-1790-0). Iowa St U Pr.

Migrant Workers. International Labour Office, Geneva. 196p. (Orig.). 1980. pap. 14.25 (ISBN 92-2-102093-2). Intl Labour Office.

Migrant Workers in Western Europe & the United States. Jonathan Power et al. LC 78-41199. 1979. 28.00 (ISBN 0-08-023385-6); pap. 12.75 (ISBN 0-08-023384-8). Pergamon.

Migrants in Aruba: Interethnic Integration. Vera Green. 154p. 1974. pap. text ed. 18.50x (ISBN 90-232-1126-X). Humanities.

Migrants of the Mountains: The Cultural Ecology of the Blue Miao (Hmong Nyua) or Thailand. William R. Geddes. (Illus.). 1976. 37.50x (ISBN 0-19-823187-3). Oxford U Pr.

Migration & Adaptation: Tzintzuntzan Peasants in Mexico City. Robert V. Kemper. LC 77-2413. (Sage Library of Social Research: Vol. 43). 1977. 18.00x (ISBN 0-8039-0687-0); pap. 8.95x (ISBN 0-8039-0688-9). Sage.

Migration & Economic Development in Rhode Island. Kurt B. Mayer & Sidney Goldstein. LC 58-10480. 1958. pap. 2.00 (ISBN 0-87057-051-X, Pub. by Brown U Pr). Univ Pr of New England.

Migration & Economic Growth in the United States: National, Regional & Metropolitan Perspectives. Michael Greenwood. (Studies in Urban Economics). 1981. price not set (ISBN 0-12-300650-3). Acad Pr.

Migration & the Labor Market in Developing Countries. Ed. by R. H. Sabot. (Westview Special Studies in Social, Political, & Economic Development). 350p. 1981. lib. bdg. 30.00x (ISBN 0-89158-763-2). Westview.

Migration in Post-War Europe: Geographical Essays. Ed. by John Salt & Hugh Clout. (Illus.). 1976. 29.95x (ISBN 0-19-874027-1). Oxford U Pr.

Migration in West Africa: The Demographic Aspects. K. C. Zachariah & Julian Conde. (World Bank Research Publication Ser.). (Illus.). 256p. 1980. 16.95 (ISBN 0-19-520186-8); pap. 6.95 (ISBN 0-19-520187-6). Oxford U Pr.

Migration of Symbols & Their Relations to Beliefs & Customs. Donald A. Mackenzie. LC 68-18029. 1968. Repr. of 1926 ed. 18.00 (ISBN 0-8103-3074-1). Gale.

Migratory-Casual Worker. John N. Webb. LC 73-165690. (FDR & the Era of the New Deal Ser.). 1971. Repr. of 1937 ed. lib. bdg. 15.00 (ISBN 0-306-70339-4). Da Capo.

Miguel Angel Asturias. Richard J. Callan. (World Authors Ser.: Guatemala: No. 122). lib. bdg. 9.95 (ISBN 0-8057-2072-3). Twayne.

Miguel Angel Asturias, Lo Ancestral En Su Obra Literaria. E. Leon Hill. 1972. 11.95 (ISBN 0-88303-007-1); pap. 9.95 (ISBN 0-685-73211-8). E Torres & Sons.

Miguel De Cervantes-Saavedra: Two Cervantes Short Novels: El Curioso impertinente & El Celoso extremeno. Miguel De Cervantes-Saavedra. Ed. by F. F. Pierce. 1970. pap. 4.30 (ISBN 0-08-015781-5). Pergamon.

Miguel De Unamuno. Demetrios Basdekis. LC 74-92029. (Columbia Essays on Modern Writers Ser.: No. 44). (Orig.). 1969. pap. 2.00 (ISBN 0-231-03259-5). Columbia U Pr.

Miguel de Unamuno. Martin Nozick. (World Authors Ser.: Spain: No. 175). lib. bdg. 9.95 (ISBN 0-8057-2906-2). Twayne.

Miguel Delibes. Janet Diaz. (World Authors Ser.: Spain: No. 186). lib. bdg. 10.95 (ISBN 0-8057-2264-5). Twayne.

Miguel Hernandez. Geraldine C. Nichols. (World Authors Ser.: No. 464). 1978. lib. bdg. 12.50 (ISBN 0-8057-6301-5). Twayne.

Miguel, Miguel, Por Que Me Odeias? Tr. by Michael Esses. (Portugese Bks.). (Port.). 1979. 1.60 (ISBN 0-8297-0826-X). Life Pubs Intl.

Miguel, Miguel, Por Que Me Odias? Tr. by Michael Esses. (Spanish Bks.). (Span.). 1977. 1.90 (ISBN 0-8297-0724-7). Life Pubs Intl.

Miguel Mihura. Douglas R. McKay. (World Authors Ser.: No. 436). 1977. lib. bdg. 12.50 (ISBN 0-8057-6191-8). Twayne.

Miguel Street. V. S. Naipaul. 1977. pap. 2.95 (ISBN 0-14-003302-5). Penguin.

Mihaly Vitez Csokonai. Anna B. Katona. (World Authors Ser.: No. 579). 1980. lib. bdg. 13.95 (ISBN 0-8057-6421-6). Twayne.

Mike. Paul B. Ricchiuti. (Uplook Ser.). 1978. pap. 0.75 (ISBN 0-8163-0207-3, 13496-5). Pacific Pr Pub Assn.

Mike Dime. Barry Fantoni. 208p. 1981. 9.95 (ISBN 0-531-09948-2). Watts.

Mike Fletcher. George Moore. Ed. by Ian Fletcher & John Stokes. LC 76-20121. (Decadent Consciousness Ser.). 1977. Repr. of 1889 ed. lib. bdg. 38.00 (ISBN 0-8240-2770-1). Garland Pub.

Mike Nichols. H. Wayne Schuth. (Theatrical Arts Ser.). 1978. lib. bdg. 12.50 (ISBN 0-8057-9255-4). Twayne.

Mike Thaler's Complete Coptic Book. Mike Thaler. (Illus.). 96p. (gr. 1 up). 1980. pap. 1.95 (ISBN 0-380-76133-5, 76133, Camelot). Avon.

Mike's Mystery. Gertrude C. Warner. LC 60-8428. (Boxcar Children Mysteries-Pilot Bk.). (Illus.). 128p. (gr. 3-7). 1960. 6.95g (ISBN 0-8075-5140-6). A Whitman.

Mike's New Bike. Rose Greydanus. (Illus.). 32p. (gr. k-2). 1980. PLB 2.96 (ISBN 0-89375-382-3); pap. 0.95 (ISBN 0-89375-282-7). Troll Assocs.

Mikhail Botvinnik: Soviet Chess Patriarch. M. M. Botvinnik. LC 80-40437. (Pergamon Russian Chess Ser.). (Illus.). 230p. 1981. pap. 19.00 (ISBN 0-08-024120-4). Pergamon.

Mikhail Bulgakov. Ellendea Proffer. 1981. 22.00 (ISBN 0-88233-198-1). Ardis Pubs.

Mikhail Bulgakov: Selected Works. Ed. by Avril Pyman. 259p. 1972. pap. text ed. 17.00 (ISBN 0-08-015506-5). Pergamon.

Mikhail Lermontov: Magic & Mystery. Helen Michailoff. 1981. 20.00. Ardis Pubs.

Mikrofiltration und andere Transfusions-Probleme in der Intensivmedizin. Ed. by H. Busch. (Beitraege zu Infusionstherapie und klinische Ernaehrung: Band 3). (Illus.). 1979. pap. 12.00 (ISBN 3-8055-3057-9). S Karger.

Mikroradiographische Untersuchungen Zur Mineralisation der Knochen Fruehgeborener und Junger Saeuglinge, 1980. G. Mueller. (Journal: Acta Anatomica: Vol. 108, Suppl. 64). (Illus.). iv, 44p. 1980. pap. 27.00 (ISBN 3-8055-1719-X). S Karger.

Mil y una Noches. (Span.). 7.50 (ISBN 84-241-5612-9). E Torres & Sons.

Milagro Beanfield War. John Treadwell Nichols. 652p. 1976. pap. 3.50 (ISBN 0-345-29533-1). Ballantine.

Milagro Del Amor Agape. Tr. by Pat Robertson. (Spanish Bks.). (Span.). 1978. 1.90 (ISBN 0-8297-0914-2). Life Pubs Intl.

Milagros De la Oracion. (Spanish Bks.). 1977. 1.75 (ISBN 0-8297-0443-4). Life Pubs Intl.

Milagros Tambien Son Parabolas. Plutarco Bonilla. LC 78-59240. 166p. (Orig., Span.). 1978. pap. 3.50 (ISBN 0-89922-114-9). Edit Caribe.

Milbourne Christopher's Magic Book. Milbourne Christopher. LC 77-9098. (Illus.). 1977. 10.95 o.s.i. (ISBN 0-690-01677-8, TYC-T). T Y Crowell.

Mild Mental Retardation: A Growing Challenge to the Physician, Vol. 6. GAP Committee on Mental Retardation. LC 62-2872. (Report No. 66). 1967. pap. 2.00 (ISBN 0-87318-091-7). Adv Psychiatry.

Mildred Murphy How Does Your Garden Grow. Phyllis Green. (gr. k-6). 1980. pap. 1.75 (ISBN 0-440-45590-1, YB). Dell.

Mildred Pierce. Ed. by Albert J. LaValley. LC 80-5107. (Wisconsin - Warner Bros. Screenplay Ser.). (Illus.). 228p. 1980. 15.00 (ISBN 0-299-08370-5); pap. 5.95 (ISBN 0-299-08374-8). U of Wis Pr.

Mile Above the Rim. Charles Rosen. 1978. pap. 1.95 o.p. (ISBN 0-345-25955-6). Ballantine.

Mile High Surprise. Chuck Partridge. (Pal Paperbacks, - Pal Skills II Ser.). (Illus.). (gr. 5-12). 1980. pap. text ed. 1.25 (ISBN 0-8374-6804-3). Xerox Ed Pubns.

Milepost: All-the-North Travel Guide. 33rd ed. Ed. by Milepost Staff. 1981. pap. 7.95 (ISBN 0-88240-151-3). Alaska Northwest.

Miles Conrad Memorial Lecture, 1977. William O. Baker. 10.00. NFAIS.

Milesian Chief. Charles R. Maturin. Ed. by Robert L. Wolff. (Ireland-Nineteenth Century Fiction Ser. Two: Vol. 12). 1979. lib. bdg. 184.00 (ISBN 0-8240-3461-9); lib. bdg. 46.00 ea. Garland Pub.

Milestones in American Literary History. Robert E. Spiller. LC 76-47170. (Contributions in American Studies Ser.: No. 27). 1977. lib. bdg. 13.50 (ISBN 0-8371-9403-2, SMI/). Greenwood.

Milestones in Cataloging: Famous Catalogers & Their Writings, 1835-1969. Donald J. Lehnus. LC 73-94030. (Research Studies in Library Science Ser.: No. 13). 1974. lib. bdg. 10.00 o.p. (ISBN 0-87287-090-1). Libs Unl.

Milestones in Development: A Cumulative Index to Industrial Development, Site Selection Handbook & Related Publications Covering a Quarter-Century of Professional Contribution. Ed. by Jane Martin. 1981. 75.00x (ISBN 0-910436-16-9). Conway Pubns.

Milestones in Microbiology. Ed. by Thomas D. Brock. 1975. Repr. of 1961 ed. 7.00 (ISBN 0-914826-06-9). Am Soc Microbio.

Milestones in Motivation: Contributions to the Psychology of Drive & Purpose. Ed. by Wallace A. Russell. 1970. 20.95 (ISBN 0-13-581686-6). P-H.

Milestones in Soil Mechanics. Thomas Telford Ltd. Editorial Staff. 338p. 1980. 40.00x (ISBN 0-7277-0010-3, Pub. by Telford England). State Mutual Bk.

Milestones in the Life of a Jew. Donald G. Frieman. LC 65-15710. 1980. pap. 3.95x (ISBN 0-8197-0002-9). Bloch.

Milford Series: Popular Writers of Today; an Index to Volumes 1 to 30. R. Reginald & Mary A. Burgess. LC 80-15340. (Borgo Reference Library: Vol. 5). 64p. 1981. lib. bdg. 8.95x (ISBN 0-89370-803-8); pap. 2.95x (ISBN 0-89370-903-4). Borgo Pr.

Milieu Therapy Program for Behaviorally Disturbed Children. Marjorie M. Monkman. (Illus.). 312p. 1972. 19.75 (ISBN 0-398-02363-8). C C Thomas.

Militant Black Writer in Africa & the United States. Mercer Cook & Stephen E. Henderson. LC 69-17324. 1969. pap. 5.25 (ISBN 0-299-05394-6). U of Wis Pr.

Militarism & Anti-Militarism. Karl Liebknecht. 1969. 11.00 (ISBN 0-86527-130-5). Fertig.

Militarism & Antimilitarism: With Special Regard to the International Young Socialist Movement. Karl Liebknecht. Tr. by Grahame Lock from Ger. 162p. 1974. text ed. 10.00x (ISBN 0-9502495-7-2); pap. text ed. 4.00x (ISBN 0-9502495-8-0). Humanities.

Militarism & Social Revolution in the Third World. Miles D. Wolpin. 256p. 1981. text ed. 25.00 (ISBN 0-86598-021-7). Allanheld.

Military. Harry H. Turney-High. 1981. pap. 12.00 (ISBN 0-8158-0403-2). Chris Mass.

Military & American Society. Ed. by Stephen E. Ambrose & James A. Barber, Jr. LC 77-163236. 1973. pap. text ed. 6.95 (ISBN 0-02-900550-7). Free Pr.

Military & American Society. Martin Hickman. (Studies in Contemporary Issues). 1971. pap. text ed. 4.95x (ISBN 0-02-474790-4, 47479). Macmillan.

Military & Naval, 6 vols. (British Parliamentary Papers Ser.). 1971. Set. 459.00x (ISBN 0-7165-1496-6, Pub. by Irish Academic Pr Ireland). Biblio Dist.

Military & Politics in Israel: Nation Building & Role Expansion. 2nd rev. ed. Amos Perlmutter. (Illus.). 161p. 1969. 23.50x (ISBN 0-7146-3100-0, F Cass Co). Biblio Dist.

Military & Politics in Israel 1948-1967. rev ed. Amos Perlmutter. 1980. 23.50x (ISBN 0-7146-3100-0, F Cass Co). Biblio Dist.

Military & Security in the Third World: Domestic & International Impacts. Ed. by Sheldon W. Simon. LC 77-29133. (Westview Special Study Ser.). 1978. lib. bdg. 28.00x (ISBN 0-89158-424-2). Westview.

Military & Society in Latin America. John J. Johnson. 1964. 15.00x (ISBN 0-8047-0198-9); pap. 4.50 o.p. (ISBN 0-8047-0199-7). Stanford U Pr.

Military Art of People's War: Selected Writings. Vo Nguyen Giap. Ed. by Russell Stetler. LC 75-105317. (Illus.). 1970. 8.50 o.p. (ISBN 0-85345-129-X, CL-129X); pap. 5.95 (ISBN 0-85345-193-1, PB-1931). Monthly Rev.

Military Balance Nineteen Eighty--Eighty-One. International Institute for Strategic Studies. 119p. 1980. 17.95x (ISBN 0-87196-446-5). Facts on File.

Military Balance, Nineteen Seventy-Nine to Nineteen Eighty. Ed. by International Institute for Strategic Studies. LC 76-617319. (Illus.). 120p. 1980. lib. bdg. 12.50x (ISBN 0-89158-920-1). Westview.

Military Balance, 1975-1976. International Institute for Strategic Studies. 114p. 1976. 20.00x (ISBN 0-89158-522-2). Westview.

Military Balance, 1980-1981. International Institute for Strategic Studies. 120p. 1980. lib. bdg. 15.00x (ISBN 0-86079-040-1). Westview.

Military Collections at the Essex Institute. John Wright. (E. I. Museum Booklet Ser.). (Illus.). 64p. 1981. pap. text ed. 4.95 (ISBN 0-88389-104-2). Essex Inst.

Military Communications Nineteen Seventy-Nine to Nineteen Eighty. Raggett. 1980. 99.50 (ISBN 0-531-03914-5). Watts.

Military Community: Fort Bragg, North Carolina. (gr. 2). 1974. pap. text ed. 3.80 (ISBN 0-205-03886-7, 8038864); tchrs'. guide 12.00 (ISBN 0-205-03884-0, 8038848). Allyn.

Military Competency Exam, with Explanations. Astro Publishers. Date not set. pap. 7.95 (Pub. by Astro). Aviation.

Military Coup in Egypt. Rashid Al-Barrawi. LC 79-2851. 269p. 1981. Repr. of 1952 ed. 21.00 (ISBN 0-8305-0027-8). Hyperion Conn.

Military Cryptanalysis, 4 vols. William F. Friedman. 1980. lib. bdg. 500.00 (ISBN 0-87700-271-1). Revisionist Pr.

Military Equation in Northeast Asia. Stuart E. Johnson. (Studies in Defense Policy). 1979. pap. 3.95 (ISBN 0-8157-4689-X). Brookings.

Military Families: Adaptation to Change. Edna Hunter & Stephen D. Nice. LC 78-13067. (Praeger Special Studies). 1978. 27.95 (ISBN 0-03-043106-9). Praeger.

Military Garden: Instructions for All Young Souldiers. James Achesone. LC 74-80157. (English Experience Ser.: No. 637). 36p. 1974. Repr. of 1629 ed. 5.00 (ISBN 90-221-0637-3). Walter J Johnson.

Military History of Germany: From the Eighteenth Century to the Present Day. Martin Kitchen. 1976. pap. 4.95 (ISBN 0-8065-0524-9). Citadel Pr.

Military History of Germany from the 18th Century to the Present Day. Martin Kitchen. LC 74-17022. 392p. 1975. 12.50x (ISBN 0-253-33838-7). Ind U Pr.

Military in Contemporary Soviet Politics: An Institutional Analysis. Edward L. Warner, III. LC 77-83476. (Praeger Special Studies). 1978. 26.95 (ISBN 0-03-040346-4). Praeger.

Military Indoctrination & United States Imperialism. M. D. Wolpin. (Occasional Papers: No. 13). 1973. 1.50 o.p. (ISBN 0-686-05790-2). Am Inst Marxist.

Military-Industrial Complex: A Historical Perspective. Paul A. C. Koistinen. LC 79-20569. 186p. 1980. 19.95 (ISBN 0-03-055766-6). Praeger.

Military Journals of Two Private Soldiers, 1758-1775. A. Tomlinson. LC 75-146146. (Era of the American Revolution Ser). 1971. Repr. of 1855 ed. lib. bdg. 17.50 (ISBN 0-306-70134-0). Da Capo.

Military Law in a Nutshell. Charles A. Shanor & Timothy P. Terrell. LC 80-165. (Nutshell Ser.). 418p. 1980. pap. text ed. 6.95 (ISBN 0-8299-2083-8). West Pub.

Military Life of Abraham Lincoln, Commander in Chief. Trevor N. Dupuy. LC 69-19688. (Military Lives Ser). (gr. 7 up). 1969. PLB 6.45 (ISBN 0-531-01874-1). Watts.

Military Life of Adolph Hitler Fuhrer of Germany. Trevor N. Dupuy. LC 69-14500. (Military Lives Ser). (gr. 7 up). 1969. PLB 4.90 o.p. (ISBN 0-531-01873-3). Watts.

Military Life of Alexander the Great of Macedon. Trevor N. Dupuy. LC 69-11604. (Military Lives Ser). (gr. 7 up). 1969. PLB 4.90 o.p. (ISBN 0-531-01875-X). Watts.

Military Life of Frederick the Great of Prussia. Trevor N. Dupuy. LC 69-17460. (Military Lives Ser). (gr. 7 up). 1969. PLB 4.90 o.p. (ISBN 0-531-01876-8). Watts.

Military Life of Genghis Khan, Khan of Khans. Trevor N. Dupuy. LC 79-80894. (Military Lives Ser). 160p. 1969. PLB 4.90 o.p. (ISBN 0-531-01877-6). Watts.

Military Life of George Washington, American Soldier. Trevor N. Dupuy. LC 69-15881. (Military Lives Ser). (gr. 7 up). 1969. PLB 4.90 o.p. (ISBN 0-531-01871-7). Watts.

Military Life of Gustavus Adolphus: Father of Modern War. Trevor N. Dupuy. LC 79-77239. (Military Lives Ser). (gr. 7 up). 1969. PLB 6.45 (ISBN 0-531-01878-4). Watts.

Military Life of Hannibal, Father of Strategy. Trevor N. Dupuy. LC 69-11602. (Military Lives Ser). (gr. 7 up). 1969. PLB 4.90 o.p. (ISBN 0-531-01879-2). Watts.

Military Life of Napoleon, Emperor of the French. Trevor N. Dupuy. LC 73-87927. (Military Lives Ser). (gr. 7 up). 1969. PLB 4.90 o.p. (ISBN 0-531-01870-9). Watts.

Military Life of Winston Churchill of Britain. Trevor N. Dupuy. LC 69-17459. (Military Lives Ser). (gr. 7 up). 1969. PLB 6.45 (ISBN 0-531-01881-4). Watts.

Military Lives of Hindenburg & Ludendorff of Imperial Germany. Trevor N. Dupuy. LC 72-80895. (Military Lives Ser). (gr. 7 up). 1969. PLB 4.90 o.p. (ISBN 0-531-01882-2). Watts.

Military Manners & Customs. James A. Farrer. LC 68-21771. 1968. Repr. of 1885 ed. 15.00 (ISBN 0-8103-3510-7). Gale.

Military Men. Ward Just. LC 76-123428. 1971. 6.95 o.p. (ISBN 0-394-43617-2). Knopf.

Military Modelling. Gerald Scarborough. (Illus.). 64p. 1974. 4.95 o.p. (ISBN 0-85059-177-5). Aztex.

Military-Naval Encyclopedia of Russia & the Soviet Union: MERSU, Vol. 1 1978. Ed. by David R. Jones. 31.50 (ISBN 0-87569-028-9). Academic Intl.

Military-Naval Encyclopedia of Russia & the Soviet Union: MERSU, Vol. 2. Ed. by David R. Jones. 31.50 (ISBN 0-87569-033-5). Academic Intl.

Military-Naval Encyclopedia of Russia & the Soviet Union: Mersu, Vol. 3. Ed. by David R. Jones. 1981. write for info. (ISBN 0-87569-041-6). Academic Intl.

Military Necessity & Civil Rights Policy: Black Citizenship & the Constitution, 1861-1868. Mary F. Berry. LC 76-53822. (National University Publications Ser. in American Studies). 1977. 10.00 (ISBN 0-8046-9166-5). Kennikat.

Military Operations in Jefferson County, Virginia & West Virginia, 1861-1865. (Illus.). 45p. Repr. of 1911 ed. 8.50x o.p. (ISBN 0-685-65081-2). Va Bk.

Military Organization & Society. Stanislav Andreski. 1968. pap. 5.85x (ISBN 0-520-00026-9, CAMPUS 7). U of Cal Pr.

Military Panorama, No. 1. Uwe Feist. (Illus.). 1969. pap. 4.95 (ISBN 0-8168-6801-8). Aero.

Military Pay Muddle. Martin Binkin. (Studies in Defense Policy). 60p. 1975. pap. 3.95 (ISBN 0-8157-0961-7). Brookings.

Military Philosophers. Anthony Powell. (Dance to the Music of Time: No.3). pap. 2.50 (ISBN 0-445-08447-2). Popular Lib.

Military Power & Policy in Asian States: Toward the 1980's. Ed. by Onkar Marwah & Jonathan D. Pollack. (Special Studies in Military Affairs Ser.). 1979. lib. bdg. 21.50x (ISBN 0-89158-407-2). Westview.

Military Roads in Scotland. William Taylor. LC 76-9239. (Illus.). 1976. 14.95 (ISBN 0-7153-7067-7). David & Charles.

Military Roles in Moderization: Civil-Military Relations in Thailand & Burma. Moshe Lissak. LC 75-5015. (Armed Forces & Society Ser.: Vol. 8). 1976. 20.00x o.p. (ISBN 0-8039-0436-3). Sage.

Military Small Arms Ammunition of the World, 1945-1980. Peter Labbett. (Illus.). 160p. 1980. 18.95 (ISBN 0-89141-116-X). Presidio Pr.

Military Strategy: A General Theory of Power Control. Joseph C. Wylie. LC 80-36885. vii, 111p. 1980. Repr. of 1967 ed. lib. bdg. 17.50x (ISBN 0-313-22679-2, WYMS). Greenwood.

Military System of the Sikhs (During the Period 1799-1899) Fauja S. Bajwa. (Illus.). 1964. 4.95 (ISBN 0-89684-280-0). Orient Bk Dist.

Military Theory & Practice in the Age of Xenophon. J. K. Anderson. LC 74-104010. 1970. 25.75x (ISBN 0-520-01564-9). U of Cal Pr.

Military Transport of World War Two. Christopher Ellis. Ed. by Alick Bartholomew. LC 70-152283. (Mechanical Warfare Ser). 1971. 9.95 (ISBN 0-02-535230-X). Macmillan.

Military Uniforms in Canada. Jack L. Summers & Rene Chartrand. (Illus.). 220p. 1981. 35.00 (ISBN 0-660-10346-X, 56434-7, Pub. by Natl Mus Canada). U of Chicago Pr.

Military Unions: U.S. Trends & Issues. Ed. by William J. Taylor, Jr. et al. LC 77-88632. (Sage Research Progress Series on War, Revolution, & Peacekeeping: Vol. 7). 1977. 20.00x (ISBN 0-8039-0934-9); pap. 9.95x (ISBN 0-8039-0935-7). Sage.

Military Utility of the U. S. Facilities in the Philippines, Vol. II. Alvin J. Cottrell & Robert J. Hanks. LC 80-83128. (Significant Issues Ser.: No.11). 34p. 1980. 5.95 (ISBN 0-89206-027-1). CSI Studies.

Milk. Sharon Shebar. Ed. by Dan Wasserman. (Illus.). (gr. k-1). 1979. PLB 4.50 (ISBN 0-89868-067-0); pap. 1.95 (ISBN 0-89868-078-6). ARO Pub.

Milk & Milk Products. (Terminology Bulletin: No. 31). 95p. 1980. pap. 6.00 (ISBN 92-5-000758-2, F 1879, FAO). Unipub.

Milk, Butter, & Cheese: The Story of Dairy Products. Carolyn Meyer. LC 73-13574. (Illus.). 96p. (gr. 5-9). 1974. PLB 6.96 (ISBN 0-688-30100-2). Morrow.

Milk-Free & Milk-Free, Egg-Free Cookbook. Isobel S. Sainsbury. 160p. 1974. pap. text ed. 14.75 (ISBN 0-398-03108-8). C C Thomas.

Milk, Milk Products & Egg Balances in OECD Member Countries, 1973-1978. May 1980. OECD. (Illus.). 140p. (Orig., Eng. & Fr.). 1980. pap. 11.50x (ISBN 92-64-02093-4). OECD.

Milk My Ewes & Weep. Joyce Fussey. (YA) 1977. 9.95 (ISBN 0-236-40031-2, Pub. by Paul Elek). Merrimack Bk Serv.

Milk of Paradise: The Effects of Opium Visions on the Works of DeQuincey, Crabbe, Frances Thompson, & Coleridge. M. H. Abrams. LC 79-120223. 1970. Repr. lib. bdg. 12.50 (ISBN 0-374-90028-0). Octagon.

Milk Production & Processing. Henry F. Judkins & H. A. Keener. LC 60-10317. 1960. 20.95 (ISBN 0-471-45276-9). Wiley.

Milk Production in Developing Countries. R. O. Whyte. (Illus.). 1967. 10.95 o.p. (ISBN 0-571-08089-8, Pub. by Faber & Faber). Merrimack Bk Serv.

Milk Proteins, Vols. 1-2. Ed. by Hugh A. McKenzie. 1971. Vol. 1. 62.00 (ISBN 0-12-485201-7); Vol. 2. 63.00 (ISBN 0-12-485202-5); Set. 101.25 (ISBN 0-685-02414-8). Acad Pr.

Milk: The Mammary Gland & Its Secretion, 2 Vols. Ed. by S. K. Kon & Alfred T. Cowie. (Illus.). 1961. Vol. 1. 49.00 (ISBN 0-12-418701-3); Vol. 2. 49.00 (ISBN 0-12-418702-1); Set. 80.00 (ISBN 0-685-05135-8). Acad Pr.

Milking Machines: A Comprehensive Guide for Farmers, Herdsmen & Students. F. R. Lowe. (Illus.). 200p. 1981. 30.00 (ISBN 0-08-024381-9); pap. 15.00 (ISBN 0-08-024382-7). Pergamon.

Milkweed Butterflies: Monarchs, Models, & Mimics. Hilda Simon. LC 68-56601. (Illus.). (gr. 4 up). 1968. 6.95 (ISBN 0-8149-0389-4). Vanguard.

Milky Way. 4th ed. Bart J. Bok & Priscilla F. Bok. LC 73-83418. (Books on Astronomy Ser.). 288p. 1974. 16.50x (ISBN 0-674-57501-6); pap. 7.95 (ISBN 0-674-57502-4). Harvard U Pr.

Milky Way. 5th ed. Bart J. Bok & Priscilla F. Bok. LC 80-22544. (Harvard Books on Astronomy Ser.). (Illus.). 384p. 1981. text ed. 20.00 (ISBN 0-674-57503-2). Harvard U Pr.

Milky Way: An Elusive Road for Science. Stanley L. Jaki. 363p. 1975. pap. 8.95 o.p. (ISBN 0-88202-022-6, Sci Hist). N Watson.

Mill. James F. Murphy, Jr. 320p. 1981. pap. 2.95 (ISBN 0-380-77198-5). Avon.

Mill Child. Ruth Holland. LC 75-92072. (Illus.). (gr. 5-9). 1970. 7.95 (ISBN 0-02-744260-8, CCPr). Macmillan.

Mill on Liberty. C. L. Ten. 464p. 1981. 31.00 (ISBN 0-19-824643-9); pap. 14.95 (ISBN 0-19-824644-7). Oxford U Pr.

Mill on the Floss. George Eliot. (Clarendon Edition of the Novels of George Eliot Ser.). (Illus.). 516p. text ed. 55.00x (ISBN 0-19-812560-7). Oxford U Pr.

Millais & the Ruskins. Mary Lutyens. LC 68-8086. (Illus.). Date not set. 10.00 (ISBN 0-8149-0149-2). Vanguard. Postponed.

Millenial Harbinger - Index. David McWhirter. LC 81-65031. (Millenial Harbinger Ser.). 864p. 1981. 19.95 (ISBN 0-89900-228-5). College Pr Pub.

Millenialism. Herman D. Seyer. 68p. 1979. pap. 1.50. H D Seyer.

Millenialism: The Two Major Views. Charles L. Feinberg. 1980. 9.95 (ISBN 0-8024-6815-2). Moody.

Millenium: Glimpses into the Twenty-First Century. Ed. by Alberto Villoldo & Kenneth Dychtwald. (Illus.). 348p. 1981. 15.00 (ISBN 0-87477-145-5); pap. 8.95 (ISBN 0-87477-166-8). J P Tarcher.

Millenium: What It Is, & What It Is Not. George P. Fletcher. pap. 2.25 (ISBN 0-685-00747-2). Reiner.

Millennial Kingdom. John F. Walvoord. 1959. 10.95 (ISBN 0-310-34090-X). Zondervan.

Millennial Kingdom of the Franciscans in the New World. 2nd rev ed. John L. Phelan. 1970. 17.50x (ISBN 0-520-01404-9). U of Cal Pr.

Millennial Women: Tales for Tomorrow. Ed. by Virginia Kidd. LC 77-86299. 1978. 8.95 o.s.i. (ISBN 0-440-05599-7). Delacorte.

Millennialism, Utopianism, & Progress. Theodore Olson. 1981. 35.00 (ISBN 0-8020-5506-0). U of Toronto Pr.

Millennium. Ben Bova. (Del Rey Bk.). 1977. pap. 1.95 (ISBN 0-685-75021-3, 345-25556-9-195). Ballantine.

Millennium Man. George Otis. 8.95; pap. 4.95 (ISBN 0-89728-043-1, 615644). Omega Pubns OR.

Miller Analogies Test: Fourteen Hundred Analogy Questions. 3rd ed. Ed. by David R. Turner. LC 72-50. 1973. lib. bdg. 8.00 (ISBN 0-668-01115-7); pap. 5.00 (ISBN 0-668-01114-9). Arco.

Miller Comprehensive Solutions to the Uniform CPA Examination. Martin A. Miller. Incl. Solutions to the May 1978 Examination. 224p. pap. (ISBN 0-15-003951-4); Solutions to the November 1978 Examination. 202p. pap. (ISBN 0-15-003953-0); Solutions to the May 1979 Examination. 203p. pap. (ISBN 0-15-003956-5); Solutions to the November 1979 Examination. 200p. pap. text ed. 15.00 ea. (HC). HarBraceJ.

Miller's Prologue & Tale. Geoffrey Chaucer. Ed. by J. Winny. LC 76-132283. (Selected Tales from Chaucer). 1970. text ed. 4.95x (ISBN 0-521-08033-9). Cambridge U Pr.

Millet. Griselda Pollock. 1977. 15.95 (ISBN 0-8467-0252-5, Pub. by Two Continents); pap. 9.95 (ISBN 0-8467-0251-7). Hippocrene Bks.

Millets: A Bibliography of the World Literature Covering the Years 1930-1963. George Washington University, Biological Sciences Communications Project. 1967. 10.00 (ISBN 0-8108-0095-0). Scarecrow.

Millets & Minor Cereals. Kenneth O. Rachie. LC 73-22142. 1974. 10.00 (ISBN 0-8108-0700-9). Scarecrow.

Millicent. Jeannie Baker. (Illus.). (ps-2). 1980. 8.95 (ISBN 0-233-97201-3). Andre Deutsch.

Millicent Maybe. Ellen Weiss. LC 78-13144. (Easy-Read Story Bks.). (Illus.). (gr. k-3). 1979. 3.95 (ISBN 0-531-02382-6); PLB 6.45 s&l (ISBN 0-531-02299-4). Watts.

Millicent Maybe. Ellen Weiss. 1980. pap. 1.50 (ISBN 0-380-49197-4, 49197, Camelot). Avon.

Millicent the Magnificent. Alice Bach. (gr. k-6). Date not set. pap. 1.25 (ISBN 0-440-45456-5, YB). Dell.

Milligan Book of Records. Spike Milligan. 1980. 7.95 (ISBN 0-7181-1377-2, Pub. by Michael Joseph). Merrimack Bk Serv.

Milligan Case. Ed. by Samuel Klaus. LC 78-118031. (Civil Liberties in American History Ser). 1970. Repr. of 1929 ed. lib. bdg. 42.50 (ISBN 0-306-71945-2). Da Capo.

Milling, Vol. 1. 2nd ed. Ed. by C. Plaster et al. (Engineering Craftsmen: No. H4). (Illus.). 1977. spiral bdg. 16.50x (ISBN 0-85083-404-X). Intl Ideas.

Milling, Vol. 2. Ed. by A. G. Spencer. (Engineering Craftsmen: No. H29). (Illus.). 1969. spiral bdg. 14.95x (ISBN 0-85083-060-5). Intl Ideas.

Milling Machine. David J. Gingery. LC 80-66142. (Build Your Own Metal Working Shop from Scrap Ser.: Bk. 4). (Illus.). 96p. (Orig.). 1981. pap. 7.95 (ISBN 0-9604330-3-1). D J Gingery.

Milling Machine Work. 1953. pap. text ed. 7.40 (ISBN 0-8273-0185-5). Delmar.

Million Dollar Diet Plan. Dan Heffron. (Illus.). 148p. (Orig.). 1980. pap. 10.00 (ISBN 0-9605104-1-9). Heffron Ent.

Million Dollar Lift. Richard Crighton. 288p. 1981. pap. 2.50 (ISBN 0-380-76604-3, 76604). Avon.

Million Dollar Secret Hidden in Your Mind. Norvell. 223p. 1973. pap. 2.95 (ISBN 0-06-463345-4, EH 345, EH). Har-Row.

Million Dollar Studs. Alice-Leone Moats. 1977. 8.95 o.p. (ISBN 0-440-05683-7). Delacorte.

Millionaire for God (C. T. Studd) John T. Erskine. 1968. pap. 1.95 (ISBN 0-87508-611-X). Chr Lit.

Millionaire's Daughter. Dorothy Eden. 1978. pap. 2.25 (ISBN 0-449-23186-0, Crest). Fawcett.

Millionairess. George B. Shaw. (Penguin Plays Ser.). 1961. pap. 2.50 (ISBN 0-14-048009-9). Penguin.

Millions & Millions of Crystals. Roma Gans. LC 72-7547. (Let's Read & Find Out Science Bk). (Illus.). (gr. k-3). 1973. PLB 7.89 (ISBN 0-690-54030-2, TYC-J). T Y Crowell.

Mills Down Below. Mabel E. Allan. LC 80-2782. 192p. (gr. 7 up). 1981. PLB 7.95 (ISBN 0-396-07926-1). Dodd.

Mills of the Gods. Daoma Winston. 1980. pap. write for info. (ISBN 0-671-81601-2). PB.

Mills of Wisconsin. Jerry Apps. LC 80-24684. (Illus., Orig.). 1980. pap. 12.50 (ISBN 0-915024-22-5). Tamarack Pr.

Mill's Pharmacy State Board Review. 29th ed. Joseph A. Romano & Matthew B. Wiener. LC 76-14721. 1977. pap. 13.00 (ISBN 0-87488-430-6). Med Exam.

Millstatter Exodus: A Crusading Epic. Dennis H. Green. 1966. 78.00 (ISBN 0-521-05139-8). Cambridge U Pr.

Millwrights & Mechanics Guide. 2nd ed. Carl A. Nelson. LC 72-75119. (Illus.). 800p. 1972. 14.95 (ISBN 0-672-23201-4). Audel.

Milly-Molly-Mandy Again. Joyce L. Brisley. LC 76-48834. (Illus.). (gr. k-3). 1977. 4.95 o.p. (ISBN 0-679-20398-2). McKay.

Milly-Molly-Mandy & Billy Blunt. Joyce L. Brisley. LC 76-48835. (Illus.). (gr. k-3). 1977. 4.95 o.p. (ISBN 0-679-20399-0). McKay.

Milton. John C. Bailey. 256p. 1980. Repr. of 1945 ed. lib. bdg. 20.00 (ISBN 0-8495-0463-5). Arden Lib.

Milton Agonistes: A Metaphysical Criticism. Edward H. Visak. 104p. 1980. Repr. of 1923 ed. lib. bdg. 17.50 (ISBN 0-8492-2834-4). R West.

Milton & Augustine: Patterns of Augustinian Thought in Milton's Paradise Lost. Peter A. Fiore. LC 80-17854. 144p. 1981. 14.50x (ISBN 0-271-00269-7). Pa St U Pr.

Milton & Sex. Edward LeComte. LC 77-1081. 1978. 15.00x (ISBN 0-231-04340-6). Columbia U Pr.

Milton & the Line of Vision. Ed. by Joseph A. Wittreich, Jr. LC 75-12215. (Illus.). 288p. 1975. 27.50x (ISBN 0-299-06910-9). U of Wis Pr.

Milton & the Literary Satan. Frank S. Kastor. LC 74-81305. 119p. (Orig.). 1976. pap. text ed. 11.50x (ISBN 90-6203-198-6). Humanities.

Milton & the Martial Muse: Paradise Lost & European Traditions of War. James A. Freeman. LC 80-7519. 1980. 17.50x (ISBN 0-691-06435-0). Princeton U Pr.

Milton Avery. Ed. by Bonnie L. Grad. (Illus.). 132p. 1981. 95.00 (ISBN 0-931554-19-5). Strathcona.

Milton Caniff, Rembrandt of the Comic Strip. rev. ed. John P. Adams & Richard Marschall. LC 80-70395. (Illus.). 64p. 1981. pap. 6.95x (ISBN 0-918348-04-8). Flying Buttress.

Milton Criticism: Selections from Four Centuries. Ed. by James Thorpe. LC 66-19730. 1969. pap. text ed. 2.45 o.s.i. (ISBN 0-02-054730-7, Collier). Macmillan.

Milton Cross More Stories of the Great Operas. Milton Cross & Karl Kohrs. LC 77-132495. 1971. 10.95 o.p. (ISBN 0-385-08546-X). Doubleday.

Milton Cross New Encyclopedia of the Great Composers & Their Music, 2 Vols. Milton Cross & David Ewen. LC 70-87097. two-volume, boxed set 24.95 (ISBN 0-385-03635-3). Doubleday.

Milton Freidman's Monetary Framework: A Debate with His Critics. Milton Friedman et al. Ed. by Robert J. Gordon. LC 73-92599. xii, 192p. 1975. pap. 4.50 (ISBN 0-226-26408-4, P619, Phoen). U of Chicago Pr.

Milton Glaser: Graphic Design. Milton Glaser. LC 73-79228. (Illus.). 240p. 1973. 45.00 (ISBN 0-87951-013-7). Overlook Pr.

Milton Reconsidered: Essays in Honour of Arthur E. Baker. Ed. by John K. Franson. (Salzburg Studies in English Literature: Elizabethan & Renaissance Studies: No. 49). (Illus.). 215p. 1976. pap. text ed. 25.00x (ISBN 0-391-01378-5). Humanities.

Milton Studies, Vol. XIV. Ed. by James D. Simmonds. LC 69-12335. (Milton Studies). (Illus.). 286p. 1981. 21.95x (ISBN 0-8229-3429-9). U of Pittsburgh Pr.

Milton the Early Riser. 2nd, abr. ed. Robert Kraus. LC 80-51358. (Windmill Board Bks.). (Illus.). 16p. (ps). 1980. 3.50 (ISBN 0-671-41203-5, Pub. by Windmill). S&S.

Milton, the Individualist in Metre. Hugh C. Candy. 49p. 1980. Repr. lib. bdg. 8.50 (ISBN 0-89987-112-7). Darby Bks.

Milton's Brief Epic: The Genre, Meaning, & Art of Paradise Regained. Barbara K. Lewalski. LC 66-10282. 436p. 1967. Repr. of 1966 ed. 16.00x (ISBN 0-87057-095-1, Pub. by Brown U Pr). Univ Pr of New England.

Milton's God. W. Empson. LC 80-40109. 320p. Date not set. pap. 15.95 (ISBN 0-521-29910-1). Cambridge U Pr.

Milton's Knowledge of Music. Sigmund G. Spaeth. LC 72-8052. (Music Ser). 186p. 1972. Repr. of 1913 ed. lib. bdg. 22.50 (ISBN 0-306-70535-4). Da Capo.

Milton's Ontology, Cosmogony & Physics. Walter C. Curry. LC 57-5833. (Illus.). 226p. 1966. pap. 4.00x (ISBN 0-8131-0102-6). U Pr of Ky.

Milton's Paradise Lost, 3 vols. Ed. by A. W. Verity. 750p. 1980. Repr. of 1921 ed. Set. lib. bdg. 85.00 (ISBN 0-8414-9349-9). Folcroft.

Milton's Paradise Lost: A Commentary on the Argument. John S. Diekhoff. 1963. Repr. of 1946 ed. text ed. 10.00x (ISBN 0-391-00447-6). Humanities.

Milton's Samson Agonistes & Lycidas. John Hunter. 92p. 1980. Repr. of 1872 ed. text ed. 17.50 (ISBN 0-8492-5271-7). R West.

Milton's Sonnets & the Ideal Community. Anna K. Nardo. LC 79-17221. 1979. 15.95x (ISBN 0-8032-3302-7). U of Nebr Pr.

Milton's Unchanging Mind: Three Essays. Edward LeComte. LC 73-83266. 132p. 1974. 11.00 (ISBN 0-8046-9060-X). Kennikat.

Milwaukee Rails. Robert P. Olmsted. LC 80-81260. (Illus.). 200p. 1980. 26.95 (ISBN 0-934228-04-3). McMillan Pubns.

Milwaukee Road East. Patrick C. Dorin. LC 78-3834. (Illus.). 1977. 15.95 o.s.i. (ISBN 0-87564-528-3). Superior Pub.

Milwaukee Road-West. 2nd ed. Charles R. Wood. LC 72-77009. (Illus.). 192p. 1981. 19.95 (ISBN 0-87564-511-9). Superior Pub.

Milwaukee Transport Era: The Trackless Trolley Years. Russell E. Schultz. Ed. by Mac Sebree. (Interurbans Special Ser.: 74). (Illus.). 160p. (Orig.). 1980. pap. 13.95 (ISBN 0-916374-43-2). Interurban.

Mimansa Nyaya Prakasa. Apadeva. Tr. by Franklin Edgerton. 1929. 65.00x (ISBN 0-685-69815-7). Elliots Bks.

Mimansa Sutras of Jaimini, 2 vols. Tr. by M. L. Sandal. 1022p. 1980. text ed. 60.00 (ISBN 0-8426-1651-9). Verry.

Mime. Tony Profumo. 1978. pap. 1.95 o.s.i. (ISBN 0-515-04255-2). Jove Pubns.

Mime Book. Claude Kipnis. Ed. by Neil Kleinman. LC 73-14266. (Illus.). 256p. (YA) 1974. 15.95 o.s.i. (ISBN 0-06-012404-0, HarpT). Har-Row.

Mime Themes & Motifs. Pat Keysell. (Illus.). 80p. 80. Repr. of 1975 ed. 9.95 (ISBN 0-8238-0245-0). Plays.

Mime Workbook. 2nd, rev. ed. Samuel Avital. Ed. by Ken Reed. LC 77-84487. (Illus.). 176p. 1977. pap. 8.95 (ISBN 0-914794-30-2). Wisdom Garden.

Mimes of Herondas. Herondas. Ed. & tr. by Guy Davenport. 100p. 1981. 12.00 (ISBN 0-912516-63-1); pap. 4.95 (ISBN 0-912516-64-X). Grey Fox.

Mimesis und Poiesis Poetologische Zum Bildungsroman. Monika Schrader. (Quellen und Forschungen zur Sprach-und Kulturgeschichte der germanischen). 367p. (Ger.). 1975. 44.70x (ISBN 3-11-005904-5). De Gruyter.

Mimi: A Norman Rockwell Character Story. Mary Moline. LC 80-52873. 1980. 12.00 (ISBN 0-913444-05-7). Rumbleseat.

Mimosa, the Sensitive Plant. Millicent E. Selsam. (Illus.). (gr. 4-6). 1978. 7.95 (ISBN 0-688-22167-X); PLB 7.63 (ISBN 0-688-32167-4). Morrow.

Mimosa Tree. Vera Cleaver & Bill Cleaver. 140p. (RL 6). Date not set. pap. 1.25 o.p. (ISBN 0-451-07406-8, Y7406, Sig). NAL.

Min-Min. Mavis T. Clark. (gr. 5-9). 1969. 8.95g (ISBN 0-02-718960-0). Macmillan.

Minamata. W. Eugene Smith & Aileen M. Smith. LC 74-15467. (Illus.). 208p. 1975. 20.00 o.p. (ISBN 0-03-013631-8); pap. 10.00 o.p. (ISBN 0-03-013636-9). HR&W.

Minangkabau Social Formations: Indonesian Peasants & the World Economy. Joel S. Kahn. LC 79-7650. (Cambridge Studies in Social Anthropology: No. 30). (Illus.). 260p. 1981. 37.50 (ISBN 0-521-22993-6). Cambridge U Pr.

Minaret of Djam: An Excursion in Afghanistan. Freya Stark. (Illus.). 99p. 1972. 19.50 (ISBN 0-7195-2066-5). Transatlantic.

Minceur Italienne: Slimming Gourmet Menus & Recipes. Beverly Cox. LC 79-63111. (Gourmet Minceur Ser.). (Illus.). 1979. 8.95 (ISBN 0-8149-0820-9). Vanguard.

Mind. John R. Wilson. LC 64-23096. (Life Science Library). (Illus.). (gr. 5 up). 1969. PLB 8.97 o.p. (ISBN 0-8094-0465-6, Pub. by Time-Life). Silver.

Mind & Art of Jonathan Swift. Richardo Quintana. 8.50 (ISBN 0-8446-1370-3). Peter Smith.

Mind & Behavior: Readings from Scientific American. Intro. by Rita L. Atkinson. LC 80-15307. (Illus.). 1980. text ed. 19.95x (ISBN 0-7167-1215-6); pap. text ed. 9.95x (ISBN 0-7167-1216-4). W H Freeman.

Mind & Body in Eighteenth Century Medicine: A Study Based on Jerome Gaub's De Regimine Mentis. L. J. Rather. (Wellcome Institute of the History of Medicine). 1965. 20.00x (ISBN 0-520-01049-3). U of Cal Pr.

Mind & Cancer Prognosis. Ed. by B. A. Stoll. LC 79-40643. 1980. 33.75 (ISBN 0-471-27644-8, Pub. by Wiley-Interscience). Wiley.

Mind & Heart of Frederick Douglass: Excerpts from Speeches of the Great Negro Orator. Frederick Douglass. Ed. by Barbara Ritchie. LC 68-13587. (gr. 7 up). 1968. 7.95 (ISBN 0-690-54206-2, TYC-J). T Y Crowell.

Mind & Image: An Essay on Art & Architecture. Herb Greene. LC 74-18932. (Illus.). 224p. 1976. 23.50x (ISBN 0-8131-1323-7). U Pr of Ky.

Mind & Madness in Ancient Greece: The Classical Roots of Modern Psychiatry. Bennett Simon. LC 77-90911. (Illus.). 1978. 19.50x (ISBN 0-8014-0859-8); pap. 9.95 1980 ed. (ISBN 0-8014-9202-5). Cornell U Pr.

Mind & Madness in Ancient Greece: The Classical Roots of Modern Psychiatry. Bennett Simon. LC 77-90911. (Cornell Paperback Ser.). (Illus.). 336p. 1980. pap. 6.95 o.p. (ISBN 0-8014-9202-5). Cornell U Pr.

Mind & Method of the Historian. Emmanuel L. Ladurie. Tr. by Sian Reynolds & Ben Reynolds. 224p. 1981. price not set (ISBN 0-226-47326-0). U of Chicago Pr.

Mind & Political Concepts. Ezra Talmor. 1979. text ed. 30.00 (ISBN 0-08-023737-1); pap. text ed. 14.00 (ISBN 0-08-024269-3). Pergamon.

Mind & Politics: An Approach to the Meaning of Liberal & Socialist Individualism. Ellen Wood. LC 74-153556. 224p. 1972. 18.50x (ISBN 0-520-02029-4). U of Cal Pr.

Mind & Spirit of India. N. K. Devaraja. 1967. 5.00 (ISBN 0-89684-281-9). Orient Bk Dist.

Mind & the Soul: An Introduction to the Philosophy of the Mind. Jenny Teichmann. (Studies in Philosophical Psychology). 120p. 1973. text ed. 7.00x (ISBN 0-391-00338-0). Humanities.

Mind & the World Order. Clarence I. Lewis. 1924. pap. 6.50 (ISBN 0-486-20359-X). Dover.

Mind Appliance: Home Computer Applications. T. G. Lewis. 1978. pap. 9.55 (ISBN 0-8104-5112-3). Hayden.

Mind at Ease. M. L. Ashton. 1961. pap. 2.25 (ISBN 0-87508-902-X). Chr Lit.

Mind at Large: Institute of Electrical & Electronic Engineers Symposia on the Nature of Extrasensory Perception. Ed. by Charles T. Tart et al. LC 79-9982. 288p. 1979. 25.95 (ISBN 0-03-050476-7). Praeger.

Mind Awake. C. S. Lewis. LC 80-14133. 1980. pap. 3.95 (ISBN 0-15-659772-1, Harv). HarBraceJ.

Mind Benders. Shirley Schwarzrock & C. Gilbert Wrenn. (Coping with Ser.). (gr. 10 up). 1971. pap. text ed. 1.30 (ISBN 0-913476-16-1). Am Guidance.

Mind-Body Effect. Herbert Benson. 1980. pap. 2.50 (ISBN 0-425-04699-0). Berkley Pub.

Mind-Body Integration: Essential Readings in Biofeedback. Ed. by Erik Peper et al. LC 78-27224. (Illus.). 606p. 1978. 25.00 (ISBN 0-306-40102-9, Plenum Pr). Plenum Pub.

Mind-Body Problem: A Psychobiological Approach. Mario Bunge. (Foundations & Philosophy of Science & Technology: Vol. 1). (Illus.). 245p. 1980. 33.00 (ISBN 0-08-024720-2); pap. 14.00 (ISBN 0-08-024719-9). Pergamon.

Mind-Boggling Brain Benders. Jessica Davidson & William C. Martin. (Illus.). (gr. 7-12). pap. 1.95 (ISBN 0-13-583336-1). P-H.

Mind Cage. A. E. Van Vogt. 1981. pap. 2.25 (ISBN 0-671-42424-6). PB.

Mind-Call. Wilanne S. Belden. LC 80-18488. 252p. (gr. 5-9). 1981. PLB 10.95 (ISBN 0-689-30796-9, Argo). Atheneum.

Mind Cure in New England: From the Civil War to World War I. Gail T. Parker. LC 72-92704. 209p. 1973. text ed. 12.50x (ISBN 0-87451-073-2). U Pr of New Eng.

Mind Design: Philosophy, Psychology, Artifical Intelligence. John C. Haugeland. LC 81-24275. Orig. Title: Mind Design. (Illus.). 368p. 1981. text ed. 21.50 (ISBN 0-89706-004-0); pap. text ed. 10.00 (ISBN 0-89706-005-9). Bradford Bks.

Mind Design: Semantic Engines. John Haugeland. 288p. 1980. text ed. cancelled (ISBN 0-89706-004-0); pap. text ed. cancelled (ISBN 0-89706-005-9). Bradford Bks.

Mind Experiments. Bill Harvey. Ed. by Jan Bertisch & Yana Bragg. (Illus.). 1977. pap. 4.00 o.p. (ISBN 0-918538-04-1). Ourobourus.

Mind Game. Norman Spinard. (Orig.). pap. 2.50 (ISBN 0-515-04847-X). Jove Pubns.

Mind in Action: An Essay in Philosophical Psychology. C. H. Whiteley. (Oxford Paperbacks University Ser). 128p. 1973. pap. 3.95x o.p. (ISBN 0-19-888092-8). Oxford U Pr.

Mind in Its Place: Wordsworth, "Michael" & the Poetry of 1800. John G. Dings. (Salzburg Studies in English Literature, Romantic Reassessment: No.8). 1973. pap. text ed. 25.00x (ISBN 0-391-01361-0). Humanities.

Mind in Nature: Essays on the Interface of Science & Philosophy. Ed. by David R. Griffin & John B. Cobb, Jr. 1977. pap. text ed. 8.75x (ISBN 0-8191-0157-5). U Pr of Amer.

Mind in Sleep: Psychology & Psychophysiology. Ed. by Arthur M. Arkin et al. LC 78-6025. 1978. 29.95 (ISBN 0-470-26369-5). Halsted Pr.

Mind in the Lower Animal in Health & Disease. William L. Lindsay. (Contributions to the History of Psychology Ser.: Pts. 6 & 7, Comparative Psychology). 1980. Repr. of 1879 ed. 30.00 ea. U Pubns Amer.

Mind in the Waters. Joan McIntyre. LC 74-13000. 1975. pap. 12.95 (ISBN 0-684-14443-3, SL614, ScribT). Scribner.

Mind Magic. 3rd ed. Bill Harvey. Orig. Title: Mind Magic: the Science of Microcosmology. (Illus.). 436p. 1980. o. p. 18.50 (ISBN 0-8290-0230-8); pap. 9.95 (ISBN 0-8290-0231-6). Irvington.

Mind, Matter, & Gravitation. Haakon Forwald. LC 72-97212. (Parapsychological Monograph No. 11). 1969. pap. 3.50 (ISBN 0-912328-15-0). Parapsych Foun.

Mind Matters. Marguerite Iwersen. LC 80-67158. 129p. (Orig.). 1981. pap. 5.50 (ISBN 0-87516-421-8). De Vorss.

Mind-Murders. Janwillem Van de Wetering. 1981. 9.95 (ISBN 0-686-69054-0). HM.

Mind of a Monarch. R. K. Karanjia. (Illus.). 1977. 18.95 o.p. (ISBN 0-04-923069-7). Allen Unwin.

Mind of America, 1820-1860. Rush Welter. 576p. 1975. 20.00x (ISBN 0-231-02963-2); pap. 10.00x (ISBN 0-231-08351-3). Columbia U Pr.

Mind of Buganda: Documents of the Modern History of an African Kingdom. Ed. by D. A. Low. (Illus.). 1971. 20.00x (ISBN 0-520-01969-5). U of Cal Pr.

Mind of Dante. Uberto Limentani. 1966. 37.50 (ISBN 0-521-05560-1). Cambridge U Pr.

Mind of Eriugena. John J. O'Meara. Ed. by L. Bieler. 208p. 1973. 19.00x (ISBN 0-7165-2158-X, Pub. by Irish Academic Pr Ireland). Biblio Dist.

Mind of John Paul II: Origins of His Thought & Action. George H. Williams. 352p. 1980. 14.95 (ISBN 0-8164-0473-9). Seabury.

Mind of Napoleon: A Selection of His Written & Spoken Words. J. Christopher Herold. LC 55-9068. 1955. pap. 6.95 (ISBN 0-231-08523-0). Columbia U Pr.

Mind of Primitive Man. rev. ed. Franz Boas. 1965. pap. text ed. 3.50 o.s.i. (ISBN 0-02-904500-2). Free Pr.

Mind of St. Paul. William Barclay. LC 75-9310. 256p. 1975. pap. 5.95 (ISBN 0-06-060471-9, RD110, HarpR). Har-Row.

Mind of the Founder: Sources of the Political Thought of James Madison. rev. ed. Marvin Meyers. 400p. 1981. 12.50 (ISBN 0-87451-201-8). U Pr of New Eng.

Mind of the Founder: Sources of the Political Thought of James Madison. Ed. by Marvin Meyers. LC 72-158723. (American Heritage Ser: No. 39). 1973. pap. 10.95 (ISBN 0-672-60054-4). Bobbs.

Mind of the Horse. R. H. Smythe. (Illus.). 10.50 (ISBN 0-85131-150-4, Dist. by Sporting Book Center). J A Allen.

Mind of the Maker. Dorothy L. Sayers. Repr. of 1941 ed. lib. bdg. 20.50x (ISBN 0-8371-3372-6, SAMM). Greenwood.

Mind of the Maker. Dorothy L. Sayers. LC 78-19503. 1979. pap. 4.95 (ISBN 0-06-067071-1, RD 295, HarpR). Har-Row.

Mind of the Middle Ages: An Historical Survey: A. D. 200-1500. 3rd rev. ed. Frederick B. Artz. LC 79-16259. 1980. lib. bdg. 20.00x (ISBN 0-226-02839-9); pap. 7.50 (ISBN 0-226-02840-2, P859, Phoen). U. of Chicago Pr.

Mind of the Old South. rev. ed. Clement Eaton. LC 67-11648. (Walter Lynwood Fleming Lectures). (Illus.). 1967. 20.00x (ISBN 0-8071-0443-4); pap. text ed. 8.95 (ISBN 0-8071-0120-6). La State U Pr.

Mind Over Matter: The Story of PK. Louisa E. Rhine. LC 70-90224. (Illus.). 1970. 11.95 (ISBN 0-02-602420-9). Macmillan.

Mind Over Murder. William X. Kienzle. (Father Koesler Mystery Ser.). 320p. 1981. 9.95 (ISBN 0-686-69587-9). Andrews & McMeel.

M.I.N.D. Over Weight: How to Stay Slim the Rest of Your Life. W. Macleod & G. Macleod. 1981. pap. 7.95 (ISBN 0-13-583385-X). P-H.

Mind Play: The Creative Uses of Fantasy. Jerome L. Singer & Ellen Switzer. 1980. 13.95 (ISBN 0-13-198069-6, Spec); pap. 4.95 (ISBN 0-13-198051-3, Spec). P-H.

Mind-Reach. Russell Targ & Harold Puthoff. 1976. 8.95 o.p. (ISBN 0-440-05688-8). Delacorte.

Mind Song. Donna Swanson. 1978. pap. text ed. 2.95x (ISBN 0-8358-0364-3). Upper Room.

Mind Stimulative Correlations in Art Education. Frederick H. Daniels. (Illus.). 110p. 1981. Repr. of 1909 ed. 37.85 (ISBN 0-89901-024-5). Found Class Reprints.

Mind Teasers: Logic Puzzles & Games of Deduction. George J. Summers. LC 77-79511. (Illus.). (gr. 6 up). 1977. 6.95 (ISBN 0-8069-4566-4); PLB 6.69 (ISBN 0-8069-4567-2). Sterling.

Mind That Found Itself. 5th ed. Clifford W. Beers. LC 80-5256. (Contemporary Communities Health Ser). 232p. 1981. 14.95 (ISBN 0-8229-3442-6); pap. 6.95 (ISBN 0-8229-5324-2). U of Pittsburgh Pr.

Mind to Murder. P. D. James. 1976. pap. 2.25 (ISBN 0-445-03154-9). Popular Lib.

Mind Tool: Computers & Their Impact on Society. 2nd ed. Neill Graham. (Illus.). 1980. pap. 13.50 (ISBN 0-8299-0272-4); instrs.' manual avail. (ISBN 0-8299-0483-2); study guide avail. (ISBN 0-8299-0350-X). West Pub.

Mind Traders. J. Hunter Holly. (YA) 5.95 (ISBN 0-685-07448-X, Avalon). Bouregy.

Mind Trips to Help You Lose Weight. Frances M. Stern et al. LC 76-44202. 192p. 1981. pap. 2.25 (ISBN 0-87216-786-0). Playboy Pbks.

Mind Unfolded: Essays on Psychology's Historic Texts. Daniel N. Robinson. 1978. 24.00 (ISBN 0-89093-207-7); pap. 8.00 (ISBN 0-89093-209-3). U Pubns Amer.

Mind Your Own Business. Michael Rosen. LC 74-9969. (Illus.). 96p. (gr. 3 up). 1974. 8.95 (ISBN 0-87599-209-9). S G Phillips.

Mind Your Own Business, Be Your Own Boss. M. Winter. 1980. 12.95 (ISBN 0-13-583468-6); pap. 6.95 (ISBN 0-13-583450-3). P-H.

Mindanao Mission: Archbishop Patrick Cronin's Forty Years in the Phillipines. Edward Fischer. 1979. 8.95 (ISBN 0-8164-0412-7). Crossroad NY.

Mindbenders. Jake Quinn. (Shannon Ser: No. 3). 1975. pap. 1.25 o.p. (ISBN 0-685-51412-9, LB226ZK, Leisure Bks). Nordon Pubns.

Mindbenders. Jack Sparks. LC 79-4290. 1977. pap. 4.95 (ISBN 0-8407-5686-0). Nelson.

Mindbreaker. Arthur Mather. 1980. 10.95 (ISBN 0-440-05294-7). Delacorte.

Mindbridge. Joe Haldeman. 1977. pap. 1.95 (ISBN 0-380-01689-3, 33605). Avon.

Minder: The Story of the Courtship, Call & Conflicts of John Ledger, Minder & Minister, 1900. Frederick R. Smith. Ed. by Robert L. Wolff. Bd. with Coming of the Preachers: A Tale of the Rise of Methodism, 1901. (Victorian Fiction Ser). 1975. lib. bdg. 66.00 (ISBN 0-8240-1590-8). Garland Pub.

Mindful Militants. T. Sheridan. LC 74-17503. 352p. 1976. 35.50 (ISBN 0-521-20680-4). Cambridge U Pr.

Minding My Own Business: Entrepreneurial Women Share Their Secrets for Success. Marjorie McVicar & Julia F. Craig. 425p. 1981. 12.95 (ISBN 0-399-90116-7). Marek.

Mindreader. C. T. Cline, Jr. LC 80-2737. 336p. 1981. 13.95 (ISBN 0-385-17372-5). Doubleday.

Minds & Machines. Ed. by Alan R. Anderson. (Orig.). 1964. pap. 7.95 ref. ed. (ISBN 0-13-583393-0). P-H.

Mind's Eye. Robert Sommer. 1978. 9.95 o.p. (ISBN 0-440-03950-9). Delacorte.

Mind's Eye of Richard Buckminster Fuller. Donald W. Robertson. 1976. 7.00 (ISBN 0-533-23314-3). Robertson.

Mind's Road to God. Saint Bonaventura. Tr. by George Boas. 1953. pap. 2.50 (ISBN 0-672-60195-8, LLA32). Bobbs.

Mindscapes: Poems for the Real World. Ed. by Richard Peck. LC 70-146821. (gr. 7 up). 1971. 5.95 o.s.i. (ISBN 0-440-05644-6). Delacorte.

Mindstorms: Children, Computers, & Powerful Ideas. Seymour Papert. LC 79-5200. 1980. 12.95 (ISBN 0-465-04627-4). Basic.

Mindszenty. Cardinal Jozsef Mindszenty. (Illus.). 480p. 1974. 10.00 o.s.i. (ISBN 0-02-585050-4). Macmillan.

Mindy. June Strong. LC 77-77429. 1977. 11.95 (ISBN 0-8127-0139-9). Southern Pub.

Mine Eyes Have Seen the Glory. Anita Bryant. (Illus.). 160p. 1970. 5.95 o.p. (ISBN 0-8007-0375-8); pap. 1.50 o.p. (ISBN 0-8007-8098-1, Spire Bks). Revell.

Mine for Keeps. Jean Little. (Illus.). (gr. 4-6). 1962. 8.95 (ISBN 0-316-52793-9). Little.

Mine for Keeps. Jean Little. (gr. 4-6). 1973. pap. 1.75 (ISBN 0-671-42455-6). Archway.

Mine Ventilation & Air Conditioning. Howard L. Hartman. (Illus.). 1961. 27.50 (ISBN 0-8260-3860-3, Pub. by Wiley-Interscience). Wiley.

Mine Will, Said John. Helen V. Griffith. LC 79-27886. (Illus.). 32p. (ps). 1980. 7.95 (ISBN 0-688-80267-2); PLB 7.63 (ISBN 0-688-84267-4). Greenwillow.

Mine, Yours, Ours. Burton Albert. LC 77-9408. (Self-Starter Books). (Illus.). (ps). 1977. 6.50g (ISBN 0-8075-5148-1). A Whitman.

Mineral & Energy Resources of the USSR: A Selected Bibliography of Sources in English. Compiled by Eugene A. Alexandrov. 160p. 1980. 10.00 (ISBN 0-913312-21-5). Am Geol.

Mineral Atlas: Pacific Northwest. Alan A. DeLucia et al. LC 80-52312. (Orig.). 1980. pap. 8.95 (ISBN 0-89301-072-3). U Pr of Idaho.

Mineral Belt: Old South Park-Across the Great Divide, Vol. 2. David S. Digerness. (Illus.). 416p. 49.00 (ISBN 0-913582-21-2). Sundance.

Mineral Belt: Old South Park-Denver to Leadville, Vol. 1. David S. Digerness. (Illus.). 416p. 49.00 (ISBN 0-913582-20-4). Sundance.

Mineral Belt: Old South Park Railroads, 2 vols. new ed. David S. Digerness. Ed. by Russ Collman. (Illus.). 1977. Vol. 1. 49.00 (ISBN 0-913582-20-4); Vol. 2. 49.00 (ISBN 0-913582-21-2). Sundance.

Mineral Chemistry of the Metal Sulfides. David J. Vaughan & James R. Craig. LC 76-62585. (Earth Science Ser). (Illus.). 1978. 59.50 (ISBN 0-521-21489-0). Cambridge U Pr.

Mineral Deposits of the Deep-Ocean Floor. K. O. Emery & Brian J. Skinner. LC 78-59181. 1978. pap. 4.95x (ISBN 0-8448-1363-X). Crane-Russak Co.

Mineral Metabolism: An Advanced Treatise, 3 vols. Ed. by C. L. Comar & Felix Bronner. Incl. Vol. 1, Pt. A. Principles, Processes & Systems. 1960. 49.00 (ISBN 0-12-183201-5); Vol. 1, Pt. B. Principles, Processes & Systems. 1961. 61.00 (ISBN 0-12-183241-4); Vol. 2, Pt. A. The Elements. 1964. 68.00 (ISBN 0-12-183202-3); Set. 52.00 (ISBN 0-686-66613-5); Vol. 2, Pt. B. The Elements. 1962. 64.00 (ISBN 0-12-183242-2); 41.00 (ISBN 0-686-66614-3); Vol. 3. Supplementary Volume. 1969. 55.00 (ISBN 0-12-183250-3). 240.75 set (ISBN 0-685-23116-X). Acad Pr.

Mineral Nutrition of Fruit Trees. Ed. by D. Atkinson et al. LC 79-41647. (Studies in the Agricultural & Food Sciences). 1980. text ed. 79.95 (ISBN 0-408-10662-X). Butterworths.

Mineral Nutrition of Legumes in Tropical & Subtropical Soils. 415p. 1978. 29.00 (ISBN 0-643-00311-8, CO14, CSIRO). Unipub.

Mineral Optics: Principles & Techniques. William R. Phillips. LC 78-134208. (Geology Ser.). (Illus.). 1971. text ed. 28.95x (ISBN 0-7167-0251-7). W H Freeman.

Mineral Processing Plant Design. 2nd ed. Ed. by A. L. Mular & R. B. Bhappu. LC 79-57345. (Illus.). 958p. 1980. text ed. 27.00x (ISBN 0-89520-269-7). Soc Mining Eng.

Mineral Processing Technology: An Introcuction to the Practical Aspects of Ore Treatment & Mineral Recovery. 2nd ed. B. A. Wills. LC 80-41698. (International Series on Materials Science & Technology: Vol. 29). (Illus.). 450p. 1981. 60.00 (ISBN 0-08-027322-X); pap. 20.00 (ISBN 0-08-027323-8). Pergamon.

Mineral Resources & the Economy of the USSR. Alexander Sutulov. LC 73-10266. (Illus.). 1973. 10.00 o.p. (ISBN 0-87930-101-5). Miller Freeman.

Mineral Resources & the Environment. National Research Council. 1975. pap. 8.25 (ISBN 0-309-02343-2). Natl Acad Pr.

Mineral Resources of South Texas: Region Served Through the Port of Corpus Christi. R. A. Maxwell. (Illus.). 140p. 1962. 3.50 (RI 43). Bur Econ Geology.

Mineral Resources of the Colorado River Industrial Development Association Area. J. W. Dietrich & J. T. Lonsdale. (Illus.). 84p. 1958. 1.50 (RI 37). Bur Econ Geology.

Mineral Studies with Isotopes in Domestic Animals. (Illus., Orig.). 1971. pap. 12.00 (ISBN 92-0-111371-4, IAEA). Unipub.

Mineral Tolerance of Domestic Animals. Subcommittee on Toxicity in Animals, Board on Agricultural & Renewable Resources. 1980. pap. text ed. 15.50 (ISBN 0-309-03022-6). Natl Acad Pr.

Mineral Tolerances of Domestic Animals. 1980. 16.00 (ISBN 0-309-03022-6). Natl Acad Pr.

Mineralogical Applications of Crystal Field Theory. R. G. Burns. LC 77-85714. (Earth Sciences Ser). (Illus.). 1969. 29.50 (ISBN 0-521-07610-2). Cambridge U Pr.

Mineralogy. 5th ed. Edward H. Kraus & W. F. Hunt. (Illus.). 1959. text ed. 23.00 o.p. (ISBN 0-07-035388-3, C). McGraw.

Mineralogy, Chemistry, & Physics of Tropical Soils with Variable Charge Clays. Goro Uehara & Gavin P. Gillman. (Tropical Agriculture Ser.). 1981. lib. bdg. 27.50x (ISBN 0-89158-484-6). Westview.

Mineralogy: Concepts, Descriptions, Determinations. Leonard G. Berry & Brian Mason. LC 59-7841. (Geology Ser.). (Illus.). 1959. 26.95x (ISBN 0-7167-0203-7). W H Freeman.

Mineralogy for Students. M. H. Battey. (Illus.). 1975. pap. text ed. 17.95 (ISBN 0-582-44159-5). Longman.

Minerals. Andrew Clark. (Illus.). 128p. 1979. 8.95 (ISBN 0-600-36313-9). Transatlantic.

Minerals & How to Study Them. 3rd ed. E. S. Dana & C. S. Hurlbut. pap. 13.50 (ISBN 0-471-19195-7). Wiley.

Minerals & Man. Cornelius Hurlbut, Jr. (Illus.). 1975. 20.00 o.p. (ISBN 0-394-43625-3). Random.

Minerals & Your Health. Len Mervyn. LC 80-84442. 144p. 1981. Repr. 9.95 (ISBN 0-686-69376-0). Keats.

Minerals: Kill or Cure. rev. ed. Ruth Adams & Frank Murray. 366p. (Orig.). 1974. pap. 1.95 (ISBN 0-915962-16-0). Larchmont Bks.

Minerals Transportion: Proceedings, Vol. 3. International Symposium on the Transportation & Handling of Minerals, 3rd British Columbia, Canada, Oct. 1979. Ed. by George O. Argall, Jr. LC 76-189985. (World Mining Bk.). 1980. pap. 50.00 (ISBN 0-87930-080-9). Miller Freeman.

Miners. Robert Wallace. LC 73-94242. (Old West). (Illus.). (gr. 5 up). 1976. kivar 12.96 (ISBN 0-8094-1539-9, Pub. by Time-Life). Silver.

Miners. Ed. by Robert Wallace. (Old West Ser.). (Illus.). 1976. 12.95 (ISBN 0-8094-1537-2). Time-Life.

Miners & Merchants in Bourbon Mexico, 1763-1810. D. Brading. LC 74-123666. (Cambridge Latin American Studies: No. 10). (Illus.). 1971. 44.50 (ISBN 0-521-07874-1). Cambridge U Pr.

Miners, Merchants & Missionaries: The Roles of Missionaries & Pioneer Churches in the Colorado Gold Rush & Its Aftermath, 1858-1870. Alice C. Cochran. LC 80-16895. (ATLA Monographs: No. 15). x, 287p. 1980. 15.00 (ISBN 0-8108-1325-4). Scarecrow.

Miners: One Union, One Industry: A History of the National Union of Mineworkers 1939-46. R. Page Arnot. (Illus.). 1979. text ed. 30.00x (ISBN 0-04-331074-5). Allen Unwin.

Miners, Quarrymen & Saltworkers. Ed. by Raphael Samuel. (History Workshop Ser.). (Illus.). 1977. 22.00 (ISBN 0-7100-8353-X); pap. 12.50 (ISBN 0-7100-8354-8). Routledge & Kegan.

Minerva Nuova Encyclopedia Universale, 8 vols. (Ital.). 1973. including 1 supplement 330.00 o.p. (ISBN 0-8277-3038-1). Maxwell Sci Intl.

Minerva's Stepchild. Helen Forrester. LC 80-26968. 320p. 1981. 9.95 (ISBN 0-8253-0017-7). Beaufort Bks NY.

Mines of Death Valley. L. Burr Belden. (Illus.). 1966. wrappers 2.95 (ISBN 0-910856-16-8). La Siesta.

Minetown, Milltown, Railtown: Life in Canadian Communities of Single Industry. Rex A. Lucas. LC 70-166934. 1971. pap. 7.95 (ISBN 0-8020-6123-0). U of Toronto Pr.

Miney & the Blessing. Miriam E. Mason. (Illus.). (gr. 2-6). 1961. 2.95 o.s.i. (ISBN 0-02-764610-6). Macmillan.

Ming & Qing: Historical Studies in the People's Republic of China. Ed. by Fredric Wakeman, Jr. (China Research Monographs: No. 17). 1981. pap. 8.00 (ISBN 0-912966-27-0). IEAS Ctr Chinese Stud.

Mingled Chime: An Autobiography. Thomas Beecham. LC 76-40182. (Lyric Stage Ser.). Repr. of 1943 ed. 22.50 (ISBN 0-306-70791-8). Da Capo.

Mingled Yarn: Chronicle of a Troubled Family. Beulah Parker. LC 72-75206. 320p. 1972. 15.00x (ISBN 0-300-01568-2); pap. 5.95x (ISBN 0-300-02292-1). Yale U Pr.

Mingling of Heaven & Earth: Yeats' Theory of Theatre. George M. Harper. (New Yeats Papers Ser: No. 10). 48p. 1975. pap. text ed. 5.00x (ISBN 0-85105-269-X, Dolmen Pr). Humanities.

Minhagim: The Customs & Ceremonies of Judaism, Their Origins & Rationale. 2nd corrected ed. Abraham Chill. LC 78-62153. (Illus.). 339p. 1980. 13.95 (ISBN 0-87203-076-8); pap. 7.95 (ISBN 0-87203-077-6). Hermon.

Mini & Microcomputer Control in Industrial Processes: Handbook of Systems Application & Strategies. Ed. by M. Robert Skrokov. 320p. 1980. text ed. 27.50 (ISBN 0-442-27643-5). Van Nos Reinhold.

Mini & Trail Bikes: How to Build Them Yourself. James C. Sparks. (Illus.). 1976. 9.95 (ISBN 0-87690-184-4); pap. 5.95 (ISBN 0-87690-190-9). Dutton.

Mini-Bike Racing. David-Linn Seaver. LC 76-38615. (Speed Sports Ser.). (Illus.). (gr. 9 up). 1972. 6.50 o.p. (ISBN 0-397-31293-8). Lippincott.

Mini Deep-Fry Cookery. Mable Hoffman. LC 77-83277. (Illus.). 1977. 7.95 (ISBN 0-912656-81-6); pap. 5.95 (ISBN 0-912656-80-8). H P Bks.

Mini-Guide to Leadership. Ernest Y. Flores. LC 80-83627. 90p. 1981. perfect bdg. 5.50 (ISBN 0-86548-037-0). Century Twenty One.

Mini-Guide to the Contents of the Books of the Bible. pap. 0.50. Reiner.

Mini-Manual on Nuclear War Survival. Laird M. Wilcox. 1980. pap. cancelled (ISBN 0-933592-12-4). Edit Res Serv.

Mini Meals for Food Service Menu Planning. Eulalia C. Blair. LC 76-7073. (Foodservice Menu Planning Ser.). 1976. 16.50 (ISBN 0-8436-2102-8). CBI Pub.

Mini Meals in Minutes. 7.95 (ISBN 0-916752-09-7). Green Hill.

Mini-Micro Soldering & Wire Wrapping. Murray P. Rosenthal. 1978. pap. 4.75 (ISBN 0-8104-0864-3). Hayden.

Mini-Microcomputer Hardware Design. George D. Kraft & Wing N. Toy. (Illus.). 1978. ref. ed. 24.95 (ISBN 0-13-583807-X). P-H.

Mini Page & Your Newspaper Activity Book. Betty Debnam & Lois Avery. 128p. (gr. k-6). 1980. pap. 5.95 (ISBN 0-8362-4209-2). Andrews & McMeel.

Mini Page Kids' Cookbook. Betty Debnam. 1978. spiral bd. 5.95 (ISBN 0-8362-4202-5). Andrews & McMeel.

Mini Sims Temporaries: Modern Office Simulations 1. Rosemarie McCauley. 1979. pap. 9.95 (ISBN 0-672-97167-4); tchr's. resource 6.67 (ISBN 0-672-97168-2). Bobbs.

Mini Sims Temporaries: Modern Office Simulations 2. Rosemarie McCauley. 1979. pap. 9.95 (ISBN 0-672-97424-X); tchr's. resource 6.67 (ISBN 0-672-97168-2). Bobbs.

Mini Value Plays. Sharon Tell. (gr. 2-3). 1977. pap. text ed. 3.25x (ISBN 0-933892-07-1). Child Focus Co.

Miniature Beer Bottles & Go-Withs: A Price Guide & Reference Manual for Miniature Beer Collectables. Robert E. Kay. LC 80-81282. (Illus.). 166p. (Orig.). 1980. pap. 13.95 (ISBN 0-9604218-0-7). K & K Pubs.

Miniature Crocheting & Knitting for Dollhouses. Rosemary Drysdale. (Illus.). 50p. 1981. pap. 2.00 (ISBN 0-486-23964-0). Dover.

Miniature Dollhouses & Dioramas. Robert Schleicher. LC 80-961. 176p. Date not set. 14.95 (ISBN 0-8019-6905-0); pap. 8.95 (ISBN 0-8019-6906-9). Chilton.

Miniature Gardens. Anne Ashberry. 1977. 9.95 o.p. (ISBN 0-7153-7289-0). David & Charles.

Miniature Gardens. 1.95 (ISBN 0-686-21152-9). Bklyn Botanic.

Miniature Lamp. Frank Smith & Ruth Smith. (Illus.). 288p. 1981. Repr. of 1968 ed. 18.95 (ISBN 0-916838-44-7). Schiffer.

Miniature Macrame for Dollhouses. Marjorie Ames. Date not set. pap. price not set (ISBN 0-486-23960-8). Dover. Postponed.

Miniature Mysteries: One Hundred Malicious Little Mystery Stories. Isaac Asimov et al. 256p. 1981. 12.95 (ISBN 0-8008-5251-6). Taplinger.

Miniature Needlepoint Rugs for Dollhouses Charted for Easy Use. Susan McBaine. (Dover Needlework Ser). (Illus., Orig.). 1976. pap. 1.75 (ISBN 0-486-23388-X). Dover.

Miniature Scenic Modelling. Jack Kine. (Illus., Orig.). 1979. pap. 7.50x (ISBN 0-85242-650-X). Intl Pubns Serv.

Miniature Schnauzer Guide. John F. Gordon. 6.98 o.p. (ISBN 0-385-01579-8). Doubleday.

Miniature Schnauzers. John F. Gordon. Ed. by Christina Foyle. (Foyle's Handbks). 1972. 3.95 (ISBN 0-685-55812-6). Palmetto Pub.

Miniature Shrubs. Royton E. Heath. (Illus.). 1978. 10.95 o.p. (ISBN 0-214-20477-4, 8053, Dist. by Arco). Barrie & Jenkins.

Miniature Trees in the Japanese Style. Gillian E. Severn. (Illus.). 1967. 6.95 (ISBN 0-571-08624-1, Pub. by Faber & Faber). Merrimack Bk Serv.

Miniatures & Bonsai. James U. Crockett & Philip Perl. (Time-Life Encyclopedia of Gardening Ser.). (Illus.). 1979. lib. bdg. 11.96 (ISBN 0-686-51066-6). Silver.

Minibeasts: Stages 1 & 2. Sheila Parker. LC 77-82989. (Science 5-13 Ser.). (Illus.). 1977. pap. text ed. 9.30 (ISBN 0-356-04106-9). Raintree Child.

Minibikes & Minicycles for Beginners. I. G. Edmonds. (gr. 5-7). 1975. pap. 1.25 (ISBN 0-671-29783-X). Archway.

Minibikes & Minicycles for Beginners. I. G. Edmonds. (Illus.). (gr. 5-7). pap. 1.25 (ISBN 0-671-29783-X). PB.

Minicalculators in the Classroom. Joseph R. Caravella. 64p. 1977. pap. 3.50 (ISBN 0-686-63710-0, 1812-5-06). NEA.

Minicomputer in the Laboratory: With Examples Using the PDP-11. James W. Cooper. LC 76-44255. 1977. 22.50 (ISBN 0-471-01883-X, Pub. by Wiley-Interscience). Wiley.

Minicomputer Simplified: An Executive's Guide to the Basics. Carol W. Brown. LC 80-1031. (Illus.). 1980. 12.95 (ISBN 0-02-905130-4). Free Pr.

Minicomputer Systems: Organization, Programming & Applications (PDP-11) 2nd ed. Richard H. Eckhouse, Jr. & L. Robert Morrison. (Illus.). 1979. text ed. 25.00 (ISBN 0-13-583914-9). P-H.

Minicomputer Systems: Structure, Implementation, & Application. Cay Weitzman. (Illus.). 384p. 1974. 24.95 (ISBN 0-13-584227-1). P-H.

Minicomputers. P. C. Sanderson. text ed. 12.95 (ISBN 0-408-00213-1). Butterworths.

Minicomputers in Data Processing & Simulation. Branko Soucek. LC 77-37436. 533p. 1972. 34.50 (ISBN 0-471-81390-7, Pub. by Wiley-Interscience). Wiley.

Minicomputers in on-Line Systems. Martin Healey & David Hebditch. (Computer Systems Ser.). (Illus.). 352p. 1981. text ed. 22.95 (ISBN 0-87626-579-4). Winthrop.

Minicomputers: Low-Cost Computer Power for Management. rev. ed. Donald P. Kennedy. (Illus.). 1979. 15.95 (ISBN 0-8144-5484-4). Am Mgmt.

Minicomputers: Structure & Programming. Theodore Lewis & Jerry Doerr. (Illus.). 1976. text ed. 16.60x (ISBN 0-8104-5642-7). Hayden.

Minigroup Science. Quentin Durham. (Illus.). 232p. (gr. 7-10). 1980. pap. 25.00 (ISBN 0-87879-244-9). Acad Therapy.

Minima Moralia: Reflexionen Aus Dem Beschaedigten Leben. Theodor W. Adorno. (Gesammelte Schriften: Vol. 4). 350p. Date not set. text ed. 24.70 (ISBN 3-518-07496-2, Pub. by Insel Verlag Germany); pap. 16.90 quality paper (ISBN 3-518-07496-2). Suhrkamp.

Minimal Art: A Critical Anthology. Ed. & intro. by Gregory Battcock. 1968. pap. 7.50 (ISBN 0-525-47211-8). Dutton.

Minimal Brain Dysfunction. Eric Denhoff & Leo Stern. LC 78-61473. (Illus.). 208p. 1979. 26.25 (ISBN 0-89352-038-1). Masson Pub.

Minimal Brain Dysfunction: A Prospective Study. Paul L. Nichols & Ta-Chuan Chen. LC 80-18739. 356p. 1981. text ed. 24.95 (ISBN 0-89859-074-4). L Erlbaum Assocs.

Minimal Brain Dysfunction in Children. Paul H. Wender. LC 77-142142. (Personality Processes Ser). 1971. 26.50 (ISBN 0-471-93362-7). Wiley.

Minimum Competency Achievement Testing: Motives, Models, Measures & Consequences. Ed. by Richard M. Jaeger & Carol K. Tittle. LC 79-88823. 1980. 19.50 (ISBN 0-685-96790-5); in copies of 10 17.50 (ISBN 0-685-96791-3). McCutchan.

Minimum Competency Achievement Testing. Ed. by Richard Jaeger & Carol K. Title. 487p. 18.25 (ISBN 0-8211-0909-X); institutional price 21.25. Am Educ Res.

Minimum Competency Testing. Rodney P. Riegel & Ned B. Lovell. LC 79-93113. (Fastback Ser.: No. 137). (Orig.). 1980. pap. 0.75 (ISBN 0-87367-137-6). Phi Delta Kappa.

Minimum Level of Unemployment & Public Policy. Frank C. Pierson. 194p. 1980. text ed. 8.50 (ISBN 0-911558-76-4); pap. text ed. 5.50 (ISBN 0-911558-75-6). Upjohn Inst.

Minimum State: Beyond Party Politics. Brian Crozier. 1979. 27.00 (ISBN 0-241-10242-1, Pub. by Hamish Hamilton England). David & Charles.

Minimum Wages: Issues & Evidence. Finis Welch. 1978. pap. 4.25 (ISBN 0-8447-3308-3). Am Enterprise.

Mining & Petroleum Legislation. Organization of American States. LC 78-16150. (Binder 1 & supplement). 1978. per. binder 75.00 (ISBN 0-379-20381-2). Oceana.

Mining & Petroleum Legislation, Release 1. Organization of American States. 1980. 35.00 (ISBN 0-379-20381-2). Oceana.

Mining & Public Policy in Alaska: Mineral Policy, the Public Lands, & Economic Development. Arlon R. Tussing & Gregg K. Erickson. LC 72-629327. (Joint Institute of Social & Economic Research Ser.: No. 21). 142p. 1969. pap. 5.00 (ISBN 0-295-95118-4). U of Wash Pr.

Mining Annual Review 1980. Mining Journal Editors. 200p. 1980. 60.00x (Pub. by Mining Journal England). State Mutual Bk.

Mining Chemicals. 1980. 850.00 (ISBN 0-89336-262-X, C-021). BCC.

Mining Coal. John Davey. (Junior Reference Ser.). (Illus.). 64p. 7.95 (ISBN 0-7136-1596-6). Dufour.

Mining Engineers' Handbook, 2 vols. 3rd ed. R. Peele. (Engineering Handbook Ser.). 1941. Set. 75.00 (ISBN 0-471-67716-7, Pub. by Wiley-Interscience). Wiley.

Mining for Development in the Third World: Multinationals, State Enterprises & the International Economy. Ed. by S. Sideri & S. Johns. LC 80-20930. (Pergamon Policy Studies on International Development). 376p. 1980. 35.00 (ISBN 0-08-026308-9). Pergamon.

Mining Frontiers of the Far West,1848-1880. Rodman W. Paul. LC 63-8818. (Histories of the American Frontier Ser). (Illus.). 256p. 1980. pap. 6.50x (ISBN 0-8263-0315-3). U of NM Pr.

Mining in the Outer Continental Shelf & in the Deep Ocean. Marine Board, Assembly of Engineering, National Research Council. 152p. 1975. pap. 6.25 (ISBN 0-309-02405-6). Natl Acad Pr.

Mining in Western Australia. Rex T. Prider. 328p. 1980. 22.50x (ISBN 0-85564-153-3, Pub. by U of West Australia Pr Australia). Intl Schol Bk Serv.

Mining Methods & Equipment. Mining Information Services. 224p. 1980. 16.50 (ISBN 0-07-039794-5). McGraw.

Miniquaternion Geometry. Thomas G. Room & P. B. Kirkpatrick. LC 79-123347. (Tracts in Mathematics: No. 60). 1971. 28.95 (ISBN 0-521-07926-8). Cambridge U Pr.

Minireviews of the Neurosciences from Life Sciences, Vols. 13-15. Ed. by Bernard B. Brodie & R. Bressler. LC 75-8733. 493p. 1975. text ed. 32.00 combined ed. (ISBN 0-08-019724-8); pap. text ed. 16.00 combined ed. (ISBN 0-08-019723-X). Pergamon.

Minister & the Care of Souls. Daniel D. Williams. LC 76-62929. (Orig.). 1977. pap. 4.95 (ISBN 0-06-318071-5, RD 213, HarpR). Har-Row.

Minister As Shepherd. Jefferson. (Orig.). 1970. pap. 1.75 (ISBN 0-87508-290-4). Chr Lit.

Minister Is Leaving: A Project Test Pattern Book in Parish Development. Celia A. Hahn. 1974. pap. 3.95 (ISBN 0-8164-2099-8). Crossroad NY.

Minister? Pastor? Prophet? Grassroots Leadership in the Churches. Lucas Grollenberg et al. 112p. (Dutch.). 1981. 9.95 (ISBN 0-8245-0017-2). Crossroad NY.

Ministerial Ethics. John W. Duggar. 1979. pap. 1.00 o.p. (ISBN 0-89114-002-6). Baptist Pub Hse.

Ministerial Ethics & Etiquette. rev. ed. Nolan B. Harmon. (Series C). (Illus.). 1978. pap. 5.95 (ISBN 0-687-27033-2). Abingdon.

Ministering Children. Maria L. Charlesworth. Ed. by Alison Lurie & Justin G. Schiller. LC 75-32166. (Classics of Children's Literature Ser.: 1621-1932). PLB 38.00 (ISBN 0-8240-2279-3). Garland Pub.

Ministering Church. Gaines S. Dobbins. LC 60-9530. 1960. 7.50 (ISBN 0-8054-2505-5). Broadman.

Ministering to the Aging. Bartholomeo J. Laurello. LC 79-90992. (Paths of Life Ser.). 90p. (Orig.). 1979. pap. 2.45 (ISBN 0-8091-2268-5). Paulist Pr.

Ministering to the Divorced Catholic. Ed. by James J. Young. LC 78-61731. 1978. pap. 6.95 (ISBN 0-8091-2142-5). Paulist Pr.

Ministering to Youth. Cecil R. Guiles. 1973. 4.50 (ISBN 0-87148-551-6); pap. 3.50 (ISBN 0-87148-552-4); instrs. kit 4.50 (ISBN 0-87148-834-5). Pathway Pr.

Ministerio Ideal, 2 vols, Vols. 1 & 2. C. H. Spurgeon. Vol. 1. 2.30 o.p. (ISBN 0-686-12558-4); Vol. 2. 2.60 o.p. (ISBN 0-686-12559-2). Banner of Truth.

Minister's Charge; Or, The Apprenticeship of Lemuel Barker. W. D. Howells. LC 77-22213. (Selected Edition of W. D. Howells: Center for Editions of American Authors: Vol. 14). (Illus.). 1978. 20.00x (ISBN 0-253-33855-7). Ind U Pr.

Minister's Guide for Special Occasions. Zeno C. Tharp. 1966. 5.25 (ISBN 0-87148-553-2). Pathway Pr.

Minister's Manual: Doran's Nineteen Eighty Edition. Charles L. Wallis. LC 25-21658. 1979. 8.95 o.p. (ISBN 0-06-069025-9, HarpR). Har-Row.

Ministrando Con Musica. Tr. by Betty L. Grahams. (Portugese Bks.). (Port.). 1979. write for info. (ISBN 0-8297-0732-8). Life Pubs Intl.

Ministrando Con Musica. Tr. by Betty J. Grams. (Spanish Bks.). 1978. 2.50 (ISBN 0-8297-0584-8). Life Pubs Intl.

Ministries for Women. (Aglow Bible Study: Bk. 8). 64p. 1975. 1.95 (ISBN 0-930756-16-9, 4220-8). Women's Aglow.

Ministries: Sharing God's Gifts. James B. Dunning. LC 80-52058. (Illus.). 136p. (Orig.). 1980. pap. 5.95 (ISBN 0-88489-123-2). St Marys.

Ministries Through Non-Parish Institutions. William E. Ramsden. LC 80-22294. (Into Our Third Century Ser.). 96p. (Orig.). 1981. pap. 3.95 (ISBN 0-687-27037-5). Abingdon.

Ministry. Edward Schillebeeckx. 160p. (Dutch.). 1981. 12.95 (ISBN 0-8245-0030-X). Crossroad NY.

Ministry & Education in Conversation. Ed. by Mary C. Boys. LC 80-53204. 160p. (Orig.). 1981. pap. 6.95 (ISBN 0-88489-126-7). St Mary's.

Ministry & Imagination. Urban T. Holmes. 1976. 10.95 (ISBN 0-8164-0292-2). Crossroad NY.

Ministry Explosion. Robert J. Hater. 96p. (Orig.). 1979. pap. 3.25 (ISBN 0-697-01709-5). Wm C Brown.

Ministry of Angels. Joy Shell. 1977. pap. 3.95 (ISBN 0-8065-0586-9). Citadel Pr.

Ministry of Culture: Politics in Art. Michael M. Mooney. 1980. 14.95 (ISBN 0-671-61021-X, Wyndham). S&S.

Ministry of Healing. Ellen G. White. 1942. pap. 4.95 o.p. (ISBN 0-8163-0123-9, 13541-8); pap. 6.50 deluxe ed. (ISBN 0-8163-0124-7, 13540-0). Pacific Pr Pub Assn.

Ministry of Healing: The History of the Alexian Brothers from the French Revolution to the Present. Christopher J. Kauffman. 1978. 15.00 (ISBN 0-8164-0387-2). Crossroad NY.

Ministry of Intercession. F. J. Huegel. LC 76-15861. (Orig.). 1971. pap. 1.75 (ISBN 0-87123-365-7, 200365). Bethany Fell.

Ministry of Music in the Church. Victor L. Delamont. 1980. pap. 5.95 (ISBN 0-8024-5673-1). Moody.

Ministry of Sovereign Authority. Dennis Hart. 1978. 4.50 o.p. (ISBN 0-682-49119-5). Exposition.

Ministry of the Spirit. Adoniran J. Gordon. 1964. pap. 2.45 (ISBN 0-87123-366-5, 210366). Bethany Fell.

Ministry to Word & Sacraments: History & Theology. Bernard Cooke. LC 75-36459. 688p. 1980. pap. 14.95 (ISBN 0-8006-1440-2, 1-1440). Fortress.

Ministry with the Aging. Ed. by William M. Clements. LC 80-7739. 288p. 1981. 11.95 (ISBN 0-06-061496-X, HarpR). Har-Row.

Ministry with Young Adults. Luella H. Slover. 1980. pap. 3.00 (ISBN 0-8309-0283-X). Herald Hse.

MiniVacations, U.S.A. Karen Cure. (Illus.). 256p. (Orig.). 1976. pap. 6.95 o.p. (ISBN 0-695-80529-0). Follett.

Minneapolis Rehearsals: Tyrone Guthrie Directs Hamlet. Alfred Rossi. LC 70-115496. 1970. 23.75x (ISBN 0-520-01719-6). U of Cal Pr.

Minnesota: A History. William E. Lass. (States & the Nation Ser.). (Illus.). 1977. 12.95 (ISBN 0-393-05651-1, Co-Pub. by AASLH); pap. 3.95 (ISBN 0-393-00937-8). Norton.

Minnesota: A State Guide. Federal Writers' Project. 545p. 1938. Repr. 49.00 (ISBN 0-403-02173-1). Somerset Pub.

Minnesota & Manitoba One Hundred Years Ago. Powell & Van Dyke. (Illus.). pap. 3.50 (ISBN 0-89540-056-1). Sun Pub.

Minnesota Birds: Where, When, & How Many. Janet C. Green & Robert B. Janssen. LC 74-16980. (Illus.). 1980. pap. 6.95 (ISBN 0-8166-0959-4). U of Minn Pr.

Minnesota Centennial Cookbook: One Hundred Years of Good Cooking. 7th print. ed. Ed. by Virginia Huck & Ann H. Andersen. LC 58-12061. 191p. 1958. pap. 3.00 (ISBN 0-87351-014-3). Minn Hist.

Minnesota Connection. Al Palmquist & John Stone. pap. cancelled o.s.i. (ISBN 0-681-12881-X, 698511). Omega Pubns OR.

Minnesota Heritage Cookbook. Ed. by Sue Zelickson et al. LC 79-52859. (Illus.). 1979. 6.00 (ISBN 0-9602796-0-1). Am Cancer Minn.

Minnesota Legal Forms: Bankruptcy. Michael P. Wagner. Ed. by Mason Publishing Staff. 150p. 1981. ring binder 15.00 (ISBN 0-917126-92-0). Mason Pub.

Minnesota Legal Forms-Commercial Real Estate. John M. Miller. Ed. by Mason Publishing Staff. 150p. 1981. ring binder 15.00 (ISBN 0-917126-89-0). Mason Pub.

Minnesota Legal Forms-Criminal Law. Mattox. 1981. ring binder 15.00 (ISBN 0-917126-84-X). Mason Pub.

Minnesota Legal Forms-Family Law. Daniels McLean. Ed. by Mason Publishing Company Staff. (Minnesota Legal Forms 1981 Ser.). 150p. 1981. ring binder 15.00 (ISBN 0-917126-85-8). Mason Pub.

Minnesota Legal Forms-Personal Injury. Gary E. Stoneking. Ed. by Mason Publishing Staff. 150p. 1981. ring binder 15.00 (ISBN 0-917126-93-9). Mason Pub.

Minnesota Legal Forms-Real Estate. Kathleen Roer. Ed. by Mason Publishing Company Staff. (Minnesota Legal Forms 1981 Ser.). 150p. 1981. ring binder 15.00 (ISBN 0-917126-86-6). Mason Pub.

Minnesota Life & Health. 1979. 15.50 (ISBN 0-930868-17-X). Merritt Co.

Minnesota Multiphasic Personality Inventory: A Comprehensive, Annotated Bibliography 1966-1975. Earl S. Taulbee et al. 1981. write for info. (ISBN 0-87875-161-0). Whitston Pub.

Minnesota Property & Casualty. 1980. 15.50 (ISBN 0-930868-18-8). Merritt Co.

Minnesota State Industrial Directory, 1980. State Industrial Directories Corp. 1980. pap. 50.00 (ISBN 0-89910-003-1). State Indus Dir.

Minnesota: State of Beauty. Charles Wechsler. (Illus.). 96p. 1981. pap. 10.95 (ISBN 0-931714-12-5). Nodin Pr.

Minnesota Strip. Peter McCurtin. 1979. pap. 1.75 (ISBN 0-505-51333-1). Tower Bks.

Minnesota Supplement for Modern Real Estate Practice. 3rd ed. Edward J. Driscoll. 184p. (Orig.). 1980. pap. 10.95 (ISBN 0-88462-324-6). Real Estate Ed Co.

Minnesota Vikings. Julian May. (NFL Today). (Illus.). (gr. 3-6). 1977. PLB 6.45 (ISBN 0-87191-594-4); pap. 2.95 (ISBN 0-686-67477-4). Creative Ed.

Minnesota Walk Book: A Guide to Hiking & Cross-Country Skiing in the Pioneer Region. James W. Buchanan. (Minnesota Walk Book Ser.: Vol. 5). (Illus.). 59p. (Orig.). 1979. pap. 4.50 (ISBN 0-931714-07-9). Nodin Pr.

Minnesota's Boundary with Canada: Its Evolution Since 1783. William E. Lass. LC 80-21644. (Minnesota Public Affairs Center Publication Ser.). 141p. 1980. 16.50 (ISBN 0-87351-147-6); pap. 8.75 (ISBN 0-87351-153-0). Minn Hist.

Minnie Muenscher's Herb Cookbook. Minnie W. Muenscher. LC 77-90908. (Illus.). 224p. 1978. 11.50 (ISBN 0-8014-1166-1). Comstock.

Minnie Pearl Cooks. Minnie Pearl. LC 73-104838. (Illus.). 1977. 4.95 o.s.i. (ISBN 0-87695-137-X). Aurora Pubs.

Minnie Santangelo & the Evil Eye. Anthony Mancini. 1979. pap. 1.75 o.p. (ISBN 0-449-23967-5, Crest). Fawcett.

Minnie Santangelo's Mortal Sin. Anthony Mancini. 1976. pap. 1.50 o.p. (ISBN 0-449-23024-4, Crest). Fawcett.

Minnow Family. Laurence Pringle. LC 75-28335. (Illus.). 64p. (gr. 3-7). 1976. 6.25 (ISBN 0-688-22060-6); PLB 6.00 (ISBN 0-688-32060-0). Morrow.

Minoan & Mycehaean Art. Reynold Higgins. (World of Art Ser.). (Illus.). 1967. pap. 9.95 (ISBN 0-19-519918-9). Oxford U Pr.

Minoan & Mycenaean Art. rev. ed. Reynold Higgins. (World of Art Ser.). (Illus.). 288p. 1981. 17.95 (ISBN 0-19-520256-2); pap. 9.95 (ISBN 0-19-520257-0). Oxford U Pr.

Minoan Distance: The Symbolism of Travel in D. H. Lawrence. L. D. Clark. LC 80-18844. 1980. text ed. 25.00x (ISBN 0-8165-0707-4); pap. 12.95 (ISBN 0-8165-0712-0). U of Ariz Pr.

Minoan Linear A. David W. Packard. (Illus.). 1974. 20.00x (ISBN 0-520-02580-6). U of Cal Pr.

Minoan Stone Vases. Peter Warren. LC 69-13794. (Cambridge Classical Studies). (Illus.). 1970. 49.50 (ISBN 0-521-07371-5). Cambridge U Pr.

Minobe Tatsukichi: Interpreter of Constitutionalism in Japan. Frank O. Miller. (Center for Japanese & Korean Studies, UC Berkeley). 1965. 23.50x (ISBN 0-520-00865-0). U of Cal Pr.

Minolta Systems Handbook. 2nd ed. J. Cooper. 1979. 34.95 (ISBN 0-13-584581-5, Spec). P-H.

Minolta XD & XG Book. Clyde Reynolds. (Camera Book Series). (Illus.). 128p. 1980. pap. 9.95 (ISBN 0-240-51035-6). Focal Pr.

Minor American Novelists. Ed. by Charles A. Hoyt. LC 70-86184. (Crosscurrents-Modern Critiques Ser.). 160p. 1970. 8.95 (ISBN 0-8093-0447-3). S Ill U Pr.

Minor Auto Body Repair. 2nd ed. (New Automotive Bks.). 208p. 1980. 10.95 (ISBN 0-8019-6939-5); pap. 7.95 (ISBN 0-8019-6940-9). Chilton.

Minor British Poetry 1680-1800: An Anthology. J. Ernest Barlough. LC 73-4878. 1973. 13.00 (ISBN 0-8108-0619-3). Scarecrow.

Minor Educational Writings of Jean-Jacques Rousseau. Ed. by William H. Boyd. LC 62-21561. 1962. pap. text ed. 3.50x (ISBN 0-8077-1113-6). Tchrs Coll.

Minor Elizabethan Drama, Vol. 2. Ed. by Thorndike. 1959. 5.00x o.p. (ISBN 0-460-00492-1, Evman). Dutton.

Minor Law-Books, Vol. 33. Ed. by F. Max Mueller. Tr. by Jolly. (Sacred Books of the East Ser.). 15.00x (ISBN 0-8426-1404-4). Verry.

Minor Poems, Pt. 1. Ed. by George B. Pace & Alfred David. LC 80-5943. (Works of Geoffrey Chaucer Ser., Variorum Ed.: Vol. V). 200p. 1981. 25.00 (ISBN 0-8061-1629-3). U of Okla Pr.

Minor Prophets. rev ed. Charles L. Feinberg. 384p. 1976. 9.95 (ISBN 0-8024-5306-6). Moody.

Minor Prophets: Hosea, Joel, Amos, Obadiah, Jonah, Micah. Gordon Lindsay. (Old Testament Ser.). 1.25 (ISBN 0-89985-156-8). Christ Nations.

Minor Prophets: Nahum, Habakkuk, Zephaniah, Haggai. Zechariah, Malachi. Gordon Lindsay. (Old Testament Ser.). 1.25 (ISBN 0-89985-157-6). Christ Nations.

Minor Prophets of Israel. Irving L. Jensen. (Bible Self-Study Guides Ser.). 112p. (Orig.). 1975. pap. 2.25 (ISBN 0-8024-1028-6). Moody.

Minor Prophets of Judah. Irving L. Jensen. (Bible Self-Study Guide Ser.). 112p. 1976. pap. 2.25 (ISBN 0-8024-1029-4). Moody.

Minor Sexual Deviance: Diagnosis & Pastoral Treatment. Dale H. Ratliff. LC 76-29284. 1976. pap. text ed. 3.95 o.p. (ISBN 0-8403-1605-4). Kendall-Hunt.

Minor Tooth Movement in Children. 2nd ed. Joseph M. Sim. LC 77-24370. (Illus.). 1977. 47.50 (ISBN 0-8016-4616-2). Mosby.

Minor White: Rites & Passages. James B. Hall. LC 77-80023. (Illus.). 144p. 1981. 25.00 (ISBN 0-89381-069-X); pap. 15.00. Aperture.

Minorities & Aging. Jacquelyne J. Jackson. 272p. 1979. pap. text ed. 8.95x (ISBN 0-534-00779-1). Wadsworth Pub.

Minorities & Community Colleges. Ed. by Fontelle Gilbert. 1979. pap. 7.50 (ISBN 0-87117-091-4). Am Assn Comm Jr Coll.

Minorities & Marketing: Research Challenges. Ed. by Alan R. Andreasen & Frederick D. Sturdivant. LC 77-6819. (Illus.). 1977. pap. text ed. 7.00 o.p. (ISBN 0-87757-095-7). Am Mktg.

Minorities & the Police. D. H. Bayley & H. Mendelsohn. LC 69-12119. 1969. 9.95 o.s.i. (ISBN 0-02-901980-X); pap. text ed. 3.50 o.s.i. (ISBN 0-02-901970-2). Free Pr.

Minorities, Gender & Work. Elizabeth M. Almquist. LC 77-4537. 1979. 19.95 (ISBN 0-669-01488-5). Lexington Bks.

Minorities in American History, 6 vols. W. L. Katz. Incl. Vol. 1. Early America: 1492-1812. LC 73-17282 (ISBN 0-531-02676-0, W39); Vol. 2. Slavery to the Civil War: 1812-1865. LC 73-17284 (ISBN 0-531-02677-9, W37); Vol. 3. Reconstruction & National Growth: 1865-1900. LC 73-22475 (ISBN 0-531-02715-5, O20); Vol. 4. From the Progressive Era to the Great Depression: 1900-1929. LC 73-23062 (ISBN 0-531-02716-3, O46); Vol. 5. Years of Strife: 1929-1956 (ISBN 0-531-02785-6, U27); Vol. 6. Modern America: 1957-Present (ISBN 0-531-02821-6). (gr. 6 up). 1974. 4.47 ea. o.p. Watts.

Minorities in the New World: Six Case Studies. Charles Wagley & Marvin Harris. LC 58-12214. 1958. 20.00x (ISBN 0-231-02280-8); pap. 6.00x (ISBN 0-231-08557-5). Columbia U Pr.

Minorities in U. S. Institutions of Higher Education. Frank Brown & Madelon D. Stent. LC 75-19768. (Special Studies). 1977. text ed. 18.95 o.p. (ISBN 0-275-55540-2). Praeger.

Minorities of Southwest China: An Introduction to the Yi - Lolo; & Related Peoples & an Annotated Bibliography. Alain Y. Dessaint. LC 80-80017. (Bibliography Ser.). viii, 373p. 1980. 18.00 (ISBN 0-87536-250-8). HRAFP.

Minority Administrator in Higher Education: Progress, Experiences, & Perspectives. Ed. by George L. Mims. 220p. 1981. text ed. 22.50x (ISBN 0-87073-161-0); pap. text ed. 8.95x (ISBN 0-87073-162-9). Schenkman.

Minority Admissions. Robert L. Bailey & Anne L. Hafner. LC 77-18360. (Illus.). 1978. 21.00 (ISBN 0-669-02095-8). Lexington Bks.

Minority-Dominant Relations: A Sociological Analysis. F. James Davis. LC 77-90659. 1978. pap. text ed. 11.95x (ISBN 0-88295-209-9). AHM Pub.

Minority Economic, Political & Social Development. Jesse E. Gloster. LC 78-62738. 1978. pap. text ed. 17.25 (ISBN 0-8191-0593-7). U Pr of Amer.

Minority Enterprise in Construction. Robert W. Glover. LC 77-10650. (Praeger Special Studies). 22.95 (ISBN 0-275-24070-3). Praeger.

Minority-Ethnic Media Guide. 1981. 65.00 (ISBN 0-685-79886-0). Directories Intl.

Minority Group Participation in Graduate Education. National Board on Graduate Education. LC 76-16850. 1976. pap. 7.00 (ISBN 0-309-02502-8). Natl Acad Pr.

Minority Group Relations. James G. Martin & Clyde W. Franklin. LC 72-97539. 1973. text ed. 14.95x (ISBN 0-675-08953-0). Merrill.

Minority Marketing. LC 80-67815. (Marketing Ser.). 1980. pap. 4.95 (ISBN 0-87251-054-9). Crain Bks.

Minority of Members: Women in the U.S. Congress. Hope Chamberlin. 408p. (RL 10). 1974. pap. 2.25 o.p. (ISBN 0-451-61316-3, ME1316, Ment). NAL.

Minority Politics in Bangladesh. Mohammad G. Kabir. LC 80-900147. 1980. text ed. 17.50x (ISBN 0-7069-1034-6, Pub. by Vikas India). Advent Bk.

Minority Press & the English Crown: A Study in Repression, 1558-1625. Leona Rostenberg. 1971. text ed. 45.75x (ISBN 90-6004-271-9). Humanities.

Minority Status: The Position of Women. Dorothy E. Lee & A. Kay Clifton. LC 79-65259. 155p. 1981. perfect bdg. 13.50 (ISBN 0-86548-044-3). Century Twenty One.

Minority Teachers As Change Agents: A Case Study. Darrell Millner. 1977. pap. text ed. 7.50x (ISBN 0-8191-0136-2). U Pr of Amer.

Minotaur. Benjamin Tammuz. 1981. price not set (H401). NAL.

Minotaur Factor. Stuart Stern. LC 76-49403. 1978. pap. 1.95 o.p. (ISBN 0-87216-370-9). Playboy Pbks.

Minou. Francoise. LC 62-9646. (Illus.). (gr. k-3). 1962. 5.95 (ISBN 0-684-13153-6, ScribJ). Scribner.

Minou: The Halfbreed. a Novel of Self-Discovery. June P. Adams. LC 77-89859. 225p. 1980. 9.95 (ISBN 0-86533-006-9). Amber Crest.

Minstrel-Show Songs. Steven Foster. (Early American Music Ser.). 1979. Repr. of 1863 ed. lib. bdg. 18.50 (ISBN 0-306-77314-7). Da Capo.

Minstrels of the Dawn: The Folk-Protest Singer As a Cultural Hero. Jerome L. Rodnitzky. LC 76-4520. 186p. 1976. 13.95 (ISBN 0-88229-284-6); pap. 7.95 (ISBN 0-88229-427-X). Nelson-Hall.

Minstrelsy Ancient & Modern. William Motherwell. LC 68-24477. 1968. Repr. of 1873 ed. 20.00 (ISBN 0-8103-3415-1). Gale.

Minstrelsy of Maine. Fanny Eckstorm. LC 79-152248. 1971. Repr. of 1927 ed. 20.00 (ISBN 0-8103-3707-X). Gale.

Minstrelsy of the Scottish Border, 4 Vols. Walter Scott. Ed. by T. F. Henderson. LC 67-23924. 1968. Repr. of 1902 ed. Set. 90.00 (ISBN 0-8103-3418-6). Gale.

Minton Pottery & Porcelain of the First Period: 1783-1850. Geoffrey A. Godden. 1978. 29.95 o.p. (ISBN 0-686-01036-1, 8034, Dist. by Arco). Barrie & Jenkins.

Minus Sign. Carlos D. Andrade. Ed. by Virginia De Araujo. 160p. 1980. 15.00x (ISBN 0-933806-03-5). Black Swan CT.

Minus Thirty-One & the Wind Blowing: 9 Reflections About Living on Land. John Haines et al. (Alaskana Book Ser.: No. 37). 150p. (Orig.). 1980. 12.95 (ISBN 0-935094-01-6); pap. 4.95 (ISBN 0-935094-03-2). Alaska Pacific.

Minute for Murder. Nicholas Blake. lib. bdg. 13.95x (ISBN 0-89966-246-3). Buccaneer Bks.

Minutemen & Their World. Robert A. Gross. 1976. 8.95 (ISBN 0-8090-6933-4, AmCen); pap. 4.95 (ISBN 0-8090-0120-9). Hill & Wang.

Minutes of the Commissioners for Detecting & Defeating Conspiracies in the State of New York, 2 vols. Albany County Sessions. Ed. by Victor H. Paltsits. LC 72-1835. (Era of the American Revolution Ser.). (Illus.). 1972. Repr. of 1909 ed. Set. lib. bdg. 95.00 (ISBN 0-306-70504-4). Da Capo.

Minutes of the Philadelphia Baptist Association from AD 1707 to AD 1807. A. D. Gillette. Repr. 15.00 (ISBN 0-686-12341-7). Church History.

Miocene Desmatophocinae (Mammalia: Carnivora) from California. Lawrence G. Barnes. (U. C. Publ. in Geological Sciences: Vol. 89). 1972. pap. 7.00x (ISBN 0-520-09384-4). U of Cal Pr.

Miocene Equidae of the Texas Gulf Coastal Plain. J. H. Quinn. (Illus.). 102p. 1955. 1.75 (PUB 5516). Bur Econ Geology.

Miocene Pinniped Allodesmus. Edward Mitchell. (U. C. Publ. in Geological Sciences: Vol. 61). 1966. pap. 5.00x (ISBN 0-520-09162-0). U of Cal Pr.

Mir iskusstva Group & Russian Art, 1898-1912. Janet Kennedy. LC 76-23633. (Outstanding Dissertations in the Fine Arts - 20th Century). (Illus.). 1977. Repr. lib. bdg. 87.00 (ISBN 0-8240-2702-7). Garland Pub.

Mira. Daoma Winston. LC 80-68544. 288p. 1981. 11.95 (ISBN 0-87795-300-7). Arbor Hse.

Mira De Amescua. James A Castaneda. LC 77-1956. (World Authors Ser.: Spain: No. 449). 1977. lib. bdg. 12.50 (ISBN 0-8057-6285-X). Twayne.

Mira Silverstein's Guide to Upright Stitches. Mira Silverstein. (Illus.). 1977. 9.95 o.p. (ISBN 0-679-50818-X); pap. 3.95 o.p. (ISBN 0-679-50784-1). McKay.

Mirabell: Books of Number. James Merrill. LC 78-4350. 1979. 10.95 (ISBN 0-689-10901-6); pap. 7.95 (ISBN 0-689-11167-3). Atheneum.

Miracle at Joaseiro. Ralph Della Cava. LC 76-127364. (Illus.). 1970. 16.00x (ISBN 0-231-03293-5). Columbia U Pr.

Miracle Cure: Organic Germanium. Kazuhiko Asai. LC 79-91512. (Illus.). 256p. 1980. 12.95 (ISBN 0-87040-474-1). Japan Pubns.

Miracle Happiness. Don Stewart. (Orig.). 1981. pap. 2.95 (ISBN 0-88270-483-4). Logos.

Miracle Hill: The Story of a Navaho Boy. Emerson B. Mitchell & T. D. Allen. 230p. 1967. 10.95 o.p. (ISBN 0-8061-0743-X); pap. 5.95 (ISBN 0-8061-1616-1). U of Okla Pr.

Miracle in the Wilderness. Paul Gallico. 48p. 1975. 4.95 o.s.i. (ISBN 0-440-05714-0). Delacorte.

Miracle Living. Arnold Prater. (Orig.). pap. 2.95 (ISBN 0-89081-125-3). Harvest Hse.

Miracle Makers. J. G. Thompson, Jr. Date not set. 22.50 (ISBN 0-915926-11-3). Magic Ltd.

Miracle Medical Foods. Rex Adams. 304p. (Orig.). 1981. pap. 2.50 (ISBN 0-446-91940-3). Warner Bks.

Miracle Medicine Foods. Rex Adams. LC 77-6245. 1977. pap. 3.95 (ISBN 0-13-585463-6, Reward). P-H.

Miracle Microwave Cookbook. Hyla O'Connor. (Illus.). 160p. 1976. pap. 4.95 o.p. (ISBN 0-89104-044-7). A & W Pubs.

Miracle Mongers & Their Methods: A Complete Expose. Harry Houdini. LC 80-84404. (Skeptic's Bookshelf Ser.). 240p. 1981. Repr. of 1920 ed. 13.95 (ISBN 0-87975-143-6). Prometheus Bks.

Miracle of Anne. Bruce Shelly. 96p. 1974. pap. 3.50 (ISBN 0-911336-55-9). Sci of Mind.

Miracle of Birth. rev. ed. Geoffrey Hodson. LC 80-53950. (Illus.). 100p. 1981. pap. 3.95 (ISBN 0-8356-0545-0). Theos Pub Hse.

Miracle of Democracy in India. N. Khanna. 124p. 1980. 4.50x (ISBN 0-89955-319-2, Pub. by Interprint India). Intl Schol Bk Serv.

Miracle of Dialogue. Reuel L. Howe. 1963. pap. 3.95 (ISBN 0-8164-2047-5, SP9). Crossroad NY.

Miracle of Haitian Art. Selden Rodman. LC 73-81447. 96p. (gr. 9 up). 1974. 6.95 o.p. (ISBN 0-385-07800-5). Doubleday.

Miracle of Love. Charles L. Allen. LC 72-5430. 128p. 1972. 6.95 (ISBN 0-8007-0543-2). Revell.

Miracle of Motivation. George Shinn. 1981. text ed. 8.95 (ISBN 0-8423-4353-9). Tyndale.

Miracle of Natural Self-Cure. Al G. Fabroni. 1981. 6.00 (ISBN 0-8062-1581-X). Carlton.

Miracle of Propolis. Mitja Vosnjak. 1978. pap. 3.95 o.s.i. (ISBN 0-7225-0408-X). Newcastle Pub.

Miracle of the Gods. Erich Von Daniken. 336p. 1976. 8.95 o.p. (ISBN 0-440-05595-4). Delacorte.

Miracle of the Scarlet Thread. Richard Booker. (Orig.). (YA) 1981. pap. 4.95 (ISBN 0-88270-499-0). Logos.

Miracle of the Tulips. Ruth Ann. (Orig.). 1980. pap. 5.50 (ISBN 0-8309-0296-1). Herald Hse.

Miracle of Vision. Arthur J. Freese. LC 76-26226. 1977. 11.95 (ISBN 0-06-011371-5, HarpT). Har-Row.

Miracle Pond. 2nd ed. Wybe J. Van Der Meer. (Illus.). 48p. (gr. 1-4). 1980. PLB 8.49x (ISBN 0-934744-01-7). Vermeer Arts.

Miracle Power for Infinite Riches. Joseph Murphy. 1972. 8.95 (ISBN 0-13-585638-8, Parker); pap. 3.45. P-H.

Miracle Protein. Wade. 10.95 (ISBN 0-13-585653-1). P-H.

Miracle Season. Linda Cline. LC 76-18070. (YA) 1976. 6.95 o.p. (ISBN 0-399-11654-0, Dist. by Putnam). Berkley Pub.

Miracle Season. Linda Cline. 1977. pap. 1.25 o.p. (ISBN 0-425-03447-X, Medallion). Berkley Pub.

Miracle Seed. Asif Currimbhoy. (Writers Workshop Bluebird Ser.). 38p. 1975. 8.00 (ISBN 0-88253-576-5); pap. text ed. 4.80 (ISBN 0-88253-575-7). Ind-US Inc.

Miracle Success. Don Stewart. 1980. pap. text ed. 2.95 (ISBN 0-88270-484-2). Logos.

Miracle to Believe in. Barry N. Kaufman. LC 80-942. 320p. 1981. 12.95 (ISBN 0-385-14991-3). Doubleday.

Miracles. H. Richard Casdorph. LC 76-2330. 1976. 5.95 o.p. (ISBN 0-88270-171-1); pap. 3.95 o.p. (ISBN 0-88270-172-X). Logos.

Miracles & Parables of the Bible. Lucile P. Johnson. (Quiz & Puzzle Bks). 1971. pap. 2.95 (ISBN 0-8010-5007-3). Baker Bk.

Miracles at Cana. Catherine Chase. LC 78-64117. (Illus.). (gr. k-5). 1979. 3.50 (ISBN 0-89799-124-9); pap. 1.50 (ISBN 0-89799-033-1). Dandelion Pr.

Miracles Don't Just Happen. Lester Sumrall. 1979. pap. 3.95 o.p. (ISBN 0-88270-369-2). Logos.

Miracles in Pinafores & Bluejeans. Ardeth G. Kapp. LC 77-4268. 81p. pap. 1.50 (ISBN 0-87747-741-8). Deseret Bk.

Miracles of Christ. A. B. Bruce. Date not set. 17.25 (ISBN 0-86524-060-4). Klock & Klock.

Miracles of Our Saviour. William M. Taylor. LC 74-79944. 1975. 10.95 (ISBN 0-8254-3806-3). Kregel.

Miracles of Rebound Exercise. Albert E. Carter. 188p. 1979. pap. 5.95 (ISBN 0-938302-00-0). NIRH.

Miracles of Survival: Canada & French Canada. Waris Shere. 160p. 1981. 7.50 (ISBN 0-682-49730-4). Exposition.

Miraculous Affair. Louise Louis. (Illus.). 75p. 1974. text ed. 12.00. Pen-Art.

Miraculous Lunacy of War. William Nuttall. 1981. 8.95 (ISBN 0-533-04665-3). Vantage.

Mirage Bar. Zay N. Smith & Pamela Zekman. LC 79-4760. (Illus.). 1979. 8.95 (ISBN 0-394-50368-6). Random.

Mirage of Power, British Foreign Policy. C. J. Lowe & M. L. Dockrill. Incl. Vol. 1. 1902-1914. 13.95x (ISBN 0-7100-7092-6); Vol. 2. 1914-1922. 18.00x (ISBN 0-7100-7093-4); Vol. 3. The Documents. 24.00x (ISBN 0-7100-7094-2). (Foreign Policies of the Great Powers Ser). 1972. Set. 50.00 (ISBN 0-685-25614-6). Routledge & Kegan.

Mirage of Safety: Food Additives & Federal Policy. Beatrice T. Hunter. LC 75-20299. 192p. 1976. 9.95 o.p. (ISBN 0-684-14426-3, ScribJ). Scribner.

Mirages of Marriage. William J. Lederer & Don D. Jackson. LC 67-16608. 1968. 14.95 (ISBN 0-393-08400-0). Norton.

Mirages: Travel Notes in the Promised Land. Stanley Burnshaw. LC 76-21513. 1977. 5.95 o.p. (ISBN 0-385-12500-3). Doubleday.

Miramar. Naguib Mahfouz. Tr. by Fatma Moussa-Mahmoud from Arabic. LC 78-72968. (Orig.). 1978. pap. 5.00 (ISBN 0-89410-020-3). Three Continents.

Miranda, No. 60. Grace L. Hill. 224p. 1981. pap. 2.25 (ISBN 0-553-14270-4). Bantam.

Miranda in the Middle. Elizabeth Winthrop. (Skylark Ser.). 128p. 1981. pap. cancelled (ISBN 0-553-15073-1). Bantam.

Miranda No. Sixty. Emilie Loring. 208p. 1981. pap. cancelled (ISBN 0-553-14294-1). Bantam.

Miranda the Great. Eleanor Estes. LC 66-10422. (Illus.). 80p. 1967. 4.95 o.p. (ISBN 0-15-254600-6, HJ). HarBraceJ.

Mirate Los Ojos. Paul Showers. Tr. by Richard J. Palmer. LC 68-29617. (Let's-Read-and-Find-Out Science Bk). Orig. Title: Look at Your Eyes. (Illus., Span.). (gr. k-3). 1968. bds. 7.95 (ISBN 0-690-50729-1, TYC-J). T Y Crowell.

Mirgorad: Four Tales. Nikolai Gogol. Tr. by David Magarshack. (Funk & W Bk.). 1969. pap. 2.50 o.s.i. (ISBN 0-308-60067-3, M62, TYC-T). T Y Crowell.

Miriam the Virgin of Nazareth. LC 63-15246. 1963. 3.50 o.p. (ISBN 0-915540-03-7). Friends-Israel-Spearhead Pr.

Mirkheim. Paul Anderson. 1979. pap. 1.75 (ISBN 0-425-04309-6). Berkley Pub.

Miro, No. 203. (Maeght Gallery: Derriere le Miroir Ser.). (Fr.). 1977. pap. 19.95 (ISBN 0-8120-0894-4). Barron.

Miro, No. 151. (Maeght Gallery: Derriere le Miroir Ser.). (Fr.). 1977. pap. 19.95 (ISBN 0-8120-0918-5). Barron.

Miro, No. 186. (Maeght Gallery: Derriere le Miroir Ser.). (Fr.). 1977. pap. 19.95 (ISBN 0-8120-0901-0). Barron.

Miro Artigas, No. 139-140. (Maeght Gallery: Derriere le Ser.). (Fr.). 1977. pap. 19.95 (ISBN 0-8120-0917-7). Barron.

Miro: Selected Paintings. Charles W. Millard. LC 79-9662. (Illus.). 94p. 1980. 20.00 (ISBN 0-87474-638-8). Smithsonian.

Mirror. Leonard Gross. LC 80-8229. 352p. 1981. 10.95 o.p. (ISBN 0-06-011642-0, HarpC). Har-Row.

Mirror. Nagib Mahfouz. (Arabic.). pap. 5.50 (ISBN 0-685-82846-8). Intl Bk Ctr.

Mirror & the Garden: Realism & Reality in the Writings of Anais Nin. Evelyn J. Hinz. LC 73-4979. 127p. 1973. pap. 2.45 o.p. (ISBN 0-15-660500-7, HB259, Harv). HarBraceJ.

Mirror & the Lamp: Romantic Theory & the Critical Tradition. Meyer H. Abrams. pap. 6.95 (ISBN 0-19-501471-5, 360, GB). Oxford U Pr.

Mirror Crack'd. Agatha Christie. 1980. pap. 2.50. PB.

Mirror Driven Through Nature: Vagrom Champ Bk. William Zaranka. (No. 18). 48p. 1981. pap. 3.95 (ISBN 0-935552-00-6). Sparrow Pr.

Mirror for Americans: Likeness of the Eastern Seaboard, 1810. Ralph H. Brown. LC 67-27449. (American Scene Ser). 1968. Repr. of 1943 ed. 35.00 (ISBN 0-306-70974-0). Da Capo.

Mirror for Gotham: New York As Seen by Contemporaries from Dutch Days to the Present. Bayrd Still. LC 80-16246. (Illus.). xix, 417p. 1980. Repr. of 1956 ed. lib. bdg. 35.00x (ISBN 0-313-22439-0, STMG). Greenwood.

Mirror for Modern Scholars: Essays in Methods of Research in Literature. Ed. by Lester A. Beaurline. LC 65-26779. (Orig.). 1966. pap. 9.50 o.p. (ISBN 0-672-63064-8). Odyssey Pr.

Mirror Image. Linda DuBreuil. 1979. pap. 1.75 (ISBN 0-505-51393-5). Tower Bks.

Mirror Magic. Seymour Simon. LC 80-13038. (Illus.). 48p. (gr. 1-4). 1980. 7.95 (ISBN 0-688-41955-0); PLB 7.63 (ISBN 0-688-51955-5). Lothrop.

Mirror Mind: Spirituality & Transformation. William Johnston. LC 80-8350. 192p. 1981. 10.95 (ISBN 0-06-064197-5, HarpR). Har-Row.

Mirror, Mirror. Donald Green. 192p. 1980. 17.95 (ISBN 0-241-10248-0, Pub. by Hamish Hamilton England). David & Charles.

Mirror Mirror: Images of Women in Popular Culture. Kathryn N. Weibel. LC 76-47835. 1977. pap. 3.95 (ISBN 0-385-11131-2, Anch). Doubleday.

Mirror, Mirror on the Wall. Stanley Ellin. 144p. 1975. pap. 1.25 o.s.i. (ISBN 0-440-15599-1). Dell.

Mirror, Mirror on the Wall. Stanley Ellin. LC 72-2709. 1972. 5.95 o.p. (ISBN 0-394-47168-7). Random.

Mirror, Mirror on the Wall. Gayelord Hauser. 1977. pap. 1.95 o.p. (ISBN 0-449-22952-1, Crest). Fawcett.

Mirror of Danger. Pamela Sykes. (gr. 5-7). 1976. pap. 1.95 (ISBN 0-671-42892-6). Archway.

Mirror of Danger. Pamela Sykes. (gr. 5-7). 1976. pap. 1.75 (ISBN 0-671-41134-9). PB.

Mirror of Her Own. Rosa Guy. LC 80-69448. 192p. (YA) (gr. 8-12). 1981. 8.95 (ISBN 0-440-05513-X). Delacorte.

Mirror of Love: A Reinterpretation of the "Romance of the Rose". Alan M. Gunn. 1952. 24.00 (ISBN 0-89672-005-5). Tex Tech Pr.

Mirror of Production. Jean Baudrillard. Tr. by Mark Poster. LC 74-82994. 1975. pap. 3.95 (ISBN 0-914386-06-9). Telos Pr.

Mirror Planet. Eve Bunting. (Science Fiction Ser.). (Illus.). (gr. 3-9). 1978. PLB 5.95 (ISBN 0-87191-628-2); pap. 2.95 (ISBN 0-89812-057-8). Creative Ed.

Mirror Within a Mirror: Ben Jonson & the Play-Within. Robert W. Witt. (Salzburg Studies in English Literature Jacobean Drama Studies: No. 46). 154p. 1976. pap. text ed. 25.00x (ISBN 0-391-01574-5). Humanities.

Mirrors. Barbara Krasnoff. 464p. (Orig.). 1980. pap. 2.75 (ISBN 0-89083-690-6). Zebra.

Mirrors. James Lipton. 352p. 1981. 12.95 (ISBN 0-312-53438-8). St Martin.

Mirrors & Magnifiers. Dorothy Diamond. LC 77-82982. (Teaching Primary Science Ser.). (Illus.). 1977. pap. text ed. 6.95 (ISBN 0-356-05078-5). Raintree Child.

Mirrors, Masks, Lies, Secrets & the Limits of Human Predictability. Karl E. Scheibe. LC 78-19791. 192p. 1979. 19.95 (ISBN 0-03-046661-X). Praeger.

Mirrors, Mice, & Mustaches. George D. Hendricks. 110p. 1981. pap. 4.95 (ISBN 0-87074-075-X). SMU Press.

Mirrors of Man in Existentialism. Nathan A. Scott, Jr. LC 78-69971. 1978. 7.95 (ISBN 0-529-05641-0, RB5641, Pub. by Collins Pubs); pap. 4.95 (ISBN 0-529-05487-6, FT5487). Abingdon.

Mirrors of Man in Existentialism. Nathan A. Scott, Jr. 1980. pap. text ed. 7.95 (ISBN 0-687-27073-1). Abingdon.

Mirrors of the Mind. Thomas Lafayette Hamm. 1977. 4.00 o.p. (ISBN 0-682-48880-1). Exposition.

Mirrour of Monsters. William Rankins. Bd. with Menaphon. Thomas Nashe; Kind Harts Dream. Henry Chettle. (English Stage Ser.: Vol. 9). lib. bdg. 50.00 (ISBN 0-8240-0592-9). Garland Pub.

MIRV & the Arms Race: An Interpretation of Defense Strategy. Ronald L Tammen. LC 73-9065. (Special Studies in International Politics & Government). 1973. 28.50x (ISBN 0-275-28749-1). Irvington.

Mirza Malkum Khan: A Biographical Essay in 19th Century Iranian Modernism. Hamid Algar. LC 78-187750. 1973. 23.50x (ISBN 0-520-02217-3). U of Cal Pr.

MIS: Concepts & Design. Robert G. Murdick. 1980. text ed. 21.00 (ISBN 0-13-585331-1). P-H.

Mis Primeros Cuentos. Pablo Ozaeta. Ed. by Marjorie Frank & Luz P. Lono. LC 75-16546. (Illus.). (gr. 4-8). 1975. pap. 4.95 student ed. (ISBN 0-88499-241-1); teachers's ed. 7.95 (ISBN 0-88499-242-X); program package (1 teacher's ed. & 10 student wkbks.) 38.95 (ISBN 0-88499-243-8). Inst Mod Lang.

Misadventures of Tim McPick: A Gay Comedy. Daniel Curzon. LC 75-32707. 1980. pap. 4.00 (ISBN 0-930650-02-6). D Brown Bks.

Misanthrope. Moliere. Ed. by G. Rudler. (French Texts Ser.). 1947. pap. text ed. 9.95x (ISBN 0-631-00520-X, Pub. by Basil Blackwell). Biblio Dist.

Miscelanea, Meditations, Memoratives. Elizabeth Grymeston. LC 79-84114. (English Experience Ser.: No. 933). 68p. 1979. Repr. of 1604 ed. lib. bdg. 8.00 (ISBN 90-221-0933-X). Walter J Johnson.

Miscellaneous Group Exhibitions. Ed. by Theodore Reff. (Modern Art in Paris 1855 to 1900 Ser.). 219p. 1981. lib. bdg. 44.00 (ISBN 0-8240-4734-6). Garland Pub.

Miscellaneous Plays. Joanna Baillie. LC 75-31146. (Romantic Context: Poetry 1789-1830 Ser.: Vol. 3). 1977. Repr. of 1804 ed. lib. bdg. 47.00 (ISBN 0-8240-2102-9). Garland Pub.

Miscellaneous Studies in the History of Music. Oscar G. Sonneck. LC 68-9192. (Music Reprint Ser). 1968. Repr. of 1921 ed. lib. bdg. 35.00 (ISBN 0-306-71163-X). Da Capo.

Miscellaneous Verse, Originally Published in Quarto, by Burges, Carv, Dyer, Lloyd, Merivale, Thelwall & Wilson. Ed. by Donald H. Reiman. Bd. with James Bland Burges: The Birth & Triumph of Love, A Poem. James B. Burges. Repr. of 1796 ed; Henry Francis Cary (1755-1844) Sonnets & Odes. Repr. of 1788 ed; Ode to General Kosciusko. Repr. of 1797 ed; George Dyer: Poems. Repr. of 1792 ed; Charles Lloyd: Poems on the Death of Priscilla Farmer (Including Poems by Coleridge & Lamb) Repr. of 1796 ed; Lines Suggested by the Fast, Appointed on Wednesday, February 27, 1799. Repr. of 1799 ed; John Herman Merivale: The Minstrel: Book the Third (Continuation of a Poem by James Beattie) Repr. of 1808 ed; John Thelwall: Poems Written in Close Confinement in the Tower & Newgate, Under a Charge of High Treason. Repr. of 1795 ed; John Wilson: The Magic Mirror. Addressed to Walter Scott, Esq. Repr. of 1812 ed. LC 75-31175. (Romantic Context Ser.: Poetry 1789-1830: No. 28). 1978. lib. bdg. 47.00 (ISBN 0-8240-2127-4). Garland Pub.

Miscellaneous Works. Charles Blount. LC 75-11197. (British Philosophers & Theologians of the 17th & 18th Centuries: Vol. 4). 1976. Repr. of 1695 ed. lib. bdg. 42.00 (ISBN 0-8240-1753-6). Garland Pub.

Miscellaneous Works. David Humphreys. LC 68-24210. 1968. Repr. of 1804 ed. 42.00x (ISBN 0-8201-1028-0). Schol Facsimiles.

Miscellaneous Works: Some Gospel Truths Opened,a Vindication of Some Gospel Truths Opened, & a Few Sighs from Hell, Vol 1. John Bunyan. Ed. by T. L. Underwood & Roger Sharrock. (Oxford English Texts Ser.). (Illus.). 458p. 1980. 69.00x (ISBN 0-19-812730-8). Oxford U Pr.

Miscellaneous Writings of Horatio Greenough. Horatio Greenough. LC 75-1118. 1975. lib. bdg. 20.00x (ISBN 0-8201-1152-X). Schol Facsimiles.

Miscellaneous Writings of Joseph Story. Joseph Story. Ed. by William W. Story. LC 79-75269. (American Constitutional & Legal History Ser). 828p. 1972. Repr. of 1852 ed. lib. bdg. 75.00 (ISBN 0-306-71314-4). Da Capo.

Miscellanies, Vol. 1. Henry Fielding. Ed. by Henry K. Miller. LC 71-184366. (Wesleyan Edition of the Works of Henry Fielding Ser). 306p. (Textual intro. by Fredson Bowers). 1973. Repr. of 1743 ed. 27.50x (ISBN 0-8195-4046-3, Pub. by Wesleyan U Pr). Columbia U Pr.

Mischianza. Henry Misrock. 1967. 4.95 o.s.i. (ISBN 0-02-585150-0). Macmillan.

Mischief. Ben Travers. Incl. Rookery Nook; Cuckoo in the Nest. LC 78-4746. 1978. 13.95 o.s.i. (ISBN 0-06-014347-9, HarpT). Har-Row.

Mischief on the Farm. Susan B. Consky. (Childrens Bks). Orig. Title: Beanie and His Friends. (Illus.). 128p. (gr. 1-5). 1970. pap. 1.50 (ISBN 0-8024-1540-7). Moody.

Mischling, Second Degree: My Childhood in Nazi Germany. Ilse Koehn. LC 77-6189. (gr. 7 up). 1977. 8.95 (ISBN 0-688-80110-2); PLB 8.59 (ISBN 0-688-84110-4). Greenwillow.

Misdirection: Opera Production in the Twentieth Century. A. M. Nagler. 134p. 1981. 15.00 (ISBN 0-208-01899-9, Archon). Shoe String.

Miser & Other Plays. Jean B. Moliere. Tr. by John Wood. Incl. Would-Be Gentleman; That Scoundrel Scapin; Don Juan; Love's the Best Doctor. (Classics Ser.). (Orig.). (YA) (gr. 9 up). 1953. pap. 2.75 (ISBN 0-14-044036-4). Penguin.

Miser Hoadley's Secret: A Detective Story. Arthur W. Marchmont. 1976. lib. bdg. 14.85x (ISBN 0-89968-067-4). Lightyear.

Miserable Aunt Bertha. John V. Lord & Fay Maschler. (gr. k-3). 1980. 8.95 (ISBN 0-224-01613-X, Pub. by Chatto Bodley Jonathan). Merrimack Bk Serv.

Miserables. Victor Hugo. (Literature Ser). (gr. 10-12). 1970. pap. text ed. 6.33 (ISBN 0-87720-732-1). AMSCO Sch.

Miserables, 2 vols. Victor Hugo. Tr. by Norman Denny from Fr. (Penguin Classics). 1160p. 1980. pap. 4.95 ea. (ISBN 0-14-044403-3). Vol. 1. Vol. 2 (ISBN 0-14-044404-1). Penguin.

Miserables. Victor Hugo. (Arabic.). pap. 8.95x (ISBN 0-686-63556-6). Intl Bk Ctr.

Miserables Notes. George Klin & Amy L. Marsland. (Orig.). 1968. pap. 2.25 (ISBN 0-8220-0735-5). Cliffs.

Miserere. Georges Rouault. LC 63-21914. (Illus.). 87p. 1963. 30.00 (ISBN 0-912158-46-8, Pub. by Boston Bk & Art Shop). Hennessey.

Miser's Manual: A Guide to Frofitable Self-Employment. Deek Gladson. 1981. pap. 4.00 (ISBN 0-686-69465-1); plastic bdg. 6.00 (ISBN 0-89316-626-X). Exanimo Pr.

Misery in Four Languages. Suzanne Heller. LC 80-15416. (Illus.). 96p. 1981. 4.95 (ISBN 0-8397-5803-0). Eriksson.

Mishmash. Molly Cone. (Illus.). (gr. 3-5). 1971. pap. 1.50 (ISBN 0-671-56083-2). PB.

Mishmash & the Robot. Molly Cone. (gr. 2-5). 1981. 6.95 (ISBN 0-395-30345-1). HM.

Mishmash & the Sauerkraut Mystery. Molly Cone. (Illus.). (gr. 3-5). 1979. pap. 1.50 (ISBN 0-671-29935-2). PB.

Mishmash & the Venus Flytrap. Molly Cone. (Illus.). (gr. 3-5). 1979. pap. 1.50 (ISBN 0-671-29936-0). PB.

Mishmash & Uncle Looey. Molly Cone. (Illus.). (gr. 3-5). 1979. pap. 1.50 (ISBN 0-671-29937-9). PB.

Mishnah. Tr. by Herbert Danby. 1933. 29.95x (ISBN 0-19-815402-X). Oxford U Pr.

Mishnah-Moed, Vol. 3. Hersh Goldwurm et al. (Art Scroll Mishnah Ser.). 1980. 16.95 (ISBN 0-89906-256-3); pap. 13.95 (ISBN 0-89906-257-1). Mesorah Pubns.

Mishpokhe: A Study of New York City Jewish Family Clubs. William E. Mitchell. 262p. 1980. text ed. 19.95 (ISBN 90-27976-95-3); pap. text ed. 5.95 (ISBN 0-202-01166-6). Aldine Pub.

Misia: The Life of Misia Sert. Arthur Gold & Robert Fizdale. (Illus.). 340p. 1981. Repr. pap. price not set (ISBN 0-688-00391-5, Quill). Morrow.

Mision Ineludible. Tr. by Corrie Ten Boom. (Spanish Bks.). (Span.). 1978. 1.95 (ISBN 0-8297-0586-4). Life Pubs Intl.

Miso Production: The Book of Miso, Vol. II. rev. ed. William Shurtleff & Akiko Aoyagi. LC 76-19599. (Soyfood Production Ser.: No. 1). (Illus.). 1979. pap. 9.95 (ISBN 0-933332-00-9). Soyfoods-New Age.

Misogonus. Anthony Rudd. Ed. by Lester E. Barber & Stephen Orgel. LC 78-66756. (Renaissance Drama Ser.). 1979. lib. bdg. 41.00 (ISBN 0-8240-9751-3). Garland Pub.

Miss Annie F. Horniman & the Abbey Theatre. James W. Flannery. (Irish Theatre Ser: No. 31). 40p. 1976. pap. text ed. 3.25x (ISBN 0-85105-182-0, Dolmen Pr). Humanities.

Miss Bianca & the Bridesmaid. Margery Sharp. (Illus.). (gr. 5 up). 1972. 6.95 o.p. (ISBN 0-316-78299-8). Little.

Miss Bianca in the Antarctic. Margery Sharp. LC 75-158484. 1971. 6.95 (ISBN 0-316-78294-7). Little.

Miss Bianca in the Orient. Margery Sharp. LC 79-119110. (Illus.). 1970. 6.95 o.p. (ISBN 0-316-78319-6). Little.

Miss Billy. Eleanor P. Porter. 1976. lib. bdg. 16.25x (ISBN 0-89968-103-4). Lightyear.

Miss Billy - Married. Eleanor H. Porter. 1976. lib. bdg. 16.75x (ISBN 0-89968-104-2). Lightyear.

Miss Billy's Decision. Eleanor H. Porter. 1976. lib. bdg. 16.25x (ISBN 0-89968-105-0). Lightyear.

Miss Brown. Vernon Lee. Ed. by Ian Fletcher & John Stokes. LC 76-20088. (Decadent Consciousness Ser.). 1978. lib. bdg. 38.00 (ISBN 0-8240-2766-3). Garland Pub.

Miss Carstairs Dress for Bloodings. Peter Redgrove. 108p. 1981. pap. 5.95 (ISBN 0-7145-2557-X, Pub. by M Boyars). Merrimack Bk Serv.

Miss Charity Comes to Stay. Alberta W. Constant. LC 59-5250. (Illus.). (gr. 5-9). 1959. 8.95 o.p. (ISBN 0-690-54490-1, TYC-J). T Y Crowell.

Miss Craig's Face-Saving Exercises. Marjorie Craig. 1970. 7.95 (ISBN 0-394-42412-3). Random.

Miss Craig's Growing-up Exercises. Marjorie Craig. (Illus.). 1973. 7.95 o.p. (ISBN 0-394-48491-6). Random.

Miss Ghost. Ruth M. Arthur. LC 79-63117. (gr. 5-9). 1979. 7.95 (ISBN 0-689-30702-0). Atheneum.

Miss Giardino. Dorothy Bryant. LC 78-54280. 1978. pap. 6.00 (ISBN 0-931688-01-9). Ata Bks.

Miss Harriet Hippopotamus & the Most Wonderful. Nancy Moore & Edward Leight. LC 63-11499. (Illus.). (gr. k-2). 5.95 (ISBN 0-8149-0369-X). Vanguard.

Miss Hungerford's Handsome Hero. Noel V. Carter. (Orig.). 1981. pap. 1.50 (ISBN 0-440-15312-3). Dell.

Miss Jellytot's Visit. Mabel L. Hunt. (Illus.). (gr. 4-6). 1955. PLB 7.89 o.p. (ISBN 0-397-30305-X). Lippincott.

Miss Julie. August Strindberg. 1965. pap. 1.75 (ISBN 0-380-01416-5, 77412, Bard). Avon.

Miss Liberty Meet Crazyhorse. Don Jones. LC 74-18916. 62p. 1972. 5.00 o.p. (ISBN 0-8040-0584-2); pap. 3.25 (ISBN 0-8040-0585-0). Swallow.

Miss Lillian & Friends: The Plains, Georgia, Family Philosophy & Recipe Book. Beth Tartan & Rudy Hayes. (Illus.). (RL 7). 1977. pap. 1.75 o.p. (ISBN 0-451-07852-7, E7852, Sig). NAL.

Miss Lonelyhearts. Nathanael West. Bd. with Day of the Locust. LC 62-16924. pap. 3.95 (ISBN 0-8112-0215-1, NDP125). New Directions.

Miss Lucy. Nola Langner. LC 74-78082. (Illus.). (gr. k-3). 1969. 4.95g o.s.i. (ISBN 0-02-751450-1). Macmillan.

Miss Margaret Ridpath & the Dismantling of the Universe. Don Robertson. 1978. pap. 2.25 o.s.i. (ISBN 0-515-04569-1). Jove Pubns.

Miss Margarida's Way. Roberto Athayde. 1979. pap. 1.95 (ISBN 0-380-40568-7, 40568, Bard). Avon.

Miss Marjoribanks. Mrs. Oliphant. LC 70-487580. (Zodiac Press Ser.). 1979. 9.95 (ISBN 0-7011-1503-3, Pub. by Chatto Bodley Jonathan). Merrimack Bk Serv.

Miss Marjoribanks, 1866. Margaret O. Oliphant. Ed. by Robert L. Wolff. (Victorian Fiction Ser.). lib. bdg. 66.00 (ISBN 0-8240-1615-7). Garland Pub.

Miss Mouse. Mira Stables. 224p. 1981. pap. 1.95 (ISBN 0-449-50178-7, Coventry). Fawcett.

Miss Nobody. Caroline Ross. 256p. 1981. 10.95 (ISBN 0-312-92536-0). St Martin.

Miss One Thousand Spring Blossoms. John Ball. 1979. pap. 1.95 (ISBN 0-380-42325-1, 42325). Avon.

Miss Osborne the Mop. Wilson Gage. (Illus.). (gr. 4-6). 1975. pap. 1.50 (ISBN 0-671-29895-X). PB.

Miss Peach. Mell Lazarus. 128p. (Orig.). 1981. pap. 1.75 (ISBN 0-553-14789-7). Bantam.

Miss Pickerell & the Geiger Counter. Ellen MacGregor. 128p. (gr. 3-6). pap. 1.75 (ISBN 0-671-56019-0). Archway.

Miss Pickerell & the Supertanker, No. 6. Ellen MacGregor & Dora Pankell. (Illus.). (gr. 4-6). 1980. pap. 1.75 (ISBN 0-671-56026-3). Archway.

Miss Pickerell & the Weather Satellite. Ellen MacGregor & Dora Pantell. (Illus.). (gr. 4-6). 1980. pap. 1.75 (ISBN 0-671-56027-1). PB.

Miss Pickerell Goes on a Dig, No. 7. Ellen MacGregor & Dora Pantell. (Illus.). (gr. 4-6). 1980. pap. 1.75 (ISBN 0-671-56022-0). Archway.

Miss Pickerell Goes to Mars, No. 9. Ellen MacGregor. (gr. 4-6). 1980. pap. 1.75 (ISBN 0-671-56018-2). Archway.

Miss Pickerell Goes to the Arctic, No. 14. Ellen McGregor. (Illus.). 1981. pap. 1.75 (ISBN 0-671-56021-2). Archway.

Miss Pickerell Goes Undersea. Ellen MacGregor. 1981. pap. 1.75 (ISBN 0-671-56020-4). PB.

Miss Pickerell Harvests the Sea, No. 8. Ellen MacGregor. (Illus.). 1980. pap. 1.75 (ISBN 0-671-56024-7). Archway.

Miss Pickerell Meets Mr. H. U. M. Ellen MacGregor & Dora Pantell. (Illus.). (gr. 4-6). 1980. pap. 1.75 (ISBN 0-671-56028-X). PB.

Miss Pickerell on the Moon. Ellen MacGregor & Dora Pantell. (Illus.). (gr. 4-6). 1965. PLB 6.95 o.p. (ISBN 0-07-044551-6, GB). McGraw.

Miss Pickerell Tackles the Energy Crisis. Ellen MacGregor & Dora Pantell. LC 79-24149. (Illus.). (gr. 4-6). 1980. 7.95 (ISBN 0-07-044589-3). McGraw.

Miss Pickerell Takes the Bull by the Horns. Ellen MacGregor & Dora Pantell. LC 75-41454. (Illus.). (gr. 4-6). 1976. 6.95 o.p. (ISBN 0-07-044582-6, GB). McGraw.

Miss Pickerell Takes the Bull by the Horns. Ellen MacGregor & Dora Pantell. (Illus.). (gr. 4-6). 1980. pap. 1.75 (ISBN 0-671-56029-8). PB.

Miss Pickerell Takes the Bull by the Horns, No. 4. Ellen MacGregor & Dora Pantell. (Illus.). (gr. 4-6). 1980. pap. 1.75 (ISBN 0-671-56029-8). Archway.

Miss Pickerell to the Earthquake Rescue, No. 5. Ellen MacGregor & Dora Pantell. (Illus.). (gr. 4-6). 1980. pap. 1.75 (ISBN 0-671-56025-5). Archway.

Miss Piggy's Guide to Life. Miss Piggy. LC 80-2708. (Illus.). 192p. 1981. 12.95 (ISBN 0-394-51912-4). Knopf.

Miss Pym Disposes. Josephine Tey. LC 79-19665. 1981. Repr. of 1948 ed. lib. bdg. 10.00x (ISBN 0-8376-0447-8). Bentley.

Miss Ravenel's Conversion from Secession to Loyalty: (Standard Ed.) Arlin Turner. LC 75-100633. 1969. pap. text ed. 2.95x (ISBN 0-675-09390-2). Merrill.

Miss Suzy. Miriam Young. LC 64-10363. (Illus.). (gr. k-3). 1964. 5.95 o.s.i. (ISBN 0-8193-0092-6, Four Winds); PLB 5.41 o.s.i. (ISBN 0-8193-0093-4). Schol Bk Serv.

Miss Suzy's Birthday. Miriam Young. LC 73-22187. (Illus.). (ps-3). 1974. 5.95 o.s.i. (ISBN 0-8193-0764-5, Four Winds); PLB 5.41 o.s.i. (ISBN 0-8193-0765-3). Schol Bk Serv.

Miss Suzy's Easter Surprise. Miriam Young. LC 80-17315. (Illus.). 48p. (ps-3). 1980. Repr. of 1972 ed. 8.95 (ISBN 0-590-07777-5, Four Winds). Schol Bk Serv.

Miss Willmott of Warley Place. Audrey Le Lievre. (Illus.). 240p. 1981. 28.00 (ISBN 0-571-11622-1, Pub. by Faber & Faber). Merrimack Bk Serv.

Missabe Road: The Duluth, Missabe & Iron Range Railway. Frank A. King. LC 74-190177. (Illus.). 200p. 1972. 19.95 (ISBN 0-87095-040-1). Golden West.

Missile Defense Controversy: Strategy, Technology, & Politics, 1955-1972. Ernest J. Yanarella. LC 76-46034. 1977. 18.00x (ISBN 0-8131-1355-5). U Pr of Ky.

Missiles and Rockets. Kenneth Gatland. LC 75-15641. (Illus.). 256p. 1975. 9.95 (ISBN 0-02-542860-8, 54286). Macmillan.

Missing Head Mystery. Carole Marsh. LC 79-55447. (HistoryMystery Ser.). (Illus.). 160p. (Orig.). 1980. pap. 3.95 (ISBN 0-935326-01-4). Gallopade Pub Group.

Missing in Action. Bill Linn. 224p. (Orig.). 1981. pap. 2.25 (ISBN 0-380-77370-8, 77370). Avon.

Missing Link. Maitland Edey. LC 72-89569. (Emergence of Man Ser). (Illus.). 1972. lib. bdg. 9.63 o.p. (ISBN 0-8094-1256-X, Pub. by Time-Life). Silver.

Missing Link. Maitland A. Edey. (Emergence of Man Ser.). (Illus.). 160p. 1972. 9.95 (ISBN 0-8094-1255-1); lib. bdg. avail. (ISBN 0-685-28517-0). Time-Life.

Missing Link. Warren Murphy. (Destroyer Ser.: No. 39). (Orig.). 1980. pap. 1.95 (ISBN 0-523-41254-1). Pinnacle Bks.

Missing Links & the Men Who Found Them. John Reader. (Illus.). 181p. 1981. 19.95 (ISBN 0-316-73590-6). Little.

Missing Man. Katharine MacLean. LC 74-16610. (YA) 1975. 6.95 o.p. (ISBN 0-399-11474-2, Dist. by Putnam). Berkley Pub.

Missing Papers. Joseph Coleman. (Pal Paperbacks, - Pal Skills II Ser.). (Illus.). (gr. 5-12). 1980. pap. text ed. 1.25 (ISBN 0-8374-6802-7). Xerox Ed Pubns.

Missing Person. Doris Grumbach. 256p. 1981. 11.95 (ISBN 0-399-12587-6). Putnam.

Missing Persons. Jack Olsen. LC 80-69375. 1981. 12.95 (ISBN 0-689-11133-9). Atheneum.

Missing Piece Meets the Big O. Shel Silverstein. LC 80-8721. (Illus.). 112p. (gr. 3 up). 1981. 8.95 (ISBN 0-06-025657-5, HarpJ); PLB 8.79 (ISBN 0-06-025658-3). Har-Row.

Missing Pony. Laura Lee Hope. Ed. by Wendy Barish. (Bobbsey Twins Ser.). (Illus.). 128p. (gr. 2-5). 1981. 7.95 (ISBN 0-671-42295-2); pap. 1.95 (ISBN 0-671-42296-0). Wanderer Bks.

Missing: Stories of Strange Disappearances. Daniel Cohen. LC 78-25729. (High Interest-Low Vocabulary Ser.). (Illus.). (gr. 4 up). 1979. 5.95 (ISBN 0-396-07651-3). Dodd.

Missing: Stories of Strange Disappearances. Daniel Cohen. 1980. pap. write for info. (ISBN 0-671-56052-2). PB.

Missing Stories of Strange Disappearances. Daniel Cohen. (Illus.). 1980. pap. write for info. (ISBN 0-671-56052-2). PB.

Mission A-Go-Go. Dorothy Applegate. LC 78-73043. (Illus.). 1979. 9.95 (ISBN 0-9602122-2-1). Apple-Gems.

Mission & Expansion of Christianity in the First Three Centuries. Adolph Harnack. 10.00 (ISBN 0-8446-2206-0). Peter Smith.

Mission-Church Dynamics. W. Harold Fuller. LC 80-83659. (Orig.). 1980. pap. 8.95 (ISBN 0-87808-176-3). William Carey Lib.

Mission Furniture: Making It, Decorating with It, Its History & Place in the Antique Market. Cynthia Rubin & Jerome Rubin. LC 79-24376. (Illus.). 160p. (Orig.). 1980. pap. 8.95 (ISBN 0-87701-169-9). Chronicle Bks.

Mission Handbook: North American Protestant Ministries Overseas. Ed. by Edward R. Dayton. 1977. 15.00 (ISBN 0-912552-06-9). MARC.

Mission Handbook: North American Protestant Ministries Overseas. Ed. by Samuel Wilson. 1980. 22.50 (ISBN 0-912552-34-4). MARC.

Mission in Burma: The Columban Fathers' Forty-Three Years in Kachin Country. Edward Fischer. 192p. 1980. 9.95 (ISBN 0-8164-0464-X). Crossroad NY.

Mission Incredible. Lawrence Cortesi. 1979. pap. 1.50 (ISBN 0-505-51346-3). Tower Bks.

Mission of Baha'u'llah and Other Literary Pieces. George Townshend. 1952. 6.50 (ISBN 0-85398-021-7, 7-31-18, Pub. by G Ronald England). Baha'i.

Mission of the Church. Edward Schillebeeckx. 250p. 1973. 9.75 (ISBN 0-8164-1144-1). Crossroad NY.

Mission of the Church & the Propagation of the Faith. Ed. by G. J. Cuming. LC 77-108105. (Cambridge Studies in Church History: Vol. 6). 1970. 36.00 (ISBN 0-521-07752-4). Cambridge U Pr.

Mission of the North American People. 2nd ed. William Gilpin. LC 68-16234. (American Scene Ser.). (Illus.). 218p. 1974. Repr. of 1874 ed. lib. bdg. 25.00 (ISBN 0-306-71013-7). Da Capo.

Mission, Possible. Gottfried Oosterwal. LC 72-95276. (Anvil Ser.). 1972. pap. 4.95 (ISBN 0-8127-0066-X). Southern Pub.

Mission River Justice. W. C. Tuttle. 256p. (YA) 1975. 5.95 (ISBN 0-685-50844-7, Avalon). Bouregy.

Mission to Asia. Christopher Dawson. (Medieval Academy Reprints for Teaching Ser.). 228p. 1981. pap. 6.00x (ISBN 0-8020-6436-1). U of Toronto Pr.

Mission to Fort No. Four. Kenneth Andler. (N. H.-Vermont Historiettes). (Illus.). 64p. (gr. 6-7). 1975. 4.95 (ISBN 0-915892-04-9); pap. 1.95 (ISBN 0-915892-15-4). Regional Ctr Educ.

Mission to Malaspiga. Evelyn Anthony. 1975. pap. 1.75 o.p. (ISBN 0-451-06706-1, E6706, Sig). NAL.

Mission to the Stars. A. E. Van Vogt. 1980. pap. write for info. (ISBN 0-671-83661-7). PB.

Mission Trends No. Five: Faith Meets Faith. Ed. by Gerald H. Anderson & Thomas F. Stransky. (Mission Trends Ser.). 320p. (Orig.). 1981. pap. 3.95 (ISBN 0-8028-1821-8). Eerdmans.

Mission Trends, No. 4: Liberation Theologies. Ed. by Thomas Stransky & Gerald H. Anderson. LC 78-70827. (Mission Trend Ser.). 1979. pap. 3.45 (ISBN 0-8091-2185-9). Paulist Pr.

Mission Trends No.5: Faith Meets Faith, No. 5. Ed. by Gerald H. Anderson & Thomas F. Stransky. (Orig.). 1981. pap. 3.95 (ISBN 0-8091-2356-8). Paulist Pr.

Mission with Mountbatten. rev. ed. Alan Campbell-Johnson. 1951. pap. 2.45 (ISBN 0-88253-129-8). Ind-US Inc.

Missionary: An Indian Tale, 3 vols. in 1. Sydney O. Morgan. LC 80-20308. 1980. Repr. of 1811 ed. 35.00x (ISBN 0-8201-1358-1). Schol Facsimiles.

Missionary Factor in East Africa. Roland Oliver. (Illus.). 1967. pap. text ed. 4.00x (ISBN 0-582-60847-3). Humanities.

Missionary Go Home? Les Pederson. 1980. pap. 3.50 (ISBN 0-8024-4881-X). Moody.

Missionary Idea in Life & Religion. J. F. McFadyen. 194p. Repr. of 1926 ed. text ed. 3.50 (ISBN 0-567-02180-7). Attic Pr.

Missionary Impact on Modern Nigeria, 1842-1914. Emmanuel A. Ayandele. (Ibadan History Ser.). 1967. pap. text ed. 13.75x (ISBN 0-582-64512-3). Humanities.

Missionary Messengers of Liberation in a Colonial Context: A Case Study of the Sudan United Mission. Jan H. Boer. 542p. 1979. pap. text ed. 51.50x (ISBN 90-6203-561-2). Humanities.

Missionary of Moderation: Henry Melchior Muhlenberg & the Lutheran Church in English America. Leonard R. Riforgiato. LC 78-75203. 256p. Date not set. 19.50 (ISBN 0-8387-2379-9). Bucknell U Pr.

Missionary Set. 1978. pap. 12.95 (ISBN 0-87747-774-4). Deseret Bk.

Missions - Which Way? Peter Beyerhaus. (Contemporary Evangelical Perspectives Ser). 128p. 1971. kivar 2.45 o.p. (ISBN 0-310-21191-3). Zondervan.

Missions of New Mexico Since 1776. John L. Kessell. LC 79-4934. (Illus.). 320p. 1980. 45.00x (ISBN 0-8263-0514-8). U of NM Pr.

Missions of San Antonio. Emilie Toepperwein & Fritz Toepperwein. pap. text ed. 1.50 (ISBN 0-910722-12-9). Highland Pr.

Missions Strategy of the Local Church. 1976. pap. 1.90 (ISBN 0-912552-14-X). MARC.

Mississippi. Susan Darell-Brown. LC 78-62982. (Rivers of the World Ser.). (Illus.). 1978. lib. bdg. 7.95 (ISBN 0-686-51135-2). Silver.

Mississippi. 28.00 (ISBN 0-89770-100-3). Curriculum Info Ctr.

Mississippi: A Guide to the Magnolia State. Federal Writers' Project. 545p. 1938. Repr. 49.00 (ISBN 0-403-02174-X). Somerset Pub.

Mississippi: America's Great River System. Corinne J. Naden. LC 73-14702. (First Bks). (Illus.). 72p. (gr. 4-6). 1974. PLB 4.90 o.p. (ISBN 0-531-00819-3). Watts.

Mississippi Bubble. Emerson Hough. 1976. lib. bdg. 19.25x (ISBN 0-89968-042-9). Lightyear.

Mississippi Heroes, Vol. 1. Ed. by Dean F. Wells & Hunter Cole. LC 80-19704. (Illus.). 250p. 1980. 15.00 (ISBN 0-87805-128-7). U Pr of Miss.

Mississippi Life & Health. 1980. 14.00 (ISBN 0-930868-19-6). Merritt Co.

Mississippi Property & Casualty. 1979. 14.70 (ISBN 0-930868-20-X). Merritt Co.

Mississippi Run. Paul D. Boles. LC 76-27875. 1977. 10.00 o.s.i. (ISBN 0-690-01158-X, TYC-T). T Y Crowell.

Mississippi State Industrial Directory, Nineteen Eighty-One. State Industrial Directories Corp. Date not set. pap. price not set (ISBN 0-89910-050-3). State Indus D.

Mississippi: Storm Center of Secession, 1856-1861. Percy L. Rainwater. LC 72-84188. (American Scene, Comments & Commentators Ser). 1969. Repr. of 1938 ed. lib. bdg. 27.50 (ISBN 0-306-71614-3). Da Capo.

Mississippi: The Closed Society. James W. Silver. LC 66-15957. (Illus.). 1966. 5.75 o.p. (ISBN 0-15-118176-4). HarBraceJ.

Mississippi Wildflowers. Lucile Parker. (Illus.). 144p. 1981. 29.95 (ISBN 0-88289-165-0). Pelican.

Mississippian Occupation of the Red Wing Area: Microfiche Edition. Guy E. Gibbon. (Minnesota Prehistoric Archaeology Ser.: No. 13). 394p. 1979. 12.50 (ISBN 0-87351-137-9). Minn Hist.

Missles of the World. 3rd, rev. ed. Michael J. Taylor. 1980. 14.95 (ISBN 0-684-16593-7, ScribT). Scribner.

Missolonghi Manuscript. Frederic Prokosch. 1968. 5.95 o.p. (ISBN 0-374-21064-0). FS&G.

Missoula-Bitterroot Memory Book: A Picture Post Card History. Stan B. Cohen & Frank Houde. LC 79-90794. (Illus.). 96p. 1979. pap. 5.95 (ISBN 0-933126-09-3). Pictorial Hist.

Missouri. 28.00 (ISBN 0-89770-101-1). Curriculum Info Ctr.

Missouri. Stanley Vestal. LC 44-5196. (Illus.). 1964. pap. 4.50 (ISBN 0-8032-5207-2, BB 186, Bison). U of Nebr Pr.

Missouri: A Guide to the 'Show Me' State. LC 72-84486. 1941. 54.00 (ISBN 0-403-02175-8). Somerset Pub.

Missouri: A History. Paul C. Nagel. (States & the Nation Ser.). (Illus.). 1977. 12.95 (ISBN 0-393-05633-3, Co-Pub. by AASLH). Norton.

Missouri Agricultural Law. 4th ed. Stephen F. Matthews & Donald R. Levi. (Lucas Text Ser). 1979. spiral bdg. 10.00x (ISBN 0-87543-132-1). Lucas.

Missouri Breaks. Thomas McGuane. (Orig.). 1976. pap. 1.75 o.p. (ISBN 0-345-25218-7). Ballantine.

Missouri Compromises & Presidential Politics, 1820-1825: From the Letters of William Plumer. Jr. Ed. by Everett S. Brown. LC 76-103942. (American Constitutional & Legal History Ser). 1970. Repr. of 1926 ed. lib. bdg. 17.50 (ISBN 0-306-71869-3). Da Capo.

Missouri Controversy, 1819-1821. Glover Moore. LC 53-5518. (Illus.). 392p. 1966. pap. 5.50x (ISBN 0-8131-0106-9). U Pr of Ky.

Missouri Heart of the Nation. Parrish Christensen et al. LC 80-66209. 1980. text ed. 16.95x (ISBN 0-88273-237-4). Forum Pr MO.

Missouri Life & Health Property & Casualty. 1980. 17.50 (ISBN 0-930868-21-8). Merritt Co.

Missouri Music. Ernst C. Krohn. LC 65-23398. (Music Ser.). xlvi, 380p. 1971. Repr. of 1924 ed. lib. bdg. 37.50 (ISBN 0-306-70932-5). Da Capo.

Missouri Notary Law Primer. Editors of The National Notary Magazine of the National Notary Assn. 1981. pap. 5.95 (ISBN 0-933134-04-5). Natl Notary.

Missouri Reader. Ed. by Frank L. Mott. LC 64-14412. 1964. 15.00 (ISBN 0-8262-0024-9). U of Mo Pr.

Missouri Supplement for Modern Real Estate Practice. David A. Roth & Dale E. Roach. 128p. (Orig.). 1980. pap. 7.95 (ISBN 0-88462-333-5). Real Estate Ed Co.

Missouri Valley. Merrill J. Mattes. 1971. pap. 2.95 (ISBN 0-8077-1718-5). Tchrs Coll.

Missouri's Black Heritage. Kremer et al. LC 79-54887. (Orig.). 1980. pap. text ed. 6.95x (ISBN 0-88273-115-7). Forum Pr MO.

Mistake Proof Earth Shelter Handbook. David Werning & Mary K. Werning. (Illus.). 160p. 1981. price not set (ISBN 0-89196-087-2, Domus Bks); pap. price not set. Quality Bks IL.

Mr. & Mrs. Thief. Naomi Kojima. LC 79-7902. (Illus.). 32p. (gr. k-4). 1980. 6.95 (ISBN 0-690-04021-0, TYC-J); PLB 6.89 (ISBN 0-690-04022-9). T Y Crowell.

Mr. Ass Comes to Town. Krishan Chander. Tr. by Helen H. Bouman. 167p. 1968. pap. 1.60 o.p. (ISBN 0-88253-026-7). Ind-US Inc.

Mr. Big Time. Elizabeth Levy. (Orig.). (gr. k-6). 1981. pap. 1.95 (ISBN 0-440-46184-7, YB). Dell.

Mr. Bill Show. Walter Williams. 80p. pap. 2.50 (ISBN 0-671-42039-9). PB.

Mr. Blood's Last Night. Martin Quigley. 167p. 1980. pap. 5.95 (ISBN 0-86629-023-0). Sunrise MO.

Mister Blue. Myles Connolly. pap. 0.75 (ISBN 0-385-02866-0, D5, Im). Doubleday.

Mister Blue. Myles Connolly. 1928. 8.95 (ISBN 0-02-527460-0). Macmillan.

Mr. Bounce. (Mr. Books). 1980. 1.00 (ISBN 0-8431-0809-6). Price Stern.

Mr. Brimble's Hobby & Other Stories. Eve Rice. LC 75-8872. (Greenwillow Read-Alone Bks.). (Illus.). 64p. (gr. 1-4). 1975. 5.95 o.p. (ISBN 0-688-80006-8); PLB 5.71 (ISBN 0-688-84006-X). Greenwillow.

Mr. Bump. (Mr. Books). 1980. 1.00 (ISBN 0-8431-0814-2). Price Stern.

Mr. Chatterbox. (Mr. Books). 1980. 1.00 (ISBN 0-8431-0808-8). Price Stern.

Mr. Clumsy. (Mr. Books). 1980. 1.00 (ISBN 0-8431-0801-0). Price Stern.

Mr. Creator's Borrowed Brown Hands. Yvonne Davy. LC 75-46424. (Panda Ser.). 1976. pap. 4.95 (ISBN 0-8163-0263-4, 13698-6). Pacific Pr Pub Assn.

Mr. Dooley & Mr. Dunne. E. Bander. 150p. 1981. text ed. 12.50 (ISBN 0-87215-329-0). Michie.

Mr. Forgetful. (Mr. Books). 1980. 1.00 (ISBN 0-8431-0805-3). Price Stern.

Mr. Fussy. (Mr. Books). 1980. 1.00 (ISBN 0-8431-0807-X). Price Stern.

Mr. Gay's London. Alan P. Herbert. LC 75-25258. (Illus.). 136p. 1975. Repr. of 1948 ed. lib. bdg. 13.50x (ISBN 0-8371-4805-7, HEGL). Greenwood.

Mr. George, 2 pts. Ed. by M. V. Callcott & Terry Peters. Incl. Pt. 1. In Victorian England; Pt. 2. In Pioneer Texas. (National History Ser.). (Illus.). Date not set. 16.95 (ISBN 0-89482-046-X); ltd. ed. 39.95 (ISBN 0-89482-048-6); pap. 8.95 (ISBN 0-89482-047-8); video cassette of Frank Callcott 165.00 (ISBN 0-89482-022-2). Stevenson Pr.

Mr. Goat's Bad Good Idea: Three Stories. Marileta Robinson. LC 77-26601. (gr. 1-4). 1979. 6.95 (ISBN 0-690-03862-3, TYC-J); PLB 7.89 (ISBN 0-690-03864-X). T Y Crowell.

Mister God, This Is Anna. Fynn. 192p. 1976. pap. 2.25 (ISBN 0-345-28910-2). Ballantine.

Mr. Gosling & the Great Art Robbery. John Cunliffe. (Illus.). (ps-3). 1979. PLB 8.95 (ISBN 0-233-96956-X). Andre Deutsch.

Mr. Gosling & the Runaway Chair. John Cunliffe. LC 80-2696. (Illus.). 32p. (gr. k-3). 1981. 8.95 (ISBN 0-233-96956-X). Andre Deutsch.

Mr. Greedy. (Mr. Books). 1980. 1.00 (ISBN 0-8431-0817-7). Price Stern.

Mr. Grumpy. (Mr. Books). 1980. 1.00 (ISBN 0-8431-0804-5). Price Stern.

Mr. Gumpy's Motor Car. John Burningham. LC 75-4582. (Illus.). 48p. (gr. k-3). 1976. 8.95 (ISBN 0-690-00798-1, TYC-J); PLB 8.79 (ISBN 0-690-00799-X). T Y Crowell.

Mr. Hamilton & Mr. Jefferson. Donald B. Chidsey. LC 74-34448. 160p. 1975. 7.95 o.p. (ISBN 0-525-66446-7). Elsevier-Nelson.

Mr. Happy. (Mr. Books). 1980. 1.00 (ISBN 0-8431-0813-4). Price Stern.

Mr. Hodge & Mr. Hazard. Elinor Wylie. 256p. 1980. Repr. of 1928 ed. lib. bdg. 20.00 (ISBN 0-89760-924-7). Telegraph Bks.

Mr. Jackson's Mushrooms. H. A. Jackson. Intro. by Mimi Cazort. (Illus.). 1979. 35.00 (ISBN 0-88884-364-X, 56430-4, Pub. by Natl Gallery Canada). U of Chicago Pr.

Mr. Jacobson's War. Richard Hammer. 1981. 9.95. HarBraceJ.

Mr. Jelly Bean. Ed D. Garehime. LC 77-82261. (Mr. Jelly Bean Adventure Ser.: No. 1). (Illus.). 64p. (gr. k-5). PLB 6.95 (ISBN 0-918822-01-7). Deem Corp.

Mister Jones, Meet the Master. Ed. by Catherine Marshall. 1966. pap. 1.50 o.s.i. (ISBN 0-515-04810-0). Jove Pubns.

Mr. Justice Brandeis. Ed. by Felix Frankfurter. LC 73-37766. (American Constitutional & Legal History Ser). (Illus.). 232p. 1972. Repr. of 1932 ed. lib. bdg. 22.50 (ISBN 0-306-70430-7). Da Capo.

Mister Justice Cardozo, a Liberal Mind in Action. Joseph P. Pollard. Repr. of 1935 ed. lib. bdg. 18.75x (ISBN 0-8371-2815-3, POJD). Greenwood.

Mister Justice Sutherland, a Man Against the State. Joel F. Paschal. Repr. of 1951 ed. lib. bdg. 15.75x (ISBN 0-8371-2517-0, PAJS). Greenwood.

Mr. Law's Unlawfulness of the Stage Entertainment Examin'd. S. Philomusus. Bd. with Entertainment of the Stage; Some Few Hints in Defence of Dramatical Entertainments. Allan Ramsay. (English Stage Ser.: Vol. 50). lib. bdg. 50.00 (ISBN 0-8240-0633-X). Garland Pub.

Mr. Lazy. (Mr. Books). 1980. 1.00 (ISBN 0-8431-0806-1). Price Stern.

Mr. Lincoln. J. G. Randall. Ed. by Richard N. Current. Date not set. 5.00 (ISBN 0-8446-0865-3). Peter Smith.

Mr. Lincoln's Camera Man: Matthew B. Brady. 2nd, rev. ed. Roy Meredith. (Illus.). 14.00 (ISBN 0-8446-5224-5). Peter Smith.

Mr. Lincoln's Inaugural Journey. Mary K. Phelan. LC 76-175110. (Illus.). (gr. 5-8). 1972. 8.95 (ISBN 0-685-24997-2, TYC-J). T Y Crowell.

Mr. Little. Robert N. Peck. LC 78-22347. (Illus.). 1979. 7.95a (ISBN 0-385-13657-9); PLB (ISBN 0-385-13658-7). Doubleday.

Mr. Lucky's Trick Dog Training Book. 4.95 (ISBN 0-87714-086-3). Green Hill.

Mister Magnolia. Quentin Blake. (gr. k-3). 1980. 8.95 (ISBN 0-224-01612-1, Pub. by Chatto Bodley Jonathan). Merrimack Bk Serv.

Mr. Meebles. Jack Kent. LC 70-117562. (Illus.). 48p. (gr. k-2). 1970. 5.95 o.s.i. (ISBN 0-8193-0408-5, Four Winds); PLB 5.41 o.s.i. (ISBN 0-8193-0409-3). Schol Bk Serv.

Mr. Mick. Steve Augarde. LC 80-65660. (Illus.). 32p. (ps-3). 1980. 9.95 (ISBN 0-233-97254-4). Andre Deutsch.

Mr. Miller the Dog. Helme Heine. LC 80-81298. (Illus.). 64p. (gr. 1 up). 1980. 8.95 (ISBN 0-689-50174-9, McElderry). Atheneum.

Mr. Mischief. (Mr. Books). 1980. 1.00 (ISBN 0-8431-0802-9). Price Stern.

Mr. Mizzen's Rocket. George Craig. (Illus.). (ps-5). 1968. 6.95 (ISBN 0-571-08669-1, Pub. by Faber & Faber). Merrimack Bk Serv.

Mr. Moto: Great Stories from the Saturday Evening Post. LC 77-90931. 1977. 5.95 (ISBN 0-89387-016-1). Sat Eve Post.

Mr. Mysterious's Secrets of Magic. Sid Fleischman. (Illus.). 96p. (gr. 4-6). 1975. 5.95 (ISBN 0-316-28584-6, Pub. by Atlantic Monthly Pr). Little.

Mr. Noisey. (Mr. Books). 1980. 1.00 (ISBN 0-8431-0810-X). Price Stern.

Mister Papadilly & Willy. Florence Slobodkin & Louis Slobodkin. LC 64-23322. (Illus.). (gr. 4-9). 4.95 (ISBN 0-8149-0391-6). Vanguard.

Mister Parker Pyne, Detective. Agatha Christie. 1971. pap. 1.95 o.s.i. (ISBN 0-440-15888-5). Dell.

Mr. Parker Pyne, Detective. Agatha Christie. 1981. pap. 2.25 (ISBN 0-440-15888-5). Dell.

Mr. Peale's Museum: Charles Willson Peale & the First Popular Museum of Natural Science. Charles C. Sellers. (Barra Bks.). 1980. 14.95 (ISBN 0-393-05700-3). Norton.

Mr. Peeknuff's Tiny People. Donna Hill. LC 80-12271. 32p. (ps-2). 1981. PLB 9.95 (ISBN 0-689-30778-0). Atheneum.

Mr. Plum's Oasis. Elisa Trimby. LC 80-17662. 32p. (gr. 1-4). 1981. 7.95 (ISBN 0-688-41991-7); PLB 7.63 (ISBN 0-688-51991-1). Morrow.

Mr. Polk's War: American Opposition & Dissent, 1846-1848. John H. Schroeder. 224p. 1973. 17.50x (ISBN 0-299-06160-4). U of Wis Pr.

Mr. President... William Heller. 260p. 1980. 10.00 (ISBN 0-8059-2753-0). Dorrance.

Mr. Quiet. (Mr. Books). 1980. 1.00 (ISBN 0-8431-0803-7). Price Stern.

Mr. Revere & I. Robert Lawson. (gr. 3-6). 1973. pap. 1.25 (ISBN 0-440-45897-8, YB). Dell.

Mr. Right. Carolyn Banks. 1980. pap. 2.50 (ISBN 0-446-91191-7). Warner Bks.

Mr. Rogers' Neighborhood: The Costume Party. Fred Rogers. (ps-1). 1976. PLB 5.38 (ISBN 0-307-68958-1, Golden Pr). Western Pub.

Mister Roger's Songbook. Fred Rogers. (gr. k-2). 1970. 4.95 o.p. (ISBN 0-394-80481-3). Random.

Mr. Rumbletum's Gumboot. Postgate & Firmin. 1975. 3.95 (ISBN 0-7207-0781-1, Pub. by Michael Joseph). Merrimack Bk Serv.

Mr. Sampath: The Printer of Malgudi. R. K. Narayan. LC 80-27352. 220p. 1981. lib. bdg. 15.00x (ISBN 0-226-56838-5); pap. 4.95 (ISBN 0-226-56839-3). U of Chicago Pr.

Mr. September. John Trengove. 1980. 10.95 (ISBN 0-8253-0018-5). Beaufort Bks NY.

Mr. Shaw's Shipshape Shoeshop. Eve Titus. LC 76-77789. (Illus.). 48p. (gr. k-3). 5.95 o.s.i. (ISBN 0-8193-0366-6, Four Winds); PLB 5.41 o.s.i. (ISBN 0-8193-0367-4). Schol Bk Serv.

Mr. Siggie Morrison with His Comb & Paper. Bill Reed. (Australian Theatre Workshop Ser.). 1972. pap. text ed. 4.25x (ISBN 0-686-65323-8, 00525). Heinemann Ed.

Mr. Silly. (Mr. Books). 1980. 1.00 (ISBN 0-8431-0811-8). Price Stern.

Mr. Silver & Mr. Gold. Dale B. Fink. 32p. (gr. 4-8). 8.95 (ISBN 0-87705-447-9). Human Sci Pr.

Mr. Skinner's Skinny House. Ann McGovern. LC 79-18360. (Illus.). 48p. (gr. 2-6). 1980. 7.95 (ISBN 0-590-07620-5, Four Winds). Schol Bk Serv.

Mr. Stubbs: Horsepainter. Constance-Anne Parker. (Illus.). 24.50 (ISBN 0-85131-123-7, Dist. by Sporting Book Center). J A Allen.

Mister Tail Gate. Glen J. Hatfield. (Illus.). 1969. pap. 2.00 (ISBN 0-9600216-0-4). Hatfield.

Mr. Terwilliger's Secret. Dave Ross & Jeanne Wilson. (Easy-Read Story Bk.). (Illus.). 32p. (gr. k-3). 1981. 3.95 (ISBN 0-531-02472-5). Watts.

Mister Tompkins in Paperback. George Gamow. (Illus., Orig.). 1967. bds. 17.95 (ISBN 0-521-06905-X); pap. 5.95x (ISBN 0-521-09355-4). Cambridge U Pr.

Mister Turtle's Magic Glasses. Jane Thayer. LC 74-118284. (Illus.). (ps-3). 1971. 7.25 (ISBN 0-688-21650-1). Morrow.

Mr. Watson's Editorials on the War Issues. Thomas E. Watson. (Studies in Populism). 1980. lib. bdg. 69.95 (ISBN 0-686-68881-3). Revisionist Pr.

Mr. William Prynn - His Defence of Stage-Plays: Retraction of a Former Book of His Called 'Histrio-Mastix' Bd. with Vindication of William Prynne. William Prynne; Theatrum Redivivum: In Answer to Mr. Pryn's Histrio-Mastix. Sir Richard Baker. (English Stage Ser.: Vol. 15). lib. bdg. 50.00 (ISBN 0-8240-0598-8). Garland Pub.

Mister Wolf & Me. Mary F. Shura. LC 78-22432. (Illus.). (gr. 5 up). 1979. 5.95 (ISBN 0-396-07666-1). Dodd.

Mr. Worry. (Mr. Books). 1980. 1.00 (ISBN 0-8431-0800-2). Price Stern.

Mr. Yowder & the Lion Roar Capsules. Glen Rounds. (gr. k-6). 1980. pap. 1.25 (ISBN 0-440-45726-2, YB). Dell.

Mr. Yowder & the Steamboat. Glen Rounds. (gr. k-6). 1980. pap. 1.25 (ISBN 0-440-45727-0, YB). Dell.

Mister Zip & U. S. Mail. Jene Barr. LC 64-16364. (Career Awareness-Community Helpers Ser.). (Illus.). (gr. k-2). 1964. 4.75g o.p. (ISBN 0-8075-5180-5). A Whitman.

Mistletoe & Sword. Anya Seton. 1974. pap. 1.25 (ISBN 0-380-00583-2, 27672). Avon.

Mistletoe & Sword. Anya Seton. 1976. lib. bdg. 11.40 (ISBN 0-89190-442-5). Am Repr-Rivercity Pr.

Mistral. Max Brand. 224p. 1971. pap. 1.95 (ISBN 0-446-90316-7). Warner Bks.

Mistral. Rob Lyle. 1953. 24.50x (ISBN 0-686-50050-4). Elliots Bks.

Mistral. Margaret MacWilliams. LC 80-2056. (Starlight Romance Ser.). 192p. 1981. 9.95 (ISBN 0-385-17390-3). Doubleday.

Mistress. Wendy James & Susan J. Kedgley. 208p. 1974. 10.00 (ISBN 0-200-72102-X). Transatlantic.

Mistress Masham's Repose. T. H. White. (Children's Literature Ser.). 1980. PLB 9.95 (ISBN 0-8398-2615-X). Gregg.

Mistress Nancy. Barbara Bentley. LC 80-14264. 384p. 1980. 12.95 (ISBN 0-07-016722-2). McGraw.

Mistress of Corey's Landing. Margaret Harmon. 256p. (Orig.). 1981. pap. 1.95 (ISBN 0-89083-711-2). Zebra.

Mistress of Glory. Lorinda Hagen. 1978. pap. 1.95 (ISBN 0-505-51279-3). Tower Bks.

Mistress of Mellyn. Victoria Holt. 240p. 1978. pap. 2.25 (ISBN 0-449-23924-1, Crest). Fawcett.

Mistress of Soundcliff Manor. Deborah Wood. 528p. (Orig.). 1980. pap. 2.95 (ISBN 0-89083-652-3). Zebra.

Mistress of the Boards. Richard Sumner. 1976. 8.95 o.p. (ISBN 0-394-40857-8). Random.

Mistress of the Boards. Richard Sumner. 1978. pap. 1.95 o.s.i. (ISBN 0-515-04422-9). Jove Pubns.

Mistress of the King. Richard Sumner. (Orig.). 1979. pap. 1.95 o.s.i. (ISBN 0-515-04836-4). Jove Pubns.

Mistress of the Morning Star. Elizabeth Lane. 1980. 2.75 (ISBN 0-515-05467-4). Jove Pubns.

Mistress of the Streets. Richard Sumner. 1978. pap. 1.95 o.s.i. (ISBN 0-515-04487-3). Jove Pubns.

Mistress of the Sun King. Sandra DuBay. (Orig.). 1980. pap. 2.25 (ISBN 0-505-51495-8). Tower Bks.

Mistress of the Western Wind. Jessica Richards. 208p. (Orig.). 1980. pap. 2.50 (ISBN 0-515-04755-4). Jove Pubns.

Mistress of Versailles, the Life of Madame Du Barry. Agnes De Stoeckl. 1967. 8.95 (ISBN 0-685-20605-X). Transatlantic.

Mistress Wilding. Rafael Sabatini. 272p. 1976. pap. 1.50 o.p. (ISBN 0-345-25062-1). Ballantine.

Misty Meadows. Marjorie K. Lawrence. 96p. 1981. 6.00 (ISBN 0-682-49742-8). Exposition.

Misty Mornings & Moonless Nights: A Waterfowler's Guide. Norman Strung. LC 74-8226. (Illus.). 256p. 1974. 9.95 o.s.i. (ISBN 0-02-615100-6). Macmillan.

Misty of Chincoteague. Marguerite Henry. LC 47-11404. (Illus.). (gr. 2-9). 1947. 6.95 (ISBN 0-528-82315-9); pap. 2.95 (ISBN 0-528-87685-6). Rand.

Misuse of Psychiatry in the Criminal Courts: Competency to Stand Trial, Vol. 8. GAP Committee on Psychiatry & Law. LC 74-170397. (Report No. 89). 1974. pap. 4.00 (ISBN 0-87318-124-7). Adv Psychiatry.

Misused Words. Ed. by E. L. Wain. 1981. 28.50 o.p. (ISBN 0-686-68306-4). Porter.

Mit Geschlossenen Augen: Ein Tagebuch. Birgit Heiderich. (Suhrkamp Taschenbuecher: No. 638). 144p. (Orig.). 1980. pap. text ed. 4.55 (ISBN 3-518-37138-X, Pub. by Insel Verlag Germany). Suhrkamp.

Mita P 'Arriba, Mita P'Abajo. Hugo Hanriot. Ed. by SLUSA. 118p. (Spanish.). 1980. pap. 4.95 (TX525-786). SLUSA.

Mitch & Amy. Beverly Cleary. (Illus.). (gr. 3-7). 1967. 8.25 (ISBN 0-688-21688-9); PLB 7.92 (ISBN 0-688-31688-3). Morrow.

Mitchell Is Moving. Marjorie W. Sharmat. LC 78-6816. (Ready-to-Read Ser.). (Illus.). (gr. 1-4). 1978. 8.95 (ISBN 0-02-782410-1, 78241). Macmillan.

Mites Injurious to Economic Plants. Lee R. Jeppson et al. LC 72-93523. (Illus.). 1975. 46.00x (ISBN 0-520-02381-1). U of Cal Pr.

Mites of Moths & Butterflies. Asher E. Treat. LC 75-7147. (Illus.). 368p. 1975. 45.00x (ISBN 0-8014-0878-4). Comstock.

Mithraic Studies, 2 vols. Ed. by J. R. Hinnels. (Illus.). 1975. Set. 52.50x o.p. (ISBN 0-87471-557-1). Rowman.

Mithras Liturgy. Marvin W. Meyer. LC 76-18288. (Society of Biblical Literature. Texts & Translation - Graeco-Roman Religion Ser.). 1976. pap. 4.50 (ISBN 0-89130-113-5, 060210). Scholars Pr Ca.

Mithras-Orion: Greek Hero & Roman Army God. Michael P. Speidel. (Illus.). 56p. 1980. pap. text ed. 16.00x (ISBN 90-04-06055-3). Humanities.

Mithridate. Jean Racine. Ed. by Gustave Rudler. (French Texts Ser.). 1965. pap. text ed. 4.50x o.p. (ISBN 0-631-00440-8, Pub. by Basil Blackwell). Biblio Dist.

Mitmachen Wollte Ich Nie: Gespraeche. Leo Loewenthal & Helmut Dubiel. (Edition Suhrkamp: Neue Folge). 240p. (Orig.). 1980. pap. text ed. 7.80 (ISBN 3-518-11014-4, Pub. by Insel Verlag Germany). Suhrkamp.

Mitochondria, Structure & Function. Ed. by L. Ernster & L. Ernster. 1970. 54.00 (ISBN 0-12-241250-8). Acad Pr.

Mitochondria: Structure, Function & Assembly. new ed. P. A. Whittaker & Susan M. Danks. (Integrated Themes in Biology Ser.). (Illus.). 1979. pap. text ed. 10.95 (ISBN 0-582-44382-2). Longman.

Mitral Valve Prolapse. Robert M. Jeresaty. LC 78-66350. 1979. 27.00 (ISBN 0-89004-230-6). Raven.

Mitre & Crook. Bryan Houghton. LC 80-52682. 1981. pap. write for info. o.p. (ISBN 0-89555-160-8). Tan Bks Pubs.

Mitred Earl. Brian Fothergill. (Illus.). 1974. 8.95 o.p. (ISBN 0-571-09736-7, Pub. by Faber & Faber). Merrimack Bk Serv.

Mittelalter. Hans Delbruck. LC 80-2677. 1981. Repr. of 1907 ed. 63.50 (ISBN 0-404-18559-2). AMS Pr.

Mittelhochdeutsche Glossare und Vokabulare in Schweizerischen Bibliotheken bis 1500. Heinrich Haenger. (Quellen und Forschungen zur Sprach-und Kulturgeschichte der Germanischen Voelker N. F. 44). 88p. 1972. 29.50 (ISBN 3-11-003542-1). De Gruyter.

Miwuyt Marriage: The Cultural Anthropology of Affinity in Northeast Arnhem Land. Warren Shapiro. (Illus.). 240p. 1981. text ed. 18.50x (ISBN 0-89727-021-5). Inst Study Hum.

Mix Butter with Love. Joyce Landorf. LC 74-18857. 1974. gift ed. 8.95 (ISBN 0-89081-035-4, 0354). Harvest Hse.

Mix or Match Storybook: 2,097,152 Silly Stories. Peter Lippman. LC 73-18934. (Illus.). 9p. 1974. 2.50 (ISBN 0-394-82808-9, BYR). Random.

Mixed Ability Grouping: An Individualized Approach. 2nd ed. A. V. Kelly. 1978. text ed. 15.70 (ISBN 0-06-318069-3, IntlDept); pap. text ed. 9.25 (ISBN 0-06-318070-7, IntlDept). Har-Row.

Mixed Bag: A New Collection for Understanding & Response. 2nd ed. Alan Casty. (Illus.). 256p. 1975. pap. text ed. 8.95 (ISBN 0-13-586016-4). P-H.

Mixed Bag of Magic Tricks. Roz Abisch & Boche Kaplan. LC 73-92656. (Illus.). 64p. (gr. 2-5). 1974. 5.95 o.s.i. (ISBN 0-8027-6189-5). Walker & Co.

Mixed Feelings. George A. Effinger. LC 74-4858. 1974. 7.95 o.s.i. (ISBN 0-06-011146-1, HarpT). Har-Row.

Mixed Singles. Douglass Wallop. 1978. pap. 1.75 o.s.i. (ISBN 0-515-04521-7). Jove Pubns.

Mixed-up Chameleon. Eric Carle. LC 75-5505. (Illus.). (gr. k-2). 1975. 8.95 (ISBN 0-690-00605-5, TYC-J); PLB 8.79 (ISBN 0-690-00924-0). T Y Crowell.

Mixed-up Twins. Carolyn Haywood. (Illus.). (ps-3). 1952. 8.25 (ISBN 0-688-21683-8). Morrow.

Mixed Use Development: New Ways of Land Use. Robert E. Witherspoon et al. LC 75-37217. (Technical Bulletin Ser: No. 71). (Illus.). 1976. pap. 22.00 (ISBN 0-87420-071-7). Urban Land.

Mixed-Valence Compounds: Theory & Applications in Chemistry, Physics, Geology & Biology. Ed. by David B. Brown. (NATO Advanced Study Institute, C. Mathematical & Physical Sciences Ser.: No. 58). 525p. 1980. lib. bdg. 60.50 (ISBN 90-277-1152-6, Pub. by D. Reidel). Kluwer Boston.

Mixer & Blender Cookery Book. Alison Denny. (Illus.). 1978. 11.95 (ISBN 0-571-09736-7, Pub. by Faber & Faber); pap. 5.95 (ISBN 0-571-11073-8). Merrimack Bk Serv.

Mixing: Principals & Applications. Shinji Nagata. LC 75-2056. 1975. 64.95 (ISBN 0-470-62863-4). Halsted Pr.

MLA Handbook for Writers of Research Papers, Theses & Dissertations. Joseph Gibaldi & Walter S. Achtert. LC 77-76954. 163p. (Orig.). 1977. 6.25 (ISBN 0-87352-450-0); pap. 4.75x (ISBN 0-87352-000-9). Modern Lang.

MLA International Bibliography of Books & Articles on the Modern Languages & Literatures, 1970. Compiled by Harrison T. Meserole. 1972. 150.00x (ISBN 0-87352-202-8). Modern Lang.

MLA International Bibliography of Books & Articles on the Modern Languages & Literatures, 1971. Compiled by Harrison T. Meserole. 1973. 150.00x (ISBN 0-87352-213-3). Modern Lang.

MLA International Bibliography of Books & Articles on the Modern Languages & Literatures, 1972. Compiled by Harrison T. Meserole. 1974. 150.00x (ISBN 0-87352-221-4). Modern Lang.

MLA International Bibliography of Books & Articles on the Modern Languages & Literatures, 1973. Compiled by Harrison T. Meserole. 1975. 150.00x (ISBN 0-87352-233-8). Modern Lang.

MLA International Bibliography of Books & Articles on the Modern Languages & Literatures, 1969. Compiled by Harrison T. Meserole. 1970. 150.00x (ISBN 0-87352-409-8). Modern Lang.

MLA International Bibliography of Books & Articles on the Modern Languages & Literatures, 1974. Compiled by Harrison T. Meserole. 1976. 150.00x (ISBN 0-87352-241-9). Modern Lang.

MLA International Bibliography of Books & Articles on the Modern Languages & Literatures, 1978. LC 64-20773. 1979. 150.00x (ISBN 0-87352-413-6). Modern Lang.

MLA International Bibliography of Books & Articles on the Modern Languages & Literatures, 1977. LC 64-20773. 1978. 150.00x (ISBN 0-87352-408-X). Modern Lang.

MLA International Bibliography of Books & Articles on the Modern Languages & Literatures, 1975. 1977. 150.00x (ISBN 0-87352-245-1). Modern Lang.

MLA International Bibliography of Books & Articles on the Modern Languages & Literatures, 1976. 1978. 150.00x (ISBN 0-87352-403-9). Modern Lang.

MLA International Bibliography of Books & Articles on the Modern Languages & Literatures, 1979. LC 64-20773. 800p. 1980. 150.00x (ISBN 0-87352-418-7). Modern Lang.

Mliss. Bret Harte. Ed. by Walter Pauk & Raymond Harris. (Classics Ser). (gr. 6-12). 1976. pap. text ed. 1.60x (ISBN 0-89061-048-7, 517); tchrs. ed. 3.00 (ISBN 0-89061-049-5, 519). Jamestown Pubs.

MMPI: An Interpretive Manual. Roger L. Greene. 1980. 21.00 (ISBN 0-8089-1279-8). Grune.

MMPI: Clinical & Research Trends. Ed. by Charles S. Newmark. LC 79-17777. (Praeger Special Studies). 464p. 1979. 35.95 (ISBN 0-03-048926-1). Praeger.

Mo-Ped: The Wonder Vehicle. Jerry Murray. (Illus.). (YA) (gr. 7-9). 1978. pap. 1.25 (ISBN 0-671-29882-8). PB.

Mob, Inc. Fred J. Cook. (gr. 7 up). 1977. PLB 7.90 (ISBN 0-531-00124-5). Watts.

Mob: The Story of Organized Crime in America. Leslie Waller. LC 73-6242. 160p. (gr. 7 up). 1973. 5.95 o.p. (ISBN 0-440-05720-5). Delacorte.

Mobil Travel Guide, 7 vols. Incl. California & the West (ISBN 0-528-84520-9); Great Lakes Area (ISBN 0-528-84521-7); Middle Atlantic States (ISBN 0-528-84522-5); Northeastern States (ISBN 0-528-84523-3); Northwest & Great Plains States (ISBN 0-528-84524-1); Southeastern States (ISBN 0-528-84525-X); Southwest & South Central Area (ISBN 0-528-84526-8). 1981. pap. 6.95 ea. Rand.

Mobil Travel Guides, 7 vols. Incl. California & the West (ISBN 0-528-84451-2); Great Lakes Area (ISBN 0-528-84452-0); Middle Atlantic States (ISBN 0-528-84453-9); Northeastern States (ISBN 0-528-84454-7); Northwest & Great Plains States (ISBN 0-528-84455-5); Southeastern States (ISBN 0-528-84456-3); Southwest & South Central Area (ISBN 0-528-84457-1). 1980. pap. 5.95 ea. o.p. Rand.

Mobile Home & Recreation Vehicle Park Operation Manual: (Two Looseleaf Volumes) David Nulsen & Robert H. Nulsen. 1978. 129.50 (ISBN 0-87593-126-X). Trail-R.

Mobile Home Park Plans & Specifications. David Nulsen. Date not set. 69.50 o.s.i. (ISBN 0-87593-009-3). Trail-R. Postponed.

Mobile Homes, 2 pts. Max Wehrly. LC 72-79132. (Illus.). 80p. 1972. Set. pap. 4.75 (ISBN 0-87420-068-7). An Analysis Of Characteristics. An Analysis Of Communities. Urban Land.

Mobile Intensive Care: A Problem Oriented Approach. Linda Baldwin & Ruth Pierce. LC 78-18240. (Illus.). 1978. pap. 12.95 (ISBN 0-8016-0428-1). Mosby.

Mobility & Community Change in Australia. Ed. by I. H. Burnley et al. (Studies in Society & Culture). (Illus.). 286p. 1981. text ed. 30.25x (ISBN 0-7022-1446-9). U of Queensland Pr.

Mobility: From There to Here. Don Fabun. 1971. pap. text ed. 2.50x (ISBN 0-02-475380-7, 47538). Macmillan.

Mobility of PhD's: Before & After the Doctorate. Office Of Scientific Personnel. LC 72-611001. (Orig.). 1971. pap. text ed. 6.75 (ISBN 0-309-01874-9). Natl Acad Pr.

Mobilization & Reassembly of Genetic Information: Vol. 17 of the Miami Winter Symposia. Ed. by Walter A. Scott et al. LC 80-18845. 1980. 35.00 (ISBN 0-12-633360-2). Acad Pr.

Mobilizing Technology for World Development. Ed. by Jairam Ramesh & Charles Weiss, Jr. LC 79-5349. 240p. 1979. pap. 6.95 (ISBN 0-03-055451-9). Overseas Dev Council.

Moby Dick. Herman Melville. 1954. 11.50x (ISBN 0-460-00179-5, Evman); pap. 4.95 (ISBN 0-460-01179-0). Dutton.

Moby Dick. Herman Melville. (Illus.). (gr. 7 up). 1962. 5.95 o.s.i. (ISBN 0-02-766830-4). Macmillan.

Moby Dick. Herman Melville. (Literature Ser). pap. text ed. 4.17 (ISBN 0-87720-710-0). AMSCO Sch.

Moby-Dick. Herman Melville. Ed. by Harold Beaver. (English Library). 1975. pap. 3.95 (ISBN 0-14-043082-2). Penguin.

Moby Dick. Herman Melville. pap. 1.95. Bantam.

Moby-Dick & Calvinism: A World Dismantled. T. Walter Herbert, Jr. 1977. 14.00 (ISBN 0-8135-0829-0). Rutgers U Pr.

Moby-Dick As Doubloon. Ed. by Harrison Hayford & Hershel Parker. 1970. pap. text ed. 6.95x (ISBN 0-393-09883-4, NortonC). Norton.

Moby Dick or, The Whale. Herman Melville. Ed. by Charles Feidelson, Jr. LC 64-16178. 1964. pap. 6.95 (ISBN 0-672-60971-1, LL5). Bobbs.

Moby Dick with Reader's Guide. Herman Melville. (Amsco Literature Program Ser.). 1970. pap. 4.67 (ISBN 0-87720-806-9); tchr's ed. 3.00 (ISBN 0-87720-906-5). AMSCO Sch.

Moccasin Meanderings. Leonora McDowell. Ed. by M. Karl Kulikowski. (Gusto Press Poetry Discovery Ser.). (Orig.). 1979. pap. 3.95 (ISBN 0-933906-02-1). Gusto Pr.

Moccasins & Sneakers. Beverly Amstutz. (Illus.). 1980. pap. 2.50 (ISBN 0-937836-02-8). Precious Res.

Moche Occupation of the Santa Valley, Peru. Christopher B. Donnan. (U. C. Publ. in Anthropology: Vol. 8). 1973. pap. 10.50x o.p. (ISBN 0-520-09410-7). U of Cal Pr.

Mock Revolt. Vera Cleaver & Bill Cleaver. LC 75-151467. 160p. (gr. 6 up). 1971. PLB 8.79 (ISBN 0-397-31238-5); pap. 1.95 (ISBN 0-397-31237-7). Lippincott.

Mockingbird. Walter Tevis. 288p. 1980. pap. 2.95 (ISBN 0-553-14144-9). Bantam.

Mockingbird Flight: Music Book & Records. Patricia H. Nielsen & Floyd Sucher. (Kindergarten Keys Ser.). (Illus.). 1975. pap. text ed. 10.80 (ISBN 0-87892-660-7); record set 49.50 (ISBN 0-87892-666-6). Economy Co.

Mockingbird Wish Me Luck. Charles Bukowski. 160p. (Orig.). 1979. 10.00 (ISBN 0-87685-139-1); pap. 5.00 (ISBN 0-87685-138-3). Black Sparrow.

Modal Counterpoint in the Style of the Sixteenth Century. Ernst Krenek. LC 59-45012. 21p. 1959. pap. 3.50 (ISBN 0-913932-11-6). Boosey & Hawkes.

Modal Logic. Brian F. Chellas. LC 76-47197. 1980. 50.50 (ISBN 0-521-22476-4); pap. 15.95x (ISBN 0-521-29515-7). Cambridge U Pr.

Modal System of Arab & Persian Music A.D. 1250-1300. O. Wright. (Illus.). 292p. 1976. 95.00x (ISBN 0-19-713575-7). Oxford U Pr.

MODCOM Modules in Speech Communication, 22 modules. Ed. by Ronald Applbaum & Roderick Hart. 1976. Individual Modules. pap. text ed. 2.25 (ISBN 0-586-68014-6); Set. pap. 49.50 (ISBN 0-574-22529-3, 13-5529). SRA.

Mode in Costume. R. Turner Wilcox. LC 58-12732. (Illus.). 1942. Repr. of 1942 ed. lib. rep. ed. 25.00x (ISBN 0-684-15165-0, ScribT). Scribner.

Mode of Action of Herbicides. 2nd ed. Floyd M. Ashton & Alden S. Crafts. 464p. 1981. 42.50 (ISBN 0-471-04847-X. Pub. by Wiley-Interscience). Wiley.

Mode of Inheritance, Interaction & Application of Genes Conditioning Resistance to Yellow Rust. Gerhard Roebbelen & Eugene L. Sharp. (Advances in Plant Breeding Ser.: Vol. 9). (Illus.). 88p. (Orig.). 1978. pap. text ed. 25.00 (ISBN 3-489-71110-6). Parey Sci Pubs.

Model A Ford: Care & Maintenance of Automobiles & Trucks. Victor W. Page. (Illus.). 1948. pap. 4.00 o.p. (ISBN 0-89287-264-0, H524). Clymer Pubns.

Model A Miseries & Cures. Mary Moline. (Illus.). 1972. pap. 6.00 (ISBN 0-913444-00-6, Pub. by Rumbleseat Press). Motorbooks Intl.

Model Aircraft. Barbara Curry. (First Bks.). (Illus.). (gr. 4 up). 1979. PLB 6.45 s&l (ISBN 0-531-02260-9). Watts.

Model Aircraft Handbook. rev. ed. Howard G. McEntee. LC 68-27317. (Funk & W Bk.). (Illus.). 240p. 1975. pap. 2.95 o.s.i. (ISBN 0-308-10150-2, F109, TYC-T). T Y Crowell.

Model Aircraft Handbook. rev. ed. Howard G. McEntee & William Winter. LC 68-27317. (Illus.). 1968. 8.95 o.s.i. (ISBN 0-690-54632-7, TYC-T). T Y Crowell.

Model Airplanes & How to Build Them. Harvey Weiss. LC 74-19451. (Illus.). 80p. (gr. 5 up). 1975. 9.95 (ISBN 0-690-00594-6, TYC-J). T Y Crowell.

Model Analysis of Plane Structures. T. M. Charlton. 1966. 9.90 o.p. (ISBN 0-08-011304-4); pap. 6.00 o.p. (ISBN 0-08-011303-6). Pergamon.

Model & Department Policy Statement with Job Descriptions for Hospitals. Frank D. Murphy. (Medical Bks.). 1980. lib. bdg. 64.95 (ISBN 0-8161-2199-0, Hall Medical). G K Hall.

Model Building Techniques for Management. John Hull et al. (Illus.). 1977. 19.95 (ISBN 0-566-00149-7, 00719-6 Pub. by Saxon Hse). Lexington Bks.

Model Business Letters. 2nd ed. I. Gartside. 416p. 1974. pap. 13.95x (Pub. by Macdonald & Evans England). Intl Ideas.

Model Cars. Richard L. Knudson. LC 80-17153. (Superwheels & Thrill Sports Bks.). (Illus.). (YA) (gr. 4 up). 1981. PLB 6.95g (ISBN 0-685-96939-8). Lerner Pubns.

Model Cars & Trucks & How to Build Them. Harvey Weiss. LC 44-7403. (Illus.). 80p. (gr. 5 up). 1974. 10.95 (ISBN 0-690-00414-1, TYC-J). T Y Crowell.

Model Cars of Gerald Wingrove. G. A. Wingrove. (Illus.). 1979. 42.95 (ISBN 0-904568-12-1, Pub. by Eyre Methuen England). Motorbooks Intl.

Model Childhood. Christa Wolf. Tr. by Ursule Molinaro & Hedwig Rappolt. 416p. 1980. 17.50 (ISBN 0-374-21170-1). FS&G.

Model Choice & the Value of Travel Time. Ian G. Heggie. (Illus.). 1976. 24.00x (ISBN 0-19-828404-7). Oxford U Pr.

Model Church. G. C. Brewer. 6.50 o.p. (ISBN 0-89225-167-0). Gospel Advocate.

Model Continuing Education Recognition System in Library & Information Science. E. Stone et al. 1979. 32.80 (ISBN 0-89664-145-7, Pub. by K G Saur). Shoe String.

Model Country: Jose Batlle y Ordonez of Uruguay, 1907-1915. Milton I. Vanger. LC 80-50489. (Illus.). 448p. (Orig.). 1980. text ed. 25.00x (ISBN 0-8745 -184-4). U Pr of New Eng.

Model Criteria Sets for Professional Standards Review Organization. Ed. by American Psychiatric Association's Ad Hoc Committee on Professional Standards Review Organization. 1974. 2.50 o.p. (ISBN 0-685-77443-0, 189). Am Psychiatric.

Model Design & Building. Boy Scouts Of America. LC 19-600. (Illus.). 44p. (gr. 6-12). 1964. pap. 0.70x (ISBN 0-8395-3280-6, 3280). BSA.

Model Flying Handbook. Ottar Stensbol. LC 75-14507. (Illus.). 128p. (gr. 6 up). 1976. 9.95 (ISBN 0-8069-0088-1); PLB 9.29 (ISBN 0-8069-0089-X). Sterling.

Model for Murder. Carter Brown. (Orig.). 1980. pap. 1.50 (ISBN 0-505-51527-X). Tower Bks.

Model for Theses & Research Papers. Stephen V. Ballou. LC 72-125125. (Illus., Orig.). 1970. pap. text ed. 6.85 (ISBN 0-395-10806-3, 3-02700). HM.

Model Jury Instructions in Virginia: Civil, 2 vols. 1980. Set. 90.00 (ISBN 0-87215-284-7); Vol. I. (ISBN 0-87215-282-0). Vol. II. Michie.

Model Jury Instructions in Virginia: Criminal, 2 vols. 1979. 90.00 set (ISBN 0-87215-281-2). Vol. 1 (ISBN 0-87215-230-8). Vol. 2 (ISBN 0-87215-231-6). 1980 suppl. 20.00 (ISBN 0-87215-333-9). Michie.

Model Locomotive Construction. 2nd ed. Martin Evans. (Illus.). 163p. 1978. pap. 9.50x (ISBN 0-85242-602-X). Intl Pubns Serv.

Model Making in Schools. Brenda B. Jackson. 1971. 15.95 o.p. (ISBN 0-7134-2298-X, Pub. by Batsford England). David & Charles.

Model Managerie: Laboratory Studies About Living Systems. Steven Vogel & Katherine C. Ewel. 1972. pap. text ed. 7.95 (ISBN 0-201-08149-0). A-W.

Model of an Ablating Solid Hydrogen Pellet in a Plasma. Paul B. Parks. LC 78-74999. (Outstanding Dissertations on Energy Ser.). 1979. lib. bdg. 14.00 (ISBN 0-8240-3989-0). Garland Pub.

Model of Interpersonal Speech Communication. Paul E. Reid. LC 79-64197. 1979. pap. text ed. 6.25 (ISBN 0-8191-0755-7). U Pr of Amer.

Model of Mass Communications & National Development: A Liberian Perspective. Abdulai Vandi. LC 79-89253. 1979. pap. text ed. 9.00 (ISBN 0-8191-0812-X). U Pr of Amer.

Model of Output, Employment, Wages & Prices in the UK. Ed. by I. F. Pearce et al. LC 75-46134. (Illus.). 1976. 29.95 (ISBN 0-521-21210-3). Cambridge U Pr.

Model of the Brain. John Z. Young. 1964. 24.50x (ISBN 0-19-857333-2). Oxford U Pr.

Model Penal Code & Commentaries, 3 vols, Pt. II. Commentary by R. Kent Greenawalt & Peter W. Low. 1427p. 105.00 set (ISBN 0-686-69005-2); postage & handling 9.00 (ISBN 0-686-69006-0). Am Law Inst.

Model Railroader Cyclopedia: Diesel Locomotives. Ed. by Bob Hayden. LC 61-21207. (Illus.). 160p. (Orig.). 1980. pap. 22.00 (ISBN 0-89024-547-9). Kalmbach.

Model Railroading: A Complete Guide. Bruce Greenberg. LC 78-61847. (Illus.). 1979. 14.95 o.p. (ISBN 0-13-586149-7). P-H.

Model Railroading: How to Plan, Build, & Maintain Your Trains & Pikes. Gil Paust. LC 80-1817. (Illus.). 160p. (gr. 4 up). 1981. 9.95a (ISBN 0-385-13033-3); PLB (ISBN 0-385-13034-1). Doubleday.

Model Rockets from Design to Launch. Douglas J. Malawicki & Donald C. Schwenn. 1976. pap. text ed. 8.00x (ISBN 0-912468-16-5); tchrs'. ed. 10.00 (ISBN 0-912468-15-7). Rockets.

Model Schemes for the Training of Adult Operators in Technical Trades, 40 vols. Ed. by Engineering Industry Training Board. (Illus.). 1968-1972. Set. 132.50x (ISBN 0-685-90166-1). Intl Ideas.

Model Soldiers. M. Windrow & Gembleton. (Illus.). 1976. 4.95 o.p. (ISBN 0-85059-234-8). Aztex.

Model Soldiers in Color. Roy Dilley. (Illus.). 1979. 12.95 (ISBN 0-7137-0907-3, Pub by Blandford Pr England). Sterling.

Model State Plan for Vocational Evaluation of Deaf Clients. Jerome Schein. 1977. pap. 2.50 o.p. (ISBN 0-913072-28-1). Natl Assn Deaf.

Model Theory of Algebra & Arithmetics: Procedings. Ed. by L. Pacholski et al. (Lecture Notes in Mathematics Ser.: Vol. 834). 410p. 1981. pap. 24.50 (ISBN 0-686-69431-7). Springer-Verlag.

Modeling & Analysis: An Introduction to System Performance Evaluation Methodology. Hisashi Kobayashi. LC 77-73946. (IBM Ser.). (Illus.). 1978. text ed. 20.95 (ISBN 0-201-14457-3). A-W.

Modeling & Analysis of Dynamic Systems. Charles M. Close & Dean K. Frederick. LC 77-74421. (Illus.). 1978. text ed. 27.95 (ISBN 0-395-25040-4); sol. manual 2.05 (ISBN 0-395-25031-5). HM.

Modeling & Analysis Using Q-Gert Networks. 2nd ed. A. Alan Pritsker. LC 78-71976. 1979. 19.50x o.p. (ISBN 0-470-26648-1). Halsted Pr.

Modeling & Other Glamour Careers. Candy Jones. LC 68-28204. (Illus.). 1969. 8.95 o.p. (ISBN 0-06-110901-0, HarpT). Har-Row.

Modeling Careers. Greta Walker. LC 76-9811. (Career Concise Guides Ser.). (Illus.). 72p. (gr. 6 up). 1976. PLB 6.45 (ISBN 0-531-01206-9). Watts.

Modeling Crop Responses to Irrigation in Relation to Soils, Climate & Salinity. R. J. Hanks & R. W. Hill. (IIIC Publication: No. 4). 71p. 1981. 17.25 (ISBN 0-08-025513-2). Pergamon.

Modeling Glass Furnace, Refiner & Forehearth Design & Operation for Energy Efficiency & Improved Control. Robert R. McConnell. LC 78-75008. (Outstanding Dissertations on Energy Ser.). 1979. lib. bdg. 28.00 (ISBN 0-8240-3976-9). Garland Pub.

Modeling in Wax for Jewelry & Sculpture. Lawrence Kallenberg. LC 80-70384. (Illus.). 288p. 1981. 18.50 (ISBN 0-686-69521-6); text ed. 18.50 (ISBN 0-686-69522-4). Chilton.

Modeling of Complex Systems. V. Vemuri. (Operation Research & Industrial Engineering). 1978. text ed. 22.00 (ISBN 0-12-716550-9). Acad Pr.

Modeling of Differential Equations in Biology. Burton. 296p. 1980. 35.00 (ISBN 0-8247-1075-4). Dekker.

Modeling of Large-scale Energy Systems: Proceedings of the IIASA-IFAC Symposium, Laxenburg, Austria, Feb. 25-29, 1980, Vol. 11. Ed. by W. Hafele & L. K. Kirchmayer. LC 80-41554. (IIASA Proceedings Ser.: Vol 11). 350p. 1980. 70.00 (ISBN 0-08-025696-1). Pergamon.

Modeling of Rivers. Hsieh W. Shen. LC 79-3913. 1979. 45.00 (ISBN 0-471-05474-7, Pub. by Wiley-Interscience). Wiley.

Modeling Seventy-Five. Compiled by American Society of Civil Engineers. 1712p. 1975. pap. text ed. 67.00 (ISBN 0-87262-124-3). Am Soc Civil Eng.

Modeling Techniques for Community Development. U. S. National Committee for the International Council for Building Research, Studies & Documentation, National Research Council. LC 75-37377. x, 86p. 1975. pap. 5.75 (ISBN 0-309-02420-X). Natl Acad Pr.

Modeling the Distribution & Intergenerational Transmission of Wealth. Ed. by James D. Smith. LC 80-15537. (National Bureau of Economic Research). 1981. lib. bdg. 28.00x (ISBN 0-226-76454-0). U of Chicago Pr.

Modeling the Multiregional Economic System: Perspectives for the Eighties. F. Gerard Adams & Norman Glickman. LC 79-48005. (Wharton Econometric Ser.). 1980. 24.95x (ISBN 0-669-03627-7). Lexington Bks.

Modeling Wastewater Renovation Land Treatment. I. K. Iskander. 343p. 1981. 20.00 (ISBN 0-471-08128-0, Pub. by Wiley-Interscience). Wiley.

Modelling & Simulation in Practice. M. Cross et al. LC 78-31375. 1979. 42.95x (ISBN 0-470-26645-7). Halsted Pr.

Modelling Jet Fighters. Bryan Philpott. (Illus.). 1976. 5.75 o.p. (ISBN 0-85059-231-3). Aztex.

Modelling Large Systems: Limits to Growth Revisited. Peter C. Roberts. LC 78-13339. (Orasa Text). 1978. pap. 19.95 (ISBN 0-470-26528-0). Halsted Pr.

Modelling Miniature Figures. Bruce Quarrie. (Illus.). 1978. pap. 11.75 (ISBN 0-85059-331-X). Aztex.

Modelling Nitrogen from Farm Wastes. Ed. by J. K. Gasser. (Illus.). 1979. 26.00x (ISBN 0-85334-869-3). Intl Ideas.

Modelling of Dynamic Systems, Vol. I, Vol. 2. Ed. by H. Nicholson. (IEE Control Engineering Ser.). (Illus.). 256p. 1981. 62.00 (ISBN 0-906048-38-9, Pub. by Peregrinus England). Inst Elect Eng.

Modelling RAF Vehicles. Gerald Scarborough. (Illus.). 1978. 6.50 o.p. (ISBN 0-85059-261-5). Aztex.

Modelling Thames Sailing Barges. Ewart Co Freeston & Bernard Kent. 96p. 1980. 15.00x (ISBN 0-85177-091-6, Pub. by Cornell England). State Mutual Bk.

Modelling with Differential Equations. D. N. Burghes & Y. M. Borrie. (Mathematics & Its Applications Ser.). 160p. 1981. 29.95 (ISBN 0-470-27101-9). Halsted Pr.

Modelling World War 2 Fighters. Bryan Philpott. (Illus.). 1977. 5.65 o.p. (ISBN 0-85059-262-3). Aztex.

Modelmaker's Handbook. Albert Jackson & David Day. LC 80-2702. (Illus.). 352p. 1981. 19.95 (ISBN 0-394-50788-6). Knopf.

Modelo de Oratoria. Moises Chavez. 144p. (Orig., Span.). 1979. pap. 3.50 (ISBN 0-89922-141-6). Edit Caribe.

Models & Mavericks: A Profile of Private Liberal Arts Colleges. Carnegie Commission on Higher Education. 1971. 6.95 o.p. (ISBN 0-07-010029-2, P&RB). McGraw.

Models & Methods: Guide to Effective Composition. J. F. Dorill & C. W. Harwell. (Illus.). 352p. 1976. pap. 9.95 (ISBN 0-13-586040-7). P-H.

Models & Systems in Architecture & Building, Vol. 2. D. Hawkes. (Land Use & Built Form Studies). 1978. text ed. 38.00x (ISBN 0-904406-09-1). Longman.

Models, Evaluations & Information Systems for Planners, Vol. 1. J. Perraton & R. Baxter. (Land Use & Built Form Studies). 1978. text ed. 38.00x (ISBN 0-904406-50-4). Longman.

Models for Concrete Structures. 1970. pap. 25.75 (ISBN 0-685-85104-4, SP-24) (ISBN 0-685-85105-2). ACI.

Models for Indicator Development: A Framework for Policy Analysis. Harvey A. Garn et al. (Institute Paper). 61p. 1976. pap. 2.50 o.p. (ISBN 0-685-99538-0, 89000). Urban Inst.

Models for Management: The Structure of Competence. Ed. by John A. Shtogren. LC 79-93291. (Illus.). 1981. pap. 17.95 (ISBN 0-937932-00-0). Teleometrics.

Models for Optimal Investment & Maintenance Decisions. Birger Rapp. LC 74-25084. 461p. 1975. 41.95 (ISBN 0-470-70911-1). Halsted Pr.

Models for the Long Distance Transport of Atmospheric Sulfur Oxides. David H. Nochumson. LC 78-74994. (Outstanding Dissertations on Energy). 1980. lib. bdg. 38.00 (ISBN 0-8240-3992-0). Garland Pub.

Models for Water Quality Management. Asit K. Biswas. (M-H Series in Water Resources & Environmental Engineering). (Illus.). 392p. 1980. text ed. 44.50 (ISBN 0-07-005481-9). McGraw.

Models in Ecology. J. M. Smith. (Illus.). 200p. 1974. 21.95 (ISBN 0-521-20262-0); pap. 8.50x (ISBN 0-521-29440-1). Cambridge U Pr.

Models in Planning. Colin Lee. LC 72-8442. 152p. 1973. text ed. 21.00 (ISBN 0-08-017020-X); pap. text ed. 9.75 (ISBN 0-08-017021-8). Pergamon.

Models in Urban & Regional Analysis. N. Oppenheim. 1980. 24.95 (ISBN 0-13-041467-0). P-H.

Models Mart Directory. 4th ed. 1980. pap. 15.00 (ISBN 0-87314-053-2). Peter Glenn.

Models of Class Domination in Plural Societies of Central Africa. Oliver V. Madu. LC 77-18595. 1978. pap. text ed. 15.45x o.p. (ISBN 0-8191-0407-8). U Pr of Amer.

Models of Disorder. J. M. Ziman. LC 77-82527. (Illus.). 1979. 71.50 (ISBN 0-521-21784-9); pap. 19.95 (ISBN 0-521-29280-8). Cambridge U Pr.

Models of Economic Growth: Proceedings. Ed. by J. Mirrlees & N. H. Stern. LC 73-531. 372p. 1973. 28.95 (ISBN 0-470-60918-4). Halsted Pr.

Models of Group Therapy & Sensitivity Training. John B. Shaffer & M. David Galinsky. (Personal, Clinical & Social Psychology Ser). 228p. 1974. 17.95 (ISBN 0-13-586081-4). P-H.

Models of High Energy Processes. J. C. Polkinghorne. LC 79-296. (Monographs on Mathematical Physics). (Illus.). 1980. 29.95 (ISBN 0-521-22369-5). Cambridge U Pr.

Models of Holiness. Ed. by Christian Duquoc & Casiano Floristan. (New Concilium: Vol. 129). 120p. (Orig.). 1980. pap. 4.95 (ISBN 0-8164-2037-8). Crossroad NY.

Models of Jesus. John F. O'Grady. LC 80-1726. 192p. 1981. 10.95 (ISBN 0-385-17320-2). Doubleday.

Models of Madness, Models of Medicine. Miriam Siegler & Humphrey Osmond. 1976. pap. 5.95x (ISBN 0-06-131953-8, TB 1953, Torch). Har-Row.

Models of Madness, Models of Medicine. Miriam Siegler & Humphry Osmond. Pref. by Paul Huston. 384p. 1974. 8.95 o.s.i. (ISBN 0-02-594000-7). Macmillan.

Models of Man: Explorations in the Western Educational Tradition. Paul Nash et al. LC 67-29011. 1968. pap. text ed. 16.95x (ISBN 0-471-63043-8). Wiley.

Models of Markets. Ed. by Alfred R. Oxenfeldt. LC 63-18435. (Illus.). 1963. 20.00x (ISBN 0-231-02643-9). Columbia U Pr.

Models of Monetary Economies. Ed. by John H. Kareken & Neil Wallace. 313p. (Orig., Avail. only from Publisher). 1980. pap. 5.00 (ISBN 0-9603936-0-9). Fed Res Bank MN.

Models of Moral Education. Richard Hersh & John Miller. 1979. pap. text ed. 7.95 (ISBN 0-582-28123-7). Longman.

Models of Spatial Processes. A. Getis & B. Boots. LC 75-17118. (Cambridge Geographical Studies Ser.: No.8). 1978. 29.95x (ISBN 0-521-20983-8). Cambridge U Pr.

Models of Teaching. Bruce Joyce & Marsha Weil. (Illus.). 368p. 1972. ref. ed. 17.95 (ISBN 0-13-586065-2). P-H.

Models of the Church. Avery Dulles. LC 77-11246. 1978. pap. 3.50 (ISBN 0-385-13368-5, Im). Doubleday.

Models on Man. M. Hollis. LC 76-49902. (Illus.). 1977. 32.95 (ISBN 0-521-21546-3); pap. 8.95x (ISBN 0-521-29181-X). Cambridge U Pr.

Models, Planning & Basic Needs: Conference on the Applicability of Global Modelling to Integrated Planning & Developing Countries. Ed. by Sam Cole. (Illus.). 1979. text ed. 28.00 (ISBN 0-08-023732-0). Pergamon.

Model's Way to Beauty, Slenderness & Glowing Health. Oleda Baker & Bill Gale. 256p. 1976. pap. 1.75 o.p. (ISBN 0-345-24444-3). Ballantine.

Modern Accident Investigation & Analysis: An Executive Guide to Accident Investigation. Ted S. Ferry. 350p. 1981. 30.00 (ISBN 0-471-07776-3, Pub. by Wiley-Interscience). Wiley.

Modern Administrative Practices in Human Services. Paul M. Dubois. 1981. write for info. (ISBN 0-398-04164-4). C C Thomas.

Modern Administrative Practices in Physical Education & Athletics. 3rd ed. Matthew C. Resick et al. LC 78-67946. (Physical Education Ser.). (Illus.). 1979. text ed. 16.95 (ISBN 0-201-06249-6). A-W.

Modern Aeromodelling. 3rd ed. R. G. Moulton. 1974. 9.95 (ISBN 0-571-04852-8, Pub. by Faber & Faber). Merrimack Bk Serv.

Modern Aesthetics: An Historical Introduction. Listowel. LC 67-14767. (Orig.). 1967. text ed. 10.25 (ISBN 0-8077-1696-0); pap. text ed. 7.00x (ISBN 0-8077-1695-2). Tchrs Coll.

Modern Africa: Change & Continuity. R. Hull. 1980. pap. 11.95 (ISBN 0-13-586305-8). P-H.

Modern African Stories. Ezekiel Mphalele. Ed. by Ellis A. Komey. (Orig.). 1966. pap. 5.95 (ISBN 0-571-11217-X, Pub. by Faber & Faber). Merrimack Bk Serv.

Modern Agricultural Management. 2nd ed. Donald Osburn & Kenneth Schneeberger. 370p. 1982. text ed. 16.95 (ISBN 0-8359-4550-2); instr's. manual free (ISBN 0-8359-4551-0). Reston.

Modern Agricultural Mechanics. T. J. Wakeman. LC 76-28839. 1977. 19.65 (ISBN 0-8134-1851-8); text ed. 14.75x (ISBN 0-685-81722-9). Interstate.

Modern Agriculture Management. Donald O. Osburn & Kenneth C. Schneeberger. 1978. 16.95 (ISBN 0-87909-495-8); instrs'. manual avail. Reston.

Modern Algebra: An Introduction. Tim Anderson. LC 73-82414. 1974. text ed. 16.95x (ISBN 0-675-08904-2). Merrill.

Modern Algebra: An Introduction. John R. Durbin. LC 78-15778. 1979. text ed. 19.50 (ISBN 0-471-02158-X); tchrs. manual avail. (ISBN 0-471-03753-2). Wiley.

Modern Algebra & Trigonometry. 3rd ed. Elbridge P. Vance. LC 72-11471. 1973. text ed. 16.95 (ISBN 0-201-08036-2). A-W.

Modern Algebra Two. Isidore Dressler & Barnett Rich. (Orig.). (gr. 11-12). 1973. text ed. 12.17 (ISBN 0-87720-233-8); pap. text ed. 6.50 (ISBN 0-87720-232-X). AMSCO Sch.

Modern Algebra with Applications. William J. Gilbert. LC 76-22756. 1976. 25.95 (ISBN 0-471-29891-3, Pub by Wiley-Interscience). Wiley.

Modern American College: Responding to the New Realities of Diverse Students & a Changing Society. Arthur W. Chickering et al. LC 80-8010. (Higher Education Ser.). 1981. text ed. 29.95x (ISBN 0-87589-466-6). Jossey-Bass.

Modern American English, 2 bks. Robert J. Dixson. (gr. 7-12). 1977. pap. text ed. 3.45 ea.; Bk. 1. pap. text ed. (ISBN 0-88345-308-8); wkbk. 2.25 (ISBN 0-88345-314-2); Bk. 2. pap. text ed. (ISBN 0-88345-309-6); wkbk. 2.25 (ISBN 0-88345-315-0); cassette 80.00 ea. Regents Pub.

Modern American English, Bk. 3. Robert J. Dixson. (Illus.). (gr. 7-12). 1977. pap. text ed. 3.45 (ISBN 0-88345-310-X); wkbk. 2.25 (ISBN 0-88345-316-9); cassettes 80.00 (ISBN 0-686-68052-9). Regents Pub.

Modern American English, Bk. 4. Robert J. Dixson. 1978. pap. text ed. 3.45 (ISBN 0-88345-311-8); tchr's manual 1 4.95 (ISBN 0-88345-319-3); tchr's manual 2 4.95 (ISBN 0-88345-321-5); wkbk. 4 2.25 (ISBN 0-88345-317-7). Regents Pub.

Modern American English, Bk. 5. Robert J. Dixson. (Illus.). 167p. (gr. 7-12). 1980. pap. text ed. 3.75 (ISBN 0-88345-312-6, 18724); tchr's manual 4.95 (ISBN 0-88345-324-X); wkbk. 2.25 (ISBN 0-88345-318-5). Regents Pub.

Modern American English, Bk. 6. Robert J. Dixson. (Illus.). 1980. pap. text ed. 3.75 (ISBN 0-88345-313-4); tchr's manual 4.95 (ISBN 0-88345-325-8); wkbk 2.25 (ISBN 0-88345-320-7). Regents Pub.

Modern American English: Teacher's Manual 3. Robert J. Dixson. (Modern American English Ser.). (Illus.). 187p. 1978. pap. text ed. 4.95 (ISBN 0-88345-322-3). Regents Pub.

Modern American Literature, 3 Vols. 4th enl. ed. Ed. by Dorothy N. Curley et al. LC 76-76599. (Library of Literary Criticism Ser.). (gr. 9-12). 1969. text ed. 90.00 (ISBN 0-8044-3046-2). Ungar.

Modern American Lyric: Lowell, Berryman, Creeley, & Plath. Arthur Oberg. 1978. 13.00 (ISBN 0-8135-0826-6). Rutgers U Pr.

Modern American Painting: 1900 - 1970. Time-Life Books Editors. (Library of Art Ser.). (Illus.). (gr. 6 up). 1970. kivar 12.96 (ISBN 0-8094-0287-4, Pub. by Time-Life). Silver.

Modern American Usage: A Guide. Wilson Follett. Ed. by Jacques Barzun. 443p. 1979. 12.95 (ISBN 0-8090-6950-4); pap. 6.95 (ISBN 0-8090-6950-4). Hill & Wang.

Modern Analytic Geometry. Tullio J. Pignani & Paul W. Haggard. 1970. text ed. 14.95x o.p. (ISBN 0-669-49536-0); instructor's guide gratis o.p. (ISBN 0-669-49544-1). Heath.

Modern & Ancient Lake Sediments. Ed. by Albert Matter & Maurice E. Tucker. (International Association of Sedimentologists & the Societas Internationalis Limnologiae Symposium Proceding Ser.). 1979. 34.95 (ISBN 0-470-26571-X). Halsted Pr.

Modern & Classic: The "Wooing Both Ways". Marden J. Clark. (Charles E. Merrill Monograph Series in the Humanities & Social Sciences: Vol. 2, No. 2). 94p. 1973. pap. 2.00 o.p. (ISBN 0-8425-0808-2). Brigham.

Modern Applications of Linear IC's. United Tech. Pubs. LC 73-90737. 1974. 12.95 o.p. (ISBN 0-8306-4708-2); pap. 9.95 (ISBN 0-8306-3708-7, 708). TAB Bks.

Modern Approach to Business English. Annie DeCaprio. LC 73-90044. 1974. pap. text ed. 10.95 (ISBN 0-672-96102-4); tchr's manual 6.67 (ISBN 0-672-96103-2). Bobbs.

Modern Approach to Chemistry. J. D. Stove & K. A. Phillips. 1971. pap. text ed. 9.50 o.p. (ISBN 0-435-64856-X). Heinemann Ed.

Modern Approach to English Grammar: An Introduction to Systemic English Grammar. James Muir. 148p. 1972. pap. text ed. 10.25x (ISBN 0-7134-2008-1). Humanities.

Modern Approach to Property: Cases, Notes, Materials. Richard H. Chused. LC 78-5110. (American Casebook Ser.). 1069p. 1978. text ed. 21.95 (ISBN 0-8299-2004-8). West Pub.

Modern Arab Dictionary. 29.00 (ISBN 2-03-020540-0, 3680). Larousse.

Modern Arab Woman: A Bibliography. Michelle Raccagni. LC 78-15528. 1978. lib. bdg. 14.50 (ISBN 0-8108-1165-0). Scarecrow.

Modern Arabic Short Stories. Ed. by Denys Johnson-Davies. Tr. by D. Johnson-Davies from Arabic. (Orig.). 1976. 9.00x (ISBN 0-914478-75-3, Co-Pub by Heinemann Educ. Bks); pap. 5.00x (ISBN 0-435-99403-4). Three Continents.

Modern Architecture. rev ed. Vincent Scully. LC 61-13689. (Illus.). 128p. 1974. 12.50 (ISBN 0-8076-0159-4); pap. 5.95 (ISBN 0-8076-0334-1). Braziller.

Modern Architecture. Manfredo Tafuri & Francesco Dal Co. (History of World Architecture Ser.). (Illus.). 1980. 45.00 (ISBN 0-8109-1006-3). Abrams.

Modern Art & Man's Search for the Self. Fritz W. Faiss. (Illus.). 30p. 1974. pap. 6.00 ltd. ed. signed (ISBN 0-916678-12-1); pap. 48.00x hand-colored, signed ltd. ed. (ISBN 0-916678-13-X). Green Hut.

Modern Art from Post Impressionisms to the Present. Hunter & Jacobus. LC 76-14611. (Illus.). 1977. 45.00 o.p. (ISBN 0-8109-1616-9). Abrams.

Modern Aspects of Electrochemistry, No. 13. Ed. by Conway & Bockris. (Illus.). 1979. 42.50 (ISBN 0-306-40256-4, Plenum Pr). Plenum Pub.

Modern Aspects of Inorganic Chemistry. 4th ed. H. J. Emeleus & A. G. Sharpe. LC 73-2577. 677p. 1973. text ed. 22.95 (ISBN 0-470-23902-6). Halsted Pr.

Modern Astronomy. Ludwig Oster. LC 72-83247. 500p. 1973. text ed. 18.95x (ISBN 0-8162-6523-2). Holden-Day.

Modern Atomic Physics. B. Cagnac & J. C. Pebay-Peyroula. Incl. Vol. 1. Fundamentals & Principles. LC 74-28161. text ed. 24.95 (ISBN 0-470-12920-4); Vol. 2. Quantum Theory & Its Application. LC 74-26875. text ed. 17.95 o.p. (ISBN 0-470-12921-2). 1975. Halsted Pr.

Modern Australian Poetry: A Guide to Information Sources. Ed. by Herbert C. Jaffa. LC 74-11535. (American Literature, English Literature, & World Literatures in English Information Guide Ser.: Vol. 24). 1979. 30.00 (ISBN 0-8103-1242-5). Gale.

Modern Australian Prose, Nineteen One to Nineteen Seventy-Five: A Guide to Information Sources, Vol. 32. A. Grove Day. Ed. by A. Grove Day. LC 74-11536. (American Literature, English Literature & World Literatures in English Information Guide Ser.). 425p. 1980. 30.00 (ISBN 0-8103-1243-3). Gale.

Modern Austrian Writing: Literature & Society After 1945. Ed. by Alan D. Best & Hans Wolfshutz. 307p. 1980. 24.50x (ISBN 0-389-20038-7). B&N.

Modern Backgammon Complete. Charles H. Goren. 208p. 1975. pap. 2.95 (ISBN 0-346-12296-1). Cornerstone.

Modern Bank Management: A Casebook. Paul F. Jessup. 1978. text ed. 15.95 (ISBN 0-8299-0207-4); instrs.' maual avail. (ISBN 0-8299-0496-4). West Pub.

Modern Biography. Ed. by David Cecil. 229p. 1980. Repr. of 1938 ed. lib. bdg. 15.00 (ISBN 0-8492-3971-0). R West.

Modern Biology & Its Human Implications. J. A. Butler. LC 76-27619. 1976. pap. 9.95x (ISBN 0-8448-1007-X). Crane-Russak Co.

Modern Biology at a Glance. Maurice Bleifeld. LC 78-154424. (Illus.). 122p. (Orig., Prog. Bk.). (YA) 1971. pap. 3.95 o.p. (ISBN 0-8120-0238-5). Barron.

Modern Biology: Its Conceptual Foundations. Ed. by Elof Axel Carlson. LC 67-12476. (Science Ser). (Illus.). 1967. 7.50 o.s.i. (ISBN 0-8076-0405-4). Braziller.

Modern Boat Building. rev. ed. Edwin Monk. LC 72-1220. (Encore Edition). (Illus.). 6.95 o.p. (ISBN 0-684-15257-6, ScribT). Scribner.

Modern Bookkeeping & Accounting. 2nd ed. Morris Miller & Arthur Janis. LC 72-109961. Orig. Title: Fundamentals of Modern Bookkeeping. (gr. 10-12). 1973. text ed. 13.28 (ISBN 0-8224-2011-2); tchrs'. manual 4.80 (ISBN 0-8224-2070-8); solutions 8.00 (ISBN 0-8224-2072-4); Workbook I (units 1-26) 5.32 (ISBN 0-8224-2068-6); Workbook II (units 27-45) 5.32 (ISBN 0-8224-2069-4); tests 40.00 (ISBN 0-8224-2071-6). Pitman Learning.

Modern Brazilian Short Stories. Ed. by William L. Grossman. LC 67-13379. 1974. 14.00x (ISBN 0-520-00523-6); pap. 2.25 (ISBN 0-520-02766-3). U of Cal Pr.

Modern Breeds of Livestock. 4th ed. Hilton M. Briggs & Dinus M. Briggs. (Illus.). 1980. text ed. 22.95 (ISBN 0-02-314730-X). Macmillan.

Modern Britain: Structure & Change. Trevor Noble. 1975. 38.00 (ISBN 0-7134-2987-9, Pub. by Batsford England); pap. 15.95 (ISBN 0-7134-2988-7). David & Charles.

Modern British Army. Terry Gander. (Illus.). 280p. 1980. 59.95 (ISBN 0-85059-435-9). Aztex.

Modern British Farming Systems. 1972. 23.95 (ISBN 0-236-17730-3, Pub. by Paul Elek); pap. 10.95 (ISBN 0-236-15455-9). Merrimack Bk Serv.

Modern Building: Its Nature, Problems & Forms. Walter C. Behrendt. LC 78-59005. (Illus.). 1981. Repr. of 1937 ed. 25.00 (ISBN 0-88355-681-2). Hyperion Conn.

Modern Business Arithmetic. 3rd ed. H. F. Hemstock & J. Costelloe. 1974. pap. text ed. 11.95x (ISBN 0-17-741005-1). Intl Ideas.

Modern Business Correspondence. 3rd ed. L Gartside. (Illus.). 480p. 1976. pap. 14.95x (ISBN 0-7121-1392-4, Pub. by Macdonald & Evans England). Intl Ideas.

Modern Business Data Processing. Daniel D. Benice. (Illus.). 416p. 1973. ref. ed. 18.95 (ISBN 0-13-589648-7). P-H.

Modern Business Law. Thomas W. Dunfee et al. LC 78-13129. (Law Ser.). 1979. text ed. 20.95 o.p. (ISBN 0-88244-179-5). Grid Pub.

Modern Business Law: An Introduction to Government & Business. 2nd ed. Thomas W. Dunfee & Frank F. Gibson. LC 76-44997. 1977. pap. text ed. 10.50 (ISBN 0-88244-146-9). Grid Pub.

Modern Business Law: An Introduction to the Legal Environment of Business. Thomas W. Dunfee et al. LC 77-71017. (Law Ser.). 1978. pap. text ed. 9.95 (ISBN 0-88244-117-5). Grid Pub.

Modern Business Law: Contracts. Thomas W. Dunfee et al. LC 77-91087. (Law Ser.). 1978. pap. text ed. 14.95 (ISBN 0-88244-166-3). Grid Pub.

Modern Business Mathematics. Wallace W. Kravitz. (Orig.). (gr. 7-12). 1973. pap. text ed. 5.33 (ISBN 0-87720-400-4). AMSCO Sch.

Modern Cabinetmaking in Solid Wood: Design for Handmade Furniture with Construction Details & Photographs. new ed. Franz Karg. (Illus.). 136p. 1980. 29.95 (ISBN 0-8038-1276-0). Hastings.

Modern Cake Decoration. 2nd ed. L. J. Hanneman. (Illus.). 1978. text ed. 28.50x (ISBN 0-85334-785-9). Intl Ideas.

Modern Camping. Alan Ryalls. LC 75-7. 1975. 2.95 o.p. (ISBN 0-7153-6996-2). David & Charles.

Modern Capital Theory. Donald Dewey. LC 65-22157. (Illus.). 1965. 16.00x (ISBN 0-231-02831-8). Columbia U Pr.

Modern Capitalism: The Changing Balance of Public & Private Power. Andrew Shonfield. 1969. pap. 7.95 (ISBN 0-19-500298-9, GB). Oxford U Pr.

Modern Capitalist Planning: The French Model. new ed. Stephen S. Cohen. 1977. 24.00x (ISBN 0-520-02793-0); pap. 7.95x (ISBN 0-520-02892-9, CAMPUS 141). U of Cal Pr.

Modern Cardiovascular Physiology. Carl R. Honig. 1981. text ed. write for info. (ISBN 0-316-37214-5); pap. text ed. write for info (ISBN 0-316-37215-3). Little.

Modern Carpentry. Willis H. Wagner. LC 79-11956. 1979. text ed. 14.00 (ISBN 0-87006-274-3); wkbk. 3.20 (ISBN 0-87006-282-4). Goodheart.

Modern CB Radio Servicing. Marvin Hobbs. 1979. pap. 7.75 (ISBN 0-8104-0865-1). Hayden.

Modern Chess Opening Theory. A. S. Suetin. Ed. by P. H. Clarke. Tr. by D. J. Richards. (Pergamon Chess Ser.). (Illus.). 1965. text ed. 18.00 (ISBN 0-08-011199-8); pap. text ed. 9.50 (ISBN 0-08-011198-X). Pergamon.

Modern Chess Openings. 11th ed. Walter Korn. 1978. 12.50 (ISBN 0-679-13056-X, 13056X). McKay.

Modern Chess Openings. 12th ed. 1981. cancelled (ISBN 0-679-13500-6). McKay.

Modern Chicano Writers: A Collection of Critical Essays. J. Sommers & T. Ybarra-Frausto. 1979. 10.95 (ISBN 0-13-589721-1); pap. 3.45 (ISBN 0-13-589713-0). P-H.

Modern Childrearing: A Behavioral Approach. Donald K. Pumroy & Shirley S. Pumroy. LC 77-26964. (Illus.). 1978. text ed. 14.95 (ISBN 0-88229-185-8). Nelson-Hall.

Modern China & a New World: K'ang Yu-Wei, Reformer & Utopian, 1858-1927. Kung-Chuan Hsiao. LC 74-28166. (Publications on Asia of School of International Studies: No. 25). 680p. 1975. 26.50 (ISBN 0-295-95385-3). U of Wash Pr.

Modern China & Traditional Chinese Medicine. G. B. Risse. 176p. 1973. 12.75 (ISBN 0-398-02816-8). C C Thomas.

Modern Chinese: A Basic Course. Peking University Faculty. LC 78-169835. Orig. Title: Modern Chinese Reader. 1971. pap. text ed. 3.50 (ISBN 0-486-22755-3); record & manual o.p. 12.95 (ISBN 0-686-66298-9). Dover.

Modern Chinese: A Second Course. rev. ed. Peking University Faculty. 500p. 1981. pap. price not set (ISBN 0-486-24155-6). Dover.

Modern Chinese Economic History: Proceedings of the Conference on Modern Chinese Economic History, Academia Sinica. Ed. by Chi-Ming Hou & Tzong-shian Yu. LC 79-4926. 694p. 1980. pap. 25.00 (ISBN 0-295-95675-5, Pub. by Coun Econ Planning Taiwan). U of Wash Pr.

Modern Chinese for the Elementary School, First Year. 2nd ed. Lucy Y. Wang. LC 66-24847. (Illus.). 242p. (gr. 4-6). 1972. perfect bdg. 8.00 (ISBN 0-9600176-0-7); classroom lab tape set 30.00 (ISBN 0-685-22813-4); student's cassette tape 10.00 (ISBN 0-685-22814-2). Ascension.

Modern Chinese for the Elementary School, Second Year. 2nd ed. Lucy Y. Wang. LC 66-24847. (Illus.). 276p. (gr. 5-7). 1979. spiral bdg. 8.00 (ISBN 0-9600176-1-5); classroom lab tape set 30.00 (ISBN 0-685-22815-0); students' record set 10.00 (ISBN 0-685-22816-9). Ascension.

Modern Chinese for the Elementary School, Third Year. 2nd ed. Lucy Y. Wang. LC 66-24847. (Illus.). 315p. (gr. 6-8). 1979. perfect bdg. 8.00 (ISBN 0-9600176-6-6). Ascension.

Modern Chinese Poetry: An Introduction. Julia C. Lin. LC 70-152330. (Washington Paperback Ser: No. 66). 278p. 1972. 11.50 (ISBN 0-295-95145-1); pap. 2.95 (ISBN 0-295-95281-4). U of Wash Pr.

Modern Chinese Stories & Novellas, Nineteen Nineteen to Nienteen Forty-Nine. Ed. by Joseph Lau et al. LC 80-27572. (Modern Asian Literature Ser.). 608p. (Eng.). 1981. 35.00x (ISBN 0-231-04202-7); pap. 15.00x (ISBN 0-231-04203-5). Columbia U Pr.

Modern Chinese Woodcuts. 1980. pap. 8.95 (ISBN 0-8351-0720-5). China Bks.

Modern Chlor-Alkali Technology. Ed. by M. O. Coulter. 280p. 1980. 89.95x (ISBN 0-470-27005-5). Halsted Pr.

Modern Churches & the Church. J. Porter Wilhite. 4.95 (ISBN 0-89315-155-6). Lambert Bk.

Modern Collector's Dolls: Second Ser. Patricia Smith. (Illus.). 1975. 17.95 (ISBN 0-517-52110-5). Collector Bks.

Modern Collector's Dolls: Third Ser. Patricia Smith. (Illus.). 1976. 17.95 (ISBN 0-517-52666-2). Collector Bks.

Modern College Algebra. 3rd ed. Elbridge P. Vance. LC 75-370. (Illus.). 320p. 1975. text ed. 15.95 (ISBN 0-201-08159-8). A-W.

Modern College Algebra & Trigonometry. 3rd ed. Edwin F. Beckenbach & Irving Drooyan. 1977. 18.95x (ISBN 0-534-00468-7). Wadsworth Pub.

Modern College Typewriting: A Basic Course. Leonard J. West. (Illus.). 1977. text ed. 7.95 spiral bdg. (ISBN 0-15-560550-X, HC); instructor's manual avail. (ISBN 0-15-560551-8); kit of student supplies 3.75 (ISBN 0-686-68519-9); timing tapes avail. (ISBN 0-15-560555-0); transparency masters avail.; Student's ProgramedGuide 3.95 (ISBN 0-686-68520-2). HarBraceJ.

Modern Commonwealth Literature. Ed. by John H. Ferres & Martin Tucker. LC 75-35425. (Library of Literary Criticism). 1977. 35.00 (ISBN 0-8044-3080-2). Ungar.

Modern Communication Systems. R. F. Coates. (Illus.). 1976. pap. text ed. 17.95x (ISBN 0-333-18560-9). Scholium Intl.

Modern Communist Chinese Usage: Chinese English Dictionary. 2nd ed. Joint Publications Research Service. pap. 56.00 (ISBN 0-686-23791-9, JPRS 20904). Natl Tech Info.

Modern Competing Ideologies. L. Earl Shaw. 1973. pap. text ed. 7.95x o.p. (ISBN 0-669-81869-0). Heath.

Modern Concepts in Biochemistry. 3rd ed. Robert C. Bohinski. 1979. text ed. 27.95 (ISBN 0-205-06521-X, 6865216); answerbook avail. (ISBN 0-205-06542-2, 6865429). Allyn.

Modern Concepts in Geomorphology. Patrick McCullagh. (Science in Geography Ser.). (Illus.). 128p. (Orig.). 1978. pap. text ed. 4.95x (ISBN 0-19-913236-4). Oxford U Pr.

Modern Concepts of Ecology. H. D. Kumar. 1977. 14.00 (ISBN 0-7069-0501-6, Pub. by Vikas India). Advent Bk.

Modern Concepts of Gynecological Oncology. Ed. by John R. Van Nagell, Jr. & Hugh R. Barber. 350p. 1981. text ed. 30.00 (ISBN 0-88416-268-0). PSG Pub.

Modern Conductor. 3rd ed. Elizabeth A. Green. (Illus.). 288p. 1981. text ed. 18.95 (ISBN 0-13-590216-9). P-H.

Modern Constitutional Law, 2 vols. Chester J. Antieau. LC 69-19951. 1969. 100.00 (ISBN 0-686-14506-2). Lawyers Co-Op.

Modern Constitutional Law. R. Cortner & C. Lytle. LC 73-122280. 1971. text ed. 14.95 (ISBN 0-02-906740-5). Free Pr.

Modern Constitutional Law: Cases & Notes. Ronald D. Rotunda. (American Casebook Ser.). 1058p. 1981. text ed. price not set (ISBN 0-8299-2136-2). West Pub.

Modern Construction Management. Frank Harris & Ronald McCaffer. (Illus.). 1977. 24.95x (ISBN 0-8464-0636-5). Beekman Pubs.

Modern Control Engineering. M. Noton. LC 72-181056. 288p. 1972. text ed. 28.00 (ISBN 0-08-016820-5). Pergamon.

Modern Control Engineering. Katsuhiko Ogata. LC 72-84843. (Electrical Engineering Ser). 1970. ref. ed. 27.95 (ISBN 0-13-590232-0). P-H.

Modern Control, System Theory & Application. 2nd ed. Stanley M. Shinners. LC 78-52497. (Electrical Engineering Ser.). 1978. text ed. 24.95 (ISBN 0-201-07494-X); instr's man. 3.00 (ISBN 0-201-07495-8). A-W.

Modern Control Systems. 3rd ed. Richard C. Dorf. LC 79-16320. (Electrical Engineering Ser.). (Illus.). 1980. text ed. 23.95 (ISBN 0-201-01258-8). A-W.

Modern Conversational Czech, 2 bks. 2nd ed. John J. Skirvanek. Ed. by James Mendl. 1977. pap. 7.25x ea. Bk. 1 (ISBN 0-934786-02-X). Bk. 2 (ISBN 0-934786-03-8). G Davis.

Modern Cooking Equipment & Its Applicaions. Roger Young. (Illus.). 1979. 18.50x (ISBN 0-7198-2684-5). Intl Ideas.

Modern Corporate State: Private Governments & the American Constitution. Arthur S. Miller. LC 75-35350. (Contributions in American Studies: No. 23). 320p. 1976. lib. bdg. 17.95 (ISBN 0-8371-8589-0, MCS/). Greenwood.

Modern Corporation Finance. 7th ed. William H. Husband & James C. Dockeray. 1972. text ed. 17.95x (ISBN 0-256-00221-5). Irwin.

Modern Corporation Law, 6 Vols. Howard L. Oleck. 1958-1960. with 1978 suppl 325.00 (ISBN 0-672-83063-9, Bobbs-Merrill Law); 1978 suppl. 115.00 (ISBN 0-672-81982-1). Michie.

Modern Corrections: The Offenders, Therapies & Community Reintegration. Harjit S. Sandhu. (Illus.). 368p. 1977. 14.00 (ISBN 0-398-03031-6); pap. 11.50 (ISBN 0-398-03032-4). C C Thomas.

Modern Course in Aeroelasticity. E. H. Dowell & H. C. Curtiss, Jr. (Mechanics: Dynamical Systems Ser.: No. 4). 479p. 1978. 85.00x (ISBN 90-286-0057-4); pap. 25.00x (ISBN 90-286-0737-4). Sijthoff & Noordhoff.

Modern Criminal Investigation. 5th ed. Harry Soderman & John J. O'Connell. Ed. by Charles E. O'Hara. LC 62-9736. (Funk & W Bk.). (Illus.). 1962. 10.00 o.s.i. (ISBN 0-308-40080-1, TYC-T). T Y Crowell.

Modern Criminal Procedure: Cases, Comments & Questions. 5th ed. Yale Kamisar et al. LC 80-36680. (American Casebook Ser.). 1813p. 1980. text ed. 25.95 (ISBN 0-8299-2101-X). West Pub.

Modern Criticism: Theory & Practice. Ed. by Walter Sutton & Richard Foster. 1963. 29.50x (ISBN 0-672-63185-7); pap. text ed. 16.95x (ISBN 0-89197-853-4). Irvington.

Modern Crystallography I. B. K. Vainshtain. (Springer Series in Solid-State Sciences: Vol. 15). (Illus.). 420p. 1981. 54.50 (ISBN 0-387-10052-0). Springer-Verlag.

Modern Cultural Anthropology. 2nd ed. Philip K. Bock. 512p. 1974. text ed. 14.95 o.p. (ISBN 0-394-31778-5). Random.

Modern Czech Grammar. William E. Harkins. LC 53-397. (Slavic Studies). (Illus.). 1953. 20.00x (ISBN 0-231-09937-1). Columbia U Pr.

Modern Dairy Cattle Management. Richard F. Davis. 1962. ref. ed. 18.95 (ISBN 0-13-590794-2). P-H.

Modern Dairy Goat. Joan Shields & Harry Shields. Date not set. 5.00 (ISBN 0-686-26683-8). Dairy Goat.

Modern Dairy Products. 3rd ed. L. M. Lampert. (Illus.). 1975. 39.50 (ISBN 0-8206-0230-2). Chem Pub.

Modern Dance. 2nd ed. Gay Cheney & Janet Strader. 100p. 1975. pap. text ed. 6.50 (ISBN 0-205-04839-0, 624839X). Allyn.

Modern Dance: A Biochemical Approach to Teaching. Joan F. Hays. (Illus.). 312p. 1981. pap. text ed. 13.95 (ISBN 0-8016-2179-8). Mosby.

Modern Dance: Building & Teaching Lessons. 5th ed. Aileene S. Lockhart & Esther E. Pease. 1977. 9.95x (ISBN 0-697-07430-7). Wm C Brown.

Modern Dance: Seven Statements of Belief. Ed. by Selma J. Cohen. LC 66-14663. (Illus.). 1969. pap. 5.95x (ISBN 0-8195-6003-0, Pub. by Wesleyan U Pr). Columbia U Pr.

Modern Data Communication: Concepts, Language & Media. W. Davenport. (Illus.). 1971. pap. 10.95 (ISBN 0-8104-5667-2). Hayden.

Modern Data Processing. 3rd ed. Robert R. Arnold et al. LC 77-14941. 1978. 21.95 (ISBN 0-471-03361-8); instructors' manual (ISBN 0-471-03405-3); wkbk. 8.50x (ISBN 0-471-03362-6). Wiley.

Modern Deer Hunter. John O. Cartier. (Funk & W Bk.). (Illus.). 1977. 10.95 o.p. (ISBN 0-308-10270-3, TYC-T). T Y Crowell.

Modern Defence. R. D. Keene & G. S. Botterill. 1979. 18.95 (ISBN 0-7134-0360-8). David & Charles.

Modern Democracy in China: Studies in Chinese Government & Law. Mingchien J. Bau. 467p. 1977. Repr. of 1923 ed. 25.00 (ISBN 0-89093-060-0). U Pubns Amer.

Modern Descriptive English Grammar. Hulton Willis. 1972. text ed. 13.95 scp (ISBN 0-352-15125-0, HarpC). Har-Row.

Modern Design in Metal. Richard Stewart. (Illus.). 1979. 18.00 (ISBN 0-7195-3537-9). Transatlantic.

Modern Design in Wood. Richard Stewart. (Illus.). 1979. 18.50 (ISBN 0-7195-3536-0). Transatlantic.

Modern Dev. Fin. Mngt. 1976. pap. 16.95 (ISBN 0-275-89360-X). Dryden Pr.

Modern Development in Audiology. 2nd ed. Ed. by James Jerger. 1973. 24.50 (ISBN 0-12-385156-4). Acad Pr.

Modern Development in Invest. Mngt. 2nd ed. Love & Brealy. 1978. pap. 15.95 (ISBN 0-03-040716-8). Dryden Pr.

Modern Development in Yacht Design. David Cannell & John Leather. LC 76-11397. (Illus.). 1976. 20.00 (ISBN 0-396-07355-7). Dodd.

Modern Developments in Fluid Dynamics, 2 Vols. Ed. by Sydney Goldstein. (Illus.). 1938. pap. text ed. 5.50 ea.; Vol. 1. pap. text ed. (ISBN 0-486-61357-7); Vol. 2. pap. text ed. (ISBN 0-486-61358-5). Dover.

Modern Developments in Heat Transfer. Ed. by Warren E. Ibele. 1963. 55.50 (ISBN 0-12-369550-3). Acad Pr.

Modern Developments in the Mechanics of Continua: Proceedings. Ed. by Salamon Eskinazi. 1967. 31.50 (ISBN 0-12-242550-2). Acad Pr.

Modern Developments in the Principles & Practice of Chiropractic. Ed. by Scott Haldeman. 480p. 1980. 28.50x (ISBN 0-8385-6350-3). ACC.

Modern Developments in Thermodynamics. Ed. by B. Gal-Or. LC 74-2399. 458p. 1974. text ed. 34.95 (ISBN 0-470-29044-7). Halsted Pr.

Modern Dictionary of Sociology. George A. Theodorson & Achilles G. Theodorson. LC 69-18672. 1969. 12.95 o.s.i. (ISBN 0-690-55058-8, TYC-T). T Y Crowell.

Modern Dictionary of Sociology. George A. Theodorson & Achilles G. Theodorson. LC 69-18672. (Apollo Eds.). 1969. pap. 3.95 o.s.i. (ISBN 0-8152-0238-5, TYC-T). T Y Crowell.

Modern Diesel Cars. Jan Norbye. (Modern Automotive Ser.). (Illus.). 1978. 9.95 (ISBN 0-8306-9899-X); pap. 7.95 (ISBN 0-8306-2046-X, 2046). TAB Bks.

Modern Diesel: Development & Design. 14th ed. Ed. by D. S. Williams. 248p. 1973. 24.00 (ISBN 0-408-00260-3). Transatlantic.

Modern Diplomacy: The Art &The Artisans. Ed. by Elmer Plischke. 1979. pap. 9.25 (ISBN 0-8447-3350-4). Am Enterprise.

Modern Display Techniques. Emily M. Mauger. LC 64-18578. 1964. 10.00 (ISBN 0-87005-045-1). Fairchild.

Modern Dowsing: The Dowser's Handbook. Raymond C. Willey. LC 75-18220. (Illus.). 1975. pap. 6.00 (ISBN 0-89861-005-2). Esoteric Pubns.

Modern Drag Racing Superstars. Ross R. Olney. LC 80-25908. (High Interest-Low Vocabulary Ser.). (Illus.). 112p. (gr. 4). 1981. PLB 5.95 (ISBN 0-396-07925-3). Dodd.

Modern Drama: Annotated Texts. Ed. by Anthony Caputi. Bd. with Desire Under the Elms. Eugene O'Neill; Devil's Disciple. George B. Shaw; Dream Play. August Strindberg; Henry Fourth. Luigi Pirandello; Three Sisters. Anton Chekhov; Wild Duck. Henrik Ibsen. (Critical Editions). 1966. pap. text ed. 9.95x (ISBN 0-393-09664-5). Norton.

Modern Drama in America & England, Nineteen Fifty-Nineteen Seventy: A Guide to Information Sources. Ed. by Richard H. Harris. (American Literature, English Literature & World Literatures in English Ser.: Vol. 34). 400p. 1981. 32.00 (ISBN 0-8103-1493-2). Gale.

Modern Drama in Theory & Practice, 3 vols. J. L. Styan. Incl. Vol. 1. Realism & Naturalism. Cloth (ISBN 0-521-22737-2); Vol. 2. Symbolism, Surrealism & the Absurd. Cloth (ISBN 0-521-22738-0); Vol. 3. Expressionism & Epic Theatre. Cloth (ISBN 0-521-22739-9). LC 79-15947. (Illus.). 250p. Date not set. 75.00 set; 29.50 ea. Cambridge U Pr. Postponed.

Modern Drug Encyclopedia & Therapeutic Index, No. 16. 16th ed. Ed. by Gertrude D. Gonzales & Arthur J. Lewis. LC 34-12823. 1100p. 1981. text ed. 40.00 (ISBN 0-914316-21-4). Yorke Med.

Modern Dunciad. Richard Nason. pap. 4.00 (ISBN 0-912292-49-0). The Smith.

Modern Economic History. Edmund Seddon. (Illus.). 384p. 1979. pap. text ed. 11.95x (ISBN 0-7121-1286-3, Pub. by Macdonald & Evans England). Intl Ideas.

Modern Economic Organization. Richard E. Low. 1970. text ed. 17.50 (ISBN 0-256-00315-7). Irwin.

Modern Economic Problems in Historical Perspective. 2nd ed. Douglas F. Dowd. (Orig.). 1965. pap. text ed. 6.95x o.p. (ISBN 0-669-25536-X). Heath.

Modern Economics. 2nd rev. ed. Robert D. Leiter. (Orig.). 1976. pap. 3.95 (ISBN 0-06-460138-2, CO 138, COS). Har-Row.

Modern Economy: A Theoretical Debate & Its Practical Implications. L. W. Stafford. LC 75-20322. (Illus.). 1976. text ed. 12.00x (ISBN 0-582-44357-1); pap. text ed. 7.95x (ISBN 0-582-44358-X). Longman.

Modern Education for the Junior High School Years. rev. ed. William Van Til et al. LC 66-26209. 1967. text ed. 13.50 (ISBN 0-672-60640-2). Bobbs.

Modern Educational Dance. Laban. (Orig.). 1980. pap. 5.95 (ISBN 0-8238-0165-9). Plays.

Modern Educational Psychology: An Historical Introduction. E. G. Evans. (Students Library of Education Ser.). 1969. pap. text ed. 2.50x (ISBN 0-7100-6515-9). Humanities.

Modern Egypt. rev. ed. Emil Lengyel. (First Bks). (Illus.). (gr. 5-7). 1978. PLB 6.45 s&l (ISBN 0-531-02240-4). Watts.

Modern Egypt: Studies in Politics & Society. Ed. by Elie Kedourie & Sylvia G. Haim. 136p. 1980. 25.00 (ISBN 0-7146-3168-X, F Cass Co). Biblio Dist.

Modern Egyptian Drama: An Anthology. Ed. & tr. by Farouk Abdel Wahab. LC 72-94939. (Studies in Middle Eastern Literatures Ser: No. 3). 1974. 25.00x (ISBN 0-88297-005-4). Bibliotheca.

Modern Electrical Communications: Theory & Systems. Henry Stark & Franz B. Tuteru. (Illus.). 1979. ref. 27.95 (ISBN 0-13-593202-5). P-H.

Modern Electrical Equipment for Automobiles. Arthur W. Judge. LC 68-31549. (Motor Manuals Ser.: Vol. 6). text ed. 10.95x o.p. (ISBN 0-8376-0002-2). Bentley.

Modern Electronic Circuit Design. David J. Comer. LC 75-9008. 704p. 1976. text ed. 25.95 (ISBN 0-201-01008-9); solutions manual 2.00 (ISBN 0-201-01009-7). A-W.

Modern Electronic Circuits Reference Manual. John Markus. (Illus.). 1980. 44.50 (ISBN 0-07-040446-1, P&RB). McGraw.

Modern Electronics Math. Martin Clifford. LC 73-86767. (Illus.). 602p. 1976. pap. 11.95 (ISBN 0-8306-5655-3, 655). TAB Bks.

Modern Elementary Differential Equations. 2nd ed. Richard Bellman & Kenneth Cooke. (Mathematics Ser). 1971. text ed. 19.95 (ISBN 0-201-00511-5). A-W.

Modern Elementary Linear Algebra. Noel Cortey. LC 78-57573. 1978. pap. text ed. 7.50 (ISBN 0-8191-0524-4). U Pr of Amer.

Modern Elementary Mathematics. 3rd ed. Malcolm Graham. 470p. 1979. text ed. 15.95 (ISBN 0-15-561041-4, HC); instructor's manual avail. (ISBN 0-15-561042-2). HarBraceJ.

Modern Elementary School Science: A Recommended Sequence. Willard J. Jacobson. LC 61-14667. (Orig.). (gr. 1-6). 1961. pap. text ed. 4.75x (ISBN 0-8077-1560-3). Tchrs Coll.

Modern Elementary Statistics. 5th ed. John E. Freund. 1979. text ed. 18.95 (ISBN 0-13-593491-5); pap. 5.95 study guide (ISBN 0-13-593517-2). P-H.

Modern Employment Function. Donald H. Sweet. 330p. 1973. text ed. 13.95 (ISBN 0-201-07388-9). A-W.

Modern Encyclopedia of Russian & Soviet History: Mersh. Ed. by Joseph L. Wieczynski. Incl. Vol. 1 (ISBN 0-87569-064-5); Vol. 2 (ISBN 0-87569-065-3); Vol. 3; Vol. 4. 1977; Vol. 5. 1977; Vol. 19. 1980. 30.50; Vol. 4. Ed. by Harry B. Weber. 1980. 31.50 (ISBN 0-87569-038-6). 30.50 ea. Academic Intl.

Modern Encyclopedia of Russian & Soviet History: Mersh, Vols. 6 & 7. Joseph L. Wieczynski. 1978. Set. 30.50 ea. (ISBN 0-685-92172-7). Academic Intl.

Modern Encyclopedia of Russian & Soviet History: Mersh, Vol. 8. Ed. by Joseph L. Wieczynski. 1978. 30.50 (ISBN 0-685-03450-X). Academic Intl.

Modern Encyclopedia of Russian & Soviet History: Mersh, 50 vols, Vols. 9, 10 & 11. Ed. by Joseph L. Wieczynski. 1979. 30.50 (ISBN 0-685-92201-4). Academic Intl.

Modern Encyclopedia of Russian & Soviet History: Mersh, Vols. 12-13. Ed. by Joseph L. Wieczynski. 1979. 30.50 (ISBN 0-686-65389-0). Academic Intl.

Modern Encyclopedia of Russian & Soviet History: Mersh, Vols. 14, Ed. by Joseph L. Wieczynski. 30.50 ea.; Vols. 15,16,17,18. 1980 30.50 ea. Academic Intl.

Modern Encyclopedia of Russian & Soviet Literature: Mersh, Vol. 1. Ed. by Harry B. Weber. 1977. 31.50 (ISBN 0-87569-070-X). Academic Intl.

Modern Encyclopedia of Russian & Soviet Literature: Mersh, Vol. 2. 31.50 (ISBN 0-685-54328-5). Academic Intl.

Modern Encyclopedia of Russian & Soviet Literature: Mersh, Vol. 3. Ed. by Harry B. Weber. 1979. 31.50 (ISBN 0-685-96303-9). Academic Intl.

Modern England: 1901-1970. A. F. Havighurst. LC 75-23844. (Conference on British Studies Bibliographical Handbooks Ser.). 118p. 1976. 15.50 (ISBN 0-521-20941-2). Cambridge U Pr.

Modern English: A Practical Reference Guide. Marcella Frank. (Illus.). 1972. pap. text ed. 10.95 (ISBN 0-13-594002-8). P-H.

Modern English Canadian Poetry: A Guide to Information Sources. Ed. by Peter Stevens. LC 73-16994. (American Literature, English Literature, & World Literatures in English Information Guide Ser.: Vol. 15). 1978. 30.00 (ISBN 0-8103-1244-1). Gale.

Modern English Handbook. 6th ed. Robert Gorrell & Charlton Laird. 1976. text ed. 12.95 (ISBN 0-13-594283-7); tchr's man. free (ISBN 0-13-594275-6). P-H.

Modern English Reader. 2nd ed. Charles Laird et al. (Illus.). 416p. 1977. pap. text ed. 9.95 (ISBN 0-13-594176-8). P-H.

Modern English Reform: From Individualism to Socialism. Edward P. Cheyney. 1962. pap. 3.95 o.p. (ISBN 0-498-04077-1, Prpta). A S Barnes.

Modern English Writers, Alfred Tennyson. Andrew Lang. 233p. 1980. Repr. lib. bdg. 25.00 (ISBN 0-89984-321-2). Century Bookbindery.

Modern Ethology. S. A. Barnett. (Illus.). 720p. 1981. text ed. 19.95x (ISBN 0-19-502780-9). Oxford U Pr.

Modern European Filmmakers & the Art of Adaption. Ed. by Andrew S. Horton & Joan Magretta. LC 79-48073. (Ungar Film Library). (Illus.). 400p. 1981. 14.95 (ISBN 0-8044-2403-9); pap. 6.95 (ISBN 0-8044-6277-1). Ungar.

Modern Experimental Chemistry. George W. Latimer & Ronald O. Ragsdale. 279p. 1971. text ed. 8.95 (ISBN 0-12-437250-3). Acad Pr.

Modern Family Law, 3 vols. Samuel Green & John V. Long. 1800p. Date not set. Set. 180.00 (ISBN 0-07-024275-5). McGraw.

Modern Fantasy: Five Studies. C. N. Manlove. LC 74-31798. 320p. 1975. 42.00 (ISBN 0-521-20746-0); pap. 9.95x (ISBN 0-521-29386-3). Cambridge U Pr.

Modern Filter Design: Active RC & Switched Capacitor. M. Ghausi & K. Laker. 1980. 34.95 (ISBN 0-13-594663-8). P-H.

Modern Fine Gentleman. (Flowering of the Novel in England 1700-1775 Ser.). 1974. Repr. of 1774 ed. lib. bdg. 50.00 (ISBN 0-8240-1203-8). Garland Pub.

Modern Fireplaces. Ernst Danz & Axel Manges. Date not set. 29.95 (ISBN 0-8038-0165-3). Hastings.

Modern Food Preservation. Margaret McWilliams & Harriett Paine. LC 77-76339. (Illus.). 1977. text ed. 11.95x (ISBN 0-916434-25-7). Plycon Pr.

Modern France: Mind, Politics, Society, 1870-1970. Barnett Singer. LC 80-24177. 212p. 1981. 16.95 (ISBN 0-686-69480-5). U of Wash Pr.

Modern French A, 2 bks. Eliane Burroughs. (gr. 8-12). 1966. pap. text ed. 7.00 each (ISBN 0-686-57756-6); tchr's manual & test avail. Learning Line.

Modern French B, 3 bks. Eliane Burroughs. (gr. 8-12). 1966. pap. text ed. 7.00 each (ISBN 0-686-57757-4); tchr's manual & test avail. Learning Line.

Modern French Cooking. Rae Spurlock. LC 79-23751. 208p. 1981. 16.95 (ISBN 0-88229-480-6). Nelson-Hall.

Modern French Course. 3rd ed. Muthurin Dondo & Camille Le Vois. 1966. text ed. 10.95x o.p. (ISBN 0-669-27144-6). Heath.

Modern French Culinary Art. rev. ed. H. P. Pellaprat. Ed. by John Fuller. Orig. Title: L'art Culinaire Moderne. (Illus.). 1974. 89.95 (ISBN 0-00-435143-6, Virtue & Co.). CBI Pub.

Modern French Culinary Art. Pelleprat. 1978. 92.50 (ISBN 0-685-47809-2). Radio City.

Modern French Masters. Ed. by John C. Van Dyke. LC 75-28885. (Art Experience in Late 19th Century America Ser.: Vol. 19). (Illus.). 1976. Repr. of 1896 ed. lib. bdg. 52.00 (ISBN 0-8240-2243-2). Garland Pub.

Modern French Masters-the Impressionists. (Illus.). 1975. Repr. 5.95 o.p. (ISBN 0-88308-007-9). Lamplight Pub.

Modern French Music. Edward B. Hill. LC 71-87491. (Music Reprint Ser). 1969. Repr. of 1924 ed. lib. bdg. 27.50 (ISBN 0-306-71497-3). Da Capo.

Modern French Philosophy. Vincent Descombes. Tr. by L. Scott-Fox & J. M. Harding. 240p. Date not set. 32.50 (ISBN 0-521-22837-9); pap. 11.50 (ISBN 0-521-29672-2). Cambridge U Pr.

Modern French Poetry: A Bilingual Anthology. Patricia Terry & Serge Garronsky. Tr. by Patricia Terry & Serge Garronsky. 192p. 1975. 15.00x (ISBN 0-231-03957-3); pap. 7.00x (ISBN 0-231-03958-1). Columbia U Pr.

Modern French Poets on Poetry. Compiled by R. Gibson. LC 78-73241. 1979. 32.50 (ISBN 0-521-05078-2). Cambridge U Pr.

Modern French Writing. Georges Lannois. 1969. pap. text ed. 2.95x o.p. (ISBN 0-435-37550-4). Heinemann Ed.

Modern Fundamentals of Golf. Ben Hogan. 128p. 1962. pap. 3.95 (ISBN 0-346-12326-7). Cornerstone.

Modern General Shop. Walter C. Brown et al. LC.74-23595. (Illus.). 1978. text ed. 12.40 (ISBN 0-87006-260-3). Goodheart.

Modern Geometry: Complete Course. John P. Ashley & E. R. Harvey. Ed. by Eugene Maier. (Mathematics for Individualized Instruction Ser). (Orig., Prog. Bk.). 1970. pap. text ed. 10.95x (ISBN 0-02-473490-X, 47349); dupl. masters 10.95x (ISBN 0-02-473400-4, 47340). Macmillan.

Modern German Authors: Johannes Bobrowski. B. Keith-Smith. Tr. by R. W. Last. (Vol. 4). 8.95 (ISBN 0-85496-044-9). Dufour.

Modern German Drama. Edgar Lohner & H. G. Hannum. LC 66-3026. 1966. text ed. 21.30 (ISBN 0-395-04808-7, 3-33585). HM.

Modern German Drama: A Study in Form. Christopher Innes. LC 78-26597. 1979. 56.00 (ISBN 0-521-22576-0); pap. 13.95 (ISBN 0-521-29560-2). Cambridge U Pr.

Modern German Music: Recollections & Criticisms, 2 vols. Henry F. Chorley. LC 79-110994. (Music Reprint Ser.). 1973. Repr. of 1854 ed. 57.50 (ISBN 0-306-71911-8). Da Capo.

Modern German Novel, 1945-1965. 2nd ed. H. M. Waidson. 176p. 1971. pap. 10.95x o.p. (ISBN 0-19-713414-9). Oxford U Pr.

Modern Germany: A Social, Cultural, & Political History. Henry M. Pachter. (Illus.). 1979. lib. bdg. 28.50x (ISBN 0-89158-166-9). Westview.

Modern Greece. rev. ed. Ruth Warren. (First Bks.). (Illus.). (gr. 4 up). 1979. PLB 5.90 s&l o.p. (ISBN 0-531-02934-4). Watts.

Modern Greek. (Teach Yourself Ser.). 1967. 3.50 (ISBN 0-679-10189-6). McKay.

Modern Greek Reference Grammar. Olga Elefteriades. (Orig.). 1981. pap. text ed. 10.00x (ISBN 0-87840-173-3). Georgetown U Pr.

Modern Guidance Practices in Teaching. C. R. Foster et al. (Illus.). 294p. 1980. 19.75 (ISBN 0-398-03990-9); pap. 14.50 (ISBN 0-398-04040-0). C C Thomas.

Modern Guide to Foodservice Equipment. Arthur C. Avery. LC 79-20831. (Illus.). 1980. text ed. 26.95 (ISBN 0-8436-2179-6). CBI Pub.

Modern Gun Values. 3rd ed. Jack Lewis. (Illus.). 384p. (Orig.). 1981. pap. 9.95 (ISBN 0-910676-19-4, 5836). DBI.

Modern Guns, Identification & Values. 2nd, rev. ed. Russel Quertermous & Steve Quertermous. (Illus.). 416p. 1980. pap. 11.95 o.p. (ISBN 0-89145-118-8). Collector Bks.

Modern Gynaecology with Obstetrics for Nurses. 6th ed. Winifred Hector & Gordon Bourne. (Illus.). 282p. 1980. pap. 14.95x (ISBN 0-433-14210-3). Intl Ideas.

Modern Handgun. Robert Hertzberg. 1977. 4.95 o.p. (ISBN 0-668-01464-4); pap. 2.50 o.p. (ISBN 0-668-04074-2). Arco.

Modern Handloading. George Nonte. (Illus.). 1972. 10.00 o.p. (ISBN 0-87691-046-0). Winchester Pr.

Modern Handmade Knives. B. R. Hughes. Date not set. price not set (ISBN 0-913150-44-4). Pioneer Pr.

Modern Hausa-English Dictionary. Compiled by Paul Newman & Roxanna M. Newman. 168p. 1979. pap. text ed. 6.95x (ISBN 0-19-575303-8). Oxford U Pr.

Modern Health & Figure Culture. Oscar Heidenstem. (Illus.). 1960. 6.50 (ISBN 0-571-03850-6, Pub. by Faber & Faber). Merrimack Bk Serv.

Modern Hebrew Poetry. Tr. & intro. by Bernhard Frank. LC 80-20037. (Iowa Translations Ser.). 240p. 1980. text ed. 15.00x (ISBN 0-87745-106-0); pap. 9.95 (ISBN 0-87745-107-9). U of Iowa Pr.

Modern Herbal. M. Grieve. Ed. by Mrs. C. F. Leyel. LC 72-169784. (Illus.). 1971. pap. 6.00 ea.; Vol. 1. pap. (ISBN 0-486-22798-7); Vol. 2. pap. (ISBN 0-486-22799-5). Dover.

Modern Herbal, 2 vols. Mrs. M. Grieve. (Illus.). Set. 22.00 (ISBN 0-8446-0302-3). Peter Smith.

Modern Heroism: Essays on D. H. Lawrence, William Empson, & J. R. R. Tolkien. Roger Sale. LC 73-186106. 1973. 20.00x (ISBN 0-520-02208-4). U of Cal Pr.

Modern Higher Algebra. Adrian A. Albert. LC 63-11397. 1937. 9.00x o.s.i. (ISBN 0-226-01176-3). U of Chicago Pr.

Modern Hinduism: An Account of the Religion & Life of the Hindus. 2nd ed. W. J. Wilkins. 1975. text ed. 12.50x (ISBN 0-7007-0046-3). Humanities.

Modern Historians on British History, 1584-1945: A Critical Bibliography, 1945-1969. G. R. Elton. LC 77-137677. 248p. 1971. 17.50x (ISBN 0-8014-0611-0). Cornell U Pr.

Modern History of Ethiopia & the Horn of Africa: A Select & Annotated Bibliography. Harold G. Marcus. LC 78-155298. (Bibliographical Ser.: No. 56). 1972. 30.00 (ISBN 0-8179-2561-9). Hoover Inst Pr.

Modern History of Europe: Men, Cultures, & Societies from the Renaissance to the Present. Eugen Weber. LC 77-133957. (Illus.). 1971. 17.95x (ISBN 0-393-09981-4). Norton.

Modern History of Somalia: Nation & State in the Horn of Africa. I. M. Lewis. (Illus.). 248p. 1980. pap. text ed. 10.95 (ISBN 0-582-64657-X). Longman.

Modern History of Tanganyika. J. Iliffe. LC 77-95445. (African Studies Ser.: No. 25). 1979. 79.50 (ISBN 0-521-22024-6); pap. 19.95x (ISBN 0-521-29611-0). Cambridge U Pr.

Modern History of Warships. William Hovgaard. 516p. 1980. 44.50x (ISBN 0-85177-040-1, Pub. by Cornell England). State Mutual Bk.

Modern Home Dictionary of Medical Words: With Descriptions, Uses & Standards of Commonly Used Tests. Fishbein, Morris, M.D. LC 74-18845. 240p. 1976. pap. 1.95 (ISBN 0-385-01105-9, Dolp). Doubleday.

Modern Hospital: International Planning Practices. (Illus.). 682p. 1980. text ed. 69.95 (ISBN 0-89443-355-5). Aspen Systems.

Modern Hotel & Motel Management. 3rd ed. Gerald W. Lattin. LC 77-10007. (Illus.). 1977. text ed. 16.95x (ISBN 0-7167-0483-8). W H Freeman.

Modern Household Equipment. Ruth E. Brasher & Carolyn L. Garrison. Date not set. 11.50 (ISBN 0-02-313540-9). Macmillan. Postponed.

Modern Human Relations. Richard M. Hodgetts. 512p. 1980. text ed. 18.95 (ISBN 0-03-054276-6). Dryden Pr.

Modern Humanistic Psychotherapy. Arthur Burton. LC 67-27947. (Social & Behavioral Science Ser.). 1967. 11.95x o.p. (ISBN 0-87589-007-5). Jossey-Bass.

Modern Hungarian Historiography. Steven B. Vardy. (East European Monographs: No. 16). 268p. 1976. 18.00x (ISBN 0-914710-08-7, Dist. by Columbia U Pr). East Eur Quarterly.

Modern Hungarian Poetry. Ed. by Miklos Vajda. 1979. pap. 7.95 (ISBN 0-231-08370-X). Columbia U Pr.

Modern Hungarian Poetry. Ed. & intro. by Miklos Vajda. LC 76-2453. (Illus.). 1977. 15.00x (ISBN 0-231-04022-9). Columbia U Pr.

Modern Ideas in Chess. Richard Reti. pap. 3.00 (ISBN 0-486-20638-6). Dover.

Modern Igneous Petrology. Mohan K. Sood. 250p. 1981. 22.50 (ISBN 0-471-08915-X, Pub. by Wiley-Interscience). Wiley.

Modern India. Percival Griffiths. 1962. pap. 2.00 (ISBN 0-88253-203-0). Ind-US Inc.

Modern India & Science & Technology. S. P. Gupta. 166p. 1979. 13.95 (ISBN 0-7069-0743-4, Pub by Vikas India). Advent Bk.

Modern India & the West: A Study of the Interaction of Their Civilizations. Ed. by L. S. O'Malley. (Royal Institute of International Affairs Ser). 1941. 17.00x o.p. (ISBN 0-19-821541-X). Oxford U Pr.

Modern Indian Poetry in English. Ed. by P. Lal. 733p. 1973. 15.00 (ISBN 0-88253-273-1); pap. text ed. 10.00 (ISBN 0-88253-986-8). Ind-US Inc.

Modern Indian Short Stories. Ed. by Suresh Kohli. (Indian Short Stories Ser.). 164p. 1975. 5.00 (ISBN 0-88253-737-7). Ind-US Inc.

Modern Indo-Anglian Love Poetry. Subhas C. Saha. (Writer's Workshop Greybird Ser.). 46p. 1975. 5.00 (ISBN 0-88253-578-1); pap. text ed. 4.00 (ISBN 0-88253-577-3). Ind-US Inc.

Modern Industrial Ceramics. Eugene C. Stafford. LC 72-14907. 1979. 19.95 (ISBN 0-672-97129-1); pap. 4.95 student's manual (ISBN 0-672-97128-3); instructor's manual 3.33 (ISBN 0-672-97127-5). Bobbs.

Modern Industrial Plastics. Terry Richardson. LC 72-92621. 17.95 (ISBN 0-672-20948-9). Bobbs.

Modern Inshore Fishing Gear. 2nd ed. John Garner. 13.75 (FN). Unipub.

Modern Intermediate Algebra. 2nd ed. Margaret F. Willerding. LC 74-16160. 368p. 1975. text ed. 21.95 (ISBN 0-471-94667-2); instructor's manual avail. (ISBN 0-471-94672-9). Wiley.

Modern Internal Auditing: An Operational Approach. 3rd ed. V. Z. Brink et al. 795p. 1973. 34.50 (ISBN 0-471-06524-2). Wiley.

Modern Internal Auditing: An Operational Approach. 3rd ed. Victor Z. Brink et al. (Illus.). 1973. 34.50 (ISBN 0-8260-1311-2). Ronald Pr.

Modern International Negotiation. Arthur Lall. LC 66-17587. 1966. 22.50x (ISBN 0-231-02935-7). Columbia U Pr.

Modern Interstitial & Intracavitary Radiation Cancer Management, Vol. 6. George. (Cancer Management Ser.). 1981. write for info. Masson Pub.

Modern Introduction to Biblical Hebrew. John F. Sawyer. (Orig.). 1976. pap. 12.50 (ISBN 0-85362-159-4, Oriel). Routledge & Kegan.

Modern Introduction to Chemistry. D. White. 1967. pap. 3.45 o.p. (ISBN 0-08-012164-0). Pergamon.

Modern Introduction to Classical Mechanics & Control Series: Mathematics & Its Applications. David N. Burghes & A. M. Downs. LC 75-16463. 300p. 1975. 43.95 (ISBN 0-470-12362-1). Halsted Pr.

Modern Introduction to International Law. 3rd ed. Michael Akehurst. (Minerva Ser. of Students' Handbooks). 1977. text ed. 29.95x (ISBN 0-04-341013-8); pap. text ed. 13.75x (ISBN 0-04-341014-6). Allen Unwin.

Modern Introduction to Philosophy. 3rd ed. Paul Edwards & A. Pap. LC 65-18470. 1973. text ed. 17.95 (ISBN 0-02-909200-0). Free Pr.

Modern Introduction to the Family. rev. ed. Ed. by Norman W. Bell & Ezra F. Vogel. LC 68-12830. 1968. text ed. 15.95 (ISBN 0-02-902330-0). Free Pr.

Modern Introductory Analysis. 2nd ed. Mary P. Dolciani et al. (gr. 11-12). 1977. text ed. 16.28 (ISBN 0-395-25157-5); tchr's ed. 17.20 (ISBN 0-395-25158-3). HM.

Modern Irish Drama IV: The Rise of the Realists. Robert Hogan et al. 1979. text ed. 45.00x (ISBN 0-391-01118-9, Dolmen Pr). Humanities.

Modern Irish Drama, No. 3: The Abbey Theatre, the Years of Synge 1905-1909. Robert Hogan & James Kilroy. (Irish Theatre Ser.: No. 8). 1978. text ed. 30.00x (ISBN 0-391-00754-8, Dolmen Pr). Humanities.

Modern Irish Drama, Vol. 2: Laying the Foundations, 1902-1904. Robert Hogan & James Kilroy. (Irish Theatre Ser: No. 7). 164p. 1976. text ed. 16.00x (ISBN 0-391-00609-6, Dolmen Pr). Humanities.

Modern Irish Drama 1: The Irish Literary Theater 1899-1901. Robert Hogan & James Kilroy. (Irish Theatre Ser.: No. 6). 160p. (Orig.). 1975. text ed. 12.00x (ISBN 0-391-00377-1, Dolmen Pr); pap. text ed. 7.50x (ISBN 0-391-00378-X). Humanities.

Modern Irish Short Stories. Ed. by Ben Forkner. 1980. pap. 5.95 (ISBN 0-14-005669-6). Penguin.

Modern Irish Short Stories. Ed. by Ben Forkner. 512p. 1980. 15.95 (ISBN 0-670-48324-9). Viking Pr.

Modern Issues in Guidance-Personnel Work. rev. ed. Ruth Barry & Beverly Wolf. LC 57-11977. 1963. pap. 4.25x (ISBN 0-8077-1050-4). Tchrs Coll.

Modern Italian Novel: From Capuana to Tozzi. Sergio Pacifici. LC 75-156786. (Crosscurrents-Modern Critiques Ser.). 1973. 10.95 (ISBN 0-8093-0614-X). S Ill U Pr.

Modern Italian Novel: From Manzoni to Svevo. Sergio Pacifici. LC 67-13047. (Crosscurrents-Modern Critiques Ser.). 215p. 1967. 10.95 (ISBN 0-8093-0267-5). S Ill U Pr.

Modern Italian Novel: From Pea to Moravia. Sergio Pacifici. LC 67-13047. (Crosscurrents Modern Critiques Ser.). 288p. 1979. 16.95 (ISBN 0-8093-0873-8). S Ill U Pr.

Modern Japan: Aspects of History, Literature & Society. Ed. by W. G. Beasley. (Campus Ser.: No. 195). 1977. pap. 6.95x (ISBN 0-520-03495-3). U of Cal Pr.

Modern Japanese Haiku: An Anthology. Compiled by Makato Ueda. LC 74-75035. 1976. pap. 7.50 (ISBN 0-8020-6245-8). U of Toronto Pr.

Modern Japanese Military System. Ed. by James H. Buck. LC 75-14628. (Sage Research Progress Ser. on War, Revolution, & Peacekeeping: Vol. 5). 1975. 20.00x (ISBN 0-8039-0513-0); pap. 9.95x (ISBN 0-8039-0514-9). Sage.

Modern Japanese Novels & the West. Donald Keene. (Illus.). 1961. 4.95x (ISBN 0-8139-0156-1). U Pr of Va.

Modern Japanese Organization & Decision-Making. Ed. by Ezra F. Vogel. 1975. 24.95x (ISBN 0-520-02857-0); pap. 5.95 o.p. (ISBN 0-520-03038-9). U of Cal Pr.

Modern Japanese Prints: A Contemporary Selection. Ed. by Yuji Abe. LC 70-120391. 1970. pap. 3.75 (ISBN 0-8048-0926-7). C E Tuttle.

Modern Japanese Prints: An Art Reborn. Oliver Statler. LC 59-8180. (Illus.). 1956. 17.50 (ISBN 0-8048-0406-0). C E Tuttle.

Modern Japanese Stories: An Anthology. Ed. by Ivan Morris. LC 61-11971. (Illus.). 1977. pap. 8.50 (ISBN 0-8048-1226-8). C E Tuttle.

Modern Jewish Problems. rev. ed. Roland B. Gittelson. (gr. 9-12). text ed. 5.00 (ISBN 0-8074-0099-8, 163303); tchrs'. guide 2.50 (ISBN 0-685-04890-X, 203303); wkbk. 1.75 (ISBN 0-685-04891-8, 163312). UAHC.

Modern Juice Therapy. Johnny Lovewisdom. pap. 2.00 (ISBN 0-933278-08-X). OMango.

Modern Junior High School. 3rd ed. William T. Gruhn & Harl R. Douglass. LC 78-110549. 424p. 1971. 18.95 (ISBN 0-8260-3695-3, 41985). Wiley.

Modern Land Use Control Course Handbook. (Real Estate Law & Practice Course Handbook Ser. 1977-78: Vol. 143). 1978. pap. 20.00 o.p. (ISBN 0-685-77709-8, N4-4307). PLI.

Modern Language Teaching in Schools & Colleges. Ed. by Seymour L. Flaxman. 72p. 1961. pap. 7.95x (ISBN 0-915432-61-7). NE Conf Teach Foreign.

Modern Latin American Literature, 2 vols. Ed. by David W. Foster & Virginia R. Foster. LC 72-81710. (A Library of Literary Criticism). 1100p. 1975. Set. 60.00 (ISBN 0-8044-3139-6). Ungar.

Modern Latin American Literature. D. P. Gallagher. 210p. 1973. pap. 3.95 (ISBN 0-19-888071-5, 400, GB). Oxford U Pr.

Modern Law Enforcement & Police Science. E. W. Williams. (Illus.). 408p. 1967. lexotone 37.50 (ISBN 0-398-02071-X). C C Thomas.

Modern Legal Glossary. Kenneth R. Redden & Enid L. Veron. 576p. 1980. 19.00 (ISBN 0-87215-237-5). Michie.

Modern Linguistics. S. Potter. (Andre Deutsch Language Library). 1977. lib. bdg. 12.50x (ISBN 0-233-95546-1). Westview.

Modern Linguistics, Its Development Methods & Problems. Manfred Bierwisch. (Janua Linguarum, Ser. Minor: No. 110). 103p. 1971. pap. text ed. 15.30x (ISBN 90-2791-657-8). Mouton.

Modern Literary Tibetan. Melvyn C. Goldstein. 1977. 13.95x (ISBN 0-685-89513-0). Himalaya Hse.

Modern Lithography. 2nd ed. Ian Faux. (Illus.). 1979. pap. 20.00 (ISBN 0-7121-1294-4). Transatlantic.

Modern Lithography. Ian Faux. (Illus.). 352p. 1978. pap. 15.95x (ISBN 0-7121-1294-4, Pub. by Macdonald & Evans England). Intl Ideas.

Modern Livestock & Poultry Production. James Gillespie. LC 79-50918. (Agriculture Ser.). 1981. pap. 18.20 (ISBN 0-8273-1688-7); instr's guide 3.15 (ISBN 0-8273-1689-5). Delmar.

Modern Logic: An Introduction. Norman L. Thomas. (Illus., Orig.). 1966. pap. 3.95 (ISBN 0-06-460103-X, CO 103, COS). Har-Row.

Modern Love Poems. Ed. by D. J. Klemer. LC 61-12542. 1961. 4.95 o.p. (ISBN 0-385-03266-8). Doubleday.

Modern Makonde Sculpture Exhibit Catalog. (Foreign & Comparative Studies-African Special Publications: No.5). 103p. 1968. pap. 3.50x. Syracuse U Foreign Comp.

Modern Man in Search of Religion. Swami Pavitrananda. pap. 1.00 o.s.i. (ISBN 0-87481-060-4). Vedanta Pr.

Modern Management Accounting. 2nd ed. Nelson & Miller. 640p. 1981. write for info. (ISBN 0-8302-5904-X). Goodyear.

Modern Management & Information Systems. Joel E. Ross. (Illus.). 288p. 1976. 15.95 (ISBN 0-87909-499-0). Reston.

Modern Management & Machiavelli. Richard H. Buskirk. LC 74-11194. 291p. 1974. 11.95 (ISBN 0-8436-0734-3). CBI Pub.

Modern Manager. Edgar F. Huse. (Illus.). 1979. text ed. 18.95 (ISBN 0-8299-0197-3); pap. study guide 7.50 (ISBN 0-686-67406-5); study guide 7.50 (ISBN 0-8299-0253-8). instrs.' manual avail. (ISBN 0-8299-0492-1); transparency masters avail. (ISBN 0-8299-0493-X). West Pub.

Modern Managerial Decision Making. K. J. Radford. 1981. text ed. 17.95 (ISBN 0-8359-4571-5); instr's. manual avail. (ISBN 0-8359-4229-5). Reston.

Modern Marine Electricity & Electronics. Percy D. Smith. LC 66-20866. (Illus.). 1966. 16.00x (ISBN 0-87033-062-4). Cornell Maritime.

Modern Marketing of Farm Products. 3rd ed. William P. Mortenson. LC 76-14650. (Illus.). (gr. 9-12). 1977. 15.35 (ISBN 0-8134-1816-X); text ed. 11.50x (ISBN 0-685-77710-3). Interstate.

Modern Marketing: Principles & Practice. Edward J. Fox & Edward W. Wheatley. 1978. 16.95x (ISBN 0-673-15045-3). Scott F.

Modern Masonry. Clois E. Kinklighter. (Illus.). 1980. text ed. 12.00 (ISBN 0-87006-296-4). Goodheart.

Modern Masonry Panel Construction Systems. J. J. Svec & P. E. Jeffers. LC 72-83307. (Illus.). 1971. 16.95 (ISBN 0-8436-0114-0). CBI Pub.

Modern Mathematical Methods in Engineering. F. S. Merritt. 1970. 28.50 o.p. (ISBN 0-07-044512-9, P&RB). McGraw.

Modern Mathematics. Charlotte M. Gemmel. LC 68-55295. (Rapid Reviews Ser.). pap. text ed. 2.75 o.s.i. (ISBN 0-8220-1757-1). Cliffs.

Modern Mathematics: An Elementary Approach, Alternative Edition. Ruric Wheeler. 585p. 1981. text ed. 18.95 (ISBN 0-8185-0413-7). Brooks-Cole.

Modern Mathematics: An Elementary Approach. 5th ed. Ruric E. Wheeler. 625p. 1981. text ed. 19.95 (ISBN 0-8185-0430-7). Brooks-Cole.

Modern Mathematics & Economic Analysis. Blaine Roberts & David L. Schulze. 1973. 16.95x (ISBN 0-393-09392-1); study guide 4.95x (ISBN 0-393-09374-3). Norton.

Modern Mathematics & the Teacher. Lucienne Felix. (Orig.). 1966. 17.95 (ISBN 0-521-04989-X); pap. 6.95x (ISBN 0-521-09385-6). Cambridge U Pr.

Modern Mathematics at Ordinary Level. L. Harwood Clarke. 1970. pap. text ed. 7.50x o.p. (ISBN 0-435-50180-1). Heinemann Ed.

Modern Mathematics Check-up. A. J. Raven & L. K. Kuan. 1977. pap. text ed. 6.50x o.p. (ISBN 0-435-50812-1). Heinemann Ed.

Modern Mathematics for Business Decision-Making. 2nd ed. Donald R. Williams. 1978. text ed. 19.95x (ISBN 0-534-00558-6). Wadsworth Pub.

Modern Mathematics in Secondary Schools. D. T. Marjoram. 1964. text ed. 6.95 (ISBN 0-08-010719-2); pap. 5.40 (ISBN 0-08-010718-4). Pergamon.

Modern Mathematics with Applications to Business & the Social Sciences. 2nd ed. Ruric E. Wheeler & W. D. Peeples. LC 74-21453. (Contemporary Undergraduate Mathematics Ser.). 1976. text ed. 16.95x o.p. (ISBN 0-685-67043-0); instructor's manual avail. o.p. (ISBN 0-685-67044-9). Brooks-Cole.

Modern Mathematics with Applications to Business & the Social Sciences. 3rd ed. Ruric E. Wheeler & W. D. Peeples, Jr. LC 79-18636. 1980. text ed. 18.95 (ISBN 0-8185-0366-1). Brooks-Cole.

Modern Medical Discoveries. 3rd ed. Irmengarde Eberle. LC 68-17084. (gr. 5-9). 1968. 7.95 (ISBN 0-690-55271-8, TYC-J). T Y Crowell.

Modern Merchant Banking: A Guide to the Workings of the Accepting Houses of the City of London & Their Services to Industry & Commerce. Ed. by C. J. Clay & B. S. Wheble. 160p. 1980. pap. 12.50 (ISBN 0-85941-044-7). Herman Pub.

Modern Metallography. R. E. Smallman & K. H. Ashbee. 1966. 13.75 (ISBN 0-08-011571-3); pap. 6.25 (ISBN 0-08-011570-5). Pergamon.

Modern Metalworking. John R. Walker. LC 76-22559. 1976. text ed. 13.92 (ISBN 0-87006-212-3); wkbk. 3.20 (ISBN 0-87006-223-9). Goodheart.

Modern Methods for Computer Security & Privacy. Lance J. Hoffman. LC 76-49896. (Illus.). 1977. 23.95x (ISBN 0-13-595207-7). P-H.

Modern Methods for the Separation of Rarer Metal Ions. J. Korkisch. 1969. text ed. 60.00 (ISBN 0-08-012921-8). Pergamon.

Modern Methods in High School Teaching. Harl R. Douglass. 544p. 1981. Repr. lib. bdg. 25.00 (ISBN 0-8495-1061-9). Arden Lib.

Modern Methods in the History of Medicine. Ed. by Edwin Clarke. 1971. text ed. 33.75x (ISBN 0-485-11121-7, Athlone Pr). Humanities.

Modern Methods of Chemical Analysis. 2nd ed. Robert L. Pecsok et al. LC 76-13894. 1976. 23.95x (ISBN 0-471-67662-4); solution manual avail. (ISBN 0-471-02878-9). Wiley.

Modern Middle East: A Guide to Research Tools in the Social Sciences. Reeva S. Simon. LC 77-27319. (Westview Special Studies on the Middle East Ser.). 1978. lib. bdg. 26.50x (ISBN 0-89158-059-X); pap. text ed. 9.50x (ISBN 0-89158-158-8). Westview.

Modern Migrations in Western Africa: Studies Presented & Discussed at the 11th Int'l African Seminar, Dakar, 4/1972. Ed. by Samir Amin. (International African Institute Ser.). 428p. 1974. 37.50x (ISBN 0-19-724193-X). Oxford U Pr.

Modern Military Dictionary: Ten Thousand Technical & Slang Terms of Military Usage. 2nd ed. Max B. Garber & P. S. Bond. LC 74-31354. 1975. Repr. of 1942 ed. 20.00 (ISBN 0-8103-4208-1). Gale.

Modern Minerology. Keith Frye. (Illus.). 336p. 1973. ref. ed. 21.95 (ISBN 0-13-595686-2). P-H.

Modern Modern Times. Reid J. Daitzman. 75p. 1981. pap. text ed. 2.95 (ISBN 0-938340-01-8). World Univ Pr.

Modern Molecular Orbital Theory for Organic Chemists. Weston T. Borden. (Illus.). 336p. 1975. 22.95 (ISBN 0-13-595983-7). P-H.

Modern Motor Bikes. Laurie Caddell. (Illus.). 1979. 12.50 (ISBN 0-7137-0989-8, Pub by Blandford Pr England). Sterling.

Modern Movements in Architecture. Charles Jencks. 432p. 1973. pap. 7.95 (ISBN 0-385-02554-8, Anch). Doubleday.

Modern Music Notation. Laszlo Boehm. 1961. pap. 5.95 (ISBN 0-02-870490-8). Schirmer Bks.

Modern Music: The Avant Garde Since 1945. Paul Griffiths. (Illus.). 308p. 1981. 37.50x (ISBN 0-460-04365-X, Pub. by J. M. Dent England). Biblio Dist.

Modern Musical Scholarship: Studies in Musical History. Ed. by Edward Olleson. (Illus.). 1980. write for info. (ISBN 0-85362-180-2, Oriel). Routledge & Kegan.

Modern Network Theory: An Introduction. R. K. Brayton et al. Ed. by G. S. Moschytz & J. Neirynck. 1978. text ed. 42.00 (ISBN 2-604-00034-2). Renouf.

Modern Newspaper Editing. 2nd ed. Gene Gilmore & Robert Root. 1976. 14.95x (ISBN 0-87835-054-3). Boyd & Fraser.

Modern Nigeria. Guy Arnold. 1977. pap. text ed. 8.95x (ISBN 0-582-64643-X). Longman.

Modern Norwegian Literature, Eighteen Eighty-Nineteen Eighteen. Brian W. Downs. 1966. 47.50 (ISBN 0-521-04854-0). Cambridge U Pr.

Modern Novel Writing, 4 vols. in 1. William Beckford. Incl. Azemia. Repr. of 1797 ed. LC 74-81366. 264p. 1970. Repr. of 1796 ed. 35.00x (ISBN 0-8201-1063-9). Schol Facsimiles.

Modern Novel Writing, or the Elegant Enthusiast: And Interesting Emotions of Arabella Bloomville, a Rhapsodical Romance, Interspersed with Poetry, by the Right Hon. Lady Harriet Marlow, 2 vols. William Beckford. (Feminist Controversy in England, 1788-1810 Ser.). 1974. Set. lib. bdg. 100.00 (ISBN 0-8240-0851-0); lib. bdg. 50.00 ea. Garland Pub.

Modern Nurseryman. Alan Toogood & John Stanley. (Illus.). 432p. 1981. 45.00 (ISBN 0-571-11544-6, Pub. by Faber & Faber); pap. 22.00 (ISBN 0-571-11547-0). Merrimack Bk Serv.

Modern Nursing: Theory & Practice. 6th ed. Winifred Hector. (Illus.). 1976. 18.95x (ISBN 0-433-14212-X). Intl Ideas.

Modern Occasions Two: New Fiction, Criticism, Poetry. Ed. by Philip Rahv. LC 66-18863. (National Univ. Pubns.). 320p. 1974. 15.00 (ISBN 0-8046-9068-5). Kennikat.

Modern Oil-Hydraulic Engineering. Jean U. Thoma. (Illus.). 1970. 52.00x (ISBN 0-85461-043-X). Intl Ideas.

Modern Ophthalmology, 4 vols. 2nd ed. Ed. by Arnold Sorsby. Incl. Vol. 1. Basic Aspects. (Illus.). 640p. 45.00 o.p. (ISBN 0-685-27023-8); Vol. 2. Systemic Aspects. (Illus.). 748p. 50.00 o.p. (ISBN 0-685-27024-6); Vols. 3 & 4. Topical Aspects. (Illus.). 1200p. Set. 95.00 o.p. (ISBN 0-685-27025-4). (Illus.). 2588p. 1972. Set. 190.00 o.p. (ISBN 0-685-27022-X). Lippincott.

Modern Organization Theory: A Symposium of the Foundation for Research on Human Behavior. Ed. by M. Haire. LC 74-30245. 334p. 1975. Repr. of 1959 ed. 15.00 o.p. (ISBN 0-88275-223-5). Krieger.

Modern Ornamentation. Christopher Dresser. Ed. by Peter Stansky & Rodney Shewan. LC 76-17771. (Aesthetic Movement & the Arts & Crafts Movements Ser.: Vol. 26). 1978. Repr. of 1886 ed. lib. bdg. 44.00 (ISBN 0-8240-2475-3). Garland Pub.

Modern Oscilloscope Handbook. Douglas Bapton. (Illus.). 1979. ref. 18.95 (ISBN 0-8359-4582-0). Reston.

Modern Painters. Joseph E. Muller & Frank Elgar. (Illus.). 172p. 1980. pap. 7.95 (ISBN 0-8120-2285-8). Barron.

Modern Painting. George Moore. 288p. 1980. cancelled (ISBN 0-8180-0130-5). Horizon.

Modern Parliamentary Procedure. Ray E. Keesey. 208p. 1974. pap. text ed. 8.95 (ISBN 0-395-17015-X). HM.

Modern Pastry Chef: Cakes, Pies & Other Baked Goods, Vol. 1. William J. Sultan. (Illus.). 1977. lib. bdg. 32.50 (ISBN 0-87055-225-2); pap. text ed. 21.50 (ISBN 0-87055-310-0). AVI.

Modern Pastry Chef: French Pastries, Cookies, Molded and Frozen Desserts, Vol. 2. William J. Sultan. (Illus.). 1977. lib. bdg. 32.50 (ISBN 0-87055-226-0); pap. text ed. 21.50 (ISBN 0-87055-311-9). AVI.

Modern Persian Prose Literature. Hassan Kamshad. 1966. 48.00 (ISBN 0-521-05464-8). Cambridge U Pr.

Modern Persian Prose Reader. Hassan Kamshad. LC 68-22663. (Persian). 1968. text ed. 48.00 (ISBN 0-521-07077-5). Cambridge U Pr.

Modern Persian Short Stories. Ed. by Minoo Southgate. LC 79-89930. 228p. (Orig.). 1980. 14.00x (ISBN 0-89410-032-7, 033-5); pap. 6.00x (ISBN 0-686-64484-0). Three Continents.

Modern Personnel Management. Sexton Adams & Adelaide Griffin. 330p. 1981. 14.95 (ISBN 0-87201-662-5). Gulf Pub.

Modern Personnel Management. Greenlaw. 1979. 19.95 (ISBN 0-03-020806-8). Dryden Pr.

Modern Perspectives in the Psychiatry of Middle Age. Ed. by John G. Howells. LC 74-78715. 375p. 1981. 30.00 (ISBN 0-87630-245-2). Brunner-Mazel.

Modern Photo-Journalism: Origin & Evolution, 1910-1933. Tim N. Gidal. Tr. by Maureen Oberli-Turner. (Men & Movements Ser.: Vol. 1). (Illus.). 96p. 1974. 10.95 o.s.i. (ISBN 0-02-544300-3). Macmillan.

Modern Photo-Journalism: Origin & Evolution, 1910-1933. Tim N. Gidal. Tr. by Maureen Oberli-Turner. (Photography, Men & Movements Ser.: Vol. 1). (Illus.). 96p. 1974. pap. 5.95 o.s.i. (ISBN 0-02-000400-1, Collier). Macmillan.

Modern Photographic Processing, 2 vols. Grant Haist. LC 78-17559. (Photographic Science & Technology & Graphic Arts Ser.). 1979. Set. 85.00 (ISBN 0-471-04286-2); Vol. 1. 50.00 (ISBN 0-471-02228-4); Vol. 2. 45.00 (ISBN 0-471-04285-4, Pub. by Wiley-Interscience). Wiley.

Modern Physical Geography. Arthur N. Strahler & Alan H. Strahler. LC 77-20242. 1978. text ed. 22.95x (ISBN 0-471-01871-6); tapes avail. (ISBN 0-471-04093-2); study guide 4.95x (ISBN 0-471-04310-9). Wiley.

Modern Physical Science: A Student Study Guide. Charles A. Payne & William R. Falls. 1976. pap. text ed. 4.95 (ISBN 0-8403-1364-0). Kendall-Hunt.

Modern Physical Techniques in Materials Technology. Ed. by T. Mulvey & R. K. Webster. (Harwell Ser.). (Illus.). 336p. 1974. text ed. 45.00x (ISBN 0-19-851708-4). Oxford U Pr.

Modern Physics. 3rd ed. R. L. Sproull & W. A. Phillips. LC 79-26680. 682p. 1980. text ed. 27.95 (ISBN 0-471-81840-2). Wiley.

Modern Physics. 2nd ed. Robert L. Sproull. LC 63-11452. 1963. text ed. 27.95x o.p. (ISBN 0-471-81845-3). Wiley.

Modern Physics. 2nd ed. Paul A. Tipler. LC 77-58725. 1977. text ed. 11.95x (ISBN 0-87901-088-6). Worth.

Modern Physics: An Introductory Survey. Arthur Beiser. LC 68-12695. (Physics Ser). (Illus., Orig.). 1968. pap. 7.95 (ISBN 0-201-00515-8). A-W.

Modern Physics for Applied Science. Barry C. Robertson. 368p. 1981. text ed. 20.95 (ISBN 0-471-05343-0). Wiley.

Modern Physics in Chemistry, Vol. 1. E. Fluck & V. I. Goldanskii. 1977. 58.00 (ISBN 0-12-261201-9). Acad Pr.

Modern Pinyin Chinese-English Dictionary. 1980. pap. 9.95 o.p. (ISBN 0-86519-001-1). Caroline Hse.

Modern Plastics Technology. Raymond B. Seymour. (Illus.). 256p. 1975. 17.95 (ISBN 0-87909-500-8). Reston.

Modern Plumbing. E. Keith Blankenbaker. LC 77-15954. (Illus.). 1978. text ed. 14.00 (ISBN 0-87006-245-X). Goodheart.

Modern Plumbing for Old & New Houses. Jay Hedden. Ed. by Shirley M. Horowitz. LC 79-26539. (Illus.). 144p. (Orig.). 1980. 12.95 (ISBN 0-932944-13-2); pap. 4.95 (ISBN 0-932944-14-0). Creative Homeowner.

Modern Plywood Techniques Vol. 3: Proceedings. Plywood Clinic, 3rd, Portland, Mar.1975. Ed. by Herbert G. Lambert. LC 74-20159. (Plywood Clinic Library: A Forest Industries Book). (Illus.). 240p. 1976. pap. 29.50 o.p. (ISBN 0-87930-048-5). Miller Freeman.

Modern Poetry & the Idea of Language: A Critical & Historical Study. Gerald L. Bruns. LC 73-86886. 1974. 20.00 o.p. (ISBN 0-300-01613-1). Yale U Pr.

Modern Poetry: Essays in Criticism. Ed. by John Hollander. (Orig.). (YA) (gr. 9 up). 1968. pap. 6.95 (ISBN 0-19-500757-3, GB). Oxford U Pr.

Modern Poetry Four. 2nd ed. Ed. by Jim Hunter. 1979. 5.95 o.p. (ISBN 0-571-08862-7, Pub. by Faber & Faber); pap. 4.95 (ISBN 0-571-04977-X). Merrimack Bk Serv.

Modern Poetry Four. 1968. 5.95 o.p. (ISBN 0-571-08862-7, Pub. by Faber & Faber); pap. 2.50 o.p. (ISBN 0-571-08863-5). Merrimack Bk Serv.

Modern Poets Five. Jim Hunter. 160p. 1981. pap. 8.95 (ISBN 0-571-11567-5, Pub. by Faber & Faber). Merrimack Bk Serv.

Modern Poets One. (Orig.). 1968. pap. 4.50 (ISBN 0-686-24616-0, Pub. by Faber & Faber). Merrimack Bk Serv.

Modern Poets Three. 1968. 5.95 o.p. (ISBN 0-571-08860-0, Pub. by Faber & Faber); pap. 4.50 (ISBN 0-571-08861-9). Merrimack Bk Serv.

Modern Poets Two. (Orig.). 1968. pap. 4.50 (ISBN 0-571-08951-8, Pub. by Faber & Faber). Merrimack Bk Serv.

Modern Police Management Organization. Victor I. Cizankas & Donald G. Hanna. (Illus.). 256p. 1977. text ed. 15.95 (ISBN 0-13-597104-7). P-H.

Modern Political Analysis. 3rd ed. Robert A. Dahl. (Foundations of Modern Political Science Ser). (Illus.). 176p. 1976. ref. ed. o.p. 8.95x (ISBN 0-13-596999-9); pap. text ed. 6.95x (ISBN 0-13-596981-6). P-H.

Modern Political Economy. N. J. Frolick & J. Oppenheimer. 1978. pap. 7.95 (ISBN 0-13-597120-9). P-H.

Modern Political Economy, Paper. Bruno S. Frey. 166p. 1980. pap. text ed. 13.95 (ISBN 0-470-26999-5). Halsted Pr.

Modern Political Geography. Richard Muir. 262p. 1975. 19.95 (ISBN 0-470-62356-X); pap. 14.95 (ISBN 0-470-99194-1). Halsted Pr.

Modern Political Systems: Europe. 4th ed. Roy C. Macridis. 1978. ref. 17.95 (ISBN 0-13-597187-X). P-H.

Modern Political Theory. S. P. Varma. 1976. 15.95 (ISBN 0-7069-0369-2, Pub. by Vikas India). Advent Bk.

Modern Politics. C. L. James. pap. 4.00 (ISBN 0-685-20861-3). Univ Place.

Modern Politics. 2nd ed. C. L. James. (Illus.). iv, 167p. 1973. pap. 3.00 (ISBN 0-935590-09-9). Bewick Edns.

Modern Politics in America: How Did It Come About? Martin W. Sandler et al. (People Make a Nation Ser.). (gr. 7-12). 1971. pap. text ed. 4.40 (ISBN 0-205-03438-1, 7834381). Allyn.

Modern Portfolio Theory. Robert Hagin. 1980. pap. 10.95x (ISBN 0-256-02379-4). Irwin.

Modern Portfolio Theory. Andrew Rudd & Henry K. Clasing, Jr. 1981. 21.50 (ISBN 0-87094-191-7). Dow Jones-Irwin.

Modern Power Transformer Practice. Ed. by R. Feinberg. LC 78-5608. 1979. 54.95 (ISBN 0-470-26344-X). Halsted Pr.

Modern Practical Neurology. 2nd ed. Peritz Scheinberg. 360p. 1981. 26.00 (ISBN 0-89004-521-6); pap. 14.95 (ISBN 0-686-69137-7). Raven.

Modern Practical Neurology: An Introduction to Diagnosis & Management of Common Neurological Disorders. Ed. by Peritz Scheinberg. LC 76-49718. 1977. 22.00 (ISBN 0-685-71561-2); pap. 13.00 (ISBN 0-685-71562-0). Raven.

Modern Practice in Servo Design. D. Wilson. 1970. 60.00 (ISBN 0-08-015812-9). Pergamon.

Modern Practice of Adult Education: Andragogy Versus Pedragogy. rev. ed. Malcolm S. Knowles. 400p. 1980. 17.95 (ISBN 0-695-81472-9, Assn Pr). Follett.

Modern Presidency. Charles Radding. (American Government Ser.). (gr. 7 up). 1979. PLB 6.90 s&l (ISBN 0-531-02266-8). Watts.

Modern Prince & Other Writings. Antonio Gramsci. LC 67-25646. 1959. 5.95 o.p. (ISBN 0-7178-0134-9); pap. 2.25 (ISBN 0-7178-0133-0). Intl Pub Co.

Modern Principles of Athletic Training. 5th ed. Carl E. Klafs & Daniel D. Arnheim. (Illus.). 580p. 1981. text ed. 21.95 (ISBN 0-8016-2682-X). Mosby.

Modern Production-Operations Management. 6th ed. Elwood S. Buffa. LC 79-17788. (Wiley Ser. in Management). 1980. text ed. 23.50 (ISBN 0-471-05672-3); tchrs'. manual avail. (ISBN 0-471-06443-2). Wiley.

Modern Products Liability Law. Richard A. Epstein. LC 80-11486. (Quorum Bk.). 210p. 1980. lib. bdg. 25.00 (ISBN 0-89930-002-2, EPL/, Quorum). Greenwood.

Modern Programming: Fortran 4. Henry Mullish. 1968. pap. 12.95x o.p. (ISBN 0-471-00388-3). Wiley.

Modern Project Management: Foundations for Quality & Productivity. Claude W. Burrill & Leon W. Ellsworth. LC 79-24457. (Data Processing Handbook Ser.). (Illus.). 576p. 1980. text ed. 39.00x (ISBN 0-935310-00-2). Burrill-Ellsworth.

Modern Psychological Novel. Leon Edel. 8.50 (ISBN 0-8446-2020-3). Peter Smith.

Modern Psychology. Phillip L. Harriman. (Quality Paperback: No. 20). (Orig.). 1975. pap. 3.95 (ISBN 0-8226-0020-X). Littlefield.

Modern Psychology: The Teachings of Carl Gustav Jung. David Cox. 1968. pap. 2.95 (ISBN 0-06-463231-8, EH 231, EH). Har-Row.

Modern Public Finance. 4th ed. Bernard P. Herber. 1979. text ed. 18.50 (ISBN 0-256-02159-7). Irwin.

Modern Quantum Mechanics with Applications to Elementary Particle Physics: An Introduction to Contemporary Physical Thinking. John Eisele. LC 69-19102. 1969. 38.95 (ISBN 0-471-23466-4, Pub. by Wiley-Interscience). Wiley.

Modern Radiation Oncology: Classic Literature & Current Management. Ed. by Harvey A. Gilbert & A. Robert Kagan. (Illus.). 1978. text ed. 52.50x (ISBN 0-06-140910-3, Harper Medical). Har-Row.

Modern Radio Broadcasting. Robert H. Coddington. LC 68-56096. 288p. 1969. 12.95 o.p. (ISBN 0-8306-9482-X, 482). TAB Bks.

Modern Railroad Roadway Maintenance & Management. Ed. by Railsearch Publishing, Inc. (Railsearch Railroad Management Ser.: No. 4). (Illus.). 600p. 1980. 147.50 (ISBN 0-937060-03-8); lib. bdg. 48.00 (ISBN 0-937060-07-0). Railsearch.

Modern Reader in the Philosophy of Religion. Ed. by Willard E. Arnett. LC 66-20470. (Century Philosophy Ser.). 1966. 29.50x (ISBN 0-89197-482-2); pap. text ed. 16.95x (ISBN 0-89197-483-0). Irvington.

Modern Reader's Bible. Ed. by Richard G. Moulton. 1943. 9.95 o.s.i. (ISBN 0-02-587860-3). Macmillan.

Modern Reader's Chaucer. John S. Tatlock & Percy MacKaye. 1966. pap. text ed. 8.95 (ISBN 0-02-932410-6). Free Pr.

Modern Reader's Japanese-English Character Dictionary. Andrew Nelson. LC 61-11973. 1962. 35.00 (ISBN 0-8048-0408-7). C E Tuttle.

Modern Real Estate Finance. 3rd ed. William Atteberry. LC 79-24627. (Grid Ser. in Finance & Real Estate). 1980. text ed. 20.95 (ISBN 0-88244-212-0). Grid Pub.

Modern Real Estate Practice in Pennsylvania. 2nd ed. Herbert J. Bellairs et al. 576p. (Orig.). 1978. pap. 25.00 (ISBN 0-88462-280-0). Real Estate Ed Co.

Modern Real Estate Practice Teacher's Manual. Fillmore W. Galaty et al. 96p. (Orig.). 1978. pap. 13.95 (ISBN 0-88462-263-0). Real Estate Ed Co.

Modern Real Estate Principles. rev. ed. William M Shenkel. 1980. 17.95x (ISBN 0-256-02291-7); study guide 5.50x (ISBN 0-256-02292-5). Business Pubns.

Modern Real Estate Principles in California. 2nd ed. B. E. Tsagris. 550p. 1980. pap. 21.95 o.p. (ISBN 0-695-81493-1). Real Estate Ed Co.

Modern Refrigeration & Air Conditioning. Andrew Althouse et al. LC 79-12403. (Illus.). 1979. text ed. 23.00 (ISBN 0-87006-275-1); lab manual 4.96 (ISBN 0-87006-265-4). Goodheart.

Modern Relay Techniques. M. L. Gayford. (Illus.). 149p. 1975. 15.00x (ISBN 0-408-06843-4). Transatlantic.

Modern Religious Lyrics. Jocelyn Hollis. LC 80-80565. (Contemporary American Traditional Poetry Ser.: Vol. 2, No. 1). 28p. (Orig.). 1980. pap. 2.95 (ISBN 0-933486-19-7). Am Poetry Pr.

Modern Religious Movements in India: New York, 1919. J. N. Farquhar. LC 78-74274. (Oriental Religions Ser.: Vol. 3). 497p. 1980. lib. bdg. 55.00 (ISBN 0-8240-3909-2). Garland Pub.

Modern Religious Situation. Edward S. Kiek. 227p. Repr. of 1926 ed. 2.95 (ISBN 0-567-02158-0). Attic Pr.

Modern Researcher. 3rd ed. Jacques Barzun & Henry F. Graff. 378p. 1977. pap. text ed. 9.95 (ISBN 0-15-562511-X, HC). HarBraceJ.

Modern Reservoir Engineering: A Simulation Approach. Henry B. Crichlow. (Illus.). 1977. 34.95 (ISBN 0-13-597468-2). P-H.

Modern Retailing Management. 9th ed. Delbert J. Duncan et al. 1977. text ed. 18.95 (ISBN 0-256-01926-6). Irwin.

Modern Retailing: Theory & Practice. J. Barry Mason & Morris L. Mayer. 1978. 18.95x (ISBN 0-256-02072-8). Business Pubns.

Modern Revision Questions in Physics. A. C. Jarvis & C. R. Gregory. 1975. pap. text ed. 5.50x o.p. (ISBN 0-435-67540-0). Heinemann Ed.

Modern Revolutions: An Introduction to the Analysis of a Political Phenomenon. John Dunn. LC 72-177942. 352p. 1972. 34.95 (ISBN 0-521-08441-5); pap. 9.95xx (ISBN 0-521-09698-7). Cambridge U Pr.

Modern Revolutions & Revolutionists: A Bibliography. Robert Blackey. LC 75-45301. (War-Peace Bibliography Ser.: No. 5). 257p. 1976. text ed. 17.00 (ISBN 0-87436-223-7). ABC-Clio.

Modern Rhetoric of Speech-Communication. 2nd ed. Raymond E. Nadeau. LC 74-167994. (Speech Ser). 1972. text ed. 11.95 (ISBN 0-201-04999-6). A-W.

Modern Riding. Albert Brandl. (EP Sports Ser.). (Illus.). 142p. 1981. 12.95 (ISBN 0-8069-9133-X, Pub. by EP Publishing England). Sterling.

Modern Roofing: Care & Repair. Donald L. Meyers. Ed. by Shirley M. Horowitz. (Illus.). 144p. (Orig.). 1981. pap. 6.95 (ISBN 0-686-69553-4). Creative Homeowner.

Modern Rope Seamanship. Colin Jarman & Bill Beavis. LC 76-20290. (Illus.). 1979. 15.00 (ISBN 0-87742-074-2). Intl Marine.

Modern Russian Composers. Leonid Sabaneyeff. Tr. by Judah A. Joffe from Rus. LC 75-14232. (Music Reprint Ser). 253p. 1975. Repr. of 1927 ed. lib. bdg. 25.00 (ISBN 0-306-70673-5). Da Capo.

Modern Russian Poets on Poetry. Ed. by Carl Proffer. 1976. 15.00 (ISBN 0-88233-185-X). Ardis Pubs.

Modern Russian Stress. R. I. Avanesov. (Pergamon Oxford Russian Ser.). 1963. pap. 4.00 o.p. (ISBN 0-08-010300-6). Pergamon.

Modern Russian Usage. D. E. Rozental. Ed. by C. V. James. 1963. 11.75 o.p. (ISBN 0-08-009811-8). Pergamon.

Modern Safety Practices. Russell De Reamer. LC 58-12708. 372p. 1958. 11.50 (ISBN 0-471-20361-0). Krieger.

Modern Saltwater Fishing. Vic Dunaway. 288p. 1975. 11.95 (ISBN 0-87691-168-8). Winchester Pr.

Modern Saltwater Fishing Tackle. Frank T. Moss. LC 76-8780. (Illus.). 1977. 22.50 (ISBN 0-87742-068-8). Intl Marine.

Modern Sawmill Techniques Vol. 5: Proceedings. Sawmill Clinic, 5th, Portland, Oregon, March 1975. Ed. by Vernon S. White. LC 73-88045. (Sawmill Clinic Library: A Forest Industries Bk.). (Illus.). 1975. 35.00 (ISBN 0-87930-047-7). Miller Freeman.

Modern Sawmill Techniques Vol. 6: Proceedings. Sawmill Clinic, 5th, Portland, Oregon, March 1975. Ed. by Vernon S. White. LC 73-88045. (Sawmill Clinic Library: A Forest Industries Bk.). (Illus.). 1976. 35.00 (ISBN 0-87930-052-3). Miller Freeman.

Modern Sawmill Techniques, Vol. 8: Proceedings. Sawmill Clinic, 8th, Portland, Oregon Mar. 1978. LC 73-88045. (Sawmill Clinic Library: A Forest Industries Bk.). (Illus.). 1978. pap. 29.50 (ISBN 0-87930-103-1). Miller Freeman.

Modern School Library. 2nd ed. Helen E. Saunders. LC 75-20377. 1975. 10.00 (ISBN 0-8108-0864-1). Scarecrow.

Modern Science & Anarchism. Peter Kropotkin. 1980. lib. bdg. 49.95 (ISBN 0-8490-3125-7). Gordon Pr.

Modern Science Fiction. Ed. by Norman Spinrad. LC 73-18782. 560p. 1974. pap. 3.50 (ISBN 0-385-02263-8, Anch). Doubleday.

Modern Scotland. James G. Kellas. (Illus.). 208p. (Orig.). text ed. 22.50x (ISBN 0-04-941008-3); pap. text ed. 9.95x (ISBN 0-04-941009-1). Allen Unwin.

Modern Scottish Short Stories. Ed. by Fred Urquhart & Giles Gordon. 1979. 19.95 (ISBN 0-241-10058-5, Pub by Hamish Hamilton). David & Charles.

Modern Sculpture: Origins & Evolution. Jean Selz. LC 63-14802. 20.00 o.s.i. (ISBN 0-8076-0245-0). Braziller.

Modern Ships: Elements of Their Design, Construction, & Operation. John H. La Dage. LC 65-21747. (Illus.). 1965. 8.50x (ISBN 0-87033-065-9). Cornell Maritime.

Modern Short Stories. 4th ed. Ed. by Arthur Mizener. 1979. pap. text ed. 8.95x (ISBN 0-393-95025-5); handbk. 2.95x (ISBN 0-393-95032-8). Norton.

Modern Short Stories in English. rev. ed. Robert J. Dixson. (Illus., Orig., Sequel to Easy Reading Selections in English). (gr. 9-11). 1971. pap. text ed. 2.75 (ISBN 0-88345-117-4, 17986); tapes o.p. 35.00 (ISBN 0-685-19799-9); cassettes 40.00 (ISBN 0-685-19800-6). Regents Pub.

Modern Short Story in Peru. Earl M. Aldrich, Jr. 1966. 17.50 (ISBN 0-299-03960-9). U of Wis Pr.

Modern Sioux: Social Systems & Reservation Culture. Ed. by Ethel Nurge. LC 71-88089. (Illus.). xvi, 352p. 1970. 15.00x (ISBN 0-8032-0715-8); pap. 4.50 (ISBN 0-8032-5812-7, BB 596, Bison). U of Nebr Pr.

Modern Socialism. Ed. by Massimo Salvadori. LC 68-27381. (Documentary History of Western Civilization Ser). 1968. 15.00x o.s.i. (ISBN 0-8027-2015-3). Walker & Co.

Modern Society with Revisions. 3rd ed. John Biesanz & Mavis Biesanz. 1971. text ed. 17.95 (ISBN 0-13-597732-0). P-H.

Modern Sound Reproduction. Harry F. Olson. LC 77-28682. 352p. 1978. Repr. of 1972 ed. lib. bdg. 21.00 (ISBN 0-88275-648-6). Krieger.

Modern Spacecraft Dynamics & Control. Marshall H. Kaplan. LC 76-14859. 1976. text ed. 29.95 (ISBN 0-471-45703-5). Wiley.

Modern Spain. Raymond Carr. 256p. 1981. 19.95 (ISBN 0-19-215828-7); pap. 11.50 (ISBN 0-19-289090-5). Oxford U Pr.

Modern Spanish A & B, 7 bks. M. W. Sullivan. (gr. 8-12). 1968. pap. text ed. 7.00 each (ISBN 0-686-57758-2). Learning Line.

Modern Spanish C, 5 vols. M. W. Sullivan. (gr. 8-12). 1972. pap. text ed. 6.00 each (ISBN 0-686-57759-0). Learning Line.

Modern Spanish D, 3 bks. M. W. Sullivan. (gr. 8-12). 1972. pap. text ed. 6.00 each (ISBN 0-686-57760-4). Learning Line.

Modern Spanish Stage for Plays. Ed. by Marion P. Holt. LC 78-106966. 388p. 1970. pap. 6.95 (ISBN 0-8090-0746-0). Hill & Wang.

Modern Spanish Syntax. Yolanda Sole & Carlos Sole. 1977. text ed. 17.95x (ISBN 0-669-00193-7). Heath.

Modern Spoken Cambodian. Franklin E. Huffman et al. LC 71-104615. 1970. text ed. 30.00x (ISBN 0-300-01315-9); pap. text ed. 12.00x (ISBN 0-300-01316-7). Yale U Pr.

Modern Spoken Spanish: An Interdisciplinary Perspective. Ronald P. Lombardi & Amalia B. De Peters. LC 80-1442. 507p. (Orig.). 1981. pap. text ed. 16.75 (ISBN 0-8191-1513-4). U Pr of Amer.

Modern Sri Lanka: A Society in Transition. Ed. by Tissa Fernando & Robert N. Kearney. LC 79-13077. (Foreign & Comparative Studies: South Asian Ser.: No. 4). (Illus.). 297p. 1979. pap. text ed. 7.50x (ISBN 0-915984-80-6). Syracuse U Foreign Comp.

Modern Statistics. Richard Goodman. LC 63-19414. (Orig.). 1964. pap. 1.45 o.p. (ISBN 0-668-01108-4). Arc Bks.

Modern Statistics: Methods & Applications. Ed. by Robert V. Hogg. (Proceedings of Symposia in Applied Mathematics: Vol. 23). 1980. 12.00 (ISBN 0-8218-0023-X, PSAPMS-23). Am Math.

Modern Stentors: Radio Broadcasters & the Federal Government,1920-1934. Philip T. Rosen. LC 79-8952. (Contributions in Economics & Economic History: No. 31). (Illus.). 267p. 1980. lib. bdg. 25.00x (ISBN 0-313-21231-7, RMS/). Greenwood.

Modern Street Ballads. John Ashton. LC 67-23926. (Illus.). 1968. Repr. of 1888 ed. 18.00 (ISBN 0-8103-3407-0). Gale.

Modern Study in the Book of Proverbs: Charles Bridges Classic Revised for Today's Reader. George F. Santa. LC 78-7667. 1978. kiver bdg. 17.95 (ISBN 0-915134-27-6); incl. study guide (ISBN 0-915134-49-7). Mott Media.

Modern Stylists: Writers on the Art of Writing. Ed. by Donald Hall. LC 68-12918. (Orig.). 1968. 5.95 o.s.i. (ISBN 0-02-913630-X); pap. text ed. 5.95 (ISBN 0-02-913640-7). Free Pr.

Modern Supermarket Operation. 2nd ed. Edward A. Brand. LC 62-19750. (Illus.). 1965. 15.00 o.p. (ISBN 0-87005-047-8). Fairchild.

Modern Supermarket Operations. 3rd. rev. ed. Faye Gold et al. (Illus.). 260p. 1981. text ed. 18.50 (ISBN 0-87005-263-2). Fairchild.

Modern Swedish Grammar. 9th, rev. ed. I. Bjorkhagen. 1966. 12.50 o.p. (ISBN 0-685-47300-7). Heinman.

Modern Swedish Grammar. 9th ed. Immanuel Bjorkhagen. 1962. 12.50x o.s.i. (ISBN 0-686-00876-6). Colton Bk.

Modern Swedish Masterpieces. Ed. by Charles W. Stork. LC 79-53464. (Short Story Index in Reprint Ser.). Date not set. Repr. of 1923 ed. 22.50x (ISBN 0-8486-5012-3). Core Collection. Postponed.

Modern Switching Theory & Digital Design. Samuel C. Lee. 1978. ref. 25.95x (ISBN 0-13-598680-X). P-H.

Modern Syllabus Algebra. D. G. Lloyd. 1971. 19.50 (ISBN 0-08-015965-6); pap. 9.75 (ISBN 0-08-015964-8). Pergamon.

Modern Synthetic Reactions. 2nd ed. Herbert O. House. LC 78-173958. 1972. text ed. 27.95 (ISBN 0-8053-4501-9). Benjamin-Cummings.

Modern Systems Research for the Behavioral Scientist. Ed. by Walter Buckley. LC 66-19888. (Illus.). 1968. 31.95x (ISBN 0-202-30011-0). Aldine Pub.

Modern Tariff History: Germany, United States, France. Percy Ashley. LC 68-9645. 1970. Repr. of 1926 ed. 17.50 (ISBN 0-86527-131-3). Fertig.

Modern Technical Physics. 3rd ed. Arthur Beiser. LC 78-31596. 1979. 22.95 (ISBN 0-8053-0680-3); instr's guide 3.95 (ISBN 0-8053-0681-1). Benjamin-Cummings.

Modern Technical Writing. 3rd ed. Theodore A. Sherman & Simon Johnson. (Illus.). 480p. 1975. 15.95 (ISBN 0-13-598763-6). P-H.

Modern Technique of Rock Blasting. 3rd ed. U. Langefors & B. Kihlstrom. LC 77-23895. 1978. 34.95 (ISBN 0-470-99282-4). Halsted Pr.

Modern Techniques in Physiological Sciences. Ed. by J. F. Gross et al. 1974. 66.00 (ISBN 0-12-304450-2). Acad Pr.

Modern Techniques of Vocal Rehabilitation. Morton Cooper. (Amer. Lec. Speech & Hearing Ser.). (Illus.). 384p. 1977. 19.75 (ISBN 0-398-02451-0). C C Thomas.

Modern Telugu Short Stories: An Anthology. Ed. by V. Patanjali & A. Muralidhar. Tr. by A. Muralidhar. 261p. 1968. pap. 2.45 (ISBN 0-88253-065-8). Ind-US Inc.

Modern Textiles. Dorothy S. Lyle. LC 75-38558. 480p. 1976. text ed. 22.95 (ISBN 0-471-55726-9); instrs'. manual avail. (ISBN 0-471-01839-2). Wiley.

Modern Theatre Practice: A Handbook of Play Production. 5th ed. Hubert C. Heffner et al. LC 72-89404. (Illus.). 656p. 1973. 21.95 (ISBN 0-13-598805-5). P-H.

Modern Theatre: Seven Plays & an Essay. Par Lagerkvist & Thomas R. Buckman. LC 64-11582. 1966. 14.95x (ISBN 0-8032-0098-6). U of Nebr Pr.

Modern Theories of Language. Philip W. Davis. (Illus.). 496p. 1973. 15.95 (ISBN 0-13-598987-6). P-H.

Modern Theory & Method in Group Training. William G. Dyer. 256p. 1981. Repr. of 1972 ed. text ed. write for info. (ISBN 0-89874-280-3). Krieger.

Modern Therapies. V. Binder et al. 1976. 11.95 (ISBN 0-13-599001-7, Spec); pap. 5.95 (ISBN 0-13-598995-7). P-H.

Modern Thin-Section Tomography. Ed. by Arnold Berrett et al. (Illus.). 352p. 1973. 39.50 (ISBN 0-398-02468-5). C C Thomas.

Modern Times. (Picture Panorama of British History Ser.). 1977. pap. 4.95 (ISBN 0-263-06246-5). Transatlantic.

Modern Times: Or, the Adventures of Gabriel Outcastt, 3 vols. in 1. Gabriel Outcast, pseud. LC 80-2493. 1981. Repr. of 1785 ed. 123.50 (ISBN 0-404-19127-4). AMS Pr.

Modern Transmission Line Theory & Applications. Lawrence N. Dworsky. LC 79-9082. 1979. 21.50 (ISBN 0-471-04086-X, Pub. by Wiley-Interscience). Wiley.

Modern Treatment of Tense Patients: Including the Neurotic & Depressed with Case Illustrations, Follow-Ups, & EMG Measurements. Edmund Jacobson. (Illus.). 484p. 1970. text ed. 45.50 photocopy ed. (ISBN 0-398-00910-4). C C Thomas.

Modern Trends in Accident Surgery & Medicine-2. P. S. London. 1970. 17.95 (ISBN 0-407-28001-4). Butterworths.

Modern Trends in Cybernetics & Systems I-III: Proceedings of the Third International Congress of Cybernetics & Systems, Bucharest, Romania, August 25-29, 1975, 3 vols. Ed. by J. Rose & C. Bilciu. Incl. Vol. 1 (ISBN 0-387-08196-8); Vol. 2 (ISBN 0-387-08197-6); Vol. 3 (ISBN 0-387-08198-4). 1977. Set. 173.20 (ISBN 3-540-08199-2); 69.30 ea. Springer-Verlag.

Modern Trends in Hinduism. Philip H. Ashby. (Lectures in the History of Religions Ser.: No. 10). 176p. 1974. 16.00x (ISBN 0-231-03768-6). Columbia U Pr.

Modern Trends in Human Genetics, Vol. 2. Emery. 1975. 54.95 (ISBN 0-407-00028-3). Butterworths.

Modern Trends in Medical Malpractice Course Handbook. (Litigation & Administrative Practice Course Handbook Ser. 1977-78: Vol. 112). 1978. pap. 20.00 o.p. (ISBN 0-685-07698-9, H4-3861). PLI.

Modern Trends in Pediatrics-4. J. Apley. 1974. 28.95 (ISBN 0-407-30803-2). Butterworths.

Modern Trigonometry. J. P. Ashley & E. R. Harvey. 1974. text ed. 10.95 kivar bdg. (ISBN 0-02-473480-2, 47348); dupl. masters 9.95x (ISBN 0-02-473390-3, 47339). Macmillan.

Modern Trigonometry. Kaj L. Nielsen. (Illus., Orig.). 1966. pap. 4.95 (ISBN 0-06-460047-5, CO 47, COS). Har-Row.

Modern Trigonometry. rev. ed. William Wooton et al. 1979. text ed. 15.64 (ISBN 0-395-21687-7, 2-60824); instructor's guide & solutions, pap. 7.40 (ISBN 0-395-21688-5, 2-60825). HM.

Modern Trombone: A Definition of Its Idioms. Stuart Dempster. (New Instrumentation Ser.: Vol. III). 1979. 16.50x (ISBN 0-520-03252-7). U of Cal Pr.

Modern Turkish Drama: An Anthology. Talat S. Halman. LC 73-79204. (Studies in Middle Eastern Literatures: No. 5). 1976. 25.00x (ISBN 0-88297-007-0). Bibliotheca.

Modern Upholstering Methods. William F. Tierney. (gr. 9 up). 1965. text ed. 14.00 (ISBN 0-87345-482-0). McKnight.

Modern Upholstery. Dorothy Cox. (Illus.). 152p. 1980. pap. 11.75x (ISBN 0-7135-1599-6, LTB). Soccer.

Modern Upholstery Techniques. Robert McDonald. 144p. 22.50 o.p. (ISBN 0-7134-2197-5). David & Charles.

Modern Urdu Stories. Tr. by A. I. Mirza from Urdu. (Writers Workshop Saffronbird Bk Ser.). 1977. flexible bdg. 4.80 (ISBN 0-89253-643-8); text ed. 10.00 (ISBN 0-89253-642-X). Ind-US Inc.

Modern Utopia. H. G. Wells. LC 67-26614. 1967. pap. 5.95x (ISBN 0-8032-5213-7, BB 393, Bison). U of Nebr Pr.

Modern Varieties of Judaism. Joseph L. Blau. LC 66-10732. 1966. 17.50x (ISBN 0-231-02867-9); pap. 5.00 (ISBN 0-231-08668-7). Columbia U Pr.

Modern Vegetable Protein Cookery. Keith Kendig & Joan Kendig. LC 79-21127. 352p. 1980. 11.95 (ISBN 0-668-04617-1). Arco.

Modern Verse Drama. Stuart R. McLeod. (Salzburg Studies in English Literature, Poetic Drama & Poetic Theory: No. 2). 345p. 1972. pap. text ed. 25.00x (ISBN 0-391-01480-3). Humanities.

Modern Verse from Taiwan. Tr. by Angela J. Palandri. LC 79-161994. 1972. 18.50x (ISBN 0-520-02061-8). U of Cal Pr.

Modern Verse Translations from French. Dorothy Aspinwall. 220p. 1980. 9.95 (ISBN 0-89962-020-5). Todd & Honeywell.

Modern View of Conveyancing. G. H. Glasgow. 1969. 22.00 (ISBN 0-08-013063-1); pap. 10.75 (ISBN 0-08-013062-3). Pergamon.

Modern View of Geometry. Leonard M. Blumenthal. (Illus.). 1980. pap. text ed. 4.00 (ISBN 0-486-63962-2). Dover.

Modern View of the Law for Builders & Surveyors. V. Powell-Smith. 1967. 25.00 (ISBN 0-08-012297-3). Pergamon.

Modern Viola Technique. Robert Dolejsi. LC 72-8343. (Music Ser). (Illus.). viii, 133p. 1973. Repr. of 1939 ed. lib. bdg. 21.50 (ISBN 0-306-70552-4). Da Capo.

Modern Warship Design & Development. Norman Friedman. (Illus.). 192p. 1980. 22.50 (ISBN 0-686-65676-8). Mayflower Bks.

Modern Watch & Clock Repairing. P. Buford Harris. LC 73-77479. 1972. 13.95 (ISBN 0-911012-05-2). Nelson-Hall.

Modern Waterskiing: A Guide for Skiers & Boat Divers. Reginald Prytherch. (Illus.). 1979. 9.95 (ISBN 0-7137-0927-8, Pub by Blandford Pr England). Sterling.

Modern Welding Technology. Howard B. Cary. LC 78-2966. (Illus.). 1979. 28.00 (ISBN 0-13-599290-7); text ed. 21.00 o.p. (ISBN 0-686-67267-4). P-H.

Modern Western Civilization: A Concise History. Gordon R. Mork. 1976. pap. text ed. 8.50 o.p. (ISBN 0-256-01804-9). Dorsey.

Modern Western Civilization: A Concise History. Gordon R. Mork. LC 80-6198. 253p. (Orig.). 1981. lib. bdg. 19.25 (ISBN 0-8191-1434-0); pap. text ed. 10.00 (ISBN 0-8191-1435-9). U Pr of Amer.

Modern Western Experience. Robert Anchor. (Illus.). 1978. pap. text ed. 12.95 (ISBN 0-13-599357-1). P-H.

Modern Witchcraft. Frank Smyth. 128p. 1973. pap. 1.25 o.p. (ISBN 0-06-087038-9, HW). Har-Row.

Modern Woodworking. Willis H. Wagner. LC 80-18994. (Illus.). 1980. text ed. 13.28 (ISBN 0-87006-301-4); wkbk. 3.20 (ISBN 0-87006-300-6). Goodheart.

Modern Word-Finder: A Living Guide to Modern Usage, Spelling, Synonyms, Pronunciation, Grammar, Word Origins, & Authorship. Paul D. Hugon. LC 73-20139. 420p. 1974. Repr. of 1934 ed. 26.00 (ISBN 0-8103-3970-6). Gale.

Modern World Rulers: A Chronology. Compiled By Alan R. Langville. LC 79-19294. 372p. 1979. 20.00 (ISBN 0-8108-1251-7). Scarecrow.

Modern World-System I. Immanuel Wallerstein. 1980. pap. 9.50 lib ed (ISBN 0-12-785919-5). Acad Pr.

Modern World-System II: Mercantilism & the Consolidation of the European World-Economy, 1600-1750. Immanuel Wallerstein. LC 73-5318. (Studies in Social Discontinuity). 1980. 22.00 (ISBN 0-12-785923-3); pap. 9.50 o.s.i. (ISBN 0-12-785924-1). Acad Pr.

Modern Written Arabic. Foreign Service Institute. 419p. (Arabic.). 1980. 165.00x (ISBN 0-88432-039-1, A269); 18 audiocassettes incl. J Norton Pubs.

Modern Yoga Handbook. Vijay Hassin. LC 77-76243. 1978. pap. 4.95 (ISBN 0-385-13001-5, Dolp). Doubleday.

Moderne Budgetierungsverfahren. Alexander Hamilton Institiue, Inc. Ed. by James M. Jenks. (Illus.). 85p. (Orig., Ger.). 1978. pap. 49.50 (ISBN 0-86604-004-8, TX-150-972). Hamilton Inst.

Moderne Deutsche Erzaehler. 3rd ed. Ed. by Robert Roseler & Audrey Duckert. 1960. 7.95x (ISBN 0-393-09536-3, NortonC). Norton.

Moderne Deutsche Sprachlehre. 3rd ed. F. Alan DuVal et al. 672p. 1980. text ed. 15.95 (ISBN 0-394-32345-9); wkbk. 6.95 (ISBN 0-394-32406-4); tapes 200.00 (ISBN 0-394-32407-2); individualized instruction program 5.95 (ISBN 0-394-32434-X). Random.

Modernes Deutsch: Eine Wiederholung der Grammatik Mit Modernes Autoren. 2nd ed. Erna Kritsch. (Illus., Ger.). (gr. 10-12). 1966. pap. text ed. 8.95 o.p. (ISBN 0-13-595033-3); tapes 75.00 o.p. (ISBN 0-13-595017-1). P-H.

Modernism: 1890-1930. Ed. by Malcolm Bradbury & James McFarlane. (Pelican Guides to European Literature). 1978. Repr. of 1974 ed. text ed. 28.50x (ISBN 0-391-00818-8). Humanities.

Modernismo: the Catalan Renaissance of the Arts. Joseph P. Cervera. LC 75-23787. (Outstanding Dissertations in the Fine Arts - 19th Century). (Illus.). 1976. lib. bdg. 48.00 (ISBN 0-8240-1983-0). Garland Pub.

Modernization & British Colonial Rule in Egypt, 1882-1914. Robert L. Tignor. (Princeton Studies on the Near East). 1966. 21.00x (ISBN 0-691-03037-5). Princeton U Pr.

Modernization & Diversity in Soviet Education: With Special Reference to Nationality Groups. Jaan Pennar et al. LC 70-105285. (Special Studies in International Economics Development). 1971. 39.50x (ISBN 0-89197-854-2); pap. text ed. 16.50x (ISBN 0-89197-855-0). Irvington.

Modernization & Its Impact Upon Korean Law. Kwun Sup Chung et al. (Korea Research Monographs: No. 3). 150p. 1981. pap. 12.50 (ISBN 0-686-69422-8). IEAS Ctr Chinese Stud.

Modernization & Social Change Among Muslims in India. Ed. by Imtiaz Ahmad. 1981. 17.50x (ISBN 0-88386-892-X). South Asia Bks.

Modernization & the Japanese Factory. Robert M. Marsh & Hiroshi Mannari. LC 75-3466. 560p. 1976. 32.50 (ISBN 0-691-09365-2); pap. 12.50 ltd. ed. (ISBN 0-691-10037-3). Princeton U Pr.

Modernization, Dislocation & Aprismo: Origins of the Peruvian Aprista Party, 1870-1932. Peter F. Klaren. LC 73-4915. (Latin American Monographs, No. 32). (Illus.). 282p. 1973. 10.00 (ISBN 0-292-76001-9). U of Tex Pr.

Modernization in a Mexican Ejido. B. R. De Walt. LC 78-3412. (Latin American Studies: No. 33). (Illus.). 1979. 29.95 (ISBN 0-521-22064-5). Cambridge U Pr.

Modernization in Brazil: Story of Political Dueling Among Politicians, Charismatic Leaders & Military Guardians. F. LaMond Tullis. (Charles E. Merrill Monograph Series in the Humanities & Social Sciences: Vol. 3, No. 1). 1973. pap. 2.00 o.p. (ISBN 0-8425-0630-6). Brigham.

Modernization in Ghana & the USSR. Robert E. Dowse. (Library of Political Studies). 1969. text ed. 7.00x (ISBN 0-7100-6171-4). Humanities.

Modernization in Romania Since World War 2. Trond Gilberg. LC 73-15187. (Special Studies). 195p. 1975. text ed. 24.95 (ISBN 0-275-09520-7). Praeger.

Modernization in Turkey Nineteen Twenty-Three to Nineteen Seventy-Nine. Walter F. Weiker. LC 80-24514. 250p. 1980. text ed. 24.00x (ISBN 0-8419-0503-7). Holmes & Meier.

Modernization of Agriculture: Rural Transformation in Hungary, 1848-1975. Ed. by Joseph Held. (East European Monographs: 3no. 67). 1980. 25.00x (ISBN 0-914710-60-5, Dist. by Columbia U Pr). East Eur Quarterly.

Modernization of American Reform: Structures & Perceptions. Steven Kesselman. Ed. by Frank Freidel. LC 78-62386. (Modern American History Ser.: Vol. 10). 550p. 1980. lib. bdg. 40.00 (ISBN 0-8240-3635-2). Garland Pub.

Modernization of French Jewry: Consistory & Community in the Nineteenth Century. Phyllis C. Albert. LC 76-50680. (Illus.). 472p. 1977. text ed. 27.50x (ISBN 0-87451-139-9). U Pr of New Eng.

Modernization of Japan & Russia. Cyril E. Black et al. LC 75-8429. (Perspectives on Modernization Ser.). 1975. 19.95 (ISBN 0-02-906850-9). Free Pr.

Modernizing Calhoun County Government. Robert W. Kaufman et al. 1975. 3.95 (ISBN 0-932826-08-3). New Issues MI.

Modernizing Racial Domination: The Dynamics of South African Politics. Heribert Adam. LC 75-132422. (Perspectives on Southern Africa: No. 2). 1971. pap. 5.50x (ISBN 0-520-02251-3, CAMPUS229). U of Cal Pr.

Modernizing the Central City: New Towns Intown... & Beyond. Harvey S. Perloff et al. LC 74-14687. 448p. 1975. text ed. 18.00 o.p. (ISBN 0-88410-414-1). Ballinger Pub.

Modernizing the Chinese Dragon: The Prospective Impact of Western Aid & Technology on Mainland China. Donald J. Senese. pap. 10.00 (ISBN 0-686-64115-9). Coun Am Affairs.

Modernizing the Strategic Bomber Force. B. Alton H. Quanbeck & Archie L. Woods. (Studies in Defense Policy). 1976. 3.95 (ISBN 0-8157-7281-5). Brookings.

Modes of Analogy in Ancient & Medieval Verse. Phillip Damon. (California Library Reprint Series: No. 33). 1973. 14.00x (ISBN 0-520-02366-8). U of Cal Pr.

Modes of Argument. Monroe C. Beardsley. LC 67-18663. 1967. pap. 2.50 (ISBN 0-672-60893-6). Bobbs.

Modes of Being. Paul Weiss. LC 57-11877. 626p. 1958. lib. bdg. 19.95x (ISBN 0-8093-0012-5); deluxe ed. 25.00x 2 vols. boxed (ISBN 0-8093-0013-3). S Ill U Pr.

Modes of Being. Paul Weiss. LC 57-11877. (Arcturus Books Paperbacks). 626p. 1968. pap. 11.95x (ISBN 0-8093-0294-2). S Ill U Pr.

Modes of Literature. J. Bard McNulty. LC 76-10896. (Illus.). 1976. text ed. 15.70 (ISBN 0-395-24249-5); inst. manual 0.50 (ISBN 0-395-24248-7). HM.

Modes of Modern Writing: Metaphor, Metonymy, & the Modern Literature. David Lodge. LC 76-51544. 1977. 19.50x o.p. (ISBN 0-8014-1046-0). Cornell U Pr.

Modes of Perceiving & Processing Information. Ed. by Herbert L. Pick, Jr. & Elliot Saltzman. LC 77-21025. 1977. 14.95 (ISBN 0-470-99342-1). Halsted Pr.

Modes of Speciation. Michael J. White. LC 77-10955. (Biology Ser.). (Illus.). 1978. text ed. 33.95x (ISBN 0-7167-0284-3). W H Freeman.

Modes of Thought. Alfred N. Whitehead. LC 38-33184. 1968. pap. text ed. 3.95 (ISBN 0-02-935210-X). Free Pr.

Modes of Transportation. Compiled by American Society of Civil Engineers. 160p. 1970. pap. text ed. 8.75 (ISBN 0-87262-021-2). Am Soc Civil Eng.

Modest Proposal: Students Can Learn. John E. Roueche & John C. Pitman. LC 73-184956. (Higher Education Ser.). 1972. 9.95x o.p. (ISBN 0-87589-116-0). Jossey-Bass.

Modest Technologies for a Complicated World. Roberto Vacca. 144p. Date not set. 26.00 (ISBN 0-08-024067-4); pap. cancelled (ISBN 0-08-024068-2). Pergamon.

Modification of Behavior of the Mentally Ill: Rehabilitation Approaches. Ed. by Richard E. Hardy & John G. Cull. (American Lectures in Social & Rehabilitation Psychology Ser.). (Illus.). 248p. 1974. text ed. 18.50 (ISBN 0-398-03052-9). C C Thomas.

Modification of Behavior of the Mentally Retarded: Applied Principles. Ed. by Richard E. Hardy & John G. Cull. (American Lectures in Social & Rehabilitation Psychology Ser.). 180p. 1975. text ed. 16.75 (ISBN 0-398-03136-3). C C Thomas.

Modification of Child & Adolescent Behavior. 3rd ed. Garth J. Blackham & Adolph Silberman. 1979. pap. text ed. 10.95x (ISBN 0-534-00725-2). Wadsworth Pub.

Modification of Radiosensitivity of Biological Systems. (Panel Proceedings Ser.). (Illus., Orig.). 1976. pap. 18.25 (ISBN 92-0-111176-2, IAEA). Unipub.

Modified Nucleosides in Nucleic Acids. Ross H. Hall. LC 73-122745. (Molecular Biology Ser). 1971. 27.50x (ISBN 0-231-03018-5). Columbia U Pr.

Modified Nucleosides of Transfer RNA: A Bibliography of Biochemical & Biophysical Studis from 1970 to 1979. Paul F. Agris. LC 80-81197. 219p. 1980. 24.00 (ISBN 0-8451-0207-9). A R Liss.

Modifiers of Chemical Carcinogenesis. Ed. by Thomas J. Slaga. LC 77-504. (Carcinogenesis: a Comprehensive Survey Ser.: Vol. 5). 1979. text ed. 32.50 (ISBN 0-89004-232-2). Raven.

Modifying Children's Behavior: A Book of Readings. Ed. by Alan R. Brown & Connie Avery. (Illus.). 296p. 1974. 16.00 (ISBN 0-398-02953-9). C C Thomas.

Modifying Children's Behavior: A Guide for Parents & Professionals. Robert E. Valett. LC 70-79239. (Orig.). 1969. pap. text ed. 3.40 o.p. (ISBN 0-8224-4495-X). Pitman Learning.

Modifying Fiberglass Boats. Jack Wiley. LC 74-25164. (Illus.). 200p. 1975. 12.50 (ISBN 0-87742-048-3). Intl Marine.

Modifying Man: Implications & Ethics. Ed. by Craig Elison. 11.25 (ISBN 0-8191-0302-0). U Pr of Amer.

Modifying Medicaid Eligibility & Benefits. Bruce Spitz & John Holashan. (Medicaid Cost Containment Ser.). 93p. 1977. pap. 3.00 (ISBN 0-87766-195-2, 17700). Urban Inst.

Modifying Retarded Behavior. John T. Neisworth & Robert M. Smith. (Illus.). 200p. 1973. text ed. 18.50 (ISBN 0-395-14049-8, 3-40420). HM.

Modifying Section Eight: Implications from Experiments with Housing Allowances. James P. Zais et al. (Institute Paper). 61p. 1979. pap. 4.50 (ISBN 0-87766-240-1, 24100). Urban Inst.

Modigliani. Carol Mann. LC 79-28336. (World of Art Ser.). (Illus.). 300p. 1980. 17.95 (ISBN 0-19-520198-1); pap. 9.95 (ISBN 0-19-520199-X). Oxford U Pr.

Modigliani & the Painters of Montparnasse. Helen I. Hubbard. (Illus.). 1975. Repr. 5.95 o.p. (ISBN 0-88308-008-7). Lamplight Pub.

Mods I've Been. Douglas Carpenter. (Contemporary Poets of Dorrance Ser.). 36p. 1977. 2.95 (ISBN 0-8059-2402-7). Dorrance.

Modsim: A Computer Program for Simulating Macroeconomic Models. Carl Van Duyne. Ed. by Molly L. Hepler. (Orig., User's man., 89 p.; instr's. man., 67 p.). 1980. User's Manual. pap. text ed. 5.00 (ISBN 0-686-27411-3); Instructor's Manual. 5.00 (ISBN 0-686-27412-1). Conduit.

Modular Electronics: An Individualized Study Program. James Staley & Jay Stryker. LC 73-91054. 1974. text ed. 11.95x o.p. (ISBN 0-675-08880-1); instructor's manual 3.95 o.p. (ISBN 0-686-66914-2). Merrill.

Modular Forms & Functions. R. A. Rankin. LC 76-11089. (Illus.). 1977. 68.50 (ISBN 0-521-21212-X). Cambridge U Pr.

Modular Functions of One Variable 2: Proceedings. International Summer School, University of Antwerp, 1972. Ed. by W. Kuyk & P. Deligne. (Lecture Notes in Mathematics: Vol. 349). v, 598p. 1974. pap. 20.50 (ISBN 0-387-06558-X). Springer-Verlag.

Modular Mathematics: Modules 1-18 Teachers Pack. Modular Mathematics Organization. 65.00 o.p. (ISBN 0-435-50899-7). Heinemann Ed.

Modular Mathematics: Modules 19-36 Teachers Pack. Modular Mathematics Organization. 80.00 o.p. (ISBN 0-435-50900-4). Heinemann Ed.

Modular Programming in COBOL. Russell M. Armstrong. LC 73-4030. (Business Data Processing Ser.). 224p. 1973. 23.95 (ISBN 0-471-03325-1, Pub. by Wiley-Interscience). Wiley.

Modular Typewriting. Louis Freeman. (gr. 10-11). 1978. wkbk. 7.58 (ISBN 0-87720-405-5). AMSCO Sch.

Modulation. F. R. Connor. (Introductory Topics in Electronics & Telecommunication Ser.). (Illus.). 1973. pap. text ed. 11.00x (ISBN 0-7131-3303-1). Intl Ideas.

Modulation of Neurochemical Transmission: Proceedings. Hungarian Pharmacological Society, 3rd Congress, Budapest, 1979. Ed. by J. Knoll & E. S. Vizi. LC 80-41281. (Advances in Pharmacological Research & Practice Ser.: Vol. II). (Illus.). 450p. 1981. 84.00 (ISBN 0-08-026387-9). Pergamon.

Module, Proportion, Symmetry, Rhythm. Ed. by Gyorgy Keppes. LC 66-13044. (Vision & Value Ser). (Illus.). 1966. 17.50 (ISBN 0-8076-0363-5). Braziller.

Module Theory: An Approach to Linear Algebra. T. S. Blyth. (Illus.). 1977. 39.00x (ISBN 0-19-853162-1). Oxford U Pr.

Modules for Basic Nursing Skills, 2 vols. 2nd ed. Janice R. Ellis et al. LC 79-89521. (Illus.). 1980. Vol. 1. pap. text ed. 10.00 (ISBN 0-395-28654-9); Vol. 2. pap. text ed. 9.50 (ISBN 0-395-28655-7). HM.

Modumath: Arithmetic. Miriam Hecht & Caroline Hecht. LC 77-75447. 1978. pap. text ed. 15.25 (ISBN 0-395-24424-2); instr's. manual 0.60 (ISBN 0-395-24421-8). HM.

Modusprobleme bei Notker: Die modalen Werte in den Nebensaetzen der Consolatio-Uebersetzung. Dieter Furrer. 201p. 1971. 34.75x (ISBN 3-11-001808-X). De Gruyter.

Moe Q McGlutch, He Smoked Too Much. Ellen Raskin. LC 73-4383. (Illus.). 48p. (gr. k-3). 1973. 5.95 o.s.i. (ISBN 0-8193-0686-X, Four Winds); PLB 5.41 o.s.i. (ISBN 0-8193-0687-8). Schol Bk Serv.

Moehler & Baur in Controversy Eighteen Thirty-Two to Thirty-Eight: Reformation & Counter-Reformation in the Age of Romantic Idealism. Joseph Fitzer. LC 74-77619. (American Academy of Religion. Studies in Religion). 1974. 7.50 (ISBN 0-88420-111-2, 010007). Scholars Pr Ca.

Moffat Road. 2nd ed. Edward T. Bollinger & Frederick Bauer. LC 62-12397. (Illus.). 359p. 1967. 33.95 (ISBN 0-8040-0207-X, SB). Swallow.

Mogul Tales: or the Dreams of Man Awake, Pt. 2. Thomas S. Gueulette. LC 73-170593. (Novel in England, 1700-1775). lib. bdg. 50.00 (ISBN 0-8240-0576-7). Garland Pub.

Mogul Tales: or the Dreams of Men Awake, Pt. 1. Thomas S. Gueulette. LC 73-170593. (Novel in England, 1700-1775). lib. bdg. 50.00 (ISBN 0-8240-0575-9). Garland Pub.

Mohammed. David S. Margoliuth. LC 79-2875. 151p. 1981. Repr. of 1939 ed. 14.50 (ISBN 0-8305-0044-8). Hyperion Conn.

Mohammed & Charlemagne. Henri Pirenne. Tr. by Bernard Miall. 293p. 1974. pap. text ed. 9.50x (ISBN 0-04-940025-8). Allen Unwin.

Mohammed: The Man & His Faith. Tor Andrae. LC 60-5489. 1977. pap. text ed. 4.95x (ISBN 0-06-130062-4, TB 62, Torch). Har-Row.

Mohammed: The Prophet of Islam, a Flame in the Desert. B. K. Narayan. 250p. 1980. text ed. 27.50x (ISBN 0-8426-1662-4). Verry.

Mohammedanism: An Historical Survey. 2nd ed. Hamilton A. Gibb. 1953. pap. 3.95x (ISBN 0-19-500245-8, 90). Oxford U Pr.

Mohave Indians. Alfred L. Kroeber. Ed. by David A. Horr. (American Indian Ethnohistory Ser.). 1978. lib. bdg. 42.00 (ISBN 0-8240-0738-7). Garland Pub.

Mohenjodaro & the Indus Civilization: Being an Official Account of Archaeological Excavations at Mohenjodaro Carried Out by the Government of India Between the Years 1922-1927, 3 vols. John Marshall. LC 73-905649. (Illus.). 716p. 1973. Repr. Set. 100.00x o.p. (ISBN 0-8364-0437-8). South Asia Bks.

Moholy-Nagy: Photographs & Photograms. Andreas Haus. (Illus.). 1980. 35.00 (ISBN 0-394-50449-6). Pantheon.

Moira. Caroline Stafford. 1978. pap. 1.75 o.p. (ISBN 0-449-23530-0, Crest). Fawcett.

Moire Fringes in Strain Analysis. P. S. Theocaris. 1969. text ed. 32.00 (ISBN 0-08-012974-9); pap. text ed. 15.00 (ISBN 0-08-012973-0). Pergamon.

Moise. Gioachino Rossini. Ed. by Charles Rosen & Philip Gossett. LC 76-49190. (Early Romantic Opera Ser.: Vol. 15). 1980. lib. bdg. 82.00 (ISBN 0-8240-2914-3). Garland Pub.

Moisture Gardening. Alan Bloom. (Illus.). 1966. 8.95 o.p. (ISBN 0-8231-6020-3). Branford.

Mojados: The Wetback Story. Julian Samora. LC 71-148190. (Illus.). 1971. text ed. 8.95x o.p. (ISBN 0-268-00442-0); pap. text ed. 3.95 o.p. (ISBN 0-268-00445-5). U of Notre Dame Pr.

Mojave Road. new ed. Dennis G. Casebier. LC 74-33063. (Illus.). 1975. 15.00 o.p. (ISBN 0-914224-04-2). Tales Mojave Rd.

Mojave Road in Newspapers. new ed. Ed. by Dennis G. Casebier. LC 75-31484. (Illus.). 1976. 7.50 o.p. (ISBN 0-914224-05-0). Tales Mojave Rd.

Mojo & the Russians. Walter D. Myers. (gr. 5 up). 1978. pap. 1.50 (ISBN 0-380-41814-2, 41814). Avon.

Molar Mass Measurements in Polymer Science. N. C. Billingham. LC 77-2823. 1977. 41.95 (ISBN 0-470-99125-9). Halsted Pr.

Molas: What They Are; How to Make Them; Ideas They Suggest for Creative Applique. Rhoda L. Auld. 136p. 1980. pap. 9.95 (ISBN 0-442-20050-1). Van Nos Reinhold.

Molding & Casting: Its Technique & Application. 3rd ed. Carl D. Clarke. (Illus.). 380p. 1972. 18.00 (ISBN 0-685-25470-4). Standard Arts.

Mole. Dan Sherman. 1978. pap. 1.75 o.p. (ISBN 0-449-23531-9, Crest). Fawcett.

Mole Cricket Called Servol: An Account of Experiences in Education & Community Development in Trinidad & Tobago, West Indies. Gerard Pantin. (Illus.). 1979. text ed. 22.00 (ISBN 0-08-024278-2). Pergamon.

Mole Family's Christmas. Russell Hoban. LC 80-17068. (Illus.). 48p. (ps-3). 1980. Repr. of 1969 ed. 8.95 (ISBN 0-590-07774-0, Four Winds). Schol Bk Serv.

Mole Notes. Michael Benedikt. LC 78-161695. (Illus.). 1971. 12.00x (ISBN 0-8195-4038-2, Pub. by Wesleyan U Pr). Columbia U Pr.

Molecular Actions & Targets for Cancer Chemotherapeutic Agents. Ed. by A. C. Sartorelli et al. (Bristol-Myers Cancer Symposia Ser.). 1981. 45.00 (ISBN 0-12-619280-4). Acad Pr.

Molecular & Cellular Aspects of Muscle Function: Proceedings of the 28th International Congress of Physiological Sciences, Budapest 1980 (Including Proceedings of the Satellite Symposium on Membrane Control of Skeletal Muscle Function) Ed. by E. Varga et al. LC 80-42101. (Advances in Physiological Sciences: Vol. 5). (Illus.). 320p. 1981. 40.00 (ISBN 0-08-026817-X). Pergamon.

Molecular & Cellular Biology of the Eye Lens. Hans Bloemendal. LC 80-26815. 400p. 1981. 45.00 (ISBN 0-471-05171-3, Pub. by Wiley-Interscience). Wiley.

Molecular & Crystal Structure Models. Anne Walton. LC 78-40227. 1978. 27.95 (ISBN 0-470-26356-3). Halsted Pr.

Molecular & Environmental Aspects of Mutagenesis. Ed. by Louise Prakash et al. (Illus.). 296p. 1975. 31.75 (ISBN 0-398-03137-1). C C Thomas.

Molecular & Hormonal Basis of Plant Growth Regulation. Y. Leshem. LC 73-6802. 168p. 1974. 14.50 (ISBN 0-08-017649-6). Pergamon.

Molecular Aspects of Bioelectricity: Proceedings of the Symposium in Honour of David Nachmansohn, Liege, May 19-20, 1980. Ed. by E. Schoffeniels & E. Neumann. (Illus.). 360p. 1980. 72.00 (ISBN 0-08-026371-2). Pergamon.

Molecular Aspects of Gene Expression in Plants. Ed. by J. A. Bryant. 1977. 46.50 (ISBN 0-12-138150-1). Acad Pr.

Molecular Aspects of Medicine, Vol. 2. Ed. by H. Baum & J. Gergely. LC 80-40473. (Illus.). 453p. 1980. 70.00 (ISBN 0-08-026355-0). Pergamon.

Molecular Aspects of Membrane Transport: Proceedings of the ICN-UCLA Symposium Held at Keystone, Col., Mar. 1977. Ed. by Dale Oxender & C. Fred Fox. LC 78-541. (Progress in Clinical & Biological Research: Vol. 22). 1978. 67.00 (ISBN 0-8451-0022-X). A R Liss.

Molecular Basis of Antibiotic Action. 2nd ed. E. F. Gale et al. 640p. 1981. 98.00 (ISBN 0-471-27915-3, Pub. by Wiley-Interscience). Wiley.

Molecular Basis of Complement Action. Herbert J. Rapp & Tibor Borsos. LC 75-110165. 164p. 1970. 19.50 (ISBN 0-306-50065-5, Plenum Pr). Plenum Pub.

Molecular Basis of Immune Cell Function. J. G. Kaplan. 780p. 1979. 70.75 (ISBN 0-444-80168-5, North Holland). Elsevier.

Molecular Basis of Microbial Pathogenicity. Ed. by H. Smith et al. (Dahlem Workshop Reports, Life Sciences Research Report Ser.: No. 16). (Illus.). 357p. (Orig.). pap. text ed. 27.50 (ISBN 0-89573-098-7). Verlag Chemie.

Molecular Basis of Odor. John E. Amoore. (American Lecture in Living Chemistry Ser). (Illus.). 216p. 1970. 21.00 (ISBN 0-398-00039-5). C C Thomas.

Molecular Beam Epitaxy. Brian R. Pamplin. (Illus.). 178p. 1980. 40.00 (ISBN 0-08-025050-5). Pergamon.

Molecular Biology & Biochemistry: Problems & Applications. David Freifelder. LC 78-18712. (Biology Ser.). (Illus.). 1978. pap. text ed. 10.95x (ISBN 0-7167-0068-9). W H Freeman.

Molecular Biology of Plants. Joe H. Cherry. 224p. 1973. text ed. 20.00x (ISBN 0-231-03642-6). Columbia U Pr.

Molecular Biology of the Gene. 3rd ed. J. D. Watson. LC 75-14791. 1976. 23.95 (ISBN 0-8053-9609-8). Benjamin-Cummings.

Molecular Cloning Lab Manual. Ed. by T. Maniatis et al. J. Sambrook. (Orig.). 1981. pap. text ed. 24.00 (ISBN 0-87969-136-0). Cold Spring Harbor.

Molecular Crystals: Their Transforms & Diffuse Scattering. J. L. Amoros & M. Amoros. 479p. 1968. text ed. 26.00 (ISBN 0-471-02555-0, Pub. by Wiley). Krieger.

Molecular Dynamics in Biosystems. Kenneth H. Norwick. 1977. 66.00 (ISBN 0-08-020420-1). Pergamon.

Molecular Energy Transfer. R. D. Levine & J. Jortner. LC 75-37726. 1976. 44.95 (ISBN 0-470-15205-2). Halsted Pr.

Molecular Evolution: Prebiological & Biological. Ed. by Duane Rohlfing & A. I. Oparin. 481p. 1972. 39.50 (ISBN 0-306-30719-7, Plenum Pr). Plenum Pub.

Molecular Gas Dynamics. G. A. Bird. (Oxford Engineering & Science Ser.). 1976. text ed. 49.50x (ISBN 0-19-856120-2). Oxford U Pr.

Molecular Genetic Regulatory Systems. V. A. Ratner. 1981. write for info. (ISBN 0-201-06190-2). A-W.

Molecular Genetics: An Introductory Narrative. 2nd ed. Gunther S. Stent & Richard Calendar. LC 78-688. (Illus.). 1978. text ed. 27.95x (ISBN 0-7167-0048-4). W H Freeman.

Molecular Genetics of Development. Ed. by Terrance Leighton & William F. Loomis. LC 80-532. (Molecular Biology Ser.). 1980. 49.50 (ISBN 0-12-441960-7). Acad Pr.

Molecular Gods: How Molecules Determine Our Behavior. Philip B. Applewhite. (Illus.). 288p. 1981. 10.95 (ISBN 0-13-599530-2). P-H.

Molecular Hydrodynamics. Jean P. Boon & Sidney Yip. (Illus.). 440p. 1980. text ed. 49.95 (ISBN 0-07-006560-8). McGraw.

Molecular Interactions. H. Ratajczak & W. J. Orville-Thomas. Vol. 1, 448 Pp. 78.00 (ISBN 0-471-27664-2, 1-500); Vol. 2. write for info. (ISBN 0-471-27681-2). Wiley.

Molecular Interactions, Vol. 2. Ed. by H. Ratajczak & W. J. Orville-Thomas. LC 79-40825. 1981. write for info. (ISBN 0-471-27681-2, Pub. by Wiley-Interscience). Wiley.

Molecular Mechanics: A Symposium. Ed. by Delos F. DeTar. LC 77-14614. 1978. pap. text ed. 33.00 (ISBN 0-08-022070-3). Pergamon.

Molecular Mechanisms of Anesthesia. Ed. by B. Raymond Fink. LC 74-14474. (Progress in Anesthesiology Ser: Vol. 1). 1975. 48.00 (ISBN 0-911216-94-4). Raven.

Molecular Mechanisms of Anesthesia. Ed. by B. Raymond Fink. (Progress in Anesthesiology Ser.: Vol. 2). (Illus.). 528p. 1980. text ed. 48.50 (ISBN 0-89004-456-2). Raven.

Molecular Mechanisms of Biological Recognition. Ed. by M. Balaban. 516p. 1979. 68.50 (ISBN 0-444-80130-8). Elsevier.

Molecular Mechanisms of Genetic Processes. Ed. by N. P. Dubinin & D. M. Gol'dfarb. Tr. by A. Mercado from Rus. LC 74-30205. 373p. 1975. 58.95 (ISBN 0-470-22330-8). Halsted Pr.

Molecular Microbiology. Ed. by J. B. Kwapinski. LC 80-11813. 494p. 1981. Repr. of 1974 ed. lib. bdg. write for info. (ISBN 0-89874-148-3). Krieger.

Molecular Motion in Polymers by ESR. Ed. by R. Boyer & S. Keinath. (MMI Press Symposium Ser.: Vol. 1). 352p. 1980. lib. bdg. 44.00 (ISBN 3-7186-0012-9). Harwood Academic.

Molecular Movements & Chemical Reactivity As Conditioned by Membranes, Enzymes & Other Macromolecules. Ed. by R. Lefever & A. Goldbeter. LC 58-9935. (Advances in Chemical Physics Ser.: Vol. 39). 1978. 46.50 (ISBN 0-471-03541-6, Pub. by Wiley-Interscience). Wiley.

Molecular Orbital Theory in Drug Research. Lemont B. Kier. LC 73-137616. (Medicinal Chemistry Ser). 1971. 40.50 (ISBN 0-12-406550-3). Acad Pr.

Molecular Pathology. Ed. by Robert A. Good et al. (Illus.). 888p. 1975. text ed. 85.50 (ISBN 0-398-02944-X). C C Thomas.

Molecular Quantum Mechanics: An Introduction to Quantum Chemistry, 2 vols. P. W. Atkins. Vol. 1, Pts. 1-2. pap. 14.95x (ISBN 0-19-855129-0); Vol. 2. pap. 19.95x (ISBN 0-19-855130-4). Oxford U Pr.

Molecular Shapes: Theoretical Models of Inorganic Stereochemistry. Jeremy K. Burdett. 270p. 1980. 29.50 (ISBN 0-471-07860-3, Pub. by Wiley-Interscience). Wiley.

Molecular Sieve Zeolites I & II, 2 pts. Ed. by E. M. Flanigen & Leonard B. Sand. LC 77-156974. (Advances in Chemistry Ser.: Nos. 101-102). 1971. Set. 59.00 (ISBN 0-8412-0617-1); Pt. 1. 39.50 (ISBN 0-8412-0114-5); Pt. 2. 35.25 (ISBN 0-8412-0115-3). Am Chemical.

Molecular Spectroscopy. Ira N. Levine. LC 74-30477. 480p. 1975. 32.50 (ISBN 0-471-53128-6, Pub. by Wiley-Interscience). Wiley.

Molecular Statistics for Students of Chemistry. L. A. Woodward. (Illus.). 232p. 1975. 28.00x (ISBN 0-19-855357-9). Oxford U Pr.

Molecular Structure & Dynamics. W. H. Flygare. LC 77-16786. (Illus.). 1978. ref. 29.95 (ISBN 0-13-599753-4). P-H.

Molecular Structure & Function of Food Carbohydrate. Ed. by G. G. Birch & L. F. Green. LC 73-16299. 308p. 1974. 44.95 (ISBN 0-470-07323-3). Halsted Pr.

Molecular Structure: The Physical Approach. 2nd ed. J. C. Brand & J. C. Speakman. Ed. by J. K. Tifer. LC 75-8507. 1975. 31.95 (ISBN 0-470-09795-7). Halsted Pr.

Molecular Theory of Radiation Biology. K. H. Chadwick & H. P. Leenhouts. (Monographs on Theoretical & Applied Genetics: Vol. 5). (Illus.). 450p. 1981. 67.50 (ISBN 0-387-10297-3). Springer-Verlag.

Molecular Thermodynamics of Fluid-Phase Equilibria. J. M. Prausnitz. LC 69-16866. 1969. ref. ed. 28.95 (ISBN 0-13-599639-2). P-H.

Molecular Vib-Rotors. H. C. Allen, Jr. 324p. 1963. text ed. 17.50 (ISBN 0-471-02325-6, Pub. by Wiley). Krieger.

Molecular Vibrations: The Theory of Infrared & Raman Vibrational Spectra. E. B. Wilson, Jr. et al. (Illus.). 1980. pap. text ed. 6.00 (ISBN 0-486-63941-X). Dover.

Molecular Weight Distribution in Polymers. Leighton H. Peebles. LC 70-143175. (Polymer Reviews Ser: Vol. 18). 1971. 30.95 o.p. (ISBN 0-471-67710-8, Pub. by Wiley-Interscience). Wiley.

Molecules & Cell Movement. Ed. by S. Inoue & R. E. Stephens. LC 75-16666. (Society of General Physiologists Ser.: Vol. 30). 350p. 1975. 36.00 (ISBN 0-89004-041-9). Raven.

Molecules & Evolution. Thomas H. Jukes. (Illus.). 1968. Repr. of 1966 ed. 18.00x (ISBN 0-231-08614-8). Columbia U Pr.

Molecules & Life: Historical Essays on the Interplay of Chemistry & Biology. Joseph S. Fruton. LC 72-3095. 579p. 1972. 17.00 (ISBN 0-471-28448-3, Pub. by Wiley-Interscience). Wiley.

Molecules, Cells & Parasites in Immunology. Ed. by Carlos Larralde et al. 1980. 19.50 (ISBN 0-12-436840-9). Acad Pr.

Molecules to Living Cells: Highlights in Molecular Biology. Readings from Scientific Americans. Intro. by Philip C. Hanawalt. LC 80-10814. (Illus.). 1980. text ed. 19.95x (ISBN 0-7167-1208-3); pap. text ed. 9.95x (ISBN 0-7167-1209-1). W H Freeman.

Moles & Shrews. Charles L. Ripper. (Illus.). (gr. 5-9). 1957. PLB 6.48 o.p. (ISBN 0-688-31513-5). Morrow.

Molesworth Back in the Jug Agane. Geoffrey Willans & Ronald Searle. (Illus.). 1959. 4.95 o.s.i. (ISBN 0-8149-0235-9). Vanguard.

Molesworth's Guide to the Atommic Age. Geoffrey Willans & Ronald Searle. (Illus.). 4.95 o.s.i. (ISBN 0-8149-0234-0). Vanguard.

Molesworth's Marathi-English Dictionary. James T. Molesworth. 1978. Repr. 32.00x o.p. (ISBN 0-8364-0233-2). South Asia Bks.

Moliere. Hallam Walker. (World Authors Ser.: France: No. 176). lib. bdg. 12.50 (ISBN 0-8057-2620-9). Twayne.

Moliere: A Collection of Critical Essays. Ed. by J. Giucharhaud. 1964. 10.95 (ISBN 0-13-599712-7, Spec). P-H.

Moliere & the Comedy of Intellect. J. D. Hubert. (California Library Reprint). 1974. 18.50x (ISBN 0-520-02520-2). U of Cal Pr.

Moliere: Stage & Study. Ed. by W. D. Howarth & J. Merlin Thomas. 1973. 29.95x (ISBN 0-19-815712-6). Oxford U Pr.

Moliere's Don Juan. Christopher Hampton. 1974. pap. 3.95 o.p. (ISBN 0-571-10193-3, Pub. by Faber & Faber). Merrimack Bk Serv.

Moline: A Pictorial History. Bess Pierce. Ed. by Donna R. Friedman. (Illus.). 208p. 1981. pap. write for info. (ISBN 0-89865-095-X). Donning Co.

Moll Flanders. Daniel Defoe. (Classics Ser). (gr. 11 up). 1969. pap. 1.95 (ISBN 0-8049-0200-3, CL-200). Airmont.

Moll Flanders. Ed. by Edward Kelly. (Critical Editions Ser.). 500p. 1973. pap. text ed. 5.95x (ISBN 0-393-09412-X). Norton.

Mollie: The Journal of Mollie Dorsey Sanford in Nebraska & Colorado Territories, 1857-1866. Mollie D. Sanford. LC 75-8764. (Pioneer Heritage Series: Vol. 1). xii, 199p. 1976. pap. 3.95 (ISBN 0-8032-5826-7, BB 607, Bison). U of Nebr Pr.

Molloy's Live for Success. John T. Molloy. LC 80-2279. (Illus.). 288p. 1981. 11.95 (ISBN 0-688-00412-1). Morrow.

Mollusca from the Upper Cretaceous Jalama Formation, Santa Barbara County, California. D. H. Dailey & W. P. Popence. (U. C. Publ. in Geological Sciences: Vol. 65). 1966. pap. 6.00x (ISBN 0-520-09166-3). U of Cal Pr.

Molluscan Nerve Cells: From Biophysics to Behavior. Ed. by John H. Byrne & John Koester. (Cold Spring Harbor Reports in the Neurosciences Ser.: Vol. 1). 250p. 1980. 26.00x (ISBN 0-87969-135-2). Cold Spring Harbor.

Molluscs. J. E. Morton. (Hutchinson Biological Sciences Ser.). (Illus.). 244p. 1979. pap. text ed. 11.25 (ISBN 0-09-134161-2, Hutchinson U Lib). Humanities.

Molly & the Giant. Kurt Werth & Mabel Watts. LC 72-6076. (Illus.). 48p. (gr. k-3). 1973. 5.95 o.s.i. (ISBN 0-8193-0638-X, Four Winds); PLB 5.41 o.s.i. (ISBN 0-8193-0639-8). Schol Bk Serv.

Molly Companion. Maura Stanton. 1978. pap. 1.95 (ISBN 0-380-40436-2, 40436). Avon.

Molly Goldberg Jewish Cookbook. Gertrude Berg & Myra Waldo. 1972. pap. 1.75 o.s.i. (ISBN 0-515-04777-5, V2398). Jove Pubns.

Molly the Mule. Hope R. Kjellerup. 1981. 5.95 (ISBN 0-533-04776-5). Vantage.

Mollyday Holiday. Margaret Storey. (Illus.). (ps-5). 1971. 6.95 (ISBN 0-571-09590-9, Pub. by Faber & Faber). Merrimack Bk Serv.

Molly's Lies. Kay Chorao. LC 78-12383. (Illus.). (gr. 1-3). 1979. 7.50 (ISBN 0-395-28951-3, Clarion). HM.

Molly's Manhattan. Molly Parkin. 200p. Date not set. cancelled (ISBN 0-686-68788-4). Riverrun NY.

Molly's Moe. Kay Chorao. LC 76-3526. (Illus.). (ps-3). 1976. 7.50 (ISBN 0-395-28784-7, Clarion). HM.

Molokan Oral Tradition: Legends & Memorates of an Ethnic Sect. Willard B. Moore. (U. C. Publ. in Folklore Studies: Vol. 28). 1974. pap. 9.00x (ISBN 0-520-09483-2). U of Cal Pr.

Molotov Cocktail. John O. Virtanen. (Orig.). 1980. pap. 2.25 (ISBN 0-505-51517-2). Tower Bks.

Molten State of Matter: Melting & Crystal Structure. A. R. Ubbelohde. LC 77-28300. 454p. 1979. 68.95 (ISBN 0-471-99626-2). Wiley.

Molybdenum & Molybdenum-Containing Enzymes. Michael P. Coughlan. (Illus.). 1980. 94.00 (ISBN 0-08-024398-3). Pergamon.

Molybdenum Chemistry of Biological Significance. Ed. by William E. Newton & Sei Otsuka. 435p. 1980. 39.50 (ISBN 0-306-40352-8, Plenum Pr). Plenum Pub.

Molyneux's Question: Vision, Touch, & the Philosophy of Perception. Michael J. Morgan. LC 76-54066. 1977. 27.50 (ISBN 0-521-21558-7). Cambridge U Pr.

Mom, I Can't Decide. Robin Worthington. (Uplook Ser.). 32p. 1973. pap. 0.75 (ISBN 0-8163-0075-5, 13640-8). Pacific Pr Pub Assn.

Mom Is an Elephant. Otto Gmelin. Tr. by Judith M. Hermann from Ger. LC 80-80651. (Illus.). Date not set. price not set (ISBN 0-89793-026-6). Hunter Hse.

Mom or Pop. Elizabeth Levy. (Orig.). (gr. k-6). pap. 1.95 (ISBN 0-440-45779-3, YB). Dell.

Mom, the Wolfman & Me. Norma Klein. (gr. 5-9). 1974. pap. 1.95 (ISBN 0-380-00791-6, 53595). Avon.

Mom the Wolfman & Me. Norma Klein. (gr. 5-9). 1977. pap. 1.95 (ISBN 0-380-01725-3, 49502, Camelot). Avon.

Mom, They Won't Let Us Pray. Rita Warren & Dick Schneider. 1975. pap. 2.50 o.p. (ISBN 0-8499-4110-5, 4110-5, Dist. by Word Bks.); 1975 5.95 o.p. (ISBN 0-912376-10-4). Chosen Bks Pub.

Mombasa Rising Against the Portuguese, Sixteen Thirty-One: From Sworn Evidence. G. S. Freeman-Grenville. (British Academy-Fontes Historiae Africanae). (Illus.). 224p. 98.00x (ISBN 0-19-725992-8). Oxford U Pr.

Moment a Day. Deborah Stansbury. 1980. 4.95 (ISBN 0-533-04420-0). Vantage.

Moment of Death: A Symposium. Arthur Winter. (Illus.). 100p. 1969. 9.50 (ISBN 0-398-02090-6). C C Thomas.

Moment of Truth for Protestant America: Interchurch Campaigns Following World War I. Eldon Ernst. LC 74-16567. (American Academy of Religion. Dissertation Ser.). 1974. pap. 7.50 (ISBN 0-88420-120-1, 010103). Scholars Pr Ca.

Moment of Vision. Ed. by Joseph M. Solan et al. LC 80-68991. 80p. (Orig.). 1980. pap. 9.50 (ISBN 0-937968-00-5). Dark Sun.

Momentos Hispanos. Robert Cabot & Louis Cabat. (gr. 11). 1978. pap. text ed. 3.92 (ISBN 0-87720-520-5). AMSCO Sch.

Momentous Event. W. J. Grier. 1976. pap. 2.45 (ISBN 0-85151-020-5). Banner of Truth.

Moments of Light. Fred Chappell. LC 80-81219. 195p. 1980. 12.95 (ISBN 0-917990-05-6). New South Co.

Moments of Reflection. L. D. Johnson. LC 80-67779. 1980. pap. 3.95 (ISBN 0-8054-5287-7). Broadman.

Moments of Vision: The Poetry of Thomas Hardy. Paul Zietlow. LC 73-85184. 304p. 1974. text ed. 16.50x (ISBN 0-674-58215-2). Harvard U Pr.

Moments with Chaplin. Lillian Ross. LC 80-80828. (Illus.). 64p. 1980. 8.95 (ISBN 0-396-07829-X). Dodd.

Momentum, Energy, & Mass Transfer in Continua. 2nd ed. John C. Slattery. LC 80-22746. 700p. 1980. text ed. 32.50 (ISBN 0-89874-212-9). Krieger.

Momentum Transfer in Boundary Layers. T. Cebeci & P. Bradshaw. LC 76-57750. (Thermal & Fluids Engineering Ser.). (Illus.). 1977. text ed. 23.95 (ISBN 0-07-010300-3, C); solutions manual 4.95 (ISBN 0-07-010301-1). McGraw.

Momism: The Silent Disease of America. Hans Sebald. LC 75-45223. 386p. 1976. 14.95 (ISBN 0-88229-275-7). Nelson-Hall.

Momma. Mell Lazarus. 128p. (Orig.). 1981. pap. 1.75 (ISBN 0-553-14788-9). Bantam.

Momma Treasury. Mell Lazarus. (Illus.). 1978. 12.95 o.p. (ISBN 0-8362-1102-2); pap. 7.95 o.p. (ISBN 0-8362-1101-4). Andrews & McMeel.

Mommies & Daddies Work. Laura Dayton. LC 78-73532. (Illus.). (ps-2). Date not set. price not set (ISBN 0-89799-158-3); pap. price not set (ISBN 0-89799-076-5). Dandelion Pr. Postponed.

Mommy, I Feel Sick. Clair Isbister. 1979. 7.95 o.p. (ISBN 0-8015-5116-1). Dutton.

Mommy's Gone. Rachel Summers. 1976. pap. 1.25 o.p. (ISBN 0-685-69144-6, LB359ZK, Leisure Bks). Nordon Pubns.

Momotaro. George Suyeoka. Ed. by Ruth Tabrah. LC 72-86744. (Illus.). (gr. 1-7). 1972. pap. 5.95 (ISBN 0-89610-009-X). Island Her.

Moms Are God's Idea. Roy Lessin. (God's Idea Books Ser.). (Illus.). 32p. (ps-4). 1981. pap. 1.25 (ISBN 0-87123-175-1, 210175). Bethany Fell.

Mom's House, Dad's House: Making Shared Custody Work. Isolina Ricci. 224p. 1980. 12.95 (ISBN 0-02-602550-7). Macmillan.

Mom's New Job. Paul Sawyer. LC 77-27982. (Moods & Emotions Ser.). (Illus.). (gr. k-3). 1978. PLB 8.95 (ISBN 0-8172-1150-0). Raintree Pubs.

Mom's Tried & True Recipes for Family Prayer. Mary A. Wolf. (Illus., Orig.). 1981. pap. 3.25 (ISBN 0-89570-199-5). Claretian Pubns.

Momus Truimphans: The Plagiaries of the English Stage-Expos'd in a Catalogue. Gerard Langbaine. Bd. with Lives & Characters of the English Dramatic Poets. (English Stage Ser.: Vol. 19). lib. bdg. 50.00 (ISBN 0-8240-0602-X). Garland Pub.

Mon Larousse en Images. Marthe Fonteneau. (Illus.). 16.75 (ISBN 0-686-65648-2). Larousse.

Mon Oncle Jules. Maupassant. (Easy Reader, D). pap. 3.75 (ISBN 0-88436-044-X, FRA301052). EMC.

Mon Premier Alphabet. A. Rosenstiehl. (Illus.). 1978. 14.25 (ISBN 2-03-051422-5, 3803). Larousse.

Mon Premier Larousse en couleurs. M. Fonteneau & S. Theureau. (Illus., Fr.). 27.25 (ISBN 2-03-051403-9, 3795). Larousse.

Mon Premier Larousse francais-anglais, anglais-francais en couleurs. Larousse And Co. (Fr. & Eng.). (gr. 6-9). 23.75 (ISBN 2-03-051431-4, 3794). Larousse.

Mon Premier Livre de chansons. (ISBN 2-03-051416-0, 3580). records incl. 21.50 (ISBN 0-685-47335-X, 3799). Larousse.

Mona Antiqua Restaurata. Henry Rowlands. Ed. by Burton Feldman & Robert D. Richardson. LC 78-60894. (Myth & Romanticism Ser.: Vol. 21). 399p. 1979. lib. bdg. 60.00 (ISBN 0-8240-3570-4). Garland Pub.

Mona Lisa Mystery. Pat Hutchins. LC 79-20263. (Illus.). 192p. (gr. 3-5). 1981. 8.95 (ISBN 0-688-80243-5); PLB 8.59 (ISBN 0-688-84243-7). Greenwillow.

Monadology & Other Philosophical Essays. Gottfried Leibniz. Tr. by Paul Schrecker & Anne Schrecker. LC 65-26531. (Orig.). 1965. pap. 4.95 (ISBN 0-672-60426-4, LLA188). Bobbs.

Monarch. Babette Rosmond. 1980. pap. 2.25 o.p. (ISBN 0-425-04147-6). Berkley Pub.

Monarch & the Princess. Diana Robinson. 1981. 5.95 (ISBN 0-533-04745-5). Vantage.

Monarch Notes on Aeschylus' Plays. Robert H. Ahrens, Jr. (Orig.). pap. 2.50 (ISBN 0-671-00801-3). Monarch Pr.

Monarch Notes on Austen's Emma & Mansfield Park. William J. Fitzpatrick. (Orig.). pap. 1.95 (ISBN 0-671-00704-1). Monarch Pr.

Monarch Notes on Bronte's Jane Eyre. (Orig.). pap. 1.95 (ISBN 0-671-00602-9). Monarch Pr.

Monarch Notes on Browning's Poetry. Ralph Ranald. (Orig.). pap. 1.75 (ISBN 0-671-00776-9). Monarch Pr.

Monarch Notes on Camus' Major Works. Austin Fowler. (Orig.). pap. 1.75 (ISBN 0-671-00552-9). Monarch Pr.

Monarch Notes on Cervantes' Don Quixote. Gregor Roy. (Orig.). pap. 1.95 (ISBN 0-671-00553-7). Monarch Pr.

Monarch Notes on Coleridge's the Rime of the Ancient Mariner & Other Poems. John Elliott. (Orig.). pap. 1.95 (ISBN 0-671-00778-5). Monarch Pr.

Monarch Notes on Conrad's Heart of Darkness & the Secret Sharer. James Weiss. (Orig.). pap. 1.95 (ISBN 0-671-00817-X). Monarch Pr.

Monarch Notes on Defoe's Moll Flanders. David Gooding. (Orig.). pap. 1.95 (ISBN 0-671-00705-X). Monarch Pr.

Monarch Notes on Dickens' David Copperfield. (Orig.). pap. 1.95 (ISBN 0-671-00609-6). Monarch Pr.

Monarch Notes on Dickens' Great Expectations. Leonard Jenkin. (Orig.). pap. 1.75 (ISBN 0-671-00610-X). Monarch Pr.

Monarch Notes on Dickens' Oliver Twist. (Orig.). pap. 2.25 (ISBN 0-671-00824-2). Monarch Pr.

Monarch Notes on Donne & the Metaphysical Poets. Joseph Grennen. (Orig.). pap. 1.95 (ISBN 0-671-00731-9). Monarch Pr.

Monarch Notes on Dostoyevsky's Crime & Punishment. Frederic Tuten. (Orig.). pap. 1.95 (ISBN 0-671-00517-0). Monarch Pr.

Monarch Notes on Dostoyevsky's Notes from the Underground. Leslie Juhasz. (Orig.). pap. 1.95 (ISBN 0-671-00558-8). Monarch Pr.

Monarch Notes on Faulkner's Absalom, Absalom. Elizabeth C. Phillips. (Orig.). pap. 1.95 (ISBN 0-671-00664-9). Monarch Pr.

Monarch Notes on Fitzgerald's Tender Is the Night. Stanley Cooperman. (Orig.). pap. 1.95 (ISBN 0-671-00668-1). Monarch Pr.

Monarch Notes on Freud's Introductory Lectures. pap. 2.25 (ISBN 0-671-00615-0). Monarch Pr.

Monarch Notes on Graham Greene's Major Novels. Gregor Roy. (Orig.). pap. 1.95 (ISBN 0-671-00838-2). Monarch Pr.

Monarch Notes on Hardy's Far from the Madding Crowd. Elizabeth R. Nelson. (Orig.). pap. 1.95 (ISBN 0-671-00890-0). Monarch Pr.

Monarch Notes on Hardy's Tess of the D'Urbervilles. Robert Ackerman. (Orig.). pap. 1.95 (ISBN 0-671-00619-3). Monarch Pr.

Monarch Notes on Heller's Catch 22. pap. 1.75 (ISBN 0-671-00905-2). Monarch Pr.

Monarch Notes on Hemingway's for Whom the Bell Tolls. Lawrence Klibbe. (Orig.). pap. 1.75 (ISBN 0-671-00672-X). Monarch Pr.

Monarch Notes on Hemingway's Major Novels. Stanley Cooperman. (Orig.). pap. 1.75 (ISBN 0-671-00621-5). Monarch Pr.

Monarch Notes on Hugo's Les Miserables. (Orig.). pap. 2.25 (ISBN 0-671-00844-7). Monarch Pr.

Monarch Notes on Hume's Philosophy. Nicholas Capaldi. (Orig.). pap. 1.95 (ISBN 0-671-00529-4). Monarch Pr.

Monarch Notes on Kafka's the Trial, the Castle & Other Works. Gregor Roy. (Orig.). pap. 1.95 (ISBN 0-671-00847-1). Monarch Pr.

Monarch Notes on Lawrence's Sons & Lovers & Other Works. Sandra Gilbert. (Orig.). pap. 1.95 (ISBN 0-671-00716-5). Monarch Pr.

Monarch Notes on Lewis' Arrowsmith. (Orig.). pap. 1.95 (ISBN 0-671-00682-7). Monarch Pr.

Monarch Notes on Lewis' Babbitt. (Orig.). pap. 1.75 (ISBN 0-671-00683-5). Monarch Pr.

Monarch Notes on Machiavelli's the Prince. Robert Sobel. (Orig.). pap. 1.95 (ISBN 0-671-00565-0). Monarch Pr.
Monarch Notes on Marlowe's Dr. Faustus & Other Writings. Peter Mullany. (Orig.). pap. 1.95 (ISBN 0-671-00717-3). Monarch Pr.
Monarch Notes on Miller's Death of a Salesman. Joan T. Nourse. (Orig.). pap. 1.95 (ISBN 0-671-00688-6). Monarch Pr.
Monarch Notes on Plath's Bell Jar. Barry Wallenstein. 1975. pap. 2.25 (ISBN 0-671-00965-6). Monarch Pr.
Monarch Notes on Plato's the Republic & Selected Dialogues. Leo Rauch. pap. 1.95 (ISBN 0-671-00505-7). Monarch Pr.
Monarch Notes on Rawlings' the Yearling. Charles A. Raines. (Orig.). pap. 1.95 (ISBN 0-671-00859-5). Monarch Pr.
Monarch Notes on Remarque's All Quiet on the Western Front. John S. White. (Orig.). pap. 1.75 (ISBN 0-671-00861-7). Monarch Pr.
Monarch Notes on Shakespeare's a Midsummer Night's Dream. Eve Leoff. (Orig.). pap. 1.95 (ISBN 0-671-00638-X). Monarch Pr.
Monarch Notes on Shakespeare's Henry Fourth, Part 2. Frances Barasch. (Orig.). pap. 1.95 (ISBN 0-671-00634-7). Monarch Pr.
Monarch Notes on Shakespeare's Julius Caesar. (Orig.). pap. 1.95 (ISBN 0-671-00632-0). Monarch Pr.
Monarch Notes on Shakespeare's Measure for Measure. Unicio J. Violi. (Orig.). pap. 1.95 (ISBN 0-671-00636-3). Monarch Pr.
Monarch Notes on Shakespeare's Midsummer's Night Dream. pap. 1.95 (ISBN 0-671-00638-X). Monarch Pr.
Monarch Notes on Shakespeare's the Tempest. Ralph A. Ranald. (Orig.). pap. 1.75 (ISBN 0-671-00644-4). Monarch Pr.
Monarch Notes on Shakespeare's Winter's Tale. Margaret L. Ranald. (Orig.). pap. 1.75 o.p. (ISBN 0-671-00656-8). Monarch Pr.
Monarch Notes on Shaw's Plays. Robert Rockman. pap. 2.25 (ISBN 0-671-00646-0). Monarch Pr.
Monarch Notes on Steinbeck's Major Novels. (Orig.). pap. 1.95 (ISBN 0-671-00647-9). Monarch Pr.
Monarch Notes on Steinbeck's Red Pony, the Pearl. (Orig.). pap. 1.95 (ISBN 0-671-00694-0). Monarch Pr.
Monarch Notes on Stendhal's the Red & the Black & Charterhouse of Parma. Patricia Plante. (Orig.). pap. 1.95 (ISBN 0-671-00570-7). Monarch Pr.
Monarch Notes on Swift's Gulliver's Travels. Richard Feingold. (Orig.). pap. 1.95 (ISBN 0-671-00648-7). Monarch Pr.
Monarch Notes on Tennessee Williams' Major Plays. Benjamin Nelson. (Orig.). pap. 1.95 (ISBN 0-671-00650-9). Monarch Pr.
Monarch Notes on Tennyson's Idylls of the King & Other Poems. David Rogers. (Orig.). pap. 2.25 (ISBN 0-671-00734-3). Monarch Pr.
Monarch Notes on the New Testament. Unicio J. Violi. (Orig.). pap. 2.50 (ISBN 0-671-00625-8). Monarch Pr.
Monarch Notes on Tolkein's Fellowship of the Ring. Louis Morrison. 1976. pap. 1.95 (ISBN 0-671-00971-0). Monarch Pr.
Monarch Notes on Tolstoy's Anna Karenina. Herbert Reaske. (Orig.). pap. 1.95 (ISBN 0-671-00571-5). Monarch Pr.
Monarch Notes on Turgenev's Fathers & Sons. Jane Wexford. (Orig.). pap. 2.25 (ISBN 0-671-00877-3). Monarch Pr.
Monarch Notes on Twain's Huckleberry Finn & Other Works. (Orig.). pap. 1.95 (ISBN 0-671-00649-5). Monarch Pr.
Monarch Notes on Twain's the Prince & the Pauper. Charles Leavitt. (Orig.). pap. 1.95 (ISBN 0-671-00878-1). Monarch Pr.
Monarch Notes on Twain's Tom Sawyer. (Orig.). pap. 2.25 (ISBN 0-671-00696-7). Monarch Pr.
Monarch Notes on Verne's 20,000 Leagues Under the Sea & Other Works. pap. 2.25 (ISBN 0-671-00763-7). Monarch Pr.
Monarch Notes on Wharton's Ethan Frome. (Orig.). pap. 1.95 (ISBN 0-671-00698-3). Monarch Pr.
Monarch Notes on Wilde's Plays. Grace H. Schwartz. (Orig.). pap. 1.95 (ISBN 0-671-00881-1). Monarch Pr.
Monarch Notes on Woolf's Mrs. Dalloway & to the Lighthouse. S. M. Gilbert. (Orgi). pap. 1.95 (ISBN 0-671-00883-8). Monarch Pr.
Monarchy & Community. A. J. Black. LC 72-108101. (Studies in Medieval Life & Thought). 1970. 32.95 (ISBN 0-521-07739-7). Cambridge U Pr.
Monarchy in Hawaii. rev., 2nd ed. John D. Holt. 1971. pap. 3.50 (ISBN 0-686-63589-2). Topgallant.
Monarchy of France. Claude De Seyssel. Tr. by J. H. Hexter & Donald H. Kelley. LC 80-23554. 1981. text ed. 16.95x (ISBN 0-300-02516-5). Yale U Pr.
Monasteries of Western Europe: The Architecture of the Orders. Wolfgang Braunfels. LC 73-2472. (Illus.). 263p. 1980. 35.00x; pap. 15.00x (ISBN 0-691-00313-0). Princeton U Pr.
Monastery. Walter Scott. 1969. 11.50x (ISBN 0-460-00136-1, Evman). Dutton.
Monastery & Cathedral in France: Medieval Architecture, Sculpture, Stained Glass, Manuscripts, the Art of the Church Treasuries. Whitney S. Stoddard. LC 66-23923. 1966. 40.00x (ISBN 0-8195-3071-9). Wesleyan U Pr.
Monastic Architecture in France from the Renaissance to the Revolution. Joan Evans. LC 79-91816. (Illus.). 822p. 1980. Repr. of 1964 ed. lib. bdg. 75.00 (ISBN 0-87817-260-2). Hacker.
Monastic Iconography in France from the Renaissance to the Revolution. Joan Evans. LC 67-12317. (Illus.). 1969. 78.00 (ISBN 0-521-06960-2). Cambridge U Pr.
Monastic Journey. Thomas Merton. Ed. by Hart, Patrick, Bro. LC 77-27714. 1978. pap. 2.95 (ISBN 0-385-14094-0, Im). Doubleday.
Monastic Journey. Thomas Merton. Ed. by Patrick Hart. 1977. 8.95 o.p. (ISBN 0-8362-0665-7). Andrews & McMeel.
Monastic Order in England. 2nd ed. David Knowles. 1963. 67.50 (ISBN 0-521-05479-6). Cambridge U Pr.
Monastic Order in South Wales, 1066-1349. F. G. Cowley. (Studies in Welsh History: Vol. 1, History & Law Committee, Univ. of Wales). 1978. text ed. 40.00x (ISBN 0-685-04716-4). Verry.
Monastic Theology of Aelred of Rievaulx: An Experiential Theology. Amedee Hallier. Tr. by Columban Heaney from Fr. (Cistercian Studies: No. 2). xxxii, 180p. 1969. 7.95 o.p. (ISBN 0-87907-802-2). Cistercian Pubns.
Monastic Tithes from Their Origins to the Twelfth Century. Giles Constable. (Cambridge Studies in Medieval Life & Thought). 46.95 (ISBN 0-521-04715-3). Cambridge U Pr.
Monastic World. Christopher Brooke. (Illus.). 1978. 49.00 (ISBN 0-236-31059-3, Pub. by Paul Elek). Merrimack Bk Serv.
Monday Horses. Jean S. Doty. LC 77-13310. (gr. 5-9). 1978. 7.95 (ISBN 0-688-80134-X); PLB 7.63 (ISBN 0-688-84134-1). Greenwillow.
Monday Horses. Jean S. Doty. (gr. 5-7). 1979. pap. 1.75 (ISBN 0-671-41856-4). Archway.
Monday I Was an Alligator. Susan Pearson. LC 78-23618. (Lippincott-I-Like-to-Read Books). (Illus.). (gr. k-2). 1979. 6.95 (ISBN 0-397-31830-8). Lippincott.
Monday Morality: Right & Wrong in Daily Life. Edward Wakin. LC 80-80871. 96p. (Orig.). 1980. pap. 3.95 (ISBN 0-8091-2317-7). Paulist Pr.
Monday Morning Imagination: Report from the Boyer Workshop on State University Systems. Ed. by Martin Kaplan. (Special Studies). 1977. text ed. 23.95 (ISBN 0-03-021481-5). Praeger.
Monday Morning Movie. Marilyn Zuckerman. LC 80-51924. (Illus.). 56p. (Orig.). 1980. write for info. (ISBN 0-935694-03-X); pap. 10.00 (ISBN 0-935694-04-8). St Edns.
Monday the Rabbi Took Off. Harry Kemelman. (Rabbi Ser.). 288p. 1978. pap. 2.25 (ISBN 0-449-23872-5, Crest). Fawcett.
Monday's God. new ed. Dwight E. Stevenson. 128p. (Orig.). 1976. pap. 1.25 (ISBN 0-8272-2309-9). Bethany Pr.
Monday's Mob. Don Pendleton. (Executioner Ser.: No. 33). pap. 1.95 (ISBN 0-523-41097-2, Dist. by Independent News Co.). Pinnacle Bks.
Monde autour de l'an 33. new ed. Ed. by Daniel Moreau. (Collection monde et histoire). (Illus.). 160p. (Fr.). 1973. 14.50x o.p. (ISBN 0-685-39577-4). Larousse.
Monde autour de 1492. new ed. Ed. by Daniel Moreau. (Collection monde et histoire). (Illus.). 160p. (Fr.). 1973. 15.00x (ISBN 2-03-053201-0). Larousse.
Monde autour de 1793. new ed. Ed. by Daniel Moreau. (Collection monde et histoire). (Illus.). 160p. (Fr.). 1973. 15.00x (ISBN 2-03-053205-3). Larousse.
Monde autour de 1871. new ed. Ed. by Daniel Moreau. (Collection monde et histoire). (Illus.). 160p. (Fr.). 1973. 15.00x (ISBN 2-03-053203-7). Larousse.
Monde autour de 1938. new ed. Ed. by Daniel Moreau. (Collection monde et histoire). (Illus.). 160p. (Fr.). 1973. 15.00x (ISBN 2-03-053204-5). Larousse.
Monde autour de 1949. new ed. Ed. by Daniel Moreau. (Collection monde et histoire). (Illus.). 160p. (Fr.). 1973. 14.50x o.p. (ISBN 2-03-053206-1). Larousse.
Monde de la nature. (Illus.). 1978. text ed. 26.95x (ISBN 2-03-019112-4). Larousse.
Monde En Marche. 1980. pap. 1.40 (ISBN 0-686-69358-2). Vida Pubs.
Monde Oriental De 395 a 1081. LC 80-2356. 1981. Repr. of 1936 ed. 72.50 (ISBN 0-404-18906-7). AMS Pr.
Mondrian. Hans L. Jaffe. (Library of Great Painters Ser). (Illus.). 1970. 35.00 (ISBN 0-8109-0325-3). Abrams.
Monerias De Darwin. Tr. by Harold Hill. (Spanish Bks.). (Span.). 1977. 1.60 (ISBN 0-8297-0771-9). Life Pubs Intl.
Monet. Michael Hoog. (Masters of Art Ser.). (Illus.). (gr. 11-12). 1979. pap. 3.95 (ISBN 0-8120-2152-5). Barron.
Monet. William C. Seitz. LC 60-7800. (Library of Great Painters Ser). (Illus.). 1960. 35.00 (ISBN 0-8109-0326-1). Abrams.
Monet & His Critics. Steven Z. Levine. LC 75-23800. (Outstanding Dissertations in the Fine Arts - 19th Century). (Illus.). 1976. lib. bdg. 45.00 (ISBN 0-8240-1995-4). Garland Pub.
Monetarism: How the Financial Crisis Can Help You Make Money in the Stock Market. Thomas R. Ireland. 1974. 7.95 o.p. (ISBN 0-87000-235-X). Arlington Hse.
Monetarism: Theory, Evidence & Policy. Howard R. Vane & John L. Thompson. 1979. pap. text ed. 10.95 (ISBN 0-470-26569-8). Halsted Pr.
Monetarists & Keynesians: Their Contributions to Monetary Theory. Brian Morgan. 1980. pap. text ed. 10.95x (ISBN 0-470-26885-9). Halsted Pr.
Monetary & Financial Policy in Nineteenth Century Britain. F. W. Fetter & D. Gregory. (Government & Society in 19th Century Britain Ser.). 106p. 1973. 15.00x (ISBN 0-7165-2217-9, Pub. by Irish Academic Pr Ireland); pap. 6.00x (ISBN 0-7165-2218-7). Biblio Dist.
Monetary Approach to International Adjustment. Ed. by Bluford H. Putnam & D. Sykes Wilford. LC 78-19753. 1979. 24.50 (ISBN 0-03-046711-X); pap. 9.95 (ISBN 0-03-056211-2). Praeger.
Monetary Correction & Housing Finance in Colombia, Brazil & Chile. Roger J. Sandilands. 182p. 1980. text ed. 41.00x (ISBN 0-566-00355-4, Pub. by Gower Pub Co England). Renouf.
Monetary Economics. G. E. Dennis. (Modern Economic Ser.). (Illus.). 320p. (Orig.). 1981. pap. text ed. 18.95x (ISBN 0-582-45573-1). Longman.
Monetary Economics in Developing Countries. Subrata Ghatak. Date not set. 25.00 (ISBN 0-312-54418-9). St Martin.
Monetary Economics: Theories, Evidence & Policy. David G. Pierce & David M. Shaw. LC 73-91530. 1974. 27.00x (ISBN 0-8448-0267-0); pap. 14.50x (ISBN 0-8448-0268-9). Crane-Russak Co.
Monetary History of the United States: 1867-1960. M. Friedman & A. J. Schwartz. (National Bureau of Economic Research, B.12). 1963. 33.00x (ISBN 0-691-04147-4); pap. 11.95 (ISBN 0-691-00354-8). Princeton U Pr.
Monetary Incentives & Work Standards in Five Cities: Impacts & Implications for Management & Labor. John M. Greiner et al. 94p. 1977. pap. 3.95 (ISBN 0-87766-187-1, 17300). Urban Inst.
Monetary Independence Under Flexible Exchange Rates. Harvey A. Poniachek. (Illus.). 1979. 18.95 (ISBN 0-669-02728-6). Lexington Bks.
Monetary Integration in Western Europe. Douglas C. Kruse. LC 80-40980. (European Studies Ser.). (Illus.). 256p. 1980. text ed. 42.95 (ISBN 0-408-10666-2). Butterworths.
Monetary Macroeconomics. Thomas M. Havrilesky & John T. Boorman. LC 77-85996. (Illus.). 1978. pap. text ed. 14.95x (ISBN 0-88295-401-6). AHM Pub.
Monetary Management Under the New Deal. Arthur W. Crawford. LC 70-173988. (FDR & the Era of the New Deal Ser.). 380p. 1972. Repr. of 1940 ed. lib. bdg. 39.50 (ISBN 0-306-70374-2). Da Capo.
Monetary Maze: Gold, the International Monetary System, & the Emerging World Economy. William P. Kinney. LC 76-52187. 1977. pap. text ed. 4.95 (ISBN 0-8403-1700-X). Kendall-Hunt.
Monetary Planning for India. Suraj B. Gupta. 252p. 1979. text ed. 14.95x (ISBN 0-19-561145-4). Oxford U Pr.
Monetary Policy. Douglas Fisher. LC 75-20330. 91p. 1976. pap. text ed. 7.95x (ISBN 0-470-25996-5). Halsted Pr.
Monetary Policy, 6 pts. Incl. Pt. 1. General, 12 vols. Set. 846.00x (ISBN 0-686-01126-0); Pt. 2. Commercial Distress, 4 vols. Set. 288.00x (ISBN 0-686-01127-9); Pt. 3. Currency, 8 vols. Set. 612.00x (ISBN 0-686-01128-7); Pt. 4. Decimal Coinage, 2 vols. Set. 153.00x (ISBN 0-686-01129-5); Pt. 5. Joint Stock Banks, 1 vol. Set. 121.00x (ISBN 0-686-01130-9); Pt. 6. Savings Banks, 4 vols. Set. 306.00x (ISBN 0-686-01131-7). (British Parliamentary Papers Ser.). 1971 (Pub. by Irish Academic Pr Ireland). Biblio Dist.
Monetary Policy & Credit Control: The Uk Experience. David Gowland. 1978. 30.00x (ISBN 0-85664-327-0, Pub. by Croom Helm Ltd England). Biblio Dist.
Monetary Policy & Economic Activity in West Germany. Ed. by S. F. Frowen et al. LC 77-2403. 1977. 52.95 (ISBN 0-470-99131-3). Halsted Pr.
Monetary Policy & the Financial System. 4th ed. P. Horvitz. 1979. 18.95 (ISBN 0-13-599944-8). P-H.
Monetary Policy & the Open Economy: Mexico's Experience. D. Sykes Wilford. LC 77-14386. (Fraeger Special Studies). 1977. 22.95 (ISBN 0-03-028156-3). Praeger.
Monetary Problems of the International Economy. Ed. by Robert A. Mundell & Alexander K. Swoboda. pap. write for info. (ISBN 0-226-55066-4). U of Chicago Pr.
Monetary Process: Essentials of Money & Banking. 2nd ed. Robert H. Marshall & Rodney B. Swanson. 450p. 1980. text ed. 17.95 (ISBN 0-395-26530-4); instructors' manual 0.65 (ISBN 0-395-26527-4). HM.
Monetary Relations & World Development. Ed. by Fabio Basagni & Pierre Uri. LC 77-15650. (Fraeger Special Studies). 1977. 19.85 (ISBN 0-03-041591-8). Praeger.
Monetary Targets. Ed. by Brian Griffiths. Geoffrey E. Wood. 27.50 (ISBN 0-312-54421-9). St Martin.
Monetary Theory & Policy. Richard S. Thorn. LC 75-41865. 1976. pap. 9.95 o.p. (ISBN 0-275-64470-7). Praeger.
Monetary Theory & Practice. 6th ed. J. L. Hanson. (Illus.). 352p. 1978. pap. text ed. 13.95x (ISBN 0-7121-1293-6, Pub. by Macdonald & Evans England). Intl Ideas.
Monetary Theory & the Demand for Money. Douglas Fisher. LC 77-15504. 278p. 1980. pap. 19.95 (ISBN 0-470-27023-3, Pub. by Halsted Pr). Wiley.
Monetary Theory Before Adam Smith. Arthur E. Monroe. 1923. 8.50 (ISBN 0-8446-1314-2). Peter Smith.
Money. 4th, rev. ed. Lawrence S. Ritter & William L. Silber. 336p. 1981. 12.95x (ISBN 0-465-04718-1); pap. 6.95x (ISBN 0-465-04720-3). Basic.
Money: A Financial Guide for Nurses. Dorothy Del Bueno. (Illus.). 208p. 1981. text ed. 12.50 (ISBN 0-86542-007-6). Blackwell Sci.
Money: A Labor Theory of Value. L. I. Rinkel. 202p. 1980. pap. text ed. 15.75x (ISBN 90-232-1744-6). Humanities.
Money & Banking. 3rd ed. Campbell. 1978. 18.95 (ISBN 0-03-020806-8). Dryden Pr.
Money & Banking. 4th ed. Colin Campbell & Rosemary Campbell. LC 80-65792. 608p. 1981. text ed. 18.95 (ISBN 0-03-058076-5). Dryden Pr.
Money & Banking. Douglas Fisher. (Irwin Ser. in Economics). 1971. text ed. 15.95x o.p. (ISBN 0-256-00152-9). Irwin.
Money & Banking. S. Herbert Frankel. 1980. pap. 4.25 (ISBN 0-8447-3398-9). Am Enterprise.
Money & Banking. G. Krishnan-Kutty. 1979. text ed. 9.25x (ISBN 0-391-01815-9). Humanities.
Money & Banking. Donald T. Savage. LC 76-56134. 1977. text ed. 23.50x (ISBN 0-471-75519-2); tchrs. manual avail. (ISBN 0-471-02578-X). Wiley.
Money & Banking. 3rd ed. Herbert Spero & Lewis E. Davids. (Orig.). 1970. pap. 3.95 (ISBN 0-06-460069-6, CO 69, COS). Har-Row.
Money & Banking. Richard H. Timerlake, Jr. & Edward B. Selby, Jr. 1972. 16.95x (ISBN 0-534-00108-4). Wadsworth Pub.
Money & Banking: An Introduction to Analysis & Policy. 3rd ed. John G. Ranlett. LC 77-23251. 1977. text ed. 23.50 (ISBN 0-471-70815-1). Wiley.
Money & Banking in Latin America. Mario Rietti. LC 79-4157. 1979. 24.95 (ISBN 0-03-049156-8). Praeger.
Money & Banking in Puerto Rico. Biaggio DiVenuti. 2.50 o.p. (ISBN 0-8477-2605-3). U of PR Pr.
Money & Capacity Growth. Jerome L. Stein. LC 73-160844. 1971. 17.50x (ISBN 0-231-03372-9). Columbia U Pr.
Money & Capital in Economic Development. Ronald I. McKinnon. 1973. 11.95 (ISBN 0-8157-5614-3); pap. 4.95 (ISBN 0-8157-5613-5). Brookings.
Money & Economic Activity. Myron B. Slovin & Marie E. Sushka. LC 76-20950. (Illus.). 1977. 21.00 o.p. (ISBN 0-669-00882-6). Lexington Bks.
Money & Empire: The International Gold Standard 1890-1914. Marcello De Cecco. 254p. 1975. 22.50x (ISBN 0-87471-625-X). Rowman.
Money & Finance in Contemporary Yugoslavia. Dimitrije Dimitrijevic & George Macesich. LC 72-92889. (Special Studies in International Economics & Development). 1973. 28.50x (ISBN 0-275-28725-4); pap. text ed. 16.50x (ISBN 0-89197-857-7). Irvington.

Money & Finance: Readings in Theory, Policy & Institutions. 2nd ed. C. Deane Carson. LC 70-37643. 1972. text ed. 18.95 (ISBN 0-471-13712-X). Wiley.

Money & Finance: Sources of Print & Nonprint Materials. Barbara Ladley. (Neal-Schuman Sourcebook Ser.). 1980. 19.95x (ISBN 0-918212-23-5). Neal-Schuman.

Money & Financial Intermediation: The Theory & Structure of Financial Systems. Paul F. Smith. LC 77-21636. (Illus.). 1978. 19.95 (ISBN 0-13-600288-9). P-H.

Money & Inflation: Monetarist Approach. J. Houston McCulloch. 121p. 1975. 7.95 (ISBN 0-12-483050-1). Acad Pr.

Money & Information for Mental Health: Descriptive Directory of Federal & Private Resources. Ed. by Paul T. Wilson & Donna Becke. 1971. pap. 3.50 o.p. (ISBN 0-685-24849-6, 174). Am Psychiatric.

Money & Man: A Survey of Monetary Experience. Elgin Groseclose. LC 75-40960. 326p. 1976. 14.95 (ISBN 0-8061-1338-3); pap. 6.95 (ISBN 0-8061-1339-1). U of Okla Pr.

Money & Monetary Policy in Communist China. Katherine H. Hsiao. LC 77-158341. (Illus.). 1971. 20.00 (ISBN 0-231-03510-1). Columbia U Pr.

Money & Monetary Policy in Interdependent Nations. Ralph C. Bryant. LC 80-19225. 584p. 1980. 29.95 (ISBN 0-8157-1130-1); pap. 12.95 (ISBN 0-8157-1129-8). Brookings.

Money & Monetary Policy in Less Developed Countries: A Survey of Issues & Evidence. Ed. by Warren L. Coats & Deena R. Khatkhate, Jr. LC 79-42703. (Illus.). 834p. 1980. 105.00 (ISBN 0-08-024041-0); pap. 25.00 (ISBN 0-08-024042-9). Pergamon.

Money & Politics 1970-74: Contributions, Campaign Abuses, & the Law. Ed. by Lester A. Sobel. LC 74-81147. 225p. 1974. lib. bdg. 15.00x o.p. (ISBN 0-87196-262-4); pap. 4.95x o.p. (ISBN 0-87196-263-2). Facts on File.

Money & the Coming World Order. David P Calleo et al. LC 75-34673. 120p. 1976. 8.95x (ISBN 0-8147-1367-X); pap. 5.00x (ISBN 0-8147-1368-8). NYU Pr.

Money & the Real World. 2nd ed. Paul Davidson. 1978. pap. text ed. 14.95 (ISBN 0-470-99217-4). Halsted Pr.

Money Answers All Things. Jacob Vanderlint. LC 72-114079. 1978. 35.00x o.p. (ISBN 0-85409-233-1). Charles River Bks.

Money at Interest: The Farm Mortgage on the Middle Border. Allan G. Bogue. LC 55-1350. 1969. pap. 4.50x (ISBN 0-8032-5018-5, BB 396, Bison). U of Nebr Pr.

Money, Banking & Credit in Mediaeval Bruges. Raymond De Roover. 1966. Repr. of 1948 ed. 15.00 o.p. (ISBN 0-910956-25-1). Medieval Acad.

Money, Banking & Economic Analysis. Thomas Simpson. (Illus.). 496p. 1976. 18.95 (ISBN 0-13-600247-1). P-H.

Money, Banking & Macroeconomics: A Guide to Information Sources. Ed. by James M. Rock. LC 73-17585. (Economics Information Guide Ser.: Vol. 11). 1977. 30.00 (ISBN 0-8103-1300-6). Gale.

Money, Banking & Monetary Policy. Douglas Fisher. 1980. 18.95x (ISBN 0-256-02365-4). Irwin.

Money, Banking, & the Economy. Thomas Mayer et al. 1981. 16.95x (ISBN 0-393-95121-9). Norton.

Money Begets Money: A Guide to Personal Finance. Hancock Irving & Gary Zimmerman. LC 75-28508. 1975. pap. 5.00 (ISBN 0-916202-02-X). Zimmerman.

Money Book. Joan W. German. (Illus.). 32p. (ps-2). 1981. 5.95 (ISBN 0-525-66726-1). Elsevier-Nelson.

Money Book of Lists. Jeffrey Feinman. LC 79-6590. 432p. 1981. pap. 7.95 (ISBN 0-385-15444-5, Dolp). Doubleday.

Money: Christ's Perspective on the Use & Abuse of Money. Andrew Murray. 1978. pap. 1.50 (ISBN 0-87123-382-7, 200382). Bethany Fell.

Money Counts: A Handbook on Local Church Finance. Claude A. Horton. 88p. 1980. pap. 4.95 (ISBN 0-89367-051-0). Light & Life.

Money, Credit, & Interest Rates: Their Gross Mismanagement by the Federal Reserve System. Leon H. Keyserling & Conference of Economic Staff. (Illus.). 1980. 3.00. Conf Econ Prog.

Money Credit & the Economy. Richard Coghlan. (Illus.). 192p. 1981. text ed. 35.00x (ISBN 0-04-332079-1, 2649). Allen Unwin.

Money, Employment & Inflation. R. J. Barro & H. I. Grossman. LC 75-13449. (Illus.). 304p. 1976. 24.50x (ISBN 0-521-20906-4). Cambridge U Pr.

Money, Expectations & Business Cycles: Essays in Macroeconomics. Robert J. Barro. (Economic Theory, Econometrics & Mathematical Economic Ser.). 1981. write for info. (ISBN 0-12-079550-7). Acad Pr.

Money, Finance & Development. Peter J. Drake. 244p. 1980. 27.95x (ISBN 0-470-26992-8). Halsted Pr.

Money, Flow of Funds, & Economic Policy. Nathaniel Jackendoff. LC 68-30892. (Illus.). 523p. 1968. 20.95 (ISBN 0-8260-4730-0) (ISBN 0-471-07469-1). Wiley.

Money Game. David Ericson. (Pacesetters Ser.). (Illus.). 64p. (gr. 4 up). 1978. PLB 7.95 (ISBN 0-516-02156-7). Childrens.

Money Game. Adam Smith. LC 68-14526. 1968. 10.00 o.p. (ISBN 0-394-43667-9). Random.

Money Hard & Soft on the International Currency Markets. Brendan Brown. LC 78-16929. 1978. 21.95 (ISBN 0-470-26466-7). Halsted Pr.

Money: How to Get It, Keep It, & Make It Grow. Michael Hayes. (Illus.). 1979. 15.95 (ISBN 0-8144-5503-4). Am Mgmt.

Money: How to Save It, Spend It, & Make It. B. D. Coleman. 1969. 22.00 (ISBN 0-08-012936-6); pap. text ed. 10.75 (ISBN 0-08-012935-8). Pergamon.

Money: How to Spend Less & Have More. David J. Juroe. 1981. pap. 4.95 (ISBN 0-8007-5056-X). Revell.

Money in a Theory of Finance. John G. Gurley & Edward S. Shaw. 1960. 18.95 (ISBN 0-8157-3322-4). Brookings.

Money in Growing. 80p. 1980. pap. 6.95x (ISBN 0-901361-39-9, Pub. by Grower Bks England). Intl Schol Bk Serv.

Money in International Exchange: The Convertible Currency System. Ronald I. McKinnon. 1979. text ed. 13.95x (ISBN 0-19-502408-7); pap. text ed. 7.95x (ISBN 0-19-502409-5). Oxford U Pr.

Money-in-the-Bank Cookbook. Marie R. Hamm. 1970. pap. 1.25 o.s.i. (ISBN 0-02-009690-9, Collier). Macmillan.

Money in the Computer Age. F. P. Thomson. 1968. 23.00 (ISBN 0-08-012856-4); pap. 11.25 (ISBN 0-08-012855-6). Pergamon.

Money Is Love. Richard Condon. 320p. 1976. pap. 1.95 o.p. (ISBN 0-345-24971-2). Ballantine.

Money Is Not Enough. Winston Howard. 1980. 8.95 (ISBN 0-914244-05-1). Epic Pubns.

Money Isn't Everything. Kathlyn Gay. LC 67-10677. (Illus.). (gr. 4-6). 1967. PLB 4.58 o.s.i. (ISBN 0-440-05784-1). Delacorte.

Money, Magic, & Marriage. Barbara Cartland. (Orig.). pap. 1.75 (ISBN 0-515-05565-4). Jove Pubns.

Money Makes Sense. 2nd ed. Charles H. Kahn & J. Bradley Hanna. (Illus., Orig.). 1972. pap. 3.96 (ISBN 0-8224-4515-8); tchrs' manual free (ISBN 0-8224-5210-3). Pitman Learning.

Money-Making Advertising: Guide to Advertising That Sells. Victor Wademan. LC 80-19059. 128p. 1980. 16.95 (ISBN 0-471-06276-6, Pub. by Ronald Pr). Wiley.

Money-Making Photography. Bill Hurter. LC 80-81784. (Petersen's Photographic Libray). (Illus.). 160p. (Orig.). (gr. 8-12). pap. 8.95 (ISBN 0-8227-4040-0). Petersen Pub.

Money Management for Women. Rosalie Minkow. LC 80-84373. 256p. (Orig.). 1981. pap. 2.50 (ISBN 0-87216-816-6). Playboy Pbks.

Money Management in the Casino. Dean Wiley. (Gambler's Book Shelf). pap. 2.95 (ISBN 0-89650-584-7). Gamblers.

Money, Marbles & Chalk. Jimmy Banks. LC 70-180195. 1971. 2.95 o.p. (ISBN 0-685-48119-0). Shoal Creek Pub.

Money Market Calculations: Yields, Swaps, & Break-Even Prices. Marcia Stigum. 1981. 27.50 (ISBN 0-87094-192-5). Dow Jones-Irwin.

Money Marriage: A Novel. Elaine Suss. LC 79-23995. 240p. 1980. 9.95 (ISBN 0-8008-5319-9). Taplinger.

Money Mountain: The Story of Cripple Creek Gold. Marshall Sprague. LC 79-13838. (Illus.). 1979. 16.50x (ISBN 0-8032-4104-6); pap. 5.95 (ISBN 0-8032-9103-5, BB696, Bison). U of Nebr Pr.

Money Plays. Morton Beckner. 1980. 10.95 (ISBN 0-686-68751-5, 25122). S&S.

Money, Questions & Answers. Charles E. Coughlin. 1978. pap. 4.00x (ISBN 0-911038-28-0). Noontide.

Money-Savers' Do-It-Yourself Car Repair. Leroy Smith. LC 73-18509. (Illus.). 320p. 1975. 12.95 (ISBN 0-02-611940-4). Macmillan.

Money Saver's Guide to Decorating. Ellen Liman. LC 74-109451. 1971. 7.95 o.s.i. (ISBN 0-02-572300-6). Macmillan.

Money Saver's Guide to Decorating. Ellen Liman. (Illus.). 296p. 1972. pap. 1.95 o.s.i. (ISBN 0-02-080530-6, Collier). Macmillan.

Money Saving Conservation Products & Projects for the Homeowner. Stephen Kokette. LC 78-55883. 1978. pap. 5.95 (ISBN 0-932314-07-4). Aylmer Pr.

Money Saving Recipes Through Sprouting & Gardening. Bruford S. Reynolds. pap. 4.95 (ISBN 0-89036-134-7). Hawkes Pub Inc.

Money Sermons. Norm Lucas. 94p. (Orig.). 1980. pap. text ed. 4.65 (ISBN 0-89536-457-3). CSS Pub.

Money Stones. Ian St. James. LC 80-65984. 1980. 9.95 (ISBN 0-689-11104-5). Atheneum.

Money Supply, Money Demand & Macroeconomic Models. John T. Boorman & Thomas M. Havrilesky. LC 79-167998. 1972. pap. 11.95x (ISBN 0-88295-400-8). AHM Pub.

Money Talks, It Says Good-by. Bill King & Pat King. 112p. 1977. 3.45 (ISBN 0-930756-31-2, 4230-K14). Women's Aglow.

Money Talks: Language & Lucre in American Fiction. Ed. by Roy R. Male. LC 80-5945. 160p. 1981. 14.95 (ISBN 0-8061-1754-0). U of Okla Pr.

Money That Money Can't Buy. James Munro. 288p. 1981. pap. 2.50 (ISBN 0-441-53698-0). Charter Bks.

Money, the Financial System, & Monetary Policy. Thomas F. Cargill. (Illus.). 1979. ref. 18.95 (ISBN 0-13-600346-X). P-H.

Money: The Price Level & Interest Rates - an Introduction to Monetary Theory. Gil Makinen. (Illus.). 1977. ref. ed. 20.95 (ISBN 0-13-600486-5). P-H.

Money: Theory, Policy & Institutions. Andrew D. Crockett. 1973. pap. text ed. 14.95x (ISBN 0-17-712206-4). Intl Ideas.

Money Today, More Tomorrow. Milton Smith. 320p. 1981. 14.95 (ISBN 0-87626-593-X); pap. text ed. 9.95 (ISBN 0-87626-592-1). Winthrop.

Money, Work & Crime: A Field Experiment in Reducing Recidivism Through Postrelease Financial Aid to Prisoners. Peter H. Rossi et al. LC 80-512. (Quantitative Studies in Social Relations Ser.). 1980. 29.00 (ISBN 0-12-598240-2). Acad Pr.

Moneylove. Jerry Gillies. 1979. pap. 2.50 (ISBN 0-446-91009-0). Warner Bks.

Moneyman. Judith Liederman. 1980. pap. 2.75 (ISBN 0-451-09164-7, E9164, Sig). NAL.

Moneywise Guide to North America: Canada - U S. A. -Mexico 1980-81. (Illus.). 328p. 1980-81. pap. 9.95 (ISBN 0-88254-545-0, Pub. by Travelaid England). Hippocrene Bks.

Moneywise Guide to North America Canada, USA, Mexico. rev. ed. Michael Von Haag & Anna Crew. (Travelaid Travel Bks.). (Illus., Orig.). 1978. pap. 5.95 (ISBN 0-8467-0438-2, Pub. by Two Continents). Hippocrene Bks.

Moneywise Guide to North America: Canada, U. S. A., Mexico. 13th ed. 1979. pap. 5.95 (ISBN 0-902743-15-5, Pub. by Two Continents). Hippocrene Bks.

Moneywise: The Prentice-Hall Book of Personal Money Management. Richard J. Stillman. LC 77-25493. (Illus.). 1978. 14.95 o.p. (ISBN 0-13-600734-1). P-H.

Mongkut, the King of Siam. Abbot L. Moffat. (Illus.). 254p. (YA) (gr. 9-12). 1968. pap. 3.95 (ISBN 0-8014-9069-3, CP69). Cornell U Pr.

Mongol World Empire, 1206-1370. J. A. Boyle. 316p. 1980. 60.00x (ISBN 0-86078-002-3, Pub. by Variorum England). State Mutual Bk.

Mongolian Language Handbook. Nicholas Poppe. LC 72-125673. (Language Handbook Ser.). 1970. pap. text ed. 5.00 (ISBN 0-87281-003-8). Ctr Appl Ling.

Mongolian Short Stories. Ed. by Henry G. Schwarz. LC 74-620031. (Program in East Asian Studies Occasional Papers Ser: No. 8). (Illus.). 190p. 1974. pap. 5.00 o.p. (ISBN 0-914584-08-1). West Wash Univ.

Mongolian Studies: Dedicated to the Second International Congress of Mongolists, to Its Organizers, the Mongolian Scholars, Budapest, 1970. Ed. by Louis Ligeti. (Bibliotheca Orientalis Hungrica). 1970. text ed. 48.50x (ISBN 90-6032-352-1). Humanities.

Mongolia's Culture & Society. Sechin Jagchid & Paul Hyer. LC 79-1438. (Illus.). 461p. 1980. 35.00x (ISBN 0-89158-390-4). Westview.

Mongols et la Papaute, 3 pts. in 1 vol. Paul Pelliot. LC 80-2365. 1981. Repr. of 1923 ed. 34.50 (ISBN 0-404-18913-X). AMS Pr.

Mongols of Manchuria. Owen Lattimore. LC 68-9626. 1969. Repr. of 1934 ed. 18.00 (ISBN 0-86527-132-1). Fertig.

Monheim's General Anesthesia in Dental Practice. 4th ed. C. Richard Bennett. LC 73-4653. (Illus.). 446p. 1974. text ed. 21.00 o.p. (ISBN 0-8016-0608-X). Mosby.

Monique. Madelyn Cunningham. (Historical Romance Ser.). (Orig.). 1979. pap. 2.50 (ISBN 0-515-05113-6). Jove Pubns.

Moniseur Jones. James C. Wyatt. 1980. 7.95 (ISBN 0-533-04457-X). Vantage.

Monitor, the Miners & the Shree. Lee Killough. (Orig.). 1980. pap. 1.95 (ISBN 0-345-28456-9). Ballantine.

Monitoring: Breakfast & Lunch Program in New York City Schools. 1976. 1.00 (ISBN 0-86671-026-4). Comm Coun Great NY.

Monitoring Cerebral Function: Long-Term Recordings of Cerebral Electrical Activity. Pamela Prior. LC 78-14390. (Illus.). 1979. text ed. 30.00x (ISBN 0-397-58251-X). Lippincott.

Monitoring Drug Therapy in the Long-Term Care Facility. LC 77-93746. 1978. 36.00 (ISBN 0-917330-19-6). Am Pharm Assn.

Monitoring for Government Agencies. John D. Waller et al. (Institute Paper). 170p. 1976. pap. 5.00 (ISBN 0-87766-142-1, 11600). Urban Inst.

Monitoring Heart Rhythm. C. P. Summerall, 3rd et al. 1976. 14.50 (ISBN 0-471-83556-0). Wiley.

Monitoring in Anesthesia. Lawrence J. Saidman & N. Ty Smith. LC 77-12506. (Anesthesiology Ser.). 1977. 33.50 (ISBN 0-471-74980-X, Pub. by Wiley Medical). Wiley.

Monitoring National Standards of Attainment in Schools. Ed. by Ray Sumner. (Council of Europe: European Trend Reports on Educational Research Ser.: No. 5). (Illus.). 1977. pap. text ed. 38.50x (ISBN 0-85633-144-9, NFER). Humanities.

Monitoring of Airborne & Liquid Radioactive Releases from Nuclear Facilities to the Environment. (Safety Ser.: No. 46). 1978. pap. 10.75 (ISBN 92-0-123178-4, ISP482, IAEA). Unipub.

Monitoring of Radioactive Contamination on Surfaces. R. F. Clayton. (Technical Reports Ser.: No. 120). (Illus., Orig.). 1970. pap. 5.00 (ISBN 92-0-125570-5, IDC 120, IAEA). Unipub.

Monitoring of Radioactive Effluents from Nuclear Facilities. 1978. pap. 62.25 (ISBN 92-0-020078-8, ISP 466, IAEA). Unipub.

Monitoring of Vital Parameters During Extracorporeal Circulation. H. P. Kimmich. (Illus.). 1981. soft cover 72.00 (ISBN 3-8055-2059-X). S Karger.

Monitoring Revenue Sharing. Richard P. Nathan et al. 394p. 1975. 14.95 (ISBN 0-8157-5984-3); pap. 5.95 (ISBN 0-8157-5983-5). Brookings.

Monitoring Surgical Patients in the Operating Room. J. S. Gravenstein et al. (Illus.). 288p. 1979. 25.75 (ISBN 0-398-03774-4). C C Thomas.

Monitoring the Inpacts of Prison & Parole Services: An Initial Examination. Louis H. Blair et al. (Institute Paper). 88p. 1977. pap. 3.95 (ISBN 0-87766-201-0, 16900). Urban Inst.

Monitoring the Marine Environment. Ed. by David Nichols. LC 78-71806. 220p. 1979. 27.95 (ISBN 0-03-050746-4). Praeger.

Monitoring the Outcome of Social Services, 2 vols. Annie Millar et al. Incl. Vol. 1. Preliminary Suggestions (ISBN 0-87766-194-4, 19100); Vol. 2. Review of Past Research & Test Activities (ISBN 0-87766-200-2, 19200). (Institute Paper). 1977. Set. pap. 7.00 (ISBN 0-686-53140-X, 20600); pap. 4.00 ea. Urban Inst.

Monitoring the Outcomes of State Chronic Disease Control Programs: Some Initial Suggestions. Alfred H. Schainblatt. (Institute Paper). 60p. 1977. pap. 4.00 (ISBN 0-87766-205-3, 19800). Urban Inst.

Monitoring the Outcomes of State Mental Health Treatment Programs: Some Initial Suggestions. Alfred H. Schainblatt. (Institute Paper). 86p. 1977. pap. 4.00 (ISBN 0-87766-202-9, 19400). Urban Inst.

Monitoring Toxic Gases in the Atmosphere. William Thain. 1980. 25.00 (ISBN 0-08-023810-6). Pergamon.

Monitoring: What Happens to Children Out of School. 1976. 2.00 (ISBN 0-86671-028-0). Comm Coun Great NY.

Monk & the Hangman's Daughter. Ambrose Bierce. 143p. 1976. Repr. of 1911 ed. lib. bdg. 8.35 (ISBN 0-89190-183-3). Am Repr-Rivercity Pr.

Monk Who Shook the World (Martin Luther) Cyril Davey. 1960. pap. 1.95 (ISBN 0-87508-614-4). Chr Lit.

Monkey & The Crocodile. Paul Galdone. LC 78-79939. (Illus.). (ps-2). 1969. 8.95 (ISBN 0-395-28806-1, Clarion). HM.

Monkey & the Pumpkin. John J. Sullivan. 1978. 4.50 o.p. (ISBN 0-533-03077-3). Vantage.

Monkey Book. Jan Pfloog. (Illus.). 24p. (ps-4). 1977. Repr. of 1969 ed. PLB 5.38 (ISBN 0-307-68953-0, Golden Pr). Western Pub.

Monkey Business. Gus Augspurg & Casey Augspurg. (Illus.). 1957. pap. 1.79 o.p. (ISBN 0-87666-211-4, AP8052). TFH Pubns.

Monkey Face. Frank Asch. LC 76-18101. (Illus.). 40p. (ps-2). 1977. 5.95 o.s.i. (ISBN 0-8193-0862-5, Four Winds); PLB 5.41 o.s.i. (ISBN 0-8193-0863-3). Schol Bk Serv.

Monkey in the Family. Louisa Johnston & Mable C. Bristle. LC 73-188431. (Illus.). 128p. (gr. 3-7). 1972. 5.95g o.p. (ISBN 0-8075-5256-9). A Whitman.

Monkey King. Timothy Mo. LC 79-7875. 288p. 1980. 10.95 (ISBN 0-385-15621-9). Doubleday.

Monkey Mountain. Craig Hiler. 1979. pap. 2.25 (ISBN 0-505-51403-6). Tower Bks.

Monkey Wrench Gang. Edward Abbey. LC 75-831. 352p. 1975. 8.95 o.s.i. (ISBN 0-397-01084-2). Lippincott.

Monkeys. Ed. by Lynn Hughes. LC 80-57619. (Illus.). 56p. 1980. 4.95 (ISBN 0-89480-098-1). Workman Pub.

Monkeys. Cynthia Overbeck. (Lerner Natural Science Bks.). (Illus.). (gr. 4-10). 1981. PLB 7.95 (ISBN 0-8225-1464-8). Lerner Pubns.

Monkeys. Herbert S. Zim. (Illus.). (gr. 3-7). 1955. PLB 6.48 (ISBN 0-688-31517-8). Morrow.

Monkeys & Apes. Jane Annixter & Paul Annixter. LC 76-9834. (First Bks.). (Illus.). 72p. (gr. 4-6). 1976. PLB 4.90 o.p. (ISBN 0-531-00322-1). Watts.

Monkeys & Apes. (Wild, Wild World of Animals Ser). 1976. 10.95 (ISBN 0-913948-03-9). Time-Life.

Monkeys & Apes. LC 75-40056. (Wild, Wild World of Animals). (Illus.). (gr. 5 up). 1976. lib. bdg. 11.97 (ISBN 0-685-73290-8). Silver.

Monkeys & Apes. Dean Morris. LC 77-8148. (Read About Animals Ser.). (Illus.). (gr. k-3). 1977. PLB 9.95 (ISBN 0-8393-0005-0). Raintree Child.

Monkey's Paw. rev. ed. Jean N. Dale. (Reading & Exercise Ser.: No. 5). 1976. pap. 2.50 (ISBN 0-89285-054-X); cassette tapes 29.50 (ISBN 0-89285-072-8). ELS Intl.

Monkey's Paw. Ed. by Jean N. Dale. (Reading & Exercise Ser.). (Illus.). (gr. k-6). 1974. pap. text ed. 2.50x (ISBN 0-19-433623-9). Oxford U Pr.

Monkey's Tail: A Study in Evolution & Parapsychology. T. C. Lethbridge. (Illus.). 1969. 12.00 (ISBN 0-7100-6598-1). Routledge & Kegan.

Monkeyshines for a Laughing Lunacy. Alfred D. Niess. 1978. pap. 4.95 (ISBN 0-686-15529-7). S&S Co OR.

Monks & Love in Twelfth-Century France: Psycho-Historical Essays. Jean Leclercq. 156p. 1979. text ed. 28.50x (ISBN 0-19-822546-6). Oxford U Pr.

Monks & Magic: An Analysis of Religious Ceremonies in Central Thailand. Bareno J. Terweil. (Scandinavian Institute of Asian Studies Monographs: No. 24). (Orig.). 1976. pap. text ed. 13.75x (ISBN 0-7007-0091-9). Humanities.

Monks, Bishops, & Pagans: Christian Culture in Gaul & Italy. Ed. by Edward Peters. Incl. Selections from the Minor Writings. Gregory Of Tours. Ed. by William C. McDermott. LC 74-33702. (Middle Ages Ser). 256p. 1975. pap. text ed. 5.95x (ISBN 0-8122-1069-7, Pa Paperbks). U of Pa Pr.

Monk's Court. Katherine W. Eyre. pap. 0.95 o.p. (ISBN 0-451-06081-4, Q6081, Sig). NAL.

Monk's-Hood. Ellis Peter. 224p. 1981. 9.95. Morrow.

Monks of Durham. Anne Boyd. LC 74-14438. (Introduction to the History of Mankind Ser). (Illus.). 48p. (gr. 6-11). 1975. text ed. 3.95 (ISBN 0-521-20647-2). Cambridge U Pr.

Monmouth Rebellion: A Social History Including the Complete Text of "Wade's Narrative," 1685 & "a Guide to the Battlefield of Sidgemoor". W. MacDonald Wigfield. (Illus.). 176p. 1980. 24.50x (ISBN 0-389-20149-9). B&N.

Monnaies Grecques Antiques et Romaines. R. Jameson. 1007p. (Fr.). 1980. Repr. 295.00 (ISBN 0-916710-65-3). Obol Intl.

Mono-Olefins: Chemistry & Technology. H. Asinger. 1969. text ed. 150.00 (ISBN 0-08-011547-0). Pergamon.

Monoamine Oxidase: Structure, Function & Altered Functions. Ed. by Thomas P. Singer et al. LC 79-24107. 1980. 39.00 (ISBN 0-12-646880-X). Acad Pr.

Monoamine Oxidases - New Vistas. Ed. by E. Costa & M. Sandler. LC 73-84113. (Advances in Biochemical Psychopharmacology Ser.: Vol. 5). (Illus.). 1972. 34.50 (ISBN 0-911216-19-7). Raven.

Monoamine Oxidases & Their Selective Inhibition: Proceedings of the Third Congress of the Hungarian Pharmacological Society, Budapest, 1979. Ed. by K. Magyar. LC 80-41281. (Advances in Pharmacological Research Practice Ser.: Vol. IV). 165p. 1981. 30.00 (ISBN 0-08-026389-5). Pergamon.

Monochromes. Ella D'Arcy. Ed. by Ian Fletcher & John Stokes. LC 76-20056. (Decadent Consciousness Ser.). 1978. lib. bdg. 38.00 (ISBN 0-8240-2754-X). Garland Pub.

Monoclonal Antibodies. Ed. by Roger H. Kennett et al. (Illus.). 375p. 1980. 29.50 (ISBN 0-306-40408-7, Plenum Pr). Plenum Pub.

Monoclonal Antibodies Against Neural Antigens. Ed. by Ron McKay et al. (Cold Spring Harbor Reports in the Neurosciences). 300p. 1981. price not set (ISBN 0-87969-138-7). Cold Spring Harbor.

Monoclonal Gammopathies: Multiple Myeloma & Related Plasma-Cell Disorders. Robert A. Kyle & Edwin A. Bayrd. (Amer. Lec. Living Chemistry Ser.). (Illus.). 432p. 1976. 48.75 (ISBN 0-398-03545-8). C C Thomas.

Monocytes, Monocytosis & Monocytic Leukemia. Lawrence Kass & Bertram Schnitzer. (Illus.). 120p. 1973. 23.75 (ISBN 0-398-02883-4). C C Thomas.

Monodromos. Marian Engel. LC 73-85572. (Anansi Fiction Ser.: No. 27). 250p. 1973. 11.95 (ISBN 0-88784-436-7, Pub. by Hse Anansi Pr Canada). U of Toronto Pr.

Monogram Close-up: Kikka. (Close-up Ser.: No. 19). (Illus.). Date not set. pap. 5.95 (ISBN 0-914144-19-7, Pub. by Monogram). Aviation.

Monogram Close-up: Mess Bf-109k. Ed. by Thomas H. Hitchcock. (Close-up Ser.: No. 16). Date not set. pap. 5.95 (ISBN 0-914144-16-2, Pub. by Monogram). Aviation.

Monogram Close-up: Taifun. Ed. by Thomas H. Hitchcock. (Close-up Ser.: No. 5). (Illus.). Date not set. pap. 5.95 (ISBN 0-914144-05-7, Pub. by Momogram). Aviation.

Monograpgh of Ceratocystis & Ceratocystiopsis. H. P. Upadhyay. (Illus.). 288p. 1981. 27.50x (ISBN 0-8203-0539-1). U of Ga Pr.

Monograph of Ramaria Subgenus Echinoramaria. R. H. Petersen. (Bibliotheca Mycologica). (Illus.). 150p. 1980. lib. bdg. 30.00x (ISBN 0-686-28365-1). Lubrecht & Cramer.

Monograph of the Genus Anaptychia. S. Kurokawa. 1962. pap. 20.00 (ISBN 3-7682-5406-2). Lubrecht & Cramer.

Monograph of the Genus Lasianthaea (Asteraceae) Kenneth M. Becker. (Memoirs Ser.: Vol. 31, No. 2). 1979. pap. 6.50 (ISBN 0-89327-211-6). NY Botanical.

Monograph of the Ithomiidae: Napeogenini, Pt. 4. R. M. Fox & H. G. Real. (Memoirs Ser: No. 15). (Illus.). 368p. 1971. 25.00 (ISBN 0-686-01270-4). Am Entom Inst.

Monographia Cladaoniarum Universalis, 3 vols. E. A. Wainio. 1278p. (Lat. & Fr.). 1978. Set. lib. bdg. 200.00x (ISBN 3-87429-135-9). Lubrecht & Cramer.

Monographic Revision of the Heliothripinae of the World - Thysanoptera. Wilson. (Memoirs Ser: No. 23). (Illus.). 354p. 1974. 25.00 (ISBN 0-686-17150-0). Am Entom Inst.

Monographic Searching on the OCLC Terminal: A Programmed Text with Teacher's Guide. Jinnie Y. Davis & Joseph B. Abrera. (Illus.). 1980. pap. 14.50x (ISBN 0-208-01843-3, Linnet). Shoe String.

Monographie der Harpacticiden. K. Lang. (Illus.). 1682p. (Ger.). 1975. Repr. of 1948 ed. lib. bdg. 240.00x (ISBN 3-87429-089-1). Lubrecht & Cramer.

Monographie von Masdevallia Ruiz et Pavon Lothiana Kraenz: Scaphosepalum Pfitzer, Cryptophorantus Bearb, Rodr., Pseudostomeria Kraenzl. R. Kraenzlin. (Feddes Repertorium: Beiheft 34). 240p. (Ger.). 1980. Repr. of 1925 ed. lib. bdg. 47.85x (Pub. by Koeltz Germany). Lubrecht & Cramer.

Monographs & Papers in Maya Archaeology. Ed. by William R. Bullard, Jr. LC 72-105721. (Peabody Museum Papers: Vol. 61). 1970. pap. text ed. 40.00 (ISBN 0-87365-175-8). Peabody Harvard.

Monographs of the Shallow-Water Indo-West Pacific Echinoderms. Ailsa M. Clark & Francis W. Rowe. (Illus.). ix, 238p. 1971. 46.00x (ISBN 0-565-00690-8, Pub. by Brit Mus Nat Hist England). Sabbot-Natural Hist Bks.

Monographs on Fragrance Raw Materials. Ed. by D. L. Opdyke. (Illus.). 1979. 140.00 (ISBN 0-08-023775-4). Pergamon.

Monographs on Plastic Surgery, Vol. 1. Robert C. Bell. (Illus.). 200p. 1973. text ed. 18.50x o.p. (ISBN 0-19-265106-4). Oxford U Pr.

Monologue to Dialogue: An Exploration of Interpersonal Commuication. 2nd ed. Charles T. Brown & Paul T. Keller. LC 78-16541. (Special Communication Ser.). 1979. pap. 11.95 (ISBN 0-13-600825-9). P-H.

Monologues for the Actor. Robert Westrom. 60p. (Orig.). 1978. pap. 2.50 (ISBN 0-938230-02-6). Westrom.

Monon Route. George W. Hilton. LC 78-52512. (Illus.). 468p. 1978. Repr. of 1978 ed. 30.00 (ISBN 0-8310-7115-X). Howell-North.

Monoprints for the Artist. Roger Marsh. (gr. 10 up). 1969. pap. 7.50 (ISBN 0-85458-549-4). Transatlantic.

Monotypes of Joseph Solman. Joseph Solman. (Illus.). 1977. lib. bdg. 18.95 (ISBN 0-306-77425-9). Da Capo.

Monroe Doctrine. Hiram Bingham. (Latin America in the 20th Century Ser.). 1976. Repr. of 1913 ed. lib. bdg. 15.00 (ISBN 0-306-70833-7). Da Capo.

Monroe Doctrine, 3 vols. Dexter Perkins. Incl. 1823-1826. 8.00 (ISBN 0-685-22731-6); 1826-1867. 9.50 (ISBN 0-685-22732-4); 1867-1907. 9.50 (ISBN 0-685-22733-2). Set (ISBN 0-8446-1346-0). Peter Smith.

Monroe Doctrine & American Expansionism 1843-1849. Frederick Merk. 320p. 1972. pap. 1.95 o.p. (ISBN 0-394-71760-0, V760, Vin). Random.

Monroe Doctrine, 1823: A Landmark in American Foreign Policy. Harold Vaughan. LC 72-8853. (Focus Bks.). (Illus.). 72p. (gr. 7 up). 1973. PLB 4.90 o.p. (ISBN 0-531-02461-X). Watts.

Monroe's Island. Gregory Brooks. LC 79-1568. (Illus.). (ps-1). 1979. 7.95 (ISBN 0-87888-140-9). Bradbury Pr.

Mons Perfectionis. John Alcock. LC 74-28823. (English Experience Ser.: No. 706). 1974. Repr. of 1497 ed. 6.00 (ISBN 90-221-0706-X). Walter J Johnson.

Monsoon Dynamics. Ed. by J. Lighthill & R. P. Pearce. LC 78-72091. (Illus.). 700p. Date not set. 130.00 (ISBN 0-521-22497-7). Cambridge U Pr.

Monsoon Murder. Brian Cooper. LC 68-8081. 1968. 6.95 (ISBN 0-8149-0042-9). Vanguard.

Monsoon-Poems. Bina Agarwal. 1976. 8.00 (ISBN 0-89253-807-4); flexible cloth 4.00 (ISBN 0-89253-808-2). Ind-US Inc.

Monster at Loch Ness. Sally Berke. LC 77-24715. (Great Unsolved Mysteries Ser.). (Illus.). (gr. 4-5). 1977. PLB 9.65 (ISBN 0-8172-1054-7). Raintree Pubs.

Monster at the End of This Book. Jon Stone. (Illus.). (gr. k-2). 1976. PLB 5.00 (ISBN 0-307-60316-4, Golden Pr). Western Pub.

Monster at the End of This Book. Jon Stone. (Illus.). (ps-2). 1977. 1.95 (ISBN 0-307-10506-7, Golden Pr); PLB 7.62 (ISBN 0-307-60506-X). Western Pub.

Monster Behind Black Rock. Varga. (Illus.). (gr. 3). 1980. pap. 3.50 incl. record (ISBN 0-590-24005-6, Schol Pap). Schol Bk Serv.

Monster Books: Set 1, 12 bks. Ellen Blance et al. Incl. Monster Comes to the City (ISBN 0-8372-0826-2); Monster Looks for a House (ISBN 0-8372-0827-0); Monster Cleans His House (ISBN 0-8372-0828-9); Monster Looks for a Friend (ISBN 0-8372-0829-7); Monster on the Bus (ISBN 0-8372-0830-0); Monster Meets Lady Monster (ISBN 0-8372-0831-9); Monster Goes to the Museum (ISBN 0-8372-0832-7); Monster Goes to School (ISBN 0-8372-0833-5); Monster at School (ISBN 0-8372-0834-3); Monster & the Magic Umbrella (ISBN 0-8372-0835-1); Monster Has a Party (ISBN 0-8372-0836-X); Monster Goes to the Zoo (ISBN 0-8372-0837-8). (Illus., Avail. in Spanish). (ps-3). 1973. pap. 1.38 ea.; pap. 141.60 set of 10 ea. of 12 titles & tchr's. guide (ISBN 0-8372-0300-7, 300); pap. 15.00 set of monster bks. - 1 ea. title & tchr's. guide (ISBN 0-8372-0301-5, 301). Bowmar-Noble.

Monster Bubbles: A Counting Book. Dennis Nolan. LC 76-10167. 1976. PLB 5.95 (ISBN 0-13-600635-3); pap. 1.95 (ISBN 0-13-600643-4). P-H.

Monster Festival: Classic Tales of the Macabre. Ed. by Eric Protter. LC 79-56028. (Illus.). (gr. 7 up). 10.00 (ISBN 0-8149-0377-0). Vanguard.

Monster Fly. Charles A. Piddock. Ed. by Patricia McCarthy. (Pal Paperbacks Kit Ser.). (Illus., Orig.). (gr. 7-12). pap. text ed. 1.25 (ISBN 0-8374-3475-0). Xerox Ed Pubns.

Monster for a Day: Or, the Monster in Gregory's Pajamas. Frank Kaff. LC 79-1866. (Illus.). (ps-3). 1979. 1.95 (ISBN 0-525-69002-6, Gingerbread Bks); PLB 5.95 (ISBN 0-525-69003-4). Dutton.

Monster Gallery. Leah Waskey. (Fantasy Ser.). (Illus.). 32p. 1973. pap. 3.50 (ISBN 0-912300-32-9, 32-9). Troubador Pr.

Monster in the Mirror: Studies in Nineteenth-Century Realism. Ed. by D. Z. Williams. 1978. 34.50x (ISBN 0-19-713433-5). Oxford U Pr.

Monster Is Coming! a Monster Is Coming! Florence P. Heide & Roxanne Heide. (gr. k-3). 1980. 3.95 (ISBN 0-531-03449-6); PLB 6.45 (ISBN 0-531-04136-0). Watts.

Monster Madness Outrageous Jokes About Weird Folks. Jack Stokes. LC 80-2068. (Illus.). 64p. (gr. 6). 1981. 8.95a (ISBN 0-385-15690-1); PLB (ISBN 0-385-15691-X). Doubleday.

Monster Madness: Riddles, Jokes, & Fun. Joseph Rosenbloom. LC 80-52339. (Illus.). 128p. (gr. 2 up). 1980. 5.95 (ISBN 0-8069-4634-2); PLB 6.69 (ISBN 0-8069-4635-0). Sterling.

Monster Masks. Chester J. Alkema. (Little Craft Book Ser.). (Illus.). 48p. (gr. 7 up). 1973. 4.95 o.p. (ISBN 0-8069-5256-3); PLB 5.89 o.p. (ISBN 0-8069-5257-1). Sterling.

Monster Masterpieces, 3 bks. Robert L. Stevenson et al. 1980. pap. 3.75 boxed set (ISBN 0-307-13621-3, Golden Pr). Western Pub.

Monster! Monster! David Harrison. (Eager Readers Ser). (gr. k-3). 1975. PLB 5.00 (ISBN 0-307-60808-5, Golden Pr). Western Pub.

Monster Myths of Ancient Greece. William Wise. (Illus.). 48p. (gr. 7-11). 1981. PLB 6.99 (ISBN 0-399-61143-6). Putnam.

Monster on Wheels. George Ancona. (Illus.). 48p. (gr. 3 up). 1974. PLB 8.95 (ISBN 0-525-35155-8). Dutton.

Monster That Wouldn't Die. Steve Otfinoski. Ed. by Mary Verdick. (Pal Paperbacks Ser., Kit A). (Illus., Orig.). (gr. 7-12). 1976. pap. text ed. 1.25 (ISBN 0-8374-3497-1). Xerox Ed Pubns.

Monsters & Medics. James White. (Del Rey Bk.). 1977. pap. 1.50 o.p. (ISBN 0-345-25623-9). Ballantine.

Monsters: Creatures of Mystery. Nancy Christensen. LC 79-55011. (Illus.). 48p. (gr. 2-8). 1980. 5.95 (ISBN 0-448-47485-9); PLB 11.85 (ISBN 0-448-13622-8). Platt.

Monsters from the Movies. Thomas G. Aylesworth. 160p. (gr. 4-6). pap. 1.95 (ISBN 0-553-15091-X, Skylark). Bantam.

Monsters, Monsters, Monsters. Helen Hoke. LC 75-6045. (Terrific Triple Titles Ser). 187p. (gr. 7 up). 1975. PLB 6.90 o.p. (ISBN 0-531-02846-1). Watts.

Monsters of Loch Ness: The First Complete Scientific Study & Its Startling Conclusions. Roy P. Mackal. LC 76-3139. (Illus.). 401p. 1980. pap. 8.95 (ISBN 0-8040-0704-7). Swallow.

Monsters of North America. Elwood D. Baumann. (Illus.). (gr. 5 up). 1978. PLB 7.90 s&l (ISBN 0-531-02246-3). Watts.

Monsters of Star Trek. Daniel Cohen. (Illus., Orig.). (gr. 4 up). 1980. pap. 1.75 (ISBN 0-671-56057-3, HI/LO). Archway.

Monsters of Star Trek. Daniel Cohen. (Illus.). 1980. pap. 1.75 (ISBN 0-671-56057-3). PB.

Monsters of the Mountains. Jon Jameson. (Easy-Read Facts Bks.). (Illus.). (gr. 2-4). 1979. PLB 6.45 s&l (ISBN 0-531-02269-2). Watts.

Monsters' Room. Campbell. (gr. 3-5). pap. 1.25 (ISBN 0-590-02076-5, Schol Pap). Schol Bk Serv.

Monsters: Their Histories, Homes & Habits. Perle Epstein. LC 72-97496. 128p. (gr. 6-9). 1973. 6.95 o.p. (ISBN 0-385-04874-2). Doubleday.

Monsters to Know & Love. Steven Otfinoski. Ed. by Mary Verdick. (Beginning Pal Paperbacks Ser.). (Illus., Orig.). (gr. 7-12). 1977. pap. text ed. 1.25 (ISBN 0-8374-3455-6). Xerox Ed Pubns.

Monstre dans le Metro et d'Autres Merveilles. Joseph F. Conroy. (gr. 7-12). 1974. wkbk. 4.58 (ISBN 0-87720-469-1). AMSCO Sch.

Monstrous Glisson Glop. Dianne R. Massie. LC 71-93856. (Illus.). (gr. k-3). 1970. 5.95 o.s.i. (ISBN 0-8193-0380-1, Four Winds); PLB 5.41 o.s.i. (ISBN 0-8193-0381-X). Schol Bk Serv.

Monstrous Races in Medieval Art & Thought. John B. Friedman. LC 80-23181. (Illus.). 272p. 1981. text ed. 20.00 (ISBN 0-674-58652-2). Harvard U Pr.

Mont Cant Gold. Paul Fisher. LC 80-23851. 264p. (gr. 5-9). 1981. PLB 10.95 (ISBN 0-689-30808-6, Argo). Atheneum.

Montagnards of South Vietnam. (Minority Rights Group: No. 18). 1974. pap. 2.50 (ISBN 0-89192-104-4). Interbk Inc.

Montagu Cave in Prehistory: A Descriptive Analysis. Charles M. Keller. (U. C. Publ. in Anthropological Records: Vol. 28). 1973. pap. 12.50x (ISBN 0-520-09401-8). U of Cal Pr.

Montague Rhodes James. Richard W. Pfaff. (Illus.). 461p. 1980. 40.00x (ISBN 0-85967-554-8, Pub. by Scolar Pr England). Biblio Dist.

Montague's Modern Bottle Identification & Price Guide. (Illus.). pap. 9.95 (ISBN 0-686-51546-3). Wallace-Homestead.

Montaigne. Marcel Tetel. LC 74-2250. (World Authors Ser.: France: No. 317). 1974. lib. bdg. 12.50 (ISBN 0-8057-2623-3). Twayne.

Montaigne: Selections from the Essays. Michel De Montaigne. Ed. & tr. by Donald M. Frame. LC 72-96557. (Crofts Classics Ser.). 1973. pap. text ed. 2.95x (ISBN 0-88295-105-X). AHM Pub.

Montana. 23.00 (ISBN 0-89770-102-X). Curriculum Info Ctr.

Montana: A History. Clark C. Spence. (States & the Nation Ser.). (Illus.). 1978. 12.95 (ISBN 0-393-05679-1, Co-Pub by AASLH). Norton.

Montana: A State Guide Book. Federal Writers' Project. 430p. 1939. Repr. 45.00 (ISBN 0-403-02176-6). Somerset Pub.

Montana Bound: An Activity Approach to Teaching Montana History. Bruce Whitehead & Charlotte Whitehead. (Illus.). 180p. (gr. 5-6). 1980. pap. text ed. 7.95x (ISBN 0-87108-235-7). Pruett.

Montana Bullwhacker. C. C. Rouse. LC 69-17694. 1969. pap. 4.95 (ISBN 0-8163-0122-0, 13644-0). Pacific Pr Pub Assn.

Montana: In Words & Pictures. Dennis Fradin. LC 80-25023. (Young People's Stories of Our States Ser.). (Illus.). 48p. (gr. 2-5). 1981. PLB 8.65g (ISBN 0-516-03926-1, Time Line). Childrens.

Montana Industrial Minerals. 1975. 15.20. Minobras.

Montana: Our Land & People. William Lang. (Illus.). 1981. pap. 11.95 (ISBN 0-87108-586-0). Pruett.

Montana Showdown. LC 77-79431. (John Slocum Ser.: No. 13). 1977. pap. 1.75 (ISBN 0-87216-741-0). Playboy Pbks.

Montana State Industrial Directory, 1980. State Industrial Directories Corp. 1980. pap. 25.00 (ISBN 0-89910-026-0). State Indus Dir.

Montanans' Fishing Guide: West of the Continental Divide, Vol. I. rev. ed. Dick Konizeski. Ed. by Dale A. Fbursk. (Illus.). 325p. 1980. pap. 7.95 (ISBN 0-87842-139-4). Mountain Pr.

Montana's Genealogical Records. Ed. by Dennis L. Richards. (Gale Genealogy & Local History Ser.: Vol. 11). 330p. 1981. 30.00 (ISBN 0-8103-1487-8). Gale.

Montana's Past: Selected Essays. Malone & Roeber. 1973. 5.95 o.p. (ISBN 0-686-23486-3). U of MT Pubns Hist.

Montauk Fault. Herbert Mitgang. LC 80-70744. 320p. 1981. 12.95 (ISBN 0-87795-320-1). Arbor Hse.

Montcalm & Wolfe. Francis Parkman. 1962. pap. 1.50 o.s.i. (ISBN 0-02-035920-9, Collier). Macmillan.

Monte Carlo. Dorothy Daniels. 1981. pap. 2.75 (ISBN 0-8439-0900-5, Leisure Bks). Nordon Pubns.

Monte Walsh. Jack Schaefer. LC 80-25036. x, 442p. 1981. 21.50x (ISBN 0-8032-4124-0); pap. 7.50 (ISBN 0-8032-9121-3, BB 755, Bison). U of Nebr Pr.

Montecassino Passion & the Poetics of Medieval Drama. Robert Edwards. LC 75-22655. 1977. 19.50x (ISBN 0-520-03102-4). U of Cal Pr.

Montenegrin Gold. Brian Ball. 1978. 7.95 o.s.i. (ISBN 0-8027-5384-1). Walker & Co.

Monterey. John Hicks & Regina Hicks. (Pictorial History: No. 2). (Illus.). 64p. 1973. pap. 3.95 (ISBN 0-914606-02-6). Creative Bks.

Monterey, a Pictorial History. Date not set. price not set. Creative Bks.

Monterey Bay Yesterday: A Nostalgic Era in Post Cards. Betty Lewis. LC 77-93856. (Illus.). 1977. 3.98 (ISBN 0-913548-48-0, Valley Calif). Western Tanager.

Monterey's Mother Lode. Randall A. Reinstedt. LC 79-110351. (Illus.). 1977. pap. 5.50 (ISBN 0-933818-01-7). Ghost Town.

Montesa Service-Repair Handbook: 123-360cc Singles, 1965-1975. Clymer Publications. (Illus.). 1975. pap. text ed. 8.50 o.p. (ISBN 0-89287-020-6, M356). Clymer Pubns.

Montesquieu: A Critical Biography. Robert Shackleton. 1961. 29.95x (ISBN 0-19-815339-2). Oxford U Pr.

Montesquieu & Rousseau: Forerunners of Sociology. Emile Durkheim. 1960. pap. 3.95x (ISBN 0-472-08291-4, AA). U of Mich Pr.

Montesquieu & Social Theory. Alan Baum. 1979. 27.50 (ISBN 0-08-024317-7). Pergamon.

Montesquieu & the Old Regime. Mark Hulliung. 1977. 18.50x (ISBN 0-520-03108-3). U of Cal Pr.

Montevarese: A Study of Peasant Society & Culture in Southern Italy. Jan Brogger. 160p. 1971. 19.50x (ISBN 8-200-06143-4, Dist. by Columbia U Pr). Universitet.

Monteverdi, Creator of Modern Music. Leo Schrade. (Music Reprint Ser.). 1979. Repr. of 1950 ed. lib. bdg. 32.50 (ISBN 0-306-79565-5). Da Capo.

Montezuma's Ball. Eugene Wildman. LC 74-112037. 183p. 1970. 8.95x (ISBN 0-8040-0211-8); pap. 4.50 (ISBN 0-8040-0212-6). Swallow.

Montgomery Bus Boycott, December, 1955: American Blacks Demand an End to Segregation. Janet Stevenson. LC 78-161072. (Focus Bks). (Illus.). (gr. 7 up). 1971. PLB 4.90 o.p. (ISBN 0-531-00994-7). Watts.

Montgomery Museum of Fine Arts: A Handbook to the Collection. C. Reynolds Brown. LC 80-80053. (Illus.). 68p. 1980. pap. 3.00 (ISBN 0-89280-014-3). Montgomery Mus.

Montgomery's Auditing. 9th ed. P. L. Defliese et al. 1975. 36.50 (ISBN 0-8260-2562-5). Ronald Pr.

Montgomery's Auditing. 9th ed. P. L. Defliese et al. 869p. 1975. 36.50 (ISBN 0-471-06527-7). Wiley.

Month of Sundays. Rose Blue. LC 72-182293. (Illus.). 64p. (gr. 3-5). 1972. PLB 6.90 (ISBN 0-531-02037-1). Watts.

Monthly Payment Direct Reduction Loan Amortization Schedules No.185. 12th ed. Financial Publishing Co. 40.00 (ISBN 0-685-02550-0). Finan Pub.

Months & Seasons. Alexander Harvey. 20p. 1980. 8.00 (ISBN 0-936198-00-1); pap. 4.00 (ISBN 0-936198-01-X). Hollow Spring Pr.

Monticelli. Andre Alauzen & Pierre Ripert. (Illus., Fr.). 1970. 60.00 (ISBN 0-685-02319-2). Newbury Bks Inc.

Monticello: A Guide Book. Frederick D. Nichols & James A. Bear, Jr. (Orig.). 1967. pap. 2.95x (ISBN 0-8139-0329-7). U Pr of Va.

Montmorillon: Portrait of a Provincial Town. I. C. Thimann. 1970. 2.75 o.p. (ISBN 0-08-016005-0); pap. 1.85 o.p. (ISBN 0-08-015821-8). Pergamon.

Montpelier: Reflections of Marion DuPont Scott. Gerald Strine. 1977. 50.00 o.p. (ISBN 0-684-14798-X, ScribT). Scribner.

Montreal Canadians. Claude Mouton. 256p. 1981. 19.95 (ISBN 0-442-29634-7). Van Nos Reinhold.

Montreal in Evolution: Historical Analysis of the Development of Montreal Architecture & Urban Environment. Jean C. Marsan. (Illus.). 488p. 1981. 27.50x (ISBN 0-7735-0339-0). McGill-Queens U Pr.

Montreal Nineteen Seventy-Nine: Tournament of Stars. M. Tal et al. Tr. by K. P. Neat. LC 80-40715. (Illus.). 200p. 1980. 19.00 (ISBN 0-08-024132-8); pap. 11.90 (ISBN 0-08-024131-X). Pergamon.

Monty. James Stevenson. LC 78-11409. (Illus.). (gr. k-3). 1979. 8.50 (ISBN 0-688-80209-5); PLB 8.16 (ISBN 0-688-84209-7). Greenwillow.

Monty. James Stevenson. (Illus.). 32p. 1980. Repr. pap. 1.95 (ISBN 0-590-30268-X, Schol Pap). Schol Bk Serv.

Monty Monkey-Shines with Speech Sounds. James N. Blake. (Illus.). 80p. 1973. pap. 8.75 (ISBN 0-398-02791-9). C C Thomas.

Monty Python's Big Red Book. (Illus.). 1975. pap. 6.95 (ISBN 0-446-97166-9). Warner Bks.

Monument Builders. Robert Wernick. (Emergence of Man Ser.). (Illus.). 160p. 1973. 9.95 (ISBN 0-8094-1312-4); lib. bdg. avail. (ISBN 0-685-48123-9). Time-Life.

Monument Builders. Robert Wernick. LC 73-88012. (gr. 6 up). 1973. PLB 9.63 o.p. (ISBN 0-8094-1313-2, Pub. by Time-Life). Silver.

Monument Protection in Europe. Ed. by Council of Europe. 1980. lib. bdg. 31.50 (ISBN 90-268-1107-1, Kluwer Law & Taxation Pubs). Kluwer Boston.

Monument to Magic. J. Dunninger. 1974. 14.95 (ISBN 0-8184-0160-5). Lyle Stuart.

Monumenta Linguae Palaeoslovenicae e Codice Supraliensi. Franz Miklosich. LC 80-2361. 1981. Repr. of 1851 ed. 57.00 (ISBN 0-404-18909-1). AMS Pr.

Monumental Brasses: The Craft. Malcolm Norris. (Illus.). 1978. 58.00 (ISBN 0-571-09891-6, Pub. by Faber & Faber). Merrimack Bk Serv.

Monumental Classic Architecture in Great Britain & Ireland. Albert E. Richardson. (Illus.). 1981. 25.00 (ISBN 0-393-01451-7); pap. 10.95 (ISBN 0-393-00053-2). Norton.

Monumental Experiences: Biography of Florence Hansen, Sculptor. Dora B. Flack. Ed. by Heather Bennett. 90p. 1980. pap. 5.95 o.p. (ISBN 0-913420-84-0). Olympus Pub Co.

Monumental Silver: Selections from the Gilbert Collection. William E. Jones. LC 76-57976. (Illus.). 1977. pap. text ed. 5.50 o.p. (ISBN 0-87587-077-5). LA CO Art Mus.

Monuments & Sculptures. Nathan Rapoport. LC 80-52914. (Illus.). 96p. 1981. 20.00 (ISBN 0-88400-073-7). Shengold.

Monumentum. Ed. by Terry B. Morton. (Illus.). 128p. (Orig.). 1976. pap. 10.00 (ISBN 0-89133-087-9). Preservation Pr.

Monun Route. 25.00. Chatham Pub CA.

Moo Duk Kwan Tae Kwon Do, Korean Art of Self-Defense. Richard Chun. Ed. by Gilbert Johnson et al. LC 75-3784. (Ser. 120). (Illus.). 1975. pap. text ed. 6.95 (ISBN 0-89750-015-6). Ohara Pubns.

Moods & Emotions. Ruth Odor. Ed. by Jane Buerger. 1980. 5.95 (ISBN 0-89565-177-7, 4934). Standard Pub.

Moods of the Mountain II. Josef Scaylea. (Illus.). 64p. 1981. 24.95 (ISBN 0-87564-017-6). Superior Pub.

Moods of the Prairie. Ed Eakin. (Illus.). 4.95 (ISBN 0-685-48785-7). Nortex Pr.

Moominhsummer Madness. Tove Jansson. (ps-8). 1976. pap. 1.25 o.s.i. (ISBN 0-380-00633-2, 39768, Camelot). Avon.

Moominland Midwinter. Tove Jansson. 1976. pap. 1.95 (ISBN 0-380-00748-7, 51789, Camelot). Avon.

Moominstroll, 7 vols. Tove Jansson. Incl. Comet in Moominland. Vol. 1 (ISBN 0-380-00436-4, 39784); Finn Family Moomintroll. Vol. 2 (ISBN 0-380-00350-3, 39776); Moominland Midwinter. Vol. 3 (ISBN 0-380-00748-7, 30205); Moominpappa at Sea. Vol. 4 (ISBN 0-380-01726-1, 34157); Moomin's Summer Madness. Vol. 5 (39768); Moominvalley in November. Vol. 6 (ISBN 0-380-00765-7, 30544); Tales from Moominvalley. Vol. 8 (ISBN 0-380-00911-0, 30544). (gr. 6 up). 1978. pap. 1.25 ea. o.s.i. (Camelot); pap. 8.75 boxed set o.s.i. (ISBN 0-380-34926-4, 34926). Avon.

Moon. Isaac Asimov. (Beginning Science Ser.). (Illus.). (gr. 2-4). 1966. 2.50 o.p. (ISBN 0-695-45875-2); lib. bdg. 3.59 o.p. (ISBN 0-685-10943-7). Follett.

Moon. Ed. by Zdenek Kopel & Z. K. Mikhailov. 1963. 49.00 (ISBN 0-12-419362-5). Acad Pr.

Moon. (MacDonald Educational Ser.). (Illus., Arabic.). 3.50 (ISBN 0-686-53081-0). Intl Bk Ctr.

Moon. David Romtvedt. 80p. 1981. write for info. (ISBN 0-931460-14-X); pap. write for info. (ISBN 0-931460-16-6). Bieler.

Moon. Henry D. Thoreau. LC 80-2521. 1981. Repr. of 1927 ed. 17.50 (ISBN 0-404-19069-3). AMS Pr.

Moon & Me. Hadley Irwin. LC 80-24053. 168p. (gr. 5-9). 1981. 8.95 (ISBN 0-689-50194-3, McElderry Bk). Atheneum.

Moon & Sixpence. W. Somerset Maugham. 1977. pap. 2.95 (ISBN 0-14-000468-8). Penguin.

Moon & the Virgin: Reflections on the Archetypal Feminine. Nor Hall. LC 78-2138. (Illus.). 1981. pap. 5.95 (ISBN 0-06-090793-2, CN 793, CN). Har-Row.

Moon by Night. Madeleine L'Engle. (YA) (gr. 7-12). 1981. pap. 1.95 (ISBN 0-440-95776-1, LE). Dell.

Moon Dancers. Mary Wibberley. (Alpha Books). 80p. 1978. pap. text ed. 2.25x (ISBN 0-19-424162-9). Oxford U Pr.

Moon Flute. Audrey Wood. 40p. (Orig.). 1980. pap. 6.95 (ISBN 0-914676-44-X). Green Tiger.

Moon in Eclipse: A Life of Mary Shelley. Jane Dunn. LC 78-850. 1978. 16.95 (ISBN 0-312-54692-0). St Martin.

Moon in Five Disguises. Joan S. Ison. LC 80-70081. (Illus.). 54p. (Orig.). 1981. pap. 4.95 (ISBN 0-938604-00-7). Foxmoor.

Moon in Rahu: A Novel. Tara A. Baig. 10.00x (ISBN 0-210-33812-1). Asia.

Moon Is Not the Son: A Close Look at the Religion of Rev. Son Myung Moon. James Bjornstad. LC 76-46208. 1977. pap. 2.50 (ISBN 0-87123-380-0, 200380). Bethany Fell.

Moon Lamp. Mark Smith. 1976. 7.95 o.p. (ISBN 0-394-49888-7). Knopf.

Moon Magic. Robert B. Ruddell et al. (Pathfinder - Allyn & Bacon Reading Program: Level 11). (gr. 2). 1978. text ed. 8.20 (ISBN 0-205-05145-6, 5451450); tchr's guide 12.20 (ISBN 0-205-05146-4, 5451469); 3.60. Allyn.

Moon, Mars & Venus. Antonin Rukl. (Concise Guides Ser.). (Illus.). 1979. 7.95 (ISBN 0-600-36219-1). Transatlantic.

Moon Men. Edgar R. Burroughs. LC 62-8706. (Illus.). 1975. Repr. 8.95 (ISBN 0-686-10382-3). Canaveral.

Moon of Aphrodite. Sara Craven. (Harlequin Presents Ser.). 192p. (Orig.). 1981. pap. 1.50 (ISBN 0-373-10411-1, Pub. by Harlequin). PB.

Moon of Popping Trees. Rex A. Smith. LC 80-24863. (Illus.). xviii, 220p. 1981. 15.50x (ISBN 0-8032-4123-2); pap. 4.95 (ISBN 0-8032-9120-5, BB 750, Bison). U of Nebr Pr.

Moon of the Big-Dog. Jay Leech & Zane Spencer. LC 79-7893. (Illus.). 64p. (gr. 2-6). 1980. 6.95 (ISBN 0-690-04001-6, TYC-J); PLB 6.89 (ISBN 0-690-04002-4). T Y Crowell.

Moon of the Lost Frenchman. Kitty Mendenhall. 192p. (YA) 1976. 4.95 o.p. (ISBN 0-685-64249-6, Avalon). Bouregy.

Moon of the Red Strawberry. Ann Irwin et al. LC 72-85163. 1977. 4.95 o.s.i. (ISBN 0-87695-159-0). Aurora Pubs.

Moon on a Rainbow Shawl. Errol John. 1958. pap. 4.95 (ISBN 0-571-05403-X, Pub. by Faber & Faber). Merrimack Bk Serv.

Moon Power. Mort Gale. (Orig.). 1980. pap. 2.25 (ISBN 0-446-82988-9). Warner Bks.

Moon Ribbon, & Other Tales. Jane Yolen. LC 75-34462. (Illus.). 64p. (gr. 3-7). 1976. 8.95 (ISBN 0-690-01044-3, TYC-J). T Y Crowell.

Moon Rocks & Minerals. A. A. Levinson & Ross Taylor. 240p. 1976. text ed. 31.00 (ISBN 0-08-016669-5). Pergamon.

Moon Seems to Change. Franklyn M. Branley. LC 60-8796. (Let's-Read-&-Find-Out Science Bk). (Illus.). (gr. k-3). 1960. PLB 7.89 (ISBN 0-690-55485-0, TYC-J). T Y Crowell.

Moon Signs. Sybil Leek. 1977. 2.25 (ISBN 0-425-04364-9, Pub. by Putnam). Berkley Pub.

Moon-Spinners. Mary Stewart. 1978. pap. 2.25 (ISBN 0-449-23941-1, Crest). Fawcett.

Moon. Stars, Frogs & Friends. Patricia MacLachlan. (Illus.). (ps-3). 1980. 6.95 (ISBN 0-394-84138-7); PLB 6.99 (ISBN 0-394-94138-1). Pantheon.

Moon Walker. Paul Showers. LC 73-17490. 48p. (ps-3). 1975. PLB 4.95 o.p. (ISBN 0-385-02042-2). Doubleday.

Moondeath. Rick Hautala. 436p. (Orig.). 1981. pap. 2.75 (ISBN 0-89083-702-3). Zebra.

Moonies. Steve Kemperman. LC 80-54091. 192p. 1981. pap. 2.95 (ISBN 0-8307-0780-8). Regal.

Moonlanders. W. C. Chalk. 1971. pap. text ed. 2.50x o.p. (ISBN 0-435-11199-X). Heinemann Ed.

Moonlight at Greystone, No. 5. Louisa Bronte. (Greystone Series). 240p. 1976. pap. 1.50 o.p. (ISBN 0-345-25060-5). Ballantine.

Moonlight Kingdom. Brian Benabo. LC 75-29608. (Illus.). 92p. (YA) 1976. 6.95 o.p. (ISBN 0-312-54705-6). St Martin.

Moonlight Standing in As Cordelia. William Lane. 1980. pap. 2.50 (ISBN 0-914610-20-1). Hanging Loose.

Moonlight: The Doge's Daughter, Ariadne, Carmen Britanicum. Edward Thurlow. Ed. by Donald H. Reiman. LC 75-31266. (Romantic Context Ser.: Poetry 1789-1830). 1978. Repr. of 1814 ed. lib. bdg. 47.00 (ISBN 0-8240-2212-2). Garland Pub.

Moonlight Variations. Florence Stevenson. 224p. (Orig.). 1981. pap. 2.50 (ISBN 0-515-05655-3). Jove Pubns.

Moonraker. Ian Fleming. (James Bond Seer.). 1981. pap. 2.25 (ISBN 0-515-06002-X). Jove Pubns.

Moon's Acceleration & Its Physical Origins: Vol. 1, As Deduced from Solar Eclipses. Robert Newton. LC 78-2059. 1979. 32.50x (ISBN 0-8018-2216-5). Johns Hopkins.

Moon's Dominion: Narrative Dichotomy & Female Dominance in the First Five Novels of D. H. Lawrence. Gavriel Ben-Ephraim. LC 78-75172. 300p. 1981. 18.50 (ISBN 0-8386-2266-6). Fairleigh Dickinson.

Moon's on Fire. Margaret Donaldson. LC 80-65664. (Illus.). 152p. (gr. 2-7). 1980. 9.95 (ISBN 0-233-97249-8). Andre Deutsch.

Moonshiner. Lucy Walker. 1976. pap. 1.25 o.p. (ISBN 0-345-25236-5). Ballantine.

Moonsong Chronicles. Jessica Stuart. 384p. (Orig.). 1981. pap. 2.75 (ISBN 0-523-41167-7). Pinnacle Bks.

Moonstone. Wilkie Collins. (World's Classics Ser.). 8.95 o.p. (ISBN 0-19-250316-2). Oxford U Pr.

Moonstone: Abridged & Adapted to Grade 2 Reading Level. Wilkie Collins. Ed. by Carli Laklan. LC 67-25786. (Pacemaker Classics Ser.). (Illus., Orig.). 1967. pap. 3.80 (ISBN 0-8224-9220-2); tchrs' manual free (ISBN 0-8224-5200-6). Pitman Learning.

Moonstruck: An Anthology of Lunar Poetry. Ed. by Robert Phillips. LC 73-83042. (Illus.). 224p. 1974. 8.95 (ISBN 0-8149-0734-2). Vanguard.

Moonwitch. Felicia Andrews. (Historical Romance Ser.). 1980. pap. 2.50 (ISBN 0-515-04781-3). Jove Pubns.

Moore's Historical, Biographical, & Miscellaneous Gatherings. John W. Moore. LC 68-17977. 1968. Repr. of 1886 ed. 30.00 (ISBN 0-8103-3312-0). Gale.

Moorings - Past & Present. Isabelle R. Algee. (Illus.). 557p. 1980. lib. bdg. 35.00 (ISBN 0-918518-18-0); pap. 20.00 (ISBN 0-918518-17-2). St Luke TN.

Moorish Culture in Spain. Titus Burckhardt. Tr. by Alisa Jaffa. (Illus.). 228p. 1972. 18.95x (ISBN 0-04-946008-0). Allen Unwin.

Moorish Novel: "El Abencerraje"& Gines Perez De Hita. Maria S. Carrasco-Urgoiti. LC 75-25977. (World Authors Ser.: No. 375). 1976. lib. bdg. 12.50 (ISBN 0-8057-6178-0). Twayne.

Moorish Spain: Cordoba, Seville, Granada. Enrique Sordo. 1971. 21.95 (ISBN 0-236-31091-7, Pub. by Paul Elek). Merrimack Bk Serv.

Moose: A Very Special Person. Chet Oden & W. Scott MacDonald. 1978. pap. 3.95 o.p. (ISBN 0-03-043936-1). Winston Pr.

Moose & Goose. Marc Brown. (Illus.). (ps-3). 1978. PLB 6.95 o.p. (ISBN 0-525-35175-2). Dutton.

Moose, Goose & Little Nobody. Ellen Raskin. LC 80-15287. (Illus.). 32p. (ps-3). 1980. Repr. of 1974 ed. 8.95 (ISBN 0-590-07775-9, Four Winds). Schol Bk Serv.

Mopac Power. Joe G. Collias. (Illus.). 352p. 1980. 30.00 (ISBN 0-8310-7117-6). Howell-North.

Mopal Power. 30.00. Chatham Pub CA.

Moped: The Wonder Vehicle. Jerry Murray. (gr. 7-9). 1978. pap. 1.25 (ISBN 0-671-29882-8). Archway.

Mopeding. Charles Coombs. (Illus.). (gr. 4-6). 1978. 6.95 (ISBN 0-688-22155-6); PLB 6.67 (ISBN 0-688-32155-0). Morrow.

Mopsa the Fairy. Jean Ingelow. LC 75-32172. (Classics of Children's Literature, 1621-1932: Vol. 35). (Illus.). 1976. Repr. of 1869 ed. PLB 38.00 (ISBN 0-8240-2284-X). Garland Pub.

Moral Action, God, & History in the Thought of Immanuel Kant. Carl A. Raschke. LC 75-11787. (American Academy of Religion. Dissertation Ser.). xiv, 236p. 1975. pap. 7.50 (ISBN 0-89130-003-1, 010105). Scholars Pr Ca.

Moral & Ethical Implications of Human Organ Transplants. George W. Miller. (Illus.). 164p. 1971. 12.75 (ISBN 0-398-01311-X). C C Thomas.

Moral & Physical Condition of the Working Classes Employed in the Cotton Manufacture in Manchester. J. P. Kay-Shuttleworth. 76p. 1971. Repr. of 1832 ed. 15.00x (ISBN 0-7165-1772-8, Pub. by Irish Academic Pr Ireland). Biblio Dist.

Moral & Political Philosophy. David Hume. Ed. by Henry D. Aiken. (Library of Classics Ser.: No. 3). 1975. pap. text ed. 6.95 (ISBN 0-02-846170-3). Hafner.

Moral & Political Thought of Mahatma Gandhi. Raghavan Iyer. 400p. 1973. 17.95 (ISBN 0-19-501692-0). Oxford U Pr.

Moral & Political Thought of Mahatma Gandhi. Raghavan N. Iyer. LC 72-96613. 1978. pap. 6.95 (ISBN 0-19-502357-9, GB527, GB). Oxford U Pr.

Moral & Political Tradition of Rome. Donald A. Earl. (Aspects of Greek & Roman Life Ser.). 1967. 18.50x (ISBN 0-8014-0110-0). Cornell U Pr.

Moral & Psychological Education. Peter Scharf. 1976. pap. text ed. 10.25x (ISBN 0-8191-0027-7). U Pr of Amer.

Moral & Religious Education in County Primary Schools. Ed. by H. J. Blackham. (General Ser.). (Orig.). 1976. pap. text ed. 5.75x (ISBN 0-85633-115-5, NFER). Humanities.

Moral & Spiritual Development for the Young Child. Doris Rouse & Sybil Waldrop. LC 79-55850. 1981. perfect bdg - 3 hole punch 6.95 (ISBN 0-8054-4923-X). Broadman.

Moral Basis of a Backward Society. Edward C. Banfield & L. F. Banfield. LC 58-9398. 1958. 12.95 (ISBN 0-02-901520-0); pap. text ed. 5.95 (ISBN 0-02-901510-3). Free Pr.

Moral Basis of Fielding's Art: A Study of Joseph Andrews. Martin C. Battestin. LC 59-10177. 1959. 15.00x (ISBN 0-8195-3007-7, Pub. by Wesleyan U Pr); pap. 6.00 (ISBN 0-8195-6038-3). Columbia U Pr.

Moral Choice. Daniel C. Maguire. 1979. pap. 9.95 (ISBN 0-03-053796-7). Winston Pr.

Moral Criticism of Law. David A. Richards. 1977. pap. text ed. 11.95x (ISBN 0-8221-0198-X). Dickenson.

Moral Development & Politics. Ed. by Richard W. Wilson & Gordon J. Schochet. LC 79-15922. 1980. 26.95 (ISBN 0-03-044231-1). Praeger.

Moral Development & Socialization. Windmiller et al. 320p. 1980. text ed. 16.95 (ISBN 0-205-06844-8, 2468441). Allyn.

Moral Development: Current Theory & Research. D. J. De Palma & J. M. Foley. LC 75-14211. 1975. 14.95 o.p. (ISBN 0-470-20950-X). Halsted Pr.

Moral Duty & Legal Responsibility: A Philosophical-Legal Casebook. 2nd ed. Ed. by Philip E. Davis. LC 66-24252. (Century Philosophy Ser). (Orig.). 1981. Repr. of 1966 ed. 14.95x. Irvington.

Moral Education. Emile Durkheim. LC 59-6815. 1961. 12.95 (ISBN 0-02-908330-3); pap. text ed. 4.95 (ISBN 0-02-908320-6). Free Pr.

Moral Education. Ed. by David E. Purpel & Kevin Ryan. LC 76-18041. 1976. 20.00 (ISBN 0-8211-1516-2); text ed. 18.00x (ISBN 0-685-71410-1). McCutchan.

Moral Education: A First Generation of Research & Development. Ed. by Ralph Mosher. LC 80-18607. 450p. 1980. 29.95 (ISBN 0-03-053961-7). Praeger.

Moral Education & the Curriculum. J. Wilson. 1969. 9.75 o.p. (ISBN 0-08-013897-7); pap. 5.25 o.p. (ISBN 0-08-013898-5). Pergamon.

Moral Education in a Changing Society. W. R. Niblett. (Orig.). 1970. pap. 3.95 (ISBN 0-571-09411-2, Pub. by Faber & Faber). Merrimack Bk Serv.

Moral Education: Theory & Practice. A. V. Kelly & Meriel Downey. 1979. text ed. 15.70 (ISBN 0-06-318079-0, IntlDept); pap. text ed. 9.25 (ISBN 0-06-318080-4, IntlDept). Har-Row.

Moral Education...It Comes with the Territory. Ed. by David Purpel & Kevin Ryan. LC 76-18041. xix, 424p. 1976. 15.75x (ISBN 0-8211-1516-2, Co-Pub. & Co-Distrib. by McCutchan). Phi Delta Kappa.

Moral Evil Under Challenge. Ed. by Johannes B. Metz. (Concilium Ser.: Religion in the Seventies: Vol. 56). 1969. pap. 4.95 (ISBN 0-8164-2512-4). Crossroad NY.

Moral Foundation & Christianity Concilium, Vol. 110. Ed. by Franz Bockle & Jacques-Marie Pohier. 1978. pap. 4.95 (ISBN 0-8164-2169-2). Crossroad NY.

Moral Foundations of Professional Ethics. Alan H. Goldman. (Philosophy & Society Ser.). 305p. 1980. 22.50x (ISBN 0-8476-6274-8); pap. 9.95x (ISBN 0-8476-6285-3). Rowman.

Moral Function of Education. Archibald H. Wells. (Illus.). 1980. 33.45 (ISBN 0-89266-226-3). Am Classical Coll Pr.

Moral Hazards: Police Strategies for Honesty & Ethical Behavior. Allan N. Kornblum. LC 75-34614. 224p. 1976. 22.95 (ISBN 0-669-00378-6). Lexington Bks.

Moral Idealists, Bureaucracy, & Catherine the Great. Walter J. Gleason. 320p. 1981. 21.00 (ISBN 0-8135-0917-3). Rutgers U Pr.

Moral Imperative: Ethical Issues for Discussion & Writing. Vincent R. Ruggiero. LC 73-78659. (Illus.). 225p. (Orig.). 1973. pap. text ed. 7.95x (ISBN 0-88284-007-X). Alfred Pub.

Moral Imperatives of Human Rights: A World Survey. Ed. by Kenneth W. Thompson. LC 79-3736. 1980. text ed. 17.50 (ISBN 0-8191-0920-7); pap. text ed. 8.75 (ISBN 0-8191-0921-5). U Pr of Amer.

Moral Issues in Business. Vincent Barry. 1979. text ed. 17.95x (ISBN 0-534-00709-0). Wadsworth Pub.

Moral Judgement from Childhood to Adolescence. Norman J. Bull. LC 71-101420. 1970. 12.00x (ISBN 0-8039-0038-4). Sage.

Moral Learning & Development. Douglas Graham. 1974. pap. 17.95 (ISBN 0-7134-2842-2, Pub. by Batsford England). David & Charles.

Moral Norms & Moral Order. William A. Banner. LC 80-24206. x, 111p. 1981. 10.00 (ISBN 0-8130-0661-9). U Presses Fla.

Moral Notions. Julius Kovesi. 1967. text ed. 7.00x (ISBN 0-7100-2984-5); pap. text ed. 5.25x (ISBN 0-7100-7167-1). Humanities.

Moral Perspective in Webster's Major Tragedies. Joseph H. Stodder. (Salzburg Studies in English Literature, Jacobean Drama Studies: No. 48). 1974. pap. text ed. 25.00x (ISBN 0-391-01536-2). Humanities.

Moral Philosopher in a Dialogue Between Philalethes, a Christian Deist, & Theophanes, a Christian Jew. Thomas Morgan. LC 75-11239. (British Philosophers & Theologians of the 17th & 18th Centuries: Vol. 39). 1977. Repr. of 1737 ed. lib. bdg. 42.00 (ISBN 0-8240-1791-9). Garland Pub.

Moral Philosophy: An Introduction. 2nd ed. Paul Fink. 1977. pap. text ed. 14.95x (ISBN 0-8221-0207-2). Dickenson.

Moral Philosophy at Seventeenth-Century Harvard: A Discipline in Transition. Norman Fiering. LC 80-18282. 368p. 1981. 24.00x (ISBN 0-8078-1459-8). U of NC Pr.

Moral Philosophy: Classic Texts & Contemporary Problems. Joel Feinberg & Henry West. 1977. pap. text ed. 16.95x (ISBN 0-8221-0196-3). Dickenson.

Moral Philosophy of Peter Abelard. Paul L. Williams. LC 80-5604. 191p. 1980. lib. bdg. 17.75 (ISBN 0-8191-1137-6); pap. text ed. 9.00 (ISBN 0-8191-1138-4). U Pr of Amer.

Moral Philosophy: Text & Readings. 2nd ed. Andrew Oldenquist. LC 77-77978. (Illus.). 1978. pap. text ed. 11.50 (ISBN 0-395-25433-7). HM.

Moral Principles in Education. John Dewey. LC 74-18472. (Arcturus Books Paperbacks). 80p. 1975. pap. 2.95 (ISBN 0-8093-0715-4). S Ill U Pr.

Moral Problem in Medicine. Samuel Gorovitz. 500p. 1976. 18.95 (ISBN 0-13-600817-8). P-H.

Moral Reasoning: A Psychological-Philosophical Integration. William D. Boyce & Larry C. Jensen. LC 78-5935. 1978. 15.95x (ISBN 0-8032-0982-7). U of Nebr Pr.

Moral Reasoning: A Teaching Handbook for Adapting Kohlberg to the Classroom. Ronald E. Galbraith & Thomas M. Jones. (Illus.). 1976. lib. bdg. 11.95 (ISBN 0-912616-23-7); pap. 6.95 (ISBN 0-912616-22-9). Greenhaven.

Moral Reasoning & Truth: An Essay in Philosophy & Jurisprudence. Thomas D. Perry. 1976. 27.00x (ISBN 0-19-824532-7). Oxford U Pr.

Moral Reasoning: Ethical Theory & Some Contemporary Moral Problems. Victor Grassian. 400p. 1981. pap. text ed. 10.95 (ISBN 0-13-600759-7). P-H.

Moral Responsibility in Prolonging Life Decisions. 200p. (Orig.). 1981. pap. text ed. price not set (ISBN 0-935372-08-3). Pope John Ctr.

Moral Situations. N. Fotion. LC 68-31034. 1968. 7.00x (ISBN 0-87338-076-2); pap. 3.50x (ISBN 0-87338-077-0). Kent St U Pr.

Moral State: A Study of the Political Socialization of Chinese & American Children. Richard W. Wilson. LC 73-2333. 1974. 19.95 (ISBN 0-02-935410-2). Free Pr.

Moral Status of Animals. Stephen R. Clark. 1977. 26.50x (ISBN 0-19-824578-5). Oxford U Pr.

Moral Tales. Lawrence P. Spingarn. (Illus.). 80p. 1981. pap. 4.00 (ISBN 0-912288-17-5). Perivale Pr. Postponed.

Moral Tales for Young People, 3 vols. Maria Edgeworth. (Feminist Controversy in England, 1788-1810 Ser.). 1974. lib. bdg. 50.00 ea. (ISBN 0-8240-0856-1). Garland Pub.

Moral Teaching of the New Testament. Rudolf Schnackenburg. pap. 7.95 (ISBN 0-8164-2557-4). Crossroad NY.

Moral Trollope. Ruth ApRoberts. LC 75-141383. 203p. 1971. 12.00x (ISBN 0-8214-0089-4). Ohio U Pr.

Morality & Foreign Policy: A Symposium on President Carter's Stance. Ed. by Ernest W. Lefever. 82p. 1977. pap. 3.00 (ISBN 0-89633-005-2). Ethics & Public Policy.

Morality & Moral Controversies. J. Arthur. 1981. pap. 10.95 (ISBN 0-13-601278-7). P-H.

Morality & the Good Life: A Commentary on Aristotle's "Nicomachean Ethics". Roger J. Sullivan. LC 77-13485. 222p. 1980. pap. text ed. 5.95x (ISBN 0-87870-111-7). Memphis St Univ.

Morality & the Law. Richard A. Wasserstrom. 1970. pap. 7.95x (ISBN 0-534-00167-X). Wadsworth Pub.

Morality & U. S. Foreign Policy. Charles Frankel. (Headline Ser.: No. 224). (Orig.). 1975. pap. 2.00 (ISBN 0-87124-029-7). Foreign Policy.

Morality, Anyone? Lester William. 1975. 7.95 o.p. (ISBN 0-87000-297-X). Arlington Hse.

Morality As a Biological Phenomenon, LSRR 9. Ed. by Gunther S. Stent. (Dahlem Wporkshop Reports Ser.). 1978. pap. 25.60 (ISBN 0-89573-093-6). Verlag Chemie.

Morality As a Biological Phenomenon: The Presuppositions of Sociobiological Research. Ed. by Gunther S. Stent. 1980. 12.95 (ISBN 0-520-04028-7, CAL 482); pap. 6.95 (ISBN 0-520-04029-5). U of Cal Pr.

Morality for Our Time. Marc Oraison. LC 68-11922. 1969. pap. 1.25 (ISBN 0-385-01490-2, D266, Im). Doubleday.

Morality: How to Live It Today. Leonard F. Badia & Ronald Sarno. LC 79-20498. 1980. pap. 7.95 (ISBN 0-8189-0391-0). Alba.

Morality in Medicine: An Introduction to Medical Ethics. Richard Warner. LC 79-23049. 1980. pap. 8.95 (ISBN 0-88284-103-3). Alfred Pub.

Morality in the Modern World. Laurence Habermehl. 1976. pap. text ed. 14.95x (ISBN 0-8221-0176-9). Dickenson.

Morality of Consent. Alexander M. Bickel. LC 75-10988. 176p. 1975. 12.50x (ISBN 0-300-01911-4); pap. 4.95x (ISBN 0-300-02119-4). Yale U Pr.

Morality of Nuclear Planning?? H. C. Dudley. LC 76-11464. 1976. pap. 7.00 (ISBN 0-917994-00-0). Kronos Pr.

Morality of Scholarship. Northrop Frye et al. Ed. by Max Black. (Studies in Humanities Ser.). 101p. 1967. 12.50 (ISBN 0-8014-0042-2). Cornell U Pr.

Morality-Religious & Secular: The Dilemma of the Traditional Conscience. Basil Mitchell. 180p. 1980. 22.50 (ISBN 0-19-824537-8). Oxford U Pr.

Morall Fabillis of Esope in Scottis Meter Be Maister Henrisone. Aesop. LC 79-25964. (English Experience Ser.: No. 282). 104p. 1970. Repr. of 1570 ed. 14.00 (ISBN 90-221-0282-3). Walter J Johnson.

Morals & Early Adolescent Education: From Apathy to Action. Ed. by Clifford H. Sweat. LC 80-80727. 1980. pap. text ed. 4.25 (ISBN 0-8134-2134-9, 2134). Interstate.

Morals & Ethics. Carl Wellman. 328p. 1975. pap. 8.95x (ISBN 0-673-05013-0). Scott F.

Morals & Law. Max Hamburger. LC 65-15244. 1965. 12.00x (ISBN 0-8196-0151-9). Biblo.

Morals & Markets. Viviana Zelizer. LC 78-31205. 1979. 17.50x (ISBN 0-231-04570-0). Columbia U Pr.

Morals & Politics: The Ethics of Revolution. William Ash. (Direct Editions Ser.). 1977. pap. 9.00 (ISBN 0-7100-8558-3). Routledge & Kegan.

Moravian & Methodist. Clifford W. Towlson. 1957. 15.00x (ISBN 0-8401-2387-6, 8401-2387-6). Allenson.

Mordida Man. Thomas Ross. 1981. 13.95 (ISBN 0-671-42186-7). S&S.

More About Little Pear. Eleanor F. Lattimore. LC 71-151939. (Illus.). (gr. 2-5). 1971. 7.25 (ISBN 0-688-21892-X). Morrow.

More About Names. Leopold Wagner. LC 68-17937. 1968. Repr. of 1893 ed. 20.00 (ISBN 0-8103-3099-7). Gale.

More Actors Guide to Monologues, Vol. 2. rev. ed. Jane Grumbach & Robert Emerson. LC 73-21893. pap. text ed. 1.95x o.p. (ISBN 0-89676-043-X). Drama Bk.

More Adventures in Cooking with Health Foods. Nancy Sutton. LC 73-90512. 1974. 6.95 (ISBN 0-8119-0229-3); pap. 4.95 (ISBN 0-8119-0390-7). Fell.

More Adventures of the Great Brain. John D. Fitzgerald. 1971. pap. 1.50 (ISBN 0-440-45822-6, YB). Dell.

More Adventures of the Superkids, Bk. 2. Pleasant Rowland. (Addison-Wesley Reading Program). (gr. 1). 1979. pap. text ed. 6.72 (ISBN 0-201-20650-1, Sch Div); reader, 3 skills bks. 3.12 (ISBN 0-201-20651-X); binder with 3 tchr. guides, tape incl. 38.52; pretest pkg. of dup. masters, gr. 1 38.52 (ISBN 0-201-20657-9); dupe masters avail. A-W.

More Aesop's Fables. Retold by Laura Dayton. LC 78-73537. (Illus.). (gr. 2-5). Date not set. price not set (ISBN 0-89799-149-4); pap. price not set (ISBN 0-89799-067-6). Dandelion Pr. Postponed.

More American Furniture Treasures. Lester Margon. Date not set. 16.50 (ISBN 0-8038-0163-7). Hastings.

More & More Ant & Bee. Angela Banner. (Ant & Bee Bks). (gr. k-3). 1970. 2.95 o.p. (ISBN 0-531-01164-X). Watts.

More Ant & Bee. Angela Banner. (Ant & Bee Bks). (gr. k-3). 1958. 2.50 o.p. (ISBN 0-531-01161-5). Watts.

More Bad News, Vol. 2. Glasgow University Media Group. (Illus.). 1980. 50.00x (ISBN 0-7100-0414-1). Routledge & Kegan.

More Ballpoint Bananas. Compiled by Charles Keller. LC 77-5356. (Illus.). (gr. 1-4). 1977. 4.95 (ISBN 0-13-600767-8); pap. 1.95 (ISBN 0-13-600775-9). P-H.

More Basic Computer Games. Ed. by David H. Ahl. LC 80-57619. (Illus.). 188p. 1980. pap. 8.95 (ISBN 0-89480-137-6). Workman Pub.

More Basics for Buyers. Somerby R. Dowst. LC 79-11755. 1979. 15.95 (ISBN 0-8436-0780-7). CBI Pub.

More Baskets & How to Make Them. Mary White. LC 76-162524. Repr. of 1912 ed. 18.00 (ISBN 0-8103-3065-2). Gale.

More Bible Puzzles & Games. M. J. Capley. 1978. pap. 1.95 (ISBN 0-8007-8320-4, Spire). Revell.

More Big Sky Cooking. Greg Patent. (Big Sky Cooking Ser.: No. 2). (Illus.). 151p. (Orig.). 1980. pap. 9.50. Eagle Comm.

More Black American Playwrights: A Bibliography. Esther S. Arata. LC 78-15231. 1978. lib. bdg. 16.50 (ISBN 0-8108-1158-8). Scarecrow.

More Blue Ribbon Systems. Ed. by GBC Editorial Staff. (Gambler's Book Shelf). (Orig.). 1979. pap. 2.95 (ISBN 0-89650-801-3). Gamblers.

More Brave New Words. Bill Sherk. LC 80-1729. (Illus.). 240p. 1981. pap. 6.95 (ISBN 0-385-17250-8). Doubleday.

More by Alison Knowles. Knowles. pap. write for info. (ISBN 0-914162-41-1). Knowles.

More Calculated Cooking: Practical Recipies for Diabetics & Dieters. Jeanne Jones. 192p. (Orig.). 1981. 10.95 (ISBN 0-89286-185-1); pap. 6.95 (ISBN 0-89286-184-3). One Hurd One Prods.

More Chapters of Opera: Being Historical & Critical Observations & Records Concerning the Lyric Drama in New York from 1908-1918. Henry E. Krehbiel. LC 78-66910. (Encore Music Editions Ser.). 1981. Repr. of 1919 ed. 45.00 (ISBN 0-686-66139-7). Hyperion Conn.

More Codes for Kids. Burton Albert, Jr. Ed. by Kathy Pacini. LC 79-245. (How-to Bks.). (Illus.). (gr. 3-6). 1979. 6.50g (ISBN 0-8075-5270-4). A Whitman.

More Collected Poems. Hugh MacDiarmid. LC 68-31076. 108p. 1970. 7.95 (ISBN 0-8040-0213-4). Swallow.

More Colonial Crafts for You to Make. Janet D'Amato & Alex D'Amato. LC 77-6333. (Illus.). (gr. 4-6). 1977. PLB 7.79 o.p. (ISBN 0-671-32841-7). Messner.

More Confederate Imprints, 2 Vols. Richard B. Harwell. LC 57-9084. (Illus.). 1957. Vol. 1. pap. 7.50x set (ISBN 0-88490-045-2, Virginia State Library); Vol. 2. pap. (ISBN 0-88490-046-0). U Pr of Va.

More Consonant Sounds. Virginia Polish. (Starting off with Phonics Ser.: Bk. 4). (Illus.). (gr. k). 1980. pap. text ed. 2.21 (ISBN 0-87895-054-0); tchrs. ed. 2.00 (ISBN 0-87895-064-8). Modern Curr.

More Cookery for Today. Joan Miller. 1974. pap. text ed. 4.95x0 o.p. (ISBN 0-435-42601-X). Heinemann Ed.

More Cooking with Love. 1978. pap. 2.95 (ISBN 0-89728-045-8, 709194). Omega Pubns OR.

More Designs. Ruth Heller. (Creative Coloring Activity Pandabacks). (Illus.). 32p. 1981. pap. 1.25 (ISBN 0-448-49622-4). G&D.

More Effective Use of Resources: An Imperative for Higher Education. Carnegie Commission on Higher Education. 256p. 1972. 7.50 o.p. (ISBN 0-07-010051-9, P&RB). McGraw.

More Essays from the World of Music. Ernest Newman. LC 77-17332. (Music Reprint Ser.: 1978). (Illus.). 1978. Repr. of 1958 ed. lib. bdg. 27.50 (ISBN 0-306-77520-4). Da Capo.

More Essays in Legal Philosophy: General Assessment of Legal Philosophies. Ed. by Robert S. Summers. 1971. 14.50x (ISBN 0-520-01971-7). U of Cal Pr.

More Fables of Aesop. Jack Kent. LC 73-13635. (Illus.). 64p. (ps up). 1974. 5.95 o.s.i. (ISBN 0-8193-0750-5, Four Winds); PLB 5.41 o.s.i. (ISBN 0-8193-0751-3). Schol Bk Serv.

More Fairy Tales for Me. Wilma D. Pepper. 180p. (gr. 1). 1967. 2.50x o.p. (ISBN 0-89039-054-1). Ann Arbor Pubs.

More Fantasy by Fabian. Ed. by Gerry De La Ree. (Illus.). 1979. 15.75 (ISBN 0-938192-05-1). De La Ree.

More Favourite Stories from Asia. Leon Comber. (Favourite Stories Ser.). pap. text ed. 1.25 (ISBN 0-686-65637-7, 00301). Heinemann Ed.

More Festivals in Asia. Compiled by Asian Cultural Centre for Unesco. LC 75-34740. (Illus.). 68p. (gr. 9-12). 1975. 7.95 (ISBN 0-87011-273-2). Kodansha.

More Flower Arrangement. Eric Roberts. (Teach Yourself Ser.). 1975. pap. 2.95 o.p. (ISBN 0-679-10429-1). McKay.

More Fortran Programs for Economists. Lucy J. Slater. (Department of Applied Economics, Occasional Papers: No. 3). (Illus.). 150p. 1972. 15.95x (ISBN 0-521-09722-3). Cambridge U Pr.

More from Hollywood! Dewitt Bodeen. LC 77-3213. (Illus.). 512p. 1977. 15.00 (ISBN 0-498-01533-5). A S Barnes.
More Games for the Super-Intelligent. James Fixx. 1977. pap. 2.25 (ISBN 0-445-04114-5). Popular Lib.
More Goops & How Not to Be Them. G. Burgess. (Peter Possum Paperbacks Ser). 1967. pap. 0.95 o.p. (ISBN 0-531-05138-2). Watts.
More Great American Mansions: And Their Stories. Merrill Folsom. (Illus.). 1979. 1.50 (ISBN 0-8038-4635-5); pap. 7.95 (ISBN 0-8038-4723-8). Hastings.
More Horse Stories. Ed. by A. L. Furman. (gr. 5-7). 1979. pap. 1.75 (ISBN 0-671-56009-3). Archway.
More Houses for Good Living. Royal Barry Wills Assoc. Date not set. 13.95 (ISBN 0-8038-0162-9). Hastings.
More How to Speak Southern. Steve Mitchell. 64p. (Orig.). 1980. pap. 1.95 (ISBN 0-553-14351-4). Bantam.
More Indian Fairy Tales. Mulk R. Anand. 80p. (gr. 5-7). 1975. 4.00 (ISBN 0-88253-684-2). Ind-US Inc.
More Jokes, Jokes, Jokes. Ed. by Helen Hoke. (Illus.). (gr. 4-6). 1965. PLB 7.90 (ISBN 0-531-01736-2). Watts.
More Joys of Living. Uffa Fox. 180p. 1980. 12.00x (ISBN 0-245-50796-5, Pub. by Nautical England). State Mutual Bk.
More Killing Defence at Bridge. H. W. Kelsey. 1972. 8.95 o.p. (ISBN 0-571-10153-4, Pub. by Faber & Faber). Merrimack Bk Serv.
More Learning in Less Time. Norma Kahn. 80p. 1979. pap. 3.90 (ISBN 0-8104-6043-2). Hayden.
More Lights on Yoga. Sri Aurobindo. 1979. pap. 2.00 (ISBN 0-89744-950-9). Auromere.
More Literary Essays. David Daiches. LC 68-16688. 1968. 11.00x o.s.i. (ISBN 0-226-13472-5). U of Chicago Pr.
More Lives Than a Cat. Goldie Down. LC 79-17814. (Crown Ser.). 1979. pap. 4.50 (ISBN 0-8127-0243-3). Southern Pub.
More Lives Than One. Claude Bragdon. 368p. 1980. Repr. of 1938 ed. lib. bdg. 35.00 (ISBN 0-89984-063-9). Century Bookbindery.
More Looking at Cooking. Mildred Swift. (Illus.). 1976. pap. 6.95 (ISBN 0-88289-096-4). Pelican.
More Mad About Sports. Frank Jacobs & Bob Clarke. (Mad Ser.). (Illus., Orig.). 1977. pap. 1.75 (ISBN 0-446-94600-1). Warner Bks.
More Mad's Snappy Answers to Stupid Questions. Al Jaffee. pap. 1.25 (ISBN 0-451-06740-1, Y6740, Sig). NAL.
More Magic of the Minimum Dose. Dorothy Shepherd. 1980. text ed. 7.00x (ISBN 0-8464-1033-8). Beekman Pubs.
More Make-A-Mix Cookery. Karine Eliason et al. (Orig.). 1980. pap. 5.95 (ISBN 0-89586-055-4). H P Bks.
More Marginalia. Albert F. Trams. 50p. 1980. Repr. of 1931 ed. lib. bdg. 12.50 (ISBN 0-8482-2740-9). Norwood Edns.
More Marine & Drawings in the Peabody Museum. Philip C. Smith. (Illus.). 192p. 1979. 35.00 (ISBN 0-87577-064-9); boxed numbered 50.00 (ISBN 0-686-68319-6). Peabody Mus Salem.
More Massachusetts Broadsides. (Massachusetts Historical Society Picture Book Ser.). 1981. price not set. Mass Hist Soc.
More Math Puzzles & Games. Michael Holt. LC 77-75319. 1978. 7.95 o.s.i. (ISBN 0-8027-0561-8); pap. 3.95 (ISBN 0-8027-7114-9). Walker & Co.
More Michigan Cooking.... & Other Things, Vol. 2. Carole Eberly. (Illus.). 112p. (Orig.). 1981. pap. 4.95 (ISBN 0-932296-07-6). Eberly Pr.
More Misinformation. Tom Burnam. 1981. pap. 2.50 (ISBN 0-345-29251-0). Ballantine.
More Mobiles: Math Shapes & Forms. Victoria S. Morris. (Mobiles Ser.: Vol. 2). (gr. 1-8). 1977. pap. 3.00 (ISBN 0-914318-03-9). V S Morris.
More Modern Women Superstars. Bill Gutman. LC 78-22433. (High Interest-Low Vocabulary Ser.). (Illus.). (gr. 4 up). 1979. 5.95 (ISBN 0-396-07680-7). Dodd.
More Mojave Myths. Alfred L. Kroeber. (U. C. Publ. in Anthropological Records: Vol. 27). 1972. pap. 11.00x (ISBN 0-520-09373-9). U of Cal Pr.
More Money for More Opportunity: Financial Support of Community College Systems. James L. Wattenbarger & Bob N. Cage. LC 74-3608. (Higher Education Ser.). 224p. 1974. 11.95x o.p. (ISBN 0-87589-233-7). Jossey-Bass.
More Money for Your Retirement. John Barnes. 320p. 1980. pap. 4.95 (ISBN 0-686-61976-5, EH 514, EH). Har-Row.
More Monster Books: Set 2, 12 bks. Ellen Blance et al. Incl. Monster & the Mural (ISBN 0-8372-2124-2); Monster, Lady Monster & the Bike Ride (ISBN 0-8372-2125-0); Lady Monster Helps Out (ISBN 0-8372-2126-9); Monster Goes to the Circus (ISBN 0-8372-2127-7); Monster Goes to the Hospital (ISBN 0-8372-2128-5); Monster Goes to the Beach (ISBN 0-8372-2129-3); Monster Gets a Job (ISBN 0-8372-2130-7); Monster & the Surprise Cookie (ISBN 0-8372-2131-5); Monster Goes Around the Town (ISBN 0-8372-2132-3); Monster Buys a Pet; Lady Monster Has a Plan (ISBN 0-8372-2135-8). (Illus., Avail in spanish). (ps-3). 1976. pap. 1.56 ea.; pap. text ed. 16.92 12 bks. 1 of ea. & tchr's guide (ISBN 0-8372-2122-6, 2122); pap. text ed. 160.20 120 bks 10 of ea. & tchr's guide (ISBN 0-8372-2123-4, 2123). Bowmar-Noble.
More Music for Sight Singing. R. Ottman. 1981. pap. 11.95 (ISBN 0-13-601211-6). P-H.
More Needlepoint by Design. Maggie Lane. LC 72-1205. (Illus.). 192p. 1972. 17.50 (ISBN 0-684-12906-X, ScribT). Scribner.
More Needlework Blocking & Finishing. Dorothy Burchette. (Illus.). 1979. 3.95 (ISBN 0-684-16892-8, ScribT). Scribner.
More Nice Poems: Special Issue 11. pap. 1.00 (ISBN 0-912292-20-2). The Smith.
More Night. Muriel Rukeyser. LC 79-2680. (Illus.). 32p. (gr. k-3). 1981. 8.95 (ISBN 0-06-025127-1, HarpJ); PLB 8.79g (ISBN 0-06-025128-X). Har-Row.
More Nineteenth-Century Studies: A Group of Honest Doubters. Basil Willey. LC 80-40635. 304p. 1981. pap. 9.95 (ISBN 0-521-28067-2). Cambridge U Pr.
More Number Games: Mathematics Made Easy Through Play. Abraham B. Hurwitz et al. LC 74-23849. (Funk & W Bk.). (gr. 5 up). 1976. 9.95 o.s.i. (ISBN 0-308-10255-X, TYC-T). T Y Crowell.
More of Paul Harvey's the Best of the Story. Paul Aurandt. 208p. 1981. pap. 2.50 (ISBN 0-553-14594-0). Bantam.
More of the Best. Gretchen Greiner. (gr. 3 up). 1978. pap. 1.25 (ISBN 0-307-21520-2, Golden Pr). Western Pub.
More of the Official Polish Italian Joke Book. Larry Wilde. 224p. (Orig.). 1975. pap. 1.95 (ISBN 0-523-41424-2). Pinnacle Bks.
More of the World's Dirty Jokes. Mr. J. 1980. pap. 3.95 (ISBN 0-8065-0689-X). Lyle Stuart.
More Other Homes & Garbage: Designs for Self-Sufficient Living. Jim Leckie et al. (Illus.). 416p. 1981. pap. 14.95 (ISBN 0-87156-274-X). Sierra.
More Pages from a Worker's Life. William Z. Foster. Ed. by Arthur Zipser. (Occasional Papers: No. 32). 1979. 1.50 (ISBN 0-89977-026-6). Am Inst Marxist.
More Perfect Union: Introduction to American Government. Samuel C. Patterson et al. 1979. 17.95x (ISBN 0-256-02095-7); study guide 5.50x (ISBN 0-256-02104-X). Dorsey.
More Perplexing Puzzles & Tantalizing Teasers. Martin Gardner. (gr. 3-6). 1981. pap. price not set. Archway.
More Perplexing Puzzles & Teasers. Martin Gardner. (Illus.). (gr. 3-6). 1977. pap. 1.25 (ISBN 0-671-29832-1). PB.
More Poems. A. Madhavan. (Redbird Bk.). 1976. 8.00 (ISBN 0-89253-698-5); pap. text ed. 4.80 (ISBN 0-89253-083-9). Ind-US Inc.
More Poems. Suniti Namjoshi. 8.00 (ISBN 0-89253-706-X); flexible cloth 4.00 (ISBN 0-89253-707-8). Ind-US Inc.
More Posters from Sesame Street. Sesame Street. (Illus.). 12p. (gr. 2-5). 1975. pap. 2.50 (ISBN 0-394-83176-4). Random.
More Powerful Reading. Wilbert J. Levy. (Orig.). (gr. 10-12). 1969. pap. text ed. 6.17 (ISBN 0-87720-325-3). AMSCO Sch.
More Precious Than Gold. Basilea Schlink. 1978. pap. 3.95 (ISBN 0-88419-178-8). Creation Hse.
More Precious Than Rubies. K. C. Chan. 1981. 8.95 (ISBN 0-533-04287-9). Vantage.
More Programs & Skits for Young Teens. Norma McPhee. 1980. pap. 3.50 (ISBN 0-8024-5669-3). Moody.
More Puppet Plays & Patter. (Hand Puppets Ser: Vol. 2). (gr. 3-8). 1980. pap. 3.00 (ISBN 0-914318-06-3). V S Morris.
More Puzzle Fun. L. H. Longley-Cook. 128p. 1977. pap. 1.25 o.p. (ISBN 0-449-13744-9, GM). Fawcett.
More Riddles, Riddles, Riddles. Helen Hoke. LC 10-696. (Illus.). (gr. 4 up). 1976. PLB 7.90 (ISBN 0-531-00351-5). Watts.
More Ripping Yarns. Michael Palin & Terry Jones. (Illus.). 1981. pap. 5.95 (ISBN 0-394-74810-7). Pantheon.
More Salt in My Kitchen. Jeanette Lockerbie. (Moody Quiet Time Ser.). 1980. pap. 1.95 (ISBN 0-8024-5668-5). Moody.
More Science Experiments You Can Eat. Vicki Cobb. LC 78-12732. (Illus.). 1979. 7.95 (ISBN 0-397-31828-6); pap. 3.95 (ISBN 0-397-31853-7). Lippincott.
More Scottish Fishing Craft & Their Work: Their Work in Great Lining, Small Lining, Seining, Pair Trawling, Drifting, Potting & Trawling. Gloria Wilson. (Illus.). 170p. 8.75 (ISBN 0-85238-048-8, FN). Unipub.
More Scrap Savers Stitchery. Sandra L. Foose. LC 80-2740. 1981. 12.95 (ISBN 0-385-17526-4). Doubleday.
More Selected Verse of Robert Service. Robert Service. LC 71-171047. pap. 2.50 (ISBN 0-396-06562-7). Dodd.
More Short Fictions. Richard Kostelanetz. LC 80-58969. (Illus.). 224p. (Orig.). 1981. 15.00 (ISBN 0-686-69408-2); pap. 6.96 (ISBN 0-686-69409-0). Assembling Pr.
More Single Shot Rifles. James J. Grant. (Illus.). 15.00 (ISBN 0-88227-006-0). Gun Room.
More Snappy Answers to Stupid Questions. Al Jaffee. (Mad Ser.). (Illus.). 1979. pap. 1.75 (ISBN 0-446-94410-6). Warner Bks.
More Songs from the Jap-Ji: Selections from the Adi-Granth. Tr. by P. Lal from Punjabi. 20p. 1975. 4.80 (ISBN 0-88253-708-3); pap. text ed. 4.00 (ISBN 0-89253-709-4). Ind-US Inc.
More Stories of Favorite Operas. Clyde R. Bulla. LC 65-18691. (Illus.). (gr. 4 up). 1965. 8.95 o.p. (ISBN 0-690-55910-0, TYC-J). T Y Crowell.
More Strange but True Baseball Stories. Howard Liss. (Major League Baseball Library: No. 16). (Illus.). (gr. 5-9). 1972. 2.95 o.p. (ISBN 0-394-82390-7, BYR); PLB 4.39 (ISBN 0-394-92390-1). Random.
More Studies in Murder. Edmund Pearson. 317p. 1980. Repr. of 1936 ed. lib. bdg. 30.00 (ISBN 0-89760-715-5). Telegraph Bks.
More Tales from Slim Ellison. Glenn R. Ellison. 1981. 17.50 (ISBN 0-8165-0715-5); pap. 9.50 (ISBN 0-8165-0681-7). U of Ariz Pr.
More Tales from Ulithi Atoll. William A. Lessa. (U. C. Publications in Folklore & Mythology Studies: Vol. 32). 1980. pap. 15.00 (ISBN 0-520-09615-0). U of Cal Pr.
More Tales of Oliver Pig. Jean Van Leeuwen. LC 80-23289. (Easy-to-Read Ser.). (Illus.). 64p. (ps-3). 1981. PLB 5.99 (ISBN 0-8037-8714-6); pap. 2.50 (ISBN 0-8037-8713-8). Dial.
More Tales of Pirx the Pilot. Stanislaw Lem. Tr. by Louis Iribarne. (Helen & Kurt Wolff Bk.). 1981. 9.95 (ISBN 0-15-162138-1). HarBraceJ.
More Technologies for Rural Health. D. A. Tyrrell et al. (Proceedings of the Royal Society, Series B.: Vol. 209). 186p. 1980. text ed. 30.00x (ISBN 0-85403-148-0, Pub. by Royal Soc London). Scholium Intl.
More Than a Cookbook. Nelson T. Offutt. LC 79-93281. 1981. pap. 5.95 (ISBN 0-89709-019-5). Liberty Pub.
More Than a Job: How to Win at Working. Robert H. Woody. LC 80-18914. 160p. (gr. 7 up). 1980. PLB 8.29 (ISBN 0-671-34048-4). Messner.
More Than a Trial: The Struggle Over Captain Dreyfus. Robert L. Hoffman. LC 80-642. (Illus.). 1980. 14.95 (ISBN 0-02-914770-0). Free Pr.
More Than Conquerers: Makers of History. Sytha Motto. (Illus.). 228p. 1980. 15.00 (ISBN 0-913270-88-1); ltd. signed 22.50 (ISBN 0-913270-94-6). Sunstone Pr.
More Than Dispensing. Cyrelle K. Gerson. LC 80-65958. 120p. 1980. 24.00 (ISBN 0-917330-31-5). Am Pharm Assn.
More Than Friends. Ruth Turk. 256p. (Orig.). 1980. pap. 2.50 (ISBN 0-553-13661-5). Bantam.
More Than Human. Theodore Sturgeon. 192p. 1981. pap. 2.25 (ISBN 0-345-28189-6, Del Rey). Ballantine.
More Than Just Me: Looking Beyond No. One. Eileen Guder. (Orig.). 1981. pap. cancelled (ISBN 0-88449-039-4). Vision Hse.
More Than Just Talk. Tim Nicholas & Ken Touchton. Ed. by Elaine S. Furlow. (Human Touch Photo-Text Ser.). (Illus.). 1977. 6.95g (ISBN 0-937170-16-X). Home Mission.
More Than Just You. Tom S. Coke. 1979. pap. 2.50 (ISBN 0-88207-578-0). Victor Bks.
More Than One Life. Hans Holzer. (Orig.). 1980. pap. 2.25 (ISBN 0-532-23127-9). Manor Bks.
More Than Two Aspirin: Help for Your Headache Problem. Seymour Diamond & William B. Furlong. 372p. 1976. 8.95 o.p. (ISBN 0-695-80612-2). Follett.
More Than Wanderers: Spiritual Disciplines for Christian Ministry. James C. Fenhagen. LC 77-17974. 1978. 6.95 (ISBN 0-8164-0386-4). Crossroad NY.
More Than You Ever Wanted to Know About Measurement & Statistics: For Reading Specialists. Donald E. Smith & Danial Fisher. (Michigan Learning Module: No. 7). (Orig.). 1978. pap. text ed. 2.95x (ISBN 0-914004-10-7). Ulrich.
More the Official Jewish-Irish Joke Book. Larry Wilde. (Larry Wilde Bestselling Humor Ser.). 1979. pap. 1.95 (ISBN 0-523-41423-4). Pinnacle Bks.
More: The Official Republican-Democrat Joke Book. Larry Wilde. 224p. (Orig.). 1980. pap. 1.95 o.p. (ISBN 0-523-40705-X). Pinnacle Bks.
More: The Official Sex Maniac's Joke Book. Larry Wilde. 176p. (Orig.). 1981. pap. 1.95 (ISBN 0-553-14623-8). Bantam.
More Time to Grow. Sharon H. Grollman. LC 76-48513. (gr. k-5). 1977. 7.95 o.p. (ISBN 0-8070-2370-1). Beacon Pr.
More Toys & Gifts for You to Make. Hermyone Fremlin-Key. (Illus.). 96p. 1971. 8.75 (ISBN 0-8231-5027-5). Branford.
More Trouble with the Obvious. Michael Van Walleghen. LC 80-24215. 76p. 1981. 10.00 (ISBN 0-252-00864-2); pap. 3.95 (ISBN 0-252-00865-0). U of Ill Pr.
More TRS-80 Basic. Don Inman. (Self-Teaching Guide Ser.). 300p. 1981. pap. text ed. 8.95 (ISBN 0-471-08010-1). Wiley.
More Truth Than Poetry. Fran Landesman. 64p. (Orig.). 1981. pap. 5.95 (ISBN 0-932966-13-6). Permanent Pr.
More Under Saturn. William Dickey. LC 70-153102. (Wesleyan Poetry Program: Vol. 58). 1971. 10.00 (ISBN 0-8195-2058-6, Pub. by Wesleyan U Pr); pap. 4.95 (ISBN 0-8195-1058-0). Columbia U Pr.
More Very First Stories with Hilary Hippo & Friends. Shreck. 117p. pap. 8.95 (ISBN 0-02-037130-6). Macmillan.
More-with-Less Cookbook. Doris Longacre. LC 75-23563. 320p. 1976. pap. 8.95 (ISBN 0-8361-1786-7). Herald Pr.
More with Less Cookbook. Doris J. Longacre. 336p. 1981. pap. 3.95 (ISBN 0-553-13930-4). Bantam.
More Women in Literature: Criticism of the Seventies. Carol Fairbanks. LC 78-26405. 1979. 19.00 (ISBN 0-8108-1193-6). Scarecrow.
Moreau. (Selected Artist Art Ser). (Illus.). 1977. pap. 5.95 (ISBN 0-8120-0812-X). Barron.
Morgan & Me. Steve Cosgrove. (Serendipity Bks). (Illus.). (gr. k-4). 1978. PLB 6.95 (ISBN 0-87191-660-6). Creative Ed.
Morgan Horse Handbook. Jeanne Mellin. LC 72-91799. 256p. 1980. pap. 8.95 (ISBN 0-8289-0390-5). Greene.
Morgan Trail: A Story of Hashknife Hartley. Wilbur C. Tuttle. 1976. lib. bdg. 14.75x (ISBN 0-89968-127-1). Lightyear.
Morgan Wade's Woman. Amii Lorin. (Orig.). 1981. pap. 1.50 (ISBN 0-440-15507-X). Dell.
Morgana's Fault. Susan Lukas. 228p. 1981. 10.95 (ISBN 0-399-12584-1). Putnam.
Morgan's Passing. Anne Tyler. (Large Print Bks.). 1980. lib. bdg. 16.95 (ISBN 0-8161-3131-7). G K Hall.
Morgantina Studies: Vol. 1, the Terracottas. Malcolm Bell. LC 80-8537. (Illus.). 416p. 1981. 55.00x (ISBN 0-691-03946-1). Princeton U Pr.
Morgenthau Diary (China, 2 vols. Committee on the Judiciary, U. S. Senate, Eighty-Ninth Congress, First Session. LC 70-167844. (FDR & the Era of the New Deal Ser.). 1693p. 1974. Repr. of 1965 ed. Set. lib. bdg. 125.00 (ISBN 0-306-70332-7). Da Capo.
Morgenthau, the New Deal & Silver. Allan S. Everest. LC 72-2368. (FDR & the Era of the New Deal Ser.). 209p. 1973. Repr. of 1950 ed. lib. bdg. 25.00 (ISBN 0-306-70469-2). Da Capo.
Mori Ogai. J. Thomas Rimer. LC 74-28163. (World Authors Ser.: No. 355). 1975. lib. bdg. 10.95 (ISBN 0-8057-2636-5). Twayne.
Mori Ogai & the Modernization of Japanese Culture. R. J. Bowring. LC 76-11074. (Oriental Publications Ser.: No. 28). (Illus.). 1979. 44.00 (ISBN 0-521-21319-3). Cambridge U Pr.
Morita Psychotherapy. David K. Reynolds. LC 74-30530. 200p. 1976. 15.95 (ISBN 0-520-02937-2). U of Cal Pr.
Mork & Mindy. Paul D. Schneck. (TV-Movie Tie-Ins Ser.). 32p. (gr. 4-8). 1980. PLB 5.95 (ISBN 0-87191-754-8); pap. 2.95 (ISBN 0-89812-223-6). Creative Ed.
Mork & Mindy Super Activity Book. Paramount Pictures Corporation. 128p. (gr. 2-6). 1980. pap. cancelled o.s.i. (ISBN 0-448-15497-8). G&D.
Mork & Mindy: The Incredible Shrinking Mork. Robin S. Wagner. (Orig.). 1980. pap. write for info. (ISBN 0-671-83677-3). PB.
Morley & India 1906-1910. Stanley A. Wolpert. 1967. 20.00x (ISBN 0-520-01360-3). U of Cal Pr.
Mormon Athletes. William T. Black. (Illus.). 6.95 (ISBN 0-87747-842-2). Deseret Bk.
Mormon Mirage. Latayne C. Scott. 1980. 11.95 (ISBN 0-310-38910-0). Zondervan.
Mormon Mother: An Autobiography. Annie C. Tanner. (Utah, the Mormons, & the West: No. 1). 1976. pap. 5.00 (ISBN 0-87480-157-5, Tanner). U of Utah Pr.

Mormon: One Hundred & Fifty Years. Ed. by Sheryl White & Robert D. Shangle. (Illus.). 72p. 1980. 14.95 (ISBN 0-89802-177-4); pap. 7.95 (ISBN 0-89802-201-0). Beautiful Am.
Mormon Revelations of Convenience. Floyd McElveen. LC 78-72945. 1978. pap. 1.75 (ISBN 0-87123-385-1, 210385). Bethany Fell.
Mormon Sisters: Women in Early Utah. Claudia L. Bushman et al. Ed. by Claudia Bushman. LC 76-53854. (Illus.). 320p. 1980. pap. 5.95 (ISBN 0-918012-01-5). Olympus Pub Co.
Mormon Trail: In Story Form. Aurelia Richards. pap. 5.95 (ISBN 0-89036-137-1). Hawkes Pub Inc.
Mormones: Sus Doctrinas Refutadas a la Luz De la Biblia. Marvin W. Cowan. Tr. by Tomas De La Fuente from Eng. 1978. pap. 2.75 (ISBN 0-311-05763-2). Casa Bautista.
Mormonism. Walter Martin. 1968. pap. 0.95 (ISBN 0-87123-367-3, 210367). Bethany Fell.
Mormonism: A Happy Way to Live! Ken Miller. (Illus.). 1977. 6.95 o.p. (ISBN 0-88290-085-4). Horizon Utah.
Mormonism & the American Experience. Klaus J. Hansen. LC 80-19312. (History of American Religion Ser.). 224p. 1981. 15.00 (ISBN 0-226-31552-5). U of Chicago Pr.
Mormonism & the Negro. John J. Stewart. LC 78-52123. 1978. 4.50 (ISBN 0-88290-098-6). Horizon Utah.
Mormonism Exposed. G. B. Hancock. 4.95 (ISBN 0-89315-157-2). Lambert Bk.
Mormonismo Refutado. Jay Jacobson. (Modern Doctrines Collection). 1978. Repr. of 1972 ed. 0.55 (ISBN 0-311-05030-1). Casa Bautista.
Mormonismo Revelacion Divina O Invencion Humana. Domingo Fernandez. 1978. 0.80 (ISBN 0-311-05762-4). Casa Bautista.
Morne-Paysan: Peasant Village in Martinique. Michael M. Horowitz. Ed. by George Spindler & Louise Spindler. (Case Studies in Cultural Anthropology). 128p. pap. text ed. 4.95x (ISBN 0-8290-0309-6). Irvington.
Morning After Death. Nicholas Blake. LC 66-22042. 212p. 1980. pap. 1.95 (ISBN 0-06-080520-X, P 520, PL). Har-Row.
Morning & Evening. Charles H. Spurgeon. 1980. 10.95 (ISBN 0-310-32920-5); large print 8.95 (ISBN 0-310-32927-2). Zondervan.
Morning by Morning. Charles H. Spurgeon. Incl. Evening by Evening. (Direction Bks). pap. 3.95 (ISBN 0-8010-8067-3). Baker Bk.
Morning Glory. Robert Bly. LC 74-15811. 96p. 1975. 8.95 (ISBN 0-06-010368-X, HarpT); pap. 3.95 (ISBN 0-06-010367-1, CN-784, HarpT). Har-Row.
Morning Glory Afternoon. Irene B. Brown. LC 80-18495. 224p. (gr. 5-9). 1981. PLB 9.95 (ISBN 0-689-30802-7). Atheneum.
Morning Is a Long Time Coming. Bette Greene. (Illus.). (YA) (gr. 7-9). 1979. pap. 1.75 (ISBN 0-671-56005-0). PB.
Morning Is a Long Time Coming. Bette Greene. (gr. 7-9). 1979. pap. 1.95 (ISBN 0-671-42456-4). Archway.
Morning Joy. Helen G. Brenneman. LC 80-26449. 80p. 1981. pap. 3.95 (ISBN 0-8361-1942-8). Herald Pr.
Morning Light. White Eagle. 1957. 3.50 (ISBN 0-85487-018-0). De Vorss.
Morning, Noon & Night Cookbook. 2nd ed. Gerald Ramsey. LC 63-16652. 272p. 8.95 (ISBN 0-87074-178-0). SMU Press.
Morning Notes of Adelbert Ames, Jr. Including a Correspondence with John Dewey. Adelbert Ames, Jr. Ed. by Hadley Cantril. 1960. 17.00 (ISBN 0-8135-0354-X). Rutgers U Pr.
Morning of America. Darrett B. Rutman. LC 77-131289. (Illus., Orig.). 1971. pap. text ed. 7.25 (ISBN 0-395-04333-6). HM.
Morning of the Massacre. Michael Cadnum. 1981. pap. price not set (ISBN 0-931460-19-0). Bieler.
Morning of the Poem. James Schuyler. 1981. pap. 6.95 (ISBN 0-374-51622-7). FS&G.
Morning Praise & Evensong. Ed. by William G. Storey et al. LC 72-91427. 200p. 1973. 8.00 o.p. (ISBN 0-8190-0601-7). Fides Claretian.
Morning Prayer & Holy Communion from the Book of Common Prayer. 1928. Large-type Ed. pap. 1.50 ea. Morehouse.
Morning Star. Denise R. Adler. 1977. pap. 1.50 (ISBN 0-89129-206-3). Jove Pubns.
Morning Was Shining. John Hetherington. 1971. 8.95 (ISBN 0-571-09569-0, Pub. by Faber & Faber). Merrimack Bk Serv.
Morning Was Starlight: My Maine Boyhood. Ernest S. Dodge. LC 80-82791. (Illus.). 224p. 1981. price not set (ISBN 0-87106-049-3); pap. 8.95 (ISBN 0-87106-047-7). Globe Pequot.
Morning Window, Evening Window. Francis Sweeney. 1980. 8.95 o.p. (ISBN 0-89182-025-6). Charles River.
Morocco. Rom Landau. 1967. 21.95 (ISBN 0-236-30866-1, Pub. by Paul Elek). Merrimack Bk Serv.
Morocco, Algeria, Tunisia & Libya. Don Lawson. (First Bks). (Illus.). (gr. 4-6). 1978. PLB 6.45 s&l (ISBN 0-531-02233-1). Watts.
Morocco & Tunisia: A Comparative History. Dwight L. Ling. LC 79-5364. 1979. pap. text ed. 9.50 (ISBN 0-8191-0873-1). U Pr of Amer.
Morotai: A Memoir of War. John Boeman. LC 80-697. 288p. 1981. 12.95 (ISBN 0-385-15586-7). Doubleday.
Morphogenesis & Malformation of the Cardiovascular System: Proceedings. International Workshop on Morphogenesis & Malformation, 4th, Grand Canyon, Ariz., 1977. Ed. by Glenn C. Rosenquist & Daniel Bergsma. LC 78-14527. (Birth Defects Original Article Ser.: Vol. 14, No. 7). 452p. 1978. 53.00x (ISBN 0-8451-1023-3). A R Liss.
Morphogenesis & Malformation of the Ear. Ed. by Robert J. Gorlin. LC 80-18892. (Birth Defects: Original Article Ser.: Vol XVI, No. 4). 367p. 1980. 44.00 (ISBN 0-8451-1038-1). A R Liss.
Morphogenesis & Malformation of the Ear. Ed. by Robert J. Gorlin. LC 80-18892. (Alan R. Liss: Vol. 16,No. 4). 1980. 44.00 (ISBN 0-8451-1038-1). March of Dimes.
Morphogenesis & Malinformation of the Cardiovascular System. Ed. by Glenn C. Rosenquist & Daniel Bergsma. LC 78-14527. (Alan R. Liss Ser.: Vol. 14, No. 7). 1978. 46.00 (ISBN 0-8451-1023-3). March of Dimes.
Morphogenesis & Pattern Formation. Ed. by Thomas G. Connelly et al. 325p. 1981. 29.50 (ISBN 0-89004-635-2). Raven.
Morphogenesis of Karst Regions: Variants of Karst Evolution. Laszlo Jakucs. LC 76-40003. 1977. 57.95 (ISBN 0-470-98952-1). Halsted Pr.
Morphogenesis of Skin. P. Sengel. LC 74-25659. (Developmental & Cell Biology Ser.: No. 2). (Illus.). 300p. 1975. 69.00 (ISBN 0-521-20644-8). Cambridge U Pr.
Morphogenesis of the Vertebrates. 4th ed. Theodore W. Torrey & Alan Feduccia. LC 78-17196. 1979. 24.95 (ISBN 0-471-03232-8). Wiley.
Morphological & Phonological Components of the Arabic Verb. M. Bakalla. (Meccan Arabic.). 1979. 20.00x. Intl Bk Ctr.
Morphological Dermatology: A Study of the Living Gross Pathology of the Skin. Robert Jackson. (Illus.). 368p. 1979. text ed. 34.50 (ISBN 0-398-03849-X). C C Thomas.
Morphological Studies of Red Algae of the Family Cryptonemiaceae. Chiang Young-Meng. (U. C. Publ. in Botany: Vol. 58). 1970. pap. 6.50x (ISBN 0-520-09354-2). U of Cal Pr.
Morphological Studies of Red Algae of the Order Gigartinales. Richard B. Searles. (U. C. Publ. in Botany: Vol. 43). 1968. pap. 7.50x (ISBN 0-520-09016-0). U of Cal Pr.
Morphological Studies of the Nymphaeaceae, Vol. 4. Structure & Development of the Flower of Brasenia schreberi Geml. F. C. Richardson. (U. C. Publ. in Botany: Vol. 47). 1969. pap. 7.00x (ISBN 0-520-09020-9). U of Cal Pr.
Morphological Study of Egyptian Colloquial Arabic. Hilmi M. Aboul-Fetouh. (Janua Linguarum, Ser. Practica: No. 33). 1969. pap. text ed. 36.50x (ISBN 90-2790-691-2). Mouton.
Morphologisch und Entwicklungsgeschichtliche Untersuchungen an Blueten und Bluetenstaenden Von Solannaceen und Von Nolana Paradoxa Lindl: Nolanaceae. K. A. Huber. (Dissertationes Botanicae: No. 55). (Illus.). 486p. (Ger.). 1980. pap. text ed. 50.00x (ISBN 3-7682-1268-8). Lubrecht & Cramer.
Morphology: An Introduction to the Theory of Word-Structure. P. H. Matthews. LC 73-91817. (Cambridge Textbooks in Linguistics Ser.). 256p. 1974. 37.50 (ISBN 0-521-20448-8); pap. 9.95x (ISBN 0-521-09856-4). Cambridge U Pr.
Morphology & Evolution of the Insect Abdomen. R. Matsuda. Ed. by Kerkut. 568p. 1976. text ed. 90.00 (ISBN 0-08-018753-6). Pergamon.
Morphology & Infrageneric Relationships of the Genus "Jatropha" (Euphorbiaceae) Bijan Deghan & Grady L. Webster. LC 77-83116. (Publications in Botany Ser.: Vol. 74). 1979. 11.50x (ISBN 0-520-09585-5). U of Cal Pr.
Morphology & Phylogenetic Relationships of the Lower Permian Tetrapod Tseajaia campi Vaughn (Amphibia: Seymouriamorpha) John Lawrence Moss. (U. C. Publ. in Geological Sciences: Vol. 98). 1973. pap. 8.00x (ISBN 0-520-09439-5). U of Cal Pr.
Morphology & Physiology of Plant Tumors. A. C. Braun & T. Stonier. (Protoplasmatologia: Vol. 10, Pt. 5a). (Illus.). 1958. 24.80 o.p. (ISBN 0-387-80492-7). Springer-Verlag.
Morphology & Taxonomy of Male Scale Insects (Homoptera: Coccoidea) M. S. Ghauri. (Illus.). vii, 221p. 1962. 19.50x (ISBN 0-565-00580-4, Pub. by British Mus Nat Hist England). Sabbot-Natural Hist Bks.
Morphology & Varietal Characteristics of the Rice Plant. (Technical Bulletin Ser.: No. 4). 40p. 1965. pap. 5.00 (R022, IRRI). Unipub.
Morphology of Gymnosperms: The Structure & Evolution of Primitive Seed Plants. K. R. Sporne. 1967. text ed. 12.50x (ISBN 0-09-077151-6, Hutchinson U Lib); pap. text ed. 9.25x (ISBN 0-09-077152-4, Hutchinson U Lib). Humanities.
Morphology of Pteridophytes: The Structure of Ferns & Allied Plants. 4th ed. K. R. Sporne. 1975. pap. text ed. 9.25x (ISBN 0-09-123861-7, Hutchinson U Lib). Humanities.
Morphology of the Liver. H. Elias & Joseph C. Sherrick. 1969. 59.75 (ISBN 0-12-237950-0). Acad Pr.
Morphology: The Descriptive Analysis of Words. 2nd ed. Eugene A. Nida. 1949. pap. 7.95x (ISBN 0-472-08684-7). U of Mich Pr.
Morphonology: The Dynamics of Derivation. Wolfgang U. Dressler. (Linguistica Extranea: Studia: No. 12). 250p. 13.50 (ISBN 0-89720-034-9); pap. 10.50 (ISBN 0-89720-035-7). Karoma.
Morphy Chess Masterpieces. Fred Reinfeld & Andy Soltis. 176p. 1974. 6.95 o.s.i. (ISBN 0-02-601980-9). Macmillan.
Morra Gambit. Janos Flesch. (Algebraic Chess Openings Ser.). (Illus.). 176p. 1981. pap. 14.50 (ISBN 0-7134-2188-6, Pub. by Batsford England). David & Charles.
Morris Approach: An Insider's Guide to Cat Care. Barbara Burn. LC 80-14051. (Illus.). 64p. 1980. 6.95 (ISBN 0-688-03693-7). Morrow.
Morris Has a Cold. Bernard Wiseman. LC 77-12030. (gr. 1-4). 1978. 6.95 (ISBN 0-396-07522-3). Dodd.
Morris Louis in the Museum of Fine Arts, Boston. Kenworth Moffett. LC 79-6360. (Illus.). 1979. pap. 6.95 (ISBN 0-87846-135-3). Mus Fine Arts Boston.
Morris on Torts. 2nd ed. Clarence Morris & C. Robert Morris. LC 80-170. (University Textbook Ser.). 457p. 1980. write for info. (ISBN 0-88277-002-0). Foundation Pr.
Morris R. Cohen & the Scientific Ideal. David A. Hollinger. LC 75-12850. 384p. 1975. text ed. 20.00x (ISBN 0-262-08084-2). MIT Pr.
Morris R. Cohen & the Scientific Ideal. David A. Hollinger. 288p. 1980. pap. 5.95 (ISBN 0-262-58041-1). MIT Pr.
Morristown: The War Years, Seventeen Seventy-Five to Seventeen Eighty-Three. Judi Benvenuti & Mary Ann Cataldo. (Illus.). 124p. 1979. 15.95 (ISBN 0-686-27870-4, Pub. by Eastern Natl Park). Eastern Acorn.
Morro Bay Meanderings. Harold Wieman. LC 72-2793. (Illus.). 1975. pap. 3.50 (ISBN 0-914598-12-0). Padre Prods.
Morrocco. Andre Launey. 1976. 19.95 (ISBN 0-7134-3182-2). David & Charles.
Mort de Pompee. Pierre Corneille. (Nouveaux Classiques Larousse). (Illus., Fr). pap. 2.95 (ISBN 0-685-13995-6, 71). Larousse.
MORT Safety Assurance Systems. Johnson. (Occupational Safety & Health Ser.: Vol. 4). 544p. 1980. 35.00 (ISBN 0-8247-6897-3). Dekker.
Mortal Engines. Stanislaw Lem. Tr. by Michael Kandel from Polish. LC 76-54758. 1977. 9.95 (ISBN 0-8164-9296-4). Continuum.
Mortal Fire. Peter Dale. LC 74-29409. ix, 181p. 1976. 16.00 (ISBN 0-8214-0185-8); pap. 5.00 (ISBN 0-8214-0187-4). Ohio U Pr.
Mortal Friends. James Carroll. 1979. pap. 2.95 (ISBN 0-440-15789-7). Dell.
Mortal Gods. Jonathan Fast. LC 77-15901. 1978. 8.95 o.p. (ISBN 0-06-011266-2, HarpT). Har-Row.
Mortal Messiah, from Bethlehem to Calvary, Bk. 3. Bruce R. McConkie. LC 79-19606. 486p. 1980. 11.95 (ISBN 0-87747-825-2). Deseret Bk.
Mortal Questions. T. Nagel. LC 78-58797. 1979. 29.95 (ISBN 0-521-22360-1); pap. 7.95x (ISBN 0-521-29460-6). Cambridge U Pr.
Mortal Worm: Shakespeare's Master Theme. Elias Schwartz. (National University Pubns. Literary Criticism Ser.). 1977. 11.00 (ISBN 0-8046-9137-1). Kennikat.
Mortal Wound. Raffaele La Capria. Tr. by M. Waldman from It. Orig. Title: Ferito a Morte. 1964. 4.75 o.p. (ISBN 0-374-21317-8). FS&G.
Mortality & Morbidity After Excessive Stress. Leo Eitinger & Axel Strom. 1973. text ed. 27.00x (ISBN 8-200-04738-5, Dist. by Columbia U Pr). Universitet.
Mortality from Diseases Associated with Smoking: United States, 1960-77. A. Joan Klebba. Ed. by Audrey Shipp. (Ser. 20, No. 17). 50p. Date not set. pap. text ed. price not set (ISBN 0-8406-0208-1). Natl Ctr Health Stats.
Mortality in Developing Countries. Julien Conde et al. Ed. by OECD Deveopment Centre. (Development Centre Studies). (Orig.). 1980. Tome 1 & 2, 1266p. pap. 85.00 (ISBN 9-2640-2097-7, 41-80-05-3); Tome 3, 550p. pap. 30.00 (ISBN 9-2640-2120-5, 41-80-06-1). OECD.
Mortality Table Construction. Robert W. Batten. LC 77-12349. (Risk, Insurance & Security Ser.). (Illus.). 1978. 17.95 (ISBN 0-13-601302-3). P-H.
Morte d'Arthur, 2 vols. Thomas Malory. 1953. 8.00x ea. (Everyman). Vol. 1 (ISBN 0-460-00045-4). Vol. 2 (ISBN 0-460-00046-2). pap. 3.75 ea. (Everyman). Vol. 1 (ISBN 0-460-01045-X). Vol. 2 (ISBN 0-460-01046-8). Dutton.
Morte Darthur. Sir Thomas Malory. Ed. by P. J. Field. LC 77-22498. (London Medieval & Renaissance Ser.). 1978. text ed. 26.50x (ISBN 0-8419-0333-6). Holmes & Meier.
Morte D'arthur: King Arthur & the Knights of the Round Table. Thomas Malory. Tr. by Keith Baines. (Orig.). 1962. pap. 2.95 (ISBN 0-451-61878-5, ME1878, Ment). NAL.
Morte Do Dolar. Tr. by Willard Cantelon. (Portuguese Bks.). 1979. 1.40 (ISBN 0-8297-0816-2). Life Pubs Intl.
Mortgage Credit & Closing. Larry Shiels, Jr. 1972. pap. 45.00 (ISBN 0-686-04915-2). Home Equity.
Mortgage Lending Fundamentals & Practices. Marshall Dennis. (Illus.). 1981. text ed. 16.95 (ISBN 0-8359-4651-7). Reston.
Mortgage Payment Table No. 291. rev ed. Financial Publishing Co. 5.00 o.p. (ISBN 0-685-41731-X). Finan Pub.
Mortgage Values Tables No. 207. Financial Publishing Co. 12.50 (ISBN 0-685-02552-7). Finan Pub.
Mortgaged Wife. Barbara Harr. LC 77-112871. (New Poetry Ser). 85p. 1970. 5.00 o.p. (ISBN 0-8040-0215-0); pap. 3.50 (ISBN 0-8040-0216-9). Swallow.
Mortgages on Paradise: Life-Centered Sermons. Walter D. Wagoner. LC 80-20138. 128p. (Orig.). 1981. pap. 4.95 (ISBN 0-687-27220-3). Abingdon.
Mortuary Science. Frederick Gale. (Illus.). 240p. 1960. pap. 14.50 photocopy ed., spiral (ISBN 0-398-04166-0). C C Thomas.
Morvern Transformed. P. Gaskell. (Illus.). 300p. 1980. 37.50 (ISBN 0-521-05060-X); pap. 14.95 (ISBN 0-521-29797-4). Cambridge U Pr.
MOS Integrated Circuits: Theory, Fabrication, Design, & Systems Applications of MOS LSI. Ed. by William M. Penney. Lillian Lau. LC 79-1039. 494p. 1979. Repr. of 1972 ed. lib. bdg. 24.50 o.p. (ISBN 0-88275-897-7). Krieger.
Mosaics. Angelica Garnett. (Oxford Paperbacks Handbooks for Artists Ser.). 1967. pap. 4.00x o.p. (ISBN 0-19-289901-5). Oxford U Pr.
Mosaics in Needlepoint. Xenia L. Parker. LC 77-5045. (Encore Edition). (Illus.). 1977. encore ed. 5.95 (ISBN 0-684-16201-6, ScribT); pap. 3.95 encore ed. (ISBN 0-684-15036-0, SL713, ScribT). Scribner.
Mosaics in Roman Britain. Anne Rainey. (Illus.). 205p. 1973. 12.00x o.p. (ISBN 0-87471-158-4). Rowman.
Mosaics of Organization Character. Robert G. Wright. LC 74-76943. 1975. lib. bdg. 11.50 (ISBN 0-8046-9297-1); pap. text ed. 5.95 (ISBN 0-8046-9278-5). Kennikat.
Mosaics of Roman North Africa: Studies in Iconography & Patronage. Katherine M. Dunbabin. (Monographs on Classical Archaeology). (Illus.). 1979. 85.00x (ISBN 0-19-813217-4). Oxford U Pr.
Mosaics of the National Shrine of the Immaculate Conception. Frank DiFederico. (Illus.). 96p. 1981. 16.95 (ISBN 0-916276-09-0). Decatur Hse.
Mosby's Comprehensive Review of Critical Care. 2nd ed. Donna A. Zschoche. LC 80-16790. (Illus.). 959p. 1980. text ed. 25.95 (ISBN 0-8016-5697-4). Mosby.
Mosby's Comprehensive Review of Nursing. 9th ed. Ed. by Dolores F. Saxton et al. Patricia M. Nugent & Phyllis K. Pelikan. 1977. text ed. 13.95 (ISBN 0-8016-3529-2). Mosby.
Mosby's Comprehensive Review of Nursing. 10th ed. Ed. by Dolores F. Saxton et al. (Illus.). 1981. text ed. cancelled (ISBN 0-8016-3530-6). Mosby.
Mosby's Comprehensive Review Series: Review of Operative Dentistry. William W. Howard. LC 72-12874. 1973. pap. text ed. 9.95 o.p. (ISBN 0-8016-2279-4). Mosby.
Mosby's Manual of Critical Care: Practices & Procedures, Nineteen Seventy-Nine. Linda F. Abels. LC 78-24358. (Illus.). 1979. pap. text ed. 16.95 (ISBN 0-8016-0055-3). Mosby.
Mosby's Manual of Emergency Care: Practices & Procedures. Janet M. Barber & Susan A. Budassi. LC 79-31708. (Illus.). 1979. pap. text ed. 19.95 (ISBN 0-8016-0447-8). Mosby.
Mosby's Manual of Nuclear Medicine Procedures. 3rd ed. D. Bruce Sodee & Paul J. Early. (Illus.). 574p. 1981. pap. text ed. 34.95 (ISBN 0-8016-4729-0). Mosby.
Mosby's Review Series: Review of Hemodialysis for Nurses & Dialysis Personnel. 3rd ed. C. F. Gutch & Martha H. Stoner. LC 79-16882. (Illus.). 1979. pap. text ed. 15.95 (ISBN 0-8016-1994-7). Mosby.

Moscow. Leo Gruliou. (The Great Cities Ser.). (Illus.). (gr. 6 up). 1977. PLB 11.97 (ISBN 0-8094-2275-1, Pub. by Time-Life). Silver.
Moscow. Ed. by Leo Gruliow. (Great Cities Ser.). 1977. 14.95 (ISBN 0-8094-2274-3). Time-Life.
Moscow Abandons Israel for the Arabs: Ten Crucial Years in the Middle East. Alden H. Voth. LC 80-5478. 275p. 1980. lib. bdg. 18.25 o.p. (ISBN 0-8191-1111-2); pap. text ed. 10.25 o.p. (ISBN 0-8191-1112-0). U Pr of Amer.
Moscow & the New Left. Klaus Mehnert. Tr. by Helmut Fischer. LC 73-90660. 1975. 20.00x (ISBN 0-520-02652-7). U of Cal Pr.
Moscow & the Roots of Russian Culture. Arthur Voyce. (Centers of Civilization Ser.: Vol. 14). 194p. 1980. pap. 3.95 (ISBN 0-8061-1701-X). U of Okla Pr.
Moscow Conference. Special Consultative Committee On Security. (Eng. & Span.). 1968. pap. 1.00 ea. o.p. OAS.
Moscow Farewell. George Feifer. 1977. pap. 1.95 o.p. (ISBN 0-425-03385-6, Medallion). Berkley Pub.
Moscow Gourmet: A Guide to Eating Out in the Soviet Capital. Lynn Fisher & Wesley Fisher. 100p. 1974. pap. 3.95 o.p. (ISBN 0-88233-066-7). Ardis Pubs.
Moscow Workers & the Nineteen Seventeen Revolution. Diane Koenker. LC 80-8557. (Studies of the Russian Institute, Columbia University). (Illus.). 456p. 1981. 30.00x (ISBN 0-691-05323-5). Princeton U Pr.
Mose in Egitto, 2 vols. Gioachino Rossini. Ed. by Phillip Gossett & Charles Rosen. LC 76-49183. (Early Romantic Opera Ser.: No. 9). 1979. lib. bdg. 82.00 (ISBN 0-8240-2908-9). Garland Pub.
Moselle. O. W. Loeb & Terence Prittie. (Illus.). 1972. 9.95 o.p. (ISBN 0-571-08199-1, Pub. by Faber & Faber). Merrimack Bk Serv.
Moses: A Man Changed by God. Hazel Offner. 72p. (Orig.). 1981. pap. 2.95 (ISBN 0-87784-617-0). Inter-Varsity.
Moses & His Contemporaries. Gordon Lindsay. (Old Testament Ser.). 1.25 (ISBN 0-89985-133-9). Christ Nations.
Moses & the Church in the Wilderness. Gordon Lindsay. (Old Testament Ser.). 1.25 (ISBN 0-89985-132-0). Christ Nations.
Moses & the Deuteronomist: A Literary Study of the Deuteronomic History. Robert M. Polzin. 224p. Date not set. 14.95 (ISBN 0-8245-4740-3); pap. 7.95 (ISBN 0-8245-4739-X). Crossroad NY.
Moses in the Letter to the Hebrews. Mary R. D'Angelo. LC 78-12917. (Society of Biblical Literature, Dissertation Ser.: No. 42). 1979. 12.00 (ISBN 0-89130-265-4, 060142); pap. 7.50 (ISBN 0-89130-333-2). Scholars Pr Ca.
Moses Maimonides on the Causes of Symptoms. Ed. by J. O. Leibowitz & Shlomo Marcus. 1974. 19.50x (ISBN 0-520-02224-6). U of Cal Pr.
Moses Maimonides: Rabbi, Philosopher, & Physician. Rebecca B. Markus. LC 69-12594. (Biography Ser). (Illus.). (gr. 7 up). 1969. PLB 6.90 (ISBN 0-531-00899-1). Watts.
Moses: Moments of Glory, Feet of Clay. Gene A. Getz. LC 75-23519. (Orig.). 1976. pap. 3.25 o.p. (ISBN 0-8307-0400-0, 54-032-00); study guide 1.39 o.p. (ISBN 0-8307-0514-7, 61-003-09). Regal.
Moses, Prince & Shepherd. Lucy Diamond. (Ladybird Ser). (Illus.). 1954. bds. 1.49 (ISBN 0-87508-850-3). Chr Lit.
Moses, The Deliverer. Gordon Lindsay. (Old Testament Ser.). 1.25 (ISBN 0-89985-131-2). Christ Nations.
Moses the Lawgiver. Gordon Lindsay. (Old Testament Ser.: Vol. 10). pap. 1.25 (ISBN 0-89985-959-3). Christ Nations.
Mosfet Circuits Guidebook: With One Hundred Tested Projects. Rufus Turner. LC 75-27483. (Illus.). 196p. 1975. 7.95 (ISBN 0-8306-5796-7); pap. 6.95 (ISBN 0-8306-4796-1, 766). TAB Bks.
MOSFET Technology--a Comprehensive Bibliography. Ed. by A. H. Agajanian. 305p. 1980. 95.00 (ISBN 0-306-65193-9). IFI Plenum.
Moshe Sharett. Menachem Z. Rosensaft. LC 66-25854. 1966. 4.95 (ISBN 0-88400-019-2). Shengold.
Moshie Cat. Helen Griffiths. (Illus.). (gr. 4-6). 1977. pap. 1.25 o.s.i. (ISBN 0-671-29816-X). Archway.
Moshie Cat. Helen Griffiths. (Illus.). (gr. 4-6). 1977. pap. 1.25 (ISBN 0-686-68484-2). PB.
Mosiac Eschatological Prophet. Howard M. Teeple. (Society of Biblical Literature, Monographs). 1957. pap. 7.50 (ISBN 0-89130-180-1, 060010). Scholars Pr Ca.
Moskauer Tagebuch. Walter Benjamin. (Edtion Suhrkamp: Neue Folge). 200p. (Orig.). 1980. pap. text ed. 6.50 (ISBN 3-518-11020-9, Pub. by Insel Verlag Germany). Suhrkamp.
Moslem Brethren: The Greatest of the Modern Islamic Movements. Ishak M. Al-Husaini. LC 79-2866. 186p. 1981. Repr. of 1956 ed. 18.00 (ISBN 0-8305-0039-1). Hyperion Conn.
Mosque & Pagoda: The Muslim Chinese. Barbara L. Pillsbury. 344p. Date not set. text ed. cancelled (ISBN 0-292-75056-0). U of Tex Pr.
Mosque of Omyad. Anthony De Perro. 23p. 1980. 4.95 (ISBN 0-533-04410-3). Vantage.
Mosquito. 2nd ed. Michael J. Bowyer & C. Martin Sharp. (Illus.). 1971. 18.95 o.p. (ISBN 0-571-04750-5, Pub. by Faber & Faber); pap. 6.95 o.p. (ISBN 0-571-09531-3). Merrimack Bk Serv.
Mosquito. Ron Reese. Ed. by Alton Jordan. (Elephant Ser.). (Illus.). (gr. k-3). 1975. PLB 3.50 (ISBN 0-89868-014-X, Read Res); text ed. 1.75 soft bd. (ISBN 0-89868-047-6). ARO Pub.
Mosquito: Classic Aircraft, No. 7. Michael J. Bowyer & Bryan Philpott. (Illus.). 128p. 1980. 29.95 (ISBN 0-85059-432-4). Aztex.
Mosquito Ecology: Field Sampling Methods. M. W. Service. 1976. 87.95 (ISBN 0-470-15191-9). Halsted Pr.
Mosquito Is Born. William White, Jr. LC 77-93319. (Sterling Nature Series). (Illus.). (gr. 5 up). 1978. 7.95 (ISBN 0-8069-3534-0); PLB 7.49 (ISBN 0-8069-3535-9). Sterling.
Mosquito Manual: The Official Air Publication for the Mosquito N.F. Mk. XIX. LC 77-80080. (RAF Museum Ser.: Vol. 6). (Illus.). 1978. 16.95 o.p. (ISBN 0-88254-446-2). Hippocrene Bks.
Mosquitoes, Malaria & Man: A History of the Hostilities Since 1880. Gordon Harrison. 320p. 1980. 40.00x (ISBN 0-7195-3580-8, Pub. by Murray Pubs England). State Mutual Bk.
Mosquitoes of Canada: Diptera; Culicidae. (Insects & Arachnids of Canada: Pt. 6). 390p. 1980. pap. 15.00 (ISBN 0-660-10402-4, SSC 143, SSC). Unipub.
Mosquitoes of North America. Stanley J. Carpenter & Walter J. Lacasse. (California Library Reprint Ser.). (Illus.). 1974. Repr. 40.00x (ISBN 0-520-02638-1). U of Cal Pr.
Moss Flora of Britain & Ireland. A. J. Smith. LC 77-71428. (Illus.). 1978. 82.50 (ISBN 0-521-21648-6). Cambridge U Pr.
Moss Rose. Day Taylor. 1980. pap. 2.75 (ISBN 0-440-15969-5). Dell.
Mossbauer Spectroscopy: An Introduction for Chemists & Geochemists. G. M. Bancroft. LC 73-3326. 252p. 1974. text ed. 29.95 (ISBN 0-470-04665-1). Halsted Pr.
Mossbauer Spectroscopy & Its Applications. (Illus.). 421p. (Orig.). 1972. pap. 26.75 (ISBN 92-0-131072-2, IAEA). Unipub.
Mosses of Eastern North America, 2 Vols. Howard A. Crum & Lewis E. Anderson. LC 79-24789. (Illus.). 576p. 1981. 60.00x (ISBN 0-231-04516-6). Columbia U Pr.
Mosses of North America. Ed. by Ronald J. Taylor & Alan E. Leviton. 170p. (Orig.). 1980. 11.95 (ISBN 0-934394-02-4). AAASPD.
Mosses of Singapore & Malaysia. Anne Johnson. 126p. 1980. pap. 7.50 (ISBN 0-8214-0547-0). Swallow.
Most Amazing Hide & Seek Counting Book. Robert Crowther. (Illus.). 14p. 1981. 8.95 (ISBN 0-670-48997-2). Viking Pr.
Most Beautiful Women in British History. Felix Barton. (Illus.). 1978. deluxe ed. 47.75 (ISBN 0-930582-07-1). Gloucester Art.
Most Common Boat Maintenance Problems. Bob Whittier. (Illus.). 256p. 1981. lib. bdg. 12.95 (ISBN 0-668-04877-8, 4877). Arco.
Most Frequently Asked Questions About Bicycling. Ed. by Bicycling Magazine. 1980. pap. 2.95 (ISBN 0-87857-300-3). Rodale Pr Inc.
Most Holy Man. Ken Noyle. Ed. by Stefan Grunwald. (Orig.). 1981. pap. price not set (ISBN 0-89865-127-1, Unilaw). Donning Co.
Most Honest People. Bill Lufburrow. LC 80-69253. (Illus., Orig.). 1980. pap. 4.95 (ISBN 0-918464-23-4). D Armstrong.
Most Important Art: East European Film After 1945. Mira Liehm & Antonin Liehm. 1977. 24.95 (ISBN 0-520-03157-1); pap. 10.95 (ISBN 0-520-04128-3, CAL 474). U of Cal Pr.
Most Important Thing in the World. Carol Farley. LC 73-9675. 256p. (gr. 5-8). 1974. PLB 4.90 o.p. (ISBN 0-531-02663-9). Watts.
Most Likely Suspects. Art Bourgeau. 196p. (Orig.). 1981. pap. 7.65 (ISBN 0-441-54376-6). Charter Bks.
Most Notorious Victory. Ben B. Seligman. 1966. 8.95 o.s.i. (ISBN 0-02-928310-8). Free Pr.
Most of All They Taught Me Happiness. Robert Muller. LC 78-52110. 1978. 8.95 (ISBN 0-385-14310-9). Doubleday.
Most Often Asked Questions & Answers About Amateur Radio. Leo G. Sands. 1979. pap. 5.50 (ISBN 0-8104-0852-X). Hayden.
Most Puzzling Situations in Bridge Play. Terence Reese. LC 78-57884. (Illus.). 1978. 6.95 o.p. (ISBN 0-8069-4936-8); lib. bdg. 6.69 o.p. (ISBN 0-8069-4937-6). Sterling.
Most Puzzling Situations in Bridge Play. Terence Reese. 1980. pap. 1.95 (ISBN 0-451-09538-3, J9538, Sig). NAL.
Most Recent Tendecies in the Socialist Orientation of Various African & Arab Countries. (Dissertationes Orientales: No. 41). 323p. (Orig.). 1979. pap. 6.00x (Pub. by Orient Inst Czechoslovakia). Paragon.
Most Revealing Book of the Bible: Making Sense Out of Revelation. Vernard Eller. 1974. pap. 4.95 (ISBN 0-8028-1572-3). Eerdmans.
Most Ridiculous Book on Gardening Ever. George Peterson. 1981. 6.95 (ISBN 0-533-04590-8). Vantage.
Most Secret. Nevil Shute. 310p. 1976. Repr. of 1945 ed. lib. bdg. 13.95x (ISBN 0-89244-084-8). Queens Hse.
Most Significant Stock Market Chart Patterns & the Amazing Anticipatory Meaning They Contain. Robert M. Elliott. (Illus.). 151p. 1981. 49.75 (ISBN 0-918968-89-5). Inst Econ Finan.
Most Splendid Men. Harold Brown. (Illus.). 192p. 1981. 12.50 (ISBN 0-7137-1107-8, Pub. by Blandford Pr England). Sterling.
Most Unvaluedst Purchase: Women in the Plays of Thomas Middleton. Caroline L. Cherry. (Salzburg Studies in English Literature, Jacobean Drama Studies: No. 34). 114p. 1973. pap. text ed. 25.00x (ISBN 0-391-01342-4). Humanities.
Most Work Measurement Systems. Ed. by K. Zandin. (Industrial Engineering Ser.). 222p. 1980. 19.50 (ISBN 0-8247-6899-X). Dekker.
Mostly Fools: A Romance of Civilization, 1886. Edmund Randolph. (Victorian Fiction Ser.). 1975. lib. bdg. 66.00 (ISBN 0-8240-1539-8). Garland Pub.
Mostly French Food Processor Cookbook. rev. ed. Colette Rossand & Jill H. Herman. 1980. pap. 2.50 (ISBN 0-451-09537-5, E9537, Sig). NAL.
Mostly Golf: A Bernard Darwin Anthology. Ed. by Peter Ryde. 1977. 15.00 (ISBN 0-7136-1687-3). Transatlantic.
Mostly Me. Gary Grimm & Don Mitchell. (gr. k-6). 1976. 10.50 (ISBN 0-916456-07-2, GA64). Good Apple.
Mostly Sitting Haiku. 2nd rev., exp. ed. Allen Ginsberg. (Xtras Ser.: No. 6). 36p. (Orig.). 1981. pap. 2.00 (ISBN 0-89120-014-2). From Here.
Mostly Tailfeathers. Gene Hill. 192p. 1975. 11.95 (ISBN 0-87691-167-X). Winchester Pr.
Motel Tapes. Mike McGrady. 352p. (Orig.). 1977. pap. 1.95 o.s.i. (ISBN 0-446-89332-3). Warner Bks.
Moth Hunters: Aboriginal Prehistory of the Australian Alps. J. Flood. (AIAS New Ser.). (Illus.). 1980. text ed. 22.00x (ISBN 0-391-00993-1); pap. text ed. 15.50x (ISBN 0-391-00994-X). Humanities.
Mother. Sri Aurobindo. 1979. pap. 1.00 (ISBN 0-89744-914-2); pap. 1.00 (ISBN 0-89744-915-0). Auromere.
Mother Bombie. John Lyly. Ed. by Harriette Andreadis. (Salzburg Studies in English Literature, Elizabethan & Renaissance Studies: No. 35). 248p. 1975. pap. text ed. 25.00x (ISBN 0-391-01465-X). Humanities.
Mother-Child Interaction Strategies. Olga K. Garnica. (Humanist Psychobiology & Psychiatry Ser.). Date not set. price not set (ISBN 0-08-024302-9). Pergamon.
Mother Courage & the Caucasian Chalk Circle Notes. Denis Calandra. 77p. 1975. pap. text ed. 1.25 o.s.i. (ISBN 0-8220-0858-0). Cliffs.
Mother Crocodile: An Uncle Amadou Tale from Senegal. Rosa Guy. LC 80-393. (Illus.). 32p. (gr. k-2). 1981. 10.95 (ISBN 0-440-06405-8); PLB 10.42 (ISBN 0-440-06406-6). Delacorte.
Mother, Daughter, Self. Veryl Rosenbaum. 1979. pap. 1.95 (ISBN 0-505-51406-0). Tower Bks.
Mother, Daughter, Sister, Lover: A Collection of Short Stories Dealing with Woman's Relations to Woman. Jan Clausen. LC 80-16386. (Crossing Press Feminist Ser.). (Orig.). 1980. 10.95 (ISBN 0-89594-034-5); pap. 4.95 (ISBN 0-89594-033-7). Crossing Pr.
Mother Earth, Father Sky, & Economic Development: Navajo Resources & Their Use. Philip Reno. (Illus.). 200p. 1981. 12.95x (ISBN 0-8263-0550-4). U of NM Pr.
Mother Earth News Alcohol Fuel Handbook. Ed. by Michael R. Kerley & The Mother Earth News Staff. 120p. (Orig.). 1980. pap. 12.95 (ISBN 0-938432-00-1). Mother Earth.
Mother Earth's Houseplant Coloring Album. Lynn Rapp & Joel Rapp. (Illus., Orig.). 1976. pap. 2.95 o.p. (ISBN 0-912300-72-8, 72-8). Troubador Pr.
Mother Florence: Biographical History. Angeline Murphy. (Biblio. Index Notes Ser.). (Illus.). 64p. 1980. 15.00 (ISBN 0-682-49625-1). Exposition.
Mother, God, & Mental Health. Lillian Maki. LC 79-92840. 1980. pap. 4.95 (ISBN 0-8323-0353-4). Binford.
Mother Goddam. rev. ed. Bette Davis. 1979. pap. 2.75 (ISBN 0-425-04119-0). Berkley Pub.
Mother Goddess in Indian Art, Archaeology & Literature. Srivastava. 1980. 32.00x (ISBN 0-686-65576-1, Pub. by Agam India). South Asia Bks.
Mother Goose. Gyo Fujikawa. (Gyo Fujikawa Tiny Board Books). (Illus.). 14p. (ps-k). 1981. 1.95 (ISBN 0-448-15091-3). G&D.
Mother Goose. Illus. by Bonnie Rutherford & Bill Rutherford. (ps-1). 1973. PLB 5.38 (ISBN 0-307-68970-0, Golden Pr). Western Pub.
Mother Goose. Zokeisha. (Puppet Story Board Bks.). (Illus.). 12p. (ps-k). Date not set. boards 2.95 (ISBN 0-671-42643-5, Little Simon). S&S.
Mother Goose Abroad: Nursery Rhymes. Ed. by Nicholas Tucker. LC 73-2831. (Illus.). (ps-3). 1975. 7.39 o.p. (ISBN 0-690-00093-6, TYC-J). T Y Crowell.
Mother Goose in French. Tr. by Hugh Latham. LC 64-10863. (Illus., Fr). (gr. 4 up). 1964. 8.79 o.p. (ISBN 0-690-56265-9, TYC-J); PLB 6.79 o.p. (ISBN 0-690-56266-7). T Y Crowell.
Mother Goose in the City. Illus. by Dora Leder. (ps-2). 1974. PLB 5.00 (ISBN 0-307-60336-9, Golden Pr). Western Pub.
Mother Goose on the Farm. Illus. by June Goldsborough. (Tell-a-Tale Readers). (Illus.). (ps-1). 1975. PLB 4.77 (ISBN 0-307-68587-X, Whitman). Western Pub.
Mother Goose Rhymes. Tr. by Editions les Belles Images Staff. (Butterfly Bks). (Illus., Orig.). (gr. 1-2). 1977. pap. 1.50 (ISBN 0-8467-0331-9, Pub. by Two Continents). Hippocrene Bks.
Mother Goose Rhymes. Illus. by Eulalie. LC 80-83934. (Illus.). 48p. (ps-1). 1981. Repr. of 1953 ed. 2.95 (ISBN 0-448-40114-2); PLB write for info. (ISBN 0-448-13946-4). Platt.
Mother Goose Rhymes for Jewish Children. Sara G. Levy. (Illus.). (ps-2). 1979. Repr. of 1945 ed. 6.95 (ISBN 0-8197-0254-4). Bloch.
Mother Goose: The Original Mother Goose's Melody As First Issued by John Newbery of London, About A.D. 1760. LC 68-31093. 1969. Repr. of 1889 ed. 15.00 (ISBN 0-686-66814-6). Gale.
Mother Goose Treasury. Raymond Briggs. (gr. k-6). 1980. pap. 7.95 (ISBN 0-440-46408-0, YB). Dell.
Mother-in-Laws Can Be Fun. Lou Beardsley. LC 80-84763. 1981. pap. 4.95 (ISBN 0-89081-281-0). Harvest Hse.
Mother India's Lighthouse: India's Spiritual Leaders. Sri Chinmoy. LC 74-189998. 288p. 1973. pap. 2.95 (ISBN 0-8334-1732-0). Steinerbks.
Mother-Infant Interaction. C. Etta Walters. LC 74-12621. 1976. text ed. 22.95 (ISBN 0-87705-240-9); pap. text ed. 9.95 (ISBN 0-87705-284-0). Human Sci Pr.
Mother Ireland. Edna O'Brien. 1976. 12.95 o.p. (ISBN 0-15-162587-5). HarBraceJ.
Mother Is Gold: A Study in West African Literature. Adrian A. Roscoe. 1971. 21.50 (ISBN 0-521-08092-4); pap. 11.95x (ISBN 0-521-09644-8). Cambridge U Pr.
Mother Jones, the Miners' Angel: A Portrait. Dale Fetherling. LC 78-16328. (Arcturus Books Paperbacks). (Illus.). 280p. 1979. pap. 8.95 (ISBN 0-8093-0896-7). S Ill U Pr.
Mother, Mother. James Stingley. 224p. 1981. 11.95 (ISBN 0-312-92543-3). Congdon & Lattes.
Mother, Mother. James Stingley. 224p. 1981. 11.95 (ISBN 0-312-92543-3). St Martin.
Mother Mother I Feel Sick Send for the Doctor Quick Quick Quick. Remy Charlip & Burton Supree. LC 80-17029. (Illus.). 48p. (ps-3). 1980. Repr. of 1966 ed. 8.95 (ISBN 0-590-07772-4, Four Winds). Schol Bk Serv.
Mother, Mother, I Want Another. Maria Polushkin. (Illus.). 1980. Repr. 1.50 (ISBN 0-590-30375-9). Schol Bk Serv.
Mother Nature's Michigan. Oscar Warbach. (Illus., Orig.). 1976. pap. 5.50 (ISBN 0-910726-70-1). Hillsdale Educ.
Mother of Sri Aurobindo Ashram. Prema Nandakumar. (National Biography Ser.). 1979. pap. 2.25 (ISBN 0-89744-198-2). Auromere.
Mother O'Possum's Problem. Udell Waters. 1980. 4.95 (ISBN 0-8062-1494-5). Carlton.
Mother Poem. Edward Brathwaite. 1977. pap. text ed. 9.95x (ISBN 0-19-211859-5). Oxford U Pr.
Mother Teresa: Caring for All God's Children. Betsy Lee. LC 80-20286. (Taking Part Ser.). (Illus.). 48p. (gr. 3 up). 1981. PLB 6.95 (ISBN 0-87518-205-4). Dillon.
Mother Teresa: Her Work & Her People. Desmond Doig. LC 75-39857. (Illus.). 176p. 1980. pap. 9.95 (ISBN 0-06-061941-4, HarpR). Har-Row.
Mother Tongue Education: The West African Experience. 153p. 1976. 14.75 (ISBN 92-3-101239-8, U392, UNESCO). Unipub.
Mother Tongue in English. Daphne M. Brown. LC 77-83987. 1979. 24.50 (ISBN 0-521-21873-X); pap. 7.95x (ISBN 0-521-29299-9). Cambridge U Pr.
Mother Tree. Ruth Whitehead. LC 75-142155. (Illus.). (gr. 3-6). 1971. 6.50 o.p. (ISBN 0-8164-3045-4, Clarion). HM.

Mother Was a Lovely Beast. Philip J. Farmer. 1976. pap. 1.25 o.s.i. (ISBN 0-515-04071-1). Jove Pubns.

Mother Wit: A Feminist Guide to Psychic Development. Diane Mariechild. (Illus.). 200p. 1981. 12.95 (ISBN 0-89594-050-7); pap. 5.95 (ISBN 0-89594-051-5). Crossing Pr.

Mother Wit from the Laughing Barrel: Readings in the Interpretation of Afro-American Folklore. Ed. by Alan Dundes. LC 80-8528. 688p. 1981. lib. bdg. 38.00 (ISBN 0-8240-9456-5). Garland Pub.

Motherhood: An up-to-Date Guide to Pregnancy & the Baby's First Nine Months. Rosemary Ellis. 1978. 6.50 o.p. (ISBN 0-214-20296-8, 8036, Dist. by Arco). Barrie & Jenkins.

Motherhood & Personality: Psychosomatic Aspects of Childbirth. Leon Chertok. 1969. 10.50 o.p. (ISBN 0-685-14245-0). Lippincott.

Motherhood Book: Adventures in Pregnancy, Birth & Being a Mother. Joan Wiener & Joyce Glick. 160p. (Orig.). 1974. pap. 1.95 o.s.i. (ISBN 0-02-078400-7, Collier). Macmillan.

Motherhood Mandate: Special Issue of Psychology of Women Quarterly. Nancy F. Russo. LC 79-88275. 148p. 1979. pap. text ed. 7.95x (ISBN 0-87705-463-0). Human Sci Pr.

Mothering Years: The Story of the Canberra Mothercraft Society 1926-79. H. Crip & L. Rudduck. (Illus.). 112p. (Orig.). 1980. pap. text ed. 7.95 (ISBN 0-9595400-0-8, 0584). Bks Australia.

Motherless Families. Victor George & Paul Wilding. (International Library of Sociology). 1972. 20.00x (ISBN 0-7100-7305-4). Routledge & Kegan.

Motherless Victim. Joyce A. Reeves. 1981. 5.95 (ISBN 0-8062-1576-3). Carlton.

Motherlode. Randy White. (Illus.). 1977. cancelled o.p. (ISBN 0-912950-35-8); pap. 4.50 o.p. (ISBN 0-912950-36-6). Blue Oak.

Mothers. Boyd K. Packer. (Illus.). 1977. pap. 0.50 o.p. (ISBN 0-87747-650-0). Deseret Bk.

Mother's Agenda, Vol. 2, 1961. Mirra Alfassa & Bernard Enginger. Orig. Title: L'agenda De Mere. 500p. (Orig.). 1981. pap. 8.95 (ISBN 0-938710-01-X). Inst Evolutionary.

Mother's Almanac. Marguerite Kelly & Elia S. Parsons. LC 73-9166. 288p. 1975. softbound 6.95 (ISBN 0-385-01806-1). Doubleday.

Mothers & Amazons. Helen Diner. 280p. 1973. pap. 2.50 o.p. (ISBN 0-385-00733-7, Anch). Doubleday.

Mothers & Daughters: A Lifelong Relationship. rev. ed. Edith G. Neisser. LC 73-4113. 412p. 1973. 11.95 o.s.i. (ISBN 0-06-013171-3, HarpT). Har-Row.

Mothers at Work. Carolyn Adams & Kathryn Winston. (Comparative Studies of Political Life). 1980. pap. text ed. 10.95 (ISBN 0-582-28064-8). Longman.

Mother's Book. Ed. by Ronnie Friedland & Carol Kort. 384p. 1981. 14.95 (ISBN 0-686-69055-9). HM.

Mothers Can Do Anything. Joe Lasker. LC 72-83684. (Concept Bks.). (Illus.). 32p. (gr. k-3). 1972. 6.95g (ISBN 0-8075-5287-9). A Whitman.

Mother's Day. Mary K. Phelan. LC 65-11646. (Holiday Ser.). (Illus.). (gr. 1-3). 1965. PLB 7.89 (ISBN 0-690-56195-4, TYC-J). T Y Crowell.

Mother's Day Is Over. Shirley L. Radl. 1974. pap. 1.95 o.s.i. (ISBN 0-446-89673-X). Warner Bks.

Mothers, Grandmothers & Daughters: Personality & Child-Care in Three Generation Families. Bertram J. Cohler & Henry U. Grunebaum. LC 80-17979. (Personality Processes Ser.). 496p. 1981. 22.50 (ISBN 0-471-05900-5, Pub. by Wiley-Interscience). Wiley.

Mother's Helper. Maureen Freely. 1981. pap. 2.95 (ISBN 0-440-15696-3). Dell.

Mother's Sourcebook of Inspiration. Eleanor Doan. Orig. Title: Sourcebook for Mothers. 192p. 1972. padded cover, gift-boxed 11.95 (ISBN 0-310-23740-8). Zondervan.

Moths. Rosalind Ashe. 1977. pap. 1.95 o.s.i. (ISBN 0-446-89447-8). Warner Bks.

Moths & How to Rear Them. 2nd, rev. ed. Paul Villiard. (Illus.). 9.50 (ISBN 0-8446-5254-7). Peter Smith.

Motices of Ecumenism. P. Schrotenboer. 1967. pap. 1.25 o.p. (ISBN 0-686-11992-4). Wedge Pub.

Motif-Index of Folk-Literature, 6 Vols. rev. ed. Stith Thompson. Incl. Vol. 1. 560p. 32.50x (ISBN 0-253-33881-6); Vol. 2. 520p. 32.50x (ISBN 0-253-33882-4); Vol. 3. 520p. 32.50x (ISBN 0-253-33883-2); Vol. 4. 500p. 32.50x (ISBN 0-253-33884-0); Vol. 5. 568p. 32.50x (ISBN 0-253-33885-9); Vol. 6. 896p. 45.00x (ISBN 0-253-33886-7). LC 55-8055. 1955-58. Set. 160.00x (ISBN 0-253-33887-5). Ind U Pr.

Motif-Index of Mediaeval Spanish Exempla. John E. Keller. 1949. pap. 5.00x o.p. (ISBN 0-87049-005-2). U of Tenn Pr.

Motility in Cell Function: Proceedings of the First John M. Marshall Symposium on Cell Biology. Ed. by Frank Pepe et al. LC 78-11880. 1979. 31.00 (ISBN 0-12-551750-5). Acad Pr.

Motion. Joel Legunn. Ed. by Gene Liberty. LC 73-128852. (Understanding Bks.). Orig. Title: Investigating Motion. (gr. 6-9). 1971. PLB 7.95 (ISBN 0-87191-041-1). Creative Ed.

Motion & Gravity. Jeanne Bendick. LC 72-4085. (Science Experiences Ser.). (Illus.). 72p. (gr. 3-5). 1972. PLB 4.90 o.p. (ISBN 0-531-01439-8). Watts.

Motion & Power. Hans M. Kolstee. (Illus.). 256p. 1981. text ed. 19.95 (ISBN 0-13-602953-1). P-H.

Motion & Time Study. 5th ed. Marvin E. Mundel. (P-H Industrial Engineering Ser.). (Illus.). 1978. ref. 24.95 (ISBN 0-13-602987-6). P-H.

Motion & Time Study. 6th ed. Benjamin W. Niebel. 1976. 20.50x (ISBN 0-256-01775-1). Irwin.

Motion & Time Study: Design & Measurement of Work. 6th ed. Ralph M. Barnes. LC 68-20097. 1968. 26.50 o.p. (ISBN 0-471-05350-3). Wiley.

Motion & Time Study: Design & Measurement of Work. 7th ed. Ralph M. Barnes. LC 80-173. 689p. 1980. text ed. 23.95 (ISBN 0-471-05905-6). Wiley.

Motion Geometry of Mechanism. E. A. Dijksman. LC 75-3977. (Illus.). 250p. 1976. 35.50 (ISBN 0-521-20841-6). Cambridge U Pr.

Motion Picture Almanac, 1981, Vol. 52. Ed. by Richard Gertner. 716p. 1981. 38.00 (ISBN 0-900610-23-9). Quigley Pub Co.

Motion Picture Camera & Lighting Equipment. David Samuelson. (Media Manuals Ser.). Date not set. pap. 8.95 (ISBN 0-8038-4685-1). Hastings.

Motion Picture Directors: A Bibliography of Magazine & Periodical Articles, 1900-1972. Mel Schuster. LC 73-780. 1973. 16.50 (ISBN 0-8108-0590-1). Scarecrow.

Motion Picture Film Editor. Rene L. Ash. LC 74-4072. 1974. 10.00 (ISBN 0-8108-0718-1). Scarecrow.

Motion Picture Performers: A Bibliography of Magazine & Periodical Articles, Supp. No. 1, 1970-74. Mel Schuster. LC 70-154300. 1976. 32.50 (ISBN 0-8108-0879-X). Scarecrow.

Motion Pictures. LaMond F. Beatty. Ed. by James E. Duane. LC 80-21340. (Instructional Media Library: Vol. 8). (Illus.). 112p. 1981. 13.95 (ISBN 0-87778-168-0). Educ Tech Pubns.

Motion Pictures from the Library of Congress Paper Print Collection 1894-1912. LC 66-28789. 1967. 45.00 (Univ. Calif. Press). Locare.

Motion Pictures from the Library of Congress Paper Print Collection, 1894-1912. Kemp R. Niver. 1967. 57.50x (ISBN 0-520-00947-9). U of Cal Pr.

Motion Pictures, Television & Radio. Ed. by Linda Mehr. (Reference Publications Ser.). 1977. lib. bdg. 27.00 (ISBN 0-8161-8089-X). G K Hall.

Motion Pictures: The Development of an Art from Silent Films to the Age of Television. Albert R. Fulton. (Illus.). 1970. Repr. of 1960 ed. 14.95 (ISBN 0-8061-0467-8). U of Okla Pr.

Motion Pictures: The Development of an Art. rev. ed. A. R. Fulton. LC 79-6711. (Illus.). 443p. 1980. 14.95x (ISBN 0-8061-1633-1). U of Okla Pr.

Motivated Mathematics. A. Evyatar & P. Rosenbloom. LC 80-40491. (Illus.). 250p. Date not set. price not set (ISBN 0-521-23308-9). Cambridge U Pr.

Motivating Administrator. David E. Lee. 128p. 1981. 6.95 (ISBN 0-88289-255-X). Pelican.

Motivating Men for the Master. Bob Harrington. LC 71-155682. 1971. 3.50 o.p. (ISBN 0-8054-2406-7). Broadman.

Motivating Your Sales Force. John Lidstone. 1978. text ed. 25.25 (ISBN 0-566-02082-3, Pub. by Gower Pub Co England). Renouf.

Motivation & Control in Organizations. Ed. by Gene W. Dalton & Paul R. Lawrence. 1971. pap. text ed. 10.95x (ISBN 0-256-00609-1). Irwin.

Motivation & Productivity. Saul W. Gellerman. LC 63-16332. 1963. 15.95 (ISBN 0-8144-5084-9). Am Mgmt.

Motivation & Productivity. Saul W. Gellerman. (AMACOM Executive Books). 1978. pap. 6.95 (ISBN 0-8144-7502-7). Am Mgmt.

Motivation, Career Striving, & Aging. Joel O. Raynor & Elliot E. Entin. LC 80-27082. (Illus.). 496p. Date not set. text ed. 24.95 (ISBN 0-89116-189-9). Hemisphere Pub. Postponed.

Motivation Techniques. Artur Kaiser. Tr. by G. Peppe & D. Birker. LC 79-89938. Orig. Title: Druck erzeugt Gegendruck. (Orig.). Date not set. pap. cancelled (ISBN 0-89793-013-4). Hunter Hse.

Motivation: Theories & Principles. Robert C. Beck. 1978. ref. ed. 18.95 (ISBN 0-13-603902-2). P-H.

Motivation: Theory & Research. Charles N. Cofer & M. H. Appley. LC 64-13214. (Illus.). 1964. 32.95 (ISBN 0-471-16317-1). Wiley.

Motivation Through the Work Itself. Robert N. Ford. LC 77-77749. 1969. 15.95 (ISBN 0-8144-5173-X). Am Mgmt.

Motivation to Work. 2nd ed. Frederick Herzberg et al. 1959. 15.95 (ISBN 0-471-37389-3, Pub. by Wiley-Interscience). Wiley.

Motivation Training Manual. William J. Wenzel. 272p. 1970. 22.50 (ISBN 0-8436-0599-5). CBI Pub.

Motivation: Understanding & Influencing Human Behavior. Walter B. Kolesnik. 1978. pap. text ed. 11.50 (ISBN 0-205-05973-2, 2459736). Allyn.

Motivational Control Systems Analysis. D. J. McFarland. 1975. 60.00 (ISBN 0-12-483860-X). Acad Pr.

Motivational Games for Mathematics. Alan Barson. (Illus.). 40p. (gr. 3-7). 1981. pap. 6.00 (ISBN 0-937138-02-9). Fabmath.

Motivational Theories & Applications for Managers. new ed. Donald Sanzotta. LC 76-41732. 1977. 11.95 (ISBN 0-8144-5430-5). Am Mgmt.

Motive. Harry Carmichael. 1977. 6.95 o.p. (ISBN 0-525-16030-2). Dutton.

Motive & Method in the Cantos of Ezra Pound. Ed. by Lewis G. Leary. LC 54-11609. 1961. 12.50x (ISBN 0-231-02060-0); pap. 4.00x (ISBN 0-231-08520-6). Columbia U Pr.

Motive Clauses in Hebrew Law: Biblical Forms & Near Eastern Parallels. Rifat Sonsino. LC 79-15024. (Society of Biblical Literature Dissertation Ser.: No. 45). 13.50x (ISBN 0-89130-317-0, 060145); pap. 9.00x. Scholars Pr CA.

Motive for Murder. Edson T. Hamill. (Ryker Ser). 1975. pap. 1.25 o.p. (ISBN 0-685-61047-0, LB315, Leisure Bks). Nordon Pubns.

Motives. Ed. by Richard Salis & Egon Larsen. Tr. by Egon Larsen from Ger. 228p. 1975. text ed. 10.00x (ISBN 0-85496-056-2). Humanities.

Motives for Adultery. (Illus.). pap. 5.00 (ISBN 0-910550-45-X). Centurion Pr.

Motivgeschichtliche Untersuchung Zur Deutschen Literatur, Insbesondere Zur Deutschen Lyrik. Verena Doebele-Fluegel. 1977. 57.65x (ISBN 3-11-005909-6). De Gruyter.

Motocourse 1977-1978. Ed. by Chris Carter. (Ser. No. 2). (Illus.). 1978. 11.95 o.p. (ISBN 0-905138-04-X, Hazelton Securities Ltd.). Motorbooks Intl.

Motocourse 1980-1981, No. 5. 208p. 1981. 36.95 (ISBN 0-905138-14-7). Motorbooks Intl.

Motor Activities for the Underachiever. David Nichols et al. (Illus.). 150p. 1980. 13.75 (ISBN 0-398-04090-7). C C Thomas.

Motor Aptitude & Intellectual Performance. Ismail. 1967. pap. text ed. 6.95 (ISBN 0-675-09680-4). Merrill.

Motor Auto Repair Manual: Fifth Early Model Edition, Nineteen Sixty-Eight to Nineteen Seventy-Four. Louis C. Forier. (Illus.). 1979. 16.95 (ISBN 0-87851-510-0). Hearst Bks.

Motor Auto Repair Manual 1981. 44th ed. (Motor Bks.). 1300p. 1981. 16.95 (ISBN 0-87851-525-9). Hearst Bks.

Motor Car: How It Works. (Illus.). Arabic 2.50x (ISBN 0-685-82848-4). Intl Bk Ctr.

Motor Car, Nineteen Forty-Six to Fifty-Six. Michael Sedgwick. (Illus.). 272p. 1980. 42.50 (ISBN 0-7134-1271-2, Pub. by Batsford England). David & Charles.

Motor Carrier Rate Structure: The Need for Basic Revision. Grant M. Davis & Eugene Shephard. LC 78-24194. 1979. 21.95 (ISBN 0-03-049136-3). Praeger.

Motor Cycle Racing Champions. Norrie Whyte. LC 75-295936. 1976. 7.95 (ISBN 0-668-03910-8). Arco.

Motor Cycles in Color. Eric E. Thompson. (Color Ser.). (Illus.). 1974. 9.95 (ISBN 0-7137-0711-9, Pub. by Blandford Pr England). Sterling.

Motor Deficit in Patients with Cerebral Palsy. Karel Bobath. (Clinics in Developmental Medicine Ser. No. 23). 54p. 1966. Repr. of 1969 ed. 6.50 o.p. (ISBN 0-685-24722-8). Lippincott.

Motor Development & Movement Experiences for Young Children. David L. Gallahue. LC 75-37676. 1976. text ed. 19.95x (ISBN 0-471-29042-4). Wiley.

Motor Development in Children Normal & Retarded. Britta Holle. 1977. pap. 24.00 (ISBN 0-397-60509-9, Pub by Blackwell Scientific). Mosby.

Motor Development in the Different Types of Cerebral Palsy. Berta Bobath & Karel Bobath. (Illus.). 1978. pap. 7.50 (ISBN 0-685-79638-8). Heinman.

Motor Development in the Different Types of Cerebral Palsy. Berta Bobath & Karel Bobath. (Illus.). 1975. pap. 11.00x (ISBN 0-433-03333-9). Intl Ideas.

Motor Development in the Preschool Years. Louise Skinner. (Illus.). 128p. 1979. pap. 11.75 (ISBN 0-398-03835-X). C C Thomas.

Motor Disturbance: "The Frank O'Hara Award Series". Kenward Elmslie. (Full Court Rebound Bk.). 1978. 14.95 (ISBN 0-231-03612-4); pap. 6.00 (ISBN 0-231-03613-2). Full Court NY.

Motor Industry As a Career. Walkerly. 10.00x (ISBN 0-392-05929-0, SpS). Soccer.

Motor Insurance & the Consumer. H. A. Cockerell & G. M. Dickinson. 192p. 1980. 30.00x (ISBN 0-85941-146-X, Pub. by Woodhead-Faulkner England). State Mutual Bk.

Motor Learning: Principles & Practices. 2nd ed. John N. Drowatzky. 1981. text ed. write for info. (ISBN 0-8087-0495-8). Burgess.

Motor Nineteen Eighty Auto Repair Manual. Louis C. Forier. (Illus.). 1979. 16.95 (ISBN 0-87851-508-9). Hearst Bks.

Motor Nineteen Seventy-Nine Truck Repair Manual. 33rd ed. (Motor Bks.). 1428p. 1980. 24.95 (ISBN 0-87851-522-4). Hearst Bks.

Motor Racing in Color. Doug Nye. (Illus.). 1978. 12.95 (ISBN 0-7137-0904-9, Pub. by Blandford Pr England). Sterling.

Motor Racing in Color. Doug Nye. (Illus.). 214p. 1980. pap. 6.95 (ISBN 0-7137-0904-9). Sterling.

Motor Skills. Richard A. Schmidt. (Scientific Perspectives of Physical Education). 192p. 1975. pap. text ed. 9.50 scp (ISBN 0-06-045784-8, HarpC). Har-Row.

Motor Sport Yearbook 1974. Ed. by Barry Gill. LC 74-2649. (Illus.). 448p. 1974. pap. 5.95 o.s.i. (ISBN 0-02-029660-6, Collier). Macmillan.

Motor Unit Types, Recruitment Patterns & Plasticity with Usage in Health & Disease. Ed. by J. E. Desmedt. (Progress in Clinical Neurophysiology Ser.: Vol. 9). (Illus.). x, 350p. 1981. 82.75 (ISBN 3-8055-1929-X). S Karger.

Motor Vehicle. 10th ed. Newton. 1981. text ed. price not set. Butterworth.

Motor Vehicle & Traffic Laws of New Jersey. Gould Editorial Staff. (Supplemented annually). looseleaf 12.50x (ISBN 0-87526-232-5). Gould.

Motor Vehicle Laws of Massachusetts. Gould Editorial Staff. (Supplemented annually). looseleaf 12.50x (ISBN 0-87526-231-7). Gould.

Motor Vehicle Mechanics Textbook. 4th ed. F. K. Sully. (Illus.). 1979. text ed. 13.95 (ISBN 0-408-00428-2). Butterworths.

Motorboat Operator License Preparation Course. rev. ed. Ed. by Richard A. Block. (Illus.). 269p. 1980. pap. text ed. 18.00 (ISBN 0-934114-29-3). Marine Educ.

Motorboat, Yacht or Canoe - You Name It. Jean E. Taggart. LC 73-14607. 1974. 10.00 (ISBN 0-8108-0661-4). Scarecrow.

Motorboating. Boy Scouts Of America. LC 19-600. (Illus.). 64p. (gr. 6-12). 1962. pap. 0.70x (ISBN 0-8395-3294-6, 3294). BSA.

Motorboating Facts & Feats. Kevin Desmond. (Illus.). 256p. 1980. 17.95 (ISBN 0-8069-9204-2, Pub by Guinness Superlatives England). Sterling.

Motorcycle: Cross-Country Racing. Gene Tardy & Al Jackson. (Sports Action Ser.). (Illus.). (gr. 3-7). 1974. PLB 5.51 (ISBN 0-914844-00-8). J Alden.

Motorcycle: Grand Prix Racing. Gene Tardy & Al Jackson. (Sports Action Ser.). (Illus.). (gr. 3-7). 1974. PLB 5.51 (ISBN 0-914844-01-6). J Alden.

Motorcycle Handbook. Bob Clampett. 1975. pap. 1.75 o.p. (ISBN 0-449-13270-6, X3270, GM). Fawcett.

Motorcycle Manual. Roy Bacon. 1977. pap. 12.50 (ISBN 0-408-00260-3). Transatlantic.

Motorcycle Milestones, Vol. 1. Richard Renstrom. LC 80-66669. (Illus.). 112p. 1980. 19.00 (ISBN 0-936660-00-7); pap. 14.00 (ISBN 0-936660-01-5). Classics Unltd.

Motorcycle: Moto-Cross Racing. Gene Tardy & Al Jackson. (Sports Action Ser.). (Illus.). (gr. 3-7). 1974. PLB 5.51 (ISBN 0-914844-02-4). J Alden.

Motorcycle Mutt. E. Radlauer & R. S. Radlauer. LC 73-942. (Sports Action Bks). (gr. 3 up). 1973. PLB 6.90 o.p. (ISBN 0-531-02091-6). Watts.

Motorcycle News Yearbook 1977-1978. 1978. pap. 11.75 o.p. (ISBN 0-85059-285-2). Aztex.

Motorcycle Panorama: A Pictorial Review of Motorcycle Development. Bob Holliday. LC 74-14052. (Illus.). 224p. 1975. 7.95 o.p. (ISBN 0-668-03647-8). Arco.

Motorcycle Pioneers: The Man, the Machines, the Events, 1860-1930. Michael Partridge. LC 76-12553. 1977. 8.95 (ISBN 0-668-04035-1). Arco.

Motorcycle Racer. John P. Covington. LC 78-121950. 144p. (gr. 6-11). 1973. 5.95 o.p. (ISBN 0-385-02325-1). Doubleday.

Motorcycle Repair Encyclopedia. 2nd ed. Tim Lockwood. Ed. by Jeff Robinson. (Illus.). 472p. 1976. pap. text ed. 10.00 o.p. (ISBN 0-89287-021-4, M430). Clymer Pubns.

Motorcycle Repair Handbook. Paul Dempsey. LC 76-24787. (Illus.). 1976. 9.95 o.p. (ISBN 0-8306-6789-X); pap. 9.95 (ISBN 0-8306-5789-4, 789). TAB Bks.

Motorcycles. D. N. Miller. (Illus.). text ed. 9.95x o.p. (ISBN 0-8464-0646-2). Beekman Pubs.

Motorcycles. M. S. Sequeira. LC 78-5963. (Easy-Read Fact Bks). (Illus.). (gr. 2-4). 1978. PLB 6.45 s&l (ISBN 0-531-01373-1). Watts.

Motorcycles & How to Manage Them: A Nineteen Twenty-Six Handbook. Ed. by Motor Cycle Magazine. 1975. Repr. of 1926 ed. 14.95x o.p. (ISBN 0-8464-0647-0). Beekman Pubs.

Motorcycles & Motorcycling. Max Alth. (First Bks.). (Illus.). (gr. 4 up). 1979. PLB 6.45 s&l (ISBN 0-531-02945-X). Watts.

Motorcycling. Charles Coombs. LC 68-23911. (gr. 5-9). 1968. PLB 7.25 (ISBN 0-688-21564-5); pap. 6.96 (ISBN 0-688-31564-X). Morrow.

Motorcycling. Ross R. Olney. LC 74-10720. (Illus.). 64p. (gr. 5 up). 1975. PLB 4.47 o.p. (ISBN 0-531-02788-0). Watts.

Motorcycling Facts & Feats. L. J. Setright. 258p. 1980. 17.95 (ISBN 0-8069-9232-8, Pub. by Guinness Superlatives England). Sterling.

Motorcycling Fundamentals. Chris Wright & Roy Bisson. (Fundamentals: A Series on Getting It Right First Time). (Illus.). 80p. (Orig.). 1979. pap. 10.25 (ISBN 0-589-50081-3, Pub. by Reed Books Australia). C E Tuttle.

Motoring in Norway. new ed. Welle-Strand. (Illus.). 1975. pap. 6.00x (ISBN 0-89918-411-1, N411). Vanous.

Motoring in the Thirties. Graham Robson. 1980. 35.95 (ISBN 0-85059-365-4). Aztex.

Motoring in the Twenties & Thirties. A. B. Demaus. 1979. 17.95 (ISBN 0-7134-1538-X, Pub. by Batsford England). David & Charles.

Motors & Engines & How They Work. Harvey Weiss. LC 69-11828. (Illus.). (gr. 5-9). 1969. 10.95 (ISBN 0-690-56478-3, TYC-J). T Y Crowell.

Motown. D. Morse. 1972. 5.95 o.s.i. (ISBN 0-02-587200-1). Macmillan.

Motown. D. Morse. 1972. pap. 1.95 o.s.i. (ISBN 0-02-061340-7, Collier). Macmillan.

Mots croises. 1978. pap. text ed. 9.75 (ISBN 2-03-029307-5). Larousse.

Mots dans le vent. Giraud. 11.25 (ISBN 0-685-36202-7, 2727). Larousse.

Mots D'Heures: Gousses, Rames. Luis Van Rooten. LC 67-21230. 1967. 8.95 (ISBN 0-670-49064-4, Grossman). Viking Pr.

Mottoes & Badges of Families, Regiments, Schools, Colleges, States, Towns, Livery Companies, Societies, Etc. W. S. Anson. LC 74-14502. 192p. 1975. Repr. of 1904 ed. 20.00 (ISBN 0-8103-4055-0). Gale.

Motueka: An Archaeological Survey. Aidan J. Challis. (New Zealand Archaeological Assn. Monographs). (Illus.). 1978. text ed. 12.50x (ISBN 0-582-71758-2). Longman.

Mouches. Jean-Paul Sartre. (Fr). 1962. pap. 1.00 o.p. (ISBN 0-685-13996-4, 3607). Larousse.

Mould & Core Material for the Steel Industry. A. D. Sarkar. 1967. 22.00 (ISBN 0-08-012486-0); pap. 9.75 (ISBN 0-08-012487-9). Pergamon.

Moulds: Their Isolation, Cultivation, & Identification. David Malloch. 88p. 1981. 12.95x (ISBN 0-8020-2418-1). U of Toronto Pr.

Moule Popular Commentary Series, 6 vols. H. C. Moule. 1980. 15.00 (ISBN 0-8254-3224-3). Kregel.

Moulin a paroles. 2nd ed. Michel Benamou & Jean Carduner. LC 71-126958. (Illus., Fr.). 1971. pap. text ed. 10.95 (ISBN 0-471-06450-5); tapes avail. (ISBN 0-471-00024-8). Wiley.

Mound Builders. Meridel Le Sueur. LC 73-22497. (First Bks). (Illus.). 72p. (gr. 5-7). 1974. PLB 4.90 o.p. (ISBN 0-531-02717-1). Watts.

Mound Builders. Robert Silverberg. 1975. pap. 1.50 o.p. (ISBN 0-345-24846-5). Ballantine.

Mount Henneth, 2 vols. Robert Bage. Ed. by Ronald Paulson. LC 78-60846. (Novel 1720-1805 Ser.: Vol. 8). 1980. Set. lib. bdg. 62.00 (ISBN 0-8240-3657-3); lib. bdg. 31.00 ea. Garland Pub.

Mount McKinley: The Story Behind the Scenery. Steve Buskirk. Ed. by Gweneth R. DenDooven. LC 78-57540. (Illus.). 1978. lib. bdg. 7.95 (ISBN 0-916122-52-2); pap. 3.50 (ISBN 0-916122-23-9). K C Pubns.

Mount Moriah: Kill a Man, Start a Cemetery. Helen Rezatto. LC 80-81127. (Illus.). 256p. 1980. 7.95 (ISBN 0-87970-150-1). North Plains.

Mount Omei Illustrated Guide. Huang Shou-Fu & T'An Chung-Yo. Tr. by Dryden L. Phelps from Chinese. (Illus.). 472p. 1981. pap. 15.00 (ISBN 0-85656-113-4). Great Eastern.

Mount Revelstoke National Park Wild Flowers. James H. Soper & Adam F. Szczawinski. (Illus.). 1976. pap. 2.95x (ISBN 0-660-00003-2, 56429-0, Pub. by Natl Mus Canada). U of Chicago Pr.

Mount Rushmore. Gilbert C. Fite. (Illus.). pap. 5.95 (ISBN 0-8061-0959-9). U of Okla Pr.

Mount Rushmore: The Story Behind the Scenery. Lincoln Borglum & Gweneth R. DenDooven. LC 76-57455. (Illus.). 1977. 7.95 (ISBN 0-916122-45-X); pap. 3.00 (ISBN 0-916122-20-4). K C Pubns.

Mount St. Helens: A Changing Landscape. Chuck Williams. (Illus.). 128p. 27.50 (ISBN 0-912856-63-7). Graphic Arts Ctr.

Mount St. Helens & Other Volcanoes of the West. Linda Kelso. Ed. by Robert D. Shangle. (Illus.). 144p. 1980. 27.50 (ISBN 0-89802-202-9). Beautiful Am.

Mount St. Helens the Volcano of Our Time. Don Roberts & Diana Roberts. (Illus.). 48p. (Orig.). pap. 5.95 (ISBN 0-936608-10-2). F Amato Pubns.

Mount St. Helens: Volcano. Linda Kelso. Ed. by Robert D. Shangle. (Illus.). 64p. 1980. pap. 7.95 (ISBN 0-89802-209-6). Beautiful Am.

Mountain Adventures. Karl Lukan. (International Library). (Illus.). 128p. (gr. 7 up). 1972. PLB 6.90 o.p. (ISBN 0-531-02110-6). Watts.

Mountain & Wilderness. Paul T. Coke. 1978. pap. 3.95 (ISBN 0-8164-2177-3). Crossroad NY.

Mountain Animals. Tony Long. LC 70-185892. (Animal Life Ser.). (Illus.). 152p. (YA) 1972. 8.95 o.s.i. (ISBN 0-06-012666-3, HarpT). Har-Row.

Mountain Artisans Quilting Book. Alfred A. Lewis. LC 72-91259. (Illus.). 120p. 1973. 15.00 o.s.i. (ISBN 0-02-571260-8). Macmillan.

Mountain Cabin. Robert S. Wood. LC 76-30878. (Illus.). 1977. pap. 4.95 o.p. (ISBN 0-87701-090-0). Chronicle Bks.

Mountain Climbing. Jerolyn Nentl. Ed. by Howard Schroeder. LC 80-415. (Funseekers Ser.). (Illus.). (gr. 3-5). 1979. lib. bdg. 5.95 (ISBN 0-89686-075-2); pap. 2.95 (ISBN 0-89686-079-5). Crestwood Hse.

Mountain Conquest. Eric Shipton & Bradford Washburn. LC 66-15087. (Horizon Caravel Bks). (Illus.). 153p. (gr. 6 up). 1966. 9.95 (ISBN 0-06-025642-7, Dist. by Har-Row); PLB 12.89 (ISBN 0-06-025643-5, Dist. by Har-Row). Am Heritage.

Mountain-Ese. Aubrey Garber. LC 76-3278. 105p. 1976. 4.95 (ISBN 0-89227-004-7); pap. 2.95 (ISBN 0-89227-038-1). Commonwealth Pr.

Mountain Fever: Historic Conquests of Rainier. Aubrey L. Haines. LC 62-63445. (Illus.). 1962. 8.95 (ISBN 0-87595-086-8); pap. 6.95 (ISBN 0-87595-007-8). Oreg Hist Soc.

Mountain, Field, & Family: The Economy & Human Ecology of an Andean Valley. Stephen B. Brush. LC 77-24364. 1977. 14.50x (ISBN 0-8122-7728-7). U of Pa Pr.

Mountain Flowers. Ira Spring & Harvey Manning. LC 79-9284. (Illus.). 1979. pap. 3.95 (ISBN 0-916890-92-9). Mountaineers.

Mountain Flowers in New Zealand. Nancy M. Adams. (Mobil New Zealand Nature Ser.). (Illus.). 80p. (Orig.). 1980. pap. 6.95 (ISBN 0-589-01328-9, Pub. by Reed Bks Australia). C E Tuttle.

Mountain Gorilla: Ecology & Behavior. George B. Schaller. LC 63-11401. (Illus.). 1976. pap. 9.00x (ISBN 0-226-73636-9, P684, Phoen). U of Chicago Pr.

Mountain King. George Ernsberger. 1979. pap. 2.25 o.p. (ISBN 0-425-04223-5). Berkley Pub.

Mountain Lion. Jean Stafford. 231p. (New preface by the author). 1972. 6.95 o.p. (ISBN 0-374-21402-6). FS&G.

Mountain Man. Vardis Fischer. 1980. pap. write for info. PB.

Mountain Man. (Sharazad Stories Ser.). (Illus., Arabic.). pap. 3.50 (ISBN 0-686-53112-4). Intl Bk Ctr.

Mountain Man Crafts & Skills. David Montgomery. LC 80-82706. (Illus.). 1981. 6.95 (ISBN 0-88290-156-7, 4024). Horizon Utah.

Mountain Meadows Massacre. Juanita Brooks. (Illus.). 1979. Repr. of 1962 ed. 14.95 (ISBN 0-8061-0549-6). U of Okla Pr.

Mountain Men. John G. Neihardt. LC 70-134770. Orig. Title: A Cycle of the West. (Illus.). 1971. pap. 5.95 (ISBN 0-8032-5733-3, BB 531, Bison). U of Nebr Pr.

Mountain Never Too High: The Story of J. E. O'Neill. Bill O'Neill. LC 77-82899. (Illus.). 1977. 7.95 (ISBN 0-913548-46-4, Valley Calif). Western Tanager.

Mountain of My Fear. David Roberts. LC 68-20393. (Illus.). (gr. 7-12). 1968. 8.95 (ISBN 0-8149-0192-1). Vanguard.

Mountain of Storms: American Expeditions to Dhaulagiri, 1969 & 1973. Andrew Harvard & Todd Thompson. LC 74-13925. (Illus.). 210p. (Co-published with Chelsea House). 1974. 15.00 (ISBN 0-8147-3366-2). NYU Pr.

Mountain of Storms: The American Expeditions to Dhaulagiri. Andrew Harvard & Todd Thompson. LC 74-13924. (Illus.). 220p. 1981. pap. 9.95 (ISBN 0-87754-146-9). Chelsea Hse.

Mountain of Winter. Shirley Schoonover. 192p. 1980. pap. 2.25 (ISBN 0-380-76513-6, 76513). Avon.

Mountain People. Colin M. Turnbull. 1972. 8.95 (ISBN 0-671-21320-2); pap. 3.95 (ISBN 0-686-68504-0). S&S.

Mountain Riders. Max Brand. 160p. 1972. pap. 1.95 (ISBN 0-446-90308-6). Warner Bks.

Mountain School Teacher. Melville D. Post. 196p. 1980. Repr. of 1922 ed. lib. bdg. 12.75x (ISBN 0-89968-199-9). Lightyear.

Mountain Sheep: A Study in Behavior & Evolution. Valerius Geist. LC 77-149596. (Wildlife Behavior & Ecology Ser). (Illus.). 1971. 15.50x o.s.i. (ISBN 0-226-28572-3). U of Chicago Pr.

Mountain Sheep: A Study in Behavior & Evolution. Valerius Geist. LC 77-149596. (Wildlife Behavior & Ecology Ser). (Illus.). xvi, 384p. 1976. pap. 9.00 (ISBN 0-226-28573-1, P666, Phoen). U of Chicago Pr.

Mountain Spirits II. Joseph E. Dabney. 1981. 4.95 (ISBN 0-932298-05-2). Green Hill.

Mountain Storm, Pine Breeze: Folk Song in Japan. Patia R. Isaku. 1981. text ed. 12.95x (ISBN 0-8165-0564-0); pap. 6.50 (ISBN 0-8165-0722-8). U of Ariz Pr.

Mountain Tasting: The Zen Haiku of Santoka Taneda. Santoka Taneda. Tr. by John Stevens from Japanese. 100p. 1980. pap. 7.95 (ISBN 0-8348-0151-5, Pub. by John Weatherhill Inc Japan). C E Tuttle.

Mountain Tasting: Zen Haiku. Santoka Taneda. Tr. by John Stevens. 112p. 1980. pap. 7.95 (ISBN 0-8348-0151-5). Weatherhill.

Mountain, the Miner & the Lord: & Other Tales from a Country Law Office. Harry M. Caudill. LC 80-51012. 192p. 1980. 12.50 (ISBN 0-8131-1403-9). U Pr of Ky.

Mountain to Climb. Eva Maxson. LC 75-30319. (Desting Ser.). 1976. pap. 4.95 (ISBN 0-8163-0223-5, 13685-3). Pacific Pr Pub Assn.

Mountain Top Mystery. Gertrude C. Warner. LC 64-7722. (Boxcar Children Mysteries-Pilot Bk.). (Illus.). 128p. (gr. 3-7). 1964. 6.95g (ISBN 0-8075-5292-5). A Whitman.

Mountain Torrent of the Tien Shan: An Ecology-Faunistic Essay. K. A. Brodsky. (Monographiae Biologicae: No. 39). (Illus.). 311p. 1980. lib. bdg. 79.00 (ISBN 90-6193-091-X). Kluwer Boston.

Mountain Trailways for Youth: Devotions for Young People. Mrs. Charles E. Cowman. 1979. pap. 4.95 (ISBN 0-310-37641-6). Zondervan.

Mountain Witch. Andrews. pap. 2.75 o.s.i. (ISBN 0-515-04780-5). Jove Pubns.

Mountain Wolf Woman, Sister of Crashing Thunder: Autobiography of a Winnebago Indian. Ed. by Nancy O. Lurie. LC 61-5019. (Illus.). 1961. 5.00 o.p. (ISBN 0-472-09109-3). U of Mich Pr.

Mountain World. David F. Costello. LC 74-34369. (Illus.). 256p. 1975. 8.95 o.s.i. (ISBN 0-690-00695-0, TYC-T). T Y Crowell.

Mountaineering: A Bibliography of Books in English to 1974. Chess J. Krawczyk. LC 76-45415. 1977. 8.50 o.p. (ISBN 0-8108-0979-6). Scarecrow.

Mountaineering: A Manual for Teachers & Instructors. D. T. Roscoe. (Illus.). 1976. 18.00 (ISBN 0-571-09456-2). Transatlantic.

Mountaineering & Its Literature. W. R. Neate. LC 80-7785. 1980. pap. 9.95 (ISBN 0-89886-004-0). Mountaineers.

Mountaineering in the Sierra Nevada. Clarence King. LC 79-116056. 1970. pap. 3.95 (ISBN 0-8032-5716-3, BB 518, Bison). U of Nebr Pr.

Mountaineering in the Tetons: The Pioneer Period, Eighteen Ninety-Eight to Nineteen Forty. 2nd ed. Fritiof Fryxell. Ed. by Phil D. Smith. LC 79-83648. (Illus.). 1978. 8.95 (ISBN 0-933160-00-3); pap. 5.95 (ISBN 0-933160-01-1). Teton Bkshop.

Mountains. rev. ed. Lorus J. Milne & Margery Milne. LC 62-11577. (Life Nature Library). (Illus.). (gr. 5 up). 1970. PLB 8.97 o.p. (ISBN 0-8094-0616-0, Pub. by Time-Life). Silver.

Mountains. 29.50. Chatham Pub CA.

Mountains & Mountaineering Facts & Feats. Edward Pyatt. (Guinness Superlatives Ser.). (Illus.). 256p. 1980. 19.95 (ISBN 0-8069-9246-8, Pub. by Guinness Superlatives England). Sterling.

Mountains & the Man: A Study of Process & Environment. Larry W. Price. (Illus.). 496p. 1981. 22.50 (ISBN 0-520-03263-2). U of Cal Pr.

Mountains & the Woman. James Mackie. 31p. (Orig.). 1980. pap. 3.00x (ISBN 0-88235-038-2). San Marcos.

Mountains of Serbia: Travels Through Inland Yugoslavia. Anna Kindersley. (Illus.). 1977. 26.00 (ISBN 0-7195-3300-7). Transatlantic.

Mountains of the World. William Bueler. LC 74-87796. (Illus.). 1977. pap. 5.95 (ISBN 0-916890-49-X). Mountaineers.

Mountains Without Handrails: Reflections on the National Parks. Joseph L. Sax. 160p. 1980. 10.00x (ISBN 0-472-09324-X); pap. 5.95 (ISBN 0-472-06324-3). U of Mich Pr.

Mountainside Reflections. Jessie Clemensen. (Illus.). 64p. 1980. 5.95 (ISBN 0-89962-022-1). Todd & Honeywell.

Mountaintops & Molehills. Tom Mullen. 1981. 6.95 (ISBN 0-8499-0193-6). Word Bks.

Mountainwitch. Felicia Andrews. 352p. (Orig.). 1980. pap. 2.75 (ISBN 0-515-05846-7). Jove Pubns.

Mountbatten. Richard Hough. 1981. 15.00 (ISBN 0-394-51162-X). Random.

Mounted Games & Gymkhanas. British Horse Society & Pony Club. LC 76-56448. 1977. 5.75 (ISBN 0-8120-5124-6). Barron.

Mountie Bison's 1st Flying Smirk Book. Mountie Bison. (gr. 3-5). pap. 1.25 o.p. (ISBN 0-590-11926-5, Schol Pap). Schol Bk Serv.

Mounting & Framing Pictures. Michael Woods. 1978. 17.95 (ISBN 0-7134-0743-3). David & Charles.

Mountolive. Lawrence Durrell. 1961. pap. 2.50 o.p. (ISBN 0-525-47082-4). Dutton.

Mourners Below. James Purdy. 1981. 13.95 (ISBN 0-670-49142-X). Viking Pr.

Mourning Glory: The Making of a Marine. David J. Regan. 1980. 8.95 (ISBN 0-8159-6218-5). Devin.

Mourning the Death of Magic. Blanche M. Boyd. LC 77-2343. 1977. 10.95 (ISBN 0-02-514270-4). Macmillan.

Mouse & His Child. Russell Hoban. 1975. pap. 1.50 (ISBN 0-380-00910-2, 31765, Camelot). Avon.

Mouse & the Egg. William Mayne. LC 80-15084. (Illus.). 32p. (gr. k-3). 1981. 9.95 (ISBN 0-688-80301-6); PLB 9.55 (ISBN 0-688-84301-8). Greenwillow.

Mouse & the Knitted Cat. Antonella Bollinger-Savelli. LC 72-93303. (Illus.). 28p. (ps-2). 1974. 7.95 (ISBN 0-02-711710-3). Macmillan.

Mouse & the Magician. Eric Houghton. LC 79-64187. (Illus.). (gr. k-4). 1979. 8.95 (ISBN 0-233-96777-X). Andre Deutsch.

Mouse & the Motorcycle. Beverly Cleary. (Illus.). (gr. 2-6). 1965. 7.75 (ISBN 0-688-21698-6); PLB 7.44 (ISBN 0-688-31698-0). Morrow.

Mouse & the Song. Marilynne K. Roach. LC 73-13877. (Illus.). 48p. (ps-3). 1974. 5.95 o.s.i. (ISBN 0-8193-0721-1, Four Winds); PLB 5.41 o.s.i. (ISBN 0-8193-0722-X). Schol Bk Serv.

Mouse at the Show. Donna L. Pape. (Illus.). 32p. (ps-2). 1981. 5.95 (ISBN 0-525-66722-9). Elsevier-Nelson.

Mouse Book. Ed. by Richard Shaw. LC 75-8104. (Illus.). 48p. (gr. 4-7). 1975. PLB 4.95 o.p. (ISBN 0-7232-6119-9). Warne.

Mouse in the Manger. Gennaro L. Gentile. LC 78-72944. (Illus.). 80p. (gr. k-4). 1978. pap. 3.95 (ISBN 0-87793-165-8). Ave Maria.

Mouse Is Miracle Enough. Myra Lockwood. 1965. 3.95 o.p. (ISBN 0-374-21429-8). FS&G.

Mouse on the Fourteenth Floor. Jane Thayer. (Illus.). (ps-3). 1977. 7.75 (ISBN 0-688-22094-0); PLB 7.44 (ISBN 0-688-32094-5). Morrow.

Mouse That Saved the West. Leonard Wibberley. LC 80-25567. 192p. 1981. 8.95 (ISBN 0-688-00364-8). Morrow.

Mouse to Be Free. Joyce W. Warren. (Illus.). (gr. 1-4). 1975. pap. 1.25 (ISBN 0-380-00349-X, 31765, Camelot). Avon.

Mouse Trouble. John Yeoman. LC 72-95190. (Illus.). 32p. (ps-3). 1973. 7.95 (ISBN 0-02-793600-7). Macmillan.

Mouse Who Didn't Believe in Santa Claus. Marguerite Atcheson. LC 80-69472. (Illus.). 64p. (Orig.). 1980. pap. 4.50x (ISBN 0-9603118-6-6). Davenport.

Mouse Woman & the Vanished Princesses. Christie Harris. LC 75-23147. (Illus.). 192p. (gr. 4-6). 1976. 7.95 (ISBN 0-689-30502-8). Atheneum.

Mouse Work. Robert Kraus. LC 80-51359. (Windmill Board Bks.). (Illus.). 16p. (ps). 1980. 3.50 (ISBN 0-671-41531-X, Pub. by Windmill). S&S.

Mouseketeer's Train Ride. Walt Disney. (Illus.). (gr. k-2). 1977. PLB 5.38 (ISBN 0-307-68894-1, Golden Pr). Western Pub.

Mousekin Takes a Trip. Edna Miller. (Illus.). (gr. k-3). 1976. 5.95 (ISBN 0-13-604363-1); pap. 1.95 (ISBN 0-13-604348-8). P-H.

Mousekin's ABC's. Edna Miller. (gr. 1-4). 1972. PLB 6.95 (ISBN 0-13-604389-5). P-H.

Mousekin's Christmas Eve. Edna Miller. (Illus.). (gr. k-3). 1965. PLB 6.95 (ISBN 0-13-604454-9); pap. 1.95 (ISBN 0-13-604447-6). P-H.

Mousekin's Close Call. Edna Miller. LC 77-27571. (Illus.). (ps-2). 1978. 6.95g (ISBN 0-13-604207-4); pap. 1.95 (ISBN 0-13-604207-4). P-H.

Mousekin's Family. Edna Miller. (Illus.). (gr. k-3). 1969. PLB 6.95 (ISBN 0-13-604462-X); pap. 1.95 (ISBN 0-13-604157-4). P-H.

Mousekin's Golden House. Edna Miller. (gr. k-3). 1964. PLB 6.95 (ISBN 0-13-604421-2); pap. 1.95 (ISBN 0-13-604439-5). P-H.

Mouse's Christmas Eve. Harry Bornstein. (Signed English Ser.). 44p. pap. 3.50 (ISBN 0-913580-28-7). Gallaudet Coll.

Mouse's Feast. Yutaka Sugita. (Illus.). (ps-6). 1980. 6.95 (ISBN 0-8120-5370-2). Barron.

Mousetrap & Other Plays. Agatha Christie. 720p. 1981. pap. 3.95 (ISBN 0-553-13024-2). Bantam.

Mouth in Sexual Orgasm. (Illus.). 4.95 (ISBN 0-910550-46-8). Centurion Pr.

Mouth of Heaven: An Introduction to Kwakiutl Religious Thought. Irving Goldman. LC 80-11163. 284p. 1981. Repr. of 1975 ed. lib. bdg. write for info. (ISBN 0-89874-136-X). Krieger.

Mouth of the Night: Gaelic Stories Retold. Iris Macfarlane. LC 75-31576. (Illus.). 160p. (gr. 4 up). 1976. 6.95 o.s.i. (ISBN 0-02-765430-3, 76543). Macmillan.

Mouth to Mouth. Deborah Metcalf. 1980. 10.95 (ISBN 0-399-90086-1). Marek.

Mouvement Du Profit En France Au XIXe Siecle: Materiaux et Etudes. Jean Bouvier et al. (Industrie et Artisanat: No. 1). 1965. pap. 40.50x (ISBN 90-279-6132-8). Mouton.

Movable Feasts: The Backpacker Magazine Cookbook. Hasse R. Bunnelle. Ed. by Backpacker Magazine. 1980. write for info. (ISBN 0-671-25032-9, Fireside); pap. write for info. (ISBN 0-671-25033-7). S&S.

Movable Insulation. Bill Langdon. (Illus.). 1980. 14.95 (ISBN 0-87857-298-8); pap. 9.95 (ISBN 0-87857-310-0). Rodale Pr Inc.

Move Ahead with Possibility Thinking. Robert H. Schuller. (Spire Bk). 1973. pap. 2.50 (ISBN 0-8007-8105-8). Revell.

Move Over, Beethoven. Julia First. (gr. 5 up). 1978. PLB 7.90 s&l (ISBN 0-531-01472-X). Watts.

Move Over, Mountain. Nancy Life. LC 74-31682. 144p. (Orig.). 1975. pap. 2.45 (ISBN 0-87123-375-4, 210375). Bethany Fell.

Move Over, Twerp. Martha Alexander. LC 80-21405. (Illus.). 32p. (ps-2). 1981. 6.95 (ISBN 0-8037-6139-2); PLB 6.46 (ISBN 0-8037-6140-6). Dial.

Move Yourself, & Save! Robert Hullinger & Robert Grosch. 1980. pap. 3.50 (ISBN 0-915644-15-0). Clayton Pub Hse.

Moveable Nest. Tom Schneider. (Orig.). 1981. pap. write for info. (ISBN 0-440-56383-6, Delta). Dell. Postponed.

Moved by Love. William Gellin. LC 80-52633. 272p. 1980. 10.00 (ISBN 0-88400-070-2). Shengold.

Movememts of the British Iron & Steel Industry, 1720 to 1951, Vol. 36. Howard G. Roepke. LC 80-23128. (Illinois Studies in the Social Sciences). (Illus.). vii, 198p. 1981. Repr. of 1956 ed. lib. bdg. 25.00x (ISBN 0-8371-9096-7, ROMB). Greenwood.

Movement Activities, Motor Ability & the Education of Children. Bryant J. Cratty et al. (Illus.). 192p. 1970. pap. 18.75 photocopy ed. spiral (ISBN 0-398-00360-2). C C Thomas.

Movement & Education in Physical Education: A Guide to Teaching & Planning. 2nd ed. Hayes Kruger & Jane M. Kruger. 1981. pap. text ed. 12.95x (ISBN 0-697-07181-2). Wm C Brown.

Movement & Phythmic Activities for the Mentally Retarded. Cynthia D. Crain. 1981. write for info. (ISBN 0-398-04174-1). C C Thomas.

Movement Approach to Acting. Nancy R. King. (P-H Ser. in Theatre & Drama). (Illus.). 288p. 1981. text ed. 13.95 (ISBN 0-13-604637-1). P-H.

Movement Awareness & Creativity. Lee Bartal & Nira Ne'eman. LC 75-36735. 1976. 7.95 o.p. (ISBN 0-685-82483-7, HarpR). Har-Row.

Movement Experience for Children: A Humanistic Approach to Elementary School Physical Education. 3rd ed. Evelyn L. Schurr. 1980. text ed. 16.95 (ISBN 0-13-604553-7). P-H.

Movement for Developing Children. Hoffman et al. 344p. 1980. 16.95 (ISBN 0-205-06953-3); tchrs'. manual free. Allyn.

Movement for International Copyright in Nineteenth Century America. Aubert J. Clark. LC 73-9209. 215p. 1973. Repr. of 1960 ed. lib. bdg. 15.00x (ISBN 0-8371-6980-1, CLIC). Greenwood.

Movement for Peace Without a Victory During the Civil War. Elbert J. Benton. LC 70-176339. (The American Scene Ser.). 1972. Repr. of 1918 ed. lib. bdg. 12.50 (ISBN 0-306-70420-X). Da Capo.

Movement for the Actor. Ed. by Lucille S. Rubin. (Illus.). 1980. pap. 7.95x (ISBN 0-89676-010-3). Drama Bk.

Movement for the Extension of Owens College, Manchester, Eighteen Sixty-Three to Seventy-Three. W. H. Chaloner. 136p. 1973. 9.00x (ISBN 0-7190-0552-3, Pub by Manchester U Pr England). State Mutual Bk.

Movement Games for Children of All Ages. Esther L. Nelson. LC 74-31710. (Illus.). 96p. (gr. 1 up). 1975. 7.95 (ISBN 0-8069-4530-3); PLB 7.49 (ISBN 0-8069-4531-1). Sterling.

Movement in Buildings. D. Lenczner. LC 73-4253. 108p. 1974. text ed. 13.25 (ISBN 0-08-017136-2). Pergamon.

Movement in Early Childhood & Primary Education. Pangrazi & Dauer. 1981. write for info. (ISBN 0-8087-1659-X); write for info. instr's guide (ISBN 0-8087-3314-1). Burgess.

Movement in Practice. John Learmouth & Keith Whitaker. LC 76-41142. (Illus.). 1977. pap. 7.95 (ISBN 0-8238-0209-4). Plays.

Movement in Psychotherapy: Psychomotor Techniques & Training. Albert Pesso. LC 69-19257. 1969. 12.00x (ISBN 0-8147-0340-2). NYU Pr.

Movement Is Life: A Holistic Approach to Exercise for Older Adults. Eva D. Garnet. (Illus.). 150p. (Orig.). 1981. pap. text ed. 12.50 (ISBN 0-916622-19-3). Princeton Bk Co.

Movement of the Young Child: Ages Two to Six. Caroline B. Sinclair. LC 72-96100. 1973. pap. text ed. 8.95 (ISBN 0-675-08975-1). Merrill.

Movement Studies & Physical Education: A Handbook for Teachers. Ed. by J. E. Kane. 1978. 18.00 (ISBN 0-7100-8775-6); pap. 9.95 (ISBN 0-7100-8684-9). Routledge & Kegan.

Movement Themes: Topics for Early Childhood Learning Through Creative Movement. Barbara S. Jones. LC 80-65608. 115p. 1981. perfect bdg. 8.50 (ISBN 0-86548-042-7). Century Twenty One.

Movements & Habits of Climbing Plants. Charles Darwin. 1979. Repr. of 1897 ed. lib. bdg. 35.00 (ISBN 0-89760-128-9, Telegraph). Dynamic Learn Corp.

Movements & Issues in American Judaism: An Analysis & Sourcebook of Developments Since 1945. Ed. by Bernard Martin. LC 77-87971. 1978. lib. bdg. 22.50 (ISBN 0-313-20044-0, MCJ/). Greenwood.

Movements in Buildings. 2nd ed. D. Lenczner. LC 80-49947. (Illus.). 105p. 1981. 18.00 (ISBN 0-08-024755-5); pap. 12.00 (ISBN 0-08-024756-3). Pergamon.

Movements in English Literature, 1900-1940. C. Gillie. LC 74-16993. 200p. 1975. 36.00 (ISBN 0-521-20655-3); pap. 8.95x (ISBN 0-521-09922-6). Cambridge U Pr.

Movers & Shakers: Young Activists of the Sixties. Helene Hanff. LC 77-110432. (Illus.). (gr. 8 up). 1970. 10.95 (ISBN 0-87599-166-1). S G Phillips.

Movie at the End of the World: Collected Poems. Thomas McGrath. LC 72-91918. 188p. 1972. 10.95 o.p. (ISBN 0-8040-0605-9); pap. 5.95 (ISBN 0-8040-0606-7). Swallow.

Movie Buff's Book. Ed. by Ted Sennett. (Orig.). 1975. pap. 3.95 o.p. (ISBN 0-515-03649-8, 3649, Harv). HarBraceJ.

Movie Collector's Catalog. Ken Weiss. (Illus.). 160p. (Orig.). 1977. pap. 5.95 (ISBN 0-938350-50-1). Cummington Pub.

Movie Comedy. Ed. by Stuart Byron & Elizabeth Weis. 1977. pap. 3.95 (ISBN 0-14-004578-3). Penguin.

Movie Comedy Teams. Leonard Maltin. 352p. (RL 10). 1974. pap. 1.75 o.p. (ISBN 0-451-06480-1, E6480, Sig). NAL.

Movie Kings. Leu Rose. (Pal Paperbacks, - Pal Skills II Ser.). (Illus.). (gr. 5-12). 1980. pap. text ed. 1.25 (ISBN 0-8374-6807-8). Xerox Ed Pubns.

Movie Makers: Artists in an Industry. Gene D. Phillips. LC 73-75524. 1973. 19.95 (ISBN 0-911012-43-5). Nelson-Hall.

Movie Making: A Guide to Film Production. new ed. Sumner Glimcher & Warren Johnson. (Illus.). 256p. 1975. 15.00x (ISBN 0-231-03962-X). Columbia U Pr.

Movie Monsters & Their Masters: The Birth of the Horror Film. Robert Quackenbush. Ed. by Kathleen Tucker. LC 79-27291. (Illus.). (gr. 3 up). 1980. 6.50g (ISBN 0-8075-5299-2). A Whitman.

Movie Murder Mystery Quiz Book. John M. Howard. (Illus.). 160p. 1980. pap. 9.95 (ISBN 0-498-02522-5). A S Barnes.

Movie Stunts & the People Who Do Them. Gloria D. Miklowitz. LC 80-7984. (Illus.). 64p. (gr. 4-6). 1980. pap. 3.95 (ISBN 0-15-256039-4, VoyB). HarBraceJ.

Moviegoer. Walker Percy. 242p. 1967. pap. 2.95 (ISBN 0-374-50596-9). FS&G.

Moviegoer. Walker Percy. 1979. pap. 2.50 (ISBN 0-380-47076-4, 47076). Avon.

Moviemaking: A Guide for Beginners. Michael L. Levine. LC 80-19314. (Illus.). 48p. (gr. 5 up). 1980. 9.95 (ISBN 0-684-16707-7). Scribner.

Moviemaking Illustrated: The Comicbook Filmbook. Murray Suid & James Morrow. (Illus.). (gr. 7-12). 1973. pap. text ed. 7.25 (ISBN 0-8104-5727-X). Hayden.

Movies & Methods. Ed. by Bill Nichols. LC 74-22968. 1977. 32.50x (ISBN 0-520-02890-2); pap. 8.95 (ISBN 0-520-03151-2, CAL 339). U of Cal Pr.

Movies As Mass Communication. Garth Jowett & James M. Linton. LC 80-13508. (Sage Comtext Ser.: Vol. 4). (Illus.). 149p. 1980. 12.50 (ISBN 0-8039-1090-8); pap. 5.95 (ISBN 0-8039-1091-6). Sage.

Movies As Social Criticism: Aspects of Their Social Psychology. I. C. Jarvie. LC 77-26778. 1978. 12.00 (ISBN 0-8108-1106-5). Scarecrow.

Movies for Kids: A Guide for Parents & Teachers on the Entertainment Film for Children. rev. ed. Ruth M. Goldstein & Edith Zornow. LC 79-6149. (Illus.). 300p. 1980. 14.95 (ISBN 0-8044-2267-2); pap. 5.95 (ISBN 0-8044-6194-5). Ungar.

Movies Grow up, Nineteen Forty to Nineteen Eighty. rev. ed. Charles Champlin. Orig. Title: Flicks; or Whatever Became of Andy Hardy? (Illus.). 300p. 1981. 19.95 (ISBN 0-8040-0363-7); pap. 10.00 (ISBN 0-8040-0364-5). Swallow.

Movies in the Age of Innocence. Edward Wagenknecht. (Illus.). 1962. 13.50x (ISBN 0-8061-0539-9); pap. 5.95 (ISBN 0-8061-1297-2). U of Okla Pr.

Movies Plus One: Seven Years of Film Reviewing. William S. Pechter. 380p. 1981. 16.95 (ISBN 0-8180-0709-5). Horizon.

Moving a Head with Attitude Research: Proceedings. Annual Attitude Research Conference, 7th, Hilton Head, S.C., Feb. 1976. Ed. by Yoram Wind & Marshall Greenberg. LC 77-5548. 1977. pap. text ed. 12.00 o.p. (ISBN 0-87757-088-4): Am Mktg.

Moving a Rocket, a Sub, & the London Bridge. David Paige. LC 80-22125. (On the Move Ser.). (Illus.). 48p. (gr. 3-6). 1980. PLB 9.25 (ISBN 0-516-03890-7). Childrens.

Moving Boundary Problems in Heat Flow & Diffusion: University of Oxford, Conference, March 25-27, 1974. Ed. by J. R. Ockendon & W. R. Hodgkins. (Illus.). 308p. 1975. 24.50x o.p. (ISBN 0-19-853345-4). Oxford U Pr.

Moving Dream. Elizabeth Renier. (Victorian Romance Ser.). 1978. pap. 1.50 o.p. (ISBN 0-449-23460-6, Crest). Fawcett.

Moving Experience. Geraldine H. Davis. (Illus.). 150p. (Orig.). 1980. pap. 5.95 (ISBN 0-89865-029-1); moving calendar 2.50 (ISBN 0-89865-098-4). Donning Co.

Moving Frontier: North America Seen Through the Eyes of Its Pioneer Discoverers. Ed. by Louis B. Wright & Elaine Fowler. (Illus.). 1972. 10.00 o.p. (ISBN 0-440-05874-0). Delacorte.

Moving Heavy Things. Jan Adkins. (gr. 5 up). 1980. reinforced bdg. 6.95 (ISBN 0-395-29206-9). HM.

Moving Home. Clare Ungerson. 99p. 1971. pap. text ed. 5.00x (Pub. by Bedford England). Renouf.

Moving in. Susan Efros. 1981. price not set. Waterfall Pr.

Moving into Adulthood: Themes & Variations in Self--Directed Development for Effective Living. Gerard Egan & Michael A. Cowan. LC 80-15876. 288p. (Orig.). 1980. pap. text ed. 8.95 (ISBN 0-8185-0406-4). Brooks-Cole.

Moving Meditation: Enlightenment of the Mind & Total Fitness. Van H. Ho. LC 79-88748. (Illus.). 214p. 1979. pap. 12.00 (ISBN 0-9602904-1-9). V H Ho.

Moving Money: An Empirical Analysis of Federal Expenditure Patterns. Thomas J. Anton et al. LC 80-21700. 272p. 1980. text ed. 20.00 (ISBN 0-89946-066-6). Oelgeschlager.

Moving Mountains: The Art & Craft of Letting Others See Things Your Way. Henry M. Boettinger. (Illus.). 1969. 7.95 o.s.i. (ISBN 0-02-512100-6). Macmillan.

Moving Pictures: Memories of a Hollywood Prince. Budd Schulberg. LC 80-9055. 448p. 1981. 16.95 (ISBN 0-8128-2817-8). Stein & Day.

Moving Places: A Life at the Movies. Jonathan Rosenbaum. LC 80-7596. (Illus.). 288p. 1980. 11.95 (ISBN 0-06-013657-X, HarpT); pap. 5.95 (ISBN 0-06-090823-8, CN823). Har-Row.

Moving Right Along: A Book of Science Experiments & Puzzlers About Motion. Robert Gardner & David Webster. LC 77-15149. (gr. 3-5). 1978. 7.95a (ISBN 0-385-11642-X); PLB (ISBN 0-385-11643-8). Doubleday.

Moving: The What, When, Where, & How of It. Patricia O. Neuman. (Illus.). 128p. 1981. pap. 5.95 (ISBN 0-89651-450-1). Icarus.

Moving Through Here. Don McNeil. 252p. 10.95 (ISBN 0-934558-08-6); pap. 5.95 (ISBN 0-934558-09-4). Entwhistle Bks.

Moving Time. Carolyn Trager. LC 78-7722. (Illus.). (gr. 5-8). 1978. PLB 6.45 s&l (ISBN 0-531-02219-6). Watts.

Moving to a New Place. Ron Schreiber. LC 74-26380. 72p. 1974. pap. 4.95 (ISBN 0-914086-07-3). Alicejamesbooks.

Moving to Metrics in Home Economics. J. Oppert. LC 77-81325. 1977. 2.50 (ISBN 0-686-20043-8, 26108430). Home Econ Educ.

Moving Toward a New Society. Susan Gowan et al. 296p. 1976. pap. 5.00 (ISBN 0-86571-007-4). Movement New Soc.

Moving Toward Change: Some Thoughts on the International Economic Order. 137p. 1976. pap. 6.00 (ISBN 92-3-101365-3, U394, UNESCO). Unipub.

Moving Toyship. Edmund Crispin. LC 80-54479. 1981. 9.95 (ISBN 0-8027-5434-1). Walker & Co.

Moving up in Style: The Successful Man's Guide to Impeccable Taste. Steven W. Naifeh & Gregory W. Smith. 1980. 10.95 (ISBN 0-312-55070-7). St Martin.

Moving up: The Successful Man's Guide to Impeccable Taste. Naifeh & Smith. 1980. 10.95 (ISBN 0-312-55070-7). St Martin.

Moving up to Supervision. Martin M. Broadwell. LC 78-21995. 1978. pap. 8.95 (ISBN 0-8436-0749-1). CBI Pub.

Mowimy Po Polski: A Beginners Course. W. Bisko. 1977. pap. 7.00x (ISBN 0-89918-519-3, P519); 3-12" l.p. records 20.00x (ISBN 0-89918-520-7). Vanous.

Mowrer, Program to Establish Fluent Speech. 1979. 19.95 (ISBN 0-675-08269-2). Merrill.

Mowry's Basic Nutrition & Diet Therapy. 6th ed. Sue R. Williams. LC 79-26165. (Illus.). 1980. pap. text ed. 9.50 (ISBN 0-8016-5556-0). Mosby.

Mozambique & Tanzania: Asking the Big Questions. Frances M. Lappe & Adele Beccar-Varela. (Illus.). 128p. 1980. pap. 4.75 (ISBN 0-935028-05-6). Inst Food & Develop.

Mozambique in the Twentieth Century: From Colonialism to Independence. Luis B. Serapiao & Mohamed A. El-Khawas. LC 79-64964. 1979. pap. text ed. 12.00 (ISBN 0-8191-0502-3). U Pr of Amer.

Mozan's Racing Numerology. Mozan. (Gambler's Book Shelf). 102p. 1972. pap. 2.95 (ISBN 0-89650-536-7). Gamblers.

Mozart. Marcia Davenport. (Illus.). 1956. lib. rep. ed. 20.00 (ISBN 0-684-14504-9, ScribT). Scribner.

Mozart. Marcia Davenport. 1979. pap. 3.50 (ISBN 0-380-45534-X, 45534, Discus). Avon.

Mozart. Wolfgang Hildesheimer. Tr. by Marion Faber from Ger. (Illus.). 1981. 20.00 (ISBN 0-374-21483-2). FS&G.

Mozart. Wolfgang Hildesheimer. (Suhrkamp Taschenbuecher: No. 598). 432p. 1980. pap. text ed. 6.50 (ISBN 3-518-37098-7, Pub. by Insel Verlag Germany). Suhrkamp.

Mozart & Haydn in London, 2 vols. in 1. C. F. Pohl. LC 70-125059. (Music Ser). 1970. Repr. of 1867 ed. lib. bdg. 35.00 (ISBN 0-306-70024-7). Da Capo.

Mozart & His Piano Concertos. Cuthbert Girdlestone. Orig. Title: Mozart's Piano Concertos,Il. 1952. pap. 7.50 (ISBN 0-486-21271-8). Dover.

Mozart & Masonry. Paul Nettl. LC 78-114564. (Music Ser). 1957. Repr. of 1957 ed. lib. bdg. 17.50 (ISBN 0-306-71922-3). Da Capo.

Mozart & the Sonata Form. Joseph R. Tobin. LC 76-125063. (Music Ser). 1970. Repr. of 1916 ed. lib. bdg. 15.00 (ISBN 0-306-70027-1). Da Capo.

Mozart: His Character, His Work. Alfred Einstein. (Orig.). 1945. 29.95x (ISBN 0-19-500538-4). Oxford U Pr.

Mozart: His Character, His Work. Alfred Einstein. 1965. pap. 7.95 (ISBN 0-19-500732-8, GB). Oxford U Pr.

Mozart: His Life & Times. Peggy Woodford. (Illustrated Lives & Times of the Composers). (Illus.). 1978. 9.95 (ISBN 0-8467-0419-6, Pub. by Two Continents); pap. 5.95 (ISBN 0-8467-0420-X). Hippocrene Bks.

Mozart on the Stage. Janos Liebner. 1980. pap. 4.95 (ISBN 0-7145-1070-X). Riverrun NY.

Mozart Piano Concertos. Philip Radcliffe. LC 75-27958. (BBC Music Guides: No. 34). (Illus.). 64p. (Orig.). 1978. pap. 2.95 (ISBN 0-295-95477-9). U of Wash Pr.

Mozart: The Man & His Works. Walter J. Turner. LC 78-20497. (Encore Music Editions Ser.). 1981. Repr. of 1938 ed. 28.50 (ISBN 0-88355-873-4). Hyperion Conn.

Mozart Wind & String Concertos. Alec H. King. LC 75-27957. (BBC Music Guides: No. 35). (Illus.). 64p. (Orig.). 1978. pap. 2.95 (ISBN 0-295-95478-7). U of Wash Pr.

Mozartian Historian: Essays on the Works of Joseph R. Levenson. Maurice Meisner & Rhoads Murphy. LC 74-82849. 250p. 1976. 15.75x (ISBN 0-520-02826-0). U of Cal Pr.

Mozart's Journey to Prague. Eduard Moerikke. Tr. by Loewenberg. 1981. pap. 3.95 (ISBN 0-7145-0389-4). Riverrun NY.

Mozart's Le Nozze Di Figaro. Siegmund Levarie. LC 77-5150. (Music Reprint Ser.). 1977. Repr. of 1952 ed. lib. bdg. 27.50 (ISBN 0-306-70897-3). Da Capo.

MRCGP Study Book. Ed. by K. Young et al. 150p. 1981. PLB 36.90 (ISBN 0-906141-13-3, Pub. by Update Books Ltd); pap. 31.50 (ISBN 0-686-28845-9). Kluwer Boston.

Mrs. Beggs & the Wizard. Mercer Mayer. LC 80-15279. (Illus.). 48p. (ps-3). 1980. Repr. of 1973 ed. 8.95 (ISBN 0-590-07773-2, Four Winds). Schol Bk Serv.

Mrs. Blackwell's Heart-of-Texas Cookbook. Louise B. Dillow & Deenie B. Carver. (Illus.). 130p. 1980. pap. 6.95 (ISBN 0-931722-06-3). Corona Pub.

Mrs. Easter's Parasol. V. H. Drummond. (Illus.). (ps-5). 1977. pap. 6.95 (ISBN 0-571-11134-3, Pub. by Faber & Faber). Merrimack Bk Serv.

Mrs. Ewing, Mrs. Molesworth, & Mrs. Hodgson Burnett. 121p. 1980. Repr. of 1950 ed. lib. bdg. 20.00 (ISBN 0-8492-1634-6). R West.

Mrs. Filbert's His & Her Cookbook. Dorothy Crandall & Jeanne Ambuter. 7.95 (ISBN 0-916752-13-5). Green Hill.

Mrs. Fish, Ape, & Me the Dump Queen. Norma F. Mazer. LC 79-20262. 144p. (gr. 4-7). 1980. PLB 8.95 (ISBN 0-525-35380-1). Dutton.

Mrs. Gaskell As Novelist. K. C. Shrivastava. (Salzburg Studies in English Literature: Romantic Reassessment Ser.: No. 70). 1977. pap. text ed. 25.00x (ISBN 0-391-01523-0). Humanities.

Mrs. Gerald's Niece: A Novel, 1869. Georgiana Fullerton. (Victorian Fiction Ser.). 1975. lib. bdg. 66.00 (ISBN 0-8240-1534-7). Garland Pub.

Mrs. J. E. De Camp Sweet's Narrative of Her Captivity in the Sioux Outbreak of 1862: The Story of Nancy McClure - Captivity Among the Sioux, the Story of Mary Schwandt - the Captivity During the Sioux Outbreak, Etc, Repr. Of 1894 Ed. Bd. with Abby Byram & Her Father. the Indian Captives. with Some Account of Their Ancestors & a Register of Their Descendants. John M. McElroy. Repr. of 1898 ed; True Story of the Lost Shackle: Or Seven Years with the Indians. Owen P. Dabney. Repr. of 1897 ed. LC 75-7126. (Indian Captivities Ser.: Vol. 99). 1977. lib. bdg. 44.00 (ISBN 0-8240-1723-4). Garland Pub.

Mrs. Jenny. Joan Tate. pap. text ed. 1.95x o.p. (ISBN 0-435-11884-6). Heinemann Ed.

Mrs. Jones, -----on You: Day-by-Day in an Inner City Preschool. Barbara S. Jones. 1977. pap. 7.95 (ISBN 0-8224-4531-X). Pitman Learning.

Mrs. Kamali Would Like to Speak to You About Cloud: Notes from a California Classroom. Melody Martin. 212p. 1980. 9.95 (ISBN 0-8037-6003-5). Dial.

Mrs. Kitching's Smith Island Cookbook. Susan S. Dowell & Frances Kitching. 1981. 9.50x (ISBN 0-686-69483-X, Pub by Tidewater). Cornell Maritime.

Mrs Man. Una Stannard. LC 76-58834. (Illus.). 1977. 14.00 (ISBN 0-914142-02-X). Germainbooks.

Mrs. Ma's Chinese Cookbook. Nancy C. Ma. LC 60-12197. (Illus.). 1960. bds. 18.50 (ISBN 0-8048-0410-9). C E Tuttle.

Mrs. Ma's Favorite Chinese Recipes. Nancy C. Ma. LC 68-13739. (Illus.). 145p. 1980. pap. 7.95 (ISBN 0-87011-427-1). Kodansha.

Mrs. NCO. Mary P. Gross. LC 71-101333. 1969. pap. 1.25 o.p. (ISBN 0-911980-02-4). Beau Lac.

Mrs. NCO. Mary P. Gross. 1980. pap. 3.45. Beau Lac.

Mrs. Overtheway's Remembrances. Juliana H. Ewing. LC 75-32171. (Classics of Children's Literature, 1621-1932: Vol. 34). (Illus.). 1976. Repr. of 1869 ed. PLB 38.00 (ISBN 0-8240-2283-1). Garland Pub.

Mrs. Periwinkle's Groceries. Pegeen Snow. LC 80-22140. (Illus.). 48p. (gr. k-3). 1981. PLB 9.25 (ISBN 0-516-03558-4). Childrens.

Mrs. Pinny & the Salty Sea Day. Helen Morgan. (Illus.). (ps-5). 1972. 7.95 (ISBN 0-571-09863-0, Pub. by Faber & Faber). Merrimack Bk Serv.

Mrs. Restino's Country Kitchen. Susan Restino. LC 74-28704. (Illus.). 304p. (Orig.). 1976. pap. 7.95 o.p. (ISBN 0-8256-3060-6, Quick Fox). Music Sales.

Mrs. Siddons: Tragic Actress. Yvonne Ffrench. LC 78-13858. (Illus.). 1981. Repr. of 1954 ed. 23.50 (ISBN 0-88355-791-6). Hyperion Conn.

Mrs. Simkin's Bed. Linda Allen. LC 80-12262. (Illus.). 32p. (gr. k-3). 1980. 6.95 (ISBN 0-688-22233-1); PLB 6.67 (ISBN 0-688-32233-6). Morrow.

Mrs. Stevens Hears the Mermaids Singing. May Sarton. 240p. 1974. 6.95 (ISBN 0-393-08695-X, Norton Lib); pap. 3.95 1975 (ISBN 0-393-00762-6). Norton.

Mrs. Vinegar. Simon Stern. (Illus.). (ps-2). 1979. 7.95g (ISBN 0-13-604488-3). P-H.

Mrs. Warren's Profession. George B. Shaw. Ed. by Margot Peters. LC 79-56701. (Bernard Shaw Early Texts: Play Manuscripts in Facsimile). 1981. lib. bdg. 50.00 (ISBN 0-8240-4577-7). Garland Pub.

Mrs. Wilson Wanders Off. Nancy W. Parker. LC 76-6112. (gr. k-5). 1976. 5.95 (ISBN 0-396-07333-6). Dodd.

Mrs. W's Last Sandwich. Edwin Denby. 1972. 6.95 o.p. (ISBN 0-685-25558-1). Horizon.

Ms. Africa: Profiles of Modern African Women. Louise Crane. LC 72-11767. (gr. 7 up). 1973. 7.95 o.p. (ISBN 0-397-31446-9). Lippincott.

Ms. Guide to a Woman's Health. Cynthia W. Cooke & Susan Dworkin. 1981. pap. 3.95 (ISBN 0-425-04796-2). Berkley Pub.

Ms. Klondike. Illus. by Jessica Ross. 1977. PLB 6.50 o.p. (ISBN 0-670-49510-7). Viking Pr.

Ms Noah Touches Earth. Susan E. Barrett. (Illus.). 1979. pap. 5.95 (ISBN 0-9603916-0-6). Artichoke.

Mt. McKinley: The Pioneer Climbs. Terris Moore. (Illus.). 224p. 1981. pap. 8.95 (ISBN 0-89886-021-0). Mountaineers.

Mt. Saint Helens, the Volcano Explodes. Leonard Palmer. 15.00; pap. 7.95 (ISBN 0-86519-004-6). Green Hill.

Much Ado About Aldo. Johanna Hurwitz. (Illus.). (gr. 4-6). 1978. 7.95 (ISBN 0-688-22160-2); PLB 7.62 (ISBN 0-688-32160-7). Morrow.

Much Ado About Nothing. Edward Grant. LC 80-13876. (Illus.). 545p. Date not set. 59.50 (ISBN 0-521-22983-9). Cambridge U Pr.

Much Ado About Nothing. William Shakespeare. Ed. by Arthur Quiller-Couch et al. (New Shakespeare Ser). 1969. 23.95 (ISBN 0-521-07548-3); pap. 4.50x (ISBN 0-521-09491-7). Cambridge U Pr.

Much Loved Books. James O. Bennett. (Black & Gold Lib). 7.95 o.p. (ISBN 0-87140-979-8). Liveright.

Much Maligned Monsters: History of European Reactions to Indian Art. Partha Mitter. (Illus.). 1978. 44.00x (ISBN 0-19-817336-9). Oxford U Pr.

Much of Jackson Pollock Is Vivid Wallpaper: An Essay in the Epistemology of Aesthetic Judgements. Graham McFee. 1978. pap. text ed. 9.50x (ISBN 0-8191-0380-2). U Pr of Amer.

Muckraker's Manual: How to Do Your Own Investigative Reporting. M. Harris. 1980. pap. 7.95. Loompanics.

Mucosal Biopsies in Gastroenterology. Yardley & Goldman. 1981. text ed. write for info. (ISBN 0-443-08059-3). Churchill.

Mucus in Health & Disease. Ed. by Dennis V. Parke & Parke. LC 77-22376. (Advances in Experimental Medicine & Biology: Vol. 89). 558p. 1977. 45.00 (ISBN 0-306-32689-2, Plenum Pr). Plenum Pub.

Mud Baths for Everyone. Denys Cazet. (Illus.). 32p. (ps-2). 1981. 8.95 (ISBN 0-87888-178-6). Bradbury Pr.

Mud Pies & Other Recipes. Marjorie Winslow. (Illus.). (gr. k-2). 1961. 5.95 o.s.i. (ISBN 0-02-793080-7). Macmillan.

Mud Pies & Other Recipes. Marjorie Winslow. LC 61-10336. (Illus.). 48p. (ps-3). 1973. pap. 1.95 o.s.i. (ISBN 0-02-045440-6, Collier). Macmillan.

Mudcrab at Gambaro's. Judith Rodriguez. (Illus.). 91p. 1981. text ed. 13.25 (ISBN 0-7022-1574-0); pap. 7.25. U of Queensland Pr.

Muddling Through: The Art of Properly Unbusinesslike Management. Roger A. Golde. LC 76-888. 1976. 12.95 (ISBN 0-8144-5411-9). Am Mgmt.

Muddling Toward Frugality. Warren A. Johnson. LC 79-5172. 1979. Repr. of 1978 ed. pap. 3.95 (ISBN 0-394-73835-7). Shambhala Pubns.

Muddy Glory: America's Indian Wars in the Phillipines, 1899 to 1935. Russell Roth. 1981. 12.95 (ISBN 0-8158-0402-4). Chris Mass.

Muddy Waters: The Army Engineers & the Nation's Rivers. Arthur Maass. LC 73-20238. (FDR & the Era of the New Deal Ser). 306p. 1974. Repr. of 1951 ed. lib. bdg. 29.50 (ISBN 0-306-70607-5). Da Capo.

Mudgrump. Jack Greene. LC 80-68130. (Illus.). 56p. (Orig.). pap. text ed. 3.95 perfect inding (ISBN 0-9601258-3-3). Golden Owl Pub.

Mudhead. Josephine R. Stone. LC 80-11982. 156p. (gr. 5-9). 1980. 8.95 (ISBN 0-689-30787-X, Argo). Atheneum.

Mudhrooms in Color: How to Know Them, Where to Find Them, & What to Avoid. Orson Miller & Hope Miller. 11.95 (ISBN 0-686-69507-0, Hawthorn). Dutton.

Mudland. Morley Adams. (Orig.). 1980. pap. 1.75 (ISBN 0-532-23146-5). Manor Bks.

Mudville's Revenge. Ted Vincent. LC 80-52410. 384p. 1981. 12.95 (ISBN 0-87223-661-7). Seaview Bks.

Muette De Portici, 2 vols. Daniel F. Auber. Ed. by Philip Grossett & Charles Rosen. LC 76-49211. (Early Romantic Opera Ser.: Vol. 30). 1980. lib. bdg. 82.00 (ISBN 0-8240-2929-1). Garland Pub.

Muffel & Plums. Lilo Fromm. LC 72-85184. (Illus.). 64p. (ps-3). 1973. 4.95g o.s.i. (ISBN 0-02-735710-4). Macmillan.

Muffie & the Birthday Party. Nixon. (ps-3). 1980. pap. 1.25 (ISBN 0-590-30064-4, Schol Pap). Schol Bk Serv.

Muffie Mouse & the Busy Birthday. Joan L. Nixon. LC 77-28866. (ps-3). 1978. 6.95 (ISBN 0-395-28868-1, Clarion). HM.

Muffin Muncher. Steve Cosgrove. (Serendipity Bks). (Illus.). (gr. k-4). 1978. PLB 6.95 (ISBN 0-87191-667-3). Creative Ed.

Muffletump Storybook. Jan Wahl. (Picture Bk.). (Illus.). 1975. 5.95 o.p. (ISBN 0-695-80477-4); lib. ed. 5.97 o.p. (ISBN 0-695-40477-6). Follett.

Muffletumps Christmas Party. Jan Wahl. (Picture Bk). (Illus.). 32p. (gr. k-3). 1975. 5.95 o.p. (ISBN 0-695-80617-3); PLB 5.97 o.p. (ISBN 0-695-40617-5). Follett.

Muffletumps' Halloween Scare. Jan Wahl. (Illus.). (ps-3). 6.95 o.p. (ISBN 0-695-80754-4); lib. bdg. 6.99 o.p. (ISBN 0-695-40754-6). Follett.

Muffletumps: The Story of Four Dolls. Jan Wahl. (gr. k-6). 1980. pap. 0.95 (ISBN 0-440-46079-4, YB). Dell.

Mugger. Ed McBain. 160p. (Orig.). 1975. pap. 2.25 o.p. (ISBN 0-345-29290-1). Ballantine.

Mugger. Ed McBain. 160p. 1981. pap. 2.25. Ballantine.

Muggers Blood: Destroyer No. 30. Warren Murphy. LC 76-42891. (Destroyer Ser.). 1977. pap. 1.50 (ISBN 0-523-40110-8). Pinnacle Bks.

Mugging As a Social Problem. Michael Pratt. 256p. 1980. 32.50 (ISBN 0-7100-0564-4). Routledge & Kegan.

Mughal Administration in Golconda. J. F. Richards. (Illus.). 360p. 1975. 45.00x (ISBN 0-19-821561-4). Oxford U Pr.

Mugs & Tankards: A Collector's Guide. Deborah Stratton. LC 76-26359. (Illus.). 1977. 9.95 o.p. (ISBN 0-684-14831-5, ScribT). Scribner.

Muhammad. Maxime Rodinson. Tr. by Anne Carter. LC 69-20189. 1980. 15.95 (ISBN 0-394-50908-0); pap. 5.95 (ISBN 0-394-73822-5). Pantheon.

Muhammad Al-Qadiris Nashr Al Mathani: The Chronicles. Ed. by Norman Cigar. (Fontes Historiae Africanae Ser.). (Illus.). 400p. 1980. 89.00 (ISBN 0-19-725994-4). Oxford U Pr.

Muhammad Ali. Kenneth Rudeen. LC 76-12093. (Biography Ser.). (Illus.). 40p. (gr. 1-4). 1976. 7.89 (ISBN 0-690-01128-8, TYC-J). T Y Crowell.

Muhammad Ali. Linda Thomas. LC 75-28194. (Creative Superstars Ser.). 1975. PLB 5.95 (ISBN 0-87191-262-7); pap. 2.95 (ISBN 0-89812-188-4). Creative Ed.

Muhammad Ali: Boxing Superstar. Julian May. LC 74-31948. (Sports Close-up Ser.). (gr. 3-9). 1975. PLB 5.95 o.p. (ISBN 0-913940-15-1); pap. 2.50 o.p. (ISBN 0-913940-22-4). Crestwood Hse.

Muhammad & the Arab Empire. John Duckworth et al. Ed. by Malcolm Yapp & Margaret Killingray. (World History Ser.). (Illus.). (gr. 10). 1980. lib. bdg. 5.95 (ISBN 0-89908-036-7); pap. text ed. 1.95 (ISBN 0-89908-011-1). Greenhaven.

Muhammad & the Course of Islam. H. M. Balyuzi. (Illus.). 1976. 18.50 (ISBN 0-85398-060-8, 7-39-01, Pub. by G Ronald England). Baha'i.

Muhammad at Medina. W. Montgomery Watt. 1956. 24.95x (ISBN 0-19-826513-1). Oxford U Pr.

Muhammad: Prophet & Statesman. W. Montgomery Watt. 255p. 1974. pap. 5.95 (ISBN 0-19-881078-4, GB409, GB). Oxford U Pr.

Muhammad: Seal of the Prophets. Muhammad Z. Khan. 400p. 1980. pap. 12.50 (ISBN 0-7100-0610-1). Routledge & Kegan.

Muhammadan Architecture in Egypt & Palestine. Martin S. Briggs. LC 74-1287. (Architecture & Decorative Arts Ser.). (Illus.). 255p. 1974. Repr. of 1924 ed. lib. bdg. 25.00 (ISBN 0-306-70590-7). Da Capo.

Muirfield & the Honorable Company. George Pottinger. 1972. 10.00x (ISBN 0-7073-0154-8, Pub. by Scottish Academic Pr Scotland). Columbia U Pr.

Mujer Encantadora. Helen B. Andelin. (Span.). 5.95 (ISBN 0-911094-02-4). Pacific Santa Barbara.

Mujer Mas Rica De la Ciudad. Tr. by Joyce Landorf. (Spanish Bks.). (Span.). 1979. 1.65 (ISBN 0-8297-0587-2). Life Pubs Intl.

Mujeres: Conversations from a Hispanic Community. Ed. by Florence Howe & John A. Rothermich. (Women's Lives - Women's Work Ser.). 192p. (Orig.). 1980. pap. text ed. 4.23 (ISBN 0-07-020445-4). Webster-McGraw.

Mujeres: Conversations from an Hispanic Community. Nan Elsasser et al. (Women's Lives - Women's Work Ser.). (Illus.). 192p. (gr. 11-12). 1981. 14.95 (ISBN 0-912670-84-3); pap. 4.95 (ISBN 0-912670-70-3). Feminist Pr.

Mukat's People: The Cahuilla Indians of Southern California. Lowell J. Bean. LC 78-145782. (Illus.). 300p. 1972. 14.00x (ISBN 0-520-01912-1); pap. 4.50x (ISBN 0-520-02627-6). U of Cal Pr.

Muktananda: Selected Essays. Paul Zweig. LC 76-9994. 1977. pap. 5.95 (ISBN 0-06-069860-8, RD185, HarpR). Har-Row.

Mukteshwari, Vol. I. Swami Muktananda. 1972. 2.95 (ISBN 0-914602-61-6). SYDA Found.

Mukteshwari, Vol. II. Swami Muktananda. 1973. 2.95 (ISBN 0-914602-62-4). SYDA Found.

Mulcaster Market. James Reeves. 1951. pap. text ed. 2.95 o.p. (ISBN 0-435-21003-3). Heinemann Ed.

Mule & Black-Tailed Deer of North America. Ed. by Olof C. Wallmo. LC 80-20128. (Illus.). xvii, 650p. 1981. 29.95 (ISBN 0-8032-4715-X). U of Nebr Pr.

Muleskinner. Robert MacLeod. 1978. pap. 1.50 o.p. (ISBN 0-449-14054-7, GM). Fawcett.

Mulga Bill's Bicycle. A. B. Paterson. LC 74-12286. (Illus.). 40p. (ps-3). 1975. 5.95 o.s.i. (ISBN 0-8193-0777-7, Four Winds); PLB 5.41 o.s.i. (ISBN 0-8193-0778-5). Schol Bk Serv.

Mulitnational Marketing Management. 2nd ed. Warren J. Keagan. (Illus.). 1980. text ed. 21.00 (ISBN 0-13-605055-7). P-H.

Mulk Raj Anand. M. K. Naik. (Indian Writers Ser.). 1976. 8.50 (ISBN 0-89253-507-5). Ind-US Inc.

Mullberry Bush. Illus. by Henrietta W. Le Mair. (Illus.). 1978. Repr. of 1911 ed. 7.50 o.p. (ISBN 0-85249-338-X, Star & Elephant). Green Tiger.

Mulroy's Magic. Marjorie-Ann Watts. (Illus.). (ps-5). 1972. 6.50 (ISBN 0-571-09645-X, Pub. by Faber & Faber). Merrimack Bk Serv.

Multi-Channel Japan. Hugh Trevor. 1980. pap. 1.00 (ISBN 0-85363-075-5). OMF Bks.

Multi-Engine Pilot Manual. 2nd ed. (Pilot Training Ser.). (Illus.). 128p. 1981. pap. text ed. 11.62 (ISBN 0-88487-070-7, JS314127A). Jeppesen Sanderson.

Multi-Hull Racing: The Hobie Cats & Other Catamarans. 3rd rev. ed. F. Miller & P. Berman. (Illus.). 1981. pap. 14.95 (ISBN 0-89404-036-7). Aztex.

Multi-Image Media. Sr. Robert V. Bullough. Ed. by James E. Duane. LC 80-21341. (Instructional Media Library: Vol. 9). (Illus.). 128p. 1981. 13.95 (ISBN 0-87778-169-9). Educ Tech Pubns.

Multi-Level Speller for Grades 3-12. Morton Botel. (gr. 3-12). 4.10 (ISBN 0-931992-15-X); pap. 3.00 (ISBN 0-931992-16-8). Penns Valley.

Multi-Level Speller Guidebook for Teachers. Morton Botel. 1961. 4.95 (ISBN 0-931992-17-6). Penns Valley.

Multi-Level Speller Student Record Book. 1960. wkbk. 2.45 (ISBN 0-931992-18-4). Penns Valley.

Multi-Party Britain. Ed. by H. M. Drucker. LC 79-52940. (Praeger Special Studies). 256p. 1979. 25.95 (ISBN 0-03-053446-1). Praeger.

Multi-Season Shrubs & Trees. Sybil C. Emberton. (Illus.). 1971. 9.95 o.p. (ISBN 0-571-08748-5, Pub. by Faber & Faber). Merrimack Bk Serv.

Multi-Sensory Educational Aids from Scrap. Kendrick Coy. (Illus.). 232p. 1980. text ed. 19.50 spiral bdg. (ISBN 0-398-03934-8). C C Thomas.

Multi-Site Tests Environments & Breeding Strategies for New Rice Technology. (IRRI Research Paper Ser.: No. 7). 30p. 1977. pap. 5.00 (R047, IRRI). Unipub.

Multi-Story Buildings in Steel. F. Hart et al. LC 74-5513. 1978. 94.95 (128p. (ISBN 0-470-35615-4). Halsted Pr.

Multichannel Time Series Analysis with Digital Computer Programs. Enders A. Robinson. LC 67-28043. 1978. pap. text ed. 17.95x (ISBN 0-8162-7254-9). Holden-Day.

Multicomponent Distillation & Rectification. S. A. Bagaturov. 10.00x (ISBN 0-210-98104-0). Asia.

Multicultural Education & the American Indian. 169p. 1979. 5.00 (ISBN 0-686-28733-9). U Cal AISC.

Multicultural Teaching: A Handbook of Activities, Information, & Resources. new ed. Pamela Tiedt & Iris M. Tiedt. 1979. text ed. 17.95 (ISBN 0-205-06445-0); pap. text ed. 9.95x (ISBN 0-205-06522-8, 2365227). Allyn.

Multicultural Transactions: A Workbook Focusing on Communication Between Groups. James S. DeLo & William A. Green. LC 80-69328. 125p. 1981. perfect bdg. 11.50 (ISBN 0-86548-030-3). Century Twenty One.

Multidimensional Analytic Geometry. Karol Borsuk. 1969. 19.25 (ISBN 0-02-841690-2). Hafner.

Multidimensional Spatial Data & Decision Analysis. Peter Nijkamp. LC 79-40518. 322p. 1980. 46.95 (ISBN 0-471-27603-0, Pub. by Wiley-Interscience). Wiley.

Multidimensional Systems: Theory & Applications. N. K. Bose. (IEEE Reprint Ser.). 1978. 29.95 (ISBN 0-471-05214-0); pap. 19.50 (ISBN 0-471-05215-9, Pub. by Wiley-Interscience). Wiley.

Multidimensional Systems: Theory & Applications. Ed. by Nirmal K. Bose. LC 78-55096. 1979. 29.95 (ISBN 0-87942-109-6). Inst Electrical.

Multidisciplinary Approach to LD: Handbook for the Classroom Teacher. 1978. non-members 5.95 (ISBN 0-917160-09-6). Am Sch Health.

Multidisciplinary Assessment of the Geriatric Patient. Ed. by Alvin J. Levenson & Susan M. Tollett. 1981. text ed. price not set (ISBN 0-89004-492-9). Raven.

Multidisciplinary Handbook of Epilepsy. B. P. Hermann. (Illus.). 388p. 1980. 34.50 (ISBN 0-398-04070-2); pap. 26.75 (ISBN 0-398-04069-9). C C Thomas.

Multiengine Airplane Rating. 7th ed. T. M Smith. LC 64-7947. (Zweng Manuals). (Illus.). 1981. soft bdg. 6.95 (ISBN 0-87219-003-X). Pan Am Nav.

Multiethnic Eduction: Theory & Practice. Banks. 300p. 1981. text ed. 17.50 (ISBN 0-205-07300-X, 2373009); pap. text ed. 10.50 (ISBN 0-205-07293-3, 2372932). Allyn.

Multifunctional Proteins. Ed. by Hans Bisswanger & Eva Schmincke-Ott. LC 79-16055. 1980. 37.50 (ISBN 0-471-04270-6, Pub. by Wiley-Interscience). Wiley.

Multihospital Systems: Strategies for Organization & Management. Montague Brown & Barbara P. McCool. LC 79-23439. (Illus.). 564p. 1979. text ed. 36.00 (ISBN 0-89443-169-2). Aspen Systems.

Multilateral Agreements. (Legal Ser.: No. 1). 1959. pap. 8.25 (ISBN 92-0-176059-0, IAEA). Unipub.

Multilateral Trade Negotiations: Toward Greater Liberalization? Robert E. Baldwin. 1979. pap. 3.75 (ISBN 0-8447-1082-2). Am Enterprise.

Multilateral Treaties & Conventions on Industrial Property in the Americas. (Treaty Ser.: No. 39). (Eng., Span., & Port.). 1973. pap. 1.00 (ISBN 0-8270-0495-8). OAS.

Multilateral Treaties in Respect of Which the Secretary General Performs Depository Functions. 677p. 1980. pap. 34.00 (ISBN 0-686-68960-7, UN80/5/10, UN). Unipub.

Multilingual Dictionary of Fish & Fish Products. 1978. 44.00 (ISBN 0-85238-086-0, FN 64, FN). Unipub.

Multilingual Dictionary of Fish & Fish Products. 2nd ed. Ed. by OECD. 446p. 1978. 42.50x (ISBN 0-85238-086-0). Intl Pubns Serv.

Multilingual Guide for Medical Personnel. Ed. by Bernard Finch. 1967. spiral bdg. 4.50 (ISBN 0-87488-961-8). Med Exam.

Multilingualism in International Law & Institutions. Mala Tabory. LC 80-51742. 304p. 1980. 32.50x (ISBN 90-286-0210-0). Sijthoff & Noordhoff.

Multimedia Library: Materials Selection & Use. James Cabeceiras. 275p. 1978. tchrs' ed. 14.00 (ISBN 0-12-153950-4). Acad Pr.

Multimedium Management of Municipal Sludge. Committee on a Multimedium Approach to Municipal Sludge Management, National Research Council. LC 77-93086. (Analytical Studies for the U. S. Environmental Protection Agency Ser.). (Illus.). 1978. pap. text ed. 8.00 (ISBN 0-309-02733-0). Natl Acad Pr.

Multimodal Therapy with Children. Donald B. Keat, II. LC 78-7044. (Pergamon General Psychology Ser.: Vol. 73). 1979. 22.00 (ISBN 0-08-022236-6). Pergamon.

Multinational Business Management. Howe Martyn. LC 75-116682. 1970. 29.50x (ISBN 0-669-58818-0). Irvington.

Multinational Businessman & Foreign Policy: Entrepreneurial Politics in East-West Trade & Investment. Jeffrey M. Brookstone. LC 76-12845. (Illus.). 1976. text ed. 22.95 (ISBN 0-275-23360-X). Praeger.

Multinational Computer Nets: The Case of International Banking. Richard H. Veith. 160p. 1981. 18.95x (ISBN 0-669-04092-4). Lexington Bks.

Multinational Cooperation for Development in West Africa. John P. Renninger. LC 78-15217. 176p. 1979. 22.00 (ISBN 0-08-022490-3). Pergamon.

Multinational Corporation. S. Hymer. Ed. by R. B. Cohen et al. LC 79-52327. (Illus.). 1979. 39.50 (ISBN 0-521-22695-3). Cambridge U Pr.

Multinational Corporation. Sanjaya Lall. 224p. 1980. 32.50 (ISBN 0-8419-5083-0). Holmes & Meier.

Multinational Corporation: A Guide to Information Sources. Ed. by Helga Hernes. LC 73-17509. (International Relations Information Guide Series: Vol. 4). 1977. 30.00 (ISBN 0-8103-1327-8). Gale.

Multinational Corporations & European Public Opinion. Georges Peninou et al. LC 78-58894. (Praeger Special Studies). 1978. 23.95 (ISBN 0-03-046191-X). Praeger.

Multinational Corporations & Governments: Business-Government Relations in an International Context. Ed. by Patrick M. Boarman & Hans Schollhammer. LC 75-8402. (Illus.). 256p. 1975. text ed. 24.95 (ISBN 0-275-00900-9). Praeger.

Multinational Corporations & National Elites: A Study in Tensions. Joseph LaPalombara & Stephen Blank. LC 76-48768. (Report Ser: No. 702). (Illus.). 1976. pap. 15.00 o.p. (ISBN 0-8237-0136-0). Conference Bd.

Multinational Corporations & National Governments: A Case Study of the United Kingdom's Experience, 1964-1970. Michael Hodges. 1974. 21.95 (ISBN 0-347-01034-2, 93500-X, Pub. by Saxon Hse England). Lexington Bks.

Multinational Corporations & the Control of Culture: The Ideological Apparatuses of Imperialism. Armand Mattelart. Tr. by Michael Chanan. LC 79-221. (Marxist Theory & Contemporary Capitalism: No. 26). 1979. text ed. 29.50x (ISBN 0-391-00978-8). Humanities.

Multinational Corporations Law, Vols. 1-2. K. Simmonds. 1979. Set. 75.00 (ISBN 0-379-20373-1). Oceana.

Multinational Corporations Law, Release 3. K. Simmonds. 1980. 50.00. Oceana.

Multinational Corporations: The ECISM Guide to Information Sources. Joseph O. Mekeirle. 71.95 (ISBN 0-03-046261-4). Praeger.

Multinational Enterprise. Ed. by John H. Dunning. 1971. text ed. 36.00x (ISBN 0-04-330189-4). Allen Unwin.

Multinational Enterprises. Ed. by J. S. Wilson. 1974. 40.00 (ISBN 9-0286-0124-4). Heinman.

Multinational Enterprises & Nation States. Michael Clapham. (Stamp Memorial Lectures). 1975. pap. text ed. 2.75x (ISBN 0-485-16429-9, Athlone Pr). Humanities.

Multinational Enterprises & U. N. Politics: The Quest for Codes of Conduct. Werner J. Feld. (Pergamon Policy Studies). (Illus.). 1980. 28.00 (ISBN 0-08-022488-1). Pergamon.

Multinational Man: The Role of the Manager Abroad. Thomas Aitken. LC 73-10602. 176p. 1973. 14.95 (ISBN 0-470-01793-7). Halsted Pr.

Multinational Management: Business Strategy & Government Policy. Yoshi Tsurumi. 622p. 1976. write for info. (ISBN 0-88410-297-1). Ballinger Pub.

Multinational Management Game. Alfred G. Edge et al. 1980. pap. 7.95x (ISBN 0-256-02362-X). Business Pubns.

Multinational Marketing & Employment Directory, 2 vols. 8th ed. 1980. Set. 125.00 (ISBN 0-8360-0019-6). World Trade.

Multinational Marketing & Employment Directory. 9th ed. 1981. 100.00. World Trade.

Multinational Oil: A Study in Industrial Dynamics. Neil H. Jacoby. LC 74-22381. (Studies of the Modern Corporation Ser.). (Illus.). 304p. 1974. 17.95 (ISBN 0-02-915990-3); pap. 3.95 (ISBN 0-02-915980-6). Macmillan.

Multinational Organization Development. David A. Heenan & Howard V. Perlmutter. 1978. pap. text ed. 6.50 (ISBN 0-201-02953-7). A-W.

Multinational Telecommunications: Opportunities, Cost & Constraint. 1979. pap. text ed. 63.50x (ISBN 0-903796-42-2, Pub. by Online Conferences England). Renouf.

Multinational Union Organizations in the Manufacturing & Processing Industries. Richard L. Rowan et al. LC 80-53989. (Multinational Industrial Relations Ser.). 213p. (Orig.). 1980. pap. 15.00 (ISBN 0-89546-021-1). Indus Res Unit-Wharton.

Multinational Union Organizations in the Public Service & White-Collar Industries. Richard L. Rowan & Rae A. O'Brien. 1980. pap. 15.00 (ISBN 0-89546-022-X). Indus Res Unit-Wharton.

Multinationals & East-West Relations: Towards Transideological Collaboration. Jozef Wilczynski. LC 76-2080. 1976. 28.50x (ISBN 0-89158-540-0). Westview.

Multinationals from Developing Countries. Ed. by Krishna Kumar & Maxwell G. McLeod. LC 80-8531. 1981. write for info. (ISBN 0-669-04113-0). Lexington Bks.

Multinationals in Africa: A Case Study of the Ivory Coast. Jean Masini et al. LC 78-19462. (Praeger Special Studies). 1978. 23.95 (ISBN 0-03-046256-8). Praeger.

Multinationals in Latin America: The Politics of Nationalization. Paul E. Sigmund. 435p. 1980. 22.50 (ISBN 0-299-08260-1); pap. 6.75 (ISBN 0-299-08264-4). U of Wis Pr.

Multinationals Under Fire: Lessons in the Management of Conflict. Thomas N. Gladwin & Ingo Walter. LC 79-21741. 1980. 34.95 (ISBN 0-471-01969-0, Pub. by Wiley-Interscience). Wiley.

Multiphase Science & Technology, Vol. 1. Ed. by Geoffrey F. Hewitt et al. (Multiphase Science & Technology Ser.). (Illus.). 400p. 1981. text ed. 49.75 (ISBN 0-89116-222-4). Hemisphere Pub.

Multiphasic Health Testing. American Society for Hospital Engineering of the American Hospital Association. LC 79-11129. (Illus.). 1979. pap. 5.00 (ISBN 0-87258-269-8, 1103). Am Hospital.

Multiplanar Anatomy of the Head & Neck: For Computed Tomography. Enrique Palacios et al. LC 80-11368. 208p. 1980. 148.00 (ISBN 0-471-05820-3, Pub. by WileyMed). Wiley.

Multiple-Beam Interferometry of Surfaces & Films. S. Tolansky. (Illus.). 1971. pap. text ed. 3.00 (ISBN 0-486-62215-0). Dover.

Multiple Choice Questions for A-Level Chemistry. D. Stebbins. LC 79-41510. (Illus.). 132p. 1980. pap. 8.95 (ISBN 0-408-10644-1). Butterworths.

Multiple-Choice Questions for Assessment in Physics. J. G. Houston et al. 1971. pap. text ed. 5.95 with answers o.p. (ISBN 0-435-67424-2). Heinemann Ed.

Multiple-Choice Questions in Biology & Human Biology. O. Kilgour. (Orig.). 1974. pap. text ed. 4.95x o.p. (ISBN 0-435-59502-4). Heinemann Ed.

Multiple-Choice Questions in Economics. Joan Chapman & Jeffrey Smith. 1973. pap. text ed. 2.95 with ans. o.p. (ISBN 0-435-84271-4); pap. text ed. 2.50 text only o.p. (ISBN 0-435-84270-6). Heinemann Ed.

Multiple-Choice Questions in O Level Chemistry. Robin A. Hillman. 1971. pap. text ed. 3.95x o.p. (ISBN 0-435-64320-7); pap. text ed. 4.95x with ans. o.p. (ISBN 0-435-64321-5). Heinemann Ed.

Multiple Choice Questions in the House & Its Services. O. F. Kilgour. 1978. pap. text ed. 4.95 o.p. (ISBN 0-435-42229-4). Heinemann Ed.

Multiple Classification Analysis: A Report on a Computer Program for Multiple Regression Using Categorical Predictors. rev. ed. Frank M. Andrews et al. LC 73-620206. 105p. 1973. cloth 9.00 (ISBN 0-87944-148-8); pap. 5.50 (ISBN 0-87944-055-4). U of Mich Soc Res.

Multiple Criteria Decision Making. Milan Zeleny. 1981. write for info instrs.' manual (ISBN 0-07-072795-3, C); price not set instr's manual (ISBN 0-07-072796-1). McGraw.

Multiple Decision Procedures: Theory & Methodology of Selecting & Ranking Populations. Shanti C. Gupta & S. Panchapakesan. LC 79-13119. (Probability & Mathematical Statistics: Applied Section). 1979. 39.95 (ISBN 0-471-05177-2, Pub. by Wiley-Interscience). Wiley.

Multiple Engine Oils. Society of Automotive Engineers. 1980. 12.00 (ISBN 0-89883-243-8). Soc Auto Engineers.

Multiple Family Housing. David Mackey. Date not set. 32.50 (ISBN 0-8038-0164-5). Hastings.

Multiple Hypergeometric Functions & Applications. Harold Exton. LC 76-20720. 1976. 37.95 (ISBN 0-470-15190-0). Halsted Pr.

Multiple Indicators: An Introduction. John L. Sullivan & Stanley Feldman. LC 79-67015. (Quantitative Applications in the Social Sciences (a Sage University Paper Ser.): No. 15). (Illus.). 1979. pap. 3.50x (ISBN 0-8039-1369-9). Sage.

Multiple Integrals. Walter Ledermann. (Library of Mathematics Ser.). (Illus.). 1966. pap. 5.00 (ISBN 0-7100-4358-9). Routledge & Kegan.

Multiple Light Scattering: Tables, Formulas & Applications, Vol.1. H. C. Van De Hulst. LC 79-51687. 1980. 33.50 (ISBN 0-12-710701-0). Acad Pr.

Multiple Orgasm. (Illus.). pap. 5.00 (ISBN 0-910550-47-6). Centurion Pr.

Multiple Regression & Analysis of Variance: An Introduction for Computer Users in Management & Economics. George O. Wesolowsky. LC 76-5884. 1976. 31.95 (ISBN 0-471-93373-2, Pub. by Wiley-Interscience). Wiley.

Multiple Regression & the Analysis of Variance & Covariance. Allen L. Edwards. LC 79-12873. (Psychology Ser.). (Illus.). 1979. pap. text ed. 8.95x (ISBN 0-7167-1081-1). W H Freeman.

Multiple Residence Inspector. Jack Rudman. (Career Examination Ser.: C-2842). (Cloth bdg. avail. on request). 1980. pap. 10.00 (ISBN 0-8373-2842-X). Natl Learning.

Multiple Sclerosis: A Disease Acquired in Childhood. J. H. Millar. (American Lecture Living Chemistry Ser.). (Illus.). 120p. 1971. text ed. 10.75 (ISBN 0-398-01307-1). C C Thomas.

Multiple Sclerosis: A Personal View. Cynthia Birrer. (Illus.). 304p. 1979. text ed. 24.75 (ISBN 0-398-03864-3); pap. text ed. 18.75 (ISBN 0-398-03886-4). C C Thomas.

Multiple Sclerosis & Me. M. H. Greenblatt. (Illus.). 86p. 1972. 8.75 (ISBN 0-398-02300-X). C C Thomas.

Multiple Sclerosis Diet Book: A Low-Fat Diet for the Treatment of M.S. Heartdisease & Stroke. Swank, Roy L., M.D., Ph.D. & Mary-Helen Pullen. LC 76-24215. 1977. 9.95 (ISBN 0-385-12092-3). Doubleday.

Multiple Skills Series: Levels Picture Level Through I. Richard A. Boning. Incl. E1 (ISBN 0-8484-0041-0); E2 (ISBN 0-8484-0042-9); E3 (ISBN 0-8484-0043-7); E4 (ISBN 0-8484-0044-5); F1 (ISBN 0-8484-0045-3); F2 (ISBN 0-8484-0046-1); F3 (ISBN 0-8484-0047-X); F4 (ISBN 0-8484-0048-8). (Also available in Span. edition-levels Picture through C). (YA) 1976. pap. 19.35 set (ISBN 0-685-69056-3); pap. 2.10 ea. Lowell & Lynwood.

Multiple Stage in Spain During the Fifteenth & Sixteenth Centuries. William H. Shoemaker. LC 78-137076. 150p. 1973. Repr. of 1935 ed. lib. bdg. 17.00x (ISBN 0-8371-5539-8, SHMS). Greenwood.

Multiple Thread Mills. Roger W. Bolz. 1950. 18.50 (ISBN 0-930220-02-1). Conquest.

Multiple Tracking: Math 2: A Self-Instruction Workbook for Visual Accuracy,Resuable Edition. Kitty Wehrli. (gr. 1). 1971. wkbk. 6.00 (ISBN 0-89039-033-9). Ann Arbor Pubs.

Multiple Trigonometric Sums. G. I. Arhipov et al. (Trudy Steklov: No. 151). Date not set. cancelled (ISBN 0-8218-3067-8). Am Math.

Multiple Uses: Positive Substitution, Problem Solutions, Relaxation, & Goal Achievements, Set-MS. rev. ed. Russell E. Mason. 1975. pap. 50.00x (ISBN 0-89533-008-3); tape-1a, t-2, t-5a t-10,t-16, t-17 incl., notes, clinical applications 1979, h.e.s.t-a, set. F I Comm.

Multiplication & Division. R. Hunt. LC 78-730962. 1978. pap. text ed. 99.00 (ISBN 0-89290-093-8, A509-SATC). Soc for Visual.

Multiplication & Energy & Construction: Division & Medicine. Learning Achievement Corporation. Ed. by Therese A. Zak. (MATCH Ser.). (Illus.). 144p. 1980. text ed. 5.28 (ISBN 0-07-037112-1, G). McGraw.

Multiplication Facts & Basic Fractions. Beverly J. Mick. (gr. 5-12). 1981. Set. price not set (ISBN 0-932786-04-9); Bk. 1. 4.25 (ISBN 0-932786-05-7); Bk. 2. 4.25 (ISBN 0-932786-06-5). Bellefontaine.

Multiplication Facts, Decimals, & Percents, 2 bks. Beverly J. Mick. (gr. 5-12). 1981. Set. price not set (ISBN 0-932786-04-9); Bk. 1. 4.25 (ISBN 0-932786-05-7); Bk. 2. 4.25 (ISBN 0-932786-06-5). Bellefontaine.

Multiplication Learning Module. Daniel Quinn & Richard G. Mills. 1975. pap. text ed. 225.00 (ISBN 0-89290-133-0). Soc for Visual.

Multiplication of Viruses. S. E. Luria. Bd. with Virus Inclusions in Plant Cells. K. M. Smith; Virus Inclusions in Insect Cells. K. M. Smith; Antibiotika Erzeugende Virus-Ahnliche Faktoren in Bakterien. P. Fredericq. (Protoplasmatologica: Vol. 4, Pts. 3, 4a, 4b, 5). (Illus.). iv, 118p. (Eng., Ger.). 1958. 32.50 o.p. (ISBN 0-387-80488-9). Springer-Verlag.

Multiplication,Level 1: Consumable Edition. Kitty Wehrli. (Michigan Arithmetic Program Ser.). (gr. 3). 1975. Repr. wkbk 7.00 (ISBN 0-89039-094-0). Ann Arbor Pubs.

Multiplicative Number Theory. H. Davenport. (Graduate Texts in Mathematics Ser.: Vol. 74). 177p. 1981. 19.80 (ISBN 0-387-90533-2). Springer-Verlag.

Multipliers on Locally Compact Groups. K. R. Parthasarathy. LC 71-84142. (Lecture Notes in Mathematics: Vol. 93). (Orig.). 1969. pap. 10.70 (ISBN 0-387-04612-7). Springer-Verlag.

Multiply. Dottie Rambo & Dave Huntsinger. (Creek Bank Kids Ser.: Vol. 8). (ps-8). 1980. 3.95 (ISBN 0-914850-91-1). Impact Tenn.

Multiply Handicapped Child. James M. Wolf & Robert Anderson. 488p. 1973. pap. 19.00 spiral (ISBN 0-398-02105-8). C C Thomas.

Multiply Your Money Trading Soybeans: A Beginner's Guide to Speculating in Soybean Futures. Merrill J. Oster et al. 198p. 1981. 14.95 (ISBN 0-914230-10-7). Investor Pubns.

Multiprocessors: A Comparative Study. M. Satyanarayanan. (Illus.). 208p. 1980. text ed. 22.95 (ISBN 0-13-605154-5). P-H.

Multiscale: Four Programs for Multidimensional Scaling by the Method of Maximum Likelihood. James O. Ramsay. pap. 9.00 (ISBN 0-89498-002-5). Natl Ed Res.

Multispeed & Standard Squirrel Cage Motors. Vol. 1 Standard (Single Sped) Motors Only: Testing, Rewinding, Reconnecting, & Redesigning. Samuel Heller. LC 75-36709. (Illus.). 704p. 1976. pap. 35.00 (ISBN 0-911740-07-4). Datarule.

Multistate Bar Exam IV. National Conference Bar Exam. 1978. text ed. 2.50x (ISBN 0-87543-144-5). Lucas.

Multistate Bar Exam V. 1980. 2.50 (ISBN 0-87543-162-3). Lucas.

Multistate Bar Examination. rev. ed. Gruber et al. (Exam Prep. Ser.). 256p. 1981. pap. text ed. 6.95 (ISBN 0-671-18965-4). Monarch Pr.

Multivalent Functions. W. K. Hayman. (Cambridge Tracts in Mathematics & Mathematical Physics: No. 48). 1958. 26.50 (ISBN 0-521-05238-6). Cambridge U Pr.

Multivariable Calculus with Linear Algebra & Series. William F. Trench & Bernard Kolman. 758p. 1972. text ed. 22.95 (ISBN 0-12-699050-6). Acad Pr.

Multivariable Mathematics: Linear Algebra, Calculus, Differential Equations. 2nd ed. Richard Williamson & Hale Trotter. (Illus.). 1979. ref. 23.95 (ISBN 0-13-604850-1). P-H.

Multivariable Technological Systems. Ed. by D. P. Atherton. 1978. text ed. 115.00 (ISBN 0-08-022010-X). Pergamon.

Multivariate Analysis. Maurice Kendall. LC 75-39882. (Griffin Statistical Monograph). 1976. 23.95 o.s.i. (ISBN 0-02-847790-1). Hafner.

Multivariate Analysis. 2nd ed. Maurice Kendall. (Griffin Statistical Monograph). 1980. 29.95 (ISBN 0-02-847570-4). Macmillan.

Multivariate Analysis. Ed. by P. Krishnaiah. 1966. 55.25 (ISBN 0-12-426650-9). Acad Pr.

Multivariate Analysis in Behavioral Research. A. E. Maxwell. LC 76-25110. 164p. 1977. pap. text ed. 13.95x o.p. (ISBN 0-412-14300-3, Pub. by Chapman & Hall). Methuen Inc.

Multivariate Analysis in Behavioral Research. A. E. Maxwell. LC 76-25110. 1977. pap. text ed. 13.95 o.p. (ISBN 0-470-98902-5). Halsted Pr.

Multivariate Analysis with Applications in Education & Psychology. Neil H. Timm. LC 74-83250. (Statistics Ser.). (Illus.). 1975. text ed. 31.95 o.p. (ISBN 0-8185-0096-4). Brooks-Cole.

Multivariate Nominal Scale Analysis: A Report on a New Analysis Technique & a Computer Program. Frank M. Andrews & Robert C. Messenger. LC 72-629721. 114p. 1973. cloth 8.00 (ISBN 0-87944-135-6); pap. 5.00 (ISBN 0-87944-134-8). U of Mich Soc Res.

Multivariate Statistical Analysis in Geography: A Primer of the General Linear Model. R. J. Johnston. (Illus.). 1980. pap. text ed. 10.95 (ISBN 0-582-30034-7). Longman.

Multivariate Statistical Methods: Among-Groups Covariation. W. R. Atchley & E. H. Bryant. LC 75-9893. (Benchmark Papers in Systematic & Evolutionary Biology: Vol. 1). 480p. 1975. 43.50 (ISBN 0-12-786085-1). Acad Pr.

Multivariate Techniques in Human Communications Research. Ed. by Peter R. Monge & Joseph N. Capella. LC 79-28430. (Human Communication Research Ser.). 1980. 45.00 (ISBN 0-12-504450-X). Acad Pr.

Multivista Cultural. Angelo M. Heptner & Sheldon Steinburg. (Orig.). (gr. 11-12). 1975. text ed. 15.60 (ISBN 0-205-04593-6, 4245938); tchrs'. guide 4.96 (ISBN 0-205-04594-4, 4245946); cassettes 172.00 (ISBN 0-205-04851-X, 4248511); dupl. masters wkbk. 32.00 (ISBN 0-205-04852-8, 424852X). Allyn.

Multum in Parvo: An Essay in Poetic Imagination. Carl Zigrosser. LC 65-19325. (Illus.). 1965. 5.00 o.s.i. (ISBN 0-8076-0309-0). Braziller.

Mulu: The Rain Forest. Robin Hanbury-Tenison. (Illus.). 176p. 1980. 22.50x (ISBN 0-297-77768-8, Pub. by Weidenfeld & Nicolson England). Biblio Dist.

Mumbo Jumbo. Ishmael Reed. 1978. pap. 2.25 (ISBN 0-380-01860-8, 36566). Avon.

Mummies, Disease & Ancient Cultures. Ed. by Aiden Cockburn & Eve Cockburn. (Illus.). 352p. 1980. 49.95 (ISBN 0-521-23020-9). Cambridge U Pr.

Mummies, Men & Madness. John J. Davis. (Illus.). pap. 3.00 o.p. (ISBN 0-88469-004-0). BMH Bks.

Mummies of Guanajuato. Ray Bradbury. LC 77-16022. (Illus.). 1978. 17.50 o.p. (ISBN 0-8109-1325-9); pap. 8.95 o.p. (ISBN 0-8109-2150-2). Abrams.

Mummy. 2nd ed. E. A. Budge. LC 64-13391. (Illus.). 1894. 15.00x (ISBN 0-8196-0139-X). Biblo.

Mummy. Carl Dreadstone. (Universal Horror Library). 1977. pap. 1.25 o.p. (ISBN 0-425-03445-3, Medallion). Berkley Pub.

Mummy Jokes & Puzzles. Rosen. (gr. 3-5). 1980. pap. 1.25 (ISBN 0-590-30052-0, Schol Pap). Schol Bk Serv.

Munchy, Crunchy, Healthy Kid's Snack Book. Roz Abisch & Boche Kaplan. LC 75-16516. (Illus.). 64p. (gr. 2-5). 1976. 6.50 o.s.i. (ISBN 0-8027-6229-8); PLB 6.39 o.s.i. (ISBN 0-8027-6234-4). Walker & Co.

Mundane Perspectives in Astrology. Marc E. Jones. LC 75-14608. 1975. 16.50 o.p. (ISBN 0-87878-014-9, Sabian). Great Eastern.

Mundo Con Palabras. Sandoval-Groce. (Illus.). (gr. k-3). 1976. pap. 6.99 (ISBN 0-87892-886-3); tchr's handbook 3.99 (ISBN 0-87892-885-5); tapes 144.30 (ISBN 0-87892-883-9); dup. masters 4.59 (ISBN 0-87892-882-0). Economy Co.

Mundo Del Nuevo Testamento. H. E. Dana. Tr. by Ildefonso Villarello. 1977. pap. 4.25 (ISBN 0-311-04342-9). Casa Bautista.

Mundo En Crisis. T. B. Maston. Tr. by Bob Adams from Eng. 224p. (Span.). 1981. pap. write for info. (ISBN 0-311-46084-4). Casa Bautista.

Mundo En Que Vivio Jesus. Douglas Feaver. Tr. by Samuel Cuadra from Eng. Orig. Title: The World to Which Jesus Came. 128p. (Orig., Span.). 1973. pap. write for info o.p. (ISBN 0-89922-023-1). Edit Caribe.

Mundo es Ancho y Ajeno. Ciro Alegria. Ed. by G. E. Wade & W. E. Stiefel. (Span.). 1945. text ed. 20.00x (ISBN 0-89197-309-5); pap. text ed. 9.50x (ISBN 0-89197-310-9). Irvington.

Mundo Fisico: Physical Science Worktext. Dissemination Center-Bilingual-Bicultural Education. 1976. pap. text ed. 1.95 o.p. (ISBN 0-8120-0681-X); tchr's manual avail. o.p. (ISBN 0-8120-0739-5). Barron.

Mundo Hispano: Lengua y Cultura. Matilde O. Castells. LC 80-23698. 416p. 1980. 13.95 (ISBN 0-471-03396-0); write for info. tapes (ISBN 0-471-03397-9); write for info. tapes (ISBN 0-471-05835-1). Wiley.

Mundo Maravilloso de las Aves. (Span.). 9.50 (ISBN 84-241-5403-7). E Torres & Sons.

Mundo Misterioso de los Peces. (Span.). 9.00 (ISBN 84-241-5404-5). E Torres & Sons.

Mundo que Dios Creo. Alyce Bergey. Tr. by Ronald Ross from Eng. (Libros Arco). (Illus.). 32p. (Orig., Span.). (gr. 1-3). 1972. pap. 0.95 o.s.i. (ISBN 0-89922-041-X). Edit Caribe.

Mundo Ufo Report. Laura Mundo. 1981. 9.95 (ISBN 0-533-04735-8). Vantage.

Mundus Symbolicus, 2 vols. Filippo Picinelli. LC 75-27878. (Renaissance & the Gods Ser.: Vol. 33). (Illus.). 1977. Repr. of 1694 ed. Set. lib. bdg. 146.00 (ISBN 0-8240-2082-0); lib. bdg. 73.00 ea. Garland Pub.

Munger Map Book: California-Alaska Oil & Gas Fields, 1979 Ed. 1979. 60.00 o.p. (ISBN 0-686-28278-7). Munger Oil.

Mungo Park: The African Traveler. Kenneth Lupton. (Illus.). 1979. 24.95x (ISBN 0-19-211749-1). Oxford U Pr.

Munich. Time-Life Books Editors & George Bailey. (Great Cities Ser.). (Illus.). 200p. 1981. 14.95 (ISBN 0-8094-3120-3). Time-Life.

Munich Air Disaster. Stanley Williamson. (Illus.). 1973. 8.95 o.p. (ISBN 0-85181-005-5, Pub. by Faber & Faber). Merrimack Bk Serv.

Munich, Before & After. Herbert Ripka. LC 68-9630. 1969. Repr. of 1939 ed. 20.00 (ISBN 0-86527-133-X). Fertig.

Munich: Nineteen Thirty-Eight Appeasement Fails to Bring Peace for Our Time. Neil Grant. LC 70-16185. (World Focus Bks). (Illus.). (gr. 7 up). 1971. PLB 6.45 (ISBN 0-531-02154-8). Watts.

Municipal Accounting & Auditing: Where We Are Now, Where We Should Be Going. (COMP Papers Ser.). 170p. 1980. pap. 18.00 (ISBN 0-916450-41-4). Coun on Municipal.

Municipal Bankruptcy Law & Its Implications. Lawrence King et al. (COMP Papers: No. P-6). 81p. (Orig.). 1980. pap. 12.00 (ISBN 0-916450-39-2). Coun on Municipal.

Municipal Bond Financing. (Corporate Law & Practice Course Handbook Ser., 1976-77: Vol. 234). 1977. pap. 20.00 o.p. (ISBN 0-685-85300-4, B4-5513). PLI.

Municipal Bonds. Jerry Oster. 288p. 1981. 10.95 (ISBN 0-395-30538-1). HM.

Municipal Control of Cable Communications. Robert E. Jacobson. LC 77-7815. (Praeger Special Studies). 1977. text ed. 22.95 (ISBN 0-03-021831-4). Praeger.

Municipal Corporations, 4 vols. 3rd ed. E. C. Yokley. 1956. with 1980 cum. suppl. 175.00 (ISBN 0-87215-063-1); 1980 cum suppl seperately 90.00 (ISBN 0-87215-340-1). Michie.

Municipal Decentralization & Neighborhood Resources: Case Studies of Twelve Cities. George J. Washnis. LC 72-80467. (Special Studies in U.S. Economic, Social & Political Issues). 1972. 29.50x (ISBN 0-685-70540-4); pap. text ed. 14.50x (ISBN 0-89197-860-7). Irvington.

Municipal Development Programs in Latin America: An Intercountry Evaluation. Pirie M. Gall et al. LC 76-23401. (Illus.). 1976. 22.95 (ISBN 0-275-23280-8). Praeger.

Municipal Government in the Calcutta Metropolitan District. M. M. Singha. 4.25x o.p. (ISBN 0-210-27114-0). Asia.

Municipal Information Systems Directory. Kenneth L. Kraemer et al. LC 75-22891. (Illus.). 1976. 41.95 (ISBN 0-669-00469-3). Lexington Bks.

Municipal Public Safety: A Guide for the Implementation of Consolidated Police-Fire Services. Esai Berenbaum. (Illus.). 104p. 1977. 15.75 (ISBN 0-398-03612-8). C C Thomas.

Municipal Securities Regulation: A Public Perspective, 10 vols. Incl. Vol. 1 & 2. Certain Legal Considerations, Vol. II: An Introduction, Vol. 1. (Bound & sold together with Vol. II). 1977. price of 2 vols. 50.00. Vol. 1 (ISBN 0-916450-08-2). Vol. 2, 129 Pages; Vol. III. Self-Regulation: Is It Working? 148p. 1977. 40.00 (ISBN 0-916450-10-4); Vol. IV. Summary of Publications & Hearings. 264p. 1977. 70.00 (ISBN 0-916450-11-2); Federal Legislative Background Vol. V, Four Legal Memoranda, Vol. VI. 224p. (Vols. V & VI are bound & sold together). 1978. price of 2 vols. 65.00. Vol. V (ISBN 0-916450-12-0). Vol. VI; Vol. VII. Municipal Disclosure Standards Sourcebook. 199p. 1978. 60.00 (ISBN 0-916450-18-X); Vol. VIII. State Laws. 204p. 1978. 50.00 (ISBN 0-916450-19-8); Vol. IX. Disclosure Guidelines. 1979. 40.00; Vol. X. Way Back: Toward Accountability in America's Cities. 231p. 1979. 25.00 (ISBN 0-916450-21-X). Set. 270.00. Coun on Municipal.

Munshi Prem Chand. Govind N. Sharma. (World Author Ser.: No. 488). 1978. 14.95 (ISBN 0-8057-6329-5). Twayne.

Muon Physics. Ed. by Vernon Hughes & C. S. Wu. Incl. Vol. 1. 47.00 (ISBN 0-12-360601-2); Vol. 2. Weak Interactions. 81.00 (ISBN 0-12-360602-0); Vol. 3. Chemistry & Solids. 58.00 (ISBN 0-12-360603-9). 1975. 150.50 set (ISBN 0-685-72444-1). Acad Pr.

Muppet Madness. Henson Associates. LC 79-5269. (Illus., Orig.). (gr. 2-6). 1980. pap. 3.95 (ISBN 0-394-84393-2). Random.

Muppet Magic. Patricia D. Frevert. (TV-Movie Tie-Ins Ser.). 32p. (gr. 4-8). 1980. PLB 5.95 (ISBN 0-87191-755-6); pap. 2.95 (ISBN 0-89812-224-4). Creative Ed.

Muppet Manners (or the Night Gonzo Gave a Party) Pat Relf. LC 80-24087. (Muppet Show Bks.). (Illus.). 32p. (gr. 1-5). 1981. pap. 1.95 (ISBN 0-394-84713-X). Random.

Mur de Jean-Paul Sarte: Techniques et contexte d'une provocation. new ed. G. Idt. (Collection themes et textes). 224p. (Orig., Fr.). 1972. pap. 6.75 (ISBN 2-03-035013-3, 2659). Larousse.

Mural Painters of Tuscany: From Cimabue to Andrea Del Sarto. Eve Borsook. (Oxford Studies in the History of Art & Architecture Ser.). (Illus.). 400p. 1981. 165.00 (ISBN 0-19-817301-6). Oxford U Pr.

Murals from the Han to the Tang Dynesties. 1974. 35.00 (ISBN 0-8351-0161-4). China Bks.

Murals of Tepantitla, Teotihaucan. Esther Pasztory. LC 75-23806. (Outstanding Dissertations in the Fine Arts - Native American Arts). (Illus.). 1976. lib. bdg. 45.00 (ISBN 0-8240-2000-6). Garland Pub.

Murat Halstead & the Cincinnati Commercial. Donald W. Curl. LC 80-12046. (Illus.). ix, 186p. 1980. 17.50 (ISBN 0-8130-0669-4). U Presses Fla.

Murder at Crome Hous. G. D. H & Margaret Cole. 1976. lib. bdg. 13.95x (ISBN 0-89968-167-0). Lightyear.

Murder at Larinum. Cicero. Ed. by Humfrey Grose-Hodge. (Latin). 1932. text ed. 5.75x (ISBN 0-521-04648-3). Cambridge U Pr.

Murder at Tall Tip. Eleanor G. Gless. (YA) 5.95 (ISBN 0-685-07449-8, Avalon). Bouregy.

Murder at the ABA. Isaac Asimov. LC 75-21206. 240p. 1976. 7.95 o.p. (ISBN 0-385-11305-6). Doubleday.

Murder at the Flea Club. Matthew Head. LC 80-8716. 272p. 1981. pap. 2.25 (ISBN 0-06-080542-0, P542, PL). Har-Row.

Murder by Contract: The People Vs. "Tough Tony" Boyle. Arthur H. Lewis. LC 75-6721. 400p. 1975. 10.95 o.s.i. (ISBN 0-02-570520-2, 57052). Macmillan.

Murder by Death. Henry Keating. (Orig.). 1976. pap. 1.50 o.s.i. (ISBN 0-446-88161-9). Warner Bks.

Murder by Mail: And Other Postal Investigations. Robert B. Clifton. LC 79-51377. (Illus.). 240p. 1979. 7.95 (ISBN 0-8059-2649-6). Dorrance.

Murder by Microphone. John Reeves. 224p. 1980. pap. 2.25 (ISBN 0-380-43729-5, 43729). Avon.

Murder by Radio. Judith A. Green. (Adult Learner Ser.). (Illus.). 191p. (Orig.). 1979. pap. text ed. 3.60x (ISBN 0-89061-152-1, 200). Jamestown Pubs.

Murder by the Book. Rex Stout. 208p. 1981. pap. 1.95 (ISBN 0-553-14450-2). Bantam.

Murder Came Late. Jeremy York. (Cock Robin Mystery Ser.). 1969. 8.95 (ISBN 0-02-633230-2). Macmillan.

Murder Cure. Ann Ross. 1978. pap. 1.50 o.p. (ISBN 0-380-40915-1, 40915). Avon.

Murder for Pleasure. Howard Haycraft. LC 68-25809. 1941. 15.00x (ISBN 0-8196-0216-7). Biblo.

Murder Go Round. Alfred Hitchcock. 1981. pap. 2.25 (ISBN 0-440-15607-6). Dell.

Murder in Luxury. Hugh Pentecost. LC 80-22250. 196p. 1981. 8.95 (ISBN 0-396-07921-0). Dodd.

Murder in Retrospect. Agatha Christie. 192p. 1981. pap. 2.25 (ISBN 0-440-16030-8). Dell.

Murder in the White House. Margaret Truman. 1980. lib. bdg. 13.95 (ISBN 0-8161-3171-6, Large Print Bks). G K Hall.

Murder in White. Hugh Zachary. 1981. pap. 1.95 (ISBN 0-8439-0876-9, Leisure Bks). Nordon Pubns.

Murder, Inequality, & the Law: Differential Treatment & the Legal Process. Victoria Swigert & Ronald A. Farrell. LC 76-22222. 1976. 15.95 (ISBN 0-669-00881-8). Lexington Bks.

Murder Is Announced. Agatha Christie. 1980. pap. 2.50 (ISBN 0-671-43284-2). PB.

Murder Is Suspected. Peter Alding. 1978. 7.95 o.s.i. (ISBN 0-8027-5389-2). Walker & Co.

Murder Machine & Other Essays. Padraic Pearse. 1976. pap. 3.50 o.p. (ISBN 0-85342-471-3). Irish Bk Ctr.

Murder Makers. Jonathan Ross. 1977. 6.95 o.s.i. (ISBN 0-8027-5371-X). Walker & Co.

Murder Most Foul: And Other Great Crime Stories from the World Press. Ed. by Rob Warden & Martha Groves. LC 78-51586. (Illus.). x, 348p. 1980. 15.00 (ISBN 0-8040-0796-9). Swallow.

Murder Most Strange. Dell Shannon. 224p. 1981. 9.95 (ISBN 0-688-00378-8). Morrow.

Murder Must Advertise. Dorothy L. Sayers. (Large Print Bks.). 1980. lib. bdg. 15.95 (ISBN 0-8161-3045-0). G K Hall.

Murder of Christ: The Emotional Plague of Mankind. Wilhelm Reich. 228p. 1953. 5.95 (ISBN 0-374-21625-8); pap. 3.95 (ISBN 0-374-50476-8, N290). FS&G.

Murder of Herodes & Other Trials from the Athenian Law Courts. Kathleen Freeman. 1963. pap. 2.95 o.p. (ISBN 0-393-00201-2, Norton Lib). Norton.

Murder of Jacob De Haan by the Zionists: A Martyr's Message. Emil Marmorstein. 1980. lib. bdg. 59.95 (ISBN 0-686-68747-7). Revisionist Pr.

Murder of Lawrence of Arabia. Matthew Eden. LC 78-69528. 1979. 9.95 o.s.i. (ISBN 0-690-01790-1, TYC-T). T Y Crowell.

Murder of Mary Steers. Brian Cooper. LC 66-16980. 5.95 (ISBN 0-8149-0043-7). Vanguard.

Murder of Roger Ackroyd. Agatha Christie. 1980. pap. 2.25 (ISBN 0-671-83050-3). PB.

Murder of the Mahatma & Other Cases from a Judge's Notebook. G. D. Khosla. 276p. 1965. pap. 2.50 (ISBN 0-88253-051-8). Ind-US Inc.

Murder on Capitol Hill. Margaret Truman. LC 80-70223. 256p. 1981. 11.95 (ISBN 0-87795-312-0). Arbor Hse.

Murder on Mars. Hugh Walters. 1978. 6.95 o.p. (ISBN 0-571-10717-6, Pub. by Faber & Faber). Merrimack Bk Serv.

Murder on the Links. Agatha Christie. 1980. pap. 1.95 (ISBN 0-440-16102-9). Dell.

Murder on the Yellow Brick Road. Stuart Kaminsky. LC 77-15825. 1978. 7.95 o.p. (ISBN 0-312-55318-8). St Martin.

Murder or Three. Laurie Mantell. LC 80-54378. 1981. 9.95 (ISBN 0-8027-5432-5). Walker & Co.

Murder Racquet. Alfred Hitchcock. 1980. pap. 2.25 (ISBN 0-440-15931-8). Dell.

Murder R.F.D. Leslie Stephan. 1978. 8.95 o.p. (ISBN 0-684-15522-2, ScribT). Scribner.

Murder Trail: Shadow No. 18. Maxwell Grant. 1977. pap. 1.25 o.s.i. (ISBN 0-515-04280-3). Jove Pubns.

Murder Ward. Warren Murphy. (Destroyer Ser., No. 15). (Orig.). 1974. pap. 1.50 (ISBN 0-523-40289-9). Pinnacle Bks.

Murder with Malice. Michael Underwood. LC 76-28064. Date not set. 7.95 (ISBN 0-312-55336-6). St Martin.

Murder with Pictures. George H. Coxe. LC 80-8410. 288p. 1981. pap. 2.25 (ISBN 0-06-080527-7, P 527, PL). Har-Row.

Murdercycles. Patricia Zonker. LC 78-12855. (Illus.). 1978. 13.95 (ISBN 0-88229-553-5); pap. 7.95 (ISBN 0-88229-610-8). Nelson-Hall.

Murderer. Roy A. Heath. 176p. 1981. pap. 5.95 (ISBN 0-8052-8072-3, Pub. by Allison & Busby England). Schocken.

Murderer. Anthony Shaffer. 96p. 1979. 9.95 (ISBN 0-7145-2544-8, Pub. by M Boyars); pap. 5.95 (ISBN 0-7145-2545-6). Merrimack Bk Serv.

Murderer Is a Fox. Ellery Queen. 1976. pap. 1.50 o.p. (ISBN 0-345-25289-6). Ballantine.

Murderer's Choice. Anna M. Wells. 256p. 1981. pap. text ed. 2.25 (ISBN 0-06-080534-X, P 534, PL). Har-Row.

Murderers' Row. Donald Hamilton. (Matt Helm Ser.). 1978. pap. 1.95 (ISBN 0-449-14088-1, GM). Fawcett.

Murdering Mind. David Abrahamsen. LC 72-9742. 256p. 1973. 6.95 o.s.i. (ISBN 0-06-010022-2, HarpT). Har-Row.

Murdering Mothers: Infanticide in England & New England, 1558-1803. Peter C. Hoffer & N. E. Hull. (NYU School of Law Ser. in Anglo-American Legal History). 208p. 1981. text ed. 22.50x (ISBN 0-8147-3412-X). NYU Pr.

Murders in the Rue Morgue. rev. ed. Edgar A. Poe. Ed. by Robert J. Dixson. Bd. with Gold Bug. (American Classics Ser.: Bk. 3). (gr. 9 up). 1973. pap. text ed. 2.75 (ISBN 0-88345-199-9, 18122); cassettes 40.00 (ISBN 0-685-38998-7); tapes 40.00 (ISBN 0-685-38999-5). Regents Pub.

Muret-Sanders, English German Dictionary. Incl. Vol. 1, A-M. 920p; Vol. 2, N-Z. 968p. 1962. 70.00x ea. Hippocrene Bks.

Muret-Sanders, German-English Dictionary. Incl. Vol. 2, A-K. 1014p; Vol. 2, L-Z. 1040p. 1975. 80.00x ea. Hippocrene Bks.

Muriel at Metropolitan. Miriam Tlali. 190p. (Orig.). 1979. 9.00 (ISBN 0-89410-101-3); pap. 5.00 (ISBN 0-89410-100-5). Three Continents.

Muriel Spark. Karl Malkoff. LC 68-54456. (Columbia Essays on Modern Writers Ser.: No. 36). (Orig.). 1968. pap. 2.00 (ISBN 0-231-03063-0, MW36). Columbia U Pr.

Muriel Spark. Derek Stanford. 10.00x (ISBN 0-87556-326-0). Saifer.

Murle: Red Chiefs & Black Commoners. B. A. Lewis. (Oxford Monographs in Social Anthropology). 1972. 11.00x o.p. (ISBN 0-19-823172-5). Oxford U Pr.

Murnau. Lotte Eisner. 1973. 18.50x (ISBN 0-520-02285-8). U of Cal Pr.

Murphy's Men. Gerald Green. LC 80-52409. 352p. 1981. 12.95 (ISBN 0-87223-662-5). Seaview Bks.

Murray Hill. Charles Mercer. 1981. pap. 2.95 (ISBN 0-440-16124-X). Dell.

Murray on Contracts. Murray. 877p. 1974. 25.00 (ISBN 0-672-81775-6, Bobbs-Merrill Law). Michie.

Murray's Handbook for Travellers in Switzerland. John Murray. (Victorian Library). 1970. Repr. of 1838 ed. text ed. 10.00x (ISBN 0-391-00111-6, Leicester). Humanities.

Murtala Muhammed. Billy J. Dudley. 1981. 27.50x (ISBN 0-7146-3130-2, F Cass Co). Biblio Dist.

Musar Movement. Zalman R. Ury. 1970. pap. 3.00x o.p. (ISBN 0-685-00969-6). Bloch.

Muscidae of California, Exclusive of Subfamily Scatophaginae (Diptera) H. C. Huckett. (Bulletin of the California Insect Survey: Vol. 12). 1974. pap. 13.50x (ISBN 0-520-09508-1). U of Cal Pr.

Muscle Biopsy: A Modern Approach. Victor Dubowitz & Michael H. Brooke. LC 72-88846. (Major Problems in Neurology Ser.: No.2). (Illus.). 490p. 1973. 30.00 o.p. (ISBN 0-7216-3220-3). Saunders.

Muscle Builders: Twelve-Week Bodybuilding Course. Jeffrey R. Weber. LC 80-66788. 112p. (gr. 10-12). 1980. pap. text ed. 11.95 (ISBN 0-9604892-1-5). Five Arms Corp.

Muscle Contraction: Its Regulatory Mechanism. Ed. by S. Ebashi et al. 549p. 1981. 64.00 (ISBN 0-387-10411-9). Springer-Verlag.

Muscle Regeneration. Ed. by Alexander Mauro. 1979. text ed. 59.50 (ISBN 0-89004-284-5). Raven.

Muscle Relaxants. 2nd. ed. Stanley A. Feldman. LC 79-88002. (Major Problems in Anesthesia Ser.: Vol. I). (Illus.). 1979. text ed. 24.00 (ISBN 0-7216-3592-X). Saunders.

Muscle Structure, Chemistry & Function. Association of Bone & Joint Surgeons. Ed. by Marshall R. Urist & Anthony F. De Palma. (Clinical Orthopaedics & Related Research Ser. No. 85). (Illus.). 12.00 o.p. (ISBN 0-685-24747-3). Lippincott.

Muscle Testing: Techniques of Manual Examination. 4th ed. Lucille Daniels & Catherine Worthingham. LC 79-67302. (Illus.). 191p. 1980. 11.95 (ISBN 0-7216-2877-X). Saunders.

Muscles, Molecules & Movement. J. R. Bendall. 1969. text ed. 6.50x o.p. (ISBN 0-435-62054-1). Heinemann Ed.

Muscles Morals & Team Sports: The Culture of City Playgrounds, Eighteen Eighty to Nineteen Twenty. Dominick Cavallo. LC 80-50689. 240p. 1980. 21.50x (ISBN 0-8122-7782-1). U of Pa Pr.

Musconetcong Valley of New Jersey: A Historical Geography. Peter O. Wacker. LC 68-18694. (Illus.). 1968. 15.00 (ISBN 0-8135-0575-5). Rutgers U Pr.

Muscovite Russia. Samuel H. Baron. 362p. 1980. 75.00x (ISBN 0-86078-063-5, Pub. by Variorum England). State Mutual Bk.

Muscular Dystrophy & Other Inherited Diseases of Skeletal Muscle in Animals, Vol. 317. Ed. by John B. Harris. LC 78-27609. (Annals Ser.). 1979. pap. 80.00x (ISBN 0-89766-005-6). NY Acad Sci.

Muscular Dystrophy in Man & Animals. Ed. by G. H. Bourne. (Illus.). 1963. 37.25 o.s.i. (ISBN 0-02-841750-X). Hafner.

Muscular Exercise in Chronic Lung Disease: Proceedings of Meeting on Factors Limiting Exercise, Nancy, France, 13-15 Sept. 1978. Ed. by P. Sadoul. LC 79-40806. (Special Issue of the Bulletin Europeen De Physiopathologie Respiratoire). (Illus.). 1980. 50.00 (ISBN 0-08-024930-2). Pergamon.

Musculoskeletal Pain: Principles of Physical Diagnosis & Physical Treatment. David A. Zohn & John M. Mennell. 1976. 19.95 (ISBN 0-316-98893-6). Little.

Musculoskeletal System. James L. Poland et al. 1981. pap. write for info. (ISBN 0-87488-667-8). Med Exam.

Museum of Anthropology 1978-79 Annual Report. Lawrence H. Feldman & Elsebet S. Rowlett. (Annual Report Ser.: No. 6). (Illus.). v, 73p. 1979. pap. 3.60 (ISBN 0-913134-84-8). Mus Anthro MO.

Museum of Early American Tools. Eric Sloane. 1973. pap. 2.95 o.p. (ISBN 0-345-24675-6). Ballantine.

Museum of Modern Art Artists' Cookbook. Madeleine Conway & Nancy Kirk. LC 77-82029. (Illus.). 1977. pap. 8.95 (ISBN 0-87070-219-X, Dist. by Harry N. Abrams, Inc.). Museum Mod Art.

Museum Studies. Ed. by John Maxon et al. (Museum Studies Ser.). (Orig.). pap. 5.00 ea.; No. 1. (ISBN 0-86559-006-0); No. 2. (ISBN 0-86559-007-9); No. 3. (ISBN 0-86559-009-5); No. 4. (ISBN 0-86559-010-9); No.5. (ISBN 0-86559-011-7); No. 6. (ISBN 0-86559-012-5); No. 7. (ISBN 0-86559-013-3). Art Inst Chi.

Museum Studies, 1-9. Ed. by John Maxon et al. (Museum Studies Ser.). (Orig.). pap. 5.00 ea; No. 8. (ISBN 0-86559-018-4); No. 9. (ISBN 0-86559-027-3). Art Inst Chi.

Museum to Instruct & Delight. Roger G. Rose. LC 80-69203. (Special Publication Ser.: No. 68). (Illus.). 96p. Date not set. pap. 6.50 (ISBN 0-910240-28-0). Bishop Mus.

Museums & Women. John Updike. 256p. 1973. pap. 1.25 o.p. (ISBN 0-449-22007-9, P2007, Crest). Fawcett.

Museums: Architecture, Technics. R. Aloi. (Illus.). 1962. 50.00 (ISBN 0-685-12032-5). Heinman.

Museums for the Nineteen Hundred & Eighties: A Survey of World Trends. Kenneth Hudson. LC 77-24930. 1978. text ed. 49.50x (ISBN 0-8419-0327-1). Holmes & Meier.

Museums, Imagination & Education. LC 72-97589. (Illus.). 148p. (Orig.). 1973. pap. 13.50 (ISBN 92-3-101036-0, U395, UNESCO). Unipub.

Museums in Crisis. Ed. by Brian O'Doherty. LC 79-183186. (Illus.). 192p. 1972. 6.95 o.s.i. (ISBN 0-8076-0629-4). Braziller.

Museums of the Andes. Elizabeth Benson & William Conklin. Ed. by Henry Lafarge. LC 80-8912. 1981. 16.95 (ISBN 0-88225-306-9). Newsweek.

Museums of the World. 3rd ed. 1981. 185.00 (ISBN 0-686-69416-3, Dist. by Gale Research). K G Saur.

Musgrave Ritual. Arthur Conan Doyle. Ed. by Walter Pauk & Raymond Harris. (Classics). (Illus.). (gr. 6-12). 1976. pap. text ed. 1.60x (ISBN 0-89061-056-8, 533); tchrs. ed. 3.00 (ISBN 0-89061-057-6, 535). Jamestown Pubs.

Mushroom Growing for Everyone. Roy Genders. 1970. 11.50 (ISBN 0-571-08992-5). Transatlantic.

Mushroom Growing To-Day. 5th ed. Frederick C. Atkins. (Illus.). 1967. 5.95 o.s.i. (ISBN 0-02-504150-9). Macmillan.

Mushroom Growing Today. 6th ed. Fred C. Atkins. (Illus.). 1973. 9.95 o.p. (ISBN 0-571-04793-9, Pub. by Faber & Faber). Merrimack Bk Serv.

Mushroom Hunter's Field Guide: All Color & Enlarged. Alexander H. Smith & Nancy Weber. (Illus.). 336p. 1980. 14.95 (ISBN 0-472-85610-3). U of Mich Pr.

Mushroom in the Rain. A. Sinsberg. LC 72-92438. (Illus.). 32p. (gr. k-2). 1974. 5.95g (ISBN 0-685-38979-0); PLB 8.95 (ISBN 0-02-736240-X). Macmillan.

Mushroom Matings: The Best in Mushroom Cookery. Jean Granger. LC 78-5407. 1978. pap. 2.95 (ISBN 0-89666-000-1). Cragmont Pubns.

Mushroom Stones of Meso-America. Karl H. Mayer. (Illus.). 1977. pap. 4.95 (ISBN 0-916552-09-8). Acoma Bks.

Mushroom Terms: Polyglot on Research & Cultivation of Edible Fungi. 312p. 1981. pap. 83.00 (ISBN 90-220-0673-5, PDC 211, Pudoc). Unipub.

Mushrooms & Molds. Robert Froman. LC 71-187936. (Let's-Read-&-Find-Out Science Book). (Illus.). (gr. k-3). 1972. PLB 7.89 (ISBN 0-690-56603-4, TYC-J). T Y Crowell.

Mushrooms & Toadstools. Ronald Rayner. (Illus.). 128p. 1980. 8.95 (ISBN 0-600-36283-3). Transatlantic.

Mushrooms Demystified. David Arora. LC 79-8513. (Illus.). 1979. 18.95 (ISBN 0-89815-010-8); pap. 11.95 (ISBN 0-89815-009-4). Ten Speed Pr.

Mushrooms in the Wild. Uberto Tosco. Ed. by Ian Tribe. LC 77-82738. (Illus.). 1977. 7.95 o.p. (ISBN 0-8467-0371-8, Pub. by Two Continents). Hippocrene Bks.

Mushrooms of Idaho & the Pacific Northwest (Discomycetes) Edmund E. Tylutki. LC 79-64127. (GEM Books-Natural History). (Illus.). 166p. (Orig.). 1979. pap. 5.95 (ISBN 0-89301-062-6). U Pr of Idaho.

Mushrooms of the Great Smokies: A Field Guide to Some Mushrooms & Their Relatives. L. R. Hesler. LC 60-12221. (Illus.). 1960. 9.95 (ISBN 0-87049-028-1). U of Tenn Pr.

Mushrooms of Western North America. Robert T. Orr & Dorothy B. Orr. (Illus.). 1980. 12.95 (ISBN 0-520-03656-5). U of Cal Pr.

Music. 2nd ed. Daniel Politaske. 1979. 17.95 (ISBN 0-13-607556-8); study guide & workbook 5.95 (ISBN 0-13-607564-9); records set 16.95 (ISBN 0-13-607580-0). P-H.

Music. Jack Rudman. (Undergraduate Program Field Test Ser.: UPFT-16). (Cloth bdg. avail. on request). pap. 9.95 (ISBN 0-8373-6016-1). Natl Learning.

Music: A Pictorial Archive of Woodcuts & Engravings. Jim Harter. (Pictorial Archive Ser.). (Illus.). 155p. (Orig.). 1981. pap. 6.00 (ISBN 0-486-24002-9). Dover.

Music & Aesthetics in the Eighteenth & Early Nineteenth Centuries. Peter Le Huray & James Day. (Cambridge Studies in Music: Readings in the Literature of Music). (Illus.). 700p. Date not set. price not set (ISBN 0-521-23426-3). Cambridge U Pr.

Music & Bugling. Boy Scouts Of America. LC 19-600. (Illus.). 48p. (gr. 6-12). 1968. pap. 0.70x (ISBN 0-8395-3336-5, 3336). BSA.

Music & Ceremonies. Edith Sitwell. LC 63-13788. 1963. 6.95 (ISBN 0-8149-0205-7). Vanguard.

Music & Language with Young Children. E. M. Chacksfield et al. (Illus.). 1975. 18.50x (ISBN 0-631-15330-6, Pub. by Basil Blackwell). Biblio Dist.

Music & Language with Young Children. E. M. Chacksfield et al. 192p. 1981. pap. 6.50x (Pub. by Basil Blackwell England). Biblio Dist.

Music & Meaning. W. Coker. LC 72-142358. 1972. 12.95 (ISBN 0-02-906350-7). Free Pr.

Music & Moonlight. Arthur O'Shaughnessy. Ed. by Ian Fletcher & John Stokes. LC 76-20153. (Decadent Consciousness Ser.: Vol. 31). 1977. Repr. of 1874 ed. lib. bdg. 38.00 (ISBN 0-8240-2781-7). Garland Pub.

Music & Musical Instruments of Japan. F. T. Piggott. LC 70-155234. (Music Ser). 1971. Repr. of 1909 ed. lib. bdg. 22.50 (ISBN 0-306-70160-X). Da Capo.

Music & Musicians in Chicago. Florence F. Ffrench. (Music Reprint Ser.). 1979. Repr. of 1899 ed. lib. bdg. 27.50 (ISBN 0-306-79542-6). Da Capo.

Music & Musket: Bands & Bandsmen of the American Civil War. Kenneth E. Olson. LC 79-6195. (Contributions to the Study of Music & Dance: No. 1). (Illus.). 296p. 1981. lib. bdg. 27.50 (ISBN 0-313-22112-X). Greenwood.

Music & Nationalism: A Study of English Opera. Cecil Forsyth. LC 80-2276. 1981. Repr. of 1911 ed. 37.00 (ISBN 0-404-18844-3). AMS Pr.

Music & Nature: A Study of Aldous Huxley. Gerald Cockshott. (Salzburger Studien: No. 11). 1980. pap. text ed. 39.00x (ISBN 0-391-02158-3). Humanities.

Music & Painting: A Study in Comparative Ideas from Turner to Schoenberg. Edward Lockspeiser. LC 73-7979. (Icon Editions). (Illus.). 208p. 1973. pap. 4.95x o.s.i. (ISBN 0-06-430040-4, IN-40, HarpT). Har-Row.

Music & Patronage in Sixteenth Century Mantua. Iain Fenlon. LC 79-41377. (Cambridge Studies in Music). (Illus.). 350p. Date not set. 57.50 (ISBN 0-521-22905-7). Cambridge U Pr.

Music & Perceptual Motor Development. Katherine Crews. (Classroom Music Enrichment Units Ser.). (Illus.). 1974. pap. text ed. 5.95x (ISBN 0-87628-213-3). Ctr Appl Res.

Music & Poetry in the Early Tudor Court. Ed. by J. E. Stevens. LC 77-90180. (Cambridge Studies in Music). (Illus.). 1979. 69.50 (ISBN 0-521-22030-0); pap. 17.95 (ISBN 0-521-29417-7). Cambridge U Pr.

Music & Poetry of the English Renaissance. Bruce Pattison. LC 70-127278. (Music Ser). (Illus.). 1970. Repr. of 1948 ed. lib. bdg. 22.50 (ISBN 0-306-71298-9). Da Capo.

Music & the Line of Most Resistance. Artur Schnabel. LC 69-12690. (Music Ser). 1969. Repr. of 1942 ed. lib. bdg. 15.00 (ISBN 0-306-71224-5). Da Capo.

Music & the Reformation in England: Fifteen Forty-Nine to Sixteen Sixty. P. Le Huray. LC 77-87383. (Studies in Music). (Illus.). 1978. 64.50 (ISBN 0-521-21958-2); pap. 14.95x (ISBN 0-521-29418-5). Cambridge U Pr.

Music & the Theater: An Introduction to Opera. Reinhard G. Pauly. 1970. 18.50 (ISBN 0-13-607002-7). P-H.

Music As Experience: Structure & Sequence for the Elementary School. Gretchen H. Beall. 352p. 1981. pap. text ed. write for info. (ISBN 0-697-03444-5). Wm C Brown.

Music at Harvard: A Historical Review of Men & Events. Walter R. Spalding. LC 76-58921. (Music Reprint Series). 1977. Repr. of 1935 ed. lib. bdg. 27.50 (ISBN 0-306-70871-X). Da Capo.

Music at Nevers Cathedral: Principal Sources of Mediaeval Chant. Nancy Van Duesen. (Musicological Studies). 430p. 1980. lib. bdg. 55.00 pt. 1 (ISBN 0-912024-34-8); lib. bdg. 55.00 pt. 2 (ISBN 0-912024-33-X). Inst Mediaeval.

Music at Your Fingertips: Advice for the Artist & Amateur on Playing the Piano. Ruth Slenczynska. LC 74-1018. (Music Ser.). 160p. 1974. lib. bdg. 19.50 (ISBN 0-306-70653-9); pap. 3.95 (ISBN 0-306-80034-9). Da Capo.

Music Business Handbook & Career Guide. 2nd ed. David Baskerville. LC 78-57949. (Illus.). 1979. 18.95 (ISBN 0-933056-00-1). Sherwood Co.

Music by Heart. Lillias Mackinnon. LC 80-26551. xi, 141p. 1981. Repr. of 1954 ed. lib. bdg. 17.50x (ISBN 0-313-22810-8, MAMB). Greenwood.

Music Criticism: An Annotated Guide to the Literature. Harold J. Diamond. LC 79-22279. 326p. 1979. 17.50 (ISBN 0-8108-1268-1). Scarecrow.

Music Cultures of the Pacific, the Near East & Asia. 2nd ed. William P. Malm. (Illus.). 1977. text ed. 13.95 (ISBN 0-13-608000-6); pap. text ed. 10.95 (ISBN 0-13-607994-6). P-H.

Music Dictation: A Stereo Taped Series. Robert G. Olson. (Orig.). 1970. pap. 9.95x (ISBN 0-534-00671-X); stereo taped s 195.00x (ISBN 0-534-00672-8). Wadsworth Pub.

Music Dictionary. Arnold Broido & Marilyn K. Davis. LC 54-9837. (gr. 1-9). 1956. 5.95 o.p. (ISBN 0-385-07594-4). Doubleday.

Music Director's Complete Handbook of Forms. Kenneth L. Neidig. 1973. 14.95 o.p. (ISBN 0-13-607135-X). P-H.

Music East & West: Essays in Honor of Walter Kaufman. Ed. by Thomas Noblitt. (Festschrift Ser.: No. 3). (Illus.). x, 386p. 1981. lib. bdg. 36.00 (ISBN 0-918728-15-0). Pendragon NY.

Music Education: A Guide to Information Sources. Ed. by Ernest E. Harris. LC 74-11560. (Education Information Guide Ser.: Vol. 1). 1978. 30.00 (ISBN 0-8103-1309-X). Gale.

Music Education in Hungary. 3rd, enl. ed. Katalin Forrai et al. Tr. by Fred Macnicol from Hungarian. LC 80-123375. 310p. 1975. 12.00 (ISBN 0-85162-025-6). Boosey & Hawkes.

Music Education Review, Vol. 2. Ed. by Michael Burnett & Ian Lawrence. 226p. 1980. pap. text ed. 15.00x (ISBN 0-85633-196-1, NFER). Humanities.

Music Engraving & Printing: Historical & Technical Treatise. W. Gamble. LC 70-155576. (Music Ser). 1971. Repr. of 1923 ed. lib. bdg. 25.00 (ISBN 0-306-70168-5). Da Capo.

Music Facts & Feats. rev. ed. Robert Dearling et al. (Illus.). 288p. 1981. 19.95 (ISBN 0-8069-9250-6, Pub. by Guinness Superlatives England). Sterling.

Music for Advanced Study. Robert A. Melcher & Willard F. Warch. (Orig.). 1964. pap. text ed. 13.95 (ISBN 0-13-607317-4). P-H.

Music for Analysis: Examples from the Common Practice Period & the Twentieth Century. Thomas Benjamin et al. LC 77-78237. 1978. pap. text ed. 12.95 (ISBN 0-395-25507-4). HM.

Music for Chameleons. Truman Capote. 1981. pap. 3.50 (ISBN 0-451-09800-5, E9800, Signet Bks). NAL.

Music for Chameleons. Truman Capote. 1980. 10.95 (ISBN 0-394-50826-2). Random.

Music for Conducting Class. James McKelvy. LC 77-76862. 1977. wire bound 11.95 (ISBN 0-916656-10-1). Mark Foster Mus.

Music for Keyboard Harmony. Robert A. Melcher & Willard F. Warch. 1966. pap. text ed. 13.95 (ISBN 0-13-607432-4). P-H.

Music for Listeners. William Thompson. (Illus.). 1978. text ed. 16.95 (ISBN 0-13-608026-X); records 16.95 (ISBN 0-13-608018-9). P-H.

Music for Mohini. 2nd ed. Bhabani Bhattacharya. 1976. pap. 2.75 (ISBN 0-89253-071-5). Ind-US Inc.

Music for Patriots, Politicans & Presidents. Vera B. Lawrence. (Illus.). 480p. 1975. 35.00 o.s.i. (ISBN 0-02-569390-5). Macmillan.

Music for Score Reading. Robert A. Melcher & Willard F. Warch. LC 78-119859. (Music Ser). 1971. pap. text ed. 12.95 (ISBN 0-13-607507-X). P-H.

Music for Shelley's Poetry. Burton Pollin. LC 74-4446. (Music Reprint Ser.). 174p. 1974. lib. bdg. 19.50 (ISBN 0-306-70640-7). Da Capo.

Music for Sight Singing. 2nd ed. Robert W. Ottman. 1967. pap. text ed. 11.95 (ISBN 0-13-607440-5). P-H.

Music for Study: A Sourcebook of Excerpts. 2nd ed. Howard A. Murphy et al. 192p. 1973. pap. text ed. 13.95 (ISBN 0-13-607515-0). P-H.

Music for the Church Year. Marion Hatchett. pap. 4.95 (ISBN 0-8164-0169-1). Crossroad NY.

Music for the Hearing Impaired. Carol Robbins & Clive Robbins. 1980. pap. 29.50 (ISBN 0-918812-11-9). Magnamusic.

Music for the Piano: A Handbook of Concert & Teaching Material from 1580 to 1952. rev. ed. James Friskin & Irwin Freundlich. LC 72-93608. 443p. 1973. pap. 5.00 (ISBN 0-486-22918-1). Dover.

Music for Two Theatre Pieces: Pizarro (1799) & Love Laughs at Locksmiths (1803) Michael Kelly. (Music Reprint Ser.: 1979). 1979. Repr. of 1803 ed. lib. bdg. 18.50 (ISBN 0-306-79562-0). Da Capo.

Music for Viola. Michael D. Williams. LC 78-70022. (Detroit Studies in Music Bibliography Ser.: No. 42). 1979. 16.50 (ISBN 0-911772-95-2). Info Coord.

Music Forum, 3 vols. Ed. by William J. Mitchell & Felix Salzer. LC 67-16204. 1967-73. Vol. 1. 20.00 o.p. (ISBN 0-231-02806-7); Vol. 2. 20.00x o.p. (ISBN 0-231-03153-X); Vol. 3. 22.50x (ISBN 0-231-03522-5). Columbia U Pr.

Music Forum, Vol. V. Ed. by Feliz Salzer. 384p. 1981. 27.50x (ISBN 0-231-04720-7). Columbia U Pr.

Music Forum, Vol. 4. Ed. by Felix Salzer. LC 67-16204. 1977. 22.50x (ISBN 0-231-03934-4). Columbia U Pr.

Music from Home: Selected Poems. Colleen J. McElroy. LC 76-14852. 118p. 1976. 8.95 o.p. (ISBN 0-8093-0774-X). S Ill U Pr.

Music from Inside Out. Ned Rorem. LC 67-12477. 1967. 4.00 o.s.i. (ISBN 0-8076-0402-X). Braziller.

Music from the Past. Kate Cameron. (Holderly Hall Ser). (Orig.). 1975. pap. 1.25 o.p. (ISBN 0-685-53904-0, LB287ZK, Leisure Bks). Nordon Pubns.

Music Fundamentals Workbook. John Hanson. 1979. pap. text ed. 13.95 (ISBN 0-582-28111-3). Longman.

Music Guide to Austria & Germany. Elaine Brody & Claire Brook. LC 75-30822. (Music Guides Ser.). 350p. 1976. 10.00 (ISBN 0-396-07217-8). Dodd.

Music Guide to Belgium, Luxembourg, Holland & Switzerland. Elaine Brody & Claire Brook. LC 77-6446. (Music Guides Ser.). (Illus.). 1977. 10.00 (ISBN 0-396-07437-5). Dodd.

Music Guide to Great Britain. Elaine Brody & Claire Brook. LC 75-30809. (Music Guides Ser.). 350p. 1976. 10.00 (ISBN 0-396-06955-X). Dodd.

Music Guide to Italy. Elaine Brody & Claire Brook. LC 78-6846. (Music Guides Ser.). 1978. 10.00 (ISBN 0-396-07436-7). Dodd.

Music in America: An Anthology from the Landing of the Pilgrims to the Close of the Civil War 1620-1865. W. Thomas Marrocco & Harold Gleason. (Illus.). 384p. 1974. pap. 12.95x (ISBN 0-393-09296-8). Norton.

Music in Ancient Arabia & Spain: Being La Musica De las Cantigas. Julian Ribera. LC 70-87614. (Music Ser). 1970. Repr. of 1929 ed. lib. bdg. 25.00 (ISBN 0-306-71622-4). Da Capo.

Music in Aztec & Inca Territory. Robert Stevenson. (California Library Reprint Ser.: No. 64). 1977. Repr. of 1968 ed. 38.50x (ISBN 0-520-03169-5). UCDLA.

Music in Bali. Colin McPhee. LC 76-4979. (Music Reprint Ser.). 1976. Repr. of 1966 ed. lib. bdg. 45.00 (ISBN 0-306-70778-0). Da Capo.

Music in Childhood Education. 2nd ed. R. L. Garretson. (Illus.). 336p. 1976. ref. ed. 14.95x (ISBN 0-13-606988-6); pap. text ed. 11.95x (ISBN 0-13-606970-3). P-H.

Music in Early Childhood. Batcheller. write for info. (ISBN 0-87628-212-5). Ctr Appl Res.

Music in Education. Malcolm Carlton. (New Education Ser.). 1978. 18.50x (ISBN 0-7130-0155-0, Woburn Pr England). Biblio Dist.

Music in Education: A Point View. Arnold Bentley. (General Ser.). 125p. 1975. pap. text ed. 10.00x (ISBN 0-85633-066-3, NFER). Humanities.

Music in Europe & the United States: A History. Edith Borroff. (Illus.). 1971. text ed. 20.95 (ISBN 0-13-608083-9). P-H.

Music in Film & Television: International Catalogue, 1964-1974. 197p. 1976. pap. 9.25 (ISBN 92-3-201273-1, U396, UNESCO). Unipub.

Music in Further Education. Inez V. Homewood. (Student's Music Library Ser). 1958. 6.95 (ISBN 0-234-77217-4). Dufour.

Music in India: The Classical Traditions. Bonnie Wade. 1979. 14.95 (ISBN 0-13-607036-1); pap. 10.95 (ISBN 0-13-607028-0). P-H.

Music in Latin America: an Introduction. Gerard Behague. (History of Music Ser.). (Illus.). 1979. text ed. 16.95 (ISBN 0-13-608919-4); pap. text ed. 14.95 (ISBN 0-13-608901-1). P-H.

Music in Medieval & Early Modern Europe: Patronage, Sources & Texts. Iain Fenlon. LC 80-40490. (Illus.). 290p. Date not set. price not set (ISBN 0-521-23328-3). Cambridge U Pr.

Music in New Hampshire, 1623-1800. L. Pichierei. LC 60-13940. 1960. 20.00x (ISBN 0-231-02377-4). Columbia U Pr.

Music in New Jersey, 1655-1860. Charles H. Kaufman. LC 78-75180. 400p. 1981. 35.00 (ISBN 0-8386-2270-4). Fairleigh Dickinson.

Music in Open Education. write for info. (ISBN 0-87628-214-1). Ctr Appl Res.

Music in Paintings of the Low Countries in the 16th & 17th Centuries. Pieter Fischer. 112p. pap. text ed. 15.50 (ISBN 90-265-0185-4, Pub. by Swets Pub Serv Holland). Swets North Am.

Music in Philadelphia & History of the Musical Fund Society. Compiled by Louis C. Madeira. LC 78-169650. (Music Reprint Ser.). (Illus.). 234p. 1973. Repr. of 1896 ed. lib. bdg. 25.00 (ISBN 0-306-70260-6). Da Capo.

Music in Shakespearean Tragedy. F. W. Sternfeld. (Illus.). 1967. Repr. of 1963 ed. 30.00x (ISBN 0-7100-2153-4). Routledge & Kegan.

Music in the Church. Sydney S. Campbell. (Student's Music Library Ser). 1951. 6.95 (ISBN 0-234-77210-7). Dufour.

Music in the Classic Period. 2nd ed. Reinhard G. Pauly. (History of Music Ser.). 224p. 1973. pap. text ed. 10.95 (ISBN 0-13-607630-0). P-H.

Music in the Education of Children. 3rd ed. Bessie R. Swanson. 1969. 18.95x (ISBN 0-534-00673-6). Wadsworth Pub.

Music in the Education of Children. 4th ed. Bessie R. Swanson. 448p. 1980. text ed. 18.95x (ISBN 0-534-00880-1). Wadsworth Pub.

Music in the English Mystery Plays. JoAnna Dutka. (Early Drama, Art, & Music Ser.). (Illus.). 171p. 1980. 18.80 (ISBN 0-918720-10-9); 11.801321. Medieval Inst.

Music in the Medieval & Renaissance Universities. Nan Cooke Carpenter. LC 70-171380. (Music Ser). (Illus.). 394p. 1972. Repr. of 1958 ed. lib. bdg. 29.50 (ISBN 0-306-70453-6). Da Capo.

Music in the Medieval World. 2nd ed. Albert Seay. (Illus.). 202p. 1975. 12.95 (ISBN 0-13-608133-9); pap. text ed. 10.95 (ISBN 0-13-608125-8). P-H.

Music in the Middle Ages. Gustave Reese. (Illus.). 1940. 24.95x (ISBN 0-393-09750-1, NortonC). Norton.

Music in the Paris Academy of Sciences. Albert Cohn & Leta E. Miller. LC 78-70025. (Detroit Studies in Music Bibliography Ser.: No. 43). 1979. 8.50 (ISBN 0-911772-96-0). Info Coord.

Music in the Renaissance. Howard M. Brown. (History of Music Ser.). (Illus.). 368p. 1976. pap. text ed. 12.95x (ISBN 0-13-608497-4). P-H.

Music in the Renaissance. rev. ed. Gustave Reese. (Illus.). 1959. 29.95x (ISBN 0-393-09530-4, NortonC). Norton.

Music in the Southwest, 1825-1950. Howard Swan. LC 77-5421. (Music Reprint Ser.). 1977. Repr. of 1952 ed. lib. bdg. 29.50 (ISBN 0-306-77418-6). Da Capo.

Music in the Theatre of Ben Jonson. Mary Chan. (Illus.). 344p. 1980. 69.00x (ISBN 0-19-812632-8). Oxford U Pr.

Music in the Twentieth Century. William Austin. (Illus.). 1966. 19.95x (ISBN 0-393-09704-8, NortonC). Norton.

Music in Theory & Practice. 2nd ed. Bruce Benward. 1980. 13.95 (ISBN 0-697-03423-2). Wm C Brown.

Music in Transition: A Study of Tonal Expansion & Atonality, 1900-1920. Jim Samson. 1977. 12.95x o.p. (ISBN 0-393-02193-9). Norton.

Music: Invent Your Own. Martha Faulhaber & Janet Underhill. LC 74-13315. (Music Involvement Ser). (Illus.). 48p. (gr. 3 up). 1974. 6.50g (ISBN 0-8075-5355-7). A Whitman.

Music Is My Faith: An Autobiography. David Mannes. (Music Reprint, 1978 Ser.). (Illus.). 1978. Repr. of 1938 ed. lib. bdg. 27.50 (ISBN 0-306-77595-6). Da Capo.

Music Is My Mistress. Ellington, Edward Kennedy "Duke". LC 73-83189. 544p. 1973. 12.95 (ISBN 0-385-02235-2). Doubleday.

Music Kit. Tom Manoff. 1976. pap. text ed. 16.95x (ISBN 0-393-09179-1); tchrs. manual avail. (ISBN 0-393-09157-0). Norton.

Music Lessons That Are Easy to Teach. Jane L. Reynolds. 1976. 11.95 (ISBN 0-13-608059-6). P-H.

Music Librarianship. Malcolm Jones. 370p. 1979. 12.00 (ISBN 0-89664-417-0, Pub. by K G Saur). Shoe String

Music Library Association Catalog of Cards for Printed Music, 1953-1972: A Supplement to the Library of Congress Catalogs, 2 vols. Ed. by Elizabeth H. Olmsted. 1974. Set. 100.00 o.p. (ISBN 0-87471-474-5). Rowman.

Music Literature for Analysis & Study. Charles Walton. 1972. pap. 13.95x (ISBN 0-534-00163-7). Wadsworth Pub.

Music Lovers' Encyclopedia. Rupert Hughes et al. LC 55-368. 1957. 7.95 o.p. (ISBN 0-385-00124-X). Doubleday.

Music Machine. Samuel Wright. LC 97-9200. (Illus.). (gr. 3-6). 1979. pap. 2.95 (ISBN 0-87123-707-5, 210707). Bethany Fell.

Music Machine: Level I. Joyce M. Burkes. LC 79-92121. (Music Machine Bks.). (Orig.). 1981. pap. 6.95 (ISBN 0-931218-07-1). Joybug.

Music Machine: Level 2. Joyce M. Burkes. LC 79-92121. (Music Machine Bks.). (Orig.). 1981. pap. 6.95 (ISBN 0-931218-08-X). Joybug.

Music Machine: Primer. Joyce M. Burkes. LC 79-92121. (Music Machine Bks.). 20p. (Orig.). 1981. pap. 6.95 (ISBN 0-931218-06-3). Joybug.

Music Makers. Bernard Rosenberg & Deena Rosenberg. 1979. 17.50 (ISBN 0-231-03953-0). Columbia U Pr.

Music Makers: Some Outstanding Musical Performers of Our Day. Roland Gelatt. LC 72-2334. (Music Ser.). Repr. of 1953 ed. lib. bdg. 25.00 (ISBN 0-306-70519-2). Da Capo.

Music Master of the Middle West: The Story of F. Melius Christiansen & the St. Olaf Choir. 2nd ed. Leola N. Bergmann. LC 68-16222. (Music Ser). 1968. Repr. of 1944 ed. 22.50 (ISBN 0-306-71057-9). Da Capo.

Music Notation in the Twentieth Century: A Practical Guidebook. Kurt Stone. (Illus.). 1981. text ed. 29.95x (ISBN 0-393-95053-0). Norton.

Music of Acoma, Isleta, Cochiti, & Zuni Pueblos. Frances Densmore. LC 72-1877. (Music Ser.). (Illus.). 142p. 1972. Repr. of 1957 ed. lib. bdg. 16.50 (ISBN 0-306-70505-2). Da Capo.

Music of Alban Berg. Douglas Jarman. 1978. 45.00x (ISBN 0-520-03485-6). U of Cal Pr.

Music of Aquarius. Canella Lewis. 1977. pap. 1.50 o.p. (ISBN 0-425-03292-2). Berkley Pub.

Music of Black Americans: A History. Eileen Southern. (Illus.). 1971. text ed. 15.00x (ISBN 0-393-02156-4); pap. text ed. 6.95x (ISBN 0-393-09899-0). Norton.

Music of Czechoslovakia. Rosa Newmarch. LC 77-26269. (Music Reprint Ser., 1978). 1978. Repr. of 1942 ed. lib. bdg. 22.50 (ISBN 0-306-77563-8). Da Capo.

Music of Finer Tone: Musical Imagery of the Major Romantic Poets. Sue E. Coffman. (Salzburg Studies in English Literature, Romantic Reassessment: No. 89). (Orig.). 1979. pap. text ed. 25.00x (ISBN 0-391-01672-5). Humanities.

Music of Hindustan. A. H. Fox Strangeways. LC 75-905015. 1975. 20.00x (ISBN 0-88386-638-2). South Asia Bks.

Music of Human Flesh. Mahmoud Darwish. Tr. by Denys Johnson-Davies from Arabic. (Modern Arab Writers Ser.). 96p. (Orig.). 1980. 9.00x (ISBN 0-89410-202-8); pap. 6.00x (ISBN 0-89410-203-6). Three Continents.

Music of Johann Sebastian Bach. Stephen Daw. LC 78-68624. (Illus.). 240p. 1981. 19.50 (ISBN 0-8386-1682-8). Fairleigh Dickinson.

Music of One Thousand Autumns: The Togaku Style of Japanese Courtly Music. Robert Garfias. LC 75-13865. 1976. 35.00x (ISBN 0-520-01977-6). U of Cal Pr.

Music of Sibelius. Ed. by Gerald Abraham. LC 74-23413. (Music Ser.). 218p. 1975. Repr. of 1947 ed. lib. bdg. 21.50 (ISBN 0-306-70716-0). Da Capo.

Music of Stockhausen: An Introduction. Jonathan Harvey. (Illus.). 1975. 22.75x (ISBN 0-520-02311-0). U of Cal Pr.

Music of Szymanowski. Natalie Houghtby. LC 80-51747. 120p. 1981. 11.95 (ISBN 0-8008-7539-7, Crescendo). Taplinger.

Music of the Baroque. Edith Borroff. LC 77-17401. (Music Reprint Ser.: 1978). (Illus.). 1978. Repr. of 1970 ed. lib. bdg. 20.00 (ISBN 0-306-77438-0). Da Capo.

Music of the Bible. John Stainer. LC 74-100657. (Music Ser). (Illus.). 1970. Repr. of 1914 ed. lib. bdg. 22.50 (ISBN 0-306-71862-6). Da Capo.

Music of the Close: The Final Scenes of Shakespeare's Tragedies. Walter C. Foreman, Jr. LC 77-75484. 240p. 1979. 16.50x (ISBN 0-8131-1366-0). U Pr of Ky.

Music of the English Parish Church, 2 vols. Nicholas Temperley. LC 77-84811. (Cambridge Studies in Music). (Illus.). 1980. Vol. 1. 79.50 (ISBN 0-521-22045-9); Vol. 2. 39.50 (ISBN 0-521-22046-7). Cambridge U Pr.

Music of the Indians of British Columbia. Frances Densmore. LC 72-1879. (Music Ser.). (Illus.). 118p. 1972. Repr. of 1943 ed. lib. bdg. 14.50 (ISBN 0-306-70507-9). Da Capo.

Music of the Medieval Church Drama. William L. Smolden. 1981. 120.00 (ISBN 0-19-316321-7). Oxford U Pr.

Music of the North American Indian, 14 vols. in 13. Frances Densmore. (Music Ser.). 1972. Set. 250.00 (ISBN 0-306-70517-6). Da Capo.

Music of the Sumerians. Francis W. Galpin. LC 78-87458. (Music Reprint Ser). 1970. Repr. of 1937 ed. lib. bdg. 25.00 (ISBN 0-306-71462-0). Da Capo.

Music of the Waters. Laura A. Smith. LC 69-16479. 1969. Repr. of 1888 ed. 20.00 (ISBN 0-8103-3552-2). Gale.

Music of the Whole Earth. David Reck. LC 76-12493. 1977. 19.95 (ISBN 0-684-14631-2, ScribT); pap. 15.95 (ISBN 0-684-14633-9, SL648, ScribT). Scribner.

Music of William Byrd, Vol. 3: Consort & Keyboard Music. Oliver Neighbour. 1979. 38.50x (ISBN 0-520-03486-4). U of Cal Pr.

Music of William Byrd, Volume 1: Latin Masses & Motets. Joseph Kerman. (California Studies in Nineteenth-Century Music Ser.). 1980. 40.00x (ISBN 0-520-04033-3). U of Cal Pr.

Music of William Walton. 2nd ed. Frank Howes. (Illus.). 1973. 24.00x (ISBN 0-19-315431-5). Oxford U Pr.

Music on My Mind: The Memoirs of an American Pianist. Willie Smith & George Hoefer. LC 74-23406. (Roots of Jazz Ser). xvi, 318p. 1975. Repr. of 1964 ed. lib. bdg. 25.00 (ISBN 0-306-70684-9). Da Capo.

Music on Record: Brass Bands. Peter Gammond. (Illus.). 184p. 1981. 39.00 (ISBN 0-85059-366-2). Aztex.

Music: Patterns & Style. R. P. DeLone. 1971. 15.95 (ISBN 0-201-01489-0). A-W.

Music Periodical Literature: An Annotated Bibliography of Indexes & Bibliographies. Joan M. Meggett. LC 77-19120. 1978. 10.00 (ISBN 0-8108-1109-X). Scarecrow.

Music, Physics & Engineering. 2nd ed. H. F. Olson. (Illus.). 10.00 (ISBN 0-8446-2680-5). Peter Smith.

Music Play--Learning Activities for Young Children. Leon Burton & William Hughes. (gr. k-6). 1980. pap. text ed. 12.25 (ISBN 0-201-00883-1, Sch Div). A-W.

Music Reading: A Comprehensive Approach, Vol. 1. Vernon L. Kliewer. LC 72-3870. (Illus.). 352p. 1973. pap. text ed. 12.95 (ISBN 0-13-607903-2). P-H.

Music Reading, a Comprehensive Approach, Vol. 2. Vernon L. Kliewer. LC 72-3870. (Illus.). 272p. 1973. pap. text ed. 12.95 (ISBN 0-13-607911-3). P-H.

Music Reading: An Ensemble Approach. R. P. DeLone & A. Winold. 1971. pap. 13.50 o.p. (ISBN 0-201-01501-3). A-W.

Music Reference & Research Materials: An Annotated Bibliography. 3rd ed. Vincent Duckles. LC 73-10697. 1974. text ed. 14.95 (ISBN 0-02-907700-1). Free Pr.

Music: Reflections in Sound. Marilyn Barnes-Ostrander. 1976. tchr's ed avail. (ISBN 0-06-371056-0, HarpC). Har-Row.

Music Room. W. E. Ross. 1978. pap. 1.50 (ISBN 0-505-51223-8). Tower Bks.

Music School. John Updike. 1977. pap. 1.75 o.p. (ISBN 0-449-23279-4, Crest). Fawcett.

Music Scores Omnibus. Ed. by William J. Starr & George F. Devine. Incl. Pt. 2. Romantic & Impressionist Music. 1964. pap. text ed. 18.95 (ISBN 0-13-608216-5). 1964. P-H.

Music Scores Omnibus, Vol. 1. 2nd ed. Ed. by William J. Starr & George F. Devine. 430p. 1974. pap. text ed. 18.95 (ISBN 0-13-608349-8). P-H.

Music, Sound & Sensation: A Modern Exposition. Fritz Winckel. Tr. by Thomas Binkley. (Illus.). 1967. pap. text ed. 3.50 (ISBN 0-486-21764-7). Dover.

Music Sources: A Collection of Excerpts & Complete Movements. M. Arlin et al. 1979. pap. 16.95 (ISBN 0-13-607168-6). P-H.

Music Stopped & Your Monkey's on Fire. David Plumb. 7.50 (ISBN 0-930324-10-2). Green Hill.

Music Stops & the Waltz Continues. David G. Smith. 256p. 1981. 10.95 (ISBN 0-8037-5719-0). Dial.

Music Study in Germany. Amy Fay. (Music Reprint Ser.: 1979). 1979. Repr. of 1880 ed. lib. bdg. 29.50 (ISBN 0-306-79541-8). Da Capo.

Music Teaching in the Junior High & the Middle School. Frederick J. Swanson. LC 72-94283. (Illus.). 304p. 1973. 14.95 (ISBN 0-13-608240-8). P-H.

Music That Is Soundless: An Introduction to God for the Graduate. Philip McShane. 1977. pap. text ed. 7.00 (ISBN 0-8191-0236-9). U Pr of Amer.

Music, the Arts, & Ideas. Leonard B. Meyer. LC 67-25515. 1969. pap. 6.95 (ISBN 0-226-52141-9, P336, Phoen). U of Chicago Pr.

Music Theatre in a Changing Society: The Influence of the Technical Media. Ed. by Jack Bornoff. 1968. pap. 6.00 (ISBN 92-3-100709-2, U397, UNESCO). Unipub.

Music Theory. George T. Jones. (Illus.). 288p. (Orig.). 1974. pap. 3.95 (ISBN 0-06-460137-4, CO 137, COS). Har-Row.

Music Therapy: An Introduction to Therapy & Special Education Through Music. Donald E. Michel. (Illus.). 152p. 1979. 12.75 (ISBN 0-398-03518-0). C C Thomas.

Music Therapy & Its Relationship to Current Treatment Theories. rev ed. Even Ruud. 1980. pap. 6.50 (ISBN 0-918812-14-3). Magnamusic.

Music Therapy for the Autistic Child. Juliette Alvin. 1979. pap. 9.95x (ISBN 0-19-317414-6). Oxford U Pr.

Music Through Sources & Documents. R. Rowen. 1979. pap. 15.95 (ISBN 0-13-608331-5). P-H.

Music Through the Centuries. Nick Rossi & Sadie Rafferty. LC 80-9066. (Illus.). 760p. 1981. lib. bdg. 27.00 (ISBN 0-8191-1498-7); pap. text ed. 16.75 (ISBN 0-8191-1499-5). U Pr of Amer.

Music to Murder by. Vernon Hinkle. 1978. pap. 1.75 (ISBN 0-505-51262-9). Tower Bks.

Music with ESN Children. Pamela I. Dickinson. (General Ser.). 144p. 1976. pap. text ed. 13.75x (ISBN 0-85633-085-X, NFER). Humanities.

Musica Aeterna: Program Notes, 1961-1967. Joseph Braunstein. LC 72-8420. (Music Ser). 332p. 1973. Repr. of 1968 ed. lib. bdg. 32.50 (ISBN 0-306-70554-0). Da Capo.

Musica Asiatica Two. Ed. by Laurence Picken. (Illus.). 195p. 1980. pap. 32.00x (ISBN 0-19-323235-9). Oxford U Pr.

Musica De la Cantigas De Santa Maria del Rey Alfonso el Sabio, 4 pts. in 3 vols. Barcelona, Biblioteca Central, Seccion De Musica. LC 80-2193. 1981. Set. 375.00 (ISBN 0-404-19046-4). Vol. 1 (ISBN 0-404-19047-2). Vol. 2 (ISBN 0-404-19048-0). Vol. 3 (ISBN 0-404-19049-9). AMS Pr.

Musica En Puerto Rico. Munoz. 1966. 12.95 (ISBN 0-87751-012-1, Pub by Troutman Press). E Torres & Sons.

Musica Folklorica De Puerto Rico. Lopez Cruz. 1967. 19.95 (ISBN 0-87751-008-3, Pub by Troutman Press). E Torres & Sons.

Musical Acoustics: An Introduction. Donald E. Hall. 528p. 1979. text ed. 17.95x (ISBN 0-534-00758-9). Wadsworth Pub.

Musical Acoustics: Violin Family Functions, 2 pts. Ed. by Carleen M. Hutchins. (Benchmark Papers in Acoustics Ser.: No. 5). 1975-76. Pt. 1. 48.50 (ISBN 0-12-786691-4); Pt. 2. 48.50 (ISBN 0-12-786692-2); Set. 85.00. Acad Pr.

Musical Adventures in Cornwall. Maisie Radford & Evelyn Radford. 1965. 6.95 o.p. (ISBN 0-685-56922-5). David & Charles.

Musical Appreciation in an Infant School. Eveline Cradock. 1.50p. (Orig.). 1977. pap. text ed. 6.75 (ISBN 0-19-321055-X). Oxford U Pr.

Musical Aptitude Profile. Edwin Gordon. write for info. (ISBN 0-395-09344-9). HM.

Musical Beginnings: For Teachers & Their Students. Gary M. Martin. 1975. pap. text ed. 12.95x (ISBN 0-534-00385-0). Wadsworth Pub.

Musical Biography, Two Vols. William Bingley. LC 70-127286. (Music Ser). 1971. Repr. of 1834 ed. Set. lib. bdg. 65.00 (ISBN 0-306-70032-8). Da Capo.

Musical Classroom: Models, Skills, & Backgrounds for Elementary Teaching. Patricia Hackett et al. 1979. pap. 15.95 ref. (ISBN 0-13-608356-0). P-H.

Musical Comedy in America: From the Black Crook Through Sweeney Todd. Cecil Smith & Glenn Litton. (Illus.). 1981. pap. 12.45 (ISBN 0-87830-564-5). Theatre Arts.

Musical Experience. 2nd ed. John Gillespie. 576p. 1972. 14.95x o.p. (ISBN 0-534-00161-0); record album 14.95x o.p. (ISBN 0-534-00674-4). Wadsworth Pub.

Musical Form: Studies in Analysis & Synthesis. Ellis B. Kohs. 1976. text ed. 19.95 (ISBN 0-395-18613-7). HM.

Musical Games for Children of All Ages. Esther L. Nelson. LC 76-19804. (Illus.). (gr. 3 up). 1976. 8.95 (ISBN 0-8069-4540-0); PLB 8.29 (ISBN 0-8069-4541-9). Sterling.

Musical Handwriting. Archibald Jacob. (Music Reprint Ser.). 1979. Repr. of 1947 ed. lib. bdg. 13.50 (ISBN 0-306-79578-7). Da Capo.

Musical History, Biography, & Criticism. George Hogarth. LC 69-12685. (Music Reprint Ser). 1969. Repr. of 1848 ed. lib. bdg. 22.50 (ISBN 0-306-71234-2). Da Capo.

Musical Houses: Homes & Secret Retreats of Music Stars. Environmental Communications. (Illus., Orig.). 1980. lib. bdg. 19.80 (ISBN 0-89471-112-1); pap. 7.95 (ISBN 0-89471-138-5). Running Pr.

Musical Instrument Collector. J. Robert Willcutt & Kenneth R. Ball. Ed. by Steven F. Brines. LC 78-68088. (Illus.). pap. 8.95 (ISBN 0-933224-00-1). Bold Strummer Ltd.

Musical Instruments. Dorothy Diamond & Robert Tiffin. LC 77-82979. (Teaching Primary Science Ser.). (Illus.). 1977. pap. text ed. 6.95 (ISBN 0-356-05077-7). Raintree Child.

Musical Instruments & Their Symbolism in Western Art. Emanuel Winternitz. (Illus.). 1979. 27.50x (ISBN 0-300-02324-3); pap. 10.95 (ISBN 0-300-02376-6). Yale U Pr.

Musical Instruments in Color. Peter Gammond. LC 75-17604. (Illus.). 176p. 1976. 6.95 o.s.i. (ISBN 0-02-542410-6). Macmillan.

Musical Instruments of India. S. Krishnaswami. (Illus.). 1967. 2.50x (ISBN 0-88253-378-9); pap. 1.00x (ISBN 0-88253-915-9). Ind-US Inc.

Musical Instruments of the World: An Illustrated Encyclopedia. The Diagram Group. (Illus.). 320p. 1978. 29.95 (ISBN 0-87196-320-5). Facts on File.

Musical Instruments Through the Ages. Ed. by Anthony Baines. LC 66-22505. (Illus.). 352p. 1975. 15.00 (ISBN 0-8027-0469-7). Walker & Co.

Musical Laughs: Jokes, Tittle-Tattle, & Anecdotes, Mostly Humorous, About Musical Celebrities. Henry T. Finck. LC 79-159955. 1971. Repr. of 1924 ed. 18.00 (ISBN 0-8103-3397-X). Gale.

Musical Letters from Abroad. 2nd ed. Lowell Mason. LC 67-13035. (Music Ser). 1967. Repr. of 1854 ed. lib. bdg. 25.00 (ISBN 0-306-70940-6). Da Capo.

Musical Manual, or Technical Directory. Thomas Busby. LC 76-20708. (Music Reprint Ser). 1976. Repr. of 1828 ed. lib. bdg. 22.50 (ISBN 0-306-70788-8). Da Capo.

Musical Memoirs, Comprising an Account of the General State of Music in England. 2 Vols. in 1. W. T. Parke. LC 77-125058. (Music Ser). 1970. Repr. of 1830 ed. lib. bdg. 55.00 (ISBN 0-306-70023-9). Da Capo.

Musical Memories. Camille Saint-Saens. LC 70-93980. (Music Reprint Ser). 1969. Repr. of 1919 ed. lib. bdg. 29.50 (ISBN 0-306-71821-9). Da Capo.

Musical Motley. Ernest Newman. LC 76-10332. (Music Reprint Ser.). 1976. lib. bdg. 22.50 (ISBN 0-306-70784-5). Da Capo.

Musical Reminiscences of the Earl of Mount Edgcumbe. Richard Edgcumbe. LC 76-125071. 294p. 1973. Repr. of 1834 ed. lib. bdg. 27.50 (ISBN 0-306-70008-5). Da Capo.

Musical Sketchbook One. Mary H. Richards. (Illus., Orig.). (gr. 1-3). 1967. pap. 1.40 (ISBN 0-8224-9011-0); tchrs' manual free (ISBN 0-8224-9015-3). Pitman Learning.

Musical Sketchbook Two. Jack W. Kukuk. (Illus., Orig.). (gr. 2-4). 1968. pap. 1.40 (ISBN 0-8224-9012-9); tchrs' manual free (ISBN 0-8224-9016-1). Pitman Learning.

Musical Structure & Design. Cedric T. Davie. (Illus.). 1966. pap. 3.25 (ISBN 0-486-21629-2). Dover.

Musical Theater Workshop. Lehman Engel. (Sound Seminars Ser.). bk., tapes, listening guide 350.00x (ISBN 0-88432-065-0, 11500). J Norton Pubs.

Musical Thought in Ancient Greece. Edward A. Lippman. LC 74-23415. (Music Reprint Ser.). 1975. Repr. of 1964 ed. lib. bdg. 22.50 (ISBN 0-306-70669-5). Da Capo.

Musical Trends in the Twentieth Century. Norman Demuth. LC 73-6258. (Illus.). 359p. 1975. Repr. of 1952 ed. lib. bdg. 30.75x (ISBN 0-8371-6896-1, DEMT). Greenwood.

Musical Voyage with Two Guitars. Vladimir Bobri & Carl Miller. LC 73-10568. (Illus.). 176p. 1974. 8.95 o.s.i. (ISBN 0-02-512000-X). Macmillan.

Musical Works of Frederick the Great, 4 Vols. Frederick The Great. Ed. by Philip Spitta. LC 67-27453. (Music Ser). 1967. Repr. of 1889 ed. lib. bdg. 115.00 (ISBN 0-306-70980-5). Da Capo.

Musicalia: Sources of Information in Music. 2nd ed. J. H. Davies. 1969. 12.25 (ISBN 0-08-006357-8); pap. 7.00 (ISBN 0-08-006356-X). Pergamon.

MusiCatalog. Resource Publications, Inc. Staff. Ed. by W. P. Cunningham. 1978. pap. 49.95 (ISBN 0-89390-013-3). Resource Pubns.

Musicatalog: The Recording Locator, 1980 Supplement. Ed. by W. Patrick Cunningham. LC 79-67309. 130p. 1980. pap. 21.95 (ISBN 0-89390-023-0). Resource Pubns.

Musicbook 0: Pulse, Pitch, Rhythm, Form, Dynamics. Erling Bisgaard & Gulle Stehouwer. Ed. by Tossi Aaron. 1976. pap. 6.00 (ISBN 0-918812-04-6). Magnamusic.

Musicians & Mummers. Hermann Klein. LC 80-2284. (Illus.). 1981. Repr. of 1925 ed. 38.50 (ISBN 0-404-18850-8). AMS Pr.

Musician's Guide. 6th ed. LC 54-14954. 990p. 1980. 59.50 (ISBN 0-8379-5601-3, 031095). Marquis.

Musician's Guide to Church Music. Joy Lawrence & John Ferguson. 280p. 1981. 16.95 (ISBN 0-8298-0424-2). Pilgrim NY.

Musician's Guide to Independent Record Production. Will Connelly. (Illus.). 1981. 12.95 (ISBN 0-8092-5969-9); pap. 6.95 (ISBN 0-8092-5968-0). Contemp Bks.

Musician's Manual: A Practical Career Guide. Beverly Hills Bar Association Barristers Committee for the Arts. Ed. by Mark Halloran. 288p. 1981. 17.95 o.p. (ISBN 0-8015-5203-6); pap. 9.95 (ISBN 0-8015-5204-4). Dutton.

Musicians of Bremen. Grimm Brothers. LC 74-78599. (Illus.). 6.95 (ISBN 0-88332-060-6). Larousse.

Musicians' Wit, Humour, & Anecdote. Frederick J. Crowest. LC 72-78131. (Illus.). 1971. Repr. of 1902 ed. 26.00 (ISBN 0-8103-3729-0). Gale.

Musiciens Polonais & Slaves. A. Sowinski. LC 77-155149. (Music Ser). 1971. Repr. of 1857 ed. lib. bdg. 55.00 (ISBN 0-306-70166-9). Da Capo.

Musicos De Brema (the Bremen-Town Musicians) Gross. (ps-3). pap. 1.95 (ISBN 0-590-10446-2, Schol Pap). Schol Bk Serv.

Musics of Many Cultures: An Introduction. Ed. by Elizabeth May. 1981. 50.00x (ISBN 0-520-03393-0). U of Cal Pr.

Musik Wozu. Ed. by Rainer Riehn. (Edition Suhrkamp: Vol. 684). (Orig.). 1980. pap. text ed. 7.80 (ISBN 3-518-10684-8, Pub. by Insel Verlag Germany). Suhrkamp.

Musings & Memories of a Musician. George Henschel. (Music Reprint Ser.). 1979. Repr. of 1919 ed. lib. bdg. 32.50 (ISBN 0-306-79540-X). Da Capo.

Musings for a Mellow Mood. Jacquie Hoffman. (Illus.). 65p. (Orig.). 1979. pap. 4.95 (ISBN 0-9604082-0-7). I J Hoffman.

Musique, 2 Vols. Ed. by N. Dufourcq. (Illus., Fr.). 62.50x ea. Vol. 1 (ISBN 2-03-014110-0). Vol. 2 (ISBN 2-03-014120-8). Larousse.

Musique au Theatre. Antoine L. Maillot. LC 80-2288. 1981. Repr. of 1863 ed. 44.00 (ISBN 0-404-18856-7). AMS Pr.

Muskets of Seventy-Six. Jonathan Scofield. 1981. pap. 2.75 (ISBN 0-440-05756-6). Dell.

Muskrat War. Larry Callen. 144p. (gr. 5 up). 1980. 8.95g (ISBN 0-316-12498-2, Pub. by Atlantic-Little Brown). Little.

Muskrats & Marsh Management. Paul L. Errington. LC 77-14177. (Illus.). 1978. 10.95x (ISBN 0-8032-0975-4); pap. 3.25 (ISBN 0-8032-5892-5, BB 664, Bison). U of Nebr Pr.

Muslim Brotherhoods in 19th Century Africa. B. G. Martin. LC 75-35451. (African Studies Ser.: No. 18). 1977. 31.95 (ISBN 0-521-21062-3). Cambridge U Pr.

Muslim Civilization in India. S. M. Ikram. Ed. by A. T. Embree. LC 64-14656. (Illus.). 1964. 17.50x (ISBN 0-231-02580-7). Columbia U Pr.

Muslim Heartlands. South Penn School Study Council. 1963. text ed. 3.50x spiral bdg. o.p. (ISBN 0-8134-0150-X, 150). Interstate.

Muslim Matrimonial Court in Singapore. Judith Djamour. (Monographs on Social Anthropology: No. 31). 1966. text ed. 20.75x (ISBN 0-485-19531-3, Athlone Pr). Humanities.

Muslim Mind. Charis Waddy. LC 76-6522. (Illus.). 216p. 1976. text ed. 20.00x (ISBN 0-582-78061-6). Longman.

Muslim Political Behaviour: A Study of the Muslim Stratagem in Indian Electoral Politics. Imtiaz Ahmad. 1981. 14.00x (ISBN 0-88386-756-7). South Asia Bks.

Muslim Puritans: Reformist Psychology in Southeast Asian Islam. James L. Peacock. LC 76-55571. 1978. 20.00x (ISBN 0-520-03403-1). U of Cal Pr.

Muslim Saints & Mystics: Episodes from the Tadhkirat Al-Auliya (Memorial of the Saints) Farid Attar. Tr. by A. J. Arberry from Persian. (Persian Heritage Ser.). 1979. pap. 7.95 (ISBN 0-7100-0169-X). Routledge & Kegan.

Muslim Society. Ernest Gellner. LC 80-41103. (Cambridge Studies in Social Anthropology: No. 32). 280p. Date not set. price not set (ISBN 0-521-22160-9). Cambridge U Pr.

Muslim Spain. D. Townson. (Introduction to the History of Mankind Ser.). (Illus.). 48p. 1973. 3.95 (ISBN 0-521-20251-5). Cambridge U Pr.

Muslim Women: A in Purdah & Out of It. Jamila Brijbhushan. 150p. 1980. text ed. 17.50 (ISBN 0-7069-1074-5, Pub. by Vikas India). Advent Bk.

Muslim World: A Historical Survey, 2 vols. Bertold Spuler. Incl. Vol. 1. Age of the Caliphs. text ed. 20.00x (ISBN 0-685-23328-6); Vol. 2. The Mongol Period. text ed. 10.00x (ISBN 0-685-23329-4). 1960. Humanities.

Muslim World: A Historical Survey, Vol. 4. Bertold Spuler. 1981. text ed. write for info. (ISBN 0-391-01209-6). Humanities.

Muslim World: A Historical Survey Part Three: The Last Great Muslim Empires. H. J. Kissling et al. 1969. text ed. 44.50x (ISBN 90-040-2104-3). Humanities.

Muslim World & the Future Economic Order. Frwd. by Salem Azzam. 383p. 1980. 29.95x (ISBN 0-906041-10-4, Pub. by Islamic Council of Europe England); pap. 14.95x (ISBN 0-906041-09-0). Intl Schol Bk Serv.

Muslims & the Congress: Correspondence of Dr. M. A. Ansari. M. A. Ansari. Ed. by M. Hasan. 1979. 18.50 (ISBN 0-8364-0381-9). South Asia Bks.

Muslims in America. E. Allen Richardson. 96p. (Orig.). 1981. pap. 4.95 (ISBN 0-8298-0449-8). Pilgrim NY.

Muslims in India. Ed. by Zafar Imam. LC 75-905301. 1975. 12.50x o.p. (ISBN 0-88386-077-5, Orient Longman). South Asia Bks.

Muslims in India: A Biographical Dictionary, 1857-1976. Ed. by N. K. Jain. 1980. 38.00x (ISBN 0-88386-886-5). South Asia Bks.

Muslims of British India. P. Hardy. LC 77-184772. (South Asian Studies: No. 13). (Illus.). 300p. 1973. 39.50 (ISBN 0-521-08488-1); pap. 11.50x (ISBN 0-521-09783-5). Cambridge U Pr.

Mussolini As Revealed in His Political Speeches: November 1914-August 1923. Benito Mussolini. Ed. by B. Quaranta Di San Severino. LC 75-16288. xxviii, 375p. 1977. Repr. of 1923 ed. 22.50 (ISBN 0-86527-134-8). Fertig.

Mussolini's March on Rome: October 30, 1922. Jerre Mangione. LC 74-9816. (World Focus Bks). (Illus.). 72p. (gr. 5-9). 1975. PLB 4.90 o.p. (ISBN 0-531-02782-1). Watts.

Mussorgsky Reader: A Life of Modeste Petrovich Mussorgsky in Letters & Documents. Ed. by Jay Leyda & Sergei Bertensson. LC 70-87393. (Music Ser). (Illus.). 1970. Repr. of 1947 ed. lib. bdg. 32.50 (ISBN 0-306-71534-1). Da Capo.

Must Corporate Income Be Taxed Twice? Charles E. McLure, Jr. LC 78-27905. (Studies of Government Finance). 1979. 14.95 (ISBN 0-8157-5620-8); pap. 5.95 (ISBN 0-8157-5619-4). Brookings.

Must Our Schools Die? A Plan to Meet the Current Crisis in Education. David H. Paynter. LC 80-23367. (Orig.). 1981. pap. 6.95 (ISBN 0-930014-41-3). Multnomah.

Must Success Cost So Much? The Human Toll of Corporate Life. Paul Evans & Fernando Bartolome. LC 81-68964. 256p. 1981. 13.95 (ISBN 0-465-04746-7). Basic.

Must the West Decline. David Harlech. LC 66-20135. 1966. 15.00x (ISBN 0-231-02976-4). Columbia U Pr.

Must Walls Divide? The Creative Witness of the Churches in Europe. James E. Will. (Orig.). 1981. pap. 3.75 (ISBN 0-377-00106-6). Friend Pr.

Must We Bus? Segregated Schools & National Policy. Gary Orfield. 1978. 18.95 (ISBN 0-8157-6638-6); pap. 9.95 (ISBN 0-8157-6637-8). Brookings.

Must We Mean What We Say? S. Cavell. LC 75-32911. 365p. 1976. 38.50 (ISBN 0-521-21116-6); pap. 11.50 (ISBN 0-521-29048-1). Cambridge U Pr.

Mustang Fever. Gary McCarthy. 1981. pap. 1.95 (ISBN 0-440-15308-5). Dell.

Mustang Men. Thorne Douglas. 1977. pap. 1.25 o.p. (ISBN 0-449-13918-2, GM). Fawcett.

Mustang Service - Repair Handbook: All Models, 1964-1973. Brick Price. Ed. by Jeff Robinson. (Illus.). 232p. 1976. pap. text ed. 10.95 (ISBN 0-89287-088-5, A167). Clymer Pubns.

Mustang: Story of the P-Fifty-One Fighter. Robert W. Gruenhagen. LC 75-30278. (Illus.). 1980. pap. 9.95 (ISBN 0-668-04884-0). Arco.

Mustangers. Owen G. Irons. (YA) 1978. 5.95 (ISBN 0-685-87345-5, Avalon). Bouregy.

Mustangs: A Return to the Wild. Hope Ryden. (Large Format Ser.). (Illus.). 1978. pap. 6.95 o.p. (ISBN 0-14-004838-3). Penguin.

Mustangs, Six-Shooters & Barbed Wire. Grant Lyons. (Illus.). 96p. (gr. 3-5). 1981. PLB 7.29 (ISBN 0-686-69299-3). Messner.

Mustard Seed: Discourses on the Sayings of Jesus from the Gospel According to Thomas. Bhagwan S. Rajneesh. LC 77-20461. 1978. pap. 6.95 (ISBN 0-06-066785-0, RD-255, HarpR). Har-Row.

Muster & Pay Rolls of the War of the Revolution, 1775-1783: Collections 1914, 1915, 2 vols. LC 16-17941. 15.00x o.p. (ISBN 0-685-73915-5, New York Historical Society). U Pr of Va.

Muster & Review: A Problem of English Military Administration, Fourteen Twenty to Fourteen Forty. Richard A. Newhall. 1940. 27.50x (ISBN 0-686-51420-3). Elliots Bks.

Mustng II Service Repair Handbook All Models, 1974-1978. Clymer Publications. (Illus., Orig.). 1979. pap. text ed. 10.95 (ISBN 0-89287-119-9, A169). Clymer Pubns.

Mutation Breeding for Disease Resistance. (Illus., Orig.). 1971. pap. 14.50 (ISBN 92-0-111071-5, IAEA). Unipub.

Mutations: Biology & Society. Ed. by Dwain N. Walcher et al. Henry L. Barnett & Norman Kretchmer. LC 78-63411. (Illus.). 432p. 1978. 31.50 (ISBN 0-89352-020-9). Masson Pub.

Mutations in Plant Breeding. 1966. pap. 13.50 (ISBN 92-0-011066-5, IAEA). Unipub.

Mutations in Plant Breeding - 2. 1968. pap. 16.25 (ISBN 92-0-111368-4, IAEA). Unipub.

Muted Consent: A Casebook in Modern Medical Ethics. Jan Wojcik. LC 77-89472. (Science & Society: a Purdue University Series in Science, Technology, & Human Values: Vol. 1). 176p. 1978. pap. 3.25 (ISBN 0-931682-02-9). Purdue Univ Bks.

Mutes. Piers Anthony. 448p. 1981. pap. 2.95 (ISBN 0-380-77578-6). Avon.

Mutholgos: Collected Lectures & Interviews, Vol. II. Charles F. Olson. Ed. by George F. Butterick. LC 77-1955. (Writing Ser.: No. 35). 1979. 12.00 (ISBN 0-87704-039-7); pap. 6.00 (ISBN 0-87704-040-0). Four Seasons Foun.

Muthologos: The Collected Lectures & Interviews, Vol. I. Charles F. Olson. Ed. by George F. Butterick. LC 77-1955. (Writing Ser.: No. 35). 1979. 12.00 (ISBN 0-87704-032-X); pap. 5.00 (ISBN 0-87704-031-1). Four Seasons Foun.

Mutiny & British Land Policy in North India, 1856-1868. Jagdish Raj. 1967. 6.25x o.p. (ISBN 0-210-22660-9). Asia.

Mutiny Does Not Happen Lightly: The Literature of the American Resistance to the Vietnam War. Ed. by G. Louis Heath. LC 76-4825. 636p. 1976. 27.50 (ISBN 0-8108-0922-2). Scarecrow.

Mutiny on the Globe. Edwin P. Hoyt. LC 75-5779. 224p. 1975. 7.95 o.p. (ISBN 0-394-49365-6). Random.

Mutiny Within. James Rieger. LC 67-12475. (Orig.). 6.50 (ISBN 0-8076-0400-3); pap. 2.50 (ISBN 0-8076-0409-7). Braziller.

Mutter Courage und Ihre Kinder. Bertolt Brecht. Ed. by H. F. Brookes & C. E. Fraenkel. 1960. pap. text ed. 3.95x (ISBN 0-435-38112-1). Heinemann Ed.

Mutual Aid: A Factor of Evolution. Peter Kropotkin. LC 79-188872. 277p. 1972. 12.00x (ISBN 0-8147-4555-5). NYU Pr.

Mutual Arrangements. Nonie C. Murphy. 1978. pap. 1.95 o.p. (ISBN 0-425-03864-5, Dist. by Putnam). Berkley Pub.

Mutual Friend. Frederick Busch. LC 77-11793. 1978. 8.95 o.s.i. (ISBN 0-06-010527-5, HarpT). Har-Row.

Mutual Ministry: New Vitality for the Local Church. James Fenhagen. 1977. 7.95 (ISBN 0-8164-0332-5). Crossroad NY.

Mutual Savings Banks & Savings & Loan Associations: Aspects of Growth. Alan Teck. LC 68-18999. (Charts). 1968. 20.00x (ISBN 0-231-03124-6). Columbia U Pr.

Mutuwhenua: The Moon Sleeps. Patricia Grace. 155p. (Orig.). 1978. pap. 6.00x (ISBN 0-582-71762-0, Pub. by Longman Paul New Zealand). Three Continents.

Muybridge's Complete Human & Animal Locomotion: All 781 Plates from the 1887 Animal Locomotion, 3 vols. Eadweard Muybridge. Incl. Vol. 1 (ISBN 0-486-23792-3); Vol. 2 (ISBN 0-486-23793-1); Vol. 3 (ISBN 0-486-23794-X). (Illus.). 1979. Repr. of 1887 ed. Set. 28.33 ea. (ISBN 0-685-92659-1). Dover.

Muzio Clementis Leben. Max Unger. LC 72-158959. (Music Ser). 1971. Repr. of 1914 ed. lib. bdg. 27.50 (ISBN 0-306-70192-8). Da Capo.

Mwindo Epic from the Banyanga (Congo Republic) Ed. by Daniel Biebuyck & Kahombo C. Mateene. 1969. 20.00x (ISBN 0-520-01502-9); pap. 2.45 (ISBN 0-520-02049-9, CAL233). U of Cal Pr.

My Adventure in the Flying Scotsman. Eden Phillpotts. Ed. by Tom Schantz. (Illus.). 40p. 1975. pap. 4.00 (ISBN 0-915230-09-7). Rue Morgue.

My Adventures in the Golden Age of Music. H. T. Finck. LC 70-87496. (Music Ser.). 462p. 1971. Repr. of 1926 ed. lib. bdg. 39.50 (ISBN 0-306-71448-5). Da Capo.

My All for Him. Basilea Schlink. 1971. pap. 2.95 (ISBN 0-87123-370-3, 200370). Bethany Fell.

My Amateur World. Peter S. Gilchrist. (Illus.). 200p. 1975. text ed. 10.00. Gilchem Corp.

My America. Louis Adamic. LC 76-2050. (FDR & the Era of the New Deal). 1976. Repr. of 1938 ed. lib. bdg. 49.50 (ISBN 0-306-70801-9). Da Capo.

My America. Eliot Wagner. 1980. 13.95 (ISBN 0-671-25332-8, Kenan Pr). S&S.

My Animal Friend. Gyo Fujikawa. (Gyo Fujikawa Tiny Board Books). (Illus.). 14p. (ps-k). 1981. 1.95 (ISBN 0-448-15079-4). G&D.

My Antonia. Willa Cather. (Keith Jennison Large Type Bks). (gr. 7 up). PLB 9.95 o.p. (ISBN 0-531-00242-X). Watts.

My Apprenticeship. Beatrice Webb. LC 79-15437. 1980. 49.95 (ISBN 0-521-22941-3); pap. 15.95 (ISBN 0-521-29731-1). Cambridge U Pr.

My April Fool Book. Arlene Popkin. (Illus.). (ps-3). 1974. PLB 5.65 (ISBN 0-914844-04-0). J Alden.

My Argument with the Gestapo: A Macaronic Journal. Thomas Merton. LC 69-20082. 256p. 1975. pap. 3.75 (ISBN 0-8112-0586-X, NDP403). New Directions.

My Baby Brother Needs a Friend. Jane B. Moncure. LC 78-21935. (Illus.). (ps-3). 1979. PLB 5.95 (ISBN 0-89565-019-3). Childs World.

My Baha'i Book. Deborah Christensen. (Sunflower Bks. for Young Children: Bk. 1). (Illus., Orig.). (ps-2). 1980. pap. 2.00 (ISBN 0-87743-141-8, 7-53-01). Baha'i.

My Barber. Anne Rockwell & Harlow Rockwell. LC 80-29467. (Ready-to-Read Ser.). (Illus.). 24p. (ps-2). 1981. PLB 7.95 (ISBN 0-02-777630-1). Macmillan.

My Battle with Low Blood Sugar. G. M. Thienell. 1971. 4.00 o.p. (ISBN 0-682-47198-4, Banner). Exposition.

My Beach Buddies of by Gone Days. 1st ed. Corrie Thompson. (Illus.). 91p. (gr. 4 up). 1974. 5.00 o.p. (ISBN 0-685-54129-0). Nortex Pr.

My Best Friend Ever. Gale Brennan. (Illus.). 48p. (Orig.). (ps-3). 1980. pap. 2.95 (ISBN 0-89542-937-3). Ideals.

My Best Friend Moved Away. Joy Zelonky. LC 79-24111. (Life & Living from a Child's Point of View Ser.). (Illus.). (gr. k-5). 1980. PLB 9.65 (ISBN 0-8172-1353-8). Raintree Child.

My Best Games of Chess, 1924-1937. Aleksandr Alekhine. 1960. text ed. 7.95 o.p. (ISBN 0-679-13026-8); pap. 5.95 (ISBN 0-679-14024-7, 19, Tartan). McKay.

My Best Games of Chess 1929-75. Arnold S. Denker. Orig. Title: If You Must Play Chess. 190p. 1981. pap. price not set (ISBN 0-486-24035-5). Dover.

My Bible Dictionary. (gr. 1-4). 1954. pap. 1.95 (ISBN 0-87239-262-7, 3040). Standard Pub.

My Bible Is Jesus. Leo G. Potter. 1976. pap. 1.25 (ISBN 0-8272-2310-2). Bethany Pr.

My Big Buck: Outdoor Stories of Maine. Gerald E. Lewis. LC 78-26185. (Illus.). 1978. lib. bdg. 9.50 o.p. (ISBN 0-89621-021-9); pap. 4.95x (ISBN 0-89621-020-0). Thorndike Pr.

My Black Me: A Beginning Book of Black Poetry. Ed. by Arnold Adoff. LC 73-16445. 96p. (gr. 3 up). 1974. PLB 8.95 (ISBN 0-525-35460-3). Dutton.

My Body, My Health. Felicia Stewart & Robert Hatcher. 592p. 1981. pap. 9.95 (ISBN 0-553-01299-1). Bantam.

My Body, My Health: The Concerned Woman's Guide to Gynecology. F. H. Stewart et al. LC 78-31499. 1979. 15.95 (ISBN 0-471-04517-9); pap. 8.95 (ISBN 0-471-04515-2, Pub. by Wiley Medical). Wiley.

My Bondage & My Freedom. Frederick Douglas. 10.00 (ISBN 0-8446-0588-3). Peter Smith.

My Bones Being Wiser. Vassar Miller. LC 60-13157. (Wesleyan Poetry Program: Vol. 19). (Orig.). 1960. 10.00x (ISBN 0-8195-2019-5, Pub. by Wesleyan U Pr); pap. 4.95 (ISBN 0-8195-1019-X). Columbia U Pr.

My Book About Abraham Lincoln. Lucille Wallower. Ed. by Patricia L. Gump. (gr. 2-4). 1967. pap. 1.85 o.p. (ISBN 0-931992-10-9). Penns Valley.

My Book of Bible Stories. Illus. by Frances Hook. (Illus.). (gr. k-2). 1964. board cover 4.95 (ISBN 0-87239-240-6, 3047). Standard Pub.

My Book of Feelings. 1977. 6.95 (ISBN 0-8065-0585-0). Citadel Pr.

My Book of Flowers. Princess Grace & Gwen Robyns. LC 78-68361. (Illus.). 224p. 1980. 24.95 (ISBN 0-385-14076-2). Doubleday.

My Book of Friends. Illus. by Frances Hook. (Illus.). (gr. k-2). 1968. pap. 4.95 board cover (ISBN 0-87239-242-2, 3045). Standard Pub.

My Book of Gospel Treasures. Rhonda Schomas. (Illus.). 63p. (Orig.). 1980. pap. 3.95 (ISBN 0-87747-839-2). Deseret Bk.

My Book of Memories & Miscellany-My Book of Autographs. Aber. (gr. 3-5). pap. 1.25 (ISBN 0-590-05390-6, Schol Pap). Schol Bk Serv.

My Book of Prayers: A Personal Prayer Book. Compiled by Melvin A. Hammarberg & Clifford A. Nelson. LC 56-10134. 192p. 1956. pap. 3.75 (ISBN 0-8006-0454-7, 1-454). Fortress.

My Book of Special Days. Marian Bennett. (Illus.). (gr. 4-8). 1977. 4.95 (ISBN 0-87239-156-6, 3049). Standard Pub.

My Book of Stories for All Seasons. Ed. by Mary Parsley. LC 74-78600. (Illus.). 120p. (gr. 1-3). 1974. 4.95 o.p. (ISBN 0-88332-063-0, 8024). Larousse.

My Brother Evelyn & Other Portraits. Alec Waugh. 1968. 6.95 o.p. (ISBN 0-374-21680-0). FS&G.

My Brother Is Special. Maureen C. Wartski. (YA) 1981. pap. 1.50 (ISBN 0-451-09578-2, W9578, Sig). NAL.

My Brother Michael. Mary Stewart. (Keith Jennison Large Type Bks). (gr. 7 up). PLB 8.95 o.p. (ISBN 0-531-00243-8). Watts.

My Brother Michael. Mary Stewart. 1978. pap. 2.25 (ISBN 0-449-24029-0, Crest). Fawcett.

My Brother Never Feeds the Cat. Reynold Ruffins. (Illus.). 32p. (gr. k-1). 1979. 7.95 (ISBN 0-684-16211-3). Scribner.

My Brother Sam Is Dead. James L. Collier & Christopher Collier. LC 74-8350. 224p. (gr. 7 up). 1974. 7.95 (ISBN 0-590-07339-7, Four Winds). Schol Bk Serv.

My Brother Steven Is Retarded. Harriet L. Sobol. LC 76-46996. (Illus.). (gr. 3-6). 1977. 7.95 (ISBN 0-02-785990-8). Macmillan.

My Brother, the Thief. Marlene F. Shyer. LC 80-343. (gr. 6 up). 1980. 8.95 (ISBN 0-684-16434-5). Scribner.

My Brother the Wind. G. Clifton Wisler. LC 78-14690. 1979. 7.95 o.p. (ISBN 0-385-14822-4). Doubleday.

My Brother Will Take the Blame. Garvey B. Bowers. 1981. 10.00 (ISBN 0-533-04929-6). Vantage.

My Brothers Keeper? Pat Boone. Orig. Title: Dr. Balaam's Talking Mule. 1975. pap. 1.50 (ISBN 0-89129-028-1). Jove Pubns.

My Burden Is Light. Robert G. Tuttle. 128p. (Orig.). 1980. pap. text ed. 5.00 (ISBN 0-89536-459-X). CSS Pub.

My Cash Register Book. Ed. by Kate Klimo. (Playboards Ser.). (Illus.). 12p. (ps-k). Date not set. boards 2.95 (ISBN 0-671-42527-7, Little Simon). S&S.

My Cat Has Eyes of Sapphire Blue. Aileen Fisher. LC 72-13925. (Illus.). (ps-3). 1973. 8.95 (ISBN 0-690-56637-9, TYC-J); PLB 7.49 o.p. (ISBN 0-690-56638-7). T Y Crowell.

My Cat Likes to Hide in Boxes. Eve Sutton. LC 73-12854. 40p. (ps-2). 1974. 5.95 o.s.i. (ISBN 0-8193-0752-1, Four Winds); PLB 5.41 o.s.i. (ISBN 0-8193-0753-X). Schol Bk Serv.

My Child on Drugs? Youth & the Drug Culture. Art Linkletter & George Gallup, Jr. (Orig.). 1981. pap. 3.50 (ISBN 0-87239-456-5, 5015). Standard Pub.

My Childhood. Maxim Gorky. Tr. by Ronald Wilks. (Classics Ser.). (Orig.). 1966. pap. 2.95 (ISBN 0-14-044178-6). Penguin.

My Choir Workbook. Kenneth W. Osbeck. 1973. pap. 3.50 o.p. (ISBN 0-8254-3409-2). Kregel.

My Clock Book. Ed. by Kate Klimo. (Playboards Ser.). (Illus.). 12p. (ps-k). Date not set. boards 2.95 (ISBN 0-671-42528-5, Little Simon). S&S.

My Color Book. Ed. by Kate Klimo. (Playboards Ser.). (Illus.). 12p. (ps-k). Date not set. boards 2.95 (ISBN 0-671-42529-3, Little Simon). S&S.

My Computer Likes Me. Bob Albrecht. LC 77-70966. 1972. pap. 4.95 (ISBN 0-918398-12-6). Dilithium Pr.

My Country & the World. Andrei D. Sakharov. 1975. pap. 1.65 o.p. (ISBN 0-394-72067-9, Vin). Random.

My Cousin Rachel. Daphne Du Maurier. LC 74-184731. 352p. 1971. Repr. lib. bdg. 12.50x (ISBN 0-8376-0413-3). Bentley.

My Dad Lives in a Downtown Hotel. Peggy Mann. 1974. pap. 1.25 (ISBN 0-380-00096-2, 50146, Camelot). Avon.

My Daddy Longlegs. Judy Hawes. LC 74-175107. (Let's-Read-&-Find-Out Science Bk). (Illus.). (gr. k-3). 1972. 7.95 (ISBN 0-690-56655-7, TYC-J); PLB 7.39 (ISBN 0-690-56656-5). T Y Crowell.

My Days As a Youngling, John Jacob Niles. Nancy N. Sexton et al. (Orig.). 1981. playscript 2.50 (ISBN 0-87602-239-5). Anchorage.

My Dentist. Harlow Rockwell. LC 75-6974. (Illus.). 32p. (ps-3). 1975. 7.95 (ISBN 0-688-80011-4); PLB 7.63 (ISBN 0-688-84011-6). Greenwillow.

My Diary. Johnston. (gr. 7-12). pap. 1.50 (ISBN 0-590-02642-9, Schol Pap). Schol Bk Serv.

My Diary - My World. Elizabeth Yates. LC 80-24977. (Illus.). (gr. 5-9). 1981. 8.95 (ISBN 0-664-32675-7). Westminster.

My Diary: Engravings by Edmund Evans. Edmund Evans. (Illus.). 1978. 6.95 (ISBN 0-374-35106-6). FS&G.

My Dish Towel Flies at Half-Mast. Mary Kuczkir. 288p. 1980. pap. 2.25 (ISBN 0-345-27855-0). Ballantine.

My Disillusionment in Russia. Emma Goldman. 8.25 (ISBN 0-8446-0115-2). Peter Smith.

My Doctor. Harlow Rockwell. LC 72-92442. (Illus.). 24p. (ps-2). 1973. 8.95 (ISBN 0-02-777480-5). Macmillan.

My Doctor Bag Book. Kathleen Daly. (Carry-Me Book). (Illus.). 24p. (ps-3). 1977. PLB 5.38 (ISBN 0-307-68851-8, Golden Pr). Western Pub.

My Dog, Your Dog. Joseph Low. LC 77-12032. (Illus.). (ps-3). 1978. 7.95 (ISBN 0-02-761400-X, 76140). Macmillan.

My Dolly. Alana Willoughby. Ed. by Dan Wasserman. (Ten Word Bks.). (Illus.). (gr. k-1). 1979. PLB 4.50 (ISBN 0-89868-075-1); pap. 1.95 (ISBN 0-89868-086-7). ARO Pub.

My Drama School. Ed. by Margaret McCall. (Illus.). 202p. 1978. 14.50x (ISBN 0-8476-3123-0). Rowman.

My Early Life: A Roving Commission. Winston S. Churchill. (Illus.). 1930. lib. rep. ed. 17.00x (ISBN 0-684-15154-5, ScribT). Scribner.

My Eighty Years in Texas. William P. Zuber. Ed. by Janis B. Mayfield. (Personal Narratives of the West Ser: No. 6). 285p. 1971. 9.95 o.p. (ISBN 0-292-70050-4); pap. 4.95 o.p. (ISBN 0-292-75022-6). U of Tex Pr.

My Enemy, My Brother. James Forman. (Illus.). 256p. (gr. 7 up). 1981. 9.95 (ISBN 0-525-66735-0). Elsevier-Nelson.

My English Journey. Sadhan K. Ghosh. 12.00 (ISBN 0-89253-670-5). Ind-US Inc.

My Everyday French Word Book. Michele Kahn. 44p. (gr. 1-6). 1980. 7.95 (ISBN 0-8120-5344-3). Barron.

My Everyday Spanish Word Book. Michel Kahn. (Illus.). 46p. (gr. 3-9). 1981. 7.95 (ISBN 0-8120-5431-8). Barron.

My Execution. Z. Bhutto. 1980. 10.00x (ISBN 0-8364-0650-8, Pub. by Muswati India). South Asia Bks.

My Experience Records in Homemaking. Mary J. Campbell. (gr. 7-12). 1963. pap. text ed. 2.60 (ISBN 0-87002-089-7). Bennett IL.

My Experiences As an Executioner. James Berry. Ed. by H. Snowden Ward. LC 70-170299. (Illus.), iv, 148p. Repr. of 1892 ed. 15.00 (ISBN 0-8103-3898-X). Gale.

My Experiences in Service, or a Nine Months Man. James F. Dargan. Ed. by Norman E. Tanis. (American Classics Facsimile Ser.: Pt. I). 416p. 1974. pap. 10.00 (ISBN 0-937048-00-3). CSUN.

My Family Heritage: Youth Genealogy Starter Kit. Duane S. Crowther. LC 78-52120. 1979. 4.50 (ISBN 0-88290-087-0). Horizon Utah.

My Father Owen Wister. Frances K. Stokes. 54p. (Orig.). 1952. pap. 5.00. South Pass Pr.

My Father Raped Me: Frances Ann Speaks Out. (gr. 6 up). 1.50. New Seed.

My Father, the Coach. Alfred Slote. (gr. 3-7). 1977. pap. 1.75 (ISBN 0-380-01724-5, 49809, Camelot). Avon.

My Father's Dragon. Stiles Gannett. (gr. k-6). 1980. pap. 1.25 (ISBN 0-440-45628-2, YB). Dell.

My Favorite Illustration. Carl G. Johnson. (Preaching Helps Ser.). 1972. pap. 1.95 o.p. (ISBN 0-8010-5016-2). Baker Bk.

My Favorite Intermissions. Victor Borge. 1971. 5.95 o.p. (ISBN 0-385-02651-X). Doubleday.

My Favorite Prayers & Passages. Deborah Christensen. (Sunflower Bks. for Young Children: Bk. 2). (Illus., Orig.). (ps-2). 1980. pap. 2.00 (ISBN 0-87743-142-6, 7-53-02). Baha'i.

My Favorite Prayers & Reflections. Daughters of St. Paul. 1973. plastic bdg. 4.00 o.s.i. (ISBN 0-8198-0276-X). Dghtrs St Paul.

My Favorites in Suspense. Ed. by Alfred Hitchcock. (YA) 1959. 10.00 o.p. (ISBN 0-394-41223-0, BYR). Random.

My Fears Are Gone. Joanne C. Yates. 1978. pap. 2.95 (ISBN 0-89728-047-4, 704083). Omega Pubns OR.

My Fifty Thousand Year at the Races. Andrew Beyer. LC 78-53918. 1978. 8.95 o.p. (ISBN 0-15-163693-1). HarBraceJ.

My First. Peggy Aldrich. 1976. pap. 1.75 o.p. (ISBN 0-685-69148-9, LB355KK, Leisure Bks). Nordon Pubns.

My First Airplane Trip. Dinah Moche. (Look Look Bk). (Illus.). 24p. 1981. pap. 1.25 (ISBN 0-307-11869-X, Golden Pr). Western Pub.

My First Book of Words. Illus. by Jan Palmer. (Illus.). (ps). 1980. 1.50 (ISBN 0-307-11982-3, Golden Pr); PLB 6.08 (ISBN 0-307-61982-6). Western Pub.

My First Books About Jesus, 4 bks. Elspeth Murphy & Wayne Hanna. Incl. Bk. 1. Jesus Does Good Things (ISBN 0-89191-334-3); Bk. 2. Jesus Is God's Son (ISBN 0-89191-332-7); Bk. 3. Jesus Loves Chilren (ISBN 0-89191-333-5); Bk. 4. Jesus Tells Us About God (ISBN 0-89191-335-1). (Illus.). 1981. write for info. board bks. Cook.

My First Days in the White House. Huey P. Long. LC 70-171695. (FDR & the Era of the New Deal Ser). (Illus.). 146p. 1972. Repr. of 1935 ed. lib. bdg. 15.00 (ISBN 0-306-70383-1). Da Capo.

My First Dictionary. (Illus.). 342p. (gr. k-3). 1980. 8.95 (ISBN 0-395-29210-7). HM.

My First Haggadah. new ed. Lois E. Rakov. (gr. k-3). 1978. 3.95 (ISBN 0-87243-075-8). Templegate.

My First Love & Other Disasters. Francine Pascal. (gr. 7-12). 1980. pap. 1.50 (ISBN 0-440-95447-9, LFL). Dell.

My First Mother Goose Book. Illus. by Jane Chambless-Rigie. (Golden Storytime Bk. of Learning). 24p. (ps). 1980. 1.50 (ISBN 0-307-11981-5); PLB 6.08 s&l (ISBN 0-307-61981-8). Western Pub.
My First Prayer Book. Ila H. Crane. LC 79-91677. 32p. (gr. k up). 1981. 5.95 (ISBN 0-89896-100-9). Larksdale.
My First Satyrnalia. Michael Rumaker. 180p. 1981. 12.95 (ISBN 0-912516-50-X); pap. 4.95 (ISBN 0-912516-51-8). Grey Fox.
My First Three Hundred Babies. Gladys W. Hendrick. LC 78-50853. 1978. 5.95 (ISBN 0-88449-030-0). Vision Hse.
My First Trip to the Library. Rasheed Mohammed & Tinamarie Mohammed. 66p. 1980. 5.95 (ISBN 0-533-04357-3). Vantage.
My First Writing Book: Manuscript Writing. rev ed. Katherine H. O'Connor. (Illus.). 57p. (gr. k-3). 1972. wkbk 1.00 (ISBN 0-910812-07-1). Johnny Reads.
My Five Senses. Aliki. LC 62-7150. (Let's-Read-&-Find-Out Science Bk). (Illus.). (gr. k-3). 1962. PLB 7.89 (ISBN 0-690-56763-4, TYC-J); filmstrip with record 11.95 (ISBN 0-690-56764-2); filmstrip with cassette 14.95 (ISBN 0-690-56766-9). T Y Crowell.
My Five Senses. Aliki. LC 62-7150. (Crocodile Paperbacks Ser.). (Illus.). 33p. (gr. k-3). 1972. pap. 2.95 (ISBN 0-690-56768-5, TYC-J). T Y Crowell.
My Flight Bag Book. Kathleen Daly. (Carry-Me Books). (Illus.). 24p. (ps-3). 1977. PLB 5.38 (ISBN 0-307-68850-X, Golden Pr). Western Pub.
My Foe Outstretch'd Beneath the Tree. Clinton Baddeley. 1981. pap. 2.25 (ISBN 0-440-15685-8). Dell.
My Friend Andrew. Patricia Collins. (Illus.). (ps-2). 1979. PLB 7.95 o.p. (ISBN 0-13-608844-9). P-H.
My Friend Carl Sandburg: The Biography of a Friendship. Lilla S. Perry. Ed. by E. Caswell Perry. LC 80-21908. 234p. 1981. 12.00 (ISBN 0-8108-1367-X). Scarecrow.
My Friend Dylan Thomas. Daniel Jones. (Illus.). 1978. 8.95 o.p. (ISBN 0-684-15917-1, ScribT). Scribner.
My Friend Fish. Mamie Hegwood. LC 75-5822. (Illus.). (gr. 1-4). 1975. reinforced bdg. 4.95 o.p. (ISBN 0-03-014731-X). HR&W.
My Friend Flicka. new ed. Mary O'Hara. LC 73-6611. (Illus.). 272p. (gr. 7-9). 1973. 9.95 (ISBN 0-397-00981-X); text ed. 3.40 (ISBN 0-397-00008-1). Lippincott.
My Friend from Limousin. Jean Girdoux. Tr. by L. C. Willcox from Fr. LC 76-27657. 1977. Repr. of 1923 ed. 15.75 (ISBN 0-86527-279-4). Fertig.
My Friend from Outer Space. Caroline Arnold. (Easy-Read Story Bks). (Illus.). 32p. (gr. k-3). 1981. 3.95 (ISBN 0-531-02473-3). Watts.
My Friend Jacob. Clifton & Di Grazia. LC 79-19168. 32p. (gr. k-2). 1980. PLB 7.95 (ISBN 0-525-35487-5). Dutton.
My Friend, Jasper Jones. Rosamond Dauer. LC 76-2459. (Illus.). 40p. (ps-4). 1977. 5.95 o.s.i. (ISBN 0-8193-0887-0, Four Winds); PLB 5.41 o.s.i. (ISBN 0-8193-0888-9). Schol Bk Serv.
My Friend the Bible. John L. Sherrill. 1978. 5.95 (ISBN 0-912376-37-6). Chosen Bks Pub.
My Friend the Computer. Jean M. Rice. (Illus.). 1976. tchrs'. guide 15.00 (ISBN 0-513-01496-9); wkbk. 3.95 (ISBN 0-513-01495-0). Denison.
My Friend the Ski Pro. Andreas Hennig. 1981. 8.95 (ISBN 0-8062-1617-4). Carlton.
My Friend William Moved Away. Martha W. Hickman. LC 78-24319. (Illus.). (gr. k-3). 1979. 7.95g (ISBN 0-687-27540-7). Abingdon.
My Friends: A Self-Portrait Autograph Book. Ruthven Tremain. (Illus.). (gr. 4 up). 1971. 2.50 o.s.i. (ISBN 0-02-789590-4). Macmillan.
My Friends & I. Maureen Curley. (Children of the Kingdom Activities Ser.). (gr. 7-9). 1978. 7.95 (ISBN 0-686-13694-2). Pflaum Pr.
My Friends Live in Many Places. Dorka Raynor. Ed. by Kathleen Tucker. LC 79-27655. (Concept Bk.: Level 1). (Illus.). (ps up). 1980. 6.95g (ISBN 0-8075-5353-0). A Whitman.
My Funny Bunny Phone Book. David L. Harrison. (Golden Play & Learn Bk.). (Illus.). 14p. (ps). 1980. pap. 2.95 (ISBN 0-307-10728-0, Golden Pr). Western Pubs OH.
My Garden: A Journal for Gardening Around the Year. Louise Murphy. LC 79-29650. (Illus.). (gr. 1-7). 1980. 8.95 (ISBN 0-684-16486-8). Scribner.
My Glimpse into Eternity. Betty Malz. 1980. pap. 1.95 (ISBN 0-425-04581-1). Berkley Pub.
My Glimpse of Eternity. B. Maltz. 2.50 (ISBN 0-8007-8363-8). Revell.
My God! Maiwand. Leigh Maxwell. (Illus.). 1979. 15.00 (ISBN 0-85052-247-1, Cooper). Shoe String.
My Golden Book of Manners. Peggy Parish. (ps-3). 1962. PLB 7.62 (ISBN 0-307-60416-0, Golden Pr). Western Pub.
My Goldfish. Herbert H. Wong & Matthew F. Vessel. LC 69-15803. (Illus.). (gr. k-2). 1969 (ISBN 0-201-08720-0, A-W Childrens). PLB 6.95 tchrs' manual o.p. (ISBN 0-685-05057-2). A-W.
My Goodnight Book. Illus. by Eloise Wilkin. (Golden Sturdy Shape Bk). (Illus.). 14p. 1981. 2.95 (ISBN 0-307-12258-1, Golden Pr). Western Pub.
My Grandfather's House: Tlingit Songs of Death & Sorrow. David Cloutier. LC 80-15499. (Illus.). 40p. (Orig.). 1980. pap. 3.00 (ISBN 0-914974-26-2). Holmgangers.
My Grandmother's Djinn. Brian Robb. LC 77-22646. (Illus.). 40p. (gr. k-4). 1978. lib. bdg. 6.95 (ISBN 0-590-07717-1, Four Winds); PLB 5.41 o.p. (ISBN 0-8193-0918-4). Schol Bk Serv.
My Guru & His Disciple. Christopher Isherwood. 338p. 1980. 12.95 (ISBN 0-374-21702-5). FS&G.
My Happy World. Fern Aldridge. (Hello World Ser.). 1976. pap. 1.65 (ISBN 0-8163-0294-4). Pacific Pr Pub Assn.
My Heart Lies South: The Story of My Mexican Marriage. 2nd ed. E. B. Trevino. LC 53-8429. (Illus.). 1972. 6.95 o.s.i. (ISBN 0-690-56905-X, TYC-T). T Y Crowell.
My Heart Turns Back. Oliver Patton. 1981. pap. 2.75 (ISBN 0-445-04241-9). Popular Lib.
My High Love Calling. Emily Cary. (YA) 1977. 5.95 (ISBN 0-685-80404-6, Avalon). Bouregy.
My Home. Renee Barkowski. (Illus.). (ps-4). 1971. PLB 5.00 (ISBN 0-307-60115-3, Golden Pr). Western Pub.
My Home, Sweet Home. Giovanni Guareschi. Tr. by Joseph Green. 1966. 4.50 o.p. (ISBN 0-374-21708-4). FS&G.
My House. Nikki Giovanni. LC 72-116. 96p. 1972. 7.95 (ISBN 0-688-00021-5); pap. 3.95 (ISBN 0-688-05021-2). Morrow.
My House. Richard Scarry. (Golden Look-Look Ser.). (Illus.). 1976. PLB 5.38 (ISBN 0-307-61820-X, Golden Pr); pap. 0.95 (ISBN 0-307-11820-7). Western Pub.
My Husband Gabrilowitsch: A History of the New York Scene. Samuel Charters & Leonard Kunstadt. 27.50 (ISBN 0-306-76055-X). Da Capo.
My Husband Ggabrilowitsch. Clara Clemens. (Music Reprint Ser.). 1979. Repr. of 1938 ed. 25.00 (ISBN 0-306-79563-9). Da Capo.
My Imagination Map. Masuo Ikeda. (Illus.). 200p. Date not set. price not set cancelled (ISBN 0-87011-243-0). Kodansha. Postponed.
My Inventions: Moji Pronalasci. Nikola Tesla. (Illus.). 112p. 1977. 35.00x (ISBN 0-686-63529-9). Heinman.
My Jesus Book. Illus. by Frances Hook. (Illus.). (gr. k-2). 1963. pap. 4.95 board cover (ISBN 0-87239-239-2, 3046). Standard Pub.
My Jesus Pocketbook of ABC's. Cynthia H. Fletcher. (Illus.). 32p. (Orig.). (ps). pap. 0.49 (ISBN 0-937420-01-8). Stirrup Assoc.
My Jesus Pocketbook of Nursery Rhymes. Cynthia H. Fletcher. LC 80-52041. (Illus.). 32p. (Orig.). (ps). pap. 0.49 (ISBN 0-937420-00-X). Stirrup Assoc.
My Job Application File. rev. ed. (Illus.). 48p. (gr. 7-12). 1980. pap. text ed. 2.25 (ISBN 0-915510-42-1). Janus Bks.
My Job, My Boss, & Me. David L. Woods. LC 80-19829. 144p. 1980. pap. 5.95 (ISBN 0-534-97982-3). Lifetime Learn.
My Kind of Rugby: Union & League. Ray French. LC 80-670268. (Illus.). 160p. 1980. 14.95 (ISBN 0-571-11422-9, Pub. by Faber & Faber). Merrimack Bk Serv.
My Kingdom for a Horse: A Owner's Manual. Carol Streeter. LC 78-69643. (Illus.). 128p. 1980. 9.95 (ISBN 0-498-02226-9). A S Barnes.
My Lady Hoyden. Jane Sheridan. 378p. 1981. 13.95 (ISBN 0-312-55776-0). St Martin.
My Lady of the North. Randall Parrish. 1976. lib. bdg. 16.30x (ISBN 0-89968-086-0). Lightyear.
My Lady of the South. Randall Parrish. 1976. lib. bdg. 16.30x (ISBN 0-89968-087-9). Lightyear.
My Lady Queen. John Cleve. pap. 1.50 o.s.i. (ISBN 0-440-15749-8). Dell.
My Ladybug. Herbert H. Wong & Matthew F. Vessel. LC 69-15802. (Illus.). (gr. k-2). 1969. PLB 6.95 (ISBN 0-201-08721-9, A-W Childrens) (ISBN 0-685-05058-0). A-W.
My Lai Four: A Report on the Massacre & Its Aftermath. Seymour M. Hersh. 1970. 10.95 o.p. (ISBN 0-394-43737-3). Random.
My Language Is Me. Beulah Parker. 352p. 1975. pap. 1.95 o.p. (ISBN 0-345-24587-3). Ballantine.
My Last Two Thousand Years. Herbert Gold. 1972. 8.95 o.p. (ISBN 0-394-47098-2). Random.
My Life. Isadora Duncan. (Black & Gold Lib). (Illus.). 1955. 10.00 (ISBN 0-87140-942-9); pap. 5.95 (ISBN 0-87140-074-X). Liveright.
My Life. Erich Raeder. Tr. by Henry W. Drexel. LC 79-6121. (Navies & Men Ser.). (Illus.). 1980. Repr. of 1960 ed. lib. bdg. 35.00x (ISBN 0-405-13075-9). Arno.
My Life. Ruby D. Reid. 1981. 4.95 (ISBN 0-8062-1694-8). Carlton.
My Life - What Shall I Do with It? Shirley Schwarzrock & C. Gilbert Wrenn. (Coping with Ser.). (Illus.). 50p. (gr. 7-12). 1973. pap. text ed. 1.30 (ISBN 0-913476-26-9). Am Guidance.
My Life & Experiences Among Our Hostile Indians. Oliver O. Howard. LC 76-87436. (The American Scente Ser.). Repr. of 1907 ed. lib. bdg. 37.50 (ISBN 0-306-71506-6). Da Capo.
My Life & Lives: The Story of a Tibetan Incarnation. Rato K. Losang. Ed. by Joseph Campbell. 1977. pap. 4.95 o.p. (ISBN 0-525-47480-3). Dutton.
My Life & Loves, Part II. Linda Van Dalen. 1976. pap. 1.50 o.p. (ISBN 0-685-72356-9, LB382DK, Leisure Bks). Nordon Pubns.
My Life & Times. Compton Mackenzie. Incl. Octave 1, 1883-1891. 253p. 8.75x (ISBN 0-7011-0933-5); Octave 2, 1891-1900. 327p. 8.75x (ISBN 0-7011-0934-3); Octave 3, 1900-1907. 294p. o.p. (ISBN 0-7011-0935-1); Octave 4, 1907-1914. 268p. 8.75x (ISBN 0-7011-0936-X); Octave 5, 1915-1923. 269p. 8.75x (ISBN 0-7011-0937-8); Octave 6, 1923-1930. 269p. 8.75x (ISBN 0-7011-0938-6); Octave 7, 1931-1938. 320p. 10.50x (ISBN 0-7011-1302-2); Octave 8, 1939-1946. 319p. 11.25x (ISBN 0-7011-1425-8); Octave 9, 1946-1953. 325p. 11.25x (ISBN 0-7011-1577-7); Octave 10, 1953-1963. 208p. 11.50x (ISBN 0-7011-1703-6). LC 63-6236. (Illus.). 1963-71. Intl Pubns Serv.
My Life As an Indian. J. W. Schultz. 208p. 1975. pap. 1.25 o.p. (ISBN 0-449-30678-X, P678, Prem). Fawcett.
My Life in Art. Constantin Stanislavski. 1952. pap. 6.95 (ISBN 0-87830-550-5). Theatre Arts.
My Life in Christ. Robert Wisdom. LC 78-68607. 1980. 5.95 (ISBN 0-533-04175-9). Vantage.
My Life in Christ: A Momento of My Confirmation. S H. Fenske. LC 76-5729. (gr. 8 up). 1976. pap. 1.95 (ISBN 0-8100-0056-3, 16*N0514). Northwest Pub.
My Life in Court. Louis Nizer. 1978. pap. 1.95 o.s.i. (ISBN 0-515-04570-5). Jove Pubns.
My Life in the Mafia. Vincent Teresa & Thomas C. Renner. 368p. 1977. pap. 1.95 o.p. (ISBN 0-449-23246-8, Crest). Fawcett.
My Life in the Russian Theatre. Vladimir Nemirovitch-Dantchenko. LC 67-18053. (Illus.). 1968. pap. 3.45 (ISBN 0-87830-520-3). Theatre Arts.
My Life Memories. Alice A. Zoerb. 1978. 10.95 (ISBN 0-9602888-0-5). Heritage Rec.
My Life, My Theater. I. Kaminska. 1973. 12.95 o.s.i. (ISBN 0-02-560490-2). Macmillan.
My Life on the Plains. George A. Custer. Ed. by Milo M. Quaife. LC 67-2618. (Illus.). 1966. pap. 6.95 (ISBN 0-8032-5042-8, BB 328, Bison). U of Nebr Pr.
My Life on the Plains. George A. Custer. 1976. pap. 1.25 o.p. (ISBN 0-685-69509-3, LB377ZK, Leisure Bks). Nordon Pubns.
My Life on the Plains: Personal Experiences with Indians. George A. Custer. (Western Frontier Library Ser.: No. 52). 1976. 10.95 (ISBN 0-8061-0523-2); pap. 6.95 (ISBN 0-8061-1357-X). U of Okla Pr.
My Life with Elvis. Becky Yance & Cliff Linedecker. LC 77-10377. (Illus.). 1977. 3.98 (ISBN 0-312-55834-1). St Martin.
My Life with Elvis. Becky Yancy & Cliff Linedecker. (Illus.). 1978. pap. 2.50 o.s.i. (ISBN 0-446-81927-1). Warner Bks.
My Life with Mikhail Bulgakov. L. E. Belozerskaya-Bulgakova. Tr. by M. Thompson from Rus. 105p. 1981. 13.50 (ISBN 0-88233-433-6). Ardis Pubs.
My Life with Sydney Laurence. Jeanne Laurence. LC 74-75661. (Illus.). 180p. 1974. 35.00 o.p. (ISBN 0-87564-010-9). Superior Pub.
My Life's Venture in Prayer. Jack M. Chisholm. (Prayer in My Life Ser.: Ser. II). 1974. pap. 1.00x (ISBN 0-8358-0316-3). Upper Room.
My Little Book About Flying. Kennon Graham. (Tell-a-Tale Readers). (Illus.). (gr. k-3). 1979. PLB 4.77 (ISBN 0-307-68646-9, Whitman). Western Pub.
My Little Book Bag. Incl. Please & Thank You. Richard Scarry; Meet Babar & His Family. Laurent De Brunhoff; Grover & the Everything in the Whole Wide World Museum. Norman Stiles & Daniel Wilcox; Five-Hundred Words to Grow on. Harry McNaught; Who's Got the Apple? Jan Loof. (ps-1). 1976. Set. pap. 4.95 (ISBN 0-394-83335-X, BYR). Random.
My Little Book of Big Animals. Jim E. Kulas. (Tell-a-Tale Readers). (Illus.). (gr. k-3). 1979. PLB 4.77 (ISBN 0-307-68645-0, Whitman). Western Pub.
My Little Book of Cars & Trucks. Kennon Graham. (Tell-a-Tale Readers). (Illus.). (gr. k-3). 1973. PLB 4.77 (ISBN 0-307-68473-3, Whitman). Western Pub.
My Little Book of Cats. N. Gretchen Greiner. (Tell-a-Tale Readers). (Illus.). (gr. k-3). PLB 4.77 (ISBN 0-307-68626-4, Whitman). Western Pub.
My Little Book of Dinosaurs. Eileen Daly. (Tell-a-Tale Readers). (Illus.). (gr. k-3). 1973. PLB 4.77 (ISBN 0-307-68482-2, Whitman). Western Pub.
My Little Book of Farm Animals. Daphne Hogstrom. (Tell-a-Tale Reader). 24p. (ps-3). 1980. PLB 4.77 (ISBN 0-307-68490-3, Golden Pr). Western Pub.
My Little Book of Horses. Jane D. Walrath. (Tell-a-Tale Reader). 32p. (ps-3). PLB 4.77 (ISBN 0-307-68410-5, Golden Pr). Western Pub.
My Little Book of Trains. Mariellen Hanrahan. (Tell-a-Tale Readers). (Illus.). (gr. k-3). 1979. PLB 4.77 (ISBN 0-307-68648-5, Whitman). Western Pub.
My Little Dinosaur. Ilse-Margret Vogel. (Illus.). 24p. (ps-2). 1971. PLB 5.00 (ISBN 0-307-60571-X, Golden Pr). Western Pub.
My Little Hen. Alice Provensen & Martin Provensen. (Illus.). (ps-1). 1973. PLB 4.99 (ISBN 0-394-92684-6, BYR). Random.
My Longest Night. Genevieve Dubosçq. Tr. by Richard S. Woodward from Fr. LC 80-23169. (Illus.). 288p. 1981. 12.95 (ISBN 0-394-51590-0). Seaver Bks.
My Lord Barbarian. Andrew J. Offutt. (Del Rey Bk.). 1978. pap. 1.50 o.p. (ISBN 0-685-75023-X, 345-25713-8-150). Ballantine.
My Lord Monleigh. Jan C. Speas. 1977. pap. 1.95 (ISBN 0-380-01847-0, 36442). Avon.
My LSE. Ed. by Joan Abse. (Illus.). 223p. 1977. 14.50x (ISBN 0-8476-3125-7). Rowman.
My Luiseno Neighbors. Eleanor Beemer. (Illus.). 91p. (Orig.). 1980. pap. 9.95 (ISBN 0-916552-20-9). Acoma Bks.
My Luke & I. Eleanor Gehrig & Joseph Durso. (RL 10). 1977. pap. 1.75 o.p. (ISBN 0-451-07818-7, E7818, Sig). NAL.
My Lunch Box Book. Kathleen Daly. (Carry-Me Books). (Illus.). (ps-3). 1977. PLB 5.38 (ISBN 0-307-68855-0, Golden Pr). Western Pub.
My Magic Garden. Ilse Klipper. (Illus., Orig.). (gr. 2-6). 1980. pap. 4.95 (ISBN 0-9605022-0-3). Pathway Pr.
My Magnificient Machine. William L. Coleman. LC 78-5035. 1978. pap. 3.95 (ISBN 0-87123-381-9, 210381). Bethany Fell.
My Maryland. Kaessman et al. (Illus.). 1971. 4.50x (ISBN 0-938420-12-7). Md Hist.
My Measuring Book. Joan C. Bowden. (Golden Play & Learn Bk). (Illus.). 14p. (ps). 1980. pap. 2.95 (ISBN 0-307-10729-9). Western Pubs OH.
My Medical School. Ed. by Dannie Abse. (Illus.). 211p. 1978. 14.50x (ISBN 0-8476-3124-9). Rowman.
My Memoirs Completed: Al-Takmilah. King Abdallah Of Jordan. (Illus.). 1978. text ed. 14.95x (ISBN 0-582-78082-9). Longman.
My Memoirs in Pictures. Birgit Nilsson. Tr. by Thomas Teal from Swedish. LC 78-22343. (Illus.). 128p. 1981. 19.95 (ISBN 0-385-14835-6). Doubleday.
My Minnie Is a Jewel. Tricia Springstubb. LC 80-66712. (Carolrhoda on My Own Bks.). (Illus.). 48p. (gr. k-3). 1980. PLB 5.95g (ISBN 0-87614-131-9). Carolrhoda Bks.
My Mom Hates Me in January. Judy Delton. LC 77-5749. (Concept Books). (Illus.). (gr. 1-3). 1977. 6.50g (ISBN 0-685-75662-9). A Whitman.
My Mom, the Truck Driver. Kathleen A. McDaniels. (Illus., Orig.). 1980. pap. 3.95 (ISBN 0-935424-01-6). Daisy.
My Mortal Enemy. Willa Cather. 1961. pap. 1.95 (ISBN 0-394-70200-X, V200, Vin). Random.
My Mother & I. Aileen Fisher. LC 67-10473. (Illus.). (ps-3). 1967. PLB 8.79 o.p. (ISBN 0-690-56976-9, TYC-J). T Y Crowell.
My Mother & I Are Growing Strong. (ps-4). 2.00. New Seed.
My Mother Didn't Kiss Me Goodnight. Charlotte Herman. LC 80-190. (Illus.). 32p. (ps-3). 1980. PLB 7.95 (ISBN 0-525-35495-6). Dutton.
My Mother Is Lost. Bernice Myers. (gr. k-3). 1971. pap. 1.25 (ISBN 0-590-04478-8, Schol Pap); pap. 3.50 bk. & record (ISBN 0-590-20694-X). Schol Bk Serv.
My Mother Is Not Married to My Father. Jean D. Okimoto. 1981. pap. price not set (ISBN 0-671-56079-4). Archway.
My Mother Lost Her Job Today. Judy Delton. Ed. by Ann Fay. LC 80-19067. (Concept Bks.). (Illus.). 32p. (gr. k-3). 1980. 6.50 (ISBN 0-8075-5359-X). A Whitman.
My Mother Made Me. Brain. (gr. 6). 1979. pap. 1.25 (ISBN 0-590-05801-0, Schol Pap). Schol Bk Serv.
My Mother, My Self. Nancy Friday. 1978. boxed gift edition 14.95 o.s.i. (ISBN 0-440-06010-9). Delacorte.
My Mother, Myself. Nancy Friday. 1981. pap. 3.25 (ISBN 0-440-15663-7). Dell.

My Mother the Witch. Rose Blue. LC 79-23950. (gr. 6-8). 1980. 8.95 (ISBN 0-07-006169-6). McGraw.
My Mother Who Fathered Me: A Study of the Family in the Selected Communities in Jamaica. Edith Clark. 1976. pap. text ed. 8.95x (ISBN 0-04-573010-5). Allen Unwin.
My Mother's House & Sido. Colette. Tr. by Una V. Troubridge & Enid McLeod. Incl. Sido. 219p. 1975. 7.95 (ISBN 0-374-21735-1); pap. 3.95 (ISBN 0-374-51218-3). FS&G.
My Mother's Welcome Home. Bette Ramsey. (Illus.). 1977. pap. 0.95 o.p. (ISBN 0-917726-10-3). Hunter Bks.
My Name Is Aram. William Saroyan. LC 40-34075. (Modern Classic Ser.). (Illus.). 1940. 4.95 (ISBN 0-15-163827-6). HarBraceJ.
My Name Is Davy: I'm an Alcoholic. Anne Snyder. LC 76-28457. (gr. 6 up). 1977. reinforced bdg. 5.95 o.p. (ISBN 0-03-017841-X). HR&W.
My Name Is Emily. Morse Hamilton & Emily Hamilton. LC 78-4537. (Illus.). (gr. k-3). 1979. 7.50 (ISBN 0-688-80181-1); PLB 7.20 (ISBN 0-688-84181-3). Greenwillow.
My Name Is Legion. Roger Zelany. 224p. (Orig.). 1981. pap. 2.25 (Del Rey). Ballantine.
My Name Is Legion. Roger Zelazny. LC 75-44242. 224p. (Orig.). 1976. pap. 2.25 (ISBN 0-345-29522-6). Ballantine.
My Name Is Million: An Illustrated History of the Poles in America. W. S. Kuniczak. LC 77-82954. 1978. 12.95 o.p. (ISBN 0-385-12228-4). Doubleday.
My Name Is Nabil. Wendy Heller. (Illus.). 59p. (gr. 3-6). 1981. price not set (ISBN 0-933770-17-0). Kalimat.
My Name on the Bullet. Brad Cordell. 1979. pap. 1.25 (ISBN 0-505-51411-7). Tower Bks.
My Nancy Drew Private Eye Diary. 416p. (gr. 3 up). 1980. pap. 6.95 (ISBN 0-671-95505-5). Wanderer Bks.
My Narrow Isle: The Story of a Modern Woman in Japan. Sumie Mishima. LC 79-2945. (Illus.). 280p. 1981. Repr. of 1941 ed. 22.50 (ISBN 0-8305-0109-6). Hyperion Conn.
My Neighbor: A Study of City Conditions, a Plan for Social Service. James S. Woodsworth. LC 77-163839. (Social History of Canada Ser.). (Illus.). xix, 216p. 1972. pap. 5.00 (ISBN 0-8020-6126-5). U of Toronto Pr.
My New Friends. Barbara J. Crane. (Crane Reading System-English Ser.). (gr. k-2). 1977. pap. text ed. 2.95 (ISBN 0-89075-102-1). Crane Pub Co.
My New Mom & Me. Betty R. Wright. LC 80-25529. (Life & Living from a Child's Point of View Ser.). (Illus.). (gr. k-5). 1981. PLB 9.65 (ISBN 0-8172-1368-6). Raintree Child.
My Nursery School. Harlow Rockwell. LC 75-25871. (Illus.). 24p. (gr. k-3). 1976. 7.95 (ISBN 0-688-80025-4); PLB 7.63 (ISBN 0-688-84025-6). Greenwillow.
My Ocean, My Love. Evelyn Barkins. LC 77-28151. 1977. pap. 2.95 (ISBN 0-8119-0391-5). Fell.
My Odyssey: An Autobiography. Nnamdi Azikiwe. 1970. 15.00 (ISBN 0-685-71645-7). Univ Place.
My Orphans of the Wild: Rescue & Home Care of Native Wildlife. Rosemary K. Collett. LC 74-1111. (Illus.). 1974. 9.95 (ISBN 0-397-01021-4). Lippincott.
My Other-Mother, My Other-Father. Harriet L. Sobol. LC 78-24165. (Illus.). 48p. (gr. 3-7). 1979. 7.95 (ISBN 0-02-785960-6). Macmillan.
My Own Book, No. 6. Dina Anastasio. 48p. (Orig.). 1981. pap. 1.75 (ISBN 0-8431-0698-0). Price Stern.
My Own Book of Feelings. Linda P. Silbert & Alvin Silbert. (Little Twirps, TM Creative Thinking Workbooks). (Illus.). (gr. k-8). 1977. 2.25 (ISBN 0-89544-017-2, 017). Silbert Bress.
My Own Book of Special Things. Linda P. Silbert & Alvin J. Silbert. (Little Twirps, TM Creative Thinking Wkbks.). (Illus.). (ps-4). 1977. wkbk. 2.25 (ISBN 0-89544-019-9, 019). Silbert Bress.
My Own Book of Wishes. Linda P. Silbert & Alvin J. Silbert. (Little Twirps Creative Thinking Workbooks). (Illus.). (gr. k-6). 1976. wkbk. 2.25 (ISBN 0-89544-016-4). Silbert Bress.
My Own Cook Book: From Stillmeadow & Cape Cod. Gladys Taber. LC 72-747. (Illus.). 1972. 8.95 (ISBN 0-397-00877-5). Lippincott.
My Own Hanukah Story. Daniel D. Stuhlman. (Illus., Orig.). (ps-1). 1980. pap. 3.95 (ISBN 0-934402-07-8); decorations 1.00 (ISBN 0-934402-08-6). BYLS Pr.
My Own Herb Garden. Allan A. Swenson. (Children's Collection Ser.). (Illus.). 72p. 1976. 6.95 (ISBN 0-87857-129-9). Rodale Pr Inc.
My Own Life: The Earlier Years. John W. Nevin. LC 64-57065. 1964. pap. 5.00 (ISBN 0-685-09356-5). Evang & Ref.
My Own Pesach Story. Daniel D. Stuhlman. (My Own Holiday Stories: No. 2). (Illus.). 1981. pap. 3.95 (ISBN 0-686-28904-8). BYLS Pr.
My Own Private Sky. Delores Beckman. LC 79-23341. 160p. (gr. 4-6). 1980. 8.95 (ISBN 0-525-35510-3). Dutton.
My Own River Kwai. Pierre Boulle. LC 67-29216. 1967. 8.95 (ISBN 0-8149-0061-5). Vanguard.
My Part in Germany's Fight. Joseph Goebbels. Tr. by Kurt Fiedler from Ger. LC 76-27871. 1979. Repr. of 1935 ed. 18.50 (ISBN 0-86527-137-2). Fertig.
My Path Through Life. Lilli Lehmann. Tr. by Alice B. Seligman. LC 80-2286. (Illus.). 1981. Repr. of 1914 ed. 54.50 (ISBN 0-404-18855-9). AMS Pr.
My Penitente Land. Angelico Chavez. LC 79-63671. 1979. Repr. of 1974 ed. 27.50 (ISBN 0-88307-568-7); pap. 13.50 o.p. (ISBN 0-88307-569-5). Gannon.
My People, My Africa. Credo V. Mutwa. (John Day Bk.). (Illus.). 1969. 7.95 o.s.i. (ISBN 0-381-98161-4, A52400, TYC-T). T Y Crowell.
My People the Sioux. Luther Standing Bear. Ed. by E. A. Brininstool. LC 74-77394. (Illus.). 1975. 14.95x (ISBN 0-8032-0874-X); pap. 3.95 (ISBN 0-8032-5793-7, BB 578, Bison). U of Nebr Pr.
My Philosophy. Benedetto Croce. 1962. pap. 0.95 o.s.i. (ISBN 0-02-064870-7, Collier). Macmillan.
My Picnic Basket Book. Kathleen Daly. (Carry-Me Books). (Illus.). 24p. 1977. PLB 5.38 (ISBN 0-307-68852-6, Golden Pr). Western Pub.
My Pilgrimage of Prayer. John Powell. (Prayer in My Life Ser.: Ser. II). 1974. pap. 1.00x (ISBN 0-8358-0313-9). Upper Room.
My Prayer Diary. Kathryn F. Garner & Christa G. Young. LC 78-17345. 1978. pap. 5.95 spiral bd (ISBN 0-8407-5657-7). Nelson.
My Private Life. Polly Webster. (Illus.). (gr. 6-10). 5.00 o.p. (ISBN 0-8313-0104-X). Lantern.
My Puppy Is Born. Joanna Cole. LC 72-14201. (Illus.). 40p. (gr. k-3). 1973. PLB 6.48 (ISBN 0-688-30078-2). Morrow.
My Recipes Are for the Birds. Irene Cosgrove & Ed Cosgrove. LC 76-23757. 62p. 1976. pap. 3.95 (ISBN 0-385-12634-4). Doubleday.
My Red Umbrella. Robert Bright. (Illus.). (ps-1). 1959. PLB 6.48 (ISBN 0-688-31619-0). Morrow.
My Reflections on Educational Psychology, Science & American Schools. William E. Roweton. LC 80-8262. 124p. 1980. lib. bdg. 15.75 (ISBN 0-8191-1329-8); pap. text ed. 7.50 (ISBN 0-8191-1330-1). U Pr of Amer.
My Reminiscences. Luigi Arditi. LC 77-5500. (Music Reprint Ser.). (Illus.). 1977. Repr. of 1896 ed. lib. bdg. 25.00 (ISBN 0-306-77417-8). Da Capo.
My Reminiscences of the Russian Revolution. Morgan P. Price. LC 79-2922. (Illus.). 402p. 1981. Repr. of 1921 ed. 27.50 (ISBN 0-8305-0091-X). Hyperion Conn.
My Robot Buddy. Alfred Slote. (Illus.). (gr. 2-7). 1978. pap. 1.75 (ISBN 0-380-40329-3, 52001, Camelot). Avon.
My Robot Buddy. Alfred Slote. LC 75-9922. (Illus.). 96p. (gr. 2-4). 1975. 7.95 (ISBN 0-397-31641-0). Lippincott.
My Roots Be Coming Back. Ed. by Nancy Lewis. (Illus.). 24p. 1973. pap. 3.50x (ISBN 0-89062-034-2, Pub. by Touchstone). Pub Ctr Cult Res.
My School the City. Mortimer Smith. LC 80-51727. 190p. 1980. 9.95 (ISBN 0-89526-674-1). Regnery-Gateway.
My Searching Heart. LC 80-83846. 242p. 1981. pap. 4.95 (ISBN 0-89081-262-4). Harvest Hse.
My Secret Hiding Place. Rose Greydanus. (Illus.). 32p. (gr. k-2). 1980. PLB 2.96 (ISBN 0-89375-383-1); pap. 0.95 (ISBN 0-89375-085-9). Troll Assocs.
My Secret Life. 1976. pap. 2.95 o.p. (ISBN 0-345-25294-2). Ballantine.
My Secret Place. Julie Gibbons. (Illus.). 20p. (Orig.). (gr. 1-4). 1975. pap. 2.50 (ISBN 0-911336-61-3). Sci of Mind.
My Secret War. Richard S. Drury. LC 79-50359. (Illus.). 1979. 10.95 (ISBN 0-8168-6841-7). Aero.
My Secrets of Natural Beauty. Virginia C. Thomas. LC 72-76464. 224p. 1972. 5.95 (ISBN 0-87983-019-0); pap. 2.25 (ISBN 0-87983-020-4). Keats.
My Shadow Ran Fast. Bill Sands. 1964. 6.95 o.p. (ISBN 0-13-608984-4). P-H.
My Side, by King Kong. Walter Wager. LC 76-49829. 1976. 7.95 o.s.i. (ISBN 0-02-622420-8). Macmillan.
My Side, by King Kong. Walter Wager. 1976. pap. 4.95 o.s.i. (ISBN 0-02-040750-5, Collier). Macmillan.
My Side of the Mountain. Jean C. George. (Illus.). (gr. 4-9). 1975. PLB 7.95 (ISBN 0-525-35530-8, Anytime Bks); pap. 3.25 (ISBN 0-525-45030-0, Anytime Bk). Dutton.
My Side: The Autobiography of Ruth Gordon. Ruth Gordon. LC 76-5124. (Illus.). 576p. 1976. 12.95 o.p. (ISBN 0-06-011618-8, HarpT). Har-Row.
My Silent War. Kim Philby. 4.95 (ISBN 0-686-28852-1). Academy Chi Ltd.
My Sister Is Different. Betty R. Wright. LC 80-25508. (Life & Living from a Child's Point of View Ser.). (Illus.). 32p. (gr. k-5). 1981. PLB 9.65 (ISBN 0-8172-1369-4). Raintree Child.
My Sister, Life. Boris Pasternak. Tr. by Olga A. Carlisle. (Helen & Kurt Wolff Bk.). 1976. 14.95 o.p. (ISBN 0-15-163964-7). HarBraceJ.
My Sister, My Love. Lucille Iremonger. LC 80-21357. 320p. 1981. 11.95 (ISBN 0-688-00055-X). Morrow.
My Sister, the Panther. Djibi Thiam. Tr. by Mercer Cook from Fr. LC 80-1016. 192p. (gr. 7 up). 1980. 6.95g (ISBN 0-396-07890-7). Dodd.
My Sister's Keeper. Beverly Butler. LC 79-6637. (gr. 7 up). 1980. 6.95 (ISBN 0-396-07803-6). Dodd.
My Son Dan. Lettie W. Moore. LC 77-94241. (Destiny Ser.). 1978. pap. 4.95 (ISBN 0-8163-0007-0, 13875-0). Pacific Pr Pub Assn.
My Sons, My England. Dougal Duncan. 1980. 11.95 (ISBN 0-684-16603-8). Scribner.
My Sports Bag Book. Kathleen Daly. (Carry-Me Bks.). (Illus.). 24p. (ps-3). 1977. PLB 5.38 (ISBN 0-307-68854-2, Golden Pr). Western Pub.
My State & Its Story: Michigan History. rev., 16th ed. Ferris E. Lewis. (Illus.). (gr. 8 up). 1972. text ed. 10.45x o.p. (ISBN 0-910726-10-8); wkbk. 2.40x o.p. (ISBN 0-910726-15-9). Hillsdale Educ.
My Stillness. Paul Griffith. LC 72-83347. 212p. 1972. 7.95 (ISBN 0-8149-0724-5). Vanguard.
My Story. Stephen M. Barooshian. 1978. 5.95 o.p. (ISBN 0-533-03000-5). Vantage.
My Summer Brother. Ilse-Margaret Vogel. LC 80-7911. (Illus.). 96p. (gr. 2-5). 1981. 8.95 (ISBN 0-06-026324-5, HarpJ); PLB 8.79g (ISBN 0-06-026325-3). Har-Row.
My Swedish Cousins. Anna Riwkin-Brick. (gr. 2-4). 1967. 4.95 o.s.i. (ISBN 0-02-776970-4). Macmillan.
My System. J. P. Muller. 5.00x o.p. (ISBN 0-392-07048-0, SpS). Soccer.
My Tang's Tungled & Other Ridiculous Situations. Compiled by Sara Brewton et al. LC 73-254. (Illus.). (gr. 4 up). 1973. 8.95 (ISBN 0-690-57223-9, TYC-J). T Y Crowell.
My Telephone Book. Ed. by Kate Klimo. (Playboards Ser.). (Illus.). 12p. (ps-k). Date not set. boards 2.95 (ISBN 0-671-42526-9, Little Simon). S&S.
My Thank You Book. Illus. by Frances Hook. (Illus.). (gr. k-2). 1964. 4.95 (ISBN 0-87239-241-4, 3048). Standard Pub.
My Theatre Life. August Bournonville. Tr. by Patricia McAndrew. LC 78-27349. (Illus.). 1979. 40.00 (ISBN 0-8195-5035-3, Pub. by Wesleyan U Pr). Columbia U Pr.
My Theodosia. Anya Seton. 1977. pap. 1.95 o.p. (ISBN 0-449-23034-1, Crest). Fawcett.
My Thoughts in Verse. Alice Landau. Date not set. 5.95 (ISBN 0-533-04817-6). Vantage.
My Threescore Years & Ten. 2nd ed. Thomas Ball. LC 75-28884. (Art Experience in Late 19th Century America Ser.: Vol. 18). (Illus.). 1976. Repr. of 1892 ed. lib. bdg. 37.00 (ISBN 0-8240-2242-4). Garland Pub.
My Time & What I've Done with It: An Autobiography, Compiled from the Diary, Notes & Personal Recollections of Cecil Colvin, 1874. Francis C. Burnard. (Victorian Fiction Ser.). 1975. lib. bdg. 66.00 (ISBN 0-8240-1535-5). Garland Pub.
My Time or Yours? William D. Blake. (Orig.). 1979. pap. 1.95 (ISBN 0-532-23286-0). Manor Bks.
My Times with Dogs. Walter R. Fletcher. LC 79-24575. (Illus.). 320p. 1980. 14.95 (ISBN 0-87605-664-8). Howell Bk.
My Toolbox Book. Jan Sukus. (Illus.). 24p. (ps-3). 1977. PLB 5.38 (ISBN 0-307-68853-4, Golden Pr). Western Pub.
My Trip to Alpha I. Alfred Slote. (Illus.). (gr. 2-5). 1980. pap. 1.95 (ISBN 0-380-51128-2, 51128, Camelot). Avon.
My Trip to Alpha 1. Alfred Slote. LC 78-6463. (Illus.). (gr. 3-5). 1978. 7.95 (ISBN 0-397-31810-3). Lippincott.
My Truth. Edda M. Ciano. Tr. by Eileen Finletter from Fr. 1977. 8.95 o.p. (ISBN 0-688-03099-8). Morrow.
My Turn, Your Turn. Pauline Watson. LC 77-25306. (Illus.). (ps-2). Date not set. 6.95g o.p. (ISBN 0-13-608703-5). P-H. Postponed.
My Twenty-Five Years in China. John B. Powell. LC 76-27721. (China in the 20th Century Ser.). 1976. Repr. of 1945 ed. lib. bdg. 35.00 (ISBN 0-306-70761-6). Da Capo.
My Two Roads. 2nd ed. J. Brian Eby. LC 75-30380. (Illus.). 1976. 7.95 (ISBN 0-88415-570-6). Pacesetter Pr.
My Uncle Dudley. Wright Morris. LC 75-5696. viii, 210p. 1975. pap. 2.95 (ISBN 0-8032-5804-6, BB 589, Bison). U of Nebr Pr.
My Uncle Oswald. Roald Dahl. 208p. 1981. pap. 2.95 (ISBN 0-345-29410-6). Ballantine.
My Uncle Sam Don't Like Me. Walter T. Coy. LC 79-56105. 1980. 8.95 (ISBN 0-533-04513-4). Vantage.
My Very Best Friend. Paul Ricchiuti. (Hello World Ser.). 1975. pap. 1.65 (ISBN 0-8163-0188-3, 13950-1). Pacific Pr Pub Assn.
My Very First Book of Colors. Eric Carle. LC 72-83776. (Illus.). 10p. (ps-2). 1974. 3.95 (ISBN 0-690-57365-0, TYC-J). T Y Crowell.
My Very First Book of Numbers. Eric Carle. LC 72-83777. (Illus.). 10p. (ps-2). 1974. 3.95 (ISBN 0-690-57366-9, TYC-J). T Y Crowell.
My Very First Book of Shapes. Eric Carle. LC 72-83778. (Illus.). 10p. (ps-2). 1974. 3.95 (ISBN 0-690-57367-7, TYC-J). T Y Crowell.
My Very First Book of Words. Eric Carle. LC 72-83779. (Illus.). 10p. (ps-2). 1974. 3.95 (ISBN 0-690-57368-5, TYC-J). T Y Crowell.
My Very Own Dictionary. Charlie Daniel & Becky Daniel. (gr. 1-4). 1978. 5.50 (ISBN 0-916456-17-X, GA81). Good Apple.
My Very Own Sukkot Book. Judyth R. Saypol & Madeline Wikler. (Illus.). 40p. (Orig.). (gr. k-6). 1980. pap. 2.95 (ISBN 0-930494-09-1). Kar Ben.
My Village in Spain. Sonia Gidal & Tim Gidal. (Illus.). (gr. 4-6). 1962. PLB 5.69 o.p. (ISBN 0-394-91922-X). Pantheon.
My Visit to the Dinosaurs. Aliki. LC 70-78255. (Let's-Read-&-Find-Out Science Bk). (Illus.). (gr. k-3). 1969. bds. 6.95 (ISBN 0-690-57401-0, TYC-J); PLB 7.89 (ISBN 0-690-57402-9); pap. 2.95 crocodile paperback ser. (ISBN 0-690-57403-7, TIYC-J). T Y Crowell.
My Wallet of Photographs: The Collected Photographs of J. M. Synge Arranged & Introduced by Lilo Stephens. J. M. Synge. (Illus.). 53p. 1971. text ed. 17.00x (ISBN 0-85105-189-8, Dolmen Pr). Humanities.
My Weakness--His Strength: The Personal Face of Renewal. Robert C. Girard. 208p. 1981. pap. 5.95 (ISBN 0-310-39081-8, 15607P). Zondervan.
My Weekly Reader Picture Word Book. Adelaide Holl. (Illus.). 128p. (ps-k). Date not set. pap. 5.95 (ISBN 0-671-42542-0, Little Simon). S&S.
My Wicked, Wicked Ways. Errol Flynn. 1976. Repr. of 1959 ed. lib. bdg. 17.95x (ISBN 0-89966-093-2). Buccaneer Bks.
My Wicked, Wicked Ways. Errol Flynn. 1981. pap. 2.75. Berkley Pub.
My Wicked, Wicked Ways. Errol Flynn. 1979. pap. 2.75 (ISBN 0-425-04686-9). Berkley Pub.
My Wife & I: The Story of Louise & Sidney Homer. Sidney Homer. LC 77-10561. (Music Reprint Ser.). (Illus.). 1978. Repr. of 1939 ed. lib. bdg. 27.50 (ISBN 0-306-77526-3). Da Capo.
My Wife, the Condesa. Felix Abelard. 1978. 9.50 o.p. (ISBN 0-682-49054-7). Exposition.
My Wild World. Joan Embery & Denise Demong. 1980. 14.95 (ISBN 0-440-05742-6). Delacorte.
My Word Book. LC 80-83586. (Illus.). 80p. (gr. k-3). 1981. PLB 11.85 (ISBN 0-448-13494-2); pap. 4.95 (ISBN 0-448-11548-4). G&D.
My Words Are Spirit & Life: Meeting Christ Through Daily Meditation. Herz, Stephanie M., T.O.C.D. LC 78-4790. 1979. pap. 3.95 (ISBN 0-385-14258-7, Im). Doubleday.
My World. Audrey Curtis & Sheelagh Hill. (General Ser.). 1978. pap. text ed. 8.25x (ISBN 0-85633-156-2, NFER). Humanities.
My World of Birds: Memoirs of an Ornithologist. George J. Wallace. 345p. 1979. 12.50 (ISBN 0-8059-2586-4). Dorrance.
My Years with General Motors. Alfred P. Sloan, Jr. LC 64-11306. 560p. 1972. pap. 3.50 (ISBN 0-385-04235-3, Anch.). Doubleday.
My Years with Ludwig Von Mises. Margit Von Mises. 1977. 9.95 o.p. (ISBN 0-87000-368-2). Arlington Hse.
Mycenae. Michael Sargent. (Aspects of Greek Life). (Illus.). 1972. pap. text ed. 2.95x (ISBN 0-582-34401-8). Longman.
Mycenaean Greece. J. T. Hooker. (States & Cities of Ancient Greece Ser.). 1976. 25.00x (ISBN 0-7100-8379-3). Routledge & Kegan.
Mycenaean Origin of Greek Mythology. enl ed. Martin P. Nilsson. LC 70-181440. (Sather Classical Lectures: Vol. 8). 258p. 1973. 17.50x (ISBN 0-520-01951-2); pap. 3.65 o.p. (ISBN 0-520-02163-0, CAMPUS76). U of Cal Pr.
Mycenaean World. J. Chadwick. (Illus.). 224p. 1976. 39.50 (ISBN 0-521-21077-1); pap. 9.95x (ISBN 0-521-29037-6). Cambridge U Pr.
Mycobacterial Infections of Zoo Animals. Ed. by Richard J. Montali. LC 77-60860. (Symposia of the National Zoological Park Ser.: No. 1). (Illus.). 275p. 1979. text ed. 19.95x (ISBN 0-87474-644-2); pap. text ed. 9.95x (ISBN 0-87474-645-0). Smithsonian.
Mycotoxin Teratogenicity & Mutagenicity. A. Wallace Hayes. 160p. 1981. 59.95 (ISBN 0-8493-5651-2). CRC Pr.
Mycotoxins in Human Health: Symposium. Ed. by I. F. Purchase. LC 72-3778. 306p. 1971. 39.95 (ISBN 0-470-70232-X). Halsted Pr.

Myelin: Chemistry & Biology. Ed. by George Hashim. LC 80-22305. (Progress in Clinical & Biological Research: Vol. 49). 130p. 1980. price not set (ISBN 0-8451-0049-1). A R Liss.

Myne Owne Ground: Race & Freedom on Virginia's Eastern Shore, 1640-1676. T. H. Breen & Stephen Innes. (Illus.). 200p. 1980. 12.95 (ISBN 0-19-502727-2). Oxford U Pr.

Myocardial Cell for the Clinical Cardiologist. Marianne J. Legato. LC 73-80701. (Illus.). 196p. 1973. 20.00 o.p. (ISBN 0-87993-024-1). Futura Pub.

Myocardial Infarction. 2nd ed. Ary L. Goldberger. LC 78-31981. (Illus.). 1979. text ed. 29.50 (ISBN 0-8016-1860-6). Mosby.

Myocardial Infarction & Psychosocial Risks. Ed. by M. J. Halhuber & J. Siegrist. (Illus.). 152p. 1981. pap. 22.50 (ISBN 0-387-10386-4). Springer-Verlag.

Myocardial Protection & Exercise Tolerance: The Role of Lidoflazine, a New Anti-Anginal Agent. Ed. by G. Towse. (Royal Society of Medicine International Congress & Symposium Ser.: No. 29). 1980. 18.50 (ISBN 0-8089-1290-9). Grune.

Myocardial Protection in Regional & Global Ischemia, Vol. 1. Ray C. Chiu. (Annual Research Reviews). 177p. 1981. 26.00 (ISBN 0-88831-097-8). Eden Med Res.

Myocardial Revascularization by Arterial Ventricular Implants. Arthur M. Vineberg. LC 80-10654. (Illus.). 624p. 1981. text ed. 49.50 (ISBN 0-88416-191-9). PSG Pub.

Myoglobin: Biochemical, Physiological & Clinical Aspects. Lawrence J. Kagen. LC 73-5658. (Molecular Biology Ser.). 144p. 1973. text ed. 17.50x (ISBN 0-231-03421-0). Columbia U Pr.

Myra. Barbara Bottner. LC 78-10417. (Illus.). (gr. k-3). 1979. 7.95 (ISBN 0-02-711740-5). Macmillan.

Myra Hess: A Portrait. Marian McKenna. (Illus.). 1978. 22.50 (ISBN 0-241-89522-7, Pub. by Hamish Hamilton England). David & Charles.

Myra Hess by Her Friends. Ed. by Denise Lassimonne & Howard Ferguson. LC 67-29444. (Illus.). 6.95 (ISBN 0-8149-0140-9). Vanguard.

Myra: The Life & Times of Myra Wolfgang, Trade-Union Leader. Jean M. Pitrone. LC 80-68386. (Illus.). 226p. 1980. 10.00 (ISBN 0-686-28855-6). Calibre Bks.

Myra Waldo's Restaurant Guide to New York City & Vicinity, 1981. Myra Waldo. 434p. 1981. pap. 6.95 (ISBN 0-02-098900-8, Collier). Macmillan.

Myra Waldo's Travel Guide to Northern Europe, 1981. Myra Waldo. (Illus.). 730p. 1981. pap. 9.95 (ISBN 0-02-098910-5, Collier). Macmillan.

Myra Waldo's Travel Guide to Southern Europe, 1981. Myra Waldo. (Illus.). 770p. 1981. pap. 9.95 (ISBN 0-02-098930-X, Collier). Macmillan.

Myra Waldo's Travel Guide to the Orient & Asia, 1981. Myra Waldo. (Illus.). 505p. 1981. pap. 9.95 (ISBN 0-02-098890-7, Collier). Macmillan.

Myra Waldo's Travel Guide to the South Pacific, 1981. Myra Waldo. (Illus.). 360p. 1981. pap. 8.95 (ISBN 0-02-098920-2, Collier). Macmillan.

Myriah. Claudette Williams. 1978. pap. 1.50 o.p. (ISBN 0-449-23577-7, Crest). Fawcett.

Myrtle for My Love. Daisy Thomson. 1977. pap. 1.25 o.s.i. (ISBN 0-515-04242-0). Jove Pubns.

Myself & I. Norma Johnston. LC 80-21855. 216p. (gr. 6 up). 1981. PLB 9.95 (ISBN 0-689-30814-0). Atheneum.

Myself Exactly. Jack Libert. (Illus., Orig.). 1971. pap. 2.00 (ISBN 0-911732-56-X). Irego.

Myself in the Rain. Tom Howe. 64p. 1980. pap. 5.95 (ISBN 0-88894-243-5, Pub. by Douglas & McIntyre Canada). Intl Schol Bk Serv.

Mystagogus Poeticus, or the Muses Interpreter. 2nd ed. Alexander Ross. Ed. by Stephen Orgel. LC 75-27875. (Renaissance & the Gods Ser.: Vol. 30). (Illus.). 1976. Repr. of 1648 ed. lib. bdg. 73.00 (ISBN 0-8240-2079-0). Garland Pub.

Mystere Frontenac. Francois Mauriac. (Documentation thematique). (Illus., Fr.). pap. 2.95 (ISBN 0-685-13998-0, 178). Larousse.

Mysteries & Secrets of Magic. C. J. Thompson. LC 78-174119. (Tower Bks). (Illus.). 1971. Repr. of 1928 ed. 24.00 (ISBN 0-8103-3213-2). Gale.

Mysteries of All Nations. James Grant. LC 79-150243. 1971. Repr. of 1880 ed. 36.00 (ISBN 0-8103-3391-0). Gale.

Mysteries of Britain. Lewis Spence. 192p. 1980. pap. 7.95 o.s.i. (ISBN 0-85030-215-3). Newcastle Pub.

Mysteries of History, with Accounts of Some Remarkable Characters & Charlatans. C. J. Thompson. LC 76-164056. (Tower Bks). 1971. Repr. of 1928 ed. 18.00 (ISBN 0-8103-3908-0). Gale.

Mysteries of Homer's Greeks. I. G. Edmonds. (Illus.). 1981. 10.95 (ISBN 0-525-66692-3). Elsevier-Nelson.

Mysteries of Identity: A Theme in Modern Literature. Robert Langbaum. LC 76-42657. 1977. 17.95 (ISBN 0-19-502189-4). Oxford U Pr.

Mysteries of Marseilles. Emile Zola. Tr. by E. Vizetelly from Fr. viii, 384p. 1976. Repr. of 1895 ed. 21.50 (ISBN 0-86527-280-8). Fertig.

Mysteries of the Deep. Ed. by Joseph J. Thorndike, Jr. LC 80-7804. (Illus.). 352p. 1980. 34.95 (ISBN 0-8281-0407-7, Dist. by Scribner); deluxe ed. 39.95 (ISBN 0-8281-0408-5, Dist. by Scribner). Am Heritage.

Mysteries of the Great Pyramids. Andre Pochan. 1977. pap. 2.25 o.p. (ISBN 0-380-00881-5, 31492). Avon.

Mysteries of the Kingdom: An Exposition of the Parables. Herman Hanko. LC 75-13930. 1975. 8.95 (ISBN 0-8254-2853-X). Kregel.

Mysteries of the Mexican Pyramids. Peter Tompkins. LC 74-15857. (Illus.). 320p. (YA) 1976. 25.00 (ISBN 0-06-014324-X, HarpT). Har-Row.

Mysteries of the Mind. Joann A. Lawless. LC 77-10726. (Great Unsolved Mysteries Ser.). (Illus.). (gr. 4-5). 1977. PLB 9.65 (ISBN 0-8172-1066-0). Raintree Pubs.

Mysteries of the Past. Lionel Casson et al. Ed. by Joseph J. Thorndike, Jr. LC 77-22838. (Illus.). 320p. 1977. 12.95 (ISBN 0-8281-0206-6, Dist. by Scribner); deluxe ed. 39.95 slipcased (ISBN 0-8281-0207-4, Dist. by Scribner). Am Heritage.

Mysteries of Time & Space. Brad Steiger. LC 74-7288. (Illus.). 224p. 1974. 8.95 o.p. (ISBN 0-13-609040-0). P-H.

Mysteries of Udolpho. rev. ed. Ann Radcliffe. Ed. by Bonamy Dobree. (World Classics Paper Ser.). 1980. pap. 5.95x. Oxford U Pr.

Mysterion. Richard Woods. 372p. 1981. 14.95 (ISBN 0-88347-127-2). Thomas More.

Mysterious Affair at Styles. Agatha Christie. 1980. pap. 8.95 (ISBN 0-8161-3105-8, Large Print Bks). G K Hall.

Mysterious Appearance of Agnes. Helen Griffiths. LC 74-21793. (Illus.). 160p. (gr. 7 up). 1975. 8.95 (ISBN 0-8234-0267-3). Holiday.

Mysterious Baba & Her Magic Caravan. Ruth Ainsworth. (Illus.). (gr. k-5). 1980. 8.95 (ISBN 0-233-97200-5). Andre Deutsch.

Mysterious Cloud. Glen J. Hatfield. 1970. pap. 4.00 (ISBN 0-9600216-3-9). Hatfield.

Mysterious Code. (Trixie Belden Mystery Stories Ser.). (gr. 4 up). 1977. PLB 5.52 (ISBN 0-307-61540-5, Golden Pr); pap. 1.25 (ISBN 0-307-21540-7). Western Pub.

Mysterious Detectives: Psychics. Tamara Wilcox. LC 77-14315. (Great Unsolved Mysteries Ser.). (Illus.). (gr. 4-5). 1977. PLB 9.65 (ISBN 0-8172-1061-X). Raintree Pubs.

Mysterious Disappearance of Leon (I Mean Noel) Ellen Raskin. (Illus.). 160p. (gr. 4-7). 1980. pap. 1.95 (ISBN 0-380-51177-0, 51177, Camelot). Avon.

Mysterious Disappearances. Daniel Cohen. LC 75-38352. (Illus.). (gr. 7 up). 1976. 5.95 (ISBN 0-396-07298-4). Dodd.

Mysterious Man. Lyumbomir Levchev. Tr. by Vladimir Phillipov. LC 80-83426. (International Poetry: Vol. 4). 40p. 1981. 10.95 (ISBN 0-8214-0594-2); pap. 6.95 (ISBN 0-8214-0595-0). Ohio U Pr.

Mysterious Marvelous Snowflake. Harvey D. Moore & Patsie S. Moore. LC 80-20996. 128p. (Orig.). 1981. pap. 4.95 (ISBN 0-687-27640-3). Abingdon.

Mysterious Moortown Bridge. Lynn Hall. 64p. 1980. PLB 4.39 (ISBN 0-695-41468-2). Follett.

Mysterious Presence: The Inner Life of Plants. Esther Bubley & Percy Knauth. LC 77-79683. 1976. 9.95 (ISBN 0-911104-98-4); pap. 5.95 (ISBN 0-911104-99-2). Workman Pub.

Mysterious Visitor. (Trixie Belden Mystery Stories Ser.). (gr. 4 up). 1977. PLB 5.52 (ISBN 0-307-61532-4, Golden Pr); pap. 1.25 (ISBN 0-307-21532-6). Western Pub.

Mysterious World of Caves. Ernest Bauer. (International Library). (Illus.). 1978. pap. 4.95 o.p. (ISBN 0-531-02378-8). Watts.

Mysterious World of Caves. Ernst W. Bauer. (International Library). (Illus.). (gr. 7 up). 1971. PLB 6.90 o.p. (ISBN 0-531-02102-5). Watts.

Mysterium Coniunctionis. C. G. Jung. 1977. pap. 9.95 (ISBN 0-691-01816-2). Princeton U Pr.

Mysterium Cosmographicum. Johannes Renchlin. Tr. by Martin Goodman. LC 77-86245. (Bilingual Editions of Classics in Philosophy & Science: Ser. 3). Date not set. 20.00 (ISBN 0-913870-56-0). Abaris Bks.

Mystery! An Illustrated History of Crime & Detective Fiction. Peter Haining. LC 80-6170. 1981. 15.95 (ISBN 0-8128-2805-4). Stein & Day.

Mystery & Art of the Apothecary. C. J. Thompson. LC 78-89294. (Illus.). 1971. Repr. of 1929 ed. 20.00 (ISBN 0-8103-3210-8). Gale.

Mystery & Lore of Apparitions, with Some Account of Ghosts, Spectres, Phantoms & Boggarts in Early Times. C. J. Thompson. LC 70-167225. (Illus.). 331p. 1975. Repr. of 1930 ed. 18.00 (ISBN 0-8103-3981-1). Gale.

Mystery & Lure of Perfume. C. J. Thompson. LC 74-75789. 1969. Repr. of 1927 ed. 15.00 (ISBN 0-8103-3842-4). Gale.

Mystery & Philosophy. Michael B. Foster. LC 79-8721. (Library of Philosophy & Theology). 96p. 1980. Repr. of 1957 ed. lib. bdg. 18.75x (ISBN 0-313-20792-5, FOMP). Greenwood.

Mystery & Romance of Astrology. C. J. Thompson. LC 71-89295. 1969. Repr. of 1929 ed. 18.00 (ISBN 0-8103-3146-2). Gale.

Mystery & Suspense from the Saturday Evening Post. LC 76-41561. 1976. 5.95 (ISBN 0-89387-005-6). Sat Eve Post.

Mystery & the Unconscious: A Study in the Thought of Paul Ricoeur. Walter J. Lowe. LC 76-44865. (ATLA Monograph: No. 9). 1977. 10.00 (ISBN 0-8108-0989-3). Scarecrow.

Mystery at Bob White Cave. (Trixie Belden Mystery Stories Ser.). (gr. 4 up). 1977. PLB 5.52 (ISBN 0-307-61586-3, Golden Pr); pap. 1.25 (ISBN 0-307-21586-5). Western Pub.

Mystery at Dark Wood. Carol B. York. LC 70-175801. (Illus.). 128p. (gr. 4-7). 1972. PLB 5.95 o.p. (ISBN 0-531-02038-X). Watts.

Mystery at Fire Island. Hope Campbell. LC 77-18311. (Illus.). 176p. (gr. 3-7). 1978. 7.95 (ISBN 0-590-07536-5, Four Winds). Schol Bk Serv.

Mystery at Indian Rocks. Ruth N. Moore. LC 80-25803. (Illus.). 192p. (gr. 5-10). 1981. pap. 4.95 (ISBN 0-8361-1944-4). Herald Pr.

Mystery at Keyhole Carnival. Florence P. Heide & Roxanne Heide. Ed. by Caroline Rubin. LC 76-45426. (Spotlight Club Mysteries & Pilot Bks). (Illus.). (gr. 3-8). 1976. 6.95g (ISBN 0-8075-5361-1). A Whitman.

Mystery at Love's Creek. Betty Cavanna. (gr. 7 up). 1965. PLB 7.44 o.p. (ISBN 0-688-31791-X). Morrow.

Mystery at Macadoo Zoo. Florence P. Heide & Sylvia Van Clief. LC 73-7316. (Pilot Bks. - Spotlight Club Mysteries Ser.). (Illus.). 128p. (gr. 3-7). 1973. 6.95g (ISBN 0-8075-5358-1). A Whitman.

Mystery at Mead's Mountain. Kathryn Kenny. (Trixie Belden Mystery Stories). (gr. 4 up). 1978. PLB 5.52 (ISBN 0-307-61593-6, Golden Pr); pap. 1.25 (ISBN 0-307-21593-8). Western Pub.

Mystery at Mouse House. Norma Q. Hare. LC 79-28254. (Mystery Ser.). 48p. (gr. k-3). 1980. PLB 5.58 (ISBN 0-8116-6412-0). Garrard.

Mystery at Old Sturbridge Village. Julia C. Mahon. LC 64-16079. (Pilot Book Ser). (Illus.). (gr. 4-7). 1964. 6.95g (ISBN 0-8075-5360-3). A Whitman.

Mystery at Poor Boy's Folly. Bernard Palmer. LC 80-65058. (Powell Family Ser.). 160p. (Orig.). (gr. 7-10). 1981. pap. 2.25 (ISBN 0-89636-049-0). Accent Bks.

Mystery at Rancho Verde. Nita Clarke. (Illus.). (gr. 1-4). 1981. 6.95 (ISBN 0-933184-13-1); pap. 4.95 (ISBN 0-933184-14-X). Flame Intl.

Mystery at Southport Cinema. Florence P. Heide & Roxanne Heide. Ed. by Kathy Pacini. LC 78-1300. (Spotlight Club Mysteries & Pilot Bks.). (Illus.). (gr. 3-8). 1978. 6.95g (ISBN 0-8075-5363-8). A Whitman.

Mystery at Star Lake. Clark. (gr. 3-5). pap. 1.25 o.p. (ISBN 0-590-11927-3, Schol Pap). Schol Bk Serv.

Mystery at the Summit of the Himalayas. Michel Garson. 1981. 8.95 (ISBN 0-8062-1625-5). Carlton.

Mystery at the Tree House. Ann Bradford & Kal Gezi. LC 80-15654. (Maple Street Five Ser.). (Illus.). 32p. (gr. k-4). 1980. PLB 5.50 (ISBN 0-89565-148-3). Childs World.

Mystery at the Treehouse. Ann Bradford & Kal Gezi. (Maple Street Five Ser.). (Illus.). 1980. 7.95g (ISBN 0-516-06494-0). Childrens.

Mystery Behind the Wall. Gertrude C. Warner. LC 72-13356. (Boxcar Children Mysteries-Pilot Bk.). (Illus.). 128p. (gr. 3-7). 1973. 6.95g (ISBN 0-8075-5364-6). A Whitman.

Mystery Dramas, 4 vols. in 1. Rudolf Steiner. 1973. pap. 16.50 (ISBN 0-919924-08-5). Anthroposophic.

Mystery Flowers, No. 61. Grace L. Hill. 256p. 1981. pap. 2.25 (ISBN 0-553-14655-6). Bantam.

Mystery for Meg. Ladd. 1977. pap. 3.50 (ISBN 0-89272-033-6). Down East.

Mystery in Arizona. (Trixie Belden Mystery Stories Ser.). (gr. 4 up). 1977. PLB 5.52 (ISBN 0-307-61533-2, Golden Pr); pap. 1.25 (ISBN 0-307-21533-4). Western Pub.

Mystery in Arles. Mabel E. Allan. LC 64-23321. (gr. 7 up). 1964. 5.95 (ISBN 0-8149-0255-3). Vanguard.

Mystery in Manhattan. Mabel E. Allan. LC 68-28342. (Illus.). (gr. 6 up). 1968. 5.95 (ISBN 0-8149-0252-9). Vanguard.

Mystery in Peru: The Lines of Nazca. David McMullen. LC 77-10456. (Great Unsolved Mysteries Ser.). (Illus.). (gr. 4-5). 1977. PLB 9.65 (ISBN 0-8172-1058-X). Raintree Pubs.

Mystery in Rome. Mabel E. Allan. LC 72-90477. (gr. 7 up). 1975. 5.95 (ISBN 0-8149-0726-1). Vanguard.

Mystery in the Desert. Jack Woolgar. (gr. 6-8). 1967. 4.25 o.p. (ISBN 0-8313-0107-4); PLB 6.19 (ISBN 0-685-13778-3). Lantern.

Mystery in the Flooded Museum. Margaret G. Clark. LC 77-16860. (Illus.). (gr. 5 up). 1978. 5.95 (ISBN 0-396-07550-9). Dodd.

Mystery in the Museum. Betty Cavanna. 240p. (gr. 7 up). 1972. PLB 7.92 (ISBN 0-688-31775-8). Morrow.

Mystery in the Old Red Barn. Helen F. Orton. LC 52-7461. (Illus.). (gr. 4-6). 1952. 5.95 o.p. (ISBN 0-397-30217-7). Lippincott.

Mystery in the Ravine. Carol Farley. 1976. pap. 1.25 (ISBN 0-380-00745-2, 30171, Camelot). Avon.

Mystery in the Sand. Gertrude C. Warner. LC 70-165823. (Boxcar Children Mysteries-Pilot Bk.). (Illus.). 128p. (gr. 3-7). 1971. 6.95g (ISBN 0-8075-5373-5). A Whitman.

Mystery in the Square Tower. Elizabeth Honness. LC 57-10325. (Illus.). (gr. 4-6). 1957. 8.95 (ISBN 0-397-30382-3). Lippincott.

Mystery in Wales. Mabel E. Allan. LC 79-89664. (gr. 7 up). 1970. 5.95 (ISBN 0-8149-0664-8). Vanguard.

Mystery in Williamsburg. (Meg Bks.). (gr. 3 up). 1978. pap. 1.25 (ISBN 0-307-21547-4, Golden Pr). Western Pub.

Mystery Mammals of the Ice Age-Great Lakes Region. J. Allan Holman & Dirk Gringhuis. LC 72-90919. (Illus.). 45p. (Orig.). (gr. 5-8). 1972. pap. 1.75 (ISBN 0-910726-74-4). Hillsdale Educ.

Mystery of Agatha Christie. Gwen Robyns. LC 77-76259. 1978. 8.95 o.p. (ISBN 0-385-12623-9). Doubleday.

Mystery of Aloha House. Lee Roddy. (Chime Gothic 202 Ser.). 1981. pap. 2.50 (ISBN 0-89191-293-2). Cook.

Mystery of Black Magic Cave. (Meg Bks.). (gr. 3 up). 1978. pap. 1.25 (ISBN 0-307-21506-7, Golden Pr). Western Pub.

Mystery of Cloomber. A Conan Doyle. LC 80-65206. (Conan Doyle Centennial Ser.). (Illus.). 195p. 1980. 11.95 (ISBN 0-934468-41-9). Gaslight.

Mystery of Commitment. Edward J. O'Toole. LC 68-55034. 1969. 3.95 o.p. (ISBN 0-8189-0098-9). Alba.

Mystery of Death. Ladislaus Boros. 216p. 1973. pap. 3.95 (ISBN 0-8164-9157-7). Crossroad NY.

Mystery of DNA Replication. Karl G. Lark. (Universsity of Utah Frederick William Reynolds Lecture Ser.: No. 43). 1980. 4.00 (ISBN 0-87480-179-6). U of Utah Pr.

Mystery of Dolphin Inlet. James Holding. (gr. 5-8). 1968. 4.95g o.s.i. (ISBN 0-02-744190-3). Macmillan.

Mystery of Edwin Drood. Charles Dickens & Leon Garfield. (Illus.). 1981. 12.95 (ISBN 0-394-51918-3). Pantheon.

Mystery of Existence: An Essay in Philosophical Cosmology. Milton K. Munitz. LC 65-14242. 270p. 1974. 13.00x (ISBN 0-8147-5419-8). NYU Pr.

Mystery of Hamlet, King of Denmark. Percy Mackaye. 1976. ltd. ed. 125.00 (ISBN 0-87027-177-6); pap. 9.95 (ISBN 0-87027-176-8). Wheelwright.

Mystery of Israel: Has God Cast Away His People? 3rd ed. H. J. Ellison. 1976. pap. 3.50 (ISBN 0-85364-169-2). Attic Pr.

Mystery of Love: How the Science of Sexual Attraction Can Work for You. Glenn Wilson & David Nias. 1980. pap. cancelled (ISBN 0-553-10876-X). Bantam.

Mystery of Matter. Ed. by Louise B. Young. 1965. pap. 9.95x (ISBN 0-19-501265-8). Oxford U Pr.

Mystery of Migration. Ed. by Robin Baker. LC 80-16839. (Illus.). 256p. 1981. 29.95 (ISBN 0-670-50286-3). Viking Pr.

Mystery of Mortimore Strange. Arthur W. Marchmont. 1976. lib. bdg. 16.70x (ISBN 0-89968-068-2). Lightyear.

Mystery of Music. Walter E. Koons. 1977. 7.50 o.p. (ISBN 0-533-02422-6). Vantage.

Mystery of Orcival. Emile Gaboriau. 320p. 1977. Repr. of 1900 ed. lib. bdg. 14.25x (ISBN 0-89968-183-2). Lightyear.

Mystery of Ovid's Exile. John C. Thibault. 1964. 15.75x (ISBN 0-520-01265-8). U of Cal Pr.

Mystery of Plum Park Pony. Lynn Hall. LC 79-28125. (Mystery Ser.). 64p. (gr. 3). 1980. PLB 5.67 (ISBN 0-8116-6414-7). Garrard.

Mystery of Preaching. James Black. 1978. pap. 4.95 (ISBN 0-310-36991-6). Zondervan.

Mystery of Providence. John Flavel. 1976. pap. 2.45 (ISBN 0-85151-104-X). Banner of Truth.

Mystery of Stonehenge. Nancy Lyon. LC 77-10044. (Great Unsolved Mysteries Ser.). (Illus.). (gr. 4-5). 1977. PLB 9.65 (ISBN 0-8172-1049-0). Raintree Pubs.
Mystery of Super People: Will They Replace Us? Jeanne Bendick. LC 79-14486. (Illus.). (gr. 7 up). 1980. 7.95 (ISBN 0-07-004503-8). McGraw.
Mystery of the Bewitched Bookmobile. Florence P. Heide & Roxanne Heide. LC 75-6763. (Pilot Bks. - Spotlight Club Mysteries Ser.). (gr. 3-8). 1975. 6.95g (ISBN 0-8075-5375-1). A Whitman.
Mystery of the Blinking Eye. (Trixie Belden Mystery Stories Ser.). (gr. 4 up). 1977. PLB 5.52 (ISBN 0-307-61587-1, Golden Pr); pap. 1.25 (ISBN 0-307-21587-3). Western Pub.
Mystery of the Blue Champ. Larry Sutton. (Carolrhoda Mini-Mysteries Ser.). (Illus.). 32p. (gr. 1-4). 1981. PLB 4.95 (ISBN 0-87614-137-8). Carolrhoda Bks.
Mystery of the Castaway Children. Kathryn Kenny. (Trixie Belden Mystery Stories Ser.). (gr. 4 up). 1978. PLB 5.52 (ISBN 0-307-61592-8, Golden Pr); pap. 1.25 (ISBN 0-307-21592-X). Western Pub.
Mystery of the Deadly Double. William Arden. LC 79-29638. (Alfred Hitchcock & the Three Investigators Ser.). 160p. (gr. 4-7). 1981. pap. 1.95 (ISBN 0-394-84491-2). Random.
Mystery of the Emerald Buddha. Betty Cavanna. LC 76-21826. (gr. 7 up). 1976. 8.25 (ISBN 0-688-22086-X); PLB 7.92 (ISBN 0-688-32086-4). Morrow.
Mystery of the Emeralds. (Trixie Belden Mystery Stories Ser.). (gr. 4 up). 1977. PLB 5.52 (ISBN 0-307-61522-7, Golden Pr); pap. 1.25 (ISBN 0-307-21522-9). Western Pub.
Mystery of the Empty House. Dorothy Martin. (Vickie Ser.). 128p. (Orig.). (gr. 6-8). Date not set. pap. 1.95 (ISBN 0-8024-5703-7). Moody.
Mystery of the Fat Cat. Frank Bonham. (Illus.). (gr. 5-9). 1968. PLB 7.95 o.p. (ISBN 0-525-35588-X). Dutton.
Mystery of the Flooded Mine. Willard B. Manus. LC 64-13844. (gr. 6-9). 1964. 5.95 o.p. (ISBN 0-385-03991-3). Doubleday.
Mystery of the Fog Man. Carol Farley. 1974. pap. 1.75 (ISBN 0-380-00102-0, 53280, Camelot). Avon.
Mystery of the Forgotten Island. Florence P. Heide & Roxanne Heide. Ed. by Kathleen Tucker. LC 79-18367. (Spotlight Club Mysteries & Pilot Bks.). (Illus.). (gr. 3-8). 1980. 6.95g (ISBN 0-8075-5376-X). A Whitman.
Mystery of the Gingerbread House. Wylly F. St. John. (Illus.). (YA) (gr. 9-12). 1977. pap. 1.95 (ISBN 0-380-01731-8, 45716, Camelot). Avon.
Mystery of the Hidden Book. Helen F. Orton. (Illus.). (gr. 4-6). 1949. 8.95 o.p. (ISBN 0-397-30245-2). Lippincott.
Mystery of the Invisible Dog. M. V. Carey. LC 79-27778. (Alfred Hitchcock & the Three Investigators Ser.). 160p. (gr. 4-7). 1981. pap. 1.95 (ISBN 0-394-84492-0). Random.
Mystery of the Jade Earring. Dorothy Martin. (Vickie Ser.). (Orig.). 1980. pap. 1.50 (ISBN 0-8024-5702-9). Moody.
Mystery of the Late News Report. Larry Sutton. (Carolrhoda Mini-Mysteries Ser.). (Illus.). 32p. (gr. 1-4). 1981. PLB 4.95 (ISBN 0-87614-136-X). Carolrhoda Bks.
Mystery of the Laughing Shadow. Arden. (gr. 5-6). Date not set. pap. cancelled (ISBN 0-590-30053-9, Schol Pap). Schol Bk Serv.
Mystery of the Lonely Lantern. Florence P. Heide & Roxanne Heide. Ed. by Caroline Rubin. LC 76-28537. (Spotlight Club Mysteries-Pilot Bks). (Illus.). 128p. 1976. 6.95g (ISBN 0-8075-5377-8). A Whitman.
Mystery of the Lost Treasure. Ruth N. Moore. LC 78-11748. (Illus.). (gr. 4-8). 1978. 4.95 o.p. (ISBN 0-8361-1870-7); pap. 3.50 (ISBN 0-8361-1871-5). Herald Pr.
Mystery of the McGilley Mansion. Florence Laughlin. (Illus.). (gr. 4-6). 1963. 6.95 (ISBN 0-688-41398-6). Lothrop.
Mystery of the Magic Circle. M. V. Carey. LC 79-27657. (Alfred Hitchcock & the Three Investigators Ser.). 160p. (gr. 4-7). 1981. pap. 1.95 (ISBN 0-394-84490-4). Random.
Mystery of the Maya, No. 11. Raymond A. Montgomery. 128p. (Orig.). 1981. pap. 1.50 (ISBN 0-553-14600-9). Bantam.
Mystery of the Maya Jade. Elizabeth Honness. LC 75-141454. 160p. (gr. 4-6). 1971. 8.95 (ISBN 0-397-31358-6). Lippincott.
Mystery of the Melting Snowman. Florence P. Heide & Roxanne Heide. LC 74-16333. (Spotlight Club Mysteries & Pilot Books Ser.). (Illus.). 128p. (gr. 3-8). 1974. 6.95g (ISBN 0-8075-5378-6). A Whitman.
Mystery of the Midnight Message. Florence P. Heide & Roxanne Heide. Ed. by Caroline Rubin. LC 77-14382. (Spotlight Club Mysteries & Pilot Books Ser.). (Illus.). (gr. 3-8). 1977. 6.95g (ISBN 0-8075-5381-6). A Whitman.
Mystery of the Missing Bracelets. Dorothy Martin. (gr. 4-7). 1980. pap. 1.50 (ISBN 0-8024-5701-0). Moody.
Mystery of the Missing Dogs. Ann Bradford & Kal Gezi. (Maple Street Five Ser.). (Illus.). 1980. 7.95g (ISBN 0-516-06492-4). Childrens.
Mystery of the Missing Heiress. (Trixie Belden Mystery Stories Ser.). (gr. 4 up). 1977. PLB 5.52 (ISBN 0-307-61542-1, Golden Pr); pap. 1.95 (ISBN 0-307-21542-3). Western Pub.
Mystery of the Missing Suitcase. Florence P. Heide & Sylvia Van Clief. LC 72-83683. (Pilot Bks. - Spotlight Club Mysteries Ser.). (Illus.). 128p. (gr. 3-8). 1972. 6.95g (ISBN 0-8075-5382-4). A Whitman.
Mystery of the Missing Totem Pole. Betty Swinford. 128p. (Orig.). (gr. 6-8). 1981. pap. 1.95 (ISBN 0-8024-5676-6). Moody.
Mystery of the Mummy Mask. Florence P. Heide & Roxanne Heide. Ed. by Kathy Pacini. LC 78-31728. (Spotlight Club Mysteries & Pilot Bks.). (Illus.). (gr. 3-8). 1979. 6.95g (ISBN 0-8075-5384-0). A Whitman.
Mystery of the Musical Umbrella. Friedrick Feld. (Illus.). (gr. 2-4). 1962. PLB 3.99 o.p. (ISBN 0-394-90124-X, BYR). Random.
Mystery of the Other Girl. Wylly F. St. John. 1977. pap. 1.50 (ISBN 0-380-01926-4, 48207, Camelot). Avon.
Mystery of the Phantom Grasshopper. (Trixie Belden Mystery Stories Ser.). (gr. 4 up). 1977. PLB 5.52 (ISBN 0-307-61589-8, Golden Pr); pap. 1.25 (ISBN 0-307-21589-X). Western Pub.
Mystery of the Pirate's Ghost. Elizabeth Honness. LC 66-10035. (Illus.). (gr. 4-6). 1966. 8.95 (ISBN 0-397-30899-X). Lippincott.
Mystery of the Plumed Serpent. Barbara Brenner. LC 80-17316. (Capers Ser.). (Illus.). 128p. (gr. 3-6). 1981. PLB 4.99 (ISBN 0-394-94531-X); pap. 1.95 (ISBN 0-394-84531-5). Knopf.
Mystery of the Screaming Clock. Arthur. (gr. 5-6). Date not set. pap. cancelled (ISBN 0-590-30330-9, Schol Pap). Schol Bk Serv.
Mystery of the Silver Tag. Florence P. Heide & Sylvia Van Clief. LC 75-188429. (Pilot Bks. - Spotlight Club Mysteries Ser.). (Illus.). 128p. (gr. 3-7). 1972. 6.95g (ISBN 0-8075-5387-5). A Whitman.
Mystery of the Singing Serpent. LC 80-18947. (Alfred Hitchcock & the Three Investigators). 160p. (gr. 4-7). 1981. pap. 1.95 (ISBN 0-394-84678-8). Random.
Mystery of the Spider Doll. Carol B. York. LC 72-6073. (Illus.). 96p. (gr. 4-6). 1973. PLB 5.88 o.p. (ISBN 0-531-02601-9). Watts.
Mystery of the Uninvited Guest. (Trixie Belden Mystery Stories Ser.). (gr. 4 up). 1977. PLB 5.52 (ISBN 0-307-61588-X, Golden Pr); pap. 1.25 (ISBN 0-307-21588-1). Western Pub.
Mystery of the Vanishing Visitor. Florence P. Heide & Roxanne Heide. Ed. by Caroline Rubin. LC 75-33634. (Pilot Books-Spotlight Club Mysteries Ser.). (Illus.). 128p. (gr. 3-8). 1975. 6.95g (ISBN 0-8075-5388-3). A Whitman.
Mystery of the Velvet Gown. Julie Campbell & Katherine Kenny. (Trixie Belden Mystery Ser.). 236p. (gr. 4-6). 1980. PLB 5.52 (ISBN 0-307-61550-2, Golden Pr); pap. 1.25 (ISBN 0-307-21550-4). Western Pub.
Mystery of the Wax Museum. Ed. by Tino Balio. LC 78-53296. (Wisconsin-Warner Bros. Screenplay Ser.). (Illus.). 1979. 15.00 (ISBN 0-299-07670-9); pap. 5.95 (ISBN 0-299-07674-1). U of Wis Pr.
Mystery of the Wheat Pirates. Bette W. Widney. LC 65-17375. (gr. 4 up). 1968. 5.95 (ISBN 0-8149-0437-8). Vanguard.
Mystery of the Whispering Voice. Florence P. Heide & Sylvia Van Clief. LC 74-8511. (Pilot Bks. - Spotlight Club Mysteries Ser.). (Illus.). 128p. (gr. 3-7). 1974. 6.95g (ISBN 0-8075-5389-1). A Whitman.
Mystery of the Yellow Room. Gaston Leroux. lib. bdg. 13.95x (ISBN 0-89966-141-6). Buccaneer Bks.
Mystery of Wealth: Political Economy, Its Development & Impact on World Events. John Hutton. LC 78-13743. 1979. 24.95 (ISBN 0-470-26515-9). Halsted Pr.
Mystery off Glen Road. (Trixie Belden Mystery Stories Ser.). (gr. 4 up). 1977. PLB 5.52 (ISBN 0-307-61534-0, Golden Pr); pap. 1.25 (ISBN 0-307-21534-2). Western Pub.
Mystery off Old Telegraph Road. Kathryn Kenny. (Trixie Belden Mystery Stories Ser.). (gr. 4 up). 1978. PLB 5.52 (ISBN 0-307-61591-X, Golden Pr); pap. 1.25 (ISBN 0-307-21591-1). Western Pub.
Mystery on Cobbett's Island. (Trixie Belden Mystery Stories Ser.). (gr. 4 up). 1977. PLB 5.52 (ISBN 0-307-61521-9, Golden Pr); pap. 1.25 (ISBN 0-307-21521-0). Western Pub.
Mystery on the Fourteenth Floor. Dorothy Martin. 128p. (Orig.). (gr. 6-9). 1980. pap. 1.50 (ISBN 0-8024-5700-2). Moody.
Mystery on the Mississippi. (Trixie Belden Mystery Stories Ser.). (gr. 4 up). 1977. PLB 5.52 (ISBN 0-307-61523-5, Golden Pr); pap. 1.25 (ISBN 0-307-21523-7). Western Pub.
Mystery Pony. Primrose Cumming. LC 57-11520. (Illus.). (gr. 7 up). 1957. 8.95 (ISBN 0-87599-024-X). S G Phillips.
Mystery Raider. Leslie Erenwein. 1975. pap. 0.95 o.p. (ISBN 0-685-54124-X, LB297NK, Leisure Bks). Nordon Pubns.
Mystery Ranch. Max Brand. 1976. pap. 1.75 (ISBN 0-446-94102-6). Warner Bks.
Mystery Ranch. Gertrude C. Warner. LC 58-9953. (Boxcar Children Mysteries-Pilot Bk.). (Illus.). 128p. (gr. 3-7). 1958. 6.95g (ISBN 0-8075-5390-5). A Whitman.
Mystery Train: Images of America in Rock 'n' Roll Music. Greil Marcus. 1976. pap. 5.50 (ISBN 0-525-47422-6). Dutton.
Mystery, Value & Awareness: Aids for Understanding Religions of the World. Wm. C. Brown Education Division Staff. (To Live Is Christ Ser.). 28p. (Orig.). 1979. wkbk. 10.95 (ISBN 0-697-01736-2). Wm C Brown.
Mystery, Value, & Awareness: Spirit Masters for Religions of the World. Religious Education Staff. (To Live Is Christ Ser.). 1979. 10.95 (ISBN 0-697-01730-3). Wm C Brown.
Mystic As a Force for Change. rev. ed. Sisirkumar Ghose. LC 80-53954. 144p. 1980. pap. 4.75 (ISBN 0-8356-0547-7, Quest). Theos Pub Hse.
Mystic Experience & Other Essays, 2 vols. Claire Macfarlane. 460p. 1981. Set. 12.95 (ISBN 0-936632-07-0); Vol. 1. 6.50 (ISBN 0-936632-08-9); Vol. 2. 6.50 (ISBN 0-936632-09-7). Mann Pubs.
Mystic in the Theatre: Eleonora Duse. Eva Le Gallienne. LC 72-11975. (Arcturus Books Paperbacks). 189p. 1973. pap. 5.45 (ISBN 0-8093-0631-X). S Ill U Pr.
Mystic Island. Renate Chapman. 1980. 5.95 (ISBN 0-686-59793-1, Avalon). Bouregy.
Mystic Journey. John W. Groff. 1980. 1.45 (ISBN 0-686-28785-1). Forward Movement.
Mystic Mandrake. C. J. Thompson. LC 74-19199. (Illus.). 253p. 1975. Repr. of 1934 ed. 20.00 (ISBN 0-8103-4138-7). Gale.
Mystic Masseur. V. S. Naipaul. 1977. pap. 2.95 (ISBN 0-14-002156-6). Penguin.
Mystic of Liberation: A Portrait of Bishop Pedro Casaldaliga of Brazil. Teofilo Cabestrero. Tr. by Donald D. Walsh. LC 80-25402. (Illus.). 176p. (Orig.). 1981. pap. 7.95 (ISBN 0-88344-324-4). Orbis Bks.
Mystic Path to Cosmic Power. Vernon Howard. 1969. pap. 2.50 (ISBN 0-446-91831-8). Warner Bks.
Mystic Rose: A Study of Primitive Marriage & of Primitive Thought in Its Bearing on Marriage, 2 Vols. rev. & enl. ed. Ernest Crawley. Ed. by Theodore Besterman. LC 72-164193. 1971. Repr. of 1927 ed. 28.00 (ISBN 0-8103-3781-9). Gale.
Mystic Spiral: Journey of the Soul. Jill Purce. (Art & Imagination Ser.). (Illus.). 128p. 1980. pap. 8.95 (ISBN 0-500-81005-2). Thames Hudson.
Mystic: The Story of a Small New England Seaport. Carl C. Cutler. (Illus.). 56p. 1980. pap. 7.00 (ISBN 0-913372-14-5). Mystic Seaport.
Mystic Warriors of the Plains. Thomas E. Mails. LC 72-76191. 608p. 1972. 35.00 (ISBN 0-385-04741-X). Doubleday.
Mystical & Political Dimension of the Christian Faith. Claude Geffre. (Concilium Ser.: Religion in the Seventies: Vol. 96). pap. 4.95 (ISBN 0-8164-2580-9). Crossroad NY.
Mystical Beast. Alison Farthing. (Illus.). (gr. 2-5). 1978. 6.95 (ISBN 0-8038-4707-6). Hastings.
Mystical Element in Heidegger's Thought. John D Caputo. LC 77-92251. xvi, 292p. 1978. 18.00x (ISBN 0-8214-0372-9). Ohio U Pr.
Mystical Element in the Metaphysical Poets of the Seventeenth Century. Itrat-Husain. LC 66-23522. 1948. 12.00x (ISBN 0-8196-0177-2). Biblo.
Mystical Lady. Cumore B. Denby. 80p. 1981. 5.95 (ISBN 0-87881-095-1). Mojave Bks.
Mystical Meaning of Jesus the Christ: Significant Episodes in the Life of the Master. Helen Brungardt. 4.00 (ISBN 0-686-69472-4). Red Earth.
Mystical Poems of Rumi. Jalal A. Rumi. Tr. by A. J. Arberry from Persian. LC 68-29935. vi, 202p. 1974. 12.50x o.s.i. (ISBN 0-226-73150-2); pap. 3.95 (ISBN 0-226-73151-0, P584, Phoen). U of Chicago Pr.
Mystical Power of Pyramid Astrology. Anthony Norvell. LC 78-18405. 1978. 9.95 (ISBN 0-8119-0289-7). Fell.
Mystical Presence & Other Writings on the Eucharist. abr. ed. John W. Nevin. Ed. by Bard Thompson & George M. Bricker. LC 66-16193. 1966. 9.95 (ISBN 0-8298-0093-X). Pilgrim NY.
Mystical Qabalah. Dion Fortune. 5.95 (ISBN 0-685-22174-1). Weiser.
Mystical Reason. William Earle. LC 79-92079. 164p. 1980. pap. 6.95 (ISBN 0-89526-677-6). Regnery-Gateway.
Mystical Vision of Existence in Islam Classical. Gerhard Boewering. (Studien zur Sprache, Geschichte und Kultur desislamischen Orients, Beihefte zur "der Islam"). 296p. 1979. text ed. 79.00x (ISBN 3-11-007546-6). De Gruyter.
Mysticism & Logic & Other Essays. 2nd ed. Bertrand Russell. 1980. pap. 5.95x. B&N.
Mysticism & Philosophical Analysis. Steven T. Katz. 1978. 15.95 (ISBN 0-19-520010-1); pap. 4.95 (ISBN 0-19-520011-X, GB 538). Oxford U Pr.
Mysticism & Religion. Robert S. Ellwood, Jr. & James W. Bashford. 1980. text ed. 10.95 (ISBN 0-13-608810-4); pap. text ed. 7.95 (ISBN 0-13-608802-3). P-H.
Mysticism & the New Physics. Michael Talbot. 224p. (Orig.). 1981. pap. 3.50 (ISBN 0-553-11908-7). Bantam.
Mysticism & Zen: An Introduction. Clemens J. Caraboolad. LC 77-18492. 1978. pap. text ed. 7.50x (ISBN 0-8191-0422-1). U Pr of Amer.
Mysticism at the Dawn of the Modern. Rudolf Steiner. (Spiritual Science Library). 256p. 1980. 12.00x (ISBN 0-8334-0753-8); pap. 6.95 (ISBN 0-8334-1786-X). Steinerbks.
Mysticism East & West. Rudolph Otto. 1970. pap. 2.95 o.s.i. (ISBN 0-02-088230-0, Collier). Macmillan.
Mysticism in the Rgveda. Trimbak G. Mainkar. 1961. text ed. 3.25x (ISBN 0-391-02012-9). Humanities.
Mysticism in the World's Religions. Geoffrey Parrinder. 1977. pap. text ed. 4.95 (ISBN 0-19-502185-1, 497, GB). Oxford U Pr.
Mysticism in World Religion. Sidney Spencer. 8.00 (ISBN 0-8446-0927-7). Peter Smith.
Mysticism: Its Meaning & Message. Georgia Harkness. LC 72-10070. 192p. 1976. pap. 3.95 (ISBN 0-687-27667-5). Abingdon.
Mysticism of Paul the Apostle. Albert Schweitzer. LC 68-28707. 1968. pap. 5.95 (ISBN 0-8164-2049-1, SP51). Crossroad NY.
Mysticism of Sound. Inayat Khan. (Sufi Message of Hazrat Inayat Khan Ser.: Vol. 2). 1979. 6.95 (ISBN 90-6077-569-4, Pub. by Servire BV Netherlands). Hunter Hse.
Mysticism, Science & Revelation. rev. ed. Glenn Shook. 1953. 6.75 o.s.i. (ISBN 0-85398-015-2, 7-31-83); pap. 3.50 o.s.i. (ISBN 0-85398-053-5, 7-31-84). Baha'i.
Mystics & Medics: A Comparison of Mystical & Psychotherapeutic Encounters. Ed. by Reuven P. Bulka. 120p. 1979. pap. 7.95 (ISBN 0-87705-377-4). Human Sci Pr.
Mystics & Men of Miracles in India. Mayah Balse. (Illus.). 1976. 4.50 (ISBN 0-913244-10-4). Hapi Pr.
Mystics & Society. S. K. Ghose. 5.00x (ISBN 0-210-98132-6). Asia.
Mystics of Islam. R. A. Nicholson. 1975. pap. 6.50 (ISBN 0-7100-8015-8). Routledge & Kegan.
Myth, Allegory, & Gospel. Ed. by John W. Montgomery. LC 74-1358. Orig. Title: Names & Titles of Christ. 160p. 1974. pap. 4.95 (ISBN 0-87123-358-4, 210358). Bethany Fell.
Myth & History in Revelation: The Book of Revelation. John M. Court. LC 79-16586. 1980. 16.50 (ISBN 0-8042-0346-6). John Knox.
Myth & Literature. William Righter. (Concepts of Literature Ser.). 1975. 12.50x (ISBN 0-7100-8137-5). Routledge & Kegan.
Myth & Literature: Contemporary Theory & Practice. Ed. by John B. Vickery. LC 65-11563. 1969. pap. 4.50x (ISBN 0-8032-5208-0, BB 500, Bison). U of Nebr Pr.
Myth & Method: Modern Theories of Fiction. Ed. by James E. Miller, Jr. LC 60-12941. 1960. pap. 2.45x (ISBN 0-8032-5134-3, BB 105, Bison). U of Nebr Pr.
Myth & Philosophy. Ed. by George F. McLean. LC 72-184483. (Proceedings of the American Catholic Philosophical Association: Vol. 45). 1971. pap. 8.00 (ISBN 0-918090-05-9). Am Cath Philo.
Myth & Reality: A Reader in Education. 2nd ed. Glenn Smith & Charles R. Kniker. 500p. 1975. pap. text ed. 7.95x o.p. (ISBN 0-205-04777-7, 2247771). Allyn.
Myth & Reality in Late Eighteenth-Century British Politics & Other Papers. Ian R. Christie. LC 73-104105. 1970. 23.50x (ISBN 0-520-01673-4). U of Cal Pr.
Myth & Symbol: Critical Approaches & Applications. Northrop Frye et al. Ed. by Bernice Slote. LC 63-9960. 1963. pap. 4.25x (ISBN 0-8032-5065-7, BB 141, Bison). U of Nebr Pr.
Myth & the American Experience, Vol. 1. 2nd ed. Nicholas Cords & Patrick Gerster. 1978. pap. text ed. 7.95x (ISBN 0-02-471880-7). Macmillan.

Myth & the Crisis of Historical Consciousness. Lee Gibbs & Taylor Stevenson. LC 75-33049. (American Academy of Religion. Section Papers). 1975. pap. 7.50 (ISBN 0-89130-053-8, 010915). Scholars Pr Ca.

Myth Conceptions. Robert Asprin. Ed. by Polly Freas & Kelly Freas. LC 79-9216. (Illus.). 1980. pap. 4.95 (ISBN 0-915442-94-9, Starblaze). Donning Co.

Myth, Faith & Hermeneutics: Toward Cross-Cultural Religious Understanding. Raimundo Panikkar. LC 77-99306. 1980. 19.95 (ISBN 0-8091-0232-3). Paulist Pr.

Myth, History & Faith: The Re-Mythologizing of Christianity. Morton Kelsey. LC 73-94216. 1974. pap. 4.95 (ISBN 0-8091-1827-0). Paulist Pr.

Myth, Honor, and History in the Secular Drama of Don Pedro Calderon. Robert Ter Horst. LC 80-5183. (Studies in Romance Languages: No. 25). 1981. price not set (ISBN 0-8131-1440-3). U Pr of Ky.

Myth in a Metal Mirror. Tilottama Rajan. (Writers Workshop Redbird Ser.). 1975. 8.00 (ISBN 0-88253-580-3); pap. text ed. 4.80 (ISBN 0-88253-579-X). Ind-US Inc.

Myth in American History. Patrick Gerster & Nicholas Cords. 1977. pap. text ed. 7.95x (ISBN 0-02-473290-7). Macmillan.

Myth in the Poetry of Ted Hughes. Stuart Hirschberg. 1980. 22.50x. B&N.

Myth: Its Meaning & Functions in Ancient & Other Cultures. G. S. Kirk. (Sather Classical Lectures: No. 40). 1970. 17.50x (ISBN 0-520-01651-3); pap. 6.95x (ISBN 0-520-02389-7). U of Cal Pr.

Myth, Literature & the African World. W. Soyinka. LC 75-38184. 180p. 1976. 27.50 (ISBN 0-521-21190-5); pap. 8.95 (ISBN 0-521-29394-4). Cambridge U Pr.

Myth of Analysis. James Hillman. 1978. pap. 5.95 (ISBN 0-06-090600-6, CN 600, CN). Har-Row.

Myth of Christian Beginnings. Robert L. Wilken. LC 80-11884. 218p. 1980. pap. text ed. 4.95 (ISBN 0-268-01348-9). U of Notre Dame Pr.

Myth of Felt. Leonardo Olschki. 1949. 12.95x (ISBN 0-520-00974-6). U of Cal Pr.

Myth of Marginality: Urban Poeverty & Politics in Rio De Janeiro. Janice E. Perlman. LC 73-87246. 250p. 1976. 22.75x (ISBN 0-520-02596-2); pap. 6.95x (ISBN 0-520-03952-1). U of Cal Pr.

Myth of Mass Culture. A. Swingewood. LC 77-4699. 1977. text ed. 18.25x (ISBN 0-391-00699-1); pap. text ed. 7.75x (ISBN 0-391-00724-6). Humanities.

Myth of Mormon Inspiration. Brodie Crouch. 6.50 (ISBN 0-89315-158-0). Lambert Bk.

Myth of Social Cost. Steven Cheung. LC 80-26083. (Cato Papers: No. 16). 150p. 1980. pap. 5.00 (ISBN 0-932790-21-6). Cato Inst.

Myth of the Britannica. Harvey Einbinder. LC 63-16997. Repr. of 1964 ed. 15.50 (ISBN 0-384-14050-5). Johnson Repr.

Myth of the Deprived Child: Poor Children's Intellect & Education. Herbert Ginsburg. LC 76-166042. 1972. pap. text ed. 10.95 (ISBN 0-13-609149-0). P-H.

Myth of the Farm Family: Agribusiness Dominance of U.S. Agriculture. Ingolf Vogeler. (Westview Special Study Ser.). 300p. 1981. lib. bdg. 22.00x (ISBN 0-89158-910-4). Westview.

Myth of the Golden Age in the Renaissance. Harry Levin. 167p. 1972. pap. 4.95 (ISBN 0-19-501602-5, GB). Oxford U Pr.

Myth of the Golden Years: A Socio-Environmental Theory of Aging. Jaber F. Gubrium. (Illus.). 244p. 1973. 14.75 (ISBN 0-398-02703-X); pap. 9.75 (ISBN 0-398-02757-9). C C Thomas.

Myth of the Jewish Race. Raphael Patai & Jennifer Wing. (Encore Edition). 1975. 6.95 o.p. (ISBN 0-684-15435-8, ScribT). Scribner.

Myth of the Lokamanya: Tilak & Mass Politics in Maharashtra. Richard I. Cashman. LC 72-97734. 1975. 20.00x (ISBN 0-520-02407-9). U of Cal Pr.

Myth of the Machine, 2 vols. Lewis Mumford. Incl. Vol. 1. Technics & Human Development. LC 67-16088. 1971. Repr. of 1967 ed. pap. 5.95 (ISBN 0-15-662341-2, HB208); Vol. 2. Pentagon of Power. LC 73-13626. 1974. Repr. of 1970 ed. pap. 5.95 (ISBN 0-15-671610-0, HB274). (Illus., Harv). HarBraceJ.

Myth of the Magus. E. M. Butler. LC 78-73950. 1979. 36.00 (ISBN 0-521-22564-7); pap. 8.95 (ISBN 0-521-29554-8). Cambridge U Pr.

Myth of the OPEC Cartel: The Role of Saudi Arabia. Ali D. Johany. 191p. 1981. 34.00 (ISBN 0-471-27864-5, Pub. by Wiley-Interscience). Wiley.

Myth of Venice & Dutch Republican Thought in the Seventeenth Century. Eco O. Mulier & G. Haitsma. 250p. 1980. pap. text ed. 20.00x (ISBN 90-232-1781-0). Humanities.

Myth of Victory: What Is Victory in War? Richard Hobbs. (Special Studies in Peace, Conflict & Conflict Resolution). 1979. lib. bdg. 32.50x (ISBN 0-89158-388-2). Westview.

Myth, Oil, & Politics: Introduction to the Political Economy of Petroleum. Charles F. Doran. LC 77-4571. (Illus.). 1979. pap. text ed. 7.95 (ISBN 0-02-907710-9). Free Pr.

Myth, Religion, & Mother Right: Selected Writings of Johann Jakob Bachofen. J. J. Bachofen. Tr. by Ralph Manheim. LC 67-22343. (Bollingen Series, No. 84). 368p. 1967. 19.00x (ISBN 0-691-09799-2); pap. 5.95 (ISBN 0-691-01797-2, 303). Princeton U Pr.

Myth, Religion & Society: Structuralist Essays by M. Detienne, L. Gernet, J. P. Vernant & P. Vidal-Naquet. Ed. by R. L. Gordon. (Illus.). 250p. Date not set. text ed. price not set (ISBN 0-521-22780-1); pap. text ed. price not set (ISBN 0-521-29640-4). Cambridge U Pr.

Mythical Image: The Ideal of India in German Romanticism. Amos L. Willson. LC 65-19449. 1964. 14.75 o.p. (ISBN 0-686-66407-8). Duke.

Mythical Man-Month: Essays on Software Engineering. Frederick P. Brooks, Jr. (Illus.). 200p. 1974. pap. text ed. 9.95 (ISBN 0-201-00650-2). A-W.

Mythical Monsters. Charles Gould. LC 74-75474. 1969. Repr. of 1886 ed. 20.00 (ISBN 0-8103-3834-3). Gale.

Mythmakers of the American Dream: The Nostalgic Vision in Popular Culture. Wiley L. Umphlett. LC 78-75342. (Illus.). Date not set. cancelled o.p. (ISBN 0-498-02288-9). A S Barnes. Postponed.

Mythologiae. Natalis Comes. LC 75-27853. (Renaissance & the Gods Ser.: Vol. 11). (Illus.). 1976. Repr. of 1567 ed. lib. bdg. 73.00 (ISBN 0-8240-2060-X). Garland Pub.

Mythologiae & Mythologia. Natale Conti & Antonio M. Tritonio. Ed. by Stephen Orgel. LC 78-68194. (Philosophy of Images Ser.: Vol. 13). (Illus.). 1980. lib. bdg. 66.00 (ISBN 0-8240-3687-5). Garland Pub.

Mythologie, 2 vols. Jean Baudouin. LC 75-27871. (Renaissance & the Gods Ser.: Vol. 26). (Illus.). 1976. Repr. of 1627 ed. Set. lib. bdg. 146.00 (ISBN 0-8240-2075-8); lib. bdg. 73.00 ea. Garland Pub.

Mythologies. Roland Barthes. Tr. by Annette Lavers. LC 75-185427. 160p. 1972. 5.95 (ISBN 0-8090-7193-2); pap. 3.95 (ISBN 0-8090-1369-X). Hill & Wang.

Mythologies of the Ancient World. Ed. by Samuel Noah Kramer. LC 60-13538. 1961. pap. 2.95 (ISBN 0-385-09567-8, A229, Anch). Doubleday.

Mythologies of the World: A Concise Encyclopedia. Rhoda A. Hendricks. Ed. by Max S. Shapiro. 240p. 1981. pap. 4.95 (ISBN 0-07-056421-3). McGraw.

Mythology. James Weigel, Jr. 210p. 1973. pap. 2.95 (ISBN 0-8220-0865-3). Cliffs.

Mythology & Fables of the Ancients, Explain'd from History, 4 vols. Antoine Banier. LC 75-27885. (Renaissance & the Gods Ser.: Vol. 40). (Illus.). 1976. Repr. of 1740 ed. Set. lib. bdg. 292.00 (ISBN 0-8240-2089-8); lib. bdg. 73.00 ea. Garland Pub.

Mythology in American Education. Harold H. Punke. 384p. 1981. pap. write for info. (ISBN 0-8134-2126-5). Interstate.

Mythology: The Voyage of the Hero. 2nd ed. David A. Leeming. (Illus.). 370p. 1980. pap. text ed. 10.50 scp (ISBN 0-06-043942-4, HarpC); avail. Har-Row.

Mythopoeic Reality: The Postwar American Nonfiction Novel. Mas ud Zavarzadeh. 271p. 1980. pap. 5.95 (ISBN 0-252-00645-3). U of Ill Pr.

Myths & Cosmos: Readings in Mythology & Symbolism. Ed. by John Middleton. LC 75-43817. (Texas Press Sourcebooks in Anthropology: No. 5). 1976. pap. 7.95x (ISBN 0-292-75030-7). U of Tex Pr.

Myths & Dreams. Edward Clodd. LC 70-159918. 1971. Repr. of 1891 ed. 18.00 (ISBN 0-8103-3776-2). Gale.

Myths & Folktales of the Alabama-Coushatta Indians. Howard N. Martin. (Illus.). 1976. 8.95 o.p. (ISBN 0-88426-052-6). Encino Pr.

Myths & Legends of Babylonia & Assyria. Lewis Spence. LC 77-167199. (Illus.). 414p. 1975. Repr. of 1916 ed. 28.00 (ISBN 0-8103-4089-5). Gale.

Myths & Legends of India: An Introduction to the Study of Hinduism. J. M. MacFie. 357p. Repr. of 1924 ed. pap. text ed. 4.95 (ISBN 0-567-22181-4). Attic Pr.

Myths & Legends of Many Lands. new ed. Compiled by Harriet Ross. LC 60-8670. (Illus.). 160p. (YA) (gr. 5 up). 1981. PLB 6.87 (ISBN 0-87460-214-9). Lion.

Myths & Legends of Our Own Land, 2 Vols. Charles M. Skinner. LC 79-76999. 1969. Repr. of 1896 ed. Set. 24.00 (ISBN 0-8103-3851-3). Gale.

Myths & Legends of the Middle Ages: Their Origin & Influence on Literature & Art. Helene A. Guerber. LC 72-2464. (Illus.). xvi, 405p. 1974. Repr. of 1909 ed. 18.00 (ISBN 0-8103-3873-4). Gale.

Myths & Legends of the North American Indian. L. Spence. LC 72-81598. (Illus.). 396p. pap. 6.50 (ISBN 0-8334-1745-2). Steinerbks.

Myths & Legends of the Polynesians. Johannes E. Anderson. LC 69-13509. (Illus.). (gr. 9 up). 1969. Repr. of 1928 ed. 15.00 (ISBN 0-8048-0414-1). C E Tuttle.

Myths & Management of Natural Resources. John Baden & Richard Stroup. (Pacific Institute for Public Policy Research Ser.). 1981. price not set professional reference (ISBN 0-88410-380-3). Ballinger Pub.

Myths & Motifs in Literature. David J. Burrows et al. LC 72-90546. 448p. (Orig.). 1973. pap. text ed. 8.95 (ISBN 0-02-905030-8). Free Pr.

Myths & Realities: Conflicting Values in America. Ed. by Berkeley Kalin & Clayton Robinson. (Mississippi Valley Collection Bulletin, No. 5). 78p. 1972. pap. 5.95x (ISBN 0-87870-081-1). Memphis St Univ.

Myths & Realities: Societies of the Colonial South. Carl Bridenbaugh. LC 52-13024. 1963. pap. text ed. 2.95x (ISBN 0-689-70023-7, 17). Atheneum.

Myths & Realities: Societies of the Colonial South. Carl Bridenbaugh. LC 80-25280. (Walter Lynwood Fleming Lectures in Southern History Ser., Louisiana State University). x, 208p. 1981. Repr. of 1952 ed. lib. bdg. 19.75x (ISBN 0-313-22770-5, BRMR). Greenwood.

Myths & the Truth About Selecting a Marine Sextant. Joel H. Jacobs. LC 75-4318. (Illus.). 1975. pap. 3.00 (ISBN 0-87033-203-1). Cornell Maritime.

Myths in Education: Beliefs That Hinder Progress & Their Alternatives. Arthur W. Combs. 1978. pap. text ed. 8.95 (ISBN 0-205-05984-8, 2359847). Allyn.

Myths of Ancient Greece. Compiled by Harriet Ross. (Illus.). 160p. 1981. PLB 7.95 (ISBN 0-87460-383-8). Lion.

Myths of Antitrust: Economic Theory & Legal Cases. D. T. Armentano. 1972. 11.95 o.p. (ISBN 0-87000-159-0). Arlington Hse.

Myths of Consciousness in the Novels of Charles Maturin. Shirley C. Scott. Ed. by Devendra P. Varma. LC 79-8479. (Gothic Studies & Dissertations Ser.). 1980. lib. bdg. 22.00x (ISBN 0-405-12661-1). Arno.

Myths of Deinstitutionalization: Policies for the Mentally Disabled. Ed. by Joseph Halpern et al. (Westview Special Studies in Health Care & Medical Science). 152p. 1980. lib. bdg. 16.50x (ISBN 0-89158-843-4). Westview.

Myths of Idaho Indians. rev. ed. Deward E. Walker, Jr. LC 79-57484. (Gem Bk. & Anthropological Monograph). (Illus.). 188p. (Orig.). 1980. pap. 7.50 (ISBN 0-89301-066-9). U Pr of Idaho.

Myths of Inflation & Investing. Steven Leuthold. LC 80-67811. 1980. 27.50 (ISBN 0-87251-048-4). Crain Bks.

Myths of Information: Technology & Postindustrial Culture. Anthony Wilden et al. Ed. by Kathleen Woodward. LC 80-23653. (Theories of Contemporary Culture Ser.: Vol. 3). 276p. (Orig.). 1980. 15.95 (ISBN 0-930956-12-5); pap. 6.95 (ISBN 0-930956-13-3). Coda Pr.

Myths of National Security: The Peril of Secret Government. Arthur M. Cox. LC 75-5288. 256p. 1975. 9.95 o.p. (ISBN 0-8070-0496-0); pap. 4.50 (ISBN 0-8070-0497-9, BP538). Beacon Pr.

Myths of Northern Lands: Narrated with Special Reference to Literature & Art. Helene A. Guerber. 1970. Repr. 26.00 (ISBN 0-8103-3862-9). Gale.

Myths of the New World: A Treatise on the Symbolism & Mythology of the Red Race in America. Daniel G. Brinton. LC 74-1038. 360p. 1974. Repr. of 1896 ed. 15.00 (ISBN 0-8103-3959-5). Gale.

Myths of the New World Indians. Daniel G. Brinton. LC 72-81594. (Illus.). 334p. pap. 6.50 (ISBN 0-8334-1742-8). Steinerbks.

Myths of the Norsemen. Roger L. Green. 1970. pap. 2.50 (ISBN 0-14-030464-9, Puffin). Penguin.

Myths of the Orient. Barbara Christesen. LC 77-22199. (Myth, Magic & Superstition Ser.). (Illus.). (gr. 4-5). 1977. PLB 9.65 (ISBN 0-8172-1043-1). Raintree Pubs.

Myths, Rites, Symbols: A Mircea Eliade Reader, 2 vols. Mircea Eliade. Ed. by Wendell C. Beane & William G. Doty. 1976. Vol. 1. pap. 5.95x (ISBN 0-06-131955-4, TB 1955, CN); Vol. 2. pap. 4.95 (ISBN 0-06-090511-5, CN511). Har-Row.

Myths That Mire the Ministry. Harold A. Carter. 1980. pap. 5.95 (ISBN 0-8170-0845-4); pap. 3.95 o.p. (ISBN 0-686-65909-0). Judson.

Myths That Rule America. Herbert I. London & Albert Weeks. LC 80-5866. 176p. 1981. lib. bdg. 13.50 (ISBN 0-8191-1446-4); pap. text ed. 6.95 (ISBN 0-8191-1447-2). U Pr of Amer.

Myxomatosis. Frank Fenner & F. N. Ratcliffe. 1966. 65.00 (ISBN 0-521-04991-1). Cambridge U Pr.

N

N & S Dakota Life & Health. 1980. 15.00 (ISBN 0-930868-22-6). Merritt Co.

N & S Dakota Property & Casualty. 1980. 15.00 (ISBN 0-930868-23-4). Merritt Co.

N. B. C. Handbook of Pronunciation. 3rd, rev. ed. James F. Bender. Ed. by Thomas Crowell, Jr. 1964. 11.95 (ISBN 0-690-57472-X, TYC-T). T Y Crowell.

N-Benzoylphenylhydroxylamine & Its Analogues. A. K. Majumdar. 224p. 1972. text ed. 50.00 (ISBN 0-08-016754-3). Pergamon.

N. F. S. Grundtvig: Selected Writings. Ed. by Johannes Knudsen. LC 76-7873. 192p. 1976. pap. 5.95 (ISBN 0-8006-1238-8, 1-1238). Fortress.

N Is for Naked. (Illus.). 5.00 o.p. (ISBN 0-685-46565-9). Elysium.

N-NMR Spectroscopy. G. J. Martin et al. (NMR-Basic Principles & Progress Ser.: Vol. 18). (Illus.). 390p. 1981. 87.30 (ISBN 0-387-10459-3). Springer-Verlag.

N or M? Agatha Christie. Date not set. pap. 2.25 (ISBN 0-440-16254-8). Dell.

N P T: Paradoxes & Problems. Ed. by Anne W. Marks. LC 75-826. 1975. pap. 1.50 (ISBN 0-87003-022-1). Carnegie Endow.

N R C Trans-Bus Study. Commission on Sociotechnical Systems. 1979. pap. 1.50 (ISBN 0-309-02929-5). Natl Acad Pr.

N. Simrock Thematic Catalog of the Works of Johannes Brahms. N. Simrock. LC 72-5954. (Music Reprint Ser.). 180p. 1973. Repr. of 1897 ed. lib. bdg. 35.00 (ISBN 0-306-70271-1). Da Capo.

Na Casa De Meu Pai. Tr. by Corrie T. Boom. (Portuguese Bks.). 1979. 1.50 (ISBN 0-8297-0894-4). Life Pubs Intl.

Na Inoa Hoku: A Catalogue of Hawaiian & Pacific Star Names. Rubellite K. Johnson & John Mahelona. LC 75-23889. 1975. pap. 4.95 (ISBN 0-914916-09-2). Topgallant.

Na Pa'i Ki'i: The Photographers in the Hawaiian Islands, 1900-1945. Lynn Davis. LC 80-70100. (Special Publication Ser.: No. 69). (Illus.). 48p. Date not set. pap. 5.50 (ISBN 0-910240-29-9). Bishop Mus.

Na Scribhinni Liteartha le Padraig Mac Pearais. Patrick Pearse. Ed. by Seamus O'Buachalla. 180p. (Irish.). 1979. pap. 4.95 (ISBN 0-85342-607-4). Irish Bk Ctr.

NAACP: Triumphs of a Pressure Group 1909-1980. Warren St. James. (Biblio. Index Notes Ser.). (Illus.). 288p. 1980. 11.95 (ISBN 0-682-49605-7, University). Exposition.

Naaman & the Little Maid. Lucy Diamond. (Ladybird Ser). (Illus.). 1959. bds. 1.49 (ISBN 0-87508-852-X). Chr Lit.

Nabis: Their History & Their Art, 1888-1896. George Mauner. LC 77-94708. (Outstanding Dissertations in the Fine Arts Ser.). 1979. lib. bdg. 45.00 (ISBN 0-8240-3240-3). Garland Pub.

Nabobs. Ed. by Percival Spear. 1980. Repr. of 1963 ed. 17.00x (ISBN 0-8364-0659-1, Pub. by Curzon Pr). South Asia Bks.

Nabob's Widow. Elsie Lee. 1976. 7.95 o.p. (ISBN 0-440-06305-1). Delacorte.

Nabob's Widow. Elsie Lee. 1977. pap. 1.75 o.s.i. (ISBN 0-440-16398-6). Dell.

Nabokov. Ed. by Alfred Appel, Jr. & Charles Newman. LC 76-96906. (Triquarterly Book). 1970. 16.95x o.p. (ISBN 0-8101-0292-7). Northwestern U Pr.

Nabokov: His Life in Part. Andrew Field. 1978. pap. 3.95 o.p. (ISBN 0-14-004784-0). Penguin.

Nabokov Translated: A Comparison of Nabokov's Russian & English Prose. Jane Grayson. (Oxford Modern Languages & Literature Monographs). 1977. 36.00x (ISBN 0-19-815527-1). Oxford U Pr.

Nabokov-Wilson Letters Nineteen Forty to Nineteen Seventy-One. Ed. by Simon Karlinsky. LC 78-69627. 1980. pap. 6.95 (ISBN 0-06-090753-3, CN 753, CN). Har-Row.

Nabokov's Deceptive World. William Woodin Rowe. LC 76-158968. 1971. 12.00x (ISBN 0-8147-7353-2). NYU Pr.

Nabokovs Quartet. Nabakov. 1968. pap. 1.75 o.s.i. (ISBN 0-515-01882-1, V1882). Jove Pubns.

Nabokov's Spectral Dimension. W. Woodin Rowe. 1981. 15.00 (ISBN 0-88233-641-X). Ardis Pubs.

Nacer a Una Nueva Vida. Billy Graham. Tr. by Rhode Ward from Eng. LC 78-52622. 191p. (Orig., Span.). 1978. pap. 3.50 (ISBN 0-89922-110-6). Edit Caribe.

Nachtwandler. Arthur Koestler. (Suhrkamp Taschenbuecher: 579). 576p. (Ger.). 1980. pap. text ed. 7.80 (ISBN 3-518-37079-0, Pub. by Insel Verlag Germany). Suhrkamp.

Naci de Nuevo. Charles Colson. Tr. by Rhode Ward from Eng. LC 77-81645. 419p. (Orig., Span.). 1977. pap. 3.95 (ISBN 0-89922-087-8). Edit Caribe.

Nackte Maedchen Auf der Strasse Erzaehlungen. Fritz R. Fries. (Suhrkamp Taschenbuecher: St 577). 192p. (Ger.). 1980. pap. text ed. 3.90 (ISBN 3-518-37077-4, Pub. by Insel Verlag Germany). Suhrkamp.

Nada. Carmen Laforet. Ed. by Edward R. Mulvihill & Roberto G. Sanchez. (Orig., Sp). 1958. pap. 5.95x (ISBN 0-19-500942-8). Oxford U Pr.

Nada. 5.00 (ISBN 0-685-78403-7); pap. 2.00 (ISBN 0-912292-24-5). The Smith.

Nada the Lily. H. Rider Haggard. Ed. by R. Reginald & Douglas Menville. LC 80-19282. (Newcastle Forgotten Fantasy Library: Vol. 20). 295p. 1980. Repr. of 1979 ed. lib. bdg. 10.95x (ISBN 0-89370-519-5). Borgo Pr.

Nadars of Tamilnad: The Political Culture of a Community in Change. Robert L. Hardgrave, Jr. (Center for South & Southeast Asia Studies, UC Berkeley). (Illus.). 1969. 20.00x (ISBN 0-520-01471-5). U of Cal Pr.

Nadia Comaneci. Thomas Braun. (Sports Superstars Ser.). (Illus.). (gr. 3-9). 1977. PLB 5.95 (ISBN 0-87191-592-8); pap. 2.95 (ISBN 0-89812-195-7). Creative Ed.

Nadine Gordimer. Robert F. Haugh. (World Authors Ser.: South Africa: No. 315). 1974. lib. bdg. 10.95 (ISBN 0-8057-2387-0). Twayne.

NAEB History, Vol. 1. Harold E. Hill. 85p. 1954. pap. 4.00 (Pub Telecomm). NAEB.

NAEB History, Vol. 2. W. Wayne Halford. 173p. 1966. pap. 2.00 (Pub Telecomm). NAEB.

Nagarjuna. K. Satchidananda Murty. (National Biography Ser.). 1979. pap. 2.00 o.p. (ISBN 0-89744-199-0). Auromere.

Nagasaki Prints & Early Copperplates. Masanobu Hosono. Tr. by Lloyd R. Craighill. LC 77-75972. (Japanese Arts Library: Vol. 6). (Illus.). 150p. 1978. 16.95 (ISBN 0-87011-311-9). Kodansha.

Nagasaki: The Necessary Bomb. Joseph L. Marx. Ed. by R. Markel. (Illus.). 1971. 11.95 o.s.i. (ISBN 0-02-580400-6). Macmillan.

Nagel Travel Guide to Italy. (Nagel Travel Guide Ser.). (Illus.). xvi, 1184p. 1975. 60.00 o.p. (ISBN 2-8263-0520-4). Hippocrene Bks.

Nahj-Albalagha: Islamic Teachings. Salhar. (Arabic.). 16.00x (ISBN 0-686-63564-7). Intl Bk Ctr.

Nahuatl in Middle Years: Language Contact Phenomena in Texts of the Colonial Period. Frances Karttunen & James Lockhart. (Publications in Linguistics Ser.: Vol. 85). 1977. pap. 10.75x (ISBN 0-520-09561-8). U of Cal Pr.

Nahum Tate. Christopher Spencer. (English Authors Ser.: No. 126). lib. bdg. 10.95 (ISBN 0-8057-1536-3). Twayne.

NAIA Official Record Book. 8.50 (ISBN 0-686-22331-4). NAIA Pubns.

Naif Aux Guarante Enfants. Paul Guth. (Easy Readers, C). 1979. pap. 3.75 (ISBN 0-88436-294-9). EMC.

Nail Biters Anonymous. Suzanne Taylor-Moore. 48p. 1981. pap. 3.00 (ISBN 0-686-28092-X). MTM Pub Co.

Nail Biter's Handbook. Judy Hyde. (Illus.). 24p. (Orig.). 1980. pap. 2.95 (ISBN 0-930380-11-8). Quail Run.

Nail-Biting: The Beatable Habit. Frederick H. Smith. LC 80-11687. (Illus., Orig.). 1980. pap. 7.95 (ISBN 0-8425-1806-1). Brigham.

Nail Diseases in Internal Medicine. P. De Nicola et al. (Illus.). 128p. 1974. 14.75 (ISBN 0-398-03178-9). C C Thomas.

Nailheads & Potato Eyes. Cynthia Basil. LC 75-23180. (Illus.). 32p. (gr. k-3). 1976. PLB 7.63 (ISBN 0-688-32056-2). Morrow.

Nailing Jelly to a Tree. Jerry Willis & William Danley, Jr. 275p. 1981. pap. 12.95 (ISBN 0-918398-42-8). Dilithium Pr.

Nailing up the Home Sweet Home. Jeanne M. Walker. (CSU Poetry Ser.: No. 9). (Orig.). 1980. pap. 4.00 (ISBN 0-914946-24-2). Cleveland St Univ Poetry Ctr.

Nailsea Glass. Keith Vincent. (Illus.). 1975. 7.50 (ISBN 0-7153-6807-9). David & Charles.

Nairn Way: Desert Bus to Baghdad. John M. Munro. LC 80-11875. 1980. 22.00x (ISBN 0-88206-035-X). Caravan Bks.

NAIS Middle School Task Force: Initial Position Paper & Accompanying Papers. 1975. pap. 3.25 (ISBN 0-934338-17-5). NAIS.

Naive Painters of Yugoslavia. Nebojsa Tomasevic. (Illus.). 1978. 22.50 o.p. (ISBN 0-8467-0467-6, Pub. by Two Continents). Hippocrene Bks.

Naj Atu Ur-Ra'ld wa-Shar Atu al-Warid Fi al-Mutaradifi. Ibrahim Yaziji. (Arabic.). 1970. 23.00x (ISBN 0-685-72052-7). Intl Bk Ctr.

Nakae Chomin & His Sansuijin Keirin Mondo, 1847-1901. Nakae Chomin. Tr. by Margaret B. Dardess from Jap. LC 76-58485. (Program in East Asian Studies Occasional Papers Ser.: No. 10). (Illus.). 1977. pap. 4.00 o.p. (ISBN 0-914584-10-3). West Wash Univ.

Nakajima Ki. 43, Hayabusha 1-3. Richard M. Bueschel. (Arco-Aircam Aviation Ser. 15). 1970. pap. 2.95 o.p. (ISBN 0-668-02292-2). Arco.

Naked & the Dead. Norman Mailer. 744p. 1980. pap. 7.95 (ISBN 0-03-059043-4, Owl Bks). HR&W.

Naked & Together. Joe Webber & Diane Webber. 5.95 (ISBN 0-910550-06-9). Elysium.

Naked Ape or Homo Sapiens: A Reply to Desmond Morris. 2nd ed. John Lewis & Bernard Towers. (Teilhard Study Library). 1972. text ed. 6.25x (ISBN 0-900391-21-9). Humanities.

Naked at the Feast: A Biography of Josephine Baker. Lynn Haney. (Illus.). 360p. 1981. 15.00 (ISBN 0-396-07900-8). Dodd.

Naked Child: The Long Range Effects of Family & Social Nudity. Dennis C. Smith. LC 80-69234. (Illus.). 180p. 1981. perfect bdg. 7.95 (ISBN 0-86548-056-7). Century Twenty One.

Naked Children. Daniel Fader. 1971. 10.95 (ISBN 0-02-536900-8). Macmillan.

Naked Civil Servant. Quentin Crisp. LC 77-73866. 1977. 7.95 o.p. (ISBN 0-03-022451-9). HR&W.

Naked-Eye Astronomy. Patrick Moore. (Illus.). 1966. 8.95 o.p. (ISBN 0-393-06303-8). Norton.

Naked Flagpole: Battle for Bataan. Richard C. Mallonee. Ed. by Richard C. Mallonee. LC 80-15538. (Illus.). 1980. 14.95 (ISBN 0-89141-094-5). Presidio Pr.

Naked I: Fictions for the Seventies. Ed. by Frederick R. Karl & Leo Hamalian. 1975. pap. 1.75 o.p. (ISBN 0-449-30757-3, X757, Prem). Fawcett.

Naked Investor. Robert Heller. 1977. 8.95 o.p. (ISBN 0-440-06257-8). Delacorte.

Naked King & Other Poems. Nirendranath Chakrabarti. Tr. by Sujit Mukherjee & Meenakshi Mukherjee. (Saffronbird Bk). 53p. 8.00 (ISBN 0-88253-833-0); pap. 4.80 (ISBN 0-88253-834-9). Ind-US Inc.

Naked Man. Claude Levi-Strauss. Tr. by John Weightman & Doreen Weightman. LC 79-3399. (Introduction to a Science of Mythology Ser.). (Illus.). 440p. 1981. 30.00 (ISBN 0-06-012584-5, HarpT). Har-Row.

Naked Masks: Five Plays. Luigi Pirandello. Ed. by Eric Bentley. Incl. It Is So If You Think So; Henry Fourth; Six Characters in Search of an Author; Each in His Own Way; Liola. 1957. pap. 4.50 (ISBN 0-525-47006-9). Dutton.

Naked Poetry: Recent American Poetry in Open Forms. Ed. by Stephen Berg & Robert Mezey. LC 69-16527. 1969. pap. 7.95 (ISBN 0-672-60669-0). Bobbs.

Naked Range. Steven C. Lawrence. Orig. Title: Thruway West. 1976. pap. 0.95 o.p. (ISBN 0-685-69152-7, LB354NK, Leisure Bks). Nordon Pubns.

Naked Society. Vance Packard. (gr. 9 up). 1964. 9.95 o.p. (ISBN 0-679-50066-9). McKay.

Naked Sword. F. W. Kenyon. 1975. pap. 1.50 o.p. (ISBN 0-685-59191-3, LB308, Leisure Bks). Nordon Pubns.

Naked Sword. F. W. Kenyon. 1979. pap. 1.95 (ISBN 0-505-51341-2). Tower Bks.

Naked Therapist. Sheldon Kopp. LC 76-17939. 1976. 11.95 (ISBN 0-912736-18-6). EDITS Pubs.

Naked Triangle. Balwant Gargi. 1980. text ed. cancelled o.p. (Pub. by Vikas India). Advent Bk.

Nam. Mark Baker. 288p. 1981. 10.95 (ISBN 0-688-00086-X). Morrow.

Nam Bok. Jack London. 250p. (Orig.). pap. 3.95 (ISBN 0-932458-03-3). Star Rover.

Nam-Bok, the Liar. Jack London. Ed. by Walter Pauk & Raymond Harris. (Classics Ser). (Illus.). (gr. 6-12). 1976. pap. text ed. 1.60x (ISBN 0-89061-042-8, 505); tchrs. ed. 3.00 (ISBN 0-89061-043-6, 507). Jamestown Pubs.

Nam Doc. Wesley G. Byerly. 1980. 6.95 (ISBN 0-533-04499-5). Vantage.

Namaqualand in Flower (Eliovson) 13.50 (ISBN 0-86954-062-9). Horticultural.

Name Authority Control for Card Catalogs in the General Libraries. (Contributions to Librarianship Ser.: No. 5). 1980. pap. 10.00 (ISBN 0-930214-07-2). U TX Austin Gen Libs.

Name Game. Chris Anderson. 1979. pap. 2.50 (ISBN 0-515-04857-7). Jove Pubns.

Nameless Sight: Selected Poems 1937-1956. Alan Swallow. 74p. 1963. pap. 3.95 (ISBN 0-8040-0223-1, 50). Swallow.

Nameless War. A. H. Ramsey. 1978. pap. 4.00x (ISBN 0-911038-38-8). Noontide.

Names & Name-Days: A Dictionary of Catholic Christian Names in Alphabetical Order with Origins & Meanings. Donald Attwater. LC 68-30595. 1968. Repr. of 1939 ed. 20.00 (ISBN 0-8103-3108-X). Gale.

Names & Numbers: A Journalist's Guide to the Most Needed Information Sources & Contacts. Rod Nordland. LC 78-18903. 560p. 1978. 28.95 (ISBN 0-471-03994-2, Pub. by Wiley-Interscience). Wiley.

Names & Structures of Organic Compounds: A Programmed Text. Otto T. Benfey. LC 66-16550. 1966. pap. 10.95 (ISBN 0-471-06575-7). Wiley.

Names & Their Histories. Isaac Taylor. LC 68-17936. 1969. Repr. of 1898 ed. 22.00 (ISBN 0-8103-4217-0). Gale.

Names & Their Meanings, a Book for the Curious. Leopold Wagner. LC 68-22060. 1968. Repr. of 1893 ed. 20.00 (ISBN 0-8103-3098-9). Gale.

Names in Pedgrees. Joe Palmer. 11.00 o.p. (ISBN 0-936032-05-7). Thoroughbred Own and Breed.

Names in Pedigrees. Date not set. lib. bdg. 11.00. Thoroughbred Own & Breed.

Names in Roman Verse: A Lexicon & Reverse Index of All Proper Names of History, Mythology & Geography Found in the Classical Roman Poets. Donald C. Swanson. 1967. 30.00x (ISBN 0-299-04560-9). U of Wis Pr.

Names in South Carolina, 1954-65: Vols. I-XII. Claude H. Neuffer. LC 76-29026. 1976. Repr. 25.00 (ISBN 0-87152-248-9). C H Neuffer.

Names of Christ: A Pocket Guide. Francis H. Derk. LC 75-44928. 1976. pap. 2.50 (ISBN 0-87123-390-8, 200390). Bethany Fell.

Names of Places in a Transferred Sense in English: A Sematological Study. Carl J. Efvergren. LC 68-17922. 1969. Repr. of 1909 ed. 15.00 (ISBN 0-8103-3233-7). Gale.

Names, Sets & Numbers. Jeanne Bendick. LC 73-137151. (Science Experiences Ser.). (Illus.). (gr. 4-6). 1971. PLB 5.90 (ISBN 0-531-01436-3); pap. 1.25 o.p. (ISBN 0-531-02321-4). Watts.

Namesakes Nineteen Fifty-Six to Ninety Eighty. John O. Greenwood. 1981. casebound 27.00 (ISBN 0-686-69468-6). Freshwater.

Namesakes of the Eighties. John D. Greenwood. 1980. 22.00. Freshwater.

Namibia. Colin Winter. (Orig.). 1977. pap. 4.95 o.p. (ISBN 0-8028-1664-9). Eerdmans.

Namibia: The Road to Independence. Jeffrey Gayner. 1979. pap. 10.00 (ISBN 0-686-60259-5). Coun Am Affairs.

Namibians of Southwest Africa. Peter Fraenkel. (Minority Rights Group: No. 19). 1974. pap. 2.50 (ISBN 0-89192-105-2). Interbk Inc.

Naming & Referring: The Semantics & Pragmatics of Singular Terms. David Schwarz. (Foundations of Communication Ser.). 194p. 1979. text ed. 45.00x (ISBN 3-11-007610-1). De Gruyter.

Naming Names. Victor Navasky. LC 80-15044. 468p. 1980. 15.95 (ISBN 0-670-50393-2). Viking Pr.

Naming Names: A Consideration of Pseudonyms & Name Changes. Adrian Room. LC 80-27801. 260p. 1981. lib. bdg. write for info. (ISBN 0-89950-025-0). McFarland & Co.

Naming the Whirlwind: The Renewal of God-Language. Landgon Gilkey. LC 68-11146. 1969. pap. 8.60 o.p. (ISBN 0-672-60796-4). Bobbs.

Naming Things. H. E. Francis. LC 80-19543. (Illinois Short Fiction Ser.). 140p. 1980. 10.00 (ISBN 0-252-00830-8); pap. 3.95 (ISBN 0-252-00831-6). U of Ill Pr.

Nan-fang ts'ao-mu chuang, a Fourth Century Flora of Southeast Asia: Introduction, Translation, Commentaries. Chi Han. Tr. by Li Hui-Lin from Chinese. LC 80-100381. (Illus.). 178p. 1980. 15.00 (ISBN 0-295-95745-X, Pub. by Chinese Univ Hong Kong). U of Wash Pr.

Nana. Emile Zola. Tr. by George Holden. (Classics Ser.). 1972. pap. 3.95 (ISBN 0-14-044263-4). Penguin.

Nanas. Ester Feliciano Mendoza. 3.10 o.s.i. (ISBN 0-8477-3200-2). U of PR Pr.

Nancy Astor. John Grigg. (Illus.). 192p. 1981. 15.00 (ISBN 0-316-32870-7). Little.

Nancy Astor: A Lady Unashamed. John Grigg. (Illus.). 192p. 1981. 15.00 (ISBN 0-316-32870-7). Little.

Nancy Drew Book of Hidden Clues. Carolyn Keene. 64p. (gr. 3-7). 1980. pap. 3.95 (ISBN 0-671-95713-9). Wanderer Bks.

Nancy Drew Date Book & Homework Planner. (gr. 3-6). 1980. 2.95 (ISBN 0-671-95609-4). Wanderer Bks.

Nancy Drew: The Secret in the Old Lace. Carolyn Keene. (Nancy Drew Mystery Stories). 192p. (gr. 3-7). 1980. PLB 7.95 (ISBN 0-671-41119-5); pap. 1.95 (ISBN 0-671-41114-4). Wanderer Bks.

Nancy Graves: A Survey 1969 to 1980. Linda L. Cathcart. LC 80-13227. (Illus.). 1980. pap. 15.00 (ISBN 0-914782-34-7). Buffalo Acad.

Nancy Graves Cabot, in Memoriam, Sources of Design for Textiles & Decorative Arts. Department of Textiles, Museum of Fine Arts, Boston. 1973. pap. 2.50 (ISBN 0-87846-175-2). Mus Fine Arts Boston.

Nancy Lieberman, Basketball's Magic Lady. Betty M. Jones. LC 80-82004. (Starpeople Ser.). (Illus.). 75p. (gr. 4-9). 1980. PLB 5.79 (ISBN 0-8178-0009-3). Harvey.

Nancy Lopez. Craig Schumacher. (Sports Superstars Ser.). (Illus.). (gr. 3-9). 1979. PLB 5.95 (ISBN 0-87191-694-0); pap. 2.95 (ISBN 0-89812-164-7). Creative Ed.

Nancy Mitford: A Memoir. Harold Acton. LC 75-34580. (Illus.). 288p. 1976. 10.00 o.p. (ISBN 0-06-010018-4, HarpT). Har-Row.

Nandini Night. Subhoranjan Dasgupta. (Writers Workshop Redbird Ser.). 1975. 8.00 (ISBN 0-88253-582-X); pap. text ed. 4.00 (ISBN 0-88253-581-1). Ind-US Inc.

Nanette. Patricia Veryan. 288p. 1981. 11.95 (ISBN 0-8027-0664-9). Walker & Co.

Nang Loi: The Floating Maiden. Pensak Chagsuchinda. (Scandinavian Institute of Asian Studies Monograph: No. 18). 80p. (Orig.). 1973. pap. text ed. 6.00x (ISBN 0-7007-0067-6). Humanities.

Nannie's Niece's Notes. Valerie Hunt. (Illus.). 32p. 1980. 5.00 (ISBN 0-934750-07-6). Jalamap.

Nanny Goat & the Fierce Dog. Charles Keeping. LC 73-19598. (Illus.). 48p. (gr. k-3). 1974. 8.95 (ISBN 0-87599-201-3). S G Phillips.

Nantucket in Color. Peter Dreyer & Edouard Stackpole. (Profiles of America Ser). (Illus.). 1974. 6.95 (ISBN 0-8038-5030-1). Hastings.

Naomi in the Middle. Norma Klein. (Illus.). (gr. 3-5). 1978. pap. 1.50 (ISBN 0-671-56070-0). PB.

Nap Master. William Kotzwinkle. LC 78-12178. (Illus.). 32p. 1979. 7.95 (ISBN 0-15-256704-6, HJ). HarBraceJ.

Napkin Notes: On the Art of Living. Gary M. Durst. LC 79-50554. (Illus.). 1979. pap. text ed. 4.95 o.p. (ISBN 0-9602552-0-6). Ctr Art Living.

Napkin Notes: On the Art of Living. Gary M. Durst. LC 79-50554. (Illus.). 200p. 1980. pap. 6.95 (ISBN 0-9602552-2-2). Ctr Art Living.

Naples & Neapolitan Opera. Michael F. Robinson. (Oxford Monographs on Music). 200p. 1972. 36.00x (ISBN 0-19-816124-7). Oxford U Pr.

Naples, Pompeii & Southern Italy. Anthony Pereira. 1977. 24.00 (ISBN 0-7134-0815-4, Pub. by Batsford England). David & Charles.

Napoleon. Richard Tames. Ed. by Malcolm Yapp & Margaret Killingray. (World History Ser.). (Illus.). (gr. 10). 1980. Repr. of 1977 ed. lib. bdg. 5.95 (ISBN 0-89908-044-8); pap. text ed. 1.95 (ISBN 0-89908-019-7). Greenhaven.

Napoleon & the Restoration of the Bourbons: The Complete Portion of Macaulay's Projected History of France from the Restoration of the Bourbons to the Accession of Louis Phillipe. Thomas B. Macaulay. LC 77-7107. 1977. 15.00x (ISBN 0-231-04376-7). Columbia U Pr.

Napoleon: From Eighteen Brumaire to Tilsit, 1799-1807. Georges Lefebvre. Tr. by Henry F. Stockhold. LC 68-29160. 1969. 20.00x (ISBN 0-231-02558-0). Columbia U Pr.

Napoleon: From Tilsit to Waterloo, 1807-1815. Georges Lefebvre. Tr. by J. E. Anderson. LC 74-79193. 1969. 20.00x (ISBN 0-231-03313-3). Columbia U Pr.

Napoleon Third & the Second Empire: Buffoon, Modern Dictator, or Sphinx. 2nd ed. Samuel M. Osgood. (Problems in European Civilization Ser). Orig. Title: Napoleon Third: Buffoon, Modern Dictator, or Sphinx. 1973. pap. text ed. 4.95x o.p. (ISBN 0-669-81653-1). Heath.

Napoleonic Empire in Southern Italy & the Rise of the Secret Societies, 2 vols. Robert M. Johnston. LC 77-156852. (Europe 1815-1945 Ser). 640p. 1973. Repr. of 1904 ed. lib. bdg. 49.50 (ISBN 0-306-70558-3). Da Capo.

Napoleonic Revolution. Robert B. Holtman. LC 67-11308. (Critical Periods of History Ser). (Illus.). 1967. pap. 4.50 o.p. (ISBN 0-397-47134-3). Lippincott.

Napoleon's Book of Fate. Richard Deacon. Orig. Title: The Book of Fate: Its Origins & Uses. 1977. 10.00 (ISBN 0-8065-0564-8); pap. 4.95 (ISBN 0-8065-0577-X). Citadel Pr.

Napoleon's Conquest of Prussia, 1806. F. Loraine Petre. LC 77-72679. 1977. 14.95 (ISBN 0-88254-435-7). Hippocrene Bks.

Napoleon's Continental Blockade: The Case of Alsace. Geoffrey Ellis. (Oxford Historical Monographs). (Illus.). 368p. 1981. 49.95 (ISBN 0-19-821881-8). Oxford U Pr.

Napoleon's Guards Cavalry. Emil Bukhari. (Men-at-Arms Ser.). (Illus.). 48p. 1979. pap. 7.95 (ISBN 0-85045-288-0). Hippocrene Bks.

Napoleon's Last Journey. Gilbert Martineau. Tr. by Frances Partridge. (Illus.). 1977. 15.00 (ISBN 0-7195-3293-0). Transatlantic.

Napoleon's Line Chasseurs. Emir Bukhari. (Men-at-Arms Ser.). (Illus.). 48p. 1977. pap. 7.95 (ISBN 0-85045-269-4). Hippocrene Bks.

Napoleon's "Little Pest" The Dutchess of Abrantes. Peter Gunn. (Illus.). 1979. 24.00 (ISBN 0-241-10183-2, Pub. by Hamish Hamilton England). David & Charles.

Napoleon's Thoughts on History, Politics & the Management of Men. Ed. by John E. Draper. (Illus.). 1980. deluxe ed. 39.75 (ISBN 0-89266-232-8). Am Classical Coll Pr.

Napper Tandy. Rupert Coughlan. (Illus.). 1976. 18.50 (ISBN 0-900068-34-5). Irish Bk Ctr.

Narayaneeyam. M. N. Bhattatiri. Tr. by Swami Tapasyananda from Sanskrit. 1976. 8.50 o.p. (ISBN 0-87481-474-X). Vedanta Pr.

Narcissa Notebook. Barbara Drake. (Illus.). 1973. 1.00 o.p. (ISBN 0-686-23603-3). Stone Pr MI.

Narcissistic Condition: A Fact of Our Lives & Times, Vol. 1. Marie Nelson. LC 76-20724. (Self in Process Ser.). 1977. text ed. 22.95 (ISBN 0-87705-250-6). Human Sci Pr.

Narcolepsy & Hypersomnia. B. Roth. Ed. by Roger Broughton. Tr. by Margaret Schierlova. Orig. Title: Czech. (Illus.). xiv, 304p. 1980. pap. 58.75 (ISBN 3-8055-0490-X). S Karger.

Narcotic Antagonists. Ed. by M. C. Braude et al. LC 73-84113. (Advances in Biochemical Psychopharmacology Ser.: Vol. 8). (Illus.). 580p. 1974. 48.00 (ISBN 0-911216-55-3). Raven.

Narcotic Officer's Notebook. 2nd ed. Malachi L. Harney & John C. Cross. (Illus.). 396p. 1975. 21.75 (ISBN 0-398-02310-7). C C Thomas.

Narcotic Plants of the Old World, Used in Rituals & Everyday Life: An Anthology of Texts from Ancient Times to the Present. Hedwig Schleiffer. (Illus., Orig.). 1979. lib. bdg. 12.50x (ISBN 0-934454-01-9); pap. text ed. 7.95x (ISBN 0-934454-00-0). Lubrecht & Cramer.

Narcotics & Drug Abuse - A to Z, 3 vols. LC 78-173860. 1971. 45.00 ea. Vol. 1 (ISBN 0-87514-004-1). Vol. 2 (ISBN 0-87514-005-X). Vol. 3 (ISBN 0-87514-006-8). Croner.

Narcotics & Narcotic Addiction. 4th ed. David W. Maurer & Victor H. Vogel. (American Lectures in Public Protection). (Illus.). 496p. 1973. 24.75 (ISBN 0-398-02906-7). C C Thomas.

Narcotics & the Hypothalamus. Ed. by E. Zimmermann & R. George. LC 74-83453. 1974. 27.00 (ISBN 0-911216-87-1). Raven.

Narcotics: Lingo & Lore. J. E. Schmidt. 216p. 1959. 7.50 (ISBN 0-398-01671-2). C C Thomas.

Nares Seamanship Eighteen Sixty-Two. 2nd ed. George S. Nares. (Illus.). 239p. 1979. 15.00x (ISBN 0-905418-37-9). Intl Pubns Serv.

Naropa Institute Journal of Psychology, Vol. 1. 71p. (Orig.). 1981. pap. 6.00 (ISBN 0-87773-751-7). Great Eastern.

Narradores De Hoy. Ed. by Edith F. Helman & Doris K. Arjona. 1966. 7.95x (ISBN 0-393-09693-9, NortonC); tapes o.p. 50.00 (ISBN 0-685-18949-X). Norton.

Narragansett Bay: A Friend's Perspective. Stu Hale. (Marine Bulletin Ser.: No. 42). 7.00 (ISBN 0-938412-19-1). URI MAS.

Narration in the German Novelle. J. M. Ellis. LC 73-82460. (Anglica Germanica Ser.: No. 2). 232p. 1974. 45.00 (ISBN 0-521-20330-9). Cambridge U Pr.

Narration in the German Novelle. J. M. Ellis. LC 78-73602. (Anglica Germanica Ser.: No. 2). 1979. pap. 10.95x (ISBN 0-521-29592-0). Cambridge U Pr.

Narrativa Hispanoamericana Actual: America y Sus Problemas. Anita Arroyo. LC 79-19468. (Mente y Palabra Ser.). v, 517p. 1980. 20.00 (ISBN 0-8477-0563-3); pap. 15.00 (ISBN 0-8477-0563-3). U of PR Pr.

Narrative & Descriptive Bibliography of New Jersey. Nelson R. Burr. 1970. 12.50 (ISBN 0-8135-0639-5). Rutgers U Pr.

Narrative & Dramatic Sources of Shakespeare, 8 vols. Ed. by Geoffrey Bullough. Incl. Vol. 1. Early Comedies, Poems, Romeo & Juliet. 1957 (ISBN 0-231-08891-4); Vol. 2. Comedies, 1597-1603. 1958 (ISBN 0-231-08892-2); Vol. 3. Earlier English History Plays: Henry Sixth, Richard Third, Richard Second. 1960 (ISBN 0-231-08893-0); Vol. 4. Later English History Plays: King John, Henry Fourth, Henry Fifth, Henry Eighth. 1962 (ISBN 0-231-08894-9); Vol. 5. Roman Plays: Julius Caesar, Antony & Cleopatra, Coriolanus. 1964 (ISBN 0-231-08895-7); Vol. 6. Other Classical Plays: Titus Adronicus, Troilus & Cressida, Timon of Athens, Pericles, Prince of Tyre. 1966 (ISBN 0-231-08896-5); Vol. 7. Major Tragedies: Hamlet, Othello, King Lear, Macbeth (ISBN 0-231-08897-3). LC 57-9969. 30.00x ea. Columbia U Pr.

Narrative & Its Discontents: Problems of Closure in the Traditional Novel. D. A. Miller. LC 80-8565. 320p. 1981. 20.00x (ISBN 0-691-06459-8). Princeton U Pr.

Narrative & Structure: Exploratory Essays. John Holloway. LC 78-20826. 1979. 19.95 (ISBN 0-521-22574-4). Cambridge U Pr.

Narrative Bible. Tr. by Alvin Boyd. 256p. 1981. 8.95 (ISBN 0-89490-047-1). Enslow Pubs.

Narrative Consciousness: Structure & Perception in the Fiction of Kafka, Beckett & Robbe-Grillet. George H. Szanto. 260p. 1972. 12.50x o.p. (ISBN 0-292-75500-7). U of Tex Pr.

Narrative Discourse: An Essay in Method. Gerard Genette. Tr. by Jane E. Lewin from Fr. LC 79-13499. (Illus.). 1979. 17.50 (ISBN 0-8014-1099-1). Cornell U Pr.

Narrative Impulse: Short Stories for Analysis. Ed. by Mary Purcell & Robert C. Wylder. LC 63-14021. (Orig.). 1963. pap. 6.50 (ISBN 0-672-63067-2). Odyssey Pr.

Narrative of Lord Byron's Last Journey to Greece. Pietro Gamba. 314p. 1980. Repr. of 1945 ed. lib. bdg. 45.00 (ISBN 0-8495-2046-0). Arden Lib.

Narrative of My Captivity Among the Sioux Indians...with a Brief Account of General Sully's Indian Expedition in 1864, Bearing Upon Events Occurring in My Captivity. Fanny W. Kelly. LC 75-7111. (Indian Captivities Ser.: Vol. 85). 1976. Repr. of 1871 ed. lib. bdg. 44.00 (ISBN 0-8240-1709-9). Garland Pub.

Narrative of the Captivity & Adventures of John Tanner (U.S. Interpreter at the Saut de Ste. Marie) During 30 Years Residence Among the Indians in the Interior of North America. LC 75-7068. (Indian Captivities Ser.: Vol. 46). 1976. Repr. of 1830 ed. lib. bdg. 44.00 (ISBN 0-8240-1670-X). Garland Pub.

Narrative of the Captivity & Sufferings of Benjamin Gilbert & His Family. William Walton. Ed. by Wilcomb E. Washburn. LC 75-7036. (Narratives of North American Indian Captivities: Vol. 15). 1975. lib. bdg. 44.00 (ISBN 0-8240-1639-4). Garland Pub.

Narrative of the Captivity... of Mrs. Clarissa Plummer... Who with Mrs. Caroline Harris... Were... Taken Prisoners by the Camanche Tribe of Indians, Repr. Of 1838 Ed. Bd. with History of the Captivity & Providential Release Therefrom of Mrs. Caroline Harris... Who with Mrs. Clarissa Plummer... Were... with Their Unfortunate Husbands Taken Prisoner by the Comanche Tribe of Indians. Repr. of 1838 ed; Narrative of the Captivity of Mrs. Horn, & Her 2 Children, with Mrs. Harris, by the Camanche Indians. E. House. Repr. of 1839 ed; Authentic & Thrilling Narrative of the Captivity of Mrs. Horn. Repr. of 1851 ed; Narrative of Ransom Clark, the Only Survivor of Major Dade's Command in Florida. Repr. of 1839 ed; Historical Sketches of Roswell Franklin & Family. Robert Hubbard. Repr. of 1839 ed. LC 75-7076. (Indian Captivities Ser.: Vol. 54). 1977. lib. bdg. 44.00 (ISBN 0-8240-1678-5). Garland Pub.

Narrative of the Captivity of Mrs. Johnson: Containing an Account of Her Sufferings During Four Years with the Indians & French, Repr. Of 1796 Ed. Bd. with glascow ed. Repr. of 1797 ed; enl. ed. Repr. of 1814 ed. LC 75-7045. (Indian Captivities Ser.: Vol. 23). 1976. lib. bdg. 44.00 (ISBN 0-8240-1647-5). Garland Pub.

Narrative of the Capture & Providential Escape of Misses Frances & Almira Hall, 2 Respectable Young Women of the Ages of 16 & 18 Who Were Taken Prisoners by the Savages, Repr. Of 1832 Ed. Bd. with History of the War Between the United States & the Sac & Fox Nations of Indians. John A. Wakefield. Repr. of 1834 ed; Indian Massacre & Captivity of Hall Girls. Charles M. Scanlan. Repr. of 1915 ed. LC 75-7071. (Indian Captivities Ser.: Vol. 49). 1976. lib. bdg. 44.00 (ISBN 0-8240-1673-4). Garland Pub.

Narrative of the Capture & Treatment of John Dodge, by the English at Detroit, Repr. Of 1779. Ed. by Wilcomb E. Washburn. Incl. Entertaining Narrative of the Cruel & Barbarous Treatment & Extreme Sufferings of Mr. John Dodge During His Captivity. Repr. of 1780 ed; Narratives of a Late Expedition Against the Indians...& the Wonderful Escape of Dr. Knight & John Slover from Captivity. Ed. by Hugh H. Brackenridge. Repr. of 1783 ed; Indian Atrocities. Repr. of 1843 ed. (Narratives of North American Indian Captivities Ser.: Vol. 12). 1978. lib. bdg. 44.00 (ISBN 0-8240-1636-X). Garland Pub.

Narrative of the Capture of Abel Janney by the Indians in 1782. from His Diary: In: Ohio State Arch. & Hist. Society Publications, Vol. 8, 465-73, Columbus, Repr. Of 1900 Ed. Abel Janney. Bd. with Shetek Pioneers & the Indians. Harry J. Hibschman. Repr. of 1901 ed; Captivity Among the Sioux, August 18 to September 26, 1862: In: Minnesota Historical Society Collections, Vol. 9, St. Paul, 1901, pp. 395-426. Mrs. N. D. White. (Illus.). Repr. of 1901 ed; Elizabeth Hicks, a True Romance of the American War of Independence, 1775 to 1783, Abridged from Her Own Manuscript by Her Daughter Fanny Bird, Completed & Ed. by Her Granddaughter Louisa J. Marriott. Elizabeth Hicks. Repr. of 1902 ed; Scout Journals, 1757. Narrative of James Johnson, a Captive During French & Indian Wars. Repr. of 1902 ed. LC 75-7132. (Indian Captivities Ser.: Vol. 104). 1976. lib. bdg. 44.00 (ISBN 0-8240-1728-5). Garland Pub.

Narrative of the Capture of Certain Americans, at Westmorland, by Savages, Repr. Of 1780 Ed. Bd. with 2nd ed. Repr. of 1784 ed; Sketches of the Life & Adventure of Moses Van Campen. John N. Hubbard. Repr. of 1841 ed. LC 75-7033. (Indian Captivities Ser.: Vol. 13). 1977. lib. bdg. 44.00 (ISBN 0-8240-1637-8). Garland Pub.

Narrative of the Chinese Embassy to the Khan of the Tourgouth Tartars, 1712-1715. Tulisen. Tr. by George L. Staunton from Chinese. (Studies in Chinese History & Civilization). 330p. Date not set. Repr. of 1821 ed. 24.00 (ISBN 0-89093-073-2). U Pubns Amer.

Narrative of the Incidents Attending the Capture, Detention & Ransom of Charles Johnston... Who Was Made Prisoner by the Indians. LC 75-7065. (Indian Captivities Ser.: Vol. 43). 1976. Repr. of 1827 ed. lib. bdg. 44.00 (ISBN 0-8240-1667-X). Garland Pub.

Narrative of the Life of Frederick Douglass. Frederick Douglass. pap. 2.95 (ISBN 0-385-00705-1, C419, Anch). Doubleday.

Narrative of the Life of Mrs. Charlotte Charke. Charlotte C. Charke. LC 70-81365. (Illus.). 1969. Repr. of 1755 ed. 32.00x (ISBN 0-8201-1065-5). Schol Facsimiles.

Narrative of the Life of Mrs. Mary Jamison Who Was Taken by the Indians in the Year 1755 When Only About 12 Years of Age & Has Continued to Reside Amongst Them to the Present Time, Repr. Of 1824 Ed. James E. Seaver. Bd. with enl. ed. Ed. by Lewis H. Morgan. Repr. of 1856 ed. LC 75-7063. (Indian Captivities Ser.: Vol. 41). 1977. lib. bdg. 44.00 (ISBN 0-8240-1665-3). Garland Pub.

Narrative of the Lord's Wonderful Dealings with John Marrant, a Black, Repr. Of 1785. Ed. by Wilcomb E. Washburn. Bd. with Very Remarkable Narrative of Luke Swetland, Who Was Taken Captive Four Times in the Space of Fifteen Months. Repr. of 1785 ed. 1875 ed. with additions incl. (ISBN 0-685-63632-1); Edward Merrifield: The Story of the Captivity & Rescue from the Indians of Luke Swetland. Edward Merrifield. Repr. of 1915 ed; Surprising Account of the Captivity & Escape of Philip M'Donald & Alexander M'Leod of Virginia from the Chickkemogga Indians. Repr. of 1786 ed. 1794 ed. incl. (ISBN 0-685-63633-X); Surprising Account of the Discovery of a Lady Who Was Taken by the Indians in the Year 1777, & After Making Her Escape, She Retired to a Lonely Cave, Where She Lived Nine Years. in: Bickerstaff's Almanack for the Year...1788. Repr. of 1787 ed. 1794 ed. incl. (ISBN 0-685-63634-8). (Narratives of North American Indian Captivities Ser.). 1979. lib. bdg. 44.00 (ISBN 0-8240-1641-6). Garland Pub.

Narrative of the Sufferings, & Surprizing Deliverance of William & Elizabeth Fleming, Repr. Of 1756 Ed. William Fleming. Incl. John Maylem: Gallic Perfidy; a Poem. John Maylem. Repr. of 1758 ed; Faithful Narrative of the Many Dangers & Sufferings, As Well As Wonderful Deliverances of Robert Eastburn, During His Late Captivity Among the Indians. Repr. of 1758 ed; Erzehlungen Von Maria le Roy und Barbara Leininger, Welche Vierthalb Jahr Unter Den Indianern Gefangen Gewesen. Repr. of 1759 ed; Plain Narrative of the Uncommon Sufferings, & Remarkable Deliverance of Thomas Brown, of Charlestown in New-England. Repr. of 1760 ed; Narrative of the Uncommon Sufferings, & Surprizing Deliverance of Briton Hammon, a Negro Man,...Servant to General Winslow. Repr. of 1760 ed; Journal of the Captivity of Jean Lowry & Her Children...in Pennsylvania. Repr. of 1760 ed; Erzehlung Eines Unter Den Indianern Gewesenger Gefangenen. Repr. of 1762 ed. (Narrative of North American Indian Captivities: Vol. 8). 1978. lib. bdg. 44.00 (ISBN 0-8240-1632-7). Garland Pub.

Narrative of the Sufferings of Massy Harbison from Indian Barbarity, Giving an Account of Her Captivity, the Murder of Her 2 Children, Her Escape, with an Infant at Her Breast, Repr. Of 1825 Ed. Incl. 4th, enl. ed. Repr. of 1836 ed. LC 75-7064. (Indian Captivities Ser.: Vol. 42). 1977. lib. bdg. 44.00 (ISBN 0-8240-1666-1). Garland Pub.

Narrative of the Tragical Death of Mr. Darius Barber, & His Seven Children, Who Were Inhumanly Butchered by the Indians... to Which Is Added an Account of the Captivity & Sufferings of Mrs. Barber, Repr. Of 1816 Ed. Incl. Shocking Murder by the Savage! of Mr. Darius Barber's Family in Georgia; Narrative of the Captivity & Sufferings of Mrs. Hannah Lewis, & Her 3 Children, Who Were Taken Prisoners by the Indians. Repr. of 1817 ed; Narrative of the Captivity & Providential Escape of Mrs. Lewis. Repr. of 1833 ed; Narrative of James Van Horne: On the Plains of Michigan. Repr. of 1817 ed; Indian Captive: Or a Narrative of the Captivity & Sufferings of Zadock Steele... to Which Is Prefixed an Account of the Burning of Royalton. Repr. of 1818 ed. LC 75-7058. (Indian Captivities Ser.: Vol. 36). 1976. lib. bdg. 44.00 (ISBN 0-8240-1660-2). Garland Pub.

Narrative Strategies: Original Essays in Film & Prose Fiction. Ed. by Syndy M. Conger & Janice R. Welsch. (Essays in Literature Ser.: Bk. 4). 140p. (Orig.). 1981. pap. 8.00x (ISBN 0-934312-03-6). Western Ill Univ.

Narratives of Sorcery & Magic, from the Most Authentic Sources. Thomas Wright. LC 73-177421. 1974. Repr. of 1851 ed. 28.00 (ISBN 0-8103-3821-1). Gale.

Narrow Boat Painting: A History & Description of the English Narrow Boats' Traditional Paintwork. A. J. Lewery. LC 74-81074. 1975. 16.95 (ISBN 0-7153-6771-4). David & Charles.

Narrow Boats at Work. Michael Ware. 144p. 1980. 23.85x (ISBN 0-86190-006-5, Pub. by Allan Pubs England). State Mutual Bk.

Narrow Cage: An American Family Saga. Kathleen S. Ryan. LC 80-687. 320p. 1980. 12.95 (ISBN 0-672-52655-7). Bobbs.

Narrow Escapes of Solomon Smart. Mabel Watts. LC 66-10021. (Illus.). (ps-3). 1966. 5.95 o.s.i. (ISBN 0-8193-0149-3, Four Winds); PLB 5.41 o.s.i. (ISBN 0-8193-0150-7). Schol Bk Serv.

Narrow Gap Semiconductors: Physics & Applications. Ed. by W. Zawadzki. (Lecture Notes in Physics Ser.: Vol. 133). 572p. 1981. pap. 37.20 (ISBN 0-387-10261-2). Springer-Verlag.

Narrow Gauge Adventure: The Story of the Craig & Mertonford Railway. P. D. Hancock. (Illus.). 1978. 19.25 o.p. (ISBN 0-900586-44-3). Aztex.

Narrow Gauge Adventure: The Story of the Craig & Mertonford Railways. 2nd ed. P. D. Hancock. (Illus.). 128p. 1980. 23.50 (ISBN 0-900586-54-0). Aztex.

Narrow Gauge into the Eighties. G. T. Heavyside. LC 79-56067. (Illus.). 96p. 1980. 16.95 (ISBN 0-7153-7979-8). David & Charles.

Narrow Ground. A. T. Stewart. (Illus.). 1977. 14.95 o.p. (ISBN 0-571-10325-1, Pub. by Faber & Faber). Merrimack Bk Serv.

Narrowing the Gap Between Intent & Practice: A Report to Policy-Makers on Community Organizations & School Decisionmaking. Kathleen Huguenin et al. 118p. (Orig.). 1979. pap. 5.00 (ISBN 0-917754-13-1). Inst Responsive.

Narzistische Figuren in Elisabethanischen Tragodien. Eckart Hammerstrom. (Salzburg Studies in English Literature Elizabethan & Renaissance Studies: No. 55). 1976. pap. text ed. 25.00x (ISBN 0-391-01397-1). Humanities.

Nascent Marxist Christian Dialogue: 1961-1967-a Bibliography. D. C. Strange. (Bibliographical Ser.: No. 5). 0.75 o.p. (ISBN 0-89977-005-3). Am Inst Marxist.

Nashville Convention: Southern Movement for Unity, Eighteen Forty-Nine to Eighteen Fifty. Thelma Jennings. LC 80-12917. 1980. 16.95x (ISBN 0-87870-097-8). Memphis St Univ.

Nashville Sound. Paul Hemphill. (Mockingbird Bks). 224p. 1975. pap. 1.50 o.p. (ISBN 0-345-24521-0). Ballantine.

Nasir-I Khusraw: Forty Poems from the Divan. Ed. by Seyyed H. Nasr. Tr. by Peter L. Wilson & Gholam R. Aavani. 1978. 12.50 (ISBN 0-87773-730-4). Great Eastern.

Naskapi: The Savage Hunters of the Labrador Peninsula. Frank G. Speck. (Civilization of the American Indian Ser: Vol. 10). (Illus.). 1935. 12.50 (ISBN 0-8061-1412-6); pap. 5.95 (ISBN 0-8061-1418-5). U of Okla Pr.

Nassau County, Long Island, in Early Photographs, 1869-1940. Bette S. Weidman & Linda B. Martin. (Illus.). 144p. (Orig.). 1981. pap. price not set (ISBN 0-486-24136-X). Dover.

NASSP Advisory List of National Contests & Activities: Annual 1980-1981. 1980. pap. 0.50 (ISBN 0-685-52530-9). Natl Assn Principals.

NASW Register of Clinical Social Workers. 2nd ed. LC 75-42777. 687p. 1978. pap. 30.00x (ISBN 0-87101-019-4, JBD-019-C). Natl Assn Soc Wkrs.

Nat Phil. Jim Jardine. Yrs. 3 & 4, 1974. text ed. 11.00x combined ed. o.p. (ISBN 0-435-67494-3); Yr. 5, 1973. text ed. 10.95x o.p. (ISBN 0-435-68220-2); Yr. 3, 1970. wkbk. 4.95 o.p. (ISBN 0-435-67491-9); Yr. 4, 1971. wkbk. 4.25x o.p. (ISBN 0-435-67492-7); wkbk. 4.25 o.p. (ISBN 0-435-67493-5). Heinemann Ed.

Nat Young's Book of Surfing: The Fundamentals & Adventures of Board-Riding. Nat Young. (Illus.). 90p. 1979. 17.95 (ISBN 0-589-50130-5, Pub. by Reed Books Australia). C E Tuttle.

Natalya. Anabel Brooke. 352p. (Orig.). 1981. pap. 2.75 (ISBN 0-345-29254-5). Ballantine.

Natasha. H. G. Gunther. (Gunther Romance Ser.: No. 6). 224p. (Orig.). 1981. pap. 1.95 o.p. (ISBN 0-515-05680-4). Jove Pubns.

Natchez. Louise MacKendrick. (Orig.). 1977. pap. 1.75 (ISBN 0-505-51138-X). Tower Bks.

Nate the Great & the Lost List. Marjorie W. Sharmat. 1981. pap. 1.25 (ISBN 0-440-46282-7, YB). Dell.

Nate the Great & the Missing Key. Marjorie W. Sharmat. (Illus.). 48p. (gr. 7-10). 1981. PLB 6.99 (ISBN 0-698-30726-7). Coward.

Nate the Great & the Phony Clue. Marjorie W. Sharmat. (gr. k-6). 1981. pap. 1.25 (ISBN 0-440-46300-9, YB). Dell.

Nate the Great & the Sticky Case. Marjorie W. Sharmat. (gr. k-6). pap. 1.25 (ISBN 0-440-46289-4). Dell.

Nathalie Sarraute. Gretchen R. Besser. (World Authors Ser.: No. 534). 1979. lib. bdg. 13.50 (ISBN 0-8057-6376-7). Twayne.

Nathalie Sarraute: The War of the Words. Valerie Minogue. 156p. 1981. 21.00x (ISBN 0-85224-405-3, Pub. by Edinburgh U Pr Sctland). Columbia U Pr.

Nathan Hale, Patriot. Martha Mann. LC 44-8683. (Illus.). (gr. 6-9). 1944. 5.00 (ISBN 0-396-02565-X). Dodd.

Nathaniel Altman's Vegetarian Book. Nathaniel Altman. LC 80-85343. 1981. pap. 2.95. Keats.

Nathaniel Branden Anthology: The Psychology of Self-Esteem, Breaking Free the Disowned Self. Nathaniel Branden. LC 80-51879. 723p. 1980. 17.50 (ISBN 0-87477-142-0), J P Tarcher.

Nathaniel Hawthorne. Terence Martin. (U. S. Authors Ser.: No. 75). 1964. lib. bdg. 11.95 (ISBN 0-8057-0348-9). Twayne.

Nathaniel Hawthorne. George E. Woodberry. LC 67-23888. 1967. Repr. of 1902 ed. 20.00 (ISBN 0-8103-3043-1). Gale.

Nathaniel Hawthorne, 30 vols. George E. Woodberry. LC 80-23480. (American Men & Women of Letters Ser.). 304p. 1981. pap. 4.95 (ISBN 0-87754-154-X). Chelsea Hse.

Nathaniel Hawthorne: A Descriptive Bibliography. C. Frazer Clark, Jr. LC 76-50885. (Pittsburgh Ser. in Bibliography). 1978. 30.00x (ISBN 0-8229-3343-8). U of Pittsburgh Pr.

Nathaniel Hawthorne: Captain of the Imagination. Seon Manley. LC 69-10907. (Illus.). (gr. 8-10). 1969. 7.95 (ISBN 0-8149-0358-4). Vanguard.

Nathaniel Hawthorne in His Time. James R. Mellow. 672p. 1980. 19.95 (ISBN 0-395-27602-0). HM.

Nathaniel Hawthorne Journal. Ed. by C. Frazer Clark, Jr. LC 75-148262. (Illus.). 1971 ed. 22.00 (ISBN 0-910972-04-4); 1972 ed. o.s.i. 22.00 (ISBN 0-910972-33-8); 1973 ed. 22.00 (ISBN 0-910972-39-7); 1974 ed. 23.00 (ISBN 0-910972-50-8); 1975 o.s.i. 23.00 (ISBN 0-910972-55-9); 1976 24.00 (ISBN 0-910972-60-5). IHS-PDS.

Nathaniel Hawthorne Journal Nineteen Seventy-Eight. Ed. by C. Frazer Clark, Jr. (Bruccoli Clark Bk.). (Illus.). 400p. 1980. 28.00 (ISBN 0-8103-0929-7). Gale.

Nathaniel Hawthorne: The English Experience 1853-1864. Raymona E. Hull. LC 79-26616. (Illus.). 1980. 21.95 (ISBN 0-8229-3418-3). U of Pittsburgh Pr.

Nathaniel Hawthorne: Transcendental Symbolist. Marjorie J. Elder. LC 69-18476. vi, 215p. 1969. 12.95x (ISBN 0-8214-0051-7). Ohio U Pr.

Nathaniel Lee. J. M. Armistead. (English Authors Ser.: No. 270). 1979. 14.50 (ISBN 0-8057-6748-7). Twayne.

Nation at War. Arthur A. Stein. LC 80-7994. 176p. 1981. text ed. 12.95x (ISBN 0-8018-2441-9). Johns Hopkins.

Nation-Building & Citizenship: Studies of Our Changing Social Order. Reinhard Bendix. 400p. 1977. 25.75x (ISBN 0-520-02676-4); pap. 6.95x (ISBN 0-520-02761-2, CAMPUS 138). U of Cal Pr.

Nation-Building in Africa: Problems & Prospects. Arnold Rivkin. Ed. by John Morrow. 1970. 22.00 (ISBN 0-8135-0618-2). Rutgers U Pr.

Nation in Crisis 1828-1865. Ed. by David R. Ross et al. LC 78-101951. (AHM Structure of American History Ser: Vol. 3). 1970. pap. 4.95x (ISBN 0-88295-757-0). AHM Pub.

Nation in Crisis, 1861-1877. Compiled by David Donald. LC 74-79169. (Goldentree Bibliographies in American History Ser.). 112p. 1969. pap. 6.95x (ISBN 0-88295-511-X). AHM Pub.

Nation Moving West: Readings in the History of the American Frontier. Ed. by Robert W. Richmond & Robert W. Mardock. LC 66-10446. 1966. 15.95x (ISBN 0-8032-0152-4); pap. 3.50x (ISBN 0-8032-5157-2, BB 336, Bison). U of Nebr Pr.

Nation of Change: The American Democratic System. 2nd ed. John P. Carney. LC 74-26600. 416p. 1975. pap. text ed. 14.95 scp (ISBN 0-06-382347-0, HarpC); scp study guide 6.50 (ISBN 0-06-382348-9). Har-Row.

Nation of Crusaders: The General Plan for the Second American Revolution. Ed. by James Ervin Norwood. LC 75-14729. 1975. 30.00 (ISBN 0-915854-01-5). Friend Freedom.

Nation of Lions...Chained. Mohammad Mehdi. LC 62-17245. 1963. pap. 5.00 (ISBN 0-911026-05-3). New World Press NY.

Nation of Nations. Ed. by Peter Marzio. LC 75-25051. (Illus.). 416p. (YA) 1976. 27.50 (ISBN 0-06-012834-8, HarpT); pap. 8.95 o.p. (ISBN 0-06-012836-4, TD-256, HarpT). Har-Row.

Nation or No Nation? Six Years in British Politics. Enoch Powell & Richard Ritchie. 1978. 24.00 (ISBN 0-7134-1542-8, Pub. by Batsford England). David & Charles.

Nation State & National Self Determination. A. Cobban. 1969. pap. 1.50 o.p. (ISBN 0-531-06014-4, Fontana Pap). Watts.

Nation Unaware: The Canadian Economic Culture. Herschel Hardin. LC 75-302646. 384p. 1974. pap. 8.95 (ISBN 0-295-95723-9). U of Wash Pr.

Nation Within a Nation: The Rise of Texas Nationalism. Mark E. Nackman. (American Studies Ser.). 183p. 1975. 15.00 (ISBN 0-8046-9131-2, Natl U). Kennikat.

Nation Without Prisons. Ed. by Calvert R. Dodge. LC 74-16928. (Illus.). 1976. 21.95 (ISBN 0-669-96438-7). Lexington Bks.

National Academy of Engineering Memorial Tributes. National Academy of Engineering. 1979. 10.00 (ISBN 0-309-02889-2). Natl Acad Pr.

National Account Marketing Handbook. Ed. by Robert S. Rogers & V. B. Chamberlain, 3rd. 426p. 1981. 24.95 (ISBN 0-8144-5618-9). Am Mgmt.

National Accounting Practices in Seventy Countries, Vol. I. (Studies in Methods Ser. F.: No. 26). 226p. 1979. pap. 15.00 (ISBN 0-686-68961-5, UN79/17/19, UN). Unipub.

National Accounting Practices in Seventy Countries, Vol. II. (Studies in Methods Ser. F: No. 26). 205p. 1979. pap. 14.00 (ISBN 0-686-68962-3, UN79/17/19, UN). Unipub.

National Accounting Practices in Seventy Countries, Vol. III. (Studies in Methods Ser. F: No. 26). 203p. 1979. pap. 14.00 (ISBN 0-686-68963-1, UN79/17/19, UN). Unipub.

National Accounts of OECD Countries, Vol. II. OECD. (Illus.). 284p. 1980. pap. 18.00x (ISBN 92-64-02094-2, 30-80-03-3). OECD.

National Accounts of OECD Countries, 1950-1978: Main Aggregates. 90p. 1980. pap. 7.50 (ISBN 92-64-02059-4). OECD.

National Agenda for the Eighties. President's Commission for a National Agenda for the Eighties. 1981. pap. 2.95 (ISBN 0-451-62011-9, ME2011, Ment). NAL.

National & International Radiation Dose Intercomparisons. (Illus.). 165p. 1973. pap. 10.75 (ISBN 92-0-011173-4, IAEA). Unipub.

National & International Standardization of Radiation Dosimetry, Vol. 1. 1978. pap. 50.00 (ISBN 92-0-010478-9, ISP471-1, IAEA). Unipub.

National & International Standardization of Radiation Dosimetry: Vol. 2. 1979. pap. 36.00 (ISBN 92-0-010578-5, ISP471-2, IAEA). Unipub.

National Archives & Foreign Relations Research. Ed. by Milton O. Gustafson. LC 74-82494. (National Archives Conferences Ser.: Vol. 4). xvii, 292p. 1974. 15.00x (ISBN 0-8214-0163-7). Ohio U Pr.

National Association Executives of the United States. Ed. by Craig Colgate, Jr. & Arthur C. Close. LC 80-20428. 1981. pap. 37.50 (ISBN 0-910416-38-9). Columbia Bks.

National Attributes & Behavior. R. J. Rummel. LC 76-50501. (Dimensions of Nations Ser.: Vol. 3). 1979. 27.50x (ISBN 0-8039-0392-8). Sage.

National Case Study: An Empirical Comparative Study of 21 Educational Systems. A. H. Passow et al. LC 76-6078. (International Studies in Evaluation: Vol. 7). 379p. 1976. pap. 29.95 (ISBN 0-470-15119-6). Halsted Pr.

National Central Library: An Experiment in Library Cooperation 1916 - 1974. S. P. Filon. 300p. 1977. lib. bdg. 22.00x (ISBN 0-85365-249-X, Pub. by Lib Assn England). Oryx Pr.

National Character in Action: Intelligence Factors in Foreign Relations. Washington Platt. 1961. 17.50x (ISBN 0-8135-0382-5). Rutgers U Pr.

National Coal Policy Project. 83p. 1979. pap. 10.00 (ISBN 0-686-68797-3, CSIS016, CSIS). Unipub.

National Communications Systems: Some Policy Issues & Options. Lloyd E. Sommerlad. (Reports & Papers on Mass Communication Ser: No. 74). 35p. 1975. pap. 2.50 (ISBN 92-3-101248-7, U398, UNESCO). Unipub.

National Communism & Popular Revolt in Eastern Europe: A Selection of Documents on Events in Poland & Hungary Feb. - Nov., 1956. Ed. by Paul E. Zinner. LC 57-13560. (Orig.). 1956. pap. 10.00x (ISBN 0-231-02200-X). Columbia U Pr.

National Computer Conference '78 Personal Computing Digest. Ed. by Jim C. Warren, Jr. (Illus.). iv, 425p. 1978. pap. 12.00 (ISBN 0-88283-011-2). AFIPS Pr.

National Conference on Catholic School Finance III. 84p. 1977. 3.00. Natl Cath Educ.

National Conference on Catholic School Finance II. 71p. 1975. 3.00. Natl Cath Educ.

National Conference on Catholic School Finance I. 75p. 1974. 3.00. Natl Cath Educ.

National Conference on Clays & Clay Minerals, 9th: Proceedings. Ed. by A. Swineford. (International Ser. on Earth Sciences: Vol. 11). 1962. 22.00 o.p. (ISBN 0-08-009664-6). Pergamon.

National Conference on Clays & Minerals, 8th: Proceedings. Ed. by A. Swineford. 1961. 28.50 o.p. (ISBN 0-08-009351-5). Pergamon.

National Conference on Construction Contracts. Compiled by American Society of Civil Engineers. 84p. 1968. pap. text ed. 11.75 o.p. (ISBN 0-87262-010-7). Am Soc Civil Eng.

National Conference on Environmental Engineering. Compiled by American Society of Civil Engineers. 480p. 1978. pap. text ed. 29.00 (ISBN 0-87262-128-6). Am Soc Civil Eng.

National Conference on Social Welfare: Social Welfare Forum 1976. National Conference on Social Welfare. Ed. by Dorothy M. Swart. LC 8-8537. 1977. 20.00x (ISBN 0-231-04268-X). Columbia U Pr.

National Construction Estimator Nineteen Eighty-One. Gary Moselle. (Illus.). 304p. (Orig.). 1980. pap. 10.75 (ISBN 0-910460-29-9). Craftsman.

National Control of Foreign Business: A Survey of Fifteen Countries. Richard D. Robinson. LC 75-44938. (Special Studies). (Illus.). 1976. text ed. 45.00 (ISBN 0-275-56500-9). Praeger.

National Costumes. Max Tilke. (Illus.). 1978. 67.50 (ISBN 0-8038-5381-5). Hastings.

National Crime Surveys: Cities Attitude Sub-Sample, 1972-1975. Law Enforcement Assistance Administration. 1979. codebook 12.00 (ISBN 0-89138-970-9). ICPSR.

National Crime Surveys: Cities, 1972-1975. Law Enforcement Assistance Administration. LC 78-71978. 1978. codebook 12.00 (ISBN 0-89138-992-X). ICPSR.

National Crime Surveys: National Sample, 1973-1978. Law Enforcement. LC 78-71979. 1979. 10.00 (ISBN 0-89138-991-1). ICPSR.

National Cyclopedia of American Biography. 1979. Index Volume. 59.50 (ISBN 0-88371-028-5). J T White.

National Cyclopedia of American Biography, Vol. 59. 1980. 69.50 (ISBN 0-88371-031-5). J T White.

National Debt. Eric L. Hargreaves. LC 66-9657. Repr. of 1930 ed. 25.00x (ISBN 0-678-05172-0). Kelley.

National Defense System. Stephen Goode. (Career Concise Guides Ser.). (Illus.). (gr. 7 up). 1977. PLB 6.90 s&l (ISBN 0-531-00398-1). Watts.

National Democratic Party: Right-Radicalism in the Federal Republic of Germany. John D. Nagle. LC 78-101340. 1970. 20.00x (ISBN 0-520-01649-1). U of Cal Pr.

National Dental Assistant Boards (NDAB) Jack Rudman. (Admission Test Ser.: AT-87). (Cloth bdg. avail. on request). 17.95 (ISBN 0-8373-5087-5). Natl Learning.

National Development 1776-1966: A Selective & Annotated Guide to the Most Important Articles in English. H. Kent Geiger. LC 77-5813. 1969. 10.00 (ISBN 0-8108-0248-1). Scarecrow.

National Directory of Arts Support by Private Foundations. Daniel Millsaps et al. LC 77-79730. (Arts Patronage Ser.: No. 6, Vol. 3). 1978. pap. 65.00 (ISBN 0-912072-07-5). Wash Intl Arts.

National Directory of Arts Support by Private Foundations, Vol. 4. Daniel Millsaps & Washington International Arts Letter Editors. (Arts Patronage Ser.: No. 9). 214p. 1980. pap. 65.00 (ISBN 0-912072-10-5). Wash Intl Arts.

National Directory of Budget Motels. Ed. by Raymond Carlson. LC 75-11992. 1981. pap. 3.50 (ISBN 0-87576-051-1). Pilot Bks.

National Directory of CB Radio Channels. ABM Service Corp. LC 78-12796. 1979. 15.00 (ISBN 0-88280-064-7); pap. 7.95 (ISBN 0-88280-065-5). ETC Pubns.

National Directory of External Degree Programs. Alfred Munzert. 1977. 8.95 o.p. (ISBN 0-9991729-2-1); pap. 4.95 (ISBN 0-9991729-3-X). Dutton.

National Directory of Four Year Colleges, Two Year Colleges & Post High School Training Programs for Young People with Learning Disabilities. 4th ed. Ed. by P. M. Fielding. 1981. 14.95 (ISBN 0-686-19675-9). PIP.

National Directory of Free Tourist Attractions. Ed. by Raymond Carlson. LC 77-3251. 1979. pap. 2.95 (ISBN 0-87576-057-0). Pilot Bks.

National Directory of Full-Service, Twenty-Four-Hour Auto-Truck Stops. 1979. pap. 2.50 (ISBN 0-918734-21-5). Reymont.

National Directory of Private Social Agencies. LC 64-20853. 1964. 45.00 (ISBN 0-87514-001-7). Croner.

National Directory of State Agencies, 1980-1981. Compiled by Nancy D. Wright & Gene P. Allen. 718p. 1975. text ed. 62.50 (ISBN 0-87815-032-3). Info Resources.

National Directory of the Safety Consultants. 1980. 7.50 (ISBN 0-686-21678-4). ASSE.

National Directory of Women's Employment Programs: Who They Are; What They Do. Women's Work Force. LC 79-117218. (Illus.). 1979. 7.50 (ISBN 0-934966-00-1). WOW Inc.

National Economic Accounting. C. O'Loughlin. 1971. 23.00 (ISBN 0-08-016395-5). Pergamon.

National Economy. J. D. Farquhar. 184p. 1975. 18.00x (ISBN 0-86003-008-3, Pub. by Allan Pubs England); pap. 9.00x (ISBN 0-86003-109-8). State Mutual Bk.

National Economy: An Introduction to Macroeconomics. Gordon A. Philpot. LC 80-20615. (Introduction to Economics Ser.). 256p. 1981. pap. text ed. 7.95 (ISBN 0-471-05591-3). Wiley.

National Education Association: The Power Base for Education. Allan M. West. LC 80-66130. 1980. 15.95 (ISBN 0-02-934880-3). Free Pr.

National Election of 1964. Ed. by Milton C. Cummings, Jr. et al. 1966. 9.95 (ISBN 0-8157-1642-7). Brookings.

National Electrical Code Questions & Answers, 1978. J. Garland. 1979. pap. 5.95 o.p. (ISBN 0-13-622779-1). P-H.

National Electrical Code Reference Book, 1981. 3rd ed. J. D. Garland. (Illus.). 640p. 1981. 21.95 (ISBN 0-13-609321-3). P-H.

National Energy Issues: How Do We Decide? Plutonium As a Test Case. Ed. by Robert G. Sachs. LC 79-18341. (American Academy of Arts & Sciences Ser.). 360p. 1980. reference 25.00 (ISBN 0-88410-620-9). Ballinger Pub.

National Energy Policy: A Continuing Assessment. Council on Energy Resources. (Illus.). 395p. 1978. 4.00. Bur Econ Geology.

National Energy Profiles. Kenneth R. Stunkel. (Praeger Special Studies Ser.). 1980. 32.95 (ISBN 0-03-050646-8). Praeger.

National Estimates of Marriage Dissolution & Survivorship. James A. Weed. Ed. by Klaudia Cox. (Ser. 3, No. 19). 50p. 1980. pap. text ed. 1.75 (ISBN 0-8406-0196-4). Natl Ctr Health Stats.

National Executive Branch. J. W. Davis, Jr. LC 72-96834. 1970. 8.95 o.s.i. (ISBN 0-02-907070-8). Free Pr.

National Faculty Directory Nineteen Eighty-One: An Alphabetical List with Addresses, of About 480,000 Members of Teaching Faculties at Junior Colleges, Colleges, & Universities in the United States & at Selected Canadian Institutions, 2 vols. 11th ed. 2700p. 1980. Set. 175.00 (ISBN 0-8103-0491-0). Gale.

National Field Trial Champions, 1956-1966. William F. Brown. (Illus.). 1966. 12.00 o.p. (ISBN 0-498-06387-9). A S Barnes.

National Finance, 3 pts. Incl. Pt. 1. General, 8 vols. 648.00x (ISBN 0-686-01123-6). Set; Pt. 2. Income Tax, 2 vols. Set. 171.00x (ISBN 0-686-01124-4); Pt. 3. Newspapers, 2 vols. Set. 135.00x (ISBN 0-686-01125-2). (British Parliamentary Papers Ser.). 1971 (Pub. by Irish Academic Pr Ireland). Biblio Dist.

National Fine Arts Exhibitions. Ed. by Theodore Reff. (Modern Art in Paris 1855 to 1900 Ser.). 396p. 1981. lib. bdg. 44.00 (ISBN 0-8240-4733-8). Garland Pub.

National Front. Nigel Fielding. (International Library of Sociology). 228p. 1980. 38.50 (ISBN 0-7100-0559-8). Routledge & Kegan.

National Gallery of Victoria. Ursula Hoff. (Illus.). 216p. 1974. 18.00 (ISBN 0-500-18139-X); pap. 6.95 (ISBN 0-500-20133-1). Transatlantic.

National Geographic Picture Atlas of Our Universe. Roy A. Gallant & Magaret Sedeen. (Illus.). 276p. (gr. 6 up). 1980. 14.95 (ISBN 0-87044-356-9); PLB 16.95 (ISBN 0-87044-357-7). Natl Geog.

National Guard in Politics. Martha A. Derthick. LC 65-11588. (Political Studies Ser). 1965. 10.00x (ISBN 0-674-60200-5). Harvard U Pr.

National Health Insurance: Benefits, Costs, & Consequences. Karen Davis. (Studies in Social Economics). 182p. 1975. 10.95 (ISBN 0-8157-1760-1); pap. 4.95 (ISBN 0-8157-1759-8). Brookings.

National Health Insurance: Can We Learn from Canada? Ed. by Spyros Andreopoulos. LC 75-2348. (Sun Valley Forum on National Health Ser.). 304p. 1975. 20.95 (ISBN 0-471-02925-4, Pub. by Wiley Medical). Wiley.

National Health Insurance: Conflicting Goals & Policy Choices. Ed. by J. Feder et al. LC 80-80045. 721p. 1980. text ed. 25.00x; pap. 12.50 (ISBN 0-87766-271-1). Urban Inst.

National Health Insurance: Costs & Distributional Effects. Gail R. Wilensky & John Holahan. 1972. pap. 3.50 o.p. (ISBN 0-87766-035-2, 70008). Urban Inst.

National Health Insurance in Ontario: Effects of a Policy Cost Control. William S. Comanor. 1980. pap. 4.25 (ISBN 0-8447-3379-2). Am Enterprise.

National Health Insurance: What Now, What Later, What Never? Ed. by Mark V. Pauly. 1980. 16.95 (ISBN 0-8447-2184-0); pap. 8.25 (ISBN 0-8447-2185-9). Am Enterprise.

National Health Service: The First Phase 1948-1974 & After. Brian Watkin. 1978. text ed. 25.00x (ISBN 0-04-362025-6); pap. text ed. 8.95x (ISBN 0-04-362026-4). Allen Unwin.

National Identity. Ed. by Kenneth Goodwin. 1970. text ed. 10.50 o.p. (ISBN 0-435-18370-2). Heinemann Ed.

National Incinerator Conference, 1974: Resource Recovery Thru Incineration. 372p. 1974. pap. text ed. 35.00 (ISBN 0-685-41501-5, 1X0083). ASME.

National Income & Outlay. Colin Clark. LC 67-33059. Repr. of 1937 ed. 22.50x (ISBN 0-678-05162-3). Kelley.

National Income & Social Accounting. Harold C. Edey & Alan Peacock. 1966. text ed. 5.50x (ISBN 0-09-036763-4, Hutchinson U Lib); pap. text ed. 3.00x (ISBN 0-09-036764-2, Hutchinson U Lib). Humanities.

National Income, Expenditure & Output of the United Kingdom, 1855-1965. C. H. Feinstein. LC 71-163055. (Studies in the National Income & Expenditure of the United Kingdom: Vol. 6). (Illus.). 1972. 71.50 (ISBN 0-521-07230-1). Cambridge U Pr.

National Income Nineteen Twenty-Four to Nineteen Thirty-One. Colin Clark. LC 67-33571. Repr. of 1932 ed. 24.00x (ISBN 0-678-05161-5). Kelley.

National Income Statistics: A Critique of Macroeconomic Aggregation. Oskar Morgenstern. (Cato Papers Ser.: No.5). 64p. 1979. pap. 2.00 (ISBN 0-932790-04-6). Cato Inst.

National Index of American Imprints Through 1800: The Short-Title Evans. Ed. by Clifford K. Shipton & James E. Mooney. xxv, 1028p. 1969. 50.00x (ISBN 0-8271-6908-6, Dist. by U Pr of Va). Am Antiquarian.

National Interests & Presidential Leadership: The Setting of Priorities. Donald E. Nuechterlein. LC 78-2764. (Westview Special Studies in International Relations & U.S. Foreign Policy). (Illus.). 1978. lib. bdg. 24.00 o.p. (ISBN 0-89158-169-3); pap. text ed. 9.75x (ISBN 0-89158-170-7). Westview.

National Job Finding Guide. Heinz Ulrich & Robert Conner. LC 79-6182. 336p. 1981. pap. 10.95 (ISBN 0-385-15782-7, Dolp). Doubleday.

National Labor Movements in the Postwar World. Ed. by Everett M. Kassalow. 1963. 11.95x o.s.i. (ISBN 0-8101-0133-5). Northwestern U Pr.

National Liberation. N. Miller & R. Aya. LC 65-11900. 1971. 12.95 (ISBN 0-02-921520-X); pap. text ed. 4.50 (ISBN 0-02-921360-6). Free Pr.

National Materials Policy. National Materials Advisory Board. LC 74-23549. 1975. pap. 11.50 (ISBN 0-309-02247-9). Natl Acad Pr.

National Music of America & Its Sources. Louis C. Elson. LC 70-159950. (Illus.). 1975. Repr. of 1911 ed. 20.00 (ISBN 0-8103-4039-9). Gale.

National Park Guide, 1981. Michael Frome. LC 77-4075. 1981. pap. 7.95 (ISBN 0-528-84544-6). Rand.

National Parks. rev.. ed. Michael Frome. (Illus.). 160p. (Orig.). 1981. pap. 9.95 (ISBN 0-528-88045-4). Rand.

National Parks. Stewart Udall. (Jackdaw Ser: No. A9). 1974. 5.95 o.s.i. (ISBN 0-670-50457-2, Grossman). Viking Pr.

National Parks of Japan. Dorothy Britton. LC 75-30181. 144p. 1981. 17.95 (ISBN 0-87011-250-3). Kodansha.

National Parks of the West. Sunset Editors. LC 79-90339. (Illus.). 256p. 1980. pap. 8.95 (ISBN 0-376-05583-9, Sunset Bks). Sunset-Lane.

National Parkways, Zion & Bryce Canyon National Parks. M. D. Yandell. (Illus.). 64p. 1972. 2.95. Zion.

National Patriotic & Typical Airs of All Lands. John P. Sousa. LC 76-52480. (Music Reprint Series). 1977. Repr. of 1890 ed. lib. bdg. 32.50 (ISBN 0-306-70861-2). Da Capo.

National Playwrights Directory. Ed. by Phyllis J. Kaye. LC 77-83135. (Illus.). 1977. 35.00 (ISBN 0-685-87023-5, O'Neill Theater Center). Gale.

National Plumbing Code Illustrated. Vincent T. Manas. LC 62-16324. (Illus.). 1968. pap. 10.75 (ISBN 0-911804-01-3). Manas.

National Policy for the Environment: NEPA & Its Aftermath. Richard A. Liroff. LC 75-28910. 288p. 1976. 10.00x (ISBN 0-253-33973-1). Ind U Pr.

National Policy for Urban & Regional Development. Ed. by Donald N. Rothblatt. LC 73-11672. (Illus.). 224p. 1974. 21.50 (ISBN 0-669-85043-8). Lexington Bks.

National Politics & Sex Discrimination in Education. Andrew Fishel & Janice Pottker. LC 75-31291. (Politics of Education Ser.). 1977. 17.95 (ISBN 0-669-00336-0). Lexington Bks.

National Portrait Gallery: Complete Illustrated Catalogue. Compiled by K. K. Yung. (Illus.). 650p. 1980. 49.50x (ISBN 0-312-15777-0). St Martin.

National Power & the Structure of Foreign Trade. Albert O. Hirschman. (California Library Reprint Ser.: No. 105). 1980. 45.50 (ISBN 0-520-04084-8); pap. 4.95 (ISBN 0-520-04082-1, CAMPUS 254). U of Cal Pr.

National Power Study Prefeasibility Investigation: Nicaragua, Environmental Impact Reconnaissance. Robert Tillman & Robert Goodland. LC 76-22812. (Illus.). 1976. pap. 5.00 o.p. (ISBN 0-89327-202-7). NY Botanical.

National Priorities for Health: Past, Present, & Projected. R. F. Rushmer. LC 79-25313. (Wiley Series in Health Service). 1980. 24.95 (ISBN 0-471-06472-6, Pub. by Wiley Med). Wiley.

National Program for Solar Heating & Cooling of Buildings: Annual Report. Department of Energy. 1979. pap. cancelled (ISBN 0-930978-22-6). Solar Energy Info.

National Program Plan for Research & Development in Solar Heating & Cooling for Buildings, Agricultural, & Industrial Applications. Department of Energy. 1979. pap. cancelled (ISBN 0-930978-23-4). Solar Energy Info.

National Psychology Boards (NPsyB) Jack Rudman. (Admission Test Ser.: AT-89). (Cloth bdg. avail. on request). pap. 19.95 (ISBN 0-8373-5089-1). Natl Learning.

National Purpose Reconsidered. Ed. by Dona Baron. 1978. 15.00x (ISBN 0-231-04472-0). Columbia U Pr.

National Question: Selected Writings by Rosa Luxembourg. Rosa Luxemburg. Ed. by Horace B. Davis. LC 74-2148. (Illus.). 320p. 1981. pap. 7.00 (ISBN 0-85345-577-5). Monthly Rev.

National Radio Publicity Directory. 9th ed. 1980. 75.00 o.p. (ISBN 0-87314-045-1). Peter Glenn.

National Radio Publicity Directory, 1980-81. 10th ed. Ed. by Peter Glenn et al. 400p. 1981. ring-binder 75.00 (ISBN 0-87314-046-X). Peter Glenn.

National Radio Publicity Directory, 1981. 11th ed. Ed. by Peter Glenn et al. 320p. 1981. 85.00 (ISBN 0-87314-047-8). Peter Glenn.

National Real Estate Examination Study Guide. Richard Beals. 1980. pap. text ed. 10.00 (ISBN 0-89764-002-0). Lincoln's Leadership.

National Recovery Administration. Leverett Lyon et al. LC 71-171386. (FDR & the Era of the New Deal Ser.). 1972. Repr. of 1935 ed. lib. bdg. 75.00 (ISBN 0-306-70385-8). Da Capo.

National Recreational, Sporting & Hobby Organizations of the United States. Craig Colgate, Jr. & Laurie Evans. LC 80-70429. 1981. pap. 25.00 (ISBN 0-910416-36-2). Columbia Bks.

National Roster of Black Judicial Officers, 1980. Ed. by George W. Crockett et al. 120p. (Orig.). 1980. pap. 2.95 (8562). Am Judicature.

National Roster of Women Judges, 1980. Ed. by Larry C. Berkson & Donna Vandenberg. 120p. (Orig.). 1980. pap. 2.95 (8563). Am Judicature.

National Science Policy & Organization of Research in Poland. (Science Policy Studies & Documents Ser., No. 21). (Illus., Orig.). 1970. pap. 6.00 (ISBN 92-3-100819-6, U406, UNESCO). Unipub.

National Science Policy & Organization of Scientific Research in India. LC 72-189984. (Science Policy Studies & Documents Ser., No. 27). (Illus.). 129p. (Orig.). 1973. pap. 6.00 (ISBN 92-3-100952-4, U804, UNESCO). Unipub.

National Security Affairs: A Guide to Information Sources. Ed. by Arthur D. Larson. LC 70-184013. (Management Information Guide Ser.: No. 27). 350p. 1973. 30.00 (ISBN 0-8103-0827-4). Gale.

National Security & Individual Freedom. Harold D. Lasswell. LC 71-139193. (Civil Liberty in American History Ser). 1970. Repr. of 1950 ed. lib. bdg. 25.00 (ISBN 0-306-70085-9). Da Capo.

National Security Policy-Making. Morton H. Halperin. LC 74-16941. 1975. 17.95 (ISBN 0-669-96578-2). Lexington Bks.

National Shark-O-Pedia. Victor R. Faughnan. LC 80-81115. (Illus.). 84p. 1980. pap. 5.95 (ISBN 0-9605532-0-7). Undersea Res.

National Specialty Conference on Disinfection. Compiled by American Society of Civil Engineers. 712p. 1971. text ed. 22.50 (ISBN 0-87262-027-1). Am Soc Civil Eng.

National Square Dance Directory. rev. ed. Gordon J. Goss. 128p. 1981. pap. 8.50 (ISBN 0-9605494-2-0). Natl Sq Dance.

National Strategy for Continuing White-Collar Crime. Ed. by Herbert Edelhertz & Charles Rogovin. LC 79-2373. (Human Affairs Research Center Ser.). 160p. 1980. 15.95x (ISBN 0-669-03166-6). Lexington Bks.

National Strategy for Improving Productivity in Building & Construction. Technology Assessment & Utilization Committee. LC 80-81951. xii, 209p. 1980. pap. text ed. 8.25 (ISBN 0-309-03080-3). Natl Acad Pr.

National Suicide: Military Aid to the Soviet Union. Antony C. Sutton. 1973. 8.95 o.p. (ISBN 0-87000-207-4). Arlington Hse.

National System of Political Economy. Friedrich List. Ed. by Stephen Colwell. Tr. by G. A. Matile. (Neglected American Economists Ser.). 1974. lib. bdg. 50.00 (ISBN 0-8240-1013-2). Garland Pub.

National Teacher Examination. 5th ed. Arco Editorial Board. LC 79-148866. 1974. pap. 6.75 (ISBN 0-668-00823-7). Arco.

National Trade & Professional Associations of the U.S. Canada & Labor Unions. 380p. 1980. 32.00 (ISBN 0-686-62468-8). B Klein Pubns.

National Trade & Professional Associations of the United States & Canada & Labor Unions 1980. 15th ed. Craig Colgate, Jr. & Patricia Broida. LC 74-647774. 1980. pap. 30.00x o.p. (ISBN 0-910416-32-X). Columbia Bks.

National Trade & Professional Associations of the U. S. & Canada & Labor Unions. 16th ed. Craig Colgate, Jr. & Patricia Broida. LC 74-647774. 624p. 1981. pap. 35.00 (ISBN 0-910416-34-6). Columbia Bks.

National Transportation Policy: A Study of Studies. new ed. Harvey A. Levine. LC 78-7156. 1978. 18.95 (ISBN 0-669-02393-0). Lexington Bks.

National Trust Studies Nineteen Seventy-Nine. Ed. by Gervase Jackson-Stops. (Illus.). 184p. 1978. 27.50x (ISBN 0-85667-051-0, Pub. by Sotheby Parke Bernet England). Biblio Dist.

National Trust Studies, 1980. Ed. by Gervase Jackson-Stops. (Illus.). 175p. 1979. 27.50x (ISBN 0-85667-065-0, Pub. by Sotheby Parke Bernet England). Biblio Dist.

National Trust Studies 1981. Ed. by Gervase Jackson-Stops. (Illus.). 160p. 1980. 32.50x (ISBN 0-85667-110-X, Pub. by Sotheby Parke Bernet England). Biblio Dist.

National Velvet. Enid Bagnold. (gr. 7-9). 1971. pap. 1.95 (ISBN 0-671-42893-4). Archway.

National Velvet. Enid Bagnold. (Illus.). (gr. 7 up). 1949. Repr. of 1935 ed. 9.50 (ISBN 0-688-21422-3); PLB 9.12 (ISBN 0-688-31422-8). Morrow.

National Veterinary Boards (NVB) Jack Rudman. (Admission Test Ser.: ATS-50). (Cloth bdg. avail. on request). pap. 25.95 (ISBN 0-8373-5050-6). Natl Learning.

Nationalised Industries: Policies & Performance. Richard Pryke. 282p. 1981. 32.50x (ISBN 0-85520-241-6, Pub. by Martin Robertson England); pap. 12.95x (ISBN 0-85520-242-4). Biblio Dist.

Nationalism. 3rd ed. E. Kedourie. 1979. pap. text ed. 6.50x (ISBN 0-391-02077-3, Hutchinson U Lib). Humanities.

Nationalism. Malcolm Yapp. Ed. by Margaret Killingray & Edmund O'Connor. (World History Ser.). (Illus.). 32p. (gr. 10). 1980. Repr. of 1977 ed. lib. bdg. 5.95 (ISBN 0-89908-227-0); pap. text ed. 1.95 (ISBN 0-89908-202-5). Greenhaven.

Nationalism & Education in Modern China. Cyrus H. Peake. LC 72-80580. 1970. Repr. of 1932 ed. 14.50 (ISBN 0-86527-138-0). Fertig.

Nationalism and Human Rights: Processes of Modernization in the USSR. Ihor Kamenetsky. LC 77-1257. (Series in Issues Studies (Ussr & East Europe): No. 1). 1977. lib. bdg. 18.50x (ISBN 0-87287-143-6). Libs Unl.

Nationalism & Imperialism in the Hither East. Hans Kohn. 1932. 17.00 (ISBN 0-86527-139-9). Fertig.

Nationalism & Revolution in Egypt: The Role O the Muslim Brotherhood. Christina Harris. LC 79-2861. 276p. 1981. Repr. of 1964 ed. 22.50 (ISBN 0-8305-0034-0). Hyperion Conn.

Nationalism & Socialism. F. Davis. 1979. 24.50 o.p. (ISBN 0-685-67810-5). Porter.

Nationalism, Communism & Canadian Labour: The CIO, the Communist Party, & the Canadian Congress of Labour, 1935-56. Irving M. Abella. LC 72-80712. 304p. 1973. pap. 6.50 (ISBN 0-8020-6150-8). U of Toronto Pr.

Nationalism: Essays in Honor of Louis L. Snyder. Ed. by Michael Palumbo & William O. Shanahan. 1981. 19.95 (ISBN 0-935764-02-X). Ark Hse NY.

Nationalism in Contemporary Europe. Franjo Tudjman. (East European Monographs: No. 76). 352p. 1981. text ed. 21.50x (ISBN 0-914710-70-2). East Eur Quarterly.

Nationalism in East Asia: An Annotated Bibliography of Selected Works. Ed. by Gilbert F. Chan. LC 80-8490. 180p. 1981. lib. bdg. 22.00 (ISBN 0-8240-9497-2). Garland Pub.

Nationalism in the Twentieth Century. Anthony D. Smith. LC 78-71404. 1979. cUSA 17.50x (ISBN 0-8147-7799-6); pap. 9.00x cusa (ISBN 0-8147-7803-8). NYU Pr.

Nationalism: Opposing Viewpoints. Ed. by Bruno Leone. (ISMS Ser.). (Illus.). (gr. 9-12). 1978. 8.95 (ISBN 0-912616-57-1); pap. 3.95 (ISBN 0-912616-56-3). Greenhaven.

Nationalist Crusade in Syria. Elizabeth P. MacCallum. LC 79-2873. (Illus.). 299p. 1981. Repr. of 1928 ed. 23.50 (ISBN 0-686-60185-8). Hyperion Conn.

Nationalist Revival in France. Eugen Weber. (California Library Reprint Series: No. 7). 1968. 21.50x (ISBN 0-520-01321-2). U of Cal Pr.

Nationalities of the Soviet East: Publications & Writing Systems, a Bibliographical Directory & Transliteration Tables for Iranian & Turkic-Language Materials Located in U.S. Libraries. Edward Allworth. LC 73-110143. (Middle East Institute Ser). (Illus.). 1971. 25.00x (ISBN 0-231-03274-9). Columbia U Pr.

Nationality & Population Change in Russia & the USSR: An Evaluation of Census Data, 1897-1970. Robert A. Lewis et al. LC 76-6942. (Special Studies). (Illus.). 465p. 1976. text ed. 31.95 o.p. (ISBN 0-275-56480-0). Praeger.

Nationality & Statelessness in International Law. rev. ed. P. Weis. 400p. 1979. 62.50x (ISBN 90-286-0329-8). Sijthoff & Noordhoff.

Nationality Group Survival in Multi-Ethnic States: Shifting Support Patterns in the Soviet Baltic Region. Ed. by Edward Allworth. LC 77-4952. 1977. text ed. 30.95 (ISBN 0-275-24040-1). Praeger.

Nationality: Its Nature & Problems. Bernard Joseph. 1923. 37.50x (ISBN 0-686-51422-X). Elliots Bks.

Nationality Question in Soviet Central Asia. Ed. by Edward Allworth. LC 72-85986. (Special Studies in International Politics & Government Ser.). 1973. 34.50x (ISBN 0-275-28659-2). Irvington.

Nationalization of State Government. Ed. by Jerome J. Hanus. LC 80-8635. (Illus.). 192p. 1981. 19.95x (ISBN 0-669-04334-6). Lexington Bks.

Nationalization of Venezuelan Oil. James F. Petras et al. LC 77-7822. (Praeger Special Studies). 1977. text ed. 24.95 (ISBN 0-03-022656-2). Praeger.

Nations & States: An Inquiry into the Origins of Nations & the Politics of Nationalism. H. Seton-Watson. LC 77-4237. 1977. lib. bdg. 32.50x (ISBN 0-89158-227-4). Westview.

Nation's Families: 1960-1990. George Masnick & Mary Jo Bane. LC 80-20531. (Illus.). 200p. (Orig.). 1980. 17.95 (ISBN 0-86569-050-2); pap. 10.00 (ISBN 0-86569-051-0). Auburn Hse.

Nation's Health. Ed. by Philip R. Lee et al. 560p. 1980. lib. bdg. 16.00x (ISBN 0-87835-107-8); pap. 8.95x (ISBN 0-87835-108-6). Boyd & Fraser.

Nation's Health. Ed. by Stephen Lewin. (Reference Shelf Ser: Vol. 43, No. 3). 1971. 6.25 (ISBN 0-8242-0448-4). Wilson.

Nations in Action: International Tensions. Educational Research Council of America. (Challenges of Our Time Ser.). (gr. 7). 1972. pap. text ed. 9.32 (ISBN 0-205-05033-6, 8050333); tchrs'. guide 6.60 (ISBN 0-205-05034-4, 8050341). Allyn.

Nations in Arms: The Theory & Practice of Territorial Defense. Adam Roberts. LC 76-10671. (Special Studies). (Illus.). 280p. 1976. text ed. 24.95 (ISBN 0-275-23170-4). Praeger.

Nations in Conflict: National Growth & International Violence. Nazli Choucri & Robert North. LC 74-23453. (Illus.). 1975. text ed. 24.95x (ISBN 0-7167-0773-X). W H Freeman.

Nations in Darkness: China, Russia, & America. 3rd ed. John G. Stoessinger. 1978. pap. text ed. 6.95x (ISBN 0-394-32126-X). Random.

Nations in Darkness: China, Russia, & America. 3rd ed. John G. Stoessinger. 263p. 1981. pap. text ed. 6.95 (ISBN 0-394-32657-1). Random.

Nations of the Indian Subcontinent. Ed. by Irwin Isenberg. (Reference Shelf Ser: Vol. 46, No. 1). 1974. 6.25 (ISBN 0-8242-0521-9). Wilson.

Nation's Psychiatrists: 1970 Survey. 38p. pap. 3.25 o.p. (ISBN 0-685-65575-X, 233). Am Psychiatric.

Nations Remembered: An Oral History of the Five Civilized Tribes, 1865-1907. Theda Perdue. LC 79-6828. (Contributions in Ethnic Studies: No. 1). xxiv, 221p. 1980. lib. bdg. 23.95 (ISBN 0-313-22097-2, PFN/). Greenwood.

Nations Without a State: Ethnic Minorities of Western Europe. Ed. by Charles R. Foster. 304p. 1980. 22.95 (ISBN 0-03-056807-2). Praeger.

Nationwide System for Animal Health Surveillance. Committee on Animal Health. LC 74-19048. 1974. pap. 4.25 (ISBN 0-309-02243-6). Natl Acad Pr.

Native American Art at Philbrook. Philbrook Art Center. LC 80-82374. (Orig.). 1980. pap. 8.00 (ISBN 0-86659-001-3). Philbrook.

Native American Christian Community: A Directory of Indian, Aleut, & Eskimo Churches. Ed. by R. Pierce Beaver. 1979. text ed. 10.95 (ISBN 0-912552-25-5). MARC.

Native American Music. new ed. Marcia Herndon. 233p. 1980. lib. bdg. 20.00 (ISBN 0-8482-4475-3). Norwood Edns.

Native American Prehistory: A Critical Bibliography. Dean R. Snow. LC 79-2168. (Newberry Library Center for the History of the American Indian Bibliographical Ser.). 96p. 1980. pap. 3.95x (ISBN 0-253-33498-5). Ind U Pr.

Native American Tribalism. new ed. D'Arcy McNickle. (Illus.). 120p. 1973. 9.95x (ISBN 0-19-501723-4). Oxford U Pr.

Native Americans of North America: A Bibliography Based on Collections in the Libraries of California State University, Northridge. David Perkins & Norman Tanis. (Illus.). 1975. 14.50 (ISBN 0-8108-0878-1). Scarecrow.

Native Americans of the Northwest Coast: A Critical Bibliography. Robert S. Grumet. LC 79-2165. (Newberry Library Center for the History of the American Indian Bibliographical Ser.). 128p. (Orig.). 1980. pap. 4.95x (ISBN 0-253-30385-0). Ind U Pr.

Native & Naturalized Woody Plants of Austin & the Hill Country. Daniel Lynch. Ed. by Jane Mosely. LC 80-53737. (Illus.). 160p. (Orig.). 1980. pap. 6.95 (ISBN 0-938472-00-3). St Edwards Univ.

Native Arts of North America. Christian F. Feest. (World of Art Ser.). (Illus.). 300p. 1980. 17.95 (ISBN 0-19-520215-5); pap. 9.95 (ISBN 0-19-520216-3). Oxford U Pr.

Native Daughter. Leslie Lacy. LC 73-10785. 256p. 1974. 9.95 o.s.i. (ISBN 0-02-567220-7). Macmillan.

Native Languages of the Americas, 2 vols. Ed. by Thomas A. Sebeok. Incl. Vol. 1. 630p. 1976. 47.50 (ISBN 0-306-37157-X); Vol. 2. 535p. 1977. 47.50 (ISBN 0-306-37158-8). LC 76-28216 (Plenum Pr). Plenum Pub.

Native Muse: Theories of American Literature from Bradford to Whitman. Richard Ruland. 1976. pap. 6.95 o.p. (ISBN 0-525-47412-9). Dutton.

Native Population of the Americas in 1492. Ed. by William N. Denevan. LC 75-32071. 1976. 22.50x (ISBN 0-299-07050-6). U of Wis Pr.

Native Races, 5 vols. Hubert H. Bancroft. LC 67-29422. (Works of Hubert Howe Bancroft Ser.). 1967. Repr. of 1888 ed. Set. 125.00x (ISBN 0-914888-00-5). Bancroft Pr.

Native Realm: A Search for Self-Definition. Czeslaw Milosz. 304p. 1981. 12.95 (ISBN 0-385-17596-5). Doubleday.

Native Sons Reader. Ed. by Edward Margolies. LC 74-103596. 1970. 6.95 o.p. (ISBN 0-397-47183-1); pap. 3.25 o.p. (ISBN 0-685-14246-9). Lippincott.

Native to the Grain. George Troy. LC 61-6646. 1961. 3.95 o.p. (ISBN 0-15-164793-3). HarBraceJ.

Native Use of Marine Invertebrates in Old Hawaii. Margaret Titcomb. 1979. pap. text ed. 6.95x (ISBN 0-8248-0715-4). U Pr of Hawaii.

Native's Return. Herbert Kubly. LC 80-5894. 408p. 1981. 14.95 (ISBN 0-8128-2768-6). Stein & Day.

Nativity Stories. Alan Howard. LC 79-20746. (Illus.). 96p. (gr. 5 up). 1980. 9.95 (ISBN 0-89742-027-6). Dawne-Leigh.

NATO After Thirty Years. Lawrence S. Kaplan & Robert W. Clawson. LC 80-53885. 250p. 1981. lib. bdg. 19.95 (ISBN 0-8420-2172-8). Scholarly Res Inc.

NATO: Alliance for Peace. David R. Mets. (Illus.). 190p. (gr. 9-12). 1981. PLB price not set (ISBN 0-671-34065-4). Messner.

Nato: An Alliance for Peace. David R. Mets. (Illus.). 1981. write for info. Messner.

NATO & the Range of American Choice. William T. Fox & Annette B. Fox. LC 67-11560. 1967. 22.50x (ISBN 0-231-03001-0). Columbia U Pr.

NATO: The Next Thirty Years. (Significant Issues Ser.: Vol. I, No. 6). 25p. 1979. pap. 5.00 (ISBN 0-89206-012-3, CSIS007, CSIS). Unipub.

Nato: the Next Thirty Years: A Report of the Conference, Vol. I. LC 79-57250. (Significant Issues Ser.: No. 6). 25p. 1979. 4.00 (ISBN 0-89206-012-3). CSI Studies.

NATO's Strategic Options: Arms Control & Defense. Ed. by David S. Yost. (Pergamon Policy Studies on International Politics). (Illus.). 275p. 1981. 30.00 (ISBN 0-08-027184-7). Pergamon.

Natucket Yesterday & Today. John McCalley. (Illus.). 176p. (Orig.). 1981. pap. price not set (ISBN 0-486-24059-2). Dover.

Natura Legis Naturae, et De Ejus Censura in Succesione Regnorum Suprema: The Works of Sir John Fortescue, London, 1869. John Fortescue. (Classics of the Modern Era: Vol. 1). 296p. 1980. lib. bdg. 50.00 (ISBN 0-8240-4600-5). Garland Pub.

Natural. Bernard Malamud. 237p. 1961. 10.95 (ISBN 0-374-21960-5); pap. 5.95 (ISBN 0-374-50200-5). FS&G.

Natural & Healthy Childhood. Jessie Thomson. 120p. 1976. pap. 6.00x (ISBN 0-8464-1034-6). Beekman Pubs.

Natural & Herbal Beauty. Sally A. Voak. LC 77-85030. (Penny Pinchers Ser.). 1978. 2.95 (ISBN 0-7153-7550-4). David & Charles.

Natural & Induced Cell-Mediated Cytotoxicity: Effector & Regulatory Mechanisms. Ed. by Gert Riethmuller et al. LC 79-14162. (Perspectives in Immunology Ser.). 1979. 19.00 (ISBN 0-12-584650-9). Acad Pr.

Natural & Synthetic Poisons. Gail K. Haines. (Illus.). (gr. 4-6). 1978. 6.95 (ISBN 0-688-22157-2); PLB 6.67 (ISBN 0-688-32157-7). Morrow.

Natural Anthraquinone Drugs. Anthraquinone Symposium, Buergenstock-Luzern, September, 1978. Ed. by J. W. Fairbairn. (Pharmacology Journal: Vol. 20, Suppl. 1). (Illus.). 140p. 1980. pap. 24.00 (ISBN 3-8055-0683-X). S Karger.

Natural Assemblages & the True Crow. Knowles. pap. write for info. (ISBN 0-914162-47-0). Knowles.

Natural Behavior in Humans & Animals. American Psychological Association. (Human Behavior Curriculum Project Ser.). 64p. (Orig.). 1981. pap. text ed. 3.95x (ISBN 0-8077-2613-3); tchrs. manual & duplication masters 9.95 (ISBN 0-8077-2614-1). Tchrs Coll.

Natural Body Building for Men & Women. Robert Kennedy. LC 79-91395. (Illus.). 160p. 1980. 10.95 (ISBN 0-8069-4144-8); lib. bdg. 9.89 (ISBN 0-8069-4145-6); pap. 5.95 (ISBN 0-8069-8920-3). Sterling.

Natural Breast Enlargement: Through Effective Relaxation Techniques. Joan Packard. (Illus.). 96p. (Orig.). 1981. pap. 6.95 (ISBN 0-915190-30-3). Jalmar Pr.

Natural Cat: A Holistic Guide for Finnicky Owners. Anitra Frazier & Norma Eckroate. (Illus.). 208p. 1981. 11.95 (ISBN 0-936602-12-0); pap. 7.95 (ISBN 0-936602-13-9). Harbor Pub CA.

Natural Cell-Mediated Immunity Against Tumors. Ronald B. Herberman. 1980. 65.00 (ISBN 0-12-341350-8). Acad Pr.

Natural Chelating Polymers. Riccardo A. Muzzarelli. 260p. 1974. text ed. 40.00 (ISBN 0-08-017235-0). Pergamon.

Natural Childbirth Book. Joyce Milburn & Lynette Smith. 224p. (Orig.). 1981. pap. 5.95 (ISBN 0-87123-399-1, 210339). Bethany Fell.

Natural Childbirth Primer. Grantly Dick-Read. (Illus.). 1956. 6.95 o.s.i. (ISBN 0-06-001320-6, HarpT). Har-Row.

Natural Convection Heat & Mass Transfer. Y. Jaluria. LC 79-41176. (HMT Ser.). (Illus.). 400p. 1980. 59.00 (ISBN 0-08-025432-2). Pergamon.

Natural Disasters. John E. Butler. 1976. pap. text ed. 7.95x (ISBN 0-435-34068-9). Heinemann Ed.

Natural Fast Food Cookbook. Gail L. Worstman. LC 80-19474. 160p. 1980. pap. 5.95 (ISBN 0-914718-52-5). Pacific Search.

Natural Fire, Its Ecology in Forests. Laurence Pringle. LC 79-13606. (Illus.). 64p. (gr. 4-6). 1979. 5.95 (ISBN 0-688-22210-2); PLB 5.71 (ISBN 0-688-32210-7). Morrow.

Natural Fission Reactors. 1979. pap. 64.25 (ISBN 92-0-051078-7, ISP 475, IAEA). Unipub.

Natural Flower Arranging. Mary Adams. (Illus.). 120p. 1981. 19.95 (ISBN 0-7134-2677-2, Pub. by Batsford England). David & Charles.

Natural Food Book. George Seddon & Jackie Burrow. LC 77-77527. (Illus.). 1977. 14.95 o.s.i. (ISBN 0-528-81002-2). Rand.

Natural Food Cookery. Eleanor Levitt. Orig. Title: Wonderful World of Natural-Food Cookery. (Illus.). 320p. 1979. pap. 3.95 (ISBN 0-486-23851-2). Dover.

Natural Foods. Barbara Fenten & D. X. Fenten. LC 73-10381. (Concise Guide Ser). (Illus.). 72p. (gr. 5 up). 1974. PLB 5.45 o.p. (ISBN 0-531-02675-2). Watts.

Natural Foods & Health Foods Calorie Counter. William I. Kaufman. (Orig.). 1973. pap. 1.25 o.s.i. (ISBN 0-515-04939-5, 9360). Jove Pubns.

Natural Foods Cookbook. Beatrice T. Hunter. 1972. pap. 2.75 o.p. (ISBN 0-515-05691-X, V2850). Jove Pubns.

Natural Foods Ice Cream Book. Robert Soman. (Orig.). 1975. pap. 1.50 o.s.i. (ISBN 0-515-03575-0, A3575). Jove Pubns.

Natural Foods Sweet Tooth Cookbook. Eunice Farmilant. 1978. pap. 2.50 (ISBN 0-515-05826-2). Jove Pubns.

Natural Gas Engineering. Chi Ikoku. 776p. 1980. 45.00 (ISBN 0-87814-141-3). Pennwell Pub.

Natural Gas Regulation Handbook. Richard J. Pierce, Jr. 1980. pap. 25.00 (ISBN 0-917386-29-9). Exec Ent.

Natural Gas: The New Energy Leader. Ernest J. Oppenheimer. 156p. (Orig.). 1981. pap. 7.50 (ISBN 0-9603982-2-8). Pen & Podium.

Natural Geography of Plants. Henry A. Gleason & Arthur Cronquist. LC 64-15448. (Illus.). (gr. 9 up). 1964. 25.00x (ISBN 0-231-02668-4). Columbia U Pr.

Natural Healer's Acupressure Handbook: G-Jo Fingertip Technique. Michael Blake. (Illus.). 1977. 9.95 (ISBN 0-916878-06-6). Falkynor Bks.

Natural Healer's Acupressure Handbook: G-Jo Fingertip Technique. Michael Blate. LC 76-45282. (Illus.). 1977. 8.95 o.p. (ISBN 0-03-020631-6); pap. 4.95 (ISBN 0-03-020626-X). HR&W.

Natural Healing Cookbook: Over Four Hundred Fifty Delicious Ways to Get Better & Stay Healthy. Mark Bricklin & Charon Claessens. (Illus.). 416p. 1981. 16.95 (ISBN 0-87857-338-0). Rodale Pr Inc.

Natural Health & Beauty. Meredith Bronwen. (Illus.). 304p. 1981. 19.95 (ISBN 0-03-057976-7). HR&W.

Natural Health Book. Dorothy Hall. LC 77-74715. (Illus.). 1977. pap. 6.95 o.p. (ISBN 0-684-15228-2, ScribT). Scribner.

Natural Health, Sugar & the Criminal Mind. Jerome I. Roddale. (Orig.). 1968. pap. 1.50 o.s.i. (ISBN 0-515-01828-7, N1828). Jove Pubns.

Natural High Fiber Diet. William I. Kaufmann. 1976. pap. 1.25 o.p. (ISBN 0-515-04121-1, Jove). BJ Pub Group.

Natural History. Eugen Kolisko. 1980. pap. 3.25x (ISBN 0-906492-21-1, Pub. by Kolisko Archives). St George Bk Serv.

Natural History & Progress in Treatment of Congenital Heart Defects. B. S. Kidd & John D. Keith. (Illus.). 360p. 1971. 26.50 (ISBN 0-398-02174-0). C C Thomas.

Natural History Auctions, Seventeen Hundred to Nineteen Seventy-Two: A Register of Sales in the British Isles. Ed. by J. M. Chalmers-Hunt. 192p. 1976. 45.00x (ISBN 0-85667-021-9, Pub. by Sotheby Parke Bernet England). Biblio Dist.

Natural History Drawings in the India Office Library. Mildred Archer. (Illus.). 116p. 1962. 22.50x (ISBN 0-85667-082-0, Pub. by Sotheby Parke Bernet England). Biblio Dist.

Natural History Manuscript Resources in the British Isles. Compiled by Gavin D. Bridson et al. LC 79-92886. 1980. 100.00 (ISBN 0-8352-1281-5). Bowker.

Natural History Notebook, 2 bks. Charles Douglas. (Illus.). 1977. No. 1. pap. 2.00 (ISBN 0-660-00092-X, 56440-1, Pub. by Natl Mus Canada); No. 2. pap. 2.00 (ISBN 0-660-00094-6, 56442-8). U of Chicago Pr.

Natural History Notebook, No. 3. Charles Douglas. (Illus.). iv, 54p. Date not set. pap. 2.00 (ISBN 0-660-10341-9, 56444-4, Pub. by Natl Mus Canada). U of Chicago Pr. Postponed.

Natural History of Infectious Disease. 4th ed. F. Macfarlane Burnet & D. O. White. LC 74-174264. (Illus.). 400p. 1972. 38.50 (ISBN 0-521-08389-3); pap. 12.95x (ISBN 0-521-09688-X). Cambridge U Pr.

Natural History of Mexican Rattlesnakes. Barry L. Armstrong & James B. Murphy. Ed. by E. O. Wiley & Joseph T. Collins. (U of KS Museum of Nat. Hist. Special Publication: No. 5). (Illus.). 88p. (Orig.). Date not set. pap. 6.00 (ISBN 0-89338-010-5). U of KS Mus Nat Hist.

Natural History of Mosquitos. Marston Bates. (Illus.). 8.25 (ISBN 0-8446-0480-1). Peter Smith.

Natural History of Raccoons. Dorcas MacClintock. (Illus.). 160p. (gr. 7 up). 1981. 10.95 (ISBN 0-684-16619-4). Scribner.

Natural History of Religion & Dialogues Concerning Natural Religion. David Hume. Ed. by A. Wayne Colver & Vladimir Price. 1976. 34.95x (ISBN 0-19-824379-0). Oxford U Pr.

Natural History of Sharks. Thomas H. Lineaweaver, 3rd & Richard H. Backus. LC 75-109174. (Illus.). 1970. 9.95 (ISBN 0-397-00660-8). Lippincott.

Natural History of the Land of the Bible. Azaria Alon. LC 77-91916. 1978. 12.95 o.p. (ISBN 0-385-14222-6). Doubleday.

Natural History of the State: An Introduction to Political Science. Henry J. Ford. LC 79-1628. 1981. Repr. of 1915 ed. 18.00 (ISBN 0-88355-932-3). Hyperion Conn.

Natural History of the Whale. Harrison L. Matthews. (Illus.). 1978. 20.00x (ISBN 0-231-04588-3). Columbia U Pr.

Natural History of the Whale. L. Harrison Matthews. (Illus.). 1980. pap. 9.95 (ISBN 0-231-04589-1). Columbia U Pr.

Natural History of Western Trees. Donald C. Peattie. LC 80-12263. (Illus.). xvi, 751p. 1980. pap. 14.95 (ISBN 0-8032-8701-1, BB 741, Bison). U of Nebr Pr.

Natural History of Wild Shrubs & Vines. Donald Stokes. LC 80-8219. (Illus.). 256p. 1981. 12.95 (ISBN 0-06-014163-8, HarpT). Har-Row.

Natural History Photography. Ed. by D. M. Turner Ettlinger. 1975. 40.50 (ISBN 0-12-703950-3). Acad Pr.

Natural Home Physician. Eric F. Powell. LC 79-50415. Date not set. 8.95 (ISBN 0-448-16558-9); pap. 5.95. G&D. Postponed.

Natural Inheritance. Francis Galton. Bd. with Darwinism. (Contributions to the History of Psychology Ser., Vol. IV, Pt. D: Comparative Psychology). 1978. Repr. of 1889 ed. 30.00 (ISBN 0-89093-173-9). U Pubns Amer.

Natural Language Information Processing: A Computer Grammmar of English & Its Applications. Naomi Sager. 1980. text ed. 37.50 (ISBN 0-201-06769-2). A-W.

Natural Law. G. W. Hegel. Tr. by T. M. Knox from Ger. LC 75-10123. 1975. pap. 3.95x (ISBN 0-8122-1083-2, Pa Paperbks). U of Pa Pr.

Natural Law: An Introduction to Legal Philosophy. 2nd rev. ed. A. P. D'Entreves. 1964. text ed. 10.25x (ISBN 0-09-102600-8, Hutchinson U Lib); pap. text ed. 8.50x (ISBN 0-09-102601-6, Hutchinson U Lib). Humanities.

Natural Likeness: Faces & Figures in Nature. John Michell. LC 79-84214. (Illus.). 1979. pap. 7.95 o.p. (ISBN 0-525-47584-2). Dutton.

Natural Logic. N. Tennant. 206p. 1979. 13.00x (ISBN 0-85224-347-2, Pub. by Edinburgh U Pr Scotland). Columbia U Pr.

Natural Order: Historical Studies of Scientific Culture. Ed. by Barry Barnes & Steven Shapin. LC 78-19650. (Sage Focus Editions: Vol. 6). 1979. 18.95x (ISBN 0-8039-0958-6); pap. 9.95x (ISBN 0-8039-0959-4). Sage.

Natural Philosophy of Love. Remy De Gourmont. Tr. by Ezra Pound. 170p. 1972. pap. 1.25 o.s.i. (ISBN 0-02-064950-9, Collier). Macmillan.

Natural Philosophy of Time. 2nd ed. G. J. Whitrow. (Illus.). 288p. 1980. 39.50x (ISBN 0-19-858212-9). Oxford U Pr.

Natural Process Analysis (NPA) A Procedure for Phonological Analysis of Continuous Speech Analysis. Lawrence D. Shribert & Joan Kwiatkowski. LC 80-51707. (Wiley Ser. on Communication Disorders). 175p. 1980. pap. 10.50x (ISBN 0-471-07893-X). Wiley.

Natural Proteinase Inhibitors. Rosemarie Vogel et al. 1969. 24.00 (ISBN 0-12-722850-0). Acad Pr.

Natural Regions of Texas. Elmer H. Johnson. (Research Monograph: No. 8). 1933. pap. 5.00 (ISBN 0-87755-005-0). U of Tex Busn Res.

Natural Regions of the United States & Canada. Charles B. Hunt. LC 73-12030. (Geology Ser.). (Illus.). 1974. text ed. 23.95x (ISBN 0-7167-0255-X); tchr's manual avail. W H Freeman.

Natural Resource Economics: Issues Analysis & Policy. Charles W. Howe. LC 78-24174. 1979. text ed. 24.95x (ISBN 0-471-04527-6). Wiley.

Natural Resources & Energy: Theory & Policy. Chennat Gopalakrishnan. (Illus.). 120p. 1980. 12.50 (ISBN 0-250-40385-4). Ann Arbor Science.

Natural Resources & National Welfare: The Case of Copper. Ed. by Ann Seidman. LC 75-60. (Illus.). 476p. 1975. text ed. 27.50 (ISBN 0-275-05450-0). Praeger.

Natural Resources & Public Relations. Douglas L. Gilbert. LC 76-143896. (Illus.). 320p. 1971. 8.00 (ISBN 0-933564-03-1). Wildlife Soc.

Natural Resources & the State: The Political Economy of Resource Management. Oran R. Young. 1981. 16.50 (ISBN 0-520-04285-9). U of Cal Pr.

Natural Resources for a Democratic Society: Public Participation in Decision-Making. Ed. by Albert E. Utton et al. LC 76-15363. (Special Studies on Natural Resources Management Ser). 1976. pap. text ed. 10.50 (ISBN 0-89158-110-3). Westview.

Natural Resources in U. S. - Canadian Relations: Patterns & Trends in Resource Supplies & Policies, Vol. 2. Ed. by Carl E. Beigie & Alfred O. Hero, Jr. 1980. lib. bdg. 27.50x (ISBN 0-89158-555-9); pap. text ed. 12.00x (ISBN 0-89158-878-7). Westview.

Natural Resources in U. S. - Canadian Relations: Perspectives, Prospects, & Policy Options, Vol. 3. Ed. by Carl E. Beigie & Alfred O. Hero, Jr. 240p. 1981. lib. bdg. 18.50x (ISBN 0-89158-556-7); pap. text ed. 8.50x (ISBN 0-89158-879-5). Westview.

Natural Resources of the Soviet Union: Their Use & Renewal, English Edition. Ed. by I. P. Gerasimov et al. LC 74-138667. (Illus.). 1971. text ed. 31.95x (ISBN 0-7167-0248-7). W H Freeman.

Natural Rights Theories. Richard Tuck. LC 78-73819. 1980. 29.95 (ISBN 0-521-22512-4). Cambridge U Pr.

Natural Rubber & the Synthetics. P. W. Allen. LC 72-5094. 255p. 1972. 22.95 (ISBN 0-470-02329-5). Halsted Pr.

Natural Science Books in English, Sixteen Hundred to Nineteen Hundred. David M. Knight. 1972. 60.00 (ISBN 0-7134-0728-X, Pub. by Batsford England). David & Charles.

Natural Selection & Heredity. 4th ed. Philip M. Sheppard. 1975. text ed. 10.75x (ISBN 0-09-036801-0, Hutchinson U Lib); pap. text ed. 7.50x (ISBN 0-09-036802-9). Humanities.

Natural Selection & Social Behavior. Ed. by Richard D. Alexander. Donald W. Tinkle. LC 80-65758. (Illus.). 550p. 1981. text ed. 49.95x (ISBN 0-913462-08-X). Chiron Pr.

Natural Selection of Population & Communities. D. S. Wilson. 1980. 16.95 (ISBN 0-8053-9560-1). A-W.

Natural Snack Cookbook. Jill Pinkwater. LC 75-11717. (Illus.). 272p. (gr. 7 up). 1975. 14.95 (ISBN 0-590-07374-5, Four Winds). Schol Bk Serv.

Natural Sulfur Compounds: Novel Biochemical & Structural Aspects. Ed. by D. Cavallini et al. 565p. 1980. 49.50 (ISBN 0-306-40335-8, Plenum Pr). Plenum Pub.

Natural Superiority of the Left-Hander. James T. Kay. LC 79-15824. (Illus.). 128p. 1979. pap. 3.95 (ISBN 0-87131-307-3). M Evans.

Natural Superiority of Women. rev. ed. Ashley Montagu. 1968. 7.95 o.s.i. (ISBN 0-02-585620-0). Macmillan.

Natural Supernaturalism: Tradition & Revolution in Romantic Literature. M. H. Abrams. 550p. 1973. pap. 6.95 (ISBN 0-393-00609-3). Norton.

Natural Sweets & Treats. new ed. Ruth Laughlin. LC 75-17275. (Illus.). 176p. (Orig.). 1975. pap. 5.95 (ISBN 0-912800-17-8). Woodbridge Pr.

Natural Tendencies. Joan Mellen. 256p. 1981. 11.95 (ISBN 0-686-69088-5). Dial.

Natural Theology. William Paley. Repr. of 1972 ed. 3.95 o.p. (ISBN 0-686-05047-9). St Thomas.

Natural Toxins: Proceedings of the 6th International Symposium on Animal, Plant & Microbial Toxins, Uppsala, August, 1979. Ed. by D. Baker & T. Wadstrom. LC 80-40898. (Illus.). 704p. 1980. 110.00 (ISBN 0-08-024952-3). Pergamon.

Natural Vegetation of North America. John L. Vankat. LC 78-31264. 1979. pap. text ed. 13.50 (ISBN 0-471-01770-1). Wiley.

Natural Victims. Stephen Lewis. 1978. pap. 1.95 o.p. (ISBN 0-449-14042-3, GM). Fawcett.

Natural Way to Beauty. 3.98. Mayflower Bks.

Natural Way to Better Eyesight. Jerome I. Rodale. (Orig.). 1968. pap. 1.50 (ISBN 0-515-01827-9, V1827). Jove Pubns.

Natural Way to Golf Power. Judy Rankin & Michael Aronstein. LC 74-20407. (Illus.). 224p. (YA) 1976. 8.95 o.s.i. (ISBN 0-06-013517-4, HarpT). Har-Row.

Natural Way to Health. Victor H. Lindlahr. LC 80-19863. 255p. 1980. Repr. of 1973 ed. lib. bdg. 9.95x (ISBN 0-89370-617-5). Borgo Pr.

Natural Wonders of America. American Heritage. pap. 4.95 (ISBN 0-686-60942-5, 24712). S&S.

Natural Wonders of America: An American Heritage Guide. American Heritage Editors. Ed. by Beverly Da Costa. LC 72-80700. (Illus.). 320p. 1972. 6.95 (ISBN 0-686-65711-X, 13065). S&S.

Natural Wonders of America: An American Heritage Guide. American Heritage Editors. Ed. by Beverley Da Costa. LC 72-80700. (Illus.). 320p. 1972. pap. 6.95 (ISBN 0-8281-0296-1, B034G). Am Heritage.

Natural Wonders of the World. Ed. by Reader's Digest. (Illus.). 464p. 1980. 19.95 (ISBN 0-89577-087-3, Pub by Reader's Digest Assoc). Norton.

Natural World Cookbook: Complete Gourmet Meals from Wild Edibles. Joe Freitus. (Illus.). 320p. 1980. 15.00 (ISBN 0-913276-33-2). Stone Wall Pr.

Natural Zeolites: Occurrence, Properties, Use. Ed. by L. B. Sand & F. A. Mumpton. LC 77-30439. 1978. text ed. 115.00 (ISBN 0-08-021922-5). Pergamon.

Naturalism & Ontology. Wilfrid Sellars. 1980. lib. bdg. 22.00 (ISBN 0-917930-36-3); pap. text ed. 7.50x (ISBN 0-917930-16-9). Ridgeview.

Naturalism & Social Science. David Thomas. LC 79-14223. (Themes in Social Sciences Ser.). 1980. 38.50 (ISBN 0-521-22821-2); pap. 13.50 (ISBN 0-521-29660-9). Cambridge U Pr.

Naturalism & the Human Spirit. Ed. by Yervant H. Krikorian. LC 44-2760. 1944. 20.00x (ISBN 0-231-01424-4). Columbia U Pr.

Naturalist Buys an Old Farm. Edwin W. Teale. LC 74-3779. (Illus.). 275p. 1974. 10.00 (ISBN 0-396-06974-6). Dodd.

Naturalist in Central Southern England: Hampshire, Berkshire, Wiltshire, Dorset & Somerset. Derrick Knowlton. (Regional Naturalist Ser.). (Illus.). 13.95 o.p. (ISBN 0-7153-5876-6). David & Charles.

Naturalist in Lakeland. Eric Hardy. (Regional Naturalist Ser.). (Illus.). 1973. 5.95 (ISBN 0-7153-5745-X). David & Charles.

Naturalist in London. John Burton. LC 74-78247. (Regional Naturalist). (Illus.). 168p. 5.95 (ISBN 0-7153-6215-1). David & Charles.

Naturalist in Majorca. James D. Parrack. (Regional Naturalist Ser). (Illus.). 208p. 1973. 5.95 (ISBN 0-7153-5948-7). David & Charles.

Naturalist in Scotland. Derrick Knowlton. LC 74-78250. 1975. 7.50 o.p. (ISBN 0-7153-6627-0). David & Charles.

Naturalist in South East England. S. A. Manning. (Regional Naturalist Ser.). (Illus.). 1973. 14.95 (ISBN 0-7153-6109-0). David & Charles.

Naturalist in the Hebrides. Derrick Knowlton. 1977. 17.95 (ISBN 0-7153-7446-X). David & Charles.

Naturalist in the Isle of Man. Larch S. Garrad. (Naturalist in...Ser.). (Illus.). 232p. 1973. 5.95 (ISBN 0-7153-5628-3). David & Charles.

Naturalist in Wales. R. M. Lockley. 232p. 1970. 14.95 (ISBN 0-7153-4900-7). David & Charles.

Naturalist on a Tropical Farm. Alexander Skutch. LC 78-64474. (Illus.). 1980. 16.95; pap. 7.95 (ISBN 0-520-04149-6, CAL 461). U of Cal Pr.

Naturalist on the Amazons. Henry W. Bates. 1969. 5.00x o.p. (ISBN 0-460-00446-8, Evman). Dutton.

Naturalistic Philosophies of Experience. D. C. Mathur. LC 79-117613. 192p. 1971. 12.00 (ISBN 0-87527-052-2). Fireside Bks.

Naturalist's Adventure in Nepal: Search for the Spiny Babbler. S. Dillon Ripley. (Illus.). 301p. 1981. Repr. of 1953 ed. 12.50 (ISBN 0-87474-810-0). Smithsonian.

Naturalist's Big Bend. Roland H. Wauer. LC 78-21776. (Illus.). 158p. 1980. 10.45 (ISBN 0-89096-069-0); pap. 5.95 (ISBN 0-89096-070-4). Tex A&M Univ Pr.

Naturalist's Handbook -- Collecting & Preparing Animals, Plants & Minerals. Mario Guerra. LC 79-91396. (Illus.). 96p. (gr. 10 up). Date not set. cancelled (ISBN 0-8069-3114-0); PLB 9.29 (ISBN 0-8069-3115-9). Sterling.

Naturalist's Seashore Guide: Common Marine Life Along the Northern California Coast & Adjacent Shores. Gary J. Brusca & Richard C. Brusca. 1978. pap. 8.50x (ISBN 0-916422-12-7). Mad River.

Naturally Italian: A Treasury of Original Stay-Slim Dishes Prepared in Minutes. Elisa Celli & Inez M. Krech. 1978. 12.95 o.p. (ISBN 0-87690-305-7). Dutton.

Naturally Powered Old Time Toys: How to Make Sun Yachts, Sail Cars, a Monkey on a String, & Other Moving Toys. Marjorie Henderson & Elizabeth Wilkinson. LC 78-8556. (Illus.). 1978. 12.95 o.p. (ISBN 0-397-01308-6); pap. 6.95 o.p. (ISBN 0-397-01316-7). Lippincott.

Naturals: Foods Organisms of the Trout. Gary A. Borger. (Illus.). 224p. 1980. 15.95 (ISBN 0-8117-1006-8). Stackpole.

Nature. Boy Scouts Of America. LC 19-600. (Illus.). 48p. (gr. 6-12). 1973. pap. 0.70x (ISBN 0-8395-3285-7, 3285). BSA.

Nature & Art in Renaissance Literature. Edward W. Tayler. LC 64-20484. (Illus.). 1964. 15.00x (ISBN 0-231-02718-4). Columbia U Pr.

Nature & Art of Motion. Ed. by Gyorgy Kepes. LC 65-10807. (Vision & Value Ser). 12.50 o.s.i. (ISBN 0-8076-0289-2). Braziller.

Nature & Art of Workmanship. David Pye. LC 68-12062. (Illus.). 1968. 24.50 (ISBN 0-521-06016-8); pap. 8.95 (ISBN 0-521-29356-1). Cambridge U Pr.

Nature & Background of Major Concepts of Divine Power in Homer. Odysseus Tsagarakis. 1977. pap. text ed. 34.25x (ISBN 90-6032-083-2). Humanities.

Nature & Culture: American Landscape & Painting Eighteen Twenty-Five to Eighteen Seventy-Five. Barbara Novak. (Illus.). 1980. 35.00 (ISBN 0-19-502606-3). Oxford U Pr.

Nature & Culture: American Landscape & Painting 1825-1875. Barbara Novak. (Illus.). 336p. 1981. pap. 18.95 (ISBN 0-19-502935-6, OPB). Oxford U Pr.

Nature & Culture in D. H. Lawrence. Aidan Burns. 137p. 1980. 19.50x (ISBN 0-389-20091-3). B&N.

Nature & Destiny of Man, Two Vols. Vol. 1, Human Nature, Vol. 2, Human Destiny. Reinhold Niebuhr. 1949. Vol. 1. pap. 5.95 o.p. (ISBN 0-684-71858-8, SL97, ScribT); Vol. 2. pap. 5.95 o.p. (ISBN 0-684-71859-6, SL98, ScribT). Scribner.

Nature & Dignity of Love. William Of St. Tierry. Ed. by E. R. Elder. Tr. by Thomas X. Davis from Lat. (Cistercian Fathers Ser.: No. 30). Orig. Title: De natura et dignitate amoris. 1981. write for info. (ISBN 0-87907-330-6). Cistercian Pubns.

Nature & Industrialization. Ed. by Alasdair Clayre. (Illus.). 1977. 19.50x (ISBN 0-19-871096-8); pap. 6.95x (ISBN 0-19-871097-6). Oxford U Pr.

Nature & Life. Alfred N. Whitehead. LC 34-9604. (Illus.). 1969. Repr. of 1934 ed. lib. bdg. 10.75x (ISBN 0-8371-0751-2, WHNL). Greenwood.

Nature & Needs of the Gifted Child. Don Sellin & Jack Birch. 350p. 1981. text ed. price not set (ISBN 0-89443-362-8). Aspen Systems.

Nature & Nurture of Behavior: Developmental Psychobiology: Readings from Scientific American. Intro. by William T. Greenough. LC 72-11800. (Illus.). 1973. pap. text ed. 7.95x (ISBN 0-7167-0867-1); multiple choice questions avail. (ISBN 0-685-99777-4). W H Freeman.

Nature & Organization of Retroviral Genes in Animal Cells. D. R. Strayer & D. H. Gillespie. (Virology Monographs: Vol. 17). (Illus.). 117p. 1980. 39.80 (ISBN 0-387-81563-5). Springer-Verlag.

Nature & Ornament: Nature the Raw Material of Design. Lewis F. Day. LC 74-137355. (Illus.). 1971. Repr. of 1930 ed. 18.00 (ISBN 0-8103-3328-7). Gale.

Nature & Properties of Engineering Materials. 2nd ed. Zbigniew D. Jastrzebski. LC 75-20431. 656p. 1975. text ed. 28.95x (ISBN 0-471-44089-2). Wiley.

Nature & Properties of Engineering Materials: SI Version. 2nd ed. Zbigniew D. Jastrzebski. LC 77-83735. 1977. text ed. 27.95 (ISBN 0-471-02859-2); solns. manual avail. (ISBN 0-471-03671-4). Wiley.

Nature & Purpose. John F. Haught. LC 80-5738. 131p. 1980. lib. bdg. 15.75 (ISBN 0-8191-1257-7); pap. text ed. 7.75 (ISBN 0-8191-1258-5). U Pr of Amer.

Nature & Religious Imagination: From Edwards to Bushnell. Conrad Cherry. LC 79-7374. 256p. 1980. 12.95 (ISBN 0-8006-0550-0, 1-550). Fortress.

Nature & Society: Later Eighteenth Century Uses of the Pastoral & Georgic. Richard Feingold. 1978. 17.00 (ISBN 0-8135-0847-9). Rutgers U Pr.

Nature & the American Mind: Louis Agassiz & the Culture of Science. Edward Lurie. 128p. 1974. pap. text ed. 4.95x o.p. (ISBN 0-88202-011-0, Sci Hist). N Watson.

Nature & the American: Three Centuries of Changing Attitudes. Hans Huth. LC 57-12393. (Illus.). 250p. 1972. 13.95x (ISBN 0-8032-0926-6); pap. 3.95x (ISBN 0-8032-5761-9, BB 554, Bison). U of Nebr Pr.

Nature & the Fibonacci's Conception of the Universe. James R. Leclerque. (Illus.). 123p. 1980. deluxe ed. 59.85 (ISBN 0-89266-263-8). Am Classical Coll Pr.

Nature & the Victorian Imagination. Ed. by U. C. Knoepflmacher & G. B. Tennyson. 1978. 27.50 (ISBN 0-520-03229-2). U of Cal Pr.

Nature & Treatment of Articulation Disorders. J. P. Johnson. (Illus.). 304p. 1980. 19.75 (ISBN 0-398-03983-6). C C Thomas.

Nature & Treatment of Depression. Frederic F. Flach & Suzanne C. Draghi. LC 74-28265. 448p. 1975. 38.95 (ISBN 0-471-26271-4, Pub. by Wiley Medical). Wiley.

Nature & Types of Sociological Theory. Don Martindale. LC 60-50843. 1960. text ed. 20.50 (ISBN 0-395-04843-5, 3-34640). HM.

Nature & Types of Sociological Theory. 2nd ed. Don A. Martindale. LC 80-68142. (Illus.). 640p. 1981. text ed. 20.50 (ISBN 0-395-29732-X). HM.

Nature As Constructor. Klaus Wunderlich & Wolfgang Gloede. Tr. by Vladimir Varecha from Ger. LC 80-18311. (Illus.). 196p. 1979. 40.00x (ISBN 0-8002-2424-8). Intl Pubns Serv.

Nature As Constructor. Klaus Wunderluch & Wolfgang Gloede. Tr. by Vladimir Varecha from Ger. LC 80-18311. (Illus.). 196p. 1981. 19.95 (ISBN 0-668-05102-7, 5102). Arco.

Nature at Work. British Museum Natural History. LC 78-66795. (Illus.). 1978. 18.95 (ISBN 0-521-22390-3); pap. 6.95 (ISBN 0-521-29469-X). Cambridge U Pr.

Nature Centers: The Pursuit of Environmental Awareness. James Shoman. 1980. 20.00 o.p. (ISBN 0-8424-0122-9). Caroline Hse.

Nature Close Up: A Fantastic Journey into Reality. rev. ed. Andreas Feininger. (Illus.). 160p. 1981. pap. price not set (ISBN 0-486-24102-5). Dover.

Nature Conservation, 2 vols. Ed. by D. A. Ratcliffe. Incl. Vol. 1. 115.00 (ISBN 0-521-21159-X); Vol. 2. 90.00 (ISBN 0-521-21403-3). LC 76-11065. (Illus.). 1977. Cambridge U Pr.

Nature Crafts. Ellsworth Jaeger. (Illus.). (gr. 9 up). 1950. 8.95 (ISBN 0-02-558770-6). Macmillan.

Nature Crafts & Projects. Beverly Frazier. (Illus.). 40p. (gr. 1-8). 1979. pap. 2.25 (ISBN 0-912300-23-X). Troubador Pr.

Nature, Culture & Gender. Ed. by Carol MacCormack & Marilyn Strathern. (Illus.). 1980. 24.95 (ISBN 0-521-23491-3); pap. 8.95 (ISBN 0-521-28001-X). Cambridge U Pr.

Nature Day & Night. Richard Adams. (Illus.). 112p. 1980. pap. 7.95 (ISBN 0-14-005345-X). Penguin.

Nature Discoveries with a Hand Lens. Richard Headstrom. (Illus.). 425p. 1981. pap. price not set (ISBN 0-486-24077-0). Dover.

Nature Ever New: Essays on the Renewal of Agriculture. George Adams. 1979. pap. 5.95 (ISBN 0-916786-40-4). St George Bk Serv.

Nature Heals: The Psychological Essays of Paul Goodman. Paul Goodman. Ed. by Taylor Stoehr. 1979. pap. 4.95 o.p. (ISBN 0-525-47569-9). Dutton.

Nature in Ornament. Lewis F. Day. LC 70-159852. (Illus.). 1971. Repr. of 1898 ed. 18.00 (ISBN 0-8103-3207-8). Gale.

Nature in Ornament. Lewis F. Day. LC 76-17768. (Aesthetic Movement Ser.: Vol. 23). (Illus.). 1977. Repr. of 1892 ed. lib. bdg. 44.00 (ISBN 0-8240-2472-9). Garland Pub.

Nature in the City: Plants. Joan E. Rahn. LC 76-44324. (Science Information Ser.). (Illus.). (gr. k-5). 1977. PLB 8.65 (ISBN 0-8172-0661-2). Raintree Pubs.

Nature, Intelligibility & Metaphysics: Studies in the Philosophy of F.J.E. Woodbridge. Hae Soo Pyun. (Philosophical Currents Ser.: No. 2). 108p. 1972. pap. text ed. 15.00x (ISBN 90-6032-004-2). Humanities.

Nature Invented It First. Ross E. Hutchins. LC 79-23791. (Illus.). (gr. 5 up). 1980. 5.95g (ISBN 0-396-07788-9). Dodd.

Nature Is Price: The Economics of Mother Earth. W. V. Dieren & M. W. Hummelinck. (Ideas in Progress Ser). 1979. 15.00 (ISBN 0-7145-2663-0, Pub. by M Boyars); pap. 6.95 (ISBN 0-7145-2664-9). Merrimack Bk Serv.

Nature, Man & Society in the Twelfth Century: Essays on New Theological Perspectives in the Latin West. abr. ed. M. D. Chenu. Tr. by Jerome Taylor. LC 68-15574. 1968. 15.00x o.s.i. (ISBN 0-226-10254-8). U of Chicago Pr.

Nature Meditations. Hazrat I. Kahn. LC 80-50829. (Collected Works of Hazrat Inayat Khan Ser.). (Illus.). 128p. (Orig.). 1980. pap. 5.00 (ISBN 0-930872-12-6). Sufi Order Pubns.

Nature of Alexander. Mary Renault. LC 74-15152. 1976. pap. 7.95 (ISBN 0-394-73254-5). Pantheon.

Nature of American Politics. H. G. Nicholas. 142p. 1980. 12.95 (ISBN 0-19-219121-7). Oxford U Pr.

Nature of Anthropology. Pelto. 1966. pap. text ed. 4.95x (ISBN 0-675-09715-0). Merrill.

Nature of Atoms. Alan Holden. (Illus.). 1971. pap. text ed. 3.95x (ISBN 0-19-501499-5). Oxford U Pr.

Nature of Biochemistry. 2nd ed. Ernest Baldwin. (Orig.). 1962. 19.50 (ISBN 0-521-04097-3); pap. 6.95x (ISBN 0-521-09177-2, 177). Cambridge U Pr.

Nature of Black Cultural Reality. Chukwulozie K. Anyanwu. 1976. pap. text ed. 16.75x o.p. (ISBN 0-8191-0013-7). U Pr of Amer.

Nature of Computation: An Introduction to Computer Science. Ira Pohl & Alan Shaw. (Illus.). 1981. text ed. 16.95 (ISBN 0-914894-12-9). Computer Sci.

Nature of Culture. Alfred L. Kroeber. (Illus.). 1952. 20.00x (ISBN 0-226-45422-3). U of Chicago Pr.

Nature of Dance As a Creative Art Activity. 1980. 12.50x (ISBN 0-912536-11-X). Mettler Studios.

Nature of Democracy, Freedom & Revolution. Herbert Aptheker. LC 67-29076. (Orig.) (YA) (gr. 9-12). 1967. pap. 1.50 o.p. (ISBN 0-7178-0137-3). Intl Pub Co.

Nature of Economic Thought. George L. Shackle. 1966. 44.50 (ISBN 0-521-06278-0). Cambridge U Pr.
Nature of Enzymology. R. L. Foster. 384p. 1980. 79.00x (ISBN 0-85664-434-X, Pub. by Croom Helm England). State Mutual Bk.
Nature of Explanation. Kenneth J. Craik. 1943. 19.95 (ISBN 0-521-04755-2); pap. 7.95 (ISBN 0-521-09445-3, 445). Cambridge U Pr.
Nature of Faith. Gerhard Ebeling. Tr. by Ronald G. Smith from Ger. LC 62-7194. 192p. 1967. pap. 5.95 (ISBN 0-8006-1914-5, 1-1914). Fortress.
Nature of Gothic: A Chapter from the Stones of Venice. John Ruskin. Ed. by William Morris. LC 76-17747. (Aesthetic Movement & the Arts & Crafts Movement Ser.: Vol. 1). 1977. Repr. of 1892 ed. lib. bdg. 44.00 (ISBN 0-8240-2450-8). Garland Pub.
Nature of Human Behaviour. Altner Gunter. Tr. by Charles Van Amerongen. 1976. text ed. 21.00x o.p. (ISBN 0-04-573012-1). Allen Unwin.
Nature of Human Consciousness: A Book of Readings. Ed. by Robert E. Ornstein. LC 73-4431. (Psychology Ser.). (Illus.). 1973. pap. text ed. 10.95x (ISBN 0-7167-0790-X). W H Freeman.
Nature of Human Intelligence. Joy P. Guilford. (Psychology Ser.). (Illus.). 1967. text ed. 34.00 o.p. (ISBN 0-07-025135-5, C). McGraw.
Nature of Human Values. Milton Rokeach. LC 72-92870. 1973. 17.95 (ISBN 0-02-926750-1). Free Pr.
Nature of Hypnosis: Selected Basic Readings. Ed. by R. E. Shor & M. T. Orne. 1981. Repr. of 1965 ed. 18.95x (ISBN 0-03-050965-3). Irvington.
Nature of International Society. C. A. Manning. LC 75-23427. 220p. 1962. 28.95 (ISBN 0-470-56760-0). Halsted Pr.
Nature of Law. Ed. by Martin P. Golding. 1966. 11.95 (ISBN 0-394-30213-3). Random.
Nature of Leadership for Hispanics & Other Minorities. Ernest Y. Flores. LC 80-69239. 140p. 1981. perfect bdg. 10.95 (ISBN 0-86548-036-2). Century Twenty One.
Nature of Life. Derry D. Koob & William E. Boggs. LC 73-140837. (Life Science Ser). 1972. text ed. 18.95 (ISBN 0-201-03815-3). A-W.
Nature of Light & Colour in the Open Air. M. Minnaert. 1948. pap. text ed. 4.00 (ISBN 0-486-20196-1). Dover.
Nature of Man. Blaise Pascal. (Illus.). 1980. 33.75 (ISBN 0-89901-007-5). Found Class Reprints.
Nature of Man: A Reader. Ed. by Erich Fromm & Ramon Xirau. (Problems of Philosophy Series, Vol. 5). 1968. 7.95 o.s.i. (ISBN 0-02-541530-1); pap. 2.95 o.s.i. (ISBN 0-02-084960-5). Macmillan.
Nature of Man: A Social Psychological Perspective. Richard L. Gorsuch & H. Newton Malony. (Illus.). 228p. 1976. 18.75 (ISBN 0-398-03327-7). C C Thomas.
Nature of Medieval Narrative. Ed. by Minnette Grunmann-Gaudet & Robin F. Jones. LC 80-66330. (French Forum Monographs: No. 22). 218p. (Orig.). 1980. pap. 12.50 (ISBN 0-917058-21-6). French Forum.
Nature of Melanoma. Vincent J. McGovern & Malcolm M. Brown. (Amer. Lec. Living Chemistry Ser.). (Illus.). 196p. 1969. pap. 17.50 spiral (ISBN 0-398-01257-1). C C Thomas.
Nature of Modern Mathematics. 2nd ed. Karl J. Smith. LC 75-19937. (Contemporary Undergraduate Mathematics Ser.). (Illus.). 1976. text ed. 15.95 o.p. (ISBN 0-8185-0171-5); instructor's manual avail. o.p. (ISBN 0-685-55263-2). Brooks-Cole.
Nature of Modern Mathematics. 3rd ed. Karl J. Smith. LC 79-20064. 1980. text ed. 16.95 (ISBN 0-8185-0352-1). Brooks-Cole.
Nature of Morality: An Introduction to Ethics. Gilbert Harman. 1977. text ed. 9.95x (ISBN 0-19-502142-8); pap. text ed. 4.95x (ISBN 0-19-502143-6). Oxford U Pr.
Nature of Narrative. Robert Scholes & Robert Kellogg. 1968. pap. 5.95 (ISBN 0-19-500773-5, GB). Oxford U Pr.
Nature of Necessity. Alvin Plantinga. 1979. pap. 9.95x (ISBN 0-19-824414-2). Oxford U Pr.
Nature of Occupational Cancer: A Critical Review of Present Problems. Bertram D. Dinman. 112p. 1974. 14.75 (ISBN 0-398-02907-5). C C Thomas.
Nature of Philosophy. John Kekes. (American Philosophical Quarterly Library of Philosophy). 226p. 1980. 24.50x (ISBN 0-8476-6247-0). Rowman.
Nature of Physics: A Physicist's Views on the History & Philosophy of His Science. Robert B. Lindsay. LC 68-10642. 212p. 1971. Repr. of 1968 ed. 10.00 (ISBN 0-87057-107-9, Pub. by Brown U Pr). Univ Pr of New England.
Nature of Proof. 2nd ed. Erwin P. Bettinghaus. LC 76-173979. (Orig.). 1972. pap. 3.50 (ISBN 0-672-61295-X, SC1). Bobbs.
Nature of Religious Knowledge. Norman MacLeish. 174p. Repr. of 1938 ed. text ed. 3.50 (ISBN 0-567-02193-9). Attic Pr.
Nature of Science. David C. Greenwood. 1960. 3.75 o.p. (ISBN 0-685-77487-2). Philos Lib.
Nature of Settle Structure & Change: A European View. M. Drewitt & R. Drewett. Date not set. 48.01 (ISBN 0-08-023157-8). Pergamon.
Nature of Sociology. C. R. Bell. LC 78-57600. (Studies in Society). 1980. text ed. cancelled o.p. (ISBN 0-86861-328-2); pap. text ed. 9.95x o.p. (ISBN 0-86861-336-3). Allen Unwin.
Nature of Solids. Alan Holden. LC 65-22156. (Illus.). 1968. 20.00x (ISBN 0-231-02785-0); pap. 7.50x (ISBN 0-231-08591-5). Columbia U Pr.
Nature of Statistics. W. Allen Wallis & Harry V. Roberts. LC 62-11024. 1965. pap. text ed. 3.95 (ISBN 0-02-933730-5). Free Pr.
Nature of System Change: Reform Impact in the Criminal Courts. Raymond T. Nimmer. Ed. by Bette Sikes. 1978. 10.00 (ISBN 0-910058-93-8); pap. 5.00 (ISBN 0-685-65361-7). Am Bar Foun.
Nature of the Bibliotheca of Photius. W. T. Treadgold. (Dumbarton Oaks Studies: Vol. 18). 1980. write for info. (ISBN 0-88402-090-8, Ctr Byzantine). Dumbarton Oaks.
Nature of the Bibliotheca of Photius. Warren T. Treadgold. (Dumbarton Oaks Studis: Vol. 18). (Illus.). 201p. 1980. write for info. (ISBN 0-88402-090-8, Ctr Byzantine). Dumbarton Oaks.
Nature of the Physical Universe: 1976 Nobel Conference. Ed. by Douglas Huff & Omer Prewett. LC 78-14788. 1979. 22.95 (ISBN 0-471-03190-9, Pub. by Wiley-Interscience). Wiley.
Nature of the Social Studies. Robert D. Barr et al. LC 77-2014. 1978. pap. 6.95 (ISBN 0-88280-049-3). ETC Pubns.
Nature of the Stratigraphical Record. 2nd ed. D. V. Ager. 136p. 1981. 17.95 (ISBN 0-470-27052-7). Halsted Pr.
Nature of the Universe. rev. ed. Fred Hoyle. LC 60-13436. (Illus.). 1960. 8.95 o.s.i. (ISBN 0-06-002820-3, HarpT). Har-Row.
Nature of the Universe. Clive W. Kilmeister. Ed. by Robin Clarke. (World of Science Lib.). 1973. pap. 3.95 o.p. (ISBN 0-525-04005-6). Dutton.
Nature of Theological Argument: A Study of Paul Tillich. Robert W. Schrader. LC 75-43784. (Harvard Dissertations in Religion). 1975. pap. 7.50 (ISBN 0-89130-071-6, 020104). Scholars Pr Ca.
Nature of Theory & Research in Social Psychology. Clyde Hendrick & Russell A. Jones. 1972. text ed. 17.95 (ISBN 0-12-340750-8). Acad Pr.
Nature of Thermodynamics. P. W. Bridgman. 8.50 (ISBN 0-8446-0512-3). Peter Smith.
Nature of Things. Anthony Quinton. 400p. 1973. 25.00x (ISBN 0-7100-7453-0). Routledge & Kegan.
Nature of Things. Anthony Quinton. 1978. pap. 8.95 (ISBN 0-7100-8903-1). Routledge & Kegan.
Nature of Thought: Essays in Honor of D. O. Hebb. Ed. by Peter W. Jusczyk & Raymond M. Klein. LC 80-18697. (Illus.). 336p. 1980. text ed. 24.95 (ISBN 0-89859-034-5). L Erlbaum Assocs.
Nature of True Virtue. Jonathan Edwards. 1960. pap. 3.95 (ISBN 0-472-06037-6, 37, AA). U of Mich Pr.
Nature of Vermont: Introduction & Guide to a New England Environment. Charles W. Johnson. LC 79-56774. (Illus.). 250p. 1980. text ed. 15.00x (ISBN 0-87451-182-8); pap. 7.50 (ISBN 0-87451-183-6). U Pr of New Eng.
Nature of Violent Storms. Louis J. Battan. LC 80-24986. (Science Study Ser.: No. S19). (Illus.). 158p. 1981. Repr. of 1961 ed. lib. bdg. 19.50x (ISBN 0-313-22582-6, BANV). Greenwood.
Nature of Woman: An Encyclopedia. Mary A. Warren. LC 79-55299. 736p. 1980. 20.00 (ISBN 0-918528-07-0); pap. 16.00 (ISBN 0-918528-06-2). Edgepress.
Nature Photography at Night. Tappan Gregory. (Museum Pictorial: No. 14). 1952. pap. 1.10 o.p. (ISBN 0-916278-41-7). Denver Mus Natl Hist.
Nature Photography: Its Art & Techniques. Heather Angel. 14.95 o.p. (ISBN 0-85242-105-2, Pub. by Fountain). Morgan.
Nature Photography with High Speed Flash. Walker V. Riper et al. (Museum Pictorial: No. 5). 1952. pap. 1.10 o.p. (ISBN 0-916278-34-4). Denver Mus Natl Hist.
Nature Photography with Miniature Cameras. Alfred M. Bailey. (Museum Pictorial: No. 1). 1951. pap. 1.10 o.p. (ISBN 0-916278-30-1). Denver Mus Natl Hist.
Nature Pleads Not Guilty: An IFIAS Report. Rolando V. Garcia. (Illus.). 330p. Date not set. 54.01 (ISBN 0-08-025823-9). Pergamon.
Nature Reserves & Wildlife. Eric Duffey. 1974. pap. text ed. 9.95x o.p. (ISBN 0-435-61256-5). Heinemann Ed.
Nature Runs Wild: True Disaster Stories. Karen O. Sweeney. (Illus.). (gr. 5-8). 1979. PLB 7.45 s&l (ISBN 0-531-02220-X). Watts.
Nature-Science Annual 1970. LC 70-99175. (Best-Selling Single Titles Ser.). (Illus.). lib. bdg. 7.65 o.p. (ISBN 0-686-51032-1). Silver.
Nature-Science Annual 1972. LC 70-99175. (Best-Selling Single Titles Ser.). (Illus.). lib. bdg. 7.65 o.p. (ISBN 0-686-51031-3). Silver.
Nature-Science Annual 1974. LC 70-99175. (Best-Selling Single Titles Ser.). (Illus.). lib. bdg. 7.65 o.p. (ISBN 0-686-51030-5). Silver.
Nature-Science Annual 1975. LC 75-24690. (Best-Selling Single Titles Ser.). (Illus.). lib. bdg. 8.94 o.p. (ISBN 0-686-51029-1). Silver.
Nature-Science Annual 1976. LC 75-18694. (Best-Selling Single Titles Ser.). (Illus.). lib. bdg. 8.94 o.p. (ISBN 0-686-51028-3). Silver.
Nature-Science Annual 1977. LC 76-25346. (Best-Selling Single Titles Ser.). (Illus.). lib. bdg. 8.94 o.p. (ISBN 0-686-51027-5). Silver.
Nature-Science Annual 1978. (Best-Selling Single Titles Ser.). (Illus.). lib. bdg. 8.94 o.p. (ISBN 0-686-51026-7). Silver.
Nature, Spirituality & Science. Sukh R. Tarneja. 240p. 1980. text ed. 27.50x (ISBN 0-7069-1203-9, Pub by Vikas India). Advent Bk.
Nature Walks in the Kikapoo Valley. Jeanne G. Smith. (Illus.). 274p. 1977. 11.95x (ISBN 0-9604694-0-0); plastic bound 8.45x (ISBN 0-9604694-1-9). Jeannes Dreams.
Nature's Colors: Dyes from Plants. Ida Grae. LC 73-11836. (Illus.). 1974. 14.95 o.s.i. (ISBN 0-02-544950-8). Macmillan.
Nature's Colors: Dyes from Plants. Ida Grae. (Illus.). 1979. pap. 8.95 (ISBN 0-02-012390-6, Collier). Macmillan.
Nature's Design: A Practical Guide to Natural Landscaping. Carol A. Smyser. (Illus.). 416p. Date not set. 16.95 (ISBN 0-87857-343-7). Rodale Pr Inc. Postponed.
Nature's Economy. Donald Worster. LC 78-8220. 1979. pap. 4.95 (ISBN 0-385-14345-1, Anch). Doubleday.
Nature's Law & the Secret of the Universe. R. N. Elliott. (Illus.). 1980. Repr. 94.75 (ISBN 0-89901-008-3). Found Class Reprints.
Nature's Light: The Story of Bioluminescence. Francine Jacobs. LC 73-18326. (Illus.). 96p. (gr. 3-7). 1974. 7.25 (ISBN 0-688-20115-6); PLB 6.96 (ISBN 0-688-30115-0). Morrow.
Nature's Medicine Chest, Sets 1-6. LeArta Moulton. (Illus.). Sets 1&2. 3.50 ea. o.p.; Sets 3-6. 4.50 ea. o.p.; file box 1.25 o.p. (ISBN 0-685-85405-1). Bi World Indus.
Nature's Oddballs. Lisbeth Zappler. LC 76-42419. (gr. 7-9). 1978. PLB 5.95 (ISBN 0-385-08355-6). Doubleday.
Nature's Own Vegetable Cookbook. Ann Williams-Heller. LC 73-183557. Orig. Title: Cooked to Your Taste. 234p. 1972. pap. 1.45 o.p. (ISBN 0-668-02586-7). Arc Bks.
Naturwissenschaft, Technik und NS-Ideologie. Ed. by Herbert Mehrtens & Steffen Richter. (Suhrkamp Taschenbuecher Wissenschaft: Vol. 303). 288p. (Orig.). 1980. pap. text ed. 8.45 (ISBN 3-518-07903-4, Pub. by Insel Verlag Germany). Suhrkamp.
Naughty but Nice. Gerry Blumenfeld & Harold Blumenfeld. 1976. pap. 1.25 o.p. (ISBN 0-685-69508-5, LB374ZK, Leisure Bks). Nordon Pubns.
Naughty Sammy. Ron Van Der Meer & Atie Van Der Meer. (Illus.). 32p. 1980. 8.95 (ISBN 0-241-10140-9, Pub. by Hamish Hamilton England). David & Charles.
Nausea. Jean-Paul Sartre. Tr. by Lloyd Alexander. LC 49-8942. 1959. pap. 3.95 (ISBN 0-8112-0188-0, NDP82). New Directions.
Nautical Etiquette & Customs. Lindsay Lord. LC 76-44659. 1976. pap. 3.00 (ISBN 0-87033-225-2). Cornell Maritime.
Nautical No-No's. Elyse Katz & Robert Katz. LC 80-50537. (Illus.). 160p. 1980. pap. 9.95 (ISBN 0-9604208-0-0). Shayna Ltd.
Nautical Rules of the Road. B. A. Farnsworth & Larry C. Young. 1981. 15.00x (ISBN 0-87033-275-9). Cornell Maritime.
Navaho Neighbors. Franc J. Newcomb. (Illus.). 1966. 12.95 (ISBN 0-8061-0704-9); pap. 5.95 (ISBN 0-8061-1040-6). U of Okla Pr.
Navahos Have Five Fingers. T. D. Allen. LC 63-17167. (Civilization of the American Indian Ser.: Vol. 68). (Illus.). 249p. 1981. 13.95 (ISBN 0-8061-0575-5). U of Okla Pr.
Navajo & Hopi Weaving Techniques. Mary Pendleton. (Illus.). 224p. 1974. 13.95 (ISBN 0-02-595500-4). Macmillan.
Navajo Architecture: Forms, History, Distributions. Stephen C. Jett & Virginia E. Spencer. 1981. text ed. 24.50x (ISBN 0-8165-0688-4); pap. text ed. 12.50x (ISBN 0-8165-0723-6). U of Ariz Pr.
Navajo Design Book. 1975. pap. 2.50 (ISBN 0-918858-04-6). Fun Pub.
Navajo: Herders, Weavers & Silversmiths. Sonia Bleeker. (Illus.). (gr. 3-6). 1958. PLB 6.67 (ISBN 0-688-31456-2). Morrow.
Navajo Indian Book. 1975. pap. 2.50 (ISBN 0-918858-03-8). Fun Pub.
Navajo Indians, Vol. 2. Incl. Navajo Activities Affecting the Acoma-Laguna Area, 1746-1910. Myra E. Jenkins; Navajo Indians. Frank D. Reeve. (American Indian Ethnohistory Ser: Indians of the Southwest). (Illus.). lib. bdg. 42.00 (ISBN 0-8240-0704-2). Garland Pub.
Navajo Indians, Vol. 3. Incl. Navajo Sacred Places. Richard Van Valkenburgh. Ed. by Clyde Kluckhohn. (Illus.); Short History of the Navajo People. Richard Van Valkenburgh; Findings of Fact, & Opinion. Indian Claims Commission. (American Indian Ethnohistory Ser: Indians of the Southwest). (Illus.). lib. bdg. 42.00 (ISBN 0-8240-0705-0). Garland Pub.
Navajo Indians, Vol. 1: Anthropological Study of the Navajo Indians. Florence H. Ellis. (American Indian Ethnohistory Ser: Indians of the Southwest). (Illus.). lib. bdg. 42.00 (ISBN 0-8240-0703-4). Garland Pub.
Navajo Language: A Grammar & Colloquial Dictionary. Robert W. Young & William Morgan. LC 79-56812. 1980. 35.00x (ISBN 0-8263-0536-9). U of NM Pr.
Navajo Mountain Community: Social Organization & Kinship Terminology. Mary Shepardson & Blodwen Hammond. LC 70-97233. 1970. 18.50x (ISBN 0-520-01570-3). U of Cal Pr.
Navajo Nation. Peter Iverson. LC 80-1024. (Contributions in Ethnic Studies: No. 3). (Illus.). 312p. 1981. lib. bdg. 25.00 (ISBN 0-313-22309-2, INN/). Greenwood.
Navajo Native Dyes. Nonobah G. Bryan & Stella Young. (Wild & Woolly West Ser: No. 34). (Illus.). 1978. 7.00 (ISBN 0-910584-49-4); pap. 2.50 (ISBN 0-910584-57-5). Filter.
Navajo Native Dyes: Their Preparation & Use. Ed. by Stella Young. LC 76-43671. (Indian Affairs Ser.: No. 2). (Illus.). Repr. of 1940 ed. 11.50 (ISBN 0-404-15504-9, E99). AMS Pr.
Navajo Symbols of Healing: Essays, Aphorisms, Autobiographical Writings. Donald Sandner. 1979. pap. 8.95 (ISBN 0-15-665445-8, Harv). HarBraceJ.
Navajo Verb Prefix Phonology. James M. Kari. LC 75-25117. (American Indian Linguistics Ser.). 1976. lib. bdg. 42.00 (ISBN 0-8240-1968-7). Garland Pub.
Navajos. rev. ed. Ruth M. Underhill. (Civilization of the American Indian Ser: No. 43). (Illus.). 1978. Repr. of 1956 ed. 12.95 (ISBN 0-8061-0341-8). U of Okla Pr.
Navajos: A Critical Bibliography. Peter Iverson. LC 76-12374. (Newberry Library Center for the History of the American Indian Bibliographical Ser.). 80p. 1976. pap. 3.95x (ISBN 0-253-33986-3). Ind U Pr.
Naval Architecture. (Teach Yourself Ser.). 1976. pap. 4.95 o.p. (ISBN 0-679-10507-7). McKay.
Naval Architecture: Examples & Theory. B. Baxter. 450p. 1978. 39.95x (ISBN 0-85264-179-6, Pub. by Griffin England). State Mutual Bk.
Naval Aristocracy. Peter Karsten. LC 76-136609. 1972. 15.95 (ISBN 0-02-917070-2). Free Pr.
Naval Battles & Heroes. Wilbur Cross & John B. Heffernan. LC 60-13854. (American Heritage Junior Library). (Illus.). 153p. (gr. 5 up). 1960. 9.95 (ISBN 0-06-021375-2, Dist. by Har-Row); PLB 12.89 (ISBN 0-06-021376-0, Dist. by Har-Row). Am Heritage.
Naval Ceremonies, Customs, & Traditions. William P. Mack & Royal W. Connell. LC 79-92236. 352p. 1980. 14.95 (ISBN 0-87021-412-8). Naval Inst Pr.
Naval Encyclopaedia. LC 73-155740. 1971. Repr. of 1884 ed. 45.00 (ISBN 0-8103-3389-9). Gale.
Naval Fast Strike Craft & Patrol Boats. Roy McLeavy. (Illus.). 1979. 10.95 (ISBN 0-7137-0866-2, Pub by Blandford Pr England). Sterling.
Naval History of the Civil War. Howard P. Nash, Jr. LC 76-146768. (Illus.). 288p. 1972. 12.00 o.p. (ISBN 0-498-07841-8). A S Barnes.
Naval Hydrodynamics: Proceedings. Symposium on Naval Hydrodynamics, 12th, Naval Studies Board. 1979. 18.75 (ISBN 0-309-02896-5). Natl Acad Pr.
Naval, Marine & Air Force Uniforms of World War 2. Andrew Mollo. LC 75-28336. (Macmillan Color Ser.). (Illus.). 232p. 1976. 9.95 (ISBN 0-02-579391-8, 57939). Macmillan.
Naval Officer's Guide. 8th ed. Arthur A. Ageton & William P. Mack. LC 43-4401. (Illus.). 1970. 12.00x o.s.i. (ISBN 0-87021-432-2). Naval Inst Pr.
Naval Officers Uniform Guide. John B. Castano. LC 74-82538. (Illus.). 1974. 10.50x o.p. (ISBN 0-87021-485-3); pap. 7.00x o.p. (ISBN 0-686-66912-6). Naval Inst Pr.

Naval Operations Analysis. 2nd ed. Ed. by Naval Science Dept., U. S. Naval Academy. LC 77-73342. 1977. 16.95x (ISBN 0-87021-440-3). Naval Inst Pr.

Naval Review Nineteen Eighty. Ed. by Frank J. Uhlig. LC 62-21028. (Illus.). 264p. 1980. 11.00x (ISBN 0-87021-490-X). Naval Inst Pr.

Naval Science, Vol. 1. Wilbur A. Sundt. LC 78-56425. (Illus.). 320p. 1980. 7.50x (ISBN 0-87021-489-6). Naval Inst Pr.

Naval Special Warfare Teams. Peter B. Mohn. LC 80-26004. (Illus.). 48p. (gr. 4-8). 1981. PLB 9.25 (ISBN 0-686-69420-1). Childrens.

Naval War with France, 1798-1800: "Millions for Defense, but Not One Cent for Tribute". David C. Knight. LC 70-119577. (Focus Books). (Illus.). (gr. 7 up). 1970. PLB 6.45 (ISBN 0-531-01017-1). Watts.

Naval Warfare. Tom Crichton. LC 77-430997. (Pegasus Books: No. 22). (Illus.). 1969. 7.50x (ISBN 0-234-77184-4). Intl Pubns Serv.

Naval Warfare in the Twentieth Century: A Festschrift in Honour of Professor Arthur J. Marder. Ed. by Gerald Jordan. LC 76-28613. 1977. 24.50x (ISBN 0-8448-1001-0). Crane-Russak Co.

Navarre: A Littel Town & Its People. 2nd ed. Clay C. Fisher. LC 74-27622. 1976. 8.00 o.p. (ISBN 0-686-14560-7). C C Fisher.

Naven. 2nd ed. Gregory Bateson. (Illus.). 1958. 17.50x (ISBN 0-8047-0519-4); pap. 6.95 (ISBN 0-8047-0520-8). Stanford U Pr.

Nave's Topical Bible. Orville J. Nave. 1979. 16.95 (ISBN 0-8407-4992-9). Nelson.

Navier-Stokes Equations. R. Teman. LC 79-15106. (Studies Inmathematics & Its Applications: Vol. 2). 520p. 1979. 68.50 (ISBN 0-444-85307-3, North Holland); pap. 24.50 (ISBN 0-444-85308-1, North-Holland). Elsevier.

Navies & Men Series, 25 bks. 1980. Repr. Set. lib. bdg. 706.00x (ISBN 0-405-13030-9). Arno.

Navies in the American Revolution: A Bibliography. Myron J. Smith, Jr. LC 72-10995. (American Naval Bibliography Ser.: Vol. 1). 1973. 10.00 (ISBN 0-8108-0569-3). Scarecrow

Navies of the World: Their Present State & Future Capabilities. Hans Busk. LC 73-82475. (Illus.). 440p. 1973. Repr. of 1859 ed. text ed. 11.00 o.s.i. (ISBN 0-87021-853-0). Naval Inst Pr.

Navigating Britain's Coastline: Land's End to Portland. Adrienne Oldale & Peter Oldale. LC 79-91496. (Illus.). 1980. 17.95 (ISBN 0-7153-7579-2). David & Charles.

Navigating Britain's Coastline: Portland to Dover. Adrienne Oldale & Peter Oldale. LC 80-68901. (Illus.). 88p. 1981. 18.50 (ISBN 0-7153-7960-7). David & Charles.

Navigating with Chart & Compass. Jeff Toghill. (Illus.). 96p. (Orig.). 1980. pap. 8.25 (ISBN 0-589-50183-6, Pub. by Reed Bks Australia). C E Tuttle.

Navigation. (Library of Boating Ser.). (Illus.). 176p. 1975. 14.95 (ISBN 0-8094-2112-7). Time-Life.

Navigation. LC 75-13778. (Library of Boating Ser.). (Illus.). (gr. 6 up). 1975. PLB 13.95 (ISBN 0-8094-2113-5, Pub. by Time-Life). Silver.

Navigation Afloat: A Manual for the Seaman. Alton B. Moody. 768p. 1981. 35.00 (ISBN 0-442-25488-1). Van Nos Reinhold.

Navigation: Finding Your Way on Sea & Land. Tony Gibbs. LC 75-12541. (Impact Bks). 96p. (gr. 8 up). 1975. PLB 6.90 (ISBN 0-531-00838-X). Watts.

Navigation for Watchkeepers. L. W. Fifield. (Illus.). 413p. 1980. 32.50 o.p. (ISBN 0-434-90564-X). Sheridan.

Navigation for Watchkeepers. L. W. Fifield. (Illus.). 416p. 1980. text ed. 32.50x. Sheridan.

Navigation Primer. (Illus.). 1978. pap. 16.00 (ISBN 0-85238-081-X, FN27, FN). Unipub.

Navigational Applications of Plane & Spherical Trigonometry. Carol A. Congleton. LC 79-9431. (Illus.). 1980. pap. 8.50x (ISBN 0-87033-256-2). Cornell Maritime.

Navigator. Morris West. LC 76-5504. 1976. 8.95 o.p. (ISBN 0-688-03061-0). Morrow.

Navigators Supply. William Barlow. LC 76-38150. (English Experience Ser.: No. 430). 100p. Repr. of 1597 ed. 16.00 (ISBN 90-221-0430-3). Walter J Johnson.

Navodenie. Evgeny Zamiatin. (Rus.). 1977. pap. 8.00 (ISBN 0-88233-240-6). Ardis Pubs.

Navy & the Industrial Mobilization in World War II. Robert Howe Connery. LC 73-166951. (FDR & the Era of the New Deal Ser). 526p. 1972. Repr. of 1951 ed. lib. bdg. 49.50 (ISBN 0-306-70322-X). Da Capo.

Navy That Beat Napoleon. Walter Brownlee. LC 78-18091. (Cambridge Introduction to the History of Mankind Ser.). 1981. 3.95 (ISBN 0-521-22145-5). Cambridge U Pr.

Navy, the Company, & Richard King: British Exploration in the Canadian Arctic, 1829-1860. Hugh N. Wallace. (Illus.). 265p. 1980. 21.95x (ISBN 0-7735-0338-2). McGill-Queens U Pr.

Nazi Cinema. Erwin Leiser. (Illus.). 1975. pap. 4.95 o.s.i. (ISBN 0-02-012400-7, Collier). Macmillan.

Nazi Culture. George L. Mosse. LC 80-26608. 432p. 1981. pap. 8.95 (ISBN 0-8052-0668-X). Schocken.

Nazi Interrogator. Raymond F. Tolliver. 464p. 1980. pap. 2.95 (ISBN 0-89083-649-3). Zebra.

Nazi Movement in the United States, Nineteen Twenty-Four to Nineteen Forty-One. Sander A. Diamond. LC 73-16654. 380p. 1973. 22.50x (ISBN 0-8014-0788-5). Cornell U Pr.

Nazi Olympics. Richard R. Mandell. (Illus.). 1971. 7.95 o.s.i. (ISBN 0-02-579290-3). Macmillan.

Nazi Organisation of Women. Jill Stephenson. 246p. 1980. 23.50x (ISBN 0-389-20113-8). B&N.

Nazi Party in Lower Saxony 1921-1933. Jeremy Noakes. (Oxford Historical Monographs). (Illus.). 312p. 1971. 29.50x (ISBN 0-19-821839-7). Oxford U Pr.

Nazi Question. Pierre Aycoberry. 1981. price not set. Pantheon.

Nazi Youth in the Weimar Republic. Peter D. Stachura. LC 74-14196. (Studies in International & Comparative Politics: No. 5). 301p. 1975. text ed. 18.80 (ISBN 0-87436-198-2); pap. text ed. 6.00 (ISBN 0-87436-199-0). ABC-Clio.

Nazis. Robert Hertzstein. Ed. by Time-Life Bks. (World War II Ser.). (Illus.). 208p. 1980. 13.95 (ISBN 0-8094-2534-3). Time-Life.

Nazism. James D. Forman. (gr. 6 up). 1978. PLB 6.90 s&l (ISBN 0-531-01473-8). Watts.

Nazism & the Pastors. James A. Zabel. LC 75-30607. (American Academy of Religion. Dissertation Ser.: No. 14). 1976. pap. 7.50 (ISBN 0-89130-040-6, 010114). Scholars Pr Ca.

NCEA-GANLEY's Catholic Schools in America. 322p. 30.00. Natl Cath Educ.

NCR Basic Electronics Course, with Experiments. NCR Corporation. LC 78-56596. 1978. pap. 11.95 (ISBN 0-672-21549-7). Sams.

NCR Data Communications Concepts. NCR Corporation. LC 78-56590. 1971. pap. 6.95 (ISBN 0-672-21548-9). Sams.

Neanderthal Planet. Brian Aldiss. 192p. 1981. pap. 2.25 (ISBN 0-380-54197-1, 54197). Avon.

Neanderthals. George Constable. (Emergence of Man Ser.). (Illus.). 1973. 9.95 (ISBN 0-8094-1263-2); lib. bdg. avail. (ISBN 0-685-30024-2). Time-Life.

Neanderthals. George Constable. LC 72-96553. (Emergence of Man Ser). (Illus.). 1973. lib. bdg. 9.63 o.p. (ISBN 0-8094-1264-0, Pub. by Time-Life). Silver.

Near Death Experience: A Christian Approach. Hill Brennan. 64p. (Orig.). 1981. pap. 3.50 (ISBN 0-697-01758-3). Wm C Brown.

Near East Readings on Agricultural Investment Projects. (Agricultural Planning Studies: No. 20). 199p. 1980. pap. 10.75 (ISBN 92-5-100917-1, F1935, FAO). Unipub.

Near East(South-West Asia & North Africa) A Bibliographic Study. Jalal Zuwiyya. LC 72-13364. 1973. 13.50 (ISBN 0-8108-0583-9). Scarecrow.

Near the Tidal River: Readings in the Historical Geography of Central Connecticut. Thomas R. Lewis. LC 80-6181. 156p. 1981. lib. bdg. 17.50 (ISBN 0-8191-1464-2); pap. text ed. 8.00 (ISBN 0-8191-1465-0). U Pr of Amer.

Nearing Case: Limitation of Academic Freedom at the Univ. of Penn. by Act of the Board of Trustees, June 14, 1915. Lightner Witmer. LC 71-122163. (Civil Liberties in American Liberty Ser.). 123p. 1974. Repr. of 1915 ed. lib. bdg. 17.50 (ISBN 0-306-71978-9). Da Capo.

Nearing the Crossroads: Contending Approaches to Contemporary American Foreign Policy. Reynold Levy. LC 74-21490. 1975. 10.95 o.s.i. (ISBN 0-02-918810-5). Free Pr.

Nearshore Sediment Dynamics & Sedimentation. Ed. by J. Hails & A. Carr. LC 75-6950. 316p. 1975. 53.50 (ISBN 0-471-33946-6, Pub. by Wiley-Interscience). Wiley.

Neat Desk Is the Sign of a Sick Mind. Mab G. Hoover. LC 80-65057. 128p. (Orig.). 1981. pap. 2.95 (ISBN 0-89636-047-4). Accent Bks.

Neat-O, the Supermarket Mouse. Tom Tichenor. LC 80-24770. 32p. (gr. k-3). 1981. 8.95g (ISBN 0-687-27690-X). Abingdon.

Neatos & Litterbugs: Mystery of the Missing Ticket. Norah Smaridge. (Illus.). 24p. (ps-2). 1952. PLB 5.00 (ISBN 0-307-60515-9, Golden Pr). Western Pub.

Nebraksa Symposium on Motivation, 1966. LC 53-11655. (Nebraska Symposia on Motivation Ser: Vol. 14). 1966. 10.95x (ISBN 0-8032-0608-9); pap. 4.95x (ISBN 0-8032-5614-0). U of Nebr Pr.

Nebraska. 28.00 (ISBN 0-89770-103-8). Curriculum Info Ctr.

Nebraska: A Guide to the Cornhusker State. Federal Writers' Project. 424p. 1939. Repr. 39.00 (ISBN 0-403-02177-4). Somerset Pub.

Nebraska: A Guide to the Cornhusker State. Federal Writer's Project of the Works Progress Administration. LC 78-26756. (Illus.). 1979. 15.95x (ISBN 0-8032-1953-9); pap. 5.50 (ISBN 0-8032-6851-3, BB690, Bison). U of Nebr Pr.

Nebraska: A History. Dorothy W. Creigh. (States & the Nation Ser.). (Illus.). 1977. 12.95 (ISBN 0-393-05598-1, Co-Pub. by Aaslh). Norton.

Nebraska Centennial Cookbook. (Illus.). 1966. pap. 6.95 (ISBN 0-8220-1620-6). Centennial.

Nebraska Curriculum for English: Grade 12, Unit 114, Rhetoric. Nebraska Curriculum Development Center. (Nebraska Curriculum for English Ser). (Orig.). 1974. pap. 3.25x student manual (ISBN 0-8032-7546-3). U of Nebr Pr.

Nebraska Curriculum for English: Grade 12, Units 109-110, Man, Society, Nature & Moral Law. Nebraska Curriculum Development Center. (Nebraska Curriculum for English Ser). (Orig.). 1973. pap. 3.95x teacher manual (ISBN 0-8032-7542-0); pap. 2.75x student manual (ISBN 0-8032-7543-9). U of Nebr Pr.

Nebraska Curriculum for English, Grade 10: Units 97-98, Man & Nature. Nebraska Curriculum Development Center. (Nebraska Curriculum for English Ser). (Orig.). 1970. pap. 4.95x student manual (ISBN 0-8032-7530-7); pap. 3.00x tch. manual (ISBN 0-8032-7529-3). U of Nebr Pr.

Nebraska Curriculum for English: Grade 7, Units 71-72, the Rhetoric of Literature. Nebraska Curriculum Development Center. (Nebraska Curriculum for English Ser). 1967. pap. 2.00x teacher manual (ISBN 0-8032-7509-9); pap. 2.75x student manual (ISBN 0-8032-7510-2). U of Nebr Pr.

Nebraska Curriculum for English, Grade 8: Units 82-84, the Hero. Nebraska Curriculum Development Center. (Nebraska Curriculum for English Ser). 1968. pap. 6.95x, student's manual (ISBN 0-8032-7519-6); 3.00x, teachers' manual (ISBN 0-8032-7518-8). U of Nebr Pr.

Nebraska Curriculum for English, Grade 9: Units 89-90, the Rhetoric of Literature. Nebraska Curriculum Development Center. (Nebraska Curriculum for English Ser). 1969. pap. 3.20x student's manual (ISBN 0-8032-7524-2); 2.00x, teachers manual (ISBN 0-8032-7523-4). U of Nebr Pr.

Nebraska Pioneer Cookbook. Compiled by Kay Graber. LC 74-77089. (Illus.). x, 164p. 1974. 8.95 (ISBN 0-8032-0945-2); pap. 3.75 (ISBN 0-8032-5801-1, BB 573, Bison). U of Nebr Pr.

Nebraska Place-Names. Lilian L. Fitzpatrick. Ed. by G. Thomas Fairclough. LC 60-15471. 1960. pap. 3.50 (ISBN 0-8032-5060-6, BB 107, Bison). U of Nebr Pr.

Nebraska State Industrial Directory, 1980. State Industrial Directories. 1980. pap. 20.00 (ISBN 0-89910-005-8). State Indus Dir.

Nebraska Symposium Motivation, 1960. LC 53-11655. (Nebraska Symposia on Motivation Ser.: Vol. 8). 1960. 12.50x (ISBN 0-8032-0601-1); pap. 4.95x (ISBN 0-8032-5608-6). U of Nebr Pr.

Nebraska Symposium on Motivation, 1953. Ed. by Judson S. Brown & James K. Cole. LC 53-11655. (Nebraska Symposia on Motivation Ser: Vol. 1). 1953. pap. 3.95x (ISBN 0-8032-5600-0). U of Nebr Pr.

Nebraska Symposium on Motivation, 1955. Ed. by Marshall R. Jones. LC 53-11655. (Nebraska Symposia on Motivation Ser: Vol. 3). 1955. pap. 4.95x (ISBN 0-8032-5602-7). U of Nebr Pr.

Nebraska Symposium on Motivation, 1956. LC 53-11655. (Nebraska Symposia on Motivation Ser: Vol. 4). 1956. pap. 5.50x (ISBN 0-8032-5603-5). U of Nebr Pr.

Nebraska Symposium on Motivation, 1957. LC 53-11655. (Nebraska Symposia on Motivation Ser: Vol. 5). 1957. pap. 6.95x (ISBN 0-8032-5604-3). U of Nebr Pr.

Nebraska Symposium on Motivation, 1958. LC 53-11655. (Nebraska Symposia on Motivation Ser: Vol. 6). 1958. pap. 4.95x (ISBN 0-8032-5605-1). U of Nebr Pr.

Nebraska Symposium on Motivation, 1959. LC 53-11655. (Nebraska Symposia on Motivation Ser: Vol. 7). 1959. 11.95x (ISBN 0-8032-0600-3). U of Nebr Pr.

Nebraska Symposium on Motivation, 1961. LC 53-11655. (Nebraska Symposia on Motivation Ser.: Vol. 9). 1962. 10.95x (ISBN 0-8032-0603-8); pap. 3.95x (ISBN 0-8032-5609-4). U of Nebr Pr.

Nebraska Symposium on Motivation, 1962. LC 53-11655. (Nebraska Symposia on Motivation Ser: Vol. 10). 1962. 13.50x (ISBN 0-8032-0604-6). U of Nebr Pr.

Nebraska Symposium on Motivation, 1963. LC 53-11655. (Nebraska Symposia on Motivation Ser: Vol. 11). 1963. 10.95x (ISBN 0-8032-0605-4); pap. 3.95x (ISBN 0-8032-5611-6). U of Nebr Pr.

Nebraska Symposium on Motivation, 1964. LC 53-11655. (Nebraska Symposia on Motivation Ser: Vol. 12). 1964. 13.50x (ISBN 0-8032-0606-2); pap. 4.25x (ISBN 0-8032-5612-4). U of Nebr Pr.

Nebraska Symposium on Motivation, 1965. LC 53-11655. (Nebraska Symposia on Motivation Ser: Vol. 13). 1966. 13.50x (ISBN 0-8032-0607-0). U of Nebr Pr.

Nebraska Symposium on Motivation, 1968. LC 53-11655. (Nebraska Symposia on Motivation Ser: Vol. 16). 1969. 13.50x (ISBN 0-8032-0610-0); pap. 5.95x (ISBN 0-8032-5616-7). U of Nebr Pr.

Nebraska Symposium on Motivation, 1979: Attitudes, Values, & Beliefs. Nebraska Symposium on Motivation, 1979. Ed. by Herbert E. Howe, Jr. & Monte M. Page. LC 53-11655. (Nebraska Symposium on Motivation Ser.: Vol. 27). xii, 365p. 1980. 19.95x (ISBN 0-8032-2313-7); pap. 9.95x (ISBN 0-8032-7207-3). U of Nebr Pr.

Nebraska Symposium on Motivation, 1974: Brain Research. Ed. by James K. Cole. LC 53-11655. (Nebraska Symposia on Motivation Ser: Vol. 22). xviii, 310p. 1975. 13.50x (ISBN 0-8032-0617-8); pap. 6.95x (ISBN 0-8032-5622-1). U of Nebr Pr.

Nebraska Symposium on Motivation, 1975: Conceptual Foundations of Psychology. Ed. by William J. Arnold & James K. Cole. LC 53-11655. (Nebraska Symposium on Motivation Ser.: Vol. 23). 1976. 22.50x (ISBN 0-8032-0618-6); pap. 11.95x (ISBN 0-8032-5624-8). U of Nebr Pr.

Nebraska Symposium on Motivation, 1978: Human Emotion. Ed. by Herbert E. Howe, Jr. & Herbert E. Howe. LC 53-11655. (Nebraska Symposia on Motivation Ser.: Vol. 26). 1979. 17.95x (ISBN 0-8032-2306-4); pap. 8.95x (ISBN 0-8032-7203-0). U of Nebr Pr.

Nebraska Symposium on Motivation, 1973: Human Sexuality. Ed. by Richard Dienstbier & James K. Cole. LC 53-11655. (Nebraska Symposia on Motivation Ser: Vol. 21). (Illus.). xvi, 323p. 1974. 13.50x (ISBN 0-8032-0615-1); pap. 5.95x (ISBN 0-8032-5621-3). U of Nebr Pr.

Nebraska Symposium on Motivation, 1976: Personal Construct Psychology. Ed. by James K. Cole & Alvin W. Landfield. LC 53-11655. (Symposia on Motivation Ser: Vol. 24). 1977. 16.95x (ISBN 0-8032-0619-4); pap. 7.95x (ISBN 0-8032-5625-6). U of Nebr Pr.

Nebraska Symposium on Motivation, 1977: Social Cognitive Development. Ed. by Charles B. Keasey, Jr. & Charles B. Keasey, Jr. LC 53-11655. (Nebraska Symposium on Motivation: Vol. 25). 1978. 16.95x (ISBN 0-8032-2701-9); pap. 7.95x (ISBN 0-8032-7750-4). U of Nebr Pr.

Nebraska Symposium on Motivation, 1970. Ed. by Monte M. Page & William J. Arnold. LC 53-11655. (Nebraska Symposia on Motivation Ser: Vol. 18). 1971. 13.50x (ISBN 0-8032-0612-7); pap. 5.50x (ISBN 0-8032-5618-3). U of Nebr Pr.

Nebraska Symposium on Motivation, 1971. Ed. by James K. Cole. LC 53-11655. (Nebraska Symposia on Motivation Ser: Vol. 19). xii, 304p. 1972. 13.50x (ISBN 0-8032-0613-5); pap. 5.50x (ISBN 0-8032-5619-1). U of Nebr Pr.

Nebraska Symposium on Motivation 1972. Ed. by Marshall R. Jones. LC 53-11655. (Nebraska Symposia on Motivation Ser: Index to Vols. 1-6). 1960. pap. 1.50x (ISBN 0-8032-7649-4). U of Nebr Pr.

Nebraska Symposium on Motivation, 1972. Ed. by Donald D. Jensen. LC 53-11655. (Nebraska Symposia on Motivation Ser: Vol. 20). xiv, 347p. 1973. 13.50x (ISBN 0-8032-0614-3); pap. 5.75x (ISBN 0-8032-5620-5). U of Nebr Pr.

Nebraska Symposium on Motivation, 1980: Human Cognition. Ed. by John H. Flowers. LC 53-11655. (Nebraska Symposium on Motivation: Vol. 28). 264p. 1981. 16.50x (ISBN 0-8032-0620-8); pap. 9.95x (ISBN 0-8032-0621-6). U of Nebr Pr.

Nebraska Wild Flowers. Robert C. Lommasson. LC 70-188343. (Illus.). x, 185p. 1973. 16.50 (ISBN 0-8032-0816-2); pap. 10.50 (ISBN 0-8032-5768-6, BB 559, Bison). U of Nebr Pr.

Nebraskan. George E. Johnson, II. 240p. 1981. write for info. (ISBN 0-89305-036-9). Anna Pub.

Nebula Award Stories Eleven. Ed. by Ursula K. LeGuin. LC 66-20974. (YA) 1977. 8.95 o.p. (ISBN 0-06-012564-0, HarpT). Har-Row.

Nebula Award Stories No. 10, Anniversary Issue. Ed. by James Gunn. LC 66-20974. 268p. (YA) 1975. 10.95 o.s.i. (ISBN 0-06-011628-5, HarpT). Har-Row.

Nebula Winners Fifteen. Ed. by Frank Herbert. LC 78-645226. 256p. 1981. 12.95 (ISBN 0-06-014830-6, HarpT). Har-Row.
Nebula Winners Fourteen. Ed. by Frederick Pohl. LC 66-20974. (Harper Science Fiction Ser.). 240p. 1980. 11.95 (ISBN 0-06-013382-1, HarpT). Har-Row.
Nebular Variables. John S. Glasby. LC 74-3354. 220p. 1974. text ed. 42.00 (ISBN 0-08-017949-5). Pergamon.
Necessarie, Fit & Conuenient Education of Gentlewoman. LC 77-26268. (English Experience Ser.: No. 168). 1969. Repr. of 1598 ed. 16.00 (ISBN 90-221-0168-1). Walter J Johnson.
Necessary Diet. Juliette Karow. (Orig.). 1981. pap. 5.95 (ISBN 0-89865-085-2). Donning Co.
Necessary Elements. 1979 ed. Louis A. Kass. 59p. 1979. 4.50 (ISBN 0-87526-242-2). Gould.
Necessary Majority: Middle America & the Urban Crisis. Robert C. Wood. LC 70-183228. (Radner Lecture Ser). 108p. 1972. 12.50x (ISBN 0-231-03617-5). Columbia U Pr.
Necessary Objects. Lois Gould. 1972. 6.95 o.p. (ISBN 0-394-46847-3). Random.
Necessities of War: A Study of Thucydides' Pessimism. Peter Pouncey. LC 80-16887. 232p. 1981. 19.50x (ISBN 0-231-04994-3). Columbia U Pr.
Necessity, Cause & Blame: Perspectives on Aristotle's Theory. Richard Sorabji. LC 79-2449. 1980. 38.50x (ISBN 0-8014-1162-9). Cornell U Pr.
Necessity for Choice. Henry A. Kissinger. LC 61-6187. 1961. 12.50 o.p. (ISBN 0-06-012410-5, HarpT). Har-Row.
Necessity for Ruins, & Other Topics. J. B. Jackson. LC 79-23212. 1980. lib. bdg. 10.00x (ISBN 0-87023-291-6); pap. 4.95 (ISBN 0-87023-292-4). U of Mass Pr.
Necessity of Social Control. I. Meszaros. 1971. text ed. 3.00x (ISBN 0-85036-154-0). Humanities.
Necessity of Social Control. Istvan Meszaros. 1971. pap. 2.95 (ISBN 0-686-23499-5, Merlin Pr). Carrier Pigeon.
Neck & Shoulder Pain. Ian Macnab. (Illus.). 300p. Date not set. lib. bdg. price not set (ISBN 0-683-05354-X). Williams & Wilkins. Postponed.
Neck or Nothing. John Welcome. (Illus.). 1970. lib. bdg. 5.95 o.p. (ISBN 0-571-08466-4, Pub. by Faber & Faber). Merrimack Bk Serv.
Neckache & Backache: Proceedings. E. S. Gurdjian & L. M. Thomas. (Illus.). 296p. 1970. 14.50 (ISBN 0-398-00747-0). C C Thomas.
Necker: Reform Statesman of the Ancien Regime. Robert D. Harris. 1979. 19.50x (ISBN 0-520-03647-6). U of Cal Pr.
Necronomicon. Simon. 288p. 1979. pap. 2.75 (ISBN 0-380-75192-5, 75192). Avon.
Nectar of Heaven. E. C. Tubbs. 1981. pap. 1.95 (ISBN 0-87997-613-6, UJ1613). DAW Bks.
Ned Harrigan: From Corlear's Hook to Herald Square. Richard Moody. LC 80-221. (Illus.). 288p. 1980. 20.95 (ISBN 0-88229-674-4); pap. 10.95 (ISBN 0-88229-755-4). Nelson-Hall.
Ned Kelly & the City of the Bees. Thomas Keneally. LC 80-66217. (Illus.). 128p. (gr. 4-8). 1980. 8.95g (ISBN 0-87923-338-9). Godine.
Ned the Lonely Donkey. (Illus.). Arabic 2.50x (ISBN 0-685-82864-6). Intl Bk Ctr.
Nedra. George B. McCutcheon. 1976. lib. bdg. 15.75x (ISBN 0-89968-063-1). Lightyear.
Need for Change: Towards the New International Economic Order. Gamani Corea. LC 80-40800. 350p. 1980. 25.00 (ISBN 0-08-026095-0). Pergamon.
Need for Chocolate: And Other Poems. Mary Cheever. LC 80-5390. 96p. 1980. 12.50 (ISBN 0-8128-2728-7). Stein & Day.
Need for National Policy for the Use of Underground Space. Compiled by American Society of Civil Engineers. 240p. 1975. pap. text ed. 14.50 (ISBN 0-87262-102-2). Am Soc Civil Eng.
Need to Fail. Bill Steele. 72p. 1974. pap. text ed. 3.50x (ISBN 0-89039-060-6). Ann Arbor Pubs.
Need to Question: An Introduction to Philosophy. Malcolm Clark. LC 72-5579. 304p. 1973. text ed. 13.95 (ISBN 0-13-610857-1). P-H.
Needed Words. Logan P. Smith et al. Ed. by Steele Commager. Incl. B.B.L.'s Recommendations for Pronouncing Doubtful Words; Bull's Bellow; Possibility of a Universal Language; Robert Bridges Recollections; Colloquial Language in Literature; Oxford English; Arabic Words in English; Best English; Index to Tracts XXI-XXIX. (Society for Pure English Ser.: Vol. 4). 1979. lib. bdg. 42.00 (ISBN 0-8240-3668-9). Garland Pub.
Needfull, New & Necessarie Treatise of Chyrugerie. John Banister. LC 73-171732. (English Experience Ser.: No. 300). 276p. Repr. of 1575 ed. 22.00 (ISBN 90-221-0300-5). Walter J Johnson.
Needle. Hal Clement. 1979. pap. 1.95 (ISBN 0-380-00635-9, 44263). Avon.
Needle Lace: Battenberg, Point & Reticella. Ed. by Jules Kliot & Kaethe Kliot. (Illus.). 1981. pap. 5.95 (ISBN 0-916896-18-8). Lacis Pubns.
Needle-Punching. A. T. Purdy. 69.00x (ISBN 0-686-63775-5). State Mutual Bk.
Needle-Watcher: The Will Adams Story, British Samurai. Richard Blaker. LC 72-89743. 1973. pap. 7.95 (ISBN 0-8048-1094-X). C E Tuttle.
Needlecraft Manual. Ana G. Lopo & Bruce Murphy. LC 77-80197. (Illus.). 1977. pap. 7.95 (ISBN 0-8069-8532-1). Sterling.
Needlecraft Projects. Patricia Riley. 1978. 14.95 (ISBN 0-7134-0745-X). David & Charles.
Needlecraft with Beads & Crystals. Marianne Stradal. (Illus.). 64p. 1975. 6.95 (ISBN 0-263-05005-X). Transatlantic.
Needleplay. Erica Wilson. LC 75-6036. (Encore Edition). 1975. 5.95 (ISBN 0-684-16556-2, ScribT). Scribner.
Needlepoint. rev. ed. Hope Hanley. LC 74-14016. (Encore Edition). (Illus.). 176p. 1975. 5.95 (ISBN 0-684-16685-2, ScribT). Scribner.
Needlepoint. 2nd ed. Sunset Editors. LC 76-46659. (Illus.). 80p. 1977. pap. 3.95 (ISBN 0-376-04584-1, Sunset Bks). Sunset-Lane.
Needlepoint. Eleanor R. Young. (Career Concise Guides Ser.). (Illus.). 96p. (gr. 6 up). 1976. PLB 4.90 o.p. (ISBN 0-531-02779-1). Watts.
Needlepoint Book: 303 Stitches with Patterns & Projects. Jo Ippolito Christensen. (Illus.). 384p. 1976. 19.95 (ISBN 0-13-610980-2, Spec); pap. 10.95 (ISBN 0-13-610972-1). P-H.
Needlepoint by Design. Maggie Lane. LC 71-123842. 1970. 17.50 (ISBN 0-684-10338-9, ScribT). Scribner.
Needlepoint Designs for Traditional Furniture. Charles Blackburn. LC 79-67255. (Illus.). 160p. 1980. 17.50 (ISBN 0-8149-0815-2); pap. 12.95 (ISBN 0-8149-0835-7). Vanguard.
Needlepoint Designs from Amish Quilts. Barbara Buchholz & Laura S. Gilberg. (Encore Editions). (Illus.). 1977. 4.95 (ISBN 0-684-16536-8, ScribT). Scribner.
Needlepoint for Everyone. Mary B. Picken & Doris White. LC 67-22543. (Illus.). 1970. 13.95 o.s.i. (ISBN 0-06-005761-0, HarpT). Har-Row.
Needlepoint: In Stitches. Nancy N. Kurten. pap. 3.95 o.p. (ISBN 0-684-13843-3, SL530, ScribT). Scribner.
Needlepoint Simplified. Jo I. Christensen & Sonie S. Ashner. LC 75-167666. (Little Craft Book Ser.). (Illus.). (gr. 6 up). 1971. 5.95 (ISBN 0-8069-5178-8); PLB 6.69 (ISBN 0-8069-5179-6). Sterling.
Needles. William Deverell. 288p. 1981. pap. 2.75 (ISBN 0-553-13974-6). Bantam.
Needleweaving-Easy As Embroidery. Esther Warner Dendel. 1976. pap. 4.95a o.p. (ISBN 0-385-12543-7). Doubleday.
Needlework As Art. M. M. Cust. Ed. by Peter Stansky & Rodney Shewan. LC 76-17770. (Aesthetic Movement & the Arts & Crafts Movement Ser.). 1978. Repr. of 1886 ed. lib. bdg. 44.00x (ISBN 0-8240-2474-5). Garland Pub.
Needlework Book of Bible Stories. Carolyn Meyer. LC 75-10135. (Illus.). 96p. (gr. 5 up). 1975. 6.95 o.p. (ISBN 0-15-256793-3, HJ). HarBraceJ.
Needlework Magic with Two Basic Stitches. Marel Harayda. (Illus.). (gr. 7 up). 1977. 6.95 o.p. (ISBN 0-679-20423-7). McKay.
Needlework Plus. new ed. Ed. by Janet DuBane & Diane Friend. (Illus.). 96p. 1980. pap. 2.00 (ISBN 0-918178-18-5). Simplicity.
Needlework Styles for Period Furniture. Hope Hanley. LC 78-3496. (Encore Edition). (Illus.). 1978. 5.95 (ISBN 0-684-16686-0, ScribT). Scribner.
Needleworker's Constant Companion. Marshall Cavandish. (Illus.). 1978. 29.95 o.p. (ISBN 0-670-50576-5, Studio). Viking Pr.
Needleworker's Dictionary. Pamela Clabburn. LC 75-45517. (Illus.). 228p. 1976. 19.95 o.p. (ISBN 0-688-03054-8). Morrow.
Needleworks Projects for All: Canvas Work Simplified. Joan Nicholson. LC 73-79196. (Illus.). 96p. 1973. 5.95 o.p. (ISBN 0-668-03320-7). Arco.
Needs Assessment: A Model for Community Planning. Keith A. Neuber et al. LC 79-27929. (Sage Human Services Guides: Vol. 14). 107p. 1980. pap. 6.50x (ISBN 0-8039-1396-6). Sage.
Needs: Of People & Their Communities & the Adult Educator. 1970. 2.30 (ISBN 0-88379-004-1). Adult Ed.
Nefertiti: An Archaeological Biography. Philipp Vandenberg. Tr. by Ruth Hein. LC 77-28107. (Illus.). 1978. 10.00 o.s.i. (ISBN 0-397-01256-X). Lippincott.
Nefertiti: The Mystery Queen. Burnham Holmes. LC 77-10445. (Great Unsolved Mysteries Ser.). (Illus.). (gr. 4-5). 1977. PLB 9.65 (ISBN 0-8172-1056-3). Raintree Pubs.
Negara: Theatre-State in 19th Century Bali. C. Geertz. LC 80-7520. 256p. 1980. 18.50 (ISBN 0-691-05316-2); pap. 5.95 (ISBN 0-691-00778-0). Princeton U Pr.
Negation & Non-Being. Ed. by Nicolas Rescher. (Monograph Ser.: No. 10). 1976. pap. 10.00x o.p. (ISBN 0-631-11540-4, Pub. by Basil Blackwell). Biblio Dist.
Negative & Positive Sides of Norweigian Life Styles: An Empirical Assessmant of Overdevelopment. 32p. 1980. pap. 5.00 (ISBN 92-808-0137-6, TUNU 069, UNU). Unipub.
Negative & Responsive Doubles in Bridge. Harold Feldheim. 64p. (Orig.). 1980. pap. 2.95 (ISBN 0-87643-031-0). Barclay Bridge.
Negative Critique of the Philosophy of Johann Gottlieb Fichte. Lee W. Sandorvan. (Essential Library of the Great Philosophers). (Illus.). 141p. 1980. deluxe ed. 49.85 (ISBN 0-89266-268-9). Am Classical Coll Pr.
Negative Dialectics. Theodor W. Adorno. LC 77-11720. 1973. 19.50 o.p. (ISBN 0-8164-9129-1). Continuum.
Negative Electron Affinity Devices. R. L. Bell. (Monographs in Electrical & Electronic Engineering). (Illus.). 148p. 1973. 29.95x (ISBN 0-19-859313-9). Oxford U Pr.
Negative Ions. 3rd ed. Harrie Massey. LC 74-31792. (Cambridge Monographs on Physics). (Illus.). 600p. 1976. 126.00 (ISBN 0-521-20775-4). Cambridge U Pr.
Negative Strand Viruses: Proceedings, 2 vols, Vols. 1 & 2. Ed. by B. W. Mahy & R. D. Barry. 1975. Vol. 1. 87.00 (ISBN 0-12-465301-4); Vol. 2. 65.50 (ISBN 0-12-465302-2). Acad Pr.
Negative Taxes & the Poverty Problem. Christopher Green. (Studies of Government Finance). 1967. 11.95 (ISBN 0-8157-3264-3); pap. 4.95 (ISBN 0-8157-3263-5). Brookings.
Neglected Aspect of Foreign Affairs: American Educational & Cultural Policy Abroad. Charles Frankel. 1966. 9.95 (ISBN 0-8157-2918-9). Brookings.
Neglected Majority: Facilities for Commuting Students. 1977. pap. 4.00 (ISBN 0-89192-232-6). Interbk Inc.
Neglected Older American: Social & Rehabilitation Services. Ed. by John G. Cull & Richard E. Hardy. (American Lectures in Social Rehabilitation Psycholology Ser.). (Illus.). 288p. 1973. 24.75 (ISBN 0-398-02835-4). C C Thomas.
Negligence Case: Comparative Fault, Vol. 1. Henry Woods. LC 78-51108. 1978. 47.50. Lawyers Co-Op.
Negligence Case: Res Ipsa Loquitur, 2 vols. Stuart M. Speiser. LC 72-84856. 1972. 85.00 (ISBN 0-686-14530-5). Lawyers Co-Op.
Negotiability in the Federal Sector. Henry H. Robinson. 1981. 18.00 (ISBN 0-87546-080-1); pap. 12.95 (ISBN 0-87546-081-X). NY Sch Indus Rel.
Negotiable Instruments Under U.C.C. 1981. 5.50 (ISBN 0-87526-183-3). Gould.
Negotiate Your Way to Success: Intenious Strategies & Techniques for Succeeding in Any Business or Personal Negotiations. David D. Seltz & Alfred J. Modica, Jr. LC 80-24058. 1980. 10.95 (ISBN 0-87863-182-8). Farnswth Pub.
Negotiated Justice: Pressure to Plead Guilty. John Baldwin & Michael J. McConville. (Law in Society Ser.). 128p. 1977. 19.00x (ISBN 0-85520-171-1, Pub. by Martin Robertson England). Biblio Dist.
Negotiating the Curriculum: A Study in Secondary Schooling. Penelope B. Weston. (Monographs in Curriculum Study: No. 4). 302p. 1980. pap. text ed. 29.00x (ISBN 0-85633-186-4, NFER). Humanities.
Negotiating the Law: Social Work & Legal Services. Clive Grace & Philip Wilkinson. (Direct Editions Ser.). 1978. pap. 14.00 (ISBN 0-7100-8851-5). Routledge & Kegan.
Negotiating to Win. Tessa A. Warschaw. 1980. 9.95 (ISBN 0-07-000780-2). McGraw.
Negotiation & Administration of Hotel Management Contracts. 2nd, rev. ed. James J. Eyster. (Illus.). 209p. 1980. text ed. 22.95 (ISBN 0-937056-04-9). Cornell U Sch Hotel.
Negotiation & Drafting of Mining Development Agreements. Mining Journal Books Ltd. 236p. 1980. 19.00x (ISBN 0-900117-11-7, Pub. by Mining Journal England). State Mutual Bk.
Negotiation & Management of Defense Contracts. Dean F. Pace. LC 69-13681. 1970. 69.95 (ISBN 0-471-65741-7, Pub. by Wiley-Interscience). Wiley.
Negotiations on Mutual & Balanced Force Reductions: The Search for Arms Control in Central Europe. John G. Keliher. LC 80-16473. (Pergamon Policy Studies on International Politics). 240p. 1980. 25.00 (ISBN 0-08-025964-2). Pergamon.
Negotiations on Two Fronts: Manufactures & Commodities. Guy F. Erb. LC 78-57199. (Development Papers: No. 25). 80p. 1978. pap. 1.50 (ISBN 0-686-28674-X). Overseas Dev Council.
Negotiations, Understanding the Bargaining Process. Neal W. Beckmann. 1981. write for info. (ISBN 0-87527-242-8). Green.
Negotiator: A Manual for Winners. Royce A. Coffin. LC 73-75768. (Illus.). 1973. 10.95 (ISBN 0-8144-5327-9). Am Mgmt.
Negotiator Out of Season: The Career of Wilhelm Egon von Furstenberg (1629-1704) John T. O'Connor. LC 77-23872. 272p. 1978. 20.00x (ISBN 0-8203-0436-0). U of Ga Pr.
Negro & Jew: An Encounter in America. Ed. by Shlomo Katz. (Orig.). 1967. 4.95 o.s.i. (ISBN 0-02-560800-2); pap. 1.45 o.s.i. (ISBN 0-02-086180-X). Macmillan.
Negro Folk Music, U.S.A. Harold Courlander. LC 63-18019. 1963. 20.00x (ISBN 0-231-02365-0); pap. 7.50x (ISBN 0-231-08634-2). Columbia U Pr.
Negro Genius. Benjamin G. Brawley. LC 66-17517. 1966. Repr. of 1937 ed. 10.50x (ISBN 0-8196-0184-5). Biblo.
Negro in America. rev. ed. Earl Spangler. LC 71-150773. (In America Bks.). (Illus.). (gr. 5-11). 1971. PLB 5.95 o.p. (ISBN 0-8225-0207-0). Lerner Pubns.
Negro in American Fiction. Sterling Brown. 1969. Repr. of 1937 ed. 12.50 (ISBN 0-87266-002-8). Argosy.
Negro in American History, 3 vols. (Illus.). 1972. 39.50 (ISBN 0-87827-007-8). Ency Brit Ed.
Negro in Art: A Pictorial Record of the Negro Artist & of the Negro Theme in Art. Ed. by Alain Locke. LC 68-9006. (Illus.). 1971. Repr. of 1940 ed. lib. bdg. 30.00 buckram (ISBN 0-87817-013-8). Hacker.
Negro in Brazilian Society. Florestan Fernandes. LC 78-76247. (Institute of Latin American Studies). 1969. 25.00x (ISBN 0-231-02979-9). Columbia U Pr.
Negro in Eighteenth-Century Williamsburg. Thad W. Tate, Jr. LC 73-153687. (Williamsburg Research Studies). 256p. (Orig.). 1965. 5.00x o.p. (ISBN 0-8139-0399-8); pap. 3.00x o.p. (ISBN 0-8139-0233-9). U Pr of Va.
Negro in the American Revolution. Benjamin Quarles. 256p. 1973. pap. 4.95 (ISBN 0-393-00674-3, Norton Lib.). Norton.
Negro in the Caribbean. Eric E. Williams. LC 74-103458. (Studies in Black History & Culture, No. 54). 1970. Repr. lib. bdg. 17.95 (ISBN 0-8383-1190-3). Haskell.
Negro in the Caribbean. Eric E. Williams. LC 71-88421. Repr. of 1942 ed. 7.50x (ISBN 0-8371-1809-3); pap. 3.95 (ISBN 0-8371-8987-X). Negro U Pr.
Negro in the Making of America. Benjamin Quarles. (Orig.). (gr. 9 up). 1964. pap. 2.95 (ISBN 0-02-036130-0, Collier). Macmillan.
Negro in the Reconstruction of Florida, 1865-1877. Joe M. Richardson. LC 73-84442. 272p. 1973. Repr. of 1965 ed. 10.00 o.p. (ISBN 0-88251-038-X). Trend House.
Negro Ironworkers in Louisiana. Marcus B. Christian. LC 72-85953. (Illus.). 64p. (Orig.). 1972. pap. 3.95 (ISBN 0-911116-74-5). Pelican.
Negro Liberation. Harry Haywood. 1978. pap. 3.95 (ISBN 0-930720-50-4). Liberator Pr.
Negro Musicians & Their Music. Maud Cuney-Hare. LC 74-4108. (Music Reprint Ser.). 1974. Repr. of 1936 ed. 35.00 (ISBN 0-306-70652-0). Da Capo.
Negro Myths from the Georgia Coast. Charles C. Jones, Jr. LC 68-21779. 1969. Repr. of 1888 ed. 18.00 (ISBN 0-8103-3836-X). Gale.
Negro Novel in America. rev. ed. Robert A. Bone. (Publications in American Studies: No. 3). 1965. 21.00x o.p. (ISBN 0-300-00316-1). Yale U Pr.
Negro Politicians: The Rise of Negro Politics in Chicago. Harold F. Gosnell. LC 66-30216. 1935. 7.95x (ISBN 0-226-30493-0). U of Chicago Pr.
Negro Politics. J. Q. Wilson. LC 60-10906. 1960. pap. 2.95 o.s.i. (ISBN 0-02-935400-5); pap. 2.95 (ISBN 0-02-935390-4). Free Pr.
Negro Potential. Eli Ginzberg. LC 56-9606. 1956. pap. 5.00x (ISBN 0-231-08546-X). Columbia U Pr.
Negro Revolt. Louis E. Lomax. LC 62-7911. 1962. 8.95 o.p. (ISBN 0-06-012660-4, HarpT). Har-Row.
Negro Revolution: From Its African Genesis to the Death of Martin Luther King. Robert Goldston. (Illus.). (gr. 7-12). 1968. pap. text ed. 2.96 o.s.i. (ISBN 0-02-296870-9). tchrs' manual 0.60 o.s.i. (ISBN 0-686-66484-1). Macmillan.
Negro Slavery in Latin America. Rolando Mellafe. 1975. 20.00x (ISBN 0-520-02106-1). U of Cal Pr.
Negro Thought in America, 1880-1915: Racial Ideologies in the Age of Booker T. Washington. August Meier. 1963. pap. 4.95 (ISBN 0-472-06118-6, 118, AA). U of Mich Pr.

Negroes & the Great Depression: The Problem of Economic Recovery. Raymond Wolters. Ed. by Stanley E. Kutler. LC 78-95510. (Contributions in American History: No. 6). 1970. lib. bdg. 19.95 (ISBN 0-8371-2341-0, WON/); pap. 3.95 (ISBN 0-8371-5961-X). Greenwood.

Nehemiah: A Man of Prayer & Persistence. Gene A. Getz. LC 80-53102. 1981. pap. 4.95 (ISBN 0-8307-0778-6). Regal.

Nehemiah: Man in Charge. Donald K. Campbell. 1979. pap. 2.50 (ISBN 0-88207-781-3). Victor Bks.

Nehru Anthology. Ed. by Sarvepalli Gopal. 648p. 1980. 29.95x (ISBN 0-19-561220-5). Oxford U Pr.

Nehrus of India: Three Generations of Leadership. Beatrice P. Lamb. (gr. 7 up). 1967. 5.95 o.s.i. (ISBN 0-02-751320-3). Macmillan.

Neidhart Von Reuenthal. Eckehard Simon. LC 75-2067. (World Authors Ser.: Germany: No. 364). 1975. lib. bdg. 12.50 (ISBN 0-8057-6215-9). Twayne.

Neighborhood Finds Itself. Julia Abrahamson. 370p. 1972. Repr. of 1959 ed. 16.00x (ISBN 0-8196-0268-X). Biblo.

Neighborhood Government: The Local Foundations of Political Life. Milton Kotler. LC 69-13097. 1969. pap. 4.50 (ISBN 0-672-60720-4). Bobbs.

Neighborhood Groups & Urban Renewal. J. Clarence Davies. LC 65-27764. 1966. 17.50x (ISBN 0-231-02792-3). Columbia U Pr.

Neighborhood Guide. Gerald Adams. Ed. by Jan Leonard. LC 80-66584. (Savvy San Francisco Ser.). (Illus.). 64p. (Orig.). 1980. pap. 2.50 (ISBN 0-89395-049-1). Cal Living Bks.

Neighborhood Law Firms for the Poor: A Comparative Study of Recent Developments in Legal Aid & in the Legal Profession. Bryant Garth. LC 80-51739. 282p. 1980. 40.00x (ISBN 90-286-0180-5). Sijthoff & Noordhoff.

Neighborhood of Baseball. Barry Gifford. 1981. 12.95 (ISBN 0-525-16457-X). Dutton.

Neighborhood Reinvestment & Displacement: A Working Paper. Michael H. Schill. LC 80-85160. 64p. 1981. pap. 2.50x (ISBN 0-938882-01-5). PURRC.

Neighborhood Renewal: Trends & Strategies. Phillip L. Clay. LC 78-14153. 1979. 14.95 (ISBN 0-669-02681-6). Lexington Bks.

Neighborhood Revitalization: Theory & Practice. Roger S. Ahlbrandt & Paul C. Brophy. LC 75-12483. 224p. 1975. 18.95 (ISBN 0-669-00026-4). Lexington Bks.

Neighborhoods in the Urban Economy. Ed. by Benjamin Goldstein & Ross Davis. LC 77-166. (Illus.). 1977. 14.95 (ISBN 0-669-01459-1). Lexington Bks.

Neighbors & Other People: More of the Best of Douglass Welch. Ed. by Ruth Welch. LC 77-20285. (Illus.). 1977. pap. 4.95 (ISBN 0-914842-24-2). Madrona Pubs.

Neighbors to the South. rev. ed. Delia Goetz. LC 56-5874. (Illus.). (gr. 7-9). 1956. 4.95 o.p. (ISBN 0-15-256885-9, HJ). HarBraceJ.

Neighbours & Networks: The Idiom of Kinship Among the Ndendeuli of Tanzania. P. H. Gulliver. LC 71-115491. 1971. 21.50x (ISBN 0-520-01722-6). U of Cal Pr.

Neighbours: Subdivision Life in England & the United States. Howard E. Bracey. LC 64-15877. 1964. 12.50 (ISBN 0-8071-0329-2). La State U Pr.

Neil Armstrong: Space Pioneer. Paul Westman. LC 80-10832. (Achievers Ser.). (Illus.). (gr. 4-9). 1980. PLB 5.95g (ISBN 0-8225-0479-0). Lerner Pubns.

Neil Diamond. Susan K. O'Regan. (Rock 'n Pop Stars Ser.). (Illus.). (gr. 3-6). 1975. PLB 5.95 (ISBN 0-87191-464-6); pap. 2.95 (ISBN 0-89812-115-9). Creative Ed.

Neil Simon's Chapter Two. Robert Grossbach. (Orig.). 1980. pap. 2.25 (ISBN 0-446-92279-X). Warner Bks.

Neither Feast nor Famine. Selwyn Enzer et al. LC 78-3128. (Illus.). 1978. 15.95 (ISBN 0-669-02317-5). Lexington Bks.

Neither Fire nor Steel: Sir Christopher Hatton. Alice G. Vines. LC 77-21424. 1978. 15.95 (ISBN 0-88229-372-9). Nelson-Hall.

Neither the Fanatics nor the Fainthearted: The Tour Leading to President Kennedy's Death & the Two Speeches He Could Not Give. John H. Jenkins. 25.00 (ISBN 0-685-13277-3); pap. 4.50 wrappers (ISBN 0-685-13278-1). Jenkins.

Neither White nor Black: The Mulatto Character in American Fiction. Judith R. Berzon. LC 77-94392. 1978. 15.00x (ISBN 0-8147-0996-6); pap. 7.00x (ISBN 0-8147-0997-4). NYU Pr.

Nellie Bly: First Woman of the News. Tim Lisker. LC 78-14382. (Famous Firsts Ser.). (Illus.). 1978. lib. bdg. 7.35 (ISBN 0-686-51113-1). Silver.

Nellie Cameron. Michele Murray. LC 75-133060. (gr. 3-6). 1971. 6.95 (ISBN 0-395-28867-3, Clarion). HM.

Nellie's Story. Nellie Grant. Ed. by Elspeth Huxley. 352p. 1981. Repr. 12.95 (ISBN 0-688-00475-X). Morrow.

Nelly's Silver Mine: A Story of Colorado Life. Helen Hunt Jackson. LC 75-32183. (Classics of Children's Literature, 1621-1932: Vol. 46). (Illus.). 1976. Repr. of 1878 ed. PLB 38.00 (ISBN 0-8240-2295-5). Garland Pub.

Nelson Algren. Martha Heasley Cox & Wayne Chatterton. (U. S. Authors Ser.: No. 249). 192p. 1975. lib. bdg. 10.95 (ISBN 0-8057-0014-5). Twayne.

Nelson Music Collection. Newton F. Tolman & Kay Gilbert. 6.00x o.p. (ISBN 0-87233-014-1). Bauhan.

Nelson's Encyclopedia for Young Readers, 2 vols. Ed. by Laurence Urdang et al. 973p. 1980. Set. 29.95 (ISBN 0-8407-5184-2). Nelson.

Nelson's Last Diary, a Facsimile. Ed. by Oliver Warner. LC 70-165752. 1972. 9.00x (ISBN 0-87338-121-1). Kent St U Pr.

Nematode Ecology & Plant Disease. H. R. Wallace. LC 73-90720. 1973. 32.50x (ISBN 0-8448-0271-9). Crane Russak Co.

Nematode Parasites of Animals & of Man. 2nd ed. Norman D. Levine. 477p. 1980. 68.95 (ISBN 0-8087-1299-3). Burgess.

Nemerteans. Ray Gibson. (Illus.). 1972. text ed. 10.50x (ISBN 0-09-111990-1, Hutchinson U Lib); pap. text ed. 5.50x (ISBN 0-09-111991-X, Hutchinson U Lib). Humanities.

Nemesis at Potsdam. rev. ed. Alfred M. DeZayas. (Illus.). 1979. pap. 9.50 (ISBN 0-7100-0170-3). Routledge & Kegan.

Nemesis of Faith, 1849. James A. Froude. Ed. by Robert L. Wolff. Bd. with Shadows of the Clouds, 1847. LC 75-1519. (Victorian Fiction Ser.). 1975. lib. bdg. 66.00 (ISBN 0-8240-1592-4). Garland Pub.

Nennius: British History & the Welsh Annals. Ed. by John Morris. (History from the Sources Ser.). 100p. 1980. 13.00x (ISBN 0-8476-6264-0). Rowman.

Nenshu & the Tiger: Parables of Life & Death. Martin Bell. 128p. 1975. 5.95 (ISBN 0-8164-0261-2). Crossroad NY.

Neo-Classical Dramatic Criticism: 1560-1771. Thora B. Jones & Nicol De Bear. LC 75-16873. 172p. 1976. 32.50 (ISBN 0-521-20857-2). Cambridge U Pr.

Neo-Classical Theory of Economic Growth. J. E. Meade. 1964. pap. text ed. 7.95x o.p. (ISBN 0-04-330062-6). Allen Unwin.

Neo-Confucian Thought in Action: Wang Yang-Ming's Youth. Wei-Ming Tu. 1976. 17.50x (ISBN 0-520-02968-2). U of Cal Pr.

Neo-Conservatives. Peter Steinfels. 1980. 5.95 (ISBN 0-686-62897-7, 41384, Touchstone). S&S.

Neo-Slavism & the Czechs, 1898-1914. P. Vysny. LC 76-4239. (Soviet & East European Studies). (Illus.). 1977. 41.00 (ISBN 0-521-21230-8). Cambridge U Pr.

Neoclassical Analysis of Macroeconomic Policy. M. Beenstock. LC 79-8961. 1981. 32.50 (ISBN 0-521-23077-2). Cambridge U Pr.

Neoclassical & Nineteenth Century Architecture. Robin Middleton & David Watkin. (History of World Architecture Ser.). (Illus.). 492p. 1980. 45.00 (ISBN 0-8109-1014-4). Abrams.

Neoclassical Theory of Production & Distribution. C. E. Ferguson. (Illus.). 1969. 27.50x (ISBN 0-521-07453-3). Cambridge U Pr.

Neoclassicism & Romanticism: 1750-1850, 2 vols. Lorenz Eitner. Incl. Vol. 1. Enlightenment-Revolution. 1970 (ISBN 0-13-610907-1); Vol. 2. Restoration-the Twilight of Humanism. (Illus.). 1970 (ISBN 0-13-610915-2). pap. 10.95 ea. ref. ed. P-H.

Neogene Mollusks from Northwestern Ecuador. Axel A. Olsson. (Illus.). 1964. 12.00 (ISBN 0-87710-367-4). Paleo Res.

Neolithic & A-Group Sites, 2 vols. Hans-Ake Nordstrom & Randi Haland. LC 73-851683. (Scandinavian Joint Expedition to Sudanese Nubia Ser). (Illus.). 420p. 1973. Set. text ed. 65.00x (ISBN 0-8419-8802-1, Africana). Holmes & Meier.

Neolithic Cattle-Keepers of Southern India. F. R. Allchin. (University of Cambridge Oriental Pubs). 1963. 38.50 (ISBN 0-521-04018-3). Cambridge U Pr.

Neolithic Levels on the Titelberg, Luxembourg. Elsebet S. Rowlett et al. LC 76-623772. (Museum Brief: No. 18). iii, 61p. 1976. pap. write for info. (ISBN 0-913134-83-X). Mus Anthro Mo.

Neolithic Revolution. D. M. Knox. Ed. by Malcolm Yapp et al. (World History Ser.). (Illus.). 32p. (gr. 10). 1980. lib. bdg. 5.95 (ISBN 0-89908-130-4); pap. text ed. 1.95 (ISBN 0-89908-105-3). Greenhaven.

Neologistic Jargon Aphasia. Hugh W. Buckingham & Andrew Kertesz. (Neurolinguistics Ser.: Vol. 3). 100p. 1976. text ed. 21.50 (ISBN 90-265-0227-3, Pub. by Swets Pub Serv Holland). Swets North Am.

Neon Distances. Joseph Awad. 1980. 5.50 (ISBN 0-8233-0320-9). Golden Quill.

Neon Gobies. Patrick Colin. (Illus.). 304p. 1976. 9.95 (ISBN 0-87666-450-8, H-957). TFH Pubns.

Neon Motorcycle. Thomas Rockwell. LC 72-10350. (Illus.). 40p. (gr. k-3). 1973. PLB 4.90 o.p. (ISBN 0-531-02561-6). Watts.

Neonatal Behavioral Assessment Scale. T. Berry Brazelton. (Illus.). 1974. 12.95x (ISBN 0-433-04030-0). Intl Ideas.

Neonatal Emergencies & Other Problems. J. Black. 288p. 1972. 27.50 (ISBN 0-407-32780-0). Butterworths.

Neonatal Intensive Care: Principles & Guidelines. Lutz Wille & Michael Obladen. (Illus.). 300p. 1981. pap. 28.40 (ISBN 0-387-10462-3). Springer-Verlag.

Neonatal Medicine. Malcolm L. Chiswick. (Illus.). 1978. text ed. 10.50x (ISBN 0-906141-01-X, Pub. by Update Pubns England). Kluwer Boston.

Neonatal Orthopaedics. Robert N. Hensinger. (Neonatology Ser.). 1981. write for info. (ISBN 0-8089-1355-7). Grune.

Neonatal Screening for Inborn Errors of Metabolism. Ed. by H. Bickel et al. (Illus.). 300p. 1980. 50.70 (ISBN 0-387-09779-1). Springer-Verlag.

Neonatal Surgery. 2nd ed. P. P. Rickham & Irene M. Irving. 1978. 149.00x (ISBN 0-407-00069-0). Butterworths.

Neonate with Congenital Heart Disease. 2nd ed. Richard D. Rowe et al. (Illus.). 450p. 1981. text ed. 42.50 (ISBN 0-7216-7775-4). Saunders.

Neonatol Behavioral Assessment Scale. Ed. by T. B. Brazleton. (Clinics in Developmental Medicine Ser.: Vol. 50). 66p. 1973. 13.00 (ISBN 0-685-59044-5). Lippincott.

Neonatology - A Practical Guide. 2nd ed. Alistair G. Philip. LC 80-21108. 1980. pap. 18.50 (ISBN 0-87488-671-6). Med Exam.

Neoplasia in the Central Nervous System. Ed. by Richard A. Thompson & John R. Green. LC 75-25113. (Advances in Neurology Ser.: Vol. 15). 394p. 1976. 41.50 (ISBN 0-89004-058-3). Raven.

Neoplasms - Comparative Pathology of Growth in Animals, Plants & Man. Hans E. Kaiser. (Illus.). 820p. 1980. lib. bdg. write for info. (ISBN 0-683-04503-2). Williams & Wilkins.

Neoplastic & Normal Cells in Culture. J. M. Vasiliev & I. M. Gelfand. LC 80-40075. (Development & Cell Biology: No. 8). (Illus.). 300p. Date not set. price not set (ISBN 0-521-23149-3). Cambridge U Pr.

Neoplastic Development. L. Foulds. Vol. 1. 1969. 58.50 (ISBN 0-12-262801-2); Vol. 2. 1975. 96.00 (ISBN 0-12-262802-0). Acad Pr.

Neostriatum: Proceedings of a Workshop Sponsored by the European Brain & Behaviour Society, Denmark, 17-19 April 1978. Ed. by Ivan Divac et al. (Illus.). 1979. 55.00 (ISBN 0-08-023174-8). Pergamon.

Neoteron Enkyklopaidikon Lexikon, 18 vols. (Greek.). 1957-1962. 925.00 (ISBN 0-8277-3040-3). Maxwell Sci Intl.

Neotestamentica et Semitica: Studies in Honor of Matthew Black. E. E. Ellis & M. Wilcox. 320p. Repr. of 1969 ed. 10.50x (ISBN 0-567-02305-2). Attic Pr.

Neotropic Mesochorinae - Hymenoptera, Ichneumonidae. Dasch. (Memoirs Ser: No. 22). (Illus.). 509p. 1974. 30.00 (ISBN 0-686-17149-7). Am Entom Inst.

Neotropical Primates: Field Studies & Conservation. Institute for Laboratory Animal Resources. Ed. by Richard Thorington, Jr. & Paul Heltne. (Illus.). 1976. pap. 10.25 (ISBN 0-309-02442-0). Natl Acad Pr.

Nepal, 2 vols. Perceval Landon. (Illus.). 27.95 o.s.i. (ISBN 0-685-89507-6). Himalaya Hse.

Nepal Art Treasures of the Himalayas. Ernest Waldschmidt & Rose L. Waldschmidt. 1969. 19.95 (ISBN 0-236-17724-9, Pub. by Paul Elek). Merrimack Bk Serv.

Nepal: Strategy for Survival. Leo E. Rose. LC 75-100022. (Center of South & Southeast Asia Studies, UC Berkeley). 1971. 22.75x (ISBN 0-520-01643-2). U of Cal Pr.

Nepal: Where the Gods Are Young. Pratapaditya Pal. LC 75-769. (Illus.). 136p. 1975. 19.95 (ISBN 0-87848-045-5). Asia Soc.

Nephew. James Purdy. 152p. 1980. pap. 3.95 (ISBN 0-14-005670-X). Penguin.

Nephrology. Philip Freedman et al. (Medical Examination Review Book: Vol. 34). 1976. spiral bdg. 15.00 (ISBN 0-87488-176-5). Med Exam.

Nephrology-A Review of Clinical Nephrology. Marvin Forland. 1977. pap. 16.00 (ISBN 0-87488-622-8). Med Exam.

Nephrology for Nurses - A Modern Approach to the Kidney. 2nd ed. J. Stewart Cameron et al. 1977. sprial bdg. 9.50 (ISBN 0-87488-869-7). Med Exam.

Nephrology for Nurses: A Modern Approach to the Kidney. 2nd ed. Stewart Cameron et al. (Illus.). 330p. 1976. pap. 16.95x (ISBN 0-433-05111-6). Intl Ideas.

Neptune Effect. Patricia Morimando. 1979. pap. 3.95 (ISBN 0-87728-487-3). Weiser.

Nereis Boreali-Americana: 1852-1858, 3 parts in 1. W. H. Harvey. (Illus.). 1976. 125.00 (ISBN 3-7682-1063-4). Lubrecht & Cramer.

Nero & Other Plays. Ed. by Herbert P. Horne et al. Havelock Ellis & Arthur Symons. Tr. by Arthur Verity & A. Wilson. 488p. 1980. Repr. of 1888 ed. lib. bdg. 17.50 (ISBN 0-89760-333-8). Telegraph Bks.

Nero Wolfe Cookbook. Rex Stout & Viking Press Eds. 224p. 1981. pap. 3.95 (ISBN 0-14-005754-4). Penguin.

Nero's Vice. James Kisner. LC 80-27484. 256p. 1981. 10.95 (ISBN 0-8253-0042-8). Beaufort Bks NY.

Nerve & Muscle Excitation. Douglas Junge. LC 75-30151. 1976. pap. text ed. 8.95x o.p. (ISBN 0-87893-408-1). Sinauer Assoc.

Nerve & Muscle Excitation. 2nd ed. Douglas Junge. LC 80-18158. (Illus.). 230p. 1981. pap. text ed. 12.95x (ISBN 0-87893-410-3). Sinauer Assoc.

Nerve & Muscle: Membranes, Cells & Systems. R. B. Stein. (Illus.). 250p. 1980. 18.95 (ISBN 0-306-40512-1, Plenum Pr). Plenum Pub.

Nerve Growth Factor & Its Antiserum. Ed. by Eleanor Zaimis. (Illus.). 384p. 1972. text ed. 24.00x (ISBN 0-485-11132-2, Athlone Pr). Humanities.

Nerve Membranes: A Study of the Biological & Chemical Aspects of Neuron Glia Relationships. P. Johnston & B. Roots. 279p. 1972. text ed. 55.00 (ISBN 0-08-013222-7). Pergamon.

Nerve, Muscle & Synapse. Bernard Katz. (New Biology Ser.). 1966. text ed. 10.95 o.p. (ISBN 0-07-033374-2, C); pap. text ed. 7.95 o.p. (ISBN 0-07-033383-1). McGraw.

Nerve Repair & Regeneration: Its Clinical & Experimental Basis. Don L. Jewett & H. Relton McCarroll, Jr. LC 79-19276. 1979. pap. text ed. 52.50 (ISBN 0-8016-2507-6). Mosby.

Nerves & Muscle, Bk. 10. M. A. Tribe & M. R. Eraut. LC 76-55511. (Basic Biology Course Ser.). (Illus.). 1977. 32.50 (ISBN 0-521-21369-X); pap. 11.95x (ISBN 0-521-21368-1). Cambridge U Pr.

Nerves in Collision. Walter C. Alvarez. 1974. pap. 1.75 o.s.i. (ISBN 0-515-03414-2, M3414). Jove Pubns.

Nerves of Government. Karl W. Deutsch et al. LC 67-4684. 1963. 12.95 (ISBN 0-02-907280-8). Free Pr.

Nervous Christians. Gilbert Little. 1956. pap. 1.50 (ISBN 0-8024-5878-5). Moody.

Nervous Disorders & Religion: A Study of Souls in the Making. John G. McKenzie. LC 79-8719. 183p. 1981. Repr. of 1951 ed. lib. bdg. 18.75x (ISBN 0-313-22192-8, MCND). Greenwood.

Nervous Splendor: Vienna 1888-1889. Frederic Morton. 1980. pap. 4.95 (ISBN 0-14-005667-X). Penguin.

Nervous System, 3 vols. Ed. by D. B. Tower. Incl. Vol. 1. Basic Neurosciences. 20.00 (ISBN 0-89004-075-3); Vol. 2. Clinical Neurosciences. 20.00 (ISBN 0-89004-076-1); Vol. 3. Human Communication & Its Disorders. 20.00 (ISBN 0-89004-077-X). LC 75-33499. 1800p. 1975. Set. 59.50 (ISBN 0-685-61107-8). Raven.

Nervous System Basic Sciences. 2nd ed. Ed. by Royce L. Montgomery et al. 1977. spiral bdg. 11.75 (ISBN 0-87488-210-9). Med Exam.

Nervous System: Disease, Diagnosis, Treatment. E. Diamond. (Clinical Monographs Ser.). (Illus.). 1976. pap. 7.95 (ISBN 0-87618-065-9). R J Brady.

Nervous System Theory: An Introductory Study. K. N. Leibovic. 1973. 33.00 (ISBN 0-12-441250-5). Acad Pr.

Nesselrode & the Russian Rapprochement with Britain, 1836-1843. Harold N. Ingle. LC 74-79764. 1976. 18.50x (ISBN 0-520-02795-7). U of Cal Pr.

Nest. Gregory A. Douglas. 1980. 2.75 (ISBN 0-89083-662-0). Zebra.

Nest of Ninnies & Other English Jestbooks of the Seventeenth Century. Ed. by P. M. Zall. LC 70-88091. 1970. 11.75x (ISBN 0-8032-0723-9). U of Nebr Pr.

Nest of Teachers. Edward Blishen. 186p. 1980. 19.95 (ISBN 0-241-10145-X, Pub. by Hamish Hamilton England). David & Charles.

Nest of the Kildeer. Ethel Van Pelt. (YA) 1976. 5.95 (ISBN 0-685-68911-5, Avalon). Bouregy.

Nesting Biology & Associates of Melitoma (Hymenoptera, Anthrophoridae) E. G. Linsley & J. W. MacSwain. (U. C. Publications in Entomolgy: Vol. 90). 1980. pap. 6.00 (ISBN 0-520-09618-5). U of Cal Pr.

Nesting Birds, Eggs & Fledglings in Color. rev. ed. Winwood Reade & Eric Hosking. (Color Ser.). (Illus.). 1974. 9.95 (ISBN 0-7137-0710-0, Pub by Blandford Pr England). Sterling.

Nestor Makhno in the Russian Civil War. Michael Malet. 1980. text ed. 37.50x (ISBN 0-333-25969-6). Humanities.

Nestorian Collection of Christological Texts, 2 vols. Ed. by Luise Abramowski & Allan E. Goodman. Incl. Vol. 1. Syriac Text. 58.00 (ISBN 0-521-07578-5); Vol. 2. Introduction, Translation & Indexes. 49.50 (ISBN 0-521-08126-2). LC 77-130904. (Oriental Publications Ser.: No. 18, 19). 1972. Cambridge U Pr.

Nests Above the Abyss. Isobel Kuhn. pap. 3.95 (ISBN 0-85363-031-3). OMF Bks.

Net-Making & Knotting. Warren Hartzell & Lura LaBarge. LC 74-82328. (Little Craft Book Ser). (Illus.). 48p. (gr. 7 up). 1974. 4.95 o.p. (ISBN 0-8069-5310-1); PLB 5.89 o.p. (ISBN 0-8069-5311-X). Sterling.

Net Migration for Mississippi's Counties, 1960-1970. E. Nolan Waller. 1975. pap. 3.00 (ISBN 0-938004-05-0). U MS Bus Econ.

Net Net. Isadore Barmash. LC 77-180292. 320p. 1972. 5.95 o.s.i. (ISBN 0-02-507200-5). Macmillan.

Net Theory & Applications Proceedings: Proceedings. W. Brauer. (Lecture Notes in Computer Science Ser.: Vol. 84). 537p. 1980. pap. 29.50 (ISBN 0-387-10001-6). Springer-Verlag.

Net-Winged Midges or Blephariceridae of California. Charles L. Hogue. (Bulletin of the California Insect Survey: Vol. 15). 1973. pap. 7.00x (ISBN 0-520-09454-9). U of Cal Pr.

Net Yield After Capital Gains Tax 25 Percent No. 344, 30 Percent No. 444, 48 Percent No. 544, 3 Vols. Financial Publishing Co. 7.50 ea. Finan Pub.

Net Yield Table for GNMA Mortgage Backed Securities, No. 710. rev ed. Financial Publishing Co. 5.00 o.p. (ISBN 0-685-02554-3). Finan Pub.

Netball Fundamentals. Toy Martin. LC 80-66418. (Illus.). 96p. 1980. 11.95 (ISBN 0-7153-7984-4). David & Charles.

Nethergate. Norah Lofts. 256p. 1977. pap. 1.75 o.p. (ISBN 0-449-23095-3, Crest). Fawcett.

Netherlandish Artists. Ed. by Mark Leach. LC 79-50679. (Illustrated Bartsch: Vol. II). 1979. 120.00 (ISBN 0-89835-002-6). Abaris Bks.

Netherlandish Masters. Ed. by Leonard Slatkes. LC 79-50679. (Illustrated Bartsch: Vol. I). 1979. 120.00 (ISBN 0-89835-001-8). Abaris Bks.

Netherlands. new ed. David Pinder. Ed. by Ian Thompson. LC 76-18924. (Westview Special Studies in Industrial Geography). (Illus.). 1976. lib. bdg. 26.00 o.p. (ISBN 0-89158-626-1). Westview.

Netherlands. Max Schuchart. LC 74-183927. (Nations & Peoples Library). 288p. 1972. 8.50x o.s.i. (ISBN 0-8027-2126-5). Walker & Co.

Netherlands. Sacheverell Sitwell. 1974. 24.00 (ISBN 0-7134-2779-5, Pub. by Batsford England). David & Charles.

Netherlands: An Historical & Cultural Survey 1795-1977. Gerald Newton. LC 77-16100. (Nations of the Modern World Ser.). 1978. lib. bdg. 28.50x (ISBN 0-89158-802-7). Westview.

Netherlands Antilles Cookbook. Jewell Fenzi. 1972. 5.00 o.p. (ISBN 0-911268-23-5). Rogers Bk.

Netherlands Economy in the Twentieth Century: An Examination of the Most Characteristic Feature in the Period 1900-1970. J. de Vries. (Aspects of Economic History, the Low Countries Ser.: No. 3). 1978. pap. text ed. 13.50x (ISBN 90-232-1594-X). Humanities.

Netherlands Yearbook of International Law: State Immunity from Attachment & Execution, Vol. X. Ed. by L. J. Bouchez et al. 650p. 1980. 40.00x (ISBN 90-286-0710-2). Sijthoff & Noordhoff.

Netsilik Eskimo Material Culture: The Roald Amundsen Collection from King William Island. J. Garth Taylor. (Illus.). 1974. pap. 17.00x (ISBN 8-200-08945-2, Dist. by Columbia U Pr). Universitet.

Netsuke: Selected Pieces. Marie-Therese Coullery & Martin S. Newstead. (Baur Collection Catalogues Ser.: Vol. 6). (Illus.). 1978. 225.00 (ISBN 0-685-39558-8). Routledge & Kegan.

Netsuke: The Collection of the Peabody Museum of Salem. Lisa A. Edwards & Margie M. Krebs. (Illus.). 160p. 1980. 30.00 (ISBN 0-87577-059-2); pap. 17.50 (ISBN 0-87577-062-2). Peabody Mus Salem.

Nettie & Sissie: A Biography of Ethel M. Dell & Her Sister Ella. Penelope Dell. (Illus.). 1978. 16.95 (ISBN 0-241-89663-0, Pub. by Hamish Hamilton England). David & Charles.

Netting Materials for Fishing Gear. Gerhard Klust. (Illus.). 184p. 8.75 (ISBN 0-85238-060-7, FN). Unipub.

Nettlewood. Mary Melwood. LC 74-19426. 352p. (gr. 6 up). 1975. 8.95 (ISBN 0-395-28919-X, Clarion). HM.

Network. Jim Lowe & Curtis B. Taylor. LC 75-44360. 304p. (Orig.). 1976. pap. 1.75 o.p. (ISBN 0-345-24970-4). Ballantine.

Network Analysis. Alan C. Dixon. LC 72-90475. 1973. text ed. 21.95 (ISBN 0-675-09024-5). Merrill.

Network Analysis. 3rd ed. M. E. Van Valkenburg. (Illus.). 699p. 1974. 27.95 (ISBN 0-13-611095-9). P-H.

Network Analysis & Feedback Amplifier Design. rev. ed. Hendrik W. Bode. LC 74-23514. 596p. 1975. Repr. of 1945 ed. 29.50 o.p. (ISBN 0-88275-242-1). Krieger.

Network Analysis & Transmission Lines. George L. Konnully. 1967. pap. 10.00x (ISBN 0-210-26907-3). Asia.

Network Analysis: Studies in Human Interaction. Ed. by Jeremy Boissevain & J. Clyde Mitchell. LC 72-77471. (Change & Continuity in Africa Monographs). 1973. 24.70x (ISBN 90-2797-187-0). Mouton.

Network Analysis: Theory & Computer Methods. Randall W. Jensen & Bruce O. Watkins. (Illus.). 544p. 1974. ref. ed. 26.95 (ISBN 0-13-611061-4). P-H.

Network-Based Management Systems. Russell D. Archibald & R. Villoria. LC 66-25216. (Information Science Ser.). 1967. 27.95 o.p. (ISBN 0-471-03250-6, Pub. by Wiley-Interscience). Wiley.

Network Flow, Transportation & Scheduling: Theory & Algorithms. M. Iri. (Mathematics in Science & Engineering Ser., Vol. 57). 1969. 47.00 (ISBN 0-12-373850-4). Acad Pr.

Network Nation: Human Communication Via Computer. Starr R. Hiltz & Murray Turoff. 1978. text ed. 34.50 (ISBN 0-201-03140-X, Adv Bk Prog); pap. text ed. 22.50 (ISBN 0-201-03141-8). A-W.

Network-Related Scheduling Models for Problems with Quasi-Adjacency & Block Adjacency Structures. Fred Glover & John M. Mulvey. 1976. 2.50 (ISBN 0-686-64194-9). U CO Busn Res Div.

Network Television & the Public Interest: A Preliminary Inquiry. Ed. by Michael Botein & David Rice. LC 79-1751. 320p. 1980. 19.95x (ISBN 0-669-02927-0). Lexington Bks.

Network Theory & Filter Design. V. K. Aatre. 432p. 1981. 18.95 (ISBN 0-470-26934-0). Halsted Pr.

Networking. Mary Scott Welch. 304p. 1981. pap. 2.95 (ISBN 0-446-93578-6). Warner Bks.

Networking Families in Crisis. Uri Rueveni. LC 78-8024. 1979. 16.95 (ISBN 0-87705-374-X). Human Sci Pr.

Networks. F. R. Connor. (Introductory Topics in Electronics & Telecommunication Ser.). (Illus.). 1972. pap. text ed. 11.00x (ISBN 0-7131-3258-2). Intl Ideas.

Networks & Places: Social Relations in the Urban Setting. Claude S. Fischer et al. LC 76-55101. (Illus.). 1977. 19.95 (ISBN 0-02-910240-5). Free Pr.

Networks, Lines, & Fields. 2nd ed. John D. Ryder. 1955. ref. ed. 23.95 (ISBN 0-13-611251-X); ans. 0.35 (ISBN 0-13-611269-2). P-H.

Neue Aspekte in der Behandlung der Herzinsuffizienz: Oberrheinisches Kardiologen - Symposium. Ed. by F. Burkhart. (Cardiology: Vol.65, Suppl. 1,1980). (Illus.). 1980. pap. 11.50 (ISBN 3-8055-0652-X). S Karger.

Neue Brockhaus, 5 vols. & atlas. 5th ed. (Ger.). 1975. 395.00 (ISBN 0-8277-3041-1). Maxwell Sci Intl.

Neue Deutsche Prosa. Ed. by Erna K. Neuse. LC 68-30796. (Illus., Orig., Ger.). 1968. pap. text ed. 5.95x (ISBN 0-89197-315-X). Irvington.

Neue Herder, 14 vols. Incl. Atlas. (Ger.). 1973-1975. 955.00 (ISBN 0-685-40123-5). Maxwell Sci Intl.

Neue Herder Bibliothek, 14 vols. (Ger.). 1968-1973. Set. 995.00 (ISBN 0-8277-3055-1). Maxwell Sci Intl.

Neuen Lieden Des Jungen W. Ulrich Plenzdorf. 1978. pap. text ed. 9.95 (ISBN 0-471-02855-X). Wiley.

Neuere Aspekte Kinderkardiology. Ed. by F. Stocker & J. W. Weber. (Paediatrische Fortbildungskurse Fuer Die Praxis: Vol. 51). (Illus.). vi, 130p. 1980. pap. 41.50 (ISBN 3-8055-0926-X). S Karger.

Neumann's Problem for Differential Forms on Riemannian Manifolds. P. E. Conner. LC 52-42839. (Memoirs: No. 20). 1979. pap. 6.40 (ISBN 0-8218-1220-3, MEMO-20). Am Math.

Neural Basis of Human Behavior. H. S. Burr. 272p. 1960. pap. 19.75 photocopy ed. spiral (ISBN 0-398-00264-9). C C Thomas.

Neural Basis of Oral & Facial Function. Ed. by Dubner et al. LC 78-4048. (Illus.). 495p. 1978. 37.50 (ISBN 0-306-31094-5, Plenum Pr). Plenum Pub.

Neural Blockade in Clinical Anesthesia & Management of Pain. Michael J. Cousins & Phillip O. Bridenbaugh. (Illus.). 1188p. 1980. text ed. 95.00 (ISBN 0-397-50439-X). Lippincott.

Neural Communication & Control: Satellite Symposium of the 28th International Congress of Physiological Sciences, Debrechen, Hungary, 1980. Ed. by Gy. Szekely et al. (Advances in Physiological Sciences: Vol. 30). (Illus.). 350p. 1981. 35.00 (ISBN 0-08-027351-3). Pergamon.

Neural Control of Circulation. Ed. by Maysie J. Hughes & Charles D. Barnes. LC 79-6784. (Research Topics in Physiology Ser.). 1980. 24.00 (ISBN 0-12-360850-3). Acad Pr.

Neural Control of Locomotion. Ed. by Robert H. Herman et al. LC 76-18949. (Advances in Behavioral Biology: Vol. 18). 822p. 1976. 55.00 (ISBN 0-306-37918-X, Plenum Pr). Plenum Pub.

Neural Growth & Differentiation. Esmail Meisami & Mary A. Brazier. (International Brain Research Organization Monographs: Vol. 5). 1979. text ed. 52.00 (ISBN 0-89004-378-7). Raven.

Neural Mechanisms in Behavior: A Texas Symposium. Ed. by D. McFadden. (Illus.). 350p. 1980. 24.90 (ISBN 0-387-90468-9). Springer-Verlag.

Neural Mechanisms in Cardiac Arrhythmias. Ed. by Peter J. Schwartz et al. LC 77-77962. (Perspectives in Cardiovascular Research Ser.: Vol. 2). 1978. 41.00 (ISBN 0-89004-209-8). Raven.

Neural Mechanisms of Goal-Directed Behavior & Learning. Ed. by Richard F. Thompson et al. LC 79-6775. 1980. 49.50 (ISBN 0-12-688980-5). Acad Pr.

Neural Mechanisms of the Auditory & Vestibular Systems. Grant L. Rasmussen & William F. Windle. 436p. 1965. pap. 20.25 spiral (ISBN 0-398-01554-6). C C Thomas.

Neural Peptides & Neural Communication. Ed. by Erminio Costa & Marco Trabucchi. (Advances in Biochemical Psychopharmacology Ser.). 1980. text ed. 61.50 (ISBN 0-89004-375-2). Raven.

Neural Regulatory Mechanisms During Aging. Ed. by Richard Adelman et al. (Modern Aging Ser.: Vol. 1). 230p. 1980. write for info. (ISBN 0-8451-2300-9). A R Liss.

Neural Substrates of Limbix Epilepsy. Makram Girgis. (Illus.). 320p. 1981. 35.00 (ISBN 0-87527-238-X). Green.

Neural Systemic Theory of Emotion: An Outline of a New Methodological Approach to Psychology & a Theory of Emotion & the Mind. Philip L. Sawyer. LC 66-29400. 57p. 1966. 2.95 o.p. (ISBN 0-911308-00-8); pap. 1.75 o.p. (ISBN 0-911308-01-6). P Sawyer.

Neural Trauma. Ed. by A. John Popp et al. LC 78-24627. (Seminars in Neurological Surgery). 1979. text ed. 38.00 (ISBN 0-89004-257-8). Raven.

Neuro-Linguistic Programming, Vol. 1. R. Dilts et al. LC 80-50147. 1980. limited boxed ed. 24.00x (ISBN 0-916990-07-9). Meta Pubns.

Neuro-Ophthalmology Focus, 1980. Ed. by J. Lawton Smith. LC 79-87484. (Illus.). 472p. 1979. text ed. 57.75 (ISBN 0-89352-071-3). Masson Pub.

Neuro-Ophthalmology: Symposium of the University of Miami & the Bascom Palmer Eye Institute, Vol. 8. Joel S. Glaser & J. Lawton Smith. (Illus.). 1975. text ed. 37.50 o.p. (ISBN 0-8016-1846-0). Mosby.

Neuro-Ophthalmology: Symposium of the University of Miami & the Bascom Palmer Eye Institute, Vol. 9. Ed. by Joel S. Glaser. LC 64-18729. (Illus.). 1977. 39.50 o.p. (ISBN 0-8016-1843-6). Mosby.

Neuro Ophthalmology: Symposium of the University of Miami & the Bascom Palmer Eye Institute, Vol. 10. Joel S. Glaser. LC 64-18729. (Illus.). 242p. 1980. text ed. 45.00 (ISBN 0-8016-1876-2). Mosby.

Neuro-Ophthalmology Update. J. Lawton Smith. LC 77-78562. (Illus.). 412p. 1977. 57.75 (ISBN 0-89352-005-5). Masson Pub.

Neuro-Psychopharmacology: Proceedings. Collegium Internationale Neuro-Psychopharmacologium 11th Congress, Vienna, July 9-14 1978. Ed. by B. Saletu et al. (Illus.). 1979. 140.00 (ISBN 0-08-023089-X). Pergamon.

Neuroactive Peptides. Sir Arnold Burgen et al. (Proceedings of the Royal & Society, Series B.: Vol. 210). (Illus.). 192p. 1980. text ed. 35.00x (ISBN 0-85403-149-9, Pub. by Royal Soc London). Scholium Intl.

Neuroanatomy. John Nolte. (Illus.). 382p. 1981. pap. text ed. 13.50 (ISBN 0-8016-3702-3). Mosby.

Neuroanatomy Laboratory Guide. Jose G. Frontera. 7.50 o.p. (ISBN 0-8477-2309-7); pap. 6.25 (ISBN 0-8477-2310-0). U of PR Pr.

Neuroanatomy Review. Alvin M. Earle & William K. Metcalf. (Basic Science Review Bks.). 1977. spiral bdg. 8.00 o.p. (ISBN 0-87488-218-4). Med Exam.

Neurobehavioral Study in Preschool Children. Alexander Kalvaboer. (Clinics in Developmental Medicine Ser.: Vol. 54). 1975. 21.00 (ISBN 0-685-59120-4). Lippincott.

Neurobiological Mechanisms of Adaptation & Behavior. Ed. by Arnold J. Mandell. LC 74-14475. (Advances in Biochemical Psychopharmacology Ser.: Vol. 13). 1975. 27.00 (ISBN 0-89004-001-X). Raven.

Neurobiology of Behavior: An Introduction. Gordon J. Mogenson. LC 77-18283. 1977. 14.95 (ISBN 0-470-99341-3). Halsted Pr.

Neurobiology of Cerebrospinal Fluid, I. Ed. by James H. Wood. 750p. 1980. 69.50 (ISBN 0-306-40369-2, Plenum Pr). Plenum Pub.

Neurobiology of Chemical Transmission. Ed. by Masanori Otsuka & Z. W. Hall. LC 78-24602. 1979. 31.50 (ISBN 0-471-03974-8, Pub. by Wiley-Medical). Wiley.

Neurobiology of Cholinergic & Adrenergic Transmitters. Ed. by E. Heldman et al. (Monographs in Neural Sciences: Vol. 7). (Illus.). xvi, 200p. 1980. pap. 53.60 (ISBN 3-8055-0828-X). S Karger.

Neurobiology of the Mauthner Cell. Ed. by Donald Faber & Henri Korn. LC 78-66351. 1978. 31.50 (ISBN 0-89004-233-0). Raven.

Neurochemical & Immunologic Components in Schizophrenia: Proceedings of a Conference Held at the University of Texas Medical Branch, Oct. 1976. Ed. by Daniel Bergsma & Allan L. Goldstein. LC 78-8534. (Birth Defects Original Article Ser.: Vol. 14, No. 5). 447p. 1978. 46.00 (ISBN 0-8451-1019-5). A R Liss.

Neurochemical Aspects of Hypothalmic Function. Ed. by L. Martini & J. Meites. 1971. 25.00 (ISBN 0-12-475560-7). Acad Pr.

Neurochemical Mechanisms of Opiates & Endorphins. Ed. by Horace H. Loh & David H. Ross. LC 78-24623. (Advances in Biochemical Pharmacology Ser.: Vol. 20). 1979. text ed. 44.50 (ISBN 0-89004-166-0). Raven.

Neurochemistry & Clinical Neurology. Ed. by Leontino Battistin et al. LC 80-7475. (Progress in Clinical & Biological Research Ser.: Vol. 39). 512p. 1980. 38.00 (ISBN 0-8451-0039-4). A R Liss.

Neurochemistry of Arthropods. J. E. Treherne. (Cambridge Monographs in Experimental Biology). 1966. 28.95 (ISBN 0-521-06645-X). Cambridge U Pr.

Neurochemistry of Cholinergic Receptors. Ed. by Eduardo DeRobertis & Jochen Schacht. LC 73-91105. 156p. 1974. 18.00 (ISBN 0-911216-66-9). Raven.

Neurochemistry of the Retina: Proceedings of the International Symposium on the Neurochemistry of the Retina, 28 August - 1 September 1979, Athens, Greece. Ed. by N. G. Bazan & R. N. Lolley. (Illus.). 584p. 1980. 70.00 (ISBN 0-08-025485-3). Pergamon.

Neurocristopathies. P. Kissel et al. LC 79-89479. (Illus.). 1980. 57.50 (ISBN 0-89352-039-X). Masson Pub.

Neuroendocrinology. Ed. by Dorothy T. Krieger & Joan Hughes. LC 79-28123. (Illus.). 1980. 25.00x (ISBN 0-87893-425-1). Sinauer Assoc.

Neuroethology. J. P. Ewert. (Illus.). 1980. pap. 24.80 (ISBN 0-387-09790-2). Springer-Verlag.

Neuroethology: An Introduction. D. M. Guthrie. 200p. 1981. pap. 24.95x (ISBN 0-470-26993-6). Halsted Pr.

Neurofibromatosis (von Recklinghausen's Disease) Ed. by John J. Mulvihill & Vincent M. Riccardi. (Advances in Neurology Ser.: Vol. 29). 225p. 1981. text ed. 22.50 (ISBN 0-686-64310-0). Raven.

Neurogenic Control of the Brain Circulation. Ed. by Christer Owman & Lars Edvinsson. LC 77-30303. 1977. text ed. 66.00 (ISBN 0-08-021553-X). Pergamon.

Neurogenic Heart Lesions. I. S. Zavodskaya et al. LC 80-40436. (Illus.). 150p. 1980. 58.00 (ISBN 0-08-025482-9). Pergamon.

Neurologic Care: A Guide for Patient Education. Marjie Van Meter. (Patient Education Series). 288p. pap. 9.50 (ISBN 0-8385-6706-1). ACC.

Neurologic Emergencies: Recognition & Management. Michael Salcman. 1980. text ed. 27.00 (ISBN 0-89004-409-0). Raven.

Neurologic Infections in Children. 2nd ed. William E. Bell & William McCormick. (Major Problems in Clinical Pediatrics Ser.: Vol. 12). (Illus.). 600p. 1981. text ed. price not set (ISBN 0-7216-1676-3). Saunders.

Neurologic Manifestations of General Diseases. John A. Aita. 936p. 1975. 69.50 (ISBN 0-398-02675-0). C C Thomas.

Neurologic Nursing. Marilyn Rubin. LC 76-6218. 300p. 1980. cancelled (ISBN 0-87527-250-9). Green.

Neurologic Problems: A Critical Care Nursing Focus. Mariah Snyder & Mary Jackle. (Critical Care Ser.). (Illus.). 352p. 1980. pap. text ed. 17.95 (ISBN 0-87619-713-6). R J Brady.

Neurological Anatomy in Relation to Clinical Medicine. 3rd ed. A. Brodal. (Illus.). 1072p. 1981. 35.00 (ISBN 0-19-502694-2). Oxford U Pr.

Neurological Clinical Pharmacology. Mervyn J. Eadie & John H. Tyrer. 470p. 1980. text ed. 47.50 (ISBN 0-909337-07-1). ADIS Pr.

Neurological Epidemiology: Principles & Clinical Applications. Ed. by Bruce S. Schoenberg. LC 77-72796. (Advances in Neurology Ser.: Vol. 19). 1978. 63.50 (ISBN 0-89004-212-8). Raven.

Neurological Examination of Children. Richmond S. Paine & Thomas E. Oppe. (Clinics in Developmental Medicine Ser. Nos. 20 & 21). 280p. 1966. 19.50 (ISBN 0-685-24720-1). Lippincott.

Neurological Examination of the Full Term Newborn Infant. 2nd ed. Heinz Prechtl & David Beintema. (Clinics in Developmental Medicine Ser.: No. 63). 68p. 1977. Repr. of 1965 ed. 21.00 (ISBN 0-685-24716-3). Lippincott.

Neurological Organization & Reading. Carl H. Delacato. 200p. 1973. pap. 16.75 photocopy ed. spiral (ISBN 0-398-00420-X). C C Thomas.

Neurological Study of Newborn Infants. David Beintema. (Clinics in Developmental Medicine Ser. No. 28). 170p. 1968. 13.00 (ISBN 0-685-24725-2). Lippincott.

Neurological Surgery. 2nd ed. James G. McMurtry, 3rd. (Medical Examination Review Bk.: Vol. 19). 1975. spiral bdg. 16.50 (ISBN 0-87488-119-6). Med Exam.

Neurology. 6th ed. Paul S. Slosberg. (Medical Examination Review Book Ser.: Vol. 8). 1977. spiral bdg. 8.50 (ISBN 0-87488-108-0). Med Exam.

Neurology & Neurosurgical Nursing: Continuing Education Review. Barbara A. Russo. 1974. spiral bdg. 8.00 o.p. (ISBN 0-87488-357-1). Med Exam.

Neurology Case Studies. 2nd ed. Sheldon M. Wolf et al. 1975. spiral bdg. 13.75 (ISBN 0-87488-006-8). Med Exam.

Neurology: Clinical Neurophysiology, Vol. 1. Stalberg. (Butterworths International Medical Reviews Ser.). 1981. text ed. price not set (ISBN 0-407-02294-5). Butterworth.

Neurology Continuing Education Review. 3rd. ed. Ed. by James H. Halsey, Jr. 1981. spiral bdg. 14.00 (ISBN 0-87488-345-8). Med Exam.

Neurology for Nurses: Including Nursing Technics in Neurology. Erwin M. Jacobs & Phyllis M. DeNault. (Illus.). 208p. 1964. 13.75 (ISBN 0-398-00908-2). C C Thomas.

Neurology Handbook. Labe C. Scheinberg et al. 1972. spiral bdg. 11.00 (ISBN 0-87488-604-X). Med Exam.

Neurology of Musculoskeletal & Rheumatic Disorders. Kenneth K. Nakano. (Illus.). 1979. 40.00x (ISBN 0-89289-401-6). HM Prof Med Div.

Neurology of Ocular Movement. R. John Leigh & David S. Zee. (Contemporary Neurology Ser.: No. 22). 350p. 1981. 35.00 (ISBN 0-8036-5524-X). Davis Co.

Neurology of the Ocular Muscles. 2nd ed. David G. Cogan. (Illus.). 320p. 1978. 18.75 (ISBN 0-398-00321-1). C C Thomas.

Neurology Specialty Board Review. 2nd ed. Ed. by Herbert H. Schaumburg & Labe C. Scheinberg. 1972. spiral bdg. 16.50 (ISBN 0-87488-306-7). Med Exam.

Neurometric Assessment of Brain Dysfunction in Neurological Patients. Thalia Harmony. (Functional Neuroscience: Vol. 3). 500p. 1981. profess. refer 29.95 (ISBN 0-89859-044-2). L Erlbaum Assocs.

Neuromuscular Blocking & Stimulating Agents, Vols. 1 & 2. J. Cheymol. 654p. 1972. text ed. 145.00 (ISBN 0-08-016277-0). Pergamon.

Neuromuscular Diseases of Infancy & Childhood. Kenneth F. Swaiman & Francis S. Wright. (Illus.). 272p. 1970. 18.00 o.p. (ISBN 0-398-01885-5). C C Thomas.

Neuromuscular Functions & Disorders. Alan McComas. 1977. 59.95 (ISBN 0-407-00058-5). Butterworths.

Neuronal Mechanisms of the Orienting Reflex. Ed. by E. N. Sokolov & O. S. Vinogradova. LC 75-23135. 302p. 1975. 19.95 (ISBN 0-470-92562-0, Pub. by Wiley). Krieger.

Neuronal Plasticity. Ed. by Carl W. Cotman. LC 77-72807. 1978. 31.50 (ISBN 0-89004-210-1). Raven.

Neurones Without Impulses. Ed. by A. Roberts & B. M. Bush. LC 79-42572. (Society for Experimental Biology Seminar Ser.). (Illus.). 250p. Date not set. 59.50 (ISBN 0-521-23364-X); pap. 19.95 (ISBN 0-521-29935-7). Cambridge U Pr.

Neurons: Building Blocks of the Brain. Leonard A. Stevens. LC 74-4399. (Illus.). 128p. (gr. 7 up). 1974. 7.95 (ISBN 0-690-00403-6, TYC-J). T Y Crowell.

Neuronuclear Medicine. Ed. by O. Juge & A. Donath. (Progress in Nuclear Medicine Ser.: Vol. 7). (Illus.). vii, 240p. 1981. 90.00 (ISBN 3-8055-2319-X). S Karger.

Neuropathology Case Studies. 2nd ed. Sydney S. Schochet, Jr. & William F. McCormick. 1979. pap. 16.50 (ISBN 0-87488-046-7). Med Exam.

Neuropeptide Influences on the Brain & Behavior. Lyle H. Miller et al. LC 76-5663. (Advances in Biochemical Psychopharmacology: Vol. 17). 1977. 31.50 (ISBN 0-89004-130-X). Raven.

Neuropeptides & Neural Transmission. Ed. by Cosimo Ajmone-Marson et al. (International Brain Research Organization (IBRO) Monograph: Vol. 7). 412p. 1980. text ed. 40.00 (ISBN 0-89004-501-1). Raven.

Neuropeptides: Biochemical & Physiological Studies. Ed. by R. P. Millar. (Illus.). 368p. 1981. lib. bdg. 55.90 (ISBN 0-443-02265-8). Churchill.

Neuropharmacology & Behavior. V. G. Longo. LC 72-75588. (Illus.). 1972. text ed. 11.95x (ISBN 0-7167-0828-0); pap. text ed. 6.95x (ISBN 0-7167-0827-2). W H Freeman.

Neuropharmacology of Central Nervous System & Behavioral Disorders. Ed. by Gene C. Palmer. LC 80-1107. 1981. 59.00 (ISBN 0-12-544760-4). Acad Pr.

Neurophysical Basis for the Treatment of Cerebral Palsy. Karel Bobath. (Clinics in Developmental Medicine Ser.: No. 75). 106p. 1980. 19.50. Lippincott.

Neurophysics. Alwyn C. Scott. LC 77-2762. 1977. 33.95 o.p. (ISBN 0-471-02998-X, Pub. by Wiley-Interscience). Wiley.

Neurophysiologic Studies in Tissue Culture. Stanley M. Crain. LC 75-14567. 1976. 29.50 (ISBN 0-89004-048-6). Raven.

Neurophysiological Basis of Normal & Abnormal Motor Activities. Ed. by Melvin D. Yahr & Dominick P. Purpura. LC 67-28247. 1967. 37.50 (ISBN 0-911216-04-9). Raven.

Neurophysiological Concepts of Patient Learning: The Tree of Learning. Margot C. Heiniger. LC 80-25454. (Illus.). 350p. 1981. text ed. 23.00 (ISBN 0-8016-2203-4). Mosby.

Neurophysiological Model of Emotional & Intentional Behavior. John L. Weil. (Illus.). 204p. 1974. 22.75 (ISBN 0-398-02497-9). C C Thomas.

Neurophysiology Study Guide. 2nd ed. Beverly Bishop. (Illus.). 1973. spiral bdg. 8.50 (ISBN 0-87488-600-7). Med Exam.

Neuropsychiatric Manifestations of Physical Disease in the Elderly. Ed. by Alvin J. Levenson & Richard C. Hall. (Aging Ser.: Vol. 14). 175p. 1980. text ed. 17.00 (ISBN 0-89004-493-7). Raven.

Neuropsychiatric Mental Status Examination: A Phenomenologic Program Text. Ed. by Michael A. Taylor. Date not set. text ed. price not set (ISBN 0-89335-130-X). Spectrum Pub.

Neuropsychiatric Side Effects of Drugs in the Elderly. Ed. by Alvin Levenson. LC 78-55806. (Aging Ser.: Vol. 9). 1979. 24.00 (ISBN 0-89004-285-3). Raven.

Neuropsychiatric Study in Childhood. William Yule et al. (Clinics in Developmental Medicine Ser.: Nos. 35 & 36). 272p. 1970. 21.00 (ISBN 0-685-24728-7). Lippincott.

Neuropsychiatry. Michael R. Trimble. 304p. 1981. 37.50 (ISBN 0-471-27827-0, Pub. by Wiley-Interscience). Wiley.

Neuropsychodiagnosis in Psychotherapy. rev. ed. Leonard Small. LC 80-19415. 480p. 1980. 25.00 (ISBN 0-87630-243-6). Brunner Mazel.

Neuropsychological & Cognitive Processes in Reading. Francis J. Pirozzolo & Merlin C. Wittrock. (Perspectives in Neurolinguistics & Psycholinguistics Ser.). 1981. price not set (ISBN 0-12-557360-X). Acad Pr.

Neuropsychological Fundamentals. 2nd ed. J. De Quiros & O. Schrager. (Illus.). 292p. 1980. 20.00 (ISBN 0-87879-240-6). Acad Therapy.

Neuropsychological Studies in Aphasia. A. R. Luria. (Neurolinguistics Ser.: Vol. 6). 184p. 1977. text ed. 26.00 (ISBN 90-265-0244-3, Pub. by Swets Pub Serv Holland). Swets North Am.

Neuropsychology: A Textbook of Systems & Psychological Functions of the Human Brain. S. J. Dimond. LC 79-40087. 1980. text ed. 72.95 (ISBN 0-407-00152-2). Butterworths.

Neuropsychology & Neurolinguistics. Egon Weigl. (Janua Linguarum, Ser. Maior: No. 78). 1980. text ed. 75.00x (ISBN 90-279-7956-1). Mouton.

Neuropsychology of Developmental Reading Disorders. Francis J. Pirozzolo. LC 78-19752. 1979. 18.95 (ISBN 0-03-046121-9). Praeger.

Neuropsychopathology of Written Language. Joseph H Rosenthal. LC 77-2825. 1977. 16.95 (ISBN 0-88229-382-6). Nelson-Hall.

Neuropsychopharmacology of Monoamines & Their Regulatory Enzymes. Ed. by Earl Usdin. LC 74-77231. (Advances in Biochemical Psychopharmacology Ser: Vol. 12). 530p. 1974. 41.50 (ISBN 0-911216-77-4). Raven.

Neuroradiology, 2 vols. E. H. Burrows & Norman E. Leeds. (Illus., Vol. 1, 800 p., vol. 2, 384 p.). 1980. text ed. 175.00x set (ISBN 0-443-08016-X). Churchill.

Neuroradiology Case Studies. Ajax E. George. 1977. sprial bdg. 17.50 (ISBN 0-87488-037-8). Med Exam.

Neuroradiology in Infants & Children, 3 vols. Derek C. Harwood-Nash. LC 76-27253. (Illus., Orig.). 1976. 175.00 set o.p. (ISBN 0-8016-2086-4). Mosby.

Neuroradiology of Sellar & Juxtasellar Lesions. K. Francis Lee & Shu-Ren Lin. (Illus.). 512p. 1979. 84.75 (ISBN 0-398-03717-5). C C Thomas.

Neuroradiology with Computed Tomography. Ramsey K. Pitcoff & Herb Powell. 575p. 1981. text ed. price not set (ISBN 0-7216-7444-5). Saunders.

Neuroreceptors Basic & Clinical Aspects: Based on Symposia Held at the American College of Neuropsychology Annual Meeting December 1979. Earl Usdih & William E. Bunney. 280p. 1981. 60.50 (ISBN 0-686-69370-1, Pub. by Wiley-Interscience). Wiley.

Neuroscience: A Clinical Perspective. Joan K. Werner. LC 79-64779. (Illus.). 225p. 1980. text ed. 13.95 (ISBN 0-7216-9116-1). Saunders.

Neuroscience Research Program Bulletins, Vol. 15 & 16. (Neurosciences Research Program Ser. 1979 & 1980). 30.00x ea. Vol. 15 (ISBN 0-262-14030-6). Vol. 16 (ISBN 0-262-14033-0). MIT Pr.

Neurosciences for Allied Health Therapies. Donald R. Brown. LC 79-19685. (Illus.). 1980. text ed. 17.95 (ISBN 0-8016-0827-9). Mosby.

Neurosciences: Second Study Program. Ed. by F. O. Schmitt. LC 78-136288. (Illus.). 1088p. (Charts, Photos, Micrographs, Tabs). 1970. ref. ed. 60.00 (ISBN 0-87470-014-0); prof. ed. 30.00 (ISBN 0-685-04785-7). Rockefeller.

Neurosecretion. Simon H. Maddrell & Jean J. Nordmann. LC 79-63655. (Tertiary Level Biology Ser.). 173p. 1979. 24.95x (ISBN 0-470-26711-9). Halsted Pr.

Neurosecretion & Brain Peptides: Implications for Brain Function & Neurological Disease. (Advances in Biochemical Psychopharmacology Ser.: Vol. 28). 725p. 1981. 58.00 (ISBN 0-89004-535-6). Raven.

Neuroses of the Nations. C. E. Playne. 468p. 1980. Repr. of 1925 ed. lib. bdg. 35.00 (ISBN 0-8495-4373-8). Arden Lib.

Neurosis & Personality Disorders. Elton B. McNeil. (Lives in Disorder Ser). 1970. pap. 8.95 ref. ed. (ISBN 0-13-611491-1). P-H.

Neurosis & Psychosis. 3rd ed. Beulah C. Bosselman. 216p. 1969. pap. 14.75 photocopy ed. spiral (ISBN 0-398-00195-2). C C Thomas.

Neurospeech Therapy for Cerebral Palsied: 2nd. Edward D. Mysak. 1980. text ed. 22.50x (ISBN 0-8077-2612-5). Tchrs Coll.

Neurosurgery. Valentine Logue. Ed. by C. Rob & R. Smith. (Operative Surgery, Vol. 14). 1970. 20.00 o.p. (ISBN 0-685-14248-5). Lippincott.

Neurosurgery. 3rd ed. Lindsay Symon. Ed. by Charles Rob & Rodney Smith. (Operative Surgery Ser). (Illus.). 1979. text ed. 135.00 (ISBN 0-407-00625-7). Butterworths.

Neurosurgery of Infancy & Childhood. 2nd ed. Donald D. Matson. (Illus.). 952p. 1969. pap. 49.00 spiral (ISBN 0-398-01236-9). C C Thomas.

Neurosurgical Anesthesia & Intensive Care. T. V. Campkin & J. M. Turner. LC 79-41659. (Illus.). 1980. text ed. 49.95 (ISBN 0-407-00185-9). Butterworths.

Neurosurgical Management of the Epilepsies. Ed. by D. P. Purpura et al. LC 74-80533. (Advances in Neurology Ser: Vol. 8). 1975. 32.00 (ISBN 0-911216-88-X). Raven.

Neurotic Personality of Our Times. Karen Horney. 1937. 6.75 (ISBN 0-393-01012-0, Norton Lib); pap. 3.95 (ISBN 0-393-00742-1). Norton.

Neurotoxicity of the Visual System. Ed. by William Merigan & Bernard Weiss. 1980. text ed. 34.50 (ISBN 0-89004-400-7). Raven.

Neurotoxicology, Vol. 1. Ed. by L. Roizin & H. Shiraki. LC 77-4632. 1977. 68.50 (ISBN 0-89004-148-2). Raven.

Neurotoxins: Tools in Neurobiology. Ed. by Bruno Ceccarelli & Francesco Clementi. LC 78-57244. (Advances in Cytopharmacology Ser.: Vol. 3). 1979. text ed. 49.00 (ISBN 0-89004-303-5). Raven.

Neurotransmitter Receptor Binding. Ed. by Henry I. Yamamura et al. LC 78-3010. 1978. 21.00 (ISBN 0-89004-231-4). Raven.

Neurotransmitters. Ed. by Irwin J. Kopin. LC 72-75942. (ARNMD Research Publications Ser: Vol. 50). 1972. 34.50 (ISBN 0-683-00244-9). Raven.

Neurotransmitters & Anterior Pituitary. Eugenio E. Muller et al. 1978. 50.00 (ISBN 0-12-510550-9). Acad Pr.

Neurotransmitters & Drug. Z. L. Kruk & C. J. Pycock. 160p. 1980. 35.00x (ISBN 0-85664-865-5, Pub. by Croom Helm England). State Mutual Bk.

Neutral Mechanism of Conditioning. B. C. X Kotliar. LC 80-25451. 205p. 1981. 11.00 (ISBN 0-08-026334-8). Pergamon.

Neutral Zone in Complete & Partial Dentures. 2nd ed. Victor E. Beresin & Frank J. Schiesser. LC 78-59658. (Illus.). 1978. text ed. 39.50 (ISBN 0-8016-0617-9). Mosby.

Neutralism. Peter Lyon. 1963. text ed. 5.75x (ISBN 0-7185-1038-0, Leicester). Humanities.

Neutrality & Impartiality. Ed. by A. Montefiore. 320p. 1975. 38.50 (ISBN 0-521-20664-2); pap. 9.95x (ISBN 0-521-09923-4). Cambridge U Pr.

Neutrinos. G. M. Lewis & G. A. Wheatley. LC 73-135382. (Wykeham Science Ser.: No. 12). 1970. 9.95x (ISBN 0-8448-1114-9). Crane-Russak Co.

Neutron Bomb: Political, Technological & Military Issues. S. T. Cohen. LC 78-63388. (Special Reports Ser.). 1978. 6.50 (ISBN 0-89549-009-9). Inst Foreign Policy Anal.

Neutron Capture Gamma-Ray Spectroscopy. (Illus., Orig.). 1969. pap. 45.00 (ISBN 92-0-130369-6, IAEA). Unipub.

Neutron Data of Structural Materials for Fast Reactors: Proceedings. Specialists Meeting Held at the Central Bureau for Nuclear Measurements, Geel, Belgium, 5-8 Dec. 1977. Ed. by K. H. Bockhoff. (Illus.). 1979. text ed. 120.00 (ISBN 0-08-023424-0). Pergamon.

Neutron Diffraction. 3rd ed. G. E. Bacon. (Monographs on the Physics & Chemistry of Materials). (Illus.). 652p. 1975. 109.00x (ISBN 0-19-851353-4). Oxford U Pr.

Neutron Fluence Measurements. (Technical Reports Ser.: No. 107). (Illus., Orig.). 1970. pap. 10.75 (ISBN 92-0-135070-8, IAEA). Unipub.

Neutron Inelastic Scattering - 1968, 2 vols. 1968. Vol. 1. pap. 36.00 (ISBN 92-0-030268-8, IAEA); Vol. 2. pap. 26.25 (ISBN 92-0-030368-4). Unipub.

Neutron Inelastic Scattering - 1972. (Illus.). 888p. (Orig.). 1973. pap. 63.75 (ISBN 92-0-030172-X, ISP 308, IAEA). Unipub.

Neutron Inelastic Scattering Nineteen Seventy-Seven, Vol. 1. 1978. pap. 55.75 (ISBN 92-0-030078-2, ISP 468-1, IAEA). Unipub.

Neutron Inelastic Scattering Nineteen Seventy-Seven, Vol. 2. 1978. pap. 47.25 (ISBN 92-0-030178-9, ISP468-2, IAEA). Unipub.

Neutron Irradiation Embrittlement of Reactor Pressure Vessel Steels. L. E. Steel. (Technical Report Ser.: No. 163). (Illus.). 235p. 1975. pap. 21.00 (ISBN 92-0-155075-8, IAEA). Unipub.

Neutron Irradiation of Seeds. (Technical Reports Ser.: No. 76). 1967. pap. 6.00 (ISBN 92-0-115267-1, IAEA). Unipub.

Neutron Irradiation of Seeds, Two. (Technical Reports Ser.: No. 92). 1968. pap. 10.25 (ISBN 92-0-015068-3, IAEA). Unipub.

Neutron Irradiaton of Seeds, Three. (Technical Reports Ser.: No. 141). (Illus.). 132p. (Orig.). 1973. pap. 9.75 (ISBN 92-0-115272-8, IAEA). Unipub.

Neutron Moisture Gauges. (Technical Reports Ser.: No. 112). (Illus., Orig.). 1970. pap. 6.00 (ISBN 92-0-165070-1, IAEA). Unipub.

Neutron Monitoring. 1967. pap. 33.25 (ISBN 92-0-020067-2, IAEA). Unipub.

Neutron Monitoring for Radiation Protection Purposes, 2 vols. (Illus.). 355p. (Orig.). 1974. Vol. 1. pap. 28.00 (ISBN 92-0-020173-3, ISP 318-1, IAEA); Vol. 2. pap. 40.25 (ISBN 92-0-020273-X, ISP 318-2). Unipub.

Neutron Nuclear Data Evaluation. (Technical Reports Ser.: No. 146). 127p. (Orig.). 1973. pap. 8.25 (ISBN 92-0-135173-9, IAEA). Unipub.

Neutron Physics. G. E. Bacon & G. R. Noakes, (Wykeham Science Ser.: Vol. 2). (Illus.). 1969. pap. 4.40 o.p. (ISBN 0-387-91046-8). Springer-Verlag.

Neutron Physics. G. E. Bacon & G. R. Noakes. (Wykeham Science Ser.: No. 2). 1969. 9.95x (ISBN 0-8448-1104-1). Crane-Russak Co.

Neutron Standard Reference Data: Proceedings. (Illus.). 369p. 1975. pap. 26.75 (ISBN 92-0-031074-5, IAEA). Unipub.

Neutron Stars. J. M. Irvine. (Oxford Studies in Physics). (Illus.). 150p. text ed. 32.00x (ISBN 0-19-851460-3). Oxford U Pr.

Neutron Thermalization & Reactor Spectra, 2 vols. (Illus., Eng., Fr. & Rus.). 1968. Vol. 1. pap. 32.25 (ISBN 92-0-050068-4, IAEA); Vol. 2. pap. 25.00 (ISBN 92-0-050168-0). Unipub.

Neutron Thermalization in Reactor Lattice Cells: An NPY-Project Report. (Technical Reports Ser.: No. 68). 1966. pap. 6.50 (ISBN 92-0-155266-1, IAEA). Unipub.

Neutron Two Is Critical. Lawrence Dunning. 1977. pap. 1.75 (ISBN 0-380-01775-X, 35089). Avon.

Nevada. Zane Grey. 304p. 1980. pap. 1.95 (ISBN 0-553-12383-1). Bantam.

Nevada. 23.00 (ISBN 0-89770-104-6). Curriculum Info Ctr.

Nevada: A Guide to the Silver State. Federal Writers' Project. 1940. Repr. 45.00 (ISBN 0-403-02178-2). Somerset Pub.

Nevada: An Annoted Bibliography. Stanley W. Paher. (Illus.). 1980. 95.00x (ISBN 0-913814-26-1). Nevada Pubns.

Nevada Constitution: Origin & Growth. 5th ed. Eleanore Bushnell & Don W. Driggs. LC 80-23682. (History & Political Science Ser.: No. 8). x, 221p. 1980. pap. text ed. 5.25x (ISBN 0-87417-060-5). U of Nev Pr.

Nevada Government. Effie M. Mack et al. 384p. 1953. octavo 5.00. Holmes.
Nevada Gun. Gordon D. Shirreffs. 1977. pap. 1.25 (ISBN 0-505-51166-5, BT51166). Tower Bks.
Nevada: In Words & Pictures. Dennis Fradin. LC 80-24179. (Young People's Stories of Our States Ser.). (Illus.). 48p. (gr. 2-5). 1981. PLB 8.65g (ISBN 0-516-03928-8, Time Line). Childrens.
Nevada Industrial Minerals. 1973. 13.40. Minobras.
Nevada Lost Mines & Buried Treasure. Douglas McDonald. (Illus.). 1981. 6.95. Nevada Pubns.
Nevada Printing History: A Bibliography of Imprints & Publications, 1858-1880. Robert D. Armstrong. (Illus.). 540p. 1981. price not set (ISBN 0-87417-063-X). U of Nev Pr.
Nevada State Industrial Directory, 1980. State Industrial Directories Corp. 1980. pap. 15.00 (ISBN 0-89910-017-1). State Indus Dir.
Nevada: This Is Our Land. Nancy C. Miluck. (Illus.). 148p. 1978. pap. 6.50 (ISBN 0-686-27941-7). Dragon Ent.
Nevada's Turbulent Fifties: Decade of Political & Economic Change. Mary E. Glass. LC 80-25651. (Nevada Studies in History & Political Science: No. 15). (Illus.). ix, 138p. (Orig.). 1981. pap. price not set (ISBN 0-87417-062-1). U of Nev Pr.
Nevada's Valley of Fire. G. William Fiero. Ed. by Gweneth R. DenDooven. LC 75-18136. (Illus.). 1975. 7.95 (ISBN 0-916122-42-5); pap. 2.50 (ISBN 0-916122-17-4). K C Pubns.
Neve Erfabrungen mit Oxazaphosphorinen Unter Bersonderer Bervecksichtigung des. Ed. by H. Burkert & G. A. Nagel. (Beitraege zur Onkologie: Band 5). (Illus.). 120p. 1980. pap. 21.00 (ISBN 3-8055-1381-X). S Karger.
Never at Rest: A Biography of Isaac Newton. R. S. Westfall. LC 77-84001. (Illus.). 850p. 1981. 49.50 (ISBN 0-521-23143-4). Cambridge U Pr.
Never Catch Colds Again. Oliver Clark. 64p. 1979. pap. 6.95x (ISBN 0-8464-1035-4). Beekman Pubs.
Never Complain, Never Explain. Victor Lasky. 338p. 1981. 15.00 (ISBN 0-399-90104-3). Marek.
Never Cry Wolf. Farley Mowat. 1963. 9.95 (ISBN 0-316-58639-0, Pub. by Atlantic Monthly Pr). Little.
Never Eat Out on a Saturday Night. Jim Quinn. 224p. 1981. pap. 6.95 (ISBN 0-525-47657-1). Dutton.
Never Get Too Personally Involved with Your Own Life. Tom Wilson. (Illus.). 96p. (Orig.). 1975. pap. 2.50 o.p. (ISBN 0-8362-0623-1). Andrews & McMeel.
Never Is a Long, Long Time. Dick Cate. LC 77-10818. (Illus.). (gr. 4-7). 1977. 5.95 o.p. (ISBN 0-525-66563-3). Elsevier-Nelson.
Never Kiss a Goat on the Lips: Tales of a Suburban Homesteader. Vic Sussman. Ed. by Carol Stoner. (Illus.). 288p. 1981. 12.95 (ISBN 0-87857-346-1); pap. 8.95 (ISBN 0-87857-347-X). Rodale Pr Inc.
Never Leave Shadow Wood. Sally T. Smith. (YA) 1977. 4.95 o.p. (ISBN 0-685-71791-7, Avalon). Bouregy.
Never Monkey with a Monkey: A Book of Homographic Homophones. Sylvia R. Tester. LC 77-9503. (Using Words Ser.). (Illus.). (gr. k-3). 1977. PLB 5.50 (ISBN 0-913778-90-7). Childs World.
Never Say Die: A Doctor & Patient Talk About Breast Cancer. Lucy Shapero & Anthony A. Goodman. (Appleton Consumer Health Guides). 170p. 1980. 10.95 (ISBN 0-8385-6718-5). ACC.
Never Say Die! A Thousand Years of Jewish Life & Letters. Ed. by Joshua A. Fishman. (Contributions to the Sociology of Language Ser.). 1980. 53.00x (ISBN 9-0279-7978-2). Mouton.
Never Say Ugh! to a Bug. Norma Farber. LC 78-13948. (Illus.). (gr. k-3). 1979. 7.50 (ISBN 0-688-80140-4); PLB 7.20 (ISBN 0-688-84140-6). Greenwillow.
Never Shake a Skeleton. A. Flett. 1978. 7.95 o.s.i. (ISBN 0-8027-5392-2). Walker & Co.
Never So Good or How Children Were Treated. Muriel Goaman. 1974. 7.95 o.p. (ISBN 0-7207-0627-0, Pub. by Michael Joseph). Merrimack Bk Serv.
Never Talk to Strangers. Irma Joyce. (gr. 4 up). 1970. 1.95 (ISBN 0-307-10876-7, Golden Pr); PLB 7.62 (ISBN 0-307-60876-X). Western Pub.
Never Tease a Weasel. Jean C. Soule. LC 64-12353. 48p. (gr. k-3). PLB 5.41 o.s.i. (ISBN 0-8193-0095-0, Four Winds). Schol Bk Serv.
Never the Twain: A Novel. G. D. Khosla. 177p. 1981. text ed. 15.00x (ISBN 0-7069-1270-5, Pub by Vikas India). Advent Bk.
Never Tickle a Turtle: Cartoons, Riddles & Funny Stories. Mike Thaler. (Illus.). (gr. 4-6). 1977. PLB 6.45 s&l (ISBN 0-531-00386-8). Watts.
Never Too Late. Kathryn Kuhlman. LC 75-32235. 80p. 1975. pap. 1.50 (ISBN 0-87123-397-5, 200387). Bethany Fell.
Never Too Old. Geri Harrington. 256p. 1981. cancelled (ISBN 0-8129-0913-5). Times Bks.
Never Too Old to Learn. 120p. 1974. pap. 5.00 o.p. (ISBN 0-89192-069-2). Interbk Inc.
Never Too Old to Teach. Judith Murphy & Carol Florio. 116p. 1978. pap. 5.00 (ISBN 0-89192-243-1). Interbk Inc.
Never Touch a Tiger. Hugh Steven. 180p. 1980. pap. 4.95 (ISBN 0-8407-5737-9). Nelson.
Never Underestimate the Selling Power of a Woman. Dottie Walters. 1978. pap. 4.95 (ISBN 0-8119-0392-3). Fell.
Neveu de rameau. Denis Diderot. (Documentation thematique). (Fr). pap. 2.95 (ISBN 0-685-13999-9, 85). Larousse.
Nevil Shute. Julian Smith. LC 76-8018. (English Authors Ser.: No. 190). 1976. lib. bdg. 10.95 (ISBN 0-8057-6664-2). Twayne.
Neville Cayley. J. H. Prince. (Illus.). 80p. 1981. 40.00x (ISBN 0-87663-355-6). Universe.
Neville Site: 8,000 Years at Amoskeag. Dina F. Dincauze. Ed. by Emily Flint. LC 75-40771. (Peabody Museum Monographs Ser.: No. 4). (Illus.). 1976. pap. 12.00 (ISBN 0-87365-903-1). Peabody Harvard.
New Abelard: A Romance. Robert Buchanan. Ed. by Robert L. Wolff. LC 75-483. (Victorian Fiction Ser.). 1975. lib. bdg. 66.00 (ISBN 0-8240-1603-3). Garland Pub.
New Adventures in Origami. Robert Harbin. (Funk & W Bk.). (Illus.). 192p. 1972. pap. 1.95 (ISBN 0-308-10040-9, F81, TYC-T). T Y Crowell.
New Age Directory. 4.95 (ISBN 0-933278-02-0). OMango.
New Age of Healing. 96p. 1980. pap. 3.50 (ISBN 0-911336-78-8). Sci of Mind.
New Age Training for Fitness & Health. Dyveke Spino. LC 78-65254. 1980. pap. 7.95 (ISBN 0-394-17738-X, E766, Ever). Grove.
New Agrarian Technology & India. Biplab Dasgupta. 1980. 17.50x (ISBN 0-8364-0635-4, Pub. by Macmillan India). South Asia Bks.
New Agricultural Crops. Ed. by Gary A. Ritchie. (AAAS Selected Symposium: No. 38). 1979. lib. bdg. 23.00x (ISBN 0-89158-473-0). Westview.
New Aikido. Yoshimitsu Yamada. 1981. 25.00 (ISBN 0-8184-0301-2). Lyle Stuart.
New Alchemy Backyard Fish Farm Book. 100p. 1981. pap. 4.95 (ISBN 0-931790-21-2). Brick Hse Pub.
New Alchemy Tree Crop Book. 96p. 1981. pap. 4.95 (ISBN 0-931790-22-0). Brick Hse Pub.
New Alchemy Water Pumping Windmill. 96p. 4.95 (ISBN 0-931790-23-9). Brick Hse Pub.
New Alignments in American Politics. Carl Lowe. (Reference Shelf Ser.). 1980. 6.25 (ISBN 0-8242-0636-3). Wilson.
New America? Ed. by Stephen R. Graubard. 1979. pap. text ed. 6.95x (ISBN 0-393-95019-0). Norton.
New American Gothic. Irving Malin. LC 62-15005. (Crosscurrents-Modern Critiques Ser.). 190p. 1962. 11.95 (ISBN 0-8093-0071-0). S Ill U Pr.
New American Justice: Ending the White Male Monopolies. Daniel C. Maguire. LC 78-20084. (Illus.). 240p. 1980. 9.95 (ISBN 0-385-14325-7). Doubleday.
New American Nudes. Ed. by Arno R. Minkkinen. (Illus.). 128p. 1981. pap. 19.95 (ISBN 0-87100-178-0). Morgan.
New American Photography. Ed. by Steven Klindt. (Illus.). 48p. 1981. pap. 10.00 (ISBN 0-932026-06-0). Chicago Contemp Photo.
New American Plays, Vol. 1. Ed. by Robert W. Corrigan. Incl. Mister Biggs. Anna M. Barlow; The Hundred & First. Kenneth Cameron; A Summer Ghost. Claude Fredericks; Blood Money. Dennis Jasudowicz; Socrates Wounded. Alfred Levinson; Constantinople Smith. Charles L. Mee, Jr; Pigeons. Lawrence Osgood; The Death & Life of Sneaky Fitch. James L. Rosenberg; Ginger Anne. Deric Washburn; The Golden Bull of Boredom. Lorees Yerby. 284p. (Orig.). 1965. pap. 5.95 (ISBN 0-8090-0734-7, Mermaid). Hill & Wang.
New American Plays, Vol. 3. Ed. by William M. Hoffmann. Incl. The Electronic Nigger. Ed Bullins; The Poet's Papers. David Starkweather; Always with Love. Tom Harris; Thank You, Miss Victoria. William M. Hoffman; The Golden Circle. Robert Patrick; An American Playground Sampler. Marc Estrin; The King of Spain. Byrd Hoffman. (Illus.). 288p. (Orig.). 1969. 5.95 (ISBN 0-8090-7252-1, Mermaid, Mermaid). Hill & Wang.
New American Revolution. R. Aya & N. Miller. LC 74-142353. 1971. 10.95 o.s.i. (ISBN 0-02-901110-8); pap. text ed. 4.50 o.s.i. (ISBN 0-02-901090-X). Free Pr.
New American Standard Bible Deluxe Cowhide Leather. 1976. Black. 48.95 (ISBN 0-8024-6231-6). Moody.
New American Standard Bible Deluxe Cowhide Leather. 1976. Brown. 48.95 (ISBN 0-8024-6233-2). Moody.
New American Standard Bible Deluxe Cowhide Leather Burgundy. 1976. 48.95 (ISBN 0-8024-6232-4). Moody.
New American Standard Bible: Deluxe Cowhide Leather Edition. (Illus.). 1977. Blue. 48.95 (ISBN 0-8024-6234-0). Moody.
New American Standard Bible Genuine Leather: Limp Black. 1976. 40.95 (ISBN 0-8024-6226-X). Moody.
New American Standard Bible Genuine Leather: Limp Blue. 1976. 40.95 (ISBN 0-8024-6227-8). Moody.
New American Standard Bible Genuine Leather: Limp Brown. 1976. 40.95 (ISBN 0-8024-6228-6). Moody.
New American Standard Bible: Red Letter, Deluxe Cowhide Leather, Black, Edition. (Illus.). 1977. 49.95 (ISBN 0-8024-6241-3). Moody.
New American Standard Bible: Red Letter, Deluxe Cowhide Leather, Blue. (Illus.). 1977. 49.95 (ISBN 0-8024-6244-8). Moody.
New American Standard Bible: Red Letter, Deluxe Cowhide Leather, Burgundy, (Illus.). 1977. 49.95 (ISBN 0-8024-6242-1). Moody.
New American Standard Bible: Red Letter, Deluxe Cowhide Leather, Brown. (Illus.). 1977. 49.95 (ISBN 0-8024-6243-X). Moody.
New American Standard Bible: Red Letter Edition, Genuine Leather Limp Black. (Illus.). 1977. 41.95 (ISBN 0-8024-6246-4). Moody.
New American Standard Bible: Red Letter Edition, Genuine Leather Limp Blue. (Illus.). 1977. 41.95 (ISBN 0-8024-6247-2). Moody.
New American Standard Bible: Red Letter Edition, Genuine Leather Limp Brown. (Illus.). 1977. 41.95 (ISBN 0-8024-6248-0). Moody.
New American Standard Bible: Red Letter Edition White Imitation Leather. (Illus.). 1977. 16.95 o.p. (ISBN 0-8024-6220-0). Moody.
New American State Papers: Complete Series, 179 vols. Ed. by Thomas C. Cochran. Set. 8125.00 (ISBN 0-8420-2161-2). Scholarly Res Inc.
New American State Papers: Labor & Slavery Subject Set, 7 vols. Ed. by Harold M. Hyman. LC 72-95577. 1973. Set. 425.00 o.p. (ISBN 0-8420-1505-1). Scholarly Res Inc.
New American State Papers: Naval Affairs, 1949 to 1979, 10 vols. Ed. by K. Jack Bauer. LC 80-53884. 3000p. 1981. Set. lib. bdg. 595.00 (ISBN 0-686-69283-7). Scholarly Res Inc.
New American State Papers: Public Lands Subject Set, 8 vols. Ed. by Margaret B. Bogue. LC 72-95582. 1972. Set. lib. bdg. 450.00 (ISBN 0-8420-1643-0). Scholarly Res Inc.
New Americans. Cecyle S. Neidle. (Immigrant Heritage of American Ser.). lib. bdg. 9.95 (ISBN 0-8057-3247-0). Twayne.
New Americans: Vietnamese Boat People. James Haskins. LC 80-14560. (Illus.). 64p. (gr. 4-6). 1980. PLB 6.95 (ISBN 0-89490-035-8). Enslow Pubs.
New & Appropriate System of Education for the Labouring People. P. Colquhoun. 98p. 1971. Repr. of 1806 ed. 15.00x (ISBN 0-7165-1773-6, Pub. by Irish Academic Pr Ireland). Biblio Dist.
New & Better Uses of Secondary Resources: Proceedings of the Second Recycling World Congress, Philippine International Conventional Center, Manila, March 1979. Ed. by M. Henstock & M. B. Bever. 278p. 1980. pap. 40.00 (ISBN 0-08-026245-7). Pergamon.
New & Controversial Aspects of Vitreoretinal Surgery. Alice McPherson. LC 77-1827. (Illus.). 1977. 52.50 o.p. (ISBN 0-8016-3321-4). Mosby.
New & Different Summer. Lenora M. Weber. LC 66-11951. (gr. 5 up). 1966. 10.95 (ISBN 0-690-58040-1, TYC-J). T Y Crowell.
New & Living Way. George A. Turner. LC 74-23104. 240p. 1974. pap. 4.95 (ISBN 0-87123-388-6, 210388); study guide 0.75 (ISBN 0-87123-522-6, 210522). Bethany Fell.
New & Selected Poems. Donald Davie. LC 61-14214. (Wesleyan Poetry Program: Vol. 12). (Orig.). 1961. 10.00x (ISBN 0-8195-2012-8, Pub. by Wesleyan U Pr); pap. 4.95x (ISBN 0-8195-1012-2). Columbia U Pr.
New & Selected Poems. William J. Smith. 1970. 6.95 o.p. (ISBN 0-440-06371-X, Sey Lawr). Delacorte.
New & Specialty Fibers. Ed. by James Economy. (Applied Polymer Symposia: No. 29). 1976. 22.50 (ISBN 0-471-02302-7, Pub. by Wiley-Interscience). Wiley.
New & the Old Criminology. Ed. by Edith E. Flynn & John P. Conrad. LC 76-14130. (Praeger Special Studies). 1978. 25.95 (ISBN 0-03-040891-1). Praeger.
New & Used Car Gas Milage & Price Guide. Mike Steele. (Orig.). 1981. pap. 3.95 (ISBN 0-933474-11-3, Gabriel Bks). Minn Scholarly.
New & Used Car Gas Mileage & Price Guide for 1981. Mike Steel. 160p. (Orig.). 1981. pap. 3.95 (ISBN 0-933474-23-7, Gabriel Bks). Minn Scholarly.
New & Used Foreign Car Prices. rev. ed. Ed. by Michael L. Green. (Buyer's Guide Ser.). 96p. (Orig.). Date not set. pap. 2.50 (ISBN 0-89552-067-2). DMR Pubns.
New Antigone. Canon W. Barry. LC 75-462. (Victorian Fiction Ser.). 1975. Repr. of 1887 ed. lib. bdg. 66.00 (ISBN 0-8240-1540-1). Garland Pub.
New Appleton's Cuyas English-Spanish & Spanish-English Dictionary. 5th ed. Ed. by A. Cuyas. 1972. 16.95 (ISBN 0-13-611749-X); thumb-indexed 17.95 (ISBN 0-13-611756-2). P-H.
New Approach for the Understanding & Interpretation of Financial Statements. Lloyd Houston. (Illus.). 1978. 51.85 (ISBN 0-918968-05-4). Inst Econ Finan.
New Approach to Capital Budgeting for City & County Governments. Richard F. Wacht. LC 80-13336. (Research Monograph: No. 87). 170p. 1980. spiral bdg. 29.00 (ISBN 0-88406-140-X). Ga St U Busn Pub.
New Approach to Ear Training. Leo Kraft. (Orig., Prog. Bk.). 1967. 5.95x (ISBN 0-393-09764-1, NortonC); tapes 185.00 (ISBN 0-393-09916-4); tchrs. manual free (ISBN 0-393-09788-9). Norton.
New Approach to Keyboard Harmony. Allen Brings et al. (Illus.). 1979. pap. text ed. 9.95x (ISBN 0-393-95001-8). Norton.
New Approach to Latin: 1. E. G. MacNaughton & T. W. McDougall. (Illus.). 1973. pap. text ed. 5.00x (ISBN 0-05-002185-0). Longman.
New Approach to Latin: 2. E. G. MacNaughton & T. W. McDougall. (Illus.). 1974. pap. text ed. 5.00x (ISBN 0-05-002365-9). Longman.
New Approach to Self-Diagnosis: Introducing Applied Kinesiology. Yoshiaki Omura. LC 79-89345. (Illus.). Date not set. 9.95 (ISBN 0-87040-468-7). Japan Pubns. Postponed.
New Approach to Teaching & Learning Anatomy: Objectives & Learning Activities for the Anatomy Course. M. Blunt. 1976. 9.95 (ISBN 0-407-00098-4). Butterworths.
New Approach to the Secondary School Health Education Curriculum: Reading Proficiency. Karen M. Lorentzen. 1981. 11.95 (ISBN 0-533-04633-5). Vantage.
New Approaches in Child Guidance. Herbert S. Strean. LC 74-15008. 1970. 10.00 (ISBN 0-8108-0330-5). Scarecrow.
New Approaches to Breeding for Improved Plant Protein. 1969. pap. 10.75 (ISBN 92-0-111069-3, IAEA). Unipub.
New Approaches to Coleridge: Biographical & Critical Essays. Ed. by Donald Sultana. (Critical Studies Ser.). 256p. 1981. 28.50x (ISBN 0-389-20060-3). B&N.
New Approaches to Ezra Pound: A Co-ordinated Investigation of Pound's Poetry & Ideas. Ed. by Eva Hesse. LC 76-78928. 1969. 16.50x (ISBN 0-520-01439-1). U of Cal Pr.
New Approaches to Family Pastoral Care. Douglas A. Anderson. LC 79-8898. (Creative Pastoral Care & Counseling Ser.). 96p. (Orig.). 1980. pap. 3.25 (ISBN 0-8006-0564-0, 1-564). Fortress.
New Approaches to Genetics. Ed. by P. W. Kent. 1978. 28.00 (ISBN 0-85362-169-1, Oriel). Routledge & Kegan.
New Approaches to Personality Classification. Ed. by Alvin R. Mahrer. LC 73-96313. 1970. 22.50x (ISBN 0-231-03296-X). Columbia U Pr.
New Approaches to the Study of Central-Local Government Relationships. Ed. by George Jones. 200p. 1980. text ed. 38.00x (ISBN 0-566-00332-5, Pub. by Gower Pr England). Renouf.
New Approaches to Urban Transportation Needs. Compiled by American Society of Civil Engineers. 218p. pap. text ed. 11.00 (ISBN 0-87262-032-8). Am Soc Civil Eng.
New Art of Living. Norman V. Peale. 160p. 1977. pap. 2.25 (ISBN 0-449-23938-1, Crest). Fawcett.
New Aspects of Naval History. Ed. by Craig L. Symonds. 1981. text ed. 32.95 (ISBN 0-87021-495-0). Naval Inst Pr.
New Aspects of Subnuclear Physics. Ed. by Antonio Zichichi. (Subnuclear Ser.: Vol. 16). 800p. 1981. 75.00 (ISBN 0-306-40459-1, Plenum Pr). Plenum Pub.
New Assertive Woman. L. Z. Bloom et al. 1976. pap. 2.25 (ISBN 0-440-16393-5, LE). Dell.
New Assertive Woman. Lynn Z. Bloom & Karen Coburn. 1975. 7.95 o.s.i. (ISBN 0-440-06439-2). Delacorte.
New Astronomy & Space Science Reader. Ed. by John C. Brandt & Stephen P. Maran. LC 76-54316. (Illus.). 1977. text ed. 19.95x (ISBN 0-7167-0350-5); pap. text ed. 9.95x (ISBN 0-7167-0349-1). W H Freeman.

New Attempts at the Monetization of Gold & Their Meaning for the Future of the World. Vernon C. Pierson. (Illus.). 127p. 1980. 49.75 (ISBN 0-918968-72-0). Inst Econ Finan.

New Australia, 1883. Edmond M. La Meslee. Tr. by Russel Ward. 1973. text ed. 13.95x o.p. (ISBN 0-435-32895-6). Heinemann Ed.

New Baby. Stanley Berenstain & Janice Berenstain. LC 74-2535. (Picturebacks Ser). (Illus.). 32p. (Orig.). (ps-1). 1974. pap. 1.25 (ISBN 0-394-82908-5, BYR). Random.

New Baby. Terry Berger. LC 75-19415. (Moods & Emotions Ser.). (Illus.). 32p. (gr. k-3). 1975. Repr. of 1974 ed. PLB 8.95 (ISBN 0-8172-0053-3). Raintree Pubs.

New Baby. Ruth Shane & Harold Shane. LC 79-10844. (Illus.). (ps-k). 1979. PLB 7.62 (ISBN 0-307-60822-0, Golden Pr); pap. 1.95 (ISBN 0-307-10822-8). Western Pub.

New Baja Handbook. rev. ed. James T. Crow. LC 73-81325. 1974. enlarged ed. 3.95 (ISBN 0-87880-020-4). Norton.

New Basic Course in Pitman Shorthand. 1961. text ed. 5.96 (ISBN 0-8224-1700-6); transcripts 2.56 (ISBN 0-8224-0041-3); wkbk. 3.32 (ISBN 0-8224-0042-1); tests A & B 0.72a (ISBN 0-8224-0124-X); accelrated speed drills, spiral bdg., 1967 4.42 (ISBN 0-8224-1703-0); tchr's. manual 5.76 (ISBN 0-8224-1704-9). Pitman Learning.

New Basketry. Ed Rossbach. 128p. 1980. pap. 7.95 (ISBN 0-442-23996-3). Van Nos Reinhold.

New Believers: Young Religion in America. (Illus.). 192p. 1976. pap. 1.75 o.p. (ISBN 0-345-24854-6). Ballantine.

New Bible Commentary. rev. ed. Donald Guthrie. 1970. 19.95 (ISBN 0-8028-2281-9). Eerdmans.

New Bible Dictionary. Ed. by J. D. Douglas. 1962. 24.95 (ISBN 0-8028-2282-7). Eerdmans.

New Bible Survey. J. Lawrence Eason. 16.95 (ISBN 0-310-24000-X). Zondervan.

New Blue Shoes. Eve Rice. LC 74-13259. (Illus.). 32p. (ps-1). 1975. 8.95 (ISBN 0-02-775960-1). Macmillan.

New Book of Chinese Lattice Designs. Daniel S. Dye. (Pictorial Archive Ser.). (Illus.). 128p. (Orig.). 1981. pap. price not set (ISBN 0-486-24128-9). Dover.

New Book of Favorite Breads from Rose Lane Farm. 2nd, rev. ed. Ada L. Roberts. (Illus.). 192p. 1981. pap. 3.00 (ISBN 0-486-24091-6). Dover.

New Book of Gymnastics. 8rev. ed. Meg Warren. (Illus.). 120p. 1980. 13.50x (ISBN 0-213-16772-7, Pub. by Weidenfeld & Nicolson England). Biblio Dist.

New Book of Gymnastics. Meg Warren. (Illus.). 120p. 1980. 13.50x (ISBN 0-213-16772-7). Biblio Dist.

New Book of Knowledge, 21 vols. Ed. by William E. Shapiro. LC 80-82958. (Illus.). 1981. write for info. (ISBN 0-7172-0512-6). Grolier Ed Corp.

New Book of Knowledge, 21 vols. Ed. by William E. Shapiro. LC 79-53915. (Illus.). 1980. write for info o.p. (ISBN 0-7172-0511-8). Grolier Ed Corp.

New Book of Knowledge Annual, 1981. Ed. by William E. Shapiro & Fern Mamberg. LC 79-26807. (Illus.). 1981. write for info. (ISBN 0-7172-0612-2). Grolier Ed Corp.

New Book of Popular Science, 6 vols. Ed. by Herbert Kondo. LC 79-55175. (Illus.). 1980. write for info o.p. (ISBN 0-7172-1210-6). Grolier Ed Corp.

New Book of Popular Science, 6 vols. Ed. by Herbert Kordo. LC 80-83090. (Illus.). 1981. write for info. (ISBN 0-7172-1211-4). Grolier Ed Corp.

New Boy in Dublin: A Story of Ireland. Clyde R. Bulla. LC 77-78257. (Stories from Many Lands Ser). (Illus.). (gr. k-3). 1969. 7.95 (ISBN 0-690-57756-7, TYC-J). T Y Crowell.

New Boy Is Blind. William E. Thomas. LC 80-349. (Illus.). 64p. (gr. 3-6). 1980. PLB 6.97 (ISBN 0-671-33094-2). Messner.

New Brahmans: Five Maharashtrian Families. D. D. Karve & Ellen E. McDonald. 1963. 21.50x (ISBN 0-520-00635-6). U of Cal Pr.

New Breed. Douglass Elliot. 1981. pap. 2.95 (ISBN 0-345-29483-1). Ballantine.

New Brew It Yourself. Leigh Beadle. 150p. 1981. 5.95 (ISBN 0-374-51529-8). FS&G.

New British Science Fiction & Fantasy Books Published During 1970 & 1971. Gerald Bishop. LC 80-20579. 1980. Repr. of 1972 ed. lib. bdg. 9.95x (ISBN 0-89370-057-6). Borgo Pr.

New Bronze Age Civilization in the USSR: Archeological Findings. Ed. by Philip L. Kohl. Tr. by William Mandell from Rus. LC 80-5454. (Illus.). 300p. 1981. 30.00x (ISBN 0-87332-169-3). M E Sharpe.

New Brooms! & The Manager in Distress. George Colman. LC 80-14205. 25.00x (ISBN 0-8201-1353-0). Schol Facsimiles.

New Burgeoning Video Industries. BCC Staff. 1980. cancelled (ISBN 0-89336-264-6, G-058). BCC.

New Business Ventures & the Entrepreneur. Patrick R. Liles. 1974. text ed. 18.50x (ISBN 0-256-01560-0). Irwin.

New Businesses Women Can Start & Successfully Operate. David D. Seltz & Mary Leslie. LC 77-608270. 1977. 9.95 (ISBN 0-87863-129-1). Farnswth Pub.

New by the Spirit. Arnold V. Wallenkampf. LC 77-91485. (Dimension Ser.). 1978. pap. 5.95 (ISBN 0-8163-0091-7, 14390-9). Pacific Pr Pub Assn.

New Calculus. Arthur W. Siddons et al. 1950. Pt. 1. text ed. 5.95x (ISBN 0-521-06465-1). Cambridge U Pr.

New Call to Holiness. J. Sidlow Baxter. 256p. 1973. pap. 5.95 (ISBN 0-310-20581-6). Zondervan.

New Calligraphic Ornaments & Flourishes. Arthur Baker. (Pictorial Archive Ser.). (Orig.). 1981. pap. price not set (ISBN 0-486-24095-9). Dover.

New Cambridge Modern History, Vol. XIII. Ed. by P. Burke. LC 57-14935. (New Cambridge Modern History Ser.). 384p. 1980. pap. 13.95 (ISBN 0-521-28017-6). Cambridge U Pr.

New Cambridge Modern History. Incl. Vol. 1. Renaissance, 1493-1520. Ed. by G. R. Potter. 1957. 49.95 (ISBN 0-521-04541-X); pap. 21.95 (ISBN 0-521-09974-9); Vol. 2. Reformation, 1520-1559. Ed. by G. R. Elton. 1958. 53.00 (ISBN 0-521-04542-8); pap. 22.95 (ISBN 0-521-09960-9); Vol. 3. Counter-Reformation & Price Revolution, 1559-1610. Ed. by R. B. Wernham. 1968. 49.95 (ISBN 0-521-04543-6); Vol. 4. Decline of Spain & the Thirty Years War, 1609-59. Ed. by J. P. Cooper. 1970. 59.95 (ISBN 0-521-07618-8); Vol. 5. Ascendary of France, 1648-88. Ed. by F. L. Carsten. 1961. 49.95 (ISBN 0-521-04544-4); Vol. 6. Rise of Great Britain & Russia, 1688-1725. Ed. by J. S. Bromley. 1970. 69.00 (ISBN 0-521-07524-6); pap. 24.95 (ISBN 0-521-29396-0); Vol. 7. Old Regime 1713-1763. Ed. by J. O. Lindsay. 1957. 79.95 (ISBN 0-521-04545-2); Vol. 8. American & French Revolutions, 1763-93. A. Goodwin. 1965. 59.50 (ISBN 0-521-04546-0); pap. 22.95 (ISBN 0-521-29108-9); Vol. 9. War & Peace in an Age of Upheaval, 1793-1830. Ed. by C. W. Crawley. 1965. 59.95 (ISBN 0-521-04547-9); Vol. 10. Zenith of European Power 1830-1870. Ed. by J. P. Bury. 1960. 59.95 (ISBN 0-521-04548-7); Vol. 11. Material Progress & World-Wide Problems, 1870-98. Ed. by F. H. Hinsley. 1962. 59.95 (ISBN 0-521-04549-5); pap. 22.95 (ISBN 0-521-29109-7); Shifting Balance of World Forces, 1898-1945. 2nd ed. Ed. by C. L. Mowat. 1960. 65.95 (ISBN 0-521-04551-7); Vol. 13. Companion Volume. Ed. by Peter Burke. 1979. 34.95 (ISBN 0-521-22128-5); pap. 13.95 (ISBN 0-521-28017-6); Vol. 14. Atlas. Ed. by H. C. Darby & Harold Fullard. (Illus.). 1970. 65.00 (ISBN 0-521-07708-7); pap. 22.95 (ISBN 0-521-09908-0). Set. 600.00 (ISBN 0-521-08787-2). Cambridge U Pr.

New Car Prices Buyer's Guide, 1981. rev. ed. Ed. by Michael L. Green. (Buyer's Guide Ser.). 128p. (Orig.). Date not set. pap. 2.50 (ISBN 0-89552-068-0). DMR Pubns.

New Careers for Older People. Ed. by Carter C. Osterbind. LC 53-12339. (Center for Gerontological Studies & Programs Ser.: Vol. 20). 1971. pap. 4.25 (ISBN 0-8130-0332-6). U Presses Fla.

New Careers for the Poor. Arthur Pearl & F. Riessman. LC 65-14910. 1965. 6.95 o.s.i. (ISBN 0-02-925200-8). Free Pr.

New Caribbean Man Poems-1972 to 1976. P. D. Sharma. (Illus.). 72p. (Orig.). 1980. pap. 5.00 (ISBN 0-936378-00-X). Carib Hse.

New Casserole Treasury. rev. enl. ed. Lousene R. Brunner. LC 74-138711. (Illus.). 1971. 8.95 o.p. (ISBN 0-06-010557-7, HarpT). Har-Row.

New Catechism. 1967. 10.00 (ISBN 0-8164-1070-4). Crossroad NY.

New Catechism: Catholic Faith for Adults. 1977. pap. 5.95 (ISBN 0-8164-2140-4). Crossroad NY.

New Caxton Encyclopedia, 20 vols. 1977. 525.00 (ISBN 0-8277-3043-8); yearbooks 10.00 ea. Maxwell Sci Intl.

New Celibacy: Why More Men & Wonen Are Abstaining from Ex & Enjoying It. Gabrielle Brown. 300p. 1980. 10.95 (ISBN 0-07-008430-0). McGraw.

New Century Bible Commentary on Isaiah 1-39. rev. ed. R. E. Clements. 320p. 1980. pap. 7.95 (ISBN 0-8028-1841-2). Eerdmans.

New Century Bible Commentary on Job. rev. ed. H. H. Rowley. Ed. by Ronald E. Clements. 304p. 1980. pap. 7.95 (ISBN 0-8028-1838-2). Eerdmans.

New Century Composition-Rhetoric. Ed. by Edward P. Corbett & Virginia M. Burke. LC 73-150594. 1971. 22.50x (ISBN 0-89197-315-X); pap. text ed. 14.95x (ISBN 0-89197-865-8). Irvington.

New Century Handbook of English Literature. rev. ed. Ed. by Clarence L. Barnhart & William D. Halsey. (gr. 9-12). 1956. 23.95 (ISBN 0-13-611962-X). P-H.

New Century Shakespeare Handbook. Ed. by Sandra Clark & T. H. Long. 304p. 1974. Repr. 13.95 (ISBN 0-13-612093-8). P-H.

New Certificate Chemistry. 5th, rev. ed. A. Holderness et al. (Illus.). 1977. pap. text ed. 9.50x o.p. (ISBN 0-435-64424-6). Heinemann Ed.

New Challenge of Soccer. rev. ed. Hubert Vogelsinger. (Illus.). 380p. 1981. 12.95 (ISBN 0-89037-179-2). Anderson World.

New Challenges to the Role of Profit: The Fourth Series of the John Diebold Lectures. Ed. by Benjamin M. Friedman. 1978. 14.95 (ISBN 0-669-02171-7). Lexington Bks.

New Chapters in the History of Greek Literature. Ed. by J. U. Powell & E. A. Barber. 1921. 15.00x (ISBN 0-8196-0286-8). Biblo.

New Chapters in the History of Greek Literature. Ed. by J. U. Powell & E. A. Barber. (Second Ser). 1929. 15.00x (ISBN 0-8196-0287-6). Biblo.

New Christian Hymnal. National Union of Christian Schools. PLB 2.95 o.p. (ISBN 0-8028-9004-0). Eerdmans.

New Christianity. Salem Bland. LC 72-95815. (Social History of Canada Ser.). 1973. pap. 2.50 (ISBN 0-8020-6179-6). U of Toronto Pr.

New Christology. Karl Rahner & Wilhelm Thusing. 256p. 1980. 12.95 (ISBN 0-8164-0211-6). Crossroad NY.

New Citizenship: Origins of Progressivism in Wisconsin, 1885-1900. David Thelen. LC 79-158075. 1972. 15.00x (ISBN 0-8262-0111-3). U of Mo Pr.

New Class. B. Bruce-Briggs. 252p. 1981. pap. 5.95 (ISBN 0-07-008573-0). McGraw.

New Code of Civil Procedure in France, Bk. 1. 1978. 32.50 (ISBN 0-379-20266-2). Oceana.

New Collector's Directory for the 1980's. rev. 2nd ed. Robert D. Connolly. (Illus.). 168p. 1980. pap. 5.95 (ISBN 0-914598-38-4). Padre Prods.

New College French & English Dictionary. Roger J. Steiner. (gr. 7-12). 1972. pap. text ed. 7.17 (ISBN 0-87720-463-2). AMSCO Sch.

New College Italian & English Dictionary. Robert C. Melzi. (Orig.). (gr. 7-12). 1976. pap. text ed. 8.50 (ISBN 0-87720-592-2). AMSCO Sch.

New College Latin & English Dictionary. John C. Traupman. (gr. 7-12). 1966. pap. text ed. 6.25 (ISBN 0-87720-560-4). AMSCO Sch.

New College Spanish & English Dictionary. Edwin B. Williams. (gr. 7-12). 1968. pap. text ed. 7.17 (ISBN 0-87720-511-6). AMSCO Sch.

New Columbia Encyclopedia. Columbia University Press. LC 74-26686. (Illus.). 1975. 79.50 o.p. (ISBN 0-397-03572-1); deluxe ed. 135.00 leather bdg. o.p. (ISBN 0-397-03977-8). Lippincott.

New Command: The Story of Bruce Medaris, Maj. Gen. Retired. Gordon Harris. LC 76-10533. 1977. pap. 3.95 o.p. (ISBN 0-88270-181-9). Logos.

New Commentaries on the Law of England, 4 vols. Henry J. Stephen. Ed. by David S. Berkowitz & Samuel E. Thorne. LC 77-86571. (Classics of English Legal History in the Modern Era Ser.: Vol. 73). 1979. lib. bdg. 55.00 ea. (ISBN 0-8240-3060-5). Garland Pub.

New Commentary on Genesis, 2 vols. Franz Delitzsch. 1978. 27.75 (ISBN 0-686-12963-6). Klock & Klock.

New Commodities & Consumer Behaviour. new ed. D. S. Ironmonger. LC 75-163056. (Department of Applied Economics Monographs: No. 20). (Illus.). 1972. 36.00 (ISBN 0-521-08337-0). Cambridge U Pr.

New Communications & Freedom. John Wicklein. 1981. 14.95 (ISBN 0-670-50658-3). Viking Pr.

New Communications & Information Technologies. 1979. pap. 8.95 (ISBN 0-9603466-1-9). NCCB.

New Compact Bible Dictionary. Al Bryant. 1967. 8.95 (ISBN 0-310-22080-7); pap. 3.95 (ISBN 0-310-22082-3). Zondervan.

New Compact Bible Dictionary. 1976. pap. 2.25 (ISBN 0-89129-098-2). Jove Pubns.

New Companion to Shakespeare Studies. K. Muir & S. Schoenbaum. LC 78-118066. (Illus.). 1971. 47.50 (ISBN 0-521-07941-1); pap. 10.95 (ISBN 0-521-09645-6). Cambridge U Pr.

New Comparative Mytholgy: An Anthropological Assessment of the Theories of Georges Dumezil. 3rd ed. C. Scott Littleton. 1980. pap. 5.95 (ISBN 0-520-04103-8, CAMPUS 216). U of Cal Pr.

New Comparative Mythology: An Anthropological Assessment of the Theories of George Dumezil. 2nd ed. C. Scott Littleton. 1974. pap. 5.95x o.p. (ISBN 0-520-02403-6). U of Cal Pr.

New Complete Book of Home Remodeling, Improvement, & Repair. Arthur M. Watkins. (Encore Edition). (Illus.). 1979. 7.95 (ISBN 0-684-16731-X, ScribT). Scribner.

New Complete Hoyle. rev. ed. Richard L. Frey et al. LC 55-11330. 1956. 9.95 (ISBN 0-385-00126-6). Doubleday.

New Comprehensive A-Z Crossword Dictionary. Redentor M. Tuazon & Edy G. Schaffer. 1974. pap. 3.95 (ISBN 0-380-00168-3, 50492). Avon.

New Concept of the Novel. Raj. Kunar. 49p. 1980. Repr. of 1959 ed. lib. bdg. 6.00 (ISBN 0-8482-1446-3). Norwood Edns.

New Concepts in Air Pollution Research. Ed. by Jan-Olaf Willums. LC 73-19210. 184p. 1974. pap. 21.95 (ISBN 0-470-94956-2). Halsted Pr.

New Concepts in Business Information. 1979. pap. text ed. 42.00x (ISBN 0-903796-39-2, Pub. by Online Conferences England). Renouf.

New Concepts in Endocrinology & Metabolism. Ed. by Leslie I. Rose & Robert L. Lavine. LC 77-9314. (39th Hahnemann Symposium on Endocrinology). 1977. 28.50 (ISBN 0-8089-1028-0). Grune.

New Concepts in Lipid Research in Honor of Stina & Einar Stenhagen, Vol. 16. new ed. Ed. by Ralph T. Holman. (Progress in the Chemistry of Fats & Other Lipids). 1978. text ed. 71.00 (ISBN 0-08-022663-9). Pergamon.

New Concepts of Cattle Growth. R. T. Berg & R. M. Butterfield. LC 75-32561. 1976. 18.95 (ISBN 0-470-06888-4). Halsted Pr.

New Conceptual Model for the Study of Political Integration in Africa. Peter Osei-Kwame. LC 80-5708. 307p. 1980. lib. bdg. 20.00 (ISBN 0-8191-1316-6); pap. 11.50 (ISBN 0-8191-1317-4). U Pr of Amer.

New Conceptualism of the Uniform Commercial Code. Donald B. King. 126p. (Orig.). 1968. pap. text ed. 8.50x (ISBN 0-8377-0726-9). Rothman.

New Concise Atlas of the Universe. Patrick Moore. 1978. 35.00 (ISBN 0-528-83031-7). Rand.

New Concrete Technologies & Building Design. Ed. by A. M. Neville & M. Chatterton. 134p. 1980. 44.95x (ISBN 0-470-26944-8). Halsted Pr.

New Congress. Stephen Goode. LC 80-19111. 224p. (gr. 7 up). 1980. PLB 9.49 (ISBN 0-671-34031-X). Messner.

New Connecticut Yankees. Trish Hall. (Illus.). (gr. 9-12). 1981. 7.95 (ISBN 0-938348-07-8); pap. 2.95 (ISBN 0-938348-08-6); limited edition 12.95 (ISBN 0-938348-06-X). Cottage Indus.

New Consciousness in Science & Religion. Harold K. Schilling. LC 72-13792. 1973. 10.95 (ISBN 0-8298-0247-9). Pilgrim NY.

New Consultants, Periodical Supplement for Consultants & Consulting Organizations Directory: Four Issues Covering the Period Between Editions, Issue 1. 4th ed. Ed. by Paul Wasserman & Janice McLean. 1979. 130.00 (ISBN 0-8103-0354-X). Gale.

New Consumer Product Electronics: Growth Trends, G-040r. Ed. by Business Communications. 1980. 725.00 (ISBN 0-89336-224-7). BCC.

New Contents, New Teachers, New Publics. Ed. by Warren C. Born & Thomas H. Geno. 1978. pap. 7.95x (ISBN 0-915432-78-1). NE Conf Teach.

New Conventional Weapons & East-West Security. Christoph Bertram. LC 78-78216. (Praeger Special Studies Ser.). 102p. 1979. 20.95 (ISBN 0-03-052091-6). Praeger.

New Cookbook for Poor Poets & Others. rev ed. Ann Rogers. (Illus.). 1979. 8.95 o.p. (ISBN 0-684-16046-3, ScribT); pap. 3.95 (ISBN 0-684-16948-7, SL837, ScribT). Scribner.

New Cosmetic Formulary. H. Bennett. 1970. 25.00 o.p. (ISBN 0-8206-0088-1). Chem Pub.

New Cosmology. James K. Feibleman. LC 77-81794. 224p. 1981. 14.50 (ISBN 0-87527-171-5). Green.

New Cosmos. A. Unsoeld. Tr. by W. H. McCrea from Ger. LC 68-8301. (Heidelberg Science Library: Vols. 5 & 6). (Illus.). 1970. 15.50 (ISBN 0-387-90017-9); pap. 11.90 o.p. (ISBN 0-387-90007-1). Springer-Verlag.

New Country: A Social History of the American Frontier 1776-1890. Richard A. Bartlett. LC 74-79619. (Illus.). 495p. 1976. pap. 8.95 (ISBN 0-19-502021-9, 452, GB). Oxford U Pr.

New Cratylus: Notes on the Craft of Poetry. Alec D. Hope. 193p. 1979. text ed. 33.00x (ISBN 0-19-550576-X). Oxford U Pr.

New Creation Story: The Creative Sprituality of Teilhard de Chardin. Donald P. Gray. 1979. pap. 2.00 (ISBN 0-89012-014-5). Anima Pubns.

New Creationism. Harold Clark. LC 79-22250. (Horizon Ser.). 1980. pap. 6.95 (ISBN 0-8127-0247-6). Southern Pub.

New Criminology: For a Social Theory of Deviance. Ian Taylor et al. 1974. pap. 6.95x (ISBN 0-06-131812-4, TB1812, Torch). Har-Row.

New Criminology: For a Social Theory of Deviance. Ian Taylor et al. (International Library of Sociology). 342p. 1973. 19.95x o.p. (ISBN 0-7100-7472-7). Routledge & Kegan.

New Critical Essays. Roland Barthes. Tr. by Richard Howard from Fr. 121p. 1980. 10.95 (ISBN 0-8090-7257-2). Hill & Wang.

New Cults. Walter Martin. (Orig.). 1980. pap. 7.95 (ISBN 0-88449-016-5). Vision Hse.

New Culture in China. Lancelot Forster. LC 79-2823. 240p. 1981. Repr. of 1936 ed. 19.75 (ISBN 0-8305-0003-0). Hyperion Conn.

New Dalda Cookbook. (Illus.). 1975. text ed. 11.50 (ISBN 0-7069-0377-3, Pub. by Vikas India). Advent Bk.

New Dark Ages Conspiracy: Britain's Plot to Destroy Civilization. Carol White. LC 80-23546. (Illus.). 400p. (Orig.). 1980. pap. 4.95 (ISBN 0-933488-05-X). New Benjamin.

New Day. Robert T. Smith. LC 72-81449. (Illus.). 32p. (gr. 5-12). 1973. PLB 4.95 (ISBN 0-87191-213-9). Creative Ed.

New Day for Dragons. Lynn Hall. 1976. pap. 1.25 (ISBN 0-380-00763-0, 30528, Camelot). Avon.

New Deal. Ed. by Bernard Sternsher. LC 78-73287. (Orig.). 1979. pap. text ed. 3.95x (ISBN 0-88273-212-9). Forum Pr MO.

New Deal: An Anthology. Ed. by Frank A. Warren & Michael Wreszin. LC 68-9745. (Orig.). 1969. pap. 4.95x o.p. (ISBN 0-88295-769-4). AHM Pub.

New Deal: Analysis & Interpretation. 2nd ed. Ed. by Alonzo L. Hamby. 224p. 1980. pap. text ed. 7.95 (ISBN 0-582-28204-7). Longman.

New Deal & American Politics: A Study in Political Change. John M. Allswang. LC 78-5733. (Critical Episodes in American Politics Ser.). 1978. text ed. 11.95 o.p. (ISBN 0-471-02515-1); pap. text ed. 8.95 (ISBN 0-471-02516-X). Wiley.

New Deal & the Problem of Monopoly. Ellis W. Hawley. LC 65-24273. (Orig.). 1966. 18.00 o.p. (ISBN 0-691-04528-3); pap. 6.95 (ISBN 0-691-00564-8). Princeton U Pr.

New Deal & War, 1933-1945. William E. Leuchtenburg. LC 63-8572. (Life History of the United States). (Illus.). (gr. 5 up). 1974. PLB 9.96 (ISBN 0-8094-0560-1, Pub. by Time-Life). Silver.

New Deal at Home & Abroad, 1929-1945. Ed. by Clarke A. Chambers. LC 65-11896. (Orig.). 1965. pap. text ed. 3.50 o.s.i. (ISBN 0-02-905300-5). Free Pr.

New Deal Collective Bargaining Policy. Irving Bernstein. LC 75-8997. (FDR & the Era of the New Deal Ser.). xi, 178p. 1975. Repr. of 1950 ed. lib. bdg. 20.00 (ISBN 0-306-70703-9). Da Capo.

New Deal for Blacks: The Emergence of Civil Rights As a National Issue; the Depression Decade. Harvard Sitkoff. 412p. 1981. pap. 6.95 (ISBN 0-19-502893-7, GB 627, OPB). Oxford U Pr.

New Deal for the World: Eleanor Roosevelt & American Foreign Policy, 1920-1962. Jason Berger. 240p. 1981. 20.00x (ISBN 0-930888-07-3). Brooklyn Coll Pr.

New Deal for Youth. Betty Lindley & E. K. Lindley. LC 72-172687. (FDR & the Era of the New Deal Ser). (Illus.). 316p. 1972. Repr. of 1938 ed. lib. bdg. 32.50 (ISBN 0-306-70382-3). Da Capo.

New Deal Thought. Ed. by Howard Zinn. LC 66-16755. (Orig.). 1966. pap. 8.50 (ISBN 0-672-60112-5). Bobbs.

New Dealers: By the Unofficial Observer. John F. Carter. LC 74-23461. (Fdr & the Era of the New Deal Ser.). ix, 414p. 1975. Repr. of 1934 ed. lib. bdg. 35.00 (ISBN 0-306-70710-1). Da Capo.

New Deal's SEC: The Formative Years. Ralph F. De Bedts. LC 64-14236. 1964. 20.00x (ISBN 0-231-02713-3). Columbia U Pr.

New Democratic Theory. K. A. Megill. LC 71-122277. 1971. 7.95 o.s.i. (ISBN 0-02-920780-0); pap. text ed. 4.50 o.s.i. (ISBN 0-02-920790-8). Free Pr.

New Demons. Jacques Ellul. 320p. (Eng.). 1975. 9.95 (ISBN 0-8164-0266-3). Crossroad NY.

New Depression in Higher Education: A Study of the Financial Conditions at 41 Colleges & Universities. Carnegie Commission On Higher Education. 1971. 9.95 o.p. (ISBN 0-07-010027-6, P&RB). McGraw.

New Design for Living. Ernest Holmes & Willis Kinnear. 1959. pap. 5.95 (ISBN 0-911336-11-7). Sci of Mind.

New Design for Nuclear Disarmament: Pugwash Symposium, Kyoto, Japan. Ed. by William Epstein & Toshiyuka Toyoda. (Illus.). 1977. 30.00x o.p. (ISBN 0-8476-2322-X). Rowman.

New Development in New Ceramics GB-058. 1981. 800.00 (ISBN 0-89336-255-7). BCC.

New Development in Topology. Ed. by G. Segal. LC 73-84323. (London Mathematical Society Lecture Notes Ser.: No. 11). 120p. 1973. 14.50 (ISBN 0-521-20354-6). Cambridge U Pr.

New Development Strategy. Robert J. Alexander. LC 75-7783. 176p. 1976. 6.95x o.p. (ISBN 0-88344-328-7). Orbis Bks.

New Developments in Clinical Instrumentation. Ed. by Leroy Hersh. 192p. 1981. 49.95 (ISBN 0-8493-5305-X). CRC Pr.

New Developments in Modelling Travel Demand & Urban Systems. Ed. by G. R. Jansen et al. 1979. 40.25x (ISBN 0-566-00269-8, Pub. by Gower Pub Co England). Renouf.

New Developments in Pediatric Research, 3 vols. Ed. by O. P. Ghai. 1330p. 1980. Set. 42.50x (ISBN 0-89955-325-7, Pub. by Interprint India); Set. pap. 25.00x (ISBN 0-89955-326-5). Intl Schol Bk Serv.

New Developments in Retail Trading Area Analysis & Site Selection. Jac L. Goldstucker et al. LC 78-8033. (Research Monograph: No. 78). 1978. pap. 9.95 (ISBN 0-88406-115-9). Ga St U Busn Pub.

New Developments with Human & Veterinary Vaccines. Ed. by A. I. Hertmann et al. A. Kohn. LC 80-19130. (Progress in Clinical & Biological Research: Vol. 47). 444p. 1980. 36.00 (ISBN 0-8451-0047-5). A R Liss.

New Diary: How to Use a Journal for Self-Guidance & Expanded Creativity. Tristine Rainer. LC 76-62677. 1979. pap. 5.95 (ISBN 0-87477-150-1). J P Tarcher.

New Diary: How to Use a Journal for Self-Guidance & Expanded Creativity. Tristine Rainer. LC 76-62677. 1978. 9.95 o.p. (ISBN 0-87477-061-0). J P Tarcher.

New Diary: Recreating Oneself Through Journal Writing. Tristine Rainer. LC 76-6277. Date not set. cancelled (ISBN 0-312-90736-2). St Martin.

New Dictionary of Americanisms. Sylvia Clapin. LC 68-17985. 1968. Repr. of 1902 ed. 24.00 (ISBN 0-8103-3244-2). Gale.

New Dictionary of Family Names. Elsdon C. Smith. LC 72-79693. 512p. 1973. 17.50 (ISBN 0-06-013933-1, HarpT). Har-Row.

New Dictionary of Physics. 2nd ed. Ed. by A. Isaacs & H. J. Gray. LC 75-307635. Orig. Title: Dictionary of Physics. (Illus.). 640p. 1975. text ed. 42.00x (ISBN 0-582-32242-1). Longman.

New Dictionary of Railroad Working Terminology. Ed. by Railsearch Publishing, Inc. (Railsearch Railroad Management Ser.). (Illus.). 400p. 1980. 28.00 (ISBN 0-686-27634-5); lib. bdg. 29.25 (ISBN 0-686-27635-3). Railsearch.

New Dictionary of Statistics: A Complement to the Fourth Edition of Mulhall's Dictionary of Statistics. Augustus D. Webb. LC 68-18017. 1971. Repr. of 1911 ed. 44.00 (ISBN 0-8103-3988-9). Gale.

New Dictionary of Strange & Ingenious Stock Market Tricks the Experts Follow in Their Search for Wealth. C. M. Flumiani. 215p. 1976. 37.50 (ISBN 0-89266-002-3). Am Classical Coll Pr.

New Dictionary of Thoughts. rev. ed. Ed. by Tryon Edwards. 1955. 12.95 (ISBN 0-385-00127-4). Doubleday.

New Dimensions in Creativity. D. Gade. LC 74-78396. 1974. pap. 5.00 (ISBN 0-686-14991-2, 261-08418). Home Econ Educ.

New Dimensions in Mental Health - Psychiatric Nursing. rev. ed. Marion Kalkman & Anne Davis. Orig. Title: Psychiatric Nursing. (Illus.). 704p. 1974. text ed. 14.95 o.p. (ISBN 0-07-033242-8, HP). McGraw.

New Dimensions in Music Education. Lloyd F. Sunderman. LC 73-189289. 1972. 10.00 (ISBN 0-8108-0482-4). Scarecrow.

New Dimensions in Puppet Ministry. Lee Garsee. 1981. pap. write for info. (ISBN 0-89137-607-0). Quality Pubns.

New Dimensions in Second Language Acquisition Research. Ed. by Roger W. Andersen. (Illus.). 280p. (Orig.). 1981. pap. text ed. 14.95 (ISBN 0-88377-180-2). Newbury Hse.

New Dimensions of Appropriate Technology: Selected Proceedings. International Association for the Advancement of Appropriate Technology for Developing Countries, 1979 Symposium. Ed. by Alfred L. Edwards & Thomas Wagner. Tr. by Thomas Wagner. xii, 251p. (Orig.). 1980. pap. 5.00 (ISBN 0-87712-208-3). U Mich Busn Div Res.

New Dimensions of Political Economy. Walter Heller. 1967. pap. 3.95x (ISBN 0-393-09755-2). Norton.

New Dimensions of Political Economy. Walter W. Heller. LC 66-23467. (Godkin Lectures Ser.: 1966). 1966. 10.00x (ISBN 0-674-61100-4). Harvard U Pr.

New Dimensions: Science Fiction No. 7. Ed. by Robert Silverberg. LC 76-26276. (Illus.). 1977. 8.95 o.p. (ISBN 0-06-013862-9, HarpT). Har-Row.

New Dimensions: The Decorative Arts of Today in Words and Pictures. Paul T. Frankl. LC 75-15851. (Architecture and Decorative Arts Ser.). (Illus.). 122p. 1975. Repr. of 1928 ed. lib. bdg. 37.50 (ISBN 0-306-70741-1). Da Capo.

New Dimensions to Energy Policy. Robert Lawrence. LC 78-389. (Policy Studies Organization Ser.). 1979. 22.95 (ISBN 0-669-02172-5). Lexington Bks.

New Dimensions: 8. Ed. by Robert Silverberg. LC 77-11774. 1978. 10.95 o.s.i. (ISBN 0-06-013792-4, HarpT). Har-Row.

New Directions for Clarinet. Phillip Rehfeldt. (New Instrumentation Ser.: Vol. 4). 1978. 17.95x (ISBN 0-520-03379-5). U of Cal Pr.

New Directions for Directors: Behind the by-Laws. Robert Kirk Mueller. LC 77-10216. 1978. 18.95 (ISBN 0-669-01889-9). Lexington Bks.

New Directions Forty-One: Anthology. Ed. by J. Laughlin et al. LC 37-1751. 192p. 1980. 15.95 (ISBN 0-8112-0770-6); pap. 5.95 (ISBN 0-8112-0771-4, NDP505). New Directions.

New Directions Forty-Two: Anthology. Ed. by J. Laughlin et al. LC 37-1751. 192p. 1981. 15.95 (ISBN 0-8112-0783-8); pap. 5.95 (ISBN 0-8112-0784-6, NDP510). New Directions.

New Directions in American Architecture. rev. ed. Robert A. Stern. LC 70-81278. (New Directions in Architecture Ser). 1978. 9.95 (ISBN 0-8076-0523-9); pap. 5.95 (ISBN 0-8076-0527-1). Braziller.

New Directions in American Psychiatry, 1944-1968. American Psychiatric Association, Committee on the History of Psychiatry. lib. bdg. 5.00 o.p. (ISBN 0-685-24847-X, 230); pap. 3.00 o.p. (ISBN 0-685-24848-8). Am Psychiatric.

New Directions in Attribution Research, 2 vols. Ed. by John H. Harvey et al. LC 76-26028. (Wiley Monographs in Applied Econometrics). Vol. 1, 1976. text ed. 19.95 (ISBN 0-470-98910-6); Vol. 2, 1978. 19.95 (ISBN 0-470-26372-5). Halsted Pr.

New Directions in Attribution Research, Vol. 3. Ed. by John H. Harvey et al. 512p. 1981. prof. - refer. 29.95 (ISBN 0-89859-098-1). L Erlbaum Assocs.

New Directions in Austrian Economics. Ed. by Louis M. Spadaro. LC 77-28611. (Studies in Economic Theory Ser.). 240p. 1978. 15.00; pap. 4.95. NYU Pr.

New Directions in Childhood Psychopathology: Vol. 2, Deviations in Development. Ed. by Saul I. Harrison & John F. McDermott. LC 78-70232. 750p. 1981. text ed. 35.00 (ISBN 0-8236-3571-6). Intl Univs Pr.

New Directions in Children's Mental Health. new ed. Ed. by Jalal Shamsie. LC 79-17844. 1979. text ed. 20.00 (ISBN 0-89335-083-4). Spectrum Pub.

New Directions in Creativity. Joseph S. Renzulli. 1976. 23.84 ea. (SchDept). Mark A (ISBN 0-06-538998-0). Mark B (ISBN 0-06-538999-9). Har-Row.

New Directions in Crochet. Anne R. Ough. LC 80-52646. (Illus.). 248p. 1981. 17.95 (ISBN 0-670-40008-4, Studio). Viking Pr.

New Directions in Dance: Proceedings. Dance in Canada Annual Conference, 7th, Waterloo, Ontario, June 27-July 2, 1979. Ed. by Taplin. (Pergamon International Series on Dance & the Related Arts). (Illus.). 200p. 1979. 35.00 (ISBN 0-08-024773-3). Pergamon.

New Directions in Development: Study of U. S. Aid. Ed. by Donald R. Mickelwait et al. Charles F. Sweet & Elliott R. Morse. 1979. lib. bdg. 22.00x (ISBN 0-89158-266-5). Westview.

New Directions in Employability: Reducing Barriers to Full Employment. Ed. by David B. Orr. LC 73-6094. (Special Studies in U.S. Economic, Social & Political Issues). 1973. 28.50x (ISBN 0-275-28838-2). Irvington.

New Directions in Ethnic Studies: Minorities in America. Ed. by David Claerbaut. LC 80-69329. 115p. 1981. perfect bdg. 8.50 (ISBN 0-86548-026-5). Century Twenty One.

New Directions in European Historiography. Georg G. Iggers. LC 75-12665. 240p. 1975. 20.00x (ISBN 0-8195-4084-6, Pub. by Wesleyan U Pr). Columbia U Pr.

New Directions in Geography Teaching. Ed. by Rex Walford. (Illus.). 197p. 1973. pap. text ed. 5.00x o.p. (ISBN 0-582-31240-X). Longman.

New Directions in Latin American Architecture. Francisco Bullrich. LC 71-85698. (New Directions in Architecture Ser). (Illus., Orig.). 1969. 7.95 o.s.i. (ISBN 0-8076-0524-7); pap. 3.95 o.s.i. (ISBN 0-8076-0528-X). Braziller.

New Directions in Legal Education. Carnegie Commission on Higher Education. Ed. by Herbert L. Packer & Thomas Ehrlich. LC 72-5311. 416p. 1972. 13.95 o.p. (ISBN 0-07-010047-0, P&RB); pap. 2.95 o.p. (ISBN 0-07-010057-8). McGraw.

New Directions in Literature: A Critical Approach to a Contemporary Phenomenon. John Fletcher. 1968. text ed. 7.75x (ISBN 0-7145-0004-6). Humanities.

New Directions in Medical Geography: Medical Geography Papers from the 75th Anniversary Meeting of the Association of American Geographers, Philadelphia Pa., April 1979. Ed. by Gerald F. Pyle. (Illus.). 86p. 1980. 14.95 (ISBN 0-08-025817-4). Pergamon.

New Directions in Memory & Aging: Proceedings. George A. Talland Memorial Conference. Ed. by Leonard W. Poon et al. LC 79-27548. (Illus.). 592p. 1980. text ed. 36.00 (ISBN 0-89859-035-3). L Erlbaum Assocs.

New Directions in Music. 3rd ed. David H. Cope. 200p. 1981. pap. text ed. 7.50x (ISBN 0-697-03448-8). Wm C Brown.

New Directions in Music. 3rd ed. David H. Cope. 286p. 1981. pap. text ed. price not set (ISBN 0-697-03448-8). Wm C Brown.

New Directions in Organizational Behavior. Ed. by Barry M. Staw & Gerald R. Salancik. LC 76-47795. (Illus.). 250p. 1976. pap. text ed. 9.95 (ISBN 0-914292-06-4). Wiley.

New Directions in Parapsychological Research. Joseph H. Rush. LC 64-22612. (Parapsychological Monograph No. 4). 1964. pap. 2.00 (ISBN 0-912328-07-X). Parapsych Foun.

New Directions in Parapsychology: With a Postscript by Arthur Koestler. Ed. by John Beloff. LC 75-15489. 1975. 10.00 (ISBN 0-8108-0866-8). Scarecrow.

New Directions in Patient Compliance. Ed. by Stuart J. Cohen. (Illus.). 1979. 16.95 (ISBN 0-669-02721-9). Lexington Bks.

New Directions in Piagetian Theory & Practice. Ed. by I. E. Sigel et al. 320p. 1981. ref. 19.95 (ISBN 0-89859-072-8). L Erlbaum Assocs.

New Directions in Political Socialization. Ed. by David C. Schwartz & Sandra K. Schwartz. LC 74-2653. (Illus.). 1975. 17.95 (ISBN 0-02-928180-6). Free Pr.

New Directions in Psychohistory: The Adelphi Papers in Honor of Erik H. Erikson. Ed. by Mel Albin et al. LC 78-4410. 240p. 1980. 25.95x (ISBN 0-669-02350-7). Lexington Bks.

New Directions in Robots for Manufacturing, G-053. Ed. by Business Communications. 1979. 750.00 (ISBN 0-89336-219-0). BCC.

New Directions in Suspension Design: Making the Fast Car Faster. Colin Campbell. LC 80-24348. (Illus.). 224p. 1981. 18.50 (ISBN 0-8376-0150-9). Bentley.

New Directions in Swiss Architecture. Jul Bachmann & Stanislaus Von Moos. LC 72-78052. (New Directions in Architecture Ser). (Illus., Orig.). 1969. 7.95 o.s.i. (ISBN 0-8076-0525-5); pap. 3.95 o.s.i. (ISBN 0-8076-0529-8). Braziller.

New Directions in the Kindergarten. Helen F. Robison. LC 65-22438. (Orig.). 1966. pap. 7.00x (ISBN 0-8077-2045-3). Tchrs Coll.

New Directions in the Law of the Sea, Vol. 7. M. Nordquist. 1980. 45.00 (ISBN 0-379-00532-8). Oceana.

New Directions in Theology Today. Colin W. Williams. LC 68-22647. (New Directions in Theology Today: Vol. 4). 1968. pap. 3.25 (ISBN 0-664-24834-9). Westminster.

New Directions in Urban-Rural Migration: The Population Turnaround in Rural America. Ed. by David L. Brown & John M. Wardwell. (Studies in Population). 1980. 29.50 (ISBN 0-12-136380-5). Acad Pr.

New Discovery Technique for Art Instruction: An Innovative Handbook for the Elementary Teacher. Billie M. Phillips & Virginia S. Brown. 1976. 13.95 o.p. (ISBN 0-13-612507-7). P-H.

New Documentary in Action: A Casebook in Film Making. Alan Rosenthal. 1972. 15.95 (ISBN 0-520-01888-5); pap. 2.95 (ISBN 0-520-02254-8, CAL249). U of Cal Pr.

New Earth Book: Our Changing Planet. Melvin Berger. LC 79-7828. (Illus.). 128p. (gr. 5 up). 1980. 7.95 (ISBN 0-690-00735-3, TYC-J); PLB 7.89 (ISBN 0-690-04074-1). T Y Crowell.

New Economic Nationalism. Ed. by Otto Hieronymi. 300p. 1980. 29.95 (ISBN 0-03-056676-2). Praeger.

New Economic Order & International Development Law. Oswaldo De Rivero. LC 79-41222. 132p. 1980. 18.50 (ISBN 0-08-024706-7). Pergamon.

New Economic Systems of Eastern Europe. Ed. by Hans-Hermann Hohmann et al. LC 74-76386. 1975. 36.50x (ISBN 0-520-02732-9). U of Cal Pr.

New Economics of Growth: A Strategy for India & the Developing World. John W. Mellor. LC 75-38430. (Illus.). 384p. 1976. 18.50x (ISBN 0-8014-0999-3); pap. 7.95 (ISBN 0-8014-9188-6). Cornell U Pr.

New Economics of Growth: A Strategy for India & the Developing World. John W. Mellor. (Twentieth Century Fund Study). 1980. 14.50 o.p. (ISBN 0-8014-1000-2); pap. 7.95 o.p. Cornell U Pr.

New Economics of the Less Developed Countries: Changing Perceptions in the North-South Dialogue. Ed. by Nake Kamrany. LC 77-14602. (Westview Special Studies in Social Political, & Economic Development Ser.). 1978. lib. bdg. 28.50x (ISBN 0-89158-449-8). Westview.

New Educational Facilities: An International Survey. Carlo Testa. LC 75-23359. (Illus.). 192p. 1976. 29.75 o.p. (ISBN 0-89158-505-2). Westview.

New Egalitarianism: Questions & Challenges. Ed. by David L. Schaefer. (National Univ. Pubns. Political Science Ser.). 1979. 17.50 (ISBN 0-8046-9220-3). Kennikat.

New Egon Ronay Pub Guide. rev. ed. 384p. 1980. pap. 4.95 o.p. (ISBN 0-14-005465-0, Pub. by Auto Assn-British Tourist Authority England). Merrimack Bk Serv.

New Emily Post's Etiquette. Elizabeth Post. LC 74-14667. (Funk & W Bk.). (Illus.). 880p. 1975. 13.95 (ISBN 0-308-10167-7, TYC-T); thumb-indexed 12.95 (ISBN 0-308-10168-5). T Y Crowell.

New Empire. Brooks Adams. (Social Science Classics Ser.). 1982. text ed. 19.95 (ISBN 0-87855-315-0); pap. text ed. 6.95 (ISBN 0-87855-691-5). Transaction Bks. Postponed.

New England & the Sea. Robert G. Albion et al. LC 72-3694. (American Maritime Library: Vol. 5). (Illus.). 303p. Date not set. 15.95 (ISBN 0-8195-4052-8); pap. 7.00 (ISBN 0-913372-23-4) (ISBN 0-8195-6046-4). Mystic Seaport.

New England Annals: History & Genealogy, Vol. 1. Ed. by Laird C. Towle. 500p. 1980. 20.00 (ISBN 0-917890-19-1). Heritage Bk.

New England Butt'ry Shelf Almanac. Mary M. Campbell. LC 76-128491. 1970. 9.95 o.s.i. (ISBN 0-690-00361-7, TYC-T). T Y Crowell.

New England Butt'ry Shelf Cookbook. M. M. Campbell. 1968. 6.95 o.s.i. (ISBN 0-690-00362-5, TYC-T). T Y Crowell.

New England Diesels. 28.95. Chatham Pub CA.

New England Guest House Book. Corinne M. Ross. LC 79-4899. (Illus.). 192p. 1979. lib. bdg. 10.25 o.p. (ISBN 0-914788-15-9). East Woods.

New England Gun: The First 200 Years. Merrill Lindsay. (Illus.). 190p. 1976. 20.00 o.p. (ISBN 0-679-50586-5); pap. 12.50 o.p. (ISBN 0-679-50621-7). McKay.

New England in the English Nation 1689-1713. Philip S. Haffenden. 328p. 1974. text ed. 22.50x (ISBN 0-19-821124-4). Oxford U Pr.

New England in the Off-Color Season. Keith Jennison. LC 80-67659. (Illus., Orig.). 1980. pap. 5.95 (ISBN 0-911764-23-2). Durrell.

New England Indians. C. Keith Wilbur. LC 78-61713. (Illus.). 1978. pap. 8.95 (ISBN 0-87106-004-3); pap. 8.95 (ISBN 0-87106-040-X). Globe Pequot.

New England Legends & Folklore. Harry Hansen. 1967. 6.95 o.s.i. (ISBN 0-8038-4998-2). Hastings.

New England Life in the Eighteenth Century: Representative Biographies from Sibley's Harvard Graduates. Clifford K. Shipton. LC 63-9562. (Illus.). 1963. 25.00x (ISBN 0-674-61250-7, Belknap Pr). Harvard U Pr.

New England Love Story: Nathaniel Hawthorne & Sophia Peabody. LouAnn Gaeddert. LC 80-16329. (Illus.). 160p. (gr. 7 up). 1980. 8.95 (ISBN 0-8037-6153-8). Dial.

New England: Off the Beaten Path, a Guide to Unusual Places. Corinne M. Ross & Ralph Woodward. (Illus.). 128p. 1981. pap. 4.95 (ISBN 0-914788-40-X). East Woods.

New England Patriots: A Pictorial History. George McGuane. LC 80-84555. (Illus.). 176p. 1981. 16.95 (ISBN 0-938694-00-6). JCP Corp VA.

New England Pattern: The History of Manchester, Connecticut. William E. Buckley. LC 73-79895. (Illus.). 376p. 1973. casebound 9.95 (ISBN 0-87106-116-3). Globe Pequot.

New England Politics. Ed. by Josephine Milburn & Victoria Shuck. LC 80-14530. 320p. 1981. text ed. 27.00x (ISBN 0-87073-356-7); pap. text ed. 10.50x (ISBN 0-87073-357-5). Schenkman.

New England Primer. Ed. by Paul L. Ford. LC 62-20977. (Orig.). 1962. pap. text ed. 4.00x (ISBN 0-8077-1368-6). Tchrs Coll.

New England Reflections, Eighteen Eighty-Two to Nineteen Seven: Photographs by the Howes Brothers. Ed. by Alan B. Newman. (Illus.). 1981. 25.00 (ISBN 0-394-51375-4); pap. 12.95 (ISBN 0-394-74912-X). Pantheon.

New England Town in Early Photographs: Illustrations of Southbridge, Massachusetts 1878 - 1930. Ed. by Edmund V. Gillon. LC 75-463. (Illus.). 176p. (Orig.). 1976. pap. 6.00 (ISBN 0-486-23286-7). Dover.

New England Trials. John Smith. LC 70-171793. (English Experience Ser.: No. 416). 1971. Repr. of 1620 ed. 7.00 (ISBN 90-221-0416-8). Walter J Johnson.

New England Village Life. Edward M. Chapman. LC 72-143643. 1971. Repr. of 1937 ed. 18.00 (ISBN 0-8103-3699-5). Gale.

New England White Water River Guide. 2nd ed. Ray Gabler. (Illus.). 250p. 1981. pap. 7.95 (ISBN 0-910146-33-0). Appalach Mtn.

New England Wilds. Ogden Tanner. (American Wilderness Ser.). (Illus.). 184p. 1974. 12.95 (ISBN 0-8094-1229-2). Time-Life.

New England Wilds. Ogden Tanner. LC 73-92887. (American Wilderness). (Illus.). (gr. 6 up). 1974. PLB 11.97 (ISBN 0-8094-1230-6, Pub. by Time-Life). Silver.

New England Year: A Journal of Vermont Farm Life. Muriel Follett. LC 73-145711. 1971. Repr. of 1939 ed. 15.00 (ISBN 0-8103-3393-7). Gale.

New England's White Mountains: At Home in the Wild. Brooks Atkinson & W. Kent Olson. LC 78-55506. 1978. 35.00 (ISBN 0-913890-18-9, 936065). NYGS.

New English Bible: Companion to the New Testament. A. E. Harvey. 1970. 49.50x (ISBN 0-19-826160-8). Oxford U Pr.

New English Bible Companion to the New Testament. rev. ed. A. E. Harvey. (Illus.). 856p. 1980. pap. 19.50 (ISBN 0-19-213229-6). Oxford U Pr.

New English Bible Companion to the New Testament. A. E. Harvey. 1979. 59.50 (ISBN 0-521-07705-2); pap. 19.50 (ISBN 0-521-50539-9). Cambridge U Pr.

New English Bible Companion to the New Testament: The Gospels. A. E. Harvey. 1972. pap. 10.95 (ISBN 0-19-826168-3). Oxford U Pr.

New English Course, 6 bks. Edwin T. Cornelius, Jr. Incl. Book 1. pap. text ed. (ISBN 0-89285-125-2); tchr's. annotated ed. 5.95 (ISBN 0-89285-137-6); wkbk. 1.50 (ISBN 0-89285-131-7); cassette 110.00 (ISBN 0-89285-119-8); cassette tape 14.95 (ISBN 0-89285-113-9); Book 2. pap. text ed. (ISBN 0-89285-126-0); tchr's annotated ed. 5.95 (ISBN 0-89285-138-4); wkbk. 1.50 (ISBN 0-89285-132-5); cassette 110.00 (ISBN 0-89285-120-1); cassette tape 14.95 (ISBN 0-89285-114-7); Book 3. pap. text ed. (ISBN 0-89285-127-9); tchr's annotated ed. 5.95 (ISBN 0-89285-139-2); wkbk. 1.50 (ISBN 0-89285-133-3); cassette 110.00 (ISBN 0-89285-121-X); cassette tape 14.95 (ISBN 0-89285-115-5); Book 4. pap. text ed. (ISBN 0-89285-128-7); tchr's annotated ed. 5.95 (ISBN 0-89285-140-6); wkbk. 1.50 (ISBN 0-89285-134-1); cassette 110.00 (ISBN 0-89285-122-8); cassette tape 14.95 (ISBN 0-89285-116-3); Book 5. pap. text ed. (ISBN 0-89285-129-5); tchr's annotated ed. 5.95 (ISBN 0-89285-141-4); wkbk. 1.50 (ISBN 0-89285-135-X); cassette 110.00 (ISBN 0-89285-123-6); cassette tape 14.95 (ISBN 0-89285-117-1); Book 6. pap. text ed. (ISBN 0-89285-130-9); tchr's annotated ed. 5.95 (ISBN 0-89285-142-2); wkbk. 1.50 (ISBN 0-89285-136-8); cassette 110.00 (ISBN 0-89285-124-4); cassette tape 14.95 (ISBN 0-89285-118-X); progress quizzes & placement tests avail.. (Illus.). 1979. pap. text ed. 3.95 ea. English Lang.

New English Course. 2nd ed. Rhodri Jones. 1976. pap. text ed. 8.50x o.p. (ISBN 0-435-10493-4). Heinemann Ed.

New English First. Rhodri Jones. (Illus.). 1977. pap. text ed. 5.95x o.p. (ISBN 0-435-10494-2). Heinemann Ed.

New English Poetry by Indian Women. Ed. by P. Lal. (Writers Workshop Redbird Ser.). 1977. flexible bdg. 8.00 (ISBN 0-89253-804-X); text ed. 14.00 (ISBN 0-89253-803-1). Ind-US Inc.

New English Second. Rhodri Jones. 1978. pap. text ed. 5.95 o.p. (ISBN 0-435-10495-0). Heinemann Ed.

New English: Structure, Form & Style. Joseph M. Williams. LC 76-7225. 1970. text ed. 10.95 (ISBN 0-02-935310-6). Free Pr.

New English Third. Rhodri Jones. 1979. pap. text ed. 5.95x o.p. (ISBN 0-435-10496-9). Heinemann Ed.

New Enlarged Anthology of Robert Frost's Poems. enl. ed. Robert Frost. Ed. by Louis Untermeyer. pap. 2.50 (ISBN 0-671-48149-5). WSP.

New Enlightenment. N. A. Smith. 1980. pap. 6.95 (ISBN 0-7145-3604-0). Riverrun NY.

New Entrepreneurs: Women Working from Home. Terri P. Tepper & Nona D. Tepper. LC 80-17578. (Illus.). 256p. 1980. 10.95 (ISBN 0-87663-342-4). Universe.

New Environmental Handbook. Garrett DeBell. LC 79-56911. (Orig.). 1980. pap. 5.95 (ISBN 0-913890-36-7). Friends Earth.

New Era Car Book & Auto Survival Guide. Bob Fendell. LC 75-5466. (Illus.). 320p. 1976. 9.95 o.p. (ISBN 0-03-014031-5); pap. 5.95 o.p. (ISBN 0-03-014036-6). HR&W.

New Era Community. 1978. Repr. of 1951 ed. softbd. 9.00 (ISBN 0-933574-03-7). Agni Yoga Soc.

New Essays in the Philosophy of Education. Ed. by Glenn Langford & D. J. O'Connor. (International Library of the Philosophy of Education). 1973. 22.50x (ISBN 0-7100-7690-8). Routledge & Kegan.

New Essays on Donne. Ed. by Gary A. Stringer. (Salzburg Studies in English Literature, Elizabethan & Renaissance Studies: No. 57). 1977. pap. text ed. 25.00x (ISBN 0-391-01538-9). Humanities.

New Essays on Human Understanding. G. W. Leibniz. Ed. by Peter Remnant & Jonathan Bennett. 610p. Date not set. price not set (ISBN 0-521-23147-7); pap. price not set (ISBN 0-521-29836-9). Cambridge U Pr.

New Essays on Plato & Aristotle. Ed. by Renford Bambrough. (International Library of Philosophy & Scientific Method). 1965. text ed. 14.50x (ISBN 0-391-00979-6). Humanities.

New Essays on Tolstoy. Ed. by M. Jones. LC 78-1158. (Illus.). 1979. 34.00 (ISBN 0-521-22091-2). Cambridge U Pr.

New Ethinics: Asian Indians in the U. S. Ed. by Parmatma Saran & Edwin Eames. 410p. 1980. 29.95 (ISBN 0-03-051121-6). Praeger.

New Euromarkets: A Theoretical & Practical Study of International Financing in the Eurobond & Eurocurrency Markets. Brian S. Quinn. LC 75-4755. 1975. 24.95 (ISBN 0-470-70266-4). Halsted Pr.

New Europe, an Economic Geography of the EEC. 2nd ed. G. N. Minshall. LC 78-6581. 288p. 1981. pap. text ed. 17.50x (ISBN 0-8419-6221-9). Holmes & Meier.

New Europe: An Introduction to Its Political Geography. Walter Fitzgerald. LC 80-24065. (Illus.). xiii, 298p. 1980. Repr. of 1946 ed. lib. bdg. 29.75x (ISBN 0-313-21006-3, FINE). Greenwood.

New Expanded Dictionary of Stock Market Charts. new ed. C. M. Flumiani. (Illus.). 1977. 43.25 (ISBN 0-89266-050-3). Am Classical Coll Pr.

New Explorers: Women in Antarctica. Barbara Land. LC 80-2778. (Illus.). 224p. (gr. 7 up). 1981. PLB 8.95 (ISBN 0-396-07924-5). Dodd.

New Face for the Church. Lawrence O. Richards. 288p. (Orig.). 1981. pap. 6.95 (ISBN 0-310-31901-3). Zondervan.

New Fashion Areas - For Designing Apparel Through the Flat Pattern. Ernestine Kopp et al. LC 72-82160. (Illus.). 350p. 1972. 14.50 (ISBN 0-87005-111-3). Fairchild.

New Fashion from Old. Maureen Goldsworth. 1978. pap. 8.95 (ISBN 0-7134-0913-4, Pub. by Batsford England). David & Charles.

New Federalism. Michael D. Reagan. 192p. 1972. 3.95 (ISBN 0-19-501585-1). Oxford U Pr.

New Federalism. Michael D. Reagan. 175p. 1972. pap. text ed. 2.95x o.p. (ISBN 0-19-501584-3). Oxford U Pr.

New Federalism. 2nd ed. Michael D. Reagan & John G. Sanzone. 208p. 1981. pap. text ed. 3.95x (ISBN 0-19-502772-8). Oxford U Pr.

New Female. (Illus.). softcover 5.00 (ISBN 0-910550-48-4). Centurion Pr.

New Feminism. Lucy Komisar. LC 70-149011. (Illus.). (gr. 7 up). 1971. PLB 6.88 o.p. (ISBN 0-531-01981-0). Watts.

New Feminism in Twentieth Century America. June Sochen. LC 71-160664. (Problems in American Civilization Ser). 1971. pap. 4.25x o.p. (ISBN 0-669-63461-1). Heath.

New Fire Is Blazing. Peter Popoff. Ed. by Don Tanner. LC 80-67993. (Illus.). 194p. (Orig.). 1980. pap. 4.95 (ISBN 0-938544-02-0). Faith Messenger.

New Fish Cookery. Marika H. Tenison. 1979. 14.95x (ISBN 0-8464-0060-X). Beekman Pubs.

New Food Book: Nutrition, Diet, Consumer Tips & Foods of the Future. Melvin Berger & Gilda Berger. LC 77-7976. (gr. 4-6). 1978. 7.95 (ISBN 0-690-01295-0, TYC-J); PLB 7.89 (ISBN 0-690-03841-0). T Y Crowell.

New Forms of Work Organisation: German Democratic Republic, India, Italy, USSR, Economic Costs & Benefits, Vol.2. International Labour Office. (Illus.). 1979. lib. bdg. 14.25 (ISBN 92-2-102110-6). Intl Labour Office.

New Forms of Work Organization. Lisl Klein. LC 75-22556. 1976. 18.95 (ISBN 0-521-21055-0). Cambridge U Pr.

New Formulation of Particle Mechanics. Reese T. Prosser. LC 52-42839. (Memoirs: No. 61). 1980. pap. 6.00 (ISBN 0-8218-1261-0, MEMO-61). Am Math.

New Foster Parents. Patricia W. Cautley. 288p. 1980. 19.95 (ISBN 0-87705-495-9). Human Sci Pr.

New Foster Parents: The First Experience. Patricia W. Cautley. LC 80-10937. 288p. 1980. 19.95x (ISBN 0-87705-495-9). Human Sci Pr.

New French-English Dictionary of Slang & Colloquialisms. Ed. by Joseph Marks et al. 1971. 8.50 o.p. (ISBN 0-525-16555-X). Dutton.

New French Feminisms. Ed. by Elaine Marks & Isabelle De Courtivron. LC 79-4698. 1979. 13.95x (ISBN 0-87023-280-0). U of Mass Pr.

New French Poetry: An Anthology. Ed. by C. A. Hackett. 1973. 18.25x (ISBN 0-631-14490-0, Pub. by Basil Blackwell); pap. 12.50x (ISBN 0-631-14500-1, Pub. by Basil Blackwell). Biblio Dist.

New Friends for the Saggy Baggy Elephant. Adelaide Holl. (Illus.). (gr. k-3). 1976. PLB 5.00 (ISBN 0-307-60131-5, Golden Pr). Western Pub.

New Frontiers in Astronomy: Readings from Scientific American. Intro. by Owen Gingerich. LC 75-8902. (Illus.). 1975. text ed. 19.95x (ISBN 0-7167-0520-6); pap. text ed. 9.95x (ISBN 0-7167-0519-2). W H Freeman.

New Frontiers in Good Health. Richard Utt. (Uplook Ser.). 1979. pap. 0.75 (ISBN 0-8163-0325-8, 14400-6). Pacific Pr Pub Assn.

New Frontiers in Second Language Learning. John H. Schumann & Nancy Stenson. 1975. pap. 9.95 (ISBN 0-912066-84-9). Newbury Hse.

New Frontiers of Interior Decoration. Adrian Lefebvre. (Illus.). 1980. deluxe ed. 41.75 (ISBN 0-930582-60-8). Gloucester Art.

New Fruit Cookbook. Cynthia Rubin & Jerome Rubin. LC 76-42442. 1977. 12.95 o.p. (ISBN 0-8092-7892-8); pap. 4.95 o.p. (ISBN 0-8092-7890-1). Contemp Bks.

New Fully Illustrated Family Book on the Life of Christ. Alexander Eaglefort. (Most Meaningful Classics in World Culture Ser.). (Illus.). 1979. 37.50 (ISBN 0-89266-190-9). Am Classical Coll Pr.

New Furniture, Vol. XI. Ed. by Gerd Hatie. Date not set. 24.95 o.p. (ISBN 0-8038-0186-6). Hastings.

New Games Book. New Games Foundation. Ed. by Andrew Fluegelman. 4.95 (ISBN 0-385-12516-X, Dolp). Doubleday.

New Generation: A Curator's Choice. Kenworth Moffett. LC 80-52831. (Illus.). 96p. (Orig., Eng., Fr., & Ger.). 1980. pap. 10.00 (ISBN 0-9604746-0-9). Rhineburgh Pr.

New Generation of Essays. James M. Salem. 1972. pap. text ed. 6.95x o.p. (ISBN 0-697-03816-5); instructor's manual 1.00 o.p. (ISBN 0-686-28510-7). Wm C. Brown.

New Genetics: Promises & Perils. Margaret O. Hyde. LC 74-916. (Illus.). (gr. 9 up). 1974. PLB 6.88 o.p. (ISBN 0-531-02672-8). Watts.

New German-Arabic Dictionary, 3 vols. Wahrmud. 1974. 50.00x (ISBN 0-685-77129-6). Intl Bk Ctr.

New German Cinema. John Sandford. (Illus.). 180p. 1980. 25.75x (ISBN 0-389-20015-8). B&N.

New Germans: Thirty Years After. John Dornberg. 320p. 1976. 11.95 o.s.i. (ISBN 0-02-532170-6). Macmillan.

New Girl. LaVada Weir. LC 74-824. (Laurie Newman Adventures Ser). 32p. (gr. 3-9). 1974. 5.95 (ISBN 0-87191-351-8). Creative Ed.

New Girls. Beth Gutcheon. 336p. 1981. pap. 2.50 (ISBN 0-380-50831-1, 50831). Avon.

New Glass: A Worldwide Survey. Corning Museum of Glass. (Illus.). 286p. 1981. pap. price not set (ISBN 0-486-24156-4). Dover.

New Glass Review 1. (Illus.). 16p. pap. 8.00 (ISBN 0-87290-074-6). Corning.

New Glass Stained Glass Pattern Book. Ed Sibbett, Jr. (Illus.). 64p. (Orig.). 1980. pap. 3.00 (ISBN 0-486-24029-0). Dover.

New Gnomes: Multinational Banks in the Third World. Howard Wachtel. LC 77-81604. 1977. pap. 3.95 o.p. (ISBN 0-89758-006-0). Inst Policy Stud.

New Gods: Psyche & Symbol in Popular Art. Harold Schechter. LC 79-92848. 1980. 13.95 (ISBN 0-87972-168-5); pap. 6.95 o.p. (ISBN 0-686-64303-8). Bowling Green.

New Golden Bough. abridged ed. James G. Frazer. Ed. by Theodor H. Gaster. LC 59-6125. 1959. 19.95 (ISBN 0-87599-036-3). S G Phillips.

New Golf for Women. Ed. by John Coyne. LC 72-94173. 192p. 1973. 4.95 o.p. (ISBN 0-385-00849-X). Doubleday.

New Golf Mind. Gary Wiren et al. 164p. 1981. pap. 4.95 (ISBN 0-346-12478-6). Cornerstone.

New Good (but Cheap) Chicago Restaurant Book: Where to Find Great Meals at Little Neighborhood Restaurants from 1.50 to 4.95. rev & enl ed. Jill Rohde & Ron Rohde. LC 76-3133. 250p. 1977. pap. 3.95 (ISBN 0-8040-0698-9). Swallow.

New Good Buy Book: Illinois, Wisconsin, Ohio, Michigan & Indiana. Annie Moldafsky. LC 76-3129. 224p. 1977. pap. 3.25 (ISBN 0-8040-0705-5). Swallow.

New Gothic Restaurant. E. B. Weinstock & Robert P. Arthur. 1978. pap. text ed. 9.25 (ISBN 0-8191-0369-1). U Pr of Amer.

New Governance Structure for OCLC: Principles & Recommendations. LC 78-2099. 1978. pap. 10.00 (ISBN 0-8108-1146-4). Scarecrow.

New Grammar of the Arabic Language, 4 vols. Julie Saide. pap. text ed. 22.00x (ISBN 0-686-63573-6). Intl Bk Ctr.

New Grammarian's Funeral. I. Robinson. LC 75-6009. (Illus.). 225p. 1975. 27.95 (ISBN 0-521-20856-4); pap. 9.95 (ISBN 0-521-29316-2). Cambridge U Pr.

New Grange & Other Incised Tumuli in Ireland. G. Coffey. (Illus.). 1978. 9.95 o.p. (ISBN 0-85642-041-7, Pub. by Blandford Pr England). Sterling.

New Green World. Josephine Herbst. (American Procession Ser.). (Illus.). 1954. 7.95 (ISBN 0-8038-5001-8). Hastings.
New Grosset Road Atlas of the United States, Canada, & Mexico. Ed. by Western Publishing Co. Editors. (Illus., Orig.). Date not set. pap. 3.95 (ISBN 0-448-16282-2). G&D.
New Grove Dictionary of Music & Musicians, 20 vols. Ed. by Stanley Sadie. 1980. 1900.00 (ISBN 0-333-23111-2). Groves Dict Music.
New Guide to Better Writing. Rudolf Flesch & A. H. Lass. 1977. pap. 1.95 (ISBN 0-445-08384-0). Popular Lib.
New Guide to Intelligent Reducing. Gayelord Hauser. 1976. pap. 1.75 o.p. (ISBN 0-449-23046-5, Crest). Fawcett.
New Guide to Popular Government Publications: For Libraries & Home Reference. Walter L. Newsome. LC 78-12412. 1978. lib. bdg. 20.00 (ISBN 0-87287-174-6). Libs Unl.
New Guide to Study Abroad, 1978-1979. rev., 6th ed. John A. Garraty et al. LC 77-11533. 1978. 15.95 o.s.i. (ISBN 0-06-011458-4, HarpT); pap. 5.95 o.s.i. (ISBN 0-06-011424-X, TD-299, HarpT). Har-Row.
New Guide to Study Abroad: 1981 to 1982. John A. Garraty & Lily Von Klemperer. LC 77-11533. 464p. 1980. 15.95 (ISBN 0-06-011423-1, CN849, HarpT); pap. 7.95 (ISBN 0-06-090849-1). Har-Row.
New Guide to the Birds of Taiwan. Sheldon R. Severinghaus et al. 222p. 1980. 7.50 (ISBN 0-89955-185-8, Spub. by Mei Ya China). Intl Schol Bk Serv.
New Guide to the Diplomatic Archives of Western Europe. Ed. by Daniel H. Thomas & Lynn M. Case. LC 75-10127. 1975. 15.00x (ISBN 0-8122-7697-3). U of Pa Pr.
New Guides for the Professional Accountant. 1980. pap. 6.00 (ISBN 0-685-58518-2). Am Inst CPA.
New Guinea. Ray MacKay. (World's Wild Places Ser.). (Illus.). 1976. 12.95 (ISBN 0-8094-2056-2). Time-Life.
New Guinea. Ray MacKay. (World's Wild Places Ser.). (Illus.). 1978. lib. bdg. 11.97 (ISBN 0-686-51022-4). Silver.
New Guineas, Our Nearest Neighbor: Australia. J. K. McCarthy. 1968. 7.50 o.p. (ISBN 0-7015-1245-8). Verry.
New Gulliver. Esme Doderidge. LC 79-63120. 220p. 1980. pap. 3.95 (ISBN 0-8008-5507-8, Pivot). Taplinger.
New Hamburger & Hot Dog Cookbook. Mettja C. Roate. LC 74-20888. 1975. Repr. 8.95 o.p. (ISBN 0-87000-299-6). Arlington Hse.
New Hampshire. Elting E. Morison & Elizabeth F. Morison. (States & the Nation Ser). (Illus.). 1976. 12.95 (ISBN 0-393-05583-3, Co-Pub by AASLH). Norton.
New Hampshire. 23.00 (ISBN 0-89770-105-4). Curriculum Info Ctr.
New Hampshire Architecture: An Illustrated Guide. Bryant F. Tolles, Jr. & Carolyn K. Tolles. LC 78-63586. (Illus.). 420p. 1979. text ed. 15.00 (ISBN 0-87451-165-8); pap. 7.50 (ISBN 0-87451-167-4). U Pr of New Eng.
New Hampshire Colony. Daniel H. Giffen. LC 76-93178. (Forge of Freedom Ser). (Illus.). (gr. 5-8). 1970. 7.95 (ISBN 0-02-735890-9, CCPr). Macmillan.
New Hampshire: In Words & Pictures. Dennis Fradin. LC 80-25421. (Young People's Stories of Our States Ser.). (Illus.). 48p. (gr. 2-5). 1981. PLB 8,65g (ISBN 0-686-69455-4, Time Line). Childrens.
New Hampshire Maps to Nineteen Hundred: An Annotated Cartobibliography. David A. Cobb. LC 78-63588. 1981. text ed. 9.00x (ISBN 0-87451-166-6). U Pr of New Eng.
New Hampshire Register: Ninteen Eighty to Nineteen Eighty-One. 1980. 65.00 (ISBN 0-89442-018-6). Tower Pub Co.
New Hampshire Seventeen Hundred & Seventy-Six Census. Jay M. Holbrook. LC 76-151110. 1976. pap. 20.00 (ISBN 0-931248-02-7). Holbrook Res.
New Hampshire's Covered Bridges. rev. ed. Thedia C. Kenyon. (Illus.). 1966. 5.00 o.p. (ISBN 0-87482-023-5). Wake-Brook.
New Hamshire Atlas & Gazatteer. 2nd ed. Ed. by Paula Lane. 67p. 1979. pap. 6.95 (ISBN 0-89933-004-5). DeLorme Pub.
New Handbook of Handgunning. Paul B. Weston. (Illus.). 112p. 1980. 12.95 (ISBN 0-398-04092-3). C C Thomas.
New Handbook of Italian Renaissance Painting. rev. ed. Laurence Schmeckebier. LC 79-50409. 1980. lib. bdg. 40.00 (ISBN 0-87817-253-X). Hacker.
New Hanover County: a Brief History. rev. ed. Lawrence Lee. (Illus.). 1977. pap. 2.00 (ISBN 0-86526-128-8). NC Archives.
New Harbinger Pubns. Sandra Heath. (Orig.). 1981. pap. 1.95 (ISBN 0-451-09771-8, J9771, Sig). NAL.
New Haven Mathematical Colloquium. Eliakim H. Moore et al. 1910. 75.00x (ISBN 0-686-51424-6). Elliots Bks.
New Health Professionals: Nurse Practitioners & Physician's Assistants. Ann Bliss & Eva Cohen. LC 76-46831. 1977. 29.95 (ISBN 0-912862-35-1). Aspen Systems.
New Healthy Trail Food Book. rev. ed. Dorcas S. Miller. LC 79-28172. (Orig.). 1980. lib. bdg. 7.25 o.p. (ISBN 0-914788-25-6). East Woods.
New Heartthrobs, Vol. II. Buddy McCaslin. (Illus.). 160p. (Orig.). (gr. 5 up). pap. 1.95 (ISBN 0-448-14152-3, Tempo). G&D.
New Heat Theorem. W. Nernst. Tr. by Guy Barr. LC 69-15365. (Illus.). 1969. pap. text ed. 3.00 (ISBN 0-486-62252-5). Dover.
New Heaven, New Earth: The Visionary Experience in Literature. Joyce C. Oates. LC 74-76438. 308p. 1974. 10.00 (ISBN 0-8149-0743-1). Vanguard.
New High Altitude Cookbook. Beverly M. Anderson & Donna M. Hamilton. LC 80-5287. (Illus.). 320p. 1980. 13.95 (ISBN 0-394-51308-8). Random.
New High Fiber Diet. Ruth Adams & Frank Murray. 319p. (Orig.). 1977. pap. 2.25 (ISBN 0-915962-21-7). Larchmont Bks.
New High School Equivalency Diploma Tests. David R. Turner. LC 77-20196. 576p. 1978. lib. bdg. 10.00 (ISBN 0-668-04447-0); pap. 5.95 (ISBN 0-668-04451-9). Arco.
New Hindu Movement, Eighteen Sixty-Six to Nineteen Eleven. Rakhal Nath. 1981. 14.50x (ISBN 0-685-59382-7). South Asia Bks.
New Historical Geography of England After 1600. Ed. by H. C. Darby. LC 76-26029. 1978. 59.50 (ISBN 0-521-22123-4); pap. 19.50 (ISBN 0-521-29145-3). Cambridge U Pr.
New Historical Geography of England Before 1600. Ed. by H. C. Darby. LC 76-26141. 1978. 49.50 (ISBN 0-521-22122-6); pap. 17.50 (ISBN 0-521-29144-5). Cambridge U Pr.
New History of India. Stanley Wolpert. LC 76-42678. (Illus.). 1977. 19.95 (ISBN 0-19-502153-3); pap. 8.95x (ISBN 0-19-502154-1). Oxford U Pr.
New History of Painting in Italy from the Second to the Sixteenth Century, 3 vols. J. A. Crowe & G. B. Cavalcaselle. Ed. by Sydney J. Freedberg. LC 77-19372. (Connoisseurship Criticism & Art History Ser.: Vol. 7). (Illus.). 1980. Set. lib. bdg. 132.00 (ISBN 0-8240-3264-0). Garland Pub.
New History of Portugal. 2nd ed. Harold U. Livermore. (Illus.). 1977. 51.95 (ISBN 0-521-21320-7); pap. 12.95x (ISBN 0-521-29103-8). Cambridge U Pr.
New History of Spanish Literature. Richard E. Chandler & Kessel Schwartz. LC 61-15756. (Illus.). 1961. text ed. 30.00x (ISBN 0-8071-0343-8). La State U Pr.
New History of the Organ: From the Greeks to the Present Day. Peter Williams. LC 79-2176. (Illus.). 264p. 1980. 27.50x (ISBN 0-253-15704-8). Ind U Pr.
New History of Wind Music. David Whitwell. 1980. pap. 9.00 (ISBN 0-686-15899-7). Instrumentalist Co.
New Holistic Way to Lose Weight & Rejuvenate. rev. ed. Sally W. Mason. (Illus.). 228p. 1980. Repr. of 1979 ed. 9.95 (ISBN 0-8119-0348-6). Fell.
New Home for Snow Ball. Joan Bowden. (Eager Readers Ser.). (Illus.). (gr. k-3). 1975. PLB 5.00 (ISBN 0-307-60800-X, Golden Pr). Western Pub.
New Hooked on Books. Daniel Fader. 1977. 8.95 o.p. (ISBN 0-399-11954-X). Berkley Pub.
New Hooked on Books. Daniel Fader. pap. 2.50 (ISBN 0-425-04359-2). Berkley Pub.
New Hope for Incurable Diseases. E. Cheraskin & W. M. Ringsdorf, Jr. LC 72-3330. 192p. 1973. pap. 1.65 o.p. (ISBN 0-668-02671-5). Arc Bks.
New Hope for the Arthritic. Collin H. Dong & Jane Banks. LC 75-16388. 184p. 1975. 7.95 (ISBN 0-690-00964-X, TYC-T). T Y Crowell.
New Hope Through Hypnotherapy: The Joe Keeton Phenomenon. Monica O'Hara. 150p. 1980. 13.50x (ISBN 0-85626-194-7, Pub. by Abacus Pr England); pap. 7.95x (ISBN 0-85626-194-7). Intl Schol Bk Serv.
New Horizon in Central Banking. Sid Mittra. 1968. 14.50x o.p. (ISBN 0-210-31161-4). Asia.
New Horizons. Ernest Holmes. Ed. by Willis Kinnear. 96p. (Orig.). 1973. pap. 4.50 (ISBN 0-911336-52-4). Sci of Mind.
New Horizons for Academic Libraries. (Invited & Contributed Papers at the ACRL Conference Nineteen Seventy-Eight). 588p. 1979. 38.00 (ISBN 0-89664-093-0, Pub. by K G Saur). Gale.
New Horizons for Human Factors in Design. Dale Huchingson. (Illus.). 512p. Date not set. text ed. 22.95 (ISBN 0-07-030815-2, C). McGraw.
New Horizons for Veterinary Medicine. Committee on Veterinary Medical Research & Education. LC 74-181827. 176p. (Orig.). 1972. pap. 5.50 (ISBN 0-309-01935-4). Natl Acad Pr.
New Horizons in Astronomy. 2nd ed. John C. Brandt & Stephen P. Maran. LC 78-11717. (Illus.). 1979. text ed. 21.95x (ISBN 0-7167-1043-9). W H Freeman.
New Horizons in English: English As a Second Language, 6 bks. L. Mellgren & M. Walker. (gr. 10-12). 1973-74. Bks.1-2. pap. 3.72 ea.; Bks. 3-6. pap. 3.84 ea.; Bks. 1-2, 5-6. tchr's guides 3.96 ea.; Bks. 3-4. tchr's guides 5.32 ea. Bk. 1 (ISBN 0-201-04415-3). Bk. 2 (ISBN 0-201-04418-8). Bk. 3 (ISBN 0-201-04421-8). Bk. 4 (ISBN 0-201-04424-2). Bk. 5 (ISBN 0-201-04427-7). A-W.
New Horizons in Industrial Microbiology: Philosophical Transactions of the Royal Society, 1980. rev. ed. Ed. by S. Brenner et al. (Ser. B: Vol. 290). (Illus.). 152p. text ed. 47,50x (ISBN 0-85403-146-4, Pub. by Dechema Germany). Scholium Intl.
New Horizons in Public Administration. Leonard D. White. 1946. 9.50 o.p. (ISBN 0-8173-4800-X). U of Ala Pr.
New Horizons in Rock Mechanics. Compiled by American Society of Civil Engineers. 800p. 1973. text ed. 25.00 (ISBN 0-87262-050-6). Am Soc Civil Eng.
New Horizons in Travel-Behavior Research. Ed. by Peter R. Stopher et al. LC 78-24830. 1981. price not set (ISBN 0-669-02850-9). Lexington Bks.
New Hospital Supervisor. Nancy Diekelmann & Martin M. Broadwell. (Illus.). 1977. pap. text ed. 8.95 (ISBN 0-201-00773-8). A-W.
New House. Deborah Manley. LC 78-31914. (Ready, Set, Look Ser.). (Illus.). (gr. k-3). 1979. PLB 9.65 (ISBN 0-8172-1306-6). Raintree Pubs.
New Humanism: A Critique of Modern America, 1900-1940. J. David Hoeveler, Jr. LC 76-25168. 1977. 13.95x (ISBN 0-8139-0658-X). U Pr of Va.
New Husbands & How to Become One. Andrew J. Dubrin. LC 76-15359. 1976. 12.95 (ISBN 0-88229-358-3). Nelson-Hall.
New Hydrogenating Catalysts: Urushibara Catalysts. Kazud Hata. LC 72-2652. 247p. 1972. 19.95 (ISBN 0-470-35890-4). Halsted Pr.
New Ice Age. Henry Gilfond. (Impact Bks). (Illus.). (gr. 7 up). 1978. PLB 6.90 s&l (ISBN 0-531-01458-4). Watts.
New Idea Book. 2nd ed. Progressive Grocer's Marketing Guidebook Staff. (Illus.). 1980. 18.95 (ISBN 0-911790-59-4). Prog Grocer.
New Ideas in Art Education: A Critical Anthology. Ed. & intro. by Gregory Battcock. 1973. pap. 2.95 o.p. (ISBN 0-525-47345-9). Dutton.
New Image of the Person: The Theory & Practice of Clinical Philosophy. Peter Koestenbaum. LC 77-84764. (Contributions in Philosophy: No. 9). 1978. lib. bdg. 22.50 (ISBN 0-8371-9888-7, KNI/). Greenwood.
New Images from Spain. Margit Rowell. Tr. by Lucy Flint. LC 79-92992. (Illus.). 144p. (Orig.). 1980. soft cover 8.50 (ISBN 0-89207-023-4). S R Guggenheim.
New Improved Sun: An Anthology of Utopian S-F. Ed. by Thomas M. Disch. LC 74-15866. (Illus.). 216p. (YA) 1975. 8.95 o.s.i. (ISBN 0-06-011052-X, HarpT). Har-Row.
New in the City. Muriel Stanek. LC 65-23888. (Illus.). 128p. (gr. 3-5). 1965. 5.95g o.p. (ISBN 0-8075-5576-2). A Whitman.
New Individualist Review. New Individualist Review Journal. LC 65-35281. 1024p. 1981. 12.00 (ISBN 0-913966-90-8). Liberty Fund.
New Industrial Society. Bernard A. Weisberger. LC 68-8953. 1969. pap. text ed. 8.95x (ISBN 0-471-92723-6). Wiley.
New Inflation: Causes, Effects, Cures. G. L. Bach. LC 72-2451. (Illus.). 103p. 1974. Repr. of 1972 ed. 7.50 (ISBN 0-87057-136-2, Pub. by Brown U Pr). Univ Pr of New England.
New Iniid Cetacean from the Miocene of California. John M. Rensberger. (Publcations in Geological Sciences Ser.: Vol. 82). 1969. pap. 5.75x (ISBN 0-520-09186-8). U of Cal Pr.
New Inquisition? The Case of Edward Schillebeeckx & Hans Kung. Peter Hebblethwaite. LC 80-7290. 160p. (Orig.). 1980. pap. 4.95 (ISBN 0-06-063795-1, RD 339, HarpR). Har-Row.
New Insurance Supervisor. Martin M. Broadwell & William F. Simpson. 168p. 1981. pap. text ed. cancelled (ISBN 0-201-00568-9). A-W.
New Interdependence: The European Community & the United States. Gordon K. Douglass. LC 79-5121. 160p. 1979. 17.95 (ISBN 0-669-03203-4). Lexington Bks.
New Interior Decoration. Dorothy Todd & Raymond Mortimer. LC 77-4444. (Architecture & Decorative Art Ser.). (Illus.). 1977. Repr. of 1929 ed. lib. bdg. 45.00 (ISBN 0-306-70899-X). Da Capo.
New International Atlas. Rand McNally. LC 80-51969. (Illus.). 568p. 1980. 60.00 (ISBN 0-528-83111-9); deluxe ed. 100.00 (ISBN 0-528-83112-7). Rand.
New International Confectioner. 3rd rev. ed. Ed. by W. J. Fance. (Illus.). 1976. 75.00 (ISBN 0-685-90333-8, Virtue & Co.). CBI Pub.
New International Confectioner. rev. ed. (Illus.). 740p. 1973. 80.00x (ISBN 0-685-41623-2). Radio City.
New International Dictionary of New Testament Theology, 3 vols. Colin Brown. Set. 92.00 (ISBN 0-310-21928-0). Zondervan.
New International Dictionary of New Testament Theology, Vol. 2. Ed. by Colin Brown. 1977. 29.95 (ISBN 0-310-21900-0). Zondervan.
New International Dictionary of Refrigeration in English, French, Russian, German, Italian, Spanish, & Norwegian. International Institute of Refrigeration. 550p. 1975. text ed. 145.00 (ISBN 0-08-020368-X). Pergamon.
New International Economic Order: A U. S. Response. Ed. by David B. Denoon. LC 79-1997. (UNA-USA Bk.). 1979. 20.00x (ISBN 0-8147-1769-1); pap. 9.00x (ISBN 0-8147-1770-5). NYU Pr.
New International Economic Order: Conflict or Cooperation Between North & South? K. Sauvant & H. Hasenpflug. LC 76-26623. 1977. lib. bdg. 28.75x (ISBN 0-89158-139-1); pap. 13.50 o.p. (ISBN 0-89158-288-6). Westview.
New International Economic Order: Toward a Fair Redistribution of the World's Resources. Jyoti S. Singh. LC 76-54508. (Special Studies). 1977. text ed. 20.95 (ISBN 0-275-24170-X). Praeger.
New International Economics. Jan S. Hogendorn & Wilson H. Brown. LC 78-67953. (Economics Ser.). (Illus.). 1979. text ed. 17.95 (ISBN 0-201-02824-7). A-W.
New International Health Order. Charles O. Pannenborg. 476p. 1979. 32.50x (ISBN 90-286-0239-9). Sijthoff & Noordhoff.
New International Monetary System. Ed. by Robert A. Mundell & Jacques J. Polak. LC 77-10485. 1977. 15.00x (ISBN 0-231-04368-6). Columbia U Pr.
New Internationalism: Strategy & Initiatives for U.S. Foreign Economic Policy. Wilbur F. Monroe. LC 75-36989. 1976. 18.95 (ISBN 0-669-00391-3). Lexington Bks.
New Introduction to Latin. Alston H. Chase. (gr. 9). text ed. 5.00x (ISBN 0-88334-001-1). Ind Sch Pr.
New Invention of Shooting Fireshafts in Long-Bowes. LC 74-80195. (English Experience Ser.: No. 674). 1974. Repr. of 1628 ed. 3.50 (ISBN 90-221-0674-8). Walter J Johnson.
New Investor's Guide to Real Estate: An Apartment House Guide. Arthur C. Simon. LC 78-55988. (Illus.). 1978 softcover 12.95 o.p. (ISBN 0-930490-05-3). Future Shop.
New Invitation to Linguistics. Joseph H. Greenberg. LC 76-42422. 1977. pap. 2.95 (ISBN 0-385-07550-2, Anch). Doubleday.
New Iris Syrett Cookery Book. Mary Lovell & Herbert Lees. (Illus.). 1973. 10.95 o.p. (ISBN 0-571-09613-1, Pub. by Faber & Faber). Merrimack Bk Serv.
New Islands. Maria L. Bombal. Tr. by Richard Cunningham from Span. 1981. 10.95 (ISBN 0-374-22118-9). FS&G.
New Israeli Architecture. Amiram Harlap. LC 73-8291. (Illus.). 355p. 1981. 40.00 (ISBN 0-8386-1425-6). Fairleigh Dickinson.
New Italian Cooking. Margaret Romagnoli & Franco G. Romagnoli. 384p. 1980. 15.00 (ISBN 0-316-75565-6). Little.
New Italian Poetry: Nineteen Forty-Five to the Present. Ed. by Lawrence R. Smith. 400p. 1981. 16.95 (ISBN 0-520-03859-2). U of Cal Pr.
New Japanese-English Dictionary of Economic Terms. Ed. by Oriental Economist. 580p. 1977. 20.00x (ISBN 0-8002-1609-1). Intl Pubns Serv.
New Japanese House: Ritual & Anti-Ritual Patterns of Dwelling. Chris Fawcett. LC 80-8224. (Illus.). 192p. 1981. 25.00 (ISBN 0-06-433010-9, HarpT). Har-Row.
New Jersey. Richard P. McCormick. LC 65-15071. 1965. pap. 2.95 (ISBN 0-8077-1734-7). Tchrs Coll.
New Jersey. 28.00 (ISBN 0-89770-106-2). Curriculum Info Ctr.
New Jersey Colony. Fred J. Cook. LC 69-10893. (Forge of Freedom Ser). (Illus.). (gr. 4-7). 1969. 8.95 (ISBN 0-02-724360-5, CCPr). Macmillan.
New Jersey Industrial Directory 1980. State Industrial Directories Corp. 1980. pap. 90.00 (ISBN 0-89910-027-9). State Indus Dir.
New Jersey Police & Fire Arbitration Databook, 1980, 2 vols. Ernest Gross et al. 2000p. 1980. Set. 100.00. Inst Mgmt & Labor.
New Jersey Supplement for Modern Real Estate Practice. 3rd ed. Joseph H. Martin & William Jackson. 130p. (Orig.). 1981. pap. 7.95 (ISBN 0-88462-281-9). Real Estate Ed Co.
New Jersey Supplement for Real Estate Principles and Practices. Vincent Hubin. (Business and Economics Ser.). 112p. 1976. 4.95 (ISBN 0-675-08561-6). Merrill.

New Jewish Yellow Pages. Mae S. Rockland. (Illus.). 288p. (Orig.). 1981. pap. 9.95 (ISBN 0-89961-016-1). SBS Pub.
New Journalism: An Historical Anthology. Nicolaus Mills. (Illus.). 512p. 1974. pap. text ed. 12.95 o.p. (ISBN 0-07-042349-0, C); pap. text ed. 9.95 o.p. (ISBN 0-07-042350-4). McGraw.
New Joy. Colleen T. Evans. (Orig.). pap. 1.50 (ISBN 0-89129-015-X). Jove Pubns.
New Juice. M. T. Brown. (Illus.). 1980. pap. 9.95 o.p. (ISBN 0-930490-32-0). Future Shop.
New Kind of Joy: The Story of the Special Olympics. James S. Haskins. LC 75-14825. 144p. 1976. 7.95 o.p. (ISBN 0-385-03902-6). Doubleday.
New Knowledge in Human Values. Ed. by Abraham H. Maslow. 1959. 9.95 o.p. (ISBN 0-06-034140-8, HarpT). Har-Row.
New Korea. Kyung C. Chung. (Illus.). 1962. 6.00 o.s.i. (ISBN 0-02-525540-1). Macmillan.
New Land, New Language: An Anthology of Australian Verse. Ed. by Judith Wright. 1958. pap. 5.95x (ISBN 0-19-550298-1). Oxford U Pr.
New Landscapes. Ed. by James Alinder. (Untitled Ser.: No. 24). (Illus.). 56p. 1981. pap. 8.95 (ISBN 0-933286-21-X). Friends Photography.
New Language of Politics. rev ed. William Safire. 544p. 1972. pap. 4.95 o.s.i. (ISBN 0-02-074700-4, Collier). Macmillan.
New Language of Psychiatry: Learning & Using DSM-III. Levy. 384p. 1981. text ed. 16.95 (ISBN 0-87626-610-3). Winthrop.
New Laokoon. Irving Babbit. 259p. 1980. Repr. of 1910 ed. lib. bdg. 40.00 (ISBN 0-89760-049-5). Telegraph Bks.
New Leads in Cancer Chemotherapeutics. Enrico Mihich. 1981. lib. bdg. 27.50 (ISBN 0-8161-2148-6, Hall Medical). G K Hall.
New Learning for Older Americans. Roger DeCrow. 1975. 5.75 (ISBN 0-685-84004-2). Adult Ed.
New Left Diplomatic Histories & Historians: The American Revisionists. Joseph M. Siracusa. LC 73-75575. (National University Publications). 1973. 12.00 (ISBN 0-8046-9037-5). Kennikat.
New Left in America: Reform to Revolution 1956-1970. Edward J. Bacciocco, Jr. LC 73-75887. (Publications Ser.: No. 130). 300p. 1974. 8.95 (ISBN 0-8179-6301-4). Hoover Inst Pr.
New Left in France: The Unified Socialist Party. Charles Hauss. LC 77-94753. (Contributions in Political Science: No. 9). (Illus.). 1978. lib. bdg. 19.95 (ISBN 0-313-20113-7, HNL/). Greenwood.
New Left Thought. Lyman T. Sargent. 1972. pap. text ed. 9.50x (ISBN 0-256-01203-2). Dorsey.
New Liberalism: An Ideology of Social Reform. Michael Freeden. 1978. 37.50x (ISBN 0-19-822463-X). Oxford U Pr.
New Liberty Bell: A Bicentennial Anthology of American Choral Music. Ed. & intro. by James G. Smith. LC 76-373. (Illus.). 1976. pap. 5.50 (ISBN 0-916656-00-4, MF276). Mark Foster Mus.
New Library Buildings: Nineteen Seventy-Four. Ed. by H. Ward. 1974. pap. 22.50x (ISBN 0-85365-397-6, Pub. by Lib Assn England). Oryx Pr.
New Library Buildings: Nineteen Seventy-Six. Ed. by H. Ward. 1976. pap. 31.00x (ISBN 0-85365-089-6, Pub. by Lib Assn England). Oryx Pr.
New Life. Compiled by Christopher J. Christianson. pap. 3.95 o.p. (ISBN 0-88270-008-1). Logos.
New Life. Bernard Malamud. 352p. 1980. pap. 2.75 (ISBN 0-380-52530-5, 52530). Avon.
New Life. rev. ed. Andrew Murray. LC 80-7531. 1965. pap. 2.95 (ISBN 0-87123-395-9, 200395). Bethany Fell.
New Life. Reginald Wallis. (gr. 3-7). Date not set. pap. 1.00 (ISBN 0-87213-912-3). Loizeaux.
New Life for Your Sunday School. Iris Culley. 1979. pap. 3.95 (ISBN 0-8164-2208-7). Crossroad NY.
New Life Hotel. Edward Hower. 1980. pap. 2.95 (ISBN 0-686-69254-3, 76372, Bard). Avon.
New Life in the Neighborhood: How Persons with Retardation & Other Disabilities Can Help Make a Good Community Better. Robert Perske. LC 80-15517. (Illus.). 80p. (Orig.). 1980. pap. 4.95 (ISBN 0-687-27800-7). Abingdon.
New Life of Grace. Peter Fransen. 384p. 1972. pap. 6.95 (ISBN 0-8164-2559-0). Crossroad NY.
New Life of Virginea: Being the Second Part of Nova Britannia. Robert Johnson. LC 73-17167. (English Experience Ser.: No. 332). 52p. 1971. Repr. of 1612 ed. 8.00 (ISBN 90-221-0332-3). Walter J Johnson.
New Light Breaks Forth. Lyndon W. Cook & Donald Q. Cannon. pap. 7.95 (ISBN 0-89036-148-7). Hawkes Pub Inc.
New Light on Ancient Carthage. Ed. by John Pedley. (Illus.). 160p. 1980. 20.00x (ISBN 0-472-10003-3). U of Mich Pr.
New Light on Byron. James Hogg et al. (Salzburg Studies in English Literature: Romantic Reassessment: No. 74). 1978. pap. text ed. 25.00x (ISBN 0-391-01419-6). Humanities.
New Light on the Rapture. Donald Meresco. LC 80-67028. (Orig.). 1980. pap. 9.95 (ISBN 0-937078-00-X). Bible Light.
New Literacy. Donald Gordon. LC 71-163816. 1971. pap. 3.50 (ISBN 0-8020-6120-6). U of Toronto Pr.
New Liturgy, New Laws. R. Kevin Seasoltz. 1980. pap. 7.95 (ISBN 0-8146-1077-3). Liturgical Pr.
New Living Spaces. Ed. by Time & Life Editors. LC 72-72104. (Home Repair & Improvement). (Illus.). (gr. 7 up). 1977. PLB 11.97 (ISBN 0-8094-2375-8, Pub by Time-Life). Silver.
New Living Spaces. Ed. by Time-Life Books. (Home Repair & Improvement Ser.). 1977. 10.95 (ISBN 0-8094-2374-X). Time-Life.
New Look at Accounting for Pension Costs. William D. Hall & David L. Landsittell. 1977. 11.50x (ISBN 0-256-01971-1). Irwin.
New Look at Biblical Crime. Ralph W. Scott. LC 78-27535. 1979. 15.95 (ISBN 0-88229-416-4). Nelson-Hall.
New Look at Earthquakes. Paul W. Arvidson. 1979. 9.55 o.p. (ISBN 0-914330-18-7). Pioneer Pub Co.
New Look at Mechanisms in Bioenergetics. Efraim Racker. 1976. 18.00 (ISBN 0-12-574670-9); pap. text ed. 10.00 (ISBN 0-12-574672-5). Acad Pr.
New Look at Microwave Cooking. Lila Chalpin. 1981. 8.95 (ISBN 0-916752-04-6). Green Hill.
New Look at Senility. Albert Fisk. write for info (ISBN 0-398-04436-8). C C Thomas.
New Look at the Commonwealth. A. M. Walker. 1978. text ed. 23.00 (ISBN 0-08-021823-7); pap. text ed. 11.25 (ISBN 0-08-021824-5). Pergamon.
New Look at the Lutheran Confession. Holsten Fagerberg. Tr. by Gene J. Lund. 336p. 1981. 14.50 (ISBN 0-570-03223-7, 15-2121). Concordia.
New Look at the Relation Between School Education and Work: Second All-European Conference for Directors of Educational Research Institutions, Madrid 11-13 Sept. 79. Ed. by M. Dino Carelli. (International Studies in Education Ser.: No. 37). vi, 164p. 1980. pap. text ed. 16.00 (ISBN 90-265-0355-5). Swets North Am.
New Look in Home Landscaping. Earl H. New. 1975. pap. 12.00 (ISBN 0-686-19191-9). Thomson Pub CA.
New Lottie Moon Story. Catherine Allen. LC 79-52336. 1980. 7.95 (ISBN 0-8054-6319-4). Broadman.
New Low Carbohydrate Diet. William I. Kaufman. 1973. pap. 1.25 o.p. (ISBN 0-515-04940-9, P101, Jove). BJ Pub Group.
New Macreme. Jane Dodge. (Step by Step Craft Ser.). Date not set. pap. 2.95 (ISBN 0-307-42023-X, Golden Pr). Western Pub.
New Male: From Self-Destruction to Self-Care. Herb Goldberg. 1980. pap. 2.95 (ISBN 0-451-09339-9, E9339, Sig). NAL.
New Man. Thomas Merton. 256p. 1962. pap. 4.95 (ISBN 0-374-51444-5). FS&G.
New Man. Reginald Wallis. Date not set. pap. 0.80 (ISBN 0-87213-913-1). Loizeaux.
New Man for Our Time. Elton Trueblood. LC 77-85059. 1970. 5.95 o.p. (ISBN 0-06-068532-8, HarpR). Har-Row.
New Manager's Guide to Success. James R. Baehler. 160p. 1980. 19.95 (ISBN 0-03-058014-5). Praeger.
New Manual of Kung Fu. Peter P. Tang. LC 75-13890. (Illus.). 1976. 7.95 o.p. (ISBN 0-668-03851-9). Arco.
New Manual of Yoga. Karen Ross. LC 74-75398. (Illus.). 1977. pap. 2.95 o.p. (ISBN 0-668-04347-4). Arco.
New Markets for Small Business Computers, G-055. Ed. by Business Communications. 1980. 750.00 (ISBN 0-89336-220-4, G-055). BCC.
New Masses: An Anthology of the Rebel Thirties. Ed. by Joseph North. (Illus.). 1980. pap. 2.25 (ISBN 0-7178-0355-4). Intl Pub Co.
New Materials in Sculpture. 2nd ed. H. M. Percy. 1966. 8.95 (ISBN 0-85458-998-8); pap. 6.50 (ISBN 0-85458-996-1). Transatlantic.
New Math Made Simple. Albert F. Kempf. LC 66-12224. pap. 3.50 (ISBN 0-385-04174-8, Made). Doubleday.
New Mathematics. rev. & enl. ed. Irving Adler. LC 72-2411. (Illus.). 224p. 1972. 9.95 (ISBN 0-381-98002-2, A55601, JD-J). John Day.
New Mathematics. J. Davidson. (Teach Yourself Ser.). 1974. pap. 4.95 (ISBN 0-679-12326-1). McKay.
New Means of Financing International Needs. Eleanor B. Steinberg & Joseph A. Yager. LC 77-21275. 1978. 14.95 (ISBN 0-8157-8116-4); pap. 5.95 (ISBN 0-8157-8115-6). Brookings.
New Media in Printmaking. John Bickford. (Illus., Orig.). 1976. 17.95 o.p. (ISBN 0-8230-3165-9). Watson-Guptill.
New Media in Public Libraries: A Survey of Current Practices. James W. Brown. pap. 12.50 (ISBN 0-88432-003-0). Gaylord Prof Pubns.
New Mediumship. Grace Cooke. 1965. 4.95 (ISBN 0-85487-013-X). De Vorss.
New Met in Profile. Stephen E. Rubin. (Illus.). 368p. 1974. 9.95 o.s.i. (ISBN 0-02-605800-6). Macmillan.
New Method Supplementary Readers. Ed. by D. K. Swan. (Illus.). write for info (ISBN 0-686-00592-9). Longman.
New Methods for Delivering Human Services. Brian Jones et al. Ed. by Garry R. Walz & Libby Benjamin. LC 77-1746. (New Vistas in Counseling: Vol. 2). 1977. 14.95 (ISBN 0-87705-309-X). Human Sci Pr.
New Methods for the Analysis of Coagulation Using Chromogenic Substrates. Ed. by I. Witt. 275p. 1977. text ed. 52.50x (ISBN 3-11007-116-9). De Gruyter.
New Methods in Social Science Research: Policy Sciences & Futures Research. T. Harrell Allen. LC 76-12840. (Praeger Special Studies). 1978. 21.95 (ISBN 0-275-23630-7). Praeger.
New Mexico. 23.00 (ISBN 0-89770-107-0). Curriculum Info Ctr.
New Mexico. Marc Simmons. (States & the Nation Ser.). (Illus.). 1977. 12.95 (ISBN 0-393-05631-7, Co-Pub by AASLH). Norton.
New Mexico: A Guide to the Colorful State. Federal Writers' Project. 1940. Repr. 49.00 (ISBN 0-403-02181-2). Somerset Pub.
New Mexico: A History of Four Centuries. Warren A. Beck. (Illus.). 1979. Repr. of 1962 ed. 11.95 (ISBN 0-8061-0533-X). U of Okla Pr.
New Mexico Chronology & Factbook, Vol. 31. R. I. Vexler. 1978. 8.50 (ISBN 0-379-16156-7). Oceana.
New Mexico Government. rev. ed. F. Chris Garcia & Paul Hain. 360p. 1981. 12.95 (ISBN 0-686-68597-0). U of NM Pr.
New Mexico: In Words & Pictures. Dennis Fradin. (Young People's Stories of Our States Ser.). (Illus.). 48p. (gr. 2-5). 1981. PLB 8.65g (ISBN 0-516-03931-8, Time Line). Childrens.
New Mexico One Hundred Years Ago. Ingersoll et al. (Sun Historical Ser.). (Illus.). pap. 3.50 (ISBN 0-89540-057-X). Sun Pub.
New Mexico Place Names: A Geographical Dictionary. T. M. Pearce. LC 64-17808. 1980. pap. 4.95 (ISBN 0-8263-0082-0). U of NM Pr.
New Mexico State Industrial Directory 1980. State Industrial Directories Corp. 1980. pap. write for info. (ISBN 0-89910-037-6). State Indus Dir.
New Mexico: The Shining Land. John L. Sinclair. 224p. 1980. 14.95 (ISBN 0-8263-0548-2). U of NM Pr.
New Milton Cross More Stories of the Great Operas. Milton Cross & Karl Kohrs. LC 79-8023. 816p. 1980. 17.95 (ISBN 0-385-14776-7). Doubleday.
New Mind. Roger Elwood. 1973. 5.95 o.s.i. (ISBN 0-686-66933-9). Macmillan.
New Mind, Vol. 2. Roger Elwood. 1973. pap. 1.50 o.s.i. (ISBN 0-02-019810-8, Collier). Macmillan.
New Ministries: The Global Context. William R. Burrows. LC 80-17261. 176p. 1980. pap. 7.95 (ISBN 0-88344-329-5). Orbis Bks.
New Model of the Universe: Principles of the Psychological Method in Its Application to Problems of Science, Religion & Art. P. D. Ouspensky. LC 35-8632. 1971. pap. 4.95 (ISBN 0-394-71524-1, Vin). Random.
New Money Dynamics. Venita Van Caspel. (Illus.). 1978. 13.95 o.p. (ISBN 0-87909-518-0); instrs'. manual avail. o.p. Reston.
New Moon Rising. Eugenia Price. LC 69-14496. 1969. 10.00 o.s.i. (ISBN 0-397-10079-5). Lippincott.
New Morality: A Profile of American Youth in the Seventies. Daniel Yankelovich. 176p. (Orig.). 1974. pap. 2.95 (P&RB). McGraw.
New Morality from Science: Beyondism. Raymond B. Cattell. 1976. 35.00 (ISBN 0-08-016956-2). Pergamon.
New Mother Goose. (Puppet Storybooks Ser.). (ps-2). 1980. pap. 2.95 (ISBN 0-448-09750-8). G&D.
New Movements in the Study & Teaching of English. Ed. by Nicholas Bagnall. 1977. 12.00 (ISBN 0-85117-044-7). Transatlantic.
New Movements in the Study & Teaching of Geography. Ed. by Norman Graves. (Illus.). 248p. 1972. text ed. 11.75x (ISBN 0-685-30108-7). Humanities.
New Music Composition. David Cope. LC 76-21376. 1977. pap. text ed. 10.95 (ISBN 0-02-870630-7). Schirmer Bks.
New Mythos: The Novel of the Artist As Heroine, 1877-1977. G. B. Stewart. LC 78-74840. 1979. 17.95 (ISBN 0-88831-030-7). EPWP.
New Myths & Old Realities: College Counseling in Transition. Charles F. Warnath. LC 77-172879. (Higher Education Ser.). 1971. 11.95x o.p. (ISBN 0-87589-114-4). Jossey-Bass.
New Naked Poetry: Recent American Poetry in Open Forms. Ed. by Stephen Berg & Robert Mezey. LC 75-12999. 1976. pap. 9... 0-672-61354-9). Bobbs.
New Nation: A History of the Uni... During the Confederation 178... Jensen. 446p. 1981. text ed. 1... 930350-15-4); pap. text ed. 9... 930350-14-6). NE U Pr.
New Nationalism. Theodore Ro... (ISBN 0-8446-0237-X). Pet...
New Nationalism & the Us... Issues in Marine Pol... of Antarctica. Ed... 420p. 1981. te... 012-8). Allanheld...
New Nationalism: Ir... Relations. new ... Werner J. Feld... Policy Studie... 08-023370-... 023369-4)...
New Natio... Kay. (I... 1970... U P...
New ... C...
New ... W. M... (ISBN 0-...
New Naturama... 400p. pap. text...
New Negro. Mathew ... 1969. Repr. of 1961 ... 0232-9). Biblo.
New Neighbors. Edmund Plan... pap. 1.95 (ISBN 0-686-68909-...
New Neighbors. Paul Sawyer. LC 7... (Moods & Emotions Ser.). (Illus.). ... 1978. PLB 8.95 (ISBN 0-8172-1156-X). Raintree Pubs.
New Neighbors for Nora. Johanna Hurwitz. LC 78-12631. (Illus.). (gr. k-3). 1979. 6.50 (ISBN 0-688-22173-4); PLB 6.24 (ISBN 0-688-32173-9). Morrow.
New Nineteen Eighty Suppressed Inventions & How They Work. 2nd ed. Mike Brown. 106p. 1974. pap. 11.95. Madison Pub.
New North-West. C. A. Dawson. (Scholarly Reprint Ser.). 1980. 45.00 (ISBN 0-8020-7105-8). U of Toronto Pr.
New Novalis? Short Brilliant Thought-Flashes & Great Unity. J. E. Von Emmichoven. Tr. by Elizabeth Spaey. 1976. pap. 2.00 o.p. (ISBN 0-916786-17-X, Pub by Elizabeth Spaey). St George Bk Serv.
New Old: Struggling for Decent Aging. Ronald Gross et al. LC 77-12857. 1978. pap. 5.95 (ISBN 0-385-12763-4, Anch). Doubleday.
New Opportunities, for Residential Development in Central Cities. ULI Research Division. (Research Report Ser.: No. 25). 1976. pap. 6.00 (ISBN 0-87420-325-2). Urban Land.
New Opportunities in Realty Trusts. Kenneth D. Campbell. 1978. 35.00 (ISBN 0-912840-03-X); pap. 40.00 (ISBN 0-685-64945-8). Audit Investment.
New Organic Chemistry. 2nd ed. H. L. Heys. (Illus.). 1973. 17.95x (ISBN 0-245-50693-4). Intl Ideas.
New Organon & Related Writings. Francis Bacon. Ed. by Fulton H. Anderson. LC 60-11682. 1960. pap. 6.95 (ISBN 0-672-60289-X, LLA97). Bobbs.
New Orientations: Essays in International Relations. Ed. by Edith Tilton Penrose et al. 136p. 1970. 24.00x (ISBN 0-7146-2593-0, F Cass Co). Biblio Dist.
New Orleans. Carolyn Kolb. LC 71-160873. 1972. pap. 3.95 (ISBN 0-385-02460-6, Dolp). Doubleday.
New Orleans: A City Guide. Federal Writers' Project. 416p. 1938. Repr. 45.00 (ISBN 0-403-02203-7). Somerset Pub.
New Orleans Architecture, Vol. 6: Faubourg Treme & the Bayou Road. Roulhac B. Toledano & Mary Louise Christovich. (New Orleans Architecture Ser.). (Illus.). 224p. 1980. 34.95 (ISBN 0-88289-166-9). Pelican.
New Orleans Mardi Gras Guide, Nineteen Eighty One. rev. ed. Arthur Hardy. (Illus.). 82p. 1981. pap. 2.95x (ISBN 0-930892-05-4). A Hardy & Assocs.
New Orleans Voter: A Handbook of Political Description, Vol. 2. L. Reisman et al. Bd. with Republicanism in New Orleans. K. N. Vines. 1955. 4.00 (ISBN 0-930598-01-6). Tulane Stud Pol.
New Orleans, 1718-1812: An Economic History. John G. Clark. LC 77-119115. (Illus.). 1970. 25.00 (ISBN 0-8071-0346-2). La State U Pr.

New Oxford Atlas. Ed. by The Cartographic Department of Oxford University Press. (Illus.). 204p. 1975. 24.00x o.p. (ISBN 0-19-891108-4). Oxford U Pr.

New Oxford Book of American Verse. Ed. by Richard Ellmann. LC 75-46354. 1976. 19.95 ...N 0-19-502058-8); deluxe ed. 65.00 ...ound (ISBN 0-19-502194-0). Oxford U

...History of Music. Ed. by Gerald ...al. Incl. Vol. 1. Ancient & ...ic. Ed. by Egon Wellesz. (15 ...4.00 (ISBN 0-19-316301-2); ...dieval Music up to 1300. Ed. ...ughes. 1954. 49.95 (ISBN ...3. Ars Nova & the ...0. Ed. by Dom Anselm ...am. 1960. 49.95 ... Vol. 4. Age of ... Ed. by Gerald ...8. 44.00x (ISBN 0-19- ...Age of Enlightenment, ... Egon Wellesz & Frederick ...). 1973. 49.95 (ISBN 0-19- ...10. Modern Age, 1890-1960. ... Cooper. 1974. 49.95x (ISBN ...1). Oxford U Pr.

...istory of Music, Vol. 5: Opera & ...usic 1630-1750. Ed. by Nigel ... Anthony Lewis. (Illus.). 800p. 1975. ...ISBN 0-19-316305-5). Oxford U Pr.

...rd Illustrated Dickens, 21 vols. Charles ...ns. Incl. Old Curiosity Shop. Illus. by ...ge Cattermole & Phiz. (Illus.). 1951. ...0x (ISBN 0-19-254506-X); Our Mutual ...d. Illus. by Marcus Stone. (Illus.). 1952. ...0x (ISBN 0-19-254510-8); Personal ...story of David Copperfield. (Illus.). 17.95x (ISBN 0-19-254502-7); Posthumous Papers of the Pickwick Club. (Illus.). 1947. 22.50x (ISBN 0-19-254501-9); Sketches by Boz: Illustrative of Every-Day Life & Every-Day People. Illus. by George Cruickshank. (Illus.). 1957. 22.50x (ISBN 0-19-254518-3); Tale of Two Cities. (Illus.). 1949. 17.95x (ISBN 0-19-254504-3); Uncommercial Traveller, & Reprinted Pieces, Etc. Illus. by G. J. Pinwell et al. (Illus.). 1958. 22.50x (ISBN 0-19-254521-3); Adventures of Oliver Twist. Illus. by George Cruickshank. 1949. 17.95x (ISBN 0-19-254505-1); American Notes & Pictures from Italy. Illus. by Marcus Stone et al. 1957. 17.95x (ISBN 0-19-254519-1); Barnaby Rudge: A Tale of the Riots of 'eighty. Illus. by George Cattermole & H. K. Browne. 1954. 21.00x (ISBN 0-19-254513-2); Bleak House. Illus. by Phiz. 1948. 22.50x (ISBN 0-19-254503-5); Christmas Books. Intro. by Eleanor Farjeon. (Illus.). 1954. 17.95x (ISBN 0-19-254514-0); Christmas Stories. Illus. by E. G. Dalziel et al. 1956. 21.00x (ISBN 0-19-254517-5); Dealings with the Firm of Dombey, & Son, Wholesale, Retail, & for Exploration. Illus. by Phiz. 1950. 22.50x (ISBN 0-19-254507-8); Great Expectations. Illus. by F. W. Pailthrope. 1953. 12.50x (ISBN 0-19-254511-6); Hard Times for These Times. Illus. by F. Walker & Maurice Greiffenhagen. 1955. 17.95x (ISBN 0-19-254515-9); Life & Adventures of Martin Chuzzlewit. Illus. by Phiz. 1951. 22.50x (ISBN 0-19-254509-4); Life & Adventures of Nicholas Nickleby. Illus. by Phiz. 1950. 22.50x (ISBN 0-19-254508-6); Little Dorrit. Illus. by Phiz. 1953. 22.50x (ISBN 0-19-254512-4); Master Humphrey's Clock & a Child's History of England. Intro. by Derek Hudson. 1958. 17.95x (ISBN 0-19-254520-5); Mystery of Edwin Drood. Illus. by Luke Fildes & Charles Collins. 1956. 17.95x (ISBN 0-19-254516-7). (Illus.). (gr. 7 up). Set. 365.00x (ISBN 0-19-254522-1); Boxed Set Ecrase. 595.00x (ISBN 0-19-195252-4). Oxford U Pr.

New Park Street Pulpit 1855-1860, 6 vols, C H. Spurgeon. 1981. 60.00 (ISBN 0-686-16847-X). Pilgrim Pubns.

New Patches for Old: A Turkish Folktale Retold. Barbara K. Walker & Ahmet E. Uysal. Tr. by Ahmet E. Uysal from Turk. LC 73-12951. (Illus.). 48p. (ps-3). 1974. 5.95 o.s.i. (ISBN 0-8193-0713-0, Four Winds); PLB 5.41 o.s.i. (ISBN 0-8193-0714-9). Schol Bk Serv.

New Paths in Criminology. Ed. by Sarnoff A. Mednick & Shlomo Shoham. LC 77-25739. 1979. 21.95 (ISBN 0-669-01510-5). Lexington Bks.

New Paths in Muslim Evangelism: Evangelical Approaches to Contextualization. Phil Parshall. 200p. (Orig.). 1980. pap. 6.95 (ISBN 0-8010-7056-2). Baker Bk.

New Pathways in Inorganic Chemistry. Ed. by E. A. Ebsworth et al. (Illus.). 1969. 46.00 (ISBN 0-521-07254-9, 68-26984). Cambridge U Pr.

New Pathways in Psychology. Colin Wilson. 280p. 1974. pap. 1.95 o.p. (ISBN 0-451-61315-5, MJ1315, Ment). NAL.

New Patterns in Genetics & Development. Conrad H. Waddington. LC 62-12875. (Illus.). 1962. 20.00x (ISBN 0-231-02509-2); pap. 6.00x (ISBN 0-231-08570-2). Columbia U Pr.

New Patterns of Defense & Development in Asia. Ed. by Sudershan Chawla & D. R. SarDesai. LC 79-22977. 272p. 1980. 23.95 (ISBN 0-03-052416-4); pap. 9.95 (ISBN 0-03-052411-3). Praeger.

New Payment Patterns & the Foster Parent Role. Draza Kline & Benson Jaffee. LC 76-129456. (Orig.). 1970. pap. 2.00 o.p. (ISBN 0-87868-044-6). Child Welfare.

New Penguin Dictionary of Electronics. E. C. Young. 1979. pap. 5.95 (ISBN 0-14-051074-5). Penguin.

New Pennsylvania Primer. Lucille Wallower & Bernice Wier. (gr. 3-4). 1970. 6.25 (ISBN 0-931992-04-4). Penns Valley.

New Pentecost? Leon J. Suenens. 1975. 8.95 (ISBN 0-8164-0276-0). Crossroad NY.

New Pentecost? Leon J. Suenens. (Orig.). 1977. pap. 1.95 (ISBN 0-8164-2139-0). Crossroad NY.

New People: Miscegenation & Mulattoes in the United States. Joel Williamson. LC 80-65201. 1980. 16.95 (ISBN 0-02-934790-4). Free Pr.

New Perspective on Psychotherapy of the Borderline Adult. Ed. by James F. Masterson. LC 77-94736. 1978. 12.50 (ISBN 0-87630-175-8). Brunner-Mazel.

New Perspectives in Archeology. Ed. by Lewis R. Binford & Sally R. Binford. LC 67-27386. 1968. 28.95x (ISBN 0-202-33022-2). Aldine Pub.

New Perspectives on Coleridge & Wordsworth: Selected Papers from the English Institute. Ed. by Geoffrey H. Hartman. LC 72-3738. 1972. 12.50x (ISBN 0-231-03679-5). Columbia U Pr.

New Perspectives on Personality Development in College Students. Florence B. Brawer. LC 73-7150. (Higher Education Ser). 256p. 1973. 14.95x o.p. (ISBN 0-87589-189-6). Jossey-Bass.

New Perspectives on Teaching Vocabulary. Howard H. Keller. (Language in Education Ser.: No. 8). 1978. pap. 2.95 (ISBN 0-87281-084-4). Ctr Appl Ling.

New Perspectives on the Old Testament. J. Barton Payne. Date not set. 14.95 (ISBN 0-88469-134-9). BMH Bks.

New Philosophy & the Philosophical Sciences, 2 vols. Apostolos Makrakis. Ed. by Orthodox Christian Educational Society. Tr. by Denver Cummings from Hellenic. Incl. Vol. 1. Introduction to Philosophy, Psychology, Logic, & Theology. 888p; Vol. 2. Introduction to Ethics. 745p. 1940. Repr. of 1890 ed. Set. 20.00x (ISBN 0-938366-01-7). Orthodox Chr.

New Phoenix Wings: Reparation in Literature. Simon Stuart. (Illus.). 1979. 25.00x (ISBN 0-7100-0179-7). Routledge & Kegan.

New Photography. Frank Webster. 1981. 29.95 (ISBN 0-7145-3798-5); pap. 14.95 (ISBN 0-7145-3801-9). Riverrun NY.

New Physical Education for Elementary School Children. Elsie C. Burton. LC 76-11981. (Illus.). 1976. text ed. 16.75 (ISBN 0-395-20658-8). HM.

New Physics. Al Zolynas. LC 79-65337. (Wesleyan Poetry Program: Vol. 97). 1979. 10.00x (ISBN 0-8195-2097-7, Pub. by Wesleyan U Pr); pap. 4.95 (ISBN 0-8195-1097-1). Columbia U Pr.

New Pilgrim's Progress; or, the Pious Indian Convert, 1748. James Walcot. LC 74-16309. (Novel in England, 1700-1775 Ser). 1974. lib. bdg. 50.00 (ISBN 0-8240-1122-8). Garland Pub.

New Plays by Women. Ed. by Susan La Tempa. L. M. Sullivan & Susan Latempa. 1979. pap. 3.95 (ISBN 0-915288-41-9). Shameless Hussy.

New Poems. Lawrence Bantleman. 8.00 (ISBN 0-89253-491-5); flexible cloth 4.00 (ISBN 0-89253-492-3). Ind-US Inc.

New Poetry Anthology One. Ed. by Michael Anania. LC 69-20470. (New Poetry Ser). 111p. (Orig.). 1969. 7.95x (ISBN 0-8040-0224-X); pap. 4.95x (ISBN 0-8040-0225-8). Swallow.

New Poets of England & America: Second Selection. Ed. by Donald Hall & Robert Pack. (Orig.). 1962. pap. 4.95 o.p. (ISBN 0-452-00135-8, F135, Mer). NAL.

New Police. J. F. Elliott. 88p. 1973. 9.75 (ISBN 0-398-02680-7). C C Thomas.

New Police Technology. V. A. Leonard. (Illus.). 360p. 1980. 29.75 (ISBN 0-398-03967-4). C C Thomas.

New Political Economy: The Public Use of Private Sector. 2nd ed. Ed. by Bruce L. Smith. 1977. pap. 9.95 (ISBN 0-470-15157-9). Halsted Pr.

New Politics. Joseph Papworth. 336p. 1980. text ed. 37.50x (ISBN 0-7069-1273-X, Pub. by Vikas India). Advent Bk.

New Politics of Food. Don Hadwiger et al. LC 77-11574. (Policy Studies Organization Ser.). 1978. 21.95 (ISBN 0-669-01986-0). Lexington Bks.

New Pregnancy: The Active Woman's Guide to Work, Legal Rights, Health Care, Travel, Sports, Dress, Sex, & Emotonal Well-Being. Susan Lichtendorf & Phyllis Gillis. 1979. 9.95 (ISBN 0-394-50210-8). Random.

New Priorities & Developments in the Construction Market in Saudi Arabia & Iran. D. Frith. 206p. 1979. 209.00x (ISBN 0-86010-135-5, Pub. by Graham & Trotman England). State Mutual Bk.

New Priorities in the Curriculum. Louise M. Berman. LC 68-28703. (International Education Ser). 1968. text ed. 16.95 (ISBN 0-675-09612-X). Merrill.

New Processes of Waste Water Treatment & Recovery. Ed. by G. Mattock. 1978. 69.95x (ISBN 0-470-26341-5). Halsted Pr.

New Product Development: A Systematic Approach to Diversification. A. G. Douglas et al. LC 78-2398. 1978. 24.95 (ISBN 0-470-26328-8). Halsted Pr.

New-Product Forecasting: Models & Applications. Yoram Wind et al. LC 80-8388. 1981. price not set (ISBN 0-669-04102-5). Lexington Bks.

New Product Planning. Ed. by Sarojini Balachandran. LC 79-24046. (Management Information Guide Ser.: No. 38). 1980. 30.00 (ISBN 0-8103-0838-X). Gale.

New Professional: An Introduction for the Human Service Worker. 2nd ed. James G. Dugger. LC 80-13324. 200p. 1980. text ed. 8.95 (ISBN 0-8185-0393-9). Brooks-Cole.

New Pronouncing Dictionary of the Spanish & English Languages. rev. ed. Ed. by Velazquez et al. LC 72-94281. 1973. thumb-indexed 17.95 (ISBN 0-13-615534-0). P-H.

New Protectionism: The Welfare State & International Trade. Melvyn B. Krauss. LC 78-19545. 1978. cOBE 10.00x (ISBN 0-8147-4570-9); pap. 5.00x cobe (ISBN 0-8147-4571-7). NYU Pr.

New Provinces: Poems of Several Authors. Intro. by Michael Gnarowski. (Literature of Canada Ser., Poetry & Prose in Reprint). 1976. pap. 5.50 (ISBN 0-8020-6299-7). U of Toronto Pr.

New Pseudonyms & Nicknames--Supplements: Supplements to Pseudonyms & Nicknames Dictionary. Jennifer Mossman. 1981. softbound 45.00 (ISBN 0-8103-0548-8). Gale.

New Public Administration. H. George Frederickson. LC 80-10569. (Illus.). 144p. 1980. 10.50 (ISBN 0-8173-0040-6); pap. 5.50 (ISBN 0-8173-0041-4). U of Ala Pr.

New Public Personnel Administration. 2nd ed. Felix A. Nigro & Lloyd G. Nigro. LC 80-83098. 420p. 1981. text ed. 14.95 (ISBN 0-87581-265-1). Peacock Pubs.

New Publications for Architectural Libraries, March Nineteen Eighty. Mary Vance. (Architecture Ser.: Bibliography A-196). 64p. 1980. pap. 7.00. Vance Biblios.

New Publications for Architecture Libraries, April Nineteen Eighty. Mary Vance. (Architecture Ser.: Bibliography A-218). 63p. 1980. pap. 7.00. Vance Biblios.

New Publications for Architecture Libraries: February 1980. Mary Vance. (Architecture Ser. Bibliography a-176). 56p. 1980. pap. 6.00. Vance Biblios.

New Publications for Architecture Libraries, May Nineteen Eighty. Mary Vance. (Architecture Ser.: Bibliography A-236). 55p. 1980. pap. 6.00. Vance Biblios.

New Publications for Architecture Libraries, November Nineteen Eighty. Mary Vance. (Architecture Ser.: Bibliography A-357). 50p. 1980. pap. 7.50. Vance Biblios.

New Publications for Architecture Libraries, September Nineteen Eighty. Mary Vance. (Architecture Ser.: Bibliography A-317). 55p. Date not set. pap. price not set. Vance Biblios.

New Quantitative Techniques for Economic Analysis: Economic Theory, Econometrics & Mathematical Economics. Giorgio Szego. 1980. write for info. (ISBN 0-12-680760-4). Acad Pr.

New Quest of the Historical Jesus. James M. Robinson. LC 59-1300. (Scholars Press Reprint Ser.: No. 2). 1979. pap. 7.50 (ISBN 0-89130-328-6, 000702). Scholars Pr Ca.

New Questions on God. Johannes B. Metz. LC 73-185752. (Concilium Ser.: Religion in the Seventies: Vol. 76). 1972. pap. 4.95 (ISBN 0-8164-2532-9). Crossroad NY.

New Readings in Philosophical Analysis. Herbert Feigl. Ed. by Keith Lehrer & Wilfred Sellars. LC 72-89406. (Century Philosophy Ser.). 784p. 1972. 22.95 (ISBN 0-13-615526-X). P-H.

New Readings in Public Administration. Jae T. Kim. 320p. 1980. pap. text ed. 9.95 (ISBN 0-8403-2245-3). Kendall-Hunt.

New Recipes for the Cuisinart Food Processor. 4th ed. James Beard & Carl Jerome. 96p. 1978. pap. 5.00 (ISBN 0-936662-00-X, FP-250). Cuisinart Cooking.

New Red Legions: A Survey Data Source Book. Richard A. Gabriel. LC 79-24458. (Contributions in Political Science: No. 44). (Illus.). xii, 252p. 1980. lib. bdg. 40.00 (ISBN 0-313-21497-2, GAP/). Greenwood.

New Red Legions: An Attitudinal Portrait of the Soviet Soldier. Richard A. Gabriel. LC 79-8956. (Contributions in Political Science: No. 44). (Illus.). xiv, 246p. 1980. lib. bdg. 22.50 (ISBN 0-313-21496-4, GAO/). Greenwood.

New Religions & Mental Health: A Guide to the Issues. Ed. by Herbert W. Richardson. (Symposium Ser.: Vol. 6). (Orig.). 1980. soft cover 11.95x (ISBN 0-88946-910-5). E Mellen.

New Religious Consciousness. Ed. by Charles Y. Glock & Robert N. Bellah. LC 75-17295. 1976. 21.50x (ISBN 0-520-03083-4); pap. 6.95 (ISBN 0-520-03472-4). U of Cal Pr.

New Robinson Crusoe, 4 vols. in 2. J. H. Campe. LC 75-32148. (Classics of Children's Literature, 1621-1932: Vol. 14). 1976. Repr. of 1788 ed. Set. PLB 70.00 (ISBN 0-8240-2262-9); PLB 38.00 ea. Garland Pub.

New Roget's Thesaurus in Dictionary Form. Ed. by Roger Lewis. 1977. pap. 1.95 (ISBN 0-425-04727-X). Berkley Pub.

New Roots for Agriculture. Wes Jackson. LC 79-56913. (Orig.). 1980. pap. 4.95 (ISBN 0-913890-38-3). Friends Earth.

New Russian-English & English-Russian Dictionary. M. A. O'Brien. pap. 6.00 (ISBN 0-486-20208-9). Dover.

New Russian Poets. bilingual ed. Ed. & tr. by George Reavey. 320p. 1981. pap. 9.95 (ISBN 0-7145-2715-7, Pub. by M. Boyars). Merrimack Bk Serv.

New Russian Tragedy. Anatole Shub. 1970. pap. text ed. 2.95x (ISBN 0-393-09910-5, NortonC). Norton.

New School Executive: A Theory of Administration. 2nd ed. Thomas J. Sergiovanni & Fred D. Carver. (Illus.). 1980. text ed. 16.50 scp (ISBN 0-06-045906-9, HarpC). Har-Row.

New Science of Management Decision. rev. ed. Herbert A. Simon. LC 76-40414. 1977. ref. ed. 15.95x (ISBN 0-13-616144-8); pap. text ed. 10.95 (ISBN 0-13-616136-7). P-H.

New Science of Organizations: A Reconceptualization of the Wealth of Nations. Alberto G. Ramos. 224p. 1981. 25.00 (ISBN 0-8020-5527-3). U of Toronto Pr.

New Science of Skin & Skuba Diving. 5th rev. ed. National Council for Cooperation in Aquatics. 320p. 1980. pap. 7.95 (ISBN 0-695-81424-9); min. purchase of 10 copies, 32p. 9.95 (ISBN 0-695-81516-4). Follett.

New Scotland. David Turnock. LC 78-58561. 1979. 24.00 (ISBN 0-7153-7560-1). David & Charles.

New Seasoning. Graham Kerr. 1976. 7.95 o.p. (ISBN 0-8007-0804-0); pap. 1.95 o. p. o.p. (ISBN 0-8007-8333-6, Spire Bks). Revell.

New Secretary's Deskbook. Ed. by Betty M. Corson. LC 78-78240. 1980. cancelled (ISBN 0-87100-160-8). Morgan.

New Self-Hypnosis. Paul Adams. pap. 4.00 (ISBN 0-87980-233-2). Wilshire.

New Sex Therapy: Active Treatment of Sexual Dysfunctions. Helen S. Kaplan. LC 73-77724. 1974. 20.00 (ISBN 0-87630-083-2, Dist. by Quadrangle). Brunner-Mazel.

New Sexuality: Myths, Fables & Hang-Ups. Kennedy, Eugene C., M.M. LC 77-180907. 160p. 1973. pap. 2.45 (ISBN 0-385-06357-1, Im). Doubleday.

New Shorter Spanish Review Grammar. Juan R. Castellano & Charles B. Brown. LC 73-1349. 225p. 1975. text ed. 9.95x (ISBN 0-684-14482-4, ScribC). Scribner.

New Simplicity Sewing Book. rev. ed. (Illus.). 256p. 1979. pap. 2.95 (ISBN 0-918178-17-7). Simplicity.

New Siwalik Primates: Their Bearing on the Question of Evolution of Man & the Anthropoidea. C. E. Pilgrim. Bd. with Sivapithecus Palate. LC 77-86436. (India Geological Survey. Records of the Geological Survey of India: Vol. 45). 1977. Repr. of 1915 ed. 15.00 (ISBN 0-404-16675-X). AMS Pr.

New Smith's Bible Dictionary. rev. ed. William Smith. Ed. by Reuel G. Lemmons et al. LC 66-20927. 1966. 8.95 (ISBN 0-385-04872-6); thumb-indexed 9.95 (ISBN 0-385-04869-6). Doubleday.

New Social Marketplace: Notes on Effecting Social Change in America's Third Century. Hewitt D. Crane. LC 80-11674. (Communication & Information Science Ser.). (Illus.). 112p. 1980. text ed. 14.95 (ISBN 0-89391-063-5). Ablex Pub.

New Social Order in China. Leang-Li T'Ang. (Studies in Chinese History & Civilization). 1977. Repr. of 1936 ed. 22.00 (ISBN 0-89093-090-2). U Pubns Amer.

New Socialist Revolution. Michael Lerner. 488p. 1973. 8.95 o.p. (ISBN 0-440-06372-8). Delacorte.

New Sociology: Essays in Social Science & Social Theory in Honor of C. Wright Mills. Ed. by Irving L. Horowitz. 1964. 19.95 (ISBN 0-19-500587-2). Oxford U Pr.

New Sociology: Essays in Social Science & Social Theory in Honor of C. Wright Mills. Ed. by Irving L. Horowitz. (YA) (gr. 9 up). 1965. pap. 6.95 (ISBN 0-19-500722-0, GB). Oxford U Pr.

New Solar Physics. Ed. by John A. Eddy. LC 78-66338. (AAAS Selected Symposium Ser.: No. 17). 1978. lib. bdg. 20.00x (ISBN 0-89158-444-7). Westview.

New Solar System. Ed. by Brian O'Leary & J. Kelly Beatty. (Illus.). 192p. 1981. 19.95 (ISBN 0-933346-26-3). Sky Pub.

New Soldier. J. F. Kerry, Jr. 1971. 7.95 o.s.i. (ISBN 0-02-562890-9). Macmillan.

New Soldier. John F. Kerry, Jr. & Vietnamese Veterans Against the War. Ed. by David Thorne & George Butler. (Illus.). 176p. 1971. pap. 3.95 o.s.i. (ISBN 0-02-073610-X, Collier). Macmillan.

New Sonnets from Shakespeare: Thirty Famous Passages & Thirty New Sonnets from Shakespeare's Best-Loved Plays. J. David Andrews. 71p. (gr. 8-12). 1979. pap. 5.00. Planetary Pr.

New Sounds for Woodwind. Bruno Bartolozzi. Ed. by Reginald S. Brindle. 80p. 1981. 22.50x (ISBN 0-19-318611-X). Oxford U Pr.

New Sources of Energy: Solar Two. Reports from the United Nations Conference in Rome. (Illus.). 1978. lib. bdg. 16.00 (ISBN 0-88930-032-1, Pub. by Cloudburst Canada); pap. 8.50 (ISBN 0-88930-031-3). Madrona Pubs.

New Sources of Self. T. R. Young. 124p. 1972. text ed. 12.25 (ISBN 0-08-016672-5). Pergamon.

New South & the "New Competition" A Case Study of Trade Association Development in the Southern Pine Industry. James E. Fickle. LC 80-12420. 300p. 1980. 17.50 (ISBN 0-252-00788-3). U of Ill Pr.

New Sovereignty. Reginald Wallis. 1974. pap. 1.25 (ISBN 0-87123-391-6, 200391). Bethany Fell.

New Soviet Empire. David J. Dallin. 1951. 27.50x (ISBN 0-685-69806-8). Elliots Bks.

New Space for Women. Ed. by Gerda R. Wekerle et al. (Westview Special Studies in Women in Contemporary Society). 352p. 1980. lib. bdg. 28.50x (ISBN 0-89158-775-6). Westview.

New Spain's Far Northern Frontier: Essays on Spain in the American West, 1540-1821. Ed. by David J. Weber. LC 78-21428. 296p. 1979. pap. 9.95x (ISBN 0-8263-0499-0). U of NM Pr.

New Special Education Administrative Training Simulator (NSEATS) Ed. by Daniel D. Sage. (Illus.). 1980. Data Bank, 1-9. 9.00 (ISBN 0-685-82631-7); 10-24 8.00 (ISBN 0-685-82632-5); 25 & over 7.00 (ISBN 0-685-82633-3); participants consumable booklet 11.00 (ISBN 0-8156-8103-8); inst. manual 9.00 (ISBN 0-8156-8104-6); package of 25 participant's booklets, 25 sets of data bank, 1 inst. manual 400.00. Syracuse U Pr.

New Spoon River Anthology. Edgar L. Masters. 1968. 10.95 (ISBN 0-02-581720-5). Macmillan.

New Stage in International Relations. N. I. Lebedev. LC 77-30488. 1978. text ed. 30.00 (ISBN 0-08-022246-3). Pergamon.

New Standard Book of Dog Care & Training. Jeannette W. Cross & Blanche Saunders. (Illus.). (gr. 9 up). 1962. 12.95 (ISBN 0-8015-5372-5, Hawthorn). Dutton.

New Standard Encyclopedia, 14 vols. Standard Education Corporation. Ed. by Douglas W. Downey. LC 80-19936. (gr. 9-12). 1981. Set. 349.50 (ISBN 0-87392-186-0). Standard Ed.

New Standard Jewish Encyclopedia. Ed. by Geoffrey Wigoder & Itzhak Karpman. LC 76-21965. 1977. 29.95 o.p. (ISBN 0-385-12519-4). Doubleday.

New Start for the Child with Reading Problems. rev. ed. Carl H. Delacato. 1977. 8.95 o.p. (ISBN 0-679-50760-4); pap. 4.95 o.p. (ISBN 0-679-50765-5). McKay.

New Steinbeck Bibliography (1929-1971) Tetsumaro Hayashi. LC 73-9982. (Author Bibliographies Ser.: No. 1). 1973. 10.00 (ISBN 0-8108-0647-9). Scarecrow.

New Steinerbooks Dictionary of the Paranormal. George Riland. (Spiritual Science Library). 370p. 1980. 20.00x (ISBN 0-8334-0719-8). Multimedia.

New Story. Thomas Berry. 1978. 2.00 (ISBN 0-89012-012-9). Anima Pubns.

New Strategic Perspectives on Social Policy. John E. Tropman & Roger M. Lind. (Policy Studies). Date not set. 47.51 (ISBN 0-08-025554-X); pap. 14.51 (ISBN 0-08-025553-1). Pergamon.

New Strategies for Public Affairs Reporting: Investigation, Interpretation & Research. Hage et al. (Illus.). 336p. 1976. 13.95 (ISBN 0-13-615831-5). P-H.

New Strategies for Social Development. International Conference On Social Welfare. LC 31-3460. 1971. 20.00x (ISBN 0-231-03580-2). Columbia U Pr.

New Strategy for North-South Negotiations. Khadija Haq. (Policy Studies). 1980. 25.00. Pergamon.

New Strategy in Indian Agriculture. C. Subramaniam. text ed. 12.50 (ISBN 0-7069-0921-6, Pub. by Vikas India). Advent Bk.

New Super-Spirituality. Francis A. Schaeffer. pap. 0.95 o.p. (ISBN 0-87784-318-X). Inter-Varsity.

New Supervisor. 2nd ed. Martin M. Broadwell. 1979. pap. text ed. 8.95 (ISBN 0-201-00565-4). A-W.

New Surgical Approaches, Vol. 91. Association of Bone & Joint Surgeons. Ed. by Marshall Urist. (Clinical Orthopaedics & Related Research Ser.). 1973. 15.00 (ISBN 0-685-34612-9). Lippincott.

New Survey of Social Sciences. Ed. by Baidya N. Varma. 1963. 8.00x o.p. (ISBN 0-210-26861-1). Asia.

New System for Public Housing: Salvaging a National Resource. Raymond J. Struyk. LC 80-53321. 254p. 1980. 20.00 (ISBN 0-87766-279-7). Urban Inst.

New System of Anatomy: Being a Dissector's Guide & Atlas. 2nd ed. Zuckerman et al. (Illus.). 650p. 1981. pap. text ed. 29.50x (ISBN 0-19-263136-5). Oxford U Pr.

New System of Slavery: The Export of Indian Labor Overseas 1830-1920. Hugh Tinker. (Illus.). 472p. 1974. 24.00x (ISBN 0-19-218410-5). Oxford U Pr.

New System, or, an Analysis of Ancient Mythology, 3 vols. Jacob Bryant. Ed. by Burton Feldman & Robert Richardson. LC 78-60881. (Myth & Romanticism Ser.: Vol. 5). (Illus.). 1980. Set. lib. bdg. 198.00 (ISBN 0-8240-3554-2); lib. bdg. 66.00 ea. Garland Pub.

New Tax Structure for the United States. Donald H. Skadden. LC 77-29249. (Key Issues Lecture Ser). 1978. 11.50 (ISBN 0-672-97222-0); pap. 5.50 (ISBN 0-672-97223-9). Bobbs.

New Teachers. Don M. Flournoy et al. LC 77-184957. (Higher Education Ser.). 1972. 11.95x o.p. (ISBN 0-87589-117-9). Jossey-Bass.

New Teaching, New Learning: Current Issues in Higher Education 1971. Ed. by G. Kerry Smith. LC 72-173856. (Higher Education Ser.). 1971. 12.95x o.p. (ISBN 0-87589-113-6). Jossey-Bass.

New Techniques & Instrumentation in Ultrasound. Ed. by P. N. T. Wells & Marvin Ziskin. (Clinics in Diagnostic Ultrasound Ser.). (Illus.). 224p. 1980. text ed. 20.50 (ISBN 0-443-08075-5). Churchill.

New Technologies of Birth & Death: Medical, Legal & Moral Dimensions. LC 80-83425. xvi, 196p. (Orig.). 1980. pap. 8.95 (ISBN 0-935372-07-5). Pope John Ctr.

New Technology & Military Power: General Purpose Military Forces for the 1980's & Beyond. Seymour J. Deitchman. (Special Studies in Military Affairs). 1979. lib. bdg. 28.00x (ISBN 0-89158-358-0). Westview.

New Tertiary Mathematics: Applied Mathematics, Vol. 1, Pt. 2: Basic Applied Mathematics. C. Plumpton & P. S. Macilwaine. (Illus.). 42.00 (ISBN 0-08-025035-1); pap. 14.00 (ISBN 0-08-021645-5). Pergamon.

New Tertiary Mathematics: Further Applied Mathematics, Vol. 2, Pt. 2. C. Plumpton & P. S. Macilwaine. (Illus.). Date not set. 42.00 (ISBN 0-08-025037-8); pap. 16.75 (ISBN 0-08-025026-2); F/non-net 14.00 (ISBN 0-08-025036-X). Pergamon.

New Tertiary Mathematics: Further Pure Mathematics, Vol. 2, Pt. 1. C. Plumpton & P. S. Macilwaine. LC 79-41454. (Illus.). 408p. 1981. 42.00 (ISBN 0-08-025033-5); pap. 16.75 (ISBN 0-08-021644-7). Pergamon.

New Tertiary Mathematics: The Core. C. Plumpton & P. S. MacIlwaine. (Pure Mathematics: Vol. 1). (Illus.). 1980. 42.00 (ISBN 0-08-025031-9); pap. 14.00 (ISBN 0-08-021643-9). Pergamon.

New Test Papers in Physics. M. Nelkon. 1974. pap. text ed. 3.95x o.p. (ISBN 0-435-68654-2). Heinemann Ed.

New Testament: A New Translation. William Barclay. 576p. (Orig.). 1980. pap. 2.95x (ISBN 0-664-24358-4). Westminster.

New Testament: An Introduction to Its History & Literature. J. Gresham Machem. 1976. 11.95 (ISBN 0-85151-240-2). Banner of Truth.

New Testament & Criticism. George E. Ladd. 1966. pap. 3.95 (ISBN 0-8028-1680-0). Eerdmans.

New Testament & Structuralism: A Collection of Essays. Ed. & tr. by Alfred M. Johnson, Jr. LC 76-25447. (Pittsburgh Theological Monographs: No. 11). 1976. pap. text ed. 7.95 (ISBN 0-915138-13-1). Pickwick.

New Testament as the Church's Book. Willi Marxsen. Tr. by James E. Mignard from Ger. LC 70-164554. 160p. (Orig.). 1972. pap. 3.95 (ISBN 0-8006-0102-5, 1-102). Fortress.

New Testament Background: Selected Documents. Ed. by Charles K. Barrett. pap. 4.95x (ISBN 0-06-130086-1, TB86, Torch). Har-Row.

New Testament Church & Its Symbols. Fred Pruitt. 131p. 1.00. Faith Pub Hse.

New Testament Church Then & Now. LeRoy Lawson. (Orig.). 1981. pap. 3.95 (ISBN 0-87239-443-3, 88585). Standard Pub.

New Testament Commentary. 7.95 o.p. (ISBN 0-686-12894-X). Schmul Pub Co.

New Testament Commentary: A General Introduction to & a Commentary on the Books of the New Testament. rev. ed. Ed. by Herbert C. Alleman. LC 44-47049. 1944. 8.95 (ISBN 0-8006-0364-8). Fortress.

New Testament Concept of Witness. A. A. Trites. LC 76-11067. (Society for New Testament Studies Monograph: No. 31). 1977. 48.00 (ISBN 0-521-21015-1). Cambridge U Pr.

New Testament Essays. Brown, Raymond E., S.S. 1968. pap. 1.95 (ISBN 0-385-05276-6, D251, Im). Doubleday.

New Testament Evidences. rev. ed. Wallace Wartick. LC 75-328412. (Bible Study Textbook Ser.). (Illus.). 1975. 10.00 o.p. (ISBN 0-89900-052-5). College Pr Pub.

New Testament Exegesis: Examples. French L. Arrington. 1977. 7.25 (ISBN 0-8191-0108-7). U Pr of Amer.

New Testament for Spiritual Reading, 25 vols. Ed. by J. L. McKenzie. Incl. Vol. 1. Gospel According to St. Matthew, Pt. 1 (ISBN 0-8164-1072-0); Vol. 2. Gospel According to St. Matthew, Pt. 2 (ISBN 0-8164-1073-9); Vol. 3. Gospel According to St. Mark, Pt. 1 (ISBN 0-8164-1074-7); Vol. 4. Gospel According to St. Mark, Pt. 2 (ISBN 0-8164-1075-5); Vol. 5. Gospel According to St. Luke, Pt. 1 (ISBN 0-8164-1076-3); Vol. 6. Gospel According to St. Luke, Pt. 2 (ISBN 0-8164-1077-1); Vol. 7. Gospel According to St. John, Pt. 1 (ISBN 0-8164-1078-X); Vol. 8. Gospel According to St. John, Pt. 2 (ISBN 0-8164-1079-8); Vol. 9. Gospel According to St. John, Pt. 3 (ISBN 0-8164-1080-1); Vol. 10. Acts of the Apostles, Pt. 1 (ISBN 0-8164-1081-X); Vol. 11. Acts of the Apostles, Pt. 2 (ISBN 0-8164-1082-8); Vol. 12. Epistle to the Romans (ISBN 0-8164-1083-6); Vol. 13. First Epistle to the Corinthians (ISBN 0-8164-1084-4); Vol. 14. Second Epistle to the Corinthians (ISBN 0-8164-1085-2); Vol. 15. Epistle to the Galatians (ISBN 0-8164-1086-0); Vol. 16. Epistle to the Ephesians (ISBN 0-8164-1087-9); Vol. 17. Epistle to the Philippians. Epistle to the Colossians (ISBN 0-8164-1088-7); Vol. 18. First Epistle to the Thessalonians. Second Epistle to the Thessalonians (ISBN 0-8164-1089-5); Vol. 19. First Epistle to Timothy. Second Epistle to Timothy (ISBN 0-8164-1090-9); Vol. 20. Epistle to Titus. Epistle to Philemon (ISBN 0-8164-1091-7); Vol. 21. Epistle to the Hebrews. Epistle to James (ISBN 0-8164-1092-5); Vol. 22. First Epistle to Peter. Second Epistle to Peter (ISBN 0-8164-1093-3); Vol. 23. Epistle to Jude. Three Epistles of John (ISBN 0-8164-1094-1); Vol. 24. Revelation of St. John, Pt. 1 (ISBN 0-8164-1095-X); Vol. 25. Revelation of St. John, Pt. 2 (ISBN 0-8164-1096-8). 6.00 ea; Set. 119.00 (ISBN 0-686-57583-0). Crossroad NY.

New Testament Greek Primer. Alfred Marshall. 176p. (Orig.). 1981. pap. 5.95 (ISBN 0-310-20401-1). Zondervan.

New Testament Greek Workbook: An Inductive Study of the Complete Text of the Gospel of John. James A. Walther. LC 80-23762. (Illus.). 1981. lib. bdg. 12.00x (ISBN 0-226-87239-4). U of Chicago Pr.

New Testament Greek Workbook: Inductive Study of the Complete Text of the Gospel of John. James A. Walther. (Illus.). 1966. 11.00x o.s.i. (ISBN 0-226-87238-6). U of Chicago Pr.

New Testament History. F. F. Bruce. LC 78-144253. 462p. 1972. pap. 5.95 (ISBN 0-385-02533-5, Anch). Doubleday.

New Testament in Current Study. Reginald H. Fuller. (Hudson River Editions). 1976. 12.50x (ISBN 0-684-14843-9, ScribT). Scribner.

New Testament in Modern English. rev ed. J. B. Phillips. student ed. 9.95 (ISBN 0-02-596970-6). student ed. 3.95 (ISBN 0-686-67531-2, 59697). Macmillan.

New Testament in Modern Speech. 3rd ed. R. F. Weymouth. LC 78-9536. 1978. kivar 10.95 (ISBN 0-8254-4025-4). Kregel.

New Testament in Shorter Form. Ed. by Samuel Terrien. LC 73-95182. Orig. Title: Reader's New Testament. 1970. 4.95 o.p. (ISBN 0-02-616980-0); pap. 2.95 (ISBN 0-02-089560-7). Macmillan.

New Testament in the Life of the Church. Eugene LaVerdiere. LC 80-67403. 1 (Orig.). 1980. pap. 4.95 (ISBN 0-87 Ave Maria.

New Testament Index. Ed. by R. G. 1963. pap. 0.50 (ISBN 0-8267-000 United Bible.

New Testament: Its Background, Gro Content. Bruce M. Metzger. 1965. 0-687-27913-5): Abingdon.

New Testament of the Jerusalem Bible: Reader's Edition. Ed. by Alexander Jones. LC 69-11018. (Illus.). 1969. pap. 2.95 (ISBN 0-385-06569-8, D253, Im). Doubleday.

New Testament Questions of Today. Ernst Kasemann. Tr. by W. J. Montague from Ger. LC 70-81531. 320p. 1979. pap. 6.95 (ISBN 0-8006-1351-1, 1-1351). Fortress.

New Testament Student, the New Testament Student at Work, Vol. II. John Skilton. kivar 5.00 o.p. (ISBN 0-87552-434-6). Presby & Reformed.

New Testament Survey. rev. ed. Merrill C. Tenney. (Illus.). 1961. 13.95 (ISBN 0-8028-3251-2). Eerdmans.

New Testament Teaching on Tongues. Merrill F. Unger. LC 70-165057. 1971. pap. 2.95 (ISBN 0-8254-3900-0). Kregel.

New Testament Theology. Donald Guthrie. 1056p. 1981. text ed. 24.95 (ISBN 0-87784-965-X). Inter-Varsity.

New Testament Theology. Joachim Jeremias. LC 70-143936. lib. rep. ed. 20.00x (ISBN 0-684-15157-X, ScribT). Scribner.

New Testament Without Illusion. John L. McKenzie. 1980. 11.95 (ISBN 0-88347-109-4). Thomas More.

New Testament Wordbook for Translators, Pt. 1. R. G. Bratcher et al. (Translational Articles Ser.). 1966. pap. 1.00 (ISBN 0-8267-0020-9, 08638). United Bible.

New Testament Wordbook for Translators, Pt. 2. R. G. Bratcher. (Exegetical Articles Ser.). 1964. pap. 2.00 (ISBN 0-8267-0019-5, 08637). United Bible.

New Testament World: Insights from Cultural Anthropology. Bruce J. Malina. (Illus.). 224p. 1981. pap. 8.95 (ISBN 0-8042-0423-3). John Knox.

New, Tested Techniques for Independent Learning. Thomas G. Lyman. (Human Development Library-Bk). (Illus.). 131p. 1981. 27.85 (ISBN 0-89266-291-3). Am Classical Coll Pr.

New Textbook of Higher Plane Geometry. S. M. Mathur. pap. 3.00x o.p. (ISBN 0-210-22652-8). Asia.

New Themes in Christian Philosophy. Ed. by Ralph M. McInerny. LC 68-20439. 1968. text ed. 29.50x (ISBN 0-268-00192-8). Irvington.

New Theory of Value: The Canadian Economics of Harold Adams Innis. Robin Neill. LC 77-185867. 184p. 1972. pap. 3.50 (ISBN 0-8020-6152-4). U of Toronto Pr.

New Theory of Vision. George Berkeley. 1954. 5.00x o.p. (ISBN 0-460-00483-2, Evman). Dutton.

New TNT - Miraculous Power Within You! rev. ed. Harold Sherman. 1979. Repr. of 1966 ed. 3.95 (ISBN 0-346-12383-6). Cornerstone.

New Tools for Urban Management. Richard S. Rosenbloom & John R. Russell. 1971. text ed. 15.00 (ISBN 0-87584-093-0). Harvard U Pr.

New Touch-Stone for Gold & Silver Wares. W. Badcock & J. Reynolds. 390p. Repr. of 1679 ed. 10.00x (ISBN 0-686-28346-5, Pub. by Irish Academic Pr). Biblio Dist.

New-Town Planning: Principles & Practice. Gideon Golany. LC 76-15958. 1976. 37.50 (ISBN 0-471-31038-7, Pub. by Wiley-Interscience). Wiley.

New Towns & the Suburban Dream. Ed. by Irving L. Allen. (Interdisciplinary Urban Ser). 1976. 17.50 (ISBN 0-8046-9161-4, Natl U); pap. 8.95 (ISBN 0-8046-9165-7). Kennikat.

New Towns in America: The Design & Development Process. American Institute of Architects. LC 73-77292. 1973. 35.95 (ISBN 0-471-00975-X, Pub. by Wiley-Interscience). Wiley.

New Towns in-Town: Why a Federal Program Failed. Martha Derthick. 102p. 1972. pap. 4.00 (ISBN 0-87766-022-0, 70006). Urban Inst.

New Towns: Planned Towns Throughout History. Ervin Y. Galantay. LC 74-81216. (Planning & Cities Ser.). (Illus.). 192p. 1975. 15.00 o.s.i. (ISBN 0-8076-0766-5); pap. 5.95 o.s.i. (ISBN 0-8076-0767-3). Braziller.

New Towns Planning & Development: A Worldwide Bibliography. Gideon Golany. LC 72-93819. (Research Reports: No. 20). (Illus.). 1973. pap. 4.75 (ISBN 0-87420-320-1). Urban Land.

New Trade Names 1980: Supplement to Trade Names Dictionary. 2nd ed. Ed. by Ellen T. Crowley. LC 79-12685. (Incl. 1981 supplement). 1980. pap. 95.00 (ISBN 0-8103-0693-X). Gale.
Ne[illegible]ining & Development Organizations: [illegible]nt to Training & Development [illegible] Directory, 2nd Edition. Ed. by [illegible]sserman. 1981. Set. pap. 48.00 (ISBN [illegible]0180-6). Gale.
[illegible]ing for Service. rev. ed. C. J. Sharp. [illegible]rig.). 1942. pap. 2.50 (ISBN 0-87239-[illegible]059). Standard Pub.
[illegible]on of Volney's Ruins, 2 vols. C. F. [illegible]by Burton Feldman & Robert D. [illegible] 78-60900. (Myth & [illegible] Vol. 25). (Illus.). 1979. Set. [illegible]N 0-8240-3574-7); lib. [illegible] and Pub.
[illegible]proaches to Juvenile Delinquency. Ed. by J. L. Khanna. (Illus.). 164p. 1975. 15.75 (ISBN 0-398-03184-3). C C Thomas.
New Treaty for Panama? Abraham F. Lowenthal et al. (AEI Defense Review). 1.50 (ISBN 0-8447-1325-2). Am Enterprise.
New Trends & New Responsibilities for Universities in Latin America. 96p. 1980. pap. 8.50 (ISBN 92-3-101830-2, U1040, UNESCO). Unipub.
New Trends in Drug Liability & Litigation Course Handbook. (Litigation & Administrative Practice Course Handbook Ser.1977-78: Vol. 109). 1978. pap. 20.00 o.p. (ISBN 0-685-07697-0, H4-3858). PLI.
New Trends in Food Retailing, GA-045. Ed. by Business Communications Co. 1980. 825.00 (ISBN 0-89336-228-X). BCC.
New Trends in Integrated Science Teaching: Education of Teachers, Vol. 3. Ed. by P. E. Richmond. (Illus.). 227p. (Orig.). 1974. pap. 18.00 (ISBN 92-3-101190-1, U419, UNESCO). Unipub.
New Trends in Securities Litigation 1977. (Corporate Law & Practice Course Handbook Ser. 1977-78: Vol. 260). 1977. pap. 20.00 o.p. (ISBN 0-685-05619-8, B4-5546). PLI.
New Trends in the Description of the General Mechanism & Regulation of Enzymes. Ed. by S. Damjanovich. (Illus.). 312p. 1978. 30.00x (ISBN 963-05-1881-3). Intl Pubns Serv.
New Trends in Thermal Physiology. Ed. by Y. Houdas & J. D. Guieu. 212p. 1978. pap. 30.00 (ISBN 2-225-49874-1). Masson Pub.
New Truck & Van Prices, 1981. rev. ed. Ed. by Michael L. Green. (Buyer's Guide Ser.). 96p. (Orig.). Date not set. pap. 2.50 (ISBN 0-89552-070-2). DMR Pubns.
New Tyranny: How Nuclear Power Enslaves Us. Robert Jungk. 1979. pap. 2.50 (ISBN 0-446-91351-0). Warner Bks.
New Unhappy Lords. A. K. Chesterton. 255p. (Orig.). 1970. pap. 4.50x (ISBN 0-911038-83-3, Christian Book Club of America). Noontide.
New Unity Inn Cookbook. 2.95 (ISBN 0-87159-112-X). Unity Bks.
New University. Ed. by John Lawlor. LC 68-8250. 1968. 15.00x (ISBN 0-231-03217-X). Columbia U Pr.
New U.S. Policy Toward China. A. Doak Barnett. LC 70-166508. 1971. 9.95 (ISBN 0-8157-0818-1); pap. 3.95 (ISBN 0-8157-0817-3). Brookings.
New Utopians: A Study of System Design & Social Change. enl. ed. Robert Boguslaw. 1981. pap. text ed. 7.95x (ISBN 0-8290-0115-8). Irvington.
New Vegetarian Restaurant Guide. 288p. pap. 6.95 (ISBN 0-686-28809-2). Daystar Pub Co.
New Venture Creation: A Guide to Small Business Development. Jeffry A. Timmons et al. 1977. pap. 18.50 (ISBN 0-256-01887-1). Irwin.
New Venture Strategies. K. Vesper. 1980. 16.95 (ISBN 0-13-615948-6); pap. 10.95 (ISBN 0-13-615930-3). P-H.
New View of a Woman's Body: A Totally Illustrated Guide. Federation of Feminist Women's Health Centers. 1981. 14.95 (ISBN 0-671-41214-0); pap. 6.95 (ISBN 0-671-41215-9). S&S.
New View of the Earth: Moving Continents & Moving Oceans. Seiya Uyeda. Tr. by Masako Ohnuki. LC 77-9900. (Geology Ser.). (Illus.). 1978. text ed. 19.95x (ISBN 0-7167-0283-5); pap. text ed. 9.95x (ISBN 0-7167-0282-7). W H Freeman.
New Views of the Constitution of the United States. John Taylor. LC 75-124903. (American Constitutional & Legal History Ser). 1971. Repr. of 1823 ed. lib. bdg. 32.50 (ISBN 0-306-71996-7). Da Capo.
New Vigilantes: Deprogrammers, Anti-Cultists & the New Religions. Anson D. Shupe, Jr. & David G. Bromley. LC 80-23276. (Sage Library of Social Research: Vol. 113). 272p. 1980. 18.00 (ISBN 0-8039-1542-X); pap. 8.95 (ISBN 0-8039-1543-8). Sage.
New Vision: Forty Years of Photography at the Institute of Design. John Grimes et al. (Illus.). Date not set. 20.00 (ISBN 0-89381-067-3). Aperture. Postponed.
New Vitamin Cures. new ed. Mark C. Marvin. LC 80-81401. 284p. 1980. 10.95 (ISBN 0-9604336-1-9); pap. 5.95 (ISBN 0-9604336-0-0). Marvanco.
New Vocational Pathways for the Mentally Retarded. (ARCA Monograph). 52p. 1966. pap. 1.50 o.p. (ISBN 0-686-11442-6). Am Personnel.
New Voice. Linda R. Weltner. LC 80-70414. 192p. Date not set. 12.95 (ISBN 0-8070-3248-4); pap. 5.95 (ISBN 0-8070-3249-2, BP 621). Beacon Pr.
New Voices I: The Campbell Award Nominees. George R. Martin. 1978. pap. 1.75 o.s.i. (ISBN 0-515-04507-1). Jove Pubns.
New Voices: Stories & Poems by Young Chinese Writers. rev. 2nd ed. Ed. by Nancy Ing. (Asian Library Ser.: No. 15). Orig. Title: New Voices: Fiction & Poetry by Young Chinese Writers. 212p. 1980. pap. 5.00 (ISBN 0-89644-580-1). Chinese Materials.
New Voyager in English, Levels 3-8. Incl. Three (ISBN 0-8294-0300-0). tchr's ed. (ISBN 0-8294-0301-9); Four (ISBN 0-8294-0298-5). tchr's ed. (ISBN 0-8294-0299-3); Five (ISBN 0-8294-0294-2). tchr's ed. (ISBN 0-8294-0295-0); Six (ISBN 0-8294-0296-9). tchr's ed. (ISBN 0-8294-0297-7); Seven (ISBN 0-8294-0288-8). tchr's ed. (ISBN 0-8294-0289-6); Eight (ISBN 0-8294-0286-1). tchr's ed. (ISBN 0-8294-0287-X). 1979-80. 5.95 ea.; tchr's eds. with ans. 5.95 ea. Loyola.
New Voyages in English One. 168p. 1981. pap. 2.50 (ISBN 0-8294-0361-2); tchrs'. ed. 2.50 (ISBN 0-8294-0362-0). Loyola.
New Voyages in English Two. 168p. 1981. pap. 2.50 (ISBN 0-8294-0363-9); tchrs'. ed. 2.50 (ISBN 0-686-69394-9). Loyola.
New Voyages in English 7. 464p. 1979. 5.95 (ISBN 0-8294-0288-8); tchr's ed. 5.95. Loyola.
New Voyages in English 8. 5.95 (ISBN 0-8294-0286-1); tchr's ed. 5.95 (ISBN 0-8294-0287-X). Loyola.
New Water Book. Melvin Berger. LC 73-3395. (Illus.). 128p. (gr. 3-6). 1973. 7.95 (ISBN 0-690-58146-7, TYC-J). T Y Crowell.
New Wave of Japanese Architecture. Ed. by Kenneth Frampton. (IAUS Exhibition Catalogues Ser.). (Illus.). 96p. 1978. pap. 12.00 (ISBN 0-932628-00-1). IAUS.
New Way to Proficiency in English. John L. Cook et al. 336p. 1980. pap. 9.95x (ISBN 0-631-12652-X, Pub. by Basil Blackwell). Biblio Dist.
New Ways in Christian Worship. Robert W. Bailey. 1981. pap. 5.95. Broadman.
New Ways in School Mental Health: Early Detection & Prevention of School Maladaptation. Emory L. Cowen et al. LC 74-11815. 396p. 1975. 22.95 (ISBN 0-87705-214-X). Human Sci Pr.
New Ways Through the Glens: Highland Road, Bridge & Canal Makers of the Early Nineteenth Century. A. R. Haldane. (Illus.). 248p. 1973. Repr. of 1962 ed. 14.95 (ISBN 0-7153-6080-9). David & Charles.
New Ways to Produce Textiles. Harrison. 12.95 (ISBN 0-87245-604-8). Textile Bk.
New Webster's English Dictionary. (Handy Reference Bks.). (Orig.). 1981. pap. 3.50 (ISBN 0-8326-0056-3, 6480). Delair.
New Webster's Medical Dictionary. (Handy Reference Bks.). (Orig.). 1981. pap. 3.50 (ISBN 0-8326-0057-1, 6483). Delair.
New Webster's Medical Dictionary: Vest Pocket Edition. Ed. by Edward G. Finnegan. 1980. pap. 1.95 (ISBN 0-8326-0048-2, 6453). Delair.
New Webster's Quick Reference Dictionary. 1981. pap. 1.95 (ISBN 0-8326-0051-2, 6604). Delair.
New Webster's Quick Reference English-Spanish Dictionary. (Quick Reference Ser.). (Orig.). 1981. pap. 1.95 (ISBN 0-8326-0054-7, 6607). Delair.
New Webster's Quick Reference Speller. (Quick Reference Ser.). (Orig.). 1981. pap. 1.95 (ISBN 0-8326-0053-9, 6606). Delair.
New Webster's Quick Reference Thesaurus. (Quick Reference Ser.). (Orig.). 1981. pap. 1.95 (ISBN 0-8326-0052-0, 6605). Delair.
New Webster's Speller. (Handy Reference Bks.). (Orig.). 1981. pap. 3.50 (ISBN 0-8326-0042-3, 6481). Delair.
New Webster's Thesaurus. (Handy Reference Bks.). (Orig.). 1981. pap. 3.50 (ISBN 0-8326-0055-5, 6482). Delair.
New Western Type Book. 334p. 1980. 38.00 (ISBN 0-241-89984-2, Pub. by Hamish Hamilton England). David & Charles.
New Wheels. Valjean McLenighan. LC 77-27052. (Moods & Emotions Ser.). (Illus.). (gr. k-3). 1978. PLB 8.95 (ISBN 0-8172-1152-7). Raintree Pubs.
New Wind Blowing. Compiled by Baha'i Committee on Music. (Illus., Orig.). 1970. pap. 3.00 (ISBN 0-87743-040-3, 7-58-04). Baha'i.
New Wine in Old Bottles? Royston Lambert. 171p. 1968. pap. text ed. 5.00x (Pub. by Bedford England). Renouf.
New Wine Is Better. Robert Thom. 1974. pap. 2.95 (ISBN 0-88368-036-X). Whitaker Hse.
New Wine: New Wineskins. James B. Dunning. 128p. (Orig.). 1981. pap. 6.80 (ISBN 0-8215-9807-4). Sadlier.
New Woman & the Victorian Novel. Gail Cunningham. LC 78-6179. 1978. text ed. 21.50x (ISBN 0-06-491347-3). B&N.
New Woman's Guide to Health & Medicine. Caroline Derbyshore. (Appleton Consumer Health Guides). (Illus.). 316p. 1980. 12.95 (ISBN 0-8385-6759-2); pap. 5.95 (ISBN 0-8385-6758-4). ACC.
New Women in Art & Dance. Kathleen Bowman. LC 76-5457. (New Women Ser.). (Illus.). (gr. 4-12). 1976. PLB 6.95 (ISBN 0-87191-512-X). Creative Ed.
New Women in Entertainment. Kathleen Bowman. LC 76-4940. (New Women Ser.). (Illus.). (gr. 4-12). 1976. PLB 6.95 (ISBN 0-87191-510-3). Creative Ed.
New Women in Media. Kathleen Bowman. LC 76-6061. (New Women Ser.). (Illus.). (gr. 4-12). 1976. PLB 6.95 (ISBN 0-87191-511-1). Creative Ed.
New Women in Medicine. Kathleen Bowman. LC 76-4873. (New Women Ser.). (Illus.). (gr. 4-12). 1976. PLB 6.95 (ISBN 0-87191-508-1). Creative Ed.
New Women in Politics. Kathleen Bowman. LC 76-5513. (New Women Ser.). (Illus.). (gr. 4-12). 1976. PLB 6.95 (ISBN 0-87191-507-3). Creative Ed.
New Women in Social Sciences. Kathleen Bowman. LC 76-5508. (New Women Ser.). (Illus.). (gr. 4-12). 1976. PLB 6.95 (ISBN 0-87191-509-X). Creative Ed.
New Work on Paper. John Elderfield. (Illus.). 56p. 1980. pap. 6.95 (ISBN 0-87070-496-6). Museum Mod Art.
New Worker. K. N. Vaid. 6.25x o.p. (ISBN 0-210-22205-0). Asia.
New World & Eurasian Cultures. The Educational Research Council. (Human Adventure Concepts and Inquiry Ser). (gr. 6). 1975. pap. text ed. 7.20 (ISBN 0-205-04454-9, 8044546); tchrs'. guide 5.20 (ISBN 0-205-04455-7, 8044554). Allyn.
New World Archaeology: Theoretical & Cultural Transformations: Readings from Scientific American. Intro. by Ezra B. Zubrow et al. LC 74-7028. (Illus.). 1974. text ed. 20.95x (ISBN 0-7167-0503-6); pap. text ed. 10.95x (ISBN 0-7167-0502-8). W H Freeman.
New World: Before 1775. Richard B. Morris. LC 63-8572. (Life History of the United States). (Illus.). (gr. 5 up). 1974. PLB 9.96 (ISBN 0-8094-0550-4, Pub. by Time-Life). Silver.
New World of Economics: Explorations into the Human Experience. rev. ed. Richard B. McKenzie & Gordon Tullock. 1978. pap. text ed. 9.95 (ISBN 0-256-02029-9). Irwin.
New World Pre-History: Archaeology of the American Indians. William T. Sanders & Joseph P. Marino. 1970. pap. 6.95 ref. ed. (ISBN 0-13-616185-5). P-H.
New Writers Eight. C. Bowler et al. (New Writing & Writers). 1968. text ed. 13.00x (ISBN 0-7145-0014-3). Humanities.
New Writers Eight. Christine Bowler et al. 1980. pap. 6.00 (ISBN 0-7145-0015-1). Riverrun NY.
New Writers Eleven. S. A. Madsen et al. (New Writing & Writers Ser.). 1974. text ed. 13.00x (ISBN 0-7145-0813-6). Humanities.
New Writers Eleven. Svend A. Madsen et al. 1980. pap. 6.00 (ISBN 0-7145-0814-4). Riverrun NY.
New Writers Five. D. Castelain et al. (New Writing & Writers Ser.). 1966. text ed. 13.00x (ISBN 0-7145-0404-1). Humanities.
New Writers Five. Daniel Castelain et al. 1980. pap. 6.00 (ISBN 0-7145-0405-X). Riverrun NY.
New Writers Four. J. J. Lebel & Charles Marowitz. 1980. pap. 6.00 (ISBN 0-7145-0403-3). Riverrun NY.
New Writers Nine. R. Rasp et al. (New Writing & Writers Ser.). 1971. text ed. 13.00x (ISBN 0-7145-0016-X). Humanities.
New Writers Nine. Renate Rasp et al. 1980. pap. 6.00 (ISBN 0-7145-0017-8). Riverrun NY.
New Writers One. Alan Burns et al. 1980. pap. 6.00 (ISBN 0-7145-0397-5). Riverrun NY.
New Writers Seven. Tina Morris et al. 1980. pap. 6.00 (ISBN 0-7145-0013-5). Riverrun NY.
New Writers Seven: Special Volume on Dreams. Tina Morris et al. (New Writing & Writers Ser.). 1969. text ed. 13.00x (ISBN 0-7145-0012-7). Humanities.
New Writers Six. C. Burns et al. (New Writing & Writers Ser.). 1967. pap. text ed. 6.00x (ISBN 0-391-02014-5). Humanities.
New Writers Six. Carol Burns et al. 1980. pap. 6.00 (ISBN 0-7145-0407-6). Riverrun NY.
New Writers Ten. F. Salas et al. (New Writing & Writers Ser.). 1971. text ed. 13.00x (ISBN 0-7145-0751-2). Humanities.
New Writers Ten. Floyd Salas et al. 1980. pap. 6.00 (ISBN 0-7145-0752-0). Riverrun NY.
New Writers Three. Alexander Trocchi et al. 1980. pap. 6.00 (ISBN 0-7145-0401-7). Riverrun NY.
New Writers Twelve. David Galloway et al. 1980. pap. 6.00 (ISBN 0-7145-3545-1). Riverrun NY.
New Writers Two. Simon Vestdijk et al. 1980. pap. 6.00 (ISBN 0-7145-0399-1). Riverrun NY.
New Writing & Writers, No. 14. Bond et al. text ed. 13.00x. Humanities.
New Writing & Writers, Vol. 17. 1980. pap. 5.95 (ISBN 0-7145-3695-4). Riverrun NY.
New Writing & Writers Eighteen. Tibor Varady et al. 1980. pap. 6.00 (ISBN 0-7145-3815-9). Riverrun NY.
New Writing & Writers Fifteen. Heinrich Boll et al. 1980. pap. 6.00 (ISBN 0-7145-3561-3). Riverrun NY.
New Writing & Writers Fifteen. 1978. pap. 4.95 (ISBN 0-7145-3561-3). Riverrun NY.
New Writing & Writers Sixteen. William Burroughs et al. 1980. pap. 6.00 (ISBN 0-7145-3638-5). Riverrun NY.
New Writing & Writers Thirteen. Samuel Beckett et al. 1980. pap. 6.00 (ISBN 0-7145-3541-9). Riverrun NY.
New Writing: From Lead to 30, with Revisions. W. Metz. 1979. 12.95 o.p. (ISBN 0-686-52159-5); pap. 11.95 o.p. (ISBN 0-13-617514-7). P-H.
New Writing from the Middle East. Ed. by Leo Hamalian & John D. Yohannan. LC 78-4411. 1978. 15.95 (ISBN 0-8044-2338-5). Ungar.
New Year's Eve - 1929. James T. Farrell. 4.50 (ISBN 0-912292-02-4). The Smith.
New Year's Mystery. Joan L. Nixon. Ed. by Kathy Pacini. LC 79-172. (First Read-Alone Mysteries Ser.). (Illus.). (gr. 1-3). 1979. 5.50g (ISBN 0-8075-5592-4). A Whitman.
New York. Anthony Burgess. (The Great Cities Ser.). (Illus.). (gr. 6 up). 1977. PLB 14.94 (ISBN 0-8094-2271-9, Pub. by Time-Life). Silver.
New York. Ed. by Anthony Burgess. (Great Cities Ser.). 1977. 14.95 (ISBN 0-8094-2270-0). Time-Life.
New York. Carole Chester. (Illus.). 1977. 10.95 o.s.i. (ISBN 0-7134-0183-4). Hippocrene Bks.
New York. Carole Chester. 1977. 24.00 (ISBN 0-7134-0183-4, Pub. by Batsford England). David & Charles.
New York, 8 vols. Ed. by David G. DeLong. Incl. Vol. 1. lib. bdg. 100.00 (ISBN 0-8240-3186-5); Vol. 2. lib. bdg. 100.00 (ISBN 0-8240-3187-3); Vol. 3. lib. bdg. 100.00 (ISBN 0-8240-3188-1); Vol. 4. lib. bdg. 100.00 (ISBN 0-8240-3189-X); Vol. 5. lib. bdg. 100.00 (ISBN 0-8240-3190-3); Vol. 6. lib. bdg. 100.00 (ISBN 0-8240-3191-1); Vol. 7. lib. bdg. 100.00 (ISBN 0-8240-3192-X); Vol. 8. lib. bdg. 100.00 (ISBN 0-8240-3193-8). (Historic American Buildings). 1979. lib. bdg. 600.00 set. Garland Pub.
New York. 33.00 (ISBN 0-89770-108-9). Curriculum Info Ctr.
New York. Marvin A. Rapp. LC 68-9256. 1968. pap. 2.95 (ISBN 0-8077-2022-4). Tchrs Coll.
New York: A City Guide. Federal Writers' Project. LC 39-27593. (Illus.). 708p. 1939. Repr. 59.00 (ISBN 0-403-02921-X). Somerset Pub.
New York: A Guide to Information & Reference Sources. Manuel D. Lopez. LC 80-18634. x, 307p. 1980. 17.50 (ISBN 0-8108-1326-2). Scarecrow.
New York at-a-Glance. Howard Hillman. 1971. pap. 2.50 o.p. (ISBN 0-679-50133-9). McKay.
New York Botanical Garden Illustrated Encyclopedia of Horticulture, 10 vols. T. H. Everett. 1980. Set. lib. bdg. 525.00 (ISBN 0-8240-7222-7). Garland Pub.
New York Casting-Survival Guide & Datebook, 1981. Ed. by Chip Brill & Peter Glenn. 124p. 1980. pap. 10.00 (ISBN 0-87314-036-2). Peter Glenn.
New York City Department of Cultural Affairs, 1976-1973: A Record of Government's Involvement in the Arts. Ryna A. Segal. LC 76-22386. 88p. 1976. pap. 1.75x (ISBN 0-89062-037-7, Pub. by NYC Cultural). Pub Ctr Cult Res.
New York City Resources for the Arts & Artists. LC 73-91956. 100p. 1973. pap. 2.00x (ISBN 0-89062-003-2). Pub Ctr Cult Res.
New York City Slicker: A Counterchic Guide to Manhattan. Didi Lorillard. (Richard Seaver Book). (Orig.). 1979. pap. 7.95 o.p. (ISBN 0-670-50911-6). Viking Pr.
New York: Civic Exploitation. Robert Goldston. LC 72-89586. (Portraits in Urban Civilization Ser). (Illus.). (gr. 9 up). 1970. 5.95g o.s.i. (ISBN 0-02-736400-3). Macmillan.

New York Colony. Thelma Nurenberg. LC 77-77966. (Forge of Freedom Ser). (Illus.). (gr. 5-8). 1969. 7.95 (ISBN 0-02-768400-8, CCPr). Macmillan.

New York Cops Talk Back: A Study of a Beleaguered Minority. Nicholas Alex. LC 76-1852. 1976. 18.95 (ISBN 0-471-02055-9, Pub. by Wiley-Interscience). Wiley.

New York Criminal Practice Under the CPL. Robert M. Pitler. LC 74-181692. 1972. with 1979 suppl. 50.00 (ISBN 0-87632-087-6). Boardman.

New York Cultural Consumer. 264p. 1976. pap. 7.50x (ISBN 0-89062-019-9, Pub. by NYSCA). Pub Ctr Cult Res.

New York Diary. Ned Rorem. LC 67-27523. (Illus.). 1967. 5.95 o.p. (ISBN 0-685-07515-X). Braziller.

New York for Nicola. Mabel E. Allan. LC 63-13791. (gr. 8-11). 5.95 (ISBN 0-8149-0256-1). Vanguard.

New York Giants. Julian May. (NFL Today). (Illus.). (gr. 3-6). 1977. PLB 6.45 (ISBN 0-87191-598-7); pap. 2.95 (ISBN 0-686-67476-6). Creative Ed.

New York in Aerial Views: Eighty-Six Photographs. William Fried & Edward B. Watson. (Illus.). 176p. (Orig.). 1981. pap. 6.50 (ISBN 0-486-24018-5). Dover.

New York Is Very Much Alive: A Manpower View. Eli Ginzberg & Conservation of Human Resources Staff. LC 73-2674. 287p. 1973. 12.95 o.p. (ISBN 0-07-023286-5, P&RB). McGraw.

New York Jets. Julian May. (NFL Today Ser.). (gr. 4-8). 1980. PLB 6.45 (ISBN 0-87191-726-2); pap. 2.95 (ISBN 0-89812-229-5). Creative Ed.

New York Jets. Julian May. LC 74-908. (Superbowl Champions Ser). 48p. 1974. PLB 6.45 (ISBN 0-87191-329-1); pap. 2.95 (ISBN 0-89812-089-6). Creative Ed.

New York Jews & the Quest for Community. Arthur A. Goren. LC 76-129961. 1979. pap. 10.00 (ISBN 0-231-08368-8). Columbia U Pr.

New York Jews' Quest of Community: The Kehillah Experiment, 1908-1922. Arthur A. Goren. LC 76-129961. 1970. 22.50 (ISBN 0-231-03422-9). Columbia U Pr.

New York Job Bank: Conprehensive Guide to Major Employers Throughout Greater New York City Including Northern New Jersey, Southwestern Connecticut, Long Island, Southeastern New York State, & All Five Boroughs of New York City. Ed. by Robert Lang Adams Associates. 450p. (Orig.). 1981. pap. 9.95 (ISBN 0-937860-03-4). Adams Inc MA.

New York Little Renaissance: Iconoclasm, Modernism, & Nationalism in American Culture, 1908-1917. Arthur Frank Wertheim. LC 75-21805. 1976. 17.50x (ISBN 0-8147-9164-6). NYU Pr.

New York Matrimonial Practice Under Equitable Distribution: Course Handbook. Ed. by Milton G. Gershenson & Paul I. Birzon. LC 80-83148. 364p. 1980. pap. 25.00 (ISBN 0-686-69170-9, F4-3706). PLI.

New York Matrimonial Practice 1978. 1978. pap. 20.00 o.p. (ISBN 0-685-90297-8, F4-2797). PLI.

New York on Twenty Dollars a Day: 1980-81 Edition. 304p. 1981. pap. 4.95 (ISBN 0-671-25427-8). Frommer-Pasmantier.

New York Panorama: A Comprehensive View of the Metropolis. LC 72-10165. 1938. 59.00 (ISBN 0-403-02152-9). Somerset Pub.

New York Places & Pleasures: An Uncommon Guidebook. rev. 4th ed. Kate Simon. LC 70-138761. (Illus.). 1972. pap. 5.95 (ISBN 0-06-013876-9, CN-0818, HarpT). Har-Row.

New York Production Manual 1979-80: The "Producer's Masterguide" for Motion Picture, Television, Commercials & Videotape Industries. Shmuel Bension. 1979. pap. 35.00 (ISBN 0-935744-00-2). NY Prod Manual.

New York Production Manual 1981: The "Producer's MasterGuide" for: Motion Picture, Television, Commercials & Videotape Industries. Shmuel Bension. 1000p. (Orig.). 1981. pap. 49.50 (ISBN 0-935744-01-0). NY Prod Manual.

New York Real Estate. New York Assn. of Realtors & Bruce Harwood. 1981. text ed. 16.95 (ISBN 0-8359-4894-3). Reston.

New York School: A Cultural Reckoning. Dore Ashton. (Illus.). 1979. pap. 6.95 (ISBN 0-14-005263-1). Penguin.

New York School: The Painters & Sculptors of the Fifties. Irving Sandler. LC 77-82357. (Icon Editions). (Illus.). 1978. 29.95 (ISBN 0-06-438505-1, HarpT); pap. 14.95 (ISBN 0-06-430094-3, HarpT). Har-Row.

New York State: A Citizen's Handbook. League of Women Voters of New York State. Ed. by Jeanne Richman. LC 79-24095. (Illus.). 119p. (Orig.). 1979. pap. 2.95 (ISBN 0-938588-03-6). LWV NYS.

New York State: A Guide to the Empire State. Federal Writers' Project. 782p. 1940. Repr. 59.00 (ISBN 0-403-02151-0). Somerset Pub.

New York State in Story, Pts. 1 & 2. Schwarz & Goldberg. 1962. comb. 7.95x (ISBN 0-88323-099-2, 280); wkbk. 2.25x (ISBN 0-88323-100-X, 283). Richards Pub.

New York State in Story, Pt. 1. rev. ed. Schwarz & Goldberg. 1962. pap. 3.00x (ISBN 0-88323-096-8, 281). Richards Pub.

New York State Industrial Directory, 1980. State Industrial Directories Corp. 1980. 95.00 (ISBN 0-89910-023-6). State Indus Dir.

New York State Regents Scholarship Exams. rev. ed. David R. Turner. LC 66-27875. (Orig.). (YA) 1975. pap. 5.00 o.p. (ISBN 0-668-00400-2). Arco.

New York Supplement for Modern Real Estate Practice. James R. Loeb & Harold L. Kahn. 130p. (Orig.). 1980. pap. 7.95 (ISBN 0-88462-375-0). Real Estate Ed Co.

New York: The Centennial Years, 1676-1976. Ed. by Milton M. Klein. (Interdisciplinary Urban Ser.). (Illus.). 250p. 1976. 13.95 (ISBN 0-8046-9143-6, Natl U). Kennikat.

New York: the Empire State. 4th ed. D. Ellis et al. 1975. 10.40 o.p. (ISBN 0-13-620385-X). P-H.

New York: The Largest City in the United States. Rene Orth. (Q Book: Famous Cities). (Illus.). (gr. 2-6). 1978. 3.95 (ISBN 0-8467-0447-1, Pub. by Two Continents). Hippocrene Bks.

New York: The States & the Nation. Bruce Bliven, Jr. (Illus.). 1981. 12.95 (ISBN 0-393-05665-1). Norton.

New York Theatre Annual: Nineteen Seventy-Seven to Seventy Eight. Ed. by Catharine R. Hughes. LC 78-50757. (Illus.). 1978. 35.00 (ISBN 0-8103-0417-1). Gale.

New York Theatre Annual: 1976-77. Ed. by Catharine R. Hughes. LC 78-50757. (Illus.). 1978. 35.00 (ISBN 0-8103-0416-3). Gale.

New York Time. Richard Peck. 1981. 9.95 (ISBN 0-440-06346-9). Delacorte.

New York Times Book of the Civil War. Ed. by Arlene Keylin & Douglas J. Bowen. LC 80-7799. (Illus.). 1980. lib. bdg. 12.98x (ISBN 0-405-13396-0). Arno.

New York Times Cook Book. Craig Claiborne. Incl. New York Times Menu Cook Book. (Illus.). 1975. boxed set 29.95 o.s.i. (ISBN 0-06-010775-8, HarpT). Har-Row.

New York Times Cumulative Subject & Personal Name Index: Environment Nineteen Sixty-Five to Nineteen Seventy-Five. Ed. by Edward A. Reno, Jr. 778p. 1978. 75.00 (ISBN 0-667-00606-0). Microfilming Corp.

New York Times Guide to Business & Finance: The American Economy & How It Works. Albert L. Kraus. LC 70-138745. (Illus.). 352p. 1972. 10.95 o.p. (ISBN 0-06-012462-8, HarpT). Har-Row.

New York Times Guide to Dining Out in New York. Mimi Sheraton. 352p. 1981. pap. 6.95 (ISBN 0-8129-0930-5). Times Bks.

New York Times Guide to Simple Home Repairs. Bernard Gladstone. LC 75-45764. (Illus.). 177p. 1976. pap. 2.95 o.p. (ISBN 0-89104-040-4). A & W Pubs.

New York Times Obituaries Index II, 1969-1978. 133p. 1980. write for info. (ISBN 0-667-00598-6). Microfilming Corp.

New York Times Oral History Guide, No. 1. LC 76-5389. 244p. 1976. 17.50 (ISBN 0-88455-996-3). Microfilming Corp.

New York Times Oral History Guide, No. 2. Ed. by Patsy A. Cook. 134p. 1979. pap. 17.50 (ISBN 0-667-00620-6). Microfilming Corp.

New York Times Sixty Minute Gourmet. Pierre Franey. 352p. 1981. pap. 6.95 (ISBN 0-686-69133-4, Columbine). Fawcett.

New York Wills & Trusts: Laws, Forms & Taxes, 2 vols. rev. 2nd ed. Elmer L. Fingar et al. LC 61-9883. 1971. looseleaf with 1979 suppl. 90.00 (ISBN 0-87632-062-0). Boardman.

New York Women's Yellow Pages 1978-1979 Edition. Boston Women's Collective. LC 76-5369. (Illus.). 1978. 12.95 (ISBN 0-312-57120-8); pap. 5.95 o.p. (ISBN 0-312-57155-0). St Martin.

New You. Harold Myra. (gr. 9-12). 1980. pap. 2.25 (ISBN 0-88207-581-0). Victor Bks.

New Zealand. K. B. Cumberland & J. S. Whitelaw. (The World's Landscapes Ser.). (Illus.). 1970. pap. text ed. 10.95x (ISBN 0-582-31157-8). Longman.

New Zealand. R. F. Grover. (World Bibliographical Ser.: No. 13). 1981. write for info. (ISBN 0-903450-31-3). ABC-Clio.

New Zealand. Ngaio Marsh. (Illus.). (gr. 7 up). 1964. 5.95g (ISBN 0-02-762380-7). Macmillan.

New Zealand. Ngaio Marsh. 1976. Repr. of 1942 ed. lib. bdg. 13.30 (ISBN 0-88411-489-9). Amereon Ltd.

New Zealand. 3rd ed. Sunset Editors. LC 77-90726. (Illus.). 128p. 1978. pap. 5.95 (ISBN 0-376-06534-6, Sunset Bks). Sunset-Lane.

New Zealand, a Travel Survival Kit. Tony Wheeler. (Illus.). 1977. pap. 2.95 o.p. (ISBN 0-9598080-9-4, Pub. by Two Continents). Hippocrene Bks.

New Zealand & the Antarctic. L. B. Quartermain. (Illus.). 1971. 11.50x o.p. (ISBN 0-8426-1477-X). Verry.

New Zealand at the Polls: The General Election of 1978. Ed. by Howard R. Penniman. 1980. pap. 7.95 (ISBN 0-8447-3376-8). Am Enterprise.

New Zealand Flora & Fauna. Glen Pownall. 60p. 1980. pap. 1.95 (ISBN 0-85467-032-7, Pub. by Viking Sevenseas New Zealand). Intl Schol Bk Serv.

New Zealand Freshwater Fishes: A Guide and Natural History. R. M. McDowall. (Illus.). 230p. 1972. text ed. 27.50x (ISBN 0-87474-632-9, Pub. by Heinemann New Zealand). Smithsonian.

New Zealand Ghost Book. Robyn Jenkin. (Illus.). 1980. 13.50 (ISBN 0-589-01118-9, Pub. by Reed Books Australia). C E Tuttle.

New Zealand in Colour, Vol. 1. James K. Baxter. (Illus.). 1961. 13.50 o.s.i. (ISBN 0-589-00259-7, Dist. by C E Tuttle). Reed.

New Zealand in Pictures. Sterling Publishing Company Editors. LC 64-24690. (Visual Geography Ser.). (Orig.). (gr. 6 up). PLB 4.99 (ISBN 0-8069-1047-X); pap. 2.95 (ISBN 0-8069-1046-1). Sterling.

New Zealand: Its Land & Its People. Michael King. (Illus.). 152p. 1979. Repr. of 1977 ed. 19.95 (ISBN 0-589-01295-9, Pub. by Reed Bks Australia). C E Tuttle.

New Zealand Journal, 1842-1844, of John B. Williams of Salem, Massachusetts. John B. Williams. Ed. by Robert W. Kenny. (Illus.). 120p. 1956. 10.00 (ISBN 0-87057-041-2, Pub. by Brown U Pr). Univ Pr of New England.

New Zealand Literature to Nineteen Seventy-Seven: A Guide to Information Sources. Ed. by John Thompson. LC 74-11537. (American Literature, English Literature, & World Literature in English Information Guide Ser.: Vol. 30). 250p. 1980. 30.00 (ISBN 0-8103-1246-8). Gale.

New Zealand Native Trees, Vol. 1. Nancy M. Adams. (Mobil New Zealand Nature Ser.). (Illus.). 84p. 1967. pap. 7.50 (ISBN 0-589-00052-7, Pub. by Reed Bks Australia). C E Tuttle.

New Zealand on Fifteen & Twenty Dollars a Day. 240p. 1981. pap. 4.95 (ISBN 0-671-25492-8). Frommer-Pasmantier.

New Zealand Shells and Shellfish. Glen Pownall. 88p. 1980. pap. 7.50 (ISBN 0-85467-033-5, Pub. by Viking Sevenseas New Zealand). Intl Schol Bk Serv.

New Zealand Ways with Flowers. Eileen Dobson. 84p. 1980. pap. 4.50 (ISBN 0-85467-012-2, Pub. by Viking Sevenseas New Zealand). Intl Schol Bk Serv.

New Zealanders: How They Live & Work. R. J. Johnston. LC 75-34976. 168p. 1976. text ed. 8.95 (HoltC). HR&W.

New Zoning Landmarks in Planned Unit Developments. Lenard L. Wolffe. LC 68-59421. (Technical Bulletin Ser: No. 62). (Orig.). 1968. pap. 4.75 (ISBN 0-87420-062-8). Urban Land.

Newbery & Caldecott Medal Books: 1956-1965. Ed. by Lee Kingman. LC 65-26759. (Illus.). 1965. 17.00 (ISBN 0-87675-002-1). Horn Bk.

Newbery & Caldecott Medal Books: 1966-1975. Ed. by Lee Kingman. LC 75-20167. (Illus.). 325p. 1975. 17.00 (ISBN 0-87675-003-X). Horn Bk.

Newbery Medal Books, 1922-1955. Ed. by Bertha M. Miller & Elinor W. Field. LC 55-13968. (Illus.). 1955. 17.00 (ISBN 0-87675-000-5). Horn Bk.

Newborn & the Nurse. 2nd ed. Mary L. Moore. (Illus.). 450p. 1981. text ed. price not set (ISBN 0-7216-6491-1). Saunders.

Newborn Behavioral Organization: Nursing Research &Implications. Ed. by Gene C. Anderson & Beverly Raff. LC 79-2597. (Alan R. Liss Ser.: Vol. 15, No. 7). 1979. 24.00 (ISBN 0-8451-1032-2). March of Dimes.

Newborn Christian. J. B. Phillips. 1978. 9.95 (ISBN 0-02-596120-9). Macmillan.

Newborn Management: Decision Trees & Management Problems. Carmi Z. Margolis & Donald L. Shapiro. (Illus., Orig., With work sheets). 1977. pap. 11.50 (ISBN 0-913178-60-8). Redgrave Pub Co.

Newborns & Parents: Parent-Infant Contact & Newborn Sensory Stimulation. Ed. by Vincent L. Smeriglio. 224p. 1981. text ed. 19.95 (ISBN 0-89859-041-8). L Erlbaum Assocs.

Newcastle: A Duke Without Money; Thomas Pelham-Holles, 1693-1768. Ray A. Kelch. 1974. 21.50x (ISBN 0-520-02537-7). U of Cal Pr.

Newcastle & Carlisle Railway. G. Whittle. LC 79-52378. (Illus.). 1979. 19.95 (ISBN 0-7153-7855-4). David & Charles.

Newcastle Disease Virus: An Evolving P[illegible] Ed. by Robert P. Hanson. (Illus.). 19[illegible] 30.00x (ISBN 0-299-03410-0). U of [illegible]

Newcomer. Anne Roiphe. 1981. price n[illegible] (ISBN 0-671-41455-0, Linden). S&S.

Newcomer. Helen I. Troyanovich. 160p. 1[illegible] 6.95 (ISBN 0-8059-2658-5). Dorrance.

Newcomer's Guide to Metropolitan Washington. 4th ed. Ed. by Marian Hoffman. LC 78-54447. (Illus.). 168p. (Orig.). 1978. pap. 2.75 (ISBN 0-915168-27-8). Washingtonian.

Newe Boke of Presidentes in Maner of a Register. Thomas Phayre. LC 73-6100. (English Experience Ser.: No. 569). 1973. Repr. of 1543 ed. 21.00 (ISBN 90-221-0569-5). Walter J Johnson.

Newer Virus Diseases. John M. Adams. (Illus.). 1960. 8.95 o.s.i. (ISBN 0-02-300490-8). Macmillan.

Newes from Italy of a Second Moses or, the Life of Galeacius Carracciolus the Noble Marquese of Vico. Niccolo Balbani. Tr. by W. Crashaw. LC 79-84085. (English Experience Ser.: No. 905). 92p. 1979. Repr. of 1608 ed. lib. bdg. 10.00 (ISBN 90-221-0905-4). Walter J Johnson.

Newes of the Complement of the Art of Navigation & of the Mightie Empire of Cataia. Anthony Linton. LC 72-215. (English Experience Ser.: No. 204). 1969. Repr. of 1609 ed. 8.00 (ISBN 90-221-0204-1). Walter J Johnson.

Newes Out of Holland, of the East India Trade There. LC 73-6145. (English Experience Ser.: No. 609). 14p. 1973. Repr. of 1622 ed. 3.50 (ISBN 90-221-0609-8). Walter J Johnson.

Newest Peruvian Poetry in Translation. Ed. by Luis A. Ramos-Garcia & Edgar O'Hara. 1979. 4.95 (ISBN 0-934840-00-8). U Tex Studia.

Newest Views on Scoliosis, Vol. 93. Association of Bone & Join Surgeons. Ed. by Marshall Urist. (Clinical Orthopaedics & Related Research Ser.). 1973. 12.00 o.p. (ISBN 0-685-34614-5). Lippincott.

Newfoundland in the Nineteenth & Twentieth Centuries. Ed. by James Hiller & Peter Neary. 1980. 20.00x (ISBN 0-8020-5486-2); pap. 7.50 (ISBN 0-8020-6391-8). U of Toronto Pr.

Newly Industrialized Countries in the World Economy. Bela Balassa. LC 80-20787. 450p. 1981. 42.50 (ISBN 0-08-026336-4); pap. 15.00 (ISBN 0-08-026335-6). Pergamon.

Newlywed Handbook. Yvonne Garrett. 1981. 8.95 (ISBN 0-8499-0276-2). Word Bks.

Newman: A Bibliography of Secondary Studies. John R. Griffin. 150p. (Orig.). 1980. pap. text ed. 12.00 (ISBN 0-931888-04-2). Christendom Pubns.

Newport: A Pictorial History. Judith A. Boss. Ed. by Donna R. Friedman. (Illus.). 208p. 1981. pap. price not set (ISBN 0-89865-097-6). Donning Co.

Newport in the Rockies: The Life & Good Times of Colorado Springs. rev. ed. 2nd ed. Marshall Sprague. LC 79-150759. (Illus.). 1971. 7.95 o.p. (ISBN 0-8040-0540-0, SB). Swallow.

Newport in the Rockies: The Life & Good Times of Colorado Spring. rev. ed. Marshall Sprague. LC 80-52995. 1981. 15.95 (ISBN 0-8040-0412-9, SB); pap. 9.95 (ISBN 0-8040-0413-7). Swallow.

News: A Consumer's Guide. Ivan Doig & Carol Doig. (Illus.). 256p. 1972. pap. text ed. 6.95 o.p. (ISBN 0-13-615617-7). P-H.

News Boy. Arch Brown. LC 80-84131. (Illus.). 80p. (Orig.). 1980. pap. 3.95 (ISBN 0-935672-02-8). JH Pr.

News Bureaus in the U. S. 6th ed. Richard Weiner. LC 80-83995. 186p. 1981. 25.00 (ISBN 0-913046-01-9). Public Relations.

News Dictionary, 1979: Annual. 1980. 14.95 (ISBN 0-87196-109-1); pap. 9.95 (ISBN 0-87196-110-5). Facts on File.

News Dictionary 1980. Donald Paneth. 400p. 1981. 14.95 (ISBN 0-87196-111-3). Facts on File.

News Editing. 3rd ed. Bruce Westley. LC 79-88796. (Illus.). 1980. text ed. 17.75 (ISBN 0-395-27993-3). HM.

News Editing. 2nd ed. Bruce H. Westley. LC 79-170163. (Illus.). 1972. text ed. 16.95 o.p. (ISBN 0-395-05529-6, 3-59706). HM.

News from Abroad & the Foreign Policy Public. W. Phillips Davison et al. LC 80-68024. (Headline Ser.: No. 250). (Illus.). 64p. (Orig.). 1980. pap. 2.00 (ISBN 0-87124-063-7). Foreign Policy.

News from Nowhere. William Morris. Ed. by James Redmond. (Routledge English Texts). 1970. pap. 6.95 (ISBN 0-7100-6799-2). Routledge & Kegan.

News Media: What Makes Them Tick? John L. Hulteng. (Topics in Mass Communications Ser.). 1979. ref. 9.95 (ISBN 0-13-621094-5); pap. 7.95 (ISBN 0-13-621086-4). P-H.

News of the Nation. R. Hoffman. 1975. kit 83.61 o.p. (ISBN 0-13-620609-3). P-H.

News of the Universe. Robert Bly. 320p. 1980. 15.95 o.p. (ISBN 0-87156-198-0); pap. 7.95 o.p. (ISBN 0-87156-199-9). Sierra.

News Reporting & Writing. 2nd ed. Melvin [illegible]cher. 500p. 1980. pap. text ed. write for [illegible] SBN 0-697-04338-X); write for info. [illegible] (ISBN 0-697-04343-6); write for info. [illegible]. manual (ISBN 0-697-04339-8). Wm C [illegible]own.
[illegible]ews Writing. George A. Hough. 1975. text ed. 13.95 o.p. (ISBN 0-395-18593-9); instructor's manual pap. 2.00 o.p. (ISBN 0-395-18788-5); wkbk. 7.25 o.p. (ISBN 0-395-18597-1). HM.
News Writing. 2nd ed. George A. Hough. LC 79-91631. (Illus.). 1980. text ed. 14.50 (ISBN 0-395-28636-0); inst. man. 0.75 (ISBN 0-395-28638-7). HM.
News Writing. M. Lyle Spencer. 357p. 1980. Repr. of 1917 ed. lib. bdg. 30.00 (ISBN 0-89760-828-3). Telegraph Bks.
News Writing for Non-Professionals. Walter C. Line. LC 78-20771. 1979. 12.95 (ISBN 0-88229-348-6). Nelson-Hall.
Newscasters: The News Business As Show Business. Ron Powers. LC 76-62789. 256p. 1977. 8.95 o.p. (ISBN 0-312-57207-7). St Martin.
Newscasters: The News Business As Show Business. Ron Powers. LC 76-62789. 1978. pap. 4.95 o.p. (ISBN 0-312-57208-5). St Martin.
Newsdeath. Ray Connolly. LC 77-15840. 1978. 8.95 o.p. (ISBN 0-689-10872-9). Atheneum.
Newsgathering. K. Metgler. pap. 14.50 (ISBN 0-13-621037-6). P-H.
Newsletter Editor's Desk Book. 2nd, rev. ed. Marvin Arth & Helen Ashmore. 168p. (Orig.). 14.95 (ISBN 0-938270-00-1); pap. 8.95 (ISBN 0-686-28910-2). Kindinger.
Newsletter Editor's Desk Book. 2nd rev. ed. Marvin Arth & Helen Ashmore. LC 80-83042. (Illus.). 168p. (gr. 11-12). 1980. pap. 9.95 (ISBN 0-938270-00-1). Kindinger.
Newsletter Editor's Deskbook. Marvin Arth & Helen Ashmore. 1981. 14.95 (ISBN 0-938270-01-X). Kindinger.
Newspaper Advertising Handbook. Don Watkins. LC 80-10996. (Illus.). 112p. 1980. 12.95 (ISBN 0-936294-01-9); pap. 7.95 (ISBN 0-936294-00-0). Newspaper Bk.
Newspaper: An Alternative Textbook. J. Rodney Short & Beverly Dickerson. LC 79-54759. (gr. 6-11). 1980. pap. 5.50 (ISBN 0-8224-4661-8). Pitman Learning.
Newspaper: An Introduction to Newswriting & Reporting. Ronald P. Lovell. 1979. pap. text ed. 12.95x (ISBN 0-534-00729-5). Wadsworth Pub.
Newspaper & You. Diane Golder. (Orig.). (gr. 9). 1980. wkbk. 5.83 (ISBN 0-87720-300-8). AMSCO Sch.
Newspaper Days. H. L. Mencken. 1955. Repr. 8.95 o.p. (ISBN 0-394-43831-0). Knopf.
Newspaper: Everything You Need to Know to Make It in the Newspaper Business. D. E. Newsom. (Illus.). 256p. 1981. 19.95 (ISBN 0-13-616045-X, Spectrum); pap. 10.95 (ISBN 0-13-616037-9). P-H.
Newspaper Game. Paul Hoch. LC 74-192811. 1979. 10.95 (ISBN 0-7145-0857-8, Pub. by M Boyars); pap. 5.95 (ISBN 0-7145-1125-0, Pub. by M Boyars). Merrimack Bk Serv.
Newspaper Indexes: A Location & Subject Guide for Researchers. Anita C. Milner. LC 77-7130. 1977. 10.00 (ISBN 0-8108-1066-2). Scarecrow.
Newspaper Indexes: A Location & Subject Guide for Researchers, Vol. II. Anita C. Milner. LC 77-7130. 303p. 1979. 11.00 (ISBN 0-8108-1244-4). Scarecrow.
Newspaper Industry in the Nineteen Eighties: An Assessment of Economics & Technology. (Communications Library). 1980. 29.95x (ISBN 0-914236-37-7). Knowledge Indus.
Newspaper Press in Kentucky. Herndon J. Evans. LC 76-24340. (Kentucky Bicentennial Bookshelf Ser.). (Illus.). 138p. 1976. 5.95 (ISBN 0-8131-0221-9). U Pr of Ky.
Newspaper: Reading Skills. Barbara Gregorich & Carol Zack. LC 78-730963. (Illus.). 1978. pap. text ed. 99.00 (ISBN 0-89290-114-4, A160). Soc for Visual.
Newspaper Story: One Hundred Years of the Boston Globe. Louis M. Lyons. LC 74-152697. (Illus.). 1971. 20.00x (ISBN 0-674-62225-1, Belknap Pr). Harvard U Pr.
Newspapers. Leonard E. Fisher. LC 80-8812. (A Nineteenth Century America Book). (Illus.). 64p. (gr. 5 up). 1981. PLB 7.95 (ISBN 0-8234-0387-4). Holiday.
Newspapers. Frank Huggett. (Liberal Studies). 1972. pap. text ed. 2.50x o.p. (ISBN 0-435-46542-2). Heinemann Ed.
Newspapers & Democracy. Ed. by Anthony Smith. 320p. 1980. text ed. 25.00x (ISBN 0-262-19184-9). MIT Pr.
Newspapers As Organisations. Lars Engwall. 1979. text ed. 29.00x (ISBN 0-566-00262-0, Pub. by Gower Pub Co England). Renouf.
Newspapers As Tools for Historians. William H. Taft. 1970. text ed. 3.75x spiral bldg. (ISBN 0-87543-064-3). Lucas.
Newswriting Exercises. Ken Metzler. (Illus.). 288p. 1981. pap. text ed. 11.95 (ISBN 0-13-617803-0). P-H.
Newton D. Baker: A Biography. C. H. Cramer. Ed. by Frank Freidel. LC 78-66521. (The History of the United States: Vol. 4). 316p. 1979. lib. bdg. 24.00 (ISBN 0-8240-9708-4). Garland Pub.
Newtonian Revolution. I. B. Cohen. LC 79-18637. 1981. 37.50 (ISBN 0-521-22964-2). Cambridge U Pr.
Next. Bob Randall. 352p. (Orig.). 1981. pap. 2.75 (ISBN 0-446-95740-2). Warner Bks.
Next Door to Danger. Charlotte MacLeod. (YA) 5.95 (ISBN 0-685-07450-1, Avalon). Bouregy.
Next Phase in Foreign Policy. Ed. by Henry Owen et al. 1973. 14.95 (ISBN 0-8157-6766-8); pap. 5.95 (ISBN 0-8157-6765-X). Brookings.
Next Room of the Dream: Poems & Two Plays. Howard Nemerov. LC 62-22328. 1962. 5.75x o.s.i. (ISBN 0-226-57249-8). U of Chicago Pr.
Next Stop, Earth. William Butterworth. LC 77-18346. (Illus.). (gr. 2-4). 1978. 5.95 o.p. (ISBN 0-8027-6322-7); PLB 5.85 (ISBN 0-8027-6323-5). Walker & Co.
Next to Nothing: Collected Poems 1926-1977. Paul Bowles. 80p. (Orig.). 1981. 14.00 (ISBN 0-87685-505-2); pap. 4.00 (ISBN 0-87685-504-4); signed edition 20.00 (ISBN 0-87685-506-0). Black Sparrow.
Next Whole Earth Catalog: Access to Tools. Ed. by Stewart Brand. (Illus.). 608p. 1980. pap. 12.95 (ISBN 0-394-73951-5). Random.
Next Year I'll Be Special. Patricia G. Giff. LC 79-19174. 32p. (gr. k-3). 1980. PLB 7.95 (ISBN 0-525-35810-2). Dutton.
Nexus Psychotherapy: Between Humanism & Behaviorism. Kenneth U. Gutsch & Jacob V. Ritenour. (Illus.). 196p. 1978. 19.75 (ISBN 0-398-03734-5). C C Thomas.
Nez Perce Grammar. Harro Aoki. (California Library Reprint). 1974. 20.00x (ISBN 0-520-02524-5). U of Cal Pr.
Nez Perce Indians. Incl. Aboriginal Territory of the Nez Perce Indians. Stuart A. Chalfant; Ethnology of the Joseph Band of the Nez Perce Indians, 1805-1905. Verne F. Ray; Findings of Fact, & Opinion. Indian Claims Commission. (American Indian Ethnohistory Ser: Indians of the Northwest). (Illus.). lib. bdg. 42.00 (ISBN 0-8240-0762-X). Garland Pub.
Nez Perce Joseph. Oliver O. Howard. LC 70-39379. (Law, Politics, & History Ser). (Illus.). 274p. 1972. Repr. of 1881 ed. lib. bdg. 37.50 (ISBN 0-306-70461-7). Da Capo.
Nez Perce Texts. Haruo Aoki. LC 77-91776. (Publications in Linguistics: Vol. 90). 1979. 12.75x (ISBN 0-520-09593-6). U of Cal Pr.
Nez Perces: Tribesmen of the Columbia Plateau. Francis Haines. LC 55-9626. (Civilization of American Indian Ser.: No. 42). (Illus.). 1955. 14.95 (ISBN 0-8061-0325-6); pap. 6.95 (ISBN 0-8061-0982-3). U of Okla Pr.
NFL Nineteen Eighty-One Media Information Book. NFL Public Relations Dept. (Illus.). 130p. 1981. pap. 7.95 (ISBN 0-89480-148-1). Workman Pub.
Ngaanyatjarra Texts. rev. ed. Amee Glass & Dorothy Hackett. (AIAS New Ser.: No. 16). 144p. 1979. pap. text ed. 9.25x (ISBN 0-391-01683-0). Humanities.
Ngiyambaa: The Language of the Wangaaybuwan. T. Donaldson. LC 79-7646. (Cambridge Studies in Linguistics: No. 29). (Illus.). 320p. 1980. 59.50 (ISBN 0-521-22524-8). Cambridge U Pr.
N'heures Souris Rames: The Coucy Castle Manuscript. Ormonde Dekay. (Clarkson N. Potter Bks.). 1980. 7.95 (ISBN 0-517-54081-9). Crown.
Niagara Escarpment: From Tobermory to Niagara Falls. William H. Gillard & Thomas R. Tooke. LC 73-84434. (Illus.). 1974. pap. 4.95 (ISBN 0-8020-6214-8). U of Toronto Pr.
NIBM: A Decade of Progress in Burn Medicine. National Institute for Burn Medicine. LC 80-82419. (Illus.). pap. write for info. Natl Inst Burn.
Nicanor's Gate. Eric A. Kimmel. 32p. (gr. k-4). 1979. 5.95 (ISBN 0-8276-0168-9). Jewish Pubn.
Nicaragua: A Profile. Thomas W. Walker. (Nations of Contemporary Latin America). 128p. 1981. lib. bdg. 16.50x (ISBN 0-89158-947-3). Westview.
Nicaragua: An Ally Under Seige. Ed. by Belden Bell. 1978. pap. 10.00 (ISBN 0-685-59450-5). Coun Am Affair.
Nicaragua Betrayed. Anastasio Somoza. 1980. 15.00 (ISBN 0-88279-235-0). Western Islands.
Nicaragua in Revolution: The Poets Speak. Ed. by Bridget Aldaraca et al. LC 80-16304. (Studies in Marxism: Vol. 5). (Bilingual: spanish & english). 1980. 12.95 (ISBN 0-930656-10-5); pap. 6.95 (ISBN 0-930656-09-1). Marxist Educ.
Nicaragua-June Nineteen Seventy-Eight to July Nineteen Seventy-Nine. Susan Meiselas. (Illus.). 1981. 20.00 (ISBN 0-394-51265-0); pap. 11.95 (ISBN 0-394-73931-0). Pantheon.
Nicaragua Traicionada. Anastasio Somoza. 1980. pap. 7.95 (ISBN 0-88279-128-1). Western Island.
Niccolo Jommelli: The Last Years, Seventeen Sixty-Nine to Seventeen Seventy-Four. Marita P. McClymonds. Ed. by George Buelow. (Studies in Musicology). 700p. 1981. 59.95 (ISBN 0-8357-1113-7, Pub. by UMI Res Pr). Univ Microfilms.
Nice & cozy. Bijou Le Tord. LC 80-11376. (Illus.). 32p. (ps-3). 1980. 8.95 (ISBN 0-590-07668-X, Four Winds). Schol Bk Serv.
Nice Day Out? Dick Cate. (Illus.). (gr. 3-6). 1981. 7.95 (ISBN 0-525-66700-8). Elsevier-Nelson.
Nice Little Girls. Elizabeth Levy. LC 73-15394. (Illus.). 48p. (gr. k-3). 1974. 6.95 o.s.i. (ISBN 0-440-06207-1); PLB 6.46 o.s.i. (ISBN 0-440-06193-8). Delacorte.
Nice New Neighbors. Brandenberg. (ps-3). 1980. pap. 1.50 (ISBN 0-590-30070-9, Schol Pap). Schol Bk Serv.
Nicene & Post Nicene Fathers. Repr. of 14 vols. 185.00 set (ISBN 0-686-12360-3); 14.50 ea. (ISBN 0-686-12362-X). Church History.
Nicene Creed Illumined by Modern Thought. Geddes MacGregor. 1981. pap. 7.95 (ISBN 0-8028-1855-2). Eerdmans.
Nichiren: Selected Readings. Laurel R. Rodd. LC 79-17054. (Asian Studies in Hawaii: No. 26). 224p. 1980. pap. text ed. 9.75x (ISBN 0-8248-0682-4). U Pr of Hawaii.
Nicholas. Ginny Cowles. LC 74-11432. (Illus.). 40p. (ps-3). 1975. 6.95 (ISBN 0-395-28785-5, Clarion). HM.
Nicholas Fernandez de Moratin. David T. Gies. (World Authors Ser.: No. 558). 1979. lib. bdg. 14.50 (ISBN 0-8057-6400-3). Twayne.
Nicholas Hilliard. Roy Strong. (Folio Miniature Ser.). 1975. 4.95 (ISBN 0-7181-1301-2, Pub. by Michael Joseph). Merrimack Bk Serv.
Nicholas I & Official Nationality in Russia, 1825-1855. Nicholas V. Riasanovsky. (Russian & East European Studies). 1959. 18.50x (ISBN 0-520-01064-7); pap. 5.95x (ISBN 0-520-01065-5, CAMPUS 120). U of Cal Pr.
Nicholas I: Emperor & Autocrat of All the Russias. W. Bruce Lincoln. LC 77-15764. 424p. 1980. pap. 7.95x (ISBN 0-253-20254-X). Ind U Pr.
Nicholas Murray Butler. Albert Marrin. (World Leaders Ser.: No. 52). 1976. lib. bdg. 10.95 (ISBN 0-8057-7706-7). Twayne.
Nicholas Murray Butler & Public Education 1862-1911. Richard Whittemore. LC 78-122749. 1970. text ed. 13.75x (ISBN 0-8077-2336-3). Tchrs Coll.
Nicholas Nickelby. Charles Dickens. 1957. 15.50x (ISBN 0-460-00238-4, Evman); pap. 4.95 o.p. (ISBN 0-460-01238-X). Dutton.
Nicholas Nickelby. Charles Dickens. Ed. by Michael Slater. (English Library). 1978. pap. 4.95 (ISBN 0-14-043113-6). Penguin.
Nicholas of Cusa on Learned Ignorance: A Translation & an Appraisal of De Docta Ignorantia. Jasper Hopkins. (Texts & Studies in Religion: Vol. 9). 256p. 1981. cancelled (ISBN 0-88946-978-4); cancelled soft cover (ISBN 0-88946-980-6). E Mellen.
Nicholas of Cusa on Learned Ignorance: A Translation & an Appraisal of De Docta Ignorantia. Jasper Hopkins. LC 80-82907. (Illus.). 216p. text ed. 27.00x (ISBN 0-938060-23-6). Banning Pr.
Nicholas of Cusa's Debate with John Wenck: A Translation & an Appraisal of De Ignota Litteratura & Apologia Doctae Ignorantiae. Jasper Hopkins. LC 80-82908. 1981. 23.00x (ISBN 0-938060-24-4). Banning Pr.
Nicholas of Cusa's Debate with John Wenck: A Translation & Appraisal of De Ignota Litteratura & Apologia Doctae Ignorantiae. Jasper Hopkins. (Texts & Studies in Religion: Vol. 10). 128p. 1981. cancelled (ISBN 0-88946-979-2); cancelled (ISBN 0-88946-981-4). E Mellen.
Nicholas Poussin. 2 Vols. Anthony Blunt. (Bollinger Ser.: No. 35). (Illus.). 1966. 60.00x, boxed o.p. (ISBN 0-691-09791-7). Princeton U Pr.
Nicholas Ray. John F. Kreidl. (Theatrical Arts Ser.). 1977. lib. bdg. 12.50 (ISBN 0-8057-9250-3). Twayne.
Nicholas Rowe. Annibel Jenkins. (English Authors Ser.: No. 200). 1977. lib. bdg. 10.95 (ISBN 0-8057-6663-4). Twayne.
Nichols File of "The Gentleman's Magazine". Ed. by Kuist. 300p. 1981. 50.00 (ISBN 0-299-08480-9). U of Wis Pr.
Nicholson at Large. Ward Just. 256p. 1976. pap. 1.95 o.p. (ISBN 0-345-25151-2). Ballantine.
Nicholson's Complete London. Nicholson Publications. 1978. pap. 5.95 (ISBN 0-684-15640-7, SL794, ScribT). Scribner.
Nichovev Plot. (Nick Carter Ser.). 1978. pap. 1.75 (ISBN 0-441-57435-1). Charter Bks.
Nicht-Euklidische Geometrie. Felix Klein. LC 59-10281. (Ger). 12.00 (ISBN 0-8284-0129-2). Chelsea Pub.
Nick Joins in. Joe Lasker. Ed. by Kathleen Tucker. LC 79-29637. (Concept Bk.: Level 1). (Illus.). (gr. 1-3). 1980. PLB 6.95g (ISBN 0-8075-5612-2). A Whitman.
Nickel. Committee on Medical & Biological Effects of Environmental Pollutants. 1975. pap. 15.00 (ISBN 0-309-02314-9). Natl Acad Pr.
Nickel & Chromium Plating. Dennis T. Such. 1972. pap. text ed. 34.95 (ISBN 0-408-00086-4). Butterworths.
Nickel & Its Alloys. W. Betteridge. (Illus.). 160p. 1977. pap. 12.95x (ISBN 0-7121-0947-1, Pub. by Macdonald & Evans England). Intl Ideas.
Nickel Chimera. Steven D. Lakey. LC 80-65824. (Illus.). 60p. 1980. 4.95 (ISBN 0-936748-00-1); pap. 2.95 (ISBN 0-936748-01-X). Fade In.
Nickel in the Environment. Jerome O. Nriagu. LC 80-16600. (Environmental Science & Technology: a Wiley Interscience Ser. of Texts & Monographs). 833p. 1980. 65.00 (ISBN 0-471-05885-8, Pub. by Wiley Interscience). Wiley.
Nickel Industry & the Developing Countries. 100p. 1980. pap. 8.00 (UN80-2A2, UN). Unipub.
Nickel Plating. Robert Brugger. LC 70-523834. 1970. 32.50x (ISBN 0-85218-031-4). Intl Pubns Serv.
Nickelodeon. E. M. Corder. 1976. pap. 1.50 o.p. (ISBN 0-345-25471-6). Ballantine.
Nickels & Dimes: The Story of F. W. Woolworth. Nina B. Baker. LC 54-9621. (gr. 4-7). 1966. pap. 0.50 o.p. (ISBN 0-15-665590-X, AVB17, VoyB). HarBraceJ.
Nickle Nackle Tree. Lynley Dodd. LC 77-12493. (Illus.). (gr. k-3). 1978. 8.95 (ISBN 0-02-732610-1, 73261). Macmillan.
Nicknames & Pseudonyms. Lawrence H. Dawson. LC 73-164216. viii, 312p. 1974. Repr. of 1908 ed. 24.00 (ISBN 0-8103-3177-2). Gale.
Nicknames & Sobriquets of U. S. Cities, States, & Counties. 3rd ed. Joseph N. Kane & Gerard L. Alexander. LC 79-20193. 445p. 1979. 19.00 (ISBN 0-8108-1255-X). Scarecrow.
Nicknames: Their Origins & Social Consequences. Jane Morgan et al. (Social Worlds of Childhood Ser.). 1979. 16.00x (ISBN 0-7100-0139-8). Routledge & Kegan.
Nicky & the Joyous Noise. Mildred Ames. LC 80-384. (gr. 4-6). 1980. 8.95 (ISBN 0-684-16524-4). Scribner.
Nicky-Sunny Letters: Letters of the Tsar to the Tsaritsa, 1914-1917 & Letters of the Tsaritsa to the Tsar, 1914-1916, 2 vols. in 1. (Russian Ser.: Vol. 2). 30.00 (ISBN 0-87569-015-7). Academic Intl.
Nicola Pisano & the Revival of Sculpture in Italy. George H. Crichton. LC 78-59011. (Illus.). 1981. Repr. of 1938 ed. 23.50 (ISBN 0-88355-686-3). Hyperion Conn.
Nicolas Malebranche: Dialogue Between a Christian Philosopher & a Chinese Philosopher on the Existence & Nature of God. Dominick A. Iorio. LC 80-5045. 115p. 1980. text ed. 16.00 (ISBN 0-8191-1027-2); pap. text ed. 7.50 (ISBN 0-8191-1028-0). U Pr of Amer.
Nicolas Roeg. Neil Feineman. (Theatrical Art Ser.). 1978. 12.50 (ISBN 0-8057-9258-9). Twayne.
Nicole Oresme & the Kinematics of Circular Motion: Tractatus De Commensurabilitate Vel Incommensurabilitate Motuum Celi. Ed. by Edward Grant. LC 79-133238. (Medieval Science Ser). 1971. 50.00 (ISBN 0-299-05830-1). U of Wis Pr.
Nicole Oresme & the Medieval Geometry of Qualities & Motions. Tr. by Marshall Clagett. (Medieval Science Pubns., No. 12). (Illus.). 1968. 50.00x (ISBN 0-299-04880-2). U of Wis Pr.
Nicomachean Ethics. Aristotle. Tr. by Martin Ostwald. LC 62-15690. (Orig.). 1962. pap. 4.50 (ISBN 0-672-60256-3, LLA75). Bobbs.
Nicomede. Pierre Corneille. (Documentation thematique). pap. 2.95 (ISBN 0-685-14000-8, 73). Larousse.
Nicomedes Guzman: Proletarian Author in Chile's Literary Generation of 1938. Lon Pearson. LC 75-19334. 320p. 1976. 15.00x (ISBN 0-8262-0178-4). U of Mo Pr.
NICSEM Master Index to Special Education Materials, 3 vols. National Information Center for Special Education Materials (NICSEM) LC 80-83854. 1980. Set. pap. 106.00 (ISBN 0-89320-049-2). Univ SC Natl Info.
NICSEM Mini-index to Special Education Materials: Functional Communication Skills. National Information Center for Special Education Materials (NICSEM) LC 80-82540. 1980. pap. 16.00 (ISBN 0-89320-045-X). Univ SC Natl Info.

NICSEM Mini-Index to Special Education Materials: Family Life & Sex Education. National Information Center for Special Education Materials (NICSEM) LC 80-82540. 1980. pap. 16.00 (ISBN 0-89320-043-3). Univ SC Natl Info.

NICSEM Mini-index to Special Education Materials: High Interests, Controlled Vocabulary Supplementary Reading Materials for Adolescents & Young Adults. National Information Center for Special Education Materials (NICSEM) LC 80-82901. 1980. pap. 16.00 (ISBN 0-89320-047-6). Univ. SC Natl Info.

NICSEM Mini-index to Special Education Materials: Independent Living Skills for Moderately & Severely Handicapped Students. National Information Center for Special Education Materials (NICSEM) LC 80-82530. 1980. pap. 16.00 (ISBN 0-89320-044-1). Univ SC Natl Info.

NICSEM Mini-index to Special Education Materials: Personal & Social Developments for Moderately & Severely Handicapped Students. National Information Center for Special Education Materials (NICSEM) LC 80-82541. 1980. pap. 16.00 (ISBN 0-89320-046-8). Univ SC Natl Info.

NICSEM Source Directory. National Information Center for Special Education Materials (NICSEM) LC 80-83757. 1980. pap. 12.50 (ISBN 0-89320-050-6). Univ SC Natl Info.

NICSEM Special Education Thesaurus. 2nd ed. National Information Center for Educational Media. LC 80-83509. 1980. pap. 16.00 (ISBN 0-89320-028-X). Univ SC Natl Info.

Nida: A Case Study in Institution Development. Choop Karnjanaprakorn et al. 1974. pap. text ed. 3.00 (ISBN 0-89249-007-1). Intl Development.

Nid's Exciting Day. Mary Gurtler. 1961. pap. 0.90 (ISBN 0-85363-033-X). OMF Bks.

Niedere Zahlentheorie, 2 Vols. in 1. Paul Bachmann. LC 66-20395. (Ger). 1968. Repr. of 1902 ed. text ed. 19.50 o.p. (ISBN 0-8284-0217-5). Chelsea Pub.

Niels Hendrik Abel, Mathematician Extraordinary. Oystein Ore. LC 73-14693. (Illus.). viii, 277p. 1974. Repr. of 1957 ed. text ed. 10.95 (ISBN 0-8284-0274-4). Chelsea Pub.

Nietzche As Philosopher. A. Danto. 1965. 9.95 (ISBN 0-02-529490-3); pap. 2.45 (ISBN 0-02-084570-7). Macmillan.

Nietzche: Philosopher, Psychologist, Architect. 4th ed. W. Kaufmann. 1975. 25.00x (ISBN 0-691-07207-8); pap. 6.95 (ISBN 0-691-01983-5). Princeton U Pr.

Nietzche und Emerson. Stanley Hubbard. LC 80-2538. 1981. Repr. of 1958 ed. 25.50 (ISBN 0-404-19264-5). AMS Pr.

Nietzsche. R. J. Hollingdale. (Author Guides Ser). 238p. 1973. 17.50x (ISBN 0-7100-7562-6); pap. 8.95 (ISBN 0-7100-7563-4). Routledge & Kegan.

Nietzsche & Eternal Recurrence: The Redemption of Time & Becoming. Lawrence J. Hatab. LC 78-62266. 1978. pap. text ed. 7.75 (ISBN 0-8191-0564-3). U Pr of Amer.

Nietzsche & Kazantzakis. B. T. McDonough. LC 78-61302. 1978. pap. text ed. 7.25 (ISBN 0-8191-0607-0). U Pr of Amer.

Nietzsche As Philosopher. Arthur Danto. 250p. 1980. pap. 6.95x (ISBN 0-231-05053-4). Columbia U Pr.

Nietzsche: Imagery & Thought. Ed. by Malcolm Pasley. 1978. 23.75x (ISBN 0-520-03577-1). U of Cal Pr.

Nietzsche in Anglosaxony: A Study of Nietzsche's Impact on English & American Literature. Patrick Bridgewater. 250p. 1972. text ed. 10.50x (ISBN 0-7185-1104-2, Leicester). Humanities.

Nietzsche on Tragedy. M. S. Silk & J. P. Stern. LC 80-40433. 500p. Date not set. price not set (ISBN 0-521-23262-7). Cambridge U Pr.

Nietzsche-Studien. Ed. by Ernst Behler et al. (Internationales Jahrbuch Fur Die Nietzsche-Forschung: Vol. 9). 400p. 1980. text ed. 92.50x (ISBN 3-11-008241-1). De Gruyter.

Nietzsche's Gift. Harold G. Alderman. LC 76-25612. xvi, 184p. 1977. 15.00x (ISBN 0-8214-0231-5); pap. 5.50 (ISBN 0-8214-0385-0). Ohio U Pr.

Nietzsche's Thought of Eternal Return. Joan Stambaugh. LC 75-171553. 144p. 1972. 10.00x o.p. (ISBN 0-8018-1288-7). Johns Hopkins.

Nigeria. Ernest Dunbar. LC 74-913. (First Bks). (Illus.). 96p. (gr. 6 up). 1974. PLB 4.90 o.p. (ISBN 0-531-02720-1). Watts.

Nigeria: Background to Nationalism. James S. Coleman. (California Library Reprint Series: No. 28). 1971. 32.50x (ISBN 0-520-02070-7). U of Cal Pr.

Nigeria in History. A. Fajana & J. Biggs. (Illus., Orig.). 1967. pap. text ed. 2.50x (ISBN 0-582-60242-4). Humanities.

Nigeria in the First World War. Akinjide Osuntokun. (Ibadan History Ser.). 1979. text ed. 30.75x (ISBN 0-391-00916-8). Humanities.

Nigerian Capitalism. Sayre P. Schatz. LC 74-16718. 1978. 27.50x (ISBN 0-520-02859-7). U of Cal Pr.

Nigerian Financial System. G. O. Nwanko. 400p. 1980. text ed. 43.50x (ISBN 0-8419-5076-8). Holmes & Meier.

Nigerian Groundnut Exports: Origins & Early Developments. J. S. Hogendorn. (Illus.). 1979. 29.95x (ISBN 0-19-575443-3). Oxford U Pr.

Nigerian Military: A Sociological Analysis of Authority & Revolt, 1960-67. Robin Luckham. (African Studies: No. 4). (Illus.). 1971. 39.95 (ISBN 0-521-08129-7); pap. 11.95x (ISBN 0-521-09882-3). Cambridge U Pr.

Nigerian Politics & Military Rule: Prelude to the Civil War. Ed. by S. K. Panter-Brick. (Athlone Commonwealth Papers: No. 13). 1970. text ed. 9.75x (ISBN 0-485-17613-0, Athlone Pr). Humanities.

Nigerian Public Finance. P. N. Okigbo. (African Studies Ser.: No. 15). 1965. 12.95x o.s.i. (ISBN 0-8101-0181-5). Northwestern U Pr.

Nigerian War: 1967-70. Zdenek Cervenka. LC 73-885548. (Illus.). 459p. 1971. pap. 40.00x (ISBN 3-7637-0210-5). Intl Pubns Serv.

Nigeria's Educator-Statesman: Selected Writings of Eyo Ita. Ed. by E. U. Oton. 1980. 25.00x (ISBN 0-7146-2731-3, F Cass Co). Biblio Dist.

Nigeria's Financial System. P. N. Okigbo. (Illus.). 320p. 1981. text ed. 25.00x (ISBN 0-582-59733-1). Longman.

Nigeria's Leadership Role in Africa. Joseph Wayas. 1979. text ed. 26.00x (ISBN 0-333-26295-6). Humanities.

Nigger: An Autobiography. Dick Gregory. Ed. by Robert Lipsyte. 1964. 7.95 o.p. (ISBN 0-525-16697-1). Dutton.

Nigger of the "Narcissus". Joseph Conrad. Ed. by Robert Kimbrough. (Norton Critical Editions). 1979. 12.95 (ISBN 0-393-04517-X); pap. 4.95 (ISBN 0-393-09019-1). Norton.

Nigger of the Narcissus. Joseph Conrad. lib. bdg. 12.95x (ISBN 0-89966-055-X). Buccaneer Bks.

Nigger Question. Thomas Carlyle. Ed. by Eugene R. August. Bd. with Negro Question. John S. Mill. LC 73-14584. (Crofts Classics Ser.). 1971. text ed. 5.95x (ISBN 0-88295-021-5); pap. text ed. 1.25x (ISBN 0-88295-020-7). AHM Pub.

Night, a Descriptive Poem, Pt. 1, 4 Bks., Repr. Of 1813. Ebenezer Elliott. Bd. with Love, a Poem in Three Parts. To Which Is Added, the Giaour, a Satirical Poem. Repr. of 1823 ed. LC 75-31200. (Romantic Context Ser.: Poetry 1789-1830: Vol. 52). 1978. lib. bdg. 47.00 (ISBN 0-8240-2151-7). Garland Pub.

Night Action. Peter Dickens. 256p. 1981. pap. 2.50 (ISBN 0-553-14764-1). Bantam.

Night After the Wedding. The Gordons. LC 78-20073. 288p. 1979. 8.95 (ISBN 0-385-14012-6). Doubleday.

Night Again. Karla Kuskin. (Illus.). 32p. (ps-1). 1981. 6.95 (ISBN 0-316-50721-0, Atlantic). Little.

Night & Day. Tom Stoppard. LC 78-73218. 1979. 10.00 (ISBN 0-394-50526-3, GP 825, Grove). Grove.

Night & Day: The Interaction Between an Academic Institution & Its Evening College. Myrtle S. Jacobson. 1970. 12.50 o.p. (ISBN 0-8108-0324-0). Scarecrow.

Night & Shift Work- Biological & Social Aspects: Proceedings of the Vth International Symposium on Night and Shift Work-Scientific Committee on Shift Work of the Permanent Commission & International Association on Occupational Health (PCIAIH, Rouen, 12-16 May 1980. Ed. by A. Reinberg et al. (Illus.). 516p. 1981. 80.00 (ISBN 0-08-025516-7). Pergamon.

Night & the Sublime in Giacomo Leopardi. Nicolas J. Perella. (U. C. Publ. in Modern Philology: Vol. 99). 1971. pap. 9.00x (ISBN 0-520-09368-2). U of Cal Pr.

Night Animals. (gr. 1). Date not set. pap. cancelled (ISBN 0-590-30058-X, Schol Pap). Schol Bk Serv.

Night Animals. Millicent E. Selsam. LC 80-13465. (Illus.). 40p. (gr. 1-5). 1980. 7.95 (ISBN 0-590-07755-4, Four Winds). Schol Bk Serv.

Night at the Vulcan. Ngaio Marsh. 1977. pap. 1.75 o.s.i. (ISBN 0-515-05293-0). Jove Pubns.

Night Before Christmas. Clement Moore. LC 79-165390. (Illus.). 1971. pap. 1.50 (ISBN 0-486-22797-9). Dover.

Night Before Christmas. Clement Moore. LC 80-11758. (Illus.). 32p. (ps up). 1980. PLB 10.95 (ISBN 0-8234-0414-5); pap. 4.95 (ISBN 0-8234-0417-X). Holiday.

Night Before Christmas. Clement C. Moore. LC 78-72136. (Illus.). (gr. k-5). Date not set. price not set (ISBN 0-89799-143-5); pap. price not set (ISBN 0-89799-061-7). Dandelion Pr. Postponed.

Night Before Christmas. Clement C. Moore. (Golden Storytime Bk.). (Illus.). 1981. 1.95 (ISBN 0-307-11956-4, Golden Pr). Western Pub.

Night Before Christmas-in Texas,That Is. Leon Harris. (Illus.). (gr. k-7). 1977. Repr. of 1952 ed. 6.95 (ISBN 0-88289-175-8). Pelican.

Night Before the Wedding. The Gordons. LC 68-22621. 1969. 5.50 o.p. (ISBN 0-385-04130-6). Doubleday.

Night Before Us. Deb K. Das. 8.00 (ISBN 0-89253-489-3); flexible cloth 4.00 (ISBN 0-89253-490-7). Ind-US Inc.

Night-Blooming Cactus. Robert Watson. LC 80-65999. 1980. 10.00 (ISBN 0-689-11090-1); pap. 5.95. Atheneum.

Night Boat. Robert A. McCammon. 1980. 2.50 (ISBN 0-380-75598-X, 75598). Avon.

Night Book. William Kotzwinkle. 1980. pap. 2.50 (ISBN 0-380-49106-0, 49106, Bard). Avon.

Night Branders. Walt Coburn. 1979. pap. 1.50 (ISBN 0-505-51348-X). Tower Bks.

Night Caller. Brennan Patrick. (Orig.). 1981. pap. 2.25 (ISBN 0-440-16674-8). Dell.

Night Chase. Cheryl Herbert. LC 77-71006. (Crown Ser.). 1977. pap. 4.50 (ISBN 0-8127-0135-6). Southern Pub.

Night Chasers. Jamey Cohen. 353p. 1981. 11.95 (ISBN 0-87223-685-4). Seaview Bks.

Night Child. Celeste De Blasis. 1979. pap. 1.95 o.p. (ISBN 0-449-23927-6, Crest). Fawcett.

Night Chills. Kirby E. McCauley. (Orig.). 1975. pap. 1.50 (ISBN 0-380-00397-X, 26856). Avon.

Night Cover. Michael Z. Lewin. 1980. pap. 1.95 o.p. (ISBN 0-425-04030-5). Berkley Pub.

Night Creature: A Journal of Jazz, 1975-1980. Whitney Balliett. (Illus.). 275p. 1981. 15.95 (ISBN 0-19-502908-9). Oxford U Pr.

Night Cries. Michael Benedikt. LC 75-32526. (Wesleyan Poetry Program: Vol. 80). 1976. 10.00x (ISBN 0-8195-2080-2, Pub. by Wesleyan U Pr); pap. 4.95 (ISBN 0-8195-1080-7). Columbia U Pr.

Night Falls Too Soon. Francesca Chimenti. 1978. pap. 1.50 o.s.i. (ISBN 0-515-04552-7). Jove Pubns.

Night Flight. Antoine De Saint-Exupery. Tr. by Stuart Gilbert from Fr. LC 73-16016. Orig. Title: Vol De Nuit. 87p. 1974. pap. 1.95 (ISBN 0-15-665605-1, HPL63, HPL). HarBraceJ.

Night Flight to Brussels. Roger J. De Wiest. LC 80-84739. 1981. 15.00 (ISBN 0-686-68869-4). Philos Lib.

Night Flyers. George R. Martin. Bd. with True Names. Vernor Vinge. (Binary Star: No. 5). (Orig.). 1981. pap. 2.50 (ISBN 0-440-10757-1). Dell.

Night Hell's Corners Died. Clay Ringold. 1978. Repr. of 1972 ed. 1.25 (ISBN 0-505-51328-5). Tower Bks.

Night Jasmine. Mary Lou Widmer. 1980. pap. 2.75 (ISBN 0-440-16558-X). Dell.

Night Jump--Cuba. Poke Runyon. 1978. 1.75 o.s.i. (ISBN 0-515-04819-4). Jove Pubns.

Night Land. W. H. Hodgson. 1976. lib. bdg. 12.95x (ISBN 0-89968-179-4). Lightyear.

Night Life: Explorations in Dreaming. Rosalind D. Cartwright. (Illus.). 1977. 10.95 (ISBN 0-13-622324-9, Spec); pap. 4.95 (ISBN 0-13-622316-8). P-H.

Night Life of Indian Tribals. S. S. Shashi. 1978. 11.00x o.p. (ISBN 0-8364-0440-8). South Asia Bks.

Night Lords. Nicolas Freeling. LC 78-55242. 1978. 7.95 (ISBN 0-394-50281-7). Pantheon.

Night Marshal. L. P. Holmes. 1981. pap. 1.75 (ISBN 0-445-00701-X). Popular Lib.

Night Monsters. Sharon Shebar. Ed. by Dan Wasserman. (Ten Word Bks.). (Illus.). (gr. k-1). 1979. PLB 4.50 (ISBN 0-89868-068-9); pap. 1.95 (ISBN 0-89868-079-4). ARO Pub.

Night Music. Charlotte Lamb. (Harlequin Presents Ser.). 192p. (Orig.). 1981. pap. 1.50 (ISBN 0-373-10404-9, Pub. by Harlequin). PB.

Night of Gaiety, No. 142. Barbara Cartland. (Orig.). 1981. pap. 1.95 (ISBN 0-553-14791-9). Bantam.

Night of Kadar. Garry Kilworth. 208p. 1979. pap. 1.95 (ISBN 0-380-50070-1, 50070-1). Avon.

Night of the Blood Moon. Grover Brinkman. 200p. (gr. 4-6). 1976. 8.00 o.p. (ISBN 0-8309-0149-3). Independence Pr.

Night of the Funny Hats. Elspeth Davie. 192p. 1980. 18.50 o.p. (ISBN 0-241-10377-0, Pub. by Hamish Hamilton England). David & Charles.

Night of the Grizzlies. Jack Olsen. 1971. pap. 1.75 (ISBN 0-451-08806-9, E8806, Sig). NAL.

Night of the Hammer. Ned O'Gorman. LC 59-6419. 1959. 4.50 o.p. (ISBN 0-15-165621-5). HarBraceJ.

Night of the Kachina. Nichole Salas. LC 78-16066. (Pacesetters Ser.). (Illus.). (gr. 4 up). 1978. PLB 7.95 (ISBN 0-516-02157-5). Childrens.

Night of the Lionhead. Ashley Saunders. 67p. 1979. 2.95 (ISBN 0-8059-2571-6). Dorrance.

Night of the Scorpion. large type ed. Saliee O'Brien. pap. 1.50 o.p. (ISBN 0-425-03238-8). Berkley Pub.

Night of the Tribades: A Play from 1889. Per Olov Enquist. Tr. by Ross Shideler from Swedish. 81p. 1977. 9.95 (ISBN 0-8090-7365-X); pap. 3.95 o.p. (ISBN 0-8090-1237-5). Hill & Wang.

Night Raid. Frank Bonham. 1978. pap. 1.50 o.p. (ISBN 0-425-03770-3, Medallion). Berkley Pub.

Night Raid. 1981. pap. 1.95 (ISBN 0-425-04814-4). Berkley Pub.

Night Raider & Other Stories. Walter D. Edmonds. 96p. (gr. 7 up). 1980. 6.95g (ISBN 0-316-21141-9). Little.

Night Riders. Keith Jarrod. 1980. pap. 1.95 (ISBN 0-440-16368-4). Dell.

Night Riders in Black Folk History. Gladys-Marie Fry. LC 74-34268. (Illus.). 264p. 1975. pap. 7.95x (ISBN 0-87049-238-1). U of Tenn Pr.

Night Riders of Reelfoot Lake. Paul J. Vanderwood. LC 79-91959. (Illus.). 1980. pap. 6.95 (ISBN 0-87870-196-6). Memphis St Univ.

Night Scenes in the Bible. Daniel March. LC 77-189204. 1972. 8.95 (ISBN 0-8254-3211-1). Kregel.

Night Screams. Bill Pronzini & Barry N. Malzberg. LC 80-83596. 304p. 1981. pap. 2.75 (ISBN 0-87216-788-7). Playboy Pbks.

Night She Died. Dorothy Simpson. 192p. 1981. 8.95 (ISBN 0-684-16869-3, ScribT). Scribner.

Night-Side. Joyce C. Oates. LC 77-77416. 1977. 10.95 (ISBN 0-8149-0793-8). Vanguard.

Night Stand: A Book of Stories. James McConkey. 207p. 1965. 12.50x (ISBN 0-8014-0280-8). Cornell U Pr.

Night Story. Ethel Kessler & Leonard Kessler. LC 80-24626. (Ready-to-Read Ser.). (Illus.). 48p. (gr. 1-4). 1981. PLB 7.95 (ISBN 0-02-750220-1). Macmillan.

Night Studies: A Novel. Cyrus Colter. LC 79-64295. 775p. 1980. 16.00 (ISBN 0-8040-0827-2). Swallow.

Night the Crayons Talked. Vick Knight. 1974. 4.95 (ISBN 0-686-64102-7). Borden.

Night the Sky Lit Up. Freida Andrews. Ed. by Mary Verdick. (Pal Paperbacks - Pal Skills Ser.). (Illus., Orig.). (gr. 7-12). 1978. pap. text ed. 1.25 (ISBN 0-8374-6704-7). Xerox Ed Pubns.

Night Thoughts: Reflections of a Sex Therapist. Avodah Offit. 284p. 1981. 11.95 (ISBN 0-312-92575-1). Congdon & Lattes.

Night Vegetable Eater. Elke Musicant & Ted Musicant. LC 80-22389. (Illus.). 48p. (gr. k-3). 1981. PLB 7.95 (ISBN 0-396-07923-7). Dodd.

Night Visitor. Laura Wylie. 1979. pap. 1.95 o.p. (ISBN 0-523-40398-4). Pinnacle Bks.

Night Voyagers: You & Your Dreams. Sybil Leek. 192p. 1976. pap. 1.50 o.p. (ISBN 0-345-24850-3). Ballantine.

Night Watch. Stephen Koch. 1979. 10.95 (ISBN 0-7145-0411-4, Pub. by M Boyars). Merrimack Bk Serv.

Night Watch. Stephen Koch. 212p. 1981. pap. 6.95 (ISBN 0-7145-2736-X, Pub. by M. Boyars). Merrimack Bk Serv.

Night Watch. Jack Olsen. 1980. pap. 2.75 (ISBN 0-445-04609-0). Popular Lib.

Night Way. Janet Dailey. (Orig.). 1981. pap. 2.75 (ISBN 0-671-83605-6). Pb.

Night Whispers. Charles Veley. 320p. 1981. pap. 2.75 (ISBN 0-345-29150-6). Ballantine.

Night with the Hants & Other Alabama Experiences. Ed. by Ray Browne. LC 76-43449. 1976. 12.95 (ISBN 0-87972-075-1); pap. 6.95 (ISBN 0-87972-167-7). Bowling Green Univ.

Night Without End. Alistair MacLean. 1978. pap. 2.25 (ISBN 0-449-14129-2, GM). Fawcett.

Nightbird. Francoise Sagan. (Clarkson N. Potter Bks.). (Illus.). 1980. 9.95 (ISBN 0-517-54224-2). Crown.

Nightbirds on Nantucket. Joan Aiken. Date not set. pap. 1.75 (ISBN 0-440-96370-2, LE). Dell.

Nightfall. John Crosby. 1977. pap. 1.95 o.s.i. (ISBN 0-446-89354-4). Warner Bks.

Nightfall & Other Stories. Isaac Asimov. 1978. pap. 2.25 (ISBN 0-449-23672-2, Crest). Fawcett.

Nightfrost in Prague: The End of Humane Socialism. Zdenek Mlynar. Tr. by Paul Wilson from Czech. Orig. Title: Mraz Prichazi Z Kremlu. 1980. 16.95x (ISBN 0-918294-08-8). Karz Pub.

Nightgleams (Sagittarius) Julia Thatcher. (Zodiac Gothics). 1976. pap. 1.25 o.p. (ISBN 0-345-25310-8). Ballantine.

Nightingale & the Rose. Oscar Wilde. (Illus.). 32p. (gr. 4 up). 1981. 9.95 (ISBN 0-19-520231-7). Oxford U Pr.

Nightingale for Love. Daisy Thomson. 1978. pap. 1.50 o.s.i. (ISBN 0-515-04488-1). Jove Pubns.

Nightingales. Mary Burchell. (Harlequin Romances Ser.). 192p. 1980. pap. 1.25 (ISBN 0-373-02359-6, Pub. by Harlequin). PB.

Nightmare. Mihaly Babits. Tr. by Eva Racz. 6.50x (ISBN 0-89918-348-4, H348). Vanous.

Nightmare. Richard Owen. LC 79-16339. 1979. 10.95 (ISBN 0-312-57328-6). St Martin.

Nightmare Blue. Gardner Dozois & George A. Effinger. (Orig.). 1975. pap. 0.95 o.p. (ISBN 0-425-02819-4, Medallion). Berkley Pub.

Nightmare Candidate. Ramona Stewart. Date not set. pap. 2.25 (ISBN 0-440-16062-6). Dell.

Nightmare Country. Marlys Millhiser. 384p. 1981. 12.95 (ISBN 0-399-12595-7). Putnam.

Nightmare Express. Isidore Haiblum. 1979. pap. 1.95 o.p. (ISBN 0-449-14204-3, GM). Fawcett.

Nightmare Factor. Thomas N. Scortia & Frank M. Robinson. LC 77-11760. 1978. 10.00 o.p. (ISBN 0-385-11462-1). Doubleday.

Nightmare Factory. Maxine Kumin. LC 77-108941. 1970. 8.95 o.p. (ISBN 0-06-012481-4, HarpT). Har-Row.

Nightmare in Pewter. Jean De Weese. LC 78-3257. 1978. 7.95 o.p. (ISBN 0-385-12097-4). Doubleday.

Nightmare in Pink. John D. MacDonald. LC 75-31753. (Travis McGee Mystery Ser.). 1976. 9.95 (ISBN 0-397-01116-4). Lippincott.

Nightmare Island. Ron Roy. LC 80-23526. (Illus.). 80p. (gr. 3-7). 1981. 7.95 (ISBN 0-525-35905-2). Dutton.

Nightmare Machine. John N. Datesh. 1979. pap. 1.75 (ISBN 0-505-51372-2). Tower Bks.

Nightmares: Poems to Trouble Your Sleep. Jack Prelutsky. LC 76-4820. (Illus.). 40p. (gr. 3 up). 1976. 8.25 (ISBN 0-688-80053-X); PLB 7.92 (ISBN 0-688-84053-1). Greenwillow.

Nightriders. Peter McCurtin. (Sundance Ser.: No. 26). 1976. pap. 1.75 (ISBN 0-8439-0653-7, LB346NK, Leisure Bks). Nordon Pubns.

Nightrunners. Michael Collins. LC 80-84369. 224p. 1981. pap. 2.25 (ISBN 0-87216-822-0). Playboy Pbks.

Nights in the Garden of Love. Peggy Aldrich. (Orig.). 1975. pap. 1.50 o.p. (ISBN 0-685-52939-8, LB256NK, Leisure Bks). Nordon Pubns.

Nights We Put the Rock Together. Clayton Eshleman. LC 79-55418. 1979. signed numbered ed. 9.00 (ISBN 0-686-59689-7); signed numbered ed. 20.00 (ISBN 0-686-59690-0); signed lettered ed. o.p. (ISBN 0-686-59691-9). Cadmus Eds.

Nights with Sasquatch. John Cotter & Judith Frankle. 1977. pap. 1.25 o.p. (ISBN 0-425-03393-7, Medallion). Berkley Pub.

Nights with Uncle Remus: Myths & Legends of the Old Plantation. Joel C. Harris. LC 70-164329. 1971. Repr. of 1883 ed. 26.00 (ISBN 0-8103-3866-1). Gale.

Nightschool for Saints. Ursule Molinaro. 128p. 1981. 10.95 (ISBN 0-89097-021-1); pap. 5.95 (ISBN 0-89097-022-X). Archer Edns.

Nightshades: The Paradoxical Plants. Charles B. Heiser, Jr. LC 70-85798. (Biology Ser.). (Illus.). 1969. text ed. 9.95x (ISBN 0-7167-0672-5). W H Freeman.

Nightside. Thomas Collins. (Orig.). 1979. pap. 2.25 (ISBN 0-532-23143-0). Manor Bks.

Nightwalker. Thomas Tessier. 1981. pap. 2.50 (ISBN 0-451-09720-3, E9720, Sig). NAL.

Nightwatch Winter. Jenny Overton. 1973. 6.50 (ISBN 0-571-09969-6, Pub. by Faber & Faber). Merrimack Bk Serv.

Nightwind. Sarah Allis. 1978. pap. 1.75 o.p. (ISBN 0-449-23693-5, Crest). Fawcett.

Nightwing. Martin C. Smith. 1978. pap. 2.50 (ISBN 0-515-05298-1). Jove Pubns.

Nightwings. Robert Silverberg. 1978. pap. 1.50 (ISBN 0-380-00571-9, 41467). Avon.

Nightwork. Irwin Shaw. 384p. 1975. 8.95 o.s.i. (ISBN 0-440-05757-4). Delacorte.

Nihilism & Culture. Johan Goudsblom. 213p. 1980. 27.50x (ISBN 0-8476-6766-9). Rowman.

Nihilist Egoist: Max Stirner. R. W. Paterson. 1971. 24.95x (ISBN 0-19-713413-0). Oxford U Pr.

Nijinsky & the Last Days of Nijinsky. Romola Nijinsky. 1980. 16.95 (ISBN 0-671-41123-3). S&S.

Nijinsky: The Film. Gelatt. 29.95 (ISBN 0-345-28899-8). Ballantine.

Nikita Sergeievich Khrushchev: Modern Dictator of the USSR. Gerald Kurland. Ed. by D. Steve Rahmas. LC 74-185668. (Outstanding Personalities Ser.: No. 12). 32p. 1972. lib. bdg. 2.75 incl. catalog cards (ISBN 0-87157-512-4); pap. 1.50 vinyl laminated covers (ISBN 0-87157-012-2). SamHar Pr.

Nikki 108. Rose Blue. LC 72-6071. (Illus.). 64p. (gr. 4-8). 1973. PLB 4.90 o.p. (ISBN 0-531-02602-7). Watts.

Nikola D. Obrechkoff: Opera, Vol. I. Ed. by Bulgarian Academy of Sciences. (Illus.). 431p. 1978. 61.50 (ISBN 3-7643-0988-1). Birkhauser.

Nikola Tesla (1856-1943) Lectures, Patents, Articles. Ed. by Popovic. 1977. 60.00 o.p. (ISBN 0-89918-639-4, Y-639). Vanous.

Nikolai Evreinov: A Photo Biography/Fotobiografiia. (Rus. & Eng.). 1981. 17.50 (ISBN 0-88233-619-3). Ardis Pubs.

Nikolai Fedorov: An Introduction. George M. Young, Sr. LC 78-78119. 400p. 1980. 29.50 (ISBN 0-913124-29-X). Nordland Pub.

Nikolai Gogol. Vladimir Nabokov. LC 44-8135. 1961. pap. 4.95 (ISBN 0-8112-0120-1, NDP78). New Directions.

Nikolai Negorev. Ivan Kuschevsky. Tr. by Bella Costello. 1980. pap. 4.95 (ISBN 0-7145-0414-9). Riverrun NY.

Nikolai Nikolaevich. Yuz Aleshkovsky. 80p. (Rus.). 1980. 12.50 (ISBN 0-88233-564-2); pap. 4.50 (ISBN 0-88233-565-0). Ardis Pubs.

Nikolay Gogol. Thais S. Lindstrom. (World Authors Ser.: Russia: No. 299). 1974. lib. bdg. 12.50 (ISBN 0-8057-2377-3). Twayne.

Nikolay Karamazin. Natalya Kochetkova. (World Authors Ser.: Russia: No. 250). 1974. lib. bdg. 12.50 (ISBN 0-8057-2488-5). Twayne.

Nikoly Leskov. Kenneth Lantz. (World Authors Ser.: No. 523). 1979. lib. bdg. 12.95 (ISBN 0-8057-6364-3). Twayne.

Nikon F-3 Book. Rex Hayman. (Camera Book Ser.). 128p. 1980. pap. 9.95 (ISBN 0-240-51073-9). Focal Pr.

Nikon FE, FM, EM Book. (Camera Book Ser.). (Illus.). 128p. 1980. pap. 9.95 (ISBN 0-240-51034-8). Focal Pr.

Nikonos Photography: The Camera & the System. 3rd ed. Fred M. Roberts. LC 77-80027. 1977. pap. 6.00 (ISBN 0-912746-00-9, Dist. by Aqua-Craft, Inc.). F M Roberts.

Nile. Helen O'Clery. LC 76-512551. (Pegasus Books: No. 30). (Illus.). 1970. 7.50x (ISBN 0-234-77483-5). Intl Pubns Serv.

Nile. Barton Worthington. LC 78-62991. (Rivers of the World Ser.). (Illus.). 1978. lib. bdg. 7.95 (ISBN 0-686-51136-0). Silver.

Nile Basin. 2nd ed. Richard F. Burton. LC 65-23403. 1967. Repr. of 1864 ed. 19.50 (ISBN 0-306-70926-0). Da Capo.

Nimbus: The Creation Story According to Mr. G. LC 78-58330. (Illus.). 1978. pap. 4.95 o.p. (ISBN 0-89556-008-9). IDHHB.

Nimzo-Indian Defence: Leningrad System. Michael MacDonald-Ross. 1979. pap. 14.95 (ISBN 0-7134-0947-9). David & Charles.

Nimzowitsch Larsen Attack. R. D. Keene. 1977. pap. 13.95 (ISBN 0-7134-0245-8). David & Charles.

Nine & a Half Weeks: A Mamoir of a Love Affair. Elizabeth McNeill. 1978. 7.95 o.p. (ISBN 0-525-16715-3). Dutton.

Nine Billion Names of God. Arthur Clarke. 204p. (RL 7). Date not set. pap. 1.75 o.p. (ISBN 0-451-08381-4, E8381, Sig). NAL.

Nine Billion Names of God. Arthur C. Clarke. LC 67-16086. 1967. 7.95 o.p. (ISBN 0-15-165890-0). HarBraceJ.

Nine Cities: The Anatomy of Downtown Renewal. Leo Adde. LC 73-85476. (Special Publications Ser.). 1969. pap. 4.25 o.p. (ISBN 0-87420-907-2). Urban Land.

Nine Classic French Plays. rev. ed. Ed. by Henri Peyre & Joseph Seronde. 1974. pap. text ed. 12.95x (ISBN 0-669-90241-1). Heath.

Nine Coaches Waiting. Mary Stewart. 1959. 9.95 o.p. (ISBN 0-688-02185-9). Morrow.

Nine Critics - Nine Photographs. Ed. by James Alinder. LC 80-68803. (Untitled Ser.: No. 23). (Illus.). 56p. (Orig.). 1980. pap. 8.95 (ISBN 0-933286-20-1). Friends Photography.

Nine Daring Adventures. Ed. by Mary Verdick. (Pal Paperbacks Kit B Ser.). (Illus., Orig.). (gr. 7-12). 1973. pap. text ed. 1.25 (ISBN 0-8374-3520-X). Xerox Ed Pubns.

Nine Days to Christmas. Marie H. Ets & Aurora Labastida. (Illus.). (ps-2). 1959. PLB 9.95 (ISBN 0-670-51350-4). Viking Pr.

Nine for Keeps. Jean Little. (Illus.). (gr. 4-6). 1974. pap. 1.75 (ISBN 0-671-29993-X). PB.

Nine Hundred Buckets of Paint. Edna Becker. (Illus.). (gr. k-2). 1949. 3.95 o.p. (ISBN 0-687-28013-3). Abingdon.

Nine Hundred Ninety-Nine Places to Eat for Around Five Pounds. rev. ed. Aoutomobile Association. (Illus.). 288p. 1981. pap. price not set (ISBN 0-86145-055-8, Pub. by Auto Assn-British Tourist Authority England). Merrimack Bk Serv.

Nine Hundred Primary School Teachers. Michael Bassey. (General Ser.). (Illus.). 1978. pap. text ed. 12.50x (ISBN 0-85633-157-0, NFER). Humanities.

Nine Investments Abroad & Their Impact at Home. Robert B. Stobaugh. 1976. text ed. 12.00 (ISBN 0-87584-113-9). Harvard U Pr.

Nine Lives of Island MacKenzie. Ursula M. Williams. LC 80-670265. 128p. (gr. 3-7). 1980. 8.95 (ISBN 0-7011-0227-6, Pub. by Chatto, Bodley Head & Jonathan). Merrimack Bk Serv.

Nine Months: A Practical Guide for Expectant Mothers. Alice Fleming. Orig. Title: Nine Months: An Intelligent Woman's Guide to Pregnancy. 192p. 1974. pap. 2.95 (ISBN 0-06-463390-X, EH 390, EH). Har-Row.

Nine Month's Reading: Medical Guide for Pregnant Women. rev. ed. Hall, Robert E., M.D. LC 72-77076. 192p. 1972. 8.95 (ISBN 0-385-03688-4). Doubleday.

Nine Nations of North America. Joel Garreau. 1981. 14.00 (ISBN 0-395-29124-0). HM.

Nine Old Men. Drew Pearson & Robert S. Allen. LC 73-21727. (American Constitutional & Legal History Ser). 325p. 1974. Repr. of 1966 ed. lib. bdg. 39.50 (ISBN 0-306-70609-1). Da Capo.

Nine Papers on Number Theory & Theory of Operators. M. S. Brodskii et al. LC 51-5559. (Translations Ser.: No. 2, Vol. 13). 1980. Repr. of 1964 ed. 35.60 (ISBN 0-8218-1713-2, TRANS 2-13). Am Math.

Nine Plays of the Modern Theater. Ed. by Harold Clurman. LC 79-52121. 912p. 1981. pap. text ed. 11.95 (ISBN 0-394-17411-9, E 773, Ever). Grove.

Nine Seventeenth Century Organ Transcriptions from the Operas of Lully. Jean B. Lully. Ed. by Almonte C. Howell, Jr. LC 62-19378. 1963. pap. 3.50x (ISBN 0-8131-1078-5). U Pr of Ky.

Nine Symphonies of Beethoven. Antony Hopkins. LC 80-27053. (Illus.). 296p. 1981. 20.00 (ISBN 0-295-95823-5). U of Wash Pr.

Nine-Thirty-Fifty-Five. John Minahan. pap. 1.75 o.p. (ISBN 0-380-00970-6, 32474). Avon.

Nine to Five. Thom Racina. 160p. (Orig.). 1980. pap. 2.25 (ISBN 0-553-14496-0). Bantam.

Nine to Five: The Complete Looks, Clothes & Personality Handbook for the Working Woman. Constance Schrader. (Illus.). 200p. 1981. 13.95 (ISBN 0-13-622555-1); pap. 6.95 (ISBN 0-13-622563-2). P-H.

Nine Tomorrows. Isaac Asimov. LC 59-6347. 1970. 4.95 o.p. (ISBN 0-385-05314-2). Doubleday.

Nine True Dolphin Stories. Margaret Davidson. 72p. (gr. 2-6). 1975. 6.95g (ISBN 0-8038-5037-9). Hastings.

Nine Ways of Bon: Excerpts from Gzi-brjid. Ed. by David L. Snellgrove. LC 78-13010. (Illus.). 1980. pap. 12.50 (ISBN 0-87773-739-8, Prajna). Great Eastern.

Nine Young Men. Wesley McCune. Repr. of 1947 ed. lib. bdg. 17.50x (ISBN 0-8371-2247-3, MCNY). Greenwood.

Nineteen-Eighteen: Gamble for Victory. Robert Cowley. (gr. 6 up). 1964. 7.95 (ISBN 0-02-724830-5). Macmillan.

Nineteen Eighties Countdown to Armageddon. Hal Lindsey. 192p. 1981. pap. 6.92 (ISBN 0-553-01303-3). Bantam.

Nineteen Eighty A. I. M. Aero Staff. LC 70-186849. 192p. 1980. 4.50 (ISBN 0-8168-1359-0). Aero.

Nineteen Eighty Aircraft & Helicopter Digest. Aviation Mechanincs Journal. (Illus.). 204p. 1980. text ed. 13.25 (ISBN 0-89100-184-0, E*A-184-0). Aviation Maintenance.

Nineteen Eighty Autos: Rating, Specifications & Best Buys. Ed. by Michael L. Green. (Buyer's Guide Ser.). 1979. pap. 2.25 (ISBN 0-89552-060-5). DMR Pubns.

Nineteen Eighty Berger Building Cost File, 4 vols. Berger. Incl. Eastern Edition (ISBN 0-442-12214-4); Western Edition; Central Edition (ISBN 0-442-12220-9); Southern Edition (ISBN 0-442-12215-2). 1980. 27.95 ea. Van Nos Reinhold.

Nineteen Eighty Car Facts. Ed. by Michael L. Green. (Buyer's Guide Ser.). 1979. pap. 2.25 (ISBN 0-89552-059-1). DMR Pubns.

Nineteen-Eighty Case Supplement, Civil Rights: Leading Cases. Date not set. 8.95 (ISBN 0-316-08819-6). Little.

Nineteen Eighty Combined Membership List. 10.00 o.p. (ISBN 0-686-61108-X). Am Math.

Nineteen Eighty Cumulative Supplement Higher Education & the Law. Harry T. Edwards & Virginia D. Nordin. LC 80-82432. 136p. (Orig.). 1980. pap. text ed. 4.95 (ISBN 0-934222-03-7). Inst Ed Manage.

Nineteen Eighty Economy Cars. Ed. by Michael L. Green. (Buyer's Guide Ser.). 1979. pap. 2.25 (ISBN 0-89552-063-X). DMR Pubns.

Nineteen Eighty-Eight: The New Wave Punk Rock Explosion. Caroline Coon. (Illus.). 1978. pap. 4.95 o.p. (ISBN 0-8015-6129-9). Dutton.

Nineteen Eighty F. A. R. Aero Staff. LC 60-10472. 112p. 1980. 3.50 (ISBN 0-8168-5736-9). Aero.

Nineteen Eighty Five Interindustry Forecasts of the American Economy. Clopper Almon et al. LC 73-21608. (Illus.). 224p. 1974. 19.95 (ISBN 0-669-92494-6). Lexington Bks.

Nineteen Eighty-Four. George Orwell. LC 66-91393. (gr. 10 up). 8.95 (ISBN 0-15-166035-2). HarBraceJ.

Nineteen Eighty New Car Prices. Ed. by Michael L. Green. (Buyer's Guide Ser.). 1979. pap. 2.25 (ISBN 0-685-95267-3). DMR Pubns.

Nineteen Eighty New Truck & Van Prices. Ed. by Michael L. Green. (Buyer's Guide Ser.). 1979. pap. 2.25 (ISBN 0-89552-061-3). DMR Pubns.

Nineteen Eighty-One Administrative Directory. 1981. cancelled (ISBN 0-686-63430-6). Am Math.

Nineteen Eighty-One Annual World's Best SF. Ed. by Donald A. Wollheim. (Science Fiction Ser.). 1981. pap. 2.50 (ISBN 0-87997-617-9, UE1617). DAW Bks.

Nineteen Eighty One Anthology of Magazine Verse & Yearbook of American Poetry. Ed. by Alan F. Pater. 650p. lib. bdg. write for info. (ISBN 0-917734-05-X); lib. bdg. price not set (ISBN 0-917734-05-X). Monitor.

Nineteen Eighty-One Building Cost File, 4 vols, Vol. 1. Berger. Incl. Eastern Edition. 34.95 (ISBN 0-442-21240-2); Western Edition. 34.95 (ISBN 0-442-21238-0); Central Edition. 34.95 (ISBN 0-442-21237-2); Southern Edition. 34.95. 1981. Van Nos Reinhold.

Nineteen Eighty-One Building Cost File, 4 vols, Vol. 2. Berger. Incl. Eastern Edition. 24.95 (ISBN 0-442-21235-6); Western Edition. 24.95 (ISBN 0-442-21234-8); Central Editin. 24.95 (ISBN 0-442-21232-1); Southern Edition. 24.95 (ISBN 0-442-21231-3). 1981. Van Nos Reinhold.

Nineteen Eighty-One Federal Employees' Almanac. Ed. by Joseph Young & Lucille Young. 156p. (Orig.). 1981. pap. 2.75 (ISBN 0-910582-01-7). Fed Employees.

Nineteen Eighty-One Guide to Coupons & Refunds. 2nd rev. ed. Martin Sloane. (Orig.). 1981. pap. 2.95 (ISBN 0-553-14617-3). Bantam.

Nineteen Eighty-One Insecticide, Herbicide, Fungicide Quick Guide. B. G. Page & W. T. Thomson. 140p. 1981. pap. 11.00 (ISBN 0-913702-11-0). Thomson Pub Ca.

Nineteen Eighty-One Labor Rates for the Construction Industry. 8th ed. Robert S. Godfrey. LC 74-75990. 300p. 1981. pap. 26.75 (ISBN 0-911950-33-8). Means.

Nineteen Eighty-One Radio Contacts. Ed. by Michael McMahon. 1981. pap. text ed. 126.00 (ISBN 0-935224-05-X). Larimi Comm.

Nineteen Eighty-One Tax Fighter's Guide. Philip Storrer & Brian Williams. 192p. 1981. pap. 6.95 (ISBN 0-936602-08-2). Harbor Pub CA.

Nineteen Eighty-One Television Contacts. Ed. by Michael McMahon. 1981. pap. text ed. 117.00 (ISBN 0-935224-04-1). Larimi Comm.

Nineteen Eighty-One World Refugee Survey. Ed. by Michael de Sherbinin. (Illus.). 64p. 1981. 5.00 (ISBN 0-936548-02-9). US Comm Refugees.

Nineteen Eighty-Our Profession: Present Status & Future Directions. Ed. by NE Conf Teach Foreign. 1980. 7.95x (ISBN 0-915432-80-3). NE Conf Teach Foreign.

Nineteen Eighty Report on Equal Employment Opportunity & Affirmative Action: The Roots Grow Deeper. Geraldine Leshin. 526p. 1980. pap. text ed. 14.00 (ISBN 0-89215-110-2). U Cal LA Indus Rel.

Nineteen Eighty to Nineteen Eighty-One TV News. Ed. by Michael McMahon. 1980. 70.00 (ISBN 0-935224-03-3). Larimi Comm.

Nineteen Eighty U. S. Income Tax Guide. Ed. by Michael L. Green. (Buyer's Guide Ser.). 1979. pap. 2.25 (ISBN 0-89552-064-8). DMR Pubns.

Nineteen Fifty-Three Production of "Venice Preserv'd". James Hogg & Robert Muller. Bd. with Zur Rezeption Von Otway's "Venice Preserv'd" in der Restaurationszeit. James Hogg; Nahum Tate's "Richard II" & Censorship During Theexclusion Bill Crisis. Robert Muller; James Elroy Flecker's "Hassan: a Near East Masterpiece?". Robert Muller. (Salzburg Studies in English Literature, Poetic Drama & Poetry Theory Ser.: No. 26). 121p. 1976. pap. text ed. 25.00x (ISBN 0-391-01416-1). Humanities.

Nineteen Forty-One. 1979. pap. 3.95 (ISBN 0-931064-11-2). Starlog.

Nineteen Forty-Three: The Victory That Never Was. John Grigg. 234p. 1980. 12.50 (ISBN 0-8090-7377-3). Hill & Wang.

Nineteen Hundred & One Album of Designs for Boats, Launches & Yachts. rev. ed. Fred W. Martin. LC 80-69290. (Illus.). 80p. 1980. pap. 5.00. Altair Pub Co.

Nineteen Hundred Eighty-One Heavy Construction Cost File: Unit Prices. Coert Engelsman. 256p. 1980. pap. text ed. 24.50 (ISBN 0-442-12223-3). Van Nos Reinhold.

Nineteen Hundred Six: Surviving the Great Earthquake & Fire. Gerstle Mack. 96p. (Orig.). pap. 5.95 (ISBN 0-87701-176-1). Chronicle Bks.

Nineteen One to Nineteen Eight. W. B. Yeats. Ed. by Samhain. 324p. Repr. of 1970 ed. 35.00x (ISBN 0-7146-2101-3, F Cass Co). Biblio Dist.

Nineteen Poems. Rakshat Puri. (Writers Workshop Redbird Ser.). 1975. 8.00 (ISBN 0-89253-521-0); pap. text ed. 4.80 (ISBN 0-88253-724-5). Ind-US Inc.

Nineteen Seventies: Best Editorial Cartoons of the Decade. Jerry Robinson. (McGraw-Hill Paperbacks Ser.). (Illus.). 192p. (Orig.). 1980. pap. 7.95 (ISBN 0-07-053281-8). McGraw.

Nineteen Seventy-Eight New Car Prices. rev. ed. (Vehicle Price Group Ser.). 1977. pap. 1.95 (ISBN 0-89552-007-9). DMR Pubns.

Nineteen Seventy Eight New Truck & Van Prices. rev. ed. (Vehicle Price Group Ser.). 1977. pap. 1.95 (ISBN 0-89552-008-7). DMR Pubns.

Nineteen Seventy-Eight Shopper's Guide. rev. ed. (Illus.). 1977. pap. 3.00 (ISBN 0-89552-009-5). DMR Pubns.

Nineteen Seventy-Eight Supplement to the Handbook of Magazine Publishing. 1978. 20.00 (ISBN 0-918110-03-3). Folio.

Nineteen Seventy-Eight U. S. Income Tax Guide. rev. ed. Ed. by Internal Revenue Service. (Illus.). 1977. pap. 1.95 (ISBN 0-89552-010-9). DMR Pubns.

Nineteen Seventy-Eight Yearbook of International Trade Statistics, 2 vols. 1178p. 1979. Set. pap. 65.00 (UN79-17-16, UN). Unipub.

Nineteen Seventy-Five Annotated Checklist of the Birds of Ceylon (Sri Lanka) rev. ed. W. W. Phillips. (Illus.). 92p. 1975. pap. text ed. 7.95x (ISBN 0-87474-761-9). Smithsonian.

Nineteen Seventy Five Calendar for Children. Ruthven Tremain. (Illus.). 14p. (gr. 1-6). 1974. pap. 2.50 o.s.i. (ISBN 0-02-789450-9). Macmillan.

Nineteen Seventy-Nine Conference on Environmental Engineering. Compiled by American Society of Civil Engineers. 840p. 1979. pap. text ed. 48.00 (ISBN 0-87262-185-5). Am Soc Civil Eng.

Nineteen Seventy-Nine Folio Annual: Supplement to the Handbook of Magazine Publishing. 1979. 20.00 (ISBN 0-918110-04-1). Folio.

Nineteen Seventy Nine Guide to Current Amerian Government. Congressional Quarterly Inc. 1979. pap. text ed. cancelled o.p. (ISBN 0-87187-175-0). Congr Quarterly.

Nineteen Seventy-Nine International Air Transportation Conference. Compiled by American Society of Civil Engineers. 836p. 1980. pap. text ed. 59.00 (ISBN 0-87262-201-0). Am Soc Civil Eng.

Nineteen Seventy-Nine Patent Law Handbook. Gerald Rose. LC 78-17713. 1979. 13.50 (ISBN 0-87632-251-8). Boardman.

Nineteen Seventy Nine Pocket Watch Price Indicator. Roy Ehrhardt. (Illus.). 1979. plastic ring bdg. 10.00 (ISBN 0-913902-29-2). Heart Am Pr.

Nineteen Seventy Six Ames Research Center (NASA) Conference on Geometric Nonlinear Wave Theory. Ed. by Robert Hermann. (Lie Groups; History, Frontiers & Applications: Vol. 6). 1977. pap. 13.00x (ISBN 0-915692-19-8). Math Sci Pr.

Nineteen Seventy Six Joint Automatic Control Conference - Productivity. 1976. pap. text ed. 50.00 (ISBN 0-685-72342-9, I00103). ASME.

Nineteen-Seventy's Divorce Revolution. Margaret McCrory. pap. 3.95. Green Hill.

Nineteen Sixteen Poets. Ed. by Desmond Ryan. LC 79-18768. 224p. 1980. Repr. of 1963 ed. lib. bdg. 17.50x (ISBN 0-313-22100-6, RYNI). Greenwood.

Nineteen Sixties: Politics & Public Policy. John C. Donovan. LC 80-5757. 142p. 1980. lib. bdg. 15.50 (ISBN 0-8191-1189-9); pap. text ed. 6.75 (ISBN 0-8191-1190-2). U Pr of Amer.

Nineteen Steps up the Mountain. Joseph P. Blank. 1977. pap. 1.95 (ISBN 0-515-04442-3). Jove Pubns.

Nineteen Ten to Nineteen Sixteen Antarctic Photographs: The Scott, Mawson, & Schackleton Expeditions. Herbert Ponting & Frank Hurley. (Illus.). 1980. 12.50 o.p. (ISBN 0-312-57443-6). Berkley Pub.

Nineteen Thirty-Two Campaign. Roy V. Peel & Thomas C. Donnelly. LC 73-454. (FDR & the Era of the New Deal Ser.). 252p. 1973. Repr. of 1935 ed. lib. bdg. 29.50 (ISBN 0-306-70567-2). Da Capo.

Nineteen-Twelve to Nineteen Twenty-Two. Roy J. Wright & Richard M. Wagner. (Cincinnati Streetcars: No.6). 1973. pap. 4.95 o.s.i. (ISBN 0-914196-14-6). Trolley Talk.

Nineteen Twenty (Feb. Seventh - April Ninth, 1920) Ed. by Richard D. Challener. (United States Military Intelligence 1917-1927 Ser.). 1979. lib. bdg. 60.50 (ISBN 0-8240-3011-7). Garland Pub.

Nineteen Twenty-Seven: Summer of Eagles. Jack Huttig. (Illus.). 1980. 22.95 (ISBN 0-88229-525-X); pap. 11.95 (ISBN 0-88229-723-6). Nelson-Hall.

Nineteenth & Twentieth Century Architecture. LC 76-14074. (Garland Library of the History of Art). 1976. lib. bdg. 50.00 (ISBN 0-8240-2421-4). Garland Pub.

Nineteenth & Twentieth Century Art: Painting, Sculpture, Architecture. George H. Hamilton. (Illus.). 492p. 1972. text ed. 21.95 (ISBN 0-13-622639-6). P-H.

Nineteenth-Century Accounts of William Blake by Benjamin Heath Malkin, Henry Crabb Robinson, John Thomas Smith, Allan Cunningham, Frederick Tatham, & William Butler Yeats. Ed. by Joseph A. Wittreich, Jr. LC 78-133330. 1970. 30.00x (ISBN 0-8201-1085-X). Schol Facsimiles.

Nineteenth Century Aether Theories. Kenneth F. Schaffner. 288p. 1972. text ed. 26.00 (ISBN 0-08-015674-6). Pergamon.

Nineteenth Century American Clocks. H. R. Harris. (Illus.). 256p. 1981. 12.95 (ISBN 0-87523-197-7). Emerson.

Nineteenth Century American Drama: A Finding Guide. Don L. Hixon & Don A. Hennessee. LC 77-12057. 1977. 24.00 (ISBN 0-8108-1083-2). Scarecrow.

Nineteenth-Century Architecture of Saratoga Springs. Stephen S. Prokopoff & Joan C. Siegfried. (Architecture Worth Saving in New York State Ser.). (Illus.). 104p. 1980. pap. write for info. (ISBN 0-89062-001-6). NYSCA.

Nineteenth Century Constitution, Eighteen Fifteen to Nineteen Fourteen. Ed. by H. J. Hanham. LC 69-11148. 1969. 44.50 (ISBN 0-521-07351-0); pap. 15.95x (ISBN 0-521-09560-3, 560). Cambridge U Pr.

Nineteenth Century Education: Selected Sources. Ed. by Victor Neuberg. (Social History of Education, Second Ser.: No. 6). 285p. 1981. 27.50x (ISBN 0-7130-0015-5, Pub. by Woburn Pr England). Biblio Dist.

Nineteenth Century English Furniture. Elizabeth Aslin. 1962. 22.50 o.p. (ISBN 0-571-05046-8, Pub. by Faber & Faber). Merrimack Bk Serv.

Nineteenth Century Foreign Office: An Administrative History. Ray Jones. (London School of Economics Research Monographs Ser: No. 9). 1971. bds. 14.00x (ISBN 0-297-00299-6). Humanities.

Nineteenth-Century Literary Criticism: Excerpts from Criticism of the Works of Nineteenth-Century Novelists, Poets, Playwrights, Short-Story Writers, & Other Creative Writers, Vol. 1. Ed. by Laurie L. Harris. 48.00 (ISBN 0-8103-5801-8). Gale.

Nineteenth Century Painters & Painting: A Dictionary. Geraldine Norman. (Illus.). 1978. 42.50 (ISBN 0-520-03328-0). U of Cal Pr.

Nineteenth Century Piano Music: A Handbook for Pianists. Kathleen Dale. LC 70-87500. (Music Ser.). Repr. of 1954 ed. 27.50 (ISBN 0-306-71414-0). Da Capo.

Nineteenth Century Readers' Guide to Periodical Literature, 1890-1899, 2 Vols. Set. 62.00 (ISBN 0-8242-0584-7). Wilson.

Nineteenth Century Romantic Bronzes. Jeremy Cooper. 1977. 23.95 o.p. (ISBN 0-7153-6346-8). David & Charles.

Nineteenth Century Romanticism in Music. 2nd ed. Rey M. Longyear. LC 72-3962. (History of Music Ser). (Illus.). 304p. 1973. pap. text ed. 10.95 (ISBN 0-13-622647-7). P-H.

Nineteenth-Century Russian Literature: Studies of Ten Russian Writers. Ed. by John Fennell. (Library Reprint Ser.). 1976. 22.75x (ISBN 0-520-03203-9). U of Cal Pr.

Nineteenth-Century Spanish Plays. Lewis E. Brett. (Span.). 1935. text ed. 18.95 (ISBN 0-13-622704-X). P-H.

Nineteenth Century Spanish Verse. Ed. by Jose Sanchez. LC 79-18739. 1979. pap. text ed. 12.95x (ISBN 0-89197-538-1). Irvington.

Nineteenth Century Studies: Coleridge to Mathew Arnold. Basil Willey. LC 49-50265. 1949. 20.00x (ISBN 0-231-01789-8). Columbia U Pr.

Nineteenth-Century Studies; Coleridge to Matthew Arnold. Basil Willey. LC 80-40634. 288p. 1981. pap. 9.95 (ISBN 0-521-28066-4). Cambridge U Pr.

Ninety Five Poems. E. E. Cummings. LC 58-10909. 1971. pap. 1.95 (ISBN 0-15-665950-6, HPL51, HPL). HarBraceJ.

Ninety Nine Advertising Layout Designs. Compiled by H. Kenwood Spriggle. (Illus.). 1980. write for info. H Spriggle.

Ninety-Nine Names of Allah. Ira Friedlander. (Orig.). 1978. pap. 3.50 (ISBN 0-06-090621-9, CN 621, CN). Har-Row.

Ninety Notes Toward Partial Images & Lovers Prints. Tom Montag. 1976. pap. 2.50x (ISBN 0-915316-37-4); signed 7.50x (ISBN 0-915316-38-2). Pentagram.

Ninety-One Prints by Childe Hassam. Childe Hassam. Ed. by Joseph S. Czestochowski. (Illus., Orig.). 1980. 6.00 (ISBN 0-486-23981-0). Dover.

Ninety-Six: The Struggle for the South Carolina Back Country. Robert D. Bass. LC 77-20551. (Illus.). 1978. 12.50 (ISBN 0-87844-039-9); ltd. signed 25.00 (ISBN 0-87844-017-8). Sandlapper Store.

Ninety-Thirty-Three Characters in Crisis. Herbert Feis. (FDR & the Era of the New Deal Ser.). 1976. Repr. of 1966 ed. lib. bdg. 32.50 (ISBN 0-306-70807-8). Da Capo.

Ninety-Two Puzzlers from Old & New Testaments. 48p. (Orig.). (gr. 6 up). 1981. pap. 1.25 (ISBN 0-87239-450-6, 2841). Standard Pub.

Ninety Two Twenty Six Kercheval: The Storefront That Did Not Burn. Nancy Milio. 1971. pap. 4.50 (ISBN 0-472-06180-1, 180, AA). U of Mich Pr.

Ninety Ways to Leave Your Lover & Survive. William Fezler & Jack Shapiro. 198p. 1980. 9.95 (ISBN 0-934810-01-X). Laurida.

Ninja. Eric Van Lustbader. 512p. 1981. pap. 3.50 (ISBN 0-449-24367-2, Crest). Fawcett.

Ninja & Their Secret Fighting Art. Stephen K. Hayes. LC 81-50105. (Illus.). 160p. 1981. 13.50 (ISBN 0-8048-1374-4). C E Tuttle.

Ninja: Clan of Death. Al Weiss. (Orig.). 1981. pap. 2.50 (ISBN 0-671-43046-7). PB.

Ninja: Spirit of the Shadow Warrior. Stephen K. Hayes. Ed. by Bill Griffeth. LC 80-84678. 1980. pap. 6.95 (ISBN 0-89750-073-3). Ohara Pubns.

Ninja, the Invisible Assasins. Andrew Adams. Ed. by Pat Alston. LC 75-130760. (Ser. 302s). (Illus.). 1970. 6.95 (ISBN 0-89750-030-X). Ohara Pubns.

Ninjutsu: The Art of Invisibility. 2nd ed. Donn Draeger. (Illus.). 1980. pap. 4.95 (ISBN 0-914778-19-6). Phoenix Bks.

Nino Benjamin y la Primera Navidad. Betty Forell. Tr. by Fernando Villalobos from Eng. (Libros Arco). (Illus.). 32p. (Orig., Span.). (gr. 1-3). 1974. pap. 0.95 o.s.i. (ISBN 0-89922-042-8). Edit Caribe.

Nino que Regalo Su Merienda. Dave Hill. Tr. by Fernando Villalobos from Eng. (Illus.). 32p. (Orig., Span.). (gr. 1-3). 1977. pap. 0.95 (ISBN 0-89922-146-7). Edit Caribe.

Nino que Salvo a su Familia. Alyce Bergey. Tr. by Fernando Villalobos from Eng. (Libros Arco). (Illus.). 32p. (Orig., Span.). (gr. 1-3). 1970. pap. 0.95 o.s.i. (ISBN 0-89922-043-6). Edit Caribe.

Nino y el Gigante. Mary Warren. Tr. by Fernando Villalobos from Eng. (Libros Arco). (Illus.). 32p. (Orig., Span.). (gr. 1-3). 1975. pap. 0.95 o.s.i. (ISBN 0-89922-044-4). Edit Caribe.

Ninos, Children of Mexico. Bob Schalkwijk & Nina Lincoln. (Illus.). 1980. 395.00 (ISBN 0-915998-08-4). Lime Rock Pr.

Ninos De la Biblia. (Span.). 9.00 (ISBN 84-241-5410-X). E Torres & Sons.

Ninteen Gifts of the Spirit. Leslie B. Flynn. LC 74-91027. 204p. 1974. pap. 3.95 (ISBN 0-88207-701-5). Victor Bks.

Ninth Asian Regional Conference, Manila, December, 1980: Report of the Director-General Asian Development in the 1980s-Growth, Employment & Working Conditions, Report I, Pt. 1. International Labour Office. iii, 100p. (Orig.). 1980. pap. 10.00 (ISBN 92-2-102497-0). Intl Labour Office.

Ninth Asian Regional Conference, Manila, December 1980: Report of the Director-General Application of ILO Standards, Report I, Pt. 2. International Labour Office. iii, 45p. (Orig.). 1980. pap. text ed. 7.15 (ISBN 92-2-102498-9). Intl Labour Office.

Ninth Configuration. William P. Blatty. LC 78-4741. 1978. 7.95 o.s.i. (ISBN 0-06-010359-0, HarpT). Har-Row.

Ninth Decade: Secret Plans for the Coming Communist Takeovers. Jean-Jacques Sensoir. 1977. 7.50 o.p. (ISBN 0-682-48801-1). Exposition.

Ninth Directive. Adam Hall. 1979. cancelled o.s.i. (ISBN 0-515-05204-3). Jove Pubns.

Ninth International Forum for Air Cargo Proceedings. Society of Automotive Engineers. 1979. 18.00 (ISBN 0-89883-049-4). Soc Auto Engineers.

Ninth Windmill Book of One-Act Plays. Margaret Wood. 1977. pap. text ed. 3.25x o.p. (ISBN 0-435-23959-7). Heinemann Ed.

Niobium: Physico-Chemical Properties of Its Compounds & Alloys. (Atomic Energy Review Ser.: Special Issue No. 2). 1968. pap. 10.75 (ISBN 92-0-149068-2, IAEA). Unipub.

Nippon: A Chartered Survey of Japan, 1980-81. 25th ed. Ed. by Tsuneta Yano Memorial Society (Tokyo) (Illus.). 347p. 1980. 37.50x (ISBN 0-8002-2748-4). Intl Pubns Serv.

Nips Poem. John M. Bennett. (Illus.). 40p. (Orig.). 1980. pap. 3.00 (ISBN 0-935350-00-4); signed & lettered 6.00. Luna Bisonte.

Niquin el Cesante. Jose Sanchez-Boudy. LC 78-74694. (Coleccion Caniqui). (Illus.). 157p. (Orig., Span.). 1980. pap. 5.95 (ISBN 0-89729-217-0). Ediciones.

Nirad C. Chaudhuri. C. P. Verghese. (Indian Writers Ser.). 1973. 8.50 (ISBN 0-89253-509-1). Ind-US Inc.

Nirad C. Chaudhuri. C. Paul Verghese. (Indian Writers Ser: No. 2). 118p. (Orig.). 1973. pap. text ed. 3.50x (ISBN 0-391-00430-1). Humanities.

Nirvana Contracts. James P. Wohl. 1979. pap. 1.75 o.s.i. (ISBN 0-515-04691-4). Jove Pubns.

Nirvana Now: Higher Consciousness in the Dawning Aquarian Age. Roland Gammon. 555p. 1980. 14.95 (ISBN 0-89975-003-6). World Authors.

Nirvana: The Last Nightmare. Bhagwan Sri Rajneesh. Ed. by Rajneesh Foundation. (Illus.). 278p. (Orig.). 1981. pap. 7.95 (ISBN 0-914794-37-X). Wisdom Garden Bks.

Nisei Daughter. Monica Sone. LC 79-4921. (Orig.). 1979. pap. 5.95 (ISBN 0-295-95688-7). U of Wash Pr.

Nissim Ezekiel. Chetan Karnani. (Indian Writers Ser.). 192p. 1975. 6.50 (ISBN 0-88253-699-0). Ind-US Inc.

Nitrates: An Environmental Assessment. Committee on Environmental Pollutants, National Research Council. (Scientific & Technical Assessments of Environmental Pollutants Ser.). 1978. pap. text ed. 15.25 (ISBN 0-309-02785-3). Natl Acad Pr.

Nitration & Aromatic Reactivity. J. G. Hoggett et al. LC 76-138374. (Illus.). 1971. 42.50 (ISBN 0-521-08029-0). Cambridge U Pr.

Nitrenes. Walter Lwowski. LC 76-97256. (Reactive Intermediates Ser). 1970. 44.95 (ISBN 0-471-55710-2, Pub. by Wiley-Interscience). Wiley.

Nitrofurans. Ed. by George T. Bryan. LC 77-72824. (Carcinogenesis-A Comprehensive Survey Ser.: Vol. 4). 1978. 25.00 (ISBN 0-89004-250-0). Raven.

Nitrogen & Rice. 499p. 1979. pap. 32.50 (R026, IRRI). Unipub.

Nitrogen, Electrolytes Water & Metabolism. Ed. by M. Rechcigl, Jr. (Comparative Animal Nutrition: Vol. 3). (Illus.). 1979. 78.00 (ISBN 3-8055-2829-9). S Karger.

Nitrogen Fixation by Free-Living Micro-Organisms. Ed. by W. D. Stewart. LC 75-2731. (International Biological Programme Ser.: Vol. 6). (Illus.). 448p. 1976. 72.00 (ISBN 0-521-20708-8). Cambridge U Pr.

Nitrogen Fixation in Plants. W. D. Stewart & Janet Sprent. 1980. cancelled (ISBN 0-485-11155-1, Athlone Pr). Humanities.

Nitrogen Fixation, Vol. 1: Ecology. W. J. Broughton. (Illus.). 350p. 1981. 59.00 (ISBN 0-19-854540-1). Oxford U Pr.

Nitrogen in the Environment, Vol. 1. D. R. Nielsen. 1978. 32.00 (ISBN 0-12-518401-8). Acad Pr.

Nitrogen-15 in Soil-Plant Studies. (Illus., Orig.). 1971. pap. 19.50 (ISBN 92-0-111171-1, ISP 278, IAEA). Unipub.

Nitroquinolines. Ed. by Takashi Sugimura. (Carcinogenesis, A Comprehensive Survey: Vol. 6). 166p. 1981. text ed. 22.00 (ISBN 0-89004-162-8). Raven.

Nitrous Oxide. H. Davy. (Illus.). 606p. 1972. 38.50 (ISBN 0-407-33150-6). Butterworths.

Nitter Pitter. Stephen Cosgrove. (Creative Fantasies Ser.). (Illus.). (gr. k-4). 1979. PLB 6.95 (ISBN 0-87191-691-6). Creative Ed.

Nitty Gritty, Rather Pretty, City: Test Package. Pleasant Rowland. (Addison-Wesley Reading Program). (gr. 2). 1979. 28.76 (ISBN 0-201-20770-2, Sch Div); avail. tchr's man. progress & pretests 1.24 (ISBN 0-201-20760-5); pretest pkg. 28.76 (ISBN 0-201-20758-3); tchr's man. & class record form & ans. key 1.24 (ISBN 0-201-20768-0). A-W.

Nitty-Gritty, Rather Pretty, City, 1st to 12th Streets. Pleasant Rowland. (Addison-Wesley Reading Program). (gr. 2). 1979. text ed. 7.32 (ISBN 0-201-20700-1, Sch Div); tchr's. guides in binder (6 booklets) 23.40 (ISBN 0-201-20702-8); student skills books 2-1 2.52 (ISBN 0-201-20701-X); tchr. skills bks. 3.32 (ISBN 0-201-20709-5). A-W.

Nitty Gritty, Rather Pretty, City: 13-24th Streets. Pleasant Rowland. (Addison-Wesley Reading Program). (gr. 2). 1979. text ed. 7.32 (ISBN 0-201-20750-8, Sch Div); skills bk., s.e. 2.52 (ISBN 0-201-20751-6); tchr's. guides in binder (6 booklets) 23.40 (ISBN 0-201-20752-4). A-W.

Nitty-Gritty Rhyming Riddle Book. Sharon Lerner. (Electric Company Ser.). (Illus.). (gr. 1-5). 1973. PLB 5.38 (ISBN 0-307-64823-0, Golden Pr). Western Pub.

NIV Complete Concordance. Edward W. Goodrick & John P. Kohlenberger. 1056p. 1981. 19.95 (ISBN 0-310-43650-8). Zondervan.

Niv Interlinear Hebrew-English Old Testament. John R. Kohlenberger, III. 544p. 1980. Vol. 1. 19.95 (ISBN 0-310-38890-2, 6281); Vol. 2. 19.95 (ISBN 0-310-38890-2). Zondervan.

NIV Triglot Old Testament. Ed. by John R. Kohlenberger. 1334p. 1981. 49.95 (ISBN 0-310-43820-9). Zondervan.

Nixon Administration Public Broadcasting Papers. Ed. by National Telecommunications & Information Administration. 124p. 1979. pap. 5.00. NAEB.

Nixon's Good Deed: Welfare Reform. Vincent Burke & Vee Burke. 224p. 1974. 15.00x (ISBN 0-231-03850-X); pap. 6.00x (ISBN 0-231-08346-7). Columbia U Pr.

Njal's Saga. Tr. by Magnus Magnusson & Hermann Palsson. (Classics Ser.). (Orig.). 1960. pap. 3.50 (ISBN 0-14-044103-4). Penguin.

Njals Saga: A Critical Approach. Lars Lonnroth. LC 73-94437. 400p. 1976. 24.50x (ISBN 0-520-02708-6). U of Cal Pr.

Njals Saga: A Literary Masterpiece. Einar Ol Sveinsson. Tr. by Paul Schach. Ed. by Paul Schach. LC 70-128914. 1971. 12.50x o.p. (ISBN 0-8032-0789-1). U of Nebr Pr.

NLRB & Secondary Boycotts. rev. ed. Ralph M. Dereshinsky & Alan D. Berkowitz. 1980. pap. 15.00 (ISBN 0-89546-027-0). Indus Res Unit-Wharton.

NLRB Elections: A Guidebook for Employers. James P. Swann, Jr. 150p. (Orig.). 1980. pap. 10.00 (ISBN 0-87179-322-9). BNA.

NLRB General Counsel: Unreviewable Power to Refuse to Issue an Unfair Labor Practice Complaint. Michael C. McClintock. LC 80-67049. (Scholarly Monographs). 180p. 1980. pap. 15.00 (ISBN 0-8408-0510-1). Carrollton Pr.

NMR Data Tables for Organic Compounds, Vol. 1. Frank A. Bovey. LC 67-20258. 1967. 149.00 (ISBN 0-470-09210-6, Pub. by Wiley-Interscience). Wiley.

NMR in Medicine. Ed. by R. Danadian. (NMR--Basic Principles & Progress Ser.). (Illus.). 230p. 1981. 57.90 (ISBN 0-387-10460-7). Springer-Verlag.

NMR Spectroscopy: A Working Manual with Exercises. E. Breitmaier & G. C. Bauer. Tr. by B. K. Cassels from Ger. 400p. 1981. 80.00 (ISBN 3-7186-0022-6). Harwood Academic.

NMR Spectroscopy Using Liquid Crystal Solvents. J. W. Emsley & J. C. Lindon. 367p. 1975. text ed. 55.00 (ISBN 0-08-019919-4). Pergamon.

No Access to Law: Alternatives to the American Judicial System. Ed. by Laura Nader. LC 80-526. 1980. 27.50 (ISBN 0-12-513560-2); pap. 12.95 (ISBN 0-12-513562-9). Acad Pr.

No, Agatha. Rachel Isadora. LC 79-26734. (Illus.). 32p. (ps-3). 1980. 7.95 (ISBN 0-688-80274-5); PLB 7.63 (ISBN 0-688-84274-7). Greenwillow.

No Appointment Needed. Bernhard Aaen. Ed. by Bobbie J. Van Dolson. 128p. 1981. pap. write for info. (ISBN 0-8280-0025-5). Review & Herald.

No Baloney Sandwich Book. Alden Robertson. LC 77-80145. 1978. pap. 4.95 o.p. (ISBN 0-385-12429-5). Doubleday.

No Bed of Roses. Faith Baldwin. 1980. pap. write for info. (ISBN 0-671-83096-1). PB.

No Bed of Roses. Joan Fontaine. 1979. pap. 2.75 (ISBN 0-425-05028-9). Berkley Pub.

No Boys Allowed. Susan Terris. LC 74-23348. 48p. (gr. 1-5). 1976. 5.95 o.p. (ISBN 0-385-04887-4); PLB write for info. o.p. (ISBN 0-385-05749-0). Doubleday.

No Bugles Tonight. Bruce Lancaster. 1977. pap. 1.95 o.p. (ISBN 0-685-78260-3, 40-074-2). Pinnacle Bks.

No Cause for Indictment: An Autopsy of Newark. Ron Porambo. 408p. 1972. pap. 3.95 o.p. (ISBN 0-03-003301-2). HR&W.

No Certain Life. Richard Neely. 1978. pap. 1.50 o.s.i. (ISBN 0-685-86780-3, 4548). Jove Pubns.

No Chance to Panic. Molly K. Rankin. LC 79-87734. (Destiny Ser.). 1980. pap. 4.95 (ISBN 0-8163-0383-5, 14484-0). Pacific Pr Pub Assn.

No Child Is Ineducable. 2nd ed. S. S. Segal. LC 73-21571. 412p. 1974. text ed. 18.75 (ISBN 0-08-017815-4). Pergamon.

No Chinese Stranger. Jade S. Wong. LC 73-14301. (Illus.). 378p. (YA) 1975. 10.95 o.s.i. (ISBN 0-06-014732-6, HarpT). Har-Row.

No Church. Frederick W. Robinson. Ed. by Robert L. Wolff. LC 75-499. (Victorian Fiction Ser.). 1975. Repr. of 1861 ed. lib. bdg. 66.00 (ISBN 0-8240-1574-6). Garland Pub.

No Comment. Nurit Karlin. LC 78-16725. (Encore Edition). (Illus.). 1978. 2.95 (ISBN 0-684-16561-9, ScribT). Scribner.

No Commercial Potential: The Saga of Frank Zappa Then & Now. David Walley. (Illus.). 192p. 1980. 6.95 (ISBN 0-525-93153-8). Dutton.

No-Cost Low Cost Energy Tips: Fifty-Two Ways to Save One Thousand Dollars a Year in Energy Cost Without Sacrifice. Stuart Diamond. 112p. 1980. pap. 1.95 (ISBN 0-553-14239-9). Bantam.

No Credentials, but Credible Counseling. 61p. (Orig.). 1981. pap. 7.00 (ISBN 0-686-28928-5). Mor Mac.

No Crystal Stair: A Bibliography of Black Literature. Office of Adult Services. 63p. 1971. pap. 2.00 o.p. (ISBN 0-87104-600-8, Branch Lib). NY Pub Lib.

NO DIET Way to Health, Beauty, Happiness, How to Have It, How to Keep It: Natures Way Cookbook & Canning with Honey. Joe M. Parkhill. 157p. 1979. spiral bdg. 6.95 (ISBN 0-936744-00-6). Country Bazaar.

No Divided Allegiance: Essays in Brownson's Thought. Ed. by Leonard Gilhooley. LC 79-56139. xiv, 193p. 1980. 20.00 (ISBN 0-8232-1056-1); pap. 8.00 (ISBN 0-8232-1057-X). Fordham.

No Earth for Foxes. Manning O'Brine. 288p. 1975. 7.95 o.p. (ISBN 0-440-06208-X). Delacorte.

No Earthly Shore. Francine Mezo. 256p. (Orig.). 1981. pap. 2.50 (ISBN 0-380-77347-3, 77347). Avon.

No Easy Answers. Enoch Powell. LC 73-17906. 1974. 6.95 (ISBN 0-8164-0251-5). Crossroad NY.

No Easy Answers: The Learning Disabled Child. Sally L. Smith. 352p. 1981. pap. 3.95 (ISBN 0-553-14138-4). Bantam.

No Easy Walk to Freedom. Nelson Mandela. (African Writers Ser.). 1973. pap. text ed. 3.25x (ISBN 0-435-90123-0). Heinemann Ed.

No Elephants Allowed. Deborah Robison. (Illus.). 32p. (ps-2). 1981. 8.95 (ISBN 0-395-30078-9, Clarion). HM.

No End of Nonsense. W. Blecher. 1968. 3.95g o.s.i. (ISBN 0-02-710900-3). Macmillan.

No End to Yesterday. Shelagh Macdonald. LC 78-74755. (Illus.). (gr. 7 up). 1979. 7.95 (ISBN 0-233-96865-2). Andre Deutsch.

No Exit. C. Raju. (Writers Workshop Redbird Ser.). 1975. 6.75 (ISBN 0-88253-586-2); pap. text ed. 4.00 (ISBN 0-88253-585-4). Ind-US Inc.

No Exit & Three Other Plays. Jean-Paul Sartre. 1955. pap. 2.95 (ISBN 0-394-70016-3, Vin). Random.

No Face in the Mirror. Hugh McLeave. 192p. 1980. 9.95 o.s.i. (ISBN 0-8027-5421-X). Walker & Co.

No-Fault Auto Insurance. Council on Law Related Studies. 1977. 24.00 (ISBN 0-379-00391-0). Oceana.

No-Fault Insurance. Willis P. Rokes. LC 72-173308. 416p. 1972. 12.50 o.p. (ISBN 0-88245-006-9). Merritt Co.

No Fear in His Presence. David Dawson. LC 80-50261. 192p. 1980. text ed. 9.95 (ISBN 0-8307-0753-0, 5108918). Regal.

No Foot of Land: Folklore of American Methodist Itinerants. Donald E. Byrne. LC 75-1097. (ATLA Monograph: No. 6). (Illus.). 370p. 1975. 15.00 (ISBN 0-8108-0798-X). Scarecrow.

No Forty-Hour Week. Goldie M. Down. LC 77-19223. (Crown Ser.). (gr. 8-12). 1978. pap. 4.50 (ISBN 0-8127-0167-4). Southern Pub.

No Golden Cities. T. Nason. 1971. 3.95 o.s.i. (ISBN 0-02-768100-9, CCPr). Macmillan.

No Graven Images. Madelon Brunson & Imogene Goodyear. LC 77-24081. 1977. 3.00 (ISBN 0-8309-0189-2). Herald Hse.

No Greater Sacrifice. Steven L. Shields. LC 80-83864. 250p. 1980. 6.95 (ISBN 0-88290-166-4, 1059). Horizon Utah.

No Grown-Ups in Heaven. Arthur E. Greer. 1977. pap. 3.95 (ISBN 0-8015-5403-9, Hawthorn). Dutton.

No He's Not a Monkey, He's an Ape & He's My Son. Hester Mundis. 1978. pap. 1.75 o.s.i. (ISBN 0-515-04748-1). Jove Pubns.

No Higher Calling. J. N. Hunt. (Horizon Ser.). 96p. 1981. pap. price not set (ISBN 0-8280-0064-6). Review & Herald.

No-Hitter. Pepe. (gr. 7 up). 1977. pap. 1.25 o.p. (ISBN 0-590-02977-0). Schol Bk Serv.

No King but Caesar? William R. Durland. LC 74-30093. 184p. 1975. 6.95 (ISBN 0-8361-1757-3). Herald Pr.

No Language but a Cry. Richard D'Ambrosio. LC 75-111154. 1970. 8.95 o.p. (ISBN 0-385-05380-0). Doubleday.

No Laughing Matter: The Autobiography of a WASP. Margaret Halsey. 1977. 8.95 o.p. (ISBN 0-397-01240-3). Lippincott.

No Laurels for De Gaulle: An Appraisal of the London Years. Robert Mengin. 1966. 6.95 o.p. (ISBN 0-374-22296-7). FS&G.

No Left Turns. Joseph L. Schott. 192p. 1976. pap. 1.50 o.p. (ISBN 0-345-25013-3). Ballantine.

No Life for a Lady. Agnes M. Cleaveland. LC 77-6825. (Illus.). 1977. pap. 4.50 (ISBN 0-8032-5868-2, BB 652, Bison). U of Nebr Pr.

No Limits to Learning: Bridging the Human Gap: the Club of Rome Report. James W. Botkin et al. LC 79-40911. 1979. 17.00 (ISBN 0-08-024705-9); pap. 7.75 (ISBN 0-08-024704-0). Pergamon.

No Little People. Francis A. Schaeffer. LC 74-78675. 276p. 1974. pap. text ed. 5.95 (ISBN 0-87784-765-7). Inter-Varsity.

No Little Plans: Fairfax County's PLUS Program with Managing Growth. Grace Dawson. 168p. 1977. pap. 3.95 (ISBN 0-87766-185-5, 17100). Urban Inst.

No Longer a Nobody. Matilda Nordvedt. (Illus.). 32p. (Orig.). (gr. 1-3). 1976. pap. 1.95 (ISBN 0-8024-5938-2). Moody.

No Longer at Ease. Chinua Achebe. 1977. pap. 2.25 (ISBN 0-449-30847-2, Prem). Fawcett.

No Longer Deprived: Using Minority Cultures & Languages in Educating Disadvantaged Children & Their Teachers. Ruth Fedder & Jacqueline Gabaldon. LC 78-76318. 1970. pap. text ed. 6.50x (ISBN 0-8077-1312-0). Tchrs Coll.

No Longer Human. Osamu Dazai. Tr. & intro. by Donald Keene. LC 58-9509. 192p. 1973. pap. 4.95 (ISBN 0-8112-0481-2, NDP357). New Directions.

No Longer Lonely. Pat Ansite. 1977. pap. 2.95 (ISBN 0-89728-048-2, 670689). Omega Pubns OR.

No Love Lost. Helen Van Slyke. 416p. 1981. pap. 2.95 (ISBN 0-553-14512-6). Bantam.

No Man Ever Spoke As This Man. A. M. Coniaris. 1969. pap. 3.50 (ISBN 0-937032-18-2). Light&Life Pub Co MN.

No Man Is an Island. Thomas Merton. LC 78-7108. 1978. pap. 4.50 (ISBN 0-15-665962-X, Harv). HarBraceJ.

No Man's Land. E. J. Leed. LC 78-73601. 1979. 21.50 (ISBN 0-521-22471-3). Cambridge U Pr.

No Mans Land, Nineteen Eighteen: The Last Year of the Great War. John Toland. LC 78-22761. (Illus.). 672p. 1980. 17.95 (ISBN 0-385-11291-2). Doubleday.

No Many Is Not a One (For the Case Is a Comparison) Francis Schwanauer. LC 80-6173. 66p. (Orig.). 1981. pap. text ed. 5.00 (ISBN 0-8191-1455-3). U Pr of Amer.

No Margin for Error: The U. S. Navy's Transpacific Flight of 1925. Dwight R. Messimer. 176p. 1981. 15.95 (ISBN 0-87021-497-7). Naval Inst Pr.

No Measles, No Mumps for Me. Paul Showers. LC 79-7106. (Let's-Read-&-Find-Out Science Book). (Illus.). 40p. (gr. k-3). 1980. 7.95 (ISBN 0-690-04017-2, TYC-J); PLB 7.89 (ISBN 0-690-04018-0). T Y Crowell.

No Metaphor, Remember. Nasima Aziz. 10.00 (ISBN 0-89253-646-2); flexible cloth 5.00 (ISBN 0-89253-647-0). Ind-US Inc.

No More A-Roving. Sylvia Thorpe. (Regency Romance Ser.). 1979. pap. 1.75 o.p. (ISBN 0-449-24080-0, Crest). Fawcett.

No More Dry Holes. James B. Bullock. LC 80-66936. (Illus.). 150p. 1981. pap. 9.95 (ISBN 0-937024-00-7). Gourmet Guides.

No More Masks: An Anthology of Poems by Women. Ed. by Florence Howe & Ellen Bass. LC 72-89675. 432p. 1973. pap. 4.50 (ISBN 0-385-02553-X, Anch). Doubleday.

No More Than Five in a Bed: Colorado Hotels in the Old Days. Sandra Dallas. (Illus.). 1967. 9.95 (ISBN 0-8061-0742-1). U of Okla Pr.

No More Vietnams: The War & the Future of American Foreign Policy. Ed. by Richard M. Pfeffer. LC 68-58302. 1968. 8.95 o.s.i. (ISBN 0-06-013324-4, HarpT). Har-Row.

No Need to Count. Leon B. Dubey, Jr. LC 79-23884. 176p. 1980. pap. 4.95 (ISBN 0-498-02465-2). A S Barnes.

No-Nibbling Book: One Hundred Twenty-Eight Things to Do at the Refrigerator Door So You Won't Open It. Robert M. Alter. 144p. 1981. 9.95 (ISBN 0-399-12581-7). Putnam.

No-No Boy. John Okada. LC 79-55834. 176p. 1978. pap. 5.95 (ISBN 0-295-95525-2). U of Wash Pr.

No, No, Sammy Crow. Lillian Hoban. LC 80-15299. (Illus.). 32p. (gr. k-3). 1981. 7.95 (ISBN 0-688-80297-4); PLB 7.63 (ISBN 0-688-84297-6). Greenwillow.

No! No! Word Bird. Jane B. Moncure. LC 80-29491. (Word Birds for Early Birds Ser.). (Illus.). 32p. (gr. k-2). 1981. PLB 5.50 (ISBN 0-89565-161-0). Childs World.

No-Nonsense Delegation. Dale D. McConkey. (Illus.). 1979. pap. 5.95 (ISBN 0-8144-7517-5). Am Mgmt.

No-Nonsense Management. Richard S. Sloma. 176p. 1981. pap. 3.50 (ISBN 0-553-20035-6). Bantam.

No-Nonsense Nutrition for Your Baby's First Year. Jo-Ann Heslin & Annette B. Natow. LC 78-12359. 1978. pap. 8.95 (ISBN 0-8436-2134-6). CBI Pub.

No-Nonsense Nutrition for Your Baby's First Year. Jo Ann Heslin et al. 288p. 1980. pap. 2.95 (ISBN 0-553-13725-5). Bantam.

No Offense: Civil Religion & Protestant Taste. John M. Cuddihy. 1978. 12.95 (ISBN 0-8164-0385-6). Crossroad NY.

No One Has to Die. Roy Masters. LC 76-20023. 1977. pap. 6.50 (ISBN 0-933900-03-1). Foun Human Under.

No One Hears But Him. Taylor Caldwell. 1977. pap. 2.25 (ISBN 0-449-24030-4, Crest). Fawcett.

No One Here Gets Out Alive. Jerry Hopkins & Daniel Sugarman. 1980. pap. 7.95 (ISBN 0-446-97133-2); pap. 2.95 (ISBN 0-446-93921-8). Warner Bks.

No One Here Gets Out Alive. Jerry Hopkins & Danny Sugerman. 400p. (Orig.). 1981. pap. 2.95 (ISBN 0-446-93921-8). Warner Bks.

No. One Home Business Book. George Delany & Sandra Delany. LC 80-84427. (Illus.). 176p. 1981. pap. 4.95 (ISBN 0-89709-022-5). Liberty Pub.

No One Writes to the Colonel & Other Stories. Gabriel Garcia-Marquez. Tr. by J. S. Bernstein from Span. LC 68-15977. 1979. pap. 3.95 (ISBN 0-06-090700-2, CN 700, CN). Har-Row.

No Other Foundation. Jeremy C. Jackson. LC 79-92017. 384p. 1979. pap. 12.95 (ISBN 0-89107-169-5, Cornerstone Bks). Good News.

No Other God. Gabriel Vahanian. LC 66-28591. (Orig.). 1966. pap. 2.50 o.s.i. (ISBN 0-8076-0389-9). Braziller.

No Other Gospels. Ed. by A. J. Koelpin. 1980. 12.95 (ISBN 0-8100-0123-3). Northwest Pub.

No Other Name. R. Leonard Small. 190p. 1966. text ed. 4.95 (ISBN 0-567-02257-9). Attic Pr.

No Pat Answers. Eugenia Price. pap. 2.95 (ISBN 0-310-31332-5); study guide 0.75 (ISBN 0-310-31333-3). Zondervan.

No Pets Allowed & Other Animal Stories. Margaret Dunnett. LC 80-2692. (Illus.). 144p. (gr. 2-7). 1981. 8.95 (ISBN 0-233-97103-3). Andre Deutsch.

No Pets Allowed & Other Animal Stories. Margaret Dunnett. LC 80-2692. 144p. (gr. 2-7). 1981. 8.95 (ISBN 0-233-97103-3). Andre Deutsch.

No Place for a Goat. Helen R. Sattler. (Illus.). 32p. (ps-3). 1981. 5.95 (ISBN 0-525-66723-7). Elsevier-Nelson.

No Place for a Hero. Niven Busch. (Illus.). 128p. Date not set. pap. 3.95 (ISBN 0-89395-027-0). Cal Living Bks.

No Place for Baseball. Alex B. Allen. LC 72-13346. (Springboard Ser.). (Illus.). 64p. (gr. 3-6). 1973. 5.75g (ISBN 0-8075-5697-1). A Whitman.

No Place for Mitty. Miriam Young. LC 75-35606. 128p. (gr. 3-7). 1976. 5.95 (ISBN 0-685-62044-1, Four Winds). Schol Bk Serv.

No Place to Run. Barbara Beasley. (YA) (gr. 7-9). 1978. pap. 1.95 (ISBN 0-671-43291-5). PB.

No Play of Japan. Arthur Waley. LC 75-28969. 1976. pap. 5.95 (ISBN 0-8048-1198-9). C E Tuttle.

No Pledge of Privacy: The Watergate Tapes Litigation, 1973-1974. Howard Ball. (National University Pubns. Multi-Disciplinary Studies in the Law). 1977. 15.00 (ISBN 0-8046-9181-9). Kennikat.

No Promises in the Wind. Irene Hunt. 224p. (gr. 5 up). 1981. pap. 1.95 (ISBN 0-448-17271-2, Tempo). G&D.

No Quittin' Sense. C. C. White & Ada M. Holland. (Illus.). 1969. 9.95x (ISBN 0-292-70002-4); pap. 5.95 (ISBN 0-292-75508-2). U of Tex Pr.

No Read Math Activities, 3vols. Donald A. Buckeye. Incl. Vol. 1. One Hundred Ninety-Eight Activities on the Lower Elementary Level; Vol. 2. One Hundred Ninety-Eight Activities on the Upper Elementary Level; Vol. 3. One Hundred Ninety-Eight Activities on the Junior High Level (ISBN 0-910974-74-8). text ed. 35.00 ea. o.p.; Midwest Pubns.

No Regrets: Memoirs of the Earl of Carnarvon. Porchey. (Illus.). 227p. 1980. Repr. 17.00x (ISBN 0-297-77246-5, Pub. by Weidenfeld & Nicolson England). Biblio Dist.

No-Return Trail. Sonia Levitin. LC 77-88964. (gr. 7 up). 1978. 6.95 (ISBN 0-15-257545-6, HJ). HarBraceJ.

No-Risk Society. Yair Aharoni. (Chatham House Series on Change in American Politics). 320p. (Orig.). 1981. pap. text ed. 9.95x (ISBN 0-934540-06-3). Chatham Hse Pubs.

No Rocking Chair for Me. Harold E. Dye. 1980. pap. 3.95 (ISBN 0-8054-5286-9). Broadman.

No Room for Man: Population & the Future Through Science Fiction. Ed. by Ralph S. Clem et al. 247p. 1979. 11.50x (ISBN 0-8476-6181-4). Rowman.

No Running on the Boardwalk. Paul Ramsey. LC 74-75941. (Contemporary Poetry Ser.). 59p. 1975. pap. 4.50 (ISBN 0-8203-0356-9). U of Ga Pr.

No Scarlet Ribbons. Susan Terris. 176p. (gr. 5 up). 1981. 9.95 (ISBN 0-374-35322-0). FS&G.

No School Today! Franz Brandenberg. LC 74-13186. (Illus.). 32p. (gr. 1-3). 1975. 7.95 o.s.i. (ISBN 0-02-711930-0). Macmillan.

No-Sew Decorating. Janet Roda. (Orig.). 1981. pap. 9.95 (ISBN 0-440-56207-4, Delta). Dell.

No Slipper for Cinderella. Mildred Lawrence. LC 65-17990. (gr. 7 up). 1965. 5.25 o.p. (ISBN 0-15-257575-8, HJ). HarBraceJ.

No Steady Job for Papa. Marion Benasutti. 1966. 7.95 o.s.i. (ISBN 0-8149-0051-8). Vanguard.

No Substitute for Madness: The Collected Stories of Ron Jones. Ron Jones. 280p. 1981. pap. 8.00 (ISBN 0-933280-06-8). Island CA.

No Tears for Mao. Kenneth O. Waterman. 1981. 4.95 (ISBN 0-8062-1698-0). Carlton.

No Thanks to the Duke. Alastair Dunnett. LC 80-1984. (Crime Club Ser.). 192p. 1981. 9.95 (ISBN 0-385-17389-X). Doubleday.

No Through Road. Roy Brown. LC 74-3484. 192p. (gr. 6 up). 1974. 5.95 (ISBN 0-395-28896-7, Clarion). HM.

No Time but Place. Jeffrey Pearson & Jessica Pearson. (Illus.). 256p. 1980. 16.95 (ISBN 0-07-049030-9). McGraw.

No Time for Neutrality. Donald K. Campbell. 144p. 1981. pap. 3.95 (ISBN 0-88207-337-0). Victor Bks.

No Time Like Tomorrow. Brian Aldiss. 160p. (RL 7). Date not set. pap. 1.25 (ISBN 0-451-06969-2, Y6969, Sig). NAL.

No Transfer. Stephen Walton. LC 66-28880. 7.95 (ISBN 0-8149-0229-4). Vanguard.

No Transfer: An American Security Principle. John A. Logan. 1961. 42.50x (ISBN 0-685-69838-6). Elliots Bks.

No Trespassing. Ray Prather. LC 73-19056. (Illus.). 32p. (gr. k-3). 1974. 4.95g o.s.i. (ISBN 0-02-775020-5). Macmillan.

No Trespassing. Sondra Stanford. 192p. (Orig.). 1980. pap. 1.50 (ISBN 0-671-57046-3). S&S.

No Two Rivers Alike: Fifty Canoeable Rivers of New York & Pennsylvania. Alec Proskine. LC 80-11648. (Illus.). 1980. 9.95 (ISBN 0-89594-020-5). Crossing Pr.

No Uncertain Sound. R. L. Small. (Scholar As Preacher Ser.). 190p. 1963. text ed. 7.75 (ISBN 0-567-04431-9). Attic Pr.

No Volvera a Mi Vacia. LC 76-55490. 365p. (Orig., Span.). 1976. pap. 2.95 (ISBN 0-89922-080-0). Edit Caribe.

No Warning. Kathleene West. 1977. 2.50 (ISBN 0-918116-11-2). Jawbone Pr.

No Way of Knowing: Dallas Poems. Myra C. Livingston. LC 80-14584. 64p. (gr. 5 up). 1980. 7.95 (ISBN 0-689-50179-X, McElderry Bk). Atheneum.

No Way Out. Jane Donnelly. (Harlequin Romances Ser.). 192p. 1980. pap. 1.25 (ISBN 0-373-02373-1, Pub. by Harlequin). PB.

No Way to Stop It. Margaret Church. LC 80-27102. (Prime Time Adventures Ser.). (Illus.). 64p. (gr. 4 up). 1981. PLB 7.95 (ISBN 0-516-02107-9). Childrens.

No Witness. Gerald A. Hausman. (Illus.). 224p. 1980. 14.95 (ISBN 0-8117-1009-2). Stackpole.

Noah. new ed. Louie J. Fant, Jr. (Illus.). 14p. 1973. pap. text ed. 2.50 (ISBN 0-917002-70-9). Joyce Media.

Noah & the Ark. (MacDonald Educational Ser.). (Illus., Arabic.). 3.50 (ISBN 0-686-53084-5). Intl Bk Ctr.

Noah & the Rainbow: An Ancient Story. Max Bolliger. Tr. by Clyde R. Bulla. LC 72-76361. (Illus.). (gr. k-3). 1972. 8.79 (ISBN 0-690-58448-2, TYC-J); pap. text ed. 2.95 (ISBN 0-690-03814-3). T Y Crowell.

Noah Builds a Big Boat. (Tell-a-Bible Story Ser.). (Illus.). 28p. bds. 0.69 (ISBN 0-686-68637-3, 3681). Standard Pub.

Noah Riddle? Ann Bishop. LC 71-115893. (Riddle Bk.). (gr. 1-3). 1970. 5.75g (ISBN 0-8075-5702-1). A Whitman.

Noah Webster. Horace E. Scudder. LC 80-20031. (American Men & Women of Letters Ser.). 310p. 1981. pap. 4.95 (ISBN 0-87754-158-2). Chelsea Hse.

Noah Webster's American Spelling Book. Henry S. Commager. LC 62-21960. 1963. text ed. 8.75 (ISBN 0-8077-1179-9); pap. text ed. 4.00x (ISBN 0-8077-1176-4). Tchrs Coll.

Noah's Ark. Judy Brook. LC 73-2024. (Illus.). (gr. k-3). 1973. PLB 5.90 o.p. (ISBN 0-531-02630-2). Watts.

Noah's Ark. Retold by Lawrence T. Lorimer. LC 77-92377. (Picturebacks Ser.). (Illus.). (ps-2). 1978. PLB 4.99 (ISBN 0-394-93861-5, BYR); pap. 1.25 (ISBN 0-394-83861-0). Random.

Noah's Ark. Peter Spier. LC 76-43630. (gr. 1-3). 1977. 8.95a (ISBN 0-385-09473-6); PLB (ISBN 0-385-12730-8). Doubleday.

Noah's Ark. Peter Spier. 48p. (ps). 1981. pap. 3.95 (ISBN 0-385-17302-4, Zephyr). Doubleday.

Noah's Ark Diorama Book. Carol Ferntheil. (gr. k-3). 1977. 3.25 (ISBN 0-87239-167-1, 3606). Standard Pub.

Noah's Ark Is Stranded. Bjorn Berglund. 1976. 12.95 o.p. (ISBN 0-440-06434-1, Sey Lawr). Delacorte.

Noam Chomsky: A Philosophic Overview. Justin Lieber. (World Leaders Ser.: No. 36). 1975. lib. bdg. 9.95 (ISBN 0-8057-3661-1). Twayne.

Nobask. Monty Creagh. 100p. 1980. 7.95 (ISBN 0-533-04510-X). Vantage.

Nobility & the Chiefly Tradition in the Modern Kingdom of Tonga. George E. Marcus. 1980. pap. text ed. 15.00x (Pub. by Polynesian Soc). U Pr of Hawaii.

Nobility of Later Medieval England: The Ford Lectures for 1953 & Related Studies. K. B. McFarlane. 1973. 29.95x (ISBN 0-19-822362-5). Oxford U Pr.

Noble Buyer: John Quinn, Patron of the Avant-Garde. Judith Zilczer. LC 78-2041. (Illus.). 198p. 1978. 25.00 (ISBN 0-87474-998-0). Smithsonian.

Noble Drama of W. B. Yeats. Liam Miller. (New Yeats Papers: No. 13). (Illus.). 500p. 1977. text ed. 52.00x (ISBN 0-391-00633-9, Dolmen Pr). Humanities.

Noble Enemy. Charles Fox. LC 78-22770. 1980. 12.50 o.p. (ISBN 0-385-14526-8). Doubleday.

Noble Enemy. Charles Fox. 1980. 12.50 (ISBN 0-385-14526-8). Doubleday.

Noble Experiment, 1920-1933: The Eighteenth Amendment Prohibits Liquor in America. James P. Barry. LC 78-180165. (Focus Books). (Illus.). 72p. (gr. 7 up). 1972. PLB 4.47 o.p. (ISBN 0-531-02454-7). Watts.

Noble Heritage: Jerusalem & Christianity - a Portrait of the Church of the Resurrection. Alistair Duncan. 1974. 10.00x (ISBN 0-685-61499-9). Intl Bk Ctr.

Noble Profession. Pierre Boulle. LC 60-15063. 1960. 8.95 (ISBN 0-8149-0066-6). Vanguard.

Noble Savages: An Essay on Charisma-the Rehabilitation of a Concept. Bryan Wilson. LC 74-81444. (Quantum Bk Ser.). 1975. 11.95x (ISBN 0-520-02815-5). U of Cal Pr.

Noble Task: The Elder. rev. ed. Andrew A. Jumper. LC 65-14420. 1965. pap. 3.00 (ISBN 0-8042-3992-4). John Knox.

Nobody. Nikolai Bokov. Tr. by April Fitzlyon. 1979. 9.95 (ISBN 0-7145-0975-2); pap. 4.95 (ISBN 0-7145-3551-6). Riverrun NY.

Nobody Asked Me, but... The World of Jimmy Cannon. Ed. by Jack Cannon & Tom Cannon. LC 77-13832. (Illus.). 1978. 10.95 o.p. (ISBN 0-03-015381-6). HR&W.

Nobody Comes to Dinner. F. Emerson Andrews. (Illus.). (gr. 1-3). 1977. 6.95 (ISBN 0-316-04221-8). Little.

Nobody Has to Be a Kid Forever. Hila Colman. (gr. 5-7). 1977. pap. 1.75 (ISBN 0-671-56098-0). PB.

Nobody Home. Jennifer L. Paul. 1978. pap. 1.95 o.s.i. (ISBN 0-446-89591-1). Warner Bks.

Nobody Knows. Jeremy Larner. 1968. 4.95 o.s.i. (ISBN 0-02-568390-X). Macmillan.

Nobody Knows but Me. Eve Bunting. (Young Romance Ser.). (gr. 3-9). 1978. PLB 5.95 (ISBN 0-87191-635-5); pap. 2.95 (ISBN 0-89812-060-8). Creative Ed.

Nobody Knows I Have Delicate Toes. Patz. (gr. k-3). 1980. 5.95 (ISBN 0-531-02392-3, C15); PLB 7.90 (ISBN 0-686-65252-5, B25). Watts.

Nobody Knows Me in Miami. Sheila S. Klass. 156p. (gr. 4-6). 1981. 8.95 (ISBN 0-684-16851-0). Scribner.

Nobody Loves a Drunken Indian. Clair Huffaker. 1980. pap. write for info. (ISBN 0-671-83058-9). PB.

Nobody Meets Bigfoot. Marian T. Place. LC 75-40030. (gr. 4-7). 1976. 4.95 (ISBN 0-396-07290-9). Dodd.

Nobody Said It Better! Two Thousand Seven Hunred Wise & Witty Quotations About Famous People. Miriam Ringo. LC 80-20404. 352p. 1980. 12.95 (ISBN 0-528-81104-5). Rand.

Nobody Said It Would Be Easy: Raising Responsible Kids -- and Keeping Them Out of Trouble. Dan Kiley. LC 77-11821. 1978. 10.95 o.s.i. (ISBN 0-06-012369-9, HarpT). Har-Row.

Nobody's Perfect. Terry Powell. 1979. pap. 1.95 (ISBN 0-88207-577-2). Victor Bks.

Nobody's Perfect. Norma Simon. Ed. by Kathleen Tucker. (Concept Bks.). (Illus.). 32p. (gr. k-3). 1981. 6.50 (ISBN 0-8075-5707-2). A Whitman.

Nobs & Snobs. Michael Nelson. 1976. 13.95 o.p. (ISBN 0-86033-028-1). Gordon-Cremonesi.

Noche Callada (Poemas) Mercedes Castro. (Illus.). 79p. (Orig., Span.). pap. 3.75 (ISBN 0-9604748-0-3). Castro.

Noche de Primavera sin Sueno: Comedia Humoristica en Tres Actos. Enrique J. Poncela. Ed. by Francisco C. Lacosta. LC 67-25113. (Span.). (YA) (gr. 9 up). 1967. pap. text ed. 3.95x (ISBN 0-89197-320-6). Irvington.

Noche, Fuente: Poesia. 2nd ed. Carlos M. Passalacqua. LC 79-23317. (Illus.). 104p. 1980. pap. write for info. (ISBN 0-8477-3226-6). U of PR Pr.

Nociones Esenciales Del Hebreo Biblico. Kyle M. Yates & J. J. Owens. Tr. by S. Daniel Daglio. 1980. Repr. of 1978 ed. 5.25 (ISBN 0-311-42056-7). Casa Bautista.

Nocturnal Learning: Theory & Practice of Sleep Learning. Don A. Clausing. 64p. (Orig.). 1980. pap. text ed. 6.95 (ISBN 0-936214-02-3). Nat Learn Res.

Nocturnal Malagasy Primates: Ecology, Physiology & Behavior. P. Charles-Dominique et al. LC 89-6799. (Communication & Behavior: an Interdisciplinary Ser.). 1980. 27.50 (ISBN 0-12-169350-3). Acad Pr.

Nocturne: From the Notes of Lt. Amiran Amilakhvari, Retired. Boulat Okudjava. Tr. by Antonina W. Bouis from Russian. LC 77-11544. 1978. 10.00 o.p. (ISBN 0-06-013289-2, HarpT). Har-Row.

Nocturnes & Pastorals. A. B. Miall. Ed. by Ian Fletcher & John Stokes. LC 76-20104. (Decadent Consciousness Ser.: Vol. 28). 1977. Repr. of 1896 ed. lib. bdg. 38.00 (ISBN 0-8240-2777-9). Garland Pub.

Noel Coward. Milton Levin. LC 68-24285. (English Authors Ser.: No. 73). 1969. lib. bdg. 10.95 (ISBN 0-8057-1120-1). Twayne.

Noelle's Brown Book. Noelle Lamperti et al. LC 79-89574. (Illus., Orig.). (ps). 1979. pap. 1.50 (ISBN 0-934678-03-0). New Victoria Pubs.

Noise. F. R. Connor. (Introductory Topics in Electronics & Telecommunication Ser.). (Illus.). 1973. pap. text ed. 11.00x (ISBN 0-7131-3306-6). Intl Ideas.

Noise Abatement Policies. 392p. 1980. 16.00 (ISBN 92-64-12084-X). OECD.

Noise Abatement: Policy Alternatives for Transportation. Assembly of Behavioral & Social Sciences. 1977. pap. 8.00 (ISBN 0-309-02648-2). Natl Acad Pr.

Noise & Fluctuations in Electronic Devices & Circuits. F. N. Robinson. (Monographs in Electrical & Electronic Engineering). (Illus.). 254p. 1975. 37.50x (ISBN 0-19-859319-8). Oxford U Pr.

Noise & Office Work. Susan T. Mackenzie. (Key Issues Ser.: No. 19). 1975. pap. 3.00 (ISBN 0-87546-232-4). NY Sch Indus Rel.

Noise & Prices. A. A. Walters. (Illus.). 160p. 1975. 24.00x (ISBN 0-19-828197-8). Oxford U Pr.

Noise, Buildings, & People. Derek J. Croome-Gale. LC 73-7982. 500p. 1975. text ed. 76.00 (ISBN 0-08-019690-X); pap. text ed. 45.00 (ISBN 0-08-019816-3). Pergamon.

Noise Control for Engineers. Harold W. Lord et al. (Illus.). 448p. 1979. text ed. 24.95x (ISBN 0-07-038738-9); solutions manual 4.95 (ISBN 0-07-038739-7). McGraw.

Noise Control for Engineers. Harold W. Lord et al. (Illus.). 1980. text ed. 24.95 (ISBN 0-07-038738-9); solutions manual 4.95 (ISBN 0-07-038739-7). McGraw.

Noise in Measurements. Aldert Van Der Ziel. LC 76-12108. 228p. 1976. 21.50 (ISBN 0-471-89895-3, Pub. by Wiley-Interscience). Wiley.

Noise in the Trees. William Heyen. 152p. 1974. 5.95 o.s.i. (ISBN 0-8149-0739-3). Vanguard.

Noise Levels in Australian Sawmills. E. P. Lhuede & W. A. Davern. 1980. 10.00x (ISBN 0-643-00348-7, Pub. by CSJRO Australia). State Mutual Bk.

Noise of the Fields. Hugh Maxton. 1976. pap. text ed. 5.00x (ISBN 0-85105-294-0, Dolmen Pr). Humanities.

Noise Pollution: A Guide to Information Sources. Ed. by Clifford R. Bragdon. LC 73-17535. (Man & the Environment Information Guide Ser.: Vol. 5). 600p. 1979. 30.00 (ISBN 0-8103-1345-6). Gale.

Noise Pollution: Impact & Countermeasures. Antony Milne. 1979. 17.95 (ISBN 0-7153-7701-9). David & Charles.

Noise Pollution: The Unquiet Crisis. Clifford R. Bragdon. LC 70-157049. (Illus.). 1972. 16.95x (ISBN 0-8122-7638-8). U of Pa Pr.

Noise: Sources, Characterization, Measurement. Albert Van Der Ziel. LC 71-112911. (Electrical Engineering Ser). 1970. ref. ed. 17.95 o.p. (ISBN 0-13-623165-9). P-H.

Noise: The New Menace. Lucy Kavaler. LC 74-9367. 224p. 1975. 9.95 (ISBN 0-381-98274-2, JD-J). John Day.

Noisy Nancy Norris. Lou Ann Gaeddert. LC 65-10180. (ps-1). 1971. Repr. of 1965 ed. PLB 7.95 (ISBN 0-385-04749-5). Doubleday.

Nolan: Bait Money, No. 1. Max Collins. 192p. pap. 1.95 (ISBN 0-523-41159-6). Pinnacle Bks.

Nolan, Number Two: Blood Money. rev. ed. Max Collins. 192p. 1981. pap. 1.95 (ISBN 0-523-41160-X). Pinnacle Bks.

Nolan Nutria's Story. Aleta R. Bogan. 1979. 4.00 o.p. (ISBN 0-8062-1192-X). Carlton.

Nolo Contendere. Judson Crews. 6.50 (ISBN 0-930324-08-0). Green Hill.

Nomad: George A. Custer in Turf, Field & Farm, Vol 3. Ed. by Brian W. Dippie. (John Fielding & Lois Lasater Maher Ser: No. 3). (Illus.). 176p. Date not set. 22.50 (ISBN 0-292-75519-8). U of Tex Pr.

Nomads, Exiles, & Emigres: The Rebirth of the Latin American Narrative, 1960-80. Ronald Schwartz. LC 80-20669. 168p. 1980. 10.00 (ISBN 0-8108-1359-9). Scarecrow.

Nomads of South Siberia: The Pastoral Economies of Tuva. Sevyan Vainshtein. Ed. by Caroline Humphrey. Tr. by M. Colenso from Russian. LC 78-504728. (Studies in Social Anthropology: No. 25). 1981. 39.50 (ISBN 0-521-22089-0). Cambridge U Pr.

Nomads of the Balkans. Alan J. B. Wace. 1973. Repr. 19.50x (ISBN 0-685-30613-5). Biblo.

Nomads of the Nomads: The Al Murrah Bedouin of the Empty Quarter. Donald P. Cole. LC 74-18211. (Worlds of Man Ser.). 192p. 1975. pap. 5.75x (ISBN 0-88295-605-1). AHM Pub.

Nome Hermopolite. Marie Drew-Bear. LC 78-13005. (American Studies in Papyrology: No. 21). 45.00x (ISBN 0-89130-258-1, 310021). Scholars Pr CA.

Nomenclature & Criteria for Diagnosis of Diseases of the Heart & Great Vessels. 8th ed. New York Heart Association. LC 78-71219. 349p. 1979. text ed. 14.95 (ISBN 0-316-60536-0); pap. text ed. 11.95 (ISBN 0-316-60537-9). Little.

Nomenclature of Organic Chemistry: The Blue Book: 1978 Ed. Sections A-F & H. Ed. by J. Rigaudy & S. P. Klesney. 1978. text ed. 82.00 (ISBN 0-08-022369-9). Pergamon.

Nomenclature of Regular Single-Strand Organic Polymers. Ed. by K. L. Loening. 1977. pap. text ed. 10.00 (ISBN 0-08-021579-3). Pergamon.

Nomie Book: Growing up from Shy. Sunnie Williams. (Illus.). 104p. (Orig.). (gr. 3-6). 1981. pap. 5.95 (ISBN 0-9605444-0-2). Wee Smile.

Nommo (the Word) Zizwe Ngafua. (Illus.). 56p. (Orig.). 1978. pap. 4.00 (ISBN 0-917886-04-6). Shamal Bks.

Non-Abelian Minimal Closed Ideals of Transitive Lie Algebras. Jack F. Conn. LC 79-5479. (Mathematical Notes Ser.: 25). 216p. 1980. pap. 7.50x (ISBN 0-691-08251-0). Princeton U Pr.

Non-Alcoholic Food Service Beverage Handbook. 2nd ed. Marvin E. Thorner & R. J. Herzberg. 1979. lib. bdg. 29.00 (ISBN 0-87055-279-1). AVI.

Non-Aqueous Electrolytes Handbook, 2 vols. George J. Janz & R. P. T. Tompkins. Vol. 1, 1972. 88.00 (ISBN 0-12-380401-9); Vol. 2, 1974. 88.00 (ISBN 0-12-380402-7); Set. 142.00 (ISBN 0-685-36102-0). Acad Pr.

Non-Being & Somethingness. Woody Allen. 96p. 1978. pap. 4.95 (ISBN 0-686-68485-0). Random.

Non-Communicating Children. L. Minski & M. J. Shepperd. (Illus.). 1970. 10.95 (ISBN 0-407-33200-6). Butterworths.

Non Compos Mentis. John Brydall & Anthony Highmore. Ed. by David S. Berkowitz & Samuel E. Thorne. LC 77-86669. (Classics of English Legal History in the Modern Era Ser.: Vol. 46). 471p. 1979. lib. bdg. 40.00 (ISBN 0-8240-3095-8). Garland Pub.

Non-Destructive Examination in Relation to Structural Integrity. Ed. by R. W. Nichols. (Illus.). x, 286p. 1980. 60.00x (ISBN 0-85334-908-8). Burgess-Intl Ideas.

Non-Destructive Testing in Nuclear Technology, 2 vols. 1965. Vol. 1. 24.25 (ISBN 92-0-530065-9, IAEA); Vol. 2. 28.00 (ISBN 92-0-530165-5). Unipub.

Non-Destructive Testing of Concrete & Timber. Thomas Telford Ltd. Editorial Staff. 126p. 1980. 80.00x (ISBN 0-901948-27-6, Pub. by Telford England). State Mutual Bk.

Non-Equilibrium Thermodynamics & Its Statistical Foundations. H. J. Kreuzer. (Monographs on the Physics & Chemistry of Materials). (Illus.). 500p. 1981. 105.00 (ISBN 0-19-851361-5). Oxford U Pr.

Non-Ferrous Extractive Metallurgy. C. B. Gill. LC 79-28696. 1980. 39.50 (ISBN 0-471-05980-3, Pub. by Wiley-Interscience). Wiley.

Non-Ferrous Motal Data Yearbook, 1979. American Bureau of Metal Statistics Inc. (Illus.). 1980. yrbk. 25.00 (ISBN 0-686-61434-8). Am Bur Metal.

Non-Fiction Film - A Critical History. Richard M. Barsam. 1973. pap. 4.95 o.p. (ISBN 0-525-47331-9). Dutton.

Non-Formal Education: An Annotated International Bibliography. Ed. by Rolland G. Paulston. LC 72-186197. (Special Studies in International Economics & Development). 1972. 34.50x (ISBN 0-275-28623-1). Irvington.

Non-Formal Education As a Strategy in Development: Comparative Analysis of Rural Development Projects. Alemneh Dejene. LC 80-5882. 131p. 1980. lib. bdg. 16.25 (ISBN 0-8191-1346-8); pap. text ed. 7.75 (ISBN 0-8191-1347-6). U Pr of Amer.

Non-Formal Education in African Development. James R. Sheffield & Victor P. Diejomack. 258p. 1972. pap. 3.00 o.p. (ISBN 0-89192-070-6). Interbk Inc.

Non-Hodgkin's Lymphomas in Children. Ed. by John Graham-Pole. LC 80-81990. (Oncology). (Illus.). 192p. 1980. 26.50 (ISBN 0-89352-068-3). Masson Pub.

Non-Invasive Measurements of Bone Mass & Their Clinical Application. Ed. by S. H. Cohn. 240p. 1980. 64.95 (ISBN 0-8493-5789-6). CRC Pr.

Non-Invasive Methods in Cardiology. Samuel Zoneraich. (Illus.). 596p. 1975. text ed. 59.75 (ISBN 0-398-03107-X). C C Thomas.

Non-Linear Problems in Stress Analysis. Ed. by P. Stanley. (Illus.). 1978. text ed. 96.80x (ISBN 0-85334-780-8). Intl Ideas.

Non Linear Systems Analysis. M. Vidyasagar. LC 77-24379. (Illus.). 1978. ref ed. 27.95x (ISBN 0-13-623280-9). P-H.

Non-Linear Waves in Dispersive Media. V. I. Karpman. Tr. by Ferdinand Cap. 1974. text ed. 30.00 (ISBN 0-08-017720-4). Pergamon.

Non-Marine Organic Geochemistry. Frederick M. Swain. (Cambridge Earth Science Ser). (Illus.). 1970. 83.50 (ISBN 0-521-07757-5). Cambridge U Pr.

Non-Nuclear Conflicts in the Nuclear Age. Ed. by Sam C. Sarkesian. 360p. 1980. 29.95 (ISBN 0-03-056138-8). Praeger.

Non-Nuclear Futures: The Case for an Ethical Energy Strategy. Amory B. Lovins & John H. Price. LC 75-20260. 1980. pap. 3.95 (ISBN 0-06-090777-0, CN777, CN). Har-Row.

Non-Orgasmic Woman. (Illus.). 4.95 (ISBN 0-910550-49-2). Centurion Pr.

Non-Profit Hospitals: Their Structure, Human Resources, & Economic Importance. Thomas A. Barocci. LC 80-22075. (Illus.). 224p. 1980. 19.95 (ISBN 0-86569-054-5). Auburn Hse.

Non-Proliferation of Nuclear Weapons. Georges Fischer. Tr. by David Willey. LC 72-189811. 270p. 1971. text ed. 21.50x (ISBN 0-8290-0190-5). Irvington.

Non-Public School Aid: The Law, Economics & Politics of American Education. E. G. West. LC 75-31289. 256p. 1976. 18.95x (ISBN 0-669-00337-9). Lexington Bks.

Non-Resident & Surplus Line Laws: Annual Edition 1980. rev. ed. Editors of the Fire Casualty & Surety Bulletins. 60p. 1980. pap. 5.00 (ISBN 0-87218-306-8). Natl Underwriter.

Non-Resident & Surplus Line Laws, Nineteen Seventy-Nine. 1979 rev. ed. Fire Casualty &Surety Bulletins Editors. pap. 4.00 o.p. (ISBN 0-87218-302-5). Natl Underwriter.

Non-Resident Students & the U. W. Madison: Summer Session. William A. Strang & Howard Feldman. (Wisconsin Economy Studies: No. 17). (Illus.). 52p. 1979. 2.50 (ISBN 0-86603-006-9). U Wis Grad Sch Bush.

Non-Resident Students & the U. W. Madison Summer Session: An Evaluation of Demand & an Estimate of Local Economic Impact. William A. Strang & Howard Feldman. (Wisconsin Economy Studies: No. 17). (Orig.). 1979. pap. 2.50. Bureau Busn Res U Wis.

Non-Ricardian Political Economy. Barry J. Gordon. (Kress Library of Business & Economics: No. 20). 1967. pap. 5.00x (ISBN 0-678-09914-6, Baker Lib). Kelley.

Non-Solar Gamma-Rays: Proceedings. COSPAR, Twenty-Second Plenary Meeting, Bangalore, India, 1979. Ed. by R. Cowsik & R. D. Wills. 254p. 1980. 50.00 (ISBN 0-08-024440-8). Pergamon.

Non-State Nations in International Politics: Comparative System Analyses. Ed. by Judy S. Bertelsen. LC 75-36404. 1978. text ed. 29.95 (ISBN 0-275-56320-0). Praeger.

Non-Stoichiometric Compounds: Tungsten Bronzes; Vanadium Bronzes; & Related Compounds. D. Bevan & P. Hagenmuller. (Pergamon Texts in Inorganic Chemistry: Vol 1). 154p. 1975. text ed. 27.00 (ISBN 0-08-018776-5); pap. text ed. 14.00 (ISBN 0-08-018775-7). Pergamon.

Non-Stop Discussion Workbook! Problems for Intermediate & Advanced Students of English. George Rooks. (Orig.). 1980. pap. text ed. 2.95 (ISBN 0-88377-171-3). Newbury Hse.

Non-Traded & Intermediate Goods & the Pure Theory of International Trade. Bharat Hazari et al. 1981. 29.95 (ISBN 0-312-57728-1). St Martin.

Non-Verbal Communication. Ed. by R. A. Hinde. LC 75-171675. (Illus.). 464p. 1972. 47.50 (ISBN 0-521-08370-2); pap. 14.95x (ISBN 0-521-29012-0). Cambridge U Pr.

Non-Violent Action & Social Change. Ed. by Severyn T. Bruyn & Paula Rayman. (Orig.). 1980. pap. text ed. 8.95x (ISBN 0-8290-0271-5). Irvington.

Non-Violent Mad. Mad Magazine Editors. (Mad Ser.: No. 33). (Illus.). 1972. pap. 1.75 (ISBN 0-446-94593-5). Warner Bks.

Non-Vocal Communication Resource Book. G. Vauderheiden. 1978. 15.95 (ISBN 0-8391-1252-1). Univ Park.

Non-Waste Technology & Production: Proceedings of an International Seminar Held in Paris, Nov.-Dec. 1976. United Nations Economic Commission for Europe. 1978. pap. 115.00 (ISBN 0-08-022028-2). Pergamon.

Nonalignment in Contemporary International Relations. Ed. by K. R. Narayanan & K. P. Misra. 275p. 1981. text ed. 27.50x (ISBN 0-7069-1286-1, Pub by Vikas India). Advent Bk.

Nonaqueous Solution Chemistry. Orest Popovych & Reginald Tomkins. LC 80-21693. 450p. 1981. 32.00 (ISBN 0-471-02673-5, Pub. by Wiley-Interscience). Wiley.

Nonbook Cataloguing Sampler. David V. Laertacher. 100p. 1975. pap. 5.00 (ISBN 0-912556-04-8). Hi Willow.

Noncommutative Ring Theory: Papers. International Conference, Kent State U., April 4-5, 1975. Ed. by J. H. Cozzens et al. (Lecture Notes in Mathematics: Vol. 545). 1976. soft cover 13.00 (ISBN 0-387-07985-8). Springer-Verlag.

Nonconformity in the Nineteenth Century. Ed. by David M. Thompson. (Birth of Modern Britain Ser.). 1972. 15.00 (ISBN 0-7100-7274-0); pap. 8.95 (ISBN 0-7100-7275-9). Routledge & Kegan.

Nondestructive Evaluation in the Nuclear Industry. Ed. by R. Natesh. 1978. 42.00 (ISBN 0-87170-029-8). ASM.

Nondiscrimination in Employment-& Beyond, Report No. 782. Ruth G. Shaeffer. vi, 108p. (Orig.). 1980. pap. 30.00 (ISBN 0-8237-0218-9). Conference Bd.

None of These Diseases. S. I. McMillen. (Orig.). pap. 1.50 (ISBN 0-515-04604-3). Jove Pubns.

None of These Diseases. S. I. McMillin. 1975. pap. 1.50 (ISBN 0-89129-011-7). Jove Pubns.

Nonesuch. Georgette Heyer. 1978. pap. 2.25 (ISBN 0-449-23716-8, Crest). Fawcett.

Nonesuch Creek: Selected Poems 1969 to 79. Al Masarik. Ed. by Kirk Robertson. 112p. (Orig.). 1980. pap. 4.50 (ISBN 0-916918-12-2). Duck Down.

Nonexistent Knight & the Clover Viscount. Italo Calvino. Ed. by J. Ferrone & H. Wolff. 1977. pap. 3.95 (ISBN 0-15-665975-1, HPL). HarBraceJ.

Nongonococcal Urethritis & Related Infections. Ed. by Derek Hobson & King K. Holmes. LC 77-24329. 1977. 14.00 (ISBN 0-914826-12-3). Am Soc Microbio.

Noninvasive Diagnostic Techniques in Vascular Disease. new ed. Ed. by Eugene F. Bernstein et al. LC 78-892. (Illus.). 1978. text ed. 45.50 (ISBN 0-8016-0670-5). Mosby.

Noninvasive Evaluation of Human Circulation. Simonyi. 1976. 17.00 (ISBN 0-9960008-0-1, Pub. by Kaido Hungary). Heyden.

Nonlinear Analysis in Chemical Engineering. Bruce A. Finlayson. (M-H Chemical Engineering Ser.). (Illus.). 384p. 1980. text ed. 44.50 (ISBN 0-07-020915-4). McGraw.

Nonlinear Analysis of Plates. C. Y. Chia. (Illus.). 448p. 1980. text ed. 46.50 (ISBN 0-07-010746-7). McGraw.

Nonlinear Differential Equations in Abstract Spaces. V. Kakshmikantham. (I.S. Nonlinear Mathematics Series; Theory, Methods and Applications: Vol. 2). 272p. 1981. 45.00 (ISBN 0-08-025038-6). Pergamon.

Nonlinear Electromagnetics. Piergiorgio Uslenghi. 1980. 30.00 (ISBN 0-12-709660-4). Acad Pr.

Nonlinear Electronic Circuits. Aldert Van Der Ziel. LC 76-48145. 1977. 22.50 (ISBN 0-471-02227-6, Pub. by Wiley-Interscience). Wiley.

Nonlinear Functional Analysis, Pts. 1 & 2. Ed. by F. Browder. LC 74-3414. (Proceedings of Symposia in Pure Mathematics Ser.). 1968. Set. 44.80. Am Math.

Nonlinear Networks: Theory & Analysis. Alan N. Willson, Jr. LC 74-19558. (IEEE Selected Reprint Ser.). 397p. 1975. 14.50 (ISBN 0-471-94953-1, Pub. by Wiley-Interscience). Wiley.

Nonlinear Operators & Differential Equations in Banach Spaces. Robert H. Martin, Jr. LC 76-15279. (Pure & Applied Mathematics Ser.). 544p. 1976. 39.95 (ISBN 0-471-57363-9, Pub. by Wiley-Interscience). Wiley.

Nonlinear Ordinary Differential Equations. D. W. Jordan & P. Smith. (Oxford Applied Mathematics & Computing Science Ser.). (Illus.). 1977. pap. 17.95x (ISBN 0-19-859621-9). Oxford U Pr.

Nonlinear Oscillations. Ali H. Nayfeh & Dean T. Mook. LC 78-27102. (Pure & Applied Mathematics Texts, Monographs & Tracts). 1979. 39.50 (ISBN 0-471-03555-6, Pub. by Wiley-Interscience). Wiley.

Nonlinear Programming Codes. K. Schittkowski. (Lecture Notes in Economics & Mathematical Systems Ser.: Vol. 183). 242p. 1981. pap. 19.00 (ISBN 0-387-10247-7). Springer-Verlag.

Nonlinear Programming for Operations Research. D. M. Simmons. (International Ser. in Management). (Illus.). 480p. 1976. ref. ed. 21.95 (ISBN 0-13-623397-X). P-H.

Nonlinear Programming: Proceedings, Vol. 9. Society for Industrial & Applied Mathematics-American Mathematical Society Symposia-New York, March 1975. Ed. by Richard W. Cottle & C. E. Lemke. LC 75-47471. 1980. Repr. of 1976 ed. 14.00 (ISBN 0-8218-1329-3, SIAMS-9). Am Math.

Nonlinear Programming: Theory & Algorithms. Mokhtar S. Bazaraa & C. M. Shetty. LC 78-986. 1979. text ed. 30.95 (ISBN 0-471-78610-1). Wiley.

Nonlinear Programming: Unconstrained Minimization Techniques. A. V. Fiacco & G. P. McCormick. LC 68-30909. 1968. 20.50 o.p. (ISBN 0-471-25810-5, Pub. by Wiley-Interscience). Wiley.

Nonlinear Vibrations in Mechanical & Electrical Systems Pure & Aplied Mechanics, Vol. 2. J. J. Stoker. 1950. 29.95 (ISBN 0-470-82830-7). Wiley.

Nonlinear Viscoelastic Solids. F. J. Lockett. 1973. 28.00 (ISBN 0-12-454350-2). Acad Pr.

Nonmetropolitan Industrial Growth & Community Change. Ed. by Gene F. Summers & Arne Selvik. LC 78-22652. (Illus.). 1979. 23.95 (ISBN 0-669-02820-7). Lexington Bks.

Nonny Poems. David Kherdian. LC 73-11832. 64p. 1974. 4.95 o.s.i. (ISBN 0-02-562990-5). Macmillan.

Nonparametric Methods for Quantitative Analysis. Jean D. Gibbons. LC 74-28910. 1976. text ed. 29.95 (ISBN 0-03-007811-3). Am Sciences Pr.

Nonparametric Methods in Multivariate Analysis. M. L. Puri & P. K. Sen. LC 79-129052. (Ser. in Probability & Mathematical Statistics). 1971. 40.95 (ISBN 0-471-70240-4, Pub. by Wiley-Interscience). Wiley.

Nonparametric Statistics: A Contemporary Approach. Richard P. Runyon. LC 76-55635. 1977. pap. text ed. 9.95 (ISBN 0-201-06547-9); avail test book 2.75 (ISBN 0-201-06548-7). A-W.

Nonparametric Techniques in Statistical Inference. Ed. by M. L. Puri. LC 74-116750. (Illus.). 1970. 86.50 (ISBN 0-521-07817-2). Cambridge U Pr.

Nonparametrics: Statistical Methods Based on Ranks. E. L. Lehmann. LC 72-93538. 1975. text ed. 29.95x (ISBN 0-8162-4994-6). Holden-Day.

Nonprint Materials on Communication: An Annotated Directory of Select Films, Videotapes, Videocassettes, Simulations & Games. June D. Buteau. LC 76-21857. 454p. 1976. 19.50 (ISBN 0-8108-0973-7). Scarecrow.

Nonprofessional Revolution in Mental Health. Francine Sobey. LC 71-118355. 1970. 15.00x (ISBN 0-231-03304-4). Columbia U Pr.

Nonprofessionals in the Human Services. Ed. by Charles Grosser et al. LC 76-92887. (Social & Behavioral Science Ser.). 1969. 14.95x o.p. (ISBN 0-87589-041-5). Jossey-Bass.

Nonprofit Organizations: A Government Management Tool. Ed. by Harold Orlans. 1980. 22.95 (ISBN 0-03-053966-8). Praeger.

Nonprofit Research & Patent Management in the United States. Committee On Patent Policy. 1956. pap. 2.75 (ISBN 0-309-00371-7). Natl Acad Pr.

Nonprofit Research Institute: Its Origin, Operation, Problems & Prospects. Carnegie Commission on Higher Education. Ed. by Harold Orlans. LC 70-37532. 256p. 1972. 9.95 o.p. (ISBN 0-07-010040-3, P&RB). McGraw.

Nonproliferation & U. S. Foreign Policy. Ed. by Joseph A. Yager. LC 80-20483. 464p. 1980. 22.95 (ISBN 0-8157-9674-9); pap. 8.95 (ISBN 0-8157-9673-0). Brookings.

Nonsense Alphabets. Edward Lear. (Peter Possum Paperbacks). (gr. k-3). 1975. pap. 0.95 o.p. (ISBN 0-531-05129-3). Watts.

Nonsense Book. Ed. by Duncan Emrich. LC 77-105339. (Illus.). 272p. (gr. 1 up). 1970. 8.95 (ISBN 0-590-07157-2, Four Winds). Schol Bk Serv.

Nonsense Rhymes. Sukumar Ray & Satyajit Ray. Tr. by Satyajit Ray from Bengali. (Writers Workshop Saffronbird Ser.). 1975. 8.00 (ISBN 0-88253-588-9); pap. text ed. 4.00 (ISBN 0-88253-587-0). Ind-US Inc.

Nonsmooth Optimization: Proceedings of an IIASA Workshop, 28 March-8 April 1977. Ed. by C Lemarechale & R. Mifflin. 1979. text ed. 37.00 (ISBN 0-08-023428-3). Pergamon.

Nonspeech Language & Communication. R. Schiefelbusch. 1979. 24.95 (ISBN 0-8391-1558-X). Univ Park.

Nonstop. Marion Winik. (Cedar Rock Poetry Ser.). 1981. pap. 3.50 (ISBN 0-930024-13-3). Cedar Rock.

Nonstriatal Dopaminergic Neurons. Ed. by E. Costa & G. L. Gessa. LC 76-5661. (Advances in Biochemical Psychopharmacology Ser.: Vol. 16). 1977. 59.50 (ISBN 0-89004-127-X). Raven.

Nontariff Distortions of International Trade. Robert E. Baldwin. 1970. 12.95 (ISBN 0-8157-0786-X). Brookings.

Nontax & Tax Aspects of Life Insurance. 53p. 1980. pap. 10.00 (T182). ALI-ABA.

Nontoxic Goiter: Concept & Controversy. Joel I Hamburger. (Illus.). 232p. 1973. 14.50 (ISBN 0-398-02723-4). C C Thomas.

Nonverbal Aspects of Psychotherapy. Peter H. Waxer. LC 78-71280. 1978. 19.95 (ISBN 0-03-046721-7). Praeger.

Nonverbal Communication. Abne M. Eisenberg & Ralph R. Smith. LC 77-160790. (Speech Communication Ser.: No. 9). 1971. pap. 4.50 (ISBN 0-672-61155-4). Bobbs.

Nonverbal Communication. Albert Mehrabian. LC 72-172859. 336p. 1972. 19.95x (ISBN 0-202-25091-1). Aldine Pub.

Nonverbal Communication. Ed. by David C. Speer. LC 73-90714. (Sage Contemporary Social Science Issues: No. 10). 1974. 4.95x (ISBN 0-8039-0339-1). Sage.

Nonverbal Communication: A Research Guide & Bibliography. Mary R. Key. LC 76-53024. 1977. lib. bdg. 21.00 (ISBN 0-8108-1014-X). Scarecrow.

Nonverbal Communication for Business Success. new ed. Ken Cooper. (Illus.). 1979. 12.95 o.p. (ISBN 0-8144-5500-X). Am Mgmt.

Nonverbal Communication: Readings with Commentary. 2nd ed. Shirley Weitz. (Illus.). 1978. text ed. 15.95x (ISBN 0-19-502447-8); pap. text ed. 9.95x (ISBN 0-19-502448-6). Oxford U Pr.

Nonverbal Communication: The State of the Art. Robert G. Harper et al. LC 77-19185. (Personality Processes Ser.). 1978. 28.95 (ISBN 0-471-02672-7, Pub. by Wiley-Interscience). Wiley.

Nonverbal Communication with Patients: Back to the Human Touch. Marion N. Blondis & Barbara Jackson. LC 76-30732. 1977. 8.95 (ISBN 0-471-01753-1, Pub. by Wiley Medical). Wiley.

Nonverbal Communications Systems. Dale Leathers. 288p. 1976. pap. text ed. 10.95 (ISBN 0-205-04894-3, 4848942). Allyn.

Nonviolence in America: A Documentary History. Ed. by Staughton Lynd. Incl. Civil Disobedience. Henry D. Thoreau; Moral Equivalent of War. William James; Pilgrimage to Nonviolence. Martin L. King. LC 65-23010. 1966. pap. 8.20 o.p. (ISBN 0-672-60092-7, AHS60). Bobbs.

Nonviolent Alternative. Thomas Merton. Date not set. 12.95 (ISBN 0-374-22312-2); pap. 6.95 (ISBN 0-374-51575-1). FS&G.

Nonwood Plant Fiber Pulping, Progress Report, No. 10. Joseph E. Atchison. (TAPPI PRESS Reports). (Illus.). 1979. pap. 38.95 (ISBN 0-89852-381-8, 01-01-R081). TAPPI.

Nonwood Pulp Fiber Pulping: Progress Report, No. 9. Joseph E. Atchinson et al. (TAPPI PRESS Reports). (Illus.). 1978. pap. 38.95 (ISBN 0-89852-375-3, 01 01 R075). TAPPI.

Nonwovens & Disposables: New Technical-Marketing Developments. ViJay M. Bhatnagar. 86p. 1978. pap. 25.00 (ISBN 0-87762-256-6). Technomic.

Nonwovens & Disposables: Proceedings of the First Canadian Symposium of Nonwovens & Disposables. Ed. by ViJay M. Bhatnagar. LC 78-68591. (Illus.). 1978. pap. 25.00 (ISBN 0-87762-268-X). Technomic.

Noodlehead Stories from Around the World. Moritz A. Jagendorf. LC 57-12266. (Illus.). (gr. 4-6). 7.95 (ISBN 0-8149-0329-0). Vanguard.

Noodles du Jour. Wally Armbruster. LC 75-42818. (Illus.). 192p. 1976. pap. 4.50 (ISBN 0-570-03729-8, 12-2631). Concordia.

Nooks & Corners of the New England Coast. Samuel A. Drake. LC 69-19883. 1969. Repr. of 1875 ed. 20.00 (ISBN 0-8103-3827-0). Gale.

Noon Sight Navigation: Simplified Celestial. A. A. Birney. LC 72-88042. (Illus.). 1972. pap. 5.00 (ISBN 0-87033-171-X). Cornell Maritime.

Nootka & Quileute Music. Frances Densmore. LC 72-1885. (Music Ser.). (Illus.). 416p. 1972. Repr. of 1939 ed. lib. bdg. 29.50 (ISBN 0-306-70513-3). Da Capo.

Nopalgarth. Jack Vance. (Science Fiction Ser.). 1980. pap. 2.25 (ISBN 0-87997-563-6, UE1563). Daw Bks.

Nora & Brs. Mind Your Own Business. Hohanna Hurwitz. (gr. k-6). Date not set. pap. price not set (ISBN 0-440-45668-1, YB). Dell.

Nora & Mrs. Mind-Your-Own-Business. Johanna Hurwitz. (Illus.). (gr. 1-5). 1977. PLB 6.00 (ISBN 0-688-32097-X). Morrow.

Norah. Pamela Hill. 1978. pap. 1.95 o.p. (ISBN 0-449-23482-7, Crest). Fawcett.

Nordic Countries Legislation on the Environment with Special Emphasis on Conservation: A Survey. (Environmental Policy & Law Paper: No. 14). 44p. 1980. pap. 10.75 (IUCN 83, IUCN). Unipub.

Nordic Model. Clive Archer & Stephen Maxwell. 1980. text ed. 28.00x (ISBN 0-566-00341-4, Pub. by Gower Pub Co England). Renouf.

Nordic Touring & Cross Country Skiing. 4th, rev. ed. M. Michael Brady. LC 77-77159. (Illus.). 92p. (Orig.). 1977. pap. 4.50x (ISBN 0-8277-7715-9, N395). Vanous.

Norfolk: A Pictorial History. 2nd ed. Carroll Walker. Ed. by Donna R. Friedman. (Illus.). 208p. 1981. pap. write for info. (ISBN 0-89865-129-8). Donning Co.

Norgil: More Tales of Prestidigitection. Maxwell Grant. LC 78-53497. (Illus.). 1979. 10.00 (ISBN 0-89296-041-8); limited ed. o.p. 25.00 (ISBN 0-89296-042-6). Mysterious Pr.

Norgil the Magician. Maxwell Grant, pseud. LC 76-16891. 1977. 10.00 (ISBN 0-89296-006-X). Mysterious Pr.

Norma, 2 vols. Vincenzo Bellini. Ed. by Charles Rosen & Philip Gossett. LC 76-49177. (Early Romantic Opera Ser.: Vol. 4). Date not set. lib. bdg. 82.00 (ISBN 0-8240-2903-8). Garland Pub. Postponed.

Norma. Norma Zimmer. 1976. 7.95 o.p. (ISBN 0-8423-4717-8); with cassette o.p. 8.95 (ISBN 0-685-80877-7); pap. 2.95 (ISBN 0-685-80878-5). Tyndale.

Normal Adolescence: Its Dynamics & Impact, Vol. 6. GAP Committee on Adolescence. LC 62-2872. (Report: No. 68). 1968. pap. 4.00 (ISBN 0-87318-093-3). Adv Psychiatry.

Normal & Abnormal Development of the Human Nervous System. Ronald J. Lemire et al. (Illus.). 1975. 34.00x o.p. (ISBN 0-06-141530-8, Harper Medical). Har-Row.

Normal & Abnormal Development: The Influence of Primitive Reflexes on Motor Development. Mary R. Fiorentino. (Illus.). 80p. 1980. 10.75 (ISBN 0-398-02278-X). C C Thomas.

Normal & Impaired Differentiation Processes in the Nervous System. Ed. by W. Lierse & F. Beck. (Bibliotheca Anatomica Ser.: No. 19). (Illus.). 1980. soft cover 112.00 (ISBN 3-8055-1039-X). S Karger.

Normal & Pathological Development of Energy Metabolism. Ed. by E. A. Hommes & C. J. Van Den Berg. 1976. 34.00 (ISBN 0-12-354560-9). Acad Pr.

Normal Christian Life. Watchman Nee. 1961-1963. pap. 2.95 (ISBN 0-87508-414-1). Chr Lit.

Normal Christian Life Study Guide. Watchman Nee. Ed. by Foster. 1978. pap. 1.25. Chr Lit.

Normal Development of Body Image. Ed. by Fay L. Bower. LC 77-3487. (Nursing Concept Modules Ser.). 1977. pap. 10.95 (ISBN 0-471-02170-9, Pub. by Wiley Medical). Wiley.

Normal Diet. Compiled by Margaret Gammon. 1976. pap. 1.95 (ISBN 0-87604-010-5). ARE Pr.

Normal Topological Spaces. R. A. Alo & H. L. Shapiro. LC 73-79304. (Tracts in Mathematics Ser.: No. 65). (Illus.). 250p. 1974. 43.00 (ISBN 0-521-20271-X). Cambridge U Pr.

Norman Achievement: 1050-1100. David C. Douglas. LC 74-88028. 1969. 20.00x (ISBN 0-520-01383-2). U of Cal Pr.

Norman Age - Commentaries of an Era. A. F. Scott. Incl. The Norman Age. (Illus.). 336p. 1976. 16.00x (ISBN 0-8476-6000-1); The Plantagenet Age. (Illus.). 328p. 1976. 13.50x (ISBN 0-8476-6001-X); The Stuart Age. (Illus.). 328p. 1974. 12.00x (ISBN 0-8476-6003-6); The Tudor Age. (Illus.). 291p. 1975. 13.50x (ISBN 0-8476-6002-8). (Everyone a Witness Ser). (Illus.). Rowman.

Norman Angell. Albert Marrin. (World Leaders Ser.: No. 79). 1979. lib. bdg. 14.50 (ISBN 0-8057-7725-3). Twayne.

Norman Castles of Britain. Derek F. Renn. 1968. text ed. 21.00x (ISBN 0-391-00276-7). Humanities.

Norman Conquerors. David Walker. (New History of Wales). (Illus.). 1977. text ed. 10.50x (ISBN 0-7154-0302-8). Humanities.

Norman Conquest in English Historiography. James M. Carter. 1980. pap. 18.00 (ISBN 0-89126-085-4). Military Aff Aero.

Norman Conquest of the North: The Region & Its Transformation, 1000-1135. William E. Kapelle. LC 79-10200. 1980. 19.00x (ISBN 0-8078-1371-0). U of NC Pr.

Norman Douglas. Lewis Leary. LC 68-19753. (Columbia Ser.: No. 32). (Orig.). 1968. pap. 2.00 (ISBN 0-231-02874-1, MW32). Columbia U Pr.

Norman Empire. John Le Patourel. (Illus.). 426p. 1977. 49.50x (ISBN 0-19-822525-3). Oxford U Pr.

Norman England. Peter Lane. (Visual Sources Ser.). (Illus.). 96p. (gr. 7 up). 1980. text ed. 14.95 (ISBN 0-7134-3356-6, Pub. by Batsford England). David & Charles.

Norman Fate, 1100-1154. David C. Douglas. LC 75-13155. 350p. 1976. 29.50x (ISBN 0-520-03027-3). U of Cal Pr.

Norman Institutions. Charles H. Haskins. LC 80-2026. 1981. Repr. of 1918 ed. 39.50 (ISBN 0-404-18568-1). AMS Pr.

Norman Learns About the Scriptures. Evelyn Maples. LC 61-9685. (Illus.). 40p. (gr. 1-3). 1972. 3.00 o.p. (ISBN 0-8309-0060-8). Herald Hse.

Norman Mailer. Philip H. Bufithis. LC 74-78438. (Modern Literature Ser.). 1978. 10.95 (ISBN 0-8044-2097-1); pap. 3.45 (ISBN 0-8044-6064-7). Ungar.

Norman Mailer. Robert Merrill. (United States Authors Ser.: No. 322). 1978. 12.50 (ISBN 0-8057-7254-5). Twayne.

Norman Mailer: A Collection of Critical Essays. Ed. by Leo Braudy. 1972. pap. 1.95 (ISBN 0-13-545541-3, STC101, Spec). P-H.

Norman Mailer: A Comprehensive Bibliography. Laura Adams. LC 74-14163. (Author Bibliographies Ser.: No. 20). 1974. 10.00 (ISBN 0-8108-0771-8). Scarecrow.

Norman Mailer: The Radical As Hipster. Robert Ehrlich. LC 78-14849. 1978. lib. bdg. 12.00 (ISBN 0-8108-1160-X). Scarecrow.

Norman Mailer's Novels. Sandy Cohen. (Costerus Ser.: No. 20). 1979. pap. text ed. 14.25x (ISBN 90-6203-912-X). Humanities.

Norman Nicholson. Philip Gardner. (English Authors Ser.: No. 153). 1973. lib. bdg. 10.95 (ISBN 0-8057-1418-9). Twayne.

Norman Rockwell. Christopher Finch. LC 79-57405. (Abbeville Library of Art: No. 5). (Illus.). 112p. 1980. pap. 4.95 (ISBN 0-89659-090-9). Abbeville Pr.

Norman Rockwell: A 60 Year Retrospective. (Large format). pap. 7.95 (ISBN 0-451-79969-0, G9969, Abrams Art Bks). NAL.

Norman Rockwell Collectibles Value Guide. 3rd ed. Mary Moline. LC 80-66161. 1980. pap. 9.95 (ISBN 0-913444-06-5). Rumbleseat.

Norman Rockwell Encylopedia. Mary Moline. LC 79-90498. (Illus.). 1979. 15.95 (ISBN 0-89387-032-3). Sat Eve Post.

Norman Rockwell: My Adventures As an Illustrator. Norman Rockwell. LC 79-55715. (Illus.). 1979. 13.95 (ISBN 0-89387-034-X). Sat Eve Post.

Norman Rockwell Review. LC 79-90499. (Illus.). 1979. 11.95 (ISBN 0-89387-033-1). Sat Eve Post.

Norman Rockwell's Americana ABC. cancelled o.p. (ISBN 0-685-63958-4); deluxe ed. cancelled o.p. (ISBN 0-685-63959-2). Bowmar-Noble.

Norman Rockwell's Diary for a Young Girl. George Mendoza. (Illus.). 1978. 17.95 (ISBN 0-89659-013-5). Abbeville Pr.

Norman Rockwell's Scrapebook for a Young Boy. George Mendoza. (Illus.). 180p. 1979. 17.95 (ISBN 0-89659-026-7); pap. 12.95 (ISBN 0-89659-162-X). Abbeville Pr.

Norman the Doorman. Don Freeman. (Illus.). (ps-2). 1959. PLB 6.95 o.s.i. (ISBN 0-670-51515-9). Viking Pr.

Norman the Doorman. Don Freeman. (Picture Puffins Ser.). (Illus.). (ps-3). 1981. pap. 1.95 (ISBN 0-14-050288-2, Puffin). Penguin.

Norman Thomas. James C. Duram. (U. S. Authors Ser.: No. 234). 1974. lib. bdg. 12.50 (ISBN 0-8057-0727-1). Twayne.

Norman Thomas: The Last Idealist. encore ed. W. A. Swanberg. LC 76-15591. (Encore Edition). (Illus.). 1976. 6.95 o.p. (ISBN 0-684-15958-9, ScribT). Scribner.

Norman Vincent Peale's Treasury of Joy & Enthusiasm. Norman V. Peale. 1981. 9.95 (ISBN 0-8007-1180-7). Revell.

Normandy Harbors & Pilotage. Edward Delmar-Morgan. 1979. 29.95x (ISBN 0-8464-0073-1). Beekman Pubs.

Normans. Patrick Rooke et al. LC 78-56586. (Peoples of the Past Ser.). (Illus.). 1978. lib. bdg. 7.95 (ISBN 0-686-51159-X). Silver.

Normans in Scotland. Robert L. Ritchie. LC 80-2216. 1980. Repr. of 1954 ed. 57.50 (ISBN 0-404-18783-8). AMS Pr.

Normative Economics: An Introduction to Microeconomic Theory & Radical Critiques. Frank J. Stilwell. 162p. 1975. pap. text ed. 10.75 (ISBN 0-08-018300-X). Pergamon.

Normative Political Theory. Fred M. Frohock. (Foundations of Modern Political Science Ser). 128p. 1973. pap. 7.95 (ISBN 0-13-623710-X). P-H.

Normative Structure of Sociology: Conservative & Emancipatory Themes in Social Thought. Hermann Strasser. (International Library of Sociology). 340p. 1976. 24.00x (ISBN 0-7100-8166-9); pap. 12.00 (ISBN 0-7100-8167-7). Routledge & Kegan.

Normy Ukrains'koi Literaturnoi Movy. Oleksa Syniavskyi. LC 78-202939. (Ukra.). 1967. text ed. 20.00 (ISBN 0-918884-14-4). Slavia Lib.

Norse Discovery of America, Vol. 1. Anne Ingstad. 1977. 40.00x (ISBN 82-00-01513-0, Dist. by Columbia U Pr). Universitet.

Norse Mythology: Legends of Gods & Heroes. rev. ed. Ed. by Peter A. Munch & Magnus Olsen. Tr. by Sigurd B. Hustuedt. LC 68-31092. (Illus.). 1968. Repr. of 1926 ed. 18.00 (ISBN 0-8103-3454-2). Gale.

Norsemen. (gr. 1). 1974. pap. text ed. 2.80 (ISBN 0-205-03878-6, 8038783); tchrs' guide 12.00 (ISBN 0-205-03866-2, 803866X). Allyn.

Norsk Allkunnebok, 10 Vols. (Norwegian.). 1950-1966. incl. 1 atlas 575.00 (ISBN 0-8277-3044-6). Maxwell Sci Intl.

North. Louis-Ferdinand Celine. 1972. 10.00 o.p. (ISBN 0-440-06420-1, Sey Lawr). Delacorte.

North. Seamus Heaney. LC 75-34888. 1976. pap. 4.95 (ISBN 0-19-519913-8, 506, GB). Oxford U Pr.

North Africa. Ed. by Ronald Steel. (Reference Shelf Ser: Vol. 38, No. 5). 1967. 6.25 (ISBN 0-8242-0092-6). Wilson.

North Africa & the Middle East: The Challenge to Western Security. Peter Duignan & L. H. Gann. (Publication Ser.: No.239). 180p. 1981. pap. 9.95 (ISBN 0-8179-7392-3). Hoover Inst Pr.

North Africa Story: An Anthropologist As OSS Agent, 1941-1943. Carleton S. Coon & Gambit Editors. 1980. 10.95 (ISBN 0-87645-108-3). Gambit.

North African Stones Speak. Paul MacKendrick. LC 79-18534. xxii, 434p. 1980. 21.00x (ISBN 0-8078-1414-8). U of NC Pr.

North America. 4th ed. F. S. Hudson. (Illus.). 464p. 1978. pap. 14.95x (ISBN 0-7121-1410-6, Pub. by Macdonald & Evans England). Intl Ideas.

North America. 6th ed. J. H. Paterson. (Illus.). 1979. text ed. 17.95 (ISBN 0-19-502484-2). Oxford U Pr.

North America in Maps: Topographical Map Studies of Canada and the USA. R. Knowles. (Illus.). 1976. pap. text ed. 12.95x (ISBN 0-582-31017-2). Longman.

North American B-Twenty-Five C-H Mitchell. LC 77-113958. (Arco-Aircam Aviation Ser., No. 32). (Illus.). 46p. 1971. pap. 3.25 o.p. (ISBN 0-668-02312-0). Arco.

North American Deserts. Edmund C. Jaeger. (Illus.). 1957. 12.50 (ISBN 0-8047-0498-8). Stanford U Pr.

North American Droughts. Ed. by Norman J. Rosenberg. LC 78-52024. (AAAS Selected Symposium Ser.). (Illus.). 1978. lib. bdg. 20.00x (ISBN 0-89158-443-9). Westview.

North American F-86A-H Sabre, Vol. 1. Ernest R. McDowell. LC 79-113953. (Arco-Aircam Aviation Ser., No. 19). 1970. pap. 2.95 o.p. (ISBN 0-668-02301-5). Arco.

North American Game Birds of Upland & Shoreline. Paul A. Johnsgard. LC 74-15274. (Illus.). xxx, 229p. 1975 (ISBN 0-8032-5811-9). pap. 7.95 (ISBN 0-8032-5811-9, BB 597, Bison). U of Nebr Pr.

North American Human Rights Directory 1980. Laurie S. Wiseberg & Harry M. Scoble. 188p. (Orig.). 1980. pap. 12.00 (ISBN 0-912048-20-4). Garrett Pk.

North American Indian Captivity. W-Ilcomb E. Washburn & John Aubrey. LC 76-7664. (Reference Library of the Humanities Ser.: Vol. 70). (Illus.). 1977. lib. bdg. 24.00 o.p. (ISBN 0-8240-1736-6). Garland Pub.

North American Indians. Marigold Coleman. (Jackdaw Ser: No. 145). (gr. 7 up). 1977. 5.95 o.s.i. (ISBN 0-670-51521-3, Grossman). Viking Pr.

North American Indians. Marie Gorsline & Douglas Gorsline. LC 77-79843. (Picturebacks Ser.). (ps-2). 1978. PLB 4.99 (ISBN 0-394-93702-3, BYR); pap. 1.25 (ISBN 0-394-83702-9). Random.

North American Indians Coloring Album. Illus. by Rita Warner. (Illus.). 32p. (Orig.). 1978. pap. 3.50 (ISBN 0-912300-95-7, 95-7). Troubador Pr.

North American Indians: Photographs by Edward S. Curtis. LC 72-87367. (Illus.). 15.00 (ISBN 0-912334-34-7); pap. 8.95 (ISBN 0-912334-35-5). Aperture.

North American Mammmals: A Photographic Album for Artists & Designers. James Spero. 1980. 9.00 (ISBN 0-8446-5667-4). Peter Smith.

North American Mustang Mk. 1-4. Christopher F. Shores & Richard Ward. LC 73-88967. (Arco-Aircam Aviation Ser., No. 3). (Illus., Orig.). 1968. lib. bdg. 5.00 o. p. (ISBN 0-668-02098-9); pap. 2.95 (ISBN 0-668-02097-0). Arco.

North American Quarternary Canis. Ronald M. Nowak. Ed. by E. O. Wiley. (U of KS Museum of Nat. Hist. Monograph: No. 6). (Illus.). 154p. 1979. pap. 10.00 (ISBN 0-89338-007-5). U of KS Mus Nat Hist.

North American Radio T. V. Station Guide. 14th ed. Jones. pap. 7.95 (ISBN 0-686-64616-9). Bobbs.

North American Radio-TV Station Guide: TV Station Guide. 13th ed. Vane A. Jones. LC 79-62993. 1979. pap. 6.95 o.p. (ISBN 0-672-21577-2). Sams.

North American Radio-T.V. Station Guide: TV Station Guide. 14th ed. Vane A. Jones. 1980. pap. 7.95 (ISBN 0-672-21725-2). Sams.

North American Sealife Coloring Album. Mal Whyte. (Wildlife Ser.). (Illus.). 1973. pap. 3.50 (ISBN 0-912300-27-2, 27-2). Troubador Pr.

North American Species of Heterosarus Robertson (Hymenoptera, Apoidea) P. H. Timberlake. (Publicaions in Entomology: Vol. 77). 1975. pap. 9.50x (ISBN 0-520-09528-6). U of Cal Pr.

North American Urban Patterns. Maurice Yeates. LC 80-17708. (Scripta Series in Geography). 168p. 1980. 27.95 (ISBN 0-470-27017-9, Pub. by Halsted Pr). Wiley.

North & South Korea: First Bks. Gene Gurney & Claire Gurney. LC 73-4278. (gr. 7 up). 1973. PLB 4.47 o.p. (ISBN 0-531-00804-5). Watts.

North Atlantic Security: The Forgotten Flank? Kenneth A. Myers. LC 78-66209. (Washington Papers: No. 62). 1979. pap. 3.50x (ISBN 0-8039-1231-5). Sage.

North Avenue Irregulars. Albert F. Hill. 1979. pap. 1.95 o.p. (ISBN 0-425-04085-2). Berkley Pub.

North Biscay Pilot. K. Adlard Coles & A. N. Black. 1979. 44.95x (ISBN 0-8464-0072-3). Beekman Pubs.

North British Railway, 2 vols. John Thomas. LC 70-469296. (Illus.). 1975. Vol. 1. 17.95 (ISBN 0-7153-4697-0); Vol. 2. 17.95 (ISBN 0-7153-6699-8). David & Charles.

North Brittainy Pilot. K. Adlard Coles. 1979. 34.95x (ISBN 0-8464-0071-5). Beekman Pubs.

North Carolina. 28.00 (ISBN 0-89770-109-7). Curriculum Info Ctr.

North Carolina: A Guide to the Old North State. Federal Writers' Project. 649p. 1939. Repr. 54.00 (ISBN 0-403-02182-0). Somerset Pub.

North Carolina & the War of 1812. Sarah M. Lemmon. (Illus.). 1971. pap. 1.00 (ISBN 0-86526-087-7). NC Archives.

North Carolina Appellate Handbook. J. Reid Potter. 1978. 28.50 (ISBN 0-87215-211-1, Bobbs-Merrill Law). Michie.

North Carolina Chronology & Factbook, Vol. 33. R. I. Vexler. 1978. 8.50 (ISBN 0-379-16158-3). Oceana.

North Carolina Civil War Documentary. Ed. by W. Buck Yearns & John G. Barrett. LC 79-17604. (Illus.). xvii, 365p. 1980. 17.95x (ISBN 0-8078-1407-5). U of NC Pr.

North Carolina Colony. William S. Powell. LC 69-11795. (Forge of Freedom Ser). (Illus.). (gr. 4-7). 1969. 5.95g o.s.i. (ISBN 0-02-775100-7, CCPr). Macmillan.

North Carolina During Recontruction. Richard L. Zuber. (Illus.). 1975. pap. 1.00 (ISBN 0-86526-089-3). NC Archives.

North Carolina Family Law, 3 vols. 3rd ed. Robert E. Lee. 1963. 1979-1980 100.00 (ISBN 0-87215-098-4). Michie.

North Carolina: From the Mountains to the Sea. Jim Doane. LC 80-80955. 72p. 1980. 10.95 (ISBN 0-936672-01-3); pap. text ed. 7.50 (ISBN 0-936672-00-5). Aerial Photo.

North Carolina in Maps. 36p. 1966. of 15 maps with booklet 12.00 set (ISBN 0-86526-137-7). NC Archives.

North Carolina Legends. Richard Walser. (Illus.). viii, 86p. (Orig.). 1980. 6.00 (ISBN 0-86526-145-8); pap. 2.50 (ISBN 0-86526-139-3). NC Archives.

North Carolina Real Estate. Bill Gobble & Bruce Harwood. 1981. text ed. 16.95 (ISBN 0-8359-4951-6). Reston.

North Carolina Research: Genealogy & Local History. Ed. by Helen F. Leary & Maurice R. Stirewalt. LC 80-50414. (Illus.). 672p. 1980. 21.50 (ISBN 0-936370-00-9). Natl Genealogical.

North Carolina State Industrial Directory, 1980. State Industrial Directories Corp. 1980. pap. 60.00 (ISBN 0-89910-033-3). State Indus Dir.

North Carolina Supplement for Modern Real Estate Practice. Ruth D. Silverman. Ed. by Patrick Hetrick. 130p. (Orig.). 1981. pap. 7.95 (ISBN 0-88462-301-7). Real Estate Ed Co.

North Carolina Trial Evidence Manual. Anthony J. Bocchino & J. Alexander Tanford. LC 76-29099. 1976. with 1978 suppl 20.00 (ISBN 0-87215-188-3); 1978 suppl. 7.50 (ISBN 0-87215-277-4). Michie.

North Carolina's Role in the First World War. Sarah M. Lemmon. (Illus.). 1975. pap. 1.00 (ISBN 0-86526-094-X). NC Archives.

North Carolina's Role in World War Two. Sarah M. Lemmon. (Illus.). 1969. pap. 1.00 (ISBN 0-86526-095-8). NC Archives.

North Carolina's Signers: Brief Sketches of the Men Who Signed the Declaration of Independence & the Constitution. Memory F. Mitchell. (Illus.). 1969. pap. 0.25 o.p. (ISBN 0-86526-097-4). NC Archives.

North Cascadians. JoAnn Roe. LC 80-21620. 200p. 1980. 14.95 (ISBN 0-914842-49-8). Madrona Pubs.

North China Villages: Social, Political & Economic Activities Before 1933. Sidney D. Gamble. 1963. 16.50x o.p. (ISBN 0-520-00452-3). U of Cal Pr.

North Country Bishop: A Biography of William Nicolson. Francis G. James. 1956. 42.50x (ISBN 0-686-51425-4). Elliots Bks.

North Dakota. 23.00 (ISBN 0-89770-110-0). Curriculum Info Ctr.

North Dakota. Robert P. Wilkins & Wynona H. Wilkins. (States & the Nation Ser.). (Illus.). 1977. 12.95 (ISBN 0-393-05655-4, Co-Pub by AASLH). Norton.

North Dakota Chronology & Factbook, Vol. 34. R. I. Vexler. 1978. 8.50 (ISBN 0-379-16159-1). Oceana.

North Dakota: Guide to the Northern Prairie State. LC 72-84498. 1938. 45.00 (ISBN 0-403-02183-9). Somerset Pub.

North Dakota: In Words & Pictures. Dennis Fradin. LC 80-26480. (Young People's Stories of Our States Ser.). (Illus.). 48p. (gr. 2-5). 1981. PLB 8.65g (ISBN 0-516-03934-2, Time Line). Childrens.

North Dakota Political Tradition. Ed. by Thomas W. Howard. 192p. 1981. 8.95 (ISBN 0-8138-0520-1). Iowa St U Pr.

North Dakota State Industrial Directory, 1980. State Industrial Directories Corp. 1980. pap. 15.00 (ISBN 0-89910-034-1). State Indus Dir.

North Dakota Supplement for Modern Real Estate Practice. James A. Gorzelany. 120p. (Orig.). 1980. pap. 7.95 (ISBN 0-88462-377-7). Real Estate Ed Co.

North Dallas Forty. Peter Gent. 1973. 7.95 o.p. (ISBN 0-688-00183-1). Morrow.

North East England. 2nd ed. J. E. Waltham & W. D. Holmes. LC 78-68119. (Geography of the British Isles). (Illus.). (YA) 1979. pap. 6.95x (ISBN 0-521-22473-X). Cambridge U Pr.

North East England: The Region's Development 1760-1914. Norman McCord. 1979. 50.00 (ISBN 0-7134-1261-5, Pub. by Batsford England). David & Charles.

North-East Frontier: A Documentary Study of the Internecine Rivalry Between India, Tibet & China, Vol. 1, 1906-14. Parshotam Mehra. 270p. 1979. text ed. 9.95x (ISBN 0-19-561158-6). Oxford U Pr.

North East Railway Book. Ken Hoole & Ken Hoole. LC 79-52354. (Illus.). 1979. 14.95 (ISBN 0-7153-7683-7). David & Charles.

North Eastern Locomotive Sheds. K. Hoole. (Illus.). 268p. 1971. 8.95 o.p. (ISBN 0-7153-5323-3). David & Charles.

North Eastern Railway 1870-1914: An Economic History. R. J. Irving. 1976. text ed. 28.75x (ISBN 0-7185-1141-7, Leicester). Humanities.

North Face. Mary Renault. 286p. 1976. Repr. of 1948 ed. lib. bdg. 13.95x (ISBN 0-89244-081-3). Queens Hse.

North for the Trade: The Life & Times of a Berber Merchant. John Waterbury. LC 70-174453. (Illus.). 200p. 1972. 20.00x (ISBN 0-520-02134-7). U of Cal Pr.

North India Between Empires: Awadh, the Mughals, & the British, 1720-1801. Richard B. Barnett. (Center for South & Southeast Asian Studies). 400p. 1981. 25.00x (ISBN 0-520-03787-1). U of Cal Pr.

North Korea's Foreign Relations: The Politics of Accomodation, 1945-75. Wayne S. Kiyosaki. LC 76-19548. (Special Studies). 1976. 24.95 (ISBN 0-275-23490-8). Praeger.

North Mexican Cattle Industry, 1910-1975: Ideology, Conflict & Change. Manuel A. Machado, Jr. LC 80-5515. (Illus.). 184p. 1980. 14.50x (ISBN 0-89096-104-2). Tex A&M Univ Pr.

North Mexican Frontier: Readings in Archaeology, Ethnohistory & Ethnography. Ed. by Basil C. Hedrick et al. LC 70-132477. 271p. 1971. 15.95x (ISBN 0-8093-0489-9). S Ill U Pr.

North Mkata Plain, Tanzania: A Study of Land Capability & Land Tenure. J. Roger Pitblado. (Department of Geography Research Publications Ser.). 200p. 1981. pap. 8.50x (ISBN 0-8020-3378-4). U of Toronto Pr.

North of Athens. John Judson. LC 80-53396. 64p. 1980. pap. 3.95 (ISBN 0-933180-20-9). Spoon Riv Poetry.

North of Boston Poems. Robert Frost. Ed. by Edward C. Lathem. LC 77-1401. (Illus.). 1977. 8.95 (ISBN 0-396-07440-5). Dodd.

North of Danger. Dale Fife. (gr. 5 up). 1978. PLB 8.95 (ISBN 0-525-36035-2). Dutton.

North of the Narrows: Story of Priest Lake Country. Claude C. Simpson & Catherine Simpson. LC 80-51781. (GEM Bks-Historical Ser.). (Illus.). 332p (Orig.). 1981. pap. 11.95 (ISBN 0-89301-069-3). U Pr of Idaho.

North of 53 Degrees: The Wild Days of the Alaska-Yukon Mining Frontier 1870-1914. William R. Hunt. LC 74-12404. (Illus.). 416p. 1975. 12.95 o.s.i. (ISBN 0-02-557510-4). Macmillan.

North Pacific Cretaceous Trigoniid Genus Yaadia. LouElla Saul. (Publications in Geological Science Ser.: Vol. 119). 1978. pap. 10.50x (ISBN 0-520-09582-0). U of Cal Pr.

North Sea Field Development: Experiences & Challenges. Norwegian Petroleum Society. 314p. 1980. 95.00x (ISBN 82-7270-012-3, Pub. by Norwegian Info Norway). State Mutual Bk.

North Sea Harbors & Pilotage. Edward Delmar-Morgan. 1979. 29.95x (ISBN 0-8464-0070-7). Beekman Pubs.

North Sea Oil & Gas. Keith Chapman. (Problems in Modern Geography). (Illus.). 240p. 1976. 18.95 (ISBN 0-7153-7183-5). David & Charles.

North Sea Oil & Gas: Implications for Future United States Development. Irvin L. White et al. LC 73-21222. (Illus.). 176p. (Orig.). 1973. pap. 5.95x (ISBN 0-8061-1182-8). U of Okla Pr.

North Sea Oil: Resource Requirements for UK Development. J. Kenneth Klitz. (Illus.). 1981. 36.00 (ISBN 0-08-024442-4). Pergamon.

North Ship. Philip Larkin. 1974. pap. 4.95 (ISBN 0-571-10503-3, Pub. by Faber & Faber). Merrimack Bk Serv.

North Ships: The Life of a Trawlerman. Steven Piper. LC 74-76187. 1974. 5.50 o.p. (ISBN 0-7153-6483-9). David & Charles.

North Shore. William D. Middleton. LC 64-16408. (Illus.). 1963. 15.95 (ISBN 0-87095-016-9). Golden West.

North, South, East, & West. Franklyn M. Branley. LC 66-14486. (Let's-Read-&-Find-Out Science Bk). (Illus.). (gr. k-3). 1966. PLB 7.89 (ISBN 0-690-58609-4, TYC-J). T Y Crowell.

North Star. Hammond Innes. 1979. pap. 1.95 o.p. (ISBN 0-345-25194-6). Ballantine.

North Star Crusade. William Katz. 1977. pap. 1.95 o.s.i. (ISBN 0-515-04356-7). Jove Pubns.

North: "the Frank O'Hara Award Series". Tony Towle. LC 70-125619. (Full Court Rebound Bk.). 1978. 14.95 (ISBN 0-231-03471-7); pap. 6.00 (ISBN 0-231-03472-5). Full Court NY.

North to Dakota. Jake Logan. LC 76-9581. (John Slocum Ser.: No. 8). 1976. pap. 1.75 (ISBN 0-87216-742-9). Playboy Pbks.

North to Lake Superior: Journal of Charles W. Penny, 1840. Ed. by James L. Carter & Ernest H. Rankin. LC 74-80875. 1970. 4.50 (ISBN 0-938746-02-2). Marquette Cnty Hist.

North to Montana! Jehus, Bullwhackers & Mule Skinners on the Montana Trail. Betty M. Madsen & Brigham D. Madsen. (University of Utah Publications in the American West). (Illus.). 1980. 20.00 (ISBN 0-87480-130-3). U of Utah Pr.

North to Oak Island. Dudley Bromley. (Pacesetters Ser.). (Illus.). 64p. (gr. 4 up). PLB 7.95 (ISBN 0-516-02171-0). Childrens.

North to Rabaul. Christopher Wood. 320p. 1980. pap. 2.75 (ISBN 0-345-28782-7). Ballantine.

North to the Horizon. Harrison J. Hunt. Ed. by Ruth H. Thompson. LC 80-69081. (Illus.). 135p. 1981. 11.95 (ISBN 0-89272-080-8). Down East.

North Vietnam & the Pathet Lao: Partners in the Struggle for Laos. Paul F. Langer & Joseph J. Zasloff. LC 73-134326. (Rand Corporation Research Studies). 1970. 12.50x (ISBN 0-674-62675-3). Harvard U Pr.

North Wales. Automobile Association - British Tourist Authority. (Regional Guide Ser.). (Illus.). 1979. pap. 2.95 o.p. (ISBN 0-900784-50-4, Pub. by B T a). Merrimack Bk Serv.

North Wales: A Shell Guide. Elizabeth Beazley & Lionel Brett. (Shell Guide Ser.). (Illus.). 1971. 14.95 (ISBN 0-571-09756-1, Pub. by Faber & Faber). Merrimack Bk Serv.

North Wales: A Tourist Guide. rev. ed. Wales Tourist Board. (Illus.). 84p. Date not set. pap. price not set (ISBN 0-900784-71-7, Pub. by Auto Assn-British Tourist Authority England). Merrimack Bk Serv.

North Wales Tramways. Keith Turner. LC 79-74089. 1979. 17.95 (ISBN 0-7153-7769-8). David & Charles.

North Wall. Roger Hubank. 1978. 8.95 o.p. (ISBN 0-670-51551-5). Viking Pr.

North West England. rev. ed. British Tourist Authority. (Illus.). 74p. 1981. pap. write for info. (ISBN 0-86143-039-5, Pub. by Auto Assn-British Tourist Authority England). Merrimack Bk Serv.

North West England. 2nd ed. W. E. Marsden. LC 78-67243. (Geography of the British Isles). 1979. pap. 5.95 (ISBN 0-521-22474-8). Cambridge U Pr.

North-Western Provinces of India: Their History, Ethnology & Administration. W. Crooke. (Illus.). 365p. 1973. Repr. text ed. 15.00x o.p. (ISBN 0-8426-0506-1). Verry.

North with the Spring. Edwin W. Teale. LC 51-13966. (Illus.). (gr. 7 up). 1951. 10.00 (ISBN 0-396-03325-3). Dodd.

North Woods. Percy Knauth. (American Wilderness Ser.). (Illus.). 1972. 12.95 (ISBN 0-8094-1164-4). Time-Life.

North Woods. Percy Knauth. LC 72-88525. (American Wilderness Ser). (Illus.). (gr. 6 up). 1972. lib. bdg. 11.97 (ISBN 0-8094-1165-2, Pub. by Time-Life). Silver.

North Yemen. Manfred W. Wenner. (Nations of the Contemporary Middle East Ser.). 128p. 1981. lib. bdg. 16.50x (ISBN 0-89158-774-8). Westview.

Northamptonshire. Ed. by Frank Thorn & Caroline Thorn. (Domesday Bk.: Vol. 21). (Illus.). 231p. 1980. 20.00x (ISBN 0-8476-3142-7). Rowman.

Northamptonshire & the Soke of Peterborough: A Shell Guide. Juliet Smith. (Shell Guide Ser.). (Illus.). 1968. 12.95 (ISBN 0-571-08420-6, Pub. by Faber & Faber). Merrimack Bk Serv.

Northanger Abbey. Jane Austen. (World's Classics Ser.). 8.95 o.p. (ISBN 0-19-250355-3). Oxford U Pr.

Northanger Abbey. Jane Austen. 1977. pap. 2.25 o.p. (ISBN 0-460-01893-0, Evman). Dutton.

Northanger Abbey. Jane Austen. (Macdonald Classics Ser.). 266p. 1974. 9.95x (ISBN 0-8464-0676-4). Beekman Pubs.

Northanger Abbey. Jane Austen. (Zodiac Press Ser.). 1978. 9.95 (ISBN 0-7011-1234-4, Pub. by Chatto Bodley Jonathan). Merrimack Bk Serv.

Northanger Abbey. Jane Austen. Ed. by James Kinsley & John Davie. Bd. with Lady Susan; Watsons; Sandition. (World's Classics Ser.). 350p. 1981. pap. 2.95 (ISBN 0-19-281525-3). Oxford U Pr.

Northcountry Cookbook: Compilation of Northcountry Recipes. 1980. 7.95 (ISBN 0-932212-17-4). Avery Color.

Northeast. rev. ed. Ed. by Jerry Jennings. LC 78-54254. (United States Ser.). (Illus.). 320p. (gr. 5 up). 1979. text ed. 9.93 ea. 1-4 copies (ISBN 0-88296-057-1); text ed. 7.94 ea. 5 or more copies; tchrs.' annotated ed. 13.68 (ISBN 0-88296-347-3). Fideler.

Northeast, Vol. 15. Bruce G. Trigger. LC 77-17162. (Handbook of North American Indians). (Illus.). 924p. 1979. text ed. 14.50 (ISBN 0-87474-195-5). Smithsonian.

Northeast Asia in Prehistory. Chester S. Chard. LC 73-2040. 1974. 15.00x (ISBN 0-299-06430-1). U of Wis Pr.

Northeast Asia in U. S. Foreign Policy. Stephen P. Gibert. LC 79-67647. (Washington Policy Papers: No. 71). 88p. 1979. pap. 3.50 (ISBN 0-8039-1427-X). Sage.

Northeast Asia: Prosperity & Vulnerability, Vol. I. Asiatic Research Center, Korea University CSIS. LC 79-65209. (Significant Issues Ser.: No. 2). 79p. 1979. 5.95 (ISBN 0-89206-008-5). CSI Studies.

Northeast Asia: Prosperity & Vulnerability. 79p. 1980. pap. 7.50 (ISBN 0-89206-008-5, CSIS003, CSIS). Unipub.

Northeast Coast. Maitland Edey. LC 70-187925. (American Wilderness Ser). (Illus.). (gr. 6 up). 1972. lib. bdg. 11.97 (ISBN 0-8094-1149-0, Pub. by Time-Life). Silver.

Northeast Coast. Maitland A. Edey. (American Wilderness Ser.). (Illus.). 184p. 1972. 12.95 (ISBN 0-8094-1148-2). Time-Life.

Northeast Retreat. Joseph S. Haas. (Cathedral of the Beechwoods Ser.: No. 1). (Illus.). 102p. (Orig.). 1980. write for info. (ISBN 0-9605552-0-X). Haas Ent NH.

Northeast Wine. Ted Meredith. LC 80-80917. (Illus.). 160p. (Orig.). 1980. pap. 6.95 (ISBN 0-936666-00-5). Nexus Pr.

Northern & Western Islands of Scotland in the Seventeenth Century. Frances J. Shaw. (Illus.). 275p. 1980. text ed. 39.00x (ISBN 0-85976-059-6). Humanities.

Northern Antiquities; or, a Description of the Manners, Customs, Religion & Laws of the Ancient Danes, & Other Northern Nations, 2 vols. Paul H. Mallet. Ed. by Burton Feldman & Robert Richardson. LC 78-60889. (Myth & Romanticism Ser.: Vol. 16). 1980. Set. lib. bdg. 132.00 (ISBN 0-8240-3565-8); lib. bdg. 66.00 ea. Garland Pub.

Northern Barbarians: 100bc-300ad. Malcolm Todd. (Illus., Orig.). 1975. text ed. 18.75x (ISBN 0-09-122220-6, Hutchinson U Lib). Humanities.

Northern California: Travel Guide. Sunset Editors. LC 79-90341. (Illus.). 128p. 1980. pap. 4.95 (ISBN 0-376-06557-5, Sunset Bks). Sunset-Lane.

Northern Colonial Frontier, 1607-1763. Douglas E. Leach. LC 66-10083. (Histories of the American Frontier Ser.). (Illus.). 282p. 1966. pap. 6.50x (ISBN 0-8263-0337-4). U of NM Pr.

Northern Crusades: The Baltic & the Catholic Frontier, 1100-1525. Eric Christiansen. (Illus.). xxii, 265p. 1981. 25.00x (ISBN 0-8166-0994-2); pap. 10.95x (ISBN 0-8166-1018-5). U of Minn Pr.

Northern Gabon Coast to 1875. K. David Patterson. (Oxford Studies in African Affairs Ser). (Illus.). 176p. 1975. 29.95x (ISBN 0-19-821696-3). Oxford U Pr.

Northern Girl. Elizabeth A. Lynn. 1981. pap. 2.25 (ISBN 0-425-04725-3). Berkley Pub.

Northern Girls. Elizabeth A. Lynn. 1979. 9.95 o.p. (ISBN 0-399-12409-8). Berkley Pub.

Northern Great Barrier Reaf. Ed. by D. R. Stoddart & Maurice Yonge. (Proceedings of the Royal Society). (Illus.). 364p. 1979. text ed. 95.75x (ISBN 0-85403-102-2, Pub. by Royal Soc London). Scholium Intl.

Northern Ireland: Between Civil Rights & Civil War. Liam O'Dowd et al. 224p. 1980. text ed. 26.00x (ISBN 0-906336-18-X); pap. text ed. 19.50x (ISBN 0-906336-19-8). Humanities.

Northern Ireland: Crises & Conflict. John Magee. (World Studies). (Illus.). 212p. 1974. 16.00x (ISBN 0-7100-7946-X); pap. 7.95 (ISBN 0-7100-7947-8). Routledge & Kegan.

Northern Ireland: Society Under Siege. Rona M. Fields. (Orig.). 1981. pap. 5.95 (ISBN 0-87855-806-3). Transaction Bks.

Northern Isles: Orkney & Shetland. Alexander Fenton. (Illus.). 1978. text ed. 39.00x (ISBN 0-85976-019-7). Humanities.

Northern Marianas Covenant & American Territorial Relations. Paul M. Leary. LC 80-10945. (IGS Research Report: No. 80-1). 55p. (Orig.). 1980. pap. 3.50x (ISBN 0-87772-269-2). Inst Gov Stud Berk.

Northern Mists. Carl O. Sauer. (Illus.). 1968. 17.50x (ISBN 0-520-01126-0). U of Cal Pr.

Northern Myth: Limits to Agricultural & Pastoral Development in Tropical Australia. B. R. Davidson. (Illus.). 320p. 1972. o.p. 2nd ed. (ISBN 0-522-83577-5, Pub. by Melbourne U Pr); pap. 11.50x 3rd ed. (ISBN 0-522-84035-3, Pub. by Melbourne U Pr). Intl Schol Bk Serv.

Northern New Spain: A Research Guide. Thomas C. Barnes et al. LC 80-24860. 1981. pap. text ed. 9.95x (ISBN 0-8165-0709-0). U of Ariz Pr.

Northern Phantom. Alan Wildsmith. (gr. 6 up). 1979. PLB 8.95 (ISBN 0-233-97002-9). Andre Deutsch.

Northern Pike Fishing: The Angler's Complete Handbook. Kit Bergh. LC 75-6532. (Illus.). 1975. 8.95 (ISBN 0-87518-096-5). Dillon.

Northern Plainsmen: Adaptive Strategy & Agrarian Life. John W. Bennett. LC 76-75043. (Worlds of Man Ser.). (Illus.). 1970. text ed. 13.95x (ISBN 0-88295-602-7); pap. text ed. 8.75x (ISBN 0-88295-603-5). AHM Pub.

Northern Rhodesia General Election, 1962. David C. Mulford. 1964. 5.00x o.p. (ISBN 0-19-690287-8); pap. 2.65x o.p. (ISBN 0-19-519606-6). Oxford U Pr.

Northern Schools, Southern Blacks, & Reconstruction: Freedmen's Education, 1862-1875. Ronald E. Butchart. LC 79-8949. (Contributions in American History: No. 87). (Illus.). xiv, 309p. 1980. lib. bdg. 25.00 (ISBN 0-313-22073-5, BNS/). Greenwood.

Northern Shoshoni. Brigham D. Madsen. LC 78-53138. (Illus., Orig.). 1980. 17.95 (ISBN 0-87004-289-0); pap. 12.95 (ISBN 0-87004-266-1). Caxton.

Northern Spy. Chase Twichell. LC 80-54061. (Pitt Poetry Ser). 80p. 1981. 9.95 (ISBN 0-8229-3437-X); pap. 4.50 (ISBN 0-8229-5328-5). U of Pittsburgh Pr.

Northern Ute Music. Frances Densmore. LC 72-1887. (Music Ser.). (Illus.). 236p. 1972. Repr. of 1922 ed. lib. bdg. 19.50 (ISBN 0-306-70515-X). Da Capo.

Northern World: The History & Heritage of Northern Europe, A. D. 400-1100. Ed. by David M. Wilson. (Illus.). 248p. 1980. 40.00 (ISBN 0-686-62715-6, 1365-8). Abrams.

Northmen. Thomas Froncek. LC 74-77815. (Emergence of Man Ser.). (gr. 6 up). 1974. lib. bdg. 9.63 o.p. (ISBN 0-8094-1275-6, Pub. by Time-Life). Silver.

Northmen. Thomas Froncek. (Emergence of Man Ser). (Illus.). 1974. 9.95 (ISBN 0-8094-1324-8); lib. bdg. avail. (ISBN 0-685-49690-2). Time-Life.

Northrop Frye: An Enumerative Bibliography. Robert D. Denham. LC 73-20345. (Author Bibliographies Ser.: No. 14). 1974. 10.00 (ISBN 0-8108-0693-2). Scarecrow.

Northumbria. rev. ed. British Tourist Authority. (Illus.). 82p. 1981. pap. write for info. (ISBN 0-86143-038-7, Pub. by Auto Assn-British Tourist Authority England). Merrimack Bk Serv.

Northumbria. Maxwell Fraser & Kenneth Elmsley. 1978. 27.00 (ISBN 0-7134-1140-6, Pub. by Batsford England). David & Charles.

Northumbrian Minstrelsy: A Collection of the Ballads, Melodies, & Small-Pipe Tunes of Northumbria. John C. Bruce & John Stokoe. LC 65-4143. xxxiv, 197p. 1965. Repr. of 1882 ed. 10.00 (ISBN 0-8103-5042-4). Gale.

Northwest Adventure Guide. Pacific Search Press. LC 80-24309. (Illus.). 1981. pap. 5.95 (ISBN 0-914718-54-1). Pacific Search.

Northwest Coast. Richard Williams. LC 73-87559. (American Wilderness Ser). (Illus.). (gr. 6 up). 1973. lib. bdg. 11.97 (ISBN 0-8094-1193-8, Pub. by Time-Life). Silver.

Northwest Coast. Richard Williams. (American Wilderness Ser.). (Illus.). 240p. 1974. 12.95 (ISBN 0-8094-1192-X). Time-Life.

Northwest Coast Indian Art: An Analysis of Form. Bill Holm. LC 65-10818. (Thomas Burke Memorial Washington State Museum Monograph: No. 1). (Illus.). 133p. 1965. 12.95 (ISBN 0-295-73855-3); pap. 7.95 (ISBN 0-295-95102-8). U of Wash Pr.

Northwest Experience Two. Ed. by Lane Morgan. 192p. 1981. lib. bdg. 10.00 (ISBN 0-686-62337-1); pap. 4.95 (ISBN 0-686-62338-X). Madrona Pubs.

Northwest Heritage. William E. Scofield. (gr. 7-9). 1978. pap. text ed. 5.83 (ISBN 0-87720-623-6). AMSCO Sch.

Northwest Kitchen: A Seasonal Cookbook. Judie Geise. LC 78-64741. 1978. 12.95 (ISBN 0-685-91736-3, Pub. by B Wright & Co). Madrona Pubs.

Northwest Mosaic: Minority Conflicts in Pacific Northwest History. Ed. by James A. Halseth & Bruce A. Glasrud. 1977. pap. 6.00x o.p. (ISBN 0-87108-208-X). Pruett.

Northwest Passage. Kenneth Roberts. 1981. pap. 2.95 (ISBN 0-449-24095-9, Crest). Fawcett.

Northwest Perspectives: Essays on the Culture of the Pacific Northwest. Ed. by Edwin R. Bingham & Glen A. Love. LC 77-15189. 264p. 1981. pap. 7.95 (ISBN 0-295-95805-7). U of Wash Pr.

Northwest Trees. Stephen F. Arno. LC 77-82369. (Illus.). 1977. 30.00 (ISBN 0-916890-55-4); pap. 6.95 (ISBN 0-916890-50-3). Mountaineers.

Northwest Wine. Ted Meredith. LC 80-80917. (Illus.). 180p. 1980. pap. 6.95 (ISBN 0-936666-00-5). Nexus Pr.

Northwestern Arizona Ghost Towns. Stanley W. Paher. (Illus.). 1981. pap. 2.95 (ISBN 0-913814-30-X). Nevada Pubns.

Northwestern Fights & Fighters. Cyrus T. Brady. LC 79-15171. (Illus.). 1979. 18.50x (ISBN 0-8032-1156-2); pap. 5.50 (ISBN 0-8032-6053-9, BB 713, Bison). U of Nebr Pr.

Northwestern Pacific Railroad. 22.00. Chatham Pub CA.

Northwestern Univ., Transportation Center. Lucille W. Ellison. (Illus.). 144p. (gr. 4-6). 1981. 8.95 (ISBN 0-684-16875-8). Scribner.

Norton Anthology of English Literature, 2 vols. 3rd ed. Ed. by M. H. Abrams et al. 5000p. 1974. text ed. 12.95x ea.; Vol. 1. (ISBN 0-393-09301-8). pap. text ed. 9.95x ea.; Vol. 1. pap. (ISBN 0-393-09304-2); Vol. 2. pap. (ISBN 0-393-09306-9). Norton.

Norton Anthology of English Literature, 2 vols. 4th ed. Ed. by M. H. Abrams et al. (Illus.). 1979. text ed. 16.95x (ISBN 0-393-95039-5); Vol. II. text ed. 16.95x (ISBN 0-393-95043-3); Vol. I. pap. text ed. 11.95x (ISBN 0-393-95048-4); Vol II. pap. text ed. 14.95x (ISBN 0-685-94872-2). Vol. II (ISBN 0-393-95051-4). Norton.

Norton Anthology of English Literature: Third Major Authors Edition. Ed. by M. H. Abrams et al. 1975. text ed. 17.95x (ISBN 0-393-09298-4); pap. text ed. 14.95x (ISBN 0-393-09299-2). Norton.

Norton Anthology of World Masterpieces, 2 vols. 4th ed. Ed. by Maynard Mack et al. 1979. text ed. 17.95x (ISBN 0-393-95036-0); Vol II. text ed. 17.95x (ISBN 0-393-95040-9); Vol I. pap. text ed. 14.95x (ISBN 0-393-95079-4); Vol II. pap. text ed. 14.95x (ISBN 0-393-95045-X). Vol. II (ISBN 0-393-95050-6). Norton.

Norton Anthology of World Masterpieces, 2 vols. in pap. 4th continental ed. Ed. by Maynard Mack et al. 1980. pap. text ed. 16.95x one vol. (ISBN 0-393-95079-4); pap. text ed. 14.95x ea. Vol. I (ISBN 0-393-95082-4). Vol. II (ISBN 0-393-95090-5). Norton.

Norton Facsimile--William Shakespeare. William Shakespeare. 1969. academic ed. 75.00x (ISBN 0-393-09843-5). Norton.

Norton Introduction to Fiction. 2nd ed. Ed. by Jerome Beaty. 640p. 1981. pap. text ed. 8.95x (ISBN 0-393-95156-1); classroom guide avail. (ISBN 0-393-95159-6). Norton.

Norton Introduction to Literature. 2nd ed. Ed. by Carl E. Bain et al. 1977. pap. 9.95 (ISBN 0-393-09119-8); tchr's manual 2.95x (ISBN 0-393-09127-9). Norton.

Norton Introduction to Literature. 3rd ed. Ed. by Carl E. Bain et al. 1536p. 1981. pap. text ed. 11.95x (ISBN 0-393-95146-4); classroom guide avail. (ISBN 0-393-95158-8). Norton.

Norton Introduction to Literature: Poetry. Ed. by J. Paul Hunter. 600p. 1973. pap. text ed. 10.95x (ISBN 0-393-09380-8); teachers guide to poetry 1.25x (ISBN 0-393-09333-6). Norton.

Norton Sampler: Short Essays for Composition. Ed. by Thomas Cooley. 1978. pap. text ed. 5.45x (ISBN 0-393-09007-8); instructor's handbook free (ISBN 0-393-95047-6). Norton.

Norton Service Repair Handbook: 750 & 850 Commandos, All Years. Mike Bishop. Ed. by Jeff Robinson. (Illus.). 1977. pap. 9.95 (ISBN 0-89287-158-X, M361). Clymer Pubns.

Norway & Europe in the Nineteen Seventies. Hilary Allen. 1979. 31.00x (ISBN 82-00-05230-3, Dist. by Columbia U Pr.). Universitet.

Norway-Brief History. 7th ed. Ed. by J. Midgaard. (Tanum of Norway Tokens Ser.). 1979. pap. 12.50x (ISBN 82-518-0053-6, N-441). Vanous.

Norway in Pictures. Sterling Publishing Company Editors. LC 67-16017. (Visual Geography Ser). (Orig.). (gr. 6 up). PLB 4.99 (ISBN 0-8069-1089-5); pap. 2.95 (ISBN 0-8069-1088-7). Sterling.

Norway: Native Art. Hauglid & Asker. 1977. deluxe ed. 39.50x (ISBN 82-09-01381-5, N-387). Vanous.

Norway, NATO & the Forgotten Soviet Challenge. Kirsten Amundsen. (Policy Papers in International Affairs: No. 14). (Illus.). iv, 60p. 1981. pap. 2.95x (ISBN 0-87725-514-8). U of Cal Pr.

Norway-Sweden-Croatia: A Comparative Study of State Secession & Formation. Margaret Omrcanin. 1976. pap. 6.95 (ISBN 0-8059-2309-8). Dorrance.

Norway 1940-45: The Resistance Movement. Olav Riste & Berit Nokleby. (Illus.). 93p. (Orig.). 1970. pap. 6.50x (ISBN 82-518-0164-8). Intl Pubns Serv.

Norway's Delights Cookbook. rev. ed. E. Sverdrup. (Tanum of Norway Tokens Ser). 1980. pap. 11.00x (ISBN 8-2518-0089-7, N429). Vanous.

Norwegian-Americans. Arlow W. Andersen. (Immigrant Heritage of American Ser). 1975. lib. bdg. 9.95 (ISBN 0-8057-3249-7). Twayne.

Norwegian Deluxe Dictionary: English-Norse. B. Berulfsen & A. Svenkerud. 1968. 90.00x (ISBN 82-02-06627-1, N461). Vanous.

Norwegian Dictionary: Engelsk-Norwegina. rev. ed. B. Berulfsen & T. Berulfsen. 433p. 1978. 18.50x (ISBN 82-573-0007-1, N481). Vanous.

Norwegian Dictionary: English-Norwegian. Ed. by L. Bjerke & H. Soraas. 1963. 26.00x (N434). Vanous.

Norwegian Dictionary: Norwegian-English. G. Haugen. 1976. pap. 13.75x (ISBN 0-299-03874-2, N533). Vanous.

Norwegian-English Dictionary. Ed. by Einar Haugen. 1967. pap. 17.50 (ISBN 0-299-03874-2). U of Wis Pr.

Norwegian-English Dictionary. T. Slette. 1977. 80.00x (ISBN 82-521-0692-7, N-537). Vanous.

Norwegian Folk Tales. P. Chr. Asbjornsen & Jorgen Moe. (Illus.). 188p. 1961. 20.00x (ISBN 82-09-01603-2, N449). Vanous.

Norwegian Painting: A Survey. J. Askeland. (Tanum of Norway Tokens Ser). (Illus.). pap. 10.00x (ISBN 82-518-1122-8, N505). Vanous.

Norwegian Penal Code. (American Series of Foreign Penal Codes: Vol. 3). 1961. 15.00x (ISBN 0-8377-0023-X). Rothman.

Norwegian Petroleum Law. Scandinavian Institute of Maritime Law. 500p. 1980. 135.00x (Pub. by Norwegian Info Norway). State Mutual Bk.

Norwegian Petroleum-Yearbook for the Norwegian Petroleum Society 1979. 211p. 1980. 60.00x (ISBN 82-7270-004-2, Pub. by Norwegian Info Norway). State Mutual Bk.

Norwegian Petroleum Yearbook for the Norwegian Petroleum Society 1980. 218p. 1980. 60.00x (ISBN 82-7270-013-1, Pub. by Norwegian Info Norway). State Mutual Bk.

Norwegian Pocket Dictionary: English-Norwegian, Norwegian-English. 7th ed. J. Dietrichson & O. Overland. 1980. 8.00x (ISBN 8-2573-0054-3, N-407). Vanous.

Norwegian Price & Income Freeze. 1980. 50.00x (Pub. by Norwegian Info Norway). State Mutual Bk.

Norwegian Printmakers: A Hundred Years of Graphic Arts. Jan Askeland. Tr. by Pat Shaw from Norwegian. LC 79-305965. (Tokens of Norway Ser.). (Illus.). 55p. (Orig.). 1978. pap. 10.50x (ISBN 82-518-0688-7). Intl Pubns Serv.

Norwegian Rosemaling: Decorative Painting on Wood. Margaret M. Miller & Sigmund Aarseth. (Illus.). 1973. pap. 12.95 (ISBN 0-684-16743-3, ScribT). Scribner.

Norwegian Silver. A. Polak. (Illus.). 158p. 1972. 30.00x (ISBN 8-2090-1050-6, N520). Vanous.

Norwegian Society. Natalie R. Ramsay. 1974. text ed. 15.00x (ISBN 82-00-04834-9, Dist. by Columbia U Pr); pap. text ed. 11.00x (ISBN 82-00-04610-9). Universitet.

Norwegian Technical Dictionary: Norwegian-English, Vol. 2. rev. ed. Ed. by J. Ansteinsson. 1954. 25.00x (ISBN 8-2702-8006-2, N432). Vanous.

Norwegian Wilderness: National Parks & Protected Areas. Arild Holt-Jensen. LC 79-321366. (Tokens of Norway Ser.). (Illus.). 78p. (Orig.). 1978. pap. 10.50x (ISBN 82-518-0719-0). Intl Pubns Serv.

Norwegians in America. Hjalmar R. Holand. LC 78-55075. (Illus.). 1978. pap. 8.95 (ISBN 0-931170-07-9). Ctr Western Studies.

Norwegisch Daenisches Etymologisches Woerterbuch: Mit Literatur-Nachweisen Strittiger Etymologien Sowie Deutschem und Altnordischen Woerterverzeichnis. 2nd ed. H. S. Falk & Alf Torp. 1722p. 1960. 80.00x (ISBN 8-200-00085-0, Dist. by Columbia U Pr). Universitet.

Norwood Tor. Michael Bradley. LC 79-24215. (gr. 5 up). 1980. 6.95 (ISBN 0-396-07790-0). Dodd.

Nose for Trouble. Barbara S. Hazen. (Golden Scratch & Sniff Bk.). (Illus.). 32p. (ps-2). 1973. PLB 9.92 (ISBN 0-307-64534-7, Golden Pr). Western Pub.

Nose Tree. Warwick Hutton. LC 79-23247. (Illus.). 32p. Date not set. price not set (ISBN 0-689-50166-8, McElderry Bk). Atheneum. Postponed.

Nosferatu: Vampyre. Monette. 1979. pap. 2.25 (ISBN 0-380-44107-1, 44107). Avon.

Nosocomial Infections. Ed. by Richard E. Dixon. (Illus.). 500p. 1981. text ed. price not set (ISBN 0-914316-24-9). Yorke Med.

Nostalgia and Nightmare: A Study in the Fiction of S. Y. Agnon. Arnold J. Band. (Near Eastern Center, UCLA). 1968. 30.00x (ISBN 0-520-00076-5). U of Cal Pr.

Nostalgia for the Present. Andrei Voznesensky. LC 72-76218. 1978. pap. 4.95 o.p. (ISBN 0-385-08368-8); pap. 4.95 Softbound o.p. (ISBN 0-385-08373-4). Doubleday.

Nostalgia Isn't What It Used to Be. Simone Signoret. Tr. by Cornelia Schaefer from French. LC 77-3773. 1978. 12.95 o.p. (ISBN 0-06-013986-2, HarpT). Har-Row.

Nostalgias for a House of Cards: Poems. Byron Vazakas. Orig. Title: Poems of Byron Vazakas. 1970. 4.95 (ISBN 0-8079-0159-8); pap. 1.95 (ISBN 0-8079-0160-1). October.

Nosy Norman. Annie Ingle. (Illus.). (ps-3). 1980. 3.95 (ISBN 0-525-69453-6, Gingerbread); PLB 5.95 (ISBN 0-525-69457-9). Dutton.

Not a Blessed Thing! Monica Quill. (Sister Mary Teresa Mystery Ser.). 224p. 1981. 9.95 (ISBN 0-8149-0849-7). Vanguard.

Not a Word About Nightingales. Maureen Howard. 196p. 1980. pap. 4.50 (ISBN 0-14-005596-7). Penguin.

Not All Our Pride. Vokes Richardson. LC 65-14600. 1965. 4.50 o.p. (ISBN 0-8076-0296-5). Braziller.

Not Alone with Cancer: A Guide for Those Who Care; What to Expect; What to Do. Ruth D. Abrams. 128p. 1976. pap. 8.75 (ISBN 0-398-02973-3). C C Thomas.

Not As a Stranger. Morton Thompson. 1971. pap. 2.25 o.p. (ISBN 0-451-07786-5, E7786, Sig). NAL.

Not at Home. Bernice Myers. (Illus.). (gr. 6-9). 6.95 (ISBN 0-688-41974-7). Lothrop.

Not at Home? Bernice Myers. LC 80-16288. (Illus.). 48p. (gr. 1-3). 1981. 6.95 (ISBN 0-688-41974-7); PLB 6.67 (ISBN 0-688-51974-1). Morrow.

Not by Bread Alone: Bible Readings for the Weekdays of Lent. (Illus.). 112p. 1972. pap. 1.95 (ISBN 0-87793-087-2). Ave Maria.

Not by War Alone: Security & Arms Control in the Middle East. Paul Jabber. 200p. 1981. 12.50x (ISBN 0-520-04050-3). U of Cal Pr.

Not Charity, but Justice: The Story of Jacob Riis. Edith P. Meyer. LC 73-83032. (gr. 6-10). 1974. 7.95 (ISBN 0-8149-0736-9). Vanguard.

Not Coming to Be Barked at. Ted Kooser. LC 76-21422. (Illus.). 1976. 15.00x (ISBN 0-915316-45-5); pap. 4.50x (ISBN 0-915316-25-0); ltd. signed ed. 5.00 (ISBN 0-915316-26-9). Pentagram.

Not Everything We Eat Is Curry. Aravinda Chakravarti & Donald C. Morizot. LC 78-52255. (Illus., Orig.). 1978. pap. 8.95 o.p. (ISBN 0-930138-01-5). Harold Hse.

Not for Bread Alone: An Appreciation of Job Enrichment. 3rd ed. Linda K. Taylor. 202p. 1980. pap. 12.25x (ISBN 0-220-67019-6, Pub. by Busn Bks England). Renouf.

Not for Doctors Only: Breakthrough Reports from the Medical Front. James E. Wasco. 12.95 (ISBN 0-201-08297-7); pap. 7.95 (ISBN 0-201-08298-5). A-W.

Not for Glory: A Personal History of the 1914-18 War. R. H. Haigh & P. W. Turner. 1969. 16.00 (ISBN 0-08-007101-5). Pergamon.

Not-for-Profit Business: Readings, Legal Documents & Commentary. Richard J. Hunter, Jr. 273p. 1980. pap. text ed. 12.95 (ISBN 0-89651-509-5). Icarus.

Not for Salads Only from Wishbone. Wishbone, Lipton Kitchens. (Orig.). Date not set. price not set (ISBN 0-87502-081-X). Benjamin Co.

Not for the Boys Only. Russ Hurn. LC 80-51432. 154p. 1980. 8.95 (ISBN 0-533-04695-5). Vantage.

Not Guilty. Jerome Frank & Barbara Frank. LC 72-138495. (Civil Liberties in American History Ser.). 1971. Repr. of 1957 ed. lib. bdg. 25.00 (ISBN 0-306-70072-7). Da Capo.

Not Here, but in Another Place. Ralph Barker. (Illus.). 352p. 1980. 13.95 (ISBN 0-312-57961-6). St Martin.

Not I but Christ. Roy Hession. 1980. pap. 2.95. Chr Lit.

Not Just Schoolwork: New Directions in Written Expression. Amy Maid & Roger Wallace. LC 76-9524. (Illus.). 201p. 1976. pap. 9.95 (ISBN 0-916250-15-6). Irvington.

Not Made of Wood: A Psychiatrist Discovers His Profession. Jan Foudraine. LC 73-6057. 480p. 1974. 9.95 o.s.i. (ISBN 0-02-540200-5). Macmillan.

Not My Daughter: Facing up to Adolescent Pregnancy. K. Oettinger & E. Mooney. 1979. 9.95 (ISBN 0-13-623850-5). P-H.

Not of the World: A History of the Commune in America. Daniel Cohen. (Illus.). 224p. (gr. 5 up). 1974. lib. ed. 5.97 o.p. (ISBN 0-695-40405-9). Follett.

Not of the World: A Living Account of the United Order. Lucy C. Parr. LC 75-5320. (Illus.). 232p. 1975. 6.95 (ISBN 0-88290-047-1). Horizon Utah.

Not of This Time, Not of This Place. Yehuda Amichai. Tr. by Shlomo Katz from Hebrew. 345p. 1973. 12.50x (ISBN 0-85303-180-0, Pub. by Vallentine Mitchell England). Biblio Dist.

Not One Man! Not One Penny! German Social Democracy, 1863-1914. Gary P. Steenson. LC 80-54058. (Illus.). 336p. 1981. 19.95 (ISBN 0-8229-3440-X); pap. 8.95 (ISBN 0-8229-5329-3). U of Pittsburgh Pr.

Not Quite Dead Enough. Rex Stout. (Adventures of Nero Wolfe). pap. 1.75 (ISBN 0-515-05119-5). Jove Pubns.

Not-Quite Puritans: Some Genial Follies & Peculiar Frailities of Our Revered New England Ancestors. Henry W. Lawrence. (Illus.). 1975. Repr. of 1928 ed. 18.00 (ISBN 0-8103-3993-5). Gale.

Not Raptured...but Resurrected. Margery Marpie. 1979. 4.00 o.p. (ISBN 0-8062-1109-1). Carlton.

Not Regina. Christmas C. Kauffman. (Giant Ser). (Illus.). 1971. pap. 2.95 (ISBN 0-8024-0072-8). Moody.

Not So Empty Nest: How to Live with Your Kids After They've Lived Someplace Else. Phillis Feuerstein & Carol Roberts. 256p. 1981. 10.95 (ISBN 0-695-81441-9). Follett.

Not So Good Book: A Resource for the Alienated. C. Edward Hopkin. 100p. 1981. 5.95 (ISBN 0-8059-2776-X). Dorrance.

Not So Long Ago. Emma Beckerman. LC 79-57538. 6.95 (ISBN 0-8197-0477-6). Bloch.

Not So Wild a Dream. Eric Sevareid. LC 76-11538. 1978. 15.00 (ISBN 0-689-10741-2); pap. 8.95 (ISBN 0-689-70578-6, 235). Atheneum.

Not the Usual Kind of Girl. Joan Tate. (gr. 7-12). 1975. pap. 1.25 o.p. (ISBN 0-590-09818-7, Schol Pap). Schol Bk Serv.

Not This Bear. Bernice Meyers. (Illus.). (gr. k-3). 1971. pap. 1.25 (ISBN 0-590-01556-7, Schol Pap); pap. 3.50 bk. & record (ISBN 0-590-20741-5). Schol Bk Serv.

Not This Pig. Philip Levine. LC 68-16006. (Wesleyan Poetry Program: Vol. 38). (Orig.). 1968. 10.00x (ISBN 0-8195-2038-1, Pub. by Wesleyan U Pr); pap. 2.45 o.p. (ISBN 0-8195-1038-6). Columbia U Pr.

Not to Be Broadcast: The Truth About the Radio. Ruth Brindze. LC 73-19802. (Civil Liberties in American History Ser.). 310p. 1974. Repr. of 1937 ed. lib. bdg. 29.50 (ISBN 0-306-70598-2). Da Capo.

Not Well Advised. Peter Szanton. LC 80-69174. 175p. 1981. text ed. 11.95x (ISBN 0-87154-874-7). Russell Sage.

Not What You Expected. Joan Aiken. LC 73-81121. 288p. 1974. 5.95 (ISBN 0-385-07518-9). Doubleday.

Not Wisely, but Too Well. Rhoda Broughton. Ed. by Herbert Van Thal. 1867-1967. 5.25 (ISBN 0-304-92524-1); pap. 3.95 (ISBN 0-685-09188-0). Dufour.

Not Without Design. Marvin J. Rosenthal. (Illus.). 1980. pap. 2.95 (ISBN 0-915540-27-4). Friends Israel-Spearhead Pr.

Not Work Alone: A Cross-Cultural View of Activities Superfluous to Survival. Ed. by Jeremy Cherfas & Roger Lewin. LC 79-3805. (Illus.). 255p. 1980. 20.00x (ISBN 0-8039-1394-X). Sage.

Not Working. Harry Maurer. 1981. pap. 6.95 (ISBN 0-452-25272-5, Z5272, Plume). NAL.

Not Yet Free. Dianna D. Booher. LC 80-69005. (gr. 9 up). 1981. 5.95 (ISBN 0-8054-7315-7). Broadman.

Not Yet Uhuru. Oginga Odinga. (African Writers Ser.). 1968. pap. text ed. 7.95x (ISBN 0-435-90038-2). Heinemann Ed.

Nota Biblica en la Literatura Castellana. Luis Salem. LC 77-163. 186p. (Orig., Span.). 1977. pap. 3.25 (ISBN 0-89922-086-X). Edit Caribe.

Notable Cross-Examinations. Ed. by Edward W. Fordham. LC 79-98759. Repr. of 1951 ed. lib. bdg. 15.00x (ISBN 0-8371-3099-9, FOCE). Greenwood.

Notable Man: The Life & Times of Oliver Goldsmith. John Ginger. (Illus.). 1978. 25.00 (ISBN 0-241-89626-6, Pub. by Hamish Hamilton England). David & Charles.

Notable Maryland Women. Ed. by Winifred G. Helmes. LC 77-966. 1977. 12.50 (ISBN 0-87033-236-8, Pub. by Tidewater); pap. 8.00 (ISBN 0-685-80908-0). Cornell Maritime.

Notable Men of Alabama: Personal & Genealogical with Portraits, 2 vols. Ed. by Joel C. Dubose. LC 75-45385. (Illus.). 1976. Repr. of 1904 ed. 25.00 ea.; Vol. 1. (ISBN 0-87152-225-X). Vol. 2 (ISBN 0-87152-226-8). Set. 50.00 (ISBN 0-87152-310-8). Reprint.

Notable Names in American History. 3rd ed. 1979. 74.00 (ISBN 0-8103-0409-0). Gale.

Notable Numbers. rev. ed. William T. Stokes. (Illus.). 1974. 5.95 (ISBN 0-914534-01-7). Stokes.

Notable Thoughts About Women: A Literary Mosaic. Maturin M. Ballou. LC 78-141602. 1971. Repr. of 1882 ed. 20.00 (ISBN 0-8103-3771-1). Gale.

Notation. Virginia Gaburo. LC 77-75432. (Illus.). 176p. 1977. soft-cover 14.45. Lingua Pr.

Notation in New Music: A Critical Guide to Interpretation & Realisation. Erhard Karkoschka. Tr. by Rush Koenig from Ger. LC 75-134522. Orig. Title: Das Schriftbild der Neuen Musik. 1972. 31.25 (ISBN 0-900938-28-5, 50-26902). Eur-Am Music.

Notations & Editions. Edith Borroff. (Music Reprint Series). 1977. Repr. of 1974 ed. lib. bdg. 25.00 (ISBN 0-306-70867-1). Da Capo.

Notations on the Arrest. Y. Y. Schneersohn. Ed. by Moshe Chaim Levin. Tr. by David A. Gurevich from Hebrew. LC 80-21987. (Illus.). 226p. (Orig.). 1980. 11.75 (ISBN 0-86639-100-2). Friends Refugees.

Note: A Handbook of Classroom Ideas to Motivate the Teaching of Elementary Music. (Spice Ser). 1973. 6.50 (ISBN 0-89273-113-3). Educ Serv.

Note by William Morris on His Aims in Founding the Kelmscott Press. William Morris. 1968. Repr. of 1898 ed. 15.00x o.p. (ISBN 0-7165-0024-8, Pub. by Irish Academic Pr Ireland). Biblio Dist.

Note by William Morris on...the Kelmscott Press. W. Morris. 76p. Repr. of 1829 ed. 15.00x (ISBN 0-7165-0620-3, Pub by Irish Academic Pr). Biblio Dist.

Notebook of Medical Physiology: Gastroenterological. Ross W. Hawker. (Illus.). 1981. pap. text ed. 12.50 (ISBN 0-443-02144-9). Churchill.

Notebook of Medical Physiology: Gastroenterology. Ross W. Hawker. (Notebooks of Medical Physiology Ser.). (Illus.). 256p. (Orig.). 1981. pap. text ed. 12.50 (ISBN 0-443-02144-9). Churchill.

Notebook on Time. Richard Zybert. LC 80-50741. (Illus.). 60p. (Orig.). 1981. pap. 4.95 (ISBN 0-9604260-0-0). Zybert.

Notebooks. B. F. Skinner. Ed. by Robert Epstein. LC 80-20094. 1981. 15.95 (ISBN 0-13-624106-9). P-H.

Notebooks of Andre Walter. Andre Gide. LC 67-24573. 1968. 4.75 o.p. (ISBN 0-8022-0586-0). Philos Lib.

Notebooks of Edgar Degas: A Catalogue of the Thirty-Eight Notebooks in the Bibliotheque Nationale & Other Collections, 2 vols. Theodore Reff. 1977. Set. 159.00x (ISBN 0-19-817333-4). Oxford U Pr.

Notebooks of Leonardo DaVinci. Ed. by Edward Maccurdy. (Illus.). 1956. 10.00 (ISBN 0-8076-0003-2). Braziller.

Notebooks: 1914-1916. Ludwig Wittgenstein. Ed. by G. E. Anscombe & G. H. Von Wright. Tr. by G. E. Anscombe. 1969. Repr. of 1961 ed. 24.50x (ISBN 0-631-06220-3, Pub. by Basil Blackwell). Biblio Dist.

Noteforms for Surveying Measurements. Russell C. Brinker & Austin Barry. 93p. 1957. pap. text ed. 3.50 scp o.p. (ISBN 0-685-01024-4, HarpC). Har-Row.

Notemaking. Diane Brown. 245p. 1977. text ed. 10.20 (ISBN 0-7715-0858-1). Forkner.

Notes & Blots from a Psychologist's Desk. Marvin Rosen. LC 77-16183. 1978. 13.95 (ISBN 0-88229-199-8). Nelson-Hall.

Notes for Breeders of Common Laboratory Animals. Ed. by George Porter & William Lane-Petter. 1964. 28.50 (ISBN 0-12-562750-5). Acad Pr.

Notes for Continuing the Performance. Anne Pitkin. 1977. 2.50 (ISBN 0-913116-04-X). Jawbone Pr.

Notes from a Distant Flute. Bruce Lawrence. LC 78-62007. 1979. 8.00 (ISBN 0-87773-735-5). Great Eastern.

Notes from an Underwater Zoo. Don C. Reed. (Illus.). 1981. 11.95. Dial.

Notes from China. Barbara W. Tuchman. LC 72-93468. 128p. 1972. pap. 2.95 (ISBN 0-02-074800-0, Collier). Macmillan.

Notes from the Castle. Howard Moss. LC 79-52417. 1979. 10.00 (ISBN 0-689-11014-6); pap. 5.95 (ISBN 0-689-11021-9). Atheneum.

Notes from the Chef's Desk. Arno B. Schmidt. LC 77-3005. 1977. 13.95 o.p. (ISBN 0-8436-2158-3). CBI Pub.

Notes from the Water Journals. Rich Ives. 1980. pap. 4.00 (ISBN 0-917652-20-7). Confluence Pr.

Notes in Hand: Miniatures of My Notebook Pages. Claes Oldenburg. 1971. pap. 2.95 o.p. (ISBN 0-525-47325-4). Dutton.

Notes of a Ten-Square Rush Mat Sized World. Kano N. Chomei. Tr. by Thomas Rowe & Anthony Kerrigan. 1980. text ed. 11.25x (ISBN 0-85105-343-2, Dolmen Pr). Humanities.

Notes of a Tour in the Manufacturing Districts of Lancashire. William C. Taylor. LC 67-131562. Repr. of 1842 ed. 17.50x (ISBN 0-678-05088-0). Kelley.

Notes of Debates in the Federal Convention of 1787 Reported by James Madison. James Madison. LC 65-18705. 1976. 20.00x (ISBN 0-8214-0011-8). Ohio U Pr.

Notes on a Social Theory: Twenty Six Annotations Related to Political Economy. T. A. Karlovich. LC 79-54249. 155p. 1979. 7.95 (ISBN 0-8059-2666-6). Dorrance.

Notes on Biblical Theology. Geerhardus Vos. 1948. pap. 6.95 (ISBN 0-8028-1209-0). Eerdmans.

Notes on Cargo Work. 4th ed. J. F. Kemp & P. Young. (Kemp & Young Ser.). (Illus., Orig.). 1981. pap. text ed. 9.50x (ISBN 0-540-07332-6). Sheridan.

Notes on Chasta Costa Phonology & Morphology. E. Sapir. (Anthropological Publications Ser.: Vol. 2-2). (Illus.). 1914. 2.00 (ISBN 0-686-24092-8). Univ Mus of U.

Notes on Conversations with the Duke of Wellington 1831-1851. P. H. Stanhope. LC 72-126611. (Modern European History Ser). 1973. Repr. of 1888 ed. lib. bdg. 35.00 (ISBN 0-306-70056-5). Da Capo.

Notes on Elementary Particle Physics. H. Muirhead. 264p. 1972. text ed. 29.00 (ISBN 0-08-016550-8). Pergamon.

Notes on Fallacies of American Protectionists. Francis Lieber. Bd. with Lectures on the History of Protection in the United States. William Sumner. (Neglected American Economists Ser.). 1974. lib. bdg. 50.00 (ISBN 0-8240-1018-3). Garland Pub.

Notes on Gogol's "The Government Inspector". Nigel Brown. 1974. pap. text ed. 1.50x o.p. (ISBN 0-435-18375-3). Heinemann Ed.

Notes on Japanese Sword Fittings. S. F. Moran. pap. 5.00 o.p. (ISBN 0-686-65148-0). Hawley.

Notes on Joseph Conrad, with Some Unpublished Letters. Arthur Symons. (Orig.). 1925. 8.00 (ISBN 0-685-13669-8). Kelly.

Notes on Labor Problems in Nationalist China. Israel Epstein. LC 78-74341. (Modern Chinese Economy Ser.). 159p. 1980. lib. bdg. 16.50 (ISBN 0-8240-4281-6). Garland Pub.

Notes on Land Tenure & Local Institutions in Old Japan. John H. Wigmore & D. B. Simmons. (Studies in Japanese History & Civilization). 1979. 21.00 (ISBN 0-89093-223-9). U Pubns Amer.

Notes on Love & Courage. Hugh Prather. LC 77-75873. 1977. pap. 4.95 (ISBN 0-385-12772-3). Doubleday.

Notes on Methods for the Narcotization, Killing, Fixation, & Preservation of Marine Organisms. H. D. Russell. 1963. 6.00 (ISBN 0-685-52861-8). Marine Bio.

Notes on Moral Theology. Richard A. McCormick. LC 80-5682. 902p. 1981. lib. bdg. 24.50 (ISBN 0-8191-1439-1); pap. text ed. 15.00 (ISBN 0-8191-1440-5). U Pr of Amer.

Notes on Novelists, with Some Other Notes. Henry James. LC 68-56451. 1969. Repr. of 1914 ed. 16.00x (ISBN 0-8196-0233-7). Biblo.

Notes on Nursing, 2 bks. Incl. Bk. 1. Science & the Art. Florence Nightingale. 50p; Bk. 2. What It Is & What It Is Not. Muriel Skeet. 75p. 1980. Set. 20.00 (ISBN 0-443-02130-9). Churchill.

Notes on Prints. William M. Ivins, Jr. LC 67-25544. (Graphic Art Ser). 1967. Repr. of 1930 ed. lib. bdg. 27.50 (ISBN 0-306-70957-0). Da Capo.

Notes on Prophecy. Ludwigson. pap. 2.95 o.p. (ISBN 0-686-12897-4). Schmul Pub Co.

Notes on Psychiatry. 4th ed. I. M. Ingram et al. LC 75-17741. (Illus.). 128p. 1976. pap. text ed. 5.75 (ISBN 0-443-01334-9). Churchill.

Notes on Stagflation. Howard S. Ellis. 1978. pap. 2.25 (ISBN 0-8447-3323-7). Am Enterprise.

Notes on the Bhagavad-Gita. William Q. Judge & Robert Crosbie. 237p. 1918. Repr. 4.00 (ISBN 0-938998-10-2). Theosophy.

Notes on the Bhagavad-Gita. T. Subba Row. LC 77-88628. 1978. 6.00 (ISBN 0-911500-81-2); softcover 3.50 (ISBN 0-911500-82-0). Theos U Pr.

Notes on the Cathedral Libraries of England. Beriah Botfield. LC 68-23138. 1969. Repr. of 1849 ed. 32.00 (ISBN 0-8103-3174-8). Gale.

Notes on the Collection of Transfers. William J. Sidis. LC 80-50701. 305p. 1981. Repr. of 1928 ed. lib. bdg. 40.00x (ISBN 0-88000-115-1). Quarterman.

Notes on the Epistles of St. Paul. J. B. Lightfoot. Date not set. 12.95 (ISBN 0-88469-137-3). BMH Bks.

Notes on the Era & Other Poems. K. P. Joseph. (Writers Workshop Redbird Ser.). 1975. 12.00 (ISBN 0-88253-590-0); pap. text ed. 4.80 (ISBN 0-88253-589-7). Ind-US Inc.

Notes on the Gynecology & Obstetrics of the Arikara Tribe of Indians, Vol. 14, No. 1. Melvin Gilmore. 1980. pap. 2.50 (ISBN 0-686-69103-2). Acoma Bks.

Notes on the Literature of the Piano. Albert Lockwood. LC 67-30400. (Music Ser). 1968. Repr. of 1940 ed. lib. bdg. 22.50 (ISBN 0-306-70983-X). Da Capo.

Notes on the Parables of Our Lord. R. C. Trench. (Twin Brooks Ser). pap. 4.95 (ISBN 0-8010-8774-0). Baker Bk.

Notes on the Puerto Rican Revolution: An Essay on American Dominance & Caribbean Resistance. Gordon K. Lewis. LC 74-7791. 192p. 1975. 9.50 o.p. (ISBN 0-85345-341-1, CL-3411). Monthly Rev.

Notes, on the Settlement & Indian Wars, of the Western Parts of Virginia & Pennsylvania, from the Year 1763 Until the Year 1783 Inclusive. Joseph Doddridge. LC 75-7062. (Indian Captivities Ser.: Vol. 40). 1977. Repr. of 1824 ed. lib. bdg. 44.00 (ISBN 0-8240-1664-5). Garland Pub.

Notes on the Tribes, Provinces, Emirates & States of the Northern Province of Nigeria. O. Temple. 595p. 1965. 35.00x (ISBN 0-7146-1728-8, F Cass Co). Biblio Dist.

Notes on Trusteeship. David Lynes & Leonard E. Opdycke. 1975. pap. 3.25 (ISBN 0-934338-29-9). NAIS.

Notes Sur le Classement Chronologique Des Monnaies D'athenes (Series Avec Noms De Magistrats) M. L. Kambanis. (Illus., Fr.). pap. 5.00 (ISBN 0-916710-78-5). Obol Intl.

Notes to the Overworld. Carroll E. Simcox. LC 72-81029. 128p. 1972. 4.50 (ISBN 0-8164-0242-6). Crossroad NY.

Notes Without Music. Darius Milhaud. LC 72-87419. (Music Ser). (Illus.). 1970. Repr. of 1953 ed. lib. bdg. 35.00 (ISBN 0-306-71565-1). Da Capo.

Notescript. Laurence F. Hawkins. (Orig.). 1964. pap. 2.95 (ISBN 0-06-463232-6, EH 232, EH). Har-Row.

Notetaking & Study Skills. Gloria H. Weber et al. (gr. 10-12). 1977. 11.20x (ISBN 0-912036-27-3); wkbk. 5.76x (ISBN 0-912036-28-1); instrs'. manual 1.76x (ISBN 0-912036-29-X); profiles pkg. of 25 5.88x (ISBN 0-912036-30-3). Forkner.

Noteworthy Paintings in American Private Collections, 2 vols. Ed. by John La Farge et al. LC 75-28888. (Art Experience in Late 19th Century America Ser.: Vol. 21). (Illus.). 1976. Repr. of 1907 ed. Set. lib. bdg. 218.00 (ISBN 0-8240-2245-9). Garland Pub.

Nothing Book. 1977. pap. 2.50 (ISBN 0-446-91907-1). Warner Bks.

Nothing but Prairie & Sky: Life on the Dakota Range in the Early Days. Walker D. Wyman. (Western Frontier Library: No. 45). 1954. 5.95 (ISBN 0-8061-0287-X). U of Okla Pr.

Nothing but Soup. Katy Hall. (Picture Bk). (Illus.). 32p. (gr. 1 up). 1976. 5.95 o.p. (ISBN 0-695-80670-X); lib. ed. 5.97 o.p. (ISBN 0-695-40670-1). Follett.

Nothing but the Best. Leslie Tonner. 160p. 1976. pap. 1.50 o.p. (ISBN 0-345-24966-6). Ballantine.

Nothing Could Be Finer Than a Crisis That Is Minor in the Morning. Charles Osgood. LC 79-14377. 204p. 1979. 9.95 (ISBN 0-03-047646-1); pap. 3.95 (ISBN 0-03-057646-6). HR&W.

Nothing-Doting-Blindness. Henry Green. 1980. pap. 6.95 (ISBN 0-14-005664-5). Penguin.

Nothing Down. Robert Allen. Date not set. 10.95 (ISBN 0-671-24748-4). S&S.

Nothing Is Impossible with God. Kathryn Kuhlman. (Orig.). pap. 1.75 (ISBN 0-89129-084-2). Jove Pubns.

Nothing Lasts Forever. Oscar Haimo. 1981. deluxe ed. 9.00x (ISBN 0-686-10361-0). Haimo.

Nothing Never Happens: Exercises to Trigger Group Discussion & Promote Self-Discovery with Selected Readings. Kenneth G. Johnson et al. LC 72-91270. 352p. 1974. pap. text ed. 10.95x (ISBN 0-02-475140-5); tchr's ed. 10.95x (ISBN 0-02-475130-8). Macmillan.

Nothing New Under the Sun. Russ Williams. 1981. 7.95 (ISBN 0-8062-1585-2). Carlton.

Nothing Said. L. M. Boston. LC 70-137756. (Illus.). (gr. 2-5). 1971. 4.95 o.p. (ISBN 0-15-257580-4, HJ). HarBraceJ.

Nothing Stops a Determined Being! Aron Breslow. 1981. 4.00 (ISBN 0-918430-03-8). Happy History.

Nothing to Do with Love. Joyce R. Kornblatt. LC 80-52006. 204p. 1981. 11.95 (ISBN 0-670-48020-7, Studio). Viking Pr.

Nothing's Fair in Fifth Grade. Barthe DeClements. 144p. (gr. 3-7). 1981. 8.95 (ISBN 0-670-51741-0). Viking Pr.

Notices of Florida & the Campaigns. Myer M. Cohen. Ed. by O. Z. Tyler, Jr. LC 64-19153. (Floridiana Facsimile & Reprint Ser). 1964. Repr. of 1836 ed. 10.75 (ISBN 0-8130-0048-3). U Presses Fla.

Noticiario: Primer Nivel-Sight Readings in Spanish. William F. Smith. (Orig.). 1981. pap. text ed. 5.95 (ISBN 0-88377-161-6). Newbury Hse.

Notion by Notion. Linda Ferreira. 96p. (Orig.). 1981. pap. text ed. 3.95 (ISBN 0-88377-199-3). Newbury Hse.

Notion De Force Dans le Systeme D' Aristote. Henri Carteron. LC 78-66622. (Ancient Philosophy Ser.). 293p. 1980. lib. bdg. 28.50 (ISBN 0-8240-9605-3). Garland Pub.

Notion of Tribe. Morton H. Fried. 1975. pap. 4.95 o.p. (ISBN 0-8465-1548-2). Benjamin-Cummings.

Notional Syllabuses. D. A. Wilkins. 1977. pap. text ed. 6.50x (ISBN 0-19-437071-2). Oxford U Pr.

Notions of the Americans. Ed. by David Grimsted. LC 77-132199. (American Culture Ser). 1970. 8.95 o.s.i. (ISBN 0-8076-0568-9); pap. 6.95 o.s.i. (ISBN 0-8076-0567-0). Braziller.

Notorious Angel. Patricia Maxwell. 1977. pap. 1.95 o.p. (ISBN 0-449-13825-9, GM). Fawcett.

Notorious Eliza. Basil Beyea. 1979. pap. 1.95 o.p. (ISBN 0-449-23998-5, Crest). Fawcett.

Notorious Grizzly Bears. W. P. Hubbard & Peggy Harris. LC 60-14583. (Illus.). 205p. 1960. pap. 4.95 (ISBN 0-8040-0617-2, Sage). Swallow.

Notorious Lady. Maggie MacKeever. 1978. pap. 1.50 o.p. (ISBN 0-449-23491-6, Crest). Fawcett.

Notpoems. Adele Aldridge. LC 72-23824. 1976. pap. 5.95 (ISBN 0-915600-01-3, 0753-5). Swallow.

Notre-Dame de Paris. Victor Hugo. (Documentation thematique). pap. 2.95 (ISBN 0-685-14001-6, 127). Larousse.

Notre Dame Football Scrapbook. Richard M. Cohen et al. LC 77-5262. (Illus.). 1977. pap. 6.95 o.p. (ISBN 0-672-52335-3). Bobbs.

Notre Dame Weight Training Program for Football. Peter P. Broccoletti & Pat Scanlon. LC 78-20947. (Illus.). 1979. 12.95 (ISBN 0-89651-502-8); pap. 9.95 (ISBN 0-89651-503-6). Icarus.

Nottinghamshire in the Eighteenth Century. Jonathan D. Chambers. LC 65-5293. Repr. of 1932 ed. 22.50x (ISBN 0-678-05036-8). Kelley.

Nourishing Self Esteem: A Parent Handbook for Nurturing Love. Earl White. (Illus.). 95p. (Orig.). 1981. pap. text ed. 5.00 (ISBN 0-686-69561-5). Whitenwife Pubns.

Nourrir En Harmonie Avec L'environment. Bergeret et al. 1977. 21.75x (ISBN 90-279-7684-8). Mouton.

Nous Valons Plus Que Des Passereaux. Tr. by Mary Welch. (French Bks.). (Fr.). 1979. 1.75 (ISBN 0-8297-0843-X). Life Pubs Intl.

Nouveau Dictionnaire etymologique. A. Dauzat et al. (Fr). 27.50 (ISBN 2-03-020210-X, 3612). Larousse.

Nouveau Dictionnaire francais-hebreu. 1973. 26.00 (ISBN 0-685-55772-3). Larousse.

Nouveau Glossaire Nautique, Lettre C: Revision De L'edition Publiee En 1848. Augustin Jal. (Fr.). 1978. pap. 57.00x (ISBN 90-279-7538-8). Mouton.

Nouveau Larousse des debutants. (Fr.). 16.25 (ISBN 2-03-020146-4, 3750). Larousse.

Nouveau Larousse elementaire. Larousse And Co. (Illus., Fr.). 23.95 (ISBN 0-685-14003-2). Larousse.

Nouveau Larousse francais-anglais, English-French. (Mars). 24.00 (ISBN 2-03-020812-4, 4083). Larousse.

Nouveau Larousse gastronomique. G. Mathiot. (Illus., Fr.). 79.75x (ISBN 0-685-14004-0, 3905). Larousse.

Nouveau Larousse universel, 2 Vols. Larousse And Co. (Illus., Fr.). 91.00x ea. Larousse.

Nouveau Petit Larousse en couleurs. Larousse And Co. (Illus., Fr.). 1974. 83.00 (ISBN 2-03-020111-1, 3676). Larousse.

Nouveau Point De Vue. James S. Noblitt. 1978. text ed. 16.95x (ISBN 0-669-96545-6); inst. manual free (ISBN 0-669-00335-2); wkbk. 5.95 (ISBN 0-669-96552-9); Sets. reels 60.00 (ISBN 0-669-96560-X); cassettes 60.00 (ISBN 0-669-00250-X). Heath.

Nouveau Roman & the Poetics of Fiction. Ann Jefferson. LC 79-41507. 225p. 1980. 29.50 (ISBN 0-521-22239-7). Cambridge U Pr.

Nouveau Roman Reader. Intro. by John Calder. 1979. 11.95 (ISBN 0-7145-3719-5); pap. 5.95 (ISBN 0-7145-3720-9). Riverrun NY.

Nouveau Traite Des Regles Pour La Composition De la Musique. 2nd ed. Charles Masson. LC 67-25446. (Music Ser). 1967. Repr. of 1699 ed. lib. bdg. 16.50 (ISBN 0-306-70941-4). Da Capo.

Nouveaux mots dans le vent. J. Giraud & J. Riverain Pamart. 271p. (Fr.). 1974. pap. 11.95 (ISBN 2-03-070334-6, 2717). Larousse.

Nouvelle Grammaire du francais. Jean Dubois & Rene Lagane. 272p. (Orig., Fr.). 1973. pap. 10.95 (ISBN 2-03-040165-X, 3772). Larousse.

Nouvelle Heloise, 2 Vols. Jean-Jacques Rousseau. (Documentation thematique). (Fr). pap. 2.95 ea. Larousse.

Nouvelles Considerations Sur les Annees Climateriques. Louis De Beausobre. (Principal French Demographic Works of the 18th Century Ser.). (Fr.). 1976. lib. bdg. 20.00x o.p. (ISBN 0-8287-0068-0); pap. text ed. 10.00x o.p. (ISBN 0-685-71511-6). Clearwater Pub.

Nouvelles Conventions De la Haye: Leur Application Par les Juges Nationaux, Vol. II. Mathilde Sumanpouw. 260p. (Fr.). 1980. 45.00x (ISBN 90-286-0870-2). Sijthoff & Noordhoff.

Nouvelles Du Quebec. 2nd ed. K. Brearley & R. McBride. (Fr). 1977. pap. text ed. 8.95 o.p. (ISBN 0-13-625467-5). P-H.

Nouvelles et Recits Du XXIeme Siecle. Ed. by G. Mernier & M. Spingler. 1971. pap. 7.95 o.p. (ISBN 0-13-625335-0). P-H.

Nouvelles Recherches Sur la Population De la France. Messance. (Principal French Demographic Works of the 18th Century Ser.). (Fr.). 1976. lib. bdg. 40.00x o.p. (ISBN 0-8287-0608-5); pap. text ed. 30.00x o.p. (ISBN 0-685-71501-9). Clearwater Pub.

Nova Scotia Statutes: Statutes at Large, Vols. 1-4. Richard J. Uniacke. LC 76-612783. 1970. Repr. Set. lib. bdg. 160.00x (ISBN 0-912004-06-1). W W Gaunt.

Nova Venturion's Bootstrap Venture Manual. Walter Zintz. 1981. softcover 14.50 (ISBN 0-915254-08-5). Nova Venturion.

Nova Venturion's Handbook for Non-Salesmen. Walter Zintz. 1981. softcover 12.50 (ISBN 0-915254-09-3). Nova Venturion.

Novak's Textbook of Gynecology. 3rd, student ed. Howard Jones, Jr. & Georgeanna S. Jones. (Illus.). 450p. 1981. write for info. softcover (4467-2). Williams & Wilkins.

Novantiqua: Rhetorics as a Contemporary Theory. Paolo Valesio. LC 79-9632. (Advances in Semiotics Ser.). 384p. 1980. 22.50x (ISBN 0-253-11055-6). Ind U Pr.

Novel & Contemporary Experience in Africa. Shatto A. Gakwandi. LC 77-1273. 1981. text ed. 22.50x (ISBN 0-8419-0306-9, Africana); pap. text ed. 8.95x (ISBN 0-8419-0642-4). Holmes & Meier.

Novel & Romance, 1700-1800: A Documentary Record. Ioan Williams. 1970. 40.00x (ISBN 0-7100-6595-7). Routledge & Kegan.

Novel Approach to Losing Weight. Hans Gandhi. 1981. 10.00 (ISBN 0-533-04724-2). Vantage.

Novel Before the Novel. Arthur Heiserman. LC 76-8102. 1977. lib. bdg. 17.50x o.s.i. (ISBN 0-226-32572-5). U of Chicago Pr.

Novel Drilling Techniques. W. C. Maurer. 1968. 26.00 (ISBN 0-08-012734-7). Pergamon.

Novel Experiments with Electricity. John P. Shields. LC 78-122966. (Illus.). 1970. pap. 3.50 o.p. (ISBN 0-672-20794-X, 20794). Sams.

Novel in India: Its Birth & Development. Ed. by T. W. Clark. LC 70-119719. 1970. 19.50x (ISBN 0-520-01725-0). U of Cal Pr.

Novel in Seventeenth-Century China. Robert E. Hegel. (Illus.). 320p. 1981. 20.00x (ISBN 0-231-04928-5). Columbia U Pr.

Novel Materials. Editors of Time-Life Books. LC 74-16950. (Art of Sewing). (Illus.). (gr. 6 up). 1974. PLB 11.97 (ISBN 0-8094-1723-5, Pub. by Time-Life). Silver.

Novel Materials. (Art of Sewing Ser). (Illus.). 1974. 9.95 (ISBN 0-8094-1721-9). Time-Life.

Novel of Adultery. Judith Armstrong. LC 76-15793. 1976. text ed. 18.50x o.p. (ISBN 0-06-490203-X). B&N.

Novel of India, 2 vols. Steven Hemenway. Incl. Vol. 1. The Anglo-Indian Novel. flexible cloth 8.00 (ISBN 0-89253-667-5); Vol. 2. The Indo-Anglian Novel. 15.00 (ISBN 0-89253-668-3); flexible cloth 8.00 (ISBN 0-89253-669-1). Ind-US Inc.

Novel of the American West. John R. Milton. LC 79-17713. xviii, 341p. 1980. 17.95 (ISBN 0-8032-0980-0). U of Nebr Pr.

Novel of the Future. Anais Nin. 1970. pap. 2.95 o.s.i. (ISBN 0-02-053100-1, Collier). Macmillan.

Novel Sources of Coherent Radiation: Adaptive Optics. Ed. by Stephen F. Jacobs et al. LC 78-3420. (Physics of Quantum Electronics: Vol. 5). (Illus.). text ed. cancelled o.s.i. (ISBN 0-201-05685-2, Adv Bk Prog). A-W.

Novel to Nineteen Hundred. Intro. by A. O. Cockshut. 320p. 1981. pap. 7.95 (ISBN 0-312-57965-9). St Martin.

Novel Writers. Emily Sisley. LC 80-81487. 78p. (Orig.). 1980. pap. 2.95 (ISBN 0-934696-01-2). Mosaic Pr.

Novela Caballeresca. (Span.). 7.95 (ISBN 84-241-5617-X). E Torres & Sons.

Novela Picaresca. (Span.). 7.95 (ISBN 84-241-5614-5). E Torres & Sons.

Novelas Ejemplares. Miguel de Cervantes. (Span.). 7.95 (ISBN 84-241-5613-7). E Torres & Sons.

Novelas Ejemplares. Miguel De Cervantes. (Span). 4.50x o.s.i. (ISBN 0-686-00878-2). Colton Bk.

Novelistica Cubana De la Revolucion. Antonio Fernandez-Vazquez. LC 79-52159. (Coleccion Polymita Ser.). 157p. (Span.). 1980. pap. 9.95 (ISBN 0-89729-228-6). Ediciones.

Novelistica de Ciro Alegria. 2nd enlarged ed. Matilde Vilarino De Olivieri. LC 79-22294. (Coleccion Mente y Palabra). Orig. Title: Novelas de Ciro Alegria. 283p. (Sp.). 1980. 6.25 (ISBN 0-8477-0566-8); pap. 5.00 (ISBN 0-686-61425-9). U of PR Pr.

Novelistica Espanola De los Sesenta. E. Guillermo & J. A. Hernandez. 1971. 12.45 (ISBN 0-88303-002-0); pap. 9.00 (ISBN 0-685-73208-8). E Torres & Sons.

Novella Box. Smith Experimental Fiction Project. Incl. Invisibles. Hugh Fox. pap. 3.00 (ISBN 0-685-78301-4); Same Thing Happened Over & Over. Leonard Chabrowe. pap. 3.00 (ISBN 0-685-78302-2); Teak. Robert Reinhold. pap. 2.00 (ISBN 0-685-78303-0). 1976. Boxed Set. pap. 5.00 (ISBN 0-912292-40-7). The Smith.

Novellen. Zweig. (Easy Reader, C). pap. 3.75 (ISBN 0-88436-042-3, GEA201053). EMC.

Novels & Novelists: From Elizabeth to Victorian, 2 vols. J. Cordy Jeaffreson. 405p. 1980. Repr. of 1858 ed. Set. lib. bdg. 85.00 (ISBN 0-8414-5416-7). Folcroft.

Novels & Travels of Camilo Jose Cela. Robert Kirsner. (Studies in the Romance Languages & Literatures: No. 43). 1964. pap. 8.50x (ISBN 0-8078-9043-X). U of NC Pr.

Novels in English by Women, 1891 to 1920: A Preliminary Checklist. Janet Grimes & Diva Daims. Ed. by Doris Robinson. LC 79-7911. 800p. 1981. lib. bdg. 75.00 (ISBN 0-8240-9522-7). Garland Pub.

Novels of Anthony Powell. James Tucker. LC 76-15201. 1976. 15.00x (ISBN 0-231-04150-0). Columbia U Pr.

Novels of August Strindberg: A Study in Theme & Structure. Eric O. Johannesson. LC 68-29156. 1968. 18.75x (ISBN 0-520-00607-0). U of Cal Pr.

Novels of George Eliot. Jerome Thale. LC 59-8377. 1959. 15.00x (ISBN 0-231-02328-6). Columbia U Pr.

Novels of Henry James: A Study of Culture & Consciousness. Brian Lee. LC 78-16902. 1979. 16.95 (ISBN 0-312-57969-1). St Martin.

Novels of Julio Cortazar. Stephen Boldy. LC 79-41579. (Cambridge Iberian & Latin American Studies). 320p. 1980. 29.50 (ISBN 0-521-23097-7). Cambridge U Pr.

Novels of Margaret Drabble: Equivocal Figures. Ellen C. Rose. (Illus.). 141p. 1980. 26.50x (ISBN 0-389-20006-9). B&N.

Novels of Mary Shelley. Safaa El Shater. (Salzburg Studies in English Literature: Romantic Reassessment Ser.: No. 59). (Orig.). 1977. pap. text ed. 25.00x (ISBN 0-391-01372-6). Humanities.

Novels of R. K. Narayan. Lakshmi Holmstrom. (Writers Workshop Greybird Ser.). 130p. 1975. 15.00 (ISBN 0-88253-584-6); pap. text ed. 8.00 (ISBN 0-88253-583-8). Ind-US Inc.

Novels of the Eighteen-Forties. Kathleen Tillotson. 1954. pap. 3.95x o.p. (ISBN 0-19-881015-6, OPB). Oxford U Pr.

Novels of Thomas Hardy: Illusion & Reality. Penelope Vigar. 236p. 1974. text ed. 17.50x (ISBN 0-391-00932-X). Humanities.

Novels of Tobias Smollett. P. G. Bouce. LC 75-31687. 1976. text ed. 32.00x (ISBN 0-582-50023-0). Longman.

Novels of William Godwin & Those of His Contemporaries. Mona Scheuermann. Ed. by Devendra P. Varma. LC 79-8477. (Gothic Studies & Dissertations Ser.). 1980. lib. bdg. 25.00x (ISBN 0-405-12678-6). Arno.

Novels of Worldliness, Crebillon, Marivaux, Laclos, Stendhal. Peter Brooks. LC 68-56303. 1969. 18.00x (ISBN 0-691-06154-8). Princeton U Pr.

November. Rolf Schneider. LC 80-22770. 240p. 1981. 11.95 (ISBN 0-394-51440-8). Knopf.

November Twenty-Second. Bryan Wooley. 448p. 1981. 12.95 (ISBN 0-87223-690-0). Seaview Bks.

Novia Hoy-Esposa Manana: Guia Para Novias. Joan L. Sutton & Leda Watson de Barros. Tr. by Olivia S. D. de Lerin. Orig. Title: Manual das Noivas. 1980. pap. 1.70 (ISBN 0-311-46056-9, Edit Mundo). Casa Bautista.

Noviazgo. Carmen LaForet. Ed. by Carolyn L. Galerstein. LC 72-85231. 100p. 1973. pap. 3.95 (ISBN 0-672-63131-8). Odyssey Pr.

Novice & General Class Amateur License Q & A Manual. 2nd ed. M. Tepper. (gr. 10 up). 1977. pap. 9.55 (ISBN 0-8104-5599-4). Hayden.

Novum Testamentum Graece. 26th ed. Ed. by E. Nestle & K. Aland. 1979. 8.65 (ISBN 3-438-05100-1, 57902). United Bible.

Novum Testamentum Latine: Editio Minor. Ed. by J Wordsworth & H. J. White. 1980. Repr. of 1920 ed. 2.95 (ISBN 0-564-02119-9, 71700). United Bible.

Now a Word from Our Creator. Leslie B. Flynn. 144p. 1976. pap. 2.25 o.p. (ISBN 0-88207-728-7). Victor Bks.

NOW Accounts. Dwight D. Crane & Michael J. Riley. LC 77-6580. 1978. 18.95 (ISBN 0-669-01612-8). Lexington Bks.

Now & Then: Poems, 1976-1978. Robert P. Warren. 1978. 8.95 (ISBN 0-394-50164-0); pap. 4.95 (ISBN 0-394-73515-3); lmtd. ed. 15.00 (ISBN 0-394-50220-5). Random.

Now Barabbas Was a Rotter: The Extraordinary Life of Corelli. Brian Masters. 1979. 22.50 (ISBN 0-241-89767-X, Pub. by Hamish Hamilton England). David & Charles.

Now: Essays & Articles. Maurice L. Sutton et al. LC 69-12305. 1969. pap. text ed. 6.95x (ISBN 0-02-478760-4, 47876). Macmillan.

Now I Can Smile. Karen M. Walden. 1981. 4.95 (ISBN 0-533-04493-6). Vantage.

Now I Have a Step-Parent, & It's Kind of Confusing. Janet S. Stenson. 1979. pap. 2.95 (ISBN 0-380-46516-7, 46516). Avon.

Now I Lay Me Down to Eat: Notes & Footnotes on the Lost Art of Living. Bernard Rudofsky. LC 80-714. (Illus.). 196p. 1980. pap. 10.95 (ISBN 0-385-15716-9, Anch). Doubleday.

Now I Lay Me Down to Eat: Notes & Footnotes on the Lost Art of Living. Bernard Rudofsky. LC 80-714. (Illus.). 160p. 1980. 19.95 (ISBN 0-385-15715-0, Anchor Pr); pap. 10.95 (ISBN 0-385-15716-9). Doubleday.

Now in Mexico. Hudson Strode. LC 47-11420. (Illus.). 5.00 o.p. (ISBN 0-15-167691-7). HarBraceJ.

Now is the Time: Integration in the Berkeley Schools. Neil V. Sullivan & Evelyn S. Stewart. LC 73-85102. 224p. 1970. 10.00x (ISBN 0-253-15841-9). Ind U Pr.

Now Is Too Soon(a Mother's Prayers As Her Daughter Nears Marriage) Star L. Courtney. 64p. 1974. 2.95 o.p. (ISBN 0-8007-0652-8). Revell.

Now It Can Be Told: The Story of the Manhattan Project. Leslie R. Groves. LC 75-1001. (FDR & the Era of the New Deal Ser). 465p. 1975. Repr. of 1962 ed. lib. bdg. 35.00 (ISBN 0-306-70738-1). Da Capo.

Now Listen Good! A Collection of Authentic West Indian Recipes. Estella F. Schulman. LC 79-19954. 1979. 6.95 (ISBN 0-88427-037-8, Dist. by Caroline Hse). North River.

Now Listen Good: A Collection of Authentic West Indian Recipes. Estella F. Schulman. 6.95 (ISBN 0-88427-037-8). Green Hill.

Now Newman Was Old. Chaim Bermant. LC 78-3993. 1978. 8.95 o.p. (ISBN 0-312-57971-3). St Martin.

Now One Foot, Now the Other. Tomie De Paola. (Illus.). 48p. (gr. 3-7). 1981. 7.95 (ISBN 0-399-20774-0); pap. 2.95 (ISBN 0-399-20775-9). Putnam.

Now or Never: A Time for Survival. Cantor M. Radzivilover. LC 78-26200. 1979. 9.95 (ISBN 0-8119-0314-1). Fell.

Now Songs: Contemporary Gospel Songs with Guitar Chords. Malcolm Stewart. Orig. Title: Gospel Song Book. 1969. pap. 2.50 (ISBN 0-687-28211-X). Abingdon.

Now Student: Reading & Study Skills. rev ed. Edward Spargo. (Illus.). (gr. 12 up). 1977. pap. text ed. 4.80x (ISBN 0-89061-120-3); instructor's guide free (ISBN 0-89061-121-1). Jamestown Pubs.

Now That Days Are Colder. Aileen Fisher. (Natue Ser). (gr. k-6). 1973. PLB 6.96 (ISBN 0-8372-0862-9); filmstrip & record 18.00 (ISBN 0-8372-0207-8); filmstrip & cassette 18.00 (ISBN 0-8372-0873-4). Bowmar-Noble.

Now That I Believe. Robert A. Cook. 1956. pap. 1.50 (ISBN 0-8024-5982-X). Moody.

Now That I'm a Christian, Vol. 1. Chuck Miller. (Orig.). 1974. pap. 3.95 (ISBN 0-8307-0326-8, 52-019-18). Regal.

Now That I'm a Christian, Vol. 2. Chuck Miller. (Orig.). 1976. pap. 2.75 (ISBN 0-8307-0327-6, 52-015-00). Regal.

Now That We're All Here...Relations in Small Groups. Lawrence Rosenfeld. (Interpersonal Communication Ser.). (Illus.). 1976. pap. text ed. 5.95x (ISBN 0-675-08642-6). Merrill.

Now That You Own a Puppy. Joan Tate. (Illus.). 1976. pap. 3.95 (ISBN 0-8119-0394-X). Fell.

Now That You're Saved. Richard Kennedy. 1977. pap. 0.60 (ISBN 0-89265-046-X). Randall Hse.

Now That You've Incorporated. S. Gorlick. 1977. 14.95 (ISBN 0-87489-138-8). Med Economics.

Now to Take Care of Yourselves Naturally. 2nd ed. John Barton & Margaret Barton. LC 77-80393. (Illus.). 158p. (Orig.). 1980. pap. 8.00 o.p. (ISBN 0-937216-00-3). J&M Barton.

Now You Can Profit from Inflation. George E. Croom, Jr. & John Van Der Wal. 264p. 1981. 14.95 (ISBN 0-442-25397-4). Van Nos Reinhold.

Now You Can Understand the Book of Revelation. Jim McKeever. 320p. 1980. 10.95 (ISBN 0-931608-07-4); pap. 5.95 (ISBN 0-931608-08-2). Omega Pubns OR.

Nowhere Boys: A Comparative Study of Open & Closed Residential Placement. Cairine Petrie. 184p. 1980. 18.50x (ISBN 0-566-00302-3, 02835-5, Pub. by Saxon Hse England). Lexington Bks.

Nowhere City. Alison Lurie. 1976. pap. 1.65 (ISBN 0-380-00230-2, 23754). Avon.

Nowhere Fast. Margoe Jane. Ed. by Craig H. Hastings. (Illus.). 64p. (Orig.). 1980. pap. 4.00 (ISBN 0-9602330-1-6). Margoe Jane.

Nowhere to Play. Buchi Emecheta. (gr. 4-8). 1981. 6.95 (ISBN 0-8052-8058-8, Pub. by Allison & Busby England). Schocken.

Nowhere to Run. Hilary Milton. LC 78-2798. (gr. 7 up). 1978. PLB 7.90 s&l (ISBN 0-531-02247-1). Watts.

NPT: The Main Political Barrier to Nuclear Weapon Proliferation. SIPRI. LC 80-16984. 1980. pap. 8.95x (ISBN 0-8448-1380-X). Crane-Russak Co.

NRA Economic Planning. C. F. Roos. LC 72-171693. (Fdr & the Era of the New Deal Ser.). 596p. 1972. Repr. of 1937 ed. lib. bdg. 55.00 (ISBN 0-306-70396-3). Da Capo.

NRMA's Advertising & Sales Promotion Budget Book. Joseph R. Rowen. 100p. 1981. text ed. 13.75 (ISBN 0-686-60193-9, 266780). Natl Ret Merch.

NSAA Economic Analysis of North American Ski Areas (79-80 Season) C. R. Goeldner & Ted Farwell. 139p. 1980. 35.00 (ISBN 0-89478-054-9). U CO Busn Res Div.

NST Story, 1944-1974. Robert H. Carleton. (Orig.). 1976. pap. 3.00 o.p. (ISBN 0-686-53818-8, 471-14700). Natl Sci Tchrs.

NSTA Energy-Environment Materials Guide. Kathryn E. Mervine & Rebecca E. Cawley. 80p. 1975. pap. text ed. 2.00 o.p. (ISBN 0-685-55989-0, 471-14694). Natl Sci Tchrs.

Nubia: Corridor to Africa. W. R. Adams. 1977. 45.00 o.p. (ISBN 0-691-09370-9). Princeton U Pr.

Nuclear Accident Dosimetry Systems. (Illus., Orig.). 1970. pap. 14.00 (ISBN 92-0-021070-8, ISP 241, IAEA). Unipub.

Nuclear Activation Cross-Section Data: Neutron, Proton, & Charged Particle Nuclear Reaction Cross-Section Data. (Technical Reports Ser., No. 156). (Illus.). 558p. (Orig.). 1974. pap. 40.75 (ISBN 92-0-135074-0, IAEA). Unipub.

Nuclear Activation Techniques in the Life Sciences. 1967. pap. 34.25 (ISBN 92-0-010267-0, IAEA). Unipub.

Nuclear Activation Techniques in the Life Sciences - 1978. 1979. pap. 92.25 (ISBN 92-0-010079-1, ISP492, IAEA). Unipub.

Nuclear Activation Techniques in the Life Sciences - 1972. (Illus.). 664p. (Orig.). 1973. pap. 41.75 (ISBN 92-0-010272-7, IAEA). Unipub.

Nuclear Analogue States. Ed. by D. Robson & J. D. Fox. LC 76-17849. (Benchmark Papers in Nuclear Physics Ser.: Vol. 1). 1976. 48.50 (ISBN 0-12-787356-2). Acad Pr.

Nuclear & Radiochemistry. 3rd ed. Gerhart Friedlander. 650p. 1981. price not set (ISBN 0-471-28021-6, Pub. by Wiley-Interscience). Wiley.

Nuclear & Radiochemistry. 2nd ed. Gerhart Friedlander et al. 1964. 29.95 (ISBN 0-471-28020-8). Wiley.

Nuclear & Relativistic Astrophysics & Nuclidic Cosmochemistry: 1963-1967, 4 vols. B. Kuchowicz. 1976. Vol. 1. 62.50 (ISBN 0-677-02760-5); Vol. 2. microform 35.00; Vol. 3. microform 32.00 (ISBN 0-677-02780-X); Vol. 4. 62.50 (ISBN 0-677-02790-7). Gordon.

Nuclear Apple & the Solar Orange: Alternatives in World Energy. M. Grenon. LC 80-40836. (Illus.). 200p. 1980. 36.00 (ISBN 0-08-026157-4); pap. 15.75 (ISBN 0-08-026156-6). Pergamon.

Nuclear Arms in the Third World: U. S. Policy Dilemma. Ernest W. Lefever. 1979. 11.95 (ISBN 0-8157-5202-4); pap. 4.95 (ISBN 0-8157-5201-6). Brookings.

Nuclear Chemical Engineering. 2nd ed. Manson Benedict et al. (Illus.). 1008p. 1981. text ed. 44.50 (ISBN 0-07-004531-3). McGraw.

Nuclear Chemistry: A Current Review. National Research Council - Committee For The Survey Of Chemistry. 1966. pap. 3.00 (ISBN 0-309-01292-9). Natl Acad Pr.

Nuclear Chemistry: Theory & Applications. Ed. by G. Choppin & J. Ryberg. (Illus.). 1980. text ed. 87.00 (ISBN 0-08-023826-2); pap. text ed. 29.50 (ISBN 0-08-023823-8). Pergamon.

Nuclear Cytology in Relation to Development. Francesco D'Amato. LC 76-46045. (Developmental & Cell Biology Ser.: No. 6). 1977. 54.00 (ISBN 0-521-21508-0). Cambridge U Pr.

Nuclear-Cytoplasmic Interactions in the Cell Cycle. Ed. by Gary Whitson. (Cell Biology Ser.). 1980. 39.00 (ISBN 0-12-747750-0). Acad Pr.

Nuclear Data for Reactors - 1966, 2 vols. 1967. Vol. 1. pap. 28.00 (ISBN 92-0-030167-3, IAEA); Vol. 2. pap. 21.50 (ISBN 92-0-030267-X). Unipub.

Nuclear Data for Reactors - 1970, 2 Vols. (Illus., Orig.). 1970. Vol. 1. pap. 51.00 (ISBN 92-0-030070-7, ISP 259-1, IAEA); Vol. 2. pap. 50.50 (ISBN 92-0-030170-3, ISP 259-2). Unipub.

Nuclear Data in Science & Technology, 2 vols. (Illus.). 1214p. (Orig.). 1974. pap. 43.50 ea. (IAEA); Vol. 1. pap. (ISBN 92-0-030073-1, ISP 343-1); Vol. 2. pap. (ISBN 92-0-030173-8, ISP 343-2). Unipub.

Nuclear Deterrence: A Short Political Analysis. Roy E. Jones. (Library of Political Studies). 1968. text ed. 6.25x (ISBN 0-7100-6537-X). Humanities.

Nuclear Electronic Instruments in Tropical Countries. (Technical Reports Ser.: No. 13). 1963. pap. 2.75 (ISBN 92-0-135063-5, IAEA). Unipub.

Nuclear Electronics - 1961, 3 vols. 1962. Vol. 1. 18.50 (ISBN 92-0-030162-2, IAEA); Vol. 2. 16.25 (ISBN 92-0-030262-9); Vol. 3. 18.50 (ISBN 92-0-030362-5). Unipub.

Nuclear Electronics - 1965. 1966. pap. 26.75 (ISBN 92-0-030266-1, IAEA). Unipub.

Nuclear Energy. Dan Halacy. LC 78-4659. (First Bks.). (Illus.). 1978. PLB 6.45 s&l (ISBN 0-531-01492-4). Watts.

Nuclear Energy. Raymond L. Murray. LC 74-8685. 296p. 1975. text ed. 24.00 o.p. (ISBN 0-08-018164-3); pap. text ed. 14.25 o.p. (ISBN 0-08-018163-5). Pergamon.

Nuclear Energy & Nuclear Proliferation: Japanese & American Views. Ryukichi Imai & Henry S. Rowen. LC 79-16589. (Special Studies in International Relations). 1979. lib. bdg. 18.50x (ISBN 0-89158-667-9). Westview.

Nuclear Energy & the Environment. Ed. by Essam E. El-Hinnawi. LC 80-40365. (Illus.). 310p. 1980. 52.00 (ISBN 0-08-024472-6). Pergamon.

Nuclear Energy Centres & Agro-Industrial Complexes. (Technical Reports Ser.: No. 140). (Illus.). 138p. (Orig.). 1973. pap. 9.75 (ISBN 92-0-145072-9, IAEA). Unipub.

Nuclear Energy Controversy. Goode. (gr. 7 up). 1980. PLB 6.90 (ISBN 0-531-04165-4, G05). Watts.

Nuclear Energy Costs & Economic Development. (Proceedings Ser.: No. 239). (Illus., Orig.). 1970. pap. 41.75 (ISBN 92-0-050070-6, IAEA). Unipub.

Nuclear Energy for Water Desalination. 1966. pap. 6.50 (ISBN 92-0-145066-4, IAEA). Unipub.

Nuclear Energy: Its Physics & Its Social Challenge. David R. Inglis. LC 78-186840. 1973. pap. text ed. 10.95 (ISBN 0-201-03199-X). A-W.

Nuclear Explosions & Earthquakes: The Parted Veil. Bruce A. Bolt. LC 75-28295. (Illus.). 1976. text ed. 18.95x (ISBN 0-7167-0276-2). W H Freeman.

Nuclear Forces. D. M. Brink. 1965. 19.50 (ISBN 0-08-011034-7); pap. 9.75 (ISBN 0-08-011033-9). Pergamon.

Nuclear Forces: Introduction to Theoretical Nuclear Physics. 2nd ed. Gernot Eder. 1974. pap. 6.95x (ISBN 0-262-55004-0). MIT Pr.

Nuclear Fuel & Energy Policy. S. Basheer Ahmed. LC 78-19673. 1979. 18.95 (ISBN 0-669-02714-6). Lexington Bks.

Nuclear Fuel Management. Harvey W. Graves. LC 78-19119. 1979. text ed. 28.95 (ISBN 0-471-03136-4). Wiley.

Nuclear Fuel Quality Assurance. (STI-PUB-435). (Illus.). 1977. pap. 39.75 (ISBN 92-0-050276-8, IAEA). Unipub.

Nuclear Fusion. H. R. Hulme & A. Collieu. (Wykeham Science Ser.: No. 4). 1969. 8.75x (ISBN 0-8448-1106-8). Crane-Russak Co.

Nuclear Heavy-Ion Reactions. P. E. Hodgson. (Oxford Studies in Nuclear Physics). (Illus.). 598p. 1978. text ed. 55.00x (ISBN 0-19-851514-6). Oxford U Pr.

Nuclear Impact: A Case Study of the Plowshare Program to Produce Natural Gas by Underground Nuclear Stimulation in the Rocky Mountains. Frank Kreith & Catherine B. Wrenn. LC 75-31708. (Special Studies on Technology, Natural Resources & the Environment). 250p. 1976. 26.75 o.p. (ISBN 0-89158-005-0). Westview.

Nuclear Isospin. Ed. by J. D. Anderson et al. 1969. 52.50 (ISBN 0-12-058150-7). Acad Pr.

Nuclear Law for a Developing World. (Legal Ser.: No. 5). pap. 21.00 (ISBN 92-0-176169-4, IAEA). Unipub.

Nuclear Lessons. Richard Curtis & Elizabeth Hogan. 288p. 1980. 16.95 (ISBN 0-8117-1851-4). Stackpole.

Nuclear Love. Eugene Wildman. LC 70-189193. 85p. 1972. 6.50 (ISBN 0-8040-0568-0); pap. 3.75 (ISBN 0-8040-0569-9). Swallow.

Nuclear Magnetic Resonance. Edwin R. Andrew. (Cambridge Monographs on Physics Ser). 1956. 49.95 (ISBN 0-521-04030-2). Cambridge U Pr.

Nuclear Magnetic Resonance. William W. Paudler. 1971. pap. text ed. 12.95 (ISBN 0-205-02888-8, 6828884). Allyn.

Nuclear Magnetic Resonance (Nmr) in Biochemistry: Applications to Enzyme Systems. Raymond A. Dwek. (Monographs on Physical Biochemistry Ser.). 387p. 1974. 42.00x (ISBN 0-19-854614-9). Oxford U Pr.

Nuclear Magnetic Resonance in Ferro & Antiferromagnetics. E. A. Turov & M. P. Petrov. 206p. 1972. 49.95 (ISBN 0-470-89323-0). Halsted Pr.

Nuclear Magnetic Resonance Shift Reagents. Robert E. Sievers. 1973. 23.00 (ISBN 0-12-643050-0). Acad Pr.

Nuclear Magnetic Resonance Spectroscopy of Nuclei Other Than Protons. Theodore Axenrod & Graham Webb. 424p. Repr. of 1974 ed. lib. bdg. write for info. (ISBN 0-89874-290-0). Krieger.

Nuclear Magnetic Resonance Spectroscopy. Frank A. Bovey. LC 68-23485. 1969. 20.95 o.p. (ISBN 0-12-119750-6). Acad Pr.

Nuclear Materials Management. 1966. 39.75 (ISBN 92-0-050066-8, IAEA). Unipub.

Nuclear Medicine. 2nd. ed. Ed. by Nathan A. Solomon. (Medical Examination Review Bk. Ser.: Vol. 25). 1977. spiral bdg. 16.50 (ISBN 0-87488-133-1). Med Exam.

Nuclear Medicine - Focus on Clinical Diagnosis. 2nd ed. Richard P. Spencer. 1980. pap. 18.00 (ISBN 0-87488-825-5). Med Exam.

Nuclear Medicine: A Comprehensive Bibliography. Compiled by Alberta D. Berton. (Biomedical Information Guides Ser.: Vol. 2). 355p. 1980. 85.00 (ISBN 0-306-65178-5, IFI). Plenum Pub.

Nuclear Medicine Annual, 1980. Ed. by Leonard Freeman. Heidi Weissmann. 440p. 1980. text ed. 42.50 (ISBN 0-89004-472-4). Raven.

Nuclear Medicine: Clinical & Technological Bases. John T. Andrews & Marvis J. Milne. LC 77-5040. 1977. 39.50 (ISBN 0-471-01594-6, Pub. by Wiley Medical). Wiley.

Nuclear Medicine: Endocrinology. Ed. by Benjamin Rothfeld. LC 78-3773. (Illus.). 1978. 43.50 (ISBN 0-397-50392-X). Lippincott.

Nuclear Medicine: Hepatolineal. Ed. by Benjamin Rothfeld. (Illus.). 288p. 1980. text ed. 45.00 (ISBN 0-397-50412-8). Lippincott.

Nuclear Medicine in Urology & Nephrology. P H O'Reilly & Shields. (Illus.). 1979. text ed. 44.95 (ISBN 0-407-00151-4). Butterworths.

Nuclear Medicine Review Syllabus. Ed. by Peter T. Kirchner. LC 79-92990. (Illus.). 619p. 1980. pap. text ed. 32.50 (ISBN 0-932004-04-0). Soc Nuclear Med.

Nuclear Medicine Science Syllabus. Ed. by Audrey V. Wegst. LC 78-68703. 1978. loose-leaf text 33.00 (ISBN 0-932004-01-6). Soc Nuclear Med.

Nuclear Medicine: Technology & Techniques. Donald R. Bernier et al. LC 80-17455. (Illus.). 450p. 1981. pap. text ed. 34.50 (ISBN 0-8016-0662-4). Mosby.

Nuclear Medicine Technology Continuing Education Review. E. V. Dubovsky et al. 1976. sprial bdg. 13.50 (ISBN 0-87488-331-8). Med Exam.

Nuclear Medicine Technology Examination Review. Stewart M. Spies et al. LC 79-17328. (Orig.). 1980. pap. text ed. 12.00 o.p. (ISBN 0-668-04724-0). Arco.

Nuclear Medicine Technology Examination Review Book. G. Donald Frey & Christopher J. Klobukowski. 1980. pap. 14.50 (ISBN 0-87488-457-8). Med Exam.

Nuclear Membrane & Nucleocytoplastic Interchange. C. M. Feldherr et al. (Protoplasmatologia: Vol. 5, Pt. 2). (Illus.). 1964. pap. 16.60 (ISBN 0-387-80690-3). Springer-Verlag.

Nuclear Merchant Ships. National Research Council, Maritime Transportation Research Board. (Illus.). xi, 125p. 1974. pap. 9.25 (ISBN 0-309-02318-1). Natl Acad Pr.

Nuclear Mysteries: Or Creation of the Parent Atoms. Sister Incarnata Marie. 1980. 9.95 (ISBN 0-533-03850-2). Vantage.

Nuclear Nightmares. Nigel Calder. 1981. pap. 3.95 (ISBN 0-14-005867-2). Penguin.

Nuclear Nightmares: An Investigation into Possible Wars. Nigel Calder. (Illus.). 188p. 1980. 10.95 (ISBN 0-670-51820-4). Viking Pr.

Nuclear Non-Proliferation Treaty, Vols. 1-3. Shaker. 1980. 40.00 ea. Oceana.

Nuclear Non-Proliferation Treaty: Origin & Implementation 1959 to 1979, 3 vols. Mohamed I. Shaker. LC 80-17359. 1980. lib. bdg. 40.00 ea. (ISBN 0-379-20470-3). Vol. 1 (ISBN 0-379-20470-3). Vol. 2 (ISBN 0-379-20471-1). Vol. 3 (ISBN 0-379-20472-X). Oceana.

Nuclear Nonproliferation: The Spent Fuel Problem. Ed. by Frederick C. Williams. David A. Deese. (Pergamon Policy Studies). 1980. 33.00 (ISBN 0-08-023887-4). Pergamon.

Nuclear or Not? Choices for Our Energy Future. Gerald Foley & E. Ariane Van Buren. 1978. text ed. 18.95x o.p. (ISBN 0-435-54770-4). Heinemann Ed.

Nuclear, Particle & Many Body Physics, 2 vols. Philip M. Morse et al. 1972. Vol. 1. 53.50 (ISBN 0-12-508201-0); Vol. 2. 50.50 (ISBN 0-12-508202-9); Set. 84.50 (ISBN 0-685-27233-8). Acad Pr.

Nuclear Particles in Cancer Treatment. John F. Fowler. (Medical Physics Handbook: No. 8). 216p. 1981. 28.00 (ISBN 0-9960020-7-3, Pub. by a Hilger England). Heyden.

Nuclear Physics. M. G. Bowler. 444p. 1973. text ed. 42.00 (ISBN 0-08-016983-X); pap. text ed. 24.00 (ISBN 0-08-018990-3). Pergamon.

Nuclear Physics. 2nd ed. Irving Kaplan. 1962. 24.95 (ISBN 0-201-03602-9). A-W.

Nuclear Physics & Interaction of Particles with Matter. Ed. by D. V. Skolbel'Tsyn. LC 70-120025. (P. N. Lebedev Physics Institute Ser.: Vol. 44). 269p. 1971. 37.50 (ISBN 0-306-10851-8, Consultants). Plenum Pub.

Nuclear Politics: America, France, & Britain. Wynfred Joshua & Walter F. Hahn. LC 73-83411. (Washington Papers: No. 9). 1973. 3.50x (ISBN 0-8039-0282-4). Sage.

Nuclear Power & Civil Liberties: Can We Have Both? 2nd ed. Ken Bossong & Scott Denman. 150p. 1981. 7.50 (ISBN 0-89988-071-1). Citizens Energy.

Nuclear Power & Its Critics: Moral Politics at M.I.T. Dorothy Nelkin. LC 70-147316. 6.50 (ISBN 0-8076-0722-3, Orig. Pub. by Cornell U. Press); pap. 1.75 o.s.i. (ISBN 0-8076-0723-1). Braziller.

Nuclear Power & Its Environmental Effects. Samuel Glasstone & Walter H. Jordan. LC 80-67303. (Illus.). 400p. 1980. 25.95 (ISBN 0-89448-022-7); pap. 17.95 (ISBN 0-89448-024-3). Am Nuclear Soc.

Nuclear Power & Its Fuel Cycle: Indexes & Lists, Vol. 8. 1978. pap. 25.75 (ISBN 92-0-050777-8, ISP 465-8, IAEA). Unipub.

Nuclear Power & Its Fuel Cycle: Nuclear Safety, Vol. 5. 1978. pap. 59.00 (ISBN 92-0-050477-9, ISP 465-5, IAEA). Unipub.

Nuclear Power & Its Fuel Cycle: Nuclear Power & Public Opinion & Safeguards, Vol. 7. (Illus.). 1978. pap. 68.50 (ISBN 92-0-050677-1, ISP 465-7, IAEA). Unipub.

Nuclear Power & Its Fuel Cycle: Nuclear Power in Developing Countries, Vol. 6. (Illus.). 1978. pap. 59.00 (ISBN 92-0-050577-5, IAEA). Unipub.

Nuclear Power & Its Fuel Cycle: Nuclear Power Prospects & Plans, Vol. 1. (Illus.). 1978. pap. 68.50 (ISBN 0-685-89402-9, ISP465-1, IAEA). Unipub.

Nuclear Power & Its Fuel Cycle: Radioactivity Management. (Vol. 4). (Illus.). 1978. pap. 79.75 (ISBN 92-0-050377-2, ISP 465-4, IAEA). Unipub.

Nuclear Power & Its Fuel Cycle: The Nuclear Fuel Cycle, Pt. 1, Vol. 2. 1978. pap. 79.75 (ISBN 92-0-050177-X, ISP465-2, IAEA). Unipub.

Nuclear Power & Its Fuel Cycle: The Nuclear Fuel Cycle, Pt. 2, Vol. 3. (Illus.). 1978. pap. 79.75 (ISBN 92-0-050277-6, ISP 465-3, IAEA). Unipub.

Nuclear Power & Its Regulation in the United States. Ed. by L. Manning Muntzing. (Illus.). 125p. 1980. pap. 30.00 (ISBN 0-08-027139-1). Pergamon.

Nuclear Power & Nuclear Weapons Proliferation, 2 vols. Atlantic Council Working Group on Nuclear Fuels Policy. Ed. by John E. Gray & Joseph W. Harned. (Atlantic Council Policy Papers). (Illus.). 1978. pap. text ed. 8.25x ea. Vol. 1 (ISBN 0-917258-13-4). Vol. 2. Westview.

Nuclear Power & Public Policy: The Social & Ethical Problems of Fission Technology. K. S. Shrader-Frechette. (Pallas Paperbacks Ser.: No. 15). 220p. 1980. lib. bdg. 19.95 (ISBN 90-277-1054-6); pap. 10.50 (ISBN 90-277-1080-5). Kluwer Boston.

Nuclear Power & Radioactive Waste. David A. Deese. LC 77-18496. (Illus.). 1978. 19.95 (ISBN 0-669-02114-8). Lexington Bks.

Nuclear Power & Safety. 1980. 50.00x (Pub. by Norwegian Info Norway). State Mutual Bk.

Nuclear Power & Social Planning: The City of the Second Sun. Gerald Garvey. LC 76-54556. 1977. 18.95 (ISBN 0-669-01303-X). Lexington Bks.

Nuclear Power Controversy. Ed. by Arthur W. Murphy. (Illus.). 1976. pap. 3.95 (ISBN 0-13-625574-4, Spec). P-H.

Nuclear Power Debate: Moral, Economic, Technical, & Political Issues. Desaix Myers. LC 75-25022. (Special Studies). 1977. text ed. 23.95 (ISBN 0-275-56440-1). Praeger.

Nuclear Power Decisions: British Policies, 1953-1978. Roger Williams. 365p. 1980. 49.00x (ISBN 0-7099-0265-4, Pub. by Croom Helm Ltd England). Biblio Dist.

Nuclear Power: From Physics to Politics. Laurence Pringle. LC 78-27180. (Science for Survival Ser.). 144p. (gr. 6 up). 1979. PLB 8.95 (ISBN 0-02-775390-5, 77539). Macmillan.

Nuclear Power Hazard Control Policy. J. C. Chicken. LC 80-40992. (Illus.). 300p. 1981. 35.00 (ISBN 0-08-023254-X); pap. 17.50 (ISBN 0-08-023255-8). Pergamon.

Nuclear Power Issue: A Guide to Who's Doing What in the U. S. & Abroad. Kimberly J. Mueller. LC 79-52430. (Who's Doing What Ser.: No. 8). (Illus., Orig.). 1981. pap. 12.00x (ISBN 0-912102-44-6). Cal Inst Public.

Nuclear Power, Man & the Environment. R. J. Pentreath. LC 80-20173. (Wykeham Science Ser.: No. 51). 250p. 1981. pap. price not set (ISBN 0-8448-1381-8). Crane-Russak Co.

Nuclear Power Planning for Hong Kong. (Illus.). 1977. pap. 16.75 (ISBN 92-0-159077-6, IAEA). Unipub.

Nuclear Power Planning Study for Indonesia. (Illus.). 1977. pap. 18.25 (ISBN 92-0-159276-0, IAEA). Unipub.

Nuclear Power Plant Control & Instrumentation - 1973. (Illus.). 886p. (Orig.). 1974. pap. 52.50 (ISBN 92-0-050173-7, IAEA). Unipub.

Nuclear Power Plant Control & Instrumentation. (Illus.). 3110p. (Orig.). 1971. pap. 20.00 (ISBN 92-0-051072-8, IAEA). Unipub.

Nuclear Power Plant Control & Instrumentation-1978, Vol. 1. 1979. pap. 44.00 (ISBN 92-0-050378-0, ISP491-1, IAEA). Unipub.

Nuclear Power Plant Control & Instrumentation-1978, Vol. 2. 1979. pap. 51.50 (ISBN 92-0-050478-7, ISP491-2, IAEA). Unipub.

Nuclear Power Plant Siting: A Handbook for the Layman. rev. ed. Ed. by Dennis L. Meredith. (Marine Bulletin Ser.: No. 6). 1972. pap. 1.00 (ISBN 0-938412-11-6). URI MAS.

Nuclear Power Plant Systems & Equipment. new ed. Kenneth C. Lish. 160p. 1972. 24.50 (ISBN 0-8311-1078-3). Indus Pr.

Nuclear Power: Technology on Trial. James Duderstadt & Chihiro Kikuchi. 1979. 16.00 (ISBN 0-472-09311-8); pap. 8.50 (ISBN 0-472-06312-X). U of Mich Pr.

Nuclear Proliferation: A Strategy for Control. Andrew J. Pierre & Claudia W. Moyne. LC 76-29317. (Headline Ser.: 232). (Illus., Orig.). 1976. pap. 2.00 (ISBN 0-87124-037-8). Foreign Policy.

Nuclear Proliferation & Safeguards. Congress of the U. S., Office of Technology Assessment. LC 77-60024. (Praeger Special Studies). 1977. 29.95 (ISBN 0-03-041601-9). Praeger.

Nuclear Properties of Heavy Elements, 3 vols. rev. ed. Earl K. Hyde et al. LC 70-153894. (Orig.). 1971. Repr. text ed. 15.00 ea. Vol. I (ISBN 0-486-62805-1). Vol. II (ISBN 0-486-62806-X). Vol. III (ISBN 0-486-62807-8). Dover.

Nuclear Quadrupole Resonance in Chemistry. G. K. Semin et al. Tr. by P. Shelnitz from Rus. 517p. 1975. 64.95 (ISBN 0-470-77580-7). Halsted Pr.

Nuclear Question. Ann E. Weiss. LC 80-8806. (Illus.). 192p. (gr. 7 up). 1981. 10.95 (ISBN 0-15-257596-0, HJ). HarBraceJ.

Nuclear Radiation Physics. 4th ed. Ralph Lapp & Howard Andrews. (Illus.). 1972. 21.95 (ISBN 0-13-625988-X). P-H.

Nuclear Radiation: What It Is, How to Detect It, How to Protect Yourself from It. Gregory H. Piesinger. (Illus.). 150p. (Orig.). 1980. pap. 9.95 (ISBN 0-937224-00-6). Dyco Inc.

Nuclear Reactions. I. E. McCarthy. 1970. text ed. 35.00 (ISBN 0-08-006630-5); pap. text ed. 10.75 (ISBN 0-08-006629-1). Pergamon.

Nuclear Reactions in Heavy Elements: A Data Handbook. V. M. Gorbachev & A. A. Zamyatnin. LC 79-40928. 460p. 1980. 115.00 (ISBN 0-08-023595-6). Pergamon.

Nuclear Reactor Analysis. James J. Duderstadt & Louis J. Hamilton. LC 75-20389. 650p. 1976. text ed. 34.95 (ISBN 0-471-22363-8). Wiley.

Nuclear Reactor Engineering. 2nd ed. Samuel Glasstone & Alexander Sesonske. 800p. 1980. text ed. 39.50 (ISBN 0-442-20057-9). Van Nos Reinhold.

Nuclear Reactor Kinetics & Control. J. Lewins. LC 77-8107. 1978. text ed. 45.00 (ISBN 0-08-021682-X); pap. text ed. 18.00 (ISBN 0-08-021681-1). Pergamon.

Nuclear Reactor Safety Heat Transfer: Proceedings of the International Centre for Heat & Mass Transfer. Ed. by Owen C. Jones. (International Centre for Heat & Mass Trans Transfer Ser.). (Illus.). 1981. text ed. 99.00 (ISBN 0-89116-224-0). Hemisphere Pub.

Nuclear Research with Low Energy Nuclear Accelerators. Ed. by Jerry B. Marion & Douglas M. Van Patter. 1967. 48.50 (ISBN 0-12-472259-8). Acad Pr.

Nuclear Revolution: International Politics Before & After Hiroshima. Michael Mandelbaum. LC 80-24194. 256p. Date not set. price not set (ISBN 0-521-23819-6); pap. price not set (ISBN 0-521-28239-X). Cambridge U Pr.

Nuclear Safeguards Technology Nineteen Seventy-Eight, Vol. 1. 1979. pap. 89.25 (ISBN 92-0-070079-9, ISP 497, IAEA). Unipub.

Nuclear Safety. M. M. Williams. (Illus.). 1979. pap. 18.50 (ISBN 0-08-024752-0). Pergamon.

Nuclear Science. P. J. Grant. (Illus.). 1971. pap. text ed. 11.95x (ISBN 0-245-50419-2). Intl Ideas.

Nuclear Science Teaching. (Technical Reports: No. 94). 1968. pap. 2.75 (ISBN 92-0-175368-3, IAEA). Unipub.

Nuclear Science Teaching III. (Technical Reports Ser. No. 162). (Illus.). 34p. 1975. pap. 4.50 (ISBN 92-0-175075-7, IAEA). Unipub.

Nuclear Science Teaching Two. (Technical Reports: No. 132). 51p. (Orig.). 1972. pap. 3.25 (ISBN 92-0-175171-0, IDC132, IAEA). Unipub.

Nuclear Ship Propulsion. Holmes F. Crouch. LC 59-13449. (Illus.). 1960. 20.00x (ISBN 0-87033-071-3). Cornell Maritime.

Nuclear Sizes & Structure. Roger C. Barrett & Daphne F. Jackson. (International Series of Monographs on Physics). 1977. 69.00x (ISBN 0-19-851272-4). Oxford U Pr.

Nuclear Spectroscopy & Reactions, 4 pts. Ed. by Joseph Cerney. Set. 199.50 (ISBN 0-685-48719-9); Pt. A 1974. 67.00 (ISBN 0-12-165201-7); Pt. B 1974. 68.00 o.s.i. (ISBN 0-12-165202-5); Pt. C 1974. 68.00 (ISBN 0-12-165203-3); Pt. D 1975. 43.50 (ISBN 0-12-165204-1). Acad Pr.

Nuclear Strategy in a Dynamic World: American Policy in the Nineteen Eighties. Donald M. Snow. LC 80-13634. 332p. 1981. 25.00 (ISBN 0-8173-0044-9); pap. 12.95 (ISBN 0-8173-0045-7). U of Ala Pr.

Nuclear Structure: Dubna Symposium, 1968. 1968. pap. 29.00 (ISBN 92-0-530068-3, IAEA). Unipub.

Nuclear Structure Theory. J. M. Irvine. 492p. 1972. text ed. 55.00 (ISBN 0-08-016401-3); pap. text ed. 27.00 (ISBN 0-08-018991-1). Pergamon.

Nuclear Structures of Protocaryotic Organisms. G. W. Fuhs. (Protoplasmatologia: Vol. 5, Pt. 4). (Illus.). 1969. 54.30 o.p. (ISBN 0-387-80917-1). Springer-Verlag.

Nuclear Techniques & Mineral Resources. 1969. pap. 29.00 (ISBN 92-0-040069-8, IAEA). Unipub.

Nuclear Techniques for Mineral Exploration & Exploitation. (Illus., Orig.). 1971. pap. 12.50 (ISBN 92-0-041071-5, IAEA). Unipub.

Nuclear Techniques for Seed Protein Improvement. (Illus.). 442p. (Orig.). 1973. pap. 33.75 (ISBN 92-0-111073-1, ISP320, IAEA). Unipub.

Nuclear Techniques for Studying Pesticide Residue Problems. (Illus., Orig.). 1970. pap. 6.50 (ISBN 92-0-111470-2, IAEA). Unipub.

Nuclear Techniques in Analytical Chemistry. A. J. Moses. LC 64-15736. (International Series on Analytical Chemistry: Vol. 20). 1965. 11.30 o.p. (ISBN 0-08-010695-1). Pergamon.

Nuclear Techniques in Animal Production & Health. (Proceedings Ser.). (Illus., Orig.). 1976. pap. 46.25 (ISBN 92-0-010276-X, IAEA). Unipub.

Nuclear Techniques in Environmental Pollution. (Illus., Orig.). 1971. pap. 57.25 (ISBN 92-0-060071-9, ISP268, IAEA). Unipub.

Nuclear Techniques in Geochemistry & Geophysics: Proceedings. (Illus.). 271p. 1976. pap. 27.50 (ISBN 92-0-041076-6, ISP425, IAEA). Unipub.

Nuclear Techniques in Groundwater Pollution Research. 285p. 1981. pap. 36.25 (ISBN 92-0-141080-8, ISP 518, IAEA). Unipub.

Nuclear Techniques in Helminthology Research. (Illus.). 187p. 1975. pap. 14.50 (ISBN 92-0-111075-8, IAEA). Unipub.

Nuclear Techniques in the Basic Metal Industries. LC 73-164980. (Proceedings Ser.). (Illus.). 634p. (Orig.). 1973. pap. 39.75 (ISBN 92-0-060073-5, IAEA). Unipub.

Nuclear Technology & Mineral Resources 1977. (Proceedings Ser). (Illus.). 1978. pap. 66.50 (ISBN 92-0-060077-8, ISP464, IAEA). Unipub.

Nuclear Theme As a Determinant of Patet in Javanese Music. Mantle Hood. LC 77-5680. (Music Reprint Ser.). 1977. Repr. of 1954 ed. lib. bdg. 32.50 (ISBN 0-306-77419-4). Da Capo.

Nuclear Tracks in Solids. Robert L. Fleischer et al. 1975. 42.50x (ISBN 0-520-02665-9); pap. 15.95x (ISBN 0-520-04096-1). U of Cal Pr.

Nuclear War: Can You Survive? John Boynton. (Illus.). 64p. pap. 4.95. Astroart Ent.

Nuclear War Films. Ed. by Jack G. Shaheen. LC 78-17984. 213p. 1978. 12.95x (ISBN 0-8093-0843-6); pap. 6.95 (ISBN 0-8093-0879-7). S Ill U Pr.

Nuclear Waste Management: The Ocean Alternative- Edited Proceedings of a Public Policy Forum Sponsored by the Oceanic Society in the Georgetown University Law Center, DC, February 6, 1980. Ed. by Thomas Jackson. (Pergamon Policy Studies on Energy). (Illus.). 100p. 15.00 (ISBN 0-08-027204-5). Pergamon.

Nuclear Well Logging in Hydrology. (Technical Reports: No. 126). (Illus., Orig.). 1971. pap. 7.50 (ISBN 92-0-145071-0, IDC126, IAEA). Unipub.

Nuclear Witnesses: Insiders Speak Out. Leslie J. Freeman. (Illus.). 1981. 14.95 (ISBN 0-393-01456-8). Norton.

Nuclei & Radioactivity: Elements of Nuclear Chemistry. Gregory R. Choppin. (Orig.). (YA) (gr. 9-12). 1964. pap. 9.95 o.p. (ISBN 0-8053-2151-9). Benjamin-Cummings.

Nucleic Acid Geometry & Dynamics. Ramaswamy H. Sarma. LC 80-10620. (Illus.). 424p. 1980. 55.00 (ISBN 0-08-024631-1); pap. 24.50 (ISBN 0-08-024630-3). Pergamon.

Nucleic Acid Metabolism, Cell Differentiation & Cancer Growth. E. V. Cowdry & S. Seno. 1968. 75.00 (ISBN 0-08-013252-9). Pergamon.

Nucleic Acid Sequence Analysis. Stanley Mandeles. LC 79-186389. (Molecular Biology Ser). 352p. 1972. 20.00x (ISBN 0-231-03130-0). Columbia U Pr.

Nucleic Acid Synthesis: Applications to Molecular Biology & Genetic Engineering. International Symposium in Chemical Synthesis of Nucleic Acids, Egestorf, West Germany, May 1980. (Nucleic Acids Symposium Ser.: No. 7). 396p. 1980. 40.00 (ISBN 0-904147-26-6). Info Retrieval.

Nucleic Acids & Nucleoproteins: Proceedings, Vol. 12. Cold Spring Harbor Symposia On Quantitative Biology. Repr. of 1947 ed. 19.50 (ISBN 0-384-42250-0). Johnson Repr.

Nucleic Acids in Immunology: Proceedings. Symposium of the Institute of Microbiology, Rutgers University, 1967. Ed. by O. J. Plescia & W. Braun. (Illus.). 1968. 62.10 o.p. (ISBN 0-387-04290-3). Springer-Verlag.

Nucleic Acids in Plants, 2 vols. Timothy C. Hall & Jeffrey W. Davies. 1979. Vol. 1, 272p. 64.95 (ISBN 0-8493-5291-6); Vol. 2, 256p. 59.95 (ISBN 0-8493-5292-4). CRC Pr.

Nucleon Simplified. Albert O. Roberts. 1980. 4.95 (ISBN 0-533-04319-0). Vantage.

Nucleotide Analogs: Synthesis & Biological Function. Karl H. Scheit. LC 79-25445. 1980. 29.50 (ISBN 0-471-04854-2, Pub. by Wiley-Interscience). Wiley.

Nucleotide Metabolism. J. Frank Henderson & A. R. Paterson. 1973. 33.50 (ISBN 0-12-340550-5). Acad Pr.

Nucleus. M. Bates et al. write for info. (ISBN 0-686-19151-X). Longman.

Nucleus & Cytoplasm. 3rd ed. Henry Harris. (Illus.). 1974. text ed. 16.00x (ISBN 0-19-854124-4); pap. text ed. 7.95x o.p. (ISBN 0-19-854125-2). Oxford U Pr.

Nude: A Study in Ideal Form. Kenneth M. Clark. (Bollingen Series, No. 35: A. W. Mellon Lectures in the Fine Arts, Vol. 2). (Illus.). 458p. 1972. 50.00 (ISBN 0-691-09792-5); pap. 14.95 (ISBN 0-691-01788-3). Princeton U Pr.

Nude Look. (Illus.). softcover 4.95 (ISBN 0-910550-07-7). Elysium.

Nude Male: A New Perspective. Margaret Walters. (Illus.). 1979. pap. 8.95 o.p. (ISBN 0-14-005188-0). Penguin.

Nude Photography Annual. (Illus.). 6.95 (ISBN 0-910550-08-5). Elysium.

Nude Photography: The French Way. Laurent Biancani. Orig. Title: Nu. (Illus.). 1980. 25.00 (ISBN 0-8174-5095-5); pap. 9.95 (ISBN 0-8174-5096-3). Amphoto.

Nudibranchs. T. E. Thompson. (Illus., Orig.). 1976. pap. 5.95 (ISBN 0-87666-459-1, PS-696). TFH Pubns.

Nudism, Obscenity & the Law. Eduard Frankhauser. Tr. by Alozis Knapp. (Illus.). 1.95 (ISBN 0-910550-09-3). Elysium.

Nudist Nudes. Ed Lange. 4.95 (ISBN 0-910550-12-3). Elysium.

Nueces County, Texas. Nueces County Historical Society. (Illus.). 9.50 o.p. (ISBN 0-8363-0122-6). Jenkins.

Nuer: A Description of the Modes of Livelihood & Political Institutions of a Nilotic People. Edward E. Evans-Pritchard. (Illus.). 1968. 24.00x (ISBN 0-19-823105-9); pap. 4.95x (ISBN 0-19-500322-5). Oxford U Pr.

Nuestra Aventura Literaria: Los Ismos En la Poesia Puertorriquena, 1913-1940. 2nd, rev. ed. Luis Hernandez Aquino. pap. 3.10 o.p. (ISBN 0-8477-3134-0). U of PR Pr.

Nuestra Natacha. Alejandro Casona. Ed. by William H. Shoemaker. (Span.). (gr. 11 up). 1979. pap. text ed. 7.95x (ISBN 0-89197-541-1). Irvington.

Nueva Ficcion Hispanoamericana A Traves De Miguel Angel Asturias Y Gabriel Garcia Marquez. L. Gonzalez Del Valle & Vicente Cabrera. 1972. 9.95 (ISBN 0-88303-008-X); pap. 6.95 (ISBN 0-685-73212-6). E Torres & Sons.

Nueva Vida. J. C. Ryle. 1.50 o.p. (ISBN 0-686-12557-6). Banner of Truth.

Nueva vista. Ruth R. Ginsburg et al. (gr. 7-12). 1978. text ed. 14.80 (ISBN 0-205-05878-7, 4258789); 4.40 (ISBN 0-205-05880-9, 4258800); 4.96 (ISBN 0-205-03662-7, 4236629). Allyn.

Nuevas Fuerzas. Werner Marx. LC 77-243. 166p. (Orig., Span.). 1976. pap. 3.25 (ISBN 0-89922-068-1). Edit Caribe.

Nuevo Auxiliar Biblica. G. T. Manley. Tr. by Jose Flores from Eng. 572p. (Span.). 1958. pap. 8.50 (ISBN 0-89922-001-0). Edit Caribe.

Nuevo Auxiliar Biblico. Manley & Robinson. Tr. by Jose Flores. 1977. pap. 8.25 (ISBN 0-311-03636-8). Casa Bautista.

Nuevo Comentario Bible. Motyer Guthrie et al. Orig. Title: New Bible Commentary Revised. 136p. 1980. pap. 29.95 (ISBN 0-311-03001-7). Casa Bautista.

Nuevo Larousse manual illustrado. Larousse And Co. (Span.). 17.95 o.p. (ISBN 2-03-020546-X, 21121). Larousse.

Nuevo Lexico Griego Espanol. McKibben-Stockwell. 1978. pap. 7.95 (ISBN 0-311-42058-3, Edit Mundo). Casa Bautista.

Nuevo Testamento De Nuestro Senor Jesucristo. Tr. by Pablo Besson from Greek. 576p. (Span.). 1980. pap. write for info. (ISBN 0-311-48710-6, Edit Mundo). Casa Bautista.

Nuevos Sofistas: La Subversion Cultural de Nietzche a Beckett. Ludwig Schajowicz. LC 78-9541. 1979. 12.00 (ISBN 0-8477-2823-4); pap. 10.00 (ISBN 0-8477-2817-X). U of PR Pr.

Nugae Canorae: Poems. 1819. Charles Lloyd. Ed. by Donald H. Reiman. LC 75-31226. (Romantic Context Ser.: Poetry 1789-1830). 1978. lib. bdg. 47.00 (ISBN 0-8240-2176-2). Garland Pub.

Nuggets of Knowledge. George W. Stimpson. LC 75-109182. 1970. Repr. of 1928 ed. 22.00 (ISBN 0-8103-3860-2). Gale.

Nuggets of Truth. Charles Hunter & Frances Hunter. 1975. pap. 1.95 (ISBN 0-917726-01-4). Hunter Bks.

Nukey Poo. Elizabeth Vienna. (Illus.). 1980. pap. 4.95 o.p. (ISBN 0-930490-30-4). Future Shop.

Number & Pattern in the Eighteen-Century Novel: Defoe, Fielding, Smollett & Sterne. Douglas Brooks. 208p. 1973. 16.50 (ISBN 0-7100-7598-7). Routledge & Kegan.

Number Families. Jane J. Srivastava. LC 78-19511. (Illus.). (gr. 2-5). 1979. PLB 7.89 (ISBN 0-690-03924-7, TYC-J). T Y Crowell.

Number Ideas Through Pictures. Mannis Charosh. LC 73-4370. (Young Math Ser.). (Illus.). 40p. (gr. 1-5). 1974. PLB 7.89 (ISBN 0-690-00156-8, TYC-J). T Y Crowell.

Number of the Beast. Robert A. Heinlein. 1980. 6.95 (ISBN 0-449-90019-3, Columbine). Fawcett.

Number One. Billy Martin. 1981. pap. 3.25 (ISBN 0-440-16229-7). Dell.

Number One. Billy Martin & Peter Golenbock. 1980. 11.95 (ISBN 0-440-06416-3). Delacorte.

Number One Nazi Jew Baiter. William Varga. 1981. 9.95 (ISBN 0-8062-1623-9). Carlton.

Number Power. Keith Ellis. 1980. pap. 4.95 (ISBN 0-312-57989-6). St Martin.

Number Stories of Long Ago. David E. Smith. LC 70-167181. (Illus.). 150p. (gr. 1 up). 1973. Repr. of 1951 ed. 18.00 (ISBN 0-8103-3273-6). Gale.

Number Symbolism. Christopher Butler. (Ideas & Forms in English Literature Ser.). 1970. 15.00x (ISBN 0-7100-6766-6). Routledge & Kegan.

Number Systems & the Foundations of Analysis. Elliot Mendelson. 1973. text ed. 19.95 (ISBN 0-12-490850-0). Acad Pr.

Number: The Language of Science. 4th ed. Tobias Dantzig. (Illus.). 1967. pap. text ed. 8.95 (ISBN 0-02-906990-4). Free Pr.

Number Theory. Z. I. Borevich & I. R. Shafarevich. (Pure and Applied Mathematics: Vol. 20). 1966. text ed. 22.50 (ISBN 0-12-117850-1). Acad Pr.

Number Theory. T. H. Jackson. (Library of Mathematics). 1975. pap. 5.00 (ISBN 0-7100-7998-2). Routledge & Kegan.

Number Theory in Digital Signal Processing. Joseph H. McClellen & Charles M. Rader. (Signal Processing Ser.). (Illus.). 1979. ref. 23.95 (ISBN 0-13-627349-1). P-H.

Number Theory: The Theory of Partitions. George E. Andrews. LC 76-41770. (Encyclopedia of Mathematics & Its Applications: Vol. 2). (Illus.). 1976. text ed. 21.50 (ISBN 0-201-13501-9). A-W.

Number to Call Is.... Raymond Thompson & Treve Daly. 288p. 1981. pap. 2.50 (ISBN 0-380-53769-9, 53769). Avon.

Number Tracking: Math 1: A Self-Instruction Workbook for Visual Accuracy, Resuable Edition. Kitty Wehrli. (gr. 1). 1971. wkbk. 5.00 (ISBN 0-89039-031-2). Ann Arbor Pubs.

Number Two: A Look at the Vice Presidency. Robert I. Alotta. (Illus.). 256p. (gr. 8 up). 1981. PLB price not set. Messner.

Numbers. G. Buchanan Gray. LC 3-31887. (International Critical Commentary Ser.). 544p. 1930. text ed. 23.00x (ISBN 0-567-05002-5). Attic Pr.

Numbers. Jan Pienkowski. LC 74-83405. (Concept Bks). (Illus.). 32p. (ps-2). 1975. PLB 5.29 (ISBN 0-8178-5242-5). Harvey.

Numbers. John J. Reiss. LC 76-151313. (Illus.). (ps-1). 1971. 8.95 (ISBN 0-87888-029-1). Bradbury Pr.

Numbers. Gillian Youldon. (Picture Play Ser.). (Illus.). (ps-2). 1979. 3.50 (ISBN 0-531-02388-5); PLB 5.90 s&l (ISBN 0-531-00440-6). Watts.

Numbers & Ideals. Abraham Robinson. LC 65-16747. (Illus.). 1965. 10.95x (ISBN 0-8162-7234-4). Holden-Day.

Numbers & Numerals. Kitty Wehrli. (Michigan Arithmetic Program). (ps-2). 1976. 1.00 (ISBN 0-89039-199-8); wkbk. 5.00 (ISBN 0-89039-102-5). Ann Arbor Pubs.

Numbers & Units for Science. Frank E. Harris. (gr. 10-12). 1972. pap. text ed. 6.00 (ISBN 0-8449-0301-9); tchr's manual & test avail. Learning Line.

Numbers & You: A Numerology Guide for Everyday Living. Lloyd Strayhorn. 154p. 1980. 9.95 (ISBN 0-937290-02-5). Yama Pub.

Numbers Book: Student Syllabus, 2 vols. Sue C. Cook. (gr. k-2). 1974. Vol. 1. pap. text ed. 11.85 ea. packs of 10 (ISBN 0-89420-081-X, 193050). Vol. 2 (ISBN 0-89420-082-8, 193051). cassette recordings 17.36 (ISBN 0-89420-208-1, 193000). Natl Book.

Numbers, Deuteronomy. Irving L. Jensen. (Bible Self Study Ser.). 1970. pap. 2.25 (ISBN 0-8024-1004-9). Moody.

Numbers: Fun & Facts. J. Newton Friend. 1972. 5.95 (ISBN 0-684-10186-6, ScribT); pap. 2.45 o.p. (ISBN 0-684-13082-3, SL399, ScribT). Scribner.

Numbers Game: Statistics in Psychology. Joan G. Snodgrass. 1977. 14.95x (ISBN 0-19-502301-3). Oxford U Pr.

Numbers in Motion: A Balanced Approach to Measurement & Evaluation in Physical Education. Dale P. Mood. LC 79-91835. (Illus.). 396p. 1980. text ed. 15.95 (ISBN 0-87484-503-3). Mayfield Pub.

Numbers Mean More Than You Think. Elsie M. Knapp & Denise Faithful. 51p. (gr. 6 up). 1974. pap. 1.50 (ISBN 0-686-05514-4). Sandollar Pr.

Numbers of Life. Kevin Quinn Avery. LC 76-45969. 354p. 1977. pap. 4.50 (ISBN 0-385-12629-8, Dolp). Doubleday.

Numbers of Things. Helen Oxenbury. LC 68-10048. (Illus.). (gr. k-3). 1968. PLB 4.90 o.p. (ISBN 0-531-01751-6). Watts.

Numbers Old & New. Irving Adler & Ruth Adler. LC 60-11126. (Reason Why Ser). (Illus.). (gr. 3-6). 1960. PLB 6.89 o.p. (ISBN 0-381-99961-0, A56400, JD-J). John Day.

Numbers, Please. 2nd enlarged ed. F. Emerson Andrews. LC 77-20492. 1977. pap. 5.25x (ISBN 0-8077-2545-5). Tchrs Coll.

Numbers Workbook Four (with the Scarecrow from Oz) Vana Earle. (Funny Face Activity Bks.). (Illus.). 48p. (ps-1). 1981. pap. 1.95 saddle-stitched (ISBN 0-394-84670-2). Random.

Numbers Workbook Three (with Daring Dog) May Svendson. (Funny Face Activity Bks.). (Illus.). 48p. (ps-1). 1981. pap. 1.95 saddle-stitched (ISBN 0-394-84458-0). Random.

Numeracy & Accounting. Terry S. McNamara. (Illus.). 370p. 1979. pap. text ed. 16.95x (ISBN 0-7121-1411-4, Pub. by Macdonald & Evans England). Intl Ideas.

Numerical Algorithms: Origins & Applications. Bruce W. Arden & Kenneth N. Astill. LC 76-100853. 1970. 17.95 (ISBN 0-201-00336-8). A-W.

Numerical Analysis. Ed. by Gene Golub & James Oliger. LC 78-11096. (Proceedings of Symposia in Applied Mathematics: Vol. 22). 1978. 14.00 o.p. (ISBN 0-8218-0122-8); softcover 10.00 o.p. (ISBN 0-685-99044-3). Am Math.

Numerical Analysis. Lee W. Johnson & R. Dean Riess. LC 76-14658. (Illus.). 1977. text ed. 18.95 (ISBN 0-201-03442-5). A-W.

Numerical Analysis. I. M. Khabaza. 1965. text ed. 25.00 (ISBN 0-08-010776-1); pap. text ed. 12.75 (ISBN 0-08-010775-3). Pergamon.

Numerical Analysis. Proceedings of the Colloquium on Numerical Analysis, Lausanne, Oct. 11-13, 1976. Ed. by J. Descloux & J. T. Marti. (International Series of Numerical Mathematics: No. 37). 248p. 1977. pap. 30.00 (ISBN 3-7643-0939-3). Birkhauser.

Numerical Analysis & Computing. Ward Cheney & David Kincaid. LC 79-17230. 1980. text ed. 18.95 (ISBN 0-8185-0357-2). Brooks-Cole.

Numerical Analysis: Proceedings of a Symposia in Applied Mathematics, Vol. 22. Ed. by Gene Golub & Joseph Oliger. write for info. o.p. (ISBN 0-8218-0122-8); pap. write for info. o.p. Am Math.

Numerical Analysis: Second Course. James M. Ortega. (Computer Science & Applied Mathematics Ser.). 201p. 1972. 19.95 o.p. (ISBN 0-12-528560-4). Acad Pr.

Numerical & Matrix Methods in Structural Mechanics, with Applications to Computers. Ping'Chun Wang. LC 66-11529. 1966. 35.95 (ISBN 0-471-91950-0, Pub. by Wiley-Interscience). Wiley.

Numerical Approximation. B. R. Morton. (Library of Mathematics). 1969. pap. 5.00 (ISBN 0-7100-4354-6). Routledge & Kegan.

Numerical Approximations to Functions & Data. Ed. by J. G. Hayes. 1970. text ed. 21.25x (ISBN 0-485-11109-8, Athlone Pr). Humanities.

Numerical Aspects of Inorganic Chemistry. R. B. Heslop. (Illus.). 1970. text ed. 18.60x (ISBN 0-444-20060-6). Intl Ideas.

Numerical Bible, 7 vols. Ed. by F. W. Grant. Incl. Vol. 1. Genesis to Deuteronomy (ISBN 0-87213-262-5); Vol. 2. Joshua to Second Samuel (ISBN 0-87213-263-3); Vol. 3. Psalms (ISBN 0-87213-264-1); Vol. 4. Ezekiel (ISBN 0-87213-265-X); Vol. 5. Matthew to John (ISBN 0-87213-266-8); Vol. 6. Acts to Philemon (ISBN 0-87213-267-6); Vol. 7. Hebrews to Revelation (ISBN 0-87213-268-4). 1890-1932. Set. 52.95 (ISBN 0-87213-261-7); 7.95 ea. Loizeaux.

Numerical Control & Computer-Aided Manufacturing. R. S. Pressman & J. E. Williams. 310p. 1977. 24.95 (ISBN 0-471-01555-5). Wiley.

Numerical Control & Computer-Aided Manufacturing. R. S. Pressman & J. E. Williams. 310p. 1977. text ed. 24.95 (ISBN 0-471-01555-5). Wiley.

Numerical Control Applications. Ed. by Jack Moorhead. LC 80-52613. (Manufacturing Update Ser.). (Illus.). 260p. 1980. 29.00 (ISBN 0-87263-058-7). SME.

Numerical Control Fundamentals. Ed. by Jack Moorhead. LC 80-52723. (Manufacturing Update Ser.). (Illus.). 242p. 1980. 29.00 (ISBN 0-87263-057-9). SME.

Numerical Control of Machine Tools. 2nd rev. ed. Wilhelm Simon. LC 72-89494. 1972. 55.00x (ISBN 0-8448-0117-8). Crane-Russak Co.

Numerical Control Part Programming. James J. Childs. (Illus.). 340p. 1973. 21.00 (ISBN 0-8311-1099-6); answer bks. avail. (ISBN 0-685-30302-0). Indus Pr.

Numerical Heat Transfer & Fluid Flow. Suhas V. Patankar. LC 79-28286. (Hemisphere Series on Computational Methods in Mechanics & Thermal Sciences). (Illus.). 208p. 1980. text ed. 22.50 (ISBN 0-07-048740-5). McGraw.

Numerical Mathematics-Numerische Mathematik. Rainer Ansorge et al. (International Series of Numerical Mathematics: No. 49). 210p. (Eng. Ger.). 1979. 28.00 (ISBN 3-7643-1099-5). Birkhauser.

Numerical Methods for Engineering Applications. J. H. Ferziger. 400p. 1981. 36.00 (ISBN 0-471-06336-3, Pub. by Wiley-Interscience). Wiley.

Numerical Methods for Stiff Equations & Singular Perturbation Problems. Willard L. Miranker. (Mathematics & Its Applications Ser.: No. 5). 216p. 1980. lib. bdg. 29.95 (ISBN 90-277-1107-0, Pub. by D. Reidel). Kluwer Boston.

Numerical Methods in Finite Element Analysis. Klaus-Jurgen Bathe & Edward L. Wilson. (Illus.). 544p. 1976. 33.95 (ISBN 0-13-627190-1). P-H.

Numerical Methods in Fluid Dynamics. H. J. Wirz & J. J. Smolderen. (McGraw-Hill - Hemisphere Series in Thermal & Fluids Engineering). (Illus.). 1978. text ed. 37.50 (ISBN 0-07-071120-8, C). McGraw.

Numerical Methods in Geomechanics. Compiled by American Society of Civil Engineers & C. S. Desai. 1568p. 1976. pap. text ed. 52.00 (ISBN 0-87262-168-5). Am Soc Civil Eng.

Numerical Methods in Heat Transfer. R. W. Lewis & K. Morgan. Ed. by O. C. Zienkiewicz. (Numerical Methods in Engineering Ser.). 1981. price not set (ISBN 0-471-27803-3, Pub. by Wiley-Interscience). Wiley.

Numerical Methods in Laminar & Turbulent Flow. Ed. by C. Taylor & K. Morgan. LC 78-16077. 1978. 68.95x (ISBN 0-470-26462-4). Halsted Pr.

Numerical Methods in Offshore Piling. Institute of Civil Engineers. 224p. 1980. 69.00x (ISBN 0-7277-0086-3, Pub. by Telford England). State Mutual Bk.

Numerical Modeling of Detonations. Charles S. Mader. (Los Alamos Ser. in Basic & Applied Sciences). 1979. 45.00x (ISBN 0-520-03655-7). U of Cal Pr.

Numerical Models of Ocean Circulation. Ocean Affairs Board. LC 74-28404. vii, 364p. 1975. 25.50 o.p. (ISBN 0-309-02225-8). Natl Acad Pr.

Numerical Ranges, No. 2. F. F. Bonsall & J. Duncan. (London Mathematical Society Lecture Note Ser.: No. 10). (Illus.). 192p. 1973. pap. text ed. 20.50x (ISBN 0-521-20227-2). Cambridge U Pr.

Numerical Ranges of Operators on Normed Spaces & of Elements of Normed Algebras. F. F. Bonsall & J. Duncan. LC 71-128498. (London Mathematical Society Lecture Note Ser.: No. 2). 1971. 16.95x (ISBN 0-521-07988-8). Cambridge U Pr.

Numerical Reactor Calculations. (Illus.). 821p. (Orig.). 1972. pap. 49.25 (ISBN 92-0-030072-3, IAEA). Unipub.

Numerical Solution of Differential Equations. Isaac Fried. (Computer Science & Applied Math. Ser.). 1979. 26.50 (ISBN 0-12-267780-3). Acad Pr.

Numerical Solution of Differential Equations. M. K. Jain. LC 78-26549. 1979. 21.95 (ISBN 0-470-26609-0). Halsted Pr.

Numerical Solution of Differential Equations. William E. Milne. 1970. pap. text ed. 5.00 (ISBN 0-486-62437-4). Dover.

Numerical Solution of Integral Equations. Ed. by L. M. Delves & J. Walsh. (Illus.). 352p. 1974. 28.00 (ISBN 0-19-853342-X). Oxford U Pr.

Numerical Solution of Partial Differential Equations. 2nd ed. Gordon D. Smith. (Oxford Mathematical Handbooks Ser.). (Illus.). 1978. text ed. 29.95x (ISBN 0-19-859625-1); pap. text ed. 14.95x (ISBN 0-19-859626-X). Oxford U Pr.

Numerical Taxonomic Study of the Genus Salix, Section Sitchenses. Theodore J. Crovello. (U. C. Publ. Botany: Vol. 44). 1968. pap. 5.00x (ISBN 0-520-09017-9). U of Cal Pr.

Numerical Taxonomy of Streptomycetes. Ed. by W. Kurylowicz et al. (Illus.). 1975. 6.00 (ISBN 0-685-88610-7). Am Soc Microbio.

Numerical Taxonomy: The Principles & Practice of Numerical Classification. Peter H. Sneath & Robert R. Sokal. LC 72-1552. (Biology Ser.). (Illus.). 1973. 36.95x (ISBN 0-7167-0697-0). W H Freeman.

Numerical Techniques in Social Anthropology. Ed. by J. Clyde Mitchell. LC 80-11082. (ASA Essays in Social Anthropology Ser.: Vol. 3). (Illus.). 1981. text ed. 22.00x (ISBN 0-915980-93-2); pap. text ed. 9.95x (ISBN 0-89727-013-4). Inst Study Human.

Numerical Trigonometry: Syllabus. Carlton W. Bryson & Allan W. Gray. 1973. pap. text ed. 7.35 (ISBN 0-89420-050-X, 355110); cassette recordings 70.50 (ISBN 0-89420-164-6, 355000). Natl Book.

Numerische Methoden bei Graphentheoretischen und Kombinatorishen Problemen: Vol. II. Ed. by L. Collatz et al. (International Series of Numerical Mathematics: No. 46). (Illus.). 255p. (Ger. & Eng.). 1979. pap. 32.50 (ISBN 3-7643-1078-2). Birkhauser.

Numero Magico, 4 bks. rev. ed. Richard M. Sharp & Seymour Mitzner. Ed. by Editorial Turabo, Inc. Incl. Libro Primero. 48p. (gr. 1-3) (ISBN 0-675-01038-1); Libro 2. 48p. (gr. 2-4) (ISBN 0-675-01039-X); Libra 3. 48p. (gr. 3-5) (ISBN 0-675-01040-3); Libra 4. 48p. (gr. 4-6) (ISBN 0-675-01041-1). (Span.). 1979. pap. 1.50 ea. Merrill.

Numero Uno. Bud Greenspan. Date not set. pap. 1.75 o.p. (ISBN 0-451-08686-4, E8686, Sig). NAL. Postponed.

Numerology. Daniel F. Brooks. (Concise Guides Ser.). (Illus.). (gr. 7 up). 1978. PLB 6.45 s&l (ISBN 0-531-02248-X). Watts.

Numerology. Austin Coates. 1980. pap. 3.95 (ISBN 0-8065-0499-4). Lyle Stuart.

Numerology Its Facts & Secrets. Ariel Taylor-Hyler. 1958. 6.95 (ISBN 0-910140-17-0). Anthony.

Numerology Made Plain. Ariel Y. Taylor. LC 80-19322. 147p. 1980. Repr. of 1973 ed. lib. bdg. 9.95x (ISBN 0-89370-612-4). Borgo Pr.

Numerology Map - Interstate System. 1978. 1.00. AASHTO.

Numerology: The Complete Guide. Mathew O. Goodwin. 1981. Repr. Set. lib. bdg. 33.00 (ISBN 0-89370-999-9); Vol. 1. lib. bdg. 16.95 ea. (ISBN 0-89370-653-1). Vol. 2 (ISBN 0-89370-654-X). Borgo Pr.

Numerology: The Complete Guide. Matthew O. Goodwin. (Orig.). 1981. Set. pap. 17.50 (ISBN 0-87877-999-X); Vol. 1. pap. 8.95 (ISBN 0-87877-053-4); Vol. 2. pap. 8.95 (ISBN 0-87877-054-2). Newcastle Pub.

Numerous Cases of Surgical Operations Without Pain in the Mesmeric State. John Elliotson. Bd. with Mesmerism in India; Philosophy of Sleep. (Contributions to the History of Psychology Ser., Vol. X, Pt. A: Orientations). 1978. Repr. of 1843 ed. 30.00 (ISBN 0-89093-159-3). U Pubns Amer.

Numismatic Index: (1888-1978, Vol. 1-99. LC 80-69614. 204p. 1980. pap. 4.95 (ISBN 0-89637-001-1). Am Numismatic.

Numismatic Literature, No. 103. Ed. by Marion T. Brady. lix, 193p. 1980. pap. 4.00x o.p. (ISBN 0-89722-185-0). Am Numismatic.

Numismatics of Massachusetts. Malcolm Storer. LC 80-52820. 317p. 1981. Repr. of 1923 ed. 35.00x (ISBN 0-88000-117-8). Quarterman.

Numismatique Grecque Falsifications Moyens Pour les Reconnaitre. O. E. Ravel. 105p. (Fr.). 1980. Repr. of 1946 ed. 20.00 (ISBN 0-916710-71-8). Obol Intl.

Numismatisc Literature, Nos. 1-99. Nos. 1-77. 1.00 ea.; Nos. 78-94. 2.00 ea.; No. 95-101. 4.00 (ISBN 0-685-88664-6); Biennial Indexes 1947-65. 2.00 ea. No. 1 (ISBN 0-89722-073-0). No. 99 (ISBN 0-89722-171-0). No. 100 (ISBN 0-89722-177-X). No. 101 (ISBN 0-89722-178-8). No. 102 (ISBN 0-89722-182-6). Am Numismatic.

Nun. Denis Diderot. Tr. by Leonard Tancock. (Classics Ser). 1977. pap. 2.75 (ISBN 0-14-044300-2). Penguin.

Nun in the Concentration Camp. C. M. Target. 1977. pap. 1.55 (ISBN 0-08-017611-9). Pergamon.

Nunchaku & Sai: Ancient Okinawan Martial Arts. Ryusho Sakagami & Setsumei Sakagami. (Okinawan Combat Arts Ser.). (Illus.). 180p. 1974. pap. 9.95 (ISBN 0-87040-333-8). Japan Pubns.

Nung Grammar. Saul Wilson & Frieberger Wilson. (SIL Publications in Linguistics Ser.). 150p. 1980. write for info. (ISBN 0-88312-081-X); price not set microfiche (ISBN 0-88312-481-5). Summer Inst Ling.

Nungu & the Elephant. Cole. 117p. Date not set. lib. bdg. 6.95 (ISBN 0-07-011696-2). McGraw.

Nuns & Soldiers. Iris Murdoch. LC 80-16935. 512p. 1981. 14.95 (ISBN 0-670-51826-3). Viking Pr.

Nun's Castle. Jennie Melville. 224p. 1975. pap. 1.25 o.p. (ISBN 0-685-51457-9, P2412-125, Crest). Fawcett.

Nun's Curse. Charlotte Riddell. (Nineteenth Century Fiction Ser.: Ireland: Vol. 63). 932p. 1979. lib. bdg. 46.00 (ISBN 0-8240-3512-7). Garland Pub.

Nun's Priest's Prologue & Tale. Geoffrey Chaucer. Ed. by M. Hussey. (Selected Tales from Chaucer). 1966. text ed. 4.95x (ISBN 0-521-04626-2). Cambridge U Pr.

Nuovissima Enciclopedia Universale Curico, 20 vols. (Ital.). 1971. 490.00 (ISBN 0-8277-3070-5). Maxwell Sci Intl.

Nuovissimo Melzi: Dizionario Enciclopedico Italiano, 2 vols. 2970p. 1979. Set. 89.00x (ISBN 0-913298-53-0). S F Vanni.

Nuremberg & Other War Crimes Trials: A New Look. Richard Harwood. (Illus.). 1978. pap. 2.50 (ISBN 0-911038-34-5, Inst Hist Rev). Noontide.

Nuremberg Diary. G. M. Gilbert. pap. 1.50 (ISBN 0-451-04551-3, W4551, Sig). NAL.

Nurse. Peggy Anderson. 1980. pap. 2.75 (ISBN 0-425-04685-0). Berkley Pub.

Nurse & Radiotherapy: A Manual for Daily Care. Irene M. Leahy et al. LC 78-12296. 1978. pap. text ed. 11.95 (ISBN 0-8016-2896-2). Mosby.

Nurse & the Cancer Patient: A Programmed Textbook. Josephine K. Craytor & Margot L. Fass. LC 71-124393. (Prog. Bk.). 1970. pap. text ed. 5.95x o.p. (ISBN 0-397-54103-1). Lippincott.

Nurse & the Childbearing Family. Deborah M. Bash & Winifred A. Gold. LC 80-22945. 800p. 1981. 17.95 (ISBN 0-471-05520-4). Wiley.

Nurse & the Mental Patient: A Study of Interpersonal Relations. Morris S. Schwartz & Emmy L. Shockley. 1956. pap. 9.95 (ISBN 0-471-76610-0, Pub. by Wiley-Medical). Wiley.

Nurse Anesthetists Continuing Education Review. Alice R. Bakutis. 1975. spiral bdg. 10.75 (ISBN 0-87488-356-3). Med Exam.

Nurse As Caregiver for the Terminal Patient & His Family. Ed. by Ann M. Earle et al. LC 76-14441. 1976. 20.00x (ISBN 0-231-04020-2). Columbia U Pr.

Nurse As Manager. Joyce F. Schweiger. LC 80-17456. 194p. 1980. 11.95 (ISBN 0-471-04343-5, Pub. by Wiley Med). Wiley.

Nurse Assistant. Lucy Brooks. LC 77-73939. 1978. pap. text ed. 7.40 (ISBN 0-8273-1620-8); instructor's guide 1.60 (ISBN 0-8273-1621-6). Delmar.

Nurse Assistant in Long Term Care: A New Era. Betty J. Walston & Walston. LC 80-12308. (Illus.). 1980. pap. text ed. 8.95 (ISBN 0-8016-5355-X). Mosby.

Nurse at Deer Hollow. Christine Bush. (YA) 1977. 5.50 o.p. (ISBN 0-685-81424-6, Avalon). Bouregy.

Nurse at Orchard Hill. Callie Buckingham. (YA) 1978. 5.95 (ISBN 0-685-87346-3, Avalon). Bouregy.

Nurse at Playland Park. Dorothy B Francis. 192p. (YA) 1976. 4.95 o.p. (ISBN 0-685-67079-1, Avalon). Bouregy.

Nurse at the Ritz. W. Ross. 1979. 5.95 (ISBN 0-686-66185-0, Avalon). Bouregy.

Nurse at Towpath Lodge. Anne Maguire. (YA) 1976. 4.95 o.p. (ISBN 0-685-68910-7, Avalon). Bouregy.

Nurse Autumn's Secret Love. Colleen L. Reece. 1979. 5.95 (ISBN 0-686-52547-7, Avalon). Bouregy.

Nurse Called Tommie. Thelma Norman. LC 59-13496. (Destiny Ser.). 1959. 4.95 (ISBN 0-8163-0140-9, 14600-1). Pacific Pr Pub Assn.

Nurse-Client Interaction: Implementing the Nursing Process. Sandra Sundeen et al. (Illus.). 260p. 1981. pap. text ed. 11.95 (ISBN 0-8016-4844-0). Mosby.

Nurse-Client Relationship in Mental Health Nursing: Workbook Guides to Understanding & Management. Janet A. Simmons. LC 75-40639. 240p. 1978. pap. 8.95 (ISBN 0-7216-8286-3). Saunders.

Nurse in Community Health. Edith P. Lewis & Mary H. Browning. (Contemporary Nursing Ser). 1972. 6.50 o.p. (ISBN 0-686-02586-5, C04). Am Journal Nurse.

Nurse in Training. Carli Laklan. LC 65-15667. 5.95 o.p. (ISBN 0-385-05816-0). Doubleday.

Nurse Jean's Strange Case. Arlene Hale. LC 80-26058. 237p. 1980. Repr. of 1970 ed. large print ed. 8.95 (ISBN 0-89621-259-9). Thorndike Pr.

Nurse Matilda. Christianna Brand. (Children's Literature Ser.). 1980. PLB 7.95 (ISBN 0-8398-2604-4). Gregg.

Nurse Molly's Search. Polly Mark. 1978. 5.95 (ISBN 0-685-86410-3, Avalon). Bouregy.

Nurse of St. John. Sue Alden. (YA) 1977. 4.95 o.p. (ISBN 0-685-75641-6, Avalon). Bouregy.

Nurse of the Crystalline Valley. Mary Collins Dunne. (YA) 1977. 4.95 o.p. (ISBN 0-685-74273-3, Avalon). Bouregy.

Nurse of the Island. Phyllis T. Pianka. 192p. (YA) 1976. 5.95 (ISBN 0-685-66476-7, Avalon). Bouregy.

Nurse of the Thousand Islands. Audrey P. Johnson. (YA) 1978. 5.95 (ISBN 0-685-85780-8, Avalon). Bouregy.

Nurse of Thorne Grotto. Jane McCarthy. (YA) 1977. 4.95 o.p. (ISBN 0-685-73809-4, Avalon). Bouregy.

Nurse on Leave. large print ed. Arlene Hale. LC 80-28022. 1981. Repr. of 1965 ed. 8.95 (ISBN 0-89621-270-X). Thorndike Pr.

Nurse Power: Unions & the Law. Karen O'Rourke & S. R. Barton. (Illus.). 420p. 1980. pap. text ed. 14.95 (ISBN 0-87619-669-5). R J Brady.

Nurse Practitioners: USA. Harry A. Sultz et al. LC 78-19728. 1979. 25.95 (ISBN 0-669-02727-8). Lexington Bks.

Nurse Recruitment: Strategies for Success. Dolores Ziff & Tina Filoromo. LC 80-14829. 1980. text ed. 25.00 (ISBN 0-89443-164-1). Aspen Systems.

Nurse Sandra's Choice. Lucy Bowdler. (YA) 1978. 5.95 (ISBN 0-685-85781-6, Avalon). Bouregy.

Nurse Staffing: A Practical Guide. Barbara Brown. 200p. 1980. 23.95 (ISBN 0-89443-291-5). Aspen Systems.

Nursery & Midwifery Sourcebook. Arnold Lancaster. 304p. 1980. 25.00x (Pub. by Beaconsfield England). State Mutual Bk.

Nursery Care of Nonhuman Primates. Ed. by G. C. Puppenthal. LC 78-322018. (Advances in Primatology Ser.). 349p. 1979. 32.50 (ISBN 0-306-40150-9, Plenum Pr). Plenum Pub.

Nursery Companion. Iona Opie & Peter Opie. (Illus.). 128p. 1980. 19.95 (ISBN 0-19-212213-4). Oxford U Pr.

Nursery Crops & Landscape Designs for Agri-Business Studies. George S Williams. LC 75-10482. 1975. 9.65 (ISBN 0-8134-1717-1); text ed. 7.25x (ISBN 0-685-65744-2). Interstate.

Nursery Management. Cohan & Yoshikawa. 1982. text ed. 16.95 (ISBN 0-8359-5051-4); instr's. manual free (ISBN 0-8359-5052-2). Reston.

Nursery Management: Administration & Culture. Harold Davidson & Roy Mechlenburg. (Illus.). 464p. 1981. text ed. 19.95 (ISBN 0-13-627455-2). P-H.

Nursery Rhymes. (Sturdy Shape Bks.). (Illus.). 14p. (ps). 1980. 2.95 (ISBN 0-307-12253-0, Golden Pr). Western Pub.

Nursery Rhymes. Ed. by A. H. Watson. (Childrens Illustrated Classics Ser). (Illus.). 1975. Repr. of 1958 ed. 9.00x o.p. (ISBN 0-460-05041-9, Pub. by J. M. Dent England). Biblio Dist.

Nursery Rhymes & Tales, Their Origin & History. Henry Bett. LC 68-21756. 1968. Repr. of 1924 ed. 18.00 (ISBN 0-8103-3474-7). Gale.

Nursery Rhymes of England. James O. Halliwell-Phillipps. LC 67-23936. 1969. Repr. of 1843 ed. 18.00 (ISBN 0-8103-3482-8). Gale.

Nursery School & Day Care Center Management Guide. rev ed. Clare Cherry et al. 1978. looseleaf bdg. 18.50 (ISBN 0-8224-4791-6). Pitman Learning.

Nurse's Almanac. Howard S. Rowland & Beatrice L. Rowland. LC 78-311. (Illus.). 1978. 32.95 (ISBN 0-89443-031-9); pap. 21.95 (ISBN 0-89443-040-8). Aspen Systems.

Nurses Drug Book. 2nd ed. Suzanne Loebl et al. LC 80-15274. 889p. 1980. 19.95 (ISBN 0-471-06092-5, Pub. by Wiley Med); pap. 14.95 (ISBN 0-471-06017-8, Pub. by Wiley-Med). Wiley.

Nurses Guide to Writing for Publication. Susan R. Mirin. LC 80-84085. (Nursing Dimension Education Ser & Nursing Dimension Administrative Ser.). 180p. 1981. text ed. 14.50 (ISBN 0-913654-71-X). Nursing Res.

Nurses in Practice: A Perspective on Work Environments. Marcella Z. Davis et al. LC 74-13232. 1975. 8.95 o.p. (ISBN 0-8016-1208-X). Mosby.

Nurse's Liability for Malpractice: A Programed Course. 3rd ed. Eli Bernzweig. 368p. 1980. pap. text ed. 11.95 (ISBN 0-07-005058-9, HP); prepub. 2.95 test bank (ISBN 0-07-005059-7). McGraw.

Nurse's Quest for a Professional Identity. Helen A. Cohen. 1980. 14.95 (ISBN 0-201-00956-0); pap. 9.95 (ISBN 0-201-01157-3). A-W.

Nursing. LC 79-18811. (Nursing PreTest Self-Assessment & Review Ser.). (Illus.). 1979. 11.95 (ISBN 0-07-051574-3). McGraw-Pretest.

Nursing: A Human Needs Approach. Janice Ellis & Elizabeth Nowlis. LC 76-12023. (Illus.). 416p. 1977. text ed. 16.75 (ISBN 0-395-24067-0); instructor's manual 1.25 (ISBN 0-395-24068-9). HM.

Nursing: A Human Needs Approach. 2nd ed. Janice R. Ellis & Elizabeth A. Nowlis. LC 80-82841. (Illus.). 528p. 1981. text ed. 17.95 (ISBN 0-395-29642-0); price not set instr's. manual (ISBN 0-395-29643-9). HM.
Nursing: A World View. Huda Abu-Saad. LC 78-25860. (Illus.). 1979. text ed. 12.50 (ISBN 0-8016-0065-0). Mosby.
Nursing Actions for Health Promotion. Colleen Smitherman. LC 80-17464. (Illus.). 415p. 1980. pap. text ed. 13.95 (ISBN 0-8036-7941-6). Davis Co.
Nursing Administration Handbook. Howard Rowland & Beatrice Rowland. LC 80-11857. 600p. 1980. text ed. 42.50 (ISBN 0-89443-275-3). Aspen Systems.
Nursing Administration in the Hospital Health Care System. 2nd ed. Edythe L. Alexander. LC 77-18114. (Illus.). 1978. text ed. 16.95 (ISBN 0-8016-0110-X). Mosby.
Nursing Administration: Theory for Practice with a Systems Approach. 2nd ed. Clara Arndt & Loucine Huckabay. LC 80-14034. (Illus.). 1980. pap. 15.95 (ISBN 0-8016-0305-6). Mosby.
Nursing Administration: Theory for Practice with a Systems Approach. Clara Arndt & Loucine M. Huckabay. LC 75-4893. (Illus.). 336p. 1975. text ed. 14.95 o.p. (ISBN 0-8016-0312-9). Mosby.
Nursing & Medical Terminology: A Workbook. Ruth K. Radcliff & Shelia J. Ogden. LC 76-17597. (Illus.). 1977. pap. text ed. 12.50 (ISBN 0-8016-3714-7). Mosby.
Nursing & Social Change. Monica E. Baly. (Illus.). 1973. pap. text ed. 13.95x (ISBN 0-433-01160-2). Intl Ideas.
Nursing & the Aged. 2nd ed. Irene M. Burnside. (Illus.). 736p. 1980. text ed. 17.95 (ISBN 0-07-009211-7, HP). McGraw.
Nursing & the American Health Care System. Joellen W. Hawkins & Loretta P. Higgins. (Illus., Orig.). 1981. pap. text ed. price not set (ISBN 0-913292-33-8). Tiresias Pr.
Nursing & the Cancer Patient. (Contemporary Nursing Ser.). 354p. 1973. 5.00 o.p. (ISBN 0-686-08732-1, C09). Am Journal Nurse.
Nursing & the Concept of Loss. F. L. Bower. 214p. 1980. 10.95 (ISBN 0-471-04790-2). Wiley.
Nursing & the Law. 3rd ed. Mary W. Cazalas. LC 78-24253. 1978. text ed. 17.50 (ISBN 0-89443-075-0). Aspen Systems.
Nursing & the Nephrology Patient: A Symposium on Current Trends & Issues. Ed. by Lowanna Schlotter. 1973. spiral bdg. 9.50 (ISBN 0-87488-376-8). Med Exam.
Nursing & the Process of Continuing Education, Nineteen Seventy-Seven. 2nd ed. Elda S. Popiel. LC 76-57997. (Illus.). 1977. pap. text ed. 10.95 (ISBN 0-8016-3969-7). Mosby.
Nursing Assessment. Ed. by Fay L. Bower & Robinetta T. Wheeler. LC 77-5160. (Wiley Nursing Concept Modules). 1977. pap. 10.95 (ISBN 0-471-02167-9, Pub. by Wiley Medical). Wiley.
Nursing Assessment & Health Promotion Through the Life Span. 2nd ed. Ruth B. Murray & Judith P. Zentner. (Illus.). 1979. ref. 15.95 (ISBN 0-13-627588-5); pap. 12.95 (ISBN 0-13-627596-6). P-H.
Nursing Assignment Patterns: User's Manual. Fred C. Munson et al. (Illus.). 300p. (Orig.). 1980. pap. text ed. 32.50 (ISBN 0-914904-40-X). Health Admin Pr.
Nursing Audit: Self-Regulation in Nursing Practice. 2nd ed. Phaneuf. (Illus.). 1976. pap. 13.50 (ISBN 0-8385-7005-4). ACC.
Nursing Care Evaluation: Concurrent & Retrospective Review Criteria. Sharon V. Davidson et al. LC 77-5069. 1977. 19.95 (ISBN 0-8016-1210-1). Mosby.
Nursing Care in Eye, Ear, Nose & Throat Disorders, Nineteen Seventy-Nine. William Saunders et al. LC 79-499. (Illus.). 1979. text ed. 19.95 (ISBN 0-8016-2113-5). Mosby.
Nursing Care of Adults with Orthopedic Conditions. Leona A. Mourad. LC 79-26251. 1980. 17.95 (ISBN 0-471-04677-9, Pub. by Wiley Med). Wiley.
Nursing Care of Children: PreTest Self-Assessment & Review. Ed. by Elizabeth Laliberte & Carol A. Daisy. LC 78-50595. (PreTest Self-Assessment & Review Ser.). (Illus.). 1978. pap. 6.95 (ISBN 0-07-051568-9). McGraw-Pretest.
Nursing Care of Infants & Children. Lucille F. Whaley & Donna Wong. LC 78-31225. (Illus.). 1979. text ed. 27.95 (ISBN 0-8016-5417-3). Mosby.
Nursing Care of Patients with Urologic Diseases. 4th ed. C. Chester Winter & Alice Morel. LC 76-14837. (Illus.). 1977. pap. 16.95 (ISBN 0-8016-5607-9). Mosby.
Nursing Care of the Cancer Patient. 4th ed. Rosemary Bouchard & Norma F. Owens. LC 80-21708. (Illus.). 496p. 1981. pap. text ed. 19.95 (ISBN 0-8016-0720-5). Mosby.
Nursing Care of the Elderly. Helen I. Weber. (Illus.). 240p. 1980. text ed. 12.95 (ISBN 0-8359-5035-2); pap. 11.95 (ISBN 0-8359-5034-4). Reston.
Nursing Care of the Older Adult. Mildred O. Hogstel. 650p. 1981. 16.95 (ISBN 0-471-06022-4, Pub. by Wiley Med). Wiley.
Nursing Care of the Patient with Burns. 2nd ed. Florence G. Jacoby. LC 75-15578. (Illus.). 176p. 1976. pap. 8.95 o.p. (ISBN 0-8016-2396-0). Mosby.
Nursing Care of the Pediatric Surgical Patient. Imelda Charles-Edwards & Harold Nixon. 1981. text ed. price not set. Butterworth.
Nursing Care Planning Guides, Set 2. 2nd ed. Margo C. Neal & Patricia F. Cohen. 1980. pap. 11.95 (ISBN 0-935236-16-3). Nurseco.
Nursing Care Planning Guides, Set 5. Margo N. Creighton & Joan Reighley. 1981. pap. 11.95 (ISBN 0-935236-14-7). Nurseco.
Nursing Care Planning Guides for Long Term Care. Margo N. Creighton & Patricia F. Cohen. 1980. pap. write for info. (ISBN 0-935236-13-9). Nurseco.
Nursing Care Planning Guides for Psychiatric & Mental Health. Margo C. Neal & Patricia F. Cohen. 1980. pap. 15.95 (ISBN 0-935236-15-5). Nurseco.
Nursing Concepts & Nursing Care. Alice R. Rines & Mildred L. Montag. LC 75-40028. 505p. 1976. 15.95 o.p. (ISBN 0-471-72245-6, Pub. by Wiley Medical). Wiley.
Nursing Concepts & Processes. Carolyn C. Clark. LC 76-14095. 1977. pap. text ed. 11.60 (ISBN 0-8273-1318-7); instructor's guide 2.75 (ISBN 0-8273-1319-5). Delmar.
Nursing Concepts for Health Promotion. 2nd ed. Ruth B. Murray & Judith P. Zentner. (Illus.). 1979. ref. 15.95 (ISBN 0-13-627638-5); pap. text ed. 12.95 (ISBN 0-13-627620-2). P-H.
Nursing: Concepts of Practice. Dorothea E. Orem. 1971. pap. 9.95 o.p. (ISBN 0-07-047691-8, HP). McGraw.
Nursing Diagnosis & Intervention in Nursing Practice. Claire Campbell. LC 77-17095. 1978. text ed. 28.50 (ISBN 0-471-13307-8, Pub. by Wiley Medical). Wiley.
Nursing Diagnosis of the Alcoholic Person. Nada J. Estes et al. LC 80-11057. (Illus.). 1980. pap. text ed. 9.95 (ISBN 0-8016-1558-5). Mosby.
Nursing Drug Handbook 81. 1000p. 1981. text ed. 15.95 (ISBN 0-916730-33-6). Intermed Comm.
Nursing Education in a Changing Society. Ed. by Mary Q. Innis. LC 70-498725. 1970. pap. 3.00 (ISBN 0-8020-6112-5). U of Toronto Pr.
Nursing Eighty Career Directory. 2nd, rev. ed. John Kelly et al. Ed. by June F. Gomez. (Illus.). 320p. 1980. pap. 10.00 (ISBN 0-916730-23-9). InterMed Comm.
Nursing Fundamentals. Ed. by Rosemarie R. Parse. (Nursing Outline Ser.). 1974. 8.00 (ISBN 0-87488-378-4). Med Exam.
Nursing Guide to Oxygen Therapy: Unit in Fundamentals of Nursing. 3rd rev. ed. Marie M. Seedor. (Nursing Education Monograph: No. 10). (Illus.). 1980. pap. 8.50 (Pub. by Columbia U Pr). Lippincott.
Nursing Home: A Caring Community Staff Manuel. Paul R. Welter. 96p. 1981. pap. 2.95 (ISBN 0-8170-0935-3). Judson.
Nursing Home: A Caring Community-Trainers' Manual. Paul R. Welter. 176p. 1981. pap. 9.95 (ISBN 0-8170-0934-5). Judson.
Nursing Home Activities for the Handicapped. Mark Laker. 98p. 1980. 9.75 (ISBN 0-398-04074-5). C C Thomas.
Nursing Home Care As a Public Policy Issue. Mary W. Bednarski & Sandra E. Florczyk. (Learning Packages in Policy Issues: No. 4). 62p. (Orig.). 1978. pap. text ed. 3.50 (ISBN 0-936826-13-4). Pol Stud Assocs.
Nursing Home Estimates for California, Illinois, Massachusetts, New York & Texas from the 1977 National Nursing Home Survey. Daniel J. Foley. Ed. by Mary Olmsted. (Ser. 13-48). 50p. 1980. pap. text ed. 1.75 (ISBN 0-8406-0190-5). Natl Ctr Health Stats.
Nursing Home Life: What It Is & What It Could Be. Clifford Bennett. LC 80-52650. (Illus.). 192p. 1980. pap. text ed. 6.95 (ISBN 0-913292-19-2). Tiresias Pr.
Nursing Home Menu Planning, Food Purchasing & Management. Bro. Herman E. Zaccarelli & Josephine Maggiore. LC 73-182087. 1972. 15.95 (ISBN 0-8436-0541-3). CBI Pub.
Nursing Home Murder. Ngaio Marsh. 1978. pap. 1.50 (ISBN 0-515-04530-6). Jove Pubns.
Nursing-Home Organization & Efficiency: Profit Versus Non Profit. Michael Koetting. LC 79-2796. 160p. 1980. 19.95 (ISBN 0-669-03290-5). Lexington Bks.
Nursing Home Organization & Operation. Dulcy B. Miller & Jane T. Barry. LC 79-183. (Illus.). 1979. text ed. 19.95 (ISBN 0-8436-0782-3). CBI Pub.
Nursing Homes in Profile: National Nursing Home Survey, 1973-74. Al Sirrocco & Hugo Koch. (Ser. 14). 1976. pap. 1.50 (ISBN 0-8406-0084-4). Natl Ctr Health Stats.
Nursing Homes in the United States: 1973-74 National Nursing Home Survey. Al Sirrocco & Hugo Koch. Ed. by Mary Rutherford. (Ser. 14: No. 17). 1977. pap. 1.50 (ISBN 0-8406-0097-6). Natl Ctr Health Stats.
Nursing in Society: A Historical Perspective. 14th ed. Josephine A. Dolan. LC 77-88313. (Illus.). 380p. 1978. 22.00 (ISBN 0-7216-3133-9). Saunders.
Nursing in the European Community. Ed. by Sheila Quinn. 192p. 1980. 25.00x (ISBN 0-7099-0080-5, Pub. by Croom Helm Ltd England). Biblio Dist.
Nursing in the Seventies. Anne K. Roe & Mary C. Sherwood. LC 73-2874. 272p. 1973. pap. text ed. 12.50 (ISBN 0-471-72962-0). Wiley.
Nursing Job Guide to Over Seven Thousand Hospitals. 1981. softcover 15.00 (ISBN 0-932834-02-7). Prime NATL Pub.
Nursing Leadership Behavior in General Hospitals. Elizabeth Hagen & Luverne Wolff. LC 61-18762. 1961. pap. text ed. 4.75x (ISBN 0-8077-1482-8). Tchrs Coll.
Nursing Leadership: Theory & Process. 2nd ed. Yura. (Illus.). 1980. pap. 11.95 (ISBN 0-8385-7028-3). ACC.
Nursing: Levels of Health Intervention. Ed. by Ann W. Burgess. (P-H General Nursing Ser.). (Illus.). 1978. ref. 19.95 (ISBN 0-13-627687-3). P-H.
Nursing Management. Joan Ganong & Warren Ganong. LC 76-29787. 1976. 15.95 o.p. (ISBN 0-912862-30-0). Aspen Systems.
Nursing Management. 2nd ed. Warren Ganong & Joan Ganong. 350p. 1980. text ed. 19.95 (ISBN 0-89443-278-8). Aspen Systems.
Nursing Management & Leadership in Action: Principles & Applications to Staff Situations. 3rd ed. Laura M. Douglass & Em O. Bevis. LC 78-31960. (Illus.). 1979. pap. text ed. 12.75 (ISBN 0-8016-1441-4). Mosby.
Nursing Management of Diabetes Mellitus. Ed. by Diana W. Guthrie & Richard A. Guthrie. LC 76-27828. (Illus.). 1977. pap. 12.95 (ISBN 0-8016-1995-5). Mosby.
Nursing Management of Renal Problems. 2nd ed. Dorothy J. Brundage. LC 80-11720. (Illus.). 1980. pap. text ed. 9.95 (ISBN 0-8016-0849-X). Mosby.
Nursing Perspectives & Issues. Gloria M. Grippando. LC 76-14090. 1977. pap. text ed. 11.60 (ISBN 0-8273-1314-4); instructor's guide 2.75 (ISBN 0-8273-1315-2). Delmar.
Nursing Pharmacology. Michael C. Gerald & Freda V. O'Bannon. (Illus.). 544p. 1981. text ed. 22.95 (ISBN 0-13-627505-2). P-H.
Nursing Process: A Humanistic Approach. Elaine L. La Monica. 1979. text ed. 13.95 (ISBN 0-201-04138-3, 04138, M&N Div). A-W.
Nursing Process: A Scientific Approach to Nursing Care. 2nd ed. Ann Marriner. LC 78-21093. (Illus.). 1979. pap. 11.50 (ISBN 0-8016-3122-X). Mosby.
Nursing Process in Later Maturity. Dorothy L. Driscoll et al. (Illus.). 1980. text ed. 18.95 (ISBN 0-13-627570-2). P-H.
Nursing Process in Practice. (Contemporary Nursing Ser.). 290p. 1974. 6.50 (ISBN 0-937126-12-8, C12). Am Journal Nurse.
Nursing Process: Proceedings. Ed. by Marie M. Seedor. LC 73-85353. 51p. 1973. pap. text ed. 3.50x (ISBN 0-8077-2405-X). Tchrs Coll.
Nursing Research: A Learning Guide. Natalie Pavlovich. LC 77-22518. 1978. pap. text ed. 9.50 (ISBN 0-8016-3763-5). Mosby.
Nursing Research: A Survey & Assessment. Simmons. 1964. 18.50 o.p. (ISBN 0-8385-7046-1). ACC.
Nursing Research: Design Statistics & Computer Analysis. Carolyn Waltz & Baker Bausell. (Illus.). 350p. 1981. pap. text ed. 13.95 (ISBN 0-8036-9040-1). Davis Co.
Nursing Research: Development, Collaboration & Utilization. Janelle C. Kruegar & Allen H. Nelson. LC 78-26215. (Illus.). 1978. text ed. 25.00 (ISBN 0-89443-082-3). Aspen Systems.
Nursing Research I. Ed. by Phyllis J. Verhonick. 1975. 13.50 (ISBN 0-316-90010-9). Little.
Nursing Research II. Phyllis Verhonick. 1977. 13.50 (ISBN 0-316-90011-7). Little.
Nursing Service Administration: Managing the Enterprise. Helen M. Donovan. LC 75-26845. (Illus.). 272p. 1975. pap. 12.95 (ISBN 0-8016-1423-6). Mosby.
Nursing Skills. Ohio State University. 1077p. 1980. pap. text ed. 18.95 (ISBN 0-8359-5039-5). Reston.
Nursing Studies Index, 4 vols. Virginia Henderson. Ed. by Yale University Index Staff. Incl. Vol. 1. 1900-1929. 900p. 35.00 o.p. (ISBN 0-397-54125-2); Vol. 2. 1930-1949. 1037p. 28.00 o.p. (ISBN 0-397-54104-X); Vol. 3. 1950-1956. 653p. 25.00 o.p. (ISBN 0-397-54053-1); Vol. 4. 1957-1959. 280p. 15.00 o.p. (ISBN 0-685-22858-4). Lippincott.
Nursing Supervision. Lee Hand. (Illus.). 368p. 1980. text ed. 16.95 (ISBN 0-8359-5044-1); pap. 13.95 (ISBN 0-8359-5043-3). Reston.
Nursing System: Issues, Ethics & Politics. G. F. Donnelly et al. LC 80-12402. 224p. 1980. 10.95 (ISBN 0-471-04441-5). Wiley.
Nursing the Critically Ill Adult. Nancy M. Holloway. LC 78-21153. 1979. 20.95 (ISBN 0-201-02948-0, 02948, M&N Div). A-W.
Nursing the Elderly. M. A. Hodkinson. 1967. 18.00 (ISBN 0-08-011987-5); pap. 7.00 (ISBN 0-686-66515-5). Pergamon.
Nursing the Law. A. Young. 1981. text ed. 19.80 (ISBN 0-06-318181-9, Pub. by Har-Row Ltd England); pap. text ed. 10.45 (ISBN 0-686-69150-4). Har-Row.
Nursing Theories: The Base for Professional Nursing Practice. Nursing Theories Conference Group. (Illus.). 1980. pap. text ed. 11.95 (ISBN 0-13-627703-9). P-H.
Nursing 81: Career Directory, Vol. 3, No. 1. 3rd ed. Ed. by June F. Gomez. (Illus., Orig.). 1981. pap. 10.00 (ISBN 0-916730-30-1). Intermed Comm.
Nurturant Task Leader: A Model of the Effective Executive. Jai B. Sinha. 1980. text ed. 11.25x (ISBN 0-391-01823-X). Humanities.
Nut Between Two Blades: The Novels of Charles Robert Maturin. Peter M. Henderson. Ed. by Devendra P. Varma. LC 79-8457. (Gothic Studies & Dissertations Ser.). 1980. lib. bdg. 25.00x (ISBN 0-405-12672-7). Arno.
Nutation & the Earth's Rotation: Proceedings. I.A.U Symposium No. 78, Kiev, USSR, May 23-28, 1977 et al. Ed. by M. L. Smith & P. L. Bender. 284p. 1980. lib. bdg. 34.00 (ISBN 90-277-1113-5); pap. 21.00 (ISBN 90-277-1114-3). Kluwer Boston.
Nutcracker. Janet Schulman. LC 79-11223. (Illus.). (gr. 1-5). 1979. 7.95 (ISBN 0-525-36245-2). Dutton.
Nutcracker. Toshiko Yamanushi. Tr. by Alvin Tresselt from Japanese. LC 74-5809. Orig. Title: Kurmi- wari Ningyo. (Illus.). 40p. (ps-2). 1974. Repr. 5.95 o.s.i. (ISBN 0-8193-0743-2, Four Winds); PLB 5.41 o.s.i. (ISBN 0-8193-0744-0). Schol Bk Serv.
Nutcracker in a Tree: A Book of Riddles. Riana Duncan. LC 80-67492. (Illus.). 32p. (gr. k-2). 1981. 8.95 (ISBN 0-440-06426-0); PLB 8.44 (ISBN 0-440-06429-5). Delacorte.
Nutrient Requirements of Beef Cattle. new 5th rev. ed. Committee on Animal Nutrition Board on Agriculture & Renewable Resources, Natl Research Council. LC 75-43977. (Nutrient Requirements of Domestic Animals Ser.). 56p. 1976. pap. 3.75 (ISBN 0-309-02419-6). Natl Acad Pr.
Nutrient Requirements of Cats. Committee on Animal Nutrition, National Research Council. LC 78-5976. (Nutrient Requirements of Domestic Animals Ser.). 1978. pap. text ed. 5.50 (ISBN 0-309-02743-8). Natl Acad Pr.
Nutrient Requirements of Dairy Cattle, 1978. 5th ed. Committee On Animal Nutrition. (Nutrient Requirements of Domestic Animals Ser). 1978. pap. text ed. 4.50 (ISBN 0-309-02749-7). Natl Acad Pr.
Nutrient Requirements of Dogs. Committee on Animal Nutrition. 1974. pap. 4.75 (ISBN 0-309-02315-7). Natl Acad Pr.
Nutrient Requirements of Horses. 1978. 3.75 (ISBN 0-309-02760-8). Natl Acad Pr.
Nutrient Requirements of Laboratory Animals. rev. 3rd ed. Agricultural Board. LC 54-60841. (Illus.). 128p. 1978. pap. 6.75 (ISBN 0-309-02767-5). Natl Acad Pr.
Nutrient Requirements of Mink & Foxes. Committee On Animal Nutrition. (Nutrient Requirements of Domestic Animals Ser.). 1968. pap. 3.50 (ISBN 0-309-01676-2). Natl Acad Pr.
Nutrient Requirements of Non Human Primates. Board on Agriculture & Renewable Resources. 1978. pap. 5.00 (ISBN 0-309-02786-1). Natl Acad Pr.
Nutrient Requirements of Poultry. 7th rev ed. Animal Nutrition. Ed. by Agricultural Board. LC 54-60841. (Nutrient Requirements of Domestic Animals Ser). 1978. pap. 4.50 (ISBN 0-309-02725-X). Natl Acad Pr.
Nutrient Requirements of Rabbits. rev. 7th ed. Committee On Animal Nutrition. LC 77-6318. 1977. pap. 4.50 (ISBN 0-309-02607-5). Natl Acad Pr.
Nutrient Requirements of Sheep. National Academy of Sciences. 1975. pap. 5.25 (ISBN 0-309-02212-6). Natl Acad Pr.
Nutrient Requirements of Swine. 8th rev. ed. Board on Agriculture & Renewable Resources. (Nutrient Requirements of Domestic Animals Ser). (Illus.). 64p. 1979. pap. 3.75 (ISBN 0-309-02870-1). Natl Acad Pr.
Nutrient Requirements of Trout, Salmon & Catfish. Agricultural Board. (Nutrient Requirements of Domestic Animals Ser). (Illus.). 64p. 1973. pap. 4.50 (ISBN 0-309-02141-3). Natl Acad Pr.
Nutrients & Toxic Substances in Water for Livestock & Poultry. National Research Council, Committee on Animal Nutrition. LC 74-2836. (Illus.). v, 93p. 1974. pap. 4.75 (ISBN 0-309-02312-2). Natl Acad Pr.

Nutrients in Natural Waters. Ed. by Herbert E. Allen & James R. Kramer. LC 72-3786. (Environmental Science & Technology Ser.). 449p. 1972. 37.50 o.p. (ISBN 0-471-02328-0, Pub by Wiley-Interscience). Wiley.

Nutrients to Age Without Senility. Abram Hoffer & Morton Walker. LC 79-93428. 265p. 1980. 10.50 (ISBN 0-87983-217-7); pap. 2.95 (ISBN 0-87983-218-5). Keats.

Nutrition. 9th ed. Margaret S. Chaney et al. LC 78-69546. (Illus.). 1979. text ed. 18.95 (ISBN 0-395-25448-5); o.p. inst. manual (ISBN 0-395-25449-3). HM.

Nutrition. Cheryl Corbin. LC 80-11138. (Illus.). 208p. 1981. 13.95 (ISBN 0-03-048281-X, Owl Bks); pap. 7.95 (ISBN 0-03-048276-3). HR&W.

Nutrition. M. Pyke. (Teach Yourself Ser.). 1974. pap. 2.95 o.p. (ISBN 0-679-10371-6). McKay.

Nutrition: A Comprehensive Treatise, 3 vols. Ed. by G. H. Beaton & E. W. McHenry. Incl. Vol. 1. Macronutrients & Nutrient Elements. 1964. 62.00 (ISBN 0-12-084101-0); Vol. 2. Vitamins, Nutrient Requirements & Food Selections. 1964. 62.00 (ISBN 0-12-084102-9); Vol. 3. Nutritional Status: Assessment & Application. 1966. 53.00 (ISBN 0-12-084103-7). 143.00 (ISBN 0-685-23127-5). Acad Pr.

Nutrition: An Applied Science. Pat B. Reed. (Illus.). 650p. 1980. text ed. 19.95 (ISBN 0-8299-0311-9); instrs.' manual avail. (ISBN 0-8299-0570-7). West Pub.

Nutrition & Aging. Ed. by Mark Ordy & Denham Harman. 1980. write for info. (ISBN 0-89004-477-5, 531). Raven.

Nutrition & Cancer. Myron Winick. LC 77-22650. (Current Concepts in Nutrition: Vol. 6). 1977. 27.50 (ISBN 0-471-03394-4, Pub. by Wiley-Interscience). Wiley.

Nutrition & Development. Ed. by Myron Winick. LC 72-5097. (Current Concepts in Nutrition Ser.: Vol. 1). 320p. 1972. 32.50 (ISBN 0-471-95440-3, Pub. by Wiley-Interscience). Wiley.

Nutrition & Diet Modifications. 3rd ed. Carolynn E. Townsend. LC 78-74166. (Health Occupations Ser.). (gr. 9). 1980. pap. text ed. 10.40 (ISBN 0-8273-1324-1); instructor's guide 1.50 (ISBN 0-686-59749-4). Delmar.

Nutrition & Diet Therapy. 2nd ed. Rose Mirenda et al. (Nursing Examination Review Book: Vol. 8). 1972. spiral bdg. 6.00 (ISBN 0-87488-508-6). Med Exam.

Nutrition & Diet Therapy. 4th ed. Sue R. Williams. (Illus.). 875p. 1981. text ed. 19.95 (ISBN 0-8016-5554-4). Mosby.

Nutrition & Diet Therapy in Gastrointestinal Diseases. Martin H. Floch. (Topics in Gastroenterology Ser.). 390p. 1981. 35.00 (ISBN 0-306-40508-3, Plenum Pr). Plenum Pub.

Nutrition & Dietectics for Nurses. 6th ed. Mary E. Beck. (Churchill Livingstone Nursing Texts Ser.). (Illus.). 288p. 1980. pap. text ed. 9.75 (ISBN 0-443-02009-4). Churchill.

Nutrition and Dietetics for Nurses. 5th ed. Mary E. Beck. LC 76-51312. (Illus.). 1977. pap. text ed. 8.25 o.p. (ISBN 0-443-01557-0). Churchill.

Nutrition & Environmental Health: The Influence of Nutritional Status on Pollutant Toxicity & Carcinogenicity, 2 vols. Edward J. Calabrese. Incl. Vol. 1. Vitamins. 60.00 (ISBN 0-471-04833-X); Vol. 2. Minerals & Macronutrients. 544p. 35.00 (ISBN 0-471-08207-4). LC 79-21089. (Environmental Science & Technology Ser.). 1980 (Pub. by Wiley-Interscience). Wiley.

Nutrition and Fertility Interrelationships. Food & Nutrition Board. 1975. pap. 4.50 (ISBN 0-309-02341-6). Natl Acad Pr.

Nutrition & Fetal Development. Ed. by Myron Winick. (Current Concepts in Nutrition, Vol. 2). 240p. 1974. 26.50 (ISBN 0-471-95435-7, Pub. by Wiley-Interscience). Wiley.

Nutrition & Food Processing. H. G. Muller & G. Tobin. 240p. 1980. 35.00x (ISBN 0-85664-540-0, Pub. by Croom Helm England). State Mutual Bk.

Nutrition & Food Processing. american ed. H. G. Muller & G. Tobin. 1980. pap. 30.00 (ISBN 0-87055-363-1). AVI.

Nutrition & Food Science: Present Knowledge & Utilization, 3 vols. Ed. by W. J. Santos et al. 1980. 195.00 set (Plenum Pr); Vol. 1, 850p. 75.00 (ISBN 0-306-40342-0); Vol. 2, 900p. 79.50 (ISBN 0-306-40343-9); Vol. 3, 760p. 69.50 (ISBN 0-306-40344-7). Plenum Pub.

Nutrition & Gastroenterology. Myron Winick. LC 80-16169. (Vol. 9). 221p. 1980. 32.50 (ISBN 0-471-08173-6, Pub. by Wiley Interscience). Wiley.

Nutrition & Good Health. Brooke Beebe et al. LC 78-731300. (Illus.). 1978. pap. text ed. 99.00 (ISBN 0-89290-099-7, A576-SATC). Soc for Visual.

Nutrition & Heart Disease. Ed. by H. Naito. (Monographs of the American College of Nutrition: Vol. 5). 1981. text ed. 25.00 (ISBN 0-89335-119-9). Spectrum Pub.

Nutrition & Its Disorders. 3rd ed. (Livingston Medical Text Ser.). (Illus.). 1981. pap. text ed. 15.00 (ISBN 0-443-02158-9). Churchill.

Nutrition & Learning. Robert H. Goldsmith. LC 80-82680. (Fastback Ser.: No. 147). (Orig.). 1980. pap. 0.75 (ISBN 0-87367-147-3). Phi Delta Kappa.

Nutrition & Medical Practice. Ed. by Lewis A. Barness et al. (Illus.). 1981. text ed. 17.00 (ISBN 0-87055-365-8). AVI.

Nutrition & Our Overpopulated Planet. S. L. Manocha. (Illus.). 488p. 1975. 31.75 (ISBN 0-398-03180-0); pap. 22.50 (ISBN 0-398-03181-9). C C Thomas.

Nutrition & the Brain: Disorders of Eating & Nutrients in Treatment of Brain Diseases. Ed. by Richard J. Wurtman & Judith J. Wurtman. (Nutrition & the Brain Ser.: Vol. 3). 1979. text ed. 32.00 (ISBN 0-89004-245-4). Raven.

Nutrition & the Brain: Toxic Effects of Food Constituents on the Brain. Ed. by Richard J. Wurtman & Judith J. Wurtman. LC 79-2073. (Nutrition & the Brain Ser.: Vol. 4). 1979. text ed. 25.00 (ISBN 0-89004-246-2). Raven.

Nutrition & the Developing Nervous System. Philip R. Dodge et al. (Illus.). 538p. 1975. 60.00 o.p. (ISBN 0-8016-1392-2). Mosby.

Nutrition & the Elderly. Barbara M. Posner. LC 77-17683. 1979. 19.95 (ISBN 0-669-02085-0). Lexington Bks.

Nutrition & the Killer Diseases. M. Winick. (Current Concepts in Nutrition Ser.: Vol. 10). 200p. 1981. 24.95 (ISBN 0-471-09130-8, Pub. by Wiley-Interscience). Wiley.

Nutrition & the Later Years. Ruth B. Weg. LC 77-91696. 1978. pap. 6.50 (ISBN 0-88474-042-0). USC Andrus Geron.

Nutrition & Therapy. Clara M. Lewis. 1981. write for info. (ISBN 0-8036-5615-7). Davis Co.

Nutrition & Vitamin Therapy. Michael Lesser. 224p. 1981. pap. 2.50 (ISBN 0-553-14437-5). Bantam.

Nutrition, Behavior & Change. Helen Gifft et al. LC 79-170033. 1972. ref. ed. 17.95 (ISBN 0-13-627836-1). P-H.

Nutrition: Concepts & Controversy. Eva M. Hamilton & Eleanor N. Whitney. (Illus.). 1979. pap. text ed. 15.50 (ISBN 0-8299-0281-3, Pub by Hartnell); study guide 6.95 (ISBN 0-686-67552-5); study guide o.p. 4.95 (ISBN 0-8299-0288-0); instrs.' manual avail. (ISBN 0-8299-0485-9). West Pub.

Nutrition Cookbook: 123 Gourmet Recipes Computer Analyzed for Your Specific Daily Requirements. Stephen Kreitzman & Susan Kreitzman. LC 76-54565. 1977. 12.95 o.p. (ISBN 0-15-167750-6). HarBraceJ.

Nutrition During Pregnancy & Breast Feeding. Bonnie Worthington & Lynda Taylor. (Illus.). 1980. pap. 2.50. Budlong.

Nutrition Factor: Its Role in National Development. Alan Berg. 1973. 14.95 (ISBN 0-8157-0914-5); pap. 5.95 (ISBN 0-8157-0913-7). Brookings.

Nutrition, Food & Weight Control. Brent Q. Hafen. 320p. 1980. pap. text ed. 9.95 (ISBN 0-205-06826-X, 6268169); tchr's ed. free (ISBN 0-205-06828-6, 6268285). Allyn.

Nutrition, Food & Weight Control. Brent Q. Hafen. 400p. 1980. text ed. 17.95 (ISBN 0-205-06825-1, 6268250). Allyn.

Nutrition for Athletics. Ellington Darden. LC 76-10811. 1975. pap. 5.95 (ISBN 0-87095-058-4). Athletic.

Nutrition for Good Health. Fredrick J. Stare & Margaret McWilliams. LC 74-81644. 1974. 8.95x (ISBN 0-916434-11-7). Plycon Pr.

Nutrition for the Elderly. Ed. by Anthony A. Albanese. LC 80-21565. (Current Topics in Nutrition & Disease: Vol. 3). 280p. 1980. 38.00 (ISBN 0-8451-1602-9). A R Liss.

Nutrition for the Growing Years. 2nd ed. Margaret McWilliams. LC 74-28180. 452p. 1975. text ed. 18.95 o.p. (ISBN 0-471-58738-9). Wiley.

Nutrition for the Growing Years. 3rd ed. Margaret McWilliams. LC 80-453. 491p. 1980. text ed. 20.50x (ISBN 0-471-02692-1). Wiley.

Nutrition in a Changing World. Lily H. O'Connell et al. (Illus.). 152p. (Orig.). (gr. 5). 1981. pap. text ed. 11.95 (ISBN 0-8425-1916-5). Brigham.

Nutrition in a Changing World: Grade Four. Pennsylvania State University Nutrition Education Curriculum Study. LC 80-20736. (Illus.). 152p. (Orig.). (gr. 4). 1981. pap. text ed. 8.95x (ISBN 0-8425-1864-9). Brigham.

Nutrition in a Nutshell. Roger J. Williams. LC 62-15322. pap. 2.50 (ISBN 0-385-03031-2, C396, Dolp). Doubleday.

Nutrition in Clinical Surgery. Mervyn Deitel. (Illus.). 284p. 1980. 43.95 (ISBN 0-683-02449-3). Williams & Wilkins.

Nutrition in Contemporary Nursing Practice. Marilyn L. Green & Joann Harry. 752p. 1981. 17.95 (ISBN 0-471-03892-X, Pub. by Wiley Med). Wiley.

Nutrition in Infancy & Childhood. Peggy Pipes. LC 76-39865. (Illus.). 1977. pap. 9.95 (ISBN 0-8016-3940-9). Mosby.

Nutrition in Infancy & Childhood. 2nd ed. Peggy L. Pipes. (Illus.). 288p. 1981. pap. text ed. 11.95 (ISBN 0-8016-3941-7). Mosby.

Nutrition in Nursing. Lorraine S. Boykin. (Nursing Outline Ser.). 1975. spiral bdg. 6.00 o.p. (ISBN 0-87488-375-X). Med Exam.

Nutrition in Perspective. Patricia Kreutler. (Illus.). 1980. text ed. 17.95 (ISBN 0-13-627752-7); wkbk. 6.95 (ISBN 0-13-627778-0). P-H.

Nutrition in Pregnancy & Lactation. Bonnie S. Worthington-Roberts et al. (Illus.). 296p. 1981. pap. text ed. 11.95 (ISBN 0-8016-5626-5). Mosby.

Nutrition in the Community: The Art of Delivering Services. Reva T. Frankle & Anita Y. Owen. LC 78-9144. 1978. text ed. 17.95 (ISBN 0-8016-1666-2). Mosby.

Nutrition in the Life Span. Virginia A. Beal. LC 79-24610. 1980. text ed. 19.95 (ISBN 0-471-03664-1). Wiley.

Nutrition in the Lower Metazoa: Proceedings. Ed. by D. C. Smith & Y. Tiffon. (Illus.). 192p. 1980. 35.00 (ISBN 0-08-025904-9). Pergamon.

Nutrition Intervention in Developing Countries: An Overview. Ed. by James E. Austin & Marian F. Zeitlin. LC 80-29223. (Nutrition Intervention in Developing Countries Ser.). 256p. 1981. lib. bdg. 20.00 (ISBN 0-89946-077-1). Oelgeschlager.

Nutrition, Lipids & Coronary Heart Disease. Ed. by Robert I. Levy et al. LC 78-67020. (Nutrition in Health & Disease Ser.: Vol. 1). 1979. 52.00 (ISBN 0-89004-181-4). Raven.

Nutrition of the Dog & Cat: Proceedings of an International Symposium 26 June 1978, Hanover. Ed. by R. S. Anderson. LC 80-40449. (Illus.). 212p. 1980. 32.00 (ISBN 0-08-025526-4). Pergamon.

Nutrition of the Oilseed Rape Crop. M. R. Holmes. (Illus.). xii, 148p. 1980. 25.00x (ISBN 0-85334-900-2). Burgess-Intl Ideas.

Nutrition, Physiology & Obesity. Rachel Schemmel. 256p. 1980. 64.95 (ISBN 0-8493-5471-4). CRC Pr.

Nutrition Policy in Transition. Ed. by Jurgen Schmandt et al. LC 79-9628. (Illus.). 320p. 1980. 22.95x (ISBN 0-669-03596-3). Lexington Bks.

Nutrition: Principles & Application in Health Promotion. Carol W. Suitor & Merrily F. Hunter. LC 79-22569. 468p. 1980. text ed. 18.25 (ISBN 0-397-54256-9). Lippincott.

Nutrition: Principles & Clinical Practice. Sara M. Hunt et al. LC 79-25899. 1980. text ed. 20.95 (ISBN 0-471-03149-6). Wiley.

Nutrition Programs in the Third World: Cases & Concepts. Ed. by James E. Austin. LC 80-21083. 464p. 1981. lib. bdg. 27.50 (ISBN 0-89946-024-0). Oelgeschlager.

Nutrition Scoreboard. Michael F. Jacobson. 1975. pap. 2.25 (ISBN 0-380-00534-4, 44537). Avon.

Nutrition, Stress & Toxic Chemicals: An Approach to Environmental Health Controversies. Arthur J. Vander. 360p. 1981. text ed. 18.00 (ISBN 0-472-09329-0); pap. 9.95 (ISBN 0-472-06329-4). U of Mich Pr.

Nutrition Survival Kit. Dinaburg & Akel. (Orig.). pap. 1.75 (ISBN 0-515-04654-X). Jove Pubns.

Nutrition, Time & Motion in Metabolism & Genetics. Sydney J. Webb. (Illus.). 426p. 1976. 39.75 (ISBN 0-398-03158-4). C C Thomas.

Nutrition, Weight Control, & Exercise. Frank I. Katch & William D. McArdle. LC 76-14695. (Illus.). 1977. pap. text ed. 12.25 (ISBN 0-395-24453-6). HM.

Nutrition Workbook for Children. Catherine J. Frompovich. 32p. (gr. 1-5). 1978. pap. 1.50x (ISBN 0-935322-00-0). C J Frompovich.

Nutritional Deficiencies in Industrialized Countries. Ed. by J. C. Somogyi & G. Varela. (Bibliotheca Nutritic et Dieta Ser.: Vol. 30). (Illus.). 1981. soft cover 48.00 (ISBN 3-8055-1994-X). S Karger.

Nutritional Disorders in Chrysanthemums. 42p. 1980. pap. 22.75 (ISBN 90-220-0718-9, Pudoc). Unipub.

Nutritional Disorders of American Women. Myron Winick. LC 76-54393. (Current Concepts in Nutrition Ser.: Vol. 5). 1977. 25.95 (ISBN 0-471-02393-0, Pub. by Wiley-Interscience). Wiley.

Nutritional Elements & Clinical Biochemistry. Ed. by Marge A. Brewster & Herbert K. Naito. 450p. 1980. 45.00 (ISBN 0-306-40569-5, Plenum Pr). Plenum Pub.

Nutritional Encyclopedia for the Elderly. Edward S. Koniecko. 1981. 12.95 (ISBN 0-8062-1676-X). Carlton.

Nutritional Evaluation of Cereal Mutants. (Illus.). 1978. pap. 16.25 (ISBN 92-0-111077-4, ISP 444, IAEA). Unipub.

Nutritional Evaluation of Food Processing. 2nd ed. Robert S. Harris & Endel Karmas. (Illus.). 1975. text ed. 39.50 (ISBN 0-87055-189-2); pap. 20.50 (ISBN 0-87055-312-7). AVI.

Nutritional Factors: Modulating Effects on Metabolic Processes. Ed. by Roland F. Beers & Edward G. Bassett. (Miles International Symposium Ser.: Vol. 13). 1981. text ed. price not set (ISBN 0-89004-592-5). Raven.

Nutritional Food Additives, GA-040. BCC Staff. 1979. 675.00 (ISBN 0-89336-119-4). BCC.

Nutritional Management of Genetic Disorders, Vol. 8. Ed. by Myron Winick. LC 79-16192. (Current Concepts in Nutrition Ser.). 1979. 28.50 (ISBN 0-471-05781-9, Pub. by Wiley-Interscience). Wiley.

Nutritional Management of the Cancer Patient. Joy J. Wollard. LC 78-68523. 1979. text ed. 17.50 (ISBN 0-89004-357-4); pap. text ed. 12.00 (ISBN 0-685-94934-6). Raven.

Nutritional Quality Index of Foods. R. Gaurth Hansen & Bonita W. Wyse. (Illus.). 1979. text ed. 26.50 (ISBN 0-87055-320-8). AVI.

Nutritional Research: An International Approach. Ed. by Brita Rolander-Chilo. (Illus.). 1979. text ed. 28.00 (ISBN 0-08-024399-1). Pergamon.

Nuts. Olive L. Earle & Michael Kantor. LC 74-26800. (Illus.). 64p. (gr. 3-7). 1975. 6.75 (ISBN 0-688-22025-8); PLB 6.48 (ISBN 0-688-32025-2). Morrow.

Nuts, Berries & Grapes. Hollis Lee. (Country Home & Small Farm Guides Ser.). (Illus.). 1978. pap. 2.95 (ISBN 0-88453-009-4). Barrington.

Nuts, Berries & Grapes. (Country Home Ser.). 96p. 2.95 (ISBN 0-88453-009-4). Berkshire Traveller.

Nuttier Nock Nocks. Louis Phillips & Karen Markoe. Ed. by Meg Schneider. (Funnybones Ser.). (Illus.). 64p. (gr. 3-7). 1981. pap. 1.50 (ISBN 0-671-42248-0, Wanderer). S&S.

Nutty for President. Dean Hughes. LC 80-36719. 144p. (gr. 4-6). 1981. PLB 8.95 (ISBN 0-689-30812-4). Atheneum.

Nutty Joke Book. Compiled by Charles Keller. (Illus.). (gr. 2-5). 1978. 6.95 (ISBN 0-13-627737-3). P-H.

Nutty Nock-Nocks. Karen Markoe & Louis Phillips. (Funnybones Ser.). (Illus.). 64p. (gr. 3-7). 1981. pap. 1.50 (ISBN 0-671-42249-9). Wanderer Bks.

Nutty Number Riddles. Rose Wyler & Eva-Lee Baird. LC 74-33695. (gr. 3-5). 1977. PLB 5.95 (ISBN 0-385-00685-3). Doubleday.

Nwandu's Child of Life Reader. Robert F. Brooks. (Illus.). 20p. (Orig.). (gr. k-4). Date not set. pap. 2.00 (ISBN 0-936868-00-7). Freeland Pubns.

Nyamwezi Today: A Tenzanian People in the Seventies. R. G. Abrahams. LC 80-41012. (Changing Cultures Ser.). (Illus.). 176p. Date not set. price not set (ISBN 0-521-22694-5); pap. price not set (ISBN 0-521-29619-6). Cambridge U Pr.

Nyerere & Nkrumah. David Killingray. Ed. by Malcolm Yapp & Margaret Killingray. (World History Ser.). (Illus.). 32p. (gr. 10). 1980. Repr. of 1977 ed. lib. bdg. 5.95 (ISBN 0-89908-129-0); pap. text ed. 1.95 (ISBN 0-89908-104-5). Greenhaven.

Nyla & the White Crocodile. Norma Youngberg. LC 65-18680. (Destiny Ser.). 1977. pap. 4.95 (ISBN 0-8163-0306-1, 14640-7). Pacific Pr Pub Assn.

Nymphomaniac's Cookbook. H. Straubing. (Illus.). 144p. 1980. 4.95 (ISBN 0-87786-003-3); pap. 2.97 (ISBN 0-686-69011-7). Gold Penny.

Nymphs. Ernest Schwiebert. LC 73-188596. (Illus.). 339p. 1973. 17.95 (ISBN 0-87691-074-6). Winchester Pr.

Nyoro State. John Beattie. 294p. 1971. 29.95x (ISBN 0-19-823171-7). Oxford U Pr.

O

O America: When You & I Were Young. Luigi Barzini. LC 76-5110. 1977. 10.00 o.p. (ISBN 0-06-010226-8, HarpT). Har-Row.

O & M for First Line Managers. Stanley Oliver. 1975. pap. 14.95x (ISBN 0-7131-3350-3). Intl Ideas.

O & M in Local Government. T. D. Sherman. 1969. 22.00 (ISBN 0-08-013317-7); pap. 11.25 (ISBN 0-08-013309-6). Pergamon.

O Beulah Land. Mary L. Settle. 304p. 1981. pap. 3.50 (ISBN 0-345-29311-8). Ballantine.

O C S Oil & Gas: An Assessment. Environmental Studies Board. 1978. pap. 7.25 (ISBN 0-309-02739-X). Natl Acad Pr.

O Cheshskom Stikhe, Preimushchestvenno V Sopostavlenii S Russkim. Roman Jakobson. LC 68-8623. (Slavic Reprint Ser.: No. 6). 125p. (Rus). 1969. pap. 3.00 (ISBN 0-87057-119-2, Pub. by Brown U Pr). Univ Pr of New England.

O Dostoevskom: Stat'i. P. M. Bitsilli et al. LC 66-23779. (Slavic Reprint Ser.: No. 4). 229p. (Rus). 1966. pap. 4.00 (ISBN 0-87057-098-6, Pub. by Brown U Pr). Univ Pr of New England.

O God, Guide Me! A Selection of Prayers Revealed. Baha'U'Llah The Bab & Abdu'l-Baha. LC 66-22165. (Illus.). (gr. 2-6). 1974. 4.00 (ISBN 0-87743-080-2, 7-52-47). Baha'i.

O Grade Questions & Worked Examples in Chemistry. Alan W. Mackaill. 1971. pap. text ed. 3.95x o.p. (ISBN 0-435-64563-3). Heinemann Ed.

O Guia Do Pastor. Tr. by Ralph M. Riggs. (Portugese Bks.). (Port.). 1979. 3.25 (ISBN 0-8297-0665-8); pap. 2.25 (ISBN 0-686-28815-7). Life Pubs Intl.

O. Henry. Eugene Current-Garcia. (U. S. Authors Ser.: No. 77). 1972. lib. bdg. 9.95 (ISBN 0-8057-0368-3). Twayne.

O. Henry. C. A. Smith. LC 80-23470. (American Men & Women of Letters Ser.). 1981. pap. 4.95 (ISBN 0-87754-167-1). Chelsea Hse.

O. Henry Almanac. Emilie Toepperwein & Fritz Toepperwein. pap. 1.00 (ISBN 0-910722-07-2). Highland Pr.

O. J. Simpson. Paul Deegan. LC 73-17056. (Creative Superstars Ser.). 1974. PLB 5.95 (ISBN 0-87191-312-7); pap. 2.95 (ISBN 0-89812-166-3). Creative Ed.

O. J. Simpson: Juice on the Gridiron. Julian May. LC 74-82745. (Sports Close-up Ser.). (Illus.). (gr. 3-5). 1974. PLB 5.95 o.p. (ISBN 0-913940-10-0); pap. 2.50 o.p. (ISBN 0-913940-72-0). Crestwood Hse.

O Jerusalem. Larry Collins & Dominique Lapierre. 1980. pap. write for info. (ISBN 0-671-83684-6). PB.

O-kee-pa: A Religious Ceremony & Other Customs of the Mandans. George Catlin. Ed. by John C. Ewers. LC 76-4522. (Illus.). 106p. 1976. pap. 7.95 (ISBN 0-8032-5845-3, BB 625, Bison). U of Nebr Pr.

O Lord, from You: Prayers & Devotions of Petition in Large Print. 1.00 o.p. (ISBN 0-685-62050-6). Augsburg.

O Master Caliban! Phyllis Gotlieb. LC 76-5540. 256p. (YA) 1976. 8.95 o.p. (ISBN 0-06-011621-8, HarpT). Har-Row.

O My Pilot Beloved. Sri Chinmoy. 54p. (Orig.). 1980. pap. 2.00 (ISBN 0-88497-502-9). Aum Pubns.

O Pioneers. Willa Cather. 10.95 (ISBN 0-395-07516-5); pap. 4.96 (ISBN 0-395-08365-6). HM.

O Rugged Land of Gold. Martha Martin. 1967. 4.95 o.s.i. (ISBN 0-02-580460-X). Macmillan.

O. S. U. Theses & Dissertations, Nineteen Seventy-One to Nineteen Seventy-Seven. Compiled by Pia T. Brown. (Bibliographic Ser.: No. 17). 128p. 1980. pap. 4.00 (ISBN 0-87071-137-7). Oreg St U Pr.

O Signo Selvagem. Cid Seixas. (Bi-Lingual Port. - Eng.). 1981. pap. 1.50. Ghost Dance.

O Sliver of Liver. Myra C. Livingston. LC 78-23681. (Illus.). (gr. 4-7). 1979. 7.95 (ISBN 0-689-50133-1, McElderry Bk). Atheneum.

O. W. O. W. Wilson & the Search for a Police Profession. William J. Bopp. (National University Publications Interdisciplinary Urban Ser.). 1977. 12.95 (ISBN 0-8046-9179-7); pap. 7.95 (ISBN 0-8046-9201-7). Kennikat.

O Ye Jigs & Juleps. Virginia C. Hudson. 1962. 6.95 (ISBN 0-02-555340-2). Macmillan.

O. Z. Brown: A True Narrative of Daniel McCollum, a Captive Among the Indians During the Revolutionary War, Repr. Of 1853. O. Z. Brown. Ed. by Wilcomb E. Washington. Incl. James Moore Brown: The Captives of Abb's Valley, a Legend of Frontier Life. By a Son of Mary Moore. James M. Brown. Repr. of 1854 ed; Jane A. Wilson: Narrative of Sufferings...Among Comanche. in "Supplement to the Courant," XIX, No. 3, p.p. 2021, Feb. 11, 1854. Jane A. Wilson; Joseph Barney: Eighteen Years a Captive Among the Indians. A Very Interesting Narrative. In: "America's Own..."New York, 1855, VII, No. 18. Joseph Barney. (Narratives of North American Indian Captivities Ser.: Vol. 65). 1978. lib. bdg. 44.00 (ISBN 0-8240-1689-0). Garland Pub.

Oak Alley, 4 vols. James Wagenvoord. (Illus.). 160p. 1981. 166.80 (ISBN 0-312-58050-9). St Martin.

Oak & Maple. Phyl Surman. 1981. 6.75 (ISBN 0-8062-1709-X). Carlton.

Oak Creek Canyon & the Red Rock Country of Arizona. Stewart W. Aitchison. LC 78-53385. (Illus., Orig.). 1978. pap. 5.95 (ISBN 0-933762-01-1). Stillwater Canyon Pr.

Oak Furniture to Pharmacist's Equipment. Time-Life Books Editors. (Encyclopedia of Collectibles Ser.). (Illus.). 1979. lib. bdg. 10.98 (ISBN 0-8094-2791-5); kivar bdg. 8.95 (ISBN 0-8094-2792-3). Silver.

Oak Tree. Paula Z. Hogan. LC 78-21183. (Life Cycles Ser.). (Illus.). (gr. k-3). 1979. PLB 9.95 (ISBN 0-8172-1251-5). Raintree Pubs.

Oakdale Affair. Edgar R. Burroughs. 1976. Repr. of 1937 ed. lib. bdg. 12.50x (ISBN 0-89966-041-X). Buccaneer Bks.

Oakfield, or Fellowship in the East. W. D. Arnold. (Victorian Library Ser.). 298p. 1973. Repr. of 1854 ed. text ed. 14.50x (ISBN 0-391-00275-9, Leicester). Humanities.

Oakfield; or, Fellowship in the East, 1854. 2nd ed. William D. Arnold. Ed. by Robert L. Wolff. LC 75-1522. (Victorian Fiction Ser.). 1975. lib. bdg. 66.00 (ISBN 0-8240-1594-0). Garland Pub.

Oakland Raiders. Julian May. (NFL Today). (Illus.). (gr. 3-6). 1977. PLB 6.45 (ISBN 0-87191-595-2); pap. 2.95 (ISBN 0-686-67475-8). Creative Ed.

Oakland Raiders Super Bowl Champions. Julian May. (Super Bowl Champions Ser.). (Illus.). (gr. 3-9). 1978. PLB 6.45 (ISBN 0-87191-614-2); pap. 2.95 (ISBN 0-89812-091-8). Creative Ed.

Oars, Sails & Steam: A Picture Book of Ships. Edwin Tunis. LC 76-25453. (Illus.). (gr. 6 up). 1977. 12.95 (ISBN 0-690-01284-5, TYC-J). T Y Crowell.

OAS Opening Doors to Opportunity. (Eng & Span.). 1975. pap. 1.00 Eng. ed. (ISBN 0-8270-6500-0); pap. 1.00 Span. ed. (ISBN 0-8270-6495-0). OAS.

Oasis of Solitude in the Sahara of Multitudes. M. K. Kaw. (Writers Workshop Redbird Ser.). 72p. 1975. 14.00 (ISBN 0-88253-592-7); pap. text ed. 4.80 (ISBN 0-88253-591-9). Ind-US Inc.

Oaten Reeds & Trumpets: Pastoral & Epic in Virgil, Spenser, & Milton. D. N. Rosenberg. LC 80-17974. 288p. 1981. 22.50 (ISBN 0-8387-5002-8). Bucknell U Pr.

Oats, Peas, Beans & Barley Cookbook: A Complete Vegetarian Cookbook Using Nature's Most Economical Foods. rev. ed. Edyth Y. Cottrell. LC 80-80794. (Illus.). 1980. pap. 4.95 (ISBN 0-912800-85-2). Woodbridge Pr.

Oats, Peas, Beans & Barley Cookbook: The Complete Vegetarian Cookbook. Edyth Y. Cottrell. LC 73-77411. (Illus.). 272p. 1974. 8.95 o.p. (ISBN 0-912800-08-9); pap. 5.95 o.p. (ISBN 0-912800-07-0). Woodbridge Pr.

Obadiah. John D. W. Watts. Date not set. pap. 4.95 (ISBN 0-88469-138-1). BMH Bks.

Obadiah Comes Fourteen. Elizbeth Spring. (N. H.-Vermont Historiettes). (Illus.). 64p. (gr. 4-5). 1976. 4.95x (ISBN 0-915892-07-3); pap. 1.95x (ISBN 0-915892-16-2). Regional Ctr Educ.

Obaldia Plays, Vol. III. 1981. 14.95 (ISBN 0-7145-3534-6). Riverrun NY.

Obaldia Plays; Plays, Vol. I. 1980. pap. 4.00 (ISBN 0-7145-0470-X). Riverrun NY.

Obaldig Plays, Vol. II. 1980. 9.95 (ISBN 0-7145-0471-8). Riverrun NY.

Obedience. rev. ed. Jane Buerger. LC 80-39520. (What Is It? Ser.). (Illus.). 32p. (gr. k-3). 1981. PLB 5.50 (ISBN 0-89565-206-4). Childs World.

Obedient Jack. Paul Galdone. LC 72-131155. (Illus.). (gr. k-3). 1971. PLB 4.90 o.p. (ISBN 0-531-01970-5). Watts.

Obelisks of Egypt: The Skyscrapers of the Past. Labib Habachi. Ed. by Charles C. Van Siclen, III. LC 76-54646. (Illus.). 1977. 12.95 o.p. (ISBN 0-684-14805-6, ScribT). Scribner.

Oberammergau, Its Environment & Tradition. R. Sattelmair. (Illus.). 1970. 6.00 o.p. (ISBN 0-911268-12-X). Rogers Bk.

Oberammergau: The Passion-Play-Village & Its Text in German-English-French. Otto Siegner. (Illus.). 1978. 15.00x (ISBN 0-686-63526-4). Heinman.

Oberon: A Poem from the German of Wieland. William Sotheby. Ed. by Donald H. Reiman. LC 75-31258. (Romantic Context Ser.: Poetry 1789-1830). 1978. Repr. of 1798 ed. lib. bdg. 47.00 (ISBN 0-8240-2205-X). Garland Pub.

Obeserver's Book of Big Bands. Mark White. (Observer Bks.). (Illus.). 1978. 3.95 (ISBN 0-684-15593-1, ScribT). Scribner.

Obesity: A Bibliography 1974-1979. Ed. by Anne Smith. 340p. 1980. 55.00 (ISBN 0-904147-17-7). Info Retrieval.

Obesity & Anorexia Nervosa: A Question of Shape. Peter Dally & Joan Gomez. 128p. 1980. 17.95 (ISBN 0-571-10542-4, Pub. by Faber & Faber); pap. 6.95 (ISBN 0-571-11472-5). Merrimack Bk Serv.

Obesity: Etiology, Treatment, & Management. Milton V. Kline et al. (Illus.). 480p. 1976. 29.50 (ISBN 0-398-03369-2). C C Thomas.

Object & Self: A Developmental Approach. Saul Tuttman. 600p. 1981. text ed. 40.00x (ISBN 0-8236-3700-X, 00-3700). Intl Univs Pr.

Object Lessons from the Bible. Wesley T. Runk. (Object Lessons Ser.). 96p. 1980. pap. 2.95 (ISBN 0-8010-7698-6). Baker Bk.

Object of My Affection: An Autobiography. Pinky Tomlin. LC 80-5938. (Illus.). 300p. 1981. 12.50 (ISBN 0-8061-1719-2). U of Okla Pr.

Object Relations Theory & Its Applications. Otto F. Kernberg. LC 75-42548. 300p. 1981. 25.00x (ISBN 0-87668-247-6, 24760). Aronson.

Objective Based Reading. Wayne Otto & Robert D. Chester. LC 75-12100. (Illus.). 288p. 1976. text ed. 7.95 (ISBN 0-201-19311-6); tchr's guide 2.95 (ISBN 0-201-19321-3). A-W.

Objective Interpretation of Test Performance: The Rasch Model Applied. Alan S. Willmott & Diane E. Fowles. (General Ser.). (Illus.). 94p. 1974. pap. text ed. 11.25x (ISBN 0-85633-041-8, NFER). Humanities.

Objective Knowledge: An Evolutionary Approach. Karl R. Popper. 360p. 1972. text ed. 14.95x o.p. (ISBN 0-19-824370-7); pap. text ed. 6.95x (ISBN 0-19-875024-2). Oxford U Pr.

Objective Mental Measurement: Individual & Program Evaluation Using the Rasch Model. Robert M. Hashway. LC 78-19739. 1978. 21.95 (ISBN 0-03-046476-5). Praeger.

Objective Methods for Food Evaluation. Committee on Food Stability, National Research Council. LC 76-26723. 1976. pap. 8.75 (ISBN 0-309-02520-6). Natl Acad Pr.

Objective Psychology of Music. 2nd ed. Robert W. Lundin. 1967. 15.95 (ISBN 0-8260-5600-8). Wiley.

Objective Questions in "A" Level Modern Mathematics. K. Austwick et al. 1973. pap. text ed. 3.95x o.p. (ISBN 0-435-51040-1). Heinemann Ed.

Objective Questions in Physics for Advanced Level. K. A. Toh & S. H. Tan. 1977. pap. text ed. 8.50x o.p. (ISBN 0-435-68826-X). Heinemann Ed.

Objective Tests for Nurses, Book 2. Janet T. Riddle & Joan Dinner. (Objective Tests for Nurses Ser.). (Illus.). 112p. 1981. pap. text ed. 6.95 (ISBN 0-443-01740-9). Churchill.

Objective Tests in Advanced Level Physics. J. H. Avery & A. W. Ingram. 1970. pap. text ed. 1.50x o.p. (ISBN 0-435-68042-0); pap. text ed. 2.95x with answers o.p. (ISBN 0-435-68043-9). Heinemann Ed.

Objective Tests in C. S. E. Mathematics. L. Harwood Clarke & F. G. Norton. 1970. pap. text ed. 3.50x o.p. (ISBN 0-435-50208-5). Heinemann Ed.

Objective Tests in Introductory Economics with Answers. Vivian Anthony. 1975. pap. text ed. 3.95x o.p. (ISBN 0-435-33150-7). Heinemann Ed.

Objective Tests in Ordinary Level Physics, Bk. 1. J. H. Avery & A. W. Ingram. 1969. pap. text ed. 2.95x with ans. o.p. (ISBN 0-435-67043-3). Heinemann Ed.

Objective Tests in Ordinary Level Physics, Bk. 2. J. H. Avery & A. W. Ingram. 1975. pap. text ed. 2.25x with ans. o.p. (ISBN 0-435-67044-1). Heinemann Ed.

Objectives & Design of Environmental Monitoring Programmes for Radioactive Contaminants. (Safety Ser. No. 41). (Illus.). 131p. 1975. pap. 13.00 (ISBN 92-0-123075-3, ISP385, IAEA). Unipub.

Objectives & Perspectives in Education: Studies in Educational Theory, 1955-70. Ben Morris. 284p. 1972. 22.00x (ISBN 0-7100-7247-3). Routledge & Kegan.

Objectives for Instruction & Evaluation. Robert Kibler et al. 225p. 1980. pap. text ed. 8.95 o.p. (ISBN 0-686-64464-6, 247174-4). Allyn.

Objectives for Instruction & Evaluation. Robert J Kibler et al. 228p. 1974. text ed. 11.95x o.p. (ISBN 0-205-04402-6, 2244020); pap. text ed. 6.95x o.s.i. (ISBN 0-205-04399-2). Allyn.

Objectives of Teacher Education. Leeds University Institute of Education. (General Ser.). 45p. 1973. pap. text ed. 5.75x (ISBN 0-85633-028-0, NFER). Humanities.

Objectives of the New International Economic Order. Ervin Laszlo et al. LC 78-14766. (Pergamon Policy Studies). 288p. 1978. 20.00 (ISBN 0-08-023697-9). Pergamon.

Objectives-Tool for Change. Peter Pipe. LC 74-83218. 1975. pap. 4.20 (ISBN 0-8224-4900-5). Pitman Learning.

Objectivity in Social Science. Frank Cunningham. LC 72-95461. 1973. 10.00x o.p. (ISBN 0-8020-1943-9). U of Toronto Pr.

Oblate. Joris K. Huysmans. Tr. by Edward Perceval from Fr. LC 77-11670. 1978. Repr. of 1924 ed. 17.50 (ISBN 0-86527-284-0). Fertig.

Obligation of Contracts Clause of the United States Constitution. Warren B. Hunting. LC 75-31433. (Johns Hopkins Univ Studies in Hist & Pol. Science, Ser.: No. 37, Pt.4). 1976. Repr. of 1919 ed. lib. bdg. 13.75x (ISBN 0-8371-8524-6, HUOC). Greenwood.

Obligations of Society in the Turlfth & Thirteenth Centuries: The Ford Lectures Delivered in the University of Oxford in Michaelmas Term. Austin L. Poole. LC 80-2007. 1981. Repr. of 1946 ed. 18.50 (ISBN 0-404-18587-8). AMS Pr.

Oblique Tomography. Arfa Khan. 1981. write for info. (ISBN 0-87527-219-3). Green.

Oblomov. Ivan Goncharov. Tr. by C. J. Hogarth from Rus. LC 79-19061. 1980. Repr. of 1915 ed. lib. bdg. 12.50x (ISBN 0-8376-0451-6). Bentley.

Oboe. 3rd ed. Philip Bate. (Instruments of the Orchestra Ser). (Illus.). 1975. 13.95x o.p. (ISBN 0-393-02166-1). Norton.

Oboe. Leon Goosens & Edwin Roxburgh. LC 77-15886. (Yehudi Menuhin Music Guides Ser.). (Illus.). 1978. 12.95 (ISBN 0-02-871450-4); pap. 6.95 (ISBN 0-02-871460-1). Schirmer Bks.

Oboe Reeds: How to Make & Adjust Them. Robert Mayer & Traugott Rohner. (Illus.). pap. 7.00 (ISBN 0-686-15900-4). Instrumentalist Co.

Oboe Technique. rev. ed. Evelyn Rothwell. (YA) (gr. 9 up). 1962. 7.75 (ISBN 0-19-318602-0). Oxford U Pr.

Obra poetica de Felix Franco Oppenheimer: Estudio Tematico-Analitico-Estilistico. Rafael A. Gonzalez Torres. LC 79-17993. (Coleccion UPREX; Ser. Estudios Literarios: No. 59). 150p. (Orig., Sp.). 1980. pap. 1.85x (ISBN 0-8477-0059-3). U of PR Pr.

Obras Completas. Cerveri De Girona. LC 80-2175. 1981. Repr. of 1947 ed. 59.50 (ISBN 0-404-19005-7). AMS Pr.

Obras: Luis Pales Matos, Nineteen Fourteen to Nineteen Fifty-Nine, 2 vols. Luis Pales Matos. Ed. by Margot Arce de Vazquez. LC 79-16469. 609p. (Sp.). 1980. Vol. I: Poetry. write for info. (ISBN 0-8477-3220-7); Vol. II: Prose. write for info (ISBN 0-8477-3221-5). Set (ISBN 0-8477-3219-3). U of PR Pr.

O'Briens & The O'Flahertys. Lady Morgan S. Owenson. Ed. by Robert L. Wolff. (Ireland-Nineteenth Century Fiction, Ser. Two: Vol. 9). 1979. lib. bdg. 184.00 (ISBN 0-8240-3458-9); lib. bdg. 46.00 ea. Garland Pub.

Obscene Bird of Night. Jose Donoso. Tr. by Hardie St. Martin & Leonard Mades. LC 79-88419. 1979. pap. 7.50 (ISBN 0-87923-191-2, Nonpareil Bks.). Godine.

Obscene Literature & Constitutional Law. Theodore A. Schroeder. LC 72-116913. (Civil Lib. in Am. Hist. Ser.). 440p. 1972. Repr. of 1911 ed. lib. bdg. 25.00 (ISBN 0-306-70156-1). Da Capo.

Obscenity. 2nd ed. Ed. by Leon Friedman. (Oral Arguments Before the Supreme Court Ser.). 365p. 1981. pap. 8.95 (ISBN 0-87754-211-2). Chelsea Hse.

Obscenity & the Law. Norman St. John-Stevas. LC 74-8011. (Civil Liberties in American History Ser.). 289p. 1974. Repr. of 1956 ed. lib. bdg. 27.50 (ISBN 0-306-70602-4). Da Capo.

Observa-Story: Portland to Cut & Color. Nancy K. Lightbody & Sarah H. Malley. LC 76-54460. (Illus.). (gr. 1-4). 1976. pap. 1.25 (ISBN 0-9600612-5-8). Greater Portland.

Observable Materials Testing Text & Workbook. Jesse R. Fairbanks. 1978. pap. text ed. 7.50x (ISBN 0-8191-0386-1). U Pr of Amer.

Observation. Jeanne Bendick. LC 72-6053. (Science Experiences Ser). (Illus.). 72p. (gr. 3-5). 1972. PLB 4.90 o.p. (ISBN 0-531-01440-1). Watts.

Observation of Savage Peoples: Considerations on Methods. Joseph-Marie Degerando. Tr. by F. C. Moore. (Illus.). 1969. 16.50x (ISBN 0-520-01500-2). U of Cal Pr.

Observational Astronomy for Amateurs. J. B. Sidgwick. (Illus.). 384p. 1981. pap. write for info. (ISBN 0-486-24033-9). Dover.

Observations. Ernest Holmes. 1968. pap. 4.50 (ISBN 0-911336-12-5). Sci of Mind.

Observations-Four. Richard Kieninger. (Orig., Forty percent discount on ten or more books). 1979. pap. 3.00 ea. Stelle.

Observations in Lower California. Johann J. Baegert. Tr. by M. M. Brandenburg & Carl L. Baumann. (Library Reprint Ser.: No. 100). 1979. Repr. of 1952 ed. 17.50x (ISBN 0-520-03873-8). U of Cal Pr.

Observations of Deviance: Deviant Situations, Styles, & Ways of Life. Ed. by Jack D. Douglas. (Orig.). 1970. pap. text ed. 5.95x (ISBN 0-394-30130-7, RanC). Random.

Observations on Life, Literature & Learning in America. Henri Peyre. LC 61-8218. 1961. 7.95x o.p. (ISBN 0-8093-0043-5). S Ill U Pr.

Observations on Man, His Frame, His Duty & His Expectations, 2 vols. David Hartley. LC 66-11026. 1966. Repr. of 1749 ed. 90.00x (ISBN 0-8201-1025-6). Schol Facsimiles.

Observations on Mental Derangement: Being an Application of the Principles of Phrenology to the Elucidation of the Causes, Symptoms, Nature, Treatment of Insanity. Andrew Combe. LC 72-161928. (History of Psychology Series). Repr. of 1834 ed. 35.00x (ISBN 0-8201-1089-2). Schol Facsimiles.

Observations on the Biology of Protozoan Gromia Oviformis Dujardin. Zach M. Arnold. (U. C. Publ. in Zoology: Vol. 100). 1973. pap. 9.50x (ISBN 0-520-09455-7). U of Cal Pr.

Observations on the Deranged Manifestations of the Mind, or Insanity. Johann C. Spurzheim. LC 78-81359. (Hist. of Psych. Ser.). (Illus.). 1970. Repr. of 1833 ed. 27.00x (ISBN 0-8201-1078-7). Schol Facsimiles.

Observations on the Florid Song. 2nd ed. Pietro F. Tosi. Repr. of 1743 ed. 25.00 (ISBN 0-384-60980-5). Johnson Repr.

Observations on the Importance & Necessity of Introducing Improved Machinery into the Woollen Manufactory. J. Anstie. 104p. 1971. Repr. of 1803 ed. 17.00x (ISBN 0-7165-1575-X, Pub. by Irish Academic Pr Ireland). Biblio Dist.

Observations on the Influence of Religion Upon the Health & Physical Welfare of Mankind, 1835: Remarks on the Influence of Mental Cultivation & Mental Excitement Upon Health, 2 vols. in 1. Amariah Brigham. LC 73-17271. (Hist. of Psych. Ser.). 1973. 48.00x (ISBN 0-8201-1125-2). Schol Facsimiles.

Observations on the Popular Antiquities of Great Britain: Chiefly Illustrating the Origin of Our Vulgar & Provincial Customs, Ceremonies & Superstitions. John Brand. LC 67-23896. 1969. Repr. of 1849 ed. 42.00 (ISBN 0-8103-3256-6). Gale.

Observer's Book of Architecture. John Penoyre & Michael Ryan. (Observer Bks.). (Illus.). 1977. 4.95 (ISBN 0-684-15208-8, ScribT). Scribner.

Observer's Book of Automobiles. The Olyslager Organization. (Observer Bks). (Illus.). 1980. 4.95 (ISBN 0-684-16516-3, ScribT). Scribner.

Observer's Book of Birds. S. Vere Benson. (Observer Bks.). (Illus.). 1977. 4.95 (ISBN 0-684-15204-5, ScribT). Scribner.

Observer's Book of Butterflies. W. J. Stokoe. (Observer Bks). (Illus.). 1979. 2.95 (ISBN 0-684-16035-8, ScribT). Scribner.

Observer's Book of Cacti & Other Succulents. S. H. Scott. (Illus.). 1977. 2.95 (ISBN 0-684-14942-7, ScribT). Scribner.

Observer's Book of Cathedrals. Anthony S. New. (Observer Bks). (Illus.). 1979. 4.95 (ISBN 0-684-16026-9, ScribT). Scribner.

Observer's Book of Cats. rev. ed. Grace Pond. (Illus.). 1979. 3.95 (ISBN 0-684-16589-9, ScribT). Scribner.

Observer's Book of Coins. Howard Linecar. (Observer Bks.). (Illus.). 1977. 4.95 (ISBN 0-684-15207-X, ScribT). Scribner.

Observer's Book of European Costume. Geoffrey Squire & Pauline Baynes. (Observer Bks.). (Illus.). 1977. 2.95 (ISBN 0-684-15213-4, ScribT). Scribner.

Observer's Book of Flags. I. O. Evans. (Illus.). 1977. 4.95 (ISBN 0-684-14941-9, ScribT). Scribner.

Observer's Book of Fossils. Rhona M. Black. (Observer Bks.). (Illus.). 1977. 4.95 (ISBN 0-684-15209-6, ScribT). Scribner.

Observer's Book of Furniture. John Woodforde. (Observer Bks.). (Illus.). 1977. 3.95 o.p. (ISBN 0-684-15217-7, ScribT). Scribner.

Observer's Book of Garden Flowers. David Pycraft. (Observer Bks.). (Illus.). 1977. 2.95 (ISBN 0-684-15219-3, ScribT). Scribner.

Observer's Book of Glass. Mary Payton & Geoffrey Payton. (Illus.). 1977. 2.95 (ISBN 0-684-14940-0, ScribT). Scribner.

Observer's Book of Golf. Tom Scott. (Observer Bks.). (Illus.). 1977. 2.95 (ISBN 0-684-15212-6, ScribT). Scribner.

Observer's Book of House Plants. Stanley B. Whitehead. (Illus.). 1977. 2.95 (ISBN 0-684-14943-5, ScribT). Scribner.

Observer's Book of Lichens. Kenneth Alvin. (Observer Bks.). (Illus.). 1977. 4.95 (ISBN 0-684-15202-9, ScribT). Scribner.

Observer's Book of Music. rev. ed. Freda Dinn. (Illus.). 1979. 3.95 (ISBN 0-684-16590-2, ScribT). Scribner.

Observer's Book of Pottery & Porcelain. Geoffrey Payton & Mary Payton. (Observer Bks.). (Illus.). 1977. 2.95 (ISBN 0-684-15215-0, ScribT). Scribner.

Observer's Book of Sea & Seashore. I. O. Evans. (Observer Bks.). (Illus.). 1977. 4.95 (ISBN 0-684-15218-5, ScribT). Scribner.

Observer's Book of Sea Fishes. T. B. Bagenal. (Observer Bks). (Illus.). 1979. 3.95 (ISBN 0-684-16032-3, ScribT). Scribner.

Observer's Book of Seashells. Nora F. McMillan. (Observer Bks.). (Illus.). 1977. 4.95 (ISBN 0-684-15206-1, ScribT). Scribner.

Observer's Book of Sewing. Meriel Tilling. (Illus.). 1977. 2.95 (ISBN 0-684-14939-7, ScribT). Scribner.

Observer's Book of Trees. Herbert L. Edlin. (Observer Bks). (Illus.). 1979. 4.95 (ISBN 0-684-16037-4, ScribT). Scribner.

Observer's Book of Zoo Animals. Jan Hatley. (Observer Bks.). (Illus.). 1977. 4.95 (ISBN 0-684-15222-3, ScribT). Scribner.

Observer's World Airlines Directory. William Green & Gordon Swanborough. LC 74-21043. 374p. 1975. 15.00 o.p. (ISBN 0-7232-1547-2). Warne.

Observing Children: A Child Development Manual. Carol Quanty & Anthony Davis. LC 74-79515. 1974. pap. text ed. 5.95x o.p. (ISBN 0-88284-016-9). Alfred Pub.

Observing Intelligence in Young Children: Eight Case Studies. J. Carew & I. Chan. (Early Childhood Education Ser.). (Illus.). 192p. 1976. 11.95x (ISBN 0-13-628990-8); pap. 9.95 (ISBN 0-13-628982-7). P-H.

Observing National Holidays & Church Festivals: A Weekday Church School Unit in Christian Citizenship Series for Grades Three & Four. Florence Martin. LC 76-174077. 1971. Repr. of 1940 ed. 24.00 (ISBN 0-8103-3804-1). Gale.

Observing the Law: Field Methods in the Study of Crime & the Criminal Justice System. George J. McCall. LC 77-99094. (Illus.). 1978. 19.95 (ISBN 0-02-920400-3). Free Pr.

Obsession. Katherine Hale. 352p. (Orig.). 1980. pap. 2.25 (ISBN 0-345-28451-8). Ballantine.

Obsessionsdelikte. Ed. by W. De Boor & G. Kohlmann. (Schriftenreihe des Instituts Fuer Konfliktforschung: No. 6). 1980. pap. 13.25 (ISBN 3-8055-3015-3). S Karger.

Obsolete Fractional Coinage of the United States. Paul Andersen. LC 79-55915. (Illus.). 67p. (Orig.). (gr. 9 up). 1980. pap. 2.95 (ISBN 0-9604720-0-2). P Andersen.

Obstacle Race. Ethel M. Dell. 160p. (Orig.). 1980. pap. 1.50 (ISBN 0-553-13912-6). Bantam.

Obstacle Race: The Fortunes of Women Painters & Their Work. Germaine Greer. (Illus.). 373p. 1979. 25.00 (ISBN 0-374-22412-9); pap. 15.00 (ISBN 0-374-51582-4). FS&G.

Obstacles to Existential Freedom. James Park. (Existential Freedom Ser.: No. 10). 1976. pap. 2.00x (ISBN 0-89231-010-3). Existential Bks.

Obstacles to Mineral Development: A Pragmatic View. John S. Carman. Ed. by Benison Varon. LC 78-26807. (Illus.). 1979. 28.00 (ISBN 0-08-023904-8). Pergamon.

Obstacles to the New International Economic Order. Ervin Laszlo et al. LC 79-28723. (Pergamon Policy Studies on the New International Economic Order). 170p. 1980. 20.00 (ISBN 0-08-025110-2); pap. 7.95 (ISBN 0-08-025970-7). Pergamon.

Obstaculo Al Evangelismo. Iain Murray. (Span.). Date not set. pap. 0.60 (ISBN 0-686-28950-1). Banner of Truth.

Obstetric & Gynecologic Pathology. Frank Vellios & W. M. Christopherson. LC 79-10733. (Anatomic Pathology Slide Seminar Ser.). (Illus.). 1979. pap. text ed. 15.00 o.p. (ISBN 0-89189-070-X, 50-1-044-00); slides 85.00 o.p. (ISBN 0-686-67536-3, 01-1-078-01). Am Soc Clinical.

Obstetric Anesthesia & Perinatology. Ermelando V. Cosmi. 500p. 1981. 33.50 (ISBN 0-8385-7196-4). ACC.

Obstetric Ultrasound for the Practitioner: Applications & Principals. William S. Van Bergen. LC 80-14969. 1980. 19.95 (ISBN 0-201-08001-X). A-W.

Obstetrical Nursing Continuing Education Review. 2nd ed. Ed. by Dolores Malo-Juvera et al. 1979. pap. 9.50 (ISBN 0-87488-350-4). Med Exam.

Obstetrical Practice. Silvio Aladjem. LC 80-17356. (Illus.). 877p. 1980. text ed. 39.50 (ISBN 0-8016-0114-2). Mosby.

Obstetrician-Gynecologist & Primary Care. Wayne F. Baden et al. (Illus.). 197p. 1980. lib. bdg. 22.00 (ISBN 0-683-00301-1). Williams & Wilkins.

Obstetrics & Gynecology. 6th ed. J. Robert Willson & Elsie R. Carrington. LC 78-31642. (Illus.). 1979. text ed. 34.50 (ISBN 0-8016-5595-1). Mosby.

Obstetrics & Gynecology Annual: 1974, Vol. 3. Ed. by Wynn. (Illus.). 1974. 22.50 o.p. (ISBN 0-8385-7178-6). ACC.

Obstetrics & Gynecology Annual: 1975, Vol. 4. Ed. by Wynn. (Illus.). 1975. 26.50 o.p. (ISBN 0-8385-7179-4). ACC.

Obstetrics & Gynecology Annual: 1976, Vol. 5. Ed. by Wynn. (Illus.). 1976. 28.50 o.p. (ISBN 0-8385-7180-8, A7180-1). ACC.

Obstetrics & Gynecology Annual 1978, Vol. 7. Ed. by Ralph M. Wynn. (Illus.). 1978. 33.50 (ISBN 0-8385-7182-4). ACC.

Obstetrics & Gynecology Annual 1979, Vol. 8. Ed. by Ralph M. Wynn. (Illus.). 1979. 29.50 (ISBN 0-8385-7183-2). ACC.

Obstetrics & Gynecology Annual 1980. Ed. by Ralph M. Wynn. (Obstetrics & Gynecology Ser.). 390p. 1980. 29.50x (ISBN 0-8385-7186-7). ACC.

Obstetrics & Gynecology Annual, 1981. Ed. by Ralph M. Wynn. (Obstetrics & Gynecology Annual Series). 1981. 33.50 (ISBN 0-8385-7188-3). ACC.

Obstetrics & Gynecology: Preterm Labor, Vol. 1. M. G. Elder & C. H. Hendricks. (Butterworths International Medical Reviews Ser.). 1981. text ed. price not set (ISBN 0-407-02300-3). Butterworths.

Obstetrics & Gynecology: PreTest Self-Assessment & Review. Ed. by Alan De Cherney. LC 77-78446. (Clinical Sciences: PreTest Self-Assessment & Review Ser.). (Illus.). 1978. pap. 9.95 (ISBN 0-07-051602-2). McGraw-Pretest.

Obstetrics & Gynecology Specialty Board Review. 5th ed. Ed. by Raymond E. Probst. 1977. spiral bdg. 16.50 (ISBN 0-87488-304-0). Med Exam.

Obstetrics: Essentials of Clinical Practice. 2nd ed. Kenneth R. Niswander. 1981. pap. text ed. price not set. Little.

Obstetrics, Family Planning & Paediatrics: A Manual of Practical Management for Doctors & Nurses. R. H. Philpott & K. E. Sapire. 1977. pap. text ed. 7.50 o.p. (ISBN 0-86980-109-0). Verry.

Obstetrics for the Nurse. Barbara Anderson & Pamela Shapiro. LC 77-83424. 1979. pap. text ed. 7.40 (ISBN 0-8273-1330-6); instructor's guide 1.60 (ISBN 0-8273-1331-4). Delmar.

Obstetrics for the Nurse. Barbara Anderson & Pamela Shapiro. 272p. 1981. text ed. 13.95 (ISBN 0-442-21840-0). Van Nos Reinhold.

Obstetrics Illustrated. 3rd ed. Matthew M. Garrey et al. (Illus.). 550p. 1980. pap. text ed. 22.00 (ISBN 0-443-02223-2). Churchill.

Obstetrics Illustrated: 2nd Edition. Matthew M. Garrey et al. LC 73-91453. (Illus.). 536p. 1974. pap. 18.75 o.p. (ISBN 0-443-01118-4). Churchill.

Obstinate Land. Harold Keith. LC 77-1826. (gr. 5 up). 1977. 9.95 (ISBN 0-690-01319-1, TYC-J). T Y Crowell.

Obtaining Citizen Feedback: The Application of Citizen Surveys to Local Governments. Kenneth Webb & Harry P. Hatry. 1973. pap. 3.50 (ISBN 0-87766-055-7, 18000). Urban Inst.

Obvious Illusion. Philip Pocock. LC 80-69634. (Illus.). 96p. 1980. 25.00 (ISBN 0-8076-0987-0); pap. 14.95 (ISBN 0-8076-0994-3). Braziller.

Occasional Horseman. George Canning. (Illus.). 8.05 (ISBN 0-85131-188-1, Dist. by Sporting Book Center). J A Allen.

Occasional Suite. Deidra Baldwin. (Jazz Press Chapbook Ser.). 20p. (Orig.). 1981. pap. 1.50 (ISBN 0-937310-08-5). Jazz Pr.

Occasions for Philosophy. James Edwards & Douglass MacDonald. 1979. pap. text ed. 13.95 (ISBN 0-13-629287-9). P-H.

Occlusal Morphology. Frank V. Celenza. 110p. 1980. pap. 18.00 (ISBN 0-931386-33-0). Quint Pub Co.

Occlusion. 2nd ed. Sigurd Ramfjord & McKinley Ash, Jr. LC 78-151682. (Illus.). 1971. 22.00 (ISBN 0-7216-7441-0). Saunders.

Occlusion, the State of the Art. Frank V. Celenza & John N. Nasedkin. (Illus.). 165p. 1978. 32.00 (ISBN 0-931386-00-4). Quint Pub Co.

Occult ABC. Kurt E. Koch. 1980. 7.95 (ISBN 0-8254-3031-3). Kregel.

Occult & Curative Powers of Precious Stones. William T. Fernie. LC 80-8894. (Harper Library of Spiritual Wisdom Ser.). 496p. 1981. pap. 7.95 (ISBN 0-06-062360-8). Har-Row.

Occult & the Third Reich. Jean Angebert & Michel Angebert. LC 73-2748. (Illus.). 288p. 1974. 8.95 o.p. (ISBN 0-02-502150-8). Macmillan.

Occult Bibliography: An Annotated List of Books Published in English, 1971 Through 1975. Thomas C. Clarie. LC 78-17156. 1978. 24.00 (ISBN 0-8108-1152-9). Scarecrow.

Occult Establishment. James Webb. LC 75-22157. (Illus.). 541p. 1976. 22.50 o.p. (ISBN 0-912050-56-X, Library Pr). Open Court.

Occult Glossary. G. De Purucker. LC 53-37086. 1972. Repr. of 1933 ed. 6.00 (ISBN 0-911500-50-2); softcover 3.50 (ISBN 0-911500-51-0). Theos U Pr.

Occult Lines Behind Life. M. P. Pandit. LC 79-63488. 1979. pap. 3.95 (ISBN 0-89744-001-3). Auromere.

Occult Philosophy. Isabella Ingalese. LC 80-23861. 321p. 1980. Repr. lib. bdg. 12.95x (ISBN 0-89370-649-3). Borgo Pr.

Occult Philosophy. Isabella Ingalese. 1980. pap. 5.95 (ISBN 0-87877-049-6). Newcastle Pub.

Occult Philosophy. Marc E. Jones. LC 48-5791. 1971. 13.50 o.p. (ISBN 0-87878-006-8, Sabian). Great Eastern.

Occult Philosophy in the Elizabethan Age. Frances A. Yates. (Illus.). 1979. 20.00 (ISBN 0-7100-0320-X). Routledge & Kegan.

Occult Revolution: A Christian Meditation. Richard Woods. 1971. pap. 2.95 (ISBN 0-8164-2584-1). Crossroad NY.

Occult Sciences in Atlantis. Lewis Spence. LC 70-16446. 1970. pap. 5.00 (ISBN 0-87728-136-X). Weiser.

Occult Sciences in the Renaissance: A Study in Intellectual Patterns. Wayne Shumaker. LC 70-153552. (Illus.). 1972. 24.50x (ISBN 0-520-02021-9); pap. 6.95 (ISBN 0-520-03840-1). U of Cal Pr.

Occult Symbolism in France: Josephin Peladan & the Salons De la Rose-Croix. Robert Pincus-Witten. LC 75-23809. (Outstanding Dissertations in the Fine Arts - 20th Century). (Illus.). 1976. lib. bdg. 41.00 (ISBN 0-8240-2003-0). Garland Pub.

Occult World. Arnulf Esterer & Louise Esterer. LC 78-18267. (gr. 7 up). 1978. PLB 8.29 (ISBN 0-671-32876-X). Messner.

Occult World. 9th ed. A. P. Sinnett. 1969. 10.25 (ISBN 0-7229-5019-5). Theos Pub Hse.

Occupation & Pay in Great Britain. 2nd, rev. ed. Guy Routh. 269p. 1981. text ed. 37.50x (ISBN 0-333-28417-8, Pub. by Macmilla, England); pap. text ed. 20.00x (ISBN 0-333-28653-7). Humanities.

Occupation: Housewife. Helena Z. Lopata. 400p. 1972. pap. 5.95 (ISBN 0-19-501564-9, GB374, GB). Oxford U Pr.

Occupation: Housewife. Helena Z. Lopata. LC 80-23658. (Illus.). xvi, 387p. 1980. Repr. of 1971 ed. lib. bdg. 25.00x (ISBN 0-313-22697-0, LOOH). Greenwood.

Occupation of Japan & Its Legacy to the Postwar World. Ed. by Lawrence H. Redford. 158p. pap. 4.00. MacArthur Memorial.

Occupation of Japan: Economic Policy & Reform. 382p. pap. 6.00. MacArthur Memorial.

Occupation of Japan: Impact of Legal Refor, Ed. by Lawrence H. Redford. 212p. pap. 5.00. MacArthur Memorial.

Occupational Activities Training Manual: For Severely Retarded Adults. Jay L. Zaetz. (Illus.). 124p. 1969. photocopy ed. spiral 12.50 (ISBN 0-398-02138-4). C C Thomas.

Occupational Alcoholism Programs. Richard L. Williams & Gene H. Moffat. (Illus.). 296p. 1975. 24.75 (ISBN 0-398-03282-3). C C Thomas.

Occupational Cancer & Carcinogenesis. Ed. by Harri Vainio et al. (Illus.). 600p. 1980. text ed. 49.50 (ISBN 0-89116-193-7). Hemisphere Pub.

Occupational Choice. Eli Ginzberg. LC 51-10961. 1951. 17.50x (ISBN 0-231-01846-0). Columbia U Pr.

Occupational Choice: A Selection of Papers from the Sociological Review. W. M. Williams. 1974. pap. text ed. 12.50x (ISBN 0-04-371026-3). Allen Unwin.

Occupational Choices & Training Needs. Leonard A. Lecht. LC 76-24356. (Special Studies). 1977. text ed. 23.95 (ISBN 0-275-23960-8). Praeger.

Occupational Disability: Causes, Prediction, Prevention. Rollard A. Martin. (Illus.). 220p. 1975. 19.75 (ISBN 0-398-03224-6). C C Thomas.

Occupational Employee Assistance Programs for Substance Abuse & Mental Health Problems. Andrea Foote & John C. Erfurt. 1977. pap. 3.50x (ISBN 0-87736-327-7). U of Mich Inst Labor.

Occupational Epidemiology. Richard R. Monson. 256p. 1980. 59.95 (ISBN 0-8493-5793-4). CRC Pr.

Occupational Exposure to Airborne Substances Harmful to Health. 44p. 1981. pap. 6.50 (ISBN 92-2-102442-3, ILO 152, ILO). Unipub.

Occupational Exposure to Mercury. S. A. Kelkar. xi, 112p. 1980. text ed. 15.95x (ISBN 0-86590-001-9). Apt Bks.

Occupational Hazards. Henry H. Roberts. 1981. pap. 2.50 (ISBN 0-8439-0904-8, Leisure Bks). Nordon Pubns.

Occupational Health & Safety Concepts. Gordon Atherly. 1978. 22.50x. Intl Ideas.

Occupational Health & Safety in Canada. G. B. Reschenthaler. 152p. 1979. pap. text ed. 5.00x (ISBN 0-920380-35-2, Pub. by Inst Res Pub Canada). Renouf.

Occupational Health & Safety Management. S. S. Chissick & R. Derricott. LC 80-41218. 720p. 1981. 117.00 (ISBN 0-471-27646-4, Pub. by Wiley-Interscience). Wiley.

Occupational Health & Safety Regulation. Ed. by Marshall L. Miller. LC 78-60849. 154p. 1980. pap. text ed. 22.50 (ISBN 0-86587-078-0). Gov Insts.

Occupational Health As Human Ecology. Stewart Wolf et al. (Illus.). 128p. 1978. 14.75 (ISBN 0-398-03793-0). C C Thomas.

Occupational Health in America. Henry B. Selleck & Albert H. Whittaker. LC 61-16777. (Illus.). 1962. 14.00x o.p. (ISBN 0-8143-1121-0). Wayne St U Pr.

Occupational Health Nursing. Mary L. Brown. LC 80-21024. 368p. 1981. text ed. 21.95 (ISBN 0-8261-2250-7); pap. text ed. cancelled (ISBN 0-8261-2251-5). Springer Pub.

Occupational Health Nursing. Ed. by Brenda Slaney. 177p. 1980. 22.00x (ISBN 0-85664-779-9, Pub. by Croom Helm Ltd England). Biblio Dist.

Occupational Health Practice. 2nd ed. Ed. by R. S. Schilling. LC 80-41044. (Illus.). 512p. 1981. text ed. 49.00 (ISBN 0-407-33701-6). Butterworths.

Occupational Home Economics Notebook. Penelope Easton Kupsinel. (gr. 9-12). text ed. 2.90 o.p. (ISBN 0-686-66739-5, 1109-1110). Interstate.

Occupational Lung Disorders. 2nd ed. W. Raymond Parkes. 1981. text ed. price not set (ISBN 0-407-33731-8). Butterworth.

Occupational Medicine: Principles & Practical Applications. Ed. by Carl Zenz. (Illus.). 944p. 1975. 65.00 (ISBN 0-8151-9864-7). Year Bk Med.

Occupational Radiation Exposure in Nuclear Fuel Cycle Facilities. 640p. 1980. pap. 79.25 (ISBN 92-0-020080-X, ISP527, IAEA). Unipub.

Occupational Safety & Health: A Guide to Information Sources. Ed. by Theodore P. Peck. LC 74-7199. (Management Information Guide Ser.: No. 28). 262p. 1974. 30.00 (ISBN 0-8103-0828-2). Gale.

Occupational Safety Management & Engineering. 2nd ed. Willie Hammar. (Illus.). 608p. 1981. text ed. 19.95 (ISBN 0-13-629410-3). P-H.

Occupational Stress. Ed. by A. McLean. (Illus.). 128p. 1974. 13.50 (ISBN 0-398-03067-7). C C Thomas.

Occupational Stress: Sources, Management & Prevention. Lennart Levi. (Occupational Stress Ser.). 143p. 1981. pap. text ed. 6.50 (ISBN 0-201-04317-3). A-W.

Occupational Survival: The Case of the Local Authority Social Worker. Carole Satyamurti. (Practice of Social Work Ser.: No. 5). 208p. 1981. 25.00x (ISBN 0-631-12441-1, Pub. by Basil Blackwell England); pap. 12.50x (ISBN 0-631-12595-7). Biblio Dist.

Occupational Therapy Case Studies. 2nd ed. Jennie A. Lucci. 1980. pap. 14.00 (ISBN 0-87488-034-3). Med Exam.

Occupational Therapy Examination Review Book, Vol. 1. 3rd ed. Ed. by Elinor Jackson & H. Dwyer Dundon. 1974. pap. 9.50 (ISBN 0-87488-475-6). Med Exam.

Occupational Therapy: Practice Skills for Physical Dysfunction. Lorraine W. Pedretti. (Illus.). 676p. 1981. pap. text ed. 23.95 (ISBN 0-8016-3772-4). Mosby.

Occupations. new ed. Trevor Griffiths. 74p. 1981. pap. 7.50 (ISBN 0-571-11667-1, Pub. by Faber & Faber). Merrimack Bk Serv.

Occupations & Society: Toward a Sociology of the Labor Market. Paul D. Montagna. LC 76-40121. 1977. text ed. 18.95x (ISBN 0-471-61383-5). Wiley.

Occupations & the Social Structure. 2nd ed. Richard H. Hall. LC 74-23243. (Illus.). 384p. 1975. text ed. 17.95 (ISBN 0-13-629345-X). P-H.

Occupations Filing Plan & Bibliography. Wilma Bennett. LC 68-56288. 138p. 1968. pap. text ed. 3.95x (ISBN 0-8134-1055-X, 1055). Interstate.

Occurance at Norman's Burger Castle. James D. Houston. (Capra Chapbook Ser.: No. 2). (Orig.). 1972. pap. 2.50 o.p. (ISBN 0-912264-41-1). Capra Pr.

Occurrence at Owl Creek Bridge. Ambrose Bierce. (Creative's Classics Ser.). (Illus.). 40p. (gr. 4-9). 1980. PLB 6.95 (ISBN 0-87191-770-X). Creative Ed.

Occurrence of Oil & Gas in West Texas. Ed. by F. A. Herald. (Illus.). 456p. 1957. 9.00 (PUB 5716). Bur Econ Geology.

Ocean. Lewis Jones. (Newbury Hse Raders Ser.: Stage 4 - Intermediate). (Illus.). 80p. (Orig.). (gr. 7-12). 1981. pap. text ed. 2.95 (ISBN 0-88377-197-7). Newbury Hse.

Ocean: A Scientific American Book. Scientific American Editors. LC 71-102897. (Illus.). 1969. pap. text ed. 7.95x (ISBN 0-7167-0997-X). W H Freeman.

Ocean & Inland Operator License Preparation Course. rev. ed. Ed. by Richard A. Block. (Illus.). 499p. 1979. pap. text ed. 42.00 (ISBN 0-934114-21-8). Marine Educ.

Ocean-Atmosphere System. A. H. Perry & J. M. Walker. (Illus.). 1977. text ed. 22.00x (ISBN 0-582-48559-2); pap. text ed. 14.95x (ISBN 0-582-48560-6). Longman.

Ocean Basins & Margins, Vol. 5: The Arctic Ocean. Ed. by Alan E. Nairn et al. 610p. 1981. 55.00 (ISBN 0-686-63459-4, Plenum Pr). Plenum Pub.

Ocean Crossing Wayfarer. Frank Dye & Margaret Dye. 1977. 14.95 (ISBN 0-7153-7371-4). David & Charles.

Ocean Energy Systems Program Summary: Fiscal Year Nineteen Seventy Nine. U.S. Dept. of Energy. 285p. 1981. pap. 30.00 (ISBN 0-89934-100-4). Solar Energy Info.

Ocean Engineering Power Systems. A. Douglas Carmichael. LC 74-4343. (Illus.). 1974. 8.00x (ISBN 0-87033-192-2). Cornell Maritime.

Ocean Environment. Ed. by Jonathan Bartlett. (Reference Shelf Ser.). 1977. 6.25 (ISBN 0-8242-0600-2). Wilson.

Ocean Flying. Louise Sacchi. (McGraw-Hill Ser. in Aviation). (Illus.). 240p. 1979. 16.50 (ISBN 0-07-054405-0). McGraw.

Ocean Freight Forwarder, the Exporter & the Law. Gerald H. Ullman. LC 67-25958. 1967. 6.00x (ISBN 0-87033-072-1). Cornell Maritime.

Ocean Laboratory. Athelstan Spilhaus. LC 66-246868. (Illus., Orig.). (gr. 6 up). 1967. PLB 7.95 (ISBN 0-87191-009-8). Creative Ed.

Ocean of Regrets. Noelle B. McCue. (Orig.). 1981. pap. 1.50 (ISBN 0-440-16592-X). Dell.

Ocean of Theosophy. William Q. Judge. (Illus.). 153p. 1915. Repr. of 1893 ed. 5.00 (ISBN 0-938998-07-2). Theosophy.

Ocean Resources: An Introduction to Economic Oceanography. Roger H. Charlier & Bernard L. Gordon. LC 78-61393. (Illus.). 1978. pap. text ed. 9.00 (ISBN 0-8191-0599-6). U Pr of Amer.

Ocean Science. Keith S. Stowe. LC 78-11962. 1979. pap. text ed. 21.95x (ISBN 0-471-04261-7); tchrs' manual avail. (ISBN 0-471-08084-5). Wiley.

Ocean Science: Readings from Scientific American. Intro. by H. W. Menard. LC 77-23465. (Illus.). 1977. text ed. 19.95x (ISBN 0-7167-0014-X); pap. text ed. 9.95x (ISBN 0-7167-0013-1). W H Freeman.

Ocean Space Rights: Developing U.S. Policy. Lawrence Juda. LC 74-1732. (Special Studies). 318p. 1975. text ed. 33.95 (ISBN 0-275-09240-2). Praeger.

Ocean Thermal Energy Conversion: Legal, Political & Institutional Aspects. Ed. by H. Gary Knight et al. LC 77-2049. 1977. 22.95 (ISBN 0-669-01441-9). Lexington Bks.

Ocean Voyaging. David M. Parker. LC 74-78837. 1975. 15.00 (ISBN 0-8286-0068-6). De Graff.

Ocean Wave Energy Conversion. Michael E. McCormick. (Alternate Energy Ser.). 300p. 1981. 30.00 (ISBN 0-471-08543-X, Pub. by Wiley-Interscience). Wiley.

Ocean Wave Measure & Analysis. Compiled by American Society of Civil Engineers. 1240p. 1974. pap. text ed. 62.00 (ISBN 0-87262-116-2). Am Soc Civil Eng.

Ocean Yearbook Two. Ed. by Elisabeth M. Borgese & Norton Ginsburg. LC 79-642855. 1981. 35.00x (ISBN 0-226-06603-7). U of Chicago Pr.

Oceania: Polynesia, Melanesia, Micronesia. Charles P. May. LC 72-13152. (World Neighbors Ser.). (Illus.). 224p. (gr. 6 up). 1973. 7.95 o.p. (ISBN 0-525-67068-8). Elsevier-Nelson.

Oceanic Lithosphere. Cesare Emiliani. LC 62-18366. (The Sea: Ideas & Observations on Progress in the Study of the Seas: Vol. 7). 1712p. 1981. 55.00 (ISBN 0-471-02870-3, Pub. by Wiley-Interscience). Wiley.

Oceanic Micropalaeontology, Vol. 1. A. T. Ramsay. 1977. 120.00 (ISBN 0-12-577301-3). Acad Pr.

Oceanic Pipeline Computations. Alex Marks. 560p. 1980. 75.00 (ISBN 0-87814-143-X). Pennwell Pub.

Oceanic Prehistory. Richard Shutler, Jr. & M. E. Shutler. 1975. pap. text ed. 5.95 (ISBN 0-8465-1938-0). Benjamin-Cummings.

Oceanic Quest: The International Decade of Ocean Exploration. Committee On Oceanography & Committee On Ocean Engineering. (Orig.). 1969. pap. 5.00 (ISBN 0-309-01709-2). Natl Acad Pr.

Oceanographer. Jack Rudman. (Career Examination Ser.: C-550). (Cloth bdg. avail. on request). pap. 10.00 (ISBN 0-8373-0550-0). Natl Learning.

Oceanographic Atlas of the Bering Sea Basin. Myron A. Sayles et al. LC 76-49165. (Illus.). 170p. 1980. 25.00 (ISBN 0-295-95545-7). U of Wash Pr.

Oceanographic Products & Methods of Analysis & Prediction. (Illus.). 1977. pap. 9.25 (ISBN 92-3-101453-6, U555, UNESCO). Unipub.

Oceanographical Engineering. Robert L. Wiegel. 1964. ref. ed. 34.95 (ISBN 0-13-629600-9). P-H.

Oceanography. Boy Scouts Of America. LC 19-600. (Illus.). 48p. (gr. 6-12). 1965. pap. 0.70x (ISBN 0-8395-3306-3, 3306). BSA.

Oceanography. Walter A. Thurber et al. (Exploring Earth Science Program Ser.). (gr. 7-12). 1976. pap. text ed. 4.60 (ISBN 0-205-04745-9, 694745X). Allyn.

Oceanography. Jerome Williams. LC 72-2336. (First Bks). (Illus.). 96p. (gr. 7-12). 1972. PLB 4.90 o.p. (ISBN 0-531-00775-8). Watts.

Oceanography: A View of the Earth. 2nd ed. M. Grant Gross. (Illus.). 1977. 19.95 (ISBN 0-13-629675-0). P-H.

Oceanography: An Introduction. 2nd ed. Dale E. Ingmanson & William J. Wallace. 1979. text ed. 19.95x (ISBN 0-534-00538-1); lab manual 8.95x (ISBN 0-534-00624-8). Wadsworth Pub.

Oceanography: An Introduction to the Marine Environment. Peter K. Weyl. 1970. 21.95 (ISBN 0-471-93744-4). Wiley.

Oceanography & Marine Biology. Ed. by H. Barnes. Incl. Vol. 8. 1970. 40.50 (ISBN 0-02-840940-X); Vol. 10. 1972. 40.50 (ISBN 0-02-840960-4); Vol. 11. 1973. 40.50 (ISBN 0-02-840970-1); Vol. 12. 1974. 40.50 (ISBN 0-02-841010-6); Vol. 13. 1975. 57.75 (ISBN 0-02-841020-3). Hafner.

Oceanography & Marine Biology: An Annual Review, Vol. 15. Ed. by Harold Barnes. 1977. 70.00 (ISBN 0-900015-39-X). Taylor-Carlisle.

Oceanography & Marine Biology: An Annual Review, Vol. 16. Ed. by Harold Barnes. 1978. 75.00 (ISBN 0-900015-44-6). Taylor-Carlisle.

Oceanography & Marine Biology: An Annual Review, Vol. 17. 1979. 80.00 (ISBN 0-08-023849-1). Taylor-Carlisle.

Oceanography & Marine Biology: An Annual Review, Vol. 18. Ed. by Margaret Barnes & Harold Barnes. (Illus.). 528p. 1980. 84.00 (ISBN 0-08-025732-1). Pergamon.

Oceanography & Marine Biology: An Annual Review, Vol. 18. 1980. 95.00. Taylor Carlisle.

Oceanography & Marine Biology: Annual Review, Vol. 14. Ed. by Harold Barnes. 1976. 70.00 (ISBN 0-900015-37-3). Taylor-Carlisle.

Oceanography & Seamanship: A Guide for Ocean Cruising. William G. Van Dorn. LC 73-15377. (Illus.). 550p. 1974. 22.50 (ISBN 0-396-06888-X). Dodd.

Oceanography: Concepts & History. Ed. by Margaret B. Deacon. (Benchmark Papers in Geology: Vol. 35). 1978. 32.00 (ISBN 0-12-786340-0). Acad Pr.

Oceanography: Contemporary Readings in Ocean Sciences. 2nd ed. Ed. by R. Gordon Pirie. (Illus.). 1977. pap. text ed. 8.95x (ISBN 0-19-502119-3). Oxford U Pr.

Oceanography for Practicing Engineers. Luis R. Capurro. LC 71-126339. 1970. 11.95 (ISBN 0-389-00503-7); pap. 9.95 (ISBN 0-8436-0323-2). CBI Pub.

Oceanography in China. 1980. 7.00 (ISBN 0-309-03046-3). Natl Acad Pr.

Oceanography Lab. Melvin Berger. LC 72-2417. (Scientists at Work Ser.). (Illus.). 128p. (gr. 2-4). 1973. PLB 9.89 (ISBN 0-381-99940-8, A56700, JD-J). John Day.

Oceanography Nineteen Sixty-Six: Achievements & Opportunites. Committee On Oceanography. 1967. pap. 6.25 (ISBN 0-309-01492-1). Natl Acad Pr.

Oceanography of the Bering Sea: With Emphasis on Renewable Resources. Ed. by D. W. Hood & E. J. Kelley. (Occasional Pub. Ser. No. 2). 20.00 (ISBN 0-914500-04-X). U of AK Inst Marine.

Oceanography: The Past. Ed. by M. Sears & D. Merriman. (Illus.). 812p. 1980. 37.50 (ISBN 0-387-90497-2). Springer-Verlag.

Oceans. Robert Barton. 336p. 1980. 19.95x (ISBN 0-87196-414-7). Facts on File.

Oceans. 2nd ed. Karl K. Turekian. (Illus.). 160p. 1976. pap. 6.95 (ISBN 0-13-630418-4); 11.95 (ISBN 0-13-630426-5). P-H.

Oceans & Continents in Motion. H. Arthur Klein. LC 72-3731. (Introducing Modern Science Ser). (Illus.). 192p. (gr. 8 up). 1972. 7.95 o.p. (ISBN 0-397-31271-7). Lippincott.

Oceans of Energy: Reservoir of Power for the Future. Augusta Goldin. LC 79-3767. (Illus.). 114p. (gr. 7 up). 8.95 (ISBN 0-15-257688-6, HJ). HarBraceJ.

Oceanus: The Marine Environment. Ruth Lebow & Tom Garrison. 204p. 1979. 7.95x (ISBN 0-534-00841-0). Wadsworth Pub.

Ochrana: The Russian Secret Police. Aleksiei T. Vasil'Ev. LC 79-2925. (Illus.). 305p. 1981. Repr. of 1930 ed. 26.50 (ISBN 0-8305-0094-4). Hyperion Conn.

Ochre Robe: An Autobiography. 2nd ed. Agahananda Bharati. 300p. 1980. 14.95 (ISBN 0-915520-40-0); pap. 7.95. Ross-Erikson.

Ochre Robe: An Autobiography. rev. ed. Agehananda Bharati. LC 80-24101. 300p. 1980. 14.95 o.p. (ISBN 0-915520-40-0); pap. 7.95 o.p. (ISBN 0-915520-28-1). Ross-Erikson.

Ocie Dixon's Miracles Through Faith. Lou Mallard. 1979. 4.50 o.p. (ISBN 0-8062-1211-X). Carlton.

Ockham, Descartes, & Hume: Self Knowledge, Substance, & Causality. Julius R. Weinberg. Ed. by William J. Courtenay. 1977. 22.50 (ISBN 0-299-07120-0). U of Wis Pr.

OCLC: An Introduction to Searching & Input. Martha L. Manheimer. LC 79-23985. 1980. text ed. 8.50x (ISBN 0-918212-38-3); text ed. 4.95x 5 or more (ISBN 0-686-66212-1). Neal-Schuman.

OCLC, Inc. Its Goverence, Function, Finance & Technique. Maruskin. 160p. 1980. 22.75 (ISBN 0-8247-1179-3). Dekker.

OCR-A Implementation Handbook. National Retail Merchants Assn. 1979. pap. text ed. 50.00 (ISBN 0-685-95732-2, U1679). Natl Ret Merch.

Ocran's Acronyms: A Dictionary of Abbreviations & Acronyms Used in Scientific & Technical Writing. Emanuel B. Ocran. 1978. 25.00 (ISBN 0-7100-8869-8). Routledge & Kegan.

Octagon Magic. Andre Norton. (Illus.). (gr. 4-6). 1978. pap. 1.75 (ISBN 0-671-56074-3). PB.

Octave of Prayer. Ed. by Minor White. LC 72-87368. (Aperture Vol. 17, No. 1). (Illus.). 96p. 1972. 12.50 o.p. (ISBN 0-912334-36-3); pap. 8.50 o.p. (ISBN 0-912334-37-1). Aperture.

Octavian, Antony & Cleopatra. rev. ed. William W. Tarn & Martin P. Charlesworth. (Orig.). 1965. pap. 6.95x (ISBN 0-521-09354-6). Cambridge U Pr.

Octavian: Prolog to Actium, Antony, Pt. 10. Mark Dunster. 50p. (Orig.). 1981. pap. 4.00 (ISBN 0-89642-074-4). Linden Pubs.

Octavio Paz. J. Wilson. LC 78-18108. 1979. 32.50 (ISBN 0-521-22306-7); pap. 9.95x (ISBN 0-521-29509-2). Cambridge U Pr.

Octavio Paz: Homage to the Poet. Ed. by Kosrof Chantikian. LC 80-82167. 256p. (Orig.). 1981. 15.00 (ISBN 0-916426-03-3); pap. 7.95 (ISBN 0-916426-04-1). Kosmos.

October Dawn. Dorothy C. Raemsch. 26p. 1980. 3.75 (ISBN 0-9605398-0-8). D C Raemsch.

October Revolution. Roy Medvedev. Tr. by George Saunders from Rus. LC 79-9854. 1979. 15.00 (ISBN 0-231-04590-5). Columbia U Pr.

October the First Is Too Late. Fred Hoyle. LC 66-20764. 1966. 7.95 o.s.i. (ISBN 0-06-002845-9, HarpT). Har-Row.

Octopus. Carol Carrick. LC 77-12769. (Illus.). (gr. 1-4). 1978. 6.95 (ISBN 0-395-28777-4, Clarion). HM.

Octopus. Frank Norris. 1976. lib. bdg. 19.50x (ISBN 0-89968-070-4). Lightyear.

Octopus: A Story of California. Frank Norris. LC 76-184737. 464p. 1971. Repr. lib. bdg. 12.50x (ISBN 0-8376-0405-2). Bentley.

Octopus & Squid: The Soft Intelligence. Jacques-Yves Cousteau & Philippe Diole. (Undersea Discoveries of Jacques-Yves Cousteau). (Illus.). 1978. pap. 8.95 (ISBN 0-89104-111-7). A & W Pubs.

Ocular Anatomy. J. D. Spooner. (Illus.). 1972. pap. 24.95 (ISBN 0-407-93412-X). Butterworths.

Ocular Fundus: Methods of Examination & Typical Findings. 4th ed. Arno Nover & Frederick C. Blodi. (Illus.). 212p. 1981. text ed. write for info. (ISBN 0-8121-0709-8). Lea & Febiger.

Ocular Inflammatory Disease. Bruce Golden. (Illus.). 352p. 1974. 32.00 (ISBN 0-398-02792-7). C C Thomas.

Ocular Microsurgery. Ed. by Arthur S. Lim. (Developments in Opthamology Ser.: Vol. 1). (Illus.). 130p. 1981. 36.00 (ISBN 3-8055-1106-X). S Karger.

Ocular Pathology Update. Ed. by Don H. Nicholson. LC 80-80967. (Illus.). 304p. 1980. 59.50 (ISBN 0-89352-051-9). Masson Pub.

Ocular Pharmacology. 4th ed. William H. Havener. LC 78-7208. 1978. text ed. 52.50 (ISBN 0-8016-2105-4). Mosby.

Ocular Therapeutics. Ed. by Dobli Srinivasan. LC 80-80728. (Illus.). 248p. 1980. 42.25 (ISBN 0-89352-084-5). Masson Pub.

Oculoplastic Surgery. Clinton D. McCord, Jr. 300p. 1981. 29.00 (ISBN 0-89004-633-6). Raven.

Ocupate En Ensenar. Crea Ridenour. 1979. pap. 0.95 (ISBN 0-311-11031-2). Casa Bautista.

Odd Animals. Susan Harris. (Easy-Read Wildlife Books). (Illus.). (gr. 2-4). 1977. PLB 4.90 s&l o.p. (ISBN 0-531-00099-0). Watts.

Odd Habitats of Land Animals. Sarah R. Reidman. (gr. 3-6). 1980. 6.95 o.p. (ISBN 0-679-20779-1). McKay.

Odd Job Man. N. J. Crisp. 208p. 1981. pap. 2.25 (ISBN 0-380-54528-4). Avon.

Odd Lot Boys & the Tree Fort War. Janes. (gr. 3-5). pap. 1.25 o.p. (ISBN 0-590-05408-2, Schol Pap). Schol Bk Serv.

Odd Number. Guy De Maupassant. 1889. 10.00 o.s.i. (ISBN 0-06-012855-0, HarpT). Har-Row.

Odd Woman. Gail Godwin. pap. 1.95 o.p. (ISBN 0-425-03167-5). Berkley Pub.

Oddball Fishes & Other Strange Creatures of the Deep. Braz Walker. LC 75-14510. (Illus.). 192p. 1975. 7.95 o.p. (ISBN 0-8069-3726-2); lib. bdg. 7.49 o.p. (ISBN 0-8069-3727-0). Sterling.

Oddballs: The Social Maverick & the Dynamics of Individuality. Bernard G. Suran. LC 77-16660. 1978. 13.95 (ISBN 0-88229-366-4); pap. 6.95 (ISBN 0-88229-557-8). Nelson-Hall.

Oddities in Modern Japan: Obeservations of an Outsider. Peter Milward. (Illus.). viii, 187p. 1980. pap. 11.50 (ISBN 0-89346-183-0, Pub. by Hokuseido Pr). Heian Intl.

Odds & Chances for Kids: A Look at Probability. Manfred Riedel. (Illus.). (gr. 5-9). 1979. PLB 8.95 (ISBN 0-13-630442-7). P-H.

Odds & Ends. Lois Brokering. (A Nice Place to Live Ser.). 1978. pap. 2.25 (ISBN 0-570-07754-0, 12-2713). Concordia.

Odds & Ends of Ward Wit. T. Canarecci. 1976. 7.50 (ISBN 0-87489-021-7). Med Economics.

Odd's End. Tim Wynne-Jones. 1980. 11.95 (ISBN 0-316-96308-9). Little.

Odds on Investing: Survival & Success in the New Stock Market. Eugene D. Brody & Betsy L. Bliss. LC 78-18222. 1978. 19.95 (ISBN 0-471-04478-4, Pub. by Wiley-Interscience). Wiley.

Odds on Miss Seeton. Heron Carvic. LC 75-9348. (Harper Novel of Suspense). 160p. (YA) 1975. 7.95 o.s.i. (ISBN 0-06-010654-9, HarpT). Har-Row.

Odds: On Virtually Everything. Richard Scammon. 1980. 12.95 (ISBN 0-399-12483-7). Putnam.

Ode, Inscribed to John Howard, Repr. Of 1780. William Hayley. Ed. by Donald H. Reiman. Bd. with Essay on Painting: in Two Epistles to Mr. Romney...Third Edition Corrected & Enlarged. Repr. of 1781 ed; Triumphs of Temper; a Poem. In Six Cantos. Repr. of 1781 ed; Essay on Epic Poetry: in Five Epistles to the Rev. Mr. Mason. With Notes... Repr. of 1782 ed. LC 75-31207. (Romantic Context Ser.: Poetry 1789-1830: Vol. 58). 1979. lib. bdg. 47.00 (ISBN 0-8240-2157-6). Garland Pub.

Ode to America's Independence: A Bilingual Edition. Vittorio Alfieri. Tr. by Adolph Caso. 60p. 1980. pap. text ed. 5.00 (ISBN 0-937832-01-4). Dante Univ Bkshlf.

Ode to the Sea & Other Poems. Howard Baker. LC 66-20097. 77p. 1966. 4.95 (ISBN 0-8040-0228-2). Swallow.

Odes. Charles Boer. LC 70-75737. (New Poetry Ser: No. 36). 51p. 1969. 5.50 (ISBN 0-8040-0229-0). Swallow.

Odes by George Dyer, M. Robinson, Anna Laetitia Barbauld, Repr. Of 1800 Ed. George Dyer. Ed. by Donald H. Reiman. Bd. with Poet's Fate, a Poetical Dialogue. Repr. of 1797 ed. LC 75-31197. (Romantic Context Ser.: Poetry 1789-1830). 1979. lib. bdg. 47.00 (ISBN 0-8240-2148-7). Garland Pub.

Odes for Odd Occasions. James Broughton. 1977. signed ed. 12.00 o.p. (ISBN 0-686-19030-0). Man-Root.

Odes on Various Subjects. Joseph Warton. LC 77-8452. 1977. Repr. of 1746 ed. 20.00x (ISBN 0-8201-1291-7). Schol Facsimiles.

Odes, Pastorals, Masques. John Milton. Ed. by Broadbent et al. LC 73-94355. (Milton for Schools & Colleges). 300p. 1975. pap. text ed. 8.50x (ISBN 0-521-20456-9). Cambridge U Pr.

Odessy of the Blithe Spirit II. Robert Schwaig. 200p. (Orig.). pap. 6.95 (ISBN 0-86629-024-9). Sunrise MO.

Odhams Knitting Encyclopaedia. Intro. by A. Mayfield. (Illus.). 1971. 8.95 (ISBN 0-600-72123-X). Transatlantic.

Odi Barbare: Italian Text with English Prose. Giosue Carducci. Tr. by William F. Smith. 1950. 6.50 o.p. (ISBN 0-913298-40-9). S F Vanni.

Odi Et Amo: The Complete Poetry of Latussus. Catullus. Tr. by Roy A. Swanson. LC 59-11685. 1959. pap. 3.95 (ISBN 0-672-60314-4, LLA114). Bobbs.

Odilon Redon. Andre Mellerio. LC 67-27461. (Graphic Art Ser). (Fr). 1968. Repr. of 1913 ed. lib. bdg. 55.00 (ISBN 0-306-70975-9). Da Capo.

Odious Commerce: Britain, Spain & the Abolition of the Cuban Slave Trade. David R. Murray. LC 79-52835. (Cambridge Latin American Studies: No. 37). 435p. Date not set. 44.50 (ISBN 0-521-22867-0). Cambridge U Pr.

Odissea Finita. Gerald Fabian. 1969. signed ed. 5.00 (ISBN 0-686-28710-X); pap. 2.00 (ISBN 0-686-28711-8). Man-Root.

Odiyan Country Cookbook. Bill Farthing. (Illus.). 1977. pap. 5.95 (ISBN 0-913546-19-4). Dharma Pub.

Odonata of Canada & Alaska, Vol. 1. Edmund M. Walker. LC 54-4344. (Illus.). 1953. 35.00x o.p. (ISBN 0-8020-7074-4). U of Toronto Pr.

Odonata of Canada & Alaska, Vol.2. Edmund M. Walker. LC 54-4344. 1958. 35.00x o.p. (ISBN 0-8020-7076-0). U of Toronto Pr.

Odor Quality & Chemical Structure. Ed. by H. R. Moskowitz & Craig Warren. (ACS Symposium Ser.: No. 148). 1981. price not set (ISBN 0-8412-0607-4). Am Chemical.

Odors from Golden Vials. C. E. Orr. 78p. pap. 0.60. Faith Pub Hse.

Odors from Stationary & Mobile Sources. Board on Toxicology & Environmental Health Hazards. 1979. pap. 20.50 (ISBN 0-309-02877-9). Natl Acad Pr.

Odysseus Elytis: Analogies of Light. Ivar Ivask. LC 80-5240. (Illus.). 130p. 1980. 12.50 (ISBN 0-8061-1715-X); pap. 5.95 (ISBN 0-8061-1692-7). U of Okla Pr.

Odysseus: The Complete Adventures. Dennis J. Hartzell. (Illus.). 92p. (Orig.). (gr. 7-9). 1978. pap. text ed. 2.75x (ISBN 0-88334-110-7). Ind Sch Pr.

Odysseus to Columbus: A Synopsis of Classical & Medieval History. C. Warren Hollister. LC 74-2428. 352p. 1974. pap. text ed. 10.95 (ISBN 0-471-40689-9). Wiley.

Odyssey. Homer. Tr. by W. H. Rouse. 1971. pap. 1.75 (ISBN 0-451-61824-6, ME1824, Ment). NAL.

Odyssey. Homer. LC 61-8886. 1961. 12.50 o.p. (ISBN 0-385-09553-8). Doubleday.

Odyssey. Homer. Tr. by S. O. Andrew. 1953. 5.00x o.p. (ISBN 0-460-00454-9, Evman). Dutton.

Odyssey. Homer. Tr by Walter Shewring. (World's Classics Ser.). 384p. 1981. pap. 4.95x (ISBN 0-19-281542-3). Oxford U Pr.

Odyssey, Bks. 6 & 7. Homer. Ed. by Gerald M. Edwards. (Gr.). 1915. text ed. 5.75x (ISBN 0-521-05322-6). Cambridge U Pr.

Odyssey: Critical Ed. Homer. Ed. & tr. by Albert Cook. 1974. 10.00 (ISBN 0-393-04161-1); pap. 4.95x (ISBN 0-393-09971-7). Norton.

Odyssey of an American Composer. Otto Luening. (Illus.). 1980. 22.50 (ISBN 0-684-16496-5, ScribT). Scribner.

Odyssey of Ben O'Neal. Theodore Taylor. LC 76-23800. (gr. 3-7). 1977. 5.95a o.p. (ISBN 0-385-00166-5); PLB (ISBN 0-385-00289-0). Doubleday.

Odyssey of Enoch: A Political Memoir. Humphry Berkeley. (Illus.). 1978. 17.95 (ISBN 0-241-89623-1, Pub. by Hamish Hamilton England). David & Charles.

Odyssey of Farah Antun: A Syrian Christian's Quest for Secularism. Donald M. Reid. LC 74-80598. (Studies in Middle Eastern History: No. 2). 1975. 23.50x (ISBN 0-88297-009-7). Bibliotheca.

Odyssey of Homer. Homer. Tr. by Ennis Rees. LC 76-55800. (Library of Liberal Arts: 225). 1977. pap. 6.50 (ISBN 0-672-61415-4). Bobbs.

Odyssey of Martin Luther King, Jr. Lee A. McGriggs. LC 77-26343. 1978. pap. text ed. 9.00x o.p. (ISBN 0-8191-0415-9). U Pr of Amer.

Odyssey Reader: Ideas & Style. Newman P. Birk & Genevieve B. Birk. LC 68-13057. 1968. 12.95 (ISBN 0-672-63187-3); pap. 7.95 (ISBN 0-672-63075-3). Odyssey Pr.

OECD Economic Survey: Austria. OECD Staff. (OECD Economic Surveys 1980 Ser.). (Illus.). 62p. (Orig.). 1980. pap. 3.50x (ISBN 92-64-12029-7). OECD.

Oedipus. Seneca. Tr. by Moses Hadas. LC 55-13616. 1955. pap. 2.50 (ISBN 0-672-60210-5, LLA44). Bobbs.

Oedipus & Ahknaton. Immanuel Velikovsky. 1980. pap. write for info. (ISBN 0-671-83193-3). PB.

Oedipus at Colonus. Sophocles. Tr. by Gilbert Murray. 1948. pap. text ed. 3.95x (ISBN 0-04-882050-4). Allen Unwin.

Oedipus Burning. David Lang. LC 80-5408. 204p. 1981. 11.95 (ISBN 0-8128-2722-8). Stein & Day.

Oedipus Cycle of Sophocles. Sophocles. Tr. by Dudley Fitts & Robert Fitzgerald. Incl. Oedipus Rex; Antigone; Oedipus at Colonus. 243p. 1955. pap. 2.95 (ISBN 0-15-683838-9, HB8, Harv). HarBraceJ.

Oedipus, King of Thebes. Sophocles. Tr. by Gilbert Murray. pap. text ed. 3.95x (ISBN 0-04-882052-0). Allen Unwin.

Oedipus: Myth & Drama. Ed. by Martin Kallich et al. LC 67-18744. 1968. pap. 7.95 (ISBN 0-672-63076-1). Odyssey Pr.

Oedipus Rex. M. Karl Kulikowski. (Orig.). 1979. pap. 4.75 (ISBN 0-933906-06-4). Gusto Pr.

Oedipus the King. Sophocles. Tr. by Stephen Berg & Diskin Clay. (Greek Tragedy in New Translations Ser.). 1978. 10.95x (ISBN 0-19-502325-0). Oxford U Pr.

Oedipus Tyrannus. Sophocles. (Norton Critical Editions Ser). (Orig.). 1970. text ed. 5.00 (ISBN 0-393-04307-X); pap. 4.95x (ISBN 0-393-09874-5). Norton.

Oedipus Tyrannus. smaller ed. Sophocles. (Gr.). text ed. 8.95x (ISBN 0-521-06527-5). Cambridge U Pr.

Oedipus Tyrannus: Lame Knowledge & the Homosporic Womb. John Hay. LC 78-57075. 1978. pap. text ed. 8.00 (ISBN 0-8191-0518-X). U Pr of Amer.

Oeuvre Complet de Eugene Delacroix: Peintures, Dessins, Gravures Lithographies. Alfred Robaut. LC 78-75310. (History & Literature of Art Ser). 1969. lib. bdg. 55.00 (ISBN 0-306-71628-3). Da Capo.

Oeuvres, 2 Vols. E. Laguerre. LC 70-125075. (Fr). 1971. Repr. of 1905 ed. text ed. 39.50 (ISBN 0-8284-0263-9). Chelsea Pub.

Oeuvres Completes d'antoine de Fevin. Ed. by Edward Clinkscale. (Gesamtausgaben - Collected Works Ser.: Vol. XI, No. 1). xvi, 134p. (Eng. & Ger.). 1980. lib. bdg. 55.00 (ISBN 0-912024-68-2). Inst Mediaeval.

Oeuvres critiques: Petits Poemes en prose. Charles Baudelaire. (Nouveaux Classiques Larousse). (Fr). pap. 2.95 (ISBN 0-685-14010-5, 20). Larousse.

Oeuvres diverses, 5 Vols. Pierre Bayle. Ed. by E. Labrousse. Orig. Title: Oeuvres completes. 1969. Repr. of 1727 ed. 780.00 set (ISBN 0-685-05263-X). Adler.

Oeuvres philosophiques. Francois M. De Voltaire. (Documentation thematique). (Fr). pap. 2.95 (ISBN 0-685-14012-1, 351). Larousse.

Oevres: Collected Papers, 2 Vols. P. L. Chebyshev. LC 61-17956. (Fr). 69.50 set (ISBN 0-8284-0157-8). Chelsea Pub.

Of a Homosexual Teacher: Beneath the Mainstream of Constitutional Equalities. Patricia B. Fry & Ronald A. Rubinstein. (Scholarly Monographs). 180p. 1981. pap. 15.00 (ISBN 0-8408-0508-X). Carrollton Pr.

Of a World That Is No More. I. J. Singer. LC 73-134665. 1970. 10.00 (ISBN 0-8149-0683-4). Vanguard.

Of Age & Innocence. George Lamming. 414p. 1981. 13.95 (ISBN 0-8052-8095-2, Pub. by Allison & Busby England); pap. 5.95 (ISBN 0-8052-8094-4). Schocken.

Of All Things Most Yielding. Marc Lappe & John C. McCurdy. Ed. by David R. Brower. Tr. by Betty L. Moulton. LC 73-8379. (Celebrating the Earth Ser). (Illus.). 128p. 1973. 14.95 o.p. (ISBN 0-913890-25-1); pap. 6.95 o.p. (ISBN 0-685-56641-2, Co-Pub. by Ballantine). Friends Earth.

Of Art & Artists. Louis Dollarhide. LC 80-52629. (Illus.). 168p. 1981. 24.95. Yoknapatawpha.

Of Being & Meaning. Hans C. Syz. 1981. 6.00 (ISBN 0-8022-2374-5). Philos Lib.

Of Bones & Stars. Evelyn Thorne. 24p. (Orig.). 1981. pap. 3.00 (ISBN 0-934996-12-1). Am Stud Pr.

Of Building: Roger North's Writings on Architects. Howard Colvin & John Newman. (Illus.). 200p. 1981. 45.00 (ISBN 0-19-817325-3). Oxford U Pr.

Of, by & for the People: State & Local Governments & Politics. Morris J. Levitt & Eleanor G. Feldbaum. 300p. 1980. lib. bdg. 27.00x (ISBN 0-89158-591-5); pap. text ed. 12.00x (ISBN 0-89158-896-5). Westview.

Of Cabbages & Kings Cookbook. Charlotte Turgeon. LC 77-85390. (Illus.). 1977. 8.95 (ISBN 0-89387-014-5). Sat Eve Post.

Of Celebration of Morning. Higgins. write for info. (ISBN 0-914162-45-4); signed & numbered ed. avail. (ISBN 0-914162-46-2). Knowles.

Of Children: An Introduction to Child Development. 3rd ed. Guy R. Lefrancois. 560p. 1979. text ed. 19.95x (ISBN 0-534-00806-2); study guide 6.95x (ISBN 0-534-00840-2). Wadsworth Pub.

Of Clouds & Sunshine. Michele F. Keegan. 36p. 1981. 3.50 (ISBN 0-8059-2772-7). Dorrance.

Of Cobblers & Kings. Aure Sheldon. LC 77-24725. (Illus.). 40p. (ps-3). 1978. lib. bdg. 6.95 (ISBN 0-590-07728-7, Four Winds); PLB 5.41 o.p. (ISBN 0-8193-0832-3). Schol Bk Serv.

Of Comfort & Despair: Shakespeare's Sonnet Sequence. Robert W. Witt. (SSEL Elizabethan & Renaissance Studies: NO. 77). 1979. pap. text ed. 25.00x (ISBN 0-391-01620-2). Humanities.

Of Corporations, Fraternities, & Guilds, or a Discourse Wherein the Learning of the Law Touching Bodies-Politique Is Unfolded...with Forms & Presidents of Charters of Corporations. William Sheppard. Ed. by David Berkowitz & Samuel Thorne. LC 77-86635. (Classics of English Legal History in the Modern Era Ser.: Vol. 88). 1979. Repr. of 1659 ed. lib. bdg. 55.00 (ISBN 0-8240-3075-3). Garland Pub.

Of Costliest Emblem: Paradise Lost & the Emblem Tradition. Shahla Anand. LC 78-59853. (Illus.). 1978. pap. text ed. 11.25 (ISBN 0-8191-0556-2). U Pr of Amer.

Of Councils & Counselors, 1570: An English Reworking by Thomas Blundeville of el Consejo I Consejeros Del Principe, 1559. Fadrique Furio Ceriol. LC 63-7083. 1963. 20.00x (ISBN 0-8201-1018-3). Schol Facsimiles.

Of Course Polly Can Do Almost Everything. Astrid Lindgren. (Illus.). 1978. 6.95 o.p. (ISBN 0-695-80967-9); lib. bdg. 6.99 o.p. (ISBN 0-695-40967-0). Follett.

Of Course Polly Can Ride a Bike. Astrid Lindgren. (Picture Bk). (Illus.). 32p. (gr. k-3). 1972. 6.95 o.p. (ISBN 0-695-40349-4). Follett.

Of Course You Can! Hoyt E. Stone. 1973. pap. 1.75 (ISBN 0-87148-654-7). Pathway Pr.

Of Course You Can Sew: Basics of Sewing for the Young Beginner. Barbara Corrigan. LC 77-110030. (gr. 5 up). 1971. 4.95 o.p. (ISBN 0-385-07697-5); PLB (ISBN 0-385-03241-2). Doubleday.

Of Delinquency & Crime: A Panorama of Years of Search & Research. S. Glueck & E. Glueck. (Criminal Law Education & Research Genter Ser.). 384p. 1974. 17.50 (ISBN 0-398-02989-X). C C Thomas.

Of Divers Arts. Naum Gabo. (Bollingen Ser. Vol. 35; A. W. Mellow Lecture Ser. No. 8). (Illus.). 1962. 21.00x (ISBN 0-691-09794-1, 224). Princeton U Pr.

Of Dope & Dervishes. Louis Gainesborough. 1981. 8.95. Green Hill.

Of Finnish Ways. Aini Rajanen. LC 80-28932. (Heritage Books). (Illus.). 232p. 1981. 8.95 (ISBN 0-87518-214-3). Dillon.

Of Holy Disobedience. A. J. Muste. 23p. 1952-1964. pap. 0.75 (ISBN 0-934676-09-7). Greenlf Bks.

Of Human Bondage. W. Somerset Maugham. 685p. Date not set. pap. 3.95 (ISBN 0-394-70137-2, Vin). Random.

Of Human Bondage Notes. Cliff's Notes Editors. (Orig.). pap. 1.95 (ISBN 0-8220-0930-7). Cliffs.

Of Human Freedom. Friedrich W. Schelling. Tr. by James Gutmann. 128p. 1936. 10.95 (ISBN 0-87548-024-1); pap. 3.95 (ISBN 0-87548-025-X). Open Court.

Of Humans: Introductory Psychology by Kongor. Guy R. Lefrancois. LC 73-91422. 1974. text ed. 13.95 o.p. (ISBN 0-8185-0120-0); instructor's manual avail. o.p. (ISBN 0-685-42222-4). Brooks-Cole.

Of Kennedys & Kings: Making Sense of the Sixties. Harris Wofford. 496p. 1980. 17.50 (ISBN 0-374-22432-3). FS&G.

Of Laws in General. Jeremy Bentham. Ed. by H. L. Hart. (Collected Works of Jeremy Bentham Ser.). 1970. text ed. 27.00x (ISBN 0-485-13210-9, Athlone Pr). Humanities.

Of Life & Love & Such. Aimee Leon. 1981. 5.95 (ISBN 0-533-04860-5). Vantage.

Of Light & Sounding Brass. V. S. Yanovsky. Tr. by Isabella Levitin from Rus. LC 72-83353. 296p. 1972. 8.95 (ISBN 0-8149-0719-9). Vanguard.

Of Love & Battle. Hugh Zachary & Elizabeth Zachary. 480p. (Orig.). 1981. pap. 2.75 (ISBN 0-345-28610-3). Ballantine.

Of Love & Death & Other Journeys. Isabelle Holland. LC 74-30012. (gr. 7 up). 1975. 9.95 (ISBN 0-397-31566-X). Lippincott.

Of Love & Intrigue. Virginia Coffman. Bd. with Chinese Door. 1980. pap. 1.95 (J9313, Sig). NAL.

Of Love & Lust. Theodore Reik. 1976. pap. 2.25 o.s.i. (ISBN 0-515-03971-3). Jove Pubns.

Of Love & Time. Joseph B. Roberts, Jr. LC 80-50319. 1980. 7.95 (ISBN 0-916624-30-7). TSU Pr.

Of Matters Great & Small. Isaac Asimov. (Isaac Asimov Collection Ser). 320p. 1976. pap. 2.25 (ISBN 0-441-61072-2). Ace Bks.

Of Men & Crabs. Josue De Castro. LC 79-139980. 1979. 7.95 (ISBN 0-8149-0667-2). Vanguard.

Of Men & Galaxies. Fred Hoyle. LC 64-25266. (Jessie & John Danz Lecture Ser). 83p. 1964. 6.95 (ISBN 0-295-73859-6). U of Wash Pr.

Of Men & Machines. Ed. by Arthur O. Lewis, Jr. 1963. pap. 3.95 o.p. (ISBN 0-525-47130-8). Dutton.

Of Men & Monsters. William Tenn. 256p. 1975. pap. 2.50 o.p. (ISBN 0-345-24884-8). Ballantine.

Of Men & Monsters. William Tenn. 256p. (Orig.). 1981. pap. 2.50 (ISBN 0-345-29523-4, Del Rey). Ballantine.

Of Men & Music. Deems Taylor. LC 80-2305. 1981. Repr. of 1937 ed. 36.00 (ISBN 0-404-18873-7). AMS Pr.

Of Men & Plants. Maurice Messegue. LC 72-81079. 384p. 1973. 6.95 o.s.i. (ISBN 0-02-584380-X). Macmillan.

Of Men & Stars: A History of Lockheed Aircraft Corporation. Lockheed Aircraft Corporation. Ed. by James Gilbert. LC 79-7280. (Flight: Its First Seventy-Five Years Ser.). (Illus.). 1979. Repr. of 1957 ed. lib. bdg. 21.00x (ISBN 0-405-12189-X). Arno.

Of Men, Matter & Me. R. V. Rama Rao. 4.50x o.p. (ISBN 0-210-34006-1). Asia.

Of Mice & Magic: A History of American Animated Cartoons. Leonard Maltin. LC 79-21923. (Illus.). 488p. 1980. 19.95 (ISBN 0-07-039835-6, P&RB). McGraw.

Of Mice & Magic: A History of American Animated Cartoons. Leonard Maltin. 1980. pap. 9.95 (ISBN 0-452-25240-7, 25240, Plume). NAL.

Of Mice & Men. John Steinbeck. 1937. 9.95 (ISBN 0-670-52071-3); large type ed. 6.50 (ISBN 0-670-52073-X, LT1). Viking Pr.

Of Mice & Mice. Jean G. Howard. LC 78-50486. (Illus., Ltd. ed. 1000 trade, 35 deluxe). (ps-3). 1978. 10.50 (ISBN 0-930954-03-3); deluxe ed. 50.00 (ISBN 0-930954-04-1). Tidal Pr.

Of Microbes & Life. Ed. by Jacques Monod & Ernest Borek. LC 71-133382. (Molecular Biology Ser). (Illus.). 1971. 20.00x (ISBN 0-231-03431-8). Columbia U Pr.

Of Molecules & Men. Francis Crick. LC 66-26994. (Jesse & John Danz Lecture Ser.). 118p. 1967. pap. 3.95 (ISBN 0-295-97869-4, WP-26). U of Wash Pr.

Of Nightingales That Weep. Katherine Paterson. Tr. by Haru Wells. (Illus.). (gr. 5 up). 1980. pap. 1.95 (ISBN 0-380-51110-X, 51110, Camelot). Avon.

Of Other Gods & Other Spirits. E. H. Wendland. 1977. pap. 4.95 (ISBN 0-8100-0034-2, 12-1711). Northwest Pub.

Of Outlaws, Whores, Politicians, Con Men & Other Artists. Larry L. King. 288p. 1981. pap. 3.95 (ISBN 0-14-005755-2). Penguin.

Of Oxygen, Energy & Nutrients, Vol. 1, Pt. 1. G. Semenza. (Evolving Life Sciences Ser: First-Hand Accounts of Scientific Ideas & Events). 440p. 1981. 90.00 (ISBN 0-471-27923-4, Pub. by Wiley-Interscience). Wiley.

Of Plymouth Plantation: The Pilgrims in America. William Bradford. 8.75 (ISBN 0-8446-1718-0). Peter Smith.

Of Prelates & Princes: A Study of the Economic & Social Position of the Tudor Episcopate. Felicity Heal. LC 79-41791. (Illus.). 368p. 1980. 47.50 (ISBN 0-521-22950-2). Cambridge U Pr.

Of Primary Importance. Maurice J. Thomas. LC 63-22538. (Illus.). 1963. pap. text ed. 1.00x o.p. (ISBN 0-8134-0151-8, 151). Interstate.

Of Quarks, Quasars & Other Quirks: Quizzical Poems for the Supersonic Age. Sara Brewton et al. LC 76-54747. (Illus.). (gr. 4 up). 1977. 8.95 (ISBN 0-690-01286-1, TYC-J). T Y Crowell.

Of Roots & Petals. Jessie S. Grigg. LC 79-57290. 1980. 10.95 (ISBN 0-89754-009-3); pap. 3.50 (ISBN 0-89754-008-5). Dan River Pr.

Of Scientists & Salmanders. Victor C. Twitty. LC 66-24954. (Biology Ser.). (Illus.). 1966. 10.95x (ISBN 0-7167-0652-0). W H Freeman.

Of Smoke & Ash - Mt. St. Helens. J. P. Jones & Betty Jones. (Illus., Orig.). 1980. pap. write for info. (ISBN 0-9604838-0-2). G & BJ's Serv.

Of Sondry Folk: The Dramatic Principles in the Canterbury Tales. R. M. Lumiansky. (Illus.). 286p. 1980. pap. 6.95 (ISBN 0-292-76017-5). U of Tex Pr.

Of Such As These: A History of Motley Country. Eleanor Traweek. 15.00 o.p. (ISBN 0-685-48803-9). Nortex Pr.

Of Swedish Ways. Lilly Lorenzen. (Illus.). 1978. pap. 3.95 (ISBN 0-06-464021-3, BN 4025, BN). Har-Row.

Of the Decorative Illustration of Books Old & New. Walter Crane. LC 68-30611. 1968. Repr. of 1905 ed. 24.00 (ISBN 0-8103-3299-X). Gale.

Of the Education of the Poor. Thomas Bernard. (Social History of Education Ser.: Second Series, No. 1). 380p. 1981. Repr. of 1809 ed. 22.50x (ISBN 0-7130-0010-4, Woburn Pr England). Biblio Dist.

Of the Farm. John Updike. 128p. 1981. pap. 2.50 (ISBN 0-686-69195-4, Crest). Fawcett.

Of the Imitation of Christ. Thomas A'Kempis. (Summit Bks). 1977. pap. 1.95 (ISBN 0-8010-0115-3). Baker Bk.

Of the Imitation of Christ. Thomas A. Kempis. 256p. 1981. pap. 2.50 (ISBN 0-88368-094-7). Whitaker Hse.

Of the Just Shaping of Letters. Albrecht Durer. Tr. by Nichol. 7.50 (ISBN 0-8446-2016-5). Peter Smith.

Of the Just Shaping of Letters: From the Applied Geometry of Albrecht Durer, Book 3. Albrecht Durer. Tr. by R. T. Nichol. (Illus.). 1917. pap. 3.00 (ISBN 0-486-21306-4). Dover.

Of the Press, by the Press, for the Press (& Others, Too) 2nd ed. Washington Post Writers Group. 1976. pap. text ed. 8.75 (ISBN 0-395-24016-6). HM.

Of the Standard of Taste & Other Essays. David Hume. Ed. by John W. Lenz. LC 64-66070. 1965. pap. 6.50 (ISBN 0-672-60269-5). Bobbs.

Of Time & Experience: Literary Themes. R. Dodge & P. Lindblom. 1972. pap. 11.95 (ISBN 0-87626-630-8, 630). P-H.

Of Time & the River, 2 vols. Thomas Wolfe. (Contemporary Classics). 1971. pap. 9.95 set (ISBN 0-684-16649-6, SL284, ScribT). Scribner.

Of Time & the River. Thomas Wolfe. 1935. lib.rep.ed. 17.50x o.p. (ISBN 0-684-14739-4, ScribT). Scribner.

Of Time & Value. Carla Vento. (Illus.). 96p. (Orig.). 1980. tchr's ed 4.95 (ISBN 0-914634-76-3, 8002). DOK Pubs.

Of Time, Space, & Other Things. Isaac Asimov. 1975. pap. 1.75 (ISBN 0-380-00325-2, 35584, Discus). Avon.

Of Walking in Ice. Werner Herzog. Tr. by Alan Greenberg from Ger. 96p. 1980. 9.95 (ISBN 0-934378-14-2); pap. 4.95 (ISBN 0-934378-01-0). Tanam Pr.

Of Water & the Spirit: A Liturgical Study of Baptism. Alexander Schmemann. LC 74-30061. 170p. 1974. pap. 4.95 (ISBN 0-913836-10-9). St Vladimirs.

Of Whom the World Was Not Worthy. Marie Chapian. LC 78-769. (Illus.). 1978. pap. 3.95 (ISBN 0-87123-250-2, 210417). Bethany Fell.

Of Wolves & Men. Barry H. Lopez. LC 78-6070. (Encore Edition). (Illus.). 1979. 5.95 (ISBN 0-684-16909-6, ScribT); pap. 7.95 (ISBN 0-684-16322-5, SL882, ScribT). Scribner.

Of Women & Their Elegance. Norman Mailer. (Illus.). 1980. 29.95 (ISBN 0-671-24020-X). S&S.

Of Wrath & Praise. Tom Taylor. 224p. (Orig.). 1981. pap. 2.95 (ISBN 0-8024-9249-5). Moody.

Off & Walking: A Hiker's Guide to American Places. Ruth Rudner. LC 76-29913. (Illus.). 1977. pap. 4.95 o.p. (ISBN 0-03-015591-6). HR&W.

Off-Beat Walks in London. rev. ed. 56p. 1980. pap. 2.95 (ISBN 0-85263-378-5, Pub. by B T A). Merrimack Bk Serv.

Off Broadway: Essays About the Theatre. Maxwell Anderson. LC 75-77699. (Theater, Film, & the Performing Arts Ser.). 92p. 1971. Repr. of 1947 ed. lib. bdg. 17.50 (ISBN 0-306-71337-3). Da Capo.

Off Center. Barbara G. Harrison. LC 81-80030. 320p. 1981. pap. 2.95 (ISBN 0-87216-870-0). Playboy Pbks.

Off Center. Barbara G. Harrison. 1980. 9.95 (ISBN 0-8037-6677-7). Dial.

Off Highway & Construction Trucks. Arthur Ingram. (Illus.). 160p. 1980. 17.50 (ISBN 0-7137-0960-X, Pub. by Blandford Pr England). Sterling.

Off Key. Betty J. Hudson. (Orig.). 1979. pap. 1.75 (ISBN 0-532-23150-3). Manor Bks.

Off Road Drivers Handbook. Robert Ames. LC 77-92562. (Illus.). 176p. 1981. pap. 6.95 (ISBN 0-89632-002-2). Del Oeste. Postponed.

Off Season. Jack Ketchum. 1981. pap. 2.50 (ISBN 0-345-29427-0). Ballantine.

Off-Stage. Doug Case & Ken Wilson. (Orig.). 1979. pap. text ed. 5.95x (ISBN 0-435-28032-5); tchr's ed. 12.95x (ISBN 0-435-28033-3); tape 28.00x (ISBN 0-435-28035-X); cassette 24.00x (ISBN 0-686-65959-7). Heinemann Ed.

Off Stage & On: An Introduction to Youth Drama. Alison Taylor. 1968. pap. text ed. 4.50 (ISBN 0-08-012968-4). Pergamon.

Off the Court. Arthur Ashe. 1981. price not set (ISBN 0-453-00400-8, H400). NAL.

Off the Middle Way: Report from a Swedish Village. Sture Kallberg. Tr. by Angela Gibbs. LC 77-139709. 1972. 28.50x (ISBN 0-394-46853-8). Irvington.

Off the Pigs! The History & Literature of the Black Panther Party. Ed. by G. Louis Heath. LC 75-45204. 429p. 1976. 18.00 (ISBN 0-8108-0901-X). Scarecrow.

Off the Record: The Private Papers of Harry S. Truman. Ed. by Robert H. Ferrell. LC 79-3390. (Illus.). 448p. 1980. 15.00 (ISBN 0-06-011281-6, HarpT). Har-Row.

Off-The-Road Locomotion: Research & Development in Terramechanics. M. G. Bekker. LC 61-5020. (Illus.). 1960. 10.00 o.p. (ISBN 0-472-04142-8). U of Mich Pr.

Off the Wall. Craig Glassman. (Illus.). 277p. 1980. 12.95 (ISBN 0-8119-0410-5, Pegasus Rex). Fell.

Off the Wall: Interviews with Philip Whalen. Philip Whalen. Ed. by Donald Allen. LC 77-1511. (Writing Ser.: No. 37). 1978. pap. 3.50 (ISBN 0-87704-035-4). Four Seasons Foun.

Off the Wall: Robert Rauschenberg & the Art World of Our Time. Calvin Tomkins. 1981. pap. 5.95 (ISBN 0-14-005812-5). Penguin.

Off Track: Bets & Pieces. Steven Crist. LC 79-6662. 168p. 1981. 9.95 (ISBN 0-385-15215-9). Doubleday.

Off Watch: A Selection of Bunkside Reading. Ed. by James Skellorn. 1979. 21.95x (ISBN 0-8464-0069-3). Beekman Pubs.

Off We Go: A Book of Transportation. William Wise. LC 73-168483. (Finding-Out Book). (Illus.). 64p. (gr. 3-4). 1972. PLB 6.95 (ISBN 0-8193-0532-4). Enslow Pubs.

Off-Wheel Pottery Book. Raymond Hull & Ida C. Larden. (Encore Edition). (Illus.). 1977. 3.95 o.p. (ISBN 0-684-14980-X, ScribT). Scribner.

Off with Their Heads: A Serio-Comic Tale of Hollywood. Frances Marion. (Illus.). 320p. 1972. 8.95 o.s.i. (ISBN 0-02-579500-7). Macmillan.

Offbeat Baja. Jim Honter. 156p. 1977. pap. 5.95 (ISBN 0-87701-093-5). Chronicle Bks.

Offbeat Canada. Gerry Hall. (Orig.). 1981. pap. 2.50 (ISBN 0-451-09842-0, E9842, Sig). NAL.

Offender Restitution in Theory & Action. Ed. by Burt Galaway & Joe Hudson. LC 78-54700. 1978. 18.95 (ISBN 0-669-02328-0). Lexington Bks.

Offenders & Corrections. Ed. by Denis Szabo & Susan Katzenelson. LC 78-8399. (Praeger Special Studies). 1978. 24.95 (ISBN 0-03-044236-2). Praeger.

Offenders in the Community. Edwin M. Lemert & Forrest Dill. LC 77-87184. 1978. 19.95 (ISBN 0-669-01981-X). Lexington Bks.

Offer. Jesse L. Lasky & Pat Silver. LC 80-1813. (Illus.). 800p. 1981. 15.95 (ISBN 0-385-15767-3). Doubleday.

Offering. James Reid. 1978. pap. 1.75 o.s.i. (ISBN 0-685-54631-4, 04768-6). Jove Pubns.

Offshore Drilling Register: A Directory of Self-Contained Mobile Seal-Going Rigs 1980. 6th ed. (Illus.). 123p. 1980. 100.00 (ISBN 0-8002-2462-0). Intl Pubns Serv.

Offical Book of Movie Lists. Gabe Essoe. (Illus.). 256p. 1981. 12.95 (ISBN 0-87000-496-4). Arlington Hse.

Offical Book of TV Lists. Gabe Essoe. (Illus.). 256p. 1981. 12.95 (ISBN 0-87000-497-2). Arlington Hse.

Office Administration Handbook. Clark Fetridge & Robert Minor. 1981. 48.50 (ISBN 0-85013-123-5). Dartnell Corp.

Office Administration Handbook. B. H. Walley. 470p. 1975. text ed. 25.75x (ISBN 0-220-66281-9, Pub. by Busn Bks England). Renouf.

Office & Administrative Management. 3rd ed. Donald L. Caruth et al. 1970. text ed. 18.95 (ISBN 0-13-630996-8). P-H.

Office & Ministry in the Church. Ed. by R. Murphy & B. Van Iersel. LC 72-3946. (Concilium Ser.: Vol. 80 Religion in the Seventies: Scripture). 156p. 1972. pap. 4.95 (ISBN 0-8164-2536-1, 73610). Crossroad NY.

Office Automation Conference Digest Nineteen-Eighty. Ed. by Ira W. Cotton. LC 80-80155. (Illus.). ix, 373p. 1980. pap. 12.00 (ISBN 0-88283-002-3). AFIPS Pr.

Office Dermatology. Henry H. Roenigk, Jr. (Illus.). 340p. 1981. write for info. (7316-8). Williams & Wilkins.

Office Dynamics Company: An Office Services & Temporary Help Practice Set. Olive Church. 250p. 1981. pap. text ed. 6.95 (ISBN 0-205-07136-8); free (ISBN 0-205-07361-1). Allyn.

Office Fun! Paul E. Bierley. LC 76-39578. (Cartoon Ser.). (Illus., Orig.). pap. 2.00 autographed ed. (ISBN 0-918048-01-X). Integrity.

Office Gynecology: An Audiovisual Book. W. Goldfarb. 1971. including three cassettes 37.95 (ISBN 0-685-54393-5). Krieger.

Office Location & the Journey to Work: A Comparative Study of Five Urban Centers. P. W. Daniels. 175p. 1980. text ed. 30.00x (ISBN 0-566-00352-X, Pub. by Gower Pub Co England). Renouf.

Office Location in Urban & Regional Development. John B. Goddard. (Theory & Practice in Geography Ser.). (Illus.). 1975. pap. text ed. 5.95x (ISBN 0-19-874033-6). Oxford U Pr.

Office Machines: A College Course. Weston C. Wilsing. 1974. pap. text ed. 9.50x o.p. (ISBN 0-256-00596-6). Irwin.

Office Management. 5th ed. J. C. Denyer. (Illus.). 528p. 1980. pap. text ed. 17.95x (ISBN 0-7121-1525-0). Intl Ideas.

Office Management & Control. 8th ed. George R. Terry & John J. Stallard. 1980. 17.95x (ISBN 0-256-02271-2). Irwin.

Office Management Handbook. 2nd ed. Ed. by Harry L. Wylie & James Q. Harty. (Illus.). 1958. 37.50 (ISBN 0-8260-9680-8). Ronald Pr.

Office Management of Low Back Pain. Harold Carron & Robert E. McLaughlin. 320p. 1981. 25.00 (ISBN 0-88416-317-2). PSG Pub.

Office of Generall Remembrance - Kept in Cursitors Court. LC 74-80217. (English Experience Ser.: No. 681). 1974. Repr. of 1617 ed. 6.00 (ISBN 90-221-0123-1). Walter J Johnson.

Office of the Future. BCC Staff. 1980. cancelled (ISBN 0-89336-242-5, G-056). BCC.

Office Organisation & Management. S. P. Arora. 1980. text ed. 18.95x (ISBN 0-7069-0795-7, Pub. by Vikas India). Advent Bk.

Office Orthopedics. 4th ed. L. Cozen. (Illus.). 588p. 1975. 39.75 (ISBN 0-398-03068-5); pap. 29.75 (ISBN 0-398-03069-3). C C Thomas.

Office Procedures. Jeffrey R. Stewart, Jr. & Wanda A. Blockhus. LC 79-9095. (Illus.). 1980. text ed. 12.95 (ISBN 0-07-061440-7); General Office Projects 5.20 (ISBN 0-07-061441-5); Administrative Projects 5.20 (ISBN 0-07-061442-3); tchrs. manual & key 5.50 (ISBN 0-07-061443-1). McGraw.

Office Procedures for the Dental Team. new ed. Betty A. Ladley & Jerry Patt. LC 77-23557. 1977. pap. text ed. 16.95 (ISBN 0-8016-2815-6). Mosby.

Office Procedures 2000. Douglas G. Westgate. 512p. 1977. text ed. 15.27 (ISBN 0-7715-0897-2); tchr's. manual 39.93 (ISBN 0-7715-0898-0). Forkner.

Office Suite. Alan Bennett. 60p. 1981. pap. 8.50 (ISBN 0-571-11744-9, Pub. by Faber & Faber). Merrimack Bk Serv.

Office Systems & Careers: A Resource for the Administrative Assistants. Church & Schatz. 780p. 1981. text ed. 18.95 (ISBN 0-205-07134-1, 087134-6); tchrs' ed. avail. (ISBN 0-205-07135-X). Allyn.

Office Without Power: Secretary-General Sir Eric Drummond 1919-1933. James Barros. 1979. 48.00x (ISBN 0-19-822551-2). Oxford U Pr.

Office Work Measurement. H. W. Nance & R. E. Nolan. 1971. 23.50 o.p. (ISBN 0-07-045880-4, P&RB). McGraw.

Officer in Trouble. Jim Viner & Brad Sagstetter. 200p. (Orig.). 1981. price not set (ISBN 0-89896-001-0). Larksdale.

Officers & Committee Directory Nineteen Seventy-Nine to Nineteen Eighty. American Water Works Association. (Rosters & Directories). (Illus.). 121p. 1979. pap. text ed. 4.00 o.p. (ISBN 0-89867-226-0). Am Water Wks Assn.

Officer's Manual of Personal Finance & Insurance. rev 3rd ed. LC 79-140746. (Illus.). 320p. 1979. pap. 11.95 (ISBN 0-8117-1154-4). Stackpole.

Officer's Wives. Thomas Fleming. LC 80-1063. 1981. 15.95 (ISBN 0-385-14805-4). Doubleday.

Offices. Cicero. Tr. by Thomas Cockman. Incl. Laelius, on Friendship; & Cato, on Old Age & Selected Letters. Tr. by W. Melmouth. 1953. 12.95x (ISBN 0-460-00345-3, Evman). Dutton.

Official & Political Manual of the State of Tennessee. Charles A. Miller. LC 73-22440. (Illus.). 380p. 1974. Repr. of 1890 ed. 18.00 (ISBN 0-87152-162-8). Reprint.

Official Boy Scout Handbook. 9th ed. William Hillcourt. LC 78-72563. (Illus.). (gr. 6-12). 1979. 3.45x (ISBN 0-8395-3227-X). BSA.

Official Catalogue of the Uffizi. Intro. by Luciano Berti. (Illus.). 1980. 350.00 (ISBN 88-7038-017-3, Centro Di). Gale.

Official Catholic Teachings, Update 1977. LC 80-82422. (Official Catholic Teachings Ser.). 350p. 1980. text ed. 35.00 (ISBN 0-8434-0742-5, Consortium). McGrath.

Official Catholic Teachings, Update 1978. LC 80-82423. (Official Catholic Teachings Ser.). 400p. 1980. text ed. 35.00 (ISBN 0-8434-0743-3, Consortium). McGrath.

Official Catholic Teachings, Update 1979. LC 80-82424. (Official Catholic Teachings Ser.). 400p. 1980. text ed. 35.00 (ISBN 0-8434-0744-1, Consortium). McGrath.

Official CB Slanguage Language Dictionary: Including Cross Reference. 4th ed. Lanie Dills. pap. 2.95 o.p. (ISBN 0-685-52921-5). L J Martin.

Official Democrat-Republican Joke Book. Larry Wilde. 224p. (Orig.). 1976. pap. 1.50 o.p. (ISBN 0-523-40535-9). Pinnacle Bks.

Official Directory of Industrial & Commercial Traffic Executives: 1981 Edition. Ed. by Callie Possinger. LC 72-626342. (Illus.). 490p. 1980. 37.50 (ISBN 0-87408-019-3). Traffic Serv.

Official Dirty Joke Book. Larry Wilde. (Illus.). 1978. pap. 1.95 (ISBN 0-523-41421-8). Pinnacle Bks.

Official Explanations. Paul Dickson. (Illus.). 225p. 1980. 9.95 (ISBN 0-440-06513-5). Delacorte.

Official Golfers Joke Book. Larry Wilde. 1977. pap. 1.95 (ISBN 0-523-41469-2). Pinnacle Bks.

Official Guide to Ballroom Dancing. Allen Dow. (Illus.). 96p. 1980. 5.98 (ISBN 0-89196-065-1, Domus Bks). Quality Bks IL.

Official Guide to Bottles, Old & New. 4th rev. ed. LC 78-72029. (Illus.). 1979. pap. 9.95 o.p. (ISBN 0-87637-106-3). Hse of Collectibles.

Official Guide to Collector Prints. rev. ed. Pollard. LC 78-72033. (Illus.). 1979. pap. 9.95 o.p. (ISBN 0-87637-108-X). Hse of Collectibles.

Official Guide to Comic & Science Fiction Books. 3rd rev. ed. Resnick. LC 78-61693. (Illus.). 1979. pap. 7.95 o.p. (ISBN 0-87637-102-0). Hse of Collectibles.

Official Guide to Detecting Altered Counterfeit Coins & Currency. Hudgeons. (Collector Ser.). (Illus.). 160p. (Orig.). 1981. pap. 4.95 (ISBN 0-87637-169-1, 169-01). Hse of Collectibles.

Official Guide to Disco Dance Steps. Jack Villari & Kathleen S. Villari. Ed. by Jim Hargrove. LC 78-9849. (Illus.). 1978. 4.95 o.p. (ISBN 0-89009-259-1, Domus Bks); PLB 4.95 o.p. (ISBN 0-89196-025-2). Quality Bks IL.

Official Guide to Jazz Dancing. Allen Dow. (Illus.). 96p. 1980. 5.98 (ISBN 0-89196-064-3, Domus Bks). Quality Bks IL.

Official Guide to Latin Dancing. Allen Dow. (Illus.). 96p. 1980. 5.98 (ISBN 0-89196-067-8, Domus Bks). Quality Bks IL.

Official Guide to Old Books. 2nd rev. ed. Rodgers. LC 78-72024. (Illus.). 1979. pap. 8.95 o.p. (ISBN 0-87637-113-6). Hse of Collectibles.

Official Guide to Pocket Knives. 2nd rev. ed. Parker & Voyles. LC 78-72038. (Illus.). 1979. pap. 9.95 o.p. (ISBN 0-87637-101-2). Hse of Collectibles.

Official Guidebook of China: 1980-1981 Edition. China Travel & Tour Service. pap. 9.95 (ISBN 0-86519-000-3). Green Hill.

Official History of Colonial Development, 5 vols. D. J. Morgan. Incl. Vol. 1. The Origins of British Aid Policy 1924-1945. 253p (ISBN 0-391-01684-9); Vol. 2. Developing British Colonial Resources 1945-1951. 398p (ISBN 0-391-01685-7); Vol. 3. Reassessment of British Aid Policy 1951-1965. 334p (ISBN 0-391-01686-5); Vol. 4. Changes in British Aid Policy 1951-1970. 275p (ISBN 0-391-01687-3); Vol. 5. Guidance Towards Self-Government on British Colonies 1941-1971. 382p (ISBN 0-391-01688-1). 1980. text ed. 37.50x ea. Humanities.

Official Indicators & the Prediction of the Economic & Stock Market Future. James D. Holmes. (Illus.). 1980. deluxe ed. 37.75 (ISBN 0-918968-61-5). Inst Econ Finan.

Official Investors Guide to Buying & Selling Gold, Silver & Diamonds. Hudgeons. (Collector Ser.). (Illus.). 160p. (Orig.). 1981. pap. 4.95 (ISBN 0-87637-171-3, 171-03). Hse of Collectibles.

Official Italian Joke Book. rev. ed. Larry Wilde. 160p. 1981. pap. 1.75 (ISBN 0-523-41196-0). Pinnacle Bks.

Official Jewish Irish Jokebook. Larry Wilde. (Orig.). 1974. pap. 1.95 (ISBN 0-523-41257-6). Pinnacle Bks.

Official Mixer's Manual. rev. ed. Patrick Gavin Duffy. LC 74-25119. 1956. 6.95 (ISBN 0-385-02328-6). Doubleday.

Official Nineteen Seventy Nine-Eighty Guide to Airline Careers: 1979-1980. rev. ed. Alexander C. Morton. (Illus.). 1979. lib. bdg. 9.00 o. p. (ISBN 0-668-04353-9); pap. 6.95 (ISBN 0-668-03955-8). Arco.

Official Papers of Francis Fauquier, Lieutenant Governor of Virginia, 1758-1768: Vol. II, 1761-1763. Ed. by George Reese. LC 80-19866. (Virginia Historical Society Documents Ser.: Vol. 15). 1981. price not set (ISBN 0-8139-0895-7). U Pr of Va.

Official Papers of Francis Fauquier, Lieutenant Governor of Virginia, Seventeen Fifty-Eight to Seventeen Sixty-Eight, Vol. 1. Ed. by George Reese. LC 80-19866. (Virginia Historical Society Documents Ser.: Vol. 14). 1981. 37.50x (ISBN 0-8139-0856-6). U Pr of Va.

Official PGA Tour Media Guide Nineteen Eighty-One. PGA Tour. 240p. 1981. pap. 5.95 (ISBN 0-89480-142-2). Workman Pub.

Official Polish Joke Book. rev. ed. Larry Wilde. 160p. 1981. pap. 1.75 (ISBN 0-523-41195-2). Pinnacle Bks.

Official Position Statements of the American Psychiatric Association in Precise Form 1948-1977. 1977. 3.00 o.p. (ISBN 0-685-77444-9, 300). Am Psychiatric.

Official Price Guide to Antique & Other Collectibles. Grace McFarland. LC 78-67961. 1979. pap. 8.95 o.p. (ISBN 0-87637-340-6). Hse of Collectibles.

Official Price Guide to Antique Jewelry. Arthur G. Kaplan. (Collector Ser.). (Illus.). 400p. 1980. pap. 9.95 (ISBN 0-87637-341-4, 341-04). Hse of Collectibles.

Official Price Guide to Bottles, Old & New. 4th ed. Carlo Sellari & Dot Sellari. (Collector Ser.). (Illus.). 400p. 1980. pap. 8.95 (ISBN 0-87637-106-3, 106-03). Hse of Collectibles.

Official Price Guide to Collector Cars. 2nd ed. Kruse Classic Auction Co. (Collector Ser.). (Illus.). 400p. 1980. pap. 9.95 (ISBN 0-87637-119-5, 119-05). Hse of Collectibles.

Official Price Guide to Collector Prints. 3rd ed. Pollard. (House of Collectibles Ser.). Date not set. 9.95 (ISBN 0-87637-147-0, 5003). Arco.

Official Price Guide to Mint Errors & Varieties. 3rd ed. Hudgeons. (Collector Ser). (Illus.). 182p. 1981. pap. 4.95 (167-05). Hse of Collectibles.

Official Price Guide to Paper Collectibles. House of Collectibles. (Collector Ser.). (Illus.). 400p. 1980. pap. 9.95 (ISBN 0-87637-114-4, 114-04). Hse of Collectibles.

Official Publishing, an Overview: An International Survey & Review of the Role, Organization & Principles of Official Publishing. J. J. Cherns. LC 78-41157. (Guides to Official Publication Ser.: Vol. 3). 1979. 60.00 (ISBN 0-08-023340-6). Pergamon.

Official Records of the Conference on the Establishment of an International Compensation Fund for Oil Pollution Damage, 1971. 742p. 1978. 33.60 (IMCO). Unipub.

Official Rummikub Book: Including Rules, Strategy & Tactics for Winning. Ephraim Hertzano. LC 77-93321. (Illus.). 1978. 6.95 (ISBN 0-8069-4944-9); lib. bdg. 6.69 (ISBN 0-8069-4945-7); pap. 2.95 (ISBN 0-8069-4946-5). Sterling.

Official Russian Joke Book. Steve Leininger. 192p. (Orig.). 1981. pap. 1.95 (ISBN 0-523-41427-7). Pinnacle Bks.

Official Scrabble Player's Dictionary. (gr. 10 up). 1979. pap. 3.75 (ISBN 0-671-43269-9). PB.

Official Soap Opera Annual. Ed. by Bryna Laub. 1977. pap. 1.95 (ISBN 0-345-25695-6, 345-25695-6). Ballantine.

Official USTA Yearbooks, 1980. (Illus.). 1980. pap. text ed. 7.50 (ISBN 0-938822-06-3). USTA.

Official Visitors Guide: Los Angeles. Camaro Editors. 1980. 2.95 (ISBN 0-913290-30-0). Camaro Pub.

Official Visitors Guide: San Francisco. Camaro Editors. 1980. 2.95 (ISBN 0-913290-32-7). Camaro Pub.

Officials of the Boards of Trade 1660-1870. Ed. & intro. by J. C. Sainty. (Office-Holders in Modern Britain Ser: No. 3). 126p. 1974. text ed. 15.00x (ISBN 0-485-17143-0, Athlone Pr). Humanities.

Offshore. (Library of Boating Ser.). (Illus.). 1976. 14.95 (ISBN 0-8094-2136-4). Time-Life.

Offshore! Ross R. Olney. LC 80-10908. (Illus.). 96p. (gr. 5-9). 1981. PLB 10.95 (ISBN 0-525-36305-X). Dutton.

Offshore Crew. Jeremy Howard-Williams. LC 79-65613. (Illus.). 190p. 1980. 12.95 (ISBN 0-396-07779-X). Dodd.

Offshore-Cruising Navigation Racing. Ed. by Time Life Books. LC 76-417. (Library of Boating Ser.). (Illus.). (gr. 6 up). 1976. lib. bdg. 13.95 (ISBN 0-685-73295-9, Pub. by Time-Life). Silver.

Offshore Ecology Investigation. Ed. by C. H. Ward et al. (Rice University Studies: Vol. 65, Nos. 4 & 5). (Illus.). 600p. (Orig.). 1980. pap. 11.00x (ISBN 0-89263-243-7). Rice Univ.

Offshore Fishing in Southern California & Baja. Chuck Garrison. (Illus.). 1977. pap. 4.95 (ISBN 0-87701-166-4). Chronicle Bks.

Offshore Fishing: In Southern California & Baja. Chuck Garrison. (Illus., Orig.). 1980. pap. 4.95 (ISBN 0-87701-166-4). Chronicle Bks.

Offshore Lending by U. S. Commercial Banks. 2nd ed. Ed. by F. John Mathis. LC 80-83082. (Illus.). 344p. 1980. 18.00 (ISBN 0-936742-01-1). R Morris Assocs.

Offshore North Sea 1978, 2 vols. Norwegian Petroleum Society. 1980. 165.00x (Pub. by Norwegian Info Norway). State Mutual Bk.

Offshore Oil & Gas Yearbook 1980-81. Ed. by Martin Beudell. 500p. 1980. 115.00x (ISBN 0-85038-336-6). Nichols Pub.

Offshore Petroleum & New England. Thomas A. Grigalunas. (Marine Technical Report Ser.: No. 39). 1975. pap. 5.00 (ISBN 0-938412-12-4). URI MAS.

Offshore Petroleum Engineering: A Bibliographic Guide to Publications & Information Sources. Ed. by Marjorie Chryssostomidis. 1978. 50.00x (ISBN 0-89397-045-X). Nichols Pub.

Offshore Seismic Data Acquisition & Quality Control. Norwegian Petroleum Society. 287p. 1980. 100.00x (ISBN 82-7270-001-8, Pub. by Norwegian Info Norway). State Mutual Bk.

Offshore Structures. Thomas Telford Ltd. Editorial Staff. 208p. 1980. 75.00x (ISBN 0-7277-0008-1, Pub. by Thomas Telford England). State Mutual Bk.

Offshore Structures: The Use of Physical Models in Their Design. Ed. by G. S. Armer & F. K. Garas. (Illus.). 420p. 1981. 55.00 (ISBN 0-86095-874-4). Longman.

Offsprings of Servagna. Servagna. (Translated rom Kannada). 12.00 (ISBN 0-89253-609-8); flexible cloth 6.75 (ISBN 0-89253-610-1). Ind-US Inc.

Ogg & Ray's Essentials of American National Government. 10th ed. W. Young. 1969. pap. 12.95 (ISBN 0-13-633651-5). P-H.

Ogg & Ray's Essentials of American State & Local Government. 10th ed. Frederic A. Ogg & P. Orman Ray. Ed. by William H. Young. (Illus.). 1969. pap. text ed. 9.95 (ISBN 0-13-633644-2). P-H.

Oggi in Italia: A First Course in Italian. Ferdinando Merlonghi et al. LC 77-83330. 1978. text ed. 16.50 (ISBN 0-395-26244-5); tchrs'. ed. 17.60 (ISBN 0-395-26243-7); wkbk. 5.50 (ISBN 0-395-26242-9); tapes 148.20 (ISBN 0-395-26245-3). HM.

OGrade Questions in Physics. B. H. Crawshaw & J. H. Ritchie. (Orig.). 1979. pap. text ed. 8.25x o.p. (ISBN 0-435-67045-X). Heinemann Ed.

Ogre & His Bride. Nami Kishi. Tr. by Alvin Tresselt from Jap. LC 73-136990. Orig. Title: Oni No Yomesan. (Illus.). (gr. k-3). 1971. 5.95 o.s.i. (ISBN 0-8193-0471-9, Four Winds); PLB 5.41 o.s.i. (ISBN 0-8193-0472-7). Schol Bk Serv.

Ogun Abibiman. Wole Soyinka. 24p. 1976. pap. 5.00x (ISBN 0-86036-031-8). Three Continents.

Ogun: An Old God for a New Age. Sandra T. Barnes. LC 79-26577. (ISHI Occasional Papers in Social Change: No. 3). 1980. pap. text ed. 4.95x (ISBN 0-89727-011-8). Inst Study Human.

Oh! Mary Robison. LC 80-2723. 1981. 10.95 (ISBN 0-394-50947-1). Knopf.

Oh Boy! Babies! Alison C. Herzig & Jane L. Mali. (Illus.). 144p. (gr. 5 up). 1980. 9.95g (ISBN 0-316-35896-7); pap. 5.95 (ISBN 0-316-35897-5). Little.

Oh, God, Not Another Beautiful Day! Debby Wood. LC 80-69857. (Illus.). 128p. 1980. pap. 3.95 (ISBN 0-89305-032-6). Anna Pub.

Oh, How Silly. William Cole. (Illus.). (gr. 4-6). 1970. PLB 3.95 o.p. (ISBN 0-670-52095-0). Viking Pr.

Oh, Lewis! Eve Rice. LC 73-19057. (Illus.). 32p. (ps-2). 1974. 7.95g (ISBN 0-02-775950-4). Macmillan.

Oh Lord, I Wish I Was a Buzzard. Polly Greenberg. LC 68-24103. (Illus.). (gr. k-2). 1968. 10.95 (ISBN 0-02-736730-4). Macmillan.

Oh Millersville! Fern Gravel, pseud. Tr. by Clarence A. Andrews. 100p. (gr. 6-12). 1980. Repr. of 1940 ed. PLB price not set (ISBN 0-934582-01-7). Midwest Heritage.

Oh, My Aching Back: A Doctor's Guide to Your Back Pain & How to Control It. Leon Root & Thomas Kiernan. LC 72-92649. 1980. 3.98 o.p. (ISBN 0-679-50384-6). McKay.

Oh, My Comet, Shine! Found Haiku and Senryu, Based on "Thought Forms" by Mirtala Bentov. J. David Andrews. 60p. (Orig.). 1979. pap. 5.00; pap. text ed. 5.00. Planetary Pr.

Oh, Ranger! rev. 14th ed. Horace M. Albright & Frank J. Taylor. Ed. by William R. Jones. (Illus.). 176p. pap. 6.95 (ISBN 0-89646-068-1). Outbooks.

Oh, Rick. Eve Bunting. (Young Romance Ser). (Illus.). (gr. 3-9). 1978. PLB 5.95 (ISBN 0-87191-634-7); pap. 2.95 (ISBN 0-89812-061-6). Creative Ed.

Oh, Riddlesticks! Ann Bishop. Ed. by Caroline Rubin. LC 76-41418. (Riddle Bk.). (Illus.). (gr. 2-6). 1976. 5.75g (ISBN 0-8075-5916-4). A Whitman.

Oh, Simple! Jane B. Zalben. (Illus.). 32p. (ps up). 1981. 8.95 (ISBN 0-374-35604-1). FS&G.

Oh, Such Foolishness! William Cole. LC 78-1622. (Illus.). (gr. 3-6). 1978. 8.95 (ISBN 0-397-31807-3). Lippincott.

Oh to Be in England. Herbert E. Bates. 167p. 1963. 4.50 o.p. (ISBN 0-374-22492-7). FS&G.

Oh, Were They Ever Happy. Peter Spier. LC 77-78144. (gr. k-3). 1978. 7.95a (ISBN 0-385-13175-5); PLB (ISBN 0-385-13176-3). Doubleday.

Oh, What Nonsense. Ed. by William Cole. (Illus.). (gr. k-6). 1966. PLB 6.95 o.p. (ISBN 0-670-52117-5). Viking Pr.

O'Hara - or Seventeen Ninety-Eight. William H. Maxwell. Ed. by Robert E. Wolff. (Ireland Nineteenth Century Fiction - Ser. Two: Vol. 50). 610p. 1979. lib. bdg. 32.00 (ISBN 0-8240-3499-6). Garland Pub.

O'Hare Story. Charles B. Cannon. LC 80-50072. 54p. 1981. 6.95 (ISBN 0-533-04585-1). Vantage.

Ohio. 33.00 (ISBN 0-89770-059-7). Curriculum Info Ctr.

Ohio: A Bicentennial History. Walter Havighurst. (States & the Nation Ser.). (Illus.). 1976. 12.95 (ISBN 0-393-05613-9, Co-Pub by AASLH). Norton.

Ohio Art & Artists. Edna M. Clark. LC 74-13860. xvi, 509p. 1975. Repr. of 1932 ed. 32.00 (ISBN 0-8103-4058-5). Gale.

Ohio Chronology & Factbook, Vol. 35. R. I. Vexler. 1978. 8.50 (ISBN 0-379-16160-5). Oceana.

Ohio Gang: The World of Warren G. Harding. Charles L. Mee, Jr. Ed. by Herbert M. Katz. 250p. 1981. 12.95 (ISBN 0-87131-340-5). M Evans.

Ohio Guide. Federal Writers' Project. 634p. 1940. Repr. 49.00 (ISBN 0-403-02184-7). Somerset Pub.

Ohio Industrial Directory: 1981. rev. ed. Ed. by Vivian Lace. LC 75-42929. (Illus., Annual). 1981. 65.00 (ISBN 0-916512-55-X). Harris Pub.

Ohio Magazine's Offical Guide to Columbus & Central Ohio. rev. ed. Marion E. Rucker & Anne LaPidus. LC 80-53248. (Illus.). 272p. (Orig.). 1980. pap. 5.95 (ISBN 0-938040-00-6). Ohio Mag.

Ohio One Hundred Years Ago. Kirke et al. (Sun Historical Ser.). (Illus.). pap. 3.50 (ISBN 0-89540-050-2). Sun Pub.

Ohio Real Estate. Bruce Harwood & Elmer Synek. (Illus.). 640p. 1980. ref. ed 19.95; pap. 16.95 (ISBN 0-8359-5189-8). Reston.

Ohio Schoolmistress: The Memoirs of Irene Hardy. Irene Hardy. Ed. by Louis Filler. LC 80-17242. (Illus.). 321p. 1980. 14.50 (ISBN 0-87338-242-0). Kent St U Pr.

Ohio Supplement for Modern Real Estate Practice. 5th ed. Margaret E. Sprencz et al. 128p. (Orig.). 1980. pap. 7.95 (ISBN 0-88462-283-5). Real Estate Ed Co.

Ohio Supplement for Real Estate Principles & Practices. Nicholas Kemock. (Business & Economics Ser.). 80p. 1976. 4.95 (ISBN 0-675-08584-5). Merrill.

Ohio Valley. R. E. Banta. LC 66-19221. (gr. 7 up). 1967. pap. 2.95x (ISBN 0-8077-1044-X). Tchrs Coll.

Ohio's Natural Heritage. Ed. by Michael B. Lafferty. LC 78-60505. 1979. 23.95 (ISBN 0-933128-01-0). Ohio Acad Sci.

Ohlin-Heckscher Theory of the Basis & Effects of Commodity Trade. James L. Ford. 6.00x (ISBN 0-210-27110-8). Asia.

Oikos, the Environment & Education. George O'Hearn. LC 74-33808. (Fastback Ser.: No. 52). (Illus.). 54p. (Orig.). 1975. pap. 0.75 (ISBN 0-87367-052-3). Phi Delta Kappa.

Oil. Barbara Lowery. (Easy-Read Fact Bks.). (Illus.). 48p. (gr. 2-4). 1977. PLB 6.45 (ISBN 0-531-00357-4). Watts.

Oil! Upton Sinclair. LC 79-24682. 1981. Repr. of 1927 ed. lib. bdg. 15.00x (ISBN 0-8376-0444-3). Bentley.

Oil. rev. ed. Harlan Wade. LC 78-27069. (Book About Ser.). (Illus.). (gr. k-3). 1979. PLB 7.30 (ISBN 0-8172-1534-4). Raintree Pubs.

Oil & Development in the Middle East. David G. Edens. LC 79-848. 1979. 22.95 (ISBN 0-03-049141-X). Praeger.

Oil & Gas: From Fossils to Fuel. Hershell H. Nixon & Joan Lowery. LC 77-1671. (Let Me Read Bk.). (Illus.). 64p. (gr. 1-4). 1977. 5.95 (ISBN 0-15-257700-9, HJ). HarBraceJ.

Oil & Gas in Comecon. J. D. Park. 1979. 39.50x (ISBN 0-89397-040-9). Nichols Pub.

Oil & Geopolitics in the Persian Gulf Area: A Center of Power. Enver M. Koury. LC 73-85565. 96p. 1973. pap. 5.00 (ISBN 0-934484-03-1). Inst Mid East & North Africa.

Oil & Its' Impact: A Case Study of Community Change. John J. Pfuhl. LC 80-5090. 164p. 1980. text ed. 17.25 (ISBN 0-8191-1043-4); pap. text ed. 9.00 (ISBN 0-8191-1044-2). U Pr of Amer.

Oil & Natural Gas. Betsy H. Kraft. (First Bks). (Illus.). (gr. 4 up). 1978. PLB 6.45 (ISBN 0-531-01411-8). Watts.

Oil & Regional Development: Examples from Algeria & Tunisia. Konrad Schliephake. LC 76-24367. (Praeger Special Studies). 1977. text ed. 25.95 (ISBN 0-275-23910-1). Praeger.

Oil & the Changed Structure of the World at the Beginning of the 21st Century. Emmanuel J. Crawford. 1980. 54.75 (ISBN 0-930008-49-9). Inst Econ Pol.

Oil Burners. 3rd ed. Edwin M. Field. LC 76-45884. (Illus.). 1977. 9.95 (ISBN 0-672-23277-4, 23277). Audel.

Oil Cartel Case: A Documentary Study of Antitrust Activity in the Cold War Era. Burton I. Kaufman. LC 77-87963. (Contributions in American History: No. 72). (Illus.). 1978. lib. bdg. 17.95x (ISBN 0-313-20043-2, KOC/). Greenwood.

Oil Companies in the International System. Louis Turner. 1978. text ed. 25.00x (ISBN 0-04-382020-4). Allen Unwin.

Oil Company Divestiture & the Press: Economic Vs. Journalistic Perceptions. Barbara Hobbie. LC 77-10627. (Praeger Special Studies). 1977. 24.95 (ISBN 0-03-022841-7). Praeger.

Oil Countries of the Middle East. Emil Lengyel. LC 73-5891. (First Bks). (gr. 6-9). 1973. PLB 4.90 o.p. (ISBN 0-531-00809-6). Watts.

Oil Crisis. Ed. by Raymond Vernon. 1976. pap. 6.95 (ISBN 0-393-09186-4). Norton.

Oil Debt & Development: OPEC in the Third World. C. Paul Hallwood & Stuart W. Sinclair. 208p. 1981. text ed. 29.95x (ISBN 0-04-382027-1, 2580). Allen Unwin.

Oil Economists' Handbook. Gilbert Jenkins. 1977. 68.30x (ISBN 0-85334-728-X). Intl Ideas.

Oil Economy of Kuwait. Y. S. F. Al-Sabah. 176p. 1981. write for info. (ISBN 0-7103-0003-4). Routledge & Kegan.

Oil from Prospect to Pipeline. 4th ed. Robert R. Wheeler & Maurine Whited. 157p. 1981. pap. 6.95 (ISBN 0-87201-635-8). Gulf Pub.

Oil Industry & Government Strategy in the North Sea. Oystein Noreng. 268p. 1980. 35.00x (ISBN 0-85664-850-7, Pub. by Croom Helm Ltd England). Biblio Dist.

Oil Machines. Christopher C. Pick. LC 78-26333. (Machine World Ser.). (Illus.). (gr. 2-4). 1979. PLB 9.95 (ISBN 0-8172-1327-9). Raintree Pubs.

Oil Mill on the Texas Plains: A Study in Agricultural Cooperation. William N. Stokes, Jr. LC 78-6372. (Illus.). 248p. 1979. 10.00 (ISBN 0-89096-059-3). Tex A&M Univ Pr.

Oil Money & the World Economy. Yoon S. Park. LC 75-40467. (Special Studies in International Economics Ser). 1976. 35.00x (ISBN 0-89158-018-2). Westview.

Oil on the Waters: Cleaning up Oil Spills. Madelyn K. Anderson. LC 80-21139. (Illus.). 128p. 1981. 8.95 (ISBN 0-8149-0842-X). Vanguard.

Oil Palm. 2nd ed. C. W. Hartley. LC 76-23180. (Tropical Agriculture Ser.). 1977. text ed. 60.00x (ISBN 0-582-46809-4). Longman.

Oil Pipelines & Public Policy: Analysis of Proposals for Industry Reform & Reorganization. Ed. by Edward J. Mitchell. 1979. 15.25 (ISBN 0-8447-2157-3); pap. text ed. 8.25 (ISBN 0-8447-2158-1). Am Enterprise.

Oil Pollution as an International Problem: A Study of Puget Sound & the Strait of Georgia. William M. Ross. LC 73-5610. (Illus.). 296p. 1973. 15.00 (ISBN 0-295-95275-X). U. of Wash Pr.

Oil, Power & Politics: Conflict in Arabia, the Red Sea & the Gulf. Mordechai Abir. 210p. 1974. 25.00x (ISBN 0-7146-2990-1, F Cass Co). Biblio Dist.

Oil Prices & Trade Deficits: U. S. Conflicts with Japan & West Germany. David Gisselquist. LC 79-20632. (Praeger Special Studies Ser.). 158p. 1980. 21.95 (ISBN 0-03-052381-8). Praeger.

Oil Reservoir Engineering. Sylvain J. Pirson. LC 76-56806. (Illus.). 746p. 1977. Repr. of 1958 ed. lib. bdg. 34.50 o.p. (ISBN 0-88275-500-5). Krieger.

Oil Revenues, Absorptive Capacity & Prospects for Accelerated Growth. Kadhim A. Al-Exd. 1979. 22.95 o.p. (ISBN 0-03-053306-6). Praeger.

Oil Revenues & Accelerated Growth: Absorptive Capacity in Iraq. Kadhim A. Al-Eyd. LC 79-18596. 206p. 1979. 22.95 (ISBN 0-03-053306-6). Praeger.

Oil Revenues in the Gulf Emirates. Ali-Khaklifa Al-Luwari. LC 78-7358. (Illus.). 1978. lib. bdg. 45.00x (ISBN 0-89158-831-0). Westview.

Oil Rig. Neil Potter. LC 78-61231. (Careers Ser.). (Illus.). 1978. lib. bdg. 7.95 (ISBN 0-686-51122-0). Silver.

Oil Search in Australia. C. E. B. Conybeare. LC 80-65047. (Illus.). 151p. 1980. pap. text ed. 14.95 (ISBN 0-7081-1164-5, 0593). Bks Australia.

Oil Shale & Tar Sands Technology. M. W. Ranney. LC 79-16122. (Energy Technology Review No. 49; Chemical Technology Review No. 137). (Illus.). 1980. 48.00 (ISBN 0-8155-0769-0). Noyes.

Oil Shale Processing Technology. Ed. by V. Dean Allred. 208p. 1981. price not set (ISBN 0-86563-001-1). Ctr Prof Adv.

Oil Shale Technical Data Handbook. Ed. by Perry Nowacki. LC 80-27547. (Energy Tech. Rev. 63 Ser.: Chemical Tech. Rev. 182). (Illus.). 309p. 1981. 48.00 (ISBN 0-8155-0835-2). Noyes.

Oil Spills. Ed. by A. A. Moghissi. 80p. 1980. pap. 12.80 (ISBN 0-08-026237-6). Pergamon.

Oil Spills: Danger in the Sea. Joseph E. Brown. LC 78-7743. (Illus.). (gr. 5 up). 1978. 5.95 (ISBN 0-396-07607-6). Dodd.

Oil States. W. B. Fisher. (Illus.). 72p. (gr. 9-12). 1980. 16.95 (ISBN 0-7134-2477-X, Pub. by Batsford England). David & Charles.

Oil Statistics Nineteen Seventy-Seven: Supply & Disposal. 1979. 20.00 (ISBN 92-64-01875-1). OECD.

Oil: The Buried Treasure. Roma Gans. LC 74-7375. (Let's-Read-&-Find-Out Science Bk). (Illus.). (gr. k-3). 1975. PLB 7.89 (ISBN 0-690-00613-6, TYC-J). T Y Crowell.

Oil, the Middle East & the World. Charles Issawi. LC 72-5301. (Policy Papers: The Washington Papers, No. 4). 1972. 3.50x (ISBN 0-8039-0278-6). Sage.

Oil Well Drilling Technology. Arthur W. McCray & Frank W. Cole. (Illus.). 1979. Repr. of 1959 ed. 15.95x (ISBN 0-8061-0423-6). U of Okla Pr.

Oildorado: Boom Times on the West Side. William Rintoul. LC 78-50141. (Illus.). 240p. 1980. pap. 7.95 (ISBN 0-934136-07-6, Valley Calif). Western Tanager.

Oilman's Oilman. James A. Clark. LC 75-5318. (Illus.). 1979. write for info. (ISBN 0-88415-633-8). Pacesetter Pr.

Oils. J. M. Parramon. (Art Ser.). (Orig.). 1980. pap. 4.95 (ISBN 0-89586-073-2). H P Bks.

Oils & Gases from Coal: A Review of the State-of-the-Art in Europe & North America Based on the Work of the Symposium on the Gasification & Liquefaction of Coal Held Under the Auspices of the UNECE, Katowice, Poland. 23-27 April 1979. United Nations Economic Commission for Europe, Geneva, Switzerland. (ECE Seminars & Symposia Ser.). (Illus.). 316p. 1980. 59.00 (ISBN 0-08-025678-3). Pergamon.

Oilseed World Handbook. Michael E. Galvin. 450p. 1981. 50.00 (ISBN 0-937358-52-5). G D L Inc.

Oinker Away: Pig Riddles, Cartoons, Jokes and Other Amusing Things from the Creator of the Letterman. Mike Thaler. (Orig.). 1981. pap. 1.50 (ISBN 0-686-69579-8). Archway.

Ojibwa Indian Legends. Wah-Be-Gwo-Nese, pseud. (Illus.). 1972. 2.95 (ISBN 0-918616-05-0). Northern Mich.

Ojibwas: A Critical Bibliography. Helen H. Tanner. LC 76-12376. (Newberry Library Center for the History of the American Indian Bibliographical Ser.). 88p. 1976. pap. 3.95x (ISBN 0-253-34165-5). Ind U Pr.

Ojibway Heritage. Basil H. Johnston. (Illus.). 1976. 14.00x (ISBN 0-231-04168-3). Columbia U Pr.

Ojo & San Juan Excavations. 1981. pap. 14.95 (ISBN 0-89013-135-X). Museum NM Pr.

Ojos Para No Ver. Matias Montes-Huidobro. LC 79-52160. (Coleccion Teatro Ser.). (Illus.). 59p. (Span.). 1980. pap. 5.95 (ISBN 0-89729-229-4). Ediciones.

OJT File Clerk Resource Materials. 2nd ed. Joyce Sherster. (Gregg Office Job Training Program). (Illus.). 104p. (gr. 11-12). soft-cover 4.80 (ISBN 0-07-056640-2, G). McGraw.

OJT Mail Clerk Resource Materials. 2nd ed. Frances French. (Gregg Office Job Training Program Ser.). (Illus.). 112p. (gr. 11-12). 1980. soft cover 4.80 (ISBN 0-07-022190-1); training manual 3.56 (ISBN 0-07-022191-X). McGraw.

OJT Payroll Clerk Resource Materials. 2nd ed. Marcia S. Foster. (Gregg Office Job Training Program). (Illus.). 112p. (gr. 11-12). 1980. soft cover 4.80 (ISBN 0-07-021641-X); training manual 3.56 (ISBN 0-07-021641-X). McGraw.

OJT Traffic Clerk Resource Materials. 2nd ed. Joy Risser. (Gregg Office Job Training Program). (Illus.). 112p. (gr. 11-12). 1980. soft cover 4.80 (ISBN 0-07-052960-4); training manual avail. (ISBN 0-07-052961-2). McGraw.

Okada, Shinoda, & Tsutaka. Illus. by Kenzo Okada et al. LC 79-84887. (Illus.). 50p. (Orig.). 1979. pap. 6.00 (ISBN 0-88397-034-1). Intl Exhibit Foun.

Okara Mask. Rex Wiseman. 1979. pap. 1.95 (ISBN 0-505-51434-6). Tower Bks.

Okefenokee Swamp. Francis Russell. LC 73-78582. (American Wilderness Ser). (Illus.). (gr. 6 up). 1973. lib. bdg. 11.97 (ISBN 0-8094-1181-4, Pub. by Time-Life). Silver.

Okefenokee Swamp. Franklin Russell. (American Wilderness Ser.). (Illus.). 1973. 12.95 (ISBN 0-8094-1201-2). Time-Life.

Okefinokee Album. Francis Harper & Delma E. Presley. LC 80-14220. (Illus.). 235p. 1981. 14.95 (ISBN 0-8203-0530-8). U of Ga Pr.

Oklahoma. 28.00 (ISBN 0-89770-112-7). Curriculum Info Ctr.

Oklahoma: A Guide to the Sooner State. Federal Writers' Project. 532p. Repr. 49.00 (ISBN 0-403-02185-5). Somerset Pub.

Oklahoma: A History. H. Morgan Morgan & Anne H. Morgan. (States & the Nation Ser.). (Illus.). 1977. 12.95 (ISBN 0-393-05642-2). Norton.

Oklahoma Adventure: Of Banks & Bankers. James M. Smallwood. LC 79-4745. (Illus.). 1979. 11.95 (ISBN 0-8061-1545-9). U of Okla Pr.

Oklahoma Chronology & Factbook, Vol. 36. R. I. Vexler. 1978. 8.50 (ISBN 0-379-16161-3). Oceana.

Oklahoma Homes: Past & Present. Charles R. Goins & John W. Morris. LC 80-5239. (Illus.). 288p. 1981. 25.00 (ISBN 0-8061-1668-4). U of Okla Pr.

Oklahoma: In Words & Pictures. Dennis Fradin. LC 80-26961. (Young People's Stories of Our States Ser.). (Illus.). 48p. (gr. 2-5). 1981. PLB 8.65g (ISBN 0-516-03936-9, Time Line). Childrens.

Oklahoma Petroleum Industry. Kenny A. Franks. LC 80-5242. (Oklahoma Horizons Ser.). (Illus.). 320p. 1980. 17.50 (ISBN 0-8061-1625-0). U of Okla Pr.

Oklahoma State Industrial Directory 1981. State Industrial Directories Corp. 1980. pap. 35.00 (ISBN 0-89910-036-8). State Indus Dir.

Oklahoma Supplement for Modern Real Estate Practice. Dwayne Wilson & John Haley. 130p. (Orig.). 1981. pap. 7.95 (ISBN 0-88462-327-0). Real Estate Ed Co.

Oklahoma: The Story of Its Past & Present. rev. ed. Edwin C. McReynolds et al. (Illus.). 1980. Repr. of 1961 ed. 12.50x (ISBN 0-8061-0509-7). U of Okla Pr.

Oklahoma Vs. Texas: When Football Becomes War. Robert Heard. LC 80-82909. (Illus.). 544p. 1980. 25.00 (ISBN 0-937642-00-2). Honey Hill.

Oktoberfest. Frank De Felitta. 208p. 1980. pap. 2.50 (ISBN 0-380-53546-7, 53546). Avon.

Ol' Paul, the Mighty Logger. Glen Rounds. LC 75-22163. 96p. (gr. 4-6). 1976. 9.95 (ISBN 0-8234-0269-X). Holiday.

Olaf Wieghorst. William Reed. LC 76-101419. (Illus.). 1976. 30.00 o.p. (ISBN 0-87358-045-1). Northland.

Olam Gadol, 2 bks. Abraham Shumsky & Adaia Shumsky. Incl. Alef: a Big World. (Preprimer). text ed. 5.00 o.p. (ISBN 0-8074-0184-6, 405250); Bet. (Primer). 1973. text ed. 5.00 o.p. (ISBN 0-8074-0185-4, 405252); wkbk. with record 4.25 o.p. (ISBN 0-8074-0186-2, 405253). (Mah Tov Hebrew Program Ser.). (gr. 1-2). tchrs'. guide 5.00 o.p. (ISBN 0-8074-0187-0, 205254). UAHC.

Old Abe Dead & Other Stories. Eston Meade. 1981. 6.95 (ISBN 0-533-04800-1). Vantage.

Old Acquaintance. Nicholas Guild. (Orig.). pap. 2.50 (ISBN 0-515-05229-9). Jove Pubns.

Old Age - a Balance Sheet. Hope L. Cahill. (Illus.). 102p. 1981. pap. 3.95 (ISBN 0-933174-13-6). Wide World.

Old Age, Handicapped & Vietnam-Era Antidiscrimination Legislation. rev. ed. James P. Northrup. 1980. pap. 15.00 (ISBN 0-89546-020-3). Indus Res Unit-Wharton.

Old Age in a Changing Society. Zena S. Blau. 285p. 1973. 9.95 o.p. (ISBN 0-531-06354-2). Watts.

Old Age on the New Scene. Robert Kastenbaum. (Springer Series on Adulthood & Aging: No. 9). 1981. pap. text ed. 19.95 (ISBN 0-8261-2361-9). Springer Pub.

Old, Alone, & Neglected: Care of the Aged in Scotland & in the United States. Jeanie S. Kayser-Jones. 160p. 1981. 14.95 (ISBN 0-520-04153-4). U of Cal Pr.

Old America Comes Alive: Our Restored Villages from Colonial Williamsburg to Dodge City. Olive W. Burt. LC 65-20734. (Illus.). (gr. 5-8). 1966. PLB 7.95 o.p. (ISBN 0-381-99904-1, A57400, JD-J). John Day.

Old & Middle English Poetry: A Guide to Information Sources. Walter H. Beale. LC 74-11538. (American Literature, English Literature & World Literatures in English Information Guide Ser.: Vol. 7). 1976. 30.00 (ISBN 0-8103-1247-6). Gale.

Old & New Architecture: Design Relationship. LC 80-13245. 280p. 1980. 25.00 (ISBN 0-89133-076-3). Preservation Pr.

Old & Rare Children's Books Offered for Sale by Walter Schatzki, Dealer in Rare Books, Prints & Autographs. Ed. by Walter Schatzki. LC 73-16044. (Illus.). 46p. 1974. Repr. of 1941 ed. 15.00 (ISBN 0-8103-3878-5). Gale.

Old & Rare: Thirty Years in the Book Business. Leona Rostenberg & Madeleine B. Stern. (Illus.). 256p. 1975. 12.00 o.p. (ISBN 0-8390-0131-2). Allanheld & Schram.

Old & the Beautiful: Living Historic Buildings; Durango Colorado. Wybe J. Van Der Meer et al. (Illus.). 110p. (Orig.). 1980. 15.00 (ISBN 0-934744-02-5). Vermeer Arts.

Old & the New: From Don Quixote to Kafka. Marthe Robert. Tr. by Carol Cosman. 1977. 19.50x (ISBN 0-520-02509-1). U of Cal Pr.

Old Believers & the World of Antichrist: The Vyg Community & the Russian State, 1694-1855. Robert O. Crummey. LC 79-98121. 1970. 25.00 (ISBN 0-299-05560-4). U of Wis Pr.

Old Black Witch! Wende Devlin & Harry Devlin. LC 80-17064. (Illus.). 32p. (ps-3). 1980. Repr. of 1966 ed. 8.95 (ISBN 0-590-07785-6, Four Winds). Schol Bk Serv.

Old Blood. Edgar Mittelholzer. 1977. pap. 1.95 o.p. (ISBN 0-449-23355-3, Crest). Fawcett.

Old Boston Taverns & Tavern Clubs. Samuel A. Drake. LC 78-162511. 132p. 1971. Repr. of 1917 ed. 18.00 (ISBN 0-8103-3293-0). Gale.

Old Boyfriends. (Orig.). 1979. pap. 1.75 o.s.i. (ISBN 0-515-04840-2). Jove Pubns.

Old Boys-New Women: The Politics of Discrimination. Joan Abramson. LC 79-65933. (Praeger Special Studies). 270p. 1979. 24.95 (ISBN 0-03-049756-6); pap. 9.95 student edition (ISBN 0-03-049751-5). Praeger.

Old Bread, New Wine: A Portrait of the Italiann-Americans. Patrick J. Gallo. LC 80-20401. 360p. 1981. 16.95 (ISBN 0-88229-146-7). Nelson-Hall.

Old Brethren. James Lehman. (Orig.). 1976. pap. 2.45 (ISBN 0-89129-155-5). Jove Pubns.

Old Buildings, Gardens & Furniture in Tidewater, Maryland. H. Chandlee Forman. LC 67-17538. (Illus.). 1967. 12.50 (ISBN 0-87033-075-6, Pub. by Tidewater). Cornell Maritime.

Old Calabor, Sixteen Hundred to Eighteen Ninety One: The Impact of the International Economy Upon a Traditional Society. A. J. Latham. 1973. 33.00x (ISBN 0-19-821687-4). Oxford U Pr.

Old Cathedral. 2nd ed. Gregory M. Franzwa. LC 80-15885. (Illus.). 1980. 14.95 (ISBN 0-935284-18-4). Patrice Pr.

Old Celtic Romances. 3rd ed. P. W. Joyce. (Sackville Library Reprint Ser.). 1978. Repr. of 1907 ed. 25.00 o.p. (ISBN 0-7171-0940-2). Irish Bk Ctr.

Old Chair. Thacher Hurd. LC 77-1581. (Illus.). (gr. k-3). 1978. 5.95 (ISBN 0-688-80104-8); PLB 5.71 (ISBN 0-688-84104-X). Greenwillow.

Old Charlie Farquharson's Testymint. Charlie Farquharson, pseud. 1978. 9.95 o.s.i. (ISBN 0-685-52805-7). Vanguard.

Old Cheque-Book, or Book of Rememberance of the Chapel Royal from 1561. Ed. by Edward F. Rimbault. LC 65-23407. (Music Ser.). 1966. Repr. of 1872 ed. lib. bdg. 25.00 (ISBN 0-306-70911-2). Da Capo.

Old Chore. John Hildebidle. LC 80-70828. 72p. (Orig.). 1981. pap. 4.95 (ISBN 0-914086-34-0). Alicejamesbooks.

Old Christmas - Bracebridge Hall. Washington Irving. (Illus.). 528p. 1980. boxed set 22.00 (ISBN 0-912882-43-3). Sleepy Hollow.

Old Church Slavonic: An Elementary Grammar. S. C. Gardiner. Date not set. price not set (ISBN 0-521-23674-6). Cambridge U Pr.

Old Church Slavonic Translation of the Andron Hagion Biblos in the Edition of Nikolas Van Wijk. D. Armstrong et al. Ed. by C. H. Van Schooneveld. (Slavistic Printings & Reprintings Ser: No. 1). 310p. 1975. text ed. 98.80x (ISBN 90-2793-196-8). Mouton.

Old Cook Books: An Illustrated History. Eric Quayle. 1978. 14.95 o.p. (ISBN 0-87690-283-2). Dutton.

Old Cookery Books & Ancient Cuisine. William C. Hazlitt. LC 68-30612. 1968. Repr. of 1886 ed. 15.00 (ISBN 0-8103-3306-6). Gale.

Old Corps. Robert H. Williams. (Illus.). 160p. Date not set. 25.95 (ISBN 0-87021-504-3). Naval Inst Pr. Postponed.

Old Country Cookbook: Recipes from Thirty-One Countries. Walter Oleksy. LC 73-81082. 1974. 16.95 (ISBN 0-88229-105-X). Nelson-Hall.

Old Country Life. Sabine Baring-Gould. LC 78-77086. 1969. Repr. of 1890 ed. 18.00 (ISBN 0-8103-3848-3). Gale.

Old Creole Days. George W. Cable. 234p. 1980. Repr. of 1897 ed. lib. bdg. 30.00 (ISBN 0-89987-111-9). Century Bookbindery.

Old Dog, New Tricks. Dick Cate. (Illus.). 96p. (gr. 3-6). 1981. 9.95 (ISBN 0-525-66730-X). Elsevier-Nelson.

Old Dominion & the New Nation, 1788-1801. Richard R. Beeman. LC 76-190531. 296p. 1972. 15.00x (ISBN 0-8131-1269-9). U Pr of Ky.

Old English & Middle English Poetry. Derek Pearsall. (History of English Poetry Ser.). 1977. 28.00x (ISBN 0-7100-8396-3). Routledge & Kegan.

Old English Anthology. Francis P. Magoun, Jr. & James A. Walker. 108p. 1980. Repr. of 1950 ed. lib. bdg. 15.00 (ISBN 0-89760-542-X). Telegraph Bks.

Old English Customs. Roy Christian. (Illus.). 1966. 7.50 o.p. (ISBN 0-8038-5342-4). Hastings.

Old English Customs. (Illus.). 1972. Repr. 11.95 (ISBN 0-7153-5741-7). David & Charles.

Old English Customs Extant at the Present Time. P. H. Ditchfield. LC 68-21765. 1968. Repr. of 1896 ed. 18.00 (ISBN 0-8103-3427-5). Gale.

Old English Exodus. J. R. Tolkien. Ed. by Joan Turville-Petre. 128p. 1981. 24.00 (ISBN 0-19-811177-0). Oxford U Pr.

Old English Furniture. Hampden Gordon. pap. 1.95 o.p. (ISBN 0-7195-0509-7). Transatlantic.

Old English Glosses in the Ephinal-Erfurt Glossary. Ed. by J. D. Pheifer. 259p. 1974. 24.95x (ISBN 0-19-811164-9). Oxford U Pr.

Old English Grammar. 3rd ed. Joseph Wright & Elizabeth M. Wright. 1925. 26.00x (ISBN 0-19-811923-2). Oxford U Pr.

Old English Home & Its Dependencies. Sabine Baring-Gould. LC 74-77085. 1969. Repr. of 1898 ed. 18.00 (ISBN 0-8103-3847-5). Gale.

Old English Libraries. Ernest A. Savage. LC 68-26177. (Illus.). 1968. Repr. of 1912 ed. 22.00 (ISBN 0-8103-3179-9). Gale.

Old English Literature in Context: Ten Essays. Ed. by John D. Niles. (Illus.). 184p. 1980. 42.50x (ISBN 0-8476-6770-7). Rowman.

Old English Orosius. Ed. by Janet Bately. (Early English Text Society Ser.). (Illus.). 558p. 1981. 65.00 (ISBN 0-19-722406-7). Oxford U Pr.

Old English Poetry: Essays on Style. Ed. by Daniel C. Calder. (Contributions of the Center for Medieval & Renaissance Studies, UCLA: No. 10). 1979. 16.50x (ISBN 0-520-03830-4). U of Cal Pr.

Old English Porcelain: A Handbook for Collectors. rev. 3rd ed. W. B. Honey. (Illus.). 1978. 35.00 o.p. (ISBN 0-571-04902-8, Pub. by Faber & Faber). Merrimack Bk Serv.

Old English Sheepdog. Jill A. Keeling. Ed. by Christina Foyle. (Foyle's Handbks). 1973. 3.95 (ISBN 0-685-55799-5). Palmetto Pub.

Old English Sheepdogs. Beverly Pisano. (Illus.). 128p. 1980. 2.95 (ISBN 0-87666-723-X, KW-093). TFH Pubns.

Old English Sheepdogs. Sylvia Woods & Ray Owen. (Illus.). 224p. 1981. 22.00 (ISBN 0-571-11620-5, Pub. by Faber & Faber). Merrimack Bk Serv.

Old English Sound Changes for Beginners. R. F. Hamer. 1967. pap. 7.25x (ISBN 0-631-10150-0, Pub. by Basil Blackwell England). Biblio Dist.

Old English Verse. T. A. Shippey. 1972. text ed. 14.50x (ISBN 0-09-111030-0, Hutchinson U Lib); pap. text ed. 7.50x (ISBN 0-09-111031-9). Humanities.

Old Enough to Feel Better: A Medical Guide for Seniors. Michael Gordon. LC 80-70351. 384p. 1981. 14.95 (ISBN 0-686-69523-2). Chilton.

Old European Order Sixteen Sixty to Eighteen Hundred. William Doyle. (Short Oxford History of the Modern World Ser.). (Illus.). 1978. 36.00x (ISBN 0-19-913073-6); pap. 12.95 (ISBN 0-19-913131-7). Oxford U Pr.

Old Farm Implements. Philip A. Wright. LC 73-168335. (Illus.). 112p. 1975. 11.95 (ISBN 0-7153-6801-X). David & Charles.

Old Farm Tools & Machinery: An Illustrated History. Percy W. Blandford. LC 75-44376. 1976. 26.00 (ISBN 0-8103-2019-3). Gale.

Old Farmer's Almanac. (Illus.). 176p. 1980. pap. 1.00. Yankee Bks.

Old Farmers's Almanac Gardner's Companion. (Illus.). 144p. 1980. pap. 1.50 (ISBN 0-911658-99-8). Yankee Bks.

Old-Fashion Fun & Games. E. O. Harbin. (Games & Party Books). 1978. pap. 3.45 (ISBN 0-8010-4184-8). Baker Bk.

Old-Fashioned Raggedy Ann ABC Book. Robert Kraus. Ed. by Pam Kraus. (Illus.). 32p. (ps-2). 1980. 4.95 (ISBN 0-671-42552-8). Windmill Bks.

Old Favorites from the McGuffey Readers. William H. McGuffey. Ed. by Harvey C. Minnich. LC 79-76081. 1969. Repr. of 1936 ed. 20.00 (ISBN 0-8103-3854-8). Gale.

Old Fishing Lures & Tackle: A Collectors Identification & Value Guide. Carl Luckey. (Illus.). pap. 14.95 (ISBN 0-686-51464-5). Wallace-Homestead.

Old Florida. Nichols & Woolson. (Sun Historical Ser.). (Illus.). pap. 3.50 (ISBN 0-89540-054-5). Sun Pub.

Old Folks at Home: A Field Study of Nursing & Board-&-Care Facilities. R. M. Glasscote et al. 148p. 1976. 8.00 (ISBN 0-685-76789-2, P222-0). Am Psychiatric.

Old French: A Concise Handbook. E. C. Einhorn. 210p. 1975. 29.50 (ISBN 0-521-20343-0); pap. 12.50x (ISBN 0-521-09838-6). Cambridge U Pr.

Old French Johannis Translation of the Pseudo-Turpin Chronicle: A Critical Edition. Ronald N. Walpole. 1976. 26.75x (ISBN 0-520-02707-8); suppl. 39.50x (ISBN 0-520-02840-6). U of Cal Pr.

Old Friend from Far Away: One Hundred Fifty Chinese Poems from the Great Dynasties. Tr. by C. H. Kwock & Vincent McHugh. 192p. 1980. 15.00 (ISBN 0-86547-017-0); pap. 6.50 (ISBN 0-86547-018-9). N Point Pr.

Old Gentlemen's Convention: The Washington Peace Conference of 1861. Robert G. Gunderson. LC 80-24747. (Illus.). xiii, 168p. 1981. Repr. of 1961 ed. lib. bdg. 17.50x (ISBN 0-313-22584-2, GUOG). Greenwood.

Old Girl. Joshua Gidding. LC 79-26850. 264p. 1980. 12.95 (ISBN 0-03-052196-3); pap. 5.95 (ISBN 0-03-057998-8). HR&W.

Old Grammar Schools. Foster Watson. (Illus.). 150p. 1968. 29.50x (ISBN 0-7146-1449-1, F Cass Co). Biblio Dist.

Old Gravois Coal Diggings. Maryjoan Boyer. 4.00 o.p. (ISBN 0-911208-12-7). Ramfre.

Old Gray Mayors of Denver. G. V. Kelly. LC 73-94191. (Illus.). 1974. 9.95 o.p. (ISBN 0-87108-078-8). Pruett.

Old Greasybeard: Tales from the Cumberland Gap. Leonard Roberts. LC 69-20398. (Illus.). 1980. pap. text ed. 7.95 (ISBN 0-933302-04-5). Pikeville Coll.

Old Harry's Bunkside Book. J. D. Sleightholme. 1979. 4.95x (ISBN 0-8464-0068-5). Beekman Pubs.

Old Hasdrubal & the Pirates. Berthe Amoss. LC 76-153787. (Illus.). (gr. k-3). 1971. 5.95 o.s.i. (ISBN 0-8193-0519-7, Four Winds); PLB 5.41 o.s.i. (ISBN 0-8193-0520-0). Schol Bk Serv.

Old Herb Doctor. 1981. Repr. lib. bdg. 13.95 (ISBN 0-89370-652-3). Borgo Pr.

Old Herb Doctor. 1981. pap. 6.95 (ISBN 0-87877-052-6). Newcastle Pub.

Old House. (Home Repair & Improvement Ser.). (Illus.). 1979. lib. bdg. 11.97 (ISBN 0-8094-2423-1); kivar bdg. 9.96 (ISBN 0-8094-2424-X). Silver.

Old House. Time-Life Books Editors. (Home Repair & Improvement Ser.). (Illus.). 1980. 10.95 (ISBN 0-8094-2422-3). Time-Life.

Old House Book of Bedrooms. Lawrence Grow. (Old House Book Ser.). (Illus.). 96p. 1980. 15.00 (ISBN 0-446-51216-8); pap. 7.95 (ISBN 0-446-97553-2). Warner Bks.

Old House Book of Living Rooms & Parlors. Lawrence Grow. (Old House Book Ser.). (Illus.). 150p. 1980. 15.00 (ISBN 0-446-51215-X); pap. 7.95 (ISBN 0-446-97552-4). Warner Bks.

Old House Book of Outdoor Living Places. Laurence Grow. (Illus., Orig.). 1981. 15.00 (ISBN 0-446-51219-2). Warner Bks.

Old House Book of Outdoor Spaces. Laurence Grow. (Orig.). 1981. 8.95 (ISBN 0-446-97556-7). Warner Bks.

Old-House Journal 1981 Catalog: A Buyer's Guide. Ed. by The Old-House Journal Staff. (Illus.). 142p. (Orig.). 1981. pap. 9.95 (ISBN 0-87951-125-7). Overlook Pr.

Old Houses: A Rebuilder's Manual. George Nash. (Illus.). 1980. 22.95 (ISBN 0-13-633875-5, Spec); pap. 12.95 (ISBN 0-13-633883-6). P-H.

Old Houses, New Homes. Roger Albright. (Illus.). 256p. 1980. 14.95 (ISBN 0-8289-0395-6); pap. 9.95 (ISBN 0-8289-0396-4). Greene.

Old Houses of Connecticut. Ed. by Berta C. Trowbridge. (Illus.). 1923. 125.00x (ISBN 0-685-89768-0). Elliots Bks.

Old Irish Reader. R. Thurneysen. 1949. 7.50x (ISBN 0-686-00879-0). Colton Bk.

Old Jake & the Pirate's Treasure. Betty Hager. LC 80-80606. (Illus.). 104p. (gr. 4 up). 1980. lib. bdg. 5.89 (ISBN 0-8178-0006-9). Harvey.

Old Joke Book. Janet Ahlberg & Allan Ahlberg. (Illus.). (gr. 2-5). 1979. pap. 2.50 (ISBN 0-14-050333-1, Puffin). Penguin.

Old Jules. Mari Sandoz. LC 35-27361. 1962. pap. 4.95 (ISBN 0-8032-5173-4, BB 100, Bison). U of Nebr Pr.

Old Kyle's Boy. Frank Roderus. LC 80-1661. (Double D Western Ser.). 192p. 1981. 9.95 (ISBN 0-385-15937-4). Doubleday.

Old Landmarks & Historic Personages of Boston. Samuel A. Drake. LC 76-99068. (Illus.). 1970. Repr. of 1900 ed. 20.00 (ISBN 0-8103-3582-4). Gale.

Old Line State: Her Heritage. Charles W. Titus & Thomas E. Jones. LC 79-180858. (Illus.). 1971. pap. 4.00 (ISBN 0-87033-159-0, Pub. by Tidewater). Cornell Maritime.

Old Lithuanian Catechism of Baltramiejus Vilentas 1579: A Phonological, Morphological, & Syntactical Investigation. Gordon B. Ford, Jr. LC 68-23807. 1969. 40.00 o.p. (ISBN 0-910198-20-9). Baltica Pr.

Old Lithuanian Texts of the Sixteenth & Seventeenth Centuries with a Glossary. Ed. by Gordon B. Ford, Jr. LC 68-17875. 1969. 10.00 o.p. (ISBN 0-910198-13-6). Baltica Pr.

Old London Street Cries. Andrew W. Tuer. (Illus.). 137p. 1978. pap. 2.50 (ISBN 0-85967-402-9, Pub. by Scolar Pr England); pkg. of 10 24.95 (ISBN 0-686-28431-3). Biblio Dist.

Old Louisiana Plantation Homes & Family Trees, Vol. 1. Herman Seebold. (Illus.). 1971. Repr. of 1941 ed. 30.00 (ISBN 0-911116-34-6). Pelican.

Old Love. Isaac B. Singer. 1980. pap. 2.50 (ISBN 0-449-24343-5, Crest). Fawcett.

Old MacDonald Had a Farm. Illus. by Mel Crawford. (Illus.). (ps-1). 1967. PLB 5.38 (ISBN 0-307-68931-X, Golden Pr). Western Pub.

Old Macdonald Had a Farm. Illus. by Abner Graboff. (Illus.). (gr. k-3). 1970. pap. 1.25 (ISBN 0-590-01622-9, Schol Pap); pap. 3.50 bk. & record (ISBN 0-590-09098-4). Schol Bk Serv.

Old Madam Yin: A Memoir of Peking Life. Ida Pruitt. LC 78-68782. 1979. 8.95x (ISBN 0-8047-1038-4); pap. 2.95 (ISBN 0-8047-1099-6, SP24). Stanford U Pr.

Old Man. Marsh. pap. 1.50 o.p. (ISBN 0-686-12917-2). Schmul Pub Co.

Old Man & the Astronauts. Ruth Tabrah. Tr. by George Suyeoka. LC 75-16524. (Illus.). (gr. 1-7). 1975. 5.95 (ISBN 0-89610-015-4). Island Her.

Old Man & the Boy. Robert Ruark. 1977. pap. 1.95 o.p. (ISBN 0-449-23151-8, Crest). Fawcett.

Old Man & the Medal. Ferdinand Oyono. (African-American Library). 1971. pap. 1.50 o.s.i. (ISBN 0-02-053190-7, Collier). Macmillan.

Old Man & the Sea. Ernest Hemingway. (Hudson River Edition). 1952. 12.50x (ISBN 0-684-15363-7, ScribT); pap. 3.25 (ISBN 0-684-71805-7, SL104); text ed. 4.80 (ISBN 0-684-51528-8); pap. text ed. 2.44 (ISBN 0-684-51529-6, SSP6, ScribC); pap. 2.25 (ISBN 0-684-16326-8, SL885, ScribC). Scribner.

Old Man in the Corner. Emmuska Orczy. 340p. 1980. Repr. of 1908 ed. lib. bdg. 15.95x (ISBN 0-89968-196-4). Lightyear.

Old Man in the Corner: Twelve Mysteries by the Baroness Orczy. Emmuska Orczy. Ed. by E. G. Bleiler. (Orig.). 1980. pap. 3.50. Dover.

Old Man of Lochnagar. Prince Of Wales. (gr. k up). 1980. 10.95 (ISBN 0-374-35613-0). FS&G.

Old Man Savarin Stories: Tales of Canada & Canadians. E. W. Thomson. LC 73-91557. (Literature of Canada Ser.). 1974. pap. 4.50 (ISBN 0-8020-6207-5). U of Toronto Pr.

Old Man Who Does As He Pleases. Yu Lu. Tr. by Burton Watson from Chinese. (Translations from the Oriental Classics Ser). (Illus.). 128p. 1973. 12.50x (ISBN 0-231-03766-X). Columbia U Pr.

Old Manor House: A Novel, 4 vols. Charlotte Smith. (Feminist Controversy in England, 1788-1810 Ser.). 1974. lib. bdg. 50.00 ea. (ISBN 0-8240-0880-4). Garland Pub.

Old Master Drawings from Christ Church, Oxford. Intro. by James B. Shaw. LC 72-83826. (Illus.). 1972. pap. 5.95 o.p. (ISBN 0-88397-061-9). Intl Exhibit Foun.

Old Men Drunk & Sober. Howard M. Bahr & Theodore Caplow. LC 72-96370. (Illus.). 407p. 1974. 20.00x (ISBN 0-8147-0965-6). NYU Pr.

Old Mike of Monk's Lagoon. Edward N. Opheim. 1981. 6.95 (ISBN 0-533-04853-2). Vantage.

Old Mobile: Fort Louis De la Louisiana, 1702-1711. Jay Higginbotham. LC 77-89698. (Illus., Orig.). 1977. 50.00 (ISBN 0-914334-04-2); pap. 25.00 (ISBN 0-914334-03-4). Museum Mobile.

Old Mother Hubbard & Her Dog. Evaline Ness. LC 74-182788. (Illus.). 40p. (ps-3). 1972. reinfoced bdg. 4.95 (ISBN 0-03-088369-5); pap. 1.45 (owlet bk.) o.p. (ISBN 0-03-005721-3). HR&W.

Old Mother Witch. Carol Carrick. LC 75-4609. (Illus.). 32p. (ps-4). 1975. 7.95 (ISBN 0-395-28778-2, Clarion). HM.

Old Myths & New Realities: And Other Commentaries. J. William Fulbright. 1964. 8.95 o.p. (ISBN 0-394-43741-1). Random.

Old Navajo Rugs: Their Development from 1900 to 1940. Marian E. Rodee. (Illus.). 96p. 1981. price not set (ISBN 0-8263-0566-0); pap. price not set (ISBN 0-8263-0567-9). U of NM Pr.

Old Neighborhood. Avery Corman. 1980. lib. bdg. 12.95 (ISBN 0-8161-3146-5, Large Print Bks). G K Hall.

Old Neighborhood. Avery Corman. 1980. 10.95 (ISBN 0-686-68758-2, 41475, Linden). S&S.

Old Niagara on the Lake. Peter J. Stokes. LC 74-151393. 1971. pap. 10.95 (ISBN 0-8020-6318-7). U of Toronto Pr.

Old North Trail; or, Life, Legends & Religion of the Blackfeet Indians. Walter McClintock. LC 68-13651. (Illus.). 1968. pap. 5.95 (ISBN 0-8032-5130-0, BB 379, Bison). U of Nebr Pr.

Old Ohio, 2 vols. Incl. Vol. I. Logan & Matthews; Vol. II. Welch & Matthews. (Sun Historical Ser.). pap. 3.50 ea. Sun Pub.

Old Order Changes. W. H. Mallock. Ed. by Robert L. Wolff. LC 75-1533. (Victorian Fiction Ser.). 1975. lib. bdg. 66.00 (ISBN 0-8240-1605-X). Garland Pub.

Old Oregon Country: A History of Frontier Trade, Transportation, & Travel. Oscar O. Winther. LC 50-63368. (Illus.). 1969. pap. 3.95 (ISBN 0-8032-5218-8, BB 388, Bison). U of Nebr Pr.

Old Paths & Legends of New England: Saunterings Over Historic Roads with Glimpses of Picturesque Fields & Old Homesteads in Massachusetts, Rhode Island & New Hampshire. Katherine M. Abbott. LC 76-75228. Repr. of 1903 ed. 18.00 (ISBN 0-8103-3564-6). Gale.

Old Paths & Legends of the New England Border: Connecticut, Deerfield, Berkshire. Katharine M. Abbott. LC 72-75227. 1970. Repr. of 1907 ed. 18.00 (ISBN 0-8103-3562-X). Gale.

Old People & London Government. Kathleen M. Slack. 82p. 1970. pap. text ed. 5.00x (ISBN 0-7135-1620-8, Pub. by Bedford England). Renouf.

Old People's Homes & the Production of Welfare. Bleddyn Davies & Martin Knapp. (Library of Social Work Ser.). 240p. 1981. 32.50 (ISBN 0-7100-0700-0). Routledge & Kegan.

Old Perisher. Diana Ross. (Illus.). (ps-5). 1965. 6.95 (ISBN 0-571-06162-1, Pub. by Faber & Faber). Merrimack Bk Serv.

Old Persian Grammar Texts Lexicon. 2nd rev. ed. Roland G. Kent. (American Oriental Ser.: Vol. 33). 1953. 13.00x (ISBN 0-686-00016-1). Am Orient Soc.

Old Pewter: Its Makers & Marks in England, Scotland & Ireland; an Account of the Old Pewterer & His Craft. Howard H. Cotterell. LC 29-22959. (Illus.). 1963. 87.50 (ISBN 0-8048-0443-5). C E Tuttle.

Old Philadelphia Houses on Society Hill. Elizabeth B. McCall. Date not set. 16.50 (ISBN 0-8038-0194-7). Hastings.

Old, Poor, Alone, & Happy: How to Live Nicely on Nearly Nothing. Katherine Dissinger. 1980. 17.95 (ISBN 0-88229-629-9). Nelson-Hall.

Old Possum's Book of Practical Cats. T. S. Eliot. LC 39-33125. 1968. pap. 1.95 (ISBN 0-15-668570-1, HPL31, HPL). HarBraceJ.

Old Pro Turkey Hunter. Gene Nunnery. LC 80-80630. (Illus.). 1980. 12.50 (ISBN 0-916620-48-4). Portals Pr.

Old Quantum Theory. D. Ter Haar. 1967. 26.00 (ISBN 0-08-012102-0); pap. 8.50 (ISBN 0-08-012101-2). Pergamon.

Old Record of the Captivity of Margaret Erskine 1779, Repr. Of 1912 Ed. Bd. with Indian Horrors of the Fifties: Story & Life of the Only Known Living Captive of the Indian Horrors of Sixty Years Ago. Jesse H. Alexander. Repr. of 1916 ed. LC 75-7136. (Indian Captivities Ser.: Vol. 108). 1977. lib. bdg. 44.00 (ISBN 0-8240-1732-3). Garland Pub.

Old Regime & the French Revolution. Alexis de Tocqueville. Ed. by J. P. Mayer & A. P. Kerr. LC 55-10160. 1955. pap. 3.50 (ISBN 0-385-09260-1, A60, Anch). Doubleday.

Old Regime in France. Frantz Funck-Brentano. LC 68-9656. 1970. Repr. 17.50 (ISBN 0-86527-141-0). Fertig.

Old Religion in the Brave New World: Reflections on the Relation Between Christendom & the Republic. Sidney Mead. (Jafferson Memorial Lecture). 1977. 11.95 (ISBN 0-520-03322-1). U of Cal Pr.

Old Rock the Fisherman. Norman C. Habel. (Purple Puzzle Tree Bk.). 1972. pap. 0.85 (ISBN 0-570-06543-7, 56-1247). Concordia.

Old Rooms for New Living. Narcissa Chamberlain. (Illus.). 1977. 12.95 (ISBN 0-8038-5346-7). Hastings.

Old Salem in Pictures. Bruce Roberts. (Illus., Orig.). 1968. 3.95 (ISBN 0-87461-951-3). McNally.

Old Santa Fe Today. 3rd, enl. ed. Historic Santa Fe Foundation. (Illus.). 128p. 1981. pap. price not set (ISBN 0-8263-0562-8). U of NM Pr.

Old School Ties, the Public Schools in British Literature. John R. Reed. LC 64-23341. 1964. 7.95x (ISBN 0-8156-2070-5). Syracuse U Pr.

Old Settlers Association of Greene County, Illinois: Coda of the Deep Snow of 1830. Ed. by Eileen S. Cunningham. 1976. 17.00 (AU00122); pap. 12.00. E S Cunningham.

Old Shrub Roses. Graham S. Thomas. (Illus.). 1965. 15.95x o.p. (ISBN 0-460-07792-9, Pub. by J. M. Dent England). Biblio Dist.

Old Shrub Roses. rev. ed. Graham St. Thomas. (Illus.). 232p. 1979. 15.95x (ISBN 0-460-04345-5, Pub. by J M Dent England). Biblio Dist.

Old-Soldier Sahib. Frank Richards. (Orig.). 1966. pap. 4.95 (ISBN 0-571-06574-0, Pub. by Faber & Faber). Merrimack Bk Serv.

Old South. Compiled by Fletcher M. Green & J. Isaac Copeland. LC 79-55730. (Goldentree Bibliographies in American History Ser.). 1980. text ed. 16.95 (ISBN 0-88295-539-X); pap. text ed. 12.95x (ISBN 0-88295-580-2). AHM Pub.

Old Steamboat Days on the Hudson River: Tales & Reminiscences of the Stirring Times That Followed the Introduction of Steam Navigation. David L. Buckman. LC 77-156931. (Illus.). 1971. Repr. of 1909 ed. 18.00 (ISBN 0-8103-3737-1). Gale.

Old Stump. John Hawkinson. LC 65-23883. (Self Starter Bks.). (Illus.). (ps-2). 1965. 6.50g (ISBN 0-8075-5969-5). A Whitman.

Old Tales for a New Day: Early Answers to Life's Eternal Questions. Sophia L. Fahs & Alice Cobb. LC 80-84076. (Library of Liberal Religion). (gr. 3-9). 1981. 9.95 (ISBN 0-87975-138-X); tchr's manual 7.95 (ISBN 0-87975-132-0). Prometheus Bks.

Old Tales of San Francisco. Arthur B. Chandler. LC 77-78491. (History Ser.). (Illus.). 1977. pap. text ed. 7.95 (ISBN 0-8403-1746-8). Kendall-Hunt.

Old Tavern Signs: An Excursion into the History of Hospitality. Fritz A. Endell. LC 68-26572. (Illus.). 1968. Repr. of 1916 ed. 18.00 (ISBN 0-8103-3505-0). Gale.

Old Testament, an Introduction. Otto Eissfeldt. LC 65-15399. 1965. 12.95x (ISBN 0-06-062171-0, RD162, HarpR). Har-Row.

Old Testament & the Archaeologist. H. Darrell Lance. Ed. by Gene M. Tucker. LC 80-2387. (Guides to Biblical Scholarship: Old Testament Ser.). 112p. (Orig.). 1981. pap. 4.50 (ISBN 0-8006-0467-9, 1-467). Fortress.

Old Testament Bible History. Alfred Edersheim. 1972. 18.95 (ISBN 0-8028-8028-2). Eerdmans.

Old Testament Charts. M. Ross Richards & Marie C. Richards. pap. 1.95 o.p. (ISBN 0-87747-447-8). Deseret Bk.

Old Testament Commentaries, 10 vols. Carl F. Keil & Franz Delitzsch. Incl. Vol. 1. Pentateuch (ISBN 0-8028-8035-5); Vol. 2. Joshua - Second Samuel (ISBN 0-8028-8036-3); Vol. 3. First Kings - Esther (ISBN 0-685-25927-7); Vol. 4. Job (ISBN 0-8028-8038-X); Vol. 5. Psalms (ISBN 0-8028-8039-8); Vol. 6. Proverbs - Song of Solomon (ISBN 0-8028-8040-1); Vol. 7. Isaiah (ISBN 0-8028-8041-X); Vol. 8. Jeremiah-Lamentations (ISBN 0-8028-8042-8); Vol. 9. Ezekiel-Daniel (ISBN 0-8028-8043-6); Vol. 10. Minor Prophets (ISBN 0-8028-8044-4). 1971. Repr. Set. 149.50 o.p. (ISBN 0-8028-8034-7); 14.95 ea. o.p. Eerdmans.

Old Testament Covenant: A Survey of Current Opinions. Dennis J. McCarthy. LC 71-37117. (Growing Points in Theology Ser). (Orig.). 1972. pap. 4.95 (ISBN 0-8042-0020-3). John Knox.

Old Testament Digest: Gen-Deut, Vol. 1. William MacDonald. 1981. pap. 7.50 (ISBN 0-937396-59-1). Walterick Pubs.

Old Testament Digest: Vol. 3, Job-Malachi. William MacDonald. 1981. pap. 6.95 (ISBN 0-937396-29-X). Walterick Pubs.

Old Testament Heroes, No. 1. LeRoy Dugan. 80p. (Orig.). (ps-4). 1981. pap. 1.49 oversized, saddle stitched (ISBN 0-87123-705-9, 220705). Bethany Fell.

Old Testament History of Redemption. Franz Delitzsch. Date not set. pap. 6.95 (ISBN 0-88469-141-1). BMH Bks.

Old Testament in Living Pictures. David S. Alexander. LC 73-85490. (Illus.). 1973. lib. bdg. 6.95 o.p. (ISBN 0-8307-0225-3, 51-062-06). Regal.

Old Testament Quotations in the New Testament. rev. ed. Ed. by R. G. Bratcher. 1980. Repr. of 1967 ed. softcover 1.25 (ISBN 0-8267-0000-4, 08503). United Bible.

Old Testament Sabbath: A Tradition-Historical Investigation. Niels-Erik A. Andreasen. LC 72-88671. (Society of Biblical Literature. Dissertation Ser.). 1974. pap. 9.00 (ISBN 0-89130-163-1, 060107). Scholars Pr Ca.

Old Testament Speaks. 3rd ed. Samuel J. Schultz. LC 80-7740. (Illus.). 448p. 1980. 11.95x (ISBN 0-06-067134-3, HarpR). Har-Row.

Old Testament Speaks: Old Testament History & Literature. Samuel J. Schultz. (Illus.). 1970. 10.50x o.p. (ISBN 0-06-067130-0, HarpR). Har-Row.

Old Testament Study Simplified. new ed. James N. Layne. LC 77-23715. 1978. pap. 3.25 (ISBN 0-87148-656-3). Pathway Pr.

Old Testament Wisdom: An Introduction. James L. Crenshaw. LC 80-82183. 262p. 1981. 16.50 (ISBN 0-8042-0143-9); pap. 9.95 (ISBN 0-8042-0142-0). John Knox.

Old Testament Without Illusion. John L. McKenzie. 1979. 11.95 o.p. (ISBN 0-88347-098-5). Thomas More.

Old Thad Stevens: A Story of Ambition. Richard N. Current. LC 80-15189. (Illus.). v, 344p. 1980. Repr. of 1942 ed. lib. bdg. 27.50x (ISBN 0-313-22569-9, CUOT). Greenwood.

Old Thinking, New Thinking: A Sufi Prism. Fazal Inayat-Khan. LC 77-7831. 1979. pap. 5.95 (ISBN 0-06-064086-3, RD 239, HarpR). Har-Row.

Old Time Agriculture in the Ads. Robert F. Karolevitz. LC 77-122596. (Illus.). 96p. 1970. pap. 2.95 (ISBN 0-87970-116-1). North Plains.

Old Time Cures - Farmers Folklore. David J. Gerrick & Doreen Dietsche. 104p. (Orig.). 1980. pap. 3.95 (ISBN 0-686-68571-7). Dayton Labs.

Old Time Gardens, Newly Set Forth. Alice M. Earle. LC 68-31219. (Illus.). 1968. Repr. of 1901 ed. 18.00 (ISBN 0-8103-3429-1). Gale.

Old-Time Parson. P. H. Ditchfield. 342p. 1980. Repr. of 1908 ed. lib. bdg. 35.00 (ISBN 0-89760-130-0). Telegraph Bks.

Old Time Punishments. William Andrews. LC 78-124585. 1970. Repr. of 1890 ed. 15.00 (ISBN 0-8103-3841-6). Gale.

Old Time Radio Hour. Peter Nicoletta. 1977. 2.50 (ISBN 0-918116-08-2). Jawbone Pr.

Old-Time Saloon: Not Wet--Not Dry, Just History. George Ade. LC 77-181797. (Illus.). xii, 176p. 1975. Repr. of 1931 ed. 18.00 (ISBN 0-8103-4076-3). Gale.

Old-Time Tools & Toys of Needlework. Gertrude Whiting. 1970. pap. 6.00 (ISBN 0-486-22517-8). Dover.

Old Times. John Ashton. LC 67-23944. (Illus.). 1969. Repr. of 1885 ed. 15.00 (ISBN 0-8103-3252-3). Gale.

Old Times. Walter C. Meller. LC 68-26592. (Illus.). 1968. Repr. of 1925 ed. 15.00 (ISBN 0-8103-3453-4). Gale.

Old Transvaal, Eighten Thirty-Four to Eighteen Ninety-Nine. 1980. 40.00x (Pub. by Bailey & Swinton South Africa). State Mutual Bk.

Old Trinity, a Story of Real Life. T. Mason Jones. (Nineteenth Century Fiction Ser.: Ireland: Vol. 64). 900p. 1979. lib. bdg. 46.00 (ISBN 0-8240-3513-5). Garland Pub.

Old Ugly. W. C. Chalk. pap. text ed. 2.75x o.p. (ISBN 0-435-11222-8). Heinemann Ed.

Old Vic Prefaces: Shakespeare & the Producer. Hugh Hunt. LC 72-6197. (Illus.). 193p. 1973. Repr. of 1954 ed. lib. bdg. 22.75x (ISBN 0-8371-6460-5, HUOV). Greenwood.

Old Walhalla: Portrait of a Gold Town. Raymond Paull. 148p. 1980. pap. 8.00x (ISBN 0-522-84212-7, Pub. by Melbourne U Pr Australia). Intl Schol Bk Serv.

Old Ways of Working Wood. rev. ed. Alex W. Bealer. (Illus.). 1980. 12.50 (ISBN 0-517-54047-9, 540479). Potter.

Old Ways of Working Wood. rev ed. Alex W. Bealer. (Illus.). 256p. 1980. 12.50 (ISBN 0-517-54047-9). Barre.

Old Westminster Bridge. R. J. Walker. LC 79-52379. (Illus.). 1980. 38.00 (ISBN 0-7153-7837-6). David & Charles.

Old Whaling Days. Robert McNab. 1977. 8.50 o.p. (ISBN 0-85558-432-7). Transatlantic.

Old Witch & the Polka-Dot Ribbon. Wende Devlin & Harry Devlin. LC 80-15284. (Illus.). 40p. (ps-3). 1980. Repr. of 1970 ed. 8.95 (ISBN 0-590-07787-2, Four Winds). Schol Bk Serv.

Old Witch Rescues Halloween. Wende Devlin & Harry Devlin. LC 80-17071. (Illus.). 48p. (ps-3). 1980. Repr. of 1972 ed. 8.95 (ISBN 0-590-07786-4, Four Winds). Schol Bk Serv.

Old Witch Rescues Halloween. Wende & Devlin. (gr. 3-4). 1980. pap. 3.50 incl. record (ISBN 0-590-24006-4, Schol Pap). Schol Bk Serv.

Old Wives' Lore for Gardeners. Maureen Boland & Bridget Boland. (Illus.). Date not set. pap. 3.25 (ISBN 0-374-51639-1). FS&G.

Old Woman and the Bird. David M. Webb. LC 79-55781. (Illus.). 45p. (gr. 3-8). 1981. 6.95 (ISBN 0-935054-04-9). Webb-Newcomb.

Old Woman & the Red Pumpkin. Adapted by Betsy Bang. LC 74-13057. (Illus.). 32p. (gr. k-3). 1975. 8.95g (ISBN 0-02-708360-8). Macmillan.

Old Woman & the Rice Thief. Betsy Bang. LC 76-30671. (Illus.). (gr. k-3). 1978. 7.95 (ISBN 0-688-80098-X); PLB 7.63 (ISBN 0-688-84098-1). Greenwillow.

Old World & the New, Fourteen Ninety-Two - Sixteen Fifty. John H. Elliott. LC 73-121362. (Studies in Early Modern History). (Illus.). 1970. 19.95 (ISBN 0-521-07937-3); pap. 5.95x (ISBN 0-521-09621-9). Cambridge U Pr.

Old World, New Horizons: Britain, Europe, & the Atlantic Alliance. Edward M. Heath. LC 71-106959. (Godkin Lecture Ser: 1967). 1970. 6.95x (ISBN 0-674-63260-5). Harvard U Pr.

Old Yeller. Fred Gipson. 1964. pap. 1.95 (ISBN 0-06-080002-X, P2, PL). Har-Row.

Old Yellow Eyes. Ed. by Thomas J. Mooney. (Pal Paperbacks - Kit A Ser.). (Illus., Orig.). (gr. 7-12). 1976. pap. text ed. 1.25 (ISBN 0-8374-3494-7). Xerox Ed Pubns.

Olde Concorde Christmas. Museum of Concord Antiquarian Society. (Illus.). 104p. 1980. 12.95 (ISBN 0-312-58421-0). St Martin.

Olden Days. Joe Mathieu. (Pictureback Ser.). (Illus.). 32p. (ps-3). 1981. PLB 4.99 (ISBN 0-394-94085-7); pap. 1.25 (ISBN 0-394-84085-2). Random.

Olden England, 2 vols. J. Frederick Hodgetts. 413p. 1981. Repr. of 1884 ed. Set. lib. bdg. 200.00 (ISBN 0-89987-364-2). Darby Bks.

Oldenbarnevelt, 2 vols. Jan Den Tex. Tr. by Ralph Powell from Dutch. LC 73-177937. (Illus.). 368p. 1973. Set. 145.00 (ISBN 0-521-08429-6). Cambridge U Pr.

Older Adult: A Process for Care. Elizabeth Forbes & Virginia Fitzsimons. 300p. 1981. pap. text ed. 11.50 (ISBN 0-8016-1631-X). Mosby.

Older Americans: An Untapped Resource. National Committee on Careers for Older Americans. LC 79-51560. 63p. (Orig.). 1979. pap. 8.50 (ISBN 0-89492-006-5). Acad Educ Dev.

Older Deaf Child: Pedagogical, Methodical & Didactical Aspects. P. Hoiberg. (Modern Approaches to the Diagnosis & Instructionsof Multi-Handicapped Children: Vol. 12). 64p. 1973. text ed. 15.00 (ISBN 90-237-4112-9, Pub. by Swets Pub Serv Holland). Swets North Am.

Older Persons & Retirement Communities: Case Studies in Social Gerontology. Jerry Jacobs. 144p. 1975. 14.75 (ISBN 0-398-03445-1); pap. 9.75 (ISBN 0-398-03446-X). C C Thomas.

Older Than the Dinosaurs: The Origin & Rise of the Mammals. Edward Ricciuti. LC 77-26606. (Illus.). 96p. (gr. 5-12). 1980. 7.95 (ISBN 0-690-01328-0, TYC-J); PLB 7.89 (ISBN 0-690-03879-8). T Y Crowell.

Older Volunteers in Church & Community. Paul B. Maves. 96p. 1981. pap. 6.95 (ISBN 0-8170-0889-6). Judson.

Older Woman. M. M. Fuller & C. A. Martin. 368p. 1980. pap. 16.75 (ISBN 0-398-03974-7). C C Thomas.

Older Women - Younger Men. Arlene Derenski & Sally Landsburg. 272p. 1981. 11.95 (ISBN 0-316-51366-0). Little.

Oldest Dance: Origins & Philosophy of Danse Orientale. Zarifa Aradoon. LC 78-67210. (Illus.). 1979. 14.95 o.p. (ISBN 0-930486-02-1); pap. 15.00 (ISBN 0-930486-03-X). Dream Place.

Oldest English Text. Henry Sweet. 668p. 1980. Repr. of 1885 ed. lib. bdg. 85.00 (ISBN 0-8482-6221-2). Norwood Edns.

Oldest God: Archaic Religion Yesterday & Today. Denise L. Carmody. LC 80-25499. 192p. (Orig.). 1981. pap. 6.95 (ISBN 0-687-28813-4). Abingdon.

Oldest Kid. Elaine Knox-Wagner. Ed. by Kathleen Tucker. (Concept Bks.). (Illus.). 32p. (gr. k-3). 1981. 6.50 (ISBN 0-8075-5986-5). A Whitman.

Oldest Revolutionary: Essays on Benjamin Franklin. Ed. by J. A. Lemay. LC 75-41618. 176p. 1976. 15.00x (ISBN 0-685-63233-4). U of Pa Pr.

Oldsmobile Cutlass: Nineteen Seventy to Nineteen Eighty Shop Manual. Jim Combs. Ed. by Eric Jorgensen. (Illus.). 342p. (Orig.). 1980. pap. text ed. 10.95 (ISBN 0-89287-324-8, A285). Clymer Pubns.

Oldtime Steam Cars. John Bentley. LC 53-4010. (Illus.). 1969. lib. bdg. 3.50 o.p. (ISBN 0-668-02073-3). Arco.

Olduvai Gorge, Vol. 1 & 2: Nineteen Fifty-One - Nineteen Sixty-One. Ed. by L. S. Leakey & P. V. Tobias. 1965. Vol. 1. 65.00 (ISBN 0-521-05527-X); Vol. 2. 72.50 (ISBN 0-521-06901-7). Cambridge U Pr.

Olduvai Gorge, Vol. 3: Nineteen Sixty - Nineteen Sixty-Three. Ed. by M. D. Leakey. 1972. 110.00 (ISBN 0-521-07723-0). Cambridge U Pr.

Ole Bull Returns to Pennsylvania: The Biography of a Norwegian Violin Virtuoso and Pioneer in the Keystone State. Inez Bull. (Illus.). 1961. 5.00 o.p. (ISBN 0-686-67700-5). Exposition.

Ole Miss Football: A Photo History. Lawrence Wells. LC 79-92411. (Illus.). 1980. 24.95 (Pub. by Sports Yearbook). Yoknapatawpha.

Oleanders. R. D. Furtado. (Redbird Bk.). 1976. lib. bdg. 8.00 (ISBN 0-89253-094-4); flexible bdg. 4.00 (ISBN 0-89253-131-2). Ind-US Inc.

Olfaction & Taste. Ed. by Yngve Zotterman. (Vol. 1). 1963. text ed. 24.75 o.p. (ISBN 0-08-009814-2). Pergamon.

Olfaction & Taste, Vol. 5. Ed. by Derek A. Denton & John P. Coghlan. 1975. 36.50 (ISBN 0-12-209750-5). Acad Pr.

Olfaction & Taste VI: Proceedings. International Symposium on Olfaction & Taste, 6th, Gif Sur Yvette, France, 1977. 500p. 25.00 (ISBN 0-904147-08-8). Info Retrieval.

Olga Carries on: More Tales of Olga Da Polga. Michael Bond. (Illus.). (gr. 3-6). 1977. 6.95 (ISBN 0-8038-5380-7). Hastings.

Olga Korbut. Jay H. Smith. LC 74-19169. (Creative Education Sports Superstars Ser.). (Illus.). 32p. (gr. 3-6). 1974. PLB 5.95 (ISBN 0-87191-384-4); pap. 2.95 (ISBN 0-89812-190-6). Creative Ed.

Olga Korbut: A Biographical Portrait. Michael Suponev. LC 73-11636. 96p. 1975. 6.95 o.p. (ISBN 0-385-09498-1). Doubleday.

Olga Meets Her Match: More Tales of Olga Da Polga. Michael Bond. (Illus.). 128p. (Orig.). (gr. 3-6). 1975. 6.95g (ISBN 0-8038-5377-7). Hastings.

Oligocene Rodents of North America, Vol. 70, Pt. 5. Albert E. Wood. 1980. 8.00 (ISBN 0-87169-705-X). Am Philos.

Oligozoospermia. Ed. by G. Frajese et al. 1981. text ed. price not set (ISBN 0-89004-589-5). Raven.

Olive. Dinah M. Craik. Ed. by Robert L. Wolff. LC 75-1521. (Victorian Fiction Ser.). 1975. Repr. of 1850 ed. lib. bdg. 66.00 (ISBN 0-8240-1593-2). Garland Pub.

Olive & Swee' Pea Wash up! Bill Pearson. Ed. by Philip Mann. (Shape Board Play Book). (Illus.). 14p. (gr. k-3). 1980. bds. 2.95 comb bdg. (ISBN 0-89828-126-1, 6008). Tuffy Bks.

Olive Schreiner: Feminism on the Frontier. Joyce Berkman. LC 78-74842. 1979. 11.95 (ISBN 0-88831-031-5). EPWP.

Oliver & Alison's Week. Jane B. Zalben. LC 80-17300. (Illus.). 32p. (gr. k-3). 1980. 9.95 (ISBN 0-374-35618-1). FS&G.

Oliver & Jonathan. Evalyne S. Grand. 32p. 1980. 8.95 (ISBN 0-86629-014-1). Sunrise MO.

Oliver Twist. Charles Dickens. (Literature Ser). (gr. 10-12). 1970. pap. text ed. 3.83 (ISBN 0-87720-747-X). AMSCO Sch.

Oliver Twist. Charles Dickens. Ed. by Harry Shefter et al. (YA) pap. 2.50 (ISBN 0-671-42073-9, Re). WSP.

Oliver Twist. Charles Dickens. 1957. 12.95x (ISBN 0-460-00233-3, Evman); pap. 2.95 (ISBN 0-460-01233-9). Dutton.

Oliver Twist. Charles Dickens. (Arabic.). pap. 8.95x (ISBN 0-686-63548-5). Intl Bk Ctr.

Oliver Wendell Holmes. Ed. by S. I. Hayakawa & Howard M. Jones. 472p. 1980. Repr. of 1939 ed. lib. bdg. 40.00 (ISBN 0-8495-2351-6). Arden Lib.

Oliver Wendell Holmes, 2 vols. John T. Morse, Jr. LC 80-21475. (American Men & Women of Letters Ser.). 700p. 1981. Set. pap. 10.95 (ISBN 0-87754-171-X). Chelsea Hse.

Oliver Wendell Holmes. Miriam R. Small. (U. S. Authors Ser.: No. 29). 1962. lib. bdg. 10.95 (ISBN 0-8057-0380-2). Twayne.

Oliver Wendell Holmes, Jr. David H. Burton. (United States Authors Ser.). 1980. lib. bdg. 10.95 (ISBN 0-8057-7262-6). Twayne.

Oliver Wiswell. Kenneth Roberts. 1977. pap. 1.95 o.p. (ISBN 0-449-30696-8, C696, Prem). Fawcett.

Olives & Olive Oil for the Gourmet. George F. Steffanides. LC 38-9182. (Illus.). iv, 49p. 1980. pap. 2.50 (ISBN 0-686-61076-8). Steffanides.

Olivia Newton-John. Ann Morse. (Rock 'n Pop Stars Ser.). (Illus.). (gr. 3-6). 1976. PLB 5.95 (ISBN -087191-475-1); pap. 2.75 o. p. (ISBN 0-89812-117-5). Creative Ed.

Olivocerebellar Projection: A Review. A. Brodal & K. Kawamura. (Advances in Anatomy, Embryology & Cell Biology Ser.: Vol. 64). (Illus.). 144p. 1981. pap. 46.10 (ISBN 0-387-10305-8). Springer-Verlag.

Ollie Owl. Suzanne Burke. Ed. by Alton Jordan. (Elephant Ser.). (Illus.). (gr. k-3). 1975. PLB 3.50 (ISBN 0-89868-015-8, Read Res); text ed. 1.75 softbd. (ISBN 0-89868-048-4). ARO Pub.

Ollie's Team & the Baseball Computer. Clem Philbrook. Date not set. 3.99 (ISBN 0-8038-5348-3). Hastings.

Ologies & Isms: A Thematic Dictionary. Ed. by Howard E. Zettler. LC 78-8328. 1978. 30.00 (ISBN 0-8103-1014-7). Gale.

Ologies & Isms: A Thematic Dictionary. 2nd ed. Ed. by Howard G. Zettler. 300p. 1981. 28.00 (ISBN 0-8103-1055-4). Gale.

OLT. Kenneth Gangemi. LC 75-476287. 1979. pap. 5.95 (ISBN 0-7145-0660-5, Pub. by M Boyars). Merrimack Bk Serv.

Olvida los Tambores. new ed. Ana Diosdado. Ed. by Angel R. Maroto. 112p. (Orig.). (gr. 11-12). 1974. pap. text ed. 3.25x (ISBN 0-88334-063-1). Ind Sch Pr.

Olvidados. Peter McCurtin. (Sundance Ser.: No. 30). 1980. 1.75. Nordon Pubns.

Olympia. Elgin Groseclose. 1981. pap. 9.95 (ISBN 0-89191-290-8). Cook.

Olympiad. Albert I. Mayer, Jr. LC 61-12875. (Illus.). (gr. 7-11). 1938. 8.50x (ISBN 0-8196-0115-2). Biblo.

Olympian & the Leprachaun: W.B. Yeats & James Stephens. Richard Finneran. (New Yeats Papers Ser.: No. 16). (Illus.). 1978. pap. text ed. 9.25x (ISBN 0-85105-338-6, Dolmen Pr). Humanities.

Olympia's Inheritance. Orlando R. Petrocelli. 1977. pap. 1.75 o.p. (ISBN 0-523-40006-3). Pinnacle Bks.

Olympic Alpine Skiing. Ice Skating Institute of America Staff. LC 79-19029. (Olympic Bks.). (Illus.). (gr. 4 up). 1979. lib. bdg. 7.95 (ISBN 0-516-02551-1); pap. 1.95 (ISBN 0-516-42551-X). Childrens.

Olympic Bobsledding. Ice Skating Institute of America Staff. LC 79-18842. (Olympic Bks.). (Illus.). (gr. 4 up). 1979. lib. bdg. 7.95 (ISBN 0-516-02552-X); pap. 1.95 (ISBN 0-516-42552-8). Childrens.

Olympic Figure Skating. Ice Skating Institute of America Staff. LC 79-16948. (Olympic Bks.). (Illus.). (gr. 4 up). 1979. lib. bdg. 7.95 (ISBN 0-516-02553-8); pap. 1.95 (ISBN 0-516-42553-6). Childrens.

Olympic Games. David Chester. LC 75-18816. (Encore Edition). 1975. 3.50 o.p. (ISBN 0-684-15688-1, ScribT). Scribner.

Olympic Games. Wolfgang Girardi. LC 72-173604. (International Library). (Illus.). 128p. (gr. 7 up). 1972. PLB 6.90 o.p. (ISBN 0-531-02111-4). Watts.

Olympic Games. Lord Killanin. 272p. 1976. 22.95 (ISBN 0-02-563050-4). Macmillan.

Olympic Games: The First Thousand Years. new ed. M. I. Finley & H. W. Pleket. LC 75-44456. (Illus.). 168p. 1976. 14.95 o.p. (ISBN 0-670-52406-9). Viking Pr.

Olympic Gymnastics. Akitomo Kaneko. LC 76-1171. (Illus.). 256p. 1980. pap. 7.95 (ISBN 0-8069-8926-2). Sterling.

Olympic Ice Hockey. Ice Skating Institute of America Staff. LC 79-16382. (Olympic Bks.). (Illus.). (gr. 4 up). 1979. lib. bdg. 7.95 (ISBN 0-516-02554-6); pap. 1.95 (ISBN 0-516-42554-4). Childrens.

Olympic Nordic Skiing. Ice Skating Institute of America Staff. LC 79-18626. (Olympic Bks.). (Illus.). (gr. 4 up). 1979. lib. bdg. 7.95 (ISBN 0-516-02555-4); pap. 1.95 (ISBN 0-516-42555-2). Childrens.

Olympic Speed Skating. Ice Skating Institute of America Staff. LC 79-16969. (Olympic Bks.). (Illus.). (gr. 4 up). 1979. lib. bdg. 7.95 (ISBN 0-516-02556-2); pap. 1.95 (ISBN 0-516-42556-0). Childrens.

Olympic Story Nineteen Eighty. Compiled by Associated Press & Grolier. (Illus.). 256p. 1981. 14.95 (ISBN 0-531-09942-3). Watts.

Olympic Story: Pursuit of Excellence. LC 80-67767. (Illus.). 1980. write for info. (ISBN 0-7172-8158-2). Grolier Ed Corp.

Olympic Story: Pursuit of Excellence. LC 79-66061. (Illus.). 1979. write for info o.p. (ISBN 0-7172-8153-1). Grolier Ed Corp.

Olympics. Julian May. LC 75-8755. (Sports Classics Ser.). (Illus.). 48p. (gr. 4-6). 1975. PLB 8.95 o.p. (ISBN 0-87191-453-0). Creative Ed.

Olympic's Film Finder: Nineteen Eighty-One Business Edition. Ed. by Walter J. Carroll. 1981. 24.00x (ISBN 0-88367-600-1). Olympic Media.

Olympie. Gasparo Spontini. Ed. by Philip Grossett & Charles Rosen. LC 76-49227. (Early Romantic Opera Ser.: Vol. 44). 1980. lib. bdg. 82.00 (ISBN 0-8240-2943-7). Garland Pub.

Olympism. Ed. by Jeffrey Segrave & Donald Chu. 1981. text ed. 17.95x (ISBN 0-931250-20-X). Human Kinetics.

OlympiX: A Spoof on the Games. Charles S. Hellman & Robert A. Tiritilli. (Illus.). 1980. 4.95x (ISBN 0-935938-01-X). Hit Ent.

Olympus on Main Street: A Process for Planning a Community Arts Facility. Joseph Golden. LC 80-16479. 248p. 1980. 9.95 (ISBN 0-8156-0156-5). Syracuse U Pr.

Om Krishna II: From the Sickroom of the Walking Eagles. Charles H. Ford. LC 80-13972. (Orig.). 1981. 35.00x (ISBN 0-916156-48-6); pap. 4.00x (ISBN 0-916156-47-8). Cherry Valley.

Om Mane Padme Hum! Hail to the Jewel in the Lotus. Asif Currimbhoy. (Bluebird Ser.). 67p. 1975. 12.00 (ISBN 0-88253-594-3); pap. text ed. 4.80 (ISBN 0-88253-593-5). Ind-US Inc.

Om, the Secret of Ahbor Valley. Mundy Talbot. 392p. 1980. pap. 7.25 (913004-39). Point Loma Pub.

Omaha Crossing. Ray Hogan. 1977. pap. 1.75 (ISBN 0-441-62341-7). Ace Bks.

Omaha Indians. G. Hubert Smith. Ed. by David A. Horr. (American Indian Ethnohistory Ser. - Plains Indians). 1974. lib. bdg. 42.00 (ISBN 0-8240-0739-5). Garland Pub.

Omaha Tribal Myths & Trickster Tales. Roger Welsch. LC 80-22636. 350p. 1981. 15.95 (ISBN 0-8040-0700-4, 0700S, SB). Swallow.

Omaha Tribe, 2 vols. Alice C. Fletcher & Francis La Flesche. Incl. Vol. 1. 312p (ISBN 0-8032-5756-2, BB 549, Bison); Vol. 2. viii, 347p (ISBN 0-8032-5757-0, BB 550, Bison). LC 72-175503. (Illus.). 686p. 1972. pap. 7.95 ea. U of Nebr Pr.

Oman a History. Wendell Phillips. 14.00x (ISBN 0-685-72053-5). Intl Bk Ctr.

Oman & Gulf-Security. B. K. Narayan. 300p. 1980. text ed. 24.00x (ISBN 0-8426-1660-8). Verry.

Oman: The Reborn Land. F. A. Clements. 1981. text ed. 25.00 (ISBN 0-582-78300-3). Longman.

Omani Silver. Ruth Hawley. LC 77-20799. (Illus.). 1977. pap. text ed. 7.50x (ISBN 0-582-78070-5). Longman.

Ombibulous Mister Mencken. Bud Johns. LC 68-8421. (Illus.). 1968. bds. 3.95 (ISBN 0-912184-01-9). Synergistic Pr.

Ombre Des Jeunes Filles En Fleurs. Marcel Proust. (Coll. Folio). 1965. pap. 4.50 (ISBN 0-685-23900-4, 1428). French & Eur.

Ombudsmen Around the World: A Comparative Chart. 2nd ed. Kent M. Weeks. LC 78-17224. 1978. pap. 7.00x (ISBN 0-87772-258-7). Inst Gov Stud Berk.

Omdurman. Philip Ziegler. 1974. 7.95 o.p. (ISBN 0-394-48936-5). Knopf.

Omega Document. J. Alexander McKenzie. LC 79-53442. (Canaan Trilogy Ser.). 1979. pap. 2.50 (ISBN 0-87123-416-5, 200416). Bethany Fell.

Omens from the Flight of Birds: The First 101 Days of Jimmy Carter. Ed. by Stephen Vincent. (Illus.). 1978. lib. bdg. o.p. (ISBN 0-917672-06-2); pap. 4.95x (ISBN 0-917672-05-4). Momos.

Omicron Process. Jack R. Gibb. LC 80-67898. 1981. pap. 8.95 (ISBN 0-89615-025-9). Guild of Tutors.

Omitted Chapters of History Disclosed in the Life & Papers of Edmund Randolph. M. D. Conway. LC 73-124041. (American Public Figures Ser). 1971. Repr. of 1888 ed. lib. bdg. 39.50 (ISBN 0-306-70995-3). Da Capo.

Omni & Horizon, Nineteen Seventy-Eight to Nineteen Eighty. Chilton's Automotive Editorial Dept. LC 78-20257. (Chilton's Repair & Tune-Up Guides). (Illus.). 1979. pap. 8.95 (ISBN 0-8019-6845-3, 6845). Chilton.

Omni Strain. Cliff Patton. 432p. (Orig.). 1980. pap. 2.75 (ISBN 0-89083-689-2). Zebra.

Omnivorous Primates: Gathering & Hunting in Human Evolution. Ed. by Robert S. Harding. Geza P. Teleki. LC 80-23726. (Illus.). 912p. 1981. 30.00x (ISBN 0-231-04024-5). Columbia U Pr.

On a Clear Day You Can See General Motors. J. Patrick Wright. 304p. 1980. pap. 2.95 (ISBN 0-380-51722-1, 51722). Avon.

On a Deserted Shore. Kathleen Raine. 1973. text ed. 6.00x (ISBN 0-85105-248-7, Dolmen Pr). Humanities.

On a General Economic Theory of Motion. M. J. Magill. LC 74-135961. (Lecture Notes in Operations Research & Mathematical Systems: Vol. 36). 1970. pap. 10.70 o.p. (ISBN 0-387-04959-2). Springer-Verlag.

On a Pincushion, 2 vols, Repr. Of 1877 Ed. Mary De Morgan. Incl. Necklace of Princess Fiorimonde, & Other Stories. Repr. of 1880 ed. LC 75-32181. (Classics of Children's Literature, 1621-1932). (Illus.). 1977. Set. PLB 76.00 (ISBN 0-8240-2293-9); PLB 38.00 ea. Garland Pub.

On a Research Program in Early Modern Physics. Paul Elzinga. (Studies in the Theory of Science). 1972. text ed. 12.00x (ISBN 0-391-00245-7). Humanities.

On a Shoestring to Coorg. Dervla Murphy. 1977. 18.50 (ISBN 0-7195-3284-1). Transatlantic.

On a Slide of Light. Greta Woodrew. 224p. 1981. 12.95 (ISBN 0-02-631390-1). Macmillan.

On Act & Scene Division in the Shakespere First Folio. T. W. Baldwin. LC 64-20255. 190p. 1965. 6.50x (ISBN 0-8093-0153-9). S Ill U Pr.

On Adolescence: A Psychoanalytic Interpretation. Peter Blos. LC 61-14110. 1962. 15.95 (ISBN 0-02-904320-4); pap. 4.95 (ISBN 0-02-904330-1). Free Pr.

On Amphetamine and in Europe: Excerpts from the Anonymous Diary of a New York Youth, Vol. 3. Taylor Mead. 1968. pap. 7.95 (ISBN 0-932430-01-5). Boss Bks.

On & Around Sydney Harbour. Lawrence Collings & Olaf Ruhen. 128p. 1980. 13.95x (ISBN 0-00-216407-8, Pub. by W Collins Australia). Intl Schol Bk Serv.

On Applied Psychoanalysis. Fritz Schmidl. LC 79-92435. 1981. 15.00 (ISBN 0-8022-2364-8). Philos Lib.

On Aristotle & Greek Tragedy. John Jones. LC 80-50895. 288p. 1980. 16.50x (ISBN 0-8047-1092-9); pap. 6.95 (ISBN 0-8047-1093-7, SP11). Stanford U Pr.

On Art. Marsden Hartley. Ed. by Gail R. Scott. (Illus.). 360p. 1981. 19.95 (ISBN 0-8180-0130-5). Horizon.

On Becoming a Counselor: A Basic Guide for Non-Professional Counselors. Eugene Kennedy. 338p. 14.95 (ISBN 0-8164-0315-5); pap. 8.95 (ISBN 0-8264-0020-5). Continuum.

On Becoming a Family: The Growth of Attachment. T. Berry Brazelton. 1981. 14.95 (ISBN 0-440-06712-X, Sey Lawr). Delacorte.

On Becoming a Rock Musician. H. Stith Bennett. LC 80-5378. 272p. 1981. lib. bdg. 15.00x (ISBN 0-87023-311-4). U of Mass Pr.

On Becoming Human. Nancy Tanner. LC 80-21526. (Illus.). 350p. Date not set. 29.95 (ISBN 0-521-23554-5); pap. 10.95 (ISBN 0-521-28028-1). Cambridge U Pr.

On Being a Bird. Philip Wills. 1977. 13.50 (ISBN 0-7153-7426-5). David & Charles.

On Being a Deacon's Wife: Study Guide. Martha Nelson. LC 72-96150. 1977. saddlewire 1.35 (ISBN 0-8054-3507-7). Broadman.

On Being a Teacher. Jonathan Kozol. 208p. 1981. 12.95 (ISBN 0-8264-0035-3). Continuum.

On Being Gifted. American Association for Gifted Children. LC 78-58622. 1979. 8.95 (ISBN 0-8027-0616-9); pap. 5.95 (ISBN 0-8027-7138-6). Walker & Co.

On Being Human. Montagu. (gr. 9-12). 1967. 4.95 (ISBN 0-8015-5508-6, Hawthorn); pap. 3.50 (ISBN 0-8015-5514-0, Hawthorn). Dutton.

On Being Jewish. Ed. by Daniel Walden. 480p. 1974. pap. 1.75 o.p. (ISBN 0-449-30696-8, X638, Prem). Fawcett.

On Being Sure in Religion. Ian T. Ramsey. 1963. text ed. 11.25x (ISBN 0-485-11063-6, Athlone Pr). Humanities.

On Beyond Koch. Phyllis A. Tickle. (Illus.). 160p. 1981. pap. 2.95 (ISBN 0-918518-20-2). St Luke TN.

On Beyond Zebra! Dr. Seuss. LC 55-9321. (Dr. Seuss Paperback Classics Ser.). (Illus.). 64p. (gr. k-3). 1980. pap. 2.95 (ISBN 0-686-64846-3). Random.

On Both Sides of the Gate. Joel Freedman. LC 79-67518. 1981. 6.95 (ISBN 0-533-04466-9). Vantage.

On Call. Miguel Algarin. LC 79-90764. (Illus., Orig.). 1980. pap. 5.00x (ISBN 0-934770-03-4). Arte Publico.

On Capitalist Underdevelopment. Andre F. Frank. 1976. pap. 3.95x (ISBN 0-19-560475-X). Oxford U Pr.

On Christian Doctrine. Saint Augustine. Tr. by D. W. Robertson. LC 58-9956. 1958. pap. 4.95 (ISBN 0-672-60262-8). Bobbs.

On Christian Doctrine. Saint Augustine. 1981. pap. 3.95 (ISBN 0-89526-887-6). Regnery-Gateway.

On Christianity: Early Theological Writings. Friedrich Hegel. Tr. by Knox. 8.50 (ISBN 0-8446-0689-8). Peter Smith.

On Christmas Day: First Carols to Play & Sing. Ed. by Mervyn Horder. LC 69-11103. (Illus.). (gr. 1-7). 1969. 5.95 o.s.i. (ISBN 0-02-744400-7). Macmillan.

On City Streets: An Anthology of Poetry. Ed. by Nancy Larrick. LC 68-30505. (Illus.). 160p. (gr. 5-8). 1968. 7.95 (ISBN 0-87131-080-5). M Evans.

On Civil Liberty & Self Government. Francis Lieber. LC 76-169655. (Civil Liberties in American History Ser). 1972. Repr. of 1877 ed. lib. bdg. 59.50 (ISBN 0-306-70284-3). Da Capo.

On Cliches: The Supersedure of Meaning by Function in Modernity. Anton C. Zijderveld. (International Library of Sociology). 1979. 18.00 (ISBN 0-7100-0186-X). Routledge & Kegan.

On Coexistence: A Causal Approach to Diversity & Stability in Grassland Vegetation. (Agricultural Research Reports Ser.: No. 902). 164p. 1981. pap. 25.75 (ISBN 90-220-0747-2, PDC 217, Pudoc). Unipub.

On Commercial Economy. E. S. Cayley. 280p. Repr. of 1830 ed. 30.00x (ISBN 0-686-28326-0, Pub. by Irish Academic Pr). Biblio Dist.

On Communications: A Fundamental Approach to Reading, Writing, Speaking & Listening. Richard W. Swanson & Charles E. Marquardt. LC 73-7370. (Illus.). 192p. 1974. pap. text ed. 5.95x (ISBN 0-02-478750-7). Macmillan.

On Consciousness, Language, & Cognition: Three Studies in Materialism. Morris Colman. (Occasional Papers: No. 31). 1978. 1.50 (ISBN 0-89977-027-4). Am Inst Marxist.

On Crime Writing. new ed. Ross MacDonald. (Capra Chapbook Ser.: No. 11). (Illus.). 1973. pap. 2.50 o.p. (ISBN 0-912264-66-7). Capra Pr.

On Crimes & Punishments. Cesare Beccaria. Tr. by Henry Paolucci. LC 61-18589. 1963. pap. 3.95 (ISBN 0-672-60302-0, LLA107). Bobbs.

On Dating Phonological Change: A Miscellany of Articles by Lennart Moberg, Axel Kock, and Ernst Wigforss. Ed. & tr. by T. L. Markey. (Linguistica Extranea Ser.: Studia 1). 113p. 1978. lib. bdg. 8.25 (ISBN 0-89720-002-0); pap. 5.50 (ISBN 0-89720-000-4). Karoma.

On Death & Dying. E. K. Ross. 1969. 9.95 (ISBN 0-685-44001-X); pap. 1.95 (ISBN 0-02-089130-X, 08913). Macmillan.

On Designing. Anni Albers. LC 62-12321. (Illus.). 1962. pap. 5.95 (ISBN 0-8195-6019-7, Pub. by Wesleyan U Pr). Columbia U Pr.

On Detective Fiction & Other Things. George F. McCleary. 161p. 1980. Repr. of 1960 ed. lib. bdg. 20.00 (0-8492-6600-9). R West.

On Difficulty & Other Essays. George Steiner. 224p. 1980. pap. 3.95 (ISBN 0-19-520222-8, G-B613). Oxford U Pr.

On Directing. Harold Clurman. 320p. 1972. 12.95 (ISBN 0-02-526410-9). Macmillan.

On Directing. Harold Clurman. (Illus.). 336p. 1974. pap. 6.95 (ISBN 0-02-013350-2, Collier). Macmillan.

On Divers Arts: The Foremost Medieval Treatise on Painting, Glassmaking, & Metalwork. Theophilus. Tr. by John G. Hawthorne & Cyril S. Smith. (Illus.). 1979. pap. text ed. 5.00 (ISBN 0-486-23784-2). Dover.

On Dying & Denying: A Psychiatric Study of Terminality. Avery D. Weisman. LC 79-174268. 208p. 1972. text ed. 22.95 (ISBN 0-87705-068-6). Human Sci Pr.

On Eagle's Wing. Martin Cecil. 1977. 2.95 (ISBN 0-686-27653-1). Cole-Outreach.

On Economic Theory & Socialism: Collected Papers. Maurice Dobb. 1965. Repr. of 1955 ed. 26.00x (ISBN 0-7100-1283-7). Routledge & Kegan.

On Education & Freedom. Harold Taylor. LC 53-13096. (Arcturus Books Paperbacks). 320p. 1967. pap. 2.65 (ISBN 0-8093-0246-2). S Ill U Pr.

On Either Side of Arrogance. Pritish Nandy. (Redbird Ser.). 1975. 4.80 (ISBN 0-88253-596-X); pap. text ed. 4.00 (ISBN 0-88253-595-1). Ind-US Inc.

On Essays: A Reader for Writers. Paul H. Connolly. 352p. 1980. pap. text ed. 7.50 scp (ISBN 0-06-041345-X, HarpC). Har-Row.

On Every Front: The Making of the Cold War. Thomas G. Paterson. 1979. 14.95 (ISBN 0-393-01238-7); pap. 4.95x (ISBN 0-393-95014-X). Norton.

On Explaining Language Change. Roger Lass. LC 79-51825. (Studies in Linguistics Ser.: No. 27). (Illus.). 1980. 29.95 (ISBN 0-521-22836-0). Cambridge U Pr.

On-Farm Maize Drying & Storage in the Humid Tropics. (FAO Agricultural Services Bulletin: No. 40). 69p. 1981. pap. 6.00 (ISBN 92-5-100944-9, F2077, FAO). Unipub.

On Fetal Growth Rate. Margaret Oonsted & Christopher Oonsted. (Clinics in Developmental Medicine Ser.: Vol. 46). 1972. 19.50 (ISBN 0-685-34617-X). Lippincott.

On Fiction: Critical Essays & Notes. Edward Loomis. LC 66-30425. 71p. 1966. 3.25 (ISBN 0-8040-0231-2). Swallow.

On First Principles: Being Koetschau's Text of the De Principiis. Origen. Tr. by G. W. Butterworth. 7.50 (ISBN 0-8446-2685-6). Peter Smith.

On Foot Through Europe: A Trail Guide to Scandinavia. Craig Evans. Ed. by Stephen Whitney. (Illus.). 480p. 1980. lib. bdg. 13.95 (ISBN 0-933710-12-7); pap. 7.95 (ISBN 0-686-26899-7). Foot Trails.

On Free Choice of the Will. Saint Augustine. Tr. by A. S. Benjamin & L. H. Hackstaff. LC 63-16932. (Orig.). 1964. pap. 4.95 (ISBN 0-672-60368-3, LLAS150). Bobbs.

On Freedom's Side: An Anthology of American Poems of Protest. Ed. by Aaron Kramer. (gr. 7up). 1972. 5.95 o.s.i. (ISBN 0-02-750950-8). Macmillan.

On Genesis. Bruce Vawter. LC 76-26354. 1977. 12.95 (ISBN 0-385-06104-8). Doubleday.

On God & Political Duty. 2nd ed. John Calvin. LC 50-4950. 1956. pap. 3.95 (ISBN 0-672-60184-2, LLA23). Bobbs.

On Going to Church. George B. Shaw. 24p. pap. 1.00 (ISBN 0-934676-13-5). Greenlf Bks.

On Golden Pond. Ernest Thompson. LC 79-12879. 1979. 7.95 (ISBN 0-396-07710-2). Dodd.

On Gramsci & Other Writings. Palmiro Togliatti. Ed. by Donald Sassoon. 1980. text ed. 24.75x (ISBN 0-391-01679-2). Humanities.

On Great Writing on the Sublime. Longinus. Tr. by G. M. Grube. LC 57-14628. 1957. pap. 2.40 o.p. (ISBN 0-672-60261-X, LLA79). Bobbs.

On Growth & Form, 2 Vols. D'Arcy W. Thompson. 1952. Set. 125.00 (ISBN 0-521-06622-0). Cambridge U Pr.

On Growth & Form. abr. ed. D'Arcy W. Thompson. Ed. by John T. Bonner. 49.50 (ISBN 0-521-06623-9); pap. 13.95x (ISBN 0-521-09390-2). Cambridge U Pr.

On Guilt & Innocence: Essays in Legal Philosophy & Moral Psychology. Herbert Morris. LC 72-89789. 1976. 11.50x o.p. (ISBN 0-520-02349-8); pap. 3.95 (ISBN 0-520-03944-0). U of Cal Pr.

On Guilt, Responsibility & Punishment. Alf Ross. LC 73-94446. 1975. 17.50x (ISBN 0-520-02717-5). U of Cal Pr.

On Heroes & Tombs. Ernesto Sabato. 1981. 17.95 (ISBN 0-87923-381-8). Godine.

On Heroes, Hero-Worship & the Heroic in History. Thomas Carlyle. Ed. by Carl Niemeyer. LC 66-12130. (Illus.). 1966. pap. 2.95x (ISBN 0-8032-5030-4, BB 334, Bison). U of Nebr Pr.

On Heroes, Hero-Worship & the Heroic in History. Thomas Carlyle. (World's Classics Ser: No. 62). 320p. 1975. 10.95 (ISBN 0-19-250062-7). Oxford U Pr.

On Higher Education: Origins & Consequences of the Academic Counterrevolution in America. David Riesman. LC 80-8007. (Carnegie Council Ser.). 1981. text ed. 15.95 (ISBN 0-87589-484-4). Jossey-Bass.

On His Majesty's Service in Uganda: The Origins of Uganda's African Civil Service, 1912-1940. Nizar Motani. (Foreign & Comparative Studies-African Ser.: No. 29). 72p. 1978. pap. text ed. 5.00x (ISBN 0-915984-51-2). Syracuse U Foreign Comp.

On History. Fernand Braudel. Tr. by Sarah Matthews from Fr. LC 80-11201. 1980. lib. bdg. 15.00x (ISBN 0-226-07150-2). U of Chicago Pr.

On History. Immanuel Kant. Ed. by Lewis W. Beck. Tr. by L. W. Beck et al. LC 62-22315. (Orig.). 1963. pap. 5.95 (ISBN 0-672-51070-7); pap. 3.95 (ISBN 0-672-60387-X, LLA162). Bobbs.

On Human Conduct. Michael Oakeshott. 350p. 1975. 34.00x (ISBN 0-19-827195-6). Oxford U Pr.

On Intelligence. Hippolyte A. Taine. (Contributions to the History of Psychology Ser.). 1978. 30.00 (ISBN 0-89093-152-6). U Pubns Amer.

On Judging Works of Visual Art. Conrad Fiedler. Tr. by Henry Schaefer-Simmern from Ger. (Library Reprint Ser.: Vol. 88). 1978. 12.95x (ISBN 0-520-03597-6). U of Cal Pr.

On Keynesian Economics & the Economics of Keynes: A Study in Monetary Theory. Axel Leijonhufvud. 1968. text ed. 12.95x (ISBN 0-19-500948-7). Oxford U Pr.

On Labour: Its Wrongful Claims & Rightful Dues: Its Actual Present & Possible Future. 2nd ed. William T. Thornton. (Development of Industrial Society Ser.). 499p. 1980. Repr. 35.00x (ISBN 0-7165-1788-4, Pub. by Irish Academic Pr). Biblio Dist.

On Language. William Safire. 1980. 13.95 (ISBN 0-8129-0937-2). Times Bks.

On Language, Culture & Religion: In Honor of Eugene A. Nida. Ed. by M. Black & W. A. Smalley. (Approaches to Semiotics Ser: No. 56). (Illus.). 386p. 1974. text ed. 45.90x (ISBN 90-2793-236-0). Mouton.

On Law & Ideology. Paul Hirst. 1979. text ed. 20.00x (ISBN 0-391-00970-2); pap. 10.25x (ISBN 0-391-01009-3). Humanities.

On Law & Justice. Alf Ross. (California Library Repr). 1975. Repr. of 1959 ed. 23.75x (ISBN 0-520-02851-1). U of Cal Pr.

On Liberty. John S. Mill. Ed. by Currin V. Shields. 1956. pap. 3.95 (ISBN 0-672-60234-2, LLA61). Bobbs.

On Linguistic Anthropology: Essays in Honor of Harry Hoijer, 1979. Ed. by J. Maquet. LC 80-50214. (Other Realities Ser.: Vol. 2). 140p. text ed. 12.00; pap. text ed. 9.00. Undena Pubns.

On Literature. Maxim Gorky. LC 72-11682. 400p. 1975. pap. 3.95 (ISBN 0-295-95453-1). U of Wash Pr.

On Love & Loving: Psychological Perspectives on the Nature & Experience of Romantic Love. Kenneth S. Pope et al. LC 80-8012. (Social & Behavioral Science Ser.). 1980. text ed. 16.95x (ISBN 0-87589-479-8). Jossey-Bass.

On Loving. George Holden. LC 75-2425. (Personal Guidance & Social Adjustment Ser.). 190p. (gr. 7-12). 1975. PLB 5.97 o.p. (ISBN 0-8239-0324-9). Rosen Pr.

On Loving God, & Selections from Sermons by St. Bernard of Clairvaux. Saint Bernard De Clairvaux. Ed. by Hugh Martin. LC 79-8706. (A Treasury of Christian Books). 125p. 1981. Repr. of 1959 ed. lib. bdg. 17.50x (ISBN 0-313-20787-9, BEOL). Greenwood.

On Loving God: Selections from Sermons by St. Bernard of Clairvaux. St. Bernard de Clairvaux. Ed. by Hugh Martin. LC 79-8706. (Treasury of Christian Books). 125p. 1981. Repr. of 1959 ed. lib. bdg. 17.50x (ISBN 0-313-20787-9, BEOL). Greenwood.

On Market Street. Arnold Lobel. LC 80-21418. (Illus.). 40p. (gr. k-3). 1981. 8.95 (ISBN 0-688-80309-1); PLB 8.59 (ISBN 0-688-84309-3); prepack. Greenwillow.

On Marriage in Norway. Eilert Sundt. Tr. by M. Drake from Norwegian. LC 79-42648. 1980. 29.50 (ISBN 0-521-23199-X). Cambridge U Pr.

On Medieval & Renaissance Slavic Writings. Henrik Birnbaum. LC 73-85243. (Slavistic Printings & Reprintings Ser.: No. 266). 381p. 1974. text ed. 76.50x (ISBN 90-2792-680-8). Mouton.

On Mime. Angna Enters. LC 65-21130. 1978. pap. 5.95 (ISBN 0-8195-6056-1, Pub. by Wesleyan U Pr). Columbia U Pr.

On Music & Musicians. Manue De Falla. 136p. 1981. pap. 7.95 (ISBN 0-7145-2735-1, Pub. by M. Boyars). Merrimack Bk Serv.

On My Way to Grandpa's. Ann Schweninger. LC 80-22729. (Illus.). 32p. (ps-2). 1981. 7.50 (ISBN 0-8037-6741-2); PLB 7.28 (ISBN 0-8037-6752-8). Dial.

On Nature. Lucretius. Tr. by Russel M. Geer. LC 63-12204. (Orig.). 1965. pap. 5.95 (ISBN 0-672-60355-1, LLA142). Bobbs.

On Neoclassicism. Mario Praz. Tr. by Angus Davidson. 1969. 19.95x o.s.i. (ISBN 0-8101-0009-6). Northwestern U Pr.

On Noam Chomsky: Critical Essays. Ed. by Gilbert Harman. LC 74-3558. 360p. 1974. pap. 4.95 (ISBN 0-385-03765-1, Anch). Doubleday.

On Not Being Good Enough: Writings of a Working Critic. Roger Sale. 1979. 14.95 (ISBN 0-19-502559-8). Oxford U Pr.

On Not Knowing How to Live. Allen Wheelis. LC 75-4294. 128p. (YA) 1975. 5.95 o.s.i. (ISBN 0-06-014562-5, HarpT). Har-Row.

On Old Age. Cicero. Bd. with On Friendship. LC 67-27680. 1967. pap. 3.50 (ISBN 0-672-60463-9, LLA213). Bobbs.

On or About the First Day in June. John Colleton. (Orig.). 1978. pap. 2.25 (ISBN 0-451-09007-1, E9007, Sig). NAL.

On Our Own. Karon W. Gibson et al. Ed. by Joy S. Catterson & Patricia Skalka. 256p. 1981. 10.95 (ISBN 0-312-58455-5). St Martin.

On Our Own: Patient Controlled Alternatives to the Mental Health System. Judi Chamberlain. LC 76-56520. 1978. 12.00 o.p. (ISBN 0-8015-5523-X). Dutton.

On Our Way. F. D. Roosevelt. LC 72-2383. (FDR & the Era of the New Deal Ser.). 216p. 1973. Repr. of 1934 ed. lib. bdg. 29.50 (ISBN 0-306-70476-5). Da Capo.

On Our Way to Christmas: A Family Activity Book for Advent. Mary P. Warren. 32p. (Orig.). 1980. pap. 3.50 (ISBN 0-8066-1784-5, 10-4768). Augsburg.

On Pain of Seeing. Erich Fried. Tr. by Georg Rapp. LC 74-97025. (Poetry Europe Ser.: No. 11). 72p. 1969. 6.95 (ISBN 0-8040-0234-7). Swallow.

On Playing the Flute. Johann J. Quantz. Tr. by Edward R. Reilly. LC 75-10986. (Illus.). 1975. 19.95 (ISBN 0-02-871940-9); pap. 8.95 (ISBN 0-02-871930-1). Schirmer Bks.

On Poetic Imagination & Reverie: Selections from the Works of Gaston Bachelard. Gaston Bachelard. Ed. by C. Gaudin. LC 73-148015. (Library of Liberal Arts Ser). 1971. pap. 3.95 (ISBN 0-672-61187-2). Bobbs.

On Poetry. Giovanni Boccaccio. Tr. by Charles G. Osgood. 1956. pap. 5.80 o.p. (ISBN 0-672-60265-2, LLA82). Bobbs.

On Poetry & Style. Aristotle. Tr. by G. M. Grube. LC 58-13827. 1958. pap. 3.95 (ISBN 0-672-60244-X, LLA68). Bobbs.

On Political Economy & Econometrics. Oskar Lange. 1965. 56.00 (ISBN 0-08-011588-8). Pergamon.

On Power: Its Nature & the History of Its Growth. Bertrand de Jouvenel. Tr. by J. F. Huntington from Fr. LC 80-24721. xix, 421p. 1981. Repr. of 1949 ed. lib. bdg. 39.75x (ISBN 0-313-22515-X, JOOP). Greenwood.

On Preaching. Robert L. Dabney. 1979. 10.95 (ISBN 0-85151-290-9). Banner of Truth.

On Psychotherapy & Casework, Vol. 7. GAP Committee on Psychiatry & Community. LC 62-2872. (Report No. 71). 1969. pap. 2.00 (ISBN 0-87318-099-2). Adv Psychiatry.

On Reading. Marcel Proust. Ed. by Jean Autret & William Burford. Tr. by Jean Autret & William Burford. 1971. 7.95 o.s.i. (ISBN 0-02-599240-6). Macmillan.

On Reflection: An Autobiography. Helen Hayes & Sandford Dody. LC 68-54122. (Illus.). 256p. 1968. 8.95 (ISBN 0-87131-082-1); autographed ed. 12.50 (ISBN 0-87131-293-X). M Evans.

On Religion: Speeches to Its Cultured Despisers. Friedrich Schleirmacher. 1959. 9.00 (ISBN 0-8446-2878-6). Peter Smith.

On Reporting the News. William E. Burrows. LC 76-16472. 345p. 1977. 15.00x (ISBN 0-8147-1009-3). NYU Pr.

On Revolutions & Progress in Economic Knowledge. T. W. Hutchinson. LC 77-82498. 1978. 44.50 (ISBN 0-521-21805-5). Cambridge U Pr.

On, Romanticism. Donald Sutherland. LC 78-145514. (Illus.). 1971. 15.00x (ISBN 0-8147-7753-8). NYU Pr.

On-Scene Traffic Accident Investigator's Manual. R. W. Rivers. (Illus.). 192p. 1981. 32.75 (ISBN 0-398-04121-0). C C Thomas.

On Scientific Thinking. Ed. by Ryan D. Tweney et al. 496p. 1981. 25.00x (ISBN 0-231-04814-9); pap. 12.50x (ISBN 0-231-04815-7). Columbia U Pr.

On Semantics. Uriel Weinreich. Intro. by William Labov & Beatrice S. Weinreich. LC 78-65114. 1979. 28.50x (ISBN 0-8122-7759-7). U of Pa Pr.

On-Shore Britain, 1976-77. Ed. by Sue Elliott. (Illus.). 1976. pap. 40.00 o.p. (ISBN 0-7161-0322-2, Gower). Unipub.

On Sigmund Freud's Dreams. Alexander Grinstein. 484p. 1968. 19.95x o.p. (ISBN 0-8143-1351-5). Wayne St U Pr.

On Site: The Construction of a High-Rise. Richard Younker. LC 79-7889. (Illus.). (gr. 5-12). 1980. 7.95 (ISBN 0-690-04003-2, TYC-J); PLB 7.89 (ISBN 0-690-04004-0). T Y Crowell.

On Social Ideas & Ideologies. Ferdinand Tonnies. Ed. & tr. by E. G. Jacoby. 1974. pap. 5.95x o.p. (ISBN 0-06-139533-1, HR1810, Torch). Har-Row.

On Social Indicators & Development. 36p. 1981. pap. 10.00 (ISBN 92-808-0147-3, TUNU 107, UNU). Unipub.

On Some of the Forms of Insanity. John Conolly. Bd. with Inquiry Concerning the Indications of Insanity. (Contributions to the History of Psychology Ser.). 1980. Repr. of 1850 ed. 30.00 (ISBN 0-89093-315-4). U Pubns Amer.

On Soviet Dissent: Interviews with Piero Ostellino. Roy Medvedev. Tr. by William A. Packer from Italian. LC 79-27877. 1980. 10.95 (ISBN 0-231-04812-1). Columbia U Pr.

On Speech Act Verbs. Jef Verschueren. (Pragmatics & Beyond: No.4). 91p. 1980. pap. text ed. 17.25x (ISBN 90-272-2508-7). Humanities.

On Spider Creek. Robert Roper. 1979. pap. 2.25 o.p. (ISBN 0-449-23903-9, Crest). Fawcett.

On Stage with Elvis Presley. Kathleen Bauman. (gr. 4-8). 1975. PLB 5.95 o.p. (ISBN 0-87191-488-3); pap. 2.95 o.p. (ISBN 0-685-61189-2). Creative Ed.

On Stonehenge. Fred Hoyle. LC 76-49469. (Illus.). 1977. pap. text ed. 8.95x (ISBN 0-7167-0363-7). W H Freeman.

On Strike Against God. Joanna Russ. pap. 3.50 (ISBN 0-918314-13-5). Out & Out.

On Synthesizing Marxism & Christianity. Dale Vree. LC 76-27706. 1976. 21.95 (ISBN 0-471-01603-9, Pub. by Wiley-Interscience). Wiley.

On Tasting Best of Baking. Annette Wolter & Christian Teubner. (Orig.). 1980. 14.95 (ISBN 0-89586-041-4); pap. 9.95 (ISBN 0-89586-071-6). H P Bks.

On Teaching Speech in Elementary & Junior High Schools. Ed. by J. Jeffery Auer & Edward B. Jenkinson. LC 73-138412. (English Curriculum Study Ser). 1971. 7.50x o.p. (ISBN 0-253-34240-6); pap. 3.25x o.p. (ISBN 0-253-34241-4). Ind U Pr.

On Text & Context: Methodological Approaches to the Context of Literature. Eduardo Forastieri-Braschi & Gerald Guiness. LC 79-18001. 1980. pap. write for info. (ISBN 0-8477-3194-4). U of PR Pr.

On the Advantage & Disadvantage of History for Life. Friedrich Nietzsche. Tr. by Peter Preuss from Ger. LC 80-16686. (Philosophical Classics Ser.). 80p. 1980. lib. bdg. 12.50 (ISBN 0-915144-95-6); pap. text ed. 1.95 (ISBN 0-915144-94-8). Hackett Pub.

On the Art of Poetry with a Supplement on Music. 2nd ed. Aristotle. Ed. by Milton C. Nahm. Tr. by S. H. Butcher. 1976. pap. 2.50 (ISBN 0-672-60168-0, LLA 6). Bobbs.

On the Art of the Theatre. Gordon Craig. (Illus.). 1925. pap. 5.95 (ISBN 0-87830-570-X). Theatre Arts.

On the Automorphisms of the Classical Groups. Jean Dieudonne & L. K. Hua. LC 52-42839. (Memoirs: No. 2). 1980. pap. 9.60 (ISBN 0-8218-1202-5, MEMO-2). Am Math.

On the Balance Beam. Nancy Robison. Ed. by Kathy Pacini. LC 78-15228. (Springboard Bks). (Illus.). (gr. 3-6). 1978. 5.75g (ISBN 0-8075-6067-7). A Whitman.

On the Banks of Plum Creek. Laura I. Wilder. (Little House Ser.). (gr. 1-5). 1976. pap. 1.25 o.p. (ISBN 0-06-080393-2, P393, PL). Har-Row.

On the Basis of Morality. Arthur Schopenhauer. Tr. by E. F. Payne. LC 65-26525. (Orig.). 1965. pap. 5.50 (ISBN 0-672-60445-0, LLA203). Bobbs.

On the Beginning of Social Inquiry. Peter McHugh et al. 1974. 15.00x (ISBN 0-7100-7765-3); pap. 7.95 (ISBN 0-7100-7766-1). Routledge & Kegan.

On the Boards. Van Milverstedt & Peter Sanders. LC 75-1128. (Venture Ser, a Reading Incentive Program). (Illus.). 80p. (gr. 7-12,RL 4.5-6.5). 1975. In Packs Of 5. text ed. 23.25 ea. pack (ISBN 0-8172-0210-2). Follett.

On the Border: Portraits of America's Southwestern Frontier. Tom Miller. LC 79-2631. 224p. 1981. 10.95 (ISBN 0-06-013039-3, HarpT). Har-Row.

On the Border with Crook. John G. Bourke. LC 74-155699. 1971. pap. 8.50 (ISBN 0-8032-5741-4, BB 535, Bison). U of Nebr Pr.

On the Brink. Dave Hunt. LC 72-76590. Orig. Title: Confessions of a Heretic. 1975. pap. 1.95 o.p. (ISBN 0-88270-099-5). Logos.

On the Christian Faith: Selections from the Institutes, Commentaries & Tracts. John Calvin. Ed. by John T. McNeill. LC 58-7660. 1957. pap. 5.50 (ISBN 0-672-60283-0, LLA93). Bobbs.

On the Commonwealth. Cicero. Tr. by George H Sabine & Stanley B Smith. LC 50-11678. 1929. pap. 5.95 (ISBN 0-672-60309-8). Bobbs.

On the Consolation of Philosophy. Boethius. 1981. pap. 3.95 (ISBN 0-89526-885-X). Regnery-Gateway.

On the Construction of Programs. Ed. by R. M. McKeag & A. M. MacNaghten. 432p. 1980. 24.50 (ISBN 0-521-23090-X). Cambridge U Pr.

On the Corner: Male Social Life in a Paramaribo Creole Neighborhood. Gary B. Shute. (Studies of Developing Countries: No. 21). 1979. pap. text ed. 13.50x (ISBN 90-232-1605-9). Humanities.

On the Creation of a Just World Order: Preferred Worlds for the 1990's. Ed. by Saul H. Mendlovitz. LC 74-28937. (Preferred Worlds for the 1990's Ser.). 1977. pap. text ed. 7.95 (ISBN 0-02-920910-2). Free Pr.

On the Cumulants of Cumulative Processes. Walter L. Smith. 48p. 1959. pap. 1.60 (1257). U of NC Pr.

On the Day of the Bulls. Robert Hedin. 1979. 3.00 (ISBN 0-918116-19-8). Jawbone Pr.

On the Different Forms of Insanity in Relation to Jurisprudence. James Prichard. Bd. with Suggestions for the Future Provision of Criminal Lunatics. W. C. Hood; Statistics of Insanity. W. C. Hood. (Contributions to the History of Psychology Ser., Vol. III, Pt. E: Insanity & Jurisprudence). 1980. Repr. of 1842 ed. 30.00 (ISBN 0-89093-328-6). U Pubns Amer.

On the Dignity of Man. Giovanni Pico Della Mirandola. Tr. by Charles G. Wallis et al. Bd. with On Being & Unity; Heptaplus. LC 65-26540. 1965. pap. 5.50 (ISBN 0-672-60483-3, LLA227). Bobbs.

On the Discrimination of Gothicisms. William E. Coleman. Ed. by Devendra P. Varma. LC 79-8447. (Gothic Studies & Dissertations Ser.). 1980. lib. bdg. 25.00x (ISBN 0-405-12651-4). Arno.

On the Divine Images: St. John of Damascus. Tr. by David Anderson from Greek. LC 80-13409. 106p. 1980. pap. 3.95 (ISBN 0-913836-62-1). St Vladimirs.

On the Drag Strip. E. Radlauer & R. S. Radlauer. LC 70-151889. (Sports Action Ser). (Illus.). (gr. 3 up). 1971. 5.20 o.p. (ISBN 0-531-01995-0). Watts.

On the Early Education of the Citizen-Orator. rev. ed. Quintilian. Tr. by John S. Watson. 1965. 5.50 (ISBN 0-672-60474-4). Bobbs.

On the Economic Identification of Social Classes. Guglielmo Carchedi. (Direct Editions Ser.). 1977. pap. 14.00 (ISBN 0-7100-8648-2). Routledge & Kegan.

On the Edge of Destruction: Jews in Poland 1918-39. Celia Heller. LC 76-22646. (Illus.). 1977. 20.00x (ISBN 0-231-03819-4). Columbia U Pr.

On the Edge of Paradise: A. C. Benson; the Diarist. David Newsome. LC 80-12747. (Illus.). 416p. 1980. lib. bdg. 25.00x (ISBN 0-226-57742-2). U of Chicago Pr.

On the Edge of Reason. Miroslav Krleza. LC 74-81810. 1977. 8.95 (ISBN 0-8149-0747-4). Vanguard.

On the Edge of the Cliff & Other Stories. V. S. Pritchett. LC 79-4805. 1979. 10.00 (ISBN 0-394-50485-2). Random.

On the Edge of the Spotlight: Celebrities' Children Speak Out About Their Lives. Kathy Cronkite. LC 80-21255. (Illus.). 320p. 1981. 12.95 (ISBN 0-688-00357-5). Morrow.

On the Eighth Day. Lawrence Okun. LC 81-80093. 208p. 1981. pap. 2.25 (ISBN 0-87216-852-2). Playboy Pbks.

On the Elements: Aristotle's Early Cosmology. A. P. Bos. 168p. 1972. text ed. 23.25x (ISBN 90-232-1027-1). Humanities.

On the Endings of Wars. Ed. by Stuart Albert & Edward C. Luck. (National University Publications, Political Science Ser.). 180p. 1980. 17.50 (ISBN 0-8046-9240-8). Kennikat.

On the European Workers' Movements and Eurocommunism. Ed. by Immanual Wallerstein. 100p. 1980. pap. 5.001311. Synthesis Pubns.

On the Evaluation of Verbal Material in Parapsychology. J. G. Pratt. LC 70-94866. (Parapsychological Monograph No. 10). 1969. pap. 2.50 (ISBN 0-912328-14-2). Parapsych Foun.

On the Eve of Invasion: A Journey Through Afghanistan. David Chaffetz. 12.95 (ISBN 0-686-68743-4). Regnery-Gateway.

On the Farm. Eugene Booth. LC 77-7965. (Raintree Spotlight Book). (Illus.). (gr. k-3). 1977. PLB 8.25 (ISBN 0-8393-0113-8). Raintree Child.

On the Farm. Richard Scarry. (Golden Look-Look Ser.). (Illus.). 1976. PLB 5.38 (ISBN 0-307-61821-8, Golden Pr); pap. 0.95 (ISBN 0-307-11821-5). Western Pub.

On the Feasibility of a Labor Market Information System, 3 vols. Malcom S. Cohen. 1974. pap. 10.95x set (ISBN 0-87736-331-5); pap. 3.95x ea. U of Mich Inst Labor.

On the Forest Edge. Carol Lerner. (Illus.). (gr. k-3). 1978. 6.95 (ISBN 0-688-22162-9); PLB 6.67 (ISBN 0-688-32162-3). Morrow.

On the Functions of the Brain & Each of Its Parts. Franz J. Gall. Tr. by W. Lewis from Ger. (Contributions to the History of Psychology Ser.). 1980. Repr. of 1835 ed. 30.00 ea. U Pubns Amer.

On the Future of Social Prediction. Richard L. Henshel. LC 75-26745. 1975. pap. 2.55 (ISBN 0-672-61334-4). Bobbs.

On the Glaubenslehre: Two Letters to Dr. Lucke. Friedrich Schleiermacher. Ed. by James A. Massey. Tr. by James Duke & Francis S. Fiorenza. LC 80-20717. (American Academy of Religion, Texts & Translations Ser.: No. 3). Orig. Title: Sendschreiben Uber Seine Glaubenslehre an Lucke. 1981. write for info. (ISBN 0-89130-419-3); pap. write for info. (ISBN 0-89130-420-7). Scholars Pr CA.

On the Gleaming Way: Navajos, Eastern Pueblos, Zunis, Hopis, Apaches & Their Land, & Their Meaning to the World. John Collier. LC 62-12407. 163p. (Photos, Orig). 1962. pap. 4.95 (ISBN 0-8040-0232-0, 8, SB). Swallow.

On the Green. E. F. Yeatman. 50p. 1980. Repr. of 1894 ed. lib. bdg. 10.00 (ISBN 0-8414-9767-2). Folcroft.

On the Hawser: A Tugboat Album. Steven Lang & Peter Spectre. LC 79-67416. (Illus.). 506p. 1980. 30.00 (ISBN 0-89272-071-9). Down East.

On the Hill, No. 17. Bessie M. Mason. (Vagrom Chap Book Ser.: No. 17). 42p. (Orig.). 1980. pap. 3.95 (ISBN 0-935552-01-4). Sparrow Pr.

On the Holy Spirit. St. Basil The Great. Tr. by David Anderson from Gr. (Orig.). 1980. pap. 3.95 (ISBN 0-913836-74-5). St Vladimirs.

On the Hoof in Nevada. Velma S. Truitt. (Illus.). 1950. 50.00 (ISBN 0-913814-06-7). Nevada Pubns.

On the Hymn to Zeus in Aeschylus' Agamemnon. Peter M. Smith. LC 80-11327. (American Classical Studies: No. 5). 12.00x (ISBN 0-89130-387-1); pap. 7.50x (ISBN 0-89130-388-X). Scholars Pr CA.

On the Ice in Antarctica. Theodore K. Mason. LC 77-16856. (gr. 7 up). 1978. 6.95 (ISBN 0-396-07535-5). Dodd.

On the Improvement of the Understanding. Benedict Spinoza. 1977. pap. text ed. 4.50 (ISBN 0-486-20250-X). Dover.

On the Independence of Matthew & Mark. J. M. Rist. LC 76-40840. (Society for New Testament Studies Monographs: No. 22). 1978. 19.95 (ISBN 0-521-21476-9). Cambridge U Pr.

On the Interpretation of Empedocles. Clara E. Millerd. LC 78-66600. (Ancient Philosopy Ser.). 98p. 1980. lib. bdg. 13.00 (ISBN 0-8240-9591-X). Garland Pub.

On the Job Training & Where to Get It. rev. ed. Robert A. Liston. LC 72-11898. (Career Bks.). (Illus.). 192p. (gr. 7 up). 1973. PLB 7.29 o.p. (ISBN 0-671-32590-6). Messner.

On the Land: The Evolution of American Agriculture. Elinor L. Horwitz. LC 79-3545. (gr. 7 up). 1980. 8.95 (ISBN 0-689-50165-X, McElderry Bk). Atheneum.

On the Law of God: To the Young People of the Church. Metropolitan Philaret. 1975. pap. 5.00 (ISBN 0-913026-76-X, Synaxis Pr). St Nectarios.

On the Laws & Customs of England: Essays in Honor of Samuel E. Thorne. Ed. by Morris S. Arnold et al. LC 80-11909. (Studies in Legal History). xx, 426p. 1981. 25.00x (ISBN 0-8078-1434-2). U of NC Pr.

On the Ledge. Ed. by Mary Verdick. (Pal Paperbacks Kit A Ser.). (Illus., Orig.). (gr. 7-12). 1976. pap. text ed. 1.25 (ISBN 0-8374-3495-5). Xerox Ed Pubns.

On the Letter Omega. Zosimos Of Panopolis. Tr. by Howard Jackson from Greek. LC 78-18264. (Society of Biblical Literature. Texts & Translations. Graeco-Roman Religion Ser.: No. 5). 1978. pap. 4.50 (ISBN 0-89130-250-6, 060214). Scholars Pr Ca.

On the Level. George Mason & William D. Sheldon. (Breakthrough Ser.). (RL 1). 1973. pap. text ed. 5.12 (ISBN 0-205-03101-3, 5231019); tchrs'. guide 2.40 (ISBN 0-205-03102-1, 5231027). Allyn.

On the Limits of Social Science Theory. Oswald Werner. (PDR Press Publication in Ethnoscience Ser.: No. 1). 1975. pap. text ed. 1.00x o.p. (ISBN 90-316-0045-8). Humanities.

On the Line. John Mitchell. 9.50x (ISBN 0-392-06594-0, SpS). Soccer.

On the Line: New Gay Fiction. Ed. by Ian Young. 224p. 1981. 11.95 (ISBN 0-89594-048-5); pap. 5.95 (ISBN 0-89594-049-3). Crossing Pr.

On the Loose. Terry Russell & Renny Russell. (Sierra Club Ser). (Illus.). 1975. pap. 4.95 o.p. (ISBN 0-345-24307-2). Ballantine.

On the Making of Americans: Essays in Honor of David Riesman. Ed. by Herbert Gans et al. LC 78-65118. (Illus.). 1979. 19.95x (ISBN 0-8122-7754-6). U of Pa Pr.

On the Margins of Science: The Social Construction of Rejected Knowledge. Ed. by Roy Wallis. (Sociological Review Monograph: No. 27). 337p. 1979. pap. 28.00x (ISBN 0-8476-2300-9). Rowman.

On the Motion & Immobility of Douve. Yves Bonnefoy. Tr. by Galway Kinnell. LC 67-24284. (Fr. & Eng.). 1968. 10.00x (ISBN 0-8214-0035-5). Ohio U Pr.

On the Move. William Sheldon et al. (Breakthrough Ser.). (gr. 7-12). 1979. pap. text ed. 4.96 (ISBN 0-205-06072-2, 5260728); tchrs'. guide 2.40 (ISBN 0-205-06073-0). Allyn.

On the Music of the North American Indians. Theodore Baker. Tr. by Ann Buckley from Ger. (Music Reprint Ser., 1977). 1977. lib. bdg. 17.50 (ISBN 0-306-70888-4). Da Capo.

On the Nature of Organizations. Peter M. Blau. LC 74-7392. 358p. 1974. 28.95 (ISBN 0-471-08037-3, Pub. by Wiley-Interscience). Wiley.

On the Night of the Seventh Moon. Victoria Holt. 1978. pap. 1.95 (ISBN 0-449-23568-8, Crest). Fawcett.

On the Objective Study of Crowd Behavior. L. S. Penrose. 78p. 1981. Repr. of 1952 ed. text ed. price not set. Krieger.

On the Old Saw: That May Be Right in Theory but It Won't Work in Practice. Immanuel Kant. Tr. by E. B. Ashton from Ger. LC 73-83291. (Works in Continental Philosophy Ser.). 1974. 8.00x (ISBN 0-8122-7677-9); pap. 3.95x (ISBN 0-8122-1058-1, Pa Paperbks). U of Pa Pr.

On the Opposition. Joseph Stalin. 1974. 6.95 (ISBN 0-8351-0549-0); pap. 4.95 (ISBN 0-8351-0214-9). China Bks.

On the Origin & Formation of Creoles: A Miscellany of Articles by Dirk Christiaan Hesseling. Dirk C. Hesseling. Ed. by T. L. Markey & Paul T. Roberge. (Linguistica Extranea Ser.: Studia 4). 120p. 1979. lib. bdg. 7.50 (ISBN 0-89720-005-5); pap. 4.50 (ISBN 0-89720-006-3). Karoma.

On the Other Side of the Gate. Yuri Suhl. LC 74-13452. 160p. (gr. 7 up). 1975. PLB 5.90 o.p. (ISBN 0-531-02792-9). Watts.

On the Other Side of the River. Joanne Oppenheim. (Illus.). 32p. (gr. k-3). 1972. PLB 4.90 o.p. (ISBN 0-531-02562-4). Watts.

On the Pententiary System in the United States & Its Application in France. Gustave De Beaumont & Alexis De Tocqueville. LC 79-431. (Arcturus Bks Paperbacks). 264p. 1979. pap. 7.95 (ISBN 0-8093-0913-0). S Ill U Pr.

On the Plantation: A Story of a Georgia Boy's Adventures During the War. Joel C. Harris. LC 79-5189. (Brown Thrasher Bks.). (Illus.). 235p. 1980. 15.00x (ISBN 0-8203-0494-8); pap. 4.95x (ISBN 0-8203-0495-6). U of Ga Pr.

On the Problem of Plateau - Subharmonic Functions. T. Rado. LC 71-160175. (Illus.). 1971. pap. 19.90 (ISBN 0-387-05479-0). Springer-Verlag.

On the Prod. Richard Wormser. 1978. pap. 1.25 o.p. (ISBN 0-449-14031-8, GM). Fawcett.

On the Psychology of Woman: A Survey of Empirical Studies. Julia A. Sherman. 320p. 1975. 15.50 (ISBN 0-398-01744-1); pap. 9.75 (ISBN 0-398-02762-5). C C Thomas.

On the Range: Cooking Western Style. Marian Pfrommer. LC 80-18380. (Illus.). 104p. 1981. 8.95 (ISBN 0-689-30826-4). Atheneum.

On the Reappraisal of Keynesian Economics. A. G. Hines. 85p. 1972. pap. 7.95x (ISBN 0-85520-004-9, Pub. by Martin Robertson England). Biblio Dist.

On the Red World. Leo P. Kelley. LC 78-68227. (Galaxy Five Ser.). (Illus.). 64p. (gr. 4 up). 1980. PLB 7.95 (ISBN 0-516-02254-7). Childrens.

On the Revolution of the Heavenly Spheres. Nicholas Copernicus. Ed. by Alistair M. Duncan. LC 76-7172. (Illus.). 1976. text ed. 26.50x o.p. (ISBN 0-06-491279-5). B&N.

On the Rise, Progress & Present State of Public Opinion, in Great Britain & Other Parts of the World. William A. MacKinnon. 343p. 1971. Repr. of 1828 ed. 30.00x (ISBN 0-686-28332-5, Pub. by Irish Academic Pr). Biblio Dist.

On the Road. Jack Kerouac. pap. 2.50 (ISBN 0-451-08198-6, E8973, Sig). NAL.

On the Road. Jack Kerouac. (Critical Library Ser.). 1979. 12.95 o.s.i. (ISBN 0-670-52513-8). Viking Pr.

On the Road to Damascus, Maryland. Enid Dame. 56p. (Orig.). 1980. pap. 2.50 (ISBN 0-917402-15-4). Downtown Poets.

On the Road to Nowhere: A History of Greer, Arizona, 1879-1979. Karen M. Applewhite. LC 79-54966. (Illus., Orig.). 1979. pap. text ed. 6.95 (ISBN 0-9603472-0-8). Applewhite.

On the Road with Andre Crouch. Allan Hartley. 1978. pap. 0.49 o.p. (ISBN 0-8007-8529-0). Revell.

On the Road with John James Audubon. Mary Durant & Michael Harwood. LC 79-22734. (Illus.). 576p. 1980. 19.95 (ISBN 0-396-07740-4). Dodd.

On the Roads to Modernity--Conscience, Science, & Civilization: Selected Writings. Benjamin Nelson. Ed. by Toby E. Huff. 1981. 27.50x (ISBN 0-8476-6209-8). Rowman.

On the Rock. Alvin Karpas. (Illus.). 368p. 1981. 12.95 (ISBN 0-8253-0019-3). Beaufort Bks NY.

On the Ropes. Otto Salassi. LC 80-20399. 224p. (gr. 5-7). 1981. 8.95 (ISBN 0-688-80313-X). Greenwillow.

On the Run. John D. MacDonald. 1978. pap. 1.95 (ISBN 0-449-13983-2, GM). Fawcett.

On the Run: Franco Harris. George Sullivan. LC 76-10357. (Sports Profiles Ser.). (Illus.). 48p. (gr. 4-11). 1976. PLB 8.50 (ISBN 0-8172-0138-6). Raintree Pubs.

On the Sand. E. Radlauer & R. S. Radlauer. LC 73-180240. (Sports Action Bks). (Illus.). 48p. (gr. 3 up). 1972. PLB 5.20 o.p. (ISBN 0-531-02035-5). Watts.

On the Semantics of Syntax: Mood & Condition in English. Eirian Davies. (Croom Helm Linguistic Ser.). 1979. text ed. 26.00x (ISBN 0-391-00936-2). Humanities.

On the Several Senses of Being in Aristotle. Franz Brentano. LC 72-89796. 210p. 1976. 16.75x (ISBN 0-520-02346-3). U of Cal Pr.

On the Silence of the Declaration of Independence. Paul Eidelberg. LC 76-8759. 148p. 1980. pap. text ed. 5.95x (ISBN 0-87023-313-0). U of Mass Pr.

On the Slain Collegians. Herman Melville. Ed. by Antonio Frasconi. (Illus.). 48p. 1971. 5.95 o.p. (ISBN 0-374-22637-7); pap. 1.95 o.p. (ISBN 0-374-50954-9). FS&G.

On the Spot. William Sheldon & Nina C. Woessner. (Breakthrough Ser). (Orig.). (RL 6). 1972. pap. text ed. 4.96 (ISBN 0-205-03097-1, 5230977); tchrs'. guide 2.40 (ISBN 0-205-03098-X, 5230985); dup. masters 20.00 (ISBN 0-205-03099-8, 5230993). Allyn.

On the Structure of the Spermathecae & Aedeagus in the Asilidae & Their Importance in the Systematics of the Family. Oskar Theodor. (Illus.). 175p. 1976. 25.00x (ISBN 0-87474-914-X, Pub. by Israel Academy of Sciences & Humanities). Smithsonian.

On the Study of Character, Including an Estimate of Phrenology. Alexander Bain. (Contributions to the History of Psychology Ser.: Orientations). 1980. Repr. of 1861 ed. 30.00 (ISBN 0-89093-316-2). U Pubns Amer.

On the Subject of Tongues: From the New Testament. Don Welborn. 56p. pap. 0.35 (ISBN 0-937396-48-6). Walterick Pubs.

On the Take. William Riordan. (Orig.). 1976. pap. 1.25 o.p. (ISBN 0-685-64015-9, LB342ZK, Leisure Bks). Nordon Pubns.

On the Texture of Brains: An Introduction to Neuroanatomy for the Cybernetically Minded. Tr. by E. H. Braitenbach from Ger. LC 77-21851. (Illus.). 1977. pap. 8.70 (ISBN 0-387-08391-X). Springer-Verlag.

On the Theory & Practice of Voice Identification. Committee on Evaluation of Sound Spectrograms, National Research Council. 1979. pap. text ed. 7.00 (ISBN 0-309-02873-6). Natl Acad Pr.

On the Track of Bigfoot. Marion T. Place. (Illus.). (gr. 5 up). 1979. pap. 1.75 (ISBN 0-671-29944-1). PB.

On the Track of Murder. Barbara Gelb. 1976. pap. 1.95 o.p. (ISBN 0-345-25228-4). Ballantine.

On the Track of the Dixie Limited. Petersen. (Illus.). 64p. 8.50 (ISBN 0-936610-00-X). Colophon.

On the Track of the Mystery Animal: The Story of the Discovery of the Okapi. Miriam Schlein. LC 78-5387. (Illus.). 64p. (gr. 3-7). 1978. 7.95 (ISBN 0-590-07488-1, Four Winds). Schol Bk Serv.

On the Trail: The Life & Trail Stories of "Lead Steer" Potter. Jean Burroughs. (Illus.). 1980. 12.95 (ISBN 0-89013-131-7). Museum NM Pr.

On the Twentieth Century. Betty Comden et al. LC 79-28365. (Illus.). 1981. 7.95 (ISBN 0-89676-033-2). Drama Bk.

On the Urban Scene: Proceedings. Meeting of the American Orthopsychiatric Assoc., 47th. Ed. by Morton Levitt & Ben Rubenstein. LC 72-1440. 1972. 13.50x (ISBN 0-8143-1478-3). Wayne St U Pr.

On the Verge. Dikkon Eberhart. LC 79-9810. 1979. 9.95 (ISBN 0-916144-40-2). Stemmer Hse.

On the Volterra & Other Nonlinear Models of Interacting Populations. N. S. Goel et al. (Reviews of Modern Physics Monographs). 1971. 21.00 (ISBN 0-12-287450-1). Acad Pr.

On the Walls of the Lower East Side. Sol LeWitt. (Illus.). 72p. (Orig.). 1981. pap. 20.00 (ISBN 0-9601068-8-X). Agrinde Pubns.

On the Water. E. Radlauer & R. S. Radlauer. LC 72-7085. (Sports Action Bks.). (Illus.). 48p. (gr. 3 up). 1973. PLB 5.20 o.p. (ISBN 0-531-02586-1). Watts.

On the Way: Thoughts for Pilgrims. Terra R. G. 1975. 3.95 o.s.i. (ISBN 0-8198-0447-9). Dghtrs St Paul.

On the Way to the Island. David Ferry. LC 60-13156. (Wesleyan Poetry Program: Vol. 7). (Orig.). 1960. 10.00x (ISBN 0-8195-2007-1, Pub. by Wesleyan U Pr); pap. 4.95 (ISBN 0-8195-1007-6). Columbia U Pr.

On the Way to the Movies. Charlotte Herman. LC 79-19015. (Illus.). 32p. (gr. k-3). 1980. PLB 7.95 (ISBN 0-525-36400-5). Dutton.

On the Wing: Rod Gilbert. Sheldon Ilowite. LC 76-12547. (Sports Profiles Ser.). (Illus.). 48p. (gr. 4-11). 1976. PLB 8.50 (ISBN 0-8172-0134-3). Raintree Pubs.

On the Wing: The Story of the Pittsburgh Sisters of Mercy. M. Jerome McHale. 284p. 1980. 15.00 (ISBN 0-8164-0466-6). Crossroad NY.

On Their Own: The Poor in Modern America. David J. Rothman & Sheila M. Rothman. LC 76-183669. 1972. pap. text ed. 6.95 (ISBN 0-201-06527-4). A-W.

On Theoretical Sociology: Five Essays, Old & New. Robert K. Merton. 1967. pap. text ed. 3.95 (ISBN 0-02-921150-6). Free Pr.

On Thinking. Gilbert Ryle. 148p. 1980. 18.00x (ISBN -08476-6203-9). Rowman.

On to Oregon. Honore Morrow. (Illus.). (gr. 5-9). 1946. Repr. of 1926 ed. 8.95 (ISBN 0-688-21639-0). Morrow.

On Translations of the Bible. H. F. Sparks. (Ethel M. Wood Lectures). 1973. pap. text ed. 2.50x (ISBN 0-485-14316-X, Athlone Pr). Humanities.

On Trotskyism. Kostas Mavrakis. 280p. (Orig.). 1976. pap. 16.00 (ISBN 0-7100-8277-0). Routledge & Kegan.

On Understanding the Supreme Court: A Series of Lectures Delivered Under the Auspices of the Julius Rosenthal Foundation at Northwestern University, School of Law. Paul A. Freund. LC 77-23550. (Illus.). 1977. Repr. of 1949 ed. lib. bdg. 13.50x (ISBN 0-8371-9699-X, FROU). Greenwood.

On University Studies. Friedrich Schelling. Ed. by Norbert Guterman. Tr. by E. S. Morgan. LC 65-15086. xxii, 166p. 1966. 10.00x (ISBN 0-8214-0015-0). Ohio U Pr.

On Vacation. Richard Scarry. (Golden Look-Look Ser.). (Illus.). 1976. PLB 5.38 (ISBN 0-307-61823-4, Golden Pr); pap. 0.95 (ISBN 0-307-11823-1). Western Pub.

On Varients & Theory of Numbers. Leonard E. Dickson. 1967. pap. 2.00 (ISBN 0-486-61667-3). Dover.

On Violence. Hannah Arendt. LC 74-95867. 1970. pap. 2.95 (ISBN 0-15-669500-6, HB177, Harv). HarBraceJ.

On Wages & Combination. Robert Torrens. (Development of Industrial Society Ser.). 133p. 1980. Repr. of 1834 ed. 10.00x (ISBN 0-7165-1595-4, Pub. by Irish Academic Pr Ireland). Biblio Dist.

On War. Raymond Aron. Tr. by Terence Kilmartin. 1968. pap. 3.45 (ISBN 0-393-00107-5, Norton Lib). Norton.

On War. Carl Von Clausewitz. Ed. by Michael Howard & Peter Paret. LC 75-30190. 1976. 23.50 (ISBN 0-691-05657-9). Princeton U Pr.

On War. Karl Von Clausewitz. Ed. by Anatol Rapoport. (Classics Ser.). 1968. pap. 3.95 (ISBN 0-14-040004-4, Pelican). Penguin.

On War: Political Violence in the International System. Manus I. Midlarsky. LC 74-9195. (Illus.). 1975. 19.95 (ISBN 0-02-921200-6). Free Pr.

On Weaving. Anni Albers. LC 65-19855. (Illus.). 1965. 20.00x (ISBN 0-8195-3059-X, Pub. by Wesleyan U Pr); pap. 7.95 (ISBN 0-8195-6031-6). Columbia U Pr.

On What Is Learned in School. Robert Dreeben. LC 68-25923. (Education Ser). (Orig.). 1968. pap. 6.95 (ISBN 0-201-01610-9). A-W.

On What There Must Be. Ross Harrison. (Illus.). 224p. 1974. 22.50x (ISBN 0-19-824507-6). Oxford U Pr.

On Wheels. John Jakes. 1973. pap. 1.95 o.s.i. (ISBN 0-446-89932-1). Warner Bks.

On Wings of Love. Lee Roddy. 128p. 1981. pap. 3.95 (ISBN 0-8407-5758-1). Nelson.

On World Government (De Monarchia) Dante. Tr. by H. W. Schneider. LC 57-1099. 1957. pap. 3.50 (ISBN 0-672-60176-1, LLA 15). Bobbs.

On Writing Well: An Informal Guide to Writing Nonfiction. 2nd ed. William K. Zinsser. 1980. text ed. 8.50 scp (ISBN 0-06-047396-7, HarpC); pap. text ed. write for info. (ISBN 0-06-047395-9). Har-Row.

On Your Feet. Elizabeth H. Roberts. 1977. pap. 1.75 o.s.i. (ISBN 0-515-04385-0). Jove Pubns.

On-Your-Own Guide to Asia: Budget Handbook to East & Southeast Asia, 1981-82. rev. ed. Ed. by John Doll & Terry George. LC 77-90889. (Illus.). 1981. pap. 4.95 (ISBN 0-8048-1353-1). C E Tuttle.

On Your Own in Europe: A Teen-Agers Travel Guide. Elizabeth McGough. (gr. 7 up). 1978. PLB 7.20 (ISBN 0-688-32163-1); pap. 5.50 (ISBN 0-688-27163-4). Morrow.

Onassis: An Extravagant Life. Frank Brady. 1978. pap. 1.95 o.s.i. (ISBN 0-515-04746-5). Jove Pubns.

Once a Mouse. Marcia Brown. LC 61-14769. (Illus.). (ps-5). 1961. reinforced bdg. 9.95 (ISBN 0-684-12662-1, ScribJ). Scribner.

Once a Slave: The Slaves' View of Slavery. Stanley Feldstein. LC 70-130535. 329p. 1971. pap. 3.50 (ISBN 0-688-07227-5). Morrow.

Once a Spy. Robert Footman. LC 80-15748. 224p. 1980. 8.95 (ISBN 0-396-07864-8). Dodd.

Once-a-Week Indoor Gardening Guide. Jack Kramer. (Orig.). pap. 1.75 (ISBN 0-515-04475-X). Jove Pubns.

Once-a-Year Witch. Judy Varga. (Illus.). 32p. (ps-3). 1973. PLB 7.92 (ISBN 0-688-31777-4). Morrow.

Once Against the Law. William Tenn & D. Westlake. 1968. 6.95 o.s.i. (ISBN 0-02-616900-2). Macmillan.

Once & Future Church. Barbara O'Dea. LC 80-82554. 96p. (Orig.). 1980. pap. 4.95 (ISBN 0-934134-08-1, Celebration Bks). Natl Cath Reporter.

Once I Was a Plum Tree. Johanna Hurwitz. LC 79-23518. (Illus.). 160p. (gr. 4-6). 1980. 7.50 (ISBN 0-688-22223-4); PLB 7.20 (ISBN 0-688-32223-9). Morrow.

Once in Golconda: A True Dream of Wall Street, Nineteen Twenty - Nineteen Thirty Eight. John Brooks. 1981. 15.95 (ISBN 0-393-01375-8). Norton.

Once in Six Thousand Years. Eloise R. Rees. (Orig.). 1980. pap. 1.95 (ISBN 0-532-23185-6). Manor Bks.

Once More from the Middle: A Philosophical Anthropology. James F. Sheridan, Jr. LC 72-85543. ix, 157p. 1973. 9.50x (ISBN 0-8214-0108-4). Ohio U Pr.

Once My Child, Now My Friend. Elinor Lenz. (Orig.). 1981. 12.95 (ISBN 0-446-51224-9). Warner Bks.

Once Saved...Always Saved. new ed. Perry Lassiter. LC 74-15289. 98p. 1975. pap. 2.95 (ISBN 0-8054-1931-4). Broadman.

Once There Was a Fat Girl. Cynthia Blair. 1981. pap. 1.95 (ISBN 0-449-14394-5, GM). Fawcett.

Once There Was a Giant Sea Cow. Bernard L. Gordon. (Illus.). (gr. k-3). 1977. 5.95 o.p. (ISBN 0-679-20410-5). McKay.

Once There Was a Giant Sea Cow. Esther Gordon & Bernard Gordon. (Illus.). (gr. k-3). 1980. pap. 1.95 o.p. (ISBN 0-679-20851-8). McKay.

Once Through the New Testament. Zola Levitt & Tom McCall. LC 80-69306. 160p. 1981. pap. 5.95 (ISBN 0-915684-78-0). Christian Herald.

Once Upon a Bible Time. Etta B. Degering. Ed. by Bobbie J. Van Dolson. LC 76-14118. (Illus.). (gr. k-3). 1976. 4.95 (ISBN 0-8280-0052-2). Review & Herald.

Once Upon a Dream. Patricia Bird. (YA) 1977. 4.95 o.p. (ISBN 0-685-73812-4, Avalon). Bouregy.

Once Upon a Galaxy: A Journal of the Making of the Empire Strikes Back. Alan Arnold. 1980. pap. 2.75 (ISBN 0-345-29075-5, Del Rey Bks). Ballantine.

Once Upon a Lifetime: A Collection of Words, Pictures, & Memorabilia of the Recent Past in America. 1979. pap. 5.50 (ISBN 0-570-03780-8, 12-2734). Concordia.

Once Upon a Molecule. George Javor. LC 78-27359. (Flame Ser.). 1979. pap. 0.95 (ISBN 0-8127-0227-1). Southern Pub.

Once Upon a Mouse. Lockie Holt. LC 79-1868. (Illus.). (ps-2). 1979. 1.95 (ISBN 0-525-69006-9, Gingerbread Bks); DLLB 5.95 (ISBN 0-525-69007-7). Dutton.

Once Upon a Star. Linda Vold. 0.95 (ISBN 0-8024-6062-3). Moody.

Once Upon a Time. Charlotte Huber et al. (Wonder-Story Books Ser). (primer). text ed. 7.16 (ISBN 0-06-517500-X, SchDept). Har-Row.

Once Upon a Time. Ed. by Malcolm Whyte. (Illus.). 40p. (gr. 1-8). 1979. pap. 2.25 (ISBN 0-912300-16-7). Troubador Pr.

Once Upon a Time in a Pig Pen. Margaret W. Brown & Ann Strugnell. LC 77-5077. (Illus.). 64p. (ps-4). 1980. PLB 10.95 (ISBN 0-201-00343-0, A-W Childrens). A-W.

Once Upon a Time: On the Nature of Fairy Tales. Max Luthi. Tr. by Lee Chadeayne & Paul Gottwald. LC 76-6992. (Midland Bks.: No. 203). 192p. 1976. pap. 3.95x (ISBN 0-253-20203-5). Ind U Pr.

Once Upon a Time Tales. new ed. Corinne Denan. LC 79-66337. (Illus.). 48p. (gr. 2-6). 1980. lib. bdg. 4.89 (ISBN 0-89375-340-8); pap. 1.50 (ISBN 0-89375-339-4). Troll Assocs.

Once Upon a Tree. Calvin Miller. 1978. pap. 3.95 (ISBN 0-8010-6050-8). Baker Bk.

Once Upon a Wilderness. Calvin Rutstrum. LC 72-91260. (Illus.). 208p. 1973. 9.95 (ISBN 0-02-606330-1). Macmillan.

Once Upon MacDonald's Farm. Stephen Gammell. LC 80-23956. (Illus.). 32p. (gr. k-3). 1981. 7.95 (ISBN 0-590-07792-9, Four Winds). Schol Bk Serv.

Once We Had a Horse. Glen Rounds. LC 76-151758. (Illus.). (ps-3). 1971. 5.95 (ISBN 0-8234-0193-6). Holiday.

Once We Went on a Picnic. Aileen Fisher. LC 75-9836. (Illus.). 32p. (gr. k-3). 1975. 8.95 (ISBN 0-690-00955-0, TYC-J); PLB 8.79 (ISBN 0-690-00956-9). T Y Crowell.

Once You Start Climbing, Don't Look Down. Richard Utt. LC 78-50438. (Redwood Ser.). 1978. pap. 3.95 (ISBN 0-8163-0092-5, 04441-2). Pacific Pr Pub Assn.

Oncogenic Herpes Viruses, Vols. 1 & 2. Ed. by Fred Rapp. 1980. Vol. 1, 240p. 59.95 (ISBN 0-8493-5619-9); Vol. 2, 160p. 49.95 (ISBN 0-8493-5620-2). CRC Pr.

Oncogenic Viruses. 2nd ed. L. Gross. 1970. 57.00 (ISBN 0-08-013236-7). Pergamon.

Oncologic Emergencies. Ed. by John Yarbro & Richard Bornstein. (Clinical Oncology Monographs). 1980. write for info. (ISBN 0-8089-1317-4). Grune.

Oncology. Ed. by Samuel G. Taylor, 3rd. (Medical Examination Review Bk. Ser.: Vol. 29). 1973. spiral bdg. 16.50 (ISBN 0-87488-146-3). Med Exam.

Oncology for Nurses & Health Care Professionals, Vol. 1. Ed. by Robert Tiffany. (Illus.). 1978. text ed. 35.00x (ISBN 0-04-610009-1); pap. text ed. 18.95x (ISBN 0-04-610010-5). Allen Unwin.

Oncology for Nurses & Health Care Professionals, Vol. 2. Ed. by Robert Tiffany. (Illus.). 1978. text ed. 25.00x (ISBN 0-04-610006-7); pap. text ed. 13.95x (ISBN 0-04-610007-5). Allen Unwin.

Oncology Nursing Case Studies. Marylin J. Dodd. 1978. spiral bdg. 10.50 (ISBN 0-87488-044-0). Med Exam.

Oncology: UCLA Postgraduate Medicine for the Internist. Jerome B. Block. (Illus.). 1981. price not set (ISBN 0-89289-376-1). HM.

One Across, Two Down. Ruth Rendell. 224p. 1981. pap. 2.25 (ISBN 0-553-14729-3). Bantam.

One Against the Storm. Stanley C. Mann. (Illus.). 221p. (Orig.). pap. write for info. (ISBN 0-938662-00-7). Quest Utah.

One & Indivisible French Republic. Jack Hayward. (Comparative Modern Government Ser.). 306p. 1974. 10.95x (ISBN 0-393-05506-X); pap. 5.95x (ISBN 0-393-09325-5). Norton.

One & Only You. Bruce Larson. (Orig.). 1976. pap. 1.50 (ISBN 0-89129-135-0). Jove Pubns.

One & the Many in the Canterbury Tales. Traugott Lawler. 209p. 1980. 17.50 (ISBN 0-208-01842-5, Archon). Shoe String.

One Arm & Other Stories. Tennessee Williams. LC 57-31974. pap. 5.95 (ISBN 0-8112-0223-2, NDP237). New Directions.

One Bad Thing About Birthdays. David R. Collins. LC 80-23104. (Let Me Read Bk.). (Illus.). 32p. (ps-3). 1981. pap. 2.95 (ISBN 0-15-258289-4, VoyB). HarBraceJ.

One Bad Thing About Birthdays. David R. Collins. LC 80-23104. (Let Me Read Bk.). (Illus.). 32p. (gr. 4-6). 1981. 6.95 (ISBN 0-15-258288-6, HJ). HarBraceJ.

One Bear, Two Bears: The Strawberry Number Book. Hefter. 118p. Date not set. 4.95 (ISBN 0-07-027825-3). McGraw.

One Best System: A History of American Urban Education. David B. Tyack. LC 74-77184. (Illus.). 368p. 1974. text ed. 16.50x (ISBN 0-674-63780-1); pap. 3.95 (ISBN 0-674-63782-8). Harvard U Pr.

One Big Yo to Go. Valerie Osborne. (Illus.). 32p. (gr. 1 up). 1981. 9.95 (ISBN 0-19-554265-7). Oxford U Pr.

One Blanket & Ten Days Rations. Charles Meketa & Jacqueline Meketa. Ed. by Earl Jackson & Carolyn Dodson. LC 79-67811. (Popular Ser.: No. 27). (Illus.). 100p. (Orig.). pap. 4.50x (ISBN 0-911408-54-1). SW Pks Mnmts.

One Book-Five Ways: The Publishing Procedures of Five University Presses. Ed. by Association of American University Presses. LC 78-9505. (Illus.). 350p. 1978. 18.75 (ISBN 0-913232-53-X); pap. 10.95 (ISBN 0-913232-54-8). W Kaufmann.

One Bowl: A Simple Concept for Controlling Body Weight. Don Gerrard. 1974. 5.95 o.p. (ISBN 0-394-49285-4); pap. 1.45 (ISBN 0-394-70690-0). Random.

One Bright Monday Morning. Arline Baum & Joseph Baum. (Illus.). (ps). 1962. pap. 0.95 (ISBN 0-394-82650-7). Random.

One-Burner Gourmet. rev. ed. Harriett Barker. (Illus.). 1981. pap. 7.95 (ISBN 0-8092-5883-8). Contemp Bks.

One Continual Cry: Walker's Appeal to the Colored Citizens of the World, 1829. Ed. by Herbert Aptheker. (Historical Ser.: No. 1). 7.50 (ISBN 0-686-19223-0). Am Inst Marxist.

One Cool Sister. Ed. by Thomas J. Mooney. (Pal Paperbacks Kit A Ser.). (Illus., Orig.). (gr. 7-12). 1976. pap. text ed. 1.25 (ISBN 0-8374-3501-3). Xerox Ed Pubns.

One Corpse Too Many. Ellis Peters. 192p. 1981. pap. 2.25 (ISBN 0-445-04653-8). Popular Lib.

One Creature. Joanne De Longchamps. (Illus.). 1977. pap. 5.00 o.p. (ISBN 0-915596-19-9). West Coast.

One Crow, Two Crow. Virginia Chase. LC 78-8164. 1978. lib. bdg. 9.50 o.p. (ISBN 0-89621-009-X); pap. 4.95x (ISBN 0-89621-008-1). Thorndike Pr.

One Culture. W. H. Davenport. LC 70-106054. 1970. 12.75 (ISBN 0-08-016322-X). Pergamon.

One Dancing Drum. Gail Kredenser. LC 79-146845. (Illus.). (gr. k-3). 1971. 8.95 (ISBN 0-87599-178-5). S G Phillips.

One Day. Wright Morris. LC 76-3766. 1976. 15.95x (ISBN 0-8032-0879-0); pap. 4.95 (ISBN 0-8032-5841-0, BB 619, Bison). U of Nebr Pr.

One Day at a Time: Making the Most Out of Life. Ed. by Susan P. Schutz. (Illus., Orig.). 1981. pap. 4.95 (ISBN 0-88396-131-8). Blue Mtn Pr CO.

One Day at Teton Marsh. Sally Carrighar. 1975. pap. 1.75 o.p. (ISBN 0-345-24821-X). Ballantine.

One Day at Teton Marsh. Sally Carrighar. LC 78-26679. (Illus.). 1979. pap. 4.25 (ISBN 0-8032-6302-3, BB 692, Bison). U of Nebr Pr.

One Day Everything Went Wrong. Elizabeth Vreeken. (Beginning-to-Read Bks). (Illus.). (ps). pap. 1.50 o.p. (ISBN 0-695-36550-9). Follett.

One Day in Aztec Mexico. G. B. Kirtland. LC 63-7897. (Illus.). (gr. 4-6). 1963. 4.50 o.p. (ISBN 0-15-258381-5, HJ). HarBraceJ.

One Day in the Life of Ivan Denisovich. Alexander Solzhenitsyn. Tr. by Aitken Gillon from Rus. 174p. 1971. 15.00 (ISBN 0-374-22642-3); pap. 1.50 o.p. (ISBN 0-686-66696-8). FS&G.

One Day on Beetle Rock. Sally Carrighar. (Walden Editions). 192p. 1976. pap. 1.50 o.p. (ISBN 0-345-24866-X). Ballantine.

One Day on Beetle Rock. Sally Carrighar. LC 78-18854. viii, 196p. 1978. pap. 3.25 (ISBN 0-8032-6301-5, BB 691, Bison). U of Nebr Pr.

One Day Scene Through a Leaf. Patrick Dowers. (Illus.). 40p. 1981. 10.95 (ISBN 0-914676-56-3); pap. 6.95 (ISBN 0-914676-55-5). Green Tiger.

One Dead Debutante. Heywood Gould. LC 75-9483. 256p. 1975. 7.95 o.p. (ISBN 0-312-58520-9). St Martin.

One Dead Debutante. Heywood Gould. 1979. pap. 1.95 o.p. (ISBN 0-345-25520-8). Ballantine.

One Dialogue or Colloquy Entitled Diversoria. Desiderius Erasmus. LC 71-26509. (English Experience Ser.: No. 244). 20p. 1970. Repr. of 1566 ed. 7.00 (ISBN 90-221-0244-0). Walter J Johnson.

One-Dimensional Compressible Flow. M. Danenshyar. 1977. text ed. 30.00 (ISBN 0-08-020414-7); pap. text ed. 10.75 (ISBN 0-08-020413-9). Pergamon.

One Dimensional Man. Herbert Marcuse. 1964. 7.50 o.p. (ISBN 0-8070-1574-1); pap. 5.95 (ISBN 0-8070-1575-X, BP221). Beacon Pr.

One Dragon's Dream. Illus. by Peter Pavey. LC 79-12008. (Illus.). (ps-2). 1979. 8.95 (ISBN 0-87888-148-4). Bradbury Pr.

One Earth, Many People: The Challenge of Human Population Growth. Laurence Pringle. LC 71-133559. (Illus.). (gr. 5 up). 1971. 4.95g o.s.i. (ISBN 0-02-775260-7); text ed. 1.96 o.s.i. (ISBN 0-02-775280-1). Macmillan.

One Eye, Two Eyes, Three Eyes, Four... The Many Ways Animals See. Dorothy Leon. LC 80-15468. (Illus.). 64p. (gr. 4-6). 1980. PLB 7.29 (ISBN 0-671-34001-8). Messner.

One-Eyed Jake. Pat Hutchins. LC 78-18346. (Illus.). (gr. k-3). 1979. 7.95 (ISBN 0-688-80183-8); PLB 7.63 (ISBN 0-688-84183-X). Greenwillow.

One Fearful Yellow Eye. John D. Macdonald. LC 77-24165. 1978. 8.95 o.p. (ISBN 0-397-01191-1). Lippincott.

One Fine Day. Nonny Hogrogian. LC 75-119834. (Illus.). (gr. k-3). 1971. 8.95 (ISBN 0-02-744000-1). Macmillan.

One Fine Day: A Novel. Leon Arden. 1981. 10.95 (ISBN 0-393-01423-1). Norton.

One Foot in the Grave. Peter Dickinson. 224p. 1981. pap. 2.95 (ISBN 0-14-005779-X). Penguin.

One for Paradise. W. C. Strader. LC 79-56873. 1981. 8.95 (ISBN 0-533-04542-8). Vantage.

One for the Price of Two. Cynthia Jameson. LC 72-705. (Illus.). 48p. (gr. k-3). 1972. 5.95 o.s.i. (ISBN 0-8193-0602-9, Four Winds); PLB 5.41 o.s.i. (ISBN 0-8193-0603-7). Schol Bk Serv.

One for the Record: The Inside Story of Hank Aaron's Chase for the Home-Run Record. George Plimpton. LC 74-7026. (Illus.). 160p. (YA) 1974. 8.95 o.p. (ISBN 0-06-013373-2, HarpT). Har-Row.

One for the Road. Clara L. Brown. 1970. 4.95 o.p. (ISBN 0-8158-0232-3). Chris Mass.

One Generation. Roy A. Heathe. 176p. 1981. 13.95 (ISBN 0-8052-8074-X); pap. 5.95 (ISBN 0-8052-8073-1). Schocken.

One God in Trinity. Peter Toon. LC 79-57395. 192p. 1980. 12.95 (ISBN 0-89107-187-3, Cornerstone Bks.). Good News.

One God or Three. LC 78-51764. 1978. pap. 1.50 (ISBN 0-915540-19-3). Friends Israel-Spearhead Pr.

One-Hander's Book: Helpful Hints for Activities of Daily Living. Veronica Washam. LC 77-155019. (John Day Bk.). (Illus.). 160p. 1973. 10.00 o.s.i. (ISBN 0-381-97096-5, TYC-T). T Y Crowell.

One Hectic Summer. George A. Dunlap. 64p. 1981. 4.95 (ISBN 0-8059-2784-0). Dorrance.

One Horse, One Hundred Miles, One Day: The Story of the Tevis Cup Endurance Ride. Sam Savitt. LC 80-2777. (Illus.). 96p. (gr. 7 up). 1981. PLB 7.95 (ISBN 0-396-07935-0). Dodd.

One Hundred American Poems. Ed. by Selden Rodman. (Orig.). pap. 1.50 (ISBN 0-451-61666-9, MW1666, Ment). NAL.

One Hundred & Fifty Years of Main Line Railways. O. S. Nock. LC 79-56455. (Illus.). 1980. 17.95 (ISBN 0-7153-7881-3). David & Charles.

One Hundred & Fifty Years of Modern Britain. S. Hopewell. 1965. 3.15 o.p. (ISBN 0-08-011254-4). Pergamon.

One Hundred & Five Art Nouveau Designs in Full Color. M. P. Verneuil & Carol B. Grafton. (Pictorial Archive Ser.). (Illus.). 48p. (Orig.). 1981. pap. price not set (ISBN 0-486-24112-2). Dover.

One Hundred & Forty Four Ways to Sell Printing by Mail. C. Owen Brantley. LC 72-6609. 1972. 24.50 (ISBN 0-912920-23-8). North Am Pub Co.

One Hundred & One Best Jazz Albums: A History of Jazz on Records. Len Lyons. 1980. 17.95 (ISBN 0-688-03720-8, Quill); pap. 9.95 (ISBN 0-688-08720-5). Morrow.

One Hundred & One Creative Uses for Yesterday's Newspaper. Max Brown & Duane Shinn. 1978. pap. 3.95 o.p. (ISBN 0-912732-48-2). Duane Shinn.

One Hundred & One Elephant Jokes. Robert Blake. (Orig.). (YA) (gr. 7-12). 1964. pap. 0.95 (ISBN 0-515-01090-1, N1090). Jove Pubns.

One Hundred & One Flowering House Plants Anyone Can Grow. T. H. Everett. 144p. 1975. pap. 2.25 o.p. (ISBN 0-449-13271-4, 3271, GM). Fawcett.

One Hundred & One Intimate Sexual Problems Answered. LeMon Clark. (Orig.). 1967. pap. 0.95 o.p. (ISBN 0-451-05519-5, Q5519, Sig). NAL.

One Hundred & One More Houseplants. T. H. Everett. 1976. pap. 1.95 o.p. (ISBN 0-449-13500-4, Gm). Fawcett.

One Hundred & One Parsi Recipes. Jeroo Mehta. (Illus.). 146p. 1975. comb. bound 4.95 (ISBN 0-88253-438-6). Ind-US Inc.

One Hundred & One Pickle Jokes. Bob Vlasic. 1974. pap. 1.25 o.s.i. (ISBN 0-515-03553-X, N3553). Jove Pubns.

One Hundred & One Prints: The History & Techniques of Printmaking. Norman R. Eppink. (Illus.). 272p. 1972. 25.00 (ISBN 0-8061-0915-7); pap. 9.95 (ISBN 0-8061-1181-X). U of Okla Pr.

One Hundred & One Ranch. Ellsworth Collings & Alma England. LC 73-167774. (Illus.). 255p. 1937. 9.95 (ISBN 0-8061-0986-6); pap. 5.95 (ISBN 0-8061-1047-3). U of Okla Pr.

One Hundred & One Successful Ways to Turn Weekends into Wealth. Dan Ramsey. 216p. 1980. 10.95 (ISBN 0-13-634808-4, Parker). P-H.

One Hundred & One Tips & Hints for Your Boat. Jacques Damour. Tr. by Jeremy Howard-Williams from Fr. (Illus.). 1981. 13.95 (ISBN 0-393-03262-0). Norton.

One Hundred & One Ways to Get Free Publicity for Yourself, Your Product or Your Organization. Bev Shinn & Duane Shinn. 1978. pap. 9.95 (ISBN 0-912732-37-7); spiral bdg. 19.95. Duane Shinn.

One Hundred & One Ways to Use Your Oscilloscope. 2nd ed. Robert G. Middleton. LC 66-24122. (Illus.). 1966. pap. 5.50 o.p. (ISBN 0-672-20416-9, 20416). Sams.

One Hundred & One Ways to Use Your Oscilloscope. 3rd ed. Robert G. Middleton. 1980. pap. 6.95 (ISBN 0-672-21794-5). Sams.

One Hundred & One Ways to Use Your VOM & VTVM. 2nd ed. Robert G. Middleton. LC 66-29409. (Illus., Orig.). 1966. pap. 4.95 o.p. (ISBN 0-672-20510-6, 20510). Sams.

One Hundred & One Ways to Use Your VOM, TVM, DVM. 3rd ed. Robert G. Middleton. LC 80-52934. 1980. pap. 9.95 (ISBN 0-672-21756-2). Sams.

One Hundred & One Ways to Win at Golf. Dick Aultman & Golf Digest Editors. LC 80-66689. 248p. (Orig.). 1980. pap. 5.95 (ISBN 0-914178-40-7, 41417-8). Golf Digest.

One Hundred & One Word Games. George P. McCallum. 176p. 1980. pap. text ed. 5.95x (ISBN 0-19-502742-6). Oxford U Pr.

One Hundred & Ten CMOS Digital IC Projects. R. M. Marston. 1976. pap. 7.15 (ISBN 0-8104-0856-2). Hayden.

One Hundred & Ten Electronic Alarm Projects. R. M. Marston. (gr. 10 up). 1977. pap. 7.25 (ISBN 0-8104-5660-5). Hayden.

One Hundred & Ten Helps for Teachers. Carolyn Lehman. 64p. (Orig.). 1980. pap. text ed. 3.50 (ISBN 0-87239-413-1, 3070). Standard Pub.

One Hundred & Ten IC Timer Projects. Jules Gilder. 1979. pap. 6.35 (ISBN 0-8104-5688-5). Hayden.

One Hundred & Ten OP-AMP Projects. R. M. Marston. (Illus.). 128p. 1975. pap. 7.15 (ISBN 0-8104-0701-9). Hayden.

One-Hundred & Thirty-Three Ski Lessons by Jean-Claude Killy. Jean-Claude Killy. 80p. 1975. pap. 3.95 o.p. (ISBN 0-695-80628-9). Follett.

One Hundred & Twenty Eight Garden Plants You Can Grow. Rob Herwig. (Illus.). 60p. 1976. pap. 1.95 o.s.i. (ISBN 0-02-063070-0, Collier). Macmillan.

One Hundred & Twenty Eight Houseplants You Can Grow. Rob Herwig. 1972. pap. 1.95 o.s.i. (ISBN 0-02-063090-5, Collier). Macmillan.

One Hundred & Two Bird Houses, Feeders You Can Make. Hi Sibley. (Illus.). 1980. pap. 4.80 (ISBN 0-87006-304-9). Goodheart.

One Hundred Ballades. Nigel Wilkins. LC 69-10342. 1969. 42.00 (ISBN 0-521-07146-1). Cambridge U Pr.

One Hundred Bible Games. Edith B. Allen. (Paperback Program Ser). (YA) 1968. pap. 2.95 (ISBN 0-8010-0033-5). Baker Bk.

One Hundred Bible Quiz Activities for Church School Classes. James H. Robinson & R. Darline. 1981. pap. 3.95 (ISBN 0-570-03829-4, 12-2794). Concordia.

One Hundred Bible Stories. rev. ed. LC 66-10838. (Illus., King James Ed). (gr. 4-6). 1966. text ed. 5.50 (ISBN 0-570-03461-2, 56-1063); wkbk. 3.10 (ISBN 0-685-03397-X, 22-1201). Concordia.

One Hundred Booming Years. George B. Anderson. Ed. by H. J. Row & D. Stupek. (Illus.). 305p. 1980. 32.50 (ISBN 0-9604136-0-X). Bucyrus-Erie Co.

One Hundred Careers: How to Pick the One That's Best for You. Durham. 1977. 10.95 (ISBN 0-13-634717-7, Spec); pap. 4.95 (ISBN 0-13-634709-6). P-H.

One Hundred Classic Houdini Tricks You Can Do. Dunninger. LC 74-14200. (Illus.). 144p. 1975. pap. 3.50 (ISBN 0-668-03617-6). Arco.

One Hundred Dollar Misunderstanding. Robert Gover. LC 62-20506. 256p. 1980. pap. 2.95 (ISBN 0-394-17764-9, B448, BC). Grove.

One Hundred Families of Flowering Plants. M. Hickey & C. King. LC 79-42670. (Illus.). 220p. Date not set. 66.00 (ISBN 0-521-23283-X); pap. 19.95 (ISBN 0-521-29891-1). Cambridge U Pr.

One Hundred Famous American Festivals & Their Food. Helen Naismith. LC 75-30398. (Illus.). 1979. 10.00 (ISBN 0-933718-30-6). Browning Pubns.

One Hundred Famous Haiku. Tr. by Daniel Buchanan. LC 72-95667. 1977. pap. 5.95 (ISBN 0-87040-222-6). Japan Pubns.

One Hundred Favorite Old Master Paintings from the Louvre Museum, Paris. Michel Laclotte & Jean-Pierre Cuzin. LC 79-64988. (Illus.). 160p. 1979. 17.95 (ISBN 0-89659-065-8). Abbeville Pr.

One Hundred Fifty Blue Ribbon Systems. Ed. by GBC Editorial Staff. (Gambler's Book Shelf). (Orig.). 1979. pap. 2.95 (ISBN 0-89650-813-7). Gamblers.

One Hundred Fifty Fantastic Fund Raisers. Laura Dunnam. LC 77-94856. 1979. 10.00 o.p. (ISBN 0-89430-018-0). Morgan-Pacific.

One Hundred Fifty Masterpieces of Drawing. Anthony Toney. (Illus., Orig.). 1963. pap. 5.00 (ISBN 0-486-21032-4). Dover.

One Hundred Fifty Progressive Exercises for Melodic Dictation. Maurice Whitney. (For use with Backgrounds in Music Theory). 1954. pap. 1.95 (ISBN 0-02-872880-7). Schirmer Bks.

One-Hundred Fifty Years of British Steam Locomotives. Brian Reed. LC 75-10514. (Illus.). 128p. 1975. 19.95 (ISBN 0-7153-7051-0). David & Charles.

One Hundred Four Ideas for Improving Your Young Child's Language Skills. Carolyn P. Lind, pseud. (Illus.). 80p. (Orig.). 1980. pap. 10.00 (ISBN 0-9604940-0-6). Lindell Pubs.

One Hundred Great Operas & Their Stories. rev. ed. Henry W. Simon. LC 68-27816. (Reference Bk.). 1968. pap. 3.95 (ISBN 0-385-05448-3, C100, Dolp). Doubleday.

One Hundred Great Science Fiction Short Short Stories. Ed. by Isaac Asimov et al. 1980. pap. 2.50 (ISBN 0-686-69237-3, 50773). Avon.

One Hundred Greatest Baseball Players of All Time. Donald Honig & Lawrence S. Ritter. Ed. by Pamela Thomas. 288p. 1981. 15.95 (ISBN 0-517-54300-1). Crown.

One Hundred Hours at Mont Saint Michel. (One Hundred Hours in Ser.). (YA) (gr. 7). 1976. pap. 5.95 o.p. (ISBN 0-88332-019-3, 4112). Larousse.

One Hundred Hours to Visit the Chateaux of the Loire. new ed. L. Larfillon. (Illus.). 95p. 1973. pap. 5.95 o.p. (ISBN 0-88332-016-9, 4103). Larousse.

One Hundred Middle English Lyrics. Ed. by Robert D. Stevick. LC 76-20862. (Orig.). 1964. pap. 5.50 (ISBN 0-672-60974-6, LL7). Bobbs.

One Hundred Million Japanese. Masataka Kosaka. LC 72-76298. (Illus.). 282p. 1972. 10.00x (ISBN 0-87011-182-5). Kodansha.

One Hundred One Basic Recipes. Beryl Ruth. 1973. pap. text ed. 4.95x o.p. (ISBN 0-435-42703-2). Heinemann Ed.

One Hundred One Best Jazz Albums: A History of Jazz on Records. Len Lyons. LC 80-20392. (Illus.). 640p. 1980. 17.95 (ISBN 0-688-03720-8). Morrow.

One Hundred One Best Magic Tricks. Guy Frederick. (Illus.). (gr. 8 up). 6.95 (ISBN 0-8069-4510-9); PLB 6.69 (ISBN 0-8069-4511-7). Sterling.

One Hundred One Heritage Homes. Waller County Historical Survey Committee. (Illus.). 224p. 1975. 14.95 (ISBN 0-89015-103-2). Nortex Pr.

One Hundred One Media Center Ideas. Eleanor Silverman. LC 80-17034. 213p. 1980. pap. 13.50 (ISBN 0-8108-1329-7). Scarecrow.

One Hundred One Microwave Favorites Plus Four. Arlene Hamernik. (Illus.). 1978. pap. 2.95x o.p. (ISBN 0-685-99246-2). Microwave Helps.

One Hundred One Microwave Favorites Plus Four. Arlene Hamernik. 128p. 1978. Repr. of 1977 ed. spiral bdg. 2.95 o.p. (ISBN 0-9602930-0-0). Microwave Helps.

One Hundred One Microwave Favorites Plus Four. rev. ed. Arlene Hamernik. (Illus.). 82p. 1979. spiral bdg. 2.95x (ISBN 0-9602930-4-3). Microwave Help.

One Hundred One Patented Solar Energy Uses. Daniel J. O'Connor. 96p. 1980. pap. 8.95 (ISBN 0-442-24432-0). Van Nos Reinhold.

One-Hundred One Practical Uses for Propane Torches. Robert Brightman. (Illus.). 1978. 6.95 o.p. (ISBN 0-8306-9976-7); pap. 3.95 (ISBN 0-8306-1030-8, 1030). TAB Bks.

One Hundred One Proven Techniques for Getting the Job Interview. Burdette Bostwick. 256p. 1981. 12.95 (ISBN 0-471-07762-3, Pub. by Wiley-Interscience). Wiley.

One Hundred One Shark Jokes. Phil Hirsch. (Orig.). 1976. pap. 0.95 o.s.i. (ISBN 0-515-04075-4). Jove Pubns.

One Hundred One Short Cuts in Math Anyone Can Do. Gordon Rockmaker. LC 65-15500. (gr. 9 up). 1965. 8.95 (ISBN 0-8119-0136-X). Fell.

One Hundred One Snappy Sermonettes for the Children's Church. Paul E. Holdcraft. 1951. pap. 2.50 (ISBN 0-687-29015-5). Abingdon.

One Hundred One Stories of the Great Ballets. George Balanchine & Francis Mason. LC 73-9140. 560p. 1975. pap. 5.95 (ISBN 0-385-03398-2, Dolp). Doubleday.

One Hundred One Ways to Learn Vocabulary. Joan D. Berbrich. (Orig.). (gr. 10-12). 1971. wkbk. 6.25 (ISBN 0-87720-343-1). AMSCO Sch.

One Hundred One Ways to Make Money at Home. R. Fern. 1978. 12.50 o.p. (ISBN 0-685-05013-0, 0-911156-28-2). Porter.

One Hundred Paintings from the Boston Museum. Intro. by Perry T. Rathbone. (Illus.). 1970. pap. 4.95 o.p. (ISBN 0-87846-176-0). Mus Fine Arts Boston.

One Hundred Plays for Children. Ed. by A. S. Burack. (gr. 1-6). 1970. 11.95 (ISBN 0-8238-0002-4). Plays.

One Hundred Pounds of Popcorn. Hazel Krantz. LC 61-15479. (Illus.). (gr. 3-6). 1961. 4.95 (ISBN 0-8149-0344-4). Vanguard.

One Hundred Questions in Auditing with Suggested Answers for Accountancy Examinees. D. Kirkby. 1968. 15.00 (ISBN 0-08-012901-3); pap. 7.75 (ISBN 0-08-012900-5). Pergamon.

One Hundred Secret Hiding Places in Your Home. Laird M. Wilcox. (Orig.). 1980. pap. 3.00 (ISBN 0-933592-11-6). Edit Res Serv.

One Hundred Seven & Three Quarters Elephant Jokes. Jack Stokes. LC 78-1223. (Illus.). 1979. 6.95a (ISBN 0-385-14101-7); PLB (ISBN 0-385-14102-5). Doubleday.

One Hundred Seventy Seven Free Oregon Campgrounds. new ed. Ed Bedrick & Christina Bedrick. LC 79-66656. (Illus., Orig.). 1980. pap. 6.95 (ISBN 0-913140-33-3). Signpost Bk Pub.

One Hundred Sixty-Eight Days. Joseph Alsop & Turner Catledge. LC 72-2362. (American Constitutional & Legal History Ser). 324p. 1973. Repr. of 1938 ed. lib. bdg. 32.50 (ISBN 0-306-70481-1). Da Capo.

One Hundred Speeches from the Theater. Ed. by Rona Laurie & Barbara Vann. LC 72-81070. 208p. (gr. 9-12). 1973. 5.95g o.s.i. (ISBN 0-02-754610-1, CCPr). Macmillan.

One Hundred-Ten Thyristor Projects Using SCR's & TRIAC's. R. M. Marston. (Illus.). 1973. pap. 7.50 (ISBN 0-8104-5096-8). Hayden.

One Hundred Thirty-Two of the Most Unusual Cars That Ever Ran at Indianapolis. Lyle K. Engel & Auto Racing Magazine Staff. LC 72-103077. 1970. lib. bdg. 4.95 o.p. (ISBN 0-668-02194-2). Arco.

One Hundred Thousand Dollar Decision: The Older American's Guide to Selling a Home & Choosing Retirement Housing. Robert Irwin. (Illus.). 192p. 1981. 14.95 (ISBN 0-07-032070-5, P&RB). McGraw.

One Hundred Three Hikes in Southwestern British Columbia. 2nd ed. Mary Macaree & David Macaree. LC 80-17573. (Illus.). 224p. (Orig.). 1980. pap. 7.95 (ISBN 0-916890-96-1). Mountaineers.

One Hundred Twenty Days of Sodom & Other Writings. Marquis De Sade. Ed. by Austryn Wainhouse & Richard Seaver. (Illus.). 1966. pap. 7.95 (ISBN 0-394-17119-5, B138, BC). Grove.

One Hundred Twenty-Eight Bulbs You Can Grow. Rob Herwig. (Illus.). 60p. 1975. pap. 1.95 o.s.i. (ISBN 0-02-065390-5, Collier); pap. 39.00 pre-pack o.s.i. (ISBN 0-02-065410-3). Macmillan.

One Hundred Twenty-Five Typical Electronic Circuits Analyzed & Repaired. Art Margolis. LC 73-78197. (Illus.). 224p. 1973. 7.95 o.p. (ISBN 0-8306-3658-7); pap. 4.95 (ISBN 0-8306-2658-1, 658). TAB Bks.

One Hundred Twenty Questions & Answers About Birds. Madeline Angell. 6.95 o.p. (ISBN 0-672-51771-X). Bobbs.

One Hundred Twenty-Seven Sales Closes That Work. Gary O'Brien 192p. 1980. pap. 4.95 (ISBN 0-8015-5517-5, Hawthorn). Dutton.

One Hundred Two Birdhouses Feeders You Can Make. Hi Sibley. (Illus.). 96p. 1980. pap. text ed. 4.80 (ISBN 0-87006-304-9). Goodheart.

One Hundred Ways to Enhance Self Concepts in the Classroom: Handbook for Teachers & Parents. Harold C. Wells & Jack Canfield. (Illus.). 288p. 1976. 14.95 (ISBN 0-13-636951-0); pap. 10.95 (ISBN 0-13-636944-8). P-H.

One Hundred Ways to Stretch Your Dollar. Mother Thompson. (Illus.). 1979. pap. 12.95 o.p. (ISBN 0-930490-16-9). Future Shop.

One Hundred Ways to Use Your Pocket Calculator. Len Buckwalter. 128p. 1978. pap. 1.95 (ISBN 0-449-13356-7, GM). Fawcett.

One Hundred White Horses. Mildred Lawrence. LC 53-7866. (Illus.). (gr. 4-6). 1953. 5.25 o.p. (ISBN 0-15-258675-X, HJ). HarBraceJ.

One Hundred Years Ago. Frank Davis & Alise D. Williams. 1980. pap. 4.95 (ISBN 0-910286-79-5). Boxwood.

One Hundred Years of Architecture in Chicago. Oswald Grube. 1977. 14.95 o.p. (ISBN 0-695-80837-0). Follett.

One Hundred Years of Collectible Jewelry. Lillian Baker. (Illus.). 1980. pap. 8.95 (ISBN 0-89145-066-1). Collector Bks.

One Hundred Years of Geosciences in Romania. Ed. by V. Mihailescu. 1976. pap. text ed. 28.00 (ISBN 0-08-019969-0). Pergamon.

One Hundred Years of Siamese Cats. May Eustace. (Illus.). 1978. 8.95 o.p. (ISBN 0-684-15783-7, ScribT). Scribner.

One Hundred Years of Solitude. Gabriel G. Marquez. 1977. pap. 2.95 o.s.i. (ISBN 0-380-01758-X, 45278, Bard). Avon.

One in a Million: The Ron LeFlore Story. Ron LeFlore & Jim Hawkins. 1978. pap. 1.95 o.s.i. (ISBN 0-446-89976-3). Warner Bks.

One in the Gospel. Friedemann Hebart. 1981. pap. 4.25 (ISBN 0-570-03830-8, 12-2796). Concordia.

One in the Middle Is the Green Kangaroo. Judy Blume. (Illus.). 40p. (ps-3). 1981. 7.95 (ISBN 0-87888-182-4). Bradbury Pr.

One Is a Whole Number. Barbara Sroka. 1978. pap. 3.95 (ISBN 0-88207-631-0). Victor Bks.

One Is More Than un. Debbie Salter. 111p. 1978. pap. 2.50 (ISBN 0-8341-0548-9, Beacon). Nazarene.

One Kind of Freedom. R. Ransom & R. Sutch. LC 76-27909. 1978. 35.50 (ISBN 0-521-21450-5); pap. 11.95x (ISBN 0-521-29203-4). Cambridge U Pr.

One Language for the World & How to Achieve It. Mario Pei. LC 68-56449. 1958. 10.00x (ISBN 0-8196-0218-3). Biblo.

One Last Season. Richard Woodley. (Orig.). 1981. pap. 2.95 (ISBN 0-440-16698-5). Dell.

One Life. C. Barnard. 1970. 7.95 o.s.i. (ISBN 0-02-507230-7). Macmillan.

One Little Kitten. Tana Hoban. LC 78-31862. (Illus.). (gr. k-3). 1979. 6.95 (ISBN 0-688-80222-2); PLB 6.67 (ISBN 0-688-84222-4). Greenwillow.

One Little World. Jane B. Moncure. LC 75-35975. (Illus.). (ps-3). 1975. 5.50 (ISBN 0-913778-31-1). Childs World.

One Lonely Night - The Twisted Thing. Mickey Spillane. 1980. pap. 2.50 (ISBN 0-451-09465-4, E9465, Sig). NAL.

One Love Lost. Helen Holt. (Aston Hall Romances Ser.). 192p. 1981. pap. 1.75 (ISBN 0-523-41130-8). Pinnacle Bks.

One Man, Hurt. Albert Martin. 288p. 1975. 8.95 o.s.i. (ISBN 0-02-580470-7). Macmillan.

One Man's Gold Rush: A Klondike Album. rev. ed. Murray Morgan. LC 67-13109. (Illus.). 224p. 1976. Repr. of 1967 ed. pap. 12.50 (ISBN 0-295-95187-7). U of Wash Pr.

One Man's Initiation: Nineteen Seventeen. John Dos Passos. LC 69-15945. (Illus.). 180p. 1970. pap. 2.95 (ISBN 0-8014-9082-0, CP82). Cornell U Pr.

One Man's Judaism. Emanuel Rackman. LC 73-100583. 1970. 8.95 o.p. (ISBN 0-8022-2323-0). Philos Lib.

One Man's Research: The Autobiography of Reginald L. Reagan. Reginald Reagan. LC 80-66703. 1980. 10.95 (ISBN 0-89754-011-5); pap. 3.50 (ISBN 0-89754-010-7). Dan River Pr.

One Man's West. David Lavender. LC 76-45450. 1977. 14.95x (ISBN 0-8032-0908-8); pap. 3.95 (ISBN 0-8032-5855-0, BB 633, Bison). U of Nebr Pr.

One Mexican Sunday. Mike Oehler. LC 80-82949. (Illus.). 112p. 1980. 8.50 (ISBN 0-9604464-1-9). Mole Pub Co.

One Million Centuries. Richard A. Lupoff. 1981. pap. 2.50 (ISBN 0-671-83226-3). PB.

One Million Men: The Civil War Draft in the North. Eugene C. Murdock. LC 80-14431. (Illus.). xi, 366p. 1980. Repr. of 1971 ed. lib. bdg. 29.75x (ISBN 0-313-22502-8, MUOM). Greenwood.

One Money for Europe. Ed. by Michele Fratianni & Theo Peeters. LC 78-67228. (Praeger Special Studies). 1979. 24.95 (ISBN 0-03-047526-0). Praeger.

One More Makes Four. Robert Gernhardt. Tr. by Elizabeth W. Taylor. (Illus.). 32p. (gr. k up). 1981. 9.95 (ISBN 0-224-01577-X, Pub. by Chatto-Bodley-Jonathan). Merrimack Bk Serv.

One-More-Na-Bob Andd & Butt. Elizbeth M. Teffault. 76p. 1979. 4.50 (ISBN 0-8059-2664-X). Dorrance.

One More: Poems. Nasima Aziz. (Redbird Bk). 43p. 1975. 8.00 (ISBN 0-88253-837-3); pap. 4.80 (ISBN 0-88253-838-1). Ind-US Inc.

One More Thing, Dad. Susan L. Thompson. Ed. by Kathleen Tucker. LC 79-27887. (Self-Starter Bk.). (Illus.). (ps-1). 1980. PLB 6.50g (ISBN 0-8075-6095-2). A Whitman.

One More Time. Don Musgraves & Dave Balsiger. LC 74-1395. 224p. 1974. pap. 2.45 (ISBN 0-87123-419-X, 210419). Bethany Fell.

One Nation: An American Government Text with Readings. Robert L. Keighton & Martin P. Sutton. 512p. 1972. text ed. 12.95x o.p. (ISBN 0-669-61192-1); tchrs. guide free o.p. (ISBN 0-669-61200-6). Heath.

One Nation Divisible: Class, Race & Ethnicity in the U.S. Since 1938. Richard Polenberg. (Pelican History of the United States Ser.). 1980. pap. 4.95 (ISBN 0-14-021246-9). Penguin.

One Nation, So Many Governments: A Ford Foundation Report. Michael N. Danielson et al. LC 76-53868. 1977. 16.95 (ISBN 0-669-01293-9). Lexington Bks.

One Night Girl. Jacques Vieux. 65p. (Orig.). 1980. pap. 2.95 (ISBN 0-89260-184-1). Hwong Pub.

One Night in Newport. Elizabeth Villars. LC 80-718. (Illus.). 360p. 1981. 12.95 (ISBN 0-385-15328-7). Doubleday.

One Night Stand & Other Stories. Jack Spicer. Ed. by Donald Allen. LC 79-28053. 136p. 1980. 12.00 (ISBN 0-912516-45-3); pap. 4.95 (ISBN 0-912516-46-1). Grey Fox.

One, None and a Hundred-Thousand. Luigi Pirandello. Tr. by S. Putnam from Ital. LC 76-50039. 268p. 1981. Repr. of 1933 ed. 19.00 (ISBN 0-686-69134-2). Fertig.

One Ocean Touching: Papers from the First Pacific Rim Conference on Children's Literature. Ed. by Sheila A. Egoff. LC 78-31308. 260p. 1979. lib. bdg. 13.00 (ISBN 0-8108-1199-5). Scarecrow.

One O'Clock at the Gotham. Rae Foley. 1978. pap. 1.75 o.s.i. (ISBN 0-515-04494-6). Jove Pubns.

One of a Kind: The Legend of Carl Joseph. Jeff Meyers. 200p. 1980. pap. 6.95 (ISBN 0-86629-028-1); 11.95 (ISBN 0-86629-025-7). Sunrise MO.

One of a Kind (the Many Faces & Voices of America) Harry Barba. LC 75-41743. 1976. 6.95 o.s.i. (ISBN 0-911906-11-8); pap. 5.95 (ISBN 0-911906-12-6). Harian Creative.

One of Cleburne's Command. Ed. by Norman D. Brown. LC 80-16447. 224p. 1980. 14.95 (ISBN 0-292-76014-0). U of Tex Pr.

One of Our Bombers Is Missing. Dan Brennan. 1977. pap. 1.50 (ISBN 0-505-51140-1). Tower Bks.

One of the Boys. Janet Dailey. (Harlequin Presents Ser.). 192p. 1980. pap. 1.50 (ISBN 0-373-10399-9, Pub. by Harlequin). PB.

One of the Crowd. Rosamond Du Jardin. LC 61-15257. (gr. 4-9). 1961. 9.89 (ISBN 0-397-30582-6). Lippincott.

One of the Raymonds. Jean Rikhoff. 1977. pap. 1.95 o.p. (ISBN 0-449-23090-2, Crest). Fawcett.

One on One. Pat Nobel. (Orig.). 1980. pap. 2.25 (ISBN 0-532-23186-4). Manor Bks.

One-Parent Families. Diana Davenport. 1979. 19.95 (ISBN 0-686-63744-5, Pub. by Batsford England). David & Charles.

One Piece of Card. George Aspden. 1973. 13.50 (ISBN 0-7134-2866-X, Pub. by Batsford England). David & Charles.

One Pig with Horns. Laurent De Brunhoff. Tr. by Richard Howard from Fr. LC 78-4917. (Illus.). (gr. k-3). 1979. 5.95 (ISBN 0-394-83673-1); PLB 6.99 (ISBN 0-394-93673-6). Pantheon.

One Plus One Equals. Palmer Gedde. Ed. by Mentor Kujath. 1979. pap. 4.95 (ISBN 0-8100-0103-9, 12-1712). Northwest Pub.

One Plus One Equals One. Phyllis J. Le Peau & Andrew T. Le Peau. 96p. (Orig.). 1981. pap. 2.95 (ISBN 0-87784-803-3). Inter-Varsity.

One-Point Embroidery & Applique. new ed. Ondori Publishing Company Staff. (Ondori Young Handicraft Ser). (Illus.). 1977. pap. 3.95 (ISBN 0-87040-397-4). Japan Pubns.

One Potato, Two Potato: The Folklore of American Children. Mary Knapp & Herbert Knapp. 1978. pap. text ed. 4.95x (ISBN 0-393-09039-6). Norton.

One Real Poem Is Life. Douglas Anderson. LC 72-93478. 1973. 5.95 o.s.i. (ISBN 0-8076-0669-3). Braziller.

One Reel a Week. Fred J. Balshofer & Arthur C. Miller. (Illus.). 1968. 17.50 (ISBN 0-520-00073-0). U of Cal Pr.

One School for All. Margaret Cox. (Exploring Education Ser.). 1969. pap. text ed. 2.50x (ISBN 0-901225-03-7, NFER). Humanities.

One-Shot War. Brian O'Connor. 1981. 9.95 (ISBN 0-8129-0939-9). Times Bks.

One Small Blue Bead. Byrd B. Schweitzer. (Illus.). (gr. k-3). 1965. 7.95 (ISBN 0-02-781330-4). Macmillan.

One Snail & Me. Emilie W. McLeod. (Illus.). (gr. k up). 1961. 6.95 o.p. (ISBN 0-316-56197-5, Pub. by Atlantic Monthly Pr). Little.

One Special Summer. Jacqueline Bouvier & Lee Bouvier. (Illus.). 70p. 1974. 7.95 o.s.i. (ISBN 0-440-06037-0, E Friede). Delacorte.

One Step at a Time. Lenor Madruga. 1980. pap. 2.25 (ISBN 0-451-09407-7, E9407, Sig). NAL.

One Step at a Time. Willie Mae Smith. 1979. 4.95 (ISBN 0-533-04046-9). Vantage.

One Step Forward, Two Steps Back. V. I. Lenin. 1976. 3.95 (ISBN 0-8351-0232-7); pap. 2.25 (ISBN 0-8351-0233-5). China Bks.

One Step Further. Evonne Delizio. LC 80-52186. 1981. 5.95 (ISBN 0-533-04748-X). Vantage.

One Step, Two... rev. ed. Charlotte Zolotow. LC 80-11749. (Illus.). 32p. (gr. k-1). 1981. 7.95 (ISBN 0-688-51971-7); PLB 7.63 (ISBN 0-686-68921-6). Morrow.

One-Stitch Stitchery. Madeleine Appell. LC 78-51063. (Little Craft Book). (Illus.). 1978. 5.95 (ISBN 0-8069-5384-5); lib. bdg. 6.69 (ISBN 0-8069-5385-3). Sterling.

One Stringed Harp. Violet S. Devieux. 1980. 6.50 (ISBN 0-8233-0311-X). Golden Quill.

One Summer Night. Eleanor Schick. LC 76-25199. (Illus.). (gr. k-3). 1977. PLB 7.92 (ISBN 0-688-84072-8). Greenwillow.

One Sunny Day. Joan Alexander. 1978. pap. 1.95 o.p. (ISBN 0-425-03619-7, Medallion). Berkley Pub.

One Thing Worth Having. Lona B. Kenney. unpublished due to cancellation of publisher's rights

One Third of a Nation: Lorena Hickok Reports on the Great Depression. Ed. by Richard Lowitt & Maurine Beasley. (Illus.). 450p. 1981. 18.95 (ISBN 0-252-00849-9). U of Ill Pr.

One Third of Our Time? An Introduction to Recreation, Behavior & Resources: An Introduction to Recreation Behavior & Resources. Michael Chubb. LC 80-25131. 600p. 1981. text ed. 16.95 (ISBN 0-471-15637-X); write for info. study guide (ISBN 0-471-02184-9). Wiley.

One Thousand & One Helpful Family Hints. Ed. by Donald D. Wolf. (Illus.). 256p. (Orig.). 1980. pap. 9.95 (ISBN 0-8326-2246-X, 7030). Delair.

One Thousand & One Pitfalls in German. Henry Strutz. (gr. 9-12). 1981. pap. 6.95 (ISBN 0-8120-0590-2). Barron.

One Thousand & One Questions Answered About Trees. Rutherford Platt. LC 59-6900. 6.50 o.p. (ISBN 0-396-04233-3). Dodd.

One Thousand & One Texas Place Names. Fred Tarpley. 256p. 1980. text ed. 14.95x (ISBN 0-292-76015-9); pap. 5.95 (ISBN 0-292-76016-7). U of Tex Pr.

One Thousand & One Ways to Have Fun with Children. rev. ed. Jeanne Scargall. LC 72-12174. (Illus.). 160p. 1978. pap. 4.95 o.p. (ISBN 0-684-15926-0, SL815, ScribT). Scribner.

One Thousand Beautiful Garden Plants & How to Grow Them. Jack Kramer. 256p. 1976. 12.95 o.p. (ISBN 0-688-03025-4). Morrow.

One Thousand Beautiful Things. Marjorie Barrows. (Library of Beautiful Things: Vol. 1). (gr. 7 up). 1955. 9.95 (ISBN 0-8015-5562-0, Hawthorn). Dutton.

One Thousand Bible Study Outlines. F. E. Marsh. LC 75-125115. 1970. 9.95 (ISBN 0-8254-3209-X). Kregel.

One Thousand Ideas for Term Papers in American History. Robert A. Farmer. LC 74-77566. (One Thousand Ideas for Term Papers Ser). 160p. 1969. pap. 1.95 o.p. (ISBN 0-668-01925-5). Arc Bks.

One Thousand Inspirational Things. Audrey S. Morris. (Library of Beautiful Things: Vol. 2). (YA) (gr. 9-12). 1956. 9.95 (ISBN 0-8015-5568-X, Hawthorn). Dutton.

One Thousand Inventions. Alan Benjamin. LC 80-80659. (Illus.). 10p. (ps up). 1980. spiral bdg. 4.95 (ISBN 0-590-07749-X, Four Winds). Schol Bk Serv.

One Thousand Monsters. Alan Benjamin. LC 79-10682. (Illus.). 10p. (ps up). 1979. spiral 4.95 (ISBN 0-590-07636-1, Four Winds). Schol Bk Serv.

One Thousand One Games for Better Writing: Writing Easily, Clearly & Enthusiastically. Priscilla Vail. LC 80-54818. (Illus.). 288p. 1981. 16.95 (ISBN 0-8027-0682-7). Walker & Co.

One Thousand One Glenwood. Annis Ward-Jackson. Ed. by Thomas Duncan. (Illus.). 117p. (gr. 6 up). 1979. PLB 6.95. Era Pr NC.

One Thousand One Pitfalls in Italian. Ragusa & Cherubini. 1980. pap. 6.95 (ISBN 0-8120-0589-9). Barron.

One Thousand One Questions About Your Car. Mort J. Schultz. LC 73-9815. (Illus.). 224p. 1973. 11.00 o.p. (ISBN 0-07-055645-8, P&RB). McGraw.

One Thousand One Questions Answered About the Oceans & Oceanography. Robert W. Taber & Harold W. Dubach. LC 73-184136. (Illus.). 352p. 1972. 7.95 o.p. (ISBN 0-396-06496-5). Dodd.

One-Thousand One Ways of Saving Money. Tony Swindells. 7.50 o.p. (ISBN 0-7153-7540-7). David & Charles.

One Thousand One Words. Bobbi Katz. LC 75-6832. 96p. (gr. 4-8). 1975. 5.90 (ISBN 0-531-02849-6). Watts.

One Thousand Quaint Cuts from Books of Other Days. Andrew W. Tuer. LC 68-31097. 1968. Repr. of 1886 ed. 18.00 (ISBN 0-8103-3494-1). Gale.

One Thousand Sayings of History, Presented As Pictures in Prose. Walter Fogg. LC 79-143634. 1971. Repr. of 1929 ed. 28.00 (ISBN 0-8103-3779-7). Gale.

One Thousand Space Monsters--"Have Landed". Alan Benjamin. LC 79-55339. (Illus.). 10p. (ps up). 1980. spiral 3.95 (ISBN 0-590-07667-1, Four Winds). Schol Bk Serv.

One Thousand Ways to Save Energy & Money: Energy Saving Handbook for Homes, Businesses & Institutions. Edwin B. Feldman. 1979. 9.95 (ISBN 0-8119-0321-4). Fell.

One Thousand Years of Irish Poetry. Ed. by Kathleen Hoagland. 832p. 1981. 12.95 (ISBN 0-517-34295-2). Devin.

One Thousand Years: Western Europe in the Middle Ages. Richard L. Demolen et al. 325p. 1974. pap. text ed. 9.75 (ISBN 0-395-14032-3). HM.

One Through Six: How to Understand & Enjoy the Years That Count. Patricia Coffin & J. Hansen. 1972. pap. 4.95 o.s.i. (ISBN 0-02-079380-4, Collier). Macmillan.

One to Another: A Guidebook for Interpersonal Communication. Richard E. Crable. (Illus.). 300p. 1980. pap. text ed. 12.50 scp (ISBN 0-06-041395-6, HarpC); avail. Har-Row.

One-to-One: Resources for Conference-Centered Writing. Dawe & Dornan. (Orig.). 1981. pap. text ed. 7.95 (ISBN 0-316-17722-9); tchrs'. manual free (ISBN 0-316-17723-7). Little.

One to Teeter-Totter. Edith Battles. LC 72-13348. (Self Starter Bks.). (Illus.). 32p. (ps-1). 1973. 6.50g (ISBN 0-8075-6103-7). A Whitman.

One to Ten Count Again. James Woodard & Linda Purdy. (Illus.). (ps). 1972. PLB 5.51 (ISBN 0-914844-07-5). J Alden.

One-Trick Pony. Paul Simon. LC 80-7636. (Illus.). 224p. 1980. 15.95 (ISBN 0-394-51381-9); pap. 8.95 (ISBN 0-394-73961-2). Knopf.

One Turn of Seasons. Elizabeth Whittle & F. A. Dockery. LC 80-65203. (Illus.). 64p. (Orig.). 1980. pap. 5.95x perfect bound (ISBN 0-9604046-0-0). E Whittle & F A Dockery.

One, Two, Buckle My Shoe. Illus. by Amye Rosenburg. (Floppies Ser.). (Illus.). 6p. (ps-k). Date not set. 3.95 (ISBN 0-671-42532-3, Little Simon). S&S.

One Two Three: An Animal Counting Book. Marc Brown. 32p. (gr. k-3). 1976. PLB 6.95 (ISBN 0-316-11064-7, Pub. by Atlantic Monthly Pr). Little.

One, Two, Three, & More. Solveig P. Russell. LC 66-18230. (ps). 1966. bds. 5.50 laminated (ISBN 0-570-03410-8, 56-1062). Concordia.

One, Two, Three for Fun. Muriel Stanek. LC 67-26519. (Concept Bks.). (Illus.). 32p. (ps-2). 1967. 6.95g (ISBN 0-8075-6106-1). A Whitman.

One-Two-Three-Four-Five-Six: How to Understand & Enjoy the Years That Count. Patricia Coffin. LC 72-76278. 160p. 1972. 8.95 o.s.i. (ISBN 0-02-526690-X). Macmillan.

One, Two, Three, Going to Sea. Alain. (gr. k-3). 1969. pap. 1.25 (ISBN 0-590-02605-4, Schol Pap). Schol Bk Serv.

One, Two, Three, John. Curtis Vaughan. (Study Guide Ser). 1970. pap. 3.50 (ISBN 0-310-33563-9). Zondervan.

One, Two, Three with Ant & Bee. Angela Banner. (Ant & Bee Bks). (Illus.). (gr. k-3). 1959. 2.95 o.p. (ISBN 0-531-01162-3). Watts.

One Way. Robert L. Brandt. (Radiant Life Ser.). 1977. pap. 1.50 (ISBN 0-88243-909-X, 02-0909); teacher's ed 2.50 (ISBN 0-88243-179-X, 32-0179). Gospel Pub.

One Way or Another. Leonardo Sciascia. Tr. by Adrienne Foulke from It. LC 76-26274. (Illus.). 1977. 7.95 o.s.i. (ISBN 0-06-013804-1, HarpT). Har-Row.

One Word at a Time: The Use of Single Word Utterances Before Syntax. Lois Bloom. LC 72-94445. (Janua Linguarum, Ser. Minor: No. 154). 262p. 1973. pap. text ed. 21.20x (ISBN 90-2793-375-8). Mouton.

One Word More on Browning. Frances T. Russell. 157p. 1980. Repr. of 1927 ed. text ed. 28.00 (ISBN 0-8492-7709-4). R West.

One Word Storybook. Ken Wagner. (Illus.). (ps-3). 1968. PLB 7.62 (ISBN 0-307-60867-0, Golden Pr). Western Pub.

One World. Brian Maegraith. (Heath Clark Lectures 1970). 250p. 1973. text ed. 18.75x (ISBN 0-485-26323-8, Athlone Pr). Humanities.

One World Divided: A Geographer Looks at the Modern World. 3rd ed. Preston E. James & Kempton Webb. LC 79-12136. 1980. text ed. 20.95 (ISBN 0-471-02687-5). Wiley.

One Year Accounting Course, 2 pts. Trevor Gambling. 1969. Pt. 1. text ed. 11.75 (ISBN 0-08-013025-9); Pt. 2. text ed. o.p. (ISBN 0-08-013027-5); pap. text ed. 6.00 ea.; Pt. 1. pap. text ed. (ISBN 0-08-013024-0); Pt. 2. pap. text ed. (ISBN 0-08-013026-7). Pergamon.

One-Year Courses in Colleges & Sixth Forms: A Report from the Sixteen Plus Education Unit. Denis Vincent & Judy Dean. 1977. pap. text ed. 8.75x (ISBN 0-85633-134-1, NFER). Humanities.

Oneida Community: An Autobiography. Constance Robertson. (Illus.). 1981. pap. 9.95 (ISBN 0-8156-0166-2). Syracuse U Pr.

O'Neill. enl. ed. Arthur Gelb & Barbara Gelb. LC 73-6760. (Illus.). 1088p. 1974. 25.00 o.p. (ISBN 0-06-011487-8, HarpT); pap. 7.95 o.p. (ISBN 0-06-011484-3, TD-202, HarpT). Har-Row.

O'Neill & His Plays: Four Decades of Criticism. Ed. by Oscar Cargill et al. LC 61-17631. (Gotham Library). 1961. 15.00x o.p. (ISBN 0-8147-0075-6); pap. 6.95 (ISBN 0-8147-0076-4). NYU Pr.

Oneness of Politics & Religion. Nicholas Eliopoulos. 126p. (Orig.). 1970. pap. 3.00x (ISBN 0-9605396-1-1). Phystiklakis & Eliopoulos.

Onesimus. Lance Webb. 374p. 1980. pap. 5.95 (ISBN 0-8407-5742-5). Nelson.

Ongoing Reform of the Church. Alois Muller. (Concilium Ser.: Religion in the Seventies: Vol. 73). 1972. pap. 4.95 (ISBN 0-8164-2529-9). Crossroad NY.

Onin War: History of Its Origins & Background with a Selective Translation of the Chronicle of Onin. H. Paul Varley. LC 66-14595. (Studies in Oriental Culture Ser.: No. 1). (Illus.). 1966. 17.50x (ISBN 0-231-02943-8). Columbia U Pr.

Onion Field: A True Story. Joseph Wambaugh. 488p. 1973. 8.95 o.s.i. (ISBN 0-440-06692-1). Delacorte.

Onion John. Joseph Krumgold. LC 59-11395. (Illus.). (gr. 5 up). 1959. 9.95 (ISBN 0-690-59957-9, TYC-J). T Y Crowell.

Onion Peel. K. M. Trishanku. (Indian Novels Ser, Vol. 2). 175p. 1974. 7.50 (ISBN 0-88253-465-3). Ind-US Inc.

Onion Production in California. Ronald E. Voss. (Illus.). 1979. pap. 5.00x (ISBN 0-931876-35-4, 4097). Ag Sci Pubns.

Onions & Cucumbers & Plums: Fourty-Six Yiddish Poems in English. Ed. by Sarah Z Betsky. Tr. by Sarah Z. Betsky from Yiddish. 280p. 1981. 12.50 (ISBN 0-8143-1080-X); pap. 6.95 (ISBN 0-8143-1674-3). Wayne St U Pr.

Onions & Roses. Vassar Miller. LC 68-27544. (Wesleyan Poetry Program: Vol. 42). 1968. 10.00x (ISBN 0-8195-2042-X, Pub. by Wesleyan U Pr); pap. 4.95 (ISBN 0-8195-1042-4). Columbia U Pr.

Onitsha Market Literature. Emmanual Obiechina. (African Writers Ser.). 1972. pap. text ed. 6.50x (ISBN 0-435-90109-5). Heinemann Ed.

Online Information Retrieval Bibliography 1964-1979. Donald Hawkins. 175p. 1980. 25.00x (ISBN 0-938734-00-8). Learned Info.

Online Searching: A Primer. Carol Fenichel & Thomas Hogan. 130p. 1981. text ed. 12.95x (ISBN 0-938734-01-6). Learned Info.

Online Searching: An Introduction. Henry et al. LC 80-40242. 1980. 31.95 (ISBN 0-408-10696-4). Butterworths.

Only a Gringo Would Die for an Anteater: The Adventures of a Veterinarian. Michael H. Milts & Carl Larsen. (McGraw-Hill Paperbacks Ser.). 240p. 1980. pap. 3.95 (ISBN 0-07-042391-1). McGraw.

Only a Little Planet. Lawrence Collins & Martin Schweitzer. Ed. & pref. by David R. Brower. LC 72-187904. (Celebrating the Earth Ser). (Illus.). 128p. 1974. 14.95 o.p. (ISBN 0-913890-27-8); pap. 6.95 o.p. (ISBN 0-685-56645-5, Co-Pub. by Ballantine). Friends Earth.

Only a Matter of Time. V. C. Clinton-Baddeley. Date not set. pap. price not set (ISBN 0-440-16055-3). Dell.

Only a Prayer Meeting. C. H. Spurgeon. pap. 3.95 (ISBN 0-686-09106-X). Pilgrim Pubns.

Only a Trillion. Isaac Asimov. (Isaac Asimov Collection Ser.). 224p. 1976. pap. 2.25 (ISBN 0-441-63121-5). Ace Bks.

Only a Woman. Evelyn M. Anderson. (Ultra Bks Ser). 1969. 3.50 (ISBN 0-8010-0062-9). Baker Bk.

Only Astrology Book You'll Ever Need. Martine. LC 80-5403. 288p. 1981. 14.95 (ISBN 0-8128-2726-0). Stein & Day.

Only Chance. Eric Jannerston. Tr. by H. W. Kelsey. (Illus.). 176p. 1981. 12.95 (ISBN 0-370-30266-4, Pub. by Chatto-Bodley-Jonathan). Merrimack Bk Serv.

Only Child's Play: Developing the Capicities of Handicapped Children. Linda Routledge. (Illus.). 1978. pap. 11.95x (ISBN 0-433-28350-5). Intl Ideas.

Only Connect: Readings on Children's Literature. Ed. by Sheila Egoff et al. 1969. pap. 7.50x o.p. (ISBN 0-19-540161-1). Oxford U Pr.

Only Connect: Readings on Children's Literature. 2nd ed. Ed. by Sheila Egoff et al. (Illus.). 496p. 1980. pap. text ed. 8.95x (ISBN 0-19-540309-6). Oxford U Pr.

Only Connect: Readings on Children's Literature. 2nd ed. Ed. by Sheila Egoff et al. (Illus.). 482p. 1980. pap. 8.95 (ISBN 0-19-540309-6). Oxford U Pr.

Only Couples Need Apply. Doris M. Disney. 160p. 1974. pap. 0.95 o.p. (ISBN 0-451-05953-0, Q5953, Sig). NAL.

Only Dance There Is: Thoughts Along the Spiritual Way. Ram Dass. LC 73-14054. 295p. 1974. pap. 4.95 (ISBN 0-385-08413-7, Anch). Doubleday.

Only Earth We Have. Laurence Pringle. LC 71-78076. (Illus.). (gr. 5-8). 1971. pap. 0.95 o.s.i. (ISBN 0-02-044880-5, Collier). Macmillan.

Only Earth We Have. Laurence Pringle. LC 71-78076. (Illus.). (gr. 4-8). 1969. 5.95g o.s.i. (ISBN 0-02-775210-0); text ed. 1.96 o.s.i. (ISBN 0-02-775250-X). Macmillan.

Only for a Day. Barbara J. Crane. (Crane Reading System-English Ser.). (Illus.). (gr. k-2). 1977. pap. text ed. 2.95 (ISBN 0-89075-101-3). Crane Pub Co.

Only for Peace. A. A. Gromyko. (Illus.). 1979. text ed. 46.00 (ISBN 0-08-023582-4); pap. text ed. 19.00 (ISBN 0-08-024513-7). Pergamon.

Only Game in Town: An Illustrated History of Gambling. Hank Messick & Burt Goldblatt. LC 75-26583. (Illus.). 224p. 1976. 12.50 o.s.i. (ISBN 0-690-01061-3, TYC-T). T Y Crowell.

Only Girl in the Game. John D. MacDonald. 1978. pap. 1.75 o.p. (ISBN 0-449-14032-6, GM). Fawcett.

Only Good Indian...the Hollywood Gospel. Ralph Friar & Natasha Friar. LC 72-78907. (Illus.). 346p. 1973. 5.00 o.p. (ISBN 0-910482-21-7). Drama Bk.

Only Hope. Felix A. Lorenz. LC 75-43059. 112p. 1976. pap. 4.50 (ISBN 0-8127-0108-9). Southern Pub.

Only Investment Guide You'll Ever Need. Andrew Tobia. 200p. 1981. pap. 2.75 (ISBN 0-553-14481-2). Bantam.

Only Just Above the Ground: Special Issues 28. Stuart Z. Perkoff. pap. 1.00 o.p. (ISBN 0-685-78406-1). The Smith.

Only Kangaroo Among the Beauty: Emily Dickinson & America. Karl Keller. LC 79-10462. 1980. text ed. 19.50x (ISBN 0-8018-2174-6); pap. text ed. 5.95 (ISBN 0-8018-2538-5). Johns Hopkins.

Only Land They Knew: The Tragic Story of the American Indians in the Old South. J. Leitch Wright, Jr. LC 80-1854. (Illus.). 1981. 16.95 (ISBN 0-02-935790-X). Free Pr.

Only Love. Susan Sallis. LC 79-2686. 256p. (YA) (gr. 7 up). 1980. 8.95 (ISBN 0-06-025174-3, HarpJ); PLB 8.79 (ISBN 0-06-025175-1). Har-Row.

Only One Ant. Leonore Klein. 32p. (gr. k-3). 1971. 5.95g (ISBN 0-8038-5362-9). Hastings.

Only One Year. Svetlana Alliluyeva. Tr. by Paul Chavchavadze. LC 79-81883. 1969. 12.50 o.p. (ISBN 0-06-010102-4, HarpT). Har-Row.

Only Revolution. Jiddu Krishnamurti. Ed. by Mary Lutyens. LC 77-109066. 1970. 5.95 o.p. (ISBN 0-06-064869-4, HarpR). Har-Row.

Only Revolution. Jiddu Krishnamurti. Ed. by Mary Lutyens. 1977. pap. 1.95 o.p. (ISBN 0-06-080410-6, P410, PL). Har-Row.

Only Silly People Waste. Norah Smaridge. LC 75-15623. (Illus.). (gr. k-4). 1976. 5.50g (ISBN 0-687-28847-9). Abingdon.

Only the Beginning. Nelson L. Price. LC 79-55662. (gr. 10 up). 1980. 4.95 (ISBN 0-8054-5331-8). Broadman.

Only the Clounds Remain: Ted Parsons of the Lafayette Escadrille. Dale L. Walker. LC 80-68357. (Illus.). 72p. 1980. pap. 6.95 (ISBN 0-937748-00-5). Alandale Pr.

Only the Dreamer Can Change the Dream: Selected Poems. John Logan. LC 80-23184. (American Poetry Ser.: Vol. 21). 256p. 1981. 14.95 (ISBN 0-912946-77-6). Ecco Pr.

Only the Present. Noelle McGue. 1981. pap. 1.50 (ISBN 0-440-16597-0). Dell.

Only Thing I've Done Wrong. John J. Osborne, Jr. 1977. pap. 1.75 (ISBN 0-380-01870-5, 36970). Avon.

Only to the House of Israel? Jesus & the Non-Jews. T. W. Manson. Ed. by John Reumann. LC 64-11860. (Facet Bks). 1964. pap. 1.00 (ISBN 0-8006-3005-X, 1-3005). Fortress.

Only Way to Cross. John Maxtone-Graham. (Illus.). 480p. 1972. 15.95 (ISBN 0-02-582350-7). Macmillan.

Only Way to Learn Astrology: Vol. 2, Math & Aftermath. 2nd, rev. ed. Marion March & Joan McEvers. (Illus.). 320p. 1981. pap. 11.95 (ISBN 0-917086-26-0). Astro Comp Serv.

Onstage Christ: Studies in the Persistence of a Theme. John Ditsky. (Critical Studies Ser.). 188p. 1980. 25.00x (ISBN 0-389-20059-X). B&N.

Ontem, a Hora Setima. Tr. by Jeanne Hale. (Portugese Bks.). (Port.). 1979. 1.50 (ISBN 0-8297-0827-8). Life Pubs Intl.

Ontogeny & Phylogeny of Hormone Receptors. (Monographs in Developmental Biology). (Illus.). 200p. 1981. pap. 72.00 (ISBN 3-8055-2174-X). S Karger.

Ontogeny of Receptors & Reproductive Hormone Action. Ed. by T. H. Hamilton et al. LC 77-92523. 1979. text ed. 42.50 (ISBN 0-89004-254-3). Raven.

Ontogeny of Social Behavior in the Gray Squirrel (Sciurus carolinensis) R. H. Horwich. (Advances in Ethology Ser.: Vol. 8). (Illus.). 103p. (Orig.). 1972. pap. text ed. 23.50. Parey Sci Pubs.

Ontological Relativity & Other Essays. Willard V. Quine. LC 72-91121. (John Dewey Lectures Ser.: No. 1). 1969. 15.00x (ISBN 0-231-03307-9); pap. 5.00x (ISBN 0-231-08357-2). Columbia U Pr.

Ontology of Humor. Bob W. Parrott. 1981. 10.95 (ISBN 0-8022-2387-7). Philos Lib.

Onward & Upward. Mildred Zeigler. 60p. 1981. pap. 4.00 (ISBN 0-86629-027-3). Sunrise MO.

Onward & Upward in the Garden. Katherine S. White. Ed. by E. B. White. 384p. 1979. 12.95 (ISBN 0-374-22654-7). FS&G.

Onward & Upward in the Garden. Katherine S. White. Ed. by E. B. White. 1981. pap. 6.95 (ISBN 0-374-51629-4). FS&G.

Onze Contes. Olin H. Moore & Walter Meiden. LC 57-674. (Fr). 1957. pap. text ed. 7.70 (ISBN 0-395-04941-5, 3-38350). HM.

Onzieme Reunion Du Conseil Interamericain Pour L'education, la Science et la Culture: Rapport Final. OAS General Secretariat. 236p. (Fr.). 1980. pap. text ed. 19.00 (ISBN 0-8270-1198-9). OAS.

Oom-Pah. William Crane. LC 80-18404. 204p. (gr. 5-9). 1981. PLB 9.95 (ISBN 0-689-30804-3). Atheneum.

Oort & the Universe. Ed. by Hugo Van Woerden et al. 210p. 1980. PLB 29.00 (ISBN 0-686-28847-5, Pub. by D. Reidel); pap. 12.95 (ISBN 90-277-1209-3). Kluwer Boston.

OP AMP Handbook. Frederick W. Hughes. (Illus.). 304p. 1981. text ed. 21.95 (ISBN 0-13-637298-8). P-H.

Opal. Jane Boulton & Opal Whitely. 152p. 1976. 6.95 o.s.i. (ISBN 0-02-513970-3). Macmillan.

Opal-Eyed Fan. Andre Norton. (gr. 7 up). 1977. 7.95 o.p. (ISBN 0-525-36440-4). Dutton.

Opal Springs. Beatrice C. Harris. 1979. 3.50 (ISBN 0-686-28896-3). Klassen.

OPEC & the Middle East: The Impact of Oil on Societal Development. Ed. by Russell A. Stone. LC 77-2920. (Special Studies). 1976. text ed. 28.95 (ISBN 0-275-24490-3). Praeger.

OPEC & the Petroleum Industry. Mana S. Al-Otaiba. LC 75-15447. 187p. 1975. 15.95 (ISBN 0-470-02252-3). Halsted Pr.

OPEC Market to Nineteen Eighty-Five. Farid Abolfathi et al. LC 76-44612. (Illus.). 1977. 24.95 (ISBN 0-669-01102-9). Lexington Bks.

OPEC Official Resolutions & Press Releases 1960-1980. LC 80-41924. 224p. 1980. pap. 40.00 (ISBN 0-08-027335-1). Pergamon.

OPEC: Policy Implications for the United States. Robin C. Landis. Ed. by Michael W. Klass. LC 78-19457. (Praeger Special Studies). (Illus.). 304p. 1980. 29.95 (ISBN 0-03-044361-X). Praeger.

OPEC: Success & Prospects. Dankwart A. Rustow & John F. Mugno. LC 75-29526. 179p. 1976. uKE 12.50x (ISBN 0-8147-7369-9); pap. 5.00x uke (ISBN 0-8147-7379-6). NYU Pr.

OPEC: Twenty Years & Beyond. Ragaei El Mallakh. 240p. 1981. lib. bdg. 25.00x (ISBN 0-86531-163-3). Westview.

Opel Service Repair Handbook: All Models, 1966-1979. Ray Hoy. Ed. by Eric Jorgensen. (Illus.). 1977. pap. 10.95 (ISBN 0-89287-171-7, A175). Clymer Pubns.

Open & Shut. Milton J. Silverman & Ron Winslow. 1981. 15.95 (ISBN 0-393-01442-8). Norton.

Open Care for the Elderly in Seven European Countries: A Pilot Study in the Possibilities & Limits of Care. Ed. by Anton Amann. LC 80-40816. 238p. 1980. 36.00 (ISBN 0-08-025215-X). Pergamon.

Open Case: The Organisational Context of Social Work. Joyce Warham. (Library of Social Work). 1977. 16.00 (ISBN 0-7100-8608-3); pap. 7.95 (ISBN 0-7100-8609-1). Routledge & Kegan.

Open Classroom: A Practical Guide for the Teacher of the Elementary Grades. Rose Sabaroff & Mary A. Hanna. LC 74-6442. (Illus.). 1974. 10.00 (ISBN 0-8108-0726-2). Scarecrow.

Open Decision. J. H. Bryant. LC 79-129473. 1970. 10.95 (ISBN 0-02-904860-5). Free Pr.

Open Door Colleges: Policies for the Community Colleges. Carnegie Commission On Higher Education. 1970. 2.95 o.p. (ISBN 0-07-010019-5, P&RB). McGraw.

Open-Door Policy & the Territorial Integretiy of China. Shutaro Tomimas. (Studies in Chinese History & Civilization). 1977. 17.00 (ISBN 0-89093-095-3). U Pubns Amer.

Open Door to French. Margarita Madrigal & Colette Dulac. (gr. 7-10). 1963. pap. text ed. 2.95 (ISBN 0-88345-121-2, 17476). Regents Pub.

Open Door to Learning: The Land-Grant System Enters Its Second Century. Herman R. Allen. LC 63-18672. 1963. 8.00 o.p. (ISBN 0-252-72590-5). U of Ill Pr.

Open Door to Spanish, 2 bks. Margarita Madrigal. (gr. 7 up). 1972. Bk. 1. pap. text ed. 3.50 o.p. (ISBN 0-88345-186-7, 18098); Bk. 2. pap. text ed. 2.75 (ISBN 0-88345-187-5, 17704); records 20.00 ea.; tapes o.p. 30.00 ea.; cassettes 40.00 ea. Regents Pub.

Open Door to Spanish, Bk. 1. new ed. Margarita Madrigal. (Illus.). 223p. (gr. 5-12). 1980. pap. text ed. 3.75 (ISBN 0-88345-420-3, 18469); cassettes 40.00. Regents Pub.

Open Door to Spanish, Bk. 2. Margarita Madrigal. (Open Door to Spanish Ser.). 200p. (gr. 5-12). 1981. pap. text ed. 3.75 (ISBN 0-88345-427-0, 18470). Regents Pub.

Open Doors. Institute of International Education. 157p. 1980. pap. 15.00 o.p. (ISBN 0-87206-098-5). Inst Intl Educ.

Open Doors Nineteen Seventy-Eight to Nineteen Seventy-Nine: Report on International Educational Exchange. rev. ed. Ed. by Douglas R. Boyan. LC 55-4594. 125p. 1980. pap. text ed. 15.00 o.p. (ISBN 0-87206-098-5). Inst Intl Educ.

Open Doors Nineteen Seventy-Nine to Nineteen Eighty: Report on International Educational Exchange. Ed. by Douglas R. Boyan. LC 55-4594. 160p. 1981. pap. 20.00 o.p. (ISBN 0-87206-106-X). Inst Intl Educ.

Open Doors Nineteen Seventy-Seven to Seventy-Eight: Report on International Educational Exchange. rev. ed. Ed. by Alfred C. Julian & Janet Lowenstein. LC 55-4594. 1979. pap. text ed. 7.50 o.p. (ISBN 0-87206-093-4). Inst Intl Educ.

Open Doors 1975: A Report on International Exchange. 1976. pap. 5.00 o.p. (ISBN 0-87206-079-9). Inst. Intl Educ.

Open Economy: Essays on International Trade & Finance. Ed. by Peter B. Kenen & Roger Lawrence. (Columbia Studies in Economics). xvi, 391p. 1968. 25.00x (ISBN 0-231-03009-6). Columbia U Pr.

Open Economy Macroeconomics. Rudiger Dornbusch. LC 80-66308. (Illus.). 293p. 1980. text ed. 17.95x (ISBN 0-465-05286-X). Basic.

Open-End Investment Funds in the European Economic Community & Switzerland. D. C. Corner & D. C. Stafford. LC 76-17101. 1977. lib. bdg. 46.50x (ISBN 0-89158-620-2). Westview.

Open Field System & Beyond. C. J. Dahlman. LC 79-7658. 1980. 27.50 (ISBN 0-521-22881-6). Cambridge U Pr.

Open Fords. Lorin Sorensen. (Fordiana Ser.). 1979. 49.50 o.p. (ISBN 0-87938-081-0). Motorbooks Intl.

Open Gates of Heaven: A Brief Introduction to Literary Analysis of the Book of Revelations. Kenneth A. Strand. 1979. pap. text ed. 2.75 o.p. (ISBN 0-89039-119-X). Ann Arbor FL.

Open Heart-Open Home. Karen B. Mains. 1980. pap. 1.95 (ISBN 0-451-09530-8, J9530, Sig). NAL.

Open Housing. Juliet Saltman. LC 78-19464. 1978. 31.95 (ISBN 0-03-022376-8). Praeger.

Open Learning & Career Mobility in Nursing. Carrie B. Lenburg. LC 74-20887. 1975. pap. 12.95 o.p. (ISBN 0-8016-2938-1). Mosby.

Open Lesson to a Bishop. Michael Davies. 1980. pap. 1.00 (ISBN 0-89555-142-X). Tan Bks Pubs.

Open Mappings in Locally Compact Spaces. Gordon T. Whyburn. LC 52-42839. (Memoirs: No. 1). 1969. pap. 4.40 (ISBN 0-8218-1201-7, MEMO-1). Am Math.

Open Marriage: A New Lifestyle for Couples. Nena O'Neill & George O'Neill. 1976. pap. 2.25 (ISBN 0-380-00271-X, 37465). Avon.

Open Minds!: The Forgotten Side of Communication. William F. Keefe. LC 75-2412. 208p. 1975. 13.95 (ISBN 0-8144-5372-4). Am Mgmt.

Open Net. George Plimpton. 300p. 1981. 11.95 (ISBN 0-399-12558-2). Putnam.

Open Path: Christian Missionaries, 1515-1914. Jack Beeching. LC 80-21270. 350p. 1981. 14.95 (ISBN 0-915520-37-0). Ross-Erikson.

Open Philosophy & the Open Society. Maurice Cornforth. LC 68-27395. (Orig.). 1968. pap. 3.45 o.p. (ISBN 0-7178-0142-X). Intl Pub Co.

Open Pit Planning & Design. Ed. by John T. Crawford, III & William A. Hustrulid. LC 79-52269. (Illus.). 367p. 1979. text ed. 27.00x (ISBN 0-89520-253-0). Soc Mining Eng.

Open Prisons. Howard Jones & Paul Cornes. (International Library of Social Policy). (Illus.). 1977. 25.00x (ISBN 0-7100-8602-4). Routledge & Kegan.

Open Road. Kenneth Grahame. LC 79-22614. (Illus.). (gr. 1 up). 1980. 9.95 (ISBN 0-684-16471-X). Scribner.

Open Sea Mariculture. Joe A. Hanson. LC 74-13103. 320p. 1974. 43.50 (ISBN 0-12-786625-6). Acad Pr.

Open Season. Norman Moser. 32p. 1980. 3.00. Illuminations Pr.

Open Shadow. Brad Solomon. LC 78-13486. 1979. 10.00 (ISBN 0-671-40057-6). Summit Bks.

Open the Book. 2nd ed. Roberta B. Freund. LC 66-13739. (Illus.). 1966. 10.00 (ISBN 0-8108-0107-8). Scarecrow.

Open the Door & See All the People. Clyde R. Bulla. LC 73-184980. (Illus.). (gr. 2-5). 1972. PLB 7.89 (ISBN 0-690-60046-1, TYC-J). T Y Crowell.

Open the Meeting with Prayer. Alfred Doerffler. LC 55-7442. 1955. 3.25 (ISBN 0-570-03147-8, 12-2531). Concordia.

Open to Change. David C. McCasland. 144p. 1981. pap. 3.95 (ISBN 0-88207-258-7). Victor Bks.

Open to the Sun: An Anthology of Latin American Poets. Ed. by Nora Weiser. 1980. 8.50 o.p. (ISBN 0-912288-16-7). Caroline Hse.

Open Your Hearts. Huub Oosterhuis. LC 74-140237. 1971. 4.50 (ISBN 0-8164-1098-4). Crossroad NY.

Openers & Temper. Nina Nyhart & Margo Lockwood. LC 78-74232. 88p. 1979. pap. 4.95 (ISBN 0-914086-26-X). Alicejamesbooks.

Opening & Closing. O. E. Klapp. LC 77-87382. (A.S.A. Rose Monograph Ser.). (Illus.). 1978. 19.95 (ISBN 0-521-21923-X); pap. 6.95x (ISBN 0-521-29311-1). Cambridge U Pr.

Opening Closed Doors: The Deinstitutionalization of Disabled Individuals. David Braddock. LC 77-72050. 1977. pap. text ed. 7.50 o.p. (ISBN 0-86586-059-9). Coun Exc Child.

Opening Five: Art for Grade Five. Sr. Carol J. Cincerelli. LC 79-3013. 192p. (gr. 5). 1980. pap. text ed. 9.00x (ISBN 0-934902-10-0). Learn Concepts OH.

Opening Leads & Signals in Contract Bridge. John Mallon. 1969. pap. 2.95 (ISBN 0-02-029210-4, Collier). Macmillan.

Opening Moves: August, 1914. John Keegan. 160p. 1975. pap. 2.00 (ISBN 0-345-24339-0, 24339-0-200). Ballantine.

Opening of the Field. rev. ed. Robert Duncan. LC 72-93976. 96p. 1973. pap. 4.95 (ISBN 0-8112-0480-4, NDP356). New Directions.

Opening of the Suez Canal, November, 1869: A Water Gateway Joins East & West. Carol Z. Rothkopf. LC 72-6893. (World Focus Bks.). (Illus.). 96p. (gr. 7 up). 1973. PLB 4.90 o.p. (ISBN 0-531-02166-1). Watts.

Opening of the Way. Isha S. De Lubicz. Tr. by Rupert Gleaolow. 1981. pap. 8.95 (ISBN 0-89281-015-7). Inner Tradit.

Opening One: Art for Grade One. Sr. Carol J. Cincerelli. LC 79-3013. 174p. (gr. 1). 1979. pap. text ed. 9.00x (ISBN 0-934902-07-0). Learn Concepts OH.

Opening Opportunities for Disadvantaged Learners. Ed. by A. Harry Passow. LC 72-178197. 1972. text ed. 12.75x (ISBN 0-8077-1886-6); pap. 8.00x (ISBN 0-8077-1894-7). Tchrs Coll.

Opening Repertoire for the Attacking Player. Raymond Keene & David Levy. (Clubplayers Library). (Illus.). 152p. (Orig.). 1980. 17.95 (ISBN 0-7134-1311-5, Pub. by Batsford England); pap. 10.50 (ISBN 0-7134-1312-3). David & Charles.

Opening the Canadian West. Bercuson. (gr. 6-10). 1980. PLB 6.90 (ISBN 0-531-00448-1). Watts.

Opening the Channels: The Changing Control of Public T. V. Mareth. cancelled (ISBN 0-8070-3214-X). Beacon Pr.

Opening the Door: Citizen Roles in Educational Collective Bargaining. Ed. by Irving Hamer et al. 194p. (Orig.). 1979. pap. 4.50 (ISBN 0-917754-11-5). Inst Responsive.

Opening the Door of Faith: The Why, When & Where of Evangelism. John R. Hendrick. LC 76-12404. 1977. pap. 4.50 (ISBN 0-8042-0675-9). John Knox.

Opening the Gates: The Rise of the Prisoners Movement. Ronald Berkman. 224p. 1979. 21.95 (ISBN 0-669-02828-2). Lexington Bks.

Opening the Old Testament. H. Robert Cowles. LC 80-65149. (Illus.). 158p. (Orig.). Date not set. pap. 4.50 (ISBN 0-87509-279-9). Chr Pubns.

Opening the Schools: Alternative Ways of Learning. Richard Saxe. LC 78-190056. 1972. 19.50 (ISBN 0-8211-1851-X); text ed. 17.50x (ISBN 0-685-24961-1). McCutchan.

Opening Three: Art for Grade Three. Sr. Carol J. Cincerelli. LC 79-3013. 195p. (gr. 3). 1980. pap. text ed. 9.00x (ISBN 0-934902-09-7). Learn Concepts OH.

Opening-Two: Art for Grade Two. Sr. Carol J. Cincerelli. LC 79-3013. (gr. 2). 1979. pap. text ed. 9.00x (ISBN 0-934902-06-2). Learn Concepts OH.

Opening VII: Art for Grade Eight. Sr. Carol J. Cincerelli. LC 79-3013. 192p. (gr. 8). 1979. pap. text ed. 9.00x (ISBN 0-934902-13-5). Learn Concepts OH.

Opening Your Class with Learning Stations. Kim Marshall. LC 75-12462. (Learning Handbooks Ser.). 1975. pap. 3.95 (ISBN 0-8224-1909-2). Pitman Learning.

Openings into Ministry. Ed. by Ross Snyder. LC 77-92707. (Studies in Ministry & Parish Life). 1977. 12.95x (ISBN 0-913552-10-0); pap. 5.50x (ISBN 0-913552-11-9). Exploration Pr.

Openness of God. Richard Rice. (Horizon Ser.). 96p. 1981. pap. write for info. (ISBN 0-8127-0303-0). Southern Pub.

Opera. Richard Capell. LC 78-66894. (Encore Music Editions Ser.). 1981. Repr. of 1948 ed. 14.50 (ISBN 0-88355-730-4). Hyperion Conn.

Opera, 5 vols. Homer. Ed. by D. B. Monro & T. W. Allen. Incl. Vol. 1. Iliad 1-12. 3rd ed. 1920. 14.95x o.p. (ISBN 0-19-814528-4); Vol. 2. Iliad 13-24. 3rd ed. 1920. 14.95x o.p. (ISBN 0-19-814529-2); Vol. 3. Odyssey, 1-12. 2nd ed. 1917. 14.95x o.p. (ISBN 0-19-814531-4); Vol. 4. Odyssey, 13-24. 2nd ed. 1919. 13.95x o.p. (ISBN 0-19-814532-2); Vol. 5. Hymns, Etc. 1911. 16.95x o.p. (ISBN 0-19-814534-9). (Oxford Classical Texts Ser.). Oxford U Pr.

Opera. 2nd ed. Horace. Ed. by E. C. Wickham & H. W. Garrod. (Oxford Classical Texts Ser). 1912. 14.95 (ISBN 0-19-814618-3). Oxford U Pr.

Opera, 5 vols. Plato. Ed. by John Burnet. Incl. Vol. 1. Euthyphro, Apologia Socratis, Crito, Phaedo, Cratylus, Theaetetus, Sophista, Politicus. 2nd ed. 1905. 17.50x (ISBN 0-19-814540-3); Vol. 2. Parmenides, Philebus, Symposium, Phaedrus, Alcibiades 1 & 2, Hipparchus, Amatores. 2nd ed. 1910. 17.50x (ISBN 0-19-814541-1); Vol. 3. Theages, Charmides, Laches, Lysis, Euthydemus, Protagoras, Gorgias, Meno, Hippias Maior, Hippas Minor, Io, Menexenus. 1903. 18.95x (ISBN 0-19-814542-X); Vol. 4. Clitopho, Respublica, Timaeus, Critias. 1905. 18.95x (ISBN 0-19-814544-6); Vol. 5. Minos, Leges, Epinomis, Epistulae, Definitiones. 1907. 22.50x (ISBN 0-19-814546-2). Oxford U Pr.

Opera. Virgil. Ed. by R. A. Mynors. (Oxford Classical Texts Ser). 1969. 14.95x (ISBN 0-19-814653-1). Oxford U Pr.

Opera, 2 vols. Virgil. LC 75-27849. (Renaissance & the Gods Ser.: Vol. 7). (Illus.). 1977. Repr. of 1544 ed. Set. lib. bdg. 146.00 (ISBN 0-8240-2056-1); lib. bdg. 73.00 ea. Garland Pub.

Opera Buffa Napoletana Durante Il Settecento: Storia Letteraria. 2nd ed. LC 80-2298. 1981. Repr. of 1917 ed. 53.50 (ISBN 0-404-18867-2). AMS Pr.

Opera Caravan. Quaintance Eaton. LC 78-9128. (Music Reprint 1978 Ser.). (Illus.). 1978. lib. bdg. 29.50 (ISBN 0-306-77596-4); pap. 6.95 (ISBN 0-306-80089-6). Da Capo.

Opera Comica Italiana nel Settecento, Studi ed Appunti, 2 vols. Andrea Della Corte. LC 80-2269. 1981. Repr. of 1923 ed. Set. 62.50 (ISBN 0-404-18830-3). Vol. 1 (ISBN 0-404-18831-1). Vol. 2 (ISBN 0-404-18832-X). AMS Pr.

Opera-Comique Connu et Inconnu: Son Histoire Depuis l'origine Jusqu'a Nos Jours. Emile Genest. LC 80-2277. 1981. Repr. of 1925 ed. 39.50 (ISBN 0-404-18845-1). AMS Pr.

Opera de Rameau. Paul Marie Masson. LC 70-168675. (Music Ser). (Illus.). 596p. 1972. Repr. of 1930 ed. lib. bdg. 55.00 (ISBN 0-306-70262-2). Da Capo.

Operá-Dead or Alive: Production, Performance, & Enjoyment of Musical Theatre. Ronald Mitchell. LC 73-121772. (Illus.). 1970. 25.00 (ISBN 0-299-05811-5); pap. 7.95 (ISBN 0-299-05814-X). U of Wis Pr.

Opera for Amateurs. Frederick Woodhouse. 1951. 6.95 (ISBN 0-234-77225-5). Dufour.

Opera for the People. Herbert Graf. LC 68-23811. (Music Reprint Ser.). 1973. Repr. of 1951 ed. lib. bdg. 27.00 (ISBN 0-306-70984-8). Da Capo.

Opera from A to Z. Elizabeth Forbes. LC 76-44554. 1977. 8.95 o.p. (ISBN 0-498-02046-0). A S Barnes.

Opera: Front & Back. Hyman H. Taubman. LC 80-2306. 1981. Repr. of 1938 ed. 51.50 (ISBN 0-404-18872-9). AMS Pr.

Opera Goers' Complete Guide. Leo L. Melitz. Rev. by Louise W. Hackney. Tr. by Richard Salinger. LC 80-2293. 1981. Repr. of 1936 ed. 54.50 (ISBN 0-404-18859-1). AMS Pr.

Opera in Chicago. Ronald L. Davis. (Illus.). 393p. 1980. Repr. of 1966 ed. text ed. 22.50x (ISBN 0-8290-0225-1). Irvington.

Opera in the High Baroque. Lesley Orrey. 1981. 27.50 (ISBN 0-7145-3658-X). Riverrun NY.

Opera Italiana Nel Secolo Xix: Dono Agli Abbonati Des Corriere Della Sera. Alfredo Colombani. LC 80-2266. 1981. Repr. of 1900 ed. 61.00 (ISBN 0-404-18819-2). AMS Pr.

Opera-Italien de 1548 a 1856. Francois H. Blaze. LC 80-2260. 1981. Repr. of 1856 ed. 52.00 (ISBN 0-686-69547-X). AMS Pr.

Opera Minora. Tacitus. Ed. by R. M. Ogilive & M. Winterbottom. (Oxford Classical Texts Ser.). 124p. 1975. text ed. 10.50x (ISBN 0-19-814658-2). Oxford U Pr.

Opera Production One: A Handbook. Quaintance Eaton. LC 73-20232. (Music Ser.). 266p. 1974. Repr. of 1961 ed. lib. bdg. 22.50 (ISBN 0-306-70635-0). Da Capo.

Opera Quae Supersunt Omnia, 59 Vols. in 58. Jean Calvin. Ed. by G. Baum et al. 1863-1900. Set. 1715.00 (ISBN 0-384-07195-3); 42.00 ea. Johnson Repr.

Opera Scenes for Class & Stage. Mary E. Wallace & Robert Wallace. LC 78-11095. 314p. 1979. 18.95x (ISBN 0-8093-0903-3). S Ill U Pr.

Opera Therapy. Gualtiero Bartalini. 176p. 1981. 8.50 (ISBN 0-682-49703-7). Exposition.

Opera Tomus III: Libelli 44-68. Lucian Macleon. (Oxford Classical Texts Ser.). 406p. 1980. text ed. 24.00x (ISBN 0-19-814592-6). Oxford U Pr.

Opera. Vol. 1, Porphyrii Vita Plotini: Enneades 1-3. Plotinus. Ed. by P. Henry & H. R. Schwyzer. (Oxford Classical Texts Ser). 1964. 31.00x (ISBN 0-19-814561-6). Oxford U Pr.

Operaciones Ginecologicas. Harold Tovell & Leonard Dank. (Span.). 1980. pap. text ed. write for info. (ISBN 0-06-319301-9, Pub. by HarLA Mexico). Har-Row.

Operant Learning: Procedures for Changing Behavior. Jon L. Williams. LC 72-91088. (Core Bks in Psychology Ser). 1973. text ed. 10.95 o.p. (ISBN 0-8185-0058-1). Brooks-Cole.

Operas of Alban Berg: Vol. I, Wozzeck. George Perle. 325p. 1980. 20.00 (ISBN 0-520-03440-6). U of Cal Pr.

Operas of Benjamin Britten. Ed. by David Herbert. LC 79-2052. (Illus.). 1979. 65.00 (ISBN 0-231-04868-8). Columbia U Pr.

Operas of Gian Carlo Menotti, 1937-1972: A Selective Bibliography. Lyndal C. Grieb. LC 74-16310. 1974. 10.00 (ISBN 0-8108-0743-2). Scarecrow.

Operas of Leos Janacek. E. Chisholm. 1976. 23.00 (ISBN 0-08-012854-8); pap. 10.75 (ISBN 0-08-012853-X). Pergamon.

Operas of Verdi, Vol. 3: From Don Carlos to Falstaff. Julian Budden. 1981. 39.95 (ISBN 0-19-520254-6). Oxford U Pr.

Operating a Successful Accounting Practice. 1979. pap. 7.50. Am Inst CPA.

Operating Costs in Public Housing: A Financial Crisis. Frank De Leeuw & Eleanor L. Tarutis. 63p. 1969. pap. 1.50 o.p. (ISBN 0-87766-002-6, 30001). Urban Inst.

Operating Experience with Nuclear Power Stations in Member States in 1977. 1979. pap. 37.50 (ISBN 92-0-159079-2, ISP512, IAEA). Unipub.

Operating Experience with Nuclear Power Stations in Member States in 1976. 1978. pap. 28.00 (ISBN 92-0-159477-1, IAEA). Unipub.

Operating Experience with Nuclear Power Stations in Member States: Performance Analysis Report 1975. 21p. 1978. pap. 4.50 (ISBN 92-0-159377-5, ISP 472, IAEA). Unipub.

Operating Experience with Nuclear Power Stations in Member States: Performance Anaysis Report 1976. 27p. 1978. pap. 4.50 (ISBN 92-0-159078-4, ISP 481, IAEA). Unipub.

Operating Experience with Nuclear Power Stations in Member States in 1975. (Illus.). 1977. pap. 24.75 (ISBN 92-0-159176-4, IAEA). Unipub.

Operating Experience with Nuclear Power Stations in Member States: Performance Analysis Report 1977. 27p. 1980. pap. 5.00 (ISBN 92-0-159179-9, ISP 543, IAEA). Unipub.

Operating Experience with Nuclear Power Stations in Member States, 1978. 366p. 1980. pap. 44.75 (ISBN 92-0-159080-6, ISP 546, IAEA). Unipub.

Operating Experience with Nuclear Power Stations in Member States: Performance Analysis Report 1978. 27p. 1980. pap. 5.50 (ISBN 92-0-659080-4, ISP570, IAEA). Unipub.

Operating Experience with Power Reactors, 2 vols. 1963. Vol 1. 20.00 (ISBN 92-0-050163-X, IAEA); Vol 2. 16.25 (ISBN 92-0-050263-6). Unipub.

Operating Losses & Tax Considerations in Insolvency 1977. (Tax Law & Estate Planning Course Handbook Ser. 1977-78: Vol. 114). 1977. pap. 20.00 o.p. (ISBN 0-685-05641-4, J4-3444). PLI.

Operating Manager: An Integrative Approach. Waino Suojanen & Richard I. Henderson. (Illus.). 480p. 1974. ref. ed. 16.95 (ISBN 0-13-637942-7). P-H.

Operating Room Guidelines: An Illustrated Manual. Reba D. Grubb & Geraldine Ondov. LC 78-31422. (Illus.). 1979. pap. text ed. 17.95 (ISBN 0-8016-1985-8). Mosby.

Operating Systems. Harold Lorin & Harvey Deitel. LC 80-10625. (Computer Science: Systems Programming (IBM) Ser.). (Illus.). 480p. 1981. text ed. 18.95 (ISBN 0-201-14464-6). A-W.

Operating Systems: A Systematic View. William S. Davis. LC 76-10414. (Illus.). 1977. text ed. 17.95 (ISBN 0-201-01118-2). A-W.

Operating Systems: An Advanced Course. Ed. by R. Bayer & R. M. Graham. (Lecture Notes in Computer Science: Vol. 60). 1978. pap. 22.50 o.p. (ISBN 0-387-08755-9). Springer-Verlag.

Operating Systems: Concepts & Principles. John Zarrella. LC 79-122639. (Microprocessor Software Engineering Concepts Ser.). (Illus., Orig.). 1979. pap. 7.95 (ISBN 0-935230-00-9). Microcomputer Apprs.

Operating Systems Techniques. Ed. by C. A. Hoare & R. H. Perrott. (Automatic Programming Information Centre Studies in Data Processing: No. 9). 1973. 55.00 (ISBN 0-12-350650-6). Acad Pr.

Operating Systems Theory. Edward G. Coffman, Jr. & Peter J. Denning. LC 73-491. 400p. 1973. ref. ed. 25.95 (ISBN 0-13-637868-4). P-H.

Operating Theatre Technique. 4th ed. Raymond J. Brigden. (Illus.). 840p. 1980. text ed. 87.50x (ISBN 0-443-01999-1). Churchill.

Operation & Control of Ion-Exchange Processes for Treatment of Radioactive Wastes. L. A. Emelity. 1967. pap. 6.50 (ISBN 92-0-125067-3, IAEA). Unipub.

Operation & Maintenance for Air Particulate Control Equipment. Ed. by Richard A. Young & Frank L. Cross. LC 80-65506. (Illus.). 184p. 1980. 37.50 (ISBN 0-250-40367-6). Ann Arbor Science.

Operation & Maintenance of Irrigation & Drainage Systems. Compiled by American Society of Civil Engineers. LC 79-55951. (Manuel & Report on Engineering Practice Ser: No. 57). 280p. 1980. pap. text ed. 28.00 (ISBN 0-87262-231-2). Am Soc Civil Eng.

Operation Apricot. Pamela Kerr. LC 77-3792. (Harper Novel of Intrigue). 1978. 7.95 (ISBN 0-06-011707-9, HarpT). Har-Row.

Operation Backlash. Leslie McManus. LC 79-88066. 1979. pap. 1.50 o.p. (ISBN 0-87216-536-1). Playboy Pbks.

Operation Bodenplatte. Lawrence Cortesi. 288p. (Orig.). 1981. pap. 2.50 (ISBN 0-89083-710-4). Zebra.

Operation Bro-Kee. Rita Puttcamp. (Bro-Kee Ser.). (gr. 5-9). 1978. pap. 3.50 (ISBN 0-570-07761-3, 39-1107). Concordia.

Operation Dixie: The C.I.O. Organizing Committee Papers 1946-1953-a Guide to the Microfilm Edition. Katherine F. Martin. 154p. 1980. pap. 25.00 (ISBN 0-667-00584-6). Microfilming Corp.

Operation Hong Kong. Peter McCurtin. (Soldier of Fortune Ser). (Orig.). 1977. pap. text ed. 1.50 (ISBN 0-505-51161-4). Tower Bks.

Operation Intercept. Lawrence A. Gooberman. 1976. 23.00 (ISBN 0-08-017837-5); pap. 10.00 (ISBN 0-08-017836-7). Pergamon.

Operation Menace: The Dakar Expedition & the Dudley North Affair. Arthur Marder. 1976. 24.95x (ISBN 0-19-215811-2). Oxford U Pr.

Operation Morning Light. Leo Heaps. 1979. pap. 2.95 (ISBN 0-345-28101-2). Ballantine.

Operation Research in World War Two. C. H. Waddington. 1973. 22.95 (ISBN 0-236-15463-X, Pub. by Paul Elek). Merrimack Bk Serv.

Operation Time Search. Andre Norton. 224p. 1981. pap. 2.25 (ISBN 0-449-24370-2, Crest). Fawcett.

Operation Wetback: The Mass Deportation of Mexican Undocumented Workers in 1954. Juan R. Garcia. LC 79-6189. (Contributions in Ethnic Studies: No. 2). (Illus.). xvii, 268p. 1980. lib. bdg. 25.00 (ISBN 0-313-21353-4, GOW/). Greenwood.

Operational Amplifier Characteristics & Applications. Robert G. Irvine. (Illus.). 416p. 1981. text ed. 24.95 (ISBN 0-13-637751-3). P-H.

Operational Amplifiers. 2nd ed. G. Clayton. 1979. text ed. 26.95 (ISBN 0-408-00370-7). Butterworths.

Operational Amplifiers & Linear Integrated Circuits. R. Coughlin & F. Driscoll. 312p. 1977. text ed. 18.95 (ISBN 0-13-637850-1). P-H.

Operational Amplifiers in Chemical Instrumentation. Robert Kalvoda. LC 75-8866. (Ser. in Analytical Chemistry). 1975. 29.95 (ISBN 0-470-45566-7). Halsted Pr.

Operational Analysis & Indian Defence. Utpal K. Banerjee. 1980. text ed. 40.50x (ISBN 0-391-01839-6). Humanities.

Operational Aspects of the Drought of 1975-76. Institute of Civil Engineers, UK. 142p. 1980. pap. 50.00x (ISBN 0-7277-0059-6, Pub. by Telford England). State Mutual Bk.

Operational Calculus. J. Mikusinskii. 1969. 46.00 (ISBN 0-08-006367-5). Pergamon.

Operational Calculus, Vol. 1. 2nd ed. Jan Mikusinski. (International Series in Pure & Applied Mathematics: Vol. 109). (Illus.). 320p. 1981. 27.00 (ISBN 0-08-025071-8). Pergamon.

Operational Distribution Research: Innovative Case Studies. A. Mercer et al. (ORASA Text Ser.: No. 2). 1978. pap. 19.95x (ISBN 0-470-26537-X). Halsted Pr.

Operational Economics of Electric Utilities. Constantine W. Bary. LC 63-9807. 1963. 22.50x (ISBN 0-231-02614-5). Columbia U Pr.

Operational Financial Management. Robert Pritchard. LC 76-25062. (Illus.). 1977. text ed. 18.95 (ISBN 0-13-637827-7). P-H.

Operational Handbook for Narcotic Law Enforcement Officers. Mitchell Ware. 128p. 1975. 16.75 (ISBN 0-398-03349-8). C C Thomas.

Operational Limits & Conditions for Nuclear Power Plants. (Safety Ser.: No. 50-SG-D2). 1979. pap. 5.50 (ISBN 92-0-123479-1, ISP 531, IAEA). Unipub.

Operational Mathematics for Business. R. C. Pierce & W. Gene Tebeaux. 512p. 1980. text ed. 16.95x (ISBN 0-534-00789-9). Wadsworth Pub.

Operational Methods for Linear Systems. Wilfred Kaplan. 1962. 24.95 (ISBN 0-201-03620-7). A-W.

Operational Organic Chemistry: A Laboratory Course. new ed. John W. Lehman. 640p. 1981. text ed. 19.95 (ISBN 0-205-07146-5, 687146-1); tchr's. ed. free (ISBN 0-205-07147-3). Allyn.

Operational Problem Solving for the Hotel & Restaurant Industry. Lothar A. Kreck. LC 78-15134. 1978. pap. 10.95 (ISBN 0-8436-2132-X). CBI Pub.

Operational Research for Management. M. J. Sargeaunt. 1965. 16.95x (ISBN 0-685-83666-5). Intl Ideas.

Operational Research for Managers. S. C. Littlechild. 256p. 1977. 33.00x (ISBN 0-86003-504-2, Pub. by Allan Pubs England); pap. 16.50 (ISBN 0-86003-604-9). State Mutual Bk.

Operational Research in Maintenance. A. K. Jardine. 242p. 1970. 45.00x (ISBN 0-7190-0389-X, Pub. by Manchester U Pr England). State Mutual Bk.

Operational Theory & Method in Regional Economics. Jean H. Paelinck & Peter Nijkamp. LC 75-28609. (Regional Science Monograph Ser.). 488p. 1975. 32.95 (ISBN 0-347-01117-9, 00199-6, Pub. by Saxon Hse). Lexington Bks.

Operations & Effects of the Generalized System of Preferences. 146p. 1979. pap. 11.00 (ISBN 0-686-68964-X, UN79/2D2., UN). Unipub.

Operations Auditing in Hospitals. Dale L. Flesher. LC 75-29936. 128p. 1976. 16.95 (ISBN 0-669-00363-8). Lexington Bks.

Operations in the Nonferrous Scrap Metal Industry. (Illus.). 45.00 o.p. (ISBN 0-686-22346-2). Natl Recycling.

Operations Management. Kostas Dervitsiotis. (Industrial Engineering & Management Science). (Illus.). 784p. 1980. text ed. 21.95x (ISBN 0-07-016537-8, C); solutions manual 9.50 (ISBN 0-07-016538-6). McGraw.

Operations Management. R. Schroeder. (Management Ser.). (Illus.). 736p. 1981. text ed. 19.95 (ISBN 0-07-055612-1, C); instr's manual 5.95 (ISBN 0-07-055613-X). McGraw.

Operations Management. Barry Shore. (Management Ser.). (Illus.). 544p. 1973. text ed. 21.00 (ISBN 0-07-057045-0, C); instructor's manual 7.95 (ISBN 0-07-057046-9). McGraw.

Operations Management: A Policy Framework. Ray Wild. (Illus.). 1979. 35.00 (ISBN 0-08-022504-7); pap. 15.00 (ISBN 0-08-022505-5). Pergamon.

Operations Management in Practice. C. D. Lewis. 304p. 1980. 36.00x (ISBN 0-86003-511-5, Pub. by Allan Pubs England); pap. 18.00x (ISBN 0-86003-611-1). State Mutual Bk.

Operations Management: Problems & Models. 3rd ed. Elwood S. Buffa. LC 78-37167. (Management & Administration Ser). 1972. 24.95 (ISBN 0-471-11867-2); tchrs. manual avail. (ISBN 0-471-11880-X). Wiley.

Operations Management: Text & Cases. Paul W. Marshall et al. 1975. text ed. 20.95 (ISBN 0-256-01682-8). Irwin.

Operations Management: The Management of Productive Systems. Elwood S. Buffa. LC 75-33179. (Management & Administration Ser.). 640p. 1976. text ed. 24.95 (ISBN 0-471-11890-7); instructor's manual avail. (ISBN 0-471-11891-5). Wiley.

Operations Manager. Roy D. Harris & Richard F. Gonzalez. (Illus.). 450p. 1981. text ed. 14.36 (ISBN 0-8299-0332-1). West Pub.

Operations of Increasing Order. J. C. Gowan. 408p. (Orig.). 1980. pap. 5.00x (ISBN 0-686-28154-3). Gowan.

Operations of the French Fleet Under the Count De Grasse. Ed. by J. G. Shea. LC 75-167946. (Era of the American Revolution Ser.). 206p. 1971. Repr. of 1864 ed. lib. bdg. 25.00 (ISBN 0-306-70246-0). Da Capo.

Operations Research. 2nd ed. Frederick S. Hillier & Gerald J. Lieberman. LC 73-94383. 816p. 1974. text ed. 27.95x (ISBN 0-8162-3856-1); solutions manual o.p. 7.50 (ISBN 0-8162-3866-9). Holden-Day.

Operations Research. James E. Shamblin & G. T. Stevens. (Illus.). 416p. 1974. text ed. 21.00 (ISBN 0-07-056378-0, C); instructor's manual 5.50 (ISBN 0-07-056379-9). McGraw.

Operations Research: A First Course. John S. Croucher. (Illus.). 320p. 1980. 27.00 (ISBN 0-08-024798-9); pap. 13.50 (ISBN 0-08-024797-0). Pergamon.

Operations Research & Management Science: An Applications Approach. P. Ramalingam. Date not set. text ed. 19.95 (ISBN 0-8162-6996-3). Holden-Day.

Operations Research for Business. Roger D. Eck. 1976. text ed. 24.95x (ISBN 0-534-00424-5). Wadsworth Pub.

Operations Research for Management Decisions. Samuel B. Richmond. LC 68-20552. (Illus.). 600p. 1968. 24.95 (ISBN 0-8260-7460-X); manual o.p. (ISBN 0-471-07476-4). Wiley.

Operations Research for Managerial Decisions. Donald R. Plane & Gary A. Kochenberger. 1972. text ed. 13.90 (ISBN 0-256-00451-X). Irwin.

Operations Research: Implications for Libraries (35th Annual Conference of the Graduate Library School, August 2-4, 1971) Ed. by Don R. Swanson & Abraham Bookstein. LC 73-185760. (University of Chicago Studies in Library Science). (Illus.). 160p. 1972. lib. bdg. 10.00 (ISBN 0-226-78466-5). U of Chicago Pr.

Operations Research in Decision Making. James P. Ignizio et al. LC 74-12829. 360p. 1975. 22.50x (ISBN 0-8448-0670-6); pap. 9.50x (ISBN 0-8448-0671-4). Crane-Russak Co.

Operations Research in Health Care: A Critical Analysis. Ed. by Larry J. Shuman et al. LC 74-24397. 440p. 1975. 20.00x o.p. (ISBN 0-8018-1642-4). Johns Hopkins.

Operations Research in Law Enforcement & Societal Security. Ed. by Sidney H. Brounstein & Murray Kamrass. (Illus.). 1976. 21.95 (ISBN 0-669-00732-3). Lexington Bks.

Operations Research Methods. Stuart S. Nagel & Marian Neef. LC 76-25693. (University Papers Ser.: Quantitative Applications in the Social Sciences, No. 2). 1976. pap. 3.50x (ISBN 0-8039-0651-X). Sage.

Operations Research Models for Public Administration. J. Jack Byrd. LC 74-31563. 192p. 1975. 19.95x o.p. (ISBN 0-669-98202-4). Lexington Bks.

Operations Research: Planning, Operating & Information Systems. Nicolai Siemens et al. LC 70-184529. 1973. text ed. 19.95 (ISBN 0-02-928740-5). Free Pr.

Operations Research: Principles & Practices. Don T. Phillips et al. LC 75-44395. 585p. 1976. text ed. 23.95 (ISBN 0-471-68707-3). Wiley.

Operations Research: Process & Strategy. David S. Stoller. 1964. 17.50x (ISBN 0-520-01222-4). U of Cal Pr.

Operations Research Techniques for Management. H. Moskowitz & G. Wright. 1979. 21.00 (ISBN 0-13-637389-5). P-H.

Operations Zapata: The "Ultrasensitive" Report & Testimony of the Board of Inquiry on the Bay of Pigs. Maxwell Taylor et al. 1980. 24.00 (ISBN 0-89093-185-2); pap. 8.00 (ISBN 0-89093-186-0). U Pubns Amer.

Operative Biliary Radiology. George Berci & J. A. Hamlin. (Illus.). 290p. 1980. lib. bdg. 37.50 (ISBN 0-683-00602-9). Williams & Wilkins.

Operative Dentistry. 3rd ed. H. William Gilmore et al. LC 76-30465. (Illus.). 1977. text ed. 32.95 (ISBN 0-8016-1822-3). Mosby.

Operative Gynecology. 4th ed. Richard W. Te Linde & Richard F. Mattingly. LC 79-97124. (Span. & Portuguese eds. avail). 1970. 35.00 o.p. (ISBN 0-397-50266-4). Lippincott.

Operative Neurosurgery, 2 vols. L. G. Kempe. Incl. Vol. 1. Cranial, Cerebral & Intracranial Vascular Disease. (Illus.). xiii, 269p. 1968. 94.70 (ISBN 0-387-04208-3); Vol. 2. Posterior Fossa, Spinal Cord & Peripheral Nerve Disease. (Illus.). viii, 281p. 1970. 94.70 (ISBN 0-387-04890-1). Springer-Verlag.

Operative Obstetrics. Martius. 1980. 16.00. Thieme Stratton.

Operative Orthopedics in Cerebral Palsy. Sidney Keats. (Illus.). 264p. 1970. photocopy ed. 19.75 (ISBN 0-398-00991-0). C C Thomas.

Operative Plastic & Reconstructive Surgery, 3 vols. J. N. Barron & M. N. Saad. 1981. text ed. 220.00 (ISBN 0-443-01600-3). Churchill.

Operative Plastic & Reconstructive Surgery, Vol. 3. Ed. by J. B. Barron & M. N. Saad. (Illus.). 352p. 1980. text ed. 59.00 (ISBN 0-443-02212-7). Churchill.
Operative Techniques in Vascular Surgery. Ed. by John J. Bergan & James S. Yao. 1980. write for info. (ISBN 0-8089-1334-4). Grune.
Operator Certification Study Guide. American Water Works Association. (AWWA Handbooks Ser.: General). (Illus.). 104p. 1979. pap. 12.00 (ISBN 0-89867-227-9). Am Water Wks Assn.
Operators Algebra & Quantum Statistical Mechanics, Vol. II: Equilibrium States; Models. Ed. by O. Bratteli & D. W. Robinson. (Texts & Monographs in Physics Ser.). 496p. 1981. 46.00 (ISBN 0-387-10381-3). Springer-Verlag.
Operator's Training Program for Powered Industrial Trucks. 2nd ed. Robert P. Drolet & John R. Dowling. 96p. 1980. pap. 13.50 (ISBN 0-8436-0797-1); of 10 79.50 set. CBI Pub.
Opere Di Dio. Robert J. Rodini. LC 75-39907. (It.). 1976. pap. text ed. 7.20 (ISBN 0-395-13399-8). HM.
Opern-Handbuch. Hugo Riemann. LC 80-2295. 1981. 75.00 (ISBN 0-404-18864-8). AMS Pr.
Operon. 2nd ed. Ed. by J. H. Miller & W. S. Reznikoff. LC 80-15490. (Monograph Ser.: No. 7). (Illus.). 469p. (Orig.). 1980. pap. text ed. 18.00x (ISBN 0-87969-133-6). Cold Spring Harbor.
Opflow, Vol. 4, 1978. American Water Works Association. (OpFlow Bound Volumes). (Illus.). 104p. 1979. text ed. 14.00 (ISBN 0-89867-221-X). Am Water Wks Assn.
Ophthalmic Drug Delivery Systems. Ed. by Joseph R. Robinson. LC 80-66335. 144p. 1980. 18.00 (ISBN 0-917330-32-3). Am Pharm Assn.
Ophthalmic Manifestations of Systemic Vascular Disease. David G. Cogan. LC 74-4556. (Major Problem in Internal Medicine Ser.: Vol. 3). (Illus.). 225p. 1974. 15.00 (ISBN 0-7216-2648-3). Saunders.
Ophthalmic Nursing: Its Practice & Management. F. E. Rooke et al. (Illus.). 256p. 1980. pap. text ed. 13.50x (ISBN 0-443-01494-9). Churchill.
Ophthalmodynamometry. E. Weigelin & A. Lobstein. 1963. 10.75 o.s.i. (ISBN 0-02-854630-X). Hafner.
Ophthalmologic Disorders: A Practitioner's Guide. Richard D. Richards. 1973. spiral bdg. 12.00 (ISBN 0-87488-703-8). Med Exam.
Ophthalmologic Nursing. Joan F. Smith & Delbert P. Nachazel. 1980. text ed. 14.95 (ISBN 0-316-80158-5). Little.
Ophthalmology. Burton Chance. (Illus.). 1962. Repr. of 1939 ed. pap. 9.75 o.s.i. (ISBN 0-02-842700-9). Hafner.
Ophthalmology: (Concise Medical Textbook) 2nd ed. Kenneth Wybar. (Illus.). 1974. text ed. 14.50 (ISBN 0-02-859840-7). Macmillan.
Ophthalmology in Internal Medicine. Lee C. Chumbley. (Illus.). 288p. 1980. write for info. (ISBN 0-7216-2578-9). Saunders.
Ophthalmology: Principles & Concepts. 4th ed. Frank W. Newell. 1978. 34.50 (ISBN 0-8016-3640-X). Mosby.
Ophthalmology Review Book. Ed. by Charles I. Thomas. 1972. spiral bdg. 13.00 (ISBN 0-87488-347-4). Med Exam.
Ophthalmology: The Essentials. David Miller. (Illus.). 1979. 16.00x (ISBN 0-89289-325-7). HM Prof Med Div.
Ophthamology. 4th ed. Charles I. Thomas. (Medical Examination Review Book: Vol. 15). 1980. pap. 16.50 (ISBN 0-87488-115-3). Med Exam.
Opiate Addiction: Theory & Process. Larry J. Kroll & Manuel S. Silverman. LC 80-8283. 199p. 1980. lib. bdg. 17.50 (ISBN 0-8191-1324-7); pap. text ed. 9.00 (ISBN 0-8191-1325-5). U Pr of Amer.
Opiate Narcotics: Neurochemical Mechanisms of Analgesia & Dependence. Ed. by Avram Goldstein. 270p. 1976. text ed. 30.00 (ISBN 0-08-019869-4). Pergamon.
Opiate Receptors & the Neurochemical Correlates of Pain: Proceedings of the Third Congress of the Hungarian Pharmacological Society, Budapest, 1979. Ed. by Susanna Furst & J. Knoll. LC 80-41281. (Advances in Pharmacological Research & Practice Ser.: Vol. V). 240p. 1981. 45.00 (ISBN 0-08-026390-9). Pergamon.
Opinions: Committees on Professional Ethics: the Association of the Bar of the City of New York, the New York County Lawyer's Association, New York State Bar Association. Meira G. Pimsleur. LC 80-14204. 1000p. 1980. Set. looseleaf bdg. 150.00 (ISBN 0-379-20670-6). Oceana.
Opinions, Committees on Professional Ethics, Release 1. Pimsleur. 1980. 150.00 (ISBN 0-379-20670-6). Oceana.
Opinions of the Attorney General of the Republic of Liberia, September, 1964-August 1968. Liberia, Republic of. Ed. by Milton R. Konvitz. LC 28-17298. (Liberian Law Reports Ser). 1969. 25.00x (ISBN 0-8014-0529-7). Cornell U Pr.
Opinions, Publics & Pressure Groups: An Essay on "Vox Populi" & Representative Government. Graeme C. Moodle & Gerald Studdert-Kennedy. (Studies in Political Science). 1970. pap. text ed. 10.95x (ISBN 0-04-322002-9). Allen Unwin.
Opioid Dependence--Mechanisms & Treatment. Abraham Wikler. 300p. 1980. 27.50 (ISBN 0-306-40591-1, Plenum Pr). Plenum Pub.
Opisanie Voiny Velikago Kniazia Sviatoslava Igorevicha Protiv Bolgar I Grekov V 967-971 Godakh. Aleksandr D. Chertkov. (Ukra.). 1972. 17.50 (ISBN 0-918884-24-1). Slavia Lib.
Opium. Rudolph Johnson, Jr. (Novel - Adventure Ser.). 232p. 1981. 11.95 (ISBN 0-938952-00-5). Mona Pub.
Opium of the Intellectuals. Raymond Aron. 1962. pap. 3.45 o.p. (ISBN 0-393-00106-7, Norton Lib). Norton.
Opium: The Diary of a Cure. Jean Cocteau. Tr. by Margaret Crosland & Sinclair Road. LC 58-5967. (Illus.). 176p. 1980. pap. 6.95 (ISBN 0-394-17737-1, E771, Ever). Grove.
Opium War in China, 1840-1842: The British Resort to War in Order to Maintain Their Opium Trade. Robin McKown. LC 74-2436. (World Focus Bks.). (Illus.). 72p. (gr. 7 up). 1974. PLB 4.47 o.p. (ISBN 0-531-02728-7). Watts.
Opium War Through Chinese Eyes. Arthur D. Waley. 1958. text ed. 12.50x (ISBN 0-04-951012-6). Allen Unwin.
Opossums. Anne LaBastille. Ed. by Russell Bourne & Natalie Rifkin. LC 73-89876. (Ranger Rick's Best Friends Ser.: No. 2). (Illus.). 32p. (gr. 1-5). 1974. 2.50 o.p. (ISBN 0-912186-08-9). Natl Wildlife.
Oppenheimer Affair: A Political Play in Three Acts. Joseph Boskin & Fred Krinsky. (Insight Series: Studies in Contemporary Issues). 1968. pap. text ed. 4.95x (ISBN 0-02-473760-7). Macmillan.
Opponents of War, 1917-1918. H. C. Peterson & Gilbert C. Fite. LC 57-5239. (Illus.). 1968. Repr. of 1957 ed. pap. 2.95 o.p. (ISBN 0-295-78560-8, WP41). U of Wash Pr.
Opportunistic Infections in Cancer Patients. D. Armstrong et al. LC 77-94828. (Illus.). 207p. 1978. 29.75 (ISBN 0-89352-014-4). Masson Pub.
Opportunities for Faith: Elements of a Modern Spirituality. Karl Rahner. 1975. 8.95 (ISBN 0-8164-1180-8). Crossroad NY.
Opportunities for Minorities in Librarianship. E. J. Josey & Kenneth E. Peeples, Jr. LC 77-375. 1977. 10.00 (ISBN 0-8108-1022-0). Scarecrow.
Opportunities for Women in Higher Education: Their Current Participation, Prospects for the Future & Recommendations for Action. Carnegie Commission on Higher Education. LC 73-14726. (Illus.). 300p. 1973. 8.50 o.p. (ISBN 0-07-010102-7, P&RB). McGraw.
Opportunities in Clothing. rev. ed. Irene E. McDermott & Jeanne L. Norris. (Illus.). (gr. 9-12). 1972. text ed. 14.60 (ISBN 0-87002-140-0). Bennett IL.
Opportunities in Life Insurance Selling. Lee Rosler. LC 65-19433. 1965. pap. 4.95 (ISBN 0-89022-006-9). Farnswth Pub.
Opportunity & the Family. John Scanzoni. LC 70-84935. 1970. 10.95 o.s.i. (ISBN 0-02-927800-7). Free Pr.
Opportunity for Skillful Reading. 3rd ed. Irwin L. Joffe. 496p. 1979. pap. text ed. 9.95x (ISBN 0-534-00774-0). Wadsworth Pub.
Opposing Absolutes: Conviction & Convention in John Ford's Plays. Florence Ali. (Salzburg Studies in English Literature, Jacobean Drama Studies: No.44). 1974. pap. text ed. 25.00x (ISBN 0-391-01295-9). Humanities.
Opposing Virtues: Two Essays. Fahmy Farag. (New Yeats Papers: No. 15). 1978. pap. text ed. 9.25x (ISBN 0-85105-323-8, Dolmen Pr). Humanities.
Opposite Odelia: A Book of Antonyms. Sylvia R. Tester. LC 78-5294. (Using Words Ser.). (Illus.). (gr. k-3). 1978. PLB 5.50 (ISBN 0-89565-036-3). Childs World.
Opposites. Gillian Youldon. (ps-2). 1980. 3.50 (ISBN 0-531-02127-0, C16); PLB 5.90 (ISBN 0-531-03416-X, B26). Watts.
Opposition & Dissent in Contemporary China. Peter R. Moody, Jr. LC 77-72054. (Publication Ser: No. 177). (Illus.). 360p. 1977. 14.95 (ISBN 0-685-80269-8). Hoover Inst Pr.
Opposition in a Dominant-Party System: A Study of the Jan Sangh, the Praja Socialist & Socialist Parties in Uttar Pradesh, India. Angela S. Burger. LC 77-76540. (Center for South & Southeast Asia Studies, UC Berkeley). 1969. 19.00x (ISBN 0-520-01428-6). U of Cal Pr.
Opposition Politics: The Anti-New Deal Tradition. Joseph Boskin. (Insight Series: Studies in Contemporary Issues). 1968. pap. text ed. 4.95x (ISBN 0-02-473770-4). Macmillan.
Oppositions in Chaucer. Peter Elbow. LC 75-16216. 192p. 1975. 15.00x (ISBN 0-8195-4087-0, Pub. by Wesleyan U Pr). Columbia U Pr.
Oppressed Middle: The Politics of Middle Management. Earl Shorris. LC 80-717. 408p. 1981. 13.95 (ISBN 0-385-14564-0, Anchor Pr). Doubleday.
Oppression. Tadeusz Grygier. LC 73-14194. (International Library of Sociology & Social Reconstruction: A Study in Social & Criminal Psychology). 362p. 1974. Repr. of 1954 ed. lib. bdg. 27.50x (ISBN 0-8371-7145-8, GROP). Greenwood.
Oppression & Liberty. Simone Weil. Tr. by Arthur Wills & John Petrie. LC 72-92284. 216p. 1973. 12.00x o.p. (ISBN 0-87023-120-0); pap. 4.95 (ISBN 0-87023-251-7). U of Mass Pr.
Oppression & Social Intervention: The Human Condition & the Problems of Change. I. Ira Goldenberg. LC 78-6869. (Illus.). 1978. 13.95 (ISBN 0-88229-349-4); pap. 6.95 (ISBN 0-88229-601-9). Nelson-Hall.
OPS Officer's Manual. P. T. Deutermann. LC 79-89179. (Illus.). 216p. 1980. 14.95x (ISBN 0-87021-505-1). Naval Inst Pr.
Opthalmic Dispensing. 3rd ed. Russel L. Stimson. (Illus.). 720p. 1979. text ed. 33.75 (ISBN 0-398-03823-6). C C Thomas.
Optical & Infrared Detectors. Ed. by R. J. Keyes. LC 77-7309. (Topics in Applied Physics Ser.: Vol. 19). (Illus.). 1977. 45.80 o.p. (ISBN 0-387-08209-3). Springer-Verlag.
Optical & Infrared Detectors. 2nd ed. Ed. by R. J. Keyes. (Topics in Applied Physics Ser.: Vol. 19). (Illus.). 325p. 1981. pap. 24.80 (ISBN 0-387-10176-4). Springer-Verlag.
Optical & Kinetic Art. Michael Compton. (Tate Gallery: Little Art Book Ser.). 1977. pap. 1.95 (ISBN 0-8120-0859-6). Barron.
Optical Communication Theory. Robert O. Harger. (Benchmark Papers in Electrical Engineering & Computer Science: Vol. 18). 1977. 34.50 (ISBN 0-12-786630-2). Acad Pr.
Optical Crystallography. 5th ed. Ernest E. Wahlstrom. LC 78-13695. 488p. 1979. text ed. 26.95 (ISBN 0-471-04791-0). Wiley.
Optical Design of Reflectors. 2nd ed. William B. Elmer. LC 79-14206. (Wiley Ser. in Pure & Applied Optics). 1980. 27.95 (ISBN 0-471-05310-4, Pub. by Wiley-Interscience). Wiley.
Optical Design of Reflectors: Condensed Extracts of Book for Engineer's Manuals & Technical Classrooms. William B. Elmer. (Illus.). 1977. pap. 3.30x (ISBN 0-9601028-2-5). Elmer.
Optical Dispensing & Workshop Practice. W. S. Topliss. 1975. 39.95 (ISBN 0-407-00025-9). Butterworths.
Optical Fiber Systems & Their Components. A. B. Sharma et al. (Springer Ser. in Optical Sciences: Vol. 24). (Illus.). 250p. 1981. 38.35 (ISBN 0-387-10437-2). Springer-Verlag.
Optical Fiber Technology II. C. K. Kao. 304p. 1980. 24.00 (ISBN 0-471-09169-3, Pub. by Wiley-Interscience); pap. 15.75 (ISBN 0-471-09171-5). Wiley.
Optical Fiber Transmission Systems. Stewart D. Personick. (Applications of Communications Theory Ser.). 210p. 1981. 25.00 (ISBN 0-306-40580-6, Plenum Pr). Plenum Pub.
Optical Fibre Communication. Centro Studi e Laboratori Telecomumicazioni. (Illus.). 928p. 1980. 39.50 (ISBN 0-07-014882-1, P&RB). McGraw.
Optical Fibre Communications. C. P. Sandbank. LC 79-40822. 1980. 49.00 (ISBN 0-471-27667-7, Pub. by Wiley-Interscience). Wiley.
Optical Fibre Communications: Devices, Circuits & Systems. M. J. Howes & D. V. Morgan. LC 79-40512. (Wiley Series in Solid State Devices & Circuits). 1980. 46.75 (ISBN 0-471-27611-1, Pub. by Wiley-Interscience). Wiley.
Optical Illusion Book. Seymour Simon. LC 75-33873. (Illus.). 80p. (gr. 2-6). 1976. 8.95 (ISBN 0-685-62042-5, Four Winds). Schol Bk Serv.
Optical Information Processing & Holography. W. Thomas Cathey. LC 73-14604. (Pure & Applied Optics Ser). 398p. 1974. 29.95 (ISBN 0-471-14078-3, Pub. by Wiley-Interscience). Wiley.
Optical Letterspacing. David Kindersley. (Illus.). pap. 12.50 (ISBN 0-913720-05-4). Sandstone.
Optical Methods in Mechanics of Solids: Proceedings. I.U.T.A.M Symposium on Optical Methods in Mechanics of Solids. Ed. by Alexis Lagarde. 692p. 1980. 50.00x (ISBN 90-286-0860-5). Sijthoff & Noordhoff.
Optical Methods of Radio-Frequency Spectroscopy. I. I. Agarbiceanu & I. M. Popescu. LC 74-22001. 310p. 1975. 62.95 (ISBN 0-470-00935-7). Halsted Pr.
Optical Mineralogy: The Nonopaque Minerals. Wm. Revell Phillips & Dana T. Griffen. LC 80-12435. (Illus.). 1981. text ed. 39.95x (ISBN 0-7167-1129-X). W H Freeman.
Optical Physics. Max Garbuny. 1965. text ed. 22.95 (ISBN 0-12-275350-X). Acad Pr.
Optical Physics. S. G. Lipson & H. Lipson. LC 67-15308. (Illus.). 1969. 39.95 (ISBN 0-521-06926-2). Cambridge U Pr.
Optical Physics. 2nd ed. S. G. Lipson & H. Lipson. LC 79-8963. (Illus.). 496p. Date not set. 55.00 (ISBN 0-521-22630-9); pap. 22.50 (ISBN 0-521-29584-X). Cambridge U Pr.
Optical Properties & Band Structures of Semiconductors. D. L. Greenaway & G. Harbeke. 1968. 34.00 (ISBN 0-08-012648-0). Pergamon.
Optical Resonance & Two-Level Atoms. A. Allen & J. H. Eberly. LC 74-18023. (Interscience Monographs & Texts in Physics & Astronomy: No. 28). 224p. 1975. 30.95 (ISBN 0-471-02327-2, Pub. by Wiley-Interscience). Wiley.
Optical Rotatory Power. T. Martin Lowry. 1935. pap. 5.00 o.p. (ISBN 0-486-61197-3). Dover.
Optical Waveguides. N. S. Kapany & J. J. Burke. (Quantum Electronics Ser). 1972. 48.00 (ISBN 0-12-396760-0). Acad Pr.
Optics. 9th rev. ed. W. H. Fincham & M. H. Freeman. LC 80-40274. (Illus.). 1980. 34.95 (ISBN 0-407-93422-7). Butterworths.
Optics. E. Hecht & A. Zajac. 1974. 24.95 (ISBN 0-201-02835-2). A-W.
Optics. Miles V. Klein. LC 73-107584. 1970. 31.95 (ISBN 0-471-49080-6). Wiley.
Optics. Isaac Newton. 1952. pap. text ed. 5.50 (ISBN 0-486-60205-2). Dover.
Optics. REA Staff. 960p. 1980. 22.85 (ISBN 0-87891-526-5). Res & Educ.
Optics. 3rd ed. Francis W. Sears. 1949. 17.95 (ISBN 0-201-06915-6). A-W.
Optics: An Introduction for Ophthalmologists. 2nd ed. Kenneth N. Ogle. (Illus.). 288p. 1979. 13.75 (ISBN 0-398-01417-5). C C Thomas.
Optics & Information Theory. Francis T. Yu. LC 76-23135. 1976. 21.50 (ISBN 0-471-01682-9, Pub. by Wiley-Interscience). Wiley.
Optics of the Atmosphere: Scattering by Molecules & Particles. Earl J. McCartney. LC 76-10941. (Pure & Applied Optics Ser). 1976. 37.95 (ISBN 0-471-01526-1, Pub. by Wiley-Interscience). Wiley.
Optics, Painting & Photography. M. H. Pirenne. LC 71-108109. (Illus.). 1970. 58.00x (ISBN 0-521-07686-2). Cambridge U Pr.
Optics, Waves & Sound. M. Nelkon. 1973. pap. text ed. 11.95x (ISBN 0-435-68662-3). Heinemann Ed.
Optimal City Size. George Karvel & Glenn H. Petry. 66p. 10.00 (ISBN 0-686-64197-3). U CO Busn Res Div.
Optimal Control by Mathematical Programming. Daniel Tabak & Benjamin C. Kuo. LC 75-137985. 1971. 24.00 (ISBN 0-13-638106-5). SRL Pub Co.
Optimal Control of Discrete Systems. V. G. Boltyanskii. LC 78-67814. 1979. 69.95 (ISBN 0-470-26530-2). Halsted Pr.
Optimal Control Systems. A. A. Feldbaum. (Mathematics in Science & Engineering Ser.: Vol. 22). 1966. 51.50 (ISBN 0-12-251950-7). Acad Pr.
Optimal Control Theory: An Introduction. D. Kirk. 1970. ref. ed. 26.95 (ISBN 0-13-638098-0). P-H.
Optimal Control Theory: Applications to Management Science. S. P. Sethi & G. L. Thompson. (International Series in Management Science - Operations Research: Vol. 1). 1981. lib. bdg. 25.00 (ISBN 0-89838-061-8, Pub. by Martinus Nijhoff). Kluwer Boston.
Optimal Decisions. Oskar Lange. 304p. 1972. text ed. 32.00 (ISBN 0-08-016053-0). Pergamon.
Optimal Economic Growth with Exhaustible Resources. Prem C. Garg. LC 78-75019. (Outstanding Dissertations on Energy Ser.). 1979. lib. bdg. 12.00 (ISBN 0-8240-4054-6). Garland Pub.
Optimal Experiment Design for Dynamic System Identification. M. B. Zarrop. (Lecture Notes in Control & Information Sciences: Vol. 21). 197p. 1980. pap. 14.50 (ISBN 0-387-09841-0). Springer-Verlag.
Optimal Filtering. Brian Anderson & John B. Moore. 1979. 27.95 (ISBN 0-13-638122-7). P-H.
Optimal Financing Decisions. Alexander A. Robichek & Stewart C. Myers. (Illus.). 1966. pap. 10.95x ref. ed. (ISBN 0-13-638114-6). P-H.
Optimal Linear Systems: Methods of Functional Analysis. Ed. by R. Gabasov & F. M. Kirillova. (Mathematical Concepts & Methods in Science & Engineering Ser.: Vol. 15). 300p. 1978. 29.50 (ISBN 0-306-40119-3, Plenum Pr). Plenum Pub.
Optimal Personality: An Empirical & Theoretical Analysis. Richard W. Coan. LC 74-11498. 216p. 1974. 17.50x (ISBN 0-231-03807-0). Columbia U Pr.

Optimal Stockpiling of Grain. Bruce Gardner. LC 78-24768. 192p. 1979. 21.00 (ISBN 0-669-02829-0). Lexington Bks.

Optimality in Nonlinear Programming: A Feasible Directions Approach. Adi Ben-Israel et al. LC 80-36746. (Wiley Pure & Applied Mathematics Ser.). 250p. 1981. 19.95 (ISBN 0-471-08057-8, Pub. by Wiley-Interscience). Wiley.

Optimality in Parametric Systems. Thomas L. Vincent & Walter J. Grantham. 250p. 1981. 30.00 (ISBN 0-471-08307-0, Pub. by Wiley-Interscience). Wiley.

Optiman. Brian M. Stableford. (Science Fiction Ser.). 1980. pap. 1.95 (ISBN 0-87997-571-7, UJ1571). DAW Bks.

Optimisation of the Working Environment: New Trends. International Labour Office, Geneva. 428p. (Orig.). 1980. pap. 22.80 (ISBN 92-2-001905-1). Intl Labour Office.

Optimism & Pessimism in Goethe's Life. Elias Metchnikoff. (Illus.). 113p. 1981. Repr. of 1908 ed. 41.85 (ISBN 0-89901-025-3). Found Class Reprints.

Optimist's Daughter. Eudora Welty. 208p. Date not set. pap. 2.95 (ISBN 0-394-72667-7, Vin). Random.

Optimists: Themes & Personalities in Victorian Liberalism. Ian Bradley. LC 80-670269. 301p. 1980. 37.00 (ISBN 0-571-11495-4, Pub. by Faber & Faber). Merrimack Bk Serv.

Optimization. Ed. by R. Fletcher. 1970. 49.00 (ISBN 0-12-260650-7). Acad Pr.

Optimization: A Simplified Approach. William Conley. (Illus.). 272p. 1980. 20.00 (ISBN 0-89433-121-3). Petrocelli.

Optimization & Industrial Experimentation. William E. Biles & James J. Swain. LC 79-9516. 1980. 35.00 (ISBN 0-471-04244-7, Pub. by Wiley-Interscience). Wiley.

Optimization by Vector Space Methods. D. G. Luenberger. (Series in Decision & Control). 1969. 29.95 (ISBN 0-471-55359-X, Pub. by Wiley-Interscience). Wiley.

Optimization in Control Theory & Practice. Igor Gumowski & C. Mira. LC 68-12059. (Illus.). 1968. 40.75 (ISBN 0-521-05158-4). Cambridge U Pr.

Optimization in Economic Theory. A. K. Dixit. (Illus.). 1977. pap. 8.95x (ISBN 0-19-877103-7). Oxford U Pr.

Optimization Methods for Engineering Design. Richard L. Fox. LC 78-127891. (Engineering Ser). 1971. 23.95 (ISBN 0-201-02078-5). A-W.

Optimization Methods in Operations Research & Systems Analysis. K. V. Mital. LC 76-56846. 1977. 14.95 (ISBN 0-470-99056-2). Halsted Pr.

Optimization Methods in Operations Research & Systems Analysis. K. V. Mital. 259p. 1980. pap. 8.95 (ISBN 0-470-27081-0). Halsted Pr.

Optimization of Natural Communication Systems. O. Akhmanova. (Juana Linguarum, Ser. Minor: No. 92). 1977. 22.35 (ISBN 90-279-3146-1). Mouton.

Optimization of Systems Reliability. Tillman. 328p. 1980. 37.50 (ISBN 0-8247-6989-9). Dekker.

Optimization Techniques with Applications to Aerospace Systems. Ed. by George Leitmann. (Mathematics in Science & Engineering,: Vol. 5). 1962. text ed. 44.50 (ISBN 0-12-442950-5). Acad Pr.

Optimization: Theory & Applications. S. S. Rao. LC 77-28171. 1980. 19.95 (ISBN 0-470-26784-4). Halsted Pr.

Optimization with Disjunctive Constraints. H. D. Sherali & C. M. Shetty. (Lecture Notes in Economics & Mathematical Systems: Vol. 181). (Illus.). 156p. 1980. pap. 15.00 (ISBN 0-387-10228-0). Springer-Verlag.

Optimizing Development Profits in Large Scale Real Estate Projects. Michael D. Wilburn & Robert M. Gladstone. LC 72-79135. (Technical Bulletin Ser.: No. 67). (Illus.). 1972. pap. 9.75 (ISBN 0-87420-067-9). Urban Land.

Optimum Book Marketing of Trade Books. George Blagowidow. (Illus.). 222p. 1980. pap. cancelled (ISBN 0-88254-522-1). Hippocrene Bks.

Optimum Design of Mechanical Elements. 2nd ed. Ray C. Johnson. LC 79-14363. 1979. 34.50 (ISBN 0-471-03894-6, Pub. by Wiley-Interscience). Wiley.

Optimum Design of Structures. Kamal I. Majid. LC 73-15015. 264p. 1974. text ed. 30.95 (ISBN 0-470-56533-0). Halsted Pr.

Optimum Management. John B. McMaster. (Illus.). 1980. 17.50 (ISBN 0-89433-120-5). Petrocelli.

Optimum Quantity of Money & Other Essays. Milton Friedman. LC 68-8148. 1969. 19.95x (ISBN 0-202-06030-6). Aldine Pub.

Optimum Structural Design. Uri Kirsch. (Illus.). 448p. 1981. text ed. write for info (ISBN 0-07-034844-8, C); write for info. solutions manual (ISBN 0-07-034845-6). McGraw.

Optimum Structural Design: Theory & Applications. R. H. Gallagher. LC 72-8600. (Numerical Methods in Engineering Ser.). 400p. 1973. 44.25 (ISBN 0-471-29050-5, Pub. by Wiley-Interscience). Wiley.

Optimum Systems Control. 2nd ed. Andrew P. Sage & Chelsea C. White. (Illus.). 1977. ref. ed. 26.95 (ISBN 0-13-638296-7). P-H.

Option Players Advanced Guidebook: Turning the Tables on the Options Markets. Kenneth R. Trester. LC 80-83175. (Illus.). 275p. 1980. 35.00 (ISBN 0-9604914-1-4). Investrek.

Option Pricing & Strategies in Investing. Richard M. Bookstaber. LC 80-15013. 256p. 1981. text ed. 18.95 (ISBN 0-201-00123-3). A-W.

Options: Apercus de la France. Francoise DeRocher & Gregory DeRocher. LC 79-27245. 1980. pap. text ed. 7.95 (ISBN 0-471-04260-9). Wiley.

Options for Community Respnse to the Safe Drinking Water Act. LC 79-90646. (Policy Research Project Ser.: No. 35). 1979. 4.95 (ISBN 0-89940-635-1). LBJ Sch Public Affairs.

Options for School Health: Meeting Community Needs. Philip R. Nader. LC 78-9628. 1978. text ed. 21.95 (ISBN 0-89443-038-6). Aspen Systems.

Options in Contemporary Christian Ethics. Norman L. Geisler. 128p. (Orig.). 1981. pap. 4.95 (ISBN 0-8010-3757-3). Baker Bk.

Options in Health & Health Care. Alfred E. Miller & Maria G. Miller. (Health Medicine & Society Ser.). 512p. 1981. 27.50 (ISBN 0-471-60409-7, Pub. by Wiley-Interscience). Wiley.

Options in Rhetoric: Writing & Reading. Sylvia Holladay & Thomas Brown. (Illus.). 416p. 1981. pap. text ed. 8.95 (ISBN 0-13-638254-1). P-H.

Options Markets. Mark Rubinstein & John J. Cox. (Illus.). 432p. 1981. 29.95 (ISBN 0-13-638205-3). P-H.

Options: Theory & Practice. Claude G. Henin & Peter J. Ryan. LC 77-2687. 1977. 21.95 (ISBN 0-669-01623-3). Lexington Bks.

Opto Electronics. Seippel. 1981. text ed. 21.95 (ISBN 0-8359-5255-X). Reston.

Optoelectronics-Fiber-Optics Applications Manual. 2nd ed. Hewlett-Packard. (Illus.). 448p. 1981. 27.50 (ISBN 0-07-028606-X, P&RB). McGraw.

Optometry Examination Review Book, Vol. 1. 2nd ed. Ed. by I. Schmidt et al. 1978. spiral bdg. 12.00 o.s.i. (ISBN 0-87488-469-1). Med Exam.

Optricks. Melinda Wentzell & D. K. Holland. (Illus.). 40p. 1973. pap. 2.25 (ISBN 0-912300-34-5, 34-5). Troubador Pr.

Optricks Two. Melinda Wentzell & D. K. Holland. (Illus.). 40p. 1974. pap. 2.25 (ISBN 0-912300-51-5, 51-5). Troubador Pr.

Opus Thirty-One, No. 3. Theodore Enslin. 1979. pap. 2.50x (ISBN 0-915316-71-4). Pentagram.

Oqua. Thomas Blair. LC 79-15861. Date not set. 10.95 (ISBN 0-87949-163-9). Ashley Bks.

Or Give Me Death. Elizabeth Armstrong. 1977. 7.95 o.p. (ISBN 0-533-02951-1). Vantage.

Or Learn to Walk on Water. Daisy Aldan. 3.50 (ISBN 0-913152-20-X). Green Hill.

Oracion. John Bunyan & Thomas Goodwin. (Span.). Date not set. pap. 2.50 (ISBN 0-686-28949-8). Banner of Truth.

Oracle Bone Collections in the United States. Hung-hsiang Chou. LC 74-34551. (Publications, Occasional Papers, Archaeology: Vol. 10). 1976. pap. 16.50x (ISBN 0-520-09534-0). U of Cal Pr.

Oracle in the Heart. Kathleen Raine. 87p. (Orig.). 1980. pap. 8.50 (ISBN 0-04-821045-5, 2487). Allen Unwin.

Oracle of Fortuna. Ophiel. pap. 6.95 (ISBN 0-685-47280-9). Weiser.

Oracle of the Coffee House: John Dunton's Athenian Mercury. Gilbert D. McEwen. LC 78-171109. 1972. 12.50 (ISBN 0-87328-056-3). Huntington Lib.

ORACLS: A Design System for Linear Multivariable Control. Armstrong. 256p. 1980. 35.00 (ISBN 0-8247-1239-0). Dekker.

Oracy in Australian Schools. S. F. Bourke et al. (Australian Council for Educational Research Ser.: No. 9). 258p. 1980. pap. text ed. 21.00x (ISBN 0-85563-212-7). Verry.

Oraisons funebres. new ed. Jacques-Benigne Bossuet. (Nouveaux Classiques Larousse Ser.). (Illus.). 168p. (Fr.). 1975. pap. 2.95 (ISBN 0-685-62360-2, 33). Larousse.

Oral & Maxillofacial Surgery, Vol. 1. 6th. ed. Daniel M. Laskin. LC 79-18723. 1979. text ed. 75.00 (ISBN 0-8016-2822-9). Mosby.

Oral Approach to Phonetics. Harvey Cromwell & C. R. Van Dusen. LC 72-84441. 1969. pap. text ed. 12.50 (ISBN 0-675-09415-1). Merrill.

Oral Arguments Before the Supreme Court, 2 vols. Ed. by Leon Friedman. LC 80-29337. 975p. 1981. Set. pap. 20.00 (ISBN 0-87754-147-7). Chelsea Hse.

Oral-Aural Communications (OAC) A Teacher's Manual. G. S. Leavitt. (Illus.). 136p. 1974. 11.75 (ISBN 0-398-03061-8); pap. 8.25 (ISBN 0-398-03063-4). C C Thomas.

Oral Book Reviewing to Stimulate Reading: A Practical Guide in Technique for Lecture & Broadcast. Evelyn Oppenheimer. LC 80-20006. 168p. 1980. 10.00 (ISBN 0-8108-1352-1). Scarecrow.

Oral Care of the Aging & Dying Patient. Austin H. Kutscher & Ivan K. Goldberg. (American Lectures in Dentistry Ser.). (Illus.). 236p. 1973. text ed. 17.50 (ISBN 0-398-02714-5). C C Thomas.

Oral Communication. Joan B. Sered. 1978. pap. text ed. 7.95x (ISBN 0-02-471260-4). Macmillan.

Oral Communication: A Short Course in Speaking. 4th ed. Donald C. Bryant & Karl R. Wallace. (Illus.). 336p. 1976. pap. text ed. 11.95 (ISBN 0-13-638429-3). P-H.

Oral Contraceptives, Vol. 1. Michael Briggs & Maxine Briggs. LC 77-670169. (Annual Research Reviews Ser.). 1977. 14.40 (ISBN 0-88831-005-6). Eden Med Res.

Oral Contraceptives, Vol. 2. Michael Briggs & Maxine Briggs. LC 77-670169. (Annual Research Reviews Ser.). 1978. 19.20 (ISBN 0-88831-020-X). Eden Med Res.

Oral Contraceptives Abstracts--a Guide to the Literature: 1977-1979. Helen K. Kolbe. (Population Information Library Ser.: Vol. 2). 565p. 1980. 75.00 (ISBN 0-306-65192-0). IFI Plenum.

Oral Contraceptives & Steroid Chemistry in People's Republic of China. Commission on International Relations. 1977. pap. 8.00 (ISBN 0-309-02638-5). Natl Acad Pr.

Oral Diagnosis. 5th ed. Donald A. Kerr et al. LC 77-10851. (Illus.). 1978. pap. text ed. 29.95 (ISBN 0-8016-2660-9). Mosby.

Oral Diagnosis. W. R. Tyldesley. 172p. 1969. 19.25 (ISBN 0-08-013038-0). Pergamon.

Oral Disease. C. E. Renson. (Illus.). 1978. text ed. 14.50x (ISBN 0-906141-04-4, Pub. by Update Pubns England). Kluwer Boston.

Oral English. Hadley A. Thomas et al. (Reading Readiness). (Illus.). (gr. k-1). 1972. text ed. 2.28 (ISBN 0-87892-725-5); tchr's manual 2.28 (ISBN 0-87892-726-3). Economy Co.

Oral Epics of Central Asia. Nora K. Chadwick & Victor Zhirmunsky. LC 68-21189. 1969. 78.00 (ISBN 0-521-07053-8). Cambridge U Pr.

Oral Histology: Development, Structure & Function. A. Richard Ten Cate. LC 79-18620. (Illus.). 500p. 1980. text ed. 29.95 (ISBN 0-8016-4886-6). Mosby.

Oral History of James Nunn: A Unique North Carolinian. W. Wilder Towle. 230p. (Orig.). 1980. pap. 5.95 (ISBN 0-86629-001-X). Sunrise MO.

Oral History Program Manual. William W. Moss. LC 73-19446. (Special Studies). 122p. 1974. text ed. 24.95 (ISBN 0-275-08370-5). Praeger.

Oral Implantology. A. Norman Cranin. (Illus.). 384p. 1970. text ed. 38.75 (ISBN 0-398-00357-2). C C Thomas.

Oral Interpretations. 5th ed. Charlotte Lee. LC 76-13095. (Illus.). 1976. text ed. 16.50 (ISBN 0-395-24547-8). HM.

Oral Language Continuum Book. Joyce Gardner & Ida La Fleur. (gr. k-3). 1975. 9.00x (ISBN 0-933892-08-X). Child Focus Co.

Oral Literature: Seven Essays. Ed. by Joseph J. Duggan. LC 74-33851. 107p. 1975. text ed. 10.00x o.p. (ISBN 0-06-491819-X). B&N.

Oral Manifestations of Inherited Disorders. H. O. Sedano et al. 1977. 22.95 (ISBN 0-409-95050-5). Butterworths.

Oral Manifestations of Systemic Disease. G. Shklar & P. McCarthy. 1976. 22.95 (ISBN 0-409-95002-5). Butterworths.

Oral Medicine. W. R. Tyldesley. (Illus.). 225p. 1981. pap. text ed. 22.95x (ISBN 0-19-261275-1). Oxford U Pr.

Oral Medicine: A Clinical Approach with Basic Science Correlation. 2nd ed. Irwin W. Scopp. LC 73-1275. 1973. text ed. 26.50 o.p. (ISBN 0-8016-4402-X). Mosby.

Oral Medicine: Patient Evaluation & Management. L. Z. Bodak-Gyovai & J. V. Manzione, Jr. (Illus.). 208p. 1980. softcover 16.95 (ISBN 0-683-00901-X). Williams & Wilkins.

Oral Microbiology. 3rd ed. William A. Nolte. LC 77-1945. (Illus.). 1977. text ed. 31.95 (ISBN 0-8016-3688-4). Mosby.

Oral Myofunctional Disorders. 2nd ed. Barrett & Marvin L. Hanson. LC 78-7029. 1978. text ed. 36.50 (ISBN 0-8016-0497-4). Mosby.

Oral Pathology. J. D. Spouge. LC 72-86010. (Illus.). 640p. 1973. text ed. 20.00 o.p. (ISBN 0-8016-4736-3). Mosby.

Oral Pattern Drills in Fundamental English. Robert J. Dixson. (gr. 9 up). 1963. pap. text ed. 3.50 (ISBN 0-88345-124-7, 17410); with cassettes 70.00 (ISBN 0-685-04777-6). Regents Pub.

Oral Physiology. N. Emmelin & Yngve Zotterman. 311p. 1972. text ed. 75.00 (ISBN 0-08-016972-4). Pergamon.

Oral Physiology & Occlusion: An International Symposium. Ed. by James H. Perryman. LC 78-17812. 268p. 1979. 30.00 (ISBN 0-08-023183-7). Pergamon.

Oral Poetry: Its Nature, Significance Social Context. Ruth Finnegan. LC 76-11077. (Illus.). 1977. 32.00 (ISBN 0-521-21316-9). Cambridge U Pr.

Oral Premalignancy: Proceedings of the First Dows Symposium. Ed. by Ian C. Mackenzie et al. LC 80-17988. (Illus.). 336p. 1980. text ed. 32.50x (ISBN 0-87745-103-6). U of Iowa Pr.

Oral Reading of the Scriptures. Charlotte E. Lee. 1974. text ed. 14.75 (ISBN 0-395-18940-3). HM.

Oral Reporting in Business & Industry. Roger P. Wilcox. 1967. text ed. 17.95 (ISBN 0-13-639302-0). P-H.

Oral Tradition: Storytelling & Creative Drama. 2nd ed. Dewey W. Chambers. (Literature for Children Ser). 1977. pap. text ed. 3.50x (ISBN 0-697-06210-4). Wm C Brown.

Orange Balloon. Penny Harter. (Xtras Ser.: No. 8). 36p. (Orig.). 1980. pap. 2.00 (ISBN 0-89120-012-6). From Here.

Orange Fairy Book. Andrew Lang. 7.00 (ISBN 0-8446-4770-5). Peter Smith.

Orange Madness: The Incredible Odyssey of the Denver Broncos. Woodrow Paige, Jr. LC 78-4767. (Illus.). 1978. 8.95 o.p. (ISBN 0-690-01776-6, TYC-T). T Y Crowell.

Orange Order. Tony Gray. 292p. 1974. 12.00 (ISBN 0-370-10371-8). Transatlantic.

Oranges. John McPhee. 1967. 7.50 (ISBN 0-374-22688-1); pap. 3.95 (ISBN 0-374-51297-3). FS&G.

Oranging of America & Other Stories. 1981. pap. 3.95 (ISBN 0-14-005849-4). Penguin.

Orangutans. Wildlife Education, Ltd. (Zoobooks). (Illus.). 20p. (Orig.). 1980. pap. 1.00 (ISBN 0-937934-02-X). Wildlife Educ.

Orationes Philippicae: 1 & 2. Cicero. Ed. & intro. by J. D. Denniston. 1926. 9.95x (ISBN 0-19-831778-6). Oxford U Pr.

Orations of Arsanes Agaynst Philip: Of the Embassadors of Venice. Arsanes. LC 70-26068. (English Experience Ser.: No. 233). 164p. Repr. of 1560 ed. 14.00 (ISBN 90-221-0233-5). Walter J Johnson.

Orator. Peter Zarlenga. LC 79-55798. (Illus.). 1980. 12.95 (ISBN 0-916728-28-5). Bks in Focus.

Oratour: Village of the Dead. Phillip Beck. 124p. 1979. 15.00. Shoe String.

Orb Weaver. Robert Francis. LC 60-7255. (Wesleyan Poetry Program: Vol. 5). (Orig.). 1960. 10.00x (ISBN 0-8195-2005-5, Pub. by Wesleyan U Pr); pap. 4.95 (ISBN 0-8195-1005-X). Columbia U Pr.

Orban's Oral Histology & Embryology. 9th ed. S. N. Bhaskar. LC 80-11972. (Illus.). 1980. pap. text ed. 29.95 (ISBN 0-8016-4609-X). Mosby.

Orban's Oral Histology & Embryology. 8th ed. Ed. by S. N. Bhasker & Harry Sicher. LC 75-31628. (Illus.). 1976. text ed. 22.50 o.p. (ISBN 0-8016-4608-1). Mosby.

Orbis Pictus of John Amos Comenius. John A. Comenius. Ed. by Charles W. Bardeen. LC 67-23933. (Illus., Eng. & Lat.). 1968. Repr. of 1887 ed. 18.00 (ISBN 0-8103-3476-3). Gale.

Orbit Fifteen. Ed. by Damon Knight. LC 74-1890. 224p. (YA) 1974. 9.95 o.p. (ISBN 0-06-012439-3, HarpT). Har-Row.

Orbit of China. Harrison E. Salisbury. LC 67-11331. (Illus.). 1967. 10.00 o.s.i. (ISBN 0-06-013731-2, HarpT). Har-Row.

Orbit Sixteen. Ed. by Damon Knight. LC 74-15875. (Illus.). 280p. (YA) 1975. 9.95 o.p. (ISBN 0-06-012437-7, HarpT). Har-Row.

Orbit Thirteen. Ed. by Damon Knight. LC 66-15585. (YA) 1974. 5.95 o.p. (ISBN 0-399-11222-7, Dist. by Putnam). Berkley Pub.

Orbit Twenty. Ed. by Damon Knight. LC 77-11784. 1978. 9.95 o.p. (ISBN 0-06-012429-6, HarpT). Har-Row.

Orbit Twenty One. Ed. by Damon Knight. LC 78-20207. 224p. 1980. 12.95 (ISBN 0-06-012426-1, HarpT). Har-Row.

Orbital Symmetry Relationships. R. E. Lehr & Alan Manchard. 1972. text ed. 12.50 (ISBN 0-12-441150-9); pap. text ed. 6.95 (ISBN 0-12-441156-8). Acad Pr.

Orbital Tumors. John W. Henderson. LC 72-90722. (Illus.). 705p. 1973. text ed. 45.00 (ISBN 0-7216-4633-6). Saunders.

Orchard Handbook. Hollis Lee. (Country Home & Small Farm Guides Ser.). 1978. pap. 2.95 (ISBN 0-88453-007-8). Barrington.

Orchard Handbook. (Country Home Ser.). 96p. 2.95 (ISBN 0-88453-007-8). Berkshire Traveller.

Orchard Upstairs. Penelope Shuttle. 64p. 1981. pap. 11.95 (ISBN 0-19-211938-9). Oxford U Pr.

Orchestra of the Language. Ernest M. Robson. 6.50 o.p. (ISBN 0-498-07111-1, Yoseloff). A S Barnes.

Orchestral Music: A Source Book. David Daniels. LC 72-6274. 1972. 10.00 (ISBN 0-8108-0537-5). Scarecrow.

Orchestral Music Catalog: Scores. Oscar G. Sonneck. LC 69-12692. (Music Reprint Ser). 1969. Repr. of 1912 ed. lib. bdg. 55.00 (ISBN 0-306-71228-8). Da Capo.

Orchestral Percussion Technique. 2nd ed. James Blades. 94p. 1973. pap. 7.75x (ISBN 0-19-318803-1). Oxford U Pr.

Orchestrating Your Career. William E. Perry. 192p. 1981. pap. 13.95 (ISBN 0-8436-0799-8). CBI Pub.

Orchestration. King C. Palmer. (Teach Yourself Ser.). 1975. pap. 2.95 o.p. (ISBN 0-679-10438-0). McKay.

Orchestration. Walter Piston. (Illus.). 1955. 15.95x (ISBN 0-393-09740-4, NortonC). Norton.

Orchid Biology: Reviews & Perspectives, I. Ed. by Joseph Arditti. LC 76-25648. (Illus.). 328p. 1977. 35.00x (ISBN 0-8014-1040-1). Comstock.

Orchid Family. Lynne Martin. LC 73-23001. (Illus.). 96p. (gr. 3-7). 1974. 6.75 o.p. (ISBN 0-688-21784-2); PLB 6.48 (ISBN 0-688-31784-7). Morrow.

Orchidaceae, 4 vols. Alfredus Cogniaux. (Flora Brasiliensis Ser.: Vol. 3, Pts. 4-6). (Illus.). 970p. (Lat.). 1975. Repr. Set. lib. bdg. 325.00x (ISBN 3-87429-080-8). Lubrecht & Cramer.

Orchidaceae: Illustrations & Studies of the Family Orchidaceae Volume IV: the Genus Habenaria in North America. Oakes Ames. (Orchid Ser.). (Illus.). 1980. Repr. of 1910 ed. text ed. 25.00 (ISBN 0-930576-23-3). E M Coleman Ent.

Orchideenflora von Rio Grande do Sul. R. Schlechter. (Feddes Repertorium: Beiheft 35). 108p. (Ger.). 1980. Repr. of 1925 ed. lib. bdg. 30.70x (ISBN 3-87429-185-5, Pub. by Koeltz Germany). Lubrecht & Cramer.

Orchids. Frank Anderson. (Abbeville Library of Art Ser.). (Illus.). 112p. 1981. pap. 4.95 (ISBN 0-89659-122-0). Abbeville Pr.

Orchids. Lee Chew Kang. (Illus.). 1979. 15.00 (ISBN 0-89860-032-4). Eastview.

Orchids. James U. Crockett & Alice F. Skelsy. (Time-Life Encyclopedia of Gardening Ser.). (Illus.). 1978. lib. bdg. 11.97 (ISBN 0-686-51061-5). Silver.

Orchids. new ed. Alice Skelsey. Ed. by Time-Life Books. (Encyclopedia of Gardening). (Illus.). 1978. 11.95 (ISBN 0-8094-2591-2). Time-Life.

Orchids As Indoor Plants. Brian Rittershausen & Wilma Rittershausen. (Illus.). 90p. 1980. 12.50 (ISBN 0-7137-0998-7, Pub. by Blandford Pr England). Sterling.

Orchids: Flowers of Romance & Mystery. concise ed. Jack Kramer. (Illus.). 1979. 20.00 o.p. (ISBN 0-8109-1401-8); pap. 9.95 o.p. (ISBN 0-8109-2171-5). Abrams.

Orchids: Flowers of Romance & Mystery. Jack Kramer. (Illus.). 156p. 1980. 20.00 (ISBN 0-686-62708-3, 1401-8); pap. 9.95 (ISBN 0-686-62709-1, 2171-5). Abrams.

Orchids for Home & Garden. rev. ed. F. A. Fennell, Jr. 1959. 6.95 o.p. (ISBN 0-03-029060-0, HR&W). HR&W.

Orchids of Britain: A Field Guide. David C. Lang. (Illus.). 256p. 1980. 26.50x (ISBN 0-19-217692-7). Oxford U Pr.

Orchids: Scientific Studies. Ed. by Carl L. Withner. LC 73-20496. (Illus.). 624p. 1974. 40.50 (ISBN 0-471-95715-1, Pub. by Wiley-Interscience). Wiley.

Orchids: Scientific Survey. C. L. Withner. (Illus.). 1959. 27.50 (ISBN 0-8260-9485-6, Pub. by Wiley-Interscience). Wiley.

Orcidaceae Perrierianae zur Orchideenkunde der Insel Madagascar. R. Schlechter. (Feddes Repertorium: Beiheft 33). 391p. (Ger.). 1980. Repr. of 1925 ed. lib. bdg. 59.80x (Pub. by Koeltz Germany). Lubrecht & Cramer.

Orde Wingate. Cristopher Sykes. (Return to Zion Ser.). 575p. 1981. Repr. lib. bdg. 35.00x (ISBN 0-87991-146-8). Porcupine Pr.

Ordeal. Henry C. Lea. (Middle Ages Ser). 224p. 1973. pap. 5.95x (ISBN 0-8122-1061-1, Pa Paperbks). U of Pa Pr.

Ordeal. Linda Lovelace & Mike McGrady. 1981. pap. 2.95 (ISBN 0-425-04749-0). Berkley Pub.

Ordeal of Byron B. Blackbear. Nancy W. Parker. LC 79-12140. (Illus.). (ps). 1979. 6.95 (ISBN 0-396-07642-4). Dodd.

Ordeal of Consciousness in Henry James. Dorothea Krook. (Orig.). 1968. pap. 13.95x (ISBN 0-521-09449-6). Cambridge U Pr.

Ordeal of Free Labour in the West Indies. 2nd ed. William Sewell. LC 67-31561. Repr. of 1862 ed. 19.50x (ISBN 0-678-05097-X). Kelley.

Ordeal of Love. Ruth McCarthy Sears. (YA) 1977. 5.95 (ISBN 0-685-73815-9, Avalon). Bouregy.

Ordeal of Love: C. F. Andrews & India. Hugh Tinker. (Illus.). 356p. 1979. text ed. 17.95x. Oxford U Pr.

Ordeal of Power: A Political Memoir of the Eisenhower Years. Emmet J. Hughes. LC 63-12783. 1975. pap. text ed. 5.95x (ISBN 0-689-70523-9, 213). Atheneum.

Ordeal of Richard Feverel. George Meredith. 1956. 5.00x o.p. (ISBN 0-460-00916-8, Evman). Dutton.

Ordeal of Southern Illinois University. George K. Plochmann. LC 59-7379. (Illus.). 1959. 693pp. 10.00x (ISBN 0-8093-0020-6); 2 vols. set boxed 704pp. 15.00x (ISBN 0-8093-0021-4). S Ill U Pr.

Ordeal of the Union, 8 vols. Allan Nevins. Incl. Vol. 1. Ordeal of the Union: Fruits of Manifest Destiny, 1847-1852. 1947 (ISBN 0-684-10423-7); Vol. 2. Ordeal of the Union: A House Dividing, 1852-1857. 1947 (ISBN 0-684-10424-5); Vol. 3. Emergence of Lincoln: Douglas, Buchanan, & Party Chaos, 1857-1859. 1950 (ISBN 0-684-10415-6). pap. o.p. Lyceum Ed. (ISBN 0-684-71851-0, 169, SL); Vol. 4. Emergence of Lincoln: Prologue to Civil War, 1859-1861. 1950 (ISBN 0-684-10416-4). pap. o.p. Lyceum Ed. (ISBN 0-684-71852-9, 170, SL); Vol. 5. War for the Union: The Improvised War, 1861-1862. LC 47-11072. 1959 (ISBN 0-684-10426-1); Vol. 6. War for the Union: War Becomes Revolution, 1862-1863. LC 59-3690. 1960 (ISBN 0-684-10427-X); Vol. 7. War for the Union: The Organized War, 1863-1864. LC 47-11072. 1971 (ISBN 0-684-10428-8); Vol. 8. War for the Union: The Organized War to Victory, 1864-1865. LC 47-11072. 1971 (ISBN 0-684-10429-6). (Illus.). 25.00 ea. Scribner.

Ordeal of Twentieth-Century America: Interpretive Readings. Jordan A. Schwarz. 464p. 1974. pap. text ed. 7.95 (ISBN 0-395-14519-8). HM.

Order & Fluctuations in Equilibrium & Nonequilibrium Statistical Mechanics: XVIIth International Solvay Conference on Physics. G. Nicolis et al. LC 80-13215. 416p. 1981. 35.00 (ISBN 0-471-05927-7, Pub. by Wiley Interscience). Wiley.

Order & Image in the American Small Town. Ed. by Michael W. Fazio & Peggy W. Prenshaw. LC 80-24300. (Southern Quarterly Ser.). 1981. price not set (ISBN 0-87805-130-9). U Pr of Miss.

Order & Reason in Politics: Theories of Absolute & Limited Monarchy in Early Modern England. Robert Eccleshall. 1978. text ed. 24.95x (ISBN 0-19-713431-9). Oxford U Pr.

Order for the Lord's Supper or the Holy Eucharist. 3rd ed. Church Of South India. 1962. 0.25x o.p. (ISBN 0-19-635177-4). Oxford U Pr.

Order of Future Events. Ray H. Hughes. 1970. pap. 2.25 (ISBN 0-87148-650-4). Pathway Pr.

Order of Melchisedech. Michael T. Brown. LC 78-55995. 1980. softcover 7.95 o.p. (ISBN 0-930490-13-4). Future Shop.

Order of Poetry: An Introduction. Ed. by Edward A. Bloom et al. (Orig.). 1961. pap. 4.95 (ISBN 0-672-63078-8). Odyssey Pr.

Order of Words in the Ancient Languages Compared with That of the Modern Languages. Henri Weil. (Amsterdam Classics in Linguistics Ser.: No. 14). 1979. text ed. 25.75x (ISBN 90-272-0871-9). Humanities.

Order Procedures. Viola Bird et al. (AALL Publications Ser.: No. 2). 62p. (Orig.). 1960. pap. 8.50x (ISBN 0-8377-0102-3). Rothman.

Order Statistics. H. A. David. LC 78-114915. (Probability & Mathematics Statisfics Ser.). 1970. 26.50 o.p. (ISBN 0-471-19675-4, Pub. by Wiley-Interscience). Wiley.

Order Statistics. 2nd ed. Ed. by H. A. David. LC 80-16928. (Probability & Mathematical Statistics Ser.). 350p. 1981. 24.95 (ISBN 0-471-02723-5, Pub. by Wiley-Interscience). Wiley.

Order to View. Rene Cutforth. 1970. 7.95 (ISBN 0-571-09103-2, Pub. by Faber & Faber). Merrimack Bk Serv.

Order Under Law-Readings in Criminal Justice. Robert G. Culbertson & Mark R. Tezak. 272p. 1981. pap. text ed. 6.95x (ISBN 0-917974-52-2). Waveland Pr.

Order Upon the Land: The U. S. Rectangular Land Survey & the Upper Mississippi Country. Hildegard B. Johnson. (Andrew H. Clark Ser in the Historical Geography of North America). (Illus.). 350p. 1976. text ed. 12.95x (ISBN 0-19-501912-1); pap. text ed. 6.95x (ISBN 0-19-501913-X). Oxford U Pr.

Ordered Groups. Ed. by J. Smith et al. (Lecture Notes in Pure & Applied Mathematics). 192p. 1980. 25.50 (ISBN 0-8247-6943-0). Dekker.

Ordered Love: Sex Roles & Sexuality in Victorian Utopias--the Shakers, the Mormons, & the Oneida Community. Louis J. Kern. LC 80-10763. xv, 430p. 1981. 24.00x (ISBN 0-8078-1443-1); pap. 12.50x (ISBN 0-8078-4074-2). U of NC Pr.

Ordering Demons. John Wheatcroft. LC 78-75343. Date not set. cancelled o.p. (ISBN 0-498-02383-4). A S Barnes. Postponed.

Ordering from Catalogs & Dining Out. Northwest Regional Educational Laboratory. (Lifeworks Ser.). (Illus.). 1980. pap. text ed. 4.00 (ISBN 0-07-047305-6). McGraw.

Ordering in Strongly Fluctuating Condensed Matter Systems. Ed. by T. Riste. (NATO Advanced Study Institute Ser.: Series B: Physics, Volume 50). 490p. 1980. 55.00 (ISBN 0-306-40341-2, Plenum Pr). Plenum Pub.

Orderly Books of Colonel William Henshaw: October 1, 1775, Through October 3, 1776. William Henshaw. 1948. pap. 4.00x (ISBN 0-912296-29-1, Dist. by U Pr of Va). Am Antiquarian.

Orders & Directions for the Better Administration of Justice. LC 72-38176. (English Experience Ser.: No. 451). 1972. Repr. of 1630 ed. 11.50 (ISBN 90-221-0451-6). Walter J Johnson.

Orders, Medals & Decorations of Britain & Europe in Color. Paul Hieronymussen. (Illus.). 256p. 1980. 11.95 (ISBN 0-7137-0445-4, Pub. by Blandford Pr England). Sterling.

Orders of Mammals. William K. Gregory. LC 78-72718. Repr. of 1910 ed. 67.50 (ISBN 0-404-18293-3). AMS Pr.

Orders Taken & Enacted, for Orphans. LC 72-6011. (English Experience Ser.: No. 537). 1973. Repr. of 1580 ed. 5.00 (ISBN 90-221-0537-7). Walter J Johnson.

Ordinance Making Powers of the President of the United States. James Hart. LC 78-87482. (Law, Politics & History Ser.). 1970. Repr. of 1925 ed. lib. bdg. 29.50 (ISBN 0-306-71487-6). Da Capo.

Ordinances of the New Testament. William G. Schell. 67p. pap. 0.50. Faith Pub Hse.

Ordinary & Differential Equations & Stability Theory: An Introduction. David A. Sanchez. 1979. pap. text ed. 3.00 (ISBN 0-486-63828-6). Dover.

Ordinary & Partial Differential Equations. Ed. by W. N. Everett. (Lecture Notes in Mathematics Ser.: Vol. 827). (Illus.). 271p. 1981. pap. 16.80 (ISBN 0-387-10252-3). Springer-Verlag.

Ordinary & the Fabulous. 2nd ed. Elizabeth Cook. LC 75-7213. 204p. 1976. 26.50 (ISBN 0-521-20825-4); pap. 7.95x (ISBN 0-521-09961-7). Cambridge U Pr.

Ordinary Daylight. Andrew Potok. 256p. 1981. pap. 2.95 (ISBN 0-553-14432-4). Bantam.

Ordinary Differential Equations. 3rd ed. Garrett Birkhoff & Gian-Carlo Rota. LC 78-8304. 1978. text ed. 21.95 (ISBN 0-471-07411-X). Wiley.

Ordinary Differential Equations. 2nd. ed. Jack K. Hale. LC 79-17238. (Pure & Applied Mathematics Ser.: Vol. 21). 350p. 1980. Repr. of 1969 ed. lib. bdg. 27.50 (ISBN 0-89874-011-8). Krieger.

Ordinary Differential Equations. Edward L. Ince. (Illus.). 1953. pap. text ed. 6.00 (ISBN 0-486-60349-0). Dover.

Ordinary Differential Equations. Wilfred Kaplan. 1958. 20.95 (ISBN 0-201-03630-4). A-W.

Ordinary Differential Equations. E. R. Lapwood. LC 68-21278. 1968. 25.00 (ISBN 0-08-012551-4). Pergamon.

Ordinary Differential Equations. Otto Plaat. LC 70-156869. 350p. 1971. 18.50x (ISBN 0-8162-6844-4). Holden-Day.

Ordinary Differential Equations: A Computational Approach. Charles E. Roberts, Jr. LC 78-13023. 1979. 19.95 (ISBN 0-13-639757-3). P-H.

Ordinary Differential Equations: A First Course. 2nd ed. F. Brauer & J. A. Nohel. 1973. 15.75 o.p. (ISBN 0-8053-1208-0). Benjamin-Cummings.

Ordinary Differential Equations in the Complex Domain. Einar Hille. LC 75-44231. (Pure & Applied Mathematics Ser.). 432p. 1976. 43.95 (ISBN 0-471-39964-7, Pub. by Wiley-Interscience). Wiley.

Ordinary Differential Equations: Solutions & Applications. Meredith E. Sperline. LC 80-6101. 584p. 1981. pap. text ed. 17.95 (ISBN 0-8191-1358-1). U Pr of Amer.

Ordinary Differential Equations-Theory & Practice. John Heading. 1974. 23.95 (ISBN 0-236-17722-2, Pub. by Paul Elek); pap. 8.95 (ISBN 0-236-17723-0). Merrimack Bk Serv.

Ordinary Differential Equations with Modern Applications. Norman Finizio & Gerasimos Ladas. 1978. text ed. 20.95x (ISBN 0-534-00552-7); solution manual 6.95x (ISBN 0-534-00586-1). Wadsworth Pub.

Ordinary Ecstasy: Humanistic Psychology in Action. John Rowan. (Orig.). 1976. pap. 10.00 (ISBN 0-7100-8344-0). Routledge & Kegan.

Ordinary Jack. Helen Cresswell. (gr. 1-4). 1979. pap. 1.50 (ISBN 0-380-43349-4, 43349, Camelot). Avon.

Ordinary Jack: Being the First Part of the Bagthorpe Saga. Helen Cresswell. LC 77-5146. (gr. 5 up). 1977. 7.95 (ISBN 0-02-725540-9, 72554). Macmillan.

Ordinary Language: Essays in Philosophical Method. Ed. by V. C. Chappell. 128p. 1981. pap. 2.75 (ISBN 0-486-24082-7). Dover.

Ordinary Level Mathematics. L. Harwood Clarke. 1978. pap. text ed. 11.95x with ans. o.p. (ISBN 0-435-50221-2). Heinemann Ed.

Ordinary Level Practical Physics. G. L. Moss. 1971. pap. text ed. 5.50x o.p. (ISBN 0-435-67604-0). Heinemann Ed.

Ordinary Level Revision Notes in Chemistry. A. Holderness. 1971. pap. text ed. 4.95x o.p. (ISBN 0-435-64423-8). Heinemann Ed.

Ordinary People. Judith Guest. LC 76-2368. 1980. pap. 2.75 o.p. (ISBN 0-345-25755-3). Ballantine.

Ordinary People. Judith Guest. 1980. pap. 2.75 (ISBN 0-345-29132-8). Ballantine.

Ordination of Women. Paul K. Jewett. LC 80-15644. 160p. (Orig.). 1980. pap. 5.95 (ISBN 0-8028-1850-1). Eerdmans.

Ordination of Women: Pro & Con. Michael P. Hamilton & Nancy S. Montgomery. (Orig.). 1975. pap. 4.95 o.p. (ISBN 0-8192-1203-2). Morehouse.

Ordnance Survey of the United Kingdom. T. P. White. 1975. pap. text ed. 15.00x (ISBN 90-6041-118-8). Humanities.

Ordovician Trilobites of Spitsbergen I. Olenidae. R. A. Fortey. (Norsk Polarinstitutt Ser: No. 160). 1974. 16.00x (ISBN 8-200-29180-4, Dist. by Columbia U Pr). Universitet.

Ordovician Trilobites of the Spitsbergen. R. A. Fortey. (Norsk Polarinstitutt Skrifter: Vol. 171). (Illus.). 163p. 1980. pap. text ed. 18.00x (ISBN 82-00-29189-8). Universitet.

Ore Deposits. 3rd ed. Charles F. Park, Jr. & Roy A. MacDiarmid. LC 75-14157. (Geology Ser.). (Illus.). 1975. text ed. 28.95x (ISBN 0-7167-0272-X). W H Freeman.

Ore Dust in Her Shoes. Claire W. Schumacher. (Illus.). 194p. (Orig.). 5.00. Schumacher Pubns.

Ore Microscopy. James R. Craig & David J. Vaughan. 325p. 1981. 32.95 (ISBN 0-471-08596-0, Pub. by Wiley-Interscience). Wiley.

Oregon. 28.00 (ISBN 0-89770-113-5). Curriculum Info Ctr.

Oregon: A History. Gordon B. Dodds. (States & the Nation Ser.). (Illus.). 1977. 12.95 (ISBN 0-393-05632-5, Co-Pub. by AASLH). Norton.

Oregon Cattleman, Governor, Congressman: Memoirs & Times of Walter M. Pierce. Walter M. Pierce. Ed. by Arthur H. Bone. LC 80-81718. (Illus.). 528p. 1981. pap. 14.95 (ISBN 0-87595-071-X). Oreg Hist Soc.

Oregon Chronology & Factbook, Vol. 37. R. I. Vexler. 1978. 8.50 (ISBN 0-379-16162-1). Oceana.

Oregon: End of the Trail. Federal Writers' Project. 548p. 1941. Repr. 49.00 (ISBN 0-403-02186-3). Somerset Pub.

Oregon Experiment. Christopher Alexander. (Illus.). 190p. 1975. 19.95 (ISBN 0-19-501824-9). Oxford U Pr.

Oregon Indians, Vol. 1. Incl. Anthropological Investigation of the Tillamook Indians. Herbert C. Taylor; Anthropological Investigation of the Chinook Indians. Herbert C. Taylor; Ethnological Report on the Identity & Localization of Certain Native Peoples of Northwestern Oregon. Robert J. Suphan; Findings of Fact, & Opinion. Indian Claims Commission. (American Indian Ethnohistory: Indians of the Northwest). (Illus.). lib. bdg. 42.00 (ISBN 0-8240-0777-8). Garland Pub.

Oregon Indians, Vol. 2. Incl. Ethnological Report on the Wasco & Tenino Indians Relative to Socio-Political Organization & Land Use. Robert J. Suphan; Ethnological Report on the Umatilla, Walla Walla & Cayuse Indians Relative to Socio-Political Organization & Land Use. Robert J. Suphan; Findings of Fact, & Opinion. Indian Claims Commission. (American Indian Ethnohistory Ser: Indians of the Northwest). (Illus.). lib. bdg. 42.00 (ISBN 0-8240-0778-6). Garland Pub.

Oregon State Industrial Directory, 1980. State Industrial Directories Corp. 1980. pap. 30.00 (ISBN 0-89910-018-X). State Indus Dir.

Oregon Trail. Frances Parkman. Ed. by E. N. Feltskog. (Illus.). 1969. 27.50 (ISBN 0-299-05070-X). U of Wis Pr.

Oregon Trail. Francis Parkman. (Keith Jennison Large Type Bks). (gr. 6 up). PLB 7.95 o.p. (ISBN 0-531-00257-8). Watts.

Oregon Trail: The Missouri River to the Pacific Ocean. Federal Writers Project. LC 70-145012. (Illus.). 1971. Repr. of 1939 ed. 35.00 (ISBN 0-403-01290-2). Somerset Pub.

Oregon: Travel Guide. 3rd ed. Sunset Editors. LC 80-53486. (Illus.). 128p. 1981. pap. 5.95 (ISBN 0-376-06615-6, Sunset Bks.). Sunset-Lane.

Oregon: Travel Guide to. 4th ed. Sunset Editors. LC 80-53486. (Illus.). 128p. 1981. pap. 5.95 (ISBN 0-376-06615-6, Sunset Bks.). Sunset-Lane.

Oregon: Wet, High, & Dry. John O. Dart & Daniel M. Johnson. 500p. (Orig.). 1981. pap. 18.95x (ISBN 0-913244-53-8). Hapi Pr.

Oregon's Salty Coast. James A. Gibbs. LC 78-11899. (Illus.). 1978. 15.95 o.p. (ISBN 0-87564-222-5). Superior Pub.

Ores to Metals: The Rocky Mountain Smelting Industry. James E. Fell, Jr. LC 79-9093. (Illus.). xvi, 341p. 1979. 21.50x (ISBN 0-8032-1951-2). U of Nebr Pr.

Oresteian Trilogy. Aeschylus. Tr. by Philip Vellacott. Incl. Agamemnon; Choephori; Eumenides. (Classics Ser.). (Orig.). (YA) (gr. 9 up). 1956. pap. 2.50 (ISBN 0-14-044067-4). Penguin.

Orestes Brownson. Thomas R. Ryan. 1976. text ed. 29.95x (ISBN 0-8290-0333-9). Irvington.

Orestes Brownson: Yankee, Radical, Catholic. Theodore Maynard. 1971. Repr. of 1943 ed. 18.00 o.s.i. (ISBN 0-02-849030-4). Hafner.

Orestia of Aeschylus. Tr. by Robert Lowell. 129p. 1978. 8.95 (ISBN 0-374-22723-3); pap. 6.95 (ISBN 0-374-51549-2). FS&G.

Organ. F. Routh. (Teach Yourself Ser.). 1974. pap. 2.95 o.p. (ISBN 0-679-10372-4). McKay.

Organ: A Guide for Student & Teacher. Thomas L. Jaynes. 27p. 1979. pap. 7.00 (ISBN 0-935514-00-7). T L Jaynes.

Organ Building & Design. Poul-Gerhard Andersen. Tr. by Joanne Curnutt. (Illus.). 359p. 1969. 28.50 (ISBN 0-04-786003-0). Allen Unwin.

Organ Culture in Biomedical Research. Ed. by M. Balls & Marjorie Monnickendam. LC 75-21034. (British Society for Cell Biology Symposium Ser.: No. 1). (Illus.). 600p. 1976. 99.00 (ISBN 0-521-21001-1). Cambridge U Pr.

Organ Handbook. Hans Klotz. LC 69-11068. 1969. 9.75 (ISBN 0-570-01306-2, 99-1187). Concordia.

Organ Improvisation for Beginners. Jan Bender. LC 75-2934. (Illus.). 71p. 1975. bds. 7.50 (ISBN 0-570-01312-7, 99-1229). Concordia.

Organ Literature: A Comprehensive Survey. Corliss R. Arnold. LC 72-8824. 1973. 18.50 (ISBN 0-8108-0559-6). Scarecrow.

Organ Music. J. S. Bach. 357p. 1970. pap. 7.95 (ISBN 0-486-22359-0). Dover.

Organ Music of J. S. Bach, 2 vols. Peter Williams. LC 77-71431. (Illus.). Vol. 1, 01/1981. 72.00 (ISBN 0-521-21723-7); Vol. 2. 57.50 (ISBN 0-521-21517-X). Cambridge U Pr.

Organ of Corti: Its Histophysiology & Histochemistry. Ya. A Vinnikov & L. K. Titova. LC 62-21544. 253p. 1964. 32.50 (ISBN 0-306-10669-8, Consultants). Plenum Pub.

Organ Preludes: An Index to Compositions on Hymn Tunes, Chorales, Plainsong Melodies, Gregorian Tunes & Carols, 2 Vols. Jean S. Edson. LC 73-8960. 1970. Set. 40.00 (ISBN 0-8108-0287-2). Scarecrow.

Organ Preludes of Johann Sebastian Bach. George B. Stauffer. Ed. by George Buelow. (Studies in Musicology: Vol. 27). 274p. 1980. 34.95 (ISBN 0-8357-1117-X, Pub. by UMI Res Pr). Univ Microfilms.

Organ Preludes: Supplement. Jean S. Edson. 1974. 12.00 (ISBN 0-8108-0663-0). Scarecrow.

Organ Regeneration in Animals: Recovery of Organ Regeneration Ability in Animals. L. V. Polezhaev. (Amer. Lec. in Living Chemistry Ser.). (Illus.). 200p. 1972. 19.75 (ISBN 0-398-02381-6). C C Thomas.

Organ Specific Alloantigens. Ed. by Parviz Lalezari & Henry Krakauer. (Transplantations Proceedings Reprint Ser.). 1980. 24.50 (ISBN 0-8089-1324-7). Grune.

Organ Today. Herbert Norman & H. John Norman. (Illus.). 224p. 1981. 25.00 (ISBN 0-7153-8053-2). David & Charles.

Organelle Heredity. Nicholas W. Gillham. LC 75-43195. 1978. 53.50 (ISBN 0-89004-102-4). Raven.

Organic Agriculture: Economic & Ecological Comparisons with Conventional Methods. Robert C. Oelhaf. 1979. 24.95 (ISBN 0-470-26427-6). Halsted Pr.

Organic & Biological Chemistry. John R. Holum. LC 78-634. 1978. text ed. 19.95x (ISBN 0-471-40872-7). Wiley.

Organic & Polymer Waste Reclaiming Encyclopedia. Marshall Sittig. LC 80-26007. (Chem. Tech. Rev. 180 Ser.: Pollution Tech. Rev. 73). (Illus.). 512p. 1981. 54.00 (ISBN 0-8155-0832-8). Noyes.

Organic Brain Syndromes: An Introduction to Neurobehavioral Disorders. Richard L. Strub & F. William Black. (Illus.). 500p. 1981. text ed. 25.00 (ISBN 0-8036-8209-3, 8209-3). Davis Co.

Organic Charge-Transfer Complexes. R. Foster. (Organic Chemistry Ser.). 1969. 65.00 o.s.i. (ISBN 0-12-262650-8). Acad Pr.

Organic Chemicals from Biomass. Irving S. Goldstein. 304p. 1981. 74.95 (ISBN 0-8493-5531-1). CRC Pr.

Organic Chemicals in the Environment. Neely. 424p. 1980. 37.50 (ISBN 0-8247-6975-9). Dekker.

Organic Chemistry. 2nd ed. Norman L. Allinger et al. LC 75-18431. 1976. 26.95x (ISBN 0-87901-050-9). Worth.

Organic Chemistry. Roger D. Barry. LC 74-79834. (Allied Health Ser). 1975. pap. text ed. 8.35 (ISBN 0-672-61378-6); lab manual 4.80 (ISBN 0-672-61379-4). Bobbs.

Organic Chemistry. 3rd ed. R. Brewster & W. McEwen. 1961. 26.95 (ISBN 0-13-640292-5). P-H.

Organic Chemistry. A. G. Catchpole et al. 1969. 17.95x (ISBN 0-245-58990-2). Intl Ideas.

Organic Chemistry. G. H. Dazeley. LC 69-10061. 1969. text ed. 15.95x (ISBN 0-521-07171-2). Cambridge U Pr.

Organic Chemistry. 6th ed. Ed. by F. Degering. 1965. pap. 4.95 (ISBN 0-06-460006-8, CO 6, COS). Har-Row.

Organic Chemistry. J. B. Hendrickson et al. 1970. text ed. 26.00 o.p. (ISBN 0-07-028150-5, C). McGraw.

Organic Chemistry. Daniel S. Kemp & Frank Vellaccio. 1980. 26.95 (ISBN 0-87901-123-8); wkbk. & solutions manual 11.95 (ISBN 0-87901-124-6). Worth.

Organic Chemistry. Bernard Miller. 1980. 16.95 (ISBN 0-8053-7071-4); study guide 6.95 (ISBN 0-8053-7073-0). Benjamin Cummings.

Organic Chemistry. James D. Morrison. 1979. text ed. 18.95x (ISBN 0-534-00605-1); study guide 7.95x (ISBN 0-534-00720-1); lab manual 8.95x (ISBN 0-534-00690-6). Wadsworth Pub.

Organic Chemistry. 3rd ed. Robert T. Morrison & Robert N. Boyd. 1280p. 1973. text ed. 28.95 (ISBN 0-205-03239-7, 6832393); study guide 15.95 (ISBN 0-205-04466-2, 6844669). Allyn.

Organic Chemistry. 2nd ed. T. W. Graham Solomons. 1980. text ed. 28.95 (ISBN 0-471-04213-7); solutions manual avail. (ISBN 0-471-05770-3); tests avail. (ISBN 0-471-05137-3). Wiley.

Organic Chemistry: A Brief Contemporary Perspective. Charles W. Spangler. (Illus.). 1980. text ed. 19.95 (ISBN 0-13-640318-2); pap. 4.95 (ISBN 0-13-640342-5). P-H.

Organic Chemistry: A Brief Course. John R. Holum. LC 74-20773. (Illus.). 528p. 1975. text ed. 19.95x (ISBN 0-471-40849-2); solutions manual 5.50 (ISBN 0-471-40861-1); instructors' manual avail. (ISBN 0-471-51716-X). Wiley.

Organic Chemistry: A Brief Course. 4th ed. Walter W. Linstromberg & Henry E. Baumgarten. 1978. text ed. 17.95x (ISBN 0-669-00637-8); study guide with problems & solutions manual 7.95x (ISBN 0-669-00640-8). Heath.

Organic Chemistry: A Brief Survey of Concepts & Applications. 2nd ed. Bailey. 500p. 1981. text ed. 19.95 (ISBN 0-205-07233-X, 6872336); free tchr's ed. (ISBN 0-205-07234-8); free student's guide (ISBN 0-205-07235-6). Allyn.

Organic Chemistry: A Brief Survey of Concepts & Applications. Philip S. Bailey & Christina A. Bailey. 1978. text ed. 19.95 (ISBN 0-205-05925-2, 6859259); study guide o.p. 5.95 (ISBN 0-205-05926-0); lab manual 8.95 (ISBN 0-205-05927-9, 6859275). Allyn.

Organic Chemistry: A Concise Approach. 2nd ed. Frederic M. Menger et al. 1975. 19.95 (ISBN 0-8053-3281-2, 33281). Benjamin-Cummings.

Organic Chemistry: A First University Course in Twelve Programs. 2nd ed. F. W. Eastwood et al. 1970. text ed. 13.95x (ISBN 0-521-07951-9). Cambridge U Pr.

Organic Chemistry: A Short Course. 5th ed. Harold Hart & Robert D. Schuetz. LC 77-75880. (Illus.). 1977. text ed. 16.95 (ISBN 0-395-25161-3); lab. manual 9.25 (ISBN 0-395-25163-X); study guide & solutions bk. 7.95 (ISBN 0-395-25162-1). HM.

Organic Chemistry: An Experimental Approach. James Swinehart. (Illus., Orig.). 1969. pap. 16.95 (ISBN 0-13-640649-1). P-H.

Organic Chemistry: An Introduction. Jack E. Fernandez. (Illus.). 528p. 1981. text ed. 19.95 (ISBN 0-686-68299-8). P-H.

Organic Chemistry for Students of Biology & Medicine. 2nd ed. G. A. Taylor. LC 77-2193. (Illus.). 1978. pap. text ed. 14.95x (ISBN 0-582-44041-6). Longman.

Organic Chemistry of Biological Compounds. Robert Barker. (Modern Biochemistry Ser). (Illus.). 1971. pap. 13.95x ref. ed. (ISBN 0-13-640623-8). P-H.

Organic Chemistry of Drug Synthesis, 2 vols. Daniel Lednicer & Lester A. Mitscher. LC 76-28387. Vol. 1, 1977. 28.50 (ISBN 0-471-52141-8, Pub. by Wiley-Interscience); Vol. 2, 1980. 28.00 (ISBN 0-471-04392-3). Wiley.

Organic Chemistry of Life: Readings from Scientific American. Intro. by Melvin Calvin & William A. Pryor. LC 73-12475. (Illus.). 1973. text ed. 19.95x (ISBN 0-7167-0884-1); pap. text ed. 9.95x (ISBN 0-7167-0883-3). W H Freeman.

Organic Chemistry of Nickel, 2 vols. P. W. Jolly & G. Wilke. (Organometallic Chemistry Ser.). Vol. 1, 1974. 80.00 (ISBN 0-12-388401-2); Vol. 2, 1975. 66.50 (ISBN 0-12-388402-0). Acad Pr.

Organic Chemistry of Stable Free Radicals. A. R. Forrester et al. 1968. 48.00 o.s.i. (ISBN 0-12-262050-X). Acad Pr.

Organic Chemistry Problem Solver: A Supplement to Any Class Text. Research & Education Association Staff. LC 78-51952. 1978. pap. text ed. 22.85 (ISBN 0-87891-512-5). Res & Educ.

Organic Chemistry: Problems & Solutions. Arthur D. Baker & Robert Engel. 1978. pap. text ed. 10.95 (ISBN 0-205-06118-4). Allyn.

Organic Chemistry: The Basis of Life. B. Miller. 1980. 19.95 (ISBN 0-8053-7071-4); instrs guide with test items 3.95 (ISBN 0-8053-7072-2); write for info. study guide (ISBN 0-8053-7073-0). A-W.

Organic Chemistry, Vol. 1. 6th rev. ed. I. L. Finar. (Illus.). 960p. 1973. text ed. 23.00x (ISBN 0-582-44221-4). Longman.

Organic Chemistry, Vol. 2. 5th rev. ed. I. L. Finar. LC 73-157839. (Illus.). 942p. 1975. text ed. 27.00x (ISBN 0-582-44312-1). Longman.

Organic Coating Technology, 2 Vols. H. F. Payne. LC 54-5971. 1954-61. Vol. 1. 45.00 (ISBN 0-471-67286-6); Vol. 2. 49.95 (ISBN 0-471-67353-6, Pub by Wiley-Interscience). Wiley.

Organic Cooking for (Not-So-Organic) Mothers. Marlene A. Bumgarner. Ed. by Sue Olson. LC 80-23089. (Illus.). 160p. (Orig.). pap. 5.50 (ISBN 0-938006-01-0); spiral bdg. 4.95 (ISBN 0-938006-00-2). Chesbro.

Organic Crystals, Germanates, Semiconductors. Ed. by H. C. Freyhardt. (Crystals, Growth, Properties & Applications: Vol. 4). (Illus.). 250p. 1980. 55.50 (ISBN 0-387-10298-1). Springer-Verlag.

Organic Dysfunction Survey Schedules. Joseph R. Cautela. LC 80-53910. 157p. (Orig.). 1981. pap. text ed. write for info. (ISBN 0-87822-223-5, 2235). Res Press.

Organic Electrochemistry. L. Eberson. LC 70-31906. (Topics in Current Chemistry: Vol. 21). (Illus.). 1971. pap. 48.40 o.p. (ISBN 0-387-05463-4). Springer-Verlag.

Organic Electronic Spectral Data. J. P. Phillips et al. LC 60-16428. Vol. 13, 1971. 66.00 (ISBN 0-471-03563-7, Pub. by Wiley-Interscience); Vol. 14, 1978. 85.00 (ISBN 0-471-05076-8); Vol. 15, 1979. 80.00 (ISBN 0-471-05572-7). Wiley.

Organic Electronic Spectral Data, Vol. 16. John P. Phillips et al. LC 60-16428. (Data Vol. Xvi, 1974). 1126p. 1980. 90.00 (ISBN 0-471-06058-5, Pub. by Wiley-Interscience). Wiley.

Organic Experiments. 4th ed. Louis F. Fieser & Kenneth L. Williamson. 1979. text ed. 16.95x (ISBN 0-669-01688-8); instructor's manual free (ISBN 0-669-01689-6). Heath.

Organic Experiments. 4th rev. ed. Walter W. Linstromberg & Henry F. Baumgarten. 1980. pap. text ed. 7.95 (ISBN 0-669-02902-5). Heath.

Organic Farming Yesterday's & Tomorrow's Agriculture. Editors of Organic Gardening Magazine. (Illus.). 352p. 1977. pap. 5.95 (ISBN 0-87857-175-2). Rodale Pr Inc.

Organic Form: The Life of an Idea. G. S. Rousseau. 1972. 8.00x (ISBN 0-7100-7246-5). Routledge & Kegan.

Organic Functional Group Analysis, Theory & Development. G. H. Schenk. LC 67-28668. 1968. 16.50 (ISBN 0-08-012626-X); pap. 7.75 (ISBN 0-08-012625-1). Pergamon.

Organic Functional Group Preparations, 4 vols. Stanley R. Sandler & Wolf Karo. (Organic Chemistry Ser.: Vol. 12). Vol.1. 1969. 50.00 (ISBN 0-12-618550-6); Vol.2. 1971. 48.00 (ISBN 0-12-618552-2); Vol. 3. 1972. 48.00 (ISBN 0-12-618553-0); 120.05 set (ISBN 0-686-66355-1). Acad Pr.

Organic Liquids As Reactor Coolants & Moderators. (Technical Reports: No. 70). 1967. pap. 7.50 (ISBN 92-0-055067-3, IAEA). Unipub.

Organic Matter in Natural Waters. Ed. by D. W. Hood. (Occasional Pub. Ser. No. 1). 8.00 (ISBN 0-914500-00-7). U of AK Inst Marine.

Organic Mental Disease. Frank R. Freemon. LC 79-23180. (Illus.). 248p. 1981. text ed. 30.00 (ISBN 0-89335-109-1). Spectrum Pub.

Organic Method Primer: A Practical Explanation, the Why & How for the Beginner & the Experienced. Bargyla Rateaver & Gylver Rateaver. LC 73-85165. (Conservation Gardening & Farming Ser). 1975. pap. 10.00 (ISBN 0-9600698-1-X). Rateavers.

Organic Molecular Crystals: Their Electronic States. E. A. Silinish. (Springer Series in Solid State Sciences: Vol. 16). (Illus.). 410p. 1980. 54.50 (ISBN 0-387-10053-9). Springer-Verlag.

Organic Organization & How to Manage It. Hawdon Hague. LC 78-23272. 1979. 24.95x (ISBN 0-470-26563-9). Halsted Pr.

Organic Phosphorus Compounds, Vols. 1-3, 5-6. Ed. by G. M. Kosolapoff & L. Maier. LC 72-1359. 2304p. 1972. Vol. 2. 50.95 (ISBN 0-471-50441-6); Vol. 5. 50.95 (ISBN 0-471-50444-0); Vol. 6. o.p. (ISBN 0-471-50445-9, Pub. by Wiley-Interscience). Wiley.

Organic Photochemistry. J. M. Coxon & B. Halton. LC 73-82447. (Chemistry Texts Ser). (Illus.). 270p. 1974. 35.50 (ISBN 0-521-20322-8); pap. 13.95x (ISBN 0-521-09824-6). Cambridge U Pr.

Organic Photochemistry. Padwa. 1981. 65.00. Dekker.

Organic Polymeric Semiconductors. Ya. M. Paushkin et al. Ed. by A. E. Sultzkin. Tr. by R. Kondor. Orig. Title: Rus. 242p. 1974. 32.95 (ISBN 0-470-67275-7). Halsted Pr.

Organic Reaction Mechanism. Ed. by A. R. Butler & J. M. Perkins. Incl. Vol. 9. 1973. 96.95 (ISBN 0-471-12690-X); Vol. 10. 1974. 119.95 (ISBN 0-471-12693-4); Reprint A. 7.50 (ISBN 0-471-01531-8); Reprint B. 8.95 (ISBN 0-471-01532-6); Vol. 11. 1975. 115.95 (ISBN 0-471-01864-3); Vol. 12. 1976. 125.50 (ISBN 0-471-99523-1). LC 66-23143. 1975-1978 (Pub. by Wiley-Interscience). Wiley.

Organic Reactions, Vol. 1-19. Incl. Vol. 1. Ed. by Roger Adams. 400p. 1978. Repr. of 1946 ed (ISBN 0-88275-729-6); Vol. 2. Ed. by Roger Adams. 460p. 1944 (ISBN 0-471-00495-2); Vol. 3. Ed. by Roger Adams. 468p. 1975. Repr. of 1946 ed (ISBN 0-88275-875-6); Vol. 4. Ed. by Roger Adams. 438p. 1948 (ISBN 0-88275-780-6); Vol. 5. Ed. by Roger Adams. 454p. 1977. Repr. of 1949 ed (ISBN 0-88275-249-9); Vol. 6. Ed. by Roger Adams. 526p. 1975. Repr. of 1951 ed (ISBN 0-88275-876-4); Vol. 7. Ed. by Roger Adams. 448p. 1975. Repr. of 1953 ed (ISBN 0-88275-877-2); Vol. 8. Ed. by Roger Adams. 446p. 1975. Repr. of 1954 ed (ISBN 0-88275-878-0); Vol. 9. 476p. 1975. Repr. of 1957 ed (ISBN 0-88275-879-9); Vol. 10. Ed. by Roger Adams. 572p. 1975. Repr. of 1959 ed (ISBN 0-88275-880-2); Vol. 11. Ed. by Arthur C. Cope. 510p. 1975. Repr. of 1960 ed (ISBN 0-88275-881-0); Vol. 12. Ed. by Arthur C. Cope. 546p. 1975. Repr. of 1962 ed (ISBN 0-88275-882-9); Vol. 13. Arthur C. Cope. 390p. 1979. Repr. of 1962 ed (ISBN 0-88275-836-5); Vol. 14. Ed. by Arthur C. Cope. 506p. 1978. Repr. of 1965 ed (ISBN 0-88275-730-X); Vol. 15. Ed. by Arthur C. Cope. 616p. 1978. Repr. of 1967 ed (ISBN 0-88275-731-8); Vol. 17. Ed. by William G. Dauben. 346p. 1975. Repr. of 1969 ed (ISBN 0-88275-884-5); Vol. 18. Ed. by William G. Dauben. 476p. 1978. Repr. of 1970 ed (ISBN 0-88275-732-6); Vol. 19. Ed. by Wlliam G. Dauben. 446p. 1975. Repr. of 1972 ed (ISBN 0-88275-885-3). LC 42-20265. 25.50 ea. Krieger.

Organic Reactions, Vols. 20-25. Ed. by William G. Dauben. LC 42-20265. (Organic Reaction Ser.). Vol. 20, 1973. 37.50 (ISBN 0-471-19621-5); Vol. 21, 1974. 34.95 (ISBN 0-471-19622-3); Vol. 22, 1975. 36.95 (ISBN 0-471-19623-1); Vol. 23, 1975. 37.50 (ISBN 0-471-19624-X); Vol. 24, 1975. 36.95 (ISBN 0-471-19625-8); Vol. 25, 1977. 33.95 (ISBN 0-471-01741-8, Pub. by Wiley-Interscience). Wiley.

Organic Reactions & Orbital Symmetry. 2nd ed. T. L. Gilchrist & R. C. Storr. LC 78-54578. (Cambridge Texts in Chemistry & Biochemistry Ser.). (Illus.). 1979. 59.50 (ISBN 0-521-22014-9); pap. 18.95x (ISBN 0-521-29336-7). Cambridge U Pr.

Organic Reagents in Inorganic Analysis. Z. Holzbecher et al. LC 75-34459. (Ser. in Analytical Chemistry). 734p. 1976. 85.95 (ISBN 0-470-01396-6). Halsted Pr.

Organic Reagents in Metal Analysis. K. Burger. 270p. 1973. text ed. 42.00 (ISBN 0-08-016929-5). Pergamon.

Organic Selenium Compounds: Their Chemistry & Biology. Daniel L. Klayman & Wolfgang H. Gunther. LC 72-5448. (Organometallic Compounds Ser.). 1024p. 1972. 105.00 (ISBN 0-471-49032-6, Pub. by Wiley-Interscience). Wiley.

Organic Small Farming. Hugh Corley. Ed. by Bargyla & Gylver Rateaver. LC 74-33122. (Conservation Gardening & Farming Ser: Ser. C). 1975. pap. 10.00 (ISBN 0-9600698-4-4). Rateavers.

Organic Spectroscopy. W. Kemp. LC 74-7675. 1975. text ed. 24.95 (ISBN 0-470-46842-4); pap. text ed. 14.95 (ISBN 0-470-99193-3). Halsted Pr.

Organic Spectroscopy: An Introduction. 2nd ed. S. F. Dyke et al. (Illus.). 1979. pap. text ed. 11.95 (ISBN 0-582-45076-4). Longman.

Organic Stereochemistry. Henri Kagan. Tr. by M. C. Whiting & U. H. Whiting. LC 79-11500. 166p. 1979. pap. text ed. 16.95x (ISBN 0-470-26725-9). Halsted Pr.

Organic Structure Determination. Daniel Pasto & Carl Johnson. 1969. ref. ed. 23.95 (ISBN 0-13-640854-0). P-H.

Organic Sulfur Chemistry: Ninth International Symposium on Organic Sulfur Chemistry, Riga, USSR, 9-14 June 1980. Ed. by R. Kh. Freidlina. (IUPAC Symposium Ser.). (Illus.). 270p. 1981. 81.00 (ISBN 0-08-026180-9). Pergamon.

Organic Syntheses. William A. Sheppard. LC 21-17747. (Organic Syntheses Ser.: Vol. 58). 1978. 16.95 (ISBN 0-471-04739-2, Pub. by Wiley-Interscience). Wiley.

Organic Syntheses, Vol. 56. George H. Buchi. LC 22-17747. (Organic Synthesis Ser.). 1977. 16.95 (ISBN 0-471-02218-7, Pub. by Wiley-Interscience). Wiley.

Organic Syntheses Collective Volumes, Vol. 4. N. Rabjohn. 1036p. 1963. 39.00 (ISBN 0-471-70470-9, 2-203). Wiley.

Organic Synthesis. A. Brossi. LC 21-17747. (Organic Synthesis Ser.: Vol. 53). 1973. 15.95 (ISBN 0-471-10615-1). Wiley.

Organic Synthesis. S. Masamune. (Organic Synthesis Ser.: Vol. 55). 1976. 16.95 (ISBN 0-471-57390-6, Pub. by Wiley-Interscience). Wiley.

Organic Synthesis - Today & Tomorrow: Third IUPAC Symposium on Organic Synthesis, Madison, Wisconsin, U.S.A., 15-20 June 1980. Ed. by Barry M. Trost & C. R. Hutchinson. (IUAC Symposium Ser.). (Illus.). 360p. 1981. 96.00 (ISBN 0-08-025268-0). Pergamon.

Organic Synthesis Collective Volumes, Vol. 2. A. H. Blatt. 1943. 32.50 (ISBN 0-471-07986-3). Wiley.

Organic Synthesis Two: Second IUPAC Symposium on Organic Synthesis, Jerusalem & Haifa, Israel, 10-15 September, 1978. Ed. by S. Sarel. (IUPAC Symposia Ser.). (Illus.). 1979. 35.00 (ISBN 0-08-022363-X). Pergamon.

Organisation & Administration of Agricultural Research. Isaac Arnon. 1968. 44.60x (ISBN 0-444-20028-2). Intl Ideas.

Organisation & Bureaucracy: An Analysis of Modern Theories. Nicos P. Mouzelis. LC 68-11361. 1968. 15.95x (ISBN 0-202-30072-2); pap. 6.95x (ISBN 0-202-30078-1). Aldine Pub.

Organisation & Impact of Social Research: Six Original Case Studies in Education & Behavioural Sciences. Ed. by Marten Shipmen. 1976. 12.00 (ISBN 0-7100-8320-3). Routledge & Kegan.

Organisation & Management of Educational Technology. Richard N. Tucker. (New Patterns of Learning Ser.). 167p. (Orig.). 1979. 26.00x (ISBN 0-85664-941-4, Pub. by Croom Helm Ltd England). Biblio Dist.

Organisation & Manpower Planning. 3rd ed. Gordon McBeath. 1974. 21.00x o.p. (ISBN 0-8464-0691-8). Beekman Pubs.

Organisation for Education. Graham Mee. 114p. 1980. pap. text ed. 25.00 (ISBN 0-582-78300-3). Longman.

Organisation of Science & Technology in France 1808-1914. Ed. by Robert Fox & George Weisz. LC 80-40227. (Maison Des Sciences De L'homme). (Illus.). 336p. 1980. 37.50 (ISBN 0-521-23234-1). Cambridge U Pr.

Organisational Aspects of Police Behaviour. J. Merryn Jonnes. 192p. 1980. 34.25x (ISBN 0-566-00402-X, Pub. by Gower Pub Co England). Renouf.

Organisational Effectiveness in a Multinational Bureaucracy. Hans J. Michelmann. LC 78-60532. 1979. 26.95 (ISBN 0-03-047211-3). Praeger.

Organisational Structure & the Care of the Mentally Retarded. Norma V. Raynes et al. LC 79-83740. (Praeger Special Studies Ser.). 240p. 1979. 24.95 (ISBN 0-03-051516-5). Praeger.

Organisational Structure & the Care of the Mentally Retarded. Norma V. Raynes et al. 192p. 1980. 25.00x (ISBN 0-85664-532-X, Pub. by Croom Helm England). State Mutual Bk.

Organising for Social Change: A Study in the Theory & Practice of Community Social Work. 2nd ed. David N. Thomas. (National Institute Social Services Library). 1977. pap. text ed. 7.50x o.p. (ISBN 0-04-361028-5). Allen Unwin.

Organising the Farmers: Cocoa Politics & National Development in Ghana. Bjorn Beckman. 1976. pap. text ed. 14.00x (ISBN 0-8419-9722-5). Holmes & Meier.

Organism As an Adaptive Control System. J. Reiner. 1968. 18.95 (ISBN 0-13-640920-2). P-H.

Organismic & Environmental Laboratory Manual. Charlene A. Jope. 144p. 1981. pap. text ed. 6.95 (ISBN 0-8403-2322-0). Kendall-Hunt.

Organismic Evolution. Verne Grant. LC 76-54175. (Illus.). 1977. text ed. 24.95x (ISBN 0-7167-0372-6). W H Freeman.

Organization. John P. Kotter et al. 1979. 18.95 (ISBN 0-256-02226-7). Irwin.

Organization & Administration of Catholic Education in Australia. P. D. Tannock. 1975. 14.50x (ISBN 0-7022-0954-6). U of Queensland Pr.

Organization & Administration of Drug Abuse Treatment Programs. Ed. by John G. Cull & Richard E. Hardy. (American Lectures in Social & Rehabilitation Psychology Ser.). (Illus.). 360p. 1974. text ed. 27.50 (ISBN 0-398-03113-4). C C Thomas.

Organization & Administration of Distributive Education. Lucy C. Crawford & Warren G. Meyer. LC 70-187803. 336p. 1972. text ed. 18.95x (ISBN 0-675-09112-8). Merrill.

Organization & Administration of Emergency Medical Care. Ed. by George Sternbach. LC 78-74611. 117p. 1979. 9.50 (ISBN 0-87762-269-8). Technomic.

Organization & Administration of Health Care: Theory, Practice, Environment. 2nd ed. Richard L. Durbin & W. Herbert Springall. LC 74-1114. 1974. 16.95 o.p. (ISBN 0-8016-1472-4). Mosby.

Organization & Administration of Pastoral Counseling Centers. Ed. by John C. Carr et al. LC 80-22416. 304p. 1980. 15.95 (ISBN 0-687-29430-4). Abingdon.

Organization & Administration of Pupil Personnel Services. Howard L. Blanchard. (Illus.). 148p. 1974. photocopy ed. spiral 14.75 (ISBN 0-398-03142-8). C C Thomas.

Organization & Administration of Service Programs for the Older American. Ed. by Richard E. Hardy & John G. Cull. (American Lectures in Social & Rehabilitation Psychology Ser.). (Illus.). 252p. 1975. 18.50 (ISBN 0-398-03286-6). C C Thomas.

Organization & Control in Prokaryotic & Eukaryotic Cells: Proceedings. Ed. by H. P. Charles & B. C. Knight. (Illus.). 1970. 49.50 (ISBN 0-521-07815-6). Cambridge U Pr.

Organization & Efficiency of Solid Waste Collection. E. S. Savas. LC 76-43606. 1977. 17.95 (ISBN 0-669-01095-2). Lexington Bks.

Organization & Environment: Managing Differentiation & Integration. Paul R. Lawrence & Jay W. Lorsch. 1969. pap. text ed. 8.50x (ISBN 0-256-00314-9). Irwin.

Organization & Expression of Chromosomes, LSRR 4. Ed. by V. G. Allfrey et al. (Dahlem Workshop Reports Ser.). 1976. pap. 36.50 (ISBN 0-89573-088-X). Verlag Chemie.

Organization & Management: A Systems & Contingency Approach. 3rd rev. ed. Fremont Kast & James Rosenzweig. (Management Ser.). (Illus.). 1979. text ed. 22.50x (ISBN 0-07-033346-7, C); instructor's manual 7.50 (ISBN 0-07-033347-5). McGraw.

Organization & Management: Experiential Exercises. Fremont E. Kast & James Rosenzweig. 1976. text ed. 12.95x (ISBN 0-07-033346-7, C); instructor's manual 4.95 (ISBN 0-07-033347-5). McGraw.

Organization & Management for Respiratory Therapists. Arthur J. McLaughlin, Jr. LC 78-1577. (Illus.). 1979. pap. text ed. 10.95 (ISBN 0-8016-3311-7). Mosby.

Organization & Management of the Resource Room: A Cookbook Approach. Howard Drucker. (Illus.). 184p. 1976. 18.75 (ISBN 0-398-03538-5). C C Thomas.

Organization & Operation of Neighborhood Councils: A Practical Guide. Howard W. Hallman. LC 77-1872. (Special Studies). 1977. text ed. 21.95 (ISBN 0-03-022716-X). Praeger.

Organization & Retrieval of Economic Knowledge. Ed. by Mark Perlman. LC 76-30513. (International Economic Association Ser). 1977. lib. bdg. 46.65x (ISBN 0-89158-721-7). Westview.

Organization & the Human Services: Cross-Disciplinary Reflections. Ed. by Herman D. Stein. 275p. 1981. 17.50x (ISBN 0-87722-209-6). Temple U Pr.

Organization Behavior in Action: Skill Building Experiences. William C. Morris & Marshal Sashkin. LC 76-490. (Illus.). 288p. 1976. pap. text ed. 11.95 (ISBN 0-8299-0080-2); instrs.' manual avail. (ISBN 0-8299-0562-6). West Pub.

Organization Design. Jay Galbraith. LC 76-10421. (Illus.). 1977. text ed. 18.95 (ISBN 0-201-02558-2). A-W.

Organization Design. Derek Newman. 1973. 16.50x (ISBN 0-7131-3292-2). Intl Ideas.

Organization Design for Primary Health Care: The Case of the Dr. Martin Luther King Jr. Health Center. Noel M. Tichy. LC 75-44941. (Praeger Special Studies). 1977. 24.95 (ISBN 0-275-23030-9). Praeger.

Organization Development: A Practical Approach. G. James Francis. 200p. 1982. text ed. 17.95 (ISBN 0-8359-5301-7). Reston.

Organization Development Approach to Management Development. Glenn H. Varney. LC 75-9007. (Illus.). 192p. 1976. text ed. 10.94 (ISBN 0-201-07982-8). A-W.

Organization Development: Behavioral Science Interventions for Organization Improvement. 2nd ed. Wendell L. French & Cecil H. Bell, Jr. 1978. ref. 15.95 (ISBN 0-13-641688-8); pap. 10.95 (ISBN 0-13-641670-5). P-H.

Organization Development for Managers. Glenn H. Varney. LC 77-73948. 1977. pap. text ed. 10.95 (ISBN 0-201-07983-6). A-W.

Organization Development: Its Nature, Origins & Prospects. Warren G. Bennis. Ed. by Edgar Schein et al. (Ser. in Organization Development). 1969. pap. text ed. 6.50 (ISBN 0-201-00523-9). A-W.

Organization Development Overview. Fordyee. 1976. 15.95 o.p. (ISBN 0-201-02104-8). A-W.

Organization Development: Strategies & Models. Richard Beckhard. Ed. by Edgar Schein et al. (Ser. in Organization Development). 1969. pap. text ed. 6.50 (ISBN 0-201-00448-8). A-W.

Organization Development: Theory, Practice, & Research. Wendell L. French, Jr. et al. 1978. pap. 16.50 (ISBN 0-256-02089-2). Business Pubns.

Organization-Environment Relationships. Ed. by Janet Kraegel. LC 79-90380. (Management Anthology Ser.). 1980. pap. text ed. 12.95 (ISBN 0-913654-58-2). Nursing Res.

Organization for Production. 5th ed. Edwin S. Roscoe et al. 1971. text ed. 18.95 (ISBN 0-256-00470-6). Irwin.

Organization for Program Management. C. Davies et al. LC 78-27660. 1980. 34.95 (ISBN 0-471-27571-9, Pub. by Wiley-Interscience). Wiley.

Organization for Rural Development: Risk Taking & Appropriate Technology. Allen D. Jedlicka. LC 77-10757. (Praeger Special Studies). 1977. 22.95 (ISBN 0-03-022341-5). Praeger.

Organization for the Library Profession. 2nd ed. Ed. by A. H. Chaplin. (IFLA Ser.: Vol. 6). 132p. 1976. text ed. 15.00 (ISBN 3-7940-4309-X, Pub. by K G Saur). Shoe String.

Organization, Functioning & Activities of National Documentary Information Systems in the Scientific, Technical & Economic Fields. V. Taraboi. LC 67-1784. 88p. 1973. pap. text ed. 35.00 (ISBN 0-08-017725-5). Pergamon.

Organization in a Changing Environment. Richard J. Roeber. LC 72-11603. 1973. pap. text ed. 6.50 (ISBN 0-201-06501-0). A-W.

Organization in Innovation, Innovation in Organization: The Matrix As a Stimulus to Renewal. Cornelius Buitenhuis. (Mensen En Organisaties in Beweging: No. 2). 1978. pap. text ed. 15.00x (ISBN 90-232-1660-1). Humanities.

Organization in Plants. 3rd ed. W. M. Baron. LC 78-12085. 1979. pap. 19.95 (ISBN 0-470-26558-2). Halsted Pr

Organization in Vision: Essays on Gestalt Perception. Gaetano Kanizsa. LC 79-11857. (Praeger Special Studies Ser.). 288p. 1979. 29.95 (ISBN 0-03-049071-5). Praeger.

Organization, Life & Systematics of Trilobites. Jan Bergstrom. (Fossils & Strata Ser: No. 2). 1973. 12.00x (ISBN 3-200-09330-1, Dist. by Columbia U Pr). Universitet.

Organization, Location & Behavior: Decision Making in Economic Geography. Peter Toyne. LC 73-22708. 285p. 1974. text ed. 17.95 (ISBN 0-470-88100-3). Halsted Pr.

Organization Mad. Mad Magazine Editors. (Mad Ser.). (Illus.). 1973. pap. 1.50 (ISBN 0-446-88897-4). Warner Bks.

Organization Management: A Macro Approach. Warrren B. Brown & Dennis G. Moberg. LC 79-18709. (Wiley Ser. in Management). 1980. text ed. 21.95 (ISBN 0-471-02023-0); tchrs'. manual avail. (ISBN 0-471-02024-9). Wiley.

Organization of Afferents from the Brain Stem Nuclei to the Cerebellar Cortex in the Cat. B. Brown Gold. (Advances in Anatomy, Embryology & Cell Biology: Vol. 62). (Illus.). 100p. 1980. pap. 28.30 (ISBN 0-387-09960-3). Springer-Verlag.

Organization of American States: A Handbook. rev. ed. (Span. & Eng.). 1977. pap. 1.00 Eng. ed. (ISBN 0-8270-0205-X); pap. 1.00 Span. ed. (ISBN 0-8270-0210-6). OAS.

Organization of Crime. Mary McIntosh. (Studies in Sociology Ser). 1977. pap. text ed. 4.00x o.p. (ISBN 0-333-15837-7). Verry.

Organization of Information Services: Alternative Approaches. Margrethe H. Olson. Ed. by Gunter Dufey. (Research for Business Decisions: Vol. 21). 290p. 1980. 27.95 (ISBN 0-8357-1105-6, Pub. by UMI Res Pr). Univ Microfilms.

Organization of Information Systems for Government & Public Administration. (Studies & Research: No. 8). 1979. pap. 10.00 (ISBN 92-3-101595-8, U919, UNESCO). Unipub.

Organization of Judicial Power in the United States. Carl McGowan. (Julius Rosenthal Memorial Lectures Ser.: 1967). 1969. 7.95x o.s.i. (ISBN 0-8101-0007-X). Northwestern U Pr.

Organization of Language. Janice Moulton & George M. Robinson. LC 80-19052. 400p. Date not set. 42.50 (ISBN 0-521-23129-9); pap. 14.95 (ISBN 0-521-29851-2). Cambridge U Pr.

Organization of Pupil Personnel Programs-Issues & Practices. Ed. by Raymond N. Hatch. 435p. 1974. 15.00x (ISBN 0-87013-186-9). Mich St U Pr.

Organization of Regulatory Activities for Nuclear Reactors. (Technical Reports). 57p. (Orig.). 1974. pap. 4.50 (ISBN 92-0-125174-2, IDC-153, IAEA). Unipub.

Organization of Sheltered Workshop Programs for the Mentally Retarded Adult. Jay L. Zaetz. (Illus.). 248p. 1971. 24.75 (ISBN 0-398-02158-9). C C Thomas.

Organization of Soviet Medical Care. Michael Ryan. (Aspects of Social Policy). 1978. 24.50x (ISBN 0-631-18140-7, Pub. by Basil Blackwell). Biblio Dist.

Organization of the Government of Canada. 635p. 1981. pap. 37.00 (ISBN 0-660-10496-2, SSC 149, SSC). Unipub.

Organization of the Government Under the Constitution. David M. Matteson. LC 72-118201. (American Constitutional & Legal History Ser). 1970. Repr. of 1943 ed. lib. bdg. 37.50 (ISBN 0-306-71935-5). Da Capo.

Organization of the Small Public Library. Ingeborg Heintze. 1963. pap. 2.50 (ISBN 92-3-100523-5, U442, UNESCO). Unipub.

Organization Theory: A Macro-Perspective for Management. J. Jackson & C. Morgan. 1978. 19.95 (ISBN 0-13-641407-9). P-H.

Organization Theory: A Structural & Behavioral Analysis. 3rd ed. William G. Scott & Terence Mitchell. 1976. text ed. 18.95 (ISBN 0-256-01788-3). Irwin.

Organization Theory: An Integrated Contingency Approach. Richard N. Osborn et al. (Wiley Ser. in Management). 1980. text ed. 21.95 (ISBN 0-471-02173-3); tchrs' manual avail. (ISBN 0-471-02174-1). Wiley.

Organization Theory & Local Government. Robert J. Haynes. (New Local Government Ser.: No. 19). (Illus.). 224p. (Orig.). 1980. text ed. 27.50x (ISBN 0-04-352088-X, 2488); pap. text ed. 12.95x (ISBN 0-04-352089-8, 2489). Allen Unwin.

Organization Theory & Policy: Notes for Analysis. Edmund P. Learned & Audrey T. Sproat. 1966. pap. text ed. 6.25x o.p. (ISBN 0-256-00310-6). Irwin.

Organization Theory & the New Public Administration. Carl J. Bellone. 336p. 1980. text ed. 18.85 (ISBN 0-205-06997-5, 766997-6). Allyn.

Organization Theory: Integrating Structure & Behavior. G. Dessler. 1980. 19.95 (ISBN 0-13-641886-4). P-H.

Organization Theory: Structures, Systems, & Environments. W. M. Evan. LC 76-22742. 1976. 24.95 (ISBN 0-471-01512-1). Wiley.

Organizational Alternatives in Soviet-Type Economies. Nicholas Spulber. LC 78-68378. 1979. 35.00 (ISBN 0-521-22393-8). Cambridge U Pr.

Organizational Behavior. Stephen J. Carroll & Henry L. Tosi. (Illus.). 1977. 21.95 (ISBN 0-914292-08-0). Wiley.

Organizational Behavior. W. Jack Duncan. LC 77-76344. (Illus.). 1978. text ed. 17.95 (ISBN 0-395-25744-1); inst. manual 0.50 (ISBN 0-395-25745-X). HM.

Organizational Behavior. 2nd ed. W. Jack Duncan. LC 80-82460. (Illus.). 464p. 1981. text ed. 18.95 (ISBN 0-395-29640-4); write for info. instr's manual (ISBN 0-395-29641-2). HM.

Organizational Behavior. 2nd ed. Jerry L. Gray & Frederick A. Starke. (Marketing & Management Ser.). 464p. 1980. text ed. 18.95 (ISBN 0-675-08141-6); instructor's manual 3.95 (ISBN 0-686-63343-1). Merrill.

Organizational Behavior. 2nd ed. Don Hellriegel & John Slocum. (Management Ser.). (Illus.). 1979. text ed. 19.50 (ISBN 0-8299-0195-7); instrs.' manual avail. (ISBN 0-8299-0487-5). West Pub.

Organizational Behavior. Hodgetts. 1979. 19.95 (ISBN 0-7216-4713-8). Dryden Pr.

Organizational Behavior. 3rd ed. Joe Kelly. 1980. 0.19.95x (ISBN 0-256-02284-4). Irwin.

Organizational Behavior. Ed. by Steven Kerr. LC 78-26718. (Grid Series in Management). 1979. text ed. 20.95 (ISBN 0-88244-182-5). Grid Pub.

Organizational Behavior. Abraham Korman. (Illus.). 1977. 19.95 (ISBN 0-13-640938-5). P-H.

Organizational Behavior. R. Dennis Middlemist & Michael A. Hitt. 512p. 1981. text ed. 18.95 (ISBN 0-574-19390-1, 13-2390); instr's. guide avail. (ISBN 0-574-19391-X, 13-2391). SRA.

Organizational Behavior. S. Anwar Rashid & Maurice Archer. 336p. 1980. pap. text ed. 17.95 (ISBN 0-8403-2221-6). Kendall-Hunt.

Organizational Behavior: A Book of Readings. 6th ed. Keith Davis & John Newstrom. (Illus.). 468p. Date not set. text ed. price not set (ISBN 0-07-015500-3, C). McGraw.

Organizational Behavior: A Book of Readings. 6th ed. Keith Davis & John Newstrom. (Illus.). 468p. text ed. 11.95 (ISBN 0-07-015500-3). McGraw.

Organizational Behavior: An Applied Psychological Approach. W. Clay Hamner & Dennis W. Organ. 1978. 16.00x (ISBN 0-256-01811-1). Business Pubns.

Organizational Behavior & Administration: Cases & Readings. 3rd ed. Ed. by Paul R. Lawrence et al. 1976. text ed. 19.50x (ISBN 0-256-01760-3). Irwin.

Organizational Behavior & Management: A Contingency Approach. rev. ed. Ed. by Henry L. Tosi & W. Clay Hamner. LC 77-77475. (Series in Critical Sociologies). 1977. pap. text ed. 15.95 (ISBN 0-914292-09-9). Wiley.

Organizational Behavior & Personal Psychology. Kenneth A. Wexley & Gary A. Yukl. 1977. pap. 11.50 (ISBN 0-256-01884-7). Irwin.

Organizational Behavior & the Practice of Management. 3rd ed. David R. Hampton et al. 1978. 19.95x (ISBN 0-673-15119-0). Scott F.

Organizational Behavior: Concepts & Controversies. Stephen P. Robbins. (Illus.). 1979. ref. 19.95 (ISBN 0-13-641464-8). P-H.

Organizational Behavior in Education. 2nd ed. Robert G. Owens. (Illus.). 368p. 1981. text ed. 17.95 (ISBN 0-13-641050-2). P-H.

Organizational Behavior in Its Context: The Aston Programme 3. Derek S. Pugh & R. L. Payne. 1977. 19.95 o.p. (ISBN 0-566-00159-4, 01086-3, Pub. by Saxon Hse England). Lexington Bks.

Organizational Behavior in Schools. Robert G. Owens. LC 78-86521. (Education Ser). 1969. ref. ed. 14.95 (ISBN 0-13-641027-8). P-H.

Organizational Behavior: Incidents & Analysis. John V. Murray & Thomas J. Van Der Embse. LC 72-95928. 1973. pap. text ed. 13.95 (ISBN 0-675-08963-8). Merrill.

Organizational Behavior Management: A Manual for Supervisors. Raul C. Martinez. (Illus.). 148p. (Orig.). 1980. pap. 8.50 (ISBN 0-937230-00-6). NPD Corp.

Organizational Behavior: The Psychology of Effective Management. 2nd ed. David J. Lawless. (Illus.). 1979. text ed. 19.95 (ISBN 0-13-640706-4). P-H.

Organizational Behavior: Theory, Research & Application. Orlando Behling & Chester A. Schriesheim. 400p. 1976. text ed. 16.95 o.p. (ISBN 0-205-04690-8, 0846902). Allyn.

Organizational Behavior: Understanding & Prediction. 2nd ed. H. R. Bobbitt et al. LC 77-25383. 1978. ref. 19.95 (ISBN 0-13-641209-2). P-H.

Organizational Behaviour. rev. ed. Joe Kelly. 1974. text ed. 16.95x o.p. (ISBN 0-256-01434-5). Irwin.

Organizational Change & Development. Ed. by Gene W. Dalton et al. 1970. pap. text ed. 10.95x (ISBN 0-256-00606-7). Irwin.

Organizational Change Sourcebook I: Cases in Organization Development. Ed. by Bernard Lubin et al. LC 79-63006. 230p. 1979. pap. 12.95 (ISBN 0-88390-150-1). Univ Assocs.

Organizational Change Sourcebook Ii: Cases in Conflict Management. Ed. by Leonard D. Goodstein et al. LC 79-63006. 234p. 1979. pap. 12.95 (ISBN 0-88390-151-X). Univ Assocs.

Organizational Change Through Effective Leadership. R. Guest et al. 1977. 14.95 (ISBN 0-13-641316-1); pap. text ed. 9.95 (ISBN 0-13-641308-0). P-H.

Organizational Choice & Constraint. Malcolm Warner. (Illus.). 1978. 24.95 (ISBN 0-566-00180-2, 01619-5, Pub. by Saxon Hse England). Lexington Bks.

Organizational Communication: Abstracts, Analysis, & Overview, Vol. 5. Raymond L. Falcione & Howard H. Greenbaum. (Illus.). 288p. 1980. 30.00x (ISBN 0-8039-1384-2); pap. 15.00 (ISBN 0-8039-1385-0). Sage.

Organizational Communication Nineteen Seventy-Six; Abstracts, Analysis, & Overview. Raymond L. Falcione & Howard H. Greenbaum. 1977. pap. 8.00 o.p. (ISBN 0-931874-03-3). Am Busn Comm Assn.

Organizational Communication Nineteen Seventy-Seven: Abstracts, Analysis, & Overview. new ed. Howard H. Greenbaum & Raymond L. Falcione. 1979. pap. 9.00 o.p. (ISBN 0-931874-08-4). Am Busn Comm Assn.

Organizational Communication: Questions & Answers. Ragan Report Editors. 124p. (Orig.). 1980. pap. 10.00 (ISBN 0-931368-04-9). Ragan Comm.

Organizational Communication: The Essence of Effective Management. 2nd ed. Phillip V. Lewis. LC 79-19572. (Management Ser.). 1980. text ed. 18.95 (ISBN 0-88244-203-1). Grid Pub.

Organizational Decision Making. Marcus Alexis & C. Wilson. 1967. text ed. 17.95 (ISBN 0-13-641043-X). P-H.

Organizational Decision Processes. R. J. Ebert & T. R. Mitchell. LC 74-13324. (Illus.). 320p. 1975. 29.50x (ISBN 0-8448-0619-6); pap. 8.75x (ISBN 0-8448-0620-X). Crane-Russak Co.

Organizational Democracy: Participation & Self-Management. Ed. by G. David Garson & Michael P. Smith. LC 75-32375. (Sage Contemporary Social Science Issues: Vol. 22). 1976. 4.95x (ISBN 0-8039-0580-7). Sage.

Organizational Design. Jeffrey Pfeffer. Ed. by Kenneth D. Mackenzie. LC 77-86024. (Organizational Behavior Ser.). (Illus.). 1978. pap. text ed. 9.95x (ISBN 0-88295-453-9). AHM Pub.

Organizational Designs for Marketing Futures. Roy Hayhurst & Gordon Wills. (Studies in Management). 1972. 18.00x o.p. (ISBN 0-8464-0692-6). Beekman Pubs.

Organizational Development in Urban School Systems. Ed. by C. Brooklyn Derr. LC 74-78559. (Sage Contempory Social Science Issues: Vol. 14). 1974. 4.95x (ISBN 0-8039-0439-8). Sage.

Organizational Development Through Teambuilding. Thomas H. Patten, Jr. LC 80-20726. 350p. 1981. 21.95 (ISBN 0-471-66945-8, Pub. by Wiley-Interscience). Wiley.

Organizational Diagnosis: A Workbook of Theory. Marvin R. Weisbord. LC 77-93328. 1978. pap. text ed. 8.95 (ISBN 0-201-08357-4). A-W.

Organizational Dynamics: Diagnosis & Intervention. John P. Kotter. 1978. pap. text ed. 6.50 (ISBN 0-201-03890-0). A-W.

Organizational Entry: Recruitment, Selection, & Socialization of Newcomers. John P. Wanous. 1980. pap. text ed. 6.95 (ISBN 0-201-08456-2). A-W.

Organizational Formality & Performance in the Motor Carrier Industry. D. Daryl Wyckoff. LC 74-298. (Illus.). 1974. 15.95 (ISBN 0-669-91710-9). Lexington Bks.

Organizational Learning: A Theory of Action Perspective. Chris Argyris & Donald A. Schon. LC 77-81195. 1978. text ed. 10.95 (ISBN 0-201-00174-8). A-W.

Organizational Life Cycle: Issues in the Creation, Transformation, & Decline of Organizations. John R. Kimberly et al. LC 79-92446. (Social & Behavioral Science Ser.). 1980. text ed. 19.95x (ISBN 0-87589-459-3). Jossey-Bass.

Organizational Management. Earl F. Lundgren. LC 73-21940. (Illus.). 512p. 1974. text ed. 21.50 scp (ISBN 0-06-385355-8, HarpC). Har-Row.

Organizational Management Through Communication. Richard K. Allen. (Illus.). 1977. text ed. 15.50 scp (ISBN 0-06-040206-7, HarpC); inst. manual avail. (ISBN 0-685-79299-4). Har-Row.

Organizational Myths. Gunnar Westerlund & Sven-Erik Sjostrand. 1979. text ed. 11.95 (ISBN 0-06-318074-X, IntlDept). Har-Row.

Organizational Planning: Cases & Concepts. Jay W. Lorsch & Paul R. Lawrence. LC 72-79316. 1972. pap. text ed. 10.95 (ISBN 0-256-00456-0). Irwin.

Organizational Policy: Strat Mgmt. Higgins. 1979. 21.95 (ISBN 0-03-022186-2). Dryden Pr.

Organizational Politica. Charles Cachenmeyer. (Analysis Ser.). 74p. (Orig.). 1979. pap. text ed. 14.95 (ISBN 0-938526-00-6). Inst Analysis.

Organizational Politics of Criminal Justice: Policy in Context. Virginia Gray & Bruce Williams. LC 77-18590. 1980. 17.50x (ISBN 0-669-02108-3). Lexington Bks.

Organizational Processes. Francis D. Tuggle. Ed. by Kenneth D. Mackenzie. LC 77-86001. (Organizational Behavior Ser.). (Illus.). 1978. pap. text ed. 9.95x (ISBN 0-88295-455-5). AHM Pub.

Organizational Psychology. 2nd ed. Bernard M. Bass & Edward C. Ryterband. 1979. text ed. 20.95 (ISBN 0-205-06010-2, 7960107). Allyn.

Organizational Psychology. 3rd ed. Edgar G. Schein. (Foundations of Modern Psychology Ser.). (Illus.). 1980. text ed. 14.95 (ISBN 0-13-641340-4); pap. text ed. 8.95 (ISBN 0-13-641332-3). P-H.

Organizational Psychology: A Book of Readings. David A. Kolb & James M. McIntyre. (Ser. in Behavior Sciences in Business). 1979. text ed. 12.95 (ISBN 0-13-641274-2). P-H.

Organizational Psychology: An Experimental Approach. 3rd ed. D. Kolb et al. 1979. pap. 14.95 (ISBN 0-13-641258-0). P-H.

Organizational Renewel in a School District: Self-Help Through a Cadre of Organizational Specialists. Philip J. Runkel et al. LC 79-57252. 168p. (Orig.). 1980. pap. 7.50 (ISBN 0-936276-12-6). Ctr Educ Policy Mgmt.

Organizational Scientist: Their Professional Careers. Frwd. by Anselm L. Strauss. LC 63-12180. 1964. pap. 2.50 (ISBN 0-672-60835-9). Bobbs.

Organizational Strategy & Policy. 2nd ed. Paine. 1978. pap. 16.95. Dryden Pr.

Organizational Structure & Design. Ed. by Gene W. Dalton et al. 1970. pap. text ed. 10.95x (ISBN 0-256-00607-5). Irwin.

Organizational Structure in Its Context: The Aston Programme One. D. S. Pugh & D. J. Hickson. LC 75-26469. 248p. 1976. 21.95 (ISBN 0-347-01114-4, 00206-2, Pub. by Saxon Hse). Lexington Bks.

Organizational Structures. Kenneth D. Mackenzie. LC 77-86209. (Organizational Behavior Ser.). 1978. pap. text ed. 9.95x (ISBN 0-88295-452-0). AHM Pub.

Organizational Survival in the Performing Arts: The Making of the Seattle Opera. Mahmound Salem. LC 74-15422. (Special Studies). (Illus.). 1976. text ed. 19.95 o.p. (ISBN 0-275-05670-8). Praeger.

Organizational Systems: General Systems Approaches to Complex Organizations. Ed. by Frank Baker. 1973. text ed. 16.50x (ISBN 0-256-00236-3). Irwin.

Organizational Transitions: Managing Complex Change. R. Beckhard & R. T. Harris. 1977. 6.50 (ISBN 0-201-00335-X). A-W.

Organizational TV News. Tom Thompson. LC 80-81874. (Illus.). 217p. (Orig.). 1980. pap. 16.95 (ISBN 0-935608-00-1); pap. text ed. 16.95 (ISBN 0-686-63501-9). Media Concepts.

Organizations & Their Managing. Bertram M. Gross. LC 68-22642. 1968. text ed. 19.95 (ISBN 0-02-913140-5). Free Pr.

Organizations: Behavior, Design, & Change. George F. Wieland & Robert A. Ullrich. 1976. text ed. 16.95x o.p. (ISBN 0-256-01847-2). Irwin.

Organizations: Behavior, Structure, Processes. 3rd ed. James L. Gibson et al. 1979. 18.50x (ISBN 0-256-02210-0). Business Pubns.

Organizations, Clubs, Action Groups: How to Start Them, How to Run Them. Elsie E. Wolfers & Virginia B. Evansen. 256p. 1981. 11.95 (ISBN 0-312-58791-0). St Martin.

Organizations, Management, & Control: An Annotated Bibliography. Russell Stout, Jr. LC 79-3639. 256p. 1980. 15.00x (ISBN 0-253-14448-5). Ind U Pr.

Organizations of the Future: Interaction with the External Environment. Ed. by Harold Leavitt et al. LC 74-1733. (Special Studies). (Illus.). 220p. 1974. text ed. 25.95 (ISBN 0-275-28864-1). Praeger.

Organizations: Rationale, Natural, & Open Systems. W. Richard Scott. (Ser. in Sociology). (Illus.). 320p. 1981. text ed. 16.95 (ISBN 0-13-641977-1). P-H.

Organizations: Size & Intensity. Henry J. Travers. LC 78-52294. 1978. pap. text ed. 6.75x (ISBN 0-8191-0483-3). U Pr of Amer.

Organizations: Structure & Behavior. 3rd ed. J. Litterer. LC 80-15645. (Wiley Series in Management). 600p. 1980. pap. 14.95 (ISBN 0-471-07786-0). Wiley.

Organizations: Structure & Process. 2nd ed. Richard S. Hall. LC 76-45743. (Illus.). 384p. 1977. text ed. 17.95 (ISBN 0-13-642025-7). P-H.

Organizations: Theory & Analysis. Arthur G. Bedeian. 350p. 1980. text ed. 19.95 (ISBN 0-03-052956-5). Dryden Pr.

Organizations: Theory & Design. Patrick E. Connor. 1979. text ed. 21.95 (ISBN 0-574-19380-4, 13-2380); instr's guide avail. (ISBN 0-574-19381-2, 13-2381). SRA.

Organized Civil Servants: Public Employer-Employee Relations in California. Winston W. Crouch. LC 77-91767. 1978. 20.00x (ISBN 0-520-03626-3). U of Cal Pr.

Organized Complexity. R. Brunner & G. Brewer. LC 79-141936. 1971. 12.95 (ISBN 0-02-904850-8). Free Pr.

Organized Crime. Howard Abadinsky. 400p. 1980. text ed. 13.95 (ISBN 0-205-07097-3, 827097X); instrs' manual (ISBN 0-205-07098-1, 827097-X). Allyn.

Organized Crime. August Bequai. LC 77-18574. 1979. 17.95 (ISBN 0-669-02104-0). Lexington Bks.

Organized Labor in Latin America: Historical Case Studies of Workers in Dependent Societies. Hobart A. Spalding, Jr. LC 77-10203. 1977. 17.50x (ISBN 0-8147-7787-2). NYU Pr.

Organized Labor Movement in Puerto Rico. Miles Galvin. LC 77-74389. 1979. 16.50 (ISBN 0-8386-2009-4). Fairleigh Dickinson.

Organized Week. Tom Eaton. (YA) (gr. 7-12). 1977. pap. 1.25 (ISBN 0-590-09858-6, Schol Pap). Schol Bk Serv.

Organizing a Cost Containment Committee in the Hospital. American Hospital Association. LC 76-26173. 104p. 1979. 15.00 (ISBN 0-87258-272-8, 1450). Am Hospital.

Organizing a Speech: A Programmed Guide. 2nd ed. Judy L. Haynes. (Speech Communication Ser.). (Illus.). 192p. 1981. pap. text ed. 9.95 (ISBN 0-13-641530-X). P-H.

Organizing African Unity. Jon Woronoff. LC 72-16716. 703p. 1979. lib. bdg. 19.00 (ISBN 0-8108-0321-6). Scarecrow.

Organizing Against Crime: Redeveloping the Neighborhood. Anthony Sorrentino. LC 76-21840. 1977. 22.95 (ISBN 0-87705-301-4). Human Sci Pr.

Organizing Agricultural Labourers in India. Abdul Aziz. 1980. 7.50x (ISBN 0-8364-0651-6, Pub. by Minerva India). South Asia Bks.

Organizing & Documenting Data Processing Information. Thomas R. Gildersleeve. 1977. pap. text ed. 9.95x (ISBN 0-8104-5739-3). Hayden.

Organizing & Operating Profitable Workshop Classes. Janet Ruhe-Schoen. LC 80-25466. 1981. pap. 2.50 (ISBN 0-87576-092-9). Pilot Bks.

Organizing China: The Problem of Bureaucracy, 1949-1976. Harry Harding. LC 79-67772. 280p. 1981. text ed. 25.00x (ISBN 0-8047-1080-5). Stanford U Pr.

Organizing Data & Dealing with Uncertainty. National Council of Teachers of Mathematics. 1979. pap. 6.25 (ISBN 0-87353-141-8). NCTM.

Organizing Dixie: Organizing Alabama Workers in the Industrial Era. Philip Taft. LC 80-546. (Contributions in Labor History: No. 9). (Illus.). xxv, 288p. 1981. lib. bdg. 35.00 (ISBN 0-313-21447-6, TAL/). Greenwood.

Organizing for Peace: A Personal History of the Founding of the United Nations. Clark M. Eichelberger. LC 76-5127. 1977. 17.95 o.s.i. (ISBN 0-06-011114-3, HarpT). Har-Row.

Organizing for Women: Issues, Strategies, & Services. Dale A. Masi. LC 78-19577. (Illus.). 1981. 22.95 (ISBN 0-669-02577-1). Lexington Bks.

Organizing Interests in Western Europe: Pluralism, Corporatism & the Transformation of Politics. Ed. by Suzanne Berger. LC 80-16378. (Cambridge Studies in Modern Political Economies). (Illus.). 464p. Date not set. price not set (ISBN 0-521-23174-4). Cambridge U Pr.

Organizing, Operating & Terminating Subchapter S Corporations, Law, Taxation & Accounting. rev. ed. D. Larry Crumbley & P. Michael Davis. 1980. text ed. 35.00 (ISBN 0-88450-063-2, 1711-B). Lawyers & Judges.

Organizing Space Activities for World Needs. Ed. by Ernst A. Steinhoff. 1971. 67.00 (ISBN 0-08-006851-0). Pergamon.

Organizing the Community to Prevent Suicide. Ed. by Jack Zusman & David L. Davidson. 112p. 1971. 11.50 (ISBN 0-398-02448-0). C C Thomas.

Organizing the Library's Support: Donors, Volunteers, Friends. Ed. by Donald W. Krummel. (Allerton Park Institute Proceedings Ser.: No. 25). 1980. 10.00 (ISBN 0-87845-054-8). U of Ill Lib Sci.

Organizing the Non-System. Daniel L. Skoler. LC 76-27023. (Illus.). 1977. 19.50 (ISBN 0-669-00941-5). Lexington Bks.

Organizing the Presidency. Stephen Hess. 1976. 11.95 (ISBN 0-8157-3588-X); pap. 4.95 (ISBN 0-8157-3587-1). Brookings.

Organo-Metallic Compounds, Vol. 2. 3rd ed. M. Green. 376p. 1968. 35.00x o.p. (ISBN 0-412-11580-8, Pub. by Chapman & Hall). Methuen Inc.

Organo-Metallic Compounds, Vol. 2. 3rd ed. M. Green. 1968. 29.95 o.p. (ISBN 0-470-32471-6). Halsted Pr.

Organo-Transition Metal Compounds & Related Aspects of Homogenous Catalysis. B. L. Shaw & N. I. Tucker. (Pergamon Texts in Inorganic Chemistry: Vol. 23). 214p. 1975. text ed. 32.00 (ISBN 0-08-018872-9); pap. text ed. 17.50 (ISBN 0-08-018871-0). Pergamon.

Organoboron Chemistry, Vol. 1, Boron-Oxygen & Boron-Sulfur Compounds. H. Steinberg. LC 62-20337. 1964. 66.95 (ISBN 0-470-82093-4, Pub. by Wiley-Interscience). Wiley.

Organofluorine Chemicals & Their Industrial Applications. R. E. Banks. LC 79-40251. (Industrial Chemistry Ser.). 255p. 1979. 54.95x (ISBN 0-470-26720-8). Halsted Pr.

Organogenesis of Flowers: Photographic Text-Atlas. Rolf Sattler. LC 73-185736. (Illus.). 1973. 35.00x (ISBN 0-8020-1864-5). U of Toronto Pr.

Organometallic Syntheses: Non-Transitional Compounds, Vol. 2. Ed. by J. J. Eich. 1981. write for info. (ISBN 0-12-234950-4). Acad Pr.

Organophosphorus Monomers & Polymers. Y. Gefter. 1962. 32.00 (ISBN 0-08-009655-7). Pergamon.

Organophosphorus Pesticides Criteria (Dose-Effect Relationships) for Organophosphorus Compounds. Commission of the European Communities. Ed. by R. Derache. 1977. pap. text ed. 37.00 (ISBN 0-08-021993-4). Pergamon.

Organs for America: The Life & Work of David Tannenberg. William H. Armstrong. LC 67-26221. 1968. 9.95x o.p. (ISBN 0-8122-7000-2). U of Pa Pr.

Organs in Mexico. John Fesperman. (Illus.). 1981. 18.50 (ISBN 0-915548-07-0). Sunbury Pr.

Organs of Equilibrium & Orientation As a Control System. Ed. by M. Valentinuzzi. (Biomedical Engineering & Computation Ser.: Vol. 2). 194p. 1980. text ed. 45.00 (ISBN 3-7186-0014-5). Harwood Academic.

Organs of Our Time Two. Ed. by Homer D. Blanchard. 154p. write for info. Praestant.

Orgasm: Black on White. (Illus.). 4.95 (ISBN 0-910550-75-1). Centurion Pr.

Orgasms of Light. Ed. by Winston Leyland. (Illus.). 264p. 1980. 20.00 (ISBN 0-917342-53-4); pap. 7.95 o.p. (ISBN 0-917342-54-2). Gay Sunshine.

Orgasms of Light: The Gay Sunshine Anthology. Winston Leyland. (Poetry, Short Fiction, Graphics). (Illus.). 1977. lib. bdg. 20.00 (ISBN 0-917342-53-4, Pub. by Gay Sunshine); pap. 5.95 o.p. (ISBN 0-917342-54-2). Bookpeople.

Orgonomischer Funktionalismus. Wilhelm Reich. 110p. 1973. 35.00 (ISBN 0-374-22724-1). FS&G.

Orgy Lovers. (Illus.). 4.95 (ISBN 0-910550-76-X). Centurion Pr.

Orielton-the Human & Natural History of a Welsh Manor. Ronald Lockley. (Illus.). 1978. 15.00 (ISBN 0-233-96928-4). Transatlantic.

Orient Express: The Life & Times of the World's Most Famous Train. E. H. Cookridge. LC 78-57119. (Illus.). 1980. pap. 5.95 (ISBN 0-06-090770-3, CN 770, CN). Har-Row.

Orient Romanesque en Frances: 1704-1789, Tomes I & II. Marie-Louise Dufrenoy. 1978. pap. text ed. 40.00x (ISBN 0-685-59420-3). Humanities.

Orientacion Sicologica Eficaz. Gary Collins. Tr. by Miguel Blanch from Eng. 206p. (Orig., Span.). 1979. pap. 4.50 (ISBN 0-89922-136-X). Edit Caribe.

Oriental Americans. H. Brett Melendy. LC 73-187154. (Immigrant Heritage of America Ser.). 1972. lib. bdg. 9.95 (ISBN 0-8057-3254-3). Twayne.

Oriental Anecdotes; or, the History of Hardun Alrachid, 1764, 2 vols. in 1. Marianne A. Fauques. (Novel in England, 1700-1775 Ser). 1974. lib. bdg. 50.00 (ISBN 0-8240-1166-X). Garland Pub.

Oriental Architecture. Mario Bussagli et al. Ed. by Mario Bussagli. LC 74-4024. (History of World Architecture Ser.). (Illus.). 436p. 1975. 45.00 (ISBN 0-8109-1016-0). Abrams.

Oriental Architecture in the West. Patrick Conner. (Illus.). 1980. 30.00 (ISBN 0-500-34079-X). Thames Hudson.

Oriental Asia: Themes Toward a Geography. Joseph E. Spencer. LC 73-5645. (Illus.). 160p. 1973. ref. ed. 9.95 (ISBN 0-13-642843-6); pap. text ed. 6.95 (ISBN 0-13-642835-5). P-H.

Oriental Barbecues: Recipes & Menus from Six Asian Countries. May W. Trent. (Illus.). 96p. 1974. pap. 2.95 o.s.i. (ISBN 0-02-010380-8, Collier). Macmillan.

Oriental Blue & White. 3rd ed. Harry Garner. 1970. 35.00 (ISBN 0-571-04702-5, Pub. by Faber & Faber). Merrimack Bk Serv.

Oriental Carpet Designs in Full Color. Friedrich Sarre & Trenkwald Sarre. (Illus.). 1980. pap. 6.00 (ISBN 0-486-23835-0). Dover.

Oriental Ceramic Art. S. W. Bushell. (Illus.). 432p. 1980. 35.00 (ISBN 0-517-52581-X). Crown.

Oriental Cook Book. Sunset Editors. LC 78-100903. (Illus.). 96p. 1970. pap. 4.95 (ISBN 0-376-02533-6, Sunset Bks.). Sunset-Lane.

Oriental Cooking in a Yankee Kitchen. Aung Thein. (Illus., Orig.). Date not set. pap. cancelled (ISBN 0-914016-54-7). Phoenix Pub.

Oriental Export Market Porcelain & Its Influence on European Wares. Geoffrey Godden. (Illus.). 384p. 1980. text ed. 65.00x (ISBN 0-246-11057-0). Humanities.

Oriental Export Porcelain & Its Influence on European Wares. Geoffrey Godden. (Illus.). 1979. 69.95x (ISBN 0-8464-0052-9). Beekman Pubs.

Oriental Herbal Wisdom. Masaru Toguchi. (Orig.). 1973. pap. 1.50 o.s.i. (ISBN 0-515-02906-8, V2906). Jove Pubns.

Oriental Methods of Mental & Physical Fitness: The Complete Book of Meditation, Kinesitherapy & Martial Arts in China, India & Japan. Pierre Huard & Ming Wong. LC 76-23163. (Funk & W Bk.). (Illus.). 1977. 16.95 o.s.i. (ISBN 0-308-10271-1, TYC-T); pap. 9.95 o.s.i. (ISBN 0-308-10277-0, TYC-T). T Y Crowell.

Oriental Rug. Luciano Coen & Louise Duncan. LC 76-5119. (Illus.). 1978. 35.00 o.s.i. (ISBN 0-06-010824-X, HarpT). Har-Row.

Oriental Rug Designs in Needlepoint. Grethe Sorenson. (Illus.). 112p. 1980. cancelled (ISBN 0-684-16622-4, ScribT). Scribner.

Oriental Rug Primer. Aram Jerrehian. (Illus.). 1980. 12.95 (ISBN 0-87196-494-5). Facts on File.

Oriental Rug Primer: Buying & Understanding New Oriental Rugs. Aram K. Jerrehian. LC 79-19724. (Illus.). 1980. lib. bdg. 12.90 (ISBN 0-89471-078-8); pap. 7.95 (ISBN 0-89471-077-X). Running Pr.

Oriental Rugs. Herman Haack. 12.25 o.p. (ISBN 0-8231-3012-6). Branford.

Oriental Rugs. Hermann Haack. (Illus.). 1960. 14.95 o.p. (ISBN 0-571-07018-3, Pub. by Faber & Faber). Merrimack Bk Serv.

Oriental Rugs & Carpets. rev. enl. ed. Authur U. Dilley. Ed. by M. S. Dimand. LC 59-13247. (Illus.). 1959. 18.25 o.s.i. (ISBN 0-397-00110-X). Lippincott.

Oriental Rugs Antique & Modern. Walter A. Hawley. (Illus.). 1970. pap. 6.95 (ISBN 0-486-22366-3). Dover.

Oriental Rugs, Antique & Modern. Walter A. Hawley. (Illus.). 12.50 (ISBN 0-8446-4551-6). Peter Smith.

Oriental Rugs in Color. Preben Liebetrau. 1963. 8.95 (ISBN 0-02-571840-1). Macmillan.

Oriental Rugs in the Metropolitan Museum of Art. M. S. Dimand & Jean Mailey. LC 73-2846. (Illus.). 1973. 65.00 (ISBN 0-87099-124-8). Metro Mus Art.

Oriental Rugs: The Illustrated Guide. Janice S. Herbert. 1978. 19.95 (ISBN 0-02-551120-3). Macmillan.

Oriental Thought: An Introduction to the Philosophical & Religious Thought of Asia. Yong C. Kim. (Littlefield, Adams Quality Paperback Ser.: No. 365). 130p. 1981. pap. 3.95 (ISBN 0-8226-0365-9). Littlefield.

Oriental Thought: An Introduction to the Philosophical & Religious Thought of Asia. Yong Choon Kim. 130p. 1981. Repr. of 1973 ed. 8.95x (ISBN 0-8476-6972-6). Rowman.

Orientalism. Edward W. Said. LC 79-10497. 1979. pap. 5.95 (ISBN 0-394-74067-X, Vin). Random.

Orientation by Disorientation: Studies on Literary Criticism & Biblical Literary Criticism Presented in Honor of William A. Beardslee. Ed. by Richard A. Spencer. (Pittsburgh Theological Monograph Ser.: No. 35). 1980. pap. text ed. 13.50 (ISBN 0-915138-44-1). Pickwick.

Orientation Effects in Solid Polymers. G. B. Bodor. (Journal of Polymer Science Symposium: No. 58). 1978. 27.95 (ISBN 0-471-04658-2, Pub. by Wiley-Interscience). Wiley.

Orientation in American English. Texts 1-4. 3.95 ea. (ISBN 0-88499-258-6); Texts 5-6. 4.95 ea.; wkbks. & tapebks. vols. 1-4 2.95 ea.; readers vols. 1-6 3.95 ea. (ISBN 0-685-70385-1); review set avail.; tapes & cassettes avail. (ISBN 0-88499-150-4); teacher's manual 6.95 (ISBN 0-88499-257-8). Inst Mod Lang.

Orientation Manual for INIS & AGRIS (OMINAS) Nineteen Seventy-Nine. 1979. pap. 10.75 (ISBN 9-2017-8279-9, IN/18/RO, IAEA). Unipub.

Orientation to Health Services. Ruth M. Lee. LC 77-15094. pap. 8.85 (ISBN 0-672-61434-0); tchr's manual 3.33 (ISBN 0-672-61435-9). Bobbs.

Orientation to Listening & Audience Analysis. rev. ed. William Colburn & Sanford Weinberg. Ed. by Ronald Applbaum & Roderick Hart. (MODCOM, Modules in Speech Communication Ser.). 1980. pap. text ed. 2.25 (ISBN 0-574-22568-4, 13-5568). SRA.

Orientation to Mental Retardation: A Programmed Text. Patrick J. Flanigan et al. (Illus.). 216p. 1973. 13.75 (ISBN 0-398-00584-2). C C Thomas.

Orientation to Professional Practice. W. D. Nilsson & Philip Hicks. (Illus.). 400p. 1980. text ed. 19.95 (ISBN 0-07-046571-1, C). McGraw.

Orientation to the Theater. 2nd ed. Theodore W. Hatlen. (Illus., Orig.). 1972. pap. text ed. 14.95 (ISBN 0-13-642090-7). P-H.

Orientation to the Theatre. 3rd ed. Theodore W. Hatlen. (Speech & Theatre Ser.). (Illus.). 512p. 1981. text ed. 14.95 (ISBN 0-13-642108-3). P-H.

Orientations in Geochemistry. U.S. National Committee for Geochemistry, Div. of Earth Sciences. (Illus.). 152p. 1974. pap. 8.00 (ISBN 0-309-02147-2). Natl Acad Pr.

Orientations to Mass Communication. rev. ed. Norman Felsenthal. Ed. by Ronald Applbaum & Roderick Hart. (Modcom, Modules in Speech Communication Ser.). 1980. pap. text ed. 2.25 (ISBN 0-574-22569-2, 13-5569). SRA.

Orientations to Researching Communication. Leathers. Ed. by Ronald Applbaum & Roderick Hart. LC 77-20988. (MODCOM - Modules in Speech Communication). 1978. pap. text ed. 2.25 (ISBN 0-574-22535-8, 13-5535). SRA.

Orienteering. Boy Scouts of America. LC 19-600. (Illus.). 32p. (gr. 6-12). 1974. pap. 0.70x (ISBN 0-8395-3385-3, 3385). BSA.

Orienteering. rev. 2nd ed. John Disley. LC 67-22990. (Illus.). 176p. 1979. lib. bdg. 6.95 (ISBN 0-8117-2023-3). Stackpole.

Orienteering. rev ed. Martin Henley. (EP Sport Ser.). (Illus.). 119p. 1978. 12.95 (ISBN 0-8069-9136-4, Pub. by EP Publishing England); pap. 6.95 (ISBN 0-8069-9138-0). Sterling.

Orienteering Handbook: Physical Education Ser. Anne Anthony. (Illus.). 64p. 1980. pap. text ed. 5.95 (ISBN 0-88839-047-5). Hancock Hse.

Origami. Georgie Davidson. LC 75-44992. (Larousse Craft Ser.). (Illus.). 1978. pap. 5.95 (ISBN 0-88332-027-4, 8036). Larousse.

Origami for Displays. Toshie Takahama. (Illus.). 32p. (Orig.). 1979. pap 3.50 (ISBN 0-8048-1350-7, Pub by Shufunotomo Co. Ltd. Japan). C E Tuttle.

Origami for Fun: Thirty-One Basic Models. Toshie Takahama. (Illus.). 32p. (Orig.). 1980. Repr. of 1973 ed. pap. 3.50 (ISBN 0-8048-1352-3, Shufuntomo Co Ltd Japan). C E Tuttle.

Origami in the Classroom. 2 vols. Chiyo Araki. LC 65-13412. (Illus.). (gr. 1 up). 1965-68. bds. 8.95 ea. Vol. 1 (ISBN 0-8048-0452-4). Vol. 2 (ISBN 0-8048-0453-2). C E Tuttle.

Origami, Japanese Paper Folding, 3 Vols. Florence Sakade. LC 57-10685. (Illus., Orig.). (gr. 2 up). pap. 2.50 ea. Vol. 1 (ISBN 0-8048-0454-0). Vol. 2 (ISBN 0-8048-0455-9). Vol. 3 (ISBN 0-8048-0456-7). C E Tuttle.

Origami Made Easy. Kunihiko Kasahara. LC 73-83956. (Illus.). 128p. 1973. pap. 4.95 (ISBN 0-87040-253-6). Japan Pubns.

Origami: The Art of Paper-Folding. Robert Harbin. (Funk & W Bk.). (Illus.). 1969. pap. 1.75 o.s.i. (ISBN 0-308-90099-5, F67, TYC-T). T Y Crowell.

Origami Toys: Fifteen Simple Models. Toshie Takahama. (Illus.). 32p. (Orig.). 1979. pap. 3.50 (ISBN 0-8048-1351-5, Pub by Shufunotomo Co. Ltd. Japan). C E Tuttle.

Origen, Prayer, Exhortation to Martyrdom. Ed. by W. J. Burghardt et al. (ACW Ser.: No. 19). 1954. 11.95 (ISBN 0-8091-0256-0). Paulist Pr.

Origin: A Biographical Novel of Charles Darwin. Irving Stone. LC 79-6655. 744p. 1980. 14.95 (ISBN 0-385-12064-8). Doubleday.

Origin & Chemistry of Petroleum: Oriceedings of the Third Annual Karcher Symposium, Oklahoma, May 4, 1979. G. Atkinson. Ed. by J. J. Zuckerman. (Illus.). 120p. 1981. 24.00 (ISBN 0-08-026179-5). Pergamon.

Origin & Cultivation of Shade & Ornamental Trees. Li Hui-Lin. LC 62-11271. (Illus.). 288p. 1974. pap. 5.95 (ISBN 0-8122-1070-0, Pa Paperbks). U of Pa Pr.

Origin & Development of Iron & Steel Technology in Japan. 81p. 1980. pap. 5.00 (ISBN 92-808-0089-2, TUNU-056, UNU). Unipub.

Origin & Development of the Bengali Language, 3 vols. Suniti K. Chatterji. 1971. Set. text ed. 47.50x (ISBN 0-685-85182-6); Vol. 1. text ed. (ISBN 0-04-491007-X). Vol. 2. text ed. (ISBN 0-04-491008-8); Vol. 3. text ed. (ISBN 0-04-491009-6). Allen Unwin.

Origin & Distribution of the Elements. L. H. Ahrens. 1979. text ed. 115.00 (ISBN 0-08-022947-6); pap. text ed. 50.00 (ISBN 0-08-022948-4). Pergamon.

Origin & Early Evolution of Angiosperms. Ed. by Charles B. Beck. (Illus.). 416p. 1976. 25.00x (ISBN 0-231-03857-7). Columbia U Pr.

Origin & Fate of Chemical Residues in Food, Agriculture & Fisheries: Proceedings. FAO IAEA. (Illus.). 189p. 1976. pap. 17.75 (ISBN 92-0-111375-7, ISP399, IAEA). Unipub.

Origin & Natural History of Cell Lines: Proceedings of a Conference Held at Accademia Nazionale Dei Lincei, Rome, Italy, October 1977. Ed. by Claudio Barigozzi. LC 78-12805. (Progress in Clinical & Biological Research: Vol. 26). 1979. 22.00 (ISBN 0-8451-0026-2). A R Liss.

Origin & Nature of Our Institutional Models. Wolf Wolfensberger. 3.50 (ISBN 0-937540-03-X, HPP-4). Human Policy Pr.

Origin & Principles of the American Revolution, Compared with the Origin & Principles of the French Revolution. Friedrich Von Gentz. Ed. by Richard Loss. LC 77-16175. 1977. Repr. of 1800 ed. lib. bdg. 20.00 (ISBN 0-8201-1302-6). Schol Facsimiles.

Origin & Relationships of the California Flora. Peter H. Raven & Daniel I. Axelrod. (Publications in Botany: No. 72). 1978. pap. 7.50x (ISBN 0-520-09573-1). U of Cal Pr.

Origin & Significance of the Frankfurt School: A Marxist Perspective. Phil Slater. (International Library of Sociology). 1976. 22.50x (ISBN 0-7100-8438-2). Routledge & Kegan.

Origin & Survival of African Folktales in the New World. Phanuel Egejuru. Date not set. 8.95 (ISBN 0-933184-23-9); pap. 4.95 (ISBN 0-933184-24-7). Flame Intl. Postponed.

Origin & the Jews. N. R. De Lange. LC 75-36293. (Oriental Publications Ser.: No. 25). 160p. 1977. 36.00 (ISBN 0-521-20542-5). Cambridge U Pr.

Origin of Adaptations. Verne Grant. LC 63-11695. (Illus.). 1963. 27.50x (ISBN 0-231-02529-7); pap. 12.50x (ISBN 0-231-08648-2). Columbia U Pr.

Origin of Aryans: From Scythis to India. G. M. Bongard-Levin. Tr. by H. C. Gupta. 124p. 1980. text ed. cancelled (ISBN 0-8426-1663-2). Verry.

Origin of Certain Place Names in the United States. Henry Gannett. LC 68-23159. 1971. Repr. of 1902 ed. 15.00 (ISBN 0-8103-3382-1). Gale.

Origin of Christology. C. F. Moule. LC 76-11087. 1977. 23.95 (ISBN 0-521-21290-1); pap. 7.50x (ISBN 0-521-29363-4). Cambridge U Pr.

Origin of Continents & Oceans. Alfred Wegener. Tr. by John Biram. (Illus.). 1966. pap. 4.50 (ISBN 0-486-61708-4). Dover.

Origin of English Surnames. P. H. Reaney. 1980. pap. 8.95 (ISBN 0-7100-0353-6). Routledge & Kegan.

Origin of Formalism in Social Science. Jeffrey T. Bergner. LC 80-17484. 160p. 1981. lib. bdg. 16.00 (ISBN 0-226-04362-2). U of Chicago Pr.

Origin of Forms & Qualities: The Theorical Part. Robert Boyle. Ed. by Bill Barger. (Orig.). 1976. pap. 5.95x o.p. (ISBN 0-917044-02-9). Sheffield Pr.

Origin of Genetics: A Mendel Source Book. Ed. by Curt Stern & Eva R. Sherwood. LC 66-27948. (Illus.). 1966. pap. text ed. 8.95x (ISBN 0-7167-0655-5). W H Freeman.

Origin of Homo Sapiens. (Ecology & Conservation Ser.). (Illus.). 321p. 1972. 24.75 (ISBN 92-3-000948-2, U443, UNESCO). Unipub.

Origin of Language: A Formal Theory of Representation. Eric Gans. 1981. 19.95x (ISBN 0-520-04202-6). U of Cal Pr.

Origin of Life: A Warm Little Pond. Clair E. Folsome. LC 78-10809. (Biology Ser.). (Illus.). 1979. text ed. 16.95x (ISBN 0-7167-0294-0); pap. text ed. 8.95x (ISBN 0-7167-0293-2). W H Freeman.

Origin of Negative Dialectics: Theodor W. Adorno, Walter Benjamin, & the Frankfurt Institute. Susan Buck-Morss. LC 76-55103. 1979. pap. text ed. 7.95 (ISBN 0-02-905150-9). Free Pr.

Origin of Our Knowledge of Right & Wrong. Franz Brentano. Tr. by R. Chisholm & E. Schneewind. (International Library of Philosophy & Scientific Method). 1976. Repr. of 1969 ed. 14.50x (ISBN 0-391-00980-X). Humanities.

Origin of Russian Communism. Nicolas Berdyaev. 1960. pap. 3.95 (ISBN 0-472-06034-1, 34, AA). U of Mich Pr.

Origin of Russian Communism. Nicolas Berdyaev. 239p. 1980. Repr. of 1937 ed. lib. bdg. 30.00 (ISBN 0-89760-047-9). Telegraph Bks.

Origin of Sedimentary Rock. 2nd ed. H. Blatt et al. 1980. 30.95 (ISBN 0-13-642710-3). P-H.

Origin of Species. abr. ed. Charles Darwin. Ed. by Philip Appleman. 1975. pap. text ed. 2.95x (ISBN 0-393-09219-4). Norton.

Origin of Table Manners. Claude Levi-Strauss. Tr. by John Weightman & Doreen Weightman. LC 77-11810. (Science of Mythology Ser.: Vol. 3). (Illus.). 1979. 30.00 o.s.i. (ISBN 0-06-012587-X, HarpT). Har-Row.

Origin of the Book of Sindbad. B. E. Perry. 1960. 17.35x (ISBN 3-11-000538-7). De Gruyter.

Origin of the Chemical Elements. R. J. Tayler & A. S. Everest. (Wykeham Science Ser.: No. 23). 1972. 9.95x (ISBN 0-8448-1150-5). Crane Russak Co.

Origin of the Upper Jurassic Limestones of the Swabian Alb (Southwest Germany) M. P. Gwinner. Ed. by H. Fuechtbauer. (Contributions to Sedimentology Ser.: Vol. 5). (Illus.). 75p. (Orig.). 1976. pap. 37.50x (ISBN 3-510-57005-7). Intl Pubns Serv.

Origin of Variation of Races of Mankind & the Cause of Evolution. Betty Y. Ho. LC 68-57933. (Illus., Orig.). 1969. pap. 4.00 (ISBN 0-9600148-1-0). Juvenescent.

Original Americans: US Indians. James Wilson. (Minority Rights Group Ser.: No. 31). 28p. 1976. pap. 2.50 (ISBN 0-89192-128-1). Interbk Inc.

Original & Sprynge of All Sectes & Orders by Whome, Wha or Where (Sic) They Beganne. Tr. by M. Coverdale from Dutch. LC 79-84127. (English Experience Ser.: No. 946). 140p. (Eng.). 1979. Repr. of 1537 ed. lib. bdg. 11.50 (ISBN 90-221-0946-1). Walter J Johnson.

Original Art Deco Designs. William Rowe. (Pictorial Archive Ser.). (Illus., Orig.). 1973. pap. 4.00 (ISBN 0-486-22567-4). Dover.
Original Descriptions of Siwalik Primates Collected Mostly by American Expeditions, Reprinted from Various Sources. LC 78-72724. 1980. 26.50 (ISBN 0-404-18299-2). AMS Pr.
Original Floating Zoo. Jim Roberts. (Action Bks). (Illus.). 12p. (ps-3). 1975. pap. 3.50 (ISBN 0-570-07107-0, 56-1284). Concordia.
Original Journals of Henry Smith Turner: With Stephen Watts Kearny to New Mexico & California. Henry S. Turner. Ed. by Dwight L. Clarke. (American Exploration & Discovery Ser.: No. 51). 1967. pap. 2.95 (ISBN 0-8061-1157-7). U. of Okla Pr.
Original Letters of Eminent Literary Men of the 16th, 17th, & 18th Centuries. Illus. by Henry Ellis. 460p. 1980. Repr. lib. bdg. 85.00 (ISBN 0-89984-199-6). Century Bookbindery.
Original Mother Goose's Melody. Ed. by John Newbery et al. LC 68-31093. 1969. Repr. of 1892 ed. 15.00 (ISBN 0-8103-3485-2). Gale.
Original Music for Men's Voices: A Selected Bibliography. 2nd ed. William Tortolano. LC 80-25917. 206p. 1981. 12.50 (ISBN 0-8108-1386-6). Scarecrow.
Original Poems for Infant Minds, Repr. Of 1805 Ed. Jane Taylor & Ann Taylor. Bd. with Rhymes for the Nursery. Repr. of 1806 ed. LC 75-32151. (Classics of Children's Literature, 1621-1932: Vol. 17). 1977. PLB 38.00 (ISBN 0-8240-2265-3). Garland Pub.
Original Sins. Lisa Alther. LC 80-22823. 608p. 1981. 13.95 (ISBN 0-394-51685-0). Knopf.
Original Thai Cookbook. Jennifer Brennan. (Illus.). 276p. 1981. 12.95 (ISBN 0-399-90110-8). Marek.
Original Vermonters: Native Inhabitants, Past & Present. William Haviland & Marjory W. Power. (Illus.). 320p. 1981. 16.50 (ISBN 0-87451-196-8). U Pr of New Eng.
Origines De L'opera Francais. C. Nuitter & E. Thoinan. LC 77-4106. (Music Reprint Ser., 1977). 1977. Repr. of 1886 ed. lib. bdg. 32.50 (ISBN 0-306-70895-7). Da Capo.
Origins: A Short Etymological Dictionary of Modern English. Eric Partridge. 1977. 45.00 (ISBN 0-02-594840-7). Macmillan.
Origins & Destinations: Family, Class & Education in Modern Britain. Albert H. Halsey & Anthony F. Heath. (Illus.). 250p. 1980. text ed. 29.50x (ISBN 0-19-827224-3); pap. 12.95x (ISBN 0-19-827249-9). Oxford U Pr.
Origins & Early Development in Shi'a Islam. Syed H. Jafri. (Arab Background Ser.). 1979. text ed. 28.00x (ISBN 0-582-78080-2). Longman.
Origins & International Economics of Space Exploration. Bernard Lovell. LC 73-18325. 104p. 1973. 7.95 (ISBN 0-470-54851-7). Halsted Pr.
Origins & Meanings of Popular Phrases & Names. Basil Hargrave. LC 68-23164. 1968. Repr. of 1925 ed. 22.00 (ISBN 0-8103-3089-X). Gale.
Origins & Rise of Ethology. W. H. Thorpe. 21.95 (ISBN 0-03-053251-5). Praeger.
Origins: Creation Texts from the Ancient Mediterranean. Ed. by Charles Doria & Harris Lenowitz. LC 74-18844. 384p. 1976. pap. 4.95 (ISBN 0-385-01922-X, Anch). Doubleday.
Origins, Initiations. Kirk Robertson. 1980. 25.00 (ISBN 0-918824-19-2); pap. 4.00 (ISBN 0-918824-18-4). Turkey Pr.
Origins of a Tragedy. Samuel Williamson. (Problems in Civilization Ser.). (Orig.). 1981. pap. text ed. 3.95x (ISBN 0-88273-409-1). Forum Pr MO.
Origins of Academic Economics in the United States. Michael J. O'Connor. (Neglected American Economists Ser.). 1974. lib. bdg. 50.00 (ISBN 0-8240-1036-1). Garland Pub.
Origins of Academic Geography in the United States. Ed. by Brian W. Blouet & Teresa L. Stitcher. 1981. 37.50 (ISBN 0-208-01881-6, Archon). Shoe String.
Origins of American Conservation. Ed. by Henry E. Clepper. 1966. 18.50 (ISBN 0-8260-2060-7, Pub. by Wiley-Interscience). Wiley.
Origins of American Critical Thought, 1810-1835. William Charvat. 1961. pap. 1.65 o.p. (ISBN 0-498-04042-9, Prpta). A S Barnes.
Origins of American Intervention in First World War. Ross Gregory. LC 70-141588. (Essays in American History Ser). 1972. pap. 4.95x (ISBN 0-393-09980-6). Norton.
Origins of American Politics. Bernard Bailyn. LC 68-12665. 1968. 5.95 o.p. (ISBN 0-394-43941-4). Knopf.
Origins of British Aid Policy Nineteen Twenty-Four to Nineteen Forty-Five. D. J. Morgan. (Official History of Colonial Development Ser.). 1980. text ed. cancelled (ISBN 0-391-01684-9). Humanities.
Origins of Cauchy's Rigorous Calculus. Judith Grabiner. 368p. 1981. text ed. 27.50x (ISBN 0-262-07079-0). MIT Pr.
Origins of Christianity: Sources & Documents. Howard C. Kee. LC 73-4830. 320p. 1973. 9.95 (ISBN 0-13-642553-4). P-H.
Origins of Economic Thought & Justice. Joseph J. Spengler. LC 79-27026. (Political & Social Economy Ser.). 192p. 1980. 15.00x (ISBN 0-8093-0947-5). S Ill U Pr.
Origins of English Feudalism. R. Allen Brown. (Historical Problems; Studies & Documents). 1973. pap. text ed. 8.95x o.p. (ISBN 0-04-901021-2). Allen Unwin.
Origins of English Individualism. A. Macfarlane. LC 78-73956. 1979. 26.95 (ISBN 0-521-22587-6); pap. 7.50x (ISBN 0-521-29570-X). Cambridge U Pr.
Origins of Entrepreneurship in Meiji Japan. Johannes Hirschmeier. LC 64-20973. (East Asian Ser: No. 17). 1964. 16.50x (ISBN 0-674-64475-1). Harvard U Pr.
Origins of Europe: Four New Studies in Archeology & History. Ed. by Desmond Collins. (Apollo Eds.). (Illus.). 384p. 1976. pap. 6.95 o.s.i. (ISBN 0-8152-0396-9, TYC-T). T Y Crowell.
Origins of Evil in Hindu Mythology. Wendy D. O'Flaherty. 1977. 20.00x (ISBN 0-520-03163-6); pap. 8.95 (ISBN 0-520-04098-8). U of Cal Pr.
Origins of Faith & Life: Genesis A. (New Horizons Bible Study Ser.). 1981. pap. 1.75 leader's guide (ISBN 0-89367-052-9); pap. 2.25 study guide (ISBN 0-89367-053-7). Light & Life.
Origins of Feedback Control. Otto Mayr. 1970. 8.95x o.p. (ISBN 0-262-13067-X); pap. 3.95 (ISBN 0-262-63056-7, 283). MIT Pr.
Origins of Field Theory. L. Pearce Williams. LC 80-5710. 160p. 1980. lib. bdg. 15.50 (ISBN 0-8191-1175-9); pap. text ed. 7.50 (ISBN 0-8191-1176-7). U Pr of Amer.
Origins of Form. Christopher Williams. (Illus.). 160p. (Orig.). 1980. pap. 12.00 (ISBN 0-8038-5394-7). Hastings.
Origins of Human Cancer, 3 bk. set, Vol. 4. Cold Spring Harbor Conferences on Cell Proliferation. Ed. by H. H. Hiatt et al. LC 76-57915. (Illus.). 1889p. 1977. 125.00 (ISBN 0-87969-119-0). Cold Spring Harbor.
Origins of Human Competence. Burton L. White et al. LC 77-81793. 1979. 19.95 (ISBN 0-669-01943-7). Lexington Bks.
Origins of Icelandic Literature. Gabriel Turville-Petre. 1953. 35.00x (ISBN 0-19-811114-2). Oxford U Pr.
Origins of Intellect: Piaget's Theory. 2nd ed. John L. Phillips, Jr. LC 75-5703. (Illus.). 1975. text ed. 14.95x (ISBN 0-7167-0579-6); pap. text ed. 7.95x (ISBN 0-7167-0580-X). W H Freeman.
Origins of Knowledge & Imagination. Jacob Bronowski. LC 77-13209. (Silliman Lectures Ser.). 1978. 10.00 (ISBN 0-300-02192-5); pap. 3.95 (ISBN 0-300-02409-6). Yale U Pr.
Origins of Life & Evolution. Ed. by Harlyn O. Halvorson & Kensal E. Van Holde. LC 80-21901. (MBL Lectures in Biology: Vol. 1). 136p. 1980. 16.00 (ISBN 0-8451-2200-2). A R Liss.
Origins of Life on the Earth. Stanley L. Miller & Leslie E. Orgel. (Concepts of Modern Biology Ser). (Illus.). 208p. 1974. pap. 11.95x ref. ed. (ISBN 0-13-642074-5). P-H.
Origins of Madness: The Psychopathology of Animal Life. J. D. Keehn. (Illus.). 1979. text ed. 52.00 (ISBN 0-08-023725-8). Pergamon.
Origins of Man: Physical Anthropology. John Buettner-Janusch. LC 66-14128. 1966. 19.95 o.p. (ISBN 0-471-11790-0). Wiley.
Origins of Military Power in Spain, 1800-1854. Eric Christiansen. (Oxford Historical Monographs). 1967. 7.95x o.p. (ISBN 0-19-821828-1). Oxford U Pr.
Origins of Modern Biology. Url N. Lanham. LC 68-24478. (gr. 11-12). 1968. 17.50x (ISBN 0-231-02872-5); pap. 4.50x (ISBN 0-231-08660-1, 123). Columbia U Pr.
Origins of Modern English Society: 1780-1880. Harold Perkin. LC 76-384509. 1969. pap. 10.95 (ISBN 0-8020-6141-9). U of Toronto Pr.
Origins of Modern German Colonialism, 1871-1885. Mary E. Townsend. LC 74-2493. (Columbia University Studies in History, Economics, & Public Law). 205p. 1975. Repr. of 1921 ed. 15.75 (ISBN 0-86527-144-5). Fertig.
Origins of Modern Science. rev. ed. Herbert Butterfield. 1965. pap. text ed. 5.95 (ISBN 0-02-905070-7). Free Pr.
Origins of Molecular Biology: A Tribute to Jacques Monod. Ed. by Andre Lwoff & Agnes Ullman. 1979. 23.50 (ISBN 0-12-460480-3). Acad Pr.
Origins of Money. Philip Grierson. 1977. pap. text ed. 4.50x (ISBN 0-485-14115-9, Athlone Pr). Humanities.
Origins of Muhammadan Jurisprudence. Joseph Schact. 364p. 1979. pap. text ed. 12.50x (ISBN 0-19-825357-5). Oxford U Pr.
Origins of Nationalism in Tunsia. Nicola Ziadeh. (Arab Background Ser.). Repr. of 1969 ed. 8.00x (ISBN 0-685-77110-5). Intl Bk Ctr.
Origins of Open Field Agriculture. Ed. by R. T. Rowley. 288p. 1981. 26.50x (ISBN 0-389-20102-2). B&N.
Origins of Peace: A Study of Peacemaking & the Structure of Peace Settlements. Robert F. Randle. LC 72-80078. (Illus.). 1973. 19.95 (ISBN 0-02-925800-6). Free Pr.
Origins of Pest, Parasite, Disease & Weed Problems. Ed. by J. M. Cherrett & G. R. Sager. (British Ecological Society Symposia Ser.). 1977. 44.95 (ISBN 0-470-99121-6). Halsted Pr.
Origins of Polish Socialism: The History & Ideas of the First Polish Socialist Party, 1878-1886. Lucjan Blit. LC 70-152642. (International Studies). 1971. 23.50 (ISBN 0-521-08192-0). Cambridge U Pr.
Origins of Popular Superstitions & Customs. Thomas S. Knowlson. LC 68-30946. 1968. Repr. of 1910 ed. 18.00 (ISBN 0-8103-3357-0). Gale.
Origins of Popular Superstitutions & Customs. T. Sharper Knowlson. LC 80-329. 242p. 1980. Repr. of 1972 ed. lib. bdg. 9.95x (ISBN 0-89370-613-2). Borgo Pr.
Origins of Prussianism. Heinrich Von Treitschke. 1942. 14.25 (ISBN 0-86527-145-3). Fertig.
Origins of Psychopharmacology: From CPZ to LSD. Anne E. Caldwell. (American Lecture in Objective Psychiatry Ser.). 240p. 1970. pap. 19.50 photocopy edition, spiral (ISBN 0-398-00271-1). C C Thomas.
Origins of Scientific Sociology. John H. Madge. LC 62-11855. 1962. 14.95 (ISBN 0-02-919700-7); pap. text ed. 9.95 (ISBN 0-02-919710-4). Free Pr.
Origins of Scientific Thought. Giorgio De Santillana. pap. 2.95 o.p. (ISBN 0-452-25006-4, Z5006, Plume). NAL.
Origins of Segregation. Ed. by Joel R. Williamson. (Problems in American Civilization Ser.). 1968. pap. text ed. 4.95x o.p. (ISBN 0-669-46201-2). Heath.
Origins of Soviet-American Diplomacy. Robert P. Browder. 1953. 16.50x (ISBN 0-691-05627-7); pap. o.p. (ISBN 0-691-01053-6). Princeton U Pr.
Origins of Spain & Portugal. Harold Livermore. 1971. text ed. 13.50x o.p. (ISBN 0-04-946005-6). Allen Unwin.
Origins of the Chavin Culture. Chiaki Kano. LC 79-89241. (Studies in Pre-Columbian Art & Archaeology: No. 22). (Illus.). 87p. 1979. pap. 5.00 (ISBN 0-88402-092-4, Ctr Pre-Columbian). Dumbarton Oaks.
Origins of the Cold War. Ed. by Lloyd C. Gardner et al. 1970. pap. 9.95 (ISBN 0-471-00188-0). Wiley.
Origins of the Cultural Revolution: Contradictions Among the People 1956-1957, Vol. 1. Roderick Macfarquhar. 428p. 1974. 22.50x (ISBN 0-231-03841-0). Columbia U Pr.
Origins of the Fifth Amendment: The Right Against Self-Incrimination. Leonard W. Levy. 1971. pap. 7.95 (ISBN 0-19-501356-5, GB34, GB). Oxford U Pr.
Origins of the First World War. Luke Trainer. 1974. pap. text ed. 3.95 (ISBN 0-435-31900-0). Heinemann Ed.
Origins of the French Labor Movement. Bernard H. Moss. LC 75-3775. 1976. 16.00x (ISBN 0-520-02982-8). U of Cal Pr.
Origins of the French Revolution. William Doyle. 272p. 1981. 37.50 (ISBN 0-19-873020-9); pap. 14.95 (ISBN 0-19-873021-7). Oxford U Pr.
Origins of the Greek Nation: The Byzantine Period 1204-1461. Apostolos E. Vacalopoulos. Tr. by Ian N. Moles. (Byzantine Ser.). (Illus.). 1970. 27.50 (ISBN 0-8135-0659-X). Rutgers U Pr.
Origins of the Industrial Revolution in the U.S. David J. Jeremy. (Illus.). 544p. 1981. text ed. 32.50x (ISBN 0-262-10022-3). MIT Pr.
Origins of the Japanese Language. Roy A. Miller. LC 80-50871. (Publications on Asia of the School for International Studies: No. 34). (Illus.). 192p. 1980. 17.50 (ISBN 0-295-95766-2). U of Wash Pr.
Origins of the Korean War: Liberation & the Emergence of Separate Regimes. Bruce Cumings. LC 80-8543. (Illus.). 552p. 1981. 35.00x (ISBN 0-691-09383-0); pap. 14.50x (ISBN 0-691-10113-2). Princeton U Pr.
Origins of the Modern European State, Fourteen Fifty to Seventeen Twenty-Five. J. H. Shennan. 1980. text ed. 14.50x (ISBN 0-09-119030-4, Hutchinson U Pr); pap. text ed. 9.25x (ISBN 0-09-119031-2). Humanities.
Origins of the Modern Jew: Jewish Identity & European Culture in Germany, 1749-1824. Michael A. Meyer. LC 67-12384. (Waynebooks Ser: No. 32). 250p. 1972. 9.95x (ISBN 0-8143-1315-9); pap. 4.95x (ISBN 0-8143-1470-8). Wayne St U Pr.
Origins of the Novel. Marthe Robert. Tr. by Sacha Rabinovitch from Fr. LC 80-7970. 256p. 1980. 19.95x (ISBN 0-253-18824-5). Ind U Pr.
Origins of the Number Concept. Charles J. Brainerd. LC 78-21223. 1979. 22.60 (ISBN 0-275-24310-9). Praeger.
Origins of the Science of Crystals. John Burke. 1966. 20.00x (ISBN 0-520-00198-2). U of Cal Pr.
Origins of the Second Republic in Spain. Shlomo Ben-Ami. (Historical Monographs). 1978. 36.00x (ISBN 0-19-821871-0). Oxford U Pr.
Origins of the Second World War. Alan J. Taylor. 1978. pap. 2.25 (ISBN 0-449-30797-2, Prem). Fawcett.
Origins of the State & Civilization: The Process of Cultural Evolution. Elman R. Service. 1975. pap. text ed. 7.95 (ISBN 0-393-09224-0). Norton.
Origins of the Turbo-Jet Revolution. Edward W. Constant, II. LC 80-11802. (JH Studies in the History of Technology). 1981. 22.50x (ISBN 0-8018-2222-X). Johns Hopkins.
Origins of the War with Mexico: The Polk-Stockton Intrigue. Glenn W. Price. 1967. pap. 5.95x (ISBN 0-292-76003-5). U of Tex Pr.
Origins of the Whig Party: A Dissertation. Malcolm E. Carroll. LC 72-112705. (Law, Politics & History Ser). 1970. Repr. of 1925 ed. lib. bdg. 32.50 (ISBN 0-306-71917-7). Da Capo.
Origins of World War One: 1871-1914. Joachim Remak. 12.50 (ISBN 0-8446-0873-4). Peter Smith.
Origins of World War Two. Keith Eubank. LC 73-77338. (AHM Europe Since 1500 Ser.). 1969. pap. 5.95x (ISBN 0-88295-733-3). AHM Pub.
Origins of Zionism. David Vital. (Illus.). 412p. 1975. 12.95x (ISBN 0-19-827439-4); pap. 12.95x (ISBN 0-19-827439-4). Oxford U Pr.
Origins, Orient & Oriana. Charles F. Morris. LC 79-28664. (Illus.). xx, 491p. 1980. 56.00 (ISBN 0-935786-00-7). McCartan & Root.
Orion Blinded: Essays on Claude Simon. Ed. by Randi Birn & Karen Gould. LC 79-17687. 320p. 1981. 18.50 (ISBN 0-8387-2420-5). Bucknell U Pr.
Orkney. Patrick Bailey. (Island Ser.). (Illus.). 245p. 1974. 16.95 (ISBN 0-7153-5000-5). David & Charles.
Orkney. Ronald Miller. 1976. 19.95 o.p. (ISBN 0-7134-3131-8, Pub. by Batsford England). David & Charles.
Orkney & Shetland: An Archaeological Guide. Lloyd Laing. LC 74-76182. 1974. 16.95 (ISBN 0-7153-6305-0). David & Charles.
Orkney & Shetland: An Historical, Geographical, Social & Scenic Survey. 3rd ed. Eric Linklater. Rev. by James R. Nicolson. (Illus.). 285p. 1980. 20.00x (ISBN 0-7091-8142-6). Intl Pubns Serv.
Orlando, a Centennial History, 2 vols. Eve Bacon. Incl. Vol. 1. (Illus.). 1975. 17.76 (ISBN 0-913122-08-4); Vol. 2. (Illus.). 1977. 19.95 (ISBN 0-913122-10-6). LC 75-21374. 35.00 set (ISBN 0-913122-13-0). Mickler Hse.
Orlando Furioso: A New Prose Translation. Ludovico Ariosto. Tr. by Guido Waldman from It. 700p. 1974. text ed. 19.25x (ISBN 0-19-212576-1); pap. text ed. 6.95 o.p. (ISBN 0-19-281161-4). Oxford U Pr.
Orlando Furioso in English Heroical Vers. Ludovico Ariosto. LC 77-25638. (English Experience Ser.: No. 259). (Illus.). 424p. Repr. of 1591 ed. 51.00 (ISBN 90-221-0259-9). Walter J Johnson.
Orlando in Roncevalles: A Poem. John H. Merivale. Ed. by Donald H. Reiman. LC 75-29781. (Romantic Context Ser.: Poetry 1789-1830: Vol. 81). 1978. Repr. of 1814 ed. lib. bdg. 47.00 (ISBN 0-8240-2180-0). Garland Pub.
Orlando the Marmalade Cat & the Water Cats. Kathleen Hale. LC 72-185736. (Illus.). (gr. k-3). 1979. 6.95 (ISBN 0-224-00662-2, Pub. by Chatto Bodley Jonathan). Merrimack Bk Serv.
Orlando the Marmalade Cat Buys a Farm. Kathleen Hale. (Illus.). 32p. (gr. 1-4). 1980. 6.95 (ISBN 0-224-00754-8, Pub. by Chatto Bodley Jonathan). Merrimack Bk Serv.
Orlando the Marmalade Cat: The Frisky Housewife. Kathleen Hale. (Illus.). (gr. k-3). 1979. 6.95 (ISBN 0-224-00753-X, Pub. by Chatto Bodley Jonathan). Merrimack Bk Serv.
Orleanais ont la Parole. P. Biggs & C. Dalwood. (Illus.). 1977. pap. text ed. 4.00x (ISBN 0-582-33121-8); tchr's ed. 4.50x (ISBN 0-582-33122-6); tapes 17.50x (ISBN 0-582-37746-3). Longman.
Ormond. Maria Edgeworth. 1972. Repr. of 1900 ed. 13.00x (ISBN 0-7165-1799-X, Pub. by Irish Academic Pr Ireland). Biblio Dist.
Ormond, 2 vols. Marie Edgeworth. Ed. by Robert L. Wolff. (Ireland Nineteenth Century Fiction - Ser. Two). 786p. 1979. lib. bdg. 64.00 (ISBN 0-8240-3454-6). Garland Pub.

Orn, No. 2. Piers Anthony. 1975. pap. 1.75 (ISBN 0-380-00266-3, 40964). Avon.

Ornament & Its Application. Lewis F. Day. LC 71-136735. (Illus.). 1971. Repr. of 1904 ed. 18.00 (ISBN 0-8103-3324-4). Gale.

Ornament of Action. P. Holland. LC 78-1157. (Illus.). 1979. 42.00 (ISBN 0-521-22048-3). Cambridge U Pr.

Ornamental Carpentry of Nineteenth-Century American Houses: One Hundred Sixty Five Photographs. rev. ed. Ben Karp. Orig. Title: Wood Motifs in American Domestic Architecture. (Illus.). 96p. 1981. pap. price not set (ISBN 0-486-24144-0). Dover.

Ornamental Conifers. Charles R. Harrison. LC 74-11229. (Illus.). 1975. 19.75 o.s.i. (ISBN 0-02-845760-9). Hafner.

Ornamental Grasses. Roger Grounds. 216p. 1981. 16.95 (ISBN 0-442-24707-9). Van Nos Reinhold.

Ornamental Grasses. Mary Meyer. LC 75-11720. (Encore Editions). (Illus.). 1975. 2.95 o.p. (ISBN 0-684-15259-2, ScribT). Scribner.

Ornamental Horticulture As a Vocation. Stanley B. Moore. (gr. 11 up). 1969. text ed. 8.00x (ISBN 0-912178-01-9). Mor-Mac.

Ornamental Shrubs. Jaroslav Hofman. (Concise Guides Ser.). (Illus.). 1979. 7.95 (ISBN 0-600-38246-X). Transatlantic.

Ornamental Waterfowl. Hartmut Kolbe. Tr. by Ilse Lindsay from Ger. (Illus.). 260p. 1979. 22.50x (ISBN 0-8002-2277-6). Intl Pubns Serv.

Ornamentation in J. S. Bach's Organ Works. Putnam Aldrich. LC 78-17258. (Music Reprint, 1978 Ser.). (Illus.). 1978. Repr. of 1950 ed. lib. bdg. 15.95 (ISBN 0-306-77590-5). Da Capo.

Ornamentation in the Works of Frederick Chopin. John Dunn. LC 78-125069. (Music Ser). (Illus.). 1970. Repr. of 1921 ed. lib. bdg. 12.50 (ISBN 0-306-70006-9). Da Capo.

Ornaments & Mirrors in Stained Glass 1. Joel Wallach. (Illus.). 1979. pap. 4.95 o.p. (ISBN 0-934280-03-7). Glass Works.

Oro y el Futuro del Pueblo. Ed. by Rose De Tevis et al. (Illus.). 155p. 1979. pap. 5.00 (ISBN 0-918358-11-6). Pajarito Pubns.

Orphan. Samantha Mellors. 224p. (Orig.). 1980. pap. 2.25 (ISBN 0-515-05402-X). Jove Pubns.

Orphan Angel. Elinor Wylie. 337p. 1980. Repr. of 1926 ed. lib. bdg. 20.00 (ISBN 0-89984-506-1). Century Bookbindery.

Orphan Brigade: The Kentucky Confederates Who Couldn't Go Home. William C. Davis. LC 79-7491. (Illus.). 336p. 1980. 12.95 (ISBN 0-385-14893-3). Doubleday.

Orphan for Nebraska. Charlene J. Talbot. LC 78-12179. (gr. 4-6). 1979. 8.95 (ISBN 0-689-30698-9). Atheneum.

Orphans. Berniece Rabe. (gr. 4-7). 1978. PLB 7.95 (ISBN 0-525-36450-1). Dutton.

Orphans: A Play in Two Acts. James Prideaux. 1980. pap. 2.50 (ISBN 0-686-68850-3). Dramatists Play.

Orphan's Experience: Or the Hunter & Trapper. Being a History of the Personal Experience of M. V. B. Morrison. LC 75-7108. (Indian Captivities Ser.: Vol. 82). 1977. Repr. of 1868 ed. lib. bdg. 44.00 (ISBN 0-8240-1706-4). Garland Pub.

Orphans of the Living: A Study of Bastardy. Diana Dewar. 1968. text ed. 6.00x (ISBN 0-09-089120-1, Hutchinson U Lib). Humanities.

Orphans on the Guadalupe. Frances Alexander. 5.95 (ISBN 0-685-48788-1). Nortex Pr.

Orphan's Tale. Jay Neugeboren. LC 75-24989. 1976. 8.95 o.p. (ISBN 0-03-015271-2). HR&W.

Orphee. Jean Cocteau. Ed. by E. Freeman. (French Texts Ser.). (Illus.). 1976. pap. 10.25x (ISBN 0-631-00720-2, Pub. by Basil Blackwell). Biblio Dist.

Orphenica Lyra (Seville, 1554) Miguel De Fuenllana. Ed. by Charles Jacobs. (Illus.). 1978. 98.00x (ISBN 0-19-816128-X). Oxford U Pr.

Orphic Hymns. Ed. by Apostolos N. Athanassakis. LC 76-54179. (Society of Biblical Literature. Texts & Translation - Graeco-Roman Religion Ser.). (Illus.). 1977. pap. text ed. 7.50 (ISBN 0-89130-119-4, 060212). Scholars Pr Ca.

Orrible Synne. E. J. Burford. LC 74-172023. (Illus.). 1979. 15.00 (ISBN 0-7145-0978-7, Pub. by M Boyars); pap. 5.95 (ISBN 0-7145-1126-9, Pub. by M Boyars). Merrimack Bk Serv.

Orrible Synne: A Look at London Lechery from Roman to Cromwellian Times. E. J. Burford. (Illus.). 256p. 1973. text ed. 12.50x (ISBN 0-7145-0978-7). Humanities.

Orsini Inventories. Gisela Rubsamen. 224p. (Orig.). 1980. pap. 44.00 (ISBN 0-89236-010-0). J P Getty Mus.

Orson Welles: A Critical View. Andre Bazin. Tr. by Jonathan Rosenbaum from Fr. LC 74-15810. (Illus.). 1978. 12.50 o.s.i. (ISBN 0-06-010274-8, HarpT). Har-Row.

Ortega As Phenomenologist. Philip Silver. LC 78-667. 1978. 15.00x (ISBN 0-231-04544-1). Columbia U Pr.

Orthodontics in Dental Practice. Viken Sassouni. LC 70-141939. (Illus.). 1971. text ed. 37.50 o.p. (ISBN 0-8016-4300-7). Mosby.

Orthodontics: Principles & Practice. 3rd ed. T. M. Graber. LC 73-186950. (Illus.). 953p. 1972. text ed. 32.00 (ISBN 0-7216-4182-2). Saunders.

Orthodontics: The State of the Art. Ed. by Harry G. Barrer. LC 79-5043. (Illus.). 448p. 1981. 60.00x (ISBN 0-8122-7767-8). U of Pa Pr.

Orthodox & Heretical Perfectionism in the Johannine Community As Evident in the First Epistle of John. John L. Bogart. LC 77-5447. (Society of Biblical Literature. Dissertation Ser.). 1977. pap. 7.50 (ISBN 0-89130-138-0, 060133). Scholars Pr Ca.

Orthodox Approach to Philosophy. Apostolos Makrakis. Ed. by Orthodox Christian Educational Society. Tr. by Denver Cummings from Hellenic. (Logos & Holy Spirit in the Unity of Christian Thought Ser.: Vol. 1). 82p. 1977. pap. 2.50x (ISBN 0-938366-06-8). Orthodox Chr.

Orthodox Christian Meditations (Spiritual Discourses for the Orthodox Christians) Apostolos Makrakis. Ed. by Orthodox Christian Educational Society. Tr. by Denver Cummings from Hellenic. 143p. (Orig.). 1965. pap. 2.00x (ISBN 0-938366-22-X). Orthodox Chr.

Orthodox Church: Its Past & Its Role in the World Today. John Meyendorff. 258p. 1981. pap. write for info. (ISBN 0-913836-81-8). St Vladimirs.

Orthodox Churches & the West. Ed. by Derek Baker. (Studies in Church History Ser.: Vol. 13). 1976. 36.00x (ISBN 0-631-17180-0, Pub. by Basil Blackwell). Biblio Dist.

Orthodox Definition of Political Science. Apostolos Makrakis. Ed. by Orthodox Christian Educational Society. Tr. by Denver Cummings from Hellenic. 163p. 1968. pap. 2.00x (ISBN 0-938366-31-9). Orthodox Chr.

Orthodox Judaism in America. (American Jewish History Ser.: Vol. 69, Pt. 2). 1979. 6.00. Am Jewish Hist Soc.

Orthodox Protestant Debate. Apostolos Makrakis. Tr. by Denver Cummings. 1949. pap. 2.00x (ISBN 0-938366-37-8). Orthodox Chr.

Orthodox Saints: Spiritual Profiles for Modern Man, Vol. 3. George Poulos. Ed. by Nomikos M. Vaporis. (Illus.). 211p. 1980. text ed. 9.50 (ISBN 0-916586-40-5); pap. text ed. 5.50 (ISBN 0-916586-41-3). Holy Cross Orthodox.

Orthodox View on Abortion. J. Kowalczyk. 1979. pap. 1.50 (ISBN 0-686-27070-3). Light&Life Pub Co MN.

Orthodoxy. G. K. Chesterton. 160p. 1973. pap. 1.95 (ISBN 0-385-01536-4, Im). Doubleday.

Orthodoxy: A Creed for Today. A. M. Coniaris. 1972. pap. 5.95 (ISBN 0-937032-19-0). Light&Life Pub Co MN.

Orthodoxy in Massachusetts 1630-1650. Perry Miller. 8.00 (ISBN 0-8446-1312-6). Peter Smith.

Orthodoxy Life & Freedom. A. J. Philippou. LC 80-20616. 160p. 1980. lib. bdg. 17.95x (ISBN 0-89370-088-6); pap. 11.95x (ISBN 0-89370-089-4). Borgo Pr.

Orthogonal Polynomials. Geza Freud. LC 76-134028. 1971. 42.00 (ISBN 0-08-016047-6). Pergamon.

Orthogonal Polynomials. Paul G. Nevai. LC 78-32112. (Memoirs: No. 213). 1980. Repr. of 1979 ed. 7.80 (ISBN 0-8218-2213-6). Am Math.

Orthographic Projection Simplified. rev. ed. Charles Quinlan, Jr. (gr. 9-10). 1969. pap. text ed. 4.48 (ISBN 0-87345-056-6). McKnight.

Orthographic Way of Writing English Prosody. 1976. pap. 1.95. Primary Pr.

Orthography Studies. W. A. Smalley et al. 1964. 3.00 (ISBN 0-8267-0027-6, 08508). United Bible.

Orthomolecular Psychiatry: Treatment of Schizophrenia. Ed. by David Hawkins & Linus Pauling. LC 73-190182. (Illus.). 1973. text ed. 36.95x (ISBN 0-7167-0898-1). W H Freeman.

Orthopaedic Biomechanics. George Van B. Cochran. (Illus.). 1981. text ed. write for info. (ISBN 0-443-08027-5). Churchill. Postponed.

Orthopaedic Biomechanics: Orthopaedic Lectures, Vol. 5. Harold M. Frost. (Illus.). 664p. 1973. 49.50 (ISBN 0-398-02824-9). C C Thomas.

Orthopaedic Physician's Assistant Techniques. Charles E. Lambert & Donald Stone. LC 74-77819. (Allied Health Ser). 1975. pap. 7.05 (ISBN 0-672-61388-3). Bobbs.

Orthopaedic Rehabilitation. Vernon M. Nickel. (Illus.). 500p. 1981. text ed. price not set (ISBN 0-443-08060-7). Churchill. Postponed.

Orthopaedic Surgery in Infancy & Childhood. 5th ed. Albert Ferguson. (Illus.). 654p. 1981. write for info. (3167-8). Williams & Wilkins.

Orthopaedically Handicapped Child: Social, Emotional & Educational Adjustment, an Annotated Bibliography to the End of 1964. Doria Pilling. (General Ser). 60p. (Orig.). 1973. pap. text ed. 6.25x (ISBN 0-85633-004-3, NFER). Humanities.

Orthopaedics. 4th ed. H. Todd Stradford. (Medical Examination Review Book: Vol. 13). 1976. spiral bdg. 16.50 (ISBN 0-87488-113-7). Med Exam.

Orthopaedics & the Arts & Letters, Vol. 89. Association of Bone & Joint Surgeons. Ed. by Marshall Urist. (Clinical Orthopaedics & Related Research Ser.). 1972. 15.00 (ISBN 0-685-34610-2). Lippincott.

Orthopaedics in Emergency Care. F. Richard Schneider. LC 80-12233. (Illus.). 1980. pap. text ed. 11.95 (ISBN 0-8016-4348-1). Mosby.

Orthopaedics Review Book: Essay Questions & Answers. Ed. by H. Todd Stradford. 1973. text ed. 12.00 o.p. (ISBN 0-87488-349-0). Med Exam.

Orthopedic & Rehabilitation Nursing Continuing Education Review. V. Barbara Hynes. 1976. sprial bdg. 9.50 (ISBN 0-87488-397-0). Med Exam.

Orthopedic Appliances. Brian H. Day. (Illus.). 1972. 7.95 o.p. (ISBN 0-571-09051-6, Pub. by Faber & Faber); pap. 4.95 o.p. (ISBN 0-571-09947-5). Merrimack Bk Serv.

Orthopedic Medicine: A New Approach to Vertebral Manipulations. Robert Maigne. Tr. by W. T. Liberson. (Illus.). 456p. 1980. 30.50 (ISBN 0-398-02349-2). C C Thomas.

Orthopedic Nursing. 9th ed. Carroll B. Larson & Marjorie Gould. LC 77-3429. (Illus.). 1978. text ed. 18.95 (ISBN 0-8016-2866-0). Mosby.

Orthopedic Nursing. Ed. by Ann P. Smith. (Nursing Outline Ser.). 1974. spiral bdg. 8.00 (ISBN 0-87488-381-4). Med Exam.

Orthopedic Nursing: A Programmed Approach. 2nd ed. Nancy A. Brunner. 1975. pap. text ed. 7.95 o.p. (ISBN 0-8016-0838-4). Mosby.

Orthopedic Nursing: A Programmed Approach. 3rd ed. Nancy A. Brunner. LC 78-32020. (Illus.). 1979. pap. text ed. 11.50 (ISBN 0-8016-0833-3). Mosby.

Orthopedic Surgery Continuing Education Review. Ed. by Joseph A. Kopta et al. LC 80-80366. 1980. pap. 14.50 (ISBN 0-87488-398-9). Med Exam.

Orthopedics, Vol. 1. G. Bentley. (Operative Surgery Ser.). 1979. 125.00 (ISBN 0-407-00630-3). Butterworths.

Orthopedics, Vol. 2. Ed. by G. Bentley. (Operative Surgery Ser.). 1979. 125.00 (ISBN 0-407-00631-1). Butterworths.

Orthoptics: Theory & Practice. Hans G. Bredemeyer & Kathleen Bullock. LC 68-31415. (Illus.). 1968. 21.50 o.p. (ISBN 0-8016-0762-0). Mosby.

Orwell Reader: Fiction, Essays, & Reportage. George Orwell. LC 61-1439. 1961. pap. 5.95 (ISBN 0-15-670176-6, HB42, Harv). HarBraceJ.

Orygone III; or, Everything You Always Wanted to Know About Oregon but Were Afraid to Find Out. James Cloutier. LC 77-90955. (Illus., Orig.). 1977. pap. 4.95 o.s.i. (ISBN 0-918966-02-7). Image West.

Orygone, Too or, a Nice Place to Visit but You Wouldn't Want to Get Stuck There. James Cloutier. LC 80-83718. (Illus.). 160p. (Orig.). (gr. 4 up). 1980. pap. 4.95 (ISBN 0-918966-05-1). Image West.

Osage Indians, Vol. 4. Incl. A Preliminary Survey of Missouri Archaeology. Carl H. Chapman; Osage Village Locations & Hunting Territories to 1808. Carl H. Chapman; Osage Village Sites & Hunting Territory 1808-1825. Carl H. Chapman; The Osage Nation 1775-1818. Dale R. Henning. (American Indian Ethnohistory Ser: Plains Indians). (Illus.). lib. bdg. 42.00 (ISBN 0-8240-0750-6). Garland Pub.

Osage Indians, Vol. Five: Findings of Fact, & Opinion. Indian Claims Commission. (American Indian Ethnohistory Ser: Plains Indians). (Illus.). lib. bdg. 42.00 (ISBN 0-8240-0751-4). Garland Pub.

Osage Indians, Vol. One: Osage Research Project. Fred W. Voget. (American Indian Ethnohistory Ser: Plains Indians). (Illus.). lib. bdg. 42.00 (ISBN 0-8240-0747-6). Garland Pub.

Osage Indians, Vol. Three: The Origin of the Osage Indian Tribe: an Ethnographical, Historical & Archaeological Study. Carl H. Chapman. (American Indian Ethnohistory Ser.: Plains Indians). (Illus.). lib. bdg. 42.00 (ISBN 0-8240-0749-2). Garland Pub.

Osage Indians, Vol. Two: Osage Research Report, & Bibliography of Basic Research References. Alice Marriott. (American Indian Ethnohistory Ser: Plains Indians). (Illus.). lib. bdg. 42.00 (ISBN 0-8240-0748-4). Garland Pub.

Osages: Children of the Middle Waters. John J. Mathews. (Civilization of the American Indian Ser.: No. 60). (Illus.). 1981. Repr. of 1961 ed. 24.95 (ISBN 0-8061-0498-8). U of Okla Pr.

Osborne Four & Eight Bit Microprocessor Handbook. Adam Osborne. 600p. 1981. pap. text ed. 19.95 (ISBN 0-931988-42-X). Osborne-McGraw.

Osborne Sixteen-Bit Microprocessor Handbook. Adam Osborne. 500p. 1981. pap. 19.95 (ISBN 0-931988-43-8). Osborne-McGraw.

Oscar Directors. I. G. Edmonds. 1980. 17.95 (ISBN 0-498-02533-0); pap. write for info. (ISBN 0-498-02444-X). A S Barnes.

Oscar Is a Mama. Bernard Wiseman. LC 79-24737. (Bernard Wiseman Bks.). (Illus.). (gr. k-4). 1980. PLB 5.49 (ISBN 0-8116-6081-8). Garrard.

Oscar Lincoln Busby Stokes. Frances C. Sayers. LC 69-13778. (Illus.). (gr. 1-4). 1970. 4.50 o.p. (ISBN 0-15-258814-0, HJ). HarBraceJ.

Oscar-the-Grouch's Alphabet of Trash. Jeffrey Moss. (Sesame Street Shape Bks.). (Illus.). (ps-2). 1977. PLB 5.38 (ISBN 0-307-68880-1, Golden Pr). Western Pub.

Oscar Wilde. Donald Eriksen. (English Authors Ser.: No. 211). 1977. lib. bdg. 9.95 (ISBN 0-8057-6680-4). Twayne.

Oscar Wilde. Sheridan Morley. LC 76-4727. 1976. 14.95 o.p. (ISBN 0-03-017586-0). HR&W.

Oscar Wilde. Kevin Sullivan. LC 73-186638. (Columbia Essays on Modern Writers Ser.: No. 64). 1972. pap. 2.00 (ISBN 0-231-03068-1, MW64). Columbia U Pr.

Oscar Wilde: The Critical Heritage. Ed. by Karl Beckson. 1970. 40.00x (ISBN 0-7100-6929-4). Routledge & Kegan.

Oscar Zariski, 4 vols. Oscar Zariski. Ed. by J. Lipman & B. Teissier. (Mathematicians of Our Time Ser.). 1979. Vol. 1. text ed. 32.50x (ISBN 0-262-08049-4); Vol. 2. text ed. 32.50x (ISBN 0-262-01038-0); Vol. 3. text ed. 40.00x (ISBN 0-262-24021-1). MIT Pr.

Oscar's Book. Jeffry Moss. (Illus.). (ps-3). 1975. PLB 5.00 (ISBN 0-307-60120-X, Golden Pr). Western Pub.

Osceola. Matthew G. Grant. LC 73-12407. 1974. PLB 5.95 (ISBN 0-87191-266-X). Creative Ed.

Osceola, Seminole Leader. Ronald Syme. LC 75-22373. (Illus.). 96p. (gr. 3-7). 1976. 6.75 (ISBN 0-688-22054-1); PLB 6.48 (ISBN 0-688-32054-6). Morrow.

Osceola's Head & Other American Ghost Stories. W. Harter. (Illus.). 1974. 4.95 (ISBN 0-13-642991-2); pap. 1.95 (ISBN 0-13-643007-4). P-H.

Oscilloscopes. Prentiss. (Illus.). 1980. text ed. 16.95 (ISBN 0-8359-5354-8); pap. text ed. 9.95 (ISBN 0-8359-5353-X). Reston.

OSHA & Accident Control Through Training. C. Richard Anderson. LC 74-16444. (Illus.). 225p. 1975. 20.00 (ISBN 0-8311-1094-5). Indus Pr.

O.S.H.A. Compliance Manual. Joseph M. Roberts. (Illus.). 272p. 1976. 16.95 (ISBN 0-87909-599-7). Reston.

OSHA for Machine Tools. Compiled by National Research & Appraisal Co. & Jane Sharninghouse. 1000p. 1980. write for info. (ISBN 0-89692-101-8). Equipment Guide.

OSHA Reference Manual. Merritt Company Staff. 1981. 197.00 (ISBN 0-930868-03-X). Merritt Co.

O'Shaughnessy's Cafe. H. W. Clune. 1969. 6.95 o.s.i. (ISBN 0-02-526370-6). Macmillan.

Osier Cage: Rhetorical Devices in Romeo & Juliet. Robert O. Evans. LC 66-16233. 120p. 1966. 6.00x (ISBN 0-8131-1123-4). U Pr of Ky.

Osip Emilievich Manelstam: An Essay in Antiphon. Arthur A. Cohen. (Ardis Essay Ser.: No. 2). 82p. 1974. pap. 2.50 o.p. (ISBN 0-88233-076-4). Ardis Pubs.

Osip Mandelstam: Fifty Poems. Osip Mandelstam. Tr. by Bernard Meares. LC 76-52274. 1977. 7.95 (ISBN 0-89255-005-8); pap. 4.95 (ISBN 0-89255-006-6). Persea Bks.

Osler's Textbook Revisited. Harvey. 1967. 16.50 o.p. (ISBN 0-8385-7546-3). ACC.

Osmonds. Delaney & Laney. 32p. (gr. 4-6). 1975. PLB 5.95 (ISBN 0-87191-461-1); pap. 2.95 (ISBN 0-89812-113-2). Creative Ed.

Osprey Suicides. Lawrence Lieberman. 1973. 6.95 o.s.i. (ISBN 0-02-571820-7). Macmillan.

Osprey Suicides: Poems. Laurence Lieberman. LC 72-87164. 96p. 1973. pap. 1.95 o.s.i. (ISBN 0-02-069790-2, Collier). Macmillan.

OSS: The Secret History of America's First Central Intelligence Agency. R. Harris Smith. LC 73-153553. (Illus.). 450p. 1972. 14.50 o.p. (ISBN 0-520-02023-5); pap. 6.95 o.p. (ISBN 0-520-04246-8). U of Cal Pr.

Ossa Service - Repair Handbook: 125-250cc Singles, 1971-1978. 2nd ed. Brick Price. Ed. by Jeff Robinson. (Illus.). 160p. 1976. pap. text ed. 9.95 (ISBN 0-89287-092-3, M362). Clymer Pubns.

Ossian House. A. C. Stewart. LC 76-9645. (gr. 6 up). 1976. PLB 9.95 (ISBN 0-87599-219-6). S G Phillips.

Ossian Ou les Bardes. Jean F. Le Seur. Ed. by Philip Geosset & Charles Rosen. LC 76-49219. (Early Romantic Opera Ser.). 1979. lib. bdg. 82.00 (ISBN 0-8240-2936-4). Garland Pub.

Ossianic Lore & Romantic Tales of Medieval Ireland. rev. ed. Gerald Murphy. (Life & Cult Ser.). 69p. 1971. pap. 1.50 o.p. (ISBN 0-85342-267-2). Irish Bk Ctr.

Ossicle Morphology of Some Recent Asteroids & Descriptions of Some West American Fossil Asteroids. Daniel B. Blake. (U. C. Publ. in Geological Sciences: Vol. 104). 1973. pap. 10.50x (ISBN 0-520-09472-7). U of Cal Pr.

Osten Sjostrand. Staffan Bergsten. (World Authors Ser.: Spain: No. 309). 174p. 1974. lib. bdg. 12.50 (ISBN 0-8057-2844-9). Twayne.

Osteology of Phlegethontia, a Carboniferous & Permian Aistopod Amphibian. H. J. McGinnis. (U. C. Publ. in Geological Sciences: Vol. 71). 1967. pap. 5.75x (ISBN 0-520-09174-4). U of Cal Pr.

Osteomalacia, Renal Osteodystrophy & Osteoporosis. Brian Morgan. (American Lectures in Living Chemistry Ser.). (Illus.). 440p. 1973. 27.75 (ISBN 0-398-02602-5). C C Thomas.

Osteomyelitis: Clinical Features, Therapeutic Considerations, & Unusual Aspects. Francis A. Waldvogel et al. (Illus.). 128p. 1971. 12.75 (ISBN 0-398-02156-2). C C Thomas.

Osteopathy: Comparative Concepts - A. T. Still & Edgar Cayce. J. Gail Cayce. 61p. (Orig.). 1973. pap. 4.95 (ISBN 0-87604-080-6). ARE Pr.

Osteotomy at the Upper End of Femur. H. Milch. 177p. 1965. 12.50 o.p. (ISBN 0-683-05988-2, Pub. by Williams & Wilkins). Krieger.

Osteotomy of Mandibular Ramus: Prognathism & Allied Problems. Marsh Robinson. (Illus.). 168p. 1977. 19.50 (ISBN 0-398-03610-1). C C Thomas.

Oster Every Day a Gourmet Cookbook. Cynthia Rubin & Jerome Rubin. 7.95 (ISBN 0-916752-29-1). Green Hill.

Ostrich Feathers. Barbara Brenner. LC 77-24284. (Illus.). 32p. (gr. k-4). 1978. lib. bdg. 5.95 (ISBN 0-590-07718-X, Four Winds). Schol Bk Serv.

Oswald Garrison Villard: The Dilemmas of the Absolute Pacifist in Two World Wars. Ed. by Anthony Gronowicz. LC 72-147764. (Library of War & Peace; Documentary Anthologies). lib. bdg. 38.00 (ISBN 0-8240-0504-X). Garland Pub.

Oswald Jacoby on Poker. rev. ed. Oswald Jacoby. 1947. 7.95 o.p. (ISBN 0-385-04781-9). Doubleday.

Oswald Jacoby on Poker. Oswald Jacoby. LC 80-70553. 192p. 1981. pap. 4.95 (ISBN 0-385-17590-6, Dolp). Doubleday.

Oswald Von Wolkenstein. George F. Jones. (World Authors Ser.: Germany: No. 236). 1973. lib. bdg. 10.95 (ISBN 0-8057-2992-5). Twayne.

Ot Legal 'nostik Podpol'-Iu (From Legality to the Underground) Boris Dvinov. LC 67-19592. (Foreign Language Ser.: No. 2). (Rus). 1968. 8.00 (ISBN 0-8179-4021-9). Hoover Inst Pr.

OTC Handbook: What to Recommend & Why. R. Harkness. 1977. 10.95 (ISBN 0-87489-071-3). Med Economics.

Otello, 2 vols. Gioachino Rossini. Ed. by Philip Gossett & Charles Rosen. LC 76-49182. (Early Romantic Opera Ser.: Vol. 8). 1979. Set. lib. bdg. 164.00 (ISBN 0-8240-2907-0); lib. bdg. 82.00 ea. Garland Pub.

Othello. Ed. by Gamini Salgado. (New Swan Shakespeare Advanced Ser.). (Illus.). 1976. pap. text ed. 5.50x (ISBN 0-582-52748-1). Longman.

Othello. William Shakespeare. Ed. by Arthur Quiller-Couch et al. (New Shakespeare Ser). 1969. 23.95 (ISBN 0-521-07549-1); pap. 4.50x (ISBN 0-521-09492-5). Cambridge U Pr.

Othello. William Shakespeare. Ed. by Mark Eccles. LC 47-25793. (Crofts Classics Ser.). 1946. pap. text ed. 2.25x (ISBN 0-88295-079-7). AHM Pub.

Othello As Tragedy: Some Problems of Judgement & Feeling. Jane Adamson. LC 79-41437. 230p. 1980. 34.50 (ISBN 0-521-22368-7); pap. 11.50 (ISBN 0-521-29760-5). Cambridge U Pr.

Othello, Macbeth, & King Lear: A Formal Approach. Frank Amon. LC 78-58445. 1978. pap. text ed. 9.00 (ISBN 0-8191-0533-3). U Pr of Amer.

Othello Notes. Cliff's Notes Editors. (Orig.). pap. 1.95 (ISBN 0-8220-0063-6). Cliffs.

Othello, The Moor of Venice. William Shakespeare. LC 73-14771. (Shakespeare Ser). 1974. 9.85 o.p. (ISBN 0-672-51483-4); pap. 7.50 (ISBN 0-672-61106-6). Bobbs.

Othello 1622. William Shakespeare. Ed. by Charlton Hinman. (Shakespeare Quarto Facsimiles Ser: No. 16). 112p. 1975. 22.00x (ISBN 0-19-818147-7). Oxford U Pr.

Other America. Michael Harrington. (YA) (gr. 11 up). 1971. pap. 3.50 (ISBN 0-14-021308-2, Pelican). Penguin.

Other America: Poverty in the United States. rev. ed. Michael Harrington. (gr. 8 up). 1970. 10.95 (ISBN 0-02-548230-0). Macmillan.

Other American Revolution. Vincent Harding. Ed. by Robert A. Hill. LC 79-54307. (Afro-American Culture & Society Monographs: Vol. 4). 1981. pap. 8.50 (ISBN 0-934934-06-1). Ctr Afro Am St.

Other Americans: Minorities in American History. Kathleen Wright. 1976. pap. 1.75 o.p. (ISBN 0-449-30674-7, X674, Prem). Fawcett.

Other Anne Fletcher. Susanne Fletcher. 1981. pap. 2.75 (ISBN 0-451-09805-6, E9805, Signet Bks). NAL.

Other Anne Fletcher. Susanne Jaffe. 1980. 9.95 (ISBN 0-453-00386-9, H386). NAL.

Other Awkward Age. Jane Page. (Illus.). 1977. 8.95 o.p. (ISBN 0-913668-67-2); pap. 4.95 o.p. (ISBN 0-913668-65-6). Ten Speed Pr.

Other Choices for Becoming a Woman: A Handbook to Help High School Women Make Decisions. Joyce S. Mitchell. LC 76-5588. (gr. 7 up). 1976. 7.95 o.s.i. (ISBN 0-440-06795-2). Delacorte.

Other Cultures. John Beattie. LC 64-16952. 1968. 9.95 o.s.i. (ISBN 0-02-902040-9); pap. text ed. 7.95 (ISBN 0-02-902050-6). Free Pr.

Other Days. John Haines. (Illus.). 52p. 1981. 40.00x (ISBN 0-915308-29-0); pap. 16.00x (ISBN 0-915308-30-4). Graywolf.

Other Door: Poetic Exhortations! Recipients of Life's Other Door; Donkeyland, Vol. I. (Illus.). 64p. 1981. 5.00 (ISBN 0-682-49716-9). Exposition.

Other Foot. D. Knight. pap. text ed. 7.00 (ISBN 0-08-007043-4). Pergamon.

Other Generation Gap: You & Your Aging Parents. Steven Cohen & Bruce Gans. 336p. 1980. pap. 2.95 (ISBN 0-446-93756-8). Warner Bks.

Other Generation: The New Power of Older People. Rochelle Jones. LC 77-22306. 1977. 10.95 (ISBN 0-13-643064-3, Spec); pap. 4.95 (ISBN 0-13-643056-2, Spec). P-H.

Other Girl, No. 7. Lucy Walker. 192p. 1981. pap. 1.75 (ISBN 0-345-29422-X). Ballantine.

Other Gods: An American Legend. Pearl S. Buck. (John Day Bk.). 1940. 8.95 o.s.i. (ISBN 0-381-98047-2, A58200, TYC-T). T Y Crowell.

Other Governments of Europe: Sweden, Spain, Italy, Yugoslavia, E. Germany. Michael Roskin. 1977. pap. text ed. 7.95 (ISBN 0-13-642959-9). P-H.

Other Helpers. Michael Gershon & Henry B. Biller. LC 76-55535. (Illus.). 1977. 22.95 (ISBN 0-669-01317-X). Lexington Bks.

Other Homes & Garbage: Designs for Self-Sufficient Living. Jim Leckie et al. LC 75-8913. (Illus.). 320p. (Orig.). 1975. pap. 9.95 (ISBN 0-87156-141-7). Sierra.

Other House. Henry James. 228p. 1976. Repr. of 1896 ed. lib. bdg. 12.95x (ISBN 0-89244-083-X). Queens Hse.

Other Mafia. Joseph Goldbach. 1977. 5.00 o.p. (ISBN 0-682-48307-9). Exposition.

Other Minorities: Nonethnic Collectivities Conceptualized As Minority Groups. Ed. by Edward Sagarin. LC 77-126631. (Orig.). 1971. pap. text ed. 10.50 (ISBN 0-471-00498-7). Wiley.

Other Nine. Colleen L. Reece. (Orig.). 1981. pap. 6.50 (ISBN 0-8309-0288-0). Herald Hse.

Other People: A Mystery Story. Martin Amis. 1981. 11.95 (ISBN 0-670-52948-6). Viking Pr.

Other People's Lives. Johanna Kaplan. 1975. 6.95 o.p. (ISBN 0-394-47174-1). Knopf.

Other People's Property. Bernard Siegan. LC 75-22884. 160p. 1976. 16.95 (ISBN 0-669-00187-2). Lexington Bks.

Other Shoe. Mary McMullen. LC 80-2751. (Crime Club Ser.). 192p. 1981. 9.95 (ISBN 0-385-17534-5). Doubleday.

Other Shore: 100 Poems. Rafael Alberti. Ed. by Kosrof Chantikian. Tr. by Jose A. Elgorriaga & Martin Paul. LC 80-84602. (Modern Poets in Translation). 208p. (Orig.). 1981. 15.00 (ISBN 0-916426-05-X); pap. 7.95 (ISBN 0-916426-06-8). Kosmos.

Other Side. Deborah Manley. LC 78-21018. (Ready, Set, Look Ser.). (Illus.). (gr. k-3). 1979. PLB 9.65 (ISBN 0-8172-1301-5). Raintree Pubs.

Other Side. Subhas C. Saha. (Redbird Ser). 35p. 1975. 8.00 (ISBN 0-88253-598-6); pap. text ed. 4.00 (ISBN 0-88253-597-8). Ind-US Inc.

Other Side of Desire. Paula Christian. 160p. 1981. pap. 6.50 (ISBN 0-931328-08-X). Timely Bks.

Other Side of Love: Two Novellas. H. C. Brashers. LC 63-11820. 88p. (Orig.). 1963. pap. 2.65 (ISBN 0-8040-0237-1, 49). Swallow.

Other Side of Midnight. Sidney Sheldon. 1974. 12.95 (ISBN 0-688-00220-X). Morrow.

Other Side of Morality. Fritz Ridenour. LC 68-8388. (Orig.). 1969. pap. 1.85 o.p. (ISBN 0-8307-0040-4, S112-1-59). Regal.

Other Side of Power. Claude Steiner. LC 80-8921. 192p. 1981. 16.50 (ISBN 0-394-51950-7, Ever); pap. 6.95 (ISBN 0-394-17926-9). Grove.

Other Side of Racism: A Philosophical Study of Black Consciousness. Anne Wortham. 237p. 1981. 12.50 (ISBN 0-8142-0318-3). Ohio St U Pr.

Other Side of the Coin. Pierre Boulle. LC 58-13675. 1958. 8.95 (ISBN 0-8149-0068-2). Vanguard.

Other Side of the Mirrow (el Rimonio) Enrique Anderson Imbert. Tr. by Isabel Reade. LC 66-11155. (Contemporary Latin American Classic). 239p. 1966. 7.95x (ISBN 0-8093-0227-6). S Ill U Pr.

Other Side of the Mountain. E. G. Valens. (Illus.). 1975. pap. 2.50 (ISBN 0-446-91320-0). Warner Bks.

Other Side of the Summer. Jean-Rene Huguenin. LC 61-12953. 1961. 4.00 o.s.i. (ISBN 0-8076-0150-0). Braziller.

Other Side of Tomorrow. Ed. by Roger Elwood. 1975. pap. 1.25 o.s.i. (ISBN 0-515-03937-3). Jove Pubns.

Other Side: Perspectives on Deviance. Ed. by Howard S. Becker. LC 64-16953. 1967. pap. 5.95 (ISBN 0-02-902210-X). Free Pr.

Other Sides of Reality: Myths, Visions & Fantasies. Walter M. Cummins et al. LC 75-182677. 400p. 1972. pap. 7.95x (ISBN 0-87835-038-1). Boyd & Fraser.

Other Silence. Sitakant Mahapatra. (Redbird Ser.). 1975. 6.75 (ISBN 0-88253-600-1); pap. text ed. 4.80 (ISBN 0-88253-599-4). Ind-US Inc.

Other South: Southern Dissenters in the Nineteenth Century. Carl N. Degler. 1975. pap. 3.95x o.p. (ISBN 0-06-131856-6, TB1856, Torch). Har-Row.

Other Stepping Stones: A Study of Learning Experiences That Contribute to Effective Performance in Early & Long-Run Jobs. Ann S. Bisconti & Jean G. Kessler. pap. 8.95 (ISBN 0-913936-15-4). Coll Placement.

Other Time & Other Poems. Vijay N. Shankar. (Writers Workshop Redbird Ser.). 53p. 1975. 10.00 (ISBN 0-88253-602-8); pap. text ed. 4.80 (ISBN 0-88253-601-X). Ind-US Inc.

Other Titanic. Simon Martin. LC 79-56252. (Illus.). 208p. 1980. 19.95 (ISBN 0-7153-7755-8). David & Charles.

Other Twenty Three Hours: Child Care Work with Emotionally Disturbed Children in a Therapeutic Milieu. Albert E. Trieschman et al. (Modern Applications of Psychology Ser.). 1969. 12.95x o.p. (ISBN 0-202-26023-2). Beresford Bk Serv.

Other Voices. Kenneth E. Read. LC 79-26194. (Anthropology Ser.). 1980. pap. 6.95 (ISBN 0-88316-534-1). Chandler & Sharp.

Other Voices: A Study of the Late Poetry of Luis Cernuda. John A. Coleman. (Studies in the Romance Languages & Literatures: No. 81). 1969. pap. 8.50x (ISBN 0-8078-9081-2). U of NC Pr.

Other Voices in American Poetry, 1980. Gary Wilding. LC 80-81203. 184p. 1981. pap. 7.95 (ISBN 0-936092-01-7, 102). Harbinger Pr.

Other Way to Better Grades. Marvin Karlins. 168p. (Orig.). 1981. pap. 4.95 (ISBN 0-449-90046-0, Columbine). Fawcett.

Other Ways of Growing Old: Anthropological Perspectives. Ed. by Pamela T. Amoss & Stevan Harrell. LC 79-66056. 1981. 18.50x (ISBN 0-8047-1072-4). Stanford U Pr.

Other Western Europe: A Political Analysis of the Smaller Democracies. Earl H. Fry & Gregory A. Raymond. (Studies in International & Comparative Politics Ser.: No. 14). 251p. 1980. 24.75 (ISBN 0-87436-267-9). Abc-Clio.

Other Words, Other Worlds: Language in Culture. Ed. by James W. Dodge. 1972. pap. 7.95x (ISBN 0-915432-72-2). NE Conf Teach.

Other Worlds. Paul Davies. 1981. 11.95 (ISBN 0-671-42227-8). S&S.

Others. Robert Ferro. LC 77-8702. 1977. 6.95 o.p. (ISBN 0-684-15137-5, ScribT). Scribner.

Otherwise & Other Poems. Shrikant Varma. (Translated from Hindi). 12.00 (ISBN 0-89253-615-2); flexible cloth 4.80 (ISBN 0-89253-616-0). Ind-US Inc.

Otherwise Girl. Keith Claire. LC 75-29789. 1976. 6.95 o.p. (ISBN 0-03-016681-0). HR&W.

Otis Spofford. Beverly Cleary. (Illus.). (gr. 3-7). 1953. 7.75 (ISBN 0-688-21720-6); PLB 7.44 (ISBN 0-688-31720-0); pap. 1.50 (ISBN 0-688-26720-3). Morrow.

Otitis Media: Proceedings. Aram Glorig. Ed. by Kenneth S. Gerwin. (Illus.). 328p. 1972. 22.50 (ISBN 0-398-02294-1). C C Thomas.

Oto & Missouri Indians. Berlin B. Chapman. Ed. by David A. Horr. (American Indian Ethnohistory Ser.). 1978. lib. bdg. 42.00 (ISBN 0-8240-0746-8). Garland Pub.

Otolaryngology. 4th ed. Stanley N. Farb. LC 70-94388. (Medical Examination Review Bk.: Vol. 16). 1977. spiral bdg. 16.50 (ISBN 0-87488-116-1). Med Exam.

Otolaryngology Case Studies. 2nd ed. Ed. by C. T. Yarington, Jr. 1974. spiral bdg. 14.00 (ISBN 0-87488-021-1). Med Exam.

Otorhinolaryngology. 2nd. ed. Stanley N. Farb. (Medical Outline Ser). 1980. pap. 16.00 (ISBN 0-87488-661-9). Med Exam.

Otosclerosis: Genetics & Surgical Rehabilitation. Vicius B. Gapany-Gapana. LC 75-8545. 1975. 34.95 (ISBN 0-470-29080-3). Halsted Pr.

Ottawa: The Capital of Canada. Shirley E. Woods. LC 79-6101. 256p. 1981. 19.95 (ISBN 0-385-14722-8). Doubleday.

Ottemiller's Index to Plays in Collections: An Author & Title Index to Plays Appearing in Collections Published Between 1900 & Early 1975. 6th. rev. enl. ed. John M. Connor & Billie M. Connor. LC 71-166073. 1976. 21.00 (ISBN 0-8108-0919-2). Scarecrow.

Otter. Angela Sheehan. (First Look at Nature Bks.). (Illus.). (gr. 2-4). 1979. 2.50 (ISBN 0-531-09099-X); PLB 6.45 s&l (ISBN 0-685-65721-3). Watts.

Otterbein (Philip William) Arthur C. Core. 1968. 4.00 (ISBN 0-687-30917-4); pap. 2.25 (ISBN 0-687-30918-2). Abingdon.

Otters. (Publications New Ser.). 158p. 1979. pap. 7.00 (ISBN 2-88032-200-6, IUCN76, IUCN). Unipub.

Ottoman Centuries: The Rise & Fall of the Turkish Empire. Lord Kinross. LC 76-28498. (Illus.). 1979. pap. 7.95 (ISBN 0-688-08093-6, Quill). Morrow.

Ottoman Empire & Its Tributary States(Expecting Egypt) With a Sketch of Greece. W. S. Cooke. (Illus.). 1968. text ed. 34.25x (ISBN 90-6032-211-8). Humanities.

Ottoman Empire: Conquest, Organization & Economy. Halil Inalcik. 362p. 1980. 60.00x (ISBN 0-86078-032-5, Pub. by Variorum England). State Mutual Bk.

Ottoman Empire, the Great Powers, & the Straits Question: 1870-1887. Barbara Jelavich. LC 72-88631. 224p. 1973. 10.00x (ISBN 0-253-34276-7). Ind U Pr.

Ottoman Imperialism During the Reformation: Europe & The Caucasus. Carl Max Kortepeter. LC 72-75005. (Illus.). 278p. 1972. 17.50x (ISBN 0-8147-4552-0). NYU Pr.

Ottuv Slovnik Naucny, 40 vols. 12 supplements. (Czech.). 1889-1943. 1465.00 (ISBN 0-8277-3047-0). Maxwell Sci Intl.

Ounce of Prevention Is Worth a Pound of Cure. Leo G. Davis. 1981. 6.50 (ISBN 0-8062-1569-0). Carlton.

Our Acoustic Environment. Frederick A. White. LC 75-8888. 501p. 1975. 37.50 (ISBN 0-471-93920-X, Pub. by Wiley-Interscience). Wiley.

Our American Artists: With Portraits, Studios & Engravings of Paintings, Repr. Of 1879 Ed. S. G. Benjamin. Bd. with Second Series. Painters, Sculptors, Illustrators, Engravers & Architects. Repr. of 1881 ed. LC 75-28870. (Art Experience in Late 19th Century America Ser.: Vol. 6). (Illus.). 1976. lib. bdg. 58.00 (ISBN 0-8240-2230-0). Garland Pub.

Our American Sisters: Women in American Life & Thought. 2nd ed. Jean E. Friedman & William G. Shade. 317p. 1976. pap. 11.95 o.p. (ISBN 0-205-05578-8, 7855788). Allyn.

Our American Trees. Ruth H. Dudley. LC 56-9800. (Illus.). (gr. 3-7). 1956. 7.95 (ISBN 0-690-60383-5, TYC-J). T Y Crowell.

Our Ancient Liberties. Leon Whipple. LC 73-175723. (Civil Liberties in American History Ser.). 1972. Repr. lib. bdg. 15.00 (ISBN 0-306-70419-6). Da Capo.

Our Animal Friends at Maple Hill Farm. Alice Provensen & Martin Provensen. LC 74-828. (Illus.). 64p. (gr. k-3). 1974. 3.95 o.p. (ISBN 0-394-82123-8, BYR); PLB 6.99 (ISBN 0-394-92123-2). Random.

Our Baha'i Holy Places. Deborah Christensen. (Sunflower Bks. for Young Children: Bk. 4). (Illus., Orig.). (ps-2). 1980. pap. 2.00 (ISBN 0-87743-144-2, 7-03-04). Baha'i.

Our Bailey & Staggers History & Genealogy. Marion B. Brunson. 1980. 10.00 (ISBN 0-916620-51-4). Portals Pr.

Our Basic Retirement Systems-Social Security: Suggestions for Improvement. (Statement of Tax Policy: No. 8). 1978. pap. 3.50 (ISBN 0-685-92044-5). Am Inst CPA.

Our Blind Children: Growing & Learning with Them. 3rd ed. Berthold Lowenfeld. (Illus.). 260p. 1977. 17.75 (ISBN 0-398-02200-3); pap. 11.75 (ISBN 0-398-03688-8). C C Thomas.

Our Blue Planet: The Story of the Earth's Evolution. Heinz Haber. LC 77-85276. 1969. 6.95 o.p. (ISBN 0-684-31048-1, ScribT); pap. 1.95 (ISBN 0-684-12735-0, SL330, ScribT). Scribner.

Our Chalet Songbook. 2nd ed. Girl Scouts of the U.S.A., Our Chalet Committee of Wagggs. 1978. 2.00 (ISBN 0-88441-364-0, 23-929); in 7 languages avail. GS.

Our Changing Planet. John Gribbin. LC 77-5547. (Illus.). 1977. 7.95 o.s.i. (ISBN 0-690-01693-X, TYC-T). T Y Crowell.

Our Changing Times: Ireland, Europe & the Modern World Since 1890. Kenneth Neill. (Illus.). 1976. pap. text ed. 5.95 large format limp bdg. o.p. (ISBN 0-7171-0761-2). Irish Bk Ctr.

Our Children Ask About God. Edith K. Battle. 1944. pap. 0.25 (ISBN 0-687-29515-7). Abingdon.

Our Children Should Be Working. William N. Stephens. (Illus.). 228p. 1979. text ed. 13.75 (ISBN 0-398-03851-1). C C Thomas.

Our Christian Faith: Answers for the Future. Karl Rahner & Karl-Heinz Weger. 208p. (Orig.). 1980. 10.95 (ISBN 0-8245-0145-4); pap. 4.95 (ISBN 0-8245-2032-7). Crossroad NY.

Our Christmas Handbook. Sandra Ziegler. (Illus.). 112p. pap. 5.95 (ISBN 0-89565-180-7, 3041). Standard Pub.

Our Church & Our Children. Sophie Koulomzin. LC 75-20215. 158p. 1975. pap. 4.95 (ISBN 0-913836-25-7). St Vladimirs.

Our City: The Jews of San Francisco. Irena Narrell. LC 80-21216. 1980. 15.00 (ISBN 0-8310-7122-2). Howell-North.

Our Client, the Planet: The Story of Ourobourus Institute. Bill Harvey. Ed. by Jan Bertisch & Yana Bragg. (Illus.). 1977. pap. 4.50 o.p. (ISBN 0-918538-05-X). Ourobourus.

Our Coal & Our Coal-Pits. 2nd ed. J. R. Leifchild. LC 68-58856. Repr. of 1856 ed. 22.00x (ISBN 0-678-05065-1). Kelley.

Our Common Language. 3rd ed. Hans P. Guth & Edgar H. Schuster. (American English Today Ser.). (Illus.). 480p. (gr. 8). 1980. text ed. 10.88 (ISBN 0-07-025018-9, W); tchrs. manual 9.60 (ISBN 0-07-025028-6). McGraw.

Our Community. (gr. 2). 1974. pap. text ed. 5.60 (ISBN 0-205-03880-8, 8038805); tchrs'. guide 5.60 (ISBN 0-205-04227-9, 8042276). Allyn.

Our Country. (gr. 1). 1974. pap. text ed. 5.12 (ISBN 0-205-03863-8, 8038632); tchrs'. guide 12.20 (ISBN 0-205-03865-4, 8038651); dup. masters 32.00 (ISBN 0-205-04357-7, 8043574); projection masters 7.20 (ISBN 0-205-04358-5, 8043582). Allyn.

Our Daily Bread. Lester R. Brown. LC 75-851. (Headline Ser.: No. 225). (Illus.). 1975. pap. 2.00 (ISBN 0-87124-030-0). Foreign Policy.

Our Daily Bread. Martin R. De Haan & H. G. Bosch. 7.95 o.p. (ISBN 0-310-23410-7). Zondervan.

Our Daily Bread. Mieczyslaw Malinski. 142p. 1979. 7.95 (ISBN 0-8164-0439-9). Crossroad NY.

Our Daily Walk. F. B. Meyer. 1970. Repr. 7.95 (ISBN 0-310-29140-2, 10213). Zondervan.

Our Developing World. 3rd ed. L. Dudley Stamp. 1969. pap. 2.95 o.p. (ISBN 0-571-04639-8, Pub. by Faber & Faber). Merrimack Bk Serv.

Our Economy: How It Works. Elmer Clawson. 1980. 12.64 (ISBN 0-201-01057-7, Sch Div); tchr's. ed. 8.24. A-W.

Our Eddie. Sulamith Ish-Kishor. (Windward Bks.). (gr. 7 up). 1969. pap. 0.75 o.p. (ISBN 0-394-82177-7, BYR). Random.

Our Elders. J. Muir Gray & Gordon Wilcock. (Illus.). 224p. 1981. text ed. 19.95x (ISBN 0-19-217698-6); pap. text ed. 10.95x (ISBN 0-19-286012-7). Oxford U Pr.

Our Enemies the French: Being an Account of the War Fought Between the French & the British - Syria 1941. Anthony Mockler. (Illus.). xix, 252p. 1976. 18.00 (ISBN 0-85052-194-7). Shoe String.

Our Energy Future: The Role of Research, Development, & Demonstration in Reaching a National Consensus on Energy Supply. Don E. Kash et al. LC 76-46402. (Illus.). 1976. 24.95x (ISBN 0-8061-1400-2); pap. 9.95 (ISBN 0-8061-1408-8). U of Okla Pr.

Our Energy-Regaining Control. Marc H. Ross & Robert H. Williams. (Illus.). 320p. 1980. 16.95 (ISBN 0-07-053894-8, P&RB). McGraw.

Our Environment: An Introduction to Physical Geography. 2nd ed. Donald K. Fellows. LC 79-18159. 1980. text ed. 18.95 (ISBN 0-471-05755-X); tchrs'. manual avail. (ISBN 0-471-06363-0). Wiley.

Our Faces, Our Words. Lillian Smith. (Illus.). 1964. pap. 1.95 o.p. (ISBN 0-393-00251-9, 4, Norton Lib). Norton.

Our Faith. Emil Brunner. (Scribner Library Edition). 1936. pap. 2.45 o.p. (ISBN 0-684-71722-0, SL87, ScribT). Scribner.

Our Faith & Fellowship. G. Raymond Carlson. LC 77-75023. (Radiant Life Ser). 1977. pap. 1.50 (ISBN 0-88243-908-1, 02-0908); teacher's ed. 2.50 (ISBN 0-88243-178-1, 32-0178). Gospel Pub.

Our Faiths. Martin E. Marty. 1976. pap. 1.75 (ISBN 0-89129-113-X). Jove Pubns.

Our Family Night in: Workbook of Convant Living. Lois Seifert. 200p. (Orig.). pap. 3.95x (ISBN 0-8358-0420-8). Upper Room.

Our Family Prepares for Mass. Sister Jean Daniel. Orig. Title: Tomorrow Is Sunday. (Illus.). 216p. 1980. pap. 6.95 (ISBN 0-03-057842-6). Winston Pr.

Our Father. Thomas Hinde. LC 75-43649. 351p. (Orig.). 1976. 8.95 o.p. (ISBN 0-8076-0821-1). Braziller.

Our Father Our King. Saul Raskin. (Illus., Heb. & eng). 1966. 15.00 (ISBN 0-8197-0288-9); deluxe ed. 25.00. Bloch.

Our Father Who Art in Heaven. Kurt Rommel. Tr. by Edward A. Cooperrider from Ger. LC 80-2373. 64p. 1981. pap. price not set (ISBN 0-8006-1448-8, 1-1448). Fortress.

Our Fathers (Eighteen Seventy to Nineteen Hundred) Alan Bott. 249p. 1980. Repr. lib. bdg. 35.00 (ISBN 0-89987-061-9). Darby Bks.

Our Fathers Had Powerful Songs. Natalia Belting. LC 73-13968. (Illus.). 32p. (gr. 2-6). 1974. PLB 7.95 o.p. (ISBN 0-525-36485-4). Dutton.

Our Flag & Other Symbols of Americanism. Robert B. Weaver. 76p. (gr. 7-8). 1972. pap. 0.50 (ISBN 0-912530-09-X); test 0.10 (ISBN 0-685-47428-3). Patriotic Educ.

Our Foolish Ways. Clifford L. Blackman. 1981. 5.75 (ISBN 0-8062-1718-9). Carlton.

Our Founders' Legacy. (Defrosting of Minnesota Ser.: Vol. 2). 1980. 7.75 (ISBN 0-9601852-2-4). H J Cichy.

Our Four Boys: Foster Parenting Retarded Teenagers. Martha U. Dickerson. 1978. 11.95x o.p. (ISBN 0-8156-0146-8); pap. 6.95 (ISBN 0-8156-0155-7). Syracuse U Pr.

Our Fragile Brains. D. Gareth Jones. (Illus.). 300p. 1980. pap. 8.95 (ISBN 0-87784-792-4). Inter-Varsity.

Our Friends the ABC's. Albert G. Miller. (ABC Serendipity Ser). (gr. 2-6). 1973. 4.35 o.p. (ISBN 0-8372-0820-3). Bowmar-Noble.

Our Future: An Upside Opportunity Scenario. Bill Harvey. (Orig.). 1980. pap. text ed. 9.95 o.p. (ISBN 0-8290-0345-2). Irvington.

Our Future Inheritance; Choice or Chance? A Study by a British Association Working Party. Alun Jones & Walter F. Bodmer. (Illus.). 156p. 1974. pap. 4.95x o.p. (ISBN 0-19-857390-1). Oxford U Pr.

Our Future: While We Still Have a Choice. Bill Harvey. Ed. by Jan Bertisch & Yana Bragg. (Illus.). 1979. pap. 6.95 (ISBN 0-918538-07-6). New Age Pr NM.

Our God: A "Sun & Shield" for Troubled Hearts. Thomas B. Warren. 1963. 4.95 (ISBN 0-934916-38-1). Natl Christian Pr.

Our Gospel's Women. Alma E. Blanton. (Illus.). 114p. (Orig.). 1979. pap. 3.00 (ISBN 0-938134-01-9). Loving Pubs.

Our Guilty Silence: The Church, the Gospel & the World. John R. Stott. 1969. pap. 2.95 (ISBN 0-8028-1287-2). Eerdmans.

Our Haunted Planet. John A. Keel. 224p. 1977. pap. 1.50 o.p. (ISBN 0-449-13580-2, GM). Fawcett.

Our Hearts Are Restless: The Prayer of St. Augustine. F. J. Sheed. 1976. pap. 4.95 (ISBN 0-8164-2127-7). Crossroad NY.

Our Hearts Were Young & Gay. Cornelia O. Skinner & Emily Kimbrough. LC 42-36388. (Illus.). 1942. 6.95 (ISBN 0-396-02401-7). Dodd.

Our Heavenly Father. Helmut Thielicke. (Minister's Paperback Library Ser.). 1974. pap. 3.95 (ISBN 0-8010-8814-3). Baker Bk.

Our Heritage. Sarvepalli Radhakrishnan. (Orient Paperback Ser.). 156p. (Orig.). 1973. pap. 2.35 (ISBN 0-88253-249-9). Ind-US Inc.

Our Heritage in Public Worship. D. H. Hislop. LC 36-2187. 350p. 7.50. Attic Pr.

Our Historic Desert. Diana E. Lindsay. Ed. by Richard F. Puurade. LC 73-11878. (Illus.). 160p. 1973. 14.50 (ISBN 0-913938-15-7). Copley Bks.

Our Home, Virginia, & the World. Raymond C. Dingledine, Jr. 1962. pap. text ed. 1.41 o.p. (ISBN 0-684-51514-8, ScribC). Scribner.

Our Host the World. Horace S. Baldwin. LC 78-66223. 1980. 6.95 (ISBN 0-533-04152-X). Vantage.

Our Human Ancestors. Ed. by Francis Clapham. (Visual World Ser.). (Illus.). (gr. 9 up). 1977. 5.95 (ISBN 0-685-74307-1, Warwick Press Book); PLB 7.90 s&l (ISBN 0-531-01279-4). Watts.

Our Hungry Earth: The World Food Crisis. Laurence Pringle. LC 76-10828. (Science for Survival Ser.). 128p. (gr. 7 up). 1976. 7.95 (ISBN 0-02-775290-9, 77529). Macmillan.

Our Hysterical Heritage: The American Presidential Election Process, Out of the Mouths of Babes. Harold Dunn. LC 79-22777. (Illus.). 1980. 7.95 (ISBN 0-916144-50-X); pap. 3.95 (ISBN 0-916144-51-8). Stemmer Hse.

Our Indian Wards. George Washington Manypenny. LC 68-54844. (American Scene Ser). 1972. Repr. of 1880 ed. lib. bdg. 25.00 (ISBN 0-306-71140-0). Da Capo.

Our Infallible Bible. David Nettleton. LC 77-15540. 1978. pap. 1.75 (ISBN 0-87227-055-6); tchr's guide 4.50 (ISBN 0-87227-056-4). Reg Baptist.

Our Inheritance in the Great Pyramid. Piazzi Smyth. LC 77-5284. (Spiritual Science Library). (Illus.). 672p. 1978. 20.00x (ISBN 0-8334-0720-1); pap. 15.00 (ISBN 0-8334-3503-5). Steinerbks.

Our Intellectual Strength & Weakness; English-Canadian Literature; French-Canadian Literature. J. G. Bourinot et al. LC 72-91693. (Literature of Canada Ser.). 1973. pap. 5.00 (ISBN 0-8020-6175-3). U of Toronto Pr.

Our Jo: A Chronicle of a Coming Man. Kenneth M. Cameron. LC 73-15145. 384p. 1974. 7.95 o.s.i. (ISBN 0-02-521010-6). Macmillan.

Our Joyful Confidence: The Lordship of Jesus in Colossians. Thomas Trevethan. 220p. (Orig.). 1981. pap. 5.95 (ISBN 0-87784-749-5). Inter Varsity.

Our Knowledge of the External-World. 2nd ed. 251p. 1926. 14.95 (ISBN 0-04-121008-5). Allen Unwin.

Our Lady of Fatima. William Thomas Walsh. pap. 3.50 (ISBN 0-385-02869-5, D1, Im). Doubleday.

Our Landed Heritage: The Public Domain, 1776-1970. 2nd rev. ed. Roy M. Robbins. LC 75-3569. (Illus.). xii, 503p. (A Bicentennial Edition). 1976. pap. 5.95x (ISBN 0-8032-5803-8, BB 588, Bison). U of Nebr Pr.

Our Lawless Police. Ernest J. Hopkins. LC 74-168829. (Civil Liberties in American History Ser.). 379p. 1972. Repr. of 1931 ed. lib. bdg. 32.50 (ISBN 0-306-70213-4). Da Capo.

Our Legal System & How It Operates. Burke Shartel. LC 73-173666. (American Constitutional & Legal History Ser.). 628p. 1972. Repr. of 1951 ed. lib. bdg. 59.50 (ISBN 0-306-70411-0). Da Capo.

Our Life Together. James Thompson. LC 77-79338. (Journey Bks.). 1977. pap. 2.35 (ISBN 0-8344-0095-2). Sweet.

Our Literary Heritage: A Pictorial History of the Writer in America. Van Wyck Brooks & Otto L. Bettman. (gr. 9 up). 1956. 12.50 o.p. (ISBN 0-525-17275-0). Dutton.

Our Lives for Ourselves: Women Who Have Never Married. Nancy L. Peterson. 320p. 1981. 13.95 (ISBN 0-399-12476-4). Putnam.

Our Long Island. 2nd ed. George Mannello. 1981. lib. bdg. write for info. (ISBN 0-88275-968-X). Krieger.

Our Lost World. Bertha Smith. LC 80-68537. 1981. pap. 3.95 (ISBN 0-8054-6324-0). Broadman.

Our Magnificent Wildlife. (Illus.). 352p. 1975. 17.95 (ISBN 0-393-21410-9, Pub. by Reader's Digest). Norton.

Our Man in Havana. Graham Greene. LC 58-11735. 248p. 1981. 14.95 (ISBN 0-670-53141-3). Viking Pr.

Our Marching Civilization. Warren D. Allen. LC 77-25408. (Music Reprint Ser., 1978). 1978. Repr. of 1943 ed. lib. bdg. 25.00 (ISBN 0-306-77568-9). Da Capo.

Our Maritime Heritage: Maritime Developments & Their Impact on American Life. James M. Morris. 1979. pap. text ed. 10.75 (ISBN 0-8191-0700-X). U Pr of Amer.

Our Mathematical Heritage. Ed. by William L. Schaaf. 1963. pap. 1.50 o.s.i. (ISBN 0-02-093960-4, Collier). Macmillan.

Our More Perfect Union: From Eighteenth-Century Principles to Twentieth-Century Practice. Arthur N. Holcombe. 1950. 20.00x (ISBN 0-674-64650-9). Harvard U Pr.

Our Most Skillful Architect Richard Taliaferro & Associated Colonial Virginia Constructions. Claude O. Lanciano, Jr. Date not set. text ed. price not set (ISBN 0-9603558-0-4). Lands End Bks.

Our Mothers. Ed. by Alan Bott. 220p. 1980. Repr. of 1932 ed. lib. bdg. 30.00 (ISBN 0-8495-0461-9). Arden Lib.

Our Murdered Presidents: The Medical Story. Stewart M. Brooks. (Illus.). 234p. 1966. 8.95. Fell.

Our Naked Frailties: Sensational Art & Meaning in Macbeth. Paul A. Jorgensen. LC 70-145788. 1971. 14.50x (ISBN 0-520-01915-6). U of Cal Pr.

Our Nation's Capital, Washington, D. C. rev. ed. Bernadine Bailey. LC 62-19727. (Illus.). (gr. 3-5). 1967. 5.50g (ISBN 0-8075-9558-6). A Whitman.

Our Nation's Heritage: A Living History, 10 pts. Incl. Nation Expands: Unit 1; Nation Divided: Unit 2; Settling the West: Unit 3; Industrial Revolution in America: Unit 4; America Becomes a World Power: Unit 5; Twentieth Century Begins: Unit 6; Nation in Prosperity & Poverty: Unit 7; America in World War II: Unit 8; America at Mid-Century: Unit 9; America Through Five Centuries - an Epilogue: Unit 10. (Lab Two, Units 1-10). (gr. 5 up). 1976. pap. text ed. 50.40 set of 30 bks, write for more price info (ISBN 0-8372-2371-7, 2371). Bowmar-Noble.

Our Nation's Heritage: A Living History Lab, 10 pts. Incl. Prologue to America: Unit 1; New World: Unit 2; Exploring the New World: Unit 3; Europe in the New World: Unit 4; English in America: Unit 5; Colonial Frontier: Unit 6; Revolutionary War: Unit 7; Cornerstones of a New Nation: Unit 8; New Nation Is Launched: Unit 9; New Nation Is Tested: Unit 10. (Lab. One). (gr. 5 up). 1976. pap. text ed. 50.40 set of 30 bks., write for more price info. (ISBN 0-8372-2370-9, 2370); lab i complete 198.00 (ISBN 0-8372-2352-0, 2352); without cassettes & student resource bks. 111.00 (ISBN 0-685-73328-9, 2425); lab ii complete 198.00 (ISBN 0-8372-2353-9, 2353); without cassettes & student resource bks. 111.00 (ISBN 0-8372-2426-8, 2426); wkbk for lab i 50.40 (ISBN 0-8372-2370-9, 2370); labs i & ii 396.00 (ISBN 0-8372-2372-5). Bowmar-Noble.

Our Natural Resources. 4th ed. Preston E. McNall & Harry B. Kircher. LC 75-14994. (Illus.). (gr. 7-12). 1976. text ed. 10.95x o.p. (ISBN 0-8134-1739-2, 1739). Interstate.

Our Natural Resources. 5th ed. Ed. by Preston E. McNall & Harry B. Kircher. LC 80-83584. (Illus.). (gr. 7-12). 1981. text ed. 10.95x (ISBN 0-8134-2166-7, 2166). Interstate.

Our Neighbors Upstairs: The Canadians. William R. Duggan. LC 79-1308. 1979. 17.95 (ISBN 0-88229-530-6); pap. 9.95 (ISBN 0-88229-667-1). Nelson-Hall.

Our Other World: A Polish Scrapbook. M. M. Coleman. (Illus.). 1978. 6.00 (ISBN 0-685-63579-1). Alliance Coll.

Our Own State, Michigan. rev., 14th ed. Ferris E. Lewis. LC 78-66800. (Illus.). (gr. 7-10). 1978. pap. text ed. 5.25x (ISBN 0-910726-21-3); questions & ans. for tchr's. 8.00x (ISBN 0-910726-23-X). Hillsdale Educ.

Our Parade. Suzanne Burke. Ed. by Alton Jordan. (Elephant Ser.). (Illus.). (gr. k-3). 1975. PLB 3.50 (ISBN 0-89868-017-4, Read Res); pap. text ed. 1.75 (ISBN 0-89868-050-6). ARO Pub.

Our Pennsylvania Heritage. William A. Cornell & Millard Altland. LC 78-50430. (gr. 7-12). 1978. 10.50 (ISBN 0-931992-21-4). Penns Valley.

Our Philosophical Traditions: A Brief History of Philosophy in Western Civilization. Sterling P. Lamprecht. LC 55-9432. (Century Philosophy Ser.). 1980. 29.50x (ISBN 0-89197-325-7); pap. text ed. 16.95x (ISBN 0-89197-873-9). Irvington.

Our Polluted Food: A Survey of the Risks. Jack Lucas. LC 75-8700. 237p. 1975. 19.95 (ISBN 0-470-55285-9). Halsted Pr.

Our Presbyterian Belief. Felix B. Gear. LC 79-23421. 90p. (Orig.). 1980. pap. 4.95 (ISBN 0-8042-0676-7). John Knox.

Our Presidents. 2nd, enl. ed. James Morgan. (Illus.). (gr. 9 up). 1958. 6.50 o.s.i. (ISBN 0-02-586950-7); 1969 updated ed 8.95 o.s.i. (ISBN 0-02-586960-4). Macmillan.

Our Profession: Present Status & Future Directions. Ed. by Thomas H. Geno. 1980. pap. 7.95x (ISBN 0-915432-80-3). NE Conf Teach.

Our Public Life. Paul Weiss. LC 59-9852. 256p. 1966. 10.95x (ISBN 0-8093-0219-5). S Ill U Pr.

Our Public Life. Paul Weiss. LC 59-9852. (Arcturus Books Paperbacks). 256p. 1966. pap. 7.95 (ISBN 0-8093-0220-9). S Ill U Pr.

Our Railway History. Rixon Bucknall. 1970. pap. 7.95 o.p. (ISBN 0-04-385064-2). Allen Unwin.

Our Reader. Jack Tancer. (Illus.). 1964. pap. 1.50x (ISBN 0-88323-060-7, 158). Richards Pub.

Our Religion & Our Neighbors. rev. ed. Milton G. Miller & Sylvan D. Schwartzman. LC 63-14742. (Illus.). (gr. 9). 1971. text ed. 7.50 (ISBN 0-8074-0145-5, 141513); tchrs'. guide 3.50 (ISBN 0-8074-0146-3, 204280). UAHC.

Our Restless Earth: The Geologic Regions of Tennessee. Edward T. Luther. LC 77-21433. (Tennessee Three Star Bks. Ser.). (Illus.). 1977. lib. bdg. 8.50x (ISBN 0-87049-293-4); pap. 3.50x (ISBN 0-87049-293-4). U of Tenn Pr.

Our Right to Love: A Lesbian Resource Book. Ed. by Ginny Vida. LC 77-20184. 1978. 12.95 (ISBN 0-13-644401-6); pap. 9.95 (ISBN 0-13-644393-1). P-H.

Our Road to Prayer. Francis Line & Helen Line. (Prayer in My Life Ser.: Ser. I). 1974. pap. 1.00x (ISBN 0-8358-0305-8). Upper Room.

Our Roots Are Still Alive: The Story of the Paliesinian People. Joy Bonds et al. LC 77-10952. (Illus.). 182p. pap. 5.45 (ISBN 0-917654-12-9). IISJ.

Our Savior Lives. A. C. Mueller. (Bible Story Booklets Ser). (Illus.). (gr. 3-5). 1971. pap. 0.69 (ISBN 0-570-06705-7, 56-1133). Concordia.

Our School. William D. Sheldon et al. (gr. 1). 1973. text ed. 7.96 (ISBN 0-205-03522-1, 5235227); tchrs'. guide 3.96 (ISBN 0-205-03523-X, 5235235); activity bk. 3.92 (ISBN 0-205-03524-8, 5235243); tchr's ed. 3.96 (ISBN 0-205-03525-6, 5235251); activ. masters 28.00 (ISBN 0-205-03526-4, 523526X). Allyn.

Our Search for Wilderness: The Story of a Sixty-Year Marriage. Edgar B. Graves. 224p. 1975. 8.00 o.p. (ISBN 0-682-48321-4, Lochinvar). Exposition.

Our Selves. Marthinus Versfeld. 175p. 1979. pap. 7.95x (ISBN 0-8476-6223-3). Rowman.

Our Senses & How They Work. Herbert S. Zim. (Illus.). (gr. 3-7). 1956. PLB 6.48 (ISBN 0-688-31550-X). Morrow.

Our Sexual Evolution. Helen Colton. LC 70-71899. (gr. 7 up). 1971 PLB 6.90 (ISBN 0-531-01996-9). Watts.

Our Sexuality. R. Crooks & K. Baur. 1980. 16.95 (ISBN 0-8053-1910-7); instrs guide 3.95 (ISBN 0-8053-1911-5); 6.95 (ISBN 0-8053-1912-3). A-W.

Our Sexuality. Robert Crooks & Karla Baur. 1980. 16.95 (ISBN 0-8053-1910-7); study guide 6.95 (ISBN 0-8053-1912-3). Benjamin Cummings.

Our Small Native Animals: Their Habits & Care. rev. ed. Robert Snedigar. (Illus.). 8.00 (ISBN 0-8446-2961-8). Peter Smith.

Our Small Native Animals: Their Habits & Care. Robert Snedigar. (Illus.). 1963. pap. 4.00 (ISBN 0-486-21022-7). Dover.

Our Snowman Had Olive Eyes. Herman. (gr. 4-5). 1980. pap. 1.25 (ISBN 0-590-30253-1, Schol Pap). Schol Bk Serv.

Our Social Bees. Andrew Wynter. LC 67-23950. (Social History Reference Ser.). (Illus.). 1969. Repr. of 1861 ed. 15.00 (ISBN 0-8103-3265-5). Gale.

Our Social Security System: How Can We Make It Sound, Successful, & Solvent. Ed. by James Neitzel. 94p. (Orig.). 1977. pap. 7.50 (ISBN 0-89154-123-3). Intl Found Employ.

Our Social Security System: How We Make It Sound, Solvent & Successful? Ed. by James J. Neitzel. 1977. spiral bdg. 7.50 o.p. (ISBN 0-89154-068-7). Intl Found Employ.

Our Sociological Eye: Personal Essays on Society & Culture. Arthur B. Shostak. LC 76-30578. 1977. pap. text ed. 9.95x (ISBN 0-88284-048-7). Alfred Pub.

Our Southern Highlanders. Horace Kephart. LC 76-18903. (Illus.). 1976. 16.50x (ISBN 0-87049-197-0); pap. 6.95 (ISBN 0-87049-203-9). U of Tenn Pr.

Our Special Child: A Guide to Successful Parenting of Handicapped Children. Bette M. Ross. LC 80-54815. 192p. 1981. 12.95 (ISBN 0-8027-0678-9). Walker & Co.

Our Spiritual Companions. Adam Bittleston. 1980. pap. 13.50 (ISBN 0-903540-39-8, Pub. by Floris Books). St George Bk Serv.

Our State: Colorado. LeRoy Hafen & Ann Hafen. pap. 9.95x (ISBN 0-933472-35-8). Johnson Colo.

Our Statue of Liberty. Thelma Nason. LC 69-10260. (Beginning-To-Read Ser). (Illus.). (gr. 2-4). 1969. 2.50 o.p. (ISBN 0-695-86700-8); PLB 3.39 o.p. (ISBN 0-685-10945-3). Follett.

Our Struggle for the Fourteenth Colony: Canada & the American Revolution, 2 vols. Justin Smith. LC 74-12272. (Era of the American Revolution Ser.). 1273p. 1974. Repr. of 1907 ed. lib. bdg. 95.00 (ISBN 0-306-70633-4). Da Capo.

Our Sweetest Songs. Srinibas Bhattacharya. LC 77-74557. 1978. 4.95 o.p. (ISBN 0-533-02900-7). Vantage.

Our Terrariums. Herbert H. Wong & Matthew F. Vessel. LC 69-15805. (Illus.). (gr. k-2). 1969. PLB 6.95 (ISBN 0-201-08722-7, A-W Childrens). A-W.

Our Threatened Planet. Joseph F. Goodavage. 1980. pap. write for info. (ISBN 0-671-81640-3). PB.

Our Times, 6 vols. Mark Sullivan. LC 70-138308. 1926. Set. 115.00 o.s.i. (ISBN 0-684-13861-1, ScribR); 23.62 ea. o.s.i. Scribner.

Our Town. new ed. William D. Sheldon et al. (gr. 1). 1973. text ed. 7.96 (ISBN 0-205-03527-2, 5235278); tchrs'. guide 7.96 (ISBN 0-205-03528-0, 5235286); activity bk. 3.92 (ISBN 0-205-03529-9, 5235294); tchrs'. ed. activity 3.92 (ISBN 0-205-03530-2, 5235308); independent activ. masters 28.00 (ISBN 0-205-03531-0, 5235316); word cards 88.00 (ISBN 0-205-03898-0, 5238986). Allyn.

Our Troubled Children: Our Community's Challenge. Edwin Gould Foundation For Children. Ed. by Russell B. Wight. LC 67-16461. 1967. 17.50x o.p. (ISBN 0-231-02841-5). Columbia U Pr.

Our Troubled Hemisphere: Perspectives on United States-Latin American Relations. Robert N. Burr. 1967. 9.95 (ISBN 0-8157-1174-3). Brookings.

Our Uncertain Heritage: Genetics & Human Diversity. Daniel L Hartl. LC 76-30509. 1977. text ed. 18.50 scp (ISBN 0-397-47366-4, HarpC); scp study guide 6.50 (ISBN 0-397-47367-2). Har-Row.

Our Unfolding World. Glee Yoder. 13.95 o.p. (ISBN 0-685-61336-4). Brethren.

Our United States...Its History in Maps. rev. ed. Edgar B. Wesley. (Illus.). 96p. 1980. pap. text ed. 9.10x (ISBN 0-87453-001-6, 81001). Denoyer.

Our Universe, Mine & Yours. Marilyn Parsons. 1980. 4.00 (ISBN 0-8062-1364-7). Carlton.

Our Urban Planet. Ellen Switzer. LC 80-12225. (Illus.). 288p. (gr. 7 up). 1980. 10.95 (ISBN 0-689-30788-8). Atheneum.

Our Wild Wetlands. Sheila Cowing. LC 80-17600. (Illus.). 96p. (gr. 4-6). 1980. PLB 7.79 (ISBN 0-671-33089-6). Messner.

Our Wildlife Legacy. rev. ed. Durward L. Allen. LC 62-7980. (Funk & W Bk). (Illus.). (YA) (gr. 9 up). 1962. 9.95 o.s.i. (ISBN 0-308-70309-X, 780100, TYC-T). T Y Crowell.

Our Wildlife Legacy. Durward L Allen. LC 62-7980. (Funk & W Bk.). 432p. 1974. pap. 4.95 o.s.i. (ISBN 0-308-10096-4, F84, TYC-T). T Y Crowell.

Our Work in Space. Willy Ley. (gr. 7 up). 4.50 o.s.i. (ISBN 0-02-758980-3). Macmillan.

Our World & Its Peoples. rev. ed. Edward R. Kolevzon & John A. Heine. (gr. 9-12). 1977. text ed. 17.24 (ISBN 0-205-04853-6, 7748531); tchrs'. guide 7.32 (ISBN 0-205-04854-4, 774854X); wkbk 44.00 (ISBN 0-205-05606-7, 7756062); tests 36.00 (ISBN 0-205-05607-5, 7756070). Allyn.

Our World: Mexico. Dorothy Witton. LC 72-81387. (Illus.). (gr. 4-6). 1969. PLB 4.29 o.p. (ISBN 0-671-32138-2). Messner.

Our Yosemite National Park. John Muir. Ed. by William R. Jones. (Illus.). 96p. (Orig.). pap. 4.95 (ISBN 0-89646-061-4). Outbooks.

Our Youngest Parents: A Study of the Use of Support Services by Adolescent Mothers. Rosalind Zitner & Shelby Hayden. (Orig.). 1980. pap. text ed. 4.95 (ISBN 0-87868-144-2). Child Welfare.

Ourika. Claire de Durfort. Tr. by John Fowles. 1977. signed ed. 110.00 (ISBN 0-935072-01-2). W Thomas Taylor.

Ours: The Making & Unmaking of a Jesuit. F. E. Peters. 192p. 1981. 11.95 (ISBN 0-399-90113-2). Marek.

Ourselves & Others. Beryl Harding. (Liberal Studies Ser.). 1965. pap. text ed. 1.75 o.p. (ISBN 0-435-46533-3). Heinemann Ed.

Ourselves-Our Past: Psychological Approaches to American History. Ed. by Robert J. Brugger. LC 80-81425. 448p. 1981. text ed. 26.50x (ISBN 0-8018-2312-9); pap. text ed. 8.95x (ISBN 0-8018-2382-X). Johns Hopkins.

Ourselves: Stages 1 & 2. Roy Richards. LC 77-83006. (Science 5-13 Ser.). (Illus.). 1977. pap. text ed. 9.30 (ISBN 0-356-04349-5). Raintree Child.

Ouse Disciplinar. Tr. by James Dobson. (Portuguese Bks.). 1979. 1.45 (ISBN 0-8297-0768-9). Life Pubs Intl.

Ouster Conspiracy. Nick Carter. (Nick Carter Ser.). 224p. (Orig.). 1981. pap. 2.25 (ISBN 0-441-16048-4). Charter Bks.

Out: A Novel. Ronald Sukenick. LC 72-96165. 295p. 1973. 10.95 (ISBN 0-8040-0630-X). Swallow.

Out: A Novel. Ronald Sukenick. LC 72-96165. 1975. pap. 4.95 (ISBN 0-8040-0631-8). Swallow.

Out in the Back Forty: A Voice from the Field. Hazel M. Bright. (Illus.). 1978. pap. 17.50 (ISBN 0-686-26607-2). Redwood Pub Co.

Out of a Dream. Jennifer Rose. (Second Chance at Love, Contemporary Ser.: No. 4). (Orig.). 1981. pap. 1.75 (ISBN 0-515-05777-0). Jove Pubns.

Out of Africa: From West African Kingdoms to Colonization. Louise D. Hutchinson. LC 78-22469. (Illus.). 223p. 1979. 25.00x o.p. (ISBN 0-87474-534-9). Smithsonian.

Out of Care: The Community Support of Juvenile Offenders. D. H. Thorpe et al. (Illus.). 224p. 1980. text ed. 27.50x (ISBN 0-04-364018-4, 2544); pap. text ed. 10.95x (ISBN 0-04-364019-2, 2545). Allen Unwin.

Out of Concern for the Church. J. H. Olthuis et al. 1970. pap. 2.95 o.p. (ISBN 0-686-11985-1). Wedge Pub.

Out of Darkness. James M. Bryant. 1971. pap. 6.50 (ISBN 0-686-27962-X). J M Bryant.

Out of Doors. Maureen Roffey. (Illus.). (ps). 1979. 1.25 (ISBN 0-370-02007-3, Pub. by Chatto Bodley Jonathan). Merrimack Bk Serv.

Out of Little Coins, Big Fortunes Grow. rev. 3rd ed. Don Bale, Jr. 1975. pap. 5.00 o.p. (ISBN 0-912070-08-0). Bale Bks.

Out of Little Coins, Big Fortunes Grow. 4th, rev. ed. Don Bale, Jr. 1980. pap. 5.00. Bale Bks.

Out of Loneliness. Fritz W. Faiss. (Illus.). 81p. 1972. pap. 8.00x ltd ed, signed (ISBN 0-916678-05-9); pap. 4.00 ltd ed (ISBN 0-916678-06-7). Green Hut.

Out of My Body. Ed. by Nancy Lewis. (Illus.). 20p. 1974. pap. 3.00x (ISBN 0-89062-035-0, Pub. by Touchtone). Pub Ctr Cult Res.

Out of My Life & Thought. Albert Schweitzer. pap. 1.50 o.p. (ISBN 0-451-61456-9, MW1456, Ment). NAL.

Out of My Life & Thought. Albert Schweitzer. 1972. pap. 2.95 o.p. (ISBN 0-03-091483-3). HR&W.

Out of My Treasure: Special Alumni Edition, Vol. V. Ed. by Don E. Boatman. LC 80-71104. (Out of My Treasure Ser.). 260p. 1981. pap. 4.95 (ISBN 0-89900-121-1). College Pr Pub.

Out of Our Past: The Forces That Shaped Modern America. rev. ed. Carl N. Degler. LC 77-88637. 1970. pap. 5.95 (ISBN 0-06-090002-4, CN2, CN). Har-Row.

Out of Our Past: The Forces That Shaped Modern America. rev. ed. Carl N. Degler. 1970. 12.50 o.s.i. (ISBN 0-06-011012-0, HarpT). Har-Row.

Out of School: Modern Perspectives in Truancy & School Refusal. Ed. by Lionel Hersov & Ian Berg. LC 79-41725. (Studies in Child Psychiatry Ser.). 320p. 1980. 45.50 (ISBN 0-471-27743-6, Pub. by Wiley-Interscience). Wiley.

Out of Season. Ian J. Burton. Ed. by Carol Baron. 192p. 1981. 10.95 (ISBN 0-517-54334-6). Crown.

Out of Sight. William D. Sheldon & Warren Wheelock. (Breakthrough Ser.). (gr. 6-12,RL 4). 1973. pap. text ed. 4.96 (ISBN 0-205-03341-5, 5233410); tchrs'. guide 2.40 (ISBN 0-205-03342-3, 5233429); dup. masters 20.00 (ISBN 0-205-03343-1, 5233437). Allyn.

Out of Step with the Dancers. Elizabeth Howard. LC 77-25928. (gr. 7 up). 1978. 8.95 (ISBN 0-688-22141-6); PLB 8.59 (ISBN 0-688-32141-0). Morrow.

Out of the Abyss. G. A. England. (YA) 5.95 (ISBN 0-685-07451-X, Avalon). Bouregy.

Out of the Bleachers. Stephanie Twin. (Women's Lives-Women's Work Ser). (Illus.). 1979. pap. 5.50 (ISBN 0-912670-59-2, Co-Pub. by McGraw). Feminist Pr.

Out of the Cauldron. Bernice Kohn. LC 74-150030. (Illus.). (gr. 5-9). 1971. reinforced bdg. 5.95 o.p. (ISBN 0-03-088367-9). HR&W.

Out of the Closets, Voices of Gay Liberation. Karla Jay & Allen Young. 1977. pap. 1.95 (ISBN 0-515-04497-0). Jove Pubns.

Out of the Cradle, Endlessly Rocking. Dominick Consolo. LC 70-138465. (Literary Casebook Ser.). 1971. pap. text ed. 2.95x (ISBN 0-675-09254-X). Merrill.

Out of the Dark. Norah Lofts. 1978. pap. 1.75 o.p. (ISBN 0-449-23479-7, Crest). Fawcett.

Out of the Darkness: The Planet Pluto. Patrick Moore & Clyde Tombaugh. (Illus.). 224p. 1980. 14.95 (ISBN 0-8117-1163-3). Stackpole.

Out of the Depths. John Newton. (Shepherd Illustrated Classics). (Illus.). 144p. 1981. pap. 5.95 (ISBN 0-87983-243-6). Keats.

Out of the Frying Pan. Karol Hope & Nancy Young. LC 78-1199. 1979. pap. 4.95 (ISBN 0-385-13198-4, Anch). Doubleday.

Out of the Ghetto: The Social Background of Jewish Emancipation, 1770-1870. Jacob Katz. LC 72-86386. 1973. 15.00 (ISBN 0-674-64775-0). Harvard U Pr.

Out of the Mist. Ralph Byrne. LC 69-11344. 1969. 5.95 o.p. (ISBN 0-8283-1007-6). Branden.

Out of the Past. William O. Kellogg. (gr. 9-12). 1969. pap. text ed. 4.95x (ISBN 0-88334-022-4) (ISBN 0-685-39240-6). Ind Sch Pr.

Out of the Past: A Topical History of the United States. 2nd ed. Donald V. Gawronski. 1975. pap. text ed. 9.95x (ISBN 0-02-474410-7, 47441); tchrs' manual free (ISBN 0-02-474420-4). Macmillan.

Out of the Past of Greece & Rome. Michael I. Rostovtzeff. LC 63-18047. (Illus.). 1960. 9.00x (ISBN 0-8196-0126-8). Biblo.

Out of the River Mist. new ed. C. Raymond Clar. LC 74-80008. (Illus.). 135p. 1974. pap. 3.50 (ISBN 0-89030-000-3). Forest Hist Soc.

Out of the Silent Planet. C. S. Lewis. 1943. 10.95 (ISBN 0-02-570790-6); large print ed. 9.95 (ISBN 0-02-489400-1). Macmillan.

Out of the Third. Beverly Dahlen. 3.00x o.p. (ISBN 0-685-46992-1); signed ed. 15.00x o.p. (ISBN 0-685-46993-X). Momos.

Out of the Treasure Chest. V. G. Beers. (Muffin Family Ser.). (Illus.). 96p. (ps-6). 1981. 8.95 (ISBN 0-8024-6099-2). Moody.

Out of the Valley. Betty Tapscott. 128p. 1981. pap. 3.95 (ISBN 0-8407-5761-1). Nelson.

Out of the Void. Leslie F. Stone. (YA) 5.95 (ISBN 0-685-07452-8, Avalon). Bouregy.

Out of Their League. Dave Meggyesy. (Illus.). 1971. pap. 1.75 o.s.i. (ISBN 0-446-59950-6). Warner Bks.

Out of This Struggle: The Filipinos in Hawaii. Ed. by Luis V. Teodoro. (Illus.). 168p. 1981. 12.95 (ISBN 0-8248-0747-2). U Pr of Hawaii.

Out of This World. Jermayne MacAgy & Etienne Sourian. (Illus.). 1964. pap. 2.00 (ISBN 0-914412-23-X). Inst for the Arts.

Out Somewhere & Back Again: The Kansas Stories. Nancy Stockwell. 1978. pap. write for info. (ISBN 0-9601714-0-1). Medusa.

Out There Where the Big Ships Go. 1980. pap. write for info. (ISBN 0-671-83501-7). PB.

Outback Runaway. Dorothy Cork. (Harlequin Romances Ser.). 192p. 1980. pap. 1.25 (ISBN 0-373-02372-3, Pub. by Harlquin). PB.

Outbreak. Robert De Maria. (Orig.). 1978. pap. 1.95 o.s.i. (ISBN 0-515-04433-4). Jove Pubns.

Outbreak of the Peloponnesian War. Donald Kagan. LC 69-18212. 438p. 1969. 25.00 (ISBN 0-8014-0501-7). Cornell U Pr.

Outcast. Beverly Byrne. (Griffin Saga Ser.: Vol. I). 512p. (Orig.). 1981. pap. 2.95 (ISBN 0-449-14396-1, GM). Fawcett.

Outcast. William W. Reade. Ed. by Robert L. Wolff. LC 75-1525. (Victorian Fiction Ser.). 1975. Repr. of 1875 ed. lib. bdg. 66.00 (ISBN 0-8240-1597-5). Garland Pub.

Outcast. Rosemary Sutcliff. (Alpha Books). 92p. (Orig.). 1979. pap. text ed. 2.25x (ISBN 0-19-424210-2). Oxford U Pr.

Outcast Capetown. John Western. (Illus.). 352p. 1981. 20.00 (ISBN 0-8166-1025-8). U. of Minn Pr.

Outcasts. Will Cook. 144p. (Orig.). 1981. pap. 1.75 (ISBN 0-553-14740-4). Bantam.

Outcasts. Joe L. Hensley. LC 80-705. (Crime Club Ser.). 192p. 1981. 9.95 (ISBN 0-385-15820-3). Doubleday.

Outcasts of Poker Flat. Bret Harte. Ed. by Walter Pauk & Raymond Harris. (Classics Ser). (Illus.). (gr. 6-12). 1976. pap. text ed. 1.60x (ISBN 0-89061-052-5, 525); tchrs. ed. 3.00 (ISBN 0-89061-053-3, 527). Jamestown Pubs.

Outcasts of Poker Flat. Bret Harte. (Creative's Classics Ser.). (Illus.). 48p. (gr. 4-9). 1980. PLB 6.95 (ISBN 0-87191-768-8). Creative Ed.

Outcasts of Poker Flat & Luck of Roaring Camp. rev. ed. Bret Harte. Ed. by Robert J. Dixson. (American Classics Ser.: Bk. 5). (gr. 9 up). 1973. pap. text ed. 2.75 (ISBN 0-88345-201-4, 18124); cassettes 40.00 (ISBN 0-685-38996-0); tapes 40.00 (ISBN 0-685-38997-9). Regents Pub.

Outcome Evaluation: How to Do It. Jerry Spicer. 1980. pap. 4.95 (ISBN 0-89486-112-3). Hazelden.

Outcome Uncertain: Science & the Political Process. Mary E. Ames. LC 77-81692. 1978. PLB 13.95x (ISBN 0-89461-028-7); pap. 7.95x (ISBN 0-89461-029-5). Comm Pr Inc.

Outcry. Henry James. LC 80-17012. xii, 261p. 1981. Repr. of 1911 ed. 20.00 (ISBN 0-86527-335-9). Fertig.

Outdoor Adventure Activities for School & Recreation Programs. Paul W. Darst & George P. Armstrong. (Orig.). pap. text ed. 13.95 (ISBN 0-8087-0489-3). Burgess.

Outdoor Adventure Book. Walt Disney Productions. LC 77-74468. (Disney's World of Adventure). (Illus.). (gr. 2-6). 1977. 3.95 (ISBN 0-394-83601-4, BYR); PLB 4.99 (ISBN 0-394-93601-9). Random.

Outdoor Cookbook. Marjorie P. Blanchard. (Cooking Plus Ser). (Illus.). (gr. 6 up). 1977. PLB 5.90 s&l o.p. (ISBN 0-531-00381-7). Watts.

Outdoor Design: A Handbook for the Architect & Planner. Olwen C. Marlowe. 301p. 1977. text ed. 76.00x (ISBN 0-258-97017-0, Pub. by Granada England). Renouf.

Outdoor Emergency Medicine. Ed. by Frank C. Madda. (Illus.). 277p. (Orig.). 1981. pap. 3.95 (ISBN 0-938278-00-2). BioServ Corp.

Outdoor Eye: A Sportsman's Guide. 2nd ed. Charles Elliott. LC 73-100358. (Funk & W Bk.). (Illus.). 1978. 9.95 o.s.i. (ISBN 0-308-10343-2, TYC-T); pap. 4.50 o.s.i. (ISBN 0-308-10344-0, TYC-T). T Y Crowell.

Outdoor Games. Frederick Alderson. (Junior Reference Ser.). (Illus.). 64p. (gr. 7 up). 1980. 7.95 (ISBN 0-7136-2031-5). Dufour.

Outdoor Games. David Buskin. (Illus.). (gr. k-4). 1966. PLB 7.95 (ISBN 0-87460-090-1). Lion.

Outdoor Garden Build-It Book. Jack Kramer. LC 76-52761. (Illus.). 1977. 14.95 o.p. (ISBN 0-684-14762-9, ScribT); pap. 7.95 o.p. (ISBN 0-684-15039-5, SL716, ScribT). Scribner.

Outdoor Handbook. Dale Cooper et al. (Illus.). 1978. 13.95 (ISBN 0-600-36743-6). Transatlantic.

Outdoor Life Gun Data Book. F. Philip Rice. LC 74-83594. (Outdoor Life Bk.). (Illus.). 576p. 1975. 12.95 o.p. (ISBN 0-06-013529-8, HarpT). Har-Row.

Outdoor Primary Education in Bangladesh. (Experiments & Innovations in Education Ser.: No. 40). 60p. 1980. pap. 4.00 (ISBN 92-3-101816-7, U1042, UNESCO). Unipub.

Outdoor Projects for Home & Garden. Family Handyman Editors. (Illus.). 1979. 12.95 o.p. (ISBN 0-8306-9832-9); pap. 8.95 (ISBN 0-8306-1116-9, 1116). TAB Bks.

Outdoor Recreation. Robert G. Schipf. LC 75-30958. (Spare Time Guides Ser.: No. 9). 1976. 12.50x o.p. (ISBN 0-87287-123-1). Libs Unl.
Outdoor Recreation. Bruce Wilkins. (Brighton Ser. in Recreation & Leisure Studies). 1981. text ed. 15.95x (ISBN 0-89832-015-1). Brighton Pub Co.
Outdoor Recreation: Forest, Park & Wilderness. J. R. McCall & V. M. McCall. (gr. 11-12). 1977. text ed. 12.95x (ISBN 0-685-71817-4, 82047). Macmillan.
Outdoor Recreation Planning, Perspectives & Research. Tel L. Napier. 288p. 1981. pap. text ed. 12.95 (ISBN 0-8403-2309-3). Kendall-Hunt.
Outdoor Recreation Projects. James L. Bright. LC 77-28410. 1978. 13.95 (ISBN 0-912336-62-5); pap. 6.95 (ISBN 0-912336-63-3). Structures Pub.
Outdoor Recreational Areas. (Home Repair and Improvement). 128p. (Orig.). 1980. 10.95 (ISBN 0-8094-3454-7). Time-Life.
Outdoor Sculpture in Grand Rapids. Fay L. Hendry. LC 80-7500. (Illus.). 145p. (Orig.). 1980. pap. 3.50 (ISBN 0-936412-00-3). Iota Pr.
Outdoor Structures. LC 78-1110. (Home Repair & Improvement Ser.). (Illus.). 1978. lib. bdg. 11.97 (ISBN 0-686-51038-0). Silver.
Outdoor Structures. Time-Life Editors. (Home Repair Ser.). (Illus.). 1978. 10.95 (ISBN 0-8094-2402-9). Time-Life.
Outdoor Survival. Charles Platt. LC 75-35883. (Career Concise Guides Ser.). (Illus.). 72p. (gr. 6 up). 1976. PLB 6.45 (ISBN 0-531-01128-3). Watts.
Outdoor Survival Handbook. David Platten. 13.50 (ISBN 0-7153-7793-0, Pub. by Batsford England). David & Charles.
Outdoor Survival Skills. 4th rev ed. Larry D. Olsen. LC 72-94938. (Illus.). 200p. 1973. 8.95 (ISBN 0-8425-0001-4); pap. 7.95 (ISBN 0-8425-0002-2). Brigham.
Outdoors Canada. Reader's Digest Association, Canada. (Illus.). 1980. 24.95 (ISBN 0-393-01366-9). Norton.
Outdoorsman's Cookbook. rev. ed. Arthur H. Carhart. 1962. pap. 0.95 o.s.i. (ISBN 0-02-009390-X, Collier). Macmillan.
Outdoorsman's Guide to Government Surplus. David LeRoy. 1978. 9.95 (ISBN 0-8092-7612-7); pap. 5.95 o.p. (ISBN 0-8092-7611-9). Contemp Bks.
Outdoorsman's Workshop. Monte Burch. 1977. 12.95 (ISBN 0-87691-239-0). Winchester Pr.
Outer City: Geographical Consequences of the Urbanization of the Suburbs. Peter O. Muller. Ed. by Salvatore J. Natoli. LC 76-29264. (Resource Papers for College Geography Ser.). (Illus.). 1976. pap. text ed. 4.00 (ISBN 0-89291-114-X). Assn Am Geographers.
Outer Continental Shelf Frontier Technology. Marine Board, Assembly of Engineering, National Research Council. LC 80-82152. 1980. pap. text ed. 8.50 (ISBN 0-309-03084-6). Natl Acad Pr.
Outer Limits of the Mind. Betty J. Burr. (Pal Paperbacks Kit B Ser.). (Illus., Orig.). (gr. 7-12). 1974. pap. text ed. 1.25 (ISBN 0-8374-3515-3). Xerox Ed Pubns.
Outer Shores One: Ed Ricketts & John Steinbeck Explore the Pacific Coast. Ed. by Joel W. Hedgpeth. 1978. pap. 7.95x (ISBN 0-916422-13-5). Mad River.
Outer Shores Two: Breaking Through. Ed. by Joel W. Hedgpeth. 1979. pap. 9.95x (ISBN 0-916422-14-3). Mad River.
Outland. Alan D. Foster. (Orig.). 1981. pap. 2.75 (ISBN 0-446-95829-8). Warner Bks.
Outland: The Movie. Richard J. Anobile. (Orig.). 1981. pap. 9.95 (ISBN 0-686-69396-5). Warner Bks.
Outlander. Jane Rule. LC 80-84221. 220p. (Orig.). 1981. pap. 6.95 (ISBN 0-930044-17-7). Naiad Pr.
Outlanders. Blaine Stevens. pap. 2.50 (ISBN 0-515-04861-5). Jove Pubns.
Outlaw. Clarence W. Anderson. (gr. 3-6). 1967. 5.95g o.s.i. (ISBN 0-02-700940-8). Macmillan.
Outlaw: Bill Mitchell, Alias Baldy Russell: His Life & Times. C. L. Sonnichsen. LC 65-25798. 1965. 9.95 (ISBN 0-8040-0238-X, SB). Swallow.
Outlaw Fury. Burt Arthur. 1976. pap. 0.95 o.p. (ISBN 0-685-72359-3, LB385NK, Leisure Bks). Nordon Pubns.
Outlaw Gunner. Harry M. Walsh. LC 71-180856. (Illus.). 1971. 12.50 (ISBN 0-87033-162-0, Pub. by Tidewater). Cornell Maritime.
Outlaw of Torn. Edgar R. Burroughs. 1975. pap. 1.95 (ISBN 0-441-64513-5). Ace Bks.
Outlaw of Torn. Edgar R. Burroughs. 1976. Repr. of 1927 ed. lib. bdg. 10.55x (ISBN 0-89966-042-8). Buccaneer Bks.
Outlaw Years: The History of the Land Pirates of the Natchez Trace. Robert M. Coates. LC 74-1087. (Illus.). 307p. 1974. Repr. of 1930 ed. 24.00 (ISBN 0-8103-3961-7). Gale.
Outlaws' Gold. Mick Clumpner. 224p. (Orig.). 1981. pap. 1.95 (ISBN 0-89083-712-0). Zebra.
Outlaws of Lost River. Paul Evans. 256p. (YA) 1974. 5.95 (ISBN 0-685-39180-9, Avalon). Bouregy.
Outlaw's Pledge. Ray Hogan. (Orig.). 1981. pap. 1.95 (ISBN 0-451-09778-5, 9778, Sig). NAL.
Outline Course of Pure Mathematics. A. F. Horadam. 1969. 23.00 (ISBN 0-08-012593-X). Pergamon.
Outline Descriptions of the Posts in the Military Division of the Missouri. P. H. Sheridan. (Illus.). 1972. Repr. of 1182 ed. 10.95 o.p. (ISBN 0-88342-004-X). Old Army.
Outline History of Spanish American Literature. 4th ed. John E. Englekirk et al. 1981. 24.50x (ISBN 0-89197-874-7); pap. text ed. 12.95x (ISBN 0-89197-326-5). Irvington.
Outline of a Theory of Practice. P. Bourdieu. LC 76-11073. (Studies in Social Anthropology: No. 16). (Illus.). 1977. 29.95 (ISBN 0-521-21178-6); pap. 9.95x (ISBN 0-521-29164-X). Cambridge U Pr.
Outline of American Government: The Continuing Experiment. Barbara Hinckley. (Illus.). 288p. 1981. pap. 7.95 (ISBN 0-13-645200-0). P-H.
Outline of Animal Development. Richard Davenport. LC 78-62548. (Life Sciences Ser.). (Illus.). 1979. text ed. 19.95 (ISBN 0-201-01814-4). A-W.
Outline of Basic Nursing Care. Elizabeth M. Welsh et al. (Illus.). 1975. pap. text ed. 11.95x (ISBN 0-433-35220-5). Intl Ideas.
Outline of Bible Study. G. Dallas Smith. pap. 2.95 (ISBN 0-89225-192-1); pap. 2.95 (ISBN 0-89225-192-1). Gospel Advocate.
Outline of Christian Theology. W. N. Clarke. 498p. 1898. text ed. 9.50x (ISBN 0-567-02069-X). Attic Pr.
Outline of Contemporary Drama. Thomas H. Dickinson. LC 70-88059. 1969. Repr. of 1927 ed. 12.00x (ISBN 0-8196-0249-3). Biblo.
Outline of Crystal Morphology. Arthur C. Bishop. 1970. pap. text ed. 5.50x (ISBN 0-09-079423-0). Humanities.
Outline of Cultural Materials. 5th, rev. ed. George P. Murdock et al. LC 80-81130. (Bibliography Ser.). Date not set. cancelled (ISBN 0-87536-652-X). HRAFP.
Outline of Developmental Physiology. 3rd ed. C. P. Raven. 1966. 15.00 (ISBN 0-08-011343-5). Pergamon.
Outline of English Costume. Doreen Yarwood. 1972. 19.95 (ISBN 0-7134-0852-9, Pub. by Batsford England). David & Charles.
Outline of French Grammar with Vocabularies. rev. ed. Henry B. Richardson. 1950. text ed. 12.50x (ISBN 0-89197-327-3); pap. text ed. 4.95x (ISBN 0-89197-328-1). Irvington.
Outline of General Psychology. rev. ed. Lester D. Crow & Alice Crow. (Quality Paperback: No. 28). (Orig.). 1976. pap. 3.95 (ISBN 0-8226-0028-5). Littlefield.
Outline of Genetic Epidemiology. N. E. Morton. (Illus.). x, 250p. 1981. pap. 25.75 (ISBN 3-8055-2269-X). S Karger.
Outline of Geriatrics. H. M. Hodkinson. 1975. 11.50 (ISBN 0-12-351450-9). Acad Pr.
Outline of Hindi Grammar. R. S. McGregor. 304p. 1977. 5.95x (ISBN 0-19-560797-X). Oxford U Pr.
Outline of Histology. rev. ed. 7th ed. Gerrit Bevelander. (Illus., Orig.). 1971. text ed. 12.95 (ISBN 0-8016-0680-2). Mosby.
Outline of History, 4 vols. H. G. Wells. 1920. Repr. 125.00 (ISBN 0-403-03082-X). Somerset Pub.
Outline of History: Being a Plain History of Life & Mankind. rev. ed. H. G. Wells. LC 75-139072. 1971. 15.95 (ISBN 0-385-02420-7). Doubleday.
Outline of Human Anatomy. Saul Wischnitzer. (Illus.). 404p. 1972. 11.75 (ISBN 0-398-02655-6). C C Thomas.
Outline of Human Genetics. 3rd ed. L. S. Penrose. 1973. text ed. 6.50x o.p. (ISBN 0-435-60701-4). Heinemann Ed.
Outline of Industrial Organic Chemistry. Alfred Rieche. 1968. 50.00 o.p. (ISBN 0-8206-0233-7). Chem Pub.
Outline of International Finance: Exchange Rates & Payments Between Countries. L. Sirc. LC 74-3259. 1974. 14.95 (ISBN 0-470-79325-2). Halsted Pr.
Outline of Irish Railway History. H. C. Casserley. (Illus.). 304p. 1974. 24.00 o.p. (ISBN 0-7153-6377-8). David & Charles.
Outline of Middle English Grammar. Margaret M. Roseborough. Repr. of 1938 ed. lib. bdg. 15.00x (ISBN 0-8371-4324-1, ROMI). Greenwood.
Outline of Monetary Theory. 4th ed. J. L. Hanson. 160p. 1980. pap. text ed. 9.95x (ISBN 0-7121-1533-1). Intl Ideas.
Outline of Occult Science. Rudolf Steiner. 352p. 1972. 9.95 (ISBN 0-910142-26-2); pap. 5.50 (ISBN 0-910142-75-0). Anthroposophic.
Outline of Pharmacology. Kee-Chang Huang. (Illus.). 420p. 1974. pap. 21.75 (ISBN 0-398-02717-X). C C Thomas.
Outline of Philosophy. Bertrand Russell. 1927. text ed. 17.95x (ISBN 0-04-192017-1). Allen Unwin.
Outline of Psychoanalysis. rev. ed. Sigmund Freud. Ed. & tr. by James Strachey. 1970. pap. 1.95 (ISBN 0-393-00151-2, Norton Lib). Norton.
Outline of Religious Literature of India. J. N. Farquhar. 1967. Repr 6.00 (ISBN 0-89684-287-8). Orient Bk Dist.
Outline of the Bible: Book by Book. Benson Y. Landis. (Orig.). 1963. pap. 3.50 (ISBN 0-06-463263-6, EH 263, EH). Har-Row.
Outline of Theatre Law. Milton C. Jacobs. LC 72-5454. 148p. 1972. Repr. of 1949 ed. lib. bdg. 12.50x (ISBN 0-8371-6436-2, JATL). Greenwood.
Outline of Vedic Literature. James A. Santucci. Ed. by M. Gerald Bradford. LC 76-27859. (American Academy of Religion. Aids for the Study of Religion Ser.). 1976. pap. 6.00 (ISBN 0-89130-085-6, 010305). Scholars Pr Ca.
Outlines for Christmas Sermons. John S. Meyer. (Sermon Outline Ser.). 48p. 1980. pap. 1.95 (ISBN 0-8010-6107-5). Baker Bk.
Outlines of a Critique of Technology. Ed. by Phil Slater. 160p. 1980. text ed. 14.50x (ISBN 0-391-01889-2). Humanities.
Outlines of a Theory of the Light Sense. Ewald Hering. LC 64-11130. (Illus.). 1964. 16.50x (ISBN 0-674-64900-1). Harvard U Pr.
Outlines of Avian Anatomy. 2nd ed. A. S. King & J. McLelland. (Illus.). 154p. 1981. text ed. write for info. (ISBN 0-8121-0779-9). Lea & Febiger.
Outlines of Biochemistry. 4th ed. Eric E. Conn & P. K. Stumpf. LC 75-34288. 1976. text ed. 25.95 (ISBN 0-471-16843-2). Wiley.
Outlines of Chinese Symbolism & Art Motives. C. A. Williams. LC 76-40397. 472p. 1976. pap. 6.00 (ISBN 0-486-23372-3). Dover.
Outlines of Jainism. S. Gopalan. LC 73-13196. 205p. 1973. pap. 8.95 (ISBN 0-470-31530-X). Halsted Pr.
Outlines of Jainism. Jagmandar L. Jaini. Ed. by F. W. Thomas. LC 78-14128. (Illus.). 1981. Repr. of 1940 ed. 19.00 (ISBN 0-88355-801-7). Hyperion Conn.
Outlines of Jurisprudence. K. Krishna Menon. 4.25x o.p. (ISBN 0-210-33910-1). Asia.
Outlines of Medieval History. 2nd ed. C. W. Previte-Orton. LC 64-25837. 1916. 14.00x (ISBN 0-8196-0147-0). Biblo.
Outlines of Modern Chinese Law. William S. Hung. (Studies in Chinese Government & Law). 317p. 1977. Repr. of 1934 ed. 23.50 (ISBN 0-89093-057-0). U Pubns Amer.
Outlines of Paint Technology, Vol. 1. W. M. Morgans. 1981. 75.00x (ISBN 0-686-68842-2, Pub. by Griffin England). State Mutual Bk.
Outlines of Psychology. Hermann Lotze. Tr. by George T. Ladd from Ger. (Contributions to the History of Psychology Ser.: Orientations). 1978. Repr. of 1886 ed. 30.00 (ISBN 0-89093-155-0). U Pubns Amer.
Outlines of Roman Law. Hamid Ali. 1964. 5.50x o.p. (ISBN 0-210-33703-6). Asia.
Outlines of Shakespeare's Plays. rev. ed. Homer A. Watt et al. (Orig.). 1969. pap. 3.95 (ISBN 0-06-460025-4, CO 25, COS). Har-Row.
Outlines of the History of Greek Philosophy. Eduard Zeller. 1980. Repr. of 1931 ed. text ed. 4.50 (ISBN 0-486-23920-9). Dover.
Outlines of the Life of Christ. 2nd ed. W. Sanday. 285p. Repr. of 1906 ed. 4.95 (ISBN 0-567-02224-2). Attic Pr.
Outlines of the Moral Philosophy. Dugald Stewart. LC 75-11255. (British Philosophers & Theologians of the 17th & 18th Centuries: Vol. 54). 1976. Repr. of 1793 ed. lib. bdg. 42.00 (ISBN 0-8240-1805-2). Garland Pub.
Outlines of Theology. A. A. Hodge. 580p. 1972. text ed. 12.95 (ISBN 0-310-26200-3). Zondervan.
Outlines on Revelation. Croft M Pentz. (Sermon Outline Ser.). 1978. pap. 1.95 (ISBN 0-8010-7030-9). Baker Bk.
Outlines on the Holy Spirit. Croft M Pentz. (Sermon Outline Ser) 1978. pap. 1.95 (ISBN 0-8010-7029-5). Baker Bk.
Outlook for Natural Gas: A Quality Fuel. Ed. by Peter Hepple. LC 73-661. 268p. 1973. 29.95 (ISBN 0-470-37303-2). Halsted Pr.
Outlook for Nuclear Power. 1980. 3.00 (ISBN 0-309-03039-0). Natl Acad Pr.
Outlook for Western Europe. Ed. by Irwin Isenberg. LC 79-95635. (Reference Shelf Ser: Vol. 42, No. 2). 1970 6.25 (ISBN 0-8242-0410-7). Wilson.
Outlook on New Jersey. new ed. Ed. by Silvio R. Laccetti. LC 79-64897. 488p. 1979. 14.95x (ISBN 0-8349-7540-8). W H Wise.
Outlook on Our Inner Western Way. William G. Gray. 1980. pap. 6.95 (ISBN 0-87728-493-8). Weiser.
Outpatient Medicine. L. M. Aledort et al. LC 78-51280. 1979. text ed. 10.50 (ISBN 0-89004-354-X). Raven.
Outpatient Services Journal Articles. 2nd ed. Vivian V. Clark. 317p. 1973. spiral bdg. 12.00 o.p. (ISBN 0-87488-797-6). Med Exam.
Outpatient Services: Journal Articles. 2nd ed. Ed. by Vivian V. Clark. 348p. 1973. 10.00 o.s.i. (ISBN 0-686-68575-X, 1498). Hospital Finan.
Outpost Encounters. Louise Johnson. LC 79-92927. (gr. 4 up). 1980. 12.95 (ISBN 0-89002-082-5); pap. 4.95 (ISBN 0-89002-081-7). Northwoods Pr.
Outpost of Hellenism: The Emergence of Heraclea on the Black Sea. Stanley M. Burstein. LC 74-620189. (Publications in Classical Studies: Vol. 14). 1975. 8.00x o.p. (ISBN 0-520-09530-8). U of Cal Pr.
Outposts of Monopoly Capitalism: Southern Africa in the Changing Global Economy. Ann Seidman & Neva S. Makgetla. 384p. (Orig.). 1980. 16.95 (ISBN 0-88208-114-4); pap. 8.95 (ISBN 0-88208-115-2). Lawrence Hill.
Outrage. Ed. by Katherine Spielman. LC 75-13420. 1976. 5.95 o.p. (ISBN 0-89110-010-5). Penthouse Pr.
Outrageous Fortunes: The Story of the Medici, the Rothschilds, & J. Pierpont Morgan. Cass Canfield. (Illus.). 1981. 10.95 (ISBN 0-15-170513-5). HarBraceJ.
Outrageous Kasimir. Achim Broger. Tr. by Hilda Van Stockum. (Illus.). (gr. 5-9). 1976. 8.25 (ISBN 0-688-22085-1); PLB 7.92 (ISBN 0-688-32085-6). Morrow.
Outreach in Counseling: Applying the Growth & Prevention Model in Schools & Colleges. David J. Drum & Howard E. Figler. LC 77-8091. 1973. pap. 7.50 (ISBN 0-910328-11-0). Carroll Pr.
Outreach of Diakonia. Adrian M. Van Peski. (Orig.). 1968. pap. text ed. 11.50x (ISBN 0-685-12466-5). Humanities.
Outrun the Dark. Cecilia Bartholomew. pap. 2.25 (ISBN 0-515-04648-5). Jove Pubns.
Outside. Andre Norton. LC 73-92454. (Illus.). 128p. (gr. 2-5). 1974. 5.95 o.s.i. (ISBN 0-8027-6185-2). Walker & Co.
Outside. Andre Norton. (gr. 4-7). 1975. pap. 1.75 (ISBN 0-380-00435-6, 52720, Camelot). Avon.
Outside Chance: Essays on Sport. Thomas McGuane. 256p. 1980. 10.95 (ISBN 0-374-10472-7). FS&G.
Outside in. Michael Z. Lewin. Date not set. pap. 2.25 (ISBN 0-425-05006-8). Berkley Pub.
Outside Man. Richard N. Patterson. 252p. 1981. 11.95 (ISBN 0-316-69362-6). Little.
Outside Over There. Maurice Sendak. LC 79-2682. (Ursula Nordstrom Bk). (Illus.). 48p. (gr. k up). 1981. 12.95 (ISBN 0-06-025523-4, HarpJ); PLB 12.89 (ISBN 0-06-025524-2). Har-Row.
Outside Shooter. Thomas Dygaard. LC 78-24002. (gr. 7-9). 1979. 7.50 (ISBN 0-688-22177-7); PLB 7.20 (ISBN 0-688-32177-1). Morrow.
Outsider. Yvonne A. Kenward. 96p. 1981. 6.95 (ISBN 0-8059-2760-3). Dorrance.
Outsiders in a Hearing World: A Sociology of Deafness. Paul C. Higgins. LC 80-12150. (Sociological Observations: Vol. 10). (Illus.). 205p. 1980. 18.95 (ISBN 0-8039-1421-0); pap. 8.95 (ISBN 0-8039-1422-9). Sage.
Outsiders on the Inside: Women & Organizations. Barbara L. Forisha & Barbara Goldman. (Illus.). 352p. 1981. 14.95 (ISBN 0-13-645382-1, Spectrum); pap. 6.95 (ISBN 0-13-645374-0). P-H.
Outsiders: Studies in the Sociology of Deviance. Howard S. Becker. LC 63-8413. 1963. 12.95 (ISBN 0-02-902200-2); pap. 3.95 (ISBN 0-02-902140-5). Free Pr.
Outsiders: The Western Experience in India & China. Rhoads Murphey. LC 76-27279. (Michigan Studies on China Ser.). 1976. 16.50x (ISBN 0-472-08679-0). U of Mich Pr.
Outstanding Dissertations in Bilingual Education. Susan G. Schneider et al. LC 8-80120. 127p. 1980. pap. 4.85 (ISBN 0-89763-020-3). Natl Clearinghse Bilingual Ed.
Outstanding Iowa Women: Past & Present. Ethel W. Hanft & Paula J. Manley. LC 80-53730. (Illus.). 135p. 1980. pap. 4.95 (ISBN 0-9605162-0-4). River Bend.
Outstanding Women Who Promoted the Concept of the Unified School Library & Audio Visual Program. Brenda Branyon. 375p. 1981. 20.00 (ISBN 0-686-69458-9). Hi Willow.
Outstretched Hand-Advances in Modern Medicine. Moira D. Reynolds. (Illus.). 140p. 1980. lib. bdg. 7.97 (ISBN 0-8239-0502-0). Rosen Pr.
Outwards from Earth. Ed. by Edmund Crispin. (Orig.). 1974. pap. 3.95 (ISBN 0-571-10489-4, Pub. by Faber & Faber). Merrimack Bk Serv.
Outwitting Arthritis: People Talk About Controlling, Conquering & Coping with Their Arthritis. Isabel Hanson. 250p. 1980. pap. 7.95 (ISBN 0-916870-30-8). Creative Arts Bk.
Ova & Parasites. Robert S. Desowitz. (Illus.). 224p. 1980. pap. text ed. 22.50 (ISBN 0-06-140688-0, Harper Medical). Har-Row.

Oval Lady. Leonora Carrington. Tr. by Rochelle Holt. (Illus.). 1975. pap. 3.75 o.p. (ISBN 0-88496-037-4). Capra Pr.

Ovarian Carcinoma. 2nd ed. 1981. price not set. Masson Pub.

Ovarian Carcinoma: Etiology, Diagnosis & Treatment. Hugh Barber. LC 77-846077. (Illus.). 1978. 41.25 (ISBN 0-89352-009-8). Masson Pub.

Ovarian Follicular Development & Function. Ed. by A. Rees Midgley & William A. Sadler. LC 77-17750. 1978. 30.00 (ISBN 0-89004-186-5). Raven.

Ovarian Gynaecology. Derek Tacchi. LC 76-26778. (Illus.). 1976. text ed. 26.00 (ISBN 0-7216-8725-3). Saunders.

Ovarian Tumors. N. A. Janovski & T. L. Paramanandhan. LC 77-176208. (Major Problems in Obstetrics & Gynecology Ser.: Vol. 4). (Illus.). 220p. 1973. 24.00 (ISBN 0-7216-5115-1). Saunders.

Ovary. 2nd ed. Ed. by Solly Zuckerman. Incl. Vol. 1. General Aspects. 1977. 49.00 (ISBN 0-12-782601-7); Vol. 2. Physiology. 1977. 53.50 (ISBN 0-12-782602-5); Vol. 3. Regulation of Oogenesis & Sleriodogenesis. 1978. 45.00 (ISBN 0-12-782603-3). 1977. Acad Pr.

Ovary: A Correlation of Structure & Function in Mammals. Hannah Peters & Kenneth P. McNatty. 1980. 36.00 (ISBN 0-520-04124-0). U of Cal Pr.

Over a Barrell: A Guide to the Canadian Energy Crisis. Jan Marmorek. LC 80-1068. 224p. 1981. 12.95 (ISBN 0-385-17192-7); pap. 6.95 (ISBN 0-385-17195-1). Doubleday.

Over & Out. Norman Rosten. LC 72-80735. 224p. 1972. 5.95 o.s.i. (ISBN 0-8076-0661-8). Braziller.

Over & Out. William D. Sheldon et al. (Breaktrough Ser.). (gr. 7-12). 1976. pap. text ed. 5.12 (ISBN 0-205-04622-3, 5246229); tchrs'. ed. 2.40 (ISBN 0-205-04620-7, 5246202); dup. masters 22.00 (ISBN 0-205-04621-5, 5246210). Allyn.

Over Fifty-Five: A Handbook on Aging. Ed. by Theodore G. Duncan. 1981. write for info. Franklin Inst Pr.

Over Fifty: The Definitive Guide to the Best Years of Your Life. Auren Uris. 624p. 1981. pap. 9.95 (ISBN 0-553-01297-5). Bantam.

Over Here. Edgar Guest. 192p. 1980. Repr. of 1918 ed. lib. bdg. 11.95x (ISBN 0-89968-192-1). Lightyear.

Over in the Meadow. Olive A. Wadsworth. (gr. k-3). 1971. pap. 1.95 (ISBN 0-590-09195-6, Schol Pap). Schol Bk Serv.

Over My Dead Body. Rex Stout. 1979. pap. 1.75 (ISBN 0-515-04865-8, 04865-8). Jove Pubns.

Over-the-Counter Securities Markets. 3rd ed. Leo M. Loll, Jr. & Julian G. Buckley. (Illus.). 560p. 1973. 19.95x (ISBN 0-13-647180-3). P-H.

Over the Dry Side. Louis L'Amour. 192p. 1981. pap. 2.25 (ISBN 0-553-14536-3). Bantam.

Over the Edge. William Sheldon & Warren H. Wheelock. (Orig.). (RL 3). 1972. pap. text ed. 4.96 (ISBN 0-205-03340-7, 5233402); tchrs'. guide 2.40 (ISBN 0-205-03338-5, 5233380). Allyn.

Over the Hills & Far Away. Lavinia Russ. LC 68-13371. (gr. 5-9). 1968. 5.50 o.p. (ISBN 0-15-258946-5, HJ). HarBraceJ.

Over the River & Through the Wood. Lydia M. Child. (Illus.). (gr. k-3). 1975. pap. 1.95 (ISBN 0-590-09937-X, Schol Pap). Schol Bk Serv.

Over the Top. Barbara J. Crane. (Crane Reading System - English Ser.). (Illus.). (gr. k-2). 1977. pap. text ed. 2.95 (ISBN 0-89075-100-5). Crane Pub Co.

Over, Under & Through & Other Spatial Concepts. Tana Hoban. LC 72-81055. (Illus.). 32p. (ps-2). 1973. 8.95 (ISBN 0-02-744820-7). Macmillan.

Overcoat, & Other Tales of Good & Evil. Nicolai V. Gogol. Tr. by David Magarshack from Rus. LC 79-17318. 1979. Repr. of 1965 ed. lib. bdg. 10.00x (ISBN 0-8376-0442-7). Bentley.

Overcomers. Russell Chandler. 1978. 6.95 o.p. (ISBN 0-8007-0944-6). Revell.

Overcoming Arthritis. Frank D. Hart. LC 80-22466. (Positive Health Guides Ser.). (Illus.). 112p. 1981. 9.95 (ISBN 0-668-04679-1); pap. 5.95 (ISBN 0-686-69380-9). Arco.

Overcoming Barriers to School Effectiveness. Jim Stanton & Ross Zerchykov. 153p. (Orig.). 1979. pap. 6.50 (ISBN 0-917754-10-7). Inst Responsive.

Overcoming Handicap. Patricia Hedley. pap. 4.50 (ISBN 0-263-05062-9). Transatlantic.

Overcoming Hurts & Anger. Dwight L. Carlson. LC 80-83852. 1981. pap. 4.95 (ISBN 0-89081-277-2). Harvest Hse.

Overcoming Learning Disabilities: A Team Approach (Parent-Teacher-Physician-Child) Martin Baren et al. 1978. text ed. 16.95 (ISBN 0-8359-5365-3). Reston.

Overcoming Murphy's Law. William C. Waddell. 618p. 1981. 14.95 (ISBN 0-8144-5628-6). Am Mgmt.

Overcoming Procrastination. Albert Ellis & William J. Knaus. LC 76-26333. 1977. pap. 4.95 (ISBN 0-917476-04-2). Rational Living.

Overcoming Procrastination. Albert Ellis & William J. Knaus. LC 76-26333. 1977. pap. 4.95 (ISBN 0-917476-04-2). Inst Rational-Emotive.

Overcoming Religion. David Mills. 1980. pap. 3.95 (ISBN 0-8065-0742-X). Lyle Stuart.

Overcoming the Fear of Death. David C. Gordon. 1970. 8.95 (ISBN 0-02-544790-4). Macmillan.

Overdentures. Allen A. Brewer & Robert M. Morrow. LC 74-28500. (Illus.). 270p. 1975. 37.50 o.p. (ISBN 0-8016-3515-2). Mosby.

Overdentures. 2nd ed. Allen A. Brewer & Robert M. Morrow. LC 80-19356. (Illus.). 426p. 1980. text ed. 47.50 (ISBN 0-8016-0785-X). Mosby.

Overdrive: A Human Maintenance Manual. Harris. 1978. 11.95 (ISBN 0-7153-7399-4). David & Charles.

Overhead Projection. Jerry D. Sparks. Ed. by James E. Duane. LC 80-21334. (Instructional Media Library: Vol. 10). (Illus.). 112p. 1981. 13.95 (ISBN 0-87778-170-2). Educ Tech Pubns.

Overheard in a Bubble Chamber & Other Sciencepoems. Lillian Morrison. (Illus.). 64p. (gr. 7 up). 1981. 7.95 (ISBN 0-688-00490-3); PLB 7.63 (ISBN 0-688-00493-8). Morrow.

Overhearing the Gospel. Fred B. Craddock. LC 77-19106. 1978. 6.95 (ISBN 0-687-29938-1). Abingdon.

Overheated Decade. Herbert I. London. LC 76-5960. 200p. 1976. 12.00x (ISBN 0-8147-4966-6); pap. 6.95x (ISBN 0-8147-4967-4). NYU Pr.

Overing Discouragement. Richard Kaiser. LC 79-84746. 128p. 1981. pap. 2.50 (ISBN 0-89081-269-1). Harvest Hse.

Overkill. John Benteen. (Sundance Ser.: No. 1). 1976. pap. 1.50 (Leisure Bks). Nordon Pubns.

Overland. Peter Fraenkel. LC 75-26358. (Illus.). 160p. 1976. 6.50 (ISBN 0-7153-7040-5). David & Charles.

Overland Expedition to California. Parker H. French. 1970. pap. 2.25 (ISBN 0-917420-03-9). Buck Hill.

Overland Journal of Amos Piatt Josselyn. Ed. by William T. Barrett, II. 129p. 1978. octavo 10.00. Holmes.

Overland Stage. Glen Dines. (gr. 4-6). 1967. 3.95g o.s.i. (ISBN 0-02-731730-7). Macmillan.

Overlook Illustrated Dictionary of Nautical Terms. Graham Blackburn. LC 80-39640. (Illus.). 416p. 1981. 19.95 (ISBN 0-87951-124-9). Overlook Pr.

Overlord. Les V. Roper, Jr. 1978. pap. 1.95 o.s.i. (ISBN 0-515-04754-6). Jove Pubns.

Overlord: Normandy, Nineteen Forty-Four. William Jackson. Ed. by Noble Frankland & Christopher Dowling. LC 79-52238. (Politics & Strategy of the Second World War Ser.). 1979. 15.00 (ISBN 0-87413-161-8). U Delaware Pr.

Overnight Mountain & Other Missionary Stories. 38p. (Orig.). (gr. 2-6). 1980. pap. 1.50 (ISBN 0-89323-004-9) (ISBN 0-89323-004-9). BMA Pr.

Overpopulation, & Its Remedy. W. T. Thornton. 446p. 1971. Repr. of 1846 ed. 25.00x (ISBN 0-686-28337-6, Pub. by Irish Academic Pr). Biblio Dist.

Override. LC 79-57122. (Feminist Novels Ser.). 100p. 1980. pap. 4.95 (ISBN 0-935772-03-0). Diotima Bks.

Overseas Bases: Problems of Projecting American Military Power Abroad. Alvin J. Cottrell & Thomas H. Moorer. LC 77-88453. (The Washington Papers: No. 47). 1977. 3.50x (ISBN 0-8039-0952-7). Sage.

Overseas Opportunities for American Educators & Students. 2nd ed. Lorraine Mathies & W. Thomas. 1973. 11.95 o.s.i. (ISBN 0-02-469370-7). Macmillan Info.

Overshoot: The Ecological Basis of Revolutionary Change. William R. Catton, Jr. LC 80-13443. (Illus.). 250p. 1980. 16.50 (ISBN 0-252-00818-9). U of Ill Pr.

Overtones. Alice Gerstenberg. (Playbooks). 1.25 o.p. (ISBN 0-679-39054-5). McKay.

Overture to Death. Ngaio Marsh. 1978. pap. 1.75 o.s.i. (ISBN 0-515-04531-4). Jove Pubns.

Overture to Death. Ngaio Marsh. (Ngaio Marsh Mysteries Ser.). 320p. 1981. pap. 2.25 (ISBN 0-515-05966-8). Jove Pubns.

Overtures to Biology: Speculations of Eighteenth Century Naturalists. Philip Ritterbush. 1964. 42.50x (ISBN 0-685-69859-9). Elliots Bks.

Overview Environmental Training. (UNEP Report Ser.: No. 9). 150p. 1980. pap. 14.00 (UNEP037, UNEP). Unipub.

Overview: Genetic Resources, 1980. (UNEP Ser.: No. 5). 132p. 1980. pap. 12.00 (UNEP 034, UNEP). Unipub.

Overview: Marine Living Resources. (UNEP Report Ser.: No. 7). 73p. 1980. pap. 8.50 (UNEP 035, UNEP). Unipub.

Overview of Communication & Interpersonal Relationships. Ed. by Ronald Applbaum. (MODCOM Modules in Speech Communication Ser.). 1976. pap. text ed. 2.25 (ISBN 0-574-22520-X, 13-5520). SRA.

Overview of Intercultural Education, Training & Research, 3 vols. Ed. by David S. Hoopes et al. Incl. Vol. I. Theory. LC 78-70690. pap. text ed. 6.50 (ISBN 0-933934-01-7); Vol. 2. Training & Research. LC 78-70690. 1978. pap. text ed. 6.50 (ISBN 0-933934-02-5); Vol. 3. Special Research Areas. LC 78-70690. 1978. pap. text ed. 6.50 (ISBN 0-933934-03-3). LC 78-70690. Set. pap. text ed. 17.95 (ISBN 0-933934-04-1). Intercult Pr.

Overview of Speech Preparation. John A. Campbell. Ed. by Ronald Applbaum & Roderick Hart. LC 13-5567. (Modcom, Modules in Speech Communication Ser.). 1980. pap. text ed. 2.25 (ISBN 0-574-22567-6, 13-5567). SRA.

Overview of the Alaska Highway Gas Pipeline. Compiled by American Society of Civil Engineers. 136p. 1978. pap. text ed. 11.00 (ISBN 0-87262-130-8). Am Soc Civil Eng.

Overview of the Experiences of the ILIR Manpower Laboratory: The Development of a Model Approach to the Retrieval, Dissemination, & Utilization of Information on Manpower Operations. Louis A. Ferman & John C. Erfurt. 1973. looseleaf 3.00x (ISBN 0-87736-332-3). U of Mich Inst Labor.

Ovid. Ed. by J. W. Binns. (Greek & Latin Studies). 1973. 20.00x (ISBN 0-7100-7639-8). Routledge & Kegan.

Ovid & the Canterbury Tales. Richard L. Hoffman. LC 67-17174. 1967. 7.50x o.p. (ISBN 0-8122-7553-5). U of Pa Pr.

Ovid As an Epic Poet. 2nd ed. Brooks Otis. LC 75-96098. 1971. 56.00 (ISBN 0-521-07615-3). Cambridge U Pr.

Ovid's Metamorphoses: An Introduction to Its Basic Aspects. G. Karl Galinsky. LC 74-84146. 1975. 20.00x (ISBN 0-520-02848-1). U of Cal Pr.

Ovid's Metamorphoses English Ed. Ovid & George Sandys. LC 75-27873. (Renaissance & the Gods Ser.: Vol. 27). (Illus.). 1976. Repr. of 1632 ed. lib. bdg. 73.00 (ISBN 0-8240-2076-6). Garland Pub.

Ovid's Metamorphoses: Selections. Ed. by A. C. Reynell et al. 1972. pap. 4.50 (ISBN 0-571-10254-9, Pub. by Faber & Faber). Merrimack Bk Serv.

Ovum Ltd: Packet Switching Networks & the Data Communications User. (Illus.). 1976. 180.00x o.p. (ISBN 0-903969-15-7). Scholium Intl.

Owen D. Young & American Enterprise: A Biography. Everett N. Case & Josephine Y. Case. 1981. 25.00 (ISBN 0-87923-360-5). Godine.

Owen Felltham. Ted-Larry Pebworth. LC 76-4863. (English Authors Ser.: No. 189). 1976. lib. bdg. 10.95 (ISBN 0-8057-6655-3). Twayne.

Owen Roe O'Neill. J. F. Taylor. 1981. Repr. 7.50 (ISBN 0-916620-27-1). Portals Pr.

Owl & Other Poems. Rajlukshmee Debee. Tr. by Rajlukshmee Debee from Bengali. (Writers Workshop Redbird Ser.). 1975. 12.00 (ISBN 0-88253-604-4); pap. text ed. 4.80 (ISBN 0-88253-603-6). Ind-US Inc.

Owl & Other Scrambles. Lisl Weil. LC 80-13742. (Illus.). (ps-3). 1980. PLB 8.95 (ISBN 0-525-36527-3, Unicorn). Dutton.

Owl & the Pussycat & Other Verses. E. Lear. (Peter Possum Paperbacks Ser). 1967. pap. 0.95 o.p. (ISBN 0-531-05119-6). Watts.

Owls. Tony Angell. 80p. text ed. 12.95 (ISBN 0-919654-25-8). Hancock Hse.

Owls. Helen Hoke & Valerie Pitt. LC 74-23981. (Illus.). 64p. (gr. 3-7). 1975. PLB 4.47 o.p. (ISBN 0-531-00832-0). Watts.

Owls. rev. ed. Herbert S. Zim. (Illus.). (gr. 3-7). 1977. PLB 6.48 (ISBN 0-688-32109-7). Morrow.

Owls Bay in Babylon. Charles Black. (American Dust Ser.: No. 13). 90p. 1980. 7.95 (ISBN 0-913218-92-8); pap. 2.95 (ISBN 0-913218-91-X). Dustbooks.

Owls Do Cry. Janet Frame. 4.50 o.s.i. (ISBN 0-8076-0116-0). Braziller.

Owls: Hunters of the Night. Margaret W. Sadoway. LC 80-27541. (Nature Books for Young Readers). (Illus.). (gr. 3-8). 1981. PLB 5.95g (ISBN 0-8225-0293-3). Lerner Pubns.

Owls in the Family. Farley Mowat. (Skylark Ser.). 96p. 1981. pap. 1.50 (ISBN 0-553-15094-4). Bantam.

Owl's Insomnia. Mark Strand. LC 73-81724. 1973. pap. 4.95. Atheneum.

Owl's Kiss: Three Stories. Mary Q. Steele. LC 78-1983. (gr. 5-9). 1978. 7.95 (ISBN 0-688-80174-9); PLB 7.63 (ISBN 0-688-84174-0). Greenwillow.

Owls of the Southwest & Mexico. Hamilton Tyler. (Illus.). 204p. 1979. 17.50 (ISBN 0-87358-219-5); pap. 9.95 (ISBN 0-87358-225-X). Northland.

Owl's Song. (YA) (gr. 7 up). 1976. pap. 1.25 (ISBN 0-380-00605-7, 28738). Avon.

Own Your Own Life. Richard G. Abell & Corliss W. Abell. (Illus.). 288p. 1976. 9.95 o.p. (ISBN 0-679-50601-2). McKay.

Owner-Built Adobe. Duane Newcomb. (Illus.). 224p. 1980. 14.95 (ISBN 0-684-16609-7, ScribT). Scribner.

Owner-Built Pole Frame House. Ken Kern. (Illus.). 192p. 1981. 14.95 (ISBN 0-684-16767-0, ScribT). Scribner.

Owner-Operators: Independent Trucker. D. Daryl Wyckoff & David H. Maister. LC 74-23978. (Illus.). 1975. 15.95x (ISBN 0-669-96800-5). Lexington Bks.

Owner's Manual for the Human Being. Mitchell Gilbert. 1980. pap. 4.95 (ISBN 0-686-69316-7). Weiser.

Ownership, Control & Ideology. Theo Nichols. (Studies in Management Ser.). (Illus.). 272p. 1970. text ed. 8.95x (ISBN 0-04-338042-5). Allen Unwin.

Ownership Theory of the Trade Union: A New Approach. Donald L. Martin. 160p. 1981. 14.50x (ISBN 0-520-03884-3). U of Cal Pr.

Owning a Horse: A Practical Guide. Diana Gregory. LC 76-9192. (Illus.). 1977. 11.95 o.s.i. (ISBN 0-06-011622-6, HarpT). Har-Row.

Owyhee Mountain Ballads & Other Poems. Mac Parkings. 1980. 4.50 o.p. (ISBN 0-8062-1086-9). Carlton.

Ox-Bow Incident. Walter V. Clark. 6.75 (ISBN 0-8446-0060-1). Peter Smith.

Ox, No. 3. Piers Anthony. 1976. pap. 1.75 (ISBN 0-380-00461-5, 41392). Avon.

Ox of the Wonderful Horns & Other African Folktales. Ashley Bryan. LC 75-154749. (Illus.). (gr. 1-5). 1971. PLB 8.95 (ISBN 0-689-20690-9). Atheneum.

Ox That Gored. J. J. Finkelstein. LC 80-65852. (Transactions Ser.: Vol. 71, Pt. 1). 1981. 12.00 (ISBN 0-87169-711-4). Am Philos.

Oxcart Trail. Herbert Krause. LC 54-6495. 1976. Repr. of 1954 ed. 9.95 (ISBN 0-88498-047-2). leatherette 12.95 (ISBN 0-88498-047-2). Brevet Pr.

Oxfod History of the American People. Samuel E. Morrison. Incl. Vol. 2 (ISBN 0-451-61890-4, M*E 1890); Vol. 3 (ISBN 0-451-61891-2, ME1891). Date not set. pap. 2.50 (Ment). NAL.

Oxford American Dictionary. Ed. by Stuart F. Berg et al. 832p. 1980. pap. 4.95 (ISBN 0-380-51052-9, 51052). Avon.

Oxford Anthology of English Literature. Ed. by Frank Kermode et al. Incl. Vol. 1. Middle Ages Through the Eighteenth Century. 2406p. (ISBN 0-19-501659-9); pap. (ISBN 0-19-501657-2); Vol. 2. 1800 to the Present. 2270p. (ISBN 0-19-501660-2); pap. (ISBN 0-19-501658-0). (Illus.). 1973. 14.95x ea.; pap. 13.95x ea. Oxford U Pr.

Oxford Book of Ballads, 2 vols in one. Ed. by Arthur Quiller-Couch. Repr. of 1955 ed. 75.00 (ISBN 0-403-08625-6). Somerset Pub.

Oxford Book of Flowerless Plants: Ferns, Fungi, Mosses, & Liverworts, Lichens, & Seaweeds. Frank H. Brightman. Ed. by B. E. Nicholson. (Illus.). 1966. 27.00 (ISBN 0-19-910004-7). Oxford U Pr.

Oxford Book of French Verse, Thirteenth Century to Twentieth Century. 2nd ed. Ed. by St. John Lucas & P. M. Jones. (Fr). 1957. 24.95 (ISBN 0-19-812109-1). Oxford U Pr.

Oxford Book of Garden Flowers. E. B. Anderson et al. (Illus.). 1963. 27.50 (ISBN 0-19-910002-0). Oxford U Pr.

Oxford Book of German Verse, Twelfth to Twentieth Century. 3rd ed. Ed. by Ernest L. Stahl. (Ger). 1967. 27.50 (ISBN 0-19-812132-6). Oxford U Pr.

Oxford Book of Insects. John Burton et al. (Illus.). 216p. 1968. 19.50x (ISBN 0-19-910005-5). Oxford U Pr.

Oxford Book of Irish Verse Seventeenth to Twentieth Century. Ed. by Donagh Macdonagh & Lennox Robinson. 1958. 24.95 (ISBN 0-19-812115-6). Oxford U Pr.

Oxford Book of Italian Verse, Thirteenth Century to Nineteenth Century. Ed. by St. John Lucas & C. Dionisotti. 1952. 24.95 (ISBN 0-19-812116-4). Oxford U Pr.

Oxford Book of Poetry for Children. Ed. by Edward Blishen. LC 63-19091. (Illus.). (gr. k-3). 1964. PLB 7.90 o.p. (ISBN 0-531-01537-8). Watts.

Oxford Book of Portuguese Verse: 12th Century to 20th Century. 2nd ed. Ed. by B. Vidigal. 1953. 11.25x o.p. (ISBN 0-19-812122-9). Oxford U Pr.

Oxford Book of Satirical Verse. Ed. by Geoffrey Grigson. 480p. 1980. 22.50 (ISBN 0-19-214110-4). Oxford U Pr.

Oxford Book of Short Stories. Ed. by V. S. Pritchett. 750p. 1981. 19.95 (ISBN 0-19-214116-3). Oxford U Pr.

Oxford Book of Verse in English Translation. Ed. by Charles Tomlinson. 750p. 1980. 37.50 (ISBN 0-19-214103-1). Oxford U Pr.

Oxford Book of Wild Flowers. Sheila Ary & Mary Gregory. (Illus.). 1970. 27.50 (ISBN 0-19-910001-2). Oxford U Pr.

Oxford Canal. Hugh J. Compton. LC 76-54077. (Inland Waterways History Ser.). (Illus.). 1977. 6.95 (ISBN 0-7153-7238-6). David & Charles.

Oxford Chekhov. Anton Chekhov. Ed. & tr. by Ronald Hingley. Incl. Vol. 1. Short Plays. 222p. 1968. 27.50x (ISBN 0-19-211349-6); Vol. 2. Platonov, Ivanov, the Seagull. 376p. 1967. 37.50x (ISBN 0-19-211347-X); Vol. 5. Stories, 1889-1891. 270p. 1970. 32.00x (ISBN 0-19-211353-4); Vol. 6. Stories, 1892-1893. 330p. 1971. 37.50x (ISBN 0-19-211363-1); Vol. 8. Stories, 1895-1897. 300p. 1965. 28.50x (ISBN 0-19-211340-2). Oxford U Pr.

Oxford Chekhov, Vol. 9: Stories 1898 - 1904. Anton Chekhov. Ed. by Ronald Hingley. 346p. 1975. 37.50x (ISBN 0-19-211383-6). Oxford U Pr.

Oxford Companion to American Literature. 4th ed. James D. Hart. (YA) 1965. 29.95 (ISBN 0-19-500565-1). Oxford U Pr.

Oxford Companion to Canadian History & Literature. Norah Story. 1967. 35.00 o.p. (ISBN 0-19-540115-8). Oxford U Pr.

Oxford Companion to Classical Literature. 2nd ed. Ed. by Paul Harvey. (Illus.). (YA) (gr. 9 up). 1937. 21.00 (ISBN 0-19-866103-7). Oxford U Pr.

Oxford Dictionary of Modern Greek. Greek-English. Ed. by Julian T. Pring. 1965. 13.50x (ISBN 0-19-864207-5). Oxford U Pr.

Oxford Dictionary of the Christian Church. F. L. Cross & Elizabeth A. Livingstone. 1512p. 1974. 49.95x (ISBN 0-19-211545-6). Oxford U Pr.

Oxford-Duden Pictorial German-English Dictionary. John Pheby. Ed. by The Dudenredaktion & German Section of Oxford Pr Dictionary Department. (Illus.). 776p. 1980. text ed. 24.95x (ISBN 0-19-864135-4). Oxford U Pr.

Oxford Economic Atlas of the World. 4th ed. Cartographic Dept. of the Clarendon Pr. (Illus.). 248p. 1972. 35.00 (ISBN 0-19-894106-4); pap. 9.95x (ISBN 0-19-894107-2). Oxford U Pr.

Oxford Encyclopedia of Trees of the World. Ed. by Bayard Hora. (Illus.). 1981. write for info. Oxford U Pr.

Oxford English-Arabic Dictionary of Current Usage. Ed. by N. S. Doniach. 1972. 48.00x (ISBN 0-19-864312-8). Oxford U Pr.

Oxford English Dictionary: Compact Edition, 2 vols. compact ed. 16569p. 1971. 75.00 (ISBN 0-918414-08-3). Readex Bks.

Oxford Essays in Jurisprudence, Vol. 2. Ed. by Alfred W. Simpson. 315p. 1973. text ed. 39.95x (ISBN 0-19-825313-3). Oxford U Pr.

Oxford History of Modern India: Seventeen Forty to Nineteen Seventy-Five. 2nd ed. Percival Spear. 1979. pap. 6.95 (ISBN 0-19-561076-8). Oxford U Pr.

Oxford History of the American People. Samuel E. Morison. 1965. text ed. 18.95x (ISBN 0-19-500997-5). Oxford U Pr.

Oxford History of the American People, Vol. 1. Samuel E. Morison. pap. 2.25 ea. (Ment). Vol. 1 (ISBN 0-451-61653-7, ME1653). Vol. 2 (ME1890). Vol. 3 (ISBN 0-451-61655-3, ME1891). NAL.

Oxford Ibsen. Henrik Ibsen. Ed. by James W. McFarlane. Incl. Vol. 2. The Vikings at Helgeland; Love's Comedy; The Pretenders. Tr. by Jens Arup. 1962. 24.00x (ISBN 0-19-211334-8); Vol. 4. The League of Youth; Emperor Galilean. Tr. by James W. McFarlane & Graham Orton. 1963. 32.00x (ISBN 0-19-211338-0); Vol. 5. Pillars of Society, a Doll's House, Ghosts. Tr. by James W. McFarlane. 1961. 18.50x (ISBN 0-19-211326-7); Vol. 7. The Lady from the Sea; Hedda Gabler; The Master Builder. Tr. by Jens Arup & James W. McFarland. 1966. 32.00x (ISBN 0-19-211342-9); Vol. 3. Brand, Peer Gynt. Tr. by James Kirkup & Christopher Fry. 1972. 24.00x (ISBN 0-19-211360-7); Vol. 1. Early Plays. Tr. by Graham Orton. 1970. 45.00x (ISBN 0-19-211357-7). Oxford U Pr.

Oxford Illustrated Jane Austen, 6 vols. 3rd ed. Jane Austen. Ed. by R. W. Chapman. Incl. Sense & Sensibility. 1933. Vol. 1. 15.95x (ISBN 0-19-254701-1); Pride & Prejudice. 1932. Vol. 2. 16.95x (ISBN 0-19-254702-X); Mansfield Park. 1934. Vol. 3. 15.95x (ISBN 0-19-254703-8); Emma. 1933. Vol. 4. 17.95x (ISBN 0-19-254704-6); Northanger Abbey & Persuasion. 1933. Vol. 5. 17.95x (ISBN 0-19-254705-4); Minor Works. (1st ed.). 1954. Vol. 6. 17.95x (ISBN 0-19-254706-2). Oxford U Pr.

Oxford Illustrated Literary Guide to Great Britain & Ireland. Ed. by Dorothy Eagle & Hilary Carnell. (Illus.). 352p. 1981. 19.95 (ISBN 0-19-869125-4). Oxford U Pr.

Oxford in Focus. Cas Oorthuys. (Illus.). 144p. 1981. pap. 7.50 (ISBN 0-85181-100-0, Pub. by Faber & Faber). Merrimack Bk Serv.

Oxford in the Age of John Locke. W. N. Hargreaves-Mawdsley. (Centers of Civilization Ser: Vol. 32). 160p. 1973. 6.95 (ISBN 0-8061-1038-4). U of Okla Pr.

Oxford Latin Dictionary, Fascicle 5. Ed. by P. G. Glare. 260p. 1975. pap. 42.00x (ISBN 0-19-864218-0). Oxford U Pr.

Oxford Latin Dictionary, Fascicle IV: Gorgonia-Libero. Ed. by G. P. Glare. 260p. 1973. pap. 39.00x (ISBN 0-19-864217-2). Oxford U Pr.

Oxford Latin Dictionary: Fascicle VI-a-Calcitro. Ed. by P. G. W. Glare. 1978. pap. 42.00x (ISBN 0-19-864219-9). Oxford U Pr.

Oxford Latin Dictionary: Fascicle VII. Ed. by P. G. Glare. 256p. (Orig.). 1980. pap. 49.50x (ISBN 0-19-864220-2). Oxford U Pr.

Oxford Latin Dictionary: Fascicle 1, a-Calcitro. Ed. by P. G. Glare. 1968. pap. 42.00x (ISBN 0-19-864209-1). Oxford U Pr.

Oxford Latin Dictionary: Fascicle 2, Calcitro-Demitto. Ed. by P. G. Glare. 1969. pap. 39.00x (ISBN 0-19-864215-6). Oxford U Pr.

Oxford Latin Dictionary: Fascicle 3: Demiurgus-Gorgoneus. Ed. by P. G. Glare. 264p. 1971. pap. 42.00x (ISBN 0-19-864216-4). Oxford U Pr.

Oxford Literary Guide to the British Iles. Dorothy Eagle & Hilary Carnell. (Illus.). 464p. 1980. pap. 8.95 (ISBN 0-19-285098-9, GB 617). Oxford U Pr.

Oxford Reader: Varieties of Contemporary Discourse. Ed. by Frank Kermode & Richard Poirier. (Orig.). 1971. text ed. 12.95x (ISBN 0-19-501365-4); pap. 8.95x (ISBN 0-19-501366-2); pap. 6.95x shorter ed. (ISBN 0-19-501402-2). Oxford U Pr.

Oxford-Russian-English Dictionary. Ed. by Marcus Wheeler & B. O. Unbegaun. 919p. 1972. 45.00 (ISBN 0-19-864111-7). Oxford U Pr.

Oxford School Music Books: Level 3. - Junior Series, 4 Bks. Roger Fiske & J. B. Dobbs. (Oxford School Music Books Ser.). (gr. 4-8). 1954. text ed. 1.00 ea.; Vol. 1. (ISBN 0-19-321141-6); Vol. 2. (ISBN 0-19-321142-4); Vol. 3. (ISBN 0-19-321143-2); Vol. 4. (ISBN 0-19-321144-0); tchrs'. manual for bk. 1 5.00 (ISBN 0-19-321121-1); tchrs'. manual for bk. 2 5.00 (ISBN 0-19-321122-X); tchrs'. manual for bks. 3 & 4 5.00 (ISBN 0-19-321122-X). Oxford U Pr.

Oxford Slavonic Papers, Vol. 13. Ed. by J. L. Fennell et al. (Illus.). 128p. 1981. 45.00 (ISBN 0-19-815656-1). Oxford U Pr.

Oxford Student's Dictionary of Current English. Compiled by A. S. Hornby. 1978. pap. text ed. 6.95x (ISBN 0-19-431114-7). Oxford U Pr.

Oxford Union Murals. John Christian. LC 79-23664. (Illus.). 84p. 1981. incl. fiche 24.00 (ISBN 0-226-68922-0). U of Chicago Pr.

Oxfordshire. Ed. by John Morris. (Domesday Bk.). (Illus.). 154p. 1978. 18.00x (ISBN 0-8476-2286-X). Rowman.

Oxidation of Organic Compounds, 3 vols. Ed. by Frank R. Mayo. LC 67-7520. (Advances in Chemistry Ser: Nos. 75, 76, 77). 1968. Set. 72.00 (ISBN 0-8412-0618-X); Vol. 1. 29.25 (ISBN 0-8412-0076-9); Vol. 2. 33.50 (ISBN 0-8412-0077-7); Vol. 3. 25.75 (ISBN 0-8412-0078-5). Am Chemical.

Oxidation of Organic Compounds: Solvent Effects in Radical Reactions. N. M. Emanuel et al. 350p. 1980. 58.01 (ISBN 0-08-022067-3). Pergamon.

Oxidation of Petrochemicals: Chemistry & Technology. T. Dumas & W. Bulani. LC 74-11232. 186p. 1974. 27.95 (ISBN 0-470-22480-0). Halsted Pr.

Oxide Magnetic Materials. 2nd ed. K. J. Standley. (Monographs on the Physics & Chemistry of Materials). (Illus.). 265p. 1972. 34.95x (ISBN 0-19-851327-5). Oxford U Pr.

Oxide Semiconductors. Z. M. Jarzebski. LC 73-6971. 304p. 1974. 42.00 (ISBN 0-08-016968-6). Pergamon.

Oxocarbons. Robert West. LC 80-515. (Organic Chemistry Ser.). 1980. 32.00 (ISBN 0-12-744580-3). Acad Pr.

Oxy-Acetylene Welding. Ed. by N. C. Balchin et al. (Engineering Craftsmen: No. F25). (Illus.). 1977. spiral bdg. 14.95x (ISBN 0-85083-396-5). Intl Ideas.

Oxyacetylene Welding. Ronald J. Baird. LC 79-6555. (Illus.). 1980. pap. text ed. 4.96 (ISBN 0-87006-290-5). Goodheart.

Oxyacetylene Weldor's Handbook. 7th ed. T. B. Jefferson. (Monticello Bks). 320p. 1972. 5.00 (ISBN 0-686-12005-1). Jefferson Pubns.

Oxygen & Ozone: Gas Solubilities. R. Battino. (Solubility Data Ser.: Vol. 5). 1981. 100.00 (ISBN 0-08-023915-3). Pergamon.

Oxygen Induced Lung Damage: The Chemistry of Oxygen Reduction. James B. Kehrer. (Lectures in Toxicology: No. 4). (Illus.). 1981. 28.00 (ISBN 0-08-025706-2). Pergamon.

Oxygen Keeps You Alive. Franklyn M. Branley. LC 73-139093. (Let's-Read-&-Find-Out Science Bk). (Illus.). (gr. k-3). 1971. 7.95 (ISBN 0-690-60702-4, TYC-J); PLB 7.89 (ISBN 0-690-60703-2); filmstrip with record 11.95 (ISBN 0-690-60704-0); filmstrip with cassette 14.95 (ISBN 0-690-60706-7). T Y Crowell.

Oxygen Measurement in Biology & Medicine. J. P. Payne & D. W. Hill. 1975. 64.95 (ISBN 0-407-00020-8). Butterworths.

Oxygen-Seventeen & Silicon-Twenty-Nine. J. P. Kintzinger & H. Marsmann. (NMR-Basic Principles & Progress Ser.: Vol. 17). (Illus.). 250p. 1981. 48.00 (ISBN 0-387-10414-3). Springer-Verlag.

Oxytocin: Vol. 1. John S. Roberts. 1977. 14.40 (ISBN 0-88831-010-2). Eden Med Res.

Oye Dios. Tr. by Frank Foglio. (Spanish Bks.). (Span.). 1978. 1.65 (ISBN 0-8297-0588-0). Life Pubs Intl.

Oyo Empire: A West African Imperialism in the Era of the Atlantic Slave Trade. Robin Law. (Oxford Studies in African Matters). (Illus.). 1977. 48.00x (ISBN 0-19-822709-4). Oxford U Pr.

Oyotunji Village: The Yoruba Movement in America. Carl M. Hunt. LC 79-51467. (Illus.). 1979. pap. text ed. 7.50 (ISBN 0-8191-0748-4). U Pr of Amer.

Oyster & the Eagle: Selected Aphorisms of Multatuli. Ed. & tr. by E. M. Beekman. LC 73-93171. 124p. 1974. lib. bdg. 8.00x (ISBN 0-87023-123-5). U of Mass Pr.

Oystering from New York to Boston. John M. Kochiss. LC 74-5965. (American Maritime Library: Vol. 7). (Illus.). 264p. 1974. 14.95 (ISBN 0-8195-4074-9); ltd. edition 30.00 (ISBN 0-8195-4075-7). Mystic Seaport.

Oz Scrapbook. David L. Greene & Dick Martin. (Illus.). 1977. 10.00 o.p. (ISBN 0-394-41054-8). Random.

Ozark, Ozark: A Hillside Reader. Ed. by Miller Williams. 200p. 1981. 15.95 (ISBN 0-8262-0331-0). U of Mo Pr.

Ozarks. Richard Rhodes. (American Wilderness Ser.). (Illus.). 240p. 1974. 12.95 (ISBN 0-8094-1196-2). Time-Life.

Ozarks. Richard Rhodes. LC 73-90480. (American Wilderness Ser). (Illus.). (gr. 6 up). 1974. lib. bdg. 11.97 (ISBN 0-8094-1197-0, Pub. by Time-Life). Silver.

Ozeanflug, Die Horatier und Die Kuriater, Die Massnahme. Bertolt Brecht. (Edition Suhrkamp: Bd. 222). 112p. (Ger.). pap. text ed. 3.90 (ISBN 3-518-10222-2, Pub. by Insel Verlag Germany). Suhrkamp.

Ozhog. Vasily P. Aksenov. (Rus.). 1980. 18.50 (ISBN 0-88233-600-2); pap. 10.50 (ISBN 0-88233-601-0). Ardis Pubs.

Ozine Conquest. C. M. Gilbert. 1981. pap. 1.75 (ISBN 0-8439-0891-2, Leisure Bks). Nordon Pubns.

Ozma of Oz: A Tale of Time. Susan Zeder. (Orig.). 1981. playscript 2.00 (ISBN 0-87602-233-6). Anchorage.

Ozone & Chlorine Dioxide Technology for Disinfection of Drinking Water. Ed. by J. Katz. LC 80-13134. (Pollution Tech. Review, No. 67; Chemical Tech. Review: No. 164). 659p. (Orig.). 1980. 36.00 (ISBN 0-8155-0809-3). Noyes.

Ozone & Other Photochemical Oxidants. Ed. by National Research Council, Division of Medical Sciences, Medical & Biologic Effects of Environmental Pollutants. LC 77-1293. 1977. pap. text ed. 18.00 (ISBN 0-309-02531-1). Natl Acad Pr.

Ozone Layer: Synthesis of Papers Based on the UNEP Meeting on the Ozone Layer, Washington DC, March 1977. Ed. by Asit K. Biswas. LC 79-42879. (Environmental Sciences & Applications Ser.: Vol. 4). 1980. 58.00 (ISBN 0-08-022429-6). Pergamon.

Ozu: His Life & Films. Donald Richie. (Illus.). 1974. 18.50 (ISBN 0-520-02445-1); pap. 5.95 (ISBN 0-520-03277-2). U of Cal Pr.

P

P A G Compendium, 9 vols. Protein-Calorie Advisory Group. LC 74-19367. 7000p. 1975. Set. 699.95 (ISBN 0-470-70107-2). Halsted Pr.

P-Adic Analysis. N. Koblitz. (London Mathematical Society Lecture Note Ser.: No. 46). 150p. 1980. pap. 14.95 (ISBN 0-521-28060-5). Cambridge U Pr.

P-adic Numbers & Their Functions. K. Mahler. LC 79-20103. (Cambridge Tracts in Mathematics Ser.: No. 76). Date not set. 45.00 (ISBN 0-521-23102-7). Cambridge U Pr.

P-Eighty Shooting Star: Evolution of a Jet Fighter. E. T. Wooldridge, Jr. LC 79-17648. (Famous Aircraft of the National Air & Space Museum Ser.: Bk. 3). (Illus.). 110p. 1979. pap. 6.95 (ISBN 0-87474-965-4). Smithsonian.

P-Fifty-One Mustang. Len Morgan. LC 63-14945. (Famous Aircraft Ser.). (Illus.). 1979. pap. 4.95 (ISBN 0-8168-5647-8). Aero.

P-Forty Seven Thunderbolt. Len Morgan. LC 63-22711. (Famous Aircraft Ser). (Illus.). 1963. pap. 4.95 (ISBN 0-668-01297-8). Arco.

P-Forty-Seven Thunderbolt. Len Morgan. LC 63-22711. (Illus.). 1979. pap. 4.95 (ISBN 0-8168-5648-6). Aero.

P-Forty-Seven Thunderbolt at War. William Hess. (Illus.). 176p. 1980. 17.50 (ISBN 0-684-16656-9, ScribT). Scribner.

P-Four Phantom in Action. pap. 4.95. Squad Sig Pubns.

P. G. Wodehouse. Joseph Connolly. (Illus.). 160p. 1980. text ed. 18.25x (ISBN 0-85613-235-7). Humanities.

P. G. Wodehouse: Portrait of a Master. David A. Jasen. (Illus.). 352p. 1981. 17.50 (ISBN 0-8264-0046-9); pap. 8.95 (ISBN 0-8264-0033-7). Continuum.

P. H. Emerson: The Fight for Photography As a Fine Art. Nancy Newhall. LC 74-76911. (Aperture Monograph). (Illus.). 30.00 (ISBN 0-912334-58-4); pap. 15.00 (ISBN 0-912334-59-2). Aperture.

P. H. Goose: A Bibliography. R. B. Freeman & Douglas Wertheimer. 148p. 1980. 30.00 (ISBN 0-7129-0935-4, Dist. by Shoe String). Dawson Pub.

P. H. Newby. E. C. Bufkin. (English Authors Ser.: No. 176). 1975. lib. bdg. 10.95 (ISBN 0-8057-1414-6). Twayne.

P. H. Pearse. Raymond J. Porter. (English Authors Ser.: No. 154). 1973. lib. bdg. 10.95 (ISBN 0-8057-1434-0). Twayne.

P. J. Janelle Viglini. 1975. 12.50 o.p. (ISBN 0-685-54023-5, 0-911156-15-5). Porter.

P. K. A Report on the Power of Psychokinesis, Mental Energy That Moves Matter. Mike Brown. LC 76-21121. (Illus.). 320p. pap. 5.95 (ISBN 0-8334-1776-2). Steinerbks.

P. L. O. Strategy & Tactics. Aryeh Yodfat & Yuval Arnon-Ohanna. 1981. write for info. (ISBN 0-312-61761-5). St Martin.

P. Lal: An Appreciation. S. Mokashi-Punekar. (Greybird Ser). 1975. 5.00 (ISBN 0-88253-721-0); flexible bdg. 4.00 (ISBN 0-89253-790-6). Ind-US Inc.

P. O. W. E. R. The Reading - Writing Connection. Joan K. Yehl & Richard F. Bandlow. (Illus.). 320p. 1981. pap. text ed. 8.95 (ISBN 0-675-08064-9); instr's. manual 3.95 (ISBN 0-686-69497-X). Merrill.

P. S. Your Cat Is Dead. James Kirkwood. 224p. 1973. pap. 2.75 (ISBN 0-446-95948-0). Warner Bks.

P-Thirty-Nine, P-Sixty-Three in Action. 1980. pap. 4.95 (ISBN 0-89747-102-4). Squad Sig Pubns.

Pa Chin. Nathan K. Mao. (World Authors Ser.: No. 496 (China)). 1978. 13.50 (ISBN 0-8057-6337-6). Twayne.

PA-Four Locomotive. Norman E. Anderson & C. G. Macdermot. (Illus.). 1978. 19.95 (ISBN 0-89685-035-8). Chatham Pub CA.

Pablo. Gordon Stowell. Tr. by S. D. de Lerin from English. (Libros Pescaditos Sobre Personajes Biblicos). (Illus.). 1978. pap. 0.40 (ISBN 0-311-38518-4, Edit Mundo). Casa Bautista.

Pablo Neruda: All Poets the Poet. Salvatore Bizzarro. LC 78-24437. 1979. lib. bdg. 10.00 (ISBN 0-8108-1189-8). Scarecrow.

Pablo Picasso. Miranda Smith. LC 74-19319. (Illus.). 40p. (gr. 4-8). 1975. PLB 5.75 o.p. (ISBN 0-87191-411-5). Creative Ed.

Pablo Picasso: A Retrospective. Ed. by William Rubin. (Illus.). 1981. pap. 25.00 (ISBN 0-686-69217-9). NYGS.

Pablo Picasso: A Retrospective. Intro. By William Rubin & Dominique Bozo. (Illus.). 1980. 50.00 (ISBN 0-87070-528-8, 707023, Pub. by Museum Mod Art); prepub. 45.00 (ISBN 0-686-65854-X). NYGS.

Pablo Picasso, Twentieth Century Genius. Patricia D. Frevert. Ed. by Ann Redpath. (People to Remember Ser.). (Illus.). 32p. (gr. 5-9). 1981. PLB 5.95 (ISBN 0-87191-800-5). Creative Ed.

Pablo, the Bullfighter & Other Stories. Jo Stanchfield. LC 72-92848. (Highway Holidays Ser). 1973. pap. text ed. 3.54 (ISBN 0-8372-0797-5). Bowmar-Noble.

Pacatus, a Trade-Mark from Antiquity. Joseph Domjan & Evelyn A. Domjan. Ed. by Jane Emig. LC 78-73444. (Illus.). 1979. 15.00 (ISBN 0-933652-13-5). Domjan Studio.

Pacemaker Core Vocabularies, One & Two. Robert L. Hillerich. LC 79-54762. (gr. 7-12). 1980. pap. 4.60 (ISBN 0-8224-5225-1). Pitman Learning.

Pacemaker Vocational Readers, (Designed for Jr. & Sr. High School Students with Severe Reading Disalities, 10 bks. Incl. And Its So Quiet: Porter-Janitor (ISBN 0-8224-7259-7); Fitting Right in: Sewing Machine Operator (ISBN 0-8224-7258-9); Give the Kid a Chance: Baker's Helper (ISBN 0-8224-7256-2); I'll Try Tomorrow: Gardener (ISBN 0-8224-7257-0); Other Side of the Counter: Short Order Cook (ISBN 0-8224-7255-4); Power on & Start Print: Duplicating Room Worker (ISBN 0-8224-7254-6); Ready to Go: Auto Mechanic's Helper (ISBN 0-8224-7251-1); Someone for the Summer: Waitress (ISBN 0-8224-7252-X); Until Joe Comes Back: Supermarket Stock Clerk (ISBN 0-8224-7253-8); You Know How Children Are: Day Care Center Aide (ISBN 0-8224-7260-0). (gr. 7-12). 1976. pap. 146.00 5 copies of 10 bks. & 2 tchr's guides in a box (ISBN 0-8224-7262-7). Pitman Learning.

Pacemakers: A Patient's Guide. David E. Sonnenberg & Michael Birnbaum. Ed. by Kathe Groom. (Illus.). 200p. 1980. write for info. (ISBN 0-935576-04-5); pap. write for info. (ISBN 0-935576-05-3). Kesend Pub Ltd.

Pachomian Koinonia I: The Life of St. Pachomius. Tr. by Armand Veilleux. (Cistercian Studies: No. 45). 524p. (Coptic Greek.). 1981. write for info.; pap. price not set (ISBN 0-87907-945-2). Cistercian Pubns.

Pacific. Charles Mercer. 1981. 12.95 (ISBN 0-671-25587-8). S&S.

Pacific & Southeast Asian Cooking. Rafael Steinberg. (Foods of the World Ser.). (Illus.). 1970. 14.95 (ISBN 0-8094-0045-6). Time-Life.

Pacific & Southeast Asian Cooking. Rafael Steinberg. LC 70-114231. (Foods of the World Ser.). (Illus.). (gr. 6 up). 1970. PLB 14.94 (ISBN 0-8094-0072-3, Pub. by Time-Life). Silver.

Pacific-Asian American Research: An Annotated Bibliography. Mary L. Doi et al. (Orig.). 1981. pap. write for info. (ISBN 0-934584-11-7). Pacific-Asian.

Pacific Boating Almanac: Pacific Northwest & Alaska Edition 1981. annual ed. William Berssen. 416p. 1981. pap. 6.95 (ISBN 0-686-66131-1). Western Marine Ent.

Pacific Boating Almanac 1981: Northern California & Nevada Edition. annual ed. William Berssen. 416p. 1981. pap. 6.95 (ISBN 0-686-66130-3). Western Marine Ent.

Pacific Boating Almanac 1981: Southern California, Arizona, Baja Edition. annual ed. William Berssen. 416p. 1981. pap. 6.95 (ISBN 0-686-66129-X). Western Marine Ent.

Pacific Carrier. Ruben P. Kitchen, Jr. (Zebra World at War Ser.: No. 23). (Orig.). 1980. pap. 2.50 (ISBN 0-89083-683-3, Kable News Co). Zebra.

Pacific Cavalcade. Virginia Coffman. LC 80-66502. 1981. 12.95 (ISBN 0-87795-277-9). Arbor Hse.

Pacific Coast Inshore Fishes. Daniel W. Gotshall. (Illus.). 112p. 1980. pap. 11.50 (ISBN 0-930118-01-4). Western Marine.

Pacific Coast Inshore Fishes. Daniel W. Gotshall. LC 80-53027. (Illus.). 96p. pap. 11.50 (ISBN 0-930118-06-5). Sea Chall.

Pacific Coast Nudibranchs. David W. Behrens. (Illus.). 112p. 1980. pap. 14.95 (ISBN 0-930118-05-7). Western Marine.

Pacific Coast Nudibranchs: A Guide to the Opisthobranchs of the Northeastern Pacific. David W. Behrens. LC 80-51439. (Illus.). 112p. 1980. 24.95 (ISBN 0-930118-04-9, Dist. by Western Marine Enterprises); pap. 14.95 (ISBN 0-930118-05-7). Sea Chall.

Pacific Coast Shay. Dan Ranger. LC 64-8046. 14.95 (ISBN 0-87095-022-3). Golden West.

Pacific Coast Subtidal Marine Invertebrates. Daniel W. Gotshall & Laurence L. Laurent. (Illus.). 112p. pap. 11.50 (ISBN 0-686-62677-X). Western Marine Ent.

Pacific Coast Wildflowers. Beth Horn. Ed. by Robert D. Shangle. LC 80-15350. (Illus.). 48p. 1980. pap. 8.95 (ISBN 0-89802-099-9). Beautiful Am.

Pacific Crest Trail: Escape to the Wilderness. Ann Sutton & Myron Sutton. LC 75-15920. (Illus.). 240p. 1975. 8.95 o.s.i. (ISBN 0-397-01061-3). Lippincott.

Pacific Crest Trail, Vol. 2: Oregon & Washington. rev ed. Jeff P. Schaffer et al. Ed. by Thomas Winnett. LC 72-96122. (Illus., Orig.). 1979. pap. 9.95 (ISBN 0-911824-82-0). Wilderness.

Pacific Crusaders. Paul T. Smith, Jr. (Illus.). 225p. 1981. 11.50 (ISBN 0-87881-094-3). Mojave Bks.

Pacific Electric. softcover 6.95 (ISBN 0-685-83367-4). Chatham Pub CA.

Pacific Islands Speaking. Armstrong Sperry. (Illus.). (gr. 7 up). 1955. 4.75g o.s.i. (ISBN 0-02-786130-9). Macmillan.

Pacific Marine Fishes, Bk. 4. Warren E. Burgess & Herbert R. Axelrod. (Illus.). 272p. 1974. 20.00 (ISBN 0-87666-126-6, PS-720). TFH Pubns.

Pacific Navigators. Oliver Allen. Ed. by Time-Life Books Editors. (Seafarers Ser.). (Illus.). 176p. 1980. 13.95 (ISBN 0-8094-2685-4). Time-Life.

Pacific Northwest: An Index to People & Places in Books. Joseph G. Drazan. LC 79-16683. 176p. 1979. 10.00 (ISBN 0-8108-1234-7). Scarecrow.

Pacific Northwest Cenozoic Biostratigraphy. Ed. by John M. Armentrout. LC 80-82937. (Special Paper Ser.: No. 184). (Illus., Orig.). 1980. pap. write for info. (ISBN 0-8137-2184-9). Geol Soc.

Pacific Overtures. Stephen Sondheim et al. LC 76-55020. 1977. 6.95 (ISBN 0-396-07414-6). Dodd.

Pacific Quest: The Concept & Scope of an Oceanic Community. Endel Kolde. LC 76-41117. (Pacific Rim Research Series: No. 1). 1976. 17.95 (ISBN 0-669-00978-4). Lexington Bks.

Pacific Salmon & Steelhead Trout. R. J. Childerhose & Marj Trim. LC 78-65830. (Illus.). 166p. 1979. 27.50 (ISBN 0-295-95642-9). U of Wash Pr.

Pacific Since Magellan: The Spanish Lake, Vol. 1. O. H. Spate. LC 78-23164. 1979. 39.50x (ISBN 0-8166-0882-2). U of Minn Pr.

Pacific Slope: A History of California, Oregon, Washington, Idaho, Utah, & Nevada. Earl S. Pomeroy. LC 65-11128. (Washington Paperback Ser: No. 69). (Illus.). 436p. 1973. Repr. of 1965 ed. 15.00 (ISBN 0-295-95303-9). U of Wash Pr.

Pacific Tugboats. Gordon Newell & J. Williamson. (Illus.). 1975. Repr. encore ed. 9.95 o.s.i. (ISBN 0-87564-221-7). Superior Pub.

Pacific Voyages. William Napier et al. 480p. 1973. 7.95 o.p. (ISBN 0-385-04335-X). Doubleday.

Pacific War Diary, 1942-1945. James J. Fahey. LC 73-21341. (Illus.). 404p. 1974. Repr. of 1963 ed. lib. bdg. 31.25x (ISBN 0-8371-6176-2, FAWD). Greenwood.

Pacific War Diary: 1942-1945. James T. Fahey. 432p. 1980. pap. 2.50 (ISBN 0-89083-673-6). Zebra.

Pacific Wilderness. David Hancock et al. 97p. 1974. pap. write for info. (ISBN 0-919654-08-8). Hancock Hse.

Pacifism in Britain Nineteen Fourteen to Nineteen Forty Five: The Defining of a Faith. Martin Ceadel. 352p. 1980. 37.50x (ISBN 0-19-821882-6). Oxford U Pr.

Pacing the Void: T'ang Approaches to the Stars. Edward H. Schafer. 1978. 34.50x (ISBN 0-520-03344-2). U of Cal Pr.

Pack of Puzzles. Donna L. Pape & Jeanette Grote. (gr. 4-6). 1976. pap. 1.25 (ISBN 0-590-10145-5, Schol Pap). Schol Bk Serv.

Pack Rat's Day & Other Poems. Jack Prelutsky. LC 73-81061. (Illus.). 32p. (gr. k-4). 1974. 5.95g o.s.i. (ISBN 0-02-775050-7). Macmillan.

Package. Laurie Anderson. 3.95 o.p. (ISBN 0-672-51604-7). Bobbs.

Package Conveyors: Design & Estimating. D. K. Smith. 136p. 1972. 25.00x (ISBN 0-85264-213-X, Pub. by Griffin England). State Mutual Bk.

Package Production Management. 2nd ed. Harold J. Raphael & David L. Olsson. (Illus.). 1976. lib. bdg. 26.50 (ISBN 0-87055-217-1); pap. text ed. 18.00 (ISBN 0-87055-307-0). AVI.

Packaging for Climatic Protection. Cairns & Oswin. 1975. text ed. 19.95 (ISBN 0-408-00146-1). Butterworths.

Packaging Information Sources. Ed. by Gwendolyn Jones. LC 67-18370. (Management Information Guide Ser.: No. 10). 1967. 30.00 (ISBN 0-8103-0811-8). Gale.

Packaging Marketplace: The Practical Guide to Packaging Sources. Ed. by Joseph Hanlon. LC 78-53442. 1978. 65.00 (ISBN 0-8103-0989-0, Norback Bk). Gale.

Packaging Media. F. A. Paine. 444p. 1978. 43.95 (ISBN 0-470-99369-3). Wiley.

Packaging of Chemicals & Other Industrial Liquids & Solids. C. Swinbank. 1973. text ed. 15.95 (ISBN 0-408-00106-2). Butterworths.

Packaging of Cosmetics & Toiletries. J. Macchesney. 1974. text ed. 16.95 (ISBN 0-408-00125-9). Butterworths.

Packaging of Pharmaceuticals. 1974. text ed. 16.95 (ISBN 0-408-00138-0). Butterworths.

Packaging Regulations. Stanley Sacharow. (Illus.). 1979. lib. bdg. 25.50 (ISBN 0-87055-274-0). AVI.

Packaging: The Sixth Sense. Ernest Dichter. LC 73-76439. 192p. 1975. 21.50 (ISBN 0-8436-1103-0). CBI Pub.

Packard: A History of the Motor Car & the Company. Ed. by Beverly R. Kimes. LC 78-71063. 1979. 75.00 (ISBN 0-915038-12-9); leather bdg. 95.00 (ISBN 0-915038-26-9). Princeton Pub.

Packard Truck: Ask the Man Who Owns One. John B. Montville. (Illus.). 128p. 1981. pap. 14.95 (ISBN 0-89404-052-9). Aztex.

Packe of Spanish Lyes, Sent Abroard in the World. LC 77-38224. (English Experience Ser.: No. 487). 1972. Repr. of 1588 ed. 5.00 (ISBN 90-221-0487-7). Walter J Johnson.

Packet Switching: Tomorrow's Communications Today. Roy D. Rosner. (Illus.). 1981. text ed. 31.50. Lifetime Learn.

Packing-Shipping Crafts. American Craft Council. 1977. 2.70 (ISBN 0-88321-031-2). Am Craft.

Packrat Press Books. Gahan Wilson. 1978. pap. 1.25 (ISBN 0-440-43824-1, YB). Dell.

Padarn & Penrhyn Railways. Susan Turner. LC 74-76199. (Railway History Ser). (Illus.). 168p. 1975. 14.95 (ISBN 0-7153-6547-9). David & Charles.

Paddington & Snow Bear Mini. (Mini Pop-up Ser.). (Illus.). 12p. (Orig.). 1981. pap. 1.95 (ISBN 0-8431-1059-7). Price Stern.

Paddington at Large. Michael Bond. (Illus.). (gr. 1-5). 1963. 8.95 (ISBN 0-395-06641-7). HM.

Paddington Birthday Treat Mini. (Mini Pop-up Ser.). (Illus.). 12p. (Orig.). 1981. pap. 1.95 (ISBN 0-8431-1060-0). Price Stern.

Paddington Goes to Town. Michael Bond. LC 68-28043. (Illus.). (gr. 1-5). 1968. 7.95 (ISBN 0-395-06635-2). HM.

Paddington Green. Claire Rayner. 1977. pap. 1.95 o.p. (ISBN 0-449-23265-4, Crest). Fawcett.

Paddington Laundromat Mini. (Mini Pop-up Ser.). (Illus.). 12p. (Orig.). 1981. pap. 1.95 (ISBN 0-8431-1061-9). Price Stern.

Paddington Marches On. Michael Bond. (Illus.). (gr. 4-6). 1965. 8.95 (ISBN 0-395-06642-5). HM.

Paddington Shopping Mini. (Mini Pop-up Ser.). (Illus.). 12p. (Orig.). 1981. pap. 1.95 (ISBN 0-8431-1058-9). Price Stern.

Paddle Wheels & Pistols. Irvin Anthony. 329p. 1980. Repr. of 1929 ed. lib. bdg. 30.00 (ISBN 0-8495-0075-3). Arden Lib.

Paddy: A Naturalist's Story of an Orphaned Beaver. R. D. Lawrence. 1978. pap. 1.95 (ISBN 0-380-42580-7, 42580). Avon.

Paddy's New Hat. John S. Goodall. LC 80-80129. (Illus.). 64p. (ps up). 1980. 6.95 (ISBN 0-689-50172-2, McElderry Bk). Atheneum.

Paderewski. Charlotte Kellogg. 1956. 4.95 o.p. (ISBN 0-670-53416-1). Viking Pr.

Paderewski: The Story of a Modern Immortal. Charles Phillips. LC 77-17399. (Music Reprint Ser.: 1978). (Illus.). 1978. Repr. of 1934 ed. lib. bdg. 35.00 (ISBN 0-306-77534-4). Da Capo.

Padre Island National Seashore-a Guide to the Geology, Natural Environments & History of a Texas Barrier Island. B. R. Wiese & W. A. White. Date not set. price not set (GB 17). Bur Econ Geology.

Padre Padrone...My Father, My Master. Gavino Ledda. Tr. by George Salamanazar. 1979. 12.95 (ISBN 0-89396-003-9); pap. 6.95 (ISBN 0-89396-006-3). Urizen Bks.

Padre Pio: The Stigmatist. Charles M. Carty. (Illus.). 1977. pap. 6.00 (ISBN 0-89555-054-7, 115). TAN Bks Pubs.

Padres se organizan para mejorar las escuelas. Happy Fernandez. Ed. by NCCE. Tr. by ASPIRA of New York. (Spanish.). 1976. 3.50 (ISBN 0-934460-03-5). NCCE.

Paduans, Medals by Giovanni Cavino. Richard H. Lawrence. (Illus.). pap. 5.00 (ISBN 0-916710-74-2). Obol Intl.

Paediatric Intensive Care. 2nd ed. Keith D. Roberts & Jennifer M. Edwards. (Illus.). 1976. 28.25 (ISBN 0-632-08020-5, Blackwell). Mosby.

Paediatric Surgery. Elizabeth D. Strathdee & Daniel G. Young. (Modern Practical Nursing Ser: No. 3). (Illus.). 81p. 1971. pap. 9.95x (ISBN 0-433-31858-9). Intl Ideas.

Paediatrics Diagnosis. Girish Srivastava & Narender K. Anand. 400p. 1980. text ed. 35.00 (ISBN 0-7069-1047-8, Pub. by Vikas India). Advent Bk.

Pagan Celtic Britain: Studies in Iconography & Tradition. Anne Ross. LC 67-16099. (Illus.). 1967. 30.00x (ISBN 0-231-03058-4). Columbia U Pr.

Pagan Hero: An Interpretation of Meursault in Camus' the Stranger. Robert Champigny. Tr. by Rowe Portis. LC 79-83139. 1970. 8.00 o.p. (ISBN 0-8122-7597-7). U of Pa Pr.

Pagan Mysteries in the Renaissance. 2nd ed. Edgar Wind. 1968. 19.95 o.p. (ISBN 0-571-04634-7, Pub. by Faber & Faber). Merrimack Bk Serv.

Pagan Origins of the Christ Myth. John G. Jackson. 1980. pap. 3.00. Am Atheist.

Pagan Place: A Play. Edna O'Brien. 1973. 8.50 (ISBN 0-571-10336-7, Pub. by Faber & Faber); pap. 4.95 (ISBN 0-571-10316-2). Merrimack Bk Serv.

Paganini. Leslie Sheppard & R. Herbert Axelrod. (Illus.). 704p. 1980. 20.00 (ISBN 0-87666-618-7, Z-28). Paganiniana Pubns.

Paganini: The Genoese, 2 vols. G. I. C. Courcy. LC 76-5892. (Music Reprint Series). 1977. Repr. of 1957 ed. lib. bdg. 57.50 (ISBN 0-306-70872-8). Da Capo.

Paganini: The Romantic Virtuoso. Jeffrey Pulver. LC 69-11669. (Music Ser). 1970. Repr. of 1936 ed. lib. bdg. 25.00 (ISBN 0-306-71199-0). Da Capo.

Paganism in the Roman Empire. Ramsay MacMullen. LC 80-54222. 221p. 1981. 23.00x (ISBN 0-300-02655-2). Yale U Pr.

Page a Day for Lent Nineteen Eighty-One. Barbara Sullivan. 100p. 1981. pap. 2.50 (ISBN 0-8091-2340-1). Paulist Pr.

Page a Day SAT Study Guide. Frances C. Bennett & Sung-wen Chang. 320p. (Orig.). 1981. pap. 3.95 (ISBN 0-668-05196-5, 5196). Arco.

Page From: The Torah, the Talmud, the Midrash, the Mishneh Torah, the Shulchan Aruch. (Orig.). (YA) 1970. pap. 1.25 (ISBN 0-8074-0056-4, 959605). UAHC.

Page Systems. Don P. Smith. (Illus.). 1976. pap. 3.00 (ISBN 0-937514-08-X, New Era). World Merch Import.

Pageant, Eighteen Ninety-Six to Ninety-Seven, 2 vols. Ed. by Peter Stansky & Rodney Shewan. (Aesthetic Movement & the Arts & Crafts Movement Ser.: Periodicals: Vol. 5). (Illus.). 1979. Set. lib. bdg. 88.00 (ISBN 0-8240-3621-2); lib. bdg. 44.00 ea. Garland Pub.

Pageant of America, 15 vols. Ed. by Ralph H. Gabriel. Incl. Vol. 1. Adventurers in the Wilderness. Clark Wissler & Constance L. Skinner (ISBN 0-911548-56-4); Vol. 2. Lure of the Frontier. Ralph H. Gabriel (ISBN 0-911548-57-2); Vol. 3. Toilers of Land & Sea. Ralph H. Gabriel (ISBN 0-911548-58-0); Vol. 4. March of Commerce. Malcolm Keir (ISBN 0-911548-59-9); Vol. 5. Epic of Industry. Malcolm Keir (ISBN 0-911548-60-2); Vol. 6. Winning of Freedom. William Wood & Ralph H. Gabriel (ISBN 0-911548-61-0); Vol. 7. In Defense of Liberty. William Wood & Ralph H. Gabriel (ISBN 0-911548-62-9); Vol. 8. Builders of the Republic. Frederic A. Ogg (ISBN 0-911548-63-7); Vol. 9. Makers of a New Nation. John S. Bassett (ISBN 0-911548-64-5); Vol. 10. American Idealism. Luther A. Weigle (ISBN 0-911548-65-3); Vol. 11. American Spirit in Letters. Stanley T. Williams (ISBN 0-911548-66-1); Vol. 12. American Spirit in Art. Frank J. Mather, Jr. et al (ISBN 0-911548-67-X); Vol. 13. American Spirit in Architecture. Talbot F. Hamlin (ISBN 0-911548-68-8); Vol. 14. American Stage. Oral S. Coad & Edwin Mims, Jr (ISBN 0-911548-69-6); Vol. 15. Annals of American Sport. John A. Krout (ISBN 0-911548-70-X). (Illus.). 22.95 ea.; Set. 330.00 (ISBN 0-911548-72-6). US Pubs.

Pageant of American History. Gerald Leinwand. (gr. 7-9). 1975. text ed. 17.24 (ISBN 0-205-03849-2, 7838492); tchrs'. guide 3.60 (ISBN 0-205-03850-6, 7838506); dup. masters 44.00 (ISBN 0-205-05391-2, 7853912). Allyn.

Pageant of Art. Vienna I. Curtiss. LC 76-280. (Illus.). 27.50 (ISBN 0-9602742-0-0). Collectors Choice.

Pageant of Early Victorian England. Elizabeth Burton. LC 74-162746. (Encore Edition). 1971. 3.50 o.p. (ISBN 0-684-15393-9, ScribT). Scribner.

Pageant of World History. new rev. ed. Gerald Leinwand. (gr. 9-12). 1977. text ed. 16.80 (ISBN 0-205-05392-0, 7853920); tchrs'. guide 5.40 (ISBN 0-205-05393-9, 7853939); wkbk 60.00 (ISBN 0-205-05657-1, 786571); tests-duplicator masters 48.00 (ISBN 0-205-05658-X, 785658X). Allyn.

Pageantry of Britain. Julian Paget. (Illus.). 1980. 25.95 (ISBN 0-686-28008-3, Pub. by Michael Joseph). Merrimack Bk Serv.

Pageants of Despair. Dennis Hamley. LC 74-10841. 180p. (gr. 7-10). 1974. 9.95 (ISBN 0-87599-205-6). S G Phillips.

Pages & Pictures from Forgotten Children's Books. Andrew W. Tuer. LC 68-31096. (Illus.). 1969. Repr. of 1899 ed. 18.00 (ISBN 0-8103-3488-7). Gale.

Pages francaises. Ed. by Georges Lannois. 1969. 14.50 (ISBN 0-08-006379-9). Pergamon.

Pages from the Life of Dmitri Shostakovich. Dmitri Sollertinsky & Ludmilla Sollertinsky. Tr. by Graham Hobbs & Charles Midgely. LC 79-3364. 1980. 12.95 (ISBN 0-15-170730-8). HarBraceJ.

Pahlavi Conjugation. Tom Jordan. LC 78-15981. Date not set. 10.95 (ISBN 0-87949-135-3). Ashley Bks.

Pahlavi Texts, Vols. 5, 18, 24, 37, 47. Ed. by F. Max Mueller. Tr. by Darmesteter & Mills. (Sacred Books of the East Ser.). 15.00 ea.; Vol. 5. (ISBN 0-8426-1405-2); Vol. 18. (ISBN 0-8426-1406-0); Vol. 24. (ISBN 0-8426-1407-9); Vol. 37. (ISBN 0-8426-1408-7); Vol. 47. (ISBN 0-8426-1409-5). Verry.

Pai, un Filho, e Uma Corrida de Amor. Keith Leenhouts. Ed. by Luiz A. Caruso. Tr. by Vera Balthazar. 156p. (Portuguese.). 1980. pap. 1.50 (ISBN 0-8297-0676-3). Vida Pubs.

Paideia: The Ideals of Greek Culture, Vol. 1. Archaic Greece & Mind Of Athens. Werner Jaeger. Tr. by Gilbert Highet. (YA) (gr. 9 up). 1965. pap. 7.95 (ISBN 0-19-500425-6, 144, GB). Oxford U Pr.
Paige. Jerry Jenkins. (Margo Ser.). 128p. 1981. pap. 2.50 (ISBN 0-8024-4314-1). Moody.
Painful of Stars. Franklin M. Segler. LC 75-178065. 128p. 1972. 2.95 o.p. (ISBN 0-8054-8224-5). Broadman.
Pain. Ed. by John J. Bonica. (Association for Research in Nervous & Mental Disease Publications Ser.: Vol. 58). 1979. text ed. 38.00 (ISBN 0-89004-376-0). Raven.
Pain: A Comprehensive View. Ed. by Nelson H. Hendler. 250p. 1981. 24.00 (ISBN 0-88416-287-7, 287). PSG Pub.
Pain: A Personal Experience. J. Blair Pace. LC 76-15951. (Illus.). 156p. 1976. 11.95 (ISBN 0-88229-238-2). Nelson-Hall.
Pain: A Spike-Interval Coded Message in the Brain. Raimond Emmers. 1981. text ed. price not set (ISBN 0-89004-650-6). Raven.
Pain & Anxiety Control in Dentistry. Ed. by Stanley R. Spiro. (Illus.). 340p. 1981. text ed. 37.50 (ISBN 0-937218-66-9, Pub. by Piccin Italy). J K Burgess.
Pain & Providence. Ladislaus Boros. 132p. 1975. pap. 2.95 (ISBN 0-8164-2110-2). Crossroad NY.
Pain & Religion: A Psychophysiological Study. Steven Brena. (Illus.). 176p. 1972. 14.75 (ISBN 0-398-02242-9). C C Thomas.
Pain & Society. Ed. by H. W. Kosterlitz & L. Y. Terenius. (Dahlem Workshop Reports, Life Sciences Research Report Ser.: No. 17). (Illus.). 523p. (Orig.). 1980. pap. text ed. 39.40 (ISBN 0-89573-099-5). Verlag Chemie.
Pain & Suffering: Selected Aspects. Benjamin L. Crue, Jr. (Illus.). 224p. 1970. pap. 19.75 photocopy ed. spiral (ISBN 0-398-00374-2). C C Thomas.
Pain & the Neurosurgeon: A Forty-Year Experience. James C. White & William H. Sweet. (Illus.). 1032p. 1969. text ed. 52.75 (ISBN 0-398-02058-2). C C Thomas.
Pain Control. Norman Trieger. (Illus.). 143p. 1974. 24.00. Quint Pub Co.
Pain Control with Transcutaneous Electrical Neuro Stimulation (Tens) Robert A. Ersek. LC 78-50175. 1980. 23.75 (ISBN 0-87527-168-5). Green.
Pain Erasure: The Bonnie Prudden Way. Bonnie Prudden. (Illus.). 288p. 1980. 14.95 (ISBN 0-87131-328-6). M Evans.
Pain in Shoulder & Arm: An Integrated View. Ed. by J. M. Greep et al. (Developments in Surgery Ser.: No. 1). 306p. 1980. lib. bdg. 47.35 (ISBN 90-247-2146-6, Pub. by Martinus Nijhoff). Kluwer Boston.
Pain Management. Ed. by J. Fletcher Lee. 1977. 21.00 (ISBN 0-683-04918-6). Williams & Wilkins.
Pain of Being Human. Kennedy, Eugene C., M.M. LC 73-83645. 280p. 1974. pap. 3.50 (ISBN 0-385-06888-3, Im). Doubleday.
Pain: Origin & Treatment -- Discussions in Patient Management. Benjamin H. Gorsky. LC 80-15857. 1980. 18.00 (ISBN 0-87488-448-9); pap. 10.00 (ISBN 0-87488-447-0). Med Exam.
Paine. David F. Hawke. LC 73-14264. (Illus.). 512p. (YA) 1974. 15.00 o.s.i. (ISBN 0-06-011784-2, HarpT). Har-Row.
Paingod & Other Delusions. Harlan Ellison. 1975. pap. 1.50 o.s.i. (ISBN 0-515-03646-3, V3646). Jove Pubns.
Paint Along with Nancy Kominsky: Landscapes. Nancy Kominsky. (Illus., Orig.). 1979. pap. 7.95 (ISBN 0-446-97880-9). Warner Bks.
Paint Along with Nancy Kominsky: Still Lifes. Nancy Kominsky. (Orig.). 1981. pap. 7.95 (ISBN 0-446-87792-1). Warner Bks.
Paint & Wallpaper. (Home Repair & Improvement Ser.). (Illus.). 1976. 10.95 (ISBN 0-8094-2354-5). Time-Life.
Paint & Wallpaper. Ed. by Time Life Books. LC 76-3377. (Home Repair & Improvement). (Illus.). (gr. 7 up). 1976. PLB 11.97 (ISBN 0-8094-2355-3, Pub. by Time-Life). Silver.
Paint Flow & Pigment Dispersion: A Rheological Approach to Coating & Ink Technology. 2nd ed. Temple C. Patton. LC 78-10774. 1979. 52.50 (ISBN 0-471-03272-7, Pub. by Wiley-Interscience). Wiley.
Paint It Yourself: The Complete Indoor House-Painting Book. Lois Libien & Margaret Strong. LC 78-6692. 1978. 9.95 o.p. (ISBN 0-688-03289-3); pap. 5.95 o.p. (ISBN 0-688-08289-0). Morrow.
Paintbox on the Frontier: The Life & Times of George Caleb Bingham. Alberta W. Constant. LC 73-6954. (Illus.). 224p. (gr. 7-9). 1974. 9.95 (ISBN 0-690-60844-6, TYC-J). T Y Crowell.
Painted Ceramics of the Western Mound at Awatovi. Watson Smith. LC 79-102785. (Peabody Museum Papers: Vol. 38). 1970. pap. text ed. 40.00 (ISBN 0-87365-114-6). Peabody Harvard.
Painted Dresses. Shelby Hearon. LC 80-69644. 1981. 11.95 (ISBN 0-689-11155-X). Atheneum.
Painted Fans of Japan: Fifteen Noh Drama Masterpieces. Reiko Chiba. LC 62-20775. (Illus., Fr., Or Eng). 1962. 15.50 (ISBN 0-8048-0468-0). C E Tuttle.
Painted Message. O. Billig & B. G. Burton-Bradley. 1978. 19.50 (ISBN 0-470-99126-7). Wiley.
Painter & the Fish. Catherine Storr. (Illus.). (ps-5). 6.95 (ISBN 0-571-10475-4, Pub. by Faber & Faber). Merrimack Bk Serv.
Painter & the Photograph: From Delacroix to Warhol. rev ed. Van Deren Coke. LC 75-129804. (Illus.). 324p. 1972. pap. 19.95 (ISBN 0-8263-0325-0). U of NM Pr.
Painter of Modern Life & Other Essays. Charles Baudelaire. Ed. by Sydney J. Freedberg. LC 77-18671. (Connoisseurship Criticism & Art History Ser.: Vol. 1). 224p. 1979. lib. bdg. 27.00 (ISBN 0-8240-3257-8). Garland Pub.
Painter of Rural America: William Sidney Mount. Alfred Frankenstein. LC 68-57955. (Illus.). 72p. (Orig.). 1968. pap. 5.00 (ISBN 0-88397-062-7). Intl Exhibit Foun.
Painterly Print: Monotypes from the Seventeenth to the Twentieth Century. Ed. by Margaret Aspinwall. (Illus.). 262p. 1980. 29.95 (ISBN 0-87099-223-6); pap. 14.95 (ISBN 0-87099-224-4). Metro Mus Art.
Painter's Craft: An Introduction to Artists' Methods & Materials. Ralph Mayer. (Penguin Handbook Ser.). (Illus.). 1979. pap. 8.95 (ISBN 0-14-046369-0). Penguin.
Painter's Mind: A Study of the Relations of Srtructure & Space in Painting a New Printing. Romare Bearden & Carl Holty. LC 80-8527. 240p. 1981. lib. bdg. 25.00 (ISBN 0-8240-9457-3). Garland Pub.
Painter's Pocket Book of Methods & Materials. 3rd ed. Hilaire Hiler. 1970. 8.95 o.p. (ISBN 0-686-28562-X, Pub. by Faber & Faber); pap. 6.95 (ISBN 0-571-04696-7). Merrimack Bk Serv.
Painter's Progress. Will H. Low. LC 75-28889. (Art Experience in Late 19th Century America Ser.: Vol. 22). (Illus.). 1976. Repr. of 1910 ed. lib. bdg. 37.00 (ISBN 0-8240-2246-7). Garland Pub.
Painter's Secret Geometry: A Study of Composition in Art. Charles Bouleau. LC 79-91815. 268p. 1980. Repr. of 1963 ed. lib. bdg. 30.00 (ISBN 0-87817-259-9). Hacker.
Painting. Boy Scouts Of America. LC 19-600. (Illus.). 32p. (gr. 6-12). 1973. pap. 0.70x (ISBN 0-8395-3372-1, 3372). BSA.
Painting & Decorating. Elizabeth Gundrey. (Orig.). 1980. pap. 6.95x (ISBN 0-8464-1036-2). Beekman Pubs.
Painting & Decorating. A. E. Hurst & J. M. Goodier. 620p. 1980. 75.00x (ISBN 0-85264-243-1, Pub. by Griffin England). State Mutual Bk.
Painting & Decorating: A Guide for Houseowner & Decorator. J. H. Goodier. (Illus.). 1977. 16.95x (ISBN 0-7114-4612-1). Intl Ideas.
Painting & Drawing Skies. Norman Battershill. 156p. 1981. 19.95 (ISBN 0-8230-3558-1). Watson-Guptill.
Painting & Experience in Fifteenth Century Italy: A Primer in the Social History of Pictorial Style. Michael Baxandall. (Illus.). 180p. 1972. 12.95 o.p. (ISBN 0-19-817321-0). Oxford U Pr.
Painting & Experience in Fifteenth Century Italy: A Primer in the Social History of Pictorial Style. Michael Baxandall. 172p. 1974. pap. 7.95 (ISBN 0-19-881329-5, GB411, GB). Oxford U Pr.
Painting & Sculpture in Europe: 1780-1880. Fritz Novotny. (Pelican History of Art Ser: No. 20). (Illus.). 1978. pap. 17.95 (ISBN 0-14-056120-X, Pelican). Penguin.
Painting & Sculpture in Germany & the Netherlands: 1500 to 1600. Von Der Osten & Vey. (Pelican History of Art Ser.: No. 31). 1969. 40.00 (ISBN 0-670-53591-5). Viking Pr.
Painting & Sculpture in Los Angeles, 1900-1945. Nancy Moure. (Illus.). 112p. (Orig.). 1980. pap. 14.95 (ISBN 0-87587-098-8). La Co Art Mus.
Painting & Understanding Abstract Art. Leonard Brooks. 144p. 1980. pap. 9.95 (ISBN 0-442-24334-0). Van Nos Reinhold.
Painting at Court. Michael Levey. LC 75-124528. (Wrightsman Lectures: Vol. 5). (Illus.). 1971. 20.00 (ISBN 0-8147-4950-X). NYU Pr.
Painting Faces, Figures & Landscapes. Everett R. Kinstler. 144p. 1981. 22.50 (ISBN 0-8230-3625-1). Watson-Guptill.
Painting from Eighteen Hundred & Fifty to the Present. LC 76-14075. (Garland Library of the History of Art). 1976. lib. bdg. 50.00 (ISBN 0-8240-2422-2). Garland Pub.
Painting in Britain 1525 to 1975. John Sunderland. LC 76-6505. (Illus.). 256p. 1976. usa 35.00x (ISBN 0-8147-7773-2). NYU Pr.
Painting in Eighteenth-Century Venice. rev. ed. Michael Levey. LC 80-549. (Cornell-Phaidon Bks.). (Illus.). 264p. 1980. 38.50 (ISBN 0-8014-1331-1). Cornell U Pr.
Painting in Opaque Watercolor. Rudy De Reyna. LC 69-12492. (Illus.). 1969. 15.95 o.p. (ISBN 0-8230-3775-4). Watson-Guptill.
Painting in Towns & Cities. Hans Schwarz. LC 79-56606. (Start to Paint Ser.). (Illus.). 1980. pap. 3.95 (ISBN 0-8008-6204-X, Pentalic). Taplinger.
Painting Landscapes in Oils. Norman Battershill. (Leisure Arts Painting Ser.). (Illus.). 32p. 1980. pap. 2.50 (ISBN 0-8008-6202-3, Pentalic). Taplinger.
Painting Materials: A Short Encyclopedia. Rutherford J. Gettens & George L. Stout. (Illus.). 1965. pap. 4.50 (ISBN 0-486-21597-0). Dover.
Painting of Eugene Delacroix: A Critical Catalogue, Vols. 1 & 2: 1816-1831. Ed. by Lee Johnson. (Illus.). 556p. 1981. Set. 195.00 (ISBN 0-19-817314-8). Oxford U Pr.
Painting Sea & Sky in Watercolor. Leslie Worth. (Leisure Arts Painting Ser.). (Illus.). 32p. 1980. pap. 2.50 (ISBN 0-8008-6206-6, Pentalic). Taplinger.
Painting Seascapes. John Raynes. LC 79-56607. (Start to Paint Ser.). (Illus.). 104p. 1980. pap. 3.95 (ISBN 0-8008-6205-8, Pentalic). Taplinger.
Painting the Nude. Ed. by J. M. Parramon. LC 77-361625. (Illus., Orig.). 1976. pap. 10.50x (ISBN 0-85242-449-3). Intl Pubns Serv.
Painting the Seasons in Watercolor. Arthur Barbour. (Illus.). 160p. 1975. 18.95 o.p. (ISBN 0-8230-3858-0). Watson-Guptill.
Painting Trees & Landscapes in Watercolor. Ted Kautzky. 1981. pap. 9.95 (ISBN 0-442-21918-0). Van Nos Reinhold.
Painting: Visual & Technical Fundamentals. Nathan Goldstein. LC 78-15907. 1979. 17.95 (ISBN 0-13-647800-X). P-H.
Painting with Cold Enamel. A. Fromenteau. LC 73-3716. (Illus.). 96p. 1980. Repr. of 1973 ed. 4.95 (ISBN 0-8069-8550-X); lib. bdg. 4.59 (ISBN 0-8069-8551-8). Sterling.
Painting Without a Brush. Roy Sparkes. 1978. 16.95 (ISBN 0-7134-0189-3). David & Charles.
Paintings & Drawings of Dante Gabriel Rossetti (1828-1882) A Catalogue Raisonne, 2 vols. Virginia Surtees. 294p. 1971. 98.00x (ISBN 0-19-817174-9). Oxford U Pr.
Paintings & Drawings of Marco Zoppo. Lilian Armstrong. LC 75-23779. (Outstanding Dissertations in the Fine Arts - 15th Century). (Illus.). 1976. lib. bdg. 60.50 (ISBN 0-8240-1976-8). Garland Pub.
Paintings & Drawings of the Gypsies of Granada. Jo Jones et al. LC 78-8842. (Illus.). 1969. 18.00 (ISBN 0-8103-5003-3). Gale.
Paintings & Drawings of William Blake. Martin Butlin. LC 80-6221. (Paul Mellon Centre for Studies in British Art). (Illus.). 1408p. 1981. 250.00x (ISBN 0-300-02550-5). Yale U Pr.
Paintings & MS of Southeast Asia. O. P. Agrawal. 1981. text ed. price not set. Butterworths.
Paintings in Dutch Museums: An Index of Oil Paintings in Public Collections in the Netherlands. Compiled by Christopher Wright. (Illus.). 591p. 1980. 75.00x (ISBN 0-85667-077-4, Pub. by Sotheby Parke Bernet England). Biblio Dist.
Paintings of Arshile Gorky: A Critical Catalogue. Jim M. Jordan & Robert Goldwater. LC 79-2248. (Illus.). 480p. 1981. 60.00x (ISBN 0-8147-4160-6). NYU Pr.
Paintings of Charles Bird King. Andrew J. Cosentino. LC 77-608258. (Illus.). 214p. 1978. 25.00 (ISBN 0-87474-336-2). Smithsonian.
Paintings of Cornelis Engebrechtsz. Walter S. Gibson. LC 76-23620. (Outstanding Dissertations in the Fine Arts - 16th Century). (Illus.). 1977. Repr. of 1969 ed. lib. bdg. 56.00 (ISBN 0-8240-2691-8). Garland Pub.
Paintings of Han Meilin. 1980. 9.95 o.p. (ISBN 0-8351-0697-7). China Bks.
Paintings of James McNeill Whistler, 2 vols. Andrew M. Young et al. LC 80-5214. (Studies in British Art Ser.). (Illus.). 670p. 1980. 150.00 (ISBN 0-300-02384-7); prepub. 125.00 pre-Dec (ISBN 0-686-62784-9). Yale U Pr.
Paintings of the High Renaissance in Rome & Florence, 2 vols. S. J. Freedberg. (Icon Eds.). (Illus.). 1232p. 1972. Vol. 1. pap. 11.00x o.s.i. (ISBN 0-06-430013-7, IN-13, HarpT); Vol. 2. pap. 10.00x o.s.i. (ISBN 0-06-430014-5, IN-14). Har-Row.
Paints & Materials. Charles Brady. LC 77-82985. (Teaching Primary Science Ser.). (Illus.). 1977. pap. text ed. 6.95 (ISBN 0-356-05075-0). Raintree Child.
Pair Trawling & Pair Seining: The Technology of Two-Boat Fishing. (Illus.). 1978. 33.00 (ISBN 0-85238-087-9, FN 73, FN). Unipub.
Pair Trawling with Small Boats. (FAO Training Ser.: No. 1). 77p. 1981. pap. 6.75 (ISBN 92-5-100627-X, F2095, FAO). Unipub.
Pairing. George R. Bach & Ronald M. Deutsch. 1971. pap. 2.50 (ISBN 0-380-00394-5, 40675). Avon.
Paisius Ligarides. Harry T. Hionides. (World Authors Ser.: Greece: No. 240). lib. bdg. 10.95 (ISBN 0-8057-2536-9). Twayne.
Paisley Butterfly. Phyllis T. Pianka. (Orig.). 1980. pap. 1.50 o.s.i. (ISBN 0-440-17105-9). Dell.
Paiute Indians, Vol. 2. Incl. Southern Paiute Ethnography. Isabel T. Kelly; Chemehuevi Notes (Notes from Informants) Richard F. Van Valkenburgh. (American Indian Ethnohistory Ser: California & Basin - Plateau Indians). (Illus.). lib. bdg. 42.00 (ISBN 0-8240-0741-7). Garland Pub.
Paiute Indians, Vol. 4. Incl. Northern Paiute Archaeology. Gordon L. Grosscup; Medicinal Uses of Plants by Indian Tribes of Nevada. Percy Train et al; Notes on Snakes, Paiutes, Nez Perces at Malheur Reservation. A. B. Meacham. (American Indian Ethnohistory Ser: California & Basin - Plateau Indians). (Illus.). lib. bdg. 42.00 (ISBN 0-8240-0743-3). Garland Pub.
Paiute Indians, Vol. Five: Findings of Fact, & Opinion. Indian Claims Commission. (American Indian Ethnohistory Ser: California & Basin - Plateau Indians). (Illus.). lib. bdg. 42.00 (ISBN 0-8240-0744-1). Garland Pub.
Paiute Indians, Vol. One: Southern Paiute & Chemehuevi: an Ethnohistorical Report. Robert A. Manners. (American Indian Ethnohistory Ser: California & Basin - Plateau Indians). (Illus.). lib. bdg. 42.00 (ISBN 0-8240-0740-9). Garland Pub.
Paiute Indians, Vol. Three: The Northern Paiute Indians. Julian H. Steward & Erminie Wheeler-Voegelin. (American Indian Ethnohistory Ser: California & Basin - Plateau Indians). (Illus,). lib. bdg. 42.00 (ISBN 0-8240-0742-5). Garland Pub.
Pajama Walking. Vicki K. Artis. (gr. k-3). 1981. 6.95 (ISBN 0-395-30343-5). HM.
Pajamas Don't Matter (or: What Your Baby Really Needs) Trish Gribben. LC 79-90081. (Illus.). 1980. pap. 5.95 (ISBN 0-915190-21-4). Jalmar Pr.
Pajaros Notables De Puerto Rico: Guia Para Observadores De Aves. Osvaldo Rivera Cianchini & Luis Mojica Sandoz. (Illus.). v, 101p. 1980. write for info. (ISBN 0-8477-2324-0); pap. write for info. (ISBN 0-8477-2325-9). U of PR Pr.
Pakistan. B. L. Johnson. LC 79-10749. 1980. text ed. 19.95 (ISBN 0-435-35484-1). Heinemann Ed.
Pakistan. S. Aleem Qureishi. (World Bibliographical Ser.: No. 10). 1981. write for info. (ISBN 0-903450-13-5). ABC-Clio.
Pakistan. Damodar P. Singhal. (Modern Nations in Historical Perspective Ser.). (Illus.). 224p. 1972. pap. 2.95 (ISBN 0-13-648469-7, Spec). P-H.
Pakistan & Bangladesh. Emil Lengyel. LC 75-8996. (First Bks.). (Illus.). 72p. (gr. 6-9). 1975. PLB 4.90 o.p. (ISBN 0-531-00762-6). Watts.
Pakistan & Bangladesh: Bibliographic Essays in Social Science. Ed. by W. Eric Gustafson 1976. 12.00x o.p. (ISBN 0-88386-794-X); text ed. 7.50x o.p. (ISBN 0-8364-0442-4). South Asia Bks.
Pakistan-China Axis. B. L. Sharma. 7.50x (ISBN 0-210-98153-9). Asia.
Pakistan: Failure in National Integration. Rounaq Jahan. LC 72-3771. 320p. 1972. 17.50x (ISBN 0-231-03625-6). Columbia U Pr.
Pakistan in Transition. Gopinath. LC 75-907273. 1975. 9.00x o.p. (ISBN 0-88386-710-9). South Asia Bks.
Pakistan: The Consolidation of a Nation. Wayne A. Wilcox. LC 63-9873. 1963. 17.50x (ISBN 0-231-02589-0). Columbia U Pr.
Pakistan: The Development of Its Laws & Constitution. Alan Gledhill. LC 80-20180. (British Commonwealth, the Development of Its Laws & Constitutions: Vol. 8). x, 263p. 1980. Repr. of 1957 ed. lib. bdg. 29.75x (ISBN 0-313-20842-5, GLPA). Greenwood.
Pakistan: The Enigma of Political Development. Lawrence Ziring. (Illus.). 256p. 1980. lib. bdg. 28.50x (ISBN 0-89158-982-1, Pub. by Dawson Pub). Westview.
Pal Paperbacks Ser., Kit A. Ed. by Mary Verdick. (Pal Paperbacks, Ser., Kit A). (Illus., Orig.). (gr. 7-12). 1976. pap. text ed. 1.25 (ISBN 0-8374-3487-4). Xerox Ed Pubns.
Pala. Marita Bodenhofer. 1981. 8.95 (ISBN 0-8062-1715-4). Carlton.
Palabra Irresistible. Tr. by Andrew Murray. (Spanish Bks.). (Span.). 1979. 1.95 (ISBN 0-8297-0520-1). Life Pubs Intl.
Palabras Griegas Del Nuevo Testamento. William Barclay. Tr. by Javier J. Marin. 1979. pap. 3.60 (ISBN 0-311-42052-4). Casa Bautista.
Palace. Claude Simon. 4.50 o.s.i. (ISBN 0-8076-0234-5). Braziller.
Palace: A Historical Horror Novel. Chelsea Q. Yarbro. LC 78-3996. 1979. 9.95 o.p. (ISBN 0-312-59474-7). St Martin.

Palace & Politics in Pre-War Japan. David A. Titus. (Studies of the East Asian Institute, Columbia University). 368p. 1974. 22.50x (ISBN 0-231-03622-1). Columbia U Pr.

Palace for a King: The Buen Retiro & the Court of Philip IV. Jonathan Brown & John H. Elliott. LC 80-13659. (Illus.). 320p. 1980. 29.95x (ISBN 0-300-02507-6). Yale U Pr.

Palace for a King: The Buen Retiro & the Court of Philip IV. Jonathan Brown & John H. Elliott. LC 79-24393. (Illus.). 320p. 1980. 29.95x (ISBN 0-300-02507-6). Yale U Pr.

Palace Guard. Charlotte MacLeod. LC 80-2750. 192p. 1981. 9.95 (ISBN 0-385-17533-7). Doubleday.

Palace of Nestor at Pylos in Western Messehia, 3 vols. C. W. Blegen & M. Rawson. Incl. Vol. 1. The Buildings & Their Contents, 2 pts. 1966. o.p. (ISBN 0-691-03525-3); Vol. 2. The Frescoes. M. Lang. 1969. 45.00 (ISBN 0-691-03531-8); Vol. 3. Acropolis & Lower Town, Tholoi, Grave Circle, & Chamber Tombs, Discoveries Outside the Citadel. 1973. 50.00 (ISBN 0-691-03529-6). LC 65-17131. (Cincinnati Classical Studies Ser.). Princeton U Pr.

Palace of Pleasure, 3 Vols. William Painter. Ed. by Joseph Jacobs. 1966. pap. text ed. 4.00 ea.; Vol. 1. pap. text ed. (ISBN 0-486-21691-8); Vol. 2. pap. text ed. (ISBN 0-486-21692-6); Vol. 3. pap. text ed. (ISBN 0-486-21693-4). Dover.

Palace of the Moon & Other Tales from Czechoslovakia. Ruzena Wood. LC 80-2687. (Illus.). 144p. (gr. 2-7). 1981. 9.95 (ISBN 0-233-97206-4). Andre Deutsch.

Palace Politics: An Inside Account of the Ford Years. Jerry Hartmann. 320p. 1980. 14.95 (ISBN 0-07-026951-3). McGraw.

Palaces of Crete. James W. Graham. (Illus.). 1962. 25.00 o.p. (ISBN 0-691-03524-5); pap. 6.95 (ISBN 0-691-00206-1, 154). Princeton U Pr.

Palaces of Desire. Karen Alexander. 1979. pap. 2.25 o.p. (ISBN 0-345-27997-2). Ballantine.

Palaces of Venice. Peter Lauritzen. (Illus.). 1978. 35.00 o.p. (ISBN 0-670-53724-1, Studio). Viking Pr.

Paladin. Brian Garfield. 1980. 12.95 (ISBN 0-686-60899-2, 24704). S&S.

Paladin. Brian Garfield. 352p. 1981. pap. 2.95 (ISBN 0-553-14261-5). Bantam.

Palaentology & Introduction. James Scott. 160p. 1980. 15.00x (ISBN 0-89771-000-2). State Mutual Bk.

Palaeoeconomy. Ed. by E. S. Higgs. LC 74-76576. (Illus.). 330p. 1975. 42.50 (ISBN 0-521-20449-6). Cambridge U Pr.

Palaeolithic of Tangier, Morroco. Bruce Howe. (American School of Prehistoric Research Bulletin Ser.: No. 22). (Orig.). 1967. pap. text ed. 10.00 (ISBN 0-87365-523-0). Peabody Harvard.

Palaeomagnetism & Plate Tectonics. M. W. McElhinney. LC 72-80590. (Earth Science Ser). (Illus.). 368p. 1973. 57.50 (ISBN 0-521-08707-4); pap. 18.50x (ISBN 0-521-29753-2). Cambridge U Pr.

Palanca. Harlan Wade. Tr. by Mamie M. Contreras from Eng. LC 78-26992. (Book About Ser.). Orig. Title: Lever. (Illus., Sp.). (gr. k-3). 1979. PLB 7.30 (ISBN 0-8172-1489-5). Raintree Pubs.

Palanpur: The Economy of an Indian Village. C. J. Bliss & N. H. Stern. (Illus.). 464p. 1981. 37.50 (ISBN 0-19-828419-5). Oxford U Pr.

Palatability & Flavor Use in Animal Feeds. Ed. by Hans Bickel. (Advances in Animal Physiology & Animal Nutrition: Vol. 11). (Illus.). 148p. (Orig.). 1980. pap. text ed. 34.10 (ISBN 3-490-41115-3). Parey Sci Pubs.

Palatinate - a Full Declaration of the Faith & Ceremonies Professed in the Dominions of Prince Fredericke, 5. Prince Elector Palatine. Tr. by J. Rolte. LC 79-84129. (English Experience Ser.: No. 947). 208p. 1979. Repr. of 1614 ed. lib. bdg. 20.00 (ISBN 90-221-0947-X). Walter J Johnson.

Palca & Pucara: A Study of the Effects of Revolution on Two Bolivian Haciendas. Roger A. Simmons. (U. C. Publ. in Anthropology: Vol. 9). pap. 12.50x (ISBN 0-520-09440-9). U of Cal Pr.

Pale Gray for Guilt. John D. MacDonald. 1971. 5.50 o.s.i. (ISBN 0-397-00792-2). Lippincott.

Paleoanthropology. Milford H. Wolpoff. 416p. 1980. text ed. 17.95 (ISBN 0-394-32197-9). Knopf.

Paleoanthropology: Morphology & Paleoecology. Ed. by Russell H. Tuttle. (World Anthropology Ser.). (Illus.). 608p. 1975. 40.50x o.p. (ISBN 0-202-90012-6). Beresford Bk Serv.

Paleobiology of Angiosperm Origins. N. F. Hughes. LC 75-3855. (Illus.). 216p. 1976. 40.50 (ISBN 0-521-20809-2). Cambridge U Pr.

Paleobiology of Plant Protists. Helen Tappan. LC 80-14675. (Geology Ser.). (Illus.). 1980. text ed. 95.00x (ISBN 0-7167-1109-5). W H Freeman.

Paleobotany: An Intro. to Plant Biology. Thomas N. Taylor. (Illus.). 576p. 1981. text ed. 29.95 (ISBN 0-07-062954-4). McGraw.

Paleobotany: An Introduction to Fossil Plant Biology. Thomas N. Taylor. (Illus.). 576p. Date not set. text ed. 29.95 (ISBN 0-07-062954-4, C). McGraw. Postponed.

Paleocene Primates of the Fort Union, with Discussion of Relationships of Eocene Primates. James W. Gidley. Bd. with Fort Union of the Crazy Mountain Field, Montana, & Its Mammalian Faunas. George G. Simpson. Repr. of 1937 ed. LC 78-72717. Date not set. Repr. of 1923 ed. 42.50 (ISBN 0-404-18292-5). AMS Pr.

Paleoecology, Concepts &Applications. Robert J. Dodd & Robert J. Stanton, Jr. LC 80-19623. 500p. 1981. 32.95 (ISBN 0-471-04171-8, Pub. by Wiley-Interscience). Wiley.

Paleoethnobotany: The Prehistoric Food Plants of the Near East & Europe. Jane Renfrew. 300p. 1973. 22.50x (ISBN 0-231-03745-7). Columbia U Pr.

Paleogene Fossil Sporomorphus of the Bokony Mountains, Vol. I. Kedves. 1973. 8.75 (ISBN 0-9960001-5-1, Pub. by Kaido Hungary). Heyden.

Paleogene Fossil Sporomorphus of the Bokony Mountains, Vol. II. Kedves. 1974. 8.00 (ISBN 0-9960001-6-X, Pub. by Kaido Hungary). Heyden.

Paleogene Fossil Sporomorphus of the Bokony Mountains, Vol. III. Kedves. 1979. 11.50 (ISBN 0-9960012-8-X, Pub. by Kaido Hungary). Heyden.

Paleogeographic Principles of Oil & Gas Prospecting. N. I. Markovskii. LC 75-12798. 256p. 1979. 54.95x (ISBN 0-470-57215-9). Halsted Pr.

Paleolithic Cultures of Singhbhum. Asok K. Ghosh. (Transactions Ser.: Vol. 60, Pt. 1). (Illus.). 1970. pap. 1.00 o.p. (ISBN 0-87169-601-0). Am Philos.

Paleontographica Americana, Vol. 2. Incl. No. 9. Devonian Brevicones of New York & Adjacent Areas. Rousseau H. Flower. 1938. 4.00 (ISBN 0-87710-310-0); No. 11. Notes on Giant Fasciolarias. Burnett Smith. 1940. 0.50 (ISBN 0-87710-312-7); No. 12. Titusvillidae, Paleozoic & Recent Branching Hexactinellida. Kenneth E. Caster. 1941. 2.00 (ISBN 0-87710-313-5). (Illus.). 30.00 set (ISBN 0-87710-354-2). Paleo Res.

Paleontographica Americana, Vol. 3. Incl. No. 13. Notes on Structure & Phylogeny of Eurysiphonate Cephalopods. Rousseau H. Flower. 1941. 2.60 (ISBN 0-87710-314-3); No. 15. Two Abnormal Busycon Shells. Burnett Smith. 1943. 0.40 (ISBN 0-87710-316-X); No. 16. Fish Remains from the Middle Devonian Bone Beds of the Cincinnati Arch Region. John W. Wells. 1944. 2.25 (ISBN 0-87710-317-8); No. 17. Two Spine Rows in a Florida Busycon Contrarium. Burnett Smith. 1944. 0.40 (ISBN 0-87710-318-6); No. 18. New Jellyfish (Kirklandia Texana Caster) from the Low Cretaceous of Texas. Kenneth E. Caster. 1945. 2.50 (ISBN 0-87710-319-4); No. 20. Some Species of Platystrophia from the Trenton of Ontario & Quebec. G. Winston Sinclair. 1946. 0.75 (ISBN 0-87710-321-6); No. 21. Observations on Gastropod Protoconchs. Burnett Smith. 1946. Pt. III. Some Protoconchs In Busycon, Fusinus, Heilprinia, Hesperisternia & Urosalpinx. 0.75 (ISBN 0-685-85237-7); No. 22. Two Marine Quarternary Localities. Burnett Smith. 1948. 1.00 (ISBN 0-87710-323-2); No. 23. Studies of Carboniferous Crinoids: Oklahoma & Nebraska, 4 pts. 2.00 (ISBN 0-87710-324-0); No. 24. Stereotoceras & Brevioceceratidae. R. H. Flower. 1950. 2.00 (ISBN 0-87710-325-9); No. 25. Pelecypod Genus Venericardia in the Paleocene & Eocene of Western North America. P. Verastegui. 1953. 8.00 (ISBN 0-87710-326-7). (Illus.). 35.00 set (ISBN 0-87710-355-0). Paleo Res.

Paleontographica Americana, Vol. 4. Incl. No. 29. Dalmanellidae of the Cincinnatian. Donald D. Hall. 1962. 2.25 (ISBN 0-87710-330-5); No. 30. Pelecypod Genus Byssonchia As It Occurs in the Cincinnatian at Cincinnati, Ohio. John Pojeta, Jr. 1962. 3.00 (ISBN 0-87710-331-3); No. 32. Upper Ordovician Eurypterids of Ohio. K. E. Caster & E. N. Kjellesvig-Waering. 1964. 4.00 (ISBN 0-87710-333-X). (Illus.). 35.00 set (ISBN 0-87710-356-9). Paleo Res.

Paleontographica Americana, Vol. 5. Incl. No. 34. Upper Tertiary Arcacea of the Mid-Atlantic Coastal Plain. S. O. Bird. 1965. 4.00 (ISBN 0-87710-335-6); No. 35. Dimyarian Pelecypods of the Mississippi Marshall Sandstone of Michigan. Egbert G. Driscoll. 1965. 4.60 (ISBN 0-87710-336-4); No. 36. North American Ambonychiidae (Pelecypoda) John Pojeta, Jr. 1977. 7.00 (ISBN 0-87710-337-2). (Illus.). 32.00 set (ISBN 0-87710-357-7). Paleo Res.

Paleontographica Americana, Vol. 6. Incl. No. 38. Lycopsid Stems & Roots & Spenopsid Fructitications & Stems from the Upper Freeport Coal of Southeastern Ohio. Maxine L. Abbot. 1968. 3.75 (ISBN 0-87710-339-9); No. 39. Cenozoic Evolution of the Alticostate Venericards in Gulf & East Coastal North America. William G. Heaslip. 1968. 5.00 (ISBN 0-87710-340-2); No. 40. Carboniferous Crinoids of Texas with Stratigraphic Implications. H. L. Strimple & W. T. Watkins. 1969. 12.00 (ISBN 0-685-85253-9). (Illus.). 35.00 (ISBN 0-87710-358-5). Paleo Res.

Paleontographica Americana, Vol. 7. Incl. No. 42. Torreites Sanchezi (Douville) from Jamaica. Peter Jung. 1970. 1.25 (ISBN 0-87710-343-7); No. 43. Cancellariid Radula & Its Interpretation. A. A. Olsson. 1970. 1.25 (ISBN 0-87710-344-5); No. 44. Ontogeny & Sexual Dimorphism of Lower Paleozoic Trilobita. Chang-Hung Hu. 1971. 12.50 (ISBN 0-87710-345-3); No. 45. Rudists of Jamaica. L. J. Chubb. 1971. 8.50 (ISBN 0-87710-346-1); No. 46. Crinoids Rom the Girardeau Limestone. J. C. Brower. 1973. 20.00 (ISBN 0-87710-347-X). (Illus.). Set. 45.00 (ISBN 0-87710-359-3). Paleo Res.

Paleontographica Americana, Vol. 8. Incl. No. 47. Revision of the Family Seraphsidae (Gastropoda: Strombacea) Peter Jung. 1974. 6.00 (ISBN 0-87710-360-7); No. 49. Comparative Morphology & Shell History of the Ordovician Strophomenacea (Brachiopod) J. K. Pope. 1976. 6.50 (ISBN 0-87710-350-X); No. 50. Evolution & Classification of Cenozoic North American & European Lucinidae (Mollusca, Bivalva) Sara Bretsky. 10.00 (ISBN 0-87710-351-8). (Illus.). Paleo Res.

Paleontology & Paleoenvironments. Ed. by Brian J. Skinner. (Earth & Its Inhabitants: Selected Readings from American Scientist Ser.). (Illus.). 250p. (Orig.). 1981. pap. 8.95 (ISBN 0-913232-93-9). W Kaufmann.

Paleontology & Stratigraphy of the Lower Chickabally Mudstone (Berremain-Aptian) in the Ono Quadrangle, Northern California. Michael A. Murphy. (Publcations in Geological Sciences Ser.: Vol. 113). 1975. pap. 9.00x (ISBN 0-520-09536-7). U of Cal Pr.

Paleopathological Diagnosis & Interpretation: Bone Diseases in Ancient Human Populations. R. Ted Steinbock. (Illus.). 440p. 1976. 30.50 (ISBN 0-398-03512-1). C C Thomas.

Palestina. Suzanne T. Moore. Date not set. 6.95 (ISBN 0-686-10451-X). MTM Pub Co. Postponed.

Palestine, a Prize Poem, Recited in the Theatre, Oxford, June 15, 1803, Repr. Of 1803. Reginald Herber. Bd. with Europe: Lines on the Present War. Repr. of 1809 ed; Palestine...to Which Is Added, the Passage of the Red Sea, a Fragment. Repr. of 1809 ed. LC 75-31211. (Romantic Context Ser.: Poetry 1789-1830: Vol. 62). 1978. lib. bdg. 47.00 (ISBN 0-8240-2161-4). Garland Pub.

Palestine & International Law: The Legal Aspects of the Arab-Israeli Conflict. 2nd ed. Henry Cattan. LC 75-42335. 1976. text ed. 22.00x (ISBN 0-582-78067-5). Longman.

Palestine & Israel in the Nineteenth & Twentieth Centuries. Ed. by Elie Kedourie & Sylvia G. Haim. 250p. 1981. 29.50x (ISBN 0-7146-3121-3, F Cass Co). Biblio Dist.

Palestine & the Bible. Ed. by M. T. Mehdi. LC 71-114557. 1971. pap. 2.00 (ISBN 0-911026-06-1). New World Press NY.

Palestine: Concordance of United Nations Resolutions, 1967-1971. 1971. pap. 3.00 o.p. (ISBN 0-911026-07-X). New World Press NY.

Palestine of the Mandate. W. Basil Worsfold. (Return to Zion Ser.). (Illus.). xii, 275p. 1980. Repr. of 1925 ed. lib. bdg. 20.00x (ISBN 0-87991-138-7). Porcupine Pr.

Palestine State: A Rational Approach. Richard J. Ward et al. 1977. 12.95 (ISBN 0-8046-9159-2). Kennikat.

Palestine, Still a Dilemma. Frank Sakran. 6.95. New World Press NY.

Palestinian Liberation Organization (P.L.O.) Organization of a Nationalise Movement. John W. Amos. (Pergamon Policy Studies). 1981. 45.00 (ISBN 0-08-025094-7). Pergamon.

Palestinian Refugees in Jordan 1948-57. A. O. Plascov. 256p. 1980. 32.50x (ISBN 0-7146-3120-5, F Cass Co). Biblio Dist.

Palestinian Resistance: Organization of a Nationalist Movement. John W. Amos, II. LC 80-16134. (Pergamon Policy Studies on International Politics). 496p. 1981. 45.00 (ISBN 0-08-025094-7). Pergamon.

Palestinians. Colin Smith. (Minority Rights Group Ser.: No. 24). 1975. pap. 2.50 (ISBN 0-89192-110-9). Interbk Inc.

Palestinians Without Palestine: A Study of Political Socialization Among Palestinian Youths. Alice K. Kuroda & Yasumasa Kuroda. LC 78-51851. 1978. pap. text ed. 10.25x (ISBN 0-8191-0479-5). U Pr of Amer.

Paling Shadows. Samir Dasgupta. (Writers Workshop Redbird Ser.). 1975. 8.00 (ISBN 0-88253-606-0); pap. text ed. 4.80 (ISBN 0-88253-605-2). Ind-US Inc.

Palinurid & Scyllarid Lobster Larvae of the Tropical Eastern Pacific & Their Distribution As Related to the Prevailing Hydrography. Martin W. Johnson. (Bulletin of the Scripps Institution of Oceanography: Vol. 19). 1971. pap. 6.00x (ISBN 0-520-09388-7). U of Cal Pr.

Palladio & Palladianism. Rudolf Wittkower. LC 73-90463. (Illus.). 192p. 1975. 22.50 o.s.i. (ISBN 0-8076-0735-5). Braziller.

Palladio's Architecture & Its Influences: A Photographic Guide. Joseph Farber & Henry Hope. (Illus.). 1980. pap. 6.95 (ISBN 0-486-23922-5). Dover.

Palladis Tamia. Francis Meres. LC 73-170413. (English Stage Ser.: Vol 10). lib. bdg. 50.00 (ISBN 0-8240-0593-7). Garland Pub.

Palliser's New Cottage Homes & Details. Palliser. LC 75-4887. (Architecture & Decorative Arts Ser). (Illus.). 180p. 1975. Repr. of 1887 ed. lib. bdg. 45.00 (ISBN 0-306-70744-6). Da Capo.

Palm & the Pleiades. S. Hugh-Jones. LC 78-5533. (Studies in Social Anthropology: No. 24). (Illus.). 1979. 24.95 (ISBN 0-521-21952-3). Cambridge U Pr.

Palm Court. Robert Overton. 1979. 17.95 (ISBN 0-241-10110-7, Pub. by Hamish Hamilton England). David & Charles.

Palm Sunday. Kurt Vonnegut. 1981. 13.95 (ISBN 0-440-06593-3). Delacorte.

Palmer Method Cursive, Consumable. new ed. Fred D. King. (Palmer Method Easy to Teach Ser.). (Illus.). (gr. 6). 1979. wkbk. 2.60 (ISBN 0-914268-68-6, 79-6C); tchr's ed. 5.32 (ISBN 0-914268-69-4, 79-6CTE). A N Palmer.

Palmer Method Cursive, Consumable. new ed. Fred M. King. (Palmer Method Easy to Teach Ser.). (Illus.). (gr. 4). 1979. wkbk 2.60 (ISBN 0-914268-64-3, 79-4C); tchr's ed. 5.32 (ISBN 0-914268-65-1, 79-4CTE). A N Palmer.

Palmer Method Cursive, Consumable. Fred M. King. (Palmer Method Easy to Teach Ser.). (Illus.). (gr. 4). 1976. wkbk. 2.60 (ISBN 0-914268-31-7, 76-4C); tchr's ed 5.32 (ISBN 0-914268-32-5, 76-4C-TE). A N Palmer.

Palmer Method Cursive, Consumable. Fred M. King. (Palmer Method Easy to Teach Ser.). (Illus.). (gr. 5). 1976. wkbk 2.60 (ISBN 0-914268-33-3, 76-5C); tchr's ed. 5.32 (ISBN 0-914268-34-1, 76-5C-TE). A N Palmer.

Palmer Method Cursive, Consumable. Fred M. King. (Palmer Method Easy to Teach Ser.). (Illus.). (gr. 6). 1976. wkbk. 2.60 (ISBN 0-914268-35-X, 76-6C); tchr's ed. 5.32 (ISBN 0-914268-36-8, 76-6C-TE). A N Palmer.

Palmer Method Cursive, Grade 5, Consumable. new ed. Fred M. King. (Palmer Method Easy to Teach Ser.). (Illus.). (gr. 5). 1979. wkbk. 2.60 (ISBN 0-914268-66-X, 79-5C); tchr's ed 5.32 (ISBN 0-914268-67-8, 79-5CTE). A N Palmer.

Palmer Method Cursive, Non-Consumable. Fred M. King. (Palmer Method Easy to Teach Ser.). (gr. 8). 1979. wkbk 3.20 (ISBN 0-914268-86-4, N79-SL2); tchr's ed. 5.32 (ISBN 0-914268-87-2, N79-SL2TE). A N Palmer.

Palmer Method Cursive, Non-Consumable. Fred M. King. (Palmer Method Easy to Teach Ser.). (Illus.). 1979. wkbk 3.20 (ISBN 0-914268-84-8, N79-SL1); tchr's ed. 5.32 (ISBN 0-914268-85-6, N79-SL1TE). A N Palmer.

Palmer Method Cursive, Non-Consumable. new ed. Fred M. King. (Palmer Method Easy to Teach Ser.). (Illus.). (gr. 6). 1979. wkbk 3.20 (ISBN 0-914268-82-1, N79-6C); tchr's ed. 5.32 (ISBN 0-914268-83-X, N79-6CTE). A N Palmer.

Palmer Method Cursive, Non-Consumable. new ed. Fred M. King. (Palmer Method Easy to Teach Ser.). 1979. wkbk. 3.20 (ISBN 0-914268-80-5, N79-5C); tchr's ed. 5.32 (ISBN 0-914268-81-3, N79-5CTE). A N Palmer.

Palmer Method Cursive, Non-Consumable. Fred M. King. (Palmer Method Easy to Teach Ser.). (Illus.). (gr. 4). 1975. wkbk. 3.20 (ISBN 0-914268-45-7, N75-4C); tchr's ed. 5.32 (ISBN 0-914268-46-5, N75-4C-TE). A N Palmer.

Palmer Method Cursive, Non-Consumable. Fred M. King. (Palmer Method Easy to Teach Ser.). (Illus.). (gr. 5). 1975. wkbk. 3.20 (ISBN 0-914268-47-3, N75-5C); tchr's ed. 5.32 (ISBN 0-914268-48-1, N75-5C-TE). A N Palmer.

Palmer Method Cursive, Non-Consumable. Fred M. King. (Palmer Method Easy to Teach Ser.). (Illus.). (gr. 6). 1975. wkbk. 3.20 (ISBN 0-914268-49-X, N75-6C); tchr's ed. 5.32 (ISBN 0-914268-50-3, N75-6C-TE). A N Palmer.

Palmer Method Cursive, Non-Consumable. Fred M. King. (Palmer Method Easy to Teach Ser.). (Illus.). (gr. 7). 1976. wkbk 3.20 (ISBN 0-914268-51-1, N75-SL1); tchr's ed. 5.32 (ISBN 0-914268-52-X, N75-SL1-TE). A N Palmer.

Palmer Method Cursive, Non-Consumable. Fred M. King. (Palmer Method Easy to Teach Ser.). (Illus.). (gr. 8). 1976. wkbk. 3.20 (ISBN 0-914268-53-8, N75-SL2); tchr's ed. 5.32 (ISBN 0-914268-54-6, N75-SL2-TE). A N Palmer.

Palmer Method Cursive, Non-Consumable. (Palmer Method Easy to Teach Ser.). (gr. 4). 1979. wkbk 3.20 (ISBN 0-914268-78-3, N79-4C); tchr's ed. 5.32 (ISBN 0-914268-79-1, N79-4CTE). A N Palmer.

Palmer Method Manuscript, Consumable. new ed. Fred M. King. (Palmer Method Easy to Teach Ser.). (Illus.). (gr. 1). 1979. 2.60 (ISBN 0-914268-56-2, 79-1M); tchr's ed. 5.32 (ISBN 0-914268-57-0, 79-1MTE). A N Palmer.

Palmer Method Manuscript, Consumable. new ed. Fred M. King. (Palmer Method Easy to Teach Ser.). (Illus.). (gr. 2). 1979. wkbk. 2.60 (ISBN 0-914268-58-9, 79-2M); tchr's ed. 5.32 (ISBN 0-914268-59-7, 79-2MTE). A N Palmer.

Palmer Method Manuscript, Consumable. Fred M. King. (Palmer Method Easy to Teach Ser.). (Illus.). (gr. 1). 1976. tchr's ed. 5.32 (ISBN 0-914268-24-4, 76-IM-TE); wkbk. 2.60 (ISBN 0-914268-23-6, 76-1M). A N Palmer.

Palmer Method Manuscript, Consumable. Fred M. King. (Palmer Method Easy to Teach Ser.). (Illus.). (gr. 2). 1976. wkbk. 2.60 (ISBN 0-914268-25-2, 76-2M); tchr's man. 5.32 (ISBN 0-914268-26-0, 76-2M TE). A N Palmer.

Palmer Method Manuscript, Non-Consumable. new ed. Fred M. King. (Palmer Method Easy to Teach Ser.). (Illus.). (gr. 2). 1979. wkbk. 3.20 (ISBN 0-914268-72-4, N79-2M); tchr's ed. 5.32 (ISBN 0-914268-73-2, N79-2MTE). A N Palmer.

Palmer Method Manuscript, Non-Consumable. new ed. Fred M. King. (Palmer Method Easy to Teach Ser.). (Illus.). (gr. 1). 1979. wkbk. 3.20 (ISBN 0-914268-70-8, N79-1M); tchr's ed. 5.32 (ISBN 0-914268-71-6, N79-1MTE). A N Palmer.

Palmer Method Manuscript, Non-Consumable. Fred M. King. (Palmer Method Easy to Teach Ser.). (Illus.). (gr. 1). 1976. wkbk. 3.20 (ISBN 0-914268-37-6, N75-1M); tchr's ed. 5.32 (ISBN 0-914268-38-4, N75-1M-TE). A N Palmer.

Palmer Method Manuscript, Non-Consumable. Fred M. King. (Palmer Method Easy to Teach Ser.). (Illus.). (gr. 2). 1976. wkbk. 3.20 (ISBN 0-914268-39-2, N75-2M); tchr's ed. 5.32 (ISBN 0-914268-40-6, N75-2M-TE). A N Palmer.

Palmer Method Transition on Cursive, Consumable. Fred M. King. (Palmer Method Easy to Teach Ser.). (Illus.). (gr. 3). 1976. wkbk. 2.60 (ISBN 0-914268-29-5, 76-3TC); tchr's ed. 5.32 (ISBN 0-914268-30-9, 76-3TC-TE). A N Palmer.

Palmer Method Transition on Cursive, Consumable. (Palmer Method Easy to Teach Ser.). (gr. 3). 1979. wkbk 2.60 (ISBN 0-914268-62-7, 79-3TC); tchr's ed. 5.32 (ISBN 0-914268-63-5, 79-3TC TE). A N Palmer.

Palmer Method Transition on Cursive, Non-Consumable. Fred M. King. (Palmer Method Easy to Teach Ser.). (gr. 3). 1979. wkbk 3.20 (ISBN 0-914268-76-7, N79-3TC); tchr's ed. 5.32 (ISBN 0-914268-77-5, N79-3TC TE). A N Palmer.

Palmer Method Transition to Cursive, Consumable. new ed. Fred M. King. (Palmer Method Easy to Teach Ser.). (Illus.). (gr. 2). 1979. wkbk. 2.60 (ISBN 0-914268-60-0, 79-2TC); tchr's ed. 5.32 (ISBN 0-914268-61-9, 79-2TCTE). A N Palmer.

Palmer Method Transition to Cursive Consumable. Fred M. King. (Palmer Method Easy to Teach Ser.). (Illus.). (gr. 2). 1976. tchr's ed. 5.32 (ISBN 0-914268-28-7, 76-2TC-TE); wkbk. 2.60 (ISBN 0-914268-27-9, 76-2TC). A N Palmer.

Palmer Method Transition to Cursive, Non-Consumable. new ed. Fred M. King. (Palmer Method Easy to Teach Ser.). (Illus.). (gr. 2). 1979. wkbk. 3.20 (ISBN 0-914268-74-0, N79-2TC); tchr's ed. 5.32 (ISBN 0-914268-75-9, N79-2TCTE). A N Palmer.

Palmer Method Transition to Cursive, Non-Consumable. Fred M. King. (Palmer Method Easy to Teach Ser.). (Illus.). (gr. 2). 1976. wkbk. 3.20 (ISBN 0-914268-41-4, N75-2TC); tchr's ed. 5.32 (ISBN 0-914268-42-2, N75-2TC-TE). A N Palmer.

Palmer Method Transition to Cursive, Non-Consumable. Fred M. King. (Palmer Method Easy to Teach Ser.). (Illus.). (gr. 3). 1975. 3.20 (ISBN 0-914268-43-0, N75-3TC); tchr's ed. 5.32 (ISBN 0-914268-44-9, N75-3TC-TE). A N Palmer.

Palmer Method Writing Readiness, Consumable. new ed. Fred M. King. (Illus.). (gr. k-1). 1979. wkbk. 2.60 (ISBN 0-914268-55-4, 79-WR). A N Palmer.

Palmer Method Writing Readiness, Consumable. Fred M. King. (Palmer Method Easy to Teach Ser.). (Illus.). (gr. k-1). 1976. wkbk 2.60 (ISBN 0-914268-22-8, 76-WR). A N Palmer.

Palmer Patch. Barbara B. Wallace. LC 76-2185. (Illus.). 128p. (gr. 3-6). 1976. 5.95 o.p. (ISBN 0-695-80668-8); lib. ed. 5.97 o.p. (ISBN 0-695-40668-X). Follett.

Palmerston, Guizot & the Collapse of the Entente Cordiale. Roger Bullen. (University of London Historical Studies: No. 36). 380p. 1974. text ed. 30.00x (ISBN 0-485-13136-6, Athlone Pr). Humanities.

Palmistry. Thomas G. Aylesworth. LC 75-38964. (Career Concise Guides Ser.). (Illus.). 96p. (gr. 7 up). 1976. PLB 4.90 o.p. (ISBN 0-531-01129-1). Watts.

Palmistry, Reincarnation & the Dream State. Sri Chinmoy. (Orig.). 1977. pap. 2.00 o.p. (ISBN 0-88497-378-6). Aum Pubns.

Palms of the World: Supplement. Arthur C. Langlois. LC 77-161006. (Illus.). 252p. 1977. 25.00 o.p. (ISBN 0-8130-0329-6). U Presses Fla.

Paloma. Theresa Conway. 672p. (Orig.). 1981. pap. 2.75 (ISBN 0-345-28706-1). Ballantine.

Palomino. Danielle Steel. (Orig.). 1981. pap. 6.95 (ISBN 0-440-56753-X, Dell Trade Pbks). Dell.

Pamela, 2 Vols. Samuel Richardson. 1955. Vol. 1. 10.50x (ISBN 0-460-00683-5, Evman); Vol. 2. 6.00x (ISBN 0-460-00684-3); Vol. 1. pap. 3.25x (ISBN 0-460-01683-0); pap. o.p. (ISBN 0-460-01684-9). Dutton.

Pamela, No. 3. Mary Mackie. (Starlight Romance Ser.). 144p. 1981. pap. cancelled (ISBN 0-553-14365-4). Bantam.

Pamela Harlech's Practical Guide to Cooking,Entertaining & Household Management. Pamela Harlech. 1981. 16.95 (ISBN 0-686-65194-4). Atheneum.

Pamela: Or Virtue Rewarded. Samuel Richardson. Ed. by Peter Sabor. (Penguin English Library). 480p. 1981. pap. 4.95 (ISBN 0-14-043140-3). Penguin.

Pamela; or, Virtue Rewarded, 1801, 4 vols. Samuel Richardson. Ed. by Michael F. Shugrue. (Flowering of the Novel, 1740-1775 Ser: Vol. 1). 1974. lib. bdg. 50.00 ea. (ISBN 0-8240-1100-7). Garland Pub.

Pamela, Shamela. Samuel Richardson & Henry Fielding. 1980. pap. 3.50 (ISBN 0-451-51366-5, CE1366, Sig Classics). NAL.

Pamiatniki Drevnerrusskago Kanonicheskago Prava. A. Pavlov. LC 80-2366. (Russkaya Istorischeskaya Biblioteka: Vol. 6). 76.00 (ISBN 0-404-18912-1). AMS Pr.

Pamphlets & the American Revolution. LC 76-41289. 1976. 80.00x (ISBN 0-8201-1280-1). Schol Facsimiles.

Pamphlets on the Constitution of the United States. Paul L. Ford. LC 68-22228. (American History, Politics & Law Ser.). 1968. Repr. of 1888 ed. lib. bdg. 25.00 (ISBN 0-306-71144-3). Da Capo.

Pan-African Movement: A History of Pan-Africanism in America, Europe & Africa. Imanuel Geiss. LC 74-78310. 546p. 1974. text ed. 37.50x (ISBN 0-8419-0161-9, Africana); pap. text ed. 15.95x (ISBN 0-8419-0215-1). Holmes & Meier.

Pan African Protest: West Africa & the Italo-Ethiopian Crisis, 1934-41. S. K. Asante. (Legon History). (Illus.). 1977. text ed. 22.00x (ISBN 0-582-64194-2). Longman.

Pan African Short Stories: An Anthology for Schools. Ed. by Neville Denny. (Illus.). 1965. pap. text ed. 3.50x (ISBN 0-17-511099-9). Humanities.

Pan-Africanism: A Short Political Guide. Colin Legum. LC 75-25492. (Illus.). 1976. Repr. of 1962 ed. lib. bdg. 22.75x (ISBN 0-8371-8420-7, LEPA). Greenwood.

Pan-Africanism & Nationalism in West Africa 1900-1945. J. Ayodele Langley. (Oxford Studies in African Affairs). 340p. 1973. 33.00x (ISBN 0-19-821689-0). Oxford U Pr.

Pan Am World Guide. Pan Am. LC 80-14222. (Illus.). 1072p. 1980. 8.95 (ISBN 0-07-048431-7, GB). McGraw.

Pan American Associations in the United States: Directory. 1971. pap. 1.00 o.p. (ISBN 0-8270-5085-2). OAS.

Pan Am's Guide to Europe. pap. 3.00 (ISBN 0-685-37577-3). Pan Am Pubns.

Pan Am's Guide to Latin America. pap. 2.50 (ISBN 0-685-37582-X). Pan Am Pubns.

Pan Am's Guide to Pacific: Hawaii to Hong Kong. pap. 2.50 (ISBN 0-685-37580-3). Pan Am Pubns.

Pan Am's U. S. A. Guide. 3rd ed. Ed. by Pan Am World Airways. (Illus.). 1980. 7.95 (ISBN 0-07-048422-8). McGraw.

Pan Am's World Guide. 24th ed. Pan Am World Airways, Inc. 1978. 7.95 o.p. (ISBN 0-07-048418-X, GB). McGraw.

Pan & the Nightmare: Two Studies. Ed. by Wilhelm Roscher & James Hillman. (Dunquin Ser.). 1972. pap. text ed. 7.50 (ISBN 0-88214-204-6). Spring Pubns.

Pan-Enciclopedia Universale, 11 vols. (It.). 1967-1969. 590.00 (ISBN 0-8277-3048-9). Maxwell Sci Intl.

Pan-Islam. George W. Bury. LC 80-1938. 1981. Repr. of 1919 ed. 30.00 (ISBN 0-404-18956-3). AMS Pr.

Pan-Turkism & Islam in Russia. Serge A. Zenkovsky. LC 60-5399. (Russian Research Center Studies: No. 36). 1960. 17.50x (ISBN 0-674-65350-5). Harvard U Pr.

Panama. Eleanor Langstaff. (World Bibliographical Ser.: No. 14). 1981. write for info. (ISBN 0-903450-26-7). ABC-Clio.

Panama Canal. rev. ed. Maloney P. Markun. (First Bks.). (Illus.). (gr. 4 up). 1979. PLB 6.45 s&l (ISBN 0-531-04075-5). Watts.

Panama Canal & Sea Power in the Pacific. Alfred T. Mahan. (Illus.). 1977. 45.15 (ISBN 0-89266-044-9). Am Classical Coll Pr.

Panama Canal Controversy: U. S. Diplomacy & Defense Interests. Paul B. Ryan. LC 77-20643. (Publications Ser.: No. 187). (Illus.). 1977. pap. 5.95 (ISBN 0-8179-6872-5). Hoover Inst Pr.

Panama Canal: The Crisis in Historical Perspective. Walter LaFeber. 1978. 13.95 (ISBN 0-19-502360-9). Oxford U Pr.

Panama Route. John Haskell Kemble. LC 79-139195. (American Scene Ser). (Illus.). 316p. 1972. Repr. of 1943 ed. lib. bdg. 29.50 (ISBN 0-306-70083-2). Da Capo.

Panay Incident, December 12, 1937: The Sinking of an American Gunboat Worsens U. S. - Japanese Relations. Joseph B. Icenhower. LC 70-161832. (Focus Bks). (Illus.). (gr. 7 up). 1971. PLB 4.90 o.p. (ISBN 0-531-00992-0). Watts.

Pancakes for Breakfast. Tomie De Paola. LC 79-18524. (Illus.). 32p. (ps-3). 1978. pap. 2.50 (ISBN 0-15-263528-9, VoyB). HarBraceJ.

Panchayati Raj Planning & Democracy. Ed. by M. V. Mathur & I. Narain. 17.50x (ISBN 0-210-22548-3). Asia.

Pancho. Berta Hader & Elmer Hader. (gr. k-3). 1942. 4.95g o.s.i. (ISBN 0-02-740120-0). Macmillan.

Pancreatic Cancer: New Directions in Therapeutic Management. Cohn. 1981. price not set (ISBN 0-89352-133-7). Masson Pub.

Panda. Illus. by Carolyn Bracken. (Floppies Ser.). (Illus.). 6p. (ps-k). Date not set. 2.95 (ISBN 0-671-42530-7, Little Simon). S&S.

Panda Cake. Rosalie Seidler. LC 78-6109. (Illus.). 40p. (ps-3). 1978. 4.95 (ISBN 0-590-17706-0, Four Winds); lib. bdg. 4.95 (ISBN 0-590-07706-6). Schol Bk Serv.

Panda's Thumb: More Reflections in Natural History. Stephen J. Gould. (Illus.). 1980. 12.95 (ISBN 0-393-01380-4). Norton.

Pandectes of the Law of Nations. William Fulbecke. LC 79-84109. (English Experience Ser.: No.928). 192p. 1979. Repr. of 1602 ed. lib. bdg. 18.00 (ISBN 90-221-0928-3). Walter J Johnson.

Pandilla En el Circo. Alain Gree & Luis Camps. (Illus., Span.). (gr. 3). 1979. 8.95 (ISBN 0-88332-112-2). Larousse.

Pandilla En el Zoo. Gree & Camps. 1980. 8.95 (ISBN 0-88332-253-6). Larousse.

Pandilla En la Carretera. Gree & Camps. 1980. 8.95 (ISBN 0-686-69157-1). Larousse.

Pandilla Va a las Tiendas. Alain Gree & Luis Camps. (Illus., Span.). (gr. 2). 1979. 8.95 (ISBN 0-88332-111-4). Larousse.

Pandora, No. 5. Jayge Carr et al. Ed. by Lois Wickstrom. (Illus.). 60p. (Orig.). 1980. pap. 2.50 (ISBN 0-916176-10-X). Sproing.

Pandora, No. 6. Jean Lorrah et al. Ed. by Lois Wickstrom. (Illus.). 60p. (Orig.). 1980. pap. 2.50 (ISBN 0-916176-11-8). Sproing.

Pandora in Pinkralia. Cynthia A. Richter. LC 79-66393. 61p. 1980. 4.95 (ISBN 0-533-04382-4). Vantage.

Pandora's Last Voyage. Geoffrey Rawson. LC 64-18291. (Illus.). 1964. 3.95 o.p. (ISBN 0-15-170826-6). HarBraceJ.

Pandurang Hari: Or, Memoirs of a Hindoo (A Novel, 3 vols. William B. Hockley. LC 80-2484. 1981. Repr. of 1826 ed. Set. 149.50 (ISBN 0-404-19140-1). AMS Pr.

Pandyan Kingdom. 2nd ed. K. Nilakanta Sastri. 252p. 1974. text ed. 7.50 (ISBN 0-88253-426-2). Ind-US Inc.

Panglor. Jeffrey A. Carver. (Orig.). 1980. pap. 1.95 (ISBN 0-440-17310-8). Dell.

Panhandle Aspect of the Chaquaqua Plateau. Robert G. Campbell. (Graduate Studies: No. 11). (Illus., Orig.). 1976. pap. 5.00 (ISBN 0-89672-021-7). Tex Tech Pr.

Panic of 1893: A Time of Strikes, Riots, Hobo Camps, Coxey's Army, Starvation, Withering Droughts & Fears of Revolution. Frank B. Latham. LC 70-132067. (Focus Bks). (Illus.). (gr. 7 up). 1971. PLB 4.90 o.p. (ISBN 0-531-01022-8). Watts.

Panics & Crashes: How You Can Make Money from Them. rev. ed. Harry D. Schultz. 256p. 1980. 12.95 (ISBN 0-87000-491-3). Arlington Hse.

Panjab, North-West Frontier Province, & Kashmir. James M. Douie. LC 74-903982. 1974. Repr. 16.00x o.p. (ISBN 0-8364-0443-2). South Asia Bks.

Panning for Gold in a Single's Bar. Peter D. Trabucco. (Illus.). 96p. (Orig.). 1980. pap. 6.95 (ISBN 0-9605106-0-5). PT Marketing.

Panoply. Robert E. Weems. 100p. 1979. 4.95 (ISBN 0-8059-2624-0). Dorrance.

Panorama. Diana Kwiatkowski. (Gusto Press Poetry Discovery Ser.). 61p. 1979. 9.00 (ISBN 0-933906-07-2). Gusto Pr.

Panorama De la Biblia. Alfred T. Eade. 1979. Repr. of 1977 ed. 3.00 (ISBN 0-311-03657-0). Casa Bautista.

Panorama del Nuevo Testamento. Richard Foulkes. LC 75-15161. 112p. (Orig., Span.). 1975. pap. 2.50 (ISBN 0-89922-048-7). Edit Caribe.

Panorama of Evil: Insights from the Behavioral Sciences. Leonard W. Doob. LC 77-87964. (Contributions in Philosophy: No. 10). 1978. lib. bdg. 16.95 (ISBN 0-313-20030-0, DPE/). Greenwood.

Panorama of Indo-European Languages. W. D. Lockwood. 1972. text ed. 14.50x (ISBN 0-09-111020-3, Hutchinson U Lib); pap. text ed. 7.50x (ISBN 0-09-111021-1, Hutchinson U Lib). Humanities.

Panorama of Pure Mathematics: As Seen by N. Bourbaki. Jean Dieudonné. Tr. by I. Macdonald. LC 80-2330. (Pure & Applied Mathematics Ser.). 1981. write for info. (ISBN 0-12-215560-2). Acad Pr.

Panorama of West Virginia. David A. Bice. LC 79-89608. 319p. (gr. 8). 1979. text ed. 12.95 (ISBN 0-934750-00-9); tchr's guide 4.00 (ISBN 0-934750-01-7); wkbk. 3.50 (ISBN 0-934750-03-3). Jalamap.

Panoramic Dental Radiography. 2nd ed. L. R. Manson-Hing. (Illus.). 224p. 1980. 41.25 (ISBN 0-398-03976-3). C C Thomas.

Panoramic Dental Radiography. Lincoln R. Manson-Hing. (Illus.). 224p. 1976. 41.25 o.p. (ISBN 0-398-03976-3). C C Thomas.

Pantera & Mangusta Nineteen Sixty-Nine to Nineteen Seventy-Four. Ed. by R. M. Clarke. (Illus.). 70p. (Orig.). 1980. pap. 8.95 (ISBN 0-907073-00-X). Motorbooks Intl.

Pantera, 1970-1973. R. M. Clarke. (Brooklands Bks.). (Illus., Orig.). 1979. pap. 8.95 (ISBN 0-906589-75-4, Pub. by Enthusiast Pubns England). Motorbooks Intl.

Pantheisticon. John Toland. Ed. by Rene Wellek. LC 75-11260. (British Philosophers & Theologians of the 17th & 18th Centuries: Vol. 59). 1977. Repr. of 1751 ed. lib. bdg. 42.00 (ISBN 0-8240-1810-9). Garland Pub.

Pantheon. Antoine Pomey. LC 75-27879. (Renaissance & the Gods Ser.: Vol. 34). (Illus.). 1976. Repr. of 1694 ed. lib. bdg. 73.00 (ISBN 0-8240-2083-9). Garland Pub.

Pantheon. Andrew Tooke. LC 75-27880. (Renaissance & the Gods Ser.: Vol. 35). (Illus.). 1976. Repr. of 1713 ed. lib. bdg. 73.00 (ISBN 0-8240-2084-7). Garland Pub.

Panther! Alan Ryan. 1981. pap. 2.25 (ISBN 0-451-09726-2, E9726, Sig). NAL.

Panther's Moon. Ruskin Bond. (Illus.). (gr. 3-5). 1969. PLB 4.69 o.p. (ISBN 0-394-91497-X). Random.

Pantomimes, Charades & Skits. rev. ed. Vernon Howard. LC 59-12983. (Illus.). 124p. (gr. 4 up). 1974. 6.95 (ISBN 0-8069-7004-9); PLB 6.69 (ISBN 0-8069-7005-7). Sterling.

Pantyhose Craft Book: Making Things from Run Pantyhose & Nylons. Jean R. Laury & Joyce Aiken. LC 76-53871. (Illus.). 1977. 12.95 (ISBN 0-8008-6235-X); pap. 5.95 (ISBN 0-8008-6234-1). Taplinger.

Panzer Fort. Robert Newton. (Orig.). 1980. pap. 1.95. Manor Bks.

Panzer Grenadiers. Heinrich Muller. 288p. (Orig.). 1980. pap. 2.25 (ISBN 0-89083-697-3). Zebra.

Panzerkampfwagen IV. Walter J. Spielberger & Uwe Feist. LC 68-56381. (Illus.). 1968. pap. 4.95 (ISBN 0-8168-7109-4). Aero.

Panzerkampfwagen V. Walter J. Spielberger & Uwe Feist. LC 68-22408. (Illus.). 1968. pap. 4.95 (ISBN 0-8168-7110-8). Aero.

Panzerkampfwagen VI. Walter J. Spielberger & Uwe Feist. LC 68-58102. (Illus.). 1968. pap. 5.95 (ISBN 0-8168-7111-6). Aero.

Panzers in North West Europe. Bruce Quarrie. (World War Two Photo Album: No. 5). (Illus.). 96p. 1981. pap. 5.95 (ISBN 0-89404-047-2). Aztex.

Panzers in Russia Nineteen Forty-Three to Forty-Five: World War Two Photo Album. (Illus.). 96p. 1981. pap. 5.95 (ISBN 0-89404-058-8). Aztex.

Panzers in Russia, 1941-1943: World War II Photo Album. Bruce Quarrie. (Illus.). 96p. 1981. pap. 5.95 (ISBN 0-89404-055-3). Aztex.

Panzers in the Desert. Bruce Quarrie. (World War Two Photo Album: No. 1). (Illus.). 96p. 1981. pap. 5.95 (ISBN 0-89404-041-3). Aztex.

Papa Nicholas Planas. Mother Martha. Ed. & tr. by Holy Transfiguration Monastery. (Orig.). 1981. pap. price not set (ISBN 0-913026-18-2). St Nectarios.

Papa Rooster & Baby Chick. Charles Manchester. LC 79-63000. 27p. 1980. 4.95 (ISBN 0-533-04207-0). Vantage.

Papacy & Political Ideas in the Middle Ages. Walter Ullmann. 408p. 1980. 60.00x (ISBN 0-902089-87-0, Pub. by Variorum England). State Mutual Bk.

Papacy in the Modern World. D. Holmes. 288p. 1981. 14.95 (ISBN 0-8245-0047-4). Crossroad NY.

Papacy Today. Francis X. Murphy. 256p. 1981. lib. bdg. 10.95 (ISBN 0-02-588240-6). Macmillan.

Papago Indians, Vol. 1. Incl. Papago Indians: Aboriginal Land Use & Occupancy. Robert A. Hackenberg; Acculturation at the Papago Village of Santa Rosa. Ruth M. Underhill; The Cattle Industry of the Southern Papago Districts with Some Information on the Reservation Cattle Industry As a Whole. Gwyneth H. Xavier. (American Indian Ethnohistory Ser: Indians of the Southwest). (Illus.). lib. bdg. 42.00 (ISBN 0-8240-0721-2). Garland Pub.

Papago Indians, Vol. 3. Incl. The Papago Indians of Arizona. William H. Kelley; The Papago Tribe of Arizona. Bernard L. Fontana; Findings of Fact, & Opinion. Indians Claims Commission. (American Indian Ethnohistory Ser: Indians of the Southwest). (Illus.). lib. bdg. 42.00 (ISBN 0-8240-0702-6). Garland Pub.

Papago Indians, Vol. Two: Papago Population Studies. William S. King & Delmos J. Jones. (American Indian Ethnohistory Ser: Indians of the Southwest). (Illus.). lib. bdg. 42.00 (ISBN 0-8240-0701-8). Garland Pub.

Papago Music. Frances Densmore. LC 72-1881. (Music Ser.). (Illus.). 276p. 1972. Repr. of 1929 ed. lib. bdg. 19.50 (ISBN 0-306-70509-5). Da Capo.

Papal Encyclicals, 5 vols. Ed. by Claudia Carlen. 1981. Set. 400.00 (ISBN 0-8434-0765-4, Consortium). McGrath.

Papal Heraldry. 2nd ed. Donald L. Galbreath. (Illus.). 156p. 1972. 34.00 (ISBN 0-685-29193-6). Gale.

Papal Ministry in the Church. Hans Kung. (Concilium Ser.: Religion in the Seventies: Vol. 64). 1971. pap. 4.95 (ISBN 0-8164-2520-5). Crossroad NY.

Papal Power: A Study of Vatican Control Over Lay Catholic Elites. Jean-Guy Vaillancourt. 375p. 1980. 16.95 (ISBN 0-520-03733-2). U of Cal Pr.

Papal Power: Human or Divine. 125p. Date not set. pap. 5.95x (ISBN 0-686-28453-4). Bolder Landry.

Papa's Pizza: A Berenstain Bear Sniffy Book. Stan Berenstain & Janice Berenstain. LC 78-55907. (Illus.). (ps-2). 1978. 0.95 (ISBN 0-394-83922-6, BYR). Random.

Paper. (MacDonald Educational Ser.). (Illus., Arabic.). 3.50 (ISBN 0-686-53102-7). Intl Bk Ctr.

Paper. Alister Warren. (Illus.). pap. 8.95 (ISBN 0-584-62051-9). Dufour.

Paper Americana: A Collector's Guide. Lou W. McCulloch. LC 78-75317. (Illus.). 1980. 17.50 (ISBN 0-498-02392-3). A S Barnes.

Paper Apples. Lyn Lifshin. 32p. 1975. pap. 2.00 (ISBN 0-935390-00-6). Wormwood Rev.

Paper Aristocracy. Howard S. Katz. LC 76-467. (Illus.). 1976. 9.95 (ISBN 0-916728-01-3); pap. 5.95 (ISBN 0-916728-00-5). Bks in Focus.

Paper-Art & Technology. World Print Council. (Illus., Orig.). 1980. pap. 11.50 (ISBN 0-87701-162-1). Chronicle Bks.

Paper Bead Book. Beverly Dieringer. LC 76-13251. (Illus.). (gr. 7 up). 1977. 9.95 o.p. (ISBN 0-679-20319-2); pap. 4.95 o.p. (ISBN 0-679-20378-8). McKay.

Paper Bullets, Propaganda Posters of WW II. Ed. by Victor Margolin. LC 77-79049. (Illus.). 64p. 1980. Repr. of 1977 ed. 15.00 (ISBN 0-87754-204-X). Chelsea Hse.

Paper by Kids. Arnold E. Grummer. LC 79-22904. (Doing & Learning Bks.). (Illus.). (gr. 5 up). 1980. PLB 7.95 (ISBN 0-87518-191-0). Dillon.

Paper Caper. Caroline B. Cooney. (Illus.). 64p. (gr. 9-12). 1981. 6.95 (ISBN 0-698-20506-5). Coward.

Paper Capers: All Kinds of Things to Make with Paper. Florence Temko. (Illus.). (gr. 4-6). 1975. pap. 1.50 (ISBN 0-590-09938-8, Schol Pap). Schol Bk Serv.

Paper Collage. Robin Capon. (Illus.). 96p. 1975. 10.95 o.p. (ISBN 0-8231-7035-7). Branford.

Paper Crafts. Linda Hetzer. LC 77-28796. (Illustrated Crafts for Beginners). (Illus.). (gr. 3-7). 1978. PLB 9.95 (ISBN 0-8172-1186-1). Raintree Pubs.

Paper Cut-Out Design Book. Ramona Jablonski. LC 76-2467. (Illus.). 1976. 15.95 (ISBN 0-916144-03-8); pap. 7.95 (ISBN 0-916144-04-6). Stemmer Hse.

Paper Cutting. Eric Hawkesworth. LC 76-30461. (Illus.). (gr. 6 up). 1977. 8.95 (ISBN 0-87599-224-2). S G Phillips.

Paper Doctors: A Critical Assessment of Medical Research. Vernon Coleman. 1977. 12.95 (ISBN 0-85117-109-5). Transatlantic.

Paper Dragon. Marietta Moskin. LC 68-11310. (gr. 7 up). 1968. 8.95 (ISBN 0-381-99749-9, A59200, JD-J). John Day.

Paper Folding & Modelling. A. Van Breda. 1964. 6.50 (ISBN 0-571-06178-8, Pub. by Faber & Faber). Merrimack Bk Serv.

Paper House. Francoise Mallet-Joris. Tr. by D. Coltman from Fr. 1971. 6.95 o.p. (ISBN 0-374-22978-3). FS&G.

Paper Landscape: The Ordnance Survey in Nineteenth-Century Ireland. J. H. Andrews. (Illus.). 366p. 1975. 75.00x (ISBN 0-19-823209-8). Oxford U Pr.

Paper Machine Steam & Condensate Systems. 2nd ed. H. P. Fishwick et al. (TAPPI PRESS Reports). (Illus.). 1979. pap. 14.95 (ISBN 0-89852-370-2, 01-01-R070). TAPPI.

Paper Making in Pioneer America. Dard Hunter. LC 78-74388. (Nineteenth Century Book Arts & Printing History Ser.: Vol. 3). 1980. lib. bdg. 22.00 (ISBN 0-8240-3877-0). Garland Pub.

Paper Money. Adam Smith, pseud. 288p. 1981. 13.95 (ISBN 0-671-44825-0). Summit Bks.

Paper Money of the United States. 10th ed. Robert Friedberg. LC 78-66813. (Illus.). 1981. write for info. (ISBN 0-87184-210-6). Coin & Curr.

Paper Movie Machines. Bud Wentz. 1975. pap. 3.50 (ISBN 0-912300-57-4, 57-4). Troubador Pr.

Paper of Pins. Illus. by Margaret Gordon. LC 74-8767. (Illus.). 32p. (ps-3). 1975. 6.95 (ISBN 0-395-28814-2, Clarion). HM.

Paper Pools. David Hockney. Ed. by Nikos Stangos. (Illus.). 100p. 1980. 22.50 (ISBN 0-686-62704-0, 1461-1); pap. 14.95 (ISBN 0-686-62705-9, 2229-0). Abrams.

Paper Review of the Year 1979. (Benn Directories Ser.). 1980. 33.75 (ISBN 0-686-60665-5, Pub. by Benn Pubns). Nichols Pub.

Paper Robots. Yoong Bae. (Illus.). 32p. (Orig.). 1981. pap. 3.50 (ISBN 0-686-69425-2). Troubador Pr.

Paper Rockets. Yoong Bae. (Illus.). 32p. 1980. pap. 3.50 (ISBN 0-89844-022-X). Troubador Pr.

Paper Sheriff. Luke Short. 176p. 1980. pap. 1.75 (ISBN 0-553-14181-3). Bantam.

Paper Things. Michael Grater. (Make & Play Ser.). (Illus.). 48p. (gr. k-6). 1976. pap. 1.50 (ISBN 0-263-05899-9). Transatlantic.

Paperback Books for Children. Ed. by Beatrice Simmons. LC 72-86489. 130p. (Orig.). 1972. pap. 0.95 (ISBN 0-590-09542-0, Citation). Schol Bk Serv.

Paperback Parnassus: The Birth, the Development, the Pending Crises of the Modern American Paperbound Book. Roger H. Smith. 100p. 1976. 18.00x (ISBN 0-89158-007-7). Westview.

Paperback Reference Set. pap. 9.95 o.p. (ISBN 0-87747-833-3). Deseret Bk.

Paperbag. Richard Russell. 1979. pap. 1.75 (ISBN 0-505-51427-3). Tower Bks.

Paperbound Books for Young People. 2nd ed. 280p. 1980. 9.95x (ISBN 0-8352-1280-7). Bowker.

Paperbound Books in Print 1981: Fall, 1981, 2 vols. 4000p. 1981. Set. 43.00 (ISBN 0-8352-1331-5). Bowker.

Paperbound Books in Print 1981: Spring & Fall, 1981 (Full Coverage, 4 vols. 8000p. 1981. Set. 75.00 (ISBN 0-8352-1329-3). Bowker.

Paperbound Books in Print 1981: Spring, 1981, 2 vols. 4000p. 1981. Set. 43.00 (ISBN 0-8352-1330-7). Bowker.

Papercraft. Pamela Woods. (Illus.). 173p. 1980. 12.95 (ISBN 0-312-59583-2). St Martin.

Paperfolding for Beginners. William D. Murray & Francis J. Rigney. Orig. Title: Introduction to Paperfolding. (Illus.). (gr. 1 up). pap. 1.75 (ISBN 0-486-20713-7). Dover.

Papermachine Clothing. W. J. Carter. LC 74-28444. 227p. 1975. 31.95 o.p. (ISBN 0-470-13847-5). Halsted Pr.

Papermakers. Leonard E. Fisher. LC 65-13683. (Colonial Americans Ser). (Illus.). (gr. 4-6). 1965. PLB 4.90 o.p. (ISBN 0-531-01030-9). Watts.

Papermaking at Home. Anthony Hopkinson. 1979. pap. 3.95 o.s.i. (ISBN 0-7225-0483-7). Newcastle Pub.

Papermaking Fibers: A Photomicroscopic Atlas. Ed. by Wilfred A. Cote. (Renewable Materials Institute Ser.). (Illus.). 200p. 1980. pap. text ed. 12.00x (ISBN 0-8156-2228-7). Syracuse U Pr.

Papermaking Machine. R. H. Clapperton. 1968. 120.00 (ISBN 0-08-010896-2). Pergamon.

Papers. International Conference on Historical Linguistics, 4th. Ed. by Elizabeth Traugott. 500p. 1980. text ed. 54.25x (ISBN 90-272-3501-5). Humanities.

Papers. International Conference on Infrared Physics, 2nd, (CIRP 2), Zurich, 1979. Ed. by Fritz Kneubuhl. 264p. 1980. 40.00 (ISBN 0-08-025055-6). Pergamon.

Papers & Proceedings of Syntopican VII. 299p. 1979. write for info. (ISBN 0-935220-00-3). Intl Word Process.

Papers & Proceedings of Syntopican VIII. 463p. 1980. write for info. (ISBN 0-935220-03-8). Intl Word Process.

Papers Concerning Robertson's Colony in Texas: Vol. VI, March 6 Through December 5, 1831; the Campaigns Against the Tawakoni, Waco, Towash, & Comanche Indians. Compiled by Malcolm D. McLean. LC 73-78014. (Illus.). 1979. lib. bdg. 25.00 (ISBN 0-932408-06-0). UTA Pr.

Papers Concerning Robertson's Colony in Texas: Vol. VII, December 6, 1831, Through October, 1833. Those Eleven-League Grants. LC 73-78014. (Illus.). 664p. 1980. lib. bdg. 25.00 (ISBN 0-932408-07-9). UTA Pr.

Papers in African Prehistory. J. D. Fage & Roland A. Oliver. LC 74-77286. (Illus.). 1970. 32.50 (ISBN 0-521-07470-3); pap. 9.95x (ISBN 0-521-09566-2, 566). Cambridge U Pr.

Papers in Cognitive-Stratificational Linguistics. Michael Bennett et al. Ed. by James E. Copeland & Philip W. Davis. (Rice University Studies: Vol. 66, No. 2). 208p. 1980. pap. 5.50x (ISBN 0-89263-245-3). Rice Univ.

Papers in Contrastive Linguistics. Ed. by Gerhard Nickel. LC 78-149434. (Illus.). 1971. 19.95 (ISBN 0-521-08091-6). Cambridge U Pr.

Papers in Economic Prehistory. Ed. by E. S. Higgs. LC 78-180019. (Illus.). 250p. 1972. 37.50 (ISBN 0-521-08452-0). Cambridge U Pr.

Papers in Economics & Sociology, 1930-1960. Oskar Lange. Tr. by P. F. Knightsfield. LC 68-22080. 1970. 50.00 (ISBN 0-08-012352-X). Pergamon.

Papers in Linguistics in Honor of Leon Dostert. Ed. by William M. Austin. (Janua Linguarum, Ser. Major: No. 25). 1967. text ed. 34.10x (ISBN 90-2790-616-5). Mouton.

Papers in Mayan Linguistics. Laura Martin. 6.00. Lucas.

Papers of Andrew Jackson: 1770-1803, Vol. 1. Ed. by Sam B. Smith & Harriet C. Owsley. LC 79-15078. (Illus.). 656p. 1980. 25.00 (ISBN 0-87049-219-5). U of Tenn Pr.

Papers of Andrew Johnson, 5 vols. Ed. by LeRoy P. Graf & Ralph W. Haskins. Incl. Vol. 1. 1822-1851. (Illus.). 744p. 1967. 20.00x (ISBN 0-87049-079-6); Vol. 2. 1852-1857. (Illus.). 608p. 1970. 20.00x (ISBN 0-87049-098-2); Vol. 3. 1858-1860. (Illus.). 800p. 1972. 20.00x (ISBN 0-87049-141-5); Vol. 4. 1860-1861. 1976. 20.00x (ISBN 0-87049-183-0); Vol. 5. 1861-1862. 1979. text ed. 20.00x (ISBN 0-87049-273-X). LC 67-25733. U of Tenn Pr.

Papers of Daniel Webster: Correspondence, Volume 1, 1798-1824. Daniel Webster. Ed. by Charles M. Wiltse & Harold D. Moser. LC 73-92705. (Papers of Daniel Webster: Series 1, Correspondence). (Illus.). 544p. 1974. text ed. 27.50x (ISBN 0-87451-096-1). U Pr of New Eng.

Papers of Daniel Webster: Correspondence, Vol. 2, 1825-1829. Daniel Webster. Ed. by Charles M. Wiltse & Harold D. Moser. LC 73-92705. (Papers of Daniel Webster: Series 1, Correspondence). (Illus.). 587p. 1976. text ed. 27.50x (ISBN 0-87451-120-8). U Pr of New Eng.

Papers of Daniel Webster, Correspondence, Vol. 3: 1830-1834. Daniel Webster. Ed. by Charles M. Wiltse & David G. Allen. LC 73-92705. (Papers of Daniel Webster: Series 1, Correspondence). (Illus.). 573p. 1977. text ed. 27.50x (ISBN 0-87451-131-3). U Pr of New Eng.

Papers of Frederick Law Olmsted: Vol. II: Slavery & the South, 1852-1857. Ed. by Charles E. Beveridge & Charles C. McLaughlin. LC 80-8881. (Papers of Frederick Law Olmsted). (Illus.). 528p. 1981. text ed. 27.50x (ISBN 0-8018-2242-4). Johns Hopkins.

Papers of General Lucius D. Clay: Germany 1945-1949, 2 vols. Ed. by Jean E. Smith. LC 73-16536. 1216p. 1975. 40.00x (ISBN 0-253-34288-0). Ind U Pr.

Papers of Henry Bouquet. S. K. Stevens et al. Incl. Vol. 1. 1756-1758. 470p. 1972 (ISBN 0-911124-66-7); Vol. 2. Forbes Expedition. 736p. 1951. LC 51-9537. 15.00 ea. Pa Hist & Mus.

Papers of Henry Bouquet: January 1 to August 31, 1759, Vol. 3. 20.00 (ISBN 0-911124-86-1). Pa Hist & Mus.

Papers of Henry Bouquet: Sept 1, 1759 to August 31, 1760, Vol. 4. Henry Bouquet. 1978. 20.00 (ISBN 0-911124-99-3). Pa Hist & Mus.

Papers of Henry Clay, 5 vols. Henry Clay. Ed. by James F. Hopkins & Mary W. Hargreaves. Incl. Vol. 1. The Rising Statesman, 1797-1814. 1060p. 1959 (ISBN 0-8131-0051-8); Vol. 2. The Rising Statesman, 1815-1820. 952p. 1961 (ISBN 0-8131-0052-6); Vol. 3. Presidential Candidate, 1821-1824. 944p. 1963 (ISBN 0-8131-0053-4); Vol. 4. Secretary of State, 1825. 1004p. 1972 (ISBN 0-8131-0054-2); Vol. 5. Secretary of State, 1826. 1104p. 1973 (ISBN 0-8131-0055-0). LC 59-13605. 35.00x ea. U Pr of Ky.

Papers of Henry Clay: Secretary of State, 1827, Vol. VI. Ed. by Mary W. Hargreaves & James F. Hopkins. LC 59-13605. (Papers of Henry Clay). Date not set. 35.00 (ISBN 0-8131-0056-9). U Pr of Ky. Postponed.

Papers of James Madison, Vol. 13: Twenty January Seventeen Ninety to Thirty-One March Seventeen Ninety-One. Ed. by Robert A. Rutland & Charles F. Hobson. LC 62-9144. (Papers of James Madison). 1981. 20.00x (ISBN 0-8139-0861-2). U Pr of Va.

Papers of Joseph Henry: The Princeton Years, January 1838-1840, Vol. 4. Ed. by Nathan Reingold. LC 72-2005. (The Papers of Joseph Henry Ser.). (Illus.). 432p. 1981. text ed. 30.00x (ISBN 0-87474-792-9). Smithsonian.

Papers of Leverett Saltonstall, 1816-1845. Ed. by Robert E. Moody. (Collections of the Massachusetts Historical Society Ser.). (Illus.). Vol. 1, 1978. 25.00 ea. Vol. 2, 1981. Mass Hist Soc.

Papers of Robert Morris, 1781-1784: Vol. 5; April 16-July 20, 1782. Ed. by E. James Ferguson & John Catanzariti. LC 72-91107. 1981. 27.50x (ISBN 0-8229-3420-5). U of Pittsburgh Pr.

Papers of Th. Stcherbatsky. T. Stcherbatsky. Ed. by D. Chattopadhyaya. Tr. by H. C. Gupta from Rus. (Soviet Indology Ser.: No. 2). 136p. 1972. 7.50x o.p. (ISBN 0-8426-1552-0). Verry.

Papers of the Texas Revolution, 10 vols. Ed. by John H. Jenkins. Set. 145.00 (ISBN 0-685-83961-3, Pub. by Presidential Press). Jenkins.

Papers of Thomas Jefferson, 60 vols. Thomas Jefferson. Ed. by J. P. Boyd et al. Incl. Vol. 1. 1760-1776. 1950 (ISBN 0-691-04533-X); Vol. 2. 1777-1779. 1950 (ISBN 0-691-04534-8); Vol. 3. 1779-1780. 1951 (ISBN 0-691-04535-6); Vol. 4. 1780-1781. 1951 (ISBN 0-691-04536-4); Vol. 5. 1781. 1952 (ISBN 0-691-04537-2); Vol. 6. 1781-1784. 1952 (ISBN 0-691-04538-0); Vol. 7. 1784-1785. 1953 (ISBN 0-691-04539-9); Vol. 8. 1785. 1953 (ISBN 0-691-04540-2); Vol. 9. 1785-1786. 1954 (ISBN 0-691-04541-0); Vol. 10. 1786-1787. 1954 (ISBN 0-691-04542-9); Vol. 11. 1787. 1955 (ISBN 0-691-04543-7); Vol. 12. 1787-1788. 1955 (ISBN 0-691-04544-5); Vol. 13. Mar.-Oct. 1788. 1956 (ISBN 0-691-04545-3); Vol. 14. Oct. 1788-Mar. 1789. 1958 (ISBN 0-691-04546-1); Vol. 15. Mar.-Nov. 1789. 1958 (ISBN 0-691-04547-X); Vol. 16. Nov. 1789-Aug. 1790. 1961 (ISBN 0-691-04548-8); Vol. 17. July to Dec. 1790. 1965 (ISBN 0-691-04549-6); Vol. 18. Nov. 1790-Jan. 1791. 1971 (ISBN 0-691-04582-8); Vol. 19. Jan. 24-March 10, 1791 (ISBN 0-691-04583-6). Vols. 1-19. 30.00 ea.; Index To Vols. 1-6. 7.50x (ISBN 0-691-04531-3); Index To Vols. 7-12. 7.50x (ISBN 0-691-04532-1); Index To Vols. 13-18. 7.50x (ISBN 0-691-04618-2). Princeton U Pr.

Papers of Thomas Jordan Jarvis, Vol. 1, 1869-1882. Ed. by Wilfred B. Yearns. (Illus.). 1969. 10.00 (ISBN 0-86526-045-1). NC Archives.

Papers of Ulysses S. Grant: Vol. 5 - April 1 to August 31, 1862. Ulysses S. Grant. Ed. by John Y. Simon & Thomas G. Alexander. LC 67-10725. (Illus.). 488p. 1973. 30.00x (ISBN 0-8093-0636-0). S Ill U Pr.

Papers of Ulysses S. Grant: Vol. 6 - September 1 to December 8, 1862. Ulysses S. Grant. Ed. by John Y. Simon. LC 67-10725. (Illus.). 516p. 1977. 30.00x (ISBN 0-8093-0694-8). S Ill U Pr.

Papers of Ulysses S. Grant, Vol. 7: December Ninth, Eighteen Sixty-Two to March Thirty First, Eighteen Sixty-Three. Ulysses S. Grant. Ed. by John Y. Simon. LC 67-10725. (Illus.). 612p. 1979. 35.00x (ISBN 0-8093-0880-0). S Ill U Pr.

Papers of Ulysses S. Grant, Vol. 8: April First to July Sixth, Eighteen Sixty-Three. Ed. by Ulysses S. Grant & John Y. Simon. LC 67-10725. (Illus.). 634p. 1979. 35.00x (ISBN 0-8093-0884-3). S Ill U Pr.

Papers of Woodrow Wilson, Vol. 18-33. Woodrow Wilson. Ed. by Arthur S. Link. Incl. Vol. 18. 1908-1909. 1974. 30.00x (ISBN 0-691-04631-X); Vol. 19. Jan.-July 1910. 1975. 30.00x (ISBN 0-691-04633-6); Vol. 20. Jauary 12 - July 15, 1910. 1975. 30.00 (ISBN 0-691-04635-2); Vol. 21. July-Nov. 1910. 1976. 30.00 (ISBN 0-691-04636-0); Vol. 22. 1911. 1976-1977. 30.00 (ISBN 0-691-04638-7); Vol. 23. 1911-1912. 1976-1977. 30.00 (ISBN 0-691-04643-3); Vol. 24. January-August, 1912. (Illus.). 1977. text ed. 30.00 (ISBN 0-691-04645-X); Vol. 25. August - November, 1912. (Illus.). 1978. text ed. 30.00 (ISBN 0-691-04650-6); Vol. 26. Contents & Index, Vols. 14-25. 1980. 25.00 (ISBN 0-691-04664-6); Vol. 27. January - June 1913. (Illus.). 1978. 30.00 (ISBN 0-691-04652-2); Vol. 28. 1913. (Illus.). 1978. text ed. 30.00 (ISBN 0-691-04653-0); Vol. 29. 1913-1914. 1979. 30.00x (ISBN 0-691-04659-X); Vol. 30. May - December 1914. 30.00x (ISBN 0-691-04663-8); Vol. 31. September - December 1914. 1979. 30.00x (ISBN 0-691-04666-2); Vol. 32. 1979. 30.00x (ISBN 0-691-04667-0); Vol. 33. April - July 1915. (Illus.). 30.00x (ISBN 0-691-04668-9). LC 66-10880. Princeton U Pr.

Papers of Woodrow Wilson: Vol. 34, July-September, 1915. Ed. by Arthur S. Link et al. LC 66-10880. (Illus.). 1980. 30.00x (ISBN 0-691-04673-5). Princeton U Pr.

Papers of Woodrow Wilson, Vol. 36: January-May, 1916. Ed. by Arthur S. Link et al. LC 66-10880. (Illus.). 648p. 1981. 30.00x (ISBN 0-691-04682-4). Princeton U Pr.

Papers of Woodrow Wilson: Volume 35, October 1915 to January 1916. Ed. by Arthur S. Link et al. LC 66-10880. (Illus.). 568p. 1981. 30.00 (ISBN 0-691-04676-X). Princeton U Pr.

Papers on Absenteeism. K. N. Vaid. 1968. 7.00 o.p. (ISBN 0-210-22512-2). Asia.

Papers on Portugese, Dutch, & Jesuit Influences in 16th & 17th Century Japan: Studies in Japanese History & Civilization. Charles R. Boxer. 1979. 29.50 (ISBN 0-89093-255-7). U Pubns Amer.

Papers on the Subfossil Primates of Madagascar, Reprinted from Various Sources. LC 78-72722. 1980. 105.00 (ISBN 0-404-18301-8). AMS Pr.

Papers Presented at the Eighth International Gas Bearing Symposium. (Orig.). 1981. pap. 60.00 library ed. (ISBN 0-686-69308-6). BHRA Fluid.

Papers Presented at the FAO-SIDA Workshop on the Use of Organic Materials As Fertilizers in Africa: Organic Recycling in Africa. 308p. 1981. pap. 16.50 (ISBN 92-5-100945-7, F2096, FAO). Unipub.

Papers Presented at the Fifth International Symposium on Jet Cutting. Ed. by H. S. Stephens & B. Jarvis. (Illus.). 438p. (Orig.). 1980. pap. 99.00x (ISBN 0-906085-41-1). BHRA Fluid.

Papers Presented at the First World Filtration Congress, Paris. First World Filtration Congress, May 14-17, 1974. 1974. 45.95 (ISBN 0-470-25965-5). Halsted Pr.

Papers Presented at the Indo-Pacific Fisheries Commission Workshop on Fish Silage Production & Its Use. (FAO Fisheries Report: No. 230). 1980. pap. 6.00 (ISBN 92-5-100921-X, F1940, FAO). Unipub.

Papers Presented at the International Conference on Hydrocyclones. Ed. by H. S. Stephens & G. Priestley. (Illus.). 247p. (Orig.). 1980. pap. 78.00 (ISBN 0-906085-48-9). BHRA Fluid.

Papers Presented at the Ninth International Conference on Fluid Sealing. H. S. Stephens & Mrs. C. A. Stapleton. (Illus., Orig.). 1981. pap. 78.00 library ed. (ISBN 0-686-69309-4). BHRA Fluid.

Papers Presented at the Sixth Fluid Power Symposium. H. S. Stephens & D. Radband. (Orig.). 1981. pap. 78.00 library ed. (ISBN 0-686-69307-8). BHRA Fluid.

Papers Presented at the Third International Symposium on Wind Energy Systems. Ed. by H. S. Stephens & C. A. Stapleton. (Illus.). 579p. 1980. pap. 99.00 (ISBN 0-906085-47-0). BHRA Fluid.

Papers Relating to the Application of the Principle of Dyarchy to the Government of India. L. G. Curtis. 667p. 1972. Repr. of 1920 ed. 45.00x (ISBN 0-7165-2117-2, Pub. by Irish Academic Pr Ireland). Biblio Dist.

Paperweights: Flowers Which Clothe the Meadows. Paul Hollister & Dwight P. Lanmon. (Illus.). 167p. 1981. pap. price not set. Dover.

Paperweights for Collectors. 2nd ed. Lawrence H. Selman & Linda Pope-Selman. LC 75-37108. 1975. 27.50 o.p. (ISBN 0-686-53122-1). Paperweight Pr.

Paperweights for Collectors. rev. ed. Lawrence H. Selman & Linda Pope-Selman. 1981. price not set (ISBN 0-933756-03-8). Paperweight Pr.

Papier Mache. Peter Rush. 1980. pap. 8.95 (ISBN 0-374-51611-1). FS&G.

Papier Mache Crafts. Mildred Anderson. LC 75-14520. (Illus.). 132p. 1975. 9.95 (ISBN 0-8069-5338-1); lib. bdg. 9.29 (ISBN 0-8069-5339-X). Sterling.

Papillon. Henri Charriere. 1970. 9.95 o.p. (ISBN 0-688-02269-3). Morrow.

Papstlichen Legaten in England Bis Zur Beendigung der Legation Gualas, 1218. Helene Tillman. LC 80-2208. 1981. Repr. of 1926 ed. 27.50 (ISBN 0-404-18795-1). AMS Pr.

Papua New Guinea. Office of Information, Gov't of Papua New Guinea. LC 75-23775. (Illus.). 68p. 1976. text ed. 9.95x (ISBN 0-8248-0400-7, Eastwest Ctr). U Pr of Hawaii.

Papyrus Reisner I: The Records of a Building Project in the Reign of Sesostris I. William K. Simpson. (Illus.). 1963. 35.00 (ISBN 0-87846-030-6). Mus Fine Arts Boston.

Papyrus Reisner II: Accounts of the Dockyard Workshop at This in the Reign of Sesostris I. William K. Simpson. (Illus.). 1965. 35.00 (ISBN 0-87846-031-4). Mus Fine Arts Boston.

Papyrus Reisner III: The Records of a Building Project N the Early Twelfth Dynasty. William K. Simpson. (Illus.). 1969. 35.00 (ISBN 0-87846-032-2). Mus Fine Arts Boston.

Par Lagerkvist. Robert D. Spector. (World Authors Ser.: Spain: No. 267). 1973. lib. bdg. 10.95 (ISBN 0-8057-2509-1). Twayne.

Par Sa Force. Tr. by Gwen Wilkerson. (French Bks.). (Fr.). 1979. 1.85 (ISBN 0-8297-0927-4). Life Pubs Intl.

Par Voce, Noiva. (Portuguese Bks.). 1979. 0.75 (ISBN 0-8297-0678-X). Life Pubs Intl.

Para-Professional in the Treatment of Alcoholism: A New Profession. George E. Staub & Leona M. Kent. 184p. 1979. 11.00 (ISBN 0-398-02860-5). C C Thomas.

Para Ses Meurtrissures. Tr. by Hugh Jeter. (French Bks.). (Fr.). 1979. 2.50 (ISBN 0-8297-0928-2). Vida Pub.

Para Voce, Moca. (Portuguese Bks.). 1979. 0.75 (ISBN 0-8297-0678-X). Life Pubs Intl.

Parable of the Beast. John N. Bleibtreu. 1967. 6.95 o.s.i. (ISBN 0-02-511500-6). Macmillan.

Parable of the Father's Heart. G. Campbell Morgan. (Morgan Library). 96p. 1981. pap. 2.95 (ISBN 0-8010-6118-0). Baker Bk.

Parable of the Happy Animals. Cynthia Watts. (Hello Worlds Ser.). 1976. pap. 1.65 (ISBN 0-8163-0295-2). Pacific Pr Pub Assn.

Parables. Madeleine I. Boucher. (New Testament Message Ser.). 9.95 (ISBN 0-89453-130-1); pap. 5.95 (ISBN 0-89453-195-6). M Glazier.

Parables. (Children of the Kingdom Activities Ser.). (gr. 5-10). 1978. 7.95 (ISBN 0-686-13696-9). Pflaum Pr.

Parables & Metaphors of Our Lord. G. Campbell Morgan. 1956. 10.95 (ISBN 0-8007-0245-X). Revell.

Parables from Nature. Margaret Gatty. LC 75-32180. (Classics of Children's Literature, 1621-1932: Vol. 43). (Illus.). 1977. Repr. of 1880 ed. PLB 38.00 (ISBN 0-8240-2292-0). Garland Pub.

Parables He Told. David A. Redding. LC 76-9972. (Harper Jubilee Book). 192p. 1976. pap. 1.95 o.p. (ISBN 0-06-066813-X, HJ-29, HarpR). Har-Row.

Parables of Christ. Date not set. 12.50 (ISBN 0-86524-059-0). Klock & Klock.

Parables of Jesus: A History of Interpretation & Bibliography. Warren S. Kissinger. (American Theological Library Association (ATLA) Bibliography Ser.: No. 4). 463p. 1979. lib. bdg. 22.00 (ISBN 0-8108-1186-3). Scarecrow.

Parables of Jesus in Matthew 13. Jack D. Kingsbury. LC 76-40850. 1976. pap. text ed. 10.50 (ISBN 0-915644-08-8). Clayton Pub Hse.

Parables of Our Lord. William Arnot. LC 80-8065. 532p. 1981. Repr. of 1865 ed. 10.95 o.p. (ISBN 0-8254-2119-5). Kregel.

Parables of Our Saviour. William M. Taylor. LC 74-79943. 1975. 10.95 (ISBN 0-8254-3805-5). Kregel.

Parables of the Kingdom. Doyle W. Brewington. 64p. 1981. 4.95 (ISBN 0-8059-2774-3). Dorrance.

Parables of the Kingdom. Charles H. Dodd. LC 80-8420. 160p. 1981. pap. cancelled o.p. (ISBN 0-06-061932-5, HarpR). Har-Row.

Parables: Their Literary & Existential Dimension. Dan O. Via, Jr. LC 67-11910. 232p. 1974. pap. 4.95 (ISBN 0-8006-1392-9, 1-1392). Fortress.

Parachute Badges & Insignia of the World. R. J. Bragg & Roy Turner. (Illus.). 1979. 12.95 (ISBN 0-7137-0882-4, Pub. by Blandford Pr England). Sterling.

Parachute Manual: A Technical Treatise on the Parachute. 2nd ed. Dan Poynter. LC 77-71447. (Illus.). 1977. lab. manual 29.95 (ISBN 0-915516-06-3). Para Pub.

Parachute Rigging Course: A Course of Study for the FAA Rigger Certificate. 2nd ed. Dan Poynter. LC 77-71448. (Illus.). 1981. pap. 11.95 (ISBN 0-915516-14-4). Para Pub.

Parachuting & Skydiving. Sally Smith. (Illus.). 1978. 14.50 (ISBN 0-7207-1063-4). Transatlantic.

Parachuting I-E Course. 3rd ed. Dan Poynter. LC 78-50571. (Illus.). 1978. pap. 9.95 (ISBN 0-915516-18-7). Para Pub.

Parachuting Manual with Log. 5th ed. Dan Poynter. LC 76-14106. (Illus.). 1980. pap. 1.50 (ISBN 0-915516-11-X). Para Pub.

Parachuting: The Skydivers' Handbook. 3rd ed. Dan Poynter. LC 77-83469. (Illus.). 1980. 11.95 (ISBN 0-915516-17-9); pap. 6.95 (ISBN 0-915516-16-0). Para Pub.

Parachutists. Ed Klein. LC 77-82953. 406p. 1981. 10.95 (ISBN 0-385-12573-9). Doubleday.

Parade: Cubism As Theater. Richard H. Axsom. LC 78-74361. (Outstanding Dissertations in the Fine Arts, Fourth Ser.). (Illus.). 1979. lib. bdg. 38.00 (ISBN 0-8240-3950-5). Garland Pub.

Parade of the Animal Kingdom. Robert W. Hegner. (Illus.). (gr. 7 up). 1967. 19.95 (ISBN 0-02-550660-9). Macmillan.

Paradigm for Management Information Systems. Phillip Ein-Dor & Eli Segev. 232p. 1980. 22.95 (ISBN 0-03-058017-X). Praeger.

Paradigms & Exercises in Syriac Grammar. 4th ed. Theodore H. Robinson. Ed. by L. H. Brockington. 1962. 14.95x (ISBN 0-19-815416-X). Oxford U Pr.

Paradigms & Revolutions: Appraisals & Applications of Thomas Kuhn's Philosophy of Science. Ed. by Gary Gutting. LC 80-20745. 256p. 1980. text ed. 18.95 (ISBN 0-268-01542-2); pap. text ed. 7.95 (ISBN 0-268-01543-0). U of Notre Dame Pr.

Paradigms in Transition: The Methodology of Social Inquiry. Ralph L. Rosnow. 176p. 1981. text ed. 12.00x (ISBN 0-19-502876-7); pap. text ed. 5.95 (ISBN 0-19-502877-5). Oxford U Pr.

Paradigms Lost: Essays on Literacy & Its Decline. John Simon. (Illus.). 256p. 1980. 12.95 (ISBN 0-517-54034-7). Potter.

Paradis Desespere: L'Amour, L'Illusion. Jacques Ehrmann. (Yale Romantic Studies). 1963. pap. 29.50x (ISBN 0-685-69816-5). Elliots Bks.

Paradise Alley. Sylvester Stallone. LC 77-22926. (Illus.). (YA) 1977. 8.95 o.p. (ISBN 0-399-12080-7, Pub. by Berkley Pub). Berkley Pub.

Paradise Island. Tracy Sinclair. 192p. (Orig.). 1980. pap. 1.50 (ISBN 0-671-57039-0). S&S.

Paradise Isle. Jacqueline Hasci. (Orig.). 1981. pap. 1.50 (ISBN 0-440-16966-6). Dell.

Paradise Lost. G. K. Hunter. (Unwin Critical Library). 232p. 1980. text ed. 15.95x (ISBN 0-04-800004-3, 2384). Allen Unwin.

Paradise Lost. John Milton. Ed. by Scott Elledge. (Critical Editions Ser). 546p. 1975. 19.95 (ISBN 0-393-04406-8); pap. 6.95x (ISBN 0-393-09230-5). Norton.

Paradise Lost, Bks. 5 & 6. John Milton. Ed. by R. I. Hodge & I. MacCaffrey. LC 75-8314. (Milton for Schools & Colleges Ser). (Illus.). 176p. 1975. pap. text ed. 6.95x (ISBN 0-521-20796-7). Cambridge U Pr.

Paradise Lost, Bks. 7 & 8. J. Milton. Ed. by D. Aers & Mary Ann Radzinowics. LC 77-181884. (Milton for Schools & Colleges Ser). 200p. 1974. pap. text ed. 6.95x (ISBN 0-521-20457-7). Cambridge U Pr.

Paradise Lost: A Concordance. Gladys W. Hudson. LC 74-127413. 1971. 28.00 (ISBN 0-8103-1002-3). Gale.

Paradise Lost, a New Edition: A Poem in Twelve Books. John Milton. Ed. by Merritt Y. Hughes. LC 62-11937. (Orig.). 1962. pap. 3.95 (ISBN 0-672-63080-X). Odyssey Pr.

Paradise Lost & Its Critics. A. J. Waldock. 1959. 6.50 (ISBN 0-8446-1463-7). Peter Smith.

Paradise Lost & Other Poems. John Milton. pap. 2.25 (ISBN 0-451-61881-5, ME1881, Ment). NAL.

Paradise Lost & the Classical Epic. Francis C. Blessington. 1979. 18.00 (ISBN 0-7100-0160-6). Routledge & Kegan.

Paradise Now & Not Yet. Andrew T. Lincoln. LC 80-41024. (Society for the New Testament Studies Monographs: No. 43). 240p. Date not set. price not set (ISBN 0-521-22944-8). Cambridge U Pr.

Paradise of the Fathers, 2 vols. Tr. by A. E. Wallis-Budge from Syriac. 1979. Repr. of 1907 ed. 20.00x set (ISBN 0-913026-21-2). St Nectarios.

Paradise of Women: Writings by Englishwomen of the Renaissance. Compiled by Betty Travitsky. LC 80-1705. (Contributions in Women's Studies: No. 22). 312p. 1981. lib. bdg. 29.95 (ISBN 0-313-22177-4, TPW/). Greenwood.

Paradise of Women: Writings by Englishwomen of the Rennaissance. Ed. by Betty Travitsky. LC 80-1705. (Contributions in Women's Studies: No. 22). 312p. 1981. lib. bdg. 29.95 (ISBN 0-313-22177-4, TPW/). Greenwood.

Paradise Plot. Ed Naha. 352p. (Orig.). 1980. pap. 2.25 (ISBN 0-553-13979-7). Bantam.

Paradise Postponed: Essays on Research & Development in the South Pacific: Proceedings. Young Nations Conference, Sydney, 1976. Ed. by Alexander Mamak & Grant McCall. 1979. text ed. 29.00 (ISBN 0-08-023005-9); pap. text ed. 11.00 (ISBN 0-08-023004-0). Pergamon.

Paradise Regained. pap. 5.95. Chatham Pub CA.

Paradise to Prison: Studies in Genesis. John J. Davis. 10.95 (ISBN 0-88469-050-4). BMH Bks.

Paradisi in Sole, Paradisus Terrestris, or a Garden of All Sorts of Pleasant Flowers Which Our English Ayre Will Permit. John Parkinson. LC 74-28880. (English Experience Ser.: No. 758). 1975. Repr. of 1629 ed. 110.00 (ISBN 90-221-0758-2). Walter J Johnson.

Paradiso. Dante Alighiere. Tr. by John Ciardi. 1970. pap. 2.75 (ISBN 0-451-61893-9, ME1893, Ment). NAL.

Paradox: A Round Trip Through the Bermuda Triangle. Nicholas R. Nelson. 112p. 1980. 5.95 (ISBN 0-8059-2707-7). Dorrance.

Paradox & Identity in Theology. R. T. Herbert. LC 78-20784. 1979. 15.00x (ISBN 0-8014-1222-6). Cornell U Pr.

Paradox of Cause & Other Essays. John W. Miller. 192p. 1981. pap. 5.95 (ISBN 0-393-00032-X). Norton.

Paradox of Helping: Introduction to the Philosophy of Scientific Practice. Martin Bloom. LC 74-13524. 283p. 1975. text ed. 20.95 (ISBN 0-471-08235-X). Wiley.

Paradox of Instruction: An Introduction to the Esoteric Spiritual Teaching of Da Free John. Da Free John. 10.95 (ISBN 0-913922-28-5); pap. 5.95 o.p. (ISBN 0-913922-32-3). Dawn Horse Pr.

Paradox of Olbers' Paradox: A Case History of Scientific Thought. Stanley L. Jaki. LC 70-80053. 1969. lib. bdg. 15.00 o.p. (ISBN 0-685-52443-4). N Watson.

Paradox of Poverty in America. Ed. by Kenneth S. Davis. (Reference Shelf Ser: Vol. 41, No. 2). 1969. 6.25 (ISBN 0-8242-0107-8). Wilson.

Paradox of the Liar. Ed. by Robert L. Martin. 1979. lib. bdg. 21.00 (ISBN 0-917930-30-4); pap. text ed. 6.00x (ISBN 0-917930-10-X). Ridgeview.

Paradoxes. J. Cargile. LC 78-67299. (Cambridge Studies in Philosophy). 1979. 32.95 (ISBN 0-521-22475-6). Cambridge U Pr.

Paradoxes & Oxymorons. John Ashbery. 64p. 1981. 8.95 (ISBN 0-670-63786-6). Viking Pr.

Paradoxes & Oxymorons: Fifty Lyrics. John Ashbery. 1981. pap. 4.95 (ISBN 0-14-042288-9). Penguin.

Paradoxes & Problems: Oxford English Texts Ser. John Donne. Ed. by Helen Peters. (Illus.). 242p. 37.50x (ISBN 0-19-812753-7). Oxford U Pr.

Paradoxes in Politics: An Introduction to the Nonobvious in Political Science. Steven J. Brams. LC 75-28568. (Illus.). 1976. pap. text ed. 9.95 (ISBN 0-02-904590-8). Free Pr.

Paradoxes of Freedom. Sidney Hook. 1962. 12.75x (ISBN 0-520-00568-6); pap. 4.95x (ISBN 0-520-00569-4, CAL100). U of Cal Pr.

Paradoxes of Legal Science. Benjamin N. Cardozo. LC 76-104241. Repr. of 1928 ed. lib. bdg. 15.00x (ISBN 0-8371-3263-0, CALS). Greenwood.

Paragon Walk. Anne Perry. 224p. 1981. 9.95 (ISBN 0-312-59598-0). St Martin.

Paragraph Composition. Wilbert J. Levy. (gr. 10-12). 1977. wkbk 5.67 (ISBN 0-87720-957-X). AMSCO Sch.

Paragraph Development: A Guide for Students of English As a Second Language. Martin L. Arnaudet & Mary E. Barrett. (ESL Ser.). (Illus.). 160p. 1981. pap. text ed. 7.95 (ISBN 0-13-648618-5). P-H.

Paragraph of Life: Killer-Your Friend? Dino Manuel. 64p. 1981. 5.00 (ISBN 0-682-49724-X). Exposition.

Paragraph Power. Wilbert J. Levy. (gr. 10-12). 1977. pap. 5.67 wkbk. (ISBN 0-87720-334-2). AMSCO Sch.

Paragraphs. Vern Rutsala. LC 77-20145. (Wesleyan Poetry Program: Vol. 91). 1978. 10.00x (ISBN 0-686-67967-9, Pub. by Wesleyan U Pr); pap. 4.95 (ISBN 0-685-86688-2). Columbia U Pr.

Paragraphs & Themes. 3rd ed. P. Joseph Canavan. 1979. pap. text ed. 9.95x (ISBN 0-669-01695-0); instructor's manual free (ISBN 0-669-01905-4). Heath.

Paraguay - in Pictures. Sterling Editors. LC 75-14513. (Visual Geography Ser.). (Illus.). 64p. (gr. 6 up). 1975. pap. 2.50 (ISBN 0-8069-1204-9). Sterling.

Paraguay & the Triple Alliance: The Post-War Decade, 1869 to 1878. Harris G. Warren. (Latin-American Monographs: No. 44). 1978. 17.95x (ISBN 0-292-76445-6); pap. 9.95 (ISBN 0-292-76444-8). U of Tex Pr.

Paraguay Under Stroessner. Paul H. Lewis. LC 79-28554. xi, 256p. 1980. 22.00x (ISBN 0-8078-1437-7). U of NC Pr.

Parakeet Guide. Cyril H. Rogers. 1971. 6.98 o.p. (ISBN 0-385-01652-2). Doubleday.

Paralanguage & Kinesics: Nonverbal Communication with a Bibliography. Mary R. Key. LC 74-30217. 1975. 10.00 (ISBN 0-8108-0789-0). Scarecrow.

Paralegal Practice & Procedure: A Practical Guide for the Legal Assistant. D. Larbalestrier. 1979. pap. 9.95 (ISBN 0-13-648691-6). P-H.

Paralegal Practice Handbook, No. 1. rev. ed. LC 77-85386. 1979. 27.50 (ISBN 0-915362-15-5). M K Heller.

Paraleipomena Jeremiou. Robert A. Kraft & Ann-Elizabeth Purintun. LC 72-88436. (Society of Biblical Literature. Texts & Translation-Psuedepigrapha Ser.). 1972. pap. 4.50 (ISBN 0-89130-169-0, 060201). Scholars Pr Ca.

Parallax View. Loren Singer. 192p. 1981. Repr. of 1970 ed. 15.95 (ISBN 0-933256-20-5). Second Chance.

Parallel Developments: A Comparative History of Ideas. Hajime Nakamura. LC 75-24947. 567p. 1975. 34.50x (ISBN 0-87011-272-4). Kodansha.

Parallel Play for Parents: A Guide to Playground Exercise. Eleanor Dinkin & Rosalind Urbont. LC 78-23450. (Illus.). 1978. 11.95 (ISBN 0-88229-424-5); pap. 6.95 (ISBN 0-88229-600-0). Nelson-Hall.

Parallel Processes & Related Automata. Ed. by W. Knoedel & H. J. Schneider. (Computing Supplementum Ser.: No. 3). 203p. 1981. pap. 59.00 (ISBN 0-387-81606-2). Springer-Verlag.

Parallelism in Early Biblical Poetry. Stephen A. Geller. LC 78-27255. (Harvard Semitic Monographs: No. 20). 1979. 12.00 (ISBN 0-89130-275-1, 040020). Scholars Pr Ca.

Parallelisms of Complete Designs. P. J. Cameron. LC 75-32912. (London Mathematical Society Lecture Note Ser.: No. 23). (Illus.). 1976. 16.95x (ISBN 0-521-21160-3). Cambridge U Pr.

Parallels from Life-Parallels from Life. Kimberleigh Ann McRae. LC 79-57180. (Illus.). 59p. 1980. pap. 4.95 (ISBN 0-935054-01-4). Webb-Newcomb.

Paralysis of International Institutions & the Remedies: A Study of Self-Determination, Concord Among the Major Powers & Political Arbitration. Istvan Bibo. LC 75-17182. 152p. 1976. 24.95 (ISBN 0-470-07208-3). Halsted Pr.

Paramedic Emergency Handbook. Steven A. Jensen. (Illus.). 128p. Date not set. text ed. 7.95 (ISBN 0-8016-2495-9). Mosby. Postponed.

Paramedic Manual. Michael K. Copass & Mickey Eisenberg. (Illus.). 304p. 1980. text ed. 11.95 (ISBN 0-7216-2716-1). Saunders.

Paramedic Procedures. 2nd ed. Jonathan Wasserberger & David Eubanks. (Illus.). 284p. 1981. pap. text ed. 12.95 (ISBN 0-8016-5353-3). Mosby.

Paramedic Skills Manual. Charles Phillips. 288p. 1980. pap. text ed. 14.95 (ISBN 0-87619-436-6). R J Brady.

Paramedical Dictionary: A Practical Dictionary for the Semi-Medical & Ancillary Medical Professions. J. E. Schmidt. 1974. 14.25 (ISBN 0-398-01672-0); pap. 10.75 (ISBN 0-398-02902-4). C C Thomas.

Parameter Estimation: Principles & Problems. Sorenson. 400p. 1980. 45.00 (ISBN 0-8247-6987-2). Dekker.

Parameters & Flow Regimes for Hydraulic Transport of Coal by Pipelines. V. V. Traynis. Ed. by W. C. Cooley & R. R. Faddick. Tr. by Albert Peabody from Rus. LC 77-77840. (Illus., Eng.). 1977. 45.00x o.p. (ISBN 0-918990-01-7). Terraspace.

Parametric Amplifiers. J. C. Decroly et al. 1973. 48.95 (ISBN 0-470-20065-0). Halsted Pr.

Parametric Statistical Inference: Basic Theory & Modern Approaches. S. Zacks. LC 80-41715. (I.S. in Nonlinear Mathematics Series; Theory & Applications: Vol. 4). 400p. 1981. 48.00 (ISBN 0-08-026468-9); pap. 19.70 (ISBN 0-08-026467-0). Pergamon.

Paramount Doctrines of Orthodoxy--the Tricompositeness of Man, Apology of A. Makrakis & the Trial of A. Makrakis. Apostolos Makrakis. Ed. by Orthodox Christian Educational Society. Tr. by Denver Cummings from Hellenic. 380p. 1954. 10.00x (ISBN 0-938366-17-3). Orthodox Chr.

Paranasal Sinuses: Anatomy & Surgical Techniques. 2nd ed. Frank N. Ritter. LC 73-7519. (Illus.). 1978. text ed. 31.50 (ISBN 0-8016-4129-2). Mosby.

Paraneoplasia: Biological Signals in the Diagnosis of Cancer. Jan G. Waldenstrom. LC 78-18494. 1978. text ed. 29.50 (ISBN 0-471-03490-8, Pub. by Wiley Medical). Wiley.

Paranoid. Ed. by David W. Swanson et al. 525p. 1970. 19.95 (ISBN 0-316-82475-5). Little.

Paranormal Perception of Colors. Yvonne Duplessis. LC 75-19563. (Parapsychological Monograph: No. 16). 1975. pap. 5.50 (ISBN 0-912328-27-4). Parapsych Foun.

Paranormal Phenomena, Science, & Life After Death. C. J. Ducasse. LC 79-76282. (Parapsychological Monographs No. 8). 1969. pap. 2.25 (ISBN 0-912328-12-6). Parapsych Foun.

Paraplegia. Michael A. Rogers. (Illus.). 1978. 11.95 o.p. (ISBN 0-571-11209-9, Pub. by Faber & Faber); pap. 7.95 (ISBN 0-571-11208-0). Merrimack Bk Serv.

Parapolitics: Toward the City of Man. Raghavan Iyer. (Illus.). 1979. 17.95 (ISBN 0-19-502596-2). Oxford U Pr.

Paraprofessionals in Education: Paraprofessionals Today, Vol. 1. Alan Gartner. LC 76-12419. 272p. 1977. text ed. 22.95 (ISBN 0-87705-258-1). Human Sci Pr.

Paraprofessionals in Special Education. Victor S. Lombardo. (Illus.). 304p. 1980. text ed. 24.50 (ISBN 0-398-04105-9). C C Thomas.

Paraprofessionals or Teacher Aides. Paul Shank & Wayne McElroy. LC 70-107603. 1970. 8.00 o.p. (ISBN 0-87812-010-6). Pendell Pub.

Parapsychology: An Insider's View of ESP. J. Gaither Pratt. LC 76-45437. 1977. Repr. of 1966 ed. 12.00 (ISBN 0-8108-0991-5). Scarecrow.

Parapsychology & Anthropology: Proceedings. International Conference London, 1973. Ed. by Allan Angoff & Diana Barth. LC 74-82959. 10.50 (ISBN 0-912328-24-X). Parapsych Foun.

Parapsychology & the Sciences: Proceedings. International Conference, Amsterdam, 1972. Ed. by Allan Angoff & Betty Shapin. LC 73-92492. 1974. 8.50 (ISBN 0-912328-23-1). Parapsych Foun.

Parapsychology: Frontier Science of the Mind. J. B. Rhine & J. G. Pratt. (Illus.). 236p. 1974. 9.75 (ISBN 0-398-01580-5). C C Thomas.

Parapsychology: Its Relation to Physics, Biology, Psychology, & Psychiatry. Ed. by Gertrude R. Schmeidler. LC 76-916. 291p. 1976. 13.50 (ISBN 0-8108-0909-5). Scarecrow.

Parapsychology-Science or Magic? A Psychological Perspective. James E. Alcock. (Foundations & Philosophy of Science & Technology Ser.). 300p. 1981. 45.00 (ISBN 0-08-025773-9); pap. 20.00 (ISBN 0-08-025772-0). Pergamon.

Parapsychology: Sources of Information. Rhea A. White & Laura A. Dale. LC 73-4853. 1973. 10.00 (ISBN 0-8108-0617-7). Scarecrow.

Parapsychology Today: A Geographic View; Proceedings. International Conference, France, 1971. Ed. by Allan Angoff & Betty Shapin. LC 72-94940. 1973. 8.00 (ISBN 0-912328-21-5). Parapsych Foun.

Parasite. A. Conan Doyle. LC 80-67704. (Conan Doyle Centennial Ser.). (Illus.). 100p. Date not set. price not set (ISBN 0-934468-45-1). Gaslight.

Parasites. Daphne Du Maurier. LC 72-184728. 320p. 1971. Repr. of 1950 ed. lib. bdg. 12.50x (ISBN 0-8376-0410-9). Bentley.

Parasites of North American Freshwater Fishes. Glenn L. Hoffman. 1967. 30.00x (ISBN 0-520-00565-1). U of Cal Pr.

Parasites We Humans Harbor. Aaron E. Klein. (Illus.). 1981. 12.95 (ISBN 0-525-66693-1). Elsevier-Nelson.

Parasitic Copepoda of British Fishes. Z. Kabata. (Illus.). 670p. 1979. 72.00x (ISBN 0-903874-05-9, Pub. by Brit Mus Nat Hist England). Sabbot-Natural Hist Bks.

Parasitic Diseases Case Studies. David N. Reifsnyder. LC 80-81733. 1980. pap. 18.50 (ISBN 0-87488-049-1). Med Exam.

Parasitic Protozoa. J. R. Baker. (Biological Sciences Ser). 1969. pap. text ed. 6.50x (ISBN 0-09-099161-3, Hutchinson U Lib). Humanities.

Parasitic Worms. D. W. Crompton & S. M. Joyner. LC 79-20223. (Wykeham Science Ser.: No. 57). 1980. pap. 15.95x (ISBN 0-8448-1342-7). Crane-Russak Co.

Parasitism & Symbiology: An Introductory Text. Clark P. Read. LC 75-110390. 320p. 1970. 17.95 o.p. (ISBN 0-8260-7355-7). Wiley.

Parched Earth: The Maharashtra Drought, 1970-73. V. Subramaniam. LC 75-903997. 1975. 16.00x o.p. (ISBN 0-88386-656-0). South Asia Bks.

Parda: A Study of Muslim Women's Life in Northern India. Cora Vreede-de Stuers. LC 70-1402. (Samenlevingen Buiten Europa--Non-European Societies Ser.: No. 8). (Illus.). xii, 128p. 1981. Repr. of 1968 ed. lib. bdg. 19.75x (ISBN 0-313-22915-5, VRPA). Greenwood.

Pardner of the Wind. N. Howard Thorp & Neil M. Clark. LC 77-7233. (Illus.). 1977. 14.50x (ISBN 0-8032-0938-X); pap. 4.75 (ISBN 0-8032-5875-5, BB 638, Bison). U of Nebr Pr.

Pardon De Ploermel. Giacomo Meyerbeer. Ed. by Phillip Gossett & Charles Rosen. LC 76-49199. (Early Romantic Opera Ser.: No. 23). 1981. lib. bdg. 82.00 (ISBN 0-8240-2922-4). Garland Pub.

Pardon My Lenten Smile: Daily Homily-Meditation Themes for the Weekdays of Lent. Michael Manning. 90p. 1976. pap. 3.95 (ISBN 0-8189-0325-2). Alba.

Pardoner's Prologue & Tale. Geoffrey Chaucer. Ed. by A. C. Spearing. (Selected Tales from Chaucer). 1966. text ed. 4.95x (ISBN 0-521-04627-0). Cambridge U Pr.

Parent -Infant Communication. Sitnick & Rushmer. 250p. 1977. 29.95 (ISBN 0-86575-035-1). Dormac.

Parent & Child. J. W. Byers. 60p. pap. 0.50. Faith Pub Hse.

Parent, Child, & Community. Mack R. Hicks et al. LC 79-13816. (Illus.). 1979. 14.95 (ISBN 0-88229-231-5). Nelson-Hall.

Parent Child Fun Kit. Robert Stafford & Carolyn Stafford. (Illus.). 318p. 1980. soft cover 10.00 (ISBN 0-933586-00-0). Book Promo Unltd.

Parent-Child Interaction: The Socialization Process Observed in Twin & Singleton Families. Hugh Lytton. 335p. 1980. 35.00 (ISBN 0-306-40521-0, Plenum Pr). Plenum Pub.

Parent-Child Interaction: Theory, Research & Projects. Ed. by Ronald W. Henderson. LC 80-2336. (Educational Psychology Ser.). 1981. write for info. (ISBN 0-12-340620-X). Acad Pr.

Parent-Child Telepathy: A Study of the Telepathy of Everyday Life. Berthold E. Schwarz. LC 70-155052. 7.95 o.p. (ISBN 0-912326-24-7). Garrett-Helix.

Parent Conferences in the Schools: Procedures for Building Effective Partnership. new ed. Stuart Losen & Bert Diament. 1978. text ed. 18.95 (ISBN 0-205-06094-3). Allyn.

Parent Education & Elementary Counseling. Jackie Lamb & Wesley Lamb. Ed. by Garry R. Walz & Libby Benjamin. LC 77-12942. (New Vistas in Counseling Ser.: Vol. 5). 1978. 14.95 (ISBN 0-87705-318-9). Human Sci Pr.

Parent Education & Intervention Handbook. Richard R. Abidin. (Illus.). 608p. 1980. 24.50 (ISBN 0-398-03937-2). C C Thomas.

Parent-Infant Intervention: Communication Disorders. A. Simmons-Martin & D. R. Calvert. 1979. 12.00 (ISBN 0-8089-1185-6). Grune.

Parent-Infant Relationship. Ed. by Paul M. Taylor. (Monographs in Neonatology). 1980. 24.50 (ISBN 0-8089-1289-5). Grune.

Parent of the Handicapped Child: The Study of Child-rearing Practices. Ray H. Barsch. (American Lecture in Special Education Ser.). (Illus.). 452p. 1976. pap. 14.75 (ISBN 0-398-03559-8). C C Thomas.

Parent Partnership Training Program, 8 bks. Mary H. Moore. Incl. Bk. 1. Introductory Guide. LC 78-68013. 128p. pap. text ed. 12.90 (ISBN 0-8027-9053-4); Bk. 2. Parent's Manual. 192p. pap. text ed. 17.80 (ISBN 0-8027-9054-2); Bk. 3. Basic Communications Skills. LC 78-68015. 288p. pap. text ed. 39.10 (ISBN 0-8027-9055-0); Bk. 4. Developing Social Acceptability. LC 78-62918. 216p. pap. text ed. 29.70 (ISBN 0-8027-9056-9); Bk. 5. Developing Responsible Sexuality. LC 78-62919. 160p. pap. text ed. 19.50 (ISBN 0-8027-9057-7); Bk. 6. Light Housekeeping & In-Home Assistance. LC 78-61387. 272p. pap. text ed. 32.60 (ISBN 0-8027-9058-5); Bk. 7. Heavy Duty Cleaning & Yards & Ground Care. LC 78-62939. 240p. pap. text ed. 32.60 (ISBN 0-8027-9059-3); Bk. 8. Skills of Daily Living. LC 78-62940. 304p. pap. text ed. 29.80 (ISBN 0-8027-9060-7). (For use with K-12 handicapped). 1979. Walker Educ.

Parent Perogatives: How to Handle Teacher Misbehavior & Other School Disorders. Richard Weinberg & Lynn G. Weinberg. LC 78-23718. 1979. 12.95 (ISBN 0-88229-442-3). Nelson-Hall.

Parent Power. Martin Buskin. 1977. pap. 1.95 o.s.i. (ISBN 0-346-12254-6). Cornerstone.

Parent Power. John Douglas. 1979. pap. 2.50 (ISBN 0-915106-11-6, Pub. by Two Continents). Hippocrene Bks.

Parent Power. Logan Wright. 240p. 1981. pap. 2.95 (ISBN 0-553-14654-8). Bantam.

Parent-Professional Partnership: Exceptional Children, Vol. 41, No. 8. 1975. pap. text ed. 3.50x o.p. (ISBN 0-86586-060-2). Coun Exc Child.

Parent Student College Planning Guide. William F. Shanahan. LC 80-24467. 224p. (Orig.). 1981. pap. 6.95 (ISBN 0-668-04996-0, 4996). Arco.

Parent Trap. Adapted by Vic Crume. (gr. 4-6). 1969. pap. 1.25 (ISBN 0-590-02961-4, Schol Pap). Schol Bk Serv.

Parentage of IRRI Crosses IR1-R30,000. 302p. pap. 14.50 (R0120, IRRI). Unipub.

Parental Care in Mammals. Ed. by David J. Gubernick & Peter H. Klopfer. 460p. 1981. 39.50 (ISBN 0-306-40533-4, Plenum Pr). Plenum Pub.

Parental Involvement in Primary Schools. R. Cyster et al. 210p. 1981. pap. text ed. 19.25x (ISBN 0-85633-211-9, NFER). Humanities.

Parenthood. Peterson & Hey. 1981. write for info. (ISBN 0-8087-1673-5). Burgess.

Parenthood: A Commitment in Faith. Kathryn W. Orso. LC 75-5219. 64p. (Orig.). 1975. pap. text ed. 2.95 (ISBN 0-8192-1198-2); tchr's ed. 3.75 (ISBN 0-8192-1204-0); wkbk. 3.95 (ISBN 0-8192-1199-0). Morehouse.

Parenting. Ed. by Patricia M. Markun. LC 73-87791. (Illus.). 64p. 1977. 2.50x o.p. (ISBN 0-87173-036-7). ACEI.

Parenting. G. Ron Norton. 1977. 12.95 (ISBN 0-13-650077-3, Spec); pap. 3.95 (ISBN 0-13-650069-2). P-H.

Parenting Advisor. Princeton Center for Infancy. 1977. pap. 6.95 (ISBN 0-385-14330-3, Anch). Doubleday.

Parenting Alone. Ed. by Paul A. Wellington. 1980. pap. 2.50 (ISBN 0-8309-0297-X). Herald Hse.

Parenting & Teaching Young Children. Verna Hildebrand. Ed. by Carol Newman. (Illus.). 432p. (gr. 10-12). 1980. text ed. 15.92 (ISBN 0-07-028775-9, W); tchrs. manual avail. (ISBN 0-07-051305-8). McGraw.

Parenting Exceptional Children: A Manual. Sheila C. Perino & Joseph Perino. 208p. 1981. 19.95 (ISBN 0-8352-1354-4). Bowker.

Parenting Happy Healthy Children. Karen Olness. 1981. 9.95 (ISBN 0-9602790-4-0). The Garden.

Parenting in an Unresponsive Society: Managing Work & Family Life. Sheila B. Kamerman. LC 80-641. 1980. 15.95 (ISBN 0-02-916730-2). Free Pr.

Parents & Children in the Inner City. Harriet Wilson & G. W. Herbert. (Direct Editions Ser.). (Orig.). 1978. pap. 16.00 (ISBN 0-7100-8715-2). Routledge & Kegan.

Parents & Children Learn Together. 2nd ed. Katharine W. Taylor. LC 67-21500. 1968. pap. text ed. 8.95x (ISBN 0-8077-2257-X). Tchrs Coll.

Parents & Children Learn Together: Parent Cooperative Nursery Schools. 3rd ed. Katharine W. Taylor. 1981. pap. 6.95 (ISBN 0-8077-2638-9). Tchrs Coll.

Parents & Teachers: A Resource Book for Home, School & Community Relations. Doreen J. Croft. 1979. pap. text ed. 9.95x (ISBN 0-534-00610-8). Wadsworth Pub.

Parents Are Lovers. Gallagher, Chuck, Fr., S.J. 1977. pap. 2.45 (ISBN 0-385-12697-2, Im). Doubleday.

Parents Are Teachers: A Child Management Program. Wesley C. Becker. LC 72-75091. (Illus.). 200p. (Orig.). 1971. pap. 6.95 (ISBN 0-87822-019-4); leader's guide 3.95 (ISBN 0-87822-020-8); Set Of 5 Review Tests. 6.95 (ISBN 0-87822-022-4). Res Press.

Parents As Partners in the Educational Process. Eugenia H. Berger. (Illus.). 360p. 1981. pap. text ed. 11.95 (ISBN 0-8016-0637-3). Mosby.

Parents As Playmates: A Games Approach to the Pre-School Years. Joan Millman & Polly Behrmann. LC 79-4547. 1979. pap. 9.95 (ISBN 0-87705-404-5). Human Sci Pr.

Parent's Assistant, 6 vols. in 2. 3rd, rev. ed. Maria Edgeworth. LC 75-32150. (Classics of Children's Literature, 1621-1932: Vol. 16). 1977. Repr. of 1800 ed. Set. PLB 60.00 (ISBN 0-8240-2264-5); PLB 38.00 ea. Garland Pub.

Parents Book About Divorce. Gardner, Richard A., M.D. LC 76-23762. 1977. 9.95 o.p. (ISBN 0-385-12237-3). Doubleday.

Parents' Book of Physical Fitness for Children. Martin I. Lorin. LC 78-3151. (Illus.). 290p. 1981. pap. 5.95 (ISBN 0-689-70608-1). Atheneum.

Parents Can Be a Problem. Shirley Schwarzrock & C. Gilbert Wrenn. (Coping with Ser.). (Illus.). (gr. 7-12). 1970. pap. text ed. 1.30 (ISBN 0-913476-33-1). Am Guidance.

Parents Can Understand Testing. Henry Dyer. LC 80-80939. 1980. pap. 3.50 (ISBN 0-934460-08-6). NCCE.

Parents, Children & Adoption. Jane Rowe. 1966. text ed. 23.50x (ISBN 0-7100-2055-4). Humanities.

Parent's Cry for Help. rev. ed. Dave Stoop. LC 78-62916. 144p. 1981. pap. 2.50 (ISBN 0-89081-270-5). Harvest Hse.

Parent's Game Power for Phonics. Cecil D. Alberts. (Illus.). 1979. pap. 25.00 (ISBN 0-915048-01-9). Spin-a-Test Pub.

Parent's Guide to Adoption. Robert S. Lasnik. LC 78-56895. 1979. 12.95 (ISBN 0-8069-8830-4); PLB 10.79 (ISBN 0-8069-8831-2). Sterling.

Parent's Guide to Adoption. Robert S. Lasnik. LC 78-56845. 192p. 1980. pap. 5.95 (ISBN 0-8069-8956-4). Sterling.

Parent's Guide to Bedwetting Control: A Step by Step Method. Nathan H. Azrin & Victoria A. Besalel. 1981. pap. price not set (ISBN 0-671-82774-X). PB.

Parent's Guide to Child Discipline. Rudolf Dreikurs & Loren Grey. 1970. pap. 3.95 (ISBN 0-8015-5736-4, Hawthorn). Dutton.

Parent's Guide to Children: The Challenge. Lawrence Zuckerman et al. LC 77-90090. (Illus., Orig.). 1978. pap. 2.75 (ISBN 0-8015-5734-8, Hawthorn). Dutton.

Parents' Guide to Education. Barry Taylor. 1978. 13.50 (ISBN 0-7153-7526-1). David & Charles.

Parent's Guide to Intelligence Testing. John A. Glover. LC 78-25991. 1979. 16.95 (ISBN 0-88229-423-7); pap. 8.95 (ISBN 0-88229-670-1). Nelson-Hall.

Parent's Guide to the First Three Years. Burton L. White. LC 80-21924. 1980. 10.95 (ISBN 0-13-649905-8). P-H.

Parents' Guide to the Montessori Classroom. Aline D. Wolf. (Illus.). 1980. 3.50x (ISBN 0-9601016-0-8). Parent-Child Pr.

Parents Guide to Weight Control for Children Ages 5 to 13 Years. B. K. Feig. (Illus.). 200p. 1980. 11.75 (ISBN 0-398-03972-0); pap. 6.95 (ISBN 0-398-04016-8). C C Thomas.

Parents Have Rights, Too! M. Donald Thomas. LC 78-63270. (Fastback Ser.: No. 120). 1978. pap. 0.75 (ISBN 0-87367-120-1). Phi Delta Kappa.

Parents in Modern America. 3rd ed. E. E. LeMasters. 1977. pap. text ed. 9.50x (ISBN 0-256-01972-X). Dorsey.

Parents Introduction to the New Mathematics. R. B. Layton. LC 65-24340. (Illus.). 43p. 1964. pap. 1.50x o.p. (ISBN 0-685-36217-5). Nature Bks Pubs.

Parents Learn Through Discussion: Principles & Practices of Parent Group Education. Aline B. Auerbach. 372p. 1980. Repr. of 1968 ed. lib. bdg. 18.75 (ISBN 0-89874-183-1). Krieger.

Parents Love Your Children. Renee Jordan. 1977. pap. 2.95 (ISBN 0-89728-049-0, 670041). Omega Pubns OR.

Parents' Magazine's Mother's Encyclopedia & Everyday Guide to Family Health. Parents Magazine Enterprises. Ed. by Isidore Rossman. 1981. pap. 9.95 (Delta). Dell.

Parent's Manual: Answers to Questions on Child Development & Child Rearing. Manfred Adler. 124p. 1971. pap. 9.50 photocopy ed. spiral (ISBN 0-398-00010-7). C C Thomas.

Parents Organizing to Improve Schools. Happy Fernandez & NCCE. Ed. by NCCE. Tr. by ASPIRA of New York. 1976. 3.50 (ISBN 0-934460-01-9). NCCE.

Parent's Power for Phonics. new ed. Cecil D. Alberts. (Illus.). 1978. pap. text ed. 25.00 (ISBN 0-915048-01-9). Spin-A-Test Pub.

Parents Speak Out: Views from the Other Side of the Two-Way Mirror. Ann Turnbull & H. R. Turnbull. 1978. pap. 7.50 (ISBN 0-675-08385-0). Merrill.

Parents: The Child's First Piano Teacher. Dasie Singletary. (Illus.). 32p. (gr. k-4). 1980. PLB 5.95 (ISBN 0-89962-042-6). Todd & Honeywell.

Parent's When-Not-to Worry Book: Straight Talk About All Those Myths You've Learned from Your Parents, Friends-- & Even Doctors. Barry Behrstock & Richard Trubo. LC 80-7894. 256p. 1981. 10.95 (ISBN 0-690-01972-6, HarpT). Har-Row.

Parents' Yellow Pages. The Princeton Center for Infancy. Ed. by Frank Caplan. LC 76-52002. 1978. pap. 7.95 (ISBN 0-385-12410-4, Anch). Doubleday.

Parerga & Paralipomena: Short Philosophical Essays, 2 vols. Arthur Schopenhauer. Tr. by E. F. Payne from Ger. 1201p. 1974. Vol. 1. 56.00x (ISBN 0-19-824508-4); Vol. 2. 63.00x (ISBN 0-19-824527-0); Vol. 1. pap. 18.50x (ISBN 0-19-824634-X); Vol. 2. pap. 21.00x (ISBN 0-19-824635-8); Set. 115.00x (ISBN 0-19-519813-1). Oxford U Pr.

Parfait Secretaire. L. Chaffurin & F. De Quericize. (Fr). pap. 10.95 (ISBN 0-685-14021-0, 3922). Larousse.

Pari Mutuel Betting. James Hillis. (Gambler's Book Shelf). (Illus.). 122p. 1972. pap. 2.95 (ISBN 0-89650-527-8). Gamblers.

Pariah Persistence in Changing Japan: A Case Study. John D. Donoghue. 1977. pap. text ed. 7.75x (ISBN 0-8191-0170-2). U Pr of Amer.

Parikh's Textbook of Medical Jurisprudence & Toxicology: For Classrooms & Courtrooms. C. K. Parikh. (Illus.). 1108p. 1980. 91.00 (ISBN 0-08-025522-1). Pergamon.

Paris. Rudy Chelminsk. (The Great Cities Ser.). (Illus.). (gr. 6 up). 1977. 14.94 (ISBN 0-8094-2279-4, Pub. by Time-Life). Silver.

Paris. Rudolph Chelminski. (Great Cities Ser.). 14.95 (ISBN 0-8094-2278-6). Time-Life.

Paris. Anne Corbierre. LC 80-50996. (Rand McNally Pocket Guide Ser.). (Illus.). 1980. pap. 3.95 (ISBN 0-528-84308-7). Rand.

Paris, a Century Change Eighteen-Seventy Eight to Nineteen Seventeen Eight. Norma Evenson. LC 78-10257. (Illus.). 399p. 1981. pap. 12.95 (ISBN 0-300-02667-6). Yale U Pr.

Paris: A Century of Change, Eighteen Seventy-Eight to Nineteen Seventy-Eight. Evenson. LC 78-10257. 1979. 35.00 (ISBN 0-300-02210-7). Yale U Pr.

Paris A to Z. Robert S. Kane. LC 73-9036. 216p. 1974. 6.95 (ISBN 0-385-08650-4); pap. 3.95 Softbound (ISBN 0-385-08635-0). Doubleday.

Paris Album. Wilander. (Illus.). 160p. (Polyglot.). 1974. 45.00 o.p. (ISBN 2-03-079902-5, 2651). Larousse.

Paris & the Provinces: The Politics of Local Government Reform in France. Peter A. Gourevitch. 256p. 1981. 18.50x (ISBN 0-520-03971-8). U of Cal Pr.

Paris: Capital City of France. Rene Orth. (Q Book: Famous Cities). (Illus.). (gr. 2-6). 1978. 3.95 (ISBN 0-8467-0445-5, Pub. by Two Continents). Hippocrene Bks.

Paris Index & Map. 4th ed. Michelin Guides & Maps. 1980. pap. 7.95 (ISBN 2-06-000112-9). Michelin.

Paris Kitchen: An Introduction to the La Varenne Cooking School. Anne Willan. LC 80-27346. (Illus.). 288p. 1981. price not set (ISBN 0-688-00411-3). Morrow.

Paris; or, the Future of War. Basil L. Hart. LC 75-148368. (Library of War & Peace; the Character & Causes of War). lib. bdg. 38.00 (ISBN 0-8240-0460-4). Garland Pub.

Paris Pendant la Commune Revolutionnaire De 1871. Georges Jeanneret. (The Paris Commune Ser.). (Fr.). 1976. lib. bdg. 22.00x o.p. (ISBN 0-8287-0463-5); pap. text ed. 12.00x o.p. (ISBN 0-685-74532-5). Clearwater Pub.

Paris Psalter & Meters of Boethius. Ed. by George P. Krapp. LC 33-2302. 1932. 17.50x (ISBN 0-231-08769-1). Columbia U Pr.

Paris Salon de 1827 with Societe Louvre de 1827. Ed. by H. W. Janson. (Catalogues of the Paris Salon, 1673 to 1881). 1978. lib. bdg. 50.00 (ISBN 0-8240-1841-9). Garland Pub.

Paris Salon de 1833. Ed. by H. W. Janson. (Catalogues of the Paris Salon, 1673 to 1881). 1977. lib. bdg. 50.00 (ISBN 0-8240-1843-5). Garland Pub.

Paris Salon de 1834. Ed. by H. W. Janson. (Catalogues of the Paris Salon, 1673 to 1881). 1977. lib. bdg. 50.00 (ISBN 0-8240-1844-3). Garland Pub.

Paris Salon de 1835. Ed. by H. W. Janson. (Catalogues of the Paris Salon, 1673 to 1881). 1977. lib. bdg. 50.00 (ISBN 0-8240-1845-1). Garland Pub.

Paris Salon de 1836. Ed. by H. W. Janson. (Catalogues of the Paris Salon, 1673 to 1881). 1977. lib. bdg. 50.00 (ISBN 0-8240-1846-X). Garland Pub.

Paris Salon De 1837. Ed. by H. W. Janson. (Catalogues of the Paris Salon, 1673 to 1881). 1977. lib. bdg. 50.00 (ISBN 0-8240-1847-8). Garland Pub.

Paris Salon de 1838. Ed. by H. W. Janson. (Catalogues of the Paris Salon, 1673 to 1881). 1977. lib. bdg. 50.00 (ISBN 0-8240-1848-6). Garland Pub.

Paris Salon de 1839. Ed. by H. W. Janson. (Catalogues of the Paris Salon, 1673 to 1881). 1977. lib. bdg. 50.00 (ISBN 0-8240-1849-4). Garland Pub.

Paris Salon de 1840. Ed. by H. W. Janson. (Catalogues of the Paris Salon, 1673 to 1881). 1977. lib. bdg. 50.00 (ISBN 0-8240-1850-8). Garland Pub.

Paris Salon de 1841. Ed. by H. W. Janson. (Catalogues of the Paris Salon, 1673 to 1881). 1977. lib. bdg. 50.00 (ISBN 0-8240-1851-6). Garland Pub.

Paris Salon de 1842. Ed. by H. W. Janson. (Catalogues of the Paris Salon, 1673 to 1881). 1977. lib. bdg. 50.00 (ISBN 0-8240-1852-4). Garland Pub.

Paris Salon De 1843. H. W. Janson. (Catalogues of the Paris Salon 1673 to 1881: Vol. 29). 1977. Repr. lib. bdg. 50.00 (ISBN 0-8240-1853-2). Garland Pub.

Paris Salon de 1844. Ed. by H. W. Janson. (Catalogues of the Paris Salon, 1673 to 1881). 1977. lib. bdg. 50.00 (ISBN 0-8240-1854-0). Garland Pub.

Paris Salon de 1845. Ed. by H. W. Janson. (Catalogues of the Paris Salon, 1673 to 1881). 1977. lib. bdg. 50.00 (ISBN 0-8240-1855-9). Garland Pub.

Paris Salon de 1846. Ed. by H. W. Janson. (Catalogues of the Paris Salon, 1673 to 1881). 1978. lib. bdg. 50.00 (ISBN 0-8240-1856-7). Garland Pub.

Paris Salon De 1847. H. W. Janson. (Catalogues of the Paris Salon 1673 to 1881: Vol. 33). 1977. Repr. lib. bdg. 50.00 (ISBN 0-8240-1857-5). Garland Pub.

Paris Salon de 1848. Ed. by H. W. Janson. (Catalogues of the Paris Salon, 1673 to 1881). 1977. lib. bdg. 50.00 (ISBN 0-8240-1858-3). Garland Pub.

Paris Salon de 1849. Ed. by H. W. Janson. (Catalogues of the Paris Salon, 1673 to 1881). 1977. lib. bdg. 50.00 (ISBN 0-8240-1859-1). Garland Pub.

Paris Salon de 1850. Ed. by H. W. Janson. (Catalogues of the Paris Salon, 1673 to 1881). 1977. lib. bdg. 50.00 (ISBN 0-8240-1860-5). Garland Pub.

Paris Salon de 1852. Ed. by H. W. Janson. (Catalogues of the Paris Salon, 1673 to 1881). 1977. lib. bdg. 50.00 (ISBN 0-8240-1861-3). Garland Pub.

Paris Salon De 1853. H. W. Janson. (Catalogues of the Paris Salon 1673 to 1881: Vol. 38). 1977. Repr. lib. bdg. 50.00 (ISBN 0-8240-1862-1). Garland Pub.

Paris Salon de 1855. Ed. by H. W. Janson. LC 77-24778. (Catalogues of the Paris Salon, 1673 to 1881: Vol. 39). 1977. lib. bdg. 50.00 (ISBN 0-8240-1863-X). Garland Pub.

Paris Salon de 1857. Ed. by H. W. Janson. LC 77-24778. (Catalogues of the Paris Salon, 1673 to 1881: Vol. 40). 1977. lib. bdg. 50.00 (ISBN 0-8240-1864-8). Garland Pub.

Paris Salon de 1859. Ed. by H. W. Janson. LC 77-24778. (Catalogues of the Paris Salon, 1673 to 1881: Vol. 41). 1978. lib. bdg. 50.00 (ISBN 0-8240-1865-6). Garland Pub.

Paris Salon de 1861. Ed. by H. W. Janson. LC 77-24778. (Catalogues of the Paris Salon, 1673 to 1881: Vol. 42). 1977. lib. bdg. 50.00 (ISBN 0-8240-1866-4). Garland Pub.

Paris Salon de 1863. Ed. by H. W. Janson. LC 77-24778. (Catalogues of the Paris Salon, 1673 to 1881: Vol. 43). 1977. lib. bdg. 50.00 (ISBN 0-8240-1867-2). Garland Pub.

Paris Salon de 1864. Ed. by H. W. Janson. LC 77-24778. (Catalogues of the Paris Salon, 1673 to 1881: Vol. 44). 1977. lib. bdg. 50.00 (ISBN 0-8240-1868-0). Garland Pub.

Paris Salon de 1865. Ed. by H. W. Janson. LC 77-24778. (Catalogues of the Paris Salon, 1673 to 1881: Vol. 45). 1977. lib. bdg. 50.00 (ISBN 0-8240-1869-9). Garland Pub.

Paris Salon de 1866. Ed. by H. W. Janson. LC 77-24778. (Catalogues of the Paris Salon, 1673 to 1881: Vol. 46). 1977. lib. bdg. 50.00 (ISBN 0-8240-1870-2). Garland Pub.

Paris Salon de 1867. Ed. by H. W. Janson. LC 77-24778. (Catalogues of the Paris Salon, 1673 to 1881: Vol. 47). 1978. lib. bdg. 50.00 (ISBN 0-8240-1871-0). Garland Pub.

Paris Salon de 1868. Ed. by H. W. Janson. LC 77-24778. (Catalogues of the Paris Salon, 1673 to 1881: Vol. 48). 1977. lib. bdg. 50.00 (ISBN 0-8240-1872-9). Garland Pub.

Paris Salon de 1869. Ed. by H. W. Janson. LC 77-24778. (Catalogues of the Paris Salon, 1673 to 1881: Vol. 49). 1977. lib. bdg. 50.00 (ISBN 0-8240-1873-7). Garland Pub.

Paris Salon de 1870. Ed. by H. W. Janson. LC 77-24778. (Catalogues of the Paris Salon, 1673 to 1881: Vol. 50). 1977. lib. bdg. 50.00 (ISBN 0-8240-1874-5). Garland Pub.

Paris Salon de 1872. Ed. by H. W. Janson. LC 77-24778. (Catalogues of the Paris Salon, 1673 to 1881: Vol. 51). 1977. lib. bdg. 50.00 (ISBN 0-8240-1875-3). Garland Pub.

Paris Salon de 1873. Ed. by H. W. Janson. LC 77-24778. (Catalogues of the Paris Salon, 1673 to 1881: Vol. 52). 1977. lib. bdg. 50.00 (ISBN 0-8240-1876-1). Garland Pub.

Paris Salon de 1874. Ed. by H. W. Janson. LC 77-24778. (Catalogues of the Paris Salon, 1673 to 1881: Vol. 53). 1978. lib. bdg. 50.00 (ISBN 0-8240-1877-X). Garland Pub.

Paris Salon de 1875. Ed. by H. W. Janson. LC 77-24778. (Catalogues of the Paris Salon, 1673 to 1881: Vol. 54). 1977. lib. bdg. 50.00 (ISBN 0-8240-1878-8). Garland Pub.

Paris Salon de 1876. Ed. by H. W. Janson. LC 77-24778. (Catalogues of the Paris Salon, 1673 to 1881: Vol. 55). 1977. lib. bdg. 50.00 (ISBN 0-8240-1879-6). Garland Pub.

Paris Salon de 1877. Ed. by H. W. Janson. LC 77-24778. (Catalogues of the Paris Salon, 1673 to 1881: Vol. 56). 1977. lib. bdg. 50.00 (ISBN 0-8240-1880-X). Garland Pub.

Paris Salon de 1878. Ed. by H. W. Janson. LC 77-24778. (Catalogues of the Paris Salon, 1673 to 1881: Vol. 57). 1977. lib. bdg. 50.00 (ISBN 0-8240-1881-8). Garland Pub.

Paris Salon de 1879. Ed. by H. W. Janson. LC 77-24778. (Catalogues of the Paris Salon, 1673 to 1881: Vol. 58). 1977. lib. bdg. 50.00 (ISBN 0-8240-1882-6). Garland Pub.

Paris Salon de 1880. Ed. by H. W. Janson. LC 77-24778. (Catalogues of the Paris Salon, 1673 to 1881: Vol. 59). 1977. lib. bdg. 50.00 (ISBN 0-8240-1883-4). Garland Pub.

Paris Salon de 1881. Ed. by H. W. Janson. LC 77-24778. (Catalogues of the Paris Salon, 1673 to 1881: Vol. 60). 1977. lib. bdg. 50.00 (ISBN 0-8240-1884-2). Garland Pub.

Paris Salons De 1673-1881, Vols. 2-5. Ed. by H. W. Janson. Incl. Vol. 2. 1737-1743, 1745-48 (ISBN 0-8240-1826-5); Vol. 3. 1751, 1755, 1757, 1759, 1761, 1763 (ISBN 0-8240-1827-3); Vol. 4. 1765, 1767, 1769, 1771, 1773 (ISBN 0-8240-1828-1); Vol. 5. 1775, 1777, 1779, 1781, 1783 (ISBN 0-8240-1829-X). 1976. Repr. lib. bdg. 50.00 ea. Garland Pub.

Paris Salons De 1785, 1787, 1789, 1791. Compiled by H. W. Janson. (Catalogues of the Paris Salon 1673 to 1881: Vol. 6). 1977. Repr. lib. bdg. 50.00 (ISBN 0-8240-1830-3). Garland Pub.

Paris Salons De 1793, 1795. Compiled by H. W. Janson. (Catalogues of the Paris Salon 1673 to 1881: Vol. 7). 1977. Repr. lib. bdg. 50.00 (ISBN 0-8240-1831-1). Garland Pub.

Paris Salons De 1796, 1797. H. W. Janson. (Catalogues of the Paris Salon 1673 to 1881: Vol. 8). 1977. Repr. lib. bdg. 50.00 (ISBN 0-8240-1832-X). Garland Pub.

Paris Salons de 1800, 1801. Ed. by H. W. Janson. (Catalogues of the Paris Salon, 1673 to 1881). 1977. lib. bdg. 50.00 (ISBN 0-8240-1834-6). Garland Pub.

Paris Salons de 1802, 1804. Ed. by H. W. Janson. (Catalogues of the Paris Salon, 1673 to 1881). 1977. lib. bdg. 50.00 (ISBN 0-8240-1835-4). Garland Pub.

Paris Salons De 1806, 1808. H. W. Janson. (Catalogues of the Paris Salon 1673 to 1881: Vol. 12). 1977. Repr. lib. bdg. 50.00 (ISBN 0-8240-1836-2). Garland Pub.

Paris Salons de 1810, 1812. Ed. by H. W. Janson. (Catalogues of the Paris Salon, 1673 to 1881). 1977. lib. bdg. 50.00 (ISBN 0-8240-1837-0). Garland Pub.

Paris Salons de 1814, 1817. Ed. by H. W. Janson. (Catalogues of the Paris Salon, 1673 to 1881). 1977. lib. bdg. 50.00 (ISBN 0-8240-1838-9). Garland Pub.

Paris Salons de 1819, 1822. Ed. by H. W. Janson. (Catalogues of the Paris Salon, 1673 to 1881). 1977. lib. bdg. 50.00 (ISBN 0-8240-1839-7). Garland Pub.

Paris Salons de 1830, 1831. Ed. by H. W. Janson. (Catalogues of the Paris Salon, 1673 to 1881). 1977. lib. bdg. 50.00 (ISBN 0-8240-1842-7). Garland Pub.

Paris Spleen. Charles Baudelaire. Tr. by Louise Varese. LC 48-5012. 1970. pap. 3.95 (ISBN 0-8112-0007-8, NDP294). New Directions.

Paris Summer. April L. Kihlstrom. (YA) 1977. 5.95 (ISBN 0-685-74270-9, Avalon). Bouregy.

Paris Talks. 11th ed. Abdu'l-Baha. 1969. 8.00 (ISBN 0-900125-07-1, 7-06-15); pap. 4.50 (ISBN 0-900125-08-X, 7-06-16). Baha'i.

Parish Chest. 3rd ed. W. E. Tate. LC 67-28686. (Illus.). 1969. 41.00 (ISBN 0-521-06603-4). Cambridge U Pr.

Parish Churches. Hugh Braun. 1974. pap. 7.95 (ISBN 0-571-10553-X, Pub. by Faber & Faber). Merrimack Bk Serv.

Parish Churches of London. Basil F. Clarke. (Illus.). 30.00 o.s.i. (ISBN 0-8038-0205-6). Architectural.

Parish Planning. Lyle E. Schaller. (Orig.). 1971. pap. 5.95 (ISBN 0-687-30102-5). Abingdon.

Parish School Boards: Voice of the Community. 67p. 1973. 3.00. Natl Cath Educ.

Parity, Parity, Parity. John D. Black. LC 72-2364. (FDR & the Era of the New Deal Ser.). 367p. 1972. Repr. of 1942 ed. 37.50 (ISBN 0-306-70482-X). Da Capo.

Park & Recreation Maintenance Management. Robert E. Sternloff & Roger M. Warren. 388p. 1977. text ed. 16.95 (ISBN 0-205-05601-6, 845601-1). Allyn.

Park City. Lewis Baltz & Gus Blaisdell. (Illus.). 252p. 1980. 75.00 (ISBN 0-9604140-0-2). Castelli-Artspace.

Park City. Gus Blaisdell. LC 80-65768. (Illus.). 252p. 1981. 75.00. Aperture.

Park Planning Handbook: Fundamentals of Physical Planning for Parks & Recreation Areas. Monty L. Christiansen. LC 77-51844. 1977. text ed. 24.95 (ISBN 0-471-15619-1). Wiley.

Parkay Margarine Cookbook. Kraft Kitchens. (Orig.). pap. 5.95 (ISBN 0-87502-074-7). Benjamin Co.

Parker Directory of Attorneys. Parker & Son Staff. LC 75-41995. 1981. 1980 suppl. incl. 11.50 (ISBN 0-911110-18-6). Parker & Son.

Parker Gun. rev. ed. Larry L. Baer. LC 77-75333. 196p. 1980. 24.95 (ISBN 0-917714-18-0). Beinfeld Pub.

Parker: The Cobra Swirl. Ray Buck. LC 80-39987. (Sports Stars Ser.). (Illus.). 48p. (gr. 2-8). 1981. PLB 7.35 (ISBN 0-516-04310-2). Childrens.

Parking Requirements for Shopping Centers. Ed. by Urban Land Institute Editors. LC 65-28845. (Technical Bulletin Ser.: No. 53). 1965. pap. 4.75 (ISBN 0-87420-053-9); pap. 3.00 uli members (ISBN 0-685-20873-7). Urban Land.

Parking Taxes As Roadway Prices: A Case Study of the San Francisco Experience. Damian J. Kulash. 46p. 1974. pap. 2.50 o.p. (ISBN 0-87766-116-2, 68000). Urban Inst.

Parking Taxes for Congestion Relief: A Survey of Related Experience. Damian J. Kulash. 1974. pap. 2.50 o.p. (ISBN 0-87766-114-6). Urban Inst.

Parkinson's Disease: A Guide for Patient & Family. Roger C. Duvoisin. LC 76-19845. 1978. 19.00 (ISBN 0-89004-205-5); pap. 12.00 (ISBN 0-685-87129-0). Raven.

Parkinson's Disease: Advances in Neurology, Vol. 5. Canadian-American Conference on Parkinson's Disease, 2nd. Ed. by F. McDowell & A. Barbeau. LC 72-93317. (Advances in Neurology Ser.: Vol. 5). 1974. 37.50 (ISBN 0-911216-63-4). Raven.

Parks & Gardens. Robert S. Lemmon. LC 60-6114. (Illus.). (gr. 4-8). 1967. PLB 7.45 (ISBN 0-87191-018-7). Creative Ed.

Parks, Politics & the People. Conrad L. Wirth. LC 79-6709. (Illus.). 450p. 1980. 19.95 (ISBN 0-8061-1605-6). U of Okla Pr.

Parlement of Paris, 1774-1789. Bailey S. Stone. LC 79-27732. xi, 227p. 1981. 19.00x (ISBN 0-8078-1442-3). U of NC Pr.

Parliament. Ivor Jennings. 1969. 53.95 (ISBN 0-521-07056-2); pap. 11.95x (ISBN 0-521-09532-8). Cambridge U Pr.

Parliament & Its Sovereignty. Christopher Hollis. 189p. 1973. 10.00 o.p. (ISBN 0-370-01358-1). Transatlantic.

Parliament for Europe. David Marquand. 1979. o.p. (ISBN 0-224-01716-0, Pub. by Chatto Bodley Jonathan); pap. 6.50 (ISBN 0-224-01717-9). Merrimack Bk Serv.

Parliament of Bees. John Day. Ed. by Stephen Orgel & William T. Cocke, III. LC 78-66742. (Renaissance Drama Ser.). 1979. lib. bdg. 16.50 (ISBN 0-8240-9748-3). Garland Pub.

Parliament of 1621: A Study in Constitutional Conflict. Robert Zaller. LC 77-104106. 1971. 20.00x (ISBN 0-520-01677-7). U of Cal Pr.

Parliamentary & Scientific Committee: The First Forty Years 1939-1979. Compiled By Christopher Powell & Arthur Butler. (Illus.). 102p. 1980. 17.50x (ISBN 0-7099-0347-2, Pub. by Croom Helm Ltd England). Biblio Dist.

Parliamentary Diary of Sir Edward Dering, 1670-73. Edward Dering. Ed. by Basil D. Henning. (Yale Historical Pubs. Miscellany Ser.: No. XVI). 1940. 42.50x (ISBN 0-685-69825-4). Elliots Bks.

Parliamentary Government in Britain. Michael Rush. 260p. 1981. pap. text ed. 30.00x (ISBN 0-8419-0680-7). Holmes & Meier.

Parliamentary Law. Henry M. Robert. 588p. 1981. pap. 19.95 (ISBN 0-686-28898-X). Lewis Pub Co.

Parliamentary Lists of the Early Eighteenth Century: Their Compilation & Use. Ed. by Aubrey Newman. 96p. 1973. text ed. 6.75x (ISBN 0-7185-1112-3, Leicester). Humanities.

Parliamentary Practice: An Introduction to Parliamentary Law. Henry M. Robert. 203p. 1981. pap. 4.95 (ISBN 0-86616-008-6). Lewis Pub Co.

Parliamentary Privilege in the American Colonies. M. P. Clarke. LC 76-166322. (American Constitutional & Legal History Ser.). 304p. 1971. Repr. of 1943 ed. lib. bdg. 29.50 (ISBN 0-306-70237-1). Da Capo.

Parliamentary Procedure & Practice in the Dominion of Canada. John G. Bourinot. 785p. 1980. Repr. 70.00x (ISBN 0-7165-2021-4, Pub. by Irish Academic Pr). Biblio Dist.

Parliamentary Procedure at a Glance. O. Garfield Jones. (gr. 9 up). 1971. pap. 3.50 o.p. (ISBN 0-8015-5766-6). Dutton.

Parliamentary Procedures Simplified. Lucille Place. LC 76-16466. 160p. 1976. 9.95 (ISBN 0-8119-0269-2); pap. 4.95 (ISBN 0-88391-049-7). Fell.

Parliamentary Reform: 1640-1832. J. Cannon. LC 72-83588. (Illus.). 288p. 1973. pap. 11.50x (ISBN 0-521-08697-3); pap. 11.50 (ISBN 0-521-09736-3). Cambridge U Pr.

Parliamentary Socialism. Ralph Miliband. pap. 9.95 (ISBN 0-686-23500-2, Merlin Pr). Carrier Pigeon.

Parliaments & Parties in Egypt. Jacob M. Landau. LC 79-1632. 1981. Repr. of 1954 ed. 19.50 (ISBN 0-88355-936-6). Hyperion Conn.

Parlo Italiano. L. Rapaccini. (It). 12.10 (ISBN 0-685-20245-3). Schoenhof.

Parlons Francais. Vols. 1-3. 7.95 (ISBN 0-88499-069-9); tapebks. vols. 1 & 2 5.95 ea.; readers vols. 1 & 2 6.95 ea.; tchr's manual o.p. (ISBN 0-88499-068-0); cassette sets vols. 1 & 2 115.00 ea.; tape sets vols. 1 & 2 225.00 ea. Inst Mod Lang.

Parmana: Prehistoric Maize & Manioc Subsistence Along the Orinoco & Amazon. Anna C. Roosevelt. (Studies in Archaeology). 1980. 29.50 (ISBN 0-12-595350-X). Acad Pr.

Parmer County History. Parmer County Historical Society. (Illus.). 414p. 1974. 17.95 (ISBN 0-89015-073-7). Nortex Pr.

Parnassus in Pillory. Augustine J. Duganne. LC 75-122648. 1971. Repr. of 1851 ed. 10.00 (ISBN 0-8046-1296-X). Kennikat.

Parnassus on Wheels. Christopher Morley. (Illus.). 1955. 6.50 o.p. (ISBN 0-397-00065-0). Lippincott.

Parnell & His Party: 1880-90. Conor C. O'Brien. 1957. 36.00x (ISBN 0-19-821237-2). Oxford U Pr.

Parochial & Plain Sermons, 8 Vols. John H. Newman. 1966-1968. Set. 10.50 o.p. (ISBN 0-87061-016-3). Vol. 1 (ISBN 0-87061-008-2). Vol. 2 (ISBN 0-87061-009-0). Vol. 3 (ISBN 0-87061-010-4). Vol. 4 (ISBN 0-87061-011-2). Vol. 5 (ISBN 0-87061-012-0). Vol. 6 (ISBN 0-87061-013-9). Vol. 7 (ISBN 0-87061-014-7). Vol. 8 (ISBN 0-87061-015-5). Chr Classics.

Parodies of the Gothic Novel. Leland C. May. Ed. by Devendra P. Varma. LC 79-8464. (Gothic Studies & Dissertations Ser.). 1980. lib. bdg. 15.00x (ISBN 0-405-12654-9). Arno.

Parody & Burlesque in the Tragicomedies of Thomas Middleton. John F. McElroy. (Salzburg Studies in English Literature, Jacobean Drama Studies: No. 19). 1972. pap. text ed. 25.00x (ISBN 0-391-01479-X). Humanities.

Parody Anthology. Carolyn Wells. 1967. pap. 2.50 o.p. (ISBN 0-486-21844-9). Dover.

Parody Anthology. Carolyn Wells. LC 67-14060. 1968. Repr. of 1904 ed. 15.00 (ISBN 0-8103-3224-8). Gale.

Parola E Pensiero: Introduzione Alla Lingua Italiana Moderna. 3rd ed. Vincenzo Traversa. (Illus.). 437p. 1980. text ed. 18.95 scp (ISBN 0-06-046653-7, HarpC); avail. instrs' manual; wkbk. scp 5.50 (ISBN 0-06-046654-5); tapes 229.00. Har-Row.

Parole-Quebec, Countersign-Ticonderoga: Second New Jersey Regimental Orderly Book, 1776. Ed. by Doyen Salsig. LC 77-74398. (Illus.). 1980. 24.50 (ISBN 0-8386-1793-X). Fairleigh Dickinson.

Paroles. Jacques Prevert. Tr. by Lawrence Ferlinghetti. LC 56-8586. (Pocket Poet Ser.: No. 9). 1958. pap. 2.50 (ISBN 0-87286-042-6, PP9). City Lights.

Parque Paquete. Arcadia Lopez & John Smith. (Illus.). 1976. pap. 86.50 teaching system (ISBN 0-913632-09-0). Am Univ Artforms.

Parrot & the Starling. Tr. by K. P. Bahadur. (UNESCO Collection of Representative Works: Indian Ser). 1977. text ed. 21.00x (ISBN 0-8426-1034-0). Verry.

Parrots. Henry Bates & Robert Busenbark. (Orig.). pap. 2.00 (ISBN 0-87666-427-3, M506). TFH Pubns.

Parrot's Death & Other Poems. P. Lal. 13p. 1973. 5.00 (ISBN 0-88253-268-5); pap. 4.00 (ISBN 0-88253-806-3). Ind-US Inc.

Parsival: Or a Knight's Tale. Richard Monaco. (Illus.). 1977. 12.95 (ISBN 0-02-585540-9). Macmillan.

Parson of the Islands. Adam Wallace. LC 61-17566. 1961. 7.00 (ISBN 0-87033-077-2, Pub. by Tidewater). Cornell Maritime.

Parson Weem's Life of Francis Marion. Peter Horry. LC 76-21439. 1976. 10.00 (ISBN 0-937684-04-X). Tradd St Pr.

Parson Weems of the Cherry-Tree. Harold Kellock. LC 75-107137. 1971. Repr. of 1928 ed. 15.00 (ISBN 0-8103-3785-1). Gale.

Parson's Son. Michael Lyne. (Illus.). signed ed 87.50 (ISBN 0-85131-176-8, Dist. by Sporting Book Center). J A Allen.

Part. Berry Wendell. 96p. 1980. 12.50 (ISBN 0-86547-007-3); pap. 6.00 (ISBN 0-86547-008-1). N Point Pr.

Part of Myself I Give to You. Doris B. Demou. 40p. 1976. pap. 2.95x (ISBN 0-9604794-0-6). M Demou & Assocs.

Part of Speech. 1981. pap. 7.95 (ISBN 0-374-51633-2). FS&G.

Part of the Dream. Eve Bunting. (Young Romance Ser.). (Illus.). (gr. 3-9). 1978. PLB 5.95 (ISBN 0-87191-638-X); pap. 2.95 (ISBN 0-89812-066-7). Creative Ed.

Part-Time Crime: An Ethnography of Fiddling & Pilferage. Jason Ditton. 1977. text ed. 35.00x o.p. (ISBN 0-333-21466-8). Verry.

Part-Time Farming in the Southeast. R. H. Allen et al. LC 74-165677. (FDR & the Era of the New Deal Ser). 1971. Repr. of 1937 ed. lib. bdg. 35.00 (ISBN 0-306-70341-6). Da Capo.

Part-Time Father. Edith Atkin & Estelle Rubin. LC 75-25146. 1976. 8.95 (ISBN 0-8149-0766-0). Vanguard.

Partakers of Divine Nature. C. Stavropoulos. 1976. pap. 3.50 (ISBN 0-937032-09-3). Light & Life Pub Co MN.

Parte of a Register, Contayninge Sundrie Memorable Matters, Written by Diuers Godly & Learned in Our Time, Which Stande for the Reformation of Our Church. Church of England. LC 72-5981. (English Experience Ser.: No. 509). 1973. Repr. of 1593 ed. 67.00 (ISBN 90-221-0509-1). Walter J Johnson.

Partera: Story of a Midwife. Fran L. Buss. 1980. 10.95 (ISBN 0-472-09322-3); pap. 6.95 (ISBN 0-472-06322-7). U of Mich Pr.

Parthenon. Ed. by Vincent J. Bruno. (Critical Studies in Art History Ser). (Illus.). 334p. 1974. 12.50 (ISBN 0-393-04373-8); pap. 6.95x (ISBN 0-393-09354-9). Norton.

Parthenon. Susan Woodford. (Cambridge Introduction to the History of Mankind Ser.). Date not set. pap. price not set (ISBN 0-521-22629-5). Cambridge U Pr.

Parti Pris Des Choses. Francis Ponge. Ed. by Ian Higgins. (Athlone French Poets Ser.). 1979. text ed. 27.50x (ISBN 0-485-14714-9, Athlone Pr); pap. text ed. 13.00x (ISBN 0-485-12212-X, Athlone Pr). Humanities.

Partial Dentures. Fritz Singer & Fritz Schon. (Illus.). 207p. 1973. 42.00. Quint Pub Co.

Partial Derivatives. P. J. Hilton. (Library of Mathematics). 1973. pap. 5.00 (ISBN 0-7100-4347-3). Routledge & Kegan.

Partial Differential Equations. Paul R. Garabedian. LC 64-11505. 1964. 35.95 (ISBN 0-471-29088-2). Wiley.

Partial Differential Equations. 2nd ed. F. John. LC 74-26827. (Applied Mathematical Sciences Ser.: Vol. 1). (Illus.). ix, 250p. 1975. pap. 9.50 o.p. (ISBN 0-387-90111-6). Springer-Verlag.

Partial Differential Equations in Engineering Problems. Kenneth S. Miller. 1953. ref. ed. 19.95 (ISBN 0-13-650408-6). P-H.

Partial Differential Equations: Proceedings, Vol. 23. Symposia in Pure Mathematics - Berkeley, Calif. - 1971. Ed. by D. C. Spencer. LC 72-4071. 1977. Repr. of 1973 ed. 26.80 (ISBN 0-8218-1423-0, PSPUM-23). Am Math.

Partial Hospitalization for the Mentally Ill: A Study of Programs & Problems. R. M. Glasscote. 187p. 1969. pap. 5.00 (ISBN 0-685-24873-9, P204-1). Am Psychiatric.

Partial Magic: The Novel As Self-Conscious Genre. Robert Alter. 1975. 15.75x (ISBN 0-520-02755-8); pap. 3.95 (ISBN 0-520-03732-4). U of Cal Pr.

Partially Ordered Rings & Semi-Algebraic Geometry. Gregory W. Brumfield. (London Mathematical Society Lecture Note Ser.: No. 37). 1980. pap. 23.95x (ISBN 0-521-22845-X). Cambridge U Pr.

Partially Ordered Topological Vector Spaces. Yau-Chuen Wong & Kung-Fu Ng. (Oxford Mathematical Monographs Ser.). 217p. 1974. 39.00x (ISBN 0-19-853523-6). Oxford U Pr.

Participating in Secondary Reading: A Practical Approach. Joseph F. Brunner & John J. Campbell. (Illus.). 1978. ref. 15.95 (ISBN 0-13-651323-9). P-H.

Participating Reader. S. Wittig et al. 1978. pap. 9.50 (ISBN 0-13-650200-8). P-H.

Participation & Democratic Theory. Carole Pateman. LC 71-120193. 1970. 17.50 (ISBN 0-521-07856-3); pap. 5.95x (ISBN 0-521-29004-X). Cambridge U Pr.

Participation & Political Equality. S. Verba et al. LC 77-88629. (Illus.). 1978. 32.50 (ISBN 0-521-21905-1); pap. 10.95x (ISBN 0-521-29721-4). Cambridge U Pr.

Participation De la Bretagne a la Conquete De l'Angleterre Par les Normands. Etienne Dupont. LC 80-2229. 1981. Repr. of 1911 ed. 17.50 (ISBN 0-404-18758-7). AMS Pr.

Participation, Decentralization & Advocacy Planning. R. E. Kasperson & M. Breitbart. LC 74-77537. (CCG Resource Papers Ser.: No. 25). 1974. pap. text ed. 4.00 (ISBN 0-89291-072-0). Assn Am Geographers.

Participation in American Politics: The Dynamics of Agenda-Building. Roger W. Cobb & Charles D. Elder. LC 74-25268. 192p. 1975. pap. 4.95x (ISBN 0-8018-1716-1). Johns Hopkins.

Participation in Learning. Barrington Kaye. 1970. text ed. 17.95x o.p. (ISBN 0-04-370028-4). Allen Unwin.

Participation in Schools? Five Case Studies. R. T. Fitzgerald et al. (Australian Council for Educational Research). 1976. pap. text ed. 20.00x o.p. (ISBN 0-85563-138-4). Verry.

Participation in Social & Political Activities: A Comprehensive Analysis of Political Involvement, Expressive Leisure Time, & Helping Behavior. David H. Smith et al. LC 80-16362. (Social & Behavioral Science Ser.). 1980. text ed. 27.95x (ISBN 0-87589-463-1). Jossey Bass.

Participation in Urban Planning. John Ferris. 95p. 1972. pap. text ed. 6.25x (ISBN 0-7135-1714-X, Pub. by Bedford England). Renouf.

Participation, Protest & Apathy: A Question of Involvement? Alvin Wolf & Jack Zevin. (Crucial Issues in American Government). (gr. 9-12). 1978. pap. text ed. 4.96 (ISBN 0-205-05522-2, 7655223). Allyn.

Participative Approach to Computer Systems Design: A Case Study of the Introduction of a New Computer System. Enid Mumford & Don Henshall. LC 78-23831. 1978. 21.95 (ISBN 0-470-26581-7). Halsted Pr.

Participative Management. William P. Anthony. LC 77-83035. 1978. pap. text ed. 8.95 (ISBN 0-201-00253-1); instr's guide 1.25 (ISBN 0-201-00219-1). A-W.

Participative Management: Concepts, Theory, & Implementation. Ed. by Ervin Williams. LC 76-13650. 285p. 1976. 14.95 (ISBN 0-88406-102-7). Ga St U Busn Pub.

Participative Management in Academic Libraries. Maurice P. Marchant. LC 76-8740. (Contributions in Librarianship & Information Science: No. 16). 320p. 1977. lib. bdg. 18.95 (ISBN 0-8371-8935-7, MPM/). Greenwood.

Participatory Approach to Urban Planning. Edmund M. Burke. LC 78-31107. 304p. 1979. text ed. 19.95 (ISBN 0-87705-393-6). Human Sci Pr.

Participatory Bureaucracy: Women & Minorities in a More Representative Public Service. Harry Kranz. LC 75-44600. (Illus.). 1976. 21.95 (ISBN 0-669-00556-8). Lexington Bks.

Participatory Democracy in Action: International Profiles of Community Development. Ed. by Dan A. Chekki. xvi, 306p. 1980. text ed. 20.00x (ISBN 0-7069-0923-2, Pub. by Vikas India). Advent Bk.

Participatory Economy: An Evolutionary Hypothesis & a Strategy for Development. Jaroslav Vanek. LC 77-148024. (Illus.). 1971. 20.00x (ISBN 0-8014-0639-0); pap. 4.95 1974 ed. (ISBN 0-8014-9148-7). Cornell U Pr.

Participatory Economy: An Evolutionary Hyposthesis & a Strategy for Development. Jaroslav Vanek. LC 77-148024. 181p. 1974. pap. 4.95 o.p. (ISBN 0-8014-9148-7, CP148). Cornell U Pr.

Particle Accelerator Design Computer Programs. John S. Colonias. 1974. 44.50 (ISBN 0-12-181550-1). Acad Pr.

Particle Accelerators & Their Uses. C. Scharf. Tr. by E. Lepa from Polish. (Accelerators & Storage Rings Ser.: Vol. 3). 500p. 1981. lib. bdg. 100.00 (ISBN 3-7186-0034-X). Harwood Academic.

Particle Play: An Account of the Ultimate Constituents of Matter. J. C. Polkinghorne. LC 79-17846. (Illus.). 1979. text ed. 13.95x (ISBN 0-7167-1177-X). W H Freeman.

Particle Size Analysis. Z. K. Jelinek. Tr. by W. A. Bryce. LC 73-14415. (Ser. in Analytical Chemistry). (Illus.). 178p. 1974. 34.95 (ISBN 0-470-44148-8). Halsted Pr.

Particle Size Analysis in Estimating the Significance of Airborne Contamination. 1978. pap. 25.25 (ISBN 92-0-125078-9, IDC 179, IAEA). Unipub.

Particle Technology Nineteen Eighty: Proceedings, Vols. A & B. European Federation of Chemical Engineering, European Symposium, Amsterdam, Holland, June 3-5, 1980. Ed. by K. Schonert et al. (E FCE Publication Ser.: No. 7). 1232p. 1980. text ed. 79.00x (ISBN 3-921567-27-0, Pub. by Dechema Germany). Scholium Intl.

Particleboard, Vol. 1: Materials. A. A. Moslemi. LC 74-2071. 256p. 1974. 18.95x (ISBN 0-8093-0655-7). S Ill U Pr.

Particleboard, Vol. 2: Technology. A. A. Moslemi. LC 74-2071. 252p. 1974. 18.95x (ISBN 0-8093-0656-5). S Ill U Pr.

Particles: An Introduction to Particle Physics. Michael Chester. LC 77-12352. (Illus.). (gr. 7 up). 1978. 9.95 (ISBN 0-02-718240-1, 71824). Macmillan.

Particles & Fields: Readings from Scientific American. Intro. by William J. Kaufmann, 3rd. LC 80-10669. (Illus.). 1980. text ed. 15.95x (ISBN 0-7167-1233-4); pap. text ed. 7.95x (ISBN 0-7167-1234-2). W H Freeman.

Particles & Nuclei. Ed. by N. N. Bogolyubov. Incl. Vol. 1, Pt. 1. 189p (ISBN 0-306-17191-0); Vol. 1, Pt. 2. 191p (ISBN 0-306-17192-9); Vol. 2, Pt. 1. 171p (ISBN 0-306-17193-7); Vol. 2, Pt. 2. 138p (ISBN 0-306-17194-5); Vol. 2, Pt. 3. 178p (ISBN 0-306-17195-3); Vol. 2, Pt. 4. 178p (ISBN 0-306-17196-1). LC 72-83510. 1972. 45.00 ea. (Consultants). Plenum Pub.

Particles, Sources & Fields, Vol. 1. Julian Schwinger. LC 73-119670. (Physics Ser). 1970. text ed. 28.50 (ISBN 0-201-06782-X, Adv Bk Prog). A-W.

Particles, Sources, & Fields, Vol. 2. Julian Schwinger. (Physics Ser.). 1973. 28.50 (ISBN 0-201-06783-8, Adv Bk Prog). A-W.

Particulate Polycyclic Organic Matter. Committee on Biologic Effects of Atmosphere Pollutants. (Biologic Effects of Atmospheric Pollutants Ser.). (Illus.). 336p. 1972. pap. 11.50 (ISBN 0-309-02027-1). Natl Acad Pr.

Particulates in Water: Characterization, Fate, Effects, & Removal. Ed. by Michael Kavanaugh & James O. Leckie. LC 80-19663. (Advances in Chemistry Ser.: No. 189). 1980. 59.50 (ISBN 0-8412-0499-3). Am Chemical.

Parties & Politics in Northern Nigeria. B. J. Dudley. 1968. text ed. 11.50 (ISBN 0-7146-1658-3). Humanities.

Parties & Politics in Northern Nigeria. B. J. Dudley. 352p. 1968. 27.50x (ISBN 0-7146-1658-3, F Cass Co). Biblio Dist.

Parties for All Occasions. large type ed. Carlson Wade. LC 76-37819. 128p. 1976. 7.95 o.p. (ISBN 0-498-01882-2). A S Barnes.

Parties in Crisis: Party Politics in America. Ruth K. Scott & Ronald J. Hrebenar. LC 78-14362. 1979. text ed. 15.95x (ISBN 0-471-01796-5). Wiley.

Parties. Interest Groups & Campaign Finance Laws. Ed. by Michael J. Malbin. 1980. 15.25 (ISBN 0-8447-2168-9); pap. 8.25 (ISBN 0-686-64314-3). Am Enterprise.

Parties: The Real Opportunity for Effective Citizen Politics. John S. Saloma & Frederick H. Sontag. 1972. 7.95 o.p. (ISBN 0-394-48097-X). Knopf.

Parties with a Purpose. S. L. Barrett. 128p. 1980. pap. 10.50 spiral (ISBN 0-398-03986-0). C C Thomas.

Partikeln der Deutschen Sprache. Ed. by Harald Weydt. 1979. 105.00x (ISBN 3-11-007833-3). De Gruyter.

Parting Breath. Catherine Aird. LC 77-12836. 1978. 7.95 o.p. (ISBN 0-385-13563-7). Doubleday.

Parting Counsels: Exposition of II Peter 1. John Brown. (Banner of Truth Geneva Series Commentaries). 1980. 11.50 (ISBN 0-85151-301-8). Banner of Truth.

Parting of the Ways: Government & the Educated Public in Russia, 1801-1855. Nicholas V. Riasanovsky. 1977. 45.00x (ISBN 0-19-822533-4). Oxford U Pr.

Partisan. Simon Watson. LC 74-20582. 144p. (gr. 5 up). 1975. 4.95 o.s.i. (ISBN 0-02-792500-5). Macmillan.

Partisan Guide to the Jewish Problem. Milton Steinberg. (Return to Zion Ser.). 308p. 1980. Repr. of 1945 ed. lib. bdg. 20.00x (ISBN 0-87991-135-2). Porcupine Pr.

Partisan Justice. Marvin Frankel. 142p. 1980. 9.95 (ISBN 0-8090-6478-2). Hill & Wang.

Partisan Justice. Marvin E. Frankel. 1981. pap. 4.95 (ISBN 0-8090-1395-9). Hill & Wang.

Partisan Realignment: Voters, Parties, & Government in American History. Jerome Clubb et al. LC 80-16474. (Sage Library of Social Research: Vol. 108). 320p. 1980. 18.00 (ISBN 0-8039-1445-8); pap. 8.95 (ISBN 0-8039-1446-6). Sage.

Partisans & Guerrillas. Ronald Bailey. (World War II Ser.). (Illus.). 1978. lib. bdg. 14.94 (ISBN 0-686-51049-6). Silver.

Partisans & Guerrillas. Ronald H. Bailey. Ed. by Time-Life Books. (World War II Ser.). 1978. 12.95 (ISBN 0-8094-2490-8). Time-Life.

Partisans of Europe in the Second World War. Kenneth MacKsey. LC 74-78526. (Illus.). 304p. 1975. 35.00x (ISBN 0-8128-1724-9). Stein & Day.

Partition of Palestine, 1947: Jewish Triumph, British Failure, Arab Disaster. Neil Grant. LC 73-4279. (World Focus Bks). (Illus.). (gr. 7-12). 1973. PLB 4.47 o.p. (ISBN 0-531-01044-9). Watts.

Partitions: Yesterday & Today. George E. Andrews. 56p. (Orig.). 1980. pap. text ed. 7.95 (ISBN 0-9597579-0-2). Bks Australia.

Partner in Empire: Dwarkanath Tagore & the Age of Enterprise in Eastern India. Blair B. Kling. LC 74-27293. 1977. 20.00x (ISBN 0-520-02927-5). U of Cal Pr.

Partners. Louis Auchincloss. 256p. 1975. pap. 1.75 o.s.i. (ISBN 0-446-59714-7). Warner Bks.

Partners. Marguerite Corbally. LC 77-74121. 1977. pap. text ed. 4.95x (ISBN 0-8134-1953-0). Interstate.

Partners. Robert H. Redding. LC 80-1660. (Double D Western Ser.). 192p. 1981. 9.95 (ISBN 0-385-17007-6). Doubleday.

Partners. Susan Washburn. LC 80-65985. 1981. 11.95 (ISBN 0-689-11103-7). Atheneum.

Partners for Educational Reform & Renewal. George E. Dickson & Richard W. Saxe. LC 73-7241. 1973. 17.00x (ISBN 0-8211-1825-0); text ed. 15.75x (ISBN 0-685-42629-7). McCutchan.

Partners in Business. Melvin Wallace. 200p. 1981. 14.95 (ISBN 0-913864-66-8); pap. 7.95 (ISBN 0-913864-67-6). Enterprise Del.

Partners in Crime. Agatha Christie. 1981. pap. 2.25 (ISBN 0-440-16848-1). Dell.

Partners in East-West Economic Relations: The Determinants of Choice. Ed. by Zbigniew M. Fallenbuchl & Charles H. McMillan. (Pergamon Policy Studies). (Illus.). 1980. 47.50 (ISBN 0-08-022497-0). Pergamon.

Partners in Love. 3rd rev. ed. Eleanor Hamilton. LC 79-51018. 1981. 9.95 (ISBN 0-498-02431-8). A S Barnes.

Partners in Play. Dorothy Singer & Jerome Singer. 1977. 10.95 o.p. (ISBN 0-06-013891-2, HarpT). Har-Row.

Partners in Pluralism: A Study Guide. Katherine Patterson. (Orig.). 1981. pap. 2.95 (ISBN 0-377-00111-2). Friend Pr.

Partners in Prayer. Ed. by Charles H. Long. 1980. 1.50 (ISBN 0-686-28786-X). Forward Movement.

Partners in Preaching. Reuel L. Howe. 1967. 6.95 (ISBN 0-8164-0175-6). Crossroad NY.

Partners in Tomorrow: Strategies for a New International Order. Ed. by Anthony J. Dolman & Jan Van Ettinger. 1978. 9.95 (ISBN 0-87690-294-8). Dutton.

Partners: Parents & Schools. Ed. by Ronald S. Brandt. LC 79-90730. 1979. pap. text ed. 4.75 (ISBN 0-87120-096-1, 611-79168). Assn Supervision.

Partnership New York. 1981 ed. 75p. 1978. 5.50 (ISBN 0-87526-187-6). Gould.

Partnership of Mind & Body: Biofeedback. Larry Kettelkamp. LC 76-24818. (Illus.). (gr. 5-9). 1976. 7.25 (ISBN 0-688-22088-6); PLB 6.96 (ISBN 0-688-32088-0). Morrow.

Parts of Speech. Philip Lutgendorf & Shirley M. James. LC 77-730079. (Illus.). (gr. 7-9). 1976. pap. text ed. 95.00 (ISBN 0-89290-118-7, A134-SAR). Soc for Visual.

Party. Trevor Griffiths. 1974. 8.50 (ISBN 0-571-10629-3, Pub. by Faber & Faber); pap. 4.95 (ISBN 0-571-10647-1). Merrimack Bk Serv.

Party & Locality in Northern Uganda, 1945-1962. Cherry Gertzel. (Commonwealth Papers Ser: No. 16). (Illus.). 100p. 1974. pap. text ed. 8.75x (ISBN 0-485-17616-5, Athlone Pr). Humanities.

Party & Politics in Israel: Three Visions of a Jewish State. Rael J. Isaac. (Professional Ser.). 256p. 1980. lib. bdg. 19.50 (ISBN 0-582-28196-2). Longman.

Party & Professionals: The Political Role of Teachers in Contemporary China. Gordon White. 350p. 1981. 25.00 (ISBN 0-87332-188-X). M E Sharpe.

Party Coalitions: Realignments & the Decline of the New Deal Party System. John R. Petrocik. LC 80-22212. (Illus.). 1981. lib. bdg. price not set (ISBN 0-226-66378-7). U of Chicago Pr.

Party, Constituency & Congressional Voting: A Study of Legislative Behavior in the United States House of Representatives. W. Wayne Shannon. LC 80-25798. (Louisiana State University Studies, Social Science Ser.: No. 14). (Illus.). xii, 202p. 1981. Repr. of 1968 ed. lib. bdg. 23.50x (ISBN 0-313-22771-3, SHPV). Greenwood.

Party Dynamics: The Democratic Coalition & the Politics of Change. Richard L. Rubin. LC 75-32352. 180p. 1976. 13.95x (ISBN 0-19-502036-7); pap. 5.95x (ISBN 0-19-502035-9). Oxford U Pr.

Party Games. Bernard S. Mason & Elmer D. Mitchell. 1962. pap. 2.95 (ISBN 0-06-463216-4, EH 216, EH). Har-Row.

Party Ideas. Patricia Shely. (Ideas Ser). (Illus.). 1977. pap. text ed. 1.75 (ISBN 0-87239-121-3, 7961). Standard Pub.

Party Ideology & Popular Politics at the Accession of George Third. J. Brewer. (Illus.). 400p. 1916. 39.00 (ISBN 0-521-21049-6). Cambridge U Pr.

Party Image & Electoral Behavior. Richard J. Trilling. LC 76-24794. 1976. 20.95 (ISBN 0-471-88935-0, Pub. by Wiley-Interscience). Wiley.

Party Leadership & Revolutionary Power in China. Ed. by J. W. Lewis. (Publications of the Contemporary China Institute Ser). 1970. 39.95 o.p. (ISBN 0-521-07792-3); pap. 11.50x (ISBN 0-521-09614-6). Cambridge U Pr.

Party of the Year. John Crosby. (gr. 7-12). 1980. PLB 13.95 (ISBN 0-8161-3067-1, Large Print Bks). G K Hall.

Party Packets: For Hospitals & Homes Shortcuts for a Single Activity Worker. Toni Merrill. (Illus.). 196p. 1970. pap. 17.50 photocopy ed. (ISBN 0-398-01295-4). C C Thomas.

Party Politics in China, Nineteen Forty-Five to Nineteen Eighty. R. K. Jain. 1000p. 1980. text ed. 41.00x (ISBN 0-391-02048-X). Humanities.

Party Politics in the Age of Caesar. Lily R. Taylor. (Sather Classical Lectures: No. 22). 1949. pap. 5.95x (ISBN 0-520-01257-7, CAMPUS53). U of Cal Pr.

Party Politics in the Continental Congress. H. J. Henderson. 1974. text ed. 17.50 o.p. (ISBN 0-07-028143-2, P&RB). McGraw.

Party Reborn: The Democrats of Iowa, 1950-1974. James C. Larew. LC 80-51855. (Illus.). 216p. 1980. 12.00x (ISBN 0-89033-002-6); pap. 6.00. State Hist Iowa.

Party Strength in the United States 1872-1970. Paul T. David. LC 77-183897. 1972. 13.95x (ISBN 0-8139-0396-3). U Pr of Va.

Party Symbol: Readings on Political Parties. Ed. by William Crotty. LC 79-22945. (Illus.). 1980. 18.95x (ISBN 0-7167-1144-3); pap. text ed. 9.95x (ISBN 0-7167-1145-1). W H Freeman.

Party Systems & Voter Alignments. Seymour M. Lipset & S. Rokkan. LC 67-25332. 1967. 12.95 o.s.i. (ISBN 0-02-919150-5). Free Pr.

Party's Choice with an Epilogue on the 1976 Nominations. William R. Keech & Donald R. Matthews. (Studies in Presidential Selection). 1977. 14.95 (ISBN 0-8157-4852-3); pap. 5.95 (ISBN 0-8157-4851-5). Brookings.

Party's Over: The Failure of Politics in America. David S. Broder. 265p. 1972. pap. 5.95x (ISBN 0-06-131919-8, TB1919, Torch). Har-Row.

Party's Over: The Failure of Politics in Amer. David S. Broder. LC 77-181608. 1972. 10.00 o.s.i. (ISBN 0-06-010483-X, HarpT). Har-Row.

Pas De Deux: Great Partnerships in Dance. Sarah Montague. LC 80-54502. (Illus.). 112p. 1981. text ed. 12.50x (ISBN 0-87663-346-7); pap. 7.95x (ISBN 0-87663-553-2). Universe.

Pa's Top Hat. Estelle Corney. LC 80-65663. (Illus.). 32p. (ps-3). 1980. 7.95 (ISBN 0-233-97255-2). Andre Deutsch.

Pasadena. 19p. Repr. of 1938 ed. pap. 2.00 (ISBN 0-8466-0172-9, SJS172). Shorey.

Pasaporte, First Year Spanish. Richard Woehr et al. LC 79-26709. 1980. text ed. 17.95 (ISBN 0-471-02758-8); tchr's ed. (ISBN 0-471-04193-9); wkbk (ISBN 0-471-02759-6); tapes (ISBN 0-471-05837-8). Wiley.

Pasargadae: A Report on the Excavations Conducted by the British Institute of Persian Studies from 1961 to 1963. David Stronach. (Illus.). 1978. 79.00x (ISBN 0-19-813190-9). Oxford U Pr.

Pascal. David L. Heiserman. (Illus.). 350p. (Orig.). 1980. 15.95 (ISBN 0-8306-9934-1); pap. 9.95 (ISBN 0-8306-1205-X, 1205). Tab Bks.

Pascal. Alban Krailsheimer. 84p. 1980. 9.95 (ISBN 0-8090-7550-4); pap. 2.95 (ISBN 0-8090-1412-2). Hill & Wang.

Pascal: An Introduction to Methodical Programming. 2nd ed. William Findlay & David A. Watt. (Illus.). Date not set. pap. text ed. price not set (ISBN 0-914894-73-0). Computer Sci.

PASCAL Compiler. Henry Davis. (Pascal Notebook Ser.: Vol. 2). 150p. 1981. pap. 9.95 (ISBN 0-918398-44-4). Dilithium Pr.

PASCAL for Programmers. S. Eisenbach & C. Sadler. (Illus.). 225p. 1981. pap. 8.80 (ISBN 0-387-10473-9). Springer-Verlag.

Pascal Programming. Laurence Atkinson. LC 80-40126. 300p. 1980. 49.50 (ISBN 0-471-27773-8); pap. 21.00 (ISBN 0-471-27774-6). Wiley.

Pascal Programming for the Apple. Theodore G. Lewis. 224p. 1981. 14.95 (ISBN 0-8359-5455-2); pap. 9.95 (ISBN 0-8359-5454-4). Reston.

Pascal: The Language & Its Implementation. D. W. Barron. 1981. price not set (ISBN 0-471-27835-1, Pub. by Wiley-Interscience). Wiley.

Pascal with Style: Programming Proverbs. Henry F. Ledgard et al. 1979. pap. text ed. 7.70 (ISBN 0-8104-5124-7). Hayden.

Paschal Cycle. Paul Bosch. 1979. pap. 6.75 (ISBN 0-570-03796-4, 12-2778). Concordia.

Pasdale Welfare. Fiore Ai. 160p. 1981. 8.95 (ISBN 0-89962-207-0). Todd & Honeywell.

Pasmore. David Storey. 1975. pap. 1.95 (ISBN 0-380-00276-0, 38547). Avon.

Paso Mas. Joni Eareckson & Stephen Estes. Ed. by Ben Mercado. Tr. by Rhode Flores. (Span.). 1979. 1.90. Vida Pubs.

Pass It on. Carol Amen. (Uplook Ser.). 1977. pap. 0.75 (ISBN 0-8163-0310-X, 16027-5). Pacific Pr Pub Assn.

Pass It on. James M. Ewens. (Orig.). pap. 1.50 (ISBN 0-89129-051-6). Jove Pubns.

Pass of the North, Vol. I. C. L. Sonnichsen. 1980. 20.00 (ISBN 0-87404-013-2). Tex Western.

Pass of the North, Vol. II. C. L. Sonnichsen. 1980. 15.00 (ISBN 0-87404-066-3). Tex Western.

Pass or Fail? A Study of Pass Rates in the G. C. E. at the "O" Level. John K. Backhouse. (General Ser.). (Illus.). 44p. 1974. pap. text ed. 5.75x (ISBN 0-85633-036-1, NFER). Humanities.

Passage. W. R. Moses. LC 75-33361. (Wesleyan Poetry Program: Vol. 81). 1976. text ed. 10.00x (ISBN 0-8195-2081-0, Pub. by Wesleyan U Pr); pap. 4.95 (ISBN 0-8195-1081-5). Columbia U Pr.

Passage. Victor Wartofsky. (Orig.). 1980. pap. 1.95 (ISBN 0-505-51506-7). Tower Bks.

Passage by Night. Jack Higgins. 1978. pap. 1.95 (ISBN 0-449-13891-7, GM). Fawcett.

Passage Makers. Michael K. Stammers. (Illus.). xx, 508p. 1980. 50.00 (ISBN 0-903662-06-X, Pub. by Teredo Bks England). McCartan & Root.

Passage of Dominion: Geoffrey of Monmouth & the Periodization of Insular History in the Twelfth Century. R. William Leckie, Jr. 184p. 1981. 20.00x (ISBN 0-8020-5495-1). U of Toronto Pr.

Passage of Time. Gillian Martin. LC 78-18479. 1978. 8.95 o.p. (ISBN 0-684-15819-1, ScribT). Scribner.

Passage Through Abortion: The Personal & Social Reality of Women's Experiences. Mary K. Zimmerman. LC 77-12742. (Praeger Special Studies). 1977. 24.95 (ISBN 0-03-029816-4). Praeger.

Passage Through the Red Sea. Zofia Romanowicz. Tr. by Virgilia Peterson. LC 62-19588. (Helen & Kurt Wolff Bk). 1962. 3.75 o.p. (ISBN 0-15-170995-5). HarBraceJ.

Passage to Mutiny. Alexander Kent. 352p. 1980. pap. 1.95 (ISBN 0-515-05437-2). Jove Pubns.

Passage to Space: The Shuttle Transportation System. Charles Coombs. LC 79-1176. (Illus.). (gr. 4-6). 1979. 7.50 (ISBN 0-688-22188-2); PLB 7.20 (ISBN 0-688-32188-7). Morrow.

Passage to the Golden Gate: A History of the Chinese in America to 1910. Daniel Chu & Samuel Chu. LC 67-10546. (Illus.). (gr. 7 up). 1967. pap. 2.50 o.p. (ISBN 0-385-05971-X, Z11, Zenith). Doubleday.

Passage West. Dallas Miller. 1980. pap. 2.75 (ISBN 0-380-50278-X, 50278). Avon.

Passagemakers Guide from San Francisco to Ensenada. Brian Fagan. (Illus.). 120p. (Orig.). 1981. pap. 12.95 (ISBN 0-88496-161-3). Capra Pr.

Passages About Earth: An Exploration of the New Planetary Culture. William I. Thompson. LC 73-14298. 192p. 1981. pap. 3.95 (ISBN 0-06-090835-1, CN 835, CN). Har-Row.

Passages for Translation from Italian. R. N. Absalom. 1967. pap. 7.50x (ISBN 0-521-09431-3, 431). Cambridge U Pr.

Passages of a Pastor. Cecil R. Paul. 128p. 1981. 6.95 (ISBN 0-310-43070-4, 11160). Zondervan.

Passages of a Working Life: During Half a Century with a Prelude of Early Reminiscences, 3 vols. Charles Knight. (Development of Industrial Society Ser.). 1026p. 1980. Repr. 50.00x (ISBN 0-7165-1568-7, Pub. by Irish Academic Pr). Biblio Dist.

Passageways. Theodore Zukoski. 1981. 4.95 (ISBN 0-8062-1672-7). Carlton.

Passenger & Immigration Lists Index: A Reference Guide to Published Lists of Passengers Who Arrived in America in the Seventeenth, Eighteenth, & Nineteenth Centuries, 3 vols. Ed. by P. William Filby. 1980. 225.00 (ISBN 0-8103-1099-6). Gale.

Passenger Cars, 1863-1904. T. R. Nicholson. LC 75-115303. (Cars of the World in Color Ser.: No. 2). (Illus.). 1970. 9.95 (ISBN 0-02-589380-7). Macmillan.

Passenger Cars, 1905-1912. T. R. Nicholson. Ed. by Alick Bartholomew. (Cars of the World in Color Ser). (Illus.). 1971. 9.95 (ISBN 0-02-589420-X). Macmillan.

Passenger Cars: 1924-42. Michael Sedgwick. LC 75-17949. (Illus.). 172p. 1976. 9.95 o.s.i. (ISBN 0-02-609000-7, 60900). Macmillan.

Passenger Psychological Dynamics. Compiled by American Society of Civil Engineers. 192p. 1969. pap. text ed. 8.75 (ISBN 0-87262-020-4). Am Soc Civil Eng.

Passenger Transport & the Environment: The Integration of Public Transport with the Urban Environment. Ed. by Roy Cresswell. (Illus.). 1977. 37.50x (ISBN 0-249-44153-5). Intl Ideas.

Passenger Transportation. Martin T. Farris. (Illus.). 256p. 1976. ref. ed. 19.95x (ISBN 0-13-652750-7). P-H.

Passing Bells. Philip Rock. 1980. pap. 2.75 o.s.i. (ISBN 0-440-16837-6). Dell.

Passing Ceremony. Helen Weinzweig. LC 72-95751. (Anansi Fiction Ser.: No. 24). 120p. 1973. pap. 4.95 (ISBN 0-88784-325-5, Pub. by Hse Anansi Pr Canada). U of Toronto Pr.

Passing for Human. Jody Scott. (Science Fiction Ser.). (Orig.). 1977. pap. 1.50 o.p. (ISBN 0-87997-330-7, UW1330). DAW Bks.

Passing Medical Exams. M. H. Pappworth. 1975. 9.95 (ISBN 0-407-00013-5). Butterworths.

Passing of the Frontier. Emerson Hough. 1976. lib. bdg. 10.95x (ISBN 0-89968-046-1). Lightyear.

Passing of the Hapsburg Monarchy, 1914-1918, 2 Vols. Arthur J. May. LC 64-22874. 1966. 20.00 o.p. (ISBN 0-8122-7463-6). U of Pa Pr.

Passing of the Irish Act of Union: A Study in Parliamentary Politics. G. C. Bolton. (Oxford Historical Ser.). 1966. 8.50x o.p. (ISBN 0-19-821827-3). Oxford U Pr.

Passing of the Manchus. Percy H. Kent. (Studies in Chinese History & Civilization). 1977. 24.00 (ISBN 0-89093-089-9). U Pubns Amer.

Passing on Sociology: The Teaching of Discipline. Charles Goldsmid & Everett Wilson. 448p. 1980. text ed. 21.95x (ISBN 0-534-00914-X). Wadsworth Pub.

Passing Strange. Catherine Aird. LC 80-1120. (Crime Club Ser.). 192p. 1981. 9.95 (ISBN 0-385-17271-0). Doubleday.

Passing Through. Corrine Gerson. (YA) (gr. 7-12). 1980. pap. 1.50 (ISBN 0-440-96958-1, LFL). Dell.

Passing Through. Edgar Guest. 190p. 1980. Repr. of 1923 ed. lib. bdg. 11.95x (ISBN 0-89968-191-3). Lightyear.

Passing Time. Michel Butot. Tr. by Jean Stewart. 1980. pap. 4.95 (ISBN 0-7145-0438-6). Riverrun NY.

Passing Times. Peter Korniss. (Illus.). 1979. 17.50x (ISBN 963-13-0733-6). Intl Pubns Serv.

Passion. Robert Steiner. Ed. by Michael Peich. (Penmaen Fiction Ser.: No. 2). 1980. 12.00 (ISBN 0-915778-33-5); ltd. signed ed. 40.00x (ISBN 0-915778-32-7). Penmaen Pr.

Passion, Action, & Politics: A Perspective on Social Problems & Social-Problem Solving. Irving Tallman. LC 75-37959. (Illus.). 1976. text ed. 20.95x (ISBN 0-7167-0540-0); pap. text ed. 10.95x (ISBN 0-7167-0539-7). W H Freeman.

Passion & Proud Hearts. Lydia Lancaster. (Orig.). 1978. pap. 2.25 o.s.i. (ISBN 0-446-82548-4). Warner Bks.

Passion & Rebellion: The Expressionist Movement & Its Heritage. Ed. by Stephen Bronner & Douglas Kellner. 400p. 1981. lib. bdg. price not set (ISBN 0-89789-016-7); pap. text ed. price not set (ISBN 0-89789-017-5). J F Bergin.

Passion Artist. John Hawkes. LC 79-1707. 192p. 1981. pap. 3.95 (ISBN 0-06-090837-8, CN837, CN). Har-Row.

Passion for Cars. Anthony Gibbs. (Encore Ed.). (Illus.). 1974. 2.95 o.p. (ISBN 0-684-14974-5, Scribner-T). Scribner.

Passion for Equality. Nick Kotz & Mary L. Kotz. 1977. pap. text ed. 3.95x (ISBN 0-393-09006-X). Norton.

Passion for Treason. Robin Nicholson. 384p. (Orig.). 1981. pap. 2.75 (ISBN 0-515-05663-4). Jove Pubns.

Passion for Truth: Hans Kung & His Theology. Robert Nowell. 376p. 1981. 17.50 (ISBN 0-8245-0039-3). Crossroad NY.

Passion in the Desert. Curt Leviant. 160p. 1980. pap. 2.50 (ISBN 0-380-76125-4, 76125). Avon.

Passion, Knowing How, & Understanding: An Essay on the Concept of Faith. Andrew J. Burgess. LC 75-31550. (American Academy of Religion. Dissertation Ser.). 1975. pap. 7.50 (ISBN 0-89130-044-9, 010109). Scholars Pr Ca.

Passion of Christ. Veselin Kesich. 84p. pap. 1.95 (ISBN 0-913836-80-X). St Vladimirs.

Passion of Loreen Bright Weasel. James Polk. 192p. 1981. 8.95 (ISBN 0-686-69056-7). HM.

Passion of Our Lord. C. C. Crawford. 6.95 (ISBN 0-89225-140-9). Gospel Advocate.

Passion of Our Lord. Tr. by Fiscar Marison. 302p. 1980. pap. 3.95 (ISBN 0-911988-37-8). AMI Pr.

Passion of Perpetua. Marie-Louise Von Franz. Tr. by Elizabeth Welsh. (Seninar Ser.). 81p. (Orig.). 1979. pap. 6.50 (ISBN 0-88214-502-9). Spring Pubns.

Passion Planets: The Astrology of Relationships. Shellie Enteen & Judy Jacobs. 288p. (Orig.). 1980. pap. 2.50 (ISBN 0-515-05269-8). Jove Pubns.

Passion Play. Jerzy Kosinski. 1980. pap. 2.95 (ISBN 0-553-13656-9). Bantam.

Passion: Program for Algebraic Sequences Specifically of Input-Output Nature. C. William Benz. LC 72-126524. (Illus.). 1971. pap. text ed. 7.95x (ISBN 0-7167-0441-2). W H Freeman.

Passion: Selected from the Fifteenth Century Cycle of York Mystery Plays in a Version by the Company with Tony Harrison. Tony Harrison. 1978. pap. 5.00x (ISBN 0-8476-3131-1). Rowman.

Passion Star. Julia Grice. 1980. pap. 2.50 (ISBN 0-446-91498-3). Warner Bks.

Passionate Amateur's Guide to Archaeology in the United States. Josleen Wilson. (Illus.). 448p. 1981. pap. 12.95 (ISBN 0-02-098670-X, Collier). Macmillan.

Passionate Enemies. Jean Plaidy. 320p. 1981. pap. 2.50 (ISBN 0-449-24390-7, Crest). Fawcett.

Passionate God. Rosemary Haughton. 308p. 1981. pap. 11.95 (ISBN 0-8091-2383-5). Paulist Pr.

Passionate Journey. Irving Stone. 10.95 (ISBN 0-385-17198-6). Doubleday.

Passionate Liberator: Theodore Dwight Weld & the Dilemma of Reform. Robert H. Abzug. LC 80-11819. (Illus.). 300p. 1980. 19.95 (ISBN 0-19-502771-X). Oxford U Pr.

Passionate People: Carriers of the Spirit. Keith Miller & Bruce Larson. 1979. pap. 5.95 (ISBN 0-8499-2832-X). Word Bks.

Passionate Pilgrims: The American Traveler in Great Britain, 1800-1914. Allison Lockwood. LC 78-66808. 600p. 1981. 25.00 (ISBN 0-8386-2272-0). Fairleigh Dickinson.

Passionate Pretenders. Diana Haviland. 1977. pap. 1.95 o.p. (ISBN 0-449-13810-0, 0-449-13810-0, GM). Fawcett.

Passionate Princess. John Cleve. pap. 1.50 o.s.i. (ISBN 0-440-16039-1). Dell.

Passionate Touch. Bonnie Drake. 1981. pap. 1.50 (ISBN 0-440-16776-0). Dell.

Passionate Wisdom of Henry Miller: The Religious Dimension of His Life & Art. Dorothy Perkins. (Orig.). 1980. pap. 3.00 (ISBN 0-9604742-1-8). D J Perkins.

Passions. Isaac B. Singer. 1978. pap. 2.95 (ISBN 0-449-24067-3, Crest). Fawcett.

Passions. Robert C. Solomon. LC 74-33691. 1977. pap. 3.95 (ISBN 0-385-12220-9, Anch). Doubleday.

Passions & Impressions. Pablo Neruda. Tr. by Margaret S. Peden from Span. 1981. 17.95 (ISBN 0-374-22994-5). FS&G.

Passions of Animals. Edward P. Thompson. (Contributions to the History of Psychology Ser.: Comparative Psychology). 1980. Repr. of 1851 ed. 30.00 (ISBN 0-89093-322-7). U Pubns Amer.

Passions of the Mind. Irving Stone. LC 75-139064. 1971. 14.95 (ISBN 0-385-02396-0); Limited edition 35.00 (ISBN 0-385-02568-8). Doubleday.

Passions of the Minde in Generall. Thomas Wright. LC 78-139807. 1971. Repr. of 1604 ed. 16.00 o.p. (ISBN 0-252-00147-8). U of Ill Pr.

Passions, Realms & Visions. Natari Shirani Kali. 1979. 4.00 o.p. (ISBN 0-682-49406-2). Exposition.

Passion's Slave. Alexis Hill. (Orig.). 1979. pap. 2.50 (ISBN 0-515-04862-3). Jove Pubns.

Passion's Wicked Torment. Melissa Hepburne. (Orig.). 1981. pap. 2.75 (ISBN 0-523-41004-2). Pinnacle Bks.

Passive & Active Network Analysis & Synthesis. Aram Budak. 600p. 1974. text ed. 26.95 (ISBN 0-395-17203-9); solutions manual 4.55 (ISBN 0-395-17835-5). HM.

Passive Solar Design: A Short Bibliography for Practitioners. AIA Research Corporation. 1979. pap. 5.50 (ISBN 0-89934-040-7). Solar Energy Info.

Passive Solar Design: A Survey of Monitored Buildings. AIA Research Corporation. 1979. pap. 19.50 (ISBN 0-930978-85-4). Solar Energy Info.

Passive Solar Energy: A Complete Guide to Heating & Cooling with Solar Power. Bruce Anderson & Malcolm Wells. LC 80-70147. (Illus.). 208p. 1980. 17.95 (ISBN 0-931790-51-4); pap. 8.95 (ISBN 0-931790-09-3). Brick Hse Pub.

Passive Solar Energy: The Homeowners Guide to Natural Heating & Cooling. Bruce Anderson & Malcolm Wells. (Illus., Orig.). 1981. 17.95 (ISBN 0-931790-51-4); pap. 8.95 (ISBN 0-931790-09-3). Brick Hse Pub.

Passive Solar Handbook. California Energy Commission. 330p. 1981. lib. bdg. 34.50 (ISBN 0-89934-101-2). Solar Energy Info.

Passive Solar Heating & Cooling Conference & Workshop Proceedings, 1976. Solar Energy Group, Los Alamos Scientific Laboratory. 355p. 1980. pap. cancelled (ISBN 0-89934-021-0). Solar Energy Info.

Passive Solar Heating Design. Ralph M. Lebens. 234p. 1980. 49.95x (ISBN 0-470-26977-4). Halsted Pr.

Passive Solar Research & Development Project Summaries. AIA Research Corporation. 1979. pap. 11.95 (ISBN 0-89934-041-5). Solar Energy Info.

Passive Solar Retrofit for Homeowners & Apartment Dwellers. Ken Bossong. (Illus.). 100p. (Orig.). 1981. pap. text ed. 5.00 (ISBN 0-89988-068-1). Citizens Energy.

Passive Voice & Agreement of the Verb Predicate with a Collective Subject. William Harrison & J. Mullen. (Studies in the Modern Russian Language Ser: Nos. 4 & 5). (Rus). 14.95 (ISBN 0-521-05218-1). Cambridge U Pr.

Passover. Norma Simon. LC 65-11644. (Holiday Ser.). (Illus.). (gr. k-3). 1965. PLB 7.89 (ISBN 0-690-61094-7, TYC-J). T Y Crowell.

Passover: A Season of Freedom. Malka Drucker. LC 80-8810. (A Jewish Holidays Book). (Illus.). 96p. (gr. 5 up). 1981. PLB 8.95 (ISBN 0-8234-0389-0). Holiday.

Passover: Festival of Freedom. Sophia Cedarbaum. (Illus.). (gr. k-2). 1960. 3.50 (ISBN 0-8074-0147-1, 301592). UAHC.

Passover Haggadah. Ed. by Herbert Bronstein. (Illus.). 1974. 50.00 set (ISBN 0-916694-66-6); 7.95 (ISBN 0-916694-71-2); lib. bdg. 17.50 (ISBN 0-916694-06-2); pap. 4.00 (ISBN 0-916694-05-4). Central Conf.

Passover Haggadah. Tr. by Aryeh Kaplan. 288p. Sephardic 10.95 (ISBN 0-686-27545-4). Maznaim.

Passover Meal. Arleen Hynes. LC 76-187207. 1972. pap. 1.95 (ISBN 0-8091-1653-7). Paulist Pr.

Passover Seder: Afikoman in Exile. Ruth G. Fredman. 1980. 18.00x (ISBN 0-8122-7788-0). U of Pa Pr.

Passport of Mallam Ilia. Cyprian O. Ekwensi. 1960. text ed. 2.95x (ISBN 0-521-04883-4). Cambridge U Pr.

Passport to Better Health Through Eating. Fred Miller. Date not set. pap. 3.95 (ISBN 0-89404-028-6). Aztex. Postponed.

Passport to German. Charles Berlitz. 1974. pap. 1.75 (ISBN 0-451-09444-1, E9444, Sig). NAL.

Password to Heaven. Susan Davis. (My Church Teaches Ser.). 32p. (gr. k-3). 1980. pap. 1.50 (ISBN 0-8127-0298-0). Southern Pub.

Past. Neil Jordan. 1980. 8.95 (ISBN 0-8076-0982-X). Braziller.

Past & Future of Presidential Debates. Ed. by Austin Ranney. 1979. pap. 7.25 (ISBN 0-8447-3330-X). Am Enterprise.

Past & Present Vegetation of the Isle of Skye. H. J. Birks. LC 76-189591. (Illus.). 300p. 1973. 99.00 (ISBN 0-521-08533-0). Cambridge U Pr.

Past & the Present. Lawrence Stone. 288p. 1981. 15.95 (ISBN 0-7100-0628-4). Routledge & Kegan.

Past & the Present of the Pike's Peak Gold Regions. Henry Villard. LC 76-87629. (American Scene Ser). (Illus.). 186p. 1972. Repr. of 1932 ed. lib. bdg. 22.50 (ISBN 0-306-71804-9). Da Capo.

Past Climate of Arroyo Hondo, New Mexico, Reconstructed from Tree Rings. Martin R. Rose et al. (Arroyo Hondo Archaeological Ser.: Vol. 4). (Illus., Orig.). 1981. pap. 6.25 (ISBN 0-933452-05-5). Schol Am Res.

Past Imperative: A Collection of Poems 1953-1964. Monika Varma. 47p. 1974. 10.00 (ISBN 0-88253-423-8); pap. text ed. 4.80 (ISBN 0-88253-422-X). Ind-US Inc.

Past in the Present: History, Ecology, and Cultural Variation in Highland Madagascar. Conrad P. Kottak. (Illus.). 406p. 1980. 18.95x (ISBN 0-472-09323-1); pap. 9.95x (ISBN 0-472-06323-5). U of Mich Pr.

Past Joys. Ken Botto. Ed. by Jane Vandenburgh. LC 78-7999. (Illus.). 1978. ltd. signed ed. 45.00 o.p. (ISBN 0-87701-116-8, Prism Editions); pap. 12.95 o.p. (ISBN 0-87701-115-X). Chronicle Bks.

Past Landscapes: A Bibliography for Historic Preservationists. rev. ed. John A. Jakle & Virginia Oliver. (Architecture Ser.: Bibliography A-314). 68p. 1980. pap. 7.50. Vance Biblios.

Past Life Hypnotic Regression Course. Dick Sutphen. 1977. 24.95 (ISBN 0-911842-13-6). Valley Sun.

Past Lives Therapy. Morris Netherton & Nancy Shiffrin. LC 77-29262. 1978. 8.95 o.p. (ISBN 0-688-03298-2). Morrow.

Past Master. R. A. Lafferty. 1977. pap. 1.95 (ISBN 0-441-65302-2). Ace Bks.

Past, Present & Future. Arthur Prior. 1967. 27.50x (ISBN 0-19-824311-1). Oxford U Pr.

Past, Present & Future of Automotive Elastomer Applications. Society of Automotive Engineers. 1980. 15.00 (ISBN 0-89883-235-7). Soc Auto Engineers.

Past, Present & Future of the Church. Fred Pruitt. 72p. 0.60. Faith Pub Hse.

Past Speaks: Sources & Problems in British History Since 1688. Ed. by Walter Arnstein. 448p. 1981. pap. text ed. 7.95 (ISBN 0-669-02919-X). Heath.

Past Speaks: Sources & Problems in English History to 1688. Ed. by Lacey B. Smith & Jean R. Smith. 368p. 1981. pap. text ed. 7.95 (ISBN 0-669-02920-3). Heath.

Past That Poets Make. Harold Toliver. LC 80-18825. 304p. 1981. text ed. 24.00 (ISBN 0-674-65676-8). Harvard U Pr.

Past We Share: The Near Eastern Ancestry of Western Folk Literature. E. L. Ranelagh. (Illus.). 288p. 1980. 21.95 (ISBN 0-7043-2234-X, Pub. by Quartet England). Horizon.

Pasta. Time-Life Books Editors. (Good Cook Ser.). (Illus.). 176p. 1981. 12.95 (ISBN 0-8094-2891-1). Time-Life.

Pasta & Noodles. Merry White. 288p. 1981. pap. 5.95 (ISBN 0-14-046504-9). Penguin.

Pasta Cook Book. Sunset Editors. LC 79-90338. (Illus.). 96p. 1980. pap. 3.95 (ISBN 0-376-02521-2, Sunset Bks). Sunset-Lane.

Pasta! Pasta! Pasta! Ursel Norman. LC 75-510. (Illus.). 64p. 1975. 7.95 o.p. (ISBN 0-688-02922-1). Morrow.

Pastel. Georgette Heyer. 1976. Repr. of 1929 ed. lib. bdg. 15.25x (ISBN 0-89966-121-1). Buccaneer Bks.

Pastel City. M. John Harrison. 1981. pap. 1.95 (ISBN 0-671-83584-X). PB.

Pastel Painting Techniques. G. Roddon. 1979. 24.00 (ISBN 0-7134-1022-1, Pub. by Batsford England). David & Charles.

Pastels Are Great. John Hawkinson. LC 68-22193. (Activity Bks.). (Illus.). (gr. 3 up). 1968. 6.50g (ISBN 0-8075-6362-5). A Whitman.

Pastels for Beginners. Ernest Savage. LC 79-56680. (Start to Paint Ser.). (Illus.). 1980. pap. 3.95 (ISBN 0-8008-6238-4, Pentalic). Taplinger.

Pasternak's "Doctor Zhivago". Harry F. Rowland & Paul Rowland. (Crosscurrents-Modern Critiques Ser.). 1968. pap. 6.95 (ISBN 0-8093-0293-4). S Ill U Pr.

Pasternak's "Doctor Zhivago". Mary F. Rowland & Paul Rowland. LC 68-10000. (Crosscurrents-Modern Critiques Ser.). 232p. 1967. 10.95 (ISBN 0-8093-0266-7). S Ill U Pr.

Pastmasters Series: Homer. Jasper Griffin. 1981. 7.95 (ISBN 0-8090-5523-6); pap. 2.95 (ISBN 0-8090-1413-0). Hill & Wang.

Paston Letters: A Selection in Modern Spelling. Ed. by Norman Davis. (World's Classics Ser: No. 591). 1975. 12.95 (ISBN 0-19-250591-2). Oxford U Pr.

Paston Letters & Papers of the Fifteenth Century, Pt. 1. Ed. by Norman Davis. 760p. 1971. 55.00x (ISBN 0-19-812415-5). Oxford U Pr.

Pastons & Their England. 2nd ed. Henry S. Bennett. LC 68-23175. (Cambridge Studies in Medieval Life & Thought). 1968. 32.95 (ISBN 0-521-07173-9); pap. 8.95x (ISBN 0-521-09513-1). Cambridge U Pr.

Pastor. H. Harvey. Tr. by Alejandro Trevifio. Orig. Title: Pastor. 232p. (Span.). 1980. pap. 2.60 (ISBN 0-311-42025-7). Casa Bautista.

Pastor & His Work. Homer A. Kent, Sr. 8.95 o.p. (ISBN 0-88469-079-2). BMH Bks.

Pastor & Parish: A Systems Approach. E. Mansell Pattison. Ed. by Howard J. Clinebell & Howard W. Stone. LC 76-62619. (Creative Pastoral Care & Counseling Ser.). 96p. 1977. pap. 3.25 (ISBN 0-8006-0559-4, 1-559). Fortress.

Pastor & Patient. Ed. by Richard Dayringer. LC 80-70247. 240p. 1981. 20.00 (ISBN 0-87668-437-1). Aronson.

Pastor Dispenses. Joseph S. Damazo. (Uplook Ser.). 1976. pap. 0.75 (ISBN 0-8163-0265-0, 16037-4). Pacific Pr Pub Assn.

Pastora. Joanna Barnes. LC 77-79533. 1980. 13.95 (ISBN 0-87795-170-5). Arbor Hse.

Pastoral Care & Counseling in Grief & Separation. Wayne E. Oates. Ed. by Howard J. Clinevell & Howard W. Stone. LC-75-13048. (Creative Pastoral Care & Counseling Ser.). 96p. 1976. pap. 3.25 (ISBN 0-8006-0554-3, 1-554). Fortress.

Pastoral Care to the Cancer Patient. Nancy Van Dyke Platt. 84p. 1980. write for info. o.p. (ISBN 0-398-04051-6). C C Thomas.

Pastoral Counseling Guidebook. Charles F. Kemp. (Orig.). 1971. pap. 6.50 o.p. (ISBN 0-687-30320-6). Abingdon.

Pastoral Counseling with People in Distress. Harold I. Haas. LC 77-99316. 1969. pap. 6.50 (ISBN 0-570-03794-8, 12-2776). Concordia.

Pastoral Counselor in Social Action. Speed Leas & Paul Kittlaus. Ed. by Howard J. Clinebell & Howard W. Stone. LC 80-8059. (Creative Pastoral Care & Counseling Ser.). 96p. (Orig.). 1981. pap. 3.25 (ISBN 0-8006-0565-9, 1-565). Fortress.

Pastoral Epistles. E. M. Blaiklock. 128p. 1972. pap. 3.50 (ISBN 0-310-21233-2). Zondervan.

Pastoral Epistles. Martin Dibelius & Hans Conzelmann. Ed. by Helmut Koester. Tr. by Philip Buttolph & Adela Yarbro. LC 71-157549. (Hermeneia: a Critical & Historical Commentary on the Bible). 1972. 15.00 (ISBN 0-8006-6002-1, 20-6002). Fortress.

Pastoral Epistles. Patrick Fairbairn. Date not set. 14.95 (ISBN 0-86524-053-1). Klock & Klock.

Pastoral Epistles. Robert J. Karris. Ed. by Wilfrid Harrington & Donald Senior. (New Testament Message Ser.: Vol. 17). 148p. 1979. 9.95 (ISBN 0-89453-139-5); pap. 4.95 (ISBN 0-89453-202-2). M Glazier.

Pastoral Epistles. Robert J. Karris. (New Testament Message Ser.). 9.95 (ISBN 0-89453-140-9); pap. 4.95 (ISBN 0-89453-205-7). M Glazier.

Pastoral Epistles. Homer Kent, Jr. 1958. 9.95 (ISBN 0-8024-6356-8). Moody.

Pastoral Epistles. W. Lock. (International Critical Commentary Ser.). 212p. 1924. text ed. 17.50x (ISBN 0-567-05033-5). Attic Pr.

Pastoral Epistles & Philemon. H. A. Moellering & V. Bartling. (Concordia Commentary Ser). 1970. 10.95 (ISBN 0-570-06285-3, 15-2067). Concordia.

Pastoral Epistles: Studies in I & II Timothy. Homer A. Kent, Jr. 10.95 (ISBN 0-88469-075-X). BMH Bks.

Pastoral Evangelism. Samuel Southard. LC 80-82196. 192p. 1981. pap. 8.95 (ISBN 0-8042-2037-9). John Knox.

Pastoral Mentor. C. David Jones. LC 80-51494. 1980. 16.95 (ISBN 0-931804-05-1). Skipworth Pr.

Pastoral Novel: Studies in George Eliot, Thomas Hardy, & D. H.Lawrence. Michael Squires. LC 74-75793. 1975. 9.75x (ISBN 0-8139-0530-3). U Pr of Va.

Pastoral Planning Book. Charles J. Keating. 96p. (Orig.). 1981. pap. 6.95 (ISBN 0-8091-2360-6). Paulist Pr.

Pastoral Pointers: Contribution by Thirteen Church of God Ministers. 1976. pap. 2.25 (ISBN 0-87148-686-5). Pathway Pr.

Pastoral Use of Hypnotic Technique. Joseph Wittkofski. 128p. 1971. pap. 7.95 spiral (ISBN 0-398-02101-5). C C Thomas.

Pastor's Complete Workbook. Ed. by Charles M. Smith. 1958. 9.95 (ISBN 0-687-30140-8). Abingdon.

Pastor's Wife Today. Donna M. Sinclair. LC 80-26076. (Creative Leadership Ser.). 128p. (Orig.). 1981. pap. 4.95 (ISBN 0-687-30269-2). Abingdon.

Pasyon & Revolution: Popular Movements in the Philippines, 1840-1910. Reynaldo C. Ileto. (Illus.). 345p. 1980. 18.75x (ISBN 0-686-28640-5); pap. 13.75x (ISBN 0-686-28641-3). Cellar.

Pat & Roald. Barry Farrell. (Illus.). 1969. 8.95 o.p. (ISBN 0-394-43997-X). Random.

Pat Boone Devotional Book. Pat Boone. 7.95 (ISBN 0-89728-050-4, 678753). Omega Pubns OR.

Pat Garrett: The Story of a Western Lawmen. Leon C. Metz. (Illus.). 305p. 1974. 14.95 (ISBN 0-8061-1067-8). U of Okla Pr.

Pat Hobby Stories. F. Scott Fitzgerald. 1962. pap. 2.95 o.s.i. (ISBN 0-684-71761-1, SL216, ScribT). Scribner.

Pat Widmer's Dog Training Book. Pat Widmer. 1980. 4.98 (ISBN 0-679-50781-7). McKay.

Pat Widmer's Dog Training Book. Patricia P. Widmer. 1980. pap. 2.25 (ISBN 0-451-09348-8, E9348, Sig). NAL.

Pat Widmer's Dog Training Book: Straight Talk for Owners of City & Suburban Dogs. Patricia P. Widmer. (Illus.). 1977. 4.98 o.p. (ISBN 0-679-50781-7). McKay.

Pataki: Leyendas Y Misterios De los Orishas Africanos. Julio Garcia-Cortez. LC 79-54684. (Coleccion Ebano Y Canela Ser.). (Illus.). 250p. (Span.). 1980. pap. 14.95 (ISBN 0-89729-236-7). Ediciones.

Patanjali's Yoga Sutras. 2nd ed. Patanjali. Tr. by Rama Prasada from Sanskrit. 321p. 1981. Repr. of 1912 ed. 15.95 (ISBN 0-89744-996-7, Pub. by Orient Reprint India). Auromere.

Patch. C. H. Frick. LC 57-6559. (gr. 7 up). 4.50 o.p. (ISBN 0-15-259570-8, HJ). HarBraceJ.

Patch and the Strings. Karen B. Winnick. LC 76-56446. 1977. 6.95 o.p. (ISBN 0-397-31749-2). Lippincott.

Patch of Blue. Grace L. Hill. (Grace Hill Ser.: No. 34). 176p. 1980. pap. 1.95 (ISBN 0-553-14172-4). Bantam.

Patch of Earth. Lani Van Ryzin. (Illus.). 64p. (gr. 3-5). 1981. PLB 6.97 (ISBN 0-686-69298-5). Messner.

Patches of Godlight: The Pattern of Thought of C. S. Lewis. Robert H. Smith. LC 80-14132. 287p. 1981. 18.00x (ISBN 0-8203-0528-6). U of Ga Pr.

Patches of Joy. Velma S. Daniels. 1979. 5.95 (ISBN 0-88289-101-4); pap. 3.95 (ISBN 0-88289-101-4). Pelican.

Patchwork (Activities in Flexible Thinking) Dianne Draze. (Illus., Orig.). 1980. pap. text ed. 7.00 (ISBN 0-931724-13-9); tchr's ed. avail. Dandy Lion.

Patchwork Man. 1978. pap. 1.50 o.s.i. (ISBN 0-515-04434-2). Jove Pubns.

Patchwork Quilts. Averil Colby. (Encore Edition). 1975. 4.95 o.p. (ISBN 0-684-15240-1, ScribT). Scribner.

Patchwork Quilts. Averil Colby. 1965. 17.95 (ISBN 0-7134-3025-7, Pub. by Batsford England). David & Charles.

Patchwork Screen for the Ladies. Jane Barker. Bd. with Prude: A Novel by a Young Lady. LC 74-170553. (Novel in England, 1700-1775 Ser). lib. bdg. 50.00 (ISBN 0-8240-0551-1). Garland Pub.

Patchwork: Technique & Design. Alice Timmins. (Illus.). 144p. 1980. 24.00 (ISBN 0-7134-3296-9, Pub. by Batsford England). David & Charles.

Patchworkbook. Judy Marti. 100p. 1981. pap. 9.95 (ISBN 0-9602970-2-2). Moon Over Mntn.

Patent & Know-How Licensing in Japan & the United States. Ed. by Teruo Doi & Warren L. Shattuck. LC 76-7785. (Asian Law Ser.: No.5). 444p. 1977. 30.00 (ISBN 0-295-95513-9). U of Wash Pr.

Patent & Trademark Forms, 4 vols. Albert L. Jacobs. LC 67-26112. 1977. looseleaf with 1979 rev. pages 210.00 (ISBN 0-87632-217-8); Vols. 4 & 4A. 110.00; Vols. 4B & 4C. 111.00; Vols. 4, 4A, 4B, & 4C. 210.00. Boardman.

Patent Claims, 3 vols. 2nd ed. Anthony W. Deller. LC 76-112643. 1971. 150.00 (ISBN 0-686-14534-8). Lawyers Co-Op.

Patent Fraud & Inequitable Conduct. rev. ed. C. Bruce Hamburg. LC 72-89458. 1978. looseleaf with 1978 rev. pages 60.00 (ISBN 0-87632-085-X). Boardman.

Patent Invalidity: A Statistical & Substantive Analysis. Gloria K. Koenig. LC 73-89532. 1974. looseleaf with 1980 rev. pages 60.00 (ISBN 0-87632-127-9). Boardman.

Patent Law Fundamentals. 2nd ed. Peter D. Rosenberg. LC 74-15799. 1980. 37.50 (ISBN 0-87632-098-1). Boardman.

Patent Law Review: Annual. Ed. by Thomas E. Costner. Incl. 1969 (ISBN 0-87632-040-X); 1970 (ISBN 0-87632-044-2); 1971 (ISBN 0-87632-047-7); 1972 (ISBN 0-87632-081-7); 1973 (ISBN 0-87632-091-4); 1974 (ISBN 0-87632-140-6); 1975 (ISBN 0-87632-141-4). LC 79-88703. except where noted 42.50 ea. o.p. Boardman.

Patent Medicine Tax Stamps: A History of the Firms Using U.S. Private Die Proprietary Medicine Tax Stamps. Henry Holcombe. LC 76-51546. 1979. 100.00x (ISBN 0-88000-098-8). Quarterman.

Patents. Gould Editorial Staff. 1981. 77.50 (ISBN 0-87526-078-0). Gould.

Patents Throughout the World. 2nd ed. 1978. looseleaf with current service 60.00 (ISBN 0-87632-125-2). Boardman.

Paternal Deprivation: Family, School, Sexuality & Society. Henry B. Biller. LC 74-928. 1974. pap. 9.95 (ISBN 0-669-02517-8). Lexington Bks.

Paternalism in Early Victorian England. David Roberts. 1979. 24.00 (ISBN 0-8135-0868-1). Rutgers U Pr.

Paternity Testing by Blood Grouping. 2nd ed. Leon N. Sussman. (Illus.). 208p. 1976. 22.50 (ISBN 0-398-03523-7). C C Thomas.

Paterson Pieces: Poems, 1969-1979. William J. Higginson. (Illus.). 80p. (Orig.). 1981. pap. 3.95 (ISBN 0-89120-018-5, Old Plate). From Here.

Pates & Terrines. Sheila Hutchins. 1979. 17.95 (ISBN 0-241-89892-7, Pub. by Hamish Hamilton England). David & Charles.

Pates for Kings & Commoners. Barbara Wilder & Maybelle Iribe. 1977. 7.95 o.p. (ISBN 0-8015-5781-X, Hawthorn); pap. 3.95 (ISBN 0-8015-5782-8, Hawthorn). Dutton.

Pates, Terrines & Potted Meats. Simone Sekers. 1978. 24.00 (ISBN 0-7134-0679-8, Pub. by Batsford England). David & Charles.

Path Integrals & Their Applications in Quantum Statistical & Solid State Physics. Ed. by G. Papadopoulos & J. T. Devreese. (NATO Advanced Study Institutes Ser.: Series B, Physics, Vol. 34). 508p. 1978. 49.50 (ISBN 0-306-40017-0, Plenum Pr). Plenum Pub.

Path of Action. Jack Schwarz. LC 77-2247. 1977. pap. 4.95 (ISBN 0-525-47466-8). Dutton.

Path of Desire. Ellen Goforth. 192p. (Orig.). 1980. pap. 1.50 (ISBN 0-671-57005-6). S&S.

Path of Economic Growth. A. Lowe. LC 75-38186. (Illus.). 1976. 44.50 (ISBN 0-521-20888-2). Cambridge U Pr.

Path of Initiation. Inayat Khan. (Sufi Message of Hazrat Inayat Khan Ser.: Vol. 10). 1979. 6.95 (ISBN 90-6325-098-3, Pub. by Servire BV Netherlands). Hunter Hse.

Path of Least Resistance. Kenneth E. Hultman. LC 79-11178. 1979. text ed. 15.95 (ISBN 0-89384-046-7). Learning Concepts.

Path of Perfection: Yoga for the Modern Age. A. C. Bhaktivedanta Swami Prabhupada. 1979. 5.95 (ISBN 0-89213-103-9). Bhaktivedanta.

Path of Sorrow (1832), Eonchs of Ruby (1851), Memoralia (1849), Virginalia (1853), Sons of Usna (1858, 5 vols. in 1. Thomas H. Chivers. LC 79-22103. 1979. 58.00x (ISBN 0-8201-1340-9). Schol Facsimiles.

Path of the Eclipse. Chelsea Q. Yarbro. 518p. 1981. 13.95 (ISBN 0-312-59802-5). St Martin.

Path of the Paddle: An Illustrated Guide to the Art of Canoeing. Bill Mason. 192p. 1980. 24.95 (ISBN 0-442-29630-4). Van Nos Reinhold.

Path of the Storm. Douglas Reeman. pap. 1.95 (ISBN 0-515-05373-2). Jove Pubns.

Path of Victory: Discourses on the Paramita. Namgyal Rinpoche. Ed. by Karma S. Gelong. LC 80-84669. (Illus.). 75p. (Orig.). 1980. pap. 5.00 (ISBN 0-9602722-1-6). Open Path.

Path Through the Bible. John H. Piet. 1981. pap. 8.95 (ISBN 0-664-24369-X). Westminster.

Path Through the Woods. B. K. Wilson. (Illus.). (gr. 6-10). 1958. 8.95 (ISBN 0-87599-128-9). S G Phillips.

Path to Biculturalism. Marlene Kramer & Claudia Schmalenberg. LC 77-7202. 1977. pap. text ed. 12.95 (ISBN 0-913654-30-2). Nursing Res.

Path to Illumination. Leonard Huett et al. LC 75-34746. softcover 4.95 o.p. (ISBN 0-912216-14-X). Angel Pr.

Path to Rome. Hilaire Belloc. 1902. text ed. 13.95x (ISBN 0-04-914017-5). Allen Unwin.

Path to Rome. Hillare Belloc. 1981. pap. text ed. 5.95 (ISBN 0-89526-884-1). Regnery-Gateway.

Path to the Peak. Louise Louis. (Illus.). 176p. 1971. pap. 2.50. Pen-Art.

Path to the Silent Country. Lynne R. Banks. 1978. 8.95 o.s.i. (ISBN 0-440-06985-8). Delacorte.

Path-Way to Knowledg, Containing the First Principles of Geometrie. Robert Record. LC 74-80206. (English Experience Ser.: No. 687). 1974. Repr. of 1551 ed. 18.50 (ISBN 90-221-0687-X). Walter J Johnson.

Path-Way to Knowledge: Containing the Whole Art of Arithmeticke. John Tapp. LC 68-54667. (English Experience Ser.: No. 66). 1968. Repr. of 1613 ed. 49.00 (ISBN 90-221-0066-9). Walter J Johnson.

Pathaway of Life & Other Poems. Ronald F. Davis. 1981. 4.75 (ISBN 0-8062-1563-1). Carlton.

Pathe Baby. Blaise Cendrars. (Pocket Poets Ser.: No. 39). 1980. pap. 3.50 o.p. (ISBN 0-87286-108-2). City Lights.

Pather Panchali, 3 vols. Vibhuti Bhushan Bandhopadyaya. Tr. by Monika Varma from Bengali. 1974. Set. 25.00 (ISBN 0-89253-783-3); Set. pap. text ed. 12.00 (ISBN 0-88253-390-8); Vol. 1. 8.00 (ISBN 0-89253-780-9). Vol. 2. 14.00 (ISBN 0-89253-781-7); pap. text ed. 8.00 (ISBN 0-88253-808-X); Vol.3. 8.00 (ISBN 0-89253-782-5); pap. text ed. 4.00 (ISBN 0-88253-809-8). InterCulture.

Pathfinder. James F. Cooper. Ed. by Robert J. Dixson. (American Classics Ser.: Bk. 4). (gr. 9 up). 1973. pap. text ed. 2.75 (ISBN 0-88345-200-6, 18123); cassettes 40.00 (ISBN 0-685-38992-8); tapes 40.00 (ISBN 0-685-38993-6). Regents Pub.

Pathfinder. James F. Cooper. 1976. lib. bdg. 14.95x (ISBN 0-89968-159-X). Lightyear.

Pathfinder Field Guide. rev. ed. Lawrence Maxwell. 1980. 6.95 (ISBN 0-8280-0053-0, 16070-5); pap. 4.95 (ISBN 0-686-62242-1, 16071-3). Review & Herald.

Pathobiology Annual. Ed. by H. L. Ioachim. LC 75-151816. 1978. 41.00 (ISBN 0-89004-277-2). Raven.

Pathobiology Annual, 1979. Ed. by Harry L. Ioachim. LC 75-151816. 1979. text ed. 38.00 (ISBN 0-89004-360-4). Raven.

Pathobiology Annual, 1980. Ed. by Harry L. Ioachim. 336p. 1980. text ed. 32.00 (ISBN 0-89004-437-6). Raven.

Pathobiology of Cell Membranes, 2 vols, Vol. 1. Ed. by Benjamin F. Trump & A. U. Arstila. 1975. 52.75 (ISBN 0-12-701501-9). Acad Pr.

Pathogenesis & Treatment of Urinary Tract Infections. Thomas A. Stamey. (Illus.). 624p. 1980. 54.00 (ISBN 0-683-07909-3). Williams & Wilkins.

Pathogenesis of Invertebrate Microbial Diseases. Ed. by Elizabeth W. Davidson. 500p. 1981. text ed. 40.00 (ISBN 0-86598-014-4). Allanheld.

Pathogenesis of Reflux Nephropathy. C. J. Hodson et al. Ed. by T. M. Maling & P. J. McManamon. 1980. 10.00x (Pub. by Brit Inst Radiology). State Mutual Bk.

Pathogenic Anaerobic Bacteria. 2nd ed. L. Smith. 444p. 1975. 35.75 (ISBN 0-398-03393-5). C C Thomas.

Pathogenic & Non-Pathogenic Amoebae. B. N. Singh. LC 75-15788. 235p. 1975. 54.95 (ISBN 0-470-79305-8). Halsted Pr.

Pathogenic Clostridia. M. Sterne & I. Batty. 1975. 24.95 (ISBN 0-407-35350-X). Butterworths.

Pathogenic Microbiology. George W. Burnett & George S. Schuster. LC 73-16028. 1973. pap. text ed. 12.50 o.p. (ISBN 0-8016-0905-4). Mosby.

Pathogenic Microbiology: The Biology & Prevention of Selected Bacterial, Fungal, Rickettsial, & Viral Diseases of Clinical Importance. Vernon T. Schuhardt. 1978. 23.75x o.p. (ISBN 0-397-47373-7); pap. text ed. 15.25x (ISBN 0-397-47370-2). Lippincott.

Pathogenic Root-Infecting Fungi. S. D. Garrett. LC 72-10024. (Illus.). 1970. 42.50 (ISBN 0-521-07786-9). Cambridge U Pr.

Pathological Basis of Renal Disease. Michael Dunnill. LC 76-26775. (Illus.). 1976. text ed. 40.00 (ISBN 0-7216-3230-0). Saunders.

Pathological Physiology for the Anesthesiologist. Robert H. Smith. (American Lecture Anestesiology Ser). (Illus.). 600p. 1974. pap. 24.75 (ISBN 0-398-03167-3). C C Thomas.

Pathology. 7th ed. W. A. D. Anderson & John M. Kissane. LC 77-1052. (Illus.). 1977. 54.50 (ISBN 0-8016-0186-X). Mosby.

Pathology. C. H. Bloor. (Illus.). 1981. pap. text ed. write for info. (ISBN 0-443-08073-9). Churchill.

Pathology. E. B. Krumbhaar. (Illus.). 1962. Repr. of 1937 ed. pap. 8.75 o.s.i. (ISBN 0-02-848090-2). Hafner.

Pathology. 2nd ed. Ed. by Ronald D. Neumann. LC 79-83716. (Basic Sciences PreTest Self-Assessment & Review Ser.). (Illus.). 1979. 9.95 (ISBN 0-07-050964-6). McGraw-Pretest.

Pathology Annual: Cumulative Index 1966-1979. Ed. by Sheldon C. Sommers & Paul P. Rosen. (Pathology Annual Ser.). 208p. 1980. 13.50x (ISBN 0-8385-7766-0). ACC.

Pathology Annual: 1975, Vol. 10. Sommers. (Illus.). 1975. 25.50 o.p. (ISBN 0-8385-7744-X). ACC.

Pathology Annual: 1976, Vol. 11. Sommers. (Illus.). 1976. 27.50 o.p. (ISBN 0-8385-7745-8). ACC.

Pathology Annual: 1977, Vol. 12, Pt. 2. Sommers. (Illus.). 1977. 32.50 (ISBN 0-8385-7749-0). ACC.

Pathology Annual: 1977, Vol. 12, Pt. 1. Sommers. (Illus.). 1977. 28.50 (ISBN 0-8385-7748-2). ACC.

Pathology Annual 1978, Pt. 2. Ed. by Sheldon C. Sommers & Paul P. Rosen. (Illus.). 1978. 32.50 (ISBN 0-8385-7752-0). ACC.

Pathology Annual: 1979, Vol. 14, Pt. 1. Ed. by Sheldon C. Sommers & Paul P. Rosen. (Illus.). 451p. 1979. 33.50x (ISBN 0-8385-7756-3). ACC.

Pathology Annual 1979, Vol. 15, Pt. 2. Ed. by Sheldon C. Sommers & Paul P. Rosen. (Illus.). 384p. 1979. 35.00x (ISBN 0-8385-7759-8). ACC.

Pathology Annual 1980, Pt. 1. Ed. by Sheldon C. Sommers & Paul P. Rosen. (Pathology Annual Ser.). 482p. 1980. 35.00x (ISBN 0-8385-7761-X). ACC.

Pathology Annual 1980, Pt. 2. Ed. by Sheldon C. Sommers & Paul P. Rosen. (Pathology Annual Ser.). 432p. 1980. 33.50x (ISBN 0-8385-7762-8). ACC.

Pathology Annual,1981: Part 1. Ed. by Sheldon C. Sommers & Paul P. Rosen. (Pathology Annual Series). 1981. 35.00 (ISBN 0-8385-7763-6). ACC.

Pathology Decennials 1966-1975, 7 vols. Ed. by Sommers. Incl. Cardiovascular Pathology Decennial 1966-1975. (Illus.). 22.50 o.p. (ISBN 0-8385-1050-7); Endocrine Pathology Decennial 1966-1975. (Illus.). 26.50 o.p. (ISBN 0-8385-2201-7); Gastrointestinal & Hepatic Pathology Decennial 1966-1975. (Illus.). 24.75 o.p. (ISBN 0-8385-3092-3); Genital & Mammary Pathology Decennial 1966-1975. (Illus.). 24.75 o.p. (ISBN 0-8385-3123-7); Hematologic & Lymphoid Pathology Decennial 1966-1975. (Illus.). 26.50 o.p. (ISBN 0-8385-3683-2); Kidney Pathology Decennial 1966-1975. (Illus.). 27.00 o.p. (ISBN 0-8385-5192-0); Pulmonary Pathology Decennial 1966-1975. (Illus.). 25.50 o.p. (ISBN 0-8385-7952-3). 1975. 137.00 set o.p. (ISBN 0-8385-7746-6). ACC.

Pathology Illustrated. Govan et al. (Illus.). 1981. text ed. 35.00 (ISBN 0-443-01647-X). Churchill.

Pathology Illustrated. Alastair D. Govan et al. (Illus.). 880p. (Orig.). 1981. pap. text ed. 35.00 (ISBN 0-443-01647-X). Churchill.

Pathology in Computed Tomography of the Brain. Scott D. Henderson. (Illus.). 216p. 1978. 22.50 (ISBN 0-398-03749-3). C C Thomas.

Pathology of Atherosclerosis. Neville Woolf. Ed. by T. Crawford. (Postgraduate Pathology Ser.). 1981. price not set (ISBN 0-407-00125-5). Butterworths.

Pathology of Cardiac Valves. M. J. Davies. LC 80-40487. (Butterworths Postgraduate Pathology Ser.). 192p. 1980. text ed. 52.95 (ISBN 0-407-00179-4). Butterworths.

Pathology of Cerebrospinal Microcirculation. Ed. by J. Cervos-Navarro et al. LC 77-84125. (Advances in Neurology Ser.: Vol. 20). 1978. 56.00 (ISBN 0-89004-237-3). Raven.

Pathology of Congenital Heart Disease. Anderson & Becker. 1981. text ed. price not set. Butterworth.

Pathology of Drug Induced & Tonic Diseases. R. M. Riddle. 1981. text ed. write for info. (ISBN 0-443-08083-6). Churchill.

Pathology of Fishes. Ed. by William E. Ribelin & George Migaki. LC 73-15261. 1975. pap. 70.00 (ISBN 0-299-06520-0, 652). U of Wis Pr.

Pathology of Homicide: A Vade Mecum for Pathologist, Prosecutor & Defense Counsel. Lester Adelson. (Illus.). 992p. 1974. text ed. 67.50 (ISBN 0-398-03000-6). C C Thomas.

Pathology of Influenza. Milton C. Winternitz. (Illus.). 1920. 100.00x (ISBN 0-685-69886-6). Elliots Bks.

Pathology of Laboratory Animals. William E. Ribelin & John R. McCoy. (Illus.). 448p. 1971. 22.50 (ISBN 0-398-02203-8). C C Thomas.

Pathology of Malignant Melanoma, Vol. I. Ackerman. (Monographs in Dermatopathology, Vol. 1). 1981. price not set (ISBN 0-89352-132-9). Masson Pub.

Pathology of Parenteral Nutrition with Lipids. Samuel W. Thompson. (Illus.). 952p. 1974. 55.75 (ISBN 0-398-02748-X). C C Thomas.

Pathology of Peripheral Nerves: A Practical Approach. R. O. Weller & J. Cervos Navarro. (Postgraduate Pathology Ser.). 1977. 39.95 (ISBN 0-407-00073-9). Butterworths.

Pathology of Politics: Violence, Betrayal, Corruption, Secrecy & Propaganda. Carl J. Friedrich. Repr. of 1972 ed. text ed. 28.50x (ISBN 0-8290-0343-6). Irvington.

Pathology of Pulmonary Hypertension. C. A. Wagenvoort & Noeke Wagenvoort. LC 76-39782. (Wiley Ser. in Clinical Cardiology). 345p. 1977. text ed. 41.95 (ISBN 0-471-91355-3, Pub. by Wiley Medical). Wiley.

Pathology of Rheumatic Diseases. H. G. Fassbender. Tr. by G. Loewi from Ger. (Illus.). 360p. 1975. 54.20 (ISBN 0-387-07289-6). Springer-Verlag.

Pathology of Sickle Cell Disease. Joseph Song. (Illus.). 472p. 1971. photocopy ed. spiral 47.50 (ISBN 0-398-01812-X). C C Thomas.

Pathology of the Ear. Vincent J. Hyams et al. (Atlases of the Pathology of the Head & Neck). 1976. 80.00 (ISBN 0-89189-095-5, 15-1-017-00); microfiche ed. 22.00 (ISBN 0-686-67784-6, 17-1-017-00). Am Soc Clinical.

Pathology of the Heart & Blood Vessels. 3rd ed. Ed. by S. E. Gould. (Illus.). 1218p. 1968. 59.75 (ISBN 0-398-00708-X). C C Thomas.

Pathology of the Oral Cavity. Patrick D. Toto et al. (Atlases of the Pathology of the Head & Neck). 1976. text & slides 76.50 (ISBN 0-89189-030-0, 15-1-018-00). Am Soc Clinical.

Pathology of the Salivary Glands. John G. Batsakis et al. LC 77-3537. (Head & Neck Atlas Ser.). (Illus.). 1977. slide atlas 95.00 (ISBN 0-89189-031-9, 15-1-0019-00). Am Soc Clinical.

Pathology of the Spleen: A Functional Approach. Pablo Enriquez & Richard S. Neiman. LC 76-43298. (Illus.). 1976. text ed. 26.50 perfect bdg (ISBN 0-89189-029-7, 16-1-016-00); slide atlas 131.50 (ISBN 0-89189-058-0, 15-1-016-00). Am Soc Clinical.

Pathology Review. 7th ed. Ali Majid et al. (Medical Exam Review Ser.). 1980. pap. 8.50 spiral bdg. (ISBN 0-87488-204-4). Med Exam.

Pathology Specialty Board Review. 4th ed. Ed. by Myron E. Tracht & Majid Ali. 1976. spiral bdg. 16.50 (ISBN 0-87488-305-9). Med Exam.

Pathophysiological Aspects of Cyclic Nucleotides, Vol. 12. Ed. by Pavel Hamet & Howard Sands. (Advances in Cyclic Nucleotide Research). 470p. 1980. text ed. 48.50 (ISBN 0-89004-454-6). Raven.

Pathophysiology: An Introduction to Mechanisms of Disease. Bernice L. Muir. LC 79-27791. 1980. 18.95 (ISBN 0-471-03202-6, Pub. by Wiley Med). Wiley.

Pathophysiology & Treatment of Drowning & Near-Drowning. Jerome H. Modell. (Illus.). 136p. 1971. 12.75 (ISBN 0-398-02361-1). C C Thomas.

Pathophysiology of Blood. 2nd ed. Allan J. Ersley & Thomas G. Gabuzda. LC 78-24813. (Illus.). 1979. pap. text ed. 15.00 (ISBN 0-7216-3403-6). Saunders.

Pathophysiology of Congenital Heart Disease. Ed. by Forrest H. Adams et al. LC 69-16626. (UCLA Forum in Medical Sciences: No. 10). (Illus.). 1970. 55.00x (ISBN 0-520-01630-0). U of Cal Pr.

Pathophysiology of Renal Disease. (Contributions to Nephrology Ser.: Vol. 23). (Illus.). vi, 234p. 1980. pap. 58.75 (ISBN 3-8055-0943-X). S Karger.

Pathophysiology of Respiration. M. Kryer. (Wiley Pathophysiology Ser.). 384p. 1981. 17.50 (ISBN 0-471-05923-4, Pub. by Wiley Med). Wiley.

Pathophysiology of Shock, Anoxia & Ischemia. R. Adams Cowley & Benjamin F. Trump. 600p. 1981. write for info. (2149-4). Williams & Wilkins.

Pathophysiology of Spinal Cord Trauma. Jewell L. Osterholm. (Illus.). 232p. 1978. 22.75 (ISBN 0-398-03705-1). C C Thomas.

Pathophysiology of the Kidney. Neil A. Kurtzman & Manuel Martinez-Maldonado. (Illus.). 1104p. 1977. 99.50 (ISBN 0-398-03600-4). C C Thomas.

Pathophysiology PreTest Self-Assessment & Review. Robert E. Howard et al. (Illus.). 200p. (Orig.). 1980. pap. 9.95 (ISBN 0-07-051575-1). McGraw Pretest.

Pathophysiology: The Biological Principles of Disease. Lloyd H. Smith & Samuel O. Thier. (International Textbook of Medical Science: Vol. 1). 1981. text ed. price not set (ISBN 0-7216-8400-9). Saunders.

Pathos of Power. Kenneth B. Clark. LC 73-14250. 224p. 1974. 10.00 o.s.i. (ISBN 0-06-010799-5, HarpT). Har-Row.

Paths of Culture: A General Ethnology. Kaj Birket-Smith. Tr. by Karin Fennow. LC 64-8488. (Illus.). 1970. 15.00 (ISBN 0-299-03381-3); pap. 7.50x (ISBN 0-299-03384-8). U of Wis Pr.

Paths of Faith. 3rd ed. John A. Hutchison. (Illus.). 608p. Date not set. text ed. 18.95 (ISBN 0-07-031532-9, C). McGraw.

Paths of Gold: A Walker's Guide to the Golden Gate National Recreation Area. Margot P. Doss. (Illus.). 176p. 1974. pap. 3.50 o.p. (ISBN 0-87701-053-6). Chronicle Bks.

Paths of Life. Mike Giammatteo & Phil Mattox. (Illus.). 1977. 5.00 (ISBN 0-918428-10-6). Sylvan Inst.

Paths of Loneliness: The Individual Isolated in Modern Society. Margaret M. Wood. LC 53-8218. 1953. pap. 5.00x (ISBN 0-231-08503-6). Columbia U Pr.

Paths of Meditation. Ed. by Staff of Vedanta Kesari. 241p. 1980. pap. write for info. o.s.i. (ISBN 0-87481-501-0). Vedanta Pr.

Paths of Poetry: Twenty-Five Poets & Their Poems. Ed. by Louis Untermeyer. (Illus.). (gr. 7 up). 1966. PLB 4.17 o.s.i. (ISBN 0-440-06825-8). Delacorte.

Paths to Excellence & the Soviet School. John Dunstan. (General Ser.). 1978. pap. text ed. 29.50x (ISBN 0-85633-150-3, NFER). Humanities.

Paths to Peace: The UN Security & Its Prsidency. Ed. by Nicole Davidson & UNITAR. LC 80-20166. (Pergamon Policy Studies on International Politics). 380p. 1981. 42.50 (ISBN 0-08-026322-4). Pergamon.

Paths to Power: A Working Woman's Guide from First Job to Top Executive. Natash Josefowitz. 1980. 11.95 (ISBN 0-201-03485-9); pap. 6.95 (ISBN 0-201-03486-7); instr's manual 2.50 (ISBN 0-201-03479-4). A-W.

Paths to the American Past. J. R. Pole. LC 79-830. 1979. 19.95 (ISBN 0-19-502579-2). Oxford U Pr.

Paths to the Ancient Past. Tom B. Jones. LC 67-12515. 1967. pap. text ed. 6.95 (ISBN 0-02-916630-6). Free Pr.

Paths to World Order. Ed. by Andrew W. Cordier. (Orig.). 1967. pap. 4.00x (ISBN 0-231-08578-8). Columbia U Pr.

Pathway of the Sun. E. V. Timms. 1977. pap. 1.50 o.s.i. (ISBN 0-515-04398-2). Jove Pubns.

Pathway to Ecstasy: The Way of the Dream Mandala. Patricia Garfield. LC 78-16806. (Illus.). 1979. 12.95 o.p. (ISBN 0-03-041996-4). HR&W.

Pathway to Power: A Concise History of the Modern Pentecost. Leslie Davison. 104p. 1972. pap. 2.95 o.p. (ISBN 0-901398-22-5). Logos.

Pathway to Prayer & Pietie. Robert Hill. LC 74-28864. (English Experience Ser.: No. 744). 1975. Repr. of 1613 ed. 26.50 (ISBN 90-221-0744-2). Walter J Johnson.

Pathway to the National Character, 1830-1861. Robert Lemelin. LC 74-80589. 1974. 12.50 (ISBN 0-8046-9087-1, Natl U). Kennikat.

Pathway to the Wild. William Condry. (Illus.). 1975. 13.95 (ISBN 0-571-09934-3, Pub. by Faber & Faber). Merrimack Bk Serv.

Pathways Back to the Community. Ernest A. Kraus. LC 71-100099. 1970. Set. pap. 18.50 (ISBN 0-8261-1093-2); 3.95 (ISBN 0-686-66539-2). Springer Pub.

Pathways from Cancer: A Directory. The G-Jo Institute. 1980. pap. 3.00 (ISBN 0-916878-08-2). Falkynor Bks.

Pathways in International Law, a Personal Narrative. Arthur K. Kuhn. Repr. of 1953 ed. lib. bdg. 15.00x (ISBN 0-8371-2211-2, KUPI). Greenwood.

Pathways in Mathematics. Mildred Keiffer & Harold Smith. Incl. Level One. rev. ed. (gr. 7). 1977. pap. text ed. 6.64 (ISBN 0-913688-31-2); tchr's guide 6.00 (ISBN 0-913688-33-9); Level Two. rev. ed. (gr. 8). 1977 (ISBN 0-913688-32-0). tchr's guide (ISBN 0-913688-34-7). pap. text ed. 6.64x ea.; tchr's guide 6.00x (ISBN 0-685-77480-5). Pawnee Pub.

Pathways in Mathematics: Level II. 3rd ed. Harold Smith & Mildred Keiffer. Ed. by Glyn Sharpe. (Illus.). (gr. 8). 1980. pap. text ed. 6.64x (ISBN 0-913688-37-1); tchr's guide 6.00x (ISBN 0-913688-34-7). Pawnee Pub.

Pathways of Pollutants in the Atmosphere. Royal Society of London, Study Group on Pollution in the Atmosphere, 1977. (Proceedings of the Royal Society). (Illus.). 170p. 1979. 37.00x (ISBN 0-85403-107-3, Pub by Royal Soc London). Scholium Intl.

Pathways of the Pulp. 2nd ed. Stephen Cohen & Richard C. Burns. LC 79-15286. 1979. pap. 42.50 (ISBN 0-8016-1009-5). Mosby.

Pathways of the Pulp. Stephen Cohen & Richard C. Burns. LC 76-15672. (Illus.). 592p. 1976. 36.50 o.p. (ISBN 0-8016-1014-1). Mosby.

Pathways to Parliament: Candidate Selection in Britain. Austin Ranney. 1965. 25.00 (ISBN 0-299-03560-3). U of Wis Pr.

Pathways to Participation. John Hebden & Graham Shaw. LC 77-8207. 1977. 24.95 (ISBN 0-470-99196-8). Halsted Pr.

Pathways to Prophetic Fulfillment. A. A. Ledford. LC 78-53118. 1978. pap. 3.25 (ISBN 0-87148-695-4). Pathway Pr.

Pathways to Spelling, Bks. A-F. (gr. 1-6). Bk. A. text ed. 4.08 (ISBN 0-06-521000-X, SchDept); Bk. B. text ed. 4.40 (ISBN 0-06-521001-8); Bk. C. text ed. 4.40 (ISBN 0-06-521002-6); Bk. D. text ed. 4.40 (ISBN 0-06-521003-4); Bk. E. text ed. 4.40 (ISBN 0-06-521004-2); Bk. F. text ed. 4.80 (ISBN 0-06-521005-0); tchr's ed. bk. a 6.04, (ISBN 0-06-521200-2) tchr's eds. bks. b-f 6.40 ea. (ISBN 0-685-57898-4). Har-Row.

Pathways to Suicide: A Survey of Self-Destructive Behaviors. Ronald W. Maris. LC 80-24520. (Illus.). 512p. 1981. text ed. 26.50x (ISBN 0-8018-2437-0). Johns Hopkins.

Pathways to the Present: The United States Since the Civil War. Robert D. Becker. LC 78-68694. 1979. pap. text ed. 10.25 (ISBN 0-8191-0696-8). U Pr of Amer.

Patience Wright: American Artist & Spy in George III's London. Charles C. Sellers. LC 76-7193. 1976. 17.50x (ISBN 0-8195-5001-9, Pub. by Wesleyan U Pr). Columbia U Pr.

Patient Account Management Techniques. H. F. M. A. Staff. 1976. 8.50 (ISBN 0-930228-01-4, 1443). Hospital Finan.

Patient & Family Education: Tools, Techniques & Theory. Rose M. McCormick & Tamar J. Parkavich. LC 79-10014. 1979. 18.50 (ISBN 0-471-04269-2, Pub by Wiley Medical). Wiley.

Patient As Person: Exploration in Medical Ethics. Paul Ramsey. LC 77-118737. 1970. 20.00x (ISBN 0-300-01357-4); pap. 4.95x (ISBN 0-300-01741-3, Y263). Yale U Pr.

Patient: Biological, Psychological, & Social Dimensions of Medical Practice. Hoyle Leigh & Morton F. Reiser. (Illus.). 370p. 1980. 19.50 (ISBN 0-306-40207-6, Plenum Pr). Plenum Pub.

Patient Care & Rehabilitation of Communication-Impaired Adults. Ralph R Leutenegger. (Illus.). 196p. 1975. 17.50 (ISBN 0-398-03473-7). C C Thomas.

Patient Care & Special Procedures in Radiologic Technology. 4th ed. John C. Watson. LC 74-1115. 360p. 1974. text ed. 17.95 (ISBN 0-8016-5358-4). Mosby.

Patient Care Flow Chart Nineteen Eighty. 573p. 1980. 40.00 (ISBN 0-471-08162-0, Pub. by Wiley Med). Wiley.

Patient Care in Cardiac Surgery. 3rd ed. Douglas M. Behrendt & W. Gerald Austen. (Little, Brown Spiral Manual Series). 1980. pap. write for info. (ISBN 0-316-08756-4). Little.

Patient Care in Radiography. Ruth A. Ehrlich & Ellen D. Givens. (Illus.). 230p. 1981. pap. text ed. 12.95 (ISBN 0-8016-1507-0). Mosby.

Patient Care Standards. 2nd ed. Susan M. Tucker et al. LC 79-24410. (Illus.). 1980. pap. text ed. 17.95 (ISBN 0-8016-5122-0). Mosby.

Patient Care Studies in Medical-Surgical Nursing. Wilma H. Phipps & Rosemary Rich. 1972. pap. 7.50 o.p. (ISBN 0-8016-3930-1). Mosby.

Patient Care Techniques. Dorothy J. Hicks. LC 74-18673. (Allied Health Ser). 1975. pap. 7.05 (ISBN 0-672-61394-8). Bobbs.

Patient Centered Audit. Christine G. Kruse. (Illus.). 180p. (Orig.). 1981. 14.50 (ISBN 0-87527-247-9). Green.

Patient Interviewing: The Human Dimension. David E. Reiser et al. (Illus.). 264p. 1980. softcover 14.95 (ISBN 0-683-07226-9). Williams & Wilkins.

Patient Management Problems: Exercises in Decision Making & Problem Solving. Bruce S. Chertow et al. 336p. 1979. pap. 28.95x (ISBN 0-8385-7769-5). ACC.

Patient Management Problems: Pediatrics. R. Rodney Howell & Frank A. Simon. LC 80-18503. (Illus.). 160p. 1981. pap. text ed. 9.00 (ISBN 0-668-04780-1, 4780). Arco.

Patient Medication Profiles. 1975. 9.00 (ISBN 0-917330-02-1). Am Pharm Assn.

Patient Power. Philip M. Margolis. 176p. 1973. 12.75 (ISBN 0-398-02839-7). C C Thomas.

Patient Records Control. A. Ziegler. (Illus.). 1979. pap. 12.00 (ISBN 0-87489-155-8). Med Economics.

Patient Representative's Participation in Risk Management. Society of Patient Representatives of the American Hospital Association. (Orig.). 1980. pap. 8.75 (ISBN 0-87258-315-5, 1532). Am Hospital.

Patient Studies in Pharmacology: A Guidebook. Mary W. Falconer. LC 75-44608. 160p. 1976. pap. text ed. 7.00 (ISBN 0-7216-3545-8). Saunders.

Patient with End Stage Renal Disease. Larry E. Lancaster. LC 78-23659. 1979. 18.50 (ISBN 0-471-03564-5, Pub. by Wiley Medical). Wiley.

Patient's Advocate. Barbara Huttman. 416p. 1981. pap. 8.95 (ISBN 0-14-046492-1). Penguin.

Patient's Advocate, the Complete Handbook of Patient's Rights' How to Get Them & How to Use Them to Save Your Time, Your Money, & Your Life. Barbara Huttmann. LC 80-52005. 400p. 1981. 16.95 (ISBN 0-670-54273-3). Viking Pr.

Patients & Healers in the Context of Culture: An Exploration of the Borderland Between Anthropology, Medicine, & Psychiatry. Arthur Kleinman. (Comparative Studies of Health Systems & Medical Care). 1979. 27.50x (ISBN 0-520-03706-5). U of Cal Pr.

Patients & Their Doctors: A Study of General Practice. Ann Cartwright. (Reports of the Institute of Community Studies). 1967. 23.50 (ISBN 0-7100-3919-0). Routledge & Kegan.

Patients Are People. 3rd ed. Minna Field. LC 67-31049. xiv, 294p. 1967. 17.50x (ISBN 0-231-03108-4). Columbia U Pr.

Patients' Guide to Doctors: How to Hire & Fire Your Doctor to Save Your Life. Richard F. Romfh. Date not set. 15.95 (ISBN 0-87949-199-X). Ashley Bks.

Patients' Guide to Medicine: From the Drugstore Through the Hospital. 9th ed. Ed. by Warren J. Brown. 1981. pap. 7.95 (ISBN 0-912522-71-2). Aero-Medical.

Patient's Guide to Surgery. Laurence Galton. 1977. pap. 2.50 o.p. (ISBN 0-380-00683-9, 32987). Avon.

Patients or Prisoners: The Mentally Ill in America. LC 75-23466. 160p. (gr. 7 up). 1976. PLB 5.90 o.p. (ISBN 0-531-01108-9). Watts.

Patient's Progress. Ed. by Felix Marti-Ibanez. LC 67-26612. 1967. 5.95 o.p. (ISBN 0-910922-17-9). MD Pubns.

Patients: The Experience of Illness. Mark L. Rosenberg. LC 79-67115. (Illus.). 208p. (Orig.). 1980. 14.95 o.p. (ISBN 0-03-056743-2); pap. 8.95 o.p. (ISBN 0-03-056742-4). HR&W.

Patient's Views of Medical Practice. Eliot Freidson. (Midway Reprint Ser.). 268p. 1980. pap. text ed. 10.00x (ISBN 0-226-26223-5). U of Chicago Pr.

Patio Roofs: How to Build. 3rd ed. Sunset Editors. LC 73-89579. (Illus.). 80p. 1974. pap. 3.95 (ISBN 0-376-01455-5, Sunset Bks.). Sunset-Lane.

Patiofarming: A Compendium of Useful Tables. Franklin W. Martin & Ruth Ruberte. (Studies in Tropical Agriculture). 1980. lib. bdg. 69.95 (ISBN 0-8490-3075-7). Gordon Pr.

Patios & Gardens of Mexico. Patricia W. O'Gorman. (Illus.). Date not set. 22.95 (ISBN 0-8038-0210-2). Hastings.

Patmowtiwn Hayots. Lazar Of Pharbi. Date not set. Repr. of 1904 ed. cancelled. Caravan Bks.

Patmowtiwn Hayots. Moses Of Chorene. Date not set. Repr. of 1913 ed. cancelled (ISBN 0-88206-032-5). Caravan Bks.

Patmowtiwn Hayots. Phaustos Of Byzantium. Date not set. Repr. of 1883 ed. cancelled (ISBN 0-88206-033-3). Caravan Bks.

Patmowtiwn Hayots: History of the Armenians. Lazar Of Pharbi. Ed. by Dickran Kouymjian. 1981. write for info. (ISBN 0-88206-031-7). Caravan Bks.

Patmowtiwn Hayots: History of the Armenians. Moses Of Chorene. Ed. by Robert W. Thomson. 1980. write for info. (ISBN 0-88206-032-5). Caravan Bks.

Patmowtiwn Hayots: History of the Armenians. Phaustos Of Byzantium. Ed. by Nina G. Garsoian. 1981. write for info. (ISBN 0-88206-033-3). Caravan Bks.

Patria: El Periodico De Jose Marti, Registro General, 1892-1895. Carlos Ripoll. 1971. 9.95 (ISBN 0-88303-011-X); pap. 6.95 (ISBN 0-685-73215-0). E Torres & Sons.

Patriarch. Chaim Bermant. 448p. 1981. 14.95 (ISBN 0-312-59804-1). St Martin.

Patriarchs & Politics. Marilyn Warenski. (McGraw-Hill Paperbacks Ser.). 352p. 1980. pap. 6.95 (ISBN 0-07-068271-2). McGraw.

Patriarchs & Prophets. Ellen G. White. 805p. 1958. deluxe ed. 9.50 (ISBN 0-8163-0038-0, 16082-0); pap. 5.95 (ISBN 0-8163-0039-9, 16083-8). Pacific Pr Pub Assn.

Patriarchs of Constantinople Between the Council of Chalcedon & Photius. K. Andreev. LC 80-2353. 1981. Repr. of 1895 ed. 38.50 (ISBN 0-404-18901-6). AMS Pr.

Patriarchs of Outer Space. Joseph H. Friedt. 1978. 5.95 o.p. (ISBN 0-533-03814-6). Vantage.

Patrice. M. E. Mountjoy. 1970. pap. text ed. 2.95x o.p. (ISBN 0-435-37621-7). Heinemann Ed.

Patricia Roberts Knitting Patterns. Patricia Roberts. (Illus.). 18.95x o.p. (ISBN 0-8464-0705-1). Beekman Pubs.

Patrician in Politics: Daniel Dewey Barnard of New York. new ed. Sharon H. Penney. LC 74-77652. 220p. 1974. 15.00 (ISBN 0-8046-9067-7, Natl U). Kennikat.

Patricide in the House Divided: A Psychological Interpretation of Lincoln & His Age. George B. Forgie. 320p. 1981. pap. 5.95 (ISBN 0-393-00035-4). Norton.

Patrick. Quentin Blake. (Illus.). 32p. (gr. 4-7). 1980. 8.95 (ISBN 0-224-61463-0, Pub. by Chatto-Bodley-Jonathan). Merrimack Bk Serv.

Patrick. Keith Hetherington. 1979. pap. 1.95 (ISBN 0-380-48363-7, 48363). Avon.

Patrick Geddes: Spokesman for Man & the Environment. Ed. by Marshall Stalley. LC 75-163963. 1972. 27.50 (ISBN 0-8135-0697-2). Rutgers U Pr.

Patrick Henry. Moses C. Tyler. LC 80-18577. (American Statesmen Ser.). 460p. 1980. pap. 6.95 (ISBN 0-87754-190-6). Chelsea Hse.

Patrick Henry: Practical Revolutionary, Vol. 2. Robert D. Meade. LC 69-16162. 1969. 10.00 o.s.i. (ISBN 0-397-00596-2). Lippincott.

Patrick Kavanagh. John Nemo. (English Authors Ser.: No. 267). 1979. lib. bdg. 14.50 (ISBN 0-8057-6770-3). Twayne.

Patrick White. Manly Johnson. LC 76-15652. (Modern Literature Ser.). Date not set. 10.95 (ISBN 0-686-64253-8). Ungar. Postponed.

Patricks: Hockey's Royal Family. Eric Whitehead. LC 79-6879. (Illus.). 288p. 1980. 11.95 (ISBN 0-385-15662-6). Doubleday.

Patrimonial Foundations of the Brazilian Bureaucratic State. Fernando Uricoechea. 248p. 1980. 18.50x (ISBN 0-520-03853-3). U of Cal Pr.

Patriot or Traitor: The Case of General Mihailovich. David Martin. LC 77-83123. (Archival Documentary Publication Ser: No. 191). (Illus.). 520p. 1978. 19.00 (ISBN 0-8179-6911-X). Hoover Inst Pr.

Patriot's Dream. Barbara Michaels. LC 76-20500. 1976. 8.95 (ISBN 0-396-07337-9). Dodd.

Patriot's Dream. Barbara Michaels. 1977. pap. 1.75 o.p. (ISBN 0-449-23342-1, Crest). Fawcett.

Patristic Greek Lexicon, Fascicle 5. Ed. by G. W. Lampe. 1968. 22.00x (ISBN 0-19-864212-1). Oxford U Pr.

Patristic Greek Lexicon Nineteen Sixty-One to Sixty-Eight. Ed. by G. W. Lampe. 165.00x (ISBN 0-19-864213-X). Oxford U Pr.

Patrol Administration: Management by Objectives. 2nd ed. Donald T. Shanahan. 1978. pap. text ed. 17.95 (ISBN 0-205-06036-6, 8260362). Allyn.

Patrol & Troop Activities. Boy Scouts of America. (gr. 6-12). pap. 3.85x (ISBN 0-8395-6543-7). BSA.

Patrol into Yesterday: My New Guinea Years (1927-1962) J. K. McCarthy. 1967. 9.00 o.p. (ISBN 0-8426-1359-5). Verry.

Patrologiae Cursus Completus. Jacques P. Migne. Incl. Patrologia Latina, 146 vols. Repr. of 1844 ed. pap. write for info.; Patrologia Graeco Latina, 60 vols. Repr. of 1857 ed. pap. write for info.. 1965-71. Adler.

Patronage & Exploitation: Changing Agrarian Relations in South Gujarat, India. Jan Breman. 1974. 23.50x (ISBN 0-520-02197-5). U of Cal Pr.

Patronage, the Crown & the Provinces in Later Medieval England. Ed. by Ralph Griffiths. 224p. 1980. text ed. 20.00x (ISBN 0-391-02096-X). Humanities.

Patrones: Profiles of Hispanic Political Leaders in New Mexico History. Maurilio Vigil. LC 79-6813. 179p. 1980. 17.75 (ISBN 0-8191-0962-2); pap. 8.75 (ISBN 0-8191-0963-0). U Pr of Amer.

Patrons & Musicians of the English Renaissance. D. C. Price. LC 80-40054. (Cambridge Studies in Music). (Illus.). 250p. Date not set. 55.00 (ISBN 0-521-22806-9). Cambridge U Pr.

Patrons & Painters: A Study in the Relations Between Italian Art & Society in the Age of the Baroque. rev. ed. Francis Haskell. LC 79-56891. (Illus.). 1980. 45.00x (ISBN 0-300-02537-8); pap. 14.95 (ISBN 0-300-02540-8). Yale U Pr.

Patrons & Partisans: A Study of Politics in Two Southern Italian Comuni. Caroline White. LC 79-53406. (Cambridge Studies in Social Anthropology: No. 31). (Illus.). 1980. 19.95 (ISBN 0-521-22872-7). Cambridge U Pr.

Pat's Problems. Aleda Renken. (Haley Adventures Ser.). 1981. pap. 2.50 (ISBN 0-570-07236-0, 39-1071). Concordia.

Patten's Foundations of Embryology. 4th, rev. ed. Bruce M. Carlson. (Organismal Biology Ser.). (Illus.). 608p. 1981. text ed. 21.95 (ISBN 0-07-009875-1, C). McGraw.

Pattern. Vincent Buckley. (Orig.). 1979. pap. text ed. 8.00x (ISBN 0-85105-357-2, Dolmen Pr). Humanities.

Pattern & Embroidery. Anne Butler & David Green. LC 71-90357. (Illus.). 1970. 8.25 o.p. (ISBN 0-8231-4024-5). Branford.

Pattern & Process in the Early Intermediate Period Pottery of the Central Coast of Peru. Thomas C. Patterson. (U. C. Publ. in Anthropology: Vol. 3). 1966. pap. 6.50x (ISBN 0-520-09002-0). U of Cal Pr.

Pattern Cutting. Margaret Melliar. 1977. 17.95 (ISBN 0-7134-2897-X, Pub. by Batsford England). David & Charles.

Pattern Cutting & Making up: Vol. 3, The Professional Approach. Martin Shoben & Janet Ward. (Illus.). 192p. 1981. 53.00 (ISBN 0-7134-3561-5, Pub. by Batsford England); pap. 30.00 (ISBN 0-7134-3562-3). David & Charles.

Pattern Cutting & Making up: Volume I, Basic Techniques & Sample Development. Shoben Ward & Janet Ward. 1980. 35.50 (ISBN 0-7134-3338-8, Pub. by Batsford England); pap. 22.50 (ISBN 0-7134-3339-6). David & Charles.

Pattern Cutting & Making up: Volume 2, Cutting & Making Skirts & Sleeves. Marten Saoben & Janet Ward. 192p. 1980. 45.00 (ISBN 0-7134-3559-3, Pub. by Batsford England); pap. 30.00 (ISBN 0-7134-3560-7). David & Charles.

Pattern Deposition Checklists. Douglas Danner. LC 73-84916. 1973. 47.50 (ISBN 0-686-14525-9, 648A). Lawyers Co-Op.

Pattern Design. Christopher Day. 1979. 24.00 (ISBN 0-7134-3299-3, Pub. by Batsford England). David & Charles.

Pattern Design for Needlepoint & Patchwork. Susan Schoenfeld & Winifred Beniner. 200p. 1981. pap. 9.95 (ISBN 0-442-20671-2). Van Nos Reinhold.

Pattern Drills for Introductory Russian. Robert D. Sholiton & Joseph A. Van Campen. 1968. pap. 3.95x (ISBN 0-393-09772-2, NortonC). Norton.

Pattern in Islamic Art. David Wade. LC 75-33464. (Illus.). 144p. 1976. 27.95 (ISBN 0-87951-042-0). Overlook Pr.

Pattern in the Material Folk Culture of the Eastern United States. rev. ed. Henry Glassie. LC 75-160630. (Folklore & Folklife Ser). (Illus.). 1971. 12.50x (ISBN 0-8122-7569-1); pap. 5.95x (ISBN 0-8122-1013-1, Pa Paperbks). U of Pa Pr.

Pattern Interrogatories: 1970-73, 5 vols. Douglas Danner. LC 75-102027. 1970. 236.00 (ISBN 0-686-14526-7). Lawyers Co-Op.

Pattern Making by the Flat Pattern Method. 5th ed. Norma R. Hollen. 1981. 12.95 (ISBN 0-8087-3173-4). Burgess.

Pattern Making Design: Skirts & Pants. Connie Littman. LC 76-14096. (gr. 9-12). 1977. pap. text ed. 4.80 (ISBN 0-8273-0583-4). Delmar.

Pattern Making Design: Sleeved & Tailored Garments. Connie Littman. LC 76-14096. (gr. 9-12). 1977. pap. text ed. 4.80 (ISBN 0-8273-0585-0). Delmar.

Pattern Making Design: Sleeveless Dresses. Connie Littman. LC 76-14096. (gr. 9-12). 1977. pap. text ed. 4.80 (ISBN 0-8273-0584-2). Delmar.

Pattern of a Man & Other Stories. James Still. LC 76-45313. (YA) 1976. pap. 5.00 (ISBN 0-917788-01-X). Gnomon Pr.

Pattern of African Decolonialization-a New Interpretation. Warren Weinstein & John J. Grotpeter. LC 73-83839. (Foreign & Comoarative Studies-Eastern African Ser.: No. 10). 123p. 1973. pap. 4.50x (ISBN 0-915984-07-5). Syracuse U Foreign Comp.

Pattern of Baha'i Life. 3rd ed. Baha'u'llah et al. 1963. pap. 1.00 (ISBN 0-900125-15-2, 7-15-30). Baha'i.

Pattern of English Building. 2nd ed. Alec Clifton-Taylor. 1981. 41.00 (ISBN 0-571-09525-9, Pub. by Faber & Faber); pap. 27.50 (ISBN 0-571-09526-7, Pub. by Faber & Faber). Merrimack Bk Serv.

Pattern of English Building. Alec Clifton-Taylor. 1972. 32.00 o.p. (ISBN 0-571-09525-9, Pub. by Faber & Faber). Merrimack Bk Serv.

Pattern of Freedom. Bruce L. Richmond. 266p. 1980. Repr. of 1911 ed. lib. bdg. 25.00 (ISBN 0-8492-7732-9). R West.

Pattern of Herbs. Meg Rutherford & Ann Warren-Davis. (Illus.). 150p. 1975. 9.50 (ISBN 0-04-635009-8). Allen Unwin.

Pattern of Human Concerns. Hadley Cantril. 1966. 27.50 (ISBN 0-8135-0510-0). Rutgers U Pr.

Pattern of Human Concerns Data, 1957-1963. Hadley Cantril. 1977. codebk. 28.00 (ISBN 0-89138-115-5). ICPSR.

Pattern of Roses. K. M. Peyton. LC 73-3387. (Illus.). 132p. (gr. 6 up). 1973. 8.95 (ISBN 0-690-61199-4, TYC-J). T Y Crowell.

Pattern of Sound in Lucretius. Rosamund E. Deutsch. Ed. by Steele Commager. LC 77-70763. (Latin Poetry Ser.). 1979. Repr. of 1939 ed. lib. bdg. 21.00 (ISBN 0-8240-2967-4). Garland Pub.

Pattern of the Chinese Past: A Social & Economic Interpretation. Mark Elvin. LC 72-78869. (Illus.). 346p. 1973. 15.00x (ISBN 0-8047-0826-6); pap. 5.95 (ISBN 0-8047-0876-2). Stanford U Pr.

Pattern of the Past. I. Hodder et al. LC 79-8497. (Illus.). 424p. Date not set. 49.50 (ISBN 0-521-22763-1). Cambridge U Pr.

Pattern Play Tennis. R. Spencer Brent. LC 72-89295. 144p. 1974. 6.95 o.p. (ISBN 0-385-05874-8). Doubleday.

Pattern Recognition. Ed. by K. S. Perdue. (Communications & Cybernetics: Vol. 10). (Illus.). 270p. 1976. 37.70 o.p. (ISBN 0-387-07511-9). Springer-Verlag.

Pattern Recognition & Signal Processing. Ed. by C. H. Chen. (NATO Advanced Study Institute Ser.). 666p. 1978. 46.00x (ISBN 90-286-0978-4). Sijthoff & Noordhoff.

Pattern Recognition in Chemistry. K. Varmuza. (Lecture Notes in Chemistry Ser.: Vol. 21). (Illus.). 217p. 1981. pap. 21.00 (ISBN 0-387-10273-6). Springer-Verlag.

Pattern Recognition, Learning & Thought: Computer-Programmed Models of Higher Mental Processes. Leonard Uhr. (Illus.). 528p. 1973. ref. ed. 18.95 (ISBN 0-13-654095-3). P-H.

Pattern Recognition Principles: Applied Mathematics & Computation Ser. 2nd ed. J. T. Tou & R. C. Gonzalez. 1975. text ed. 28.50 (ISBN 0-201-07587-3); instr's man. 3.50 (ISBN 0-201-07588-1). A-W.

Pattern Under the Plough. George E. Evans. (Illus.). 1966. 9.95 (ISBN 0-571-06886-3, Pub. by Faber & Faber); pap. 4.95 (ISBN 0-571-08977-1). Merrimack Bk Serv.

Patternless Fashions: How to Design & Make Your Own Fashions. Diehl Lewis & May Loh. (Illus.). 1980. 14.95 (ISBN 0-87491-416-7); pap. 8.95 (ISBN 0-87491-413-2). Acropolis.

Patternmaking & Founding. Robert E. Smith. (gr. 9 up). 1959. pap. 5.00 (ISBN 0-87345-020-5). McKnight.

Patternmaster. Octavia E. Butler. 1978. pap. 1.75 (ISBN 0-380-41806-1, 41806). Avon.

Patternmaster. Octavia E. Butler. LC 76-2759. 1976. 5.95 o.p. (ISBN 0-385-12197-0). Doubleday.

Patterns & Effects of Diet & Disease Today. Ed. by John J. Hefferren & Mary L. Moller. (AAAS Selected Symposium: No. 59). 225p. 1981. lib. bdg. 18.75x (ISBN 0-89158-844-2). Westview.

Patterns & Processes: An Introduction to Anthropological Strategies for the Study of Sociocultural Change. Robert L. Bee. LC 73-10791. 1974. pap. text ed. 6.95 (ISBN 0-02-902090-5). Free Pr.

Patterns & Systems of Elementary Mathematics. Jonathan Knaupp et al. LC 76-13087. (Illus.). 1977. pap. text ed. 17.75 (ISBN 0-395-20638-3); instructors' manual 3.25 (ISBN 0-395-20639-1). HM.

Patterns for Canvas Embroidery. Diana Jones. 1977. 17.95 (ISBN 0-7134-3285-3). David & Charles.

Patterns for Composition. Joseph Collignon. 312p. (Orig.). 1969. text ed. 6.95x (ISBN 0-02-474020-9, 47402). Macmillan.

Patterns for Distribution of Patient Education. Ed. by Barbara K. Redman. (Patient Education Series). 176p. 1981. pap. 11.50 (ISBN 0-8385-7776-8). ACC.

Patterns for Guernseys, Jerseys & Arans: Fishermans' Sweaters from the British Isles. Gladys Thompson. (Illus.). 1971. pap. 4.50 (ISBN 0-486-22703-0). Dover.

Patterns for Patchwork Quilts & Cushions. Suzy Ives. (Illus.). 63p. 1977. pap. 6.50 (ISBN 0-8231-5050-X). Branford.

Patterns for Power. D. Stuart Briscoe. LC 78-68850. (Bible Commentary for Laymen Ser.). 1979. pap. 2.50 (ISBN 0-8307-0701-8, S331101). Regal.

Patterns for Practical Communications: Composition Package. D. Weddington. 1977. text ed. 180.00 (ISBN 0-13-653881-9); tchrs manual 10.00 (ISBN 0-13-653865-7). P-H.

Patterns for Practical Communications: Combined Sentence & Composition Packages. Doris C. Weddington. 1976. 40 wkbks.,20 cassettes,2 scripts,2 tchrs' manuals 350.00 (ISBN 0-13-653899-1). P-H.

Patterns for Practical Communications: Sentence Package. D. Weddington. 1977. text ed. 180.00 (ISBN 0-13-653790-1); script sentences 13.00 (ISBN 0-13-653816-9). P-H.

Patterns for Uncertainty? Planning for the Greater Medical Profession. Ed. by Gordon McLachlan et al. 1979. pap. 14.95 (ISBN 0-19-721223-9). Oxford U Pr.

Patterns in Biology. David Harrison. LC 75-16300. 250p. 1975. text ed. 18.95 (ISBN 0-470-35555-7). Halsted Pr.

Patterns in Crystals. Noel F. Kennon. LC 78-4531. 1978. text ed. 31.95 (ISBN 0-471-99748-X); pap. text ed. 15.00 (ISBN 0-471-99652-1, Pub. by Wiley-Interscience). Wiley.

Patterns in History. D. W. Bebbington. LC 79-3062. 1980. pap. 7.25 (ISBN 0-87784-737-1). Inter-Varsity.

Patterns in Household Demand & Saving. Constantino Lluch et al. (World Bank Research Publications Ser.). (Illus.). 1977. 14.95x (ISBN 0-19-920097-1); pap. 7.95x (ISBN 0-19-920100-5). Oxford U Pr.

Patterns in Human Geography. David Smith. LC 75-21520. 1976. 19.50x (ISBN 0-8448-0764-8). Crane-Russak Co.

Patterns in Medical Parasitology. 2nd ed. Haig H. Majarian. 160p. 1980. Repr. of 1975 ed. lib. bdg. write for info. (U Pr of Pacific). Intl Schol Bk Serv.

Patterns in Oral Literature. Ed. by Heda Jason & Dimitri Segal. (World Anthropology Ser.). 1977. text ed. 33.00x (ISBN 90-279-7969-3). Mouton.

Patterns in Physics. W. Bolton. 1974. 12.95 o.p. (ISBN 0-07-094396-6). McGraw.

Patterns in Plant Development. Taylor A. Steeves & Ian M. Sussex. (Foundations of Developmental Biology Ser). (Illus.). 1972. ref. ed. 15.95x (ISBN 0-13-653998-X). P-H.

Patterns in Popular Culture: A Sourcebook for Writers. Harold Schechter & Jonna G. Semeiks. (Illus.). 1980. pap. text ed. 10.95 scp (ISBN 0-06-045761-9, HarpC); instructor's manual free. Har-Row.

Patterns in Space. Richard Slade. 1969. 8.50 (ISBN 0-571-08327-7, Pub. by Faber & Faber). Merrimack Bk Serv.

Patterns in the Sand: An Exploration in Mathematics. Maurice Bosstick & John L. Cable. 1971. text ed. 10.95x o.p. (ISBN 0-02-473720-8); ans. bklt free o.p. (ISBN 0-685-03675-8). Glencoe.

Patterns in the Sand: An Exploration in Mathematics. 2nd ed. Maurice Bosstick & John L. Cable. (Illus.). 1975. text ed. 13.95x (ISBN 0-02-471960-9); ans. bk free (ISBN 0-02-471970-6). Macmillan.

Patterns of Adaptation & Variation in the Great Basin Kangaroo Rat. Blair Csuti. LC 78-54792. (Publications in Zoology Ser.: Vol. III). 1979. 8.00x o.p. (ISBN 0-520-09597-9). U of Cal Pr.

Patterns of Administrative Development in Independent India. E. N. Mangat Rai. (Commonwealth Papers Ser.: No. 19). 182p. 1976. pap. text ed. 22.25x (ISBN 0-485-17619-X, Athlone). Humanities.

Patterns of American Government. 2nd ed. Harvey M. Karlen. 1975. pap. text ed. 7.95x (ISBN 0-02-475320-3, 47532); tchrs' manual free (ISBN 0-02-475330-0). Macmillan.

Patterns of Anti-Democratic Thought: An Analysis & Criticism, with Special Reference to the American Political Mind in Recent Times. David Spitz. LC 80-22640. 347p. 1981. Repr. of 1965 ed. lib. bdg. 27.50x (ISBN 0-313-22392-0, SPPD). Greenwood.

Patterns of Attachment: A Psychological Study of the Strange Situation. Mary D. Ainsworth et al. LC 78-13303. 1979. 24.95 (ISBN 0-470-26534-5). Halsted Pr.

Patterns of Authority: A Structural Basis for Political Inquiry. Harry Eckstein & Ted R. Gurr. LC 75-19003. (Comparative Studies in Behavioral Science Ser). 488p. 1975. 28.95 (ISBN 0-471-23076-6, Pub. by Wiley-Interscience). Wiley.

Patterns of Business Organization. J. O'Shaughnessy. LC 76-26116. 1976. 21.95 (ISBN 0-470-98927-0). Halsted Pr.

Patterns of Care for the Mentally Subnormal. M. Craft & L. Miles. 1967. 22.00 (ISBN 0-08-012265-5); pap. 10.75 (ISBN 0-08-012264-7). Pergamon.

Patterns of Change in the Nepal Himalaya. Mark Poffenberger. 111p. 1981. lib. bdg. 15.50x (ISBN 0-86531-184-6). Westview.

Patterns of Civilizations. James H. Lawler. LC 77-18670. 1978. pap. text ed. 6.75x (ISBN 0-8191-0431-0). U Pr of Amer.

Patterns of Control in Post-Industrial Society: Magnificent Myth. A. Wiener. 1978. text ed. 45.00 (ISBN 0-08-021474-6); pap. text ed. 15.00 (ISBN 0-08-023100-4). Pergamon.

Patterns of Creativity Mirrored in Creation Myths. Marie-Louise Von Franz. Ed. by James Hillman. (Seminar Ser). 1972. pap. text ed. 11.50 (ISBN 0-88214-106-6). Spring Pubns.

Patterns of Decision Making in State Legislatures. Eric M. Uslaner & Ronald E. Weber. LC 76-12884. (Special Studies). 1977. text ed. 23.95 (ISBN 0-275-23230-1). Praeger.

Patterns of Derivational Affixation in the Cabraniego Dialect of East-Central Asturian. Yakov Malkiel. (U. C. Publ. in Linguistics: Vol. 64). 1970. pap. 6.50x (ISBN 0-520-09261-9). U of Cal Pr.

Patterns of Diplomatic Thinking: A Cross National Study of Structural & Social-Psychological Determinants. Luc Reychler. LC 78-19774. (Praeger Special Studies). 1979. 24.95 (ISBN 0-03-046636-9). Praeger.

Patterns of Discovery: An Enquiry into the Conceptual Foundations of Science. Norwood R. Hanson. 1958-1965. 35.50 (ISBN 0-521-05197-5); pap. 9.95x (ISBN 0-521-09261-2, 261). Cambridge U Pr.

Patterns of Discovery in the Social Sciences. Paul R. Diesing. LC 72-106978. 1971. 20.50x (ISBN 0-202-30101-X). Aldine Pub.

Patterns of Education in the British Isles. Robert Bell & Nigel Grant. (Unwin Education Books). 1977. text ed. 21.00x (ISBN 0-04-370082-9); pap. text ed. 9.95x (ISBN 0-04-370083-7). Allen Unwin.

Patterns of Equality: New Structures in European Higher Education. Guy Neave. (General Ser.). 1976. pap. text ed. 16.50x (ISBN 0-85633-114-7, NFER). Humanities.

Patterns of European Urbanisation Since 1500. Ed. by Henk Schmal. 400p. 1981. 31.00x (ISBN 0-7099-0365-0, Pub. by Croom Helm LTD England). Biblio Dist.

Patterns of Fashion: 1660-1860, Vol. 1. 3rd rev. ed. Janet Arnold. LC 76-189820. (Illus.). 1977. text ed. 12.50x (ISBN 0-89676-026-X). Drama Bk.

Patterns of Fashion: 1860-1940, Vol. 2. 3rd rev. ed. Janet Arnold. LC 76-189820. (Illus.). 1977. text ed. 12.50x (ISBN 0-89676-027-8). Drama Bk.

Patterns of Fear in the Gothic Novel: 790-1830. Ann B. Tracy. Ed. by Devendra P. Varma. LC 79-8487. (Gothic Studies & Dissertations Ser.). 1980. lib. bdg. 35.00x (ISBN 0-405-12682-4). Arno.

Patterns of Government Revenue & Expenditure in Developing Countries & Their Relevance to Policy. Panayiotis C. Afxentiou. LC 80-119979. (Center for Planning & Economic Research Ser.: No. 35). 70p. (Orig.). 1979. pap. 7.50x (ISBN 0-8002-2319-5). Intl Pubns Serv.

Patterns of Government: The Major Political Systems of Europe. 3rd ed. Samuel Beer et al. 1972. 16.95 (ISBN 0-394-31387-9). Random.

Patterns of Indian Thought. John B. Chethimattam. LC 77-164418. 1971. 4.95x o.p. (ISBN 0-88344-375-9). Orbis Bks.

Patterns of Industrial Bureaucracy: A Case Study of Modern Factory Administration. Alvin W. Gouldner. 1954. 12.95 (ISBN 0-02-912730-0); pap. text ed. 6.95 (ISBN 0-02-912740-8). Free Pr.

Patterns of Japanese Policy-Making: Experiences from Higher Education. T. J. Pempel. 1978. lib. bdg. 21.50 o.p. (ISBN 0-89158-270-3). Westview.

Patterns of Mammalian Reproduction. 2nd ed. S. A. Asdell. (Illus.). 1964. 35.00x (ISBN 0-8014-0021-X). Comstock.

Patterns of Management in Local Government. Royston Greenwood et al. (Government & Administration Ser.). 192p. 1981. 27.50x (ISBN 0-85520-244-0, Pub. by Martin Robertson England). Biblio Dist.

Patterns of Market Behavior: Essays in Honor of Philip Taft. Ed. by Michael J. Brennan. LC 65-12932. 258p. 1965. 10.00x (ISBN 0-87057-087-0, Pub. by Brown U Pr). Univ Pr of New England.

Patterns of Meaning. Wilbert J. Levy & Carol R. Farber. 1977. pap. text ed. 6.92 (ISBN 0-87720-956-1). AMSCO Sch.

Patterns of Mobility. Sidney Goldstein. LC 57-7221. 1958. 9.00x o.p. (ISBN 0-8122-7092-4). U of Pa Pr.

Patterns of Organization in the Central Nervous System. Association for Research in Nervous Mental Disease. 1968. 30.25 (ISBN 0-02-846370-6). Hafner.

Patterns of Paradise. Anne Leonard & John Terrell. Ed. by Tanisse Bushman. (Illus.). 76p. 1980. pap. 9.95 (ISBN 0-914868-05-5). Field Mus.

Patterns of Problem Solving. Mashe F. Rubinstein. LC 74-20721. (Illus.). 640p. 1975. text ed. 22.95 ref. ed. (ISBN 0-13-654251-4). P-H.

Patterns of Pulmonary Interstitial Disease. H. Johnson. (Illus.). 320p. 1981. 15.00 (ISBN 0-87527-218-5). Green. Postponed.

Patterns of Race in the Americas. Marvin Harris. 144p. 1974. pap. 4.95 (ISBN 0-393-00727-8, Norton Lib). Norton.

Patterns of Reproduction of Four Species of Vespertiliohia Bats in Paraguay. Philip Myers. (Publ. in Zoology Ser: Vol. 107). 1977. pap. 9.75x (ISBN 0-520-09554-5). U of Cal Pr.

Patterns of Reproductive Behavior. Demond Morris. (Illus.). 528p. 1980. 12.95 (ISBN 0-224-61795-8, Pub. by Chatto Bodley Jonathan). Merrimack Bk Serv.

Patterns of Residential Care: Sociological Studies in Institutions for Handicapped Children. Roy D. King et al. (International Library of Sociology). 1978. Repr. of 1971 ed. 23.50 (ISBN 0-7100-7038-1). Routledge & Kegan.

Patterns of Skin ph from Birth Through Adolescene: With a Synopsis on Skin Growth. Hans Behrendt & Marvin Green. (Illus.). 116p. 1971. 14.75 (ISBN 0-398-00125-1). C C Thomas.

Patterns of Urban & Rural Population Growth. (Population Studies: No. 68). 1980. 13.00 (E.79.XIII9). UN.

Patterns of Urban & Rural Population Growth. (Population Studies: No.68). 175p. 1979. pap. 13.00 (UN79-13-9, UN). Unipub.

Patterns of Urban Life. R. E. Pahl. (Aspects of Modern Sociology Ser). 1970. pap. text ed. 5.25x (ISBN 0-582-48803-6). Humanities.

Patterns of Verbal Communication in Mathematics Classes. James T. Fey. Ed. by Arno A. Bellack. LC 74-103135. (Illus.). 1970. text ed. 7.50x (ISBN 0-8077-1342-2). Tchrs Coll.

Patterson's American Education, Vol. 76. Ed. by Norman F. Elliott. 1979. 37.50x o.s.i. (ISBN 0-910536-25-2). Ed Direct.

Patterson's American Education, Vol. 77. Ed. by Norman F. Elliott & Mary E. Kustra. 1980. 40.00x (ISBN 0-910536-27-9). Ed Direct.

Pattersons & the Goat Men. Brenda K. Graham. (gr. 5-9). 1981. 5.95 (ISBN 0-8054-4803-9). Broadman.

Pattersons & the Mysterious Airplane. Brenda K. Graham. LC 79-6022. (gr. 5-9). 1980. 5.95 (ISBN 0-8054-4802-0). Broadman.

Patton: A Study in Command. H. Essame. LC 73-15498. 1976. 12.95 (ISBN 0-684-13671-6, ScribT); pap. 3.95 (ISBN 0-684-14692-4, SL660, ScribT). Scribner.

Patton on Armor. George S. Patton, Jr. Ed. by Charles M. Province. (Patton Ser.: Vol. 8). 60p. 1980. pap. 2.00 (ISBN 0-932348-12-2). Province Pub.

Patton's Best: An Informal History of the Fourth Armored Division. Nat Frankel & Laurence J. Smith. LC 77-79918. (Illus.). 1978. 9.95 o.p. (ISBN 0-8015-5797-6). Dutton.

Patton's Principles. Porter B. Williamson. LC 77-70779. (Illus.). 1979. 9.95 (ISBN 0-918356-04-0); pap. 5.95 (ISBN 0-918356-03-2). MSC Inc.

Patton's Third Army at War. George Forty. (Illus.). 1979. 17.50 (ISBN 0-684-16076-5, ScribT). Scribner.

Patty! Patricia Berg. James Hahn & Lynn Hahn. Ed. by Howard Schroeder. (Sports Legends Ser.). (Illus.). 48p. (Orig.). (gr. 3-5). PLB 5.95 (ISBN 0-89686-127-9); pap. text ed. 2.95 (ISBN 0-89686-142-2). Crestwood Hse.

Patty's Industrial Hygiene & Toxicology: General Principles, Vol. 1. 3rd rev. ed. George D. Clayton & Florence E. Clayton. LC 77-17515. 1978. 99.50 (ISBN 0-471-16046-6, Pub. by Wiley-Interscience). Wiley.

Pattys Industrial Hygiene & Toxicology, 4 vols. 3rd ed. G. D. Clayton & F. E. Clayton. 1981. 305.00 (ISBN 0-471-08431-X). Wiley.

Patty's Industrial Hygiene & Toxicology: Toxicology, Vol. IIA. 3rd rev. ed. George D. Clayton & Florence Clayton. LC 77-17515. 1675p. 1980. 100.00 (ISBN 0-471-16042-3, Pub. by Wiley Interscience). Wiley.

Paul. Gunther Bornkamm. Tr. by D. M. Stalker from Ger. LC 70-85068. 1971. 12.95x (ISBN 0-06-060933-8, HarpR). Har-Row.

Paul Among Jews & Gentiles & Other Essays. Krister Stendahl. LC 75-36450. 144p. 1976. pap. 3.75 (ISBN 0-8006-1224-8, 1-1224). Fortress.

Paul: An Example for Christian Teachers. Richard Grunze. 1979. pap. text ed. 2.50 (ISBN 0-8100-0108-X). Northwest Pub.

Paul & Arthur & the Little Explorer. Anne Rockwell. LC 72-463. (Illus.). 64p. (gr. k-3). 1972. 5.95 o.s.i. (ISBN 0-8193-0592-8, Four Winds); PLB 5.41 o.s.i. (ISBN 0-8193-0593-6). Schol Bk Serv.

Paul & Juhl's Essentials of Roentgen Interpretation. 4th ed. John H. Juhl. (Illus.). 1184p. 1981. text ed. price not set (ISBN 0-06-142143-X, Harper Medical). Har-Row.

Paul & Philippians. James P. Berkeley. (Orig.). 1969. pap. 1.50 o.p. (ISBN 0-8170-0434-3). Judson.

Paul & Power: The Structure of Authority in the Primitive Church Reflected in the Pauline Epistles. Bengt Holmberg. LC 79-8905. 240p. 1980. 14.95 (ISBN 0-8006-0634-5, 1-634). Fortress.

Paul & Rabbinic Judaism: Some Rabbinic Elements in Pauline Theology. W. D. Davies. LC 80-8049. 448p. 1980. pap. 13.95 (ISBN 0-8006-1438-0, 1-1438). Fortress.

Paul & the Anatomy of Apostolic Authority. J. H. Schutz. LC 74-76573. (Society for New Testament Studies, Monographs: No. 26). 1975. 47.50 (ISBN 0-521-20464-X). Cambridge U Pr.

Paul & the Intellectuals. A. T. Robertson. LC 59-5859. pap. 2.50 (ISBN 0-8054-1344-8). Broadman.

Paul & the Salvation of Mankind. Johannes Munck. LC 60-5412. 1977. pap. 6.95 (ISBN 0-8042-0373-3). John Knox.

Paul: Apostle of the Heart Set Free. F. F. Bruce. LC 77-26127. 1978. 15.95 (ISBN 0-8028-3501-5). Eerdmans.

Paul Bourget. Armand Singer. LC 76-2548. (World Authors Ser.: No. 393: France). 1976. lib. bdg. 10.95 (ISBN 0-8057-6235-3). Twayne.

Paul Broca, Eighteen Twenty-Four to Eighteen Eighty: Founder of French Anthropoogy, Explorer of the Brain. Francis Schiller. 1979. 27.50x (ISBN 0-520-03744-8). U of Cal Pr.

Paul Bunyan. James Stevens. 1975. pap. 1.75 o.p. (ISBN 0-345-24423-0). Ballantine.

Paul Bunyan Swings His Axe. Dell McCormick. (gr. 4-6). 1972. pap. 1.25 (ISBN 0-590-01327-0, Schol Pap). Schol Bk Serv.

Paul Celan. Jerry Glenn. (World Authors Ser.: Germany: No. 262). 1973. lib. bdg. 10.95 (ISBN 0-8057-2205-X). Twayne.

Paul Celan: Poems. Tr. by Michael Hamburger & Michael Hamburger. LC 79-9117. 286p. 1980. 20.00 (ISBN 0-89255-043-0). Persea Bks.

Paul Celan: Poems. 156p. (Orig.). 1980. pap. 7.95 (ISBN 0-85635-292-6, Pub. by Carcanet New Pr England). Persea Bks.

Paul: Crisis in Galatia. G. Howard. LC 77-82498. (Society for New Testament Studies Monographs: No. 35). 1979. 17.95 (ISBN 0-521-21709-1). Cambridge U Pr.

Paul Davis: Posters & Paintings. Paul Davis. 1977. pap. 7.95 o.p. (ISBN 0-525-47484-6). Dutton.

Paul De Lamerie, Citizen & Goldsmith of London 1688-1751. Philip A. Phillips. 75.00x (ISBN 0-87556-510-7). Saifer.

Paul Delaroche: A Study in 19th Century French History Painting. Norman D. Ziff. LC 76-23663. (Outstanding Dissertations in the Fine Arts - 19th Century). (Illus.). 1977. Repr. of 1974 ed. lib. bdg. 56.00 (ISBN 0-8240-2741-8). Garland Pub.

Paul Eluard. Robert Nugent. LC 74-4132. (World Authors Ser.: France: No. 322). 152p. 1974. lib. bdg. 10.95 (ISBN 0-8057-2299-8). Twayne.

Paul Elvstrom Explains the Yacht Racing Rules. rev. ed. Paul Elvstrom. 1981. 7.95 (ISBN 0-8286-0088-0). De Graff.

Paul-Emile Borduas. Francois-Marc Gagnon. (Canadian Artists Ser.). (Illus.). 1980. pap. 3.95 (ISBN 0-88884-386-0, 56470-3, Pub. by Natl Gallery Canada). U of Chicago Pr.

Paul et Remi. R. J. Cazziol. (Illus.). 40p. (Fr.). 1974. pap. text ed. 2.25x (ISBN 0-521-20433-X). Cambridge U Pr.

Paul et Virginie. Jacques H. Bernardin De Saint-Pierre. (Documentation thematique). (Illus., Fr.). pap. 2.95 (ISBN 0-685-14023-7, 29). Larousse.

Paul Faber, Surgeon. George MacDonald. Ed. by Robert L. Wolff. LC 75-1513. (Victorian Fiction Ser.). 1975. Repr. of 1879 ed. lib. bdg. 66.00 (ISBN 0-8240-1586-X). Garland Pub.

Paul Gauguin: The Paintings of the First Voyage to Tahiti. Richard S. Field. LC 76-23617. (Outstanding Dissertations in the Fine Arts Ser.). 1977. lib. bdg. 63.00 (ISBN 0-8240-2688-8). Garland Pub.

Paul, God's Special Missionary. Bessie Dean. (Story Books to Color.). 72p. (Orig.). (gr. k-5). 1980. pap. 3.95 (ISBN 0-88290-152-4). Horizon Utah.

Paul Hamilton Hayne. Rayburn S. Moore. (U. S. Authors Ser.: No. 202). lib. bdg. 10.95 (ISBN 0-8057-0352-7). Twayne.

Paul Harvey's the Rest of the Story. Paul Aurandt. LC 77-75381. 1977. 8.95 (ISBN 0-385-12768-5). Doubleday.

Paul Hogarth's Walking Tour of Old Boston. Paul Hogarth. (Illus.). 1978. pap. 7.95 (ISBN 0-87690-295-6). Dutton.

Paul Hogarth's Walking Tours of Old Washington. Paul Hogarth. 1979. 14.95 o.p. (ISBN 0-87690-347-2); pap. 7.95 o.p. (ISBN 0-87690-326-X). Dutton.

Paul Kane's Frontier. J. Russell Harper. LC 79-146522. (Illus.). 1971. 35.00 o.p. (ISBN 0-292-70110-1). Amon Carter.

Paul Klee. Paul Klee. Ed. by Will Grohmann. (Library of Great Painters Ser). 1967. 35.00 (ISBN 0-8109-0228-1). Abrams.

Paul Klee & Primitive Art. James S. Pierce. LC 75-23807. (Outstanding Dissertations in the Fine Arts - 20th Century). 1976. lib. bdg. 31.00 (ISBN 0-8240-2001-4). Garland Pub.

Paul Klee on Modern Art. Paul Klee. 1966. pap. 5.95 (ISBN 0-571-06682-8, Pub. by Faber & Faber). Merrimack Bk Serv.

Paul Laurence Dunbar. Peter Revell. (United States Authors Ser.: No. 298). 1979. lib. bdg. 12.50 (ISBN 0-8057-7213-8). Twayne.

Paul Laurence Dunbar: A Bibliography. E. W. Metcalf, Jr. LC 75-14466. (Author Bibliographies Ser.: No. 23). 202p. 1975. 10.00 (ISBN 0-8108-0849-8). Scarecrow.

Paul Little's Why & What Book. Paul E. Little. 240p. 1980. text ed. 8.95 (ISBN 0-88207-814-3). Victor Bks.

Paul McCartney: In His Own Words. Paul Gambaccini. LC 76-8068. 1976. pap. 5.95 (ISBN 0-8256-3910-7, Quick Fox). Music Sales.

Paul Meets Jesus. Jenny Robertson. (Ladybird Bible Ser.). (Illus.). 32p. (ps-4). 1980. Repr. 1.95 (ISBN 0-310-42880-7). Zondervan.

Paul Nash. Andrew Causey. (Illus.). 532p. 1980. 98.00x (ISBN 0-19-817348-2). Oxford U Pr.

Paul Newman. David Paige. (Stars of Stage & Screen Ser.). (Illus.). (gr. 4-12). 1977. PLB 5.95 (ISBN 0-87191-553-7). Creative Ed.

Paul of Venice: Logica Magna, Pt. 1, Fascicule 7. Ed. by Patricia Clarke. (Classical & Medieval Logic Texts Ser.). 232p. 1981. 149.00 (ISBN 0-19-726003-9). Oxford U Pr.

Paul of Yugoslavia. Neil Balfour & Sally Mackay. (Illus.). 364p. 1980. 45.00 (ISBN 0-241-10392-4, Pub. by Hamish Hamilton England). David & Charles.

Paul Reps: Letters to a Friend (Writings & Drawings), 1939 to 1980. Paul Reps. (Illus.). 186p. 1981. 60.00 (ISBN 0-938286-01-3); ltd. ed. 175.00 (ISBN 0-938286-00-5). Stillgate.

Paul Revere. Matthew G. Grant. LC 73-18076. 1974. PLB 5.95 (ISBN 0-87191-303-8). Creative Ed.

Paul Revere. Irwin Shapiro. (Illus.). (gr. 1-3). 1957. PLB 5.00 (ISBN 0-307-60064-5, Golden Pr). Western Pub.

Paul Revere & the Minutemen. Carole Charles. LC 75-33204. (Stories of the Revolution Ser.). (Illus.). (gr. 2-6). 1975. PLB 5.50 (ISBN 0-913778-19-2). Childs World.

Paul Revere's Boston: Seventeen Thirty-Five to Eighteen Eighteen. Department of American Decorative Arts & Sculpture, Museum of Fine Arts, Boston. (Illus.). 1975. 16.00 (ISBN 0-87846-088-8). Mus Fine Arts Boston.

Paul Revere's Boston 1735-1818. Intro. by Walter M. Whitehill. LC 74-21766. (Illus.). 300p. 1975. 29.50 (ISBN 0-87846-088-8, 694622). NYGS.

Paul Robeson. Eloise Greenfield. LC 74-13663. (Biography Ser.). (Illus.). (gr. 1-5). 1975. PLB 7.89 (ISBN 0-690-00660-8, TYC-J). T Y Crowell.

Paul Robeson: All American. Dorothy B. Gilliam. LC 76-23233. (Illus.). 1976. 8.95 o.p. (ISBN 0-915220-15-6); pap. 3.95 o.s.i. o.p. (ISBN 0-915220-39-3). New Republic.

Paul Robeson Rediscovered. Lloyd L. Brown. 1976. 1.00 (ISBN 0-89977-028-2). Am Inst Marxist.

Paul Robeson: The Great Forerunner. Ed. by Freedomways Editors. LC 78-7917. (Illus.). 1978. 12.95 (ISBN 0-396-07545-2). Dodd.

Paul the Apostle: The Triumph of God in Life & Thought. J. Christiaan Beker. LC 79-8904. 468p. 1980. 22.95 (ISBN 0-8006-0633-7, 1-633). Fortress.

Paul the Traveler. Jenny Robertson. (Ladybird Bible Ser.). (Illus.). 32p. (ps-4). 1980. Repr. 1.95 (ISBN 0-310-42890-4). Zondervan.

Paul Thek - Processions. Suzanne Delehanty. LC 77-92423. 1977. pap. 8.00 (ISBN 0-88454-023-5). U of Pa Contemp Art.

Paul Tillich. J. Heywood Thomas. Ed. by D. E. Nineham & E. H. Robertson. LC 66-11072. (Makers of Contemporary Theology Ser). 1966. pap. 3.45 (ISBN 0-8042-0678-3). John Knox.

Paul Tillich: An Essay on the Role of Ontology in His Philosophical Theology. Allstair MacLeod. (Contemporary Religious Thinkers Ser.). 1973. text ed. 17.95x o.p. (ISBN 0-04-111005-6); pap. text ed. 7.50x o.p. (ISBN 0-04-111006-4). Allen Unwin.

Paul Valery. Charles G. Whiting. (Athlone French Poets Ser.). 1978. text ed. 22.50x (ISBN 0-485-14609-6, Athlone Pr); pap. text ed. 10.75x (ISBN 0-485-12209-X). Humanities.

Paul Valery: Conciousness & Nature. Christine Crow. LC 71-160088. 300p. 1972. 47.50 (ISBN 0-521-08257-9). Cambridge U Pr.

Paul Verlaine. A. E. Carter. (World Authors Ser.: France: No. 158). lib. bdg. 10.95 (ISBN 0-8057-2944-5). Twayne.

Paulevala: Land of Hurrahs. Frederick A. Callarman. 88p. (Orig.). 1981. pap. 1.98 (ISBN 0-930092-01-5). Callarman Hse.

Pauli Lectures on Physics. Wolfgang Pauli. Ed. by C. P. Enz. Tr. by S. Marguilies & H. R. Lewis. Incl. Vol. 1. Electrodynamics. LC 76-155320 (ISBN 0-262-66033-4); Vol. 2. Optics & the Theory of Electronics. LC 72-7802 (ISBN 0-262-66034-2); Vol. 3. Thermodynamics & the Kinetic Theory of Gases. LC 72-7803 (ISBN 0-262-66035-0); Vol. 4. Statistical Mechanics. LC 72-7804 (ISBN 0-262-66036-9); Vol. 5. Wave Mechanics. LC 72-7805 (ISBN 0-262-66037-7); Vol. 6. Selected Topics in Field Quantization. LC 72-7807 (ISBN 0-262-66038-5). 1977. pap. text ed. 25.00x set (ISBN 0-262-66032-6); pap. text ed. 4.95x ea. MIT Pr.

Pauline & the Peacock. Doris T. Daniel. LC 80-50301. (Illus.). 64p. (Orig.). (ps-8). 1980. pap. 4.95 (ISBN 0-936650-00-1). E C Temple.

Pauline Epistles: Their Meaning & Message. James T. Hudson. 1958. 6.00 (ISBN 0-227-67558-4). Attic Pr.

Pauline Parallels. Ed. by Fred O. Francis & J. Paul Sampley. LC 74-26346. 400p. 1975. pap. 10.95x spiral bdg. (ISBN 0-8006-1206-X, 1-1206). Fortress.

Pauline Partnership in Christ: Christian Community & Commitment in Light of Roman Law. J. Paul Sampley. LC 79-8895. 144p. 1980. 9.95 (ISBN 0-8006-0631-0, 1-631). Fortress.

Pauline Studies: Essays Presented to Prof. F. F. Bruce on His 70th Birthday. Ed. by Donald Hagner & Murray Harris. LC 80-16146. 336p. 1981. 17.95 (ISBN 0-8028-3531-7). Eerdmans.

Pauline Theology: A Brief Sketch. Joseph F. Fitzmyer. (Orig.). 1967. pap. text ed. 7.25 (ISBN 0-13-654525-4). P-H.

Pauline's. Pauline Tabor. 256p. 1973. pap. 1.25 o.p. (ISBN 0-449-21842-2, P1842, Crest). Fawcett.

Paul's Aeon Theology in First Corinthians. French L. Arrington. 1977. pap. text ed. 9.00x (ISBN 0-8191-0119-2). U Pr of Amer.

Paul's Awakening. Frederik Van Eeden. Tr. by H. S. Lake from Dutch. LC 78-70615. 1980. pap. cancelled (ISBN 0-89793-000-2). Hunter Hse.

Paul's Christmas Birthday. Carol Carrick. LC 77-28408. (Illus.). (gr. k-3). 1978. 7.95 (ISBN 0-688-80159-5); PLB 7.63 (ISBN 0-688-84159-7). Greenwillow.

Paul's Idea of Community: The Early House Churches in the Historical Setting. Robert Banks. 1980. pap. 5.95 (ISBN 0-8028-1830-7). Eerdmans.

Paul's Intercessory Prayers. G. P. Wiles. (Society for New Testament Studies Monographs: No. 24). 360p. 1974. 47.50 (ISBN 0-521-20274-4). Cambridge U Pr.

Paul's Letters. Bessie Dean. (Story Books to Color). (Illus.). 72p. (Orig.). (gr. k-5). 1980. pap. 3.95 (ISBN 0-88290-170-2). Horizon Utah.

Paul's Letters to Churches. Gerald Dye. (Double Trouble Puzzles Ser). (Illus.). 1977. pap. 1.25 (ISBN 0-87239-152-3, 2823). Standard Pub.

Paul's Letters to His Friends. Gerald Dye. (Double Trouble Puzzles Ser). (Illus.). 1977. pap. 1.25 (ISBN 0-87239-153-1, 2824). Standard Pub.

Paul's Prison Prayers. W. Graham Scroggle. LC 80-8077. 124p. 1981. pap. 2.95 (ISBN 0-8254-3737-7). Kregel.

Paulus Vladimiri & His Doctrine Concerning International Law & Politics, 2 Vols. Stanislaus F. Belch. 1965. Set. text ed. 247.00x (ISBN 90-2790-977-6). Mouton.

Paupers: The Making of the New Claiming Class. Bill Jordan. 1973. 9.00x (ISBN 0-7100-7547-2); pap. 3.95 (ISBN 0-7100-7548-0). Routledge & Kegan.

Pausological Implications of Speech Production: An Interdisciplinary Workshop. Ed. by Hans Dechert & Manfred Raupach. (Janua Linguarum, Series Maior: No. 86). 1979. text ed. 47.00x (ISBN 90-279-7946-4). Mouton.

Pavane. Keith Roberts. pap. 1.50 o.p. (ISBN 0-425-03142-X). Berkley Pub.

Pavanne for a Fading Memory. William Pillin. LC 63-16650. 82p. 1963. 5.00 (ISBN 0-8040-0240-1). Swallow.

Pavarotti: My Own Story. Luciano Pavarotti & William Wright. LC 80-1990. (Illus.). 240p. 1981. 14.95 (ISBN 0-385-15340-6). Doubleday.

Paved with Good Intentions: The American Experience & Iran. Barry Rubin. (Illus.). 320p. 1980. 17.50 (ISBN 0-19-502805-8). Oxford U Pr.

Pavement Relections. Lionel Gardner. 6.75 (ISBN 0-89253-688-8). Ind-US Inc.

Pavements & Surfacings for Highways & Airports. Michael Sargious. LC 75-11891. 619p. 1975. 54.95 (ISBN 0-470-75418-4). Halsted Pr.

Pavese: Prison de l'imaginaire, lieu de l'ecriture. new ed. (Collection themes et textes). 192p. (Orig., Fr.). 1972. pap. 6.75 (ISBN 2-03-035007-9, 2695). Larousse.

Pavlova & Nijinsky Paper Dolls in Full Color. Tom Tierney. (Illus.). 32p. (Orig.). 1981. pap. price not set (ISBN 0-486-24093-2). Dover.

Pavlova: Repertoire of a Legend. John Lazzarini & Roberta Lazzarini. LC 80-5560. (Illus.). 1980. 35.00 (ISBN 0-02-871970-0). Schirmer Bks.

Pavlovian Approach to Psychopathology. W. H. Gantt et al. 1970. 52.00 (ISBN 0-08-013016-X). Pergamon.

Pavlovian Conditioning & American Psychiatry, Vol. 5. Group for the Advancement of Psychiatry Conference. (Symposium No. 9). 1964. pap. 3.00 (ISBN 0-87318-079-8). Adv Psychiatry.

Pawdie. Irene Cory. LC 68-21586. 1968. 5.95 (ISBN 0-8149-0047-X). Vanguard.

Pawn Endings. Yuri Averbakh & I. Maizelis. 1974. 22.50 (ISBN 0-7134-2797-3). David & Charles.

Pawn in Frankincense. Dorothy Dunnett. 576p. 1981. pap. 2.75 (ISBN 0-445-08472-3). Popular Lib.

Pawn Power in Chess. Hans Kmoch. (Illus.). 1959. pap. 5.95 (ISBN 0-679-14028-X, Tartan). McKay.

Pawnee & Kansa (KAW) Indians. Incl. Notes on the Pawnee. John L. Champe & Franklin Fenenga; Historical & Economic Geography of the Pawnee Lands. Thomas M. Griffiths; Findings of Fact, & Opinion. Indian Claims Commission; The Prehistoric & Historic Habitat of the Kansa Indians. Waldo R. Wedel. (American Indian Ethnohistory Ser: Plains Indians). (Illus.). lib. bdg. 42.00 (ISBN 0-8240-0733-6). Garland Pub.

Pawnee Bill: A Biography of Major Gordon W. Lillie. Glenn Shirley. LC 58-6870. (Illus.). 1965. pap. 5.95 (ISBN 0-8032-5185-8, BB 331, Bison). U of Nebr Pr.

Pawnee Ghost Dance Hand Game: A Study of Cultural Change. Alexander Lesser. LC 79-82340. (Illus.). 1978. 20.00 (ISBN 0-299-07480-3); pap. 7.95 (ISBN 0-299-07484-6). U of Wis Pr.

Pawnee Hero Stories & Folktales with Notes on the Origin, Customs & Character of the Pawnee People. George B. Grinnell. LC 61-10153. (Illus.). 1961. 14.95x (ISBN 0-8032-0896-0); pap. 7.50 (ISBN 0-8032-5080-0, BB 116, Bison). U of Nebr Pr.

Pawnee Music. Frances Densmore. LC 72-1880. (Music Ser.). 160p. 1972. Repr. of 1929 ed. lib. bdg. 14.50 (ISBN 0-306-70508-7). Da Capo.

Pawns in the Game. William G. Carr. 1978. pap. 4.00x (ISBN 0-911038-29-9). Noontide.

Pax Britannica. Ed. by Milton Israel. LC 68-113032. (Selections from History Today Ser.: No. 9). (Illus.). 1968. 5.00 (ISBN 0-05-001653-9); pap. 3.95 (ISBN 0-685-09189-9). Dufour.

Pax Romana. Peter Amey. Ed. by Malcolm Yapp et al. (World History Ser.). (Illus.). 32p. (gr. 10). 1980. Repr. of 1977 ed. lib. bdg. 5.95 (ISBN 0-89908-027-8); pap. text ed. 1.95 (ISBN 0-89908-002-2). Greenhaven.

Pax Romana. Paul Petit. Tr. by James Willis. 1976. 27.50x (ISBN 0-520-02171-1). U of Cal Pr.

Paxton Pride. Shana Carroll. (Orig.). 1976. pap. 1.95 (ISBN 0-515-04019-3). Jove Pubns.

Pay & Organization Development. Edward E. Lawlor, III. 230p. 1981. pap. text ed. 6.95 (ISBN 0-201-03990-7). A-W.

Pay Board's Progress: Wage Controls in Phase II. Arnold R. Weber & Daniel J. B. Mitchell. (Studies in Wage-Price Policy). 1978. 16.95 (ISBN 0-8157-9266-2); pap. 7.95 (ISBN 0-8157-9265-4). Brookings.

Pay Less Tax Legally: 1981 Edition. Barry R. Steiner. (Orig.). 1980. pap. 3.95 (ISBN 0-451-09522-7, E9522, Sig). NAL.

Pay-off in Switzerland. Noah Webster. LC 77-74271. 1977. 6.95 o.p. (ISBN 0-385-13246-8). Doubleday.

Pay TV: Markets, Developments. 1980. 750.00 (ISBN 0-89336-264-6, G-060). BCC.

Pay Your Respects. R. Graber. (gr. 7 up). 1981. pap. 1.95 (ISBN 0-440-97317-1, LE). Dell.

Paying the Modern Military. Martin Binkin & Irene Kyriakopoulos. LC 80-70080. (Studies in Defense Policy). 100p. 1981. pap. 3.95 (ISBN 0-8157-0971-4). Brookings.

Payless Tax Legally-1980: Edition for 1979 Tax Return. Barry Steiner. (Orig.). 1980. pap. cancelled o.p. (ISBN 0-451-82058-4, XE2058, Sig). NAL.

Payment Deferred. C. S. Forester. 1978. 7.95 (ISBN 0-370-00657-7, Pub. by Chatto Bodley Jonathan). Merrimack Bk Serv.

Payment for Pain & Suffering: Who Wants What, When & Why? Jeffrey O'Connell & Rita J. Simon. 1972. 10.00 o.p. (ISBN 0-88245-013-1). Merritt Co.

Payment in Full. Anne Hampson. 192p. (Orig.). 1980. pap. 1.50 (ISBN 0-671-57001-3). S&S.

Payne Hollow: Life on the Fringe of Society. Harlan Hubbard. LC 75-34720. (Illus.). 168p. 1976. 6.95 o.s.i. (ISBN 0-690-01023-0, TYC-T); pap. 3.95 (ISBN 0-690-01024-9, TYC-T). T Y Crowell.

Payoff. Attilio Veraldi. Tr. by Isabel Quigley from Italian. LC 77-11775. 1978. 8.95 o.s.i. (ISBN 0-06-014493-9, HarpT). Har-Row.

Payoff in the Park. Ed. by Robert Vitarelli. (Pal Paperbacks Kit A Ser.). (Illus., Orig.). (gr. 7-12). 1972. pap. text ed. 1.25 (ISBN 0-8374-3481-5). Xerox Ed Pubns.

Payroll: COM-PET Edition. Ed. by Lon Poole. 180p. (Orig.). 1980. pap. cancelled (ISBN 0-931988-41-1). Osborne-McGraw.

Payroll Tax for Social Security. John A. Brittain. LC 72-142. (Studies of Government Finance). 336p. 1972. 11.95 (ISBN 0-8157-1080-1). Brookings.

Payroll with Cost Accounting-CBASIC. Lon Poole et al. 364p. (Orig.). 1979. pap. 20.00 (ISBN 0-931988-22-5). Osborne-McGraw.

Paysan Parvenu: Or, the Fortunate Peasant. Pierre C. De Chamblain De Marivaux. LC 78-60836. (Novel 1720-1805 Ser.: Vol. 2). 1979. lib. bdg. 45.00 (ISBN 0-8240-3651-4); lib. bdg. 31.00 ea. Garland Pub.

Paysans Arakanais Du Pakistan Oriental: L'histoire le Monde Vegetal et L'organisation Sociale Des Refugies Marma (Mog, 2 vols. Lucien Bernot. (Le Monde D'outre-Mer Passe et Present, Etudes: No. 16). (Illus.). 1967. pap. text ed. 95.30x (ISBN 90-2796-172-7). Mouton.

Paz. Cheli D. Ryan. LC 73-139444. (Illus.). (gr. 1-3). 1971. 4.95 o.s.i. (ISBN 0-02-777980-7). Macmillan.

Paz Con Dios. Billy Graham. Tr. by Carrie Muntz from Eng. Orig. Title: Peace with God. 272p. 1980. pap. 2.95 (ISBN 0-311-43037-6). Casa Bautista.

PCC: The Car That Fought Back. Steve Carlson & Fred W. Schneider. Ed. by Mac Sebree. LC 80-81312. (Interurbans Special Ser.: No. 64). (Illus.). 256p. 1980. 29.95 (ISBN 0-916374-41-6). Interurban.

PCP Phencyclidine: Historical & Current Perspectives. Ed. by E. F. Domino. LC 80-81498. (Illus.). 300p. 1980. 30.00x (ISBN 0-916182-03-7). NPP Bks.

PDP-11 Assembler Language Programming & Machine Organization. Michael Singer. 1980. text ed. 13.95 (ISBN 0-471-04905-0). Wiley.

Peace. Aristophanes. Tr. by Robert H. Webb. LC 64-22630. 1964. pap. 2.95 (ISBN 0-8139-0013-1). U Pr of Va.

Peace. Anthony S. Pitch. (Illus.). 200p. 1979. 18.95 (ISBN 0-89961-001-3). SBS Pub.

Peace Against War: The Ecology of International Violence. Francis A. Beer. LC 80-27214. (International Relations Ser.). (Illus.). 1981. text ed. 18.95x (ISBN 0-7167-1250-4); pap. text ed. 9.95x (ISBN 0-7167-1251-2). W H Freeman.

Peace & Pieces: An Anthology of Contemporary American Poetry. 2nd ed. Ed. by Maurice Custodio. LC 73-83883. (Illus.). 216p. Date not set. pap. cancelled o.p. (ISBN 0-914024-09-4). SF Arts & Letters.

Peace & World Order Systems: Teaching & Research. Paul Wehr & Michael Washburn. LC 75-23614. (Sage Library of Social Research: Vol. 25). 1976. 18.00x (ISBN 0-8039-0552-1); pap. 8.95x (ISBN 0-8039-0553-X). Sage.

Peace Breaks Out. John Knowles. LC 80-19678. 192p. 1981. 9.95 (ISBN 0-03-056908-7). HR&W.

Peace by Revolution, Mexico After 1910. Frank Tannenbaum. LC 33-35455. (Illus.). 1933. pap. 7.50x (ISBN 0-231-08568-0). Columbia U Pr.

Peace Conference of Nineteen Nineteen: Organization & Procedure. Frank S. Marston. LC 80-28997. xi, 276p. 1981. Repr. of 1944 ed. lib. bdg. 25.00x (ISBN 0-313-22910-4, MAPEC). Greenwood.

Peace Corps. Ed. by Pauline Madow. (Reference Shelf Ser: Vol. 36, No. 2). 1964. 6.25 (ISBN 0-8242-0080-2). Wilson.

Peace Corps: Kindlers of the Spark. Edna McGuire. (gr. 7 up). 1966. 4.95g o.s.i. (ISBN 0-02-765450-8). Macmillan.

Peace Denied: The United States, Vietnam, & the Paris Agreement. Gareth Porter. LC 75-3890. (Illus.). 384p. 1976. 15.00x (ISBN 0-253-16160-6). Ind U Pr.

Peace Endangered: The Reality of Detente. R. J. Rummel. LC 76-17372. (Illus.). 1976. 17.50x (ISBN 0-8039-0387-1); pap. 7.95x (ISBN 0-8039-0828-8). Sage.

Peace from Nervous Suffering. Claire Weekes. 1972. 7.95 o.p. (ISBN 0-8015-5802-6); pap. 3.95 o.p. (ISBN 0-8015-5804-2). Dutton.

Peace Handbooks, 25 vols. Ed. by George W. Prothero. LC 73-82619. 1973. Repr. of 1920 ed. Set. 875.00 (ISBN 0-8420-1704-6). Scholarly Res Inc.

Peace in Palestine. M. T. Mehdi. LC 75-43266. 1976. pap. 3.00 (ISBN 0-911026-08-8). New World Press NY.

Peace in the Ancient World. Matthew Melko & Richard D. Weigel. LC 80-20434. 225p. 1981. lib. bdg. 15.95x (ISBN 0-89950-020-X). McFarland & Co.

Peace in the Middle East. Mohammad T. Mehdi. (Illus.). 1967. pap. 3.00 o.p. (ISBN 0-911026-09-6). New World Press NY.

Peace Is Our Profession: Poems & Passages of War Protest. Ed. by Jan Barry. LC 80-70115. 1981. pap. 5.95 (ISBN 0-917238-03-6). East River Anthol.

Peace Lagoon. Premka Kaur. (Illus.). 1972. 8.95 o.p. (ISBN 0-913852-04-X); pap. 5.50 (ISBN 0-913852-03-1). Spiritual Comm.

Peace Marshal. Frank Gruber. 160p. (Orig.). 1981. pap. 1.75 (ISBN 0-553-14539-8). Bantam.

Peace, Mommy, Peace. Bill Keane. (Family Circus Ser.). (Illus.). 1978. pap. 1.50 (ISBN 0-449-14145-4, GM). Fawcett.

Peace of Mind in Earthquake Country: How to Save Your Home & Life. Peter Yanev. LC 74-7406. (Illus.). 320p. 1974. 9.95 (ISBN 0-87701-050-1); pap. 5.95 (ISBN 0-87701-049-8). Chronicle Bks.

Peace of Mind Through Possibility Thinking. Robert H. Schuller. 1978. pap. 2.25 (ISBN 0-515-05671-5). Jove Pubns.

Peace of Mind Through Possibility Thinking. Robert H. Schuller. LC 72-76203. 1977. 7.95 (ISBN 0-385-00673-X). Doubleday.

Peace of Paris Eighteen Fifty Six. Ed. by Ann P. Saab & Winfried Baumgart. 1981. write for info. (ISBN 0-87436-309-8). Abc-Clio.

Peace of Soul. Fulton J. Sheen. 1954. pap. 1.95 (ISBN 0-385-02871-7, D8, Im). Doubleday.

Peace, Power & Happiness. George Otis. Orig. Title: Like a Roaring Lion. pap. 1.95 (ISBN 0-89728-051-2, 658302). Omega Pubns OR.

Peace Reform in American History. Charles DeBenedetti. LC 79-2173. 274p. 1980. 18.50x (ISBN 0-253-13095-6). Ind U Pr.

Peace Ship: Henry Ford's Pacifist Adventure in the First World War. Barbara S. Kraft. 1978. 17.95 o.s.i. (ISBN 0-02-566570-7). Macmillan.

Peace with Justice. Dwight D. Eisenhower. 20.00x (ISBN 0-231-02472-X). Columbia U Pr.

Peace Without Promise: Britain & the Peace Conferences 1919-1923. Michael Dockrill & Douglas Gould. 320p. 1981. 25.00 (ISBN 0-208-01909-X, Archon). Shoe String.

Peaceable Classroom: Activities to Calm & Free Student Energies. Merrill Harmin & Saville Sax. 1977. pap. 5.95 (ISBN 0-03-021256-1). Winston Pr.

Peaceable Kingdom. Jan de Hartog. 1978. pap. 2.50 o.p. (ISBN 0-449-23463-0, Crest). Fawcett.

Peaceable Kingdom: The Shaker Abecedarius. Illus. by Alice Provensen & Martin Provensen. (Picture Puffins Ser.). (Illus.). (gr. k-3). pap. 2.95 (ISBN 0-14-050370-6, Puffin). Penguin.

Peaceable Kingdoms: New England Towns in the Eighteenth Century. Michael Zuckerman. 1978. pap. 5.95 (ISBN 0-393-00895-9, N895, Norton Lib). Norton.

Peaceable Kitchen Cookbook: Cooking for Personal & Global Well-Being. Kate C. Easterday. LC 79-92912. (Orig.). 1980. pap. 8.95 (ISBN 0-8091-2225-1). Paulist Pr.

Peaceful Nuclear Explosions - Four: Proceedings. Technical Committee, Vienna Jan. 20-24, 1975. (Illus.). 479p. 1975. pap. 36.50 (ISBN 92-0-061075-7, IAEA). Unipub.

Peaceful Nuclear Explosions - Three: Applications, Characteristics & Effects. (Illus.). 488p. (Eng., Fr., Rus. & Span.). 1974. pap. 31.25 (ISBN 92-0-061074-9, IAEA). Unipub.

Peaceful Nuclear Explosions - Two: Their Practical Application. (Illus.). 355p. (Orig.). 1972. pap. 21.50 (ISBN 92-0-061071-4, IAEA). Unipub.

Peaceful Nuclear Explosions: Phenomenology & Status Report, 1970. (Illus., Orig.). 1970. pap. 26.75 (ISBN 92-0-061070-6, ISP-273, IAEA). Unipub.

Peaceful Nuclear Explosions V. 1978. pap. 18.25 (ISBN 92-0-061078-1, ISP 473, IAEA). Unipub.

Peaceful Poems & Photography: Including the Veiled Reef of Saudi Arabia. Judith M. Rudderham. 1981. 4.95 (ISBN 0-8062-1716-2). Carlton.

Peaceful Uses of Atomic Energy in Africa. (Illus., Orig.). 1970. pap. 33.25 (ISBN 92-0-070070-5, IAEA). Unipub.

Peaceful Uses of Atomic Energy: Proceedings, 15 vols. International Conference on the Peaceful Uses of Atomic Energy, 4th, Geneva, 1971. (Orig., Eng., Fr., Rus. & Span., Vols. 1, 4, 5, 6, 8, 10, 12 avail. only). 1972. pap. 15.00 ea. (IAEA); pap. 10.75 ea. discussion vols. in Fr., Rus. & Span. Unipub.

Peacekeeping in America: A Developmental Study of American Law Enforcement: Philosophy & Systems. James P. Hall. 1978. pap. text ed. 11.95 (ISBN 0-8403-1143-5). Kendall-Hunt.

Peacekeeping: Police, Prisons & Violence. Hans Toch. LC 76-5622. 1976. 16.95 (ISBN 0-669-00652-1). Lexington Bks.

Peacemaker. Frank Allnutt. 1977. pap. 1.95 (ISBN 0-89728-052-0, 693561). Omega Pubns OR.

Peach Boy & Other Stories. Florence Sakade. (Illus.). (gr. 1-5). 1958. pap. 5.25 (ISBN 0-8048-0469-9). C E Tuttle.

Peaches Point. Tim Shepard. LC 76-4521. (Illus.). 1976. 8.95 o.s.i. (ISBN 0-690-01168-7, TYC-T). T Y Crowell.

Peacock Displayed: A Satirist in His Context. Marilyn Butler. 1979. 30.00 (ISBN 0-7100-0293-9). Routledge & Kegan.

Peacock Festival: Selected Color Woodcuts. John F. Mills. LC 64-8130. (Illus.). 1964. pap. 8.00 (ISBN 0-933652-00-3). Domjan Studio.

Peacock, His Circle & His Age. Howard W. Mills. LC 68-23183. (Illus.). 1969. 49.50 (ISBN 0-521-07262-X). Cambridge U Pr.

Peacock Pie. Walter De La Mare. 1958. 8.95 (ISBN 0-571-04683-5, Pub. by Faber & Faber); pap. 3.50 (ISBN 0-571-05609-1). Merrimack Bk Serv.

Peacock Pie. Walter De La Mare. (Fanfares Ser.). (gr. 4 up). 1980. pap. 3.25 (ISBN 0-571-18014-0, Pub. by Faber & Faber). Merrimack Bk Serv.

Peacock Poems (& Others) Shirley Williams. LC 75-12531. (Wesleyan Poetry Program: Vol. 79). 87p. (Orig.). 1975. pap. 4.95 (ISBN 0-8195-1079-3, Pub. by Wesleyan U Pr). Columbia U Pr.

Peacock Smiles. Mary A. Dasgupta. 8.00 (ISBN 0-89253-471-0); flexible cloth 4.00 (ISBN 0-89253-472-9). Ind-US Inc.

Peacocks Are Very Special. Sue Alexander. 32p. (gr. 1-3). 1976. PLB 5.95 (ISBN 0-385-02169-0). Doubleday.

Peacocks, Vultures & Nightingales. Mary-Ruth C. Mundy. Ed. by Joseph Lawrence. 56p. (Orig.). 1980. pap. write for info. (ISBN 0-89144-113-1). Crescent Pubns.

Peacock's Wedding. Alfred Koenner. (Illus.). 1978. 7.95 (ISBN 0-7011-5019-X, Pub. by Chatto Bodley Jonathan). Merrimack Bk Serv.

Peafowl of the World. Josef Bergmann. 142p. 1980. 29.95x (ISBN 0-904558-52-5, Pub. by Saiga England). State Mutual Bk.

Peak Beneath the Moon. Hope Campbell. LC 78-20427. 144p. (gr. 3-7). 1979. 6.95 (ISBN 0-590-07565-9, Four Winds). Schol Bk Serv.

Peak District. Roy Christian. LC 75-26358. (British Topographical Ser.). (Illus.). 224p. 1976. 14.95 (ISBN 0-7153-7094-4). David & Charles.

Peak District Companion: A Walker's Guide. Rex Bellamy. LC 80-70294. (Illus.). 208p. 1981. 24.00. David & Charles.

Peak in Darien. Freya Stark. 1977. 12.00 (ISBN 0-7195-3291-4). Transatlantic.

Peak to Peek Principle. Robert H. Schuller. LC 80-1693. 192p. 1980. 9.95 (ISBN 0-385-17319-9). Doubleday.

Peake's Progress: Selected Writings & Drawings of Mervyn Peake. Mervyn Peake. Ed. by Maeve Gilmore. LC 80-83054. (Illus.). 576p. 1981. 25.00 (ISBN 0-87951-121-4). Overlook Pr.

Peaks & Pioneers. Francis Keenlyside. 1975. 23.95 o.p. (ISBN 0-236-31042-9, Pub. by Paul Elek). Merrimack Bk Serv.

Peanut. Millicent E. Selsam. LC 70-81886. (Illus.). (gr. 2-5). 1969. PLB 7.92 (ISBN 0-688-31803-7). Morrow.

Peanut Butter & Jelly Guide to Computers. Jerry Willis. LC 78-70238. 225p. 1978. pap. 8.95 (ISBN 0-918398-13-4). Dilithium Pr.

Peanuts Paint with Water Book. (Illus.). 48p. (ps-5). 1979. pap. 1.25 (ISBN 0-448-16769-7). G&D.

Peanuts: Production, Processing, Products. 2nd ed. J. G. Woodroof. (Illus.). 330p. 1973. text ed. 29.50 (ISBN 0-87055-135-3). AVI.

Pear Tree. Charlotte M. Stein. Ed. by Nancy Rubenstein. LC 79-54652. (Illus.). 200p. 1980. pap. 6.00 (ISBN 0-916634-03-5). Double M Pr.

Pearl. Ed. by A. C. Cawley. Incl. Sir Gawain & the Green Knight. 1962. 5.00x o.p. (ISBN 0-460-00346-1, Evman). Dutton.

Pearl. Maximo De Aragon. LC 80-83435. (Illus.). 50p. (Orig.). (gr. 7-12). 1981. pap. 2.95 (ISBN 0-932906-08-7). Pan-Am Publishing Co.

Pearl. 1977. pap. 2.95 o.p. (ISBN 0-345-25293-4). Ballantine.

Pearl Buck. Paul A. Doyle. (U. S. Authors Ser.: No. 85). 1965. lib. bdg. 8.50 o.p. (ISBN 0-8057-0112-5). Twayne.

Pearl Harbor: A Narrative Poem. John Guenther. (Illus.). 64p. (Orig.). 1980. pap. 4.95 (ISBN 0-938266-00-4). Purchase Pr.

Pearl Harbor As History: Japanese-American Relations, 1931-1941. Ed. by Dorothy Borg & Shumpei Okamoto. 830p. 1973. 35.00x (ISBN 0-231-03734-1); pap. 14.00x (ISBN 0-231-03890-9). Columbia U Pr.

Pearl Harbor December 7, 1941. Robert G. Goldston. LC 72-1339. (World Focus Bks). (Illus.). (gr. 7-12). 1972. PLB 4.47 o.p. (ISBN 0-531-02163-7). Watts.

Pearl Harbor Periscopes. J. Farragut Jones. (Orig.). 1981. pap. 2.95 (ISBN 0-440-16711-6). Dell.

Pearl Harbor: The Way It Was--December 7, 1941. Scott C. Stone. LC 77-82234. (Illus.). 1977. pap. 4.95 (ISBN 0-89610-039-1). Island Her.

Pearl in Its Setting: A Critical Study of the Structure & Meaning of the Middle English Poem. Ian Bishop. 24.00x (ISBN 0-631-11410-6, Pub. by Basil Blackwell). Biblio Dist.

Pearl Is in the Oyster. Marilyn C. Donahue. 1980. pap. text ed. 3.95 (ISBN 0-8423-4808-5). Tyndale.

Pearl Millet. Kenneth O. Rachie & J. V. Majmudar. LC 79-5144. (Illus.). 320p. 1980. lib. bdg. 29.75x (ISBN 0-271-00234-4). Pa St U Pr.

Pearl of Potentiality. Ed. by Dottie Walters. LC 79-91548. 296p. 1980. 11.95 (ISBN 0-8119-0338-9, Pub. by Royal CBC). Fell.

Pearl Pagoda. Susannah Broome. 1980. 12.95 (ISBN 0-671-25535-5). S&S.

Pearl, Sir Gawain & Cleanness. A. C. Cawley. 1977. pap. 4.50 (ISBN 0-686-63595-7, Everyman). Dutton.

Pearls in Diagnostic Radiology, Vol. 1. Harold D. Rosenbaum. (Illus.). 240p. 1980. pap. 32.50x (ISBN 0-443-08097-6). Churchill.

Pearls of Wisdom 1968, Vol. 11. Ed. by Elizabeth C. Prophet. LC 78-64502. 9.95 (ISBN 0-916766-33-0). Summit Univ.

Pears All-the-Year-Round Quiz Book. Gyles Brandeth. (Illus.). 1978. 10.95 (ISBN 0-7207-1018-9, Pub. by Michael Joseph); pap. 5.95 (ISBN 0-7207-1019-7). Merrimack Bk Serv.

Pears Book of Words. Cyles Brandreth. Ed. by Oxford English Dict. 204p. 1981. 13.95 (ISBN 0-7207-1186-X). Merrimack Bk Serv.

Pears Cyclopedia. 88th ed. Ed. by Chris Cook. (Illus.). 976p. 1980. 11.95 o.p. (ISBN 0-7207-1159-2, Pub. by Michael Joseph). Merrimack Bk Serv.

Pears Encyclopedia of Gardening: Flowers, Trees & Shrubs, Vol. 1. Roy Genders. 1972. 9.95 (ISBN 0-7207-0249-6, Pub. by Michael Joseph). Merrimack Bk Serv.

Pears Encyclopedia of Gardening: Fruits & Vegetables, Vol. 2. Roy Genders. 1973. 9.95 (ISBN 0-7207-0537-1, Pub. by Michael Joseph). Merrimack Bk Serv.

Pears Shilling Cyclopaedia. Ed. by Giles Brandreth et al. (Illus.). 1978. 12.95 (ISBN 0-7207-1032-4, Pub. by Michael Joseph). Merrimack Bk Serv.

Pearson, a Harbor Seal Pub. Susan Meyers. LC 80-13041. (Illus.). 64p. (gr. 3-7). 1980. 9.95 (ISBN 0-525-36845-0). Dutton.

Peary & Henson. (gr. 1). 1974. pap. text ed. 2.80 (ISBN 0-205-03873-5, 8038732); tchrs'. guide 12.00 (ISBN 0-205-03866-2, 803866X). Allyn.

Peas, Beans, & Licorice. Olive L. Earle. LC 77-126737. (Illus.). (gr. 3-7). 1971. 6.25 o.p. (ISBN 0-688-21570-X). Morrow.

Peasant & the Fly. Osmond Molarsky. LC 80-11609. (Illus.). 48p. (gr. k-3). 1980. pap. 3.95 (ISBN 0-15-260153-8, VoyB). HarBraceJ.

Peasant & the Raj: Studies in Agrarian Society & Peasant Rebellion in Colonial India. E. T. Stokes. LC 77-77731. (Cambridge South Asian Studies: No. 23). 304p. 1980. pap. 12.95x (ISBN 0-521-29770-2). Cambridge U Pr.

Peasant Chic. Esther Holderness. (Illus.). 1977. pap. 7.95 o.p. (ISBN 0-8015-5811-5). Dutton.

Peasant China in Transition: The Dynamics of Development Toward Socialism 1949 to 1956. Vivienne Shue. 500p. 1980. 25.75x (ISBN 0-520-03734-0). U of Cal Pr.

Peasant Cooperation & Capitalist Expansion in Central Peru. Ed. by Norman Long & Bryan R. Roberts. (Latin American Monographs: No. 46). 1978. pap. text ed. 9.95x (ISBN 0-292-76451-0); pap. text ed. 9.95x (ISBN 0-292-76452-9). U of Tex Pr.

Peasant Cooperatives & Political Change in Peru. Cynthia McClintock. LC 80-8563. (Illus.). 480p. 1981. 30.00x (ISBN 0-691-07627-8); pap. 7.95x (ISBN 0-691-02202-X). Princeton U Pr.

Peasant Farming in Muscovy. R. F. Smith. LC 75-23843. (Illus.). 1977. 41.95 (ISBN 0-521-20912-9). Cambridge U Pr.

Peasant Life in China: A Field Study of Country Life in the Yangtze Valley. Hsiao-Tung Fei. (Studies in Chinese History & Civilization). (Illus.). 296p. 1977. Repr. of 1939 ed. 21.00 (ISBN 0-89093-081-3). U Pubns Amer.

Peasant Marketing System of Oaxaca, Mexico. Ralph L. Beals. 1975. 30.00x (ISBN 0-520-02435-4). U of Cal Pr.

Peasant Mobilization & Rural Development. Edgar G. Nesman. 160p. 1981. text ed. 14.50x (ISBN 0-87073-717-1); pap. text ed. 8.95x (ISBN 0-87073-718-X). Schenkman.

Peasant Mobilization & Solidarity. B. F. Galjart. (Studies of Developing Countries: No. 19). (Illus.). 1976. pap. text ed. 14.00x (ISBN 90-232-1381-5). Humanities.

Peasant Nationalism & Communist Power: The Emergence of Revolutionary China, 1937-1945. Chalmers A. Johnson. 1962. 12.50x (ISBN 0-8047-0073-7); pap. 4.95 (ISBN 0-8047-0074-5). Stanford U Pr.

Peasant Revolt in Malabar. Robert Hardgrave. 1981. Repr. 25.00x (ISBN 0-8364-0010-0). South Asia Bks.

Peasant Revolts in China 1840-1949. Jean Chesneaux. Ed. by Geoffrey Barraclaugh. Tr. by C. A. Curwen from Fr. LC 72-13015. (Library of the World Civilization). (Illus.). 180p. 1973. 7.95 (ISBN 0-393-05485-3); pap. 5.95x (ISBN 0-393-09344-1). Norton.

Peasant Sage of Japan: The Life & Work of Sontoku Ninomiya. Kokei Tomita. (Studies in Japanese History & Civilization). 1979. Repr. of 1912 ed. 24.00 (ISBN 0-89093-258-1). U Pubns Amer.

Peasant State & Society in Medieval South India. Burton Stein. (Illus.). 550p. 1980. text ed. 31.00x (ISBN 0-19-561065-2). Oxford U Pr.

Peasant Wisdom: Cultural Adoption in a Swiss Village. Daniela Weinberg. (Illus.). 226p. 1975. 21.50x (ISBN 0-520-02789-2). U of Cal Pr.

Peasantry of Eastern Europe: Roots of Rural Transformation, Vol. I. Ed. by Ivan Volgyes. LC 78-18483. 200p. 1979. 22.50 (ISBN 0-08-023124-1). Pergamon.

Peasantry of Eastern Europe: Twentieth Century Developments. Ivan Volgyes. LC 78-18483. 240p. 1979. 28.00 (ISBN 0-08-023125-X). Pergamon.

Peasants. Eric R. Wolf. (Illus., Orig.). 1966. pap. 6.95 ref. ed. (ISBN 0-13-655456-3). P-H.

Peasants in Africa: Historical & Contemporary Perspectives. Ed. by Martin A. Klein. LC 79-23415. (Sage Series on African Modernization & Development: Vol. 4). (Illus.). 1980. 20.00x (ISBN 0-8039-1406-7); pap. 9.95x (ISBN 0-8039-1407-5). Sage.

Peasants in Revolt: A Chilean Case Study, 1965-1971. James Petras & Hugo Zemelman Merino. Tr. by Thomas Flory. LC 72-1578. (Latin American Monographs: No. 28). 164p. 1973. 8.50 (ISBN 0-292-76404-9). U of Tex Pr.

Peasants in the Pacific: A Study of Fiji Indian Rural Society. 2nd, rev. ed. Adrian C. Mayer. LC 72-91618. (Illus.). 1973. 18.50x (ISBN 0-520-02333-1). U of Cal Pr.

Peasants in Transition: The Changing Economy of the Peruvian Aymara: a General Systems Approach. Theodore C. Lewellen. LC 78-343. (Westview Replica Edition Ser.). 1978. lib. bdg. 24.00x (ISBN 0-89158-076-X). Westview.

Peasants, Knights & Heretics. R. H. Hilton. LC 76-1137. (Past & Present Publications Ser.). 320p. 1976. 29.95 (ISBN 0-521-21276-6). Cambridge U Pr.

Peasants of Mahrles: Economic Development & Family Organization in Nineteenth-Century France. James R. Lehning. LC 79-18707. 280p. 1980. 19.50x (ISBN 0-8078-1411-3). U of NC Pr.

Peasants Pea Patch. Tr. by Guy Daniels from Rus. LC 70-132355. (Illus.). (gr. k-2). 1971. PLB 5.47 o.s.i. (ISBN 0-440-06826-6). Delacorte.

Peasants, Power, & Applied Social Change: Vicos As a Model. Ed. by Henry F. Dobyns et al. LC 76-162437. 1971. 17.50x (ISBN 0-8039-0049-X). Sage.

Peasants, Primitives, & Proletariats: The Struggle for Identity in South America. Ed. by David L. Browman & Ronald A. Schwartz. (World Anthropology Ser.). 1979. text ed. 48.25x (ISBN 90-279-7880-8). Mouton.

Pebbles & Bamm-Bamm. (Play & Learn Shape Board Bks). 14p. (gr. k-3). 1981. bds. 2.95 comb bdg. (ISBN 0-89828-102-4, 6003, Ottenheimer Pubs Inc). Tuffy Bks.

Pebbles on the Beach. 2nd ed. Clarence Ellis. (Illus.). 1954. 8.95 (ISBN 0-571-06543-0, Pub. by Faber & Faber); pap. 3.95 (ISBN 0-571-06814-6). Merrimack Bk Serv.

Pecos: A History of the Pioneer West, Vol. 2. Alton Hughes. (Illus.). 232p. 1981. 16.95 (ISBN 0-933512-34-1). Pioneer Bk Tx.

Peculiar Forms of Ancient Religious Cults. Rudolf E. Cushman. (Illus.). 1980. deluxe ed. 41.50 (ISBN 0-89266-234-4). Am Classical Coll Pr.

Peculiar Music. Emily Bronte. Ed. by Naomi Lewis. (gr. 5 up). 1972. 4.95 o.s.i. (ISBN 0-02-714750-9). Macmillan.

Peculiar Truth. Duvie Clark. LC 78-55206. 1978. 9.95 o.p. (ISBN 0-689-10909-1). Atheneum.

Pedagogia Fructifera. Findley B. Edge. Tr. by Alberto Lopez. 1977. pap. 2.95 (ISBN 0-311-11025-8). Casa Bautista.

Pedagogia Ilustrada: Tomo I Principios Generales. Leroy Ford. Orig. Title: A Primer for Teachers & Leaders. (Illus.). 1979. pap. 2.10 (ISBN 0-311-11001-0, Edit Mundo). Casa Bautista.

Pedagogical Seminary: (Selections) Ed. by G. Stanley Hall. (Contributions to the History of Psychology Ser.: Psychometric & Educational Psychology). 1980. 30.00 (ISBN 0-89093-320-0). U Pubns Amer.

Pedagogy of the Oppressed. Paulo Freire. Tr. by Myra B. Ramos from Port. LC 70-110074. 1970. pap. 4.95 (ISBN 0-8164-9132-1). Continuum.

Pedahohichna Pratsia D-Ra Ivan Franke. Wasyl Luciw. (Ob'ednania Ukrains'kykh Pedahohiv U Kanadi). (Ukra.). 1956. pap. text ed. 1.50 (ISBN 0-918884-06-3). Slavia Lib.

Pedahohichna Pratsia Tarasa Shevchenka. Wasyl Luciw. (Ob'ednannia Ukrains'kykj Pedahohiv U Kanadi). (Ukra.). 1959. pap. text ed. 1.50 (ISBN 0-918884-07-1). Slavia Lib.

Peddlers. Leonard E. Fisher. LC 68-10335. (Colonial Americans Ser). (Illus.). (gr. 4-6). 1968. PLB 4.90 o.p. (ISBN 0-531-01031-7). Watts.

Pedegrewe of Heretiques. John Barthlet. LC 79-76432. (English Experience Ser.: No. 76). 180p. 1969. Repr. of 1566 ed. 21.00 (ISBN 90-221-0076-6). Walter J Johnson.

Pedestrian Malls. Klaus Uhlig. Date not set. 40.00 (ISBN 0-8038-0209-9). Hastings.

Pediatric Allergic Diseases - Focus on Clinical Diagnosis. Lloyd V. Crawford. 1977. spiral bdg. 16.50 (ISBN 0-87488-826-3). Med Exam.

Pediatric Allergy. 2nd ed. Michael R. Sly. (Medical Outline Ser.). 1980. pap. price not set (ISBN 0-87488-624-4). Med Exam.

Pediatric Allergy Case Studies. Stanley P. Galant et al. LC 80-18937. 1980. pap. 14.50 (ISBN 0-87488-195-1). Med Exam.

Pediatric & Adolescent Echocardiography: A Handbook. 2nd ed. Stanley J. Goldberg et al. (Illus.). 480p. 1980. 39.50 (ISBN 0-8151-3720-6). Year Bk Med.

Pediatric Anesthesia. Gray & Rees. 1981. text ed. price not set (ISBN 0-407-00114-X). Butterworths.

Pediatric Anesthesia: A Guide to Its Administration. Bernard W. Mayer. (Illus.). 192p. 1981. pap. text ed. 16.50 (ISBN 0-397-50478-0). Lippincott.

Pediatric Anesthesia Case Studies. John G. Adams. 1976. spiral bdg. 14.00 (ISBN 0-87488-042-4). Med Exam.

Pediatric Anesthesia Handbook. 2nd. ed. Ed. by Richard M. Levin. (Illus.). 1980. pap. 14.75 (ISBN 0-87488-637-6). Med Exam.

Pediatric Approach to Learning Disorders. Melvin D. Levine et al. LC 79-21839. 1980. 20.00 (ISBN 0-471-04736-8, Pub. by Wiley-Medical). Wiley.

Pediatric Assessment of Self Care Activities. Ida L. Coley. LC 77-2252. (Illus.). 1978. pap. text ed. 13.95 (ISBN 0-8016-1022-2). Mosby.

Pediatric Audiology. Ed. by Frederick N. Martin. (Illus.). 1978. ref. 29.95 (ISBN 0-13-655472-5). P-H.

Pediatric Cancer Chemotherapy. Rashid A. Al-Rashid. (Medical Outline Ser.). 1979. 26.00 (ISBN 0-87488-685-6); pap. 17.00 (ISBN 0-87488-663-5). Med Exam.

Pediatric Cardiac Dysrhythmias. Ed. by Paul C. Gillette et al. (Clinical Cardiology Monographs). 1981. price not set (ISBN 0-8089-1332-8). Grune.

Pediatric Cardiology. Courtney L. Anthony et al. (Medical Outline Ser.). 1979. pap. 18.00 (ISBN 0-87488-607-4). Med Exam.

Pediatric Cardiology. P. Syamasundar Rao & Max D. Miller. LC 61-66847. (Medical Examination Review Ser.: Vol. 37). 1980. pap. 19.50 (ISBN 0-87488-140-4). Med Exam.

Pediatric Cardiovascular Disease. Ed. by Mary A. Engle. LC 80-15616. (Cardiovascular Clinics Ser.: Vol. 11, No. 2). (Illus.). 475p. 1980. text ed. 48.00 (ISBN 0-8036-3204-5). Davis Co.

Pediatric Clinical Chemistry. rev. ed. Ed. by Samuel Meites. LC 80-66259. 400p. 1981. 35.00 (ISBN 0-915274-12-4). Am Assn Clinical Chem.

Pediatric Clinical Gastroenterology. 2nd ed. Roy et al. LC 75-22272. (Illus.). 1975. 41.50 (ISBN 0-8016-4613-8). Mosby.

Pediatric Critical Care Nursing. Katherine W. Vestal. 464p. 1981. 17.95 (ISBN 0-471-05674-X, Pub. by Wiley Med). Wiley.

Pediatric Dental Medicine. Ed. by Donald J. Forrester et al. LC 80-10694. (Illus.). 692p. 1981. text ed. write for info. (ISBN 0-8121-0663-6). Lea & Febiger.

Pediatric Dentistry. Ed. by Thomas K. Barber. 1981. 44.00 (ISBN 0-88416-167-6). PSG Pub.

Pediatric Diagnostic Procedures. Susan C. Droske. 272p. 1981. pap. 11.95 (ISBN 0-471-04928-X, Pub. by Wiley Med). Wiley.

Pediatric Differential Diagnosis: A Problem-Oriented Approach. Stephen Sheldon. 1979. softcover 7.50 (ISBN 0-89004-351-5). Raven.

Pediatric Dosage Handbook. Harry C. Shirkey. 1980. 18.00 (ISBN 0-917330-05-6). Am Pharm Assn.

Pediatric Emergency Management: Guidelines for Rapid Diagnosis. new ed. Ed. by Stanley Cohen. (Illus.). 250p. 1981. pap. text ed. 55.00 (ISBN 0-87619-665-2). R J Brady.

Pediatric Endocrinology. Ed. by Robert Collu et al. (Comprehensive Endocrinology Ser.). 1981. text ed. price not set (ISBN 0-89004-543-7). Raven.

Pediatric Endocrinology. S. Douglas Frasier. 1980. 29.50 (ISBN 0-8089-1272-0). Grune.

Pediatric Endocrinology. Wellington Hung et al. (Medical Outline Ser.). 1978. pap. 16.50 (ISBN 0-87488-674-0). Med Exam.

Pediatric Endocrinology. J. C. Job. 700p. 1981. 75.00 (ISBN 0-471-05257-4, Pub. by Wiley Med). Wiley.

Pediatric Gastroenterology Case Studies. William Liebman. 1980. pap. 18.50 (ISBN 0-87488-084-X). Med Exam.

Pediatric Hematology & Oncology Continuing Educaion Review. Thomas R. Walters & Franklin Desposito. 1975. spiral bdg. 12.00 o.p. (ISBN 0-87488-360-1). Med Exam.

Pediatric Hematology Case Studies. Rashid A. Al-Rashid. 1972. spiral bdg. 14.00 (ISBN 0-87488-018-1). Med Exam.

Pediatric Infectious Diseases. Cheng Cho & Burton Dudding. (Medical Outline Ser.). 1978. pap. 21.00 (ISBN 0-87488-659-7). Med Exam.

Pediatric Infectious Diseases Case Studies. Thomas E Frothingham et al. 1978. pap. 15.00 (ISBN 0-87488-048-3). Med Exam.

Pediatric Nephrology. Charles E. Hollerman. (Medical Outline Ser.). 1979. pap. 18.00 (ISBN 0-87488-590-6). Med Exam.

Pediatric Nephrology. Pierre Royer et al. LC 74-4585. (Major Problem in Clinical Pediatrics Ser.: Vol. 11). (Illus.). 415p. 1974. text ed. 25.00 (ISBN 0-7216-7776-2). Saunders.

Pediatric Nephrology, Vol. 5. Ed. by Jose Strauss. 1979. lib. bdg. 30.00 (ISBN 0-8240-7031-3). Garland Pub.

Pediatric Neurologic Nursing. Barbara L. Conway. (Illus.). 1977. text ed. 16.95 o.p. (ISBN 0-8016-1029-X). Mosby.

Pediatric Neurological Surgery. Ed. by Mark S. O'Brien. LC 78-3005. (Seminars in Neurological Surgery Ser.). 1978. 26.00 (ISBN 0-89004-178-4). Raven.

Pediatric Neurology. Michael J. Bresnan et al. (Medical Examination Review Book: Vol. 35). 1976. spiral bdg. 15.00 o.p. (ISBN 0-87488-175-7). Med Exam.

Pediatric Neurology: A Practitioner's Guide. Lester L. Lansky. 1975. spiral bdg. 12.00 o.p. (ISBN 0-87488-712-7). Med Exam.

Pediatric Neurology Case Studies. Kenneth Swaiman & Stephen Ashwal. 1978. spiral 19.50 (ISBN 0-87488-007-6). Med Exam.

Pediatric Neurology Handbook. 2nd ed. Ed. by J. T. Jabbour et al. (Illus.). 1976. pap. 19.50 (ISBN 0-87488-636-8). Med Exam.

Pediatric Neuromuscular Diseases. Kenneth F. Swaiman & Francis S. Wright. LC 79-20238. 1979. text ed. 42.50 (ISBN 0-8016-4846-7). Mosby.

Pediatric Nurse Practitioner: Guidelines for Practice. 2nd ed. Fernando J. De Castro et al. LC 75-42493. (Illus.). 240p. 1976. pap. 9.50 (ISBN 0-8016-1221-7). Mosby.

Pediatric Nursing. L. Brunner & D. Suddarth. 1981. pap. text ed. 18.35 (ISBN 0-06-318183-5, Pub. by Har-Row Ltd England). Har-Row.

Pediatric Nursing: A Self Study Guide. 3rd ed. Norma J. Anderson. LC 77-26632. (Illus.). 1978. pap. text ed. 10.50 (ISBN 0-8016-0195-9). Mosby.

Pediatric Nursing: An Introductory Text. Eleanor D. Thompson. 400p. 1981. pap. text ed. price not set (ISBN 0-7216-8843-8). Saunders.

Pediatric Nursing Continuing Education Review. Gloria C. Essoka et al. 1975. spiral bdg. 9.50 (ISBN 0-87488-361-X). Med Exam.

Pediatric Nutrition in Developmental Disorders. Sushma Palmer & Shirley Ekvall. (Illus.). 640p. 1978. 54.50 (ISBN 0-398-03652-7). C C Thomas.

Pediatric Ocular Tumors. Nicholson. 1981. price not set (ISBN 0-89352-125-6). Masson Pub.

Pediatric Oculo-Neural Diseases Case Studies. Ed. by J. A. McCrary. 1973. spiral bdg. 14.50 (ISBN 0-87488-023-8). Med Exam.

Pediatric Oncologic Radiology. Bruce R. Parker & Ronald A. Castellino. LC 77-23952. (Illus.). 1977. 47.50 o.p. (ISBN 0-8016-3756-2). Mosby.

Pediatric Oncology. Patricia Konrad & John Ertl. (Medical Outline Ser.). 1978. spiral 14.50 (ISBN 0-87488-673-2). Med Exam.

Pediatric Oncology Case Studies. Rashid A. Al-Rashid. 1975. spiral bdg. 15.00 o.p. (ISBN 0-87488-033-5). Med Exam.

Pediatric Opthalmology Practice. Eugene M. Helveston & Forrest D. Ellis. LC 79-18469. 1979. text ed. 49.50 (ISBN 0-8016-2129-1). Mosby.

Pediatric Orthopedic Nursing. Nancy E. Hilt & E. William Schmitt, Jr. LC 74-13222. (Illus.). 1975. text ed. 16.95 (ISBN 0-8016-2188-7). Mosby.

Pediatric Otolaryngology Case Studies. Ed. by W. Frederick McGuirt. LC 80-80367. 1980. pap. 18.50 (ISBN 0-87488-094-7). Med Exam.

Pediatric Otorhinolaryngology: A Review of Ear, Nose, & Throat Problems in Children. Ed. by Basharat Jazbi. 320p. 1980. 24.50x (ISBN 0-8385-7799-7). ACC.

Pediatric Pharmacology: Therapeutic Principles in Practice. Ed. by Sumner J. Yaffe. 1980. 44.50 (ISBN 0-8089-1251-8). Grune.

Pediatric Play Program: Developing a Therapeutic Play Program for Children in Medical Settings. Pat Azarnoff & Sharon Flegal. (Illus.). 112p. 1980. pap. 9.75 (ISBN 0-398-03272-6). C C Thomas.

Pediatric Priorities in the Developing World. D. Morley. 1976. 9.95 (ISBN 0-407-35113-2). Butterworths.

Pediatric Procedures. 2nd ed. Walter T. Hughes & E. Stephen Buescher. (Illus.). 400p. 1980. text ed. 24.95 (ISBN 0-7216-4826-6). Saunders.

Pediatric Radiology. 2nd ed. Alan E. Oestreich. (Medical Outline Ser.). 1980. pap. 16.50 (ISBN 0-87488-658-9). Med Exam.

Pediatric Radiology Case Studies. Howard A. Wexler & Catherine A. Poole. 1977. spiral bdg. 17.50 (ISBN 0-87488-064-5). Med Exam.

Pediatric Respiratory Disease. Jacques Gerbeaux. 875p. 1981. 45.00 (ISBN 0-471-03456-8, Pub. by Wiley-Med). Wiley.

Pediatric Respiratory Intensive Care Handbook. Richard M. Levin. 1976. spiral bdg. 13.75 (ISBN 0-87488-649-X). Med Exam.

Pediatric Rheumatology Case Studies. Aram Hanissian. 1979. pap. 19.00 (ISBN 0-87488-060-2). Med Exam.

Pediatric Surgery. 3rd ed. H. H. Nixon. Ed. by Rob & Smith. (Operative Surgery Ser.). 1978. 125.00 (ISBN 0-407-00634-6). Butterworths.

Pediatric Surgery Case Studies. John R. Lilly et al. 1978. spiral bdg. 19.50 (ISBN 0-87488-069-6). Med Exam.

Pediatric Surgery Continuing Education Review. John D. Burrington. 1976. spiral bdg. 14.00 (ISBN 0-87488-332-6). Med Exam.

Pediatric Telephone Advice. Barton D. Schmitt. 1980. pap. write for info. (ISBN 0-316-77386-7). Little.

Pediatric Therapy. 6th ed. Harry C. Shirkey. LC 80-14601. (Illus.). 1321p. 1980. text ed. 57.50 (ISBN 0-8016-4596-4). Mosby.

Pediatrician's Guide to Child Behavior Problems. Ed. by Ester Cava et al. 1979. text ed. 21.50 (ISBN 0-89352-075-6). Masson Pub.

Pediatrician's Psychological Handbook. Charles Toback. LC 79-92916. 1980. pap. 10.50 (ISBN 0-87488-687-2). Med Exam.

Pediatrics. Medical Economics Company. (Illus.). 1974. pap. 5.95 (ISBN 0-87489-052-7). Med Economics.

Pediatrics. 16th ed. Rudolph. (Illus.). 1977. 42.95 (ISBN 0-8385-7794-6). ACC.

Pediatrics. 5th ed. Hershel P. Wall. LC 61-66847. (Medical Examination Review Book: Vol. 11). 1980. pap. 8.50 (ISBN 0-87488-111-0). Med Exam.

Pediatrics - A Problem-Oriented Approach. Edward D. Wasserman & Donald S. Gromisch. 1980. spiral bdg. 9.75 (ISBN 0-87488-050-5). Med Exam.

Pediatrics Continuing Education Review. Richard D. Krugman & Thomas R. Welch. 1976. spiral bdg. 12.00 o.p. (ISBN 0-87488-342-3). Med Exam.

Pediatrics for the Practical Nurse. Catherine M. Brigley. LC 72-9384. (Illus.). 224p. 1973. pap. 7.40 (ISBN 0-8273-0332-7); instructor's guide 1.60 (ISBN 0-8273-0333-5). Delmar.

Pediatrics: PreTest Self-Assessment & Review. Ed. by Richard Lipman. LC 77-78444. (Clinical Sciences: PreTest Self-Assessment & Review Ser.). (Illus.). 1978. pap. 9.95 (ISBN 0-07-051603-0). McGraw-Pretest.

Pediatrics Specialty Board Review. 4th ed. Ed. by Marvin I. Gottlieb et al. 1974. spiral bdg. 16.50 (ISBN 0-87488-301-6). Med Exam.

Pedigree & Progress: Essays in the Genealogical Interpretation of History. Anthony Wagner. 333p. 1975. 35.00x (ISBN 0-87471-782-5). Rowman.

Pedigree Cats & Kittens: How to Choose & Care for Them. Christina Payne & Paddy Cutts. (Illus.). 64p. 1981. pap. 5.95 (ISBN 0-7134-3915-7, Pub. by Batsford England). David & Charles.

Pedigrees. Ann Shively. LC 80-7888. 408p. 1980. 12.95 (ISBN 0-690-02002-3). Lippincott & Crowell.

Pedlar of Swaffham. Kevin Crossley-Holland. LC 70-129208. (Illus.). (gr. 1-4). 1971. 6.95 (ISBN 0-395-28786-3, Clarion). HM.

Pedlar's Pack of Ballads & Songs. William H. Logan. LC 67-23929. 1968. Repr. of 1869 ed. 21.00 (ISBN 0-8103-3534-4). Gale.

Pedology. Jacob S. Joffe. 1949. 40.00 (ISBN 0-8135-0103-2). Rutgers U Pr.

Pedology, Weathering & Geomorphological Research. Peter W. Birkeland. (Illus.). 304p. 1974. text ed. 15.95x (ISBN 0-19-501730-7). Oxford U Pr.

Pedrini Supplementary Aid to the Administration of the Stanford-Binet Intelligence Scale (Form L-M) A Handbook. Duilio T. Pedrini & Lura N. Pedrini. LC 74-95256. (Professional Handbk Ser). 1970. pap. 8.75x (ISBN 0-87424-114-6). Western Psych.

Pedro. Gordon Stowell. Tr. by S. D. de Lerin from English. (Libros Pescaditos Sobre Personajes Biblicos). 1978. pap. 0.40 (ISBN 0-311-38516-8, Edit Mundo). Casa Bautista.

Pedro Antonio de Alarcon. Cyrus C. DeCoster. (World Authors Ser.: No. 549). 1979. lib. bdg. 13.50 (ISBN 0-8057-6391-0). Twayne.

Pedro Books Series. Phyllis Flowerdew. Incl. Hat for Pedro; Hats for Donkeys; Mr. Carlos & the Baby; Mrs. Carlos Wants a Car; Pedro; Pedro & the Cars; Pedro & the Kitten; Wrong Donkey. (Illus., Ea. bk 24p.). (gr. k-2). 1978. pap. 53.40 5 ea. of 8 titles incl. reproducible shts. (ISBN 0-8372-2590-6). Bowmar-Noble.

Pedro Calderon De la Barca: Los Cabellos de Absalon. Ed. by R. A. Edwards & G. Edwards. LC 73-4292. 168p. 1973. text ed. 19.50 (ISBN 0-08-017161-3); pap. text ed. 7.00 (ISBN 0-08-017162-1). Pergamon.

Pedro Menendez De Aviles. Gonzalo Solis De Meras. Ed. by Lyle N. McAlister. Tr. by Jeannette T. Connor. LC 64-19155. (Floridiana Facsimile & Reprint Ser). 1964. Repr. of 1567 ed. 16.00 (ISBN 0-8130-0214-1). U Presses Fla.

Pedro Prado. John R. Kelly. (World Authors Ser.: Chile: No. 304). 1974. lib. bdg. 10.95 (ISBN 0-8057-2712-4). Twayne.

Pedro Salinas. John Crispin. (World Authors Ser.: Spain: No. 283). 1974. lib. bdg. 10.95 (ISBN 0-8057-2784-1). Twayne.

Pee Dee Epiphany. W. Stanley Hoole. LC 79-65561. 1981. 7.50 (ISBN 0-916620-32-8). Portals Pr.

Peek-a-Boo! Judith York. (Illus.). (ps). 1979. 2.50 (ISBN 0-525-69503-6, Gingerbread). Dutton.

Peel. Norman Gash. LC 75-25695. (Illus.). 328p. 1976. 21.00x (ISBN 0-582-48083-3). Longman.

Peel's England. J. H. Peel. LC 77-73586. 1977. 14.95 (ISBN 0-7153-7380-3). David & Charles.

Peep-Larssons Go Sailing. Edith Unnerstad. (Illus.). (gr. 4-6). 1966. 4.50g o.s.i. (ISBN 0-02-789730-3). Macmillan.

Peep-Show. Pamela Blake. LC 72-80750. (Illus.). 32p. (ps-3). 1973. 3.95g o.s.i. (ISBN 0-02-710700-0). Macmillan.

Peeper, First Voice of Spring. Robert M McClung. LC 77-2410. (Illus.). (gr. 1-5). 1977. PLB 6.96 (ISBN 0-688-32116-X). Morrow.

Peer Counseling & Students Tutoring Students. Ed. by Fred Streit. 23p. 1977. pap. 8.00 o.p. (ISBN 0-686-00911-8, D-101). Essence Pubns.

Peer Gynt. Henrik Ibsen. Tr. by R. Farquharson. 1956. 7.95x (ISBN 0-460-00747-5, Evman). Dutton.

Peer Gynt. rev. ed. Henrik Ibsen. Tr. by Rolf Fjelde from Norwegian. (Vol. 2). 260p. 1981. 15.00x (ISBN 0-8166-0912-8); pap. 5.95 (ISBN 0-8166-0915-2). U of Minn Pr.

Peer-Mediated Instruction. Peter Rosenbaum. LC 72-92363. 272p. 1973. text ed. 10.25x (ISBN 0-8077-2368-1). Tchrs Coll.

Peer Review in the National Science Foundation: Phase One of a Study. Jonathan Cole et al. 1978. pap. text ed. 10.75 (ISBN 0-309-02788-8). Natl Acad Pr.

Peer Tutoring for Individual Instruction. Stewart W. Ehly & Stephen C. Larsen. 247p. 1980. text ed. 16.95 (ISBN 0-205-06878-2). Allyn.

Peerage Law in England: A Practical Treatise for Lawyers & Laymen. with an Appendix of Peerage Charters & Letters Patent (in English) Sir Francis B. Palmer. Ed. by David Berkowitz & Samuel Thorne. LC 77-89217. (Classics of English Legal History in the Modern Era Ser.: Vol. 128). 1979. Repr. of 1907 ed. lib. bdg. 55.00 (ISBN 0-8240-3165-2). Garland Pub.

Pegasus Descending: A Treasury of the Best Bad Poems in English. James Camp et al. 1971. pap. 2.45 o.s.i. (ISBN 0-02-069280-3, Collier). Macmillan.

Pegasus, the Winged Horse. new ed. Adapted by C. J. Naden. LC 80-50069. (gr. 3-5). 1980. PLB 5.89 (ISBN 0-89375-361-0); pap. 2.50 (ISBN 0-89375-365-3). Troll Assocs.

Peggy Fleming. Charles Morse. LC 74-18429. (Sports Superstars Ser). (Illus.). 32p. (gr. 3-6). 1974. PLB 5.95 o.p. (ISBN 0-87191-380-1); pap. 2.75 o.p. (ISBN 0-89812-192-2). Creative Ed.

Peggy's New Brother. Eleanor Schick. LC 70-99124. (Illus.). (gr. k-2). 1970. 4.95g o.s.i. (ISBN 0-02-781140-9). Macmillan.

Pegmes: The Renaissance & the Gods. Pierre Cousteau. Ed. by Stephen Orgel. LC 78-68181. (Philosophy of Images Ser.). (Illus.). 1980. lib. bdg. 66.00 (ISBN 0-8240-3677-8). Garland Pub.

Peiping Municipality & the Diplomatic Quarter. Robert Duncan. LC 78-74355. (Modern Chinese Economy Ser.). 146p. 1980. lib. bdg. 16.50 (ISBN 0-8240-4271-9). Garland Pub.

Peirce's Logic of Relations & Other Studies. R. M. Martin. (Studies in Semiotics: No. 12). (Orig.). 1980. pap. text ed. 10.50x (ISBN 90-316-0133-0). Humanities.

Peirol, Troubadour of Auvergne. Peirol D'Auvergne & S. C. Aston. LC 80-2185. 1981. Repr. of 1953 ed. 32.00 (ISBN 0-404-19012-X). AMS Pr.

Peking. David Bonavia. Ed. by Time-Life Books. (Great Cities Ser.). (Illus.). 1978. 14.95 (ISBN 0-8094-2327-8). Time-Life.

Peking. David P. Jones. (Great Cities Ser.). (Illus.). 1978. lib. bdg. 14.94 (ISBN 0-686-51005-4). Silver.

Peking Man Is Missing. Claire Taschdjian. LC 77-3806. 1977. 10.00 o.p. (ISBN 0-06-014219-7, HarpT). Har-Row.

Peking, Moscow & Beyond. William E. Griffith. LC 72-10375. (Washington Papers: No. 6). 1973. 3.50x (ISBN 0-8039-0280-8). Sage.

Peking Payoff. Ian Stewart. 252p. 1975. 8.95 o.s.i. (ISBN 0-02-614700-9). Macmillan.

Peking Politics, 1918-1923: Factionalism & the Failure of Constitutionalism. Andrew Nathan. LC 74-79769. 1976. 22.75x (ISBN 0-520-02784-1). U of Cal Pr.

Pekingese. Herminie W. Hill. Ed. by Christina Foyle. (Foyles Handbks). 1973. 3.95 (ISBN 0-685-55813-4). Palmetto Pub.

Pekingese Guide. Frances Sefton. 6.98 o.p. (ISBN 0-385-01580-1). Doubleday.

Pel & the Faceless Corpse. Mark Hebden. 1979. 17.95 (ISBN 0-241-10085-2, Pub. by Hamish Hamilton England). David & Charles.

Pelargoniums. Henry J. Wood. (Illus.). 1966. 9.95 o.p. (ISBN 0-571-06888-X, Pub. by Faber & Faber). Merrimack Bk Serv.

Peldanos. 2nd ed. R. L. Politzer & H. N. Urrutibeheity. LC 72-75117. 1972. pap. text ed. 17.95x (ISBN 0-471-00848-6); wkbk. 6.50x (ISBN 0-471-00854-0). Wiley.

Pele' Paula Taylor. LC 76-5818. (Sports Superstars Ser.). (Illus.). (gr. 3-9). 1976. PLB 5.95 o.p. (ISBN 0-87191-513-8); pap. 2.75 o.p. (ISBN 0-89812-193-0). Creative Ed.

Pele'! Edson do Nascimento. James Hahn & Lynn Hahn. Ed. by Howard Schroeder. (Sports Legends Ser.). (Illus.). 48p. (Orig.). (gr. 3-5). 1981. PLB 5.95 (ISBN 0-89686-125-2); pap. text ed. 2.95 (ISBN 0-89686-140-6). Crestwood Hse.

Pele: World Soccer Star. Julian May. LC 75-28935. (Sports Close-up Ser.). (gr. 3-9). 1975. PLB 5.95 o.p. (ISBN 0-913940-34-8); pap. 2.95 o.p. (ISBN 0-89686-000-0). Crestwood Hse.

Pelecypoda from the Type Locality of the Stone City Beds (Middle Eocene) of Texas. H. B. Stenzel et al. (Illus.). 237p. 1957. 3.75 (PUB 5704). Bur Econ Geology.

Pelham Golf Year. Louis Stanley. 448p. 1981. 19.95 (ISBN 0-7207-1290-4). Merrimack Bk Serv.

Pelican Chorus & Quangle Wangle's Hat. Edward Lear. LC 80-53511. (Illus.). 32p. 1981. 7.95 (ISBN 0-670-54613-5). Viking Pr.

Pelican Guide to Hillsborough: Historic Orange County, North Carolina. Lucile N. Dula. LC 78-26081. (Pelican Guide Ser). (Illus.). 1979. pap. 4.95 (ISBN 0-88289-208-8). Pelican.

Pelican Guide to Historic Homes & Sites of Revolutionary America. Adelaide Hechtlinger. Incl. Vol. 1. New England. (Illus.). 1976. pap. 3.95 (ISBN 0-88289-090-5). LC 76-20434. (Pelican Guide Ser.). Pelican.

Pelican Guide to New Orleans. 4th, rev. ed. Thomas K. Griffin. LC 74-182889. (Pelican Guide Ser.). (Illus.). 160p. 1980. pap. 3.95 (ISBN 0-88289-010-7). Pelican.

Pelican Guide to Old Homes of Mississippi, 2 vols. Helen Kempe. Incl. Vol. 1. Natchez & the South (ISBN 0-88289-134-0); Vol. 2. Columbus & the North (ISBN 0-88289-135-9). LC 76-20434. (Pelican Guide Ser.). (Illus.). 1977. pap. 3.95 ea. Pelican.

Pelican Guide to Virginia. Shirley Morris. (Pelican Guide Ser.). 1981. pap. 4.95 (ISBN 0-88289-206-1). Pelican.

Pelican History of England: Tudor England, Vol. 5. S. T. Bindoff. 1950. pap. 3.50 (ISBN 0-14-020212-9, Pelican). Penguin.

Pelican History of Music, Vol. 3, Classical & Romantic. Hugh Ottaway & Arthur Hutchings. Ed. by Denis Stevens & Alec Robertson. (Orig.). 1968. pap. 2.50 o.p. (ISBN 0-14-020494-6, Pelican). Penguin.

Pelican Mystery. Ruth Hooker. LC 77-7330. (Pilot Books). (Illus.). (gr. 3-7). 1977. 6.95g (ISBN 0-8075-6395-1). A Whitman.

Pelicans. Lester Cooper. (Animals Animals Animals Library: Second Ser.). (Illus.). (gr. 1-9). 1979. 6.95 (ISBN 0-917080-11-4). Handel & Sons.

Pelicans Are Scarce. Kathy Friedel. Date not set. 5.95 (ISBN 0-533-04865-6). Vantage.

Pella of the Decapolis, Vol. 1. Robert H. Smith. LC 72-619700. (Illus.). 248p. 1973. 50.00 (ISBN 0-9604658-0-4). Coll Wooster.

Pelo Lacio, Pelo Rizo. Augusta Goldin. Tr. by Richard J. Palmer. LC 68-27324. (Let's-Read-&-Find-Out Science Bk). (Illus., Span.). (gr. k-3). 1968. PLB 7.89 (ISBN 0-690-77923-2, TYC-J). T Y Crowell.

Peloubet's Notes 1980-81. Ralph Earle. 1980. pap. 4.95 (ISBN 0-8010-3361-6). Baker Bk.

Peloubet's Notes 1981-82. Ralph Earle. 408p. (Orig.). 1981. pap. 4.95 (ISBN 0-8010-3363-2). Baker Bk.

Pemato Jayati Soko (Love Is the Bringer of Sorrow) D. M. De Silva. Tr. by D. M. De Silva from Singhalese. (Salzburg Studies in English Literature: Poetic Drama & Poetic Theory: No. 25). 55p. 1976. pap. text ed. 25.00x (ISBN 0-391-01524-9). Humanities.

Pembroke College in Brown University: The First Seventy-Five Years, 1891-1966. Grace E. Hawk. LC 67-19656. (Illus.). 324p. 1967. 12.50 (ISBN 0-87057-101-X, Pub. by Brown U Pr). Univ Pr of New England.

Pembroke Colors. Stephen Longstreet. 320p. 1981. 12.95 (ISBN 0-399-12582-5). Putnam.

Pembrokeshire. Brian John. (Illus.). 192p. 1976. 14.95 (ISBN 0-7153-7171-1). David & Charles.

Pen & Ink Themes. Frank J. Lohan. (Illus.). 1981. 12.95 (ISBN 0-8092-7016-1); pap. 5.95 (ISBN 0-8092-7015-3). Contemp Bks.

Pen & the Sword: War & Peace in the Prose & Plays of Bernard Shaw. Gordon N. Bergquist. (Salzburg Studies in English Literature, Poetic Drama & Poetic Theory: No. 28). 1977. pap. text ed. 25.00x (ISBN 0-391-01325-4). Humanities.

Pen: Emperor Penguin. Sally Glendinning. LC 80-13212. (Young Animal Adventures Ser.). 40p. (gr. 2). 1980. PLB 5.88 (ISBN 0-8116-7500-9). Garrard.

Pen Names & Personalities. Annie R. Marble. 256p. 1980. Repr. of 1930 ed. lib. bdg. 30.00 (ISBN 0-89987-563-7). Century Bookbindery.

Penal Code of Sweden. (American Series of Foreign Penal Codes: Vol. 17). x, 114p. 1972. 15.00x (ISBN 0-8377-0037-X). Rothman.

Penal Code of the Polish People's Republic. (American Series of Foreign Penal Codes: Vol. 19). 1973. 17.50x (ISBN 0-8377-0039-6). Rothman.

Penal Code of the Romanian Socialist Republic. Tr. by Simone-Marie Kleckner from Romanian. LC 76-17385. (American Series of Foreign Penal Codes: Vol. 20). 1976. text ed. 17.50x (ISBN 0-8377-0040-X). Rothman.

Penal Law of Islam. M. I. Siddiqui. 1980. 9.95 (ISBN 0-686-64662-2). Kazi Pubns.

Penal Law of New York. (Supplemented annually). looseleaf 5.75 (ISBN 0-87526-145-0); pap. 4.50 (ISBN 0-87526-261-9). Gould.

Penal Law of New York Quizzer. Gould Editorial Staff. 1981. looseleaf 5.50 (ISBN 0-87526-225-2). Gould.

Penalty Killer: A Hockey Story. Sheldon Ilowite. (Illus.). (gr. 4-6). 1974. 5.95g (ISBN 0-8038-5799-3). Hastings.
Penalty of Death: The Canadian Experiment. C. H. Jayewardene. LC 77-167. (Illus.). 1977. 15.95 (ISBN 0-669-01464-8). Lexington Bks.
Pence. Beverly Hightower. 1981. 4.95 (ISBN 0-8062-1447-3). Carlton.
Pencil & Paper Tricks. Geoffrey Lamb. LC 77-12102. (Illus.). (gr. 5 up). 1977. Repr. 6.95 o.p. (ISBN 0-525-66565-X). Elsevier-Nelson.
Pencil Drawing for the Architect. Charles I. Hobbis. (gr. 10-12). 1954. 5.95 (ISBN 0-85458-100-6); pap. 3.95 (ISBN 0-85458-101-4). Transatlantic.
Pencil Pastimes, No. 8. (Orig.). 1979. pap. 2.50 (ISBN 0-89104-157-5). A & W Pubs.
Pencil Pastimes, No. 9. James F. Minter. 128p. 1981. pap. 2.50 (ISBN 0-89104-172-9). A & W Pubs.
Pencil, Pen, & Brush. Harvey Weiss. (Illus.). (gr. 4-6). 1974. pap. 1.50 (ISBN 0-590-02229-6, Schol Pap). Schol Bk Serv.
Pencourt File. Barry Penrose & Roger Courtiour. LC 78-2152. (Illus.). 1978. 12.95 o.s.i. (ISBN 0-06-013343-0, HarpT). Har-Row.
Pendergast Machine. Lyle W. Dorsett. LC 80-11581. (Illus.). xvi, 163p. 1980. 13.50x (ISBN 0-8032-1655-6); pap. 3.95 (ISBN 0-8032-6554-9, BB 744, Bison). U of Nebr Pr.
Pendex: An Index of Pen Names & House Names in Fantastic, Thriller & Series Literature. Susannah Bates. LC 80-8486. 200p. 1981. lib. bdg. 22.50 (ISBN 0-8240-9501-4). Garland Pub.
Pendragon. Catherine Christian. 624p. 1980. pap. 2.95 (ISBN 0-446-83820-9). Warner Bks.
Pendulum. Anthony Rossiter. LC 67-27440. 1967. 7.50 o.p. (ISBN 0-912326-22-0). Garrett-Helix.
Pendulum Power. Joseph Polansky & Greg Nielsen. (Warner Destiny Bk.). (Orig.). 1977. pap. 1.95 o.s.i. (ISBN 0-446-89348-X). Warner Bks.
Pendulum, Radiesthesia & You. Phyllis Harrison & Paul Collins. (Illus., Orig.). 1981. pap. 6.95 (ISBN 0-89407-033-9). Strawberry Hill.
Penelope. Norman Thelwell. 1973. 4.95 o.p. (ISBN 0-525-17722-1). Dutton.
Penelope Now. John Crosby. LC 80-6149. 256p. 1981. 12.95 (ISBN 0-8128-2793-7). Stein & Day.
Penelope's Pen Pal. Linda P. Silbert & Alvin J. Silbert. (Little Twirps, TM Understanding People Books). (Illus.). (gr. k-4). 1978. pap. 2.25 (ISBN 0-89544-053-9). Silbert Bress.
Penetrance & Variability in Malformation Syndromes. Ed. by James J. O'Donnell & Bryan D. Hall. LC 79-5115. (Alan R. Liss Ser.: Vol. 15, No. 5b). 1979. 42.00 (ISBN 0-8451-1029-2). March of Dimes.
Penetrating the Magic Bubble. Pat Hurley. 1978. pap. 3.50 (ISBN 0-88207-183-1). Victor Bks.
Penetration of Arabia: A Record of the Development of Western Knowledge Concerning the Arabian Peninsula. David G. Hogarth. LC 79-2863. (Illus.). 359p. 1981. Repr. of 1904 ed. 35.00 (ISBN 0-8305-0037-5). Hyperion Conn.
Penetrator: Hell's Hostages, No. 41. Lionel Derrick. 192p. (Orig.). 1981. pap. 1.75 (ISBN 0-523-41116-2). Pinnacle Bks.
Penetrators. Pat Hurley. 1978. pap. 3.50 (ISBN 0-88207-184-X). Victor Bks.
Penguin. Paula Z. Hogan. LC 78-21225. (Life Cycles Ser.). (Illus.). (gr. k-3). 1979. PLB 9.95 (ISBN 0-8172-1257-4). Raintree Pubs.
Penguin. Angela Sheehan. LC 78-68537. (First Look at Nature Ser.). (Illus.). (gr. 2-4). 1979. 2.50 (ISBN 0-531-09142-2, Warwick Press); PLB 6.45 s&l (ISBN 0-531-09153-8, Warwick Pr). Watts.
Penguin Book of Chess Positions. Hugh Alexander. (Handbook Ser.). 1974. pap. 2.50 o.p. (ISBN 0-14-046199-X). Penguin.
Penguin Book of Daily Telegraph Quick Crosswords. Alan Cash. 1980. pap. 2.95 (ISBN 0-14-005089-2). Penguin.
Penguin Book of Hebrew Verse. T. Carmi. 1981. 25.00 (ISBN 0-670-36507-6). Viking Pr.
Penguin Book of Russian Short Stories. Ed. by David Richards. 1981. pap. 4.50 (ISBN 0-14-004816-2). Penguin.
Penguin Book of Zen Poetry. Ed. by Lucien Stryk & Takashi Ikemoto. LC 77-83237. 159p. 1978. 9.95 (ISBN 0-8040-0792-6). Swallow.
Penguin Book of Zen Poetry. Ed. by Lucien Stryk & Takashi Ikemoto. Tr. by Lucien Stryk & Takashi Ikemoto. 1981. pap. 4.95 (ISBN 0-14-042247-1). Penguin.
Penguin Books of Pets: A Practical Guide to Animal Keeping. Emil P. Dolensek & Barbara Burn. (Handbooks Ser). (Illus.). 1978. pap. 4.95 o.p. (ISBN 0-14-046318-6). Penguin.
Penguin Dictionary of Architecture. rev. ed. John Fleming et al. (Reference Ser.). 1973. pap. 4.95 (ISBN 0-14-051013-3). Penguin.
Penguin Dictionary of English & European History 1485-1789. E. N. Williams. 480p. 1980. pap. 6.95 (ISBN 0-14-051084-2). Penguin.
Penguin Dictionary of Modern Quotations. J. M. Cohen & M. J. Cohen. Date not set. pap. 3.95 (ISBN 0-14-051038-9). Penguin. Postponed.
Penguin Dictionary of Quotations. J. M. Cohen & M. J. Cohen. 1978. 15.00 o.p. (ISBN 0-670-27226-4). Viking Pr.
Penguin Film Review 1946-1949, 2 vols. Ed. by Roger Manvell et al. (Illus.). 1978. Repr. of 1946 ed. Set. 49.50x (ISBN 0-8476-6029-X). Rowman.
Penguin Stereo Record Guide. 2nd ed. Edward Greenfield et al. (Handbooks Ser). 1978. pap. 8.95 o.p. (ISBN 0-14-046223-6). Penguin.
Penguin Year. Susan Bonners. LC 79-53595. (Illus.). 48p. (gr. 1-3). 1981. 9.95 (ISBN 0-440-00166-8); PLB 9.43 (ISBN 0-440-00170-6). Delacorte.
Penguins. Sylvia A. Johnson. LC 80-2880. (Lerner Natural Science Bks.). (gr. 4-10). 1981. PLB 7.95 (ISBN 0-8225-1453-2). Lerner Pubns.
Penguins. Richard Tenaza. (gr. 4 up). 1980. PLB 6.90 (ISBN 0-531-04104-2). Watts.
Penguins. Ralph Whitlock. LC 77-14042. (Animals of the World Ser.). (Illus.). (gr. 4-8). 1977. PLB 10.65 (ISBN 0-8172-1078-4). Raintree Pubs.
Penguins Live Here. Irmengarde Eberle. LC 74-1383. (gr. 1-5). 1975. 4.95 o.p. (ISBN 0-385-05715-6). Doubleday.
Penguins: The Birds with Flippers. Elizabeth S. Austin. (gr. 3-6). 1968. PLB 5.99 (ISBN 0-394-90148-7); pap. 1.95. Random.
Penicillin Fifty Years After Fleming. 2nd ed. Ed. by James Baddiley & E. P. Abraham. (Royal Society Ser.). 378p. 1980. lib. bdg. 62.00x (ISBN 0-85403-140-5, Pub. by Royal Soc London). Scholium Intl.
Peninsular General: Sir Thomas Picton, Seventeen Fifty-Eight to Eighteen Fifteen. Frederick Myatt. LC 79-56256. (Illus.). 224p. 1980. 28.00 (ISBN 0-7153-7923-2). David & Charles.
Peninsular Malaysia. 2nd ed. Ooi Jin-Bee. LC 75-42166. (Geographies for Advanced Study). Orig. Title: Land, People & Economy in Malaysia. 1976. text ed. 23.00x (ISBN 0-582-48185-6). Longman.
Penjerdel Location & Market Guide. Ed. by Jody G. Miller et al. LC 77-78304. (Illus.). 1981. pap. 20.00 (ISBN 0-918964-00-8). Greater Phila.
Penmarric. Susan Howatch. 704p. 1978. pap. 2.75 (ISBN 0-449-24090-8, Crest). Fawcett.
Pennell's New York City Etchings: Ninety-One Prints. Joseph Pennell & Edward Bryant. (Illus.). 112p. (Orig.). 1981. pap. write for info. (ISBN 0-486-23913-6). Dover.
Pennies for the Piper. Susan H. McLean. 132p. (gr. 5 up). 1981. 9.95 (ISBN 0-374-35791-9). FS&G.
Penniless Billionaires. Max Shapiro. 1981. 15.00 (ISBN 0-8129-0923-2). Times Bks.
Pennington's Last Term. K. M. Peyton. LC 75-13099. (Illus.). (gr. 7-9). 1971. 8.95 (ISBN 0-690-61271-0, TYC-J). T Y Crowell.
Penn's Woods: A Love Story. Bernard C. Barnick. 64p. 1980. 10.00x (ISBN 0-682-49660-X, Banner). Exposition.
Pennsylvania. Thomas C. Cochran. (States & the Nation Ser.). (Illus.). 1978. 12.95 (ISBN 0-393-05635-X, Co-Pub by AASLH). Norton.
Pennsylvania. 33.00 (ISBN 0-89770-114-3). Curriculum Info Ctr.
Pennsylvania. Photos by Clyde Smith. LC 78-51218. (Belding Imprint Ser.). (Illus.). 192p. (Text by Cronan Minton). 1978. 29.50 (ISBN 0-912856-40-8). Graphic Arts Ctr.
Pennsylvania: A Bicentennial Workshop. Lucille Wallower. Ed. by Annette Brookshire. LC 74-26216. (gr. 3-4). 1975. pap. 3.30 o.p. (ISBN 0-931992-03-6). Penns Valley.
Pennsylvania ABC. Lucille Wallower. Ed. by Patricia L. Gump. (Illus.). (gr. 2-5). 1964. pap. 3.50 (ISBN 0-931992-08-7). Penns Valley.
Pennsylvania Agriculture & Country Life: 1640-1840. Stevenson W. Fletcher. LC 50-9470. 1971. 9.00 (ISBN 0-911124-33-0). Pa Hist & Mus.
Pennsylvania Agriculture & Country Life: 1840-1940. Stevenson W. Fletcher. LC 50-9470. 1955. 9.00 (ISBN 0-911124-34-9). Pa Hist & Mus.
Pennsylvania & the Federal Constitution 1787-1788, 2 vols, Vol. 1. John McMaster & Frederick B. Stone. LC 74-87406. (American Constitutional & Legal History Ser). 1970. Repr. of 1888 ed. lib. bdg. 65.00 (ISBN 0-306-71550-3). Da Capo.
Pennsylvania & the War of Eighteen Twelve. Victor A. Sapio. LC 70-94070. (Illus.). 216p. 1970. 11.00x (ISBN 0-8131-1193-5). U Pr of Ky.
Pennsylvania Atlas: A Thematic Atlas of the Keystone State. Paul F. Rizza et al. 1976. pap. 6.95x o.p. (ISBN 0-686-23264-X). Ptolemy Pr.
Pennsylvania Chronology & Factbook, Vol. 38. R. I. Vexler. 1978. 8.50 (ISBN 0-379-16163-X). Oceana.
Pennsylvania Citizen. Millard Altland. (gr. 8-12). 1964. 4.50 o.p. (ISBN 0-931992-22-2). Penns Valley.
Pennsylvania Constitution of 1776. J. P. Selsam. LC 77-124925. (American Constitutional & Legal History Ser.). 1971. Repr. of 1936 ed. lib. bdg. 29.50 (ISBN 0-306-71994-0). Da Capo.
Pennsylvania Dutch. Fredric Klees. 1950. 9.95 o.s.i. (ISBN 0-02-563820-3). Macmillan.
Pennsylvania Dutch. William T. Parsons. LC 75-22044. (Immigrant Heritage of America Ser.). 1976. lib. bdg. 10.95 (ISBN 0-8057-8408-X). Twayne.
Pennsylvania Dutch American Folk Art. rev. & enl. ed. Henry J. Kauffman. (Illus.). 10.00 (ISBN 0-8446-2354-7). Peter Smith.
Pennsylvania Dutch American Folk Art. rev. & enl. ed. Henry J. Kauffman. (Illus.). pap. 5.00 (ISBN 0-486-21205-X). Dover.
Pennsylvania Dutch & Their Furniture. John C. Shea. 240p. 1980. 19.95 (ISBN 0-442-27546-3). Van Nos Reinhold.
Pennsylvania Dutch Cook Book. J. George Frederick. 7.00 (ISBN 0-8446-0099-7). Peter Smith.
Pennsylvania Dutch Cookbook. abr. ed. J. George Frederick. Orig. Title: Pennsylvania Dutch & Their Cookery. 1971. pap. 2.75 (ISBN 0-486-22676-X). Dover.
Pennsylvania Dutch Farm: To Cut Out & Assemble. Edmund V. Gillon, Jr. (Orig.). 1979. pap. 6.95 (ISBN 0-684-16341-1). Scribner.
Pennsylvania-Encyclopedia of the United States. 1980. lib. bdg. 75.00 (ISBN 0-686-58139-3). Somerset Pub.
Pennsylvania German Illuminated Manuscripts: A Classification of Fraktur-Schriften & an Inquiry into Their History & Art. Henry S. Borneman. (Illus.). 8.50 (ISBN 0-685-56779-6). Peter Smith.
Pennsylvania Government in Action: Governor Leader's Administration, 1955-1959. M. Nelson McGeary. LC 72-78442. (gr. 8-12). 1972. 7.00 (ISBN 0-931992-27-3); pap. 3.95 (ISBN 0-931992-28-1). Penns Valley.
Pennsylvania Historical Bibliography: III. Additions Through 1976. John B. Trussell, Jr. 100p. (Orig.). 1980. pap. 4.00 (ISBN 0-89271-014-4). Pa Hist & Mus.
Pennsylvania Historical Bibliography: III. Additions Through 1973. John B. Trussell, Jr. 87p. (Orig.). 1979. pap. 4.00 (ISBN 0-89271-004-7). Pa Hist & Mus.
Pennsylvania Historical Bibliography: I Additions Through 1970. Compiled by John B. Trussell, Jr. 1979. 4.00 (ISBN 0-89271-003-9). Pa Hist & Mus.
Pennsylvania Iron Manufacture in the Eighteenth Century. rev. ed. Arthur C. Bining. (Illus.). 214p. 1973. 8.50 (ISBN 0-911124-72-1); pap. 4.50 (ISBN 0-911124-71-3). Pa Hist & Mus.
Pennsylvania Landscapes: A Geography of the Commonwealth. Raymond E. Murphy & Marion F. Murphy. LC 73-77560. (gr. 8-10). 1974. 7.95 (ISBN 0-931992-19-2); teachers guide 1.00 (ISBN 0-931992-20-6). Penns Valley.
Pennsylvania Line: Regimental Organization & Operations, 1775-1783. John B. Trussell, Jr. LC 78-621999. 1976. 12.00 (ISBN 0-911124-85-3). Pa Hist & Mus.
Pennsylvania Local Government 1681-1974: Bicentennial Edition. Harold F. Alderfer. LC 73-93891. 1975. pap. 2.95 o.p. (ISBN 0-931992-26-5). Penns Valley.
Pennsylvania Main Line Canal. McCullough & Leuba. 1976. 4.75 o.p. (ISBN 0-933788-26-6). Am Canal & Transport.
Pennsylvania Navy, Seventeen Seventy-Five to Seventeen Eighty-One: The Defense of the Delaware. 2nd ed. John W. Jackson. (Illus.). 528p. 1974. 27.50 (ISBN 0-8135-0766-9). Rutgers U Pr.
Pennsylvania Notary Law Primer. Editors of The National Notary Magazine of the National Notary Assn. 1981. pap. 5.95 (ISBN 0-933134-07-X). Natl Notary.
Pennsylvania Place Names. Abraham H. Espenshade. LC 68-30591. 1969. Repr. of 1925 ed. 18.00 (ISBN 0-8103-3234-5). Gale.
Pennsylvania Politics & the Growth of Democracy: 1740-1776. Theodore Thayer. LC 54-9746. 1953. 8.00 (ISBN 0-911124-23-3). Pa Hist & Mus.
Pennsylvania Politics Today & Yesterday: The Tolerable Accomodation. Paul B. Beers. LC 79-65826. (Keystone Bks.). (Illus.). 416p. 1980. 16.75 (ISBN 0-271-00238-7). Pa St U Pr.
Pennsylvania State Industrial Directory, 1980. State Industrial Directories Corp. 1980. 90.00 (ISBN 0-89910-024-4). State Indus Dir.
Pennsylvanian Depositional Systems in North-Central Texas: A Guide for Interpreting Terrigenous Clastic Facies in a Cratonic Basin. L. F. Brown et al. (Illus.). 122p. 1973. Repr. 3.50 (GB 14). Bur Econ Geology.
Pennsylvania's Black History. Charles Blockson. (Illus.). 1981. pap. 5.95 (ISBN 0-933184-15-8). Flame Intl.
Penny a Look: An Old Story. Harve Zemach. LC 71-161373. (Illus.). (ps-3). 1971. 6.95 (ISBN 0-374-35793-5). FS&G.
Penny Ante & up. Oswald Jacoby. LC 76-40882. 1979. pap. 3.95 (ISBN 0-385-11173-8, Dolp). Doubleday.
Penny-Box. Alice Dwyer-Joyce. 192p. 1981. 8.95 (ISBN 0-312-60002-X). St Martin.
Penny Goes to Camp. Carolyn Haywood. (Illus.). (gr. 1-5). 1948. 8.25 (ISBN 0-688-21728-1). Morrow.
Penny Murders. Lionel Black. 1979. pap. 1.95 (ISBN 0-380-48090-5, 48090). Avon.
Penny-Pinching Guide to Bigger Fish & Better Hunting. Clair Rees & Hartt Wixom. (Illus.). 256p. 1980. 9.95 (ISBN 0-87691-319-2). Winchester Pr.
Penny Tales. Virginia Schone. LC 76-17827. (Illus.). (ps-3). 1977. 5.95 o.s.i. (ISBN 0-8193-0850-1, Four Winds); PLB 5.41 o.s.i. (ISBN 0-8193-0851-X). Schol Bk Serv.
Penny: The Story of a Free-Soul Basset Hound. Hal Borland. LC 74-37927. (Illus.). (YA) 1972. 7.95 (ISBN 0-397-00864-3). Lippincott.
Penny Wise. Sarah Carlisle. 224p. 1981. pap. 1.95 (ISBN 0-449-50176-0, Coventry). Fawcett.
Pennypincher Householder Handbook. Rosemary Wadey et al. LC 79-52368. (Illus.). 1979. 17.95 (ISBN 0-7153-7844-9). David & Charles.
Penny's Poodle Puppy, Pickle. Bernard Wiseman. LC 79-26403. (Bernard Wiseman Bks.). (Illus.). (gr. k-4). 1980. PLB 5.49 (ISBN 0-8116-6080-X). Garrard.
Penny's Worth of Character. Jesse Stuart. (Illus.). (gr. 3-5). 1964. PLB 7.95 o.p. (ISBN 0-07-062301-5, GB). McGraw.
Penology: A Realistic Approach. Clyde B. Vedder & Barbara A. Kay. (Illus.). 360p. 1973. 15.50 (ISBN 0-398-01975-4). C C Thomas.
Penquin Dictionary of Architecture. John Fleming & Nikolaus Pevsner. 1980. pap. 4.95 (ISBN 0-14-051013-3). Penguin.
Penrose Seventy-Nine to Eighty. Ed. by Clive Goodacre. (International Review of the Graphic Arts Ser.; Vol. 72). 1979. 49.50 o.p. (ISBN 0-8038-5881-7). Hastings.
Penrose 1980-1981: International Review of the Graphic Arts, Vol.73. Ed. by Clive Goodacre. (Illus.). 200p. 1981. 59.50 (ISBN 0-8038-5892-2, Visual Communication). Hastings.
Pensamento Da Possiblilidade, O. Tr. by Robert Schuller. (Portugese Bks.). (Port.). 1979. 1.50 (ISBN 0-8297-0727-1). Life Pubs Intl.
Pensando Con Dios. Norman Camp. 128p. (Span.). 1981. pap. 1.95 (ISBN 0-8024-6593-5). Moody.
Pensativa. Jesus Goytortua. Ed. by Donald D. Walsh. (Orig., Span.). (gr. 10-12). 1962. pap. text ed. 8.95 (ISBN 0-13-655605-1). P-H.
Pensee & Structure. 2nd ed. John Darbelnet. LC 68-19906. (Fr). 1977. text ed. 9.95x (ISBN 0-684-14882-X, ScribC); wkbk. 6.95x (ISBN 0-684-15932-5, ScribC); wkbk. 5.95 (ISBN 0-684-15091-3, ScribC). Scribner.
Pensees. Blaise Pascal. Tr. by W. F. Trotter. 1958. pap. 3.25 (ISBN 0-525-47018-2, Evman). Dutton.
Pensees. Blaise Pascal. Tr. by A. J. Krailsheimer. (Classics Ser.). (Orig.). 1966. pap. 3.50 (ISBN 0-14-044171-9). Penguin.
Pensees de Pascal: De l'anthropologie a la theologie. M. Le Guern & M. R. Le Guern. (Collection themes et textes). 244p. (Fr.). 1972. pap. 6.75 (ISBN 2-03-035005-2, 2697). Larousse.
Penseurs de l'Islam, 5 vols. Bernard Carra de Vaux. LC 80-2197. 1981. Repr. of 1926 ed. Set. 200.00 (ISBN 0-404-18990-3). AMS Pr.
Pension & Institutional Portfolio Management. Martin J. Schwimmer & Edward Malca. LC 76-6473. (Special Studies). (Illus.). 120p. 1976. text ed. 22.95 (ISBN 0-275-56730-3). Praeger.
Pension Fund Operations & Expenses: The Technical Report. Robert D. Cooper & Melody A. Carlsen. (Illus.). 149p. (Orig.). 1980. pap. 15.00 (ISBN 0-89154-139-X). Intl Found Employ.
Pension Mathematics: With Numerical Illustrations. Howard E. Winklevoss. 1977. 12.00x (ISBN 0-256-01886-3). Irwin.
Pension Planning: Pensions, Profit Sharing & Other Deferred Compensation Plans. 3rd ed. Everett T. Allen et al. 1976. text ed. 17.50x (ISBN 0-256-01857-X). Irwin.
Pension Planning Within a Major Company. Ronald J. Lucas. 1979. 35.00 (ISBN 0-08-024045-3). Pergamon.
Pension Plans & Public Policy. William C. Greenough & Francis P. King. 336p. 1976. 17.50x (ISBN 0-231-04070-9). Columbia U Pr.
Pension Reform Update. (Tax Law & Estate Planning Course Handbook Ser. 1977-78: Vol. 116). 1977. pap. 20.00 o.p. (ISBN 0-685-05642-2, J4-3445). PLI.
Pension Schemes. Michael Pilch & V. Wood. 1979. text ed. 34.25x (ISBN 0-566-02117-X, Pub. by Gower Pub Co England). Renouf.

Pensions: An Accounting & Management Guide. Felix Pomeranz et al. LC 75-35288. 1976. 31.95 (ISBN 0-8260-7199-6). Ronald Pr.

Pensions & Industrial Relations: A Practical Guide for All Involved in Pensions. Harry Lucas. 1977. text ed. 26.00 (ISBN 0-08-021947-0); pap. text ed. 11.25 (ISBN 0-08-021946-2). Pergamon.

Pentacoordinated Phosphorus. Robert R. Holmes. Incl. Structure & Spectroscopy. (No. 175). Vol. I. 92.00 (ISBN 0-8412-0458-6); Reaction Mechanisms. (176). Vol. II. 52.00 (ISBN 0-8412-0528-0); Set. 144.00 (ISBN 0-8412-0529-9). LC 80-26302. (Acs Monograph). 1980. Am Chemical.

Pentacoordinated Phosphorus. Robert R. Holmes. Incl. Vol. 1, Structure & Spectroscopy. (No. 175). 92.00 (ISBN 0-8412-0458-6); Vol. 2, Reaction Mechanisms. (No. 176). 52.00 (ISBN 0-8412-0528-0). (ACS Monograph). 1980. Set. 144.00 (ISBN 0-8412-0529-9). Am Chemical.

Pentagram As a Medical Symbol: An Iconological Study. Jan Schouten. 1979. text ed. 17.25x (ISBN 90-6004-166-6). Humanities.

Pentateuch. Samson Hirsch. 4257p. (Eng. & Hebrew.). 1962. 60.00 (ISBN 0-910818-12-6). Judaica Pr.

Pentateuch in Its Cultural Environment. G. Herbert Livingston. 1974. 11.95 (ISBN 0-8010-5540-7). Baker Bk.

Pentateuco. Tr. by Pablo Hoff. (Spanish Bks.). 1979. 2.95 (ISBN 0-8297-0876-6). Life Pubs Intl.

Pentatonic Songs for Young Children. Mary H. Richards. LC 67-29156. (Orig.). (gr. 1-3). 1967. pap. 0.96x (ISBN 0-8224-9013-7). Pitman Learning.

Pentax Guide. Fred Swartz. (Illus.). 136p. 1980. 11.95 (ISBN 0-8174-2471-7); pap. 6.95 (ISBN 0-8174-2143-2). Amphoto.

Pentax SLR Cameras. Carl Shipman. LC 76-51908. (Illus.). 1977. pap. 9.95 (ISBN 0-912656-57-3). H P Bks.

Pentecost Behind the Iron Curtain. Steve Durasoff. LC 72-93080. 170p. (Orig.). 1973. pap. 2.95 o.p. (ISBN 0-88270-018-9). Logos.

Pentecost 1. Howard C. Kee & Peter J. Gomes. Ed. by Elizabeth Achtemeier et al. LC 79-7377. (Proclamation 2: Aids for Interpreting the Lessons of the Church Year, Ser. C). 64p. 1980. pap. 2.50 (ISBN 0-8006-4081-0, 1-4081). Fortress.

Pentecost 1. Morris Niedenthal & Andre Lacocque. LC 74-76929. (Proclamation 1: Aids for Interpreting the Lessons of the Church Year, Ser. A). 64p. 1975. pap. 1.95 (ISBN 0-8006-4066-7, 1-4066). Fortress.

Pentecost 1. David Randolph & Jack D. Kingsbury. LC 75-24959. (Proclamation 1: Aids for Interpreting the Lessons of the Church Year, Ser. B). 64p. 1975. pap. 1.95 (ISBN 0-8006-4076-4, 1-4076). Fortress.

Pentecost 1. Ronald E. Sleeth & John R. Donahue. LC 73-88347. (Proclamation 1: Aids for Interpreting the Lessons of the Church Year, Ser. C). 64p. 1974. pap. 1.95 (ISBN 0-8006-4056-X, 1-4056). Fortress.

Pentecost 1. David L. Tiede & Aidan Kavanagh. Ed. by Elizabeth Achtemeier et al. LC 79-7377. (Proclamation 2: Aids for Interpreting the Lessons of the Church Year, Ser. A). 64p. (Orig.). 1981. pap. 2.50 (ISBN 0-8006-4096-9, 1-4096). Fortress.

Pentecost 2. George W. Hoyer & Wolfgang Roth. LC 73-88347. (Proclamation 1: Aids for Interpreting the Lessons of the Church Year, Ser. C). 64p. 1974. pap. 1.95 (ISBN 0-8006-4057-8, 1-4057). Fortress.

Pentecost 2. Donald H. Juel & David Buttrick. Ed. by Elizabeth Achtemeier et al. LC 79-7377. (Proclamation 2: Aids for Interpreting the Lessons of the Church Year, Ser. C). 64p. 1980. pap. 2.50 (ISBN 0-8006-4083-7, 1-4083). Fortress.

Pentecost 2. Donald Macleod & J. T. Forestell. LC 74-76929. (Proclamation 1: Aids for Interpreting the Lessons of the Church Year, Ser. C). 64p. 1975. pap. 1.95 (ISBN 0-8006-4067-5, 1-4067). Fortress.

Pentecost 2. Paul S. Minear & Harry B. Adams. Ed. by Elizabeth Achtemeier et al. LC 79-7377. (Proclamation 2: Aids for Interpreting the Lessons of the Church Year, Ser. A). 64p. (Orig.). 1981. pap. 2.50 (ISBN 0-8006-4097-7, 1-4097). Fortress.

Pentecost 2. Eduard Riegert & Richard H. Hiers. LC 75-24960. (Proclamation 1: Aids for Interpreting the Lessons of the Church Year, Ser. B). 64p. 1965. pap. 1.95 (ISBN 0-8006-4077-2, 1-4077). Fortress.

Pentecost 3. Fred Craddock & Leander Keck. LC 75-24971. (Proclamation 1: Aids for Interpreting the Lessons of the Church Year, Ser. B). 64p. 1975. pap. 1.95 (ISBN 0-8006-4078-0, 1-4078). Fortress.

Pentecost 3. O. C. Edwards, Jr. & Gardner C. Taylor. Ed. by Elizabeth Achtemeier et al. LC 79-7377. (Proclamation 2: Aids for Interpreting the Lessons of the Church Year, Ser. C). 64p. (Orig.). 1980. pap. 2.50 (ISBN 0-8006-4084-5, 1-4084). Fortress.

Pentecost 3. Victor P. Furnish & Richard L. Thulin. Ed. by Elizabeth Achtemeier et al. LC 79-7377. (Proclamation 2: Aids for Interpreting the Lessons of the Church Year, Ser. A). 64p. (Orig.). 1981. pap. 2.50 (ISBN 0-8006-4098-5, 1-4098). Fortress.

Pentecost 3. Gerard S. Sloyan & Howard C. Kee. LC 73-88347. (Proclamation 1: Aids for Interpreting the Lessons of the Church Year, Ser. C). 64p. 1974. pap. 1.95 (ISBN 0-8006-4058-6, 1-4058). Fortress.

Pentecost 3. Bruce Vawter & John H. Elliott. LC 74-76929. (Proclamation 1: Aids for Interpreting the Lessons of the Church Year, Ser. A). 64p. 1975. pap. 1.95 (ISBN 0-8006-4068-3, 1-4068). Fortress.

Pentecostal Grace: A Theology of Christian Experience. Laurence W. Wood. 256p. 1980. pap. text ed. 8.95 (ISBN 0-937336-00-9). F Asbury Pub Co.

Pentecostal Movement in the Catholic Church. Edward D. O'Connor. LC 70-153878. (Illus.). 304p. 1971. pap. 2.45 (ISBN 0-87793-035-X). Ave Maria.

Pentecostal Movement: Its Origin, Development & Distinctive Character. Nils Bloch-Hoell. 1964. text ed. 19.00x (ISBN 8-200-06004-7, Dist. by Columbia U Pr). Universitet.

Pentecostal Worship. Cecil B. Knight. 1974. pap. 2.25 (ISBN 0-87148-684-9). Pathway Pr.

Pentecostals Around the World. Karl Roebling. (Illus.). 1978. cancelled (ISBN 0-682-49109-8). Exposition.

Pentecostes. Tr. by Don A. Gee. (Spanish Bks.). 1979. 1.25 (ISBN 0-8297-0552-X). Life Pubs Intl.

Penthouse Letters. Ed. by Edward Springer. LC 75-10029. 1976. 8.95 o.p. (ISBN 0-89110-007-5). Penthouse Pr.

Penthouse Letters. Ed. by Edward Springer. 1977. pap. 2.50 (ISBN 0-446-91329-4). Warner Bks.

Pentimento. Christopher Buckley. 1980. pap. 24.00x (ISBN 0-931460-10-7). Bieler.

Pentimento. Lillian Hellman. pap. 4.95 (ISBN 0-452-25107-9, ZS107, Plume). NAL.

Pentjak-Silat: The Indonesian Fighting Art. Donn F. Draeger et al. LC 73-82659. (Illus.). 150p. 1970. 8.95 o.p. (ISBN 0-87011-104-3). Kodansha.

Peony Pavilion (Mudan Ting) Xianzu Tang. Tr. by Cyril Birch. LC 79-9631. (Chinese Literature in Translation Ser.). 352p. 1980. 22.50x (ISBN 0-253-35723-3). Ind U Pr.

People! rev ed. Population Reference Bureau. Ed. by Robert C. Cook & Jane Lecht. LC 68-20456. (Illus.). 63p. (gr. 7-9). 1973. pap. text ed. 2.50 o.p. (ISBN 0-910416-21-4). Columbia Bks.

People. Peter Spier. (Illus.). 48p. (gr. 1-3). 1980. 10.00 (ISBN 0-385-13181-X); PLB (ISBN 0-385-13182-8). Doubleday.

People: An International Choice. R. M. Salas. LC 76-11610. (Span.). 1979. 13.75 (ISBN 0-08-021952-7); pap. 8.25 (ISBN 0-08-021951-9). Pergamon.

People & a Nation. 2nd ed. Ver Steeg & Hofstadster. 1977. 18.44 (ISBN 0-06-552070-X, SchDept); tchr's ed. 15.72 (ISBN 0-06-552252-4); wkbk. 4.08 (ISBN 0-06-552301-6); tchr's wkbk. 7.92 (ISBN 0-06-552452-7); test sets 4.52 ea. Har-Row.

People & Cities. Stephen Verney. 1971. pap. 2.45 o.p. (ISBN 0-8007-0437-1). Revell.

People & Food Tomorrow: The Scientific, Economic, Political, & Social Factors Affecting Food Supplies in the Last Quarter of the 20th Century. Ed. by Dorothy Hollingsworth & Elisabeth Morse. 1976. 40.90x (ISBN 0-85334-701-8). Intl Ideas.

People & Housing in Third World Cities. D. J. Dwyer. LC 74-84346. (Illus.). 30p. 1979. pap. text ed. 13.95x (ISBN 0-582-49017-0). Longman.

People & Information. Harold B. Pepinsky. 1970. 28.00 (ISBN 0-08-015624-X). Pergamon.

People & Land in Africa South of the Sahara: Readings in Social Geography. Ed. by R. Mansell Prothero. (Illus.). 1972. pap. text ed. 9.95x (ISBN 0-19-501287-9). Oxford U Pr.

People & Music. new ed. Alice D. Nelson. (gr. 9-12). 1973. text ed. 14.80 (ISBN 0-205-03292-3, 5832926); tchrs'. guide 2.40 (ISBN 0-205-03646-5, 5836468). Allyn.

People & Organizations. G. Salaman & K. Thompson. 384p. 1974. text ed. 10.95x (ISBN 0-582-48669-6). Longman.

People & Other Mammals. George Laycock. LC 74-4874. 160p. (gr. 4-5). 1975. 5.95 o.p. (ISBN 0-385-00227-0). Doubleday.

People & Parliament. Ed. by John Mackintosh. LC 78-60433. 1978. 22.95 (ISBN 0-03-046231-2). Praeger.

People & Performance: The Best of Peter Drucker on Management. Peter Drucker. 1977. pap. text ed. 9.50 sep (ISBN 0-06-166400-6, HarpC). Har-Row.

People & Politics. 2nd ed. Herbert R. Winter & Thomas J. Bellows. LC 80-20518. 525p. 1981. text ed. 16.95 (ISBN 0-471-08153-1). Wiley.

People & Project Management. Rob Thomsett. LC 80-51921. (Illus., Orig.). 1980. pap. 10.50 (ISBN 0-917072-21-9). Yourdon.

People & the Communities in the Western World, 2 vols. Gene Brucker. 1979. pap. text ed. 9.95x ea.; Vol. 1. (ISBN 0-256-02111-2); Vol. 2. (ISBN 0-256-02186-4). Dorsey.

People & the King: The Comunero Revolution in Colombia, 1781. John L. Phelan. LC 76-53654. 1978. 27.50 (ISBN 0-299-07290-8). U of Wis Pr.

People & the Land. rev. ed. Illus. by Mac Conner et al. (Bowmar-Noble Social Studies Program). Orig. Title: Man & His World. (Illus.). 349p. (gr. 4). 1979. text ed. 7.98 (ISBN 0-686-64536-7); tchrs. ed. 11.55 (ISBN 0-8372-3687-8); test 9.00 (ISBN 0-8372-3728-9). Bowmar-Noble.

People & the Promise. Ursula Synge. LC 74-10661. 192p. (gr. 7-10). 1974. 9.95 (ISBN 0-87599-208-0). S G Phillips.

People & Weather. P. J. Kavanagh. 1980. pap. 5.95 (ISBN 0-7145-3666-0). Riverrun NY.

People & Weather. P. J. Kavanagh. 1980. pap. 5.95 (ISBN 0-686-68794-9). Riverrun NY.

People Are Crazy Here. Rex Reed. (Illus.). 352p. 1974. 7.95 o.p. (ISBN 0-440-07365-0). Delacorte.

People Called Shakers. new & enl. ed. Edward D. Andrews. 8.75 (ISBN 0-8446-1535-8). Peter Smith.

People Choose a President: Influences on Voter Decision Making. Harold Mendelsohn & Garrett J. O'Keefe. LC 75-23983. (Special Studies). 1976. text ed. 24.95 (ISBN 0-275-56110-0). Praeger.

People Create Technology. Carol W. Heiner & Wayne R. Hendrix. LC 79-53802. (Technology Series). (Illus.). 256p. (gr. 5-9). 1980. text ed. 12.95 (ISBN 0-87192-109-X, 000-2); tchr's guide 10.60 (ISBN 0-87192-111-1); activity manual 4.95 (ISBN 0-87192-110-3). Davis Pubns.

People Development in Developing Countries. R. Matheson. LC 77-28208. 1978. 29.95x (ISBN 0-470-99382-0). Halsted Pr.

People, Environment & Place: An Introduction to Human Geography. Robert P. Larkin et al. (Illus.). 368p. 1981. text ed. 20.95 (ISBN 0-675-08085-1); instr's. manual 3.95 (ISBN 0-686-69496-1). Merrill.

People, Families, & God. Mac N. Turnage & Anne S. Turnage. 1976. pap. 3.95 (ISBN 0-8042-8077-0). John Knox.

People from the Sea. Velda Johnston. 208p. 1980. pap. 2.25 (ISBN 0-553-13915-0). Bantam.

People God Chose. A. C. Mueller. LC 56-1129. (Bible Story Booklets Ser). (Illus.). (gr. 3-5). 1971. pap. 0.69 (ISBN 0-570-06701-4, 56-1129). Concordia.

People Heaters: A People's Guide to Keeping Warm in Winter. Alexis Parks. LC 80-21930. (Illus.). 128p. (Orig.). 1980. pap. 4.95 (ISBN 0-931790-16-6). Brick Hse Pub.

People Helper Growthbook. Gary Collins. 1976. pap. 4.95 (ISBN 0-88449-056-4). Vision Hse.

People Ideology-People Theology: New Perspectives on Religious Dogma. Dario Lisiero. 64p. 1980. 10.95 (ISBN 0-682-49664-2, Banner). Exposition.

People in Books. Ed. by Margaret Nicholsen. LC 69-15811. 1969. 16.00 (ISBN 0-8242-0394-1). Wilson.

People in Crisis: Understanding & Helping. Lee A. Hoff. LC 77-79466. 1978. 11.95 (ISBN 0-201-02939-1, M&N Div). A-W.

People in Culture: A Survey of Cultural Anthropology. Ino Rossi et al. LC 79-11842. (Praeger Special Studies) 640p. 1980. 32.50 (ISBN 0-02-752235-0); pap. 15.95 student ed. (ISBN 0-03-051021-X). Praeger.

People in Glass Houses: Growing up at Government House. Adelaide Lubbock. 1978. 19.95 (ISBN 0-241-10059-3, Pub. by Hamish Hamilton England). David & Charles.

People in My Camera. Michael Gnade. 1978. 21.95 o.p. (ISBN 0-8038-5876-0, Pub. by Fountain). Morgan.

People in My Family. Jeffrey Moss. (Illus.). 24p. (gr. k-2). 1976. PLB 5.38 (ISBN 0-307-68968-9, Golden Pr). Western Pub.

People in Pain: A Guide to Pastoral Care. James A. Vanderpool. 208p. 1979. 16.50 (ISBN 0-398-03846-5). C C Thomas.

People in Your Neighborhood. Jeffrey Moss. (Illus.). (ps-2). 1971. PLB 5.38 (ISBN 0-307-68969-7, Golden Pr). Western Pub.

People Lobby: The SST Story. Elizabeth Levy. LC 72-1385. 160p. (gr. 7 up). 1973. 4.95 o.s.i. (ISBN 0-440-07234-4). Delacorte.

People Make a Nation. Martin W. Sandler & Edwin C. Rozwenc. (gr. 10). 1975. text ed. 17.20 (ISBN 0-205-04236-8, 7842368); tchrs. guide 3.20 (ISBN 0-205-04237-6, 7842376). Allyn.

People Make a Nation, Vols. 1 & 2. Martin W. Sandler et al. (Orig.). (gr. 7-12). 1971. pap. text ed. 9.60 ea. Vol. 1 (ISBN 0-205-03227-3, 7832273). Vol. 2 (ISBN 0-205-03228-1, 7832281). tchrs'. ed. 5.12 (ISBN 0-205-02701-6, 7827016); activity bk. 5.12 (ISBN 0-205-02700-8, 7827008). Allyn.

People Make It Happen: The Possibilities of Outreach in Every Phase of Public Library Service. Patricia B. Hanna. LC 78-5923. 1978. lib. bdg. 10.00 (ISBN 0-8108-1136-7). Scarecrow.

People Management for Small Business. W. L. Siegel. 130p. 1978. 5.95 (ISBN 0-471-04030-4, 1-382). Wiley.

People Named Hanes. Jo W. Linn. LC 80-52426. (Illus.). 300p. 1980. 25.00 (ISBN 0-918470-12-9). J W Linn.

People Not Cases. N. M. Ragg. (International Library of Welfare & Philosophy). 1977. 15.00x (ISBN 0-7100-8482-X). Routledge & Kegan.

People Numerous & Armed: Reflections on the Military Struggle for American Independence. John Shy. LC 75-32353. 300p. 1976. 17.95 (ISBN 0-19-502012-X). Oxford U Pr.

People Numerous & Armed: Reflections on the Military Struggle for American Independence. John Shy. 1976. pap. 5.95 (ISBN 0-19-502013-8, GB). Oxford U Pr.

People of Africa. Jean Hiernaux. LC 74-26003. (Peoples of the World Ser.). 1975. 12.50 o.p. (ISBN 0-684-14040-3, ScribT); pap. 4.95 o.p. (ISBN 0-684-14043-8, SL565, ScribT). Scribner.

People of America. T. D. Stewart. LC 73-1371. (Illus.). 272p. 1973. 10.00 o.p. (ISBN 0-684-13539-6, ScribT). Scribner.

People of Coal Town. Herman R. Lantz. LC 58-7169. (Arcturus Books Paperbacks). 332p. 1971. pap. 2.85 (ISBN 0-8093-0531-3). S Ill U Pr.

People of God in Ministry. William K. McElvaney. LC 80-26077. 176p. (Orig.). 1981. pap. 6.95 (ISBN 0-687-30660-4). Abingdon.

People of Nepal. Dor Bahadur Bista. (Illus.). 1976. 8.95x (ISBN 0-685-89509-2). Himalaya Hse.

People of Old Jerusalem. William Papas. LC 80-197. (Illus.). 216p. 1980. 34.95 (ISBN 0-03-057483-8); prepub. 29.95 pre-Jan. HR&W.

People of Paradox: An Inquiry Concerning the Orignis of American Civilization. Michael Kammen. (Illus.). 368p. 1980. pap. 5.95 (ISBN 0-19-502803-1, GB 616). Oxford U Pr.

People of Rimrock: A Study of Values in Five Cultures. Ed. by Evon Z. Vogt & Ethel M. Albert. LC 66-23469. (Illus.). 1966. 17.50x (ISBN 0-674-66150-8). Harvard U Pr.

People of Roman Britain. Anthony Birley. 240p. 1980. 22.50x (ISBN 0-520-04119-4). U of Cal Pr.

People of That Book. Mary Willis. Ed. by Bobbie J. Van Dolson. 128p. 1981. pap. price not set (ISBN 0-8280-0033-6). Review & Herald.

People of the Abyss. rev. ed. Jack London. Ed. by Myron Simon. (Mind of Man Ser.). (Illus.). 224p. 1980. text ed. 25.00x (ISBN 0-686-64380-1). J Simon.

People of the Center: American Indian Religions & Christianity. Carl Starkloff. 1974. 5.95 o.p. (ISBN 0-8164-9207-7). Continuum.

People of the Covenant: An Introduction to the Old Testament. 2nd ed. Henry J. Flanders, Jr. et al. (Illus.). 539p. 1973. 18.95 (ISBN 0-8260-3140-4). Wiley.

People of the Deer. Farley Mowat. (Orig.). pap. 1.95 (ISBN 0-515-05131-4). Jove Pubns.

People of the First Cities. Ruth Goode. LC 77-6279. (gr. 5-9). 1977. 9.95 (ISBN 0-02-736430-5, 73643). Macmillan.

People of the Ice Age. Ruth Goode. LC 72-85191. (Illus.). 144p. (gr. 5-8). 1973. 8.95 (ISBN 0-02-736420-8, CCPr). Macmillan.

People of the Lord. Harry M. Buck. 1977. 8.95 o.p. (ISBN 0-89012-003-X). Anima Pubns.

People of the Magic Waters: The Cahuilla Indians of Palm Springs. John R. Brumgardt & Larry L. Bowles. (Illus.). 1981. 9.95 (ISBN 0-88280-060-4). ETC Pubns. Postponed.

People of the Mediterranean: An Essay in Comparative Social Anthropology. John Davis. (Library of Man). 1976. 17.00x (ISBN 0-7100-8412-9). Routledge & Kegan.

People of the Planet Clarion. Truman Bethurum. 1975. 6.95 o.p. (ISBN 0-685-20199-6). Saucerian.

People of the Polar North. Knud Rasmussen. LC 75-167126. 1975. Repr. of 1908 ed. 18.00 (ISBN 0-685-52348-9). Gale.

People of the Sierra. 2nd ed. Julian Pitt-Rivers. LC 70-153710. 1972. pap. 5.50 (ISBN 0-226-67010-4, P55, Phoen). U of Chicago Pr.

People of the Valley. Frank Waters. LC 78-137435. 201p. 1941. 10.95 (ISBN 0-8040-0242-8, SB); pap. 5.95 (ISBN 0-8040-0243-6). Swallow.

People of Three Mile Island. Robert Del Tredici. LC 80-13558. (Illus.). 124p. (Orig.). 1980. pap. 7.95 (ISBN 0-87156-237-5). Sierra.

People on the Move: A United States History, 2 vols. Ray Ginger & Victoria Ginger. Incl. Vol. 1. To 1877. pap. text ed. 9.50x o.p. (ISBN 0-205-04732-7); Vol. 2. Since 1860. pap. text ed. 9.50x o.p. (ISBN 0-685-99087-7). 1975. Combined Ed. text ed. 14.95x o.p. (ISBN 0-685-50569-3). Allyn.

People Parables. James E. Carter. (Pocket Pulpit Library). 128p. 1981. pap. 2.95 (ISBN 0-8010-2348-3). Baker Bk.

People, Pattern & Processes: An Introduction to Human Geography. Keith Chapman. LC 79-18917. 334p. 1980. 44.95x (ISBN 0-470-26719-4); pap. 18.95x (ISBN 0-470-26806-9). Halsted Pr.

People, Peregrines, & Arctic Pipelines: The Critical Battle to Build Canada's Northern Gas Pipelines. Donald Peacock. LC 77-375197. (Illus.). 224p. 1977. pap. 5.95 (ISBN 0-295-95722-0). U of Wash Pr.

People Planning. Norman Dennis. (Society Today & Tomorrow Ser.). (Illus.). 1970. 12.95 o.p. (ISBN 0-571-09011-7, Pub. by Faber & Faber). Merrimack Bk Serv.

People, Poverty, & Politics: Pennsylvanians During the Great Depression. Thomas H. Coode & John F. Bauman. LC 78-75198. 280p. 1981. 24.50 (ISBN 0-8387-2320-9). Bucknell U Pr.

People, Power & Politics: An Introduction to Political Science. John C. Donovan et al. (Illus.). 384p. 1981. pap. text ed. 11.95 (ISBN 0-201-03246-5). A-W.

People, Power, Change: Movements of Social Transformation. Luther P. Gerlach & Virginia H. Hine. LC 70-109434. 1970. pap. 6.50 (ISBN 0-672-60613-5). Bobbs.

People-Processing. Jeffrey M. Prottas. LC 78-19567. 1979. 18.95 (ISBN 0-669-02628-X). Lexington Bks.

People Puzzle: Understanding Yourself & Others. Morris E. Massey. (Illus.). 1980. text ed. 13.95 (ISBN 0-8359-5477-3). Reston.

People-Reading: How We Control Others, How They Control Us. Ernst G. Beier & Evans G. Valens. 320p. 1976. pap. 2.95 (ISBN 0-446-93642-1). Warner Bks.

People Reborn. Christian Keysser. Tr. by Alfred Allin & John Kuder. LC 79-23623. 306p. (Orig.). 1980. pap. 9.95x (ISBN 0-87808-174-7). William Carey Lib.

People Skills: How to Assert Yourself, Listen to Others & Resolve Conflicts. Robert H. Bolton. (Illus.). 1979. 13.95 (ISBN 0-13-655779-1, Spec); pap. 4.95 (ISBN 0-13-655761-9). P-H.

People, Society & Mass Communications. Ed. by Lewis A. Dexter & David M. White. LC 64-11222. 1964. text ed. 15.95 (ISBN 0-02-907400-2). Free Pr.

People Space: The Making & Breaking of Human Boundaries. Norman Ashcraft & Albert E. Scheflen. LC 76-2844. 1976. pap. 2.50 o.p. (ISBN 0-385-11229-7, Anch). Doubleday.

People, States, & World Order. Louis R. Beres. LC 80-83099. 300p. 1981. pap. text ed. 7.95 (ISBN 0-87581-267-8). Peacock Pubs.

People Studying People: The Human Element in Fieldwork. Robert A. Georges & Michael O. Jones. 1980. 14.95x (ISBN 0-520-03989-0); pap. 3.95x (ISBN 0-520-04067-8, CAMPUS NO. 250). U of Cal Pr.

People That Time Forgot. Edgar R. Burroughs. 1977. pap. 1.95 (ISBN 0-441-65947-0). Ace Bks.

People, Their Needs, Environment, Ecology: Vol. 1, Essays in Social Biology. Ed. by Bruce Wallace. LC 79-167789. 1972. pap. 10.95 (ISBN 0-13-656827-0). P-H.

People Therein. Mildred Lee. 320p. (gr. 7 up). 1980. 10.95 (ISBN 0-395-29434-7, Clarion). HM.

People to People Therapy. John W. Drakeford. LC 77-20447. 1978. 7.95 o.p. (ISBN 0-06-062062-5, HarpR). Har-Row.

People Vs. Jesus. Louis H. Evans, Sr. 128p. 1980. pap. 5.95 (ISBN 0-8499-2909-1). Word Bks.

People vs. Monopoly: Nineteen Eighty Draft Program of the Communist Part, USA. CPUSA. 62p. (Orig.). 1980. pap. 0.50 (ISBN 0-87898-142-X). New Outlook.

People Who Couldn't Be Stopped. Ethel Barrett. LC 79-96703. (Orig.). (gr. 4-8). 1970. pap. 1.95 (ISBN 0-8307-0007-2, S063107). Regal.

People Who Help People. Jane B. Moncure. LC 75-29225. (Illus.). (ps-3). 1975. 5.95 (ISBN 0-913778-16-8). Childs World.

People Who Live Alone in New York City: An Analysis of 1970 Census Facts. 1974. pap. 2.00 (ISBN 0-86671-021-3). Comm Coun Great NY.

People Who Pull You Down. Thomas Baird. 1978. pap. 1.75 (ISBN 0-380-39339-5, 39339). Avon.

People with Out a Country: The Kurds & Kurdistan. Ed. & intro. by Gerard Chaliand. 292p. (Orig.). 1980. 19.95 (ISBN 0-905762-69-X, Pub. by Zed Pr); pap. 8.50 (ISBN 0-905762-74-6). Lawrence Hill.

People, Work & Organizations: An Introduction to Industrial & Organizational Psychology. 2nd ed. Bass & Barrett. 1980. text ed. 18.95 (ISBN 0-205-06809-X, 7968094). Allyn.

Peopled Parables. Louise Louis. (Illus.). 100p. text ed. 6.50. Pen-Art.

People's Action Party of Singapore: Emergence of a Dominant Party System. Thomas J. Bellows. (Mongraph: No. 14). (Illus.). xii, 195p. 1970. 5.75 o.p. (ISBN 0-686-63728-3). Yale U Pr.

People's Almanac. David Wallechinsky & Irving Wallace. LC 75-2856. 1536p. 1975. 15.95 (ISBN 0-385-04186-1); pap. 10.95 (ISBN 0-385-04060-1). Doubleday.

People's Almanac Presents the Book of Lists, No. 2. Irving Wallace et al. 576p. 1981. pap. 2.95 (ISBN 0-553-13101-X). Bantam.

Peoples & Cultures of Ancient Peru. Luis G. Lumbreras. LC 74-2104. (Illus.). 248p. 1974. 19.95 o.p. (ISBN 0-87474-151-3); pap. 9.95x (ISBN 0-87474-151-3). Smithsonian.

Peoples & Cultures of Early Florida. W. B. Skinner et al. (Florida Social Studies Ser.). (Illus.). 90p. (gr. 4-9). 1971. pap. text ed. 1.50 (ISBN 0-913122-01-7); teacher's guide avail. (ISBN 0-913122-02-5); package of 25 texts & 1 tchrs' guide 24.70 (ISBN 0-913122-15-7). Mickler Hse.

People's Budget Nineteen Hundred & Nine to Nineteen Hundred & Ten: Lloyd George & Liberal Politics. Bruce K. Murray. 360p. 1980. 49.95 (ISBN 0-19-822626-8). Oxford U Pr.

Peoples' Capitalism: The Economics of the Robot Revolution. James S. Albus. LC 75-44585. 157p. 1976. 10.50 (ISBN 0-685-66376-0); pap. 5.95 (ISBN 0-685-66377-9). New World Bks.

People's Choice: How the Voter Makes up His Mind in a Presidential Campaign. Paul F. Lazarsfeld et al. LC 68-20443. (Illus.). 15.00x (ISBN 0-231-03158-0); pap. 5.00 (ISBN 0-231-08583-4, 83). Columbia U Pr.

People's Cookbook. Huquette Couffignal. 1977. 10.00 o.p. (ISBN 0-312-60007-0). St Martin.

People's England. Alan Ereira. (Illus.). 288p. 1981. 24.95 (ISBN 0-7100-0596-2). Routledge & Kegan.

People's Films: A Political History of U. S. Government Motion Pictures. Richard D. MacCann. (Studies in Public Communication). 1973. 11.50 o.s.i. (ISBN 0-8038-5795-0); pap. text ed. 6.75x (ISBN 0-8038-5796-9). Hastings.

People's Guide to Camping in Mexico. Carl Franz. (Illus.). 400p. (Orig.). 1981. pap. 9.50 (ISBN 0-912528-18-4). John Muir.

People's Health: A History of Public Health in Minnesota to 1948. Philip D. Jordan. LC 53-38147. 524p. 1953. 5.00 (ISBN 0-87351-010-0). Minn Hist.

People's Herbal. Michael Weiner. (Orig.). 1981. pap. 8.95 (ISBN 0-446-97574-5). Warner Bks.

People's History & Socialist Theory. Ed. by Raphael Samuel. (History Workshop Ser.). 425p. 1981. price not set (ISBN 0-7100-0765-5); pap. price not set (ISBN 0-7100-0652-7). Routledge & Kegan.

People's History of England. A. L. Morton. (Illus.). 1980. pap. 2.95 (ISBN 0-7178-0150-0). Intl Pub Co.

People's Liberation Army: Communist China's Armed Forces. Angus M. Fraser. LC 73-76898. 72p. 1973. pap. 2.45x (ISBN 0-8448-0223-9). Crane-Russak Co.

Peoples of Connecticut Multinational Ethnic Heritage Studies, 6 bks. Incl. Armenian Studies for Secondary Students. Frank A. Stone. 1975. 2.50 (ISBN 0-685-55887-8); Irish: In Their Homeland, In America, In Connecticut. Frank A. Stone. 1975. 4.00 (ISBN 0-685-55888-6); Italians: In Their Homeland, In America, In Connecticut. Patricia S. Weibust. 1976. 4.00 (ISBN 0-685-55889-4); Jews: Their Origins, In America, In Connecticut. Sally I. Gould. 1976. 4.00 (ISBN 0-685-55890-8); Puerto Ricans: On the Island, on the Mainland, In Connecticut. Barbara Burdette. 1976. 4.00 (ISBN 0-685-55891-6); Learning About the Peoples of Connecticut. Patricia S. Weibust. 1977. tchrs. manual 2.00 (ISBN 0-685-55892-4). Set. 24.00 (ISBN 0-685-55886-X). World Educ Proj.

Peoples of Old Testament Times. Ed. by D. J. Wiseman. (Illus.). 419p. 1973. 23.95x (ISBN 0-19-826316-3). Oxford U Pr.

Peoples of the World in Color. Francis Huxley. LC 70-77361. (Illus.). 1970. 7.50 (ISBN 0-8023-1215-2). Dufour.

Peoples of Utah. Ed. by Helen Z. Papanikolas. LC 76-12311. (Illus.). 498p. 7.50 o.p. (ISBN 0-913738-26-3). Utah St Hist Soc.

People's Panel: The Grand Jury in the United States, 1634-1941. Richard D. Younger. LC 63-12993. 263p. 1965. Repr. of 1963 ed. 10.00 (ISBN 0-87057-076-5). Univ Pr of New England.

People's Perception About Family Planning: A Study of Andhra Pradesh & Bihar. M. E. Khan & C. V. Prasad. 156p. 1980. text ed. 10.00x (ISBN 0-391-02131-1). Humanities.

People's Pharmacy - Two. Joe Graedon. 1980. pap. 5.95 (ISBN 0-380-76059-2, 76059). Avon.

People's President: The Electoral College in American History & the Direct Vote Alternative. rev. ed. Neal R. Peirce & Lawrence D. Longley. LC 80-24260. (Illus.). 416p. 1981. text ed. 40.00x (ISBN 0-300-02612-9); pap. 9.95 (ISBN 0-300-02704-4). Yale U Pr.

People's Railway. Anthony Perles. Ed. by Jim Walker. (Interurbans Special Ser.: 69). (Illus.). 300p. 1980. write for info. (ISBN 0-916374-42-4). Interurban.

People's Republic of China: A Basic Handbook. 2nd, rev. ed. Compiled by James R. Townsend & Richard C. Bush. (Illus., Orig.). 1980. pap. text ed. 4.50 (ISBN 0-936876-13-1). Learn Res Intl Stud.

People's Republic of China: A Handbook. Harold C. Hinton. (Illus.). 1979. lib. bdg. 30.00x (ISBN 0-89158-419-6, Dawson). Westview.

People's Republic of China, Nineteen Forty-Nine to Nineteen Seventy-Nine: A Documentary Survey, 5 vols. Ed. by Harold C. Hinton. LC 80-5228. 3000p. 1980. Set. lib. bdg. 295.00 (ISBN 0-8420-2166-3). Scholarly Res Inc.

People's Travel Book. Compiled by Frieda Carroll. LC 80-70869. 115p. 1981. 17.95; pap. 12.95. Biblio Pr Ga.

Pepi. Linda Roberts. (Illus.). 32p. (gr. 4-6). 1977. 2.95 (ISBN 0-8059-2459-0). Dorrance.

Peple's Money Pages. 1st ed. Frieda Carrol. LC 80-70419. 50p. 1980. 16.50 (ISBN 0-9605246-3-0); pap. 9.95. Biblio Pr GA.

Pepper. H. Pyle. (Peter Possum Paperbacks). (gr. k-3). 1975. pap. 0.95 o.p. (ISBN 0-531-05123-4). Watts.

Pepper & All the Legs. Dick Gackenbach. LC 78-5084. (ps-3). 1978. 6.95 (ISBN 0-395-28797-9, Clarion). HM.

Pepper Face & Other Stories. Ann Staden. (Illus.). (ps-5). 1972. 4.95 (ISBN 0-686-24619-5, Pub. by Faber & Faber). Merrimack Bk Serv.

Peppermint Dreams. gift ed. Linda Wilkinson. LC 77-81667. 1977. lib. bdg. 8.95 (ISBN 0-89081-070-2). Harvest Hse.

Peppermints in the Parlor. Barbara B. Wallace. LC 80-12326. 216p. (gr. 4-6). 1980. 8.95 (ISBN 0-689-30790-X). Atheneum.

Peppertree III. Shyree A. Latham. (Illus.). 100p. (Orig.). 1981. pap. 12.95 (ISBN 0-86663-600-5). Ide Hse.

Peptide Synthesis. M. Bodanszky & Miklos A. Ondetti. (Interscience Monographs on Chemistry, Organic Chemistry Section). 1966. text ed. 15.75 (ISBN 0-470-08450-2, Pub. by Wiley). Krieger.

Peptides: Analysis, Synthesis, Biology, Part A, Major Methods Of Peptide Bond Formation. Ed. by Erhard Gross & Johannes Meienhofer. LC 78-31958. 1979. 42.50, by subscription 36.50 (ISBN 0-12-304201-1). Acad Pr.

Peptides: Analysis, Synthesis, Biology: Vol. 3 Protection of Functional Groups in Peptides Synthesis. Ed. by Erhard Gross. 1980. 45.00 (ISBN 0-12-304203-8). Acad Pr.

Peptides & Proteins. D. T. Elmore. LC 68-21392. (Cambridge Chemistry Texts Ser). (Illus.). 1968. 27.95 (ISBN 0-521-07107-0); pap. 8.95x (ISBN 0-521-09535-2). Cambridge U Pr.

Peptides: Integrators of Cell & Tissue Function, Vol. 35. Ed. by Floyd E. Bloom. (Society of General Physiologists Ser.). 250p. 1980. text ed. 25.00 (ISBN 0-89004-485-6). Raven.

Peptides Nineteen Seventy-Four: Proceedings of the Thirteenth European Peptide Symposium, Israel, April, 1974. Y. Wolman. LC 75-8603. 1975. 44.95 (ISBN 0-470-95957-6). Halsted Pr.

Peptides: Proceedings. Ed. by Murray Goodman & Johannes Meienhofer. American Peptide Symposium, Fifth. LC 77-88855. 1977. 39.95 (ISBN 0-470-99384-7). Halsted Pr.

Pepysian Garland: Black-Letter Broadside Ballads of the Years 1595-1639, Chiefly from the Collection of Samuel Pepys. Samuel Pepys. Ed. by Hyder E. Rollins. LC 74-176041. (Illus.). 491p. 1971. 22.50x (ISBN 0-674-66185-0). Harvard U Pr.

Pequena Bella Durmiente. Brenda G. Prior. Tr. by Ronald Ross from Eng. (Libros Arco). (Illus.). 32p. (Orig., Span.). (gr. 1-3). 1972. pap. 0.95 o.s.i. (ISBN 0-89922-045-2). Edit Caribe.

Pequeno Larousse de ciencias y tecnicas. new ed. Tomas De Galiana Mingot. 1056p. 1975. 23.00 (ISBN 0-685-55467-8, 21115). Larousse.

Per Modo Di Dire: A First Course in Italian. Pietro Frassica & Antonio Carrara. 1981. text ed. 16.95 (ISBN 0-669-02068-0); wkbk. 5.95 (ISBN 0-669-02069-9); cassette 65.00 (ISBN 0-669-02073-7); tapes-reels 65.00 (ISBN 0-669-02072-9); instructor's guide (ISBN 0-669-02069-9); tapescript (ISBN 0-669-02074-5); demo tape (ISBN 0-669-02075-3). Heath.

Per Saecula. H. McArdle & G. Suggitt. 1974. write for info. (ISBN 0-686-19161-7); Pt. 1. pap. 3.50; Pt. 2. pap. 3.50; Pt. 3. pap. 3.50. Longman.

Per-Se Award Plays, 1969: Special Issue 5. William J. Watkins & Grace Cavalieri. 38p. pap. 1.00 (ISBN 0-912292-06-7). The Smith.

Per-Se Award Plays, 1970: Special Issue 14. Bernard Diamond & Stuart Oderman. pap. 1.00 o.p. (ISBN 0-685-78408-8). The Smith.

Per-Se Award Plays, 1971: Special Issue 24. Jane Roberts & Barry Knower. pap. 1.00 o.p. (ISBN 0-685-78409-6). The Smith.

Per Se Award Plays, 1972-1973: Special Issue 29 - the Smith. Clayelle Dalferes & David Young. 44p. pap. 1.00 o.p. (ISBN 0-685-78410-X). The Smith.

Perceiving & Behaving. Dale Lake. LC 72-77891. (Illus.). 1970. text ed. 10.50x (ISBN 0-8077-1658-8). Tchrs Coll.

Perceiving Artworks. Ed. by John Fisher. (Philosophical Monographs: 3rd Ser.). 1980. 17.50x (ISBN 0-87722-164-2). Temple U Pr.

Perceiving Structure: How Are the Ideas Organized? Walter Pauk. (Skill at a Time Ser). 64p. (gr. 9-12). 1975. pap. text ed. 2.40x (ISBN 0-89061-030-4). Jamestown Pubs.

Perceiving the Arts: An Introduction to the Humanities. Dennis Sporre. (Illus.). 256p. 1981. text ed. 9.95 (ISBN 0-13-657031-3). P-H.

Perceiving the Author's Intent: What Is the Author's Real Message? Walter Pauk. (Skill at a Time Ser). 64p. (gr. 9-12). 1975. pap. text ed. 2.40x (ISBN 0-89061-029-0). Jamestown Pubs.

Perceiving Women. Ed. by Shirley Ardener. LC 75-12662. 1975. 22.95 (ISBN 0-470-03309-6); pap. 10.95 (ISBN 0-470-99264-6). Halsted Pr.

Percent. Robert Burleigh & Raymond Matlak. LC 79-730248. (Illus.). 1979. pap. 99.00 (ISBN 0-89290-096-2, A512-SATC). Soc for Visual.

Perception. Ed. by S. Chennakesavan & K. P. Rao. 1966. 5.00x (ISBN 0-210-27196-5). Asia.

Perception. 2nd ed. Julian Hochberg. LC 77-27274. (Foundations of Modern Psychology Ser.). (Illus.). 1978. 12.95 o.p. (ISBN 0-13-657106-9); pap. text ed. 10.95 (ISBN 0-13-657098-4). P-H.

Perception. Daniel J. Weintraub & Edward L. Walker. LC 66-26288. (Basic Concepts in Psychology Ser). (Orig.). 1966. pap. text ed. 5.95 (ISBN 0-8185-0310-6); perceptual demonstration kit, 1972 15.95 (ISBN 0-8185-0049-2). Brooks-Cole.

Perception: A Representative Theory. F. Jackson. LC 76-30316. 1977. 26.95 (ISBN 0-521-21550-1). Cambridge U Pr.

Perception: An Applied Approach. William Schiff. LC 79-88717. 1980. text ed. 18.50 (ISBN 0-395-27054-5). HM.

Perception & Cosmology in Whitehead's Philosophy. Paul F. Schmidt. 1967. 13.00 (ISBN 0-8135-0557-7). Rutgers U Pr.

Perception & Design in Tennyson's "Idylls of the King". John R. Reed. LC 77-122100. 270p. 1969. 12.00x (ISBN 0-8214-0078-9). Ohio U Pr.

Perception & Identity: Essays Presented to A. J. Ayer with His Responses. Intro. by G. F. Macdonald. LC 79-52503. (Illus.). 1979. 32.50 (ISBN 0-8014-1265-X). Cornell U Pr.

Perception & Its Disorders. Ed. by David A. Hamburg et al. (ARNMD Research Publications Ser: Vol. 48). 1970. 24.50 (ISBN 0-683-00241-4). Raven.

Perception & Personal Identity: Proceedings of the 1967 Oberlin Colloquium in Philosophy. Ed. by Norman S. Care & Robert H. Grimm. LC 68-9427. (Oberlin Colloquia in Philosophy Ser). 1969. 15.00 (ISBN 0-8295-0145-2). UPBS.

Perception & Pictorial Representation. Ed. by Calvin F. Nodine & Dennis Fisher. LC 79-4613. (Praeger Special Studies Ser.). 448p. 1979. 39.95 (ISBN 0-03-049816-3). Praeger.

Perception & the Physical World. David M. Armstrong. (International Library of Philosophy & Scientific Method). 1961. text ed. 14.50x (ISBN 0-7100-3603-5). Humanities.

Perception, Consciousness, Memory: Reflections of a Biologist. G. Adam. LC 73-20153. 215p. 1980. 22.50 (ISBN 0-306-30776-6, Plenum Pr). Plenum Pub.

Perception, Decision Making & Conflict. Robert Mandel. LC 78-65350. 1978. pap. text ed. 8.50 (ISBN 0-8191-0652-6). U Pr of Amer.

Perception, Development, Communication. Ed. by Internationales Zentratinstitut Fundas Jugend- Und Bildungsfernsehen. 118p. 1978. pap. 13.00 (ISBN 0-89664-025-6, Pub. by K G Saur). Shoe String.

Perception in Criminology. Richard L. Henshel & Robert A. Silverman. LC 74-23621. 384p. 1975. 25.00x (ISBN 0-231-03760-0); pap. 9.00x (ISBN 0-231-03761-9). Columbia U Pr.

Perception: Mechanisms & Models: Readings from Scientific American. Intro. by Richard Held & Whitman Richards. LC 70-190437. (Illus.). 1972. text ed. 19.95x (ISBN 0-7167-0853-1); pap. text ed. 9.95x (ISBN 0-7167-0852-3). W H Freeman.

Perception of Desertification. 134p. 1981. pap. 22.75 (ISBN 92-808-0190-2, TUNU 104, UNU). Unipub.

Perception of Other People. Franz From. Tr. by Brendan A. Maher & Erik Kvan. LC 76-138295. 1971. 15.00x (ISBN 0-231-03402-4). Columbia U Pr.

Perception of Police Power: A Study in Four Cities. Anastassios D. Mylonas. (New York University Criminal Law Education & Research Center Monograph: No. 8). (Illus.). x, 131p. (Orig.). 1974. pap. text ed. 8.50x (ISBN 0-8377-0418-9). Rothman.

Perception, Sensation & Verification. Bede Rundle. 1972. 22.50x (ISBN 0-19-824390-1). Oxford U Pr.

Perception Stimulators. Maden Mohan & Victoria Risko. (Illus.). 64p. (Orig.). 1980. tchr's ed. 2.50 (ISBN 0-914634-80-1, 6932). DOK Pubs.

Perception: The World Transformed. Lloyd Kaufman. (Illus.). 1979. 22.50x (ISBN 0-19-502464-8); text ed. 15.95x (ISBN 0-19-502463-X). Oxford U Pr.

Perceptions & Evocations: The Art of Elihu Vedder. Joshua C. Taylor et al. LC 78-9915. (Illus.). 246p. 1979. 27.50 (ISBN 0-87474-902-6); pap. 15.50 (ISBN 0-87474-903-4). Smithsonian.

Perceptions of Reality: A Sourcebook for the Social History of Western Civilization. Edward Anson et al. LC 80-81665. 240p. 1980. pap. text ed. 10.95 (ISBN 0-8403-2224-0). Kendall-Hunt.

Perceptrons: An Introduction to Computational Geometry. Marvin L. Minsky & Seymour Papert. 1969. pap. 8.95x (ISBN 0-262-63022-2). MIT Pr.

Perceptual Activities: A Multitude of Perceptual Actitivies,Level 2-Advanced,Consumerable (Coloring) Edition. Paul McCreary. (gr. 2-8). 1972. wkbk. 4.00 (ISBN 0-89039-049-5). Ann Arbor Pubs.

Perceptual Activities: A Multitude of Reusable Perceptual Activities, Level 1-Primary. Paul McCreary. (gr. 2-8). 1972. 5.00 (ISBN 0-89039-C46-0). Ann Arbor Pubs.

Perceptual & Learning Disabilities in Children. Ed. by William M. Cruickshank & Daniel P. Hallahan. Incl. Vol. 1. Psychoeducational Practices. LC 74-24303. 496p. 20.50x (ISBN 0-8156-2165-5); Vol. 2. Research & Theory. LC 74-24303. 498p. 25.00x (ISBN 0-8156-2166-3). (Illus.). 1975. Set. 40.00x (ISBN 0-685-51977-5). Syracuse U Pr.

Perceptual & Motor Development in Infants & Young Children. 2nd ed. Bryant S. Cratty. 1979. 14.95 (ISBN 0-13-657023-2). P-H.

Perceptual Approach to College English: Experiments in Composition. J. Burl Hogins & Gerald A. Bryant, Jr. 1970. pap. text ed. 6.95x o.p. (ISBN 0-02-474860-9, 47486). Glencoe.

Perceptual Motor Development Equipment: Inexpensive Ideas & Activities. Peter H. Werner & Lisa Rini. LC 75-43744. 160p. 1976. text ed. 12.50 (ISBN 0-471-93371-6). Wiley.

Perceptual Motor Development Series, 5 bks. Jack Capon. Incl. Balance Activities (ISBN 0-8224-5302-9); Ball, Rope, Hoop Activities (ISBN 0-8224-5301-0); Basic Movement Activities (ISBN 0-8224-5300-2); Beanbag, Rhythm-Stick Activities (ISBN 0-8224-5303-7); Tire, Parachute Activities (ISBN 0-8224-5304-5). (ps-3). 1975. pap. 3.95 ea. Pitman Learning.

Perceptual Organization. Ed. by Michael Kubovy & James Pomerantz. 608p. 1981. text ed. 39.95 (ISBN 0-89859-056-6). L Erlbaum Assocs.

Perceptual Processing: Stimulus, Equivalence & Pattern Recognition. Peter C. Dodwell. (Century Psychology Ser.). (Illus.). 1981. Repr. of 1971 ed. text ed. 24.50x (ISBN 0-8290-0063-1). Irvington.

Perceptual Psychology. M. S. Lindauer. 1978. text ed. 23.50 o.p. (ISBN 0-08-019517-2); pap. text ed. 17.00 o.p. (ISBN 0-08-019516-4). Pergamon.

Perceptual Psychology: A Humanistic Approach to the Study of Persons. Arthur W. Combs et al. 492p. 1976. pap. text ed. 16.50 scp (ISBN 0-06-041346-8, HarpC). Har-Row.

Perceptual Skills Curriculum, 4 programs. Jerome Rosner. Incl. Introductory Guide. LC 73-83888. 96p. tchr's ed. 7.50 (ISBN 0-8027-8025-3); Prog. 1. Visual-Motor Skills. 327p. pap. text ed. 24.90 (ISBN 0-8027-8026-1); Prog. 2. Auditory Motor Skills. 304p. pap. text ed. 15.95 (ISBN 0-8027-8027-X); Prog. 3. General Motor Skills. 144p. pap. text ed. 7.95 (ISBN 0-8027-8028-8); Prog. 4. Introducing Letters & Numerals, Pts. 1 & 2. 562p. pap. text ed. 46.90 (ISBN 0-8027-8029-6). 1973. Walker Educ.

Perceptual Training Activities. rev ed. Betty Van Witsen. LC 79-17371. 1979. pap. 7.95x (ISBN 0-8077-2568-4). Tchrs Coll.

Perchance of Death. Elizabeth Linington. LC 76-52221. 1977. 6.95 o.p. (ISBN 0-385-13081-3). Doubleday.

Perchance to Dream: The Patient's Guide to Anesthesia. Robert C. Brown. 96p. 1981. 10.95 (ISBN 0-686-69375-2). Nelson-Hall.

Percieving the Arts: An Introduction. Dennis J. Sporre. (Illus.). 1978. pap. text ed. 8.25 o.p. (ISBN 0-8403-1884-7). Kendall-Hunt.

Percolation Processes: Theory & Applications. Ed. by A. Rodriques & D. Tondeur. (NATO Advanced Study Institute Ser.: Applied Science, No. 33). 594p. 1980. 65.00x (ISBN 90-286-0579-7). Sijthoff & Noordhoff.

Percursor Processing in the Biosynthesis of Proteins. Ed. by Morris Zimmerman et al. LC 80-16863. 449p. 1980. 79.00x (ISBN 0-89766-072-2). NY Acad Sci.

Percussion. James Holland. (Yehudi Menuhin Music Guides Ser.). (Illus.). 1981. 12.95 (ISBN 0-02-871600-0); pap. 6.95 (ISBN 0-02-871610-8). Schirmer Bks.

Percussion Anthology. 1980. 24.00 (ISBN 0-686-15892-X). Instrumentalist Co.

Percussion Instruments & Their History. new ed. James Blades. (Illus.). 1978. 46.00 (ISBN 0-571-04832-3, Pub. by Faber & Faber); pap. 15.95 o.p. (ISBN 0-571-10360-X). Merrimack Bk Serv.

Percussion Manual. Combs. 1977. 13.95x (ISBN 0-534-00504-7). Wadsworth Pub.

Percutaneous Needle Biopsies: A Radiological Approach. Jesus Zornosa. (Illus.). 200p. 1981. lib. bdg. write for info. (ISBN 0-683-09400-9). Williams & Wilkins.

Percy Bysshe Shelley. Donald H. Reiman. (English Authors Ser.: No. 81). lib. bdg. 9.95 (ISBN 0-8057-1488-X). Twayne.

Percy Grainger: The Inveterate Innovator. Thomas C. Slattery. (Illus.). 12.50 (ISBN 0-686-15893-8). Instrumentalist Co.

Perdita. Joan Smith. 224p. 1981. pap. 1.95 (ISBN 0-449-50173-6, Coventry). Fawcett.

Perdition Express. Brad Lang. (Orig.). 1976. pap. 1.25 o.p. (ISBN 0-685-62587-7, LB328, Leisure Bks). Nordon Pubns.

Pere Duchesne. Repr. of 1790 ed. 633.00 o.p. (ISBN 0-8287-0678-6). Clearwater Pub.

Pere Duchesne, 1790 - 1794: Reimpression Des 385 Numeros Du Celebre Journal De Jacques - Rene Hebert, 10 vols. Ed. by Jacques - Rene Hebert. (Fr.). 1977. Repr. of 1790 ed. lib. bdg. 687.50x o.p. (ISBN 0-8287-0679-4). Clearwater Pub.

Pere Goriot. Balzac. (Easy Reader, D). pap. 3.75 (ISBN 0-88436-043-1, FRA301051). EMC.

Pere Goriot de Balzac: Ecriture, structures, significations. new ed. P. Barberis. (Collection themes et textes). 296p. (Orig., Fr.). 1972. pap. 6.75 (ISBN 2-03-035010-9, 2681). Larousse.

Peregrinations of Jeremiah Grant, Esq., the West-Indian, 1763. (Novel in England, 1700-1775 Ser). 1974. lib. bdg. 50.00 (ISBN 0-8240-1163-5). Garland Pub.

Peregrine: Primus. Avram Davidson. 1977. pap. 1.95 (ISBN 0-441-65951-9). Ace Bks.

Peregrine: Secundus. Avram Davidson, (Orig.). 1981. pap. 2.25 (ISBN 0-425-04829-2). Berkley Pub.

Peregrino. Juan Bunyan. 1966. 2.95x (ISBN 0-8361-1112-5). Herald Pr.

Perelandra. C. S. Lewis. 1968. 10.95 (ISBN 0-02-570840-6); pap. 1.95 (ISBN 0-02-086900-2). Macmillan.

Perennial Bachelor. Anne Parrish. 1976. lib. bdg. 13.95x (ISBN 0-89968-153-0). Lightyear.

Perennial Pentecost. Frank W. Lemons. 1971. pap. 2.25 (ISBN 0-87148-679-2). Pathway Pr.

Perennial Philosophy. Aldous Huxley. 1970. pap. 4.95 (ISBN 0-06-090191-8, CN191, CN). Har-Row.

Perennial Promise: First Lillibook Anthology. Louise Louis. 48p. pap. 3.95. Pen-Art.

Perennials. James U. Crockett. (Encyclopedia of Gardening Ser). (Illus.). 1972. 11.95 (ISBN 0-8094-1109-1). Time-Life.

Perennials. James U. Crockett. LC 78-140420. (Time-Life Encyclopedia of Gardening). (Illus.). (gr. 6 up). 1972. lib. bdg. 11.97 (ISBN 0-8094-1110-5, Pub. by Time-Life). Silver.

Perennials for the Western Garden. Margaret K. Coates. (Illus.). 1976. 9.95 o.p. (ISBN 0-87108-088-5). Pruett.

Perennials for Your Garden. Alan Bloom. LC 75-4057. (Encore Edition). (Illus.). 1974. 3.95 o.p. (ISBN 0-684-15236-3, ScribT). Scribner.

Perennials in the Garden. Charles H. Potter. LC 59-6124. (Illus.). 1959. 10.95 (ISBN 0-87599-094-0). S G Phillips.

Perez & Martina. rev. ed. Pura Belpre. (Illus.). (gr. 2-5). 1961. 7.95 (ISBN 0-7232-6017-6). Warne.

Perfect Age. F. E. Baily. 187p. 1981. Repr. of 1946 ed. lib. bdg. 30.00 (ISBN 0-89987-064-3). Darby Bks.

Perfect Chocolate Chip Cookie. Claudia S. Scheckman. LC 80-67918. (Illus.). 44p. (ps-6). Date not set. pap. 4.95 (ISBN 0-916634-09-4). Double M Pr. Postponed.

Perfect Circle of the Sun. Linda Pastan. LC 76-171879. (New Poetry Ser.: No. 44). 1971. 5.00 o.p. (ISBN 0-8040-0553-2); pap. 2.75 o.p. (ISBN 0-8040-0621-0). Swallow.

Perfect Crane. Anne Laurin. LC 80-7912. (Illus.). 32p. (gr. 1-4). 1981. 8.95 (ISBN 0-06-023743-0, HarpJ); PLB 8.79g (ISBN 0-06-023744-9). Har-Row.

Perfect Fit: Charting & Finishing Knitted Garments. Cherie Palmer. LC 74-8427. (Encore Edition). (Illus.). 1975. 4.95 o.p. (ISBN 0-684-15260-6, ScribT). Scribner.

Perfect Game. Herman Weiskopf. LC 77-19111. (Illus.). 1978. text ed. 15.95 o.p. (ISBN 0-13-657015-1). P-H.

Perfect Joy of St. Francis. Felix Timmermans. 280p. 1974. pap. 2.50 (ISBN 0-385-02378-2, Im). Doubleday.

Perfect Love. Diana Chang. (Orig.). 1978. pap. 1.95 (ISBN 0-515-04355-9). Jove Pubns.

Perfect Needlepoint Projects from Start to Finish. Kathy Archer & Pat Feeley. LC 75-40786. (Illus.). 1977. 12.95 o.p. (ISBN 0-312-60070-4). St Martin.

Perfect Pitch. Beman Lord. (Children's Literature Ser.). 1981. PLB 7.95 (ISBN 0-8398-2724-5). Gregg.

Perfect Place to Be. Bijou Le Tord. LC 75-33098. (Illus.). 40p. (ps-3). 1976. 5.95 o.s.i. (ISBN 0-8193-0842-0, Four Winds); PLB 5.41 o.s.i. (ISBN 0-8193-0843-9). Schol Bk Serv.

Perfect Puddings. Christine Collins. 1976. 5.95 (ISBN 0-571-10859-8, Pub. by Faber & Faber). Merrimack Bk Serv.

Perfect Put-Down. Mosesson. (Illus.). (gr. 7-12). 1975. pap. 1.25 (ISBN 0-590-09940-X, Schol Pap). Schol Bk Serv.

Perfect Squelch: Last Laughs from the Saturday Evening Post. LC 80-67061. (Illus.). 1980. 5.95 (ISBN 0-89387-042-0). Sat Eve Post.

Perfect Stranger. Danielle Steel. (Orig.). Date not set. pap. 2.75 (ISBN 0-440-17221-7). Dell.

Perfect the Pig. Susan Jeschke. LC 80-39998. (Illus.). 48p. (gr. k-3). 1981. 9.95 (ISBN 0-03-058622-4). HR&W.

Perfect Thief. Ronald J. Bass. (Orig.). 1978. pap. 1.75 o.s.i. (ISBN 0-515-04622-1). Jove Pubns.

Perfect Wheel: An Illustrated Guide to Bicycle Wheelbuilding. Richard P. Talbot. (Illus.). Date not set. 17.95 (ISBN 0-9602418-2-5). Manet Guild. Postponed.

Perfect Wife & Mother. Nicola Thorne. 266p. 1981. 11.95 (ISBN 0-312-60077-1). St Martin.

Perfect Will of God. G. Christian Weiss. 1950. pap. 1.50 (ISBN 0-8024-6468-8). Moody.

Perfectability of Man. John Passmore. LC 77-129625. 1970. 20.00x (ISBN 0-684-15521-4, ScribT). Scribner.

Perfecting Social Skills: A/Guide to Interpersonal Behavior Development. Richard M. Eisler & Lee W. Frederiksen. (Applied Clinical Psycholgy Ser.). 225p. 1981. 18.95 (ISBN 0-306-40592-X, Plenum Pr). Plenum Pub.

Perfecting Your Card Memory. Charles Edwards. (Gambler's Book Shelf). 64p. 1974. pap. 2.95 (ISBN 0-89650-545-6). Gamblers.

Perfection & Enforcement of Security Devices 1980. (Commercial Law & Practice Course Handbook Ser. 1979-80: Vol. 235). 1979. pap. 25.00 (ISBN 0-685-92231-6, A4-3078). PLI.

Perfection in the Head World. Sri Chinmoy. 55p. (Orig.). 1980. pap. 2.00 (ISBN 0-88497-492-8). Aum Pubns.

Perfection of Exile: Fourteen Contemporary Lithuanian Writers. Rimvydas Silbajoris. LC 72-108798. (Illus.). 1970. 15.95x (ISBN 0-8061-0907-6). U of Okla Pr.

Perfection of Technology. Friedrich G. Juenger. LC 79-92076. 192p. 1980. pap. cancelled (ISBN 0-89526-896-5). Regnery-Gateway.

Perfection of Wisdom in Eight Thousand Lines & Its Verse Summary. Tr. & pref. by Edward Conze. LC 72-76540. (Wheel Ser.: No. 1). 348p. 1973. 12.00 (ISBN 0-87704-023-0); pap. 6.00 (ISBN 0-87704-024-9). Four Seasons Foun.

Perfection of Yoga. A. C. Bhaktivedanta. (Illus.). 123p. 1973. pap. 1.50 o.s.i. (ISBN 0-02-083610-4, Collier). Macmillan.

Perfection of Yoga. Swami A. C. Bhaktivedanta. LC 72-76302. (Illus.). 1972. pap. 1.50 (ISBN 0-912776-36-6). Bhaktivedanta.

Perfection Perception. O. Devivre & Joe Devivre. (Illus.). 128p. 1981. pap. 5.00 (ISBN 0-933280-08-4). Island CA.

Perfectionism. Benjamin B. Warfield. 7.95 (ISBN 0-87552-528-8). Presby & Reformed.

Perfectionist Persuasion: The Holiness Movement & American Methodism, 1867-1936. Charles E. Jones. LC 74-1376. (ATLA Monograph: No. 5). (Illus.). 1974. 10.00 (ISBN 0-8108-0747-5). Scarecrow.

Perfidious Brethren. Bd. with Love in Its Empire: Illustrated in Seven Novels. Paul Chamberlen. (Novel in England, 1700-1775 Ser). 1973. Repr. of 1720 ed. lib. bdg. 50.00 (ISBN 0-8240-0547-3). Garland Pub.

Perfidious P. Bd. with Glorious Life & Actions of St. Whigg; Life & Adventures of Captain John Avery, the Famous English Pirate... Now in Possession of Madagascar. (Novel in England, 1700-1775 Ser). lib. bdg. 50.00 (ISBN 0-8240-0518-X). Garland Pub.

Perforated Mood-Swing Book. Ronald Redder. LC 76-186644. (Illus.). 100p. (Orig.). (YA) 1972. pap. 2.50 (ISBN 0-570-03134-6, 12-2381). Concordia.

Performance Accountability System for School Administrators. Terrel H. Bell. 1974. 11.95 o.p. (ISBN 0-13-657189-1). P-H.

Performance Activities in Mathematics, 6 bks. Terry Shoemaker. Incl. Bk. 1 (ISBN 0-913688-10-X); Bk. 2 (ISBN 0-913688-11-8); Bk. 3 (ISBN 0-913688-12-6); Bk. 4 (ISBN 0-913688-13-4); Bk. 5 (ISBN 0-913688-14-2); Bk. 6 (ISBN 0-913688-15-0). 1974. pap. 6.64x ea. Pawnee Pub.

Performance & Politics in Popular Drama: Aspects of Popular Entertainment in Theatre, Film & Television, 1800-1976. Ed. by David Bradby et al. LC 79-12036. (Illus.). 1980. 32.50 (ISBN 0-521-22755-0). Cambridge U Pr.

Performance & Testing of Gear Oils & Transmission Fluids. Tourret. 1980. write for info. (ISBN 0-85501-326-5). Heyden.

Performance Appraisal: A Guide to Greater Productivity. Richard F. Olson. (Self-Teaching Guide Ser.). 200p. 1981. pap. text ed. 8.95 (ISBN 0-471-09134-0). Wiley.

Performance Appraisal & Human Development. Howard P. Smith et al. LC 76-52663. 1977. pap. text ed. 8.95 (ISBN 0-201-07455-9). A-W.

Performance Appraisal: Keys to Effective Supervision. G. L. Morrisey. 1981. pap. write for info. (ISBN 0-201-04831-0). A-W.

Performance Art Memoirs, Vol. I. Jeff Nuttall. 1981. 13.95 (ISBN 0-7145-3788-8); pap. 6.95 (ISBN 0-7145-3711-X). Riverrun NY.

Performance Art Scripts, Vol. II. Jeff Nuttall. 1981. 13.95 (ISBN 0-7145-3789-6); pap. 6.95 (ISBN 0-7145-3712-8). Riverrun NY.

Performance Budgeting for Planned Development. K. S. Sastry. (Illus.). 235p. 1980. text ed. 12.50x (ISBN 0-391-02170-2). Humanities.

Performance Goals Record. Julia S. Molloy. (John Day Bk.). 1972. 2.50 o.s.i. (ISBN 0-381-97073-6, TYC-T). T Y Crowell.

Performance in a World of Change: Perspective on Learning Environments. Robert Howard. LC 79-65294. 1979. pap. text ed. 8.75 (ISBN 0-8191-0785-9); lib. bdg. 17.75 (ISBN 0-8191-1275-5). U Pr of Amer.

Performance Measurement of the Petroleum Industry: Functional Profitability & Alternatives. Alan Beckenstein et al. LC 79-1951. (Illus.). 1979. 19.95 (ISBN 0-669-03017-1). Lexington Bks.

Performance Objectives for School Principals. Jack A. Culbertson & Curtis Henson. LC 74-75367. 1974. 16.00x (ISBN 0-8211-0223-0); text ed. 14.50x (ISBN 0-685-42628-9). McCutchan.

Performance of American Government. Gerald M. Pomper. LC 71-163607. 416p. 1972. text ed. 9.95 o.s.i. (ISBN 0-02-925270-9). Free Pr.

Performance of Concrete in Marine Environment. 1980. 32.95 (SP-65). ACI.

Performance of Earth & Earth-Supported Structures. Compiled by American Society of Civil Engineers. 1972. pap. text ed. 75.00 (ISBN 0-87262-046-8). Am Soc Civil Eng.

Performance of Indian Agriculture: A Districtwise Study. G. S. Bhalla & Y. K. Alagh. (Illus.). 239p. 1979. 15.00x (ISBN 0-8002-0994-X). Intl Pubns Serv.

Performance of Nuclear Power Reactor Components. (Illus., Orig.). 1970. pap. 38.75 (ISBN 92-0-050170-2, IAEA). Unipub.

Performance of Paper Made with Thermomechanical Pulp: A Workshop on Thermomechanical Pulp. A. Arjas et al. (TAPPI PRESS Reports). (Illus.). 1978. pap. 14.95 (ISBN 0-89852-374-5). TAPPI.

Performance of Soldiers As Governors: African Politics & the African Military. Ed. by Isaac J. Mowoe. LC 79-5511. 1980. text ed. 23.00 (ISBN 0-8191-0903-7); pap. text ed. 13.50 (ISBN 0-8191-0904-5). U Pr of Amer.

Performance of Textiles. Dorothy S. Lyle. LC 76-54110. 1977. 26.95x (ISBN 0-471-01418-4). Wiley.

Performance Testing of Lubricants for Automotive Engines & Transmissions. Ed. by C. F. McCue et al. (Illus.). 1974. 89.50x (ISBN 0-85334-468-X). Intl Ideas.

Performance Under Sub-Optimal Condition. Ed. by P. R. Davis. 1971. pap. text ed. 12.95x (ISBN 0-85066-044-0). Intl Ideas.

Performance Zoning. Lane Kendig. LC 79-93346. (Illus.). 358p. 1980. 36.95 (ISBN 0-918286-18-2). Planners Pr.

Performing Arts in America. Ed. by Diana Reische. (Reference Shelf Ser.). 1973. 6.25 (ISBN 0-8242-0505-7). Wilson.

Performing Arts in Asia. Ed. by James R. Brandon. 168p. 1972. pap. 6.00 (ISBN 92-3-100902-8, U445, UNESCO). Unipub.

Performing Arts: Music & Dance. Ed. by John Blacking & Joann W. Kealiinohomoku. (World Anthropology Ser.). 1979. text ed. 44.00x (ISBN 90-279-7870-0). Mouton.

Performing Arts Research: A Guide to Information Sources. Ed. by Marion K. Whalon. LC 75-13828. (Performing Arts Information Guide Ser.: Vol. 1). 240p. 1976. 30.00 (ISBN 0-8103-1364-2). Gale.

Performing Arts 1876-1981. 1981. 150.00 (ISBN 0-8352-1372-2). Bowker.

Performing for Others. Daniels. write for info. (ISBN 0-87628-215-X). Ctr Appl Res.

Performing G. I. Procedures. (Nursing Photobook Ser.). (Illus.). 1981. 12.95 (ISBN 0-916730-31-X). Intermed Comm.

Performing Self: Compositions & Decompositions in the Languages of Contemporary Life. Richard Poirier. 1971. 11.95 (ISBN 0-19-501368-9). Oxford U Pr.

Performing Urologic Procedures. (Nursing Photobook Ser.). (Illus.). 160p. 1981. text ed. 12.95 (ISBN 0-916730-32-8). Intermed Comm.

Perfumed Garden. Tr. by Richard Burton. 1978. pap. 2.25 o.p. (ISBN 0-425-03657-X, Medallion). Berkley Pub.

Perfumery. Glen Pownall. (New Crafts Books Ser.). 72p. 1980. 7.50 (ISBN 0-85467-026-2, Pub. by Viking Sevenseas New Zealand). Intl Schol Bk Serv.

Perfumery Technology. 2nd ed. F. V. Wells. 400p. 1981. 110.00 (ISBN 0-470-26958-8). Halsted Pr.

Perfumery Technology: Art, Science, Industry. Marcel Billot & F. V. Wells. LC 75-5768. (Illus.). 353p. 1975. 54.95 (ISBN 0-470-07298-9). Halsted Pr.

Perfumery with Herbs. Ivan Day. 1980. 30.00x (ISBN 0-232-51414-3, Pub. by. Darton-Longman-Todd England). State Mutual Bk.

Perfusion of Signs. Ed. by Thomas A. Sebeok. LC 76-29318. (Advance in Semiotics Ser.). 224p. 1977. 15.00x (ISBN 0-253-34352-6). Ind U Pr.

Pergamon World Atlas: An Atlas to Supplement All Encyclopedias. 1968. 98.00 o.p. (ISBN 0-8277-3071-3). Maxwell Sci Intl.

Perhaps It Was Never the Same. Russel Hardin. 1980. write for info.; pap. write for info. Latitudes Pr.

Pericardial Disease. Ed. by P. S. Reddy et al. 1981. text ed. price not set (ISBN 0-89004-586-0). Raven.

Pericles. William Shakespeare. Ed. by Arthur Quiller-Couch et al. (New Shakespeare Ser). 1969. 23.95 (ISBN 0-521-07550-5); pap. 4.50x (ISBN 0-521-09494-1). Cambridge U Pr.

Pericles. William Shakespeare. 1969. pap. text ed. 3.50x o.p. (ISBN 0-471-00537-1). Wiley.

Pericyclic Reactions: A Mechanistic Study. S. M. Mukherji. 1980. 16.00x (ISBN 0-8364-0637-0, Pub. by Macmillan India). South Asia Bks.

Peridontal Instrumentation: A Clinical Manual. Gordon Pattison & Anna Pattison. (Illus.). 1979. text ed. 21.95 (ISBN 0-87909-604-7). Reston.

Periglacial Environment, Permafrost & Man. L. W. Price. LC 79-188229. (CCG Resource Papers Ser.: No. 14). (Illus.). 1972. pap. text ed. 4.00 (ISBN 0-89291-061-5). Assn Am Geographers.

Perilous Ascent, Stories of Mountain Climbing. Compiled by Phyllis R. Fenner. (Illus.). (gr. 7 up). 1970. 7.75 (ISBN 0-688-21734-6). Morrow.

Perilous Homecoming. Shirley A. Franklin. 192p. (YA) 1975. 5.95 (ISBN 0-685-53497-9, Avalon). Bouregy.

Perilous Planets. Brian Aldiss. 1979. pap. 2.50 (ISBN 0-380-47100-0, 47100). Avon.

Perilous Waters. Jane Blackmore. 1981. pap. 1.50 (ISBN 0-440-17309-4). Dell.

Perils & Prospects of Southern Black Leadership: Gordon Blaine Hancock, 1884-1970. Raymond Gavins. LC 76-44090. 1977. 11.75 (ISBN 0-8223-0381-7). Duke.

Perils of Democracy. Herbert Agar. LC 66-11684. (Background Ser.). 95p. 1965. 6.25 (ISBN 0-8023-1001-X). Dufour.

Perils of Probation. C. L. Erickson. (Illus.). 238p. 1980. pap. 10.75 (ISBN 0-398-04013-3). C C Thomas.

Perils of Prosperity: Nineteen Fourteen - Thirty Two. William E. Leuchtenburg. LC 58-5680. (Chicago History of America Civilization Ser). pap. 5.50 (ISBN 0-226-47369-4, CHAC12). U of Chicago Pr.

Perils of the Ocean & Wilderness: Or, Narratives of Shipwreck & Indian Captivity, Gleaned from Early Missionary Annals. John G. Shea. LC 75-7098. (Indian Captivities Ser.: Vol. 73). 1976. Repr. of 1857 ed. lib. bdg. 44.00 (ISBN 0-8240-1697-1). Garland Pub.

Perimeters. Charles Levendosky. LC 78-105508. (Wesleyan Poetry Program: Vol. 49). 1970. 10.00x (ISBN 0-8195-2049-7, Pub. by Wesleyan U Pr); pap. 4.95 (ISBN 0-8195-1049-1). Columbia U Pr.

Perimetry: Principles, Techniques, & Interpretations. Carl Ellenberger, Jr. 128p. 1980. text ed. 12.00 (ISBN 0-89004-504-6). Raven.

Perinatal Diseases. Richard L. Naeye et al. (International Academy of Pathology Monograph: No. 22). (Illus.). 300p. 1981. write for info. (6301-4). Williams & Wilkins.

Perinatal Medicine. Ed. by Peter J. Huntingford et al. 1970. 32.00 (ISBN 0-12-362550-5). Acad Pr.

Perinatal Medicine, Vol. 2. Ed. by Manohar Rathi & Sudhir Kumar. 224p. 1981. text ed. 35.00 (ISBN 0-89116-181-3). Hemisphere Pub.

Perinatal Medicine: Clinical & Biochemical Aspects of the Evaluation, Diagnosis & Management of the Fetus & Newborn. Ed. by S. Kumar & M. Rathi. LC 78-40219. 1978. text ed. 45.00 (ISBN 0-08-021517-3). Pergamon.

Perinatal Medicine: Review & Comments. 2nd ed. Frederick C. Battagila & Dwain D. Hagerman. Ed. by Giacomo Meschia & E. J. Quilligan. (Illus.). 1978. text ed. 25.00 o.p. (ISBN 0-8016-0513-X). Mosby.

Perinatal Medicine Today: Proceedings. Ed. by Bruce K. Young. LC 80-17343. (Progress in Clinical & Biological Research Ser.: Vol. 44). 244p. 1980. 20.00 (ISBN 0-8451-0044-0). A R Liss.

Perinatal Nursing: Reproductive Health, Vol. 1. Glenda F. Butnaurescu. LC 77-25924. 1978. 19.95 (ISBN 0-471-04361-3, Pub. by Wiley Medical). Wiley.

Perinatal Thyroid Physiology & Disease. Ed. by D. A. Fisher & G. N. Burrow. LC 75-14333. 291p. 1975. 27.00 (ISBN 0-89004-044-3). Raven.

Perinatology Case Studies. Leslie Iffy & Alvin Langer. 1978. pap. 18.75 (ISBN 0-87488-043-2). Med Exam.

Period Patterns. Lucy Barton & Doris Edson. (Illus.). 1942. 5.95 (ISBN 0-685-06788-2). Baker's Plays.

Period Style for the Theatre. Douglas A. Russell. 1980. text ed. 23.95 (ISBN 0-205-06450-7, 4864506). Allyn.

Periodate Oxidation of Diol & Other Functional Groups. G. Dryhurst. LC 72-101490. 1970. 25.00 (ISBN 0-08-006877-4). Pergamon.

Periodic Flow of Groundwater: A Systematic Study of Wave Propagation Under Confined, Semiconfined & Unconfined Flow Conditions. Garth S. Van Der Kamp. LC 73-90103. (Illus.). 121p. (Orig.). 1976. pap. text ed. 14.25x (ISBN 90-6203-387-3). Humanities.

Periodic Supplement Three to Minister's Library. Cyril J. Barber. 1980. pap. 4.95 (ISBN 0-8010-0787-9). Baker Bk.

Periodic Table of the Elements. R. J. Puddephatt. (Oxford Chemistry Ser.). (Illus.). 108p. 1972. pap. text ed. 8.50x (ISBN 0-19-855407-9). Oxford U Pr.

Periodical Indexes in the Social Sciences & Humanities: A Subject Guide. Lois A. Harzfeld. LC 78-5230. 1978. lib. bdg. 10.00 (ISBN 0-8108-1133-2). Scarecrow.

Periodical Title Abbreviations. 2nd ed. Ed. by Leland G. Alkire, Jr. LC 76-52617. 1977. 50.00 (ISBN 0-8103-0336-1). Gale.

Periodical Title Abbreviations. 3rd ed. Ed. by Leland G. Alkire, Jr. 500p. 1981. 50.00 (ISBN 0-8103-0337-X). Gale.

Periodicals Collection. 2nd ed. Donald Davinson. (Grafton Book). 1978. lib. bdg. 25.50x (ISBN 0-89158-883-3). Westview.

Periodicals on the Socialist Countries & on Marxism: A New Annotated Index of English Language Publications. Harry G. Shaffer. LC 75-36907. 1977. text ed. 24.95 (ISBN 0-275-24010-X). Praeger.

Periodontal Disease: Clinical Radiographic & Histopathologic Features. Irving Glickman & Jerome B. Smulow. LC 71-145558. (Illus.). 230p. 1974. 47.00 o.p. (ISBN 0-7216-4138-5). Saunders.

Periodontal Point of View: A Practical Expression of Current Problems, Integrating Basic Science with Clinical Data. Howard L. Ward. (American Lectures in Dentistry Ser.). (Illus.). 496p. 1973. 27.75 (ISBN 0-398-02815-X). C C Thomas.

Periodontal Surgery: Biological Basis & Technique. S. Sigmund Stahl. (American Lectures in Dentistry Ser.). (Illus.). 480p. 1976. 54.50 (ISBN 0-398-03431-1). C C Thomas.

Periodontal Therapy. 6th ed. Henry M. Goldman & D. Walter Cohen. LC 77-22523. (Illus.). 1979. 47.50 (ISBN 0-8016-1875-4). Mosby.

Periodontics in General Practice. William C. Hurt. (American Lectures in Dentistry Ser.). (Illus.). 528p. 1976. 42.75 (ISBN 0-398-03495-8). C C Thomas.

Periodontics in the Tradition of Orban & Gottlieb: A Concept-Theory & Practice. 5th ed. Daniel A. Grant et al. LC 79-10615. (Illus.). 1979. text ed. 39.50 (ISBN 0-8016-1961-0). Mosby.

Periodos Biblicos. (Spanish Bks.). 1977. 1.50 (ISBN 0-8297-0590-2). Life Pubs Intl.

Periods in German Literature, Vol. 1. Ed. by James M. Ritchie. 1967. 15.95 (ISBN 0-85496-031-7); pap. 12.95 (ISBN 0-85496-032-5). Dufour.

Peripatetic, 3 vols. in 2. John Thelwall. Ed. by Donald H. Reiman. LC 75-31262. (Romantic Context Ser.: Poetry 1789-1830). 1978. Set. lib. bdg. 47.00 (ISBN 0-8240-2208-4). Garland Pub.

Peripatetic Diabetic. Margaret Bennett. LC 69-16019. (Illus.). 1969. pap. 5.95 (ISBN 0-8015-5840-9, Hawthorn). Dutton.

Peripatetic University, Cambridge Local Lectures, 1873-1973. E. Welch. LC 72-91961. (Illus.). 204p. 1973. 26.50 (ISBN 0-521-20152-7). Cambridge U Pr.

Peripheral American: Destiny for the Coming Century. Matthew Carney. LC 80-68315. 278p. 1981. 16.95 (ISBN 0-937444-00-6); pap. 11.95 (ISBN 0-937444-01-4). Caislan Pr.

Peripheral & Joint Arthrography. Rolf D. Arndt et al. (Illus.). 188p. 1981. write for info. (0253-8). Williams & Wilkins.

Peripheral Arterial Chemoreceptors. Ed. by M. J. Purves. LC 74-16996. (Illus.). 500p. 1975. 77.00 (ISBN 0-521-20522-0). Cambridge U Pr.

Peripheral Circulation. Paul C. Johnson. LC 77-26858. 1978. 41.50 (ISBN 0-471-44637-8, Pub. by Wiley Medical). Wiley.

Peripheral Driver Data Book for Design Engineers, Nineteen Eighty One. rev. ed. Texas Instruments, Inc. Engineering Staff. LC 80-54795. 144p. 1981. pap. write for info. (ISBN 0-89512-107-7, LCC4280A). Tex Instr Inc.

Peripheral Metabolism & Action of Thyroid Hormones, Vol. 1. David Ramsden. 1977. 19.20 (ISBN 0-904406-54-7). Eden Med Res.

Peripheral Metabolism & Action of Thyroid Hormones, Vol. 2, 1977. David B. Ramsden. (Annual Research Reviews). 1978. 28.80 (ISBN 0-88831-029-3). Eden Med Res.

Peripheral Worker. Dean Morse. LC 73-76251. 1969. 20.00x (ISBN 0-231-03278-1). Columbia U Pr.

Peripherals & Interconnects. Dave Jenkins. 300p. 1982. text ed. 12.95 (ISBN 0-8359-5501-X). Reston.

Periphyseon: On the Division of Nature. John The Scot. Ed. & tr. by Myra Uhlfelder. LC 75-16475. (LLA Ser: No. 157). 408p. 1975. pap. 7.95 (ISBN 0-672-60377-2). Bobbs.

Periscope Red. Richard Rohmer. 352p. 1980. 12.95 (ISBN 0-8253-0020-7). Beaufort Bks NY.

Perishing Republic. Jerome Bahr. LC 79-129182. 148p. 1971. 8.00 o.p. (ISBN 0-686-63593-0). Trempealeau.

Peristome of Fissidens limbatus Sullivant. Dale M. J. Mueller. (U. C. Publ. in Botany: Vol. 63). 1973. pap. 9.50x (ISBN 0-520-09446-8). U of Cal Pr.

Perkin Warbeck. John Ford. Ed. by Donald K. Anderson, Jr. LC 65-15338. (Regents Renaissance Drama Ser). 1965. 7.50x (ISBN 0-8032-0260-1); pap. 1.65x (ISBN 0-8032-5260-9, BB 213, Bison). U of Nebr Pr.

Permafrost. 2nd ed. Building Research Advisory Board. (Illus.). 744p. 1973. 44.50 (ISBN 0-309-02115-4). Natl Acad Pr.

Permafrost: Russian Papers. Building Research Advisory Board. 1978. pap. 18.00 (ISBN 0-309-02746-2). Natl Acad Pr.

Permanence & Change: An Anatomy of Purpose. Kenneth Burke. LC 64-66067. 1965. pap. 7.50 (ISBN 0-672-60452-3, LLA207). Bobbs.

Permanent Address: New Poems 1973-1980. Ruth Whitman. LC 80-66182. 72p. 1980. pap. 4.95 (ISBN 0-914086-30-8). Alicejamesbook.

Permanent Collection, Vol. 1. Erna Gunther. LC 75-32053. (Whatcom Museum). (Illus.). 64p. 1975. pap. 5.00 (ISBN 0-295-95579-1). U of Wash Pr.

Permanent Element. Stanley E. Rajiva. 8.00 (ISBN 0-89253-720-5); flexible cloth 4.80 (ISBN 0-89253-721-3). Ind-US Inc.

Permanent Errors. Reynolds Price. LC 70-124974. 1970. 6.50 o.p. (ISBN 0-689-10357-3). Atheneum.

Permanent Errors. Reynolds Price. LC 70-124974. 1980. pap. 4.95 (ISBN 0-689-70599-9, 258). Atheneum.

Permanent Fires: Reviews of Poetry 1958-1973. Ray Smith. LC 74-22230. 1975. 10.00 (ISBN 0-8108-0757-2). Scarecrow.

Permanent Magnet Design & Application Handbook. Lester R. Moskowitz. LC 75-28109. 1976. 45.00 (ISBN 0-8436-1800-0). CBI Pub.

Permanent Magnets & Their Applications. Rollin J. Parker & R. J. Studders. LC 62-10930. 1962. 43.50 (ISBN 0-471-66264-X, Pub. by Wiley-Interscience). Wiley.

Permanent Magnets in Theory & Practice. M. McCaig. LC 77-23949. 1977. 39.95 (ISBN 0-470-99269-7). Halsted Pr.

Permanent Part-Time Employment: The Manager's Perspective. Stanley D. Nollen et al. LC 78-17767. 1978. 23.95 (ISBN 0-03-043071-2). Praeger.

Permanent Weight Loss Program. The G-Jo Institute. 1980. pap. 4.50 (ISBN 0-916878-11-2). Falkynor Bks.

Permissible Dose for Internal Radiation. International Commission on Radiological Protection. (ICRP Publication Ser.: No. 2). 1960. pap. 10.45 (ISBN 0-08-009254-3). Pergamon.

Permission to Speak. Steve Orlen. LC 77-89038. (Wesleyan Poetry Program: Vol. 90). 1978. 10.00x (ISBN 0-8195-2090-X, Pub. by Wesleyan U Pr); pap. 4.95 (ISBN 0-8195-1090-4). Columbia U Pr.

Permit Explosion. Fred Bosselman et al. LC 76-55844. (Management & Control of Growth Ser.). 86p. 1976. pap. text ed. 11.00 (ISBN 0-87420-570-0). Urban Land.

Permutation Groups & Combinatorial Structures. N. L. Biggs & A. T. White. LC 78-21485. (London Mathematical Society Lecture Note: No. 33). (Illus.). 1979. pap. 17.95x (ISBN 0-521-22287-7). Cambridge U Pr.

Peroff: The Man Who Knew Too Much. L. H. Whittemore. 368p. 1976. pap. 1.95 o.p. (ISBN 0-345-25104-0). Ballantine.

Peroneal Atrophy & Related Disorders. Ed. by G. Serratrice. H. Roux. LC 78-62593. (Illus.). 376p. 1979. 45.50 (ISBN 0-89352-028-4). Masson Pub.

Peroxisomes & Related Particles in Animal Tissues. P. Boeck et al. (Cell Biology Monographs: Vol. 7). (Illus.). 250p. 1980. 79.00 (ISBN 0-387-81582-1). Springer-Verlag.

Perpetual Curate. Margaret O. Oliphant. Ed. by Robert L. Wolff. LC 75-1544. (Victorian Fiction Ser). 1975. Repr. of 1864 ed. lib. bdg. 66.00 (ISBN 0-8240-1614-9). Garland Pub.

Perpetual Dilemma: Jewish Religion in the Jewish State. S. Zalman Abramov. 1979. pap. 15.00 (ISBN 0-8074-0088-2, 382500, WUPJ). UAHC.

Perpetual Peace. Immanuel Kant. Tr. by Lewis W. Beck. LC 57-3588. 1957. pap. 2.50 (ISBN 0-672-60227-X, LLA54). Bobbs.

Perpetuities Law in Action: Kentucky Case Law & the 1960 Reform Act. Jesse Dukeminier, Jr. LC 62-13459. (Illus.). 180p. 1962. 8.50x (ISBN 0-8131-1070-X). U Pr of Ky.

Perplexing Puzzles & Tantalizing Teasers. Martin Gardner. (Illus., Orig.). (gr. 3-6). 1971. pap. 1.25 (ISBN 0-671-29927-1). PB.

Perplexing Puzzles & Tantalizing Teasers. Martin Gardner. 1981. pap. 1.50 (ISBN 0-686-69007-9). Archway.

Perrault's Fairy Tales. Charles Perrault. LC 72-79522. (Illus.). (gr. 4-6). 1969. pap. 3.50 (ISBN 0-486-22311-6). Dover.

Perry & the Open Door to Japan, July, 1853: An American Commander Ends Centuries of Japanese Isolation. Joseph B. Icenhower. LC 72-10423. (World Focus Bks). (Illus.). 72p. (gr. 7 up). 1973. PLB 4.47 o.p. (ISBN 0-531-02167-X). Watts.

Perscription Drugs in Short Supply. Schwartz. 144p. 1980. 17.50 (ISBN 0-686-60253-6). Dekker.

Persecuted Drug: The Story of DMSO. Pat McGgrady. 312p. (Orig.). 1981. pap. 2.50 (ISBN 0-441-15101-9). Charter Bks.

Persecuted Prophets. Karen W. Carden & Robert W. Pelton. LC 74-10322. (Illus.). 192p. 1976. 9.95 o.p. (ISBN 0-498-01511-4). A S Barnes.

Persia: An Archaeological Guide. new ed. Sylvia A. Matheson. (Illus.). 1976. pap. 13.95 (ISBN 0-571-04888-9, Pub. by Faber & Faber). Merrimack Bk Serv.

Persian & the Turkish Tales, Pt. 1. Francois Petis De La Croix. LC 77-170535. (Novel in England, 1700-1775 Ser). lib. bdg. 50.00 (ISBN 0-8240-0535-X). Garland Pub.

Persian & the Turkish Tales, Pt. 2. Francois Petis De La Croix. LC 77-170535. (Novel in England, 1700-1775 Ser). lib. bdg. 50.00 (ISBN 0-8240-0536-8). Garland Pub.

Persian Cats. Grace Pond. Ed. by Christina Foyle. (Foyle's Handbks). 1973. 3.95 (ISBN 0-685-55820-7). Palmetto Pub.

Persian Cats. Jeanne Ramsdale. (Orig.). 1962. pap. 2.00 (ISBN 0-87666-178-9, M507). TFH Pubns.

Persian Designs & Motifs for Artists & Craftsmen. Ali Dowlatshahi. (Illus.). 1979. pap. 4.00 (ISBN 0-486-23815-6). Dover.

Persian Grammar. Ann K. Lambton. 1953-1960. pap. 16.95x (ISBN 0-521-09124-1). Cambridge U Pr.

Persian Gulf: An Historical Sketch from the Earliest Times to the Beginning of the Twentieth Century. Arnold T. Wilson. LC 79-2888. (Illus.). 327p. 1981. Repr. of 1928 ed. 27.50 (ISBN 0-8305-0055-3). Hyperion Conn.

Persian Gulf: An Introduction to Its Peoples, Politics, & Economics. rev. ed. David E. Long. LC 76-6531. (Westview Special Studies on the Middle East Ser.). (Illus.). 1978. lib. bdg. 20.00 o.p. (ISBN 0-89158-826-4). Westview.

Persian Gulf & the Strait of Hormuz. P. K. Ramazani. (International Straits of the World Ser.: No. 3). 200p. 1979. 35.00x (ISBN 90-286-0069-8). Sijthoff & Noordhoff.

Persian Gulf States. Ed. by Alvin J. Cottrell. LC 79-19452. 736p. 1980. text ed. 37.50x (ISBN 0-8018-2204-1). Johns Hopkins.

Persian Gulf States. Rupert Hay. LC 80-1926. 1981. Repr. of 1959 ed. 23.50 (ISBN 0-404-18966-0). AMS Pr.

Persian Letters, Pt. 1. Charles D. Montesquieu. LC 73-170550. (Novel in England, 1700-1775 Ser). lib. bdg. 50.00 (ISBN 0-8240-0549-X). Garland Pub.

Persian Letters, Pt. 2. Charles D. Montesquieu. LC 73-170550. (Novel in England, 1700-1775 Ser). lib. bdg. 50.00 (ISBN 0-8240-0550-3). Garland Pub.

Persian Metres. L. P. Elwell-Sutton. 200p. 1976. 44.50 (ISBN 0-521-21089-5). Cambridge U Pr.

Persian Paintings in the John Rylands Library: A Descriptive Catalog. B. W. Robinson. (Illus.). 365p. 1980. 87.50x (ISBN 0-85667-072-3, Pub. by Sotheby Parke Bernet). Biblio Dist.

Persian Poetry in Kashmir, 1339-1846: An Introduction. G. L. Tikku. (U. C. Publ. in Occasional Papers: No. 4). 1971. pap. 15.00x (ISBN 0-520-09312-7). U of Cal Pr.

Persian Sufi Poem: Vocabulary & Terminology. Concordance, Frequency Word-List, Statistical Survey, Arabic Loan-Words & Sufi-Religious Terminology in Tariq Ut-Tajqiq. Bo Utas. (Scandinavian Institute of Asian Studies Monographs: No. 36). 1978. pap. text ed. 13.75x (ISBN 0-7007-0116-8). Humanities.

Persian Vocabulary. Ann K. Lambton. 1954-1962. pap. 18.95x (ISBN 0-521-09154-3, 154). Cambridge U Pr.

Persian Words in English. A. A. Daryusl et al. Ed. by Steele Commager. Incl. German Influence on the English Vocabulary; H.W. Fowler; Dutch Influence on English Vocabulary; American Variations; Fine Writing; Names, Designations, & Appelations; Linguistic Self-Criticism; Formation & Use of Compound Epithets in English Poetry; Northern Words in Modern English. (Society for Pure English Ser.: Vol. 5). 1979. lib. bdg. 42.00 (ISBN 0-8240-3669-7). Garland Pub.

Persians. Jim Hicks. (Emergence of Man Ser.). (Illus.). 1975. 9.95 (ISBN 0-8094-1297-7). Time-Life.

Persians. Jim Hicks. LC 75-10727. (Emergence of Man Ser.). (gr. 6 up). 1975. PLB 9.63 o.p. (ISBN 0-8094-1298-5, Pub. by Time-Life). Silver.

Persians. E. Denison Ross, Jr. 142p. 1980. Repr. lib. bdg. 30.00 (ISBN 0-89987-713-3). Darby Bks.

Persistence of Religion. Ed. by Andrew Greeley & Gregory Baum. (Concilium Ser.: Religion in the Seventies: Vol. 81). 156p. 1973. pap. 4.95 (ISBN 0-8164-2537-X). Crossroad NY.

Persistence of the Old Regime: Europe to the Great War. Arno Mayer. 1981. 16.95 (ISBN 0-394-51141-7). Pantheon.

Persistent Inflation. Phillip Cagan. LC 79-1017. 1979. 20.00x (ISBN 0-231-04728-2); pap. 10.00 (ISBN 0-231-04729-0). Columbia U Pr.

Persistent Pianist: A Book for the Late Beginner & Adult Re-Starter. Eileen D. Robilliard. 1967. pap. 8.95x (ISBN 0-19-318416-8). Oxford U Pr.

Persistent Poppy: A Computer-Aided Search for Heroin Policy. Gilbert Levin et al. LC 75-4656. 184p. 1975. text ed. 17.50 o.p. (ISBN 0-88410-031-6). Ballinger Pub.

Persius & the Programmatic Satire. J. C. Bramble. LC 72-83579. (Cambridge Classical Studies). 192p. 1973. 19.95 (ISBN 0-521-08703-1). Cambridge U Pr.

Person - Perception & Stereotyping. R. A. Stewart et al. 1979. 21.95 (ISBN 0-347-01072-5, 96768-8, Pub. by Saxon Hse). Lexington Bks.

Person & Community in American Philosophy. Jacquelyn A. Kegley et al. Ed. by Konstantin Kolenda. (Rice University Studies: Vol. 66, No. 4). (Orig.). 1981. pap. 5.50 (ISBN 0-89263-247-X). Rice Univ.

Person & Power of Satan. Herbert Lockyer, Sr. 1980. pap. 5.95 (ISBN 0-8499-2921-0). Word Bks.

Person from Britain: Whose Head Was the Shape of a Mitten & Other Limericks. N. M. Bodecker. (Illus.). (gr. 8 up). 1980. PLB 6.95 (ISBN 0-689-50152-8, McElderry Bk). Atheneum.

Person-in-Distress: On the Biosocial Dynamics of Adaptation. Norris Hansell. LC 74-8096. 252p. 1976. text ed. 22.95 (ISBN 0-87705-213-1). Human Sci Pr.

Person in the Potting Shed. Barbara Corcoran. LC 80-12299. 132p. (gr. 5-9). 1980. 8.95 (ISBN 0-689-30774-8). Atheneum.

Person Perception. 2nd ed. David J. Schneider et al. LC 78-67455. (Topics in Social Psychology). (Illus.). 1979. pap. text ed. 9.50 (ISBN 0-201-06768-4). A-W.

Person-Perception & Stereotyping. R. A. Stewart et al. 1979. 21.95 (ISBN 0-566-00072-5, 96768-8, Pub. by Saxon Hse England). Lexington Bks.

Person-Planet: The Creative Disintegration of Industrial Society. Theodore Roszak. 1978. 10.95 o.p. (ISBN 0-385-00063-4). Doubleday.

Person to Person. Robert B. Ruddell et al. (Pathfinder - Allyn & Bacon Reading Program: Level 15). (gr. 4). 1978. text ed. 9.12 (ISBN 0-205-05187-1, 5451876); tchrs. ed. 14.60 (ISBN 0-205-05189-8, 5451892). Allyn.

Person to Person. Sasse. (gr. 9-12). 1978. text ed. 10.60 (ISBN 0-87002-266-0); student's guide 5.12 (ISBN 0-87002-202-4); tchr's guide 7.96 (ISBN 0-87002-209-1). Bennett IL.

Person to Person Evangelism. new ed. R. Edward Davenport. LC 77-23716. 1978. pap. 2.25 (ISBN 0-87148-691-1). Pathway Pr.

Person to Person: Ways of Communicating. Michael Argyle & Peter Trower. (Life Cycle Ser.). 1979. pap. text ed. 4.95 scp (ISBN 0-06-384746-9, HarpC). Har-Row.

Person Who Chairs the Meeting. Paul O. Madsen. (Illus.). 96p. (Orig.). 1973. tanalin 2.50 (ISBN 0-8170-0582-X). Judson.

Person You Are. Linda Anderson. 1978. text ed. 11.15 (ISBN 0-913310-42-5). PAR Inc.

Persona: A Style Study for Readers & Writers. Walker Gibson. 1969. pap. text ed. 3.95 (ISBN 0-394-30198-6). Random.

Personal Adjustment: Selected Readings. Valerian Derlega & Louis H. Janda. 1979. pap. text ed. 8.95x (ISBN 0-673-15288-X). Scott F.

Personal Adjustment: The Psychology of Everyday Life. 2nd ed. Valerian J. Derlega & Louis Janda. 1981. text ed. 16.95x (ISBN 0-673-15470-X). Scott F.

Personal Aircraft Business at Airports. L. L. Bollinger & J. R. Tully. 1970. Repr. of 1946 ed. 28.00 (ISBN 0-08-018742-0). Pergamon.

Personal Aircraft Maintenance. Kas Thomas. (Aviation Ser.). (Illus.). 256p. 1980. 19.50 (ISBN 0-07-064241-9, P&RB). McGraw.

Personal & Controversial: An Autobiography. Paul Blanshard. LC 72-6225. 320p. 1973. 7.95 o.p. (ISBN 0-8070-0514-2). Beacon Pr.

Personal & Interpersonal Appraisal Techniques: For Counselors, Teachers, Students. M. A. Kiley. (Illus.). 264p. 1975. 17.50 (ISBN 0-398-03219-X); pap. 12.50 (ISBN 0-398-03240-8). C C Thomas.

Personal & Professional Recollections. George G. Scott. LC 77-1202. (Architecture & Decorative Arts Ser.). 1977. Repr. of 1879 ed. lib. bdg. 35.00 (ISBN 0-306-70873-6). Da Capo.

Personal & Public Speaking. Donald W. Klopf & Ronald E. Cambra. 208p. 1981. pap. text ed. 8.95 (ISBN 0-89582-042-0). Morton Pub.

Personal Appearance Identification. Ed. by Albert Zavala & James J. Paley. (Illus.). 352p. 1972. pap. 23.75 (ISBN 0-398-02447-2). C C Thomas.

Personal Applications in Typewriting. Farmer et al. 272p. 1976. text ed. 13.27 (ISBN 0-7715-0875-1); Set Of 26 =cassettes. tchr's. manual 6.67 (ISBN 0-7715-0876-X); 269.50 (ISBN 0-7715-0882-4); book of resource materials 39.93 (ISBN 0-7715-0831-X); typing facts & tips 3.00 ea. (ISBN 0-7715-0889-1); typing facts & tips, package of 10 21.33 (ISBN 0-7715-0896-4); certificate of proficiency (personal, 1 per student) free (ISBN 0-7715-0865-4); roll of honor for production efficiency (1 per classroom) free (ISBN 0-7715-0864-6). Forkner.

Personal Awareness: A Psychology of Adjustment. 2nd ed. Richard G. Warga. LC 78-69531. (Illus.). 1979. pap. text ed. 12.95 (ISBN 0-395-26795-1); inst. manual 1.10 (ISBN 0-395-26796-X). HM.

Personal Bible Study. William C. Lincoln. LC 75-2345. 160p. 1975. pap. 4.95 (ISBN 0-87123-458-0, 210458). Bethany Fell.

Personal Change & Reconstruction: Research on a Treatment of Stuttering. F. Fransella. 1973. 34.50 (ISBN 0-12-266150-8). Acad Pr.

Personal Choice in Ethnic Identity Maintenance: Serbs, Croats & Slovenes in Washington, D. C. Linda A. Bennett. LC 77-93261. 230p. 1978. soft cover 10.00 (ISBN 0-918660-06-8). Ragusan Pr.

Personal Column. Charles Belgrave. (Arab Background Ser.). (Illus.). 13.00x (ISBN 0-685-72054-3). Intl Bk Ctr.

Personal Computers in Business. Ed. by Online Conferences Ltd. 1978. pap. text ed. 42.00x (ISBN 0-903796-33-3, Pub. by Online Conferences England). Renouf.

Personal Computers in Chemistry. Peter Lykos. 250p. 1980. 25.00 (ISBN 0-471-08508-1, Pub. by Wiley-Interscience). Wiley.

Personal Computing. Jim Huffman. (Illus.). 1979. text ed. 15.95 (ISBN 0-8359-5516-8); pap. 11.95 (ISBN 0-8359-5515-X). Reston.

Personal Computing: A Beginner's Guide. David Bunnell. LC 77-99078. (Illus.). 1978. 11.95 o.p. (ISBN 0-8015-5843-3). Dutton.

Personal Computing Digest. Ed. by Larry Press & Lou Whittaker. (Illus.). vi, 211p. 1980. pap. 12.00 (ISBN 0-88283-012-0). AFIPS Pr.

Personal Computing: Home, Professional & Small Business Applications. Daniel R. McGlynn. LC 79-1005. 1979. pap. 10.95 (ISBN 0-471-05380-5, Pub. by Wiley-Interscience). Wiley.

Personal Computing: Proceedings. Ed. by Jay P. Lucas & Russell E. Adams. (Illus.). viii, 439p. 1979. pap. 12.00 (ISBN 0-88283-020-1). AFIPS Pr.

Personal Construct Psychology: Psychotherapy & Personality. Ed. by A. W. Landfield. L. M. Leitner. LC 80-16938. (Personality Processes Ser.). 400p. 1980. 28.00 (ISBN 0-471-05859-9, Pub. by Wiley-Interscience). Wiley.

Personal Counseling. J. H. Wallis. 1973. text ed. 10.95x o.p. (ISBN 0-04-361015-3); pap. text ed. 5.95x o.p. (ISBN 0-04-361016-1). Allen Unwin.

Personal Declension & Revival of Religion in the Soul. Octavius Winslow. 1978. pap. 2.95 (ISBN 0-85151-261-5). Banner of Truth.

Personal Development Series, 12 bks. Incl. Alcohol & Health, 2 bks. Bk. 1 (ISBN 0-8273-0522-2). Bk. 2 (ISBN 0-8273-0523-0); Drug Abuse, 2 bks. Bk. 1 (ISBN 0-8273-0524-9). Bk. 2 (ISBN 0-8273-0525-7); Facts About Sex, 2 bks. Bk. 1 (ISBN 0-8273-0526-5). Bk. 2 (ISBN 0-8273-0527-3); Facts About Venereal Disease (ISBN 0-8273-0528-1); Finding Your Way (ISBN 0-8273-0518-4); Keeping Your Body Healthy (ISBN 0-8273-0519-2); Telephone Talk (ISBN 0-8273-0517-6); Tobacco & Health, 2 bks. Bk. 1 (ISBN 0-8273-0520-6). Bk. 2 (ISBN 0-8273-0521-4). 1970. Set. pap. 19.20 o.s.i. (ISBN 0-8273-0515-X); pap. 1.80 ea. o.s.i.; ans. key 0.35 o.s.i. (ISBN 0-8273-0516-8). Delmar.

Personal Distribution of Incomes. Ed. by A. B. Atkinson. (Illus.). 1977. pap. text ed. 25.00x (ISBN 0-04-332065-1). Allen Unwin.

Personal Distribution of Incomes. Ed. by Anthony B. Atkinson. LC 75-34050. 1976. 35.00x (ISBN 0-89158-526-5). Westview.

Personal Effectiveness: Guiding People to Assert Themselves & Improve Their Social Skills. Robert P. Liberman et al. (Illus., Orig.). 1975. basic manual 7.95 (ISBN 0-87822-163-8); program guide 3.95 (ISBN 0-87822-164-6); client's introduction set 5.95 (ISBN 0-87822-165-4). Res Press.

Personal Effects. Robin Becker et al. LC 75-46406. 88p. 1976. pap. 4.95 (ISBN 0-914086-15-4). Alicejamesbooks.

Personal Evangelism Among Roman Catholics. Aniceto Sparagna. (Orig.). 1978. pap. 3.95 (ISBN 0-89900-122-X). College Pr Pub.

Personal Experiences of S. O. Susag. S. O. Susag. 191p. pap. 1.75. Faith Pub Hse.

Personal Fertitlity Guide: How to Avoid or Achieve Pregnancy Naturally. Terrie Guay. 192p. (Orig.). 1980. pap. 7.95 (ISBN 0-936602-04-X). Harbor Pub CA.

Personal Filmmaking. James Piper. (Illus.). 368p. 1975. 9.95 (ISBN 0-87909-612-8); instrs' manual avail. Reston.

Personal Finance. 2nd ed. Charles L. Barngrover et al. LC 80-18010. (Finance Ser.). 520p. 1981. text ed. 19.95 (ISBN 0-88244-216-3). Grid Pub.

Personal Finance. 6th ed. Jerome B. Cohen. 1979. text ed. 17.95x (ISBN 0-256-02154-6). Irwin.

Personal Finance. 7th ed. David T. Crary et al. LC 79-27578. 1980. text ed. 20.95 (ISBN 0-471-05639-1); tchr's ed. (ISBN 0-471-07802-6); study guide (ISBN 0-471-07919-7). Wiley.

Personal Finance. 6th ed. E. F. Donaldson et al. LC 77-71238. 1977. 18.95 o.p. (ISBN 0-8260-2766-0); instructors' manual avail. o.p. (ISBN 0-471-07561-2). Wiley.

Personal Finance. Gitman. 1978. 18.95 (ISBN 0-03-020821-1). Dryden Pr.

Personal Finance. 2nd ed. Lawrence J. Gitman. LC 80-65798. 672p. 1981. text ed. 18.95 (ISBN 0-03-058094-3). Dryden Pr.

Personal Finance. 6th ed. Harold Wolf. 700p. 1981. 19.95 (ISBN 0-205-07298-4, 1072986); tchr's ed. free (ISBN 0-205-07299-2, 1072994). Allyn.

Personal Finance. 5th ed. Harold A. Wolf. 1978. text ed. 18.95 o.p. (ISBN 0-205-06047-1, 1060473); instr's man. avail. o.p. (ISBN 0-205-06048-X, 1060481). Allyn.

Personal Finance & Money Management. Robert S. Rosefsky. LC 77-20283. 1978. text ed. 15.95 (ISBN 0-471-01740-X); tchr.'s manual avail. (ISBN 0-471-03762-1); study guide by M. H. Ivener avail. Wiley.

Personal Finance: Getting Along & Getting Ahead. J. Norman Swaton. 1980. text ed. 15.95 (ISBN 0-442-28116-1); instr's. manual 3.95 (ISBN 0-442-26236-1). D Van Nostrand.

Personal Finance Today. Roger L. Miller. (Illus.). 1979. text ed. 18.50 (ISBN 0-8299-0233-3); pap. study guide & wkbk. by Grant J. Wells 7.50 (ISBN 0-8299-0256-2); instrs.' manual avail. (ISBN 0-8299-0561-8). West Pub.

Personal Financial Management. David West & Glenn Wood. LC 75-172124. 80p. (Orig.). 1972. text ed. 18.95 (ISBN 0-395-12428-X, 3-59690); tchr's. manual. pap. 1.75 (ISBN 0-395-13495-1, 3-59691). HM.

Personal Fitness. Boy Scouts Of America. LC 19-600. (Illus.). 48p. (gr. 6-12). 1971. pap. 0.70x (ISBN 0-8395-3286-5, 3286). BSA.

Personal God. Ed. by E. Schillebeeckx & B. Van Iersel. (Concilium Ser.: Vol. 103). 1977. pap. 4.95 (ISBN 0-8164-2149-8). Crossroad NY.

Personal Health: Confronting Your Health Behavior. Phyllis G. Ensor et al. 1977. pap. text ed. 14.95x (ISBN 0-205-05737-3, 6257372); instr's manual avail. (ISBN 0-205-05738-1, 6257380). Allyn.

Personal History of Samuel Johnson. Christopher Hibbert. Repr. of 1970 ed. 10.95 (ISBN 0-911660-26-7). Yankee Peddler.

Personal History of the "Boom". Jose Donoso. LC 76-53747. 1977. pap. 5.00x (ISBN 0-231-04164-0); pap. 4.95 (ISBN 0-231-04165-9). Columbia U Pr.

Personal Identity. Ed. by John Perry. 246p. 1975. pap. 4.95x (ISBN 0-520-02960-7). U of Cal Pr.

Personal Impressions. Isaiah Berlin. Ed. by Henry Hardy. LC 79-56278. (Illus.). 240p. 1981. 13.95 (ISBN 0-670-54833-2). Viking Pr.

Personal Income Distribution: A Multicapability Theory. Joop Hartog. 208p. 1980. lib. bdg. 22.00 (ISBN 0-89838-047-2). Kluwer Boston.

Personal Influence: The Part Played by People in the Flow of Mass Communications. Elihu Katz & Paul Lazarsfeld. LC 55-7334. 1964. pap. text ed. 6.95 (ISBN 0-02-917150-4). Free Pr.

Personal Information: Privacy at the Workplace. Jack L. Osborn. LC 78-18223. 1978. pap. 7.50 o.p. (ISBN 0-8144-2223-3). Am Mgmt.

Personal Integrity. Ed. by William M. Schutte & Erwin R. Steinberg. (Illus., Orig.). 1961. pap. 3.95x (ISBN 0-393-09571-1, NortonC). Norton.

Personal Inventory: For Antiques. 1977. loose leaf bdg. 9.95 (ISBN 0-685-84410-2). Warman.

Personal Investing. rev. ed. Wilbur W. Widicus & Thomas E. Stitzel. 1976. text ed. 15.50x o.p. (ISBN 0-256-01832-4). Irwin.

Personal Law. Norbert J. Mietus & Bill W. West. LC 74-34192. (Consumer Education Ser). (Illus.). 464p. 1975. text ed. 16.95 (ISBN 0-574-18215-2, 13-2215); instr's guide avail. (ISBN 0-574-18216-0, 13-2216). SRA.

Personal Law. 2nd ed. Norbert J. Mietus & Bill W. West. 512p. 1981. text ed. 16.95 (ISBN 0-574-19505-X, 13-2505); instr's. guide avail. (ISBN 0-574-19506-8, 13-2506). Sci Res Assoc Coll.

Personal Liabilities of Corporate Officers & Directors. 2nd ed. Morton Feuer & Joseph E. Johnston. 1974. 24.95 o.p. (ISBN 0-13-657593-5). P-H.

Personal Liberty & Education. Ed. by Monroe D. Cohen. LC 76-2511. 288p. 1976. 8.95 (ISBN 0-590-07462-8, Citation); pap. text ed. 4.95 (ISBN 0-590-09406-8). Schol Bk Serv.

Personal Life Notebook. David Gustaveson. 1980. pap. 8.95 spiral bdg. (ISBN 0-87123-467-X, 210467). Bethany Fell.

Personal Management. Boy Scouts of America. LC 19-600. (Illus.). 32p. (gr. 6-12). 1972. pap. 0.70x (ISBN 0-8395-3270-9, 3270). BSA.

Personal Marriage Contract. John Whitaker. LC 76-9623. (Illus.). 1976. 5.95 o.p. (ISBN 0-917278-02-X); pap. 3.95 o.p. (ISBN 0-685-73029-8). OK Street.

Personal Models of Teaching: Expanding Your Teaching Repertoire. Marsha Weil et al. LC 77-7738. (Illus.). 1978. ref 13.95 (ISBN 0-13-657767-9); pap. text ed. 9.95 (ISBN 0-13-657759-8). P-H.

Personal Money Management. 3rd ed. Thomas E. Bailard et al. 1979. text ed. 16.95 (ISBN 0-574-19395-2, 13-2395); instr's guide avail. (ISBN 0-574-19396-0, 13-2396); study guide 6.50 (ISBN 0-574-19397-9, 13-2397). SRA.

Personal Money Management: A Consumer Guide. Hurley. 1976. 16.95 (ISBN 0-13-657650-8); instr. manual o.p. free (ISBN 0-685-78800-8). P-H.

Personal Money Management: An Objectives & Systems Approach. Roger H. Nelson. LC 77-190163. 1973. text ed. 16.95 (ISBN 0-201-05255-5). A-W.

Personal Money Management for Physicians. T. D. Rhodabarger. 1973. 16.50 (ISBN 0-87489-027-6). Med Economics.

Personal Name Index to Orton's Records of California Men in the War of the Rebellion, 1861 to 1867. Compiled by J. Carlyle Parker. LC 78-15674. (Gale's Genealogy & Local History Ser.: Vol. 5). 1978. 30.00 (ISBN 0-8103-1402-9). Gale.

Personal Name Index to the Eighteen Fifty-Six City Directories of Iowa. LaVerne Sopp. (Genealogy & Local History Ser.: Vol. 13). 400p. 1980. 30.00 (ISBN 0-8103-1486-X). Gale.

Personal Name Index to the 1856 City Directories of California. Ed. by Nathan C. Parker. LC 79-24246. (Gale Genealogy & Local History Ser.: Vol. 10). 250p. 30.00 (ISBN 0-8103-1414-2). Gale.

Personal Names: A Bibliography. Elsdon C. Smith. LC 66-31855. 1965. Repr. of 1952 ed. 15.00 (ISBN 0-8103-3134-9). Gale.

Personal Names from Cuneiform Inscriptions of Cappadocia. Ferris J. Stephens. (Yale Oriental Researches Ser.: No. XIII). 1928. pap. 22.50x (ISBN 0-685-69868-8). Elliots Bks.

Personal Names in Palmyrene Inscriptions. Jurgen K. Stark. 1971. 19.25x o.p. (ISBN 0-19-815443-7). Oxford U Pr.

Personal Narrative of a Pilgrimage to Al-Madinah & Meccah, 2 Vols. Richard F. Burton. Ed. by Isabel Burton. Set. 21.00 (ISBN 0-8446-1781-4). Peter Smith.

Personal Narrative of James O. Pattie of Kentucky During... Journeyings of 6 Years. LC 75-7070. (Indian Captivities Ser.: Vol. 48). 1976. Repr. of 1831 ed. lib. bdg. 44.00 (ISBN 0-8240-1672-6). Garland Pub.

Personal Narrative of the Irish Revolutionary Brotherhood. Joseph Denieffe. (Illus.). 1969. Repr. of 1906 ed. 17.00x (ISBN 0-686-28341-4, Pub. by Irish Academic Pr). Biblio Dist.

Personal Notebooks of Thomas Hardy. Richard H. Taylor. 1979. 25.00x (ISBN 0-231-04696-0). Columbia U Pr.

Personal Poetry of Love & Life. Betty L. Winnen. 1981. 4.50 (ISBN 0-8062-1638-7). Carlton.

Personal Politics: The Psychology of Making It. Ellen J. Langer & Carol S. Dweck. (Illus.). 192p. 1973. pap. text ed. 9.95x (ISBN 0-13-657247-2). P-H.

Personal Promise Pocketbook. Ed. by Harold Shaw Publishers. LC 80-52398. 107p. (Orig.). 1980. pap. 1.95 (ISBN 0-87788-673-3). Shaw Pubs.

Personal Pronoun Photo Book. Bonita H. Peck. (Illus.). 64p. 1980. pap. 7.50x (ISBN 0-8134-2135-7). Interstate.

Personal Property Security Interests Under the Revised UCC Course Handbook. (Commercial Law & Practice Course Handbook Ser. 1977-78: Vol. 175). 1978. pap. 20.00 o.p. (ISBN 0-685-07685-7, A4-2099). PLI.

Personal Recollections & Observations of General Nelson A. Miles. rev. ed. Nelson A. Miles. LC 68-23812. (American Scene Ser). (Illus.). Repr. of 1896 ed. lib. bdg. 55.00 (ISBN 0-306-71020-X). Da Capo.

Personal Recollections of Arnold Dolmetsch. Mabel Dolmetsch. (Music Reprint Ser.). (Illus.). 1980. Repr. of 1957 ed. lib. bdg. 19.50 (ISBN 0-306-76022-3). Da Capo.

Personal Recollections of Joan of Arc by the Sieur Louis De Conte. Samuel L. Clemens. LC 80-23663. (Illus.). xiv, 461p. 1980. Repr. of 1906 ed. lib. bdg. 45.00x (ISBN 0-313-22373-4, CLPR). Greenwood.

Personal Recollections of Wagner. Angelo Neumann. (Music Reprint Ser.). 329p. 1976. Repr. of 1906 ed. 25.00. Da Capo.

Personal Records Directory. Herman McDaniel. 1978. text ed. 8.95 (ISBN 0-89433-088-8); pap. 7.50 (ISBN 0-89433-089-6). Petrocelli.

Personal Relationships, the Handicapped & the Community: Some European Thoughts & Solutions. Ed. by Derek Lancaster-Gaye. (Illus.). 156p. 1972. 12.00 (ISBN 0-7100-7478-6). Routledge & Kegan.

Personal Reminiscences of Early Days in California. Stephen J. Field. LC 68-29601. (American Scene Ser). 1968. Repr. of 1893 ed. lib. bdg. 35.00 (ISBN 0-306-71157-5). Da Capo.

Personal Resume Preparation. M. P. Jaquish. LC 68-20098. (Wiley Series on Human Communication). 1968. 15.95 (ISBN 0-471-44025-6, Pub. by Wiley-Interscience). Wiley.

Personal Selling. Ronald Marks. 576p. 1981. text ed. 17.95 (ISBN 0-205-07327-1); free (ISBN 0-205-07328-X). Allyn.

Personal Selling. Young. 1978. 19.95 (ISBN 0-03-020836-X). Dryden Pr.

Personal Selling: An Introduction. Robin T. Peterson. LC 77-10979. (Marketing Ser.). 1978. text ed. 20.95 (ISBN 0-471-01743-4); tchrs. manual avail. (ISBN 0-471-01744-2). Wiley.

Personal Shorthand, 3 pts. Carl W. Salser & Theo Yerian. Incl. Pt. 1. pap. text ed. 6.85 (ISBN 0-89420-106-9, 241050); Cassette Recordings. 314.05 (ISBN 0-89420-167-0, 241000); Pt. 2. pap. text ed. 7.50 (ISBN 0-89420-107-7); cassette recordings 311.45 (ISBN 0-89420-168-9); Pt. 3. pap. text ed. (ISBN 0-89420-108-5). Cassette Recordings (ISBN 0-89420-169-7). (Personal Shorthand Cardinal Ser.). 1980. Set. text ed. write for info (ISBN 0-89420-105-0). cassette recordings 936.00 (ISBN 0-89420-170-0). Natl Book.

Personal Shorthand Master Dictionary. Joanne Piper. 1978. pap. 10.75 (ISBN 0-89420-043-7, 212000). Natl Book.

Personal Shorthand: Syllabus. Joanne Piper & Theo Yerian. 1975. pap. text ed. 8.95 (ISBN 0-89420-083-6, 217000); cassette recordings 246.90 (ISBN 0-89420-172-7, 178000). Natl Book.

Personal Shorthand: Teacher's Manual & Key to Syllabus. Joanne Piper & Theo Yerian. 1975. tchr's ed. 4.95 (ISBN 0-89420-094-1, 217007). Natl Book.

Personal Shorthand: Thirty Lesson Edition. Carl W. Salser & Theodore Yerian. 1967. pap. text ed. 4.95 (ISBN 0-89420-004-6, 216701); cassette recordings 241.35 (ISBN 0-686-67952-0, 176700). Natl Book.

Personal Shorthand: 70 Lesson Edition. Carl W. Salser & Theo Yerian. 1968. text ed. 7.45 (ISBN 0-89420-047-X, 216707); cassette recordings 241.35 (176700). Natl Book.

Personal Skill Building for the Emerging Manager. Dick Pinkstaff & Marlene A. Pinkstaff. LC 79-16920. 1979. pap. 8.95 (ISBN 0-8436-0785-8). CBI Pub.

Personal Styles in Neurosis: Implications for Small Group Psychotherapy & Behavior Therapy. Tom Caine et al. (International Library of Group Psychotherapy & Group Process). 224p. write for info. (ISBN 0-7100-0617-9). Routledge & Kegan.

Personal Touch. Ed. by Time Life Books. LC 74-77030. (Art of Sewing Ser.). (gr. 6 up). 1974. lib. bdg. 11.97 (ISBN 0-8094-1727-8, Pub. by Time-Life). Silver.

Personal Typing. Louis C. Nanassay et al. (gr. 9-12). 1970. pap. 8.20 (ISBN 0-8224-0272-6); tchrs'. manual 3.80 (ISBN 0-8224-2001-5). Pitman Learning.

Personal Typing in Thirty Days. Lieberman & Schimmel. 1981. pap. 3.75 (ISBN 0-8120-2284-X). Barron.

Personal Universe: Essays in Honor of John Macmurray. Intro. by Thomas Wren. 120p. 1975. Repr. text ed. 8.00x (ISBN 0-391-00398-4). Humanities.

Personal Values in Primary Education. N. Kirbya. 1981. text ed. 18.35 (ISBN 0-06-318130-4, Pub. by Har-Row Ltd England); pap. 9.25 (ISBN 0-06-318131-2). Har-Row.

Personal Vitality. Donald B. Miller. LC 76-55638. (Illus.). 1977. text ed. 12.95 (ISBN 0-201-04739-X); wkbk. 4.50 (ISBN 0-201-04738-1). A-W.

Personalidades Quebrantadas. Gary Collins. Tr. by Jose Flores from Eng. LC 78-62403. 215p. (Orig., Span.). 1978. pap. 4.50 (ISBN 0-89922-116-5). Edit Caribe.

Personalism. Emmanuel Mounier. Tr. by Philip Mairet. LC 75-122050. 1970. pap. 3.95 (ISBN 0-268-00434-X). U of Notre Dame Pr.

Personalities of the Eighteenth Century: (Samuel Foote, Christopher Smart, William Hazlitt) Grace A. Murray. 230p. 1980. Repr. of 1927 ed. lib. bdg. 25.00 (ISBN 0-8495-3772-X). Arden Lib.

Personalities of the South. 9th ed. Ed. by J. S. Thomson. 641p. 1980. 44.95x (ISBN 0-686-28826-2, Pub. by Intl Biog). Biblio Dist.

Personalities of the South. 10th ed. Ed. by J. S. Thomson. 634p. 1981. 49.95x (ISBN 0-934544-03-4, Pub. by Intl Biog). Biblio Dist.

Personalities of the West & Midwest. 6th ed. J. S. Thomson. 579p. 1980. 44.95x (ISBN 0-934544-07-7, Pub. by Intl Biog). Biblio Dist.

Personality. rev. ed. David C. McClelland. 672p. 1980. text ed. 34.50x (ISBN 0-8290-0400-9); pap. text ed. 18.50x (ISBN 0-8290-0243-X). Irvington.

Personality: A Cognitive View. Bernard H. Shulman & Ronald Forgus. 1979. text ed. 19.95 (ISBN 0-13-657882-9). P-H.

Personality: A New Look at Metatheories. Ed. by Harvey London. LC 78-7022. (Series in Clinical Community Psychology). 1976. 12.95 (ISBN 0-470-26381-4). Halsted Pr.

Personality: An Introduction. John Lamberth et al. 1978. 14.95x (ISBN 0-394-31190-6). Random.

Personality: An Objective Approach. 2nd ed. Irwin G. Sarason. LC 79-175797. 1972. text ed. 21.95 (ISBN 0-471-75406-4). Wiley.

Personality & Assessment. W. Mischel. LC 67-31183. 1968. 23.95 (ISBN 0-471-60925-0). Wiley.

Personality & Democratic Politics. Paul M. Sniderman. 1975. 20.00x (ISBN 0-520-02324-2). U of Cal Pr.

Personality & Leadership Behavior. Henry P. Knowles & Borje O. Saxberg. LC 73-125609. (Business Ser). (Illus.). 1971. pap. text ed. 8.95 (ISBN 0-201-03781-5). A-W.

Personality & National Character. R. Lynn. 1971. 27.00 (ISBN 0-08-016516-8). Pergamon.

Personality & Second Language Learning. Virginia Hodge. (Language in Education Ser.: No. 12). 1978. pap. 2.95 (ISBN 0-87281-086-0). Ctr Appl Ling.

Personality & Social Encounter: Selected Essays. Gordon W. Allport. LC 77-13911. x, 388p. 1981. pap. text ed. 17.00x (ISBN 0-226-01494-0). U of Chicago Pr.

Personality Assessment. R. I. Lanyon & L. D. Goodstein. LC 75-140552. 1971. 23.95 (ISBN 0-471-51740-2). Wiley.

Personality: Basic Aspects & Current Research. Ed. by Ervin Staub. (Illus.). 1980. text ed. 20.95 (ISBN 0-13-657932-9). P-H.

Personality Characteristics & Disciplinary Attitudes of Child-Abusing Mothers. Alan L. Evans. LC 80-69240. 145p. 1981. perfect bdg. 11.95 (ISBN 0-86548-033-8). Century Twenty One.

Personality Characteristics of College & University Faculty: Implications for the Community College. Florence B. Brawer. 1968. 3.00 (ISBN 0-87117-076-0). Am Assn Comm Jr Coll.

Personality, Cognition, & Social Interaction. Ed. by N. Cantor & J. Kihlstrom. 580p. 1981. text ed. 24.95 (ISBN 0-89859-057-4). L Erlbaum Assocs.

Personality Development & Psychopathology: A Dynamic Approach. Norman Cameron. LC 63-6438. 1963. text ed. 20.95 (ISBN 0-395-04251-8, 3-08130); tchrs. manual by K.E.Renner 1.75 (ISBN 0-395-04252-6, 3-08131). HM.

Personality Development Through the Lifespan. Barbara M. Newman & Philip R. Newman. LC 80-14291. (Life-Span Human Development Ser.). 150p. 1980. pap. text ed. 6.95 (ISBN 0-8185-0380-7). Brooks-Cole.

Personality Differences & Biological Variations: A Study of Twins. Gordon S. Claridge et al. LC 72-10132. 1973. text ed. 28.00 (ISBN 0-08-017124-9). Pergamon.

Personality: Inquiry & Application. Mark Sherman. LC 78-13540. (Pergamon General Psychology Ser.: Vol. 74). 560p. 1979. 18.50 (ISBN 0-08-019585-7). Pergamon.

Personality, Learning & Teaching. George D. Handley. (Students Library of Education). 126p. 1973. 10.00x (ISBN 0-7100-7625-8); pap. 5.00 (ISBN 0-7100-7628-2). Routledge & Kegan.

Personality: Measurement of Dimensions. Paul Horst. LC 68-54939. (Social & Behavioral Science Ser.). 1968. 14.95x o.p. (ISBN 0-87589-020-2). Jossey-Bass.

Personality, Motivation & Achievement. abr. ed. John W. Atkinson & Joel O. Raynor. LC 77-24985. 1978. Repr. of 1974 ed. text ed. 10.95 (ISBN 0-470-99336-7). Halsted Pr.

Personality of Ireland. E. E. Evans. LC 72-83667. (Wiles Lectures, 1971). (Illus.). 176p. 1973. 18.95 (ISBN 0-521-08684-1). Cambridge U Pr.

Personality of Thoreau. Franklin B. Sanborn. LC 80-2516. 1981. Repr. of 1901 ed. 18.50 (ISBN 0-404-19064-2). AMS Pr.

Personality, Politics & Planning: How City Planners Work. Ed. by Anthony J. Catanese & W. Paul Farmer. LC 77-17780. 1978. 17.50x (ISBN 0-8039-0961-6). Sage.

Personality Projection in the Drawing of the Human Figure: A Method of Personality Investigation. Karen Machover. (American Lecture Psychology Ser). (Illus.). 192p. 1978. 11.75 (ISBN 0-398-01184-2). C C Thomas.

Personality Research Manual. F. L. Geis. 227p. 1978. 10.95 (ISBN 0-471-29519-1). Wiley.

Personality: Searching for the Sources of Human Behavior. William S. Samuel. (Illus.). 544p. 18.95 (ISBN 0-07-054520-0); instr's manual 4.95 (ISBN 0-07-054521-9). McGraw.

Personality, Self-Esteem & Prejudice. Christopher Bagley et al. 1979. 18.50 (ISBN 0-566-00265-5, 02836-3, Pub. by Saxon Hse England). Lexington Bks.

Personality Signs. Max Luscher. (Orig.). pap. cancelled (ISBN 0-446-81317-6). Warner Bks.

Personality, Situation & Persistence. Roald Nygard. 1977. pap. 22.50x (ISBN 82-00-01563-7, Dist. by Columbia U Pr). Universitet.

Personality: Strategies for the Study of Man. 3rd ed. Ed. by Robert M. Liebert & Michael D. Spiegler. 1978. text ed. 18.95x (ISBN 0-256-02059-0). Dorsey.

Personality Structure & Measurement. H. J. Eysenck & Sybil B. G. Eysenck. LC 68-15875. 1968. text ed. 11.95 (ISBN 0-912736-08-9). EDITS Pubs.

Personality: The Human Potential. M. L. Weiner. 200p. 1973. 21.00 (ISBN 0-08-016946-5). Pergamon.

Personality: The Skein of Behavior. Russell G. Geen. LC 75-4786. (Illus.). 292p. 1976. text ed. 15.50 (ISBN 0-8016-1794-4). Mosby.

Personality Theories. 2nd, rev. ed. Larry A. Hjelle & Daniel J. Ziegler. (Illus.). 512p. 1981. text ed. 17.95 (ISBN 0-07-029063-6, C); write for info instrs.' manual (ISBN 0-07-029064-4). McGraw.

Personality Theories: A Comparative Analysis. 4th ed. by Salvatore R. Maddi. 1980. text ed. 18.95x (ISBN 0-256-02299-2). Dorsey.

Personality Theories: An Introduction. Barbara O. Engler. LC 78-69596. (Illus.). 1979. text ed. 17.50 (ISBN 0-395-26772-2); inst. manual 0.65 (ISBN 0-395-26773-0). HM.

Personality Theories: Comparisons & Syntheses. Robert Massey. 1981. text ed. write for info. (ISBN 0-442-23892-4). D Van Nostrand.

Personality Theory & Social Work Practice. Herbert S. Strean. LC 75-1132. 190p. 1975. 10.00 (ISBN 0-8108-0797-1). Scarecrow.

Personality Theory in Action: Handbook for the Objective-Analytic Test Kit. Raymond B. Cattell & James M. Schuerger. LC 78-50146. 1978. 26.50 (ISBN 0-918296-11-0). Inst Personality Ability.

Personalized Computational Skills Program. Bryce R. Shaw. LC 79-90570. 544p. 1980. Set. pap. text ed. 14.75 (ISBN 0-395-29032-5); Mod. A. pap. text ed. 5.75 (ISBN 0-395-29033-3); Mod. B. pap. text ed. 5.75 (ISBN 0-395-29034-1); Mod. C. pap. text ed. 5.50 (ISBN 0-395-29035-X); pap. 1.00 inst. manual (ISBN 0-395-29036-8). HM.

Personalized Data Base Systems. Benjamin Mittman & Lorraine Borman. 326p. 1981. Repr. of 1975 ed. lib. bdg. price not set (ISBN 0-89874-298-6). Krieger.

Personalizing Teaching in the Elementary School. Kenneth T. Henson & James E. Higgins. 1978. text ed. 13.95 (ISBN 0-675-08427-X). Merrill.

Personas Escogidas De Dios. Margaret Ralph. (Serie Jirafa). Orig. Title: God's Special People. 1979. 2.95 (ISBN 0-311-38535-4, Edit Mundo). Casa Bautista.

Personnages Historiques Figurant Dans la Poesie Lyrique Francaise Des XII et XIIIe Siecles. LC 80-2166. 1981. 67.50 (ISBN 0-404-19031-6). AMS Pr.

Personnel: A Book of Readings. Ed. by William F. Glueck. 1979. pap. 11.95x (ISBN 0-256-02078-7). Business Pubns.

Personnel: A Diagnostic Approach. rev. ed. William F Glueck. 1978. 18.95x (ISBN 0-256-01951-7). Business Pubns.

Personnel Administration: A Point of View & a Method. 9th ed. Paul Pigors & Charles A. Myers. (Illus.). 560p. 1981. text ed. 18.95x (ISBN 0-07-049971-3, C); instructor's manual 7.95 (ISBN 0-07-049972-1). McGraw.

Personnel Administration: An Experiential Skill-Building Approach. Richard W. Beatty & Craig E. Schneier. 576p. 1981. pap. text ed. 14.95 (ISBN 0-201-00172-1). A-W.

Personnel Administration & Human Resources Management. Andrew F. Sikula. LC 75-8691. (Management & Administration Ser.). 456p. 1976. 21.95 (ISBN 0-471-79140-7). Wiley.

Personnel Administration in the Courts. Harry O. Lawson et al. (Westview Special Study). 1979. lib. bdg. 32.50x (ISBN 0-89158-588-5). Westview.

Personnel Administration Today. Craig E. Schneier & Richard W. Beatty. 1978. pap. text ed. 10.95 (ISBN 0-201-00503-4). A-W.

Personnel & Human Resource Management. Andrew DuBrin. 1980. text ed. 18.95 (ISBN 0-442-25407-5); instr's. manual 2.00 (ISBN 0-442-25406-7). D Van Nostrand.

Personnel & Human Resource Management. Randall S. Schuler. (Management Ser.). (Illus.). 600p. 1981. text ed. 15.96 (ISBN 0-8299-0406-9). West Pub.

Personnel & Human Resources Administration. 3rd. ed. Leon C. Megginson. 1977. text ed. 18.95 (ISBN 0-256-01909-6). Irwin.

Personnel & Training Management Yearbook & Directory: United Kingdom 1980. Michael Armstrong. 1979. 35.00x (ISBN 0-686-60659-0, Pub by Kogan Pg). Nichols Pub.

Personnel: Contemporary Perspectives & Applications. 2nd ed. Robert L. Mathis & John H. Jackson. (Illus.). 1979. text ed. 17.95 (ISBN 0-8299-0199-X); readings & exercises by Sally Coltrin 6.95 (ISBN 0-686-67441-3); instrs.' manual avail. (ISBN 0-8299-0555-3); study guide 6.95 (ISBN 0-8299-0282-1). West Pub.

Personnel Dosimetry for Radiation Accidents. 1965. 29.00 (ISBN 92-0-020065-6, IAEA). Unipub.

Personnel Dosimetry Systems for External Radiation Exposures. (Technical Reports: No. 109). (Illus.). 1970. pap. 10.75 (ISBN 92-0-125270-6, IDC109, IAEA). Unipub.

Personnel for the New Diplomacy: Report of the Committee on Foreign Affairs Personnel. LC 62-22365. 1962. 3.75 (ISBN 0-87003-024-8); pap. 2.25 (ISBN 0-686-65451-X). Carnegie Endow.

Personnel Function in a Changing Environment. T. P. Lyons. (Times Management Library). 1971. 13.95x (ISBN 0-8464-0709-4); pap. 7.95 (ISBN 0-8464-0710-8). Beekman Pubs.

Personnel-Human Resource Management. Herbert G. Heneman, Jr. et al. 1980. 18.95x (ISBN 0-256-02279-8). Irwin.

Personnel-Industrial Relations Report, Pt. III: Departmental Budgets & Staffing Ratios. Steven Langer. 1980. pap. 85.00 (ISBN 0-916506-35-5). Abbott Langer Assocs.

Personnel-Industrial Relations Report, Pt. II: Income by Type & Size of Employer. Steven Langer. 1980. pap. 85.00 (ISBN 0-916506-53-3). Abbott Langer Assocs.

Personnel-Industrial Relations Report, Pt. I: Income by Individual Variables. Ed. by Steven Langer. 1980. pap. 85.00 (ISBN 0-916506-54-1). Abbott Langer Assocs.

Personnel Management. Byars. 1979. 19.95. Dryden Pr.

Personnel Management. 2nd ed. Gary Dessler. 500p. 1981. text ed. 18.95 (ISBN 0-8359-5518-4); study guide 7.95 (ISBN 0-8359-5521-4); instr's. manual free. Reston.

Personnel Management. 9th ed. Michael J. Jucius. 1979. text ed. 18.50x (ISBN 0-256-01644-5). Irwin.

Personnel Management. A. W. Savage. Ed. by A. Wilson. (Management Pamphlet Ser.). 1977. pap. 3.95x (ISBN 0-85365-580-4, Pub. by Lib Assn England). Oryx Pr.

Personnel Management. William Werther & Keith Davis. (Illus.). 528p. (Orig.). text ed. 18.95x (ISBN 0-07-069436-2); instructor's manual & test bank. write for info. (ISBN 0-07-069437-0). McGraw.

Personnel Management: A Computer Based System. Ed. by Sang M. Lee. Cary Thorp. 1979. text ed. 17.50 (ISBN 0-89433-052-7); pap. 14.00 (ISBN 0-89433-053-5). Petrocelli.

Personnel Management: A Human Resource Systems Approach. Elmer H. Burack & Robert D. Smith. 500p. 1977. text ed. 18.95 (ISBN 0-8299-0130-2); IM avail. (ISBN 0-8299-0462-X). West Pub.

Personnel Management & Human Relations. 1st ed. John R. Zabka. LC 73-142500. 1971. 12.30 o.p. (ISBN 0-672-96095-8); tchrs' manual 6.67 o.p. (ISBN 0-672-96097-4); wkbk 6.75 o.p. (ISBN 0-672-96096-6). Bobbs.

Personnel Management & Industrial Relations. 6th ed. D. Yoder. 1970. 19.95 (ISBN 0-13-659201-5). P-H.

Personnel Management & Productivity in City Government. Selma J. Mushkin & Frank H. Sandifer. (Illus.). 1979. 19.95 (ISBN 0-669-02805-3). Lexington Bks.

Personnel Management & Supervision. Richard P. Calhoon. (Orig.). 1967. pap. text ed. 12.95 (ISBN 0-13-658260-5). P-H.

Personnel Management: Cases & Exercises. Elmer H. Burack. (Illus.). 1978. pap. text ed. 11.50 (ISBN 0-8299-0203-1); IM avail. (ISBN 0-8299-0461-1); exam questions avail. (ISBN 0-8299-0463-8). West Pub.

Personnel Management Game. Jerald R. Smith. 1980. pap. text ed. 4.95 (ISBN 0-933836-14-7). Simtek.

Personnel Management, Human Resource Accounting & Human Capital Theory. Eric G. Flamholtz & John M. Lacey. (Monograph: No. 27). 100p. 1980. 7.50 (ISBN 0-89215-111-0). U Cal LA Indus Rel.

Personnel Management in Action, Skill Building Experiences. 2nd ed. Nelson L. Kelley & Arthur A. Whatley. (West Ser. in Management). 300p. 1981. pap. text ed. 13.95 (ISBN 0-8299-0389-5). West Pub.

Personnel Management in Action: Skill Building Experiences. Arthur Whatley & Lane Kelley. (Management Ser). (Illus.). 1977. pap. text ed. 11.95 (ISBN 0-8299-0123-X); instrs.' manual avail. (ISBN 0-8299-0582-0). West Pub.

Personnel Management in India: The Practical Approach to Human Relations in Industry. 2nd ed. Ed. by R. M. Gupta. 346p. 1974. pap. text ed. 5.95x o.p. (ISBN 0-210-33913-6). Asia.

Personnel Management in Libraries. Sheila Creth & Fred Duda. 300p. 1980. 17.95 (ISBN 0-918212-25-1). Neal-Schuman.

Personnel Management in Merchant Ships. D. H. Moreby. 1968. 27.00 (ISBN 0-08-012993-5); pap. 14.00 (ISBN 0-08-012992-7). Pergamon.

Personnel Management Process. 4th ed. Wendell L. French. LC 77-73992. (Illus.). 1978. text ed. 18.95 (ISBN 0-395-25529-5); inst. manual 0.50 (ISBN 0-395-25530-9). HM.

Personnel Management Process: Cases on Human Resources Administration. Wendell L. French et al. LC 77-74422. (Illus.). 1977. pap. text ed. 9.25 (ISBN 0-395-25531-7); inst. manual 0.50 (ISBN 0-395-26087-6). HM.

Personnel Management: Reaching Organizational & Human Goals. new ed. Joseph P. Yaney. (Business Ser). 448p. 1975. text ed. 17.95 (ISBN 0-675-08760-0); instructor's manual 3.95 (ISBN 0-685-50978-8). Merrill.

Personnel of Fairyland: A Short Account of the Fairy People of Great Britain for Those Who Tell Stories to Children. Katharine M. Briggs. LC 70-147084. (Illus.). 1971. Repr. of 1953 ed. 15.00 (ISBN 0-8103-3372-4). Gale.

Personnel Policies in Libraries. Ed. by Nancy Van Zant. LC 80-11734. 350p. 1980. 19.95 (ISBN 0-918212-26-X). Neal-Schuman.

Personnel Policies in Nonunion Companies. Fred K. Foulkes. 350p. 1981. 19.95 (ISBN 0-686-69329-9). P-H.

Personnel Policy in the City: The Politics of Jobs in Oakland. Frank J. Thompson. 1975. 18.50x (ISBN 0-520-02797-3); pap. 4.95x (ISBN 0-520-03509-7). U of Cal Pr.

Personnel Requirements for an Advanced Shipyard Technology. 1980. 7.50 (ISBN 0-309-02949-X). Natl Acad Pr.

Personnel: The Management of Human Resources. Mondy & Noe. 750p. 1980. text ed. 20.95 (ISBN 0-205-07217-8, 0872172); free tchr's ed. (ISBN 0-205-07218-6). Allyn.

Personnel: The Management of Human Resources. Stephen P. Robbins. LC 77-23046. (Illus.). 1978. text ed. 19.95 (ISBN 0-13-657833-0). P-H.

Persons & Institutions in Early Rabbinic Judaism. Ed. by William S. Green. LC 76-52503. (Brown University. Brown Judaic Studies: No. 3). 1977. pap. 9.00 (ISBN 0-89130-131-3, 140003). Scholars Pr Ca.

Persons & Personality: An Introduction to Psychology. Sr. Annette Walters & Sr. Kevin O'Hara. LC 52-13695. (Century Psychology Ser). 1953. 24.00x (ISBN 0-89197-550-0). Irvington.

Persons Communicating. D. K. Darnell & W. Brockriede. (Speech Communication Ser.). (Illus.). 256p. 1976. pap. text ed. 14.95 (ISBN 0-13-657387-8). P-H.

Persons in Relation. John MacMurray. 1979. pap. text ed. 4.95x (ISBN 0-571-09404-X). Humanities.

Persons Injured & Disability Days by Detailed Type & Class of Accident, U. S., 1971 & 1972. Charles S. Wilder. Ed. by Audrey M. Shipp. LC 75-35509. (Ser. 10: No. 105). 53p. 1976. pap. text ed. 1.25 (ISBN 0-8406-0055-0). Natl Ctr Health Stats.

Perspectiva Humoristica En la Trilogia De Gironelia. J. D. Suarez-Torres. 1975. 12.95 (ISBN 0-88303-021-7); pap. 10.95 (ISBN 0-685-73222-3). E Torres & Sons.

Perspectivas Politicas, Vol. 1. 2nd, rev. ed. Lynn D. Bender. (Illus.). 116p. pap. text ed. 4.55 (ISBN 0-913480-50-9). Inter Am U Pr.

Perspective. William Backus & Paul Malte. pap. 4.85 (ISBN 0-933350-06-6). Morse Pr.

Perspective. Pierre Descargues. (Illus.). 1977. 15.00 o.p. (ISBN 0-8109-1454-9); pap. 6.95 o.p. (ISBN 0-8109-2075-1). Abrams.

Perspective. J. M. Parramon. (Art Ser.). (Orig.). 1981. pap. 4.95 (ISBN 0-89586-082-1). H P Bks.

Perspective: A Guide for Artists, Architects & Designers. Gwen White. 1974. pap. 16.95 (ISBN 0-7134-2873-2, Pub. by Batsford England). David & Charles.

Perspective: An Introduction to Boarding School for Prospective Candidates. Edward T. Hall. (gr. 6-12). pap. text ed. 1.50x o.p. (ISBN 0-88334-083-6). Ind Sch Pr.

Perspective & Challenge in College Personnel Work. James F. Penney. 108p. 1972. 9.75 (ISBN 0-398-02378-6). C C Thomas.

Perspective: Community Colleges in the Nineteen Eighties. Joseph P. Cosand. (ERIC Monographs Ser.). (Orig.). pap. 5.00 (ISBN 0-87117-049-3). Am Assn Comm Jr Coll.

Perspective Drawing. H. F. Hollis. (Teach Yourself Ser.). 1974. pap. 2.95 o.p. (ISBN 0-679-10405-4). McKay.

Perspective: Fundamentals, Controversials, History. G. Ten Doesschate. 1964. text ed. 25.75x (ISBN 90-6004-042-2). Humanities.

Perspective in Biomechanics, Vol. I. Ed. by D. N. Ghista et al. (Perspectives in Biomechanics Ser.). 902p. 1981. 205.00 (ISBN 3-7186-0006-4). Harwood Academic.

Perspective of Environmental Pollution. M. W. Holdgate. LC 78-8394. (Illus.). 1979. 42.50 (ISBN 0-521-22197-8). Cambridge U Pr.

Perspective of Environmental Pollution. M. W. Holdgate. LC 78-8394. (Illus.). 288p. 1981. pap. 13.95 (ISBN 0-521-29972-1). Cambridge U Pr.

Perspective of Physics: Volume 4, Selections from Nineteen Seventy-Nine Comments on Modern Physics. H. Massey. 1980. write for info. (ISBN 0-677-16190-5). Gordon.

Perspective on Energy Modeling. Ed. by Bruce A. Smith. 1977. pap. text ed. 22.00 (ISBN 0-08-019985-2). Pergamon.

Perspective on Mycotoxins. (FAO Food & Nutrition Paper Ser.: No. 13). 171p. 1980. pap. 9.25 (ISBN 92-5-100870-1, F1957, FAO). Unipub.

Perspectives De France. abr. rev. ed. Arthur Bieler et al. (Illus.). 1972. text ed. 16.95 (ISBN 0-13-660571-0); wkbk. 7.95 (ISBN 0-13-660803-5); tapes 175.00 (ISBN 0-13-660779-9). P-H.

Perspectives: Discussion Starters on Attitudes & Values for Church Groups. Ann Billups. 224p. 1981. pap. 11.95 (ISBN 0-8170-0905-1). Judson.

Perspectives Drawing with the Computer. Mark A. Willis. pap. text ed. 14.95 (ISBN 0-87567-041-5). Entelek.

Perspectives for Change in Communist Societies. Ed. by Teresa Rakowska-Harmstone. (Special Studies on the Soviet Union & Eastern Europe). 1979. lib. bdg. 22.50x (ISBN 0-89158-336-X). Westview.

Perspectives for Moral Decisions. John Howie. LC 80-6102. 192p. 1981. lib. bdg. 17.50 (ISBN 0-8191-1375-1); pap. text ed. 9.00 (ISBN 0-8191-1376-X). U Pr of Amer.

Perspectives for Public Policy: An Environmental View on Human Ecology. Simone Clemhout. 1977. pap. text ed. 8.50x o.p. (ISBN 0-8191-0182-6). U Pr of Amer.

Perspectives for the Future: Social Work Practice in the 80's. Ed. by Kay Dea. LC 80-83988. (Professional Conference Vols. Ser.). 192p. (Orig.). 1980. pap. text ed. 12.50x (ISBN 0-87101-089-5, CBO-089-C). Natl Assn Soc Wkrs.

Perspectives Francaises One. Sarah Vaillancourt. LC 80-12737. (Illus.). 1980. text ed. 8.95 (ISBN 0-88436-754-1); pap. text ed. 5.95 (ISBN 0-88436-755-X). EMC.

Perspectives in Abnormal Behavior. Ed. by Richard J. Morris. 570p. 1976. text ed. 26.00 (ISBN 0-08-017738-7); pap. text ed. 10.50 (ISBN 0-08-017739-5); test items 0.50 (ISBN 0-686-67339-5). Pergamon.

Perspectives in Aesthetics: Plato to Camus. Ed. by Peyton E. Richter. LC 66-19066. (Orig.). 1967. pap. 8.50 (ISBN 0-672-63082-6). Odyssey Pr.

Perspectives in Asian Cross-Cultural Psychology: Selected Papers of the First Asian Regional Conference of the IACCP, March 19-23, 1979. Ed. by J. L. Dawson & G. H. Blowers. 1981. pap. write for info. (ISBN 90-265-0359-8). Swets North Am.

Perspectives in Bank Management: A Book of Readings. Roger T. King. LC 79-63851. 1979. pap. text ed. 10.50 (ISBN 0-8191-0745-X). U Pr of Amer.

Perspectives in Behavior Modification with Deviant Children. Ivar Lovaas & Bradley Bucker. LC 7-18357. (Illus.). 512p. 1974. 20.95 (ISBN 0-13-657130-1). P-H.

Perspectives in Biomechanics: Proceedings, Vol. 1. International Conference on Mechanics in Medicine & Biology, 1st, Aachen, Germany, 1978. Ed. by I. H. Reul et al. 1300p. 1980. lib. bdg. 205.00 (ISBN 3-7186-0006-4). Harwood Academic.

Perspectives in Child Psychology: Research & Review. T. D. Spencer & N. Kass. 1970. text ed. 17.95 o.p. (ISBN 0-07-060194-1, C). McGraw.

Perspectives in Clinical Endocrinology. Ed. by Walter B. Essman. (Illus.). 390p. 1980. text ed. 45.00 (ISBN 0-89335-077-X). Spectrum Pub.

Perspectives in Constitutional Law with Revisions. C. Black, Jr. 1970. pap. 5.95 o.p. (ISBN 0-13-660746-2). P-H.

Perspectives in Consumer Behavior. Harold Kassarjian & Thomas Robertson. 1981. pap. text ed. 10.95x (ISBN 0-673-15394-0). Scott F.

Perspectives in Creativity. Ed. by Irving A. Taylor & Jacob W. Getzels. LC 74-22645. 392p. 1975. lib. bdg. 20.95x (ISBN 0-202-25121-7). Aldine Pub.

Perspectives in Endocrine Psychobiology. F. Brambilla & Bridges. LC 76-27305. 650p. 1977. 55.00 o.p. (ISBN 0-471-99434-0, Pub. by Wiley-Interscience). Wiley.

Perspectives in Ethology: Advantages of Diversity, Vol. 4. Ed. by P. P. Bateson & Peter H. Klopfer. 230p. 1980. 25.00 (ISBN 0-306-40511-3, Plenum Pr). Plenum Pub.

Perspectives in Experimental Biology: Zoology & Botany, 2 pts. P. Spencer Davies & N. Sunderland. 1090p. 1976. text ed. 230.00 (ISBN 0-08-019939-9); Pt. 1. text ed. 130.00 (ISBN 0-08-018767-6); Pt. 2. text ed. 130.00 (ISBN 0-08-019868-6). Pergamon.

Perspectives in Hemostasis: Proceedings of a Symposium Held 11 May 1979 at Loyola University, Maywood, Ill., U. S. A. Ed. by Jawed Fareed. (Illus.). 400p. 1981. 50.00 (ISBN 0-08-025092-0). Pergamon.

Perspectives in Higher Education. Joseph Cangemi & Casimir Kowalski. 1981. write for info. Philos Lib.

Perspectives in Human Reproduction: Human Reproductive Physiology, Vol. 5. E. S. Hafez. LC 78-50311. (Illus.). 1978. 28.00 (ISBN 0-250-40244-0). Ann Arbor Science.

Perspectives in Italian Immigration & Ethnicity. Ed. by S. M. Tomasi. LC 77-74178. 1977. pap. text ed. 9.95x (ISBN 0-913256-26-9, Dist. by Ozer). Ctr Migration.

Perspectives in Marketing Theory. Ed. by Jerome B. Kernan & Montrose S. Sommers. LC 68-19476. 1968. 24.50x (ISBN 0-89197-333-8); pap. text ed. 7.95x (ISBN 0-89197-334-6). Irvington.

Perspectives in Marxist Anthropology. M. Godelier. Tr. by R. Brain. LC 76-11081. (Studies in Social Anthropology: No. 18). (Illus.). 1977. 29.95 (ISBN 0-521-21311-8); pap. 8.95x (ISBN 0-521-29098-8). Cambridge U Pr.

Perspectives in Metascience. Ed. by Jan Barmark. (Regiae Societatis-Interdisciplinaria: No. 2). 199p. 1980. text ed. 19.75x (ISBN 91-85252-21-2). Humanities.

Perspectives in Music Theory: An Historical-Analytical Approach. 2nd ed. Paul Cooper. LC 78-26448. 1980. text ed. 15.50 scp (ISBN 0-06-041373-5, HarpC); Vol. 1. pap. text ed. 10.50 scp (ISBN 0-06-041374-3); Vol. 2. pap. text ed. 10.50 scp (ISBN 0-06-041375-1). Har-Row.

Perspectives in Paedophilia. Brian Taylor. 160p. 1981. 42.50 (ISBN 0-7134-3718-9, Pub. by Batsford England); pap. 16.95 (ISBN 0-7134-3719-7). David & Charles.

Perspectives in Pediatric Pathology, Vol. 5. Ed. by Harvey S. Rosenberg & Robert P. Bolande. (Illus.). 309p. 1979. 43.50 (ISBN 0-89352-061-6). Masson Pub.

Perspectives in Pediatrics. Ed. by O. P. Ghai. 158p. 1980. 8.50x (ISBN 0-89955-323-0, Pub. by Interprint India). Intl Schol Bk Serv.

Perspectives in Phytochemistry: Proceedings. Phytochemical Society. Ed. by J. B. Harborne & T. Swain. 1969. 29.00 (ISBN 0-12-324660-1). Acad Pr.

Perspectives in Political Sociology. Andrew Effrat. LC 73-4329. 1973. 24.50x (ISBN 0-672-51746-9). Irvington.

Perspectives in Political Sociology. Ed. by Andrew Effrat. LC 73-4329. 320p. 1973. pap. text ed. 6.50 (ISBN 0-672-61322-0). Bobbs.

Perspectives in Political Theory. Ed. by J. S. Bain & R. B. Jain. 275p. 1980. text ed. 13.25 (ISBN 0-391-01900-7). Humanities.

Perspectives in Quantum Theory. Ed. by Wolfgang Yourgrau & Alwyn Van Der Merwe. LC 78-74119. 1979. pap. text ed. 5.00 (ISBN 0-486-63778-6). Dover.

Perspectives in Schizophrenia Research. Ed. by Claude Baxter & Theodore Melnechuk. 463p. 1980. text ed. 42.00 (ISBN 0-89004-517-8). Raven.

Perspectives in State School Support Programs. American Education Finance Association. Date not set. price not set prof. reference (ISBN 0-88410-197-5). Ballinger Pub.

Perspectives in Steroid Receptor Research. Ed. by Francesco Bresciani. 334p. 1980. text ed. 30.00 (ISBN 0-89004-490-2). Raven.

Perspectives in Toxicology. Ed. by Alan W. Bernheimer. LC 80-11261. 218p. 1981. Repr. of 1977 ed. lib. bdg. write for info. (ISBN 0-89874-131-9). Krieger.

Perspectives in Virology: The Gustav Stern Symposium, Vol. 10. Ed. by Morris Pollard. LC 77-84126. (Gustav Stern Symposium Ser.). 1978. 31.50 (ISBN 0-89004-214-4). Raven.

Perspectives in Virology, Vol. 11: Proceedings. Eleventh Gustave Stern Symposium on Perspectives in Virology, New York, February 1980. Ed. by Morris Pollard. 324p. 1981. 40.00x (ISBN 0-8451-0800-X). A R Liss.

Perspectives in World Agriculture. 532p. 1981. 82.50 (ISBN 0-85198-458-4, CAB 12, CAB). Unipub.

Perspectives in Zoology. A. A. Boyden. LC 73-1279. 294p. 1973. text ed. 32.00 (ISBN 0-08-017122-2). Pergamon.

Perspectives of a Political Ecclesiology. Ed. by Johannes B. Metz. LC 79-150306. (Concilium Ser.: Religion in the Seventies: Vol. 66). 1971. pap. 4.95(ISBN 0-8164-2522-1). Crossroad NY.

Perspectives of Fundamental Physics. Ed. by C. Schaerf. (Studies in High Energy Physics: Vol. 1). 470p. 1979. lib. bdg. 40.75 flexicover (ISBN 3-7186-0007-2). Harwood Academic.

Perspectives on a Changing China: Essays in Honor of Prof. C. Martin Wilbur. Ed. by Joshua A. Fogel & William T. Rowe. (Westview Special Studies on China & East Asia). 1979. lib. bdg. 26.50x (ISBN 0-89158-091-3, Dawson). Westview.

Perspectives on a Regional Culture: Essays About the Coimbatore Area of South India. Brenda E. Beck. 1979. text ed. 17.95x (ISBN 0-7069-0723-X, Pub. by Vikas India). Advent Bk.

Perspectives on a Regional Culture: Essays About the Coimbatore Area of South India. Ed. by Brenda E. Beck. 211p. 1980. 18.00x (ISBN 0-7069-0723-X, Pub. by Croom Helm Ltd England). Biblio Dist.

Perspectives on Aging & Human Development, 3 vols. Ed. by Robert J. Kastenbaum. Incl. Vol. 1. Being & Becoming Old (ISBN 0-89503-014-4); Vol. 2. In the Country of the Old (ISBN 0-89503-015-2); Vol. 13. Institutionalization & Alternative Futures. 160p. softcover 17.95x o.p. (ISBN 0-686-68242-4). Baywood Pub.

Perspectives on American English. J. L. Dillard. (Contributions to the Sociology of Language Ser.). 1980. 40.50x (ISBN 90-279-3367-7). Mouton.

Perspectives on American Folk Art. Ed. by Ian M. Quimby & Scott T. Swank. (Winterthur Bk.). (Illus.). 1980. 21.95 (ISBN 0-393-01273-5); pap. 9.95x (ISBN 0-393-95088-3). Norton.

Perspectives on Attribution Research & Theory: The Bielefeld Symposium. Ed. by Dietmar Gorlitz. 1981. 19.50 (ISBN 0-88410-375-7). Ballinger Pub.

Perspectives on Attributional Processes. John H. Harvey & Gifford Weary. 250p. 1981. pap. text ed. write for info. (ISBN 0-697-06637-1). Wm C Brown.

Perspectives on Behavioral Medicine 1980, Vol. I. Ed. by Stephen M. Weiss et al. (Serial Publication). 1981. price not set (ISBN 0-12-532101-5). Acad Pr.

Perspectives on Brazilian History. E. Bradford Burns. LC 67-13779. 1967. 17.50x (ISBN 0-231-02992-6). Columbia U Pr.

Perspectives on Canada's Foreign Policy. Ed. by Denis Stairs & Don Munton. (Pergamon Policy Studies). 280p. Date not set. price not set (ISBN 0-08-025972-3). Pergamon.

Perspectives on Canadian Airline Regulation. G. B. Reschenthaler & B. Roberts. 266p. 1979. pap. text ed. 13.50x (ISBN 0-409-88604-1, Pub. by Inst Res Pub Canada). Renouf.

Perspectives on Canadian Health & Social Services Policy: History & Emerging Trends. Carl A. Meilicke & Janet L. Storch. (Illus.). 522p. text ed. 38.95 (ISBN 0-914904-42-6). Health Admin Pr.

Perspectives on Cognitive Science. Ed. by Donald A. Norman. 320p. 1981. 19.95 (ISBN 0-89391-071-6). Ablex Pub.

Perspectives on Communication. Louis Forsdale. LC 80-16616. (Speech Ser.). (Illus.). 400p. 1981. text ed. 12.95 (ISBN 0-201-04571-0). A-W.

Perspectives on Communication in Social Conflict. Ed. by Gerald R. Miller & Herbert W. Simons. LC 74-3263. (Speech Communication Ser.). 1974. 16.95 (ISBN 0-13-660399-8). P-H.

Perspectives on Continuing Education in Nursing. Ed. by Margo C. Neal & Signe S. Cooper. 1980. pap. text ed. 11.95 (ISBN 0-935236-12-0). Nurseco.

Perspectives on Crime Victims. Burton Galaway & Hamilton C. Hudson. (Illus.). 435p. 1980. pap. 16.95 (ISBN 0-8016-1733-2). Mosby.

Perspectives on Death & Dying, 3 vols. Ed. by Richard A. Kalish. Incl. Vol. 1. Death & Dying: Views from Many Cultures (ISBN 0-89503-012-8); Vol. 2. Caring Relationships (ISBN 0-89503-010-1); Vol. 15. Death, Dying, Transcending (ISBN 0-89503-011-X). 160p. soft cover 17.95x o.p. (ISBN 0-686-68243-2). Baywood Pub.

Perspectives on Education. Ed. by Allen Calvin. LC 76-20019. (Illus.). 1977. pap. text ed. 9.95 (ISBN 0-201-00878-5). A-W.

Perspectives on Education As Educology. Ed. by James E. Christensen. LC 80-6078. 396p. 1981. lib. bdg. 25.50 (ISBN 0-686-69075-3); pap. text ed. 14.75 (ISBN 0-8191-1394-8). U Pr of Amer.

Perspectives on Foster Care. Hilary Prosser. (General Ser.). 1978. pap. text ed. 20.75x (ISBN 0-85633-147-3, NFER). Humanities.

Perspectives on General System Theory. Ludwig Von Bertalanffy. Ed. by Edgar Taschdjian & Maria Von Bertalanffy. LC 75-10993. 220p. 1976. 8.95 (ISBN 0-8076-0797-5); pap. 3.95 o.s.i. (ISBN 0-8076-0798-3). Braziller.

Perspectives on Geomorphic Processes. G. H. Drury. LC 78-80970. (CCG Resource Papers Ser.: No. 3). (Illus.). 1969. pap. text ed. 3.50 o.p. (ISBN 0-89291-050-X). Assn Am Geographers.

Perspectives on God: Sociological, Theological & Philosophical. Charles Curtis et al. LC 78-62943. 1978. pap. text ed. 9.25 (ISBN 0-8191-0605-4). U Pr of Amer.

Perspectives on Human Learning: An Introduction to Educational Anthropology. J. Hansen. 1979. pap. 9.95 o.p. (ISBN 0-13-660951-1). P-H.

Perspectives on Inflation: Models & Policies. Ed. by David Heathfield. (Illus.). 1979. 21.00 (ISBN 0-582-44189-7); pap. 11.95 (ISBN 0-582-44190-0). Longman.

Perspectives on Insurance. Irving Pfeffer & David R. Klock. (Illus.). 448p. 1974. ref. ed. 18.95 (ISBN 0-13-661066-8). P-H.

Perspectives on Latin America, Vol. 1. Ed. by Samuel L. Baily & Ronald T. Hyman. LC 73-10689. (Latin America Series). (Illus.). 128p. 1974. 5.95 o.p. (ISBN 0-02-505830-4). Macmillan.

Perspectives on Marginality: Understanding Deviance. James R. McIntosh. 320p. 1974. pap. text ed. 8.95x o.p. (ISBN 0-205-04419-0). Allyn.

Perspectives on Marriage. LC 80-67039. 64p. 1980. pap. 2.25 (ISBN 0-915388-08-1). Buckley Pubns.

Perspectives on Modernization: Toward a General Theory of Third World Development. M. Francis Abraham. LC 79-6811. 262p. 1980. pap. text ed. 10.25 (ISBN 0-8191-0961-4). U Pr of Amer.

Perspectives on Non-Sexist Early Childhood Education. Ed. by Barbara Sprung. LC 78-6251. 1978. pap. 9.50x (ISBN 0-8077-2547-1). Tchrs Coll.

Perspectives on Nursing Leadership: Proceedings. Stewart Conference on Research in Nursing, Sixteenth. Ed. by Shake Ketefian. LC 80-27464. (Orig.). 1981. pap. text ed. 10.95 (ISBN 0-8077-2637-0). Tchrs Coll.

Perspectives on Peirce: Critical Essays on Charles Sanders Peirce. Ed. by Richard J. Bernstein. LC 80-13703. 157p. 1980. Repr. of 1965 ed. lib. bdg. 15.75x (ISBN 0-313-22414-5, BEPP). Greenwood.

Perspectives on Pentecostalism: Case Studies from the Caribbean & Latin America. Ed. by Stephen D. Glazier. LC 80-7815. 207p. 1980. lib. bdg. 17.25 (ISBN 0-8191-1071-X); pap. text ed. 9.50 (ISBN 0-8191-1072-8). U Pr of Amer.

Perspectives on Personnel - Human Resource Management. Ed. by Herbert G. Heneman & Donald P. Schwab. 1978. pap. text ed. 11.95x (ISBN 0-256-02071-X). Irwin.

Perspectives on Plowden. Ed. by Richard S. Peters. (Students Library of Education). 1969. pap. text ed. 2.00x (ISBN 0-7100-6387-3). Humanities.

Perspectives on Political Science. Sorauf. 1966. pap. text ed. 4.95 (ISBN 0-675-09714-2). Merrill.

Perspectives on Presidential Selection. Ed. by Donald R. Matthews. (Studies in Presidential Selection). 1973. 14.95 (ISBN 0-8157-5508-2); pap. 5.95 (ISBN 0-8157-5507-4). Brookings.

Perspectives on Public Bureaucracy. 3rd ed. Fred A. Kramer. (Illus.). 236p. 1981. pap. text ed. 7.95 (ISBN 0-87626-659-6). Winthrop.

Perspectives on Public Management: Cases & Learning Designs. 2nd ed. Ed. by Robert T. Golembiewski. LC 75-17317. 1976. text ed. 12.50 (ISBN 0-87581-186-8, 186). Peacock Pubs.

Perspectives on Publishing. Philip G. Altbach & Sheila McVey. LC 75-3516. 272p. 1976. 24.95 (ISBN 0-669-99564-9). Lexington Bks.

Perspectives on Radio & Television: An Introduction to Broadcasting in the United States. F. Leslie Smith. (Illus.). 1979. text ed. 19.50 scp (ISBN 0-06-046309-0, HarpC); inst. manual avail. (ISBN 0-685-63493-0). Harper-Row.

Perspectives on Residential Child Care: An Annotated Bibliography. Hilary Prosser. (National Children's Bureau Report). 1976. pap. text ed. 8.75x (ISBN 0-85633-113-9, NFER). Humanities.

Perspectives on Retail Strategic Decision Making. Stanton G. Cort. 112p. 1979. pap. text ed. 30.00 (ISBN 0-686-60195-5, G28679). Natl Ret Merch.

Perspectives on Romanticism: A Transformational Analysis. David Morse. 362p. 1981. 29.50x (ISBN 0-389-20164-2). B&N.

Perspectives on School at Seven Years Old. John Newson & Elizabeth Newson. 1977. text ed. 25.00x (ISBN 0-04-136017-6). Allen Unwin.

Perspectives on Social Change. 2nd ed. Robert H. Lauer. 1977. text ed. 16.95 (ISBN 0-205-05846-9, 8158460). Allyn.

Perspectives on State & Local Politics. Ed. by W. P. Collins. LC 74-5202. (Illus.). 288p. 1974. pap. text ed. 9.95 (ISBN 0-13-660548-6). P-H.

Perspectives on Strategic Marketing Management. Kerin & Peterson. 100p. 1980. text ed. 17.95 (ISBN 0-205-06722-0, 0867225). Allyn.

Perspectives on Technical Information for Environmental Protection. Commission on Natural Resources. 1977. pap. 6.25 (ISBN 0-309-02623-7). Natl Acad Pr.

Perspectives on Technology. N. Rosenberg. LC 75-14623. 336p. 1976. 42.95 (ISBN 0-521-20957-9); pap. 12.50x (ISBN 0-521-29011-2). Cambridge U Pr.

Perspectives on the Academic Discipline of Physical Education. Ed. by George A. Brooks. 1981. text ed. 17.95 (ISBN 0-931250-18-8). Human Kinetics.

Perspectives on the Computer Revolution. Ed. by Z. Pylyshyn. ref. ed. 13.95x o.p. (ISBN 0-13-660761-6). P-H.

Perspectives on the Economics Problem. 2nd ed. A. MacEwan & T. Weisskopf. 1973. pap. 6.95 o.p. (ISBN 0-13-660928-7). P-H.

Perspectives on the Group Process: A Foundation for Counseling with Groups. 2nd ed. C. Gratton Kemp. LC 64-346. 1970. text ed. 18.50 (ISBN 0-395-04723-4, 3-29410). HM.

Perspectives on the Preparation of Student Affairs Professionals. Knock. (ACPA Monograph). 1977. pap. 7.25 (ISBN 0-686-23072-8). Am Personnel.

Perspectives on the Royal Commission on Corporate Concentration. P. K. Gorecki & W. T. Stanbury. 308p. 1979. pap. text ed. 15.95x (ISBN 0-409-88606-8, Pub. by Inst Res Pub Canada). Renouf.

Perspectives on the Social Sciences in Canada. Ed. by T. N. Guinsburg & Grant Reuber. LC 74-78508. 1974. pap. 4.00 (ISBN 0-8020-6248-2). U of Toronto Pr.

Perspectives on the Study of Speech. Ed. by Peter D. Eimas & Joanne L. Miller. 464p. 1981. text ed. 29.95 (ISBN 0-89859-052-3). L Erlbaum Assocs.

Perspectives on the T'ang. Ed. by Arthur F. Wright. Twitchett. LC 72-91310. 542p. 1981. pap. 10.95x (ISBN 0-300-02674-9). Yale U Pr.

Perspectives on U. S. Energy Policy: A Critique of Regulation. Ed. by Edward J. Mitchell. LC 76-23093. (American Enterprise Institute Perspectives: Vol. 3). (Illus.). 1976. 24.95 (ISBN 0-275-23640-4). Praeger.

Perspectives on Victimology. Ed. by William H. Parsonage. LC 79-15524. (Sage Research Progress Series in Criminology: Vol. 11). 1979. 12.95x (ISBN 0-8039-1323-0); pap. 6.50x (ISBN 0-8039-1324-9). Sage.

Perspectives on World Politics. Ed. by Michael Smith et al. 224p. 1981. 32.50x (ISBN 0-7099-2302-3, Pub. by Croom Helm Ltd England). Biblio Dist.

Perspectives on Writing in Grades 1-8. Ed. by Shirley Haley-James. 1981. pap. price not set (ISBN 0-8141-3519-6). NCTE.

Perspectives Seventy Six, a Compendium of Useful Knowledge About Old-Time Vermont & New Hampshire. Ed. by Del Goodwin & Dorcas Chaffee. (Illus.). (gr. 6-12). 1975. pap. text ed. 4.95 (ISBN 0-915892-02-2); 6.95 (ISBN 0-686-64804-8). Regional Ctr Educ.

Perspectives: The Alabama Heritage. Ed. by Rosemary Canfield. LC 78-64441. 1978. 15.00 (ISBN 0-916624-27-7). TSU Pr.

Perspecture, Optics, & Delft Artists Around 1650. Arthur K. Wheelock, Jr. LC 76-23661. (Outstanding Dissertations in the Fine Arts - 17th Century). (Illus.). 1977. Repr. of 1973 ed. lib. bdg. 56.00 (ISBN 0-8240-2740-X). Garland Pub.

Persuasion. Jane Austen. (World's Classics Ser.). 5.95 o.p. (ISBN 0-19-250356-1). Oxford U Pr.

Persuasion. Jane Austen. (Zodiac Press Ser.). 1978. 9.95 (ISBN 0-7011-1235-2, Pub. by Chatto Bodley Jonathan). Merrimack Bk Serv.

Persuasion. Jane Austen. Ed. by James Kinsley & John Davie. (World's Classics Ser.). 256p. 1981. pap. 2.95 (ISBN 0-19-281546-6). Oxford U Pr.

Persuasion: A Means of Social Influence. 2nd ed. Winston L. Brembeck & William S. Howell. (Illus.). 384p. 1976. 15.95 (ISBN 0-13-661090-0). P-H.

Persuasion & Healing: A Comparative Study of Psychotherapy. rev. ed. Jerome D. Frank. LC 72-4015. (Illus.). 398p. 1973. 18.50x o.p. (ISBN 0-8018-1443-X). Johns Hopkins.

Persuasion De la Charite: Themes, Formes et Structure Dans les Jornaux et Oeuvres Diverses De Marivaux. W. Pierre Jacoebee. (Orig., Fr.). 1976. pap. text ed. 20.00x (ISBN 90-6203-239-7). Humanities.

Persuasion in Marketing: The Dynamics of Marketing's Great Untapped Resource. Horace S. Schwerin & Henry H. Newell. 280p. 1981. 23.95 (ISBN 0-471-04554-3, Pub. by Wiley-Interscience). Wiley.

Persuasion in the Courtroom. John A. Burgess & Robert B. Huber. (Orig.). 1981. text ed. write for info (ISBN 0-316-11635-1). Little.

Persuasion: New Directions in Theory & Research. Ed. by Michael E. Roloff & Gerald R. Miller. LC 79-21202. (Sage Annual Reviews of Communication Research: Vol. 8). 311p. 1980. 20.00x (ISBN 0-8039-1213-7); pap. 9.95x (ISBN 0-8039-1214-5). Sage.

Persuasion: Reflection & Responsibility. 2nd ed. Charles U. Larson. 1979. pap. text ed. 11.95x (ISBN 0-534-00689-2). Wadsworth Pub.

Persuasion: Speech & Behavioral Change. Gary Cronkhite. LC 73-75140. (Speech Communication Ser.). 1969. pap. 5.50 (ISBN 0-672-61075-2, SC4). Bobbs.

Persuasion: Theory & Practice of Manipulative Communication. George Gordon. (Studies in Public Communication). 1971. 16.50 o.s.i. (ISBN 0-8038-5774-8); pap. text ed. 10.00x (ISBN 0-8038-5777-2). Hastings.

Persuasion: Understanding, Practice & Analysis. Herbert W. Simons. LC 75-9015. (Speech Communication Ser.). (Illus.). 400p. 1976. text ed. 15.50 (ISBN 0-201-07082-0). A-W.

Persuasive Writing: A Manager's Guide to Effective Letters & Reports. Robert G. Weaver & Patricia C. Weaver. LC 76-7178. 1977. 12.95 (ISBN 0-02-934020-9). Free Pr.

Pertaining to Thoreau. Samuel A. Jones. 171p. 1980. Repr. of 1901 ed. text ed. 20.00 (ISBN 0-8492-1280-4). R West.

Pertaining to Thoreau. Ed. by Samuel A. Jones. LC 80-2509. 1981. Repr. of 1901 ed. 26.00 (ISBN 0-404-19057-X). AMS Pr.

Pertinence of the Paradox: A Study of the Dialectics of Reason-In-Existence. Howard A. Slaatte. LC 68-27100. 1967. text ed. 8.50x o.p. (ISBN 0-391-00469-7). Humanities.

Perturbation Methods. Ali-Hasan Nayfeh. LC 72-8068. (Pure & Applied Mathematics Ser). 496p. 1973. 29.95 (ISBN 0-471-63059-4, Pub. by Wiley-Interscience). Wiley.

Perturbation Methods in Applied Mathematics. J. Kevorkian & J. D. Cole. (Applied Mathematical Sciences Ser.: Vol. 34). (Illus.). 512p. 1981. 42.00 (ISBN 0-387-90507-3). Springer-Verlag.

Perturbation of Spectra in Hilbert Space. K. O. Friedrichs. LC 60-12712. (Lectures in Applied Mathematics Ser.: Vol. 3). 1967. Repr. of 1965 ed. 15.20 (ISBN 0-8218-1103-7, LAM-3). Am Math.

Perturbation Theory for Linear Operators. T. Kato. (Grundlehren der Mathematischen Wissenschaften: Vol. 132). 1966. 35.70 o.p. (ISBN 0-387-03526-5). Springer-Verlag.

Perturbation Theory for Linear Operators. 2nd ed. T. Kato. (Grundlehren der Mathematischen Wissenschaften: Vol. 132). (Illus.). 619p. 1980. 72.00 (ISBN 0-387-07558-5). Springer-Verlag.

Perturbed Spirit: The Life & Personality of Samuel Taylor Coleridge. Oswald Doughty. LC 78-66792. 450p. Date not set. price not set (ISBN 0-8386-2353-0). Fairleigh Dickinson. Postponed.

Pertwee's Promenades & Pierrots: One Hundred Years of Seaside Entertainment. Bill Pertwee. LC 79-51084. (Illus.). 1979. 10.50 (ISBN 0-7153-7794-9). David & Charles.

Peru. Victor Alba. 1977. lib. bdg. 21.00x (ISBN 0-89158-111-1). Westview.

Peru. Grace Halsell. LC 69-11299. (Nations Today Books). (Illus.). (gr. 7 up). 1969. 4.95g o.s.i. (ISBN 0-02-742030-2). Macmillan.

Peru: A Cultural History. Henry F. Dobyns & Paul L. Doughty. LC 76-9224. (Latin American Histories). (Illus.). 1976. 15.95x (ISBN 0-19-502089-8); pap. 5.95x (ISBN 0-19-502091-X). Oxford U Pr.

Peru: A Short History. David P. Werlich. LC 77-17107. (Illus.). 447p. 1978. 24.95 (ISBN 0-8093-0830-4). S Ill U Pr.

Peruvian Designs for Cross-Stitch. Ellen Jessen. 64p. 1980. pap. 6.95 (ISBN 0-442-21926-1). Van Nos Reinhold.

Peruvian Painting by Unknown Artists: 800 B. C. to 1700 A. D. Intro. by Junius B. Bird. (Illus.). 1973. pap. 3.00 (ISBN 0-913456-20-9). Interbk Inc.

Perversion; or, the Causes & Consequences of Infidelity, 1856. William J. Conybeare. Ed. by Robert L. Wolff. LC 75-497. (Victorian Fiction Ser.). 1975. lib. bdg. 66.00 (ISBN 0-8240-1572-X). Garland Pub.

Peshitta of Exodus, the Development of Its Text in the Course of Fifteen Centuries. M. D. Koster. (Studia Semitica Neerlandica: No. 19). 1977. text ed. 116.85x (ISBN 90-232-1503-6). Humanities.

Pest & Disease Control Handbook. Ed. by Nigel Scopes. 250p. 1979. 35.00x (ISBN 0-901436-42-9, Pub. by Brit Crop Protection England). Intl Schol Bk Serv.

Pest & Diseases. Ed. by Time-Life Books Editors. (Encyclopedia of Gardening Ser.). (Illus.). 1978. 11.95 (ISBN 0-8094-2566-1). Time-Life.

Pest Control: An Assesssment of Present & Alternative Technologies, Vols. 1-5. Environmental Studies Board, Natl Research Council. 1976. pap. 26.00 set o.p. (ISBN 0-309-02409-9). Natl Acad Pr.

Pest Control & Public Health. Environmental Studies Board, Natl Research Council. LC 75-45777. (Pest Control Ser.: Vol.5). 282p. 1976. pap. 8.00 (ISBN 0-309-02414-5). Natl Acad Pr.

Pest Control: Cultural & Environmental Aspects. Ed. by David Pimentel & John H. Perkins. LC 79-18516. (AAAS Selected Symposium: No. 43). (Illus.). 243p. 1980. lib. bdg. 22.00x (ISBN 0-89158-753-5). Westview.

Pest Control: Strategies for the Future. Agricultural Board. LC 79-188497. (Illus.). 1972. pap. 7.00 (ISBN 0-309-01945-1). Natl Acad Pr.

Pest Management in Transition. Ed. by Peter DeJong. LC 79-53138. (Westview Replica Edition Ser.). 1979. lib. bdg. 19.00x (ISBN 0-89158-679-2). Westview.

Pest Management: Proceedings of an International Conference, 25-29 October 1976, Laxenburg, Austria. Ed. by G. A. Norton & C. S. Hollings. LC 78-40825. 1979. text ed. 60.00 (ISBN 0-08-023427-5). Pergamon.

Pest Resistance to Pesticides in Agriculture. 38p. 1970. pap. 6.00 (F1984, FAO). Unipub.

Pest War. W. W. Fletcher. LC 74-11440. 1978. pap. 11.95 (ISBN 0-470-26345-8). Halsted Pr.

Pestalozzi's Educational Writings. Johann H. Pestalozzi. Tr. by John A. Green from Ger. Bd. with How Gertrude Teaches Her Children. (Contributions to the History of Psychology Ser., Vol. II, Pt. B: Psychometrics). 1978. Repr. of 1898 ed. 30.00 (ISBN 0-89093-163-1). U Pubns Amer.

Pesticide Application & Safety Training. rev. ed. Michael Stimmann. (Illus.). 98p. (Orig.). 1980. pap. text ed. 4.00. Ag Sci Pubns.

Pesticide Application Methods. new ed. G. A. Matthews. LC 77-26033. (Illus.). 1979. text ed. 55.00 (ISBN 0-582-46054-9). Longman.

Pesticide Book. George W. Ware. LC 78-16220. (Illus.). 1978. pap. text ed. 11.95x (ISBN 0-7167-0198-7). W H Freeman.

Pesticide Chemistry in the Twentieth Century. Ed. by Jack R. Plimmer. LC 76-51748. (ACS Symposium Ser: No. 37). 1977. 23.00 (ISBN 0-8412-0364-4). Am Chemical.

Pesticide Decision Making. Committee on Pesticide Decision Making, National Research Council. LC 77-94524. (Analytical Studies for the U. S. Environmental Protection Agency Ser.). (Illus.). 1978. pap. text ed. 6.00 (ISBN 0-309-02734-9). Natl Acad Pr.

Pesticide Handbook - Entoma. 1975. pap. 6.00 o.p. (ISBN 0-686-11685-2). Entomol Soc.

Pesticide Handbook-Entoma. Ed. by Caswell. 1979. 9.00 (ISBN 0-686-23164-3); pap. 7.50 (ISBN 0-686-23165-1). Entomol Soc.

Pesticide Index. 5th ed. Ed. by Wiswesser. LC 76-21894. 1976. 20.00 (ISBN 0-686-15427-4). Entomol Soc.

Pesticide Manual. 6th ed. Ed. by Charles R. Worthing. 655p. 1979. 59.95x (ISBN 0-901436-44-5, Pub. by Brit Crop Protection England). Intl Schol Bk Serv.

Pesticide Manufacturing & Toxic Materials Control Encyclopedia. Ed. by Marshall Sittig. LC 80-19373. (Chemical Tech. Rev. 168; Env. Health Rev. 3; Pollution Tech. Rev. 69). (Illus.). 810p. 1981. 96.00 (ISBN 0-8155-0814-X). Noyes.

Pesticide Residues: A Contribution to Their Interpretation, Relevance & Legislation. Ed. by H. Frehse & H. Geissbuhler. (International Union of Pure & Applied Chemistry). 1979. text ed. 37.00 (ISBN 0-08-023931-5). Pergamon.

Pesticide Residues in Food 1979. (FAO Plant Production & Protection Paper Ser.: No. 20). 97p. 1980. pap. 6.00 (ISBN 92-5-100922-8, F1936, FAO). Unipub.

Pesticide Residues in Food-1979 Evaluations. 568p. 1981. pap. 30.25 (ISBN 92-5-100958-9, F2089, FAO). Unipub.

Pesticides. James R. Critser, Jr. (Ser. 13-78). 1979. 150.00 (ISBN 0-914428-63-2). Lexington Data.

Pesticides & Human Welfare. Donald L. Gunn & John G. R. Stevens. (Illus.). 1977. text ed. 19.95x (ISBN 0-19-854522-3); pap. text ed. 9.95x (ISBN 0-19-854526-6). Oxford U Pr.

Pesticides & the Living Landscape. Robert L. Rudd. 1964. pap. 7.95x (ISBN 0-299-03214-0). U of Wis Pr.

Pesticides: Preparation & Mode of Action. R. Cremlyn. LC 77-28590. 1978. 35.00 (ISBN 0-471-99631-9, Pub. by Wiley-Interscience); pap. 18.50 (ISBN 0-471-27669-3). Wiley.

Pests & Diseases. James U. Crockett & Richard Cravens. (Time-Life Encyclopedia of Gardening Ser.). (Illus.). 1977. lib. bdg. 11.97 (ISBN 0-686-51062-3). Silver.

Pests & Diseases of Forest Plantation Trees: An Annotated List of the Principle Species Occurring in the British Commonwealth. Frances G. Browne. 1968. 89.00x (ISBN 0-19-854367-0). Oxford U Pr.

Pests & People: The Search for Sensible Pest Control. Laurence Pringle. LC 71-165104. (Illus.). (gr. 7up). 1972. 7.95 (ISBN 0-02-775270-4). Macmillan.

PET & the IEEE 488 Bus (GPIB) Eugene Fisher & C. William Jensen. 1980. pap. 15.99 (ISBN 0-931988-31-4). Osborne-McGraw.

Pet Basic I: Training Your Pet. Zamora et al. 1981. 14.95 (ISBN 0-8359-5525-7); pap. 7.95 (ISBN 0-8359-5524-9). Reston.

Pet Basics. D. J. David. 225p. 1981. pap. 9.95 (ISBN 0-918398-47-9). Dilithium Pr.

Pet Birds. Joan Joseph. LC 75-11902. (Career Concise Guides Ser.). (Illus.). 72p. (gr. 8 up). 1975. PLB 4.90 o.p. (ISBN 0-531-02837-2). Watts.

PET-CBM Personal Computer Guide. Carroll Donaghue & Janice Enger. (Orig.). 1980. pap. 15.99 (ISBN 0-931988-30-6). Osborne-McGraw.

PET-CBM Personal Computer Guide. 2nd ed. Adam Osborne. 530p. 1980. pap. 15.00 (ISBN 0-931988-55-1). Osborne-McGraw.

Pet Friends. (Photo Board Bks.). (Illus.). 12p. (ps). 1980. 1.50 (ISBN 0-307-06070-5, Golden Pr). Western Pub.

Pet Games & Recreation. Mac Ogelsby et al. 1981. text ed. 14.95 (ISBN 0-8359-5530-3); pap. 9.95 (ISBN 0-8359-5529-X). Reston.

Pet in the Jar. Judy Stang. (Eager Readers Ser.). (Illus.). (gr. k-3). 1975. PLB 5.00 (ISBN 0-307-60801-8, Golden Pr). Western Pub.

Pet Industry: Outlook. BCC Staff. 1981. 750.00 (ISBN 0-89336-164-X, GA-034). BCC.

Pet Names. Jean E. Taggart. LC 62-19730. 1962. 10.00 (ISBN 0-8108-0111-6). Scarecrow.

Pet-Oriented Child Psychotherapy. Boris M. Levinson. 228p. 1969. 13.75 (ISBN 0-398-01118-4). C C Thomas.

Pet Safety. J. J. McCoy. (Illus.). (gr. 3 up). 1979. PLB 6.90 (ISBN 0-531-02926-3). Watts.

Pet Set, Bk II. Doug Borgstedt & Jean Borgstedt. 1979. pap. 2.00 (ISBN 0-87666-637-3, PS-766). TFH Pubns.

Pet Show! Ezra J. Keats. LC 73-156843. (Illus.). 32p. (gr. k-3). 1972. 7.95 (ISBN 0-02-749560-4). Macmillan.

Petals in the Wind. V. C. Andrews. 1980. Repr. 14.95 (ISBN 0-671-41125-X). S&S.

Petals of Blood. Ngugi Wa Thiong'O. 1978. 9.95 o.p. (ISBN 0-525-17828-7); pap. 4.95 (ISBN 0-525-04195-8). Dutton.

Petals of the Rose. Juliana Davison. 192p. (Orig.). 1980. pap. 1.75 (ISBN 0-446-94272-3). Warner Bks.

Petals on the Wind. V. C. Andrews. 1980. pap. 2.95 (ISBN 0-671-82977-7). PB.

Pete Maravich. Robert Armstrong. (Sports Superstars Ser.). (Illus.). (gr. 3-9). 1978. PLB 5.95 (ISBN 0-87191-669-X); pap. 2.95 (ISBN 0-89812-183-3). Creative Ed.

Pete Rose. Nathan Aaseng. LC 79-27377. (Achievers Ser.). (Illus.). (gr. 4-9). 1981. PLB 5.95 (ISBN 0-8225-0480-4). Lerner Pubns.

Pete Rose. James P. Smith. (Sports Superstars Ser.). (Illus.). (gr. 3-9). 1977. PLB 5.95 (ISBN 0-87191-540-5); pap. 2.95 (ISBN 0-89812-174-4). Creative Ed.

Pete the Parakeet. Sharon Gordon. (Illus.). 32p. (gr. k-2). 1980. PLB 2.96 (ISBN 0-89375-384-X); pap. 0.95 (ISBN 0-89375-284-3). Troll Assocs.

Peter Abelard: His Place in History. Kathleen M. Starnes. LC 80-8298. 161p. 1981. lib. bdg. 17.50 (ISBN 0-8191-1510-X); pap. text ed. 8.75 (ISBN 0-8191-1511-8). U Pr of Amer.

Peter & Mr. Brandon. Eleanor Schick. LC 75-165105. (Illus.). 32p. (ps-2). 1973. 5.95g o.s.i. (ISBN 0-02-781120-4). Macmillan.

Peter & the Wolf. Sergei Prokofiev. LC 79-92902. (Illus.). 32p. (ps-5). 1980. 10.00g (ISBN 0-87923-331-1). Godine.

Peter Arbiter: The Adventures of a Young Man in Texas. Edwin Shrake. (Illus.). 152p. 1973. 7.95 o.s.i. (ISBN 0-88426-030-5). Encino Pr.

Peter Arno. Peter Arno. LC 79-19540. (Illus.). 1979. 10.95 (ISBN 0-396-07772-2). Dodd.

Peter Buchan, & Other Papers on Scottish & English Ballads & Songs. William Walker. 1980. Repr. of 1915 ed. lib. bdg. 15.00 (ISBN 0-8414-2838-7). Folcroft.

Peter Calvay -- Hermit: A Personal Rediscovery of Prayer. Rayner Torkington. LC 80-13188. 107p. (Orig.). 1980. pap. 3.95 (ISBN 0-8189-0404-6). Alba.

Peter Drucker: Contributions to Business Enterprise. Ed. by Tony H. Bonaparte & John E. Flaherty. LC 70-133013. 1970. 15.00x (ISBN 0-8147-0951-6). NYU Pr.

Peter Handke. Nicholas Hern. LC 76-190349. (Modern Literature Ser.). 1972. 10.95 (ISBN 0-8044-2380-6). Ungar.

Peter Kapitsa on Life & Science. Albert Parry. 1968. 7.50 o.s.i. (ISBN 0-02-594810-5). Macmillan.

Peter Kropotkin. Stephen Osofsky. (World Leaders Ser.: No. 77). 1979. lib. bdg. 13.50 (ISBN 0-8057-7724-5). Twayne.

Peter Learns to Crochet. (gr. k-3). 1.50. New Seed.

Peter McArthur. Alec Lucas. (World Authors Ser.: Canada: No. 363). 1975. lib. bdg. 12.50 (ISBN 0-8057-6214-0). Twayne.

Peter Martyr in Italy: An Anatomy of Apostasy. Philip McNair. 1967. 12.00x o.p. (ISBN 0-19-821459-6). Oxford U Pr.

Peter Miller's Ski Almanac. Peter Miller. LC 79-7660. (Nick Lyons Bk.). (Illus.). 1979. pap. 9.95 (ISBN 0-385-15713-4, NLB). Doubleday.

Peter One, 2 vols. John Brown. (Geneva Commentaries Ser.). 1980. Set. 29.95 (ISBN 0-85151-204-6). Vol. 1 (ISBN 0-85151-205-4). Vol. 2 (ISBN 0-85151-206-2). Banner of Truth.

Peter Pan. Barrie. Ed. by Frank Josette. (gr. 3). Date not set. pap. cancelled (ISBN 0-590-30054-7, Schol Pap). Schol Bk Serv.

Peter Pan. abridged ed. James M. Barrie. Adapted by Josette Frank. (Illus.). (gr. 1-4). 1957. 3.95 (ISBN 0-394-80749-9, BYR); PLB 4.79 (ISBN 0-394-90749-3). Random.

Peter Pan. James M. Barrie. Ed. by Noras Unwin. (Illus.). (gr. 4-6). 1950. 8.95 (ISBN 0-684-13214-1, ScribJ). Scribner.

Peter Pig. Althea Braithwaite. (Dinosaur Ser.). (Illus.). (gr. k-3). 1978. pap. 7.25 pack of 5 o.p. (ISBN 0-85122-036-3, Pub. by Dino Pub); pap. 1.45 ea. o.p. Merrimack Bk Serv.

Peter Pitseolak's Escape from Death. Peter Pitseolak. Ed. by Dorothy Eber. LC 77-83236. 1978. 7.95 o.s.i. (ISBN 0-440-06894-0, Sey Lawr); PLB 7.45 (ISBN 0-440-06896-7). Delacorte.

Peter Porcupine. Majorie Bowen. LC 78-145715. 1971. Repr. of 1935 ed. 20.00 (ISBN 0-8103-3677-4). Gale.

Peter Principle: Why Things Always Go Wrong. Laurence J. Peter & Raymond Hull. (Illus.). 1969. 7.95 (ISBN 0-688-02289-8); pap. 3.95 (ISBN 0-688-27544-3). Morrow.

Peter Rabbit. Illus. by T. Izawa & S. Hijkata. (Puppet Storybooks). (Illus.). 18p. (gr. k-2). 1981. 3.50 (ISBN 0-448-09755-9). G&D.

Peter Schlemihl. Adelbert Von Chamisso. Tr. by Loewenberg-Wertheim. 1980. pap. 3.95 (ISBN 0-7145-0440-8). Riverrun NY.

Peter Schwed's Tennis Quiz. Peter Schwed. (Illus.). 224p. (Orig.). 1981. pap. 8.95 (ISBN 0-914178-46-6, 42907-8). Tennis Mag.

Peter Sellers: The Mask Behind the Mask. Peter Evans. 1980. pap. 2.50 (ISBN 0-451-09758-0, E9758, Sig). NAL.

Peter Shaffer. Dennis A. Klein. (English Authors Ser.: No. 261). 1979. lib. bdg. 12.50 (ISBN 0-8057-6738-X). Twayne.

Peter Sinks in the Water. Joyce Morse. (Books I Can Read). 32p. (Orig.). (gr. 2). 1980. pap. 1.25 (ISBN 0-8127-0281-6). Southern Pub.

Peter the Great: His Life & His World. Robert K. Massie. LC 80-7635. (Illus.). 864p. 1980. 17.95 (ISBN 0-394-50032-6). Knopf.

Peter the Great: The Reformer-Tsar. Douglas Liversidge. LC 68-18579. (Biography Ser). (Illus.). (gr. 7 up). 1968. PLB 5.90 o.p. (ISBN 0-531-00914-9). Watts.

Peter: The White Cat of Trenarren. A. L. Rowse. 1974. 4.95 o.p. (ISBN 0-7181-1228-8, Pub. by Michael Joseph). Merrimack Bk Serv.

Peter Watkins. Joseph A. Gomez. (Theatrical Arts Ser.). 1979. lib. bdg. 10.95 (ISBN 0-8057-9267-8). Twayne.

Peter Weiss. Otto F. Best. Tr. by Ursule Molinaro from Ger. LC 75-10104. (Modern Literature Ser.). 170p. 1976. 10.95 (ISBN 0-8044-2038-6). Ungar.

Peterborough Abbey Ten Eighty-Six to Thirteen Ten. Edmund King. LC 72-91959. (Cambridge Studies in Economic History). (Illus.). 232p. 1972. 32.95 (ISBN 0-521-20133-0). Cambridge U Pr.

Peter's Angel: A Story About Monsters. Hope Campbell. LC 75-9517. (Illus.). 160p. (gr. 3-7). 1976. 6.95 (ISBN 0-590-07404-0, Four Winds). Schol Bk Serv.

Peter's Portrait of Jesus. J. B. Phillips. 1976. 7.95 (ISBN 0-00-215628-8, A1154, Pub. by Collins Pubs). Abingdon.

Peter's Principles, from I & II Peter. Harold L. Fickett, Jr. LC 73-90620. 1977. pap. 2.95 (ISBN 0-8307-0455-8, S281-1-20). Regal.

Peterson's Guide to Undergraduate Engineering Study. David R. Reyes-Guerra & Alan M. Fischer. (Orig.). 1981. pap. 14.00 (ISBN 0-87866-163-8). Petersons Guides.

Peterson's Travel Guide to Colleges: Middle Atlantic States. (Illus.). 1977. pap. 4.95 o.p. (ISBN 0-8437-3450-7). Hammond Inc.

Peterson's Travel Guide to Colleges: Northeastern States. (Illus.). 1977. pap. 4.95 o.p. (ISBN 0-8437-3445-0). Hammond Inc.

Pete's First Day at School. Jorgen Clevin. (Illus.). (ps-k). 1973. PLB 4.69 (ISBN 0-394-92652-8, BYR). Random.

Pete's House. Harriet L. Sobol. LC 77-12564. (Illus.). (gr. 3-6). 1978. 8.95 (ISBN 0-02-785980-0, 78598). Macmillan.

Petit Atlas Des Champignons, 3 vols. H. Romagnesi. (Illus.). 1964. Vols. 1 & 2. 25.00 (ISBN 0-934454-91-4). Lubrecht & Cramer.

Petit Dictionnaire bilingue Larousse, francais-anglais et English-French. L. Chauffurin. (Adonis). (Fr. & Eng.). plastic bdg. 5.95 (ISBN 0-685-14032-6, 3768). Larousse.

Petit Dictionnaire bilingue Larousse, francais-espagnol, espanol-frances. Larousse And Co. (Adonis). (Fr & Span). plastic bdg. 5.95 (ISBN 0-685-14033-4, 3775). Larousse.

Petit Dictionnaire francais Larousse. Larousse And Co. (Illus., Fr.). 10.50 (ISBN 0-685-14034-2, 3754). Larousse.

Petit Larousse Illustre 1981. (Illus.). 1981. 39.95 (ISBN 2-0330-1381-2, 3381). Larousse.

Petit Prince. Antoine De St-Exupery. (Illus., Fr.). pap. 1.95 (ISBN 0-685-20246-1). Schoenhof.

Petit Prince. rev. ed. Antoine De Saint-Exupery. Ed. by John R. Miller. LC 47-151. (Fr). (gr. 11). 1975. pap. 5.00 (ISBN 0-395-24005-0). HM.

Petit Prince. Antoine de Saint-Exupery. LC 43-5812. (Illus., Fr.). (gr. 3-7). 1943. 7.95 (ISBN 0-15-243818-1, HJ); pap. 1.95 (ISBN 0-15-650300-X). HarBraceJ.

Petite Bebe Eighteen Eighty Three to Eighteen Eighty-Seven, Vol.2. Susan B. Sirkis. (Wish Booklets). 48p. 1973. pap. 5.50x (ISBN 0-913786-11-X). Wish Bklets.

Petite Suzanne. Marguerite De Angeli. (gr. 1-5). 3.50 o.p. (ISBN 0-385-07447-6). Doubleday.

Petition & Remonstrance of the Governor & Company, Etc. East India Company. LC 78-25744. (English Experience Ser.: No. 305). 38p. Repr. of 1628 ed. 8.00 (ISBN 90-221-0305-6). Walter J Johnson.

Petrarch. Thomas G. Bergin. (World Authors Ser.: Italy: No. 81). lib. bdg. 10.95 (ISBN 0-8057-2694-2). Twayne.

Petrarch His Life & Times. H. C. Holloway-Calthrop. 319p. 1980. Repr. of 1907 ed. lib. bdg. 45.00 (ISBN 0-89984-274-7). Century Bookbindery.

Petrarch: His Life & Times. H. C. Hollway-Calthrop. LC 75-187413. (Illus.). xi, 319p. 1972. Repr. of 1907 ed. lib. bdg. 13.75x (ISBN 0-8154-0406-9). Cooper Sq.

Petrarch's Poetics & Literary History. Marguerite R. Waller. LC 80-12893. 176p. 1980. lib. bdg. 13.50x (ISBN 0-87023-305-X). U of Mass Pr.

Petri Diaconi: Ortus et Vita Iustorum Casinensis. Ed. by R. H. Rodgers. (Publications in Classical Studies Ser.: Vol. 10). 1973. pap. 13.50x (ISBN 0-520-09393-3). U of Cal Pr.

Petriel Reading Comprehension Test. Neila T. Pettit & Irwin W. Cockriel. 1973. 1.00 (ISBN 0-87543-097-X); 0.75 (ISBN 0-87543-091-0). Lucas.

Petrochemical Feedstocks: The Next Crisis? 1981. 850.00 (ISBN 0-89336-066-X, C-003). BCC.

Petrochemical Technology Assessment. Dale F. Rudd et al. 325p. 1981. 32.95 (ISBN 0-471-08912-5, Pub. by Wiley-Interscience). Wiley.

Petrogenesis of Metamorphic Rocks. 4th ed. H. G. Winkler. LC 76-3443. 1976. pap. 14.10 o.p. (ISBN 0-387-07473-2). Springer-Verlag.

Petrograd Consignment. Owen Sela. 1980. pap. 2.50 o.s.i. (ISBN 0-440-16885-6). Dell.

Petrography: An Introduction to the Study of Rocks in Thin Sections. Howel Williams et al. LC 54-5872. (Geology Ser.). (Illus.). 1954. 26.95x (ISBN 0-7167-0206-1). W H Freeman.

Petrography of Tills: A Study from Ringsaker, Southeastern Norway. Sylvi Haldorsen. (Geological Survey of Norway Ser: No. 336, Bulletin 44). 32p. 1978. pap. 12.00x (ISBN 82-00-31370-0, Dist. by Columbia U Pr). Universitet.

Petroleum & Global Tectonics. Ed. by Alfred G. Fischer & Sheldon Judson. LC 72-9946. 280p. 1975. 30.00x (ISBN 0-691-08124-7); pap. 9.95 (ISBN 0-691-08128-X). Princeton U Pr.

Petroleum & Hard Minerals from the Sea. Fillmore C. Earney. LC 80-17653. (Scripta Series in Geography). 1438p. 1980. 29.95 (ISBN 0-470-27009-8, Pub. by Halsted Pr). Wiley.

Petroleum & the Continental Shelf of North-West Europe, Vol. I: Geology. Ed. by A. W. Woodland. LC 75-14329. 501p. 1975. 65.95 (ISBN 0-470-95993-2). Halsted Pr.

Petroleum Drilling Equipment Terms & Phrases: English-Spanish, Spanish-English. Arthur E. Thomann. 423p. 1980. lib. bdg. 50.00x (ISBN 0-930624-02-5). Marlin.

Petroleum Engineering. Alfred Mayer-Gurr. LC 76-6449. (Geology of Petroleum Ser: Vol. 3). 208p. 1976. pap. text ed. 13.95x (ISBN 0-470-15082-3). Halsted Pr.

Petroleum Engineering: Drilling & Well Completion. Carl Gatlin. 1960. ref. ed. 31.95 (ISBN 0-13-662155-4). P-H.

Petroleum Evaluations & Economic Decision. A. W. McCray. (Illus.). 544p. 1975. 33.95 (ISBN 0-13-662213-5). P-H.

Petroleum: Gas, Oil, & Asphalt. Irving Adler. LC 78-2431. (Reason Why Ser.). (Illus.). (gr. 3-6). 1975. PLB 7.89 (ISBN 0-381-99624-7, JD-J). John Day.

Petroleum Geochemistry & Geology. John M. Hunt. LC 79-1281. (Illus.). 1979. text ed. 32.95x (ISBN 0-7167-1005-6). W H Freeman.

Petroleum Geology. Kenneth K. Landes. LC 74-26700. 458p. 1975. Repr. of 1959 ed. 22.50 (ISBN 0-88275-226-X). Krieger.

Petroleum in the Marine Environment. Ocean Affairs Board. LC 74-18572. 1975. pap. 9.00 (ISBN 0-309-02311-4). Natl Acad Pr.

Petroleum Measurement Manual: Tank Calibration Section - Liquid Calibration Methods, Pt. II, Pt. Ii. Institute of Petroleum. 1980. 22.00 (ISBN 0-85501-433-4). Heyden.

Petroleum Price Regulation: Should We Decontrol? Kenneth J. Arrow & Joseph P. Kalt. 1979. pap. 4.25. Am Enterprise.

Petroleum Regulations: Handbook. Bell. 1980. pap. 75.00 (ISBN 0-917386-37-X). Exec Ent.

Petrologic Phase Equilibria. W. G. Ernst. LC 76-3699. (Illus.). 1976. text ed. 31.95x (ISBN 0-7167-0279-7). W H Freeman.

Petrology for Students. 8th ed. S. T. Nockolds et al. LC 76-52186. (Illus.). 1978. 67.50 (ISBN 0-521-21553-6); pap. 16.95x (ISBN 0-521-29184-4). Cambridge U Pr.

Petrology of Sedimentary Rocks. 4th ed. Robert L. Folk. (Illus.). 1980. pap. 11.95x (ISBN 0-914696-14-9). Hemphill.

Petrology of the Metamorphic Rocks. R. Mason. (Textbook of Petrology Ser.). (Illus.). 1978. text ed. 27.50x (ISBN 0-04-552013-5); pap. text ed. 14.95x (ISBN 0-04-552014-3). Allen Unwin.

Petrology of the Sedimentary Rocks. 6th ed. J. T. Greensmith. (Textbook of Petrology Ser.). (Illus.). 1978. text ed. 27.50x (ISBN 0-04-552011-9); pap. text ed. 14.95x (ISBN 0-04-552012-7). Allen Unwin.

Petrology, Structure, & Geologic History of the Catalina Schist Terrain, Southern California. John Platt. LC 74-22941. (Publications in Geological Sciences: Vol. 112). 1976. pap. 11.00x (ISBN 0-520-09525-1). U of Cal Pr.

Petronius: Cena Trimalchionis. rev. ed. Ed. by Thomas Cutt & Jacob E. Nyenhuis. LC 73-105090. (Classical Text Ser). (Latin). 1970. pap. text ed. 4.95x (ISBN 0-8143-1410-4). Wayne St U Pr.

Petronius Leader of Fashion. J. M. Mitchell. 364p. 1981. Repr. of 1922 ed. lib. bdg. 35.00 (ISBN 0-89987-565-3). Darby Bks.

Petros Brailas-Armenis. Evanghelos Moutsopoulos. (World Authors Ser.: Greece: No. 261). 1974. lib. bdg. 10.95 (ISBN 0-8057-2170-3). Twayne.

Petrucci's Harmnica Musices Odhecation-A. Ed. by Helen Hewitt. LC 77-25989. (Music Reprint Ser., 1978). 1978. Repr. of 1942 ed. lib. bdg. 42.50 (ISBN 0-306-77562-X). Da Capo.

Petrus Abaelardus Dialectica. 2nd ed. Ed. by L. M. De Rijk. 1970. text ed. 82.75x (ISBN 0-685-12392-8). Humanities.

Petrushka. Igor Stravinsky. Ed. by Charles Hamm. (Illus., Orig., Critical Score). 1967. pap. 5.95x (ISBN 0-393-09770-6, NortonC). Norton.

Pets. Boy Scouts Of America. LC 19-600. (Illus.). 48p. (gr. 6-12). 1969. pap. 0.70x (ISBN 0-8395-3281-4, 3281). BSA.

Pets. rev. 3rd ed. Frances N. Chrystie. (Illus.). (gr. 4 up). 1974. 8.95 (ISBN 0-316-14051-1). Little.

Pets. Lois Vanderhoef. (Illus.). (ps-2). PLB 5.38 (ISBN 0-307-68995-6, Golden Pr). Western Pub.

Pets & Human Development. Boris M. Levinson. 256p. 1972. 14.75 (ISBN 0-398-02358-1). C C Thomas.

Pets & More Pets. Child Study Association of America. LC 69-11825. (Illus.). (gr. 1-5). 1969. 7.95 (ISBN 0-690-61661-9, TYC-J). T Y Crowell.

Pets Are Smart. Jane B. Moncure. LC 76-4834. (Illus.). (ps-3). 1976. 5.95 (ISBN 0-913778-39-7). Childs World.

Pets, People, Plagues. Allan Magie. LC 79-19321. (Better Living Ser.). 1979. pap. 0.95 (ISBN 0-8127-0233-6). Southern Pub.

Petticoat Medic in Vietnam: Adventures of a Woman Doctor. Diane L. Trembly. 6.95 (ISBN 0-533-01937-0). Vantage.

Petticoat Patriots of the Revolution. Edith P. Meyer. LC 75-25139. (Illus.). 1978. 7.95 (ISBN 0-8149-0771-7). Vanguard.

Petticoat Surgeon. Bertha Van Hoosen. Ed. by Annette K. Baxter. LC 79-8820. (Signal Lives Ser.). 1980. Repr. of 1947 ed. lib. bdg. 30.00x (ISBN 0-405-12864-9). Arno.

Pettranella. Betty Waterton. (Illus.). 32p. (gr. 1-4). 1981. 8.95 (ISBN 0-8149-0844-6). Vanguard.

Peugeot Moped Owners Service-Repair, 1976-1978. Ed Scott. Ed. by Eric Jorgensen. (Illus.). 1978. pap. 6.00 (ISBN 0-89287-202-0, M436). Clymer Pubns.

Pew for One, Please. William Lyon. LC 76-41976. 1977. 6.95 (ISBN 0-8164-0374-0). Crossroad NY.

Pew Group. Anthony Oliver. LC 80-2079. (Crime Club Ser.). 192p. 1981. 9.95 (ISBN 0-385-17412-8). Doubleday.

Pewter Jewellery. Miriam Browne. 1979. 19.95 (ISBN 0-7134-1608-4, Pub. by Batsford England). David & Charles.

Pewter to Quilts. Time-Life Books Editors. (Encyclopedia of Collectibles Ser.). (Illus.). 1979. lib. bdg. 10.98 (ISBN 0-8094-2795-8); kivar bdg. 8.95 (ISBN 0-8094-2796-6). Silver.

Pewter Wares from Sheffield. Jack L. Scott. LC 80-68670. (Illus.). 260p. 1980. 28.00 (ISBN 0-937864-00-5). Antiquary Pr.

Peyote Dance. Antonin Artaud. Tr. by Helen Weaver from Fr. LC 75-26919. 105p. 1976. 7.95 o.p. (ISBN 0-374-23090-0); pap. 2.45 (ISBN 0-374-51100-4). FS&G.

Peyote Hunt: The Sacred Journey of Huichol Indians. Barbara G. Myerhoff. LC 73-16923. (Symbol, Myth & Ritual Ser.). (Illus.). 288p. 1974. 22.50x (ISBN 0-8014-0817-2); pap. 5.95 1976 ed. (ISBN 0-8014-9137-1). Cornell U Pr.

Pfaff's Problem & Its Generalizations. Jan A. Schouten & W. Van Der Kulk. LC 75-77140. 1969. Repr. of 1949 ed. 19.50 (ISBN 0-8284-0221-3). Chelsea Pub.

PGA: The Official History of the Professional Golfers' Association of America. Herb Graffis. LC 75-9967. 1975. 16.95 o.s.i. (ISBN 0-690-00919-4, TYC-T). T Y Crowell.

PH of Plant Cells. J. Small. Bd. with PH of Animal Cells. F. J. Wiercinski. (Protoplasmatologica: Vol. 2B, Pt. 2c). (Illus.). iv, 172p. 1955. pap. 40.20 o.p. (ISBN 0-387-80386-6). Springer-Verlag.

Phacoemulsification. Franco Verzella et al. write for info. (ISBN 0-8067-2051-4). Urban & S.

Phacoemulsification & Aspiration of Cataracts: Surgical Techniques, Complications & Results. Jared M. Emery & James H. Little. LC 79-13047. 1979. text ed. 45.00 (ISBN 0-8016-3028-2). Mosby.

Phaedo. Plato. Tr. by F. J. Church. LC 51-10496. 1951. pap. 2.95 (ISBN 0-672-60192-3, LLA30). Bobbs.

Phaedo. Plato. Ed. by R. Hackforth. 200p. 1972. 23.95 (ISBN 0-521-08458-X); pap. 6.50x (ISBN 0-521-09702-9). Cambridge U Pr.

Phaedo. Plato. Tr. & notes by David Gallop. (Clarendon Plato Ser). 224p. 1975. pap. 17.95x (ISBN 0-19-872049-1). Oxford U Pr.

Phaedo. Plato. Ed. by John Burnet. 1979. pap. 11.95x (ISBN 0-19-814014-2). Oxford U Pr.

Phaedra Complex. Jeannette Eyerly. (YA) (gr. 3-6). 1979. pap. 1.50 (ISBN 0-671-29915-8). PB.

Phaedrus. Plato. Tr. by W. C. Helmbold & W. G. Rabinowitz. 1956. pap. 2.50 (ISBN 0-672-60207-5, LLA40). Bobbs.

Phaedrus. Plato. Ed. by R. Hackforth. 200p. 1972. 23.95 (ISBN 0-521-08459-8); pap. 6.50x (ISBN 0-521-09703-7). Cambridge U Pr.

Phage & the Origins of Molecular Biology. Ed. by J. Cairns et al. LC 66-26455. (Illus.). 352p. 1966. 25.00 (ISBN 0-87969-104-2); pap. 8.50 o.p. (ISBN 0-87969-105-0). Cold Spring Harbor.

Phagocytic Cell in Host Resistance. Ed. by J. A. Bellanti & D. H. Dayton. LC 74-14147. 365p. 1975. 31.50 (ISBN 0-911216-90-1). Raven.

Phaidon Art Collection, 3 vols. Incl. Vol. 1. Painters of Fantasy. 9.40 (ISBN 0-87827-224-0); Vol. 2. Gallery of Masterpieces. 9.40 (ISBN 0-87827-225-9); Vol. 3. Van Gogh. 9.40 (ISBN 0-87827-226-7). 29.50 set (ISBN 0-87827-220-8). Ency Brit Ed.

Phaidon Guide to Silver. Margaret Holland. (Illus., Orig.). 1979. pap. 5.95 o.p. (ISBN 0-8467-0538-9, Pub. by Two Continents). Hippocrene Bks.

Phanerozoic Paleocontinental World Maps. A. G. Smith et al. LC 79-42669. (Cambridge Earth Science Ser.). 96p. Date not set. 29.50 (ISBN 0-521-23257-0); pap. 13.95 (ISBN 0-521-23258-9). Cambridge U Pr.

Phanerozoic Stromatolites: Case Histories. Ed. by C. Monty. (Illus.). 260p. 1981. 52.60 (ISBN 0-387-10474-7). Springer-Verlag.

Phanomenologische Idealismus Husserls. Theodor Celms. Ed. by Natanson. LC 78-66733. (Phenomenology: Vol. 3). 192p. 1979. lib. bdg. 20.00 (ISBN 0-8240-9567-7). Garland Pub.

Phantasies of a Love-Thief: The Caurapancasika Attributed to Bilhana. Tr. by Barbara S. Miller. LC 77-122947. (Studies in Oriental Culture: No. 6). 1971. 17.50x (ISBN 0-231-03451-2). Columbia U Pr.

Phantasmagoria: Tales of Fantasy & the Supernatural. Ed. by Jane Mobley. LC 76-52007. 1977. pap. 3.50 (ISBN 0-385-12329-9, Anch). Doubleday.

Phantasms of the Living, 2 Vols. Edmund Gurney. LC 71-119868. (Hist. of Psych. Ser.). 1970. Repr. of 1886 ed. Set. 120.00x set (ISBN 0-8201-1075-2). Schol Facsimiles.

Phantom Conspiracy. Michael Barak. LC 80-13591. 324p. 1980. 11.95 (ISBN 0-688-03689-9). Morrow.

Phantom Cyclist & Other Ghost Stories. Ruth Ainsworth. (gr. 4-7). 1977. pap. 1.25 (ISBN 0-590-10311-3, Schol Pap). Schol Bk Serv.

Phantom Detective. Ed. by Robert Weinberg. LC 80-8668. 80p. 1980. Repr. of 1979 ed. lib. bdg. 11.95 (ISBN 0-89370-085-1); pap. 5.95 (ISBN 0-89370-084-3). Borgo Pr.

Phantom Fisherboy. Ruth Ainsworth. LC 79-92493. (Illus.). 168p. (gr. 1-5). 1980. 7.95 (ISBN 0-233-96569-6). Andre Deutsch.

Phantom Lady. Carter Brown. (Orig.). 1980. pap. 1.50 (ISBN 0-505-51516-4). Tower Bks.

Phantom Limb Phenomenon - A Medical, Folkloric, & Historical Study: Texts & Translations of 10th to 20th Century Miracle Accounts. Douglas B. Price & Neil J. Twombly. Tr. by Mary C Osborne et al. 526p. 1979. pap. text ed. 6.95 (ISBN 0-87840-168-7). Georgetown U Pr.

Phantom of Edgewater Hall. W. Ross. 1980. 5.95 (ISBN 0-686-59799-0, Avalon). Bouregy.

Phantom of the Card Table. Eddie McGuire. (Gambler's Book Shelf Ser.). 1969. pap. 2.95 (ISBN 0-89650-512-X). Gamblers.

Phantom of the Open Hearth. Jean Shepherd. LC 77-76280. 1978. pap. 4.95 o.p. (ISBN 0-385-12976-9, Dolp). Doubleday.

Phantom of the Opera. David Bischoff. (gr. 7 up). 1977. pap. 1.25 (ISBN 0-590-10312-1, Schol Pap). Schol Bk Serv.

Phantom, Son of the Gray Ghost. Clarence W. Anderson. LC 69-18233. (Illus.). (gr. 4-6). 1969. 6.95g (ISBN 0-02-701350-2). Macmillan.

Phantom Wires. Arthur Stringer. 1976. lib. bdg. 14.35x (ISBN 0-89968-120-4). Lightyear.

Pharaohs of Ancient Egypt. Elizabeth Payne. LC 80-21392. (Landmark Bks.). (Illus.). 192p. (gr. 5-9). 1981. pap. 2.95 (ISBN 0-394-84699-0). Random.

Pharisee Among Philistines: The Diary of Judge Matthew P. Deady, 1871-1892, 2 vols. Matthew P. Deady. Intro. by Malcolm Clark, Jr. LC 74-75363. (Illus.). 712p. 1975. 27.95 (ISBN 0-87595-046-9); deluxe ed. 30.00 (ISBN 0-87595-080-9); pap. 21.95 (ISBN 0-87595-080-9). Oreg Hist Soc.

Pharmaceutical Calculations. 7th ed. Mitchell J. Stoklosa & Howard C. Ansel. LC 80-10333. (Illus.). 385p. 1980. text ed. 15.00 (ISBN 0-8121-0725-X). Lea & Febiger.

Pharmaceutical Calculations. 2nd ed. Joel L. Zatz. LC 80-23382. 375p. 1981. 15.00 (ISBN 0-471-07757-7, Pub. by Wiley-Interscience). Wiley.

Pharmaceutical Codex. 11th ed. Ed. by Pharmaceutical Society of Great Britain. 1125p. 1979. 68.00 (ISBN 0-85369-129-0, Pub. by Pharmaceutical). Rittenhouse.

Pharmaceutical Dictionary & Reference for Prescription Drugs. David Mason & Fran Dyller. LC 80-82854. (Illus.). 256p. 1981. pap. 3.50 (ISBN 0-87216-783-6). Playboy Pbks.

Pharmaceutical Dosage Forms: Tablets, Vol. 1. Ed. by H. Lieberman & L. Lachman. 536p. 1980. 59.75 (ISBN 0-8247-6918-X). Dekker.

Pharmaceutical Handbook. 19th ed. Ed. by Pharmaceutical Society of Great Britain. 800p. 1980. 35.00 (ISBN 0-85369-130-4, Pub. by Pharmaceutical). Rittenhouse.

Pharmaceutical Industry: Economics, Performance & Government Regulation. Ed. by Cotton M. Lindsay. LC 77-27062. 1978. 17.50 (ISBN 0-471-04077-0, Pub. by Wiley Medical). Wiley.

Pharmaceutical Services in the Long Term Care Facility. 57th ed. 1975. 3.00 (ISBN 0-917330-01-3). Am Pharm Assn.

Pharmaceuticals & Health Policy: An International Perspective on Provision & Control. Ed. by Blum et al. 387p. 1981. text ed. 38.00x (ISBN 0-8419-0682-3). Holmes & Meier.

Pharmaceuticals & Health Policy: International Perspectives on Provision & Control of Medicine. Richard Blum et al. 1981. write for info. (ISBN 0-312-60402-5). St Martin.

Pharmaceuticals for Developing Countries. Institute of Medicine. 1979. pap. 13.50 (ISBN 0-309-02891-4). Natl Acad Pr.

Pharmacist & the Law. Steven Strauss. 135p. 1980. softcover 9.95 (ISBN 0-683-08008-3). Williams & Wilkins.

Pharmacist's Guide to Liability. R. F. Steeves. 1974. pap. 3.50 (ISBN 0-87489-057-8). Med Economics.

Pharmacokinetics 1981. Ed. by H. Schoenfeld. (Antibiotics & Chemotherapy Ser.: Vol. 31). (Illus.). 200p. 1981. 72.00 (ISBN 3-8055-2448-X). S Karger.

Pharmacologic Basis of Patient Care. 4th ed. Mary K. Asperheim & Laurel A. Eisenhauer. (Illus.). 624p. 1981. text ed. write for info. (ISBN 0-7216-1438-8). Saunders.

Pharmacological & Biochemical Properties of Drug Substances. Ed. by Morton E. Goldberg. LC 77-88184. 30.00 (ISBN 0-917330-17-X). Am Pharm Assn.

Pharmacological & Chemical Synonyms. E. E. Marler. LC 73-161638. 1976. 87.50x (ISBN 0-8002-1789-6). Intl Pubns Serv.

Pharmacological & Therapeutic Aspects of Hypertension. Austin E. Doyle. LC 78-27898. 1980. Vol. 1, 224p. 64.95 (ISBN 0-8493-5385-8); Vol. 2, 256p. 66.95 (ISBN 0-8493-5386-6). CRC Pr.

Pharmacological Basis of Patient Care. 3rd ed. Mary K. Asperheim & Laurel A. Eisenhauer. LC 76-28937. (Illus.). 1977. text ed. 15.00 (ISBN 0-7216-1437-X). Saunders.

Pharmacological Control of Heart & Circulation: Proceedings of the Third Congress of the Hungarian Pharmacological Society, Budapest, 1979. Ed. by. Tardos et al. LC 80-41281. (Advances in Pharmacological Research & Practice Ser.: Vol. I). 445p. 1981. 84.00 (ISBN 0-08-026386-0). Pergamon.

Pharmacological Methods in Toxicology. Ed. by G. Zbinden & F. Gross. 1979. text ed. 160.00 (ISBN 0-08-024900-0); pap. text ed. 80.00 (ISBN 0-08-021544-0). Pergamon.

Pharmacological Modulation of Steroid Action. Ed. by E. Genazzani et al. 1980. text ed. 32.00 (ISBN 0-89004-373-6). Raven.

Pharmacological Testing in a Correctional Institution. S. H. Wells et al. 76p. 1975. 11.75 (ISBN 0-398-03202-5). C C Thomas.

Pharmacology. 3rd ed. Maurice B. Feinstein & Harriet Levine. (Nursing Examination Review Bk.: Vol. 6). 1974. spiral bdg. 6.00 (ISBN 0-87488-506-X). Med Exam.

Pharmacology. 2nd ed. Ed. by Robert E. Humphreys et al. LC 79-83721. (Basic Sciences PreTest Self-Assessment & Review Ser.). (Illus.). 1980. 9.95 (ISBN 0-07-050965-4). McGraw-Pretest.

Pharmacology: A Comprehensive Guide to Drug Therapy. Sandra Wardell. 1979. text ed. 12.95 (ISBN 0-8359-5542-7). Reston.

Pharmacology: An Introduction Text. 5th ed. Mary K. Asperheim. (Illus.). 272p. 1981. text ed. 10.50 (ISBN 0-7216-1446-9). Saunders.

Pharmacology: An Introduction to Drugs. Michael C. Gerald. (Illus.). 576p. 1974. 18.95 (ISBN 0-13-662080-9). P-H.

Pharmacology: An Introduction to Drugs. Michael C. Gerald. (Illus.). 720p. 1981. 19.95 (ISBN 0-13-662098-1). P-H.

Pharmacology & Therapeutics for Dentistry. Enid A. Neidle. LC 80-10522. (Illus.). 736p. 1980. text ed. 29.50 (ISBN 0-8016-3635-3). Mosby.

Pharmacology & Toxicology of Naturally Occurring Toxins, 2 vols. Ed. by H. Raskova. LC 77-130797. 1972. Vol. 1. 60.00 (ISBN 0-08-016319-X); Vol. 2. 52.00 (ISBN 0-08-016798-5); Set. 81.00 (ISBN 0-08-016797-7). Pergamon.

Pharmacology: Drug Actions & Reactions. 2nd ed. Ruth R. Levine. (Illus.). 1978. 18.95 (ISBN 0-316-52226-0); pap. 12.95 (ISBN 0-316-52227-9). Little.

Pharmacology: Drugs Affecting Behavior. Conan Kornetsky. LC 76-6062. 1976. 25.95 (ISBN 0-471-50410-6, Pub. by Wiley-Interscience). Wiley.

Pharmacology for Dental Students & Practioners. Thomas J. Pallasch. LC 79-16786. (Illus.). 458p. 1980. text ed. 27.00 (ISBN 0-8121-0689-X). Lea & Febiger.

Pharmacology for Respiratory Therapists. 2nd ed. Hugh S. Mathewson. (Illus.). 105p. 1981. pap. text ed. 10.95 (ISBN 0-8016-3161-0). Mosby.

Pharmacology in Critical Care. Joyce B. Comer. Ed. by R. Craig Percy. (Fleschner Series in Critical Care Nursings). (Illus.). 175p. (Orig.). 1981. pap. text ed. 9.95 (ISBN 0-937878-03-0). Fleschner.

Pharmacology in Nursing. 14th ed. Betty S. Bergersen. LC 66-10935. (Illus.). 1979. text ed. 22.95 (ISBN 0-8016-0632-2). Mosby.

Pharmacology Learning Guide. Mildred F. Marion et al. (Illus.). 100p. 1981. pap. text ed. 7.95 (ISBN 0-8016-3109-2). Mosby.

Pharmacology of Adrenal Cortical Hormones. Ed. by Gordon N. Gill. LC 78-40135. 1978. text ed. 55.00 (ISBN 0-08-019619-5). Pergamon.

Pharmacology of Antiarrhythmic Agents. Ed. by L. Szekeres. (Intermnational Encyclopedia of Pharmacology & Therapeutics Ser.: Section 105). (Illus.). 328p. 1980. 70.00 (ISBN 0-08-025897-2). Pergamon.

Pharmacology of Antihypertensive Drugs. Ed. by Alexander Scriabine. 1980. text ed. 39.50 (ISBN 0-89004-329-9). Raven.

Pharmacology of Central Synapses. V. V. Zakusov. (Illus.). 1980. 48.00 (ISBN 0-08-020549-6). Pergamon.

Pharmacology of Cerebral Circulation. Ed. by Amilcare Carpi. LC 70-182263. 370p. 1972. text ed. 110.00 (ISBN 0-08-016209-6). Pergamon.

Pharmacology of Ganglionic Transmission. Ed. by D. A. Kharkevich. LC 79-9406. (Handbook of Experimental Pharmacology: Vol. 53). (Illus.). 1980. 134.75 (ISBN 0-387-09592-6). Springer-Verlag.

Pharmacology of Gastrointestinal Secretion. Ed. by Pamela Holton & N. Emmelin. 700p. 1974. Set. 125.00 (ISBN 0-08-016552-4). Pergamon.

Pharmacology of Hearing: Experimental & Clinical Bases. R. Don Brown & Ernest A. Daigneault. 360p. 1980. 45.00 (ISBN 0-471-05074-1, Pub. by Wiley-Interscience). Wiley.

Pharmacology of Intestinal Absorption: Gastrointestinal Absorption of Drugs. Ed. by W. Forth & W. Rummel. 1976. text ed. 140.00 (ISBN 0-08-016210-X). Pergamon.

Pharmacology of Lipid Transport & Atherosclerotic Processes. Ed. by E. J. Masoro. 1974. text ed. 105.00 (ISBN 0-08-017762-X). Pergamon.

Pharmacology of Marihuana, 2 vols. Ed. by Monique C. Braude & Stephen Szara. LC 75-14562. (National Institute on Drug Abuse Monograph). 901p. 1976. Set. 68.50 (ISBN 0-89004-067-2). Raven.

Pharmacology of Pain: Proceedings - Vol. 9. Ed. by R. K. Lim. 1968. 27.25 o.p. (ISBN 0-08-012374-0). Pergamon.

Pharmacology of Reproduction, Vol. 2. Ed. by E. Diczfalusy. LC 67-19416. 1968. 32.00 (ISBN 0-08-012368-6). Pergamon.

Pharmacology of Respiratory Care. Bruce E. Lehnert & E. Neil Schachter. LC 79-28446. (Illus.). 1980. pap. text ed. 13.95 (ISBN 0-8016-2921-7). Mosby.

Pharmacology of Steroid Contraceptive Drugs. Ed. by S. Garattini & H. W. Berendes. LC 77-6100. (Monographs of the Mario Negri Institute for Pharmacological Research). 1977. 35.00 (ISBN 0-89004-187-3). Raven.

Pharmacology of Synapses. J. W. Phillis. 376p. 1970. 55.00 (ISBN 0-08-015558-8). Pergamon.

Pharmacology Review. 4th ed. Robert A. Woodbury et al. 1981. pap. 8.50 (ISBN 0-87488-205-2). Med Exam.

Pharmacopoeia for Chiropodists. 8th ed. J. N. Le Rossignol & C. B. Holliday. 1971. 5.95 o.p. (ISBN 0-571-04723-9, Pub. by Faber & Faber). Merrimack Bk Serv.

Pharmacotherapy in Otolaryngology. W. Saunders & R. Gardier. LC 76-1858. (Illus.). 1976. 19.50 o.p. (ISBN 0-8016-4310-4). Mosby.

Pharmacy: A Profession in Search of a Role. Jack Robbins. LC 79-90142. (Illus.). 164p. 1980. 14.95 (ISBN 0-686-65738-1). Technomic.

Pharmacy & the Law. Ed. by Carl DeMarco. LC 75-34698. 412p. 1975. 27.50 (ISBN 0-912862-16-5). Aspen Systems.

Pharmacy: Career Planning & Professional Opportunities. Ed. by T. D. Rucker. (Illus.). 360p. 1981. pap. write for info. (ISBN 0-914904-52-3). Health Admin Pr.

Pharmacy Computer Handbook. Business Systems Research Group. 141p. 1980. 29.95 (ISBN 0-9603584-1-2). Busn Systems Res.

Pharmacy, Drugs & Medical Care. 3rd ed. Mickey C. Smith & David A. Knapp. 345p. 1981. write for info. softcover (7761-9). Williams & Wilkins.

Pharmacy Examination Review Book Vol. 1. 7th ed. Ed. by Robert J. Gerraughty. 1979. pap. 9.50 (ISBN 0-87488-421-7). Med Exam.

Pharmacy in Health Care & Institutional Systems. Pedro J. Lecca & C. Patrick Tharp. LC 77-27655. (Illus.). 1978. text ed. 17.95 (ISBN 0-8016-2904-7). Mosby.

Pharmacy Law Digest: 1980-1981 Edition. rev. ed. Eugene L. Kaluzny. LC 72-115322. 1980. loose-leaf 34.95 (ISBN 0-915712-10-5). Douglas-McKay.

Pharmacy Practice. 2nd ed. A. Wertheimer. 1981. 24.50 (ISBN 0-8391-0801-X). Univ Park.

Pharmacy Review. Walter Singer et al. LC 74-80957. (Arco Medical Review Ser.). 288p. 1976. pap. 9.00 o.p. (ISBN 0-668-03611-7). Arco.

Pharsamond; or, the New Knight-Errant, 1750, 2 vols. in 1. Pierre Marivaux. LC 74-17039. (Novel in England, 1700-1775 Ser). 1974. lib. bdg. 50.00 (ISBN 0-8240-1129-5). Garland Pub.

Phase Blue. rev. ed. James B. Hogins & Robert E. Yarber. LC 73-87858. (Illus.). 464p. 1974. pap. text ed. 8.95 (ISBN 0-574-18370-1, 13-1370); instr's guide avail. (ISBN 0-574-18371-X, 13-1371); student guide 3.95 (ISBN 0-574-18395-7, 13-1395); instructor's guide 2.50 (ISBN 0-574-18372-8, 13-1372). SRA.

Phase Diagrams: Materials Science & Technology. Ed. by Allen Alper. Incl. Part 1. Theory, Principles & Techniques of Phase Diagrams. 1970. 51.50 (ISBN 0-12-053201-8); Part 2. Use of Phase Diagrams in Metals, Refractories, Ceramics, Glass & Electronic Materials. 1970. 51.50 (ISBN 0-12-053202-6); Part 3. Use of Phase Diagrams in Electronic Materials & Glass Technology. 1970. 51.50 (ISBN 0-12-053203-4); Part 4. Use of Phase Diagrams in Technical Materials. 1976. 49.00 (ISBN 0-12-053204-2). (Refractory Materials Ser: Vol. 6). Acad Pr.

Phase Diagrams: Materials Science & Technology Vol. 5: Crystal Chemistry, Stoichiometry, Spinodal Decomposition, Properties of Inorganic Phases. Ed. by Allan M. Alper. (Refractory Materials Ser.: Vol. 6-V). 1978. 43.50 (ISBN 0-12-053205-0). Acad Pr.

Phase Equilibria & Fluid Properties in the Chemical Industry: Proceedings, Pts. 1 & 2. European Federation of Chemical Engineering, 2nd Intl. Conference on Phase Equilibria & Fluid Properties in the Chemical Industry, Berlin, 1980. (EFCE Publication Ser.: No. 11). 1012p. 1980. text ed. 82.50x (ISBN 3-921567-35-1, Pub. by Dechema Germany). Scholium Intl.

Phase Transitions & Critical Phenomena. Ed. by C. Domb & M. Green. Vol. 1. 1973. 72.00 (ISBN 0-12-220301-1); Vol. 2. 1972. 74.00 (ISBN 0-12-220302-X); Vol. 5a. 1976. 59.00 (ISBN 0-12-220305-4); Vol. 5B. 1976. 56.00 (ISBN 0-12-220351-8); Vol. 6. 1977. 79.50 (ISBN 0-12-220306-2). Acad Pr.

Phase Transitions & Their Applications in Materials Science. Ed. by H. K. Henisch et al. LC 73-14411. 300p. 1974. text ed. 38.00 (ISBN 0-08-017955-X). Pergamon.

Phase Transitions in Surface Films. Ed. by J. G. Dash & J. Ruvalds. (NATO Advanced Studies Institutes Ser., Series B- Physical Sciences: Vol. 51). 375p. 1980. 42.50 (ISBN 0-306-40348-X). Plenum Pub.

Phaselock Loops for DC Motor Control. Dana F. Geiger. 140p. 1981. 22.00 (Pub. by Wiley-Interscience). Wiley.

Phases of Faith. Francis Newman. (Victorian Library). 1970. Repr. of 1860 ed. text ed. 5.75x (ISBN 0-391-00109-4, Leicester). Humanities.

Ph.D's & the Academic Labor Market. Allan M. Cartter. LC 75-38700. (Carnegie Commission on Higher Education Ser). 1976. 15.95 o.p. (ISBN 0-07-010132-9, P&RB). McGraw.

Pheasant Run Pubns. James M. Torrey. LC 77-4567. (Illus.). 1977. 15.95 (ISBN 0-669-01372-2). Pheasant Run.

Pheasants: Their Breeding & Management. K. C. Howman. (Illus.). 126p. 1980. 9.95 (ISBN 0-903264-35-8, 4903-0, Pub. by K & R Bks England). Arco.

Phedre De Racine: Pour une Semiotique De la Representation Classique. new ed. D. Kaisergruber et al. (Collection L Ser.). 288p. (Orig., Fr.). 1972. pap. 13.95 (ISBN 2-03-036001-5). Larousse.

Phelon's Discount Jobbing 1981-1982. 9th ed. Ed. by Phelon, Sheldon & Marsar Inc. 1980. 70.00 (ISBN 0-686-27107-6). P S & M Inc.

Phenolic Compounds & Metabolic Regulation. Ed. by Bernard J. Finkle & Victor C. Runeckles. LC 66-29065. 157p. 1967. 19.50 (ISBN 0-306-50023-X, Plenum Pr). Plenum Pub.

Phenomenological Sense of John Dewey: Habit & Meaning. Victor Kestenbaum. 1977. text ed. 8.50x (ISBN 0-391-00668-1). Humanities.

Phenomenological Sociology: Issues & Applications. Ed. by George Psathas. LC 73-2805. 384p. 1973. 20.95 (ISBN 0-471-70152-1, Pub. by Wiley-Interscience). Wiley.

Phenomenology & Education: Self-Consciousness & Its Development. Ed. by Bernard Curtis & Wolfe Mays. 150p. 1978. pap. 9.95 (ISBN 0-416-70960-5, 6368). Methuen Inc.

Phenomenology & Existentialism. Ed. by Robert C. Solomon. LC 79-66420. 1979. pap. text ed. 10.50 (ISBN 0-8191-0826-X). U Pr of Amer.

Phenomenology & Philisophical Understanding. Ed. by E. Pivcevic. LC 74-19533. 304p. 1975. 38.50 (ISBN 0-521-20637-5); pap. 11.50x (ISBN 0-521-09914-5). Cambridge U Pr.

Phenomenology & Religion: Structures of the Christian Institution. Henry Dumery. Tr. by Paul Barrett. (Hermeneutics Series: Studies in the History of Religion). 1975. 14.00x (ISBN 0-520-02714-0). U of Cal Pr.

Phenomenology & the Crisis of Philosophy. Edmund Husserl. Tr. by Quentin Lauer. (Orig.). pap. 4.95x (ISBN 0-06-131170-7, TB1170, Torch). Har-Row.

Phenomenology & the Foundations of the Sciences. Edmund Husserl. Tr. by Ted Klein & William Pohl. (Edmund Husserl, Collected Works: Vol. 1). 152p. 1980. lib. bdg. 29.00 (ISBN 90-247-2093-1). Kluwer Boston.

Phenomenology & the Science of Behaviour. George Thines. 1977. text ed. 30.00x (ISBN 0-04-121018-2). Allen Unwin.

Phenomenology & the Social World: The Philosophy of Merleau-Ponty & Its Relation to the Social Sciences. Laurie Spurling. (International Library of Sociology Ser.). 1978. 22.50x (ISBN 0-7100-8712-8). Routledge & Kegan.

Phenomenology in Modern African Studies, No. 5. Sunday O. Anozie et al. (Studies in African Semiotics). 1981. 25.00 (ISBN 0-914970-69-0); pap. text ed. 12.95 (ISBN 0-914970-70-4). Conch Mag.

Phenomenology of Mind. G. W. Hegel. Tr. by J. B. Baillie. 1967. pap. 8.95x (ISBN 0-06-131303-3, TB 1303, Torch). Har-Row.

Phenomenology of Perception. Maurice Merleau-Ponty. Tr. by Colin Smith. 1962. text ed. 26.00x (ISBN 0-391-00070-5). Humanities.

Phenomenology, Role, & Reason: Essays on the Coherence & Deformation of Social Reality. Maurice Natanson. (Amer. Lec. in Philosophy Ser.). 368p. 1974. 27.95 (ISBN 0-398-02904-0). C C Thomas.

Phenomenon of Architecture in Cultures in Change. D. Oakley. 1971. 32.00 (ISBN 0-08-016075-1). Pergamon.

Phenomenon of Control of Growth in Neoplastic & Differentiative Systems. Ed. by G. V. Sherbet. (Illus.). xii, 184p. 1981. 58.75 (ISBN 3-8055-2305-X). S Karger.

Phenomenon of Man. Pierre Teilhard De Chardin. pap. 4.95 (ISBN 0-06-090495-X, CN495, CN). Har-Row.

Phenomenon of Obedience. Michael Esses. LC 73-92248. 1974. pap. 4.95 (ISBN 0-88270-085-5). Logos.

Phenomenon of Religion. Ninian Smart. Ed. by John Hick. (Philosophy of Religion Ser). 168p. 1973. 8.95 (ISBN 0-8164-1102-6). Crossroad NY.

Phenomenon of Science. Valentin F. Turchin. Tr. by Brand Frentz from Russian. LC 77-4330. 1977. 20.00x (ISBN 0-231-03983-2). Columbia U Pr.

Phenomenon of Sociology: A Reader in the Sociology of Sociology. Ed. by Edward A. Tiryakian. LC 76-130794. 1981. 24.50x (ISBN 0-89197-882-8); pap. text ed. 12.95x (ISBN 0-89197-339-7). Irvington.

Phenothiazines & Structurally Related Drugs. Ed. by Irene S. Forrest et al. LC 73-88571. (Advances in Biochemical Psychopharmacology Ser.: Vol. 9). 840p. 1974. 61.50 (ISBN 0-911216-61-8). Raven.

Phenoxyalkanoic Herbicides: Volume 1 Chemistry, Analysis & Environmental Pollution. Shane S. Que Hee & Ronald G. Sutherland. 272p. 1981. 62.95 (ISBN 0-8493-5851-5). CRC Pr.

Phenytoin-Induced Teratology & Gingival Pathology. Ed. by Thomas Hassell et al. 252p. 1980. text ed. 27.00 (ISBN 0-89004-412-0). Raven.

Phil Donahue: A Man for All Women. Joyce Wadler. (Illus., Orig.). 1980. pap. 2.50 (ISBN 0-515-05434-8). Jove Pubns.

Phil Drabble's Country Scene. Phil Drabble. 1974. 8.95 (ISBN 0-7207-0779-X, Pub. by Michael Joseph). Merrimack Bk Serv.

Phil Esposito: The Big Bruin. Julian May. LC 74-31950. (Sports Close-up Ser.). (gr. 3-9). 1975. PLB 5.95 o.p. (ISBN 0-913940-13-5); pap. 2.50 o.p. (ISBN 0-913940-20-8). Crestwood Hse.

Phil Swing & Boulder Dam. Beverley B. Moeller. LC 71-633550. (Illus.). 1971. 18.50x (ISBN 0-520-01932-6). U of Cal Pr.

Philadelphia: A Guide to the Nation's Birthplace. LC 39-4271. 1939. 49.00 (ISBN 0-403-02204-5). Somerset Pub.

Philadelphia & Erie Railroad: Its Place in American Economic History. Homer T. Rosenberger. LC 74-75110. (Illus.). 748p. 1975. lib. bdg. 22.50 (ISBN 0-914932-02-0). Rose Hill.

Philadelphia-Baltimore Trade Rivalry: 1780-1860. James W. Livingood. LC 47-29. 195p. 1947. 5.00 (ISBN 0-911124-35-7). Pa Hist & Mus.

Philadelphia Experiment. William Moore & Charles Berlitz. 224p. 1980. pap. 2.50 (ISBN 0-449-24280-3, Crest). Fawcett.

Philadelphia Georgian: The City House of Samuel Powel & Some of Its 18th-Century Neighbors. George B. Tatum. LC 75-39905. (Illus.). 1976. 22.50x (ISBN 0-8195-4095-1, Pub. by Wesleyan U Pr); pap. 10.95 (ISBN 0-8195-6044-8). Columbia U Pr.

Philadelphia Magazines & Their Contributors 1741-1850. Albert H. Smyth. LC 77-140401. 1970. Repr. of 1892 ed. 24.00 (ISBN 0-8103-3596-4). Gale.

Philadelphia: Patricians & Philistines 1900-1950. John Lukacs. (Illus.). 1981. 15.00 (ISBN 0-374-23161-3). FS&G.

Philadelphia: Port of History 1609-1837. Charles L. Chandler et al. (Illus.). 82p. 1976. pap. 3.25 (ISBN 0-913346-02-0). Phila Maritime Mus.

Philadelphia: Seventeen Seventy-Six to Two Thousand Seventy-Six, a Three Hundred Year View. Ed. by Dennis J. Clark. (Interdisciplinary Urban Ser.). 130p. 1975. 11.50 (ISBN 0-8046-9141-X, Natl U). Kennikat.

Philadelphia Treasures in Bronze & Stone. Fairmont Park Associates. LC 75-36536. (Illus.). 192p. 1976. pap. 4.95 o.s.i. (ISBN 0-8027-7100-9). Walker & Co.

Philadelphia: Work, Space, Family & Group Experience in the Nineteenth Century. Essays Toward an Interdisciplinary History of the City. Ed. by Theodore Hershberg. (Illus.). 608p. 1981. 29.95 (ISBN 0-19-502752-3). Oxford U Pr.

Philadelphia: Work, Space, Family & Group Experience in the Nineteenth Century. Essays Toward an Interdisciplinary History of the City. Ed. by Theodore Hershberg. (Illus.). 608p. 1981. pap. 8.95 (ISBN 0-19-502753-1, 619, GB). Oxford U Pr.

Philander Priestley Claxton: Crusader for Public Education. Charles L. Lewis. 1948. 10.00x o.p. (ISBN 0-87049-002-8). U of Tenn Pr.

Philanderer. George B. Shaw. Ed. by Julius Novick. LC 79-56700. (Bernard Shaw Early Texts: Play Manuscripts in Facsimile). 1981. lib. bdg. 85.00 (ISBN 0-8240-4576-9). Garland Pub.

Philanthropist. Christopher Hampton. 1970. pap. 5.95 o.p. (ISBN 0-571-09520-8, Pub. by Faber & Faber). Merrimack Bk Serv.

Philanthropy in the Seventies: An Anglo-American Discussion. Ed. by John J. Corson & Harry V. Hodson. 128p. 1973. pap. 3.00 (ISBN 0-913456-54-3). Interbk Inc.

Philanthropy in the Shaping of American Higher Education. Gurti & Nash. LC 65-19399. 8.50 (ISBN 0-910294-27-5). Brown Bk.

Philanthropy in Victorian Scotland. Olive Checkland. (Illus.). 1980. text ed. 52.00x (ISBN 0-85976-041-3). Humanities.

Philaster. Francis Beaumont & John Fletcher. Ed. by Dora J. Ashe. LC 75-127980. (Regents Renaissance Drama Ser). xxxii, 152p. 1974. 9.95x (ISBN 0-8032-0291-1); pap. 2.75x (ISBN 0-8032-5290-0, BB 236, Bison). U of Nebr Pr.

Philatelist's Companion. Bill Gunston. (Illus.). 240p. 1975. 8.95 (ISBN 0-7153-6384-0). David & Charles.

Philebus. Plato. Ed. by R. Hackforth. 200p. 1972. 23.95 (ISBN 0-521-08460-1); pap. 6.50x (ISBN 0-521-09704-5). Cambridge U Pr.

Philebus. Plato. Tr. & notes by J. C. Gosling. (Clarendon Plato Ser). 256p. 1975. 15.50x (ISBN 0-19-872044-0); pap. 17.95x (ISBN 0-19-872054-8). Oxford U Pr.

Philip Couston. Ross Feld. LC 79-27425. (Illus.). 152p. 1980. 25.00 (ISBN 0-8076-0962-5); pap. 11.95 (ISBN 0-8076-0962-5). Braziller.

Philip Freneau. Mary W. Bowden. (U. S. Authors Ser.: No. 260). 1976. lib. bdg. 9.95 (ISBN 0-8057-7161-1). Twayne.

Philip Freneau, the Poet of the Revolution. Mary S. Austin. Ed. by Helen K. Vreeland. LC 67-23885. 1968. Repr. of 1901 ed. 15.00 (ISBN 0-8103-3040-7). Gale.

Philip Gilbert Hamerton. 591p. 1980. Repr. of 1896 ed. lib. bdg. 50.00. Telegraph Bks.

Philip Johnson & John Burgee: Architecture. Philip Johnson & John Burgee. LC 79-4786. 1979. 40.00 (ISBN 0-394-50744-4). Random.

Philip Johnson: Processes. Giorgio Ciucci et al. (IAUS Exhibition Catalogues Ser.). (Illus.). 1979. pap. 10.00 (ISBN 0-932628-01-X). IAUS.

Philip Jose Farmer. Mary Brizzi. LC 80-19171. (Starmont Reader's Guide Ser.: No. 3). 80p. 1980. Repr. of 1980 ed. lib. bdg. 9.95x (ISBN 0-89370-034-7). Borgo Pr.

Philip Jose Farmer: The Authorized Bibliography. George Scheetz. 112p. 1981. pap. 11.95 (ISBN 0-933180-16-0). Ellis Pr.

Philip Larkin. Bruce K. Martin. (English Author Ser.: No. 234). 1978. 12.50 (ISBN 0-8057-6705-3). Twayne.

Philip McCracken. Tacoma Art Museum. LC 80-51071. (Illus.). 136p. 1980. 14.95 (ISBN 0-295-95771-9). U of Wash Pr.

Philip of Macedon. Manolis Andronicos et al. Ed. by Miltiades B. Hatzopoulos & Louisa D. Loukopoulos. (Illus.). 254p. 1980. 45.00 (ISBN 0-89241-330-1). Caratzas Bros.

Philip of Macedon. George Cawkwell. (Illus.). 1978. 19.95 (ISBN 0-686-08751-8, Pub. by Faber & Faber). Merrimack Bk Serv.

Philip Paternoster: A Tractarian Love Story, 1858. Charles M. Davies. Ed. by Robert L. Wolff. LC 75-477. (Victorian Fiction Ser.). 1975. lib. bdg. 66.00 (ISBN 0-8240-1555-X). Garland Pub.

Philip Roth. Judith Jones & Guinevera Nance. LC 80-53701. (Modern Literature Ser.). 160p. 1981. 9.95 (ISBN 0-8044-2438-1); pap. 4.95 (ISBN 0-8044-6320-4). Ungar.

Philip Roth. Bernard F. Rodgers, Jr. (United States Authors Ser.: No. 318). 1978. 9.95 (ISBN 0-8057-7249-9). Twayne.

Philip Roth: A Bibliography. Bernard F. Rodgers, Jr. LC 74-16224. (Author Bibliographies Ser.: No. 19). 1974. 10.00 (ISBN 0-8108-0754-8). Scarecrow.
Philip Roth Reader. Philip Roth. 1980. 17.50 (ISBN 0-374-23170-2); pap. 7.95 (ISBN 0-374-51604-9). FS&G.
Philip Wylie. Truman F. Keefer. (US. Authors Ser.). 1977. lib. bdg. 10.95 (ISBN 0-8057-7187-5). Twayne.
Philip Wylie: The Man & His Work. Robert H. Barshay. LC 79-63682. 1979. pap. text ed. 7.50 (ISBN 0-8191-0733-6). U Pr of Amer.
Philippe Pinel, Unchainer of the Insane. Bernard Mackler. LC 68-11330. (Biography Ser). (gr. 7 up). 1969. PLB 6.90 (ISBN 0-531-00915-7). Watts.
Philippians, Notes. H. A. Ironside. Date not set. 4.95 (ISBN 0-87213-381-8). Loizeaux.
Philippians. Irving L. Jensen. (Bible Self-Study Ser). 80p. 1973. pap. 2.25 (ISBN 0-8024-1051-0). Moody.
Philippians: A Study Commentary. Howard F. Vos. (Study Guide Commentary Ser.). 96p. (Orig.). 1980. pap. 2.95 (ISBN 0-310-33863-8). Zondervan.
Philippians: An Expositional Commentary. James M. Boice. LC 79-146573. 1971. 12.95 (ISBN 0-310-21500-5). Zondervan.
Philippians & Philemon. Mary A. Getty. (New Testament Message Ser.). 9.95 (ISBN 0-89453-137-9); pap. 4.95 (ISBN 0-89453-202-2). M Glazier.
Philippians & Philemon. M. R. Vincent. LC 4-1629. (International Critical Commentary Ser.). 248p. Repr. of 1904 ed. text ed. 17.50x (ISBN 0-567-05031-9). Attic Pr.
Philippians: Joy & Peace. John F. Walvoord. (Everyman's Bible Commentary). 1971. pap. 2.95 (ISBN 0-8024-2050-8). Moody.
Philippians: Joy in Jesus. Preston Taylor. 1976. pap. 1.75 (ISBN 0-8024-6507-2). Moody.
Philippians, the Epistle of Christian Joy. Keith L. Brooks. (Teach Yourself the Bible Ser). 1964. pap. 1.75 (ISBN 0-8024-6506-4). Moody.
Philippine-American Chamber of Commerce Special Report. 10.00 o.p. (ISBN 0-686-51339-8). Am Sports Sales.
Philippine Independence: Motives, Problems & Prospects. Grayson L. Kirk. LC 72-2377. (FDR & the Era of the New Deal Ser.). 278p. 1974. Repr. of 1936 ed. lib. bdg. 29.50 (ISBN 0-306-70486-2). Da Capo.
Philippine Insurrection, 1899-1902: America's Only Try for an Overseas Empire. John E. Walsh. LC 72-8817. (Focus Bks.). (Illus.). 72p. (gr. 7 up). 1973. PLB 6.45 (ISBN 0-531-02462-8). Watts.
Philippine Island World: A Physical, Cultural & Regional Geography. Frederick L. Wernstedt & Joseph E. Spencer. (California Library Reprint Ser.). 1978. 38.50x (ISBN 0-520-03513-5). U of Cal Pr.
Philippines. Denise Adler. 1980. pap. 1.95 (ISBN 0-8423-4844-1). Tyndale.
Philippines. Richard Z. Chesnoff. LC 77-99197. (Illus.). 1978. 125.00 o.p. (ISBN 0-8109-1458-1). Abrams.
Philippines. Keith Lightfoot. (Nations of the Modern World). 1977. lib. bdg. 19.75x (ISBN 0-89158-735-7). Westview.
Philippines. Raymond Nelson. LC 66-22509. (Nations & Peoples Library). (Illus.). (YA) 1968. 8.50x o.s.i. (ISBN 0-8027-2115-X). Walker & Co.
Philippines. John H. Power & Gerardo P. Sicat. (Organization for Economic Cooperation & Development Industry & Trade in Some Developing Countries Ser). 1971. pap. 9.00x (ISBN 0-19-215337-4). Oxford U Pr.
Philippines. Albert Roland. (Illus.). (gr. 7 up). 1967. 7.95 (ISBN 0-02-777850-9). Macmillan.
Philippines & Southeast Asia. Man M. Kaul. 1978. text ed. 14.50x (ISBN 0-391-01010-7). Humanities.
Philippines in Pictures. Sterling Publishing Company Editors. LC 64-24692. (Visual Geography Ser). (Orig.). (gr. 6 up). pap. 2.95 (ISBN 0-8069-1048-8). Sterling.
Philippines: Public Policy & National Economic Development. Frank H. Golay. 473p. 1968. 25.00x (ISBN 0-8014-0153-4); pap. 5.95 1968 ed. (ISBN 0-8014-9075-8, CP75). Cornell U Pr.
Philips Paper Trade Directory. 1979. 95.00 (ISBN 0-686-27092-4). State Mutual Bk.
Phillips Collection. Horace Pippin. LC 76-52613. (Illus.). 64p. (Orig.). 1981. pap. 10.00 (ISBN 0-295-95818-9, Pub. by Phillips). U of Wash Pr.
Phillips Conveyances. Stanton Phillips. 136p. (Orig.). 1980. pap. 4.66 (ISBN 0-9605268-0-3). A J Phillips.
Phillips Paper Trade Directory 1980. 1979. 82.50x (ISBN 0-510-49010-7). Nichols Pub.
Phillis Wheatley: A Bio-Bibliography. William H. Robinson. (Reference Books Ser.). 1981. 18.00 (ISBN 0-8161-8318-X). G K Hall.
Phillis Wheatley: Negro Slave. Marilyn Jensen. 288p. 1981. PLB 8.95 (ISBN 0-87460-326-9). Lion.
Phillis Wheatley, Negro Slave of John Wheatley. Marilyn Jensen. pap. 9.95. Lion.
Philo of Alexandria: An Introduction. Samuel Sandmel. 1979. 13.95 (ISBN 0-19-502514-8); pap. 5.95 (ISBN 0-19-502515-6). Oxford U Pr.
Philobiblon: Of the Advantages of the Love of Books. Richard De Bury. Ed. by Michael Maclagan. Tr. by E. C. Thomas. Repr. of 1970 ed. 20.00x o.p. (ISBN 0-631-12620-1, Pub. by Basil Blackwell). Biblio Dist.
Philocalia of Origen. Origen. Rev. by & intro. by J. Armitage Robinson. LC 80-2359. 1981. Repr. of 1893 ed. 39.50 (ISBN 0-404-18911-3). AMS Pr.
Philoctetes. Sophocles. Ed. by Webster. 1970. pap. 9.95x (ISBN 0-521-09890-4). Cambridge U Pr.
Philology of the Gospels. Friedrich Blass. 1969. Repr. of 1898 ed. text ed. 28.50x (ISBN 90-6032-391-2). Humanities.
Philosopher & Music. Julius Portnoy. (Music Reprint Ser.: 1980). 1980. Repr. of 1954 ed. lib. bdg. 25.00 (ISBN 0-306-76006-1). Da Capo.
Philosopher at Large: An Intellectual Autobiography. Mortimer J. Adler. LC 77-1383. 1977. 14.95 (ISBN 0-02-500490-5, 50049). Macmillan.
Philosopher in the City: The Moral Dimensions of Urban Politics. Hadley Arkes. LC 80-8536. 496p. 1981. 27.50x (ISBN 0-691-09356-3); pap. 6.95x (ISBN 0-691-02822-2). Princeton U Pr.
Philosophers & Kings: Studies in Leadership. Ed. by Dankwart A. Rustow. LC 77-7778. (Daedalus Library Ser). 1970. 7.50 o.s.i. (ISBN 0-8076-0540-9); pap. 3.75 (ISBN 0-8076-0539-5). Braziller.
Philosophers & Philosophies. Frederick Copleston. 272p. 1976. Repr. of 1955 ed. 13.50x (ISBN 0-06-491278-7). B&N.
Philosopher's Annual, 1978, Vol. 1. Ed. by David L. Boyer et al. 223p. 1978. 22.50x (ISBN 0-8476-6105-9); pap. 10.95x (ISBN 0-8476-6106-7). Rowman.
Philosopher's Annual 1980, Vol. III. Ed. by David L. Boyer et al. xii, 225p. (Orig.). 1980. lib. bdg. 22.00 (ISBN 0-917930-38-X); pap. text ed. 8.50x (ISBN 0-917930-18-5). Ridgeview.
Philosophers As Educational Reformers: The Influence of Idealism on British Educational Thought & Practice, 1875-1925. Peter Gordon & John White. (International Library of the Philosophy of Education). (Illus.). 1979. 26.00x (ISBN 0-7100-0214-9). Routledge & Kegan.
Philosophers at War. A. R. Hall. LC 79-15724. 1980. 29.95 (ISBN 0-521-22732-1). Cambridge U Pr.
Philosophers of China. Clarence B. Day. LC 61-12618. 1962. pap. 6.00 (ISBN 0-8022-0366-3). Philos Lib.
Philosophers of the Earth: Talking with Ecologists. Anne Chisholm. 1972. 8.95 o.p. (ISBN 0-525-17890-2). Dutton.
Philosopher's Stone. Colin Wilson. 320p. 1974. pap. 1.95 o.s.i. (ISBN 0-446-89442-7). Warner Bks.
Philosophia: Studies in Greek Philosophy, Pt. 1. C. J. De Vogel. (Philosophical Texts & Studies: No. 19). 1970. text ed. 40.50x (ISBN 90-232-0733-5). Humanities.
Philosophic Classics, 2 vols. 2nd ed. Walter Kaufman. Incl. Vol. 1. Thales to Ockham. text ed. 19.50 (ISBN 0-13-662403-0); Vol. 2. Bacon to Kant. text ed. 18.95 (ISBN 0-13-662411-1). LC 68-15350. 1968. text ed. (ISBN 0-685-73716-0). P-H.
Philosophic Inquiry: An Introduction to Philosophy. 2nd ed. L. Beck & R. Holms. 1968. 16.50 (ISBN 0-13-662494-4). P-H.
Philosophic Researches for Advancement of Science & Technology. Georg Schuzy. 1980. 6.95 (ISBN 0-8062-1469-4). Carlton.
Philosophic Systems & Education. Rosen. 1968. pap. text ed. 7.95x (ISBN 0-675-09592-1). Merrill.
Philosophical Alternatives in Education. Gerald L. Gutek. LC 73-76802. 1974. pap. 11.50x (ISBN 0-675-08926-3). Merrill.
Philosophical Analysis & Education. Ed. by Reginald D. Archambault. 1972. text ed. 9.50x (ISBN 0-7100-1021-4); pap. text ed. 3.75x (ISBN 0-391-00239-2). Humanities.
Philosophical & Mathematical Correspondence. Gottlob Frege. Ed. by Brian McGuinness. Tr. by Hans Kaal. LC 79-23199. 1980. lib. bdg. 31.00x (ISBN 0-226-26197-2). U of Chicago Pr.
Philosophical Basis of Medical Practice: Toward a Philosophy & Ethic of the Healing Professions. Edmund D. Pellegrino & David C. Thomasma. (Illus.). 368p. 1981. 19.95x (ISBN 0-19-502790-6). Oxford U Pr.
Philosophical Basis of Medical Practice: Toward a Philosophy & Ethic of the Healing Professions. Edmund D. Pellegrino & David C. Thomasma. (Illus.). 368p. 1981. text ed. 11.95x (ISBN 0-19-502789-2). Oxford U Pr.
Philosophical Dimension of Parapsychology. James Wheatley & Hoyt L. Edge. (Illus.). 520p. 1976. 39.75 (ISBN 0-398-03310-2). C C Thomas.
Philosophical Essays: Discourse on Method; Meditations; Rules for the Direction of the Mind. Rene Descartes. Tr. by Laurence J. Lafleur. LC 63-16951. (Orig.). 1964. 5.50 (ISBN 0-672-60292-X, LLA99). Bobbs.
Philosophical Essays: From Ancient Creed to Technological Man. Hans Jonas. 14.00 (ISBN 0-226-40591-5, Phoen). U of Chicago Pr.
Philosophical Essence of the Oriental World. Georg W. Hegel. (Most Meaningful Classics in World Culture Ser.). 1979. 49.75 (ISBN 0-89266-176-3). Am Classical Coll Pr.
Philosophical Foundations for the Curriculum. Allen Brent. (Unwin Education Books). 1978. text ed. 19.50x (ISBN 0-04-370084-5); pap. text ed. 8.95x (ISBN 0-04-370085-3). Allen Unwin.
Philosophical Foundations of Economic Doctrines. Nicholas Chirovsky & Vincent Mott. 1978. 7.95 (ISBN 0-912598-18-2); pap. 4.50 (ISBN 0-912598-16-6). Florham.
Philosophical Foundations of Education. new ed. Howard Ozmon & Samuel Craver. (Coordinated Teacher Preparation Ser.). 240p. 1976. text ed. 14.95x (ISBN 0-675-08669-8). Merrill.
Philosophical Foundations of Education. 2nd ed. Howard Ozmon & Samuel Craver. (General Education Ser.). 320p. Date not set. text ed. 14.95 (ISBN 0-675-08049-5). Merrill.
Philosophical Foundations of Education. Larry K Whytes. (Illus.). 127p. 1980. deluxe ed. 39.75 (ISBN 0-89266-237-9). Am Classical Coll Pr.
Philosophical Foundations of Guidance. Carleton E. Beck. 1963. pap. text ed. 9.95 (ISBN 0-13-662262-3). P-H.
Philosophical Foundations of the Three Sociologies. Ted Benton. (International Library of Sociology). 1978. pap. 8.95 (ISBN 0-7100-0045-6). Routledge & Kegan.
Philosophical Foundations of the Three Sociologies. Ted Benton. (International Library of Sociology Ser). 1977. 21.00x (ISBN 0-7100-8593-1). Routledge & Kegan.
Philosophical Grammar. Ludwig Wittgenstein. Tr. by A. J. Kenny. 1974. 27.50x (ISBN 0-520-02664-0); pap. 6.95 (ISBN 0-520-03725-1). U of Cal Pr.
Philosophical Issues in Law: Cases & Materials. Kenneth Kipnis. 1977. pap. text ed. 12.95 (ISBN 0-13-662296-8). P-H.
Philosophical Issues in Religious Thought. Geddes MacGregor. LC 78-65851. pap. text ed. 11.50 (ISBN 0-8191-0677-1). U Pr of Amer.
Philosophical Knowledge. Ed. by John B. Brough. LC 80-69505. (Proceedings: Vol. 54). 250p. (Orig.). 1981. pap. 8.00 (ISBN 0-918090-14-8). Am Cath Philo.
Philosophical Law: Authority, Equality, Adjudication, Privacy. Ed. by Richard Bronaugh. (Contributions in Legal Studies: No. 2). 1978. lib. bdg. 19.95 (ISBN 0-8371-9809-7, BPL/). Greenwood.
Philosophical Letters. Francois M. De Voltaire. Tr. by Ernest N. Dilworth. LC 60-53370. 1961. pap. 4.50 (ISBN 0-672-60326-8, LLA124). Bobbs.
Philosophical Papers, 2 vols. H. Putnam. Incl. Vol. 1. Mathematics, Matter & Method. (Illus.). 32.95 (ISBN 0-521-20665-0); Vol. 2. Mind, Language & Reality. 38.50 (ISBN 0-521-20668-5); pap. 12.95x (ISBN 0-521-29551-3). 1975. Cambridge U Pr.
Philosophical Papers: Mathematics, Matter & Methods, Vol. 1. 2nd ed. H. Putnam. LC 75-8315. 1979. 38.50 (ISBN 0-521-22553-1); pap. 11.95 (ISBN 0-521-29550-5). Cambridge U Pr.
Philosophical Papers: Mathematics, Science & Epistemology, Vol. 2. Imre Lakatos. Ed. by J. Worrall & G. Currie. LC 77-14374. 295p. 1980. pap. 13.50 (ISBN 0-521-28030-3). Cambridge U Pr.
Philosophical Papers: The Methodology of Scientific Research Programmes, Vol. 1. Imre Lakatos. Ed. by J. Worrall & G. Currie. LC 77-71415. 258p. 1980. pap. 12.50 (ISBN 0-521-28031-1). Cambridge U Pr.
Philosophical Perspectives: History of Philosophy. Wilfrid Sellars. 1979. lib. bdg. 21.00 (ISBN 0-917930-24-X); pap. text ed. 6.50x (ISBN 0-917930-04-5). Ridgeview.
Philosophical Perspectives: Metaphysics & Epistemology. Wilfrid Sellars. 1979. lib. bdg. 21.00 (ISBN 0-917930-25-8); pap. text ed. 6.50x (ISBN 0-917930-05-3). Ridgeview.
Philosophical Poetry of W. B. Yeats. R. Snukal. LC 72-87440. 240p. 1972. 44.00 (ISBN 0-521-20057-1). Cambridge U Pr.
Philosophical Problems in Physical Science. rev. ed. Herbert Hoerz et al. Ed. by Erwin Marquit. Tr. by Salomea Genin from Ger. (Studies in Marxism: Vol. 7). Orig. Title: Philosophische Probleme der Physik. 1980. 15.95 (ISBN 0-930656-14-8); pap. 8.50 (ISBN 0-930656-13-X). Marxist Educ.
Philosophical, Psychological & Moral Degeneration of the American Pragmatists. Alexander S. Abbot. (Illus.). 114p. 1980. 41.75 (ISBN 0-89266-257-3). Am Classical Coll Pr.
Philosophical Radicals: Nine Studies in Theory & Practice, 1817 to 1841. William Thomas. (Illus.). 506p. 1979. text ed. 45.00x (ISBN 0-19-822490-7). Oxford U Pr.
Philosophical Remarks. Ludwig Wittgenstein. Ed. by Rush Rhees et al. LC 80-14296. 1980. pap. 8.95 (ISBN 0-226-90431-8, P912, Phoen). U of Chicago Pr.
Philosophical Studies in Education: Proceedings. Annual Meeting of the Ohio Valley Philosophy of Educ. Society, August 1979. Ed. by John E. Carter. 1980. write for info. (ISBN 0-686-22976-2). Ind St Univ.
Philosophical Study of Religion. David Freeman. 1976. pap. 4.95 o.p. (ISBN 0-934532-12-5). Presby & Reformed.
Philosophical Style: An Anthology About the Writng & Reading of Philosophy. Berel Lang. LC 79-20424. 1980. 27.95 (ISBN 0-88229-230-7). Nelson-Hall.
Philosophical Subjects: Essays Presented to P. F. Strawson. Ed. by Zak Van Straaten. 304p. 1980. 37.50 (ISBN 0-19-824603-X). Oxford U Pr.
Philosophical Tasks. Graham Bird. 1972. text ed. 7.00x (ISBN 0-09-113250-9, Hutchinson U Lib). Humanities.
Philosophical Theology. James F. Ross. LC 68-17707. 326p. 1980. 17.50 (ISBN 0-915144-67-0); pap. text ed. 9.95 (ISBN 0-915144-68-9). Hackett Pub.
Philosophical Theology. James F. Ross. 1969. text ed. 24.50x (ISBN 0-8290-0335-5). Irvington.
Philosophical Works, 5 vols. Henry Viscount Bolingbroke. Ed. by Rene Wellek. LC 75-11198. (British Philosophers & Theologians of the 17th & 18th Centuries: Vol. 5). 1976. Repr. of 1777 ed. Set. lib. bdg. 165.00 (ISBN 0-8240-1754-4); lib. bdg. 42.00 ea. Garland Pub.
Philosophical Works, 2 Vols. Rene Descartes. Ed. by E. S. Haldane & G. R. Ross. 1967. Vol. 1. 47.50 (ISBN 0-521-06943-2); Vol. 2. 47.50 (ISBN 0-521-06944-0); Vol. 1. pap. 8.95x (ISBN 0-521-09416-X); Vol. 2. pap. 9.95x (ISBN 0-521-09417-8). Cambridge U Pr.
Philosophical Works: Including the Works on Vision. George Berkeley. 1981. 18.50; pap. 8.75. Rowman.
Philosophical Writings. Rene Descartes. Ed. by Elizabeth Anscombe & Peter T. Geach. Tr. by Elizabeth Anscombe & Peter T. Geach. LC 79-171798. 1971. pap. 4.95 (ISBN 0-672-61274-7, LLA198). Bobbs.
Philosophical Writings. William Of Ockman. Tr. by Philotheus Boehner. LC 64-16710. pap. 4.95 (ISBN 0-672-60431-0, LLA193). Bobbs.
Philosophical Writings of John Duns Scotus. John Duns Scotus. Tr. by Allan Wolter. 1964. pap. 4.95 (ISBN 0-672-60432-9, LLA194). Bobbs.
Philosophicall Discourse Concerning Speech (1668) & a Discourse Written to a Learned Frier (1670) Geraud de Cordemoy. LC 72-6400. (History of Psychology Ser.). 224p. 1972. Repr. 23.00x (ISBN 0-8201-1106-6). Schol Facsimiles.
Philosophiches Woerterbuch. 6th ed. Max Apel & Peter Luds. (Sammlung Goeschen: 2202). (Ger). 1976. pap. 5.80x (ISBN 3-11-006729-3). De Gruyter.
Philosophie des Images, 2 vols. Claude Menestrier. Ed. by Stephen Orgel. LC 78-68189. (Renaissance & the Gods: the Philosophy of Images Ser.). 1980. lib. bdg. 66.00 (ISBN 0-8240-3691-3). Garland Pub.
Philosophie Des Lebendigen Kants Begriff Des Organischen, Seine Wurzlen und Seine Aktualiat. Reinhard Loew. 360p. 1980. text ed. 31.20 (ISBN 0-686-64717-3, 3-518-7499, Pub. by Insel Verlag Germany); pap. 22.40 quality paper (ISBN 3-518-07540-3). Suhrkamp.
Philosophie Franz Brentanos: Beitrage Zur Brentano-Konferenz Graz 4-8, September 1977. Ed. by R. Chisholm & R. Haller. (Grazer Philosophische Studien: No. 5). 1978. pap. text ed. 29.00x (ISBN 90-6203-692-9). Humanities.
Philosophie und Mythos. Hans Poser. 1979. text ed. 52.00x (ISBN 3-11-007601-2). De Gruyter.
Philosophies & Cultures. Frederick Copleston. 208p. 1980. 16.95x (ISBN 0-19-213960-6). Oxford U Pr.
Philosophies of American Education. Max G. Wingo. 1974. text ed. 15.95x (ISBN 0-669-84400-4). Heath.

Philosophies of Education. 2nd ed. William H. Howick. 150p. 1980. pap. 8.95x (ISBN 0-8134-2146-2). Interstate.

Philosophies of Essence: An Examination of the Category of Essence. 2nd ed. David H. Degrood. (Praxis Ser.: No. 1). 1976. pap. text ed. 17.25x (ISBN 90-6032-076-X). Humanities.

Philosophies of Life of Ancient Greeks & Israelites. Ben F. Kimpel. LC 80-81697. 1981. 17.50 (ISBN 0-8022-2371-0). Philos Lib.

Philosophische Grammatik. Ludwig Wittgenstein. Ed. by Rush Rhees. 1969. 20.00x o.p. (ISBN 0-631-12350-4, Pub. by Basil Blackwell). Biblio Dist.

Philosophy. Jack Rudman. (Undergraduate Program Field Test Ser.: UPFT-17). (Cloth bdg. avail. on request). pap. 9.95 (ISBN 0-8373-6017-X). Natl Learning.

Philosophy: A Modern Encounter. Robert Wolff. LC 76-25427. 1976. text ed. 12.50 (ISBN 0-13-663385-4); pap. text ed. 14.50 (ISBN 0-13-663377-3). P-H.

Philosophy: A Text with Readings. Vincent Barry. 544p. 1980. text ed. 17.95x (ISBN 0-534-00767-8). Wadsworth Pub.

Philosophy: Advanced Test for the G. R. E. Mark Steiner. LC 66-28209. (Orig.). 1966. lib. bdg. 5.50 o. p. (ISBN 0-668-01574-8); pap. 4.95 (ISBN 0-668-01472-5). Arco.

Philosophy After Darwin: Chapters for the Career of Philosophy & Other Essays, Vol. 3. John H. Randall, Jr. Ed. by Beth J. Singer. LC 62-10454. 1977. 20.00x (ISBN 0-231-04114-4). Columbia U Pr.

Philosophy: An Introduction. Antony Flew. LC 79-93076. 194p. 1980. pap. text ed. 6.95 (ISBN 0-87975-127-4). Prometheus Bks.

Philosophy: An Introduction. rev. ed. John H. Randall, Jr. & Justus Buchler. 1971. pap. 3.95 (ISBN 0-06-460041-6, CO 41, COS). Har-Row.

Philosophy: An Orthodox Christian Understanding. Apostolos Makrakis. Ed. by Orthodox Christian Educational Society. Tr. by Denver Cummings from Hellenic. (Logos & Holy Spirit in the Unity of Christian Thought Ser.: Vol. 5). 279p. 1977. pap. 3.50x (ISBN 0-938366-02-5). Orthodox Chr.

Philosophy: An Outline for the Intending Student. Ed. by R. J. Hirst. (Outlines Ser). 1968. cased 15.00x (ISBN 0-7100-2038-4); pap. 6.95 (ISBN 0-7100-6099-8). Routledge & Kegan.

Philosophy & Education. Ed. by Jonas Soltis. LC 80-83743. (National Society for the Study of Education 80th Yearbooks: Pt. I). 288p. 1981. lib. bdg. price not set. U of Chicago Pr.

Philosophy & Educational Research. John Wilson. (NFER General Ser.). (Orig.). 1979. pap. text ed. 13.75x (ISBN 0-85633-005-1). Humanities.

Philosophy & Human Movement. David Best. (Unwin Education Bks.). 1979. text ed. 21.95x (ISBN 0-04-370088-8); pap. text ed. 7.95x (ISBN 0-04-370089-6). Allen Unwin.

Philosophy & Humanism: Renaissance Essays in Honor of Paul Oskar Kristeller. Ed. by Edward P. Mahoney. LC 75-42285. 600p. 1976. 50.00x (ISBN 0-231-03904-2). Columbia U Pr.

Philosophy & Its Past. J. Ree. (Philosophy Now Ser.). 1978. text ed. 20.00x (ISBN 0-391-00544-8); pap. text ed. 9.25x (ISBN 0-391-00556-1). Humanities.

Philosophy & Language. Steven Davis. LC 75-15910. (Traditions in Philosophy Ser.). 1976. pap. 7.95 (ISBN 0-672-63674-3). Pegasus.

Philosophy & Myth in Karl Marx. 2nd ed. Robert C. Tucker. LC 70-180022. 250p. 1972. 32.95 (ISBN 0-521-08455-5); pap. 8.95x (ISBN 0-521-09701-0). Cambridge U Pr.

Philosophy & Parapsychology. Ed. by Jan K. Ludwig. LC 77-91852. 454p. 1978. 16.95 (ISBN 0-87975-075-8); pap. 8.95 (ISBN 0-87975-076-6). Prometheus Bks.

Philosophy & Political Action. Ed. by Virginia Held et al. 288p. 1972. pap. text ed. 4.95x (ISBN 0-19-501503-7). Oxford U Pr.

Philosophy & Political Economy: In Some of Their Historical Relations. 3rd ed. James Bonar. (Muirhead Library of Philosophy). 1967. Repr. of 1922 ed. 15.00x (ISBN 0-04-320056-7). Humanities.

Philosophy & Practical Education. John Wilson. (Students Library of Education). 1977. 16.50x (ISBN 0-7100-8675-X). Routledge & Kegan.

Philosophy & Psychoanalysis. John Wisdom. 1969. pap. 14.25x (ISBN 0-631-04410-8, Pub. by Basil Blackwell). Biblio Dist.

Philosophy & Psychology in the Abhidharma. 2nd rev. ed. H. V. Guenther. 1974. 12.50 o.p. (ISBN 0-87773-048-2). Orient Bk Dist.

Philosophy & Psychology in the Abhidharma. Herbert V. Guenther. LC 75-40259. 282p. 1981. pap. 6.95 (ISBN 0-87773-081-4). Great Eastern.

Philosophy & Religious Belief. Thomas McPherson. Ed. by S. Korner. (Illus.). 132p. 1974. text ed. 11.00x (ISBN 0-09-118750-8, Hutchinson U Lib); pap. text ed. 7.00x (ISBN 0-09-118751-6). Humanities.

Philosophy & Revolution. Raya Dunayevskaya. 320p. 1973. 8.95 o.s.i. (ISBN 0-440-07253-0). Delacorte.

Philosophy & Schooling. Charles D. Marler. 1975. text ed. 17.95 (ISBN 0-205-04491-3, 2244918); student manual 5.95 (ISBN 0-205-04493-X, 2244934); instr's manual free (ISBN 0-205-04492-1, 2244926). Allyn.

Philosophy & Science As Modes of Knowing: Selected Essays. Ed. by Alden L. Fisher & George B. Murray. LC 69-18680. (Orig.). 1969. pap. text ed. 6.95 (ISBN 0-89197-340-0). Irvington.

Philosophy & Scientific Realism. John J. Smart. 1963. text ed. 8.00x (ISBN 0-7100-3617-5). Humanities.

Philosophy & Sex. Ed. by Robert Baker & Frederick Elliston. LC 75-21670. 397p. 1975. 11.95 (ISBN 0-87975-055-3); pap. 6.95 (ISBN 0-87975-050-2). Prometheus Bks.

Philosophy & Social Issues: Five Studies. Richard Wasserstrom. LC 79-9486. 224p. 1980. pap. text ed. 6.95 (ISBN 0-268-01536-8). U of Notre Dame Pr.

Philosophy & the American School. 2nd ed. Van C. Morris & Young Pai. LC 75-26083. (Illus.). 544p. 1976. text ed. 17.50 (ISBN 0-395-18620-X). HM.

Philosophy & the Human Condition. Tom L. Beauchamp et al. (Illus.). 640p. 1980. text ed. 15.95 (ISBN 0-13-662528-2). P-H.

Philosophy & the Meaning of Life. K. Britton. LC 69-12926. 1969. 27.95 (ISBN 0-521-07456-8); pap. 7.95x (ISBN 0-521-09593-X, 593). Cambridge U Pr.

Philosophy & the Oriental Mind. Georg W. Hegel. (Illus.). 1980. 49.75 (ISBN 0-89266-212-3). Am Classical Coll Pr.

Philosophy & the Science of Behavior. Merle B. Turner. LC 66-25267. (Century Psychology Ser.). (Illus.). 1967. 28.50x (ISBN 0-89197-341-9); pap. text ed. 9.50x (ISBN 0-89197-342-7). Irvington.

Philosophy & the Teacher. Ed. by D. I. Lloyd. (Students' Library of Education). 180p. 1975. 16.00 (ISBN 0-7100-8282-7); pap. 7.95 (ISBN 0-7100-8288-6). Routledge & Kegan.

Philosophy & Unified Science. George R. Talbott. (Illus.). 1978. 40.00 (ISBN 0-89744-126-5, Pub. by Ganesh & Co. India). Auromere.

Philosophy & Women. Sharon Bishop & Marjorie Weinzweig. 1979. pap. text ed. 12.95x (ISBN 0-534-00609-4). Wadsworth Pub.

Philosophy (Concepts) of Scientific & Technological Development. 17p. 1981. pap. 6.75 (ISBN 92-808-0176-7, T*U*N*U 109, UNU). Unipub.

Philosophy in & Out of Europe & Other Essays. Marjorie Grene. LC 75-27924. 1976. 12.50x (ISBN 0-520-03121-0). U of Cal Pr.

Philosophy in Process. Paul Weiss. Incl. Vol. 1. June 24, 1955 - December 25, 1960. 800p. 1966 (ISBN 0-8093-0190-3); Vol. 2. December 26, 1960-March 6, 1964. 736p. 1966. o.p. (ISBN 0-8093-0231-4); Vol. 3. March-November 1964. 700p. 1968 (ISBN 0-8093-0329-9); Vol. 4. November 26, 1964-September 2, 1965. 634p. 1969 (ISBN 0-8093-0401-5); Vol. 5. September 3, 1965-August 27, 1968. 832p. 1971 (ISBN 0-8093-0465-1); Vol. 6. August 28, 1968-May 22, 1971. 761p. 1975 (ISBN 0-8093-0678-6); Vol. 7. April 13, 1975 - June 21, 1976. 643p. 1978 (ISBN 0-8093-0821-5). LC 63-14293. 25.00x ea. S Ill U Pr.

Philosophy in Social Work. Ed. by Noel Timms & David Watson. (International Library of Welfare & Philosophy Ser.). 1978. 17.50 (ISBN 0-7100-8786-1); pap. 8.95 (ISBN 0-7100-8787-X). Routledge & Kegan.

Philosophy in the Middle Ages. Paul Vignaux. Tr. by E. C. Hall. LC 72-8244. 223p. 1973. Repr. of 1959 ed. lib. bdg. 13.00x o.p. (ISBN 0-8371-6546-6, VIPM). Greenwood.

Philosophy Looks to the Future: Confrontation, Commitment & Utopia. 2nd ed. Walter L. Fogg & Peyton E. Richter. 1978. pap. text ed. 13.95 (ISBN 0-205-06030-7, 6060307). Allyn.

Philosophy Made Simple. Richard H. Popkin & Avrum Stroll. 1956. pap. 3.50 (ISBN 0-385-01217-9, Made). Doubleday.

Philosophy Matters. Lisska. 1977. 12.95 (ISBN 0-675-08592-6). Merrill.

Philosophy Now: An Introductory Reader. Ed. by Paula R. Struhl & J. Karsten. 1972. pap. text ed. 8.95 o.p. (ISBN 0-394-31978-8). Random.

Philosophy of Abraham Shalom: A Fifteenth-Century Exposition & Defense of Maimonides. H. A. Davidson. (U. C. Publ. in Near Eastern Studies: Vol. 5). 1964. pap. 6.75x (ISBN 0-520-09298-8). U of Cal Pr.

Philosophy of Accounts. Charles E. Sprague. LC 72-81869. 1972. Repr. of 1919 ed. text ed. 10.00 (ISBN 0-914348-09-4). Scholars Bk.

Philosophy of Adult Education. Paul Bergevin. 1970. pap. 4.95 (ISBN 0-8164-2056-4, SP62). Crossroad NY.

Philosophy of Art. Virgil Aldrich. (Illus.). 1963. pap. 7.95x ref. ed. (ISBN 0-13-663765-5). P-H.

Philosophy of Art & Aesthetics: From Plato to Wittgenstein. Ed. by Frank A. Tillman & Steven M. Cahn. LC 69-12552. 1969. text ed. 24.50 scp o.p. (ISBN 0-06-046628-6, HarpC). Har-Row.

Philosophy of Biological Science. David L. Hull. LC 73-12981. (Foundations of Philosophy Ser). (Illus.). 192p. 1974. ref. ed. o.p. 11.95 (ISBN 0-13-663617-9); pap. text ed. 7.95x (ISBN 0-13-663609-8). P-H.

Philosophy of Charles S. Peirce: A Critical Introduction. Robert Almeder. Ed. by Nicholas Rescher. (American Philosophical Quarterly Library of Philosophy). 224p. 1980. 27.50x (ISBN 0-8476-6854-1). Rowman.

Philosophy of Christ. D. Rayford Bell. LC 80-67408. 104p. 1980. 6.95 (ISBN 0-9604820-0-8); pap. 4.95 (ISBN 0-9604820-1-6). D R Bell.

Philosophy of Civilization. Albert Schweitzer. Tr. by C. T. Campion from Ger. LC 80-27122. xvii, 347p. 1981. pap. 6.00 (ISBN 0-8130-0694-5). U Presses Fla.

Philosophy of Composition. E. D. Hirsch, Jr. LC 77-4944. xiv, 200p. 1981. pap. 4.95 (ISBN 0-226-34243-3). U of Chicago Pr.

Philosophy of Divine Nutrition. Donald Thomas. 1977. 6.95 o.p. (ISBN 0-533-02744-6). Vantage.

Philosophy of Economics. Linda Andrews. (Foundations of Philosophy Ser.). (Illus.). 200p. 1981. pap. text ed. 7.95 (ISBN 0-13-663336-6). P-H.

Philosophy of Education. John Dewey. (Quality Paperback: No. 126). 1971. pap. 3.50 (ISBN 0-8226-0126-5). Littlefield.

Philosophy of Education: A Guide to Information Sources. Ed. by Charles A. Baatz. (Education Information Guide Ser.: Vol. 6). 1980. 30.00 (ISBN 0-8103-1452-5). Gale.

Philosophy of Education: An Introduction. Harry Schofield. (Unwin Education Bks.). text ed. 18.95x (ISBN 0-04-370039-X); pap. text ed. 8.95x (ISBN 0-04-370040-3). Allen Unwin.

Philosophy of Education & Third World Perspective. Ed. by Festus C. Okafor. LC 80-50732. 346p. (Orig.). 1981. 15.00x (ISBN 0-931494-06-0); pap. 10.00x (ISBN 0-931494-07-9). Brunswick Pub.

Philosophy of Educational Research. Ed. by Harry S. Broudy et al. LC 72-2332. (Readings in Educational Research Ser.). 1973. 25.00 (ISBN 0-471-10625-9); text ed. 22.50 10 or more copies (ISBN 0-686-67151-1). McCutchan.

Philosophy of Existence. Karl Jaspers. Tr. by Richard F. Grabau. LC 79-133203. 1971. 10.00x (ISBN 0-8122-7629-9); pap. 4.95x (ISBN 0-8122-1010-7, Pa Paperbks). U of Pa Pr.

Philosophy of Grammar. Otto Jespersen. 1924. text ed. 25.00x (ISBN 0-04-400009-X). Allen Unwin.

Philosophy of Hegel: A Systematic Exposition. Walter T. Stace. 1923. pap. text ed. 6.00 (ISBN 0-486-20254-2). Dover.

Philosophy of Henri Bergson. Daniel J. Herman. LC 80-5044. 117p. 1979. text ed. 16.75 (ISBN 0-8191-1029-9); pap. text ed. 7.50 (ISBN 0-8191-1030-2). U Pr of Amer.

Philosophy of History. William H. Dray. (Orig.). 1964. pap. 7.95x ref. ed. (ISBN 0-13-663849-X). P-H.

Philosophy of History in Schematic Representations. Sterling Atwell. (Illus.). 1980. deluxe ed. 39.55 (ISBN 0-89266-230-1). Am Classical Coll Pr.

Philosophy of Human Nature. Joseph Buchanan. LC 71-90941. (History of Psychology Ser). (Illus.). 1969. Repr. of 1812 ed. 36.00x (ISBN 0-8201-1064-7). Schol Facsimiles.

Philosophy of Human Nature. George P. Klubertanz. LC 53-6357. 1953. 34.50x (ISBN 0-89197-343-5). Irvington.

Philosophy of Human Rights: International Perspectives. Ed. by Alan S. Rosenbaum. LC 79-6191. (Contributions in Philosophy: No. 15). xv, 272p. 1980. lib. bdg. 27.50 (ISBN 0-313-20985-5, RHR/). Greenwood.

Philosophy of Indian Monotheism. M. P. Christanand. 132p. 1980. text ed. 12.00x (ISBN 0-333-90313-7). Humanities.

Philosophy of Integralism. Haridas Chaudhuri. 184p. (Orig.). pap. 3.50 (ISBN 0-686-64766-1, Pub. by Sri). Auromere.

Philosophy of Jesus. Ernest Holmes. Ed. by Willis Kinnear. 96p. (Orig.). 1973. pap. 3.50 (ISBN 0-911336-51-6). Sci of Mind.

Philosophy of Kant Explained. John Watson. Ed. by Lewis W. Beck. LC 75-32047. (Philosophy of Immanual Kant Ser.: Vol. 11). 1977. Repr. of 1908 ed. lib. bdg. 40.00 (ISBN 0-8240-2335-8). Garland Pub.

Philosophy of Language. William P. Alston. (Orig.). 1964. pap. 7.95x ref. ed. (ISBN 0-13-663799-X). P-H.

Philosophy of Language Primer. Thomas S. Vernon. LC 80-489. 136p. 1980. text ed. 15.75 (ISBN 0-8191-1023-X); pap. text ed. 7.50 (ISBN 0-8191-1024-8). U Pr of Amer.

Philosophy of Law. 2nd ed. Joel Feinberg & Hyman Gross. 656p. 1980. text ed. 20.95x (ISBN 0-534-00835-6). Wadsworth Pub.

Philosophy of Law. Martin P. Golding. (Foundation of Philosophy Ser.). 176p. 1975. text ed. 13.50 (ISBN 0-13-664136-9); pap. text ed. 7.95x (ISBN 0-13-664128-8). P-H.

Philosophy of Law. Jeffrie G. Murphy. (Philosophy & Society Ser.). 1981. 18.50x (ISBN 0-8476-6277-2); pap. 9.95x (ISBN 0-8476-6278-0). Rowman. Postponed.

Philosophy of Law in Historical Perspective. rev. ed. Carl J. Friedrich. LC 57-9546. 1963. 11.50x o.s.i. (ISBN 0-226-26465-3). U of Chicago Pr.

Philosophy of Life & the Philosophy of Death: Considerations & Anticipations of the Future Universe & of Man's Existence in It. 2nd ed. (Illus.). 1977. 17.20 (ISBN 0-89266-058-9). Am Classical Coll Pr.

Philosophy of Literary Form. Kenneth Burke. 1974. pap. 7.95x (ISBN 0-520-02483-4). U of Cal Pr.

Philosophy of Logic. Ed. by Stephan Korner. 1976. 25.00x (ISBN 0-520-03235-7). U of Cal Pr.

Philosophy of Logic. W. V. Quine. 1970. pap. 7.95x ref. ed. (ISBN 0-13-663625-X). P-H.

Philosophy of Logics. Susan Haack. LC 77-17071. (Illus.). 1978. 42.00 (ISBN 0-521-21988-4); pap. 10.95x (ISBN 0-521-29329-4). Cambridge U Pr.

Philosophy of Mahatma Gandhi. Dhirendra M. Datta. 1953. pap. 5.45 (ISBN 0-299-01014-7). U of Wis Pr.

Philosophy of Manufactures. Andrew Ure. LC 66-21697. Repr. of 1835 ed. 30.00x (ISBN 0-678-05092-9). Kelley.

Philosophy of Mathematics: An Introductory Essay. Stephen Korner. 1979. pap. text ed. 5.75x (ISBN 0-09-056642-4, Hutchinson U Lib). Humanities.

Philosophy of Meditation. 2nd ed. Haridas Chaudhuri. 88p. 1974. pap. 3.50 (ISBN 0-89744-994-0, Pub. by Cultural Integration). Auromere.

Philosophy of Mind. Ed. by J. C. B. Glover. (Oxford Readings in Philosophy). 1977. pap. text ed. 5.95x (ISBN 0-19-875038-2). Oxford U Pr.

Philosophy of Mind. Jerome A. Shaffer. LC 68-24352. (Foundations of Philosophy Series), (Orig.). 1968. pap. 7.95x ref. ed. (ISBN 0-13-663724-8). P-H.

Philosophy of Modern Art. Herbert Read. 1964. pap. 7.50 (ISBN 0-571-06506-6, Pub. by Faber & Faber). Merrimack Bk Serv.

Philosophy of Money. Georg Simmel. Tr. by Tom Bottomore & David Frisby. 1978. 40.00x (ISBN 0-7100-8874-4). Routledge & Kegan.

Philosophy of Moral Development: Essays in Moral Development, Vol. 1. Lawrence Kohlberg. LC 80-8902. 256p. 1981. 17.95 (ISBN 0-06-064760-4). Har-Row.

Philosophy of Music Education. Bennett Reimer. (Contemporary Perspectives in Music Education Ser). 1970. pap. text ed. 10.50 (ISBN 0-13-663872-4). P-H.

Philosophy of Natural History, 2 vols. William Smellie. LC 78-67541. Repr. 125.00 set (ISBN 0-404-17230-X, QL50). AMS Pr.

Philosophy of Natural Science. Carl Hempel. (Orig.). 1966. pap. 7.95x ref. ed. (ISBN 0-13-663823-6). P-H.

Philosophy of Nietzsche in Dramatic Representational Expressions. Larry N. Richardson. (Essence of the Great Philosophers Ser.). (Illus.). 97p. 1981. 19.75 (ISBN 0-89266-277-8). Am Classical Coll Pr.

Philosophy of Parapsychology: Proceedings of an International Conference, Copenhagen, 1976. Ed. by Betty Shapin & Lisette Coly. LC 77-75663. 1977. 14.00 (ISBN 0-912328-29-0). Parapsych Foun.

Philosophy of Praxis. Adolfo S. Vazquez. Tr. by Mike Gonzalez. LC 76-23235. (International Library of Social & Political Thought). 1977. text ed. 19.50x (ISBN 0-391-00650-9). Humanities.

Philosophy of Primary Education: An Introduction. R. F. Dearden. LC 68-21589. (Students' Library of Education). 1968. text ed. 5.75x (ISBN 0-7100-4223-X); pap. text ed. 3.00x (ISBN 0-7100-6648-1). Humanities.

Philosophy of Quantum Mechanics: The Interpretations of Quantum Mechanics in Historical Perspective. Max Jammer. LC 74-13030. 672p. 1974. 32.95 (ISBN 0-471-43958-4, Pub. by Wiley-Interscience). Wiley.

Philosophy of Railroads. T. C. Keefer. LC 72-163835. (Social History of Canada Ser.). 1972. pap. 4.50 (ISBN 0-8020-6157-5). U of Toronto Pr.

Philosophy of Religion. Christopher J. Bostrom. 1962. 32.50x (ISBN 0-685-69791-6). Elliots Bks.

Philosophy of Religion. 2nd ed. John Hick. LC 72-5429. (Foundations of Philosophy). 144p. 1973. pap. 7.95x ref. ed. (ISBN 0-13-663948-8). P-H.

Philosophy of Religion. M. D. Lewis. (Teach Yourself Ser.). 1975. pap. 4.95 o.p. (ISBN 0-679-10441-0). McKay.

Philosophy of Religion. Ninian Smart. 1979. 13.95 (ISBN 0-19-520138-8); pap. 4.50 (ISBN 0-19-520139-6). Oxford U Pr.

Philosophy of Religion. David E. Trueblood. LC 75-31446. 324p. 1976. Repr. of 1957 ed. lib. bdg. 25.25x (ISBN 0-8371-8514-9, TRPHR). Greenwood.

Philosophy of Religion: An Introduction. William L. Rowe. 1978. pap. text ed. 10.95x (ISBN 0-8221-0208-0). Dickenson.

Philosophy of Religion & Theology: 1975 Proceedings. Ed. by James W. McClendon. LC 75-26618. (American Academy of Religion. Section Papers). 1975. pap. 7.50 (ISBN 0-89130-024-4, 010916). Scholars Pr Ca.

Philosophy of Responsibility. Edgar Bodenheimer. LC 79-26020. x, 147p. 1980. text ed. 18.50x (ISBN 0-8377-0309-3). Rothman.

Philosophy of Rhetoric. George Campbell. Ed. by Lloyd F. Bitzer. LC 63-14291. (Landmarks in Rhetoric & Public Address Ser.). 476p. 1963. 12.95x (ISBN 0-8093-0100-8). S Ill U Pr.

Philosophy of Rhetoric. Ivor A. Richards. (YA) (gr. 9 up). 1965. pap. 3.95 (ISBN 0-19-500715-8, GB). Oxford U Pr.

Philosophy of Right. G. W. Hegel. Tr. by T. M. Knox. 1942. 31.00x (ISBN 0-19-824128-3); pap. 6.95x (ISBN 0-19-500276-8). Oxford U Pr.

Philosophy of Sartre. Mary Warnock. 1972. pap. text ed. 8.00x (ISBN 0-09-073752-0, Hutchinson U Lib). Humanities.

Philosophy of Schopenhauer in Dramatic Representational Expressions. Bruce R. Miller. (Illus.). 101p. 1981. 19.75 (ISBN 0-89266-279-4). Am Classical Coll Pr.

Philosophy of Science for Personality Theory. 2nd ed. Joseph F. Rychlak. 528p. 1981. Repr. of 1968 ed. write for info. (ISBN 0-88275-889-6). Krieger.

Philosophy of Science: The Historical Background. Ed. by Joseph J. Kockelmans. LC 68-14108. 1968. pap. text ed. 6.95 o.s.i. (ISBN 0-02-917530-5). Free Pr.

Philosophy of Sex: Contemporary Readings. Ed. by Alan Soble. 412p. 1980. 17.50x (ISBN 0-8476-6292-6). Rowman.

Philosophy of Sleep. Robert Macnish. (Contributions to the History of Psycholgy Ser.: Orientations). 1978. Repr. of 1834 ed. 30.00 (ISBN 0-89093-159-3). U Pubns Amer.

Philosophy of Social Science. Richard S. Rudner. (Orig.). 1966. pap. 7.95x ref. ed. (ISBN 0-13-664300-0). P-H.

Philosophy of Space & Time. Hans Reichenbach. Tr. by Maria Reichenbach. 1957. pap. text ed. 3.50 (ISBN 0-486-60443-8). Dover.

Philosophy of Spiritual Activity. Rudolf Steiner. (Spiritual Science Library). 304p. 1980. 13.00x (ISBN 0-8334-0728-7); pap. 6.95 (ISBN 0-8334-1786-X). Steinerbks.

Philosophy of Spiritual Activity As a Path to Self-Knowledge. Rita Stebbing. 1980. pap. 2.95 (ISBN 0-916786-50-1). St George Bk Serv.

Philosophy of Sport: A Collection of Original Essays. Ed. by Robert G. Osterhoudt. 374p. 1973. 18.75 (ISBN 0-398-02871-0). C C Thomas.

Philosophy of Symbolic Forms, Vol. 2, Mythical Thought. Ernst Cassirer. Tr. by Ralph Manheim. 1955. 19.50x (ISBN 0-300-00354-4); pap. 5.95 1965 (ISBN 0-300-00038-3, Y147). Yale U Pr.

Philosophy of Symbolic Forms, Vol. 3, The Phenomenolgy Of Knowledge. Ernst Cassirer. Tr. by Ralph Manheim. 1965. pap. 7.95 (ISBN 0-300-00039-1, Y148). Yale U Pr.

Philosophy of the American Constitution: A Reinterpretation of the Intentions of the Founding Fathers. Paul Eidelberg. 1968. 8.50 o.s.i. (ISBN 0-02-909360-0). Free Pr.

Philosophy of the American Revolution. Morton White. LC 77-18081. (American Social Thought Ser.). 1978. 17.95x (ISBN 0-19-502381-1). Oxford U Pr.

Philosophy of the American Revolution. Morton White. 321p. 1981. pap. 6.95 (ISBN 0-19-502891-0, GB 625, OPB). Oxford U Pr.

Philosophy of the Future. Ernst Bloch. LC 79-110785. 1970. 5.95 o.p. (ISBN 0-8164-9134-8). Continuum.

Philosophy of the Humanistic Society. Ed. by Alfred E. Koenig et al. LC 80-1425. 290p. (Orig.). 1981. lib. bdg. 22.50 (ISBN 0-8191-1414-6); pap. text ed. 11.75 (ISBN 0-8191-1415-4). U Pr of Amer.

Philosophy of the Practical. Benedetto Croce. Tr. by Douglas Ainslie. LC 66-30790. 1913. 15.00x (ISBN 0-8196-0192-6). Biblo.

Philosophy of the Present. George H. Mead. Ed. by Arthur E. Murphy. LC 80-16334. 240p. 1980. pap. 5.95 (ISBN 0-226-51670-9, P909, Phoen). U of Chicago Pr.

Philosophy of the Sixteenth & Seventeenth Centuries. Richard H. Popkin. LC 66-10365. (Orig.). 1966. pap. text ed. 6.95 (ISBN 0-02-925490-6). Free Pr.

Philosophy of Thomas Jefferson. Adrienne Koch. 8.00 (ISBN 0-8446-1270-7). Peter Smith.

Philosophy of Urban Existence: A Prolegomenon. A. K. Bierman. LC 72-96393. x, 194p. 1973. 12.00x (ISBN 0-8214-0123-8). Ohio U Pr.

Philosophy: Paradox & Discovery. 2nd ed. Arthur J. Minton & Thomas A. Shipka. 496p. 1982. pap. text ed. 11.95 (ISBN 0-07-042413-6, C). McGraw.

Philosophy, Poetry, History: An Anthology of Essays. Benedetto Croce. Tr. by Cecil Sprigge. 1966. 55.00x (ISBN 0-19-711621-3). Oxford U Pr.

Philosophy, Politics & Society. Ed. by Peter Laslett. Incl. First Series. 1975. Repr. of 1956 ed (ISBN 0-631-16810-9); Second Series. 1979 (ISBN 0-631-04880-4); Third Series. 1978. Repr. of 1956 ed (ISBN 0-631-17730-2); Fourth Series (ISBN 0-631-17740-X). pap. 12.50 ea. (Pub. by Basil Blackwell England). Biblio Dist.

Philosophy, Politics & Society: Second Series. Ed. by Peter Laslett. 1980. 27.50x (ISBN 0-686-28141-1, Pub. by Basil Blackwell England); pap. 12.50x (ISBN 0-631-04880-4, Pub. by Basil Blackwell England). Biblio Dist.

Philosophy, Psychology & Mysticism. Inayat Khan. (Sufi Message of Hazrat Inayat Khan Ser.: Vol. 11). 1979. 6.95 (ISBN 90-6325-099-1, Pub. by Servire BV Netherlands). Hunter Hse.

Philosophy, Science & the Sociology of Knowledge. Irving L. Horowitz. LC 76-27756. 1976. Repr. of 1961 ed. lib. bdg. 16.75x (ISBN 0-8371-9051-7, HOPS). Greenwood.

Philosophy: Something to Believe in. Richard P. Janaro. 1975. pap. text ed. 7.95x (ISBN 0-02-475800-0, 47580). Macmillan.

Philosophy's Journey: An Historical Introduction. Konstantin Kolenda. LC 73-9126. 1974. text ed. 14.95 (ISBN 0-201-03811-0). A-W.

Phiz!: Illustrator of Dickens' World. John Buchanan-Brown. (Encore Editions). (Illus.). 1978. 4.95 (ISBN 0-684-16675-5, ScribT). Scribner.

Phloem. Katherine Esau. LC 75-566979. (Encyclopedia of Plant Anatomy Ser.). (Illus.). 1969. 126.00x (ISBN 0-8002-0226-0). Intl Pubns Serv.

Phloem Transport in Plants. Alden S. Crafts & Carl E. Crisp. LC 71-125130. (Biology Ser.). (Illus.). 1971. text ed. 31.95x (ISBN 0-7167-0683-0). W H Freeman.

Phobia Free. E. Ann Sutherland & Zalman Amit. (Orig.). pap. 1.95 (ISBN 0-515-04700-7). Jove Pubns.

Phobia: Psychological and Pharmacological Treatment. Ed. by Matig Mavissakalian & David H. Barlow. 260p. 1981. 20.00 (ISBN 0-89862-602-1). Guilford Pr.

Phobias: Their Nature & Control. 136p. 1968. pap. 7.50 spiral (ISBN 0-398-01535-X). C C Thomas.

Phoebe & the Hot Water Bottles. Terry Furchgott & Linda Dawson. LC 78-74756. (Illus.). (gr. k-3). 1979. 7.95 (ISBN 0-233-96860-1). Andre Deutsch.

Phoebe Dexter Has Harriet Peterson's Sniffles. Laura J. Numeroff. LC 76-54661. (Illus.). (ps-3). 1977. 7.25 (ISBN 0-688-80091-2); PLB 6.96 (ISBN 0-688-84091-4). Greenwillow.

Phoebe, Junior: A Last Chronicle of Carlingford, 1876. Margaret O. Oliphant. Ed. by Robert L. Wolff. LC 75-1548. (Victorian Fiction Ser). 1975. lib. bdg. 66.00 (ISBN 0-8240-1616-5). Garland Pub.

Phoenicia & Carthage: A Thousand Years to Oblivion. Orville H. Bullitt. LC 78-67741. (Illus.). 260p. 1978. 10.00 (ISBN 0-8059-2562-7). Dorrance.

Phoenix: A Pictorial History. Roslyn Hoffman. Ed. by Donna R. Friedman. (Illus.). 208p. 1981. pap. write for info. (ISBN 0-89865-090-9). Donning Co.

Phoenix Assault. John Kerrigan. (Orig.). 1980. pap. 2.50 (ISBN 0-451-09522-7, E9522, Sig). NAL.

Phoenix by Thomas Middleton: A Critical, Modernized Edition. Ed. by John B. Brooks & Stephen Orgel. LC 78-66762. (Renaissance Drama Ser.). 424p. 1980. lib. bdg. 44.00 (ISBN 0-8240-9750-5). Garland Pub.

Phoenix Formula. Thomas Leighton. (Orig.). 1980. pap. 2.50 (ISBN 0-440-14649-6). Dell.

Phoenix I. M. K. Wren. (Orig.). 1981. pap. 2.75 (ISBN 0-425-04746-6). Berkley Pub.

Phoenix Island. Charlotte Paul. 1976. pap. 2.50 (ISBN 0-451-09413-1, E9413. Sig). NAL.

Phoenix Man. Glen Cunningham. 1980. write for info. o.p. (ISBN 0-912376-52-X). Chosen Bks Pub.

Phoenix Nest. Margaret Hermes. 1981. 8.95 (ISBN 0-8092-5905-2). Contemp Bks.

Phoenix Over the Galilee. Ka-Tzetnik. 1977. pap. 1.75 o.s.i. (ISBN 0-515-04192-0). Jove Pubns.

Phoenix Riddle: A Study of Irony in Comedy. Robert L. Tener. (SSEL Poetic Drama Ser.: No. 44). (Orig.). 1979. pap. text ed. 25.00x (ISBN 0-391-01612-1). Humanities.

Pholoem Translocation. M. J. Canny. 1973. 65.00 (ISBN 0-521-20047-4). Cambridge U Pr.

Phone. Jackson Mac Low. 1979. pap. 4.00 (ISBN 0-914162-29-2). Printed Edns.

Phone Calls from the Dead. Beth Bentley. LC 76-122096. 78p. 1970. 7.00 (ISBN 0-8214-0076-2). Ohio U Pr.

Phoneme: Introduction to the History & Theories of a Concept. Jiri Kramsky. 1974. 25.00 (ISBN 3-7705-0945-5); pap. 16.25 (ISBN 0-686-67210-0). Adler.

Phoneme: Its Nature & Use. 3rd ed. D. Jones. LC 70-377868. 1976. Repr. of 1976 ed. 29.50 (ISBN 0-521-21351-7). Cambridge U Pr.

Phonemics: A Technique for Reducing Language to Writing. Kenneth L. Pike. 1947. pap. 6.50x (ISBN 0-472-08732-0). U of Mich Pr.

Phonetic Context Drill Book. Jerry Griffith & Lynn E. Miner. 1979. pap. 11.95 (ISBN 0-13-665398-7). P-H.

Phonetic Description of Voice Quality. J. Laver. LC 77-82501. (Cambridge Studies in Linguistics: No. 31). (Illus.). 225p. 1980. 34.50 (ISBN 0-521-23176-0). Cambridge U Pr.

Phonetic Music. Ernest Robson. 1981. 19.00. Primary Pr.

Phonetic Processing: The Dynamics of Speech. Donald Dew & Paul J. Jensen. 1977. text ed. 14.95 (ISBN 0-675-08594-2). Merrill.

Phonetic Rules in Reading. Mary H. Manoni & Robert Cienkus. LC 78-730055. (Illus.). 1978. pap. text ed. 99.00 (ISBN 0-89290-103-9, A329-SATC). Soc for Visual.

Phonetic Science: A Program of Instruction. Samuel R. Faircloth & Marjorie A. Faircloth. (Illus.). 144p. 1973. pap. text ed. 11.95 (ISBN 0-13-664565-8). P-H.

Phonetic Spelling for College Students. Ralph M. Williams. LC 80-24084. 180p. 1980. Repr. of 1960 ed. lib. bdg. 27.50x (ISBN 0-313-22650-4, WIPS). Greenwood.

Phonetic Transcription. 2nd ed. Donald Dew & Alfred D. Jensen. 1979. text ed. 7.95 (ISBN 0-675-08309-5); instructors manual 3.95 (ISBN 0-686-67278-X). Merrill.

Phonetic Transcription: A Programmed Introduction. L. S. Harms. 1964. pap. 5.95x (ISBN 0-673-05707-0). Scott F.

Phonetics: A Critical Analysis of Phonetic Theory & a Technic for the Practical Description of Sounds. Kenneth L. Pike. 1943. pap. 6.50x (ISBN 0-472-08733-9). U of Mich Pr.

Phonetics in Linguistics: A Book of Readings. Ed. by W. E. Jones & J. Laver. (Linguistics Library, No. 12). 355p. 1973. text ed. 16.95x (ISBN 0-582-52451-2). Longman.

Phonetics of Russian. D. Jones & Dennis Ward. 1969. text ed. 58.00 (ISBN 0-521-06736-7). Cambridge U Pr.

Phonic Dictionary. Linda Hayward. (Illus.). 96p. (gr. k-4). 1981. PLB 11.85 (ISBN 0-448-13923-5); pap. 3.95 (ISBN 0-448-47336-4). Platt.

Phonics Crossword Puzzles Series. Kramer. Incl. Early Phonics Crossword Puzzle Book. (gr. k). 1974. pap. text ed. 1.60 (ISBN 0-8009-0438-9); tchr's. ed. 3.00 (ISBN 0-8009-0450-8); spirit masters (ISBN 0-8009-0440-0); Bk. A. (gr. 1-2). 1971. pap. text ed. (ISBN 0-8009-0441-9); tchr's. ed. (ISBN 0-8009-0443-5); spirit masters (ISBN 0-8009-0442-7); Bk. B. (gr. 3-4). 1970. pap. text ed. (ISBN 0-8009-0445-1); tchr's. ed. (ISBN 0-8009-0447-8); spirit masters (ISBN 0-8009-0444-3); Bk. C. (gr. 5-6). 1971. pap. text ed. (ISBN 0-8009-0449-4); tchr's. ed. (ISBN 0-8009-0451-6); spirit masters (ISBN 0-8009-0448-6). (gr. k-6). Bks. A-C. pap. text ed. 1.76 ea.; tchr's. eds. Bks. A-C 3.32 ea.; spirit masters Early Phonics-Bk. C 6.88 ea. McCormick-Mathers.

Phonics for the Teacher of Reading. 3rd ed. Marion Hull. (Illus.). 144p. 1981. pap. text ed. 5.95 (ISBN 0-675-08074-6). Merrill.

Phonics for the Teacher of Reading. 2nd ed. Marion A. Hull. Ed. by Heilman. (Elementary Education Ser.). 128p. 1976. pap. text ed. 7.95x (ISBN 0-675-08655-8). Merrill.

Phonics Guidelines: An Introduction. Paul C. Holmes. 320p. 1980. pap. text ed. 12.95 (ISBN 0-8403-2225-9). Kendall-Hunt.

Phonics in Proper Perspective. 4th ed. Arthur W. Hailman. (Illus.). 128p. 1981. pap. text ed. 6.50 (ISBN 0-675-08065-7). Merrill.

Phonics in Proper Perspective. 3rd ed. Arthur W. Heilman. (Elementary Education Ser.). 144p. 1976. pap. text ed. 7.50x (ISBN 0-675-08681-7). Merrill.

Phonics Review. rev. ed. P. A. R. Editorial Staff. 59p. 1973. pap. text ed. 3.95 (ISBN 0-913310-12-3). PAR Inc.

Phonics Workbook, Level D. Jane Ervin. (MCP Basic Phonics Program). (gr. 4). 1977. 3.40 (ISBN 0-87895-441-4). Modern Curr.

Phono-Graphic Translation. W. Haas. 98p. 1970. 24.00x (ISBN 0-7190-0394-6, Pub. by Manchester U Pr England). State Mutual Bk.

Phonograph & Our Musical Life: Proceedings of a Centennial Conference. Ed. by H. Wiley Hitchcock. LC 80-82409. (I. S.A.M Monograph: No. 14). 1980. pap. 7.50 (ISBN 0-914678-14-0). Inst Am Music.

Phonological Aspects of Modern English. John Nist. LC 78-53426. 1978. pap. text ed. 8.25x (ISBN 0-8191-0495-7). U Pr of Amer.

Phonological Investigation of Aphasic Speech. Sheila E. Blumstein. (Janua Linguarum Ser. Minor: No. 153). 1973. pap. text ed. 20.50x (ISBN 90-2792-448-1). Mouton.

Phonological Rules & Dialect Variation: A Study of the Phonology of Lumasaaba. G. Brown. LC 70-184904. (Studies in Linguistics: No. 7). (Illus.). 200p. 1972. 34.50 (ISBN 0-521-08485-7); pap. 10.95x (ISBN 0-521-29063-5). Cambridge U Pr.

Phonological Variation in the Jamaican Continuum. Glenn A. Akers. 158p. 1981. pap. 8.50 (ISBN 0-89720-038-1). Karoma.

Phonology & Prosody of Modern English. Hans Kurath. LC 64-13467. 1949. 10.00x (ISBN 0-472-08530-1). U of Mich Pr.

Phonology & Speech Remediation: A Book of Readings. Ed. by Harry H. Walsh. LC 78-32109. (Illus.). 268p. text ed. 18.95 (ISBN 0-933014-52-X). College-Hill.

Phonology, Morphonology, Morphology. Olga Akhmanova. LC 72-159459. (Janua Linguarum, Ser. Minor: No. 101). 135p. 1971. pap. text ed. 23.50x (ISBN 90-2791-748-5). Mouton.

Phonology of Catalan. Max Wheeler. 1979. 42.25x (ISBN 0-631-11621-4, Pub. by Basil Blackwell England). Biblio Dist.

Phonology of the Nineteen Eighties. D. Goyvaerts. (Story-Scientia Linguistics Ser.: No. 4). 1980. text ed. write for info. (ISBN 90-6439-150-5). Humanities.

Phonometrie, Teil 1: Grundfragen der Phonometrie. 3rd ed. E. Zwirner & K. Zwirner. Ed. by E. Zwirner & K. Ezawa. (Bibliotheca Phonetica Ser.: No. 3). (Illus.). vi, 218p. 1981. pap. 49.75 (ISBN 3-8055-2370-X). S Karger.

Phonon Scattering in Condensed Matter. Ed. by Humphrey J. Maris. 500p. 1980. 52.50 (ISBN 0-306-40355-2, Plenum Pr). Plenum Pub.

Phony Phone Book. Milford S. Poltroon. 1979. pap. 4.95 (ISBN 0-87691-280-3). Winchester Pr.

Phony War. Oscar Rosenfeld. Date not set. 8.95 (ISBN 0-533-04782-X). Vantage.

Phosphates in Food Processing: Symposium. J. M. DeMan & P. Melnychyn. (Illus.). 1971. 25.50 o.p. (ISBN 0-87055-105-1). AVI.

Phospholipases & Prostaglandins. Ed. by Claudio Galli et al. LC 77-87457. (Advances in Prostaglandin & Thromboxane Research Ser.: Vol. 3). 1978. 27.00 (ISBN 0-89004-201-2). Raven.

Phosphorous Chemistry Directed Towards Biology: International Symposium on Phosphorus Chemistry Directed Towards Biology, Burzenin, Poland, 25-28 September 1979. W. J. Stec. (IUPAC Symposium Ser.). 240p. 1980. 69.00 (ISBN 0-08-023969-2). Pergamon.

Phosphors. M. S. Waite & A. Vecht. (Illus.). 320p. 1981. write for info. (Pub. by Peregrinus London). Inst Elect Eng. Postponed.

Phosphorus Management Strategies for Lakes. Ed. by Raymond C. Loehr. LC 79-55150. (Illus.). 1980. 39.95 (ISBN 0-250-40332-3). Ann Arbor Science.

Phosphorylated Proteins & Related Enzymes: Proceedings. Biochemical Societies of France, Great Britain, Italy, & the Netherlands. Joint Meeting, Venice, 1976. 121p. 8.00. Info Retrieval.

Photian Schism. F. Dvornik. 1970. 70.00 (ISBN 0-521-07770-2). Cambridge U Pr.

Photic Field. Parry Moon & Donna E. Spencer. 272p. 1981. text ed. 25.00x (ISBN 0-262-13166-8). MIT Pr.

Photo & Thermoelectric Effects in Semiconductors. J. Tauc. 1962. 27.00 (ISBN 0-08-009611-5); pap. 15.00 (ISBN 0-08-013636-2). Pergamon.

Photo Filters. Ed. by Mike Stensvold. LC 76-5980. (Petersen's How-to Photographic Library Ser.). (Illus.). 80p. 1976. pap. 3.95 o.p. (ISBN 0-8227-4012-5). Petersen Pub.

Photo Filters & Lens Attachments. Kathryn Yahue. (Petersen's Photographic Library). (Illus.). 160p. 1981. pap. 8.95 (ISBN 0-8227-4044-3). Petersen Pub.

Photo Finish. Ngaio Marsh. 1981. lib. bdg. 14.95 (ISBN 0-8161-3149-X, Large Print Bks). G K Hall.

Photo Fun: An Idea Book for Shutterbugs. David Webster. LC 72-8112. (Illus.). 96p. (gr. 4 up). 1973. PLB 5.90 o.p. (ISBN 0-531-02620-5). Watts.

Photo Graphics. Sam Haskins. (Illus.). 1981. 30.00 (ISBN 2-88046-016-6, Pub. by Roto-Vision Switzerland). Norton.

Photo Lighting Techniques. Ben Helprin & PhotoGraphic Magazine Editors. LC 73-82538. (PhotoGraphic's Basic Ser.). (Illus.). 80p. (Orig.). 1973. pap. 3.95 o.p. (ISBN 0-8227-0022-0). Petersen Pub.

Photo-Offset Fundamentals. 4th ed. John E. Cogoli. (Illus.). (gr. 10-12). 1980. text ed. 15.72 (ISBN 0-87345-235-6); study guide 4.48 (ISBN 0-87345-236-4); filmstrips & ans. avail. 336.00 (ISBN 0-685-42198-8). McKnight.

Photo One: Basic Photo Text. Ken Muse. (Illus.). 240p. 1973. pap. text ed. 11.95 (ISBN 0-13-665331-6). P-H.

Photoabsorption, Photoionization & Photoelectron Spectroscopy. Joseph Berkowitz. (Pure & Applied Physics Ser.). 1979. 42.50 (ISBN 0-12-091650-9). Acad Pr.

Photoacoustics & Photoacoustic Spectroscopy. Allan Rosencwaig. LC 80-17286. (Chemical Analysis Ser.). 352p. 1980. 35.00 (ISBN 0-471-04495-4, Pub. by Wiley-Interscience). Wiley.

Photochemical & Photobiological Reviews, Vols. 1-5. Ed. by Kendric C. Smith. Incl. Vol. 1. 391p. 1976. 39.50 (ISBN 0-306-33801-7); Vol. 2. 329p. 1977. 29.50 (ISBN 0-306-33802-5); Vol. 3. 315p. 1978. 27.50 (ISBN 0-306-33803-3); Vol. 4. 343p. 1979. 35.00 (ISBN 0-306-40225-4); Vol. 5. 375p. 1980. 35.00 (ISBN 0-306-40360-9). LC 75-43689 (Plenum Pr). Plenum Pub.

Photochemistry of Dyed & Pigmented Polymers. Ed. by N. S. Allen & J. F. McKellar. (Illus.). xii, 296p. 1980. 50.00x (ISBN 0-85334-898-7). Burgess-Intl Ideas.

Photochemistry of Heterocyclic Compounds. O. Buchard. LC 75-33855. 1976. 80.95 (ISBN 0-471-11510-X). Wiley.

Photochemistry of Proteins & Nucleic Acids. A. D. McLaren & D. Shugar. 1964. 46.00 (ISBN 0-08-010139-9); pap. text ed. 22.00 (ISBN 0-08-013569-2). Pergamon.

Photochemistry Seven: Seventh IUPAC Symposium on Photochemistry, Leuven, Belgium, 24-28 July, 1978. Ed. by A. Reiser. (IUPAC Symposia Ser.). 1979. 37.00 (ISBN 0-08-022358-3). Pergamon.

Photocomposition with Kodak Phototypesetting Products. Eastman Kodak Company. LC 75-36853. (Illus.). 40p. 1978. 4.00 o.p. (ISBN 0-87985-168-6, Q-5). Eastman Kodak.

Photoconductivity in Polymers. A. V. Patsis & D. A. Seanor. LC 74-80461. (Illus.). 349p. (Orig.). 1976. 30.00x (ISBN 0-87762-136-5). Technomic.

Photocrafts Book of Guides, Vol. 2. Mark Baczynsky. LC 78-70581. (Illus.). 104p. 1980. pap. 19.95 (ISBN 0-89816-002-2). Embee Pr.

Photodegradation & Photostabilization of Coatings. Ed. by S. Peter Pappas & F. H. Winslow. (ACS Symposium Ser: No. 151). 1981. price not set (ISBN 0-8412-0611-2). Am Chemical.

Photodiscovery: Masterworks of Photography 1840-1940. Bruce Bernard. (Illus.). 256p. 1980. 35.00 (ISBN 0-8109-1453-0, 1453-0). Abrams.

Photoeffects at Semiconductor-Electrolyte Interfaces. Ed. by Art J. Nozik. LC 80-27773. (Symposium Ser.: No. 146). 1981. 39.00 (ISBN 0-8412-0604-X). Am Chemical.

Photoelastic & Electro-Optic Properties of Crystals. T. S. Narasimhamurty. (Illus.). 490p. 1981. 37.50 (ISBN 0-306-31101-1, Plenum Pr). Plenum Pub.

Photoelasticity, Vol. 2. M. M. Frocht. 1948. 49.50 (ISBN 0-471-28281-2, Pub. by Wiley-Interscience). Wiley.

Photoelasticity for Designers. R. B. Heywood. (International Series in Mechanical Engineering: Vol. 2). 1969. 24.00 o.p. (ISBN 0-08-013005-4). Pergamon.

Photoelasticity: Principles & Methods. H. T. Jessop & F. C. Harris. (Illus.). 1950. pap. text ed. 3.00 (ISBN 0-486-60720-8). Dover.

Photoelectron Spectroscopy. J. H. Eland. LC 73-17763. 1974. 28.95 (ISBN 0-470-23485-7). Halsted Pr.

Photoelectron Spectroscopy & Molecular Orbital Theory. R. E. Ballard. LC 78-40817. 1979. 57.95 (ISBN 0-470-26542-6). Halsted Pr.

Photoelectron Spectroscopy: Chemical & Analytical Aspects. A. D. Baker & D. Betteridge. 190p. 1972. text ed. 27.00 (ISBN 0-08-016910-4). Pergamon.

Photoemission & the Electronic Properties of Surfaces. B. Feuerbacher et al. 540p. 1978. 61.95 (ISBN 0-471-99555-X). Wiley.

Photofabrication Methods with Kodak Photo Resists. Ed. by Eastman Kodak Company. 1979. pap. 3.75 (ISBN 0-87985-013-2, P246). Eastman Kodak.

Photofact Television Course. 5th ed. Howard W. Sams Engineering Staff. LC 80-50060. (Illus.). 1980. pap. 8.95 (ISBN 0-672-21630-2). SAMS.

Photofinish. Alex Morrison. 144p. 1981. 16.95 (ISBN 0-442-21262-3). Van Nos Reinhold.

Photogeology & Regional Mapping. J. A. Allum. 1966. 21.00 (ISBN 0-08-012033-4); pap. 9.75 (ISBN 0-08-012032-6). Pergamon.

Photograph A-V Program Directory. LC 80-83469. (Illus.). 224p. 1980. 24.50 (ISBN 0-936524-00-6). PMI Inc.

Photograph Collector's Guide. Lee D. Witkin & Barbara London. 448p. 1981. pap. 19.95 (ISBN 0-8212-1124-2). NYGS.

Photographed Cat. Ed. by Jean C. Suares. LC 80-665. (Illus.). 128p. 1980. 15.95 (ISBN 0-385-17081-5). Doubleday.

Photographed Cat. Ed. by Jean C. Suares. LC 80-665. (Illus.). 128p. 1980. pap. 8.95 (ISBN 0-385-17080-7, Dolp). Doubleday.

Photographer. Pierre Boulle. Tr. by Xan Fielding. LC 68-8085. 1968. 8.95 (ISBN 0-8149-0060-7). Vanguard.

Photographer in Lebanon: The Story of Said Jureidini. Jane C. McRae. LC 69-19024. (Illus.). (gr. 4-5). 1969. pap. 0.75 (ISBN 0-8054-4313-4). Broadman.

Photographer's Assistant. Peter Gambaccini. (Illus.). Date not set. pap. 10.95 o.p. (ISBN 0-8256-3201-3, Quick Fox). Music Sales. Postponed.

Photographer's Business Handbook. Ed. by John Stockwell & Herbert Holtje. (Illus.). 320p. 1980. 14.95 (ISBN 0-07-061585-3, P&RB). McGraw.

Photographer's Market Nineteen Eighty. 3rd ed. Melissa Milar. (Illus.). 1979. 12.95 o.p. (ISBN 0-89879-001-8). Writers Digest.

Photographic Action of Ionizing Radiation in Dosimetry & Medical, Industrial, Neutron, Auto & Microradiography. R. H. Herz. 629p. 1969. text ed. 29.50 o.p. (ISBN 0-471-37430-X, Pub. by Wiley). Krieger.

Photographic Careers. E. G. Southey. 1978. pap. 7.95 o.p. (ISBN 0-85242-641-0, Pub. by Fountain). Morgan.

Photographic Gadgets. Carl Holzman & Phoebe Holzman. (Illus.). 160p. 1980. pap. 7.95 (ISBN 0-89586-043-0). H P Bks.

Photographic Illustration for Medical Writing. Donald J. Currie & Arthur Smialowski. (Illus.). 132p. 1962. 14.75 (ISBN 0-398-00379-3). C C Thomas.

Photographic Information Recording. H. Frieser. 1975. 80.00 (ISBN 0-240-50754-1). Focal Pr.

Photographic Information Recording. Hellmut Frieser. LC 75-20097. 592p. 1975. 82.95 (ISBN 0-470-28117-0). Halsted Pr.

Photographic Modeling. Valerie Cragin. LC 75-10066. (Photography How-to Ser.). 1977. pap. 4.50 (ISBN 0-8227-0102-2). Petersen Pub.

Photographic Notations. Robert Leverant. LC 80-8094. (Illus.). 1980. 54.50 (ISBN 0-9600374-6-2). Images Pr.

Photographic Processing Chemistry. 2nd ed. L. F. Mason. LC 75-20098. 326p. 1975. 39.95 (ISBN 0-470-57535-2). Halsted Pr.

Photographic Recording of High-Speed Processes. A. S. Dubovik. 1968. 60.00 (ISBN 0-08-012017-2). Pergamon.

Photographic Recording of High-Speed Processes. 2nd ed. Alexander Dubovik. Tr. by Arthur Aksenov. LC 80-17318. 624p. 1981. 35.00 (ISBN 0-471-04204-8, Pub. by Wiley-Interscience). Wiley.

Photographic Retouching & Airbrush Techniques. John Podracky. (Illus.). 1980. text ed. 13.95 (ISBN 0-13-665257-3). P-H.

Photographic Seeing. Andreas Feininger. LC 73-7567. (Illus.). 200p. 1973. 9.95 o.p. (ISBN 0-13-665372-3). P-H.

Photographic Supplement to the Diary of Anais Nin. Anais Nin. LC 77-2085. 80p. (Orig.). 1974. pap. 2.95 (ISBN 0-15-626024-7, HB293, Harv). HarBraceJ.

Photographic Techniques in Scientific Research, Vol. 3. Ed. by A. A. Newman. 1979. 89.00 (ISBN 0-12-517963-4). Acad Pr.

Photographic Theory for the Motion Picture Cameraman. Compiled by Russell Campbell. (Illus.). 160p. 1981. pap. 6.95 (ISBN 0-498-07776-4). A S Barnes.

Photographic Vision: Pictorial Photography. new ed. Ed. by Peter Bunnell. (Illus.). 124p. 1980. cancelled o.p. (ISBN 0-87905-075-6). Peregrine Smith.

Photographic Vision: Pictorial Photography. Ed. by Peter C. Bunnell. (Illus.). 1980. pap. 17.50 (ISBN 0-87905-081-0). Peregrine Smith.

Photographica: A Guide to the Value of Historic Cameras & Images. Charles Klamkin. LC 77-2849. (Funk & W Bk.). (Illus.). 1978. 17.95 (ISBN 0-308-10298-3, TYC-T). T Y Crowell.

Photographica Collector's Price Guide. George Gilbert. LC 75-28698. (Illus.). 1977. pap. 4.95 o.p. (ISBN 0-8015-1409-6). Dutton.

Photographics. Robert Routh. LC 76-15436. (Petersen's How-to Photographic Library). (Illus.). 80p. 1976. pap. 3.95 o.p. (ISBN 0-8227-4001-X). Petersen Pub.

Photographing Action Sports. Ross R. Olney. LC 75-34250. (Illus.). 160p. (gr. 7 up). 1976. PLB 5.90 o.p. (ISBN 0-531-01139-9). Watts.

Photographing Children. Kalton C. Lahue et al. LC 74-78333. (Illus.). 1974. pap. 3.95 o.p. (ISBN 0-8227-0063-8). Petersen Pub.

Photographing Children. (Life Library of Photography). (Illus.). 1971. 14.95 (ISBN 0-8094-1045-1). Time-Life.

Photographing Crafts. American Craft Council. 66p. 1974. 6.20 (ISBN 0-88321-006-1). Am Craft.

Photographing Indoors with Your Automatic Camera. Barbara London & Richard Boyer. (Your Automatic Camera Ser.). (Illus.). 144p. (Orig.). 1981. pap. 6.95 (ISBN 0-930764-18-8). Curtin & London.

Photographing Mexico City & Acapulco. Albert Moldvay & Erika Fabian. (Amphoto Travel Guide Ser.). Orig. Title: Photographer's Guide to Mexico City & Alcapulco. (Illus.). 1980. pap. 5.95 (ISBN 0-8174-2122-X). Amphoto.

Photographing Nature. (Life Library of Photography). (Illus.). 1971. 14.95 (ISBN 0-8094-1044-3). Time-Life.

Photographing Nudes. Charles F. Hamilton. (Illus.). 1980. 18.95 (ISBN 0-13-665273-5, Spec); pap. 9.95 (ISBN 0-13-665265-4). P-H.

Photographing Outtdoors with Your Automatic Camera. Barbara London & Richard Boyer. (Your Automatic Camera Ser.). (Illus.). 144p. (Orig.). 1981. pap. 6.95 (ISBN 0-930764-19-6). Curtin & London.

Photographing the West a State-by-State Guide. Erwin Bauer & Peggy Bauer. LC 80-81770. (Illus.). 192p. 1980. 27.50 (ISBN 0-87358-269-1); pap. 14.95 (ISBN 0-87358-268-3). Northland.

Photographis '81: The International Annual of Advertising, Editorial & Television Photography. Ed. by Walter Herdeg. (Illus.). 264p. 1981. 59.50 (ISBN 0-8038-5893-0, Visual Communication). Hastings.

Photographs. Christian Vogt. 1980. 35.00. Norton.

Photographs for the Tsar: The Pioneering Color Photography of Sergei Mikhailovich Prokudin-Gorskii Commissioned by Tsar Nicholas II. Ed. by Robert H. Allshouse. (Illus.). 240p. 1980. 35.00 (ISBN 0-8037-6996-2). Dial.

Photographs of Chachaji: The Making of a Documentary Film. Ved Mehta. (Illus.). 300p. 1980. 15.95 (ISBN 0-19-502792-2). Oxford U Pr.

Photographs of the Columbia River & Oregon. Carleton E. Watkins. Ed. by James Alinder. LC 79-54978. (Illus.). 1979. 29.50 o.p. (ISBN 0-933286-13-9); pap. 16.50 (ISBN 0-933286-14-7). Friends Photography.

Photography. Boy Scouts Of America. LC 19-600. (Illus.). 64p. (gr. 6-12). 1971. pap. 0.70x (ISBN 0-8395-3334-9, 3334). BSA.

Photography. Sr. Robert V. Bullough. Ed. by James E. Duane. LC 80-21333. (Instructional Media Library: Vol. 11). (Illus.). 104p. 1981. 13.95 (ISBN 0-87778-171-0). Educ Tech Pubns.

Photography. Ed. by P. Elliston. (Fundamentals of Senior Physics Ser.). 1979. pap. text ed. 7.95x (ISBN 0-686-65410-2). Heinemann Ed.

Photography. Richard Greenhill et al. (Ideals Guidelines). (Illus.). 1980. pap. 2.95 (ISBN 0-89542-900-4). Ideals.

Photography. McKnight Staff Members & Wilbur R. Miller. LC 78-53393. (Basic Industrial Arts Ser.). (Illus.). 1978. 6.00 (ISBN 0-87345-797-8); softbound 4.48 (ISBN 0-87345-789-7). McKnight.

Photography. Charles Swedlund. (Illus.). 384p. 1981. 25.00 (ISBN 0-686-69125-3). HR&W.

Photography. 2nd ed. Upton & Upton. 1981. pap. text ed. 15.95 (ISBN 0-316-88747-1). Little.

Photography: A Manual for Shutterbugs. Eugene Kohn. (Illus.). (gr. 3-7). 1965. pBL o.p. 4.95 (ISBN 0-13-665000-7); pap. 1.25 (ISBN 0-13-665018-X). P-H.

Photography Album No. One. Ed. by Pierre De Fenoyl. LC 79-20063. (Illus.). 232p. (Fr. & Eng.). 50.00 (ISBN 0-9601068-3-9). Agrinde Pubns.

Photography & Film. Jonathan Rutland. LC 78-64659. (Fact Finders Ser.). (Illus.). 1979. lib. bdg. 3.96 (ISBN 0-686-51129-8). Silver.

Photography: Art & Technique. Alfred A. Blaker. LC 79-23536. (Illus.). 1980. text ed. 28.95x (ISBN 0-7167-1115-X); pap. text ed. 16.95x (ISBN 0-7167-1116-8); reference manual incl. W H Freeman.

Photography As a Tool. (Life Library of Photography). (Illus.). 1970. 14.95 (ISBN 0-8094-1023-0). Time-Life.

Photography: Close-up. D. J. Herda. LC 76-45947. (Photography Ser.). (Illus.). (gr. 4-6). 1977. PLB 8.65 (ISBN 0-8172-0019-3). Raintree Pubs.

Photography: Essays & Images; Illustrated Readings in the History of Photography. Ed. by Beaumont Newhall. 1981. 29.95 (ISBN 0-87070-387-0, 706949); pap. 14.95 (ISBN 0-87070-385-4, 706957). NYGS.

Photography: Experiments & Projects. Dwight R. Dixon & Paul B. Dixon. (Illus.). 1976. pap. text ed. 9.95 (ISBN 0-02-329840-5). Macmillan.

Photography for Aquarists. Herbert R. Axelrod. (Illus.). 1970. pap. 2.95 o.p. (ISBN 0-87666-132-0, PS664). TFH Pubns.

Photography for Student Publications. Carl Vandermeulen. LC 79-89332. 1979. pap. 12.95 (ISBN 0-931940-01-X). Middleburg Pr.

Photography for Student Publications. Carl Vandermeulen. LC 79-89332. 1980. 16.95 (ISBN 0-931940-02-8). Middleburg Pr.

Photography for the Scale Modeller. Pieter Stroethoff. LC 78-55052. (Illus.). 1978. 8.95 (ISBN 0-8069-8558-5); PLB 7.49 (ISBN 0-8069-8559-3). Sterling.

Photography: How to Improve Your Technique. Catherine Noren. LC 73-5687. (Career Concise Guides Ser.). (gr. 5 up). 1973. PLB 4.90 o.p. (ISBN 0-531-02640-X). Watts.

Photography in America: The Formative Years, 1839-1900. William Welling. LC 77-1983. (Illus.). 1977. 29.95 o.s.i. (ISBN 0-690-01421-X, TYC-T). T Y Crowell.

Photography in Medicine. Arthur Smialowski & Donald J. Currie. (Illus.). 340p. 1960. 20.50 (ISBN 0-398-01780-8). C C Thomas.

Photography in School. Robert Leggat. 1975. 16.95 o.p. (ISBN 0-85242-404-3, Pub. by Fountain). Morgan.

Photography Index for 1980, Vol. IV. Ed. by Damon B. Flowers. LC 80-640225. 160p. (Orig.). 1981. pap. 8.95 (ISBN 0-934918-03-1). Photo Res.

Photography: Made in Philadelphia 4. Paula Marincola. LC 80-84551. (Illus.). 1979. pap. 4.00 (ISBN 0-88454-059-6). U of Pa Contemp Art.

Photography Notes. James Wagenvoord. (Illus.). 160p. 1981. 6.95 (ISBN 0-312-60840-3). St Martin.

Photography: Picture Perfect. D. J. Herda. LC 76-46369. (Photography Ser.). (Illus.). (gr. 3-5). 1977. PLB 8.65 (ISBN 0-8172-0017-7). Raintree Pubs.

Photography: Simple Truths. Philip Krejcarek. (Illus.). 1978. pap. 4.00 (ISBN 0-686-15968-3). P Krejcarek.

Photography: Take A Look. D. J. Herda. LC 76-46367. (Photography Ser.). (Illus.). (gr. k-3). 1977. 8.65 (ISBN 0-8172-0015-0). Raintree Pubs.

Photography: The Early Years a Historical Guide for Collectors. George Gilbert. LC 78-20163. (Illus.). 181p. 1980. 19.95 (ISBN 0-06-011497-5, HarpT). Har-Row.

Photography: Through the Lens. D. J. Herda. LC 76-45778. (Photography Ser.). (Illus.). (gr. 4-7). 1977. PLB 8.65 (ISBN 0-8172-0003-7). Raintree Pubs.

Photography Through the Microscope. Ed. by Eastman Kodak Company. (Illus.). 96p. 1980. pap. 9.95 (ISBN 0-87985-248-8, P-2). Eastman Kodak.

Photography Year Book 1981. 45th ed. LC 36-13575. (Illus.). 271p. 1980. text ed. 30.00x (ISBN -085242-732-8). Intl Pubns Serv.

Photography Year: 1979. Ed. by Time-Life Books. (Illus.). 1979. 14.95 (ISBN 0-8094-1671-9). Time-Life.

Photography Year: 1980. Ed. by Time-Life Books Editors. (Illus.). 1980. 14.95 (ISBN 0-8094-1685-9). Time-Life.

Photography Yearbook 1978. Ed. by John Sanders. 1977. 21.95 o.p. (ISBN 0-85242-552-X, Pub. by Fountain). Morgan.

Photojournalism. (Life Library of Photography). (Illus.). 1971. 14.95 (ISBN 0-8094-1074-5). Time-Life.

Photojournalism: Making Pictures for Publication. 2nd ed. Philip C. Geraci. (Illus.). 1978. pap. text ed. 13.95 (ISBN 0-8403-1422-1). Kendall-Hunt.

Photojournalism: Photography with a Purpose. Robert L. Kerns. (Illus.). 1980. text ed. 16.95 (ISBN 0-13-665695-1). P-H.

Photojournalism: The Professionals' Approach. Ken Kobre. (Illus.). 368p. (Orig.). 1980. 24.95 (ISBN 0-930764-16-1); pap. text ed. 15.95 (ISBN 0-930764-15-3). Curtin & London.

Photomicrographic Technique for Medical & Biological Scientists. Ralph Gander. Tr. by Roy H. Freere from Ger. (Illus., Eng.). 1969. 9.75 o.s.i. (ISBN 0-02-845100-7). Hafner.

Photomicrographs of Invertebrates. A. C. Shaw et al. (Illus.). 1976. pap. text ed. 4.50x o.p. (ISBN 0-582-32279-0). Longman.

Photomicrography. D. Lawson. 1973. 69.50 (ISBN 0-12-439750-6). Acad Pr.

Photomicrography, 2 vols. Roger P. Loveland. LC 80-12428. 1981. Vol. 1. lib. bdg. write for info.; Vol. 2. lib. bdg. write for info. (ISBN 0-89874-209-9). Krieger.

Photomontage: Barbara Morgan. Ed. by Barbara Morgan. LC 80-81142. 64p. (Orig.). pap. 9.95 (ISBN 0-87100-171-3). Morgan.

Photon-Photon Collisions: Proceedings. Ed. by G. Cochard & P. Kessler. (Lecture Notes in Physics Ser.: Vol. 134). 400p. 1981. pap. 27.70 (ISBN 0-387-10262-0). Springer-Verlag.

Photonuclear Reactions. Ed. by E. G. Fuller & E. Hayward. (Benchmark Papers in Nuclear Physics: Vol. 2). 1976. 48.50x (ISBN 0-12-786495-4). Acad Pr.

Photophysiology. Ed. by A. C. Giese. Incl. Vol. 1. General Principles - Action of Light on Plants. 1964. 46.50 (ISBN 0-12-282601-9); Vol. 2. Action of Light on Animals & Microorganisms, Photobiochemical Mechanisms, Bioluminescence. 1964. 46.50 (ISBN 0-12-282602-7); Vols. 3 & 4. Current Topics. 1968. Vol. 3. 46.50 (ISBN 0-12-282603-5); Vol. 4. 46.50 (ISBN 0-12-282604-3); Vols. 5-7. Current Topics in Photobiology & Photochemistry. 1970-72. Vol. 5. 46.50 (ISBN 0-12-282605-1); Vol. 6. 46.50 (ISBN 0-12-282607-8); Vol. 7. 46.50 (ISBN 0-12-282608-6); Vol. 8. 1973. 46.50 (ISBN 0-12-282608-6). Acad Pr.

Photorealism. Louis K. Meisel. (Illus.). 528p. 1980. 125.00 (ISBN 0-686-62703-2, 1464-6). Abrams.

Photoreception & Sensory Transduction in Aneural Organisms. Ed. by Francesco Lenci & Giuliano Colombetti. (Nato Advanced Study Institutes Ser., Ser. A: Life Sciences: Vol. 33). 430p. 1980. 45.00 (Plenum Pr). Plenum Pub.

Photoselective Chemistry, Pt. 1. Ed. by Joshua Jortner et al. (Advances in Chemical Physics Ser.). 736p. 1981. 49.50 (ISBN 0-471-06275-8, Pub. by Wiley-Interscience). Wiley.

Photoselective Chemistry, Pt. 2. Ed. by Joshua Jortner et al. (Advances in Chemical Physics Ser.). 550p. 1981. 50.00 (ISBN 0-471-06274-X, Pub. by Wiley-Interscience). Wiley.

Photosensitivity & Epilepsy. Ed. by M. Newmark & J. K. Penry. 1979. 19.50 (ISBN 0-89004-393-0). Raven.

Photosynthesis, Bk. 6. M. A. Tribe et al. LC 75-12162. (Basic Biology Course Ser). (Illus.). 88p. (Prog. Bk.). 1975. text ed. 23.95 (ISBN 0-521-20820-3); pap. text ed. 9.50x (ISBN 0-521-20821-1). Cambridge U Pr.

Photosynthesis & Productivity in Different Environments. Ed. by J. P. Cooper. (International Biological Programme Ser.: No. 3). (Illus.). 550p. 1975. 99.00 (ISBN 0-521-20573-5). Cambridge U Pr.

Photosynthesis: Physical Mechanisms & Chemical Patterns. R. K. Clayton. LC 79-27543. (IUPAB Biophysics Ser.: No. 4). 295p. Date not set. 32.50 (ISBN 0-521-22300-8); pap. 11.95 (ISBN 0-521-29443-6). Cambridge U Pr.

Phototherapy in the Newborn: An Overview. Division of Medical Sciences. LC 74-31207. 1975. pap. 12.50 (ISBN 0-309-02313-0). Natl Acad Pr.

Photovoltaics: Sunlight to Electricity in One Step. Paul D. Maycock & Edward N. Stirewalt. 224p. (Orig.). 1981. 19.95 (ISBN 0-931790-24-7); pap. 9.95 (ISBN 0-931790-17-4). Brick Hse Pub.

Phra the Phoenician. Edwin P. Arnold. 1976. lib. bdg. 12.95x (ISBN 0-89968-174-3). Lightyear.

Phrase & Word Origins: A Study of Familiar Expressions. 2nd ed. Alfred H. Holt. Orig. Title: Phrase Origins. 1961. pap. 4.00 (ISBN 0-486-20758-7). Dover.

Phrase de Proust. Jean Milly. (Collection L). (Orig., Fr.). 1976. pap. text ed. 19.95 (ISBN 0-685-66286-1). Larousse.

Phrase Dictionaries for the American Tourist, 6 bks. Frederick Stark. Incl. German for the American Tourist. pap. (ISBN 0-8326-2409-8, 6570); Spanish for the American Tourist. pap. (ISBN 0-8326-2410-1, 6571); French for the American Tourist. pap. (ISBN 0-8326-2411-X, 6572); Italian for the American Tourist. pap. (ISBN 0-8326-2412-8, 6573); Greek for the American Tourist. pap. (ISBN 0-8326-2413-6, 6574); Russian for the American Tourist. pap. (ISBN 0-8326-2414-4, 6575). 128p. (Orig.). 1981. pap. 1.95 ea. Delair.

Phraseology for Civil Engineers, 2 vols. Ed. by Central Electricity Generating Board. 1970. Set. ring binder 58.00x (ISBN 0-685-83867-6). Intl Ideas.

Phrenology. Sybil Leek. 1970. pap. 2.95 o.s.i. (ISBN 0-02-077250-5, Collier). Macmillan.

Phrenology Applied to Marriage & to the Major Social Relations of Mankind. L. N. Fowler. (Illus.). 1978. Repr. of 1842 ed. 39.75 (ISBN 0-89266-109-7). Am Classical Coll Pr.

Phulkari from Bhatinda. Harjeet S. Gill. 1980. 17.50x (ISBN 0-89955-322-2, Pub. by Interprint India). Intl Schol Bk Serv.

Phycology. R. E. Lee. LC 79-25402. (Illus.). 450p. 1980. 49.50 (ISBN 0-521-22530-2); pap. 16.95 (ISBN 0-521-29541-6). Cambridge U Pr.

Phyla Sipuncula & Echiura. A. C. Stephen & S. J. Edmonds. 1972. 62.50x (ISBN 0-565-00717-3, Pub. by Brit Mus Nat Hist England). Sabbot-Natural Hist Bks.

Phylaster: Or, Love Lyes a Bleeding. Francis Beaumont & John Fletcher. LC 68-54617. (English Experience Ser.: No. 18). 66p. 1968. Repr. of 1620 ed. 8.00 (ISBN 90-221-0018-9). Walter J Johnson.

Phylogenetic Analysis & Paleonology. Ed. by Joel Cracraft & Niles Eldredge. LC 78-31404. (Illus.). 1979. 25.00x (ISBN 0-231-04692-8); pap. 10.00x (ISBN 0-231-04693-6). Columbia U Pr.

Phylogenetics: Theory & Practice of Phylogenetic Systematics. Edward O. Wiley. 552p. 1981. price not set (ISBN 0-471-05975-7, Pub. by Wiley-Interscience). Wiley.

Physica. Aristotle. Ed. by W. David Ross. (Oxford Classical Texts Ser). 1950. 17.50x (ISBN 0-19-814514-4). Oxford U Pr.

Physica Aspects of Radioisotopic Organ Imaging. K. G. Leach. 1980. 10.00x (Pub. by Brit Inst Radiology). State Mutual Bk.

Physical Acoustics. Ed. by R. Bruce Lindsay. (Benchmark Papers in Acoustics Ser). 480p. 1974. 44.50 (ISBN 0-12-786964-6). Acad Pr.

Physical Acoustics: Principles & Methods, Vol. 15. Ed. by Warren P. Mason & Robert N. Thurston. 1981. 48.50 (ISBN 0-12-477915-8). Acad Pr.

Physical Activities for Individuals with Handicapping Conditions. 2nd ed. Dolores Geddes. LC 77-26228. (Illus.). 1978. pap. text ed. 10.50 (ISBN 0-8016-1793-6). Mosby.

Physical Activity & Health: An Epidemiologic Study of an Entire Community. Henry J. Montoye. (Intl. Physical Education Research Monograph). (Illus.). 209p. 1975. ref. ed. 13.50 (ISBN 0-13-665604-8). P-H.

Physical Agents for Physical Therapists. James E. Griffin & Terence C. Karselis. (Illus.). 388p. 1979. 26.25 (ISBN 0-398-03706-X). C C Thomas.

Physical & Creative Activities for the Mentally Handicapped. Ed. by G. Upton. LC 77-82519. (Illus.). 1979. 13.95x (ISBN 0-521-21778-4). Cambridge U Pr.

Physical & Mental Suffering of Experimental Animals. Jeff Diner. Ed. by Animal Welfare Institute. 195p. (Orig.). 1979. pap. text ed. 4.00 (ISBN 0-938414-03-8). Animal Welfare.

Physical & Solid State Electronics. Kanaan Kano. LC 77-145408. 1972. text ed. 22.95 (ISBN 0-201-03580-4). A-W.

Physical Anthropology - Laboratory Approach. rev. ed. Dave Racowsky & Thomas Hay. LC 79-65361. (Illus.). 256p. 1979. pap. text ed. 13.50x (ISBN 0-686-63523-X). U MO-St Louis.

Physical Anthropology: A Perspective. John Buettner-Janusch. LC 72-14093. (Illus.). 600p. 1973. text ed. 19.50x o.p. (ISBN 0-471-11785-4). Wiley.

Physical Anthropology & Archaeology. Jurmain et al. (Illus.). 1981. pap. text ed. 11.96 (ISBN 0-8299-0388-7). West Pub.

Physical Anthropology: Human Evolution. Ivan G. Pawson. LC 77-2412. (Self-Teaching Guides). 1977. pap. text ed. 4.95 o.p. (ISBN 0-471-67280-7). Wiley.

Physical Anthropology of Afghanistan. G. F. Debets. LC 72-116739. (Russian Translation Ser.: Vol. 5, No. 1). 1970. pap. text ed. 15.00 (ISBN 0-87365-763-2). Peabody Harvard.

Physical Anthropology of European Populations. Ed. by Ilse Schwidetzky et al. (World Anthropology Ser.). 1979. text ed. 54.00x (ISBN 90-279-7900-6). Mouton.

Physical Aspects of Radioisotope Brachytherapy. (Technical Reports: No. 75). 1967. pap. 3.25 (ISBN 92-0-115167-5, IAEA). Unipub.

Physical Assessment: A Programmed Unit in the Fundamantals of Nursing. Marie M. Seedor. LC 73-85804. (Illus.). 301p. 1974. pap. text ed. 7.50x (ISBN 0-8077-2424-6). Tchrs Coll.

Physical Assessment & Diagnosis in Primary Care. Bille Klaus & Raymond J. Stefan. (Illus.). 704p. 1981. text ed. 24.95 (ISBN 0-86542-003-3). Blackwell Sci.

Physical Assessment of the Gerontologic Client. Rosine Carotenuto & John Bullock. LC 80-15247. 1981. pap. text ed. 7.95 (ISBN 0-8036-1680-5). Davis Co.

Physical Attraction & the Theory of Homosexuality. Otto Weininger. (Illus.). 1979. deluxe ed. 49.85 (ISBN 0-930582-36-5). Gloucester Art.

Physical Basis of Electronics. rev. ed. D. J. Harris & P. D. Robson. LC 74-996. 1974. text ed. 19.50 (ISBN 0-08-017900-2); pap. text ed. 13.25 (ISBN 0-08-017901-0). Pergamon.

Physical Basis of Medical Imaging. Craig M. Coulam. 416p. 1981. 35.00 (ISBN 0-8385-7844-6). ACC.

Physical Behavior of Macromolecules with Biological Functions. S. P. Spragg. (Biophysics & Biochemistry Monographs). 208p. 1981. write for info. (ISBN 0-471-27784-3, Pub. by Wiley-Interscience). Wiley.

Physical Behaviour of Radioactive Contaminants in the Atmosphere. (Illus.). 532p. (Orig., Eng. & Fr.). 1974. pap. 40.75 (ISBN 92-0-020274-8, IAEA). Unipub.

Physical Biochemistry: Applications to Biochemistry & Molecular Biology. David Freifelder. LC 76-6495. (Illus.). 1976. text ed. 31.95x (ISBN 0-7167-0560-5); pap. text ed. 17.95x (ISBN 0-7167-0559-1). W H Freeman.

Physical Ceramics for Engineers. Lawrence H. Van Vlack. (Illus.). 1964. 22.95 (ISBN 0-201-08068-0). A-W.

Physical, Chemical & Biological Changes in Food Caused by Thermal Processing. Ed. by T. Hoyem & O. Kvale. (Illus.). 1977. 104.40x (ISBN 0-85334-729-8). Intl Ideas.

Physical Chemical Properties of Drugs. Yalkowsky & Sinkula. 384p. 1980. 45.00 (ISBN 0-8247-1008-8). Dekker.

Physical Chemistry. P. W. Atkins. LC 77-21208. (Illus.). 1978. text ed. 26.95x (ISBN 0-7167-0187-1); solutions manual 6.95x (ISBN 0-7167-1071-4). W H Freeman.

Physical Chemistry. R. Stephen Berry et al. LC 79-790. 1980. comb. text ed. 34.95 (ISBN 0-471-04829-1); solutions manual 10.95 (ISBN 0-471-04844-5). Wiley.

Physical Chemistry. 2nd ed. Gilbert W. Castellan. LC 75-133375. (Chemistry Ser). (Illus.). 1971. text ed. 23.95 (ISBN 0-201-00912-9). A-W.

Physical Chemistry. Frank T. Gucker & Ralph T. Seifert. (Illus.). 1966. 16.95x (ISBN 0-393-09691-2, NortonC). Norton.

Physical Chemistry. 5th ed. H. L. Heys. (Illus.). 1975. pap. text ed. 16.95x (ISBN 0-245-52675-7). Intl Ideas.

Physical Chemistry. 3rd ed. Scott L. Kittsley. LC 68-26399. (Orig.). 1969. pap. 3.95 (ISBN 0-06-460097-1, CO 97, COS). Har-Row.

Physical Chemistry. 2nd rev. ed. E. A. Moelwyn-Hughes. 1964. 60.00 (ISBN 0-08-010846-6). Pergamon.

Physical Chemistry. 3rd ed. S. C. Wallwork & D. J. Grant. (Longman Text Series). (Illus.). 1977. pap. text ed. 23.00x (ISBN 0-582-44254-0). Longman.

Physical Chemistry: An Advanced Treatise in Eleven Volumes. Ed. by H. Eyring et al. Incl. Vol. 1. Thermodynamics. Ed. by W. Jost. 1971. 68.75, by subscription 55.50 (ISBN 0-12-245601-7); Vol. 2. Statistical Mechanics. Ed. by H. Eyring. 55.50, by subscription 45.50 (ISBN 0-12-245602-5); Vol. 3. Electronic Structure of Atoms & Molecules. Ed. by D. Henderson. 68.75, by subscription 55.50 (ISBN 0-12-245603-3); Vol. 4. Molecular Properties. Ed. by D. Henderson. 77.50, by subscription 62.50 (ISBN 0-12-245604-1); Vol. 5. Valency. Ed. by H. Eyring. 68.75, by subscription 55.50 (ISBN 0-12-245605-X); Vol. 6A. General Introduction & Gas Reactions. Ed. by W. Jost. Pt. A. 64.75, subscription 52.50 (ISBN 0-12-245606-8); Pt. B. 68.75, by subscription 55.50; Vol. 7. Reactions in Condensed Phases. Ed. by H. Eyring. 79.50, subscription 64.25 (ISBN 0-12-245607-6); Vol. 8. Liquid State. Ed. by D. Henderson. Pt. A. 51.50, by subscription 41.75 (ISBN 0-12-245608-4); Pt. B. 55.50, by subscription 45.00 (ISBN 0-12-245658-0); Vol. 9. Electrochemistry. Ed. by H. Eyring. Pt. A. 55.50, by subscription 45.00 (ISBN 0-12-245609-2); Pt. B. 55.50, by subscription 45.00 (ISBN 0-12-245659-9). Pt. B; Vol. 10. Solid State Chemistry. Ed. by W. Jost. 68.75, by subscription 55.50 (ISBN 0-12-245610-6); Vol. 11 Pt. A. Mathematical Applications. Ed. by D. Henderson. 68.75, by subscription 55.50 (ISBN 0-12-245611-4); Pt. B. 64.75 (ISBN 0-12-245661-0). Acad Pr.

Physical Chemistry & Its Biological Applications. Wallace Brey. 589p. 1978. tchrs' ed. 18.95 (ISBN 0-12-133150-4); solutions manual 4.95 (ISBN 0-12-133152-0). Acad Pr.

Physical Chemistry & Mineralogy of Soils: Soils in Place, Vol. II. C. Edmund Marshall. LC 64-20074. 1977. 32.95 (ISBN 0-471-02957-2, Pub. by Wiley-Interscience). Wiley.

Physical Chemistry for the Life Sciences. Paul Barrante. (Illus.). 1977. text ed. 18.95 (ISBN 0-13-665984-5). P-H.

Physical Chemistry Laboratory Experiments. John M. White. (Illus.). 576p. 1975. ref. ed. 17.95 (ISBN 0-13-665927-6). P-H.

Physical Chemistry of Fast Reactions: Vol. 2: Reaction Dynamics. Ed. by I. W. Smith. (Illus.). 290p. 1980. 32.50 (ISBN 0-306-40227-0, Plenum Pr). Plenum Pub.

Physical Chemistry: Principles & Applications in Biological Sciences. Ignacio Tinoco, Jr. et al. LC 77-25417. 1978. text ed. 22.95 (ISBN 0-13-665901-2); solutions 4.95 (ISBN 0-13-665919-5). P-H.

Physical Chemistry Problems & Solutions. L. C. Labowitz & J. S. Arents. 1969. text ed. 12.95 (ISBN 0-12-432150-X). Acad Pr.

Physical Climatology. William D. Sellers. LC 65-24983. 1965. 15.00x (ISBN 0-226-74699-2). U of Chicago Pr.

Physical Conditioning & Cardiovascular Rehabilitation. Lawrence S. Cohen et al. 344p. 1981. 25.00 (ISBN 0-471-08713-0, Pub. by Wiley-Med). Wiley.

Physical Constants. 9th ed. W. H. Childs. 107p. 1972. pap. text ed. 7.95x o.p. (ISBN 0-412-21050-9, Pub. by Chapman & Hall). Methuen Inc.

Physical Constants. 9th ed. W. H. Childs. 1972. pap. 7.95x o.p. (ISBN 0-470-15578-7). Halsted Pr.

Physical Control of the Mind: Toward a Psychocivilized Society. Jose M. Delgado. Ed. by Ruth N. Anshen. LC 71-89871. (World Perspectives). (Illus.). 1969. 10.00 o.s.i. (ISBN 0-06-011016-3, HarpT). Har-Row.

Physical Diagnosis in Medicine. A. E. Davis & T. D. Bolin. 122p. 1974. pap. 12.00 (ISBN 0-08-017376-4). Pergamon.

Physical Diagnosis Review. John H. Holbrook. LC 79-88046. 1979. pap. 8.50 (ISBN 0-87488-135-8). Med Exam.

Physical Disabilities. Gilda Berger. LC 78-10106. (Illus.). 1979. s&l 7.45 (ISBN 0-531-02927-1). Watts.

Physical Disabilities Manual. Beatriz Abreu. 362p. 1981. text ed. 26.50 (ISBN 0-89004-505-4). Raven.

Physical Disability & Human Behavior. 2nd ed. James W. McDaniel. 232p. 1976. text ed. 16.00 (ISBN 0-08-019722-1); pap. text ed. 9.25 (ISBN 0-08-019721-3). Pergamon.

Physical Distribution Case Studies. Jack W. Farrell. LC 72-91987. 1973. 14.95 (ISBN 0-8436-1404-8). CBI Pub.

Physical Distribution Forum. Ed. by Jack Farrell et al. LC 72-91981. 1973. 14.95 (ISBN 0-8436-1403-X). CBI Pub.

Physical Education. Jack Rudman. (Undergraduate Program Field Test Ser.: UPFT-18). (Cloth bdg. avail. on request). pap. 9.95 (ISBN 0-8373-6018-8). Natl Learning.

Physical Education Activities Handbook for Men & Women. 3rd ed. Dennis K. Stanley et al. 352p. 1973. text ed. 18.95x o.p. (ISBN 0-205-03640-6, 6236405). Allyn.

Physical Education: An Overview. 2nd ed. Beverly L. Seidel & Matthew C. Resnick. LC 77-79453. (Physical Education Ser.). (Illus.). 1978. text ed. 13.50 (ISBN 0-201-06988-1). A-W.

Physical Education & Sport: Change & Challenge. Charles A. Bucher & Nolan A. Thaxton. LC 80-25237. (Illus.). 311p. 1981. pap. text ed. 11.95 (ISBN 0-8016-0876-7). Mosby.

Physical Education & Sports: An Introduction to Alternative Careers. Sheldon L. Fordham & Carol A. Leaf. LC 77-19115. 1978. text ed. 18.95 (ISBN 0-471-26622-1). Wiley.

Physical Education & the Physical Educator. 2nd ed. James A. Baley & David A. Field. 400p. 1976. text ed. 17.95x (ISBN 0-205-05052-2, 6250521). Allyn.

Physical Education As a Career: A Text for the Introductory Course. James H. Humphrey. (Illus.). 216p. 1978. 16.75 (ISBN 0-398-03801-5); pap. 12.25 (ISBN 0-398-03802-3). C C Thomas.

Physical Education Curriculum. 8th ed. John M. Cooper & Clinton Strong. 1973. saddle stitched 2.95x (ISBN 0-87543-099-6). Lucas.

Physical Education for Blind Children. Charles E. Buell. (Illus.). 244p. 1974. pap. 24.50 (ISBN 0-398-03141-X). C C Thomas.

Physical Education for Children with Perceptual-Motor Learning Disabilities. Robert W. Harvat. LC 78-158072. 1971. pap. text ed. 6.95x (ISBN 0-675-09901-3). Merrill.

Physical Education for Elementary School Children. 5th ed. Glenn Kirchner et al. 1981. text ed. 15.95x (ISBN 0-697-07175-8); instrs.' manual 1.00 (ISBN 0-697-07179-0); unit lesson plans avail. (ISBN 0-697-07180-4). Wm C Brown.

Physical Education for Special Needs. Ed. by L. Groves. LC 78-68389. 1979. 19.95 (ISBN 0-521-22391-1); pap. 8.95 (ISBN 0-521-29471-1). Cambridge U Pr.

Physical Education: Foundations, Principles, & Practices. Reuben B. Frost. LC 74-10351. 528p. 1975. text ed. 17.95 (ISBN 0-201-02107-2). A-W.

Physical Education Handbook. 6th ed. Donald C. Seaton et al. (Illus.). 438p. 1974. text ed. 17.95 (ISBN 0-13-667501-8); pap. text ed. 11.95 (ISBN 0-13-667493-3). P-H.

Physical Education in a Changing Society. William Freeman. LC 76-10898. (Illus.). 1977. text ed. 15.75 (ISBN 0-395-24408-0); inst. manual 1.25 (ISBN 0-395-24409-9). HM.

Physical Education: Teaching Human Movement in the Elementary Schools. Arthur G. Miller et al. (Illus.). 420p. 1974. 16.95 (ISBN 0-13-668301-0). P-H.

Physical Education Teaching Problems for Analysis & Solution. John H. Healey & William A. Healey. 196p. 1975. 14.75 (ISBN 0-398-03206-8). C C Thomas.

Physical Education: The Profession. Janet B. Parks. LC 79-24507. (Illus.). 1980. pap. text ed. 8.95 (ISBN 0-8016-3759-7). Mosby.

Physical Electronics. David K. Ferry & D. R. Fannin. LC 73-128907. (Engineering Science Ser). 1971. text ed. 20.95 (ISBN 0-201-02105-6); ans. bk 2.00 (ISBN 0-201-02106-4). A-W.

Physical Examination of the Spine & Extremities: Slide Package. Hoppenfeld. (Illus.). 621p. 1976. 19.50 (ISBN 0-8385-7853-5); 35 mm b-w slides 385.00 (ISBN 0-8385-7854-3). ACC.

Physical Fitness & Mental Health Before & After Retirement. Helen Hall Peters. 1977. 6.50 o.p. (ISBN 0-682-48837-2, Banner). Exposition.

Physical Fitness Assessment: Principles, Practice & Application. Roy J. Shephard & Hugues Lavallee. (Illus.). 320p. 1978. 33.75 (ISBN 0-398-03701-9). C C Thomas.

Physical Fitness in Law Enforcement: A Guide to More Efficient Service. Robert R. Spackman, Jr. & William F. Vincent. LC 70-83663. (Illus.). 123p. 1969. pap. 3.95 (ISBN 0-8093-0406-6). S Ill U Pr.

Physical Fitness Skill Book. Boy Scouts of America. (Illus.). 32p. (gr. 3-4). 1975. pap. 0.50x (ISBN 0-8395-6590-9, 6590); tchr's guide 0.30x (ISBN 0-685-51280-0, 18-330). BSA.

Physical Fitness: The Pathway to Healthful Living. Robert V. Hockey. (Illus.). 195p. 1981. pap. text ed. 8.95 (ISBN 0-8016-2216-6). Mosby.

Physical Foundations of the Psyche. Charles M. Fair. LC 63-8861. 1963. 20.00x (ISBN 0-8195-3037-9, Pub. by Wesleyan U Pr). Columbia U Pr.

Physical Geography. Phillip Gersmehl et al. LC 78-12212. 415p. 1980. text ed. 15.95 (ISBN 0-03-014476-0, HoltC). HR&W.

Physical Geography. Cuchlaine A. King. (Illus.). 332p. 1980. 34.50x (ISBN 0-389-20089-1). B&N.

Physical Geography. 3rd ed. Michael P. McIntyre. LC 79-19207. 1980. text ed. 18.95 (ISBN 0-471-05629-4); study guide 7.95 (ISBN 0-471-05933-1); tchrs'. manual avail. (ISBN 0-471-06367-3). Wiley.

Physical Geography. 4th ed. Arthur N. Strahler. LC 74-9994. 651p. 1975. text ed. 24.95x (ISBN 0-471-83160-3). Wiley.

Physical Geography: A Multimedia Approach. Richard S. Palm. (Geography Ser.). 1978. pap. text ed. 15.95 (ISBN 0-675-08403-2); media 595.00 (ISBN 0-675-08402-4); instructor's manual 3.95 (ISBN 0-686-66344-6); 2-4 sets 350.00 (ISBN 0-686-66345-4); 5-9 sets 250.00 (ISBN 0-686-66346-2); 10-14 sets 200.00 (ISBN 0-686-66347-0); 15 sets or more 165.00. Merrill.

Physical Geography: A Survey of Man's Physical Environment. Ross N. Pearson. (Maps, Orig). 1971. pap. 4.25 (ISBN 0-06-460074-2, CO 74, COS). Har-Row.

Physical Geography: An Introduction. James S. Gardner. (Illus.). 1977. text ed. 21.50 scp (ISBN 0-06-167411-7, HarpC); inst. manual free (ISBN 0-06-167414-1). Har-Row.

Physical Geography Manual. Mary T. Dooley & James F. Goff. 1969. spiral bdg. 9.95 (ISBN 0-8087-0420-6). Burgess.

Physical Geography of Wisconsin. 3rd ed. Lawrence Martin. (Illus.). 1965. text ed. 27.50 (ISBN 0-299-03472-0); pap. text ed. 8.95 (ISBN 0-299-03475-5). U of Wis Pr.

Physical Geography Workbook. rev. ed. John A. Carthew. (Illus.). 68p. 1981. pap. text ed. 4.70x (ISBN 0-89179-218-X). Tam's Bks.

Physical Geology. John R. Allen. (Introducing Geology Ser.). 1975. pap. text ed. 9.95x (ISBN 0-04-550022-3). Allen Unwin.

Physical Geology. 2nd ed. Richard F. Flint & Brian J. Skinner. LC 76-23206. 1977. text ed. 21.95x (ISBN 0-471-26442-3); study guide 7.50 (ISBN 0-471-02593-3). Wiley.

Physical Geology. 3rd ed. Robert J. Foster. (Science Ser.). 1979. text ed. 19.95 (ISBN 0-675-08312-5); study guide avail. Merrill.

Physical Geology. S. Judson et al. (Illus.). 592p. 1976. text ed. 19.95 (ISBN 0-13-669655-4); study guide 5.95 (ISBN 0-13-669630-9). P-H.

Physical Geology. 5th ed. L. Don Leet et al. 1978. ref. ed. 20.95 (ISBN 0-13-669739-9); study guide 5.95 (ISBN 0-13-669747-X). P-H.

Physical Geology. John E. Sanders et al. 1976. text ed. 21.50 scp (ISBN 0-06-163403-4, HarpC); instr. manual & test bank avail. (ISBN 0-06-361160-0). Har-Row.

Physical Geology Laboratory Manual. 3rd ed. H. E. Eveland & A. C. Tennissen. 96p. 1979. pap. text ed. 7.95 (ISBN 0-8403-2061-2). Kendall-Hunt.

Physical Geology: Principles & Perspectives. A. Lee McAlester & Edward A. Hay. (Illus.). 448p. 1975. 18.95 (ISBN 0-13-669523-X); study guide 4.25 (ISBN 0-13-669531-0). P-H.

Physical Knowledge in Preschool Education: Implications of Piaget's Theory. Constance Kamli & Rheta DeVries. (Illus.). 1978. ref. ed. 15.95 (ISBN 0-13-669804-2). P-H.

Physical Landscape in Pictures. Albert V. Hardy & F. J. Monkhouse. 1964. text ed. 6.95 (ISBN 0-521-05201-7). Cambridge U Pr.

Physical Management of Developmental Disorders. Errington Ellis. (Clinics in Developmental Medicine Ser. No. 26). 50p. 1967. 3.50 o.p. (ISBN 0-685-24740-6). Lippincott.

Physical Medicine & Rehabilitation. 3rd ed. Kate H. Kohn et al. (Medical Examination Review Bk.: Vol. 20). 1979. spiral bdg. 19.50 (ISBN 0-87488-128-5). Med Exam.

Physical Medicine & Rehabilitation Approaches in Spinal Cord Injury. Ed. by John G. Cull & Richard E. Hardy. (American Lectures on Social & Rehabilitation Psychology Ser.). (Illus.). 336p. 1977. 24.75 (ISBN 0-398-03609-8). C C Thomas.

Physical Medicine & Rehabilitation Continuing Education Review. 2nd ed. Paul E. Kaplan et al. 1980. pap. 13.00x (ISBN 0-87488-335-0). Med Exam.

Physical Metallurgy. Peter Haasen. Tr. by Janet Mordike. LC 76-53517. (Illus.). 1978. 71.50 (ISBN 0-521-21548-X); pap. 18.50x (ISBN 0-521-29183-6). Cambridge U Pr.

Physical Metallurgy & Design of Steels. F. B. Pickering. (Illus.). 1978. text ed. 62.60x (ISBN 0-85334-752-2). Intl Ideas.

Physical Metallurgy of Iron & Steel. Rajendra Kumar. 1968. 20.00x (ISBN 0-210-22658-7). Asia.

Physical Metallurgy of Steels. William C. Leslie. (M-H Materials Science & Engineering Ser.). 368p. 1981. text ed. 29.50 (ISBN 0-07-037780-4). McGraw.

Physical Metallurgy: Techniques & Applications, 2 vols. K. W. Andrews. LC 72-11309. 1973. Vol. 1. 34.95 (ISBN 0-470-03150-6); Vol. 2. 30.95 (ISBN 0-470-03151-4). Halsted Pr.

Physical Methods in Chemical Analysis, 4 vols. Ed. by Walter G. Berl. Incl. Vol. 1. 2nd rev. ed. 1960. 62.00 (ISBN 0-12-092061-1); Vol. 2. 1951. 51.00 (ISBN 0-12-092002-6); Vol. 3. 1956. 51.00 (ISBN 0-12-092003-4); Vol. 4. 1961. 51.00 (ISBN 0-12-092004-2). Acad Pr.

Physical Methods in Determinative Mineralogy. 2nd ed. Ed. by J. Zussman. 1978. 73.50 (ISBN 0-12-782960-1). Acad Pr.

Physical Performance, Fitness & Diet. Donald R. Young. (Amer. Lec. Environmental Studies). (Illus.). 128p. 1977. 13.50 (ISBN 0-398-03642-X). C C Thomas.

Physical, Political & International Value of the Panama Canal. William H. Taft. (Illus.). 1979. deluxe ed. 39.75 (ISBN 0-930008-29-4). Inst Econ Pol.

Physical Principles & Techniques of Protein Chemistry. Ed. by Sidney J. Leach. (Molecular Biology Ser.). 1969-1973. Pt. A. 59.00 (ISBN 0-12-440101-5); Pt. B. 55.25 (ISBN 0-12-440102-3); Pt. C. 68.50 (ISBN 0-12-440103-1); 148.25 set (ISBN 0-686-57487-7). Acad Pr.

Physical Principles of Audiology. Haughton. (Medical Physics Handbook: Vol. 3). 1980. 28.00 (ISBN 0-9960019-1-3, Pub. by a Hilger England). Heyden.

Physical Principles of Chemical Engineering. Peter Grassman. 928p. 1971. text ed. 105.00 (ISBN 0-08-012817-3). Pergamon.

Physical Principles of Exploration Methods: An Introduction Text for Geology & Geophysics Students. A. E. Beck. 256p. 1981. 39.95 (ISBN 0-470-27124-8); pap. 18.95 (ISBN 0-470-27128-0). Halsted Pr.

Physical Principles of the Quantum Theory. Werner Heisenberg. 1930. pap. text ed. 3.00 (ISBN 0-486-60113-7). Dover.

Physical Principles of Ultrasonic Technology, 2 vols. Ed. by L. D. Rozenberg. Incl. Vol. 1. 515p. 49.50 (ISBN 0-306-35041-6); Vol. 2. 544p. 47.50 (ISBN 0-306-35042-4). (Ultrasonic Technology Monographs Ser.). (Illus.). 1973 (Plenum Pr). Plenum Pub.

Physical Processes in the Interstellar Medium. Lyman Spitzer, Jr. LC 77-14273. 1978. 19.95 (ISBN 0-471-02232-2, Pub. by Wiley-Interscience). Wiley.

Physical Properties of Crystals: Their Representation by Tensors & Matrices. J. F. Nye. 1957. 37.50x (ISBN 0-19-851105-1). Oxford U Pr.

Physical Properties of Food & Agricultural Materials: A Teachin Manual. Nuri N. Mohsenin. 1981. price not set (ISBN 0-677-05630-3). Gordon.

Physical Properties of Graphite. W. N. Reynolds. (Illus.). 1968. text ed. 29.90x (ISBN 0-444-20012-6). Intl Ideas.

Physical Properties of Hydrocarbons, Vol. 2. 2nd ed. Robert W. Gallant & Jay M. Railey. 1981. cancelled (ISBN 0-87201-690-0). Gulf Pub.

Physical Properties of Rocks & Minerals, Vol. II. U. S. Touloukian & C. Y. Ho. (M-H-CINDAS Data Series on Material Properties). (Illus.). 576p. 1981. text ed. 44.50 (ISBN 0-07-065032-2). McGraw.

Physical Properties of Textile Fibres. 2nd ed. W. E. Morton & J. W. Hearle. LC 74-30834. 660p. 1975. 68.95x (ISBN 0-470-61850-7). Halsted Pr.

Physical Rehabilitation: Evaluation & Treatment Procedures. Susan B. O'Sullivan et al. LC 80-10890. (Illus.). 521p. 1980. pap. text ed. 23.50 (ISBN 0-8036-6697-7). Davis Co.

Physical Resources Investigations for Economic Development. 1970. Eng. ed. 10.00 (ISBN 0-8270-3935-2); Span ed. 10.00 (ISBN 0-8270-3885-2). OAS.

Physical Science. Fred Bueche. LC 73-182927. (Illus.). 1972. 16.95x (ISBN 0-87901-019-3). Worth.

Physical Science for Biologists. J. K. Edginton & H. J. Sherman. 1971. text ed. 6.25x (ISBN 0-09-107860-1, Hutchinson U Lib); pap. text ed. 3.50x (ISBN 0-09-107861-X, Hutchinson U Lib). Humanities.

Physical Science for Technicians I. Randall McMullan. 1978. pap. text ed. 9.95 (ISBN 0-408-00332-4). Butterworths.

Physical Science in the Middle Ages. E. Grant. LC 77-8393. (History of Science Ser.). (Illus.). 1978. 19.95 (ISBN 0-521-21862-4); pap. 6.50x (ISBN 0-521-29294-8). Cambridge U Pr.

Physical Science: Intermediate Level. Jules Weisler. (gr. 7-10). 1971. wkbk. 7.17 (ISBN 0-87720-009-2). AMSCO Sch.

Physical Science with Consumer & Environmental Applications: Laboratory Investigations. Frank Fazio et al. 1978. pap. text ed. 7.25 (ISBN 0-8403-1075-7). Kendall-Hunt.

Physical Science with Environmental Applications. Arthur W. Wiggins. 384p. 1974. text ed. 17.75 (ISBN 0-395-17072-9); instructors' manual .75 (ISBN 0-395-17852-5); study guide 5.00 (ISBN 0-395-17071-0); Set. 20-35mm slides 11.75 (ISBN 0-395-18187-9). HM.

Physical Sciences: Inquiry & Investigation. Donald Stafford & John Renner. 1977. text ed. 14.95x (ISBN 0-02-478900-3). Macmillan.

Physical Sciences: The Royal Institution Library of Science, 10 vols. plus index. Ed. by William L. Bragg & George Porter. (Illus.). 1969. Set. 396.00x (ISBN 0-444-20048-7); Set. pap. 216.00x (ISBN 0-85334-615-1). Intl Ideas.

Physical Sensors for Biomedical Applications. Ed. by Michael R. Neuman et al. 160p. 1980. 49.95 (ISBN 0-8493-5975-9). CRC Pr.

Physical Settings & Organization Development. F. I. Steele. LC 70-172802. 1973. pap. text ed. 6.50 (ISBN 0-201-07211-4). A-W.

Physical Stratigraphy of the John Day Formation, Central Oregon. Richard V. Fisher & John M. Rensberger. (U. C. Publ. in Geological Sciences: Vol. 101). 1972. pap. 6.50x (ISBN 0-520-09460-3). U of Cal Pr.

Physical Structure in Systems Theory: Network Approaches Engineering & Economics. Ed. by J. J. Van Dixhoorn & F. J. Evans. 1975. 46.00 (ISBN 0-12-712450-0). Acad Pr.

Physical Techniques in Medicine, 2 vols. J. T. McMullan. Incl. Vol. 1. LC 76-30281. 1977. 59.75 (ISBN 0-471-99468-5); Vol. 2. LC 79-42909. 160p. 1980. 45.00 (ISBN 0-471-27695-2). Pub. by Wiley-Interscience). Wiley.

Physical Theory of Neutron Chain Reactors. Alvin M. Weinberg & Eugene P. Wigner. LC 58-8507. (Illus.). 1958. 30.00x (ISBN 0-226-88517-8). U of Chicago Pr.

Physical Therapy Examination Review Book Clinical Application, Vol. 2. 2nd ed. Ronald A. Hershey. 1973. pap. 9.50 (ISBN 0-87488-482-9). Med Exam.

Physical Therapy Examination Review Book: Vol. 1, Basic Sciences. 3rd ed. Ronald A. Hershey. Ed. by Helen K. Seibert. 1976. pap. 9.50 (ISBN 0-87488-481-0). Med Exam.

Physical Therapy for Animals: Selected Techniques. Ann H. Downer. (Illus.). 196p. 1978. 14.75- (ISBN 0-398-03702-7). C C Thomas.

Physical Therapy Services in the Developmental Disabilities. Ed. by Paul H. Pearson & Carol E. Williams. (Illus.). 448p. 1980. 25.50 (ISBN 0-398-02377-8). C C Thomas.

Physical Work Effort. Ed. by Gunnar Borg. LC 76-45405. 1977. text ed. 49.00 (ISBN 0-08-021373-1). Pergamon.

Physical World of the Greeks. S. Sambursky. Tr. by Merton Dagut. 1956. pap. 8.95 (ISBN 0-7100-4637-5). Routledge & Kegan.

Physicalism. Kathleen Wilkes. (Studies in Philosophical Psychology). 1978. text ed. 12.50x (ISBN 0-391-00741-6). Humanities.

Physically Handicapped & the Community: Some Challenging Breakthroughs. 132p. 1970. pap. 8.75 sprial (ISBN 0-398-01304-7). C C Thomas.

Physically Handicapped Child in Your Classroom: A Handbook for Teachers. Dorothy Edgington. (Illus.). 92p. 1976. pap. 10.75 (ISBN 0-398-03496-6). C C Thomas.

Physician. Sarel Eimerl & Russell V. Lee. LC 67-20331. (Life Science Library). (Illus.). (gr. 5 up). 1967. PLB 8.97 o.p. (ISBN 0-8094-0480-X, Pub. by Time-Life). Silver.

Physician & Sportsmedicine Guide to Running. Allan J. Ryan. (Physician & Sportsmedicine Guides). (Illus.). 1980. 7.95 (ISBN 0-07-054358-5). McGraw.

Physician As Manager. John J. Aluise. (Illus.). 357p. 1979. 29.95 (ISBN 0-89303-006-6). Charles.

Physician Compensation. new ed. David Pieroni. LC 78-59104. 1978. text ed. 26.00 (ISBN 0-89443-049-1). Aspen Systems.

Physician Extraordinary. David Weiss. 512p. 1975. 8.95 o.s.i. (ISBN 0-440-05916-X). Delacorte.

Physician-Patient Communication: Readings & Recommendations. write for info (ISBN 0-398-04465-1). C C Thomas.

Physician Recruitment & the Hospital. Harry E. Olson, Jr. (Illus.). 160p. (Orig.). 1980. 15.00 (ISBN 0-87258-301-5, 1035). Am Hospital.

Physician Supply, Peer Review, & Use of Health Services in Medicaid. John Holahan. (Institute Paper). 70p. 1976. pap. 3.50 (ISBN 0-87766-159-6, 13800). Urban Inst.

Physician to the West: Selected Writings of Daniel Drake on Science & Society. Daniel Drake. Ed. by Henry D. Shapiro & Zane L. Miller. LC 73-94071. (Illus.). 464p. 1970. 18.00x (ISBN 0-8131-1197-8). U Pr of Ky.

Physicians' & Pharmacists' Guide to Your Medicines. U. S. Pharmacopeial Convention. 544p. (Orig.). 1981. pap. 9.95 (ISBN 0-345-29635-4). Ballantine.

Physicians & Their Careers. Betty H. Mawardi. LC 79-25421. 524p. (Orig.). 1980. 38.25 (ISBN 0-8357-0497-1, SS-00130). Univ Microfilms.

Physician's Assistant. Eugene S. Schneller. LC 76-11974. 1978. 18.95 (ISBN 0-669-00715-3). Lexington Bks.

Physician's Assistant Examination Review Book. Bernard Challenor et al. 1975. pap. 12.50 (ISBN 0-87488-422-5). Med Exam.

Physician's Assistant: Today & Tomorrow: Issues Confronting New Health Practitioners. Alfred M. Sadler, Jr. et al. LC 75-22407. 1975. 16.50 (ISBN 0-88410-125-8); pap. text ed. 8.95 (ISBN 0-88410-124-X). Ballinger Pub.

Physician's Business Manual. Richard A. Klass. 400p. 1980. 23.50x (ISBN 0-8385-7850-0). ACC.

Physicians' Desk Reference for Nonprescription Drugs. 12.25 (ISBN 0-87489-957-5). Med Economics.

Physician's Guide to Managing Emotional Problems. Arthur H. Chapman. (Illus.). 1969. 13.95 o.p. (ISBN 0-397-50238-9, 70-78609). Lippincott.

Physician's Guide to Microcomputers. Mark Spohr. 1981. 18.95 (ISBN 0-8359-5548-6). Reston.

Physician's Handbook on Orthomolecular Medicine. Ed. by Roger J. Williams & Dwight K. Kalita. LC 77-8304. 1977. text ed. 19.95 (ISBN 0-08-021533-5). Pergamon.

Physicians' Licensure & Discipline. Frank P. Grad & Noelia Marti. LC 79-21925. 471p. 1980. lib. bdg. 45.00 (ISBN 0-379-20463-0). Oceana.

Physicians of Essex County (Mass.) Russell L. Jackson. (Illus.). 152p. 1948. 10.00 o.p. (ISBN 0-88389-009-7). Essex Inst.

Physicians of the Soul. Desmond Ford. LC 79-25555. (Horizon Ser.). 1980. pap. 4.95 (ISBN 0-8127-0262-X). Southern Pub.

Physician's Posy. Dorothy Shepherd. 1980. text ed. 7.95 o.p. (ISBN 0-8464-1037-0). Beekman Pubs.

Physicians Practice. John M. Eisenberg & Sarkey V. Williams. LC 80-13691. 274p. 1980. 18.50 (ISBN 0-471-05469-0, Pub. by Wiley Med). Wiley.

Physician's Primer on Computers: Private Practice. Jan F. Brandejs & Graham Pace. LC 75-39315. (Illus.). 1979. 18.50 (ISBN 0-669-00431-6). Lexington Bks.

Physicke Against Fortune. Francesco Petrarca. Tr. by Thomas Twyne. LC 80-22768. 1980. Repr. of 1579 ed. 75.00x (ISBN 0-8201-1359-X). Schol Facsimiles.

Physico-Chemical Diagnostics of Plasma: Proceedings. Gas Dynamics Symposium - 5th Biennial - 1964. Ed. by Thomas P. Anderson et al. 1964. 8.95x o.s.i. (ISBN 0-8101-0041-X). Northwestern U Pr.

Physico-Chemical Factors of Biological Evolution. S. E. Shnol. 327p. 1981. 65.50 (ISBN 3-7186-0044-7). Harwood Academic.

Physico-Chemical Methodologies in Psychiatric Research. Ed. by Israel Hanin & Stephen Koslow. 1980. text ed. 28.50 (ISBN 0-89004-411-2). Raven.

Physico-Chemical Processes in Mixed Aqueous Solvents. Ed. by F. Franks. 1967. text ed. 14.95x o.p. (ISBN 0-435-66320-8). Heinemann Ed.

Physico Chemical Techniques of Analysis, 2 vols. Pandarinath Janardhan. Vol. 1. 15.00x (ISBN 0-210-26919-7); Vol. 2. 15.00x (ISBN 0-210-22530-0). Asia.

Physicochemical Aspects of Protein Denaturation. Savo Lapanje. LC 78-1919. 1978. 34.50 (ISBN 0-471-03409-6, Pub. by Wiley-Interscience). Wiley.

Physicochemical Measurements: Catalogue of Reference Materials from National Laboratories. Ed. by J. P. Cali. 1977. pap. text ed. 10.00 (ISBN 0-08-021578-5). Pergamon.

Physics. 3rd ed. Kenneth R. Atkins. LC 75-11677. 818p. 1976. text ed. 24.95 (ISBN 0-471-03629-3); instr's manual 2.75 (ISBN 0-471-01824-4). Wiley.

Physics. 2nd ed. Arthur Beiser. LC 77-87340. 1978. 22.95 (ISBN 0-8053-0379-0); instr's guide 7.95 (ISBN 0-8053-0380-4). Benjamin-Cummings.

Physics. D. Bryant. (Teach Yourself Ser.). 1974. pap. 2.95 (ISBN 0-679-10406-2). McKay.

Physics. Herman Gewirtz. LC 56-39359. (Regents Exams & Answer Ser.). (gr. 10-12). 1976. pap. 3.95 (ISBN 0-8120-0201-6). Barron.

Physics. new ed. William Lichten. (Orig.). (gr. 7-12). 1973. 6.44 (ISBN 0-201-04242-8, Sch Div); tchr's manual 2.84 (ISBN 0-201-04243-6). A-W.

Physics. 4th ed. Arthur E. McKenzie. 1970. 17.95x (ISBN 0-521-07698-6). Cambridge U Pr.

Physics. Jack Rudman. (Undergraduate Program Field Test Ser.: UPFT-19). (Cloth bdg. avail. on request). pap. 9.95 (ISBN 0-8373-6019-6). Natl Learning.

Physics, 2 vols. Paul A. Tipler. LC 74-82693. 1976. Set. 26.95 (ISBN 0-87901-041-X); 15.95x ea. Vol. 1 (ISBN 0-87901-094-0). Vol. 2 (ISBN 0-87901-095-9). study guide 7.95x (ISBN 0-87901-055-X). Worth.

Physics. C. Zafiratos. LC 75-14034. 911p. 1976. 27.95x (ISBN 0-471-98104-4); instructor's manual avail. (ISBN 0-471-01854-6). Wiley.

Physics, Pts. 1 & 2. 3rd combined ed. Robert Halliday & David Resnick. 1978. text ed. 29.95x (ISBN 0-471-34530-X); answer bklt. 2.50 (ISBN 0-471-03710-9). Wiley.

Physics: A Descriptive Analysis. A. J. Read. 1970. 14.95 (ISBN 0-201-06304-2). A-W.

Physics & Applications of the Josephson Effect. Antonio Barone & Gianfranco Paterno. 450p. 1981. 40.00 (ISBN 0-471-01469-9, Pub. by Wiley-Interscience). Wiley.

Physics & Archaeology. 2nd ed. M. J. Aitken. (Illus.). 320p. 1975. 39.50x (ISBN 0-19-851922-2). Oxford U Pr.

Physics & Beyond. Werner Heisenberg. (World Perspectives Ser.). pap. 5.50x (ISBN 0-06-131622-9, TB1622, Torch). Har-Row.

Physics & Chemistry of Baking. K. J. Dean et al. (Illus.). vii, 225p. 1980. pap. 22.50x (ISBN 0-85334-867-7). Intl Ideas.

Physics & Chemistry of Fission. (Proceedings Ser.). 629p. 1980. pap. 77.25 (ISBN 92-0-030080-4, ISP-526-1, IAEA). Unipub.

Physics & Chemistry of Fission - 1969. (Illus., Orig.). 1969. pap. 50.50 (ISBN 92-0-030269-6, IAEA). Unipub.

Physics & Chemistry of Fission - 1973, 2 vols. (Illus.). 579p. (Orig.). 1974. Vol. 1. pap. 36.50 (ISBN 92-0-030074-X, IAEA); Vol. 2. pap. 33.25 (ISBN 92-0-030174-6). Unipub.

Physics & Chemistry of Fission, Nineteen Seventy-Nine, Vol. 11. 501p. 1980. pap. 58.75 (ISBN 92-0-030180-0, ISP526-2, IAEA). Unipub.

Physics & Chemistry of Liquid Crystal Devices. Ed. by Gerald J. Sprokel. (IBM Research Symposia Ser.). 362p. 1980. 42.50 (ISBN 0-306-40440-0, Plenum Pr). Plenum Pub.

Physics & Chemistry of Surfaces. Jacques Oudar. (Illus.). 1975. 24.00x (ISBN 0-216-90020-4). Intl Ideas.

Physics & Computers: Problems, Simulations, & Data Analysis. Robert Ehrlich. LC 72-5640. 125p. (Orig.). 1973. pap. text ed. 10.50 (ISBN 0-395-18010-4). HM.

Physics & Its Fifth Dimension: Society. Dietrich Schroeer. LC 75-184158. 1972. pap. text ed. 9.95 (ISBN 0-201-06767-6). A-W.

Physics & Man. new ed. Robert Karplus. 1970. pap. 7.95 o.p. (ISBN 0-8053-5211-2). Benjamin-Cummings.

Physics & Material Problems of Reactor Control Rods. 1964. 32.25 (ISBN 92-0-050364-0, IAEA). Unipub.

Physics & Mathematics of the Nervous Systems. Ed. by M. Conrad et al. (Lecture Notes in Biomathematics Ser.: Vol. 4). (Illus.). xii, 584p. 1975. pap. 22.40 o.p. (ISBN 0-387-07014-1). Springer-Verlag.

Physics & Philosophy. James Jeans. 232p. 1981. pap. price not set (ISBN 0-486-24117-3). Dover.

Physics Applied to Anaesthesia. 3rd ed. D. W. Hill. 320p. 1976. 39.95 (ISBN 0-407-00039-9). Butterworths.

Physics Applied to Anesthesia. 4th ed. D. W. Hill. LC 80-40011. (Illus.). 420p. 1980. text ed. 52.95 (ISBN 0-407-00188-3). Butterworths.

Physics Around You. Dale D. Long. 608p. 1980. text ed. 17.95x (ISBN 0-534-00770-8). Wadsworth Pub.

Physics As a Liberal Art. James S. Trefil. LC 77-6729. 1978. text ed. 16.95 (ISBN 0-08-019863-5). Pergamon.

Physics-Astronomy Frontier. Fred Hoyle & Jayant V. Narlikar. LC 80-11708. (Illus.). 1980. text ed. 21.95x (ISBN 0-7167-1160-5). W H Freeman.

Physics: Classical Mechanics & Introductory Statistical Mechanics, Vol. 1. D. G. Ivey & J. N. P. Hume. 1974. 24.95x (ISBN 0-471-06756-3). Wiley.

Physics: Concepts & Aplications. 2nd ed. Jerry D. Wilson. (Illus.). 884p. 1981. text ed. 22.95 (ISBN 0-669-03373-1); instr's guide avail. (ISBN 0-669-01948-8); student guide 7.95 (ISBN 0-669-03362-6); lab guide 12.95 (ISBN 0-669-01947-X). Heath.

Physics: Concepts & Applications. Jerry D. Wilson. 1977. text ed. 20.95x o.p. (ISBN 0-669-96180-9); instructor's manual free o.p. (ISBN 0-669-00243-7). Heath.

Physics Demonstration Experiments, 2 Vols. Ed. by Harry F. Meiners. (Illus.). 1400p. 1970. Set. 59.95 (ISBN 0-8260-5990-2, 66923, Pub. by Wiley-Interscience). Wiley.

Physics Experiments for Laboratory & Life. Philip R. Hetland. 1978. pap. text ed. 8.95 (ISBN 0-8403-1907-X). Kendall-Hunt.

Physics Fifty Years Later. U. S. National Committee for the International Union of Pure & Applied Physics. (Illus.). 416p. 1973. 15.25 (ISBN 0-309-02138-3). Natl Acad Pr.

Physics for Biologists. George Duncan. LC 74-18621. 1975. pap. 12.95 (ISBN 0-470-22568-8). Halsted Pr.

Physics for College Students. alt. ed. Donald E. Tilley & Walter Thumm. 1976. 23.95 (ISBN 0-8465-7534-5); 3.95 o.p. instr's guide (ISBN 0-8465-7533-7). Benjamin-Cummings.

Physics for Engineering Technology. 2nd ed. Alexander Joseph et al. LC 76-55696. 1978. 21.95 (ISBN 0-471-45075-8); solutions manual avail. (ISBN 0-471-02536-4). Wiley.

Physics for Engineers & Scientists. 2nd ed. D. Elwell & A. J. Pointen. 1978. 52.95 o.p. (ISBN 0-470-99335-9). Halsted Pr.

Physics for Engineers & Scientists. 2nd ed. D. Elwell & A. J. Pointon. LC 77-16193. 356p. 1979. pap. 19.95x (ISBN 0-470-26872-7). Halsted Pr.

Physics for Technology. 2nd ed. John E. Betts. (Illus.). 675p. 1981. text ed. 22.95 (ISBN 0-8359-5544-3); solutions manual free (ISBN 0-8359-5545-1). Reston.

Physics, Foundations & Applications, Vol. I. Robert M. Eisberg & Lawrence S. Lerner. 720p. 1981. text ed. 21.95x (ISBN 0-07-019091-7, C); write for info study guide (ISBN 0-07-019111-5). McGraw.

Physics: Foundations & Applications, Vol. II. Robert M. Eisberg & Lawrence S. Lerner. (Illus.). 864p. 1981. text ed. 21.95 (ISBN 0-07-019092-5, C); solutions maual avail. (ISBN 0-07-019119-0); numerical calculations, suppl. avail. (ISBN 0-07-019120-4). McGraw.

Physics: Foundations & Applications, Combined Vol. Robert M. Eisberg & Lawrence S. Lerner. (Illus.). 1552p. 1981. text ed. 28.95x (ISBN 0-07-019110-7, C); price not set instrs'. manual (ISBN 0-07-019110-7); price not set numerical calculation supplement (ISBN 0-07-019120-4). McGraw.

Physics: Foundations & Frontiers. 3rd ed. G. Gamow & John Cleveland. 640p. 1976. 21.95 (ISBN 0-13-672535-X). P-H.

Physics from the Ground up, 3 parts. Herman Y. Carr & Richard T. Weidner. LC 78-22000. 1980. Repr. of 1971 ed. Vol. 2. write for info. (ISBN 0-89874-021-5); Vol. 2. write for info. (ISBN 0-89874-213-7). Krieger.

Physics: Fundamental & Frontiers. rev. ed. Robert Stollberg & Faith F. Hill. 1975. 18.20 (ISBN 0-395-18243-3); tchr's guide 9.32 (ISBN 0-395-18241-7); lab. supplement 2.64 (ISBN 0-395-18242-5). HM.

Physics: Health & the Human Body. Daniel R. Gustafson. 528p. 1979. text ed. 17.95x (ISBN 0-534-00756-2). Wadsworth Pub.

Physics in My Generation. 2nd rev. ed. M. Born. LC 68-59281. (Heidelberg Science Lib: Vol. 7). (Illus.). 1969. pap. 7.30 (ISBN 0-387-90008-X). Springer-Verlag.

Physics in Nuclear Medicine. James A. Sorenson & Michael E. Phelps. 1980. 39.50 (ISBN 0-8089-1238-0). Grune.

Physics in Perspective: The Nature of Physics and the Subfields of Physics (Student Edition) Physics Survey Committee. (Illus.). 368p. 1973. pap. 7.00x (ISBN 0-309-02118-9). Natl Acad Pr.

Physics in Perspective, Vol. 1. Division of Physical Sciences. (Illus.). 1024p. 1972. pap. 28.00 (ISBN 0-309-02037-9). Natl Acad Pr.

Physics in Perspective Vol. 2 Pt. a: The Core Subfields of Physics. Physics Survey Committee. (Illus.). 768p. 1972. pap. 18.75 (ISBN 0-309-02100-6). Natl Acad Pr.

Physics in Perspective, Volume 2, Part B: The Interfaces. Physics Survey Committee. (Illus.). 728p. 1973. pap. 18.75 (ISBN 0-309-02101-4). Natl Acad Pr.

Physics in the Modern World. 2nd ed. Jerry Marion. 1980. 20.95 (ISBN 0-12-472280-6). Acad Pr.

Physics: Including Human Application. Harold Q. Fuller et al. 1978. text ed. 20.50 scp (ISBN 0-06-042214-9, HarpC); scp lab manual 6.50 (ISBN 0-06-042212-2); scp study guide 6.50 (ISBN 0-06-042213-0). Har-Row.

Physics Investigations. Jay Walker. (gr. 11-12). 1973. pap. text ed. 6.42 (ISBN 0-87720-180-3). AMSCO Sch.

Physics Is Fun, 4 bks. Jim Jardine. 1972. Bk. 1. text ed. 5.50x o.p. (ISBN 0-435-67470-6); Bk. 2. pap. text ed. 6.50x o.p. (ISBN 0-435-67496-X); Bk. 3. text ed. 9.50x o.p. (ISBN 0-435-67474-9); Bk. 4. text ed. 9.50x o.p. (ISBN 0-435-67476-5); tchr's guide to bks. 1 & 2 5.50x o.p. (ISBN 0-435-67480-3); tchr's guide to bk.3 3.95x o.p. (ISBN 0-435-67481-1); tchr's guide to bk.4 3.95x o.p. (ISBN 0-435-67482-X). Heinemann Ed.

Physics Is Fun. Gerhard Niese. LC 60-7489. (Illus.). 1960. 5.00 (ISBN 0-910172-01-3). Astro Comp Serv.

Physics: Its Methods & Meanings. new ed. Alexander Taffel. (gr. 9-12). 1973. text ed. 17.88 (ISBN 0-205-03780-1, 7337809); tchrs' guide 7.20 (ISBN 0-205-03783-6, 7337833); tests 4.00 (ISBN 0-205-02350-9, 7323506); tchrs'. guide 7.20 (ISBN 0-205-02351-7, 7323514); lab manual 5.12 (ISBN 0-205-03781-X, 7337817). Allyn.

Physics Laboratory Manual. Ralph W. Alexander & Don M. Sparlin. 176p. 1981. pap. text ed. 11.95 (ISBN 0-8403-2289-5). Kendall-Hunt.

Physics Laboratory Manual. Stanley Farr. 1977. wire coil bdg. 4.95 o.p. (ISBN 0-685-99415-5). Paladin Hse.

Physics Laboratory Textbook. Roy G. Goodrich. (Illus.). 442p. 1980. pap. text ed. 13.95 (ISBN 0-89892-031-0). Contemp Pub Co of Raleigh.

Physics Literature. 2nd ed. Robert H. Whitford. LC 68-12636. 1968. 11.50 (ISBN 0-8108-0112-4). Scarecrow.

Physics Made Simple. rev. ed. Ira M. Freeman. LC 65-13090. pap. 3.50 (ISBN 0-385-08727-6, Made). Doubleday.

Physics, Mathematics, Biology & Applied Science. William F. Hawkins & Ronald Mackin. 1966. pap. 6.00x o.p. (ISBN 0-19-437713-X). Oxford U Pr.

Physics of Atmospheres. J. T. Houghton. LC 76-26373. (Illus.). 1979. pap. 10.95x (ISBN 0-521-29656-0). Cambridge U Pr.

Physics of Atmospheres. J. T. Houghton. LC 76-26373. (Illus.). 1977. 32.95 (ISBN 0-521-21443-2). Cambridge U Pr.

Physics of Charged-Particle Beams. J. D. Lawson. (International Series of Monographs on Physics). (Illus.). 1977. 67.00x (ISBN 0-19-851278-3). Oxford U Pr.

Physics of Deformation & Flow. E. W. Billington & A. Tate. (Illus.). 720p. 1981. text ed. 59.00 (ISBN 0-07-005285-9, C). McGraw.

Physics of Drop Formation in the Atmosphere. Yu. S. Sedunov. Ed. by P. Greenberg. Tr. by D. Lederman from Rus. LC 74-8198. 234p. 1974. 29.95 (ISBN 0-470-77111-9). Halsted Pr.

Physics of Everyday Phenomena: Readings from Scientific American. Intro. by Jearl Walker. LC 79-9287. (Illus.). 1979. text ed. 10.00x o.p. (ISBN 0-7167-1125-7); pap. text ed. 5.95x o.p. (ISBN 0-7167-1126-5). W H Freeman.

Physics of Fast & Intermediate Reactors, 3 vols. 1962. Vol. 1. 16.25 (ISBN 92-0-050062-5, IAEA); Vol. 2. 16.25 (ISBN 92-0-050162-1); Vol. 3. 21.50 (ISBN 92-0-050262-8). Unipub.

Physics of Fully Ionized Gases. 2nd ed. L. Spitzer. 1962. 14.50 (ISBN 0-470-81723-2). Wiley.

Physics of Geomagnetic Phenomena, 2 Vols. Ed. by S. Matsushita & W. H. Campbell. (International Geophysics Ser.: Vol. 11). 1967. Vol. 1. 59.00 (ISBN 0-12-480301-6); Vol. 2, 1968. 68.50 (ISBN 0-12-480302-4). Acad Pr.

Physics of Glaciers. W. S. Paterson. LC 71-82909. 1970. 37.00 (ISBN 0-08-013972-8); pap. 7.75 (ISBN 0-08-013971-X). Pergamon.

Physics of High Temperature Reactors. L. Massimo. 1975. text ed. 37.00 (ISBN 0-08-019616-0). Pergamon.

Physics of Laser Driven Plasmas. Heinrich Hora. 325p. 1981. 30.00 (ISBN 0-471-07880-8, Pub. by Wiley-Interscience). Wiley.

Physics of Liquid & Solid Helium, 2 pts. Ed. by Karl H. Bennemann & J. B. Ketterson. LC 75-20235. (Interscience Monographs & Texts in Physics & Astronomy). Pt. 1, 1976, 608p. 43.50 (ISBN 0-471-06600-1, Pub. by Wiley-Interscience); Pt. 2, 1978. 80.95 (ISBN 0-471-06601-X). Wiley.

Physics of Liquid Crystals. P. G. De Gennes. (International Series of Monographs on Physics). (Illus.). 367p. 1974. 55.00x (ISBN 0-19-851285-6). Oxford U Pr.

Physics of Magmatic Processes. Ed. by R. B. Hargraves. LC 80-7525. (Illus.). 800p. 1980. 40.00x (ISBN 0-691-08259-6); pap. 15.00x (ISBN 0-691-08261-8). Princeton U Pr.

Physics of Medical Radiography. A. Ridgway & W. Thumm. 1968. 21.95 (ISBN 0-201-06460-X). A-W.

Physics of Metals, Vol. 1: Electrons. John M. Ziman. LC 69-10436. (Illus.). 1969. 49.50 (ISBN 0-521-07106-2). Cambridge U Pr.

Physics of Metals, Vol. 2: Defects. P. B. Hirsch. LC 74-14439. (Illus.). 304p. 1976. 68.50 (ISBN 0-521-20077-6). Cambridge U Pr.

Physics of Modern Electronics. rev. ed. Werner A. Gunther. Tr. by David Antin. (Illus.). 1966. pap. text ed. 3.50 (ISBN 0-486-61749-1). Dover.

Physics of Modern Materials, Vol. II. 690p. 1980. pap. 84.00 (ISBN 92-0-130180-4, ISP 538-2, IAEA). Unipub.

Physics of Modern Materials, Vol. 1. 530p. 1980. pap. 63.00 (ISBN 92-0-130080-8, ISP 538, IAEA). Unipub.

Physics of MOS Insulators. Lucovsky et al. 400p. 1980. 50.00 (ISBN 0-08-025969-3). Pergamon.

Physics of Music. Neville Fletcher. (Fundamentals of Senior Physics Ser.: Textbook 2). 1976. pap. text ed. 4.95x (ISBN 0-686-65411-0, 00509); cassette 6.95x (ISBN 0-686-65412-9, 00510). Heinemann Ed.

Physics of Music. 7th ed. Alexander Wood. Ed. by J. M. Bowsher. LC 80-20967. (Illus.). xiv, 258p. 1981. Repr. of 1975 ed. lib. bdg. 28.50x (ISBN 0-313-22644-X, WOPM). Greenwood.

Physics of Music: Readings from Scientific American. Intro. by Carleen M. Hutchins. LC 77-28461. (Illus.). 1978. pap. 7.95x (ISBN 0-7167-0095-6). W H Freeman.

Physics of Nonlinear Transport in Semiconductors. Ed. by D. K. Ferry et al. (NATO Advanced Study Institutes Ser.: Series B: Physics, Volume 52). 634p. 1980. 65.00 (ISBN 0-306-40356-0, Plenum Pr). Plenum Pub.

Physics of Nuclear Reactions. W. Martin Gibson. LC 79-40063. (Illus.). 288p. 1980. 45.00 (ISBN 0-08-023078-4); pap. 16.75 (ISBN 0-08-023077-6). Pergamon.

Physics of Nuclei & Particles, Vols. 1-2. Pierre Marmier & Eric Sheldon. 1969-70. 25.95 ea. Vol. 1 (ISBN 0-12-473101-5). Vol. 2 (ISBN 0-12-473102-3). Acad Pr.

Physics of Quantum Electronics, 4 vols. Ed. by Stephen F. Jacobs et al. Incl. Vol. 1. High Energy Lasers & Their Applications. cancelled o.s.i. (ISBN 0-201-05681-X); Vol. 2. Laser Applications to Optics & Spectroscopy. LC 75-1438. cancelled o.s.i. (ISBN 0-201-05682-8); Vol. 3. Laser Induced Fusion & X-Ray Studies. cancelled o.s.i. (ISBN 0-201-05683-6); Vol. 4. Laser Photochemistry, Tunable Lasers & Topics. LC 76-8326. cancelled (ISBN 0-201-05684-4). (Illus., Adv Bk Prog). A-W.

Physics of Radiology. 3rd ed. Harold E. Johns & John R. Cunningham. (Illus.). 816p. 1980. 30.75 (ISBN 0-398-03007-3). C C Thomas.

Physics of Rubber Elasticity. 3rd ed. L. R. G. Treloar. (Monographs on the Physics & Chemistry of Materials). (Illus.). 322p. 1975. 55.00x (ISBN 0-19-851355-0). Oxford U Pr.

Physics of Selenium & Tellurium. W. C. Cooper. 1969. 60.00 (ISBN 0-08-013895-0). Pergamon.

Physics of Semiconductor Devices. 2nd ed. D. A. Fraser. (Oxford Physics Ser.). 1979. 29.95x (ISBN 0-19-851850-1); pap. 11.95x (ISBN 0-19-851851-X). Oxford U Pr.

Physics of Semimetals & Narrow-Gap Semiconductors. D. L. Carter & R. T. Bate. 1971. 105.00 (ISBN 0-08-016661-X). Pergamon.

Physics of Silicon Dioxide & Its Interfaces: An International Topical Conference. Ed. by Sokrates T. Pantelides. 1978. text ed. 43.00 (ISBN 0-08-023049-0). Pergamon.

Physics of Sound for Musicians. Christian N. Swenson & Eugene I. Holdsworth. LC 80-80008. (Illus.). 208p. (Orig.). 1980. pap. 15.00x (ISBN 0-916030-05-9). Bethany Coll Ks.

Physics of Speech. D. B. Fry. LC 78-56752. (Textbooks in Linguistics Ser.). (Illus.). 1979. 27.95 (ISBN 0-521-22173-0); pap. 8.95x (ISBN 0-521-29379-0). Cambridge U Pr.

Physics of Stellar Interiors. V. C. Reddish. 1975. 19.50x (ISBN 0-8448-0610-2). Crane-Russak Co.

Physics of the Atom. 3rd ed. M. Russell Wehr et al. LC 77-77752. (Physics Ser.). (Illus.). 1978. text ed. 19.95 (ISBN 0-201-08587-9). A-W.
Physics of the Earth. 2nd ed. Frank D. Stacey. LC 76-41891. 1977. text ed. 26.95 (ISBN 0-471-81956-5). Wiley.
Physics of the Earth & the Planets. A. H. Cook. LC 72-12261. 316p. 1973. text ed. 34.95 (ISBN 0-470-16910-9). Halsted Pr.
Physics of the Interstellar Medium. J. E. Dyson & D. A. Williams. LC 80-13713. 194p. 1980. 24.95x (ISBN 0-470-26983-9). Halsted Pr.
Physics of Thin Films: Advances in Research & Development, Vol. 11. Ed. by Georg Hass & Maurice H. Francombe. (Serial Publication Ser.). 1980. 42.00 (ISBN 0-12-533011-1); lib. ed 48.50 (ISBN 0-12-533080-4); microfiche 35.50 (ISBN 0-12-533081-2). Acad Pr.
Physics of Time Asymmetry. P. C. Davies. LC 74-81536. 1974. 20.00x (ISBN 0-520-02825-2); pap. 4.95x (ISBN 0-520-03247-0). U of Cal Pr.
Physics of Vibration, Vol. 1. Brian Pippard. LC 77-85685. (Illus.). 1978. 78.00 (ISBN 0-521-21899-3). Cambridge U Pr.
Physics of Vibrations & Waves. 2nd ed. H. J. Pain. 357p. 1976. 32.50 (ISBN 0-471-99407-3); pap. 16.50 (ISBN 0-471-99408-1). Wiley.
Physics: Principle with Applications. Douglas C. Giancoli. 1979. text ed. 21.95 (ISBN 0-13-672600-3). P-H.
Physics: Principles & Life Science Applications. William Buckman. Date not set. text ed. price not set (ISBN 0-442-20844-8). D Van Nostrand.
Physics Problems & How to Solve Them. 2nd ed. Clarence E. Bennett. (Orig.). 1973. pap. 3.95 (ISBN 0-06-460149-8, CO 149, COS). Har-Row.
Physics Programs. A. D. Boardman. Incl. Applied Physics. LC 80-40121. 136p (ISBN 0-471-27740-1); Magnetism. LC 80-40124. 106p (ISBN 0-471-27733-9); Optics. LC 80-40123. 134p (ISBN 0-471-27729-0); Solid State Physics. LC 80-40125. 144p (ISBN 0-471-27734-7). 1980. 13.50 ea. Wiley.
Physics: Relativity, Electromagnetism, & Quantum Physics, Vol. 2. J. N. Hume & D. G. Ivey. 1974. 24.95x (ISBN 0-471-07173-0). Wiley.
Physics Reviews Vol.III. I. M. Khalatnikov. (Soviet Scientific Reviews Ser.). 484p. 1980. 98.00 (ISBN 0-686-69597-6). Harwood Academic.
Physics, SI Version. Joseph W. Kane & Morton M. Sternheim. LC 80-17205. 680p. 1980. text ed. 24.95 (ISBN 0-471-08036-5). Wiley.
Physics Through Experiment, Vol. 1. B. Saraf et al. 1978. 10.00 (ISBN 0-7069-0643-8, Pub. by Vikas India). Advent Bk.
Physics Through Experiment: Mechanical Systems, Vol. II. Ed. by B. Saraf. 1980. text ed. 17.50x (ISBN 0-7069-0771-X, Pub. by Vikas India). Advent Bk.
Physics with Applications in Life Sciences. G. K. Strother & Robert L. Weber. (Illus.). 1977. text ed. 20.95 (ISBN 0-395-21718-0); inst. manual 0.75 (ISBN 0-395-21719-9); ans. to selected probs. avail. (ISBN 0-685-79300-1). HM.
Physics with the Computer: Teacher's Edition. Shawhan Douglas. 288p. (Orig.). 1980. 19.95 (ISBN 0-87567-037-7). Entelek.
Physics Without Mathematics. rev. ed. Clarence E. Bennett. LC 76-124362. 1970. pap. 3.95 (ISBN 0-06-460067-X, CO 67, COS). Har-Row.
Physics Workbook, 3 bks. Jim Jardine. 1970. pap. text ed. 4.25x ea. o.p.; Yr. 3. pap. text ed. (ISBN 0-435-67485-4); Yr. 4. pap. text ed. (ISBN 0-435-67486-2); Yr. 5. pap. text ed. (ISBN 0-435-67487-0). Heinemann Ed.
Physikalisch-Mathematische Monographien, 3 vols. in 1. W. Von Ignatowsky. (Ger). 9.95 (ISBN 0-8284-0201-9). Chelsea Pub.
Physiochemical Applications of Gas Chromatography. Richard J. Laub & Robert L. Pecsok. LC 78-5493. 1978. 31.95 (ISBN 0-471-51838-7, Pub. by Wiley-Interscience). Wiley.
Physiochemical Hydrodynamics. V. Levich. 1962. ref. ed. 35.95 (ISBN 0-13-674440-0). P-H.
Physiochemical Properties of Submerged Soils in Relationship to Fertility. (IRRI Research Paper Ser.: No. 5). 32p. 1977. pap. 5.00 (R045, IRRI). Unipub.
Physioengineering Principles. George E. Merva. (Illus.). 1975. pap. text ed. 20.50 (ISBN 0-87055-304-6). AVI.
Physiognomics in the Ancient World. Elizabeth C. Evans. LC 73-85468. (Transactions Ser.: Vol. 59, Pt. 5). 1969. pap. 2.00 o.p. (ISBN 0-87169-595-2). Am Philos.
Physiography of Southern Ontario. 2nd ed. L. J. Chapman & D. F. Putnam. LC 66-6736. (Illus.). 1966. 20.00x (ISBN 0-8020-1944-7); pap. 5.95 (ISBN 0-8020-6071-4); maps 7.50x (ISBN 0-8020-2107-7). U of Toronto Pr.
Physiography of the Lower Chambal Valley & Its Agricultural Development. H. S. Sharma. 1979. text ed. 15.00x (ISBN 0-391-01927-9). Humanities.
Physiologic Basis of Abdominal Organ Imaging. Marcus A. Rothschild. LC 78-55281. (Illus.). 1979. 24.50 (ISBN 0-88416-193-5). PSG Pub.
Physiological Aesthetics. Grant Allen. Ed. by Ian Fletcher & John Stokes. LC 76-20038. (Decadent Consciousness Ser.: Vol. 3). 1977. Repr. of 1877 ed. lib. bdg. 38.00 (ISBN 0-8240-2752-3). Garland Pub.
Physiological Aesthetics. Grant Allen. 283p. 1980. Repr. of 1877 ed. lib. bdg. 35.00 (ISBN 0-8495-0064-8). Arden Lib.
Physiological & Biochemical Basis for Perinatal Medicine. Ed. by A. Minkowski & M. Monset-Couchard. (Illus.). x, 370p. 1981. 72.00 (ISBN 3-8055-1283-X). S Karger.
Physiological & Pathological Aspects of Prolactin Secretion, Vol. 1, 1977. Steven W. Lamberts & Robert M. MacLeod. Ed. by David F. Horrobin. (Annual Research Reviews Ser.). 1978. 19.20 (ISBN 0-88831-034-X). Eden Med Res.
Physiological & Regulatory Functions of Adenosine & Adenine Nucleotides. Hans P. Baer & George I. Drummond. LC 78-55809. 1979. text ed. 44.50 (ISBN 0-89004-305-1). Raven.
Physiological & Toxicological Aspects of Combustion Products. Committee on Fire Research, National Research Council. LC 76-24955. 1976. pap. 8.00 (ISBN 0-309-02521-4). Natl Acad Pr.
Physiological Approach in Psychology. Charles F. Levinthal. (Illus.). 1979. 19.95 (ISBN 0-13-674796-5). P-H.
Physiological Approach to Clinical Neurology. 2nd ed. J. G. Lance & J. G. McLeod. LC 80-49872. 1975. 32.95 (ISBN 0-407-00022-4). Butterworths.
Physiological Approach to Clinical Neurology. 3rd ed. James W. Lance & James G. McLeod. (Illus.). 368p. 1981. text ed. 49.95 (ISBN 0-407-00196-4). Butterworth.
Physiological Approach to the Lower Animals. 2nd ed. James A. Ramsay. LC 68-21398. (Illus.). 1968. text ed. 29.50 (ISBN 0-521-07185-2); pap. 8.50x (ISBN 0-521-09537-9). Cambridge U Pr.
Physiological Aspects of Dryland Farming. U. S. Gupta. LC 76-42138. 392p. 1977. text ed. 18.00 (ISBN 0-916672-94-8). Allanheld.
Physiological Bases of Motivation. Jack E. Hokanson. 192p. 1981. pap. write for info. (ISBN 0-89874-187-4). Krieger.
Physiological Basis for Personality Traits: A New Theory of Personality. David Lester. (Illus.). 138p. 1974. 13.75 (ISBN 0-398-03078-2). C C Thomas.
Physiological Chemistry of Exercise & Training. Ed. by P. E. Di Prampero & J. Poortsmans. (Medicine & Sport Ser.: Vol. 13). (Illus.). xii, 200p. 1981. 76.75 (ISBN 3-8055-2028-X). S Karger.
Physiological Effects of Exercise Programs on Adults. Thomas K. Cureton. (American Lectures in Sportsmedicine Ser.). (Illus.). 228p. 1971. 19.75 (ISBN 0-398-00377-7). C C Thomas.
Physiological Effects of Immunity Against Reproductive Hormones. Ed. by R. G. Edwards & M. H. Johnson. LC 75-12470. (Clinical & Experimental Immunoreproduction Ser.: No. 3). (Illus.). 300p. 1976. 42.50 (ISBN 0-521-20914-5). Cambridge U Pr.
Physiological Effects of Wheat Germ Oil on Humans in Exercise: Forty-two Physical Training Programs Utilizing 894 Humans. Thomas K. Cureton. (Illus.). 552p. 1972. 46.50 (ISBN 0-398-02270-4). C C Thomas.
Physiological Mammalogy, 2 vols. Ed. by William V. Mayer & R. G. Van Gelder. Incl. Vol. 1 (ISBN 0-12-481001-2); Vol. 2 (ISBN 0-12-481002-0). 1964. 46.00 ea. Acad Pr.
Physiological Mechanics of Piano Technique. Otto Ortmann. (Music Ser.). (Illus.). xvi, 396p. 1981. Repr. of 1929 ed. lib. bdg. 39.50 (ISBN 0-306-76058-4). Da Capo.
Physiological Pharmacology: A Comprehensive Treatise, 4 vols. Ed. by W. S. Root & F. G. Hoffman. Incl. Vol. 1. The Nervous System, Part A. 1963. 62.50 (ISBN 0-12-595701-7); Vol. 2. The Nervous System, Part B. 1965. 49.25 (ISBN 0-12-595702-5); Vol. 3. The Nervous System, Part C. 1967. 51.00 (ISBN 0-12-595703-3); Vol. 4. The Nervous System, Part D. 1967. 51.00 (ISBN 0-12-595704-1); Vol. 5. The Nervous System, Part E. 1974. 62.50 (ISBN 0-12-595705-X). Acad Pr.
Physiological Plant Anatomy. 4th ed. G. Haberlandt. Tr. by M. Drummond from Ger. 398p. 1979. Repr. of 1928 ed. lib. bdg. 17.50x (ISBN 0-934454-89-2). Lubrecht & Cramer.
Physiological Plant Ecology. rev. ed. W. Larcher. Tr. by M. A. Biederman-Thorson from Ger. LC 79-26396. (Illus.). 340p. 24.00 (ISBN 3-540-09795-3). Springer-Verlag.
Physiological Processes in Plant Ecology: Towards a Synthesis with Atriplex. C. B. Osmond et al. (Ecololgical Studies: Vol. 36). (Illus.). 500p. 1980. 49.80 (ISBN 0-387-10060-1). Springer-Verlag.
Physiological Processes Limiting Plant Productivity. Christopher B. Johnson. 1981. text ed. price not set (ISBN 0-408-10649-2). Butterworth.
Physiological Psychology. Thomas S. Brown & Patricia Wallace. 1980. tchrs' ed. 20.95 (ISBN 0-12-136660-X). Acad Pr.
Physiological Psychology. rev. ed. J. Anthony Deutsch & Diana Deutsch. 1973. text ed. 18.95x (ISBN 0-256-01081-1). Dorsey.
Physiological Psychology. Daniel P. Kimble. LC 63-13008. (Psychology Ser). (Orig., Prog. Bk.). 1963. 9.95 (ISBN 0-201-03683-5); manual with tests 1.00 (ISBN 0-201-03686-X). A-W.
Physiological Psychology. 2nd ed. Marvin Schwartz. LC 77-17438. (Century Psychology Ser.). (Illus.). 1978. ref. ed. 20.95 (ISBN 0-13-674895-3). P-H.
Physiological Psychology: A Study Guide. 2nd ed. Francis Leukel. 208p. 1976. pap. text ed. 8.00 (ISBN 0-8016-2968-3). Mosby.
Physiological Psychology: An Introduction. William C. Watson. LC 80-82838. (Illus.). 592p. 1981. text ed. 16.95 (ISBN 0-395-30221-8); price not set instr's manual (ISBN 0-395-30222-6); study guide 6.95 (ISBN 0-395-30223-4). HM.
Physiological Psychology: The Biology of Human Behavior. Richard A. McFarland. (Illus.). 600p. 1981. text ed. price not set (ISBN 0-87484-500-9). Mayfield Pub.
Physiological Researches on Life & Death. Xavier Bichat. Tr. by F. Gold from Fr. Bd. with Outlines of Phrenology; Phrenology Examined. (Contributions to the History of Psychology, Vol. II, Pt. E: Physiological Psychology). 1978. Repr. of 1827 ed. 30.00 (ISBN 0-89093-175-5). U Pubns Amer.
Physiological Techniques in Behavioral Research. Devendra Singh & David D. Avery. LC 74-82037. 1975. pap. text ed. 8.95x o.p. (ISBN 0-8185-0110-3). Brooks-Cole.
Physiological Variation & Its Genetic Basis: Proceedings, Vol. 17. Ed. by J. S. Weiner & J S. Weiner. (Society for the Study of Human Biology, Symposia). 1977. 24.95 (ISBN 0-470-99314-6). Halsted Pr.
Physiology. 4th ed. Ewald E. Selkurt. LC 75-36762. 1976. text ed. 18.50 o.p. (ISBN 0-316-78039-1); pap. text ed. 15.95 (ISBN 0-316-78040-5). Little.
Physiology. 2nd ed. Ed. by Judy A. Spitzer. LC 79-83722. (Basic Sciences PreTest Self-Assessment & Review Ser.). (Illus.). 1980. 9.95 (ISBN 0-07-050962-X). McGraw-Pretest.
Physiology & Behaviour of Marine Organisms: Proceedings. European Symposium on Marine Biology, 12th Ed. by D. S. McLusky & A. J. Berry. LC 77-30559. 1978. text ed. 60.00 (ISBN 0-08-021548-3). Pergamon.
Physiology & Biochemistry of Haemocyanins. Ed. by F. Ghiretti. LC 68-17675. (Illus.). 1968. 18.00 (ISBN 0-12-281550-5). Acad Pr.
Physiology & Biochemistry of Muscle As a Food: Proceedings, 1965, 2 vols. Ed. by Ernest J. Briskey et al. (Illus.). 1966. Vol. 1. 35.00x (ISBN 0-299-04110-7); Vol. 2. 50.00 (ISBN 0-299-05680-5). U of Wis Pr.
Physiology & Biochemistry of the Domestic Fowl, 3 vols. Ed. by D. J. Bell & B. M. Freemon. 1972. Vol. 1. 96.00 (ISBN 0-12-085001-X); Vol. 2. 94.50 (ISBN 0-12-085002-8); Vol. 3. 67.50 (ISBN 0-12-085003-6). Acad Pr.
Physiology & Cell Biology of Aging. Ed. by Arthur Cherkin et al. LC 77-94148. (Aging Ser.: Vol. 8). 1979. text ed. 26.00 (ISBN 0-89004-283-7). Raven.
Physiology & Pathobiology of Axons. Ed. by Stephen G. Waxman. LC 77-17751. 1978. 41.00 (ISBN 0-89004-215-2). Raven.
Physiology & Pathology of Adaptation Mechanisms: Neural-Neuroendocrine-Hormonal. Ed. by E. Bajusz. 598p. 1968. text ed. 90.00 (ISBN 0-08-012023-7). Pergamon.
Physiology & Pathology of Bed Rest. Norman L. Browse. (Illus.). 240p. 1965. 22.50 (ISBN 0-398-00243-6). C C Thomas.
Physiology & Pathology of Dendrites. Ed. by G. W. Kreutzberg. LC 74-14474. (Advances in Neurology Ser: Vol. 12). 523p. 1975. 43.50 (ISBN 0-911216-99-5). Raven.
Physiology & Pathology of the Mind. Henry Maudsley. (Contributions to the History of Psychology Ser.: Medical Psychology). 1978. Repr. of 1867 ed. 30.00 (ISBN 0-89093-168-2). U Pubns Amer.
Physiology & Pathophysiology of Plasma Protein Metabolism. Ed. by G. Birke et al. 1968. 40.00 (ISBN 0-08-012965-X). Pergamon.
Physiology & Pathophysiology of the Skin, 3 vols. Ed. by A. Jarrett. Incl. Vol. 1. The Epidermis. 1973. 51.00 (ISBN 0-12-380601-1); Vol. 2. The Nerves & Blood Vessels. 1973. 64.50 (ISBN 0-12-380602-X); Vol. 3. 64.50 (ISBN 0-12-380603-8). 150.50 set (ISBN 0-686-66931-2). Acad Pr.
Physiology & Pharmacology of the Brain Stem. Shih-Chun Wang. LC 79-89753. (Illus.). 320p. 1980. 29.50 (ISBN 0-87993-127-2). Futura Pub.
Physiology & Psychology of Stock Market Charts. C. M. Flumiani. (Illus.). 103p. 1981. 47.85 (ISBN 0-918968-84-4). Inst Econ Finan.
Physiology in Sleep. Ed. by J. Orem & C. D. Barnes. (Research Topics in Physiology Ser.). 1981. write for info. (ISBN 0-12-527650-8). Acad Pr.
Physiology Laboratory Manual. Byron A. Schottelius et al. (Illus.). 1978. pap. text ed. 9.50 (ISBN 0-8016-4354-6). Mosby.
Physiology of Adequate Perfusion. Edward G. Berger. LC 78-15591. (Illus.). 1979. 21.95 (ISBN 0-8016-0618-7). Mosby.
Physiology of Aggression & Implications for Control: An Anthology of Readings. Ed. by Kenneth E. Moyer. LC 74-14476. 1976. pap. 15.50 (ISBN 0-89004-003-6). Raven.
Physiology of Behavior. Neil Carlson. 1977. text ed. 19.95x (ISBN 0-205-05706-3, 7957068); instr's manual avail. (ISBN 0-205-05707-1, 7957676); wkbk 8.95 (ISBN 0-686-68513-X, 7957580). Allyn.
Physiology of Behavior. 2nd ed. Neil R. Carlson. 704p. 1981. text ed. 20.95 (ISBN 0-205-07262-3, 797262-8); free (ISBN 0-205-07263-1); write for info. study guide (ISBN 0-205-07264-X). Allyn.
Physiology of Cartilaginous, Fibrous, & Bony Tissue: Orthopaedic Lectures, Vol. 2. Harold M. Frost. (Illus.). 264p. 1972. 29.75 (ISBN 0-398-02562-2). C C Thomas.
Physiology of Cestodes. J. D. Smyth. (Illus.). 1969. 13.95x (ISBN 0-7167-0676-8). W H Freeman.
Physiology of Crustacea, 2 vols. Ed. by T. H. Waterman. Incl. Vol. 1. Metabolism & Growth. 1960. 48.00 (ISBN 0-12-737601-1); Vol. 2. Sense Organs, Integration & Behavior. 1961. 48.00 (ISBN 0-12-737602-X). Set. 90.00 (ISBN 0-685-23209-3). Acad Pr.
Physiology of Echinoderms. J. Binyon. 212p. 1972. text ed. 36.00 (ISBN 0-08-016991-0). Pergamon.
Physiology of Excitable Cells. 2nd ed. D. J. Aidley. LC 77-87375. (Illus.). 1979. 65.50 (ISBN 0-521-21913-2); pap. 17.95x (ISBN 0-521-29308-1). Cambridge U Pr.
Physiology of Excitable Membranes: Proceedings of the 28th International Congress of Physiological Sciences, Budapest, 1980. Ed. by J. Salanki et al. LC 80-41853. (Advances in Physiological Sciences: Vol. 4). (Illus.). 350p. 1981. 40.00 (ISBN 0-08-026816-1). Pergamon.
Physiology of Exercise. Ernst Jokl. (American Lecture Sportsmedicine Ser). (Illus.). 156p. 1971. photocopy ed. 14.75 (ISBN 0-398-02152-X). C C Thomas.
Physiology of Exercise. 7th ed. Laurence E. Morehouse & Augustus T. Miller. LC 75-22186. (Illus.). 320p. 1976. text ed. 15.95 (ISBN 0-8016-3485-7). Mosby.
Physiology of Flowering Plants. 2nd ed. H. E. Street & H. Opik. (Contemporary Biology Ser.). 1976. 18.50 (ISBN 0-444-19505-X); pap. 18.50 (ISBN 0-686-67620-3). Univ Park.
Physiology of Giant Algal Cells. A. B. Hope & N. A. Walker. LC 74-77832. (Illus.). 224p. 1975. 42.50 (ISBN 0-521-20513-1). Cambridge U Pr.
Physiology of Insect Reproduction. F. Engelmann. LC 70-114850. 1970. 59.00 (ISBN 0-08-015559-6). Pergamon.
Physiology of Mammals & Other Vertebrates. 2nd ed. P. T. Marshall & G. M. Hughes. LC 78-73810. (Illus.). 1981. 39.50 (ISBN 0-521-22633-3); pap. 16.95 (ISBN 0-521-29586-6). Cambridge U Pr.
Physiology of Membrane Disorders. Ed. by Thomas E. Andreoli et al. LC 78-4071. (Illus.). 1148p. 1978. 75.00 (ISBN 0-306-31054-6, Plenum Pr). Plenum Pub.
Physiology of Mollusca, Vol. 2. Ed. by Karl M. Wilbur & C. M. Yonge. 1966. Vol. 1. 55.00 (ISBN 0-12-751302-7). Acad Pr.
Physiology of Nematodes. 2d ed. Donald Lewis Lee & H. J. Atkinson. LC 77-1232. (Illus.). 1977. 20.00x (ISBN 0-231-04358-9). Columbia U Pr.
Physiology of Non-Excitable Cells: Proceedings of the 28th International Congress of Physiological Sciences, Budapest, 1980. Ed. by J. Salanki et al. LC 80-41874. (Advannces in Physiological Sciences: Vol. 3). (Illus.). 350p. 1981. 40.00 (ISBN 0-08-026815-3). Pergamon.
Physiology of Peripheral Nerve Disease. Austin J. Sumner. (Illus.). 544p. 1980. text ed. 35.00 (ISBN 0-7216-8639-7). Saunders.

Physiology of Reproduction & Artificial Insemination of Cattle. 2nd ed. G. W. Salisbury et al. LC 77-13598. (Animal Science Ser.). (Illus.). 1978. text ed. 37.95x (ISBN 0-7167-0025-5). W H Freeman.

Physiology of Sense Organs. DeForest Mellon, Jr. (Illus.). 1968. 8.95x (ISBN 0-7167-0669-5). W H Freeman.

Physiology of Smooth Muscle. Ed. by E. Bulbring & M. F. Shuba. LC 75-14566. 440p. 1976. 41.50 (ISBN 0-89004-051-6). Raven.

Physiology of Speech & Hearing: An Introduction. R. Daniloff. 1980. 20.95 (ISBN 0-13-674747-7). P-H.

Physiology of Spinal Anesthesia. 3rd ed. Nicholas M. Greene. 265p. 1981. write for info. (3554-1). Williams & Wilkins.

Physiology of the Cerebral Circulation. M. J. Purves. LC 70-169577. (Physiological Society Monographs: No. 28). (Illus.). 40p. 1972. 72.00 (ISBN 0-521-08300-1). Cambridge U Pr.

Physiology of the Eye. 3rd ed. Hugh Davson. 1972. 36.50 o.p. (ISBN 0-12-206740-1). Acad Pr.

Physiology of the Eye: An Introduction to the Vegetative Functions. new ed. Irving Fatt. 1978. 21.95 (ISBN 0-409-95080-7). Butterworths.

Physiology of the Gastro-Intestinal Lymphatic System. J. A. Barrowman. LC 77-22823. (Physiological Society Monographs: No. 33). (Illus.). 1978. 59.50 (ISBN 0-521-21710-5). Cambridge U Pr.

Physiology of the Gastrointestinal Tract, 2 vols. Ed. by Leonard Johnson et al. 1600p. 1981. 130.00 (ISBN 0-89004-440-6). Raven.

Physiology of the Heart. Arnold M. Katz. LC 75-14580. 1977. 31.00 (ISBN 0-89004-053-2); pap. 15.95 (ISBN 0-686-67627-0). Raven.

Physiology of the Human Body. 2nd ed. J. Robert McClintic. LC 77-27066. 1978. text ed. 23.95x (ISBN 0-471-02664-6). Wiley.

Physiology of the Hypothalmus, Vol. 2. Morgane & Panksepp. 672p. 1980. 145.00 (ISBN 0-8247-6904-X). Dekker.

Physiology of the Mouth. 4th ed. G. Neil Jenkins. (Illus.). 508p. 1970. 42.50 (ISBN 0-632-00138-0, Blackwell). Mosby.

Physiology of the Newborn Infant. 4th ed. Ed. by Clement A. Smith & Nicholas M. Nelson. (Illus.). 784p. 1976. 68.50 (ISBN 0-398-03232-7). C C Thomas.

Physiology of Thirst & Sodium Appetite. J. T. Fitzsimons. LC 78-16212. (Physiological Society Monographs: No. 35). 1979. 83.50 (ISBN 0-521-22292-3). Cambridge U Pr.

Physiology: Past, Present, & Future: A Symposium in Honour of Yngve Zotterman, University of Bristol, July 11 & 12, 1979. Ed. by D. J. Anderson. LC 80-40957. (Illus.). 168p. 1980. 27.00 (ISBN 0-08-025480-2). Pergamon.

Physiology Review. 5th ed. Ed. by Kalman Greenspan & John A. Giddings. 1972. spiral bdg. 8.50 (ISBN 0-87488-206-0). Med Exam.

Physiopathology & Therapy of Human Blood Diseases. E. Kelemen. LC 68-18525. 1968. 90.00 (ISBN 0-08-012786-X). Pergamon.

Physiotherapy in Pediatric Practice. D. R. Scrutton & M. P. Gilbertson. (Postgraduate Pediatric Ser.). 1975. 19.95 (ISBN 0-407-00017-8). Butterworths.

Physyke of the Soule. Thomas Becon. LC 74-28831. (English Experience Ser.: No. 713). 1975. Repr. of 1549 ed. 3.50 (ISBN 90-221-0713-2). Walter J Johnson.

Phytochemical Phylogeny: Proceedings. Phytochemical Society. Ed. by J. B. Harborne. 1970. 47.50 (ISBN 0-12-324666-0). Acad Pr.

Phytohormones. R. W. Went et al. (Landmark Reprint in Plant Science Ser.). 1937. text ed. 22.50 (ISBN 0-86598-004-7). Allanheld.

Phytophthora & Forest Management in Australia. K. M. Old. 1980. 13.00x (ISBN 0-643-02523-5, Pub. by CSJRO Australia). State Mutual Bk.

Phytophthora Cinna Moni & the Diseases It Causes. Ed. by George A. Zentmyer. (Monograph Ser.: No. 10). 96p. 1980. 8.00 (ISBN 0-89054-030-6). Am Phytopathol Soc.

Phytophthora Disease of Cocoa. P. H. Gregory. LC 73-85686. (Illus.). 300p. 1974. text ed. 53.00x (ISBN 0-582-46658-X). Longman.

P'I Jih-Hsiu. William H. Nienhauser, Jr. (World Authors Ser.: No. 530). 1979. lib. bdg. 14.95 (ISBN 0-8057-6372-4). Twayne.

Pia Desideria. Philip J. Spener. Ed. & tr. by Theodore G. Tappert. LC 64-12995. 1964. pap. 4.50 (ISBN 0-8006-1953-6, 1-1953). Fortress.

Piaffer & Passage. Decarpentry. Tr. by Patricia Galvin. (Illus.). 9.75 o.p. (ISBN 0-85131-095-8, Dist. by Sporting Book Center). J A Allen.

Piaget: A Practical Consideration. G. A. Helmore. LC 75-94933. 1970. pap. 6.05 o.p. (ISBN 0-08-006893-6). Pergamon.

Piaget & Knowing. B. Geber. 1977. 20.00 (ISBN 0-7100-8500-1). Routledge & Kegan.

Piaget & Knowledge: Theoretical Foundations. Hans G. Furth. LC 80-26284. (Illus., Orig.). 1981. pap. price not set (ISBN 0-226-27420-9). U of Chicago Pr.

Piaget: Dictionary of Terms. Ed. by E. R. Hermann et al. 1973. text ed. 26.00 (ISBN 0-08-017039-0). Pergamon.

Piaget for Teachers. Hans G. Furth. (Illus.). 1970. 10.95 o.p. (ISBN 0-13-674945-3); pap. text ed. 13.95 (ISBN 0-13-674937-2). P-H.

Piaget, Philosophy & the Human Sciences. Hugh Silverman. 1980. text ed. 17.50 (ISBN 0-391-00958-3). Humanities.

Piaget Sampler: An Introduction to Jean Piaget Through His Own Words. S. F. Campbell. LC 75-34129. 154p. 1976. pap. text ed. 10.95 (ISBN 0-471-13344-2). Wiley.

Piaget Systematized. Gilbert Voyat. (Illus.). 300p. 1981. text ed. 24.95 (ISBN 0-89859-026-4). L Erlbaum Assocs.

Piagetian Research: A Handbook of Recent Studies. Sohan Modgil. 476p. 1974. text ed. 30.25x (ISBN 0-85633-030-2, NFER). Humanities.

Piagetian Research, Compilation & Commentary, No. 1: Jean Piaget, Theory of Cognitive Development & Sensorimotor Intelligence. Sohan Modgil & Celia Modgil. (Orig.). 1976. pap. text ed. 12.50x (ISBN 0-85633-089-2, NFER). Humanities.

Piagetian Research, Compilation & Commentary, No. 4: School Curriculum & Test Development. Sohan Modgil & Celia Modgil. (Orig.). 1976. pap. text ed. 18.75x (ISBN 0-85633-103-1, NFER). Humanities.

Piagetian Research, Compilation & Commentary, No. 5: Personality, Socialization & Emotionality Reasoning Among Handicapped Children. Sohan Modgil & Celia Modgil. 1976. pap. text ed. 25.75 (ISBN 0-85633-098-1, NFER). Humanities.

Piagetian Research, Compilation & Commentary, No. 6: The Cognitive-Development Approach to Morality. Sohan Modgil & Celia Modgil. (Piagetian Research). 1976. pap. text ed. 15.75x (ISBN 0-85633-106-6, NFER). Humanities.

Piagetian Research-Compilation & Commentary, No. 7: Training Techniques. Sohan Modgil. (Orig.). 1976. pap. text ed. 16.00x (ISBN 0-85633-107-4, NFER). Humanities.

Piagetian Research, Compilation & Commentary, No. 8: Cross-Cultural Studies. Sohan Modgil & Celia Modgil. (Piagetian Research Ser.). 1976. pap. text ed. 16.00x (ISBN 0-85633-108-2, NFER). Humanities.

Piagetian Research: Compilation & Commentary, Nos. 2 & 3. Sohan Modgil & Celia Modgil. Incl. Experimental Validation of Conservation. pap. text ed. 15.75x (ISBN 0-685-92662-1); Early Growth of Logic. pap. text ed. 20.75x (ISBN 0-85633-098-1). 1976 (NFER). Humanities.

Piagetian Tests for the Primary School. K. R. Fogelman. (General Ser.). 72p. 1970. pap. text ed. 5.75x (ISBN 0-901225-50-9, NFER). Humanities.

Piaget's Theory: A Primer. John L. Phillips, Jr. LC 80-20800. (Psychology Ser.). (Illus.). 1981. text ed. 12.95x (ISBN 0-7167-1235-0); pap. text ed. 5.95x (ISBN 0-7167-1236-9). W H Freeman.

Piaget's Theory of Cognitive Development: An Introduction for Students of Psychology & Education. Barry J. Wadsworth. LC 73-151157. 1979. pap. 7.95 (ISBN 0-679-30314-6). Longman.

Piaget's Theory of Cognitive Development. 2nd ed. Barry J. Wadsworth. LC 79-12347. 1979. pap. 7.95 (ISBN 0-582-28124-5). Longman.

Piaget's Theory of Intellectual Development. 2nd ed. Herbert Ginsburg & Sylvia Opper. (Illus.). 1979. 13.95 (ISBN 0-13-675140-7); pap. 8.95 (ISBN 0-13-675132-6). P-H.

Piaget's Theory of Intelligence. Charles J. Brainerd. (Illus.). 1978. 17.95 (ISBN 0-13-675108-3). P-H.

Pianist's Progress. Helen D. Ruttencutter. LC 78-22464. 1979. 9.95 (ISBN 0-690-01761-8, TYC-T). T Y Crowell.

Piankashaw & Kaskaskia Indians. Ed. by David A. Horr. Incl. An Anthropological Report on the Piankashaw Indians. Dorothy Libby; Report on the Piankashaw & Kaskaskia & the Treaty of Greene Ville. David B. Stout. (American Indian Ethnohistory Ser: North Central & Northeastern Indians). (Illus.). lib. bdg. 42.00 (ISBN 0-8240-0760-3). Garland Pub.

Piano. Louis Kentner. LC 76-329. (Yehudi Menuhin Music Guide Ser). 1976. 12.95 (ISBN 0-02-871420-2); pap. 6.95 (ISBN 0-02-871370-2). Schirmer Bks.

Piano Album. Higgins. pap. write for info. (ISBN 0-914162-42-X). Knowles.

Piano: An Introduction to the Instrument. William Ballantine. LC 79-114926. (Keynote Bks). (Illus.). (gr. 7 up). 1971. PLB 4.90 o.p. (ISBN 0-531-01843-1). Watts.

Piano Breakthrough: How to Revolutionize Your Playing Through Chords & Broken Chords. Duane Shinn. 1978. pap. 25.00 (ISBN 0-912732-44-X). Duane Shinn.

Piano for Classroom Music. 2nd ed. Robert Pace. LC 71-98966. (Music Ser). (Illus.). 1970. pap. text ed. 12.95 (ISBN 0-13-674994-1). P-H.

Piano-Forte. Rosamund E. Harding. LC 69-15634. (Music Ser.). 1973. Repr. of 1933 ed. lib. bdg. 29.50 (ISBN 0-306-71084-6). Da Capo.

Piano: Guided Sight-Reading: A New Approach to Piano Study. Leonhard Deutsch. (Illus.). 1978. 10.95 (ISBN 0-88229-555-1); pap. 7.95 (ISBN 0-88229-556-X). Nelson-Hall.

Piano in Chamber Ensemble: An Annotated Guide. Maurice Hinson. LC 77-9862. 1978. 19.50x (ISBN 0-253-34493-X). Ind U Pr.

Piano Makers. David Wainwright. (Illus.). 1975. text ed. 16.00x (ISBN 0-09-122950-2). Humanities.

Piano Music of Robert Schumann: Series III. Robert Schumann. Ed. by Clara Schumann. 1980. Repr. of 1887 ed. 6.50 (ISBN 0-486-23906-3). Dover.

Piano Music 1888-1905. Claude Debussy. 175p. 1972. pap. 5.50 (ISBN 0-486-22771-5). Dover.

Piano-Owner's Guide. Carl D. Schmeckel. LC 74-7362. (Illus.). 120p. 1974. 6.95 o.p. (ISBN 0-684-13869-7, ScribT); pap. 3.95 (ISBN 0-684-13872-7, SL548, ScribT). Scribner.

Piano Paperback. Ian McCombie. (Illus.). 1980. 12.50 (ISBN 0-684-16444-2, ScribT). Scribner.

Piano Pieces, (Opus 51, 55, 61, 62) Edward MacDowell. LC 70-170391. (Earlier American Music Ser.: No. 8). 144p. 1972. Repr. lib. bdg. 25.00 (ISBN 0-306-77308-2). Da Capo.

Piano Study for Beginners. Dallen. 1981. pap. 14.95 (ISBN 0-13-675603-4). P-H.

Piano Tuning: A Simple & Accurate Method for Amateurs. Cree J. Fischer. 7.25 (ISBN 0-8446-5477-9). Peter Smith.

Pianoforte Sonata: Its Origin & Development. 2nd ed. J. S. Shedlock. LC 64-18993. (Music Ser). 1964. Repr. of 1895 ed. lib. bdg. 19.50 (ISBN 0-306-70900-7). Da Capo.

Pianos & Their Makers. Alfred Dolge. (Illus.). 581p. 1972. pap. 6.00 (ISBN 0-486-22856-8). Dover.

Pianos & Their Makers: A Comprehensive History of the Development of the Piano from the Monochord to the Concert Grand Player Piano. Alfred Dolge. (Illus.). 10.00 (ISBN 0-8446-4540-0). Peter Smith.

Piaroa People of the Orinoco Basin: A Study in Kinship & Marriage. Joanna O. Kaplan. (Illus.). 256p. 1975. 37.50x (ISBN 0-19-823189-X). Oxford U Pr.

Pia's Journey to the Holy Land. Sven Gillsater & Pia Gillsater. Tr. by Annabelle MacMillan. LC 61-2285. (Illus.). (gr. 1 up). 1961. bds. 4.95 o.p. (ISBN 0-15-261360-9, HJ). HarBraceJ.

Piazza of the Decameron. Luigi Fusco. Tr. by Marion Fusco & Luigi Fusco. LC 76-56615. 1977. 8.95 o.p. (ISBN 0-8076-0862-9). Braziller.

Picaresque Hero in European Fiction. Richard Bjornson. LC 76-11312. 1977. 25.00x (ISBN 0-299-07100-6); pap. 8.95 (ISBN 0-299-07104-9). U of Wis Pr.

Picaro or Me. Arindam Basu. (Writers Workshop Greenbird Ser.). 90p. 1975. 12.00 (ISBN 0-88253-608-7); pap. text ed. 4.80 (ISBN 0-88253-607-9). Ind-US Inc.

Picasso. Timothy Hilton. (World of Art Ser.). (Illus.). 1975. pap. 9.95 (ISBN 0-19-519935-9). Oxford U Pr.

Picasso. Pablo Picasso. Ed. by Hans L. Jaffe. (Library of Great Painters Ser). 1964. 35.00 (ISBN 0-8109-0368-7). Abrams.

Picasso. Gertrude Stein. (Illus.). 1959. pap. 3.95 o.p. (ISBN 0-8070-6687-7, BP90). Beacon Pr.

Picasso, a Catalogue Raisonne of the Paintings & Related Works. Pierre Daix & Joan Rosselet. LC 78-71109. (Illus.). 1979. 125.00 (ISBN 0-8212-0672-9, 706981). NYGS.

Picasso & the Cubists. (Illus.). 1975. Repr. 5.95 o.p. (ISBN 0-88308-010-9). Lamplight Pub.

Picasso: Art As Autobiography. Mary M. Gedo. LC 80-11126. (Illus.). 288p. 1980. lib. bdg. 20.00 (ISBN 0-226-28482-4). U of Chicago Pr.

Picasso: Birth of a Genius. Juan-Eduardo Cirlot. Ed. by Roland Penrose. 1972. 29.95 o.p. (ISBN 0-236-15419-2, Pub. by Paul Elek). Merrimack Bk Serv.

Picasso Criticism, Nineteen One to Nineteen Thirty-Nine: The Making of an Artist-Hero. Eunice Lipton. LC 75-23801. (Outstanding Dissertations in the Fine Arts - 20th Century). (Illus.). 1976. lib. bdg. 45.00 (ISBN 0-8240-1996-2). Garland Pub.

Picasso: His Life & Work. rev ed. Roland Penrose. LC 72-180702. (Icon Editions). (Illus.). 544p. 1973. pap. 6.95 o.s.i. (ISBN 0-06-430016-1, IN-16, HarpT). Har-Row.

Picasso: His Life & Work. Roland Penrose. 1980. pap. 8.95 (ISBN 0-520-04207-7, CAL 487). U of Cal Pr.

Picasso on Art. Dore Ashton. 1977. pap. 5.95 (ISBN 0-14-004528-7). Penguin.

Picasso's Guernica: The Labyrinth of Narrative and Vision. Frank D. Russell. LC 79-52472. 350p. 1980. text ed. 35.00 (ISBN 0-8390-0243-2). Allanheld.

Picasso's "Vollard Suite". Anita C. Costello. LC 78-74365. (Outstanding Dissertations in the Fine Arts, Fourth Ser.). 1979. lib. bdg. 47.00 (ISBN 0-8240-3953-X). Garland Pub.

Pick a New Dream. Lenora M. Weber. LC 61-10488. (gr. 7-11). 1961. 10.95 (ISBN 0-690-62016-0, TYC-J). T Y Crowell.

Pick & the Pen. A. J. Wilson Mining Journal Books Ltd. 318p. 1980. 26.00x (ISBN 0-900117-16-8, Pub. by Mining Journal England). State Mutual Bk.

Pick Me Up: A Book of Short, Short Poems. Ed. by William Cole. LC 78-165103. (gr. 5 up). 1972. 4.95 o.s.i. (ISBN 0-02-722810-X). Macmillan.

Pick of the Crop: The Best of Vegetable Cooking. Gail Duff. 1979. 19.95 (ISBN 0-241-10175-1, Pub. by Hamish Hamilton England). David & Charles.

Pick up Sticks. Emma Lathen. 1981. pap. 2.50 (ISBN 0-671-83674-9). PB.

Pick Your Job & Land It. Sidney Edlund & Mary Edlund. 1973. 5.00 (ISBN 0-686-17213-2). Sandollar Pr.

Picked on Pat. Aleda Renken. LC 73-75864. (gr. 3-7). 1973. pap. 0.95 (ISBN 0-570-03601-1, 39-1024). Concordia.

Picking a Partner. William S. Deal. (Orig.). 1972. pap. 2.25 (ISBN 0-87123-456-4, 200456). Bethany Fell.

Picking & Weaving. Bijou Le Tord. LC 79-23457. (Illus.). 32p. (gr. k-3). 1980. 8.95 (ISBN 0-590-07642-6, Four Winds). Schol Bk Serv.

Picking up the Pieces. Betty Bates. LC 80-8811. 160p. 1981. 8.95 (ISBN 0-8234-0390-4). Holiday.

Pickle Creature. Manus M. Pinkwater. LC 78-11157. (Illus.). 32p. (gr. k-3). 1979. 8.95 (ISBN 0-590-07579-9, Four Winds). Schol Bk Serv.

Pickling of Steels. E. W. Mulcahy. LC 74-154842. (Illus.). 95p. 1973. 13.50x (ISBN 0-901994-20-0). Intl Pubns Serv.

Pick's Currency Yearbook 1977-1979. 22nd ed. Franz Pick. 1981. 180.00 (ISBN 0-87551-277-1). Pick Pub.

Picnic Gourmet. Joan Hemingway & Connie Maricich. (Illus.). 1978. pap. 6.95 (ISBN 0-394-72164-0, Vin). Random.

Picnics. Joan Chatfield-Taylor. LC 79-64872. (Illus.). 1980. pap. 4.95 (ISBN 0-394-73760-1). Taylor & NG.

Picnics with Pizzazz. Nancy A. Morton. (Orig.). 1981. pap. 5.95 (ISBN 0-8092-5922-2). Contemp Bks.

Picolata Treasure. Ruth Burnett. 192p. (YA) 1974. 5.95 (ISBN 0-685-50326-7, Avalon). Bouregy.

Picosecond Phenomena II: Proceedings. Ed. by R. M. Rochstrasser et al. (Springer Series in Chemical Physics: Vol. 14). (Illus.). 382p. 1981. 38.00 (ISBN 0-387-10403-8). Springer-Verlag.

Picto-Cabulary Series, 7 sets. Richard A. Boning. Incl. Basic Word Set-A. (gr. 1-2). 104.45 (ISBN 0-87965-409-0); Words to Eat. (gr. 4-6). 77.95 (ISBN 0-87965-401-5); Words to Wear. (gr. 4-6). 77.95 (ISBN 0-87965-402-3); Words to Meet. (gr. 4-6). 77.95 (ISBN 0-87965-403-1); Descriptive Words. (gr. 5-9). 77.95 (ISBN 0-87965-421-X); Words Around the House. (gr. 4-6). 54.95 (ISBN 0-87965-405-8); Words Around the Neighborhood. (gr. 4-6). 54.95 (ISBN 0-87965-404-X). 1976. B Loft.

Pictoral Memoir. Sylvia R. Miller. LC 80-81146. (Illus.). 120p. 1980. 20.00 (ISBN 0-913504-57-2). Lowell Pr.

Pictorial Astronomy. 4th, rev. ed. Dinsmore Alter et al. LC 73-15577. (Illus.). 352p. 1974. 14.95 (ISBN 0-690-00095-2, TYC-T). T Y Crowell.

Pictorial Autobiography. rev. ed. Barbara Hepworth. Ed. by A. Adams. (Illus.). 1978. text ed. 10.00x o.p. (ISBN 0-239-00179-6). Humanities.

Pictorial Biography of C. H. Spurgeon. Bob L. Ross. 1976. 3.95 (ISBN 0-686-16830-5); pap. 2.25 (ISBN 0-686-16831-3). Pilgrim Pubns.

Pictorial Dictionary of Ancient Rome, 2 vols. Ernest Nash. LC 79-91827. (Illus.). 1076p. 1980. Repr. of 1968 ed. Set. lib. bdg. 150.00 (ISBN 0-87817-265-3). Hacker.

Pictorial Encyclopedia of Dogs. Michael Geary. (Illus.). 192p. 1979. 14.95 (ISBN 0-528-81092-8). Rand.

Pictorial Field Book of the Revolution, 2 vols. Benson J. Lossing. LC 72-77516. (Illus.). (gr. 9 up). 1972. Repr. of 1859 ed. Set. 25.00 o.p. (ISBN 0-8048-1046-X). C E Tuttle.

Pictorial Guide to CB Radio Installation & Repair. Forest H. Belt. LC 73-85407. 1973. 8.95 o.p. (ISBN 0-8306-3683-8); pap. 5.95 (ISBN 0-8306-2683-2, 683). TAB Bks.

Pictorial Guide to the Mammals of North America. Leonard L. Rue, 3rd. (gr. 7 up). 1967. 11.95 o.s.i. (ISBN 0-690-62371-2, TYC-T). T Y Crowell.

Pictorial Guide to the Planets. 3rd ed. Joseph H. Jackson & John H. Baumert. LC 80-7897. (Illus.). 256p. 1981. 19.95 (ISBN 0-06-014869-1, HarpT). Har-Row.

Pictorial Guide to the Planets. rev. & enl. ed. Joseph H. Jackson, III. LC 72-7573. (Illus.). 256p. 1973. 13.95 o.s.i. (ISBN 0-690-62443-3, TYC-T). T Y Crowell.

Pictorial Guide to the Stars. Henry C. Kingh. (Illus.). 1967. 10.95 o.s.i. (ISBN 0-690-62513-8, TYC-T). T Y Crowell.

Pictorial Handbook of Technical Devices. Paul Grafstein & Otto B. Schwarz. LC 77-15620. (Illus.). 1978. pap. 6.95 o.p. (ISBN 0-668-04494-2, 4494). Arco.

Pictorial History, 8 vols. R. J. Unstead. Incl. Vol. 1. Invaded Island. LC 78-169914. 1972 (ISBN 0-382-06063-6); Vol. 2. Kings, Barons, & Serfs. LC 71-169915. 1972 (ISBN 0-382-06064-4); Vol. 3. Years of the Sword. LC 75-169916. 1972 (ISBN 0-382-06065-2); Vol. 4. Struggle for Power. LC 72-172430. 1972 (ISBN 0-382-06066-0); Vol. 5. Emerging Empire. LC 76-172431. 1972 (ISBN 0-382-06067-9); Vol. 6. Freedom & Revolution. LC 70-172432. 1972 (ISBN 0-382-06068-7); Vol. 7. Age of Machines. LC 73-172433. 1973 (ISBN 0-382-06069-5); Vol. 8. Incredible Century. LC 77-172434. 1975 (ISBN 0-382-06070-9). (Illus.). (gr. 4 up). lib. bdg. 7.95 (ISBN 0-685-36802-5). Silver.

Pictorial History of Black Servicemen: Air Force, Army, Navy, Marines. Jesse J. Johnson. LC 70-130752. (Illus.). 10.00 (ISBN 0-915044-09-9). Carver Pub.

Pictorial History of Canals. David Gladwin. 1977. 19.95 (ISBN 0-7134-0554-6, Pub. by Batsford England). David & Charles.

Pictorial History of Delta State University. Jack W. Gunn & Gladys C. Castle. LC 80-19085. 216p. 1980. 25.00 (ISBN 0-87805-112-0). U Pr of Miss.

Pictorial History of Florida. 3rd ed. Richard J. Bowe. 1970. 10.00 (ISBN 0-913122-14-9). Mickler Hse.

Pictorial History of Grand Rapids. Lynn G. Mapes & Anthony Travis. LC 75-8015. 1976. 14.95 (ISBN 0-8254-3213-8). Kregel.

Pictorial History of Indiana. Dwight W. Hoover. LC 80-7806. 224p. 1980. 19.95x (ISBN 0-253-14693-3). Ind U Pr.

Pictorial History of the American Theatre 1860-1980. rev. ed. Daniel Blum. Ed. by Brandt Aymar. 464p. 1981. 19.95 (ISBN 0-517-54262-5). Crown.

Pictorial History of the Black Soldier in the United States (1619-1969) in Peace & War. Jesse J. Johnson. 1976. 10.00 (ISBN 0-915044-08-0); pap. 3.00 (ISBN 0-915044-07-2). Carver Pub.

Pictorial History of the R.A.F, 3 vols. John W. Taylor. Incl. Vol. 1. 1918-1939. 202p. 1969. 5.95 (ISBN 0-668-01857-7); Vol. 2. 1939-1945. Philip J. Moyes. 240p. 1968. o. p. 5.95 (ISBN 0-668-02137-3); Vol. 3. 1945-1969. Philip J. Moyes. 208p. 1970. 5.95 o.p. (ISBN 0-668-02421-6). LC 69-12569. (Illus.). Arco.

Pictorial History of the Sub-Machine Gun. F. W. Hobart. LC 74-19683. 1975. 14.95 o.p. (ISBN 0-684-14186-8, ScribT). Scribner.

Pictorial Key to Genera of Plant-Parasitic Nematodes. 4th ed. W. F. Mai & H. H. Lyon. LC 74-14082. (Illus.). 224p. 1975. 14.50x (ISBN 0-8014-0920-9). Comstock.

Pictorial Library of Landscape Plants. 2nd ed. M. Jane Helmer. Ed. by John L. Threlkeld. (Illus.). 352p. 1979. 60.00 (ISBN 0-89484-008-8, 11101). Merchants Pub Co.

Pictorial Mementoes of the Romantic Age. George F. Kleber. (Illus.). 1979. deluxe ed. 29.75 (ISBN 0-930582-34-9). Gloucester Art.

Pictorial Mode: Space & Time in the Art of Bryant, Irving, & Cooper. Donald A. Ringe. LC 71-147859. (Illus.). 256p. 1971. 14.50x (ISBN 0-8131-1250-8). U Pr of Ky.

Pictorial Pilgrim's Progress. John Bunyan. 1960. pap. 2.50 (ISBN 0-8024-0019-1). Moody.

Pictorial Press, Its Origin & Progress. Mason Jackson. LC 68-21776. (Illus.). 1968. Repr. of 1885 ed. 15.00 (ISBN 0-8103-3355-4). Gale.

Pictorial Price Guide to American Antiques. 4th ed. Dorothy Hammond. (Illus.). 224p. 1981. pap. 9.95 (ISBN 0-525-47660-1). Dutton.

Pictorial Price Guide to American Antiques. 3rd ed. Dorothy Hammond. (Illus.). 1980. pap. 9.95 (ISBN 0-525-47625-3). Dutton.

Pictorial Sources of Mythological & Scientific Illustrations in Hrabanus Maurus' De rerum naturis. Diane O. Le Berrurier. LC 77-94732. (Outstanding Dissertations in the Fine Arts Ser.). (Illus.). 263p. 1980. lib. bdg. 31.00 (ISBN 0-8240-3234-9). Garland Pub.

Pictorial World Atlas. Brian Price. LC 79-50872. (Illus.). 224p. 1980. 29.95 (ISBN 0-528-83105-4). Rand.

Pictorial World History. W. H. Ha & C. L. Hallward. (Illus.). 1973. Bk. 1. pap. 6.00x (ISBN 0-582-67039-X); Bk. 2. pap. 7.00x (ISBN 0-582-67040-3); Bk. 3. pap. 7.75x (ISBN 0-582-67041-1). Longman.

Picture Atlas of Animals. Michael Chinery. LC 79-29657. (Illus.). 48p. (gr. 3-7). 1980. 6.95 (ISBN 0-528-82371-X). Rand.

Picture Bible, 4 vols. Incl. Vol. 1. Adam & Eve to Joshua (ISBN 0-89191-350-5); Vol. 2. Samson to Elijah (ISBN 0-89191-351-3); Vol. 3. Elijah to Jesus (ISBN 0-89191-352-1); Vol. 4. Jesus to Paul (ISBN 0-89191-353-X). Date not set. 14.95 ea. Cook.

Picture Book of Alabama. rev. ed. Bernadine Bailey. LC 59-9658. (Illus.). (gr. 3-5). 1975. 5.50g (ISBN 0-8075-9501-2). A Whitman.

Picture Book of Alaska. rev. ed. Bernadine Bailey. LC 57-7143. (Illus.). (gr. 3-5). 1968. 5.50g (ISBN 0-8075-9502-0). A Whitman.

Picture Book of American Interiors: From Colonial Times to the Late Victorians. Harold L. Peterson. (Encore Edition). (Illus.). 1979. pap. 4.95 (ISBN 0-684-16918-5, SL861, ScribT). Scribner.

Picture Book of Animal Families. (Animal Picture Bks.). (Illus.). 10p. (ps). 1979. 1.95 (ISBN 0-89346-177-6, TA05, Pub. by Froebel-Kan Japan). Heian Intl.

Picture Book of Animals of All Lands. (Children's Library of Picture Bks.). (Illus.). 10p. (ps). 1979. 1.95 (ISBN 0-89346-171-7, TA09, Pub. by Froebel-Kan Japan). Heian Intl.

Picture Book of Annuals. Arno Nehrling & Irene Nehrling. LC 76-45745. (Illus.). 1977. pap. 3.95 o.p. (ISBN 0-668-04158-7). Arco.

Picture Book of Arizona. rev. ed. Bernadine Bailey. LC 57-7146. (Illus.). (gr. 3-5). 1967. 5.15g (ISBN 0-8075-9503-9). A Whitman.

Picture Book of Arkansas. rev. ed. Bernadine Bailey. LC 66-2711. (Illus.). (gr. 3-5). 1967. 5.50g (ISBN 0-8075-9504-7). A Whitman.

Picture Book of California. rev. ed. Bernadine Bailey. LC 66-687. (Illus.). (gr. 3-5). 1968. 5.00g o.p. (ISBN 0-8075-9505-5). A Whitman.

Picture Book of California. rev ed. Bernadine Bailey. (gr. 3-5). 1981. 5.50g. A Whitman.

Picture Book of Colorado. rev. ed. Bernadine Bailey. LC 55-8827. (Illus.). (gr. 3-5). 1971. 5.50g (ISBN 0-8075-9506-3). A Whitman.

Picture Book of Connecticut. rev. ed. Bernadine Bailey. LC 60-11567. (Illus.). (gr. 3-5). 1974. 5.50g (ISBN 0-8075-9507-1). A Whitman.

Picture Book of Delaware. rev. ed. Bernadine Bailey. LC 68-4252. (Illus.). (gr. 3-5). 1977. 5.50g (ISBN 0-8075-9509-8). A Whitman.

Picture Book of Farmyard Friends. (Children's Library of Picture Bks.). (Illus.). 10p. (ps). 1979. 1.95 (ISBN 0-89346-172-5, TA12, Froebel-Kan Japan). Heian Intl.

Picture Book of Fisheries. Anita Brooks. (Picture Aids to World Geography Ser). (Illus.). (gr. 4-7). 1961. 6.89 (ISBN 0-381-99935-1, A61210, JD-J). John Day.

Picture Book of Florida. rev. ed. Bernadine Bailey. LC 68-4252. (Illus.). (gr. 3-5). 1980. 5.50g (ISBN 0-8075-9510-1). A Whitman.

Picture Book of Georgia. rev. ed. Bernadine Bailey. LC 60-11566. (Illus.). (gr. 3-5). 1966. 5.00g o.p. (ISBN 0-8075-9512-8). A Whitman.

Picture Book of Hawaii. rev. ed. Bernadine Bailey. LC 62-10660. (Illus.). (gr. 3-5). 1978. 5.50g (ISBN 0-8075-9513-6). A Whitman.

Picture Book of Idaho. rev. ed. Bernadine Bailey. LC 62-10660. (Illus.). (gr. 3-5). 1967. 5.50g (ISBN 0-8075-9514-4). A Whitman.

Picture Book of Illinois. rev. ed. Bernadine Bailey. LC 66-5264. (Illus.). (gr. 3-5). 1967. 5.50g (ISBN 0-8075-9515-2). A Whitman.

Picture Book of Indiana. rev. ed. Bernadine Bailey. LC 66-705. (Illus.). (gr. 3-5). 1974. 5.50g (ISBN 0-8075-9516-0). A Whitman.

Picture Book of Iowa. rev. ed. Bernadine Bailey. LC 62-19727. (Illus.). 32p. (gr. 3-5). 1969. 5.50g (ISBN 0-8075-9517-9). A Whitman.

Picture Book of Kansas. rev. ed. Bernadine Bailey. LC 65-29625. (Illus.). (gr. 3-5). 1969. 5.50g (ISBN 0-8075-9518-7). A Whitman.

Picture Book of Kentucky. rev. ed. Bernadine Bailey. LC 55-8828. (Illus.). (gr. 3-5). 1967. 5.50g (ISBN 0-8075-9519-5). A Whitman.

Picture Book of Louisiana. rev. ed. Bernadine Bailey. LC 54-9944. (Illus.). (gr. 3-5). 1967. 5.50g (ISBN 0-8075-9520-9). A Whitman.

Picture Book of Maine. rev. ed. Bernadine Bailey. LC 57-7144. (Illus.). (gr. 3-5). 1967. 5.50g (ISBN 0-8075-9521-7). A Whitman.

Picture Book of Maryland. rev. ed. Bernadine Bailey. LC 55-8829. (Illus.). (gr. 3-5). 1970. 5.50g (ISBN 0-8075-9522-5). A Whitman.

Picture Book of Massachusetts. rev. ed. Bernadine Bailey. LC 65-5509. (Illus.). (gr. 3-5). 1969. 5.50g (ISBN 0-8075-9523-3). A Whitman.

Picture Book of Metals. Anita Brooks. LC 78-147271. (Pictures Aids to World Geography Ser). (Illus.). (gr. 4-7). 1972. 6.89 (ISBN 0-381-99933-5, A61225, JD-J). John Day.

Picture Book of Michigan. rev. ed. Bernadine Bailey. (Illus.). (gr. 3-5). 1967. 5.50g (ISBN 0-8075-9524-1). A Whitman.

Picture Book of Minnesota. rev. ed. Bernadine Bailey. (Illus.). (gr. 3-5). 1967. 5.50g (ISBN 0-8075-9526-8). A Whitman.

Picture Book of Mississippi. rev. ed. Bernadine Bailey. LC 68-4457. (Illus.). (gr. 3-5). 1972. 5.00g o.p. (ISBN 0-8075-9527-6). A Whitman.

Picture Book of Missouri. rev. ed. Bernadine Bailey. LC 66-31256. (Illus.). (gr. 3-5). 1974. 5.50g (ISBN 0-8075-9528-4). A Whitman.

Picture Book of Montana. rev. ed. Bernadine Bailey. LC 65-8994. (Illus.). (gr. 3-5). 1969. 5.50g (ISBN 0-8075-9529-2). A Whitman.

Picture Book of Nebraska. rev. ed. Bernadine Bailey. LC 56-7756. (Illus.). (gr. 3-5). 1966. 5.50g (ISBN 0-8075-9530-6). A Whitman.

Picture Book of Nevada. rev. ed. Bernadine Bailey. LC 73-89402. (Illus.). (gr. 3-5). 1974. 5.50g (ISBN 0-8075-9531-4). A Whitman.

Picture Book of New Hampshire. rev. ed. Bernadine Bailey. LC 61-9971. (Illus.). (gr. 3-5). 1971. 5.50g (ISBN 0-8075-9532-2). A Whitman.

Picture Book of New Jersey. rev. ed. Bernadine Bailey. LC 65-9016. (Illus.). (gr. 3-5). 1968. 5.00g o.p. (ISBN 0-8075-9533-0). A Whitman.

Picture Book of New Mexico. rev. ed. Bernadine Bailey. LC 60-11568. (Illus.). (gr. 3-5). 1966. 5.50g (ISBN 0-8075-9534-9). A Whitman.

Picture Book of New York. rev. ed. Bernadine Bailey. LC 66-1262. (Illus.). (gr. 3-5). 1968. 5.50g (ISBN 0-8075-9535-7). A Whitman.

Picture Book of North Carolina. rev. ed. Bernadine Bailey. LC 74-134956. (Illus.). (gr. 3-5). 1970. 5.50g (ISBN 0-8075-9536-5). A Whitman.

Picture Book of North Dakota. rev. ed. Bernadine Bailey. LC 58-12319. (Illus.). (gr. 3-5). 1971. 5.50g (ISBN 0-8075-9537-3). A Whitman.

Picture Book of Ohio. rev. ed. Bernadine Bailey. (Illus.). (gr. 3-5). 1967. 5.50g (ISBN 0-8075-9538-1). A Whitman.

Picture Book of Oil. Anita Brooks. LC 65-19738. (Picture Aids to World Geography Ser.). (Illus.). (gr. 4-7). 1965. 6.89 (ISBN 0-381-99932-7, A61230, JD-J). John Day.

Picture Book of Oklahoma. rev. ed. Bernadine Bailey. (Illus.). (gr. 3-5). 1967. 5.50g (ISBN 0-8075-9540-3). A Whitman.

Picture Book of Oregon. rev. ed. Bernadine Bailey. LC 54-9942. (Illus.). (gr. 3-6). 1967. 5.50g (ISBN 0-8075-9541-1). A Whitman.

Picture Book of Pennsylvania. rev. ed. Bernadine Bailey. LC 66-2707. (Illus.). (gr. 3-5). 1972. 5.00g o.p. (ISBN 0-8075-9543-8). A Whitman.

Picture Book of Perennials. Arno Nehrling & Irene Nehrling. LC 76-46317. (Illus.). 1977. pap. 3.95 o.p. (ISBN 0-668-04163-3). Arco.

Picture Book of Rhode Island. rev. ed. Bernadine Bailey. LC 58-12320. (Illus.). (gr. 3-5). 1971. 5.50g (ISBN 0-8075-9545-4). A Whitman.

Picture Book of Salt. Anita Brooks. LC 64-10451. (Picture Aids to World Geography Ser). (Illus.). (gr. 4-7). 1964. 6.89 (ISBN 0-381-99931-9, A61240, JD-J). John Day.

Picture Book of San Antonio. David Bowen. 32p. (English & Spanish.). pap. 2.50 (ISBN 0-931722-02-0). Corona Pub.

Picture Book of South Carolina. rev. ed. Bernadine Bailey. LC 56-7757. (Illus.). (gr. 3-5). 1975. 5.50g (ISBN 0-8075-9546-2). A Whitman.

Picture Book of South Dakota. rev. ed. Bernadine Bailey. LC 60-11569. (Illus.). (gr. 3-5). 1966. 5.00g o.p. (ISBN 0-8075-9547-0). A Whitman.

Picture Book of Tennessee. rev. ed. Bernadine Bailey. LC 66-5266. (Illus.). (gr. 3-5). 1974. 5.50g (ISBN 0-8075-9548-9). A Whitman.

Picture Book of Texas. rev. ed. Bernadine Bailey. (Illus.). (gr. 3-5). 1967. 5.50g (ISBN 0-8075-9549-7). A Whitman.

Picture Book of Timber. Anita Brooks. LC 67-14617. (Picture Aids to World Geography Ser). (Illus.). (gr. 4-7). 1967. 6.89 (ISBN 0-381-99929-7, A61250, JD-J). John Day.

Picture Book of Utah. rev. ed. Bernadine Bailey. LC 57-7145. (Illus.). (gr. 3-5). 1967. 5.50g (ISBN 0-8075-9550-0). A Whitman.

Picture Book of Vermont. rev. ed. Bernadine Bailey. LC 65-9015. (Illus.). (gr. 3-5). 1968. 5.50g (ISBN 0-8075-9551-9). A Whitman.

Picture Book of Virginia. rev. ed. Bernadine Bailey. LC 66-4792. (Illus.). (gr. 3-5). 1970. 5.50g (ISBN 0-8075-9552-7). A Whitman.

Picture Book of Washington. rev. ed. Bernadine Bailey. LC 62-10660. (Illus.). (gr. 3-5). 1966. 5.50g (ISBN 0-8075-9553-5). A Whitman.

Picture Book of West Virginia. rev. ed. Bernadine Bailey. LC 56-7755. (Illus.). (gr. 3-6). 1970. 5.00g o.p. (ISBN 0-8075-9554-3). A Whitman.

Picture Book of Wisconsin. rev. ed. Bernadine Bailey. (Illus.). (gr. 3-5). 1975. 5.50g (ISBN 0-8075-9555-1). A Whitman.

Picture Book of Wyoming. rev. ed. Bernadine Bailey. LC 58-12321. (Illus.). (gr. 3-5). 1972. 5.50g (ISBN 0-8075-9557-8). A Whitman.

Picture Book One. (Ladybird Stories Ser.). (Illus., Arabic.). 2.50x (ISBN 0-686-53061-6). Intl Bk Ctr.

Picture Book Two. (Ladybird Stories Ser.). (Illus., Arabic.). 2.50x (ISBN 0-686-53062-4). Intl Bk Ctr.

Picture Charlie. Joan Tate. pap. text ed. 1.95x o.p. (ISBN 0-435-11874-9). Heinemann Ed.

Picture Encyclopedia of Small Plants. Jack Kramer. LC 78-1089. 192p. 1981. pap. 8.95 (ISBN 0-8128-6083-7). Stein & Day.

Picture for Harold's Room. Crockett Johnson. (Illus.). (gr. k-3). 1974. pap. 1.25 (ISBN 0-590-02396-9, Schol Pap); pap. 3.50 (ISBN 0-590-20795-4). Schol Bk Serv.

Picture History of Ancient Rome. Richard Erdoes. (gr. 4-6). 1967. 4.95 o.s.i. (ISBN 0-02-733550-X). Macmillan.

Picture History of the Boston Celtics. George Sullivan. LC 80-689. 256p. 1981. 19.95 (ISBN 0-672-52654-9). Bobbs.

Picture It. Donald R. Byrd. (Illus.). 232p. (gr. 10-12). 1981. pap. text ed. 5.95 (ISBN 0-88345-413-0). Regents Pub.

Picture Librarianship. Hilary Evans. (Outlines of Modern Librarianship Ser.). 1980. text ed. 12.00 (ISBN 0-89664-428-6, Pub. by K G Saur). Shoe String.

Picture Life of Bobby Orr. Audrey Edwards & Gary Wohl. (Picture Lives Ser.). (Illus.). 48p. (gr. k-3). 1976. PLB 4.90 o.p. (ISBN 0-531-01208-5). Watts.

Picture Life of Herman Badillo. Paul Allyn. LC 79-185925. (Picture Life Bks). (Illus.). 48p. (gr. k-3). 1972. PLB 6.45 (ISBN 0-531-00985-8). Watts.

Picture Life of Jesse Jackson. Warren Halliburton. LC 74-186937. (Picture Life Bks). (Illus.). 48p. (gr. k-3). 1972. PLB 4.90 o.p. (ISBN 0-531-00986-6). Watts.

Picture Life of Malcolm X. James S. Haskins. LC 74-7441. (Picture Life Bks). (Illus.). 48p. (gr. k-3). 1975. PLB 6.45 (ISBN 0-531-02771-6). Watts.

Picture Life of Martin Luther King, Jr. Margaret B. Young. LC 67-20866. (Picture Life Bks). (Illus.). (gr. k-3). 1968. PLB 6.45 (ISBN 0-531-00981-5). Watts.

Picture Life of Muhammad Ali. A. Edwards & G. Wohl. 1977. pap. 1.75 (ISBN 0-380-01904-3, 51623, Camelot). Avon.

Picture Life of Muhammad Ali. Audrey Edwards & Gary Wohl. LC 76-10999. (Picture Lives Ser.). (Illus.). 48p. (gr. k-3). 1976. PLB 4.90 o.p. (ISBN 0-531-00327-2). Watts.

Picture Life of O. J. Simpson. J. Jameson. 1978. pap. 1.75 (ISBN 0-380-01906-X, 51649, Camelot). Avon.

Picture Life of O. J. Simpson. Jon Jameson. (Picture Life Bks.). (Illus.). (gr. 2 up). 1977. PLB 5.90 (ISBN 0-531-01270-0). Watts.

Picture Life of Reggie Jackson. Bill Gutman. (Illus.). (gr. 1 up). 1978. pap. 1.75 (ISBN 0-380-40345-5, 51631, Camelot). Avon.

Picture Life of Stevie Wonder. A. Edwards & G. Wohl. 1977. pap. 1.75 (ISBN 0-380-01907-8, 51656, Camelot). Avon.

Picture Life of Stevie Wonder. Audrey Edwards & Gary Wohl. (Picture Life Bks.). (Illus.). (gr. k-3). 1977. PLB 6.45 s&l (ISBN 0-531-01271-9). Watts.

Picture Life of Thurgood Marshall. Margaret B. Young. LC 79-131154. (Picture Life Bks). (Illus.). (gr. k-3). 1971. PLB 4.90 o.p. (ISBN 0-531-00984-X). Watts.

Picture of a Papist: Whereunto Is Annexed a Certain Treatise, Intituled Pagano-Papismus. Oliver Ormerod. LC 74-28878. (English Experience Ser.: No. 756). 1975. Repr. of 1606 ed. 18.50 (ISBN 90-221-0756-6). Walter J Johnson.

Picture of a Puritane: Or, a Relation of the Opinions - of the Anabaptists in Germanie, & of the Puritanes in England. Oliver Ormerod. LC 74-28879. (English Experience Ser.: No. 757). 1975. Repr. of 1605 ed. 9.50 (ISBN 90-221-0757-4). Walter J Johnson.

Picture of Dorian Gray. Oscar Wilde. (Literature Ser). (gr. 10-12). 1970. pap. text ed. 3.50 (ISBN 0-87720-734-8). AMSCO Sch.

Picture of Dorian Gray. Oscar Wilde. Ed. by Isobel M. Murray. (Oxford English Novels Ser.). 256p. 1974. 13.50x (ISBN 0-19-255368-2). Oxford U Pr.

Picture of Dorian Gray. Oscar Wilde. 1976. pap. 2.95 (ISBN 0-460-01198-7, Evman). Dutton.

Picture Play: The Japanese Twins' Lucky Day. Florence Sakade. LC 64-20367. (Illus.). 3.50 o.p. (ISBN 0-8048-0322-6). C E Tuttle.

Picture Printing. Lothar Kampmann. 1970. 19.95 (ISBN 0-7134-2280-7, Pub. by Batsford England). David & Charles.

Picture Processing & Digital Filtering. T. S. Huang. LC 75-5770. (Illus.). 270p. 1975. 39.60 o.p. (ISBN 0-387-07202-0). Springer-Verlag.

Picture Processing & Reconstruction: Dimensional & Structural Analysis. Sheldon S. Sandler. LC 74-25087. (Illus.). 128p. 1975. 22.95 (ISBN 0-669-97683-0). Lexington Bks.

Picture Report of the Custer Fight. William Reusswig. (Illus.). 192p. (gr. 6-9). 1967. 12.50 (ISBN 0-8038-5737-3). Hastings.

Picture Searching: Tools & Techniques. Compiled by Renata V. Shaw. LC 72-13234. (Bibliography Ser.: No. 6). 1973. pap. 2.25 (ISBN 0-87111-207-8). SLA.

Picture Stories. Queenie B. Mills & Rosalie Mower. (ps-k). 1973. pap. text ed. 3.92 (ISBN 0-205-03510-8, 5235103); tchrs'. guide 8.20 (ISBN 0-205-03511-6, 5235111). Allyn.

Picture Stories & Words. new ed. William D. Sheldon et al. (Sheldon Reading Ser.). (gr. k-1). 1973. pap. text ed. 3.92 (ISBN 0-205-03512-4, 523512X); tchrs'. guide 8.20 (ISBN 0-205-03513-2, 5235138). Allyn.

Picture Story of Nancy Lopez. Betty L. Phillips. LC 79-25344. (Illus.). 64p. (gr. 4-6). 1980. PLB 6.97 (ISBN 0-671-33050-0). Messner.

Picture Story of Rod Carew. Anne M. Mueser. LC 80-420. (Illus.). 64p. (gr. 4-6). 1980. PLB 6.97 (ISBN 0-671-33049-7). Messner.

Picture Theory of Meaning: An Interpretation of Wittgenstein's Tractatus Logico-Philosophicus. Scott R. Stripling. LC 78-62176. 1978. pap. text ed. 7.50 (ISBN 0-8191-0109-5). U Pr of Amer.

Picture Yourself a Winner. R. Eugene Nichols. 1978. pap. 4.95 (ISBN 0-87707-206-X). CSA Pr.

Pictures & Patterns. Janet Margrie. LC 77-8005. (Beginning Crafts Ser.). (Illus.). (gr. k-3). 1977. PLB 9.30 (ISBN 0-8393-0117-0). Raintree Child.

Pictures & Stories from Forgotten Children's Books. Arnold Arnold. (Illus., Orig.). (gr. k-6). 1970. pap. 5.00 (ISBN 0-486-22041-9). Dover.

Pictures from an Institution. Randall Jarrell. 1980. pap. 2.95 (ISBN 0-686-69257-8, 49650, Bard). Avon.

Pictures from the Past. Ruth Geller. LC 80-82075. 205p. 1980. pap. 7.95 (ISBN 0-9603008-1-3). Imp Pr.

Pictures in Patchwork. Marie-Janine Solvit. LC 76-51189. (Illus.). 1977. 16.95 (ISBN 0-8069-5380-2); lib. bdg. 14.99 (ISBN 0-8069-5381-0). Sterling.

Pictures in Patchwork. Marie-Janine Solvit. LC 76-51189. (Illus.). 120p. 1981. pap. 8.95. Sterling.

Pictures in the Cave. George M. Brown. (Illus.). 136p. (gr. 4-7). 1980. 9.95 (ISBN 0-7011-5081-5, Pub. by Chatto Bodley Jonathan). Merrimack Bk Serv.

Pictures of the New Kingdom. David A. Hubbard. 110p. (Orig.). 1981. pap. 2.95 (ISBN 0-87784-471-2). Inter-Varsity.

Pictures of Truth. Ralph W. Harris. LC 76-58081. (Radiant Life Ser). 1977. pap. 1.50 (ISBN 0-88243-905-7, 02-0905); teacher's ed 2.50 (ISBN 0-88243-175-7, 32-0175). Gospel Pub.

Pictures on a Page: Photojournalism & Picture Editing. Harold Evans & Edwin Taylor. 320p. 1979. text ed. 14.95x (ISBN 0-534-00812-7). Wadsworth Pub.

Pictures, Their Preservation & Restoration. Carl D. Clarke. (Illus.). 250p. 1959. 18.00 (ISBN 0-685-25472-0). Standard Arts.

Pictures Will Talk: The Life & Films of Joseph L. Mankiewicz. Kenneth L. Geist. LC 78-1104. (Encore Edition). (Illus.). 1978. 4.95 (ISBN 0-684-16560-0, ScribT). Scribner.

Picturesque America: The Mountains, Rivers, Lakes, Forests, Waterfalls, Shores, Canyons, Valleys, Cities, & Other Picturesque Features of Our Country by Eminent American Artists. facsimile ed. Ed. by Oliver Jensen. LC 73-21908. (Illus.). 1974. 25.00 (ISBN 0-8281-0337-2, M013). Am Heritage.

Picturesque & Descriptive View of the City of Dublin. James Malton. (Illus.). 1799. Repr. of 1799 ed. text ed. 23.00x (ISBN 0-85105-336-X, Dolmen Pr). Humanities.

Picturesque Expressions: A Thematic Dictionary. Ed. by Nancy LaRoche & Laurence Urdang. LC 80-22705. 300p. 1980. 35.00 (ISBN 0-8103-1122-4). Gale.

Picturesque Images from Taos & Santa Fe. Patricia Trenton. (Illus.). 1974. pap. 12.95 (ISBN 0-914738-20-8). Denver Art Mus.

Picturing: Description & Illusion in the Nineteenth Century Novel. Michael Irwin. 1979. text ed. 22.50x (ISBN 0-04-801021-9). Allen Unwin.

Pidgey & P. J. Holly Smith. 1981. 4.50 (ISBN 0-8062-1670-0). Carlton.

Pidgin & Creole Languages. Ed. by G. G. Gilbert. LC 79-15866. 320p. 1980. 32.95 (ISBN 0-521-22789-5). Cambridge U Pr.

Pidginization & Creolization of Languages: Proceedings. Dell Hymes. LC 77-123672. 1971. 42.50 (ISBN 0-521-07833-4); pap. 14.95x (ISBN 0-521-09888-2). Cambridge U Pr.

Pidgins & Creoles. Loreto Todd. (Language & Society Ser.). 1974. 12.00x (ISBN 0-7100-7865-X); pap. 4.95 (ISBN 0-7100-7927-3). Routledge & Kegan.

Pie & the Patty Pan. Beatrix Potter. (Peter Possum Paperbacks). (gr. k-3). 1975. pap. 0.95 o.p. (ISBN 0-531-05115-3). Watts.

Piece & Pieces: An Anthology of Contemporary American Poetry. Ed. by Maurice Custodio et al. LC 73-83883. 216p. 1973. pap. 5.00 o.p. (ISBN 0-914024-08-6). SF Arts & Letters.

Piece of the Fox's Hide. Katherine Boling. 1974. pap. 1.75 o.p. (ISBN 0-89176-871-8, 6871). Mockingbird Bks.

Piece of the Pie: Blacks & White Immigrants Since 1880. Stanley Lieberson. 420p. 1981. 19.95 (ISBN 0-520-04123-2). U of Cal Pr.

Pieced Quilt: An American Design Tradition. Jonathon Holstein. LC 73-79991. (Illus.). 1975. pap. 12.95 (ISBN 0-8212-0686-9, 707317). NYGS.

Pieces a une et a Deux Violes, 1686-89: The Instrumental Works, Vol. 1. Marin Marais. Ed. by John Hsu. xxvii, 191p. 1980. lib. bdg. 67.50x (ISBN 0-8450-7201-3). Broude.

Pieces for Glass Piano. Gerard Lee. (Paperback Prose Ser.). 1978. pap. 7.25x (ISBN 0-7022-1169-9). U of Queensland Pr.

Pieces of Another World: The Story of Moon Rocks. Franklyn M. Branley. LC 71-158684. (Illus.). (gr. 5-8). 1972. PLB 9.89 (ISBN 0-690-62566-9, TYC-J). T Y Crowell.

Pieces of Christmas. Ruth E. Hillman. (Illus.). 96p. (Orig.). 1975. pap. 0.75 (ISBN 0-8272-2923-2). Bethany Pr.

Pieces of Eight Channel Islands: A Bibliographical Guide & Source Book. Adelaide L. Doran. LC 80-66447. (Illus.). 341p. 1981. 26.50 (ISBN 0-87062-132-7). A H Clark.

Pieces of Life. LC 79-93017. 1981. pap. 10.00 (ISBN 0-933830-07-6). Poly Tone.

Pieces of Life. Mark Schorer. 1977. 8.95 o.p. (ISBN 0-374-23280-6). FS&G.

Pieces of the Frame. John McPhee. 1975. 10.00 (ISBN 0-374-23281-4); pap. 4.95 (ISBN 0-374-51498-4). FS&G.

Piecework Bargaining. William Brown. 1973. text ed. 8.95x o.p. (ISBN 0-435-85125-X). Heinemann Ed.

Pied Peper of Hamelin. (Illus.). 32p. (ps-3). 1981. PLB 7.95 (ISBN 0-8234-0415-3). Holiday.

Piedmont & Northern Railway. Thomas T. Fetters & Peter W. Swanson. LC 74-14801. (Illus.). 170p. 18.95 (ISBN 0-87095-051-7). Golden West.

Piedmont Garden: How to Grow by the Calendar. Juanita B. Garrison. LC 80-23218. 1981. pap. text ed. 4.95 mechanical (ISBN 0-87249-403-9). U of SC Pr.

Piemakers. Helen Cresswell. LC 80-14433. (Illus.). 128p. (gr. 3-7). 1980. 8.95 (ISBN 0-02-725410-0). Macmillan.

Pier Fishing on San Francisco Bay. Mike Hayden. (Illus.). 116p. (Orig.). 1981. pap. 5.95 (ISBN 0-87701-138-9). Chronicle Bks.

Pier Luigi Nervi. Ada Louise Huxtable. LC 60-6076. (Masters of World Architecture Ser). (Illus.). 7.95 o.s.i. (ISBN 0-8076-0106-3); pap. 3.95 o.s.i. (ISBN 0-8076-0223-X). Braziller.

Pier Paolo Pasolini. Stephen Snyder. (Theater Arts Ser.). 1980. lib. bdg. 13.95 (ISBN 0-8057-9271-6). Twayne.

Pierce Arrow. Mark A. Ralston. LC 80-15214. (Illus.). 366p. 1980. 25.00 (ISBN 0-498-02451-2). A S Barnes.

Piero Della Francesca's Mathematical Treatises: The "Trattato d'Abaco" & "Libellus de Quinque Corporibus Regularibus". Margaret D. Davis. (Speculum Artium: No. 1). (Illus.). 165p. (It.). 1977. pap. 17.50x (ISBN 0-8150-0912-7). Wittenborn.

Piero Dorazio: A Retrospective. Ed. by Douglas G. Schultz & Edward F. Fry. LC 79-55355. (Illus.). 1979. pap. 15.00 (ISBN 0-914782-30-4). Buffalo Acad.

Pierpont Morgan Library: A Review of Acquisitions, 1949-1968. Compiled by Morgan Library Curators. (Illus.). 1969. 22.50 (ISBN 0-87598-022-8); pap. 10.00 (ISBN 0-87598-005-8). Pierpont Morgan.

Pierpont Morgan Library: Gifts in Honor of the Fiftieth Anniversary. Pref. by Charles Ryskamp. 1974. pap. 6.00 (ISBN 0-87598-048-1). Pierpont Morgan.

Pierre Attaingnant, Royal Printer of Music: A Historical Study & Bibliographical Catalogue. Daniel Heartz. LC 68-13959. 1970. 46.50x (ISBN 0-520-01563-0). U of Cal Pr.

Pierre-Auguste Renoir. Ernest Raboff. LC 72-93205. (gr. 3-7). 1970. PLB 6.95 (ISBN 0-385-03775-9). Doubleday.

Pierre Corneille. Claude Abraham. (World Authors Ser.: France: No. 214). lib. bdg. 10.95 (ISBN 0-8057-2244-0). Twayne.

Pierre Larousse et son oeuvre. new ed. Andre Retif. 335p. 1975. pap. 19.50x (ISBN 2-03-079950-5). Larousse.

Pierre Loti. Michael G. Lerner. (World Authors Ser.: France: No. 277). 1974. lib. bdg. 12.50 (ISBN 0-8057-2546-6). Twayne.

Pierre Louys Eighteen Seventy to Nineteen Twenty-Five: A Biography. H. P. Clive. 1978. 37.50x (ISBN 0-19-815751-7). Oxford U Pr.

Piers Plainnes Seauen Yeres Prentship. Henry Chettle. LC 80-2476. 1981. Repr. of 1595 ed. 32.50 (ISBN 0-404-19108-8). AMS Pr.

Piers Plowman. Dorothy L. Owen. 173p. 1980. Repr. of 1912 ed. lib. bdg. 30.00 (ISBN 0-8495-4226-X). Arden Lib.

Piers Plowman: An Interpretation of the A Text. 2nd ed. Ed. by Thomas Dunning & T. P. Dolan. 192p. 1980. 34.95x (ISBN 0-19-812446-5). Oxford U Pr.

Piers Plowman: The B Version. Ed. by George Kane & E. Talbot Donaldson. (Piers Plowman: The Three Versions Ser). 681p. 1975. text ed. 72.50x (ISBN 0-485-13502-7, Athlone Pr). Humanities.

Piers Plowman: The Evidence for Authorship. George Kane. 1965. text ed. 23.50x (ISBN 0-485-11073-3, Athlone Pr). Humanities.

Piers the Ploughman. William Langland. Tr. by J. F. Goodridge. (Classics Ser.). (Orig.). 1959. pap. 3.50 (ISBN 0-14-044087-9). Penguin.

Pies & Pastries. Ed. by Time-Life Bks. Eds. (Good Cook Ser.). (Illus.). 176p. 1981. 12.95 (ISBN 0-8094-2895-4). Time-Life.

Piet Mondrian's Early Career: The Naturalistic Periods. Robert P. Welsh. LC 76-23659. (Outstanding Disserations in the Fine Arts Ser.). 1977. lib. bdg. 56.00x (ISBN 0-8240-2738-8). Garland Pub.

Pieter Aertsen, Joachim Beuckelaer & the Rise of Secular Painting in the Context of the Reformation. Keith P. Moxey. LC 76-23656. (Outstanding Dissertations in the Fine Arts - 16th Century). (Illus.). 1977. Repr. of 1974 ed. lib. bdg. 48.00 (ISBN 0-8240-2715-9). Garland Pub.

Pieter De Hooch: Complete Edition with a Catalogue Raisonne. Peter C. Sutton. LC 80-7667. (Illus.). 312p. 1980. slipcased 95.00x (ISBN 0-8014-1339-7). Cornell U Pr.

Piety & Perservance: The Hassidic Jewish Communities of Hungary & Their Descendants in the United States. Herman Dicker. (Illus.). 208p. 1981. 12.95 (ISBN 0-87203-094-6). Hermon.

Piety & Power: The Role of Italian Parishes in the New York Metropolitan Area (1880-1930) Silvano M. Tomasi. LC 74-79913. 201p. 1975. 14.95x (ISBN 0-913256-16-1, Dist. by Ozer). Ctr Migration.

Piety & the Princeton Theologians. W. Andrew Hoffecker. (Orig.). 1981. pap. 5.95 (ISBN 0-8010-4253-4). Baker Bk.

Piety in the Public School: Trends & Issues in the Relationship Between Religion & the Public School in the United States. Robert Michaelson. LC 72-87896. 1970. 6.95 o.s.i. (ISBN 0-02-584460-1). Macmillan.

Piety of Thinking: Essays. Martin Heidegger. Ed. by James G. Hart & John C. Maraldo. LC 75-3889. (Studies in Phenomenology & Existential Philosophy). 224p. 1976. 10.95x (ISBN 0-253-34498-0). Ind U Pr.

Piezoelectric Ceramics. 2nd ed. Ed. by J. Van Randeraat & R. E. Setterington. (Mullard Publications Ser.). (Illus.). 211p. 1974. text ed. 24.50x (ISBN 0-901232-75-0). Scholium Intl.

Pig & the Blue Flag. Carla Stevens. LC 76-58384. (Illus.). (gr. k-3). 1977. 6.95 (ISBN 0-395-28825-8, Clarion). HM.

Pig Appeal. Laurie P. Winfrey. (Illus.). 96p. Date not set. postponed 15.95 (ISBN 0-8027-0668-1); pap. 9.95 (ISBN 0-8027-7166-1). Walker & Co. Postponed.

Pig at Thirty-Seven Pinecrest Drive. Susan Fleming. (Illus.). (gr. 3-5). 1981. 9.95 (ISBN 0-664-32676-5). Westminster.

Pig Grows up. David McPhail. LC 80-350. (Illus.). 24p. (ps-3). 1980. PLB 8.95 (ISBN 0-525-37027-7, Unicorn). Dutton.

Pig Iron, Number 7: Special Woman Issue. Ed. by Rose Sayre. (Literary & Art Anthology Ser.). 1980. pap. 4.95 (ISBN 0-917530-15-2). Pig Iron Pr.

Pig Iron, Number 8: The New Beats. Ed. by Jim Villani & Rose Sayre. (Literary & Art Anthology Ser.). 96p. 1980. pap. 4.95 (ISBN 0-917530-16-0). Pig Iron Pr.

Pig Party. Carol Adorjan. (Prime Time Adventures Ser.). (Illus.). 64p. (gr. 4 up). 1981. PLB 7.95 (ISBN 0-516-02108-7). Childrens.

Pig Pig Grows up. David McPhail. LC 80-377. (Illus.). 32p. (ps-2). 1980. 8.95 (ISBN 0-525-37027-7). Dutton.

Pig Production: The Scientific & Practical Principles. Colin T. Whittemore. (Longman Handbooks in Agriculture Ser.). (Illus.). 160p. (Orig.). 1980. pap. text ed. 13.50 (ISBN 0-582-45590-1). Longman.

Pig Tale. Helen Oxenbury. LC 73-6357. (Illus.). 32p. (gr. k-3). 1973. PLB 7.92 (ISBN 0-688-30092-8). Morrow.

Pig Who Saw Everything. Dick Gackenbach. LC 77-12741. (Illus.). 1978. 6.95 (ISBN 0-395-28798-7, Clarion). HM.

Pigeon. Wendell M. Levi. 1981. Repr. 42.50 (ISBN 0-910876-01-0). Levi Pub.

Pigeon Racing. Jan Aerts. 1973. 14.95 (ISBN 0-571-08287-4, Pub. by Faber & Faber). Merrimack Bk Serv.

Pigeon Racing. Herbert R. Axelrod & Edwin C. Welty, Jr. LC 72-81050. 160p. (gr. 10 up). 1973. 11.95 (ISBN 0-8069-3720-3); PLB 10.79 (ISBN 0-8069-3721-1). Sterling.

Pigeon Racing: Advanced Techniques. Jan Aerts. (Illus.). 192p. 1981. pap. 7.95 (ISBN 0-571-11572-1, Pub. by Faber & Faber). Merrimack Bk Serv.

Pigeons. Mervin F. Roberts. (Orig.). pap. 2.00 (ISBN 0-87666-432-X, M512). TFH Pubns.

Pigeons & Doves of the World. 2nd ed. Derek Goodwin. LC 76-55484. (Illus.). 464p. 1977. 32.50x (ISBN 0-8014-1100-9). Comstock.

Piggy in the Puddle. Charlotte Pomerantz. LC 73-6047. (Illus.). 32p. (ps-2). 1974. 7.95 (ISBN 0-02-774900-2). Macmillan.

Pigkeeper's Guide. Peter Mitchelmore. LC 80-68686. (Illus.). 136p. 1981. 14.95 (ISBN 0-7153-7995-X). David & Charles.

Pigman's Legacy. Paul Zindel. LC 79-2684. 192p. (YA) (gr. 7 up). 1980. 8.95 (ISBN 0-06-026853-0, HarpJ); PLB 8.79 (ISBN 0-06-026854-9). Har-Row.

Pigments: An Introduction to Their Physical Chemistry. Ed. by David Patterson. (Illus.). 1967. 33.60x (ISBN 0-444-20009-6). Intl Ideas.

Pignight & Blowjob. Snoo Wilson. 1980. pap. 4.95 (ISBN 0-7145-3509-5). Riverrun NY.

Pigors Incident Process of Case Study. Paul Pigors & Faith Pigors. LC 79-23530. 1980. 13.95 (ISBN 0-87778-149-4). Educ Tech Pubns.

Pigs Have Wings. P. G. Wodehouse. 1977. pap. 1.95 o.p. (ISBN 0-345-25516-X). Ballantine.

Pigs Say Oink. Martha Alexander. (Illus.). 32p. (ps-3). 1981. PLB 4.99 (ISBN 0-394-93838-0); pap. 1.25 (ISBN 0-394-83838-6). Random.

Pigsticking. William Rushton. (Illus.). 14.95x o.p. (ISBN 0-8464-0719-1). Beekman Pubs.

Pilates Method of Physical & Mental Conditioning. Philip Friedman & Gail Eisen. 1981. pap. 7.95 (ISBN 0-446-97859-0). Warner Bks.

Pilchard. M. B. Culley. 1972. 55.000 (ISBN 0-08-016523-0). Pergamon.

Pile Design & Construction Practice. M. J. Tomlinson. (Viewpoint Ser.). (Illus.). 1978. 52.50x (ISBN 0-7210-1013-X). Scholium Intl.

Pile Neutron Research in Physics. 1962. 22.50 (ISBN 92-0-030062-6, IAEA). Unipub.

Piles in Weak Rock. Institute of Civil Engineers. 244p. 1980. 35.00x (ISBN 0-7277-0034-0, Pub. by Telford England). State Mutual Bk.

Pilgrim. Ray Hogan. 1981. pap. 1.75 (ISBN 0-451-09576-6, E9576, Sig). NAL.

Pilgrim at Tinker Creek. Annie Dillard. LC 73-18655. 232p. 1974. 10.00 (ISBN 0-06-121980-0). Har-Row.

Pilgrim Children on the Mayflower. Ida DeLage. LC 79-21812. (Ida DeLage Bks.). (Illus.). (gr. 1-5). 1980. PLB 5.58 (ISBN 0-8116-4315-8). Garrard.

Pilgrim Fathers. Peach. (Ladybird Ser.). 1972. 1.49 (ISBN 0-87508-855-4). Chr Lit.

Pilgrim Hymnal. organist's ed. Ethel Porter & Hugh Porter. 596p. 8.00. Pilgrim Pr.

Pilgrim Hymnal. Ed. by Ethel Porter & Hugh Porter. 596p. 1931. 6.50 (ISBN 0-8298-0107-3). Pilgrim Pr.

Pilgrim: John Bunyan's Pilgrim's Progress Retold. Ronald Fuller. LC 80-156. (Illus.). 48p. (gr. 5 up). 1980. 10.95 (ISBN 0-916144-44-5); pap. 5.95 (ISBN 0-916144-45-3). Stemmer Hse.

Pilgrim; or, a Picture of Life, 1775, 2 vols. in 1. Charles Johnstone. LC 74-16216. (Novel in England, 1700-1775 Ser). 1974. lib. bdg. 50.00 (ISBN 0-8240-1208-9). Garland Pub.

Pilgrim: or the Stranger in His Own Country, Vol. 69. Lope De Vega. LC 71-170598. (Novel in England, 1700-1775 Ser). lib. bdg. 50.00 (ISBN 0-8240-0581-3). Garland Pub.

Pilgrim to Poland: Pope John Paul. 1979. 5.00 (ISBN 0-686-63640-6); pap. 3.50 (ISBN 0-8198-0627-7). Dghtrs St Paul.

Pilgrimage. Zenna Henderson. 1973. pap. 1.50 (ISBN 0-380-01507-2, 36681). Avon.

Pilgrimage. Drew Mendelson. 1981. pap. 2.25 (ISBN 0-87997-612-8, UE1612). DAW Bks.

Pilgrimage: An Image of Mediaeval Religion. Jonathan Sumption. (Illus.). 390p. 1975. 17.50x (ISBN 0-87471-677-2). Rowman.

Pilgrimage in Faith: An Introduction to the Episcopal Church. rev. ed. Franklin C. Ferguson. LC 75-5220. 180p. (Orig.). 1979. pap. 5.95 (ISBN 0-8192-1277-6). Morehouse.

Pilgrimage of Faith: The Legacy of the Otterbeins. J. Steven O'Malley. LC 73-5684. (ATLA Monograph: No. 4). 1973. 10.00 (ISBN 0-8108-0626-6). Scarecrow.

Pilgrimage to Russia: The Soviet Union & the Treatment of Foreigners, 1924-1937. Sylvia R. Margulies. 1968. 22.50 (ISBN 0-299-04720-2). U of Wis Pr.

Pilgrimage to the Holy Land. Alphonse de Lamartine. LC 78-14368. 1978. Repr. of 1838 ed. 40.00x (ISBN 0-8201-1323-9). Schol Facsimiles.

Pilgrims, Heretics & Lovers: A Medieval Journey. Claude Marks. (Illus.). 320p. 1975. 14.95 o.s.i. (ISBN 0-02-579770-0). Macmillan.

Pilgrims in a Strange Land: Hausa Communities in Chad. John A. Works, Jr. LC 76-23138. 1976. 17.50x (ISBN 0-231-03976-X). Columbia U Pr.

Pilgrim's Notebook: Guide to Western Wildlife. Buddy Mays. LC 77-22043. (Illus., Orig.). 1977. pap. 5.95 (ISBN 0-87701-103-6). Chronicle Bks.

Pilgrims of Plymouth. Barbara L. Beck. LC 79-187970. (First Bks). (Illus.). 96p. (gr. 4-6). 1972. PLB 4.47 o.p. (ISBN 0-531-00776-6). Watts.

Pilgrims of the Pacific. F. Edward Butterworth. LC 73-87643. 1974. 5.50 o.p. (ISBN 0-8309-0106-X). Herald Hse.

Pilgrims of the Stars. Dilip K. Roy & Indira Devi. LC 72-93632. 324p. 1973. 7.95 o.s.i. (ISBN 0-02-605660-7). Macmillan.

Pilgrim's Progress. John Bunyan. 1957. 10.50x (ISBN 0-460-00204-X, Evman); pap. 2.95 (ISBN 0-460-01204-5, Evman). Dutton.

Pilgrim's Progress. abr. ed. John Bunyan. (Illus.). (gr. 7-9). 1939. pap. 2.95 o.p. (ISBN 0-397-31705-0). Lippincott.

Pilgrim's Progress. John Bunyan. pap. 2.50 (ISBN 0-8024-0012-4). Moody.

Pilgrim's Progress. John Bunyan. 256p. 1973. pap. 2.25 (ISBN 0-310-22142-0). Zondervan.

Pilgrim's Progress. John Bunyan. 1979. Repr. 16.95 (ISBN 0-85151-259-3). Banner of Truth.

Pilgrim's Progress. John Bunyan. (Giant Summit Bks). pap. 6.95 (ISBN 0-8010-0732-1). Baker Bk.

Pilgrim's Progress. John Bunyan. 288p. 1981. pap. 2.95 (ISBN 0-88368-096-3). Whitaker Hse.

Pilgrims Progress. John Bunyan. 1976. lib. bdg. 15.95x (ISBN 0-89968-156-5). Lightyear.

Pilgrim's Progress. Ralph Vaughan Williams. 36p. (Libretto only). 1961. 2.25 (ISBN 0-19-339227-5). Oxford U Pr.

Pilgrim's Progress: Critical & Historical Views. Ed. by Vincent Newey. (English Texts & Studies). 302p. 1980. 30.00x (ISBN 0-389-20016-6). B&N.

Pilgrim's Progress: From This World to That Which Is to Come. 2nd ed. John Bunyan. Ed. by James B. Wharey & Roger Sharrock. (Oxford English Texts Ser). 1960. 45.00x (ISBN 0-19-811802-3). Oxford U Pr.

Pilgrim's Progress from This World, to That Which Is to Come. 2nd ed. John Bunyan. 1974. 14.95x o.p. (ISBN 0-8277-2157-9); pap. text ed. 6.50x o.p. (ISBN 0-8277-3744-0). British Bk Ctr.

Pilgrim's Progress: From This World to That Which Is to Come. John Bunyan. Ed. by James B. Wharey. (World's Classics Ser.: No. 12). 1902. 5.95 o.p. (ISBN 0-19-250012-0). Oxford U Pr.

Pilgrim's Regress: Cartoons from the CRITIC. Ed. by Joel Wells. (Illus.). 1979. 10.95 (ISBN 0-88347-093-4). Thomas More.

Pilgrims Through Space & Time: Trends & Patterns in Scientific & Utopian Fiction. James O. Bailey. LC 76-38126. 341p. 1972. lib. bdg. 25.75x (ISBN 0-8371-6323-4, BAPS); pap. 4.95 (ISBN 0-8371-7351-5). Greenwood.

Piling: Model Procedures & Specifications. Institute of Civil Engineers. 168p. 1980. pap. 40.00x (ISBN 0-7277-0036-7, Pub. by Telford England). State Mutual Bk.

Pill. John Gillebaud. (Illus.). 196p. 1980. 16.95 (ISBN 0-19-217675-7); pap. 6.95 (ISBN 0-19-286002-X). Oxford U Pr.

Pillar of Iron. Taylor Caldwell. 768p. 1978. pap. 2.75 (ISBN 0-449-23952-7, Crest). Fawcett.

Pillars of Marriage. H. Norman Wright. LC 78-68849. 1979. pap. 4.95 (ISBN 0-8307-0698-4, 5412501); leader's guide 9.95 (ISBN 0-8307-0699-2, 5202418). Regal.

Pillars of Society. Henrik Ibsen. 1979. 7.95x (ISBN 0-8464-0096-0). Beekman Pubs.

Pillow Book. Charles Blackburn. LC 77-93302. (Illus.). 1979. 12.95 (ISBN 0-8149-0799-7); pap. 7.95 (ISBN 0-87480-0801-2). Vanguard.

Pillow Book. Nik Douglas & Penny Slinger. (Illus.). 1981. 24.95 (ISBN 0-686-69423-6, Destiny Bks). Inner Tradit.

Pillow Book of Carol Tinker. Carol Tinker. Ed. by Jeffrey Miller. LC 79-57557. 100p. 1980. signed ltd. 20.00 (ISBN 0-932274-09-9); pap. 5.00 (ISBN 0-932274-08-0). Cadmus Eds.

Pillow Face & Other Stories. Robert G. Oana. (Illus.). (ps-7). 1978. pap. 2.95 (ISBN 0-8100-0067-9, 17-1619). Northwest Pub.

Pillow Ideas. Ed. by Janet DuBane & Alexandra Kuman. (Illus.). 64p. (Orig.). 1980. pap. 1.75 (ISBN 0-918178-19-3). Simplicity.

Pillows: How to Make. Sunset Editors. LC 80-80859. (Illus.). 80p. 1980. pap. 3.95 (ISBN 0-376-01431-8, Sunset Bks). Sunset-Lane.

Pills & the Public Purse. Milton Silverman et al. 300p. 1981. 14.95 (ISBN 0-520-04381-2). U of Cal Pr.

Pills, Petticoats, & Plows: The Southern Country Store. Thomas D. Clark. (Illus.). 1964. 9.95 (ISBN 0-8061-0593-3); pap. 5.95 (ISBN 0-8061-1093-7). U of Okla Pr.

Pills, Profits, & Politics. Milton Silverman & Philip R. Lee. 1974. 15.95 (ISBN 0-520-02616-0); pap. 4.95 (ISBN 0-520-03050-8). U of Cal Pr.

Pilot Error: A Professional Study of Contributory Factors. Ed. by Ronald Hurst. (Illus.). Date not set. 14.95 o.p. (ISBN 0-258-97072-3, ScribT). Scribner. Postponed.

Pilot Flight Log Book - Aero PL-6. padded lea.-like bdg. 6.00 o.p. (ISBN 0-8168-7176-0). Aero.

Pilot for Spaceship Earth: R. Buckminster Fuller, Architect, Inventor & Poet. Athena V. Lord. LC 77-12629. (Illus.). (gr. 5 up). 1978. 8.95 (ISBN 0-02-761420-4, 76142). Macmillan.

Pilot Instruction Manual. Federal Aviation Agency. 7.95 (ISBN 0-385-01046-X). Doubleday.

Pilot Logbook. Aviation Maintenance Publishers. 72p. 1979. text ed. 3.95 (ISBN 0-89100-112-3, E*A-P*L*O-2). Aviation Maintenance.

Pilot Plants, Models, & Scale-up Methods in Chemical Engineering. Robert E. Johnstone & Meredith W. Thring. (Chemical Engineering Ser.). (Illus.). 1957. 39.50 o.p. (ISBN 0-07-032693-2, P&RB). McGraw.

Pilot Reference Manual. Lawrence Turner. Date not set. pap. 10.00x cancelled (ISBN 0-685-85020-X). Scientific Pr.

Pilot Series in Literature. National Union of Christian Schools. pap. 5.00 ea. Bk. 1, Gr. 7b (ISBN 0-8028-1720-3). Bk. 2, Gr. 8 (ISBN 0-8028-1721-1). Bk. 3, Gr. 9 (ISBN 0-8028-1722-X). Eerdmans.

Piloting, Seamanship & Small Boat Handling. 54th ed. Charles F. Chapman & E. S. Maloney. (Illus.). 13.95 (ISBN 0-910990-46-8); Presentation ed. 19.95 (ISBN 0-910990-47-6). Hearst Bks.

Pilots & Aircraft Owners Legal Guide. 3rd ed. Jay C. White. 1979. pap. 9.95 (ISBN 0-911721-57-6, Pub. by Taxlogs Unlimited); pap. 5.95 (ISBN 0-686-65933-3). Taxlogs.

Pilots & Management. A. N. Blain. 1972. 21.00x o.p. (ISBN 0-8464-0720-5). Beekman Pubs.

Pilot's Bahamas Aviation Guide 1980. Dale R. Cady. (Illus.). 442p. 1979. ring bdg. 16.95 (ISBN 0-911721-68-1). Pilot Pubns.

Pilot's Handbook of Aeronautical Knowledge: Ac 61-23b. Federal Aviation Administration. pap. 11.00 (ISBN 0-685-46359-1, Pub. by Cooper). Aviation.

Pilot's Handbook of Aeronautical Knowledge. 2nd ed. Federal Aviation Administration. (Pilot Training Ser.). (Illus.). 207p. 1971. pap. 7.50 (ISBN 0-89100-100-X, E*A-A*C61-23A). Aviation Maintenance.

Pilot's Manual for the Grumman F6F Hellcat. Ed. by Michael S. Rice. (Illus.). 60p. 1975. pap. 4.95 (ISBN 0-87994-033-6, Pub. by AvPubns). Aviation.

Pilot's Radio Communications Manual. B. Sherman. 1977. pap. 6.95 (ISBN 0-911721-26-6, Pub. by Mease Assocs). Aviation.

Pilot's Ready Reference. rev ed. Caroline T. Harnsberger. LC 62-20288. (Illus.). 1980. pap. 4.50 (ISBN 0-8168-7402-6). Aero.

Pilot's Sketchbook. Joseph Tracy. LC 80-66116. 1981. pap. 8.95 (ISBN 0-8168-7408-5). Aero.

Pilot's Voice. Isabel Byrum. (Illus.). 146p. pap. 1.50. Faith Pub Hse.

Pilots Weight & Balance Handbook: FAA AC 91-23A. Federal Aviation Administration. (Illus.). 1977. pap. 3.25 (ISBN 0-685-53322-0, Pub. by Cooper). Aviation.

Piltdown Forgery. J. S. Weiner. (Illus.). 240p. 1981. pap. 4.00 (ISBN 0-486-24075-4). Dover.

Pima Bajo (Nevome) of Central Sonora, Mexico: Vocabulario en la Lengua Nevome. Ed. by Campbell W. Pennington. 1979. 16.00x (ISBN 0-87480-125-7). U of Utah Pr.

Pima Bajo of Central Sonora, Mexico: Vol. 1, The Material Culture. Campbell W. Pennington. (Illus.). 372p. 1981. 25.00 (ISBN 0-87480-126-5). U of Utah Pr.

Pima-Maricopa Indians, 2 vols. Incl. Aboriginal Land Use & Occupancy of the Pima-Maricopa Indians. Robert Hackenberg; Findings of Fact, & Opinion. Indian Claims Commission. (American Indian Ethnohistory Ser: Indians of the Southwest). (Illus.). Set. lib. bdg. 84.00 (ISBN 0-8240-0730-1); lib. bdg. 42.00 ea. Garland Pub.

Piman Shamanism & Staying Sickness: Ka: cim Mumkidag. Donald M. Bahr et al. LC 72-92103. 400p. 1974. pap. 9.95x (ISBN 0-8165-0303-6). U of Ariz Pr.

Pin. Andrew Neiderman. 1981. pap. 2.50 (ISBN 0-671-41501-8). PB.

Pin Money. Jana Harris. 1977. 5.00 o.p. (ISBN 0-686-24337-4). Jungle Garden.

Pin Pictures with Wire & Thread. Marie-Claude Riviere. Tr. by E. W. Egan from Fr. LC 75-14521. (Little Craft Book Ser.). (Illus.). 48p. 1975. 5.95 (ISBN 0-8069-5340-3); PLB 6.69 (ISBN 0-8069-5341-1). Sterling.

Pin Prick Press Annual Index of Serial & Chapbook Publications, 1980. Ed. by Roberta Mendel. (Orig.). 1981. pap. 3.00 (ISBN 0-936424-07-9, 007). Pin Prick.

Pin up. Jacques Sternberg & Pierre Chapelot. LC 74-83498. (Illus.). 104p. 1975. pap. 8.95 o.p. (ISBN 0-312-61215-X). St Martin.

Pinball. Roger C. Sharpe. LC 77-6283. 1977. 37.50 o.p. (ISBN 0-525-17975-5); pap. 8.95 o.p. (ISBN 0-525-47481-1). Dutton.

Pincher Martin. William Golding. LC 57-10059. Orig. Title: Two Deaths of Christopher Martin. 1968. pap. 2.95 (ISBN 0-15-671833-2, HPL32, HPL). HarBraceJ.

Pinckney Benton Stewart Pinchback: A Biography. James Haskins. (Illus.). 304p. 1973. 12.95 (ISBN 0-02-548890-2). Macmillan.

Pincushions. Averil Colby. 1975. 24.00 (ISBN 0-7134-3030-3, Pub. by Batsford England). David & Charles.

Pindar. Gilbert Norwood. (Sather Classical Lectures: Vol. 19). 1974. 20.00x (ISBN 0-520-01952-0). U of Cal Pr.

Pindar's Odes. Ed. by Roy A. Swanson. LC 72-90908. (Library of Liberal Arts Ser.). (Illus.). 1974. 10.35 o.p. (ISBN 0-672-51543-1, LLA178); pap. text ed. 7.50 (ISBN 0-672-61245-3). Bobbs.

Pindar's Olympian I: A Commentary. Douglas E. Gerber. (Phoenix Supplementary Volumes Ser.). 264p. 1981. 47.50 (ISBN 0-8020-5507-9). U of Toronto Pr.

Pine. Jeffrey Weiss. LC 80-7832. (Illus.). 128p. (Orig.). 1980. pap. 8.95 (ISBN 0-06-090814-9, CN 814, CN). Har-Row.

Pine Barrens. John McPhee. 1976. pap. 1.95 o.p. (ISBN 0-345-25788-X). Ballantine.

Pine Barrens Legends, Lore & Lies. William McMahon. LC 80-23518. (Illus.). 1980. 10.95 (ISBN 0-912608-12-9). Mid Atlantic.

Pine Furniture of Early New England. Russell H. Kettell. 1929. 15.00 (ISBN 0-486-20145-7). Dover.

Pineal, Vol. 1. Richard Relkin. 1976. 21.60 (ISBN 0-904406-26-1). Eden Med Res.

Pineal, Vol. 2. Russel Reiter. 1977. 21.60 (ISBN 0-88831-006-4). Eden Med Res.

Pineal, Vol. 3. Russel J. Reiter. Ed. by D. F. Horrobin. 1979. 28.80 (ISBN 0-88831-039-0). Eden Med Res.

Pineal Chemistry: In Cellular & Physiological Mechanisms. W. B. Quay. (American Lectures in Living Chemistry). (Illus.). 448p. 1974. 33.50 (ISBN 0-398-02802-8). C C Thomas.

Pineal Gland: Volume 1, Anatomy & Biochemistry. Ed. by Russel J. Reiter. 288p. 1981. 72.95 (ISBN 0-8493-5714-4). CRC Pr.

Pineal Organ. L. E. Vollrath. (Hanbuch der Mikroskopischen Anatomie: Vol. VI-7). (Illus.). 600p. 1981. 259.60 (ISBN 0-387-10313-9). Springer-Verlag.

Pineal Tumors. Henry H. Schmidek. LC 77-78560. 152p. 1977. 36.25 (ISBN 0-89352-007-1). Masson Pub.

Pineapple Child & Other Tales from Ashanti. Peggy Appiah. (Illus.). 176p. (gr. 2-7). 1981. 7.95 (ISBN 0-233-95875-4). Andre Deutsch.

Pineapple Hold 'Em. Brian Smith. (Gambler's Book Shelf). 1979. pap. 2.95 (ISBN 0-89650-827-7). Gamblers.

Piney Woods. Nell Cotten. LC 62-11221. (gr. 4-8). 3.50 (ISBN 0-8149-0292-8). Vanguard.

Pink Camellia. Louise Bergstrom. (YA) 1968. 5.95 (ISBN 0-685-07453-6, Avalon). Bouregy.

Pink Motel. Carol R. Brink. LC 59-12838. 224p. (gr. 4-6). 1972. pap. 1.95 (ISBN 0-02-041940-6, Collier). Macmillan.

Pink Panther Book. Linda Presto. (Golden Book for Early Childhood Ser.). (Illus.). (gr. k-3). 1979. PLB 5.38 (ISBN 0-307-68944-1, Golden Pr). Western Pub.

Pink Phaeton. Juliana Davison. (Orig.). 1980. pap. 1.75 (ISBN 0-446-94270-7). Warner Bks.

Pinkey. Florence A. Hasenav. (Illus.). 1975. 6.00 (ISBN 0-913042-02-1). Holland Hse Pr.

Pinky in Persia. Kay Boyle. LC 68-18472. (Illus.). (gr. 1-3). 1968. 3.50g o.s.i. (ISBN 0-02-711820-7, CCPr). Macmillan.

Pinky, the Cat Who Liked to Sleep. Kay Boyle. (Illus.). (gr. 1-3). 1968. 4.50g o.s.i. (ISBN 0-02-711770-7, CCPr). Macmillan.

Pinnacle Jake. A. B Snyder & Nellie S. Yost. LC 51-14574. (Illus.). 1962. pap. 2.95 (ISBN 0-8032-5189-0, BB 132, Bison). U of Nebr Pr.

Pinnacle: The Contemporary American Presidency. John F. Murphy. LC 74-3164. 1974. pap. text ed. 2.95 o.p. (ISBN 0-397-47312-5). Lippincott.

Pinnacled Tower: Selected Poems of Thomas Hardy. Thomas Hardy. Ed. by Helen Plotz. (Illus.). 160p. (gr. 7 up). 1975. 8.95 (ISBN 0-02-742630-0). Macmillan.

Pinnell & Talifson: Last of the Great Brown Bear Men. Marvin H. Clark, Jr. (Illus.). 224p. 1980. 15.00x (ISBN 0-937708-00-3). Great Northwest.

Pinocchio. Carlo Collodi. (Childrens Illustrated Classics Ser). (Illus.). 1975. Repr. of 1972 ed. 5.50x o.p. (ISBN 0-460-06923-3, Pub. by J. M. Dent England). Biblio Dist.

Pinocchio. Margaret Hillert. (Just Beginning-to-Read Ser.). (Illus.). 32p. (gr. 1-6). 1981. PLB 4.39 (ISBN 0-695-41551-4); pap. 1.50 (ISBN 0-695-31551-X). Follett.

Pinocchio. Littledale. (ps-3). pap. 1.95 (ISBN 0-590-12070-0, Schol Pap). Schol Bk Serv.

Pinocchio Was Nosy: Grandson of Puns, Gags, Quips & Riddles. Roy Doty. LC 76-57873. (gr. 4-7). 1977. PLB 4.95 (ISBN 0-385-12920-3). Doubleday.

Pinon Mesa. Lee Floren. 1978. pap. 1.50 (ISBN 0-505-51266-1). Tower Bks.

Pinon Pine: A Natural & Cultural History. Ronald M. Lanner. (Illus.). 160p. 1981. price not set (ISBN 0-87417-065-6). U of Nev Pr.

Pint of Murder. Alisa Craig. LC 80-22948. 318p. 1980. Repr. of 1980 ed. large print ed. 9.95 (ISBN 0-89621-255-6). Thorndike Pr.

Pinto. LC 80-80771. (Saturday Mechanic Car Care Guides). (Illus.). 176p. 12.95 (ISBN 0-87851-934-3); pap. 6.95 (ISBN 0-87851-926-2). Hearst Bks.

Pinto & Bobcat Nineteen Eighty-One to Eighty. LC 80-70340. (Illus.). 280p. 1980. pap. 8.95. Chilton.

Pinto Service Repair Handbook: All Models 1971-1979. Alan Ahlstrand. Ed. by Eric Jorgensen. (Illus.). 1978. pap. 10.95 (ISBN 0-89287-211-X, A171). Clymer Pubns.

Pinto Tune-up & Repair. Ed. by Al Hall. LC 79-64837. (Tune-up & Repair Ser.). (Illus.). 198p. (Orig.). 1979. pap. 4.95 (ISBN 0-8227-5047-3). Petersen Pub.

Pioneer: A History of the Johns Hopkins University 1874-1889. Hugh Hawkins. 368p. 1960. 22.50x o.p. (ISBN 0-8014-0181-X). Cornell U Pr.

Pioneer America. John R. Alden. (History of Human Society Ser.). (Illus.). 1966. 7.95 o.p. (ISBN 0-394-44089-7). Knopf.

Pioneer Arts & Crafts. 2nd ed. Edwin C. Guillet. LC 72-415879. (Photos). 1968. pap. 2.95 (ISBN 0-8020-6081-1). U of Toronto Pr.

Pioneer Cattleman in Montana: The Story of the Circle C Ranch. Walt Coburn. LC 68-15691. (Illus.). 1972. 14.95 o.p. (ISBN 0-8061-0815-0). U of Okla Pr.

Pioneer Conservationists of Eastern America. Peter Wild. 1981. 15.95 (ISBN 0-87842-126-2); pap. 7.95 (ISBN 0-87842-124-6). Mountain Pr.

Pioneer Evangelists of the Church of God in the Pacific Northwest. John L. Green. 164p. pap. 2.00. Faith Pub Hse.

Pioneer Family in Colonial Pennsylvania. Roger C. Heimer. 144p. 1979. 6.95 (ISBN 0-8059-2588-0). Dorrance.

Pioneer Merchant in Mid-America. Lewis E. Atherton. LC 75-77700. (American Scene Ser). 1969. Repr. of 1939 ed. 19.50 (ISBN 0-306-71338-1). Da Capo.

Pioneer Miner & the Pack Mule Express. Ernest A. Wiltsee. LC 76-4134. (Illus.). 160p. 1976. Repr. 35.00x (ISBN 0-88000-084-8). Quarterman.

Pioneer of the Third Level: A History of Air Midwest. I. E. Quastler. (Illus.). 174p. 1980. pap. 7.50 (ISBN 0-9602554-1-9). Commuter Airlines.

Pioneer Settlement in Northeast Argentina. Robert C. Eidt. LC 71-138058. 1971. 22.50x (ISBN 0-299-05920-0). U of Wis Pr.

Pioneer Settlements in Upper Canada. Edwin C. Guillet. (Illus.). 1970. pap. 4.50 (ISBN 0-8020-6110-9). U of Toronto Pr.

Pioneer Women in Texas. Annie D. Pickrell. 1970. 15.00 (ISBN 0-8363-0126-9). Jenkins.

Pioneering. Boy Scouts Of America. LC 19-600. (Illus.). 48p. (gr. 6-12). 1974. pap. 0.70x o.p. (ISBN 0-8395-3382-9, 3382). BSA.

Pioneering in Education Requires Pioneering in Community. Community Service Editors. 1973. pap. 1.50 (ISBN 0-910420-15-7). Comm Serv.

Pioneering in Montana: The Making of a State 1864-1887. Granville Stuart. Ed. by Paul C. Phillips. LC 77-7651. Orig. Title: Forty Years on the Frontier. (Illus.). 1977. 12.50x (ISBN 0-8032-0933-9); pap. 5.25 (ISBN 0-8032-5870-4, BB 648, Bison). U of Nebr Pr.

Pioneering in the Faith. Annette M. Ludeman. 6.95 (ISBN 0-685-48819-5). Nortex Pr.

Pioneers. James F. Cooper. 1976. lib. bdg. 15.95x (ISBN 0-89968-157-3). Lighthouse Pr NY.

Pioneers. Huston Horn. (Old West Ser.). (Illus.). 1974. 12.95 (ISBN 0-8094-1475-9). Time-Life.

Pioneers. Huston Horn. LC 73-94242. (Old West). (Illus.). (gr. 5 up). 1974. kivar 12.96 (ISBN 0-8094-1477-5, Pub. by Time-Life). Silver.

Pioneers & Patroits: The Lives of Six Negroes of the Revolutionary Era. Lavinia G. Dobler & Edgar A. Toppin. LC 65-17241. (gr. 6-12). pap. 2.50 o.p. (ISBN 0-385-04191-8, Z6, Zenith). Doubleday.

Pioneers & Preachers: Stories of the Old Frontier. Robert W. Mondy. (Illus.). 1980. 21.95 (ISBN 0-88229-619-1); pap. 11.95 (ISBN 0-88229-722-8). Nelson-Hall.

Pioneers in Marketing. John S. Wright & Parks B. Dimsdale. LC 73-620235. 162p. 1974. pap. 8.95 (ISBN 0-88406-016-0). Ga St U Busn Pub.

Pioneers in Print. Alice Fleming. (Adventures in Courage Ser). (Illus.). (gr. 4-7). 1971. 5.95 o.p. (ISBN 0-8092-8647-5); PLB avail o.p. (ISBN 0-685-02311-7). Contemp Bks.

Pioneers in the Tropics. Philip Staniford. (London School of Economics Monographs on Social Anthropology Ser: No. 45). (Illus.). 210p. 1973. text ed. 23.50x (ISBN 0-391-00267-8, Athlone Pr). Humanities.

Pioneers of Alcohol Fuels. Ken Bossong et al. 125p. (Orig.). 1981. 7.50 (ISBN 0-89988-067-3). Citizens Energy.

Pioneers of Australian Education, Vol. 3. Ed. by C. Turney. (Pioneers of Australian Education Ser). (Illus.). 1981. write for info. (ISBN 0-686-16294-3, Pub. by Sydney U Pr). Intl Schol Bk Serv.

Pioneers of Modern Design. Nikolaus Pevsner. 1961. pap. 4.95 (ISBN 0-14-020497-0, Pelican). Penguin.

Pioneers of Modern Economics in Britain. Ed. by D. P. O'Brien & John R. Presley. LC 79-55496. (Illus.). 392p. 1981. text ed. 26.50x (ISBN 0-06-495230-4). B&N.

Pioneers of Modern Education in the Seventeenth Century. John W. Adamson. LC 79-165366. 1971. text ed. 9.75 (ISBN 0-8077-1006-7); pap. text ed. 5.25x (ISBN 0-8077-1008-3). Tchrs Coll.

Pioneers of New France in New England. James P. Baxter. 450p. 1980. Repr. of 1894 ed. 20.00 (ISBN 0-917890-20-5). Heritage Bk.

Pioneers of Science: Nobel Prize Winners in Physics. Robert L. Weber. Ed. by J. M. Lenihan. 285p. 1980. 23.00 (ISBN 0-9960020-1-4, Pub. by a Hilger England). Heyden.

Pioneers of the French Revolution. Marius Roustan. LC 68-9659. 1970. Repr. of 1926 ed. 15.75 (ISBN 0-86527-150-X). Fertig.

Pioneers, Peddlers, & Tsadikim: The Story of the Jews in Colorado. 2nd ed. Ida L. Uchill. LC 57-57817. 327p. 1979. pap. 10.00 (ISBN 0-9604468-0-X). Uchill.

Pious Brief Narrative in Medieval Castilian & Galician Verse: From Berceo to Alfonso X. John E. Keller. LC 77-84064. (Studies in Romance Languages: No. 21). 152p. 1979. 16.00x (ISBN 0-8131-1381-4). U Pr of Ky.

Pious Prentice, or, the Prentices Piety. Abraham Jackson. LC 74-28866. (English Experience Ser.: No. 746). 1975. Repr. of 1640 ed. 7.00 (ISBN 90-221-0746-9). Walter J Johnson.

Pip Stories. Leon Steinmetz. (Illus.). 48p. (gr. k-2). 1980. 8.95 (ISBN 0-316-78738-8). Little.

Pipe & Tube Fabrication. 2nd ed. Ed. by D. Anderson et al. (Engineering Craftsmen: No. D3). (Illus.). 1978. spiral bdg. 16.50x (ISBN 0-85083-415-5). Intl Ideas.

Pipe Dream of Peace: The Story of the Collapse of Disarmament. John W. Wheeler-Bennett. LC 76-80601. 1971. Repr. 19.00 (ISBN 0-86527-151-8). Fertig.

Pipe Protection: A Review of Current Practice in the U. K. V. Hassan et al. (Illus.). 183p. 1979. pap. 104.00 lib. ed. (ISBN 0-900983-92-2, Dist. by Air Sciencec Co.). BHRA Fluid.

Pipe Welding Procedures. Hoobasar Rampaul. (Illus.). 208p. 1973. 18.50 (ISBN 0-8311-1100-3). Indus Pr.

Pipe Welding Techniques. 2nd ed. I. H. Griffin et al. LC 76-51121. 1978. pap. text ed. 5.80 (ISBN 0-8273-1256-3). Delmar.

Pipefitters Handbook. 3rd ed. Forrest R. Lindsey. (Illus.). 1967. text ed. 15.00 (ISBN 0-8311-3019-9). Indus Pr.

Pipeline. Milt Machlin. (Orig.). 1976. pap. 2.50 (ISBN 0-515-05408-9). Jove Pubns.

Pipeline Across Alaska. Charles Coombs. LC 77-28986. (Illus.). (gr. 5-9). 1978. 6.50 (ISBN 0-688-22139-4); PLB 6.24 (ISBN 0-688-32139-9). Morrow.

Pipeline & Energy Plant Piping--Design & Construction: Proceedings of the International Conference on Pipeline & Energy Plant Piping, Calgary, Alberta, Nov. 10-13, 1980. Ed. by Welding Institute of Canada, Toronto, Ontario. (Illus.). 360p. 1980. 40.00 (ISBN 0-08-025368-7). Pergamon.

Pipeline Design for Hydrocarbon Gases & Liquids. Compiled by American Society of Civil Engineers. 88p. 1975. pap. text ed. 6.00 (ISBN 0-87262-118-9). Am Soc Civil Eng.

Pipeline Design for Water & Wastewater. Compiled by American Society of Civil Engineers. 136p. 1975. pap. text ed. 7.50 (ISBN 0-87262-106-5). Am Soc Civil Eng.

Pipeline Glossary & Directory. C. D. Shann. (Orig.). 1978. pap. 32.00 (ISBN 0-914082-05-1). Syentek Bks.

Pipeline Rates on Crude Petroleum Oil. Ed. by Mary A. Crespe. 800p. Date not set. 95.00. CSG Pr.

Pipeline Rates on Gasoline & Petroleum Products. Ed. by Thresa Whipp. 700p. pap. 95.00 (ISBN 0-686-28100-4). CSG Pr.

Pipelines in Adverse Environments. Compiled by American Society of Civil Engineers. 564p. 1979. pap. text ed. 39.50 (ISBN 0-87262-176-6). Am Soc Civil Eng.

Pipelines in the Oceans. Compiled by American Society of Civil Engineers. 120p. 1974. pap. text ed. 6.00 (ISBN 0-87262-062-X). Am Soc Civil Eng.

Pipes & Plumbing Systems. Herbert S. Zim & James R. Skelly. LC 73-14589. (Illus.). 64p. (gr. 3-7). 1974. 6.75 (ISBN 0-688-20101-6); PLB 6.48 (ISBN 0-688-30101-0); pap. 1.25 (ISBN 0-688-25101-3). Morrow.

Pipesmoker. John P. Beaumier & Lewis Camp. LC 79-1770. (Illus.). 144p. 1980. 9.95 (ISBN 0-06-250376-6, HarpR). Har-Row.

Piping Design for Process Plants. H. F. Rase & M. H. Barrow. LC 63-17483. 1963. 36.95 (ISBN 0-471-70920-4, Pub. by Wiley-Interscience). Wiley.

Pippa Mouse. Betty Boeghold. 64p. 1976. pap. 1.25 (ISBN 0-440-47148-6, YB). Dell.

Pippi Goes on Board. Astrid Lindgren. (Illus.). (gr. 4-6). 1957. PLB 6.95 (ISBN 0-670-55677-7). Viking Pr.

Pippin. Roger O. Hirson & Stephen Schwartz. 1977. pap. 2.25 (ISBN 0-380-01635-4, 45740, Bard). Avon.

Piracy and the Decline of Venice, 1580-1615. Alberto Tenenti. Tr. by Janet Pullan & Brian Pullan. (Illus.). 1967. 20.00x (ISBN 0-520-01263-1). U of Cal Pr.

Pirandello: Fantasmes et logique du double. new ed. J. M. Gardair. (Collection themes et textes). 160p. (Orig., Fr.). 1972. pap. 6.75 (ISBN 2-03-035003-6, 2688). Larousse.

Piranesi. Jonathan Scott. LC 74-81701. (Illus.). 400p. 1975. 29.98 (ISBN 0-312-61355-5). St Martin.

Piranhas. George Myers. pap. 4.95 (ISBN 0-87666-133-9, M539). TFH Pubns.

Pirate Coast. Charles Belgrave. (Arab Background Ser.). 13.00x (ISBN 0-685-72055-1). Intl Bk Ctr.

Pirate Island Adventure. Peggy Parish. LC 75-12946. (Illus.). 176p. (gr. 2-5). 1975. 6.95 o.s.i. (ISBN 0-02-769900-5, 76990). Macmillan.

Pirate Island Adventure. Peggy Parish. (gr. k-6). 1981. pap. 1.50 (ISBN 0-440-47394-2, YB). Dell.

Pirate Picture. Rayner Thrower. (Illus.). 171p. 1980. 12.50x (ISBN 0-8476-6267-5). Rowman.

Pirate Royal. John Beatty & Patricia Beatty. (gr. 5-8). 1969. 4.95g o.s.i. (ISBN 0-02-708600-3). Macmillan.

Pirate Treasure. Angela Marsh. LC 78-26275. (Raintree Great Adventures). (Illus.). (gr. 3-6). 1979. PLB 8.95 (ISBN 0-8393-0155-3). Raintree Child.

Pirates. new ed. Douglas Botting. Ed. by Time-Life Books. (Seafarers Ser.). (Illus.). 1978. 13.95 (ISBN 0-8094-2650-1). Time-Life.

Pirates. Douglas Botting. LC 77-91928. (Seafarers Ser.). (Illus.). 1978. lib. bdg. 11.97 (ISBN 0-686-50988-9). Silver.

Pirate's Island. John R. Townsend. LC 68-14619. (Illus.). (gr. 4-7). 1968. PLB 5.53 o.p. (ISBN 0-397-31425-6). Lippincott.

Pirates of Colonial North Carolina. Hugh F. Rankin. (Illus.). 1979. pap. 1.00 (ISBN 0-86526-1G0-8). NC Archives.

Pirates of Colonial Virginia. Lloyd H. Williams. LC 73-78670. (Illus.). 1972. Repr. of 1937 ed. 15.00 (ISBN 0-8103-3817-3). Gale.

Pirates of the Spanish Main. Hamilton Cochran & Robert I. Nesmith. LC 61-10676. (American Heritage Junior Library). (Illus.). 153p. (gr. 5 up). 1961. 9.95 (ISBN 0-8281-0355-0, J005-0); PLB 6.89 o.p. (ISBN 0-06-021346-9). Am Heritage.

Pirate's Promise. Clyde R. Bulla. LC 58-8209. (Illus.). (gr. 2-5). 1958. PLB 7.89 (ISBN 0-690-62656-8, TYC-J). T Y Crowell.

Pirc for the Tournament Player. John Nunn. (Algebraic Chess Openings Ser.). (Illus.). 128p. 1980. 17.95 (ISBN 0-7134-3588-7, Pub. by Batsford England); pap. 10.50 (ISBN 0-7134-3589-5). David & Charles.

Piro (Arawakan) Language. Esther Matteson. (U. C. Publ. in Linguistics: Vol. 42). 1965. pap. 11.00x (ISBN 0-520-09237-6). U of Cal Pr.

Pisanello. Giovanni Paccagnini. Tr. by Jane Carroll. LC 72-86573. (Illus.). 298p. (It.). 1973. 45.00x o.p. (ISBN 0-7148-1556-X, Pub. by Phaidon Pr England). Hennessey.

Pisces. Paula Harris. (Sun Signs Ser.). (Illus.). (gr. 4-12). 1978. PLB 5.95 (ISBN 0-87191-652-5); pap. 2.95 (ISBN 0-89812-082-9). Creative Ed.

Pisces. Julia Parker. (Pocket Guide to Astrology Ser.). (Orig.). 1980. pap. write for info. (ISBN 0-671-25558-4, Fireside). S&S.

Piskies, Spriggans, & Other Magical Beings: Tales from the Droll-Teller. Shirley Climo. LC 79-7839. (Illus.). 128p. (gr. 4-7). 1981. 8.95 (ISBN 0-690-04063-6, TYC-J); PLB 8.79 (ISBN 0-690-04064-4). T Y Crowell.

Pissarro: His Life & Work. Ralph E. Shikes & Paula Harper. 1980. 30.00 (ISBN 0-8180-0128-3). Horizon.

Pissarro in Venezuela. Intro. by Stanton L. Catlin. LC 68-21908. (Illus.). 1968. pap. 2.00 o.p. (ISBN 0-913456-05-5). Interbk Inc.

Pistachio Prescription. Paula Danziger. LC 77-86330. (gr. 7 up). 1978. 7.95 (ISBN 0-440-06936-X). Delacorte.

Pistol Guide. George C. Nonte. 256p. 1980. pap. 7.95 (ISBN 0-695-81122-3). Follett.

Pistoleros. John Benteen. (Sundance: No. 5). 1979. pap. 1.75 (ISBN 0-8439-0706-1, Leisure Bks). Nordon Pubns.

Pistolsmithing. George C. Nonte, Jr. LC 74-10783. (Illus.). 560p. 1974. 19.95 (ISBN 0-8117-1265-6). Stackpole.

Piston Engine: Meeting the Challenge of the 1980's. Society of Automotive Engineers. 1980. 8.95 (ISBN 0-89883-238-1). Soc Auto Engineers.

Pit. Frank Norris. (Literature Ser). (gr. 10-12). 1970. pap. text ed. 3.67 (ISBN 0-87720-735-6). AMSCO Sch.

Pit. Frank Norris. 1976. lib. bdg. 18.25x (ISBN 0-89968-069-0). Lightyear.

Pit: A Story of Chicago. Frank Norris. LC 70-184738. 432p. 1971. Repr. of 1903 ed. lib. bdg. 12.50x (ISBN 0-8376-0407-9). Bentley.

Pit & the Pendulum. Edgar A. Poe. (Creative's Classics Ser.). (Illus.). 48p. (gr. 4-9). 1980. PLB 6.95 (ISBN 0-87191-771-8). Creative Ed.

Pit-Men, Preachers & Politics. R. Moore. LC 73-88307. 39.50x (ISBN 0-521-20356-2, 1974); pap. 12.95x (ISBN 0-521-29752-4, 1979). Cambridge U Pr.

Pitch Notation & Equal Temperament: A Formal Study. Eric Regener. (U. C. Publ: Occasional Papers: No. 6). pap. 14.50x (ISBN 0-520-09453-0). U of Cal Pr.

Pitchers. Jay H. Smith. LC 76-8485. (Stars of the NL & AL Ser.). (Illus.). (gr. 4-12). 1976. PLB 7.95 (ISBN 0-87191-518-9). Creative Ed.

Pitching. Bob Shaw. (Illus.). 1981. pap. 6.95 (ISBN 0-8092-5913-3). Contemp Bks.

Pitching Championship Horseshoes. rev. ed. Ottie W. Reno. 1975. 8.95 o.p. (ISBN 0-498-01408-8); pap. 4.95 o.p. (ISBN 0-498-01410-X). A S Barnes.

Pitching in: How to Teach Your Children to Work Around the House. Charles M. Spellmann & Rachel Williams. (Illus.). 1981. pap. 4.95 (ISBN 0-915190-31-1). Jalmar Pr.

Pitfalls in Development. H. McKinley Conway. LC 78-62198. 1980. pap. 29.00 (ISBN 0-910436-19-3). Conway Pubns.

Pitfalls of Analysis. Giandomenico Majone & Edward S. Quade. LC 79-41700. (Wiley IIASA International Series on Applied Systems Analysis). 224p. 1980. 34.90 (ISBN 0-471-27746-0, Pub. by Wiley-Interscience). Wiley.

Pithy Sayings from FORMAT Interviews, Vol. II. Ed. by C. L. Morrison. 1980. pap. 2.50 (ISBN 0-932508-07-3). Seven Oaks.

Pitman Accelerated Speed Drill Book. (Program correlates with The New Basic Course). 1967. text ed. 4.24 spiral bdg (ISBN 0-8224-1703-0); tchr's manual 5.76 (ISBN 0-8224-1704-9); tapes avail. Pitman Learning.

Pitman Secretarial Shorthand for Colleges with Student's Transcript. Evelina Thompson et al. LC 77-80300. 1978. pap. 15.00 (ISBN 0-8224-2121-6); instr's. handbk. & supplementary dictation 8.80 (ISBN 0-8224-2123-2). Pitman Learning.

Pitman Shorterhand. G. A. Reid & Evelina Thompson. Ed. by M. Angus. LC 72-88594. 1972. text ed. 7.96 (ISBN 0-8224-1007-9); Drillbook One, spiral bdg. 4.60 (ISBN 0-8224-1735-9); 15 cassettes, tape program one 220.00 (ISBN 0-8224-1026-5). Pitman Learning.

Pitman Shorthand Rules & Vocabularies. (New Era Edition). 1956. pap. 2.20 (ISBN 0-8224-0059-6). Pitman Learning.

Pits Exercises: A Manual-Anthology for Teachers & Students. Ross Talarico. (Poetry in the Schools Programs). 64p. (Orig.). (gr. 10-12). 1981. pap. 3.95 (ISBN 0-933362-05-6). Assoc Creative Writers.

Pittsburgh Steelers. Julian May. (Super Bowl Champions Ser.). (Illus.). (gr. 3-8). 1977. PLB 6.45 (ISBN 0-87191-454-9); pap. 2.95 (ISBN 0-89812-090-X). Creative Ed.

Pittsburgh Steelers. Julian May. (NFL Today Ser.). (gr. 4-8). 1980. PLB 6.45 (ISBN 0-87191-731-9); pap. 2.95 (ISBN 0-89812-234-1). Creative Ed.

Pittsburgh Steelers: A Pictorial History. Pat Livinston. LC 79-91292. 198p. 1980. 14.95 (ISBN 0-918908-11-6). Jordan & Co.

Pittsburgh's Commercial Development: 1800-1850. Catherine L. Reiser. LC 51-9480. 247p. 1951. 6.00 (ISBN 0-911124-36-5). Pa Hist & Mus.

Pituitary Adenoma. Ed. by Kalmon D. Post et al. 530p. 1980. 59.50 (ISBN 0-306-40382-X, Plenum Pr). Plenum Pub.

Pituitary Adenomas. Glenn E. Sheline et al. (Oncologic Multidisciplinary Decisions in Onology Ser.). (Illus.). 248p. 1981. pap. 50.00 (ISBN 0-08-027463-3). Pergamon.

Pituitary & Parapituitary Tumours. John Hankinson & M. Banna. LC 76-24953. (Major Problems in Neurology Ser.: Vol. 6). (Illus.). 1976. text ed. 30.00 (ISBN 0-7216-4495-3). Saunders.

Pituitary Diseases. Kalman Kovacs et al. 256p. 1980. lib. bdg. 69.95 (ISBN 0-8493-5435-8). CRC Pr.

Pituitary Gland. R. L. Holmes & J. N. Ball. LC 73-75856. (Biological Structure & Function Ser.: No. 4). (Illus.). 300p. 1974. 79.00 (ISBN 0-521-20247-7). Cambridge U Pr.

Pity & Tears: The Tragedies of Nicholas Rowe. Landon C. Burns. (Salzburg Studies in English Literature, Poetic Drama & Poetic Theory: No. 8). 256p. 1974. pap. text ed. 25.00x (ISBN 0-391-01333-5). Humanities.

Pivot. John Van Zwienen. 1980. 2.25 (ISBN 0-515-05639-1). Jove Pubns.

Pixie. Matthew Lipman. (Philosophy for Children). 90p. (Orig.). (gr. 3-4). pap. 6.00 (ISBN 0-916834-17-4). Inst Adv Philo.

PKD: A Pictorial Philip K. Dick Bibliography. Compiled by Daniel J. Levack. (Illus.). 144p. 1980. 17.50 (ISBN 0-934438-34-X); pap. 6.95 (ISBN 0-934438-33-1). Underwood-Miller.

PL-One for Business Applications. Leonard E. Edwards. LC 72-97178. (Illus.). 320p. 1973. ref. ed. 15.95 o.p. (ISBN 0-87909-631-4). Reston.

PL-One for Programmers. R. C. Scott & N. E. Sondak. 1970. pap. 11.95 (ISBN 0-201-07081-2). A-W.

PL One for Scientific Programmers. C. T. Fike. 1970. ref. ed. 17.95x (ISBN 0-13-676502-5). P-H.

PL-One Structured Programming. 2nd ed. Joan K. Hughes. LC 78-15665. 1979. text ed. 21.95 (ISBN 0-471-01908-9); tchrs. manual avail. (ISBN 0-471-03051-1). Wiley.

Placable Colonel Corby. Charles Rodda. 1981. 4.95 (ISBN 0-8062-1639-5). Carlton.

Place & People: An Ecology of a New Guinean Community. William C. Clarke. LC 78-126764. (Illus.). 1971. 23.50x (ISBN 0-520-01791-9). U of Cal Pr.

Place & Things for Experimental Schools. LC 72-75056. (Illus.). 134p. 1972. pap. 2.00 o.p. (ISBN 0-89192-059-5). Interbk Inc.

Place Beyond Man. Cary Neeper. 1977. pap. 1.50 o.s.i. (ISBN 0-440-16931-3). Dell.

Place Called Hope: Caring for Children in Distress. Tom O'Neill. (Practice of Social Work Ser.: No. 7). 128p. 1981. 22.50x (ISBN 0-631-12963-4, Pub. by Basil Blackwell England); pap. 8.95x (ISBN 0-631-12654-6). Biblio Dist.

Place Called Ugly. Avi. LC 80-23326. (Illus.). 224p. (YA) (gr. 7-9). 1981. 8.95 (ISBN 0-394-84755-5); PLB 8.99 (ISBN 0-394-94755-X). Pantheon.

Place for God to Live. (Aglow Bible Study: Bk. 11). 64p. 1977. 1.95 (ISBN 0-930756-28-2, 4220-11). Women's Aglow.

Place-Name Changes Since Nineteen Hundred: A World Gazetteer. Compiled by Adrian Room. LC 79-4300. 1979. 11.00 (ISBN 0-8108-1210-X). Scarecrow.

Place-Names in Imprints: An Index to the Latin & Other Forms Used on Title-Pages. Robert A. Peddie. LC 68-30594. 1968. Repr. of 1932 ed. 15.00 (ISBN 0-8103-3239-6). Gale.

Place-Names of Great Britain & Ireland. John Field. (Illus.). 208p. 1980. 15.00x (ISBN 0-389-20154-5). B&N.

Place-Names of Greater London. John Field. LC 79-56447. (Illus.). 168p. 1980. 19.95 (ISBN 0-7134-2538-5, Pub. by Batsford England). David & Charles.

Place Names of the Death Valley Region in California & Nevada. T. S. Palmer. LC 80-51783. (Illus.). 1980. wrappers 5.00 (ISBN 0-930704-04-5). Sagebrush Pr.

Place of Astronomy in the Ancient World: A Joint Symposium of the Royal Society & the British Academy. Ed. by F. R. Hodson. (Illus.). 280p. 1974. 69.00x (ISBN 0-19-725944-8). Oxford U Pr.

Place of Birth. Ed. by Sheila Kitzinger & John A. Davis. (Illus.). 1978. text ed. 29.50x (ISBN 0-19-261125-9); pap. text ed. 15.95x (ISBN 0-19-261238-7). Oxford U Pr.

Place of Bonhoeffer: Problems & Possibilities in His Thought. Ed. by Martin E. Marty. LC 79-8718. 224p. 1981. Repr. of 1962 ed. lib. bdg. 22.50x (ISBN 0-313-20812-3, MAPL). Greenwood.

Place of Commonsense in Educational Thought. Lionel Elvin. (Unwin Educational Books). 1977. text ed. 19.95x (ISBN 0-04-370078-0); pap. text ed. 8.95x (ISBN 0-04-370079-9). Allen Unwin.

Place of Franklin D. Roosevelt in History. Allan Nevins. (Sir George Watson Lectures). (Orig.). 1965. pap. text ed. 1.75x (ISBN 0-7185-1046-1, Leicester). Humanities.

Place of Information in Educational Development. 135p. 1981. pap. 9.25 (ISBN 92-3-101822-1, U1059, UNESCO). Unipub.

Place of Musicology in American Institutions of Higher Learning, 2 vols. in one. Ed. by Manfred Bukofzer et al. Incl. Some Aspects of Musicology. LC 77-4226. (Music Reprint Ser.). 1977. Repr. of 1957 ed. lib. bdg. 19.50 (ISBN 0-306-77407-0). Da Capo.

Place of Ravens. Pamela Hill. 224p. 1981. 9.95 (ISBN 0-312-61373-3). St Martin.

Place of Sodium Valproate in the Treatment of Epilepsy. Ed. by M. J. Parsonage & A. D. Caldwell. (Royal Society of Medicine International Congress & Symposium Ser.: No. 30). 1980. 29.00 (ISBN 0-8089-1293-3). Grune.

Place of Stones. Constance Heaver. 1976. pap. 1.50 o.p. (ISBN 0-451-07046-1, W7046, Sig). NAL.

Place of Stones. Ruth J. Ruck. (Orig.). 1970. pap. 5.95 (ISBN 0-571-09392-2, Pub. by Faber & Faber). Merrimack Bk Serv.

Place of the Circle in Elementary Geometry. William G. McMenemy. LC 66-22004. 1967. 3.00 o.p. (ISBN 0-8022-1023-6). Philos Lib.

Place of Wesley in the Christian Tradition: Essays Delevered at Drew University in Celebration of the Commencement of the Publication of the Oxford Edition of the Works of John Wesley. Ed. by Kenneth E. Rowe. LC 76-27659. 1976. 10.00 (ISBN 0-8108-0981-8). Scarecrow.

Place on the Corner. Elijah Anderson. LC 78-1879. (Studies of Urban Society). 248p. 1981. pap. 5.50 (ISBN 0-226-01954-3). U of Chicago Pr.

Place, Taste, & Tradition: A Study of Australian Art Since Seventeen Eighty-Eight. 2nd ed. Bernard Smith. (Illus.). 304p. 1979. text ed. 39.50x (ISBN 0-19-550561-1). Oxford U Pr.

Place to Live: A Study of Ecology. Jeanne Bendick. LC 74-99133. (Finding-Out Book). (Illus.). 64p. (gr. 1-4). 1970. PLB 6.95 (ISBN 0-686-64141-8). Enslow Pubs.

Placebo Effect in Healing. Michael L. Jospe. LC 77-6582. 1978. 18.95 (ISBN 0-669-01611-X). Lexington Bks.

Placebo Response: An Experimental & Theoretical Model. N. William Winkelman, Jr. Date not set. 20.00 (ISBN 0-87630-229-0). Brunner-Mazel. Postponed.

Placebo Therapy: A Practical Guide to Social Influence in Psychotherapy. Jefferson Fish. LC 73-9068. (Social & Behavioral Science Ser.). 176p. 1973. 13.95x o.p. (ISBN 0-87589-190-X). Jossey-Bass.

Placement & Improvement of Soils. Compiled by American Society of Civil Engineers. 448p. 1971. text ed. 19.75 (ISBN 0-87262-031-X). Am Soc Civil Eng.

Placement of Engineering & Technology Graduates. Date not set. 25.00 (210-80). AAES.

Placenta-a Neglected Experimental Animal. P. Beaconsfield. 1979. 68.00 (ISBN 0-08-024430-0); pap. 28.00 (ISBN 0-08-024435-1). Pergamon.

Placenta: Biological & Clinical Aspects. Ed. by Kamran S. Moghissi & E. S. Hafez. (Illus.). 412p. 1974. text ed. 38.75 (ISBN 0-398-02999-7). C C Thomas.

Placenta in Twin Pregnancy. S. J. Strong & G. Corney. 1967. 50.00 (ISBN 0-08-012223-X). Pergamon.

Placental Vasculature & Circulation. Elizabeth M. Ramsey & Martin W. Donner. LC 79-65527. (Illus.). 101p. 1980. text ed. 65.00 (ISBN 0-7216-7446-1). Saunders.

Placer De Estudiar la Biblia. Miguel Berg. 127p. (Orig., Span.). 1973. pap. 2.50 o.s.i. (ISBN 0-89922-026-6). Edit Caribe.

Placer Miner's Manual, Vol. 1. Karl Von Mueller. 1980. pap. 5.00 (ISBN 0-89316-611-1); plastic bdg. 7.50 (ISBN 0-89316-612-X). Exanimo Pr.

Placer Miner's Manual, Vol. 2. Karl Von Mueller. 1980. pap. 5.00 (ISBN 0-89316-613-8); plastic bdg 7.50 (ISBN 0-89316-614-6). Exanimo Pr.

Placer Miner's Manual, Vol. 3. Karl Von Mueller. 1980. pap. 5.00 (ISBN 0-89316-615-4); plastic bdg. 7.50 (ISBN 0-89316-616-2). Exanimo Pr.

Places: An Anthology of Britain. Ed. by Ronald Blythe. (Illus.). 270p. 1981. 19.95 (ISBN 0-19-211575-8). Oxford U Pr.

Places & Things for Experimental Schools. LC 72-75056. (Illus.). 134p. 1972. pap. 2.00 (ISBN 0-89192-059-5). Interbk Inc.

Places of Discovery I--Asheville. Lou Harshaw. 1981. 10.95. Green Hill.

Places to Take a Crowd: Three to Three Thousand. Elizabeth B. Gaylord & V. T. Abercrombie. LC 79-66213. (Orig.). 1979. pap. 5.95 (ISBN 0-933988-01-X). Brown Rabbit.

Places Where They Sing. Simon Raven. LC 73-508962. (Alms for Oblivion Ser.: No. 6). 1970. 8.50x (ISBN 0-85634-997-6). Intl Pubns Serv.

Placid Man; or, Memoirs of Sir Charles Beville, 1770, 2 vols. in 1. Charles Jenner. Ed. by Michael F. Shugrue. (Flowering of the Novel, 1740-1775 Ser: Vol. 91). 1974. lib. bdg. 50.00 (ISBN 0-8240-1190-2). Garland Pub.

Placita Anglo - Normannica: Law Cases from William First to Richard First. Melville M. Bigelow. 328p. 1970. Repr. of 1881 ed. text ed. 15.00x (ISBN 0-8377-1928-3). Rothman.

Plague & Fire of London. John Langdon-Davies. (Jackdaw Ser: No. 2). (Illus.). 1968. 5.95 o.p. (ISBN 0-670-55770-6, Grossman). Viking Pr.

Plague Notes. Gary Carey. (Orig.). pap. 2.25 (ISBN 0-8220-1039-9). Cliffs.

Plague of Demons. John Creasey. 1977. 6.95 o.p. (ISBN 0-03-017541-0). HR&W.

Plague of Europeans. David Killingray. (Education Ser.). 1974. pap. 3.65 o.p. (ISBN 0-14-080671-7). Penguin.

Plague of Plagues. Ralph Venning. 1965. pap. 2.45. Banner of Truth.

Plague, Population & the English Economy, 1348-1530. John Hatcher. (Studies in Economic & Social History). 1977. pap. 4.75x (ISBN 0-333-21293-2). Humanities.

Plague Ship. Andre Norton. 1976. pap. 1.95 (ISBN 0-441-66835-6). Ace Bks.

Plagues & People. William H. McNeill. LC 76-2798. 10.00 (ISBN 0-385-11256-4); pap. 4.50 (ISBN 0-385-12122-9). Doubleday.

Plaid for Accounting for Governmental & Nonprofit Entities. Hay & Engstrom. 1981. price not set (ISBN 0-256-02567-3, 01-1454-01). Learning Syst. Postponed.

Plaid for Advanced Accounting. Deitrick & Bizzell. 1981. price not set (ISBN 0-256-02398-0, 01-1435-01). Learning Syst. Postponed.

Plaid for American Government. Luttbeg. 1976. pap. 5.50 (ISBN 0-256-01484-1, 09-1033-00). Learning Syst.

Plaid for Auditing. Meigs & Meigs. 1975. pap. 5.50 (ISBN 0-256-01758-1, 01-1172-00). Learning Syst.

Plaid for Auditing. rev. ed. Meigs et al. 1981. write for info. (ISBN 0-256-02399-9, 01-1172-02). Learning Syst.

Plaid for Basic Algebra. E. Wainwright Martin, Jr. 1970. pap. 5.50 (ISBN 0-256-01286-5, 15-0852-00). Learning Syst.

Plaid for Basic Programming Language. rev. ed. Brady & Richardson. 1981. write for info. (ISBN 0-256-02124-4, 14-1037-02). Learning Syst.

Plaid for Basic Programming Language. Allen H. Brady & James T. Richardson. 1974. pap. 4.95 (ISBN 0-256-01485-X, 08-1037-00). Learning Syst.

Plaid for Business & Consumer Mathematics. Mason et al. 1978. pap. 5.50 (ISBN 0-256-01272-5, 15-0599-01). Learning Syst.

Plaid for Business & Economic Statistics. rev. ed. Mason. 1978. 5.50 (ISBN 0-256-00119-7, 10-0506-02). Learning Syst.

Plaid for Business Communications. Himstreet & Baty. 1976. pap. 5.50 (ISBN 0-256-01769-7, 12-1175-00). Learning Syst.

Plaid for Business Communications. rev. ed. Himstreet & Baty. 1981. price not set (ISBN 0-256-02720-X, 12-1175-02). Learning Syst. Postponed.

Plaid for Business Law. 3rd ed. Barnes. 1978. 5.50 (ISBN 0-256-02123-6, 02-0816-03). Learning Syst.

Plaid for COBOL: A First Course. Lott. 1977. 5.50 (ISBN 0-256-01981-9, 14-1262-01). Learning Syst.

Plaid for College Mathematics: With Applications in Business & Economics. Robert D. Mason. 1976. pap. 5.50 (ISBN 0-256-01267-9, 15-0498-00). Learning Syst.

Plaid for CPA Review Package. Di Antonio. 1981. price not set (ISBN 0-256-02400-6, 01-1436-01). Learning Syst. Postponed.

Plaid for Cultural Anthropology. rev. ed. Barnouw. 1978. 4.95 (ISBN 0-256-02100-7, 01-0356-02). Learning Syst.

Plaid for Developmental Psychology. Hiram E. Fitzgerald & Ellen Strommen. 1972. pap. 5.50 (ISBN 0-256-01258-X, 11-0165-00). Learning Syst.

Plaid for Elementary Accounting, 2 vols. rev ed. Pyle & Larson. 1979. Vol. 1. 5.50 (ISBN 0-256-02130-9, 01-0589-02); Vol. 2. 5.50 (ISBN 0-256-02131-7, 01-0590-02). Learning Syst.

Plaid for Financial Management. Weston. 1975. pap. 5.50 (ISBN 0-256-01285-7, 06-0848-00). Learning Syst.

Plaid for Financial Management. rev ed. Weston. 1981. write for info. (ISBN 0-256-02135-X, 06-0848-02). Learning Syst. Postponed.

Plaid for Fortran: A Beginners Approach. Daniel Couger & Loren E. Shannon. 1977. pap. 5.50 (ISBN 0-256-01986-X, 14-0826-02). Learning Syst.

Plaid for Intermediate Accounting, 2 vols. Glenn A. Welsch & Walter T. Harrison, Jr. 1977. Vol. 1. pap. 5.50 (ISBN 0-256-02005-1, 01-0776-02); Vol. 2. pap. 4.95 (ISBN 0-256-01988-6, 01-0880-02). Learning Syst.

Plaid for Introduction to Business. 3rd ed. Perlick. 1980. 5.50 (ISBN 0-256-02352-2, 08-0566-03). Learning Syst.

Plaid for Introduction to Business. Walter W. Perlick. 1976. pap. 5.50 (ISBN 0-256-01269-5, 08-056600). Learning Syst.

Plaid for Introduction to Data Processing. 3rd ed. Elliott. 1979. 5.50 (ISBN 0-256-02128-7, 14-0841-03). Learning Syst.

Plaid for Introduction to Environmental Science. Phillips Foster. 1977. pap. 5.50 (ISBN 0-256-01262-8, 08-0313-00). Learning Syst.

Plaid for Introduction to Psychology. rev. ed. Cofer. 1979. 5.50 (ISBN 0-256-02127-9, 11-0829-02). Learning Syst.

Plaid for Introductory Sociology. Paul B. Horton & Robert L. Horton. 1977. pap. 5.50 (ISBN 0-256-01987-8, 17-0302-02). Learning Syst.

Plaid for Life Insurance. Mehr. 1979. pap. 5.50 (ISBN 0-256-02101-5, 03-1293-01). Learning Syst.

Plaid for Linear Programming. Wainwright E. Martin, Jr. 1974. pap. 5.50 (ISBN 0-256-01594-5, 15-1086-00). Learning Syst.

Plaid for Management Accounting. Robert N. Anthony. 1974. pap. 5.50 (ISBN 0-256-01277-6, 01-0814-00). Learning Syst.

Plaid for Personal Finance. 3rd ed. Cohen. 1981. write for info. (ISBN 0-256-02126-0, 06-0117-03). Learning Syst.

Plaid for Personnel Administration. George S. Odiorne. 1973. pap. 5.50 (ISBN 0-256-01287-3, 08-0864-00). Learning Syst.

Plaid for Physical Anthropology & Archaeology. rev. ed. Barnouw. 1978. 4.95 (ISBN 0-256-02117-1, 01-0355-02). Learning Syst.

Plaid for Principles of Economics: Macro. 3rd ed. Reynolds & Michas. 1979. 5.50 (ISBN 0-256-02132-5, 05-0865-03). Learning Syst.

Plaid for Principles of Economics: Micro. 3rd ed. Reynolds & Michas. 1979. 5.50 (ISBN 0-256-02133-3, 05-0866-03). Learning Syst.

Plaid for Principles of Insurance. rev. ed. Mehr. 1978. 5.50 (ISBN 0-256-02097-3, 03-0859-02). Learning Syst.

Plaid for Principles of Investments. Fred Amling. 1977. pap. 5.50 (ISBN 0-256-02003-5, 06-0815-02). Learning Syst.

Plaid for Principles of Management. 3rd ed. Terry. 1978. 5.50 (ISBN 0-256-02134-1, 11-0757-03). Learning Syst.

Plaid for Principles of Salesmanship. rev. ed. Howland. 1978. 5.50 (ISBN 0-256-02102-3, 09-0303-02). Learning Syst.

Plaid for Production & Operations Management. rev. ed. Buffa & Newman. Date not set. price not set (ISBN 0-256-02222-4, 11-1035-02). Learning Syst.

Plaid for Production & Operations Management. Elwood S. Buffa. 1973. pap. 5.50 (ISBN 0-256-01481-7, 11-1035-00). Learning Syst.

Plaid for Quantitative Methods. Harwood. 1979. pap. 5.50 (ISBN 0-256-02084-1, 18-1285-01). Learning Syst.

Plaid for Retailing. 3rd ed. Duncan & Hollander. 1979. 6.95 (ISBN 0-256-02245-3, 09-0838-03). Learning Syst.

Plaid for Social Problems. Horton. 1975. pap. 5.50 (ISBN 0-256-01483-3, 17-1036-00). Learning Syst.

Plaid for Supervision. Terry. 1975. pap. 5.50 (ISBN 0-256-01265-2, 08-0388-00). Learning Syst.

Plaid for The Basic Accounting Cycle. Edwards et al. 1975. pap. 6.95 (ISBN 0-256-01707-7, 01-1137-00). Learning Syst.

Plaid for U. S. History Since Eighteen Sixty-Five. James P. Shenton & Alan Meckler. 1975. pap. 5.50 (ISBN 0-256-01274-1, 06-0643-00). Learning Syst.

Plaid for U. S. History to Eighteen Seventy-Seven. James P. Shenton & Alan Meckler. 1973. pap. 5.50 (ISBN 0-256-01273-3, 06-0641-00). Learning Syst.

Plaid for Using the Metric System. Mason & Lange. 1976. pap. 4.95 (ISBN 0-256-01772-7, 15-1178-00). Learning Syst.

Plaid for Writing Resumes, Locating Jobs, Handling Job Interviews. Freeman. 1976. pap. 4.95 (ISBN 0-256-01871-5, 11-1219-00). Learning Syst.

Plaid on the Constitution of the United States. Joseph T. Keenan. 1975. pap. 4.95 (ISBN 0-256-01615-1, 06-1099-00). Learning Syst.

Plaideurs. Jean Racine. (Documentation thematique). (Illus., Fr). pap. 2.95 (ISBN 0-685-14041-5, 269). Larousse.

Plain & Elegant, Rich & Common: Documented New Hampshire Furniture, 1750-1850. LC 79-13568. (Illus.). 153p. 1979. pap. 7.50 (ISBN 0-915916-09-6). U Pr of New Eng.

Plain & Fancy: American Women & Their Needlework, 1700-1850. Susan B. Swan. LC 77-1627. (Illus.). 1977. 14.95 o.p. (ISBN 0-03-015121-X). HR&W.

Plain Cookery Book for the Working Classes. Charles E. Francatelli. 105p. 1978. pap. 1.95 (ISBN 0-85967-390-1, Pub. by Scolar Pr England). Biblio Dist.

Plain Dealer. William Wycherley. Ed. by Leo Hughes. LC 67-10670. (Regents Restoration Drama Ser). 1967. 9.95x (ISBN 0-8032-0372-1); pap. 3.50x (ISBN 0-8032-5372-9, BB 263, Bison). U of Nebr Pr.

Plain-Language Law Dictionary. Robert Rothenberg. 1981. pap. 7.95 (ISBN 0-14-051109-1). Penguin.

Plain Man's Guide to Second-Hand Furniture. Frank Davis. 1972. 8.95 (ISBN 0-7181-0936-8). Transatlantic.

Plain Man's Guide to Second Hand Furniture. Frank Davis. 1971. 6.95 (ISBN 0-7181-0936-8, Pub. by Michael Joseph). Merrimack Bk Serv.

Plain Murder. C. S. Forester. 1978. 7.95 (ISBN 0-370-00650-X, Pub. by Chatto Bodley Jonathan). Merrimack Bk Serv.

Plain People of Boston, 1830-1860: A Study in City Growth. Peter R. Knights. (Urban Life in America Ser.). 1973. 14.95 (ISBN 0-19-501488-X). Oxford U Pr

Plain Song. Jim Harrison. 1965. 4.50 o.p. (ISBN 0-393-04240-5). Norton.

Plain Speaking: An Oral Biography of Harry S. Truman. Merle Miller. (Illus.). 288p. (YA) 1974. 8.95 o.p. (ISBN 0-399-11261-8, Dist. by Putnam). Berkley Pub.

Plain Talk on Genesis. Manford G. Gutzke. 160p. 1975. pap. 3.95 (ISBN 0-310-25531-7). Zondervan.

Plain Talk on Isaiah. Manford G. Gutzke. 1977. pap. 5.95 (ISBN 0-310-25551-1). Zondervan.

Plain Talk on Leviticus & Numbers. Manford G. Gutzke. 144p. 1981. pap. 4.95 (ISBN 0-310-41951-4, 9872P). Zondervan.

Plain Talk on Luke. Manford G. Gutzke. 1966. pap. 3.95 (ISBN 0-310-25581-3). Zondervan.

Plain Talk on Philippians. Manford G. Gutzke. 288p. 1973. pap. 5.95 (ISBN 0-310-25611-9). Zondervan.

Plain Talk on the Minor Prophets. Manford G. Gutzke. (Plain Talk Ser. of Bible Study Bks.). 160p. (Orig.). 1980. pap. 3.95 (ISBN 0-310-41941-7, 9868P). Zondervan.

Plain X-Ray in the Diagnosis of the Acute Abdomen. Malcolm Gough & Michael Gear. (Illus.). 194p. 1971. 9.50 (ISBN 0-632-08380-8, Blackwell). Mosby.

Plains Apache. John U. Terrell. LC 75-9601. 224p. (YA) 1975. 10.95 o.s.i. (ISBN 0-690-00969-0, TYC-T). T Y Crowell.

Plains Indian Book. 1974. pap. 2.50 (ISBN 0-918858-02-X). Fun Pub.

Plains Indian Raiders: The Final Phases of Warfare from the Arkansas to the Red River. Wilbur S. Nye. LC 67-24624. (Illus.). 1974. 22.50 (ISBN 0-8061-0803-7); pap. 8.95 o.p. (ISBN 0-8061-1175-5). U of Okla Pr.

Plains Indians. Christopher Davis. (Illus.). (gr. 5-8). 1978. PLB 6.90 s&l (ISBN 0-531-01429-0). Watts.

Plains Indians: A Critical Bibliography. E. Adamson Hoebel. LC 77-6914. (Newberry Library Center for the History of the American Indian Bibl. Ser.). 88p. 1977. pap. 3.95x (ISBN 0-253-34509-X). Ind U Pr.

Plains Indians: Their Origins, Migrations, & Cultural Development. F. Haines. LC 75-23259. (Illus.). 224p. 1976. 10.95 o.s.i. (ISBN 0-690-01031-1, TYC-T). T Y Crowell.

Plains Rifle. Hanson. 15.00 (ISBN 0-88227-015-X). Gun Room.

Plains Song. Wright Morris. (Contemporary American Fiction Ser.). 241p. 1981. pap. 3.95 (ISBN 0-14-005778-1). Penguin.

Plains Woman. Anne Jordan. (Orig.). 1980. pap. 1.75 (ISBN 0-505-51545-8). Tower Bks.

Plainsmen of the Yellowstone: A History of the Yellowstone Basin. Mark H. Brown. LC 60-5262. (Illus.). 1969. pap. 8.75 (ISBN 0-8032-5026-6, BB 397, Bison). U of Nebr Pr.

Plaintes et Representations. Francois-Joseph Lange. (Fr.). 1977. lib. bdg. 13.75x o.p. (ISBN 0-8287-0506-2); pap. text ed. 3.75x o.p. (ISBN 0-685-77006-0). Clearwater Pub.

Plainville Fifteen Years Later. Art Gallaher, Jr. LC 61-15104. 1961. 17.50x (ISBN 0-231-02481-9). Columbia U Pr.

Plainville, USA. James West. LC 45-1863. 1945. pap. 5.00x (ISBN 0-231-08514-1). Columbia U Pr.

Plan-Ahead Cookbook. Ceil Dyer. 1970. pap. 1.50 o.s.i. (ISBN 0-02-009440-X, Collier). Macmillan.

Plan & Market Under Socialism. Ota Sik. LC 66-23896. 1967. 17.50 o.p. (ISBN 0-87332-012-3). M E Sharpe.

Plan De Dios y los Vencedores. Ed. by Esteban Marosi. Tr. by Rhode Flores. 112p. (Span.). 1980. pap. 1.40 (ISBN 0-8297-0605-4). Vida Pubs.

Plan De Dios y los Vencedores. 1980. pap. 1.40 (ISBN 0-686-69349-3). Vida Pubs.

Plan for Promotion: Advancement & the Manager. Tom Watling. 237p. 1977. text ed. 19.75x (ISBN 0-220-66327-0, Pub. by Busn Bks England). Renouf.

Plan of Chicago Prepared Under the Direction of the Commercial Club During the Years 1906, 1907, 1908. Daniel H. Burnham & Edward H. Bennett. Ed. by Charles Moore. LC 71-75303. (Architecture & Decorative Art Ser.: Vol. 29). (Illus.). 1970. Repr. of 1909 ed. lib. bdg. 95.00 (ISBN 0-306-71261-X). Da Capo.

Plan of Chicago: 1909-1979. John Zukowsky. LC 79-55997. (Illus.). 52p. (Orig.). 1979. pap. 4.95x (ISBN 0-86559-039-7). Art Inst Chi.

Plan of Salvation. Ostis B. Wilson. 64p. pap. 0.50. Faith Pub Hse.

Plan Para Memorizar las Escrituras. J. W. Alexander. Orig. Title: Fire in My Bones. 1979. 1.45 (ISBN 0-311-03660-0). Casa Bautista.

Plan Paris, No. 12. pap. 4.95 (ISBN 2-06000-120-X). Michelin.

Plan to Planet. Haki Madhubuti. 1980. pap. 3.95 (ISBN 0-88378-066-6). Third World.

Planagement: Moving Concept into Reality. Robert M. Randolph. LC 79-17075. 1979. Repr. of 1975 ed. 17.95 (ISBN 0-89384-056-4). Learning Concepts.

Plane Algerbraic Curves. Orzech. 224p. 1981. 29.75 (ISBN 0-8247-1159-9). Dekker.

Plane Analytic Geometry. Walter W. Graham & William H. Rowan. (Quality Paperback: No. 47). (Orig.). 1968. pap. 3.50 (ISBN 0-8226-0047-1). Littlefield.

Plane & Spherical Trigonometry. rev. ed. Kaj L. Nielsen & John H. Vanlonkhuyzen. (Orig.). 1954. pap. 4.95 (ISBN 0-06-460045-9, CO 45, COS). Har-Row.

Plane Geometry Problems with Solutions. Marcus Horblit & Kaj L. Nielsen. (Orig.). 1947. pap. 3.89 (ISBN 0-06-460063-7, CO 63, COS). Har-Row.

Plane Talk: Aviators' & Astronauts' Own Stories. Carl Oliver. (gr. 7 up). 1980. 7.95 (ISBN 0-395-29743-5). HM.

Plane Trees. Monique Lange. Tr. by J. M. Calder. 1980. pap. 2.95 (ISBN 0-7145-0446-7). Riverrun NY.

Plane Trees. Monique Lange. Tr. by J. M. Calder. pap. 2.95 (ISBN 0-7145-0446-7). Riverrun NY.

Plane Trigonometry. 3rd ed. Raymond W. Brink. (Century Mathematics Ser). 1959. 32.50x (ISBN 0-89197-627-2). Irvington.

Plane Trigonometry. Walter Fleming & Dale E. Varberg. 1980. text ed. 16.95 (ISBN 0-13-679043-7). P-H.

Plane Trigonometry. Richard Miller & Patricia Henry. LC 80-18403. 275p. 1981. text ed. 15.95 (ISBN 0-8185-0421-8). Brooks-Cole.

Plane Trigonometry. 3rd ed. Nathan O. Niles. LC 75-28337. 394p. 1976. text ed. 18.95x (ISBN 0-471-64025-5); solutions manual avail. (ISBN 0-471-01716-7). Wiley.

Plane Trigonometry. Allyn J. Washington & Carolyn E. Edmond. LC 76-7883. 1977. 17.95 (ISBN 0-8465-8622-3); instr's guide 7.95 (ISBN 0-8465-8623-1). Benjamin-Cummings.

Plane Trigonometry: A New Approach. 2nd ed. Carol Johnston. LC 77-16841. 1978. text ed. 16.95 (ISBN 0-13-677666-3). P-H.

Plane Trigonometry with Tables. 7th ed. Charles Rees et al. (Illus.). 1977. text ed. 16.95 (ISBN 0-13-679209-X). P-H.

Planeamiento Nacional De Servicios Bibliotecarios, Vol. 2. (Span.). 1972. pap. 1.00 (ISBN 0-8270-3055-X). OAS.

Planecraft. C. W. Hampton & E. Clifford. LC 79-57129. (Illus.). 1980. pap. 6.00 (ISBN 0-918036-00-3). Woodcraft Supply.

Planes & Airports. Chris McAllister. (Illus.). 64p. 1981. pap. 5.95 (ISBN 0-7134-3911-4, Pub. by Batsford England). David & Charles.

Planes & Copter. Frank Ronan. (gr. 4-6). 1977. pap. 0.59 o.p. (ISBN 0-590-05420-1, Schol Pap). Schol Bk Serv.

Planet Earth in Color. Brown P. Lancaster. (Macmillan Color Ser.). (Illus.). 1976. 9.95 (ISBN 0-02-567710-1). Macmillan.

Planet Earth: Readings from Scientific American. Intro. by Frank Press & Raymond Siever. LC 74-14919. (Illus.). 1974. text ed. 19.95x (ISBN 0-7167-0507-9); pap. text ed. 9.95x (ISBN 0-7167-0506-0). W H Freeman.

Planet in Arms. Donald Barr. 288p. 1981. pap. 2.25 (ISBN 0-449-24407-5, Crest). Fawcett.

Planet in Trouble: The UFO Assault on Earth. Jerome Eden. 1973. 8.50 (ISBN 0-682-47822-9). Exposition.

Planet of Fear. Diane Detzer. (YA) 4.95 o.p. (ISBN 0-685-07454-4, Avalon). Bouregy.

Planet of Junior Brown. Virginia Hamilton. (Illus.). (gr. 7 up). 1971. 8.95 (ISBN 0-02-742510-X). Macmillan.

Planet of Junior Brown. Virginia Hamilton. LC 71-155264. 224p. (gr. 5-9). 1974. pap. 0.95 o.s.i. (ISBN 0-02-043530-4, 04353, Collier). Macmillan.

Planet of the Apes. Pierre Boulle. LC 63-21843. 1963. 8.95 (ISBN 0-8149-0064-X). Vanguard.

Planet Pluto. Anthony J. Whyte & Herbert A. Wise. LC 79-23998. 1980. 19.50 (ISBN 0-08-024648-6). Pergamon.

Planet Probable: A One-Act Poetic Play. J. Hollis. (Orig.). 1981. pap. 2.95 (ISBN 0-933486-20-0). Am Poetry Pr.

Planet Savers. Marion Z. Bradley. (Science Fiction Ser.). 1979. lib. bdg. 8.95 (ISBN 0-8398-2514-5). Gregg.

Planet to Choose. Alan S. Miller. 192p. (Orig.). 1978. pap. 6.95 (ISBN 0-8298-0348-3). Pilgrim NY.

Planet Tours. Ron Miller et al. LC 80-54620. (Illus.). 192p. 19.95 (ISBN 0-89480-147-3); pap. 9.95 (ISBN 0-89480-146-5). Workman Pub.

Planetarium. Nathalie Sarraute. Tr. by Maria Jolas from Fr. 1980. pap. 4.95 (ISBN 0-7145-0444-0). Riverrun NY.

Planetary Astronomy: An Appraisal of Ground-Based Opportunities. Space Science Board. 1968. pap. 4.75 (ISBN 0-309-01688-6). Natl Acad Pr.

Planetary Effects on Stock Market & Commodity Prices: The Influence of Certain Planetary Positions & Commodity Futures Prices, 2 vols. in 1. James M. Langham. (Illus.). 1979. Repr. deluxe ed. 135.85 (ISBN 0-918968-42-9). Inst Econ Finan.

Planetary Encounters. Robert M. Powers. 1980. pap. 2.95 (ISBN 0-446-93330-9). Warner Bks.

Planetary Geology. Nicholas M. Short. (Illus.). 384p. 1975. ref. ed. 28.95 (ISBN 0-13-679290-1). P-H.

Planets & Cataclysm. Robert R. Humula. LC 79-67520. 1980. 7.95 (ISBN 0-533-04469-3). Vantage.

Planets & Moons. William J. Kaufmann, 3rd. LC 78-21156. (Illus.). 1979. text ed. 15.50x o.p. (ISBN 0-7167-1041-2); pap. text ed. 8.95x (ISBN 0-7167-1040-4). W H Freeman.

Planets & Planetarians: A History of Theories of the Origin of Planetary Systems. Stanley L. Jaki. LC 77-4200. 1978. 21.95 (ISBN 0-470-99149-6). Halsted Pr.

Planets & Satellites. Ed. by Gerard P. Kuiper & Barbara M. Middlehurst. LC 54-7183. (Solar System Ser: Vol. 3). 1961. 23.00x (ISBN 0-226-45927-6). U of Chicago Pr.

Planets in Transit: Life Cycles for Living. Robert Hand. LC 76-12759. (Planets Ser.). 1980. pap. 18.95 (ISBN 0-914918-24-9). Para Res.

Planets, Stars, & Galaxies. 4th ed. Stuart J. Inglis. LC 75-31542. 352p. 1976. pap. text ed. 18.95x (ISBN 0-471-42738-1). Wiley.

Planets X & Pluto. William G. Hoyt. LC 79-15665. 1980. 17.95x o.s.i. (ISBN 0-8165-0684-1); pap. 9.50 (ISBN 0-8165-0664-7). U of Ariz Pr.

Plank Bridge by a Pool. Norman Thelwell. (Encore Edition). (Illus.). 1979. 3.95 (ISBN 0-684-16695-X, ScribT). Scribner.

Plank on Frame: The Who, What & Where of 150 Boatbuilders. Paul Lipke. LC 80-80779. (Illus.). 320p. 1980. pap. 19.95 (ISBN 0-87742-121-8). Intl Marine.

Plankton & Productivity in the Oceans. J. E. Raymont. 1963. 36.00 (ISBN 0-08-010185-2); pap. 15.00 (ISBN 0-08-019009-X). Pergamon.

Plankton & Productivity in the Oceans: Vol. 1, Phytoplankton. 2nd ed. John E. Raymont et al. (Illus.). 1980. text ed. 75.00 (ISBN 0-08-021552-1); pap. text ed. 19.95 (ISBN 0-08-021551-3). Pergamon.

Planktonic Diatoms of Northern Seas. M. V. Lebour. (Ray Society Publication: No. 116). (Illus.). 244p. 1978. Repr. of 1930 ed. lib. bdg. 30.00x (ISBN 3-87429-147-2). Lubrecht & Cramer.

Planned Behavior Change: Behavior Modification in Social Work. Joel Fischer & Harvey L. Gochros. LC 74-34554. (Illus.). 1979. pap. text ed. 9.95 (ISBN 0-02-910230-8). Free Pr.

Planned Press & Public Relations. Frank Jefkins. 1977. text ed. 29.95x (ISBN 0-7002-0264-1); pap. text ed. 17.95x (ISBN 0-7002-0272-2). Intl Ideas.

Planned Speaking & Your Career. Vera Gough & B. R. Grier. 1967. 12.25 (ISBN 0-08-012589-1); pap. 4.20 (ISBN 0-08-012588-3). Pergamon.

Planned Unit Development Ordinances. American Society of Planning Officials. 1973. 8.00 o.s.i. (ISBN 0-685-71649-X). Urban Land.

Planned Variation in Education: Should We Give up or Try Harder? Ed. by Alice M. Rivlin & P. Michael Timpane. (Studies in Social Experimentation). 184p. 1975. 11.95 (ISBN 0-8157-7480-X); pap. 4.95 (ISBN 0-8157-7479-6). Brookings.

Planner & Lifelong Education. (Fundamentals of Educational Planning: No. 25). 1978. pap. 4.75 (ISBN 92-803-1077-1, U762, UNESCO). Unipub.

Planner in Society. David Eversley. 1973. 14.50 o.p. (ISBN 0-686-24620-9, Pub. by Faber & Faber). Merrimack Bk Serv.

Planners & Local Politics: Impossible Dreams. Anthony James Catanese. LC 73-94287. (Sage Library of Social Research: Vol. 7). 1974. 18.00x (ISBN 0-8039-0397-9); pap. 8.95x (ISBN 0-8039-0378-2). Sage.

Planners, Politics & Health Services. Gregory Parston. 196p. 1980. 25.50x (ISBN 0-85664-909-0, Pub. by Croom Helm Ltd England). Biblio Dist.

Planning a Christian Wedding. Paul M. Krause. 1963. pap. 0.95 (ISBN 0-570-03504-X, 14-2010). Concordia.

Planning a Corrugated Container Plant. Walter G. Paulson et al. (Tappi Press Reports). (Illus.). 125p. 1980. 93.95 (ISBN 0-89852-387-7, 01-01-R087). Tappi.

Planning a Country Place. Hollis Lee. (Country Home & Small Farm Guides Ser.). (Illus.). 1978. pap. 2.95 (ISBN 0-88453-003-5). Barrington.

Planning a Country Place. (Country Home Ser.). 96p. 2.95 (ISBN 0-88453-003-5). Berkshire Traveller.

Planning a Performance Improvement Project: A Practical Guide. LC 80-8175. (Guideline Ser.). 60p. (Orig.). 1981. pap. write for info. (ISBN 0-931816-26-2); wkbk. avail.; tapes 4.95x. Kumarian Pr.

Planning a Town Garden. Jacquey Visick. (Design Centre Bks.). 1978. pap. 6.95 o.p. (ISBN 0-8256-3096-7). Music Sales.

Planning African Development: The Kenya Experience. Ed. by Glen Norcliffe. Tom Pinfold. 224p. 1981. lib. bdg. 25.00x (ISBN 0-86531-161-7). Westview.

Planning Alternative World Futures: Values, Methods, & Models. Ed. by Louis R. Beres & Harry R. Targ. LC 74-33030. (Illus.). 342p. 1975. text ed. 25.95 o.p. (ISBN 0-275-05340-7); pap. text ed. 8.95 o.p. (ISBN 0-275-89420-7). Praeger.

Planning Ambulatory Surgery Facilities. Reba D. Grubb & Geraldine Ondov. LC 79-10123. (Illus.). 1979. 17.95 (ISBN 0-8016-1986-6). Mosby.

Planning an Instructional Sequence. James Popham & Eva Baker. (Illus.). 1970. pap. text ed. 8.95 (ISBN 0-13-679704-0). P-H.

Planning & Administering Early Childhood Programs. 2nd ed. Cecil A. Decker & John R. Decker. (Elementary Education Ser.: No. C22). 480p. 1980. pap. text ed. 15.95 (ISBN 0-675-08160-2). Merrill.

Planning & Budgeting in Poor Countries. Naomi Caiden & Aaron Wildavsky. LC 73-12312. (Comparative Studies in Behavioral Science). 416p. 1974. 28.95 (ISBN 0-471-12925-9, Pub. by Wiley-Interscience). Wiley.

Planning & Conservation: The Emergence of the Frugal Society. Peter W. House & Edward R. Williams. LC 77-7584. (Praeger Special Studies). 1977. text ed. 28.95 (ISBN 0-03-021946-9); pap. 9.95 (ISBN 0-03-022281-8). Praeger.

Planning & Control Guides & Forms for Small Book Publishers. John Huenefeld & Virginia Wiley. LC 80-21051. 72p. 1980. 44.00 (ISBN 0-931932-01-7). Huenefeld Co.

Planning & Control with PERT-CPM. Richard I. Levin & C. A. Kirkpatrick. 1966. 20.95 (ISBN 0-07-037364-7, C); pap. 12.95 (ISBN 0-07-037365-5). McGraw.

Planning & Design of Townhouses & Condominiums. Robert E. Engstrom & Marc Putman. LC 79-64813. (Illus.). 256p. 1979. pap. text ed. 26.75 (ISBN 0-87420-587-5). Urban Land.

Planning & Designing a Burn Care Facility. I. Feller et al. LC 80-83418. (Illus.). 350p. 1981. 75.00 (ISBN 0-917478-21-5). Natl Inst Burn.

Planning & Educational Inequality. Eileen M. Byrne. (General Ser.). 384p. 1974. pap. text ed. 22.50x (ISBN 0-85633-039-6, NFER). Humanities.

Planning & Implementing Nursing Intervention: Stress & Adaptation Applied to Patient Care. 2nd ed. Dolores F. Saxton & Patricia A. Hyland. LC 78-31818. (Illus.). 1979. pap. 10.50 (ISBN 0-8016-4337-6). Mosby.

Planning & Managing Housing for the Elderly. M. Powell Lawton. LC 74-28099. 304p. 1975. 32.50 (ISBN 0-471-51894-8, Pub. by Wiley-Interscience). Wiley.

Planning & Organisation of National Research Programs in Information Science. Ed. by V. Slamecka & H. Borka. (Illus.). 83p. 1980. pap. 27.50 (ISBN 0-08-026472-7). Pergamon.

Planning & Organizing Career Curricula. Ronald Stadt & Dennis Nystrom. LC 72-92619. 1975. 13.95 (ISBN 0-672-97533-5). Bobbs.

Planning & Organizing for Social Change. Jack Rothman. LC 74-4434. 1974. text ed. 27.00x (ISBN 0-231-03774-0); pap. text ed. 12.00x (ISBN 0-231-08335-1). Columbia U Pr.

Planning & Organizing Instruction. rev. ed. G. Harold Silvius & Ralph C. Bohn. Orig. Title: Organizing Course Materials for Industrial Education. 1976. text ed. 16.09 (ISBN 0-87345-720-X). McKnight.

Planning & Paying Your Way to College. Clodus R. Smith. (Illus., Orig.). 1968. pap. 1.95 o.s.i. (ISBN 0-02-082050-X, Collier). Macmillan.

Planning & Productivity Under Soviet Socialism. Abram Bergson. LC 68-24703. 1968. 15.00x (ISBN 0-231-03116-5). Columbia U Pr.

Planning & Reviewing Employee Performance. rev. ed. Glenn H. Varney. 46p. 1974. pap. 4.95 (ISBN 0-686-05625-6). Mgmt Advisory.

Planning & Using the Blackboard. Patricia Mugglestone. (Practical Language Teaching Ser.). (Illus.). 96p. (Orig.). 1980. pap. text ed. 6.95x (ISBN 0-04-371062-X, 2368). Allen Unwin.

Planning Audit: A Framework with Special References to River Basin Planning. Holtan P. Odegard. 1974. 9.00 o.p. (ISBN 0-9600524-2-9). Advance Planning.

Planning Better Programs. Patrick G. Boyle. Ed. by Alan Pardoen & Don Seaman. (Adult Education Association Professional Development Ser.). (Illus.). 272p. 1980. text ed. 13.95 (ISBN 0-07-000552-4, C). McGraw.

Planning by Network. H. S. Woodgate. 330p. 1977. text ed. 24.50x (ISBN 0-220-66312-2, Pub. by Busn Bks England). Renouf.

Planning Challenges of the Seventies in Space. Ed. by George W. Morgenthaler & Robert Morra. LC 57-43769. (Advances in the Astronautical Sciences Ser.: Vol. 26). (Illus.). 1970. lib. bdg. 35.00 (ISBN 0-87703-053-7); microfiche suppl. 15.00 (ISBN 0-87703-130-4). Am Astronaut.

Planning Challenges of the 70's in the Public Domain. Ed. by W. Bursnall. (Science & Technology Ser.: Vol. 22). (Illus.). 1969. lib. bdg. 40.00 (ISBN 0-87703-050-2); microfiche suppl 20.00 (ISBN 0-87703-131-2). Am Astronaut.

Planning Community Information Utilities. Ed. by Harold Sackman & Barry W. Boehm. LC 72-83727. (Illus.). viii, 501p. 1972. 15.00 (ISBN 0-88283-000-7). AFIPS Pr.

Planning Community Services for Children in Trouble. Alfred J. Kahn. LC 63-10417. (Illus.). 1963. 22.50x (ISBN 0-231-02611-0). Columbia U Pr.

Planning, Conducting, Evaluating Workshops. Larry N. Davis. LC 74-82809. 1975. 17.95 (ISBN 0-89384-001-7); pap. 9.95 (ISBN 0-89384-002-5). Learning Concepts.

Planning Crime Prevention. William Clifford. LC 74-42910. (Illus.). 1976. 16.95 (ISBN 0-669-00560-6). Lexington Bks.

Planning, Design & Implementation of Bicycle & Pedestrian Facilities. Compiled by American Society of Civil Engineers. 656p. 1976. pap. text ed. 20.00 (ISBN 0-87262-170-7). Am Soc Civil Eng.

Planning Design: The Systems Approach. Steven L. Dickerson & Joseph E. Robertshaw. LC 74-23977. (Illus.). 1975. 24.95 (ISBN 0-669-96602-9). Lexington Bks.

Planning, Engineering, & Constructing the Super Projects. Compiled by American Society of Civil Engineers. 536p. 1979. pap. text ed. 27.00 (ISBN 0-87262-178-2). Am Soc Civil Eng.

Planning for a Family. John Marshall. 1969. pap. 5.95 (ISBN 0-571-06260-1, Pub. by Faber & Faber). Merrimack Bk Serv.

Planning for Agricultural Area Development: The Asian Experience. 246p. 1973. 7.25 (APO53, APO). Unipub.

Planning for an Individual Water System. G. E. Henderson. 7.95 (ISBN 0-914452-45-2). Green Hill.

Planning for Better Imposition. Daniel Mecher. LC 76-102070. 1977. 26.95 (ISBN 0-912920-55-6). North Am Pub Co.

Planning for Better Learning. Ed. by Peter Wolff. (Clinics in Developmental Medicine Ser. No. 33). 159p. 1969. 15.50 (ISBN 0-685-24741-4). Lippincott.

Planning for Career Options. 1978. pap. 2.95 o.s.i. (ISBN 0-89584-014-6). Hippocrene Bks.

Planning for Catholic Education. 62p. 1971. 2.00. Natl Cath Educ.

Planning for Computing in Higher Education. James C. Emery. (EDUCOM Ser. in Computing & Telecommunications in Higher Education: No. 5). 218p. 1980. lib. bdg. 25.00x (ISBN 0-86531-025-4). Westview.

Planning for Conservation: An International Perspective. Roger Kain. 1980. 30.00 (ISBN 0-312-61400-4). St Martin.

Planning for Creative Learning. 2nd ed. Bruce M. Mitchell et al. 176p. 1981. pap. text ed. 9.95 (ISBN 0-8403-2302-6). Kendall-Hunt.

Planning for Data Communications. John E. Bingham & Garth W. Davies. 218p. 1979. pap. 17.95x (ISBN 0-470-26843-3). Halsted Pr.

Planning for Data Communications. John E Bingham & Garth W. Davies. LC 77-7193. 1978. 29.95 (ISBN 0-470-99187-9). Halsted Pr.

Planning for Economic Development: The Construction & Use of a Multisectoral Model for Tunisia. Oli Hawrylyshyn et al. LC 76-12857. 1976. text ed. 24.95 (ISBN 0-275-02300-1). Praeger.

Planning for Educational Mass Media. Alan Hancock. LC 76-22496. (Illus.). 1977. text ed. 28.00x (ISBN 0-582-41055-X). Longman.

Planning for Engineers & Surveyors. F. D. Hobbs & J. F. Doling. LC 80-41553. (Illus.). 230p. 1980. 30.00 (ISBN 0-08-025459-4); pap. 15.00 (ISBN 0-08-025458-6). Pergamon.

Planning for Freedom. 4th, enl. ed. Ludwig Von Misses. LC 80-10765. 296p. 1980. pap. 6.00 (ISBN 0-910884-13-7). Libertarian.

Planning for Health Education in Schools. Clair E. Turner. 1966. 6.50 (ISBN 92-3-100626-6, U452, UNESCO). Unipub.

Planning for Higher Education: Background & Application. Allan O. Pfnister. LC 76-5906. (Special Studies in Higher Education Ser). 1976. 23.75x (ISBN 0-89158-035-2). Westview.

Planning for Man & Motor. Paul Ritter. 1964. 37.00 (ISBN 0-08-010417-7). Pergamon.

Planning for Non-Planners. Darryl J. Ellis & Peter P. Pekar. 1981. 12.95 (ISBN 0-8144-5593-X). Am Mgmt.

Planning for People. Maurice Broady. 119p. 1968. pap. text ed. 4.00x (ISBN 0-7199-0765-9, Pub. by Bedford England). Renouf.

Planning for Play: A Developmental Approach. Gail Bjorklund. 1978. pap. text ed. 5.95 (ISBN 0-675-08434-2); filmstrips or cassettes avail. 60.00, 2-4 sets (ISBN 0-686-52447-0) manual 3.95 (ISBN 0-686-67983-0). Merrill.

Planning for Services to Handicapped Persons: Community, Education, Health. Ed. by Phyllis R. Magrab & Jerry O. Elder. LC 79-21474. 1979. text ed. 14.50 (ISBN 0-933716-04-4). P H Brookes.

Planning for Social Recreation. Israel C. Heaton & Clark T. Thorstenson. LC 77-85148. (Illus.). 1978. pap. text ed. 11.50 (ISBN 0-395-25052-8). HM.

Planning for Social Welfare: Issues, Models & Tasks. N. Gilbert & H. Specht. 1977. text ed. 17.95 (ISBN 0-13-679555-2). P-H.

Planning for Standby. National Computing Centre. Ed. by L. P. Waring. LC 77-351948. 1976. pap. 16.50x (ISBN 0-85012-183-3). Intl Pubns Serv.

Planning for Standby. L. P. Waring. 112p. 1977. pap. 12.95 (ISBN 0-85012-183-3, 5465-3, Pub. by Natl Computing Centre England). Hayden.

Planning for the Elderly: Alternative Community Analysis Techniques. Victor Regnier. LC 79-90975. 152p. 1980. pap. 6.00 (ISBN 0-88474-093-5). USC Andrus Geron.

Planning for the Elderly in New York City: Report of a Research Utilization Workshop. 1980. 4.00. Comm Coun Great NY.

Planning for the Handling of Radiation Accidents. (Safety Ser.: No. 32). 1970. pap. 7.50 (ISBN 92-0-123269-1, IAEA). Unipub.

Planning for Welfare: Social Policy & the Expenditure Process. Ed. by Timothy A. Booth. (Aspects of Social Policy Ser.). 1979. 29.50x (ISBN 0-631-19560-2, Pub. by Basil Blackwell); pap. 12.95 (ISBN 0-631-11571-4). Biblio Dist.

Planning for Your Own Apartment. Virginia S. Belina. (gr. 7 up). 1975. pap. 3.96 (ISBN 0-8224-5420-3); tchrs manual free (ISBN 0-8224-5421-1). Pitman Learning.

Planning Grain-Feed Handling for Live-Stock & Cash-Grain Farms. Midwest Plan Service Personnel. (Illus.). 1974. pap. 2.50 (ISBN 0-89373-007-6, MWPS-13). Midwest Plan Serv.

Planning Home Care for the Elderly. Alan Sager. Date not set. pns professional reference (ISBN 0-88410-725-6). Ballinger Pub.

Planning, Implementing & Evaluating Career Preparation Programs. Dwight Davis & Joe Borgen. 1974. 50.00 (ISBN 0-87345-590-8). McKnight.

Planning in a Dutch & a Yugoslav Steelworks: A Comparative Study. H. C. Dekker et al. (Illus.). 1976. pap. text ed. 23.00x (ISBN 90-6032-078-6). Humanities.

Planning in East Europe. Michael Kaserand & J. Zielinski. 1971. 7.50 (ISBN 0-370-00397-7). Transatlantic.

Planning in Education. B. W. Vaughan. LC 77-82520. (Illus.). 1979. 26.50 (ISBN 0-521-21817-9); pap. 10.95x (ISBN 0-521-29285-9). Cambridge U Pr.

Planning in State Courts: Trends & Developments 1976-78. (State Court Planning Capabilities Project Ser.). 1978. pap. 5.50 (ISBN 0-89656-028-7, R0040). Natl Ctr St Courts.

Planning in the Soviet Union. Judith Pallot & Denis Shaw. LC 80-24723. 320p. 1981. lib. bdg. 25.00x (ISBN 0-8203-0550-2). U of Ga Pr.

Planning Manual for Academic Library Buildings. Ralph E. Ellsworth. LC 73-14896. (Illus.). 1973. 8.00 o.p. (ISBN 0-8108-0680-0). Scarecrow.

Planning Manual for Colleges. rev. ed. National Association of College & University Business Officers et al. 73p. 1980. pap. text ed. 15.00 (ISBN 0-915164-09-4). Natl Assn Coll.

Planning Meals & Shopping. Ann A. Weaver. (Young Homemakers at Work Ser). (Special Education Ser. for slow learners). (gr. 7-12,RL 2.5). 1970. pap. 2.80 (ISBN 0-8224-5450-5); tchrs.' manual free (ISBN 0-8224-7676-2). Pitman Learning.

Planning Models for Colleges & Universities. David S. Hopkins & William F. Massy. LC 78-66176. (Illus.). 576p. 1981. 28.50x (ISBN 0-8047-1023-6). Stanford U Pr.

Planning My Career, Occupational Guidance. Vincent Capozziello, Jr. LC 75-20074. (gr. 7 up). 1979. 2.25 (ISBN 0-912486-43-0). Finney Co.

Planning of Aquaculture Development. 1979. pap. 10.00 (ISBN 0-85238-089-5, FN66, FN). Unipub.

Planning of Investment Programs in the Fertilizer Industry. Armeane Choksi et al. LC 78-8436. (World Bank Ser: No. 2). 1978. text ed. 19.50x (ISBN 0-8018-2138-X); pap. text ed. 6.95x (ISBN 0-8018-2153-3). Johns Hopkins.

Planning of Ornament. Lewis F. Day. Ed. by Peter Stansky & Rodney Shewan. LC 76-17766. (Aesthetic Movement & the Arts & Crafts Movement Ser.). 1977. Repr. of 1887 ed. lib. bdg. 44.00x (ISBN 0-8240-2470-2). Garland Pub.

Planning of Radiotherapy Departments. Ed. by T. J. Deeley. 1980. 50.00x (Pub. by Brit Inst Radiology). State Mutual Bk.

Planning of Subsurface Use. B. Jansson & T. Winqvist. 1978. text ed. 42.00 (ISBN 0-08-022689-2). Pergamon.

Planning of Water Quality Systems. William J. Whipple. LC 76-47336. 1977. 23.95 (ISBN 0-669-01144-4). Lexington Bks.

Planning or Prevention: The New Face of Family Planning. Peter Diggory & John McEwan. (Ideas in Progress Ser.). 1978. 11.95 (ISBN 0-7145-2552-9, Pub. by M Boyars); pap. 5.95 (ISBN 0-7145-2553-7). Merrimack Bk Serv.

Planning Physical Education & Athletic Facilities in Schools. Kenneth A. Penman. LC 76-18134. 1977. text ed. 21.95 (ISBN 0-471-67915-1). Wiley.

Planning, Politics, & the Public Interest. Ed. by Waller Goldstein. LC 78-1720. 1978. 15.00x (ISBN 0-231-04538-7). Columbia U Pr.

Planning Problems in the USSR: The Contribution of Mathematical Economics to Their Solution, 1960-1971. M. Ellman. LC 73-75861. (Department of Applied Economics Monographs: No. 24). (Illus.). 240p. 1973. 35.50 (ISBN 0-521-20249-3). Cambridge U Pr.

Planning Profits in the Food and Lodging Industry. Peter Dukas. 180p. 1976. 12.95 (ISBN 0-8436-2080-3). CBI Pub.

Planning, Programming, Budgeting Systems in Academic Libraries: An Exploratory Study of PPBS in University Libraries Having Membership in the Association of Research Libraries. Harold C. Young. LC 76-10667. 180p. 1976. 26.00 (ISBN 0-8103-0264-0). Gale.

Planning Small-Scale Research: A Practical Guide for Teachers & Students. rev. ed. K. M. Evans. (Exploring Education Ser.). 1978. pap. text ed. 5.00x (ISBN 0-85633-149-X, NFER). Humanities.

Planning Smaller Cities. Herrington J. Bryce. LC 78-14154. (Urban Round Table Ser.: No. 1). 1979. 23.95 (ISBN 0-669-02680-8). Lexington Bks.

Planning Strategies for Evangelism. pap. 3.00 (ISBN 0-912552-15-8). MARC.

Planning Teacher Demand & Supply. (Fundamentals of Educational Planning Ser.: No. 27). 1979. pap. 4.75 (ISBN 92-803-1079-8, U899, UNESCO). Unipub.

Planning, Teaching & Evaluating: A Competency Approach. Clifford H. Edwards et al. LC 76-41903. 1977. 18.95 (ISBN 0-88229-204-8). Nelson-Hall.

Planning the Development of Universities - 2: Analysis of the Questionnaire. (Illus.). 267p. (Orig.). 1974. pap. 15.75 (ISBN 92-803-1058-5, U458, UNESCO). Unipub.

Planning the Development of Universities -3. 454p. (Orig.). 1975. pap. 20.75 (ISBN 92-803-1068-2, U459, UNESCO); Vol. 4. pap. 18.50 (ISBN 0-685-53183-X). Unipub.

Planning the Future of Saudi Arabia: A Model for Achieving National Priorities. Robert D. Crane. LC 78-5730. (Praeger Special Studies). 1978. 28.95 (ISBN 0-03-042276-0). Praeger.

Planning the Health Sector: The Tanzanian Experience. Oscar Gish. 209p. 1976. text ed. 24.50x (ISBN 0-8419-9722-5). Holmes & Meier.

Planning the Location of Schools: An Instrument of Educational Policy. (Illus.). 1977. pap. 20.75 (ISBN 92-803-1071-2, U465, UNESCO). Unipub.

Planning the Post-Industrial City. Harvey S. Perloff. LC 80-67753. (Illus.). 328p. 1980. 23.95 (ISBN 0-918286-21-2). Planners Pr.

Planning the Purchase & Use of Data Base Management Systems. 1981. pap. 5.00 (ISBN 0-918734-29-0). Reymont.

Planning the School Curriculum. (Fundamentals of Educational Planning: No. 23). 1977. pap. 4.75 (ISBN 92-803-1075-5, U467, UNESCO). Unipub.

Planning the Social Services. Nicholas Falk & James Lee. 1978. 17.95 (ISBN 0-347-01135-7, 00559-2, Pub. by Saxon Hse England). Lexington Bks.

Planning the Total Landscape: A Guide to Intelligent Land Use. Julius G. Fabos. (Illus.). 1979. lib. bdg. 20.00x (ISBN 0-89158-172-3). Westview.

Planning Theory. Andreas Faludi. LC 73-11236. 312p. 1973. 28.00 (ISBN 0-08-017741-7); pap. 12.75 (ISBN 0-08-017756-5). Pergamon.

Planning to Stay Together. Ed. by Paul A. Wellington. 1980. pap. 4.00 (ISBN 0-8309-0308-9). Herald Hse.

Planning Useful Evaluations: Evaluability Assessment. Leonard Rutman. LC 79-24116. (Sage Library of Social Research: Vol. 96). (Illus.). 1980. 18.00x (ISBN 0-8039-1252-8); pap. 8.95x (ISBN 0-8039-1253-6). Sage.

Planning Without Prices. Bernard Siegan. 160p. 1977. 16.95 (ISBN 0-669-00247-X). Lexington Bks.

Planning Your Future: A Workbook for Personal Goal Setting. George A. Ford & Gordon L. Lippitt. LC 76-11357. Orig. Title: Life Planning Workbook. 50p. 1976. 8.50 (ISBN 0-88390-120-X). Univ Assocs.

Planning Your Garden. Walter S. Brett. (Illus.). 14.95x o.p. (ISBN 0-392-04148-0, SpS). Soccer.

Planning Your New Home. Sunset Editors. LC 67-15741. (Illus.). 128p. 1967. pap. 2.95 o.p. (ISBN 0-376-01283-8, Sunset Bks.). Sunset-Lane.

Planning Your Office. Geoffrey Slamon. (Design Centre Bks.). 1978. 15.95 o.p. (ISBN 0-8256-3100-9); pap. 8.95 o.p. (ISBN 0-685-88353-1). Music Sales.

Plans. Yaedi Ignatow. 80p. 1981. pap. 4.95 (ISBN 0-935296-19-0). Sheep Meadow.

Plans Book. Henry D. Norris. LC 77-86203. 1977. pap. 12.50 (ISBN 0-930560-01-9, Pub. by Two Continents). Hippocrene Bks.

Plans for America. Bill Harvey. Ed. by Jan Bertisch & Yana Bragg. (Illus.). (gr. 7-12). 1977. pap. 3.00 o.p. (ISBN 0-918538-03-3). Ourobourus.

Plans of Education, with Remarks on the Systems of Other Writers: In a Series of Letters Between Mrs. Darnford & Her Friends. Clara Reeve. (Feminist Controversy in England, 1788-1810 Ser.). 1974. lib. bdg. 50.00 (ISBN 0-8240-0877-4). Garland Pub.

Plans of War: The General Staff & British Military Strategy c. 1900-1916. John Gooch. LC 74-511. 348p. 1974. 21.95 (ISBN 0-470-31321-8). Halsted Pr.

Plant a Tree: A Working Guide to Re-Greening America. Michael A. Weiner. LC 73-19048. (Illus.). 224p. 1975. 15.95 o.s.i. (ISBN 0-02-625660-6). Macmillan.

Plant a Tree Book: A Working Guide to Re-Greening America. Michael A. Weiner. (Illus.). 224p. 1975. pap. 6.95 o.s.i. (ISBN 0-02-063780-2, Collier). Macmillan.

Plant Anatomy. 2nd ed. Abraham Fahn. LC 73-5808. 616p. 1974. text ed. 45.00 o.p. (ISBN 0-08-017241-5); pap. text ed. 18.00 (ISBN 0-08-017242-3). Pergamon.

Plant & Animal Products in the U. S. Food System. Committtee on Animal Production. 1978. pap. 10.75 (ISBN 0-309-02769-1). Natl Acad Pr.

Plant Biology: A Concise Introduction. 4th ed. Ross H. Arnett & George F. Bazinet. LC 76-26531. (Illus.). 1977. text ed. 15.95 (ISBN 0-8016-0316-1). Mosby.

Plant Biology Lab Manual for a One Semester Course Form & Function. Jean Gerrath et al. 144p. 1980. pap. text ed. 6.95 (ISBN 0-8403-2272-0). Kendall-Hunt.

Plant Breeding & Genetics in Horticulture. C. North. LC 79-10436. 1980. pap. 16.95 (ISBN 0-470-26661-9). Halsted Pr.

Plant Breeding II. Ed. by Kenneth J. Frey. 1981. 30.00 (ISBN 0-8138-1550-9). Iowa St U Pr.

Plant Cell. 2nd ed. William A. Jensen. 1970. pap. 7.95x (ISBN 0-534-00273-0). Wadsworth Pub.

Plant Cell Biology: An Ultrastructural Approach. B. E. Gunning & M. Steer. LC 75-13749. 1975. 10.50x o.p. (ISBN 0-8448-0669-2). Crane-Russak Co.

Plant Cell Structure & Metabolism. J. L. Hall et al. LC 73-85204. (Illus.). 360p. (Orig.). 1974. pap. text ed. 18.95x (ISBN 0-582-44119-6). Longman.

Plant Conversion Potential to Fuel Alcohol Production. Davy McKee Corp. 125p. 1981. pap. 24.50 (ISBN 0-89934-095-4). Solar Energy Info.

Plant Disease. Russell B. Stevens. (Illus.). 459p. 1974. 22.95 (ISBN 0-8260-8503-2). Wiley.

Plant Disease: An Advanced Treatise, Vol. 3: How Plants Suffer from Disease. Ed. by James G. Horsfall & Ellis B. Cowling. 1979. 48.50 (ISBN 0-12-356403-4); by subscription 42.00 (ISBN 0-686-66289-X). Acad Pr.

Plant Disease Control. Eric Sharvelle. (Illus.). 1979. text ed. 28.00 (ISBN 0-87055-335-6). AVI.

Plant Disease Epidemiology. Ed. by P. R. Scott & A. Bainbridge. LC 78-15056. 1978. 30.95 (ISBN 0-470-26505-1). Halsted Pr.

Plant Diseases & Vectors: Ecology & Epidemiology. Karl Maramorosch & Kerry Harris. 1981. price not set (ISBN 0-12-470240-6). Acad Pr.

Plant Diseases Attributed to Botryodiplodia Theobromae Pat. E. Punithalingham. (Bibliotheca Mycologica: No. 71). (Illus.). 200p. 1980. lib. bdg. 20.00 (ISBN 3-7682-1256-4). Lubrecht & Cramer.

Plant Diseases: Epidemics & Control. J. E. Van Der Plank. 1964. 37.50 (ISBN 0-12-711450-5). Acad Pr.

Plant Diversity: An Evolutionary Approach. Robert F. Scagel et al. 1969. 19.95x o.p. (ISBN 0-534-00677-9). Wadsworth Pub.

Plant Evolution Through Amphiploidy & Autoploidy, with Examples from the Madiinae. Jens Clausen. (Experimental Studies on the Nature of Species: Vol. 2). (Illus.). 564p. 1945. pap. 7.25 (ISBN 0-87279-575-6). Carnegie Inst.

Plant Form Studies: Design Characteristics of Plant Materials. Gary O. Robinette. LC 80-68358. (Illus.). 244p. pap. text ed. 19.50 (ISBN 0-918436-12-5). Environ Des VA.

Plant Growth Substances in Agriculture. Robert J. Weaver. LC 71-166964. (Plant Science Ser.). (Illus.). 1972. text ed. 39.95x (ISBN 0-7167-0824-8). W H Freeman.

Plant Growth Substances, Nineteen Seventy-Nine: Proceedings. Ed. by F. Skoog. (Proceedings in Life Sciences Ser.). (Illus.). 580p. 1981. 57.90 (ISBN 0-387-10182-9). Springer-Verlag.

Plant Growth Substances, 1970: Proceedings. International Conference on Plant Growth Substances, 7th, Canberra, 1970. Ed. by D. J. Carr. LC 72-80291. (Illus.). 849p. 1972. pap. 27.90 (ISBN 0-387-05850-8). Springer-Verlag.

Plant Hunters in the Andes. 2nd rev. & enl. ed. T. Harper Goodspeed. 1961. 21.50x (ISBN 0-520-00495-7). U of Cal Pr.

Plant Kingdom. 4th ed. Harold C. Bold & C. L. Hundell. (Foundation of Modern Biology Ser.). (Illus.). 1977. pap. 12.95 (ISBN 0-13-680389-X). P-H.

Plant Kingdom. Jonathan Rutland. LC 76-13651. (Modern Knowledge Library). (Illus.). 48p. (gr. 5 up). 1976. 3.95 o.p. (ISBN 0-531-02445-8); PLB 5.90 o.p. (ISBN 0-531-01194-1). Watts.

Plant Layout for Chemical Engineers. J. C. Mecklenburgh. 1974. 18.95x (ISBN 0-249-44125-X). Intl Ideas.

Plant Life of the Pacific World. Elmer D. Merrill. (Illus.). 1945. 12.50x (ISBN 0-686-51288-X). Elliots Bks.

Plant Life of the Pacific World. Elmer D. Merrill. LC 80-51195. (Illus.). 312p. 1981. Repr. of 1945 ed. 13.50 (ISBN 0-8048-1370-1). C E Tuttle.

Plant Medicine & Folklore. Mildred Fielder. 1977. pap. 4.95 (ISBN 0-87691-228-5). Winchester Pr.

Plant Metabolism. Gerhard Richter. 450p. 1980. 60.95x (ISBN 0-85664-955-4, Pub. by Croom Helm England). State Mutual Bk.

Plant Metabolism. 2nd ed. H. E. Street & W. Cockburn. LC 76-174629. 332p. 1972. 25.00 (ISBN 0-08-016752-7); pap. 13.25 (ISBN 0-08-016753-5). Pergamon.

Plant Mutations & Radiations: Genetics for the Layman. F. R. Paulsen. 1960. 6.50 (ISBN 0-911268-25-1). Rogers Bk.

Plant Names. Thomas Lindsay. LC 75-16423. viii, 93p. 1976. Repr. of 1923 ed. 18.00 (ISBN 0-8103-4160-3). Gale.

Plant Nutrient Supply & Movement. (Technical Reports: No. 48). 1965. pap. 8.75 (ISBN 92-0-115265-5, IAEA). Unipub.

Plant Organelles. Ed. by E. Reid. LC 79-40730. (Methodological Surveys in Biochemistry Ser.: Vol. 9). 1979. 59.95 (ISBN 0-470-26810-7). Halsted Pr.

Plant Pathology. 2nd ed. George N. Agrios. 1978. 23.95 (ISBN 0-12-044560-3). Acad Pr.

Plant Pathology & Plant Pathogens. C. H. Dickinson & J. A. Lucas. LC 77-8689. (Basic Microbiology Ser.: Vol. 6). 1977. pap. 11.95 (ISBN 0-470-99212-3). Halsted Pr.

Plant People. Dale Carlson. (Triumph Books). (Illus.). (gr. 4 up). 1977. PLB 6.90 s&l (ISBN 0-531-00380-9). Watts.

Plant Physiology. S. N. Pandey & B. K. Sinha. 1978. 17.50 (ISBN 0-7069-0720-5, Pub. by Vikas India). Advent Bk.

Plant Physiology. 2nd ed. Ed. by Frank B. Salisbury & Cleon W. Ross. 1978. text ed. 22.95x (ISBN 0-534-00562-4). Wadsworth Pub.

Plant Physiology: A Treatise, 6 vols. Ed. by F. C. Steward. Incl. Vol. 1A. Cellular Organization & Respiration. 1960. 41.00 (ISBN 0-12-668601-7); Vol. 1B. Photosynthesis & Chemosynthesis. 1960. 40.50 (ISBN 0-12-668641-6); Vol. 2. Plants in Relation to Water & Solutes. 1959. 59.00 (ISBN 0-12-668602-5); Vol. 3. Inorganic Nutrition of Plants. 1963. 59.00 (ISBN 0-12-668603-3); Vol. 4A. Metabolism: Organic Nutrition & Nitrogen Metabolism. 1965. 59.00 (ISBN 0-12-668604-1); Vol. 4B. Metabolism: Intermediary Metabolism & Pathology. 1966. 59.00 o.s.i. (ISBN 0-12-668644-0); Vol. 5A. Analysis of Growth: Behavior of Plants & Their Organs. 1969. 59.00 (ISBN 0-12-668605-X); Vol. 5B. Analysis of Growth: The Responses of Cells & Tissues in Culture. 1969. 47.00 (ISBN 0-12-668645-9); Vol. 6A. Physiology of Development: Plants & Their Reproduction. 1972. 59.00 (ISBN 0-12-668606-8); Vol. 6B. Physiology of Development: the Hormones. 1972. 48.00 (ISBN 0-12-668646-7); Vol. 6C. From Seeds to Sexuality. 1972. 47.00 (ISBN 0-12-668656-4). Set. 897.80 (ISBN 0-685-23211-5). Acad Pr.

Plant Physiology in Relation to Horticulture. J. K. Bleasdale. 1978. text ed. 11.00 (ISBN 0-87055-239-2). AVI.

Plant Physiology Laboratory Manual. Cleon Ross. 1974. 10.95x (ISBN 0-534-00351-6). Wadsworth Pub.

Plant Propagation. John P. Mahlstede & E. S. Haber. LC 57-5924. 1957. 23.50 (ISBN 0-471-56364-1). Wiley.

Plant Propagation & Cultivation. William A. Hutchinson. (Illus.). 1980. pap. text ed. 18.00 (ISBN 0-87055-340-2). AVI.

Plant Propagation in Pictures. Adrienne Oldale & Peter Oldale. LC 75-4062. (Illus.). 96p. 1975. 14.95 (ISBN 0-7153-6875-3). David & Charles.

Plant Propagation Laboratory Manual. 3rd rev. ed. Thomas A. Fretz et al. 1979. text ed. 9.95 (ISBN 0-8087-0668-3). Burgess.

Plant Propagation Practices. James S. Wells. (Illus.). 1955. 12.95 (ISBN 0-02-625900-1). Macmillan.

Plant Propagation: Principles & Practices. 3rd ed. Dale E. Kester & Hudson T. Hartmann. (Illus.). 704p. 1975. ref. ed. 22.95 (ISBN 0-13-680991-X). P-H.

Plant Protection Discipline: Problems. Webster H. Sill, Jr. LC 78-59171. 1978. text ed. 25.00x (ISBN 0-470-26443-8). Allanheld.

Plant Proteins. LC 77-30099. (Nottingham Easter Schools Ser.). 1978. text ed. 54.95 (ISBN 0-408-70918-9). Butterworths.

Plant Psysiology. Irwin P. Ting. LC 80-16448. (Illus.). 635p. 1981. text ed. 19.95 (ISBN 0-201-07406-0). A-W.

Plant Relations in Pastures. 475p. 1980. pap. 45.00 (ISBN 0-643-00264-2, CO05, CSIRO). Unipub.

Plant Root & Its Environment. Ed. by E. W. Carson, Jr. LC 72-92877. 1974. 15.00x (ISBN 0-8139-0411-0). U Pr of Va.

Plant Science. Boy Scouts of America. LC 19-600. (Illus.). 48p. (gr. 6-12). 1975. pap. 0.70x (ISBN 0-8395-3396-9, 3396). BSA.

Plant Science: An Introduction to World Crops. 2nd ed. Jules Janick et al. LC 73-13921. (Illus.). 1974. text ed. 23.95x (ISBN 0-7167-0713-6). W H Freeman.

Plant Science: Growth, Development & Utilization of Cultivated Plants. William J. Flocker & Hudson T. Hartmann. (Illus.). 688p. 1981. text ed. 25.95 (ISBN 0-13-681056-X). P-H.

Plant Sculptures: Making Miniature Indoor Topiaries. Jack Kramer. (Illus.). (gr. 3-12). 1978. 6.95 (ISBN 0-688-22144-0); PLB 6.67 (ISBN 0-688-32144-5). Morrow.

Plant Sitter. Gene Zion. (Illus.). (gr. k-3). 1972. pap. 1.50 (ISBN 0-590-08752-5, Schol Pap). Schol Bk Serv.

Plant Sociology of Alpine Tundra, Trail Ridge, Rocky Mountain National Park, Colorado. Beatrice L. Willard & Jon W. Raese. LC 79-26590. (CSM Quarterly Ser.: Vol. 74, No. 4). (Illus.). 119p. 1979. pap. 10.00x (ISBN 0-686-63162-5). Colo Sch Mines.

Plant Speciation. Verne Grant. 1971. 25.00x (ISBN 0-231-03208-0); pap. 12.50x (ISBN 0-231-08326-2). Columbia U Pr.

Plant Studies in the People's Republic of China: A Trip Report of the American Plant Studies Delegation. American Plant Studies Delegation, National Academy of Science. LC 75-13564. (Illus.). 1975. pap. 9.75 o.p. (ISBN 0-309-02348-3). Natl Acad Pr.

Plant Taxonomic Literature in Australian Libraries. 520p. 1978. pap. 31.50 (ISBN 0-643-00286-3, CO15, CSIRO). Unipub.

Plant Tissue & Cell Culture. 2nd ed. Ed. by H. E. Street. (Botanical Monographs: Vol. 11). 1978. 60.00x (ISBN 0-520-03473-2). U of Cal Pr.

Plant Virology. 2nd ed. R. E. Matthews. 1981. write for info. (ISBN 0-12-480560-4). Acad Pr.

Plant Wizard: The Life of Lue Gim Gong. Marian Murray. LC 77-119131. (Illus.). (gr. 4 up). 1970. 3.95g o.s.i. (ISBN 0-02-767750-8, CCPr). Macmillan.

Plant World. Jean Vallin. (Basic Biology in Color Ser.). (gr. 7-12). 10.95 o.p. (ISBN 0-8069-3552-9); PLB 10.79 o.p. (ISBN 0-8069-3553-7). Sterling.

Plantagenet Age. A. F. Scott. LC 75-4880. (Everyone a Witness Ser.). (Illus.). 328p. 1976. 9.95 (ISBN 0-690-01002-8, TYC-T); pap. 4.95 o.p. (ISBN 0-8152-0393-4, A-393). T Y Crowell.

Plantagenet "Rich & Beautiful..." A History of the Shire of Plantagenet, Western Australia. Rhoda Glover et al. 429p. 1980. 21.00x (ISBN 0-85564-175-4, Pub. by U of West Australia Pr Australia). Intl Schol Bk Serv.

Plantation Agriculture. 2nd rev. ed. P. P. Courtenay. 250p. 1980. lib. bdg. 30.00x (ISBN 0-86531-090-4). Westview.

Plantation Cookbook. Junior League of New Orleans. LC 72-84921. 256p. 1972. 11.95 (ISBN 0-385-01157-1). Doubleday.

Plantation South. W. Holley et al. LC 78-166955. (FDR & the Era of the New Deal Ser). 1971. Repr. of 1940 ed. lib. bdg. 15.00 (ISBN 0-306-70354-8). Da Capo.

Plantation Trilogy: Incl. Deep Summer, the Handsome Road, This Side of Glory. Gwen Bristow. LC 62-9363. 812p. 1962. 9.95 o.s.i. (ISBN 0-690-62868-4, TYC-T). T Y Crowell.

Planters & the Making of a "New South" Class, Politics, & Development in North Carolina, 1865-1900. Dwight B. Billings, Jr. LC 78-25952. xiii, 284p. 1979. 15.00x (ISBN 0-8078-1315-X). U of NC Pr.

Planters: Make Your Own Containers for Indoor & Outdoor Plants. Jack Kramer. 1977. pap. 3.95 o.p. (ISBN 0-345-25534-8). Ballantine.

Plantin Press at Antwerp: 1555-1589. Leon Vost & Jenny Voet-Griselle. 500p. (Dutch.). 1981. 250.00 ea.; Vol. 1. (ISBN 0-8390-0264-5); Vol. 2. (ISBN 0-8390-0265-3). Allanheld & Schram.

Planting by the Moon - Nineteen Eighty-One. rev. ed. Simon Best & Nick Lollerstrom. (Illus.). 128p. 1981. pap. 2.95 (ISBN 0-917086-25-2). Astro Comp Serv.

Planting Churches Cross-Culturally. David J. Hesselgrave. 1980. pap. 12.95 (ISBN 0-8010-4219-4). Baker Bk.

Planting Details. Gary O. Robinette. 200p. 1980. pap. text ed. 20.00 (ISBN 0-918436-14-1). Environ Design.

Planting of Civilization in Western Pennsylvania. Solon J. Buck & Elizabeth H. Buck. LC 39-25307. (Illus.). 1939. 20.00 (ISBN 0-910294-28-3). Brown Bk.

Plants. Ed. by Daniel B. Ward & Peter C. Pritchard. LC 78-12121. (Rare & Endangered Biota of Florida Ser.: Vol. 5). 1979. pap. 10.50 o.p. (ISBN 0-8130-0638-4). U Presses Fla.

Plants. Frits W. Went. LC 63-20048. (Life Nature Library). (Illus.). (gr. 5 up). 1963. PLB 8.97 o.p. (ISBN 0-8094-0626-8, Pub. by Time-Life). Silver.

Plants, Agriculture, & Human Society. Norman Richardson & Thomas Stubbs. LC 77-72644. 1978. pap. text ed. 9.95 (ISBN 0-8053-8215-1). Benjamin-Cummings.

Plants & Archeology. 2nd ed. Geoffrey W. Dimbleby. LC 67-23020. (Illus.). 1978. 15.00x (ISBN 0-391-00926-5). Humanities.

Plants & Civilization. 3rd ed. Herbert G. Baker. (Fundamentals of Botany Ser.). 1978. pap. text ed. 7.95x (ISBN 0-534-00575-6). Wadsworth Pub.

Plants & Flowers for Your Garden. Stanley Russell. (Illus.). 1978. 12.95 o.p. (ISBN 0-688-03332-6). Morrow.

Plants & Man on the Seychelles Coast: A Study in Historical Biogeography. Jonathan D. Sauer. (Illus.). 1967. 15.00x (ISBN 0-299-04300-2). U of Wis Pr.

Plants & People: Aboriginal Uses of Plants on Groote Eylandt. Dulcie Levitt. (Australian Institute of Aborigianl Studies). 1981. text ed. price not set (ISBN 0-391-02195-8); pap. text ed. write for info. Humanities.

Plants, & the Ecosystem. 3rd ed. W. D. Billings. 1978. pap. 7.95x (ISBN 0-534-00571-3). Wadsworth Pub.

Plants & Their Atmospheric Enviroment. J. Grace et al. (British Ecological Society Symposia Ser.). 428p. 1981. 89.95 (ISBN 0-470-27125-6). Halsted Pr.

Plants Are Some of My Favorite People. Tom Wilson. (Illus.). 96p. (Orig.). 1976. pap. 2.50 (ISBN 0-8362-0674-6). Andrews & McMeel.

Plants As Organisms, Laboratory Studies of Plant Structure & Function. Robert M. Page. 1967. 7.95x (ISBN 0-7167-0710-1); individual studies 0.50 ea.; instr's manual avail. W H Freeman.

Plants at Work. Frederick C. Steward. (gr. 10-12). 1964. pap. 7.95 (ISBN 0-201-07286-6). A-W.

Plants, Chemicals & Growth. F. C. Steward & A. D. Krikorian. 1971. text ed. 21.50 (ISBN 0-12-668662-9); pap. 8.95 (ISBN 0-12-668660-2). Acad Pr.

Plants, Food, & People. Maarten J. Chrispeels & David Sadava. LC 76-46498. (Illus.). 1977. text ed. 19.95x (ISBN 0-7167-0378-5); pap. text ed. 9.95x (ISBN 0-7167-0377-7). W H Freeman.

Plants for Dry Climates. Mary R. Duffield & Warren Jones. (Orig.). 1981. pap. 7.95 (ISBN 0-89586-042-2). H P Bks.

Plants for Ground Cover. Graham S. Thomas. 1970. 12.50 o.p. (ISBN 0-8231-6037-8). Branford.

Plants for Kids to Grow Indoors. Adele Millard. LC 75-14509. 128p. 1975. 6.95 o.p. (ISBN 0-8069-3070-5); PLB 6.69 o.p. (ISBN 0-8069-3071-3). Sterling.

Plants for Man. 2nd ed. Robert W. Schery. (Illus.). 608p. 1972. ref. ed. 25.95 (ISBN 0-13-681254-6). P-H.

Plants for the Home. Ed. by Ernest Roth. LC 77-82737. (Illus.). 1977. 7.95 (ISBN 0-8467-0370-X, Pub. by Two Continents). Hippocrene Bks.

Plants from Plants: How to Grow New Houseplants for Next to Nothing. Suzanne Crayson. LC 76-12559. (Illus.). 1976. pap. 6.95 (ISBN 0-397-01175-X). Lippincott.

Plants Give Us Many Kinds of Food. Jane B. Moncure. LC 75-29268. (Illus.). (ps-3). 1975. 5.95 (ISBN 0-913778-17-6). Childs World.

Plants in the Landscape. Carpenter et al. 1975. 18.50 (ISBN 0-7167-0778-0). Thomson Pub CA.

Plants in the Landscape. Philip L. Carpenter et al. LC 74-32292. (Illus.). 1975. text ed. 24.95x (ISBN 0-7167-0778-0). W H Freeman.

Plants in the Service of Man. Edward Hyams. LC 71-147891. (Illus.). 1972. 7.75 o.p. (ISBN 0-397-00781-7). Lippincott.

Plants in Winter. Joanna Cole. LC 73-1771. (Let's-Read-&-Find-Out Science Bk). (Illus.). (ps-3). 1973. 7.95 (ISBN 0-690-62885-4, TYC-J); PLB 7.89 (ISBN 0-690-62886-2). T Y Crowell.

Plants of Big Basin Redwooods State Park & the Northern Coastal Mountains of California. Mary B. Lozaneo et al. (Illus.). 160p. (Orig.). 1981. pap. 6.95 (ISBN 0-87842-135-1). Mountain Pr.

Plants of Quetico & the Ontario Shiels. Shan Walshe. (Illus.). 216p. 1980. 25.00 (ISBN 0-8020-3370-9); pap. 7.95 (ISBN 0-8020-3371-7). U of Toronto Pr.

Plants of Rocky Mountain National Park. rev. ed. Ruth A. Nelson. LC 80-522. 1981. pap. 6.95 (ISBN 0-87081-092-8). Colo Assoc.

Plants of Southern New Jersey. Witmer Stone. LC 72-93855. (Illus.). 944p. 1973. Repr. of 1910 ed. 30.00x o.p. (ISBN 0-88000-011-2). Quarterman.

Plants of the Bible. G. Henslow. 294p. 1981. Repr. of 1900 ed. lib. bdg. 75.00 (ISBN 0-8495-2375-3). Arden Lib.

Plants of the Bible. H. N. Moldenke & A. L. Moldenke. (Illus.). 1952. 15.50 o.p. (ISBN 0-8260-6170-2, Pub. by Wiley-Interscience). Wiley.

Plants of the World, 3 vols. H. C. De Wit. Tr. by A. J. Pomerans. LC 66-25815. 1966-69. Vol. 1. o.p.; Vol. 2. 19.95 o.p. (ISBN 0-525-18040-0); Vol. 3. o.p. Dutton.

Plants of Waterton-Glacier National Parks & the Northern Rockies. Richard J. Shaw & Danny On. Orig. Title: Plants of Waterton-Glacier National Parks. 160p. 1981. pap. 6.95 (ISBN 0-87842-137-8). Mountain Pr.

Plants, People, & Environmental Quality: Syllabus. 1977. pap. text ed. 5.55 (ISBN 0-89420-021-6, 140014); cassette recordings 70.80 (ISBN 0-89420-173-5, 140000). Natl Book.

Plants to Grow Indoors. George Sullivan. (Beginning-to-Read Bks). (Illus.). (ps). pap. 1.50 o.p. (ISBN 0-695-37114-2). Follett.

Plants We Eat. Millicent E. Selsam. (Illus.). (gr. 2-5). 1955. PLB 6.96 (ISBN 0-688-31567-4). Morrow.

Plants We Eat & Wear. H. E. Jaques. LC 74-12656. (Illus.). 192p. 1975. pap. 2.50 o.p. (ISBN 0-486-22563-1). Dover.

Planus. Blaise Cendrars. Tr. by Nina Rootes from Fr. 1979. 18.00x (ISBN 0-8464-0046-4). Beekman Pubs.

Planus. Blaise Cendrars. LC 80-9057. 220p. 1981. 12.95 (ISBN 0-8128-2816-X). Stein & Day.

Plasma & Current Instabilities in Semiconductors. J. Pozhela. Tr. by O. A. Germogenova. (International Series in the Science of the Solid State: Vol. 18). (Illus.). 314p. 1981. 54.00 (ISBN 0-08-025048-3). Pergamon.

Plasma Astrophysics. S. A. Kaplan & V. N. Tsytovich. LC 73-5785. 316p. 1974. text ed. 72.00 (ISBN 0-08-017190-7). Pergamon.

Plasma Chemistry: Volume III. Ed. by S. Veprek & M. Venugopalan. (Topics in Current Chemistry: Vol. 94). (Illus.). 160p. 1980. 42.50 (ISBN 0-387-10166-7). Springer-Verlag.

Plasma Phenomena in Gas Discharges. Raoul N. Franklin. (Oxford Engineering Science Ser.). (Illus.). 1976. 59.00x (ISBN 0-19-856113-X). Oxford U Pr.

Plasma Physics. 1965. 32.25 (ISBN 92-0-030265-3, ISP89, IAEA). Unipub.

Plasma Physics & Controlled Nuclear Fusion Research, 3 vols. (Illus.). 1977. Vol. 1. pap. 53.50 (ISBN 92-0-130077-8, IAEA); Vol. 2. pap. 54.75 (ISBN 92-0-130177-4); Vol. 3. pap. 52.50 (ISBN 92-0-130277-0). Unipub.

Plasma Physics & Controlled Nuclear Fusion Research - 1968, 2 Vols. 1968. Vol. 1. pap. 50.50 (ISBN 92-0-530168-X, IAEA); Vol. 2. pap. 43.00 (ISBN 92-0-530268-6). Unipub.

Plasma Physics & Controlled Nuclear Fusion Research - 1971, 3 vols. (Illus.). 673p. (Orig.). 1972. pap. 39.75 ea. (IAEA); Vol. 1. pap. (ISBN 92-0-030071-5); Vol. 2. pap. (ISBN 92-0-030171-1); Vol. 3. pap. (ISBN 92-0-030271-8). Unipub.

Plasma Physics & Controlled Nuclear Fusion Research - 1972: Supplement. (Illus.). 357p. (Orig.). 1973. pap. 24.25 (ISBN 92-0-139072-6, 1WFS72, IAEA). Unipub.

Plasma Physics & Controlled Nuclear Fusion Research: Nuclear Fusion, Supplement 1975. International Conference on Plasma Physics & Controlled Nuclear Fusion. (Illus.). 186p. 1976. pap. 14.50 (ISBN 92-0-139075-0, IAEA). Unipub.

Plasma Physics & Controlled Nuclear Fusion Research 1978, 2 vols. 1979. Vol. 1. pap. 92.25 (ISBN 92-0-130079-4, ISP 495-1, IAEA); Vol. 2. pap. 77.25 (ISBN 92-0-130179-0, ISP 495-2). Unipub.

Plasma Physics & Controlled Nuclear Fusion Research 1978, Vol. 3. 552p. 1980. pap. 66.00 (ISBN 92-0-130279-7, ISP 495-3, IAEA). Unipub.

Plasma Physics Controlled Nuclear Fusion Research 1974, Vol. 1. (Illus.). 710p. 1975. pap. 60.50 (ISBN 92-0-030075-8, ISP381-1, IAEA). Unipub.

Plasma State. J. L. Shohet. 1971. text ed. 22.95 (ISBN 0-12-640550-6). Acad Pr.

Plasma Transport Meeting & MHD Theory: Proceedings of a Workshop at Varenna, Italy, 12-16 Sept. 1977. T. Stringer. Ed. by R. Rozzoli. LC 78-40822. 1979. pap. text ed. 66.00 (ISBN 0-08-023426-7). Pergamon.

Plasma Wall Interaction: Proceedings of the International Symposium EUR 5782e, Kernsfoschungsanlage Julich, 1976. Commission of the European Communities. LC 77-75794. 1977. pap. 110.00 (ISBN 0-08-021989-6). Pergamon.

Plasmapheresis & Plasma Exchange, Vol. 1. T. J. Hamblin. Ed. by D. F. Horrobin. (Annual Research Reviews). 1979. 18.00 (ISBN 0-88831-065-X, Dist. by Pergamon). Eden Med Res.

Plasmapheresis & the Immunobiology of Myasthenia Gravis. Peter C. Dau. (Illus.). 1979. 35.00x (ISBN 0-89289-404-0). HM Prof Med Div.

Plasmids. Paul Broda. LC 79-10665. (Illus.). 1979. text ed. 19.95x (ISBN 0-7167-1111-7). W H Freeman.

Plaster Art: Step by Step. Dorothy S. Allen. Ed. by Tom Cole. LC 80-70317. (Illus.). 130p. (Orig.). (gr. 5). 1981. 15.95 (ISBN 0-686-28860-2); pap. 12.95 (ISBN 0-686-28861-0). Dots Pubns.

Plaster Mold & Model Making. Charles Chaney & Stanley Skee. 144p. 1981. Repr. of 1973 ed. text ed. write for info. (ISBN 0-89874-282-X). Krieger.

Plaster Sinners. Colin Watson. LC 80-1989. (Crime Club Ser.). 192p. 1981. 9.95 (ISBN 0-385-17338-5). Doubleday.

Plastering. 3rd ed. J. B. Taylor. (Illus.). 257p. 1980. 27.50x (ISBN 0-7114-5588-0). Intl Ideas.

Plastering: A Practical Handbook. 3rd ed. J. B. Taylor. (Illus.). 1980. 27.50x. Intl Ideas.

Plastic Age. Ed. by Robert Sklar. LC 70-104698. (American Culture Ser). 386p. 1970. 8.95 (ISBN 0-8076-0571-9); pap. 4.95 (ISBN 0-8076-0570-0). Braziller.

Plastic Age: A Novel. Percy Marks. LC 80-17959. (Lost American Fiction Ser.). 352p. 1980. Repr. of 1924 ed. 12.95 (ISBN 0-8093-0984-X). S Ill U Pr.

Plastic Analysis of Concrete Frames: With Particular Reference to Limit States Des. M. Tichy & J. Rakosnik. Tr. by Dagmar et al from Czech. (Illus.). 320p. 1977. text ed. 35.00x (ISBN 0-569-08199-8, Pub. by Collets England). Scholium Intl.

Plastic & Reconstructive Surgery. 2nd ed. Lars M. Vistnes et al. Ed. by Donald R. Laub & Richard F. Ott. (Medical Examination Review Ser.: Vol. 27). 1977. spiral bdg. 19.50 (ISBN 0-87488-129-3). Med Exam.

Plastic & Reconstructive Surgery of the Face: Cosmetic Surgery. Frank W. Pirruccello. (Illus.). 200p. 1981. write for info. (6891-1). Williams & Wilkins.

Plastic Design in Steel-A Guide & Commentary. Compiled by American Society of Civil Engineers. (ASCE Manual & Report of Energy Practice Ser.: No. 41). 352p. 1971. pap. text ed. 15.00 (ISBN 0-87262-217-7). Am Soc Civil Eng.

Plastic Design of Frames, 2 vols. John Baker & J. Heyman. Incl. Vol. 1. Fundamentals. 32.95 (ISBN 0-521-07517-3); pap. 15.95 (ISBN 0-521-29778-8); Vol. 2. Applications. 33.95 (ISBN 0-521-07984-5). LC 69-19370. (Illus.). 1969-1971. Cambridge U Pr.

Plastic Design of Steel Frames. Lynn S. Beedle. LC 58-13454. 1958. 34.50 (ISBN 0-471-06171-9, Pub by Wiley-Interscience). Wiley.

Plastic Films. J. H. Briston & L. L. Katan. LC 74-2295. 1974. 30.95 (ISBN 0-470-10472-4). Halsted Pr.

Plastic-Packed Trickling Filters. new ed. Sarner. 1980. text ed. 12.50 (ISBN 0-250-40371-4, Butterworths). Ann Arbor Science.

Plastic Surgery & Burn Treatments. E. S. Macallan & Ian T. Jackson. (Modern Practical Nursing Ser.: No. 6). (Illus.). 159p. 1971. pap. 9.95x (ISBN 0-686-65687-3). Intl Ideas.

Plastic Surgery of the Abdomen. Jean S. Elbaz & G. Flageul. Tr. by William T. Keavy. LC 79-84907. (Illus.). 120p. 1979. 31.75 (ISBN 0-89352-036-5). Masson Pub.

Plastic Surgery of the Hand & Pulp. Raymond Vilain & Jacques Michon. LC 78-61477. (Illus.). 184p. 1979. 31.25 (ISBN 0-89352-037-3). Masson Pub.

Plastic Surgery of the Orbit & Eyelids. Paul A. Tessier. Tr. by S. Anthony Wolfe. (Illus.). 320p. 1980. 40.00 (ISBN 0-89352-041-1). Masson Pub.

Plastic Surgery: Operative Surgery Ser. 3rd ed. R. M. McCormack & J. Watson. LC 79-40787. (Illus.). 1979. 160.00 (ISBN 0-407-00637-0). Butterworths.

Plastic Technology, Basic Materials & Processes: Basic Materials & Processes. Robert S. Swanson. (gr. 11-12). 1965. text ed. 14.64 (ISBN 0-87345-483-9). McKnight.

Plastic Theory of Structures: In SI-Metric Units. 2nd ed. M. R. Horne. 1979. text ed. 19.50 (ISBN 0-08-022737-6); pap. text ed. 23.00 (ISBN 0-08-022738-4). Pergamon.

Plasticity: Proceedings, Symposium on Naval Structural Mechanics - 2nd - Brown Univ. - 1960. Ed. by E. H. Lee & P. S. Symonds. 1960. 17.00 o.p. (ISBN 0-08-009459-7). Pergamon.

Plastics. John Briston. LC 75-19357. (Pegasus Books: No. 23). 1969. 7.50x (ISBN 0-234-77186-0). Intl Pubns Serv.

Plastics. Dwight W. Cope & Lee E. Schoude. LC 77-21618. (Illus.). 1977. text ed. 4.80 (ISBN 0-87006-239-5). Goodheart.

Plastics. 6th ed. J. Harry Dubois. 480p. 1981. text ed. 32.00 (ISBN 0-442-26263-9). Van Nos Reinhold.

Plastics. Lynn Hahn & James Hahn. LC 73-21944. (First Bks). (Illus.). 96p. (gr. 4-7). 1974. PLB 4.90 o.p. (ISBN 0-531-02702-3). Watts.

Plastics. McKnight Staff Members & Wilbur R. Miller. LC 78-53391. (Basic Industrial Arts Ser.). (Illus.). 1978. 6.00 (ISBN 0-87345-796-X); softbound 4.48 (ISBN 0-87345-788-9). McKnight.

Plastics & Rubbers: World Sources of Information. E. R. Yescombe. 1976. 79.20x (ISBN 0-85334-675-5). Intl Ideas.

Plastics As a Metal Substitute, P-007r. rev. ed. 69p. 1976. 500.00 (ISBN 0-89336-134-8). BCC.

Plastics for Schools: Applied Polymer Science. Peter J. Clarke. 191p. (gr. 9 up). 1973. pap. 9.95 (ISBN 0-263-05380-6). Transatlantic.

Plastics History, U. S. A. J. Harry DuBois. LC 79-156480. (Illus.). 1972. 23.95 (ISBN 0-8436-1203-7). CBI Pub.

Plastics in Aircraft P-059: How? Where? 1980. cancelled (ISBN 0-89336-260-3). BCC.

Plastics in Building Illumination. National Academy Of Sciences. 1958. pap. 3.00 o.p. (ISBN 0-309-00114-5). Natl Acad Pr.

Plastics in Food Packaging P-034. BCC Staff. 1980. 975.00 (ISBN 0-89336-163-1). BCC.

Plastics Industry Safety Handbook. Society of the Plastics Industry. Ed. by D. V. Rosato & John R. Lawrence. LC 72-91982. 1973. 17.95 (ISBN 0-8436-1207-X). CBI Pub.

Plastics Manufacturing Handbook & Buyers Guide. Ed. by Plastics Technology Editors. 250p. (Annual). Date not set. pap. 22.95x (ISBN 0-89047-049-9). Herman Pub.

Plastics Materials. 3rd ed. John A. Brydson. 744p. 1975. 49.50 (ISBN 0-88275-288-X). Krieger.

Plastics Technology. Robert V. Milby. (Illus.). 576p. 1973. text ed. 22.95x (ISBN 0-07-041918-3, G); instructor's manual 3.00 (ISBN 0-07-041919-1). McGraw.

Plastics Technology: Theory, Design & Manufacture. W. J. Patton. (Illus.). 1976. 17.95 o.p. (ISBN 0-87909-635-7). Reston.

Plastics Vs. Other Pipes, P-043R. Business Communications Co. 1980. 750.00 (ISBN 0-89336-270-0). BCC.

Plate Glass. limited ed. John Kay. 1980. 2.00 (ISBN 0-917554-17-5). Maelstrom.

Plate Inspection Programme, PISC: November, 1979. Nuclear Energy Agency & Organization for Economic Cooperation & Development. (Illus.). 78p. (Orig.). 1980. pap. text ed. 7.50x (ISBN 92-64-12028-9, 66 80 02 1). OECD.

Plate Tectonics & Crustal Evolution. K. C. Condie. LC 75-4690. 35.00 (ISBN 0-08-019594-6). Pergamon.

Plate Tectonics & Geomagnetic Reversals. Ed. by Allan Cox. LC 73-4323. (Geology Ser.). (Illus.). 1973. text ed. 33.95x (ISBN 0-7167-0259-2); pap. text ed. 21.95x (ISBN 0-7167-0258-4). W H Freeman.

Plateau Tonga of Northern Rhodesia. Elizabeth Colson. (Rhodes Livingston Inst. Publications). 1970. text ed. 8.75x o.p. (ISBN 0-7190-1011-X). Humanities.

Platelets: A Multidisciplinary Approach. Ed. by Giovanni De Gaetano & Silvio Garattini. LC 78-66352. (Monographs of the Mario Negri Institute for Pharmacological Research). 1978. 43.00 (ISBN 0-89004-252-7). Raven.

Platelets & Prostaglandins in Cardiovascular Disease. Ed. by Jawahar Mehta & Paulette Mehta. 300p. 1981. write for info. (ISBN 0-87993-089-6). Futura Pub.

Platelets: Cellular Response Mechanisms & Their Biological Significance: Proceedings. EMBO Workshop, Weizmann Institute of Science, Rehovot, Israel, 1980 et al. 340p. 1980. 52.50 (ISBN 0-471-27896-3, Pub. by Wiley-Interscience). Wiley.

Plates & Shells with Cracks: A Collection of Stress Intensity Factor Solutions for Cracks in Plates & Shells. Ed. by G. C. Sih. (Mechanics of Fracture Ser.: No. 3). 352p. 1976. 62.50x (ISBN 90-286-0146-5). Sijthoff & Noordhoff.

Platform Sutra of the Sixth Patriarch. Tr. by Philip B. Yampolsky. LC 67-11847. (Records of Civilization, Studies & Sources: No. 76). 1967. 18.00x (ISBN 0-231-02994-2); pap. 10.00x (ISBN 0-231-08361-0). Columbia U Pr.

Platform Tennis. Bob Callaway & Michael Hughes. 1979. pap. 4.95 o.p. (ISBN 0-397-01198-9). Lippincott.

Platform Tennis. Bob Callaway & Michael Hughes. (Illus.). 1977. 9.95 o.s.i. (ISBN 0-397-01183-0). Lippincott.

Platicas: Conversational Spanish. Marta Andrews et al. LC 80-84024. 304p. 1981. pap. text ed. 11.95 (ISBN 0-8403-2328-X). Kendall-Hunt.

Plating on Plastics. rev. 2nd ed. G. Mueller. (Illus.). 206p. 1971. 27.50x (ISBN 0-85218-038-1). Intl Pubns Serv.

Platinum-Group Metals: Medical & Biological Effects, Environmental Pollutants. 1977. pap. 9.75 (ISBN 0-309-02640-7). Natl Acad Pr.

Platinum Print. John Hafey & Tom Shillea. LC 79-55710. (Illus.). 1979. (Orig.). 1979. pap. 14.95 (ISBN 0-89938-000-X). Graph Arts Res RIT.

Plato. J. C. Gosling. (Arguments of the Philosophers Ser). 1973. 21.00x (ISBN 0-7100-7664-9). Routledge & Kegan.

Plato. William Sahakian & Mabel Sahakian. (World Leaders Ser.: No. 66). 1977. lib. bdg. 9.95 (ISBN 0-8057-7690-7). Twayne.

Plato. Eric Voegelin. LC 57-11670. 1966. pap. text ed. 6.95 (ISBN 0-8071-0102-8). La State U Pr.

Plato & Modern Morality. Pamela Huby. 135p. 1972. text ed. 6.25x (ISBN 0-333-12053-1). Humanities.

Plato & Parmenides: Way of Truth & Plato's Parmenides. Plato. Tr. by Francis M. Cornford. 1957. pap. 5.95 (ISBN 0-672-60297-0, LLA102). Bobbs.

Plato & the Metaphysics of the State. Allan Rightridge. (Most Meaningful Classics in World Culture). (Illus.). 108p. 1981. 43.75 (ISBN 0-89266-297-2). Am Classical Coll Pr.

Plato: His Life & Teaching. W. Norman Pittenger. LC 76-150375. (Biography Ser). (gr. 7 up). 1971. PLB 5.90 o.p. (ISBN 0-531-00964-5). Watts.

Plato on Punishment. Mary M. Mackenzie. 272p. 1981. 22.50x (ISBN 0-520-04169-0). U of Cal Pr.

Plato: Protagoras. Plato. Tr. by C. C. Taylor. (Clarendon Plato Ser.). 1976. 22.00x (ISBN 0-19-872045-9); pap. 11.50 o.p. (ISBN 0-19-872088-2). Oxford U Pr.

Plato: Selections. Raphael Demos. 1927. pap. text ed. 6.95 (ISBN 0-684-14321-6, ScribC). Scribner.

Plato: The Written & Unwritten Doctrines. J. N. Findlay. (International Library of Philosophy & Scientific Method). 350p. 1974. text ed. 30.00x (ISBN 0-391-00334-8). Humanities.

Plato: Theaetetus. (Clarendon Plato Ser.). 272p. 1974. pap. 16.95x (ISBN 0-19-872083-1). Oxford U Pr.

Plato to Alexander Pope: Backgrounds of Modern Criticism. Walter Sutton & Vivian Sutton. LC 66-12945. 1966. pap. text ed. 8.95x (ISBN 0-672-63084-2). Irvington.

Plato, Utilitarianism & Education. Robin Barrow. (International Library of the Philosophy of Education Ser.). 1975. 20.00x (ISBN 0-7100-8044-1). Routledge & Kegan.

Platonic Myth & Platonic Writing. Robert Zaslavsky. LC 80-5563. 306p. 1981. lib. bdg. 20.50 (ISBN 0-8191-1381-6); pap. text ed. 11.50 (ISBN 0-8191-1382-4). U Pr of Amer.

Platonic Studies. 2nd ed. Gregory Vlastos. LC 80-8732. 520p. 1981. 35.00x; pap. 12.50. Princeton U Pr.

Platonis Sophista: Recentsuit, Prolegomenis et Commentariis Instruxit. Otto Apelt. Ed. by Leonardo Taran. LC 78-66612. (Ancent Philosophy Ser.: Vol. 1). 225p. lib. bdg. 20.00 (ISBN 0-8240-9611-8). Garland Pub.

Platonism of Philo Judaeus. Thomas H. Billings. Ed. by Leonardo Taran. LC 78-66560. (Ancient Philosophy Ser.: Vol. 3). 117p. 1979. lib. bdg. 13.00 (ISBN 0-8240-9608-8). Garland Pub.

Platonism of Plutarch & Selected Papers. Roger M. Jones. Ed. by Leonardo Taran. LC 78-66589. (Ancient Philosophy Ser.). 250p. 1980. lib. bdg. 24.00 (ISBN 0-8240-9593-6). Garland Pub.

Platonismus und hellenistische Philosophie. Hans Joachim Kraemer. 368p. 1971. 60.60x (ISBN 3-11-003643-6). De Gruyter.

Platons Ideenlehre. Gottfried Martin. LC 72-81562. 1973. 41.75x (ISBN 3-1100-4135-9). De Gruyter.

Plato's Analytic Method. Kenneth M. Sayre. LC 69-15496. 1969. 12.50x (ISBN 0-226-73555-9). U of Chicago Pr.

Plato's Cosmology: The Timaeus of Plato. Plato. Tr. by Francis M. Cornford. LC 57-4253. 1957. pap. 7.95 (ISBN 0-672-60296-2, LLA101). Bobbs.

Plato's Dialogue on Friendship: An Interpretation of the "Lysis," with a New Translation. David Bolotin. LC 79-4041. 1979. 15.00x (ISBN 0-8014-1227-7). Cornell U Pr.

Plato's Epistemology & Related Logical Problems. Gwynneth Matthews. (Selections from Philosophers Ser.). 263p. 1972. text ed. 15.00x (ISBN 0-391-00260-0); pap. text ed. 7.25x (ISBN 0-571-09909-2). Humanities.

Plato's Moral Theory: The Early & Middle Dialogues. Terence Irwin. 1979. pap. 13.50x (ISBN 0-19-824614-5). Oxford U Pr.

Plato's Phaedo. Plato. Tr. by R. S. Bluck. 1959. pap. 5.50 (ISBN 0-672-60308-X, LLA110). Bobbs.

Plato's Philosophy of History. Daniel A. Dombrowski. LC 80-5853. 225p. 1981. lib. bdg. 17.75 (ISBN 0-8191-1356-5); pap. text ed. 9.50 (ISBN 0-8191-1357-3). U Pr of Amer.

Plato's Republic. Plato. Tr. by Benjamin Jowett. (Classics Ser). (gr. 11 up). 1968. pap. 1.95 (ISBN 0-8049-0172-4, CL-172). Airmont.

Plato's Republic. Ivor A. Richards. (Orig.). 23.95 (ISBN 0-521-05965-8); pap. 6.50x (ISBN 0-521-09359-7). Cambridge U Pr.

Plato's Theory of Knowledge. Francis Cornford. (International Library of Psychology, Philosophy & Scientific Method). 1967. text ed. 21.00x (ISBN 0-7100-3119-X). Humanities.

Plato's Theory of Knowledge: The Theaetetus & the Sophist of Plato. Plato. Tr. by Francis M. Cornford. LC 57-4254. 1957. pap. 6.95 (ISBN 0-672-60294-6, LLA100). Bobbs.

Plato's Thought. G. M. Grube. Ed. by Donald J. Zeyl. 240p. 1980. 18.50 (ISBN 0-915144-79-4); pap. text ed. 7.95 (ISBN 0-915144-80-8). Hackett Pub.

Plattertales. Daniel R. Burow. Incl. Bushy-Tailed Helper (ISBN 0-570-07021-X, 56-1162); Say & Do Thanks (ISBN 0-570-07022-8, 56-1163); Conrad the Cobbler (ISBN 0-570-07025-2, 56-1166); Valley That Didn't Wake (ISBN 0-570-07026-0, 56-1167); Little King of All (ISBN 0-570-07024-4, 56-1165); Lester the Jester (ISBN 0-570-07023-6, 56-1164). 16p. (ps-3). 1974. pap. 2.69 ea.; record incl. Concordia.

Plautus: Three Comedies. Tr. by Erich Segal. 1969. pap. 5.95x (ISBN 0-06-131932-5, TB1932, Torch). Har-Row.

Play a Lone Hand. Luke Short. 160p. 1981. pap. 1.95 (ISBN 0-553-13751-4). Bantam.

Play & Aggression: A Study of Rhesus Monkeys. Donald Symons. LC 77-24638. 1978. 22.50x (ISBN 0-231-04334-1). Columbia U Pr.

Play & Education: The Basic Tool for Early Childhood Learning. Otto Weininger. 196p. 1979. 15.75 (ISBN 0-398-03845-7). C C Thomas.

Play & Sing..It's Christmas! A Piano Book of Easy-to-Play Carols. Brooke M. Varnum. LC 80-15967. (Illus.). 48p. 1980. PLB 10.95 (ISBN 0-02-791400-3); pap. 5.95 (ISBN 0-02-045420-1). Macmillan.

Play & the Reader. alt. ed. Ed. by Stanley Johnson et al. (English Ser). 1971. pap. text ed. 9.50 (ISBN 0-13-682286-X). P-H.

Play As Context. Alyce T. Cheska. (Illus., Orig.). 1981. pap. text ed. 12.95 (ISBN 0-918438-66-7). Leisure Pr.

Play As Development. Annie L. Butler et al. 1978. pap. text ed. 9.95 (ISBN 0-675-08422-9). Merrill.

Play As Exploratory Learning. Ed. by Mary Reilly. LC 72-98044. 1974. 20.00x (ISBN 0-8039-0159-3); pap. 8.95x (ISBN 0-8039-0845-8). Sage.

Play Backgammon Tonight. Dave Thompson. (Gamblers Book Shelf). (Illus.). 61p. 1976. pap. 2.95 (ISBN 0-89650-558-8). Gamblers.

Play Ball, Snoopy: Selected Cartoons from "Win a Few, Lose a Few, Charlie Brown", Vol. I. Charles M. Schulz. (Peanuts Ser.). 1979. pap. 1.50 (ISBN 0-449-23222-0, Crest). Fawcett.

Play Begins. Warren Kenton. 1971. 4.50 o.p. (ISBN 0-236-15401-X, Pub. by Paul Elek). Merrimack Bk Serv.

Play Behavior. Joseph Levy. LC 77-12504. 1978. pap. text ed. 19.95 (ISBN 0-471-01712-4). Wiley.

Play Better Golf. Jack Nicklaus. (Orig.). 1981. pap. price not set (ISBN 0-671-83624-2). PB.

Play Better Tennis. Tony Mottram. LC 70-161216. (Illus.). 127p. 1972. pap. 1.65 o.p. (ISBN 0-668-02494-1). Arc Bks.

Play Better Tennis. Tony Mottram. LC 70-161213. (Illus.). 1971. 4.50 o.p. (ISBN 0-668-02502-6). Arco.

Play Bridge Tonight. Edwin Silberstang. (Gamblers Book Shelf). 64p. 1976. pap. 2.00 o.p. (ISBN 0-911996-59-1). Gamblers.

Play Chess: Combinations & Sacrifices. David Levy. 256p. 1980. pap. cancelled o.p. (ISBN 0-19-217589-0). Oxford U Pr.

Play Chess Tonight. Edwin Silberstang. (Gambler's Book Shelf). (Illus.). 1976. pap. 2.95 (ISBN 0-911996-68-0). Gamblers.

Play Directing: Analysis, Communication & Style. Francis Hodge. LC 75-143030. (Theatre & Drama Ser). 1971. ref. ed. 15.95 (ISBN 0-13-682815-9). P-H.

Play Direction for the High School Theatre. John W. Young. LC 73-78885. 1973. 9.95 (ISBN 0-8046-9040-5); pap. 4.95 (ISBN 0-8046-9085-5). Kennikat.

Play Ebony Play Ivory. Henry Dumas. LC 74-4126. 1974. 5.95 o.p. (ISBN 0-394-48970-5); pap. 2.95 o.p. (ISBN 0-394-70948-9). Random.

Play Environments for Movement Experience. Janet Smith. (Illus.). 64p. 1980. pap. 9.50 (ISBN 0-398-04073-7). C C Thomas.

Play Gin to Win. rev. ed. Irwin Steig. 1971. 3.95 (ISBN 0-346-12172-8). Cornerstone.

Play Helps: Toys & Activities for Handicapped Children. Roma Lear. 1977. pap. 12.95x (ISBN 0-433-19085-X). Intl Ideas.

Play in Hospital. Susan Harvey & Ann Hales-Tooke. 1972. 7.95 o.p. (ISBN 0-571-09827-4, Pub. by Faber & Faber); pap. 4.95 (ISBN 0-571-10174-7). Merrimack Bk Serv.

Play in Preschool Mainstreamed & Handicapped Settings. Anne C. Federlin. LC 80-65612. 135p. 1981. perfect bdg. 10.50 (ISBN 0-86548-035-4). Century Twenty One.

Play It Again. William D. Sheldon & Nina Woessner. (Breakthrough Ser.). (gr. 7-12). 1976. pap. text ed. 5.12 (ISBN 0-205-04109-4, 524109X); dup. masters 22.00 (ISBN 0-205-02921-3, 5254396). Allyn.

Play It Again, Charlie Brown. Charles M. Schulz. 1972. pap. 1.50 (ISBN 0-451-09217-1, W9217, Sig). NAL.

Play It Again: Historic Board Games You Can Make & Play. Asterie B. Provenzo & Eugene F. Provenzo. (Illus.). 288p. 1981. 17.95 (ISBN 0-13-683367-5, Spec); pap. 8.95 (ISBN 0-13-683359-4, Spec). P-H.

Play Like a Grandmaster. Alexander Kotov. 1978. pap. 12.50 (ISBN 0-7134-1807-9). David & Charles.

Play Little Victims. Kenneth Cook. 1978. text ed. 7.75 (ISBN 0-08-023123-3). Pergamon.

Play Mas. David Gershator. 92p. (Orig.). 1981. pap. 3.00 (ISBN 0-917402-14-6). Downtown Poets.

Play Mathematics: Mathematical Puzzler with Graded Exerciser. Harry Langman. 1962. 7.50 o.p. (ISBN 0-02-848360-X). Hafner.

Play of Love. John Heywood. Ed. by Frank E. La Rosa. LC 78-66855. (Renaissance Drama Ser.). 1979. lib. bdg. 33.00 (ISBN 0-8240-9743-2). Garland Pub.

Play of the Gods: Locality, Ideology, Structure & Time in the Festivals of a Bengali Town. Akos Ostor. LC 79-25661. 264p. 1980. lib. bdg. 27.00x (ISBN 0-226-63954-1). U of Chicago Pr.

Play of the Royal Astrologers. Willis Hall. pap. text ed. 2.50x o.p. (ISBN 0-435-21007-6). Heinemann Ed.

Play of the Weather & Other Tudor Comedies. John Heywood. Ed. by Maurice Hussey & Surendra Agarwala. LC 68-18403. 1968. 1.15x (ISBN 0-87830-101-1). Theatre Arts.

Play of the World. James S. Hans. LC 80-39630. 224p. 1981. lib. bdg. 15.00x (ISBN 0-87023-324-6); pap. 7.95 (ISBN 0-87023-325-4). U of Mass Pr.

Play-Off. Benjamin Swift. (Sportellers Ser.). (Illus.). 64p. (gr. 5 up). 1981. PLB 7.95 (ISBN 0-516-02265-2). Childrens.

Play on Words. Alice Provensen & Martin Provensen. (ps-2). 1972. 2.95 (ISBN 0-394-82124-6, BYR); PLB 4.69 (ISBN 0-394-92124-0). Random.

Play Pinochle Tonight. Edwin Silberstang. (Gambler's Book Shelf). 64p. 1976. pap. 2.95 (ISBN 0-89650-562-6). Gamblers.

Play Production. rev. ed. Henning Nelms. 1958. pap. 3.95 (ISBN 0-06-460073-4, CO 73, COS). Har-Row.

Play Production. Milton M. Smith. (Illus.). 1948. 29.50x (ISBN 0-89197-345-1); pap. text ed. 16.95x (ISBN 0-89197-346-X). Irvington.

Play Strindberg. Friedrich Durrenmatt. Tr. by James Kirkup. 1973. pap. 1.95 (ISBN 0-394-17798-3, E-612, Ever). Grove.

Play the Game, 4 bks. Robert McAdam. Incl. Forty for Sixty. (RL 2.5) (ISBN 0-8372-2264-8); Viva Gonzales. (RL 3) (ISBN 0-8372-2265-6); Chief Cloud of Dust. (RL 3.5) (ISBN 0-8372-2267-2); Bull on Ice. (RL 4) (ISBN 0-8372-2266-4). (gr. 3-8). pap. text ed. 2.52 ea. o.p.; tchrs' guide 2.10 o.p. (ISBN 0-8372-0728-2). cassettes 8.49 ea. o.p.; 48 bks, 6 ea. of 8 titles with 8 cassettes & spiritmasters avail. o.p. (ISBN 0-8372-2262-1). Bowmar-Noble.

Play the Game, 4 bks. Robert McAdam. Incl. Climb Any Mountain (ISBN 0-8372-2268-0); The Skillful Rider (ISBN 0-8372-2269-9); Holdup at the Crossover (ISBN 0-8372-2270-2); More Than Speedy Wheels (ISBN 0-8372-2271-0). (gr. 3-8). 1976. pap. text ed. 2.52 ea. o.p.; cassette for ea. title 8.49 ea. o.p.; 6 ea. of 8 titles, spiritmasters 102.12 o.p. (ISBN 0-8372-3741-6). Bowmar-Noble.

Play the Man: Defenseman's Journal. Brad Park & Stan Fischler. LC 73-181824. (Illus.). 1971. 6.95 (ISBN 0-396-06433-7). Dodd.

Play the Piano Drunk Like a Percussion Instrument Until the Fingers Begin to Bleed a Bit. Charles Bukowski. 140p. 1979. 14.00 (ISBN 0-87685-438-2); pap. 5.00 (ISBN 0-87685-437-4). Black Sparrow.

Play to Win: A Profile of Princeton Basketball Coach Pete Carril. Dan White. LC 77-20143. 1978. 8.95 o.p. (ISBN 0-13-683904-5). P-H.

Play Winning Poker. Jack King, pseud. (Gambler's Book Shelf). 64p. 1979. pap. 2.95 (ISBN 0-89650-542-1). Gamblers.

Play with A & T. Jane B. Moncure. LC 73-4740. (Alphabet Books). (Illus.). (gr. k-2). 1973. PLB 4.95 (ISBN 0-913778-02-8); pap. 2.75 (ISBN 0-89565-135-1). Childs World.

Play with Dots. 2nd ed. Isobel R. Beard. (Activity Fun Books). (Illus.). (ps-3). 1969. 0.99 o.p. (ISBN 0-695-90625-9). Follett.

Play with E & D. Jane B. Moncure. LC 73-4743. (Alphabet Books). (Illus.). (ps-2). 1973. PLB 4.95 (ISBN 0-913778-03-6); pap. 2.75 (ISBN 0-89565-133-5). Childs World.

Play with I & G. Jane B. Moncure. LC 73-4739. (Alphabet Books). (Illus.). (ps-2). 1973. PLB 4.95 (ISBN 0-913778-04-4); pap. 2.75 (ISBN 0-89565-134-3). Childs World.

Play with O & G. Jane B. Moncure. LC 73-4742. (Alphabet Books). (Illus.). (ps-2). 1973. PLB 4.95 (ISBN 0-913778-05-2); pap. 2.75 (ISBN 0-89565-131-9). Childs World.

Play with Paper. Thea Bank-Jensen. (gr. 1-4). 1962. 4.95g o.s.i. (ISBN 0-02-708240-7). Macmillan.

Play with Plants. rev. ed. Millicent E. Selsam. LC 78-8509. (Illus.). (gr. 4-6). 1978. PLB 7.63 (ISBN 0-688-32167-4). Morrow.

Play with Seeds. Millicent E. Selsam. (Illus.). (gr. 5-9). 1957. PLB 6.96 (ISBN 0-688-31489-9). Morrow.

Play with U & G. Jane B. Moncure. LC 73-4741. (Alphabet Books). (Illus.). (ps-2). 1973. PLB 4.95 (ISBN 0-913778-06-0); pap. 2.75 (ISBN 0-89565-132-7). Childs World.

Play Within a Play. R. J. Nelson. LC 72-87356. (Theater, Film & the Performing Arts Ser.). 182p. 1971. Repr. of 1958 ed. lib. bdg. 22.50 (ISBN 0-306-71580-5). Da Capo.

Playboy of the Western World. John M. Synge. Bd. with Riders to the Sea. 93p. 1968. pap. 3.50 (ISBN 0-06-463226-1, EH 226, EH). Har-Row.

Playboy of the Western World & Riders to the Sea. John M. Synge. (Unwin Paperbacks Ser). 1962. pap. 2.95 (ISBN 0-04-822041-8). Allen Unwin.

Playboy Riots. James Kilroy. (Irish Theatre Ser.: No. 4). (Orig.). 1971. pap. text ed. 4.00x (ISBN 0-85105-199-5, Dolmen Pr). Humanities.

Playboy's Book of Real Running. Marty Liquori & John L. Parker. 1980. 10.95 (ISBN 0-87223-625-0). Playboy.

Playboy's Book of Sports Car Repair. Arthur Darack. LC 79-90917. (Playboy's Lifestyles Library). (Illus.). 224p. 1980. 14.95 (ISBN 0-87223-602-1, Dist by Har-Row). Playboy.

Playboy's Elite Runner's Manual. Marty Liquori & John L. Parker. LC 80-7728. (Playboy's Lifestyles Library). 224p. 1980. 10.95 (ISBN 0-87223-625-0, Dist. by Har-Row). Playboy.

Playboy's Guide to Casino Gambling: Craps, Blackjack, Roulette, & Baccarat. Edwin Silberstang. LC 80-7727. (Playboy's Lifestyles Library). (Illus.). 512p. 1980. 15.95 (ISBN 0-87223-618-8, Dist. by Har-Row). Playboy.

Playboys Guide to Good Times: Europe. Stan McGahey. LC 80-84372. 256p. (Orig.). 1981. pap. 2.95 (ISBN 0-87216-819-0). Playboy Pbks.

Playboy's Guide to Real Estate Investing for the Single Person. Jack Cummings. LC 80-7790. (Playboy's Lifestyles Library). 288p. 1980. 13.95 (ISBN 0-87223-621-8, Dist. by Har-Row). Playboy.

Playboy's Hefner. Frank Brady. 230p. 1980. 28.50 (ISBN 0-686-68307-2). Porter.

Playboy's Party Jokes. Playboy Editors. 192p. (Orig.). 1980. pap. 1.95 (ISBN 0-87216-710-0). Playboy Pbks.

Playboy's Party Jokes, No. 2. Playbody Editors. (Illus.). 192p. 1980. pap. 1.95 (ISBN 0-87216-715-1). Playboy Pbks.

Playboy's Party Jokes, No. 6. Playboy Magazine Editors. (Party Joke Ser.). 160p. 1980. pap. 1.95 (ISBN 0-87216-735-6). Playboy Pbks.

Playboy's Party Jokes No. 3. Playboy Editors. 192p. 1980. pap. 1.95 (ISBN 0-87216-720-8). Playboy Pbks.

Playboy's Party Jokes, No. 5. Playboy Magazine Editors. (Party Joke Ser.: No. 5). (Illus.). 160p. 1980. pap. 1.95 (ISBN 0-87216-730-5). Playboy Pbks.

Player Piano. Kurt Vonnegut, Jr. 320p. pap. 2.75 (ISBN 0-440-17037-0). Dell.

Player Piano Treasury. 2nd ed. Harvey N. Roehl. LC 73-77327. (Illus.). 1972. 15.00 (ISBN 0-911572-00-7). Vestal.

Players at the Game of People. John Brunner. 1980. pap. 2.25 (ISBN 0-345-29235-9). Ballantine.

Player's Boy Is Dead. Leonard Tourney. LC 80-7611. 208p. 1980. 10.95 (ISBN 0-06-014341-X, HarpT). Har-Row.

Player's Manual for International Operations Simulation. Hans B. Thorelli et al. LC 63-13249. 1963. pap. text ed. 7.95 (ISBN 0-02-932530-7). Free Pr.

Playes Confuted in Fiue Actions. Stephen Gosson. LC 74-170407. (English Stage Ser.: Vol. 6). lib. bdg. 50.00 (ISBN 0-8240-0589-9). Garland Pub.

Playfair: Everybody's Guide to Noncompetitive Play. Matt Weinstein & Joel Goodman. LC 80-12591. (Orig.). 1980. pap. 8.95 (ISBN 0-915166-50-X). Impact Pubs Cal.

Playful Fictions & Fictional Players: Game, Sport & Survival in Contemporary American Fiction. Neil D. Berman. (National University Publications, Literary Criticism Ser.). 125p. 1981. 13.50 (ISBN 0-8046-9265-3). Kennikat.

Playgirls of Yesteryear. Robert Lebeck. (Illus.). 176p. 1981. pap. 6.95 (ISBN 0-312-61553-1). St Martin.

Playground. John Buell. 1977. pap. 1.75 o.p. (ISBN 0-345-25616-6). Ballantine.

Playground. H. V. Elkin. 1979. pap. 2.25 (ISBN 0-505-51423-0). Tower Bks.

Playground Book. Donna Kelly. (Illus.). (gr. k-2). 1978. PLB 5.38 (ISBN 0-307-68992-1, Golden Pr). Western Pub.

Playground of Death. John B. Hilton. 224p. 1981. 9.95 (ISBN 0-312-61559-0). St Martin.

Playgrounds of Our Minds. John Barell. LC 79-27084. 1980. pap. text ed. 9.95x (ISBN 0-8077-2580-3). Tchrs Coll.

Playgrounds: Their Administration & Operation. 3rd ed. George D. Butler. (Illus.). 1960. 19.95 (ISBN 0-8260-1610-3). Wiley.

Playing. Helen Oxenbury. (Baby Board Bks.). (Illus.). 12p. (ps-k). Date not set. boards 3.50 (ISBN 0-671-42109-3, Little Simon). S&S.

Playing & Composing on the Recorder. Ruth Etkin. LC 74-31711. (Illus.). 64p. (gr. 2 up). 1975. 7.95 (ISBN 0-8069-4528-1); PLB 7.49 (ISBN 0-8069-4529-X). Sterling.

Playing & Teaching Stringed Instruments, Pt. 1. Ralph Matesky & Ralph E. Rush. (Orig.). 1963. pap. text ed. 12.95 (ISBN 0-13-683789-1). P-H.

Playing & Teaching the Strings. Vincent Oddo. 208p. 1979. pap. text ed. 14.95x (ISBN 0-534-00614-0). Wadsworth Pub.

Playing Blackjack As a Business: 1977 Edition. Lawrence Revere. (Illus.). 1977. 12.50 (ISBN 0-686-67857-5); pap. 8.95 (ISBN 0-8184-0064-1). Lyle Stuart.

Playing for Change. Bruce Pollock. (gr. 7-9). 1978. pap. 1.50 o.s.i. (ISBN 0-671-29877-1). Archway.

Playing for Change. Bruce Pollock. (YA) (gr. 7-9). 1978. pap. 1.50 (ISBN 0-671-29877-1). PB.

Playing for Keeps. Brooke Hastings. 192p. (Orig.). 1980. pap. 1.50 (ISBN 0-671-57013-7). S&S.

Playing from Memory. David Milofsky. 1981. 12.95 (ISBN 0-671-25252-6). S&S.

Playing God: Genetic Engineering & the Manipulation of Life. June Goodfield. 1977. 8.95 o.p. (ISBN 0-394-40692-3). Random.

Playing House. Gerald Nachman. LC 76-56323. 1978. 6.95 o.p. (ISBN 0-385-12341-8). Doubleday.

Playing My Part. Frida Leider. Tr. by Charles Osborne. LC 77-26171. (Music Reprint Ser., 1978). (Illus.). 1978. Repr. of 1959 ed. lib. bdg. 22.50 (ISBN 0-306-77535-2). Da Capo.

Playing of Chamber Music. George Stratton & Alan Frank. (Student's Music Library). 1951. 6.95 (ISBN 0-234-77197-6). Dufour.

Playing Slow Pitch Softball. Robert G. Hoehn. LC 78-66319. (Illus.). 1979. 8.95 (ISBN 0-8069-4136-7); lib. bdg. 8.29 (ISBN 0-8069-4137-5). Sterling.

Playing Social & Recreational Instruments. Robert W. John & Charles N. Douglas. (Illus.). 144p. 1972. pap. text ed. 9.95 (ISBN 0-13-683680-1). P-H.

Playing String Quartets. Athol Page. 4.95 (ISBN 0-8283-1407-1). Branden.

Playing Tahoe. Sandra Hochman. 1981. 13.95 (ISBN 0-671-25358-1, Wyndham Bks). S&S.

Playing the Game: A Psychopolitical Strategy for Your Career. Raymond Blank. (Illus.). 224p. 1981. 10.95 (ISBN 0-688-00354-0). Morrow.

Playing the Guitar. 3rd ed. Frederick M. Noad. LC 80-5494. (Illus.). 1981. pap. 7.95 (ISBN 0-02-871990-5). Schirmer Bks.

Playing the String Game: Strategies for Teaching Cello & Strings. Phyllis Young. (Illus.). 1978. 15.00x o.p. (ISBN 0-292-73814-5); pap. text ed. 9.95x (ISBN 0-292-73815-3). U of Tex Pr.

Playing Urban Games: The Systems Approach to Planning. Martin Kuenzlen. LC 75-189032. 8.95x (ISBN 0-262-11069-5); pap. 4.95x (ISBN 0-262-61028-0, Pub. by I Pr). MIT Pr.

Playing with a Football. Morris A. Shirts & Thomas R. Kingsford. (Illus.). 128p. (gr. 4-8). 1973. 4.95 o.p. (ISBN 0-8069-4524-9); PLB 4.99 o.p. (ISBN 0-8069-4525-7). Sterling.

Playing with Fire. Bob Veder. 1980. 10.95 (ISBN 0-671-25354-9, Linden). S&S.

Playing with Grown Ups. Fritz A. Callies. 1978. pap. 6.95 (ISBN 0-8100-0007-5, 11N0623). Northwest Pub.

Playing with Infinity: Mathematical Explorations & Excursions. Rozsa Peter. LC 75-26467. 288p. 1976. pap. text ed. 3.50 (ISBN 0-486-23265-4). Dover.

Playleader's Handbook. Bernard S. Mc Govern. 1976. 14.95 o.p. (ISBN 0-571-10643-9, Pub. by Faber & Faber). Merrimack Bk Serv.

Playleadership. Bernard S. Mc Govern. 1973. 12.95 (ISBN 0-571-10184-4, Pub. by Faber & Faber). Merrimack Bk Serv.

Playlets & Skits. Ruth Vaughn. (Orig.). 1973. pap. 2.25 (ISBN 0-87239-374-7, 3093). Standard Pub.

Playmaker. Mike Neigoff. LC 73-7314. (Pilot Book Ser.). (Illus.). 128p. (gr. 4-7). 1973. 6.95g (ISBN 0-8075-6543-1). A Whitman.

Playmakers. Stuart Little & Arthur Cantor. 1971. pap. 2.95 o.p. (ISBN 0-525-47278-9). Dutton.

Playmaking with Children from Kindergarten Through Junior High School. 2nd ed. Winifred Ward. (Illus.). 1957. text ed. 14.95 (ISBN 0-13-683888-X). P-H.

Playmates. Jean Bethell. LC 80-20542. 32p. (gr. k-2). 1981. 7.95 (ISBN 0-03-053821-1). HR&W.

Playmates. Barbara J. Crane. (Crane Reading System-English Ser.). (Illus.). (gr. k-2). 1977. pap. text ed. 2.80 (ISBN 0-89075-096-3). Crane Pub Co.

Plays. Aeschylus. Tr. by G. M. Cookson. 1956. 10.50x (ISBN 0-460-00062-4, Evman). Dutton.

Plays. Aristophanes. Tr. by Patric Dickinson. (Oxford Paperbacks Ser.). 1971. pap. 4.95x; Vol. 1. pap. (ISBN 0-19-281054-5); Vol. 2. pap. o.p. (ISBN 0-19-281093-6). Oxford U Pr.

Plays, 2 vols. Ben Jonson. 1953. Vol. 1. 6.00x ea. (ISBN 0-460-00489-1, Evman); Vol. 2. 6.00x (ISBN 0-460-00490-5). Dutton.

Plays. H. W. Manson. Ed. by C. Van Heyningen. Incl. Festival. o.p. (ISBN 0-685-22958-0); Magnus (ISBN 0-8426-1375-7); Counsellors (ISBN 0-8426-1376-5); Potluck (ISBN 0-8426-1377-3). 1971. 8.50x ea. o.p. (ISBN 0-8426-1374-9). Verry.

Plays, Vol. I. Robert Pinget. 1980. pap. 4.95 (ISBN 0-7145-0474-2). Riverrun NY.

Plays, Vol. II. Robert Pinget. 1980. pap. 4.95 (ISBN 0-7145-0036-4). Riverrun NY.

Plays & Poems of Mercy Otis Warren. Mercy Otis Warren. LC 80-16625. 1980. 40.00x (ISBN 0-8201-1344-1). Schol Facsimiles.

Plays & Prose Writings & Poems. Oscar Wilde. 1955. 12.95x (ISBN 0-460-00858-7, Evman); pap. 4.95 (ISBN 0-460-01858-2). Dutton.

Plays & Stories. Barrie. 1975. pap. 2.25 o.p. (ISBN 0-460-01184-7, Evman). Dutton.

Plays As Experience: One-Act Plays for the Secondary Schools. rev. ed. Ed. by Irwin J. Zachar. LC 62-13411. 1962. pap. 7.50 (ISBN 0-672-73228-9). Odyssey Pr.

Plays by American Women: The Early Years. Ed. by Judith Barlow. 368p. 1981. pap. 3.95 (ISBN 0-380-76620-5, 76620, Bard). Avon.

Plays of Arthur Murphy, 4 vols. Ed. by Paula R. Backscheider. LC 78-66610. (Eighteenth-Century English Drama Ser.: Vol. 30). 1980. Set. lib. bdg. 200.00 (ISBN 0-8240-3604-2); lib. bdg. 50.00 ea. Garland Pub.

Plays of Charles Gildon. Ed. by Paula R. Backscheider. LC 78-66609. (Eighteenth-Century English Drama Ser.: Vol. 17). 1979. lib. bdg. 50.00 (ISBN 0-8240-3591-7). Garland Pub.

Plays of Colley Cibber, 2 vols. Ed. by Rodney Hayley. LC 78-66634. (Eighteenth Century English Drama Ser.). 1980. Set. lib. bdg. 50.00 (ISBN 0-8240-3582-8). Garland Pub.

Plays of Confession & Therapy: To Damascus I, to Damascus II, & to Damascus III. August Strindberg. Tr. by Walter Johnson from Swedish. LC 78-20962. (Illus.). 260p. 1979. 19.50 (ISBN 0-295-95567-8). U of Wash Pr.

Plays of Cyril Tourneur. Ed. by G. Parfitt. LC 77-77014. (Plays by Renaissance & Restoration Dramatists Ser.). 1978. 29.95 (ISBN 0-521-21697-4); pap. 7.50x (ISBN 0-521-29235-2). Cambridge U Pr.

Plays of David Garrick: A Complete Collection of the Social Satires, French Adaptations, Pantomimes, Christmas & Musical Plays, Preludes, Interludes, & Burlesques, to Which Are Added the Alterations & Adaptations of the Plays of Shakespeare & Other Dramatists from the Sixteenth & Seventeenth Centuries: Vol. 3, Garrick's Adaptations of Shakespeare, 1744-1756. Ed. by Harry W. Pedicord & Fredrick L. Bergmann. LC 79-28443. 496p. write for info. (ISBN 0-8093-0968-8). S Ill U Pr.

Plays of David Garrick, Vol. 1: Garrick's Own Plays, 1740-1766. Ed. by Harry W. Pedicord & Frederick L. Bergmann. LC 79-28443. (Plays of David Garrick). (Illus.). 480p. 1980. 35.00x (ISBN 0-8093-0862-2). S Ill U Pr.

Plays of David Garrick, Vol. 2: Garrick's Own Play's 1767-1775. Ed. by Harry W. Pedicord & Frederick L. Bergmann. LC 79-28443. (Illus.). 444p. 1980. 35.00x (ISBN 0-8093-0863-0). S Ill U Pr.

Plays of David Mallet. Ed. by Felicity Nussbaum & Paula R. Backscheider. LC 78-66605. (Eighteenth-Century English Drama Ser.: Vol. 28). 1980. lib. bdg. 50.00 (ISBN 0-8240-3602-6). Garland Pub.

Plays of George Fitzmaurice. George Fitzmaurice. Incl. Realistic Plays. Intro. by Howard Slaughter. 164p. (Fitzmaurice plays 3). 1970. text ed. 4.50x (ISBN 0-85105-174-X); Folk Plays. Intro. by Howard Slaughter. 153p. (Fitzmaurice plays 2). 1969. text ed. 4.50x (ISBN 0-85105-013-1). Dolmen Pr). Humanities.

Plays of George Lillo. Ed. by Trudy Drucker & Paula R. Backscheider. LC 78-66658. (Eighteenth-Century English Drama Ser.: Vol. 27). 1980. lib. bdg. 50.00 (ISBN 0-8240-3601-8). Garland Pub.

Plays of Grillparzer. G. A. Wells. 1969. 16.50 (ISBN 0-08-012950-1); pap. 7.75 (ISBN 0-08-012949-8). Pergamon.

Plays of Hannah Cowley, 2 vols. Ed. by Frederick M. Link & Paula R. Backscheider. LC 78-66646. (Eighteenth-Century English Drama Ser.: Vol. 12). 1980. Set. lib. bdg. 100.00 (ISBN 0-8240-3586-0); lib. bdg. 50.00 ea. Garland Pub.

Plays of Henry Carey. Samuel C. Macey. LC 78-66613. (Eighteenth Century English Drama Ser.). 1980. lib. bdg. 50.00 (ISBN 0-8240-3580-1). Garland Pub.

Plays of Henry Medwall. Ed. by Alan H. Nelson. (Tudor Interludes Ser.). (Illus.). 237p. 1980. 33.50x (ISBN 0-8476-6243-8). Rowman.

Plays of Honore De Balzac, 2 vols. in 1. Honore De Balzac. 1976. Repr. of 1901 ed. 35.00 (ISBN 0-86527-291-3). Fertig.

Plays of Hugh Kelly. Ed. by Larry Carver. LC 78-66653. (Eighteenth Century English Drama Ser.). 1980. lib. bdg. 50.00 (ISBN 0-8240-3600-X). Garland Pub.

Plays of J. M. Synge: A Critical Study. K. S. Misra. 1978. 10.00x (ISBN 0-210-40622-4). Asia.

Plays of James Thomson. Ed. by Paula R. Backscheider. LC 78-66637. (Eighteenth-Century English Drama Ser.: Vol. 35). 1980. lib. bdg. 50.00 (ISBN 0-8240-3609-3). Garland Pub.

Plays of John Dennis. Ed. by Paula R. Backscheider. LC 78-66657. (Eighteenth-Century English Drama Ser.: Vol. 14). 1980. lib. bdg. 50.00 (ISBN 0-8240-3588-7). Garland Pub.

Plays of John Galsworthy. John Galsworthy. 1150p. 1980. Repr. of 1929 ed. lib. bdg. 40.00 (ISBN 0-8492-4960-0). R West.

Plays of John Home. Ed. by James S. Malek & Paula R. Backscheider. LC 78-66641. (Eighteenth-Century English Drama Ser.: Vol. 22). 1980. lib. bdg. 50.00 (ISBN 0-8240-3596-8). Garland Pub.

Plays of John Hoole. Ed. by Donald T. Siebert & Paula R. Backscheider. LC 78-66635. (Eighteenth-Century English Drama Ser.: Vol. 21). 1980. lib. bdg. 50.00 (ISBN 0-8240-3595-X). Garland Pub.

Plays of John Osborne: An Assessment. Simon Trussler. 1969. pap. text ed. 4.00x (ISBN 0-575-00267-0). Humanities.

Plays of Menander. Ed. by Lionel Casson. LC 76-171347. 1971. 12.00x (ISBN 0-8147-1353-X). NYU Pr.

Plays of Negro Life: A Sourcebook of Native American Drama. Alain L. Locke. LC 77-132077. Repr. of 1927 ed. 25.00x (ISBN 0-8371-5037-X). Negro U Pr.

Plays of Oscar Wilde. Alan Bird. (Critical Studies Ser.). 220p. 1977. 18.50x (ISBN 0-06-490415-6). B&N.

Plays of Our Forefathers & Some of the Traditions Upon Which They Were Founded. Charles M. Gayley. LC 68-25810. (Illus.). 1968. Repr. of 1907 ed. 15.00x (ISBN 0-8196-0209-4). Biblo.

Plays of Robert Jephson. Ed. by Temple Maynard & Paula R. Backscheider. LC 78-66647. (Eighteenth-Century English Drama Ser.: Vol. 24). 1980. lib. bdg. 50.00 (ISBN 0-8240-3598-4). Garland Pub.

Plays of Samuel Beckett. I. K. Masih. 236p. 1980. text ed. write for info. (ISBN 0-391-02074-9). Humanities.

Plays of Samuel Beckett. Eugene Webb. LC 72-2901. (Washington Paperback Ser., No. 71). 160p. 1972. 10.50 (ISBN 0-295-95202-4); pap. 2.95 (ISBN 0-295-95314-4). U of Wash Pr.

Plays of the Year, Vol. 46. Ed. by J. C. Trewin. 1978. 15.95 (ISBN 0-8044-2924-3). Ungar.

Plays of the Year, Vol. 47. Ed. by J. C. Trewin. 1979. 15.95 (ISBN 0-8044-2925-1). Ungar.

Plays of the Year, Vol. 48. Ed. by J. C. Trewin. 1980. 15.95 (ISBN 0-8044-2926-X). Ungar.

Plays of the Year Series: Selections from the London Theatre Season, 2 vols. a year, starting with vol. 42, 1972. Ed. by John C. Trewin. 10.50 ea. (ISBN 0-686-66561-9). Ungar.

Plays of Thomas Holcroft, 2 vols. Ed. by Joseph Rosenblum. LC 78-66630. (Eighteenth Century English Drama Ser.). 1980. Set. lib. bdg. 50.00 (ISBN 0-8240-3594-1). Garland Pub.

Plays of Thomas Love Peacock. Thomas L. Peacock. 157p. 1980. Repr. of 1910 ed. lib. bdg. 25.00 (ISBN 0-8495-4374-6). Arden Lib.

Plays of William Wycherley. P. Holland. (Plays by Renaissance & Restoration Dramatists). (Illus.). 400p. Date not set. price not set (ISBN 0-521-23250-3); pap. price not set (ISBN 0-521-29880-6). Cambridge U Pr.

Plays of William Wycherley. William Wycherley. Ed. by Arthur Friedman. (Oxford English Texts Ser.). 1979. 79.00x (ISBN 0-19-811861-9). Oxford U Pr.

Plays, Poems, & Prose. John M. Synge. 1968. 6.00x (ISBN 0-460-00968-0, Evman); pap. 5.95 (ISBN 0-460-01968-6). Dutton.

Play's the Thing. Lawrence Langner. 1960. text ed. 7.95 o.p. (ISBN 0-87116-036-6). Writer.

Plays Unpleasant. George B. Shaw. Incl. Widowers' Houses; Philanderer; Mrs. Warren's Profession. (Penguin Plays Ser.). 1950. pap. 2.75 (ISBN 0-14-048012-9). Penguin.

Playtime! Americans at Leisure. Mark Jury. LC 77-73123. (Illus.). 1977. pap. 5.95 o.p. (ISBN 0-15-672037-X, Harv). HarBraceJ.

Playtime Crafts. Linda Hetzer. LC 77-28790. (Illustrated Crafts for Beginners). (Illus.). (gr. 3-7). 1978. PLB 9.95 (ISBN 0-8172-1182-9). Raintree Pubs.

Playtime in Africa. Efua Sutherland. (Illus.). (gr. 2-6). 1962. PLB 6.95 o.p. (ISBN 0-689-20589-9). Atheneum.

Playtime to Bedtime, 6 bks. Margaret W. Brown. (Illus.). (ps). Date not set. boxed set 4.95 (ISBN 0-307-15515-3, Golden Pr). Western Pub.

Playtime with Music. rev. ed. Marion Abeson & Charity Bailey. (Illus.). 1952. 4.95 o.p. (ISBN 0-87140-999-2). Liveright.

Playtraining Your Dog. Patricia G. Burnham. (Illus.). 256p. 1980. 11.95 (ISBN 0-312-61689-9). St Martin.

Playwright & Historical Change: Dramatic Strategies in Brecht, Hauptmann, Kaiser, & Wedekind. Leroy R. Shaw. LC 75-106042. 1970. 17.00x (ISBN 0-299-05500-0). U of Wis Pr.

Playwrights for Tomorrow: A Collection of Plays. Ed. by Arthur H. Ballet. Incl. Vol. 3. 1967. 7.95x (ISBN 0-8166-0430-4); Vol. 4. (Orig.). 1967. 7.95x (ISBN 0-8166-0432-0); Vol. 5. (Orig.). 1969. 5.50x (ISBN 0-8166-0534-3); Vol. 6. (Orig.). 1969. o.p. (ISBN 0-8166-0537-8); Vol. 7. 10.00x (ISBN 0-8166-0579-3); Vol. 8. 10.00x (ISBN 0-8166-0650-1); Vol. 9. 10.00x (ISBN 0-8166-0653-6); Vol. 10. 1973. 10.00x (ISBN 0-8166-0693-5); Vol. 11. 1973. 10.00x (ISBN 0-8166-0695-1). LC 66-19124. U of Minn Pr.

Playwrights, Preachers & Politicians: A Study of Four Tudor Old Testament Dramas. Naomi Pasachoff. (Salzburg Studies in English Literature, Elizabethan & Renaissance Studies Ser.: No. 45). 162p. (Orig.). 1975. pap. text ed. 25.00x (ISBN 0-391-01493-5). Humanities.

Playwrights' Theatre: The English State Company at the Royal Court. Terry Browne. 1975. 8.00x (ISBN 0-273-00757-2, Pitman Pub); pap. 5.00 (ISBN 0-273-00758-0). Columbia U Pr.

Playwriting. Bernard Grebanier. (Apollo Eds.). pap. 4.95 o.s.i. (ISBN 0-8152-0111-7, A111, TYC-T). T Y Crowell.

Playwriting: The Structure of Action. Sam Smiley. LC 78-125077. (Theatre & Drama Ser). 1971. pap. 11.95 ref. ed. (ISBN 0-13-684530-4). P-H.

Plea Bargaining & Guilty Pleas. James E. Bond. LC 75-15655. 1975. looseleaf with 1978 rev. pages & supplement 45.00 (ISBN 0-87632-105-8). Boardman.

Plea for Art in the House & House Decoration & Dress & Music in the House. W. J. Loftie et al. Ed. by Peter Stansky & Rodney Shewan. LC 76-18320. (Aesthetic Movement & the Arts & Crafts Movement Ser.). 1978. Repr. lib. bdg. 44.00x (ISBN 0-8240-2460-5). Garland Pub.

Plea for the Liberty of Interpreting. Lascelles Abercrombie. 51p. 1980. Repr. of 1930 ed. lib. bdg. 5.50 (ISBN 0-89987-007-4). Darby Bks.

Plea of Puerto Rico. Luis A. Ferre. (Studies in Puerto Rican History, Literature & Culture). 1980. lib. bdg. 59.95 (ISBN 0-8490-3087-0). Gordon Pr.

Pleasant Commodie Called Looke About You. Ed. by Richard S. Hirsch & Stephen Orgel. LC 79-54343. (Renaissance Drama Second Ser.). 130p. 1980. lib. bdg. 16.50 (ISBN 0-8240-4460-6). Garland Pub.

Pleasant Dreams: Nightmares. Robert Bloch. 1979. pap. 1.75 o.s.i. (ISBN 0-515-04743-0). Jove Pubns.

Pleasant History of Lazarillo de Tormes, His Fortunes & Adversities, Containing the Strange Adventures That Befell Him in the Service of Sundry Masters, As Written Supposedly by Diego Hurtado de Mendoza: Together with the Pursuit or Second Part of His Life, As Related by Juan de Luna. Lazarillo de Tormes. LC 80-2487. 1981. Repr. of 1926 ed. 35.00 (ISBN 0-404-19121-5). AMS Pr.

Pleasant Memoirs of the Marquis De Bradomin. Ramon Valle-Inclan. Tr. by May Heywood Broun & Thomas Walsh. LC 76-28508. 1980. Repr. of 1924 ed. 20.00 (ISBN 0-86527-294-8). Fertig.

Pleasant Places. Samuel A. Schreiner, Jr. 1978. pap. 1.95 o.p. (ISBN 0-449-23769-9, Crest). Fawcett.

Pleasant Vintage of Till Eulenspiegel. Tr. by Paul Oppenheimer from Ger. LC 73-184361. (Illus.). 336p. 1972. 20.00x (ISBN 0-8195-4043-9, Pub. by Wesleyan U Pr). Columbia U Pr.

Please Don't Kiss Me Now. Merrill J. Gerber. 224p. (YA) (gr. 8 up). 1981. 9.95 (ISBN 0-8037-6792-7). Dial.

Please Don't Shoot My Dog: The Autobiography of Jackie Cooper with Dick Kleiner. Jackie Cooper & Dick Kleiner. (Illus.). 288p. 12.95 (ISBN 0-688-03659-7). Morrow.

Please Give a Devotion for All Occasions. Amy Bolding. 1967. pap. 2.95 (ISBN 0-8010-0519-1). Baker Bk.

Please Give a Devotion: For Women's Groups. Amy Bolding. (Paperback Program Ser.). 108p. 1976. pap. 2.95 (ISBN 0-8010-0583-3). Baker Bk.

Please Keep on Smoking: We Need the Money. Alvyn M. Freed & Herb Michelson. (Orig.). 1980. pap. 2.95 saddle stitch (ISBN 0-915190-27-3). Jalmar Pr.

Please Listen God! Vera Wimberly. (Illus.). (gr. k-3). 1977. pap. 2.50 (ISBN 0-570-03467-1, 56-1299). Concordia.

Please, Lord, Don't Put Me on Hold! Jane Graver. 1979. pap. 2.25 (ISBN 0-570-03790-5, 12-2753). Concordia.

Please Pass the Guilt. Rex Stout. 1979. pap. 6.95 (ISBN 0-8161-6737-0, Large Print Bks). G K Hall.

Please Quote Me: Selected Poems. Alice G. Gaydos. 64p. 1980. 5.00 (ISBN 0-682-49626-X). Exposition.

Please Remember Me. Mari Brady. (YA) 1978. pap. 1.50 (ISBN 0-686-68479-6). PB.

Please Understand Me: An Essay on Temperament Styles. David Keirsey & Marilyn Bates. 1978. write for info. Prometheus Nemesis.

Pleasurable Instruction: Form & Convention in Eighteenth-Century Travel Literature. Charles L. Batten, Jr. LC 76-14316. 1978. 16.50x (ISBN 0-520-03260-8). U of Cal Pr.

Pleasure. Alec Waugh. LC 79-53467. (Short Story Index in Reprint Ser.). Date not set. Repr. of 1921 ed. 24.50x (ISBN 0-8486-5013-1). Core Collection. Postponed.

Pleasure: A Creative Approach to Life. Alexander Lowen. 1975. pap. 3.50 (ISBN 0-14-004033-1). Penguin.

Pleasure Addicts. Lawrence J. Hatterer. LC 79-50769. 392p. 1981. 12.00 (ISBN 0-498-02285-4). A S Barnes.

Pleasure & Business in Western Pennsylvania: The Journal of Joshua Gilpin, 1809. Ed. by Joseph E. Walker. (Illus.). 156p. 1975. 7.50 (ISBN 0-911124-78-0). Pa Hist & Mus.

Pleasure & Pain. J. L. Cowan. LC 68-13019. 1968. 18.95 (ISBN 0-312-61705-4). St Martin.

Pleasure & Privilege: Life in France, Naples & America. Olivier Bernier. LC 79-6174. (Illus.). 304p. 1981. 14.95 (ISBN 0-385-15780-0). Doubleday.

Pleasure Areas: A New Theory of Behavior. H. J. Campbell. 288p. 1973. 8.95 o.p. (ISBN 0-440-07226-3). Delacorte.

Pleasure Garden. Anne Scott-James & Osbert Lancaster. LC 77-84332. 1980. pap. 5.95 (ISBN 0-87645-109-1). Gambit.

Pleasure Horse. Hollis Lee. (Country Home & Small Farm Guides Ser.). (Illus.). 1978. pap. 2.95 (ISBN 0-88453-004-3). Barrington.

Pleasure Horse. 96p. 2.95 (ISBN 0-88453-004-3). Berkshire Traveller.

Pleasure in Words. Eugene Maleska. 1981. 15.95 (ISBN 0-671-24881-2). S&S.

Pleasure of Birds: An Audubon Treasury. Ed. by Les Line. LC 75-17948. (Illus.). 240p. 1975. 14.95 o.p. (ISBN 0-397-01065-6). Lippincott.

Pleasure of Cities. Doone Beal. 1975. 10.95 o.p. (ISBN 0-7181-1430-2, Pub. by Michael Joseph). Merrimack Bk Serv.

Pleasure of Their Company: How to Have More Fun with Your Children. Ed. by William Hooks et al. LC 80-70382. 480p. (Orig.). 1981. pap. 9.95 (ISBN 0-686-69524-0). Chilton.

Pleasure Packing. Robert Wood. (Encore Edition). 1972. pap. 1.95 (ISBN 0-684-16935-5, SL577, ScribT). Scribner.

Pleasure Packing for the Eighties. 2nd rev. ed. Robert S. Wood. (Illus.). 256p. 1981. pap. 6.95 (ISBN 0-89815-035-3). Ten Speed Pr.

Pleasure Tube. Robert Onopa. 1979. pap. 1.75 o.p. (ISBN 0-425-03941-2). Berkley Pub.

Pleasure with Paper. A. Van Breda. 1954. 6.50 (ISBN 0-571-05172-3, Pub. by Faber & Faber). Merrimack Bk Serv.

Pleasures & Days: & Other Writings. Marcel Proust. Tr. by L. Varese et al from Fr. LC 78-2432. 1978. Repr. of 1957 ed. 18.50 (ISBN 0-86527-293-X). Fertig.

Pleasures & People of Bath. Kenneth Hudson. (Folio Miniature Ser.). (Illus.). 1978. 6.95 (ISBN 0-7181-1588-0, Pub. by Michael Joseph). Merrimack Bk Serv.

Pleasures of Being a Catholic, 2 vols. new ed. Leo Panzion. (Human Development Library Bk.). (Illus.). 1979. Set. 39.75 o.p. (ISBN 0-89266-155-0). Am Classical Coll Pr.

Pleasures of Italian Cooking. Romeo Salta. 1962. 12.95 (ISBN 0-02-606790-0). Macmillan.

Pleasures of Sketching Outdoors. rev. ed. Clayton Hoagland. (Illus.). 1970. pap. 4.50 (ISBN 0-486-22229-2). Dover.

Pleasures of Sociology. Lewis A. Coser. (Orig.). 1980. pap. 2.75 (ISBN 0-451-61825-4, ME1825, Ment). NAL.

Pleasures of the Table. George Ellwanger. LC 70-82031. 1969. Repr. of 1902 ed. 20.00 (ISBN 0-8103-3560-3). Gale.

Pleasures of Walking. Ed. by Edwin V. Mitchell. LC 48-11993. (Illus.). 1979. 8.95 (ISBN 0-8149-0825-X). Vanguard.

Plebejer Proben Den Aufstand. Gunter Grass. Ed. by H. F. Brookes & C. E. Fraenkel. 1971. pap. text ed. 4.50x (ISBN 0-435-38372-8). Heinemann Ed.

Plees Del Coron. William Staunford & Samuel Romilly. Ed. by David S. Berkowitz & Samuel E. Thorne. LC 77-86634. (Classics of English Legal History in the Modern Era Ser.: Vol. 28). 484p. 1979. lib. bdg. 40.00 (ISBN 0-8240-3077-X). Garland Pub.

Pleine Victoire. Tr. by Harold Hill. (French Bks.). (Fr.). 1979. 1.95 (ISBN 0-8297-0942-8). Life Pubs Intl.

Pleiocene Fossils of South Carolina. Michael Tuomey & Francis S. Holmes. (Illus.). 1974. Repr. of 1857 ed. 9.00 (ISBN 0-87710-365-8). Paleo Res.

Pleistocene Geology & Biology. 2nd ed. R. G West. LC 76-28353. (Illus.). 1977. pap. text ed. 18.95x (ISBN 0-582-44620-1). Longman.

Pleistocene Soboba Flora of Southern California. Daniel Axelrod. (U. C. Publ. in Geological Sciences: Vol. 60). 1966. pap. 6.00x (ISBN 0-520-09161-2). U of Cal Pr.

Pleneurethic: Its Evolution & Scientific Basis, Vol. 2. Richard B. Collier. 64p. 1980. 15.00 (ISBN 0-682-49623-5). Exposition.

Plenty & Want: A Social History of Diet in England from 1815 to the Present Day. John Burnett. 387p. 1979. Repr. of 1966 ed. 15.95 (ISBN 0-85967-461-4, Pub. by Scolar Pr England); pap. 7.95 (ISBN 0-85967-462-2). Biblio Dist.

Plenty-coups, Chief of the Crows. Frank B. Linderman. LC 30-11369. (Illus.). 1962. pap. 3.95 (ISBN 0-8032-5121-1, BB 128, Bison). U of Nebr Pr.

Plenty of Puppets to Make. Robyn Supraner & Lauren Supraner. LC 80-23785. (Illus.). 48p. (gr. 2-5). 1980. PLB 6.92 (ISBN 0-89375-432-3); pap. 1.75 (ISBN 0-89375-433-1). Troll Assocs.

Pleural Effusion: Some Infrequently Emphasized Causes. Stephen Sulavik & Sol Katz. 104p. 1963. pap. 6.50 spiral (ISBN 0-398-01876-6). C C Thomas.

Pliegos Poeticos de la Biblioteca Colombiana. Antonio Rodriguez-Monino. (Publications in Modern Philology: Vol. 110). 1976. pap. 12.00x (ISBN 0-520-09521-9). U of Cal Pr.

Plight of Pamela Pollworth. Margaret SeBastian. 224p. (Orig.). 1980. pap. 1.75 (ISBN 0-449-50119-1, Coventry). Fawcett.

Plimoth Plantation: Then & Now. Jean P. Colby. (Famous Museum Ser). (Illus.). 1970. 6.95g (ISBN 0-8038-5757-8). Hastings.

Pliny. Tr. by C. Greig from Lat. LC 77-91088. (Illus.). 1979. 3.95x (ISBN 0-521-21978-7). Cambridge U Pr.

Plippen's Palace. Madye L. Chastain. LC 61-6346. (Illus.). (gr. 4-7). 1961. 4.50 o.p. (ISBN 0-15-262792-8, HJ). HarBraceJ.

Ploetzlich Brach der Schulrat in Traenen Aus: Verstaendigungstexte Von Schuelern und Lehrern. Ed. by Ulrich Zimmermann & Christine Eigel. (Edition Suhrkamp). 429p. (Orig.). 1980. pap. text ed. 6.50 (ISBN 3-518-10429-2, Pub. by Insel Verlag Germany). Suhrkamp.

Plombieres: Secret Diplomacy & the Rebirth of Italy. Ed. by Mack Walker. (Problems in European History Series). (Orig.). 1968. pap. 4.95x (ISBN 0-19-501096-5). Oxford U Pr.

Plonk & Super-Plonk. John Baldwinson. 1975. 7.95 o.p. (ISBN 0-7181-1407-8, Pub. by Michael Joseph). Merrimack Bk Serv.

Plot Against Christianity. Elizabeth Dilling. 1978. pap. 10.00x (ISBN 0-911038-35-3). Noontide.

Plot Against the Church. Maurice Pinay. 1978. 15.00x (ISBN 0-911038-39-6). Noontide.

Plot of Satire. Alvin B. Kernan. LC 65-22327. 1965. 15.00x o.p. (ISBN 0-300-00621-7). Yale U Pr.

Plot Outlines of One Hundred Famous Plays. Ed. by Van H. Cartmell. 8.50 (ISBN 0-8446-0539-5). Peter Smith.

Plot Outlines of One Hundred One Best Novels. Ed. by Edwin A. Grozier & Margaret Gillet. 1962. pap. 4.95 (ISBN 0-06-463215-6, EH 215, EH). Har-Row.

Plot Summary Index. Carol L. Koehmstedt. LC 72-13726. 1973. 11.50 (ISBN 0-8108-0584-7). Scarecrow.

Plot Summary Index. 2nd rev. & enl. ed. Compiled by Carol K. Kolar. LC 80-27112. 544p. 1981. 25.00 (ISBN 0-8108-1392-0). Scarecrow.

Plot That Failed: Nixon & the Administrative Presidency. Richard P. Nathan. LC 74-30272. 176p. 1975. pap. text ed. 8.95x (ISBN 0-471-63065-9). Wiley.

Plot to Kill the President. G. Robert Blakey & Richard N. Billings. 320p. 1981. 12.95 (ISBN 0-8129-0929-1). Times Bks.

Plotinus: The Road to Reality. J. M. Rist. 1977. 38.00 (ISBN 0-521-06085-0); pap. 9.95 (ISBN 0-521-29202-6). Cambridge U Pr.

Plots & Characters in Classic French Fiction. Benjamin E. Hicks. (Plots & Characters Ser.). 1981. 27.50 (ISBN 0-208-01703-8, Archon). Shoe String.

Plots and Counterplots: More Unknown Thrillers of Louisa May Alcott. Louisa May Alcott. Intro. by Madeleine Stern. (Illus.). 320p. 1976. 9.95 o.p. (ISBN 0-688-03046-7). Morrow.

Plotting & Writing Suspense Fiction. rev. ed. Patricia Highsmith. 1972. 8.95 o.p. (ISBN 0-87116-072-2). Writer.

Plotting & Writing Suspense Fiction. rev. ed. Patricia Highsmith. 1981. 10.95 (ISBN 0-87116-125-7). Writer.

Plotting & Writing Suspense Fiction. Ed. by Patricia Highsmith. 1981. 10.95 (ISBN 0-87116-125-7). Writer.

Plotunus: The Enneads. 4th ed. Tr. by Stephen McKenna. 1970. 19.95 o.p. (ISBN 0-571-04688-6, Pub. by Faber & Faber). Merrimack Bk Serv.

Plovers. Richard Vaughan. 160p. 1980. 25.00x (ISBN 0-900963-36-0, Pub. by Terence Dalton England). State Mutual Bk.

Plow Women Rather Than Reapers: An Intellectual History of Feminism in the United States. Sarah S. Schramm. LC 78-10907. 1979. lib. bdg. 19.00 (ISBN 0-8108-1183-9). Scarecrow.

Plowden Children Four Years Later. G. F. Peaker. (General Ser.). 50p. 1971. pap. text ed. 7.00x (ISBN 0-901225-80-0, NFER). Humanities.

Plowman's Folly. Edward H. Faulkner. 154p. 1943. 7.95 (ISBN 0-8061-0124-5); pap. 3.95 (ISBN 0-8061-1169-0). U of Okla Pr.

Plucked Chickens. James Magorian. LC 80-68263. 32p. 1981. 5.00 (ISBN 0-930674-04-9). Black Oak.

Plum Jelly & Stained Glass & Other Prayers. Jo Carr & Imogene Sorley. (Festival Bks). 1981. pap. 1.95 (ISBN 0-687-31660-X). Abingdon.

Plum Plum Pickers. Raymond Barrio. (Orig.). 1970. 8.50 (ISBN 0-917438-04-3); pap. 3.75 (ISBN 0-917438-04-3). Ventura Pr.

Plumber's Bible. Scott Wilson. LC 76-42420. (Homeowner's Bible Ser.). (Illus.). 160p. 1981. pap. 4.95 (ISBN 0-385-11211-4). Doubleday.

Plumbers' Handbook. 5th ed. Joseph P. Almond. LC 79-64811. (Illus.). 1979. pap. 8.95 (ISBN 0-672-23339-8, 23339). Audel.

Plumbing. Boy Scouts Of America. LC 19-600. (Illus.). 40p. (gr. 6-12). 1965. pap. 0.70x (ISBN 0-8395-3386-1, 3386). BSA.

Plumbing. J. H. Innes. (Teach Yourself Ser.). 1975. pap. 3.95 o.p. (ISBN 0-679-10484-4). McKay.

Plumbing. (Home Repair & Improvement Ser.). (Illus.). 1976. 10.95 (ISBN 0-8094-2366-9). Time-Life.

Plumbing. Ed. by Time Life Books. LC 76-46139. (Home Repair & Improvement). (Illus.). (gr. 7 up). 1976. PLB 11.97 (ISBN 0-8094-2367-7, Pub. by Time-Life). Silver.

Plumbing Estimators Handbook. Howard C. Massey. 256p. (Orig.). 1981. pap. 15.25 (ISBN 0-910460-82-5). Craftsman.

Plumbing Fundamentals. James L. Thiesse. (Contemporary Construction Ser.). (Illus.). 192p. (gr. 10-12). 1981. 16.95x (ISBN 0-07-064191-9, G). McGraw.

Plumbing: Installation & Design. James A. Sullivan. (Illus.). 480p. 1980. text ed. 17.95 (ISBN 0-8359-5552-4); instr's manual avail. Reston.

Plumbing Repairs Simplified. rev. ed. Donald R. Brann. LC 67-27691. 1976. pap. 5.95 (ISBN 0-87733-750-0). Easi-Bild.

Plumbing with Plastic. S. Blackwell Duncan. (Illus., Orig.). 1980. 15.95 (ISBN 0-8306-9958-9); pap. 9.95 (ISBN 0-8306-1214-9, 1214). TAB Bks.

Plumes in the Dust: The Love Affair of Edgar Allen Poe & Fanny Osgood. John E. Walsh. LC 79-27534. (Illus.). 1980. 14.95 (ISBN 0-88229-683-3). Nelson-Hall.

Plummers of Harmony Grove. new ed. Eogar Z. Palmer. LC 74-8976. 1974. pap. 3.95 o.p. (ISBN 0-913408-12-3). Friends United.

Plums, Stones, Kisses & Hooks: Poems by Ronald Wallace. Ronald Wallace. LC 80-15907. 80p. 1981. text ed. 10.00x (ISBN 0-8262-0314-0). U of Mo Pr.

Plunkitt of Tammany Hall. William Riordan. 98p. 1976. Repr. of 1905 ed. lib. bdg. 12.95x (ISBN 0-89244-088-0). Queens Hse.

Plural Society in the British West Indies. M. G. Smith. (California Library Repr). 1975. Repr. of 1965 ed. 24.50x (ISBN 0-520-02853-8). U of Cal Pr.

Plural Society in the Southwest. Ed. by Edward H. Spicer & Raymond H. Thompson. 380p. 1972. 5.95 (ISBN 0-913456-53-5). Interbk Inc.

Pluralism & Personality: William James & Some Contemporary Cultures of Psychology. Don S. Browning. LC 78-75196. 280p. Date not set. 22.50 (ISBN 0-8387-2265-2). Bucknell U Pr.

Pluralism & Truth in Religion. John F. Kane. Ed. by Wendell Dietrich. LC 80-20659. (American Academy of Religion Dissertation Ser.). 1981. write for info. (ISBN 0-89130-413-4); pap. write for info. (ISBN 0-89130-414-2). Scholars Pr CA.

Pluralism in a Democratic Society. Ed. by Melvin M. Tumin & Walter Plotch. LC 76-12877. 1977. text ed. 22.95 (ISBN 0-275-23310-3). Praeger.

Pluralism in Education: Conflict, Clarity, & Commitment. Richard Pratte. (Illus.). 232p. 1979. text ed. 16.50 (ISBN 0-398-03911-9); pap. text ed. 10.50 (ISBN 0-398-03912-7). C C Thomas.

Pluralism, Similarities, & Contract: Aids to Understanding Religion in North America. Wm. C. Brown Education Division Staff. (To Live Is Christ Ser.). 28p. (Orig.). 1979. wkbk. 10.95 (ISBN 0-697-01735-4). Wm C Brown.

Pluralism, Similarities, & Contrast: Spirit Masters for Religion in North America. Religious Education Staff. (To Live Is Christ Ser.). 1979. 10.95 (ISBN 0-697-01735-4). Wm C Brown.

Pluralist & Possibilist Aspect of the Scientific Enterprise. Arne Naess. 1972. text ed. 30.00x (ISBN 8-200-04609-5, Dist. by Columbia U Pr). Universitet.

Plurality of Ministries. Ed. by Hans Kung. (Concilium Ser.: Religion in the Seventies: Vol. 74). 1972. pap. 4.95 (ISBN 0-8164-2530-2). Crossroad NY.

Pluri Dictionnaire. new ed. C. Dubois. (Illus.). 1974. 31.50x (ISBN 2-03-020124-3, 3677). Larousse.

Plus: A Handbook of Classroom Ideas to Motivate the Teaching of Elementary Mathematics. (Spice Ser). 1975. 6.50 (ISBN 0-89273-103-6). Educ Serv.

Plus & Minus of Fluids & Electrolytes. Esther Nicksic. 1981. text ed. 14.95 (ISBN 0-8359-5561-3); pap. text ed. 12.95 (ISBN 0-8359-5560-5). Reston.

Plus Duplicating Masters: Elementary Math, 2 vols. (Spice Ser.). 1975. 5.95 ea. Vol. 1, Grades K-2 (ISBN 0-89273-533-3). Vol. 2, Grades 2-4 (ISBN 0-89273-534-1). Educ Serv.

Plus Fort Des Pamphlets: L'ordre Des Paysans Aux Etats - Generaux. Restif De la Bretonne, Nicolas - Edme. 80p. (Fr.). 1977. lib. bdg. 20.00x o.p. (ISBN 0-8287-0720-0); pap. text ed. 10.00x o.p. (ISBN 0-685-75616-5). Clearwater Pub.

Plus Heureux Gouvernement...Servant D'introduction a la Theorie Des Loix Civiles. S. N. H. Linguet. (Fr.). 1977. Repr. of 1774 ed. lib. bdg. 41.25x o.p. (ISBN 0-8287-0548-8). Clearwater Pub.

Plus Petit Larousse. Larousse And Co. (Fr). plastic bdg. 6.25 (ISBN 0-685-14044-X, 3756). Larousse.

Plutarch. C. J. Gianakaris. (World Authors Ser.: Greece: No. 111). lib. bdg. 9.95 (ISBN 0-8057-2706-X). Twayne.

Plutarch Revisited. A Study of Shakespeare's Last Roman Tragedies & Their Source. David G. Green. (SSEL Jacobean Drama Studies: No. 78). (Orig.). pap. text ed. 25.00x (ISBN 0-391-01608-3). Humanities.

Plutarch's Lives. Plutarch. Ed. by John S. White. LC 66-28487. (Illus.). 468p. (gr. 7 up). 1900. 9.50x (ISBN 0-8196-0174-8). Biblo.

Plutarch's Lives. Alan Wardman. 1979. 19.95 o.p. (ISBN 0-236-17622-6, Pub. by Paul Elek). Merrimack Bk Serv.

Plutarch's Themistocles: A Historical Commentary. Frank J. Frost. LC 79-3208. 1980. 17.50x (ISBN 0-691-05300-6). Princeton U Pr.

Pluto. Pat Bemis. 1978. pap. 3.50 (ISBN 0-686-68270-X). Macoy Pub.

Plutonium As a Reactor Fuel. (Illus., Eng., Fr. & Rus.). 1967. pap. 47.75 (ISBN 92-0-050167-2, IAEA). Unipub.

Plutonium Culture from Hiroshima to Harrisburg. James Garrison. 224p. 1981. 14.95 (ISBN 0-8264-0029-9). Continuum.

Plutonium, Health Implications for Man: Proceedings of the 2nd Los Alamos Life Sciences Symposium. J. W. Healy. 1976. 32.00 (ISBN 0-08-019751-5). Pergamon.

Plutonium Ode: Poems 1977-1980. Allen Ginsberg. (Pockets Poets Ser.: No. 40). 80p. 1981. 8.50 (ISBN 0-87286-125-2); pap. 3.50 (ISBN 0-87286-126-0). City Lights.

Plutonium: Physico-Chemical Properties of Its Compounds & Alloys. (Atomic Energy Rev., Special Issue No. 1). 1966. pap. 6.50 (ISBN 92-0-149066-6, IAER1, IAEA). Unipub.

Plutonium, Power, & Politics: International Arrangements for the Disposition of Spent Nuclear Fuel. Gene I. Rochlin. 1979. 24.95x (ISBN 0-520-03887-8). U of Cal Pr.

Plymouth: A New History, 2 vols. Crispin Gill. Incl. Vol. 1. Ice Age of Elizabethans (ISBN 0-7153-4018-2); Vol. 2. Sixteen Hundred & Three to Present Day (ISBN 0-7153-7617-9). LC 66-6718. (Illus.). 1979. 22.50 ea. David & Charles.

Plymouth Arrow: 1976-1977 Shop Manual. Alan Ahlstrand. Ed. by Eric Jorgensen. (Illus.). 1979. pap. 10.95 (ISBN 0-89287-275-6, A178). Clymer Pubns.

Plymouth Horizon: 1978 Shop Manual. Jim Combs. Ed. by Eric Jorgensen. (Illus.). 1979. pap. text ed. 10.95 (ISBN 0-89287-298-5, A177). Clymer Pubns.

Plymouth Tune-up - Maintenance, 1967-1978 Models. Jim Combs. Ed. by Jeff Robinson. (Illus.). 1977. pap. 7.95 (ISBN 0-89287-142-3, A-179). Clymer Pubns.

Plymouth Volare: 1976-1979 Shop Manual. Jim Combs. Ed. by Eric Jorgensen. (Illus.). 328p. (Orig.). 1980. pap. text ed. 10.95 (ISBN 0-89287-312-4, A236). Clymer Pubns.

Plywood. Rolf Hartung. 1971. 17.95 (ISBN 0-7134-2380-3, Pub. by Batsford England). David & Charles.

Plywood Planbook. American Plywood Association. (Illus.). 1980. pap. 5.95 (ISBN 0-89586-034-1). H P Bks.

p,n Reaction & the Nucleon-Nucleon Force. Ed. by Charles D. Goodman et al. 550p. 1980. 55.00 (ISBN 0-306-40351-X, Plenum Pr). Plenum Pub.

Pneumatic & Hydraulic Components & Instruments in Automatic Control: Proceedings of the IFAC Symposium, Warsaw, Poland, 20-23 May 1980. Ed. by H. J. Laskiewicz & M. Zaremba. (IFAC Proceedings Ser.). (Illus.). 308p. 1981. 75.00 (ISBN 0-08-027317-3). Pergamon.

Pneumatic Circuits & Low Cost Automation. J. R. Fawcett. (Illus.). 1968. 27.50x (ISBN 0-85461-029-4). Intl Ideas.

Pneumatic Conveying. H. A. Stoess, Jr. LC 79-105393. 1970. 32.95 (ISBN 0-471-82680-4, Pub. by Wiley-Interscience). Wiley.

Pneumatic Conveying of Bulk Materials. Chemical Engineering Magazine. Ed. by Milton N. Kraus. (Chemical Engineering Bks). 352p. 1980. 24.50 (ISBN 0-07-010724-6, P&RB). McGraw.

Pneumatic Data, Vol. 2. Trade & Technical Press Editors. 130p. 1967. 20.00x (ISBN 0-85461-012-X, Pub by Trade & Tech England). Renouf.

Pneumatic Data, Vol. 3. Trade & Technical Press Editors. 100p. 1978. 21.00x (ISBN 0-85461-069-3, Pub by Trade & Tech England). Renouf.

Pneumatic Engineering Calculations. Trade & Technical Press Editors. 120p. 1969. 16.00x (ISBN 0-85461-038-3, Pub by Trade & Tech England). Renouf.

Pneumatic Engineering Calculations. R. H. Warring. 1969. 24.95x (ISBN 0-85461-038-3). Intl Ideas.

Pneumatic Handbook. 5th ed. Ed. by Trade & Technical Press Ltd. (Illus.). 1978. 115.00x (ISBN 0-85461-068-5). Intl Ideas.

Pneumatic Mechanisation. F. S. Van Dijen. 296p. 1980. 20.25x (ISBN 0-686-64954-0, Pub. by Thornes England). State Mutual Bk.

Pneumatic Power Glossary. Trade & Technical Press Editors. 80p. 1970. 17.00x o.p. (ISBN 0-686-65529-X, Pub by Trade & Tech England). Renouf.

Pneumatic Technical Data, Vol. 3. Ed. by Trade & Technical Press Ltd. 27.50x (ISBN 0-85461-069-3). Intl Ideas.

Pneumatics & Hydraulics. 3rd ed. Harry L. Stewart. LC 75-36658. (Illus.). 1976. 10.95 (ISBN 0-672-23237-5, 23237). Audel.

Pneumatikos-Psychikos Terminology in First Corinthians. Birger A. Pearson. LC 73-92202. (Society of Biblical Literature. Dissertation Ser.). 1975. pap. 7.50 (ISBN 0-88414-034-2, 060112). Scholars Pr Ca.

Pneumoencephalography. 2nd ed. E. Graeme Robertson. (Illus.). 832p. 1967. 42.75 (ISBN 0-398-01596-1). C C Thomas.

Pneumonia & Pneumococcal Infections. Ed. by A. D. Caldwell & H. P. Lambert. (Royal Society of Medicine International Congress & Symposium Ser.: No. 27). 1980. 15.50 (ISBN 0-8089-1287-9). Grune.

Pneumotransport Bibliography. Ed. by Wendy A. Thorton. 1972. text ed. 28.00 (ISBN 0-900983-17-5, Dist. by Air Science Co.). BHRA Fluid.

Pneumotransport Five: Proceedings. (International Conference on Pneumatic Transport of Solids in Pipes Ser.). (Illus.). 467p. 1980. pap. 104.00 (Dist. by Air Science Co.). BHRA Fluid.

Poacher from Stratford: A Partial Account of the Controversy Over the Authorship of Shakespeare's Plays. Frank W. Wadsworth. (California Library Reprint Series: No. 13). 1969. Repr. of 1958 ed. 18.50x (ISBN 0-520-01311-5). U of Cal Pr.

Pocho. Jose Antonio Villarreeal. LC 71-11196. 1970. pap. 1.95 (ISBN 0-385-06118-8, Anch). Doubleday.

Pocket Acquinas. Thomas Acquinas. pap. 2.95 (ISBN 0-671-42141-7, 48131-2). WSP.

Pocket Atlas. Rand McNally. LC 80-83201. (Illus.). 160p. 1980. pap. 4.95 (ISBN 0-528-83097-X). Rand.

Pocket Atlas of Human Histology. Robert Meadows. (Illus.). 465p. 1981. text ed. 29.50x (ISBN 0-19-261248-4); pap. text ed. 16.95x (ISBN 0-19-261177-1). Oxford U Pr.

Pocket Bi-Lingual French-English English-French. 5.95 (ISBN 2-03-020410-2, 3768). Larousse.

Pocket Book of Baseball. Howard Liss. 1981. pap. 2.75 (ISBN 0-671-41862-9). PB.

Pocket Book of British Ceramic Marks. new ed. J. P. Cushion. 1976. 19.95 (ISBN 0-571-04869-2, Pub. by Faber & Faber). Merrimack Bk Serv.

Pocket Book of Crossword Puzzles, No. 22. Ed. by Margaret Farrar. (Orig.). 1980. pap. write for info. (ISBN 0-671-82919-X). PB.

Pocket Book of Daily Prayer. Compiled By Fergus Mulligan. 128p. 1980. pap. 3.50 (ISBN 0-03-057848-5). Winston Pr.

Pocket Book of Pro Basketball 1980. John Devaney. 1980. pap. 2.75 (ISBN 0-671-41863-7). PB.

Pocket Calculator Fun & Games. Ross Olney & Pat Olney. (Illus.). (gr. 4 up). 1977. PLB 6.45 s&l (ISBN 0-531-00387-6). Watts.

Pocket Calculator Game Book, No. 2. Edwin Schlossberg & John Brockman. LC 77-7054. (Illus.). 1977. 6.95 (ISBN 0-688-03234-6); pap. 3.95 (ISBN 0-688-08234-3). Morrow.

Pocket Calculators: How to Use & Enjoy Them. Arnold Madison & David L. Drotar. LC 78-707. (Illus.). (gr. 6 up). 1978. 7.95 (ISBN 0-525-66580-3). Elsevier-Nelson.

Pocket Dictionary: Chinese-English, & Pekingese Syllabary. Chauncey Goodrich. 341p. 1981. pap. 2.50 (ISBN 0-85656-131-2). Great Eastern.

Pocket Dictionary of Art Terms. Ed. by Julia M. Ehresmann. LC 74-143464. (Illus.). 1971. pap. 2.95 (ISBN 0-8212-0748-2, 712019). NYGS.

Pocket Dictionary of Synonyms & Antonyms. 1960. pap. 2.50 (ISBN 0-394-40066-6). Random.

Pocket Dictionary of the German & English Languages. K. Wichmann. 1952. 12.00 (ISBN 0-7100-2290-5). Routledge & Kegan.

Pocket Diesel & Electric Guide. (Illus.). 1974. 5.00 (ISBN 0-913556-11-4). Spec Pr NJ.

Pocket Encyclopedia of Cacti in Color. Edgar Lamb & Brian Lamp. (Illus.). 217p. 1980. 9.95 (ISBN 0-7137-0506-X, Pub. by Blandford Pr England). Sterling.

Pocket Encyclopedia of California Wine. William I. Kaufman. Ed. by Maurice T. Sullivan. Tr. by S. Titus. 128p. (Orig.). 1980. 4.95 (ISBN 0-932664-09-1); pap. 3.95 (ISBN 0-932664-11-3). Wine Appreciation.

Pocket Encyclopedia of Dogs. Ivan Swedrup. LC 75-23131. (Macmillan Color Series). (Illus.). 256p. 1976. 8.95 (ISBN 0-02-615610-5, 61561). Macmillan.

Pocket Encyclopedia of Indoor Plants in Color. Age Nicolaisen. Ed. by Richard Goren. LC 77-91385. 1970. 9.95 (ISBN 0-02-589500-1). Macmillan.

Pocket Encyclopedia of Ocean Life. Norman Marshall. (Illus.). (gr. 7 up). 1971. 8.95 (ISBN 0-02-580180-5). Macmillan.

Pocket Encyclopedia of Roses in Color. H. Edland. (Illus.). 1963. 9.95 (ISBN 0-7137-0632-5, Pub by Blandford Pr England). Sterling.

Pocket Encyclopedia of Seaplanes & Flying Boats. Kenneth Munson. Ed. by John W. Wood. (World Aircraft in Color Ser). (Illus.). 1971. 8.95 (ISBN 0-02-587990-1). Macmillan.

Pocket Encyclopedia of Wild Flowers. M. Skytte Christiansen. (European Ecology Ser.). (Illus.). 1965. 9.95 (ISBN 0-7137-0374-1, Pub by Blandford Pr England). Sterling.

Pocket English-Chinese Dictionary. 1980. pap. 4.95 (ISBN 0-8351-0727-2). China Bks.

Pocket Fishing Guide. Tom McNally. 1981. pap. 1.95 (ISBN 0-528-84548-9). Rand.

Pocket Full of Dead. John Wyllie. LC 77-89882. 1978. 6.95 o.p. (ISBN 0-385-13483-5). Doubleday.

Pocket Guide of Movement Activities for the Elementary School. 2nd ed. Marjorie Latchaw. 1970. pap. 10.95 (ISBN 0-13-684852-4). P-H.

Pocket Guide to Cheese. Barbara Ensrud. 144p. 1981. pap. 4.95 (ISBN 0-399-50518-0, Perigee). Putnam.

Pocket Guide to Chess Openings. R. C. Griffith & H. Golomber. (Illus.). 128p. 1974. 9.50 (ISBN 0-7135-0515-X). Transatlantic.

Pocket Guide to Guns. (Illus.). 1980. pap. 1.95 (ISBN 0-89145-154-4). Collector Bks.

Pocket Guide to Health Assessment. Karen Berger & Willa Fields. (Illus.). 1980. pap. text ed. 11.95 (ISBN 0-8359-5582-6). Reston.

Pocket History of Freemasonry. 5th ed. Fred L. Pick & Norman Knight. 1969. 13.50x (ISBN 0-584-10256-9). Intl Pubns Serv.

Pocket History of the United States. 2nd, rev. ed. Allan Nevins & Henry S. Commager. 1981. pap. write for info. PB.

Pocket in a Petticoat: Memoirs. Florence E. Barrett. 1974. 4.00 o.p. (ISBN 0-682-48075-4, Lochinvar). Exposition.

Pocket Knives, Value & Identification Guide. (Illus.). 2.95 o.p. (ISBN 0-89689-004-X). Wallace-Homestead.

Pocket Lexicon to the Greek New Testament. Ed. by Alexander Souter. 1916. 14.95x (ISBN 0-19-864203-2). Oxford U Pr.

Pocket Liturgikon: Pastoral Ministrations. abr. ed. Walter J. Schmitz. LC 80-81346. 96p. 1980. 4.95 (ISBN 0-87973-674-7, 674). Our Sunday Visitor.

Pocket Mad. Mad Magazine Editors. (Mad Ser.). (Illus.). 1974. pap. 1.75 (ISBN 0-446-94594-3). Warner Bks.

Pocket Map of London. 1978. pap. 1.50 o.p. (ISBN 0-905522-14-1, 8015, Pub. by R. Nickelson). Barrie & Jenkins.

Pocket of Prose & Verse. Alexander Kellet. Ed. by Wilcomb E. Washburn. LC 75-7031. (Narratives of North American Indian Captivities: Vol. 11). 1975. lib. bdg. 44.00 (ISBN 0-8240-1635-1). Garland Pub.

Pocket Oxford Dictionary of Current English. 6th ed. Ed. by J. B. Sykes. 1978. 11.95 (ISBN 0-19-861129-3). Oxford U Pr.

Pocket Park Problem. M. Blount Christian. (The Goosehill Gang Series: No. 2). (gr. 2-5). 1977. pap. 1.10 (ISBN 0-570-07353-7, 39-1043). Concordia.

Pocket Patches. 2nd ed. Ann L. Bradford & Harold M. Murai. (Cornerstone Ser.). (gr. 1). 1978. pap. text ed. 4.52 (ISBN 0-201-41020-6, Sch Div); tchr's. ed. 5.56 (ISBN 0-201-41021-4). A-W.

Pocket Promise Book. gift ed. David Wilkerson. LC 72-86208. 96p. 1981. imitation leather 3.95 (ISBN 0-8307-0782-4). Regal.

Pocket Treasury of Daily Devotions. Al Bryant. LC 77-82183. 1978. pap. 1.75 (ISBN 0-87123-464-5, 200464). Bethany Fell.

Pocket Treasury of Devotional Verse. Compiled by Al Bryant. (Orig.). 1980. pap. 2.95 (ISBN 0-87123-466-1, 200466). Bethany Fell.

Pocket Vacation Guide. Rand McNally. 1981. pap. 3.95 (ISBN 0-528-84547-0). Rand.

Pocket Watch Price Indicator. Roy Ehrhardt. (Illus.). 1980. plastic ring bdg. 12.00 (ISBN 0-913902-32-2). Heart Am Pr.

Pocketbook for Writers: A Guide to Writing & Revision. Earl G. Bingham. 416p. 1980. pap. text ed. 8.95x (ISBN 0-534-00773-2). Wadsworth Pub.

Pocketful of Prayers. Ralph Woods. 1976. pap. 1.50 (ISBN 0-89129-217-9). Jove Pubns.

Pocketguide to Health & Health Problems in School Physical Activities. 1981. pap. 3.00 (ISBN 0-917160-13-4). Am Sch Health.

Poder De la Alabanza. Tr. by David Wilkerson. (Spanish Bks.). (Span.). 1978. 1.90 (ISBN 0-8297-0444-2). Life Pubs Intl.

Poder De la Oracion Tenaz. Juan Bisagno. Tr. by Olivia S. D. De Lerin from Eng. Orig. Title: Power of Positive Praying. 96p. (Span.). 1980. pap. 1.70 (ISBN 0-311-40029-9). Casa Bautista.

Poder Espiritual. Ted Lindwall. 1978. Repr. of 1977 ed. 0.60 (ISBN 0-311-46068-2). Casa Bautista.

Podiatric Medicine. 2nd ed. Irving Yale. (Illus.). 368p. 1980. 39.00 (ISBN 0-683-09318-5). Williams & Wilkins.

Podiatric Resource Guide for Preventive & Rehabilitative Foot & Leg Care. Michael Le Bendig & Elliot Diamond. LC 75-45780. 1976. m0n0graph 18.25 (ISBN 0-87993-080-2). Futura Pub.

Podopediatrics. Herman R. Tax. (Illus.). 376p. 1980. lib. bdg. 40.00 (ISBN 0-683-08117-9). Williams & Wilkins.

Pods: Wildflowers & Weeds in Their Final Beauty. Jane Embertson. (Illus.). 1979. pap. 9.95 (ISBN 0-684-15543-5, SL 752, ScribT). Scribner.

Poe Papers. N. L. Zaroulis. 1978. pap. 1.75 o.s.i. (ISBN 0-515-04457-1). Jove Pubns.

Poem a Day. Thomas M. Sheaffer. 58p. 1980. 3.50 (ISBN 0-8059-2721-2). Dorrance.

Poem from a Single Pallet. Fanny Howe. 1980. 4.50 (ISBN 0-932716-10-5). Kelsey St Pr.

Poem in Four Movements. Honor Moore. (Out & Out Pamphlet Ser.). pap. 1.00 (ISBN 0-918314-11-9). Out & Out.

Poem of the Cid. Edmund De Chasca. LC 75-30597. (World Authors Ser.,: Spain: No.378). 1976. lib. bdg. 12.50 (ISBN 0-8057-6194-2). Twayne.

Poem of the Cid. Tr. by Lesley B. Simpson. (YA) (gr. 9 up). 1957. pap. 3.50 (ISBN 0-520-01176-7, CAL10). U of Cal Pr.

Poem Portraits for All Occasions. James J. Metcalfe. LC 61-9537. 5.95 o.p. (ISBN 0-385-08938-4). Doubleday.

Poemes Pour le Cours Avance Nineteen Eighty to Nineteen Eighty-Three. Ed. by Andre O. Hurtgen. (Illus.). 65p. (Orig.). 1979. pap. text ed. 4.95x (ISBN 0-88334-117-4). Ind Sch Pr.

Poems. Yehuda Amichai. Tr. by Assia Gutman. LC 69-15293. 1969. 6.95 o.s.i. (ISBN 0-06-010111-3, HarpT). Har-Row.

Poems. Richard Bartholomew. (Writers Workshop Redbird Ser.). 1975. 8.00 (ISBN 0-88253-610-9); pap. text ed. 4.00 (ISBN 0-88253-609-5). Ind-US Inc.

Poems. 2nd ed. M. R. Bhagavan. (Redbird Bk.). 1976. lib. bdg. 8.00 (ISBN 0-89253-125-8); flexible bdg. 4.80 (ISBN 0-89253-139-8). Ind-US Inc.

Poems. Sukanta Chaudhuri. 8.00 (ISBN 0-89253-500-8); flexible cloth 4.00 (ISBN 0-89253-501-6). Ind-US Inc.

Poems. Elizabeth Coatsworth. (Illus.). (gr. 4-6). 1957. 4.95g o.s.i. (ISBN 0-02-721490-7). Macmillan.

Poems. Samuel T. Coleridge. Ed. by John Bierre. 1963. 11.50 (ISBN 0-460-00043-8, Evman); pap. 4.50 (ISBN 0-460-01043-3). Dutton.

Poems. Jatin Das. (Redbird Bk.). 1976. 8.00 (ISBN 0-89253-537-7); flexible bdg. 4.00 (ISBN 0-89253-098-7). Ind-US Inc.

Poems. John Donne. Ed. by Herbert J. Grierson. (Oxford Standard Authors Ser.). 1933. 23.00 (ISBN 0-19-254123-4); pap. 7.50x (ISBN 0-19-281113-4). Oxford U Pr.

Poems. William Dunbar. Ed. by James Kinsley. (Clarendon Medieval & Tudor Ser.). 1958. pap. 9.95x (ISBN 0-19-871017-8). Oxford U Pr.

Poems, 2 vols. in 1. George Dyer. LC 75-31198. (Romantic Context Ser.: Poetry 1789-1830: Vol. 50). 1978. Repr. of 1802 ed. lib. bdg. 47.00 (ISBN 0-8240-2149-5). Garland Pub.

Poems. Rachel Field. (gr. k-3). 1957. 3.95g o.s.i. (ISBN 0-02-735060-6). Macmillan.

Poems. Philip Freneau. Ed. by Harry H. Clark. (Library of Classics Ser.: No. 19). 1960. pap. text ed. 8.75 o.s.i. (ISBN 0-02-844850-2). Hafner.

Poems. M. C. Gabriel. 8.00 (ISBN 0-89253-479-6); flexible cloth 4.00 (ISBN 0-89253-480-X). Ind-US Inc.

Poems. C. L. Gammon. 1981. 4.50 (ISBN 0-8062-1710-3). Carlton.

Poems. Jean Genet. 1980. pap. 6.95 (ISBN 0-686-28714-2). Man-Root.

Poems. Heinrich Heine. Ed. by Kathleen Webber. 1952. pap. 9.95x (ISBN 0-631-01550-7, Pub. by Basil Blackwell). Biblio Dist.

Poems. John Keats. Ed. by Gerald Bullett. 1957. 12.95x (ISBN 0-460-00101-9, Evman); pap. 4.95 (ISBN 0-460-01101-4). Dutton.

Poems. John Keats. 336p. 1980. Repr. of 1897 ed. text ed. 15.75x (ISBN 0-8419-7301-6). Holmes & Meier.

Poems. Anne Killigrew. LC 67-10177. 1967. Repr. of 1686 ed. 20.00x (ISBN 0-8201-1030-2). Schol Facsimiles.

Poems. Emily Lawless. Ed. by Padraic Fallon. (Arts Council Ser). 1964. 4.25 (ISBN 0-85105-090-5). Dufour.

Poems. Charles Lloyd. Ed. by Donald H. Reiman. Incl. Blank Verse by Charles Lloyd & Charles Lamb. Repr. of 1798 ed; Poetical Essays on the Character of Pope. Repr. of 1821 ed; Poems. Repr. of 1823 ed. LC 75-31225. (Romantic Context Ser.: Poetry 1789-1830). 1978. lib. bdg. 47.00 (ISBN 0-8240-2175-4). Garland Pub.

Poems. A. Madhavan. 8.00 (ISBN 0-89253-772-8); flexible cloth 4.00 (ISBN 0-89253-773-6). Ind-US Inc.

Poems. complete ed. John Masefield. 1953. 19.95 (ISBN 0-02-580940-7). Macmillan.

Poems. John Milton. Ed. by B. A. Wright. 1956. 6.00x (ISBN 0-460-00384-4, Evman); pap. 9.25 (ISBN 0-460-01384-X). Dutton.

Poems. Eduard Morike. Ed. by Lionel Thomas. (Blackwell's German Text Ser.). 1970. pap. 9.95x (ISBN 0-631-01660-0, Pub. by Basil Blackwell). Biblio Dist.

Poems. Suniti Namjoshi. 5.00 (ISBN 0-89253-704-3); flexible cloth 4.00 (ISBN 0-89253-705-1). Ind-US Inc.

Poems. Leslie De Noronha. (Redbird). 1976. lib. bdg. 5.00 (ISBN 0-89253-127-4); flexible bdg. 4.80 (ISBN 0-89253-141-X). Ind-US Inc.

Poems. Amelia Opie. Ed. by Donald H. Reiman. LC 75-31242. (Romantic Context Ser.: Poetry 1789-1830 Ser.). 1978. Repr. of 1802 ed. lib. bdg. 47.00 (ISBN 0-8240-2191-6). Garland Pub.

Poems. Sultan Padamsee. (Redbird Bk.). 1976. 9.00 (ISBN 0-89253-123-1); flexible bdg. 6.75 (ISBN 0-89253-138-X). Ind-US Inc.

Poems. Edgar A. Poe. 225p. 1980. Repr. of 1900 ed. text ed. 14.00x (ISBN 0-8419-7300-8). Holmes & Meier.

Poems. Rakshat Puri. 8.00 (ISBN 0-89253-718-3); flexible cloth 4.80 (ISBN 0-89253-719-1). Ind-US Inc.

Poems. Raghavendra Rao. 8.00 (ISBN 0-89253-722-1); flexible cloth 4.00 (ISBN 0-89253-723-X). Ind-US Inc.

Poems. Rainer M. Rilke. Ed. by G. W. McKay. (Clarendon German Ser.). (gr. 9 up). 1965. pap. 2.95x (ISBN 0-19-500366-7). Oxford U Pr.

Poems. William Shakespeare. Ed. by Arthur Quiller-Couch et al. (New Shakespeare Ser). 1969. 23.95 (ISBN 0-521-07551-3); pap. 4.50x (ISBN 0-521-09493-3). Cambridge U Pr.

Poems. L. B. Strawn. 1981. 6.50 (ISBN 0-8062-1637-9). Carlton.

Poems. John Theobald. 8.00 (ISBN 0-89253-741-8); flexible cloth 4.80 (ISBN 0-89253-742-6). Ind-US Inc.

Poems, 2 Vols. Theocritus. Tr. by A. S. Gow. 1952. Set. 130.00 (ISBN 0-521-06616-6). Cambridge U Pr.

Poems. Gautam Vohra. (Writers Workshop Redbird Ser.). 1975. 9.00 (ISBN 0-88253-612-5); pap. text ed. 4.80 (ISBN 0-88253-611-7). Ind-US Inc.

Poems, Repr. Of 1789. Thomas Dermody. Ed. by Donald H. Reiman. Bd. with Poems, Consisting of Essays, Lyric, Elegiac, Etc. Repr. of 1792 ed; Poems, Moral & Descriptive. Repr. of 1800 ed; Histroniade: or, Theatric Tribunal; a Poem...by Marmaduke Myrtle (Pseud.) Repr. of 1802 ed; Poems on Various Subjects. Repr. of 1802 ed. LC 75-31196. (Romantic Context Ser.: Poetry 1789-1830). 1979. lib. bdg. 47.00 (ISBN 0-8240-2147-9). Garland Pub.

Poems After Martial. Philip Murray. LC 67-24109. 1967. 10.00x (ISBN 0-8195-3083-2, Pub. by Wesleyan U Pr). Columbia U Pr.

Poems Against Death. Karl Krolow. Tr. by Herman Salinger. LC 71-82716. 1980. 7.50 (ISBN 0-685-39468-9). Charioteer.

Poems & Ballads & Atalanta in Calydon. Algernon C. Swinburne. Ed. by Morse Peckham. LC 79-117333. (Library of Literature Ser). 1970. 9.50 (ISBN 0-672-51119-3); text ed. 3.55 o.p. (ISBN 0-672-61000-0). Bobbs.

Poems & Critics. Ed. by Christopher Ricks. 1966. pap. 1.95 o.p. (ISBN 0-531-06037-3, Fontana Pap). Watts.

Poems & Essays. Joseph Howe. LC 73-78943. (Literature of Canada Ser.). 1973. pap. 4.95 (ISBN 0-8020-6208-3). U of Toronto Pr.

Poems & Essays. Edgar A. Poe. 1955. 11.50x (ISBN 0-460-00791-2, Evman); pap. 7.95 (ISBN 0-460-01791-8). Dutton.

Poems & Fables of John Dryden. John Dryden. Ed. by James Kinsley. (Oxford Paperbacks Ser). 1970. pap. 12.95x (ISBN 0-19-281073-1). Oxford U Pr.

Poems & Fables of John Dryden. John Dryden. Ed. by James Kinsley. (Oxford Standard Authors Ser.). 1962. 27.50 (ISBN 0-19-254124-2). Oxford U Pr.

Poems & Hymns of Christ's Sweet Singer: Frances Ridley Havergal. Compiled by Tacey Bly. LC 77-86549. 1977. 7.95 (ISBN 0-87983-163-4); pap. 3.95 (ISBN 0-87983-164-2). Keats.

Poems & Prophecies. William Blake. Ed. by Max Plowman. 1954. 6.00x (ISBN 0-460-00792-0, Evman); pap. 4.50 (ISBN 0-460-01792-6). Dutton.

Poems & Prose: 1949-1977. Harold Pinter. LC 78-56046. 1978. pap. 5.95 (ISBN 0-394-17070-9, E722, Ever). Grove.

Poems & Romances. G. A. Simcox. Ed. by Ian Fletcher & John Stokes. LC 76-24392. (Decadent Consciousness Ser.). 1978. lib. bdg. 38.00 (ISBN 0-8240-2779-5). Garland Pub.

Poems & Songs. Robert Burns. Ed. by James Kinsley. (Oxford Standard Authors Ser.). 1969. 29.50 (ISBN 0-19-254164-1); pap. 11.50x (ISBN 0-19-281114-2). Oxford U Pr.

Poems & Translations. Clive Hawthorne. LC 79-51457. (Illus.). 1981. pap. 8.00 (ISBN 0-912908-07-6). Tamal Land.

Poems & Translations, Repr. Of 1812 Ed. Reginald Heber. Ed. by Donald H. Reiman. Bd. with Hymns, Written & Adapted to the Weekly Church Service of the Year. Repr. of 1827 ed. LC 75-31212. (Romantic Context Ser.: Poetry 1789-1830). 1979. lib. bdg. 47.00 (ISBN 0-8240-2162-2). Garland Pub.

Poems by a Slave in the Island of Cuba. Edward J. Mullen. 1981. 25.00 (ISBN 0-208-01900-6, Archon). Shoe String.

Poems, by an Amateur, Repr. Of 1818 Ed. Bernard Barton. Bd. with Poems. Repr. of 1820 ed. LC 75-31152. (Romantic Context: Poetry 1789-1830 Ser.: Vol. 8). 1977. lib. bdg. 47.00 (ISBN 0-8240-2107-X). Garland Pub.

Poems by Members of the Louise Bogen Poetry Society. 1980. write for info. Crambruck.

Poems by Richard Thomas. Richard Thomas. 1975. pap. 2.95 (ISBN 0-380-01106-9, 45286). Avon.

Poems by Three Friends. (Thomas Raffles, Baldwin Brown, & J. H. Wiffen), Repr. Of 1813 Ed. Jeremiah H. Wiffen. Ed. by Donald H. Reiman. Bd. with Aonian Hours, & Other Poems. Repr. of 1819 ed. LC 75-31272. (Romantic Ser.: Poetry 1789-1830). 1979. lib. bdg. 47.00 (ISBN 0-8240-2218-1). Garland Pub.

Poems Chosen. Henry Chapin. 1981. pap. 5.95 (ISBN 0-87233-056-7). Bauhan.

Poems, Eighteen Ninety to Eighteen Ninety-Six, 3 Vols. in 1. Emily Dickinson. LC 67-25640. 1967. 55.00x (ISBN 0-8201-1014-0). Schol Facsimiles.

Poems, Eighteen Thirty-Five to Eighteen Eighty-Nine. Robert Browning. Ed. by Humphrey Milford. (World's Classics Ser.). 1954. 10.95 (ISBN 0-19-250513-0). Oxford U Pr.

Poems for a Lazy Evening. Sheran A. Cisneros. 1981. 5.95 (ISBN 0-533-04823-0). Vantage.

Poems for All Occasions. Doris M. Brown. Date not set. 5.95 (ISBN 0-533-04888-5). Vantage.

Poems for All the Annettes. Al Purdy. LC 72-357343. (House of Anansi Poetry Ser.: No. 7). 108p. 1973. 10.95 (ISBN 0-88784-107-4, Pub. by Hse Anansi Pr Canada); pap. 4.95 (ISBN 0-88784-007-8). U of Toronto Pr.

Poems for Children & Other People. rev. & expanded ed. Ed. by George Hornby. (Illus.). 1980. 6.95 (ISBN 0-517-52588-7). Crown.

Poems for Goya's Disparates. Dale Jacobson. (Illus.). 48p. (Orig.). 1981. pap. 4.95 (ISBN 0-937310-00-X). Jazz Pr.

Poems for Holidays & Special Days. Frances Grover. LC 80-52667. (Illus.). 90p. 1980. 6.95 (ISBN 0-533-04779-X). Vantage.

Poems for Today. Christee Modica. 1981. 4.50 (ISBN 0-8062-1666-2). Carlton.

Poems. Fourth Edition, Repr. Of 1807. Samuel E. Brydges. Bd. with Odo, Count of Lingen. A Poetical Tale: in Six Cantos. LC 75-31170. (Romantic Context Ser.: Poetry 1789-1830: Vol. 24). 1978. lib. bdg. 47.00 (ISBN 0-8240-2123-1). Garland Pub.

Poems from Angola. Michael Wolfers. (African Writers Ser.). 1980. pap. text ed. 5.50x (ISBN 0-435-90215-6). Heinemann Ed.

Poems from Korea: A Historical Anthology. rev. ed. Ed. & tr. by Peter H. Lee. LC 73-80209. 196p. 1974. 8.50x (ISBN 0-8248-0263-2, Eastwest Ctr). U Pr of Hawaii.

Poems from Life Within. Lyme Webb. 1981. 4.95 (ISBN 0-8062-1648-4). Carlton.

Poems from Prison. Jack Murray et al. 1973. 6.25x (ISBN 0-7022-0875-2). U of Queensland Pr.

Poems from the Asylum. Bobby J. Johnson. 34p. 1978. 2.95 (ISBN 0-8059-2496-5). Dorrance.

Poems from the Diwan of al Mutanabbi. Tr. by Arthur Wormhoudt. (Arab Translation Ser.: No. 1). 85p. 1968. pap. 2.50 (ISBN 0-916358-51-8). Wormhoudt.

Poems from the Fifties. P. K. Saha. 8.00 (ISBN 0-89253-726-4). Ind-US Inc.

Poems from the Hebrew. Ed. by Robert Mezey. LC 75-132299. (Poems of the World Ser.). (Illus.). 156p. (gr. 9-12). 1973. 8.95 (ISBN 0-690-63685-7, TYC-J). T Y Crowell.

Poems from the Old English. 2nd, rev & enl. ed. Tr. by Burton Raffel. LC 60-14776. 1964. 7.95x (ISBN 0-8032-0150-8); pap. 1.95x (ISBN 0-8032-5154-8, BB 106, Bison). U of Nebr Pr.

Poems from the Oregon Sea Coast. Marilyn R. Riddle. (Illus.). 24p. (Orig.). 1979. pap. 3.00 large type ed. (ISBN 0-9603748-0-9). Sandpiper OR.

Poems in English. Michael Hartnett. 1977. text ed. 15.75x (ISBN 0-85105-313-0, Dolmen Pr). Humanities.

Poems in Praise of the Man. Francesca Guli. 1980. 6.50 (ISBN 0-8233-0309-8). Golden Quill.

Poems: Jules Laforgue. Ed. by J. A. Hiddleston. (Blackwell's French Text Ser.). 1975. pap. 7.00x o.p. (ISBN 0-631-15940-1, Pub. by Basil Blackwell). Biblio Dist.

Poems New & Selected. Jon Silkin. LC 66-14661. (Wesleyan Poetry Program: Vol. 30). (Orig.). 1966. 10.00x (ISBN 0-8195-2030-6, Pub. by Wesleyan U Pr); pap. 6.95x (ISBN 0-8195-1030-0). Columbia U Pr.

Poems, Nineteen Eighteen to Nineteen Thirty-Six: The Complete Poems of Charles Reznikoff, Vol. 1. Charles Reznikoff. Ed. by Seamus Cooney. 222p. (Orig.). 1978. 14.00 (ISBN 0-87685-262-2); pap. 5.00 (ISBN 0-87685-261-4). Black Sparrow.

Poems, Nineteen Fifty-Seven to Nineteen Sixty-Seven. James Dickey. LC 67-15230. 1978. pap. 7.95 (ISBN 0-8195-6055-3, Pub. by Wesleyan U Pr). Columbia U Pr.

Poems, Nineteen Fifty to Nineteen Sixty-Six: A Selection. Thom Gunn. 41p. 1969. pap. 3.95 (ISBN 0-571-08845-7, Pub. by Faber & Faber). Merrimack Bk Serv.

Poems, Nineteen Sixty-Two to Nineteen Seventy-Eight. Derek Mahon. 128p. (Orig.). 1979. pap. 8.95x (ISBN 0-19-211897-8). Oxford U Pr.

Poems, Nineteen Thirty-Four to Nineteen Sixty-Nine. David Ignatow. LC 79-105500. 1979. pap. 8.95 (ISBN 0-8195-6059-6, Pub. by Wesleyan U Pr). Columbia U Pr.

Poems, Nineteen Thirty-Seven to Nineteen Seventy-Five: The Complete Poems of Charles Reznikoff, Vol. 2. Charles Reznikoff. Ed. by Seamus Cooney. 1978. 14.00 (ISBN 0-87685-301-7); pap. 6.00 (ISBN 0-87685-300-9). Black Sparrow.

Poems, Nineteen Thirty-Three to Nineteen Forty-Five. Robert Graves. 58p. 1946. 4.95 (ISBN 0-374-23472-8). FS&G.

Poems of a Jew. Karl Shapiro. 1958. 7.50 o.p. (ISBN 0-394-40412-2). Random.

Poems of Alfred, Lord Tennyson. Alfred Tennyson. Ed. by Ruth G. Rausen. LC 64-13910. (Poets Ser). (Illus.). (gr. 6 up). 1964. 8.95 (ISBN 0-690-64146-X, TYC-J). T Y Crowell.

Poems of Ancient Tamil: Their Milieu & Their Sanskrit Counterparts. George L. Hart, III. 300p. 1975. 23.75x (ISBN 0-520-02672-1). U of Cal Pr.

Poems of Andrew Marvell. Ed. by James Reeves & Martin Seymour-Smith. (Poetry Bookshelf). 1969. pap. text ed. 4.95 (ISBN 0-435-15064-2). Heinemann Ed.

Poems of Bishop Henry King. Ed. by James H. Baker. LC 60-8067. 138p. 1960. 5.95 (ISBN 0-8040-0249-5); pap. 3.95 o.p. (ISBN 0-8040-0249-5). Swallow.

Poems of Charles Sackville, Sixth Earl of Dorset. Brice Harris. LC 78-61562. 1979. lib. bdg. write for info. (ISBN 0-8240-9753-X). Garland Pub.

Poems of Christmas. Myra C. Livingston. LC 80-13627. 132p. (gr. 5 up). 1980. 9.95 (ISBN 0-689-50180-3, McElderry Bk). Atheneum.

Poems of Cicero. William W. Ewbank. Ed. by Steele Commager. LC 77-70814. (Latin Poetry Ser.). 1978. lib. bdg. 28.00 (ISBN 0-8240-2955-0). Garland Pub.

Poems of Edgar Allan Poe. Ed. by Thomas D. Mabbott. (Harvard Paperbacks: No. 166). 512p. 1980. pap. 8.95 (ISBN 0-674-67780-3). Harvard U Pr.

Poems of Edgar Allan Poe. Edgar A. Poe. Ed. by Dwight Macdonald. LC 65-21417. (Apollo Eds.). (Illus.). 1971. pap. 1.95 o.p. (ISBN 0-8152-0311-X, A311, TYC-T). T Y Crowell.

Poems of Edgar Allan Poe. Edgar A. Poe. Ed. by Floyd Stovall. LC 65-23455. 1977. Repr. 12.95x (ISBN 0-8139-0194-4). U Pr of Va.

Poems of Edward Taylor. Edward Taylor. Ed. by Donald Stanford. LC 60-6432. 1977. pap. 6.95x (ISBN 0-300-02134-8). Yale U Pr.

Poems of Emerson: Selected Criticism from the Coming Age & the Arena, 1899-1905. Charles Malloy. LC 80-2539. 1981. 32.50 (ISBN 0-404-19265-3). AMS Pr.

Poems of Ernest Dowson. Ernest Dowson. Ed. by Mark Longaker. LC 62-14213. 1963. 9.00x o.p. (ISBN 0-8122-7331-1). U of Pa Pr.

Poems of Faith. Beverly Kittrell. 1981. 5.95 (ISBN 0-533-04798-6). Vantage.

Poems of Govindagraj. 2nd ed. Govindagraj. Tr. by Sarojini Namjoshi & Suniti Namjoshi. 1976. lib. bdg. 8.00 (ISBN 0-89253-099-5); flexible bdg. 4.80 (ISBN 0-89253-145-2). Ind-US Inc.

Poems of Gray, Collins & Goldsmith. Roger Lonsdale. LC 76-4543. (Longman Annotated English Poets Ser.). 1976. pap. text ed. 18.00x (ISBN 0-582-48495-2). Longman.

Poems of Inspiration. Thalia T. Bryan. 1981. 5.95. Vantage.

Poems of James Shirley. Ray L. Armstrong. 108p. 1980. Repr. of 1941 ed. lib. bdg. 27.50 (ISBN 0-8495-0062-1). Arden Lib.

Poems of John Audelay. Ed. by Ella K. Whiting. (EETS, OS Ser.: No. 184). Repr. of 1931 ed. 16.00 (ISBN 0-527-00183-X). Kraus Repr.

Poems of John Cleveland. John Cleveland. Ed. by Brian Morris & Eleanor Withington. (Oxford English Texts Ser). 1967. 29.00x (ISBN 0-19-811839-2). Oxford U Pr.

Poems of John Collop. John Collop. Ed. by Conrad Hilberry. 1962. 21.50x (ISBN 0-299-02490-3). U of Wis Pr.

Poems of John Keats. Ed. by Miriam Allott. (Longman Annotated English Poets Ser.). (Illus.). 1972. pap. text ed. 15.95x (ISBN 0-582-48457-X). Longman.

Poems of John Keats. John Keats. Ed. by Stanley Kunitz. LC 64-22174. (Poets Ser). (Illus.). (gr. 6 up). 1964. 8.95 (ISBN 0-690-63933-3, TYC-J). T Y Crowell.

Poems of John Milton. John Milton. Ed. by Helen Darbishire. 1961. 29.00x o.p. (ISBN 0-19-811421-4). Oxford U Pr.

Poems of Jonathan Swift. Jonathan Swift. Ed. by Padraic Colum. 1962. pap. 0.95 o.s.i. (ISBN 0-02-070810-6, Collier). Macmillan.

Poems of Joseph Campbell. Joseph Campbell. 1963. 3.95 (ISBN 0-900372-66-4). Irish Bk Ctr.

Poems of Lewis Carroll. Lewis Carroll. Compiled by Myra C. Livingston. LC 73-7914. (Poets Ser.). (Illus.). (gr. 6 up). 1973. 8.95 (ISBN 0-690-00178-9, TYC-J). T Y Crowell.

Poems of Li Ho, 791-817. Li Ho. Tr. by J. D. Frodsham. (Oxford Library of East Asian Literature Ser). 1970. 24.95x (ISBN 0-19-815436-4). Oxford U Pr.

Poems of Love & Death. George MacBeth. LC 79-55591. 1980. 9.95 (ISBN 0-689-11049-9); pap. 5.95 (ISBN 0-689-11064-2). Atheneum.

Poems of Love & Understanding. Lenard D. Moore. 1981. 4.50 (ISBN 0-8062-1549-6). Carlton.

Poems of Love & War. William H. Crall. 112p. 1979. 4.95 (ISBN 0-8059-2505-8). Dorrance.

Poems of Maria Lowell, with Unpublished Letters & a Biography. Maria Lowell. Ed. by Hope J. Vernon. (Brown University Studies: No. 2). (Illus.). 187p. 1936. 7.50x (ISBN 0-87057-015-3, Pub. by Brown U Pr). Univ Pr of New England.

Poems of Max Ehrmann. Max Ehrmann. Ed. by Bertha K. Ehrmann. 1948. 6.50 (ISBN 0-9602450-1-4). R L Bell.

Poems of Meleager. Meleager. Tr. by Peter Whigham. LC 75-7196. 128p. 1976. 14.50x (ISBN 0-520-03003-6). U of Cal Pr.

Poems of Morris Rosenfield Transliterated. Mortimer T. Cohen. LC 79-54799. 140p. pap. 7.50 (ISBN 0-686-28499-2). Retriever.

Poems of Nature. Frances Grover. 1981. 7.95 (ISBN 0-533-04780-3). Vantage.

Poems of Our Moment: Contemporary Poets of the English Language. Ed. by John Hollander. LC 67-25507. (Orig.). 1968. pap. 6.55 o.p. (ISBN 0-672-63575-5). Pegasus.

Poems of Patrick Cary. Patrick Cary. Ed. by Veronica Delany. 1978. 29.50x (ISBN 0-19-812566-6). Oxford U Pr.

Poems of Queen Elizabeth First. Elizabeth First. Ed. by Leicester Bradner. LC 64-17778. 91p. 1964. 8.00x (ISBN 0-87057-082-X, Pub. by Brown U Pr). Univ Pr of New England.

Poems of Reality. Gaye DeWindt. 1981. 6.00 (ISBN 0-8062-1615-8). Carlton.

Poems of Robert Henryson. Ed. by Denton Fox. (Oxford English Texts Ser.). 704p. 1980. 89.00 (ISBN 0-19-812703-0). Oxford U Pr.

Poems of Robert Louis Stevenson. Robert L. Stevenson. Ed. by Helen Plotz. LC 72-78282. (Poets Ser.). (Illus.). 128p. (gr. 7 up). 1973. 8.95 (ISBN 0-690-64395-0, TYC-J). T Y Crowell.

Poems of St. John of the Cross. 3rd ed. Tr. by John F. Nims. LC 79-12943. 1979. lib. bdg. 15.50x (ISBN 0-226-40108-1); pap. 4.50 (ISBN 0-226-40110-3, P845). U of Chicago Pr.

Poems of Samuel Taylor Coleridge. Samuel T. Coleridge. Ed. by E. H. Coleridge. 1912. pap. 9.95x (ISBN 0-19-281051-0). Oxford U Pr.

Poems of Samuel Taylor Coleridge. Samuel T. Coleridge. Ed. by E. H. Coleridge. (Oxford Standard Authors Ser.). 1912. 27.50 (ISBN 0-19-254120-X). Oxford U Pr.

Poems of Sappho. Sappho. Tr. by Suzy Q. Groden. LC 65-26542. (Orig.). 1966. pap. 4.95 (ISBN 0-672-60464-7, LLA214). Bobbs.

Poems of Sextus Propertius. Sextus Propertius. Tr. by J. P. McCulloch. LC 78-115490. (Bilingual ed.). 1975. 22.75x (ISBN 0-520-01714-5); pap. 2.95 (ISBN 0-520-02774-4). U of Cal Pr.

Poems of Sidney Lanier. Ed. by Mary Lanier. LC 80-29576. 262p. 1981. Repr. of 1884 ed. 12.50 (ISBN 0-8203-0560-X). U of Ga Pr.

Poems of Sir Philip Sidney. Philip Sidney. Ed. by William A. Ringler, Jr. (Oxford English Texts Ser). 1962. 49.00x (ISBN 0-19-811834-1). Oxford U Pr.

Poems of Stephen Crane. Stephen Crane. Ed. & compiled by Gerald D. McDonald. (Apollo Eds.). (Illus.). 1971. pap. 1.25 o.p. (ISBN 0-8152-0310-1, A310, TYC-T). T Y Crowell.

Poems of the Ancients. Porter. 3.50 o.s.i. (ISBN 0-8027-6054-6). Walker & Co.

Poems of the Pearl Manuscript. Ed. by Malcolm Andrew & Ronald Waldron. LC 78-64464. (York Medieval Texts). 1979. 35.00x (ISBN 0-520-03794-4). U of Cal Pr.

Poems of the Troubadour Raimbaut De Vaqueiras. Ed. by Joseph Linskill. LC 80-2190. 1981. Repr. of 1964 ed. 45.00 (ISBN 0-404-19014-6). AMS Pr.

Poems of the Vikings: The Elder Edda. Ed. by Patricia Terry. LC 69-16528. (Library of Liberal Arts Ser). 1969. text ed. 8.95 (ISBN 0-672-60332-2, LLA128). Bobbs.

Poems of Thomas Carew. Thomas Carew. Ed. by Rhodes Dunlap. (Oxford English Texts Ser). 1949. 36.00x (ISBN 0-19-811804-X). Oxford U Pr.

Poems of Thomas Hardy. K. Marsden. 1969. text ed. 19.00x (Athlone Pr). Humanities.

Poems of Trumbull Stickney. Trumbull Stickney. Ed. by Amberys Whittle. 368p. (Index of first lines). 1972. 17.50 o.p. (ISBN 0-374-23537-6). FS&G.

Poems of Walt Whitman. Walt Whitman. Ed. & compiled by Lawrence C. Powell. LC 64-20689. (Apollo Eds.). (Illus.). 1971. pap. 1.95 o.p. (ISBN 0-8152-0312-8, A312, TYC-T). T Y Crowell.

Poems of William Blake. W. H. Stevenson. (Longman Annotated English Poets Ser.). (Illus.). 1972. pap. text ed. 13.95x (ISBN 0-582-48459-6). Longman.

Poems of William Cowper, Vol. I: 1748 - 1782. William Cooper. Ed. by John D. Baird & Charles Ryskamp. (English Texts Ser.). (Illus.). 636p. 1980. 74.00 (ISBN 0-19-811875-9). Oxford U Pr.

Poems of William Dunbar. William Dunbar. Ed. by W. Mackay Mackenzie. 1933. 8.95 (ISBN 0-571-06896-0, Pub. by Faber & Faber). Merrimack Bk Serv.

Poems of William Dunbar. William Dunbar. Ed. by W. Mackay Mackenzie. 1970. pap. 3.95 o.p. (ISBN 0-571-09239-X, Pub. by Faber & Faber). Merrimack Bk Serv.

Poems Old & New, Nineteen Eighteen to Nineteen Seventy-Eight. Janet Lewis. LC 80-26209. xvi, 112p. 1981. 11.00 (ISBN 0-8040-0371-8); pap. 5.95 (ISBN 0-8040-0372-6). Swallow.

Poems Old & New: 1918-1978. Janet Lewis. LC 80-26209. xvi, 112p. 1981. 11.00 (ISBN 0-8040-0371-8); pap. 5.95 (ISBN 0-8040-0372-6). Swallow.

Poems Retrieved. Frank O'Hara. Ed. by Donald Allen. LC 77-554. 250p. 1977. 12.00 (ISBN 0-912516-18-6); pap. 5.00 (ISBN 0-912516-19-4). Grey Fox.

Poems That Bless. Ed. by Al Bryant. 96p. 1972. pap. 1.95 (ISBN 0-310-22092-0). Zondervan.

Poems That Live Forever. Ed. by Hazel Felleman. LC 65-13987. 1965. 7.95 (ISBN 0-385-00358-7). Doubleday.

Poems That Tell Me Who I Am. Margaret L. McWhorter. LC 80-51481. (Illus.). 57p. 1980. pap. 3.95 (ISBN 0-9604342-0-8). Ransom Hill.

Poems: The Location of Things. Barbara Guest. 1962. 7.95 (ISBN 0-911660-06-2). Yankee Peddler.

Poems to Hear & See. Ian H. Finlay. LC 71-133557. (Illus.). (gr. 5 up). 1971. 3.95 o.s.i. (ISBN 0-02-735210-2). Macmillan.

Poems to Shape Lives: Inspirational Verse on the Gospel, Life Love & Family. Joseph D. Rees. LC 76-3993. (Illus.). 112p. 1976. pap. 3.95 o.p. (ISBN 0-88290-059-5). Horizon Utah.

Poems to the Child-God: Structures & Strategies in the Poetry of Surdas. Kenneth E. Bryant. LC 77-80467. (Center for South & Southeast Asian Studies). 1978. 20.00x (ISBN 0-520-03540-2). U of Cal Pr.

Poems to the Eighties. Joan Fox. 1979. 6.95 (ISBN 0-533-04540-1). Vantage.

Poems Without Names: The English Lyric, 1200-1500. Raymond Oliver. LC 77-82617. 1970. 16.50x (ISBN 0-520-01403-0). U of Cal Pr.

Poems. 1809. Sir John Carr. Ed. by Donald H. Reiman. LC 75-31177. (Romantic Context Ser.: Poetry 1789-1830). 1977. lib. bdg. 47.00 (ISBN 0-8240-2129-0). Garland Pub.

Poesia Chilena: Origenes y desarrollo del siglo xvi al xix. Fernando Alegria. 1954. 14.00x (ISBN 0-520-00009-9). U of Cal Pr.

Poesia De Jose Gautier Benitez. Miriam Curet de De Anda. LC 80-17629. (Coleccion Mente y Palabra Ser.). (Illus.). 232p. Date not set. 6.25 (ISBN 0-8477-0570-6); pap. 5.00 (ISBN 0-8477-0571-4). U of PR Pr.

Poesia Espanola Del Siglo Veinte: Antologia. Ed. by Gustavo Correa. (Span.). 1972. 17.95 (ISBN 0-13-684506-1). P-H.

Poesia Hispanoamericano Desde el Modernismo. Ed. by E. Florit & J. Jemenez. 1968. 17.95 o.p. (ISBN 0-13-521807-1). P-H.

Poesia in Voz Alta in the Theater of Mexico. Roni Unger. 184p. 1981. text ed. 15.00x (ISBN 0-8262-0333-7). U of Mo Pr.

Poesia y Profecia del Antiquo Testamento. C. H. Benson. Tr. by Fernando P. Villalobos from Eng. (Curso Para Maestros Cristianos: No. 2). Orig. Title: Old Testament Survey - Poetry & Prophecy. 122p. (Span.). 1972. pap. 2.50 (ISBN 0-89922-010-X); instructor's manual 1.50 (ISBN 0-89922-011-8). Edit Caribe.

Poesie baroque, 1560-1600, Vol. I. (Nouveaux Classiques Larousse). (Illus., Fr.). pap. 2.95 o.p. (ISBN 0-685-14046-6, 241). Larousse.

Poesie Di Peire Raimon De Tolosa. Peire Raimon. Ed. by Alfredo Cavaliere. LC 80-2181. 1981. Repr. of 1935 ed. 29.50 (ISBN 0-404-19010-3). AMS Pr.

Poesie: Edizione Critica e Commento a Cura Di D'Arco Silvio Avalle, 2 vols. in 1. Peire Vidal. LC 80-2186. 1981. Repr. of 1960 ed. 72.50 (ISBN 0-404-19011-1). AMS Pr.

Poesies. Alfred De Musset. (Documentation thematique). (Fr). pap. 2.95 (ISBN 0-685-14019-9, 226). Larousse.

Poesies choisies de Malherbe, Racan & Mainard. Francois De Malherbe. (Nouveaux Classiques Larousse). (Illus., Fr.). pap. 2.95 o.p. (ISBN 0-685-14053-9, 163). Larousse.

Poesies Du Troubadour Aimeric De Belenoi. Aimeric De Belenoi. Ed. by Maria Dumitrescu. LC 80-2174. 1981. Repr. of 1935 ed. 33.50 (ISBN 0-404-19000-6). AMS Pr.

Poesies Du Troubadour Albertet. Albertet De Sestero. Ed. by Jean Boutiere. LC 80-2173. 1981. Repr. of 1937 ed. 24.50 (ISBN 0-404-19001-4). AMS Pr.

Poesies Du Troubadour Guilhem Ademar. Guilhem Ademar. LC 80-2180. 1981. Repr. of 1951 ed. 37.50 (ISBN 0-404-19006-5). AMS Pr.

Poesies Du Troubadour Guillem de Saint-Didier. Guillem De Saint-Didier. LC 80-2179. 1981. Repr. of 1956 ed. 31.00 (ISBN 0-404-19007-3). AMS Pr.

Poesies: 1830. Theophile Gautier. Ed. by H. Cockerham. 1973. text ed. 10.25x (ISBN 0-485-14705-X, Athlone Pr). Humanities.

Poet. new ed. Ed. by Doris I. Nemeth & Peggy Kenzie. (Illus.). 446p. (gr. 5 up). 1980. pap. 9.50 (ISBN 0-932192-02-5). Fine Arts Soc.

Poet & the Donkey. May Sarton. LC 72-80024. (Illus.). 1969. 4.50 o.p. (ISBN 0-393-08590-2). Norton.

Poet & the Mystic: A Study of the Cantico Espiritual of San Juan de la Cruz. Colin P. Thompson. (Oxford Modern Languages & Literature Monographs). 1978. 33.00x (ISBN 0-19-815531-X). Oxford U Pr.

Poet & the Natural World in the Age of Gongora. M. J. Woods. (Modern Languages & Literature Monographs). 1978. 37.50x (ISBN 0-19-815533-6). Oxford U Pr.

Poet & the Poem. rev ed. Judson Jerome. LC 79-10828. 330p. 1979. 11.95x (ISBN 0-911654-70-4). Writers Digest.

Poet & the Puppets: A Travestie Suggested by "Lady Windermere's Fan". Charles Brookfield & J. M. Glover. Ed. by Ian Fletcher & John Stokes. Bd. with Aristophanes at Oxford. LC 76-20012. (Decadent Consciousness Ser.). 1978. lib. bdg. 38.00 (ISBN 0-8240-2784-1). Garland Pub.

Poet & the Revolution: Aleksandr Blok's the Twelve. Sergei Hackel. 272p. 1975. 37.50x (ISBN 0-19-815645-6). Oxford U Pr.

Poet As Analyst: Essays on Paul Valery. James R. Lawler. 1974. 22.75x (ISBN 0-520-02450-8). U of Cal Pr.

Poet As Critic. Ed. by Frederick P. McDowell. 1967. 7.95x o.s.i. (ISBN 0-8101-0151-3); pap. 4.95x o.s.i. (ISBN 0-8101-0150-5). Northwestern U Pr.

Poet As Ice-Skater. Robert Peters. pap. 10.00 signed ed. o.p. (ISBN 0-686-18852-7). Man-Root.

Poet As Journalist: Life at the New Republic. Reed Whittemore. LC 76-14897. 220p. 1976. 8.95 o.p. (ISBN 0-915220-16-4). New Republic.

Poet of Exile: A Study of Milton's Poetry. Louis L. Martz. LC 79-64079. 1980. 22.50x (ISBN 0-300-02393-6). Yale U Pr.

Poet Philosophers of the Rig Veda. C. Kunhan Raja. (Sanskrit & eng.). 8.95 (ISBN 0-89744-121-4, Pub. by Ganesh & Co. India). Auromere.

Poet Pope. Ed. by Diana Kwiatkowski. 67p. 1981. 9.50 (ISBN 0-933906-16-1); pap. 4.50 (ISBN 0-933906-15-3). Gusto Pr.

Poet President of Texas. new ed. Stanley Siegel. 1977. 12.50 (ISBN 0-8363-0153-6). Jenkins.

Poetae Latini Minores, Leipzig, 1879-1883, 5 vols. Aemilius Bae Hrens. Ed. by Steele Commager. LC 77-70775. (Latin Poetry Ser.). 1979. Set. lib. bdg. 170.00 (ISBN 0-8240-2950-X). Garland Pub.

Poete Gerard Manley Hopkins, S. J. (1844-1889) Jean-Georges Ritz. 726p. 1980. Repr. of 1963 ed. lib. bdg. 100.00 (ISBN 0-8492-7748-5). R West.

Poetic Achievement of Ezra Pound. Michael Alexander. 1979. 16.00 (ISBN 0-520-03739-1). U of Cal Pr.

Poetic Closure: A Study of How Poems End. Barbara H. Smith. LC 68-15034. 1971. pap. 6.95 (ISBN 0-226-76343-9, P381, Phoen). U of Chicago Pr.

Poetic Communications & Rational Discourse: Methods of Linguistics, Literary & Philosophical Analysis. Roland Posner. (Janua Linguarum, Series Minor). 1979. pap. text ed. 17.50x (ISBN 90-279-3138-0). Mouton.

Poetic Diction: A Study in Meaning. 3rd ed. Owen Barfield. LC 72-10631. 232p. 1973. pap. 7.50 (ISBN 0-8195-6026-X, Pub. by Wesleyan U Pr). Columbia U Pr.

Poetic Drama Interviews: Robert Speaight, E Martin Browne & W. H. Auden. William B. Wahl. (Salzburg Studies in English Literature, Poetic Drama & Poetic Theory: No. 24). (Illus., Orig.). 1976. pap. text ed. 25.00x (ISBN 0-391-01553-2). Humanities.

Poetic Edda Vol. 1: Heroic Poems. Ed. by Ursula Dronke. 1969. 27.00x (ISBN 0-19-811497-4). Oxford U Pr.

Poetic Experience. Thomas Gilby. 114p. 1980. Repr. of 1934 ed. lib. bdg. 20.00 (ISBN 0-8492-4976-7). R West.

Poetic Image in Six Genres. David Madden. LC 76-76189. (Arcturus Books Paperbacks). 271p. 1969. pap. 7.45 (ISBN 0-8093-0394-9). S Ill U Pr.

Poetic Memoirs of Lady Daibu. Tr. by Phillip T. Harries from Japanese. LC 79-65519. 336p. 1980. 17.50x (ISBN 0-8047-1077-5). Stanford U Pr.

Poetic Meter & Poetic Form. Paul Fussell, Jr. LC 78-14548. 1978. pap. text ed. 4.50 (ISBN 0-394-32120-0). Random.

Poetic Potentials in Information of Astronomy. Polish Academy of Science. 1976. pap. 1.95. Primary Pr.

Poetic Printshop Past-Times. LC 74-84505. 1976. Repr. 8.50 (ISBN 0-9605622-1-4). Graphic Crafts.

Poetic Self: Towards a Phenomenology of Romanticism. Meena Alexander. 280p. 1980. text ed. 14.00x (ISBN 0-391-01754-3). Humanities.

Poetic Sketches; a Collection of Miscellaneous Poems, Repr. Of 1808 Ed. 2nd ed. Thomas Gent. Ed. by Donald H. Reiman. Bd. with Poems. Repr. of 1820 ed; Poems. Repr. of 1828 ed. LC 75-31205. (Romantic Context Ser.: Poetry 1789-1830). 1979. lib. bdg. 47.00 (ISBN 0-685-63648-8). Garland Pub.

Poetic Statement & Critical Dogma. Gerald Graff. LC 80-14318. 208p. 1980. lib. bdg. 7.00x (ISBN 0-226-30601-1). U of Chicago Pr.

Poetic Unreason & Other Studies. Robert Graves. LC 68-59244. 1968. Repr. of 1925 ed. 12.00x (ISBN 0-8196-0227-2). Biblo.

Poetic Vision of Robert Penn Warren. Victor H. Strandberg. LC 76-9503. 304p. 1977. 16.00x (ISBN 0-8131-1347-4). U Pr of Ky.

Poetic World of Boris Pasternak. Olga R. Hughes. LC 73-2467. (Princeton Essays in Literature). 196p. 1974. text ed. 12.50 (ISBN 0-691-06262-5). Princeton U Pr.

Poetical Epistle to an Eminent Painter, Repr. Of 1778. William Hayley. Ed. by Donald H. Reiman. Bd. with Elegy, on the Ancient Greek Model. Addressed to the Right Reverend Robert Lowth. Repr. of 1779 ed; Epistle to Admiral Keppel. Repr. of 1779 ed; Epistle to a Friend, on the Death of John Thornton Esq. 2nd, corrected ed. Repr. of 1780 ed; Essay on History; in Three Epistles to Edward Gibbon, Esq. with Notes. Repr. of 1780 ed. LC 75-31206. (Romantic Context Ser.: Poetry 1789-1830: Vol. 57). 1979. lib. bdg. 47.00 (ISBN 0-8240-2156-8). Garland Pub.

Poetical Histories, Repr. Of 1671 Ed. Pierre Gautruche. Tr. by Marius D'Assigny. Bd. with Appendix De Diis et Heroibus Poeticis. Joseph de Jouvency. Repr. of 1705 ed. LC 75-27877. (Renaissance & the Gods Ser.: Vol. 32). (Illus.). 1976. lib. bdg. 73.00 (ISBN 0-8240-2081-2). Garland Pub.

Poetical Memories from the Pen of Hayden R. Nesmith. Hayden R. Nesmit. 5.75 (ISBN 0-8062-1630-1). Carlton.

Poetical Recreations of the Champion & His Literary Correspondents. John Thelwall. Ed. by Donald H. Reiman. LC 75-31263. (Romantic Context Ser.: Poetry 1789-1830). 1978. Repr. of 1822 ed. lib. bdg. 47.00 (ISBN 0-8240-2209-2). Garland Pub.

Poetical Theory in Republican Rome. Lawrence Richardson. Ed. by Steele Commager. LC 77-70825. (Latin Poetry Ser.). 1978. lib. bdg. 22.00 (ISBN 0-8240-2977-1). Garland Pub.

Poetical Vagaries, Repr. Of 1812 Ed. George Colman. Bd. with Vagaries Vindicated: Or, Hypocritick Hypocritics: a Poem Addressed to the Reviewers. Repr. of 1813 ed. LC 75-31182. (Romantic Context: Poetry 1789-1830 Ser.: Vol. 34). 1976. lib. bdg. 47.00 (ISBN 0-8240-2133-9). Garland Pub.

Poetical Works. Matthew Arnold. Ed. by C. B. Tinker & H. F. Lowry. (Standard Authors Ser). 1950. 24.95 (ISBN 0-19-254110-2). Oxford U Pr.

Poetical Works. Lord George G. Byron. (Oxford Standard Authors). 936p. 1979. french morocco bdg. 45.00 o.p. (ISBN 0-19-192822-4). Oxford U Pr.

Poetical Works. Charles Churchill. Ed. by Douglas Grant. 1956. 49.00x (ISBN 0-19-811316-1). Oxford U Pr.

Poetical Works, 2 Vols. Giles Fletcher & Phineas Fletcher. Ed. by F. S. Boas. 1970. 58.00 ea. Vol. 1 (ISBN 0-521-07773-7). Vol. 2 (ISBN 0-521-07827-X). Cambridge U Pr.

Poetical Works. Robert Herrick. Ed. by L. C. Martin. (Oxford English Texts). 1956. 55.00x o.p. (ISBN 0-19-811813-9). Oxford U Pr.

Poetical Works, 2 vols. John Milton. Ed. by Helen Darbishire. Incl. Vol. 1. Paradise Lost. 1952. 42.00x (ISBN 0-19-811819-8); Vol. 2. Paradise Regained, Samson Agonistes, Poems Upon Several Occasions. 1955. 39.00x (ISBN 0-19-811820-1). (Oxford English Texts Ser). Oxford U Pr.

Poetical Works. Richard Savage. Ed. by C. Tracy. 1962. 58.00 (ISBN 0-521-06197-0). Cambridge U Pr.

Poetical Works. Percy Bysshe Shelley. Ed. by Thomas Hutchinson & G. M. Matthews. (Oxford Standard Authors Ser). 948p. 1971. 26.00 (ISBN 0-19-254143-9); pap. 11.50x (ISBN 0-19-281069-3, OPB); leather bd. 45.00 (ISBN 0-19-192852-6). Oxford U Pr.

Poetical Works. Edmund Spenser. Ed. by J. C. Smith & Ernest De Selincourt. (Oxford Standard Authors Ser.). 1912. 24.95 (ISBN 0-19-254144-7); pap. 9.95x (ISBN 0-19-281070-7). Oxford U Pr.

Poetical Works. Jonathan Swift. Ed. by Herbert Davis. (Oxford Standard Authors Ser). 1967. 23.00 (ISBN 0-19-254161-7). Oxford U Pr.

Poetical Works of Alain Chartier. Ed. by J. C. Laidlaw. LC 73-77177. 576p. 1974. 110.00 (ISBN 0-521-07940-3). Cambridge U Pr.

Poetical Works of Alexander McLachlan: 1818-1896. Alexander McLachlan. LC 73-82589. (Literature of Canada Ser.). (Illus.). 1974. pap. 5.95 (ISBN 0-8020-6235-0). U of Toronto Pr.

Poetical Works of Christopher Smart, Volume I: Jubilate Agno. Christopher Smart. Ed. by Karina Williamson. (English Texts Ser.). (Illus.). 168p. 1980. 39.95 (ISBN 0-19-811869-4). Oxford U Pr.

Poetical Works of Edward Taylor. Edward Taylor. Ed. by Thomas H. Johnson. 1944. pap. 4.95 (ISBN 0-691-01275-X). Princeton U Pr.

Poetical Works of John Keats. John Keats. Ed. by H. W. Garrod. (Oxford Standard Authors). 1956. pap. 6.95x (ISBN 0-19-281067-7). Oxford U Pr.

Poetical Works of John Keats. John Keats. Ed. by Heathcote W. Garrod. (Oxford Standard Authors Ser.). 1956. 21.00x (ISBN 0-19-254132-3). Oxford U Pr.

Poetical Works of John Keats. 2nd ed. John Keats. Ed. by Heathcote W. Garrod. (Oxford English Texts Ser). 1958. 45.00x (ISBN 0-19-811815-5). Oxford U Pr.

Poetical Works of Lord Byron. George G. Byron. Ed. by E. H. Coleridge. (Illus.). 1120p. 1972. Repr. of 1905 ed. text ed. 18.25x (ISBN 0-7195-0171-7). Humanities.

Poetical Works of Mrs. Leprohon. Rosanna E. Leprohon. (Toronto Reprint Library of Canadian Prose & Poetry). 1973. Repr. of 1881 ed. 16.75x (ISBN 0-8020-7523-1). U of Toronto Pr.

Poetical Works of Rupert Brooke. Rupert Brooke. 1970. 13.95 (ISBN 0-571-04708-4, Pub. by Faber & Faber); pap. 6.95 (ISBN 0-571-04704-1). Merrimack Bk Serv.

Poetical Works of Thomas Moore, 10 vols. Thomas Moore. 1980. Repr. of 1840 ed. lib. bdg. 300.00 (ISBN 0-89987-599-8). Century Bookbindery.

Poetical Works with Introd. & Notes. new rev ed. William Wordsworth. Ed. by Thomas Hutchinson & Ernest De Selincourt. (Oxford Standard Authors Ser.). 810p. 1950. 23.95 (ISBN 0-19-254152-8); pap. 8.95x (ISBN 0-19-281052-9, OPB). Oxford U Pr.

Poetics. Aristotle. 1970. pap. 3.95 (ISBN 0-472-06166-6, 166, AA). U of Mich Pr.

Poetics for Sociology. R. H. Brown. LC 75-35454. (Illus.). 1977. 34.50 (ISBN 0-521-21121-2); pap. 8.95x (ISBN 0-521-29391-X). Cambridge U Pr.

Poetics of Aristotle. Lane Cooper. LC 63-10307. (Our Debt to Greece & Rome Ser). 157p. 1963. Repr. of 1930 ed. 16.50x (ISBN 0-8154-0053-5). Cooper Sq.

Poetics of Aristotle in England. Marvin T. Herrick. LC 76-12455. 1976. Repr. of 1930 ed. 9.00x (ISBN 0-87753-061-0, Phaeton). Gordian.

Poetics of Augustan Elegy: Studies of Poems by Dryden, Pope, Prior, Swift, Gray & Johnson. Donald C. Mell. 116p. (Orig.). 1974. pap. text ed. 11.50x (ISBN 90-6203-278-8). Humanities.

Poetics of Composition: Structure of the Artistic Text & the Typology of Compositional Forms. Boris Uspensky. Tr. by Valentina Zavarin & Susan Wittig. LC 72-85517. 1974. 15.75x (ISBN 0-520-02309-9). U of Cal Pr.

Poetics of Disguise: The Autobiography of the Work in Homer, Dante, & Shakespeare. Franco Ferrucci. Tr. by Ann Dunnigan from It. LC 80-11242. 178p. 1980. 12.50x (ISBN 0-8014-1262-5). Cornell U Pr.

Poetics of Roman Ingarden. Eugene H. Falk. LC 79-29655. 272p. 1980. 20.00x (ISBN 0-8078-1436-9); pap. 11.00x (ISBN 0-8078-4068-8). U of NC Pr.

Poetry After Symbolism: Rimbaud to Cage. Marjorie Perloff. LC 80-8569. (Illus.). 360p. 1981. 20.00x (ISBN 0-691-06462-8). Princeton U Pr.

Poetry: An Introduction & Anthology. Edward Proffitt. LC 80-80842. 384p. 1981. pap. text ed. 8.95 (ISBN 0-395-29486-X); instr's. manual 0.40 (ISBN 0-395-29487-8). HM.

Poetry & a Principle. Gene Montague. LC 76-37397. 280p. 1972. pap. text ed. 3.95 o.p. (ISBN 0-397-47216-1). Lippincott.

Poetry & Anthropology. Paul Friedrich. 1978. 1.00 (ISBN 0-934528-01-2). B & M Waite Pr.

Poetry & Career of Li Po. Arthur Waley. (Ethical & Religious Classics of East & West Ser.). 1951. 13.50 (ISBN 0-04-895012-2). Allen Unwin.

Poetry & Change: Donne, Milton, Wordsworth, & the Equilibrium of the Present. Josephine Miles. 1974. 16.75 (ISBN 0-520-02554-7). U of Cal Pr.

Poetry & Fiction: Essays. Howard Nemerov. 1963. 22.00 (ISBN 0-8135-0438-4). Rutgers U Pr.

Poetry & Poets. Amy Lowell. LC 77-162298. 1971. Repr. of 1930 ed. 10.50x (ISBN 0-8196-0274-4). Biblo.

Poetry & Politics. M. Bowra. 1966. 29.95x (ISBN 0-521-04294-1). Cambridge U Pr.

Poetry & Politics in the Work of Rainer Maria Rilke. Egon Schwarz. Tr. by David E. Wellbery from Ger. LC 80-53704. 160p. 1981. 9.95 (ISBN 0-8044-2811-5). Ungar.

Poetry & Politics Under the Stuarts. Cicely V. Wedgwood. 1960. 32.00 (ISBN 0-521-06762-6). Cambridge U Pr.

Poetry & Speculation of the Rg Veda. Willard Johnson, Jr. 175p. 1981. 25.00 (ISBN 0-520-02560-1). U of Cal Pr.

Poetry & the Common Life. M. L. Rosenthal. 1974. 12.95 (ISBN 0-19-501838-9). Oxford U Pr.

Poetry & the Sociological Idea. J. P. Ward. 256p. 1981. 23.50x (ISBN 0-389-20188-X). B&N.

Poetry Anthology. Ed. by Marlies K. Danziger & Wendell S. Johnson. (Orig.). 1967. pap. text ed. 8.95 (ISBN 0-394-30187-0). Random.

Poetry As a Performance Art on & off the Page. 1976. pap. 1.95. Primary Pr.

Poetry by American Women, 1900-1975: A Bibliography. Joan Reardon & Kristine A. Thorsen. LC 78-11944. 1979. 27.50 (ISBN 0-8108-1173-1). Scarecrow.

Poetry Chronicle: Essays & Reviews. Ian Hamilton. 1973. 7.95 o.p. (ISBN 0-571-10175-5, Pub. by Faber & Faber); pap. 4.95 (ISBN 0-571-10228-X). Merrimack Bk Serv.

Poetry for Crazy Cowboys & Zen Monks. Raymond Coffin. (Illus.). 128p. 1980. pap. 4.95 (ISBN 0-915520-26-5). Ross-Erikson.

Poetry for Peace of Mind. Alison Wyrley Birch. LC 77-76959. 1978. 6.95 o.p. (ISBN 0-385-13253-0). Doubleday.

Poetry Handbook: A Dictionary of Terms. 4th ed. Babette Deutsch. (Funk & W Bk.). 1976. pap. 4.95 (ISBN 0-308-10248-7, M8, TYC-T). T Y Crowell.

Poetry Handbook: Dictionary of Terms. 4th ed. Babette Deutsch. (Funk & W Bk.). 224p. 1974. 10.95 (ISBN 0-308-10088-3, TYC-T). T Y Crowell.

Poetry in the Making. Ted Hughes. 1967. pap. 4.95 (ISBN 0-571-09076-1, Pub. by Faber & Faber). Merrimack Bk Serv.

Poetry: Introduction 1. 1969. pap. 4.50 (ISBN 0-571-09014-1, Pub. by Faber & Faber). Merrimack Bk Serv.

Poetry: Introduction 2. 1972. 9.95 (ISBN 0-571-09789-8, Pub. by Faber & Faber); pap. 4.50 (ISBN 0-686-28563-8). Merrimack Bk Serv.

Poetry Makers: A Graded Anthology for Secondary Schools, 4 bks. Ed. by James McGrath. 1969. Bk. 1. text ed. 3.95x o.p. (ISBN 0-435-14570-3); Bk. 2. text ed. 3.95x o.p. (ISBN 0-435-14571-1); Bk. 3. text ed. 3.95x o.p. (ISBN 0-435-14572-X); Bk. 4. text ed. 3.95x o.p. (ISBN 0-435-14573-8). Heinemann Ed.

Poetry of A. E. Ed. by Alan Denson. (Collected Edition of the Writings of G.W. Russell Ser. V). 1980. text ed. write for info. (ISBN 0-391-01144-8). Humanities.

Poetry of American Women from 1632 to 1945. Emily S. Watts. LC 76-43282. 1977. text ed. 13.95 o.p. (ISBN 0-292-76435-9); pap. 7.95x (ISBN 0-292-76450-2). U of Tex Pr.

Poetry of Baruch: A Reconstruction & Analysis of the Original Hebrew Text of Baruch 3: 9-5: 9. Ed. by David G. Burke. LC 80-10271. (Society of Biblical Literature, Septuagint & Cognate Studies: No. 10). 22.50x (ISBN 0-89130-381-2, 06 04 10); pap. 18.00x (ISBN 0-89130-382-0). Scholars Pr CA.

Poetry of Ben Jonson. J. G. Nichols. 1969. 18.00x (ISBN 0-7100-6448-9). Routledge & Kegan.

Poetry of Cats. Samuel Carr. 1979. 14.95 (ISBN 0-7134-2861-9, Pub. by Batsford England). David & Charles.

Poetry of Chaucer. John C. Gardner. LC 76-22713. 445p. 1977. 15.00 (ISBN 0-8093-0772-3); pap. 9.95 (ISBN 0-8093-0871-1). S Ill U Pr.

Poetry of Dante Gabriel Rossetti. Joan Rees. 150p. Date not set. 39.95 (ISBN 0-521-23537-5). Cambridge U Pr.

Poetry of Edward Thomas. Andrew Motion. 192p. 1981. 27.50 (ISBN 0-7100-0471-0). Routledge & Kegan.

Poetry of Ezra Pound: Forms & Renewal, 1908-1920. Hugh Witemeyer. 1969. 16.50x (ISBN 0-520-01542-8). U of Cal Pr.

Poetry of Flowers. Samuel Carr. 1977. 14.95 (ISBN 0-7134-0427-2, Pub. by Batsford England). David & Charles.

Poetry of George Crabbe. B. B. Jain. (Salzburg Studies in English Literature, Romantic Reassessment Ser.: No. 37). 340p. 1976. pap. text ed. 25.00x (ISBN 0-391-01434-X). Humanities.

Poetry of H: A Lost Poet of Lincoln's Illinois. Ed. by John Hallwas. 192p. 1981. 16.95 (ISBN 0-933180-23-3). Kickapoo.

Poetry of History: The Contribution of Literature & Literary Scholarship to the Writing of History Since Voltaire. Emery E. Neff. LC 47-30933. 1947. pap. 6.00x (ISBN 0-231-08525-7). Columbia U Pr.

Poetry of Horses. Ed. by Samuel Carr. (Illus.). 128p. 1980. 17.95 (ISBN 0-7134-2594-6, Pub. by Batsford England). David & Charles.

Poetry of Jean de la Ceppede: A Study in Text & Content. P. A. Chilton. (Oxford Modern Languages & Literature Monographs). 1977. 37.50x (ISBN 0-19-815529-8). Oxford U Pr.

Poetry of John Berryman. Gary Q. Arpin. (National University Publications Literary Criticism Ser.). 1977. 8.95 o.p. (ISBN 0-8046-9205-X). Kennikat.

Poetry of John Donne: A Study in Explication. Doniphan Louthan. LC 75-40927. 193p. 1976. Repr. of 1951 ed. lib. bdg. 19.25x (ISBN 0-8371-8693-5, LOPJ). Greenwood.

Poetry of Julian Del Casal: A Critical Edition, 3 vols. Ed. by Robert J. Glickman. Incl. Vol. 1. 1976. 15.00 (ISBN 0-8130-0540-X); pap. 6.50 (ISBN 0-8130-0572-8); Vol. 2. 1978. 20.00 (ISBN 0-8130-0596-5); Vol.iII. 1977. 17.50 (ISBN 0-8130-0576-0). LC 76-22800. U Presses Fla.

Poetry of Llywarch Hen: Introduction, Text & Translation. Patrick K. Ford. LC 73-87249. 1974. 15.75x (ISBN 0-520-02601-2). U of Cal Pr.

Poetry of Louis MacNeice. D. B. Moore. 272p. 1972. text ed. 11.50x (ISBN 0-7185-1105-0, Leicester). Humanities.

Poetry of Michelangelo. Robert J. Clements. LC 65-19514. (Gotham Library). 368p. (Orig.). 1965. 15.00x (ISBN 0-8147-0085-3); pap. 7.00 (ISBN 0-8147-0086-1). NYU Pr.

Poetry of Nature: Rural Perspectives in Poetry from Wordsworth to the Present. W. J. Keith. 1980. 20.00x (ISBN 0-8020-5494-3). U of Toronto Pr.

Poetry of Northeast Scotland. James Alison. 1976. pap. text ed. 8.95x o.p. (ISBN 0-435-14021-3). Heinemann Ed.

Poetry of Robert Browning. Robert Browning. Ed. by Jacob Korg. LC 77-122683. (Library of Literature Ser). (Illus.). 630p. 1971. pap. 7.50 (ISBN 0-672-61002-7, LL25). Bobbs.

Poetry of Robert Graves. Michael Kirkham. 1969. text ed. 15.00x (ISBN 0-485-11103-9, Athlone Pr). Humanities.

Poetry of Rock: The Golden Years. David R. Pichaske. 192p. (Orig.). 1981. pap. 5.95 (ISBN 0-933180-17-9). Ellis Pr.

Poetry of Samual Traylor Coleridge: An Annotated Bibliography of Criticism, 1935 to 1970. Mary Lee Milton. LC 80-83650. 250p. 1981. lib. bdg. 30.00 (ISBN 0-8240-9451-4). Garland Pub.

Poetry of Scotland. Ed. by Douglas Dunn. (Illus.). 127p. 1980. 17.95 (ISBN 0-7134-1414-6, Pub. by Batsford England). David & Charles.

Poetry of Sir Thomas Wyatt: A Selection & Study by E. M. W. Tillyard. Thomas Wyatt. Repr. of 1929 ed. 19.00 (ISBN 0-403-08614-0). Somerset Pub.

Poetry of Stephen Crane. Daniel G. Hoffman. LC 57-11017. 1957. 20.00x (ISBN 0-231-02195-X); pap. 7.50x (ISBN 0-231-08662-8). Columbia U Pr.

Poetry of T. S. Eliot. Desmond E. Maxwell. (Orig.). 1970. pap. text ed. 2.00x o.p. (ISBN 0-7100-4602-2). Humanities.

Poetry of T'ao Ch'ien. T'Ao Ch'Len. Ed. by James R. Hightower. (Illus.). 24.95x (ISBN 0-19-815440-2). Oxford U Pr.

Poetry of the Minor Connecticut Wits, 1791-1818. Ed. by Benjamin Franklin. LC 68-17015. 1970. 85.00x (ISBN 0-8201-1066-3). Schol Facsimiles.

Poetry of the Netherlands in Its Euroean Context: 1170-1930. Theodor Weevers. 1960. text ed. 20.00x (ISBN 0-485-11041-5, Athlone Pr). Humanities.

Poetry of the Old Testament. Theodore H. Robinson. LC 48-10111. (Studies in Theology: No. 49). 1947. pap. 8.50x (ISBN 0-8401-6049-6). Allenson.

Poetry of the Railways. Samuel Carr. 1978. 14.95 (ISBN 0-7134-0222-9). David & Charles.

Poetry of Thomas Hardy. Ed. by Patricia Clements & Juliet Grindle. (Critical Studies Ser.). 194p. 1980. 26.00x (ISBN 0-389-20057-3). B&N.

Poetry of Thomas Hardy, 2 vols. Birjadish Prasad. (Salzburg Studies in English Literature, Romantic Reassessment Ser: 57). 1977. Set. pap. text ed. 50.25x (ISBN 0-391-01501-X). Humanities.

Poetry of Thomas Kinsella. Maurice Harmon. 126p. 1975. text ed. 8.50x (ISBN 0-391-00386-0); pap. text ed. 4.95x (ISBN 0-391-00387-9). Humanities.

Poetry of W. B. Yeats: Myth As Metaphor. Ashok Bhargava. 1979. text ed. 11.50x (ISBN 0-391-01006-9). Humanities.

Poetry of Wang Wei: New Translations & Commentary. Pauline Yu. LC 79-3623. (Chinese Literature in Translation Ser.). 288p. Date not set. 27.50x (ISBN 0-253-17772-3); pap. 9.95x (ISBN 0-253-20252-3). Ind U Pr.

Poetry of Yevgeny Yevtushenko. bilingual ed. Yevgeny Yevtushenko. 312p. 1981. pap. 8.95 (ISBN 0-7145-0482-3, Pub. by M. Boyars). Merrimack Bk Serv.

Poetry on the Stage William Poel Producer of Verse Drama. Bernice L. Webb. (Salzburg Institute for English Literature Poetic Drama Studies: 45). (Orig.). 1979. pap. text ed. 25.00x (ISBN 0-391-01726-8). Humanities.

Poetry Pack Rat. Schurr. (Choose-a-Card Ser.). (gr. 2-6). 1979. pap. text ed. 5.95 (ISBN 0-913916-86-2, IP86-2). Incentive Pubns.

Poetry Reading. Ed. by Stephen Vincent & Ellen Zweig. 1981. lib. bdg. 20.00 (ISBN 0-917672-36-4); pap. 7.95 (ISBN 0-917672-35-6). Momos.

Poets & Critics: Essays from Canadian Literature 1966-1974. Ed. by George Woodcock. 256p. 1974. pap. 7.50x (ISBN 0-19-540224-3). Oxford U Pr.

Poets & Poems of the First World War: The English. Michael D. Smith. LC 78-65845. 1979. pap. text ed. 4.50 o.p. (ISBN 0-8191-0672-0). U Pr of Amer.

Poets & Story-Tellers. David Cecil. 201p. 1980. Repr. of 1968 ed. lib. bdg. 30.00 (ISBN 0-8495-0852-5). Arden Lib.

Poet's Choice: One Hundred American Poets' Favorite Poems. Ed. by George E. Murphy, Jr. 176p. 1980. 10.95 (ISBN 0-937504-01-7); pap. 5.95 (ISBN 0-937504-00-9). Tendril.

Poet's Handbook. Judson Jerome. LC 80-17270. 88p. 1980. 10.95 (ISBN 0-89879-021-2). Writers Digest.

Poets in the Garden. Compiled by Denis Wood. (Illus.). 127p. 1979. 15.00 (ISBN 0-7195-3562-X). Transatlantic.

Poets in the Nursery. Charles Powell. 79p. Repr. of 1920 ed. lib. bdg. 25.00 (ISBN 0-8492-4221-5). R West.

Poet's Journal: Days of 1945-1951. George Seferis. Tr. by Athan Angnostopoulos from Gr. LC 73-92634. 208p. 1974. 8.95 (ISBN 0-674-68040-5, Belknap Pr); pap. 3.95 (ISBN 0-674-68041-3). Harvard U Pr.

Poets Laureate of England. Walter Hamilton. LC 68-30621. 1968. Repr. of 1879 ed. 22.00 (ISBN 0-8103-3150-0). Gale.

Poet's Madness: A Reading of George Trakl. Francis M. Sharp. (Illus.). 264p. 1981. 17.50x (ISBN 0-8014-1297-8). Cornell U Pr.

Poets of America 1979. 72p. 1979. 7.50 (ISBN 0-8059-2669-0). Dorrance.

Poets of Darkness. James B. Goode. LC 80-29653. (Center for the Study of Southern Culture Ser.). 1981. price not set (ISBN 0-87805-133-3). U Pr of Miss.

Poets of Ireland. David J. O'Donoghue. LC 68-30622. 1968. Repr. of 1912 ed. 28.00 (ISBN 0-8103-3152-7). Gale.

Poets of Ohio. Emerson Venable. LC 73-18459. 1974. Repr. of 1909 ed. 26.00 (ISBN 0-8103-3622-7). Gale.

Poets of Our Time: An Anthology. Compiled by F. E. S. Finn. 160p. 1976. pap. 7.95 (ISBN 0-7195-3243-4). Transatlantic.

Poets of the Church: A Series of Biographical Sketches of Hymn-Writers, with Notes on Their Hymns. Edwin F. Hatfield. 1979. Repr. of 1884 ed. 68.00 (ISBN 0-8103-4291-X). Gale.

Poets of the Cities: New York & San Francisco, 1950-65. Ed. by Neil A. Chassman & Robert Murdock. 150p. 1975. pap. 9.95 o.p. (ISBN 0-525-47388-2). Dutton.

Poets of the Early Seventeenth Century. Ed. by Bernard Davis & Elizabeth Davis. (Boutledge English Texts). 1967. pap. 3.95 (ISBN 0-7100-4512-3). Routledge & Kegan.

Poets of the River City. Ed. by Marilou B. Thompson. LC 78-15274. 1978. pap. 1.00 (ISBN 0-918518-08-3). St Luke TN.

Poets on Street Corners. Olga Carlisle. (YA) 1968. 7.95 o.p. (ISBN 0-394-44073-0). Random.

Poet's Riddles: Essays in Seventeenth Century Explication. Edward LeComte. LC 74-77656. 1975. 12.50 (ISBN 0-8046-9065-0, Natl U). Kennikat.

Poet's Self & the Poem: Essays on Goethe, Nietzsche & Thomas Mann. Erich Heller. 1976. text ed. 12.50x (ISBN 0-485-11164-0, Athlone Pr). Humanities.

Poet's Story. Ed. by Howard Moss. 352p. 1973. 7.95 o.s.i. (ISBN 0-02-587560-4). Macmillan.

Poets Teaching: The Creative Process. Ed. by Alberta Turner. (English & Humanities Ser.). 1980. pap. 9.95 (ISBN 0-582-28105-9). Longman.

Poets Tree. Ed. by Georgene Curry & Larry Pearson. (Anthology Ser.: Vol. 1). (Illus.). 104p. (Orig.). 1980. pap. 4.50. Pikes Peak.

Poets' War: British Poets & the Spanish Civil War. Hugh D. Ford. LC 64-10899. 1964. 10.00x o.p. (ISBN 0-8122-7484-9). U of Pa Pr.

Poggenpuhls. Theodor Fontane. Ed. by Derrick Barlow. pap. 10.00x (ISBN 0-631-01640-6, Pub. by Basil Blackwell). Biblio Dist.

Pogonomyrmex Harvester Ants: A Study of the Genus in North America. Arthur C. Cole, Jr. LC 68-17144. (Illus.). 1968. 16.50x (ISBN 0-87049-085-0). U of Tenn Pr.

Poiesis: Structure & Thought. H. D. Kitto. (Sather Classical Lectures: No. 36). 1966. 21.50x (ISBN 0-520-00651-8). U of Cal Pr.

Poil de Carotte. Renard. (Easy Reader, A). pap. 2.90 (ISBN 0-88436-046-6, FRA110051). EMC.

Poinciana. Phyllis Whitney. 1981. lib. bdg. 15.95 (ISBN 0-8161-3148-1, Large Print Bks). G K Hall.

Poindexter of Washington: A Study in Progressive Politics. Howard W. Allen. LC 80-20123. 352p. 1981. price not set (ISBN 0-8093-0952-1). S Ill U Pr.

Poineer Photographers of Brazil, 1840-1920. Gilberto Ferrez & Weston J. Naef. LC 76-25710. (Center for Inter-American Relations &The American Federation of Arts). (Illus.). 144p. 1980. 16.95 (ISBN 0-295-95737-9). U of Wash Pr.

Point & Counterpoint in Organizational Behavior. Barbara Karmel. 168p. 1980. pap. 8.95 (ISBN 0-03-054686-9). Dryden Pr.

Point & Line to Plane. Wassily Kandinsky. LC 79-50616. (Illus.). 1979. pap. text ed. 3.50 (ISBN 0-486-23808-3). Dover.

Point & Pillow Lace: A Short Account of Various Kinds, Ancient & Modern, & How to Recognize Them. Mary Sharp. LC 72-141752. (Tower Bks). (Illus.). 1971. Repr. of 1905 ed. 18.00 (ISBN 0-8103-3912-9). Gale.

Point-Counterpoint: Readings in American Government. Herbert M. Levine. 1979. pap. text ed. 8.95x (ISBN 0-673-15297-9). Scott F.

Point Defects in Crystals. R. K. Watts. LC 76-43013. 1977. 35.50 (ISBN 0-471-92280-3, Pub by Wiley-Interscience). Wiley.

Point Group Character Tables & Related Data. J. A. Salthouse & M. J. Ware. (Illus.). 64p. 1972. 10.95 (ISBN 0-521-08139-4). Cambridge U Pr.

Point in Time. William D. Sheldon & Nina Woessner. (Breakthrough Ser.). (gr. 9-12). 1976. pap. text ed. 4.96 (ISBN 0-205-04502-2, 5245028); tchrs'. ed. 2.40 (ISBN 0-205-04503-0, 5245036). Allyn.

Point, Line, Plane & Solid: A Basic Text Workbook for Engineering Graphics. 2nd ed. Lawrence E. Kundis. 368p. 1980. pap. text ed. 16.95 (ISBN 0-8403-2310-7). Kendall-Hunt.

Point of Departure. Robert Gold. (gr. 7-12). 1981. pap. 1.50 (ISBN 0-440-96983-2, LE). Dell.

Point of Entry: A Study of Client Reception in the Social Services. Anthony Hall. (National Institute Social Services Library). 1974. text ed. 17.95x o.p. (ISBN 0-04-360031-X). Allen Unwin.

Point of Honour. Alan Scholefield. LC 79-51250. 1979. 9.95 (ISBN 0-688-03454-3). Morrow.

Point of Honour. Alan Scholefield. 208p. 1980. pap. 2.25 (ISBN 0-345-28713-4). Ballantine.

Point of No Return. Wilbur H. Morrison. LC 80-81000. (World War II Ser.). (Illus.). 272p. (Orig.). 1980. pap. 2.50 (ISBN 0-87216-716-X). Playboy Pbks.

Point of Reference. Richard Russell. 1979. pap. 1.50 (ISBN 0-505-51394-3). Tower Bks.

Point of View. Ralph Steiner. LC 77-20513. (Illus.). 1978. 29.95 (ISBN 0-8195-5019-1, Pub. by Wesleyan U Pr); ltd. ed. o.p. 150.00 (ISBN 0-8195-8037-6). Columbia U Pr.

Point Reyes. Dorothy L. Whitnah. Ed. by Thomas Winnett. LC 79-57597. (Illus., Orig.). 1981. pap. 6.95 (ISBN 0-911824-95-2). Wilderness.

Point Virtue. Anne T. Brooks. 1979. pap. 1.95 (ISBN 0-505-51370-6). Tower Bks.

Pointed Spade Coins of the Chou Dynasty. Arthur B. Coole. LC 72-86806. (Encyclopedia of Chinese Coins Ser.: Vol. 4). (Illus.). 464p. 1975. 35.00x (ISBN 0-88000-012-0). Quarterman.

Pointing the Way 1959-1961. Harold Macmillan. LC 72-79682. (Illus.). 487p. 1972. 20.00 o.p. (ISBN 0-06-012741-4, HarpT). Har-Row.

Points & Lines. Seicho Matsumoto. LC 72-117385. 159p. 1970. 8.95x (ISBN 0-87011-126-4). Kodansha.

Points for Emphasis, Nineteen Eighty-One to Eighty Two. William J. Fallis. 1981. pap. 1.95 (ISBN 0-8054-1467-3). Broadman.

Points for Emphasis, Nineteen Eighty-One T0 Eighty-Two. larger type ed. William J. Fallis. 1981. pap. 2.75 (ISBN 0-8054-1466-5). Broadman.

Points for Emphasis, Nineteen Eighty to Eighty-One. W. J. Fallis. LC 35-3640. 1980. kivar 1.75 (ISBN 0-8054-1453-3). Broadman.

Points for Emphasis, Nineteen Eighty to Eighty-One. large type ed. William J. Fallis. LC 35-3640. 1980. pap. 2.50 (ISBN 0-8054-1454-1). Broadman.

Points of Chinese Acupuncture. J. Lavier. Tr. by Philip Chancellor from Fr. 115p. 1974. text ed. 10.95x (ISBN 0-8464-1038-9). Beekman Pubs.

Points of Discord: Studies in Tension & Conflict. Mokwugo Okoye. 225p. 1974. 13.50x o.p. (ISBN 0-584-10221-6). Intl Pubns Serv.

Points of Entry. Renate Wood. 20p. (Orig.). 1981. pap. price not set (ISBN 0-936600-01-2). Riverstone Foothills.

Points of Modern English Syntax. P. A. Erades. Ed. by N. J. Robat. (Contributions to English Studies). 260p. 1975. pap. text ed. 17.75 (ISBN 90-265-0184-6, Pub. by Swets Pub Serv Holland). Swets North Am.

Points of My Compass. E. B. White. LC 62-15742. 1979. pap. 2.95 (ISBN 0-06-080475-0, P 475, PL). Har-Row.

Points of View: An Anthology of Short Stories. Ed. by James Moffett & Kenneth R. McElheny. pap. 2.95 (ISBN 0-451-61880-7, ME1880, Ment). NAL.

Points to Watch in Elementary Russian. Roger G. Adams & T. F. Woods. 1968. pap. text ed. 1.95x o.p. (ISBN 0-435-39301-4). Heinemann Ed.

Points to Watch in 'o' Level French. F. Gubb. (Fr.). 1965. pap. text ed. 3.50x (ISBN 0-435-37380-3). Heinemann Ed.

Poison Detection in Human Organs. 3rd ed. Alan Curry. (American Lectures in Living Chemistry Ser.). (Illus.). 376p. 1976. 34.50 (ISBN 0-398-03433-8). C C Thomas.

Poison in the Pen. Patricia Wentworth. 208p. 1980. pap. 1.95 (ISBN 0-553-14237-2). Bantam.

Poison in the System. David Highsmith. 1979. pap. 5.00. Black Stone.

Poison People. William Haggard. 1979. 8.95 o.s.i. (ISBN 0-8027-5401-5). Walker & Co.

Poison-Proof Your Body. Robert A. Shakman. 192p. 1980. 12.95 (ISBN 0-87000-478-6). Arlington Hse.

Poison Sky: Myth & Apocalypse in Ruskin. Raymond E. Fitch. LC 70-122097. (Illus.). 500p. 1981. 25.00x (ISBN 0-8214-0090-8). Ohio U Pr.

Poison Tree. Stuart Stern. LC 78-51092. 1978. pap. 1.95 o.p. (ISBN 0-87216-463-2). Playboy Pbks.

Poisoned Kiss. Joyce Carol Oates. 1977. pap. 1.95 o.p. (ISBN 0-449-23299-9, Crest). Fawcett.

Poisoned Kiss & Other Portuguese Stories. Joyce C. Oates. LC 75-385. 196p. 1975. 10.95 (ISBN 0-685-52407-8). Vanguard.

Poisoned Land: The Problem of Hazardous Waste. Irene Kiefer. LC 80-22120. (Illus.). 96p. (gr. 5-9). 1981. PLB 8.95 (ISBN 0-689-30837-X). Atheneum.

Poisoned Lands. new ed. John Montague. 1977. pap. text ed. 6.00x (ISBN 0-85105-319-X, Dolmen Pr). Humanities.

Poisoned Orchard. Ursula Curtiss. LC 79-25977. 192p. 1980. 7.95 (ISBN 0-396-07807-9). Dodd.

Poisoners. Donald Hamilton. (Matt Helm Ser.). 1979. pap. 1.95 (ISBN 0-449-14163-2, GM). Fawcett.

Poisoning: Diagnosis & Treatment. Ed. by J. A. Vale & T. J. Meredith. (Illus.). 1981. PLB 37.75 (ISBN 0-906141-81-8, Pub. by Update Books Ltd); pap. 30.75 (ISBN 0-906141-82-6). Kluwer Boston.

Poisoning Emergencies: A Guide for Emergency Medical Personnel. Peter A. Czajka & James P. Duffy. LC 79-20542. 1980. pap. text ed. 8.95 (ISBN 0-8016-1205-5). Mosby.

Poisoning Misadventures: Narrative Excerpts on Food-Borne Diseases & Poisoning for the Physician, Microbiologist, Attorney & Nutritionist. Lloyd B. Jensen. 212p. 1970. 15.75 (ISBN 0-398-00927-9). C C Thomas.

Poisonous & Hallucinogenic Mushrooms. 2nd ed. Richard Haard & Karen Haard. (Illus.). 1977. lib. bdg. 11.95 (ISBN 0-88930-014-3, Pub. by Cloudburst Canada); pap. 5.95 (ISBN 0-88930-018-6, Pub. by Cloudburst Canada). Madrona Pubs.

Poisonous & Hallucinogenic Mushrooms. 2nd ed. Richard Haard & Karen Haard. (Illus.). 164p. 1980. pap. 7.95 (ISBN 0-930180-05-4). Homestead Bk.

Poisonous Plants. Robert E. Arnold. LC 77-84881. (Orig.). 1979. pap. 5.95 (ISBN 0-8467-0585-0, Pub. by Two Continents). Hippocrene Bks.

Poisonous Plants & Animals. Horst Altmann. (Illus.). 144p. 1981. pap. 5.95 (ISBN 0-7011-2526-8, Pub. by Chatto-Bodley-Jonathan). Merrimack Bk Serv.

Poisonous Plants & Fungi. (Illus.). 1976. 25.00 o.p. (ISBN 0-685-65613-6, Pub. by Pharmaceutical). Rittenhouse.

Poisonous Plants of the United States & Canada. 3rd ed. John M. Kingsbury. 1964. 25.95 (ISBN 0-13-685016-2). P-H.

Poisonous Snakebites in the United States. Henry M. Parrish. LC 78-18625. 1980. 15.00 (ISBN 0-533-03838-3). Vantage.

Poisonous Snakes. Tony Phelps. (Illus.). 320p. 1981. 27.50 (ISBN 0-7137-0877-8, Pub. by Blanford Pr England). Sterling.

Poisonous Snakes. Seymour Simon. LC 80-23938. (Illus.). 80p. (gr. 2-6). 1981. 11.95 (ISBN 0-590-07513-6, Four Winds). Schol Bk Serv.

Poisons & Toxins. Joan Arehart-Treichel. LC 76-15034. (Illus.). 160p. (gr. 5 up). 1976. 8.95 (ISBN 0-8234-0288-6). Holiday.

Poisons, Antidotes & Anectodes. William Tichy. LC 76-51188. (Illus.). (gr. 7 up). 1977. 8.95 (ISBN 0-8069-3738-6); PLB 8.29 (ISBN 0-8069-3739-4). Sterling.

Poisons Around Us: Toxic Metals in Food, Air, & Water. Henry A. Schroeder. LC 73-15283. 160p. 1974. 8.50x (ISBN 0-253-16675-6). Ind U Pr.

Poitou touristique. (Beautes de la France). (Illus.). 1978. 14.25x (ISBN 2-03-013926-2, 3157). Larousse.

Poker. Theo. Hardison. (Gambler's Book Shelf). pap. 2.95 (ISBN 0-89650-571-5). Gamblers.

Poker: A Guaranteed Income for Life. Frank R. Wallace. 1978. pap. 7.95 (ISBN 0-446-97455-2). Warner Bks.

Poker Face. Ulvis Alberts. LC 80-70464. (Illus.). 144p. limited ed. 125.00 (ISBN 0-9605416-0-8); pap. 30.00 (ISBN 0-9605416-1-6). Angel City.

Poker Power. Frank R. Wallace. Date not set. cancelled (ISBN 0-911752-28-5). I & O Pub.

Poker Strategy. Nesmith Ankeny. LC 80-68177. 272p. 1981. 11.95 (ISBN 0-465-05839-6). Basic.

Poker: The Small-Limit Game. Scotty Barclay. 64p. (Orig.). 1980. pap. 2.95 (ISBN 0-89650-835-8). Gamblers.

Poker to Win. Al Smith. (Gambler's Book Shelf). 64p. 1975. pap. 2.95 (ISBN 0-89650-544-8). Gamblers.

Poker Troubleshooting Guide & Answer Book. Frank R. Wallace & Eric Savage. Date not set. 100.00 (ISBN 0-911752-26-9). I & O Pub. Postponed.

Poky Little Puppy. Janette S. Lowrey. (Illus.). (gr. 1-3). 1942. 1.95 (ISBN 0-307-10418-4, Golden Pr); PLB 7.62 (ISBN 0-307-60418-7). Western Pub.

Poky Little Puppy Follows His Nose Home. Adelaide Holl. (Illus.). (gr. k-3). 1977. PLB 5.00 (ISBN 0-307-60030-0, Golden Pr). Western Pub.

Pol Bury. Dore Ashton. (Maeght Gallery Ser.). (Illus.). 1977. Repr. 39.95 (ISBN 0-8120-5178-5). Barron.

Pol Bury. (Maeght Gallery: Derriere le Miroir Ser.: No. 209). (Illus.). 1978. pap. 19.95 (ISBN 0-8120-2005-7). Barron.

Poland. Vaclav Benes & Norman J. Porends. (Nations of the Modern World Ser.). 1976. 19.00x (ISBN 0-510-38911-2). Westview.

Poland. 3rd ed. LC 77-644959. (Illus.). 80p. (Orig.). 1979. pap. 7.50x (ISBN 0-686-63735-6). Intl Pubns Serv.

Poland: A Handbook. (Illus.). 613p. 1977. 20.00x o.p. (ISBN 0-8002-2273-3). Intl Pubns Serv.

Poland: Communism Adrift. Jan B. De Weydenthal. LC 79-67732. (The Washington Papers: Vol. 72). 88p. 1979. pap. 3.50 (ISBN 0-8039-1430-X). Sage.

Poland in Pictures. Sterling Publishing Company Editors. LC 71-90811. (Visual Geography Ser). (Illus., Orig.). (gr. 6 up). 1969. PLB 4.99 (ISBN 0-8069-1127-1); pap. 2.95 (ISBN 0-8069-1126-3). Sterling.

Poland in the Twentieth Century. M. K. Dziewanowski. (Illus.). 309p. 1980. pap. 9.00x (ISBN 0-231-08372-6). Columbia U Pr.

Poland in the 20th Century. M. K. Dziewanowski. LC 76-51216. (Illus.). 1977. 20.00x (ISBN 0-231-03577-2). Columbia U Pr.

Poland: The Country & Its People. Tr. by Ryszard Wojna. LC 80-451948. 208p. (Orig.). 1979. pap. 6.00x (ISBN 0-8002-2278-4). Intl Pubns Serv.

Poland's Ghettos at War. Alfred Katz. LC 78-120535. 1978. text ed. 23.00x (ISBN 0-8290-0194-8); pap. text ed. 10.95x (ISBN 0-8290-0195-6). Irvington.

Poland's International Affairs 1919-1960. Stephan Horak. LC 64-63009. (Russian & East European Ser.: Vol. 31). 268p. 1964. pap. 7.50x (ISBN 0-253-39031-1). Ind U Pr.

Polanski: Three Films; Knife in the Water; Repulsion; Cul-De-Sac. Intro. by Boleslaw Sulik. LC 74-24656. (Icon Editions, Masterworks Film Ser). (Illus.). 216p. 1975. pap. 4.95x o.s.i. (ISBN 0-06-430062-5, IN-62, HarpT). Har-Row.

Polar. Elaine Moss. (Illus.). (ps-1). 1979. PLB 8.95 (ISBN 0-233-96695-1). Andre Deutsch.

Polar & Magnetospheric Substorms. S. I. Akasofu. (Astrophysics & Space Science Library: Vol. 11). (Illus.). 1969. 18.00 o.p. (ISBN 0-387-91024-7). Springer-Verlag.

Polar Bears Like It Hot. Joseph Rosenbloom. LC 79-91397. (Illus.). 160p. (gr. 8 up). 1980. 6.95 (ISBN 0-8069-4612-1); PLB 8.29 (ISBN 0-8069-4613-X). Sterling.

Polar Deserts. Wally Herbert. LC 73-153825. (International Library). (Illus.). (gr. 7 up). 1971. PLB 6.90 o.p. (ISBN 0-531-02101-7). Watts.

Polar Dielectrics & Their Applications. J. C. Burfoot & G. W. Taylor. 1979. 45.00x (ISBN 0-520-03749-9). U of Cal Pr.

Polar Research: To the Present & the Future. Ed. by Mary A. McWhinnie. LC 78-52068. (AAAS Selected Symposium Ser.: No. 7). (Illus.). 1978. lib. bdg. 28.50x (ISBN 0-89158-435-8). Westview.

Polar Rosses. Ernest S. Dodge. (Great Travellers Ser.). (Illus.). 1973. 6.95 o.p. (ISBN 0-571-08914-3, Pub. by Faber & Faber). Merrimack Bk Serv.

Polar Structures in the Book of Qohelet. Jamer A. Loader. (Beihefte aur Zeitschrift fuer die alttestamentliche Wissenschaft). 150p. 1979. text ed. 34.50x (ISBN 3-11-007636-5). De Gruyter.

Polaris. Sheldon Perkins. 1979. pap. 1.75 (ISBN 0-505-51386-2). Tower Bks.

Polaris & the Immortals. Charles B. Stilson. (YA) 5.95 (ISBN 0-685-07455-2, Avalon). Bouregy.

Polaris Snowmobile Service-Repair: 1973-1977. Mike Bishop. Ed. by Eric Jorgensen. (Illus.). 1977. pap. 8.95 (ISBN 0-89287-177-6, X952). Clymer Pubns.

Polaritons: Proceedings, Taormina Research Conference on the Structure of Matter, 1st, Taormina, Italy, Oct, 1972. Ed. by Elias Burstein & Francesco De Martini. LC 73-12845. 1974. text ed. 45.00 (ISBN 0-08-017825-1). Pergamon.

Polarity & Analogy. Geoffrey E. Lloyd. 1966. 59.50 (ISBN 0-521-05578-4). Cambridge U Pr.

Polarity Sensitivity As Inherent Scope Relations. William A. Ladusaw & Jorge Hankamer. LC 79-6614. (Outstanding Dissertations in Linguistics Ser.). 236p. 1980. lib. bdg. 27.50 (ISBN 0-8240-4555-6). Garland Pub.

Polarization in the Church. Ed. by Hans Kung & Walter Kasper. LC 73-6435. (Concilium Ser.: Religion in the Seventies: Vol. 88). 156p. 1973. pap. 4.95 (ISBN 0-8164-2572-8). Crossroad NY.

Polarization Microscopy of Dental Tissues. W. J. Schmidt & A. Keil. Tr. by P. Middle. 604p. 1971. 87.00 (ISBN 0-08-010787-7). Pergamon.

Polarization Phenomena in Nuclear Reactions: Proceedings. Symposium - 3rd - Madison - 1970. Ed. by Henry H. Barschall & Willy Haeberli. LC 71-143762. 1971. text ed. 60.00 (ISBN 0-299-05890-5). U of Wis Pr.

Polarized Light & Optical Measurements. D. Clarke & J. F. Grainger. 1971. text ed. 28.00 (ISBN 0-08-016320-3). Pergamon.

Polarographic Techniques. 2nd ed. Louis Meites. LC 65-19735. (Electrochemical Data Ser.). (Illus.). 1965. 50.00 (ISBN 0-470-59205-2, Pub. by Wiley-Interscience). Wiley.

Pole House Construction. Len Feldheym. 224p. (Orig.). 1981. pap. 15.75 (ISBN 0-910460-85-X). Craftsman.

Polemaischen Munz-und Rechnugswerte. F. Hultsch. 66p. (Ger.). 15.00 (ISBN 0-916710-81-5). Obol Intl.

Poles. Willy Ley. LC 62-13534. (Life Nature Library). (Illus.). (gr. 5 up). 1962. PLB 8.97 o.p. (ISBN 0-8094-0617-9, Pub. by Time-Life). Silver.

Pole's History of Adult Schools. Thomas Pole. Ed. by Coolie Verner. 1967. 11.50 (ISBN 0-88379-005-X). Adult Ed.

Poles in Oklahoma. Richard M. Bernard. LC 79-6714. (Newcomers to a New Land Ser.). (Illus.). 96p. (Orig.). 1980. pap. 2.95 (ISBN 0-8061-1630-7). U of Okla Pr.

Poles on the High Seas. Jerzy Pertek. Tr. by Alexander Jordan. (Library of Polish Studies: Vol. 9). text ed. 8.95 (ISBN 0-917004-13-2). Kosciuszko.

Police Administration & Management. Sam Souryal. (Criminal Justice Ser.). 1977. text ed. 17.50 (ISBN 0-8299-0141-8); instrs.' manual avail. (ISBN 0-8299-0371-2). West Pub.

Police Administration: Organization & Performance. Anthony V. Bouza. LC 77-24748. 1978. text ed. 18.25 (ISBN 0-08-022220-X). Pergamon.

Police & Community in Japan. Walter L. Ames. (Illus.). 300p. 1981. 16.50 (ISBN 0-520-04070-8). U of Cal Pr.

Police & People: A Five Country Comparison. Paul G. Shane. (Illus.). 1980. pap. text ed. 11.00 (ISBN 0-8016-4556-5). Mosby.

Police & the Behavioral Sciences. Ed. by J. Leonard Steinberg & Donald McEvoy. 176p. 1974. text ed. 16.75 (ISBN 0-398-02957-1). C C Thomas.

Police and the Community. Louis Radelet. 1977. text ed. 14.95x (ISBN 0-02-477510-X). Macmillan.

Police & the Community: Studies. Louis A. Radelet. LC 72-11489. (Criminal Justice Ser.). 240p. 1973. text ed. 8.95x o.p. (ISBN 0-02-476710-7). Glencoe.

Police & the Elderly. Ed. by Arnold P. Goldstein et al. LC 78-27400. (Pergamon General Psychology Ser.: Vol. 78). 1979. 16.50 (ISBN 0-08-023894-7); pap. 8.00 (ISBN 0-08-023893-9). Pergamon.

Police & the People: French Popular Protest, 1789-1820. Richard C. Cobb. 414p. 1970. 34.50x (ISBN 0-19-821479-0); pap. 5.95x (ISBN 0-19-881297-3, OPB). Oxford U Pr.

Police & the Public. Richard L. Holcomb. (Illus.). 1975. pap. 4.25 (ISBN 0-398-00857-4). C C Thomas.

Police & the Public. D. W. Warwell. 128p. 1978. 13.95x (ISBN 0-7121-1683-4, Pub. by Macdonald & Evans England). Intl Ideas.

Police & the Underprotected Child. C. J. Flammang. 324p. 1970. 18.50 (ISBN 0-398-00583-4). C C Thomas.

Police & Their Many Publics. Donald W. McEvoy. LC 76-6851. 154p. 1976. 10.00 (ISBN 0-8108-0925-7). Scarecrow.

Police & Violence. Ed. by Lawrence W. Sherman & Richard D. Lambert. (Annals of the American Academy of Political & Social Science Ser.: No. 452). 1980. 7.00 (ISBN 0-87761-256-0); pap. text ed. 6.00 (ISBN 0-87761-257-9). Am Acad Pol Soc Sci.

Police at the Bargaining Table. Charles Salerno. 1981. write for info (ISBN 0-398-04462-7). C C Thomas.

Police Careers: Constructing Career Paths for Tomorrow's Police Force. David I. Sheppard & Albert S. Glickman. (Illus.). 164p. 1973. 11.75 (ISBN 0-398-02811-7). C C Thomas.

Police Communications. Marc W. Tobias. (Illus.). 650p. 1974. text ed. 39.50 (ISBN 0-398-02970-9); pap. text ed. 27.75 (ISBN 0-398-02994-6). C C Thomas.

Police Communications System. V. A. Leonard. 96p. 1970. 8.75 (ISBN 0-398-01106-0). C C Thomas.

Police-Community Relations. 3rd ed. H. H. Earle. 116p. 1980. pap. 5.75 spiral (ISBN 0-398-04468-6); instrs' guide avail. (ISBN 0-398-03900-3). C C Thomas.

Police Community Relations. Hale. LC 73-11827. 208p. 1974. pap. 8.80 (ISBN 0-8273-1423-X); instructor's guide 1.60 (ISBN 0-8273-1424-8). Delmar.

Police, Crime, & Society. Ed. by Clarence H. Patrick. 320p. 1972. 14.75 (ISBN 0-398-02376-X). C C Thomas.

Police Crime Prevention. V. A. Leonard. (Illus.). 210p. 1972. text ed. 14.75 (ISBN 0-398-02339-5). C C Thomas.

Police Crisis Intervention. Arnold P. Goldstein et al. LC 76-48283. (Pergamon General Psychology Ser.: Vol. 80). 175p. 1979. 22.00 (ISBN 0-08-023873-4); pap. 8.75 (ISBN 0-08-023874-2). Pergamon.

Police Department Psychologist. Martin Reiser. 136p. 1972. 10.75 (ISBN 0-398-02483-9). C C Thomas.

Police Detective Function. V. A. Leonard. 124p. 1970. 9.75 (ISBN 0-398-01099-4). C C Thomas.

Police Disaster Operations. Allen P. Bristow. (Illus.). 240p. 1972. 18.50 (ISBN 0-398-02244-5); pap. 18.50 o.p. (ISBN 0-398-02244-5). C C Thomas.

Police Enterprise: Its Organization & Management. V. A. Leonard. (Illus.). 104p. 1969. 8.75 (ISBN 0-398-01100-1). C C Thomas.

Police Ethics. David A. Hansen. (Illus.). 96p. 1973. pap. 6.75 spiral (ISBN 0-398-02648-3). C C Thomas.

Police Family. Arthur Niederhoffer & Elaine Niederhoffer. LC 73-11678. 1978. 16.95 (ISBN 0-669-90498-8). Lexington Bks.

Police Guide to Bomb Search Techniques. Frank A. Moyer. (Illus.). 198p. (Orig.). 1980. pap. text ed. 12.95 (ISBN 0-87364-196-5). Paladin Ent.

Police in Trouble: Our Frightening Crisis in Law Enforcement. James F. Ahern. 256p. 1971. 9.95 (ISBN 0-8015-5928-6, Hawthorn). Dutton.

Police in Urban America, Eighteen Hundred Sixty to Nineteen Twenty. Eric Monkkonen. LC 80-16762. (Interdisciplinary Perspectives on Modern History Ser.). (Illus.). 256p. Date not set. price not set (ISBN 0-521-23454-9). Cambridge U Pr.

Police Interrogation & Confessions: Essays in Law & Policy. Yale Kamisar. 1980. 17.50x (ISBN 0-472-09318-5). U of Mich Pr.

Police Ju Jitsu. J. McCauslin Moynahan, Jr. (Illus.). 132p. 1962. 8.75 (ISBN 0-398-01366-7). C C Thomas.

Police Juvenile Enforcement. C. J. Flammang. 284p. 1972. 18.75 (ISBN 0-398-02280-1). C C Thomas.

Police Lab. Melvin Berger. LC 75-33198. (Illus.). 1976. PLB 9.89 (ISBN 0-381-99620-4, JD-J). John Day.

Police Labor Movement: Problems & Perspectives. John H. Burpo. 224p. 1971. 14.75 (ISBN 0-398-00262-2). C C Thomas.

Police Leader: A Handbook. David A. Hansen & Thomas R. Culley. (Illus.). 128p. 1971. 10.50 (ISBN 0-398-02192-9). C C Thomas.

Police Leadership. Arthur R. Pell. (Illus.). 152p. 1967. 8.75 (ISBN 0-398-01471-X). C C Thomas.

Police Management & Organizational Behavior: A Contingency Approach. Roy R. Roberg. (Criminal Justice Ser.). (Illus.). 1979. text ed. 18.50 (ISBN 0-8299-0275-9); instrs.' manual avail. (ISBN 0-8299-0599-5). West Pub.

Police Management of Traffic Accident Prevention Programs. W. L. Booth. 384p. 1980. 29.50 (ISBN 0-398-04008-7). C C Thomas.

Police Medical Dictionary. J. E. Schmidt. 256p. 1968. 19.75 (ISBN 0-398-01673-9). C C Thomas.

Police of America: A Personal View, Introduction & Commentary. Harold K. Becker & Jack E. Whitehouse. (Illus.). 108p. 1979. 11.75 (ISBN 0-398-03895-3). C C Thomas.

Police Officer. 8th ed. Joseph A. Murray. LC 80-24919. 352p. 1981. lib. bdg. 10.00 (ISBN 0-668-05128-0); pap. 6.00 (ISBN 0-668-05130-2). Arco.

Police Officer's Memorandum Book. Charles L. Kuhn. (Illus.). 80p. 1964. pap. 5.00 spiral (ISBN 0-398-01062-5). C C Thomas.

Police Operations. Gwynne Peirson. LC 75-44334. (Nelson-Hall Law Enforcement Ser.). 182p. 1976. 17.95 (ISBN 0-911012-86-9). Nelson-Hall.

Police Operations-Tactical Approaches to Crimes in Progress. Andrew P. Sutor. LC 76-16911. (Criminal Justice Ser.). 1976. 12.50 (ISBN 0-685-71453-5); pap. text ed. write for info. (ISBN 0-8299-0609-6); instrs.' manual avail. (ISBN 0-8299-0611-8). West Pub.

Police: Organisation & Command. R. S. Bunyard. (Illus.). 400p. 1978. 21.95x (ISBN 0-7121-1671-0, Pub. by Macdonald & Evans England). Intl Ideas.

Police Patrol. Richard L. Holcomb. (Amer. Lec. Public Protection Ser). (Illus.). 128p. 1971. 6.75 (ISBN 0-398-00856-6). C C Thomas.

Police Patrol: Operations & Management. Charles D. Hale. LC 80-36814. 300p. 1981. text ed. 16.95 (ISBN 0-471-03291-3). Wiley.

Police Patrol Organization. V. A. Leonard. (Illus.). 116p. 1970. 11.50 (ISBN 0-398-01102-8). C C Thomas.

Police Patrol Readings. 2nd. ed. Samuel G. Chapman. (Illus.). 788p. 1972. pap. 49.75 photocopy ed. spiral (ISBN 0-398-00304-1). C C Thomas.

Police Patrol: Tactics & Techniques. T. Adams. LC 71-138484. (Essential of Law Enforcements Ser). 1971. ref. ed. 16.95x (ISBN 0-13-684662-9). P-H.

Police: Perpectives, Problems, Prospects. Ed. by Donal E. Macnamara & Marc Reidei. (Special Studies). (Illus.). 150p. 1974. text ed. 17.95 o.p. (ISBN 0-275-09660-2). Praeger.

Police Personnel Administration. V. A. Leonard. 144p. 1970. 12.75 (ISBN 0-398-01103-6). C C Thomas.

Police Personnel Selection Process. Leonard Territo et al. LC 76-30889. (Illus.). 1977. pap. text ed. 10.95 (ISBN 0-672-61403-0). Bobbs.

Police Photography. Harold Pountney. (Illus.). 1971. 26.00x (ISBN 0-85334-621-6). Intl Ideas.

Police Planning. 2nd ed. O. W. Wilson. (Illus.). 562p. 1977. 21.75 (ISBN 0-398-02081-7). C C Thomas.

Police Pre-Disaster Preparation. V. A. Leonard. (Illus.). 344p. 1973. 15.75 (ISBN 0-398-02693-9). C C Thomas.

Police Procedures & Defense Tactics Training Manual. Harry Aziz. Ed. by Sydney S. Halet. (Illus.). 1979. 19.95 (ISBN 0-87040-451-2). Japan Pubns.

Police Professionalism. Barbara R. Price. LC 76-58246. 1977. 14.95 (ISBN 0-669-01341-2). Lexington Bks.

Police Programs for Preventing Crime & Delinquency. Ed. by Dan G. Pursuit et al. (Illus.). 512p. 1972. 24.75 (ISBN 0-398-02456-1); pap. 14.75 (ISBN 0-398-02488-X). C C Thomas.

Police Records System. V. A. Leonard. (Illus.). 104p. 1977. 10.75 (ISBN 0-398-01104-4). C C Thomas.

Police Reform in the United States: The Era of August Vollmer, 1905-1932. Gene E. Carte & Elaine A. Carte. LC 73-87248. 390p. 1976. 14.50x (ISBN 0-520-02599-7). U of Cal Pr.

Police Revitalization. Gerald E. Caiden. LC 77-3111. (Illus.). 1977. 23.95 (ISBN 0-669-01477-X). Lexington Bks.

Police Revolution. Peter Evans. 1974. text ed. 16.95x (ISBN 0-04-350048-X). Allen Unwin.

Police Roadblock Operations. John I. Schwarz. (Police Science Ser.). (Illus.). 96p. 1962. 9.75 (ISBN 0-398-01700-X). C C Thomas.

Police Role in Alcohol-Related Crises. Gerald W. Garner. 168p. 1979. text ed. 14.75 (ISBN 0-398-03853-8). C C Thomas.

Police Roles in the Seventies, Vol. 1. Ed. by Jack F. Kinton. LC 75-271. (Society in Transition Ser.). 1975. 10.95 o.p. (ISBN 0-685-56482-7); pap. 6.95 o.p. (ISBN 0-685-56483-5). Soc Sci & Soc Res.

Police Science for the Young American. V. A. Leonard. (Illus.). 80p. 1968. 6.75 (ISBN 0-398-01105-2). C C Thomas.

Police Selection & Evaluation: Issues & Techniques. Charles D. Spielberger. LC 78-9958. (Praeger Special Studies Ser.). 1979. 27.95 (ISBN 0-03-050976-9). Praeger.

Police Shotgun Manual. Roger H. Robinson. (Illus.). 168p. 1973. 14.75 (ISBN 0-398-02630-0). C C Thomas.

Police-Social Work Team. Harvey Treger. (Illus.). 308p. 1975. pap. 21.75 (ISBN 0-398-03317-X). C C Thomas.

Police Supervision. Robert C. Trojanowicz & John Trojanowicz. (Illus.). 1980. text ed. 13.95 o.p. (ISBN 0-13-684043-4). P-H.

Police Supervision: A Common Sense Approach. Gerald W. Garner. 296p. 1981. write for info. (ISBN 0-398-04127-X). C C Thomas.

Police Supervision Readings. Allen P. Bristow. 488p. 1971. pap. 29.75 photocopy ed. spiral (ISBN 0-398-00227-4). C C Thomas.

Police Supervision: Theory & Practice. 2nd ed. P. M. Whisenand. (Illus.). 576p. 1976. 17.95 (ISBN 0-13-686311-6). P-H.

Police Supervisory Practice. William J. Osterloh. LC 74-23482. 1975. text ed. 15.95x o.p. (ISBN 0-471-65712-3). Wiley.

Police Systems in the United States. rev. & enl. ed. Bruce Smith. Ed. by Bruce Smith, Jr. LC 60-11498. 1960. 9.95x o.s.i. (ISBN 0-06-036090-9, HarpT). Har-Row.

Police Systems of Europe: A Survey of Selected Police Organizations. 2nd ed. Harold K. Becker. (Illus.). 256p. 1980. pap. 13.75 (ISBN 0-398-04023-0). C C Thomas.

Police Tactics in Hazardous Situations. San Diego Police Dept. (Criminal Justice Ser.). 1976. pap. text ed. 8.95 (ISBN 0-8299-0628-2). West Pub.

Police Telecommunications. Alan Burton. (Illus.). 452p. 1973. 19.75 (ISBN 0-398-02251-8). C C Thomas.

Police Terminology: Programmed Manual for Criminal Justice Personnel. Jack M. Seitzinger & Thomas M. Kelley. (Illus.). 152p. 1974. pap. 11.75 (ISBN 0-398-02947-4). C C Thomas.

Police: The Exercise of Power. Don Campbell. 128p. 1978. 13.95x (ISBN 0-7121-1678-8, Pub. by Macdonald & Evans Engalnd). Intl Ideas.

Police: The Investigation of Violence. Keith Simpson. (Illus.). 240p. 1978. 17.95x (ISBN 0-7121-1689-3, Pub. by Macdonald & Evans England). Intl Ideas.

Police, the Judiciary, & the Criminal. 2nd ed. V. A. Leonard. (Illus.). 320p. 1975. 18.75 (ISBN 0-398-03332-3). C C Thomas.

Police Traffic Control. V. A. Leonard. 176p. 1971. 11.75 (ISBN 0-398-01107-9). C C Thomas.

Police Traffic Control Function. 4th ed. Paul B. Weston. (Illus.). 420p. 1978. 16.25 (ISBN 0-398-03764-7). C C Thomas.

Police Training for Tough Calls. Frank J. Vandall. LC 75-33489. 1976. pap. 5.00 (ISBN 0-89937-009-8). Ctr Res Soc Chg.

Police Training for Tough Calls: Discretionary Situations. Frank J. Vandell. 140p. 1980. pap. 9.95 o.p. (ISBN 0-686-64815-3). Carrollton Pr.

Police Training Officer. David A. Hansen & Thomas R. Culley. (Illus.). 244p. 1973. 13.75 (ISBN 0-398-02493-6). C C Thomas.

Police Unarmed Defense Tactics. D. O. Schultz & M. Slepecky. 102p. 1973. pap. 7.50 (ISBN 0-398-02666-1). C C Thomas.

Police Unionism: Power & Impact in Public-Sector Bargaining. Hervey A. Juris & Peter Feuille. LC 73-1565. (Illus.). 208p. 1973. 19.95 (ISBN 0-669-86801-9). Lexington Bks.

Police Unions. Allen Z. Gammage & Stanley L. Sachs. 204p. 1972. 14.75 (ISBN 0-398-02467-7). C C Thomas.

Police Work. Leonard Freed. 1981. 19.95 (ISBN 0-671-25202-X, Touchstone Bks); pap. 9.95 (ISBN 0-671-25203-8). S&S.

Police Work: The Social Organization of Policies. Peter K. Manning. 1979. 23.00 (ISBN 0-262-13130-7); pap. 8.95 (ISBN 0-262-63070-2). MIT Pr.

Police Your Planet. Lester Del Rey. 224p. 1975. pap. 1.50 o.p. (ISBN 0-345-24465-6). Ballantine.

Policeman's Utopia: An Interview with the Director of the West German FBI, with an Essay by Hans Magnus Enzensberger. Sebastian Cobler. Tr. by Tonia Taubes & Sophie Wilkins. (Orig.). 1981. pap. 4.95 (ISBN 0-89396-044-6). Urizen Bks.

Policewoman's Manual. Lois L. Higgins. (Illus.). 196p. 1972. 11.75 (ISBN 0-398-00836-1). C C Thomas.

Policies of Publishers: A Handbook for Order Librarians, 1978 Edition. Ung Chon Kim. LC 77-25063. 1978. pap. 10.00 (ISBN 0-8108-1098-0). Scarecrow.

Policies of Survival. Edwin Tapp. (Studies in Twentieth Century History). 1979. pap. text ed. 4.50 (ISBN 0-686-65413-7, 00549). Heinemann Ed.

Policies Underlying Corporate Giving. Ralph L. Thomas. LC 65-25263. 1965. 17.50 (ISBN 0-686-10124-3). R L Thomas.

Policing. Adrian Kinnane. LC 78-2314. 1979. 15.95 (ISBN 0-88229-327-3). Nelson-Hall.

Policing a Perplexed Society. Ed. by Robert Mark. 1977. pap. text ed. 8.95x o.p. (ISBN 0-04-363006-5). Allen Unwin.

Policing Freedom. John Alderson. 288p. 1979. 22.95x (ISBN 0-7121-1815-2, Pub. by Macdonald & Evans England). Intl Ideas.

Policing the City. Rob Mawby. 1979. text ed. 28.25x (ISBN 0-566-00277-9, Pub. by Gower Pub Co England). Renouf.

Policy Alternatives for a New International Economic Order. William Cline. LC 79-87553. 1979. 26.95 (ISBN 0-03-049471-0); pap. 9.95 (ISBN 0-03-049466-4). Praeger.

Policy Alternatives for a New International Economic Order: An Economic Analysis. Ed. by William R. Cline. LC 79-87553. 410p. 1979. pap. 7.95 (ISBN 0-03-049466-4). Overseas Dev Council.

Policy Analysis & Deductive Reasoning. Ed. by Gordon Tullock & Richard Wagner. LC 77-18380. (Policy Studies Organization Ser.). 1978. 19.95 (ISBN 0-669-02080-X). Lexington Bks.

Policy Analysis in Local Government. Kenneth L. Kraemer. LC 73-83294. (Municipal Management Ser.). 1973. pap. 12.50 o.p. (ISBN 0-87326-003-1). Intl City Mgt.

Policy Analysis in Social Science Research. Stuart S. Nagel & Marian Neef. LC 78-11463. (Sage Library of Social Research: Vol. 72). 1979. 18.00x (ISBN 0-8039-1156-4); pap. 8.95x (ISBN 0-8039-1157-2). Sage.

Policy Analysis: Introduction & Applications to Health Programs. Marvin R. Burt. LC 74-81587. (Illus.). 136p. 1974. text ed. 18.00 (ISBN 0-87815-013-7). Info Resources.

Policy & Government in Northern Ireland: Lessons of Devolution. Derek Birrell & Alan Murie. 353p. 1980. 32.50x (ISBN 0-389-20019-0). B&N.

Policy & Police: The Enforcement of the Reformation in the Age of Cromwell. Geoffrey R. Elton. LC 79-172831. 400p. 1972. 41.95 (ISBN 0-521-08383-4). Cambridge U Pr.

Policy & Politics: Essays in Honour of Norman Chester. Ed. by David Butler & A. H. Halsey. 1978. text ed. 26.00x (ISBN 0-333-23561-4). Humanities.

Policy & Politics in Britain: The Limits of Consensus. Douglas E. Ashford. (Policy & Politics in Industrial States Ser.). 400p. 1980. 19.50 (ISBN 0-87722-194-4); pap. text ed. 9.95 (ISBN 0-87722-195-2). Temple U Pr.

Policy & Practice in Rural Development. Ed. by Guy Hunter et al. LC 76-15078. 526p. text ed. 19.50 (ISBN 0-86598-002-0). Allanheld.

Policy & Procedure Manual for Church & Synagogue Libraries: A Do-It-Yourself Guide. Martin Ruoss. LC 79-28676. 1980. pap. 3.75 (ISBN 0-915324-17-2). CSLA.

Policy & Program Research in a University Setting: A Case Study. Advisory Committee For Assessment Of University Based Institutes For Research On Poverty. LC 70-174752. 1971. pap. text ed. 3.00 (ISBN 0-309-01929-X). Natl Acad Pr.

Policy, Bureaucracy, & the Public's Health. Frank J. Thompson. 288p. 1981. text ed. 19.95x (ISBN 0-262-20041-4). MIT Pr.

Policy Decision Making in Education: An Introduction to Calculation & Control. Dale Mann. LC 74-13962. 1975. text ed. 11.95x (ISBN 0-8077-2440-8); pap. text ed. 8.50x (ISBN 0-8077-2468-8). Tchrs Coll.

Policy Dilemma: Federal Crime Policy & the Law Enforcement Assistance Administration. Malcolm Feely & Austin Sarat. 1981. 17.50x (ISBN 0-8166-0901-2); pap. 7.95x (ISBN 0-8166-0904-7). U of Minn Pr.

Policy Exploration Through Microanalytic Stimulation. Guy H. Orcutt et al. 370p. 1976. 12.50 (ISBN 0-87766-170-7, 15100); pap. 5.95 (ISBN 0-87766-169-3, 15300). Urban Inst.

Policy for Action: A Symposium on the Planning of a Comprehensive District Psychiatric Service. Ed. by Robert Cawley & Gordon McLachlan. 190p. 1973. pap. 9.50x o.p. (ISBN 0-19-721376-6). Oxford U Pr.

Policy Formulation & Administration: A Casebook of Top-Management Problems in Business. 7th ed. C. Roland Christensen et al. 1976. text ed. 19.95x (ISBN 0-256-01820-0). Irwin.

Policy Formulation & Strategy Management. Robert E. Schellenberger & Glenn F. Boseman. LC 77-2758. (Wiley Series in Management & Administration). 1978. text ed. 22.95 (ISBN 0-471-75903-1); tchrs. manual avail. (ISBN 0-471-03725-7). Wiley.

Policy Implementation in the Federal System: National Goals & Local Implementors. Carl E. Van Horn. LC 78-19929. (Illus.). 1979. 19.95 (ISBN 0-669-02435-X). Lexington Bks.

Policy Implementation: Penalties or Incentives? Ed. by John Brigham & Don W. Brown. LC 80-16765. (Sage Focus Editions: Vol. 25). (Illus.). 284p. 1980. 18.95 (ISBN 0-8039-1350-8). Sage.

Policy Implementation: Penalties or Incentives? Ed. by John Brigham & Don W. Brown. LC 80-16765. (Sage Focus Editions: Vol. 25). (Illus.). 284p. 1980. pap. 9.95 (ISBN 0-8039-1351-6). Sage.

Policy Implications of Data Network Developments in the OECD Area. OECD. (Information Computer Communications Policy: No. 3). (Illus.). 206p. (Orig., Fr.). 1980. pap. 12.50 (ISBN 92-64-12005-X, 93-79-02-1). OECD.

Policy in Urban Planning: Structure Plans, Local Plans, & Urban Development. William Solesbury. 1974. 18.00 (ISBN 0-08-017758-1). Pergamon.

Policy Instructions to Build up an Infrastructure for the Generation of Technology. (Science & Technology for Development Ser.: STPI Module 5). 57p. 1981. pap. 5.00 (ISBN 0-88936-263-7, IDRC TS26, IDRC). Unipub.

Policy-Making in a Nuclear Program: The Case of the West German Fast-Breeder Reactor. Otto Keck. LC 79-3831. 1981. write for info. (ISBN 0-669-03519-X). Lexington Bks.

Policy-Making in American Public Education: A Framework for Analysis. John T. Thompson. LC 75-5841. (Illus.). 304p. 1975. 16.95 (ISBN 0-13-685370-6). P-H.

Policy-Making in the American System: The Case of the Manpower, Development & Training Program. George T. Menake. LC 77-18584. 1978. pap. text ed. 11.50x (ISBN 0-8191-0409-4). U Pr of Amer.

Policy-Making in the Federal Executive Branch. Ed. by Randall B. Ripley & Grace A. Franklin. LC 74-33093. (Illus.). 1975. 17.95 (ISBN 0-02-926490-1). Free Pr.

Policy Making Process. 2nd ed. C. Lindblom. 1980. pap. 6.95 (ISBN 0-13-686543-7). P-H.

Policy-Making Process. J. J. Richardson. (Library of Political Studies). 1969. text ed. 5.25x (ISBN 0-7100-6523-X). Humanities.

Policy of the Entente: The Determinants of British Foreign Policy, 1904-1914. Keith Wilson. 1981. text ed. 15.00 (ISBN 0-391-02198-2). Humanities.

Policy on Land Use & Source Control Aspects of Traffic Noise Attenuation. 1980. 0.50. AASHTO.

Policy Perspectives. Henry M. Wriston. LC 64-17776. 178p. 1964. 7.50 (ISBN 0-87057-081-1). Univ Pr of New England.

Policy Predicament: Making & Implementing Public Policy. George C. Edwards, 3rd & Ira Sharkansky. LC 77-28212. (Illus.). 1978. text ed. 15.95x (ISBN 0-7167-0019-0). W H Freeman.

Policy Reform in Developing Countries. Bela Balassa. 1977. text ed. 27.00 (ISBN 0-08-021477-0); pap. text ed. 16.25 (ISBN 0-08-021478-9). Pergamon.

Policy Science: Methodologies & Cases. Ed. by Arie Y. Lewin & Melvin F. Shakum. 450p. 1975. 50.00 (ISBN 0-08-019601-2); pap. text ed. 24.00 (ISBN 0-08-019600-4). Pergamon.

Policy Simulations with an Econometric Model. Gary Fromm & Paul Taubman. 1968. 10.95 (ISBN 0-8157-2944-8). Brookings.

Policy Studies & the Social Sciences. Stuart S. Nagel. LC 75-2292. (Policy Studies Organization Policy Study Ser.). 192p. 1975. 22.95 (ISBN 0-669-99531-2). Lexington Bks.

Policy Studies in America & Elsewhere. Stuart S. Nagel. (Policy Studies Organization Ser.). 256p. 1975. 19.95 (ISBN 0-669-99549-5). Lexington Bks.

Policy Studies Personnel Directory. Ed. by Stuart Nagel & Nancy Munshaw. 1979. pap. 5.00 (ISBN 0-918592-33-X). Policy Studies.

Policy Studies Review Annual, Vol. 4. Ed. by Bertram H. Raven. LC 77-72938. (Illus.). 768p. 1980. 35.00 (ISBN 0-8039-1119-X). Sage.

Policymaking for Social Security. Martha Derthick. LC 78-24811. 1979. 19.95 (ISBN 0-8157-1816-0); pap. 8.95 (ISBN 0-8157-1815-2). Brookings.

Polish-American Folktales. Catherine H. Ainsworth. LC 77-80771. (Folklore Bks.). x, 102p. 1980. 5.00 (ISBN 0-933190-04-2). Clyde Pr.

Polish Analytical Philosophy: A Survey & a Comparison with British Analytical Philosophy. Henryk Skolimowski. 1967. text ed. 10.25x (ISBN 0-7100-3632-9). Humanities.

Polish Brethren. George H. Williams. (Harvard Theological Studies: No. 30). 16.00; pap. 11.00 (ISBN 0-89130-201-8). Scholars Pr CA.

Polish Complex. Konwicki. 1981. 10.00 (ISBN 0-374-23548-1). FS&G.

Polish Detroit & the Kolasinski Affair. Lawrence D. Orton. (Illus.). 268p. 1981. 17.95 (ISBN 0-8143-1671-9). Wayne St U Pr.

Polish-Jewish Relations During the Second World War. Emmanuel Ringelblum. Tr. by Dafna Allon et al. LC 76-1394. 330p. 1976. 24.00 (ISBN 0-86527-155-0). Fertig.

Polish Land. rev. ed. Marion M. Coleman. LC 74-81566. iv, 152p. 1974. pap. text ed. 5.00 (ISBN 0-910366-18-7). Alliance Coll.

Polish Memoirs of William John Rose. William J. Rose. Ed. by Daniel Stone. LC 74-79986. 1975. 17.50x o.p. (ISBN 0-8020-5306-8). U of Toronto Pr.

Polish Practical Dictionary (English-Polish) J. Stanislawski & K. Billip. 1976. 15.00x (ISBN 0-89918-533-9, P-533). Vanous.

Polish Prose & Verse. Ed. by J. Peterkiewicz. 1956. text ed. 13.25x (ISBN 0-485-17502-9, Athlone Pr). Humanities.

Polish Question in the Russian State Duma. Edward Chmielewski. LC 77-100411. 1970. 11.50x (ISBN 0-87049-110-5). U of Tenn Pr.

Polish Underground State. Stefan Korbonski. 288p. 1981. pap. 7.95 (ISBN 0-88254-517-5). Hippocrene Bks.

Polished Pilgrim. George Otis, Jr. pap. 1.50 (ISBN 0-89728-053-9, 533180). Omega Pubns OR.

Polishes & Waxes: Shifts & Changes, C-024. Ed. by Business Communications. 1981. 850.00 (ISBN 0-89336-211-5). BCC.

Politica. Aristotle. Ed. by W. David Ross. (Oxford Classical Texts). 1957. 18.95x (ISBN 0-19-814515-2). Oxford U Pr.

Politica Tributaria como Instrumento del Desarrolo: Documentos y Conclusiones De la III Conferencia Interamericana Sobre Tributacion. 554p. (Span.). 1973. 25.00 (ISBN 0-8270-3785-6). OAS.

Political Administration in the Soviet Union & the United States. James C. Thompson & Richard F. Vidmer. 240p. 1981. 22.95 (ISBN 0-89789-009-4). J F Bergin.

Political Analysis: An Introduction. 2nd ed. Margaret M. Conway & Frank B. Feigert. 1972. pap. text ed. 10.45 (ISBN 0-205-05512-5, 7655126). Allyn.

Political Anatomy of Ireland. W. Petty. 260p. 1970. Repr. of 1691 ed. 30.00x (ISBN 0-7165-0093-0, Pub. by Irish Academic Pr Ireland). Biblio Dist.

Political & Civil History of the United States of America from the Year 1763 to the Close of the Administration of President Washington in March, 1797, 2 Vols. Timothy Pitkin. LC 79-109613. (Ear of the American Revolution Ser). 1970. Repr. of 1823 ed. lib. bdg. 95.00 (ISBN 0-306-71908-8). Da Capo.

Political & Military Laws of War. Julian Lider. 1979. text ed. 29.00x (ISBN 0-566-00231-0, Pub. by Gower Pub Co England). Renouf.

Political & Social Doctrines of the Unity of Czech Brethren in the Fifteenth & Early Sixteenth Centuries. Peter Brock. (Slavistic Printings & Reprintings). 1957. text ed. 34.25x (ISBN 0-391-01607-5). Humanities.

Political & Social Economy of Commodity Control. Christopher P. Brown. LC 79-88568. 394p. 1979. 39.95 (ISBN 0-03-053351-1). Praeger.

Political & Social Essays. Paul Ricoeur. Ed. by David Stewart & Joseph Bien. LC 74-82500. ix, 293p. 1974. 15.00x (ISBN 0-8214-0169-6). Ohio U Pr.

Political & Social Foundations of Education. 2nd ed. Frederick Wirt & Michael Kirst. LC 75-20297. 1975. 17.50 (ISBN 0-8211-1016-0); text ed. 15.75x (ISBN 0-685-57428-8). McCutchan.

Political & Social History of Khurasan Under Abbasid Rule 747-820. Elton L. Daniel. LC 79-53302. 1979. 28.00x (ISBN 0-88297-025-9). Bibliotheca.

Political & Social Ideas of St. Augustine. Herbert A. Deane. LC 63-9809. 1963. pap. 7.00x (ISBN 0-231-08569-9). Columbia U Pr.

Political & Social Inquiry. Dickinson L. McGaw & George Watson. LC 75-31913. 336p. 1976. text ed. 18.95 (ISBN 0-471-58403-7); instructor's manual avail. (ISBN 0-471-01579-2). Wiley.

Political & Strategic Importance of Exports, Vol. I. Penelope Hartland-Thunberg. LC 79-2785. (Significant Issues Ser.: No. 3). 35p. 1979. 4.00 (ISBN 0-89206-009-3). CSI Studies.

Political & Strategic Importance of Exports. (Significant Issues Ser.: Vol. I, No. 3). 35p. 1979. pap. 5.00 (ISBN 0-89206-009-3, CSIS004, CSIS). Unipub.

Political Anthropology. Ed. by Marc J. Swartz et al. LC 66-15210. 1966. 23.95x (ISBN 0-202-01026-0). Aldine Pub.

Political Bargaining: An Introduction to Modern Politics. Thomas A. Reilly & Michael W. Sigall. LC 75-38837. (Illus.). 1976. text ed. 16.95x (ISBN 0-7167-0538-9); pap. text ed. 8.95x (ISBN 0-7167-0537-0). W H Freeman.

Political Behavior & Public Opinion: Comparative Analysis. Lewis Bowman & G. R. Boynton. 512p. 1974. pap. text ed. 13.95 (ISBN 0-13-685065-0). P-H.

Political Behavior of the American Electorate. 3rd ed. William H. Flanigan & Nancy Zingale. 175p. 1975. pap. text ed. 5.95x o.s.i. (ISBN 0-205-04770-X). Allyn.

Political Behavior of the American Electorate. 4th ed. William H. Flanigan & Nancy H. Zingale. 1979. pap. text ed. 8.35 (ISBN 0-205-06524-4, 7665245). Allyn.

Political Buttons, Bk 2: 1920-1976. Theodore L. Hake. LC 73-93793. (Illus.). 1977. 25.00 (ISBN 0-918708-00-1); pap. 18.00 (ISBN 0-918708-01-X). Hake.

Political Buttons, 1789-1916, Bk 3. Theodore L. Hake. LC 73-93793. (Illus.). 1978. 25.00 (ISBN 0-918708-02-8); pap. 18.00 (ISBN 0-918708-03-6). Hake.

Political Campaign Communication: A Bibliography & Guide to the Literature. Lynda L. Kaid et al. LC 73-22492. 1974. 10.00 (ISBN 0-8108-0704-1). Scarecrow.

Political Campaign Handbook. Arnold Steinberg. LC 75-43130. 1976. 21.95 (ISBN 0-669-00481-2). Lexington Bks.

Political Campaign Management: A Systems Approach. Arnold Steinberg. LC 75-36014. 320p. 1976. 23.95 (ISBN 0-669-00374-3). Lexington Bks.

Political Campaigning. Roy Hoopes. (Impact Ser.). (Illus.). (gr. 7 up). 1979. PLB 6.90 s&l (ISBN 0-531-02858-5). Watts.

Political Campaigning: Problems in Creating an Informed Electorate. Stanley Kelley, Jr. 1960. 9.95 (ISBN 0-8157-4878-7). Brookings.

Political Caricature in the United States in Separately Published Cartoons. Ed. by Frank Weitenkampf. LC 79-137698. (Illus.). 1971. Repr. of 1953 ed. 15.00 (ISBN 0-87104-506-0, Co-Pub. by Arno). NY Pub Lib.

Political Cartoons. Charles Press. LC 76-2309. (Illus.). 360p. 1981. 18.00 (ISBN 0-8386-1901-0). Fairleigh Dickinson.

Political Change in France Under Richelieu & Mazarin, 1624-1661. Richard Bonney. (Illus.). 1977. text ed. 49.95x (ISBN 0-19-822537-7). Oxford U Pr.

Political Change in India, Nineteen Seventy-Seven: Elections & the Emergency Aftermath. Surindar Suri. 1981. 11.00x (ISBN 0-8364-0017-8); pap. text ed. 7.00x (ISBN 0-8364-0019-4). South Asia Bks.

Political Change in the Metropolis. 2nd ed. Harrigan. 1981. pap. text ed. 9.95 (ISBN 0-316-34744-2); training manual free (ISBN 0-316-34745-0). Little.

Political Changes & the Economic Future of East Asia. Ed. by Robert B. Hewett. 208p. 1981. pap. write for info. (ISBN 0-8248-0750-2). U Pr of Hawaii.

Political Commitment & Christian Community. Ed. by Norbert Greinacher & Alois Mueller. (Concilium Ser.: Religion in the Seventies: Vol. 84). 156p. 1973. pap. 4.95 (ISBN 0-8164-2540-X). Crossroad NY.

Political Communication. Ed. by Steven H. Chaffee. LC 75-14629. (Sage Annual Reviews of Communication Research: Vol. 4). 1975. 20.00x (ISBN 0-8039-0505-X); pap. 9.95x (ISBN 0-8039-0507-6). Sage.

Political Concepts: A Reconstruction. Felix Oppenheim. LC 80-23846. (Illus.). 1981. lib. bdg. price not set (ISBN 0-226-63184-2). U of Chicago Pr.

Political Conflict & Ethnic Strategies: A Case Study of Burundi. Warren Weinstein & Robert Schire. LC 76-22649. (Foreign & Comparative Studies-Eastern African Ser.: No. 23). 68p. 1976. pap. text ed. 4.50x (ISBN 0-915984-20-2). Syracuse U Foreign Comp.

Political Consequences of Modernization. John H. Kautsky. LC 80-16087. 286p. 1980. Repr. lib. bdg. 11.50 (ISBN 0-89874-215-3). Krieger.

Political Continuity & Change. rev ed. Peter H. Merkl. 1972. pap. text ed. 15.50 scp o.p. (ISBN 0-685-03002-4, 06-044413-4, HarpC); instructors' manual. avail. o.p. (ISBN 0-06-364406-1). Har-Row.

Political Corruption in America. George C. Benson et al. LC 77-88815. 1978. write for info. (ISBN 0-669-02008-7). Lexington Bks.

Political Creature: An Evolutionary Reorientation. Peter Zollinger. LC 67-27525. 1967. 7.50 o.s.i. (ISBN 0-8076-0432-1). Braziller.

Political Crime in Europe: A Comparative Study of France, Germany, & England. Barton Ingraham. 1979. 25.00 (ISBN 0-520-03562-3). U of Cal Pr.

Political Crime in the United States: Analyzing Crimes by & Against Government. Julian Roebuck & Stanley C. Weeber. LC 78-19463. (Praeger Special Studies). 1978. 25.95 (ISBN 0-03-044241-9). Praeger.

Political Criminal Trials: How to Defend Them. John M. Sink. LC 73-89533. 1974. with 1978 rev. pages 40.00 (ISBN 0-87632-103-1). Boardman.

Political Crisis of the 1850's. Michael F. Holt. LC 77-13564. (Critical Episodes in American Politics Ser.). 1978. text ed. 11.95 o.p. (ISBN 0-471-40840-9); pap. text ed. 8.95 (ISBN 0-471-40841-7). Wiley.

Political Culture & Group Conflict in Communist China. Alan P. Liu. LC 74-14195. (Studies in International & Comparative Politics: No. 4). 205p. 1976. text ed. 19.40 (ISBN 0-87436-196-6); pap. text ed. 6.00 (ISBN 0-87436-197-4). ABC-Clio.

Political Culture in Israel: Cleavage & Integration Among Israeli Jews. Eva Etzioni-Halevy & Rina Shapira. LC 76-24350. (Special Studies). 1977. text ed. 26.95 (ISBN 0-275-23790-7). Praeger.

Political Culture of Japan. Bradley Richardson. 1974. pap. 7.95x (ISBN 0-520-03049-4); pap. 6.95x (ISBN 0-520-03049-4). U of Cal Pr.

Political Development & Bureaucracy in Libya. Omar I. Fathaly et al. LC 77-713. 1977. 15.95 (ISBN 0-669-01426-5). Lexington Bks.

Political Development & Change. Ed. by Garry D. Brewer & Ronald D. Brunner. LC 74-482. (Illus.). 1975. 25.00 (ISBN 0-02-904710-2). Free Pr.

Political Development & Social Change in Libya. Omar I. Fathaly & Monte Palmer. LC 77-712. 240p. 1980. 22.95 (ISBN 0-669-01427-3). Lexington Bks.

Political Development & Social Change. 2nd ed. J. L. Finkle & R. W. Gable. LC 72-149769. 1971. pap. 16.50 o.p. (ISBN 0-471-25891-1). Wiley.

Political Development in Eastern Europe. Ed. by Jan G. Triska & Paul M. Cocks. LC 76-19551. (Special Studies). 1977. text ed. 39.95 (ISBN 0-275-23600-5); pap. 8.95 (ISBN 0-275-89640-4). Praeger.

Political Development in Modern Japan. Ed. by Robert E. Ward. (Studies in the Modernization of Japan). 1968. 25.00 (ISBN 0-691-03045-6); pap. 9.95 (ISBN 0-691-00017-4). Princeton U Pr.

Political Development of Japan: 1867 to 1909. George E. Uyehara. (Illus.). 296p. 1972. Repr. of 1910 ed. 31.00x (ISBN 0-686-28325-2, Pub. by Irish Academic Pr). Biblio Dist.

Political Diaries of C. P. Scott, 1911-1928. Ed. by Trevor Wilson. LC 75-110993. 512p. 1970. 22.50 (ISBN 0-8014-0569-6). Cornell U Pr.

Political Disquisitions, 3 Vols. James Burgh. LC 78-146144. (American Constitutional & Legal History Ser). 1971. Repr. of 1775 ed. lib. bdg. 135.00 (ISBN 0-306-70101-4). Da Capo.

Political Dynamics: Impact on Nurses & Nursing. Grace L. Deloughery & Kristine M. Gebbie. LC 74-22120. 1975. text ed. 11.50 o.p. (ISBN 0-8016-1245-4). Mosby.

Political Ecology of the Brazilian National Bank for Development. (Span. & Eng.). 1969. pap. 1.00 ea. Span. Ed (ISBN 0-8270-6515-9). Eng. Ed (ISBN 0-8270-6510-8). OAS.

Political, Economic & Labor Climate in Colombia. Grace F. Hemphill. 1980. pap. 15.00 (ISBN 0-89546-025-4). Indus Res Unit-Wharton.

Political, Economic, & Labor Climate in the Philippines. Jaime T. Infante. LC 80-53988. (Multinational Industrial Relations Ser.: No. 8a). (Illus.). 147p. 1980. pap. 15.00 (ISBN 0-89546-024-6). Indus Res Unit-Wharton.

Political Economists & the English Poor Laws: A Historical Study of the Influence of Classical Economics on the Formation of Social Welfare Policy. Raymond G. Cowherd. LC 76-8301. xvii, 300p. 1977. 16.95x (ISBN 0-8214-0233-1). Ohio U Pr.

Political Economy, 2 vols. Oskar Lange. LC 65-367. Vol. 1, 1963. text ed. 13.75 (ISBN 0-08-013561-7); Vol. 2, 1972. text ed. 26.00 (ISBN 0-08-016572-9). Pergamon.

Political Economy: A Critique of American Society. Scott McNall. 1981. pap. text ed. 7.95x (ISBN 0-673-15424-6). Scott F.

Political Economy & Soviet Socialism. Alec Nove. 1979. text ed. 27.50x (ISBN 0-04-335037-2). Allen Unwin.

Political Economy of Advertising. Ed. by David G. Tuerck. 1978. 13.25 (ISBN 0-8447-2120-4); pap. 4.75 (ISBN 0-685-25906-4). Am Enterprise.

Political Economy of Africa. D. Cohen & J. Daniel. (Illus.). 1981. text ed. 25.00x (ISBN 0-582-64284-1); pap. text ed. 11.95x (ISBN 0-582-64285-X). Longman.

Political Economy of Antitrust: Principal Paper by William Baxter. Ed. by Robert D. Tollison. LC 80-7928. 1980. 16.95x (ISBN 0-669-03876-8). Lexington Bks.

Political Economy of Change. Ed. by K. J. Alexander. 1975. 29.50x (ISBN 0-631-16540-1, Pub. by Basil Blackwell). Biblio Dist.

Political Economy of Change. Warren F. Ilchman & Norman T. Uphoff. LC 71-81743. 1969. 17.50x (ISBN 0-520-01390-5); pap. 4.95x (ISBN 0-520-02033-2, CAMPUS58). U of Cal Pr.

Political Economy of Colonialism in Ghana: A Collection of Documents and Statistics, 1900-1960. Ed. by Geoffrey Kay. S. Hymer. (Illus.). 1971. 47.50 (ISBN 0-521-07952-7). Cambridge U Pr.

Political Economy of Development. Charles K. Wilber. 1973. pap. text ed. 7.50 o.p. (ISBN 0-394-31756-4). Random.

Political Economy of Development: Theoretical & Empirical Contributions. Ed. by Norman T. Uphoff & Warren F. Ilchman. LC 77-161999. 1972. 24.50 o.p. (ISBN 0-520-02062-6); pap. 9.95x (ISBN 0-520-02314-5, CAMPUS84). U of Cal Pr.

Political Economy of East-West Trade. Connie M. Friesen. LC 76-14395. 1976. text ed. 23.95 (ISBN 0-275-56920-9). Praeger.

Political Economy of Education: A Symposium on Regional Problems in Britain & Ireland. John Vaizey et al. LC 72-10688. 297p. 1973. 21.95 (ISBN 0-470-89780-5). Halsted Pr.

Political Economy of EEC Relations with African, Caribbean & Pacific States: Contributions to the Understanding of the Lome Convention on North-South Relations. Ed. by Frank Long. 192p. 1980. 26.00 (ISBN 0-08-024077-1). Pergamon.

Political Economy of Food. Ed. by Vilho Harle. 346p. 1978. text ed. 30.00x (ISBN 0-566-00206-X, Pub. by Gower Pub Co England). Renouf.

Political Economy of Food & Energy. Ed. by Louis J. Junker. (Michigan Business Papers: No. 62). 1977. pap. 6.00 o.p. (ISBN 0-87712-177-X). U Mich Busn Div Res.

Political Economy of Germany in the Twentieth Century. Karl Hardach. 240p. 1980. 22.50x (ISBN 0-520-03809-6). U of Cal Pr.

Political Economy of Income Distribution in Nigeria. Ed. by Henry Bienen & V. P. Diejomaoh. LC 80-16860. (Political Economy of Income Distribution in Developing Countries Ser.: No. 2). 500p. 1981. text ed. 45.00x (ISBN 0-8419-0618-1). Holmes & Meier.

Political Economy of Income Distribution in Egypt. Ed. by Robert L. Tignor & Goudal Abdel-Khalek. LC 80-26932. (Political Economy of Income Distribution in Developing Countries Ser.). 500p. 1981. text ed. 45.00x (ISBN 0-8419-0633-5). Holmes & Meier.

Political Economy of Interest Groups in the Legislative Process in Canada. Fred Thompson & W. T. Stanbury. 53p. 1979. pap. text ed. 3.00x (ISBN 0-920380-27-1, Pub. by Inst Res Pub Canada). Renouf.

Political Economy of Latin America. Wendell C. Gordon. LC 65-19444. 1965. 20.00x (ISBN 0-231-02675-7); pap. write for info. (ISBN 0-231-08572-9). Columbia U Pr.

Political Economy of Marx. Michael Howard & John King. (Modern Economics Ser.). (Illus.). 376p. 1976. text ed. 17.95x (ISBN 0-582-44610-4); pap. text ed. 10.95 (ISBN 0-582-44611-2). Longman.

Political Economy of Modern Iran: Despotism & Pseudo-Modernism, 1926-1979. Homa Katouzian. 448p. 1981. 40.00x (ISBN 0-8147-4577-6); pap. 19.50x (ISBN 0-8147-4578-4). NYU Pr.

Political Economy of Modern Spain: Policy-Making in an Authoritarian System. Charles W. Anderson. LC 72-106036. (Illus.). 1970. 25.00 (ISBN 0-299-05611-2); pap. 7.95 (ISBN 0-299-05614-7). U of Wis Pr.

Political Economy of Monetary Reform. Ed. by Robert Z. Aliber. LC 76-26692. 320p. 1977. text ed. 21.00 (ISBN 0-86598-001-2). Allanheld.

Political Economy of Monetary Reform. Ed. by Robert Z. Aliber. LC 76-26692. 320p. Date not set. 21.00 o.s.i. (ISBN 0-87663-810-8). Allanheld & Schram.

Political Economy of Nasserism. M. Abdel-Fadil. LC 80-49995. (Cambridge Department of Applied Economics, Occasional Papers: No. 52). (Illus.). 140p. 1980. 24.95 (ISBN 0-521-22313-X); pap. 13.95 (ISBN 0-521-29446-0). Cambridge U Pr.

Political Economy of North Sea Oil. Donald I. MacKay & George A. Mackay. LC 75-25633. 208p. 1976. 26.50x (ISBN 0-89158-515-X). Westview.

Political Economy of Oil. Ferdinand E. Banks. LC 79-3340. 1980. 25.95 (ISBN 0-669-03402-9). Lexington Bks.

Political Economy of Peru Nineteen Fifty-Six to Seventy-Seven. E. V. FitzGerald. LC 78-72086. (Illus.). 1980. 42.50 (ISBN 0-521-22289-3). Cambridge U Pr.

Political Economy of Producer Associations. Helge Hveem. 1978. pap. 19.00x (ISBN 82-00-01671-4, Dist. by Columbia U Pr). Universitet.

Political Economy of Race & Class in South Africa. Bernard Magubane. LC 78-13917. 1979. 18.50 o.p. (ISBN 0-85345-463-9, CL-4639). Monthly Rev.

Political Economy of Social Class. Charles Anderson. 384p. 1974. text ed. 17.95 (ISBN 0-13-685149-5). P-H.

Political Economy of Social Policy. A. J. Culyer. 1980. 27.50 (ISBN 0-312-62242-2). St Martin.

Political Economy of South Africa: The Making of Poverty. Bethuel Setai. 1977. pap. text ed. 9.50x (ISBN 0-8191-0171-0). U Pr of Amer.

Political Economy of the American Revolution. Ed. by Nancy B. Spannaus & Christopher White. 1977. pap. text ed. 5.95 (ISBN 0-918388-01-5, Univ Edns). New Benjamin.

Political Economy of the Cotton South. Ed. by Gavin Wright. (Illus.). 1978. 10.95 (ISBN 0-393-05686-4); pap. 5.95x (ISBN 0-393-09038-8). Norton.

Political Economy of the New Left: An Outsider's View. 2nd ed. Assar Lindbeck. LC 77-83267. 1977. 15.00x (ISBN 0-8147-4979-8). NYU Pr.

Political Economy of the Northern Ireland Crisis. Belinda Drobert. 1979. 24.50 o.p. (ISBN 0-685-65705-1). Porter.

Political Economy of the Oil Import Quota. Yoram Barzel & Christopher D. Hall. LC 76-41087. (Publications Ser.: No. 172). 1977. 8.95 (ISBN 0-8179-6721-4). Hoover Inst Pr.

Political Economy of the Third Sector: Co-Operation & Participation. Ed. by Alasdair Clayre. 240p. 1980. 29.50x (ISBN 0-19-877137-1); 29.50x (ISBN 0-19-877138-X). Oxford U Pr.

Political Economy of Tolerable Survival. Ed. by Maxwell Gaskin. 224p. 1981. 30.00x (ISBN 0-7099-0266-2, Pub. by Croom Helm Ltd England). Biblio Dist.

Political Economy of Urban Poverty. Charles Sackrey. 172p. 1972. pap. 4.95x (ISBN 0-393-09410-3, NortonC). Norton.

Political Economy of Urban Transportation. Delbert A. Taebel & James V. Cornehls. LC 77-23150. (National University Publications Interdisciplinary Urban Ser). (Illus.). 1977. 15.00 (ISBN 0-8046-9178-9); pap. 8.95 (ISBN 0-8046-9200-9). Kennikat.

Political Economy of War & Peace. Richard K. Ashley. 320p. 1980. 30.00 (ISBN 0-89397-087-5). Nichols Pub.

Political Economy: Past & Present. Robbins. 1976. 15.00x (ISBN 0-231-04128-4). Columbia U Pr.

Political, Electoral, & Spatial Systems. R. J. Johnston. (Contemporary Problems in Geography Ser.). (Illus.). 1979. 29.95x (ISBN 0-19-874071-9); pap. 11.95x (ISBN 0-19-874072-7). Oxford U Pr.

Political Elites in Japan. Masalaki Takane. (Japan Research Monographs: No.1). 180p. 1981. pap. price not set (ISBN 0-912966-33-5). IEAS Ctr Chinese Stud.

Political Elites in the Middle East. Ed. by George Lenczowski. LC 75-10898. 1975. 13.25 (ISBN 0-8447-3164-1); pap. 7.25 (ISBN 0-8447-3163-3). Am Enterprise.

Political Evolution of the Mexican People. Justo Sierra. Tr. by Charles Ramsdell. LC 69-63009. (Pan American Paperbacks Ser.: No. 3). 1966. 17.50x (ISBN 0-292-78382-5); pap. 8.95 (ISBN 0-292-70071-7). U of Tex Pr.

Political Experience: A Preface to the Study of Politics. William J. Meyer. LC 76-17254. 286p. 1978. Repr. of 1977 ed. lib. bdg. 12.95 o.p. (ISBN 0-88275-716-4). Krieger.

Political Fictions. Michael Wilding. 1980. 25.00x (ISBN 0-7100-0457-5). Routledge & Kegan.

Political Finance. Ed. by Herbert E. Alexander. LC 78-24439. (Sage Electoral Studies Yearbook: Vol. 5). (Illus.). 1979. 20.00x (ISBN 0-8039-1175-0); pap. 9.95x (ISBN 0-8039-1176-9). Sage.

Political Forces in Argentina. rev ed. Peter G. Snow. LC 78-19779. 1979. 17.95 (ISBN 0-03-043496-3); pap. 9.95 student ed. (ISBN 0-03-045316-X). Praeger.

Political Generations & Political Development. Richard J. Samuels. LC 77-168. 1977. 16.95 (ISBN 0-669-01463-X). Lexington Bks.

Political Geography. Robert E. Norris & L. Lloyd Haring. (Geography Ser.). 328p. 1980. text ed. 21.95 (ISBN 0-675-08223-4). Merrill.

Political Geography of Africa. E. A. Boateng. LC 77-80828. 1978. 37.95 (ISBN 0-521-21764-4); pap. 12.95x (ISBN 0-521-29269-7). Cambridge U Pr.

Political Geography of the Oceans. J. R. Prescott. LC 74-31813. 247p. 1975. 19.95 (ISBN 0-470-69672-9). Halsted Pr.

Political Groups in Chile: The Dialogue Between Order & Change. Ben G. Burnett. (Latin American Monographs Ser.: No. 21). 1970. 14.95 (ISBN 0-292-70084-9). U of Tex Pr.

Political Handbook of the World: Nineteen Eighty. 6th ed. Ed. by Arthur S Banks. (Political Handbook of the World Ser.). 1980. 34.95 (ISBN 0-07-003626-8). McGraw.

Political History of Finland: 1809-1966. L. A. Puntila. 248p. 1976. 22.50x (ISBN 0-8448-0913-6). Crane-Russak Co.

Political History of Ghana: The Rise of Gold Coast Nationalism, 1850-1928. David Kimble. 1963. 37.50x (ISBN 0-19-821623-8). Oxford U Pr.

Political History of Newfoundland, 1832-1864. Gertrude E. Gunn. LC 67-397. 1966. pap. 8.50 (ISBN 0-8020-6323-3). U of Toronto Pr.

Political History of the Ancient World. Gwynne E. H. Thomas. 1981. 7.95 (ISBN 0-8062-1680-8). Carlton.

Political History of the Chalukyas of Badami. D. P. Dikshit. 1980. 26.00x (ISBN 0-8364-0645-1, Pub. by Abhinav India). South Asia Bks.

Political History of the Cherokee Nation, 1838-1907. Morris L. Wardell. (Civilization of the American Indian Ser.: Vol. 17). (Illus.). 1938. 15.95 (ISBN 0-8061-1411-8). U of Okla Pr.

Political History of the Olympic Games. David B. Kanin. (Replica Edition Ser.). 160p. 1981. lib. bdg. 17.00x (ISBN 0-86531-109-9). Westview.

Political History of the U. S. A. During the Period of Reconstruction. Edward McPherson. Ed. by Harold Hyman & Hans Trefousse. LC 77-127288. (Studies in American History & Government Ser.). 648p. 1972. Repr. of 1871 ed. lib. bdg. 55.00 (ISBN 0-306-71206-7). Da Capo.

Political History of the United States of America During the Great Rebellion. Edward McPherson. LC 73-127287. (American Constitutional & Legal History Ser). 1972. Repr. of 1865 ed. lib. bdg. 55.00 (ISBN 0-306-71207-5). Da Capo.

Political Ideas & Movements in India. Sankar Ghose. LC 75-908962. 1975. 13.00x o.p. (ISBN 0-88386-732-X). South Asia Bks.

Political Ideas of St. Thomas Aquinas. Saint Thomas Aquinas. Ed. by Dino Bigongiari. (Library of Classics Ser.: No. 15). 1973. pap. text ed. 4.95 (ISBN 0-02-840380-0). Hafner.

Political Ideas of the Utopian Socialists. Keith Taylor. 1981. 27.50x (ISBN 0-7146-3089-6, F Cass Co). Biblio Dist.

Political Identity: A Case Study from Uganda. Marshall H. Segall et al. LC 76-21273. (Foreign & Comparative Studies-Eastern Africa: No. 24). 179p. 1976. pap. text ed. 5.50x (ISBN 0-915984-21-0). Syracuse U Foreign Comp.

Political Identity in South Asia. Ed. by David Taylor & Michael Yapp. (Collected Papers on South Asia Ser.: No. 2). 1979. text ed. 11.75x (ISBN 0-391-01005-0). Humanities.

Political Impact of Mass Media. Colin Seymour-Ure. LC 73-90038. (Communication & Society: Vol. 4). 1974. 20.00x (ISBN 0-8039-0347-2); pap. 9.95x (ISBN 0-8039-0713-3). Sage.

Political Implications of Human Genetic Technology. Robert H. Blank. (Special Studies in Science, Technology, & Public Policy). 209p. (Orig.). 1981. lib. bdg. 24.00x (ISBN 0-89158-975-9); pap. text ed. 12.00x (ISBN 0-86531-193-5). Westview.

Political Influence. Edward C. Banfield. LC 60-12182. 1965. pap. text ed. 7.95 (ISBN 0-02-901590-1). Free Pr.

Political Institutions & Social Change in Continental Europe in the Nineteenth Century. Eugene N. Anderson & Pauline R. Anderson. 1967. 23.50x (ISBN 0-520-00022-6). U of Cal Pr.

Political Institutions of West Africa. 2nd ed. J. H. Price. (Illus.). 288p. 1975. pap. text ed. 5.75x (ISBN 0-09-123111-6, Hutchinson U Lib). Humanities.

Political Involvement of Adolescents. Roberta S. Sigel & Marilyn Hoskin. 320p. 1981. 22.00 (ISBN 0-8135-0897-5). Rutgers U Pr.

Political Issues & Community Work. Ed. by Paul Curno. 1978. 23.00x (ISBN 0-7100-8975-9); pap. 12.50 (ISBN 0-7100-8976-7). Routledge & Kegan.

Political Justice: The Use of Legal Procedure for Political Ends. Otto Kirchheimer. LC 80-14279. xiv, 452p. 1980. Repr. of 1961 ed. lib. bdg. 34.50x (ISBN 0-313-22509-5, KIPJ). Greenwood.

Political Leadership. Glenn Paige. LC 76-169237. 1972. 15.95 (ISBN 0-02-923610-X). Free Pr.

Political Leadership Among Swat Pathans. Fredrik Barth. (Monographs on Social Anthropology: No. 19). 1970. pap. text ed. 7.50x (ISBN 0-485-19619-0, Athlone Pr). Humanities.

Political Leadership in NATO: A Study in Multilateral Diplomacy. Robert S. Jordan. 1979. lib. bdg. 27.50 (ISBN 0-89158-355-6). Westview.

Political Liberty: A History of the Conception in the Middle Ages & Modern Times. Alexander J. Carlyle. LC 80-18967. viii, 220p. 1980. Repr. of 1963 ed. lib. bdg. 19.75x (ISBN 0-313-21482-4, CAPL). Greenwood.

Political Life. Robert E. Lane. LC 58-6485. 1965. pap. text ed. 3.00 (ISBN 0-02-917870-3). Free Pr.

Political Man: The Social Bases of Politics. Seymour M. Lipset. LC 80-8867. 584p. 1981. pap. text ed. 7.50x (ISBN 0-8018-2522-9). Johns Hopkins.

Political Manipulation & Administrative Power: A Comparative Study. Eva Etzioni-Halevy. (International Library of Sociology). 1980. 30.00x (ISBN 0-7100-0352-8). Routledge & Kegan.

Political Memoranda: Revision of Instruction to Political Officers on Subjects Chiefly Political & Administrative, 1913-1918. 3rd rev. ed. Frederick J. Lugard. 480p. 1970. 35.00x (ISBN 0-7146-1693-1, F Cass Co). Biblio Dist.

Political Messianism: The Romantic Phase. J. L. Talmon. LC 60-14071. 1960. 34.50x (ISBN 0-89197-892-5). Irvington.

Political-Military Systems. Ed. by Catherine M. Kelleher. LC 74-77094. (Sage Research Progress Ser. on War, Revolution & Peacekeeping: Vol. 4). 1974. 20.00x (ISBN 0-8039-0414-2); pap. 9.95x (ISBN 0-8039-0415-0). Sage.

Political Mobilization. J. P. Nettl. (Society Today & Tomorrow Ser.). (Illus.). 1967. 9.95 o.p. (ISBN 0-571-08053-7, Pub. by Faber & Faber). Merrimack Bk Serv.

Political Mobilization & Economic Extraction: Chinese Communist Agrarian Policies During the Kiangi Period. Hsu King-Yi. LC 78-74335. (Modern Chinese Economy Ser.). 400p. 1980. lib. bdg. 44.00 (ISBN 0-8240-4275-1). Garland Pub.

Political Mobilization of Peasants: A Study of an Egyptian Community. Iliya F. Harik. LC 73-16535. (International Development Research Center, Studies in Development: No. 8). 320p. 1974. 12.50x (ISBN 0-253-34535-9). Ind U Pr.

Political Mobilization of the Venezuelan Peasant. John D. Powell. LC 70-134947. (Center for International Affairs Ser). (Illus.). 1971. 12.50x (ISBN 0-674-68626-8). Harvard U Pr.

Political Nature of a Ruling Class Capital & Ideology in South Africa, 1890-1933. Belinda Bozzoli. (International Library of Sociology). 356p. 1981. price not set (ISBN 0-7100-0722-1). Routledge & Kegan.

Political Obligation. Thomas McPherson. (Library of Political Studies). 1967. text ed. 5.00x (ISBN 0-7100-3158-0); pap. text ed. 2.25x (ISBN 0-7100-3159-9). Humanities.

Political Obligation in Its Historical Context. J. Dunn. LC 80-40037. (Illus.). 360p. 1980. 34.50 (ISBN 0-521-22890-5). Cambridge U Pr.

Political Offence Exception to Extradition. Christine Van den Wijngaert. 260p. 1980. lib. bdg. 53.00 (ISBN 90-268-1185-3, Pub. by Kluwer Law & Taxation). Kluwer Boston.

Political Operas 2: Attack Upon Excise. Ed. by Walter H. Rubsamen. (Ballad Opera Ser.). 1974. lib. bdg. 50.00 (ISBN 0-8240-0920-7). Garland Pub.

Political Opinion Polls. F. Teer & J. D. Spence. 1973. text ed. 10.50x (ISBN 0-09-115230-5, Hutchinson U Lib); pap. text ed. 6.00x (ISBN 0-09-115231-3). Humanities.

Political Opposition & Local Politics in Japan. Ed. by Kurt Steiner et al. LC 80-7555. 480p. 1980. 30.00 (ISBN 0-691-07625-1); pap. 9.95 (ISBN 0-691-10109-4). Princeton U Pr.

Political Organization of Native North Americans. Ed. by Ernest L. Schusky. LC 79-3715. 1980. text ed. 18.25 (ISBN 0-8191-0909-6); pap. text ed. 11.25 (ISBN 0-8191-0910-X). U Pr of Amer.

Political Organization of Space. E. W. Soja. LC 70-135471. (CCG Resource Papers Ser.: No. 8). (Illus.). 1971. pap. text ed. 4.00 (ISBN 0-89291-055-0). Assn Am Geographers.

Political Palate: A Feminist Vegetarian Cookbook. Ed. by Betsey Beaven et al. (Illus.). 352p. (Orig.). 1980. pap. 8.95 (ISBN 0-9605210-0-3, Dist. by Crossing Press). Sanguinaria.

Political Participation in Communist China. James R. Townsend. (Center for Chinese Studies, UC Berkeley). 1967. 19.50x (ISBN 0-520-01279-8); pap. 5.95x (ISBN 0-520-01416-2, CAMPUS83). U of Cal Pr.

Political Participation in Communist Systems. Donald E. Schulz. (Pergamon Policy Studies). 1981. 32.51 (ISBN 0-08-024665-6). Pergamon.

Political Participation of Asian-Americans-Problems and Strategies. Ed. by Jo Young-Hawn. LC 80-25074. (Occasional Papers Ser.: No. 6). (Orig.). 1980. pap. 12.00 (ISBN 0-934584-14-1). Pacific-Asian.

Political Participation of Women in the United States: A Selected Bibliography, 1950-1976. Kathy Stanwick & Christine Li. LC 77-23036. 1977. 10.00 (ISBN 0-8108-1075-1). Scarecrow.

Political Parties: A Cross-National Survey. Kenneth Janda. LC 80-15430. (Illus.). 1980. 100.00 (ISBN 0-02-916120-7). Free Pr.

Political Parties: An Introduction. R. Blank. 1980. 16.95 (ISBN 0-13-684761-7). P-H.

Political Parties & National Integration in Tropical Africa. Ed. by James S. Coleman & Carl G. Rosberg, Jr. (African Studies Center, UCLA). 1964. 30.00x (ISBN 0-520-00253-9). U of Cal Pr.

Political Parties & System Flexibility. Charles J. Nagy, Jr. LC 80-5846. 196p. 1981. lib. bdg. 18.00 (ISBN 0-8191-1453-7); pap. text ed. 9.00 (ISBN 0-8191-1454-5). U Pr of Amer.

Political Parties in American History. Keith I. Polakoff. LC 80-21505. 550p. 1981. pap. text ed. 14.95 (ISBN 0-471-07747-X). Wiley.

Political Parties in China. Jermyn Chi-Mung Lynn. (Studies in Chinese Government & Law). 255p. 1977. Repr. of 1930 ed. 19.50 (ISBN 0-89093-069-4). U Pubns Amer.

Political Parties in Europe. Theo Stamm. 1981. 42.50 (ISBN 0-930466-28-4). Meckler Bks.

Political Parties in Europe. Theo Stammen. 350p. 1980. 22.50x (ISBN 0-906237-08-4). Nichols Pub.

Political Parties in French-Speaking West Africa. Ruth S. Morgenthau. (Oxford Studies in African Affairs Ser). 1964. 37.50x (ISBN 0-19-821624-6). Oxford U Pr.

Political Parties in Revolutionary Massachusetts. Stephen E. Patterson. LC 72-7991. 320p. 1973. 25.00 (ISBN 0-299-06260-0). U of Wis Pr.

Political Parties in the Eighties. Ed. by Robert A. Goldwin. 1980. 10.25 (ISBN 0-8447-3377-6); pap. 5.25 (ISBN 0-686-64315-1). Am Enterprise.

Political Parties: Interest Groups & Public Policy: Group Influence in American Politics. Dennis S. Ippolito & Thomas G. Walker. 431p. 1980. text ed. 16.95 (ISBN 0-13-684357-3). P-H.

Political Partnerships: Neighborhood Residents & Their Council Members. Jeffrey L. Davidson. LC 79-13107. (The City & Society: Vol. 5). (Illus.). 231p. 1979. 18.00 (ISBN 0-8039-1050-9). Sage.

Political Partnerships: Neighborhood Residents & Their Council Members. Jeffrey L. Davidson. LC 79-13107. (The City & Society: Vol. 5). (Illus.). 231p. 1979. pap. 8.95 (ISBN 0-8039-1051-7). Sage.

Political Partnerships: Neighborhood Residents & Their Council Members. Jeffrey L. Davidson. LC 79-13107. (City & Society Ser.: Vol. 5). (Illus.). 231p. 1979. pap. 8.95 (ISBN 0-8039-1051-7); pap. 8.95 (ISBN 0-8039-1051-7). Sage.

Political Patterns in America: Conflict Representation & Resolution. Dan Nimmo & Thomas Ungs. LC 78-11419. (Illus.). 1979. text ed. 16.95x (ISBN 0-7167-1009-9). W H Freeman.

Political Philosophy & Social Welfare: Essays on the Normative Basis of Welfare Provision. Raymond Plant et al. (International Library of Welfare & Philosophy). 280p. 1981. 27.50 (ISBN 0-7100-0611-X); pap. 15.00 (ISBN 0-7100-0631-4). Routledge & Kegan.

Political Philosophy of Bakunin. Mikhail A. Bakunin. Ed. by G. P. Maximoff. 1964. 10.95 o.s.i. (ISBN 0-02-901200-7); pap. text ed. 8.95 (ISBN 0-02-901210-4). Free Pr.

Political Philosophy of Confucianism: An Interpretation of the Social & Political Ideas of Confucius, His Forerunners & His Early Disciples. L. Shihlien Hsu. (Illus.). 1975. text ed. 11.75x (ISBN 0-7007-0079-X). Humanities.

Political Philosophy of Luis De Molina, S. J. Frank B. Costello. 1974. pap. 12.00 (ISBN 0-8294-0360-4). Jesuit Hist.

Political Philosophy of Martin Luther King Jr. Hanes Walton, Jr. LC 76-111260. (Contributions in Afro-American & African Studies: No. 10). 1971. text ed. 13.95 (ISBN 0-8371-4661-5); pap. 4.95 (ISBN 0-8371-8931-4). Negro U Pr.

Political Philosophy of the American Revolution. Aldo Tassi. LC 78-59127. 1978. pap. text ed. 6.75 (ISBN 0-8191-0547-3). U Pr of Amer.

Political Philosophy of the Frankfurt School. George Friedman. LC 80-66890. 320p. 1981. 17.50x (ISBN 0-8014-1279-X). Cornell U Pr.

Political Philosophy of the Orthodox Church. Apostolos Makrakis. Ed. by Orthodox Christian Educational Society. Tr. by Denver Cummings from Hellenic. Orig. Title: The Orthodox Definition of Political Science. 163p. (Orig.). 1965. pap. 2.00x (ISBN 0-938366-11-4). Orthodox Chr.

Political Philosophy: Six Essays. Leo Strauss. Ed. by Hilail Gildin. LC 74-16290. (Traditions in Philosophy Ser). 1975. text ed. 17.95 (ISBN 0-672-63659-X). Pegasus.

Political Poetry & Idealogy of F. I. Tiutchev. Roger Conant. (Ardis Essay Ser.: No. 6). 1981. 10.00. Ardis Pubs.

Political Poetry & Ideology of Fyodor Tyutchev. Roger Conant. (Ardis Essay Ser.: No. 7). 82p. 1981. text ed. 10.00. Ardis Pubs.

Political Power & Personal Freedom: Critical Studies in Democracy, Communism & Civil Rights. Sidney Hook. 1962. pap. 1.50 o.s.i. (ISBN 0-02-073540-5, Collier). Macmillan.

Political Power & the Urban Crisis. 3rd ed. Alan Shank. 570p. 1976. pap. text ed. 11.95 (ISBN 0-205-05491-9, 765491X). Allyn.

Political Power in Birmingham, 1871-1921. Carl V. Harris. LC 77-1110. (Twentieth Century America Ser.). (Illus.). 1977. 16.50x (ISBN 0-87049-211-X). U of Tenn Pr.

Political Power in Ecuador. Osvaldo Hurtado. Tr. by Nick D. Mills, Jr. LC 79-56822. (Illus.). 328p. 1980. 25.00x (ISBN 0-8263-0533-4). U of NM Pr.

Political Power in the Soviet Union: A Study of Decision-Making in Stalingrad. Philip D. Stewart. LC 68-17706. 1968. pap. 5.50 (ISBN 0-672-60764-6). Bobbs.

Political Power in the Soviet Union: A Study of Decision-Making in Stalingrad. Philip D. Stewart. LC 68-17706. 1968. 24.50x (ISBN 0-672-51163-0). Irvington.

Political Principles of Mencius. Cho-Min Wei. (Studies in Chinese Government & Law). 99p. 1977. Repr. of 1916 ed. 11.50 (ISBN 0-89093-063-5). U Pubns Amer.

Political Process & Foreign Policy: The Making of the Japanese Peace Settlement. Bernard C. Cohen. LC 80-19832. x, 293p. 1980. Repr. of 1957 ed. lib. bdg. 37.50x (ISBN 0-313-22715-2, COPF). Greenwood.

Political Process in Modern Organization. Rolf E. Rogers. LC 79-171712. (Illus.). 158p. 1971. 6.50 o.p. (ISBN 0-682-47350-2, University). Exposition.

Political Radicalism in Late Imperial Vienna: Origins of the Christian Social Movement, 1848-1897. John W. Boyer. LC 80-17302. (Illus.). 1981. lib. bdg. price not set (ISBN 0-226-06957-5). U of Chicago Pr.

Political Reconstruction of China. Eu-Yang Kwang. (Studies in Chinese Government & Law). 190p. 1977. Repr. of 1922 ed. 18.50 (ISBN 0-89093-058-9). U Pubns Amer.

Political Reform in California: Evaluation & Perspective. Ed. by Phil Mullins et al. LC 77-26850. (Research Report 78-3). 1978. pap. 6.50x (ISBN 0-87772-252-8). Inst Gov Stud Berk.

Political Representation in England & the Origins of the American Republic. J. R. Pole. 1971. pap. 5.95x (ISBN 0-520-01903-2, CAMPUS50). U of Cal Pr.

Political Repression in Modern America. Robert J. Goldstein. (Orig.). 1978. pap. 6.95 o.p. (ISBN 0-8467-0511-7, Pub. by Two Continents). Hippocrene Bks.

Political Research: A Methodological Sampler. Betty Zisk. 352p. 1981. pap. text ed. 8.95 (ISBN 0-669-02338-8). Heath.

Political Research Methods: Foundations & Techniques. Barbara L. Smith et al. (Illus.). 352p. 1976. text ed. 16.95 (ISBN 0-395-20363-5). HM.

Political Risks in International Business: Investment Behavior of Multinationals. Lars H. Thunell. LC 77-2940. (Special Studies). 1977. text ed. 16.95 o.p. (ISBN 0-275-24500-4). Praeger.

Political Role of Minorities in the Middle East. Ed. by R. D. McLaurin. LC 79-20588. (Praeger Special Studies). 328p. 1979. 27.95 (ISBN 0-03-052596-9). Praeger.

Political Role of Mongol Buddhism. Larry W. Moses. (Indiana University Uralic & Altaic Ser.: Vol. 133). x, 299p. 1977. 14.95 (ISBN 0-933070-01-2). Ind U Res Inst.

Political Role of the General Assembly. Henry F. Haviland. LC 78-2808. (Carnegie Endowment for International Peace, United Nation Studies: No. 7). 1978. Repr. of 1951 ed. lib. bdg. 17.75x (ISBN 0-313-20334-2, HAPG). Greenwood.

Political Roles & Military Rulers. Amos Perlmutter. 314p. 1980. 24.00x (ISBN 0-7146-3122-1, F Cass Co). Biblio Dist.

Political Science. rev. ed. Gertrude A. Jacobsen & Miriam H. Lipman. (Orig.). 1965. pap. 3.50 o.p. (ISBN 0-06-460022-X, 22, COS). Har-Row.

Political Science. 2nd ed. Gertrude A. Jacobsen & Miriam H. Lipman. (Illus.). 1979. pap. 3.95 (ISBN 0-06-460178-1, CO 178, COS). Har-Row.

Political Science. Jack Rudman. (Undergraduate Program Field Test Ser.: UPFT-20). (Cloth bdg. avail. on request). pap. 9.95 (ISBN 0-8373-6020-X). Natl Learning.

Political Science: A Bibliographical Guide to the Literature, 2nd Supplement. Robert B. Harmon. LC 65-13557. 1972. 20.50 (ISBN 0-8108-0479-4). Scarecrow.

Political Science: A Bibliographical Guide to the Literature, 3rd Supplement. Robert B. Harmon. LC 65-13557. 1974. 15.00 (ISBN 0-8108-0675-4). Scarecrow.

Political Science: An Introduction. Robert L. Cord et al. 688p. 1974. Repr. text ed. 17.95 (ISBN 0-13-687889-X); study guide & access wkbk. 4.95 (ISBN 0-13-687913-6). P-H.

Political Science: An Introduction. Oscar Ibele. LC 72-103933. 546p. 1971. text ed. 20.50 scp o.p. (ISBN 0-685-03947-1, HarpC); inst. manual free o.p. (ISBN 0-06-363175-X). Har-Row.

Political Science & School Politics: The Princes & Pundits. Ed. by Samuel K. Gove & Frederick M. Wirt. (Policy Studies Organization Bk). 1976. 16.95 (ISBN 0-669-00739-0). Lexington Bks.

Political Science Bibliographies, Vol. 1. Robert B. Harmon. LC 72-8849. 1973. 10.00 (ISBN 0-8108-0558-8). Scarecrow.

Political Science Bibliographies, Vol. 2. Robert B. Harmon. LC 72-8849. 1976. 11.00 (ISBN 0-8108-0903-6). Scarecrow.

Political Science Laboratory. Oliver E. Benson. LC 69-10596. 1969. 11.95 o.p. (ISBN 0-675-09593-X). Merrill.

Political Socialization. Kenneth P. Langton. (Studies in Behavioral Political Science Ser). 1969. pap. 5.95x (ISBN 0-19-500945-2). Oxford U Pr.

Political Socialization in Eastern Europe: A Comparative Framework. Ed. by Ivan Volgyes. LC 72-83575. (Special Studies). 202p. 1975. text ed. 24.95 (ISBN 0-275-09550-9). Praeger.

Political Socialization in India. Sachida N. Mishra. (Illus.). 156p. 1980. pap. text ed. 8.75x (ISBN 0-391-02207-5). Humanities.

Political Socialization in the New Nations of Africa. Penelope Roach. LC 66-24873. (Orig.). pap. text ed. 3.50x (ISBN 0-8077-2042-9). Tchrs Coll.

Political Socialization of Black Americans: A Critical Evaluation of Research on Efficacy & Trust. Paul R. Abramson. LC 76-25343. (Illus.). 1977. 16.95 (ISBN 0-02-900170-6). Free Pr.

Political Society: A Macrosociology of Politics. Edward W. Lehman. LC 77-23887. 1977. 17.50x (ISBN 0-231-04003-2). Columbia U Pr.

Political South in the Twentieth Century. Monroe L. Billington. LC 73-1312. 1975. pap. text ed. 8.95x o.p. (ISBN 0-684-13986-3, ScribT). Scribner.

Political Spectrum: Opposing Viewpoints. David L. Bender. (Opposing Viewpoints Ser.). (gr. 12). 1981. lib. bdg. 8.95 (ISBN 0-89908-325-0); pap. text ed. 3.95 (ISBN 0-89908-300-5). Greenhaven.

Political Strategies for Industrial Order: State, Market, & Industry in France. John Zysman. 1977. 20.00x (ISBN 0-520-02889-9). U of Cal Pr.

Political Structure. 2nd ed. Grace Jones. LC 76-7409. (Aspects of Modern Sociology). (Illus.). 1977. pap. text ed. 7.50x (ISBN 0-582-48193-7). Longman.

Political Structure of the Chinese Community in Cambodia. W. E. Willmott. (Monographs on Social Anthropology Ser: No. 42). (Illus.). 1970. text ed. 18.75x (ISBN 0-391-00114-0, Athlone Pr). Humanities.

Political Studies from Spatial Perspectives: Anglo-American Essays on Political Geography. Alan D. Burnett & Peter J. Taylor. 1981. price not set (ISBN 0-471-27909-9, Pub. by Wiley-Interscience); pap. price not set (ISBN 0-471-27910-2). Wiley.

Political Succession in the U.S.S.R. Myron Rush. LC 65-14778. xv, 223p. 1965. 17.50x (ISBN 0-231-02825-3); pap. 5.00x (ISBN 0-231-08585-0). Columbia U Pr.

Political System of Brazil. Ronald M. Schneider. LC 75-154860. 431p. 1973. 22.50x (ISBN 0-231-03506-3); pap. text ed. 10.00x (ISBN 0-231-08324-6). Columbia U Pr.

Political Systems of Highland Burma: A Study of Kachin Social Structure. E. R. Leach. (Monographs on Social Anthropology Ser: No. 44). 1977. text ed. 15.00x (ISBN 0-391-00147-7, Athlone Pr); pap. text ed. 13.00x (ISBN 0-391-00975-3). Humanities.

Political Systems of the United States. John D. Lees. (Orig.). 1975. pap. 9.95 (ISBN 0-571-04878-1, Pub. by Faber & Faber). Merrimack Bk Serv.
Political Terrorism. Paul Wilkinson. LC 74-18470. 1976. pap. text ed. 12.95 (ISBN 0-470-98957-2). Halsted Pr.
Political Terrorism & Business: The Threat & the Response. Ed. by Yonah Alexander & Robert A. Kilmarx. LC 79-16374. 360p. 1979. 26.95 (ISBN 0-03-046686-5). Praeger.
Political Testament of Cardinal Richelieu: The Significant Chapters & Supporting Selections. Tr. by Henry B. Hill. (Illus.). 1961. 15.00x (ISBN 0-299-02420-2); pap. 5.95 (ISBN 0-299-02424-5). U of Wis Pr.
Political Theology. Dorothee Soelle. Tr. by John Shelley from Ger. LC 73-88349. 128p. 1974. pap. 3.50 (ISBN 0-8006-1065-2, 1-0165). Fortress.
Political Theory As Public Confession. Peter D. Bathory. 307p. 1981. 24.95 (ISBN 0-87855-405-X); text ed. 24.95 (ISBN 0-686-68058-8). Transaction Bks.
Political Theory of John Dewey. A. H. Somjee. LC 67-19028. 1968. text ed. 14.65x (ISBN 0-8077-2191-3). Tchrs Coll.
Political Theory of Montesquieu. Ed. by M. Richter. LC 76-4753. 400p. 1977. 29.95 (ISBN 0-521-21156-5); pap. 9.95x (ISBN 0-521-29061-9). Cambridge U Pr.
Political Thinking of Indonesian Chinese: Nineteen Hundred to Nineteen Seventy-Seven. Leo Suryadinata. 270p. 1980. 18.00 (ISBN 0-8214-0548-9); pap. 11.00 (ISBN 0-8214-0549-7). Swallow.
Political Thought in England, Eighteen Forty-Eight to Nineteen Fourteen. 2nd ed. Ernest Barker. LC 80-19766. (Home University Library of Modern Knowledge: 104). 256p. 1980. Repr. of 1928 ed. lib. bdg. 22.50x (ISBN 0-313-22216-9, BAPL). Greenwood.
Political Thought in England: The Utilitarians, from Bentham to J. S. Mill. William L. Davidson. LC 79-1624. 1981. Repr. of 1916 ed. 21.50 (ISBN 0-88355-929-3). Hyperion Conn.
Political Thought in England: Tyndale to Hooker. Christopher Morris. LC 79-1638. 1981. Repr. of 1953 ed. 19.50 (ISBN 0-88355-941-2). Hyperion Conn.
Political Thought of Abraham Lincoln. Richard N. Current. LC 67-30069. 1967. pap. 6.95 (ISBN 0-672-60068-4, AHS46). Bobbs.
Political Thought of American Statesmen: Selected Writings & Speeches. Ed. by Morton J. Frisch & Richard G. Stevens. LC 72-89723. 350p. 1973. 11.00 o.p. (ISBN 0-87581-141-8); pap. text ed. 10.95 (ISBN 0-87581-142-6). Peacock Pubs.
Political Thought of Benjamin Franklin. Ed. by Ralph Ketcham. LC 65-22344. 1965. pap. 8.95 (ISBN 0-672-60100-1, AHS64). Bobbs.
Political Thought of John Locke. John Dunn. 1969. 34.95 (ISBN 0-521-07408-8). Cambridge U Pr.
Political Thought of Pierre D'Ailly. Francis Oakley. (Yale Historical Pubs. Miscellany Ser.: No. 81). 1964. 42.50x (ISBN 0-685-69849-1). Elliots Bks.
Political Thought of Pierre-Joseph Proudhon. Alan Ritter. LC 80-19558. (Illus.). xii, 222p. 1980. Repr. of 1969 ed. lib. bdg. 23.50x (ISBN 0-313-22719-5, RIPT). Greenwood.
Political Thought of Plato & Aristotle. Ernest Barker. 11.50 (ISBN 0-8446-1594-3). Peter Smith.
Political Thought of William of Ockham. A. S. McGrade. LC 73-86044. (Studies in Medieval Life & Thought). 264p. 1974. 35.50 (ISBN 0-521-20284-1). Cambridge U Pr.
Political Thought Since World War 2. W. J. Stankiewicz. LC 64-13234. 1964. text ed. 11.50 o.s.i. (ISBN 0-02-930630-2). Free Pr.
Political Transformation of Spain After Franco. John F. Coverdale. LC 78-19777. (Praeger Special Studies). 1979. 22.95 (ISBN 0-03-044326-1). Praeger.
Political Transformation of the Brazilian Catholic Church. T. C. Bruneau. LC 73-79318. (Perspectives on Development Ser.: No. 2). 302p. 1974. 41.50 (ISBN 0-521-20256-6); pap. 11.50x (ISBN 0-521-09848-3). Cambridge U Pr.
Political Trials. Ed. by Theodore L. Becker. LC 78-126303. 1971. 9.50 (ISBN 0-672-60744-1). Bobbs.
Political Unconscious: Narrative As a Socially Symbolic Act. Fredric Jameson. 320p. 1981. 19.50 (ISBN 0-8014-1233-1). Cornell U Pr.
Political Values & the Educated Class in Africa. Ali A. Mazrui. 1978. 24.00x (ISBN 0-520-03292-6). U of Cal Pr.
Political Women in Japan: The Search for a Place in Political Life. Susan J. Pharr. 275p. 1981. 17.50x (ISBN 0-520-04071-6). U of Cal Pr.
Political Works of James Harrington. Ed. by J. G. Pocock. LC 75-41712. (Studies in the History and Theory of Politics: No. 27). 1977. 72.50 (ISBN 0-521-21161-1). Cambridge U Pr.
Political Writings. Ogyu Sorai. Ed. by J. R. McEwan. 1962. 29.95 (ISBN 0-521-05627-6). Cambridge U Pr.
Political Writings of James Harrington: Representative Selections. James Harrington. Ed. by Charles Blitzer. LC 80-21163. (Library of Liberal Arts: No. 38). xlii, 165p. 1980. Repr. of 1955 ed. lib. bdg. 22.50x (ISBN 0-313-22670-9, HAWR). Greenwood.
Political Writings of John Adams: Representative Selections. Ed. by George A. Peek. LC 54-4998. 1954. 24.50x (ISBN 0-672-50965-2). Irvington.
Political Writings of John Dickinson, 1764-1774. John Dickinson. Ed. by P. L. Ford. LC 70-119061. (Era of the American Revolution Ser). 1970. Repr. of 1895 ed. lib. bdg. 35.00 (ISBN 0-306-71950-9). Da Capo.
Politically Mad. Lou Silverstone & Jack Rickard. (Mad Ser.). (Illus.). 1976. pap. 1.75 (ISBN 0-446-94601-X). Warner Bks.
Politically Speaking: Cross-Cultural Studies of Rhetoric. Ed. by Robert Paine. LC 80-25411. 256p. 1981. text ed. 17.50x (ISBN 0-89727-017-7). Inst Study Human.
Politician Primeval: From the Amoeba to the White House. Edgar Berman. LC 73-22527. 256p. 1974. 6.95 o.s.i. (ISBN 0-02-510060-2). Macmillan.
Politicians, Planters, & Plain Folk: Courthouse & Statehouse in the Upper South, 1850-1860. Ralph A. Wooster. LC 75-32339. 204p. 1975. 12.50x (ISBN 0-87049-166-0). U of Tenn Pr.
Politicians, Socialism & Historians. A. J. Taylor. LC 80-6217. 252p. 1981. 15.95 (ISBN 0-8128-2796-1). Stein & Day.
Politicized Economy. Michael H. Best & William E. Connolly. 1976. pap. text ed. 5.95x (ISBN 0-669-97162-6). Heath.
Politicizing the Poor: The Legacy of the War on Poverty in a Mexican American Community. Biliana C. Ambrecht. LC 74-31501. 1976. 29.95 (ISBN 0-275-05900-6). Praeger.
Politics. Aristotle. Tr. by Ernest Barker. (YA) (gr. 9 up). 1946. pap. 6.95x (ISBN 0-19-500306-3). Oxford U Pr.
Politics: A Case for Christian Action. Robert D. Linder & Richard V. Pierard. LC 73-77850. 160p. 1973. pap. 1.95 o.p. (ISBN 0-87784-356-2). Inter-Varsity.
Politics: A Study of Control Behavior. Neil A. McDonald. 1965. 16.50 (ISBN 0-8135-0488-0). Rutgers U Pr.
Politics & Administration in Brazil. Ed. by Jean-Claude Garcia-Zamor. LC 78-58823. 1978. pap. text ed. 17.50 (ISBN 0-8191-0544-9). U Pr of Amer.
Politics & Anti-Politics of the Young. Michael Brown. Ed. by Fred Krinsky & Joseph Boskin. LC 71-75965. (Insight Ser: Studies in Contemporary Issues). (Orig.). 1969. pap. text ed. 3.95x (ISBN 0-02-473640-6, 47364). Macmillan.
Politics & Constitution in the History of the United States, 3 vols. W. W. Crosskey & William Jeffrey, Jr. 2040p. 1981. lib. bdg. 100.00x (ISBN 0-226-12134-8). U of Chicago Pr.
Politics & Economic Policy in the UK Since 1964: The Jekyll & Hyde Years. Michael Stewart. 1978. pap. 12.00 (ISBN 0-08-022469-5). Pergamon.
Politics & Economics of Public Policy: An Introductory Analysis with Cases. Grover Starling. 1979. 18.50x (ISBN 0-256-02067-1). Dorsey.
Politics & Economics of Public Spending. Charles. L Schultze. 1969. pap. 4.95 (ISBN 0-8157-7751-5). Brookings.
Politics & Economics of the Transition Period. Nikolai I. Bukharin. Ed. by Kenneth J. Tarbuck. Tr. by Oliver Field from Russian. 1979. 30.00 (ISBN 0-7100-0114-2). Routledge & Kegan.
Politics & Education in Puerto Rico: A Documentary Survey of the Language Issue. Erwin H. Epstein. LC 73-15379. 1970. 9.50 o.p. (ISBN 0-8108-0309-7). Scarecrow.
Politics & Exegesis: Origen & the Two Swords. Gerard E. Caspary. 1979. 24.50x (ISBN 0-520-03445-7). U of Cal Pr.
Politics & Force Levels: The Strategic Missile Program of the Kennedy Administration. Desmond J. Ball. 400p. 1981. 27.50x (ISBN 0-520-03698-0). U of Cal Pr.
Politics & Government: How People Decide Their Fate. 2nd ed. Karl W. Deutsch. 650p. 1974. text ed. 17.95 o.p. (ISBN 0-395-17840-1); instructor's manual .90 o.p. (ISBN 0-395-17866-5, 3-13707). HM.
Politics & Government: How People Decide Their Fate. 3rd ed. Karl W. Deutsch. LC 79-90262. (Illus.). 1980. text ed. 18.95 (ISBN 0-395-28486-4); instrs'. manual 0.90 (ISBN 0-395-28487-2). HM.
Politics & Government in Japan. 2nd ed. Theodore McNelly. LC 74-186377. (Contemporary Government Ser.). (Illus.). 256p. (Orig.). 1972. pap. text ed. 9.50 (ISBN 0-395-12649-5, 3-37419). HM.
Politics & Government in Turkey. C. H. Dodd. LC 78-85453. 1969. 20.00x (ISBN 0-520-01430-8). U of Cal Pr.
Politics & History: Selected Essays. Raymond Aron. Ed. by Miriam B. Conant. LC 78-54122. 1978. 19.95 (ISBN 0-02-901000-4). Free Pr.
Politics & Ideology in the Age of the Civil War. Eric Foner. 256p. 1981. pap. 5.95 (ISBN 0-19-502926-7, GB 646, GB). Oxford U Pr.
Politics & International Relations in the Middle East: An Annotated Bibliography. Clement M. Henry. 114p. (Orig.). 1980. pap. 4.00 (ISBN 0-932098-18-5). Ctr for NE & North Aafrican Stud.
Politics & International Relations in the Middle East: An Annotated Bibliography. Clement M. Henry. 114p. (Orig.). 1980. pap. text ed. 8.00 (ISBN 0-932098-18-5). Ctr for NE & North African Stud.
Politics & Language: Spanish & English in the United States. Ed. by D. J. Bruckner. (Orig.). 1980. pap. 4.00x (ISBN 0-686-28732-0). U Chi Ctr Policy.
Politics & Leadership in Municipal Government. S. N. Mishra. 1979. text ed. 9.00x (ISBN 0-391-01845-0). Humanities.
Politics & Liturgy. Ed. by Herman Schmidt & David Power. LC 73-17912. (Concilium Ser.: Religion in the Seventies: Vol. 92). 1974. pap. 4.95 (ISBN 0-8164-2576-0). Crossroad NY.
Politics & Parties Between Elections. National Journal. Ed. by Nelson W. Polsby. (National Journal Reprints Ser). 1977. pap. text ed. 2.35 o.p. (ISBN 0-685-59296-0). Natl Journal.
Politics & Personality Seventeen Sixty-Eighteen Twenty-Seven. Ed. by Michael J. Barnes. LC 68-97214. (Selections from History Today Ser.: No. 6). (Illus.). 1967. 5.00 (ISBN 0-05-001533-8); pap. 3.95 (ISBN 0-685-09195-3). Dufour.
Politics & Planners: Economic Development Policy in Central America. Gary W. Wynia. 296p. 1972. 21.50x (ISBN 0-299-06210-4). U of Wis Pr.
Politics & Planning. B. Dimitriou. 1977. text ed. 12.50 o.p. (ISBN 0-08-016867-1). Pergamon.
Politics & Policy Implementation in the Third World. Ed. by Merilee S. Grindle. LC 79-3213. 1980. 20.00x (ISBN 0-691-07617-0); pap. 7.95 (ISBN 0-691-02195-3). Princeton U Pr.
Politics & Policy in Australia. Geoffrey Hawker et al. 1979. pap. 14.50 (ISBN 0-7022-1307-1). U of Queensland Pr.
Politics & Policy: The Eisenhower, Kennedy, & Johnson Years. James L. Sundquist. LC 68-31837. 1968. 16.95 (ISBN 0-8157-8222-5); pap. 6.95 (ISBN 0-8157-8221-7). Brookings.
Politics & Political Systems. J. W. Ellsworth & A. A. Stahnke. 1976. text ed. 14.95x (ISBN 0-07-019250-2, C); instructor's manual 3.95 (ISBN 0-07-019251-0). McGraw.
Politics & Power I. Mike Prior et al. Ed. by David Purdy et al. 240p. (Orig.). 1980. pap. 12.50 (ISBN 0-7100-0593-8). Routledge & Kegan.
Politics & Power in American Government: An Introductory Text with Readings. Sam C Sarkesian & Krish Nanda. LC 75-1244. (Illus.). 555p. 1976. pap. text ed. 11.50x (ISBN 0-88284-026-6). Alfred Pub.
Politics & Power: Problems in Labour Politics. Ed. by Diana Adlam et al. (Politics & Power Ser.). 220p. (Orig.). 1981. pap. price not set (ISBN 0-7100-0716-7). Routledge & Kegan.
Politics & Programs of Family Policy: United States & European Perspectives. Ed. by Joan Aldous et al. LC 80-50270. 224p. (Orig.). 1980. pap. text ed. 8.95 (ISBN 0-268-01539-2). U of Notre Dame Pr.
Politics & Public Libraries in England & Wales, 1850 - 1970. J. E. Pemberton. 1977. 13.25x (ISBN 0-85365-109-4, Pub. by Lib Assn England). Oryx Pr.
Politics & Public Policy in Kenya & Tanzania. Joel D. Barkan & John J. Okumu. LC 78-19470. (Praeger Special Studies). 1979. 27.95 (ISBN 0-03-023206-6); pap. 10.95 student edition (ISBN 0-03-052336-2). Praeger.
Politics & Social Conflict in South India: The Non-Brahman Movement & Tamil Separatism, 1916-1929. Eugene F. Irschick. (Center for South & Southeast Asia Studies, UC Berkeley). (Illus.). 1969. 21.50x (ISBN 0-520-00596-1). U of Cal Pr.
Politics & Social Equality: A Comparative Analysis. Robert W. Jackman. LC 74-24725. (Comparative Studies in Behavioral Science Ser). 256p. 1975. 23.95 (ISBN 0-471-43128-1, Pub. by Wiley-Interscience). Wiley.
Politics & Social Forces in Chilean Development. James Petras. 1969. 19.50x (ISBN 0-520-01463-4). U of Cal Pr.
Politics and Social Structure. Talcott Parsons. LC 75-88631. 1969. 15.50 o.s.i. (ISBN 0-02-923960-5). Free Pr.
Politics & Society in America 1607-1877. Donald C. Swift. 1976. pap. text ed. 2.95x o.p. (ISBN 0-88273-240-4). Forum Pr MO.
Politics & Society in Contemporary France, 1789-1971: A Documentary History. Eric Cahm. 716p. 1972. 42.50x (ISBN 0-8448-0248-4). Crane-Russak Co.
Politics & Society in Rural India: A Case Study of Darauli Gram Panchayat, Siwan District, Bihar. S. N. Mishra. 184p. 1980. text ed. 11.25x (ISBN 0-391-02123-0). Humanities.
Politics & Society in the U.S.S.R. 2nd ed. David Lane. LC 78-53993. 1978. uSA 25.00x (ISBN 0-8147-4988-7); pap. 13.00x usa (ISBN 0-8147-4989-5). NYU Pr.
Politics & the Biblical Drama. Richard Mouw. 1976. pap. 2.95 o.p. (ISBN 0-8028-1657-6). Eerdmans.
Politics & the Constitution in the History of the United States: Vol. III, The Political Background of the Federal Convention. William W. Crosskey & William Jeffrey, Jr. LC 53-7433. 1981. lib. bdg. 27.00x (ISBN 0-226-12138-0). U of Chicago Pr.
Politics & the Expanding Physician Supply. Michael L. Millman. LC 78-73591. (Conservation of Human Resources: No. 11). (Illus.). 176p. 1980. text ed. 22.50 (ISBN 0-916672-84-0). Allanheld.
Politics & the International System. 2nd ed. Ed. by Robert L. Pfaltzgraff. LC 70-161414. 612p. 1972. pap. text ed. 7.50 o.p. (ISBN 0-397-47218-8). Lippincott.
Politics & the Nation, Fourteen Fifty-Sixteen Sixty: Obedience, Resistance & Public Order. D. M. Loades. Ed. by Y. R. Elton. (Fontana Library of English History). 484p. 1974. text ed. 22.25 (ISBN 0-901759-34-1). Humanities.
Politics & the Nation 1450-1660: Obedience, Resistance & Public Order. D. M. Loades. 1974. pap. 4.95 o.p. (ISBN 0-531-06053-5, Fontana Pap). Watts.
Politics & the Power Structure: A Rural Community in the Dominican Republic. Malcolm T. Walker. LC 72-89624. 1972. text ed. 11.50x (ISBN 0-8077-2302-9). Tchrs Coll.
Politics & the Professors: The Great Society in Perspective. Henry J. Aaron. LC 77-91809. (Studies in Social Economics). 1978. 11.95 (ISBN 0-8157-0026-1); pap. 4.95 (ISBN 0-8157-0025-3). Brookings.
Politics & the Social Sciences. Ed. by Seymour M. Lipset. LC 70-75604. 1969. 17.95 (ISBN 0-19-500628-3). Oxford U Pr.
Politics & the Warren Court. Alexander M. Bickel. LC 73-398. (American Constitutional & Legal History Ser.). 314p. 1973. Repr. of 1955 ed. lib. bdg. 27.50 (ISBN 0-306-70573-7). Da Capo.
Politics & Urban Policies. Brett Hawkins. LC 77-151612. (Policy Analysis Ser). 1971. 7.95 (ISBN 0-672-51474-5); pap. 4.95 (ISBN 0-672-61060-4). Bobbs.
Politics & Voters. 5th ed. Hugh A. Bone & Austin Ranney. Ed. by Eric M. Munson. (Harris Ser.). 144p. 1981. pap. text ed. 6.95 (ISBN 0-07-006492-X, C). McGraw.
Politics As Communications. Robert G. Meadow. LC 79-25176. (Communication & Information Sciences Ser.). 1980. text ed. 24.95 (ISBN 0-89391-031-7). Ablex Pub.
Politics, Bureaucracy, & Rural Development in Senegal. Edward J. Schumacher. 1975. 29.50x (ISBN 0-520-02087-1). U of Cal Pr.
Politics, Cultures & Communications: European Vs. American Approaches to Communications Policy Making. Roland Homet. LC 79-53594. (Praeger Special Studies Ser.). 1979. 19.95 (ISBN 0-03-049786-8). Praeger.
Politics, Economics & Society in Argentina in the Revolutionary Period. T. Halperin-Donghi. LC 74-79133. (Latin American Studies: No. 18). 552p. 1975. 63.95 (ISBN 0-521-20493-3). Cambridge U Pr.
Politics, Economics, & the Public Welfare. A. Dobelstein. 1980. 15.95 (ISBN 0-13-683979-7). P-H.
Politics for Human Beings. 2nd ed. Ralph P. Hummel & Robert Isaak. (Illus.). 1980. pap. text ed. 10.95 (ISBN 0-87872-229-7). Duxbury Pr.
Politics, Geography & Behavior. Ed. by Richard Muir & Ronan Paddison. (Illus.). 196p. 1980. lib. bdg. cancelled (ISBN 0-86531-058-0). Westview.
Politics, Ideology & the State: Papers from the Communist University of London. Ed. by Sally Hibbin. 1978. pap. text ed. 6.50x (ISBN 0-85315-462-7). Humanities.
Politics in Africa. Dennis Austin. LC 77-95397. 212p. 1978. text ed. 12.50x (ISBN 0-87451-150-X); pap. text ed. 7.50x (ISBN 0-87451-152-6). U Pr of New Eng.

Politics in Africa: The Former British Territories. J. F. Maitland-Jones. (Comparative Modern Government Ser.). (Illus.). 236p. 1974. pap. 4.95x (ISBN 0-393-09305-0). Norton.

Politics in America. Joseph Alvarez. Ed. by Gene Liberty. LC 76-128850. (Understanding Bks.). (Illus.). (gr. 4-9). 1971. PLB 7.95 (ISBN 0-87191-068-3). Creative Ed.

Politics in America. Ed. by Congressional Quarterly. 1979. pap. text ed. 7.25 (ISBN 0-87187-148-3). Congr Quarterly.

Politics in Brazil, Nineteen Thirty - Nineteen Sixty-Four: An Experiment in Democracy. Thomas E. Skidmore. LC 67-20406. (YA) (gr. 9 up). 1969. pap. 6.95 (ISBN 0-19-500784-0, GB). Oxford U Pr.

Politics in Camera: Film & Television for the Political Scientist & Historian. M. J. Clark. (Audio-Visual Media Education & Research: Vol. 1). 1979. 28.00 (ISBN 0-08-022483-0); pap. 14.00 (ISBN 0-08-022484-9). Pergamon.

Politics in China. 2nd ed. (Comparative Politics Ser.). 1980. pap. text ed. 7.95 (ISBN 0-316-85131-0). Little.

Politics in Czechoslovakia. Otto Ulc. LC 74-11106. (Illus.). 1974. text ed. 17.95x (ISBN 0-7167-0779-9). W H Freeman.

Politics in England. Richard Rose. 1974. 17.00 (ISBN 0-571-10297-2, Pub. by Faber & Faber); pap. 10.95 (ISBN 0-571-10534-3). Merrimack Bk Serv.

Politics in Hungary. Peter A. Toma & Ivan Volgyes. LC 76-29613. (Illus.). 1977. text ed. 17.95x (ISBN 0-7167-0557-5). W H Freeman.

Politics in Industrial Societies: A Comparative Perspection. Lawrence C. Mayer & John H. Burnett. LC 76-54694. 1977. text ed. 19.95x (ISBN 0-471-57986-6). Wiley.

Politics in Industrial Society: The Experience of the British System Since 1911. Keith Middlemas. 512p. 1979. 37.50x (ISBN 0-8476-6872-X). Rowman.

Politics in Leadership: A Comparative Perspective. Ed. by William A. Shack & Percy S. Cohen. (Illus.). 310p. 1979. text ed. 29.95x (ISBN 0-19-823193-8). Oxford U Pr.

Politics in New Brunswick. 1961 ed. Hugh G. Thorburn. LC 63-25108. 17.50x o.p. (ISBN 0-8020-7057-4). U of Toronto Pr.

Politics in Newfoundland. S. J. Noel. LC 73-151382. 1971. pap. 5.50 (ISBN 0-8020-6187-7). U of Toronto Pr.

Politics in Public Service Advertising on Television. David L. Paletz et al. LC 76-24363. (Special Studies). 1977. text ed. 23.95 (ISBN 0-275-23880-6). Praeger.

Politics in Rural America: People, Parties, & Policy. Frank M. Bryan. (Special Study Ser.). 320p. (Orig.). lib. bdg. 26.50x (ISBN 0-89158-561-3); pap. text ed. 10.00x (ISBN 0-89158-984-8). Westview.

Politics in Sierra Leone, Nineteen Forty-Seven to Nineteen Sixty-Seven. John R. Cartwright. (Scholarly Reprint Ser.). 35.00x (ISBN 0-8020-7103-1). U of Toronto Pr.

Politics in States & Communities. 4th ed. Thomas R. Dye. (Illus.). 512p. 1981. text ed. 16.95 (ISBN 0-13-685131-2). P-H.

Politics in the Age of Peel: A Study in the Technique of Parliamentary Representation, 1830-1850. 2nd ed. Norman Gash. 518p. 1977. text ed. 23.50x (ISBN 0-391-00676-2). Humanities.

Politics in the Congo: Decolonization & Independence. Crawford Young. 1965. 25.00x (ISBN 0-691-03050-2); pap. 6.50 o.p. (ISBN 0-691-00005-0, 73). Princeton U Pr.

Politics in the Poetry of Coleridge. Carl R. Woodring. 1961. 25.00 (ISBN 0-299-02440-7). U of Wis Pr.

Politics in the Post Welfare State: Responses to the New Individualism. Ed. by M. Donald Hancock & Gideon Sjoberg. LC 79-165181. 1972. text ed. 22.50x (ISBN 0-231-03127-0). Columbia U Pr.

Politics in the Sudan: Parliamentary & Military Rule in an Emerging African Nation. Peter K. Bechtold. LC 76-6466. (Special Studies). (Illus.). 375p. 1976. text ed. 33.95 (ISBN 0-275-22730-8). Praeger.

Politics in Western Europe. 3rd ed. Gordon Smith. LC 80-81211. 344p. 1980. 24.75 (ISBN 0-8419-0627-0); pap. 9.75 (ISBN 0-8419-0628-9). Holmes & Meier.

Politics, Law & Ritual in Tribal Society. Max Gluckman. 1977. pap. 15.95x (ISBN 0-631-08750-8, Pub. by Basil Blackwell). Biblio Dist.

Politics, Law, & Social Change: Selected Essays. Otto Kircheimer. LC 69-16955. 1969. 22.50x (ISBN 0-231-03191-2). Columbia U Pr.

Politics, Medicine & Social Science. David Mechanic. 306p. 1974. 21.00 (ISBN 0-471-59008-8, Pub. by Wiley-Interscience). Wiley.

Politics, Minerals, & Survival. Ed. by Ralph W. Marsden. LC 74-27310. 1975. 10.00 (ISBN 0-299-06810-2); pap. 5.95 (ISBN 0-299-06814-5). U of Wis Pr.

Politics of a Colonial Career: Jose Baquijano & the Audencia of Lima. Mark A. Burkholder. 198p. 1981. 20.00 (ISBN 0-8263-0545-8). U of NM Pr.

Politics of a Periurban Community in India. A. H. Somjee. 1966. 2.50x o.p. (ISBN 0-210-27091-8). Asia.

Politics of Abolition: Scandanavian Studies in Criminology. Thomas Mathiesen. LC 74-1601. 1974. 18.95x (ISBN 0-470-57627-8). Halsted Pr.

Politics of Accommodation: Pluralism & Democracy in the Netherlands. new ed. Arend Lijphart. 1976. 20.00x (ISBN 0-520-02918-6); pap. 6.95x (ISBN 0-520-02900-3). U of Cal Pr.

Politics of Administration: The Malaysian Experience. Mavis Puthucheary. 1978. 29.00x (ISBN 0-19-580386-8). Oxford U Pr.

Politics of Adoption. Mary K. Benet. LC 76-14287. 1976. 12.95 (ISBN 0-02-902500-1). Free Pr.

Politics of Aid, Trade & Investment. Ed. by S. Raichur & C. T. Liske. LC 75-31886. (Comparative Political Economics & Public Policy Ser.). 218p. 1976. 25.95 (ISBN 0-470-54117-2). Halsted Pr.

Politics of Alternative Technology. David Dickson. LC 75-7919. 224p. 1975. 8.00x o.s.i. (ISBN 0-87663-224-X). Universe.

Politics of American Democracy. 6th ed. Marion D. Irish et al. (Illus.). 1977. text ed. 17.95 (ISBN 0-13-685453-2). P-H.

Politics of American Foreign Policy: The Social Contexts of Decisions. M. Berkowitz et al. (Illus.). 1977. pap. text ed. 10.50 (ISBN 0-13-685073-1). P-H.

Politics of American National Government. 4th ed. David C. Saffell. (Illus.). 560p. 1981. pap. text ed. 12.95 (ISBN 0-87626-641-3). Winthrop.

Politics of Antipolitics: The Military in Latin America. Ed. by Brian Loveman & Thomas M. Davies, Jr. LC 77-25256. 1978. 19.95x (ISBN 0-8032-0954-1); pap. 5.95x (ISBN 0-8032-7900-0, BB 672, Bison). U of Nebr Pr.

Politics of Arms Control: The Role & Effectiveness of the U. S. Arms Control & Disarmament Agency. Duncan L. Clarke. LC 79-1955. 1979. 17.95 (ISBN 0-02-905700-0). Free Pr.

Politics of Assimilation: A Study of the French-Jewish Community at the Time of the Dreyfus Affair. Michael R. Marrus. (Illus.). 1971. text ed. 27.00x (ISBN 0-19-821482-0). Oxford U Pr.

Politics of Attraction: Four Middle Powers & the United States. Annette B. Fox. LC 76-27291. (Institute of War & Peace Studies of Columbia). 1977. 21.00x (ISBN 0-231-04116-0). Columbia U Pr.

Politics of Belief in Nineteenth-Century France. Philip Spencer. LC 77-80592. 284p. 1973. Repr. of 1954 ed. 16.00 (ISBN 0-86527-156-9). Fertig.

Politics of Bilingual Education: A Study of Four Southwest Texas Communities. Robert L. Hardgrave, Jr. & Santiago N. Hinojosa. LC 75-43748. 110p. (Orig.). 1975. pap. text ed. 4.95 (ISBN 0-88408-041-2). Sterling Swift.

Politics of Bureaucracy: A Comparative Perspective. B. Guy Peters. LC 77-24584. (Comparative Studies of Political Life Ser.). (Illus.). 1978. text ed. 15.95x (ISBN 0-582-28001-X); pap. text ed. 9.95x (ISBN 0-582-28000-1). Longman.

Politics of Change in Venezuela, 3 vols. Frank Bonilla & Jose A. Silva-Michelena. Incl. Vol. 1. Strategy for Research on Social Policy. 1967. o.p. (ISBN 0-262-02028-9); Vol. 2. Failure of Elites. 1970. 23.00x (ISBN 0-262-02058-0); Vol. 3. Illusion of Democracy in Dependent Nations. 1971. (ISBN 0-262-19069-9). 23.00x ea. MIT Pr.

Politics of Chile: A Socio-Geographical Assessment. Cesar Caviedes. (Special Studies on Latin America). 1979. lib. bdg. 27.50x (ISBN 0-89158-311-4). Westview.

Politics of Chinese Communism: Kiangi Under Soviet Rule. Ilpyong Kim. 1974. 20.00x (ISBN 0-520-02438-9). U of Cal Pr.

Politics of City-County Merger: The Lexington-Fayette County Experience. W. E. Lyons. LC 77-73706. (Illus.). 192p. 1978. 14.00x (ISBN 0-8131-1363-6). U Pr of Ky.

Politics of City Revenue. Arnold J. Meltsner. LC 70-129610. (Oakland Project). 1971. 18.50x (ISBN 0-520-01812-5); pap. 5.95x (ISBN 0-520-02773-6). U of Cal Pr.

Politics of Communication: A Study in the Political Sociology of Language, Socialization, & Legitimation. Claus Mueller. LC 73-83937. 256p. 1975. pap. 4.95 (ISBN 0-19-501961-X, 443, GB). Oxford U Pr.

Politics of Community Health. Ralph W. Conant. 2.00 (ISBN 0-8183-0193-7). Pub Aff Pr.

Politics of Confrontation. Ed. by Samuel Hendel. LC 75-148865. 1971. pap. text ed. 6.95x (ISBN 0-89197-893-3). Irvington.

Politics of Congress. 3rd ed. Vogler. 364p. 1980. pap. 8.95 (ISBN 0-205-06975-4, 7669755). Allyn.

Politics of Consumer Protection. Mark Nadel. LC 78-170712. (Policy Analysis Ser). 1971. pap. 6.25 (ISBN 0-672-61223-2). Bobbs.

Politics of Cultural Despair: A Study in the Rise of the Germanic Ideology. Fritz R. Stern. (California Library Reprint Ser.). 1974. 21.50x (ISBN 0-520-02643-8); pap. 6.95x (ISBN 0-520-02626-8). U of Cal Pr.

Politics of Cultural Pluralism. Crawford Young. LC 74-27318. 1976. 35.00 (ISBN 0-299-06740-8). U of Wis Pr.

Politics of Cultural Pluralism. Crawford Young. (Illus.). 1979. pap. 7.95 (ISBN 0-299-06744-0). U of Wis Pr.

Politics of Decision-Making: Strategy, Cooperation, & Conflict. Allan W. Lerner. LC 76-22632. (Sage Library of Social Research: Vol. 34). 1976. 18.00x (ISBN 0-8039-0694-3); pap. 8.95x (ISBN 0-8039-0695-1). Sage.

Politics of Decline. Andrew Gamble. (Critical Social Studies). 1980. text ed. write for info. (ISBN 0-391-01179-0); pap. text ed. write for info. (ISBN 0-391-01180-4). Humanities.

Politics of Defeat: America's Decline in the Middle East. Joseph Churba. (Illus.). 1977. text ed. 12.50x (ISBN 0-8290-0391-6). Irvington.

Politics of Development: Sugar Cooperatives in Rural Maharashtra. B. S. Baviskar. (Illus.). 240p. 1981. 18.95 (ISBN 0-19-561206-X). Oxford U Pr.

Politics of Deviance: Stigma Contests & the Uses of Power. Edwin M. Schur. 256p. 1980. text ed. 11.95 (ISBN 0-13-684753-6, Spec); pap. text ed. 5.95 (ISBN 0-13-684746-3). P-H.

Politics of Diversity: Essays in the History of Colonial New York. new ed. Milton M. Klein. LC 74-77647. (National University Publications Ser.). 212p. 1974. 17.50 (ISBN 0-8046-9081-2). Kennikat.

Politics of Division, Partition, & Unification. Ed. by Ray E. Johnston. LC 75-23973. (Special Studies). (Illus.). 1976. text ed. 21.95 (ISBN 0-275-55660-3). Praeger.

Politics of Domesticity: Women, Evangelism, & Temperance in Nineteenth-Century America. Barbara L. Epstein. 224p. 1981. 17.95x (ISBN 0-8195-5050-7). Wesleyan U Pr.

Politics of East Asia: China, Japan, Korea. John E. Endicott & William P. Heaton. LC 77-1346. 1978. lib. bdg. 26.50x (ISBN 0-89158-127-8); pap. text ed. 10.75x (ISBN 0-89158-128-6). Westview.

Politics of Ecology. James Ridgeway. 1971. 6.95 o.p. (ISBN 0-525-18108-3); pap. 2.25 (ISBN 0-525-47304-1). Dutton.

Politics of Economic & Human Resource Development. Randall B. Ripley. LC 79-173977. (Policy Analysis Ser). 1972. 8.95 (ISBN 0-672-51479-6); pap. 4.35 o.p. (ISBN 0-672-61070-1). Bobbs.

Politics of Economic Planning. Alan Budd. LC 78-66341. 1978. 20.95 (ISBN 0-03-046211-8). Praeger.

Politics of Economic Reform in the Soviet Union. Abraham Katz. LC 74-180846. (Special Studies in International Economics & Development). 1972. 38.50x (ISBN 0-275-28260-0); pap. text ed. 18.50x (ISBN 0-89197-894-1). Irvington.

Politics of Education: A Bibliographical Guide. Ed. by G. S. Harman. LC 74-194763. 1974. 32.50x (ISBN 0-8448-0405-3). Crane-Russak Co.

Politics of Education at the Local, State & Federal Levels. Michael W. Kirst. LC 75-100956. 1971. 19.50 (ISBN 0-8211-1009-8); text ed. 17.50x (ISBN 0-685-14294-9). McCutchan.

Politics of Educational Change. Maurice Kogan. LC 78-66344. 1978. 19.95 (ISBN 0-03-046246-0). Praeger.

Politics of Educational Innovation. Ernest R. House. LC 74-12822. 324p. 1974. 17.90x (ISBN 0-8211-0754-2); text ed. 16.20x (ISBN 0-685-57222-6). McCutchan.

Politics of Efficiency: Municipal Administration & Reform in America, 1880-1920. Martin Schiesl. LC 75-17285. 1977. 18.50x (ISBN 0-520-03067-2); pap. 6.95x (ISBN 0-520-04086-4). U of Cal Pr.

Politics of Elite Culture: Explorations in the Dramaturgy of Power in a Modern African Society. Abner Cohen. 200p. 1981. 18.50x (ISBN 0-520-04120-8); pap. 6.95x (ISBN 0-520-04275-1, 270). U of Cal Pr.

Politics of Environmental Concern. 2nd ed. Walter A. Rosenbaum. LC 76-41964. 1977. pap. 8.95 (ISBN 0-275-64820-6). Praeger.

Politics of Environmental Policy. Ed. by Lester W. Milbrath & Frederick R. Inscho. LC 75-27013. (Contemporary Social Science Issues Ser.: Vol. 18). 1975. 4.95x (ISBN 0-8039-0567-X). Sage.

Politics of Exclusion. Michael N. Danielson. LC 76-7609. 384p. 1976. 22.50x (ISBN 0-231-03697-3); pap. 9.00x (ISBN 0-231-08342-4). Columbia U Pr.

Politics of Expertise. 2nd ed. Guy Benveniste. 1977. text ed. 14.00x (ISBN 0-87835-067-5); pap. text ed. 7.95x (ISBN 0-87835-060-8). Boyd & Fraser.

Politics of Extinction: The Shocking Story of the World's Endangered Wildlife. Lewis Regenstein. (Illus.). 400p. 1975. 9.95 o.s.i. (ISBN 0-02-601910-8). Macmillan.

Politics of Family Planning Policy: Thailand--A Case of Successful Implementation. Caryl R. Krannich & Ronald L. Krannich. 1980. 12.50. UC Ctr for S&SE Asian.

Politics of Family Planning Policy: Thailand--a Case of Successful Implementation. Ronald L. Krannich & Caryl R. Krannich. (Monograph: No. 19). 115p. 1980. pap. 9.00x (Pub. by Northern Ill Univ Ctr S E Asian Stud); pap. text ed. 9.00. Cellar.

Politics of Fear: Joseph R. McCarthy & the Senate. Robert W. Griffith. 1971. pap. 8.35 (ISBN 0-8104-6100-5). Hayden.

Politics of Federalism: Ontario's Relations with the Federal Government 1867-1942. Christopher Armstrong. (Ontario Historical Studies). 316p. 1981. 20.00 (ISBN 0-8020-3374-1). U of Toronto Pr.

Politics of Financial Control: The Role of the House of Commons. Gordon Reid. (Orig.). 1966. text ed. 5.00x (ISBN 0-09-079260-2, Hutchinson U Lib); pap. text ed. 2.50x (ISBN 0-09-079261-0, Hutchinson U Lib). Humanities.

Politics of Formosan Nationalism. Douglas Mendel. LC 78-94982. (Illus.). 1970. 21.50x (ISBN 0-520-01557-6). U of Cal Pr.

Politics of German Protestantism: The Rise of the Protestant Church Elite in Prussia, 1815-1848. Robert M. Bigler. 1972. 24.50x (ISBN 0-520-01881-8). U of Cal Pr.

Politics of Global Economic Relations. O. Blake & R. Walters. (Illus.). 272p. 1976. pap. 9.95x (ISBN 0-13-684712-9). P-H.

Politics of Grandeur. Phillip G. Cerny. LC 79-50232. 1980. 35.50 (ISBN 0-521-22863-8). Cambridge U Pr.

Politics of Gulliver's Travels. F. P. Lock. 166p. 1980. text ed. 22.00x (ISBN 0-19-812656-5). Oxford U Pr.

Politics of Higher Education in Brazil. Jerry Haar. LC 75-23967. 1977. text ed. 19.95 o.p. (ISBN 0-275-55630-1). Praeger.

Politics of Homosexuality. Toby Marotta. 384p. 1981. 15.00 (ISBN 0-686-69057-5). HM.

Politics of Housing in Older Urban Areas. Ed. by Robert E. Mendelson & Michael A. Quinn. LC 75-23984. (Special Studies). 1976. text ed. 32.50 (ISBN 0-275-56120-8). Praeger.

Politics of Human Rights. Ed. by Paula R. Newberg. LC 79-1998. (UNA-USA Bk.). 1981. 22.50x (ISBN 0-8147-5754-5); pap. 9.00x (ISBN 0-8147-5755-3). NYU Pr.

Politics of Identity. Peter Dupreez. 1980. 25.00 (ISBN 0-312-62697-5). St Martin.

Politics of Industrial Relations. Colin Grouch. (Political Issues of Modern Britain Ser.). 1979. text ed. 5.00x (ISBN 0-391-01163-4). Humanities.

Politics of Information: Problems of Policy of Modern Media. Anthony Smith. (Communication & Culture Ser.). 1978. text ed. 25.00x (ISBN 0-333-23610-6); pap. text ed. 10.50x (ISBN 0-333-23611-4). Humanities.

Politics of Interconnection: A History of Public Television at the National Level. Robert K. Avery & Robert Pepper. 66p. 1979. pap. 3.00 (Pub Telecom). NAEB.

Politics of International Air Transport. Betsy Gidwitz. LC 79-2706. 1980. 23.95 (ISBN 0-669-03234-4). Lexington Bks.

Politics of International Cooperation: A Comparison of U. S. Experience in Space & in Security. Stephen M. Shaffer & Lisa R. Shaffer. (Monograph Series in World Affairs). 73p. Date not set. pap. 4.00 (ISBN 0-87940-063-3). U of Denver Intl.

Politics of International Fisheries Management. Arild Underal. 234p. 1981. pap. 20.00x. Universitet.

Politics of International Monetary Reform: The Exchange Crisis. Michael J. Brenner. LC 75-45458. 128p. 1976. text ed. 16.50 o.p. (ISBN 0-88410-292-0). Ballinger Pub.

Politics of Irish Literature: From Thomas Davis to W. B. Yeats. Malcolm Brown. LC 72-152328. (Washington Paperback Ser.: No. 67). 443p. 1972. 12.00 (ISBN 0-295-95170-2); pap. 3.95 (ISBN 0-295-95280-6). U of Wash Pr.

Politics of Jesus. John H. Yoder. 176p. 1972. pap. 4.95 (ISBN 0-8028-1485-9). Eerdmans.

Politics of John W. Dafoe & The Free Press. Ramsey Cook. 1963. 20.00x o.p. (ISBN 0-8020-5119-7). U of Toronto Pr.

Politics of Justice: A Study in Law, Social Science & Public Policy. William C. Louthan. (National University Pubns. Legal Series). 1979. 12.95 (ISBN 0-8046-9218-1). Kennikat.

Politics of Justice: Lower Federal Judicial Selection & the Second Party System, 1829-1861. Kermit L. Hall. LC 79-9238. 1979. 19.50x (ISBN 0-8032-2302-1). U of Nebr Pr.

Politics of Kinship: A Study in Social Manipulation Among the Lakeside Tonga of Malawi. J. Van Velsen. (Institute for African Studies). (Illus.). 338p. 1964. pap. text ed. 13.75x (ISBN 0-7190-1036-5). Humanities.

Politics of Labor. T. Philips Thompson. LC 75-9924. (Social History of Canada Ser.). 1975. pap. 5.95 (ISBN 0-8020-6270-9). U of Toronto Pr.

Politics of Labor Legislation in Japan: National-International Interaction. Ehud Harari. LC 72-78945. 1973. 20.00x (ISBN 0-520-02264-5). U of Cal Pr.

Politics of Land: The Report on Land Use in California. Robert C. Fellmeth. LC 79-184471. (Ralph Nader Study Group Reports). 1973. pap. 5.95 o.p. (ISBN 0-670-56327-7, N10, Grossman). Penguin.

Politics of Land-Use Reform. Frank Popper. 312p. 1981. 20.00 (ISBN 0-299-08530-9); pap. text ed. 7.50 (ISBN 0-299-08534-1). U of Wis Pr.

Politics of Language: The Dilemma of Bilingual Education for Puerto Ricans. Pastora San Juan Cafferty & Carmen Rivera-Martinez. (Replica Edition Ser.). 200p. 1981. lib. bdg. 20.00x (ISBN 0-86531-170-6). Westview.

Politics of Latin American Development. G. W. Wynia. LC 77-87395. (Illus.). 1978. 32.95 (ISBN 0-521-21922-1); pap. 9.95x (ISBN 0-521-29310-3). Cambridge U Pr.

Politics of Legitimacy: Struggles in a Belfast Community. Frank Burton. (International Library of Sociology). 1978. 21.00 (ISBN 0-7100-8966-X). Routledge & Kegan.

Politics of Literature: Dissenting Essays in the Teaching of English. Ed. by Louis Kampf & Paul Lauter. 1972. 24.50x (ISBN 0-8290-0039-9). Irvington.

Politics of Marriage in Contemporary China. Elisabeth Croll. LC 80-40586. (Contemporary China Institute Publications Ser.). (Illus.). 224p. Date not set. 36.00 (ISBN 0-521-23345-3). Cambridge U Pr.

Politics of Mass Society. William Kornhauser. LC 59-6820. 1959. text ed. 15.95 (ISBN 0-02-917620-4). Free Pr.

Politics of Medicare. Theodore R. Marmor. LC 76-169517. 160p. 1973. 15.95x (ISBN 0-202-24036-3); pap. 5.95 (ISBN 0-202-24037-1). Aldine Pub.

Politics of Mental Health: Organizing Community Mental Health in Metropolitan Areas. Robert H. Connery et al. LC 68-28396. (Illus.). 1968. 22.50x (ISBN 0-231-03029-0). Columbia U Pr.

Politics of Mexican Oil. George W. Grayson. LC 80-5253. (Pitt Latin American Ser.). (Illus.). 1981. 21.95 (ISBN 0-8229-3425-6); pap. 6.95 (ISBN 0-8229-5323-4). U of Pittsburgh Pr.

Politics of Migration Policies: The First World in the 1970's. Ed. by Daniel Kubat. LC 77-93185. 1979. pap. 9.95x (ISBN 0-913256-34-X, Dist. by Ozer). Ctr Migration.

Politics of Military Unification: A Study of Conflict & the Policy Process. Demetrios Caraley. LC 66-15762. 1966. 21.00x (ISBN 0-231-02885-7). Columbia U Pr.

Politics of Minorities. Moin Shakir. 1980. 16.00x (ISBN 0-8364-0622-2, Pub. by Ajanta). South Asia Bks.

Politics of Modernization in Eastern Europe: Testing the Soviet Model. Ed. by Charles Gati. LC 73-15185. (Special Studies). (Illus.). 410p. 1974. text ed. 32.95 (ISBN 0-275-09440-5). Praeger.

Politics of Motherhood: Child & Maternal Welfare in England, 1900-1939. Jane Lewis. 240p. 1980. 27.95 (ISBN 0-7735-0521-0). McGill-Queens U Pr.

Politics of Motion: The World of Thomas Hobbes. Thomas A. Spragens, Jr. LC 72-81318. 1973. 12.00x (ISBN 0-8131-1278-8). U Pr of Ky.

Politics of National Despair: French Royalism in the Post-Reformation Era. George D. Balsama. 1977. pap. text ed. 7.75x (ISBN 0-8191-0142-7). U Pr of Amer.

Politics of Natural Disaster: The Case of the Sahel Drought. Ed. by Michael H. Glantz. LC 75-8474. (Illus.). 1976. text ed. 25.95 o.p. (ISBN 0-275-01180-1). Praeger.

Politics of New Town Planning: The Newfields, Ohio, Story. Frederick Steiner. LC 80-12783. (Illus.). xiv, 266p. 1981. 16.95 (ISBN 0-8214-0414-8, 0414E). Ohio U Pr.

Politics of Nonpartisanship: A Study of California City Elections. Eugene C. Lee. 1960. 18.50x (ISBN 0-520-00719-0). U of Cal Pr.

Politics of Pacific Islands Fisheries. George Kent. (Westview Replica Edition Ser.). 1980. lib. bdg. 22.00x (ISBN 0-89158-683-0). Westview.

Politics of Pain Management: Staff-Patient Interaction. Shizuko Fagerhaugh & Anselm Strauss. LC 77-75114. 1977. pap. text ed. 14.95 (ISBN 0-201-06909-1, M&N Div). A-W.

Politics of Palestinian Nationalism. William B. Quandt et al. 1973. 15.95x (ISBN 0-520-02336-6); pap. 3.95 (ISBN 0-520-02372-2, CAMPUS 93). U of Cal Pr.

Politics of Panchaytirai Administration. Niranjan Pant. 1979. text ed. 8.00x (ISBN 0-391-01850-7). Humanities.

Politics of Participation in Poverty: A Case Study of the Board of Economic & Youth Opportunities Agency of Greater Los Angeles. Dale R. Marshall. LC 79-121192. 1971. 20.00x (ISBN 0-520-01741-2). U of Cal Pr.

Politics of Peace: An Evaluation of Arms Control. John H. Barton. LC 79-67776. 296p. 1981. text ed. 18.50x (ISBN 0-8047-1081-3). Stanford U Pr.

Politics of People-Power: Interest Groups & Lobbies in New York State. new ed. Joseph G. Metz. Ed. by Mary E. Dillon. LC 76-184891. (Politics of Government Ser.). 110p. (Orig.). 1972. pap. 2.50 o.p. (ISBN 0-8120-0453-1). Barron.

Politics of Philo Judaeus. Erwin R. Goodenough & H. L. Goodhart. 1938. 50.00x (ISBN 0-685-69822-X). Elliots Bks.

Politics of Planning. Francis Gladstone. 1977. 15.00 (ISBN 0-85117-106-0). Transatlantic.

Politics of Policy Making in America: Five Case Studies. Ed. by David A. Caputo. LC 77-24516. (Illus.). 1977. text ed. 18.95x (ISBN 0-7167-0194-4); pap. text ed. 9.95x (ISBN 0-7167-0193-6). W H Freeman.

Politics of Pollution. 2nd ed. Barbara S. Davies & J. Clarence Davies, 3rd. LC 74-20996. (Studies in Contemporary America Ser.). 256p. 1975. 6.50 (ISBN 0-672-53720-6); pap. 5.95 (ISBN 0-672-63720-0). Pegasus.

Politics of Population in Brazil: Elite Ambivalence & Public Demand. Peter McDonough & Amaury Desouza. (Texas Pan American Ser). 190p. 1981. 19.95x (ISBN 0-292-76466-9). U of Tex Pr.

Politics of Poverty. 2nd ed. John C. Donovan. LC 72-10008. (Studies in Contemporary American Politics Ser). 1973. pap. 2.95 (ISBN 0-672-63715-4). Pegasus.

Politics of Poverty. 3rd ed. John C. Donovan. LC 80-5046. 201p. 1980. text ed. 17.50 (ISBN 0-8191-1025-6); pap. text ed. 7.25 (ISBN 0-8191-1026-4). U Pr of Amer.

Politics of Prejudice: The Anti-Japanese Movement in California & the Struggle for Japanese Exclusion. Roger Daniels. (California Library Reprint Ser). 1978. 16.00x (ISBN 0-520-03412-0); pap. 3.45 (ISBN 0-520-03411-2). U of Cal Pr.

Politics of Presidential Appointments. G. Calvin Mackenzie. LC 80-1029. (Illus.). 1980. 19.95 (ISBN 0-02-919670-1). Free Pr.

Politics of Privacy, Computers, & Criminal Justice Records: Controlling the Social Costs of Technological Change. Donald A. Marchand. LC 80-80675. xvi, 433p. 1980. text ed. 34.95 (ISBN 0-87815-030-7). Info Resources.

Politics of Private Desires. Michael Laver. 272p. 1981. pap. 3.95 (ISBN 0-14-022316-9, Pelican). Penguin.

Politics of Progress. R. Wolfinger. 1974. pap. text ed. 11.95 (ISBN 0-13-685024-3). P-H.

Politics of Protection: Lord Derby & the Protectionist Party, 1841-1852. Robert Stewart. LC 77-152628. 1971. 35.50 (ISBN 0-521-08109-2). Cambridge U Pr.

Politics of Race & International Sport: The Case of South Africa. Richard E. Lapchick. LC 74-11705. (Studies in Human Rights: No. 1). 268p. 1975. lib. bdg. 16.95 (ISBN 0-8371-7691-3, LPR/). Greenwood.

Politics of Race: Comparative Studies. Ed. by Donald G. Baker. 324p. 1975. 24.95 (ISBN 0-347-01076-8, 97311-4, Pub. by Saxon Hse). Lexington Bks.

Politics of Race Relations. Dipak Nandy. (Political Issues of Modern Britain Ser.). 1980. text ed. write for info. o.p. (ISBN 0-391-01147-2). Humanities.

Politics of Raising State & Local Revenue. Richard D. Bingham et al. LC 78-8392. (Praeger Special Studies). 1978. 23.95 (ISBN 0-03-022306-7); pap. 9.95 (ISBN 0-03-041471-7). Praeger.

Politics of Religion in America. Ed. by Fred Krinsky. 128p. 1968. pap. text ed. 4.95x (ISBN 0-02-476020-X, 47602). Macmillan.

Politics of Religious Conflict: Church & State in America. 2nd ed. Richard E. Morgan. LC 79-48094. 118p. 1980. text ed. 15.50 (ISBN 0-8191-1007-8); pap. text ed. 7.25 (ISBN 0-8191-1008-6). U Pr of Amer.

Politics of Reproductive Ritual. Karen E. Paige. Ed. by Jeffrey M. Paige. 416p. 1981. 25.00 (ISBN 0-520-03071-0). U of Cal Pr.

Politics of Rescue: The Roosevelt Administration & the Holocaust, 1938-1945. Henry L. Feingold. LC 75-127049. 1970. 25.00 (ISBN 0-8135-0664-6). Rutgers U Pr.

Politics of Riot Behavior. L. Alex Swan. LC 79-5510. 1980. pap. text ed. 10.25 (ISBN 0-8191-0905-3). U Pr of Amer.

Politics of Riot Commissions. Ed. by Anthony M. Platt. 1971. pap. 3.95 o.s.i. (ISBN 0-02-074590-7, Collier). Macmillan.

Politics of Rural Russia, 1905-1914. Ed. by Leopold H. Haimson. LC 78-62420. (Studies of the Russian Institute, Columbia University). 320p. 1979. 19.50x (ISBN 0-253-11345-8). Ind U Pr.

Politics of Samuel Johnson. Donald A. Greene. LC 72-85311. 376p. 1973. Repr. of 1960 ed. 17.50 o.p. (ISBN 0-8046-1697-3). Kennikat.

Politics of School Accountibility. Edward Wynne. LC 74-190055. 300p. 1972. 17.50x (ISBN 0-8211-2250-9); text ed. 15.75x (ISBN 0-685-24960-3). McCutchan.

Politics of School Government. Ed. by G. Baron. (International Studies in Education & Social Change). 260p. Date not set. 36.01 (ISBN 0-08-025213-3). Pergamon.

Politics of Schools: A Crisis in Self-Government. Robert Bendiner. LC 73-83585. 1969. 10.00 o.p. (ISBN 0-06-010301-9, HarpT). Har-Row.

Politics of Secularization in the USSR. Shamsuddin. 336p. 1980. text ed. 27.50x (ISBN 0-7069-1274-8, Pub. by Vikas India). Advent Bk.

Politics of Self-Sufficiency. Michael Allaby & Peter Bunyard. 208p. 1980. 21.00 (ISBN 0-19-217695-1). Oxford U Pr.

Politics of Social Services. Jeffrey Galper. 272p. 1975. pap. text ed. 10.95 (ISBN 0-13-685214-9). P-H.

Politics of Starvation. Jack Shepherd. LC 75-40831. 101p. 1975. 3.00 o.p. (ISBN 0-87003-002-7). Carnegie Endow.

Politics of Taxation. Thomas J. Reese. LC 79-8413. (Illus.). xxv, 237p. 1980. lib. bdg. 25.00 (ISBN 0-89930-003-0, RPT/, Quorum Bks). Greenwood.

Politics of Technology. G. Boyle et al. LC 77-5678. (Open University Set Book). (Illus.). 1978. pap. text ed. 11.95x (ISBN 0-582-44373-3). Longman.

Politics of the Barrios of Venezuela. rev. ed. Talton F. Ray. (Illus.). 1969. 19.50x (ISBN 0-520-01461-8). U of Cal Pr.

Politics of the Chaco Peace Conference, 1935-1939. Leslie B. Rout, Jr. (Latin American Monographs: No. 19). (Illus.). 1970. 12.50 (ISBN 0-292-70049-0). U of Tex Pr.

Politics of the Chinese Cultural Revolution: A Case Study. Hong Y. Lee. 1978. 22.75x (ISBN 0-520-03297-7); pap. 7.95x (ISBN 0-520-04065-1). U of Cal Pr.

Politics of the Corporate Economy. Trevor Smith. 229p. 1979. 30.50x (ISBN 0-85520-202-5, Pub by Martin Robertson England). Biblio Dist.

Politics of the Equal Rights Amendment: Conflict & the Decision Process. Janet K. Boles. LC 78-11052. 1979. pap. text ed. 8.95 (ISBN 0-582-28090-7). Longman.

Politics of the Federal Bureaucracy. 2nd ed. Ed. by Alan A. Altshuler & Norman C. Thomas. 1977. pap. text ed. 15.50 (ISBN 0-06-040246-6, HarpC). Har-Row.

Politics of the Judiciary. J. A Griffith. LC 77-88391. (Political Issues of Modern Britain). 1977. text ed. 19.50x (ISBN 0-391-00551-0). Humanities.

Politics of the Media. John Whale. LC 77-88395. (Political Issues of Modern Britain). 1977. text ed. 13.00x (ISBN 0-391-00550-2). Humanities.

Politics of the New Left. Matthew Stolz. (Studies in Contemporary Issues). 1971. pap. text ed. 4.95x (ISBN 0-02-478700-0, 47870). Macmillan.

Politics of the Prussian Army Sixteen Forty - Nineteen Forty-Five. Gordon A. Craig. 1964. pap. 7.95 (ISBN 0-19-500257-1, GB). Oxford U Pr.

Politics of the Second Front: American Military Planning & Diplomacy in Coalition Warfare, 1941-1943. Mark A. Stoler. LC 76-47171. (Contributions in Military History Ser.: No 12). 1977. lib. bdg. 18.95 (ISBN 0-8371-9438-5, SPF/). Greenwood.

Politics of the Solar Age: The Alternative to Economics. Hazel Henderson. LC 80-1723. (Illus.). 312p. 1981. pap. 5.95 (ISBN 0-385-17150-1, Anchor Pr); pap. 5.95 (ISBN 0-385-17151-X). Doubleday.

Politics of the Soviet Cinema: Nineteen Seventeen to Nineteen Twenty-Nine. R. Taylor. LC 78-67809. (International Studies). 1979. 27.50 (ISBN 0-521-22290-7). Cambridge U Pr.

Politics of the Sword: A Personal Memoir on Military Involvement in Ghana & of Problems of Military Government. A. K. Ocran. 167p. 1977. 16.50x (ISBN 0-8476-3101-X). Rowman.

Politics of the Vets Legislation in New York State, 2 vols. Frank W. Prescott & Joseph F. Zimmerman. LC 79-9696. 649p. 1980. Vol. 1. pap. 17.50 (ISBN 0-8191-0985-1); softcover set 33.50 (ISBN 0-8191-0986-X); Vol. 2. 26.75 (ISBN 0-8191-0983-5); text ed. 51.50 hardback set (ISBN 0-8191-0984-3). U Pr of Amer.

Politics of Trade Negotiations Between Africa & the European Economic Community. I. William Zartman. LC 76-120765. (Center for International Studies, NYU Ser.). 1971. 13.50 (ISBN 0-691-05642-0). Princeton U Pr.

Politics of Union: Northern Politics During the Civil War. James A. Rawley. LC 80-17173. vi, 202p. 1980. 15.50x (ISBN 0-8032-3856-8); pap. 3.95x (ISBN 0-8032-8902-2, BB 743, Bison). U of Nebr Pr.

Politics of United States Decision-Making in United Nations Specialized Agencies: The Case of the International Labor Organization. Gregory T. Kruglak. LC 80-5318. 300p. 1980. lib. bdg. 18.50 (ISBN 0-8191-1075-2); pap. text ed. 10.75 (ISBN 0-8191-1076-0). U Pr of Amer.

Politics of U. S. Labor: From the Great Depression to the New Deal. David Milton. LC 80-8934. 352p. 1981. 18.00 (ISBN 0-85345-569-4). Monthly Rev.

Politics of Untouchability: Social Mobility & Social Change in a City of India. Owen M. Lynch. LC 76-87148. (Illus.). 1969. 17.50x (ISBN 0-231-03230-7). Columbia U Pr.

Politics of Urbanism: The New Federalism. new ed. George C. Benson. Ed. by Mary E. Dillon. LC 70-189864. (Politics of Government Ser.). 142p. (Orig.). 1972. pap. 2.50 o.p. (ISBN 0-8120-0445-0). Barron.

Politics of Violence: A Case Study of West Bengal. Sajal Basu. 1981. 11.00x (ISBN 0-685-59390-8). South Asia Bks.

Politics of Violence: Revolution in the Modern World. Carl Leiden & Karl M. Schmitt. LC 80-23161. x, 244p. 1980. Repr. of 1968 ed. lib. bdg. 27.50x (ISBN 0-313-22463-3, LEPV). Greenwood.

Politics of Wartime Aid: American Economic Assistance to France & French Northwest Africa, 1940-1946. James J. Dougherty. LC 77-84770. (Contributions in American History: No. 71). 1978. lib. bdg. 18.95 (ISBN 0-8371-9882-8, DPW/). Greenwood.

Politics of Weapons Innovation: The Thor-Jupiter Controversy. Michael H. Armacost. LC 70-90213. 1969. 22.00x (ISBN 0-231-03206-4). Columbia U Pr.

Politics of Women's Liberation: A Case Study of an Emerging Social Movement & Its Relation to the Policy Process. Jo Freeman. LC 74-25208. 1975. 9.95x (ISBN 0-679-30284-0); pap. 9.95x (ISBN 0-582-28009-5). Longman.

Politics of Work & Occupations. Ed. by Geoff Esland & Graeme Salaman. 416p. 1981. pap. 11.00x (ISBN 0-8020-6429-9). U of Toronto Pr.

Politics of Working-Class Education in Britain, 1830-1850. D. G. Paz. 199p. 1981. lib. bdg. 30.00x (ISBN 0-87023-326-2). U of Mass Pr.

Politics of Zoning: New York, 1916-1960. Stanislaw J. Makielski. LC 65-25662. (Metropolitan Politics Ser.: No. 4). 1966. 17.50x (ISBN 0-231-02789-3). Columbia U Pr.

Politics, Oil, & the Western Mediterranean. R. Michael Burrell & Alvin J. Cottrell. LC 73-638. (The Washington Papers: No. 7). 1973. write for info. (ISBN 0-8039-0259-X). Sage.

Politics, Parties & Power. John Goldbach & Michael J. Ross. LC 79-47991. 382p. 1980. 15.95 (ISBN 0-913530-21-2); pap. 10.95 (ISBN 0-686-64356-9). Palisades Pub.

Politics, Parties & 1980. National Journal. Ed. by Nelson W. Polsby. (National Journal Reprints). 56p. (Orig.). 1979. pap. 3.95 o.p. (ISBN 0-89234-023-1). Natl Journal.

Politics, Planning & the Public Interest. Martin Meyerson & Edward C. Banfield. LC 55-7335. 1964. pap. text ed. 5.95 (ISBN 0-02-921230-8). Free Pr.

Politics, Power, Polls, & School Elections. Ralph B. Kimbrough & Michael Y. Nunnery. LC 70-146308. 1971. 15.25x (ISBN 0-8211-1012-8); text ed. 13.75x (ISBN 0-685-04201-4). McCutchan.

Politics, Programs, & Bureaucrats. William P. Browne. (National University Publications, Political Science Ser.). 184p. 1980. 17.50 (ISBN 0-8046-9263-7). Kennikat.

Politics, Public Enterprise & the Industrial Development Agency: Industrialisation Policies & Practices. N. S. Carey-Jones et al. 248p. 1975. 22.50x (ISBN 0-8419-5500-X). Holmes & Meier.

Politics, Rationality, & the Urban Services: The Police. Peter F. Nardulli & Jeffrey M. Stonecash. LC 80-27169. 228p. 1981. lib. bdg. 20.00 (ISBN 0-89946-076-3). Oelgeschlager.

Politics, Science, & Cancer: The Laetrile Phenomenon. Ed. by Gerald E. Markle & James C. Peterson. (AAAS Selected Symposium: No. 46). 250p. 1980. lib. bdg. 20.00 (ISBN 0-89158-854-X); pap. 9.50 (ISBN 0-86531-046-7). Westview.

Politics, Society & Nationhood, Vol. 1. A. Norman Jeffares. (Collected Edition of the Writings of G. W. Russell Ser.: VI-1). 1980. text ed. write for info. (ISBN 0-391-01185-5). Humanities.

Politics, Society & Nationhood, Vol. 2. A. Norman Jeffares. (Collected Edition of the Writings of G. W. Russell Ser.: VI-2). 1980. text ed. write for info. (ISBN 0-391-01183-9). Humanities.

Politics: The American Way. rev. ed. Abraham Ribicoff & Jon O. Newman. (Illus.). (gr. 7-9). 1974. pap. text ed. 4.80 o.p. (ISBN 0-205-03973-1, 7639732). Allyn.

Politics, Values, & Public Policy. Frank Fischer. (Westview Special Study Ser.). 275p. 1980. lib. bdg. 23.50x (ISBN 0-89158-799-3). Westview.

Politics: Who Gets What, When & How. Harold D. Lasswell. 7.25 (ISBN 0-8446-1277-4). Peter Smith.

Politics Within: A Primer in Political Attitudes & Behavior. Jarol B. Manheim. (Illus.). 176p. 1975. text ed. 6.95 (ISBN 0-13-685362-5); pap. text ed. 8.95 (ISBN 0-13-685354-4). P-H.

Politics Within Nations. Joseph LaPalombra. (Contemporary Comparative Politics Ser.). 608p. 1974. text ed. 17.95 (ISBN 0-13-687814-8). P-H.

Politocal Economy of Botswana: A Study of Growth & Distribution. Christopher Colclough & Stephen McCarthy. (Illus.). 308p. 1980. 37.50 (ISBN 0-19-877136-3). Oxford U Pr.

Polity & Theatre in Historical Perspective. Karen Hermassi. 1977. 16.50x (ISBN 0-520-03294-2). U of Cal Pr.

Polity of the School. Ed. by Frederick M. Wirt. LC 74-26311. (Politics of Education Ser.). 384p. 1975. 22.95 (ISBN 0-669-97618-0). Lexington Bks.

Polka Dotted Pals, Pt. 1. Sheila Jenkins et al. 100p. (gr. k-1). 1980. pap. write for info (ISBN 0-932970-13-3). Prinit Pr.

Polka Dotted Pencil Pushers: Math. Irene Goodwin & Ruth Silvers. LC 79-63129. 156p. (Orig.). 1979. pap. 8.95 (ISBN 0-932970-08-7). Prinit Pr.

Pollen-Collecting Bees of the Anthidiini of California (Hymenoptera: Megachilidae) A. A. Grigarick & L. A. Stange. (Bulletin of the California Insect Survey: Vol. 9). 1968. pap. 6.50x (ISBN 0-520-09034-9). U of Cal Pr.

Polling on the Issues. Burns W. Roper et al. LC 80-23439. 224p. 1980. 11.95 (ISBN 0-932020-02-X); pap. 7.95 (ISBN 0-932020-03-8). Seven Locks Pr.

Pollock Painting. new ed. Hans Namuth. Ed. by Barbara Rose. LC 79-57621. (Illus.). 112p. 1980. 25.00 (ISBN 0-9601068-6-3); pap. 14.95 (ISBN 0-9601068-5-5). Agrinde Bks.

Polls & Surveys: A Look at Public Opinion Research. Ann E. Weiss. (Impact Bks.). (Illus.). (gr. 7 up). 1979. PLB 6.90 s&l (ISBN 0-531-02859-3). Watts.

Polls: Their Use & Misuse in Politics. rev. ed. Charles W. Roll, Jr. & Albert H. Cantril. LC 80-50359. (Illus.). 224p. 1980. pap. 5.95 (ISBN 0-932020-01-1). Seven Locks Pr.

Pollutant Effects on Marine Organisms. C. S. Giam. LC 77-2475. (Illus.). 1977. 19.95 (ISBN 0-669-01518-0). Lexington Bks.

Pollutants & High Risk Groups: The Biological Basis of Increased Human Susceptibility to Environmental & Occupational Pollutants. Edward J. Calabrese. LC 77-13957. (Environmental Science & Technology: Wiley-Interscience Series of Texts & Monographs). 1977. 27.00 (ISBN 0-471-02940-8, Pub. by Wiley-Inerscience). Wiley.

Polluted Homes. Peter Gregory. 64p. 1965. pap. text ed. 3.75x (Pub. by Bedford England). Renouf.

Polluted Nursery Rhymes. Jerry B. German. 1974. pap. 2.50 o.p. (ISBN 0-682-47864-4). Exposition.

Polluted Rain. Ed. by T. Y. Toribara et al. (Environmental Science Research Ser.: Vol. 17). 510p. 1980. 49.50 (ISBN 0-306-40353-6, Plenum Pr). Plenum Pub.

Pollution. Herta S. Breiter. LC 77-26886. (Read About Science Ser.). (Illus.). (gr. k-3). 1978. PLB 9.95 (ISBN 0-8393-0081-6). Raintree Child.

Pollution: A Selected Bibliography of U.S. Government Publications on Air, Water, & Land Pollution 1965-1970. Compiled by Louis Kiraldi & Janet L. Burk. 1971. 3.00 (ISBN 0-932826-09-1). New Issues MI.

Pollution & Water Resources. Ed. by Halasi-Kun. (Columbia University Seminar Ser.). Date not set. 20.00 (ISBN 0-08-025988-X). Pergamon.

Pollution & Water Resources: Pollution & Hydrology of Surface & Groundwater -- Selected Reports. George J. Halasi-Kun. LC 78-100896. (Columbia University Seminar Ser.: Vol. XIII, Pt. 3). (Illus.). 205p. 1981. 25.00 (ISBN 0-08-027511-7). Pergamon.

Pollution & Water Resourses: Pollution & Hydrology of Surface & Ground Water - Selected Reports. Ed. by George J. Halasi-Kun. (Columbia University Seminar Ser.: Vol. XIII-2, 1980). (Illus.). 187p. 1981. 20.00 (ISBN 0-08-027215-0). Pergamon.

Pollution by the Food Processing Industries in the EEC. Institut National De Recherche Chimique Appliguee. 193p. 1977. 33.00x (ISBN 0-86010-074-X, Pub. by Graham & Trotman England). State Mutual Bk.

Pollution Charges in Practice. (Document Ser.). 118p. 1980. 7.50 (ISBN 92-64-12042-4). OECD.

Pollution Control Costs in Industry: An Economic Study. M. H. Atkins & J. F. Lowe. text ed: 23.00 (ISBN 0-08-021851-2); pap. text ed. 13.75 (ISBN 0-08-021841-5). Pergamon.

Pollution Control Policy of the EEC. Stanley P. Johnson. 224p. 1979. 26.00x (ISBN 0-86010-136-3, Pub. by Graham & Trotman England). State Mutual Bk.

Pollution Criteria for Estuaries. Ed. by P. R. Helliwell & J. Bossanji. LC 74-26695. 1975. 44.95 (ISBN 0-470-36920-5). Halsted Pr.

Pollution Detection & Monitoring Handbook. M. Sittig. LC 74-75905. (Environmental Technology Handbook Ser: No. 1). (Illus.). 401p. 1974. 36.00 o.p. (ISBN 0-8155-0529-9). Noyes.

Pollution in the Air: Problems, Policies & Priorities. R. S. Scorer. 156p. 1973. 12.00 (ISBN 0-685-30197-4). Routledge & Kegan.

Pollution Japan: Historical Chronology. Nobuku Iijima. 401p. 1980. 64.00 (ISBN 0-08-026242-2). Pergamon.

Pollution Lab. Melvin Berger. LC 73-18542. (Illus.). 128p. (gr. 3-5). 1974. lib. bdg. 9.89 (ISBN 0-381-99629-8, JD-J). John Day.

Pollution Prevention Pays. Michael G. Royston. 1979. 28.00 (ISBN 0-08-023597-2); pap. 8.50 (ISBN 0-08-023572-7). Pergamon.

Pollution, Prices & Public Policy. Allen V. Kneese & Charles L. Schultze. 125p. 1975. 11.95 (ISBN 0-8157-4994-5); pap. 4.95 (ISBN 0-8157-4993-7). Brookings.

Pollution-Pricing: Industrial Response to Wastewater Charges. James F. Hudson et al. LC 80-8363. 1981. price not set (ISBN 0-669-04033-9). Lexington Bks.

Pollution, Resources & the Environment. new ed. Ed. by Alain C. Enthoven & A. Myrick Freeman, 3rd. 1973. pap. 5.95x (ISBN 0-393-09933-4). Norton.

Pollution: The Air We Breathe. Claire Jones et al. LC 70-156364. (Real World of Pollution Ser). (Illus.). 100p. (gr. 5-11). 1971. PLB 4.95 o.p. (ISBN 0-8225-0628-9). Lerner Pubns.

Pollution: The Dangerous Atom. Claire Jones et al. LC 75-165322. (Real World of Pollution Ser). (Illus.). (gr. 5-12). 1972. PLB 4.95 o.p. (ISBN 0-8225-0630-0). Lerner Pubns.

Pollyanna. Eleanor H. Porter. 1976. lib. bdg. 14.75x (ISBN 0-89968-106-9). Lightyear.

Pollyanna Grows up. Eleanor Porter. 308p. 1980. Repr. of 1915 ed. lib. bdg. 14.50x (ISBN 0-89968-193-X). Lightyear.

Polnoe Sobranie Sochinenii, Vol. I. Aleksandr Vvendenskii. Ed. by M. Meilakh. (Rus.). 1980. 15.00 (ISBN 0-88233-321-6); pap. 7.50 (ISBN 0-88233-322-4). Ardis Pubs.

Polo for the Pony Club. British Horse Society & Pony Club. LC 76-54905. 1977. pap. 1.95 (ISBN 0-8120-0785-9). Barron.

Polonaise. Piers P. Read. LC 76-15306. 1976. 10.00 o.p. (ISBN 0-397-01150-4). Lippincott.

Poltava Affair: A Russian Warning - an American Tragedy. Glenn Infield. LC 72-93628. 256p. 1973. 7.95 o.s.i. (ISBN 0-02-558140-6). Macmillan.

Poltergeist. William G. Roll. LC 76-25880. (Illus.). 224p. 1976. 10.00 (ISBN 0-8108-0984-2). Scarecrow.

Poltergeists: An Annotated Bibliography of Works in English, Circa 1880-1975. Compiled by Michael Goss. LC 78-11492. 1979. 16.50 (ISBN 0-8108-1181-2). Scarecrow.

Poltergeists: Hauntings & the Haunted. David C. Knight. LC 72-2449. (Illus.). 160p. (gr. 5-9). 1972. 7.95 o.p. (ISBN 0-397-31488-4); pap. 1.95 o.p. (ISBN 0-397-31416-7, LSC-19). Lippincott.

Poly (N-Vinylcarbazole) J. M. Pearson & M. Stolka. (Polymer Monographs Ser.). 1981. price not set. Gordon.

Poly (Tetrahydrofuran) P. Dreyfuss. (Polymer Monographs Ser.). Date not set. price not set (ISBN 0-677-03330-3). Gordon.

Polyamines As Biochemical Markers of Normal & Malignant Growth. D. H. Russell & G. M. Durie. LC 75-43340. (Progress in Cancer Research & Therapy Ser.: Vol. 8). 1978. 21.50 (ISBN 0-89004-116-4). Raven.

Polyamines in Biomedical Research. Ed. by Joseph M. Gaugas. LC 79-40651. 1980. 85.00 (ISBN 0-471-27629-4, Pub. by Wiley-Interscience). Wiley.

Polyamines in Normal & Neoplastic Growth. Ed. by Diane H. Russell. LC 72-96336. (Illus.). 1973. 34.50 (ISBN 0-911216-44-8). Raven.

Polyamino Acids, Polypeptides, & Proteins: Proceedings. International Symposium On Poly-A-Amino Acids - 1st - University Of Wisconsin - 1961. Ed. by Mark C. Stahmann. (Illus.). 1962. 45.00 (ISBN 0-299-02620-5). U of Wis Pr.

Polybius. F. W. Walbank. LC 72-189219. (Sather Classical Lectures, No. 42). 1973. 18.50x (ISBN 0-520-02190-8). U of Cal Pr.

Polychlorinated Biphenyls. Environmental Studies Board. 1979. pap. 7.25 (ISBN 0-309-02885-X). Natl Acad Pr.

Polychrome Historical Haggadah. Meir Ai-Nai-Yim. (Illus.). 30.00 (ISBN 0-686-10317-3). J Freedman Liturgy.

Polychrome Historical Prayerbook: Siddur 'bet Yosef' Jacob Freedman. (Illus.). 400p. Date not set. 75.00 (ISBN 0-686-12113-9). J Freedman Liturgy. Postponed.

Polycyclic Aromatic Hydrocarbons in the Aquatic Environment. Jerry M. Neff. (Illus.). 1979. 51.80x (ISBN 0-85334-832-4). Intl Ideas.

Polycyclic Hydrocarbons & Cancer, 2 vols. Ed. by Harry V. Gelboin. Incl. Vol. 1. Environment, Chemistry & Metabolism. 46.50 (ISBN 0-12-279201-7); Vol. 2. Molecular & Cell Biology. 51.50 (ISBN 0-12-279202-5). 1978. Acad Pr.

Polycythemia: Theory & Management. Ed. by Herman Klein. (American Lectures in Hematology). (Illus.). 280p. 1973. text ed. 19.75 (ISBN 0-398-02684-X). C C Thomas.

Polyelectrolytes. Kurt C. Frisch et al. LC 76-177446. (Illus.). 1976. 25.00x (ISBN 0-87762-076-8). Technomic.

Polyelectrolytes for Water & Wastewater Treatment. Ed. by William E. Schwoyer. 304p. 1981. 74.95 (ISBN 0-8493-5439-0). CRC Pr.

Polyeucte. Pierre Corneille. Ed. by R. A. Sayce. 1962. pap. 10.25x (ISBN 0-631-00480-7, Pub. by Basil Blackwell). Biblio Dist.

Polygamist. B. H. Friedman. 228p. 1981. 11.95 (ISBN 0-316-29357-1, An Atlantic Monthly Press Bk). Little.

Polygamist's Wife. Melissa Merrill. LC 74-29659. (Illus.). 168p. (Orig.). 1975. 5.95 o.p. (ISBN 0-913420-52-2). Olympus Pub Co.

Polygamous Species of the Genus Galium (Rubiaceae), Section Lophogalium, of Mexico & Southwestern United States. Lauramay T. Dempster. (U. C. Publ. in Botany: Vol. 64). 1973. pap. 6.50x (ISBN 0-520-09457-3). U of Cal Pr.

Polyglot of Foreign Proverbs - with English Translations. Ed. by Henry G. Bohn. LC 67-23915. (Polyglot). 1968. Repr. of 1857 ed. 22.00 (ISBN 0-8103-3197-7). Gale.

Polyglotta Africana. Sigismund W. Koelle. LC 65-82544. 1963. Repr. of 1854 ed. 42.50x (ISBN 3-201-00766-8). Intl Pubns Serv.

Polygraph Dictionary for the Graphic Industries in Six Languages. 38th ed. Ed. by K. Collet. LC 68-117537. (Ger. Eng. Fr. Span. It. Swedish.). 1967. 65.00x (ISBN 3-87641-150-5). Intl Pubns Serv.

Polygraph for the Defense. Robert J. Ferguson, Jr. & Allan L. Miller. 312p. 1974. 24.50 (ISBN 0-398-02877-X). C C Thomas.

Polygraph Handbook for Attorneys. Stanley Abrams. LC 77-6074. (Illus.). 1977. 19.95 (ISBN 0-669-01598-9). Lexington Bks.

Polygraph in Court. Robert T. Ferguson, Jr. & Allan L. Miller. (Illus.). 372p. 1973. pap. 28.75 photocopy ed. spiral (ISBN 0-398-02679-3). C C Thomas.

Polygraph in Private Industry. Robert J. Ferguson, Jr. (Illus.). 352p. 1966. pap. 27.75 photocopy ed. spiral (ISBN 0-398-00557-5). C C Thomas.

Polyhedra: A Visual Approach. Anthony Pugh. LC 74-27297. 150p. 1976. 14.50x (ISBN 0-520-02926-7); pap. 4.95 (ISBN 0-520-03056-7, CAL 324). U of Cal Pr.

Polyhedron Models. M. J. Wenninger. LC 69-10200. (Illus.). 1971. 27.50 (ISBN 0-521-06917-3); pap. 11.95x (ISBN 0-521-09859-9). Cambridge U Pr.

Polymer Alloys: Blends, Grafts, & Interpenetrating Networks. Ed. by K. C. Frisch & Frisch. (Polymer Science & Technology Ser.: Vol. 10). 501p. 1977. 47.50 (ISBN 0-306-36410-7, Plenum Pr). Plenum Pub.

Polymer Alloys II: Blends, Blocks, Grafts, & Interpenetrating Networks. Ed. by D. Klempner & K. C. Frisch. (Polymer Science & Technology Ser.: Vol. 11). 290p. 1980. 35.00 (ISBN 0-306-40346-3, Plenum Pr). Plenum Pub.

Polymer Analytics. M. Hoffman et al. Tr. by H. Stahlberg from Ger. (MMI Press Polymer Monographs). 623p. 1981. 124.00 (ISBN 3-7186-0024-2). Harwood Academic.

Polymer Blends, Vols. 1 & 2. Ed. by D. R. Paul & Seymour Newman. 1978. Vol. 1. 50.50 (ISBN 0-12-546801-6); Vol. 2. 51.50 (ISBN 0-12-546802-4); 86.50 set (ISBN 0-685-80434-8). Acad Pr.

Polymer Characterization by ESR & NMR. Ed. by Arthur E. Woodward & Frank Bovey. LC 80-21840. (ACS Symposium Ser.: No. 142). 1980. 32.00 (ISBN 0-8412-0594-9). Am Chemical.

Polymer Chemistry. D. B. V. Parker. (Illus.). 1974. text ed. 22.30x (ISBN 0-85334-571-6). Intl Ideas.

Polymer Chemistry: An Introduction. Malcolm P. Stevens. 1975. text ed. 23.50 (ISBN 0-201-07312-9, Adv Bk Prog); pap. text ed. 21.50 (ISBN 0-201-07313-7, Adv Bk Prog). A-W.

Polymer Colloids. Ed. by Robert M. Fitch. LC 70-153721. 187p. 1971. 24.50 (ISBN 0-306-30536-4, Plenum Pr). Plenum Pub.

Polymer Colloids, II. Ed. by Robert M. Fitch. 695p. 1980. 69.50 (ISBN 0-306-40350-1, Plenum Pr). Plenum Pub.

Polymer Conversion. W. A. Holmes-Walker. LC 74-11510. 286p. 1975. 41.95 (ISBN 0-470-40767-0). Halsted Pr.

Polymer Engineering Composites. Ed. by M. O. Richardson. (Illus.). 1977. 102.60x (ISBN 0-85334-722-0). Intl Ideas.

Polymer Films in Electrical Applications. J. G. Tapley & N. Parkman. (Iee Electrical & Electronic Materials & Devices Ser.). (Illus.). 192p. Date not set. write for info. (Pub. by Peregrinus London). Inst Elect Eng. Postponed.

Polymer Handbook. 2nd ed. Ed. by Johannes Brandrup & E. H. Immergut. LC 74-11381. 1408p. 1975. 50.50 (ISBN 0-471-09804-3, Pub. by Wiley-Interscience). Wiley.

Polymer Materials: An Introduction for Technologists & Scientists. Christopher Hall. LC 80-19341. 250p. 1981. 29.95 (ISBN 0-470-27028-4). Halsted Pr.

Polymer Materials Science. Jerold Schultz. (P-H Int'l Series in the Physical & Chemical Engineering Sciences). (Illus.). 496p. 1973. ref. ed. 29.95 (ISBN 0-13-687038-4). P-H.

Polymer-Polymer Miscibility. Olagoka Olabisi & Lloyd Robeson. 1979. 45.60 (ISBN 0-12-525050-9). Acad Pr.

Polymer Processing. James M. McKelvey. LC 62-8780. 1962. 22.50 o.p. (ISBN 0-471-58443-6). Wiley.

Polymer Products. Ed. by H. J. Cantow et al. (Advances in Polymer Science Ser.: Vol. 39). (Illus.). 230p. 1981. 57.80 (ISBN 0-387-10218-3). Springer-Verlag.

Polymer Science & Engineering. David J. Williams. (Physical & Chemical Engineering Sciences Ser). (Illus.). 1971. ref. ed. 29.95 (ISBN 0-13-685636-5). P-H.

Polymer Structure, Properties & Applications. Rudolph D. Deanin. LC 70-156478. 1972. 29.95 o.p. (ISBN 0-8436-1202-9). CBI Pub.

Polymer Surfaces. B. W. Cherry. LC 80-40013. (Cambridge Solid State Science Ser.). (Illus.). 150p. Date not set. 37.50 (ISBN 0-521-23082-9); pap. 14.95 (ISBN 0-521-29792-3). Cambridge U Pr.

Polymeric Amines & Ammonium Salts: International Symposium on Polymeric Amines & Ammonium Salts, Ghent, Belgium, 24-26 September 1979. Ed. by Eric J. Goethals. LC 80-40324. (IUPAC Symposium Ser). 424p. 1980. 98.00 (ISBN 0-08-023941-2). Pergamon.

Polymeric Drugs. Ed. by L. Guy Donaruma & Otto Vogl. 1978. 25.50 (ISBN 0-12-220750-5). Acad Pr.

Polymerization of Heterocycles (Ring-Opening) Ed. by S. Penczek. LC 76-44623. 1977. text ed. 30.00 (ISBN 0-08-021367-7). Pergamon.

Polymerization Processes. Ed. by H. J. Cantow et al. (Advances in Polymer Sciences Ser.: Vol. 38). (Illus.). 180p. 1981. 46.00 (ISBN 0-387-10217-5). Springer-Verlag.

Polymerization Processes. Ed. by C. E. Schildknecht & I. Skeist. LC 76-17108. (High Polymer Ser.: Vol. 29). 1977. 53.50 (ISBN 0-471-39381-9, Pub. by Wiley-Interscience). Wiley.

Polymers: Chemistry & Physics of Modern Materials. J. M. Cowie. (Illus.). 1973. pap. text ed. 21.00x (ISBN 0-7002-0222-6). Intl Ideas.

Polymers in Nature. A. MacGregor & C. T. Greenwood. LC 79-41787. 328p. 1980. 53.75 (ISBN 0-471-27762-2, Pub. by Wiley-Interscience); pap. write for info. (ISBN 0-471-27794-0). Wiley.

Polymetis. Joseph Spence. LC 75-27886. (Renaissance & the Gods Ser.: Vol. 41). (Illus.). 1976. Repr. of 1747 ed. lib. bdg. 73.00 (ISBN 0-8240-2090-1). Garland Pub.

Polynesian Family System in Kau, Hawaii. E. S. Handy & Mary K. Pukui. LC 75-171998. 1972. 15.00 (ISBN 0-8048-1031-1). C E Tuttle.

Polynesian Journal of Henry Byam Martin. Henry B. Martin. Ed. by Edward Dodd. (Illus.). 200p. 1981. write for info. (ISBN 0-87577-060-6). Peabody Mus Salem.

Polynesian Twilight. Juanita Ritchie. (Illus.). 170p. (Orig.). 1980. pap. 3.95 (ISBN 0-89260-179-5). Hwong Pub.

Polynesians Knew. new ed. Tillie S. Pine & Joseph Levine. (Illus.). (ps-4). 1974. PLB 7.95 o.p. (ISBN 0-07-050090-8, GB). McGraw.

Polynesia's Sacred Isle. Edward Dodd. LC 75-26513. (The Ring of Fire Ser.: Vol. 3). (Illus.). 1976. 10.00 (ISBN 0-396-07227-5). Dodd.

Polynomial Representations of GLN. J. A. Green. (Lecture Notes in Mathematics: Vol. 830). 118p. 1981. pap. 9.80 (ISBN 0-387-10258-2). Springer-Verlag.

Polynomial Rings & Affine Spaces. M. Nagata. LC 78-8264. (Conference Board of the Mathematical Sciences Ser.: No. 37). 1980. Repr. of 1978 ed. 7.40 (ISBN 0-8218-1687-X, CBMS 37). Am Math.

Polynuclear Aromatic Hydrocarbons. International Symposium on Analysis, Chemistry, & Biology, No. 2. Ed. by Peter W. Jones & Ralph I. Freudenthal. LC 77-87456. (Carcinogenesis-A Comprehensive Survey Ser.: Vol. 3). 1978. 49.00 (ISBN 0-89004-241-1). Raven.

Polynuclear Aromatic Hydrocarbons: Chemistry, Metabolism, & Carcinogenesis. Ed. by Ralph I. Freudenthal & Peter Jones. LC 75-43194. 1976. 48.00 (ISBN 0-89004-103-2). Raven.

Polyoraceae of North America: The Genus Tyromyces, No. 97. write for info. o.p. (ISBN 0-686-20707-6). SUNY Environ.

Polyp (A Quetzalcoatl Production) Tych: Polyptych Striking Camp. Fred Truck. 1.00 (ISBN 0-938236-01-6). Cookie Pr.

Polypeptide Hormones: Proceedings. Miles International Symposium, 12th. Ed. by Roland F. Beers & Edward Bassett. 544p. 1980. text ed. 49.00 (ISBN 0-89004-462-7). Raven.

Polyphase Flow & Transport Technology. Ed. by R. A. Bajura. 270p. 1980. 40.00 (H00158). ASME.

Polyphenols in Cereals & Legumes. 72p. 1980. pap. 5.00 (ISBN 0-88936-234-3, IDRC 145, IDRC). Unipub.

Polyphonie Du XIIIe Siecle, 4 vols. University of Montpellier Faculty of Medicine. LC 80-2191. (Illus.). 1981. Repr. of 1939 ed. 365.00 (ISBN 0-404-19040-5). AMS Pr.

Polyploidy & Induced Mutations in Plant Breeding. (Illus.). 413p. (Orig.). 1974. pap. 26.75 (ISBN 92-0-011074-6, IAEA). Unipub.

Polyploidy: Biological Relevance. Ed. by Walter H. Lewis. (Basic Life Sciences Ser.: Vol. 13). 590p. 1980. 55.00 (ISBN 0-306-40358-7, Plenum Pr). Plenum Pub.

Polypoid Lesions of the Gastrointestinal Tract. 2nd ed. Claude E. Welch & Stephen E. Hedberg. (Mpcs Ser.: Vol. 2). (Illus.). 220p. 1975. text ed. 16.00 (ISBN 0-7216-9171-4). Saunders.

Polysaccharide Metabolism. R. W. Stoddart. 224p. 1980. 35.00x (ISBN 0-85664-807-8, Pub. by Croom Helm England). State Mutual England.

Polysaccharide-Protein Complexes in Invertebrates. S. Hunt. 1970. 44.00 (ISBN 0-12-362050-3). Acad Pr.

Polysaccharides in Food. new ed. J. M. Blanshard & J. R. Mitchell. LC 79-40370. (Studies in the Agricultural & Food Sciences). (Illus.). 1979. text ed. 55.95 (ISBN 0-408-10618-2). Butterworths.

Polytechnics & Colleges. Alan Matterson. (Illus.). 320p. 1981. text ed. 34.00 (ISBN 0-582-49095-2). Longman.

Polyunsaturated Fatty Acids in Nutrition: Proceedings of a Round Table in Polyunsaturated Fatty Acids in Nutrition, Milan, Italy, April 1979. Ed. by C. Galli & P. Avogaro. (Progress in Food & Nutrition Sciences Ser.: Vol. 4, No. 5). (Illus.). 80p. 1980. pap. 26.00 (ISBN 0-08-027362-9). Pergamon.

Polyurethane Technology. Ed. by Paul F. Bruins. LC 68-54598. (Polymer Engineering & Technology Ser). 1969. 30.00 (ISBN 0-471-11395-6, Pub by Wiley-Interscience). Wiley.

Polyurethanes: Looking Ahead to the Eighties. LC 80-65994. 133p. 1980. 25.00 (ISBN 0-87762-284-1). Technomic.

Polywater: The History of an Artifact. Relix Franks. 100p. 1981. 17.50x (ISBN 0-262-06073-6). MIT Pr.

Pomeranian. Hilary Harmar. Ed. by Christina Foyle. (Foyle's Handbks). (Illus.). 1973. 3.95 (ISBN 0-685-55796-0). Palmetto Pub.

Pompeii. I. Andrews. (Introduction to the History of Mankind Ser.). 1978. 3.95 (ISBN 0-521-20973-0). Cambridge U Pr.

Pompeii Scroll. Jacqueline La Tourrette. 256p. 1975. 7.95 o.p. (ISBN 0-440-06091-5). Delacorte.

Pompey: A Political Biography. Robin Seager. 1980. 27.50x (ISBN 0-520-03909-2). U of Cal Pr.

Pompey, Vol. I: The Roman Alexander. Peter Greenhalgh. 288p. 1981. text ed. 23.00 (ISBN 0-8262-0335-3). U of Mo Pr.

POMR: Application to Nursing Records. Gael C. Ulisse. LC 78-60718. 1978. 7.95 (ISBN 0-201-07880-5, 07880, M&N Div). A-W.

Pon My Honor Hit's the Truth: Tales from the South Western Virginia Mountains. Hubert J. Davis. (Illus.). 1973. 4.95 (ISBN 0-930230-19-1). Johnson NC.

Ponapean Reference Grammar. Kenneth L. Rehg & Damian G. Sohl. LC 80-13276. (Pali Language Texts: Micronesia). 1980. pap. text ed. 16.00x (ISBN 0-8248-0718-9). U Pr of Hawaii.

Ponca Chiefs: An Account of the Trial of Standing Bear. Thomas H. Tibbles. Ed. by Kay Graber. LC 73-181595. xiv, 143p. 1972. 9.50x (ISBN 0-8032-0814-6); pap. 2.25 (ISBN 0-8032-5763-5, BB 547, Bison). U of Nebr Pr.

Ponca Indians. Joseph Jablow. Ed. by David A. Horr. Incl. Ethnology of the Ponca. Joseph Jablow; Findings of Fact, & Opinion. Indian Claims Commission. (American Indian Ethnohistory Ser: Plains Indians). (Illus.). 1974. lib. bdg. 42.00 (ISBN 0-8240-0734-4). Garland Pub.

Pond. Carol Carrick. (ps-2). 1970. 5.95g o.s.i. (ISBN 0-02-717310-0). Macmillan.

Pond Life. Charles O. Masters. pap. 2.95 o.p. (ISBN 0-87666-135-5, PS651). TFH Pubns.

Ponder Heart. Eudora Welty. LC 54-5248. (Illus.). 1954. 6.95 o.p. (ISBN 0-15-173073-3). HarBraceJ.

Ponds & Lakes. T. T. Macan. LC 73-91602. (Illus.). 148p. 1974. pap. 8.95x (ISBN 0-8448-0773-7). Crane-Russak Co.

Ponds & Streams. Nancy Scott. LC 76-511006. (Pegasus Books: No. 26). (Illus.). 1969. 10.50x (ISBN 0-234-77188-7). Intl Pubns Serv.

Ponds & Water Gardens. Bill Heritage. (Illus.). 176p. 1981. 12.95 (ISBN 0-7137-1015-2, Pub. by Blandford Pr England); pap. 6.95 (ISBN 0-7137-1141-8). Sterling.

Ponies for Hire. Margaret M. MacPherson. LC 67-10208. (Illus.). (gr. 6-7). 1967. 4.50 o.p. (ISBN 0-15-263165-8, HJ). HarBraceJ.

PONS (Profile of Nonverbal Sensitivity) Test Manual. Robert Rosenthal et al. (Illus.). 1979. pap. text ed. 8.95x (ISBN 0-89197-647-7). Irvington.

Pont Neuf. 3rd ed. E. Stack. (Fr.). 1978. 15.95 (ISBN 0-13-530394-X); wkbk. 4.95 (ISBN 0-13-530402-4). P-H.

Pontiac. Matthew G. Grant. LC 73-12193. 1974. PLB 5.95 (ISBN 0-87191-268-6). Creative Ed.

Pontiac Firebird Nineteen Seventy to Nineteen Eighty Shop Manual. Jim Combs. Ed. by Eric Jorgensen. (Illus., Orig.). 1980. pap. text ed. 10.95 (ISBN 0-89287-306-X, A235). Clymer Pubns.

Pontiac: The Complete History, 1926-79. Thomas E. Bonsall. LC 79-56550. (Illus.). 1980. 26.95 (ISBN 0-934780-02-1). Bookman Dan.

Pontiac: The Postwar Years. Jan P. Norbye & Jim Dunne. LC 79-17430. (Illus.). 205p. 1980. 18.95 (ISBN 0-87938-060-8). Motorbooks Intl.

Pontius Pilate, Vol. 2. Charles Babb. 1981. 9.75 (ISBN 0-8062-1564-X). Carlton.

Pontius Pilate Papers. Warren Kiefer. 1977. pap 1.95 o.s.i. (ISBN 0-515-04441-5). Jove Pubns.

Pontius the Pilot. W. C. Chalk. 1971. pap. text ed. 2.95x o.p. (ISBN 0-435-11194-9). Heinemann Ed.

Pontormo's Diary. Rosemary Mayer. (Illus.). 200p. 1981. pap. price not set (ISBN 0-915570-17-3). Oolp Pr.

Pontryagin Duality & the Structure of Locally Compact Abelian Groups. S. A. Morris. LC 76-53519. (London Mathematical Society Lecture Note Ser.: No. 29). 1977. 16.95x (ISBN 0-521-21543-9). Cambridge U Pr.

Pony Birthday Book. Norman Thelwell. (Illus.). 192p. 1979. 6.95 (ISBN 0-684-16235-0). Scribner.

Pony Called Lightning. Miriam E. Mason. (gr. 2-4). 1948. 3.95g o.s.i. (ISBN 0-02-764820-6). Macmillan.

Pony Care. Jay Swallow. (Illus.). 128p. 1976. 9.50 o.p. (ISBN 0-04-636009-3). Allen Unwin.

Pony Club Book. James K. Lewis. LC 79-87794. (Illus.). 128p. 1981. 8.95 (ISBN 0-498-02257-9). A S Barnes.

Pony Express. Samuel H. Adams. (Landmark Ser.: No. 7). (Illus.). (gr. 4-6). 1950. PLB 5.99 (ISBN 0-394-90307-2, BYR). Random.

Pony Express. Fred Reinfeld. LC 64-21330. (Illus.). 127p. 1973. pap. 2.95 (ISBN 0-8032-5786-4, BB 572, Bison). U of Nebr Pr.

Pony Express, Carry My Message. Rudolph Mellard. (Illus.). 1979. 15.00. A Jones.

Pony Express War. Gary McCarthy. 176p. 1980. pap. 1.75 (ISBN 0-553-14185-6). Bantam.

Pony for Linda. Clarence W. Anderson. (Illus.). (gr. k-3). 1951. 7.95 (ISBN 0-02-705050-5). Macmillan.

Pony for the Winter. Helen Kay. (gr. 2-3). pap. 1.25 (ISBN 0-590-08082-2, Schol Pap). Schol Bk Serv.

Pony for Three. Clarence W. Anderson. (Illus.). (gr. 1-3). 1958. 7.95 (ISBN 0-02-705160-9). Macmillan.

Pony Owner's Encyclopedia. C. E. Hope & G. N. Jackson. 1975. 10.95 (ISBN 0-7207-0848-6, Pub. by Michael Joseph). Merrimack Bk Serv.

Pony Problem. Barbara Holland. (gr. 4-7). 1977. PLB 6.95 (ISBN 0-525-37345-4). Dutton.

Pony Riders Book. George Wheatley. 1970. 7.50x (ISBN 0-87556-407-0). Saifer.

Pony Tracks. Frederick Remington. (Western Frontier Library: No. 19). (Illus.). 1977. 6.95 (ISBN 0-8061-0499-6); pap. 3.95 (ISBN 0-8061-1248-4). U of Okla Pr.

Pony Trekking. Glenda Spooner. (Illus.). pap. 4.35 (ISBN 0-85131-246-2, Dist. by Sporting Book Center). J A Allen.

Poodle Guide. Lockwood & Sheldon. 6.98 o.p. (ISBN 0-385-01598-4). Doubleday.

Poodle Handbook. Ernest H. Hart. 7.95 (ISBN 0-87666-359-5, H924). TFH Pubns.

Pooh & Piglet's Book of Big & Little. Walt Disney Studio. (Golden Story Book Ser.). (Illus.). (gr. k-3). 1979. PLB 9.15 (ISBN 0-307-62368-8, Golden Pr); pap. 1.95 (ISBN 0-307-12368-5). Western Pub.

Pooh Craft Book. Carol Friedrichson. (Illus.). (gr. 4 up). 1976. 6.95 o.p. (ISBN 0-525-37410-8). Dutton.

Pooh Sleepytime Stories. Walt Disney Studio. (Golden Story Book Ser.). (Illus.). (gr. k-3). 1979. PLB 9.15 (ISBN 0-307-63735-2, Golden Pr); pap. 3.95 (ISBN 0-307-13735-X). Western Pub.

Pool of Dreams. Lucy Walker. 1973. pap. 0.95 o.p. (ISBN 0-345-26518-1). Ballantine.

Pool of Fire. John Christopher. LC 68-23062. (gr. 5-7). 1968. 8.95 (ISBN 0-02-718350-5). Macmillan.

Pool of Tears. John Wainwright. 1977. 7.95 o.p. (ISBN 0-312-63008-5). St Martin.

Pool Simplified--Somewhat. George Fels. LC 77-23697. 1978. 7.95 (ISBN 0-8092-7771-9); pap. 4.95 o.p. (ISBN 0-8092-7770-0). Contemp Bks.

Pooled Data for Financial Markets. Terry E. Dielman. Ed. by Gunter Dufey. (Research for Business Decisions). 148p. 1980. 24.95 (ISBN 0-8357-1130-7, Pub. by UMI Res Pr). Univ Microfilms.

Poole's Index to Periodical Literature. Incl. Vol. 1. 1802-1881, 2 pts (ISBN 0-8446-1353-3); Vol. 2. 1882-1887 (1st Suppl. (ISBN 0-8446-1354-1); Vol. 3. 1887-1892 (2nd Suppl. (ISBN 0-8446-1355-X); Vol. 4. 1892-1896 (3rd Suppl. (ISBN 0-8446-1356-8); Vol. 5. 1897-1902 (4th Suppl. (ISBN 0-8446-1357-6); Vol. 6. 1902-1906 (5th Suppl. (ISBN 0-8446-1358-4). 30.00 ea.; Set. 210.00 (ISBN 0-8446-5695-X). Peter Smith.

Poop & Other Poems. Gerald Locklin. 1980. 3.00 (ISBN 0-917554-13-2). Maelstrom.

Poor & the Church. Norbert Greinacher. Ed. by Alois Muller. (Concilium Ser: Vol. 104). 1978. pap. 4.95 (ISBN 0-8164-2147-1). Crossroad NY.

Poor & the Poorest. Brian Abel-Smith. 78p. 1965. pap. text ed. 5.00x (Pub. by Bedford England). Renouf.

Poor Doubting Christian Drawn to Christ. Thomas Hooker. (Summit Bks). 168p. 1981. pap. 2.95 (ISBN 0-8010-4246-1). Baker Bk.

Poor Elizabeth's Almanac. Elizabeth Fuller. 1980. pap. 2.25 (ISBN 0-425-04603-6). Berkley Pub.

Poor Fellow My Country. Xavier Herbert. 1466p. 1980. 17.95 (ISBN 0-312-63015-8). St Martin.

Poor Folk. Fedor Dostoyevsky. Tr. by C. J. Hogarth. Incl. Gambler. 1956. 6.00x (ISBN 0-460-00711-4, Evman); pap. 5.95 (ISBN 0-460-01711-X, Evman). Dutton.

Poor Law, 30 vols. (British Parliamentary Papers Ser.). 1973. Set. 2421.00x (ISBN 0-7165-1457-5, Pub. by Irish Academic Pr Ireland). Biblio Dist.

Poor Law: The English Citizen: His Rights & Responsibilities. T. W. Fowle. vi, 175p. 1980. Repr. of 1893 ed. lib. bdg. 17.50x (ISBN 0-8377-0534-7). Rothman.

Poor Little Rich Girl. Eleanor Gates. LC 75-32203. (Classics of Children's Literature, 1621-1932: Vol. 64). (Illus.). 1976. Repr. of 1912 ed. PLB 38.00 (ISBN 0-8240-2313-7). Garland Pub.

Poor Little Rich King. LC 73-87128. (Illus.). 96p. (Orig.). (gr. 1-3). 1973. pap. 1.25 o.p. (ISBN 0-912692-26-X). Cook.

Poor Man's Route to Rich Man's Stock Market Wealth. Jordan Levenson. 120p. 1980. pap. 18.00x (ISBN 0-914442-08-2). Levenson Pr.

Poor Mouth: A Bad Story About the Hard Life. Flann O'Brien. Tr. by Patrick Power from Gaelic. LC 80-54558. (Illus.). 128p. 1981. pap. 4.95 (ISBN 0-394-17849-1). Seaver Bks.

Poor No More. Robert C. Ruark. 1978. pap. 2.50 o.p. (ISBN 0-449-23218-2, Crest). Fawcett.

Poor of the Earth. John Cole. LC 75-46616. 1976. 22.00x (ISBN 0-89158-538-9). Westview.

Poor Parents: Social Policy & the Cycle of Deprivation. Bill Jordan. 1974. 15.00 (ISBN 0-7100-7852-8); pap. 8.95 (ISBN 0-7100-7853-6). Routledge & Kegan.

Poor Pay More: Consumer Practices of Low Income Families. David Caplovitz. LC 63-18312. 1967. pap. text ed. 7.95 (ISBN 0-02-905250-5). Free Pr.

Poor Richard. James Daugherty. (Illus.). (gr. 9 up). 1941. 6.50 o.p. (ISBN 0-670-56450-8). Viking Pr.

Poor Richard's Politicks: Benjamin Franklin & His New American Order. Paul W. Conner. LC 80-21490. xiv, 285p. 1980. Repr. of 1965 ed. lib. bdg. 27.50x (ISBN 0-313-22695-4, COPRP). Greenwood.

Poore Orphans Court. LC 72-6025. (English Experience Ser.: No. 551). 1973. Repr. of 1636 ed. 6.00 (ISBN 90-221-0551-2). Walter J Johnson.

Poore Vicars Plea. Declaring That a Competencie of Means Is Due to Them Out of the Tithes..Notwithstanding the Impropriations. Thomas Ryves. LC 79-84135. (English Experience Ser.: No. 953). 164p. 1979. Repr. of 1620 ed. lib. bdg. 17.00 (ISBN 90-221-0953-4). Walter J Johnson.

Poorhouse Fair. John Updike. 1977. pap. 1.50 o.p. (ISBN 0-449-23314-6, Crest). Fawcett.

Poorhouse Waif & His Divine Teacher. Isabel Byrum. 223p. pap. 2.00. Faith Pub Hse.

Pop. S. Wilson. LC 77-80183. (Modern Movements in Art Ser.). 1978. pap. 1.95 (ISBN 0-8120-0883-9). Barron.

Pop Art. Lucy R. Lippard. (World of Art Ser.). (Illus.). 1966. pap. text ed. 9.95 (ISBN 0-19-519937-5). Oxford U Pr.

Pop Art in School. Florian Merz. 1970. 16.95 (ISBN 0-7134-2288-2, Pub. by Batsford England). David & Charles.

Pop Culture Tradition. Edward M. White. 240p. (Orig.). 1972. pap. text ed. 4.95x (ISBN 0-393-09969-5). Norton.

Pop Music in School. 2nd ed. Ed. by Graham Vulliamy & Ed Lee. LC 79-7708. (Resources of Music Ser.: No. 13). (Illus.). 1980. 22.95 (ISBN 0-521-22930-8); pap. 8.95x (ISBN 0-521-29727-3). Cambridge U Pr.

Pop-Rock Crossword Puzzles. Dean Spotts. (gr. 7-12). 1972. pap. 0.95 o.p. (ISBN 0-590-04490-7, Schol Pap). Schol Bk Serv.

Pop-Rock Question & Answer Book. Ed. by David Dachs. (YA) (gr. 7-12). 1977. pap. 1.25 (ISBN 0-590-11893-5, Schol Pap). Schol Bk Serv.

Pop-up Aladdin & the Wonderful Lamp. Ed. by Albert G. Miller. (Pop-up Classics Ser.: No. 7). (Illus.). 1970. 3.95 o.p. (ISBN 0-394-81105-4, BYR). Random.

Pop-up Books. Larry Shapiro. Incl. Pop-up Colors. (ISBN 0-525-61594-6); Pop-up Numbers. (ISBN 0-525-61591-1); Pop-up Opposites. (ISBN 0-525-61593-8); Pop-Up Shapes (ISBN 0-525-61592-X). (Illus.). (gr. 3-7). 1979. 2.95 ea. (Pub. by Gingerbread Bks.). Dutton.

Pop-up Hide & Seek: A Child's First Counting Book. Ed. by Albert G. Miller. (Pop-up Books Ser). (Illus.). (ps). 1966. 4.95 o.p. (ISBN 0-394-81590-4, BYR). Random.

Pop-up Story of the Nativity. Ed. by Albert G. Miller. (Pop-up Books Ser). (Illus.). 1970. 3.95 o.p. (ISBN 0-394-80498-8, BYR). Random.

Popcorn. Millicent E. Selsam. (Illus.). (gr. 2-5). 1976. 7.25 (ISBN 0-688-22083-5); PLB 6.96 (ISBN 0-688-32083-X). Morrow.

Popcorn Book. Tomie De Paola. (gr. k-3). 1979. pap. 1.50 (ISBN 0-590-03142-2, Schol Pap). Schol Bk Serv.

Popcorn Cookery. Larry Kusche. LC 77-83276. 1977. pap. 7.95 (ISBN 0-912656-62-X). H P Bks.

Popcorn Dragon. Jane Thayer. (Illus.). (ps-3). 1953. PLB 6.48 (ISBN 0-688-31630-1). Morrow.

Pope Alexander III & the Council of Tours (1163) A Study of Ecclesiastical Politics & Institutions in the Twelfth Century. Robert Somerville. (UCLA Center for Medieval & Renaissance Studies: Vol. 12). 1978. 14.50x (ISBN 0-520-03184-9). U of Cal Pr.

Pope & Human Nature. Geoffrey Tillotson. 1958. 19.50x (ISBN 0-19-811581-4). Oxford U Pr.

Pope John Paul II in America. Lucius Annese. LC 79-56497. (Orig.). 1980. 10.00 (ISBN 0-933402-10-4); pap. 4.95 (ISBN 0-933402-09-0). Charisma Pr.

Pope John Twenty Third: The Good Shepherd. Jeanette Struchen. LC 73-79671. (Biography Ser). (gr. 7 up). 1969. PLB 6.90 (ISBN 0-531-00951-3). Watts.

Pope Pius IX. Frank J. Coppa. (World Leaders Ser.: No. 81). 1979. lib. bdg. 14.95 (ISBN 0-8057-7727-X). Twayne.

Pope, the Council, & the Mass. James Likoudis & K. D. Whitehead. 1981. 14.95 (ISBN 0-8158-0400-8). Chris Mass.

Pope: The Critical Heritage. Ed. by John Barnard. (Critical Heritage Ser). 550p. 1973. 42.00x (ISBN 0-7100-7390-9). Routledge & Kegan.

Pope: The Rape of the Lock. Ed. by John D. Hunt. (Casebook Ser.). 1970. 2.50 o.s.i. (ISBN 0-87695-045-4). Aurora Pubs.

Popeiana, 25 vols. Incl. Vol. 1. Early Criticism, Seventeen Eleven to Seventeen Sixteen (ISBN 0-8240-1239-9); Vol. 2. Pope's Homer, One (ISBN 0-8240-1240-2); Vol. 3. Pope's Homer, Two (ISBN 0-8240-1241-0); Vol. 4. On Literary Farces (ISBN 0-8240-1242-9); Vol. 5. Pope's Shakespeare (ISBN 0-8240-1243-7); Vol. 6. Dunciad, One. Repr. of 1728 ed (ISBN 0-8240-1244-5); Vol. 7. Dunciad, Two. Repr. of 1728 ed (ISBN 0-8240-1245-3); Vol. 8. Dunciad, Three. Repr. of 1729 ed (ISBN 0-8240-1246-1); Vol. 9. Attack of Thomas Cooke (ISBN 0-8240-1247-X); Vol. 10. Dunciad & Other Matters. Repr. of 1730 ed (ISBN 0-8240-1248-8); Vol. 11. On Taste, Seventeen Thirty-Two to Seventeen Thirty-Five (ISBN 0-8240-1249-6); Vol. 12. Essay on Man, Crousaz (ISBN 0-8240-1250-X); Vol. 13. Essay on Man, Crousaz Two (ISBN 0-8240-1251-8); Vol. 14. Essay on Man, Warburton, Etc (ISBN 0-8240-1252-6); Vol. 15. Cibber & the Dunciad (ISBN 0-8240-1253-4); Vol. 16. Dunciad. Repr. of 1742 ed (ISBN 0-8240-1254-2); Vol. 17. Pope's Death & the Critical Aftermath (ISBN 0-8240-1255-0); Vols. 18-19. Warton on Pope (ISBN 0-8240-1256-9); Vols. 20-21. Biography (ISBN 0-8240-1257-7); Vol. 22. Biography (ISBN 0-8240-1258-5); Vol. 23. Biography (ISBN 0-8240-1259-3); Vol. 24. Biography (ISBN 0-8240-1260-7); Vol. 25. Folio Verse: Attacks, Defences, & Imitations (ISBN 0-8240-1261-5). (Life & Times of Seven Major British Writers Ser). 1974. lib. bdg. 47.00 ea. Garland Pub.

Popery & Politics in England, 1660-1688. J. Miller. LC 73-79306. (Illus.). 278p. 1973. 41.50 (ISBN 0-521-20236-1). Cambridge U Pr.

Popes & Princes Fourteen Seventeen to Fifteen Seventeen: Politics & Polity in Late Medieval Church. J. A. Thomson. (Early Modern Europe Today Ser.). 256p. 1980. text ed. 19.50x (ISBN 0-04-901027-1, 2546). Allen Unwin.

Popes & the Papacy in the Early Middle Ages, 476-752. Jeffrey Richards. 1979. 40.00 (ISBN 0-7100-0098-7). Routledge & Kegan.

Pope's Once & Future Kings: Satire & Politics in the Early Career. John M. Aden. LC 78-16618. 1978. 14.00x (ISBN 0-87049-252-7). U of Tenn Pr.

Popes Through the Ages. 3rd rev. ed. Joseph S. Brusher. (Illus.). 530p. 1980. 30.00 (ISBN 0-89141-110-0, Neff-Kane). Presidio Pr.

Popeye: A Photo-Storybook Based on the Movie. Adapted by Stephanie Spinner. LC 80-623. (Movie Storybooks Ser.). (Illus.). 64p. (gr. 6-9). 1981. PLB 6.99 (ISBN 0-394-94668-5); pap. 5.95 boards (ISBN 0-394-84668-0). Random.

Popeye: A Pop-up Book. Ib Penick. LC 80-52840. (Pop-up Bks.: No. 42). (Illus.). 16p. (ps-3). 1981. pap. 4.95 boards (ISBN 0-394-84584-6). Random.

Popeye & His Pals Stay in Shape. Bill Pearson. Ed. by Philip Mann. (Shape Board Play Book). (Illus.). 14p. (gr. k-3). 1980. bds. 2.95 comb bdg. (ISBN 0-89828-125-3, 6007). Tuffy Bks.

Popeye Mix or Match Storybook. Illus. by George Wildman. LC 80-52869. (Mix or Match Ser.). (Illus.). 9p. (ps-3). 1981. spiral wire 3.50 (ISBN 0-394-84585-4). Random.

Popeye Story. Bridget Terry. 1980. pap. 2.75 (ISBN 0-440-06561-5). Dell.

Popinjay Stairs: An Historical Adventure About Samuel Pepys. Geoffrey Trease. LC 74-30873. (gr. 3-6). Date not set. 5.95 (ISBN 0-8149-0758-X). Vanguard. Postponed.

Poplars & Willows. (Forestry Ser.: No. 10). 328p. 1958. pap. 36.75 (ISBN 92-5-100500-1, F2046, FAO). Unipub.

Popo. Rosser Reeves. LC 79-56380. (Illus.). 196p. 1980. 10.00 (ISBN 0-8149-0838-1). Vanguard.

Popol Vuh: The Sacred Book of the Ancient Quiche: Spanish Version of the Original Maya. Tr. by Adrian Recinos & Delia Goetz. (Civilization of the American Indian Ser.: No. 29). (Eng). 1978. Repr. of 1950 ed. 9.95 (ISBN 0-8061-0205-5). U of Okla Pr.

Popper & After: Four Modern Irrationalists. David Stove. 192p. 1981. 20.50 (ISBN 0-08-026792-0); pap. 10.75 (ISBN 0-08-026791-2). Pergamon.

Poppy. Linda Dubreuil. 1976. pap. 1.50 o.p. (ISBN 0-685-69146-2, LB357ZK, Leisure Bks). Nordon Pubns.

Poppy & the Outdoors Cat. Dorothy Haas. Ed. by Kathleen Tucker. (Illus.). 100p. (gr. 2-5). 1981. 5.95g (ISBN 0-8075-6621-7). A Whitman.

Poppy Seeds. Clyde R. Bulla. LC 55-5835. (Illus.). (gr. k-3). 1955. 8.95 (ISBN 0-690-64856-1, TYC-J). T Y Crowell.

Popski's Private Army. Vladimir Peniakoff. 368p. 1980. pap. 2.50 (ISBN 0-553-13048-X). Bantam.

Popular Abstracts. Ray B. Browne. 1978. 12.95 (ISBN 0-87972-166-9); pap. 6.95 (ISBN 0-87972-165-0). Bowling Green Univ.

Popular American Composers. Ed. by David Ewen. (Illus.). 1962. 9.00 (ISBN 0-8242-0040-3). Wilson.

Popular & the Political: Essays on Socialism in the 1980's. Ed. by Mike Prior. 220p. 1981. pap. price not set (ISBN 0-7100-0627-6). Routledge & Kegan.

Popular Appeal in English Drama to Eighteen Fifty. Peter Davison. LC 79-55528. 1981. text ed. 26.00x (ISBN 0-06-491618-9). B&N.

Popular Architecture. Marshall Fishwick. 1975. pap. 2.50 (ISBN 0-87972-164-2). Bowling Green Univ.

Popular Belief & Practice. Ed. by G. J. Cuming & Derek Baker. LC 77-155583. (Studies in Church History: Vol. 8). 1972. 47.50 (ISBN 0-521-08220-X). Cambridge U Pr.

Popular Biographies Master Index. Ed. by Annie Brewer. (Gale Biographical Index Ser.: No. 8). 1000p. 1980. write for info. (ISBN 0-8103-1076-7). Gale.

Popular Book: A History of America's Literary Taste. James D. Hart. 1950. pap. 4.95 (ISBN 0-520-00538-4, CAL49). U of Cal Pr.

Popular Careers. Marilyn Funes & Alan Lazarus. Ed. by Benjamin Piltch. 64p. (gr. 5-12). 1980. wkbk 3.50 (ISBN 0-934618-01-1). Skyview Pub.

Popular Christianity & the Early Theologians. H. J. Carpenter. Ed. by Clarence L. Lee. LC 66-12387. (Orig.). 1966. pap. 1.00 (ISBN 0-8006-3025-4, 1-3025). Fortress.

Popular Commencement Book. Effa E. Preston. LC 70-175776. 434p. 1975. Repr. of 1931 ed. 20.00 (ISBN 0-8103-4034-8). Gale.

Popular Consent & Popular Control: Whig Political Theory in the Early State Constitutions. Donald S. Lutz. LC 78-17876. (Illus.). 1980. 21.50x (ISBN 0-8071-0596-1). La State U Pr.

Popular Culture in Early Modern Europe. Peter Burke. 1978. pap. 7.95x (ISBN 0-06-131928-7, TB 1928, Torch). Har-Row.

Popular Disturbances in Scotland, 1780-1815. Kenneth J. Logue. (Illus.). 1979. text ed. 21.00x (ISBN 0-85976-037-5). Humanities.

Popular Education & Democratic Thought in America. Rush Welter. LC 62-19909. 1963. 25.00x (ISBN 0-231-02560-2); pap. 12.50x (ISBN 0-231-08563-X). Columbia U Pr.

Popular Election of United States Senators. J. Haynes. Bd. with Local Government in the South & Southwest. E. W. Bemis. 1973. Repr. of 1893 ed. pap. 10.00 (ISBN 0-384-03886-7). Johnson Repr.

Popular Entertainments. Corner. pap. write for info. (ISBN 0-914162-56-X). Knowles.

Popular Fallacies, a Book of Common Errors: Explained & Corrected with Copious References to Authorities. 4th ed. A. S. Ackermann. LC 79-121184. 1970. Repr. of 1950 ed. 38.00 (ISBN 0-8103-3295-7). Gale.

Popular Fly Patterns. Terry Hellekson. LC 76-49452. (Illus.). 1975. 15.95 o.p. (ISBN 0-87905-066-7); pap. 10.95 (ISBN 0-87905-065-9). Peregrine Smith.

Popular French Romanticism: Authors, Readers, & Books in the Nineteenth Century. James S. Allen. LC 80-27129. (Illus.). 304p. 1981. 20.00x (ISBN 0-8156-2232-5). Syracuse U Pr.

Popular French Romanticism: Authors, Readers, & Books in the 19th Century. James S. Allen. (Illus.). 1980. 20.00 (ISBN 0-8156-2232-5). Syracuse U Pr.

Popular Guide to Government Publications. 4th ed. W. Philip Leidy. LC 76-17803. 384p. 1976. 27.50x (ISBN 0-231-04019-9). Columbia U Pr.

Popular Guide to New Testament Criticism. H. P. Hamann. 1977. pap. 3.50 (ISBN 0-570-03760-3, 12-2671). Concordia.

Popular Guide to the Preserved Steam Railways of Britain. Colin Garratt. (Illus.). 1979. 12.95 (ISBN 0-7137-0978-2, Pub by Blandford Pr England). Sterling.

Popular Lectures on Mathematical Logic. Wang Hao. 286p. 1981. text ed. 24.95 (ISBN 0-442-23109-1). Van Nos Reinhold.

Popular Literature: Poe's Not So Soon Forgotten Lore. J. Lasley Dameron. Ed. by Averil J. Kadis. 1980. pap. 2.50 (ISBN 0-910556-16-4). Enoch Pratt.

Popular Management & Pay in China. Roberto M. Bernardo. 1977. pap. text ed. 8.00x (ISBN 0-8248-0741-3). U Pr of Hawaii.

Popular Mechanics Complete Car Repair. 336p. 1978. pap. 5.95 (ISBN 0-380-01902-7, 49726). Avon.

Popular Mood of Pre-Civil War America. Lewis O. Saum. LC 79-8281. (Contributions in American History: No. 46). xxiv, 336p. 1980. lib. bdg. 29.95 (ISBN 0-313-21056-X, SPM/). Greenwood.

Popular Movement for Law Reform 1640-1660. Donald Veall. 1970. 12.50x o.p. (ISBN 0-19-825191-2). Oxford U Pr.

Popular Music Periodicals Index: 1973. Dean Tudor & Nancy Tudor. LC 74-11578. 1974. 14.50 (ISBN 0-8108-0763-7). Scarecrow.

Popular Music Periodicals Index, 1974. Dean Tudor & Andrew Armitage. LC 74-11578. 1975. 18.00 (ISBN 0-8108-0867-6). Scarecrow.

Popular Music Periodicals Index, 1975. Compiled by Dean Tudor & Andrew D. Armitage. LC 74-11578. 376p. 1976. 18.00 (ISBN 0-8108-0927-3). Scarecrow.

Popular Music Periodicals Index, 1976. Dean Tudor & Linda Biesenthal. LC 74-11578. 1977. 12.00 (ISBN 0-8108-1079-4). Scarecrow.

Popular Novel in England, 1770-1800. J. M. Tompkins. LC 32-24699. 1961. pap. 4.95x (ISBN 0-8032-5201-3, BB 121, Bison). U of Nebr Pr.

Popular Questions Answered. George W. Stimpson. LC 74-109601. 1970. Repr. of 1930 ed. 26.00 (ISBN 0-8103-3859-9). Gale.

Popular Recreations in English Society: Seventeen Hundred to Eighteen Fifty. Robert W. Malcolmson. LC 72-91958. (Illus.). 1980. pap. 10.50 (ISBN 0-521-29595-5). Cambridge U Pr.

Popular Recreations in English Society, 1700-1850. R. W. Malcolmson. LC 72-91958. (Illus.). 300p. 1973. 29.95 (ISBN 0-521-20147-0). Cambridge U Pr.

Popular Religions in America. Peter W. Williams. (P-H Studies on Religions Ser.). 1980. pap. text ed. 9.95 (ISBN 0-13-686113-X). P-H.

Popular Rhymes & Nursery Tales. James O. Halliwell-Phillipps. LC 68-23470. 1968. Repr. of 1849 ed. 18.00 (ISBN 0-8103-3484-4). Gale.

Popular Rhymes of Scotland. Robert Chambers. LC 68-58902. 1969. Repr. of 1870 ed. 18.00 (ISBN 0-8103-3828-9). Gale.

Popular Science Guide to Ingenious Devices. Herbert Shuldner. Ed. by Herbert Michaelman. Date not set. 12.95 (ISBN 0-517-54280-3, Michelman Books). Crown.

Popular Song Index. Patricia P. Havlice. LC 75-9896. 1975. 35.00 (ISBN 0-8108-0820-X). Scarecrow.

Popular Song Index: First Supplement. Patricia P. Havlice. LC 77-25219. 1978. 18.00 (ISBN 0-8108-1099-9). Scarecrow.

Popular Staffordshire Pottery. David Sekers. (Folio Miniature Ser.). (Illus.). 1978. 6.95 (ISBN 0-7181-1590-2, Pub. by Michael Joseph). Merrimack Bk Serv.

Popular Stars. Benjamin Piltch. 64p. (gr. 3-7). 1980. 3.50 (ISBN 0-934618-02-X). Skyview Pub.

Popular Superstitions. Charles Platt. LC 70-167114. 244p. 1973. Repr. of 1925 ed. 24.00 (ISBN 0-8103-3170-5). Gale.

Popular Survey of the Old Testament. Norman L. Geisler. LC 77-78578. 1977. pap. 7.95 (ISBN 0-8010-3684-4). Baker Bk.

Popular Tales & Fictions, Their Migrations & Transformations, 2 Vols. William A. Clouston. LC 67-23920. 1968. Repr. of 1887 ed. Set. 54.00 (ISBN 0-8103-3460-7). Gale.

Popular Tales from the Norse: With an Introductory Essay on the Origin & Diffusion of Popular Tales. 3rd ed. George W. Dasent. LC 74-136733. clii, 443p. 1971. Repr. of 1888 ed. 20.00 (ISBN 0-8103-3796-7). Gale.

Popular Tales of the West Highlands, 4 Vols. John F. Campbell. LC 67-23921. 1969. Repr. of 1890 ed. 92.00 (ISBN 0-8103-3458-5). Gale.

Popular Titles & Subtitles of Musical Compositions. 2nd ed. Freda P. Berkowitz. LC 75-4751. 217p. 1975. 10.00 (ISBN 0-8108-0806-4). Scarecrow.

Popular Tribunals, 2 vols. Hubert H. Bancroft. LC 67-29422. (Works of Hubert Howe Bancroft Ser.). 1967. Repr. of 1888 ed. 50.00x (ISBN 0-914888-39-0). Bancroft Pr.

Popular Tube-Transistor Substitution Guide. TAB Editorial Staff. LC 74-105968. (Illus.). 1971. pap. 3.95 (ISBN 0-8306-0570-3, 570). TAB Bks.

Popular Yoga Asanas. Swami Kuvalayananda. LC 76-130420. (Illus.). (gr. 9 up). 1972. Repr. of 1931 ed. 12.50 (ISBN 0-8048-0673-X). C E Tuttle.

Population. I. Bowen. (Cambridge Economic Handbook Ser.). 1954. pap. 10.95x (ISBN 0-521-08753-8). Cambridge U Pr.

Population. rev. ed. R. K. Kelsall. (Aspects of Modern Sociology, the Social Structure of Modern Britain Ser). 1967. text ed. 4.25x (ISBN 0-582-48771-4); pap. text ed. 3.00x (ISBN 0-582-48709-9). Humanities.

Population. David Killingray. Ed. by Edmund O'Connor. (World History Ser.). (Illus.). 32p. (gr. 10). 1980. Repr. of 1977 ed. lib. bdg. 5.95 (ISBN 0-89908-141-X); pap. text ed. 1.95 (ISBN 0-89908-116-9). Greenhaven.

Population. Robert J. Lowenherz. Ed. by Gene Liberty. LC 74-104928. (Creative Understanding Bks). (Illus.). (gr. 5-9). 1970. PLB 7.95 (ISBN 0-87191-042-X). Creative Ed.

Population, 25 vols. (British Parliamentary Papers Ser.). 1971. Set. 2142.00x (ISBN 0-7165-1497-4, Pub. by Irish Academic Pr Ireland). Biblio Dist.

Population Activist's Handbook. Population Institute. (Illus.). 192p. 1974. pap. 4.95 o.s.i. (ISBN 0-02-053270-9, Collier). Macmillan.

Population Activist's Handbook. Population Institute. LC 73-21298. (Illus.). 192p. 1974. 8.95 o.s.i. (ISBN 0-02-598350-4). Macmillan.

Population: An Introduction to Concepts & Issues. John R. Weeks. 1978. text ed. 17.95x (ISBN 0-534-00549-7). Wadsworth Pub.

Population Analysis in Geography. Robert Woods. (Illus.). 1979. pap. text ed. 15.95x (ISBN 0-582-48696-3). Longman.

Population & Economic Development. Yves Bizien. LC 78-19768. 202p. 1979. 22.95 (ISBN 0-03-048896-6). Praeger.

Population & Emigration in Nineteenth Century Britain. D. V. Glass & P. A. Taylor. (Commentaries on British Parlimentary Papers). 132p. 1976. 15.00x (ISBN 0-7165-2219-5, Pub. by Irish Academic Pr Ireland). Biblio Dist.

Population & Family Planning Programs. 10th ed. Dorothy Nortman & Ellen Hofstatter. LC 80-52443. (Illus.). 96p. (Orig.). 1980. pap. 4.50 (ISBN 0-87834-041-6). Population Coun.

Population & Industrialization: The Evolution of a Concept & Its Practical Application. Ed. by N. L. Tranter. (Documents in Economic History Ser.). 1973. text ed. 15.75x (ISBN 0-7136-1310-6). Humanities.

Population & Its Problems. George V. Zito. LC 79-581. 1979. text ed. 22.95 (ISBN 0-87705-396-0); pap. text ed. 9.95 (ISBN 0-87705-414-2). Human Sci Pr.

Population & Its Problems: A Plain Man's Guide. Ed. by H. B. Parry. 432p. 1974. text ed. 34.95x (ISBN 0-19-857380-4). Oxford U Pr.

Population & Political Systems in Tropical Africa. Robert F. Stevenson. LC 68-11435. (Illus.). 1968. 17.50x (ISBN 0-231-03052-5). Columbia U Pr.

Population & Society in Norway, 1735-1865. Michael Drake. LC 69-14393. (Cambridge Studies in Economic History). (Illus.). 1969. 35.50 (ISBN 0-521-07319-7). Cambridge U Pr.

Population & Society in the Arab East. Gabriel Baer. Tr. by Hanna Szoke. LC 76-16835. (Illus.). 1976. Repr. of 1964 ed. lib. bdg. 21.25x (ISBN 0-8371-8963-2, BAPSA). Greenwood.

Population & Technological Change: A Study of Long-Term Trends. Ester Boserup. LC 80-21116. (Illus.). 1981. lib. bdg. 17.50x (ISBN 0-226-06673-8). U of Chicago Pr.

Population, Capital & Growth. Simon Kuznets. 1974. 14.95x (ISBN 0-393-05497-7). Norton.

Population Challenge: A Handbook for Non-Specialists. Johannes Overbeek. LC 76-5328. (Contributions in Sociology: No. 19). (Illus.). 224p. 1976. lib. bdg. 16.95 (ISBN 0-8371-8896-2, OPC/). Greenwood.

Population Change: A Case Study of Puerto Rico. (gr. 9-12). 1973. Sets Of 10 Plus Tchr's Guide. pap. text ed. 16.40 (ISBN 0-205-02546-3, 8125465); tchrs'. guide 4.80 (ISBN 0-205-02547-1, 8125473). Allyn.

Population Concepts in Home Management Courses. 1979. pap. 7.50 (ISBN 92-5-100847-7, F1965, FAO). Unipub.

Population Control by Social Behavior. Ed. by F. J. Ebling. D. M. Stoddart. LC 78-70352. 1978. 27.95 (ISBN 0-03-048981-4). Praeger.

Population Control for Zero Growth in Singapore. Saw S. Hock. 250p. 1981. 29.95 (ISBN 0-19-580430-9). Oxford U Pr.

Population Dispersal: A National Imperative. John Oosterbaan. LC 79-9672. 1980. 18.95 (ISBN 0-669-03615-3). Lexington Bks.

Population Dose Evaluation & Standards for Man & His Environment. (Illus.). 646p. (Orig.). 1975. pap. 54.25 (ISBN 92-0-020374-4, ISP375, IAEA). Unipub.

Population Dynamics & International Violence: Propositions, Insights & Evidence. Nazli Choucri. LC 74-11227. 1974. 22.95 (ISBN 0-669-94037-2). Lexington Bks.

Population Dynamics of the Waterbuck, Kobus ellipsiprymnus (Ogilby, 1833), in the Sabi-Sand Wildtuin. Harry J. Herbert. (Mammalia Depicta Ser.). (Illus.). 68p. (Orig.). 1972. pap. text ed. 20.00. Parey Sci Pubs.

Population Dynamics, Reproduction, & Activities of the Kangaroo Rat, Dipodomys ordii, in Western Texas. Herschel W. Garner. (Graduate Studies: No. 7). (Illus.). 28p. 1974. pap. 2.00 (ISBN 0-89672-014-4). Tex Tech Pr.

Population Dynamics: (the Twentieth Symposium of the British Ecological Society) Ed. by R. M. Anderson et al. 1980. 76.95x (ISBN 0-470-26816-6). Halsted Pr.

Population Ecology. Horace F. Quick. LC 73-19664. (Biological Sciences Curriculum Ser). 1974. pap. 4.95 (ISBN 0-672-63678-6). Pegasus.

Population Ecology of Cycles in Small Mammals: Mathematical Theory & Biological Fact. James P. Finerty. LC 79-23774. (Illus.). 1981. text ed. 18.50x (ISBN 0-300-02382-0). Yale U Pr.

Population Ecology, Water Relations & Social Behavior of a Southern California Semidesert Rodent Fauna. Richard E. MacMillen. (U. C. Publ. in Zoology: Vol. 71). 1964. pap. 4.50x (ISBN 0-520-09326-7). U of Cal Pr.

Population Economics. T. Paul Schulz. LC 80-36830. (Perspectives in Economics Ser.). 224p. 1981. pap. text ed. price not set (ISBN 0-201-08371-X). A-W.

Population Education: A Knowledge Base. Willard J. Jacobson. LC 78-13398. 1979. text ed. 15.95 (ISBN 0-8077-2533-1). Tchrs Coll.

Population, Education, & Children's Futures. Robert M. Bjork & Stewart E. Fraser. LC 80-82683. (Fastback Ser.: No. 150). (Orig.). 1980. pap. 0.75 (ISBN 0-87367-150-3). Phi Delta Kappa.

Population Education Workshop Proceedings. 62p. 1974. 2.75. Natl Cath Educ.

Population, Employment, & Inequality: The Bachue Model Applied to the Philippines. Gerry Rodgers et al. LC 78-60535. (Praeger Special Studies). 1978. 28.95 (ISBN 0-03-047216-4). Praeger.

Population Energy Relationships of the Agrimi (Capra Aegagrus Cretica) on Theodorou Island, Greece. Nikolaos Papageorgiou. (Illus.). 56p. (Orig.). pap. text ed. 14.10 (ISBN 3-490-21518-4). Parey Sci Pubs.

Population, Environment & the Quality of Life. Ed. by P. G. Marden & D. Hodgson. LC 74-579. 328p. 1975. pap. 9.95 (ISBN 0-470-56868-2). Halsted Pr.

Population Environment Relations in Tropical Islands: The Case of Eastern Fiji. (MAB Technical Notes Ser.: No. 13). 233p. 1981. pap. 18.00 (ISBN 92-3-101821-3, U1054, UNESCO). Unipub.

Population, Evolution, & Birth Control: A Collage of Controversial Ideas. 2nd ed. Ed. by Garrett Hardin. LC 69-16921. (Biology Ser.). (Illus.). 1969. pap. text ed. 10.95x (ISBN 0-7167-0670-9). W H Freeman.

Population Explosion. C. W. Park. (Liberal Studies Ser.). 1965. pap. text ed. 3.00x o.p. (ISBN 0-435-46532-5). Heinemann Ed.

Population Factor in African Studies: Proceedings. African Studies Association of the United Kingdom, 1972. Ed. by R. P. Moss & R. J. Rathbone. 240p. 1975. text ed. 17.00 (ISBN 0-8419-6200-6). Holmes & Meier.

Population: Facts & Methods of Demography. Nathan Keyfitz & Wilhelm Flieger. LC 70-141154. (Illus.). 1971. text ed. 33.95x (ISBN 0-7167-0931-7). W H Freeman.

Population Fallacies. Jack Parsons. 1977. 14.95 o.p. (ISBN 0-301-74031-3, Pub. by Paul Elek); pap. 9.95 o.p. (ISBN 0-301-74032-1). Merrimack Bk Serv.

Population Genetics. J. S. Gale. LC 80-12675. (Tertiary Level Biology Ser.). 189p. 1980. 41.95x (ISBN 0-470-26970-7); pap. text ed. 19.95x (ISBN 0-470-26969-3). Halsted Pr.

Population Genetics & Evolution. Lawrence E. Mettler & Thomas G. Gregg. LC 69-16809. (Foundations of Modern Genetics Ser). (Illus.). 1969. pap. 10.95x ref. ed. (ISBN 0-13-685289-0). P-H.

Population Geography. 2nd ed. J. I. Clarke. LC 70-183339. 187p. 1972. text ed. 18.00 (ISBN 0-08-016853-1); pap. text ed. 7.75 (ISBN 0-08-016854-X). Pergamon.

Population Geography. H. R. Jones. 1981. text ed. 25.85 (ISBN 0-06-318188-6, Pub. by Har-Row Ltd England); pap. text ed. 13.10 (ISBN 0-06-318189-4). Har-Row.

Population Geography & Developing Countries. J. I. Clarke. 1971. 17.25 (ISBN 0-08-016445-5); pap. 7.75 (ISBN 0-08-016446-3). Pergamon.

Population Growth & Agrarian Change. D. B. Grigg. LC 79-4237. (Cambridge Geographical Studies: No. 13). 368p. 1981. 47.50 (ISBN 0-521-22760-7); pap. 17.95 (ISBN 0-521-29635-8). Cambridge U Pr.

Population Growth & Economic Development Since 1750. H. J. Habakkuk. 1971. pap. text ed. 3.75x (ISBN 0-391-00211-2, Leicester). Humanities.

Population Growth & Justice: An Examination of Moral Issues Raised by Population Growth. Ronald M. Green. LC 76-44233. (Harvard Dissertations in Religion). 1976. pap. 7.50 (ISBN 0-89130-099-6, 020105). Scholars Pr Ca.

Population Growth & the Complex Society. Sociological Resources for the Social Studies. (Readings in Sociology Ser.). (gr. 9-12). 1972. pap. text ed. 4.96 (ISBN 0-205-02577-3, 8125775). Allyn.

Population Growth & Urban Systems Development. G. A. Van Der Knaap. (Studies in Applied Regional Science: Vol. 18). 245p. 1980. lib. bdg. 16.00 (ISBN 0-89838-024-3, Martinus Nijhoff Pubs). Kluwer Boston.

Population Growth, Society & Culture: An Inventory of Cross-Culturally Tested Causal Hypotheses. Richard G. Sipes. LC 80-81242. (Comparative Studies Ser.). 1981. 12.00x (ISBN 0-87536-337-7); pap. 6.00 (ISBN 0-87536-338-5). HRAFP.

Population Growth: The Human Dilemma, An NSTA Environmental Materials Guide. Kathryn M. Fowler. 1977. pap. 3.50 (ISBN 0-87355-008-0). Natl Sci Tchrs.

Population Handbook: A Quick Guide to Population Dynamics for Journalists, Policymakers, Teachers, Students & Other People Interested in People. Arthur Haupt & Thomas T. Kane. LC 77-82142. (Illus.). 64p. 1978. 3.00 (ISBN 0-917136-02-0). Population Ref.

Population in Perspective. Ed. by Louise B. Young. 1968. pap. 8.95x (ISBN 0-19-501111-2). Oxford U Pr.

Population of Israel. Dov Friedlander & Calvin Goldscheider. 1979. 20.00x (ISBN 0-231-04572-7). Columbia U Pr.

Population of Latin America. Nicolas Sanchez-Albornoz. 1974. 28.50x (ISBN 0-520-01766-8); pap. 6.95x (ISBN 0-520-02745-0). U of Cal Pr.

Population of the California Indians 1769-1970. Sherburne F. Cook. LC 74-27287. 1976. 18.50x (ISBN 0-520-02923-2). U of Cal Pr.

Population of the Mixteca Alta, 1520-1960. Sherburne F. Cook & Woodrow Borah. (U. C. Publ in Ibero-Americana: Vol. 50). 1968. pap. 6.00x (ISBN 0-520-09203-1). U of Cal Pr.

Population of the South: Structure & Change in Social Demographic Context. Ed. by Dudley L. Poston, Jr. & Robert H. Weller. 288p. 1981. text ed. 25.00x (ISBN 0-292-76467-7). U of Tex Pr.

Population Patterns of Southwestern Michigan. Charles F. Heller et al. 1974. 5.00 (ISBN 0-932826-10-5). New Issues MI.

Population Perils. Ed. by George W. Forell & William H. Lazareth. LC 78-54548. (Justice Books Ser.). 64p. 1978. pap. 2.25 (ISBN 0-8006-1554-9, 1-1554). Fortress.

Population Policy Analysis. Ed. by Michael E. Kraft & Mark Schneider. LC 77-221. (Policy Studies Organization Ser.). 1978. 18.95 (ISBN 0-669-01456-7). Lexington Bks.

Population, Politics, & the Future of Southern Asia. Ed. by W. Howard Wriggins & James F. Guyot. 400p. 1973. 15.00x (ISBN 0-231-03756-2); pap. 7.00x (ISBN 0-231-03757-0). Columbia U Pr.

Population Pressure & Cultural Adjustment. Virginia Abernethy. LC 78-11676. 1979. 16.95 (ISBN 0-87705-329-4). Human Sci Pr.

Population Problems of the Age of Malthus. Grosvenor T. Griffith. LC 67-16350. Repr. of 1926 ed. 25.00x (ISBN 0-678-05054-6). Kelley.

Population, Public Policy, & Economic Development. Ed. by Michael C. Keeley. LC 75-23975. (Praeger Special Studies). 24.95 (ISBN 0-275-55670-0). Praeger.

Population: Quantity Versus Quality. Shirley F. Hartley. 352p. 1972. pap. text ed. 9.95 o.p. (ISBN 0-13-686600-X). P-H.

Population Redistribution & Public Policy. 1980. 13.00 (ISBN 0-309-02926-0). Natl Acad Pr.

Population Redistribution in the USSR: Its Impact on Society 1897-1977. Robert A. Lewis & Richard H. Rowland. LC 79-18076. (Praeger Special Studies Ser.). 510p. 1979. 41.50 (ISBN 0-03-050641-7). Praeger.

Population Reference Bureau's Population Handbook, in Arabic. Arthur Haupt & Thomas T. Kane. (Illus.). 80p. (Orig., Arabic.). 1980. pap. 3.00 (ISBN 0-917136-07-1). Population Ref.

Population Reference Bureau's Population Handbook: International Edition. Arthur Haupt & Thomas T. Kane. LC 79-9638. (Illus.). 80p. (Orig.). 1980. pap. 3.00 (ISBN 0-917136-04-7). Population Ref.

Population Since the Industrial Revolution: The Case of England & Wales. Neil L. Tranter. 1973. text ed. 10.50x (ISBN 0-85664-012-3). Humanities.

Population Strategy for the Nineteen Eighties: Health, Mortality, & Development. Davidson R. Gwatkin. 224p. 1981. write for info. Overseas Dev Council.

Population Structure & Human Variation. Ed. by G. A. Harrison. LC 76-22987. (International Biological Programme Ser.: No. 11). (Illus.). 1977. 72.00 (ISBN 0-521-21399-1). Cambridge U Pr.

Population: The Dynamics of Change. Charles B. Nam & Susan O. Gustavus. LC 75-31031. (Illus.). 352p. 1976. text ed. 16.75 (ISBN 0-395-20627-8). HM.

Population: un choix international: Approche multilaterale au probleme demographique. Rafael M. Salas. LC 71-11610. 1977. text ed. 26.00 (ISBN 0-08-021818-0); pap. text ed. 16.50 (ISBN 0-08-021819-9). Pergamon.

Populations De L'est-Aquitain Au Debut De L'epoque Contempoaine: Recherche Sur une Region Moins Developpee, 1845-1871. Andre Armengaud. (Societe, Mouvements Sociaux et Ideologis, Etudes: No. 3). 1961. pap. 51.20x (ISBN 90-2796-236-7). Mouton.

Populations: Experiments in Ecology. A. Harris Stone & Steven Collins. LC 72-2303. (Illus.). 96p. (gr. 5 up). 1973. 6.45 (ISBN 0-531-02579-9). Watts.

Populism: A Psychohistorical Perspective. James M. Youngdale. (National University Publications Ser. in American Studies). 1975. 17.50 (ISBN 0-8046-9102-9, Natl U). Kennikat.

Populism & Politics: William Alfred Peffer & the People's Party. Peter H. Argersinger. LC 73-86400. (Illus.). 352p. 1974. 20.00x (ISBN 0-8131-1306-7). U Pr of Ky.

Populism in Peru: The Emergence of the Masses & the Politics of Social Control. Steve Stein. LC 79-5415. (Illus.). 300p. 1980. 21.50 (ISBN 0-299-07990-2). U of Wis Pr.

Populism, Progressivism, & the Transformation of Nebraska Politics: 1885 - 1915. Robert W. Cherny. LC 80-11151. (Illus.). xviii, 227p. 1981. 17.50x (ISBN 0-8032-1407-3). U of Nebr Pr.

Populist Manifestos. Lawrence Ferlinghetti. LC 80-22105. 56p. 1981. pap. 3.95 (ISBN 0-912516-52-6). Grey Fox.

Populist Mind. Ed. by Norman Pollack. (Orig.). 1967. pap. 8.50 (ISBN 0-672-60076-5, AHS50). Bobbs.

Populist Mind. Ed. by Norman Pollack. LC 66-16752. 539p. 1967. text ed. 28.50x (ISBN 0-8290-0197-2). Irvington.

Populist Moment: A Short History of the Agrarian Revolt in America. Lawrence Goodwyn. 1978. pap. 6.95 (ISBN 0-19-502417-6, GB 536, GB). Oxford U Pr.

Populist Revolt: A History of the Farmers' Alliance & the People's Party. John D. Hicks. LC 61-7237. 1961. pap. 2.75x (ISBN 0-8032-5085-1, BB 111, Bison). U of Nebr Pr.

Por el Tunel De la Depresion. Tr. by Matilda Nordvedt. (Spanish Bks.). (Span.). 1979. 1.60 (ISBN 0-8297-0796-4). Life Pubs Intl.

Por Eso Me Gustas. Luis Salem. LC 77-17649. 78p. (Orig., Span.). 1978. pap. 1.95 (ISBN 0-89922-107-6). Edit Caribe.

Por Esta Cruz Te Matare. Tr. by Bruce Olson. (Spanish Bks.). (Span.). 1979. 1.90 (ISBN 0-8297-0592-9). Life Pubs Intl.

Por Esta Cruz Te Matarei. Tr. by Bruce Olson. (Portuguese Bks.). 1979. 1.40 (ISBN 0-8297-0797-2). Life Pubs Intl.

Por Fronteras Culturales. Anthony Papalia & Jose A. Mendoza. (Orig.). (gr. 11). 1976. pap. text ed. 6.25 (ISBN 0-87720-518-3). AMSCO Sch.

Por Que Esperar Hasta el Matrimonio? Evelyn M. Duval. Tr. by Pablo A. Deiros from Eng. Orig. Title: Why Wait till Marriage? 1979. pap. 2.25 (ISBN 0-311-46044-5, Edit Mundo). Casa Bautista.

Por Que, Senor? 1980. pap. 1.60 (ISBN 0-686-69362-0). Vida Pubs.

Por Sendas Biblicas. T. E. Quiros. 162p. (Span.). Date not set. pap. price not set (ISBN 0-311-08753-1). Casa Bautista.

Por Su Llaga. Tr. by Hugo Jeter. (Spanish Bks.). (Span.). 1978. 2.50 (ISBN 0-8297-0858-8). Life Pubs Intl.

Porcelain Marks of the World. Emanuel Poche. LC 73-92270. (Illus.). 256p. 1975. 6.95 o.p. (ISBN 0-668-03403-3). Arco.

Porcelain of Paris, 1770-1850. Regine P. De Guillebon. LC 72-80541. (Illus.). 376p. 1972. 35.00 o.s.i. (ISBN 0-8027-0395-X). Walker & Co.

Porcelain: Traditions & New Visions. Jan Azel & Karen McCready. 200p. 1981. 30.00 (ISBN 0-8230-4091-7). Watson-Guptill.

Porches & Patios. Time-Life Books Editors. (Home Repair & Improvement Ser). (Illus.). 128p. 1981. 10.95 (ISBN 0-8094-3474-1). Time-Life.

Porcupine Book of Verse. Clayton et al. (Illus.). 48p. (ps-2). 1974. 6.95 (ISBN 0-570-06995-5, 56-1186). Concordia.

Pork. Ed. by Time-Life Bks. (Good Cook Ser.). (Illus.). 176p. 1980. 12.95 (ISBN 0-8094-2875-X). Time-Life.

Porky Pig & Bugs Bunny - Just Like Magic. Stella Nathan. (Illus.). (ps-3). PLB 5.00 (ISBN 0-307-60146-3, Golden Pr). Western Pub.

Porno-Graphics: The Shame of Our Art Museums. Dan Greenburg. (Illus.). 1969. 2.95 o.p. (ISBN 0-394-42483-2). Random.

Pornography. John H. Court. Ed. by Klaus Bockmuehl. LC 80-7668. (World Evangelical Fellowship Outreach & Identity Theological Monograph: No. 5). 96p. (Orig.). 1980. pap. 2.95 (ISBN 0-87784-494-1). Inter-Varsity.

Pornography & Sexual Deviance. Michael J. Goldstein et al. 1973. 16.50x (ISBN 0-520-02406-0); pap. 2.45 (ISBN 0-520-02619-5). U of Cal Pr.

Pornography & Silence: Culture's Revolt Against Nature. Susan Griffin. LC 80-8206. 320p. 1981. 11.95 (ISBN 0-06-011647-1, HarpT). Har-Row.

Pornography Explosion. (Illus.). 4.95 (ISBN 0-910550-77-8). Centurion Pr.

Pornography in Art. Poul Gerhard. 1969. 18.50 (ISBN 0-910550-11-5). Elysium.

Pornography: Men's Graphic Depiction of Whores. Andrea Dworkin. 288p. 1981. 12.95 (ISBN 0-399-12619-8, Perigee); pap. 5.95 (ISBN 0-399-50532-6). Putnam.

Pornography, Psychedelics & Technology: Essays on the Limits to Freedom. E. J. Mishan. 184p. 1980. text ed. 22.50x (ISBN 0-04-300081-9, 2547). Allen Unwin.

Pornography: The Conflict Over Sexually Explicit Materials in the United States. an Annotated Bibliography. Greg Byerly & Rick Rubin. LC 80-14336. (Garland Reference Library of Social Science). 162p. 1980. 20.00 (ISBN 0-8240-9514-6). Garland Pub.

Porphyrins. Ed. by David Dolphin. Incl. Vol. 1, Pt. A. 59.00 (ISBN 0-12-220101-9); Physical Chemistry. Vol. 3, Pt. A. 71.00 (ISBN 0-12-220103-5); Vol. 4, Pt. B. 50.00 (ISBN 0-12-220104-3); Vol. 5, Pt. C. 57.50 (ISBN 0-12-220105-1). LC 77-14197. 1978-79. Acad Pr.

Porphyrins Vol. 6: Biochemistry Part A. Ed. by David Dolphin. 1979. 93.00 (ISBN 0-12-220106-X); 79.50 set (ISBN 0-12-220106-X). Acad Pr.

Porpoises & Sonar. Winthrop N. Kellogg. LC 61-11294. (Illus.). xiv, 178p. 1961. 8.00x o.s.i. (ISBN 0-226-43004-9). U of Chicago Pr.

Porsche Cars in the 60's. R. M. Clarke. (Brooklands Bks.). (Illus.). 100p. (Orig.). 1980. pap. 11.95 (ISBN 0-906589-81-9, Pub. by Enthusiast England). Motorbooks Intl.

Porsche Cars, 1964-1968. R. M. Clarke. (Brooklands Bks.). (Illus., Orig.). 1979. pap. 11.95 (ISBN 0-906589-61-4, Pub. by Enthusiast Pubns. England). Motorbooks Intl.

Porsche Cars 1968-1972. R. M. Clarke. (Brooklands Bks.). (Illus., Orig.). 1979. pap. 11.95 (ISBN 0-906589-62-2, Pub. by Enthusiast England). Motorbooks Intl.

Porsche: Excellence Was Expected. Ed. by Karl Ludvigsen. LC 77-83507. 1977. text ed. 64.95 (ISBN 0-915038-09-9). Princeton Pub.

Porsche Nine Eleven Story. 2nd ed. Paul Frere. (Illus.). 200p. 1981. 37.95 (ISBN 0-85059-482-0). Aztex.

Porsche Nine Fourteen: Nineteen Sixty-Nine to Nineteen Seventy-Five. R. M. Clarke. (Brooklands Bks.). (Illus.). 100p. (Orig.). 1980. 11.95 (ISBN 0-906589-84-3). Motorbooks Intl.

Porsche Nine-Fourteen Series. 1970-1976: Service, Repair Handbook: 914 Series, 1970-1976--Service, Repair Handbook. 3rd ed. Eric Jorgensen. Ed. by Jeff Robinson. (Illus.). 1978. pap. 10.95 (ISBN 0-89287-203-9, A184). Clymer Pubns.

Porsche: Nine Twenty-Four Series, 1976-1978. Service Repair Handbook. Ray Hoy. Ed. by Eric Jorgensen. (Illus.). 1978. pap. 10.95 (ISBN 0-89287-204-7, A182). Clymer Pubns.

Porsche Owners Handbook & Service Manual: Covers All Porsche Models up to 356c. Clymer Publications. (Illus.). 1967. pap. 7.95 (ISBN 0-89287-251-9, A181). Clymer Pubns.

Porsche Racing Cars of the Seventies. Paul Frere. LC 80-23773. (Illus.). 256p. 1981. 16.95 (ISBN 0-668-05113-2, 5113). Arco.

Porsche Service-Repair Handbook: 911 & 912 Series, 1965-1978. Eric Jorgensen. Ed. by Jeff Robinson. (Illus.). 1978. pap. text ed. 10.95 (ISBN 0-89287-060-5, A183). Clymer Pubns.

Porsche Sport 72. Joe Rusz. LC 72-97717. 1973. 4.95 (ISBN 0-87880-015-8). Norton.

Porsche Sport 73. Joe Rusz. LC 73-89096. 1974. 5.95 (ISBN 0-87880-023-9). Norton.

Porsche; The Four-Cylinder, Four-Cam Sports & Racing Cars. Jerry Sloniger. (Illus.). 120p. (Orig.). 1977. pap. 10.95 (ISBN 0-914792-03-2, Pub. by DB Pubns). Motorbooks Intl.

Porsche 356. Denis Jenkinson. (AutoHistory Ser.). (Illus.). 128p. 1980. 12.95 (ISBN 0-85045-363-1, Pub. by Osprey England). Motorbooks Intl.

Porsche 911: Collector's Guide. Michael Cotton. (Illus.). 128p. 1980. 17.50 (ISBN 0-900549-52-1, Pub. by Motor Racing Pubns. England). Motorbooks Intl.

Porsche 914: 1969-1975. R. M. Clarke. (Brooklands Bks.). (Illus.). 100p. (Orig.) 1980. pap. 11.95 (ISBN 0-906589-84-3, Pub. by Enthusiast Pubns England). Motorbooks Intl.

Port & Ocean Engineering Under Arctic Conditions: Selected Papers from the 3rd International Conference. Ed. by Michael E. McCormick. 1977. pap. text ed. 24.00 (ISBN 0-08-021421-5). Pergamon.

Port Development in the United States. Maritime Transportation Research Board, National Research Council. LC 76-5180. xv, 244p. 1976. pap. 6.50 (ISBN 0-309-02448-X). Natl Acad Pr.

Port Dues, Charges & Accommodation Throughout the World. 37th ed. Ed. by M. C. Andrews. 1978-79. 80.00 (ISBN 0-540-07386-5). Heinman.

Port Engineering. 3rd ed. Per Bruun. 750p. 1981. text ed. 50.00 (ISBN 0-87201-739-7). Gulf Pub.

Port of Houston: A History. Marilyn M. Sibley. (Illus.). 1968. 15.00 (ISBN 0-292-73619-3). U of Tex Pr.

Port Philip Gentlemen. Paul De Serville. (Illus.). 256p. 1980. 49.00x (ISBN 0-19-554212-6). Oxford U Pr.

Port Planning & Development As Related to Problems of US Ports & US Coastal Environment. Ed. by Eric Schenker & Harry C. Brockel. LC 74-22183. (Illus.). 1974. 12.50x (ISBN 0-87033-196-5). Cornell Maritime.

Port Pricing & Investment Policy for Developing Countries. Esra Bennathan & Alan A. Walters. 1979. 16.95x (ISBN 0-19-520092-6); pap. 7.95x (ISBN 0-19-520093-4). Oxford U Pr.

Port-Royal. Henry de Montherlant. Ed. by Richard Griffiths. (French Texts Ser.). 1976. pap. text ed. 11.25x (ISBN 0-631-00730-X, Pub. by Basil Blackwel). Biblio Dist.

Port Structure Costs. Compiled by American Society of Civil Engineers. 188p. 1974. pap. text ed. 39.50 o.p. (ISBN 0-87262-072-7). Am Soc Civil Eng.

Port Tropique. Barry Gifford. LC 80-15440. (Black Lizard Bks, Fiction Ser.). 200p. 1980. pap. 5.95 (ISBN 0-916870-31-6). Creative Arts Bk.

Port Tropique. Barry Gifford. LC 80-15440. (Black Lizard Fiction Ser.). 200p. 1980. 9.95 (ISBN 0-916870-32-4). Creative Arts Bk.

Port Valdez, Alaska: Environmental Studies, Nineteen Seventy-Six to Nineteen Seventy-Nine. Ed. by J. M. Colonell & H. K. Stockholm. (Occasional Publications Ser.: No. 5). (Illus.). 500p. 1980. write for info. (ISBN 0-914500-09-0). U of AK Inst Marine.

Portability of Numerical Software: Proceedings. Ed. by W. Crowell. LC 77-13623. (Lecture Notes in Computer Science: Vol. 57). 1977. pap. text ed. 21.90 (ISBN 0-387-08446-0). Springer-Verlag.

Portable Arthur Miller. Arthur Miller. Ed. by Harold Clurman. LC 77-119777. (Viking Portable Library: No. 71). 1977. pap. 5.95 (ISBN 0-14-015071-4). Penguin.

Portable Barbara Baynton. Barbara Baynton. Ed. by Sally Krimmer & Alan Lawson. (Portable Australian Authors Ser.). 340p. 1981. text ed. 30.25 (ISBN 0-7022-1377-2); pap. 12.00 (ISBN 0-7022-1469-8). U of Queensland Pr.

Portable Bernard Shaw. Ed. by Stanley Weintraub. (Viking Portable Library Ser: P90). 1977. pap. 5.95 (ISBN 0-14-015090-0). Penguin.

Portable Cosmos: Effigies, Ornaments & Incised Stone from the Chumash Area. Georgia Lee. (Ballena Press Anthropological Papers: No. 21). (Illus.). 114p. (Orig.). 1981. pap. 6.95 (ISBN 0-87919-093-0). Ballena Pr.

Portable Energy Sources, E-001r. rev. ed. 1980. 825.00 (ISBN 0-89336-095-3). BCC.

Portable Greek Reader. Ed. by W. H. Auden. (Viking Portable Library: No. 39). 1955. pap. 5.95 (ISBN 0-14-015039-0, P39). Penguin.

Portable Mad. Mad Magazine Editors. (Mad Ser.). (Illus.). 1977. pap. 1.50 (ISBN 0-446-88765-X). Warner Bks.

Portable Nietzsche. F. Nietzsche. Ed. by Walter Kaufman. (Viking Portable Library: No. 62). 1980. 14.95 (ISBN 0-670-51119-6). Viking Pr.

Portable Oscar Wilde. rev. ed. Ed. by Stanley Weintraub. 1981. 14.95 (ISBN 0-670-76743-3). Viking Pr.

Portable Pensions. Jozetta H. Srb. (Key Issues Ser.: No. 4). 1969. pap. 3.00 (ISBN 0-87546-245-6). NY Sch Indus Rel.

Portable Redhouse Turkish-English, English-Turkish Dictionary. 1975. 9.00x (ISBN 0-686-16857-7). Intl Learn Syst.

Portable Steinbeck. 2nd ed. John Steinbeck. Ed. by Pascal Covici, Jr. (Portable Library: No. 2). 1971. 14.95 (ISBN 0-670-66960-1). Viking Pr.

Portable Stephen Crane. Stephen Crane. Ed. by Joseph Katz. (Portable Library: No. 68). 1969. 10.00 o.p. (ISBN 0-670-67041-3). Viking Pr.

Portal Hypertension: As Seen Today by Seventeen Authorities. Charles G. Child. LC 73-81829. (Major Problem in Clinical Surgery Ser.: Vol. 14). (Illus.). 283p. 1974. text ed. 17.00 (ISBN 0-7216-2541-X). Saunders.

Portal Venous System. Charles Marks. (Illus.). 160p. 1973. 17.75 (ISBN 0-398-02708-0). C C Thomas.

Portals & Photographs. William Morgan. 1981. pap. 5.95 (ISBN 0-87233-057-5). Bauhan.

Portals to Freedom. Howard C. Ives. 1937. 7.95 (ISBN 0-85398-012-8, 7-31-21, Pub. by George Ronald England); pap. 4.95 o.s.i. (ISBN 0-87743-056-X, 7-31-22, Pub. by George Ronald England). Baha'i.

Porte Etroite. Andre Gide. Ed. by M. Shackleton. 1962. pap. text ed. 4.95x o.p. (ISBN 0-669-27391-0). Heath.

Portent. Marilyn Harris. 324p. 1980. 11.95 (ISBN 0-686-68352-8). Putnam.

Portent of Milton: Some Aspects of His Genius. E. H. Visiak. 1969. Repr. of 1958 ed. text ed. 8.00x (ISBN 0-391-00473-5). Humanities.

Portentous Signs Which Indicate That the World Has Entered into One of the Last Phases of Its Existence. Eugenio V. Novello. (Illus.). 149p. 1980. deluxe ed. 73.45 (ISBN 0-930008-71-5). Inst Econ Pol.

Porter-Waters Debate. W. Curtis Porter & J. Erwin Waters. pap. 4.50 (ISBN 0-89315-205-6). Lambert Bk.

Porterfield Legacy. Casey Stephens. (Orig.). 1980. pap. 1.95 (ISBN 0-89083-684-1, Kable News Co). Zebra.

Portfolio Analysis. 2nd ed. Clark Francis & Stephen H. Archer. (Foundations of Finance Ser.). (Illus.). 1979. text ed. 19.95 (ISBN 0-13-686675-1). P-H.

Portfolio Analysis a Practical Approach. E. J. Elton & M. J. Gruber. LC 80-19517. 450p. 1981. text ed. 20.95 o.p. (ISBN 0-471-04690-6). Wiley.

Portfolio Aspects of Corporate Capital Budgeting: Method of Analysis, Survey of Applications and a Model. E. Eugene Carter. LC 74-4514. 1974. 19.95 (ISBN 0-669-93161-6). Lexington Bks.

Portfolios of Ansel Adams. Ansel Adams. 1981. 14.95 (ISBN 0-686-68992-5, 713953). NYGS.

Portia in Distress. Felicia Bryce. (YA) 1977. 5.95 (ISBN 0-685-74267-9, Avalon). Bouregy.

Portion for Foxes. Anthony Thwaite. 1977. pap. 6.95x (ISBN 0-19-211872-2). Oxford U Pr.

Portland. Josephine Detmer & Patricia Pancoast. Ed. by Martin Dibner. LC 72-172820. (Illus.). 1973. collector's 25.00x (ISBN 0-9600612-0-7). Greater Portland.

Portland. 2nd ed. Patricia Pancoast et al. LC 72-172820. (Illus.). 236p. 1973. 15.00 (ISBN 0-9600612-2-3); pap. 6.95 (ISBN 0-9600612-1-5). Greater Portland.

Portland: A Historical Sketch & Guide. Terence O'Donnell & Thomas Vaughan. LC 72-251. (Illus.). 161p. 1976. pap. 2.95 o.p. (ISBN 0-87595-051-5). Oreg Hist Soc.

Portland & Vicinity. Edward H. Elwell. (Illus.). 138p. 1975. pap. 4.95 (ISBN 0-9600612-3-1). Greater Portland.

Portland Cement Paste & Concrete. I. Soroka. 1980. 48.00 (ISBN 0-8206-0281-7). Chem Pub.

Portland Guidebook. Linda Lampman & Julie Sterling. LC 78-17274. (Illus.). 1978. pap. 3.95 o.p. (ISBN 0-916076-25-3). Writing.

Portland Super Shopper. Connie Hofferber & Terry Hofferber. LC 80-51868. (Illus.). 128p. 1980. pap. 3.50 (ISBN 0-916076-40-7). Writing.

Portland Symphony Cookbook. Ed. by Adele J. Robinson. LC 74-84052. 1974. 8.95 (ISBN 0-9601266-1-9). Portland Symphony.

Portland Walkbook. Peggy Robinson. (Illus., Maps by Judith Farmer). 1978. pap. 5.95 o.p. (ISBN 0-918480-09-4). Victoria Hse.

Portrait du vocabulaire francais. A. Sauvageot. (Langue vivante). (Fr). pap. 8.25 (ISBN 0-685-14055-5, 3627). Larousse.

Portrait in Shadows. Jane Peart. (Orig.). 1981. pap. 1.50 (ISBN 0-440-16693-4). Dell.

Portrait of a Lady. rev. ed. Henry James. Ed. by Robert J. Dixson. (American Classics Ser.: Bk. 7). (gr. 9 up). 1974. pap. text ed. 2.75 (ISBN 0-88345-203-0, 18126); cassettes 40.00 (ISBN 0-685-38927-8); tapes 40.00 (ISBN 0-685-38928-6). Regents Pub.

Portrait of a Lady. Henry James. Ed. by Robert D. Bamberg. (Norton Critical Edition Ser.). 1975. pap. text ed. 5.95 (ISBN 0-393-09259-3). Norton.

Portrait of a Man Unknown. Nathalie Sarraute. Tr. by Maria Jolas. 1958. 4.50 o.p. (ISBN 0-8076-0061-X). Braziller.

Portrait of a Marriage. Nigel Nicolson. LC 79-25497. 1973. 10.00 (ISBN 0-689-10574-6); pap. 6.95 (ISBN 0-689-70597-2). Atheneum.

Portrait of a Place, Some American Landscape Painters in Gloucester. Intro. by James F. O'Gorman. (Illus.). 1973. 7.50 (ISBN 0-930352-03-3). Nelson B Robinson.

Portrait of a Psychic Healer. Dean Kraft. 192p. 1981. 10.95 (ISBN 0-686-69592-5). Putnam.

Portrait of "All the President's Men". Jack Hirshberg. 1976. pap. 6.95 o.s.i. (ISBN 0-446-87105-2). Warner Bks.

Portrait of an Age. Erich Saloman. (Illus.). 216p. 1975. pap. 7.50 o.s.i. (ISBN 0-02-000820-1, Collier). Macmillan.

Portrait of an Artist with Twenty-Six Horses. Ed. by William Eastlake. (Zia Bks.). 224p. 1980. pap. 5.95 (ISBN 0-8263-0558-X). U of NM Pr.

Portrait of an English Churchman, 1838. William Gresley. Ed. by Robert L. Wolff. Bd. with Charles Lever; or, the Man of the Nineteenth Century, 1841; Church Clavering; or, the Schoolmaster, 1843. LC 75-468. (Victorian Fiction Ser). 1975. lib. bdg. 66.00 (ISBN 0-8240-1546-0). Garland Pub.

Portrait of Birmingham. V. Bird. LC 70-546349. (Portrait Bks.). 1970. 10.50x (ISBN 0-7091-4582-9). Intl Pubns Serv.

Portrait of Britain Between the Exhibitions: 1851-1951. Donald Lindsay & E. S. Washington. (Oxford Introduction to British History Ser.). (Illus.). 1952. 6.95x o.p. (ISBN 0-19-831513-9). Oxford U Pr.

Portrait of Cambridge. C. R. Benstead. LC 68-99210. (Portrait Bks.). (Illus.). 1968. 10.50x (ISBN 0-7091-0112-0). Intl Pubns Serv.

Portrait of Chicago. Les Krantz. Ed. by Douglas Pfeiffer. (Portrait of America Ser.). (Illus.). 80p. (Orig.). 1981. pap. text ed. 5.95 (ISBN 0-912856-70-X). Graphic Arts Ctr.

Portrait of Cornwall. Claude Berry. LC 64-2200. (Portrait Bks.). (Illus.). 1964. 10.50x (ISBN 0-7091-1872-4). Intl Pubns Serv.

Portrait of County Durham. Peter A. White. LC 67-95176. (Portrait Bks.). (Illus.). 1967. 10.50x (ISBN 0-7091-2420-1). Intl Pubns Serv.

Portrait of Dartmoor. Vian Smith. LC 66-72759. (Portrait Bks.). (Illus.). 206p. 1966. 10.50x (ISBN 0-7091-0919-9). Intl Pubns Serv.

Portrait of Devon. Douglas St. Leger-Gordon. LC 66-4363. (Portrait Bks.). (Illus.). 192p. 1966. 10.50x (ISBN 0-7091-1858-9). Intl Pubns Serv.

Portrait of Dora Simone Bennussa: The Singular Life of Albert Nobbs. Helen Cixous. Tr. by Anita Barrows & Barbara Wright. 1980. pap. 4.95 (ISBN 0-7145-3764-0). Riverrun NY.

Portrait of Dorset. Ralph Wightman. LC 66-4364. (Portrait Bks.). (Illus.). 1966. 10.50x (ISBN 0-7091-6446-7). Intl Pubns Serv.

Portrait of Edinburgh. Ian Nimmo. LC 71-401261. (Portrait Bks.). (Illus.). 1969. 10.50x (ISBN 0-7091-5350-3). Intl Pubns Serv.

Portrait of Elie Halevy. Michele B. Bramsen. 1978. pap. text ed. 28.50x (ISBN 90-6032-100-6). Humanities.

Portrait of Elizabeth I: In the Words of the Queen & Her Contemporaries. Ed. by Roger Pringle. (Illus.). 128p. 1980. 10.75x (ISBN 0-389-20088-3). B&N.

Portrait of Emily Dickinson: The Poet & Her Prose. David Higgins. LC 67-28132. (Orig.). 1967. 15.00 (ISBN 0-8135-0542-9); pap. 3.95 (ISBN 0-8135-0798-7). Rutgers U Pr.

Portrait of Exmoor. J. H. Peel. LC 75-522868. (Portrait Bks.). (Illus.). 1970. 10.50x (ISBN 0-7091-1600-4). Intl Pubns Serv.

Portrait of Gloucestershire. T. A. Ryder. LC 66-73378. (Portrait Bks.). (Illus.). 1966. 10.50x (ISBN 0-7091-3318-9). Intl Pubns Serv.

Portrait of Inequality: Black & White Children in America. Marian W. Edelman. LC 80-68585. 144p. (Orig.). 1980. pap. 5.00 (ISBN 0-938008-00-5). Childrens Defense.

Portrait of Jane Austen. David Cecil. 208p. 1980. text ed. 25.00 (ISBN 0-8090-7811-2); pap. text ed. 9.95 (ISBN 0-8090-1392-4). Hill & Wang.

Portrait of Karl Barth. George Casalis. Tr. by Robert M. Brown. LC 80-25829. viii, 135p. 1981. Repr. of 1963 ed. lib. bdg. 17.50x (ISBN 0-313-22775-6, CAKB). Greenwood.

Portrait of Lancashire. Jessica Lofthouse. LC 67-92282. (Portrait Bks.). (Illus.). 1967. 10.50x (ISBN 0-7091-6359-2). Intl Pubns Serv.

Portrait of Liverpool. Howard Channon. LC 72-550617. (Portrait Books Ser). 1970. 10.50x (ISBN 0-7091-5575-1). Intl Pubns Serv.

Portrait of London River: The Tidal Thames from Teddington to the Sea. Basil E. Cracknell. LC 68-115971. (Portrait Bks.). (Illus.). 1968. 7.50x (ISBN 0-7091-0300-X). Intl Pubns Serv.

Portrait of Lord Nelson. Oliver Warner. (Illus.). 1979. 8.95 (ISBN 0-7011-1809-1, Pub. by Chatto Bodley Jonathan). Merrimack Bk Serv.

Portrait of Love. Lynna Cooper. (Orig.). 1980. pap. 1.75 (ISBN 0-451-09495-6, E9495, Sig). NAL.

Portrait of Love. Jean Hager. (Orig.). 1981. pap. 1.50 (ISBN 0-440-17013-3). Dell.

Portrait of Maine. Clyde Smith. Ed. by Douglas Pfeiffer. (Portrait of America Ser.). (Illus.). 80p. (Orig.). 1981. pap. 5.95 (ISBN 0-912856-71-8). Graphic Arts Ctr.

Portrait of Manchester. Michael Kennedy. LC 70-550611. (Portrait Bks.). 1970. 10.50x (ISBN 0-7091-1812-0). Intl Pubns Serv.

Portrait of Marginality: The Political Behavior of the American Woman. Ed. by Marianne Githens & Jewel L. Prestage. LC 76-58484. 1977. pap. 11.95x (ISBN 0-582-28129-6). Longman.

Portrait of Morris. Vern Haddick. LC 78-31684. Date not set. 9.95 (ISBN 0-87949-152-3). Ashley Bks.

Portrait of Nationalised Banks. H. N. Agrawal. 334p. 1980. text ed. 18.00x (ISBN 0-391-02130-3). Humanities.

Portrait of Northumberland. Nancy Ridley. LC 66-5457. (Portrait Bks.). (Illus.). 1966. 10.50x (ISBN 0-7091-6070-4). Intl Pubns Serv.

Portrait of Oregon. Photos by Ray Atkeson & Ray Atkeson. LC 79-91507. (Portrait of America Ser.). (Illus., Orig., Photos by ray atkeson) 1980. pap. 5.95 (ISBN 0-912856-52-1). Graphic Arts Ctr.

Portrait of Orkney. George M. Brown. (Illus.). 128p. 1981. 23.00 (ISBN 0-7012-0513-X, Pub. by Chatto-Bodley-Jonathan). Merrimack Bk Serv.

Portrait of Perfection: A Pictorial Biography of Kirpal Singh. Intro. by Darshan Singh. LC 79-92472. (Illus.). 300p. 1981. 18.00 (ISBN 0-918224-08-X). Sawan Kirpal.

Portrait of Puerto Rico. Louise C. Samoiloff. 1981. text ed. price not set. Schenkman.

Portrait of Skye & the Outer Hebrides. W. Douglas Simpson. LC 67-74411. (Portrait Bks.). 1967. 10.50x (ISBN 0-7091-0650-5). Intl Pubns Serv.

Portrait of Somerset. Bryan Little. LC 77-444966. (Portrait Bks.). (Illus.). 224p. 1976. 10.50x (ISBN 0-7091-5791-6). Intl Pubns Serv.

Portrait of the Artist As a Young Man: A Facsimile of the Manuscript Fragments of Stephen Hero. James Joyce. Ed. by Michael Groden. LC 78-12105. (James Joyce Archive Ser.: Vol. 7-10). 1979. lib. bdg. 415.00 (ISBN 0-8240-2807-4). Garland Pub.

Portrait of the Artist As a Young Superman: A Study of Shaw's Novels. R. F. Dietrich. LC 75-77613. 7.50 (ISBN 0-8130-0277-X). Brown Bk.

Portrait of the Artist: The Plays of Tennessee Williams. Foster Hirsch. (National Univ. Pubns. Literary Criticism Ser.). 1979. 10.00 (ISBN 0-8046-9230-0). Kennikat.

Portrait of the Bay Area. Lee Foster. Ed. by Douglas A. Pfeiffer. (Portrait of America Ser.). (Illus.). 80p. (Orig.). 1981. pap. text ed. 5.95 (ISBN 0-912856-69-6). Graphic Arts Ctr.

Portrait of the Burns Country. Hugh Douglas. LC 68-117106. (Portrait Bks.). (Illus.). 1968. 10.50x (ISBN 0-7091-5368-6). Intl Pubns Serv.

Portrait of the Channel Islands. Raoul Lempriere. LC 70-515033. (Portrait Bks.). (Illus.). 1970. 10.50x (ISBN 0-7091-5152-7). Intl Pubns Serv.

Portrait of the Clyde. Jack House. LC 79-448420. (Portrait Bks.). (Illus.). 1969. 10.50x (ISBN 0-7091-4994-8). Intl Pubns Serv.

Portrait of the Cotswolds. Edith Brill. LC 66-4352. (Portrait Bks.). (Illus.). 1964. 10.50x (ISBN 0-7091-2498-8). Intl Pubns Serv.

Portrait of the Free State. Donald M. Dozer. LC 76-47023. (Illus.). 1976. 17.50 (ISBN 0-87033-226-0, Pub. by Tidewater). Cornell Maritime.

Portrait of the Highlands. W. Douglas Simpson. LC 75-376702. (Portrait Bks.). 1969. 10.50x (ISBN 0-7091-0415-4). Intl Pubns Serv.

Portrait of the Isle of Man. 3rd ed. E. H. Stenning. LC 66-4371. (Portrait Bks.). (Illus.). 192p. 1975. 12.50x (ISBN 0-7091-5190-X). Intl Pubns Serv.

Portrait of the Isles of Scilly. Clive Mumford. LC 67-98842. (Portrait Bks.). (Illus.). 1967. 10.50x (ISBN 0-7091-1718-3). Intl Pubns Serv.

Portrait of the Lakes. Norman Nicholson. LC 64-4949. (Portrait Bks.). (Illus.). 1964. 10.50x (ISBN 0-7091-2897-5). Intl Pubns Serv.

Portrait of the New Forest. Brian Vesey-Fitzgerald. LC 67-70400. (Portrait Bks.). (Illus.) 1966. 10.50x (ISBN 0-7091-6400-9). Intl Pubns Serv.

Portrait of the Pennines. Roger A. Redfern. LC 75-434154. (Portrait Bks.). (Illus.). 192p. 1969. 10.50x (ISBN 0-7091-0872-9). Intl Pubns Serv.

Portrait of the Quantocks. Vincent Waite. LC 66-4372. (Portrait Bks.). (Illus.). 1965. 10.50x (ISBN 0-7091-1158-4). Intl Pubns Serv.

Portrait of the River Trent. Peter Lord. LC 68-117316. (Portrait Bks.). (Illus.). 1968. 10.50x (ISBN 0-7091-0210-0). Intl Pubns Serv.

Portrait of the Scott Country. Marion Lochhead. LC 68-119619. (Portrait Bks.). (Illus.). 1968. 10.50x (ISBN 0-7091-3957-8). Intl Pubns Serv.

Portrait of the Severn. J. H. Peel. LC 79-365046. (Portrait Bks.). (Illus.). 1968. 10.50x (ISBN 0-7091-0432-4). Intl Pubns Serv.

Portrait of the Shakespeare Country. John C. Trewin. LC 75-503070. (Portrait Bks.). (Illus.). 1970. 10.50x (ISBN 0-7091-1342-0). Intl Pubns Serv.

Portrait of the Thames from Teddington to the Source. J. H. Peel. LC 67-84564. (Portrait Books Ser). (Illus.). 1967. 10.50x (ISBN 0-7091-0748-X). Intl Pubns Serv.

Portrait of the Wye Valley. H. L. Fletcher. LC 68-115674. (Portrait Bks.). (Illus.). 1968. 10.50x (ISBN 0-7091-0409-X). Intl Pubns Serv.

Portrait of Washington D. C. Tom Worcester & James Cary. LC 79-55979. (Portrait of America Ser.). (Illus., Orig., Photos by robert reynolds). 1980. pap. 6.95 (ISBN 0-912856-55-6). Graphic Arts Ctr.

Portrait of Yorkshire. Harry J. Scott. LC 66-4438. (Portrait Bks.). (Illus.). 1965. 10.50x (ISBN 0-7091-1842-2). Intl Pubns Serv.

Portrait of Youth Ministry: Young People & the Church. Maria Harris. 224p. (Orig.). 1981. pap. 7.95 (ISBN 0-8091-2354-1). Paulist Pr.

Portrait Painting. Derek Chittock. 1979. 24.00 (ISBN 0-7134-3293-4, Pub. by Batsford England). David & Charles.

Portraits. Yury Annenkov. Tr. by David Lowe from Rus. (Illus.). 1981. 60.00 (ISBN 0-931554-18-7). Strathcona.

Portraits. Cynthia Freeman. 608p. 1980. pap. 3.50 (ISBN 0-553-13641-0). Bantam.

Portraits: Friends & Strangers. Michael Mathers. LC 79-336. (Illus.). 1979. 14.95 (ISBN 0-914842-36-6); pap. 9.95 (ISBN 0-914842-35-8). Madrona Pubs.

Portraits from a Shooting Gallery: Life Styles from the Drug Addict World. Seymour Fiddle. LC 67-13711. 1967. 10.00 o.p. (ISBN 0-06-032065-6, HarpT). Har-Row.

Portraits from Memory. Richard Kostelanetz. 1975. 7.95 (ISBN 0-932360-21-1); signed & numbered, 1-10 75.00 (ISBN 0-685-58447-X); pap. 3.00 (ISBN 0-932360-20-3). RK Edns.

Portraits from North American Indian Life. Edward S. Curtis. 192p. 1981. pap. 10.95 (ISBN 0-89104-003-X). A & W Pubs.

Portraits in British History. Ed. by Ronald Pollitt & Herbert F. Curry. 1975. pap. text ed. 9.95x (ISBN 0-256-01679-8). Dorsey.

Portraits in Music I. David Jenkins & Mark Visocchi. 66p. 1980. 6.00 (ISBN 0-19-321400-8). Oxford U Pr.

Portraits in the Collection of the Virginia Historical Society: A Catologue. Virginius C. Hall, Jr. LC 80-14079. 1981. price not set (ISBN 0-8139-0813-2). U Pr of Va.

Portraits in Words: An Introduction to the Study of Biography. Ed. by Donald C. Rehkopf. LC 62-13410. 1962. 4.95 (ISBN 0-672-73251-3); pap. 3.50 o.p. (ISBN 0-672-73229-7). Odyssey Pr.

Portraits of Dutch Painters & Other Artists of the Low Countries: Specime of an Iconography, Reportorium. H. Van Hall. 432p. 1963. text ed. 92.00 (ISBN 90-265-0027-0, Pub. by Swets Pub Serv Holland). Swets North Am.

Portraits of John & Abigail Adams. Andrew Oliver. (Adams Papers, Ser. 4, Adams Family Portraits). (Illus.). 1967. 15.00x (ISBN 0-674-69150-4). Harvard U Pr.

Portraits of John Quincy Adams & His Wife. Andrew Oliver. LC 70-128349. (Adams Papers, Ser. 4, Adams Family Portraits). (Illus.). 1970. 17.50x (ISBN 0-674-69152-0). Harvard U Pr.

Portraits of Mexican Birds: Fifty Selected Paintings. George M. Sutton. LC 74-15911. (Illus.). 120p. 1975. 35.00 o.p. (ISBN 0-8061-1236-0). U of Okla Pr.

Portraits of Mexican Birds: Fifty Selected Paintings. George M. Sutton. (Illus.). 106p. 1980. pap. 14.95 (ISBN 0-8061-1685-4). U of Okla Pr.

Portraits of T.E. Lawrence. Charles Grosvenor. (Illus.). 1975. pap. 15.00 o.s.i. (ISBN 0-918868-00-9). Otterden.

Portraits of the American University: 1890-1910. Ed. by James C. Stone & Donald P. DeNevi. LC 72-146783. (Higher Education Ser.). (Illus.). 1971. 17.95x o.p. (ISBN 0-87589-087-3). Jossey-Bass.

Portraits of the Whiteman. Keith H. Basso. LC 78-31535. 1979. 17.95 (ISBN 0-521-22640-6); pap. 4.95 (ISBN 0-521-29593-9). Cambridge U Pr.

Portraits of White Racism. Ed. by D. T. Wellman. LC 76-47187. 1977. 29.95 (ISBN 0-521-21514-5); pap. 7.95x (ISBN 0-521-29179-8). Cambridge U Pr.

Portraiture at Home. R. H. Mason. 1977. 14.95 o.p. (ISBN 0-85242-488-4, Pub. by Fountain). Morgan.

Portraying the President: The White House & the News Media. Michael B. Grossman & Martha J. Kumar. 380p. 1981. text ed. 26.50 (ISBN 0-8018-2375-7); pap. 9.95 (ISBN 0-8018-2537-7). Johns Hopkins.

Ports Around the World. Yehuda Karmon. (Illus.). 1979. 15.95 (ISBN 0-517-53378-2). Crown.

Ports, Inland Waterways & Civil Aviation. R. E. Baxter & C. Phillips. Ed. by W. F. Maunder. 1979. text ed. 55.00 (ISBN 0-08-022460-1). Pergamon.

Ports of the World, Nineteen Eighty. 33rd ed. John Riethmuller. LC 48-3083. (Illus.). 1076p. 1980. 100.00x (ISBN 0-510-49156-1). Intl Pubns Serv.

Ports of the World 1980. (Benn Directories Ser.). 1979. 85.00x (ISBN 0-686-60660-4, Pub by Benn Pubns). Nichols Pub.

Ports Seventy-Seven. Compiled by American Society of Civil Engineers. 1024p. 1977. pap. text ed. 36.00 (ISBN 0-87262-084-0). Am Soc Civil Eng.

Portugal. Dorothy Carew. LC 68-12087. (Nations Today Books). (Illus.). (gr. 7 up). 1969. 4.95 o.s.i. (ISBN 0-02-716490-X). Macmillan.

Portugal. new ed. Ed. by Daniel Moreau. (Collection monde et voyages). (Illus.). 159p. (Fr.). 1973. 21.00x (ISBN 2-03-053113-8). Larousse.

Portugal. Henry Myhill. (Illus.). 1972. 14.00 (ISBN 0-571-09640-9). Transatlantic.

Portugal in Revolution. Michael Harsgor. LC 76-2250. (Washington Papers: No. 32). 1976. 3.50x (ISBN 0-8039-0647-1). Sage.

Portugal Political Struggle & the Mass Media. new ed. Ed. by Fernando Perrone. (Marxism & the Mass Media Ser.: No. 8). (Illus.). 1981. pap. 5.00 (ISBN 0-88477-012-5). Intl General.

Portugal Since the Revolution: Economic & Political Perspectives. Jorge Braga de Macedo. Ed. by Simon Serfaty. (Westview Special Studies in West European Politics & Society). 128p. 1981. lib. bdg. 12.50x (ISBN 0-89158-972-4). Westview.

Portugal: The Last Empire. Neil Bruce. LC 75-1034. 160p. 1975. 11.95 o.p. (ISBN 0-470-11366-9). Halsted Pr.

Portugal's African Wars. Humbaraci & Mucnik. LC 72-93676. 1974. 10.00 (ISBN 0-89388-072-8). Okpaku Communications.

Portugues Contemporaneo, 2 vols. Maria I. Abreu & Clea Rameh. Incl. Vol. 1. 256p. pap. 6.50 (ISBN 0-87840-025-7); 11 cassettes 55.00 (ISBN 0-87840-048-6); 22 reel-to-reel tapes 120.00 (ISBN 0-87840-075-3); Vol. 2. 346p. pap. 7.00 (ISBN 0-87840-026-5); 10 cassettes 65.00 (ISBN 0-87840-049-4); 20 tapes 120.00 (ISBN 0-87840-076-1). LC 66-25520. 1971. Georgetown U Pr.

Portuguese. Holloway Staff. (Harper Phrase Books for the Traveler Ser.). (Orig.). 1977. pap. 1.00 o.p. (ISBN 0-8467-0313-0, Pub. by Two Continents). Hippocrene Bks.

Portuguese-Americans. Leo Pap. (Immigrant Heritage of America Ser.). 1981. lib. bdg. 14.95 (ISBN 0-8057-8417-9). Twayne.

Portuguese Armed Forces & the Revolution. Douglas Porch. (Publications Ser.: No. 188). (Illus.). 11.00 (ISBN 0-85664-391-2). Hoover Inst Pr.

Portuguese Brazil: The King's Plantation. James Lang. (Studies in Social Discontinuity). 1979. 24.00 (ISBN 0-12-436480-2). Acad Pr.

Portuguese Embassy to Japan (1644-1647) Charles R. Boxer. Bd. with Embassy of Captain Concalo de Siqueria de Souza to Japan in 1644-7. (Studies in Japanese History & Civilization). 172p. 22.00 (ISBN 0-89093-256-5). U Pubns Amer.

Portuguese Grammar. Raul D'Eca & Eric V. Greenfield. 1979. pap. 3.95 (ISBN 0-06-460185-4, CO 185, COS). Har-Row.

Portuguese Literature. Aubrey F. Bell. (Reprints Ser). 1922. 24.00x (ISBN 0-19-815396-1). Oxford U Pr.

Portuguese of the Arabian Coast. W. B. Stevenson. (Arab Background Ser.). 1968. 14.00x (ISBN 0-685-77105-9). Intl Bk Ctr.

Portuguese Rule on the Gold Coast, 1469-1682. John Vogt. LC 77-18831. 288p. 1978. 19.50x (ISBN 0-8203-0443-3). U of Ga Pr.

Posada's Popular Mexican Prints. Jose G. Posada. Ed. by Robert Berdecio & Stanley Appelbaum. LC 77-178994. (Illus.). 192p. (Orig.). 1972. pap. 6.00 (ISBN 0-486-22854-1). Dover.

Poseidon's Shadow. A. P. Kobryn. 1980. pap. 2.75 (ISBN 0-440-16899-6). Dell.

Posidonius: Vol. 1, The Fragments. Ed. by L. Edelstein & I. G. Kidd. LC 77-145609. (Classical Texts & Commentaries Ser., No. 13). 352p. 1972. 59.00 (ISBN 0-521-08046-0). Cambridge U Pr.

Posies of G. Gascoigne, Corrected & Augmented. George Gascoigne. LC 79-84110. (English Experience Ser.: No. 929). 532p. 1979. Repr. of 1575 ed. lib. bdg. 50.00 (ISBN 90-221-0929-1). Walter J Johnson.

Position of Blacks in Brazilian Society. Anani Dzidzienyo. (Minority Rights Group: No. 7). 1971. pap. 2.50 (ISBN 0-89192-096-X). Interbk Inc.

Position of Duchamp's Glass in the Development of His Art. Lawrence D. Steefel, Jr. LC 76-23647. (Outstanding Dissertations in the Fine Arts Ser.). 1977. lib. bdg. 63.00x (ISBN 0-8240-2730-2). Garland Pub.

Position of Ultimate Trust. William Beechcroft. LC 80-26561. 256p. 1981. 8.95 (ISBN 0-396-07933-4). Dodd.

Position of Women in Contemporary France. Francis I. Clark. LC 79-5210. 250p. 1981. Repr. of 1937 ed. 19.75 (ISBN 0-8305-0101-0). Hyperion Conn.

Position of Women in Hindu Civilization. A. S. Altekar. 1978. 12.50 (ISBN 0-8426-0713-7); pap. 9.00 (ISBN 0-686-67760-9). Orient Bk Dist.

Position of Women in Primitive Societies. Pritchard E. Evans. (Illus.). 1965. 10.95 (ISBN 0-571-06196-6, Pub. by Faber & Faber). Merrimack Bk Serv.

Positional Astronomy. D. McNally. LC 74-4819. 1975. text ed. 19.95 o.p. (ISBN 0-470-58980-9). Halsted Pr.

Positioning & Technique Handbook for Radiologic Technologists. Sylvester B. Conte & Douglas H. Kemmee. LC 78-5245. 1978. pap. text ed. 13.50 (ISBN 0-8016-1031-1). Mosby.

Positioning: The Battle for Your Mind. Al Ries & Jack Trout. 224p. 1980. 10.95 (ISBN 0-07-065263-5, P&RB). McGraw.

Positions. Jacques Derrida. Tr. by Alan Bass from Fr. LC 80-17620. 1981. 11.95 (ISBN 0-226-14332-5). U of Chicago Pr.

Positive Analysis of Social Phenomena. August Comte. (The Essential Library of the Great Philosophers). (Illus.). 129p. (Fr.). 1981. 37.85 (ISBN 0-89901-027-X). Found Class Reprints.

Positive Awareness (Experiential Extension), Purposeful Relaxati0n, & (Differentiated Psychophysiological) "Feeling" States, Set-PA. Russell E. Mason. 1975. pap. 25.00x (ISBN 0-89533-012-1); tape-1a, t-3, t-4 incl., notes, feeling training. F I Comm.

Positive Discipline. James M. Black. LC 70-121834. 1970. 12.95 o.p. (ISBN 0-8144-5227-2). Am Mgmt.

Positive Discipline & Classroom Interaction: A Part of the Teaching-Learning Process. Hermine H. Marshall. (Illus.). 144p. 1972. pap. 14.75 (ISBN 0-398-02457-X). C C Thomas.

Positive Economics & Policy Objectives. Terence W. Hutchison. LC 64-55440. 1964. 10.00x (ISBN 0-674-69300-0). Harvard U Pr.

Positive Emotional Power: How to Manage Your Feelings. Stanley Ainsworth. (Illus.). 256p. 1981. 12.95 (ISBN 0-13-687616-1); pap. 6.95 (ISBN 0-686-69330-2). P-H.

Positive Fishing. Robert G. Deindorfer. LC 79-67600. 224p. 1981. 10.95 (ISBN 0-87223-660-9). Seaview Bks.

Positive Magic. rev. ed. Marion Weinstein. (Illus.). 320p. 1981. pap. 5.95 (ISBN 0-919345-00-X). Cerridwen & Co.

Positive Parenting. Roger C. Rinn & Allan Markle. (Illus.). 1977. pap. text ed. 4.95 (ISBN 0-89147-052-2). CAS.

Positive Peer Culture. Harry H. Vorrath & Larry K. Brendtro. LC 73-89515. 288p. 1974. 14.95x (ISBN 0-202-36020-2). Aldine Pub.

Positive Personality Fulfillment, Set-PPF. Russell E. Mason. 1975. 25.00x (ISBN 0-89533-048-2); tape-1a, 1-5a incl., positive personalities: joy significance & sexual feeling & values. F I Comm.

Positive Plan for a Revolutionary Change in the Political Structure of the United States. Joseph B. Rice. (American Culture Library Bk). (Illus.). 128p. 1981. 28.15 (ISBN 0-89266-290-5). Am Classical Coll Pr.

Positive Power of Jesus Christ. Norman V. Peale. 8.95 (ISBN 0-8423-4874-3). Tyndale.

Positive Power of Sex. Rose A. Garretson & Jack Fry. LC 80-68666. 120p. 1980. pap. 5.95 (ISBN 0-89708-025-4). And Bks.

Positive Salvation. Marshall Henley. Date not set. 6.95 (ISBN 0-533-04861-3). Vantage.

Positive Substitution, Purposeful Relaxation, & Goal Achievement Training: A Beginning, Set-PS. rev. ed. Russell E. Mason. 1975. pap. 50.00x (ISBN 0-89533-014-8); Clinical Applications 1979, Relaxation Training, Substitution Training incl.; tape-1A; t-2; t-4; t-5 (ISBN 0-89533-035-0); t-6 avail. (ISBN 0-89533-036-9); t-10. F I Comm.

Positive Therapy: Making the Very Best of Everything. Allen E. Wiesen. LC 76-14849. 288p. 1977. 14.95 (ISBN 0-88229-269-2); pap. 7.95 (ISBN 0-88229-463-6). Nelson-Hall.

Positive Way to Good Health. Fergus Moynihan & Liz Moynihan. 1977. 8.95 (ISBN 0-236-40030-4, Pub. by Paul Elek). Merrimack Bk Serv.

Positively No Pets Allowed. Nathan Zimelman. LC 80-377. (Illus.). 32p. (gr. k-2). 1980. 7.95g (ISBN 0-525-37560-0). Dutton.

Positively Pregnant. Madeleine Kenefick. (Illus.). 224p. 1981. pap. 2.75 (ISBN 0-523-41182-0). Pinnacle Bks.

Positivism in Latin America, 1850-1960. Ed. by Ralph L. Woodward, Jr. LC 72-152809. (Problems in Latin American Civilization Ser.). 1971. pap. text ed. 4.95x o.p. (ISBN 0-669-52431-X). Heath.

Positron Annihilation: Proceedings. Positron Annihilation Conference - Wayne State University - 1965. Ed. by Alec Stewart & Leonard Roellig. 1967. 52.50 o.p. (ISBN 0-12-669350-1). Acad Pr.

Posse from Poison Creek. Lewis B. Patten. Bd. with Red Runs the River. 1980. pap. 1.95 (ISBN 0-451-09534-0, Sig). NAL.

Possession of Amber. Nicholas Jose. 285p. 1981. text ed. 13.25 (ISBN 0-7022-1537-6); pap. 7.25 (ISBN 0-7022-1538-4). U of Queensland Pr.

Possession of Immanuel Wolf & Other Improbable Tales. Marvin Kaye. LC 79-6865. 192p. 1981. 9.95 (ISBN 0-385-15862-9). Doubleday.

Possessors & the Possessed. Samuel A. Schreiner, Jr. LC 79-54009. 1980. 12.95 (ISBN 0-87795-229-9). Arbor Hse.

Possibilities & Limitations of Functional Literacy: The Iranian Experiment. Pierre Furter. LC 73-781021. (Educational Studies & Documents, No. 9). (Illus.). 59p. (Orig.). 1973. pap. 2.50 (ISBN 92-3-101075-1, U472, UNESCO). Unipub.

Possibilities of Charting Modern Life. S. Erixon. 1970. 27.00 (ISBN 0-08-013308-8). Pergamon.

Possibilities of Civilian Defence in Western Europe: Proceedings. Polemological Centre of the Free University of Brussels. Ed. by Gustaff Geeraerts. (Vol. 6). 180p. 1977. pap. text ed. 19.25 (ISBN 90-265-0252-4, Pub. by Swets Pub Serv Holland). Swets North Am.

Possibility of Naturalism: Social Science & Social Ideologies. Roy Bhaskar. (Philosophy Now Ser.). 1978. text ed. 28.75x (ISBN 0-391-00843-9); pap. text ed. 11.75x (ISBN 0-391-00844-7). Humanities.

Possible & the Actual: Readings in the Metaphysics of Modality. Intro. by Michael J. Loux. LC 79-7618. 1979. 19.50x (ISBN 0-8014-1238-2); pap. 6.95x (ISBN 0-8014-9178-9). Cornell U Pr.

Possible She. Susan Jacoby. 160p. 1980. pap. 2.50 (ISBN 0-345-28735-5). Ballantine.

Possum. Robert M. McClung. (gr. 1-5). 1963. PLB 7.44 (ISBN 0-688-31508-9). Morrow.

Post Accident Heat Removal. V. Coen & H. Holtbecker. (European Applied Research Reports Special Topics Ser.). 402p. 1980. pap. text ed. 92.00 (ISBN 3-7186-0025-0). Harwood Academic.

Post-Augustan Poetry. Harold E. Butler. (Latin Poetry Ser.: Vol. 15). (LC 77-070766). 1977. Repr. of 1909 ed. lib. bdg. 33.00 (ISBN 0-8240-2964-X). Garland Pub.

Post-Captain: Or, the Wooden Walls Well Manned; Comprehending a View of Naval Society & Manners, Repr. Of 1806 Ed. John Davis. Bd. with Struggle of Capt. Thomas Keith in America, Including the Manner in Which He, His Wife & Child Were Decoyed by the Indians. Repr. of 1808 ed. LC 75-7048. (Indian Captivities Ser.: Vol. 26). 1977. lib. bdg. 44.00 (ISBN 0-8240-1650-5). Garland Pub.

Post Card Views & Other Souvenirs. Marcia M. Miller. (Illus.). 64p. 1973. pap. 2.95 (ISBN 0-913270-24-5). Sunstone Pr.

Post Communication: Criticism & Evaluation. Robert Cathcart. LC 66-19701. (Orig.). 1966. pap. 5.95 (ISBN 0-672-61073-6, SC2). Bobbs.

Post Communication: Rhetorical Analysis & Evaluation. Robert Cathcart. LC 80-36842. (Speech Communication Ser.). 144p. 1981. pap. text ed. 5.95 (ISBN 0-672-61520-7). Bobbs.

Post-Compulsory Education: A New Analysis in Western Europe. Ed. by Edmund J. King et al. LC 74-76709. (Sage Studies in Social & Educational Change: Vol. 1). 1974. 22.50x (ISBN 0-8039-9900-3). Sage.

Post Compulsory Education II. Edmund J. King et al. LC 74-31574. (Sage Studies in Social & Educational Change: Vol. 2). 1975. 17.50x (ISBN 0-8039-9953-4); pap. 8.95x (ISBN 0-8039-9950-X). Sage.

Post-Ecumenical Christianity. Ed. by Hans Kung. (Concilium Ser.: Religion in the Seventies: Vol. 54). 1970. pap. 4.95 (ISBN 0-8164-2510-8). Crossroad NY.

Post-Graduate Teacher Training: A Negerian Alternative. (Experiments & Innovations in Education Ser: No. 20). (Illus.). 53p. 1976. pap. 2.50 (ISBN 92-3-101320-3, U473, UNESCO). Unipub.

Post-Harvest Prevention of Waste & Loss of Food Grains. 358p. 1974. 11.75 (APO54, APO). Unipub.

Post Hypnotic Instructions. Arnold Furst. pap 3.00 (ISBN 0-87980-119-0). Wilshire.

Post Imperial Presidency. Ed. by Vincent Davis. 288p. 1980. 19.95 (ISBN 0-03-055741-0). Praeger.

Post-Impressionist Group Exhibitions. Ed. by Theodore Reff. (Modern Art in Paris Ser.). 302p. 1981. lib. bdg. 44.00 (ISBN 0-8240-4728-1). Garland Pub.

Post-Kantian Anthropology. Johnemery Konecsni. 1978. pap. text ed. 9.00x (ISBN 0-8191-0374-8). U Pr of Amer.

Post-Man Robb'd of His Mail: Or, the Packet Broke Open. Charles Gildon. LC 73-170542. (Foundations of the Novel Ser.: Vol. 31). lib. bdg. 50.00 (ISBN 0-8240-0543-0). Garland Pub.

Post-Mao China & U.S. China Trade. Ed. by Shao-Chuan Leng. LC 77-20811. 1978. 10.95x (ISBN 0-8139-0733-0). U Pr of Va.

Post-Mastectomy Reconstruction. Thomas Gant & Luis Vasconez. (Illus.). 196p. 1980. softcover 27.00 (ISBN 0-683-03419-7). Williams & Wilkins.

Post Mortem. Liam MacUlsten. (Irish Play Ser.). pap. 2.50 (ISBN 0-912262-43-5). Proscenium.

Post Mortem Estate Planning 1980. (Tax Law & Estate Planning Course Handbook Series 1980-81: Vol. 117). 1980. pap. 25.00 (ISBN 0-685-90314-1, D4-5134). PLI.

Post-Natal Depression. Wellburn. 1980. text ed. 19.50x (ISBN 0-7190-0792-5). Humanities.

Post O-Level Studies in Modern Languages. C. V. Russell. 1971. 17.25 (ISBN 0-08-016194-4). Pergamon.

Post Office Clerk-Carrier. 13th ed. Arco Editorial Board. LC 76-23985. 1980. pap. 6.00 (ISBN 0-668-04846-8, 4846-8). Arco.

Post Partum Book: How to Cope with & Enjoy the First Year of Parenting. Hank Pizer & Christine Garfink. LC 78-19710. 1979. 9.95 (ISBN 0-394-50524-7, GP821). Grove.

Post-Physician Era: Medicine in the 21st Century. Jerrold S. Maxmen. LC 76-2442. (Health, Medicine & Society Ser.). 1976. 24.50 (ISBN 0-471-57880-0, Pub. by Wiley-Interscience). Wiley.

Post Scripts: Humor from the Saturday Evening Post. LC 78-53039. (Illus.). 1978. 4.95 (ISBN 0-89387-022-6). Sat Eve Post.

Post-Symbolist Bibliography. Henry Krawitz. LC 73-1181. 1973. 10.00 (ISBN 0-8108-0594-4). Scarecrow.

Post-War British Theater. J. Elsom. 1976. 18.00 (ISBN 0-7100-8350-5). Routledge & Kegan.

Post-War Drama: Extracts from Eleven Plays. Ed. by John Hale. 1967. 7.95 (ISBN 0-571-06858-8, Pub. by Faber & Faber). Merrimack Bk Serv.

Post-War Europe: A Political Geography. Mark Blacksell. LC 77-82814. (Illus.). 1978. lib. bdg. 22.00x (ISBN 0-89158-822-1). Westview.

Post-War History of the Stock Market. A. G. Ellinger & T. H. Stewart. 80p. 1980. 30.00x (ISBN 0-85941-153-2, Pub. by Woodhead-Faulkner England). State Mutual Bk.

Post-War Immigrants in Canada. Anthony H. Richmond. LC 67-100218. 352p. 1967. 17.50x o.p. (ISBN 0-8020-1673-1). U of Toronto Pr.

Post War International Money Crisis: An Analysis. Victor Argy. 472p. (Orig.). 1981. text ed. 38.95x (ISBN 0-04-332075-9, 2576); pap. text ed. 17.50x (ISBN 0-04-332076-7, 2577). Allen Unwin.

Post War Planning Experience in Guyana. new ed. Kempe R. Hope. LC 77-27492. (Special Studies: No. 16). 1978. pap. text ed. 3.50x o.p. (ISBN 0-87918-041-2). ASU Lat Am St.

Post-Watergate Morality. Lester A. Sobel. lib. bdg. 15.00x o.p. (ISBN 0-87196-261-6). Facts on File.

Post-Yield Fracture Mechanics. Ed. by D. G. Latzko. (Illus.). 1979. 72.50x (ISBN 0-85334-775-1). Intl Ideas.

Postage Stamp Price Index U. S. & Canada from 1845: 1980-1981 Edition. Ed. by Joseph M. Heery. (Illus.). 192p. (Orig.). 1980. pap. 2.95 (ISBN 0-937458-01-5). Harris & Co.

Postage Stamps & Postal History of Newfoundland. Winthrop S. Boggs. LC 75-1791. (Illus.). 288p. 1975. Repr. 35.00x (ISBN 0-88000-066-X). Quarterman.

Postage Stamps of Mexico 1856-1868. Samuel Chapman. LC 75-40501. (Illus.). 1976. Repr. 35.00x (ISBN 0-88000-079-1). Quarterman.

Postage Stamps of the United States. John N. Luff. LC 80-54039. 320p. 1981. Repr. of 1940 ed. lib. bdg. 35.00 (ISBN 0-88000-121-6). Quarterman.

Postal Applications of Operations Research. J. N. D. Gupta. 1978. text ed. 34.50 (ISBN 0-08-023011-3). Pergamon.

Postal Business Nineteen Sixty-Nine to Nineteen Seventy-Nine: A Study in Public Sector Management. Michael Corby. 1979. 28.75x (ISBN 0-85038-227-0). Nichols Pub.

Postal Reorganization: Managing the Public's Business. John T. Tierney. 200p. 1981. 19.95 (ISBN 0-86569-061-8). Auburn Hse.

Postal Service Officer. Arco Editorial Board. LC 67-22817. (Orig.). 1967. pap. 5.00 o.p. (ISBN 0-668-01658-2). Arco.

Postcard Poems: A Collection of Poetry for Sharing. Ed. by Paul B. Janeczko. LC 79-14192. (gr. 6 up). 1979. 9.95 (ISBN 0-87888-155-7). Bradbury Pr.

Postcards of Alphonse Mucha. Q. David Bowers & Mary L. Martin. (Illus.). 100p. 1980. 9.95 (ISBN 0-911572-18-X). Vestal.

Poster Packet & Teaching Guide for Elementary Classrooms. Ed. by Lynne G. Miller & Miriam Brammer. (Illus.). 1975. pap. text ed. 9.95 (ISBN 0-590-09597-8, Citation). Schol Bk Serv.

Posterior Analytics. Aristotle. Ed. by Jonathan Barnes. (Clarendon Aristotle Ser). 1975. 19.95x (ISBN 0-19-872066-1); pap. 17.95x (ISBN 0-19-872067-X). Oxford U Pr.

Postern of Fate. Agatha Christie. 288p. 1980. pap. 2.25 (ISBN 0-553-13775-1). Bantam.

Posters. Joanne Marxhausen. (A Nice Place to Live Ser.). 1978. pap. 2.25 (ISBN 0-570-07752-4, 12-2711). Concordia.

Posters of Jules Cheret. Jules Cheret & Lucy Broido. (Illus.). 128p. (Orig.). 1980. pap. 8.95 (ISBN 0-486-24010-X). Dover.

Postgraduate Obstetrical & Gynaecological Pathology. H. Fox & F. A. Langley. 596p. 1973. 90.00 (ISBN 0-08-016992-9). Pergamon.

Postharvest Biology & Handling of Fruits & Vegetables. Norman F. Haard & D. K. Salunkhe. (Illus.). 1975. text ed. 27.50 (ISBN 0-87055-187-6). AVI.

Postharvest Physiology, Handling & Utilization of Tropical & Subtropical Fruits & Vegetables. E. B. Pantistico. (Illus.). 1975. lib. bdg. 45.00 (ISBN 0-87055-156-6). AVI.

Posthumous Pieces. Wei Wu-Wei. 245p. 1981. pap. 5.00 (ISBN 0-85656-027-8). Great Eastern.

Posthumous Works, 4 vols. Mary Wollstonecraft. Ed. by William Godwin. (Feminist Controversy in England, 1788-1810 Ser.). 1974. Set. lib. bdg. 200.00 (ISBN 0-8240-0889-8); lib. bdg. 50.00 ea. Garland Pub.

Postman. Roger Martin Du Gard, pseud. Tr. by John Russell from Fr. LC 74-13052. 156p. 1975. Repr. of 1955 ed. 13.50 (ISBN 0-86527-333-2). Fertig.

Postmen the World Over. Floyd J. Torbert. (Illus.). (gr. 4-6). 1966. 4.95g o.s.i. (ISBN 0-8038-5722-5). Hastings.

Postminimalism: American Art of the Decade. Robert Pincus-Witten. LC 77-77010. (Illus.). 1981. pap. text ed. 11.95 (ISBN 0-915570-07-6). Oolp Pr.

Postmoderns: The New American Poetry Revised. rev. ed. Ed. by Donald Allen & George F. Butterick. LC 79-52054. 512p. 1981. pap. 9.95 postponed (ISBN 0-394-17458-5, Ever). Grove.

Postscript to Preaching: After Forty Years, How Will I Preach Today? Gene E. Bartlett. 88p. 1981. pap. 3.95 (ISBN 0-8170-0909-4). Judson.

Postscript with a Chinese Accent: Memoirs & Diaries, 1972-73. C. L. Sulzberger. LC 74-10507. (Illus.). 400p. 1974. 10.00 o.s.i. (ISBN 0-02-615320-3, 61532). Macmillan.

Postural Development of Infant Chimpanzees. Austin H. Riesen & E. F. Kinder. 1952. 42.50x (ISBN 0-685-69858-0). Elliots Bks.

Postural Variations in Childhood. C. Asher. (Postgraduate Pediatric Ser.). 1975. 14.95 (ISBN 0-407-00032-1). Butterworths.

Posture & Movement: Perspective for Integrating Sensory & Motor Research on the Mammalian Nervous System. Ed. by Richard E. Talbott & Donald R. Humphrey. LC 77-85515. 1979. text ed. 32.50 (ISBN 0-89004-259-4). Raven.

Postwar America: Readings & Reminiscences. E. Rosenberg & N. Rosenberg. 336p. 1976. pap. 10.95 (ISBN 0-13-685495-8). P-H.

Postwar America: The Search for Identity. Donald G. Baker & Charles H. Sheldon. (Insight Series: Studies in Contemporary Issues). 1969. pap. 4.95x (ISBN 0-02-473840-9, 47384). Macmillan.

Postwar America: 1945-1971. Howard Zinn. LC 72-88273. (History of American Society Ser). 260p. (Orig.). 1973. pap. 5.95 (ISBN 0-672-60936-3). Bobbs.

Postwar British Theatre Criticism. Ed. by John Elsom. 224p. 1980. 25.00 (ISBN 0-7100-0535-0); pap. 14.95 (ISBN 0-7100-0536-9). Routledge & Kegan.

Postwar Germans. David Rodnick. 1948. 37.50x (ISBN 0-685-89773-7). Elliots Bks.

Postwar Population Transfers in Europe, 1945-1955. Joseph B. Schechtman. LC 62-7200. 1962. 12.50x o.p. (ISBN 0-8122-7298-6). U of Pa Pr.

Pot -- What It Is, What It Does. Ann Tobias. LC 78-10817. (Read-Alone Bk.). (Illus.). 48p. (gr. 1-3). 1981. pap. 2.95 (ISBN 0-688-00463-6). Greenwillow.

Pot & the Kettle. T. Starr Terrill. LC 79-66885. 128p. 1980. pap. 8.95 o.p. (ISBN 0-935560-00-9). D Varden Pubns.

Pot au Feu. Theodore P. Fraser & Alan L. Whipple. (Illus.). 218p. (gr. 7-10). 1975. pap. text ed. 4.75x (ISBN 0-88334-068-2). Ind Sch Pr.

Pot of Gold: A Juvenile Fantasy Novel. John Wiessner, Jr. 160p. (gr. 5). 1981. 5.95 (ISBN 0-8059-2769-7). Dorrance.

Potassium-Argon Dating, Principles, Techniques, & Applications to Geochronology. G. Brent Dalrymple & Marvin A. Lanphere. LC 71-84047. (Geology Ser.). (Illus.). 1969. text ed. 22.95x (ISBN 0-7167-0241-X). W H Freeman.

Potato Book. Myrna Davis. LC 73-7890. (Illus.). 1978. pap. 2.95 (ISBN 0-688-05186-3, Quill). Morrow.

Potato Cookbook. Gwen McIver. 1977. 11.95 (ISBN 0-7134-0477-9, Pub. by Batsford England). David & Charles.

Potato Cookbook: From Thinning to Sinning Deliciously from Soups to Desserts. Gwen Robyns. LC 76-43322. (Illus.). 136p. 1976. 9.95 (ISBN 0-916144-11-9). Stemmer Hse.

Potato Processing. 3rd ed. Ed. by W. F. Talburt & Ora Smith. 1975. lib. bdg. 49.50 (ISBN 0-87055-180-9). AVI.

Potato World Handbook. Ed. by E. Michael Galvin. 400p. 1980. perfect bdg 19.95 (ISBN 0-937358-45-2). G D L Inc.

Potatoes: Production, Storing, Processing. 2nd ed. Ora Smith. (Illus.). 1977. lib. bdg. 39.50 (ISBN 0-87055-224-4). AVI.

Potboilers. Gaylon Duke. 64p. 1980. pap. text ed. 15.00 (ISBN 0-87879-275-9). Acad Therapy.

Potent Image: Art in the Western World from Cave Paintings to the 1970's. Frederick S. Wight. 512p. 1976. pap. 9.95 o.s.i. (ISBN 0-02-000970-4, Collier). Macmillan.

Potent Prayers. Harriete Curtiss & F. Homer. pap. 1.00 o.p. (ISBN 0-87516-362-9). De Vorss.

Potential Collapse of Western Civilization & Solutions for One of the Major Crises in World History. Henry Figerot. (Institute for Economic & Political World Strategic Studies Bk). (Illus.). 87p. 1975. 49.40 (ISBN 0-913314-55-2). Am Classical Coll Pr.

Potential Energy. M. Kenward. LC 75-36174. (Illus.). 256p. 1976. 35.50 (ISBN 0-521-21086-0); pap. 9.95x (ISBN 0-521-29056-2). Cambridge U Pr.

Potential Energy Surfaces. Ed. by K. Lawley. (Advances in Chemical Physics: Vol. 42). 1980. 90.25 (ISBN 0-471-27633-2, Pub. by Wiley-Interscience). Wiley.

Potential for Increasing Production of Natural Gas from Existing Fields in the Near Term. Committee on Gas Production Opportunities. 1978. pap. 6.25 (ISBN 0-309-02784-5). Natl Acad Pr.

Potential for Liquid Fuels from Agriculture & Forestry in Australia. G. A. Stewart et al. 147p. 1980. pap. 7.50 (ISBN 0-643-00353-3, Pub. by SIRO Australia). Intl Schol Bk Serv.

Potential for Substituting Manpower for Energy. Walter R. Stahel. Date not set. 12.50 (ISBN 0-533-04799-4). Vantage.

Potential Low-Grade Iron Ore & Hydraulic-Fracturing Sand in Cambrian Sandstones, Northwestern Llano Region, Texas. V. E. Barnes & D. A. Schofield. (Illus.). 58p. 1964. 2.00 (RI 53). Bur Econ Geology.

Potential of Lignocellulosic Materials for the Production of Chemicals, Fuels, & Energy. National Academy of Sciences. 1979. pap. 14.95 (ISBN 0-930978-92-7). Solar Energy Info.

Potential Problems for Second Language & Second Dialect Speakers in Mastering Standard English. Sheilah Bobo. LC 79-54950. 1979. pap. text ed. 7.25 o.p. (ISBN 0-8191-0871-5). U Pr of Amer.

Potential Theory in Modern Function Theory. 2nd ed. Masatugu Tsuji. LC 74-4297. 600p. 1975. text ed. 19.50 (ISBN 0-8284-0281-7). Chelsea Pub.

Potestas Clavium. Lev Shestov. Tr. by Bernard Martin. LC 67-24282. 1968. 16.00 (ISBN 0-8214-0040-1). Ohio U Pr.

Potomac Program. Sarah Hyde & Engle. 439p. 1977. 34.95 (ISBN 0-86575-037-8). Dormac.

Potomac: The Nation's River. Frank Graham, Jr. (Illus.). 1976. 15.95 o.p. (ISBN 0-397-01139-3). Lippincott.

Potomac Wind & Wisdom: Jokes, Lies & True Stories About America's Politics & Politicians. Dick Hyman. LC 80-13482. (Illus.). 1980. 6.95 (ISBN 0-8289-0372-7). Greene.

Potted Plant Book. Sue Tarsky. (Illus.). 48p. (gr. 5 up). 1981. 9.95 (ISBN 0-316-83206-5). Little.

Potter Brownware. Sarah Garland. LC 77-70271. (Illus.). (gr. k-3). 1977. 6.95 (ISBN 0-684-15044-1, ScribJ). Scribner.

Potters. Leonard E. Fisher. LC 69-14499. (Colonial Americans Ser). (Illus.). (gr. 4-6). 1969. PLB 4.90 o.p. (ISBN 0-531-01032-5). Watts.

Potter's Book. Bernard Leach. (gr. 9-12). 20.00 (ISBN 0-693-01117-3); pap. 10.00 (ISBN 0-693-01157-2). Transatlantic.

Potter's Book of Glaze Recipes. Emanuel Cooper. 1980. 15.95 (ISBN 0-684-16670-4, ScribT). Scribner.

Potter's Companion: The Complete Guide to Pottery Making. Tony Birks. (Illus.). 1977. pap. 4.95 (ISBN 0-87690-246-8). Dutton.

Potters in Ireland. Sheila Murray. Ed. by Alan Beesley. 80p. 1974. pap. text ed. 3.95 (ISBN 0-8277-2529-9). British Bk Ctr.

Potters' Kitchen. Rachel Isadora. LC 76-47666. (Illus.). (gr. 1-4). 1977. 7.25 (ISBN 0-688-80089-0); PLB 6.96 (ISBN 0-688-84089-2). Greenwillow.

Potter's New Cyclopaedia of Botanical Drugs & Preparations. R. C. Wren. 1980. text ed. 23.95x (ISBN 0-8464-1039-7). Beekman Pubs.

Potter's Primer. Eleanor Chroman. 1974. pap. 5.95 (ISBN 0-8015-5959-6, Hawthorn). Dutton.

Potters' Quarter: The Pottery. Agnes N. Stillwell & J. L. Benson. (Corinth: Results of Excavations Conducted by the School of Classical Studies at Athens: Vol. XV, iii). 1981. price not set (ISBN 0-87661-153-6). Am Sch Athens.

Potter's Wheel Projects. Ed. by Thomas Sellers. 2.95 (ISBN 0-934706-04-2). Prof Pubns Ohio.

Pottery. Boy Scouts Of America. LC 19-600. (Illus.). 64p. (gr. 6-12). 1969. pap. 0.70x (ISBN 0-8395-3314-4, 3314). BSA.

Pottery & Ceramics: A Guide to Information Sources. Ed. by James E. Campbell. LC 74-11545. (Art & Architecture Information Guide Ser,: Vol. 7). 1978. 30.00 (ISBN 0-8103-1274-3). Gale.

Pottery & Porcelain Tablewares. John P. Cushion. LC 75-45518. (Illus.). 1976. 22.50 o.p. (ISBN 0-688-03055-6). Morrow.

Pottery: Materials & Techniques. David Green. 1967. 13.95 (ISBN 0-571-08080-4, Pub. by Faber & Faber). Merrimack Bk Serv.

Pottery of Mayapan: Including Studies of Ceramic Material from Uxmal, Kabah, & Chichen Itza. Robert E. Smith. LC 73-158899. (Peabody Museum Papers: Vol. 66, Nos. 1 & 2). 1971. pap. 40.00 (ISBN 0-87365-187-1). Peabody Harvard.

Pottery of San Ildefonso Pueblo. Kenneth M. Chapman & Francis H. Harlow. LC 76-99565. (School of American Research). (Illus.). 260p. 1977. Repr. of 1970 ed. 29.95x o.p. (ISBN 0-8263-0157-6). U of NM Pr.

Pottery: Step-by-Step. Macmillan. LC 76-8826. (Step-by-Step Craft Ser.). (Illus.). 1976. pap. 5.95 o.s.i. (ISBN 0-02-011810-4, 01181, Collier). Macmillan.

Pottery Style & Society in Ancient Peru: Art As a Mirror of History in the Ica Valley, 1350-1570. Dorothy Menzel. LC 74-29797. 1976. 36.50x (ISBN 0-520-02970-4). U of Cal Pr.

Pottery Technology: Principles & Reconstruction. Owen S. Rye. LC 80-53439. (Manuals on Archeology Ser.: No. 4). (Illus.). 1981. 18.00x (ISBN 0-9602822-2-X). Taraxacum.

Pottery Treasures. Photos by Jerry Jacka. LC 76-657. (Illus.). 96p. (Text by Spencer Gill). 1976. pap. 9.95 (ISBN 0-912856-28-9); 19.50 o.p. (ISBN 0-686-67419-7). Graphic Arts Ctr.

Potworks: A First Book of Clay. Billie Luisi. (Illus.). 1973. 6.95 o.p. (ISBN 0-688-00157-2). Morrow.

"Poulains" De Corinthe. O. E. Ravel. (Illus.). 1979. text ed. 80.00 (ISBN 0-916710-47-5). Obol Intl.

Poultice for Each Season. David Brewster. 1979. 2.00 (ISBN 0-918116-16-3). Jawbone Pr.

Poultry. (Good Cook Ser.). (Illus.). 1979. lib. bdg. 11.97 (ISBN 0-686-50995-1). Silver.

Poultry Cookbook. Mary Norwak. 1979. 19.95 (ISBN 0-241-89807-2, Pub. by Hamish Hamilton England). David & Charles.

Poultry: Feeds & Nutrition. 2nd ed. Homer Patrick & P. J. Schaible. (Illus.). 1980. 39.50 (ISBN 0-87055-353-4); pap. 25.00 (ISBN 0-87055-349-6). AVI.

Poultry Keeping for Beginners. David Kay. 1977. 11.95 (ISBN 0-7153-7395-1). David & Charles.

Poultry Products Technology. 2nd ed. George J. Mountney. (Illus.). 1976. text ed. 29.00 (ISBN 0-87055-199-X). AVI.

Poultry Science. 2nd ed. M. E. Ensminger. (Illus.). (gr. 9-12). 1980. 26.00 (ISBN 0-8134-2087-3, 2087); text ed. 19.50x (ISBN 0-686-60698-1). Interstate.

Pound Era. Hugh Kenner. LC 72-138349. 1971. 22.00x (ISBN 0-520-01860-5); pap. 6.95 (ISBN 0-520-02427-3). U of Cal Pr.

Poupliniere et la Musique De Chambre Au Xv111 Siecle. G. Cucuel. LC 70-158961. (Music Ser). 1971. Repr. of 1913 ed. lib. bdg. 49.50 (ISBN 0-306-70186-3). Da Capo.

Pour Lire et Parler. Elizabeth Peters & Sr. Jerome Keeler. (Illus.). (gr. 9-12). 1950. text ed. 2.00 o.p. (ISBN 0-8294-0132-6). Loyola.

Pour toi. Louis Untermeyer. (Illus., Fr.). 1968. 1.95 (ISBN 0-88332-128-9, 4420). Larousse.

Pouring Down Words. Suzette H. Elgin. 256p. 1975. pap. 7.95 (ISBN 0-13-686352-3). P-H.

Poverty: A New Perspective. Ed. by George L. Wilber. LC 74-7884. (Illus.). 208p. 1975. 14.00x (ISBN 0-8131-1321-0). U Pr of Ky.

Poverty: A Study of Town Life, London Nineteen Ten. 2nd ed. B. Seebohm Rountree. LC 79-56969. (English Working Class Ser.). 1980. lib. bdg. 38.00 (ISBN 0-8240-0120-6). Garland Pub.

Poverty: America's Enduring Paradox. Sidney Lens. LC 69-11085. 1969. 8.95 o.s.i. (ISBN 0-690-64927-4, TYC-T). T y Crowell.

Poverty Amid Plenty: A Political & Economic Analysis. Harrell R. Rodgers, Jr. LC 78-18642. (Political Science Ser.). (Illus.). 1979. pap. text ed. 7.50 (ISBN 0-201-06471-5). A-W.

Poverty & Discrimination. Lester C. Thurow. (Studies in Social Economics). 1969. 10.95 (ISBN 0-8157-8444-9). Brookings.

Poverty & Inequality in Common Market Countries. Ed. by Vic George & Roger Lawson. 1980. 27.00x (ISBN 0-7100-0424-9); pap. 15.00 (ISBN 0-7100-0517-2). Routledge & Kegan.

Poverty & Malnutrition in Latin America: Early Childhood Intervention Programs. Ernesto Pollitt. LC 80-18811. 150p. 1980. 21.95 (ISBN 0-03-058031-5). Praeger.

Poverty & Mental Health: PRR 21. Ed. by M. Greenblatt et al. 275p. 1967. pap. 5.00 (ISBN 0-685-24868-2, P021-0). Am Psychiatric.

Poverty & Piety in an English Village: Terling, 1525-1700. Keith Wrightson & David Levine. LC 78-1102. (Studies in Social Discontinuity Ser.). 1979. 17.00 (ISBN 0-12-765950-1). Acad Pr.

Poverty & Progress in Britain, 1953-1973: A Statistical Study of Low Income Households. Guy Fiegehen et al. LC 77-2143. (NIESR, Occasional Paper: No. 29). (Illus.). 1977. 29.95 (ISBN 0-521-21683-4). Cambridge U Pr.

Poverty & Prostitution. Frances Finnegan. LC 78-68123. (Illus.). 1979. 29.95 (ISBN 0-521-22447-0). Cambridge U Pr.

Poverty & Revolution in Iran: The Migrant Poor, Urban Marginality & Politics. Farhad Kazemi. 180p. 1981. text ed. 17.50x (ISBN 0-8147-4576-8). NYU Pr.

Poverty & Social Casework Services: Selected Papers. Ben A. Orcutt. LC 74-14917. 1974. 8.00 o.p. (ISBN 0-8108-0751-3). Scarecrow.

Poverty & Social Change. Kirsten Gronbjerg et al. LC 78-876. viii, 248p. 1980. lib. bdg. 9.00x (ISBN 0-226-30963-0). U of Chicago Pr.

Poverty & Social Inequality in Wales. Ed. by Gareth Rees & Teresa L. Rees. 279p. 1980. 30.00x (ISBN 0-7099-2200-0, Pub. by Croom Helm Ltd England). Biblio Dist.

Poverty & Transfers In-Kind: A Re-Evaluation of Poverty in the United States. Morton Paglin. LC 79-88586. (Publication: No. 219). 108p. 1980. pap. 6.95 (ISBN 0-8179-7192-0). Hoover Inst Pr.

Poverty Business: Britain & America. Joan M. Higgins. (Aspects of Social Policy Ser.). 1978. 22.00x (ISBN 0-631-16260-7, Pub. by Basil Blackwell). Biblio Dist.

Poverty Curtain: Choices for the Third World. Haq Mahbub Ul. 256p. 1976. 17.50x (ISBN 0-231-04062-8); pap. 9.00x (ISBN 0-231-04063-6). Columbia U Pr.

Poverty, Economics, & Society. Ed. by Helen Ginsburg. LC 80-6115. 361p. 1981. lib. bdg. 21.50 (ISBN 0-8191-1385-9); pap. text ed. 11.95 (ISBN 0-8191-1386-7). U Pr of Amer.

Poverty Establishment. Ed. by Pamela Roby. (Illus.). 224p. 1974. 7.95 o.p. (ISBN 0-13-693705-5, Spec); pap. 2.95 o.p. (ISBN 0-13-693697-0, S334, Spec). P-H.

Poverty in America: The Welfare Dilemma. Ralph Segalman & Asoke Basu. LC 79-6568. (Contributions in Sociology: No. 39). (Illus.). 446p. 1981. lib. bdg. 35.00 (ISBN 0-313-20751-8, BPO/). Greenwood.

Poverty in Britain & the Reform of Social Security. A. B. Atkinson. LC 76-85711. (Department of Applied Economic, Occasional Papers Ser). 1969. 15.95 (ISBN 0-521-07522-X); pap. 8.50 (ISBN 0-521-09607-3, 607). Cambridge U Pr.

Poverty in Israel: Economic Realities & the Promise of Social Justice. Harold I. Greenberg & Samuel Nadler. LC 76-58558. (Special Studies). 1977. text ed. 22.95 (ISBN 0-275-24300-1). Praeger.

Poverty in New York, 1783-1825. Raymond A. Mohl. (Urban Life in America Ser). 1971. 15.95 (ISBN 0-19-501367-0). Oxford U Pr.

Poverty in Rural America: A Cast Study. Janet M. Fitchen. (Special Studies in Contemporary Social Issues). 266p. (Orig.). 1981. lib. bdg. 20.00x (ISBN 0-89158-868-X); pap. text ed. 9.50x (ISBN 0-89158-901-5). Westview.

Poverty in the United Kingdom: A Survey of Household Resoures & Standards of Living. Peter Townsend. 1980. 40.00x (ISBN 0-520-03871-1); pap. 16.95x (ISBN 0-520-03976-9, CAMPUS NO. 242). U of Cal Pr.

Poverty, Inequality, & Development. Gary S. Fields. LC 79-21017. (Illus.). 256p. 1980. 29.50 (ISBN 0-521-22572-8); pap. 7.95 (ISBN 0-521-29852-0). Cambridge U Pr.

Poverty: Its Illegal Causes & Legal Cure. L. Spooner. LC 78-156804. (Studies in American History & Government Ser.). 108p. 1971. Repr. of 1846 ed. lib. bdg. 17.50 (ISBN 0-306-70207-X). Da Capo.

Poverty of Historicism. Karl R. Popper. 1977. pap. text ed. 5.95x (ISBN 0-06-131126-X, TB1126, Torch). Har-Row.

Poverty of Progress: Latin America in the Nineteenth Century. E. Bradford Burns. 224p. 1980. 12.95x (ISBN 0-520-04160-7). U of Cal Pr.

Poverty Policy: A Compendium of Cash Transfer Proposals. Ed. by Theodore R. Marmor. LC 71-140011. 1971. 17.50x (ISBN 0-202-32004-9). Aldine Pub.

Poverty, Politics & Change. Dorothy James. (Illus.). 224p. 1972. pap. text ed. 8.95 (ISBN 0-13-686584-4). P-H.

Poverty: Wealth of Mankind. Albert Tevoedjre. 1979. text ed. 30.00 (ISBN 0-08-023367-8); pap. text ed. 14.00 (ISBN 0-08-023366-X). Pergamon.

Powder Box Lady. Anita Xhafer. (Illus.). 32p. (ps-6). 1981. 10.95 (ISBN 0-19-554263-0). Oxford U Pr.

Powder Burns. Al Cody. 256p. (YA) 1973. 5.95 (ISBN 0-685-31777-3, Avalon). Bouregy.

Powder Coating: Recent Developments. Ed. by M. T. Gillies. LC 80-26426. (Chemical Tech. Rev. Ser.: 183). (Illus.). 326p. 1981. 48.00 (ISBN 0-8155-0836-0). Noyes.

Powder Metallurgy in Defense Technology: Proceedings, Vol. 5. Defense Technology Seminar, Yuma, Arizona, 1979. (Orig.). 1980. pap. text ed. 40.00 (ISBN 0-918404-50-9). Metal Powder.

Powder Metallurgy: Principles & Applications. Fritz V. Lenel. LC 80-81830. (Illus.). 608p. 1980. 55.00 (ISBN 0-918404-48-7). Metal Powder.

Powell's Canyon Voyage. W. L. Rusho. LC 70-64908. (Wild & Woolly West Ser., No. 11). (Illus., Orig.). 1969. 7.00 (ISBN 0-910584-86-9); pap. 2.00 (ISBN 0-910584-12-5). Filter.

Power. Richard M. Stern. 352p. 1976. pap. 1.95 o.p. (ISBN 0-345-25003-6). Ballantine.

Power & Class in Africa: An Introduction to Change & Conflict in African Politics. Irving L. Markowitz. 1977. pap. text ed. 11.95 (ISBN 0-13-686642-5). P-H.

Power & Control: Social Structures & Their Transformation. Ed. by Tom R. Burns & Walter Buckley. LC 76-22900. (Sage Studies in International Sociology: Vol. 6). 1976. 18.00x (ISBN 0-8039-9959-3); pap. 9.95x (ISBN 0-8039-9978-X). Sage.

Power & Diplomacy in Northern Nigeria, 1804-1906. R. A. Adeleye. (Ibadan History Ser). (Illus.). 1971. text ed. 11.50x (ISBN 0-391-00169-8). Humanities.

Power & Discontent. William A. Gamson. (Orig.). 1968. pap. text ed. 9.50x (ISBN 0-256-01101-X). Dorsey.

Power & Dissent in the Medical School. Samuel W. Bloom. LC 73-8356. 1973. pap. text ed. 4.95 (ISBN 0-02-904250-X). Free Pr.

Power & Empowerment in Higher Education: Studies in Honor of Louis Smith. Ed. by D. B. Robertson. LC 77-76333. 168p. 1978. 13.00x (ISBN 0-8131-1373-3). U Pr of Ky.

Power & Energy. Noemie Benczer-Koller & Earl L. Koller. LC 59-13619. (Illus.). (gr. 4-6). 1960. PLB 6.95 (ISBN 0-87396-009-2). Stravon.

Power & Form of Emerson's Thought. Jeffrey L. Duncan. LC 73-85043. 150p. 1974. 7.95x (ISBN 0-8139-0510-9). U Pr of Va.

Power & Identity: Tribalism in World Politics. Harold R. Isaacs. LC 79-55304. (Headline Ser.: No. 246). (Orig.). 1979. pap. 2.00 (ISBN 0-87124-057-2). Foreign Policy.

Power & Impotence of Certitude. Georg Muschalek. 150p. (Orig.). 1981. pap. text ed. price not set (ISBN 0-935780-01-7). Herbert Pubs.

Power & Independence: Urban Africans' Perception of Social Inequality. P. C. Lloyd. (International Library of Anthropology Ser). (Illus.). 1974. 24.00x (ISBN 0-7100-7973-7). Routledge & Kegan.

Power & Influence in a Southern City: Compared with the Classic Community Power Studies of the Lynds, Hunter, Vidich & Bensman, & Dahl. James B. Haugh. LC 80-5231. (Illus.). 160p. 1980. lib. bdg. 17.50 (ISBN 0-8191-1060-4); pap. text ed. 7.25 (ISBN 0-8191-1061-2). U Pr of Amer.

Power & International Relations. Inis L. Claude, Jr. 1962. text ed. 10.95 (ISBN 0-394-30133-1). Random.

Power & Manoeuvrability. T. Carty & A. Smith. 1978. text ed. 18.25x (ISBN 0-905470-04-4). Humanities.

Power & Market: Government & the Economy. Murray N. Rothbard. LC 70-111536. (Studies in Economic Theory). 304p. 1977. 15.00; pap. 4.95. NYU Pr.

Power & Market: Government & the Economy. Murray N. Rothbard. 1977. write for info. NYU Pr.

Power & Opposition in Post Revolutionary Societies. Ed. by Patrick Camiller & Jon Rothschild. 288p. 1980. text ed. 17.50x (ISBN 0-906133-18-1); pap. text ed. 9.25x (ISBN 0-906133-19-X). Humanities.

Power & Order: Henry Adams & the Naturalist Tradition in American Fiction. Harold Kaplan. LC 80-23414. 1981. lib. bdg. price not set (ISBN 0-226-42424-3). U of Chicago Pr.

Power & Parliament. Timothy Raison. 1979. 20.00x (ISBN 0-631-11301-0, Pub. by Basil Blackwell England); pap. 8.50x (ISBN 0-631-12892-1). Biblio Dist.

Power & Party in an English City. David G. Green. (New Local Government Ser.: No. 20). 256p. 1981. text ed. 37.50x (ISBN 0-04-352094-4, 2548). Allen Unwin.

Power & Politics in California. John H. Culver & John C. Syer. LC 79-18497. 1980. pap. text ed. 8.95 (ISBN 0-471-04866-6); tchrs' manual (ISBN 0-471-08076-4). Wiley.

Power & Politics in Labor Legislation. Alan K. McAdams. LC 64-11813. 1964. 20.00x (ISBN 0-231-02644-7). Columbia U Pr.

Power & Politics in Late Imperial China: Yuan Shi-kai in Beijing & Tianjin, 1901-1908. Stephen R. MacKinnon. (Center for Chinese Studies Ser.). (Illus.). 400p. 1981. 18.50x (ISBN 0-520-04025-2). U of Cal Pr.

Power & Politics in the School System: A Guidebook. Michael Locke. 192p. 1974. 16.00x (ISBN 0-7100-7732-7); pap. 7.95 (ISBN 0-7100-7733-5). Routledge & Kegan.

Power & Powerlessness: Quiescence & Rebellion in an Appalachian Valley. John Gaventa. LC 80-12988. (Illus.). 284p. 1980. 16.50 (ISBN 0-252-00772-7). U of Ill Pr.

Power & Process. Harry L. Summerfield. LC 73-17614. 1974. 16.25x o.p. (ISBN 0-8211-1826-9); text ed. 12.40x o.p. (ISBN 0-685-42642-4). McCutchan.

Power & Process, a Commentary on Eminent Domain & Condemnation. Dexter D. MacBride. LC 70-77921. (ASA Monograph: No. 1). 1969. 5.00 (ISBN 0-937828-10-6). Am Soc Appraisers.

Power & Protest in American Life. Alec Barbrook & Christine Bolt. 1980. write for info. (ISBN 0-312-63369-6). St Martin.

Power & Security. Edward Teller et al. LC 75-44722. (Critical Choices for Americans Ser.: Vol. 4). 1976. 15.95 (ISBN 0-669-00416-2). Lexington Bks.

Power & Speed in Reading. Doris W. Gilbert. 1956. text ed. 10.95 (ISBN 0-13-685040-5). P-H.

Power & the Frailty: The Future of Medicine & the Future of Man. Jean Hamburger. Tr. by Joachim Neugroschel. 192p. 1973. 4.95 o.s.i. (ISBN 0-02-547600-9). Macmillan.

Power & the Pursuit of Peace. Francis H. Hinsley. (Orig.). 1968. 31.50 (ISBN 0-521-05274-2); pap. 13.95x (ISBN 0-521-09448-8). Cambridge U Pr.

Power & the Wisdom: An Interpretation of the New Testament. John L. McKenzie. 320p. 1972. pap. 2.45 (ISBN 0-385-08082-4, Im). Doubleday.

Power & the Word of God. Franz Bockle & Jacques-Marie Pohier. LC 73-6431. (Concilium Ser.: Religion in the Seventies: Vol. 90). 156p. (Orig.). 1973. pap. 4.95 (ISBN 0-8164-2574-4). Crossroad NY.

Power & Weakness. William Breault. LC 73-86209. 1973. 4.50 o.s.i. (ISBN 0-8198-0270-0); gift edition 6.00 o.s.i. (ISBN 0-8198-0271-9). Dghtrs St Paul.

Power, Authority & Restrictive Practices: A Sociological Essay on Industrial Relations. Alan Aldridge. 1976. 25.00x (ISBN 0-631-17230-0, Pub. by Basil Blackwell). Biblio Dist.

Power Behind Aston Martin. Geoff Courtney. (Illus.). 1979. 16.95 (ISBN 0-902280-58-9, Pub. by Oxford Ill Pr Ltd. England). Motorbooks Intl.

Power Bright & Shining. Rod McKuen. 1980. 8.95 (ISBN 0-686-62883-7, 41392); deluxe ed. 19.95 (ISBN 0-686-62884-5, 41393). S&S.

Power Cable Handbook. Knox. 1981. text ed. price not set. Butterworths.

Power Development in India. K. Venkataraman. LC 72-10341. 178p. 1972. 12.95 (ISBN 0-470-90578-6). Halsted Pr.

Power Electronics: Solid Stare Motor Control. Richard Pearman. (Illus.). 1980. text ed. 19.95 (ISBN 0-8359-5585-0); instr's manual avail. Reston.

Power Elite. C. Wright Mills. 1956. 17.50 (ISBN 0-19-500020-X). Oxford U Pr.

Power Elite. C. Wright Mills. 1959. pap. 5.95 (ISBN 0-19-500680-1, GB). Oxford U Pr.

Power for Abundant Living. V. P. Wierwille. 1980. 6.95 (ISBN 0-910068-01-1). Devin.

Power for the Church in the Midst of Chaos. Harry N. Huxhold. LC 73-82078. 1973. pap. 2.25 (ISBN 0-570-03160-5, 12-2557). Concordia.

Power for the Use of Man. 128p. 1980. 35.00x (ISBN 0-7277-0067-7, Pub. by Telford England). State Mutual Bk.

Power Game. Stephen Kral. LC 78-78052. 1979. pap. 1.95 o.p. (ISBN 0-87216-548-5). Playboy Pbks.

Power Generation Alternatives. 2nd ed. Seattle City Light. (Illus.). 180p. 1974. pap. 5.00 o.p. (ISBN 0-686-05739-2). Cone-Heiden.

Power Handbook: A Strategic Guide to Personal & Organizational Effectiveness. Pamela Cuming. LC 80-14039. 340p. 1980. pap. 12.95 (ISBN 0-8436-0778-5). CBI Pub.

Power Handtool Handbook. Dave Case. (Illus.). 1980. pap. 5.95 (ISBN 0-89586-027-9). H P Bks.

Power Ideas for a Happy Family. Phyllis Schafly. (Orig.). pap. 1.75 (ISBN 0-515-05104-7). Jove Pubns.

Power Ideas for a Happy Family. Robert Schuller. 1976. pap. 1.50 (ISBN 0-89129-111-3). Jove Pubns.

Power Ideas for a Happy Family. Robert H. Schuller. 128p. 1972. 5.95 o.p. (ISBN 0-8007-0525-4). Revell.

Power in American Society: Burden or Blessing. David A. Durfee. Ed. by Jack R. Fraenkel. (Crucial Issues in American Government Ser.). (gr. 9-12). 1976. pap. text ed. 4.96 (ISBN 0-205-04907-9, 764907X). Allyn.

Power in Britain: Sociological Readings. J. Urry & J. Wakeford. 1973. text ed. 19.95 (ISBN 0-435-82900-9); pap. text ed. 15.95 (ISBN 0-435-82901-7). Heinemann Ed.

Power in Families. Ed. by R. Cromwell & D. E. Olson. LC 75-17648. 264p. 1975. 17.95 (ISBN 0-470-18846-4); pap. 9.95 (ISBN 0-470-18847-2). Halsted Pr.

Power in Penance. Michael Scanlan. 64p. 1972. pap. 0.75 (ISBN 0-87793-092-9). Ave Maria.

Power in Perception for the Young Child: A Comprehensive Program for the Development of Pre-Reading Visual Perceptual Skills. Ronnie S. Goodfriend. LC 72-189232. 1972. pap. text ed. 7.75x (ISBN 0-8077-1430-5); pap. text ed. 5.25x suppl. (ISBN 0-8077-1429-1). Tchrs Coll.

Power in the City: Decision Making in San Francisco. Frederick M. Wirt. LC 73-90662. 1975. 19.95 (ISBN 0-520-02654-3); pap. 6.95 (ISBN 0-520-03640-9). U of Cal Pr.

Power in the Helping Professions. Adolf Guggenbuhl-Craig. Ed. by James Hillman. 155p. 1971. text ed. 7.00 (ISBN 0-88214-304-2). Spring Pubns.

Power in the People. 3rd ed. Felix Morley. LC 72-81839. 1976. 10.00x o.p. (ISBN 0-916054-37-3, Caroline Hse Inc). Green Hill.

Power in the People. Felix Morley. LC 72-81839. 293p. 1972. 10.00x o.p. (ISBN 0-8402-1296-8); pap. 5.95x o.p. (ISBN 0-686-65431-5). Nash Pub.

Power Is You. Alfreda Oliver. 1976. pap. 1.75 o.p. (ISBN 0-449-13640-X, GM). Fawcett.

Power: Its Forms, Bases, & Uses. Dennis H. Wrong. LC 78-24703. (Orig.). 1979. pap. 5.95 (ISBN 0-06-090702-9, CN 702, CN). Har-Row.

Power: Its Forms, Bases, & Uses. Dennis H. Wrong. 1979. text ed. 28.50 o.p. (ISBN 0-06-136181-X, Torch Lib). Har-Row.

Power: Its Nature, Its Uses, Its Limits. Ed. by Donald W. Harward. 1981. pap. text ed. 8.95 (ISBN 0-87073-895-X). Schenkman.

Power Lovers. Myra MacPherson. 1976. pap. 1.95 o.p. (ISBN 0-345-25245-4). Ballantine.

Power Maps: Comparative Politics of Constitutions. Ivo D. Duchacek. LC 72-95265. (Studies in International & Comparative Politics: No. 2). (Illus.). 252p. 1973. pap. text ed. 2.85 (ISBN 0-87436-115-X). ABC-Clio.

Power Mechanics. Pat H. Atteberry. LC 77-16075. (Illus.). 1978. text ed. 4.80 (ISBN 0-87006-243-3). Goodheart.

Power Mechanics. Pat H. Atteberry. LC 80-20581. (Illus.). 112p. 1980. text ed. 4.40 (ISBN 0-87006-307-3). Goodheart.

Power Mechanics. McKnight Staff Members & Wilbur R. Miller. LC 78-53394. (Basic Industrial Arts Ser.). (Illus.). 1978. 6.00 (ISBN 0-87345-798-6); softbound 4.48 (ISBN 0-87345-790-0). McKnight.

Power: Mechanics of Energy Control. Angus J. MacDonald. (gr. 9-12). 1970. text ed. 14.64 (ISBN 0-87345-486-3); mechanical control man. 4.48 (ISBN 0-87345-484-7); fluid control man. 4.48 (ISBN 0-87345-488-X); electric control man. 4.48 (ISBN 0-87345-487-1); optional experiments 4.48 (ISBN 0-87345-489-8); wkbk. & tests 4.48 (ISBN 0-87345-498-7); tchr's guide 40.00 (ISBN 0-87345-497-9); lab manual set 17.16 (ISBN 0-685-04238-3). McKnight.

Power, Money & Sex: Towards a New Social Balance. James Robertson. (Ideas in Progress Ser.). 1978. 11.95 (ISBN 0-7145-2554-5, Pub. by M Boyars); pap. 7.95 (ISBN 0-7145-2555-3). Merrimack Bk Serv.

Power Motive. David G. Winter. LC 72-92869. 1973. 17.95 (ISBN 0-02-935460-9). Free Pr.

Power of an Idea. Ernest Holmes. 1965. pap. 3.50 (ISBN 0-911336-31-1). Sci of Mind.

Power of Autosuggestion & How to Master It. Patrick L. Sackett. (Illus.). 1979. deluxe ed. 37.55 (ISBN 0-930582-61-6). Gloucester Art.

Power of Belief. Ernest Holmes. Ed. by Willis H. Kinnear. 1970. pap. 4.50 (ISBN 0-911336-13-3). Sci of Mind.

Power of Biblical Thinking. Ralph L. Keiper. 1977. 5.95 o.p. (ISBN 0-8007-0862-8). Revell.

Power of Blackness. Jack Williamson. LC 75-29508. 192p. (YA) 1976. 6.95 o.p. (ISBN 0-399-11467-X, Dist. by Putnam). Berkley Pub.

Power of Blackness: Hawthorne, Poe, Melville. Harry Levin. LC 80-83221. xxii, 263p. 1980. pap. 6.95x (ISBN 0-8214-0581-0). Ohio U Pr.

Power of Calculus. 3rd ed. K. L. Whipkey & Mary N. Whipkey. LC 78-24067. 1979. 18.50 (ISBN 0-471-03140-2); tchrs. manual 2.00 (ISBN 0-471-05500-X). Wiley.

Power of God Within You. W. W. VauDell. 1980. 5.50 o.p. (ISBN 0-682-49157-8). Exposition.

Power of Goodness. Cesare Zappulli. 1980. 3.00 (ISBN 0-8198-5800-5); pap. 2.00 (ISBN 0-8198-5801-3). Dghtrs St Paul.

Power of His Resurrection: The Mystical Life of Christians. Arthur A. Vogel. 150p. 1976. 6.95 (ISBN 0-8164-0298-1). Crossroad NY.

Power of Hypnosis. Hans Holzer. LC 72-7841. 1973. 5.95 o.p. (ISBN 0-672-51584-9). Bobbs.

Power of Kindness. Harry M. Tippett. (Uplook Ser.). 32p. 1955. pap. 0.75 (ISBN 0-8163-0076-3, 16415-2). Pacific Pr Pub Assn.

Power of Light: Eight Stories for Hanukkah. Isaac B. Singer. (Illus.). (gr. 1 up). 1980. 10.95 (ISBN 0-374-36099-5). FS&G.

Power of Limits: Proportional Harmony in Art, Architecture, Nature, & Man. Gyorgy Doczi. LC 77-90883. (Illus.). 224p. 1981. 19.95 (ISBN 0-394-51352-5); pap. 9.95 (ISBN 0-394-73580-3). Shambhala Pubns.

Power of Love. Fulton J. Sheen. 1968. pap. 1.95 (ISBN 0-385-01090-7, D235, Im). Doubleday.

Power of Mathematics: Applications to Management & the Social Sciences. Kenneth L. Whipkey et al. LC 77-27365. 1978. text ed. 18.95 (ISBN 0-471-93785-1); tchrs. manual 4.50 (ISBN 0-471-03760-5); study guide 7.95 (ISBN 0-471-03759-1). Wiley.

Power of Mathematics: Applications to the Management & the Social Sciences. 2nd ed. Kenneth L. Whipkey et al. LC 80-19576. 512p. 1981. text ed. 19.95 (ISBN 0-471-07709-7). Wiley.

Power of Movement in Plant. 2nd ed. Charles Darwin. LC 65-23402. 1966. Repr. of 1881 ed. lib. bdg. 39.50 (ISBN 0-306-70921-X). Da Capo.

Power of Myth in Literature & Film. Ed. by Victor Carrabino. LC 80-21998. (Florida State University Bk.). 136p. 1980. 12.25 (ISBN 0-8130-0673-2, IS-00116, Pub. by U Presses Fla). Univ Microfilms.

Power of Oil: Economic, Social, Political. Richard Walton. LC 76-43985. (gr. 6 up). 1977. 7.95 (ISBN 0-395-28929-7, Clarion). HM.

Power of One. new ed. James L. Merrell. 128p. 1976. pap. text ed. 1.25 (ISBN 0-8272-2925-9). Bethany Pr.

Power of Perception. Marcus Bach. 1973. pap. 2.95 (ISBN 0-8015-5976-6, Hawthorn). Dutton.

Power of Play. Frank Caplan & Theresa Caplan. LC 68-10557. 336p. 1973. pap. 4.50 (ISBN 0-385-09935-5, Anch). Doubleday.

Power of Positive Praying. John Bisagno. 1965. pap. 1.95 (ISBN 0-310-21212-X). Zondervan.

Power of Positive Thinking. Norman V. Peale. 1954. 7.95 (ISBN 0-13-686402-3). P-H.

Power of Protest: A National Study of Student & Faculty Disruptions with Implications for the Future. Alexander W. Astin et al. LC 75-24007. (Higher Education Ser.). (Illus.). 224p. 1975. 14.95x o.p. (ISBN 0-87589-266-3). Jossey-Bass.

Power of Relevant Mathematics: The Basic Concept. Mary N. Whipkey et al. (Illus.). 1977. text ed. 17.95 (ISBN 0-13-687202-6). P-H.

Power of Teaching with New Techniques. rev. ed. Charles R. Hobbs. LC 72-92037. 357p. 1979. 6.95 (ISBN 0-87747-805-8). Deseret Bk.

Power of the Christian Woman. Phyllis Schlafly. (Orig.). 1981. pap. 3.50 (ISBN 0-87239-457-3, 2972). Standard Pub.

Power of the Holy Spirit, Vol. II. Don DeWelt. (Orig.). 1971. pap. 3.95 (ISBN 0-89900-124-6). College Pr Pub.

Power of the Modern Presidency. Erwin C. Hargrove. 1974. pap. text ed. 6.50x o.p. (ISBN 0-394-31724-6). Random.

Power of the Pendulum. T. C. Lethbridge. 1976. 12.00 (ISBN 0-7100-8337-8). Routledge & Kegan.

Power of the Positive Women. Phyllis Schlafly. 1978. pap. 2.95 (ISBN 0-515-05840-8). Jove Pubns.

Power of the Presidency. 2nd ed. Ed. by Robert S. Hirschfield. 464p. 1981. 24.95 (ISBN 0-202-24159-9); pap. text ed. 14.95 (ISBN 0-202-24160-2). Aldine Pub.

Power of the Presidency: Concepts & Controversy. 2nd ed. Ed. by Robert S. Hirschfield. LC 71-169513. 350p. 1973. text ed. 23.95x (ISBN 0-202-24137-8); pap. text ed. 12.95x (ISBN 0-202-24138-6). Aldine Pub.

Power of the Purse: A Symposium on the Role of European Parliaments in Budgetary Decisions. Ed. by David Coombes. LC 75-23959. (Special Studies). (Illus.). 380p. 1976. text ed. 28.95 (ISBN 0-275-05790-9). Praeger.

Power of the Spirit. William Law. Ed. by Andrew Murray. LC 76-57110. (Classics of Devotions Ser). 1977. pap. 2.50 (ISBN 0-87123-463-7, 200463). Bethany Fell.

Power of the Visible. Robert Dana. LC 79-171877. 71p. 1971. 7.50 (ISBN 0-8040-0551-6); pap. 3.95 (ISBN 0-8040-0646-6). Swallow.

Power of Three. Diana W. Jones. LC 77-3028. (gr. 5-9). 1977. 8.25 (ISBN 0-688-80106-4); PLB 7.92 (ISBN 0-688-84106-6). Greenwillow.

Power of Total Living. Marcus Bach. LC 77-13279. (Illus.). 1977. 7.95 (ISBN 0-396-07510-X). Dodd.

Power of Will. Frank C. Haddock. 9.95 (ISBN 0-912576-03-0). R Collier.

Power Packed Pronouncements. A. F. Schneider. (Anthology of Familiar Quotes Ser.). 88p. (Orig.). 1980. pap. 1.75 (ISBN 0-938784-00-5). Dicul Pub.

Power, Paradigms, & Community Research. Ed. by Roland J. Liebert & Allen W. Imershein. LC 76-54539. (Sage Studies in International Sociology: Vol. 9). 1977. 18.00x (ISBN 0-8039-9850-3); pap. 9.95x (ISBN 0-8039-9875-9). Sage.

Power, Persistence & Change: A Second Study of Banbury. Margaret Stacey. (International Library of Sociology Ser.). 1975. 20.00x (ISBN 0-7100-7995-8). Routledge & Kegan.

Power Places. Sheila Knoll. (Illus.). 40p. (Orig.). 1980. pap. 4.95 (ISBN 0-937962-00-7). Indian Feather.

Power Plant Chlorination: A Biological & Chemical Assessment. Lenwood W. Hall et al. 302p. 1981. text ed. 39.95 (ISBN 0-250-40396-X). Ann Arbor Science.

Power Plant Engineers Guide. 2nd ed. Frank Graham. LC 74-98686. (Illus.). 816p. 1974. 15.95 (ISBN 0-672-23329-0). Audel.

Power Plant Theory & Design. 2nd ed. Philip J. Potter. (Illus.). 1959. 25.95 (ISBN 0-8260-7205-4). Wiley.

Power Plant Waste Heat Utilization in Aquaculture. Ed. by Bruce L. Godfriaux. LC 78-73590. 288p. 1979. text ed. 35.00 (ISBN 0-916672-24-7). Allanheld.

Power Plants: Effects on Fish & Shellfish Behavior. Charles H. Hocutt et al. 1980. 25.00 (ISBN 0-12-350950-5). Acad Pr.

Power Play. Warren Murphy. (Destroyer: No. 36). 1979. pap. 1.75 (ISBN 0-523-40912-5). Pinnacle Bks.

Power Players. Arelo Sederberg. 480p. 1981. pap. 2.75 (ISBN 0-553-14141-4). Bantam.

Power Plays. Tom Bass. (Illus.). 40p. (Orig.). Date not set. pap. 3.00 (ISBN 0-934996-07-5). Am Stud Pr. Postponed.

Power Plays. John M. Striker & Andrew Shapiro. 1981. pap. 2.95 (ISBN 0-440-17203-9). Dell.

Power Politics. Margaret Atwood. LC 73-146455. (House of Anansi Poetry Ser.: No. 20). 56p. 1971. 8.95 (ISBN 0-88784-120-1, Pub. by Hse Anansi Pr Canada); pap. 3.95 (ISBN 0-88784-020-5). U of Toronto Pr.

Power, Politics & American Democracy. Halper. 368p. (Orig.). 1981. pap. write for info. (ISBN 0-8302-7130-9). Goodyear.

Power, Politics, & American Democracy. Thomas Halper. 1981. pap. text ed. write for info. (ISBN 0-8302-7130-9). Goodyear.

Power, Politics, & People. C. Wright Mills. Ed. by Irving L. Horowitz. 1963. 22.50 (ISBN 0-19-500021-8). Oxford U Pr.

Power, Politics & People: The Collected Essays of C. Wright Mills. C. Wright Mills. Ed. by Irving L. Horowitz. (YA) (gr. 9 up). 1967. pap. 6.95 (ISBN 0-19-500752-2, GB). Oxford U Pr.

Power, Poverty & Urban Policy. Ed. by Warner Bloomberg, Jr. & Henry J. Schmandt. LC 68-24710. (Urban Affairs Annual Reviews: Vol. 2). 1968. 25.00x (ISBN 0-8039-0006-6); pap. 9.95x (ISBN 0-8039-0031-7). Sage.

Power: Prime Mover of Technology. rev. ed. Joseph Duffy. (gr. 11-12). 1972. text ed. 17.16 (ISBN 0-87345-420-0). McKnight.

Power Profane. Robert Calhoun & Barry Schneider. 1979. pap. 2.25 o.p. (ISBN 0-449-14113-6, GM). Fawcett.

Power Punch: Bruce Lee's 1 & 3 Power Punch. James W. DeMile. (Illus.). 1980. pap. 3.95 (ISBN 0-918642-02-7). Tao of Wing.

Power, Racism & Privilege: Race Relations in Theoretical & Sociohistorical Perspectives. William J. Wilson. LC 72-87160. 1976. pap. text ed. 6.95 (ISBN 0-02-935580-X). Free Pr.

Power Racquetball Featuring PST. Ellington Darden. LC 80-84215. (Illus.). 128p. (Orig.). 1981. pap. text ed. 4.95 (ISBN 0-918438-65-9). Leisure Pr.

Power Reactors in Member States. 1975. pap. 8.25 (ISBN 92-0-152075-1, ISP423-75, IAEA). Unipub.

Power Reactors in Member States. 1978. pap. 10.25 (ISBN 92-0-152078-6, ISP423-78, IAEA). Unipub.

Power Reactors in Member States. 1977. pap. 13.50 (ISBN 92-0-152077-8, ISP423-77, IAEA). Unipub.

Power Reactors in Member States Nineteen Seventy-Nine. 1979. pap. 16.75 (ISBN 92-0-152079-4, ISP 423-79, IAEA). Unipub.

Power Reactors in Member States, 1976. 1976. pap. 9.75 (ISBN 92-0-152176-6, IAEA). Unipub.

Power Reactors in Member States 1980. 147p. 1980. pap. 19.50 (ISBN 92-0-152080-8, ISP423-80, IAEA). Unipub.

Power Relations Within the Chinese Communist Movement, 1930-34: Vol. 1-a Study of Documents. Tso-liang Hsiao. (Publications on Asia of the School of International Studies: No. 9). 416p. 1961. 11.50 (ISBN 0-295-73891-X). U of Wash Pr.

Power, Rule & Domination: A Critical & Empizical Understanding of Power in Sociological Theory & Organizational Life. Stewart Clegg. (International Library of Sociology). 272p. 1975. pap. 12.95 (ISBN 0-7100-8238-X). Routledge & Kegan.

Power Skating the Hockey Way. Ed. by Laura Stamm et al. LC 76-19759. (Illus.). 1978. pap. 5.95 (ISBN 0-8015-4435-1, Hawthorn). Dutton.

Power Structure Research. Ed. by G. William Domhoff. (Sage Focus Editons: No. 17). (Illus.). 270p. 1980. 18.95x (ISBN 0-8039-1431-8); pap. 9.95x (ISBN 0-8039-1432-6). Sage.

Power System Control & Stability. P. M. Anderson & A. A. Fouad. 1977. 45.95 (ISBN 0-8138-1245-3). Iowa St U Pr.

Power System Monitoring Control. (IEE Conference Publication: No. 187). (Illus.). 234p. 1980. softcover 47.00 (ISBN 0-85296-219-3). Inst Elect Eng.

Power System Protection & Switchgear. B. Ravindranath & M. Chander. 1978. 16.95 (ISBN 0-470-99311-1). Halsted Pr.

Power Systems Engineering & Mathematics. U. G. Knight. 304p. 1972. 40.00 (ISBN 0-08-016603-2); pap. 23.00 (ISBN 0-08-018294-1). Pergamon.

Power Technology. Stephenson. LC 77-85745. 1979. 16.52 (ISBN 0-8273-1023-4); instructor's guide 1.50 (ISBN 0-8273-1024-2). Delmar.

Power: The Inner Experience. David C. McClelland. LC 75-35603. (Social Relations Ser.). 436p. 1975. 16.95 o.p. (ISBN 0-470-58169-7). Halsted Pr.

Power Through Prayer. E. M. Bounds. pap. 0.95 (ISBN 0-8024-6721-0). Moody.

Power Through Prayer. Ed. by E. M. Bounds. 1979. mass 1.95 (ISBN 0-8024-6722-9). Moody.

Power Through Prayer. Edward M. Bounds. pap. 1.95 (ISBN 0-310-21612-5). Zondervan.

Power Thyristor & Its Applications. David Finney. (Illus.). 320p. 1980. 22.50 (ISBN 0-07-084533-6, P&RB). McGraw.

Power to Be. Thomas Olbricht. LC 79-67136. (Journey Bks.). 1979. pap. 2.35 (ISBN 0-8344-0108-8). Sweet.

Power to Be Human: Toward a Secular Theology. Charles C. West. 1971. 7.95 o.s.i. (ISBN 0-02-626060-3). Macmillan.

Power to Govern. W. H. Hamilton & D. Adair. LC 77-37759. (American Constitutional & Legal History Ser). 252p. 1972. Repr. of 1937 ed. lib. bdg. 27.50 (ISBN 0-306-70433-1). Da Capo.

Power to Tax. G. Brennan & J. Buchanan. LC 79-56862. (Illus.). 300p. 1980. 22.50 (ISBN 0-521-23329-1). Cambridge U Pr.

Power to the Parents. Joseph W. Bird & Lois F. Bird. LC 77-176346. 240p. 1974. pap. 1.95 (ISBN 0-385-08423-4, Im). Doubleday.

Power to the People: A Pictorial History. Peder Gouwenius. (Illus.). 240p. (Orig.). 1981. cancelled (ISBN 0-905762-72-X, Pub. by Zed Pr); pap. 6.95 (ISBN 0-905762-66-5). Lawrence Hill.

Power Transmission & Automation for Ships & Submersibles. I. Mortimer Datz. (Illus.). 190p. 30.00 (ISBN 0-85238-074-7, FN). Unipub.

Power, Values, & Society: An Introduction to Sociology. C. Michael Otten. 1981. pap. text ed. 11.95x (ISBN 0-673-15260-X). Scott F.

Power-Waters, Brian, Margin for Error, None. Brian Power-Waters. LC 80-22289. (Illus.). 250p. 1980. 12.95 (ISBN 0-9603980-0-7). Pierce Pubs.

Power with Words. rev. ed. Norman Lewis. (Apollo Eds.). pap. 4.50 o.s.i. (ISBN 0-8152-0079-X, A79, TYC-T). T Y Crowell.

Powerboat Maintenance. Eric Jorgensen. Ed. by Jeff Robinson. (Illus.). 288p. 1975. pap. text ed. 9.00 (ISBN 0-89287-069-9, B620). Clymer Pubns.

Powerboat Maintenance. (Illus.). 288p. 9.00 o.p. (ISBN 0-89287-069-9, B620). Western Marine Ent.

Powereading, 4 vols. rev. ed. Barry M. Smith et al. (Powereading Program Ser.: Bk. 1). (Illus.). 1974. Set Of 3 Bks. pap. text ed. 21.30 set of 4 bks. (ISBN 0-913310-00-X). PAR Inc.

Powerful Long Ladder. Owen Dodson. 103p. 1970. 4.95 (ISBN 0-374-23668-2); pap. 1.95 o.p. (ISBN 0-374-50880-1, N395). Fs&G.

Powerhouse. Robert L. Sumner. 1978. pap. 3.95 (ISBN 0-87398-662-8, Pub. by Bibl Evang Pr). Sword of Lord.

Powerlift. Bill Ashpaugh & Holly Miller. LC 80-81758. 150p. 1981. pap. 4.95 (ISBN 0-914850-67-9). Impact Tenn.

Powerlifting: A Scientific Approach. Frederick C. Hatfield. (Illus.). 1981. 12.95 (ISBN 0-8092-7002-1); pap. 6.95 (ISBN 0-8092-7001-3). Contemp Bks.

Powerline: The First Battle of America's Energy War. Barry M. Casper & Paul D. Wellstone. 336p. 1981. lib. bdg. 18.50x (ISBN 0-87023-320-3); pap. 7.95 (ISBN 0-87023-321-1). U of Mass Pr.

Powers of Poetry. Gilbert Highet. 1960. 19.95 (ISBN 0-19-500573-2). Oxford U Pr.

Powers of Tamil Women. Ed. by Susan S. Wadley. LC 80-25410. (South Asian Foreign & Comparative Studies Program: No. 6). xix, 170p. (Orig.). 1980. pap. 8.00x (ISBN 0-915984-82-2). Syracuse U Foreign Comp.

Powers of the President As Commander-in-Chief of the Army & Navy of the United States. Dorothy Schaffter & Dorothy Mathews. LC 76-172099. (American Constitution & Legal History Ser.). xi, 145p. 1974. Repr. of 1974 ed. lib. bdg. 19.50 (ISBN 0-306-70615-6). Da Capo.

Powers of the President During Crises. John Malcolm Smith & Cornelius P. Cotter. LC 71-39371. (American Constitutional & Legal History Ser). 1972. Repr. of 1960 ed. lib. bdg. 19.50 (ISBN 0-306-70462-5). Da Capo.

Powers That Be. David Halberstam. 1980. pap. 3.50 o.s.i. (ISBN 0-440-16997-6). Dell.

Practical Accounting. 3rd ed. Del Stanley & John Black. 1980. pap. text ed. write for info. (ISBN 0-8302-7305-0). Goodyear.

Practical Accounting for Lawyers. Robert O. Berger. (Modern Accounting Perspectives & Practice Ser.). 450p. 1981. 25.00 (ISBN 0-471-08486-7, Pub. by Wiley-Interscience). Wiley.

Practical Air Navigation. rev ed. Thoburn C. Lyon. Ed. by Jeppesen Sanderson. 1978. pap. text ed. 8.95 (ISBN 0-88487-053-7, JE314531). Jeppesen Sanderson.

Practical Algebra. George C. Loveday. LC 73-18336. (Self-Teaching Guides Ser). 384p. 1974. pap. text ed. 7.95x (ISBN 0-471-77557-6). Wiley.

Practical Ampelography: Grapevine Indentification. Pierre Galet. Tr. by Lucie Morton. LC 78-59631. (Illus.). 192p. 1979. 28.50x (ISBN 0-8014-1240-4). Comstock.

Practical & Decorative Concrete. Robert Wilde. LC 77-2833. (Illus.). 144p. 1977. 13.95 (ISBN 0-912336-38-2); pap. 6.95 (ISBN 0-912336-39-0). Structures Pub.

Practical Angler's Guide to Successful Fishing. Kenn Oberrecht. (Illus.). 1978. 12.95 (ISBN 0-87691-250-1). Winchester Pr.

Practical Anthropology. George Oliver. Tr. by M. A. MacConaill. 344p. 1969. pap. 16.00 spiral (ISBN 0-398-01424-8). C C Thomas.

Practical Antimicrobial Therapy. Herbert L. DuPont. (Illus.). 1978. 8.75 (ISBN 0-8385-7869-1). ACC.

Practical Apartment Management. 2nd ed. Edward N. Kelley. Ed. by Nancye J. Kirk. 400p. 1980. write for info. (ISBN 0-912104-49-X). Inst Real Estate.

Practical Application of Science of Mind. Ernest Holmes & Willis Kinnear. 1958. pap. 3.50 (ISBN 0-911336-24-9). Sci of Mind.

Practical Applications in Mathematics. new ed. Edwin I. Stein. Orig. Title: Refresher Workbook in Arithmetic. (gr. 7-12). 1972. 4.80 (ISBN 0-205-03385-7, 5633850); answer bk 2.40 (ISBN 0-205-03386-5, 5633869). Allyn.

Practical Applications of Data Communications: A User's Guide. Electronics Magazine. Ed. by Harry R. Karp. LC 79-27239. (Illus.). 418p. 1980. pap. text ed. 13.95 (ISBN 0-07-606653-3, R-005). McGraw.

Practical Approach to Adapted Physical Education. Douglas C. Wiseman. (Physical Education Ser.). (Illus.). 544p. 1981. text ed. 17.95 (ISBN 0-201-08347-7). A-W.

Practical Approach to Arm Pain. Ed. by Meredith S. Hale. (Illus.). 116p. 1971. photocopy ed. spiral 11.75 (ISBN 0-398-00754-3). C C Thomas.

Practical Approach to Communicating in Writing & Speech. Margaret P. Griffin. 1969. text ed. 7.95x (ISBN 0-02-474220-1, 47422); tchrs' manual free (ISBN 0-685-03677-4). Macmillan.

Practical Approach to Computer Simulation in Business. L. R. Carter & E. Huzan. LC 73-11017. 1973. 25.95 (ISBN 0-470-13729-0). Halsted Pr.

Practical Approach to Computing. W. Y. Arms et al. LC 75-15787. 376p. 1976. 38.50 (ISBN 0-471-03324-3); pap. 21.95 (ISBN 0-471-99736-6). Wiley.

Practical Approach to Gastroenterology & Procedures in Childhood. Walker & Smith. (Postgraduate Pediatric Ser.). 1981. text ed. price not set. Butterworth.

Practical Approach to Organization Development Through MBO: Selected Readings. Arthur C. Beck, Jr. & Ellis D. Hillmar. LC 71-183665. (Illus.). 280p. 1972. pap. text ed. 8.95 (ISBN 0-201-00447-X). A-W.

Practical Approach to Quality Control. 3rd ed. R. H. Caplen. 310p. 1978. pap. text ed. 14.75x (ISBN 0-220-66368-8, Pub. by Busn Bks England). Renouf.

Practical Approaches to Effective Functioning of the Department of Nursing Service: A Guide for Administrators of Nursing Service. American Hospital Association. (Illus.). 96p. 1972. loose-leaf bdg. 12.50 o.p. (ISBN 0-87258-076-8, 1375). Am Hospital.

Practical Approaches to Patient Teaching. Donald A. Bille. 1981. pap. text ed. write for info (ISBN 0-316-09498-6). Little.

Practical Arabic. George Scott. 13.00x (ISBN 0-685-77113-X). Intl Bk Ctr.

Practical Arithmetic: The Third "R". C. Johnson. (Illus.). 1977. pap. 14.95 (ISBN 0-13-689273-6). P-H.

Practical Aspects of Mental Health Consultation. Ed. by Jack Zusman & David L. Davidson. (Illus.). 176p. 1972. 11.75 (ISBN 0-398-02449-9). C C Thomas.

Practical Aspects of Ophthalmic Optics. Margaret Dowaliby. 222p. 1980. 27.00, leatherette (ISBN 0-87873-010-9). Prof Press.

Practical Astrology. C. De Saint-Germain. LC 80-19738. 257p. 1980. Repr. of 1973 ed. lib. bdg. 10.95x (ISBN 0-89370-618-3). Borgo Pr.

Practical Astronomy with Your Calculator. Peter Duffett-Smith. LC 79-4632. (Illus.). 1980. 26.95 (ISBN 0-521-22761-5); pap. 7.50 (ISBN 0-521-29636-6). Cambridge U Pr.

Practical Atomic Absorption Spectrometry. J. M. Ottaway & A. M. Ure. Date not set. 30.00 (ISBN 0-08-023800-9). Pergamon.

Practical Baking. 3rd ed. William J. Sultan. (Illus.). 1976. text ed. 19.50 (ISBN 0-87055-214-7). AVI.

Practical Baking Manual. William J. Sultan. (Illus.). 1976. pap. text ed. 10.50 (ISBN 0-87055-213-9). AVI.

Practical BASIC Programs. Ed. by Lon Poole. 250p. (Orig.). 1980. pap. 15.99 (ISBN 0-931988-38-1). Osborne-McGraw.

Practical Bible Doctrine Course. Keith L. Brooks. (Teach Yourself the Bible Ser). 1962. pap. 1.75 (ISBN 0-8024-6733-4). Moody.

Practical Boat Handling on Rivers & Canals. C. L. Colborne. 1977. 8.95 (ISBN 0-7153-7061-8). David & Charles.

Practical Boiler Firing. 4th ed. H. C. Armstrong & C. V. Lewis. 387p. 1954. 10.95x (ISBN 0-85264-065-X, Pub. by Griffin England). State Mutual Bk.

Practical Boiler Water Treatment: Including Air-Conditioning Systems. Leo I. Pincus. 284p. 1981. Repr. lib. bdg. price not set (ISBN 0-89874-255-2). Krieger.

Practical Bonsai for Beginners. Kenji Murata. LC 64-7611. (Illus.). 1977. pap. 7.95 (ISBN 0-87040-230-7). Japan Pubns.

Practical Book of Guns. Ken Warner. (Illus.). 1978. 13.95 (ISBN 0-87691-274-9). Winchester Pr.

Practical Book of Knives. Ken Warner. 1976. 12.95 (ISBN 0-87691-218-8). Winchester Pr.

Practical Business Education, 2 vols. R. D. Anstis et al. (Illus.). 576p. 1978. pap. text ed. 21.00x (ISBN 0-7121-2336-9, Pub. by Macdonald & Evans England). Intl Ideas.

Practical Business Models. J. E. Mulvaney & C. W. Mann. LC 75-33219. 1976. 13.95 o.p. (ISBN 0-470-62386-1). Halsted Pr.

Practical Chemistry for Schools. Cecil Jenkins. 1958. text ed. 5.95x (ISBN 0-521-05427-3). Cambridge U Pr.

Practical Chemistry in the Twelfth Century. Muhammad Ibn Zakariya. Ed. by Robert R. Steele. Tr. by Gerard Of Cremona. LC 79-8590. Repr. of 1929 ed. 12.50 (ISBN 0-404-18444-8). AMS Pr.

Practical Chinese Letter Writing. Dian Wen K. Chinn. xii, 124p. (Orig.). 1980. pap. text ed. 9.50x (ISBN 0-89644-642-5). Chinese Materials.

Practical Clinical Enzymology: Techniques & Interpretations & Biochemical Profiling. Paul L. Wolf et al. LC 80-12468. 592p. 1981. Repr. of 1973 ed. lib. bdg. price not set (ISBN 0-89874-162-9). Krieger.

Practical Clinical Neurology. John K. Wolf. LC 79-91846. 1980. pap. 13.75 (ISBN 0-87488-728-3). Med Exam.

Practical Composition. Axel Bruck. LC 80-40759. (Practical Photography Ser.). (Illus.). 164p. 1981. 19.95 (ISBN 0-240-51060-7). Focal Pr.

Practical Concepts in Human Disease. 2nd ed. Harmon C. Bickley. (Illus.). 335p. 1980. softcover 18.95 (ISBN 0-683-00914-1). Williams & Wilkins.

Practical Considerations for Successful Crown and Bridge Therapy: Biologic Considerations-Psychologic Considerations-Preventive Factors. Harold R. Horn. LC 76-8577. (Illus.). 1976. text ed. 29.00 (ISBN 0-7216-4783-9). Saunders.

Practical Controllership. 3rd ed. David R. Anderson et al. 1973. text ed. 18.50x o.p. (ISBN 0-256-00008-5). Irwin.

Practical Cookery. 4th ed. Victor Ceserani & Ronald Kinton. 1974. 16.50x (ISBN 0-7131-1853-9). Intl Ideas.

Practical Cookery: A Compilation of Principles of Cookery & Recipes. 24th ed. Kansas State University, College of Home Economics, Dept. of Foods & Nutrition. LC 20-21946. 304p. 1975. text ed. 15.50 (ISBN 0-471-45641-1). Wiley.

Practical Counseling in the Schools. Gary S. Belkin. 480p. 1975. text ed. 12.95x o.p. (ISBN 0-697-06006-3). Wm C Brown.

Practical Course in Modern Locksmithing. Whitcomb Crichton. 1943. 13.95 (ISBN 0-911012-06-0). Nelson-Hall.

Practical Course in Modern Shoe Repairing. Ralph Sarlette. Orig. Title: Shoe Repairing Course. 1956. 13.95 (ISBN 0-911012-44-3). Nelson-Hall.

Practical Criticism, a Study of Literary Judgment. Ivor A. Richards. LC 56-13740. 1956. pap. 4.95 (ISBN 0-15-673626-8, HB16, Harv). HarBraceJ.

Practical Dermatology of the Genital Region. Korting. 1981. text ed. price not set (ISBN 0-7216-5498-3). Saunders.

Practical Design of Simple Steel Structures, 2 vols. David S. Stewart. Incl. Vol. 1. Shop Practice, Riveted Connections, Beams, Tables. 6.50 o.p. (ISBN 0-8044-4906-6); Vol. 2. Plate Girders, Columns, Trusses. 8.50 o.p. (ISBN 0-8044-4907-4). Set (ISBN 0-8044-4905-8). Ungar.

Practical Diagnosis: Endocrine Diseases. Stanley G. Korenman et al. (Illus.). 1978. pap. 14.00x (ISBN 0-89289-201-3). HM Prof Med Div.

Practical Diagnosis: Gastrointestinal & Liver Disease. Gary L. Gitnick. 1979. kouverflex bdg. 14.00x (ISBN 0-89289-202-1). HM Prof Med Div.

Practical Diagnosis: Hematologic Disease. William C. Maslow et al. 1980. kroydenflex bdg. 16.00 (ISBN 0-89289-203-X). HM Prof Med Div.

Practical Diagnosis: Renal Disease. Michael A. Kirschenbaum. (Illus.). 1978. kroydenflex 14.00x (ISBN 0-89289-200-5). HM Prof Med Div.

Practical Dictation & Transcription: Shorterhand Edition. Dorothy Haydon & Elayne Gordon. Ed. by M. Angus. LC 75-14357. 1975. text ed. 11.20 (ISBN 0-8224-1021-4); transcript 8.60 (ISBN 0-8224-1702-2). Pitman Learning.

Practical Digital Design Using ICs. Joseph D. Greenfield. LC 76-54282. (Electronic Engineering Technology Ser.). 1977. text ed. 22.95 (ISBN 0-471-32505-8); tchr's manual avail. (ISBN 0-471-02532-1). Wiley.

Practical Directions for Portrait Painting. M. Merrifield. (Library of the Arts Ser.). (Illus.). 1977. 27.35 (ISBN 0-89266-069-4). Am Classical Coll Pr.

Practical Diving: A Complete Manual for Compressed Air Divers. Tom Mount & Akira J. Ikehara. LC 75-1059. (Illus.). 192p. 1975. pap. 5.95 o.p. (ISBN 0-87024-299-7). U of Miami Pr.

Practical Education, 2 vols. Maria Edgeworth & Richard L. Edgeworth. Ed. by Gina Luria. (Feminist Controversy in England, 1788-1810 Ser.). 1974. Set. lib. bdg. 100.00 (ISBN 0-685-40809-4); lib. bdg. 50.00 ea. Garland Pub.

Practical Effects in Photography. Carl Bernard & Karen Norquay. LC 80-40794. (Practical Photography Ser.). (Illus.). 168p. 1981. 19.95 (ISBN 0-240-51082-8). Focal Pr.

Practical Electricity. 3rd ed. Robert Middleton. LC 73-94187. (Illus.). 1974. 10.95 (ISBN 0-672-23218-9). Audel.

Practical English-Cantonese Dictionary. Chiang Ker-Chiu. 25.00x (ISBN 0-686-00881-2). Colton Bk.

Practical English Grammar. 3rd ed. A. J. Thomson & A. V. Martinet. 384p. 1980. pap. 7.95 (ISBN 0-19-431336-0). Oxford U Pr.

Practical English Grammar: Combined Exercises. A. J. Thomson & A. V. Martinet. 240p. 1979. pap. text ed. 3.95x o.p. (ISBN 0-19-432753-1). Oxford U Pr.

Practical English Grammar: Exercise One. A. J. Thomson & A. V. Martinet. 176p. 1980. 5.50x (ISBN 0-19-431337-9). Oxford U Pr.

Practical English Grammar: Exercises Two. A. J. Thomson & A. V. Martinet. 205p. 1980. 5.50x (ISBN 0-19-431338-7). Oxford U Pr.

Practical English Handbook. 5th ed. Floyd C. Watkins & William B. Dillingham. LC 77-75888. (Illus.). 1977. pap. text ed. 7.50 (ISBN 0-395-25825-1); inst. annot. ed. 8.75 (ISBN 0-395-25824-3); wkbk. 6.75 (ISBN 0-395-25830-8); inst. manual 0.40 (ISBN 0-395-25831-6); diagnostic test 1.50 (ISBN 0-395-29305-7). HM.

Practical English-Mandarin Dictionary. Chiang Ker-Chiu. 8.50x o.s.i. (ISBN 0-686-00882-0). Colton Bk.

Practical English One, Two, & Three, 3 bks. Tim Harris. (Illus.). 1980. Bks. 1-3. pap. text ed. write for info. (HC); write for info. instructor's manuals 1-3; write for info. Whiting Practical English 1-3 wkbks.; write for info. tapes. HarBraceJ.

Practical English Structure. Marcia Beth Bordman et al. (Practical English Structure Ser: ol. 1). (Illus.). 224p. 1981. text ed. 6.95 (ISBN 0-913580-65-1). Gallaudet Coll.

Practical English-Vietnamese Idioms for Teachers & Students. Ed. by Nguyen-Trung Hieu. 1981. 6.50 (ISBN 0-533-04431-6). Vantage.

Practical Ethics. Peter Singer. LC 79-52328. 1980. 32.95 (ISBN 0-521-22920-0); pap. 6.95 (ISBN 0-521-29720-6). Cambridge U Pr.

Practical Experiences with Flow-Induced Vibrations: Symposium Proceedings. Ed. by E. Naudascher & D. Rockwell. (International Association for Hydraulic Research - International Union of Theoretical & Applied Mechanics). (Illus.). 850p. 1980. 82.60 (ISBN 0-387-10314-7). Springer-Verlag.

Practical Experiment Designs for Engineers & Scientists. William J. Diamond. 400p. 1981. text ed. 28.00x (ISBN 0-534-97992-0). Lifetime Learn.

Practical Exposure. Leonard Gaunt. LC 80-40793. (Practical Photography Ser.). (Illus.). 192p. 1981. 19.95 (ISBN 0-240-51058-5). Focal Pr.

Practical Fiberoptic Bronchoscopy. Kenkichi Oho. LC 79-92553. (Illus.). 1980. 36.00 (ISBN 0-89640-041-7). Igaku-Shoin.

Practical Finite Mathematics. Gareth Williams. 1979. text ed. 17.80 (ISBN 0-205-06525-2, 566525-6). Allyn.

Practical Fire Precautions. George W. Underwood. 1979. text ed. 50.50x (ISBN 0-566-02124-2, Pub. by Gower Pub Co England). Renouf.

Practical Food Microbiology & Technology. 2nd ed. H. H. Weiser et al. 1971. 19.50 o.p. (ISBN 0-87055-064-0). AVI.

Practical Formulas for Hobby & Profit. Henry Goldschmiedt. LC 77-21301. (Illus.). 1978. pap. 5.95 o.p. (ISBN 0-668-04495-0). Arco.

Practical Foundations of Physical Geography. Ed. by B. J. Knapp. (Illus.). 152p. 1981. pap. text ed. 11.50x (ISBN 0-04-551035-0, 2590); tchr's ed. 13.50x (ISBN 0-04-551034-2, 2589). Allen Unwin.

Practical Gemcutting. Nance Perry & Ron Perry. (Illus.). 96p. (Orig.). 1980. pap. 13.50 (ISBN 0-589-50192-5, Pub. by Reed Bks Australia). C E Tuttle.

Practical Genetics. Ed. by P. M. Sheppard LC 73-9709. 337p. 1973. text ed. 44.95 (ISBN 0-470-78360-5). Halsted Pr.

Practical Geometry & Engineering Graphics. 8th ed. W. Abbot. (Illus.). 1971. pap. text ed. 16.50x (ISBN 0-216-89450-6). Intl Ideas.

Practical Geostatistics. Isobel Clark. 1979. 28.50x (ISBN 0-85334-843-X). Intl Ideas.

Practical Geostatistics. Isobel Clark. (Illus.). 1979. 28.50x (ISBN 0-85334-843-X, Pub. by Applied Science). Burgess-Intl Ideas.

Practical Grammar for Classical Hebrew. 2nd ed. Jacob Weingreen. 1959. 11.95x (ISBN 0-19-815422-4). Oxford U Pr.

Practical Guidance for Office Pediatric & Adolescent Practice. Byron B. Oberst. (Illus.). 280p. 1973. 18.75 (ISBN 0-398-02552-5); pap. 12.75 (ISBN 0-398-02553-3). C C Thomas.

Practical Guide for Handling Drug Crises. Jonathan W. Lehrman et al. 134p. 1980. text ed. 12.75 (ISBN 0-398-04095-8); pap. text ed. 7.50 (ISBN 0-398-04100-8). C C Thomas.

Practical Guide in the Use & Implementation of Bibliotherapy. Jacquelyn W. Stephens. 64p. 1981. PLB 6.95 (ISBN 0-89962-045-0). Todd & Honeywell.

Practical Guide to Budgetary & Management Control Systems. Lewis D. Houck, Jr. LC 78-14716. 272p. 1979. 22.95 (ISBN 0-669-02705-7). Lexington Bks.

Practical Guide to Computer Methods for Engineers. T. Shoup. 1979. 21.95 (ISBN 0-13-690651-6). P-H.

Practical Guide to Creditors' Committees. Ed. by Nacm. 29p. 1968. pap. 3.50 (ISBN 0-934914-12-5). NACM.

Practical Guide to Early Childhood Curriculum. 2nd ed. Claudia Eliason & Loa T. Jenkins. (Illus.). 330p. 1981. pap. text ed. 12.95 (ISBN 0-8016-1511-9). Mosby.

Practical Guide to Far-Eastern Macrobiotic Medicine. George Ohsawa. Ed. by Herman Alhara. (Illus.). 260p. 1973. pap. 7.50 o.p. (ISBN 0-918860-21-0). G Ohsawa.

Practical Guide to Farm & Ranch Taxation. John L. Kramer & Ted D. Englebrecht. 1978. pap. text ed. 10.50 o.p. (ISBN 0-88450-550-2, 1716-B). Lawyers & Judges.

Practical Guide to Foster Family Care. Bert L. Kaplan & Martin Seitz. 112p. 1980. lexotone 9.75 (ISBN 0-398-04033-8). C C Thomas.

Practical Guide to Home Landscaping. (Illus.). 1972. 16.95 (ISBN 0-89577-005-9, Pub. by Reader's Digest). Norton.

Practical Guide to Home Restoration. Editors of Hudson Home Magazine. 144p. 1980. 12.95 (ISBN 0-442-25400-8). Van Nos Reinhold.

Practical Guide to Integral Yoga. 7th ed. Sri Aurobindo. Ed. by Manibhai. 1979. 6.00 o.p. (ISBN 0-89744-941-X); pap. 4.50 (ISBN 0-89744-942-8). Auromere.

Practical Guide to Landscape Painting. Colin Hayes. 120p. 1981. 15.95 (ISBN 0-8230-0322-1). Watson-Guptill.

Practical Guide to Management of the Painful Neck & Back: Diagnosis, Manipulation, Exercises, Prevention. James W. Fisk. (Illus.). 248p. 1977. 22.50 (ISBN 0-398-03640-3). C C Thomas.

Practical Guide to Medical & Veterinary Mycology. R. Vanbreuseghem et al. LC 77-94829. (Illus.). 288p. 1978. text ed. 47.75 (ISBN 0-89352-018-7). Masson Pub.

Practical Guide to Microbial & Parasitic Diseases. Gerhard H. Schwebach. (Illus.). 256p. 1980. lexotone 19.75 (ISBN 0-398-03980-1). C C Thomas.

Practical Guide to Minicomputer Applications. F. F. Coury. LC 70-182820. (IEEE Press Selected Reprint Ser). 1972. pap. text ed. 10.50 (ISBN 0-471-18051-3, Pub. by Wiley-Interscience). Wiley.

Practical Guide to Multi-Level Modular ESL. Dorthea Canzano & Phyllis Canzano. 1975. pap. 12.95 (ISBN 0-87789-130-3); cassettes intermediate 70.00; cassettes advanced 75.00. Eng Language.

Practical Guide to Pediatric Intensive Care. Daniel L. Levin et al. LC 79-13793. (Illus.). 1979. pap. text ed. 24.50 (ISBN 0-8016-3011-8). Mosby.

Practical Guide to Preaching. George Fitzgerald. LC 79-67742. (Orig.). 1980. pap. 4.95 (ISBN 0-8091-2281-2). Paulist Pr.

Practical Guide to Preparation of Partnership & Partner's Tax Returns. 2nd ed. Eugene Seago. 1978. pap. 9.50 (ISBN 0-88450-061-6, 1707-B). Lawyers & Judges.

Practical Guide to Preparing a Federal Estate Tax Return. 7th ed. D. Larry Crumbley. 1980. pap. 8.50 (ISBN 0-88450-057-8, 1703-B). Lawyers & Judges.

Practical Guide to Preparing a Federal Gift Tax Return. 5th ed. D. Larry Crumbley. 1980. pap. text ed. 8.50 (ISBN 0-88450-058-6, 1705-B). Lawyers & Judges.

Practical Guide to Program Planning: A Teaching Models Approach. Adrianne Bank et al. (Orig.). 1981. pap. 14.95 (ISBN 0-8077-2641-9). Tchrs Coll.

Practical Guide to Real Estate Law. Phyllis D. Hemphill & Charles F. Hemphill. (Illus.). 272p. 1980. text ed. 14.95 (ISBN 0-13-691022-X, Spec); pap. text ed. 7.95 (ISBN 0-13-691014-9). P-H.

Practical Guide to Remedial Reading. 2nd ed. Hap Gilliland. Ed. by Arthur Heilman. (Elementary Education Ser.). 1978. text ed. 15.95 (ISBN 0-675-08359-1). Merrill.

Practical Guide to Small Computers for Business & Professional Use. Robert M. Rinder. 288p. 1981. pap. 6.95 (ISBN 0-671-09259-6). Monarch Pr.

Practical Guide to Structured Systems Design. Meilir Page-Jones. LC 79-67259. (Illus., Orig.). 1980. pap. 22.50 (ISBN 0-917072-17-0). Yourdon.

Practical Guide to the Care of the Surgical Patient. McEntyre. LC 79-16116. 1979. pap. 11.50 (ISBN 0-8016-3056-8). Mosby.

Practical Guide to the Conduct of Field Research in the Social Sciences. Elliot J. Feldman. 120p. 1981. lib. bdg. 13.75x (ISBN 0-89158-980-5); pap. text ed. 6.95x (ISBN 0-89158-981-3). Westview.

Practical Guide to the Dogs. Kay White & Joan Joshua. 1976. 11.95 (ISBN 0-600-37046-1). Transatlantic.

Practical Guide to the Teaching of English As a Foreign Language. Robert J. Dixson. 1975. pap. text ed. 3.25 (ISBN 0-88345-244-8, 18132). Regents Pub.

Practical Guide to the Teaching of English: As a Second or Foreign Language. Wilga M. Rivers & Mary S. Temperley. 1977. pap. 8.95x (ISBN 0-19-502210-6). Oxford U Pr.

Practical Guide to Value Clarification. Maury Smith. LC 76-20047. 322p. 1977. pap. 16.95 (ISBN 0-88390-124-2). Univ Assocs.

Practical Guidebook in "Spontaneous" Art. Calvin N. Otis. (A Promotion of the Arts Library Book). (Illus.). 123p. 1981. 29.85 (ISBN 0-930582-99-3). Gloucester Art.

Practical Guidelines for the Teaching of Physical Education. Gerald S. Insley. LC 71-186841. 1973. pap. text ed. 7.50 (ISBN 0-201-03155-8). A-W.

Practical Handbook of Industrial Traffic Management. 6th ed. Leon W. Morse. LC 77-9240. 552p. 1980. text ed. write for info. (ISBN 0-87408-020-7). Traffic Serv.

Practical Handbook of Psychiatry. Ed. by Joseph R. Novello. (Amer. Lec. in Clinical Psychiatry Ser.). (Illus.). 648p. 1974. 24.75 (ISBN 0-398-02868-0). C C Thomas.

Practical Handbook of Public Relations. Robert S. Cole. (Illus.). 224p. 1981. text ed. 18.95 (ISBN 0-13-691162-5, Spec); pap. text ed. 9.95 (ISBN 0-13-691154-4). P-H.

Practical Handgun Ballistics. M. Williams. (Illus.). 232p. 1980. 17.50 (ISBN 0-398-04032-X). C C Thomas.

Practical Harmonist at the Harpsichord. Francesco Gasparini. Ed. by David L. Burrows. Tr. by Frank S. Stillings from It. (Music Reprint Ser.: 1980). (Illus.). 1980. Repr. of 1963 ed. lib. bdg. 17.50 (ISBN 0-306-76017-7). Da Capo.

Practical Heat Recovery. J. L. Boyen. LC 75-17735. 254p. 1975. 21.95 o.p. (ISBN 0-471-09376-9, Pub. by Wiley-Interscience). Wiley.

Practical Herb Growing. Hewer & Senecki. 12.50x (ISBN 0-392-05980-0, LTB). Soccer.

Practical Hermeneutics. Charles E. Winquist. LC 79-22848. (Scholars Press General Ser.: No. 1). 12.00x (ISBN 0-89130-363-4); pap. 7.50x (ISBN 0-89130-364-2). Scholars Pr CA.

Practical Highway Esthetics. Compiled by American Society of Civil Engineers. 80p. 1977. pap. text ed. 17.50 (ISBN 0-87262-096-4). Am Soc Civil Eng.

Practical Home Construction-Carpentry Handbook. TAB Editorial Staff. LC 76-1552. 448p. 1976. pap. 5.95 (ISBN 0-8306-5900-5, 900). TAB Bks.

Practical Homicide Investigation. Edward A. Dieckmann. 96p. 1961. 10.50 (ISBN 0-398-00450-1). C C Thomas.

Practical Hors d'oeuvre & Canape Art. Charles Mok. LC 78-1066. (Illus.). 1978. spiral bdg. 22.95 (ISBN 0-8436-2159-1). CBI Pub.

Practical Human Relations. Robert M. Fulmer. 1977. 16.95x (ISBN 0-256-01908-8). Irwin.

Practical Hunter's Dog Book. John R. Falk. (Illus.). 1971. 10.95 (ISBN 0-87691-037-1). Winchester Pr.

Practical Hunter's Handbook. Anthony J. Acerrano. (Illus.). 1978. 11.95 (ISBN 0-87691-276-5). Winchester Pr.

Practical Hydraulics. 2nd ed. Andrew L. Simon. 416p. 1981. text ed. 18.95 (ISBN 0-471-05381-3); tchrs.' ed. 7.50 (ISBN 0-471-07783-6). Wiley.

Practical Hypnotism. Philip Magonet. pap. 3.00 (ISBN 0-87980-123-9). Wilshire.

Practical Ice Carving. Joseph F. Durocher. 112p. 1981. pap. text ed. 9.95 (ISBN 0-8436-2206-7). CBI Pub.

Practical Immunology. Leslie Hudson & Frank C. Hay. (Blackwell Scientific Pubns.). (Illus.). 1976. softcover 16.25 (ISBN 0-632-00353-7). Mosby.

Practical Implications of Calvinism. Albert N. Martin. 1979. pap. 0.75 (ISBN 0-85151-296-8). Banner of Truth.

Practical Industrial Management: Insights for Managers. Carl R. Pacifico & Daniel B. Witwer. 550p. 1981. 19.95 (ISBN 0-471-08190-6, Pub. by Wiley-Interscience). Wiley.

Practical Inferences. R. M. Hare. 132p. 1972. 11.95x (ISBN 0-520-02179-7). U of Cal Pr.

Practical Inorganic Chemistry: Preparations, Reactions & Instrumental Methods. 2nd ed. G. Pass & H. Sutcliffe. 256p. 1979. pap. 9.95x (ISBN 0-412-16150-8, Pub. by Chapman & Hall). Methuen Inc.

Practical Insect Pest Management. rev. ed. M. Curtis Wilson et al. (Insects of Livestock & Agronomic Crops Ser: No.2). (Illus.). 208p. 1980. pap. text ed. 7.95x (ISBN 0-917974-39-5). Waveland Pr.

Practical Insect Pest Management: A Self-Instructional Manual. Theo F. Watson et al. (Illus.). 1976. pap. text ed. 9.95x (ISBN 0-7167-0558-3). W H Freeman.

Practical Insect Pest Management: Insects of Man's Household & Health, No. 5. M. Curtis Wilson et al. LC 77-82251. (Illus.). 1977. 6.95x (ISBN 0-917974-07-7). Waveland Pr.

Practical Insect Pest Management: Insects of Ornamental Plants, No. 4. M. Curtis Wilson et al. LC 77-82602. (Illus.). 1977. 6.50x (ISBN 0-917974-06-9). Waveland Pr.

Practical Insect Pest Management: Insects of Vegetables & Fruits, No. 3. M. Curtis Wilson et al. LC 77-71174. 1977. 5.95x (ISBN 0-917974-05-0). Waveland Pr.

Practical Instruction in Figure Drawing. Stanley N. Carter. (A Promotion of the Arts Library Book). (Illus.). 103p. 1981. 27.45 (ISBN 0-86650-002-2). Gloucester Art.

Practical Introduction to Business. rev. ed. Harold Koontz & Robert M. Fulmer. 1978. text ed. 17.95 (ISBN 0-256-02012-4). Irwin.

Practical Introduction to Electric Circuits. M. H. Jones. LC 76-11083. (Illus.). 1977. 38.50 (ISBN 0-521-21291-X); pap. 13.95x (ISBN 0-521-29087-2). Cambridge U Pr.

Practical Larder Work. F. C. Centre. 15.00x (ISBN 0-392-06305-0, LTB). Soccer.

Practical Laundrywork. M. E. Cox. 147p. 1961. 11.50x (ISBN 0-85264-080-3, Pub. by Griffin England). State Mutual Bk.

Practical Law: A Layperson's Handbook. Chester S. Weinerman. LC 77-26164. 1978. 13.95 (ISBN 0-13-691113-7, Spec); pap. 4.95 (ISBN 0-13-691105-6, Spec). P-H.

Practical Law Enforcement Guide to Writing Field Reports, Grant Proposals, Memos, & Resumes. T. J. Agnos & S. Schatt. 136p. 1980. pap. 11.75 (ISBN 0-398-04042-7). C C Thomas.

Practical Law for Correctional Personnel: A Resource Manual & a Training Curriculum (by the National Street Law Institute) Edward L. O'Brien & Margaret E. Fisher. Ed. by David T. Austern. (Illus.). 205p. 1980. pap. text ed. write for info. (ISBN 0-8299-1034-4). West Pub.

Practical Layout for Sheet Metal Shop. C. J. Zinngrabe & F. W. Schumacher. LC 75-6063. 1975. pap. text ed. 7.40 (ISBN 0-8273-0224-X); instructor's guide 1.60 (ISBN 0-8273-0225-8). Delmar.

Practical Logic. Monroe Beardsley. 1950. text ed. 14.95 (ISBN 0-13-692111-6). P-H.

Practical Low Protein Cookery. Laura P. Krawitt & Emily K. Weinberger. (Illus.). 128p. 1971. pap. 10.50 (ISBN 0-398-01049-8). C C Thomas.

Practical Magic: Poems. Carl Bode. LC 80-17597. 52p. 1981. 8.95 (ISBN 0-8040-0362-9); pap. 4.95 (ISBN 0-8040-0373-4). Swallow.

Practical Management of Chronic Neurologic Problems. Margaret Seiden. 1981. 25.00 (ISBN 0-8385-7871-3). ACC.

Practical Management of the Developmentally Disabled Child. Albert P. Scheiner & Abroms. LC 80-13725. (Illus.). 1980. text ed. 37.50 (ISBN 0-8016-0061-8). Mosby.

Practical Manual for Patient-Teaching. Ed. by Karen S. Zander & Kathleen A. Bower. LC 78-7039. 1978. pap. text ed. 15.95 (ISBN 0-8016-5678-8). Mosby.

Practical Manual in Urban Design. Andrew Mackie. Date not set. 30.01 (ISBN 0-08-023362-7); pap. 15.01 (ISBN 0-08-023361-9). Pergamon.

Practical Map Protection. John Loxton. LC 80-40118. 1980. 24.95 (ISBN 0-471-27782-7, Pub. by Wiley-Interscience); pap. 14.50 (ISBN 0-471-27783-5). Wiley.

Practical Marketing Audits: A Guide to Increased Profitability. John Naylor & Alan Wood. LC 78-2948. 1978. 24.95x (ISBN 0-470-26327-X). Halsted Pr.

Practical Marketing for Your Small Retail Business. William H. Brannen. (Illus.). 272p. 1981. 16.95 (ISBN 0-13-692764-5, Spec); pap. 8.95 (ISBN 0-13-692756-4). P-H.

Practical Mathematics. Russell V. Person & Vernon J. Person. LC 76-21732. 400p. 1977. 19.95 (ISBN 0-471-68216-0). Wiley.

Practical Meat Cutting & Merchandising: Beef, Vol. 1. 2nd ed. Thomas Fabbricante & William J. Sultan. (Illus.). 1978. pap. text ed. 14.50 (ISBN 0-87055-273-2). AVI.

Practical Meat Cutting & Merchandising, Vol. 2: Pork, Lamb & Veal. Thomas Fabbricante & William J. Sultan. (Illus.). 242p. 1975. pap. text ed. 14.50 (ISBN 0-87055-177-9). AVI.

Practical Medical Dictionary of Sex. Armando DeMoya et al. LC 80-5799. 304p. 1981. 16.95 (ISBN 0-8128-2794-5). Stein & Day.

Practical Medico-Legal Guide for the Physician. Everett J. Gordon. (Illus.). 360p. 1973. 14.95 (ISBN 0-398-02688-2). C C Thomas.

Practical Merchandising Math for Everyday Use. Murray Krieger. 700p. 1980. pap. text ed. 21.75 (ISBN 0-686-60196-3, M47680). Natl Ret Merch.

Practical Metal Projects. M. J. Ruley. (gr. 9 up). text ed. 13.28 (ISBN 0-87345-137-6). McKnight.

Practical Methods for Social Studies. Gilliom. 1977. 11.95x (ISBN 0-534-00486-5). Wadsworth Pub.

Practical Methods of Optimization: Unconstrained Optimization, Vol. 1. R. Fletcher. LC 79-41486. 128p. 1980. 24.50 (ISBN 0-471-27711-8, Pub. by Wiley-Interscience). Wiley.

Practical Microscopic Hematology: A Manual for the Clinical Laboratory & Clinical Practice. Fritz Heckner. Ed. by H. Peter Lehmann & Yuan Kao. Tr. by H. L. Lehmann from Ger. LC 79-28562. (Illus.). 127p. 1980. pap. 19.50 (ISBN 0-8067-0811-5). Urban & S.

Practical Modern Basketball. 2nd ed. John R. Wooden. LC 79-13731. 1980. text ed. 17.95 (ISBN 0-471-05865-3). Wiley.

Practical Musical Criticism. Oscar Thompson. (Music Reprint Ser.: 1979). 1979. Repr. of 1934 ed. lib. bdg. 19.50 (ISBN 0-306-79514-0). Da Capo.

Practical Navigation. William S. Kals. LC 72-76175. 312p. 1972. 9.95 o.p. (ISBN 0-385-00246-7). Doubleday.

Practical Neurology for the Primary Care Physician. William H. Olson. (Illus.). 360p. 1981. lexotone spiral bdg. 21.75 (ISBN 0-398-04135-0). C C Thomas.

Practical Nonparametric Statistics. 2nd ed. W. J. Conover. LC 80-301. (Probability & Mathematical Statistics Ser.). 493p. 1980. 25.95 (ISBN 0-471-02867-3). Wiley.

Practical Nonparametric Statistics. William J. Conover. LC 74-126223. (Illus.). 1971. 23.95 o.p. (ISBN 0-471-16851-3). Wiley.

Practical Nuclear Cardiology. James Sprengelmeyer & Calvin L. Weisberger. (Illus.). 1979. text ed. 34.50 (ISBN 0-06-142470-6, Harper Medical). Har-Row.

Practical Nurse in Supervisory Roles. Marion K. Stevens. LC 73-80982. (Illus.). 160p. 1973. text ed. 7.50x (ISBN 0-7216-8591-9). Saunders.

Practical Nurses' Medical Dictionary: A Cyclopedic Medical Dictionary for Practical Nurses, Vocational Nurses, & Nurses' Aides. J. E. Schmidt. 300p. 1968. 11.75 (ISBN 0-398-01675-5). C C Thomas.

Practical Nursing: A Textbook for Students & Graduates. 5th ed. Dorothy R. Meeks et al. LC 73-20244. 1974. text ed. 15.95 (ISBN 0-8016-3390-7). Mosby.

Practical Nursing Examination Review. Sr. Mary Redempta. LC 74-76633. (Arco Nursing Review Ser.). 288p. 1976. pap. 5.00 o.p. (ISBN 0-668-03488-2). Arco.

Practical Nursing Examination Review Book Vol. 1. 3rd ed. Marguerite C. Holmes et al. 1973. spiral bdg. 6.00 (ISBN 0-87488-711-9). Med Exam.

Practical Nursing: PreTest Self-Assessment & Review. Alberta P. Catlin & Shirley Bachand. LC 78-70622. (Nursing: Pretest Self-Assessment & Review Ser.). (Illus.). 1979. pap. 6.95 (ISBN 0-07-051571-9). McGraw-Pretest.

Practical Nursing Study Guide & Review. 3rd ed. Zella Von Gremp & Lucile Broadwell. 1971. pap. text ed. 8.95 o.p. (ISBN 0-397-54117-1). Lippincott.

Practical Nutritional Support. S. J. Karran. LC 79-56645. 351p. 1980. 27.95 (ISBN 0-471-08024-1, Pub. by Wiley Medical). Wiley.

Practical Occultism. William Q. Judge. LC 78-63320. 1979. 10.00 (ISBN 0-911500-29-4); softcover 6.00 (ISBN 0-911500-30-8). Theos U Pr.

Practical Oncology. Ed. by Gregory P. Sarna. (UCLA Postgraduate Medicine Ser.). 1980. text ed. 18.00 (ISBN 0-89289-350-8). HM Prof Med Div.

Practical Pediatric & Adolescent Gynaclogy. Dewhurst. 344p. 1980. 35.00 (ISBN 0-8247-6978-3). Dekker.

Practical Pediatrics in Less-Developed Countries. Karen Olness. 1980. pap. 9.95 (ISBN 0-9602790-2-4). The Garden.

Practical Pediatrics in Less-Developed Countries. Karen Olness. 1980. pap. 7.95 (ISBN 0-9602790-2-4). The Garden.

Practical Pediatrics: Selected Abstracts. Ed. by Richard H. Rapkin. 234p. 1981. 22.50 (ISBN 0-88416-342-3, 342). PSG Pub.

Practical Petroleum Reservoir Engineering Methods. H. C. Slider. LC 74-33712. 1976. 39.50 (ISBN 0-87814-061-1). Pennwell Pub.

Practical Pharmaceutical Chemistry, 2 pts. A. H. Beckett & J. B. Stenlake. 1975-76. Pt. 1 3rd Ed. text ed. 35.00x (ISBN 0-485-11156-X, Athlone Pr); Pt.2 3rd Ed. text ed. 43.75x (ISBN 0-485-11159-4). Humanities.

Practical Photographer. E. A. Weber. 1974. 17.95 o.p. (ISBN 0-85242-002-1, Pub. by Fountain). Morgan.

Practical Photographic Enlarging. Derek Watkins. 224p. 1974. 9.95 o.p. (ISBN 0-13-692269-4, Spec); pap. 4.95 (ISBN 0-13-692251-1, Spec). P-H.

Practical Photographic Lighting. Ted Schwarz. (Popular Photography Workshop Ser.). (Illus.). 128p. 1980. 10.95 (ISBN 0-87165-056-8). Ziff-Davis Pub.

Practical Photography. rev ed. Robert A. McCoy. (Illus.). (gr. 10-12). 1972. text ed. 13.00 (ISBN 0-87345-431-6). McKnight.

Practical Plant Physiology. J. Roberts & D. G. Whitehouse. LC 75-46566. 1977. pap. text ed. 13.95x (ISBN 0-582-44127-7). Longman.

Practical Pointer Training. Sherman Webb. (Illus.). 1974. 9.95 (ISBN 0-87691-131-9). Winchester Pr.

Practical Points in Allergy. 2nd. ed. Ed. by Nathan Weiss et al. 1979. pap. 14.75 (ISBN 0-87488-731-3). Med Exam.

Practical Points in Anesthesiology. 2nd. ed. Ed. by David C. Stark & R. B. Roberts. LC 79-89168. 1980. 13.50 (ISBN 0-87488-700-3). Med Exam.

Practical Points in Gastroenterology. 3rd. ed. Eddy D. Palmer. LC 80-17916. 1980. 14.50 (ISBN 0-87488-733-X). Med Exam.

Practical Points in Pediatrics. 3rd ed. Ed. by Raymond Russo et al. LC 80-20380. 1980. write for info. (ISBN 0-87488-727-5). Med Exam.

Practical Points in Plastic Surgery. Stephen H. Miller et al. LC 79-91201. 1980. pap. 20.00 (ISBN 0-87488-719-4). Med Exam.

Practical Points in Pulmonary Diseases. Daniel J. Stone et al. 1978. spiral bdg. 14.00 (ISBN 0-87488-724-0). Med Exam.

Practical Points in Radiation Oncology. Larry E. Mulkerin. 1979. spiral bdg. 17.00 (ISBN 0-87488-726-7). Med Exam.

Practical Points on Boat Engines. Hans Donat. 204p. 1980. 8.00x (ISBN 0-245-53333-8, Pub. by Nautical England). State Mutual Bk.

Practical Pony Keeping. Catherine Harris. LC 64-16608. (Illus.). 1964. lib. bdg. 4.50 o. p. o.p. (ISBN 0-668-01191-2); pap. 2.95 o.p. (ISBN 0-668-04260-5). Arco.

Practical Pregnancy. Maxine G. Wolfe & Margot Goldsmith. LC 79-22003. (Illus.). 320p. (Orig.). 1980. 12.50 (ISBN 0-446-51204-4); pap. 5.95 (ISBN 0-446-97032-8). Warner Bks.

Practical Princess. Jay Williams. LC 69-12606. (Illus.). (gr. k-3). 1969. PLB 5.95 o.s.i. (ISBN 0-8193-0233-3, Four Winds); PLB 5.41 o.s.i. (ISBN 0-8193-0234-1). Schol Bk Serv.

Practical Princess & Other Liberating Fairy Tales. Jay Williams. LC 78-6998. (Illus.). 112p. 1978. lib. bdg. 8.95 (ISBN 0-590-07725-2, Four Winds); PLB 7.61 (ISBN 0-8193-0969-9). Schol Bk Serv.

Practical Problems in Math Automotive Technicians. LC 77-82372. 1979. pap. 4.40 (ISBN 0-8273-1273-3); instructor's guide 1.60 (ISBN 0-8273-1274-1). Delmar.

Practical Problems in Mathematics--Metric System. F. Schell. LC 78-73133. 1975. pap. text ed. 5.00 (ISBN 0-8273-1418-3); instructor's guide 1.60 (ISBN 0-8273-1419-1). Delmar.

Practical Problems in Mathematics for Electricians. Garrard & Boyd. LC 79-56247. 1981. pap. text ed. 5.00 (ISBN 0-8273-1277-6); instructor's guide 2.00 (ISBN 0-8273-1278-4). Delmar.

Practical Problems in Mathematics for Heating & Cooling Technicians. Russell B. DeVore. LC 79-57141. (Practical Problems in Mathematics Ser.). 175p. 1981. pap. text ed. 6.60 (ISBN 0-8273-1682-8); instr's. guide 2.10 (ISBN 0-8273-1683-6). Delmar.

Practical Problems in Mathematics for Mechanical Drafting. LC 77-78236. 1979. pap. 7.00 (ISBN 0-8273-1670-4); instructor's guide 1.60 (ISBN 0-8273-1671-2). Delmar.

Practical Problems in Mathematics for Office Workers. Joan Briggaman. LC 76-54051. 1977. pap. text ed. 4.20 (ISBN 0-8273-1612-7); instructor's guide 1.60 (ISBN 0-8273-1613-5). Delmar.

Practical Problems in Mathematics for Carpenters. LC 77-82373. 1979. pap. text ed. 5.72 (ISBN 0-685-30196-6); instructor's guide 1.60 (ISBN 0-8273-1276-8). Delmar.

Practical Problems in Mathematics for Consumers. LC 74-24811. 1975. pap. 6.00 (ISBN 0-8273-0266-5); instructor's guide 1.60 (ISBN 0-8273-0267-3). Delmar.

Practical Problems in Mathematics for Masons. John E. Ball. LC 78-74431. (Mathematics - Construction Ser.). 112p. 1980. 5.00 (ISBN 0-8273-1283-0); instructor's guide 2.00 (ISBN 0-8273-1284-9). Delmar.

Practical Problems in Mathematics for Machinists. E. Hoffman. LC 78-74432. (Mathematics Ser.). (gr. 8). 1980. 6.60 (ISBN 0-8273-1281-4); instr's guide 1.75 (ISBN 0-8273-1282-2). Delmar.

Practical Problems in Mathematics for Printers. J. DeLuca. LC 76-3942. 1976. pap. 6.00 (ISBN 0-8273-1285-7); instructor's guide 1.60 (ISBN 0-8273-1286-5). Delmar.

Practical Problems in Mathematics for Welders. Frank R. Schell & Bill J. Matlock. LC 74-24810. 1975. pap. text ed. 6.60 (ISBN 0-8273-0262-2); instructor's guide 1.60 (ISBN 0-8273-0263-0). Delmar.

Practical Problems in Mathematics for Sheet Metal Technicians. F. Schumacher. LC 71-74885. 1973. pap. text ed. 5.20 (ISBN 0-8273-0287-8); instructor's guide 1.60 (ISBN 0-8273-0288-6). Delmar.

Practical Problems of a Private Psychotherapy Practice. Ed. by George D. Goldman & George Stricker. (Illus.). 284p. 1972. 13.25 o.p. (ISBN 0-398-02296-8). C C Thomas.

Practical Procedures in Clinical Medicine. Michael J. Ford & John F. Munro. (Illus.). 144p. 1981. pap. text ed. 9.95 (ISBN 0-443-02120-1). Churchill.

Practical Process Instrumentation & Control. Jay Matley & Chemical Engineering Magazine. (Chemical Engineering Ser.). 512p. 1980. 29.50 (ISBN 0-07-010712-2). McGraw.

Practical Processing in Black & White Photography: P-229. Ed. by Eastman Kodak Company. 1978. pap. 2.50 (ISBN 0-87985-014-0). Eastman Kodak.

Practical Program Evaluation for State & Local Government Officials. Harry P. Hatry et al. 1973. pap. 4.50 (ISBN 0-87766-054-9, 17000). Urban Inst.

Practical Programming. 2nd ed. P. N. Corlett. LC 75-161295. (School Mathematics Project Handbooks). (Illus.). 1971. 23.95 (ISBN 0-521-08198-X); pap. 10.95x (ISBN 0-521-09740-1). Cambridge U Pr.

Practical Projects for the Blacksmith. Ted Tucker. (Illus.). 1980. 11.95 (ISBN 0-87857-312-7); pap. 7.95 (ISBN 0-87857-294-5). Rodale Pr Inc.

Practical Psychiatry for the Primary Physician. James R. Hodge. LC 75-9857. 368p. 1975. 19.95 (ISBN 0-88229-157-2). Nelson Hall.

Practical Psychology for Police Officers. Martin Reiser. 196p. 1973. 13.50 (ISBN 0-398-02846-X). C C Thomas.

Practical Psychology of Leadership for Criminal Justice Officers: A Basic Programmed Text. Robert J. Wicks & Ernest H. Josephs, Jr. 128p. 1973. pap. 8.75 (ISBN 0-398-02783-8). C C Thomas.

Practical Public Relations for the Businessman. William E. Farley. 7.95 o.s.i. (ISBN 0-8119-0144-0). Fell.

Practical Public Relations for the Public Schools. John Bitter. LC 77-71467. 1977. text ed. 9.95 (ISBN 0-916624-08-0). TSU Pr.

Practical Real Estate Brokerage. Robert W. Kent & D. A. Corb. 1961. 12.95 o.p. (ISBN 0-13-693671-7). P-H.

Practical Reasoning in Natural Language. Stephen Thomas. (Illus.). 352p. 1981. pap. text ed. 9.95 (ISBN 0-13-692137-X). P-H.

Practical Reference Work. Denis Grogan. (Outlines of Modern Librarianship Ser.). 144p. 1979. text ed. 12.00 (ISBN 0-686-65492-7, Pub. by K G Saur). Shoe String.

Practical Religion. J. C. Ryle. (Summit Bks). 1977. pap. 3.95 (ISBN 0-8010-7657-9). Baker Bk.

Practical Rhetoric for College Writers. Renee Hausmann & Evelyn Taylor. 272p. 1980. pap. text ed. 7.95x (ISBN 0-534-00783-X). Wadsworth Pub.

Practical Sailor. R. F. Duncan. (Illus.). 224p. 1981. 14.95 (ISBN 0-684-16621-6, ScribT). Scribner.

Practical Salad & Dessert Art. Charles Mok. 1973. spiral bdg. 22.95 (ISBN 0-8436-0570-7). CBI Pub.

Practical Sanskrit-English Dictionary. rev. ed. V. S. Apte. 1978. Repr. 24.00 (ISBN 0-89684-294-0). Orient Bk Dist.

Practical Sanskrit-English Dictionary. new ed. Vaman S. Apte. 1975. 30.00x (ISBN 0-8426-0996-2). Verry.

Practical Security in Commerce & Industry. Eric Oliver & John Wilson. 1979. pap. text ed. 36.00x (ISBN 0-566-02033-5, Pub. by Gower Pub Co England). Renouf.

Practical Selling. Ralph D. Shipp, Jr. LC 79-88039. 1980. text ed. 15.50 (ISBN 0-395-28181-4); instrs'. manual 1.10 (ISBN 0-395-28182-2); dialogue tape 1.50 (ISBN 0-395-29303-0). HM.

Practical Sensitometry. George Wakefield. 1970. 11.95 o.p. (ISBN 0-85242-310-1, Pub. by Fountain). Morgan.

Practical Sermons of Persuasive Power. Horace W. Busby. pap. 3.50 (ISBN 0-89315-206-4). Lambert Bk.

Practical Sermons That Motivate. J. J. Turner. pap. 2.95 (ISBN 0-89315-211-0). Lambert Bk.

Practical Sewing. Ann Ladbury. LC 78-50819. 1978. pap. 7.95 (ISBN 0-528-88198-1); pap. 7.95 (ISBN 0-528-88198-1). Rand.

Practical Social Sciences. Adam Podgorecki. (International Library of Sociology). 200p. 1975. 16.00x (ISBN 0-7100-8175-8). Routledge & Kegan.

Practical Solar Heating Manual Wih Blueprints: For Air & Water Systems. Dewayne Coxon. 150p. 1981. text ed. 19.95 (ISBN 0-250-40446-X). Ann Arbor Science.

Practical Solid-State Circuit Design. 2nd ed. Jerome E. Oleksy. LC 73-90284. 1980. pap. 8.95 (ISBN 0-672-21787-2). Sams.

Practical Spanish Dictionary & Phrasebook. new ed. Marguerite D. Bomse. 1978. pap. text ed. 7.50 (ISBN 0-08-023020-2). Pergamon.

Practical Spanish for Medical & Hospital Personnel. 2nd ed. Marguerite D. Bomse & Julian H. Alfaro. 1978. pap. text ed. 16.55 (ISBN 0-08-023001-6). Pergamon.

Practical Spanish for School Personnel, Firemen, Policemen & Community Agencies. 2nd ed. Marguerite D. Bomse & Julian H. Alfaro. 1978. pap. text ed. 6.55 (ISBN 0-08-023002-4). Pergamon.

Practical Spanish for the Health Professions. Frank Benitez & Sharon Benitez. 1973. 9.95 o.p. (ISBN 0-914330-01-2). Pioneer Pub Co.

Practical Spanish Grammar. Marguerite D. Bomse. 1978. pap. 7.50 (ISBN 0-08-021859-8). Pergamon.

Practical Spanish Grammar. John G. Friar & George W. Kelly. 1960. pap. 3.50 (ISBN 0-385-00977-1). Doubleday.

Practical Speech for Modern Business. Robert C. Martin et al. LC 63-7333. 1963. 24.50x (ISBN 0-89197-353-2); pap. text ed. 16.95x (ISBN 0-89197-899-2). Irvington.

Practical Statistics & Probability. R. Loveday. 256p. 1974. pap. text ed. 6.95x (ISBN 0-521-20291-4). Cambridge U Pr.

Practical Statistics for Petroleum Engineers. Lyn T. Stanley. LC 72-95444. 150p. 1973. 14.00 (ISBN 0-87814-019-0). Pennwell Pub.

Practical Stylist. 4th ed. S. Baker. 1977. pap. text ed. 7.50 scp (ISBN 0-690-00873-2, HarpC). Har-Row.

Practical Stylist. 5th ed. Sheridan Baker. 224p. 1980. pap. text ed. 7.50 scp (ISBN 0-06-040454-X, HarpC); avail. Har-Row.

Practical Surveying. 16th ed. Ed. by K. M. Hart. (Illus.). 1973. 21.00x (ISBN 0-291-39418-3). Intl Ideas.

Practical Systems & Procedures Manual. J. Vanduyn. LC 74-31160. (Illus.). 240p. 1975. 16.95 (ISBN 0-87909-634-9). Reston.

Practical Tables, Vol. 1: Six-Figure Trigonometrical Functions of Angles in Degrees & Minutes. 5th ed. Ed. by C. Attwood. 1965. 8.50 (ISBN 0-08-009894-0); pap. 4.20 (ISBN 0-08-009893-2). Pergamon.

Practical Theorist: The Life & Work of Kurt Lewin. Alfred J. Marrow. LC 77-1400. 1977. pap. text ed. 7.50x (ISBN 0-8077-2525-0). Tchrs Coll.

Practical Therapeutics for Nursing & Related Professions. 3rd ed. James Boyle. Orig. Title: Lectures Notes in Pharmacology & Therapeutics for Nurses. 288p. 1980. pap. text ed. 14.00x (ISBN 0-443-01540-6). Churchill.

Practical Transactional Analysis in Management. James H. Morrison & John O'Hearne. (Illus.). 168p. 1977. pap. text ed. 7.95 (ISBN 0-201-04898-1). A-W.

Practical Treatise on Engine Crankshaft Torsional Vibration Control. Society of Automotive Engineers. 1979. pap. 7.50 (ISBN 0-89883-216-0). Soc Auto Engineers.

Practical Treatise on the Criminal Law; Comprising the Practice, Pleadings & Evidence Which Occur in the Course of Criminal Prosecutions Whether by Indictment or Information; with a Copious Collection of Precedents, 5 vols, Vol.93. Joseph Chitty. Ed. by David Berkowitz & Samuel Thorne. LC 77-86637. (Classics of English Legal History in the Modern Era Ser.). 1979. Repr. of 1816 ed. lib. bdg. 55.00 (ISBN 0-8240-3080-X). Garland Pub.

Practical Treatise on the Law of Contracts. Joseph Chitty, Jr. Ed. by David S. Berkowitz & Samuel E. Thorne. LC 77-86636. (Classics of English Legal History in the Modern Era Ser.: Vol. 25). 807p. 1979. lib. bdg. 40.00 (ISBN 0-8240-3074-5). Garland Pub.

Practical Troubleshooting for Microprocessors. James W. Coffron. (Illus.). 256p. 1981. text ed. 19.95 (ISBN 0-13-694273-3). P-H.

Practical Use of the Microscope. George H. Needham. (Illus.). 520p. 1977. 28.75 (ISBN 0-398-03645-4). C C Thomas.

Practical Ways to Teach the Basic Mathematical Skills. Virginia Council of Teachers of Mathematics. 1979. pap. 7.50 (ISBN 0-686-65437-4). NCTM.

Practical Weaving Course. P. R. Jarvis. 6.00 o.p. (ISBN 0-87245-157-7). Textile Bk.

Practical Wildlife Photography. Ken Preston-Mafham. LC 80-40792. (Practical Photography Ser.). (Illus.). 144p. 1981. 19.95 (ISBN 0-240-51081-X). Focal Pr.

Practical Will Drafting 1979. (Tax Law & Estate Planning Course Handbook Series 1979-80: Vol. 93). 1978. pap. 20.00 (ISBN 0-685-90307-9, D4-5120). PLI.

Practical Wine Knowledge. Bruce H. Axler. 1974. pap. 3.95 (ISBN 0-672-26119-7). Bobbs.

Practical Wiring, 2 vols. Henry A. Miller. 1969. Vol. 1. pap. 4.40 (ISBN 0-08-013288-X); Vol. 2. pap. 4.40 (ISBN 0-08-013403-3). Pergamon.

Practical Wiring in SI Units, Vols. 1 & 2. rev. ed. Henry A. Miller. LC 68-57882. (Pergamon International Library, Electrical Engineering Division). 108p. 1975. Vol. 1. 1975. pap. text ed. 5.75 (ISBN 0-08-019754-X); Vol. 2. 1976. pap. text ed. 5.75 (ISBN 0-08-020573-9). Pergamon.

Practical Wood Turner. rev. ed. F. Pain. LC 74-6436. (Illus.). 1979. pap. 5.95 (ISBN 0-8069-8580-1). Sterling.

Practical Woodwork. Charles H. Hayward. (Illus.). 192p. 1978. pap. 5.95 (ISBN 0-8069-8582-8). Sterling.

Practical Woodwork for Laboratory Technicians. A. S. Eyers. LC 79-117463. 1970. 12.25 (ISBN 0-08-015962-1). Pergamon.

Practical Word Choice in Business Writing. 4th ed. Charles B. Smith. 1978. saddle stitch 2.95 o.p. (ISBN 0-8403-1867-7). Kendall-Hunt.

Practical Yoga: A Pictorial Approach. Masahiro Oki. LC 76-115846. (Illus.). 1973. pap. 6.95 (ISBN 0-87040-224-2). Japan Pubns.

Practical Zoology. 6th ed. C. J. Wallis. 1974. 19.95x (ISBN 0-433-34704-X). Intl Ideas.

Practically Painless English. Sally F. Wallace. (English Composition Ser.). 1979. pap. text ed. 7.50 (ISBN 0-13-692194-9). P-H.

Practically Seventeen. Rosamond Du Jardin. (gr. 4-9). 1949. 9.89 (ISBN 0-397-30153-7). Lippincott.

Practically Speaking: In Business, Industry, & Government. Robert Hays. LC 71-100868. 1969. pap. 8.75 (ISBN 0-201-02825-5). A-W.

Practicas de Laboratorio de Fisica. Gregorio Morones. (Span.). 1979. pap. text ed. 4.20 (ISBN 0-06-315700-4, Pub. by HarLA Mexico). Har-Row.

Practice. Alan E. Nourse. LC 75-25094. 1978. 10.95 o.p. (ISBN 0-06-013194-2, HarpT). Har-Row.

Practice. Stanley Winchester. pap. 1.50 o.s.i. (ISBN 0-440-17081-8). Dell.

Practice & Procedure Before the National Labor Relations Board. 3rd ed. 219p. 1980. pap. 15.00 (L027B). ALI-ABA.

Practice & Procedure for the Quantity Surveyor. 8th ed. Arthur J. Willis & Christopher J. Willis. 239p. 1980. text ed. 30.00x (ISBN 0-246-11172-0, Pub. by Granada England); pap. text ed. 16.75x (ISBN 0-246-11242-5, Pub. by Granada England). Renouf.

Practice & Progress: A German Grammar for Review & Reference. Karl S. Weimar & Werner G. Hoffmeister. 1970. text ed. 14.95x (ISBN 0-471-00619-X); tapes avail. (ISBN 0-471-00621-1). Wiley.

Practice & Theory Manual. 10th ed. A. M. Partington & Arthur C. Nieminsky. 19.50 (ISBN 0-932788-11-4). Bradley CPA.

Practice & Theory of Bolshevism. Bertrand Russell. (Unwin Books). 1962. text ed. 5.50x (ISBN 0-04-335017-8); pap. 3.95 (ISBN 0-04-335018-6). Allen Unwin.

Practice & Theory of Electrochemical Machining. John F. Wilson. 266p. 1981. Repr. of 1971 ed. lib. bdg. write for info. (ISBN 0-89874-229-3). Krieger.

Practice & Theory of Individual Psychology. Alfred Adler. Tr. by P. Radin. (International Library of Psychology Philosophy & Scientific Method Ser.). 1971. Repr. of 1929 ed. text ed. 27.50x (ISBN 0-7100-3015-0). Humanities.

Practice & Theory of Probation & Parole. David Dressler. 1969. 15.00x (ISBN 0-231-02956-X). Columbia U Pr.

Practice Book on English Stress & Intonation. Kenneth Croft. 81p. 1961. pap. 4.95 (ISBN 0-87789-013-7); cassette tapes 90.00 (ISBN 0-87789-125-7). Eng Language.

Practice Exercises in Everyday English. Robert J. Dixson. (Orig.). (gr. 9 up). 1957. pap. text ed. 2.95 (ISBN 0-88345-131-X, 17414); answer key 1.00 (ISBN 0-685-19801-4). Regents Pub.

Practice Exercises in News Writing. 2nd ed. George A. Hough, 3rd. 1980. pap. text ed. 7.95 (ISBN 0-395-28637-9); instrs'. manual .75 avail. (ISBN 0-395-28638-7). HM.

Practice FCC-Type Exams for Radiotelephone Operator's License-1st Class. Richard J. Smith & Victor F. Veley. (gr. 10 up). 1977. pap. 5.95 (ISBN 0-8104-5974-4). Hayden.

Practice FCC-Type Exams for Radiotelephone Operator's License-2nd Class. Richard J. Smith & Victor F. Veley. (Illus.). 180p. 1975. pap. 7.25 (ISBN 0-8104-5965-5). Hayden.

Practice for Officer Candidate Tests. 4th ed. LC 74-20760. (Military Examination Ser.). 1974. lib. bdg. 8.00 (ISBN 0-668-01507-1); pap. 6.00 (ISBN 0-668-01304-4). Arco.

Practice for the Army Classification & Placement: The Armed Services Vocational Aptitude Battery-Asuab. LC 75-13421. (Military Examination Ser.). 1975. lib. bdg. 10.00 (ISBN 0-668-03844-6); pap. 8.00 (ISBN 0-668-03845-4). Arco.

Practice for the B.S.E. Katharine Stone et al. 170p. 1980. pap. text ed. 5.95 (ISBN 0-89892-037-X). Contemp Pub Co Raleigh.

Practice for Understanding & Using English: Eighty Exercises. 2nd ed. Newman P. Birk & Genevieve B. Birk. LC 71-189751. 1972. pap. 4.95 (ISBN 0-672-63291-8). Odyssey Pr.

Practice for Uniform Product Disclosure for Unitized Microform Readers (Microfiche, Jackets & Image Cards) NMA MS22-1979. National Micrographics Assn. 1980. 3.00 (ISBN 0-89258-057-7). Natl Micrograph.

Practice in Computers & Mathematics. James Poirot et al. 227p. (Orig.). (gr. 11-12). 1980. pap. text ed. 5.95 (ISBN 0-88408-126-5). Sterling Swift.

Practice in Data Processing. David N. Groves et al. 217p. (Orig.). (gr. 11-12). 1979. wkbk 4.95x (ISBN 0-88408-114-1). Sterling Swift.

Practice in English: Test Papers for Foreign Students. M. Posner. 1971. pap. 11.00x (ISBN 0-17-555059-X). Intl Ideas.

Practice in Exposition: Supplementary Exercises for the Practical Stylist. 2nd ed. Sheridan Baker. 160p. 1980. pap. text ed. 6.50 scp (ISBN 0-690-00875-9, HarpC). Har-Row.

Practice in Medical English. Kenneth Methold. 1975. pap. text ed. 4.75x (ISBN 0-582-55057-2). Longman.

Practice in Real Estate Mathematics. 3rd ed. Marilyn Floberg. 1975. text ed. 13.50 scp (ISBN 0-06-453617-3, HarpC). Har-Row.

Practice Made Perfect: How to Design, Establish, & Maintain Your Medical Office or Diagnose & Prescribe for Your Ailing One. rev. ed. David J. Sullivan. Ed. by Robert Russo. LC 78-65989. (Illus.). 304p. 1979. 39.95 (ISBN 0-9605606-0-2). Medi-Pub.

Practice Makes Perfect. Edward Vernon. LC 77-10174. 1978. 8.95 o.p. (ISBN 0-312-63535-4). St Martin.

Practice of Advertising. Ed. by James O'Connor & Norman A. Hart. 1978. pap. 16.50x (ISBN 0-434-90362-0). Intl Ideas.

Practice of Anthropology: A Manual for Professionals. Rena C. Gropper. LC 76-19136. 1981. 20.00 (ISBN 0-87850-029-4). Darwin Pr.

Practice of Aromatherapy. Jean Valonet. (Illus.). 1981. pap. 8.95 (ISBN 0-89281-026-2). Inner Tradit.

Practice of Behavior Therapy. 2nd ed. Joseph Wolpe. LC 72-11653. 1974. text ed. 19.75 (ISBN 0-08-017089-7); pap. text ed. 8.75 (ISBN 0-08-017090-0). Pergamon.

Practice of Cardiology. Ed. by Robert A. Johnson et al. 1980. text ed. 59.95 (ISBN 0-316-46945-9). Little.

Practice of Clinical Casework. Gertrude Sackheim. LC 73-19787. 212p. 1974. text ed. 14.95 (ISBN 0-87705-141-0). Human Sci Pr.

Practice of Collective Bargaining. 5th ed. Edwin F. Beal et al. 1976. text ed. 19.50x (ISBN 0-256-01821-9). Irwin.

Practice of Community-Oriented Primary Health Care. Sidney L. Kark. 288p. 1980. pap. 13.50x (ISBN 0-8385-7865-9). ACC.

Practice of Comparative Politics: A Reader. 2nd ed. Ed. by Paul G. Lewis & David C. Potter. (Open University Set Bk.). 1979. pap. text ed. 10.95 (ISBN 0-582-49033-2). Longman.

Practice of Conjoint Therapy: Combining Individual & Group Treatment. Louis Ormont & Herbert S. Strean. LC 77-17079. 1978. text ed. 19.95 (ISBN 0-87705-355-3). Human Sci Pr.

Practice of Criticism. D. H. Rawlinson. 1968. 34.00 (ISBN 0-521-06045-1); pap. 8.95x (ISBN 0-521-09540-9). Cambridge U Pr.

Practice of Electrocardiography. Thomas M. Blake. LC 80-13084. 1980. 18.95 (ISBN 0-87488-903-0); pap. 12.00 (ISBN 0-87488-997-9). Med Exam.

Practice of Emergency Nursing. James H. Cosgriff, Jr. & Diann Anderson. 1975. 21.00 (ISBN 0-397-54169-4). Lippincott.

Practice of Equine Stud Medicine. 2nd ed. P. D. Rossdale & S. W. Ricketts. (Illus.). 425p. 1980. text ed. write for info. (ISBN 0-8121-0750-0). Lea & Febiger.

Practice of Fiction in America: Writers from Hawthorne to the Present. Jerome Klinkowitz. 140p. (gr. 9-12). 1980. text ed. 10.95 (ISBN 0-8138-1420-0). Iowa St U Pr.

Practice of Group Work. Ed. by William Schwartz & Serapio R. Zalba. LC 75-127101. 1971. 17.50x (ISBN 0-231-03241-2); pap. 5.00x (ISBN 0-231-08674-1). Columbia U Pr.

Practice of Intramedullary Nailing. Gerhard Kuntscher. (Illus.). 388p. 1967. photocopy ed. 35.75 (ISBN 0-398-01067-6). C C Thomas.

Practice of Karma Yoga. Swami Sivananda. 1974. 5.00 (ISBN 0-8426-0675-0); pap. 3.50 (ISBN 0-686-67764-1). Orient Bk Dist.

Practice of Local Government Planning, Vol. 1. Ed. by Frank S. So et al. LC 79-21380. (Municipal Management Ser.). (Illus.). 1979. text ed. 35.00 (ISBN 0-87326-020-1). Intl City Mgt.

Practice of Management. R. W. Morell & M. Daniel Henry. LC 80-8136. 510p. 1981. lib. bdg. 26.00 (ISBN 0-8191-1489-8); pap. text ed. 16.75 (ISBN 0-8191-1490-1). U Pr of Amer.

Practice of Management Science. Martin K. Starr & Irving Stein. (Illus.). 208p. 1976. 12.95 (ISBN 0-13-693630-X). P-H.

Practice of Managerial Psychology. Andrew J. Du Brin. 1972. 23.00 (ISBN 0-08-016764-0); pap. 14.50 (ISBN 0-08-018126-0). Pergamon.

Practice of Marketing. Douglas W. Smallbone. (Illus.). 400p. 1972. 16.50x o.p. (ISBN 0-8464-0745-0). Beekman Pubs.

Practice of Medical Radiesthesia. Vernon D. Wethered. 150p. 1977. 9.15x (ISBN 0-8464-1040-0). Beekman Pubs.

Practice of Medicine, 10 vols. Loose Leaf Reference Services. loose leaf bdg. 325.00 o.p. (ISBN 0-06-148005-3, Harper Medical); revision pages 55.00 o.p. (ISBN 0-685-57890-9). Har-Row.

Practice of Medicine: A Self Assessment Guide. 2nd ed. Margolis. (Illus.). 1980. pap. 14.95 (ISBN 0-8385-7877-2). ACC.

Practice of Mental Health Nursing: A Community Approach. 1st ed. Arthur J. Morgan & Judith W. Moreno. 225p. 1973. 8.50 o.p. (ISBN 0-397-54142-2); pap. 7.50 (ISBN 0-397-54148-1). Lippincott.

Practice of Multimodal Therapy. Arnold A. Lazarus. (Illus.). 256p. 1981. 18.95 (ISBN 0-07-036813-9, P&R&B). McGraw.

Practice of Palmistry for Professional Purposes. C. De Saint-Germain. LC 80-23774. 416p. 1980. Repr. of 1973 ed. lib. bdg. 11.95x (ISBN 0-89370-619-1). Borgo Pr.

Practice of Planning in Health Care Institutions. LC 73-77589. 112p. 1973. pap. 15.00 (ISBN 0-87258-120-9, 2765). Am Hospital.

Practice of Planning in Health Care Institutions. 100p. 1973. 11.25 (ISBN 0-686-68593-8, 2765). Hospital Finan.

Practice of Planning: Strategic, Administrative, Operational. Leon Reinharth et al. 352p. 1980. text ed. 19.95. Van Nos Reinhold.

Practice of Politics. K. W. Watkins. 1975. 15.95x (ISBN 0-17-711127-5). Intl Ideas.

Practice of Prayer. G. Campbell Morgan. (Morgan Library). pap. 3.45 (ISBN 0-8010-5896-1). Baker Bk.

Practice of Printing. rev. ed. Ralph W. Polk & Edwin Polk. (Illus.). (gr. 9-12). 1971. text ed. 11.80 (ISBN 0-87002-101-X); elem. ptg. job sheets. 2.60 (ISBN 0-87002-029-3). Bennett IL.

Practice of Process Meditation: The Intensive Journal Way to Spiritual Experience. Ira Progoff. 1980. 12.95 (ISBN 0-87941-008-6). Dialogue Hse.

Practice of Real Estate. O'Donnell. 1978. 17.95 (ISBN 0-7216-6913-1). Dryden Pr.

Practice of Real Estate in California. Donald C. Driscoll & Homer C. Davey. (Illus.). 304p. 1981. 18.95 (ISBN 0-13-693606-7). P-H.

Practice of Real Estate Management: For the Experienced Property Manager. William Walters, Jr. Ed. by Nancye J. Kirk. LC 79-84053. 1979. 21.95 (ISBN 0-912104-37-6). Inst Real Estate.

Practice of Recollection: A Guide to Buddhist Meditation. Bhikkhu Mangalo. 32p. 1978. pap. 1.50 o.p. (ISBN 0-87773-704-5, Prajna). Great Eastern.

Practice of Sacred Music. Carl Halter. 1955. 3.95 (ISBN 0-570-01319-4, 99-1095). Concordia.

Practice of Social Intervention: Goals, Roles & Strategies: a Book of Readings in Social Work Practice. Ed. by Frank Loewenberg & Ralph Dolgoff. LC 74-174169. 1972. pap. text ed. 11.50 (ISBN 0-87581-121-3). Peacock Pubs.

Practice of Social Research. 2nd ed. Earl R. Babbie. 1979. text ed. 19.95x (ISBN 0-534-00630-2); wkbk. 7.95x (ISBN 0-534-00702-3). Wadsworth Pub.

Practice of Social Work. 2nd ed. Robert W. Klenk & Robert M. Ryan. 1974. pap. 11.95x (ISBN 0-534-00341-9). Wadsworth Pub.

Practice of Speech Pathology: A Clinical Diary. Robert W. Blakeley. (Illus.). 240p. 1973. 14.75 (ISBN 0-398-02575-4). C C Thomas.

Practice of Supervising: Making Experience Pay. Martin M. Broadwell. LC 76-23982. (Illus.). 1977. pap. text ed. 8.95 (ISBN 0-201-00789-4). A-W.

Practice of Supervision: Achieving Results Through People. Andrew J. Dubrin. 1980. 16.95x (ISBN 0-256-02272-0). Business Pubns.

Practice of Teaching. Ken Martin & Bill Bennett. 1980. text ed. 15.70 (ISBN 0-06-318116-9, IntlDept); pap. text ed. 7.80 (ISBN 0-06-318117-7). Har-Row.

Practice of the Presence of God. Brother Lawrence. Ed. by Donald E. Demaray. (Devotional Classics Ser). 64p. 1975. pap. 1.95 (ISBN 0-8010-2844-2). Baker Bk.

Practice of the Presence of God. Tr. by John J. Delaney. LC 77-70896. 1977. pap. 2.25 (ISBN 0-385-12861-4, Im). Doubleday.

Practice of Urban Economics. Alfred J. Watkins. LC 80-13809. (Sage Library of Social Research: Vol. 107). (Illus.). 248p. 1980. 18.00 (ISBN 0-8039-1380-X); pap. 8.95 (ISBN 0-8039-1381-8). Sage.

Practice-Oriented Medical Record. Gerald S. Lang & Kenneth J. Dickie. LC 78-1931. (Illus.). 1978. text ed. 27.95 (ISBN 0-89443-032-7). Aspen Systems.

Practice Set-Basic Accounting. 2nd ed. Calvin Engler. 1969. pap. 6.00 o.p. (ISBN 0-672-26020-4). Bobbs.

Practice Set to Accompany Introduction to Accounting. Joseph DeFatta & Pierre Titard. 1976. pap. 4.95 o.p. (ISBN 0-7216-3014-6). Saunders.

Practice Through Pictures. J. B. Heaton. 1975. pap. text ed. 2.50x (ISBN 0-582-52135-1); teacher's bk. 2.25x (ISBN 0-582-52136-X). Longman.

Practice with Idioms. Ronald E. Feare. 192p. 1980. pap. text ed. 5.95x (ISBN 0-19-502782-5). Oxford U Pr.

Practicebook for Aphasics. Milfred R. McKeown. (Illus.). 236p. 1976. pap. 19.75 (ISBN 0-398-03484-2). C C Thomas.

Practices & Procedures Under the Taylor Law: A Practical Guide in Narrative Form. Grace S. Aboud & Robert E. Doherty. 1974. pap. 2.00 (ISBN 0-87546-203-0). NY Sch Indus Rel.

Practices in the Treatment of Low- & Intermediate-Level Radioactive Wastes. 1966. pap. 47.75 (ISBN 92-0-020166-0, IAEA). Unipub.

Practicing Educational Psychology. Margaret M. Clifford. (Illus.). 752p. 1981. pap. text ed. write for info. (ISBN 0-395-29921-7); write for info. set test bank (ISBN 0-395-29925-X); write for info. instr's manual (ISBN 0-395-29923-3). HM.

Practicing Management: A Guide to Accompany Tansik, Chase, & Aquilano's Management: a Life Cycle Approach. Lawrence Chase et al. 1980. pap. 6.50x (ISBN 0-256-02354-9). Irwin.

Practicing Plant Parenthood. Maggie Baylis. LC 75-22361. (Illus.). 192p. (Orig.). 1975. 4.95 (ISBN 0-912238-62-3); pap. 4.95 (ISBN 0-912238-61-5). One Hund One Prods.

Practicing Psychotherapy. Edmund C. Neuhaus & William Astwood. LC 79-25464. 208p. text ed. 18.95 (ISBN 0-87705-467-3). Human Sci Pr.

Practicing Texas Politics. 4th ed. Eugene W. Jones et al. LC 79-88888. 1980. pap. text ed. 9.95 (ISBN 0-395-28257-8); instrs' manual 1.25 (ISBN 0-395-28258-6); student guide 6.25 (ISBN 0-395-28259-4). HM.

Practicing the Piano. Franck Merrick. 1978. lib. bdg. 9.95 o.p. (ISBN 0-214-15726-1, 8025, Dist. by Arco). Barrie & Jenkins.

Practicum Manual for Counseling & Psychotherapy. 4th rev. ed. Kenneth Dimick & Frank Krause. 1980. pap. 9.95 (ISBN 0-915202-26-3). Accel Devel.

Practiquemos el Evangelio. William M. Pinson. Orig. Title: Applying the Gospel. 1976. pap. 1.85 (ISBN 0-311-46071-2). Casa Bautista.

Practiquemos la Visitacion. J. T. Sisemore. Ed. by Ananias Gonzalez. Tr. by Josue Grijalva. Orig. Title: Ministry of Visitation. 1979. 1.95 (ISBN 0-311-11034-7). Casa Bautista.

Practising Dentistry. K. Kimmel & R. O. Walker. (Illus.). 258p. 1972. 46.00. Quint Pub Co.

Practitioner-Teacher Role. Lorraine Machan. LC 80-80814. (Nursing Dimensions Education Ser.). 1980. pap. text ed. 9.50 (ISBN 0-913654-65-5). Nursing Res.

Practitioner's Guide to School Business Management. new ed. John Greenhalgh. 1978. 15.95 (ISBN 0-205-07128-7). Allyn.

Practitioners Handbook of Ambulatory OB-GYN. Jean D. Neeson & Connie R. Stockdale. 400p. 1981. 17.95 (ISBN 0-471-05670-7, Pub. by Wiley Medical). Wiley.

Practitioners of Love. Ethel Mannin. 1970. 5.95 o.p. (ISBN 0-8180-1900-X). Horizon.

Praetorius Organ. Paul G. Bunjes. (Illus.). 1966. 57.00 (ISBN 0-570-01307-0, 99-1192). Concordia.

Praeventive Aspekte in der Paediatrie. Ed. by G. Stalder & C. P. Fliegel. (Paediatrische Fortbildungskurse Fuer Die Praxis Ser.: Vol. 52). (Illus.). 1981. soft cover 48.00 (ISBN 3-8055-1980-X). S Karger.

Pragmatic a Priori. Sandra Rosenthal. LC 75-41707. 104p. 1975. 10.00 (ISBN 0-87527-142-1). Fireside Bks.

Pragmatic Federalism: An Intergovernmental View of American Government. Parris N. Glendening & Mavis M. Reeves. LC 76-29891. (Illus.). 1977. 13.50 (ISBN 0-913530-10-7); pap. 8.50x (ISBN 0-913530-09-3). Palisades Pub.

Pragmatic Illusions: The Presidential Politics of John F. Kennedy. Bruce Miroff. LC 76-7554. 1976. 10.95x (ISBN 0-679-30298-0, Pub. by MacKay); pap. 8.95x (ISBN 0-582-28130-X). Longman.

Pragmatic Logic for Commands. Melvin J. Adler. (Pragmatics & Beyond Ser.: No.3). 139p. 1980. pap. text ed. 17.25x (ISBN 90-272-2501-X). Humanities.

Pragmatic Movement in American Philosophy. Charles Morris. LC 79-119642. 1970. 6.50 o.s.i. (ISBN 0-8076-0564-6); pap. 3.25 (ISBN 0-8076-0563-8). Braziller.

Pragmatic Naturalism: An Introduction. S. Morris Eames. LC 76-58441. 256p. 1977. pap. 7.95x (ISBN 0-8093-0803-7). S Ill U Pr.

Pragmatic Programming & Sensible Software. Ed. by Online Conferences Ltd. 1978. text ed. 94.00x (ISBN 0-903796-20-1, Pub by Online Conferences England). Renouf.

Pragmatics of Public Communication. Ronald R. Allen & Ray McKerrow. (Speech and Drama Ser.). 1977. pap. text ed. 8.95 (ISBN 0-675-08487-3); manual 3.95 (ISBN 0-686-67617-3). Merrill.

Pragmatism. William James. Ed. by Bruce Kuklick. (Philosophical Classics Ser.). 152p. 1980. lib. bdg. 13.50 (ISBN 0-915145-04-9); pap. text ed. 2.95 (ISBN 0-915145-05-7). Hackett Pub.

Pragmatism & Phenomenology: A Philosophic Encounter. Sandra Rosenthal & Patrick L. Bourgeois. 199p. 1980. text ed. 23.00x (ISBN 90-6032-179-0). Humanities.

Pragmatism & Purpose: Essays Presented to T. A. Goudge. Ed. by L. W. Sumner et al. 376p. 1981. 25.00x (ISBN 0-8020-5481-1). U of Toronto Pr.

Pragmatism & the American Mind: Essays & Reviews in Philosophy & Intellectual History. Morton White. 288p. 1973. 15.95 (ISBN 0-19-501623-8). Oxford U Pr.

Pragmatism As Humanism: The Philosophy of William James. Patrick K. Dooley. LC 73-86935. 200p. 1974. 15.95 (ISBN 0-88229-125-4); pap. 7.95x (ISBN 0-88229-582-9). Nelson-Hall.

Pragmatism: Its Sources & Prospects. Ed. by Robert J. Mulvaney & Philip M. Zeltner. LC 80-26475. 1981. text ed. 9.95 (ISBN 0-87249-404-7). U of SC Pr.

Prague. Time-Life Books Editors & Geoffrey Moorehouse. (Great Cities Ser.). (Illus.). 200p. 1981. 14.95 (ISBN 0-8094-3116-5). Time-Life.

Prairie. James F. Cooper. 1976. lib. bdg. 14.95x (ISBN 0-89968-160-3). Lightyear.

Prairie Albion: An English Settlement in Pioneer Illinois. Charles Boewe. LC 62-15000. (Illus.). 1962. 10.00x o.p. (ISBN 0-8093-0074-5). S Ill U Pr.

Prairie Baroness. Robert J. Steelman. LC 80-2348. 192p. 1981. 9.95 (ISBN 0-385-17015-7). Doubleday.

Prairie Dogs in Prairie Dog Town. Irmengarde Eberle. LC 73-9921. (Illus.). 64p. (gr. 3-6). 1974. 7.95 (ISBN 0-690-00069-3, TYC-J). T Y Crowell.

Prairie Ducks: A Study of Their Behavior, Ecology & Management. Lyle K. Sowls. LC 77-14153. (Illus.). 1978. 11.50x (ISBN 0-8032-0978-9); pap. 3.50 (ISBN 0-8032-5895-X, BB 665, Bison). U of Nebr Pr.

Prairie Empire. Clayton Fox. 1977. pap. 1.50 (ISBN 0-505-51215-7). Tower Bks.

Prairie Garden: Seventy Plants You Can Grow in Town or Country. J. Robert Smith. 120p. 1980. 22.50 (ISBN 0-299-08300-4); pap. 9.95 (ISBN 0-299-08304-7). U of Wis Pr.

Prairie Has an Endless Sky. Julian May. Ed. by Publication Associates. LC 75-156061. (Investigating the Earth Ser). (Illus.). (gr. 4-8). 1972. PLB 5.95 o.p. (ISBN 0-87191-062-4). Creative Ed.

Prairie Provinces. Ed. by P. J. Smith. (Studies in Canadian Geography). 1972. pap. 5.50x (ISBN 0-8020-6161-3). U of Toronto Pr.

Prairie Vengeance. M. L. Warren. (Orig.). 1980. pap. 1.75 (ISBN 0-505-51532-6). Tower Bks.

Prairie Voices: A Collection of Illinois Poets. Ed. by Lucien Stryk. 64p. 1980. pap. 4.00 (ISBN 0-933180-21-7). Spoon Riv Poetry.

Prairie Wife. Arthur Stringer. 1976. lib. bdg. 14.85x (ISBN 0-89968-122-0). Lightyear.

Prairie World. David F. Costello. LC 69-15413. (Illus.). 1969. 8.95 o.s.i. (ISBN 0-690-65211-9, TYC-T). T Y Crowell.

Praise & Lament in the Psalms. rev. enl. ed. Claus Westermann. Tr. by Keith Crim & Richard Soulen. 1981 (ISBN 0-8042-1791-2). pap. 9.50 (ISBN 0-8042-1792-0). John Knox.

Praise from Famous Men: An Anthology of Introductions. Ed. by Guy R. Lyle. LC 76-55402. 1977. 10.00 (ISBN 0-8108-1002-6). Scarecrow.

Praise the Bridge That Carries You Over: The Life of Joseph L. Sutton. Shepard Krech, III. (University Books Ser.). 1981. lib. bdg. 18.50 (ISBN 0-8161-9038-0). G K Hall.

Praise the Bridge That Carries You Over: The Life of Joseph Sutton. Shepard Krech, 3rd. 1981. pap. text ed. 11.25x (ISBN 0-87073-650-7). Schenkman.

Praise the Lord. Leslie Brandt. 48p. 1976. pap. 1.50 (ISBN 0-570-03042-0, 6-1165). Concordia.

Praise the Lord, I'm Under Construction. Jo Anne Sekowsky. 112p. 1978. pap. 2.95 (ISBN 0-930756-40-1, 4230-SE3). Women's Aglow.

Praise to the Morning Koel. Deepak Dubey. 8.00 (ISBN 0-89253-477-X); flexible cloth 4.00 (ISBN 0-89253-478-8). Ind-US Inc.

Prajna - Paramita - Guna - Samcaya - Gatha. Ed. by Yuyama Akira. LC 75-32910. 285p. 1976. 49.50 (ISBN 0-521-21081-X). Cambridge U Pr.

Prajnaparamita & Related Systems. Ed. by Lewis Lancaster & Luis O. Gomez. 1980. 20.00 (ISBN 0-89581-150-2). Lancaster-Miller.

Praktica Book. 2nd ed. Leonard Gaunt. 120p. 1979. 8.95 (ISBN 0-240-50749-5). Focal Pr.

Praktische Anwendung Von Energie Spartechniken. 1976. pap. 7.50 o.p. (ISBN 0-89192-172-9). Interbk Inc.

Pranks, Tricks & Practical Jokes. Gyles Brandreth. LC 79-65291. (Illus.). (gr. 3 up). 1979. 5.95 (ISBN 0-8069-4606-7); PLB 6.69 (ISBN 0-8069-4607-5). Sterling.

Pratique du Francais Parle. Leon-Francois Hoffman. LC 72-7530. 93p. 1973. pap. text ed. 6.50 (ISBN 0-684-13208-7); cassettes 4.95 (ISBN 0-684-13696-1). Scribner.

Pratt Collection of Egyptian Amulets. (Illus.). 1964. pap. text ed. 3.95x (ISBN 0-87451-035-X). U Pr of New Eng.

Praxis & Action: Contemporary Philosophies of Human Activity. Richard J. Bernstein. LC 77-157048. 1971. 15.00x (ISBN 0-8122-7640-X); pap. 7.95x (ISBN 0-8122-1016-6, Pa Paperbks). U of Pa Pr.

Pray for Joy. Martin H. Franzmann. LC 73-98298. 1970. 2.95 (ISBN 0-570-03001-3, 12-2910). Concordia.

Pray: God Is Listening. Richard W. DeHaan. 80p. (Orig.). 1980. pap. 1.95 (ISBN 0-310-23542-1). Zondervan.

Pray, Praise & Hooray. Rich Bimler. LC 77-175306. (Illus.). 150p. (Orig.). (YA) 1972. pap. 3.95 (ISBN 0-570-03130-3, 12-2380). Concordia.

Pray to Live: Thomas Merton: a Contemplative Critic. Henri J. Nouwen. LC 72-10395. 1972. pap. 2.95 o.p. (ISBN 0-8190-0620-3). Fides Claretian.

Pray to Win: God Wants You to Succeed. Pat Boone. 1980. 8.95 (ISBN 0-399-12494-2). Putnam.

Pray Today's Gospel: Reflections on the Day's Good News. Bernard C. Mischke & Fritz Mischke. LC 80-14186. 358p. (Orig.). 1980. pap. 9.95 (ISBN 0-8189-0403-8). Alba.

Prayer. Olive Wyon. LC 78-2965. 72p. 1978. pap. 1.75 (ISBN 0-8006-1335-X, 1-1335). Fortress.

Prayer & Action. Tom Boone & Edna Boone. (Prayer in My Life Ser.: Ser. II). 1974. pap. 1.00x (ISBN 0-8358-0309-0). Upper Room.

Prayer & Community. Ed. by Herman Schmidt. (Concilium Ser.: Religion in the Seventies: Vol. 52). pap. 4.95 (ISBN 0-8164-2508-6). Crossroad NY.

Prayer & Modern Man. Jacques Ellul. Tr. by C. Edward Hopkins from Fr. 192p. 1973. pap. 3.95 (ISBN 0-8164-2081-5). Crossroad NY.

Prayer & Praying Men. E. M. Bounds. (Direction Bks). 1977. pap. 1.95 (ISBN 0-8010-0721-6). Baker Bk.

Prayer & the Christian's Devotional Life. G. Raymond Carlson. (Radiant Life Ser.). 128p. (Orig.). 1981. write for info. Gospel Pub.

Prayer & Worship. Douglas V. Steere. LC 78-70480. 1978. pap. 2.50 (ISBN 0-913408-44-1). Friends United.

Prayer Attitude in the Eastern Church. Gabriele Winkler. 1978. pap. 1.25 (ISBN 0-937032-01-8). Light & Life Pub Co MN.

Prayer Book Office. Ed. by Howard Galley. 800p. 1980. 24.50 (ISBN 0-8164-0370-8). Crossroad NY.

Prayer Book Renewal: Worship & the New Book of Common Prayer. Ed. by Barry Evans. 1978. pap. 3.95 (ISBN 0-8164-2157-9). Crossroad NY.

Prayer, Common Sense & the Bible. Eric S. Fife. 1977. pap. 1.50 o.p. (ISBN 0-310-24332-7). Zondervan.

Prayer: Conversing with God. Rosalind Rinker. pap. 2.75 (ISBN 0-310-32092-5); pap. youth edition o.p. (ISBN 0-310-32101-8). Zondervan.

Prayer for Katerina Horovitzova. A. Lustig. 1975. pap. 1.50 o.s.i. (ISBN 0-380-00300-7, 23408). Avon.

Prayer for Katerina Horovitzova. Arnost Lustig. Tr. by Jeanne Nemcova from Czech. LC 73-4153. 172p. (YA) 1973. 9.95 o.s.i. (ISBN 0-06-012726-0, HarpT). Har-Row.

Prayer for the Ship. Douglas Reeman. 256p. 1981. pap. 2.50 (ISBN 0-515-05783-5). Jove Pubns.

Prayer in My Life Series, 2 vols. 1974. pap. 3.50 ea. Vol. I (ISBN 0-8358-0324-4). Vol. II (ISBN 0-8358-0325-2). Upper Room.

Prayer in the Contemporary World. Douglas V. Steere. LC 80-82942. 32p. Repr. of 1966 ed. pap. 1.25 (ISBN 0-87574-907-0). Pendle Hill.

Prayer Life. Ed. by Christian Duquoc & Claude Geffre. LC 72-3944. (Concilium Ser.: Religion in the Seventies: Vol. 79). 156p. 1972. pap. 4.95 (ISBN 0-8164-2535-3). Crossroad NY.

Prayer Life. Andrew Murray. pap. 1.95 (ISBN 0-8024-6806-3). Moody.

Prayer Life. Andrew Murray. 160p. 1981. pap. 2.50 (ISBN 0-88368-102-1). Whitaker Hse.

Prayer of Faith. Ed. by J. D. Fraser & Mary E. Allbutt. pap. 0.90 (ISBN 0-85363-106-9). OMF Bks.

Prayer of Love: The Art of Aspiration. Venard Poslusney. 128p. (Orig.). 1975. pap. 1.95 (ISBN 0-914544-07-1). Living Flame Pr.

Prayer of the Heart. George A. Maloney. LC 80-69095. 208p. (Orig.). 1981. pap. 3.95 (ISBN 0-87793-216-6). Ave Maria.

Prayer That Heals. Francis MacNutt. LC 80-69770. 120p. (Orig.). 1981. pap. 2.95 (ISBN 0-87793-219-0). Ave Maria.

Prayer That Releases Power. Glenn Egli. (Orig.). 1981. pap. 4.95 (ISBN 0-88270-506-7). Logos.

Prayer That Teaches Us to Pray. Marcus Dods. LC 80-82323. (Shepherd Classic Ser.). 1980. pap. 5.95 (ISBN 0-87983-232-0). Keats.

Prayer Works! Robert Collier. 3.25 (ISBN 0-912576-01-4). R Collier.

Prayerbook Reform in Europe: The Liturgy of European Liberal & Reform Judaism. Jakob J. Petuchowski. LC 68-8262. 1969. 13.50 (ISBN 0-8074-0091-2, 387580, Pub. by World Union). UAHC.

Prayerobics: Getting Started & Staying Going. Cecil Murphey. 1979. 7.95 (ISBN 0-8499-0146-4). Word Bks.

Prayers & Graces. Ed. by Michael Jones. 1980. 5.50 (ISBN 0-903540-33-9, Pub. by Flores Books). St George Bk Serv.

Prayers & Meditations. Baha'u'llah. Tr. by Shoghi Effendi. LC 53-10767. 1938. 10.00 (ISBN 0-87743-024-1, 7-03-10). Baha'i.

Prayers & Meditations. rev. ed. The Mother. Tr. by Sri Aurobindo from Fr. 380p. (Orig.). 1979. pap. 10.00 (ISBN 0-89744-998-3, Sri Aurobindo Ashram Trust India). Auromere.

Prayers & Meditations: An Anthology of the Spiritual Writings of Karl Rahner. Karl Rahner. Ed. by John Griffiths. 128p. 1980. pap. 3.95 (ISBN 0-8245-2619-8). Crossroad NY.

Prayers & Meditations for Healing. Charles Toye. LC 80-82813. 96p. (Orig.). 1981. pap. 3.95 (ISBN 0-8091-2342-8). Paulist Pr.

Prayers by & for the Elderly. Compiled by Mary C. White. 1979. 0.60 (ISBN 0-686-28787-8). Forward Movement.

Prayers for All Occasions. 1951. 0.60 (ISBN 0-686-28788-6). Forward Movement.

Prayers for Dark People. W. E. Du Bois. Ed. by Herbert Aptheker. LC 80-12234. 88p. 1980. lib. bdg. 10.00x (ISBN 0-87023-302-5); pap. 4.50 (ISBN 0-87023-303-3). U of Mass Pr.

Prayers for Every Need. William H. Kadel. LC 57-11747. 1957. 3.85 (ISBN 0-8042-2496-X). John Knox.

Prayers for Every Occasion. Ed. by Frank Colquhoun. Orig. Title: Parish Prayers. 445p. 1974. Repr. of 1967 ed. kival 12.95 (ISBN 0-8192-1280-6). Morehouse.

Prayers for Every Occasion. Don Sanford. (Orig.). pap. 2.50 (ISBN 0-310-32582-X). Zondervan.

Prayers for Help & Healing. William Barclay. LC 74-25682. 128p. 1975. pap. 2.95 (ISBN 0-06-060481-6, RD-89, HarpR). Har-Row.

Prayers for Little People. Sarah Fletcher. (Illus.). 32p. (ps-3). 1974. pap. 0.99 (ISBN 0-570-03429-9, 56-1184). Concordia.

Prayers for the Christian Year. 2nd ed. Church Of Scotland - General Assembly - Committee On Public Worship And Aids To Devotion. 1952. 8.50x (ISBN 0-19-145602-0). Oxford U Pr.

Prayers for the Time Being. Max Pauli. 1971. pap. 1.75 o.p. (ISBN 0-89243-017-6, 42500). Liguori Pubns.

Prayers for the Young Child. Don Roberts. 1981. pap. 5.95 (ISBN 0-570-04051-5, 56-1717). Concordia.

Prayers for Worship Leaders. Arnold Kenseth & Richard P. Unsworth. LC 77-15249. 132p. (Orig.). 1978. pap. 3.95 (ISBN 0-8006-1331-7, 1-1331). Fortress.

Prayers from Prison. Dietrich Bonhoeffer. Tr. by Johann C. Hampe from Ger. LC 77-15228. 1978. pap. 3.50 (ISBN 0-8006-1334-1, 1-1334). Fortress.

Prayers New & Old. 1937. 0.60 (ISBN 0-686-28789-4). Forward Movement.

Prayers of Jesus. Joachim Jeremias. Tr. by John Bowden et al from Ger. LC 77-10427. 132p. 1978. pap. 3.75 (ISBN 0-8006-1322-8, 1-1322). Fortress.

Prayers of Jesus. LC 80-65438. (Illus.). 64p. 1980. 5.95 (ISBN 0-915684-70-5). Christian Herald.

Prayers That Are Answered. Betty Malz. 1980. 6.95 (ISBN 0-912376-50-3). Chosen Bks Pub.

Prayers That Make a Difference. rev. ed. Marjorie Soderholm. Orig. Title: Study Guide to Bible Prayers. 96p. 1980. pap. 2.50 (ISBN 0-911802-49-5). Free Church Pubns.

Praying Church. Donald M. Hultstrand. LC 77-8337. 1977. pap. 3.95 (ISBN 0-8164-2159-5). Crossroad NY.

Praying for Inner Healing. Robert Faricy. LC 79-92857. (Orig.). 1980. pap. 3.50 (ISBN 0-8091-2250-2). Paulist Pr.

Praying for the Government. Derek Prince. 1970. pap. 0.75 o.p. (ISBN 0-934920-11-7, B-20). Derek Prince.

Praying: How to Start & Keep Going. Bobb Biehl & James W. Hagelganz. 144p. 1981. pap. text ed. 2.50 (ISBN 0-8307-0781-6). Regal.

Praying Hyde. Francis A. McGaw. 1970. pap. 1.95 (ISBN 0-87123-454-8, 200454). Bethany Fell.

Praying Our Way Through Life. Basilea Schlink. 1970. pap. 0.79 (ISBN 0-87123-455-6, 260455). Bethany Fell.

Praying Together. rev. ed. Rosalind Rinker. 96p. 1980. pap. 2.95 (ISBN 0-310-32111-5). Zondervan.

Praying with the Family of God. Urban T. Holmes. 1979. pap. 7.50 (ISBN 0-03-043931-0); 3.95 (ISBN 0-03-049551-2). Winston Pr.

Praying with the Family of God: Leader Guide. Urban T. Holmes. 1980. pap. 3.95 (ISBN 0-03-049551-2). Winston Pr.

Pre- & Postoperative Evaluation of Surgical Patients. Teuro Matsumoto. 1979. pap. 15.50 (ISBN 0-87488-735-6). Med Exam.

Pre-Adolescents: What Makes Them Tick? Fritz Redl. 17p. 1974. pap. 1.00 (ISBN 0-686-12276-3). Jewish Bd Family.

Pre-Algebra Mathematics. new ed. Gerald S. Lieblich & Charles Leake. LC 72-92569. (Illus.). 318p. (gr. 8-10). 1973. text ed. 13.95 (ISBN 0-675-09007-5). Merrill.

Pre-Calculus Mathematics. 2nd ed. Hal G. Moore. LC 76-18678. 1977. text ed. 20.95x (ISBN 0-471-61454-8). Wiley.

Pre-Calculus Mathematics. 4th ed. Merrill Shanks et al. (gr. 11-12). 1981. text ed. 15.24 (ISBN 0-201-07684-5, Sch Div); tchr's ed. 7.12 (ISBN 0-201-07685-3); solution manual 13.08 (ISBN 0-201-07686-1). A-W.

Pre-Capitalist Economic Formations. Karl Marx. Ed. by Eric J. Hobsbawm. Tr. by Jack Cohen. LC 65-16393. 1965. 4.50 o.p. (ISBN 0-7178-0166-7); pap. 2.25 (ISBN 0-7178-0165-9). Intl Pub Co.

Pre-Capitalist Modes of Production. Barry Hindess & Paul Hirst. 1975. 28.00x (ISBN 0-7100-8168-5). Routledge & Kegan.

Pre-Capitalist Modes of Production. Barry Hindess & Paul Q. Hirst. 1977. pap. 11.00 (ISBN 0-7100-8169-3). Routledge & Kegan.

Pre-Clinical Carcinoma of the Cervix Uteri. M. Coppleson & B. Reid. 1967. 50.00 (ISBN 0-08-012433-X). Pergamon.

Pre-Columbian Archaeology: Readings from Scientific American. Gordon R. Willey. LC 79-26329. (Illus.). 1980. text ed. 19.95x (ISBN 0-7167-1182-6); pap. text ed. 9.95x (ISBN 0-7167-1183-4). W H Freeman.

Pre-Columbian Architecture. Donald Robertson. LC 63-7513. (Great Ages of World Architecture Ser). (Illus.). 1963. 7.95 o.p. (ISBN 0-8076-0213-2); pap. 3.95 o.p. (ISBN 0-8076-0342-2). Braziller.

Pre-Columbian Architecture of Mesoamerica. Paul Gendrop & Doris Heyden. LC 75-8993. (History of World Architecture Ser.). (Illus.). 340p. 1976. 45.00 (ISBN 0-8109-1018-7). Abrams.

Pre-Columbian Art from the Land Collection. H. B. Nicholson & Alana Cordy-Collins. Ed. by L. K. Land. LC 78-78330. (Illus.). 280p. (Orig.). 1981. pap. 24.95 (ISBN 0-295-95809-X, Pub. by Calif Acad Sci). U of Wash Pr.

Pre-Columbian Literatures of Mexico. Miguel Leon-Portilla. Tr. by Grace Lobanov. (Civilization of the American Indian Ser: No. 92). (Illus.). 1969. 9.95 (ISBN 0-8061-0818-5). U of Okla Pr.

Pre-Columbian Man Finds Central America. Doris Stone. Ed. by Emily Flint. LC 72-801668. (Peabody Museum Press Ser.). (Illus.). 1972. 18.00 (ISBN 0-87365-776-4); pap. 12.00 (ISBN 0-685-84984-8). Peabody Harvard.

Pre-Columbian Man in Costa Rica. Doris Stone. Ed. by Emily Flint. LC 77-86538. (Peabody Museum Press Books). (Illus.). 1978. pap. 12.00 (ISBN 0-87365-792-6). Peabody Harvard.

Pre-Columbian Metallurgy of South-America: Proceedings. Conference at Dumbarton Oaks, October 18 & 19, 1975. Ed. by Elizabeth P. Benson. LC 79-49261. (Illus.). 107p. 1979. 11.00 (ISBN 0-88402-094-0, Ctr Pre-Columbian). Dumbarton Oaks.

Pre-Columbian Mind. F. Guerra. LC 75-183465. 350p. 1972. 46.50 (ISBN 0-12-785286-7). Acad Pr.

Pre-Columbian Pottery of the Americas. David M. Boston. Ed. by Robert J. Charleston. LC 78-55079. (Masterpieces of Western & Near Eastern Ceramics Ser.: Vol. 3). (Illus.). 318p. 1980. thru dec. 31 165.00 (ISBN 0-87011-344-5); thereafter 200.00 (ISBN 0-87011-344-5). Kodansha.

Pre-Columbian Shell Engravings from the Craig Mound at Spiro, Oklahoma, 4 vols. Philip Phillips & James A. Brown. Ed. by Emily Flnt & Lorna Condon. LC 74-77557. (Illus.). 1978. Limited Ed. lib. bdg. 240.00 (ISBN 0-87365-777-2). Peabody Harvard.

Pre-Columbian Shell Engravings from the Craig Mound at Spiro, Oklahoma, Pt. 1. Philip Phillips & James A. Brown. (Illus.). 1978. pap. 35.00 (ISBN 0-87365-795-0). Peabody Harvard.

Pre-Existence of Christ in Justin Martyr. Demetrius C. Trakatellis. LC 76-44913. (Harvard Theological Review Ser.). 1976. pap. 7.50 (ISBN 0-89130-098-8, 020106). Scholars Pr Ca.

Pre-existence, Wisdom & the Son of Man: A Study of the Idea of Pre-Existence in the New Testament. R. G. Hamerton-Kelly. LC 72-78890. (New Testament Studies Monographs: No. 21). 340p. 1973. 42.00 (ISBN 0-521-08629-9). Cambridge U Pr.

Pre-Faces & Other Writings. Jerome Rothenberg. LC 80-24031. 224p. 1981. 14.95 (ISBN 0-8112-0785-4); pap. 6.95 (ISBN 0-8112-0786-2, NDP511). New Directions.

Pre-Glacial Pleistocene of the Norfolk & Suffolk Coasts. R. G. West. LC 77-90191. (Illus.). 1980. 95.00 (ISBN 0-521-21962-0). Cambridge U Pr.

Pre-History of the Armenian People. Iger M. Diakonoff. 1980. write for info. o.p. (ISBN 0-88206-039-2). Caravan Bks.

Pre-Imperial Coinage of Roman Antioch. Edward F. Newell. 45p. 1980. pap. 5.00 (ISBN 0-916710-66-1). Obol Intl.

Pre-Invasion Bombing Strategy: General Eisenhower's Decision of March 25, 1944. W. W. Rostow. 176p. 1981. text ed. 18.00 (ISBN 0-292-76470-7); pap. 8.95 (ISBN 0-686-69545-3). U of Tex Pr.

Pre-Raphaelite Drawings of Edward Burne-Jones. Edward Burne-Jones. (Dover Art Library). (Illus.). 48p. (Orig.). 1981. pap. price not set (ISBN 0-486-24113-0). Dover.

Pre-Raphaelite Landscape. Allen Staley. (Oxford Studies in the History of Art & Architecture Ser.). (Illus.). 1973. 54.00x (ISBN 0-19-817307-5). Oxford U Pr.

Pre-Raphaelites. Timothy Hilton. (World of Art Ser.). (Illus.). 1977. pap. 9.95 (ISBN 0-19-519929-4). Oxford U Pr.

Pre-Raphaelites. Leslie Parris. (Tate Gallery: Little Art Book Ser.). (Illus.). 1977. pap. 1.95 (ISBN 0-8120-0856-1). Barron.

Pre-Romanesque Art. H. Busch & B. Lohse. 1966. 14.95 o.s.i. (ISBN 0-686-66485-X). Macmillan.

Pre-School Story Hour. 2nd ed. Vardine Moore. LC 78-188549. 1972. 10.00 (ISBN 0-8108-0474-3). Scarecrow.

Pre-Schooling in the Community. G. A. Poulton & Terry James. 160p. 1975. 12.95x (ISBN 0-7100-8245-2); pap. 6.95 (ISBN 0-7100-8246-0). Routledge & Kegan.

Pre-Scription: A TA Look at Child Development. Ken Ernst. LC 75-28755. 1976. pap. 4.95 o.p. (ISBN 0-89087-158-2). Celestial Arts.

Pre-Socratics: A Collection of Critical Essays. Ed. by Alexander P. D. Mourelatos. LC 73-11729. 576p. 1974. pap. 5.95 (ISBN 0-385-05480-7, Anch). Doubleday.

Pre-Text, Text, Context: Essays on Nineteenth-Century French Literature. Ed. by Robert L. Mitchell. 302p. 1980. 29.00 (ISBN 0-8142-0305-1). Ohio St U Pr.

Pre-Trial Criminal Procedure: A Survey of Constitutional Rights. Marc W. Tobias & R. David Petersen. (Illus.). 448p. 1972. 23.75 (ISBN 0-398-02613-0). C C Thomas.

Pre-Tribulation Rapture. Allen Beechick. LC 79-53291. 256p. (Orig.). 1980. pap. 4.95 (ISBN 0-89636-040-7). Accent Bks.

Pre-Trig. Rudolph M. MeShane. LC 61-13070. (Illus.). (gr. 10-12). 1961. pap. 1.00 (ISBN 0-910172-02-1). Astro Comp Serv.

Preach the Word. Billy Apostolon. (Sermon Outline Ser). 1978. pap. 1.95 (ISBN 0-8010-0039-4). Baker Bk.

Preacher Aflame. Donald E. Demaray. 1972. pap. 1.25 o.p. (ISBN 0-8010-2816-7). Baker Bk.

Preacher & His Work. Jack Meyer, Sr. 6.50 (ISBN 0-89315-207-2). Lambert Bk.

Preacher & the Strumpet: And Other Short Stories. George Bascombe. 1978. 4.50 o.p. (ISBN 0-533-03499-X). Vantage.

Preacher's Kid. Rose Blue. LC 74-19154. (gr. 4-6). 1975. PLB 5.90 o.p. (ISBN 0-531-02804-6). Watts.

Preachers of Culture: A Study of English & Its Teachers. Margaret Mathieson. (Unwin Education Bks.). 1975. text ed. 25.00x (ISBN 0-04-370067-5); pap. text ed. 10.95x (ISBN 0-04-370068-3). Allen Unwin.

Preaching. G. Campbell Morgan. (Morgan Library). 1974. pap. 2.95 (ISBN 0-8010-5953-4). Baker Bk.

Preaching & Preachers. D. Martyn Lloyd-Jones. 325p. 1972. 10.95 (ISBN 0-310-27870-8). Zondervan.

Preaching As Communication: An Interpersonal Perspective. Myron R. Chartier. LC 80-21304. (Abingdon Preacher Library). 128p. (Orig.). 1981. pap. 4.95 (ISBN 0-687-33826-3). Abingdon.

Preaching Biblically: Exegesis & Interpretation. William D. Thompson. (Abingdon Preacher's Library). (Orig.). 1981. pap. 4.95 (ISBN 0-687-33840-9). Abingdon.

Preaching for Today. Clyde E. Fant. LC 74-4640. 1977. pap. 4.95 o.p. (ISBN 0-06-062332-2, RD 204, HarpR). Har-Row.

Preaching from the Bible. J. Solomon Benn. (Resources for Black Ministries Ser.). 80p. (Orig.). 1981. pap. 2.95 (ISBN 0-8010-0801-8). Baker Bk.

Preaching from the Types & Metaphors of the Bible. Benjamin Keach. LC 78-165059. (Kregel Reprint Library). 1975. 19.95 (ISBN 0-8254-3008-9). Kregel.

Preaching in Ebony. J. Solomon Benn. (Resources for Black Ministries Ser.). 128p. (Orig.). 1981. pap. 3.45 (ISBN 0-8010-0803-4). Baker Bk.

Preaching in the Spanish Golden Age: A Study of Some Preachers of the Reign of Philip III. Hilary D. Smith. (Modern Language & Literature Monographs). 1979. 29.95 (ISBN 0-19-815532-8). Oxford U Pr.

Preaching the Cross (Six Different Speakers) 2.00 o.p. (ISBN 0-89315-208-0); pap. 1.50 o.p. (ISBN 0-89315-209-9). Lambert Bk.

Preaching the Good News. George E. Sweazey. 368p. 1976. 15.95 (ISBN 0-13-694802-2). P-H.

Preaching Through Matthew. Robert E. Luccock. LC 80-12575. 240p. (Orig.). 1980. pap. 8.95 (ISBN 0-687-33908-1). Abingdon.

Preaching Through the Year. David Steel. LC 80-82191. 168p. 1980. pap. 6.50 (ISBN 0-8042-1801-3). John Knox.

Preaching Tradition: A Brief History. DeWitte T. Holland. LC 80-16339. (Abingdon Preacher's Library). 128p. (Orig.). 1980. pap. 4.95 (ISBN 0-687-33875-1). Abingdon.

Precalculus. Mike Grady et al. 464p. 1979. text ed. 18.95x (ISBN 0-534-00733-3); solns. manual for students 5.95x (ISBN 0-534-00831-3). Wadsworth Pub.

Precalculus. 3rd ed. Mustafa Munem & James P. Yizze. LC 77-81759. (Illus.). 1978. text ed. 17.95x (ISBN 0-87901-086-X); study guide 6.95x (ISBN 0-87901-092-4). Worth.

Precalculus. 2nd ed. Saturnino L. Salas & Charles G. Salas. LC 78-23236. 1979. text ed. 18.95x (ISBN 0-471-03124-0); solutions manual avail. (ISBN 0-471-05515-8). Wiley.

Precalculus: A Short Course. S. L. Salas & C. G. Salas. 250p. 1975. text ed. 15.95x (ISBN 0-471-01049-9). Wiley.

Precalculus Algebra & Trigonometry. Daniel D. Benice. (Illus.). 348p. 1976. text ed. 17.95 (ISBN 0-13-695072-8); study guide 3.95 (ISBN 0-13-695171-6). P-H.

Precalculus Mathematics. David G. Crowdis & Brandon W. Wheeler. 1976. text ed. 13.95x (ISBN 0-02-472030-5). Macmillan.

Precalculus Mathematics. 2nd ed. F. Lane Hardy. LC 75-148246. 1971. text ed. 15.95 (ISBN 0-675-09251-5). Merrill.

Precalculus Mathematics: A Functional Approach. Karl J. Smith. Ed. by Robert J. Wisner. LC 78-6279. (Contemporary Undergraduate Mathematics Ser.). (Illus.). 1979. text ed. 16.95 (ISBN 0-8185-0269-X). Brooks-Cole.

Precalculus Mathematics with Elementary Functions. Lawrence P. Runyan. 1977. text ed. 18.85 o.p. (ISBN 0-205-05573-7); instr's manual avail. o.p. (ISBN 0-205-05574-5). Allyn.

Precalculus Primer. George F. Simmons. (Illus.). 176p. (Orig.). Date not set. pap. 7.95 (ISBN 0-86576-009-8). W Kaufmann.

Precambrian Geochronology of North America: An Annotated Bibliography,1951-1977. R. G. Vugrinovich. LC 80-68063. (Special Paper Ser.: No. 11). 1980. 4.00x (ISBN 0-8137-6011-9). Geol Soc.

Precarious Truce. Gorodetsky. LC 76-2279. (Soviet & East European Studies). 1977. 36.00 (ISBN 0-521-21226-X). Cambridge U Pr.

Precast Concrete: Handling & Erection. Joseph J. Waddell. (Monograph: No. 8). 1974. 15.75 (ISBN 0-685-85142-7, M-8) (ISBN 0-685-85143-5). ACI.

Precedence Networks for Project Planning & Control. P. J. Burman. 20.00 (ISBN 0-686-27928-X). Blitz Pub Co.

Precedent in English Law. 3rd ed. Rupert Cross. 252p. 1977. pap. 11.95x (ISBN 0-19-876073-6). Oxford U Pr.

Precedent in English Law & Other Essays. J. L. Montrose. 374p. 1968. 25.00x (ISBN 0-7165-0503-7, Pub. by Irish Academic Pr Ireland). Biblio Dist.

Preceramic Sites. Anthony E. Marks. Ed. by Torgny Save-Soderbergh. (Scandinavian Joint Expedition to Sudanese Nubia). (Illus.). 1970. text ed. 13.50x (ISBN 0-8419-8801-3). Holmes & Meier.

Precio Del Pentecostes. (Spanish Bks.). 1979. 2.00 (ISBN 0-686-28806-8). Life Pubs Intl.

Precious Bane. Mary Webb. 290p. 1978. o. p. 18.00x (ISBN 0-686-28566-2, Pub. by Duckworth); pap. 4.50x (ISBN 0-7156-1336-7). Biblio Dist.

Precious Garland & the Song of the Four Mindfulnesses. Nagarjuna. Tr. by Jeffrey Hopkins & Lati Rimpoche. (Wisdom of Tibet Ser.). (Illus.). 1975. pap. 6.95 (ISBN 0-04-294089-3). Allen Unwin.

Precious Harvest. Helen Oswald. LC 79-88027. (Destiny Ser.). 1979. pap. 4.95 (ISBN 0-8163-0326-6, 16496-2). Pacific Pr Pub Assn.

Precious Metals. (Slide Ser.). 40.00 (ISBN 0-686-23292-5). Natl Recycling.

Precious Metals: Proceedings of the Fourth International Precious Metals Conference, Toronto Canada, June 3-5, 1980. Ed. by R. O. McGachie. 400p. 1981. 50.01 (ISBN 0-08-025369-5). Pergamon.

Precious Parables for Tiny Tots. Wanda J. Groves. 27p. 1980. 4.50 (ISBN 0-533-04417-0). Vantage.

Precious Pearl: A Translation from the Arabic. Ed. by Jane I. Smith. LC 79-140. (Studies in World Religions: No. 1). 1979. 12.00 (ISBN 0-89130-278-6, 030001); pap. 7.50 (ISBN 0-89130-305-7). Scholars Pr Ca.

Precious Present. Spencer Johnson. LC 80-46478. (Illus.). 80p. 1981. 7.95 (ISBN 0-89087-286-4). Celestial Arts.

Precipice. Sergio Galindo. Tr. by John Brushwood & Carolyn Brushwood. (Texas Pan American Series). Orig. Title: El Bordo. (Illus.). 1969. 9.95x (ISBN 0-292-78408-2); pap. 4.95x (ISBN 0-292-76426-X). U of Tex Pr.

Precipice. Ivan Goncharov. Tr. by M. Bryant from Rus. LC 73-21714. vii, 320p. 1975. Repr. of 1915 ed. 17.50 (ISBN 0-86527-295-6). Fertig.

Precipitation Hardening. J. W. Martin. LC 67-31505. 1968. text ed. 22.00 (ISBN 0-08-012731-2); pap. text ed. 10.75 (ISBN 0-08-012730-4). Pergamon.

Precipitation History of the Rocky Mountains. Raymond S. Bradley. Ed. by Jack Ives. LC 75-45279. (Special Studies in High Altitude Geo-Ecology Ser). 1976. 25.50x (ISBN 0-89158-026-3). Westview.

Precis de Civilisation Francaise. Minnie M. Miller et al. (Fr.). (gr. 10 up). 1979. pap. text ed. 8.95x o.p. (ISBN 0-89197-354-0). Irvington.

Precis in Conventional Obligations. Alain A. Levasseur. 300p. 1980. text ed. 18.00 (ISBN 0-87215-334-7). Michie.

Precision Approach to Voice Disorders. T. Johnson. Date not set. price not set (ISBN 0-685-32516-4). Univ Park.

Precision Attachment in Dentistry. 3rd ed. H. W. Preiskel. (Illus.). 1979. text ed. 45.00 (ISBN 0-8016-8424-2). Mosby.

Precision Bidding for Acol. Eric Crowhurst. 1974. 13.95 (ISBN 0-7207-0765-X, Pub. by Michael Joseph). Merrimack Bk Serv.

Precision Bowling for Higher Scores. H. Vermes. (Quick & Easy Ser). 1968. pap. 3.95 o.s.i. (ISBN 0-02-082160-3, Collier). Macmillan.

Precision Bridge. Eric Jannersten. LC 73-7165. 224p. 1973. pap. 3.45 o.p. (ISBN 0-684-13541-8, SL485, ScribT). Scribner.

Precision Bridge for Everyone. Charles H. Goren & C. C. Wei. LC 78-62636. 1978. 6.95 o.p. (ISBN 0-385-14709-0). Doubleday.

Precision Gearing: Theory & Practice. George W. Michalec. LC 66-21045. 1966. 46.95 (ISBN 0-471-60142-X, Pub. by Wiley-Interscience). Wiley.

Precision, Language & Logic. F. H. George. 224p. 1977. text ed. 29.00 (ISBN 0-08-019650-0). Pergamon.

Precision Sheet Metal Mathematics. Richard S. Budzik. LC 71-83129. 1969. 9.70 o.p. (ISBN 0-672-97591-2); tchr's guide 6.67 o.p. (ISBN 0-672-97593-9); student wkbk 4.80 o.p. (ISBN 0-672-97592-0). Bobbs.

Precision Sheet Metal Shop Practice. Richard S. Budzik. LC 78-97566. 1969. 4.55 o.p. (ISBN 0-672-97594-7); instructor's guide 6.67 o.p. (ISBN 0-672-97596-3); student guide 4.80 o.p. (ISBN 0-672-97595-5). Bobbs.

Precision Sheet Metal Shop Theory. Richard Budzik. LC 79-77586. 1969. 9.20 o.p. (ISBN 0-672-20679-X); pap. 5.00 instructor's guide o.p. (ISBN 0-672-20681-1); student wkbk 4.80 o.p. (ISBN 0-672-20680-3). Bobbs.

Precision System of Contract Bridge Bidding. Charles H. Goren. 225p. 1972. pap. 2.95 (ISBN 0-346-12061-6). Cornerstone.

Precision Teaching: Teaching Exceptional Children, Vol. 3, No. 3. 1971. pap. text ed. 3.50x o.p. (ISBN 0-86586-063-7). Coun Exc Child.

Preclinical Teaching of Psychiatry, Vol. 5. GAP Committee on Medical Education. (Report: No. 54). 1962. pap. 2.00 (ISBN 0-87318-073-9). Adv Psychiatry.

Precognition & the Philosophy of Science: An Essay on Backward Causation. Bob Brier. LC 73-12754. 105p. 1974. text ed. 6.50x (ISBN 0-391-00325-9). Humanities.

Predation & Freshwater Communities. Thomas M. Zaret. LC 80-5399. (Illus.). 208p. 1980. text ed. 15.00x (ISBN 0-300-02349-9). Yale U Pr.

Predestination Primer. John Gerstner. Date not set. pap. 1.95 (ISBN 0-88469-145-4). BMH Bks.

Predicacion Expositiva. D. M. White. Tr. by Francisco E. Estrello. Orig. Title: Excellence of Exposition. 1980. 3.25 (ISBN 0-311-42061-3). Casa Bautista.

Predicador: Platicas a Mis Estudiantes. Alejandro Trevino. 155p. 1980. pap. 2.30 (ISBN 0-311-42016-8). Casa Bautista.

Predicate-Oriented Database Search Algorithms. Dan E. Willard. LC 79-50230. (Outstanding Dissertations in the Computer Sciences). 1980. lib. bdg. 34.00 (ISBN 0-8240-4405-3). Garland Pub.

Predictability, Correlation & Contiguity. Peter Harzem & Michael D. Zeiler. 400p. 1981. 48.00 (ISBN 0-471-27847-5, Pub. by Wiley-Interscience). Wiley.

Predictability in Psychopharmacology: Preclinical & Clinical Correlations. Ed. by A. Sudilovsky et al. LC 74-14483. 350p. 1975. 39.50 (ISBN 0-89004-017-6). Raven.

Predicting Academic Performance in College. A. Astin. LC 78-128470. 1971. 19.95 (ISBN 0-02-901100-0). Free Pr.

Predicting Achievement: A Ten-Year Followup of Black & White Adolescents. Joseph Lowman et al. LC 80-17139. (IRSS Research Ser.). (Illus.). 102p. (Orig.). 1980. pap. text ed. 7.00 (ISBN 0-89143-100-4). U NC Inst Res Soc Sci.

Predicting Adolescent Drug Use: Utility Structure & Marijuana. Carl E. Bauman. 192p. 1980. 22.95 (ISBN 0-03-050636-0). Praeger.

Predicting Dangerousness. Stephen J. Pfohl. LC 77-25742. (Illus.). 1978. 21.50 (ISBN 0-669-01509-1). Lexington Bks.

Predicting Earthquakes: A Scientific and Technical Evaluation--with Implications for Society. Committee on Seismology, National Research Council. LC 76-40493. 1976. pap. 5.25 (ISBN 0-309-02527-3). Natl Acad Pr.

Predicting Effects of Power Plant One-Through Cooling on Aquatic Systems. (Technical Papers in Hydrology: No. 20). 1979. pap. 17.00 (ISBN 92-3-101704-7, U939, UNESCO). Unipub.

Predicting Fertility. Gerry E. Hendershot. Ed. by Paul J. Placek. LC 79-9686. 352p. 1981. 23.95x (ISBN 0-669-03618-8). Lexington Bks.

Predicting Photosynthesis for Ecosystem Models, 2 vols. John D. Hesketh & J. W. Jones. 1980. Vol. 2, 304p. 69.95 (ISBN 0-8493-5337-8); Vol. 2. (ISBN 0-8493-5336-X). CRC Pr.

Predicting Reading Failure. Katrine De Hirsch et al. (Illus.). 1966. 8.95 o.s.i. (ISBN 0-06-031630-6, HarpT). Har-Row.

Predicting Sociocultural Change. Ed. by Susan Abbott & John Van Willigen. LC 79-10193. (Southern Anthropological Society Proceedings Ser.: No. 13). 156p. 1980. 12.00x (ISBN 0-8203-0477-8); pap. 5.25 (ISBN 0-8203-0484-0). U of Ga Pr.

Predicting Teaching Success. A. C. Crocker. (General Ser.). 230p. 1974. pap. text ed. 17.00x (ISBN 0-85633-037-X, NFER). Humanities.

Predicting the Behavior of the Educational System. Thomas Green et al. (Illus.). 224p. 1980. 15.95x (ISBN 0-8156-2223-6); pap. 8.95x (ISBN 0-8156-2224-4). Syracuse U Pr.

Prediction Analysis of Cross Classifications. David K. Hildebrand et al. LC 76-25575. (Probability & Mathematical Statistics Ser.). 1977. 30.95 (ISBN 0-471-39575-7, Pub. by Wiley-Interscience). Wiley.

Prediction of Communist Economic Performance. Ed. by P. Wiles. LC 75-123677. (Soviet & East European Studies). (Illus.). 1971. 37.50 (ISBN 0-521-07885-7). Cambridge U Pr.

Prediction of Organizational Behavior. N. Frederiksen et al. 344p. 1972. text ed. 27.00 (ISBN 0-08-016967-8); pap. text ed. 14.50 (ISBN 0-08-017189-3). Pergamon.

Preface & Introduction to a Contribution to the Critque of Political Economy. Karl Marx. 1.25 (ISBN 0-8351-0263-7). China Bks.

Preface to a Neo-Firthian Linguistics. William M. Christie, Jr. LC 80-21016. (Edward Sapir Monograph Series in Language, Culture, & Cognition: No. 7). viii, 70p. (Orig.). 1980. pap. 6.00x (ISBN 0-933104-11-1). Jupiter Pr.

Preface to Coleridge. Allan Grant. (Preface Bks.). (Illus.). 1977. pap. text ed. 5.95x (ISBN 0-582-31516-6). Longman.

Preface to Democratic Theory. Robert A. Dahl. LC 56-6642. (Walgreen Foundation Lecture Ser). 1963. pap. 3.95 (ISBN 0-226-13426-1, P115, Phoen). U of Chicago Pr.

Preface to Donne. James Winny. (Preface Bks). (Illus.). 1977. pap. text ed. 5.95x (ISBN 0-582-31504-2). Longman.

Preface to Literary Analysis. Sheldon P. Zitner et al. 1964. pap. 6.95x (ISBN 0-673-05216-8). Scott F.

Preface to Marketing Management. Lawrence X. Tarpey et al. 1979. pap. 8.95x (ISBN 0-256-02207-0). Business Pubns.

Preface to Philosophy. 2nd ed. Mark Woodhouse. 1979. pap. text ed. 6.95x (ISBN 0-534-00738-4). Wadsworth Pub.

Preface to Politics. 2nd ed. David Schuman. 1977. pap. 5.95x o.p. (ISBN 0-669-00348-4). Heath.

Preface to Pope. I. R. Gordon. LC 75-25572. (Preface Books). (Illus.). 136p. 1976. text ed. 11.95x (ISBN 0-582-31505-0); pap. text ed. 5.95x (ISBN 0-582-31506-9). Longman.

Preface to Scripture: A Guide to the Understanding of the Bible in Accordance with the Jewish Tradition. Solomon B. Freehof. 1950. pap. 4.95x o.p. (ISBN 0-87441-261-7, Union of American Hebrew Congregations). Behrman.

Preface to Shakespeare: Volume 1, Hamlet. Harley Granville-Baker. 1977. pap. 10.50 (ISBN 0-7134-2050-2, Pub. by Batsford England). David & Charles.

Preface to Spenser. Helena Shire. Ed. & frwd. by Maurice Hussey. (Preface Books). (Illus.). 1979. text ed. 11.95x (ISBN 0-582-31511-5); pap. text ed. 7.50x (ISBN 0-582-31512-3). Longman.

Preface to the Philosophy of Education. John Wilson. (International Library of the Philosophy of Education). 1979. 26.00x (ISBN 0-7100-0283-1). Routledge & Kegan.

Preface to Wordsworth. John Purkis. (Preface Bks). (Illus.). 1970. pap. text ed. 5.95x (ISBN 0-582-31503-4). Longman.

Preface to Yeats. Edward Malins. (Preface Bks). (Illus.). 1977. pap. text ed. 5.95x (ISBN 0-582-35106-5). Longman.

Prefaces to Byron. Leslie A. Marchand. 131p. 1980. Repr. of 1979 ed. lib. bdg. 30.00 (ISBN 0-8414-5876-6). Folcroft.

Prefaces to Shakespeare, 6 vols. in 1. Harley Granville-Barker. 1972. 42.50 o.p. (ISBN 0-7134-2070-7, Pub. by Batsford England). David & Charles.

Preference Behaviour & Chemoreception: Proceedings. European Chemoreception Research Organisation, Symposium, Netherlands, 1979. (ECRO Minisymposium Ser.). 350p. 1979. 26.00 (ISBN 0-904147-12-6). Info Retrieval.

Prefinishing of Exterior Building Components. National Academy Of Sciences. 1962. 6.00 o.p. (ISBN 0-309-00993-6). Natl Acad Pr.

Prefrontal Cortex. Joaquin M. Fuster. 232p. 1980. text ed. 22.00 (ISBN 0-89004-524-0). Raven.

Pregnancy After Thirty-Five. Carole S. McCauley. 1976. 7.95 (ISBN 0-87690-219-0). Dutton.

Pregnancy After Thirty Workbook. Ed. by Gail S. Brewer. 1978. pap. 10.95 (ISBN 0-87857-215-5). Rodale Pr Inc.

Pregnancy & Birth: Pleasure & Problems. Frank Falkner & Christopher Macy. (Life Cycle Ser.). 1980. pap. text ed. write for info. (ISBN 0-06-384741-8, HarpC). Har-Row.

Pregnancy & Parenthood. Compiled by Anne Loader. (Illus.). 226p. 1980. 16.95 (ISBN 0-19-217684-6); pap. 8.95 (ISBN 0-19-286006-2). Oxford U Pr.

Pregnancy As a Disease: The Pill in Society. Donald H. Merkin. 1976. 12.95 (ISBN 0-8046-9138-X, Natl U). Kennikat.

Pregnancy, Birth, & Parenthood: Adaptations of Mothers, Fathers, & Infants. Frances K. Grossman et al. LC 80-16518. (Social & Behavioral Science Ser.). 1980. text ed. 15.95x (ISBN 0-87589-465-8). Jossey-Bass.

Pregnancy Metabolism, Diabetes & the Fetus. CIBA Foundation. (CIBA Foundation Symposium: No. 63). 1979. 39.50 (ISBN 0-444-90054-3, Excerpta Medica). Elsevier.

Pregnant Teen-Ager: A Medical, Educational, & Social Analysis. Howard J. Osofsky. (Illus.). 136p. 1972. 9.75 (ISBN 0-398-01434-5). C C Thomas.

Pregnant Too Soon: Adoption Is an Option. Jeanne W. Lindsay. LC 79-93356. (Illus.). 208p. (gr. 8-12). 1980. write for info. Morning Glory.

Pregnant Too Soon: Adoption Is an Option. Jeanne W. Lindsay. LC 79-93356. (Illus.). (gr. 7-12). 1980. pap. text ed. 5.95 (ISBN 0-88436-778-9); tchr's ed. avail. (ISBN 0-88436-780-0); wkbk. avail. (ISBN 0-88436-779-7). EMC.

Preguntas Practicas y Dificiles. Reuben A. Torrey. Orig. Title: Practical & Perplexing Questions Answered. (Span). 1909. pap. 1.50 (ISBN 0-8024-6810-1). Moody.

Prehispanic Cookbook(Cocina Prehispanica) Ana M. De Benitez. 1960. pap. 8.50 o.p. (ISBN 0-911268-24-3). Rogers Bk.

Prehistoric America. Anne T. White. (Landmark Ser: No. 38). (Illus.). (gr. 4-6). 1951. PLB 5.99 (ISBN 0-394-90311-0, BYR). Random.

Prehistoric America: An Ecological Perspective. 2nd ed. Betty J. Meggers. LC 78-169504. 1979. text ed. 15.95 (ISBN 0-202-33078-8); pap. 8.50 (ISBN 0-202-33079-6). Aldine Pub.

Prehistoric Andean Ecologys, Vol. 1. Ed. by Frederic-Andre Engel. 1980. text ed. 45.00x (ISBN 0-391-01873-6). Humanities.

Prehistoric Animals. Peter Zallinger. (Pictureback Ser.). (Illus.). 32p. (ps-3). 1981. PLB 4.99 (ISBN 0-394-93737-6); pap. 1.25 (ISBN 0-394-83737-1). Random.

Prehistoric Animals & Plants. Josef Benes. (Illus.). 311p. 1979. 13.95 (ISBN 0-600-30341-1). Transatlantic.

Prehistoric Animals & Their Hunters. I. W. Cornwall. (Illus.). 1968. 6.95 (ISBN 0-571-08340-4, Pub. by Faber & Faber). Merrimack Bk Serv.

Prehistoric Antiquities of the Maltese Island: A Survey. J. D. Evans. 1971. 80.00x (ISBN 0-485-11093-8, Athlone Pr). Humanities.

Prehistoric Art. T. G. Powell. (World of Art Ser.). (Illus.). 1966. pap. 9.95 (ISBN 0-19-519920-0). Oxford U Pr.

Prehistoric Bibliography. Wilfred Bonser. Ed. by June Troy. 1976. 155.00x (ISBN 0-631-17090-1, Pub. by Basil Blackwell England). Biblio Dist.

Prehistoric Carrying Capacity: A Model. E. Zubrow. LC 74-8415. 1975. 7.95 o.p. (ISBN 0-8465-8779-3, 58779). Benjamin-Cummings.

Prehistoric Cooking. Ana M. De Benitez. 8.50 o.p. (ISBN 0-685-82108-0). Rogers Bk.

Prehistoric Cordage: Identification of Impressions on Pottery. William M. Hurley. (Manuals on Archaeology Ser.: No. 3). (Illus.). xii, 154p. 1979. 18.00x (ISBN 0-9602822-0-3). Taraxacum.

Prehistoric Greece. F. H. Stubbings. 1979. 10.95x (ISBN 0-8464-0104-5). Beekman Pubs.

Prehistoric Indians of the Southwest. H. M. Wormington. (Popular Ser.: No. 7). (Illus.). 192p. 1947. pap. 4.75 o.p. (ISBN 0-916278-15-8). Denver Mus Natl Hist.

Prehistoric Kivas of Antelope Mesa, Northeastern Arizona. Watson Smith. LC 72-92005. (Peabody Museum Papers: Vol. 39, No. 1). 1972. pap. text ed. 15.00 (ISBN 0-87365-115-4). Peabody Harvard.

Prehistoric Life. Christopher Maynard. (Modern Knowledge Library). (Illus.). 48p. (gr. 5 up). 1976. 3.95 (ISBN 0-531-02446-6); PLB 6.90 (ISBN 0-531-01193-3). Watts.

Prehistoric Man in Europe. Frank C. Hibben. (Illus.). 1958. 13.95x (ISBN 0-8061-0415-5). U of Okla Pr.

Prehistoric Man on the Great Plains. Waldo R. Wedel. (Illus.). 1961. 15.95 (ISBN 0-8061-0501-1). U of Okla Pr.

Prehistoric Men. 8th ed. Robert J. Braidwood. 213p. 1975. pap. 7.95x (ISBN 0-673-07851-5). Scott F.

Prehistoric of Central Anatolia I: The Neolithic Period. Ian Todd. (Studies in Mediterranean Archaeology: Vol. LX). 177p. 1981. pap. text ed. 42.00x (ISBN 91-85058-87-4, Pub. by Astroms, Sweden). Humanities.

Prehistoric Peoples of Scotland. Ed. by Stuart Piggott. LC 80-27371. (Studies in Ancient History & Archaeology). (Illus.). ix, 165p. 1981. Repr. of 1962 ed. lib. bdg. 25.00x (ISBN 0-313-22916-3, PIPR). Greenwood.

Prehistoric Pottery Analysis & the Ceramics of Barton Ramie in the Belize Valley. James C. Gifford. LC 75-40772. (Peabody Museum Memoirs: Vol. 18). 1976. pap. text ed. 35.00 (ISBN 0-87365-691-1). Peabody Harvard.

Prehistoric Pueblo Settlement Patterns: The Arroy Hondo, New Mexico, Site Survey. D. Bruce Dickson. (Arroyo Hondo Archaeological Ser.: Vol. 2). (Illus.). 1979. pap. 6.25 (ISBN 0-686-65919-8). Schol Am Res.

Prehistoric Rock Art of Argyll. R. W. Morris. 1978. 9.95 o.p. (ISBN 0-85642-043-3, Pub. by Blandford Pr England); pap. 3.50 o.p. (ISBN 0-85642-059-X). Sterling.

Prehistoric Rock Art of Galloway & the Isle of Man. Ronald W. Morris. (Illus.). 1979. 25.00 (ISBN 0-7137-0974-X, Pub by Blandford Pr England); pap. 19.95 (ISBN 0-7137-0975-8). Sterling.

Prehistoric Rock Art of Nevada & California. Robert F. Heizer & Martin A. Baumhoff. (California Library Reprint). (Illus.). 430p. 1976. Repr. 36.50x (ISBN 0-520-02911-9). U of Cal Pr.

Prehistoric Settlement of Britain. Richard Bradley. (Archaeology of Britain Ser.). (Illus.). 1978. 24.00 (ISBN 0-7100-8993-7). Routledge & Kegan.

Prehistoric Settlement Patterns in the Southern Valley of Mexico: The Chalco-Xochimilco Region. Jeffrey R. Parsons. (Memoir Ser.: No. 14). (Orig.). 1981. pap. write for info. (ISBN 0-932206-88-3). U Mich Mus Anthro.

Prehistoric Trails of Atacama. Ed. by Clement Meighan & D. L. True. (Monumenta Archaeologica: No. 7). (Illus.). 258p. 1980. 32.65 (ISBN 0-917956-10-9). UCLA Arch.

Prehistoric Woman. Frederick A. Ide & Charles A. Ide. LC 79-19011. (Woman in History Ser.: Vol. 1). (Illus.). 49p. (Orig.). 1980. 8.00 (ISBN 0-86663-002-3); pap. 5.00 (ISBN 0-86663-003-1). Ide Hse.

Prehistory: An Introduction. Derek Roe. LC 70-81799. 1970. 17.50x (ISBN 0-520-01406-5); pap. 3.25 (ISBN 0-520-02252-1). U of Cal Pr.

Prehistory & Protohistoric Antiquities of India. R. B. Foote. 1979. text ed. 21.50x (ISBN 0-391-01865-5). Humanities.

Prehistory of Eastern Europe: Part I: Mesolitic, Neolitic & Copper Age Cultures in Russia & the Baltic Area. Marija Gimbutas. LC 57-1393. (ASPR Bulletin: No. 20). 1956. pap. text ed. 25.00 (ISBN 0-87365-521-4). Peabody Harvard.

Prehistory of Europe. Patricia Phillips. LC 79-3787. 352p. 1980. 17.50x (ISBN 0-253-11956-1). Ind U Pr.

Prehistory of the Ayacucho Basin, Peru, Vol. II: Excavations & Chronology. Richard S. MacNeish et al. LC 80-13960. (Illus.). 368p. 1981. text ed. 45.00 (ISBN 0-472-04907-0). U of Mich Pr.

Prehistory of the Ayacucho Basin, Peru: Vol. Three: Nonceramic Artifacts. Richard S. MacNeish et al. (Illus.). 360p. 45.00x (ISBN 0-472-02707-7). U of Mich Pr.

Prehospital Emergency Care & Crisis Intervention. Brent Q. Hafen & Keith J. Karren. 570p. 1981. pap. 13.95x (ISBN 0-89582-057-9); wkbk. 5.95x (ISBN 0-89582-058-7); text & wkbk. 17.00x. Morton Pub.

Prejudice & Discrimination. Educational Research Council of America. (Challenges of Our Time Ser.). (gr. 7). 1973. pap. text ed. 9.32 (ISBN 0-205-05031-X, 8050317); tchrs'. guide 6.60 (ISBN 0-205-05032-8, 8050325). Allyn.

Prejudice & Property, an Historic Brief Against Racial Convenants. U. S. Department of Justice. Ed. by Tom C. Clark & Philip B. Perlman. Repr. of 1948 ed. lib. bdg. 11.50x (ISBN 0-8371-2221-X, PRPR). Greenwood.

Prejudice & Racism. James M. Jones. 1972. pap. text ed. 6.95 (ISBN 0-201-03376-3). A-W.

Prejudice & Your Child. 2nd ed. Kenneth B. Clark. 6.75 (ISBN 0-8446-1863-2). Peter Smith.

Prejudice in Children. Ed. by Alan R. Brown. 224p. 1972. text ed. 17.50 (ISBN 0-398-02247-X). C C Thomas.

Prejudice, War, & the Constitution: Causes & Consequences of the Evacuation of the Japanese Americans in World War II. Jacobus TenBroek et al. 1954. pap. 6.95x (ISBN 0-520-01262-3). U of Cal Pr.

Preliminaries to Linguistic Phonetics. Peter Ladefoged. LC 75-179318. 1972. 6.95x o.s.i. (ISBN 0-226-46786-4). U of Chicago Pr.

Preliminaries to Linguistic Phonetics. Peter Ladefoged. pap. 5.00 (ISBN 0-226-46787-2). U of Chicago Pr.

Preliminary & Interim Report on the Hebrew Old Testament Text Project, Vol. 1. Ed. by UBS Committee. (Pentateuch Ser.). (Eng. & Fr.). 1973. pap. 2.60 (ISBN 0-8267-0008-X, 08520). United Bible.

Preliminary & Interim Report on the Hebrew Old Testament Text Project, Vol. 2. Ed. by UBS Committee. (Historical Bks.). (Eng. & Fr.). 1976. pap. 4.35 (ISBN 0-8267-0009-8, 08521). United Bible.

Preliminary & Interim Report on the Hebrew Old Testament Text Project, Vol. 3. (Poetical Books Ser.). (Eng. & Fr.). 1977. pap. 4.40 (ISBN 0-8267-0010-1, 08522). United Bible.

Preliminary Announcement. Robert Bridges et al. Ed. by Steele Commager. Incl. On English Homophones; Few Practical Suggestions; Pronunciation of English Words; Englishing of French Words; On Hyphens & Shall & Will, Should & Would; English Influence on the French Vocabulary; What Is Pure French; Language of Anatomy; On Grammatical Inversion. (Society for Pure English Ser.: Vol. 1). 1979. lib. bdg. 42.00 (ISBN 0-8240-3665-4). Garland Pub.

Preliminary Bibliography of Mexican Cave Biology with a Checklist of Published Records. James R. Reddell. (Association for Mexican Cave Studies: Bulletin 3). 184p. 1971. 10.00. Speleo Pr.

Preliminary Discourse on Philosophy in General. Christian Wolff. Tr. by Richard Blackwell. LC 63-20239. (Orig.). 1963. pap. 2.50 (ISBN 0-672-60395-0, LA167). Bobbs.

Preliminary Discourse to the Encyclopedia of Diderot. Jean L. D'Alembert. Tr. by Richard Schwab & Walter Rex. LC 63-21831. (Orig.). 1963. 6.50 (ISBN 0-672-51037-5); pap. 5.50 (ISBN 0-672-60276-8, LLA88). Bobbs.

Preliminary Environmental Assessment of Biomass Conversion to Synthetic Fuels. Battelle Columbus Laboratories. 346p. 1980. pap. 24.95 (ISBN 0-89934-049-0, B049-PP). Solar Energy Info.

Preliminary Guide to the Holdings of the Minnesota Regional Research Centers. Compiled by James E. Fogerty. LC 76-1287. (Guide Ser.: No. 1). 1975. 1.00x (ISBN 0-87351-093-3). Minn Hist.

Preliminary Investigation & Police Reporting: A Complete Guide to Police Written Communication. John Nelson. (Criminal Justice Ser.). 1970. text ed. 14.95x (ISBN 0-02-476530-9, 47653). Macmillan.

Preliminary Mathematics. Isidore Dressler. (gr. 8). 1981. text ed. 17.92 (ISBN 0-87720-243-5). AMSCO Sch.

Preliminary Mathematics. Isidore Dressler. (Orig.). 1980. pap. text ed. 10.83 (ISBN 0-87720-242-7). AMSCO Sch.

Preliminary Mathematics Review Guide. Isidore Dressler. (Illus.). (gr. 8-10). 1965. pap. text ed. 5.00 (ISBN 0-87720-205-2). AMSCO Sch.

Preliminary Practical Physics. P. N. Okebe. 1981. price not set (ISBN 0-471-27852-1, Pub. by Wiley-Interscience); pap. price not set (ISBN 0-471-27851-3). Wiley.

Preliminary Practice for the High School Equivalency Diploma Test. 5th ed. David R. Turner. LC 75-34848. (gr. 9-12). 1972. pap. 5.00 (ISBN 0-668-01441-5). Arco.

Preliminary Scholastic Aptitude Test: National Merit Scholarship Qualifying Test (PSAT-NMSQT) rev. ed. David R. Turner. LC 80-18207. 285p. (Orig.). 1981. pap. 6.00 (ISBN 0-668-04980-4, 4980-4). Arco.

Preliminary Scholastic Aptitude Test Preparation Guide. Jerry Bobrow & William A. Covino. (Cliffs Test Preparation Guide). (Illus.). (gr. 10-11). 1979. pap. 2.50 (ISBN 0-8220-2002-5). Cliffs.

Preliminary Studies in Turkic Historical Phonology. Vilhelm Gronbech. Tr. by John Krueger. (Indiana University Uralic & Altaic Ser.: Vol. 135). 162p. 1979. 8.00. Ind U Res Inst.

Preliminary Studies in Turkic Historical Phonology. Vilhelm Gronbech. Ed. by Denis Sinor. Tr. by John R. Krueger from Danish. (Indiana University Uralic & Altaic Ser.: Vol. 135). Orig. Title: Forstudier Til Turkisk Lyndhistorie. 162p. 1979. pap. text ed. 8.00 (ISBN 0-933070-03-9). Ind U Res Inst.

Preliminary Survey of the French Collection. C. Russell Jensen. (Finding Aids to the Microfilmed Manuscript Collection of the Genealogical Society of Utah). (Orig.). 1981. pap. 20.00x (ISBN 0-87480-171-0). U of Utah Pr.

Preliminary Survey of the Mexican Collection: Finding Aids to the Microfilmed Manuscript Collection of the Genealogical Society of Utah. Susan M. Cottler et al. LC 78-71761. (Orig.). 1978. pap. 12.00 (ISBN 0-87480-151-6). U of Utah Pr.

Prelude. Madeleine L'Engle. LC 68-56600. (gr. 7 up). 6.95 (ISBN 0-8149-0351-7). Vanguard.

Prelude, Bks. 1-4. William Wordsworth. Ed. by P. M. Yarker. (Routledge English Texts). 1968. 7.50x (ISBN 0-7100-6096-3); pap. 3.95 (ISBN 0-7100-6097-1). Routledge & Kegan.

Prelude: A Parallel Text. William Wordsworth. Ed. by J. C. Maxwell. (Poets Ser.). 1977. pap. 3.95 (ISBN 0-14-042214-5). Penguin.

Prelude: After Baldina. Valerie J. Sutton. (Illus.). 1974. pap. text ed. 2.00x o.p. (ISBN 0-914336-12-6). Move Short Soc.

Prelude: Or, Growth of a Poet's Mind. William Wordsworth. Ed. by Ernest De Salincourt. (Oxford Standard Authors Ser). 1960. 21.00 (ISBN 0-19-254153-6). Oxford U Pr.

Prelude to Aesthetics. Eva Schaper. 1969. Repr. of 1949 ed. text ed. 7.50x (ISBN 0-04-160006-1). Humanities.

Prelude to Appeasement: East European Central Diplomacy in the Early 1930's. Lisanne Radice. (East European Quarterly Ser.: No. 80). 256p. 1981. text ed. 17.50x (ISBN 0-914710-74-5). East Eur Quarterly.

Prelude to Chemistry: An Outline of Alchemy, Its Literature & Relationships. John Read. LC 79-8622. (Illus.). Repr. of 1937 ed. 39.50 (ISBN 0-404-18488-X). AMS Pr.

Prelude to Civil War: The Nullification Controversy in South Carolina, 1816-1836. William Freehling. (Illus.). 1968. pap. 5.95x (ISBN 0-06-131359-9, TB1359, Torch). Har-Row.

Prelude to Disaster: The American Role in Vietnam, 1940-1963. Weldon A. Brown. 1975. 18.50 (ISBN 0-8046-9122-3, Natl U). Kennikat.

Prelude to Empire: Portugal Overseas Before Henry the Navigator. Bailey W. Diffie. LC 60-14301. (Illus., Orig.). 1960. pap. 2.25x (ISBN 0-8032-5049-5, BB 108, Bison). U of Nebr Pr.

Prelude to Glory. Herbert Krause & Gary D. Olson. LC 74-80769. (Illus.). 279p. (Orig.). 1974. 19.95 (ISBN 0-88498-018-9); ltd. lea. ed. 75.00 (ISBN 0-685-50460-3); pap. 10.95 (ISBN 0-88498-019-7); pap. text ed. 7.45 o.p. (ISBN 0-685-50461-1). Brevet Pr.

Prelude to Independence: The Newspaper War on Britain 1764-1776. Arthur M. Schlesinger. LC 80-22830. 340p. 1980. pap. text ed. 8.95x (ISBN 0-930350-13-8). NE U Pr.

Prelude to Love. Daisy Thomson. pap. 1.50 o.s.i. (ISBN 0-515-04445-8). Jove Pubns.

Prelude to Revolution: Mao, the Party, & the Peasant Question, 1962-66. Richard Baum. LC 74-23894. 240p. 1975. 17.50x (ISBN 0-231-03900-X). Columbia U Pr.

Prelude to Riot: A View of Urban America from the Bottom. Paul Jacobs. 1968. pap. 2.45 o.p. (ISBN 0-394-70433-9, Vin). Random.

Prelude to the Radicals: The North & Reconstruction During 1865. J. Michael Quill. LC 79-9674. 179p. 1980. text ed. 17.75 (ISBN 0-8191-0978-9); pap. text ed. 9.00 (ISBN 0-8191-0979-7). U Pr of Amer.

Prelude to the Russian Campaign: From the Moscow Pact (August 21st 1939) to the Opening of Hostilities in Russia (June 22nd 1941) Grigore Gafencu. LC 79-5207. 348p. 1981. Repr. of 1945 ed. 26.50 (ISBN 0-8305-0072-3). Hyperion Conn.

Prelude to War. Robert Elson. (World War II Ser.). (Illus.). 1976. 12.95 (ISBN 0-8094-2450-9). Time-Life.

Prelude to War. Robert Elson et al. LC 76-10024. (World War II). (Illus.). (gr. 6 up). 1976. PLB 14.94 (ISBN 0-8094-2451-7, Pub by Time-Life). Silver.

Prelude to World Power: American Diplomatic History, 1860-1900. Foster R. Dulles. 1971. pap. 2.95 o.s.i. (ISBN 0-02-031780-8, Collier). Macmillan.

Prelude to Yesterday. Ursula Bloom. 1978. pap. 1.95 o.p. (ISBN 0-523-40212-0). Pinnacle Bks.

Preludes. Maurits I. Boas. LC 78-855. 1978. 8.95 (ISBN 0-8119-0305-2). Fell.

Preludes to Growth: An Experiential Approach. Richard Katz. LC 72-94013. 1973. pap. text ed. 7.95 (ISBN 0-02-917190-3). Free Pr.

Preludes to Vision: The Epic Venture in Blake, Keats, Wordsworth, & Hart Crane. Thomas A. Vogler. LC 70-107662. (No. 22). 1971. 15.75x (ISBN 0-520-01687-4). U of Cal Pr.

Premachining Planning & Tool Presetting. Ed. by Robert R. Runck. LC 67-28208. (Manufacturing Data Ser). (Illus.). 1967. pap. 8.25x (ISBN 0-87263-008-0). SME.

Premarital Counseling: A Manual for Clergy & Counselors. John L. C. Mitman. 144p. 1980. 9.95 (ISBN 0-8164-0467-4). Seabury.

Premarital Counseling: Education for Marriage. Robert F. Stahmann & William Hiebert. LC 78-19727. 192p. 1980. 19.95 (ISBN 0-669-02726-X). Lexington Bks.

Premarital Guide for Couples & Their Counselors. David A. Thompson. 1979. pap. 3.95 (ISBN 0-87123-465-3, 210465). Bethany Fell.

Premarital Sexual Standards in America. Ira L. Reiss. LC 60-7095. 1960. 12.95 (ISBN 0-02-926190-2); pap. text ed. 5.95 (ISBN 0-02-926200-3). Free Pr.

Premchand: His Life & Work. V. S. Naravane. 280p. 1980. text ed. 18.95x (ISBN 0-7069-1091-5, Pub. by Vikas India). Advent Bk.

Premenstrual Syndrome & Progesterone Therapy. Katharina Dalton. 1979. 19.95x (ISBN 0-433-07091-9). Intl Ideas.

Premier Guide de France: The First Year Reader. Colette D. Brichant. (Illus.). 1978. pap. text ed. 10.50 (ISBN 0-13-695460-X). P-H.

Premiers Textes Litteraires. 2nd ed. D. Gourevitch & E. M. Stadler. LC 74-83346. 242p. 1975. text ed. 8.95 (ISBN 0-471-00811-7). Wiley.

Prenatal & Postnatal Mortality in Cattle. Committee On Animal Health. (Orig.). 1968. pap. 5.75 o.p. (ISBN 0-309-01685-1). Natl Acad Pr.

Prenatal Diagnosis & Selective Abortion. Harry Harris. LC 75-3847. 112p. 1975. text ed. 7.95x (ISBN 0-674-70080-5). Harvard U Pr.

Prenatal Diagnosis of Hereditary Disorders. Aubrey Milunsky. (Illus.). 276p. 1973. text ed. 16.75 (ISBN 0-398-02747-1). C C Thomas.

Prentice-Hall CPA Review Course. C. Horngren et al. 1979. 43.95 (ISBN 0-13-695510-X). P-H.

Prentice-Hall Federal Tax Course. students ed. P-H Staff. Ed. by A. Rubin. 1981. 21.00 (ISBN 0-13-312488-6); pap. 7.95 study guide (ISBN 0-13-312496-7). P-H.

Prentice-Hall Federal Tax Course: Nineteen Seventy-Nine Student's Edition. P-H Staff. 1979. 17.95 o.p. (ISBN 0-13-312413-4). P-H.

Prentice-Hall Handbook for Writers. 7th ed. Glenn H. Leggett et al. 1978. text ed. 10.50 (ISBN 0-13-695767-6). P-H.

Prentice-Hall Workbook for Writers. 2nd ed. Donald C. Rigg & Melinda G. Kramer. LC 77-26898. 1978. pap. text ed. 7.95 (ISBN 0-13-696039-1). P-H.

Preology: The Scientific Study of the Planning of Human Development. Norman Barraclough. LC 80-40600. 265p. 1980. pap. 13.25 (ISBN 0-08-026083-7). Pergamon.

Preoperative & Postoperative Care in Neurological Surgery. 2nd ed. Burton L. Wise. (Illus.). 208p. 1978. 19.75 (ISBN 0-398-03825-2). C C Thomas.

Prepaid Legal Services: Socio-Economic Impacts. Lillian Deitch & David Weinstein. LC 76-5582. 1976. 19.50 (ISBN 0-669-00659-9). Lexington Bks.

Preparacion Para el Examen de Equivalencia de la Escuela Superior. 3rd ed. Susan Lanzano & Rosendo Abreu. Ed. by Martin Ringel & William K. Banks. LC 80-17685. 368p. (Span.). 1981. pap. 6.95 (ISBN 0-668-05095-0, 50950). Arco.

Preparation & Control of Radiopharmaceuticals in Hospitals. (Technical Reports Ser.: No. 194). 119p. 1980. pap. 16.25 (ISBN 92-0-145279-9, IDC194, IAEA). Unipub.

Preparation for Breastfeeding. Rodger Ewy & Donna Ewy. LC 74-33606. 144p. 1975. pap. 4.50 (ISBN 0-385-08962-7, Dolp). Doubleday.

Preparation for Counseling. 2nd ed. William C. Cottle & N. M. Downie. 1970. text ed. 17.95 (ISBN 0-13-697227-6). P-H.

Preparation for Criterion-Referenced Tests: A Brief Review of Mathamatical Competencies for Teachers of Early Childhood. Mary O. Miklos. LC 80-5430. 88p. 1980. pap. text ed. 6.25 (ISBN 0-8191-1092-2). U Pr of Amer.

Preparation for the New Mathematics Test (GED) rev. ed. Edward C. Gruber. (Exam Preparation Ser.). (gr. 11). 1980. pap. text ed. 5.95 (ISBN 0-671-09240-5). Monarch Pr.

Preparation for the New Science Test (GED) rev ed. Edward C. Gruber. (Exam Preparation Ser.). (gr. 11). 1980. pap. text ed. 5.95 (ISBN 0-671-09241-3). Monarch Pr.

Preparation for the New Social Studies Test: (GED) Edward C. Gruber. (Orig.). 1980. pap. 5.95 (ISBN 0-671-09246-4). Monarch Pr.

Preparation for Total Consecration. pap. 2.00 (ISBN 0-910984-10-7). Montfort Pubns.

Preparation for Work: A Cross-Country Analysis. Beatrice G. Reubens. LC 77-84454. (Conservation of Human Resources Ser.: No. 4). 1981. text ed. 25.00x (ISBN 0-86598-028-4). Allanheld.

Preparation of a Hospital Food Service Department Budget. American Society for Hospital Food Service Administrators of the American Hospital Association. LC 78-24399. 56p. 1978. pap. 9.50 (ISBN 0-87258-254-X, 1615). Am Hospital.

Preparation of Guidance Associates & Professional Counselors Within the Framework of a Competency Based Program. Ed. by North Texas State University Guidance & Counseling Staff. (ACES Monograph: No. 1). 1973. 6.50 (ISBN 0-686-05522-5, 051). Am Personnel.

Preparation of Human Service Professionals. Alan Gartner. LC 75-11004. 272p. 1976. 22.95 (ISBN 0-87705-259-X). Human Sci Pr.

Preparation of the Federal Estate Tax Return 1980 Course Handbook, 2 vols. (Tax Law & Estate Planning Course Handbook Ser., 1979-80: Vol. 110 & 111). 1980. pap. 25.00 (ISBN 0-685-59703-2, D6-5129). PLI.

Preparation of the Normal Karyotype. Barbara Kaplan. LC 78-720409. (Illus.). 1979. 55.00 (ISBN 0-89189-057-2, 21-9-015-00); student ed. 9.00 (ISBN 0-89189-071-8, 21-9-015-20). Am Soc Clinical.

Preparation to Deathe: A Boke As Devout As Eloquent. Desiderius Erasmus. LC 74-28852. (English Experience Ser.: No. 733). 1975. Repr. of 1538 ed. 6.00 (ISBN 90-221-0762-0). Walter J Johnson.

Preparations for Cast Gold Restorations. Herbert Shillingburg. (Illus.). 168p. 1974. 48.50. Quint Pub Co.

Preparative & Optical Technology Ser. Theoretical & Applied, Vol. 1. 4th ed. A. Everson Pearse. (Preperative & Optical Technology Ser.). (Illus.). 480p. 1980. text ed. 62.50 (ISBN 0-443-01998-3). Churchill.

Preparative to Mariage: Whereunto Is Annexed a Treatise of the Lords Supper, & Another of Usurie. Henry Smith. LC 74-28885. (English Experience Ser.: No. 762). 1975. Repr. of 1591 ed. 16.00 (ISBN 90-221-0762-0). Walter J Johnson.

Preparatory Latin, 2 bks. William J. Buehner & John W. Ambrose. (gr. 6-9). 1970. pap. text ed. 5.25x ea.; Bk. 1. (ISBN 0-88334-007-0); Bk. 2. (ISBN 0-88334-028-3) (ISBN 0-685-39239-2). Ind Sch Pr.

Preparatory Techniques in Histology. Jocelyn P. Germain & David J. Turvey. 1981. text ed. price not set. Butterworth.

Preparatory to Anglo-Saxon England: Being the Collected Papers of Frank Merry Stenton. Frank M. Stenton. Ed. by Doris M. Stenton. 1970. 29.95x (ISBN 0-19-822314-5). Oxford U Pr.

Prepare for Science. new ed. Ed. by C. B. Hansson. (Illus.). 1980. text ed. 30.00 (ISBN 0-08-024263-4); pap. text ed. 9.75 (ISBN 0-08-024262-6). Pergamon.

Prepare Your Own Partnership Agreements. John C. Howell. 144p. 1980. pap. 5.95 (Spec). P-H.

Prepared Childbirth. Carol Horos. Date not set. pap. 2.25 (ISBN 0-440-07087-2). Dell.

Prepared Variations. Heinrich Fraenkel & Kevin J. O'Connell. 1981. 15.61 (ISBN 0-08-024095-X); pap. 7.71 (ISBN 0-08-024096-8). Pergamon.

Preparing Administrative Manuals. Susan Z. Diamond. 199p. 1981. 17.95 (ISBN 0-8144-5631-6). Am Mgmt.

Preparing Artwork for Reproduction. David Cherry. 1976. 24.00 (ISBN 0-7134-3097-4, Pub. by Batsford England). David & Charles.

Preparing, Designing & Leading Workshops: A Humanistic Approach. Cathy Heenan & Susan Cooper. LC 79-9465. 1979. pap. 10.95 (ISBN 0-8436-0779-3). CBI Pub.

Preparing Effective Presentations. rev. ed. Ray J. Friant, Jr. LC 74-133853. 1980. pap. 3.50 (ISBN 0-87576-033-3). Pilot Bks.

Preparing Feasibility Studies in Asia. John E. Walsh, Jr. LC 72-323074. 168p. 1971. 15.00 (ISBN 92-833-1001-2, APO55, APO). Unipub.

Preparing for Confirmation: Program Outline. Michael H. Smith & Mary K. Persse. LC 72-92730. 80p. (Orig., Prog. Bk.). (gr. 6-8). 1972. pap. 1.95 (ISBN 0-87793-050-3). Ave Maria.

Preparing for Effective Bible Teaching. H. C. Brown, Jr. & Velma Brown. LC 76-157404. 1971. pap. 2.50 o.p. (ISBN 0-8054-3417-8). Broadman.

Preparing for Parenthood. Norman H. Wright & Marvin N. Inmon. LC 79-92949. 192p. 1980. pap. 4.95 (ISBN 0-8307-0743-3, 5412218); wkbk. 10.95 (ISBN 0-8307-0755-7, 80-50263). Regal.

Preparing for Retirement: A Program for Survival - A Participants Workbook. Leland P. Bradford. LC 80-52897. 106p. 1981. pap. write for info. (ISBN 0-88390-160-9). Univ Assocs.

Preparing for Retirement: A Program for Survival - A Trainers Kit. Leland P. Bradford. LC 80-2897. 196p. 1981. looseleaf bdg. 39.95 (ISBN 0-88390-161-7). Univ Assocs.

Preparing for Sabbath. Nessa Rapoport. LC 80-21539. 304p. 1981. 10.95 (ISBN 0-688-00294-3). Morrow.

Preparing for Standardization Certification & Quality Control. 298p. 1979. 15.25 (APO80, Apo). Unipub.

Preparing for the Greatest Two Years of Your Life. Mark A. Dennison. pap. 3.95 (ISBN 0-89036-128-2). Hawkes Pub Inc.

Preparing for the Latter Rain. DeWitt S. Osgood. LC 73-75219. 144p. 1973. pap. 4.50 (ISBN 0-8127-0070-8). Southern Pub.

Preparing for the Messiah. Doris Williams & Patricia Griggs. (Griggs Educational Resources Ser.). 1979. pap. 4.95 (ISBN 0-687-33920-0). Abingdon.

Preparing for Ulysses: Politics & Veterans During World War Two. Davis R. Ross. (Contemporary American History Ser). 1969. 22.50x (ISBN 0-231-03222-6). Columbia U Pr.

Preparing for Work. John W. Zehring. 1980. pap. 2.50 (ISBN 0-88207-582-9). Victor Bks.

Preparing for Your Marriage. William J. McRae. 160p. (Orig.). 1980. pap. 5.95 (ISBN 0-310-42761-4, 9366P). Zondervan.

Preparing Instructional Objectives. 2nd. ed. Robert F. Mager. LC 75-16518. 1975. pap. 4.95 (ISBN 0-8224-5601-X). Pitman Learning.

Preparing Preschoolers. Susan W. Allen & Karen H. Talbot. 150p. (Orig.). 1981. pap. 9.95 (ISBN 0-88290-160-5, 2047). Horizon Utah.

Preparing Teachers for Bilingual Education: Basic Readings. Octavio A. Ballesteros. LC 78-68567. 1979. pap. text ed. 9.50 (ISBN 0-8191-0695-X). U Pr of Amer.

Preparing Young Children for Science: A Book of Activities. Lois B. Arnold. LC 79-26119. (Illus.). 128p. (Orig.). 1980. text ed. 11.95x (ISBN 0-8052-3740-2); pap. 6.95 (ISBN 0-8052-0641-8). Schocken.

Prepodobny Feodor, Igumen Studiisky, 2 vols. in 1. Andreevich Dobrovol'Skii. LC 80-2355. 1981. Repr. of 1913 ed. 115.00 (ISBN 0-404-18907-5). AMS Pr.

Prepositions & Adverbial Particles. J. B. Heaton. 1975. pap. text ed. 5.75x (ISBN 0-582-52121-1). Longman.

Preprosthetic Oral & Maxillofacial Surgery. Thomas J. Starshak. LC 80-17921. (Illus.). 351p. 1980. 47.50 (ISBN 0-8016-4757-6). Mosby.

Prerogative of Parliaments in England, Proved in a Dialogue, 4 vols. in 1. Sir Walter Raleigh et al. Ed. by David S. Berkowitz & Samuel E. Thorne. LC 77-89209. (Classics of English Legal History in the Modern Era Ser.: Vol. 123). 1979. lib. bdg. 55.00 (ISBN 0-8240-3160-1). Garland Pub.

Prerogative of the Harlot: Press Barons & Power. Hugh Cudlipp. (Illus.). 304p. 1981. 13.50 (ISBN 0-370-30238-9, Pub. by Chatto-Bodley-Jonathan). Merrimack Bk Serv.

Preromantic Imagination of L. S. Mercier. Henry P. Majewski. LC 70-135985. 1971. text ed. 8.75x (ISBN 0-391-00122-1). Humanities.

Presbyterian Heritage. A. Mervyn Davies. LC 65-10136. (Orig.). 1965. pap. 2.25 (ISBN 0-8042-0972-3). John Knox.

Presbyterian Worship: Its Meaning & Method. rev. ed. Donald MacLeod. LC 80-82226. (Illus.). 176p. 1981. 12.50 (ISBN 0-8042-1813-7). John Knox.

Presbyterians in the South, 3 vols. Ernest T. Thompson. Incl. Vol. 1. 1607-1861. 1963 (ISBN 0-8042-0996-0); Vol. 2. 1861-1890. 1973 (ISBN 0-8042-0997-9); Vol. 3. 1890-1972. 1973. 15.00 (ISBN 0-8042-0998-7). LC 63-19121. 15.00 ea.; Set. 39.95 (ISBN 0-8042-0999-5). John Knox.

Presbyterians: Their History & Beliefs. Walter L. Lingle & John W. Kuykendall. LC 77-15750. 1978. pap. 4.50 (ISBN 0-8042-0985-5). John Knox.

Presbyteries & Profits: Calvinism & the Development of Capitalism in Scotland, 1560 - 1707. Gordon Marshall. 400p. 1980. 54.00x (ISBN 0-19-827246-4). Oxford U Pr.

Preschool Behavior Rating Scale. William F. Barker & Annick M. Doeff. LC 80-11444. (Orig.). 1980. pap. text ed. 3.95 instructions & scoring sample (ISBN 0-87868-148-5); blank scale 0.50 (ISBN 0-87868-185-X); Methodology 2.25 (ISBN 0-87868-187-6). Child Welfare.

Preschool in Action: Exploring Early Childhood Programs. 2nd ed. Mary C. Day & Ronald K. Parker. 1977. text ed. 19.95 o.p. (ISBN 0-205-05513-3). Allyn.

Preschool Language Assessment Instrument: Language of Learning in Practice. Marion Blank et al. 1978. 17.00 (ISBN 0-8089-1072-8); record forms 9.75 (ISBN 0-8089-1107-4). Grune.

Preschool Programming of Children with Disabilities. Roger Reger. (Illus.). 136p. 1974. 13.75 (ISBN 0-398-01564-3). C C Thomas.

Prescott: A Pictorial History. Melissa Weiner. Ed. by Donna R. Friedman. (Illus.). 208p. 1981. pap. write for info. (ISBN 0-89865-092-5). Donning Co.

Prescott & Dunn's Industrial Microbiology. 4th ed. Gerald Reed. (Illus.). 1981. lib. bdg. 59.00 (ISBN 0-87055-374-7). AVI.

Prescriber. 11th ed. John H. Clarke. 382p. 1972. 11.95x (ISBN 0-8464-1041-9). Beekman Pubs.

Prescriber's Guide to Drug Interactions. J. Rosenberg. 1978. pap. 12.95 (ISBN 0-87489-143-4). Med Economics.

Prescribing, Practice & Drug Usage. Ed. by Roy Mapes. 217p. 1980. 32.50x (ISBN 0-7099-0378-2, Pub. by Croom Helm Ltd England). Biblio Dist.

Prescription Drugs. Ed. by F. Glenn. 287p. 1981. 28.50 o.p. (ISBN 0-686-68308-0). Porter.

Prescription for Living. 2nd rev. ed. Ruhiyyih Rabbani. 1978. 7.95 (ISBN 0-85398-002-0, 7-31-23, Pub. by G Ronald England); pap. 2.50 (ISBN 0-85398-003-9, 7-31-24, Pub. by G. Ronald England). Baha'i.

Prescription for Today. Quinton J. Everest. pap. 4.95 (ISBN 0-686-12669-6, BE-173). Evangel Indiana.

Prescription for Tommorow. Harold J. Cummings. LC 80-25723. 112p. 1980. write for info. (ISBN 0-87863-034-1). Farnswth Pub.

Prescription: Murder. Ann Kurth. (Illus.). 1981. pap. 2.50 (ISBN 0-451-09997-4, E9997, Sig). NAL.

Prescription Pharmacy: Dosage Formulation & Pharmaceutical Adjuncts. 2nd ed. Ed. by Joseph B. Sprowls, Jr. LC 70-109958. (Illus.). 1970. text ed. 22.50 o.p. (ISBN 0-397-52050-6). Lippincott.

Prescriptions for Child Mental Health & Education. Arnold P. Goldstein. 1978. text ed. 44.00 (ISBN 0-08-022250-1); pap. text ed. 10.95 (ISBN 0-08-022249-8). Pergamon.

Prescriptions for Children with Learning & Adjustment Problems. Ralph F. Blanco. 320p. 1980. 13.75 (ISBN 0-685-02633-7). C C Thomas.

Prescriptions for Happiness. Ken Keyes, Jr. LC 80-84855. (Illus.). 132p. 1981. pap. 2.00 (ISBN 0-915972-02-6); pocketbook edition 0.95 (ISBN 0-915972-03-4). Living Love.

Prescriptions for Parishes. Jean M. Haldane et al. 128p. 1973. pap. 2.95 (ISBN 0-8164-2080-7). Crossroad NY.

Prescriptions for Survival. Frieda Carrol. LC 78-72312. 148p. 1981. pap. text ed. 14.95 (ISBN 0-9605246-1-4). Biblio Pr GA.

Prescriptive Psychotherapies. Arnold P. Goldstein & Norman Stein. LC 75-5620. 1977. text ed. 32.00 (ISBN 0-08-019506-7, 75-5620); pap. text ed. 14.50 (ISBN 0-08-019505-9). Pergamon.

Prescripton for Justice: The Theory & Practice of Sentencing Guidelines. Jack M. Kress. 368p. 1980. reference 25.00 (ISBN 0-88410-792-2). Ballinger Pub.

Presdestinacion of Saintes. Saint Augustine. Bd. with Perserveraunce Unto Thende. LC 68-54611. (English Experience Ser.: No. 32). Repr. of 1556 ed. 20.00 (ISBN 90-221-0032-4). Walter J Johnson.

Presence. Ed. by Shirley Burden. (Illus.). 92p. 1981. 20.00 (ISBN 0-89381-075-4). Aperture.

Presence in an Empty Room. Velda Johnston. 1981. lib. bdg. 12.95 (ISBN 0-8161-3158-9, Large Print Bks). G K Hall.

Presence in an Empty Room. Velda Johnston. LC 79-25431. 256p. 1980. 8.95 (ISBN 0-396-07796-X). Dodd.

Presence of Faulkner in the Writings of Garcia Marquez. Harley D. Oberhelman. (Graduate Studies, Texas Tech Univ.: No. 22). (Illus.). 1980. pap. 7.00 (ISBN 0-89672-080-2). Tex Tech Pr.

Presence of God. Elisabeth-Paule Labat. Tr. by N. D. Smith from Fr. LC 80-82089. Orig. Title: Presences De Dieu. 224p. 1980. pap. 7.95 (ISBN 0-8091-2336-3). Paulist Pr.

Presence of Siva. Stella Kramrisch. LC 80-8558. (Illus.). 550p. 1981. 37.50x (ISBN 0-691-03964-X); pap. 16.50x (ISBN 0-691-10115-9). Princeton U Pr.

Presence of the Actor. Joseph Chaikin. LC 70-175287. (Illus.). 1972. pap. text ed. 4.95x (ISBN 0-689-70338-4, 194). Atheneum.

Presence of the Future: The Eschatology of Biblical Realism. George E. Ladd. 1973. pap. 7.95 (ISBN 0-8028-1531-6). Eerdmans.

Presence of the Kingdom. Jacques Ellul. 1967. pap. 3.95 (ISBN 0-8164-2058-0, SP41). Crossroad NY.

Presence of the Past: A History of the Preservation Movement in the United States Before Williamsburg. Charles B. Hosmer, Jr. LC 65-13292. (Illus.). 386p. 1965. text ed. 12.95 (ISBN 0-89133-085-2). Preservation Pr.

Presence of the Word: Some Prolegomena for Cultural & Religious History. Walter J. Ong. 1967. 22.50x o.p. (ISBN 0-300-00810-4). Yale U Pr.

Presence of the Word: Some Prolegomena for Cultural & Religious History. Walter J. Ong. xvi, 360p. 1981. pap. 8.95x (ISBN 0-8166-1043-6). U of Minn Pr.

Presence, Power, Praise; Documents on Charismatic Renewal: International Documents, Vol. 3. Ed. by Kilian McDonnell. 1980. 35.00 (ISBN 0-8146-1065-X). Liturgical Pr.

Presence, Power, Praise: Documents on Charismatic Renewal: National Documents, Vol. 1. Ed. by Kilian McDonnell. 1980. 35.00 (ISBN 0-8146-1066-8). Liturgical Pr.

Presence, Power, Praise: Documents on Charismatic Renewal: National Documents, Vol. 2. Kilian McDonnell. 1980. 35.00 (ISBN 0-8146-1189-3). Liturgical Pr.

Presence with Secrets. W. M. Spackman. LC 80-11406. 176p. 1980. 8.95 (ISBN 0-394-51279-0). Knopf.

Present Age. Soren Kierkegaard. Ed. & tr. by Alexander Dru. pap. 3.95x (ISBN 0-06-130094-2, TB94, Torch). Har-Row.

Present & Future Civil Uses of Underwater Sound. Committee On Underwater Telecommunications Division Of Physical Sciences. LC 76-606666. (Illus., Orig.). 1970. pap. 4.25 (ISBN 0-309-01771-8). Natl Acad Pr.

Present & Future of Counseling Psychology. John M. Whiteley & Bruce R. Fretz. LC 80-315. (Counseling Psychology Ser.). 256p. (Orig.). 1980. pap. text ed. 8.95 (ISBN 0-8185-0396-3). Brooks-Cole.

Present & Past in Middle Life. Ed. by Dorothy Eichorn et al. 1981. price not set (ISBN 0-12-233680-1). Acad Pr.

Present Danger: Towards a Foreign Policy. Robert Conquest. LC 79-2086. (Publication Ser.: 216). 170p. 1979. 12.00 (ISBN 0-8179-7161-0). Hoover Inst Pr.

Present-Day Historical & Comparative Linguistics: An Introductory Guide to Theory & Method Part One General Background-Phonological Change. D. L. Goyvaerts. 231p. 1975. pap. text ed. 21.75x (ISBN 0-391-01588-5). Humanities.

Present-Day Parties in the State & Church. Friedrich J. Stahl. Tr. by Timothy D. Taylor. LC 76-54054. 502p. 1976. 35.75 o.p. (ISBN 0-918288-01-0); pap. 26.75 lmt. ed. o.p. (ISBN 0-918288-08-8). Slavia Lib.

Present Day Russian Psychology. Ed. by N. O'Connor. 1967. 25.00 (ISBN 0-08-012099-7); pap. 12.75 (ISBN 0-08-012098-9). Pergamon.

Present Day Spanish. J. R. Scarr. Vol. 1. 1966. 4.39 (ISBN 0-08-011551-9). Pergamon.

Present from a Bird. Jay Williams. LC 72-153786. (Illus.). (gr. k-3). 1971. 5.95 o.s.i. (ISBN 0-8193-0500-6, Four Winds); PLB 5.41 o.s.i. (ISBN 0-8193-0501-4). Schol Bk Serv.

Present from...Holiday Souvenirs of the British Isles. Larch S. Garrad. (Illus.). 157p. 1976. 5.95 (ISBN 0-7153-7080-4). David & Charles.

Present of Things Future: Exploring of Time in Human Experience. Thomas J. Cottle & Stephen L. Klineberg. LC 73-5292. 1974. 9.95 o.s.i. (ISBN 0-02-906820-7). Free Pr.

Present Problems in the Democratization of Secondary & Higher Education. A. Le Gall et al. LC 72-97137. (Development of Higher Education Ser.). (Illus.). 238p. (Orig.). 1973. pap. 9.25 (ISBN 92-3-101068-9, U477, UNESCO). Unipub.

Present Realities: Future Imperatives in Nursing Education. Ed. by M. Louise Fitzpatrick. LC 76-55404. 1977. pap. text ed. 5.25x (ISBN 0-8077-2513-7). Tchrs Coll.

Present Revelation: In Quest of Religious Foundations. Gabriel Moran. 204p. 1972. 8.95 (ISBN 0-8164-1105-0). Crossroad NY.

Present Situation of Science & Technology in the STPI Countries. (Science & Technology for Development Ser.: STPI Module 4). 65p. pap. 5.00 (IDRC TS22, IDRC). Unipub.

Present State of French Studies: A Collection of Research Reviews. Charles B. Osburn. LC 78-149990. 1971. 30.00 (ISBN 0-8108-0373-9). Scarecrow.

Present State of the Cape of Good-Hope: Or, a Particular Account of the Several Nations of the Hottentots, 2 vols. Peter Kolb. (Anthropology Ser.). 1969. Repr. of 1731 ed. Vol. 1. 27.00 (ISBN 0-384-30100-2); Vol. 2. 34.50 (ISBN 0-685-13553-5). Johnson Repr.

Present State of the European Settlements on the Mississippi. facsimile, new ed. Philip Pittman. Ed. by John Francis McDermott. LC 76-44247. (Illus.). 221p. 1977. 24.95x (ISBN 0-87870-011-0). Memphis St Univ.

Present Status of Calciphylaxis. Association of Bone & Joint Surgeons. Ed. by Marshall R. Urist. (Clinical Orthopaedics Ser., Vol. 69). 1970. 15.00 (ISBN 0-685-22849-5); new subscribers 8.00 (ISBN 0-685-22850-9). Lippincott.

Presentamos Al Pueblo Bautista. Cyril E. Bryant. Tr. by Federico A. Mariotti. (Illus.). 1976. pap. 0.40 (ISBN 0-311-17019-6). Casa Bautista.

Presentation Drawings by American Architects. Alfred M. Kemper. LC 76-40891. 1977. 37.50 (ISBN 0-471-01369-2, Pub. by Wiley-Interscience). Wiley.

Presentation of Ideas in Technical Writing. A. Neelameghan. 1975. 12.50 (ISBN 0-7069-0340-4, Pub. by Vikas India). Advent Bk.

Presentation of Self in Everyday Life. Erving Goffman. LC 59-9138. 1959. pap. 3.50 (ISBN 0-385-09402-7, A174, Anch). Doubleday.

Presentations of Groups. David Johnson. LC 74-31803. (London Mathematical Society Lecture Note Ser.: No. 22). 140p. 1976. 18.95x (ISBN 0-521-20829-7). Cambridge U Pr.

Presenting Entertainment Arts: Stage, Film, Television. William H. Shaw. 192p. 1980. pap. text ed. 9.95 (ISBN 0-8403-2226-7). Kendall-Hunt.

Presenting Folk Culture: A Handbook on Folk Festival Organization & Management. Joseph T. Wilson. Ed. by Lee Udall. Date not set. write for info. (ISBN 0-87049-300-0). U of Tenn Pr. Postponed.

Presenting Shakespeare. R. C. Peat. 1947. pap. 10.00x (ISBN 0-245-53047-9). Intl Ideas.

Presenting Technical Ideas: A Guide to Audience Communication. W. A. Mambert. LC 67-28335. (Wiley Series on Human Communication). 1968. 20.95 (ISBN 0-471-56629-2, Pub. by Wiley-Interscience). Wiley.

Presents. (MacDonald Educational Ser.). (Illus., Arabic.). 3.50x (ISBN 0-686-53099-3). Intl Bk Ctr.

Preservation & Conservation: Principles & Practices. LC 75-13331. (Illus.). 547p. 1976. text ed. 17.95 (ISBN 0-89133-029-1). Preservation Pr.

Preservation Comes of Age: From Williamsburg to the National Trust, 1926-1949, 2 vols. Charles B. Hosmer, Jr. 1981. Set. 37.50x (ISBN 0-8139-0712-8). U Pr of Va.

Preservation Hall. Scott Spencer. 1978. pap. 2.50 (ISBN 0-380-01877-2, 49262). Avon.

Preservation Hall. Scott Spencer. 1980. pap. 2.50 (ISBN 0-686-69266-7, 52209). Avon.

Preservation of Client Rights: A Handbook for Practitioners Providing Therapeutic, Educational, & Rehabilitative Services. Ed. by Gerald T. Hannah et al. LC 80-1644. (Illus.). 1981. 22.95 (ISBN 0-02-913820-5). Free Pr.

Preservation of Fish by Irradiation. (Illus., Orig.). 1970. pap. 10.75 (ISBN 92-0-111070-7, IAEA). Unipub.

Preservation of Fruit & Vegetables by Radiation. 1968. pap. 8.25 (ISBN 92-0-111068-5, IAEA). Unipub.

Preservation of Library Materials. Ed. by Joyce Russell. 1980. pap. write for info. (ISBN 0-87111-270-1). SLA.

Preservation of Red Blood Cells. Division of Medical Sciences, NRC. (Illus.). 384p. 1973. pap. 9.75 (ISBN 0-685-31902-4). Natl Acad Pr.

Preservation: Reusing America's Energy. National Trust for Historic Preservation. (Illus.). 128p. (Orig.). 1981. pap. 9.95 (ISBN 0-89133-095-X). Preservation Pr.

Preservation: Toward an Ethic in the Nineteen Eighties. LC 80-17564. 1980. pap. 8.95 (ISBN 0-89133-079-8). Preservation Pr.

Preservation Vs. Development: An Economic Analysis of San Francisco Bay Wetlands. Ralph A. Luken. LC 76-2907. (Special Studies). (Illus.). 150p. 1976. text ed. 24.95 (ISBN 0-275-56590-4). Praeger.

Preserving & Pickling. Rosemary Wadey. LC 77-85031. (Penny Pinchers Ser.). 1978. 2.95 (ISBN 0-7153-7551-2). David & Charles.

Preserving & Pickling: Putting Foods by in Small Batches. Jacqueline Heriteau & Thalia Erath. (Illus.). 1976. pap. 2.95 (ISBN 0-307-42019-1, Golden Pr). Western Pub.

Preserving & Restoring Monuments & Historic Buildings. LC 73-189463. (Museums & Monuments Ser., No. 14). (Illus.). 267p. 1972. 24.75 (ISBN 92-3-100985-0, U479, UNESCO); pap. (U480). Unipub.

Preserving Paper & Photographic Materials: A Handbook for Curators & Librarians. Marcella Averkamp. LC 80-26028. (Illus.). 88p. (Orig.). 1981. pap. 7.95x (ISBN 0-87020-203-0). State Hist Soc Wis.

Preserving the Past. E. R. Chamberlin. (Illus.). 205p. 1979. 17.50x (ISBN 0-460-04364-1, Pub. by J. M. Dent England). Biblio Dist.

Preserving Your American Heritage: A Guide to Family & Local History. rev. ed. Norman E. Wright. (Illus.). 1981. pap. text ed. 12.95 (ISBN 0-8425-1863-0). Brigham.

Presidencies of James A. Garfield & Chester A. Arthur. Justus D. Doenecke. LC 80-18957. (American Presidency Ser.). 232p. 1981. 15.00x (ISBN 0-7006-0208-9). Regents Pr KS.

Presidency. Gerald W. Johnson. (Illus.). (gr. 5-9). 1962. 7.75 (ISBN 0-688-21465-7). Morrow.

Presidency. Dale Vinyard. pap. 2.65 o.p. (ISBN 0-684-12534-X, SL292, ScribT). Scribner.

Presidency: An Introduction. Robert J. Sickels. 1980. pap. text ed. 10.95 (ISBN 0-13-697433-3). P-H.

Presidency & the Mass Media in the Age of Television. William C. Spragens. LC 78-51149. 1978. pap. text ed. 11.75x (ISBN 0-8191-0476-0). U Pr of Amer.

Presidency in Flux. George Reedy. 200p. 1973. 12.50x (ISBN 0-231-03736-8). Columbia U Pr.

Presidency in the Courts. Glendon A. Schubert. LC 72-8122. (American Constitutional & Legal History Ser). 408p. 1973. Repr. of 1957 ed. lib. bdg. 35.00 (ISBN 0-306-70529-X). Da Capo.

Presidency of John Adams. Stephen G. Kurtz. LC 57-7764. 1957. 10.00x o.p. (ISBN 0-8122-7101-7). U of Pa Pr.

Presidency of the Continental Congress 1774-89: A Study in American Institutional History. Jennings B. Sanders. 6.00 (ISBN 0-8446-0889-0). Peter Smith.

Presidency of William McKinley. Lewis L. Gould. LC 80-16022. (American Presidency Ser.). 298p. 1981. 15.00x (ISBN 0-7006-0206-2). Regents Pr KS.

President & Congress. Louis Fisher. LC 78-142362. 1972. 14.95 (ISBN 0-02-910320-7); pap. text ed. 4.95 (ISBN 0-02-910340-1). Free Pr.

President & Congress: Toward a New Power Balance. James W. Davis & Delbert Ruigquist. LC 74-26595. (Politics of Government Ser). 224p. 1975. pap. 2.95 o.p. (ISBN 0-8120-0965-7). Barron.

President & His Powers. William H. Taft. LC 38-32819. Orig. Title: Our Chief Magistrate & His Powers. 1967. pap. 5.00x (ISBN 0-231-08574-5, 74). Columbia U Pr.

President & the Constitution. Ed. by George A. Nikolaieff. (Reference Shelf Ser: Vol. 46, No. 4). 1974. 6.25 (ISBN 0-8242-0523-5). Wilson.

President Carter Nineteen Seventy Nine. Congressional Quarterly Inc. Ed. by Congressional Quarterly Inc. (Presidency Ser.). 240p. 1980. pap. text ed. 7.95 (ISBN 0-87187-150-5). Congr Quarterly.

President Castello Branco: Brazilian Reformer. John W. Dulles. LC 79-5281. (Illus.). 536p. 1980. 27.50x (ISBN 0-89096-092-5). Tex A&M Univ Pr.

President Edvard Benes, Between East & West: 1938-1948. Edward Taborsky. LC 80-83829. (Publication Ser.: No. 246). (Illus.). 280p. 1981. 19.95 (ISBN 0-8179-7461-X). Hoover Inst Pr.

President Eisenhower & Strategy Management: A Study in Defense Politics. Douglas Kinnard. LC 76-46031. 184p. 1977. 14.50x (ISBN 0-8131-1356-3). U Pr of Ky.

President in Love: The Courtship Letters of Woodrow Wilson & Edith Bolling Galt. Ed. by Edwin Tribble. (Illus.). 1981. 12.95 (ISBN 0-395-29482-7). HM.

President Lincoln's Attitude Toward Slavery & Emancipation. Henry W. Wilbur. 1914. 12.00x (ISBN 0-8196-0267-1). Biblo.

President Must Die. Rick Raphael. 1981. 12.95 (ISBN 0-393-01445-2). Norton.

President of India. B. C. Das. 1977. text ed. 22.50x o.p. (ISBN 0-8426-1043-X). Verry.

President: Office & Powers, 1787-1957: History & Analysis of Practice & Opinion. 4th rev. ed. Edward S. Corwin. LC 57-11573. (Stokes Lectureship on Politics Ser.). 1974. 14.50x (ISBN 0-8147-0100-0); pap. 7.00x (ISBN 0-8147-0101-9). NYU Pr.

President, the Budget, & Congress: Impoundment & the 1974 Budget Act. James P. Pfiffner. (Special Studies in Public Policy & Public Systems Management). 1979. lib. bdg. 19.50x (ISBN 0-89158-468-4); pap. text ed. 8.00x (ISBN 0-89158-495-1). Westview.

Presidenta. Lois Gould. 1981. price not set (ISBN 0-671-24930-4, Linden). S&S.

Presidential Advisory Commissions: Truman to Nixon. Thomas R. Wolanin. LC 74-27317. 368p. 1975. 27.50 (ISBN 0-299-06860-9). U of Wis Pr.

Presidential Campaign. rev. ed. Stephen Hess. 1978. pap. 3.95 (ISBN 0-8157-3591-X). Brookings.

Presidential Campaign of Eighteen Thirty-Two. Samuel R. Gammon, Jr. LC 78-96952. (Law, Politics & History Ser). 1969. Repr. of 1922 ed. lib. bdg. 20.00 (ISBN 0-306-71830-8). Da Capo.

Presidential Campaign Politics: Coalition Strategies & Citizen Response. John H. Kessel. 1980. pap. 9.95x (ISBN 0-256-02369-7). Dorsey.

Presidential Campaign Politics: Coalition Strategies & Citizen Response. John H. Kessel. LC 79-56080. 1980. 14.95 o.p. (ISBN 0-87094-211-5). Dow Jones-Irwin.

Presidential Character: Predicting Performance in the White House. 2nd ed. James D. Barber. LC 77-4094. 1977. 11.95 o.p. (ISBN 0-13-697466-X); pap. 10.95 (ISBN 0-13-697847-9). P-H.

Presidential Commissions. Carl Marcy. LC 72-8109. (Studies in American History & Government Ser.). 156p. 1973. Repr. of 1945 ed. lib. bdg. 19.50 (ISBN 0-306-70532-X). Da Capo.

Presidential Debates: Media Electeral & Policy Perspective. Ed. by George F. Bishop et al. Robert G. Meadow & Marilyn Jackson-Beeck. LC 78-70323. (Praeger Special Studies). 1978. 32.95 (ISBN 0-03-044271-0); pap. 11.95 (ISBN 0-03-057707-1). Praeger.

Presidential Decisionmaking in Foreign Policy. Alexander George. (Westview Special Studies in International Relations). 1980. lib. bdg. 24.50x (ISBN 0-89158-380-7); pap. text ed. 10.50x (ISBN 0-89158-510-9). Westview.

Presidential Election & Transition of 1960-61: Brookings Lectures & Additional Papers. Ed. by Paul T. David et al. 1961. 10.95 (ISBN 0-8157-1746-6). Brookings.

Presidential Election of Nineteen Sixteen. S. D. Lovell. LC 79-25689. 288p. 1980. 22.50x o.p. (ISBN 0-8093-0965-3). S Ill U Pr.

Presidential Elections & American Politics: Voters, Candidates, & Campaigns Since 1952. Herbert Asher. 1980. pap. 10.95x (ISBN 0-256-02322-0). Dorsey.

Presidential Elections: Strategies of American Electoral Politics. 5th ed. Nelson Polsby & Aaron Wildavsky. LC 70-162761. 1976. 12.50 (ISBN 0-684-16415-9). Scribner.

Presidential Emergency. Walter Stovall. 1978. 8.95 o.p. (ISBN 0-525-18325-6). Dutton.

Presidential Influence in Congress. George C. Edwards, III. LC 79-21975. (Illus.). 1980. text ed. 14.95x (ISBN 0-7167-1161-3); pap. text ed. 7.95x (ISBN 0-7167-1162-1). W H Freeman.

Presidential Nation. Joseph Califano, Jr. 1975. 5.95x (ISBN 0-393-09135-X). Norton.

Presidential Nominating Process: Can It Be Improved? Ed. by Austin Ranney. 1980. pap. 3.25 (ISBN 0-8447-3397-0). Am Enterprise.

Presidential Politics & Science Policy. James E. Katz. LC 77-14024. (Praeger Special Studies). 1978. 28.95 (ISBN 0-03-040941-1). Praeger.

Presidential Power in Latin American Politics. Ed. by Thomas V. Dibacco. LC 77-4727. (Special Studies). 1977. text ed. 21.95 (ISBN 0-03-021816-0). Praeger.

Presidential Power: The Politics of Leadership from FDR to Carter. Richard E. Neustadt. LC 79-19474. 1979. pap. text ed. 8.95 (ISBN 0-471-05988-9). Wiley.

Presidential Promises & Performance. McGeorge Bundy & Edmund S. Muskie. LC 80-1855. (Charles C. Moskowitz Memorial Lectures). 1980. 10.95 (ISBN 0-02-904290-9). Free Pr.

Presidential Transcripts. Ed. by Bernstein et al. 736p. 1974. 10.00 o.s.i. (ISBN 0-440-06056-7). Delacorte.

Presidential Transitions. Laurin L. Henry. 1960. 13.95 (ISBN 0-8157-3576-6). Brookings.

Presidential Zero-Year Mystery. David A. Lewis & Darryl E. Hicks. (Orig.). 1980. pap. 2.95 (ISBN 0-88270-490-7). Logos.

Presidents. Harold Coy. (First Bks.). (Illus.). (gr. 4-6). 1977. PLB 6.45 s&l (ISBN 0-531-02906-9). Watts.

Presidents. LC 79-57491. (Illus.). 1980. 13.95 (ISBN 0-89387-038-2). Sat Eve Post.

Presidents. Roland Stone. (Orig.). 1979. pap. 1.95 (ISBN 0-532-23284-4). Manor Bks.

Presidents & Prime Ministers. Ed. by Richard Rose & Ezra N. Suleiman. 1980. pap. 8.25 (ISBN 0-8447-3386-5). Am Enterprise.

President's Cabinet: And How It Grew. Nancy W. Parker. LC 77-10090. (Illus.). 40p. (gr. 1 up). 1978. 7.95 (ISBN 0-590-17711-7, Four Winds); lib. bdg. 7.95 (ISBN 0-590-07711-2). Schol Bk Serv.

Presidents Day. Jack Winder. Ed. by Alton Jordan. (Holdays Ser). (Illus.). (gr. k-3). 1977. PLB 3.50 (ISBN 0-89868-028-X, Read Res); pap. text ed. 1.75 (ISBN 0-89868-061-1). ARO Pub.

Presidents of the United States. Cornel Lengyel. (Illus.). PLB 12.23 (ISBN 0-307-67863-6, Golden Pr). Western Pub.

Presidents of the United States & Their Administrations from Washington to the Present. Maxim Armbruster. (Illus.). 400p. 1981. 14.95 (ISBN 0-8180-0812-1). Horizon.

Presidents of the United States & Their Administrations from Washington to Ford. 6th ed. Maxim E. Armbruster. (Illus.). 1975. 10.00 o.p. (ISBN 0-8180-0815-6). Horizon.

Presidents, Secretaries of State & Crisis Management in U.S. Foreign Relations: A Model & Predictive Analysis. Lawrence Falkowski. LC 77-27049. (Westview Special Studies in International Relations & U.S. Foreign Policy Ser.). (Illus.). 1978. lib. bdg. 22.50x (ISBN 0-89158-072-7); pap. text ed. 9.50x (ISBN 0-89158-073-5). Westview.

Presley: Entertainer of the Century. Antony James. 1976. pap. 1.95 (ISBN 0-505-51239-4). Tower Bks.

Presocratic Philosophers. Geoffrey S. Kirk & John E. Raven. 1957. 47.50 (ISBN 0-521-05891-0); pap. 9.95x (ISBN 0-521-09169-1). Cambridge U Pr.

Presocratics. Edward Hussey. (Classical Life & Letters Ser.). 1972. 40.50x (ISBN 0-7156-0630-1, 477, Pub. by Duckworth England); pap. 13.50x (ISBN 0-7156-0824-X, 478, Pub. by Duckworth England). Biblio Dist.

Presocratics. Ed. & tr. by Philip Wheelwright. LC 66-12944. (Orig.). 1966. pap. 7.50 (ISBN 0-672-63091-5). Odyssey Pr.

Press. A. J. Liebling. 1981. pap. 6.95 (ISBN 0-394-74849-2). Pantheon.

Press: A Handbook of Elementary Classroom Ideas to Motivate Teaching Through the Use of the Newspaper. (Spice Ser.). 1978. 6.50 (ISBN 0-89273-126-5). Educ Serv.

Press & America. 4th ed. Edwin Emery & Michael Emery. (Illus.). 1978. ref. 19.95 (ISBN 0-13-697979-3) P-H.

Press & Foreign Policy. Bernard C. Cohen. 1963. 15.00 (ISBN 0-691-07519-0); pap. 5.95 o.p. (ISBN 0-691-02157-0) Princeton U Pr.

Press & Politics in Nigeria Eighteen Eighty-Nineteen Thirty Seven. Fred I. Omu. (Ibadan History Ser.). 1978. text ed. 20.75x (ISBN 0-391-00561-8). Humanities.

Press & Public. Leo Bogart. LC 80-18357. 304p. 1980. text ed. 24.95 (ISBN 0-89859-077-9). L Erlbaum Assocs.

Press & Society: From Caxton to Northcliffe. Geoffrey A. Cranfield. LC 77-21904. (Themes in British Social History). 1978. text ed. 22.00x (ISBN 0-582-48983-0); pap. text ed. 11.50x (ISBN 0-582-48984-9). Longman.

Press Brake & Shear Handbook. rev. ed. Harold R. Daniels. LC 74-13643. 184p. 1974. 17.95 (ISBN 0-8436-0815-3). CBI Pub.

Press in the French Revolution. Ed. by W. Gilchrist & W. J. Murray. LC 77-150256. 1971. 28.50x (ISBN 0-89197-596-9). Irvington.

Press, Politics, & Power: Egypt's Heikal & Al-Ahram. Munir K. Nasser. 1979. text ed. 15.50 (ISBN 0-8138-0955-X); pap. text ed. 9.50 (ISBN 0-8138-1290-9). Iowa St U Pr.

Press Toolmaking. 2nd ed. Ed. by F. Ballard et al. (Engineering Craftsmen: No. H21). (Illus.). 1972. spiral bdg. 16.50x (ISBN 0-85083-168-7). Intl Ideas.

Press Tools & Presswork. John A. Waller. (Illus.). 1980. 39.95 (ISBN 0-86108-005-X). Herman Pub.

Presse: A Reader & Workbook. Klaus A. Mueller & Susanne Hoppmann-Liecty. 192p. 1976. pap. text ed. 7.95x (ISBN 0-669-92536-5). Heath.

Presse Deux. 2nd ed. Brian N. Morton & Jacqueline Morton. 1977. pap. text ed. 7.95x (ISBN 0-669-01636-5). Heath.

Pressure-Enthalpy Diagram for Ammonia. D. C. Hickson & F. R. Taylor. 1978. pap. 3.95x (ISBN 0-631-94210-6, Pub. by Basil Blackwell England). Biblio Dist.

Pressure-Enthalpy Diagram for Refrigerant 12. D. C. Hickson & F. R. Taylor. 1977. pap. 3.95x (ISBN 0-631-94220-3, Pub. by Basil Blackwell England). Biblio Dist.

Pressure Groups & Political Culture: A Comparative Study. Francis G. Castles. (Library of Political Studies). (Orig.). 1967. pap. text ed. 2.50x (ISBN 0-7100-6526-4). Humanities.

Pressure Groups & Politics in Antebellum Tariffs. J. J. Pincus. LC 76-51733. 1977. 17.50x (ISBN 0-231-03963-8). Columbia U Pr.

Pressure Groups in Indian Politics. Babulal Fadia. (Illus.). 295p. 1980. text ed. 21.50x (ISBN 0-391-01795-0). Humanities.

Pressure Man. Zach Hughes. (Orig.). 1980. pap. 1.95 (ISBN 0-451-09498-0, J9498, Sig). NAL.

Pressure Politics in Contemporary Britain. Graham Wootton. LC 77-26372. 1978. 21.95x (ISBN 0-669-02167-9). Lexington Bks.

Pressure Relieving Systems for Marine Bulk Liquid Cargo Containers. Committee on Hazardous Materials. (Illus.). 168p. 1973. pap. 10.25 (ISBN 0-309-02122-7). Natl Acad Pr.

Pressure Ulcers: Principles & Techniques in Management. Ed. by Mark B. Constantian. 320p. 1980. text ed. 32.50 (ISBN 0-316-15330-3). Little.

Pressure Vessel Codes: Their Application to Nuclear Reactor Systems. (Technical Reports: No. 56). 1966. pap. 2.75 (ISBN 92-0-155066-9, IAEA). Unipub.

Pressure Vessel Engineering Technology. Ed. by R. W. Nichols. (Illus.). 1970. 89.50x (ISBN 0-444-20061-4). Intl Ideas.

Pressure Vessel Handbook. 5th ed. Eugene F. Magyesy. (Illus.). Date not set. 35.00 (ISBN 0-914458-07-8). Pressure.

Pressworking: Stampings & Dies. Ed. by Karl Keyes. LC 80-53009. (Manufacturing Update Ser.). (Illus.). 260p. 1980. 29.00 (ISBN 0-87263-061-7). SME.

Prestige & Association in an Urban Community: An Analysis of an Urban Stratification System. Edward O. Laumann. LC 66-29709. (Orig.). 1966. pap. 4.95 (ISBN 0-672-60620-8). Bobbs.

Prestige & Profit: The Development of Entrepreneurial Abilities in Taiwan 1880-1972. Manfred Steinhoff. (Development Studies Centre Monograph: No. 20). (Illus.). 153p. (Orig.). 1980. pap. text ed. 11.95 (ISBN 0-909150-94-X, 0588). Bks Australia.

Preston Smith: The Making of a Texas Governor. Jerry D. Conn. (Illus.). 173p. 8.50 (ISBN 0-8363-0078-5). Jenkins.

Prestressed Concrete Designers Handbook. 2nd ed. P. W.. Abeles et al. (C & CA Viewpoint Publication Ser.). (Illus.). 467p. 1976. pap. text ed. 42.50 (ISBN 0-7210-1028-8). Scholium Intl.

Prestressed Concrete Pressure Vessels. Thomas Telford Ltd. Editorial Staff. 762p. 1980. 79.00x (ISBN 0-901948-45-4, Pub. by Telford England). State Mutual England.

Presumption of Atheism & Other Philosophical Essays on God, Freedom & Immortality. Antony Flew. LC 75-43411. 183p. 1976. text ed. 22.50x (ISBN 0-06-492119-0). B&N.

Presupposition & the Delinitation of Semantic. Ruth M. Kempson. LC 74-25078. (Studies in Linguistics Monographs: No. 15). 260p. 1975. 39.95 (ISBN 0-521-20733-9); pap. 11.95x (ISBN 0-521-09938-2). Cambridge U Pr.

Presuppositions of Human Communication. Ramchandra Gandhi. 156p. 1974. 4.50x o.p. (ISBN 0-19-560310-9). Oxford U Pr.

Presynadtic Receptors: Proceedings of the Satellite Symposium, Paris, July 22-23 1978, 7th International Congress of Pharmacology. S. Z. Langer et al. (Illus.). 414p. 1979. 65.00 (ISBN 0-08-023190-X). Pergamon.

Pret a Lire. Gustave W. Andrian & Jane Davies. 1980. pap. write for info. (ISBN 0-02-303440-8). Macmillan.

Pretend the World Is Funny & Forever: A Psychological Analysis of Comedians, Clowns, & Actors. Seymour Fisher & Rhoda L. Fisher. LC 80-7777. 288p. 1981. profess. & reference 19.95 (ISBN 0-89859-073-6). L Erlbaum Assocs.

Pretender. S. Mokashi-Punekar. 6.75 (ISBN 0-89253-702-7); flexible cloth 4.00 (ISBN 0-89253-703-5). Ind-US Inc.

Preterm Birth & Psychological Development. Ed. by Sarah L. Friedman & Marian Sigman. LC 80-980. (Developmental Psychology Ser.). 1980. 34.00 (ISBN 0-12-267880-X). Acad Pr.

PreTest for Physicians Preparing for the ECFMG Examination. 2nd ed. (Pretest Series). (Illus.). 1976. pap. 25.00 (ISBN 0-07-079140-6). McGraw-Pretest.

PreTest for Students Preparing for the National Board Examinafion, Pt. II. 4th ed. Ed. by Pretest Series. LC 77-78442. 1978. pap. 17.50 (ISBN 0-07-079139-2). McGraw-Pretest.

PreTest for Students Preparing for the National Board Examination, Pt. 1. 4th ed. Pretest Series. LC 77-78442. (Illus.). 1977. pap. 17.50 (ISBN 0-07-079138-4). McGraw-Pretest.
PreTest for Students Preparing for the State Board Examinations for Practical Nurse Licensure. 2nd ed. Ed. by Pretest Series. LC 78-56568. 1979. pap. 13.95 (ISBN 0-07-079132-5). McGraw-Pretest.
PreTest for Students Preparing for the State Board Examinations for Registered Nurse Licensure. 4th ed. Ed. by Pretest Series. LC 78-51705. 1979. pap. 13.95 (ISBN 0-07-079130-9). McGraw-Pretest.
Pretrial Conference & Effective Justice: A Controlled Test in Personal Injury Litigation. Maurice Rosenberg. LC 64-8492. (Illus.). 1964. 20.00x (ISBN 0-231-02780-X). Columbia U Pr.
Pretrial Delay: A Review & Bibliography. National Center for State Courts. 1978. pap. 4.00 (ISBN 0-89656-024-4, R0036). Natl Ctr St Courts.
Pretrial Intervention Strategies: An Evaluation of Policy-Related Research & Policymaker Perceptions. Roberta Rovner-Pieczník. LC 75-43473. (Illus.). 1976. 18.95 (ISBN 0-669-00566-5). Lexington Bks.
Prettier Than the Black Pea Flower. Prithvindra Chakravarti. (Redbird Bk.). 1976. lib. bdg. 8.00 (ISBN 0-89253-092-8); flexible bdg. 4.80 (ISBN 0-89253-147-9). Ind-US Inc.
Pretty Kitty. Zabrina Faire. 192p. (Orig.). 1981. pap. 1.75 (ISBN 0-446-94465-3). Warner Bks.
Pretty Penny. John D. Scott. LC 64-22672. 1964. 3.95 o.p. (ISBN 0-15-173951-X). HarBraceJ.
Pretty-shield, Medicine Woman of the Crows. Frank B. Linderman. LC 72-3273. (Illus.). 256p. 1974. pap. 4.95 (ISBN 0-8032-5791-0, BB 580, Bison). U of Nebr Pr.
Prevailing Prayer. Dwight L. Moody. pap. 1.50 (ISBN 0-8024-6814-4). Moody.
Prevailing Spirits: A Book of Scottish Ghost Stories. Ed. by Giles Gordon. 1979. 17.95 (ISBN 0-241-89403-4, Pub. by Hamish Hamilton England). David & Charles.
Prevent: A Handbook of Classroom Ideas to Motivate the Teaching of Elementary Safety. (Spice Ser.). (gr. k-8). 1975. 6.50 (ISBN 0-89273-115-X). Educ Serv.
Prevent Duplicating Masters: Elementary Safety, 2 vols. (Spice Ser.). 1975. 5.95 ea. Vol. 1, Grades K-4 (ISBN 0-89273-519-8). Vol. 2, Grades 4-8 (ISBN 0-89273-520-1). Educ Serv.
Prevent That Heart Attack. Tom R. Blaine. 6.95 (ISBN 0-8065-0299-1). Citadel Pr.
Preventing Aging. McCance. 1981. write for info. (ISBN 0-87527-223-1). Green.
Preventing Arterial Lipidoses. Med P. Schwandt. 300p. 1981. 27.50 (ISBN 0-87527-232-0). Green.
Preventing Burnout: The Nutritional Approach. Catherine J. Frompovich. (Illus.). 145p. Date not set. pap. 50.00 course materials (ISBN 0-935322-14-0). C J Frompovich.
Preventing Crime. Ed. by James A. Cramer. LC 78-8400. (Sage Criminal Justice System Annuals: Vol. 10). 1978. 20.00x (ISBN 0-8039-1047-9); pap. 9.95x (ISBN 0-8039-1048-7). Sage.
Preventing Dental Caries. G. Neil Jenkins. 1981. write for info (ISBN 0-87527-217-7). Green.
Preventing Hypertension. Herbert G. Langford & Robert Watson. 280p. 1981. 22.50 (ISBN 0-87527-185-5). Green. Postponed.
Preventing Legal Malpractice. Jeffery M. Smith. 160p. 1981. pap. text ed. 7.95 (ISBN 0-8299-2118-4). West Pub.
Preventing Mental Depression. Michael R. Lowry. 300p. 1981. 22.50 (ISBN 0-87527-186-3). Green.
Preventing Misbehavior in Children. Dewey J. Moore. 184p. 1972. 13.50 (ISBN 0-398-02364-6); pap. 6.75 (ISBN 0-398-02487-1). C C Thomas.
Preventing Neurologic Syndromes. James R. Merikangas. 250p. 1981. 22.50 (ISBN 0-87527-224-X). Green. Postponed.
Preventing Nuclear Theft: Guidelines for Industry & Government. Ed. by Robert B. Leachman & Philip Althoff. LC 72-76452. (Special Studies in U.S. Economic, Social & Political Issues). 1972. 28.50x (ISBN 0-275-28618-5). Irvington.
Preventing Reactive Hypoglycemia. Fred D. Hofeldt. 300p. 1981. 27.50 (ISBN 0-87527-214-2). Green.
Preventing Viral Hepatitis. Richard E. Sampliner. 300p. 1981. 22.50 (ISBN 0-87527-229-0). Green. Postponed.
Prevention & Control of Fires in Ships. Ed. by Royal Institution of Naval Architects & Institute of Marine Engineering. (Illus.). 1976. 15.00 (ISBN 0-686-16691-4, Pub. by Inst Marine Eng). Intl Schol Bk Serv.
Prevention & Rehabilitation in Ischemic Heart Disease. Charles Long. (Rehabilitation Medicine Library Ser.). (Illus.). 424p. 1980. 39.95 (ISBN 0-683-05150-4). Williams & Wilkins.
Prevention in Mental Health: Research, Policy, & Practice. Ed. by Richard H. Price et al. LC 80-14676. (Sage Annual Reviews of Community Mental Health: Vol. 1). (Illus.). 320p. 1980. 20.00x (ISBN 0-8039-1468-7); pap. 9.95x (ISBN 0-8039-1469-5). Sage.
Prevention of Alcoholism Through Nutrition. Roger J. Williams. 176p. (Orig.). 1981. pap. 2.50 (ISBN 0-553-14502-9). Bantam.
Prevention of Breast Cancer. A. N. Papsioannou. 1981. write for info. (ISBN 0-87527-227-4). Green.
Prevention of Crime & Delinquency. Alan R. Coffey. (Illus.). 400p. 1975. 16.95 (ISBN 0-13-699157-2). P-H.
Prevention of Food Poisoning. Jill Trickett. 1980. 11.85x (ISBN 0-85950-084-5, Pub. by Thornes England). State Mutual Bk.
Prevention of Genetic Disease & Mental Retardation. Aubrey Milunsky. LC 74-21015. (Illus.). 450p. 1975. 29.00 (ISBN 0-7216-6395-8). Saunders.
Prevention of Handicap & the Health of Women. Margaret Wynn & Arthur Wynn. (Inequality in Society Ser.). (Illus.). 1979. 27.00 (ISBN 0-7100-0284-X). Routledge & Kegan.
Prevention of Mental Retardation & Other Developmental Disabilities. McCormack. 680p. 1980. 49.75 (ISBN 0-8247-6950-3). Dekker.
Prevention of Microbial & Parasitic Hazard Associated with Processed Foods: A Guide for the Food Processor. Food & Nutrition Board, National Research Council. 1975. pap. 5.75 (ISBN 0-309-02345-9). Natl Acad Pr.
Prevention of Obstruction of Coronary & Vital Arteries. new ed. William Dock. 316p. 1981. 38.50 (ISBN 0-87527-202-9). Green.
Prevention of Occupational Cancer. Ed. by Charles R. Shaw. 256p. 1981. 72.95 (ISBN 0-8493-5625-3). CRC Pr.
Prevention of Oil Pollution. J. Wardley-Smith. LC 79-63534. 1979. 49.95x (ISBN 0-470-26718-6). Halsted Pr.
Prevention of Psychiatric Disorders in Children. Thomas Stapleton. 244p. 1981. 16.00 (ISBN 0-87527-234-7). Green.
Prevention of Structural Failures. 1978. 32.00 (ISBN 0-87170-006-9). ASM.
Prevention of Venous Thrombosis & Pulmonary Thromboembolism. J. G. Sharnoff. (Medical Publicatons Ser.). 1980. lib. bdg. 25.00 (ISBN 0-8161-2223-7). G K Hall.
Prevention Through Political Action & Social Change. Ed. by Justin M. Joffe. (Primary Prevention of Psychopathology Ser.: No. 5). 330p. 1981. 20.00 (ISBN 0-87451-187-9). U Pr of New Eng.
Preventive & Community Medicine. 2nd ed. Ed. by Duncan W. Clark & Brian Macmahon. 1981. pap. text ed. price not set (ISBN 0-316-14596-3). Little.
Preventive Dentistry. Leon Silverstone. (Illus.). 1978. text ed. 12.50x (ISBN 0-906141-06-0, Pub. by Update Pubns. England). Kluwer Boston.
Preventive Dentistry for the Patient. J. Edward Shephard. (Illus.). 136p. 1972. pap. 3.75 (ISBN 0-398-02480-4). C C Thomas.
Preventive Intervention in Social Work. National Association of Social Workers. Ed. by Carol H. Meyer. LC 74-83318. (NASW Modulr Ser.). 128p. 1974. Set. pap. text ed. 6.00x (ISBN 0-87101-001-1, CAO-001-I). Natl Assn Soc Wkrs.
Preventive Maintenance in a Corrugated Container Plant. Clinton C. Bell. (TAPPI Press Reports Ser.). (Illus.). 56p. 1981. pap. write for info. (ISBN 0-89852-388-5, 01-01-R088). Tappi.
Preventive Point of View. Howard L. Ward. (Amer. Lec in Dentistry Ser.). (Illus.). 600p. 1978. 43.75 (ISBN 0-398-03616-0). C C Thomas.
Preventive Primary Medicine: Reducing the Major Causes of Mortality. Robert Lewy. 1980. pap. text ed. 9.95 (ISBN 0-316-52401-8). Little.
Preventive Psychiatry in the Armed Forces: With Some Implications for Civilian Use, Vol. 4. GAP Committee on Governmental Agencies. (Report No. 47). 1960. pap. 2.00 (ISBN 0-87318-062-3). Adv Psychiatry.
Prevert Vous Parle. Ed. by A. Bergens & D. Noakes. (Fr.). 1968. pap. 8.50 (ISBN 0-13-699231-5). P-H.
Prevocational Series, 13 bks. Incl. Air Conditioning-Refrigeration Repairman (ISBN 0-8273-0506-0); Automobile Mechanic (ISBN 0-8273-0507-9); Building Maintenance Worker (ISBN 0-8273-0508-7); Choosing Your Job (ISBN 0-8273-0505-2); Electronics Technician (ISBN 0-8273-0509-5); Finding a Job Through the Newspaper (ISBN 0-8273-0504-4); Finding & Holding a Job (ISBN 0-8273-0503-6); Food Service Worker (ISBN 0-8273-0510-9); Heating Technician (ISBN 0-8273-0511-7); Household Appliance Repairman (ISBN 0-8273-0512-5); Office Machine Repairman (ISBN 0-8273-0513-3); Office Occupations (ISBN 0-8273-0514-1); Starting in the Right Direction (ISBN 0-8273-0502-8). 1970. Set. pap. 20.60 o.p. (ISBN 0-8273-0500-1); pap. 1.80 ea. o.p.; ans. key 0.35 o.p. (ISBN 0-8273-0501-X). Delmar.
Prevocational Training for Retarded Students. Dennis E. Mithang. (Illus.). 304p. 1981. text ed. 29.50 (ISBN 0-398-04111-3). C C Thomas.
Prey. Robert A. Smith. 1978. pap. 1.95 o.p. (ISBN 0-449-13923-9, GM). Fawcett.
Price. David Chacko. LC 78-21360. 1979. pap. 3.95 o.p. (ISBN 0-312-64211-3). St Martin.
Price & Value in the Aristotelian Tradition: A Study in Scholastic Economics. Odd Langholm. 1979. 28.00x (ISBN 82-00-01840-7, Dist. by Columbia U Pr.). Universitet.
Price Controls, Physician Fees, & Physician Incomes from Medicare & Medicaid. John Holahan & William Scanlon. (Institute Paper). 110p. 1978. pap. 4.50 (ISBN 0-87766-219-3, 21800). Urban Inst.
Price Determination & Prices Policy. Joan Mitchell. (Economic & Society Ser.). 1977. text ed. 19.95x (ISBN 0-04-338084-0); pap. text ed. 8.95x (ISBN 0-04-338085-9). Allen Unwin.
Price Formation & Marging Behaviour of Meat in the Netherlands & the Federal Republic of Germany. (Agricultural Research Reports: No. 856). 1979. pap. 40.00 (ISBN 90-220-0610-7, PDC140, PUDOC). Unipub.
Price Guide for Composition Dolls. 3rd ed. 1981. 6.50 (ISBN 0-686-69470-8). R Shoemaker.
Price Guide for Madame Alexander Dolls. 3rd ed. 1981. 7.50 (ISBN 0-686-69471-6). R Shoemaker.
Price Guide to American Country Pottery. Don Raycraft & Carol Raycraft. 1976. 1.50 o.p. (ISBN 0-87069-150-3). Wallace-Homestead.
Price Guide to Antique & Classic Still Cameras 1981-1982. James M. McKeown & Joan C. McKeown. LC 81-65028. (Illus.). 176p. 1981. pap. 12.95 (ISBN 0-931838-01-0). Centennial Photo Serv.
Price Guide to Antiques & Pattern Glass. 6th ed. Ed. by Robert W. Miller. (Illus.). 9.95 o.p. (ISBN 0-87069-281-X). Wallace-Homestead.
Price Guide to Country Antiques & American Primitives. Dorothy Hammond. (Funk & W Bk.). (Illus.). 1975. pap. 6.95 o.s.i. (ISBN 0-308-10184-7, TYC-T). T Y Crowell.
Price Guide to Madame Alexander Dolls. Patricia Smith. (No. 6). (Illus.). 1980. 3.95 o.p. (ISBN 0-89145-136-6). Collector Bks.
Price Guide to Madame Alexander Dolls, No. 7. Patricia Smith. (Illus.). 1981. 3.95 (ISBN 0-89145-167-6). Collector Bks.
Price Index. S. N. Afriat. LC 77-2134. (Illus.). 1978. 29.50 (ISBN 0-521-21665-6). Cambridge U Pr.
Price of Detente. Allan C. Brownfeld. 180p. 1981. 10.00 (ISBN 0-8159-6517-6). Devin.
Price of Free Land. Treva A. Strait. LC 78-24287. (Illus.). (gr. 4-6). 1979. 8.95 (ISBN 0-397-31836-7). Lippincott.
Price of Freedom. Howard Temperley. 1981. text ed. 16.50x (ISBN 0-391-01148-0). Humanities.
Price of International Justice. Philip C. Jessup. LC 76-158460. (Jacob Blaustein Lectures in International Affairs Ser.: No. 2). 1971. 17.50x (ISBN 0-231-03545-4). Columbia U Pr.
Price of Liberty. Alan Barth. LC 74-176486. (Civil Liberties in American History Ser.). 1972. Repr. of 1961 ed. lib. bdg. 25.00 (ISBN 0-306-70416-1). Da Capo.
Price of Liberty. Rosemary Thomson. 1978. 3.95 (ISBN 0-88419-183-4, Pub by Mansions Pr). Creation Hse.
Price of Liberty: Perspectives on Civil Liberties by Member of the A.C.L.U. Ed. by Alan Reitman. 1968. 6.95x (ISBN 0-393-05284-2, Norton Lib); pap. 1.95 1969 (ISBN 0-393-00505-4). Norton.
Price of Progress: Cobbett's England Seventeen Eighty to Eighteen Thirty-Five. John Clarke. 224p. 1980. text ed. 18.25x (ISBN 0-246-10604-2). Humanities.
Price of Reindeer. John Elsberg. (WEP Poetry Ser.: No. 2). 1979. pap. 1.50 (ISBN 0-917976-05-3). White Ewe.
Price of Vengeance. Freda Michel. 1977. pap. 1.50 o.p. (ISBN 0-449-23211-5, Crest). Fawcett.
Price Systems Res. Alloc. Leftwich. 1979. 20.95 (ISBN 0-03-045421-2). Dryden Pr.
Price Tags of Life. C. Roy Angell. LC 59-9692. 1959. 3.95 (ISBN 0-8054-5108-0). Broadman.
Price-Theory: A Policy-Welfare Approach. Richard K. Armey. (Illus.). 1977. 17.95 (ISBN 0-13-699694-9). P-H.
Price Theory & Applications. 2nd ed. Jack Hirshleifer. (Illus.). 1980. text ed. 19.95 (ISBN 0-13-699710-4). P-H.
Price Theory & Its Uses. 5th ed. Donald S. Watson & Malcolm Getz. LC 80-82461. (Illus.). 480p. 1981. text ed. 18.95 (ISBN 0-395-30056-8); write for info. instr's manual (ISBN 0-395-30057-6). HM.
Price Theory & Its Uses. 4th ed. Donald S. Watson & Mary A. Holman. LC 76-14003. (Illus.). 1976. text ed. 18.50 (ISBN 0-395-24422-6); inst. manual 1.25 (ISBN 0-395-24423-4). HM.
Price Theory & Price Policy. M. A. Van Meerhaeghe. 1969. text ed. 7.00x (ISBN 0-582-50005-2). Humanities.
Price Theory in Action. 4th ed. Donald S. Watson & Malcolm Getz. 448p. 1981. pap. text ed. 9.95 (ISBN 0-395-30058-4); write for info. instr's manual (ISBN 0-395-30057-6). HM.
Price Theory in Action: A Book of Readings. 3rd ed. Ed. by Donald S. Watson. LC 72-85910. 450p. (Orig.). 1973. pap. text ed. 12.50 (ISBN 0-395-15073-6, 3-58884). HM.
Price Warung (William Astley) Barry Andrews. (World Authors Ser.: Australia: No. 383). 1976. lib. bdg. 12.50 (ISBN 0-8057-6225-6). Twayne.
Priceless Cats & Other Italian Folk Stories. Moritz A. Jagendorf. LC 56-12039. (Illus.). (gr. 4-6). 7.95 (ISBN 0-8149-0330-4). Vanguard.
Priceless Gifts: A Psychologist Guide to Loving & Caring. Daniel A. Sugarman. 1978. 9.95 (ISBN 0-02-615270-3). Macmillan.
Priceless Heritage: The Future of Museums. Ian Finlay. 1977. 12.95 o.p. (ISBN 0-571-09107-5, Pub. by Faber & Faber). Merrimack Bk Serv.
Priceless Pearl. Ruhiyyih Rabbani. (Illus.). 1969. pap. 8.00 (ISBN 0-900125-03-9, 7-31-48). Baha'i.
Prices & Profits in the Pharmaceutical Industry. M. H. Cooper. 1967. 25.00 (ISBN 0-08-012178-0); pap. 12.75 (ISBN 0-08-012177-2). Pergamon.
Prices & Quantities: A Macroeconomic Analysis. Arthur M. Okun. 400p. 1981. 19.95 (ISBN 0-8157-6480-4); pap. 7.95 (ISBN 0-8157-6479-0). Brookings.
Prices & Wages in England: From the Twelfth to the Nineteenth Century, Vol. 1 Price Tables-mercantile Era. William H. Beveridge. LC 66-6277. 1939. 45.00x (ISBN 0-678-05154-2). Kelley.
Prices for Dolls 1977. Dorothy Coleman. (Illus.). 1976. pap. 3.00 o.p. (ISBN 0-87588-134-3). Hobby Hse.
Prices of Agricultural Products & Selected Inputs in Europe & North America 1978-79. 88p. 1980. pap. 13.00 (ISBN 0-686-68965-8, UN80/2E7, UN). Unipub.
Prices Through the Years: A Model for Preparing Your Family Roots. Jean Ivey. Ed. by Moseqelle White. 120p. 1980. pap. 9.95x (ISBN 0-936026-07-3). R&M Pub Co.
Pricing & Promotion: A Guide for Craftspeople. American Craft Council. Ed. by Patrick McGuire & Lois Moran. 93p. 1979. 7.20 (ISBN 0-88321-024-X). Am Craft.
Pricing Decisions: A Practical Guide to Interdivisional Transfer Pricing Policy. Alexander Young. 223p. 1979. text ed. 36.75x (ISBN 0-220-67002-1, Pub. by Busn Bks England). Renouf.
Pricing Function: A Pragmatic Approach. Ed. by Ivan Vernon, Jr. & Charles Lamb. LC 75-34945. 320p. 1976. 22.95 (ISBN 0-669-00440-5). Lexington Bks.
Pricing in Regulated Industries Theory & Application Two. Mountain States Telephone & Telegraph Company. Ed. by John T. Wenders. LC 79-83623. (Illus.). 1979. 5.00 o.p. (ISBN 0-9602580-1-9). Mountain St Tel.
Pricing: Principles & Practices. Andre Gabor. 1977. text ed. 36.95x (ISBN 0-435-84365-6); pap. text ed. 15.95x (ISBN 0-435-84366-4). Heinemann Ed.
Pricing Strategies. Alfred R. Oxenfeldt. LC 74-78207. (Illus.). 272p. 1975. 18.95 (ISBN 0-8144-5368-6). Am Mgmt.
Priciples & Methods of Adapted Physical Education & Recreation. 4th ed. Walter C. Crowe et al. (Illus.). 602p. 1981. text ed. 20.95 (ISBN 0-8016-0327-7). Mosby.
Prick up Your Ears. John Lahr. 1979. pap. 3.50 (ISBN 0-380-48629-6, 48629, Discus). Avon.
Prickly Pig. Gillian McClure. (Illus.). (ps-1). 1980. 6.95 (ISBN 0-233-96780-X). Andre Deutsch.
Prickly Plant Book. Sue Tarsky. (Illus.). 48p. (gr. 5 up). 1981. 9.95 (ISBN 0-316-83207-3). Little.

Pride: A Handbook of Classroom Ideas to Motivate the Teaching of Elementary Black Studies. (Spice Ser). 1971. 5.25 o.p. (ISBN 0-89273-110-9). Educ Serv.

Pride Against Prejudice: Work in the Lives of Older Blacks & Young Puerto Ricans. Dean W. Morse. LC 78-65534. (Conservation of Human Resources Ser.: No. 9). 260p. 1980. text ed. 21.00 (ISBN 0-916672-67-0). Allanheld.

Pride & Prejudice. Jane Austen. (Literature Ser). (gr. 7-12). 1969. pap. text ed. 3.50 (ISBN 0-87720-711-9). AMSCO Sch.

Pride & Prejudice. Jane Austen. (Illus.). (gr. 9 up). 1962. PLB 5.25 o.s.i. (ISBN 0-02-707710-1). Macmillan.

Pride & Prejudice. Jane Austen. 1976. pap. 2.95 (ISBN 0-460-01022-0, Evman). Dutton.

Pride & Prejudice. Jane Austen. lib. bdg. 15.95x (ISBN 0-89966-243-9). Buccaneer Bks.

Pride & Prejudice. Jane Austen. pap. 1.50. Bantam.

Pride & Prejudice. Jane Austen. 1980. lib. bdg. 13.95 (ISBN 0-8161-3076-0, Large Print Bks). G K Hall.

Pride & Prejudice. Jane Austen. Ed. by Tony Tanner. Date not set. pap. 1.95 (ISBN 0-14-005774-9). Penguin.

Pride & Solace: The Functions & Limits of Political Theory. Norman Jacobson. 1978. 12.95 (ISBN 0-520-03438-4). U of Cal Pr.

Pride & Splendor. Jean Pedrick. LC 75-23818. 72p. 1976. pap. 4.95 (ISBN 0-914086-10-3). Alicejamesbooks.

Pride & the Anguish. Douglas Reeman. pap. 1.95 (ISBN 0-515-05357-0). Jove Pubns.

Pride & the Poor Princes, No. 134. Barbara Cartland. 160p. (Orig.). 1981. pap. 1.75 (ISBN 0-553-13032-3). Bantam.

Pride Is for Peacocks, Young Readers Ser. Kelly L. Segraves. (Young Readers Ser.). (Illus.). Date not set. pap. 2.95 (ISBN 0-89293-078-0). Beta Bk.

Pride of Monsters. James H. Schmitz. LC 72-85788. 248p. 1973. pap. 1.25 o.s.i. (ISBN 0-02-024860-1, Collier). Macmillan.

Pride of Perth: The Story of Arthur Bell & Sons Ltd. Scotch Whiskey Distillers. Jack House. (Illus.). 1976. text ed. 9.25x (ISBN 0-09-127320-X). Humanities.

Pride of the Golden Bear. Betty S. Gibson. 560p. 1981. text ed. 23.75 (ISBN 0-8403-2397-2). Kendall-Hunt.

Pride of the Trevallions. Carola Salisbury. 240p. 1978. pap. 1.75 o.p. (ISBN 0-449-23722-2, Crest). Fawcett.

Pride of the Wineries: The California Living Wine Report. Ed. by Harold I. Silverman. LC 80-66282. (Illus.). 192p. (Orig.). 1980. pap. 5.95 (ISBN 0-89395-042-4). Cal Living Bks.

Pride's Purge. David Underdown. 1971. 37.50x (ISBN 0-19-822342-0). Oxford U Pr.

Pridolian & Early Gedinnian Age Brachiopods from the Roberts Mountains Formation of Central Nevada. J. G. Johnson et al. (U. C. Publ. in Geological Sciences: Vol. 100). 1973. pap. 11.00x (ISBN 0-520-09447-6). U of Cal Pr.

Priest. Don Gold. LC 80-22752. 320p. 1981. 13.95 (ISBN 0-03-053981-1). Hr&W.

Priest & Bishop. Raymond E. Brown. LC 78-139594. 1970. pap. 2.95 (ISBN 0-8091-1661-8). Paulist Pr.

Priest Forever. Carter Heyward. LC 75-38932. (Illus.). 160p. 1976. 6.95 o.p. (ISBN 0-06-063893-1, HarpR). Har-Row.

Priest in Community: Exploring the Roots of Ministry. Urban Holmes. LC 78-17645. 1978. 8.95 (ISBN 0-8164-0400-3). Crossroad NY.

Priest in the House. Emile Zola. 1957. 13.95 (ISBN 0-236-30964-1, Pub. by Paul Elek). Merrimack Bk Serv.

Priest of Love: A Life of D. H. Lawrence. rev ed. Harry T. Moore. LC 77-5714. (Illus.). 516p. 1977. pap. 12.95 (ISBN 0-8093-0839-8). S Ill U Pr.

Priesthood. Karl Rahner. Tr. by Edward Quinn from German. LC 72-94304. 288p. 1973. Repr. of 1970 ed. 8.95 (ISBN 0-8164-1106-9). Crossroad NY.

Priesthood of Christ & His Ministers. Andre Feuillet. LC 74-9446. 312p. 1975. 8.95 o.p. (ISBN 0-385-06009-2). Doubleday.

Priesthood, Old & New. Edward Laity. 1980. 1.95 (ISBN 0-86544-012-3). Salvation Army.

Priests & People: A No-Rent Romance. Ed. by Robert L. Wolff. (Ireland-Nineteenth Century Fiction Ser.: Vol. 77). 1979. lib. bdg. 126.00 (ISBN 0-8240-3526-7); lib. bdg. 46.00 ea. Garland Pub.

Priests in Council: Initiatives Toward a Democratic Church. Francis F. Brown. 1979. 20.00 o.p. (ISBN 0-8362-3301-8). Andrews & McMeel.

Priests of Ancient Egypt. Serge Sauneron. LC 59-10792. (Illus.). 192p. 1980. pap. 3.50 (ISBN 0-394-17410-0, B433, BC). Grove.

Priests, Warriors & Cattle: A Study in the Ecology of Religions. Bruce Lincoln. LC 78-68826. (Hermeneutics: Studies in the History of Religions). 240p. 1981. 20.00x (ISBN 0-520-03880-0). U of Cal Pr.

Prigionia Di un Artistaa: Il Romanzo Di Luigi Cherubini, 2 vols. Giulio Confalonieri. LC 80-2267. 1981. Repr. of 1948 ed. 78.00 (ISBN 0-404-18820-6). AMS Pr.

Prima Donna. Nancy Freedman. LC 80-21568. 320p. 1981. 10.95 (ISBN 0-688-03730-5). Morrow.

Prima Donna: Her History & Surroundings from the 17th to the 19th Century, 2 vols, Vol. 1. H. Sutherland Edwards. LC 77-17875. (Music Reprint Ser.). 1978. Repr. of 1888 ed. Set. lib. bdg. 45.00 (ISBN 0-306-77558-1). Da Capo.

Primacy of Practice: Essays Towards a Pragmatically Kantian Theory of Empirical Knowledge. Nicholas Rescher. 1973. 25.00x (ISBN 0-631-15020-X, Pub. by Basil Blackwell). Biblio Dist.

Primal Man: The New Consciousness. Arthur Janov & E. Michael Holden. LC 75-20416. (Illus.). 522p. 1976. 10.00 o.s.i. (ISBN 0-690-01015-X, TYC-T). T Y Crowell.

Primal Scream. Arthur Janov. 448p. 1981. pap. 6.95 (ISBN 0-399-50537-7, Perigee). Putnam.

Primaries & Conventions. Roy Hoopes. (Impact Bks.). (Illus.). (gr. 7 up). 1978. PLB 6.90 s&l (ISBN 0-531-01356-1). Watts.

Primarily BASIC. George L. Miller. 160p. (Orig.). pap. text ed. 9.95 (ISBN 0-8403-2177-5). Kendall-Hunt.

Primarily Me. Irene Hubbard & Lori Soderstrom. (gr. k-3). 1976. 9.50 (ISBN 0-916456-09-9, GA65). Good Apple.

Primarily Time. Lou Soderstrom. (gr. k-3). 1978. 7.95 (ISBN 0-916456-28-5, GA92). Good Apple.

Primary Acoustic Nuclei. Ed. by Raphael Lorente De No. Orig. Title: Cochlear Nuclei. (Illus.). 189p. 1981. text ed. 25.00 (ISBN 0-89004-318-3). Raven.

Primary Aeronautical Language Manual. Deborah J. Balter. Date not set. pap. 30.95. Aviation.

Primary Care of Young Adults: A Practitioner's Manual. Katharine E. Reichert. 1976. pap. 13.00 (ISBN 0-87488-986-3). Med Exam.

Primary Care Techniques: Laboratory Tests in Ambulatory Facilities. 1st ed. Ed. by Rita A. Fleming. LC 79-20295. (Illus.). 1980. pap. text ed. 9.50 (ISBN 0-8016-1592-5). Mosby.

Primary Commodities in International Trade. John W. Rowe. (Orig.). 1966. 41.50 (ISBN 0-521-06144-X); pap. 14.95x (ISBN 0-521-09277-9). Cambridge U Pr.

Primary Curriculum. Geva Blenkin & A. V. Kelly. 1981. text ed. 21.00 (ISBN 0-06-318121-5, IntlDept); pap. text ed. 11.90 (ISBN 0-06-318121-5). Har-Row.

Primary Dictionary Series, 4 bks. Incl. Bk. 1. (ps-1). pap. text ed. 1.50 (ISBN 0-515-05226-4); Bk. 2. (gr. 1-3). pap. text ed. 1.95 (ISBN 0-515-05837-8); Bk. 3. (gr. 3-5). text ed. 1.95 (ISBN 0-515-05836-X); Bk. 4. (gr. 5-7). text ed. 2.50 (ISBN 0-515-05969-2). Jove Pubns.

Primary Elections in the South: A Study in Uniparty Politics. Cortez A. Ewing. LC 80-12616. (Illus.). xii, 112p. 1980. Repr. of 1953 ed. lib. bdg. 14.75x (ISBN 0-313-22452-8, EWPR). Greenwood.

Primary French in the Balance: Main Report. Clare Burstall. (Research Reports Ser.). 304p. 1974. pap. text ed. 16.25x (ISBN 0-85633-052-3, NFER). Humanities.

Primary Health Care of the Young. Jane Fox. (Illus.). 1024p. 1980. text ed. 25.95 (ISBN 0-07-021741-6). McGraw.

Primary Homotopy Theory. Joseph Neisendorfer. LC 80-12109. (Memoirs of the American Mathematical Society Ser.). 1980. 4.00 (ISBN 0-8218-2232-2, MEMO-232). Am Math.

Primary Language of Poetry in the 1640's. Josephine Miles. LC 78-11614. (Univ. of California Publications in English: Vol. 19, No. 1). (Illus.). 160p. 1979. Repr. of 1948 ed. lib. bdg. 16.50x (ISBN 0-313-20661-9, MIPP). Greenwood.

Primary Metabolism: A Mechanistic Approach. J. Staunton. (Illus.). 1978. text ed. 24.00x (ISBN 0-19-855460-5). Oxford U Pr.

Primary Multi-Level Speller & First Dictionary. Morton Botel. (gr. k-2). 1959. pap. 3.00 (ISBN 0-931992-14-1). Penns Valley.

Primary Nursing. Ed. by Karen Ciske & Gloria Mayer. LC 79-90370. (Nursing Dimensions Ser.: Vol. VIII, No. 4). 1980. pap. text ed. 6.95 (ISBN 0-913654-60-4). Nursing Res.

Primary Nursing: Development & Management. Karen S. Zander. LC 79-28837. 361p. 1980. text ed. 25.95 (ISBN 0-89443-170-6). Aspen Systems.

Primary Prevention of Chronic Disease Beginning in Childhood. Christine L. Williams. 250p. 1981. 18.50 (ISBN 0-87527-237-1). Green.

Primary Prevention: The Possible Science. Martin Bloom. (P-H Ser. in Social Work). (Illus.). 288p. 1981. pap. text ed. 7.95 (ISBN 0-13-700062-6). P-H.

Primary Processes in Photosynthesis. Martin D. Kamen. (Advanced Biochemistry Ser). (Orig.). 1964. pap. 10.00 (ISBN 0-12-394856-8). Acad Pr.

Primary Productivity in Aquatic Environments. Ed. by Charles R. Goldman. 1966. 22.50x (ISBN 0-520-01425-1). U of Cal Pr.

Primary Productivity in the Sea: Environmental Science Research Ser. Ed. by Paul G. Falkowski. (Vol. 19). 335p. 1980. 49.50 (ISBN 0-306-40623-3). Plenum Pub.

Primary Readers. 1978. Set 4 Digraphs 10 Bks. pap. text ed. 7.68 (ISBN 0-87895-040-0). Modern Curr.

Primary Readers. Janis Raabe. 1978. Set 3 Blends 10 Bks. pap. text ed. 7.68 (ISBN 0-87895-039-7). Modern Curr.

Primary Readers, Set 1: Short Vowels. Janis A. Raabe. (Illus.). (gr. k-1). 1974. pap. text ed. 7.68 incl. tchrs' guide (ISBN 0-87895-011-7). Modern Curr.

Primary Readers, Set 2: Long Vowels. Janis A. Raabe. (Illus.). (gr. k-1). 1975. pap. text ed. 7.68 (ISBN 0-87895-026-5); tchrs. guide avail. Modern Curr.

Primary School Management. Roy Jones. 160p. 1980. 14.95 (ISBN 0-7153-7843-0). David & Charles.

Primary Trigonometric Ratios: Unit 3. Rudolph A. Zimmer. 49p. 1980. pap. text ed. 4.50 (ISBN 0-8403-2276-3). Kendall-Hunt.

Primary Wood Use in New York, No. 40. 1957. 0.70 o.p. (ISBN 0-686-20713-0). SUNY Environ.

Primate Behavior: Developments in Field & Laboratory Research, 4 vols. Ed. by Leonard A. Rosenblum. Vol. 2, 1971. 40.50 (ISBN 0-12-534002-8); Vol. 3, 1974. 32.50 (ISBN 0-12-534003-6); Vol. 4, 1975. 49.00 (ISBN 0-12-534004-4). Acad Pr.

Primate Models of Neurological Disorders. Ed. by B. S. Meldrum & C. D. Marsden. LC 74-21980. (Advances in Neurology: Vol. 10). 378p. 1975. 36.00 (ISBN 0-89004-002-8). Raven.

Primate Societies: Group Techniques of Ecological Adaptations. Hans Kummer. LC 78-140010. (Worlds of Man Ser.). 1971. text ed. 11.00x (ISBN 0-88295-612-4); pap. text ed. 5.75x (ISBN 0-88295-613-2). AHM Pub.

Primates. Irven De Vore & Sarel Eimerl. LC 65-17071. (Life Nature Library). (Illus.). (gr. 5 up). 1965. PLB 8.97 o.p. (ISBN 0-8094-0635-7, Pub. by Time-Life). Silver.

Primates. Sarel Eimerl & Irven DeVore. (Young Readers Library). (Illus.). 1977. lib. bdg. 7.98 (ISBN 0-686-51092-5). Silver.

Primavera, Vols. VI & VII. Harriet Susskind et al. Ed. by Janet R. Heller et al. LC 76-647540. (Illus.). 120p. (Orig.). 1981. pap. 5.00 (ISBN 0-916980-06-5). Primavera.

Primavera, I: Women Writers & Artists Anthology. Ed. by Janet R. Heller. (Illus.). 90p. 1975. pap. 4.00 (ISBN 0-916980-00-6). Primavera.

Primavera, II. Ed. by Janet R. Heller et al. LC 76-647540. (Illus., Orig.). 1976. pap. 4.00 (ISBN 0-916980-02-2). Primavera.

Primavera, III. Ed. by Janet R. Heller et al. LC 76-647540. (Illus.). 1977. pap. 4.00 (ISBN 0-916980-03-0). Primavera.

Primavera, IV. Lisel Mueller et al. Ed. by Janet R. Heller et al. LC 76-647540. (Illus.). 1978. pap. 4.00 (ISBN 0-916980-04-9). Primavera.

Primavera, V. Felicia Cotich et al. Ed. by Janet R. Heller et al. LC 76-647540. (Illus.). 1979. pap. 4.00 (ISBN 0-916980-05-7). Primavera.

Prime Ministers. George M. Thomson. LC 80-83530. (Illus.). 304p. 1981. 15.95 (ISBN 0-688-00432-6). Morrow.

Prime Ministers of Britain. Eileen Hellicar. LC 77-85014. 1978. 14.95 (ISBN 0-7153-7486-9). David & Charles.

Prime Movers: The Makers of Modern Dance in America. Joseph H. Mazo. LC 76-15375. (Illus.). 1978. pap. 6.95 o.p. (ISBN 0-688-08078-2, Quill). Morrow.

Prime Movers: The Makers of Modern Dance in America. Joseph H. Mazo. 1977. 12.50 o.p. (ISBN 0-688-03078-5); pap. 6.95 o.p. (ISBN 0-686-67558-4). Morrow.

Prime of Miss Jean Brodie. Muriel Spark. LC 62-7182. 1962. 3.95 o.p. (ISBN 0-397-00232-7). Lippincott.

Prime of Your Life. Joe Michaels. 288p. 1981. 17.50 (ISBN 0-87196-478-3). Facts on File.

Prime of Your Life: The Book That Makes Old Age Obsolete. Arthur S. Freese. Orig. Title: End of Senility. 192p. 1981. pap. 5.95 (ISBN 0-87795-316-3). Arbor Hse.

Prime Time. Herb Barks. 144p. 1981. pap. 3.95 (ISBN 0-8407-5768-9). Nelson.

Prime Time. Marlo Lewis & Mina B. Lewis. LC 79-89529. 1979. 10.00 o.p. (ISBN 0-312-90785-0). St Martin.

Prime Time... Marlo Lewis & Mina B. Lewis. LC 79-89529. (Illus.). 1979. 10.00 (ISBN 0-87477-107-2). J P Tarcher.

Prime Time. William D. Sheldon et al. (Breakthrough Ser.). (gr. 7-12). 1976. pap. text ed. 5.12 (ISBN 0-205-04619-3, 5246199); tchrs'. ed. 2.40 (ISBN 0-205-04620-7, 5246202); dup. masters 22.00 (ISBN 0-205-04621-5, 5246210). Allyn.

Prime-Time Television: Content & Control. Muriel G. Cantor. LC 80-12288. (The Sage Commtext Ser: No. 3). 143p. 1980. 12.50 (ISBN 0-8039-1316-8); pap. 5.95 (ISBN 0-8039-1317-6). Sage.

Primer Dia de Clases. Bill Binzen. LC 76-23788. (ps-k). 1977. PLB 4.95 (ISBN 0-385-12007-9). Doubleday.

Primer for Agricultural Libraries. 91p. 1980. pap. 15.25 (ISBN 90-220-0727-8, PDC-165, PUDOC). Unipub.

Primer for Calculus. Leonard Holder. 1978. text ed. 18.95x (ISBN 0-534-00554-3); solutions manual 6.95x (ISBN 0-534-00590-X). Wadsworth Pub.

Primer for Change. Clair B. Betteridge. 1981. 8.95 (ISBN 0-8062-1717-0). Carlton.

Primer for Film-Making: A Complete Guide to 16mm & 35mm Film Production. Kenneth H. Roberts & Win Sharples, Jr. LC 70-91620. (Illus.). 1971. 16.50 o.p. (ISBN 0-672-53582-3); pap. 11.95 (ISBN 0-672-63582-8). Pegasus.

Primer for FORTRAN IV: On-Line. Oliver Selfridge. 1972. 7.95x (ISBN 0-685-27126-9). MIT Pr.

Primer for Movement Description Using Effort Shape & Supplementary Concepts. 2nd rev. ed. Cecily Dell. LC 78-111086. (Illus.). 1970. pap. text ed. 8.95x (ISBN 0-932582-03-6). Dance Notation.

Primer for Pickles & a Reader for Relishes. Ruby C. Guthrie & Jack S. Guthrie. LC 74-18029. (Illus.). 144p. 1974. 4.95 (ISBN 0-912238-53-4); pap. 4.95 (ISBN 0-912238-52-6). One Hund One Prods.

Primer for Teachers & Leaders. LeRoy Ford. LC 63-19069. (Orig.). 1963. pap. 3.50 (ISBN 0-8054-3404-6). Broadman.

Primer in Family Therapy. W. M. Walsh. (Illus.). 152p. 1980. 13.50 (ISBN 0-398-03992-5). C C Thomas.

Primer in Neurological Staining Procedures. George Clark & Margaret P. Clark. (Illus.). 84p. 1971. text ed. 12.75 (ISBN 0-398-02176-7). C C Thomas.

Primer in Theory Construction. Paul D. Reynolds. 194p. (Orig.). 1971. pap. 4.95 (ISBN 0-672-61196-1). Bobbs.

Primer of Cardiac Arrhythmias: A Self Instructional Program. Cecelia C. Harris. LC 78-27022. 1979. pap. text ed. 9.50 (ISBN 0-8016-2070-8). Mosby.

Primer of Clinical Radiology. Thomas T. Thompson. (Illus.). 1973. pap. 13.95 o.p. (ISBN 0-316-84169-2). Little.

Primer of Clinical Radiology. 2nd ed. Thomas T. Thompson. 1980. pap. text ed. 14.95 (ISBN 0-316-84184-6). Little.

Primer of Clinical Symptoms. Robert B. Taylor. (Illus.). 1973. 12.95x o.p. (ISBN 0-06-142542-7, Harper Medical). Har-Row.

Primer of Drug Action. 2nd ed. Robert M. Julien. LC 77-13824. (Psychology Ser.). (Illus.). 1978. text ed. 16.50x o.p. (ISBN 0-7167-0053-0); pap. text ed. 8.95x (ISBN 0-7167-0052-2). W H Freeman.

Primer of Epidemiology. Gary D. Friedman. (Illus.). 256p. 1974. pap. text ed. 8.50 o.p. (ISBN 0-07-022425-0, HP). McGraw.

Primer of Gastrointestinal Fiberoptic Endoscopy. Choichi Sugawa & Bernard M. Schuman. 1981. text ed. write for info (ISBN 0-316-82150-0). Little.

Primer of Heraldry for Americans. Edward S. Holden. LC 73-2815. (Illus.). 129p. 1973. Repr. of 1898 ed. 15.00 (ISBN 0-8103-3271-X). Gale.

Primer of Infant Development. T. G. Bower. LC 76-27827. (Psychology Ser.). (Illus.). 1977. text ed. 16.95x (ISBN 0-7167-0499-4); pap. text ed. 7.95x (ISBN 0-7167-0498-6). W H Freeman.

Primer of Jungian Psychology. Calvin S. Hall & Vernon J. Nordby. 144p. 1973. pap. 1.75 (ISBN 0-451-61865-3, ME1865, Ment). NAL.

Primer of Linear Algebra. Gerald L. Bradley. (Illus.). 448p. 1975. text ed. 17.95 (ISBN 0-13-700328-5). P-H.

Primer of Medicine. 4th ed. Pappworth. LC 77-30428. (Primer Ser.). 1978. 27.50 (ISBN 0-407-62603-4). Butterworths.

Primer of Misbehavior: An Introduction to Abnormal Psychology. George R. Wesley. LC 70-185995. 216p. 1972. 12.95 (ISBN 0-911012-21-4). Nelson-Hall.

Primer of Misbehavior: An Introduction to Abnormal Psychology. George R. Wesley. (Quality Paperback: No. 262). 203p. 1975. pap. 3.50 (ISBN 0-8226-0262-8). Littlefield.

Primer of Multivariate Statistics. Richard J. Harris. 1974. text ed. 22.95 (ISBN 0-12-327250-5). Acad Pr.

Primer of Neurology & Neurophysiology. James P. Chaplin & Aline Demers. LC 78-6680. 1978. pap. text ed. 10.95 (ISBN 0-471-03027-9, Pub. by Wiley Medical). Wiley.

Primer of Population Biology. Edward O. Wilson & William H. Bossert. LC 73-155365. (Illus.). 192p. (Orig.). 1971. pap. text ed. 6.50x (ISBN 0-87893-926-1). Sinauer Assoc.

Primer of Population Genetics. Daniel L. Hartl. LC 80-23009. (Illus.). 175p. (Orig.). 1981. pap. text ed. 8.00x (ISBN 0-87893-271-2). Sinauer Assoc.

Primer of Psychobiology: Brain & Behavior. Timothy J. Teyler. LC 74-20989. (Psychology Ser.). (Illus.). 1975. text ed. 13.95x (ISBN 0-7167-0749-7); pap. text ed. 6.95x (ISBN 0-7167-0748-9); tchr's manual avail. W H Freeman.

Primer of Psychophysiology. James Hassett. LC 77-20913. (Psychology Ser.). (Illus.). 1978. text ed. 18.95x (ISBN 0-7167-0038-7); pap. text ed. 9.95x (ISBN 0-7167-0037-9). W H Freeman.

Primer of Social Casework. Elizabeth Nicholds. LC 60-12810. 1960. 17.50x (ISBN 0-231-02406-1). Columbia U Pr.

Primer of Social Psychological Theories. Stephen G. West & Robert A. Wicklund. LC 80-16292. 320p. 1980. text ed. 14.95 (ISBN 0-8185-0395-5). Brooks-Cole.

Primer of Sports Injuries. John P. Curran. (Illus.). 112p. 1968. pap. 11.75 photocopy ed. spiral (ISBN 0-398-00378-5). C C Thomas.

Primer of Structured Program Design. Gary L. Richardson et al. 1980. 17.50 (ISBN 0-89433-110-8); pap. 14.00 (ISBN 0-89433-085-3). Petrocelli.

Primer of Venous Pressure. George E. Burch. (Illus.). 176p. 1972. 14.75 (ISBN 0-398-02556-8). C C Thomas.

Primer of Verbal Behavior: An Operant View. Stephen Winokur. (Prentice Hall Experimental Psychology Ser). (Illus.). 192p. 1976. text ed. 13.95 (ISBN 0-13-700609-8). P-H.

Primer on Economic Geography. Robert B. McNee. 1970. pap. text ed. 3.95 o.p. (ISBN 0-394-31019-5). Random.

Primer on Labor Relations. Howard J. Anderson. 160p. pap. 7.50. BNA.

Primer on Monopoly & Competition. Willard F. Mueller. 1970. pap. text ed. 3.95 (ISBN 0-394-30738-0). Random.

Primer on Refraction. Ernst H. Christman. (Illus.). 128p. 1972. pap. 11.75 spiral bd. (ISBN 0-398-02258-5). C C Thomas.

Primer on Sleep & Dreaming. Rosalind D. Cartwright. LC 77-79453. (Topics in Clinical Psychology). (Illus.). 1978. pap. text ed. 7.50 (ISBN 0-201-00941-2). A-W.

Primer on Social Dynamics. K. E. Boulding. LC 70-123192. 1970. 8.95 o.s.i. (ISBN 0-02-904580-0); pap. text ed. 3.50 o.s.i. (ISBN 0-02-904570-3). Free Pr.

Primer on Teaching Reading: Basic Concepts & Skills of the Early Elementary Years. George E. Mason. LC 80-52458. 234p. 1981. pap. text ed. 7.50 (ISBN 0-87581-262-7). Peacock Pubs.

Primer on the Rorshach Technique: A Method of Administration, Scoring & Interpretation. Eugene E. Levitt. (Illus.). 116p. 1980. 14.50 (ISBN 0-398-04048-6); pap. 8.95 (ISBN 0-398-04081-8). C C Thomas.

Primer Set Furth by the Kinges Maiestie & His Clergie (1545) LC 74-5335. 175p. 1974. Repr. of 1546 ed. 20.00x (ISBN 0-8201-1129-5). Schol Facsimiles.

Primero Benavides. Lope F. Vega Capiro. Ed. by Arnold G. Reichenberger & Augusta E. Foley. LC 74-103336. (Haney Foundation Ser.). (Illus.). 406p. 1973. text ed. 27.50x (ISBN 0-8122-7637-X). U of Pa Pr.

Primeval Mechanisms. Doris Jonas & David Jonas. Date not set. 14.95 (ISBN 0-89793-006-1). Hunter Hse.

Primitive & Early Breads. Florence Laffal. LC 77-9240. (Illus.). Date not set. pap. cancelled (ISBN 0-913622-06-0). Gallery Pr. Postponed.

Primitive & Pioneer Sports for Recreation Today: Rope Spinning, Lariat Throwing, Tumblesticks, Whip Cracking, Boomerangs, Log Rolling, Boomabirds, Tomahawks, Darts, Blowguns, & Many Others. Bernard S. Mason. LC 76-162516. (Illus.). 342p. 1975. Repr. of 1937 ed. 20.00 (ISBN 0-8103-4029-1). Gale.

Primitive Architecture. Enrico Guidoni. (History of World Architecture Ser.). (Illus.). 1978. 45.00 (ISBN 0-8109-1026-8). Abrams.

Primitive Art. Franz Boas. (Illus.). 1962. 8.75 (ISBN 0-8446-1695-8). Peter Smith.

Primitive Art: Its Traditions & Styles. Paul S. Wingert. (Illus.). 1965. pap. 5.95 (ISBN 0-452-00545-0, F545, Mer). NAL.

Primitive Art: Pre-Columbian, American Indian, African, Oceanic. Ferdinand Anton et al. (Illus.). 1979. 35.00 (ISBN 0-8109-1459-X). Abrams.

Primitive Arts & Crafts. Roderick U. Sayce. (Illus.). 1963. Repr. of 1933 ed. 10.50x (ISBN 0-8196-0124-1). Biblo.

Primitive Church. Lanslots. LC 79-67862. 291p. 1980. write for info. o.p. (ISBN 0-89555-134-9). Tan Bks Pubs.

Primitive Family in Its Origin & Development. Carl N. Starcke. Ed. by Rodney Needham. LC 75-12232. 336p. pap. 14.00x (ISBN 0-226-77133-4, Midway). U of Chicago Pr.

Primitive Government. Lucy Mair. 8.00 (ISBN 0-8446-2513-2). Peter Smith.

Primitive Music. Richard Wallaschek. LC 72-125062. (Music Ser). 1970. Repr. of 1893 ed. lib. bdg. 25.00 (ISBN 0-306-70028-X). Da Capo.

Primitive Ordeal & Modern Law. H. Goitein. xvii, 302p. 1980. Repr. of 1923 ed. lib. bdg. 32.50x (ISBN 0-8377-0612-2). Rothman.

Primitive Paintings. Dimitrije Basicevic. (Alpine Fine Arts Collection). (Illus.). 300p. 1981. 85.00 (ISBN 0-933516-12-6, Pub by Alpine Fine Arts). Hippocrene Bks.

Primitive Reader: An Anthology of Myths, Tales, Songs, Riddles, & Proverbs of Aboriginal Peoples Around the World. John Greenway. LC 65-21986. viii, 211p. Repr. of 1965 ed. 15.00 (ISBN 0-8103-5014-9). Gale.

Primitive Religion & Healing: A Study of Folk Medicine in North East Brazil. Paul V. Williams. (Folklore Society Mistletoe Ser.). (Illus.). 212p. 1979. 32.50x (ISBN 0-8476-6222-5). Rowman.

Primitive Religion: Its Nature & Origin. Paul Radin. 1937. pap. text ed. 3.50 (ISBN 0-486-20393-X). Dover.

Primitive Views of the World. Ed. by Stanley Diamond. Orig. Title: Culture in History. 1964. pap. 6.00x (ISBN 0-231-08552-4). Columbia U Pr.

Primitve Ukiyo-E: From the James A. Michener Collection in the Honolulu Academy of Arts. Howard A. Link et al. LC 79-6397. (Illus.). 384p. 1980. 55.00 (ISBN 0-8248-0483-X). U Pr of Hawaii.

Primordial Bond: Exploring Connections Between Man & Nature Through the Humanities & Sciences. Stephen H. Schneider & Lynne Morton. (Illus.). 200p. 1981. 15.95 (ISBN 0-306-40519-9, Plenum Pr). Plenum Pub.

Prince. R. M. Koster. LC 78-155996. 1979. pap. 5.95 (ISBN 0-688-05108-1, Quill). Morrow.

Prince. Machiavelli. pap. 1.50. Bantam.

Prince. Niccolo Machiavelli. 1952. pap. 1.95 (ISBN 0-451-61857-2, MJ1857, Ment). NAL.

Prince. Niccolo Machiavelli. Ed. by James Atkinson. LC 75-15946. (LLA Ser: Vol. 172). 448p. 1975. pap. 9.50 (ISBN 0-672-61244-5). Bobbs.

Prince. Niccolo Machiavelli. Ed. & tr. by Robert M. Adams. 1977. 12.95 (ISBN 0-393-04448-3); pap. 3.95x (ISBN 0-393-09149-X). Norton.

Prince & I. Rosemarie Buschow. LC 80-938. 264p. 1981. 12.95 (ISBN 0-385-17111-0). Doubleday.

Prince & the Pink Blanket. Barbara Brenner. LC 80-10950. (Illus.). 32p. (gr. k-3). 1980. 8.95 (ISBN 0-590-07614-0, Four Winds). Schol Bk Serv.

Prince Caspian. C. S. Lewis. (Illus.). (gr. 4-6). 1951. 8.95 (ISBN 0-02-758550-6). Macmillan.

Prince Consort. Godfrey Scheele & Margart Scheele. 1977. 15.95 (ISBN 0-8467-0321-1, Pub. by Two Continents); pap. 9.95 (ISBN 0-8467-0322-X). Hippocrene Bks.

Prince George's Heritage. Louise J. Hienton. LC 72-86376. (Illus.). 1972. 12.50 (ISBN 0-938420-13-5). Md Hist.

Prince Henry: Duke of Gloucester. Noble Frankland. (Illus.). 343p. 1980. 25.00x (ISBN 0-297-77705-X, Pub. by Weidenfeld & Nicolson England). Biblio Dist.

Prince Henry: Duke of Gloucester. Noble Frankland. (Illus.). 343p. 1980. 25.00x (ISBN 0-297-77705-X). Biblio Dist.

Prince Henry the Navigator. W. J. Jacobs. (Visual Biography Ser). (Illus.). 64p. (gr. 4-5). 1973. PLB 4.90 o.p. (ISBN 0-531-00972-6). Watts.

Prince in Waiting. John Christopher. LC 70-119838. (gr. 5-9). 1970. 4.95 o.s.i. (ISBN 0-02-718410-2). Macmillan.

Prince in Waiting. John Christopher. LC 70-119838. 224p. (gr. 5-9). 1974. pap. 2.75 (ISBN 0-02-042400-0, 04240, Collier). Macmillan.

Prince Ito. Kengi Hamada. (Studies Injapanese History & Civilzation). 1979. Repr. of 1936 ed. 22.00 (ISBN 0-89093-267-0). U Pubns Amer.

Prince Jack. Frank Spiering. 224p. 1980. pap. 2.25 (ISBN 0-515-05496-8). Jove Pubns.

Prince: Les Delices Des Coeurs Ou Trait Des Qualites D'un Grand Roi et Systeme General D'un Sage Gouvernement. Morelly. 390p. (Fr.). 1977. Repr. of 1751 ed. lib. bdg. 47.50x o.p. (ISBN 0-8287-0639-5). Clearwater Pub.

Prince Lichnowsky & the Great War. Harry F. Young. LC 75-11448. (Illus.). 256p. 1977. 15.00x (ISBN 0-8203-0385-2). U of Ga Pr.

Prince of Abissinia: A Tale, 1759, 2 vols. in 1. Samuel Johnson. Bd. with Candide; or, All for the Best, 1759. Francois M. Voltaire. LC 74-17303. (Novel in England, 1700-1775 Ser). 1974. lib. bdg. 50.00 (ISBN 0-8240-1150-3). Garland Pub.

Prince of Carency. Marie C. Aulnoy. LC 70-170541. (Novel in England, 1700-1775 Ser). lib. bdg. 50.00 (ISBN 0-8240-0542-2). Garland Pub.

Prince of Darkness. Jean Plaidy. 320p. 1981. 10.95 (ISBN 0-686-69594-1). Putnam.

Prince of Dublin Printers: The Letters of George Faulkner. Robert E. Ward. LC 71-160053. 160p. 1972. 10.00x (ISBN 0-8131-1258-3). U Pr of Ky.

Prince of Judah & Other Stories of a Great Journey. 1962 ed. Rufus Learsi. LC 62-21985. (Illus.). (gr. 5-9). 5.95 (ISBN 0-88400-031-1). Shengold.

Prince of Librarians: The Life & Times of Antonio Panizzi of the British Museum. Edward Miller. LC 67-26123. (Illus.). 356p. 1967. 15.00x (ISBN 0-8214-0030-4). Ohio U Pr.

Prince of Martyrs: A Brief Account of Imam Husayn. A. Q. Faizi. 1977. pap. 2.25 (ISBN 0-85398-073-X, 7-39-03, Pub. by G Ronald England). Baha'i.

Prince of the Dolomites. Tomie De Paola. LC 79-18524. (Illus.). 48p. (ps-3). 1980. pap. 4.50 (ISBN 0-15-263529-7, VoyB). HarBraceJ.

Prince of the Dolomites. Tomie De Paola. LC 79-18524. (Illus.). (gr. k-3). 1980. 8.95 (ISBN 0-15-263528-9, HJ). HarBraceJ.

Prince of the Golden Apple. Michael Parks. 1975. 6.50 (ISBN 0-571-10702-8, Pub. by Faber & Faber). Merrimack Bk Serv.

Prince of the House of David. F. Ingraham & Eric Anderson. Orig. Title: Three Years in the Holy City. 363p. 1980. Repr. text ed. 9.95 (ISBN 0-89841-003-7). Zoe Pubns.

Prince of the Renaissance: The Life of Francois I. Desmond Seward. LC 73-2331. (Illus.). 264p. 1973. 14.95 o.s.i. (ISBN 0-02-609700-1). Macmillan.

Prince Philip, Duke of Edinburgh. Denis Judd. LC 80-22691. 1981. 16.95 (ISBN 0-689-11131-2). Atheneum.

Prince Prigio, Repr. Of 1889 Ed. Andrew Lang. Bd. with Prince Ricardo of Pantouflia. Repr. of 1893 ed. LC 75-32195. (Classics of Children's Literature, 1621-1932: Vol. 57). (Illus.). 1976. PLB 38.00 (ISBN 0-8240-2306-4). Garland Pub.

Prince Prigio & Prince Ricardo of Pantouflia. Andrew Lang. (Illus.). 156p. (gr. 1-6). 1980. 10.00 (ISBN 0-87923-390-7). Godine.

Prince Valium. Anton Holden. LC 80-6148. 256p. 1981. 12.95 (ISBN 0-8128-2795-3). Stein & Day.

Princes & Paupers in the English Church. Rosemary O'Day & Felicity Heal. 1981. 27.50x (ISBN 0-389-20200-2). B&N.

Princesa y el Ninito. Janice Kramer. Tr. by Fernando Villalobos from Eng. (Libros Arco Ser.). (Illus.). 32p. (Orig., Span.). (gr. 1-3). 1978. pap. 0.95 (ISBN 0-89922-127-0). Edit Caribe.

Princess. Lane. (gr. 4-6). 1980. pap. 0.95 (ISBN 0-590-30383-X, Schol Pap). Schol Bk Serv.

Princess & Curdie. George MacDonald. (New Children's Classics). (Illus.). (gr. 4-6). 1954. 3.95 o.s.i. (ISBN 0-02-761750-5). Macmillan.

Princess & Curdie. George MacDonald. Ed. by Jean Watson. (Family Library Ser.). (Illus.). 128p. 1980. 6.95 (ISBN 0-310-42310-4, 9062). Zondervan.

Princess & the Frog. (Illus.). Arabic 2.50x (ISBN 0-685-82866-2). Intl Bk Ctr.

Princess & the Goblin. George MacDonald. Ed. by Jean Watson. (Family Library Ser.). 128p. 1980. 6.95 (ISBN 0-310-42300-7, 9061). Zondervan.

Princess & the Pea. Hans C. Andersen. LC 77-12707. (Illus.). (ps-2). 1978. 8.95 (ISBN 0-395-28807-X, Clarion). HM.

Princess & the Pea. (Illus.). Arabic 2.50 (ISBN 0-685-82867-0). Intl Bk Ctr.

Princess & the Thorn. Paul Fisher. LC 80-12309. 256p. (gr. 4-8). 1980. 9.95 (ISBN 0-689-30776-4). Atheneum.

Princess Bride. William Goldman. 1977. pap. 2.50 (ISBN 0-345-29412-2, 345-25483-X-195). Ballantine.

Princess Casamassima. Henry James. (Apollo Eds.). 608p. 1976. pap. 5.95 o.s.i. (ISBN 0-8152-0395-0, A-395, TYC-T). T Y Crowell.

Princess Daisy. Judith Krantz. 512p. 1981. pap. 3.95 (ISBN 0-553-14200-3). Bantam.

Princess in the Tower. Joan Forman. (Illus.). (gr. 1-4). 1978. 7.50 (ISBN 0-571-09911-4, Pub. by Faber & Faber). Merrimack Bk Serv.

Princess Mary of Maryland. Nan H. Agle. LC 70-12561. (Illus.). viii, 109p. 1967. Repr. 15.00 (ISBN 0-8103-5029-7). Gale.

Princess of Thunder. Justin Jurs. 1980. pap. 2.50 (ISBN 0-686-69251-9, 75861). Avon.

Princess Remembers: The Memoirs of the Maharani of Jaipur. Gayatri Devi & Santha Rama Rau. LC 75-33293. (Illus.). 1977. 12.50 o.p. (ISBN 0-397-01103-2). Lippincott.

Princesse de Cleves. Marie-Madeleine De La Fayette. (Documentation thematique). (Illus., Fr.). pap. 2.95 (ISBN 0-685-14059-8, 143). Larousse.

Princesse de Cleves: Le Roman paradoxal. new ed. (Collection themes et textes). 192p. (Orig., Fr.). 1972. pap. 6.75 (ISBN 2-03-035017-6, 2663). Larousse.

Princeton Sermons. Charles Hodge. 1979. 11.95 (ISBN 0-85151-285-2). Banner of Truth.

Princeton Story: An Example of Community Tennis Planning & Programming. 1977. 5.50 (ISBN 0-938822-07-1). USTA.

Princeton Symposium of Social Insurance: Its Philosophy, Impact & Future Development. Bowen, Harbison, Lester & Somers et al. 1968. text ed. 16.95 o.p. (ISBN 0-07-006730-9, C). McGraw.

Princetonians, Seventeen Sixty-Nine to Seventeen Seventy-Five: A Biographical Dictionary. Richard A. Harrison. LC 80-7526. (Illus.). 576p. 1981. 40.00x (ISBN 0-691-04675-1). Princeton U Pr.

Principal: Change-Agent in Desegregation. Turnage. LC 72-87658. pap. 2.75 (ISBN 0-912008-07-5). Integrated Ed Assoc.

Principal Drug & Alcohol Counselor. Jack Rudman. (Career Examination Ser.: C-2743). (Cloth bdg. avail. on request). 1980. pap. 16.00 (ISBN 0-8373-2743-1). Natl Learning.

Principal Drugs: An Alphabetical Guide. 6th ed. S. J. Hopkins. 176p. 1980. pap. 5.50 (ISBN 0-571-18006-X, Pub. by Faber & Faber). Merrimack Bk Serv.

Principal Drugs: An Alphabetical Guide. rev. 5th ed. Ed. by S. J. Hopkins. 1977. pap. 3.95 o.p. (ISBN 0-571-04938-9, Pub. by Faber & Faber). Merrimack Bk Serv.

Principal Ecclesiastical Judgments Delivered in the Court of Arches 1867 to 1875. Robert Phillimore. xiii, 420p. 1981. Repr. of 1876 ed. lib. bdg. 35.00x (ISBN 0-8377-2504-6). Rothman.

Principal Grounds & Maxims with an Analysis of the Laws of England. 3rd ed. William Noy. xxviii, 219p. 1980. Repr. of 1845 ed. lib. bdg. 25.00x (ISBN 0-8377-0906-7). Rothman.

Principal in Metropolitan Schools. new ed. Ed. by Donald A. Erickson & Theodore L. Reller. LC 78-62641. (Contemporary Educational Issues Ser.). 1978. 17.50 (ISBN 0-8211-0417-9); text ed. 15.75 ten or more copies (ISBN 0-686-52389-X). McCutchan.

Principal of Oral Surgery. J. R. Moore. (Pergamon Series on Dentistry: Vol. 3). 11.00 o.p. (ISBN 0-08-011395-8). Pergamon.

Principal Winners Abroad of 1978. 10.00 (ISBN 0-936032-06-5). Thoroughbred Own and Breed.

Principal Winners Abroad of 1979. Ed. by Blood-Horse. (Annual Supplement, the Blood-Horse). (Orig.). 1980. pap. 10.00 (ISBN 0-936032-07-3). Thoroughbred Own & Breed.

Principal Winners Abroad of 1980. Blood-Horse Editors. (Annual Supplement of the Blood-Horse). (Orig.). 1981. pap. 10.00 (ISBN 0-936032-38-3). Thoroughbred Own & Breed.

Principal Works of Simon Stevin, 5 vols. Incl. General Introduction--Mechanism. Ed. by E. J. Dijksterhuis. 617p. 1955 (ISBN 90-265-0070-X); Vol. 2. A & B Mathematics. Ed. by D. J. Struik. 973p. 1958 (ISBN 90-265-0071-8); Astronomy & Navigation. Ed. by A. Pannekoek & E. Croone. 632p. 1961 (ISBN 90-265-0073-4); Vol. 4. Art of War. Ed. by W. H. Schukking. 525p. 1964 (ISBN 90-265-0074-2); Vol. 5. Engineering - Music - Civic Life. Ed. by R. J. Forbes et al. 609p. 1967 (ISBN 90-265-0075-0). text ed. 105.00 ea. (ISBN 0-686-27833-X, Pub. by Swets Pub Serv Holland). Swets North Am.

Principalities & Powers. John W. Montgomery. LC 74-29081. 256p. 1973. pap. 1.75 (ISBN 0-87123-460-2, 200460). Bethany Fell.

Principals: An Organized Force for Leadership. Benjamin Epstein. 48p. 1974. pap. text ed. 2.00 o.p. (ISBN 0-88210-052-1). Natl Assn Principals.

Principal's Handbook on the School Media Center. Betty Martin & Ben Carson. 212p. 1981. pap. 12.50x (ISBN 0-208-01912-X, Lib Prof Pubns). Shoe String.

Principals of Interferometric Spectroscopy. J. Chamberlain. LC 78-13206. 360p. 1979. 58.00 (ISBN 0-471-99719-6). Wiley.

Principal's Role in Improving Instruction. Floyd Sucher et al. (Illus.). 112p. 1980. 11.75 (ISBN 0-398-04123-7). C C Thomas.

Principalship: New Perspectives. Paul B. Jacobson et al. 512p. 1973. ref. ed. 18.95 (ISBN 0-13-700856-2). P-H.

Principe. Niccolo Machiavelli. Ed. by L. Arthur Burd. 1891. 14.95x (ISBN 0-19-815388-0). Oxford U Pr.

Principe Caspian. C. S. Lewis. Tr. by Julio Orozco from Eng. LC 77-14649. (Cronicas De Narnia Ser.). 223p. (Orig., Span.). (gr. 4 up). 1978. pap. 2.95 (ISBN 0-89922-105-X). Edit Caribe.

Principia Mathematica, 3 Vols. Alfred N. Whitehead & Bertrand Russell. Set. 270.00 (ISBN 0-521-06791-X). Cambridge U Pr.

Principia Mathematica to Fifty-Six. 2nd ed. Alfred N. Whitehead & Bertrand Russell. 1925-27. pap. 19.95x (ISBN 0-521-09187-X). Cambridge U Pr.

Principios Generales De Microbiologia. (Serie De Biologia: No. 7). (Span.). 1970. pap. 1.00 o.p. (ISBN 0-8270-6070-X). OAS.

Principios Generales De Microbiologia: Serie De Biologia No. 7. 2nd ed. OAS Gerneral Secretariat Department of Scientific & Technological Affairs. (Biology Ser.: No. 7). 143p. 1980. text ed. 2.00 (ISBN 0-8270-1097-4). OAS.

Principito. Antoine De Saint-Exupery. Tr. by Bonifacio Del Carril from Fr. LC 73-5511. (Illus.). 113p. (Span.). 1973. pap. 1.75 (ISBN 0-15-628450-2, HPL61, HPL). HarBraceJ.

Principle of Poetic Justice Illustrated in Restoration Tragedy. John D. Ebbs. (Salzburg Studies in English Literature, Poetic Drama & Poetic Theory Ser.: No. 4). 211p. 1973. pap. text ed. 25.00x (ISBN 0-391-01370-X). Humanities.

Principle of Protestantism. Philip Schaff. Ed. by Bard Thompson & George H. Bricker. 1964. pap. 6.95 (ISBN 0-8298-0348-3). Pilgrim NY.

Principles & Applications of Electricity. R. Sivaramakrishnan. 1967. pap. 10.00x (ISBN 0-210-22551-3). Asia.

Principles & Applications of Metal Chelation. Colin F. Bell. (Oxford Chemistry Ser.). (Illus.). 1977. 21.00x (ISBN 0-19-855485-0). Oxford U Pr.

Principles & Applications of Quantity Food Management. Vera C. Crusius. (Orig.). 1981. pap. text ed. pns (ISBN 0-8087-2966-7). Burgess.

Principles & Applications of Tribology. D. F. Moore. 1974. text ed. 44.00 (ISBN 0-08-017902-9); pap. text ed. 18.50 (ISBN 0-08-019007-3). Pergamon.

Principles & Applications or Organotransition Metal Chemistry. James P. Collman & Louis S. Hegedus. LC 79-57228. 725p. 1980. 24.00 (ISBN 0-935702-03-2). Univ Sci Bks.

Principles & Art of Cure by Homoeopathy. Herbert A. Roberts. 286p. 1942. 14.95x (ISBN 0-8464-1042-7). Beekman Pubs.

Principles & Methods of Contemporary Structural Linguistics. Ju. D. Apresjan. Tr. by Dina B. Crockett from Dutch. LC 72-94441. (Janua Linguarum, Ser. Minor: No. 144). (Illus.). 349p. (Orig.). 1973. pap. text ed. 38.25x (ISBN 90-2792-386-8). Mouton.

Principles & Methods of Musical Criticism. M. D. Calvocoressi. (Music Reprint Ser.). 1979. Repr. of 1931 ed. 20.00 (ISBN 0-306-79557-4). Da Capo.

Principles & Methods of Pharmacy Management. 2nd ed. Harry A. Smith. LC 80-17560. (Illus.). 413p. 1980. text ed. 19.50 (ISBN 0-8121-0765-9). Lea & Febiger.

Principles & Methods of Social Psychology. 4th ed. Edwin P. Hollander. (Illus.). 548p. 1981. text ed. 18.95x (ISBN 0-19-502822-8). Oxford U Pr.

Principles & Methods of Social Psychology. 3rd ed. Robert Lawson. (Illus.). 750p. 1976. text ed. 13.95x (ISBN 0-19-501850-8). Oxford U Pr.

Principles & Methods of Sterilization in Health Sciences. 2nd ed. John J. Perkins. (Illus.). 584p. 1980. 23.75 (ISBN 0-398-01478-7). C C Thomas.

Principles & Practice of Cooperative Banking in India. B. N. Choubey. 12.50x o.p. (ISBN 0-210-22556-4). Asia.

Principles & Practice of Experiments with Nucleic Acids. J. H. Parish. LC 72-6424. 511p. 1972. 43.95 (ISBN 0-470-65922-X). Halsted Pr.

Principles & Practice of Health Visiting. R. Hale et al. 1968. 12.25 (ISBN 0-08-012700-2). Pergamon.

Principles & Practice of Infectious Diseases, 2 vols. G. L. Mandell et al. LC 79-17984. 1979. Set. 95.00 (ISBN 0-471-03489-4, Pub. by Wiley Medical). Wiley.

Principles & Practice of Management in the Hospitality Industry. James Keiser. LC 80-12866. 1980. text ed. 16.95 (ISBN 0-8436-2182-6). CBI Pub.

Principles & Practice of Operative Dentistry. 2nd ed. Ed. by Gerald T. Charbeneau et al. LC 80-21029. (Illus.). 500p. 1981. text ed. write for info. (ISBN 0-8121-0775-6). Lea & Febiger.

Principles & Practice of Ophthalmology, 3 vols. Ed. by Gholam A. Peyman et al. (Illus.). 2000p. Date not set. Set. text ed. 250.00 (ISBN 0-7216-7228-0); Vol. 1. text ed. 82.50 (ISBN 0-7216-7211-6); Vol. 2. text ed. 82.50 (ISBN 0-7216-7212-4); Vol. 3. text ed. 85.00 (ISBN 0-7216-7213-2). Saunders.

Principles & Practice of Periodontics: With an Atlas of Treatment. Frank M. Wentz. (American Lecture in Dentistry). (Illus.). 320p. 1978. 42.75 (ISBN 0-398-03672-1). C C Thomas.

Principles & Practice of Public Administration in Nigeria. Augustus Adebayo. 192p. 1981. 27.00 (ISBN 0-471-27897-1, Pub. by Wiley-Interscience); pap. 13.50 (ISBN 0-471-27898-X). Wiley.

Principles & Practice of Rational-Emotive Therapy. Ruth A. Wessler & Richard L. Wessler. LC 80-8319. (Social & Behavioral Science Ser.). 1980. text ed. 14.95x (ISBN 0-87589-473-9). Jossey-Bass.

Principles & Practice of Spinal Anesthesia. P. C. Lund. (Illus.). 892p. 1971. pap. 48.00 spiral (ISBN 0-398-01164-8). C C Thomas.

Principles & Practice of Supervision. D. A. Peters. 1967. 15.00 (ISBN 0-08-012684-7); pap. 5.75 (ISBN 0-08-012683-9). Pergamon.

Principles & Practice of Surveying, 2 vols. C. B. Breed & G. L. Hosmer. Incl. Vol. 1. Elementary Surveying. 11th ed. 717p. 1977. 23.95 (ISBN 0-471-02979-3); Vol. 2. Higher Surveying. 8th ed. 543p. 1962. 22.95 (ISBN 0-471-10164-8). Wiley.

Principles & Practice of Teaching. Adjai Robinson. (Illus.). 176p. (Orig.). 1980. pap. text ed. 10.50x (ISBN 0-04-370098-5, AU449). Allen Unwin.

Principles & Practice of Textual Analysis. Vinton A. Dearing. 1975. 22.50x (ISBN 0-520-02430-3). U of Cal Pr.

Principles & Practice of the Civil Code of Japan: A Complete Theoretical & Practical Exposition of the Motifs of the Japanese Civil Code. Joseph E. De Becker. (Studies in Japanese Law & Government). 852p. 1979. Repr. of 1921 ed. Set. 60.00 (ISBN 0-89093-216-6). U Pubns Amer.

Principles & Practice of Urban Planning. 4th ed. Ed. by William I. Goodman & Eric C. Freund. LC 67-30622. (Municipal Management Ser.). 1968. text ed. 22.00 (ISBN 0-87326-006-6). Intl City Mgt.

Principles & Practices of Dryland Farming. Kenneth G. Brengle. 1981. price not set (ISBN 0-87081-095-2). Colo Assoc.

Principles & Practices of Grading, Drainage & Road Alignment: An Ecological Approach. Richard Untermann. (Illus.). 1978. ref. ed. 20.95 (ISBN 0-87909-641-1); instrs'. manual avail. Reston.

Principles & Practices of Light Construction. 2nd ed. Ronald C. Smith. LC 78-95754. (Engineering Technology Ser). (Illus.). 1970. 18.95 o.p. (ISBN 0-13-701961-0). P-H.

Principles & Practices of Outdoor-Environment Education. Phyllis M. Ford. LC 80-23200. 350p. 1981. text ed. 15.95 (ISBN 0-471-04768-6). Wiley.

Principles & Practices of Real Estate. Mary A. Hines. 1976. text ed. 17.95 (ISBN 0-256-01845-6); student workbook 5.25 (ISBN 0-256-01855-3). Irwin.

Principles & Practices of Rice Production. Surajit K. De Datta. 704p. 1981. 40.00 (ISBN 0-471-08074-8, Pub. by Wiley-Interscience). Wiley.

Principles & Practices of Secondary Education. 2nd ed. Vernon E. Anderson & William T. Gruhn. LC 62-11648. 1962. 13.50x o.p. (ISBN 0-8260-0470-9). Wiley.

Principles & Practices of Teaching Reading. 5th ed. Arthur Heilman et al. (Illus.). 544p. 1981. text ed. 16.95 (ISBN 0-675-08150-5); instr's. manual 3.75 (ISBN 0-686-69498-8). Merrill.

Principles & Practices of Teaching Reading. 4th ed. Arthur W. Heilman. (Elementary Education Ser.). 1977. text ed. 17.95 (ISBN 0-675-08537-3). Merrill.

Principles & Problems in Physical Chemistry for Biochemists. 2nd ed. Nicholas Price & Raymond Dwek. (Illus.). 1980. 23.00x (ISBN 0-19-855511-3); pap. 9.95x (ISBN 0-19-855512-1). Oxford U Pr.

Principles & Problems of Coaching. John D. Massengale. 392p. 1975. 19.75 (ISBN 0-398-03258-0); pap. 15.50 (ISBN 0-398-03259-9). C C Thomas.

Principles & Problems of Music Education. Thomas A. Regelski. (Illus.). 328p. 1975. ref. ed. 16.95 (ISBN 0-13-709840-5); pap. 13.95 ref. ed. (ISBN 0-13-709832-4). P-H.

Principles & Procedures for Evaluating the Toxicity of Household Substances. 1977. pap. 7.00 (ISBN 0-309-02644-X). Natl Acad Pr.

Principles & Procedures of Tour Management. Patrick J. Curran. LC 77-16399. 1978. 14.95 (ISBN 0-8436-0754-8). CBI Pub.

Principles & Recommendations for Population & Housing Censuses. (Statistical Papers Ser.: No. 67). 330p. 1980. pap. 20.00 (UN80/17/8, UN). Unipub.

Principles & Standards of Reactor Safety. (Illus.). 650p. (Orig.) 1974. pap. 51.00 (ISBN 92-0-020373-6, ISP342, IAEA). Unipub.

Principles & Styles of Acting. Everett M. Schreck. (Speech & Drama). 1970. text ed. 19.95 (ISBN 0-201-06765-X). A-W.

Principles & Techniques of Engineering Estimating. G. Calder. 180p. 1976. text ed. 23.00 (ISBN 0-08-019704-3); pap. 10.75 (ISBN 0-08-019703-5). Pergamon.

Principles & Techniques of Guidance. S. S. Chauhan. 300p. Date not set. text ed. 17.50 (ISBN 0-7069-1183-0, Pub. by Vikas India). Advent Bk.

Principles & Techniques of Histochemistry. Henry Troyer. LC 80-80592. 1980. text ed. 22.95 (ISBN 0-316-85310-0). Little.

Principles & Techniques of Intervention with Hyperactive Children. Marvin J. Fine. (Illus.). 328p. 1977. 29.50 (ISBN 0-398-03570-9). C C Thomas.

Principles & Techniques of Stock Market Manipulation. A. T. Miller. (New Stock Market Reference Library Ser.). (Illus.). 117p. 1981. 39.85 (ISBN 0-918968-95-X). Inst Econ Finan.

Principles & Techniques of Supervision in Physical Education. 3rd ed. James H. Humphrey et al. LC 79-92383. 272p. 1980. Repr. of 1972 ed. text ed. 15.00x (ISBN 0-916622-14-2). Princeton Bk Co.

Principles & Techniques of Vocational Guidance. H. H. London. LC 73-78475. 1973. text ed. 18.95 (ISBN 0-675-08949-2). Merrill.

Principles & Trends in Business Education. Louis C. Nanassy et al. LC 76-57995. 1977. text ed. 19.50 (ISBN 0-672-97092-9). Bobbs.

Principles, Dialogues & Philosophical Correspondence. George Berkeley. Tr. by Colin M. Turbayne. LC 64-66065. 1965. pap. 5.95 (ISBN 0-672-60453-1, LLA208). Bobbs.

Principles for a Catholic Morality. Timothy E. O'Connell. 1978. 11.95 (ISBN 0-8164-0404-6). Crossroad NY.

Principles for a Catholic Morality. Timothy E. O'Connell. 256p. 1980. pap. 7.95 (ISBN 0-8164-2031-9). Crossroad NY.

Principles for Establishing Limits for the Release of Radioactive Material into the Environment. (Safety Ser: No. 45). 1978. pap. 10.75 (ISBN 92-0-123078-8, ISP 477, IAEA). Unipub.

Principles for Evaluating Chemicals in the Environment. Division of Chemistry & Chemical Technology. 1975. pap. 16.00 (ISBN 0-309-02248-7). Natl Acad Pr.

Principles in Geology, 3 vols. Charles Lyell. (Illus.). 1970. Repr. of 1833 ed. Set. text ed. 130.00 (ISBN 3-7682-0685-8). Lubrecht & Cramer.

Principles of Accounting. James J. Benjamin et al. LC 80-67313. 1100p 1981. text ed. 18.95x (ISBN 0-931920-24-8); study guide 5.95 (ISBN 0-686-68562-8); working papers 6.95 (ISBN 0-686-68563-6); practice problem 4.95 (ISBN 0-686-68564-4). Dame Pubns.

Principles of Accounting. Belverd E. Needles et al. LC 80-80503. (Illus.). 1008p. 1981. text ed. 20.95 (ISBN 0-395-29527-0); study guide 6.95 (ISBN 0-395-29529-7); price not set test bank (ISBN 0-395-29538-6); practice set 1 5.95 (ISBN 0-395-29534-3); price not set achievement tests 1-14A (ISBN 0-395-29539-4); price not set achievement tests 1-14B (ISBN 0-395-29540-8); price not set achievement tests 14-28A (ISBN 0-395-29541-6); price not set achievement tests 14-28B (ISBN 0-395-29542-4). HM.

Principles of Accounting. K. Fred Skousen et al. 1981. text ed. write for info. (ISBN 0-87901-137-8); write for info. study guide (ISBN 0-87901-147-5); write for info. practie set, vol. 1 (ISBN 0-87901-150-5); write for info. practice set, vol. 2 (ISBN 0-87901-151-3); write for info. practice set, vol. 3 (ISBN 0-87901-152-1); write for info. working papers, vol. 1 (ISBN 0-87901-148-3); write for info. working papers, vol. 2 (ISBN 0-87901-149-1). Worth.

Principles of Accounting. William L. Ventolo, Jr. Ed. by Sidney Davidson. (Illus.). 350p. (gr. 12). 1980. text ed. 13.95 (ISBN 0-686-28726-6); pap. text ed. 11.95 (ISBN 0-686-28727-4). Performance Pub.

Principles of Accounting. 2nd ed. Paul H. Walgenbach et al. 1065p. 1980. text ed. 19.95 (ISBN 0-686-64997-4, HC); study guide 7.50 (ISBN 0-686-64998-2); solutions manual avail.; practice set A, practice set A with business papers, practice sets B&C & solutions manual avail.; working papers. set 1 8.95 (ISBN 0-686-64999-0); write for info. working papers set 2; test item file, achievement tests & ans. key avail.; transparencies avail. HarBraceJ.

Principles of Accounting. 2nd ed. Rufus Wixon & Robert G. Cox. LC 69-14676. 827p. 1969. 25.95 (ISBN 0-8260-9500-3); instructors' manual avail. (ISBN 0-471-07488-8). Wiley.

Principles of Accounting: Advanced. 6th ed. Ed. by J Gentry & G. Johnson. 1971. 17.95 o.p. (ISBN 0-13-317578-2). P-H.

Principles of Accounting & Financial Reporting for Nonprofit Organizations. Malvern J. Gross & Stephen F. Jablonsky. LC 79-4559. 1979. 21.95 (ISBN 0-471-05719-3, Pub. by Wiley-Interscience); instr's manual avail. Wiley.

Principles of Accounts. 5th ed. E. F. Castle & N. P. Owens. 448p. 1978. pap. text ed. 12.95x (ISBN 0-7121-1687-7, Pub. by Maconald & Evans England). Intl Ideas.

Principles of Active Network Synthesis & Design. Gobind Daryanani. LC 76-20659. 495p. 1976. text ed. 28.95 (ISBN 0-471-19545-6). Wiley.

Principles of Air Conditioning. V. Paul Lang. LC 77-78900. (Air Conditioning, Refrigeration Ser.). 1979. text ed. 14.52 (ISBN 0-8273-1001-3); pap. text ed. 12.20 (ISBN 0-8273-1009-9); instructor's guide 1.50 (ISBN 0-8273-1002-1). Delmar.

Principles of American Government. 8th ed. Albert B. Saye & John F. Allums. (Illus.). 1978. pap. 12.50 ref. (ISBN 0-13-701128-8). P-H.

Principles of American Nuclear Chemistry: A Novel. Thomas McMahon. 224p. 1981. pap. 2.95 (ISBN 0-380-54122-X, 54122, Bard). Avon.

Principles of Animal Environment. Merle L. Esmay. 1978. text ed. 22.50 (ISBN 0-87055-263-5). AVI.

Principles of Animal Physiology. 2nd ed. Dennis W. Wood. LC 74-4090. (Contemporary Biology Ser.). 329p. 1975. 19.50 o.p. (ISBN 0-444-19534-3); pap. text ed. 18.95 (ISBN 0-444-19533-5). Univ Park.

Principles of Animal Taxonomy. George G. Simpson. LC 60-13939. (Columbia Biological Ser.: No. 20). (Illus.). 1961. 22.50x (ISBN 0-231-02427-4). Columbia U Pr.

Principles of Animal Virology. Wolfgang K. Joklik. 320p. 1980. text ed. 21.95x (ISBN 0-8385-7920-5). ACC.

Principles of Applied Biomedical Instrumentation. 2nd ed. L. A. Geddes & L. E. Baker. LC 74-34390. (Biomedical Engineering & Health Systems Ser.). 616p. 1975. 31.95 (ISBN 0-471-29496-9, Pub. by Wiley-Interscience). Wiley.

Principles of Applied Climatology. Keith Smith. LC 74-20976. 233p. 1975. text ed. 24.95 (ISBN 0-470-80169-7). Halsted Pr.

Principles of Applied Clinical Chemistry: Plasma Protein, Vol. 3. Samuel Natelson & Ethan A. Natelson. (Illus.). 575p. 1980. 42.50 (ISBN 0-306-40276-9, Plenum Pr). Plenum Pub.

Principles of Applied Clinical Chemistry. Ed. by Samuel Natelson & Ethan A. Natelson. Incl. Vol. 1, Maintenance of Fluid & Electrolyte Balance. LC 75-4798. 393p. 1975. 22.50 (ISBN 0-306-35231-1); Vol. 2, the Erythrocyte. 584p. 1978. 39.50 (ISBN 0-306-35232-X). (Illus., Plenum Pr). Plenum Pub.

Principles of Applied Statistics. Myron Melnyk. LC 73-7943. 1974. text ed. 23.00 (ISBN 0-08-017108-7). Pergamon.

Principles of Art. Robin G. Collingwood. 1958. pap. 5.95 (ISBN 0-19-500209-1, GB). Oxford U Pr.

Principles of Art History: The Problem of the Development of Style in Later Art. Heinrich Wolfflin. (Illus.). 8.50 (ISBN 0-8446-3205-8). Peter Smith.

Principles of Artificial Intelligence. Nils J. Nilsson. LC 79-67584. (Illus.). 1980. text ed. 27.50 (ISBN 0-935382-01-1). Tioga Pub Co.

Principles of Astrometry: With Special Emphasis on Long-Focus Photographic Astrometry. Peter Van De Kamp. LC 66-22077. (Illus.). 1967. 21.95x (ISBN 0-7167-0318-1). W H Freeman.

Principles of Astronomy. 3rd ed. Stanley P. Wyatt. 1977. text ed. 20.95 (ISBN 0-205-05679-2, 7356794); answer bk. o.p. avail. (ISBN 0-205-05680-6). Allyn.

Principles of Astronomy: A Short Version. Stanley P. Wyatt & James B. Kaler. 592p. 1974. pap. text ed. 16.95x o.p. (ISBN 0-205-04205-8, 7342055). Allyn.

Principles of Astronomy: A Short Version. Stanley P. Wyatt & James B. Kaler. 550p. 1981. text ed. 18.95 (ISBN 0-205-07315-8); instructor's manual free (ISBN 0-205-07316-6). Allyn.

Principles of Atomic Physics & Electronics. M. Nelkon. 1976. text ed. 9.95x o.p. (ISBN 0-435-68656-9). Heinemann Ed.

Principles of Auditing. 6th ed. Walter B. Meigs et al. 1977. text ed. 20.95x (ISBN 0-256-01902-9). Irwin.

Principles of Auditing. canadian ed. Walter B. Meigs et al. 1978. 21.90x (ISBN 0-256-02092-2). Irwin.

Principles of Aural Rehabilitation. Mark Ross. LC 78-183116. (Studies in Communicative Disorders Ser.). 1972. pap. 2.50 (ISBN 0-672-61283-6). Bobbs.

Principles of Auto-Body Repairing & Repainting. 2nd ed. A. C. De Roche et al. (Illus.). 1976. 18.95x (ISBN 0-13-705699-0). P-H.

Principles of Autobody Repairing & Repainting. 3rd ed. Andre Deroche & Nicholas Huldebrand. (Illus.). 672p. 1981. text ed. 18.95 (ISBN 0-686-63447-0). P-H.

Principles of Behavior Therapy. G. Terence Wilson & K. Daniel O'Leary. (Ser. in Social Learning Theory). (Illus.). 1980. text ed. 18.95 (ISBN 0-13-701102-4). P-H.

Principles of Biochemical Tests in Diagnostic Microbiology. Ed. by Donna J. Blazevic & Grace M. Ederer. LC 75-17591. (Techniques in Pure & Applied Microbiology Ser.). 136p. 1975. 19.95 (ISBN 0-471-08040-3, Pub. by Wiley Medical). Wiley.

Principles of Biology Laboratory Manual. Lauren D. Howard. (Illus.). 1980. pap. 12.50 (ISBN 0-87055-354-2). AVI.

Principles of Biology Laboratory Manual. Laraine Unbehaun et al. 222p. (Orig.). 1980. pap. text ed. 10.95 (ISBN 0-8087-2115-1). Burgess.

Principles of Biomedical Instrumentation & Monitoring. Robert Traister. 300p. 1981. text ed. 24.95 (ISBN 0-8359-5611-3). Reston.

Principles of Bone X-Ray Diagnosis. 3rd ed. G. Simon. 1973. 49.95 (ISBN 0-407-36319-X). Butterworths.

Principles of Business Data Processing. 4th ed. V. Thomas Dock & Edward Essick. 512p. 1980. text ed. 15.95 (ISBN 0-574-21295-7, 13-4295); instr's guide avail. (ISBN 0-574-21296-5, 13-4296); transparency masters 30.00 (ISBN 0-574-21303-1, 13-4303); study guide 5.95 (ISBN 0-574-21297-3). SRA.

Principles of Business Data Processing: (with MIS Including BASIC) 4th ed. V. Thomas Dock & Edward Essick. 1980. text ed. 16.95 (ISBN 0-574-21305-8, 13-4305); instructor's guide avail. (ISBN 0-574-21301-5); study guide 5.95 (ISBN 0-574-21302-3, 13-4303). SRA.

Principles of Business Law. 11th ed. Robert N. Corley & William J. Robert. 1979. 21.95 (ISBN 0-13-701318-3); pap. 7.95 student guide & wkbk., 3rd ed. (ISBN 0-13-701326-4). P-H.

Principles of Catholic Theology: A Synthesis of Dogma & Morals. Edward Gratsch et al. LC 80-26272. 401p. (Orig.). 1981. pap. 10.95 (ISBN 0-8189-0407-0). Alba.

Principles of Celestial Mechanics. Philip M. Fitzpatrick. 1970. text ed. 18.95 (ISBN 0-12-257950-X). Acad Pr.

Principles of Championship Wrestling. Ray F. Carson & Buel R. Patterson. LC 73-169070. (Illus.). 192p. 1972. pap. 8.95 o.p. (ISBN 0-498-07930-9). A S Barnes.

Principles of Chemical Equilibrium. K. G. Denbigh. (Illus.). 506p. Date not set. 59.50 (ISBN 0-521-23682-7); pap. 19.95 (ISBN 0-521-28150-4). Cambridge U Pr.

Principles of Chemical Metallurgy. Moore. 1981. text ed. price not set (ISBN 0-408-00567-X); pap. text ed. price not set (ISBN 0-408-00430-4). Butterworth.

Principles of Chemical Weathering. rev ed. Walter D. Keller. 1957. text ed. 3.50x spiral bdg. (ISBN 0-87543-033-3). Lucas.

Principles of Chemistry. Frank E. Harris. (gr. 10-12). 1977. pap. text ed. 15.00 each incl. 8 texts, 1 tchrs' manual & 1 test (ISBN 0-8449-0400-7). Learning Line.

Principles of Chemistry: A Model Approach. Terrence J. Swift. 730p. 1975. text ed. 15.95x o.p. (ISBN 0-669-93021-0); instructor's manual free o.p. (ISBN 0-669-94540-4). Heath.

Principles of Chemistry with Practical Perspectives. 2nd ed. Russell S. Drago. 1977. text ed. 21.95 (ISBN 0-205-05568-0, 6855687); student guide 7.95 (ISBN 0-205-05570-2, 6855709); tchr's manual 1.50x (ISBN 0-205-05569-9, 6855695). Allyn.

Principles of Chest Roentgenology: A Programed Text. Benjamin Felson et al. LC 65-23091. (Illus.). 1965. 11.95 (ISBN 0-7216-3605-5). Saunders.

Principles of Child Psychotherapy. Donald J. Carek. 240p. 1972. text ed. 19.75 (ISBN 0-398-02254-2). C C Thomas.

Principles of Childhood Language Disabilities. J. Irwin & M. Marge. 1972. 19.95 (ISBN 0-13-708180-4). P-H.

Principles of Chinese Painting. rev ed. G. Rowley. (Monographs in Art & Archaeology: No. 24). 1959. 26.50x (ISBN 0-691-03834-1); pap. 7.50 (ISBN 0-691-00300-9). Princeton U Pr.

Principles of Cinematography. 4th ed. Leslie J. Wheeler. 1978. 17.95 o.p. (ISBN 0-85242-080-3, Pub. by Fountain). Morgan.

Principles of Clinical Pharmacy Illustrated by Clinical Case Studies. Ed. by Margaret M. McCarron. LC 74-18578. 200p. 1974. pap. 6.50 (ISBN 0-914768-12-3). Drug Intl Pubns.

Principles of Color Technology. Fred W. Billmeyer, Jr. & Max Saltzman. LC 80-21561. 272p. 1980. 19.95 (ISBN 0-471-03052-X, Pub. by Wiley-Interscience). Wiley.

Principles of Communciations: Systems Modulation & Noise. Rodger E. Ziemer & William Tranter. LC 75-25015. (Illus.). 736p. 1976. text ed. 27.50 (ISBN 0-395-20603-0); solutions manual 4.30 (ISBN 0-395-20604-9). HM.

Principles of Compiler Design. Alfred V. Aho & Jeffrey D. Ullman. LC 77-73953. (Illus.). 1977. text ed. 21.95 (ISBN 0-201-00022-9). A-W.

Principles of Computer Structures. Daniel Siewiorek et al. (Computer Science Ser.). (Illus.). 768p. 1981. text ed. 29.95 (ISBN 0-07-057302-6, C). McGraw.

Principles of Continuous System Simulation. W. K Giloi. (Illus.). 1976. pap. 19.50 (ISBN 3-5190-2336-9). Adler.

Principles of Cosmology and Gravitation. M. Berry. LC 75-22559. (Illus.). 200p. 1976. 34.95 (ISBN 0-521-21061-5); pap. 11.95x (ISBN 0-521-29028-7). Cambridge U Pr.

Principles of Cost Accounting with Managerial Implications. L. Gayle Rayburn. 1979. 19.95 (ISBN 0-256-02144-9). Irwin.

Principles of County Jail Administration Management. David P. Kalinich & Frederick J. Postill. 1981. write for info (ISBN 0-398-04140-7). C C Thomas.

Principles of Creative Selling. Kenneth B. Haas & John Ernest. 1978. text ed. 14.95 (ISBN 0-02-474980-X). Macmillan.

Principles of Criminal Law. abr. ed. Wayne R. LaFave. (Criminal Justice Ser.). 1978. text ed. 17.95 (ISBN 0-8299-0215-5); instrs.' manual avail. (ISBN 0-8299-0595-2). West Pub.

Principles of Crop Improvement. N. W. Simmonds. LC 78-40726. (Illus.). 1979. text ed. 32.00 (ISBN 0-582-45586-3); pap. text ed. 19.95 (ISBN 0-582-44630-9). Longman.

Principles of Cultural Cooperation. Sulwyn Lewis. (Orig.). 1971. pap. 2.50 (ISBN 92-3-100810-2, U482, UNESCO). Unipub.

Principles of Dairy Science. Glen H. Schmidt & L. Dale Van Vleck. LC 73-2860. (Animal Science Ser.). (Illus.). 1974. text ed. 25.95x (ISBN 0-7167-0830-2). W H Freeman.

Principles of Data Base Management. James Martin. (Illus.). 320p. 1976. Ref. Ed. 25.00 (ISBN 0-13-708917-1). P-H.

Principles of Data Collection. Robert M. Thorndike. (Gardner Press Ser. on Measurement & Statistics). 350p. 1981. text ed. 22.00 (ISBN 0-89876-022-4). Gardner Pr.

Principles of Data Processing. Steven L. Mandell. (West Ser. in Mass Communication). (Illus.). 1978. pap. text ed. 7.95 (ISBN 0-8299-0212-0); instrs.' manual avail. (ISBN 0-8299-0554-5). West Pub.

Principles of Data Processing. 2nd ed. Steven L. Mandell. (West Series in Data Processing & Information Systems). (Illus.). 165p. 1981. pap. text ed. write for info. (ISBN 0-8299-0392-5). West Pub.

Principles of Data Processing. 2nd ed. Robert Stern & Nancy Stern. LC 78-16178. 1979. text ed. 21.95x (ISBN 0-471-01696-9); tchrs.' manual avail. (ISBN 0-471-03143-7); study guide 8.50 (ISBN 0-471-05431-3). Wiley.

Principles of Desalination. Ed. by K. S. Spiegler. 1966. 51.00 o.p. (ISBN 0-12-656750-6). Acad Pr.

Principles of Desalination. 2nd ed. Ed. by K. S. Spiegler & A. D. Laird. 1980. Pt. A. 41.00 (ISBN 0-12-656701-8); Pt. B. 52.00 (ISBN 0-12-656702-6); Set. 85.00. Acad Pr.

Principles of Descartes' Philosophy. Benedictus De Spinoza. Tr. by Halbert H. Britan from Lat. LC 74-3096. 1974. pap. 3.95 (ISBN 0-87548-053-5). Open Court.

Principles of Design & Operation of Catering Equipment. american ed. A. Milson & D. Kirk. (Illus.). 1980. pap. text ed. 30.00 (ISBN 0-87055-357-7). AVI.

Principles of Diachronic Syntax. D. W. Lightfoot. LC 78-54717. (Cambridge Studies in Linguistics Monograph: No. 23). (Illus.). 1979. 69.50 (ISBN 0-521-22082-3); pap. 17.50x (ISBN 0-521-29350-2). Cambridge U Pr.

Principles of Differential & Integral Equations. 2nd ed. Constantin Corduneanu. LC 77-2962. 1977. text ed. 10.95 (ISBN 0-8284-0295-7). Chelsea Pub.

Principles of Digital Communication & Coding. Andrew J. Viterbi & James K. Omura. (Electrical Engineering Ser.). (Illus.). 1979. text ed. 31.95 (ISBN 0-07-067516-3, C); solution manual avail. (ISBN 0-07-067517-1). McGraw.

Principles of Digital Computer Design, Vol. 1. A. C. Meltzer et al. (Illus.). 624p. 1976. 26.95 (ISBN 0-13-701524-0). P-H.

Principles of Digital Data Transmission. A. P. Clark. LC 76-23217. 1976. 21.95 (ISBN 0-470-98913-0). Halsted Pr.

Principles of Drug Action: The Basis of Pharmacology. 2nd ed. Avram Goldstein et al. LC 73-15871. 1974. 35.00 (ISBN 0-471-31260-6, Pub. by Wiley-Medical). Wiley.

Principles of Dynamics. M. B. Glauert. (Library of Mathematics). 1969. pap. 5.00 (ISBN 0-7100-4348-1). Routledge & Kegan.

Principles of Dynamics. Ed. by Donald T. Greenwood & Y. Fung. 1965. text ed. 27.95 (ISBN 0-13-708974-0). P-H.

Principles of Dynamics. R. Hill. 1964. 22.00 (ISBN 0-08-010571-8); pap. 7.50 o.p. (ISBN 0-08-013540-4). Pergamon.

Principles of Economic Appraisal in Health Care. M. F. Drummond. (Illus.). 130p. 1980. pap. 12.95 (ISBN 0-19-261273-5). Oxford U Pr.

Principles of Economics. 2nd ed. Roger Chisholm & Marilu McCarty. 1981. text ed. 18.95x (ISBN 0-673-15492-0). Scott F.

Principles of Economics. rev. 9th ed. Clifford L. James. (Orig.). 1972. pap. 4.95 (ISBN 0-06-460008-4, CO 8, COS). Har-Row.

Principles of Economics. Carl Menger. Tr. by James Dingwall & Bert F. Hoselitz. (Institute for Humane Studies Ser. in Economic Theory). 328p. 1981. text ed. 20.00x (ISBN 0-8147-5380-9); pap. text ed. 7.00x (ISBN 0-8147-5381-7). NYU Pr.

Principles of Economics, 2 vols. 3rd. ed. Willis L. Peterson. 1977. pap. text ed. 9.50x macro o.p. (ISBN 0-256-01912-6); pap. text ed. 9.50x micro o.p. (ISBN 0-256-01914-2). study guide macro 2.95x o.p. (ISBN 0-256-01913-4); study guide micro 2.95x o.p. (ISBN 0-256-01915-0). Irwin.

Principles of Economics, 2 vols. 4th ed. Willis L. Peterson. Incl. Vol. 1. Macro. pap. 10.50x (ISBN 0-256-02335-2); study guide 4.50x (ISBN 0-256-02336-0); Vol. 2. Micro. pap. 10.50x (ISBN 0-256-02337-9); study guide 4.50x (ISBN 0-256-02338-7). 1980. Irwin.

Principles of Economics. rev. 13th ed. K. P. Sundharam & M. C. Vaish. 1980. text ed. 27.50x (ISBN 0-7069-0285-8, Pub. by Vikas India). Advent Bk.

Principles of Education. J. C. Chapman et al. Ed. by Ellwood P. Cubberley. 645p. 1980. Repr. of 1924 ed. lib. bdg. 25.00 (ISBN 0-8495-0851-7). Arden Lib.

Principles of Education. Elsa H. Walters & E. B. Castle. 1967. pap. text ed. 8.95x (ISBN 0-04-370018-7). Allen Unwin.

Principles of Educational & Psychological Measurement & Evaluation. 2nd ed. Gilbert Sax. 704p. 1980. text ed. 19.95x (ISBN 0-534-00832-1); wkbk 7.95x (ISBN 0-534-00833-X). Wadsworth Pub.

Principles of Educational Measurement & Evaluation. Gilbert Sax. 1974. 16.95x o.p. (ISBN 0-534-00338-9); study guide 6.95x o.p. (ISBN 0-534-00384-2). Wadsworth Pub.

Principles of Electric Circuits. Thomas L. Floyd. (Illus.). 768p. 1981. text ed. 19.95 (ISBN 0-675-08081-9); tchr's. ed. 3.95 (ISBN 0-686-69499-6). Merrill.

Principles of Electrical Transmission Lines in Power & Communication. J. H. Grindley. 1967. 25.00 (ISBN 0-08-012111-X); pap. 13.25 (ISBN 0-08-012112-8). Pergamon.

Principles of Electricity & Magnetism. 2nd ed. Emerson M. Pugh & Emerson W. Pugh. LC 70-87043. (Physics Ser). 1970. text ed. 22.95 (ISBN 0-201-06014-0). A-W.

Principles of Electricity for Students of Physics & Engineering. Eugene Key. (Orig.). 1967. pap. 4.50 (ISBN 0-06-460118-8, CO 118, COS). Har-Row.

Principles of Electronic Data Processing Management. Alex Gaydasch. 300p. 1982. text ed. 18.95 (ISBN 0-8359-5604-0); instr's. manual free (ISBN 0-8359-5605-9). Reston.

Principles of Electroplating & Electroforming. 3rd ed. William Blum & George B. Hogaboom. (Illus.). 1949. 32.50 o.p. (ISBN 0-07-006179-3, P&RB). McGraw.

Principles of Engineering Materials. C. Barrett et al. 1973. 26.95 (ISBN 0-13-709394-2). P-H.

Principles of Engineering Organization. S. H. Wearne. (Illus.). 1973. pap. text ed. 11.95x (ISBN 0-7131-3290-6). Intl Ideas.

Principles of Ethics, 2 vols, Vol. 2. Herbert Spencer. LC 77-1274. 550p. 1980. 9.00 (ISBN 0-913966-76-2); Set. pap. 6.00 (ISBN 0-913966-75-4). Liberty Fund.

Principles of Ethics: An Introduction. Paul W. Taylor. 1975. pap. 11.95x (ISBN 0-8221-0142-4). Dickenson.

Principles of Everyday Behavior Analysis. 2nd ed. L. Keith Miller. LC 79-27797. 1980. pap. text ed. 15.95 (ISBN 0-8185-0373-4). Brooks-Cole.

Principles of Examining. J. M. Thyne. LC 74-4381. 278p. 1974. text ed. 15.95 (ISBN 0-470-86700-0). Halsted Pr.

Principles of Experimentation & Measurement. Gordon M. Bragg. (Illus.). 192p. 1974. 18.95 (ISBN 0-13-701169-5). P-H.

Principles of Expression in Pianoforte Playing. Adolph Christiani. LC 74-1348. (Music Reprint Ser.). 303p. 1974. Repr. of 1886 ed. lib. bdg. 21.50 (ISBN 0-306-70623-7). Da Capo.

Principles of Family Medicine. Robert E. Rakel. LC 76-41541. (Illus.). 1977. text ed. 19.95 (ISBN 0-7216-7449-6). Saunders.

Principles of Farm Machinery. 3rd ed. R. A. Kepner & Roy Bainer. (Illus.). 1978. text ed. 23.50 (ISBN 0-87055-252-X). AVI.

Principles of Field Ionization & Field Desorption Mass Spectrometry. H. D. Beckey. LC 77-33014. 1978. text ed. 52.00 (ISBN 0-686-67953-9). Pergamon.

Principles of Figure Drawing. Alexander Dobkin. LC 74-16373. (Funk & W Bk.). (Illus.). 272p. 1975. 10.00 o.s.i. (ISBN 0-308-10084-0, TYC-T). T Y Crowell.

Principles of Finite Mathematics. William Swift & D. Wilson. (Illus.). 1977. ref. ed. 18.95 (ISBN 0-13-701359-0). P-H.

Principles of Firthian Linguistics. T. F. Mitchell. (Illus.). 232p. 1975. text ed. 19.50x (ISBN 0-582-52455-5). Longman.

Principles of Fishery Science. W. Harry Everhart et al. (Illus.). 1975. 14.50x o.p. (ISBN 0-8014-0918-7). Cornell U Pr.

Principles of Fluid Mechanics. Wen-Hsiung Li & Sau-Hai Lam. 1964. 20.95 (ISBN 0-201-04240-1). A-W.

Principles of Food, Beverage & Labor Cost Control for Hotels & Restaurants. 2nd ed. Paul R. Dittmer & Gerald C. Griffin. LC 79-20301. 1979. text ed. 15.95 (ISBN 0-8436-2177-X). CBI Pub.

Principles of Food Chemistry. rev. ed. J. M. DeMan. (Illus.). 1980. lib. bdg. 32.00 o.p. (ISBN 0-87055-216-3); pap. text ed. 19.00 (ISBN 0-87055-287-2). AVI.

Principles of Food Packaging. 2nd ed. Stanley Sacharow & Roger C. Griffin. (Illus.). 1980. lib. bdg. 28.00 (ISBN 0-87055-347-X). AVI.

Principles of Food Processing Sanitation. The Food Processors Institute. Ed. by Allen Katsuyama. LC 79-57624. 303p. (Orig.). 1980. pap. 40.00 (ISBN 0-937774-03-0). Food Processors.

Principles of Forest Yield Study. E. Assmann. 1971. text ed. 79.00 (ISBN 0-08-006658-5). Pergamon.

Principles of Fortran Seventy-Seven Programming. Jerrold L. Wagener. LC 79-17421. 1980. pap. text ed. 14.95 (ISBN 0-471-04474-1); tchr's manual (ISBN 0-471-07831-X). Wiley.

Principles of Gene Manipulation: An Introduction to Genetic Engineering. R. W. Old & S. B. Primrose. (Studies in Microbiology: Vol. 2). 1980. 32.75x (ISBN 0-520-04143-7); pap. 12.75 (ISBN 0-520-04151-8). U of Cal Pr.

Principles of General Psychology. 5th ed. Gregory A. Kimble et al. LC 79-23269. 1980. 18.95x (ISBN 0-471-04469-5, Pub by Ronald Pr). Wiley.

Principles of Genetic Toxicology. David Brusick. 300p. 1980. 25.00 (ISBN 0-306-40414-1, Plenum Pr). Plenum Pub.

Principles of Genetics. 6th ed. Eldon J. Gardner & D. Peter Snustad. LC 80-12114. 704p. 1980. text ed. 23.95 (ISBN 0-471-04412-1). Wiley.

Principles of Genetics. Tamarin. 608p. 1981. text ed. 21.95 (ISBN 0-87872-281-5). Duxbury Pr.

Principles of Geology. 4th ed. James Gilluly et al. LC 74-23076. (Geology Ser.). (Illus.). 1975. text ed. 21.95x (ISBN 0-7167-0269-X). W H Freeman.

Principles of Gynecology. 4th ed. N. Jeffcoate. 1975. 67.50 (ISBN 0-407-00000-3). Butterworths.

Principles of Harmony & Contrast of Colors & Their Applications to the Arts. M. E. Chevreul. Ed. by Sydney J. Freedberg. LC 77-18673. (Connoisseurship Criticism & Art History Ser.: Vol. 5). (Illus.). 1980. lib. bdg. 72.00 (ISBN 0-8240-3262-4). Garland Pub.

Principles of Head & Neck Surgery. 2nd ed. H. R. Freund. (Illus.). 1979. 43.50 (ISBN 0-8385-7922-1). ACC.

Principles of Heredity. 5th ed. Laurence H. Snyder & Paul R. David. (Illus.). text ed. 16.95x o.p. (ISBN 0-669-25312-X). Heath.

Principles of Heterocyclic Chemistry. Ed. by Alan R. Katritzky & J. M. Lagowski. 1968. 29.50 (ISBN 0-12-401150-0). Acad Pr.

Principles of Hindu Reckoning. Kushyar Ibn Labban. Ed. by Martin Levey. Tr. by Marvin Petruck. (Medieval Science Pubns., No. 8). 1965. 17.50x (ISBN 0-299-03610-3). U of Wis Pr.

Principles of Hospital Business Office Management. Beaufort B. Longest, Jr. 1975. 11.75 (ISBN 0-930228-02-2); instr's manual 23.50 (1448). Hospital Finan.

Principles of Host-Plant Resistance to Insect Pests. N. Panda. LC 78-59169. (Illus.). 400p. 1980. text ed. 32.50 (ISBN 0-87663-836-1). Allanheld.

Principles of Human Genetics. 3rd ed. Curt Stern. LC 72-4357. (Illus.). 315p. 1973. text ed. 25.95x (ISBN 0-7167-0597-4); answers to problems avail. (ISBN 0-685-27915-4). W H Freeman.

Principles of Hydraulics. Ed. by Trade & Technical Press Ltd. (Illus.). 24.00x (ISBN 0-685-90212-9). Intl Ideas.

Principles of Ideal-Fluid Aerodynamics. Krishnamurty Karamcheti. LC 79-26876. 654p. 1980. Repr. of 1966 ed. lib. bdg. 32.50 (ISBN 0-89874-113-0). Krieger.

Principles of Immunodiagnostics. Ralph M. Aloisi. (Illus.). 1979. pap. text ed. 15.95 (ISBN 0-8016-0118-5). Mosby.

Principles of Inductive Logic. 2nd ed. John Venn. LC 72-119162. Orig. Title: Principles of Empirical, or Inductive Logic. 643p. 1973. 18.50 (ISBN 0-8284-0265-5). Chelsea Pub.

Principles of Industrial Facility Location. Howard A. Stafford. LC 80-26737. (Illus.). 1980. pap. 25.00 (ISBN 0-910436-18-5). Conway Pubns.

Principles of Industrial Microbiology. A. Rhodes & D. L. Fletcher. 1966. 19.50 (ISBN 0-08-011906-9); pap. 15.00 (ISBN 0-08-011905-0). Pergamon.

Principles of Information Retrieval. Manfred Kochen. LC 74-1204. (Information Sciences Ser). 256p. 1974. 23.95 (ISBN 0-471-49697-9, Pub. by Wiley-Interscience). Wiley.

Principles of Inorganic & Theoretical Chemistry. Ed. by C. T. Rawcliffe & D. H. Rawson. 1974. pap. text ed. 15.95x (ISBN 0-435-66747-5). Heinemann Ed.

Principles of Insurance. 6th ed. Robert I. Mehr & Emerson Cammack. 1976. text ed. 16.95x o.p. (ISBN 0-256-01833-2). Irwin.

Principles of Insurance. 7th ed. Robert I. Mehr & Emerson Cammack. 1980. 18.95x (ISBN 0-256-02321-2). Irwin.

Principles of Intermediate Algebra. John Ashley. 1977. text ed. 13.95x (ISBN 0-02-473170-6). Macmillan.

Principles of International Economics. Miltiades Chacholiades. (Illus.). 656p. 1980. text ed. 19.95 (ISBN 0-07-010345-3, C). McGraw.

Principles of Investigation. John P. Kenney & Harry W. More, Jr. (Criminal Justice Ser.). (Illus.). 1979. text ed. 17.95 (ISBN 0-8299-0284-8); wkbk. 5.50 (ISBN 0-686-67621-1); instrs. manual avail. (ISBN 0-8299-0592-8). West Pub.

Principles of Investments: Text & Cases. 2nd ed. Leonard T. Wright. LC 76-5618. (Finance & Real Estate Ser.). 1977. text ed. 19.95 o.p. (ISBN 0-88244-083-7). Grid Pub.

Principles of Isotope Geology. Gunter Faure. LC 77-4479. (Intermediate Geology Ser.). 1977. text ed. 30.95 (ISBN 0-471-25665-X). Wiley.

Principles of Lasers. Orazio Svelto. (Illus.). 376p. 1976. 25.00 (ISBN 0-306-30860-6, Plenum Pr). Plenum Pub.

Principles of Learning & Memory. B. R. Bugelski. LC 78-19760. 1979. 21.95 (ISBN 0-03-046596-6). Praeger.

Principles of Learning & Memory. Robert G. Crowder. (Experimental Psychology Ser.). 1976. 19.95 o.p. (ISBN 0-470-15027-0). Halsted Pr.

Principles of Life Insurance, Vol. 1. rev. ed. Janice E. Greider & William T. Beadles. 1973. pap. text ed. 9.00 (ISBN 0-256-01396-9). Irwin.

Principles of Light & Color. Edwin D. Babbitt. (Illus.). 578p. Date not set. 20.00 (ISBN 0-89540-060-X). Sun Pub. Postponed.

Principles of Light and Color. Edwin S. Babbitt. 1980. pap. text ed. 7.95 (ISBN 0-8065-0748-9). Lyle Stuart.

Principles of Lubrication. 2nd ed. A. Cameron. Date not set. text ed. write for info. (ISBN 0-582-47000-5). Longman. Postponed.

Principles of Macroeconomics. 2nd ed. Roger Chisholm & Marilu McCarty. 1981. pap. text ed. 10.95x (ISBN 0-673-15493-9). Scott F.

Principles of Magnesium Technology. E. F. Emley. 1966. 110.00 o.p. (ISBN 0-08-010673-0). Pergamon.

Principles of Magnetic Resonance. 2nd rev ed. C. P. Slichter. (Springer Series in Solid State Science: Vol 1). 1978. pap. 24.80 (ISBN 0-387-08476-2). Springer-Verlag.

Principles of Magnetic Resonance 1980: Second Corrected Printing of the Second Revised & Expanded Edition. C. P. Slichter. (Springer Ser. in Solid-State Sciences: Vol. I). 397p. 1980. 24.80 (ISBN 0-387-08476-2). Springer-Verlag.

Principles of Mammalian Aging. 2nd ed. Robert R. Kohn. (Illus.). 1978. 21.95 (ISBN 0-13-709352-7). P-H.

Principles of Management. David L. Kurtz & Louis E. Boone. Incl. Student Mastery Guide. James Baird et al. 265p. wkbk. 5.95 (ISBN 0-394-32697-0). 624p. 1981. pap. text ed. 18.95 (ISBN 0-394-32246-0). Random.

Principles of Management. 7th ed. George R. Terry. 1977. text ed. 18.95 (ISBN 0-256-00562-1). Irwin.

Principles of Management & Organizational Behavior. 4th ed. Justin G. Longenecker. 1977. text ed. 19.95 (ISBN 0-675-08556-X); instructor's manual 3.95 (ISBN 0-686-67528-2). Merrill.

Principles of Management: Process & Behavior. 2nd ed. Daniel A. Wren & Dan Voich, Jr. LC 75-43472. 1976. 21.95x (ISBN 0-8260-9640-9, Pub. by Wiley-Hamilton). Wiley.

Principles of Management Science: With Applications to Executive Decisions. 2nd ed. Harvey M. Wagner. (Illus.). 576p. 1975. 21.95 (ISBN 0-13-709535-X). P-H.

Principles of Management: Text & Cases. William L. Dejon. LC 77-75123. 1978. 18.95 (ISBN 0-8053-2336-8); instr's man. 8.95 (ISBN 0-8053-2337-6). Benjamin-Cummings.

Principles of Marketing. Richard H. Buskirk. LC 74-29144. 1975. text ed. 17.45 (ISBN 0-913310-46-8). Par Inc.

Principles of Marketing. 2nd ed. Jay Diamond & Gerald Pintel. (Illus.). 1980. 15.95 (ISBN 0-13-701417-1); pap. text ed. 6.95 study guide (ISBN 0-13-701425-2). P-H.

Principles of Marketing Channel Management. Bruce Mallen. LC 76-27923. (Illus.). 1977. 23.95 (ISBN 0-669-00985-7). Lexington Bks.

Principles of Mathematical Logic. David Hilbert & W. Ackermann. LC 50-4784. 9.50 (ISBN 0-8284-0069-5). Chelsea Pub.

Principles of Mathematical Modeling. Clive L. Dym & Elizabeth Ivey. LC 79-65441. (Computer Science & Applied Mathematics Ser.). 261p. 1980. tchrs' ed. 18.95 (ISBN 0-12-226550-5); solutions manual 3.00 (ISBN 0-12-226560-2). Acad Pr.

Principles of Mathematics. 3rd ed. Paul Rees & Charles Rees. (Illus.). 1977. 17.95 (ISBN 0-13-709683-6). P-H.

Principles of Meat Science. John C. Forrest et al. LC 75-8543. (Food & Nutrition Ser.). (Illus.). 1975. text ed. 26.95x (ISBN 0-7167-0743-8). W H Freeman.

Principles of Medicinal Chemistry. 2nd ed. Ed. by William O. Foye. (Illus.). 931p. 1981. text ed. write for info. (ISBN 0-8121-0722-5). Lea & Febiger.

Principles of Medicine in Africa. E. H. Parry. (Illus.). 1976. text ed. 29.95x (ISBN 0-19-264223-5). Oxford U Pr.

Principles of Membrane Transport. Stanley G. Schultz. LC 79-54015. (IUPAB Biophysics Ser.: No. 2). (Illus.). 1980. 22.50 (ISBN 0-521-22992-8); pap. 8.50x (ISBN 0-521-29762-1). Cambridge U Pr.

Principles of Metabolic Control in Mammalian Systems. Ed. by Robert H. Herman et al. (Illus.). 690p. 1980. 35.00 (ISBN 0-306-40261-0, Plenum Pr). Plenum Pub.

Principles of Metal Surface Treatment & Protection. 2nd ed. D. R. Gabe. (International Ser. on Materials Science & Technology: Vol. 28). (Illus.). 1978. text ed. 36.00 (ISBN 0-08-022703-1); pap. text ed. 14.00 (ISBN 0-08-022707-4). Pergamon.

Principles of Microbe & Cell Cultivation. S. John Pirt. LC 74-28380. 1975. 46.95 (ISBN 0-470-69038-0). Halsted Pr.

Principles of Microbiology. 8th ed. Alice L. Smith. LC 76-30332. (Illus.). 1977. text ed. 18.95 (ISBN 0-8016-4681-2). Mosby.

Principles of Microbiology. 9th ed. Alice L. Smith. (Illus.). 816p. 1981. text ed. 19.95 (ISBN 0-8016-4682-0). Mosby.

Principles of Microeconomics. 2nd ed. Roger Chisholm & Marilu McCarty. 1981. pap. text ed. 10.95x (ISBN 0-673-15402-5). Scott F.

Principles of Microeconomics. 2nd ed. Edwin Mansfield. (Illus.). 1977. pap. text ed. 9.95x (ISBN 0-393-09113-9); readings, issues & cases 4.95x (ISBN 0-393-09102-3); study guide 4.95x (ISBN 0-393-09109-0); test item file gratis (ISBN 0-393-09105-8); transparency masters gratis (ISBN 0-393-09099-X). Norton.

Principles of Modern Algebra. 2nd ed. J. Eldon Whitesitt. LC 74-184163. 1973. text ed. 14.95 (ISBN 0-201-08706-5). A-W.

Principles of Modern Biology. Armitage. (gr. 9-12). 1972. pap. text ed. 9.00 each incl. 9 texts & tchrs' manual (ISBN 0-8449-0450-3). Learning Line.

Principles of Modern Investments. Charles A. D'Ambrosio. LC 75-34094. (Illus.). 512p. 1976. text ed. 19.50 (ISBN 0-574-19210-7, 13-2210); instr's guide avail. (ISBN 0-574-19211-5, 13-2211). SRA.

Principles of Modern Soccer. George Beim. LC 76-11986. (Illus.). 1977. pap. text ed. 15.75 (ISBN 0-395-24415-3). HM.

Principles of Monetary Economics. James M. Boughton & Elmus R. Wicker. 1975. text ed. 15.95x o.p. (ISBN 0-256-01667-4). Irwin.

Principles of Moral & Political Philosophy. William Paley. Ed. by Rene Wellek. LC 75-11246. (British Philosophers & Theologians of the 17th & 18th Centuries: Vol. 45). 1977. Repr. of 1785 ed. lib. bdg. 42.00 (ISBN 0-8240-1797-8). Garland Pub.

Principles of Moral & Political Science, 2 vols. Adam Ferguson. Ed. by Rene Wellek. LC 75-11218. (British Philosophers & Theologians of the 17th & 18th Centuries Ser.: Vol. 21). 1978. Repr. of 1792 ed. Set. lib. bdg. 66.00 (ISBN 0-8240-1772-2); lib. bdg. 42.00 ea. Garland Pub.

Principles of Muhammadan Jurisprudence According to the Hanali, Maliki, Shafi'i & Hanbali Schools. Abdur Rahim. LC 79-2879. 443p. 1981. Repr. of 1911 ed. 33.50 (ISBN 0-8305-0047-2). Hyperion Conn.

Principles of Musical Theory. Renee Longy-Miquelle. 1925. 5.00 (ISBN 0-911318-06-2). E C Schirmer.

Principles of Musik, in Singing & Setting. Charles Butler. LC 68-13273. (Music Ser). 1970. Repr. of 1636 ed. lib. bdg. 17.50 (ISBN 0-306-70939-2). Da Capo.

Principles of Natural Lighting. J. A. Lynes. (Illus.). 1968. 22.30x (ISBN 0-444-20030-4). Intl Ideas.

Principles of Neuroanatomy. Jay B. Angevine & Carl W. Cotman. (Illus.). 300p. 1981. text ed. 18.95x (ISBN 0-19-502885-6); pap. text ed. 11.95x (ISBN 0-19-502886-4). Oxford U Pr.

Principles of Nuclear Magnetism. A. Abragam. (International Series of Monographs on Physics). 1961. 89.00x (ISBN 0-19-851236-8). Oxford U Pr.

Principles of Numerical Control. 2nd ed. James J. Childs. (Illus.). (gr. 11 up). 1969. text ed. 18.00 (ISBN 0-8311-1051-1); ans. bks. avail. (ISBN 0-685-03852-1). Indus Pr.

Principles of Nutrition. 4th ed. E. D. Wilson et al. LC 78-11710. 1979. text ed. 21.95 (ISBN 0-471-02695-6); tchrs. manual avail. (ISBN 0-471-04786-4); wkbk. 6.95 (ISBN 0-471-05766-5). Wiley.

Principles of Oceanography. 2nd ed. Richard A. Davis. LC 76-10436. (Illus.). 1977. text ed. 18.95 (ISBN 0-201-01464-5). A-W.

Principles of Operations Research for Management. Frank S. Budnick et al. 1977. 21.95x (ISBN 0-256-01796-4). Irwin.

Principles of Operations Research: With Applications to Managerial Decisions. 2nd ed. Harvey M. Wagner. (Illus.). 1088p. 1975. 29.95 (ISBN 0-13-709592-9). P-H.

Principles of Optical Fiber Measurement. D. Marcuse. LC 80-2339. 1981. write for info. (ISBN 0-12-470980-X). Acad Pr.

Principles of Optics: Electromagnetic Theory of Propagation, Interference & Diffraction of Light. 6th ed. M. Born & E. Wolf. (Illus.). 808p. 1980. 50.00 (ISBN 0-08-026482-4); pap. 27.50 (ISBN 0-08-026481-6). Pergamon.

Principles of Orchestration. Nikolay Rimsky-Korsakov. 1922. pap. text ed. 6.00 (ISBN 0-486-21266-1). Dover.

Principles of Organic Chemistry. 4th ed. T. A. Geissman. LC 76-13891. (Illus.). 1977. 29.95x (ISBN 0-7167-0177-4); tchrs. manual avail. W H Freeman.

Principles of Organic Chemistry. Peter R. Murray. 1977. pap. text ed. 12.95x (ISBN 0-435-65643-0). Heinemann Ed.

Principles of Package Development. Roger Griffin & Stanley Sacharow. (Illus.). 1972. text ed. 28.50 (ISBN 0-87055-118-3). AVI.

Principles of Paediatric Clinical Pharmacology. Lars O. Boreus. (Monographs in Clinical Pharmacology). (Illus.). 1981. text ed. write for info. (ISBN 0-443-03006-2). Churchill.

Principles of Paleontology. 2nd ed. David M. Raup & Steven M. Stanley. LC 77-17443. (Illus.). 1978. text ed. 24.95x (ISBN 0-7167-0022-0). W H Freeman.

Principles of Pediatrics: Pretest Self-Assessment & Review. Robert A. Hoekelman. (Illus.). 248p. 1980. 25.00 (ISBN 0-07-079159-7, HP). McGraw.

Principles of Personal Selling. 1st ed. 1968. pap. 7.60 (ISBN 0-672-96052-4); tchrs' manual 6.67 (ISBN 0-672-96053-2). Bobbs.

Principles of Personality. Jerry S. Wiggins et al. LC 75-28729. 1976. text ed. 19.95 (ISBN 0-201-08618-2). A-W.

Principles of Pharmaceutical Accounting. Francis A. Marino et al. LC 79-20380. (Illus.). 241p. 1980. text ed. 19.50 (ISBN 0-8121-0634-2). Lea & Febiger.

Principles of Physical Geology. John E. Sanders. 608p. 1981. text ed. 19.95 (ISBN 0-471-08424-7). Wiley.

Principles of Physical Geology Laboratory Manual. Eastern Kentucky University, Dept. of Geology. 80p. 1930. pap. text ed. 5.50 (ISBN 0-8403-2285-2). Kendall-Hunt.

Principles of Physical Oceanography. Gerhard Neumann & W. J. Fierson. (Illus.). 1966. 35.95 (ISBN 0-13-709741-7). P-H.

Principles of Physics. James P. Hurley & Claude Garrod. LC 77-75475. (Illus.). 1978. text ed. 23.95 (ISBN 0-395-25036-6); sol. manual 0.35 (ISBN 0-395-25037-4). HM.

Principles of Physiology. 2nd ed. Jensen. (Illus.). 1980. text ed. 29.50 (ISBN 0-8385-7931-0). ACC.

Principles of Planned Maintenance. R. H. Clifton. 1974. pap. 14.95x (ISBN 0-7131-3317-1). Intl Ideas.

Principles of Plant & Animal Pest Control, Vol. 1, Plant-Disease Development & Control. Agricultural Board. 1968. pap. 6.00 (ISBN 0-309-01596-0). Natl Acad Pr.

Principles of Plant & Animal Pest Control, Vol. 2, Weed Control. Agricultural Board. 1968. pap. 9.25 (ISBN 0-309-01597-9). Natl Acad Pr.

Principles of Plant & Animal Pest Control, Vol. 3, Insect-Pest Management & Control. Agricultural Board Division of Biology and Agriculture. 1969. pap. 11.75 (ISBN 0-309-01695-9). Natl Acad Pr.

Principles of Plant & Animal Pest Control, Vol. 4, Control Of Plant Parasitic Nematodes. Division of Biology and Agriculture - Agricultural Board. 1968. pap. 10.00 (ISBN 0-309-01696-7). Natl Acad Pr.

Principles of Plant & Animal Pest Control, Vol. 5, Vertebrate Pests. National Academy Of Sciences. 1970. pap. 6.00 (ISBN 0-309-01697-5). Natl Acad Pr.

Principles of Plant & Animal Pest Control, Vol. 6, Effects Of Pesticides On Fruit & Vegetable Physiology. Agriculture Board. 1968. pap. 4.50 (ISBN 0-309-01698-3). Natl Acad Pr.

Principles of Plant Breeding. Robert W. Allard. LC 60-14240. 1960. 22.95 (ISBN 0-471-02310-8). Wiley.

Principles of Pneumatics. Ed. by Trade & Technical Press Ltd. (Illus.). 24.00x (ISBN 0-685-90213-7). Intl Ideas.

Principles of Police Interrogation. C. H. Van Meter. (Illus.). 148p. 1973. 11.75 (ISBN 0-398-02634-3). C C Thomas.

Principles of Political Economy. Kuzo Uno. (Marxist Theory & Contemporary Capitalism Ser.: No. 24). 1980. text ed. 50.00x (ISBN 0-391-01210-X). Humanities.

Principles of Political Economy & Taxation. David Ricardo. 1972. 5.00x (ISBN 0-460-00590-1, Evman); pap. 5.95 (ISBN 0-460-01590-7). Dutton.

Principles of Political Economy, Applied to the Condition, the Resources, & the Institutions of the American People. Francis Bowen. (Neglected American Economists Ser.). 1974. lib. bdg. 50.00 (ISBN 0-8240-1011-6). Garland Pub.

Principles of Political Thought. S. I. Benn & R. S. Peters. 1965. pap. text ed. 5.95 o.s.i. (ISBN 0-02-902670-9). Free Pr.

Principles of Politics & Government. Coulter. 336p. 1980. text ed. 9.95 (ISBN 0-205-07177-5, 767177-6). Allyn.

Principles of Poly Merization. 2nd ed. George Odian. 700p. 1981. 27.50 (ISBN 0-471-05146-2, Pub. by Wiley-Interscience). Wiley.

Principles of Polymer Morphology. D. C. Bassett. (Cambridge Solid State Science Ser.). (Illus.). 220p. Date not set. price not set (ISBN 0-521-23270-8); pap. price not set (ISBN 0-521-29886-5). Cambridge U Pr.

Principles of Polymer Processing. R. T. Fenner. 1980. 35.00 (ISBN 0-8206-0285-X). Chem Pub.

Principles of Polymer Processing. Zehev Tadmor & Costas G. Gogos. LC 78-17859. (SPE Monographs). 1979. 42.50 (ISBN 0-471-84320-2, Pub. by Wiley-Interscience). Wiley.

Principles of Polymerization. George Odian. LC 78-78958. (Illus.). 1970. 42.50 o.p. (ISBN 0-07-047585-7, P&RB). McGraw.

Principles of Population & Production. J. Weyland. 493p. 1971. Repr. of 1816 ed. 38.00x (ISBN 0-7165-1777-9, Pub. by Irish Academic Pr Ireland). Biblio Dist.

Principles of Practical Cost-Analysis. Robert Sugden & Alan Williams. (Illus.). 290p. 1978. text ed. 33.00x (ISBN 0-19-877040-5); pap. text ed. 14.50x (ISBN 0-19-877041-3). Oxford U Pr.

Principles of Prayer. Charles G. Finney. Ed. by L. G. Parkhurst. 112p. (Orig.). 1980. pap. 2.95 (ISBN 0-87123-468-8, 210468). Bethany Fell.

Principles of Programming Languages. R. Tennent. 1981. 21.00 (ISBN 0-13-709873-1). P-H.

Principles of Protein Structure. G. E. Schulz & R. H. Schirmer. LC 78-11500. (Springer Advanced Texts in Chemistry). (Illus.). 1979. 29.80 o.p. (ISBN 0-387-90386-0); pap. 14.80 (ISBN 0-387-90334-8). Springer-Verlag.

Principles of Psychology, 2 Vols. William James. 1890. Vol. 1. pap. text ed. 6.50 (ISBN 0-486-20381-6); Vol. 2. pap. text ed. 6.50 (ISBN 0-486-20382-4). Dover.

Principles of Psychopathology. Brendan A. Maher. (Psychology Ser.). 1966. text ed. 19.95 o.p. (ISBN 0-07-039610-8, C); instructor's manual 2.95 o.p. (ISBN 0-07-039613-2). McGraw.

Principles of Psychotherapy. Pierre Janet. Tr. by H. M. Guthrie & E. R. Guthrie. 322p. 1980. Repr. of 1924 ed. lib. bdg. 40.00 (ISBN 0-8495-2760-0). Arden Lib.

Principles of Psychotherapy with Children. J. M. Reisman. (Ser. on Personality Processes). 1973. 25.50 o.p. (ISBN 0-471-71568-9). Wiley.
Principles of Psychotherapy with Children. John M. Reisman. LC 80-29581. 354p. 1981. Repr. of 1973 ed. lib. bdg. price not set (ISBN 0-89874-317-6). Krieger.
Principles of Public Utility Rates. James C. Bonbright. LC 61-6569. 1961. 24.00x (ISBN 0-231-02441-X). Columbia U Pr.
Principles of Pyrometallurgy. C. B. Alcock. 1977. 48.00 (ISBN 0-12-048950-3). Acad Pr.
Principles of Quantum Chemistry. D. V. George. 280p. 1973. text ed. 21.00 (ISBN 0-08-016925-2). Pergamon.
Principles of Quantum Mechanics. 4th ed. Paul A. Dirac. (Int'l Series of Monographs on Physics). 1958. 29.95x (ISBN 0-19-851208-2). Oxford U Pr.
Principles of Quantum Mechanics. R. Shankar. (Illus.). 630p. 1980. 29.50 (ISBN 0-306-40397-8, Plenum Pr). Plenum Pub.
Principles of Radiation Therapy. Thomas J. Deeley. 160p. 1976. 17.95 (ISBN 0-407-00030-5). Butterworths.
Principles of Radiological Physics. Robin J. Wilks. (Illus.). 528p. 1981. pap. text ed. 37.50 (ISBN 0-443-02035-3). Churchill.
Principles of Radiopharmacology, 2 vols. Ed. by Lelio G. Columbetti. 1979. Vol. 1, 304p. 69.95 (ISBN 0-8493-5465-X); Vol. 2, 288p. 64.95 (ISBN 0-8493-5466-8). CRC Pr.
Principles of Real Estate. O'Donnell. 576p. 1975. 19.95 (ISBN 0-7216-6911-5). Dryden Pr.
Principles of Real Estate Decisions. Donald R. Epley & Joseph Rabianski. LC 80-21354. 1981. text ed. 18.95 (ISBN 0-201-03188-4). A-W.
Principles of Refrigeration. 2nd ed. Roy J. Dossat. LC 78-2938. 1978. text ed. 25.95 (ISBN 0-471-03550-5); solutions manual 4.00 (ISBN 0-471-03771-0). Wiley.
Principles of Refrigeration. Olivo & Marsh. LC 76-14089. 1979. 14.32 (ISBN 0-8273-1014-5); pap. text ed. 12.20 (ISBN 0-686-60690-6); instructor's guide 1.50 (ISBN 0-8273-1004-8). Delmar.
Principles of School Health. Jack Smolensky & Richard Bonvechio. 1966. text ed. 9.95x o.p. (ISBN 0-669-20198-7). Heath.
Principles of School Law: With Cases. Robert L. Drury & Kenneth C. Ray. 1965. 18.95 (ISBN 0-13-709949-5). P-H.
Principles of Scientific Management. Frederick W. Taylor. 1967. pap. 4.95 (ISBN 0-393-00398-1, Norton Lib). Norton.
Principles of Scientific Management. Frederick W. Taylor. 1923p. 1980. lib. bdg. 30.00 (ISBN 0-8495-5162-5). Arden Lib.
Principles of Scottish Private Law, 2 vols. 2nd ed. David M. Walker. 2000p. 1975. 78.00x o.p. (ISBN 0-19-825336-2). Oxford U Pr.
Principles of Security: An Introduction. Truett A. Ricks et al. (Illus.). 400p. 1981. text ed. price not set (ISBN 0-87084-744-9). Anderson Pub Co.
Principles of Sedation, Local & General Anesthesia in Denistry. S. M. Shane. (Illus.). 384p. 1975. 25.75 (ISBN 0-398-03387-0). C C Thomas.
Principles of Silviculture. 2nd ed. Theodore W. Daniel et al. (Illus.). 1979. text ed. 22.95x (ISBN 0-07-015297-7). McGraw.
Principles of Social Psychology. 2nd ed. Kelly G. Shaver. (Psychology Ser.). (Illus.). 656p. 1981. text ed. 19.95 (ISBN 0-87626-634-0). Winthrop.
Principles of Social Reconstruction. Bertrand Russell. (Unwin Bks.). 1960. pap. 3.95 (ISBN 0-04-320073-7). Allen Unwin.
Principles of Social Structure: Southeast Asia. D. E. Brown. LC 76-25889. 1977. lib. bdg. 26.75x (ISBN 0-89158-643-1). Westview.
Principles of Sociology. 3rd ed. Ed. by Alfred M. Lee et al. LC 75-89671. 1969. pap. 5.50 (ISBN 0-06-460026-2, CO 26, COS). Har-Row.
Principles of Software Engineering & Design. Marvin V. Zelkowitz et al. LC 78-27315. (Illus.). 1979. text ed. 22.95 (ISBN 0-13-710202-X). P-H.
Principles of Solar Engineering. Frank Kreith & Jan F. Kreider. LC 77-27861. (McGraw-Hill - Hemisphere Thermal & Fluids Engineering Ser). (Illus.). 1978. pap. 24.95 (ISBN 0-07-035476-6, C). McGraw.
Principles of Spaceflight Propulsion. E. M. Goodger. LC 77-88306. 1970. 19.55 o.p. (ISBN 0-08-013884-5). Pergamon.
Principles of Speaking. 3rd ed. Kenneth G. Hance et al. 1974. 13.95x (ISBN 0-534-00373-7). Wadsworth Pub.
Principles of Specification Design Workbook. Robert Marcus. Ed. by Gerald Weinberg. (Illus.). 284p. 1979. pap. text ed. 19.95 (ISBN 0-87619-459-5). R J Brady.
Principles of Speedwriting: College Edition. LC 76-41045. (Landmark Ser.). 1977. pap. text ed. 9.95 (ISBN 0-672-98048-7); tchr's manual 3.33 (ISBN 0-672-98049-5); wkbk. 8.95x (ISBN 0-672-98050-9). Bobbs.
Principles of Statistical Mechanics. Richard C. Tolman. LC 79-52649. 1980. pap. text ed. 8.95 (ISBN 0-486-63896-0). Dover.
Principles of Statistical Techniques. P. G. Moore. LC 75-85731. (Illus.). 280p. 1976. 29.95 (ISBN 0-521-07631-5); pap. 12.50x (ISBN 0-521-29055-4). Cambridge U Pr.
Principles of Stratigraphy. Carl O. Dunbar & John Rodgers. LC 57-8883. 1957. 21.50 o.p. (ISBN 0-471-22539-8). Wiley.
Principles of Structural Stability Theory. Alexander Chajes. (Civil Engineering & Engineering Mechanics Ser.). (Illus.). 288p. 1974. 25.95 (ISBN 0-13-709964-9). P-H.
Principles of Surgery Patient Management Problems Pretest Self-Assessment & Review. Ed. by John H. Morton. (Illus., Orig.). 1981. pap. 25.00 (ISBN 0-07-050968-9). McGraw-PreTest.
Principles of Surgery PreTest Self-Assessment & Review. Ed. by Seymour I. Schwartz et al. (Illus., Orig.). 1981. pap. 25.00 (ISBN 0-07-051649-9). McGraw-PreTest.
Principles of Surplus Disposal & Consultative Obligations of Member Nations. 81p. 1981. pap. 6.00 (ISBN 92-5-100899-X, F2078, FAO). Unipub.
Principles of Survey Analysis. Travis Hirschi & Hanan C. Selvin. LC 67-15058. Orig. Title: Delinquency Research. 1973. pap. text ed. 5.95 (ISBN 0-02-914740-9). Free Pr.
Principles of Surveying. 2nd ed. Charles A. Herubin. (Illus.). 1978. text ed. 16.95 (ISBN 0-87909-620-9); instrs's. manual avail. Reston.
Principles of Tantra, 2 vols. John Woodroffe. 1979. 29.50 (ISBN 0-89744-129-X, Pub. by Ganesh & Co India). Auromere.
Principles of Teaching for Christian Teachers. Charles B. Eavey. 1940. 11.95 (ISBN 0-310-24030-1). Zondervan.
Principles of Technical Writing. Robert Hays. 1965. 13.95 (ISBN 0-201-02807-7). A-W.
Principles of Telegraphy. N. N. Biswas. 1968. Repr. pap. 5.00x (ISBN 0-210-98177-6). Asia.
Principles of Textual Criticism. James Thorpe. LC 72-179135. 1972. 8.50 (ISBN 0-87328-054-7); pap. 4.00 (ISBN 0-87328-055-5). Huntington Lib.
Principles of the Economic Philosophy of Society, Government & Industry. Van Buren Denslow. (Neglected American Economists Ser.). 1974. lib. bdg. 50.00 (ISBN 0-8240-1023-X). Garland Pub.
Principles of the Flute, Recorder & Oboe. Jacques H. Le Romain. Ed. by David Lasocki. 1978. 7.50 o.p. (ISBN 0-214-65942-9, 8026, Dist. by Arco). Barrie & Jenkins.
Principles of the Human Mind. Alfred Smee. LC 80-68665. (Illus.). 96p. 1980. pap. 5.95 (ISBN 0-89708-030-0). And Bks.
Principles of the Theory of Solids. 2nd ed. J. M. Ziman. (Illus.). 456p. 1972. text ed. 33.95 (ISBN 0-521-08382-6); pap. 15.95x (ISBN 0-521-29733-8). Cambridge U Pr.
Principles of the Use of Radioisotope Tracers in Clinical & Research Investigations. Ray Oliver. 1971. pap. 10.75 (ISBN 0-08-015718-1). Pergamon.
Principles of Total Hip Arthroplasty. new ed. Nas S. Eftekhar. LC 78-18471. (Illus.). 1978. text ed. 67.50 (ISBN 0-8016-1496-1). Mosby.
Principles of Tribology. Ed. by J. Halling. (Illus.). 1978. pap. text ed. 27.50x (ISBN 0-333-24686-1). Scholium Intl.
Principles of Turfgrass Culture. John H. Madison. 412p. 1981. Repr. of 1971 ed. lib. bdg. price not set (ISBN 0-89874-197-1). Krieger.
Principles of Ultraviolet Photoelectron Spectroscopy. J. Wayne Rabalais. LC 76-28413. (Wiley-Interscience Monographs in Chemical Physics). 1977. 42.50 (ISBN 0-471-70285-4, Pub by Wiley-Interscience). Wiley.
Principles of Unit Construction. Arthur J. Jones et al. 232p. 1980. Repr. of 1939 ed. lib. bdg. 20.00 (ISBN 0-89984-261-5). Century Bookbindery.
Principles of Unit Operations. 2nd ed. A. S. Foust et al. 768p. 32.95 (ISBN 0-471-26897-6). Wiley.
Principles of Veterinary Radiography. 3rd ed. S. W. Douglas & H. D. Williamson. 296p. 1980. text ed. write for info. (ISBN 0-8121-0737-3). Lea & Febiger.
Principles of Violin Playing & Teaching. Ivan Galamian. 1962. text ed. 13.95 (ISBN 0-13-710780-3). P-H.
Principles of Water Quality Control. T. H. Tebbutt. 1971. 14.30 (ISBN 0-08-016128-6); pap. 7.70 (ISBN 0-08-016127-8). Pergamon.
Principles of Water Quality Management. Walter W. Eckenfelder. LC 79-20509. (Illus.). 1980. 29.95 (ISBN 0-8436-0338-0). CBI Pub.
Principles of World Politics. George Modelski. LC 70-163237. 1972. 16.95 (ISBN 0-02-921440-8). Free Pr.
Principles of X-Ray Diagnosis. D. H. Trapnell. 1967. 29.95 (ISBN 0-407-36560-5). Butterworths.
Principles of X-Ray Diagnosis of the Skull. 2nd ed. G. H. Du Boulay. (Illus.). 384p. 1979. text ed. 115.00x. Butterworths.
Principles of Zoophysiology, Vol. 1. B. Rybak. 1969. 79.00 (ISBN 0-08-012158-6). Pergamon.
Principles, Practices & Positions in Neuropsychiatric Research. J. Brady & W. J. Nauta. 320p. 1973. text ed. 59.00 (ISBN 0-08-017007-2). Pergamon.
Principles, Promises & Powers. Sterling W. Sill. LC 73-87714. 352p. 1973. 5.95 o.p. (ISBN 0-87747-506-7). Deseret Bk.
Principless of Learning. Hill. 1981. 7.95 (ISBN 0-88284-123-8). Alfred Pub.
Print. LC 70-124382. (Life Library of Photography). (Illus.). 1970. 14.95 (ISBN 0-8094-1015-X). Time-Life.
Print-Collector's Handbook. Alfred Whitman. LC 72-177279. (Tower Bks). (Illus.). xii, 152p. 1972. Repr. of 1901 ed. 24.00 (ISBN 0-8103-3938-2). Gale.
Print for the Visually Handicapped Reader: Proceedings. Library Association & National Association for Partially Handicapped Conference. 1971. 5.50x (ISBN 0-85365-394-1, Pub. by Lib Assn England). Oryx Pr.
Print Quality Evaluation: A Bibliography. W. C. Walker et al. Ed. by C. T. Ray & J. M. Fetsko. (TAPPI PRESS Reports). 1973. pap. 37.95 (ISBN 0-89852-350-8, 01-01-R050). TAPPI.
Print Quality Factor Classification. new ed. W. C. Walker. Ed. by W. O. Walker. (TAPPI PRESS Reports). (Illus.). 1979. pap. 14.95 (ISBN 0-89852-379-6, 01-01-R079). TAPPI.
Printcrafts for Fun & Profit. Seymour Fleishman. Ed. by Caroline Rubin. LC 76-78907. (How to Ser.). (Illus.). (gr. 3-6). 1977. 6.50g (ISBN 0-8075-6633-0). A Whitman.
Printed Art: A View of Two Decades. Riva Castleman. LC 79-56089. (Illus.). 144p. 1979. 17.50 (ISBN 0-87070-531-8); pap. 9.95 (ISBN 0-87070-541-5). Museum Mod Art.
Printed for Children. Compiled by Rosemarie Rauter. 448p. 1978. pap. 28.00 (ISBN 0-89664-111-2, Pub. by K G Saur). Gale.
Printed Music in the British Museum: A Guide to the Catalogues & Their Construction. Alec H. King. 208p. 1979. 33.00 (ISBN 0-89664-409-X, Pub. by K G Saur). Shoe String.
Printed Portraits. Clifford S. Ackley. LC 79-52929. (Illus.). 1979. pap. 3.95 (ISBN 0-87846-139-6). Mus Fine Arts Boston.
Printed Textiles: English & American Cottons & Linens, 1700-1850. Florence M. Montgomery. (Illus.). 1970. 16.95 o.p. (ISBN 0-670-57722-7). Viking Pr.
Printed Word: Its Impact & Diffusion (Primarily in the 15th & 16th Centuries) Rudolf Hirsch. 338p. 1980. 70.00x (ISBN 0-86078-026-0, Pub. by Variorum England). State Mutual Bk.
Printers. Leonard E. Fisher. (Colonial Americans Ser). (Illus.). (gr. 4-6). 1965. PLB 6.45 (ISBN 0-531-01033-3). Watts.
Printers' Price List, a Manual for the Use of Clerks & Book-Keepers in Job Printing Offices. Theodore L. De Vinne. Ed. by John Bidwell. LC 78-74396. (Nineteenth-Century Book Arts & Printing History Ser.: Vol. 10). 1980. lib. bdg. 38.00 (ISBN 0-8240-3884-3). Garland Pub.
Printers' Vocabulary. Charles T. Jacobi. LC 68-30613. 1975. Repr. of 1888 ed. 15.00 (ISBN 0-8103-3309-0). Gale.
Printing. Boy Scouts Of America. LC 19-600. (Illus.). 64p. (gr. 6-12). 1965. pap. 0.70x (ISBN 0-8395-3377-2, 3377). BSA.
Printing & Computer Technology. Harold C. Durbin. LC 80-65655. 206p. (Orig.). 1980. pap. 9.50 (ISBN 0-936786-00-0); pap. text ed. 8.50 (ISBN 0-936786-01-9). Durbin Assoc.
Printing & Embroidery. Mary Newland & Carol Walklin. 1977. 19.95 (ISBN 0-7134-0136-2, Pub. by Batsford England). David & Charles.
Printing & Publishing in Medieval China. Denis Twitchett. (Illus.). 1981. pap. 14.50 (ISBN 0-913720-08-9). Sandstone.
Printing As a Hobby. 2nd ed. J. Ben Lieberman. (Illus.). 1981. write for info. (ISBN 0-918142-08-3); pap. write for info. (ISBN 0-918142-07-5). Myriade.
Printing As a Hobby. 3rd ed. J. Ben Lieberman. 1980. pap. 5.95 o.p. (ISBN 0-918142-07-5). Caroline Hse.
Printing Estimating. Philip K. Ruggles. LC 79-13008. 1979. text ed. 16.95 (ISBN 0-534-00747-3, Breton Pubs). Wadsworth Pub.
Printing in Calcutta to Eighteen Hundred: A Description & Checklist. Graham W. Shaw. (Illus.). 144p. 1981. 79.00 (ISBN 0-19-721792-3). Oxford U Pr.
Printing in Spain, 1501-20. Frederick J. Norton. 1966. 84.00 (ISBN 0-521-05842-2). Cambridge U Pr.
Printing Inks: Developments Since 1975. J. I. Duffy. LC 79-16231. (Chemical Technology Review Ser.: No. 139). (Illus.). 1980. 42.00 (ISBN 0-8155-0772-0). Noyes.
Printing It! Clifford Burke. (Illus.). 128p. 1974. pap. 3.95 (ISBN 0-914728-03-2). Wingbow Pr.
Printing Layout & Design. 1968. pap. text ed. 6.60 o.p. (ISBN 0-8273-0374-2). Delmar.
Printing Plant. Melvin Berger. LC 78-2529. (Industry at Work Ser.). (Illus.). (gr. 4-6). 1978. PLB 5.90 s&l (ISBN 0-531-02207-2). Watts.
Printing Poetry. Clifford Burke. LC 80-52171. 168p. 1980. 50.00 (ISBN 0-912962-01-1); unbound 37.50 (ISBN 0-686-63315-6). Scarab Pr.
Printing Press As an Agent of Change, 2 vols. Elizabeth Eisenstein. LC 77-91083. 1979. Vol. 1. 43.50 (ISBN 0-521-21967-1); Vol. 2. 37.50 (ISBN 0-521-21969-8); Set. 69.00 (ISBN 0-521-22044-0). Cambridge U Pr.
Printing Press As an Agent of Change, 2 vols. in 1. Elizabeth Eisenstein. LC 77-91083. 852p. 1980. pap. 16.95 (ISBN 0-521-29955-1). Cambridge U Pr.
Printing Presses: History & Development from the Fifteenth Century to Modern Times. James Moran. (Illus.). 1973. 30.00x (ISBN 0-520-02245-9); pap. 7.95 (ISBN 0-520-02904-6). U of Cal Pr.
Printing Trades Blue Book: 1978-79 Northeastern Edition. 1978. pap. 45.00 o.p. (ISBN 0-910880-02-6). Lewis.
Printing Trades Blue Book: 1980 New York Metropolitan Edition. 1980. pap. 50.00 o.p. (ISBN 0-910880-05-0). Lewis.
Printing Trades Blue Book: 1980-81 Northeastern Edition. 700p. 1980. pap. 50.00 (ISBN 0-910880-07-7). Lewis.
Printing Trades Blue Book: 1981 New York Metropolitan Edition. 1981. pap. 50.00 (ISBN 0-910880-08-5). Lewis.
Printing Trades Directory 1980. (Benn Directories Ser.). 1980. 65.00 (ISBN 0-686-60667-1, Pub. by Benn Pubns). Nichols Pub.
Printing Types: Their History, Forms & Use, 2 vols. Daniel B. Updike. 1980. pap. 8.95 ea. Vol. 1 (ISBN 0-486-23928-4). Vol. 2 (ISBN 0-486-23929-2). Dover.
Printing Unwins. Philip Unwin. (Illus.). 159p. 1976. 14.50 (ISBN 0-913720-14-3). Sandstone.
Printmaking. rev. & expanded ed. Gabor Peterdi. LC 80-12888. (Illus.). 336p. 1980. 24.95 (ISBN 0-02-596060-1). Macmillan.
Printmaking. Harlow Rockwell. LC 73-78479. 64p. (gr. 3-7). 1974. 4.95 o.p. (ISBN 0-385-01816-9). Doubleday.
Printmaking: A Beginning Handbook. W. Maxwell & Unger. 1977. 18.95 (ISBN 0-13-710699-8, Spec); pap. 9.95 (ISBN 0-13-710681-5, Spec). P-H.
Prints & Books. William M. Ivins, Jr. LC 76-75295. (Graphic Art Ser). 1969. Repr. of 1927 ed. lib. bdg. 32.50 (ISBN 0-306-71288-1). Da Capo.
Prints & Drawings of Kathe Kollwitz. Kathe Kollwitz. (Illus.). 12.50 (ISBN 0-8446-0745-2). Peter Smith.
Prints & Patterns. (MacDonald Educational Ser.). (Illus., Arabic.). 3.50 (ISBN 0-686-53101-9). Intl Bk Ctr.
Prints & People: A Social History of Printed Pictures. A. H. Mayor. 1980. 37.50 (ISBN 0-691-03958-5); pap. 12.95 (ISBN 0-691-00326-2). Princeton U Pr.
Prints & People: A Social History of Printed Pictures. rev. ed. A Hyatt Mayor. LC 80-7817. (Illus.). 496p. 1980. 37.50x; pap. 12.50. Princeton U Pr.
Prints & Printmaking: An Introduction to the History & Techniques. Antony Griffiths. 152p. 1981. text ed. 12.95 (ISBN 0-394-32673-3). Knopf.
Prints & Visual Communication. William M. Ivins, Jr. LC 68-31583. (Graphic Art Ser). (Illus.). 1969. Repr. of 1953 ed. lib. bdg. 25.00 (ISBN 0-306-71159-1). Da Capo.
Prints in the Public Library. Donald L. Foster. LC 72-13056. (Illus.). 1973. 10.00 (ISBN 0-8108-0579-0). Scarecrow.
Prints of James Ensor. James Ensor. LC 76-184012. 1972. Repr. of 1952 ed. lib. bdg. 25.00 (ISBN 0-306-70439-0). Da Capo.
Prints of LeRoy Neiman. LeRoy Neiman. (Illus.). 364p. 1980. 100.00. Control Data.
Prints of the Twentieth Century: A History. Riva Castleman. LC 76-9219. (Illus.). 1976. 15.95 (ISBN 0-19-519887-5); pap. 9.95 (ISBN 0-19-519888-3). Oxford U Pr.
Prints: Processing & Enlarging in Black & White. Hans Gotze. Ed. by R. H. Mason. Tr. by Mike Shields from Ger. (Illus.). 83p. (Orig.). 1980. pap. 7.50x (ISBN 0-85242-704-2). Intl Pubns Serv.
Prinzessin Brambilla. E. T. Hoffman. Ed. by M. Raraty. (Blackwell's German Text Ser.). 1972. pap. 9.95x (ISBN 0-631-01880-8, Pub. by Basil Blackwell). Biblio Dist.

Prior & Posterior Analytics. Aristotle. Tr. by John Warrington. 1964. 5.00x o.p. (ISBN 0-460-00450-6, Evman). Dutton.
Priorities & People. Harry Baker Adams. 128p. 1975. pap. 0.65 (ISBN 0-8272-2924-0). Bethany Pr.
Priorities for Action. Carnegie Commission on Higher Education. (Illus.). 256p. 1973. 7.95 o.p. (ISBN 0-07-010072-1, P&RB); Brief Ed. pap. 3.95 o.p. (ISBN 0-07-010105-1). McGraw.
Priorities for Alleviating Soil-Related Constraints to Food Production in the Tropics. 468p. 1981. pap. 31.50 (R133, IRRI). Unipub.
Priorities for Space Research 1971-1980. Space Science Board. LC 75-610526. (Orig.). 1971. pap. text ed. 5.25 (ISBN 0-309-01872-2). Natl Acad Pr.
Priorities for Survival. William P. Lineberry. (Reference Shelf Ser: Vol. 44, No. 6). 223p. 1972. 6.25 (ISBN 0-8242-0469-7). Wilson.
Priorities in Adult Education. David Rauch. 1972. 10.00 o.p. (ISBN 0-88379-006-8). Adult Ed.
Priorities in Biomedical Ethics. James F. Childress. (Orig.). 1981. pap. price not set (ISBN 0-664-24368-1). Westminster.
Priorities in Multiple Trauma. Harvey W. Meislin. 176p. 1980. text ed. 21.95 (ISBN 0-89443-287-7). Aspen Systems.
Priorities in Psychiatric Research. Malcolm Lader. LC 80-40583. 256p. 1980. 37.00 (ISBN 0-471-27833-5, Pub. by Wiley-Interscience). Wiley.
Priority Toxic Pollutants: Health Impacts & Allowable Limits. Ed. by Marshall Sittig. LC 80-311. (Environmental Health Review Ser.: No. 1). 370p. 1980. 54.00 (ISBN 0-8155-0797-6). Noyes.
Prirucni Slovnik Naucny, 4 vols. (Czech.). 1963-1967. 195.00 (ISBN 0-8277-3051-9). Maxwell Sci Intl.
Prisling. Susan Eastwood. 1977. pap. 1.00 o.p. (ISBN 0-931832-07-1). No Dead Lines.
Prism. Valerie Taylor. 180p. (Orig.). 1981. pap. 5.95 (ISBN 0-930044-18-5). Naiad Pr.
Prisms. Marianne Mackay. LC 80-52415. 384p. 1981. 11.95 (ISBN 0-87223-655-2). Seaview Bks.
Prison & Plantation: Crime, Justice, & Authority in Massachusetts & South Carolina, 1767-1878. Michael S. Hindus. LC 79-19493. (Studies in Legal History). (Illus.). 1980. 20.00x (ISBN 0-8078-1417-2). U of NC Pr.
Prison Before Trial. A. Keith Bottomley. 117p. 1970. pap. text ed. 5.00x (ISBN 0-7135-1816-2, Pub. by Bedford England). Renouf.
Prison-Breakers: A Book of Escapes from Captivity. Alban M. Phillip. LC 76-174093. (Illus.). 1971. Repr. of 1927 ed. 18.00 (ISBN 0-8103-3803-3). Gale.
Prison Crisis. Peter Evans. 192p. (Orig.). 1980. text ed. 18.95 (ISBN 0-04-365003-1, 2549); pap. text ed. 8.95x (ISBN 0-04-365004-X, 2562). Allen Unwin.
Prison English. Jerome M. Spevack. 180p. (Orig.). pap. 7.95 (ISBN 0-9604448-0-7). Spevack.
Prison Experience: An Anthology. Ed. by Karl Weiss. LC 75-32920. 352p. (gr. 6 up). 1976. 9.95 o.p. (ISBN 0-440-06017-6). Delacorte.
Prison of Ice. David Axton. 1977. pap. 1.75 o.p. (ISBN 0-449-23345-6, Crest). Fawcett.
Prison of My Mind. Barbara F. Benziger. LC 80-54811. 184p. 1981. pap. 5.95 (ISBN 0-8027-7172-6). Walker & Co.
Prison of Night: Dumarest No. 7. E. C. Tubb. (Science Fiction Ser). (Orig.). 1977. pap. 1.50 o.p. (ISBN 0-87997-346-3, UW1346). DAW Bks.
Prison or Paradise? The New Religious Cults. A. James & Marcia R. Rudin. 1980. 8.95 (ISBN 0-529-05737-9, RB 5737, Pub. by Collins Pubs). Fortress.
Prison or Paradise? The New Religious Cults? A. James Rudin & Marcia R. Rudin. LC 80-10210. 168p. 1980. 8.95 (ISBN 0-8006-0637-X, 1-637). Fortress.
Prison Organization & Inmate Subcultures. Charles W. Thomas & David M. Petersen. 1977. pap. text ed. 4.00 (ISBN 0-672-61404-9). Bobbs.
Prison Poems. Daniel Berrigan. LC 73-76683. 124p. 1973. 10.00 (ISBN 0-87775-049-1). Unicorn Pr.
Prison Profiles. M. S. Richmond. 1965. 9.00 (ISBN 0-379-00238-8). Oceana.
Prison Satellite. Leo P. Kelley. LC 79-51075. (Space Police Bks.). (Illus.). 64p. (gr. 4 up). 1980. PLB 7.95 (ISBN 0-516-02234-2). Childrens.
Prison Story. Marti Sinclair et al. 1981. pap. 3.95 (ISBN 0-89191-110-3). Cook.
Prison Violence. Ed. by Albert K. Cohen et al. LC 75-24561. 1976. 19.50 o.p. (ISBN 0-669-00185-6). Lexington Bks.
Prisoner--Cell Block H: The Karen Travers Story, No. 3. Maggie O'Shell. 224p. (Orig.). 1981. pap. 2.25 (ISBN 0-523-41176-6). Pinnacle Bks.
Prisoner & Yet. Corrie T. Boom. (Orig.). pap. 1.95 (ISBN 0-515-05334-1). Jove Pubns.
Prisoner, Cell Block H: Number 4, The Frustrations of Vera. Robert Hoskins. 224p. (Orig.). 1981. pap. 2.25 (ISBN 0-523-41215-0). Pinnacle Bks.
Prisoner Education: Project Newgate & Other College Programs. Marjorie J. Seashore & Steven Haberfeld. LC 75-23991. (Special Studies). (Illus.). 1976. 23.95 o.p. (ISBN 0-275-56040-6). Praeger.
Prisoner in Paradise. Marjorie Lewty. (Harlequin Romances Ser.). 192p. (Orig.). 1981. pap. 1.25 (ISBN 0-373-02382-0, Pub. by Harlequin). PB.
Prisoner of Grace. Joyce Cary. 301p. 1976. Repr. of 1952 ed. lib. bdg. 14.95x (ISBN 0-89244-072-4). Queens Hse.
Prisoner of Passion. Nancy John. 192p. 1981. pap. 1.50 (ISBN 0-671-57057-9). S&S.
Prisoner of War: History of the "Lost Battalion". Clyde Fillmore. 5.95 o.p. (ISBN 0-685-48815-2). Nortex Pr.
Prisoner of War Ship Models 1775-1825. Ewart C. Freeston. LC 73-77883. 1973. 22.50 o.s.i. (ISBN 0-87021-858-1). Naval Inst Pr.
Prisoner of Zenda. Anthony Hope. 1962. pap. 0.95 o.s.i. (ISBN 0-02-043710-2, Collier). Macmillan.
Prisoner of Zenda. Anthony Hope. lib. bdg. 14.95x (ISBN 0-89966-226-9). Buccaneer Bks.
Prisoner Subcultures. Lee H. Bowker. LC 77-6182. 1977. 17.95 (ISBN 0-669-01429-X). Lexington Bks.
Prisoners of Childhood. Alice Miller. LC 80-50535. 1981. 11.95 (ISBN 0-465-06347-0). Basic.
Prisoners of Culture. George A. Pettitt. LC 68-57070. 1970. 8.50 o.p. (ISBN 0-684-31100-3, ScribT). Scribner.
Prisoners of England. Miriam Kochan. 288p. 1980. text ed. 37.50x (ISBN 0-391-01738-1). Humanities.
Prisoners of Pain: Unlocking the Power of the Mind to End Suffering. Arthur Janov. LC 79-8501. 288p. 1980. 11.95 (ISBN 0-385-15791-6, Anchor Pr). Doubleday.
Prisoners of Progress: American Industrial Cities, 1850-1920. Maury Klein & Harvey A. Kantor. (Illus.). 1976. 13.95 o.s.i. (ISBN 0-02-563880-7). Macmillan.
Prisoners of Psychiatry. Bruce Ennis. LC 72-79923. 252p. 1972. 7.95 o.p. (ISBN 0-15-173084-9). HarBraceJ.
Prisoners of Society: Attitudes & After-Care. Martin Davies. (International Library of Sociology Ser.). 1974. 18.50 (ISBN 0-7100-7989-3). Routledge & Kegan.
Prisoners of Space? Exploring the Geographical Experience of Older People. Graham D. Rowles. (Replica Edition Ser.). 216p. 1980. pap. text ed. 10.00x (ISBN 0-86531-072-6). Westview.
Prisoners' Rights Sourcebook: Theory-Litigation-Practice. Michele G. Hermann & Marilyn G. Haft. LC 73-82906. 1973. 40.00 (ISBN 0-87632-100-7). Boardman.
Prisoner's Self Help Litigation Manual. James L. Potts et al. LC 77-6191. 1977. 15.95 (ISBN 0-669-01640-3). Lexington Bks.
Prisonization, Friendship & Leadership. John A. Slosar, Jr. LC 77-14698. (Illus.). 1978. 16.95 (ISBN 0-669-02023-0). Lexington Bks.
Prisons. Mary L. Settle. 244p. 1981. pap. 3.50 (ISBN 0-345-29312-6). Ballantine.
Prisons for Women: A Practical Guide to Administration Problems. Joy S. Eyman. 200p. 1971. 14.50 (ISBN 0-398-00537-0). C C Thomas.
Prisons: Houses of Darkness. Leonard Orland. LC 75-8428. 1975. 14.95 (ISBN 0-02-923430-1). Free Pr.
Prisons: Houses of Darkness. Leonard Orland. LC 75-8428. (Illus.). 1978. pap. text ed. 6.95 (ISBN 0-02-923420-4). Free Pr.
Prisons: Present & Possible. Ed. by Martin E. Wolfgang. LC 77-3860. 1979. 18.95 (ISBN 0-669-01674-8). Lexington Bks.
Pritish Nandy. Subhoranjan Dasgupta. (Indian Writers Ser.: Vol. XII). 1977. 8.50 (ISBN 0-89253-450-8). Ind-US Inc.
Pritkin Program for Diet & Exercise. Nathan Pritkin & Patrick McGrady, Jr. 1979. 14.95 (ISBN 0-448-14302-X). G&D.
Privacy & Confidentiality As Factors in Survey Response. Committee on National Statistics. 1979. pap. 12.75 (ISBN 0-309-02878-7). Natl Acad Pr.
Privacy & Disclosure of Personnel Records: Staff Study. 1980. 4.75 (ISBN 0-9602426-1-9). Trends Pub.
Privacy & the Mental. George W. Bailey. (Elementa Ser.: No. 6). 1979. pap. text ed. 23.00x (ISBN 90-6203-862-X). Humanities.
Privacy & the Press: The Law, the Mass Media, & the First Amendment. Don R. Pember. LC 79-152335. (Washington Paperback Ser.: No. 64). (Illus.). 312p. 1972. 11.50 (ISBN 0-295-95152-4); pap. 3.45 (ISBN 0-295-95265-2). U of Wash Pr.
Privacy in Colonial New England, 1630-1776. David H. Flaherty. LC 76-154804. (Illus.). 350p. 1972. 17.50x (ISBN 0-8139-0339-4). U Pr of Va.
Privacy, Its Legal Protection. rev. ed. H. Gross. 1976. 5.95 (ISBN 0-379-11099-7). Oceana.
Privacy, Law & Public Policy. David M. O'Brien. LC 79-14131. (Praeger Special Studies Ser.). 278p. 1979. 25.95 (ISBN 0-03-050406-6). Praeger.
Privacy, Security, & Computers: Guidelines for Municipal & Other Public Information Systems. O. E. Dial & Edward M. Goldberg. LC 74-13617. (Special Sutdies). (Illus.). 186p. 1975. text ed. 23.95 (ISBN 0-275-09890-7). Praeger.
Private Affairs of George Washington. Stephen Decatur. LC 77-86596. (American Scene Ser). 1969. Repr. of 1933 ed. 37.50 (ISBN 0-306-71416-7). Da Capo.
Private Army. J. Jones. 1969. pap. 1.95 o.s.i. (ISBN 0-02-073600-2, Collier). Macmillan.
Private Assumption of Public Responsibilities: The Role of American Business in Urban Manpower Programs. Peter Kobrak. LC 72-83571. (Special Studies in U.S. Economic, Social & Political Issues). 1973. 29.50x (ISBN 0-275-07030-1). Irvington.
Private Aviation: A Guide to Information Sources. Ed. by Floyd N. Reister. LC 79-84660. (Sports, Games, & Pastimes Information Guide Ser.: Vol. 3). 1979. 30.00 (ISBN 0-8103-1440-1). Gale.
Private Choice: Abortion in America in the Seventies. John T. Noonan, Jr. LC 78-67752. 1979. 14.95 (ISBN 0-02-923160-4). Free Pr.
Private Churches & Public Money: Church-Government Fiscal Relations. Paul J. Weber & Dennis A. Gilbert. LC 80-1793. (Contributions to the Study of Religion: No. 1). (Illus.). 256p. 1981. lib. bdg. 27.95 (ISBN 0-313-22484-6, WCM/). Greenwood.
Private City: Philadelphia in Three Periods of Its Growth. Sam B. Warner, Jr. LC 68-21557. (Illus.). 1968. 10.00x (ISBN 0-8122-7575-6); pap. 4.95x (ISBN 0-8122-1003-4, Pa Paperbks). U of Pa Pr.
Private Diaries of Sir H. Rider Haggard, Nineteen Fourteen to Nineteen Twenty-Five. Ed. by D. S. Higgins. LC 80-5496. 326p. 1980. 19.95 (ISBN 0-8128-2738-4). Stein & Day.
Private Dispute Settlement. Merton C. Bernstein. LC 68-17521. (Illus.). 1969. 20.95 o.s.i. (ISBN 0-02-903030-7). Free Pr.
Private Economic Power in India: A Study in Genesis & Concentration. Asim Chaudhuri. LC 76-900858. 1976. 10.00x (ISBN 0-88386-717-6). South Asia Bks.
Private Elvis. Ed. by Diego Cortez. (Illus.). 1978. pap. 6.00 (ISBN 0-8467-0537-0, Pub. by Two Continents). Hippocrene Bks.
Private Enterprise & Public Purpose. S. Prakash Sethi & Carl L. Swanson. (Management & Administration Ser.). 480p. 1981. pap. text ed. 12.95 (ISBN 0-471-07697-X). Wiley.
Private Enterprise in Developing Countries. W. M. Clarke. 1966. pap 4.20 (ISBN 0-08-012142-X). Pergamon.
Private Fire Protection & Detection Systems, No. 210. IFSTA Committee. Ed. by Gene P. Carlson. LC 79-55670. (Illus., Orig.). 1979. pap. 7.00 (ISBN 0-87939-036-0). Intl Fire Serv.
Private Gold Coins & Patterns of the United States. Donald H. Kagin. LC 79-21041. (Illus.). 400p. 1980. lib. bdg. 24.95 (ISBN 0-668-04830-1). Arco.
Private Government of Public Money: Community & Policy in British Political Administration. Hugh Heclo & Aaron Wildavsky. 1974. 25.75x (ISBN 0-520-02497-4). U of Cal Pr.
Private Hell. H. G. Gunther. (Gunther Romance Ser.: No. 5). 208p. (Orig.). 1981. pap. 1.95 (ISBN 0-515-05677-4). Jove Pubns.
Private Independent Schools: The Bunting & Lyon Blue Book, 1980. 33rd ed. LC 72-122324. (Illus.). 1980. 35.00x o.p. (ISBN 0-913094-33-1). Bunting.
Private Independent Schools: The Bunting & Lyon Book, 1981. 34th ed. LC 72-122324. (Illus.). 1981. 40.00x (ISBN 0-913094-34-X). Bunting.
Private Investigation. Karl Alexander. 1980. 10.95 (ISBN 0-440-06834-7). Delacorte.
Private Investigator. Gene Blackwell. LC 79-4560. (Illus.). 1979. 16.95 (ISBN 0-913708-34-8). Butterworths.
Private Investment in India & Pakistan, 1900-1939. Amiya K. Bagchi. LC 79-152631. (South Asian Studies: No. 10). (Illus.). 1971. 53.50 (ISBN 0-521-07641-2). Cambridge U Pr.
Private Jurisdiction in England. Warren O. Ault. LC 80-1998. 1981. Repr. of 1923 ed. 37.00 (ISBN 0-404-18550-9). AMS Pr.
Private Landlords in England. John Greve. 54p. 1965. pap. text ed. 3.75x (Pub. by Bedford England). Renouf.
Private Lending for Balance of Payments Purpose. Ed. by Benjamin Cohen & Fabio Basagni. (Atlantic Institute for International Affairs Ser.: No. 4). 265p. 1981. text ed. 31.50 (ISBN 0-86598-038-1). Allanheld.
Private Letters from an American in England to His Friends in America, 1769. (Novel in England, 1700-1775 Ser). 1974. lib. bdg. 50.00 (ISBN 0-8240-1186-4). Garland Pub.
Private Letters of the Marquess of Dalhousie. Ed. by J. G. Baird. (Illus.). 448p. 1972. Repr. of 1910 ed. 30.00x (ISBN 0-686-28317-1, Pub. by Irish Academic Pr). Biblio Dist.
Private Lies. M. K. Cooper. 1980. pap. 2.25 (ISBN 0-445-04566-3). Popular Lib.
Private Life of Henry the Eighth. N. Brysson Morrison. LC 63-13796. (Illus.). 1964. 8.95 (ISBN 0-8149-0162-X). Vanguard.
Private Life of Sherlock Holmes. Vincent Starrett. (Illus.). 224p. 1975. pap. 1.95 o.p. (ISBN 0-523-00695-0, 25-695-7). Pinnacle Bks.
Private Life of the Otter. Philip Wayre. 1979. 17.95 (ISBN 0-7134-0833-2, Pub. by Batsford England). David & Charles.
Private Life of the Rabbit. R. M. Lockley. (Illus.). 1975. pap. 4.95 (ISBN 0-380-00447-X, 38224). Avon.
Private Life of the Rabbit: An Account of the Life History & Social Behavior of the Wild Rabbit. R. M. Lockley. LC 74-8855. (Illus.). 1974. 8.95 o.s.i. (ISBN 0-02-573900-X). Macmillan.
Private Lives & Public Surveillance: Social Control in the Computer Age. James B. Rule. LC 73-90685. 1974. 8.00x (ISBN 0-8052-3542-6). Schocken.
Private Lives of Orchids. Hilda Simon. LC 74-18331. (Illus.). 1975. 15.00 o.p. (ISBN 0-397-01075-3). Lippincott.
Private Lives of Our Natural Neighbors. Ames. Date not set. 15.00 (ISBN 0-8076-0960-9). Braziller.
Private Management & Public Policy: The Principle of Public Responsibility. Lee E. Preston & James E. Post. (Illus.). 192p. 1975. pap. text ed. 10.95 (ISBN 0-13-710970-9). P-H.
Private Market Housing Renovation in Older Urban Areas. J. Thomas Black et al. LC 77-80214. (ULI Research Report: No. 26). (Illus.). 40p. 1977. pap. text ed. 9.75 (ISBN 0-87420-326-0). Urban Land.
Private Morality in Greece & Rome: Some Historical Aspects. Den W. Boer. 1980. text ed. 45.75x (ISBN 90-04-05976-8). Humanities.
Private Physicians & Public Programs. Frank Sloan et al. LC 77-18330. (Illus.). 1978. 18.95 (ISBN 0-669-02093-1). Lexington Bks.
Private Pictures. Photos by Daniel Angeli & Jean-Paul Dousset. 96p. 1980. pap. 9.95 (ISBN 0-670-57849-5, Studio). Viking Pr.
Private Pieces. Tom Johnson. LC 76-14367. 1976. pap. 2.95 (ISBN 0-938690-01-9). Two Eighteen.
Private Pilot - Airplane Written Test Questions Including Answers & Explanations. combined ed. John King & Martha King. (Pilot Training Ser.). (Illus.). 206p. 1979. pap. 8.95 (ISBN 0-89100-197-2, E*A-A*C61-32C-1). Aviation Maintenance.
Private Pilot, Airplane, Question & Answer Book: For Ac 61-32c. Ed. by Wallace E. Manning, Jr. 1979. pap. 7.95 o.p. (ISBN 0-685-95909-0, Pub. by AvTest). Aviation.
Private Pilot-Airplane Written Test Guide. 4th ed. Federal Aviation Administration. (Pilot Training Ser.). (Illus.). 148p. 1979. pap. 3.00 (ISBN 0-89100-166-2, E*A-A*C61-32C). Aviation Maintenance.
Private Pilot Flight Test Guide. 2nd ed. Federal Aviation Administration. (Pilot Training Ser.). 92p. 1975. pap. 1.35 (ISBN 0-89100-171-9, E*A-A*C61-54A). Aviation Maintenance.
Private Pilot Manual. 7th ed. (Pilot Training Ser.). (Illus.). 400p. 1981. text ed. 12.95 (ISBN 0-88487-067-7, JS314301). Jeppesen Sanderson.
Private Pilot Written Exam Course. Thomas B. Gallagher. LC 80-70132. (Illus.). 68p. (Orig.). 1981. pap. 19.95 (ISBN 0-938706-00-4). Fed Aviation.
Private Pilot's Dictionary & Handbook. Kirk Polking. LC 72-95274. (Illus.). 280p. 1974. lib. bdg. 5.95 o. p. o.p. (ISBN 0-668-02932-3); lib. bdg. 5.95 o.p. (ISBN 0-668-02931-5). Arco.
Private Placements & Restricted Securities, 2 vols. rev. ed. Stuart C. Goldberg. LC 70-163723. 1978. looseleaf with 1979 rev. pages 110.00 (ISBN 0-87632-078-7). Boardman.
Private Police. Hilary Draper. 1978. text ed. 19.50x (ISBN 0-391-00852-8). Humanities.
Private Police: Security & Danger. James Kakalik & Sorrel Wildhorn. LC 76-10072. 500p. 1977. 37.50x (ISBN 0-8448-0365-0). Crane-Russak Co.
Private Power: Multinational Corporations for the Survival of Our Planet. Axel Madsen. LC 80-19372. 256p. 1980. 12.95 (ISBN 0-688-03735-6). Morrow.

Private Practice. Linda Pubreuil. 1976. pap. 1.50 o.p. (ISBN 0-685-69158-6, LB366DK, Leisure Bks). Nordon Pubns.

Private Practice in Britain. Samuel Mencher. 95p. 1967. pap. text ed. 5.00x (Pub. by Bedford England). Renouf.

Private Practice in Nursing. Charles J. Koltz. LC 79-9311. 1979. text ed. 25.50 (ISBN 0-89443-158-7). Aspen Systems.

Private Practice in Social Casework. Sidney Levenstein. LC 64-18471. 1964. 20.00x (ISBN 0-231-02712-5). Columbia U Pr.

Private Practices. Linde Wolfe. 1981. pap. 3.25 (ISBN 0-440-17185-7). Dell.

Private Press Books, 1975. Ed. by David Chambers. LC 60-31492. (Illus.). 1978. pap. 13.50x (ISBN 0-900002-53-0). Intl Pubns Serv.

Private Press Books, 1976. Ed. by David Chambers. LC 60-31492. (Illus.). 117p. (Orig.). 1979. pap. 13.50x (ISBN 0-900002-83-2). Intl Pubns Serv.

Private Presses & Publishing in England Since 1945. B. E. Bellamy. 1980. text ed. 30.00 (ISBN 0-89664-180-5, Pub. by K G Saur). Shoe String.

Private Pressure on Public Law: Legal Career of Justice Thurgood Marshall. Randall W. Bland. LC 72-91170. 1973. 15.00 (ISBN 0-8046-9035-9, Natl U). Kennikat.

Private Pressure on Public Law: The Legal Career of Justice Thurgood Marshall. Randall W. Bland. LC 72-91170. (Illus.). 220p. 1973. pap. 7.50 (ISBN 0-8046-9048-0, Natl U). Kennikat.

Private Property & the Constitution. Bruce A. Ackerman. LC 76-47667. 1977. 15.00x (ISBN 0-300-02065-1); pap. 7.95x (ISBN 0-300-02237-9). Yale U Pr.

Private Provision of Public Services: An Overview. Donald Fisk et al. (Institute Paper). 105p. 1978. pap. 6.00 (ISBN 0-87766-221-5, 18300). Urban Inst.

Private Psychiatric Hospitals - a National Survey. C. K. Kanno & R. M. Glasscote. 1966. pap. 3.00 o.p. (ISBN 0-685-24855-0, 162). Am Psychiatric.

Private Real Estate Limited Partnerships 1980: A Course Handbook. Don Augustine & Peter M. Fass. LC 80-81320. (Real Estate Law & Practice Course Handbook Ser.). 950p. 1980. pap. text ed. 25.00 (ISBN 0-686-68828-7, N4-4353). PLI.

Private Realities: Recent American Photography. Clifford S. Ackley. (Illus.). 1974. 15.00 (ISBN 0-87846-077-2); pap. 6.95 (ISBN 0-87846-089-6). Mus Fine Arts Boston.

Private Sector. Jeff Millar. 288p. 1981. pap. 2.95 (ISBN 0-449-24368-0, Crest). Fawcett.

Private Sector in Soviet Agriculture. 2nd enl. & rev ed. Karl-Eugen Wadekin. Ed. by George Karcz. Tr. by Keith Bush from Ger. LC 76-95322. Orig. Title: Privatproduzenten in der Sowjetischen Landwirtschaft. 350p. 1973. 29.50x (ISBN 0-520-01558-4). U of Cal Pr.

Private Sector Participation in Federal Energy RD&D Planning. Committee on Private Sector Participation in Government Energy RD&D Planning. 1978. pap. 6.50 (ISBN 0-309-02783-7). Natl Acad Pr.

Private Stable. James A. Garland. 50.00 (ISBN 0-88427-018-1). Green Hill.

Private Thoughts. F. Donald Williams. 1980. 4.00 o.p. (ISBN 0-8062-1198-9). Carlton.

Private Truce. Anthony Lawman. 1981. 11.95 (ISBN 0-671-25408-1). S&S.

Private Tucker's Boer War Diary. Pamela Todd & David Fordham. (Illus.). 192p. 1980. 27.00 (ISBN 0-241-10272-3, Pub. by Hamish Hamilton England). David & Charles.

Private Urban Renewal: A Different Residential Trend. Zeitz. LC 78-19568. (Illus.). 1979. 15.95 (ISBN 0-669-02627-1). Lexington Bks.

Private Vendetta. Roderick Grant. 1979. 7.95 o.p. (ISBN 0-684-15801-9, ScribT). Scribner.

Private World of Ballet. John Gruen. 1976. pap. 4.95 o.p. (ISBN 0-14-004343-8). Penguin.

Private Wound. Nicholas Blake. LC 68-15980. 224p. 1981. pap. 2.25 (ISBN 0-06-080531-5, PL). Har-Row.

Private Yankee Doodle. J. P. Martin. Ed. by George F. Scheer. Orig. Title: Being a Narrative of Some of the Adventures, Dangers, & Sufferings of a Revolutionary Soldier. 305p. 1979. pap. 2.95 (ISBN 0-89062-047-4, Pub. by Eastern Natl Par). Pub Ctr Cult Res.

Privateer. Jon Williams. (Orig.). 1981. pap. 2.75 (ISBN 0-440-16811-2). Dell.

Privateers & Volunteers, 1766-1866. R. E. Stivers. LC 75-20749. 502p. 1975. 17.00x (ISBN 0-87021-395-4). Naval Inst Pr.

Privateers in Charleston, 1793 to 1796. Melvin H. Jackson. (Illus.). 160p. 1969. 17.50x (ISBN 0-87474-158-0). Smithsonian.

Privateer's Woman. June Wetherell. 1978. pap. 1.95 o.p. (ISBN 0-523-40186-8). Pinnacle Bks.

Privatised World. Arthur Brittan. (International Library of Sociology Ser.). 1978. 18.50x (ISBN 0-7100-8769-1); pap. 8.95 (ISBN 0-7100-8768-3). Routledge & Kegan.

Priviledges & Practice of Parliaments in England. LC 74-80218. (English Experience Ser.: No. 654). 1974. Repr. of 1628 ed. 5.00 (ISBN 90-221-0654-3). Walter J Johnson.

Privilege & Burden. Robert G. Middleton. 1969. 4.95 o.p. (ISBN 0-8170-0440-8). Judson.

Privilege in America: An End to Inequality? Arthur B. Shostak et al. 160p. 1974. pap. 6.95 (ISBN 0-13-711119-3, Spec). P-H.

Privy Council. Albert V. Dicey. LC 79-1625. 1981. Repr. of 1887 ed. 16.00 (ISBN 0-88355-930-7). Hyperion Conn.

Prize Homes. Hiawatha T. Estes. (Illus.). 1981. 2.00 (ISBN 0-911008-22-5). H Estes.

Prize Stories of the Seventies from O'Henry Awards. Ed. by William Abrahams. LC 80-22790. 408p. 1981. 12.95 (ISBN 0-385-17158-7). Doubleday.

Prize Stories 1981: The O'henry Awards. William Abrahams. 360p. 1981. text ed. 13.95 (ISBN 0-385-15977-3). Doubleday.

Prize-Winning American Drama: A Bibliographical & Descriptive Guide. Jane F. Bonin. LC 73-3111. 1973. 10.00 (ISBN 0-8108-0607-X). Scarecrow.

Pro Baseball: An Almanac of Facts & Records. David Paige. (Sports Records Ser.). (Illus.). (gr. 3-12). 1977. lib. bdg. 6.75 (ISBN 0-87191-607-X). Creative Ed.

Pro Basketball: An Almanac of Facts & Records. David Paige. (Sports Records Ser.). (Illus.). 40p. (gr. 3-12). 1977. lib. bdg. 6.75 (ISBN 0-87191-605-3). Creative Ed.

Pro Basketball: Its Superstars & History. Ed. by Zander Hollander. (gr. 9 up). 1971. pap. 1.50 (ISBN 0-590-09157-3, Schol Pap). Schol Bk Serv.

Pro Basketball, 1976-1977. Barry Larit. 1976. pap. 1.75 o.p. (ISBN 0-345-25442-2). Ballantine.

Pro Basketball, 1977-78. 1977. pap. 1.95 o.p. (ISBN 0-345-25823-1). Ballantine.

Pro Football A to Z. George Sullivan. LC 75-43128. 1976. pap. 4.50 o.p. (ISBN 0-684-14641-X, SL652, ScribT). Scribner.

Pro Football: An Almanac of Facts & Records. David Paige. LC 77-857. (Sports Records Ser.). (Illus.). (gr. 3-12). 1977. PLB 6.75 (ISBN 0-87191-604-5). Creative Ed.

Pro Football Heroes. Steve Gelman. (gr. 4-6). 1969. pap. 0.95 o.p. (ISBN 0-590-02965-7, Schol Pap). Schol Bk Serv.

Pro Football Rookie. Haskel Frankel. LC 64-19297. (gr. 7-9). 5.95 o.p. (ISBN 0-385-04061-X). Doubleday.

Pro Football, 1976. (Illus.). 288p. (Orig.). 1976. pap. 1.95 o.p. (ISBN 0-345-25440-6). Ballantine.

Pro Football, 1977. 1977. pap. 1.95 o.p. (ISBN 0-345-25822-3). Ballantine.

Pro Hockey, 1976-1977. Barry Larit. 1976. pap. 1.75 o.p. (ISBN 0-345-25443-0). Ballantine.

Pro M. Caelio Oratio. 3rd ed. Cicero. Ed. by R. G. Austin. 1960. 11.95x (ISBN 0-19-814401-6). Oxford U Pr.

Pro Milone. Cicero. Ed. by J. S. Reid. 1895. text ed. 5.25x (ISBN 0-521-04650-5). Cambridge U Pr.

Pro Roscio. Cicero. Ed. by J. C. Nicol. (Latin). text ed. 5.75x (ISBN 0-521-04652-1). Cambridge U Pr.

Pro Sports Champions. Bill Gutman. (Illus.). 192p. 1981. PLB price not set (ISBN 0-671-34028-X). Messner.

Pro Sports Trivia. Lee Pretner. LC 74-34548. (Illus.). 160p. (gr. 4 up). 1975. 5.88 o.p. (ISBN 0-531-01091-0). Watts.

Probabalistic Mechanics & Structural Reliability. Compiled by American Society of Civil Engineers. 436p. 1979. pap. text ed. 32.50 (ISBN 0-87262-138-3). Am Soc Civil Eng.

Probabalistic Models for Some Intelligence & Attainment Tests. G. Rasch. LC 80-16546. 208p. 1980. lib. bdg. 9.00x (ISBN 0-226-70554-4). U of Chicago Pr.

Probabilistic Mechanical Design. Edward B. Haugen. LC 80-13428. 688p. 1980. 36.95 (ISBN 0-471-05847-5, Pub. by Wiley Interscience). Wiley.

Probabilistic Number Theory One: Mean-Value Theorems. P. D. Elliot. (Grundlehren der Mathematischen Wissenschaften: Vol. 239). 1980. 35.00 (ISBN 0-387-90437-9). Springer-Verlag.

Probabilistic Number Theory Two: Central Limit Theorems. P. D. Eliott. (Grundlehren der Mathematischen Wissenschaften: Vol. 240). 1980. 35.00 (ISBN 0-387-90438-7). Springer-Verlag.

Probabilistic Programming. S. Vajda. (Probability & Mathematical Statistics Ser.). 1972. 18.00 (ISBN 0-12-710150-0). Acad Pr.

Probabilistic Study of Linear Elliptic-Parabolic Equations of Second Order. I. Johnstone. (Notes on Pure Mathematics Ser.: No. 12). 217p. (Orig.). 1980. pap. text ed. 14.95 (ISBN 0-908160-32-1, 0564). Bks Australia.

Probabilistic System Analysis: An Introduction to Probabilistic Models, Decisions & Applications of Random Processes. Arthur M. Breipohl. LC 77-94920. 1970. 28.95 (ISBN 0-471-10181-8). Wiley.

Probability. Leo Breiman. (Illus.). 1968. text ed. 23.95 (ISBN 0-201-00646-4). A-W.

Probability. Charles F. Linn. LC 79-171006. (Young Math Ser.). (Illus.). 40p. (gr. 1-4). 1972. PLB 7.89 (ISBN 0-690-65602-5, TYC-J). T Y Crowell.

Probability: An Introduction. Samuel Goldberg. (gr. 11 up). 1960. ref. ed. 19.95 (ISBN 0-13-711580-6); pap. 0.50 ans. bk. (ISBN 0-13-711572-5). P-H.

Probability & Concepts in Engineering Planning & Design: Basic Principles, Vol. 1. A. H. Ang & W. H. Tang. LC 75-5892. 409p. 1975. text ed. 24.95x (ISBN 0-471-03200-X); solutions manaul avail. (ISBN 0-471-03198-4). Wiley.

Probability & Design: Concepts in Engineering Planning & Design, Vol. 2. A. H. Ang & W. H. Tang. 1982. 15.95 (ISBN 0-471-03201-8). Wiley.

Probability & Evidence. Alfred J. Ayer. LC 71-185572. (John Dewey Lecture Ser). 1972. 12.50x (ISBN 0-231-03650-7). Columbia U Pr.

Probability & Evidence: The John Dewey Lectures in Philosophy, No. 2. A. J. Ayer. 1979. pap. 6.00x (ISBN 0-231-04767-3). Columbia U Pr.

Probability & Expectation Inequalities. Stamatis Cambanis & Gordon Simons. 49p. 1980. pap. 1.60 (1263). U of NC Pr.

Probability & Mathematical Statistics: An Introduction. Eugene Lukacs. 1972. text ed. 19.95 (ISBN 0-12-459850-1). Acad Pr.

Probability & Measure. Patrick Billingsley. LC 78-25632. (Probability & Mathematical Statistics Ser.). 1979. 28.95 (ISBN 0-471-03173-9, Pub. by Wiley-Interscience). Wiley.

Probability & Random Processes for Engineers & Scientists. A. B. Clarke & R. L. Disney. 1970. 24.95 (ISBN 0-471-15980-8). Wiley.

Probability & Related Topics in Physical Sciences. Mark Kac. LC 59-10443. (Lectures in Applied Mathematics Ser.: Vol. 1A). 1980. Repr. of 1977 ed. 24.00 (ISBN 0-8218-0047-7, LAM-1.1). Am Math.

Probability & Statistical Inference I. J. G. Kalbfleisch. (Universitexts). (Illus.). 342p. 1980. pap. 15.00 (ISBN 0-387-90457-3). Springer-Verlag.

Probability & Statistical Inference II. J. G. Kalbfleisch. (Universitexts). (Illus.). 316p. 1980. pap. 15.00 (ISBN 0-387-90458-1). Springer-Verlag.

Probability & Statistical Inference for Scientists & Engineers. Isaac Gibra. (Industrial Engineering Ser.). (Illus.). 608p. 1973. ref. ed. 23.95 o.p. (ISBN 0-13-711622-5). P-H.

Probability & Statistics. Morris Degroot. LC 74-19691. (Behavioral Science Quantitative Methods Ser). (Illus.). 624p. 1975. text ed. 20.95 (ISBN 0-201-01503-X); sol. manual 7.95 (ISBN 0-201-01509-9). A-W.

Probability & Statistics for Business Decisions. Robert Schlaifer. 1959. text ed. 22.95 (ISBN 0-07-055309-2, C); tchr's manual 5.95 (ISBN 0-07-055313-0); student's manual 7.95 (ISBN 0-07-055314-9). McGraw.

Probability & Statistics for Business Decisions. Robert Schlaifer. LC 79-23042. 744p. 1980. Repr. of 1959 ed. lib. bdg. write for info. (ISBN 0-89874-029-0). Krieger.

Probability & Statistics for Engineers. 2nd ed. I. Miller & J. Freund. (Illus.). 1977. 23.95 (ISBN 0-13-711945-3). P-H.

Probability & Statistics in Particle Physics. A. G. Frodesen et al. 1979. pap. 39.00x (ISBN 8-2000-1906-3, Dist. by Columbia U. Pr.). Universitet.

Probability & Stochastic Processes, with a View Toward Applications. Leo Breiman. LC 78-3566. (Illus.). 1969. text ed. 22.50 (ISBN 0-395-04231-3, 3-05970). HM.

Probability Based on Radon Measures. Tue Tjur. LC 80-40503. (Wiley Series in Probability & Mathematical Statistics Ser.). 256p. 1980. 55.50 (ISBN 0-471-27824-6, Pub. by Wiley-Interscience). Wiley.

Probability, Decision, Statistics. J. Bradley. 1976. 23.95 (ISBN 0-13-711556-3). P-H.

Probability: Elements of the Mathematical Theory. C. R. Heathcote. LC 70-142998. 1971. 15.95 (ISBN 0-471-36675-7). Halsted Pr.

Probability for Practicing Engineers. Henry L. Gray & Patrick Odell. LC 78-109531. 1970. 11.95 (ISBN 0-389-00501-0); pap. 9.95 (ISBN 0-8436-0315-1). CBI Pub.

Probability for Statistical Decision Making. Park J. Ewart et al. (Illus.). 400p. 1974. ref. ed. 19.95 (ISBN 0-13-711614-4). P-H.

Probability, Logic & Management Decisions. J. Braverman. text ed. 17.95 o.p. (ISBN 0-07-007345-7, C); solutions manual 4.95 o.p. (ISBN 0-07-007346-5). McGraw.

Probability, Statistics, & Decision Making in Meterology. Ed. by Allan H. Murphy & Richard W. Katz. 450p. (Orig.). 1981. lib. bdg. 28.50x (ISBN 0-86531-152-8); pap. text ed. 15.00x (ISBN 0-86531-153-6). Westview.

Probability, Statistics & Queueing Theory: With Computer Science Application. Arnold O. Allen. (Computer Science & Applied Math Ser.). 1978. 29.50 (ISBN 0-12-051050-2). Acad Pr.

Probability, Statistics & Time: A Collection of Essays. M. S. Bartlett. LC 75-24171. 148p. 1976. text ed. 15.95x o.p. (ISBN 0-412-14150-7, Pub. by Chapman & Hall); pap. 12.95x o.p. (ISBN 0-412-22260-4). Methuen Inc.

Probability, Statistics & Time: A Collection of Essays. M. S. Bartlett. LC 75-24171. (Monographs on Applied Probability & Statistics). 1975. text ed. 15.95 o.p. (ISBN 0-470-05466-2). Halsted Pr.

Probability Theory. A. M. Arthurs. (Library of Mathematics). 1965. pap. 4.50 (ISBN 0-7100-4359-7). Routledge & Kegan.

Probability Theory: A Concise Course. rev. ed. Y. A. Rozanov. Tr. by Richard A. Silverman from Russian. LC 77-78592. 1977. pap. text ed. 3.00 (ISBN 0-486-63544-9). Dover.

Probability Theory an Vector Spaces II: Proceedings. Ed. by A. Weron. (Lecture Notes in Mathematics Ser.: Vol. 828). 324p. 1981. pap. 19.50 (ISBN 0-387-10253-1). Springer-Verlag.

Probable & the Marvelous: Blake, Wordsworth, & the Eighteenth-Century Critical Tradition. Wallace Jackson. LC 77-17807. 1978. 16.00x (ISBN 0-8203-0439-5). U of Ga Pr.

Probable & the Provable. L. Jonathan Cohen. (Clarendon Library of Logic & Philosophy). 1977. 36.00x (ISBN 0-19-824412-6). Oxford U Pr.

Probado Por Fuego. Tr. by Merril Womack & Virginia Womack. (Spanish Bks.). (Span.). 1977. 1.60 (ISBN 0-8297-0773-5). Life Pubs Intl.

Probalistic Models for Some Intelligence & Attainment Tests. G. Rasch. LC 80-16546. 208p. 1980. lib. bdg. 21.00x (ISBN 0-226-70553-6). U of Chicago Pr.

Probate Laws of Arkansas. 1961. with 1979-80 suppl. 35.00 (ISBN 0-672-83316-6, Bobbs-Merrill Law); 1978-79 17.50 (ISBN 0-672-81167-7). Michie.

Probation & Parole. Barbara A. Kay & Clyde B. Vedder. 224p. 1980. 11.00 (ISBN 0-398-00986-4). C C Thomas.

Probation & Parole: Principles & Practices. Reed K. Clegg. 196p. 1979. pap. 11.75 (ISBN 0-398-03036-7). C C Thomas.

Probation & Parole: Theory & Practice. Howard Abadinsky. (Illus.). 1977. text ed. 17.95 (ISBN 0-13-715953-6). P-H.

Probation, Parole, & Community Corrections. 2nd ed. Ed. by Robert M. Carter & Leslie T. Wilkins. LC 75-44332. 1976. text ed. 22.95 (ISBN 0-471-13845-2). Wiley.

Probe. abridged ed. Marvin D. Glock & David Bender. (Communication Skills Ser.). 1978. pap. text ed. 6.95x (ISBN 0-675-08373-7); instructor's manual 3.95 (ISBN 0-675-08372-9); 1 set 80.00 (ISBN 0-675-08372-9); 2-7 sets 55.00 (ISBN 0-686-67985-7); 8 or more 45.00 (ISBN 0-686-67986-5). Merrill.

Probe: A Handbook of Classroom Ideas to Motivate the Teaching of Primary Science. (Spice Ser). 1976. 6.50 (ISBN 0-89273-102-8). Educ Serv.

Probe Duplicating Masters: Primary Science, 2 vols. (Spice Ser.). 1977. 5.95 ea. Vol. 1, Grades K-2 (ISBN 0-89273-546-5). Vol. 2, Grades 2-4 (ISBN 0-89273-547-3). Educ Serv.

PROBES: A Prospectus on Processes & Resources of the Bering Sea Shelf Nineteen Seventy-Five to Nineteen Eighty-Five. write for info. (ISBN 0-914500-05-8). U of AK Inst Marine.

Probing Hadrons with Leptons. Ed. by G. Preparata & J. J. Aubert. (Ettore Majorana International Science Ser., Physical Sciences: Vol. 5). 502p. 1980. 59.50 (ISBN 0-306-40438-9, Plenum Pr). Plenum Pub.

Probing the Earth: Contemporary Land Projects. John Beardsley. LC 77-12419. (Illus.). 112p. 1978. 17.50 (ISBN 0-87474-232-3). Smithsonian.

Probing the Past: A Guide to the Study & Teaching of History. Stephens. 19.95 (ISBN 0-205-04196-5, 224196X). Allyn.

Probit Analysis. 3rd ed. D. J. Finney. LC 78-134618. (Illus.). 1971. 57.50 (ISBN 0-521-08041-X). Cambridge U Pr.

Problem Behaviour in the Secondary School. Bill Gillha. 192p. 1981. 26.00x (ISBN 0-7099-0129-1, Pub. by Croom Helm LTD England). Biblio Dist.

Problem Book in the Theory of Functions, 2 vols. Konrad Knopp. Incl. Vol. 1. Problems in the Elementary Theory of Functions. Tr. by Lipman Bers (ISBN 0-486-60158-7); Vol. 2. Problems in the Advanced Theory of Functions (ISBN 0-486-60159-5). 1968. pap. text ed. 3.00 ea. Dover.

Problem-Finding in Educational Administration: Trends in Research & Theory. Ed. by Glenn L. Immegart & William L. Boyd. LC 78-19912. 320p. 1979. 23.95 (ISBN 0-669-02438-4). Lexington Bks.

Problem Horse. R. S. Summerhays. (Illus.). pap. 6.10 (ISBN 0-85131-225-X, Dist. by Sporting Book Center). J A Allen.

Problem Horses - Tested Guide for Curing Most Common & Serious Horse Behavior Habits. Reginald S. Summerhays. pap. 3.00 (ISBN 0-87980-200-6). Wilshire.

Problem of Cheating in Schools: Its Psychological Meaning & the Future of the American Society. Charles Yardumian. (American Culture Library Bk.). (Illus.). 107p. 1981. 29.95 (ISBN 0-89266-293-X). Am Classical Coll Pr.

Problem of China. Bertrand Russell. 1922. text ed. 9.95x (ISBN 0-04-951009-6). Allen Unwin.

Problem of "Curse" in the Hebrew Bible. Herbert Brichto. (Society of Biblical Literature, Monographs). 1963. pap. 9.00 (ISBN 0-89130-183-6, 060013). Scholars Pr Ca.

Problem of Form in Painting and Sculpture. Adolf Hildebrand. Ed. by Sydney J. Freedberg. LC 77-19375. (Connoisseurship & Art History Ser.: Vol. 11). (Illus.). 141p. 1979. lib. bdg. 20.00 (ISBN 0-8240-3269-1). Garland Pub.

Problem of History in Mark. James M. Robinson. LC 57-857. (Scholars Press Reprint Ser.). pap. 6.00 (ISBN 0-89130-334-0, 000703). Scholars Pr CA.

Problem of International Investment. Royal Institute Of International Affairs. LC 67-55858. Repr. of 1937 ed. 30.00x (ISBN 0-678-05195-X). Kelley.

Problem of Life: An Essay of Biological Thought. C. U. Smith. LC 75-20106. 1976. 24.95 (ISBN 0-470-80188-3). Halsted Pr.

Problem of Metaphysics. D. M. MacKinnon. LC 73-79309. 180p. 1974. 23.50 (ISBN 0-521-20275-2). Cambridge U Pr.

Problem of Military Readiness. Melvin R. Laird & Lawrence J. Korb. 1980. pap. 3.75 (ISBN 0-8447-1087-3). Am Enterprise.

Problem of Organic Form. Edmund G. Sinnott. 1963. 27.50x (ISBN 0-685-69864-5). Elliots Bks.

Problem of Pain. C. S. Lewis. 1943. 7.95 (ISBN 0-02-570910-0); pap. 1.65 (ISBN 0-02-086840-5). Macmillan.

Problem of Party Government. Richard Rose. LC 74-30329. (Illus.). 1975. 17.95 (ISBN 0-02-926780-3). Free Pr.

Problem of Proof: Especially As Exemplified in Disputed Documents Trials. Albert S. Osborn. LC 75-20212. 1975. Repr. of 1926 ed. 38.95 (ISBN 0-88229-300-1). Nelson-Hall.

Problem of Purity. Dion Fortune. 1980. pap. 4.95 (ISBN 0-87728-506-3). Weiser.

Problem of Restoration: A Study in Comparative Political History. Robert A. Kann. 1967. 28.50x (ISBN 0-520-00630-5). U of Cal Pr.

Problem of Style. John M. Murry. LC 80-21463. x, 133p. 1980. Repr. of 1960 ed. lib. bdg. 19.50x (ISBN 0-313-22523-0, MUPR). Greenwood.

Problem of the Contingency of the World in Husserl's Phenomenology. Sang Ki Kim. (Philosophical Currents: No. 17). 1976. pap. text ed. 17.25x (ISBN 90-6032-054-9). Humanities.

Problem of the Economic & Political Survival of the United States. Duncan D. Macmillan. (The Major Currents in Contemporary World History Library). (Illus.). 117p. 1981. 37.85 (ISBN 0-930008-80-4). Inst Econ Pol.

Problem of the Historical Jesus. Joachim Jeremias. Ed. by John Reumann. Tr. by Norman Perrin from Ger. LC 64-23064. (Facet Bks.). 1964. pap. 1.95 (ISBN 0-8006-3015-7, 1-3015). Fortress.

Problem of Verse Language. Yury Tynyanov. Tr. by Michael Sosa & Brent Harvey. 1981. 15.00 (ISBN 0-88233-464-6); pap. 6.50x (ISBN 0-88233-465-4). Ardis Pubs.

Problem of War: A Global Issue. Roberta Moore & Joseph Moore. 144p. (gr. 10 up). 1980. pap. text ed. 6.19x (ISBN 0-8104-6073-4). Hayden.

Problem of Wineskins: Church Renewal in Technological Age. Howard A. Snyder. LC 74-31842. (Illus.). 216p. 1975. pap. text ed. 4.95 (ISBN 0-87784-769-X); study guide 0.95 (ISBN 0-87784-460-7); study guide 0.95 (ISBN 0-87784-460-7). Inter-Varsity.

Problem-Oriented Approach to Stroke Rehabilitation. Philip L. Mossman. 480p. 1976. pap. 44.00 spiral (ISBN 0-398-03427-3). C C Thomas.

Problem-Oriented Medical Record Implementation: Allied Health Peer Review. 2nd ed. Rosemarian Berni & Helen Readey. LC 77-18278. (Illus.). 1978. pap. text ed. 10.00 (ISBN 0-8016-0648-9). Mosby.

Problem-Oriented Psychiatric Index & Treatment Plans. 1st ed. Monte J. Meldman. Ed. by Edith Johnson. LC 76-200. (Illus.). 1976. pap. text ed. 10.50 (ISBN 0-8016-3393-1). Mosby.

Problem-Oriented Record in Psychiatry & Mental Health Care. 2nd ed. Ralph S. Ryback et al. 1981. write for info. (ISBN 0-8089-1308-5). Grune.

Problem-Oriented System in Nursing: A Workbook. Beth C. Vaughan-Wrobel & Betty Henderson. (Illus.). 184p. 1976. pap. 9.00 (ISBN 0-8016-5221-9). Mosby.

Problem Oriented System in Psychiatry. (Task Force Report: No. 12). 97p. 1977. 5.00 (ISBN 0-685-88006-0, P224-0). Am Psychiatric.

Problem Play in British Drama, Eighteen Ninety to Nineteen Fourteen. Elliott M. Simon. (Salzburg Studies in English Literature, Poetic Drama & Poetic Theory: No. 40). 1978. pap. text ed. 25.00x (ISBN 0-391-01525-7). Humanities.

Problem Seeking: An Architectural Programming Primer. William Pena et al. LC 77-73637. 1977. 16.95 (ISBN 0-8436-2172-9). CBI Pub.

Problem Solver in Strength of Materials & Mechanics of Solids. Research & Education Association Staff. LC 80-83305. (Illus.). 896p. (Orig.). pap. text ed. 22.85x (ISBN 0-87891-522-2). Res & Educ.

Problem Solving. F. H. George. 194p. 1980. 19.50x (ISBN 0-7156-1004-X, Pub. by Duckworth England). Biblio Dist.

Problem-Solving: A Logical & Creative Approach. Harvey J. Brightman. LC 80-25078. 256p. 1980. 14.95 (ISBN 0-88406-131-0). Ga St U Busn Pub.

Problem Solving: A Systems Approach. Joseph E. Robertshaw & Stephen J. Mecca. (Illus.). 1979. text ed. 19.25 (ISBN 0-89433-075-6). Petrocelli.

Problem Solving & Structured Programming in BASIC. Elliot B. Koffman & Frank L. Friedman. LC 78-65355. 1979. pap. text ed. 13.95 (ISBN 0-201-03888-9). A-W.

Problem Solving & Structured Programming in Fortran. 2nd ed. Frank Friedman & Elliot Koffman. LC 80-20943. (First Course in Computers Ser.). 450p. 1981. pap. text ed. 11.95 (ISBN 0-201-02461-6). A-W.

Problem Solving & the Computer: A Structured Concept with PL 1 (PLC) 2nd ed. Joseph Shortt & Thomas C. Wilson. 1979. pap. text ed. 13.95 (ISBN 0-201-06916-4). A-W.

Problem Solving Approach to Nursing Care Plans: A Program. Barbara A. Vitale et al. LC 77-14222. (Illus.). 1978. pap. text ed. 9.50 (ISBN 0-8016-5243-X). Mosby.

Problem Solving Arts: Part One Syllabus. Norman H. Crowhurst. 1976. pap. text ed. 9.95 (ISBN 0-89420-085-2, 256040); cassette recordings 227.10 (ISBN 0-89420-175-1, 256000). Natl Book.

Problem Solving Arts: Part Three Syllabus. Norman E. Crowhurst. 1978. pap. text ed. 10.45 (ISBN 0-89420-040-2, 256130); cassette recordings 196.20 (ISBN 0-89420-177-8, 256090). Natl Book.

Problem Solving Arts: Part Two Syllabus. Norman H. Crowhurst. 1977. pap. text ed. 10.25 (ISBN 0-89420-029-1); cassette recordings 195.80 (ISBN 0-89420-176-X, 256050). Natl Book.

Problem Solving in a Project Environment: A Consulting Process. L. Thomas King. 168p. 1981. 19.95 (ISBN 0-471-08115-9, Pub. by Wiley-Interscience). Wiley.

Problem Solving in Basic: A Modular Approach. Frances Gustavson & Marian Sackson. LC 78-21904. 1979. pap. text ed. 9.95 (ISBN 0-574-21240-X, 13-4240); instr's guide avail. (ISBN 0-574-21241-8, 13-4241). SRA.

Problem Solving in General Chemistry. Ronald LeLorenzo. 496p. 1980. pap. text ed. 10.95 (ISBN 0-669-02924-6). Heath.

Problem-Solving in General Chemistry. Christopher Willis. LC 76-14004. (Illus.). 1977. pap. text ed. 9.50 (ISBN 0-395-24532-X). HM.

Problem Solving in Immunohematology. 2nd ed. Israel Davidsohn & Kurt Stern. LC 77-93058. 1978. pap. text ed. 20.00 (ISBN 0-89189-035-1, 45-6-012-00). Am Soc Clinical.

Problem Solving in Medical Technology & Microbiology. Robert G. Tischer et al. LC 79-11337. (Illus.). 1979. pap. text ed. 25.00 (ISBN 0-89189-068-8, 45-7-010-00). Am Soc Clinical.

Problem Solving in Recreation & Parks. Joseph J. Bannon. LC 70-38797. (Illus.). 336p. 1972. pap. text ed. 16.50 (ISBN 0-13-711648-9). P-H.

Problem Solving in School Mathematics, 1980 Yearbook. National Council of Teachers of Mathematics. 1980. 12.00 (ISBN 0-87353-162-0). NCTM.

Problem Solving, Systems Analysis, & Medicine. Ralph Raymond Grams. (Illus.). 244p. 1972. Set. 31.00 (ISBN 0-398-02298-4); companion volume - Systems Analysis wkbk. incl. (ISBN 0-398-02566-5). C C Thomas.

Problem-Solving Therapy with Socially Anxious Children. J. J. Meijers. 290p. 1978. pap. text ed. 22.75 (ISBN 90-265-0282-6, Pub. by Swets Pub Serv Holland). Swets North Am.

Problem Solving Using Pl-C: An Introduction for Business & the Social Sciences. Gary L. Richardson & Stanley J. Birkin. LC 75-4724. 480p. 1975. 17.95 (ISBN 0-471-72048-8); instructor's manual avail. (ISBN 0-471-72049-6). Wiley.

Problem Solving with Calculators. Karen Billings & David Moursund. 150p. 1979. pap. 7.95 (ISBN 0-918398-30-4). Dilithium Pr.

Problem Solving with FORTRAN. Donald D. Spencer. LC 76-26040. (Illus.). 1977. pap. text ed. 13.95 (ISBN 0-13-720094-3). P-H.

Problem Solving with the Calculator. Russell F. Jacobs. (gr. 6-9). 1977. pap. text ed. 4.25 (ISBN 0-918272-00-9); tchr's guide with ans. key 0.75 (ISBN 0-918272-01-7); answer key 0.75 (ISBN 0-918272-02-5). Jacobs.

Problema del Dolor. C. S. Lewis. Tr. by Ernesto S. Vilela from Eng. LC 77-16715. 156p. (Orig., Span.). 1977. pap. 2.95 (ISBN 0-89922-097-5). Edit Caribe.

Problemas De Actualidad. Foy Valentine. Tr. by Ana M. Swenson. 1978. Repr. of 1975 ed. 0.95 (ISBN 0-311-46039-9). Casa Bautista.

Problematic Characters. Friedrich Spielhagen. Tr. by S. DeVere from Ger. LC 76-28509. viii, 507p. 1977. Repr. of 1888 ed. 18.50 (ISBN 0-86527-296-4). Fertig.

Probleme De la Sexualite Chez les Champignons: Recherches Sur le Genre Coprinus. A. Quintanilha. (Illus.). 1968. pap. 20.00 (ISBN 3-7682-0556-8). Lubrecht & Cramer.

Probleme der Krebsnachsorge. Ed. by A. Pfleiderer. (Beitraege zur Onkologie: Band 4). (Illus.). 112p. 1980. pap. 24.00 (ISBN 3-8055-1378-X). S Karger.

Probleme Unserer Zeit. Ed. by Edmund P. Kurz & Karl H. Ruhleder. LC 72-130785. (Orig., Ger.). 1971. pap. text ed. 4.95x (ISBN 0-89197-359-1). Irvington.

Problemes De la Guerre a Rome. Jean P. Brisson. (Civilisations et Societes: No. 12). 1969. pap. 14.10x (ISBN 0-686-20921-4). Mouton.

Problems. John Updike. 288p. 1981. pap. 2.95 (ISBN 0-449-24360-5, Crest). Fawcett.

Problems & Issues in Social Casework. Scott Briar & Henry Miller. LC 79-170924. 1971. 17.50x (ISBN 0-231-02771-0). Columbia U Pr.

Problems & Issues in the Education of Exceptional Children. Reginald L. Jones. LC 74-142329. 1971. pap. text ed. 11.95 (ISBN 0-395-11228-1, 3-28340). HM.

Problems & Materials on Negotiable Instruments. Whaley. Date not set. text ed. price not set (ISBN 0-316-93214-0). Little.

Problems & Methods of Literary History. Andre Morize. LC 66-13475. 1922. 12.00x (ISBN 0-8196-0168-3). Biblo.

Problems & Models in Operations Management. 2nd ed. Richard J. Tersine & Fredrick Davidson. LC 79-21810. (Management Ser.). 1980. pap. text ed. 10.50 (ISBN 0-88244-207-4). Grid Pub.

Problems & Opportunities in Economic Development. Alan H. Leader. (Illus.). 1977. pap. text ed. 2.95x (ISBN 0-932826-11-3). New Issues MI.

Problems & Practice of Pastoral Care. Ed. by Douglas H. Hamblin. 1981. 29.50x (ISBN 0-631-12921-9, Pub. by Basil Blackwell); pap. 10.95x (ISBN 0-631-12931-6). Biblio Dist.

Problems & Principles in English Teaching. Christopher Brumfit. LC 79-40706. (Language Teaching Methodology Ser.). (Illus.). 168p. 1980. 13.95 (ISBN 0-08-024559-5); pap. 7.95 (ISBN 0-08-024558-7). Pergamon.

Problems & Principles of Human Organization in Educational Systems. Gale E. Jensen. (Educational Ser.). 239p. 1969. pap. text ed. 5.00 o.p. (ISBN 0-89039-005-3). Ann Arbor FL.

Problems & Prospects of American East Asian Relations. John Chay. LC 76-27694. (Special Studies on China & East Asia). 1977. lib. bdg. 24.50x (ISBN 0-89158-113-8). Westview.

Problems & Prospects of LSD. Ed. by J. Thomas Ungerleider. (Illus.). 132p. 1972. 9.75 (ISBN 0-398-01952-5). C C Thomas.

Problems & Solutions in Logic Design. 2nd ed. D. Zissos. (Illus.). 1980. 29.95x (ISBN 0-19-859362-7). Oxford U Pr.

Problems & Solutions in Quantum Chemistry. Charles S. Johnson & L. G. Pedersen. 1974. pap. text ed. 13.95 (ISBN 0-201-03415-8). A-W.

Problems & Teaching Strategies in ESL Composition. Ann Raimes. (Language in Education Ser.: No. 14). (Orig.). 1979. pap. text ed. 2.95x (ISBN 0-87281-100-X). Ctr Appl Ling.

Problems & Theories of Philosophy. K. Ajdukiewicz. Tr. by A. Quinton & H. Skolimowski. LC 72-97878. 160p. 1973. 23.95 (ISBN 0-521-20219-1); pap. 6.95x (ISBN 0-521-09993-5). Cambridge U Pr.

Problems & Worked Examples in Chemistry to Advanced Level. 3rd ed. A. Holderness & J. Lambert. 1978. pap. text ed. 4.95x o.p. (ISBN 0-435-65438-1). Heinemann Ed.

Problems Associated with Export of Nuclear Power Plants. 1979. pap. 41.75 (ISBN 92-0-020178-4, ISP488, IAEA). Unipub.

Problems, Cases & Materials on Bioethics & Law. Michael H. Shapiro & Roy G. Spece, Jr. (American Casebook Ser.). 915p. 1981. text ed. 23.95 (ISBN 0-8299-2134-6). West Pub.

Problems for Chemistry. Kiesel & Gore. 3.95x o.p. (ISBN 0-205-04244-9, 6842445); instr's manual free o.p. (ISBN 0-685-47255-8, 6842453). Allyn.

Problems for Computer Solution. F. J. Gruenberger & G. Jaffray. LC 65-24303. 1965. pap. 16.95 (ISBN 0-471-32908-8). Wiley.

Problems for Computer Solution. 2nd ed. Donald Spencer. 128p. 1979. pap. 6.60 (ISBN 0-8104-5191-3). Hayden.

Problems for Exploration Geophysics. C. Ronald Seeger. LC 78-62263. 1978. pap. text ed. 4.25 (ISBN 0-8191-0573-2). U Pr of Amer.

Problems for General Chemistry & Qualitative Analysis. 4th ed. C. J. Nyman et al. LC 79-24489. 342p. 1980. pap. text ed. 9.95 (ISBN 0-471-05299-X). Wiley.

Problems in Advanced Organic Chemistry. Toshio Goto et al. LC 67-13842. (Illus.). 1968. pap. 8.95x (ISBN 0-8162-3411-6). Holden-Day.

Problems in American Foreign Policy. 2nd ed. Martin B. Hickman. 1975. pap. text ed. 4.95x (ISBN 0-02-474270-8, 47427). Macmillan.

Problems in Basic Business Finance. Stanley B. Block & Joseph G. Louderback. LC 73-9359. 240p. 1973. pap. text ed. 13.50 scp o.p. (ISBN 0-06-380585-5, HarpC); tchrs. ed. avail. o.p. (ISBN 0-06-371067-6). Har-Row.

Problems in Biology. Carol Knox & Katheryn Rowsey. (Illus.). 90p. (Orig.). (gr. 10-11). 1980. lab manual 2.95 (ISBN 0-88334-132-8). Ind Sch Pr.

Problems in Business Communications. C. J. Parsons. 1977. pap. 11.00x (ISBN 0-7131-0107-5). Intl Ideas.

Problems in Constitutional Law: A Symposium. K. E. Vanlandingham et al. LC 70-152835. (Symposia on Law & Society Ser). 1971. Repr. of 1968 ed. lib. bdg. 22.50 (ISBN 0-306-70148-0). Da Capo.

Problems in Economic & Social Archaeology. G. Sievking et al. LC 76-49652. 1977. lib. bdg. 60.00 o.p. (ISBN 0-89158-713-6). Westview.

Problems in Electronics. J. Auvray & M. Fourrier. LC 73-7617. 444p. 1974. text ed. 46.00 (ISBN 0-08-016982-1); pap. text ed. 17.50 (ISBN 0-08-017871-5). Pergamon.

Problems in Engineering Drawing for Design & Communications. 8th ed. pap. 8.95 ea. Vol. 1 (ISBN 0-13-716373-8). Vol. 2 (ISBN 0-13-716381-9). P-H.

Problems in Evidence. 2nd ed. Kenneth S. Broun & Robert Meisenholder. (American Casebook Ser.). 1981. pap. text ed. 6.95 (ISBN 0-8299-2125-7). West Pub.

Problems in French Syntax: Transformational - Generative Studies. Nicolas Ruwet. Tr. by Sheila M. Robins from Fr. (Linguistics Library). 1976. text ed. 22.00x (ISBN 0-582-55058-0). Longman.

Problems in Heat & Mass Transfer. J. R. Backhurst et al. (Illus.). 1974. pap. text ed. 14.95x (ISBN 0-7131-3327-9). Intl Ideas.

Problems in Higher Algebra. D. K. Faddeev & I. S. Sominskii. Tr. by Joel L. Brenner. LC 65-18946. 1965. pap. 7.95x (ISBN 0-7167-0426-9). W H Freeman.

Problems in Hospital Law. 3rd. ed. David G. Warren. LC 78-15865. 1978. text ed. 21.50 (ISBN 0-89443-045-9). Aspen Systems.

Problems in International Comparative Research in the Social Sciences. Jan Berting et al. 186p. 1979. 28.00 (ISBN 0-08-025247-8). Pergamon.

Problems in Labor Relations: Text & Cases. William E. Fulmer. 1980. 22.00x (ISBN 0-256-02366-2). Irwin.

Problems in Literary Research: A Guide to Selected Reference Works. Dorothea Kehler & Fidelia Dickinson. LC 75-16427. 169p. 1975. 10.00 (ISBN 0-8108-0841-2); tchrs. index incl. (ISBN 0-8108-0842-0). Scarecrow.

Problems in Marketing. 6th ed. Corey E. Raymond et al. (Illus.). 832p. 20.95 (ISBN 0-07-013141-4); instrs'. 4.95 (ISBN 0-07-013142-2). McGraw.

Problems in Materialism & Culture: Selected Essays. Raymond Williams. 288p. 1981. 19.50x (ISBN 0-8052-7093-0, Pub. by NLB England); pap. 8.75 (ISBN 0-8052-7092-2). Schocken.

Problems in Microeconomics. Marcia L. Stigum. 1975. pap. text ed. 10.95 (ISBN 0-256-01734-4). Irwin.

Problems in Middle & High School Teaching: A Handbook for Student Teachers & Beginning Teachers. new ed. Adam M. Drayer. 1980. text ed. 16.95 (ISBN 0-205-06146-X, 2361310); pap. text ed. 10.95 (ISBN 0-205-06131-1). Allyn.

Problems in National Income Analysis & Forecasting. rev. ed. Robert H. Scott. 1972. pap. 6.95x (ISBN 0-673-07793-4). Scott F.

Problems in Optics. M. Rousseau & Jean P. Mathieu. 376p. 1973. text ed. 32.00 (ISBN 0-08-016980-5). Pergamon.

Problems in Pediatric Drug Therapy. Ed. by Louis A. Pagliaro et al. LC 78-50204. 313p. 1979. text ed. 19.50 (ISBN 0-914768-29-8, 16). Drug Intl Pubns.

Problems in Philosophical Inquiry. Julius R. Weinberg & Keith Yandell. LC 73-148058. 1971. 29.50x (ISBN 0-03-083380-9); pap. text ed. 18.95x (ISBN 0-89197-905-0). Irvington.

Problems in Philosophy: West & East. Ed. by A. L. Herman & R. T. Blackwood. 544p. 1975. 17.95 (ISBN 0-13-719708-X). P-H.

Problems in Physical Chemistry. Alexander Wood. 170p. 1974. pap. text ed. 8.50x (ISBN 0-19-855134-7). Oxford U Pr.

Problems in Price Theory. David De Meza & Michael Osborne. LC 80-16597. (Illus.). xiv, 302p. 1980. lib. bdg. 25.00 (ISBN 0-226-14293-0). U of Chicago Pr.

Problems in Public Expenditure Analysis. Ed. by Samuel B. Chase, Jr. et al. (Studies of Goverment Finance). 1967. 14.95 (ISBN 0-8157-1382-7); pap. 5.95 (ISBN 0-8157-1381-9). Brookings.

Problems in Public-Utility Economics & Regulation. Ed. by Michael A. Crew. 192p. 1979. 17.95 (ISBN 0-669-02775-8). Lexington Bks.

Problems in Quantum Mechanics. F. Constantinescu & E. Magyari. 1971. 42.00 (ISBN 0-08-006826-X); pap. text ed. 18.50 (ISBN 0-08-019008-1). Pergamon.

Problems in Quantum Mechanics. I. Goldman & V. D. Krivchenkov. 1961. text ed. 24.00 (ISBN 0-08-009462-7). Pergamon.

Problems in Soil Mechanics. Shamsher Prakash & Gopal Ranjan. 150p. 1972. 8.00x (ISBN 0-210-27101-9). Asia.

Problems in Technical Mathematics for Electricity-Electronics. Forrest Barker. LC 76-12728. 1976. pap. 8.95 (ISBN 0-8465-0403-0). Benjamin-Cummings.

Problems in the Description of Modal Verbs: An Investigation of Latin. A. M. Bolkestein. (Studies in Greek & Latin Linguistics). 180p. 1980. pap. text ed. 21.00x (ISBN 90-232-1764-0). Humanities.

Problems in the History & Philosophy of Physical Education & Sport. Earle F. Zeigler. LC 68-18594. (Foundations of Physical Education Series). (Orig.). 1969. pap. 7.95 ref. ed. (ISBN 0-13-716787-3). P-H.

Problems in the Literary Biography of Mikhail Sholokhov. R. A. Medvedev. Tr. by A. D. Briggs. LC 76-14032. 1977. 32.50 (ISBN 0-521-21333-9). Cambridge U Pr.

Problems in the Strength of Materials. N. M. Belyayev. 1966. text ed. 34.00 (ISBN 0-08-010306-5); pap. 21.00 (ISBN 0-08-013664-8). Pergamon.

Problems Manual. 4th ed. Robert D. Mason. (To Accompany Statistical Techniques In Business & Economics). 1978. pap. text ed. 6.95 (ISBN 0-256-02026-4). Irwin.

Problems of a Displaced Minority: The New Position of East Africa's Asians. Yash Tandon. (Minority Rights Group: No. 16). 1973. pap. 2.50 (ISBN 0-89192-102-8). Interbk Inc.

Problems of Abortion. Joel Feinberg. 1973. pap. 7.95x (ISBN 0-534-00334-6). Wadsworth Pub.

Problems of Accelerating Aircraft Production During World War II. T. Lilley. (Harvard Graduate School of Business Administration: Studies in Aviation Research). 1970. Repr. of 1957 ed. 16.00 (ISBN 0-08-018743-9). Pergamon.

Problems of Adolescents: Social & Psychological Approach. Ed. by Richard E. Hardy & John G. Cull. (Amer. Lec. in Social & Rehabilitation Psychology Ser.). (Illus.). 296p. 1974. 19.75 (ISBN 0-398-03163-0). C C Thomas.

Problems of American Foreign Policy. Martin Hickman. Ed. by Fred Krinsky & Joseph Boskin. (Insight Series: Studies in Contemporary Issues). (Illus.). 128p. 1968. pap. text ed. 4.95x o.p. (ISBN 0-02-474800-5, 47480). Macmillan.

Problems of an Industrial Society. 2nd ed. William Faunce. Ed. by Eric M. Munson. 256p. 1981. pap. text ed. 8.95 (ISBN 0-07-020105-6, C). McGraw.

Problems of an Urban Society: Vol. 1, the Social Framework of Planning. J. B. Cullingworth. (Urban & Regional Studies Ser.). 1973. pap. text ed. 8.95x o.p. (ISBN 0-04-352045-6). Allen Unwin.

Problems of an Urban Society: Vol. 2, Social Content of Planning. J. B. Cullingworth. (Urban & Regional Studies Ser.). 1973. pap. text ed. 8.95x o.p. (ISBN 0-04-352043-X). Allen Unwin.

Problems of an Urban Society: Vol. 3, Planning for Social Change. J. B. Cullingworth. (Urban & Regional Studies Ser.). 1973. pap. text ed. 8.95x o.p. (ISBN 0-04-352047-2). Allen Unwin.

Problems of Antibiotic Therapy. Ed. by H. C. Neu & A. D. Caldwell. (Royal Society of Medicine International Congress & Symposium Ser.: No. 13). 1979. 11.50 (ISBN 0-8089-1218-6). Grune.

Problems of Aphasia. Ed. by Yvan Lebrun & Richard Hoops. (Neurolinguistics Ser.: Vol. 9). 198p. 1979. text ed. 36.00 (ISBN 90-265-0309-1, Pub. by Swets Pub Serv Holland). Swets North Am.

Problems of Art. Suzanne K. Langer. 1957. pap. text ed. 5.95x (ISBN 0-684-15346-7, ScribC). Scribner.

Problems of Biological Physics. L. A. Blumenfeld. (Springer Series in Synergetics: Vol. 7). (Illus.). 300p. 1981. 36.00 (ISBN 0-387-10401-1). Springer-Verlag.

Problems of Christian Discipleship. J. Oswald Sanders. 1977. pap. 2.10 o.p. (ISBN 0-85363-046-1). OMF Bks.

Problems of Cooperation for Development. Gerald M. Meier. 272p. 1974. pap. text ed. 5.95x (ISBN 0-19-501867-2). Oxford U Pr.

Problems of Death: Opposing Viewpoints. Ed. by David L. Bender. (Opposing Viewpoints Ser.: Vol. 8). (Illus.). 1974. lib. bdg. 8.95 (ISBN 0-912616-32-6); pap. text ed. 3.95 (ISBN 0-912616-13-X). Greenhaven.

Problems of Development in Tribal Areas. S. G. Deogaonkar. 192p. 1980. text ed. 13.50x (ISBN 0-391-02132-X). Humanities.

Problems of Disadvantaged & Deprived Youth. Ed. by John G. Cull & Richard Hardy. (Amer. Lec. Social & Rehabilitation Psychology). 272p. 1975. 22.75 (ISBN 0-398-03171-1). C C Thomas.

Problems of Doctor A. Elizabeth Seifert. LC 79-11017. 1979. 7.95 (ISBN 0-396-07686-6). Dodd.

Problems of Document Delivery for the Euronet User. Paul D. Gillespie. Ed. by Franklin Institute Gmbh. 1979. 20.00 (Pub. by K G Saur). Shoe String.

Problems of Dostoevsky's Poetics. M. M. Bakhtin. Tr. by R. W. Rotsel from Rus. (Illus.). 340p. (Orig.). 1973. 10.00 o.p. (ISBN 0-88233-040-3); pap. 3.95 o.p. (ISBN 0-88233-041-1). Ardis Pubs.

Problems of Drug Dependence 1975: Proceedings. Thirty-Seventh Annual Scientific Meeting of the Committee on Problems of Drug Dependence Division of Medical Sciences, National Research Council. LC 75-29630. vii, 1212p. 1975. pap. 22.50 (ISBN 0-309-02417-X). Natl Acad Pr.

Problems of Economic Policy. Keith Hartley. (Economics & Society Ser.). 1977. text ed. 18.95x (ISBN 0-04-339008-0). Allen Unwin.

Problems of Estimating Changes in Frequency of Mental Disorders, Vol. 4. GAP Committee on Preventive Psychiatry. (Report No. 50). 1961. pap. 2.00 (ISBN 0-87318-067-4). Adv Psychiatry.

Problems of Financing the Thai Educational System in the Nineteen Sixties & Nineteen Seventies. (Financing Educational Systems: Country Case Studies: No. 3). 235p. 1976. pap. 11.50 (ISBN 0-685-65020-0, 92-803-1069-0, U483, UNESCO). Unipub.

Problems of Indian Historiography. Devahuti. 1979. text ed. 11.50x (ISBN 0-391-01862-0). Humanities.

Problems of Industrial Society. Ed. by William J. Chambliss. LC 72-578. 1973. pap. text ed. 8.95 (ISBN 0-201-00958-7). A-W.

Problems of Knowledge. Herman Tennessen. 88p. 1980. pap. text ed. 10.25x (ISBN 90-232-1762-4). Humanities.

Problems of Linear Electron Transport Theory in Semiconductors. M. I. Klinger. LC 78-40821. 1979. text ed. 190.00 (ISBN 0-08-018224-0). Pergamon.

Problems of Listeriosis: Proceedings of the 5th International Symposium. Ed. by M. Woodbine. (Illus.). 320p. 1975. text ed. 16.25x (ISBN 0-7185-1143-3, Leicester). Humanities.

Problems of Mass Transportation. Ed. by Diana Reische. (Reference Shelf Ser: Vol. 42, No. 5). 1970. 6.25 (ISBN 0-8242-0413-1). Wilson.

Problems of Mind & Matter. John Wisdom. (Orig.). 26.95 (ISBN 0-521-08508-X); pap. 6.95x (ISBN 0-521-09197-7). Cambridge U Pr.

Problems of Moral Philosophy. 3rd ed. Paul W. Taylor. LC 75-167903. 1978. text ed. 17.95x (ISBN 0-534-00592-6). Wadsworth Pub.

Problems of Nuclear Science & Technology: The Soviet Union As a World Nuclear Power. 4th rev. & enl. ed. A. M. Petrosy'Ants. LC 80-40818. (Illus.). 400p. 1981. 56.00 (ISBN 0-08-025462-4). Pergamon.

Problems of Our Physical Environment: Energy - Transportation - Pollution. Joseph Priest. LC 72-9317. 1973. text ed. 16.95 (ISBN 0-201-05972-X). A-W.

Problems of Perception. R. J. Hirst. (Muirhead Library of Philosophy). 1978. Repr. of 1959 ed. text ed. 15.00x (ISBN 0-391-00566-9). Humanities.

Problems of Philosophy. Bertrand Russell. 1959. pap. 3.95 (ISBN 0-19-500212-1, GB). Oxford U Pr.

Problems of Philosophy & Psychology. Jay Eacker. LC 75-17548. 160p. 1975. 14.95 (ISBN 0-88229-202-1); pap. 8.95 (ISBN 0-88229-489-X). Nelson-Hall.

Problems of Philosophy: Introductory Readings. 2nd ed. William P. Alston & Richard B. Brandt. 804p. 1974. text ed. 18.50 o.p. (ISBN 0-205-03982-0, 6039820). Allyn.

Problems of Philosophy: Introductory Readings. 3rd ed. William P. Alston & Richard B. Brandt. 1978. text ed. 18.50 (ISBN 0-205-06110-9, 6061109). Allyn.

Problems of Planning, East & West. Rudolf Bicanic. (Publications of the Institute of Social Studies: No. 15). 1967. text ed. 17.05x (ISBN 90-2790-112-0). Mouton.

Problems of Product Design & Development. C. H. Buck. 1963. 13.75 (ISBN 0-08-009794-4); pap. 6.25 (ISBN 0-08-009793-6). Pergamon.

Problems of Psychiatric Leadership, Vol. 8. GAP Committee on Therapy. LC 74-170958. (Report No. 90). 1974. pap. 2.00 (ISBN 0-87318-125-5). Adv Psychiatry.

Problems of Psychotherapy. H. Zucker. LC 67-19235. 1967. 12.95 (ISBN 0-02-935700-4). Free Pr.

Problems of Recurrent Hernia. Robert C. Kimberly. (Illus.). 76p. 1975. pap. 9.50 (ISBN 0-398-03374-9). C C Thomas.

Problems of Reflexivity & Dialectics in Sociological Inquiry: Language Theorizing Difference. B. Sandywell & D. Silverman. 1975. 15.00x (ISBN 0-7100-8304-1). Routledge & Kegan.

Problems of Relative Growth. Julian Huxley. 312p. 1972. pap. 3.50 o.p. (ISBN 0-486-61114-0). Dover.

Problems of Runaway Youth. Ed. by John G. Cull & Richard E. Hardy. (American Lectures in Social & Rehabilitation Psychology Ser.). (Illus.). 184p. 1976. pap. 16.75 (ISBN 0-398-03425-7). C C Thomas.

Problems of Rural Education. V. L. Griffiths. (Fundamentals of Educational Planning Ser). (Orig.). 1968. pap. 6.00 (ISBN 92-803-1022-4, U484, UNESCO). Unipub.

Problems of Smaller Territories. Ed. by Burton Benedict. 1967. text ed. 8.75x (ISBN 0-485-17610-6, Athlone Pr). Humanities.

Problems of Suffering in the Religions of the World. John Bowker. LC 77-93706. 1975. 39.50 (ISBN 0-521-07412-6); pap. 9.95x (ISBN 0-521-09903-X). Cambridge U Pr.

Problems of the Agricultural Development of Less-Favoured Areas. United Nations Economic Commission for Europe. (European Committee for Economic Perspectives). 1979. 48.00 (ISBN 0-08-024456-4). Pergamon.

Problems of the Carless. Robert E. Paaswell & Wilfred W. Recker. LC 77-13730. (Praeger Special Studies). 1978. 23.95 (ISBN 0-03-040926-8). Praeger.

Problems of the Feminine in Fairytales. Mary-Louise Von Franz. Ed. by James Hillman. (Seminar Ser). 1972. pap. text ed. 8.50 (ISBN 0-88214-105-8). Spring Pubns.

Problems of the Middle-Aged. Ed. by Clyde B. Vedder. 216p. 1965. photocopy ed. spiral 15.75 (ISBN 0-398-01974-6). C C Thomas.

Problems of the Regulations of Activity. Ed. by Lajos Kardos & Csaba Pleh. (Illus.). 733p. 1980. write for info. (ISBN 963-05-2447-3). Intl Pubns Serv.

Problems of the Self: Philosophical Papers, 1956-1972. B. A. Williams. 240p. 1973. 35.50 (ISBN 0-521-20225-6); pap. 9.95x (ISBN 0-521-29060-0). Cambridge U Pr.

Problems of Theology. B. L. Hebblethwaite. LC 79-41812. 176p. 1980. 21.50 (ISBN 0-521-23104-3); pap. 6.95 (ISBN 0-521-29811-3). Cambridge U Pr.

Problems of Theory in Policy Analysis. Philip M. Gregg. LC 75-16626. (Policy Studies Organization Ser.). 208p. 1976. 18.95 (ISBN 0-669-00057-4). Lexington Bks.

Problems of U. S. Uranium Resources & Supply to the Year 2010. Committee on Nuclear & Alternative Energy Systems. 1978. pap. 6.00 (ISBN 0-309-02782-9). Natl Acad Pr.

Problems of Wage Policy for Economic Development. S. A. Palekar. 16.00x o.p. (ISBN 0-210-33924-1). Asia.

Procedings. Power Computation Conference, 7th, Lausanne, Switzerland, July 12-17, 1980. 1981. text ed. price not set (ISBN 0-86103-025-7). Butterworth.

Procedural Aspects of International Law Series, 13 vols. Incl. Vol. 1. International Claims: Their Adjudication by National Commission. Richard B. Lillich. LC 62-7735 (ISBN 0-8139-0834-5); Vol. 2. International Claims: Their Preparation & Presentation. Richard B. Lillich & Gordon A. Christenson. LC 62-18891 (ISBN 0-8139-0835-3); Vol. 3. Role of Domestic Courts in International Legal Order. Richard A. Falk. LC 64-16924 (ISBN 0-8139-0836-1); Vol. 4. Use of Experts by International Tribunals. Gillian White. LC 65-15853 (ISBN 0-8139-0837-X); Vol. 5. Protection of Foreign Investment: Six Procedural Studies. Richard B. Lillich. LC 65-15855 (ISBN 0-8139-0838-8); Vol. 6. International Claims: Postwar British Practice. Richard B. Lillich. LC 72-80016 (ISBN 0-8139-0850-7); Vol. 7. Law-Making in the International Civil Aviation Organization. Thomas Buergenthal. LC 72-80016; Vol. 8. UN Protection of Civil & Political Rights. John Carey. LC 71-104674 (ISBN 0-8156-2146-9); Vol. 9. International Claims: Postwar French Practice. Burns H. Weston. LC 79-134507 (ISBN 0-8156-2153-1); Vol. 10. International Law, National Tribunals & the Rights of Aliens. Frank G. Dawson & Ivan L. Head. LC 76-155828 (ISBN 0-8156-2152-3); Vol. 11. Austrian-German Arbitral Tribunal. Ignaz Seidl-Hohenveldern. LC 72-8526 (ISBN 0-8156-2159-0); Vol. 12. International Claims: Their Settlement by Lump Sum Agreements. Richard B. Lillich & Burns H. Weston. 37.50x (ISBN 0-8139-0642-3); Vol. 13. Evidence Before International Tribunals. Durward V. Sandifer. 27.50 (ISBN 0-8139-0616-4). 10.00x ea. U Pr of Va.

Procedural Justice: A Psychological Analysis. J. Thibaut & L. Walker. LC 75-15944. 1975. text ed. 9.95x o.p. (ISBN 0-470-85868-0); pap. 4.95 (ISBN 0-470-85869-9). Halsted Pr.

Procedural Terminology for Psychiatrists. 16p. 1981. pap. 1.75 (ISBN 0-685-65576-8, P199-0). Am Psychiatric.

Procedure, Extent & Limits of the Human Understanding. Peter Browne. Ed. by Rene Wellek. LC 75-11201. (British Philosophers & Theologians of the 17th & 18th Centuries: Vol. 8). 1976. Repr. of 1728 ed. lib. bdg. 42.00 (ISBN 0-8240-1757-9). Garland Pub.

Procedure of the UN Security Council. Sydney D. Bailey. (Illus.). 438p. 1975. 34.50x (ISBN 0-19-827199-9). Oxford U Pr.

Procedures & Policies of the New York State Labor Relations Board. Kurt L. Hanslowe. LC 63-63909. (Cornell Studies Ser.: No. 12). 224p. 1964. 4.00 o.s.i. (ISBN 0-87546-005-4). NY Sch Indus Rel.

Procedures for the Control of Ships & Discharges. 22p. 1978. 7.00 (IMCO). Unipub.

Procedures in the Justice System. 2nd ed. Gilbert B. Stuckey. (Public Service Technology Ser.). 280p. 1980. text ed. 16.95 (ISBN 0-675-08173-4); instructor's manual 3.95 (ISBN 0-686-63345-8). Merrill.

Proceeding of Second International Symposium on Alcohol Fuel Technology: Methanol & Ethanol U. S. Department of Energy. U. S. Department of Energy. 1979. 49.95 (ISBN 0-89934-000-8); pap. 34.95 (ISBN 0-930978-86-2). Solar Energy Info.

Proceedings. AASHTO Annual Committee Meeting, 1974. 10.00 o.p. (ISBN 0-686-20946-X, P-74). AASHTO.

Proceedings. Academy of Management, 40th Annual Meeting, 1980. Ed. by Richard C. Huseman. LC 40-2886. 436p. (Orig.). 1980. pap. text ed. 11.00 (ISBN 0-915350-19-X). Acad of Mgmt.

Proceedings. The American Society of Hospital Pharmacists Institute on Oncology Pharmacy Practice. Ed. by J. P. Caro. 128p. 1979. 23.00 (ISBN 0-444-00369-X); pap. 15.00 (ISBN 0-444-00373-8). Elsevier.

Proceedings, 2 vols. Analytical Chemical Conference, 3rd, Budapest, 1970. Ed. by I. Buzas. Incl. Vol. 1. Separation Methods; Vol. 2. Organic Analysis. LC 72-184389. 777p. 1970. Set. 25.00x (ISBN 0-8002-1840-X). Intl Pubns Serv.

Proceedings. Annual Asse Professional Development Conference, 1968, 70, 72, 78 & 79. 1980. 20.00 (ISBN 0-686-21675-X). ASSE.

Proceedings. Annual Uranium Seminar, 3rd. LC 79-48044. (Illus.). 177p. 1980. pap. 15.00x (ISBN 0-89520-260-3). Soc Mining Eng.

Proceedings. Biogas & Other Rural Energy Resources Workshop, Suva. Bd. with Proceedings: Rural Energy Development Roving Seminar; Bangkok, Manila, Tehran & Jakarta. (Energy Resources Development Ser.: No. 19). 152p. 1979. pap. text ed. 10.00 (79/2F10, UN). Unipub.

Proceedings, Vol. LXV. The British Academy, 1979. (Illus.). 500p. 1981. 175.00 (ISBN 0-19-725998-7). Oxford U Pr.

Proceedings. British Pumps Manufacturers Association, 6th Technical Conference. 270p. 1979. pap. 60.00 (ISBN 0-906085-27-6, Dist. by Air Science Co.). BHRA Fluid.

Proceedings. C. S. Peirce Bicentennial International Congress. Ed. by Kenneth Ketner et al. (Graduate Studies, Texas Tech Univ.: No. 23). 420p. (Orig.). 1981. price not set (ISBN 0-89672-075-6); pap. price not set (ISBN 0-89672-074-8). Tex Tech Pr.

Proceedings. Cairo International Workshop on Applications of Science & Technology for Desert Development September 9-15, 1978. Ed. by A. Bishay & W. B. McGinnies. (Advances in Desert & Arid Land Technology & Development: Vol. 1). 630p. 1979. lib. bdg. 73.00 (ISBN 3-7186-0002-1). Harwood Academic.

Proceedings. Caribbean Seminar on Science & Technology Policy & Planning, 2nd. (Studies on Scientific & Technological Development: No. 28). 1977. pap. text ed. 4.00 (ISBN 0-8270-6000-9). OAS.

Proceedings. Carnahan Conference on Crime Countermeasures, May 14-16, 1980. 1980. 22.50 (ISBN 0-89779-030-8). U of Ky OES Pubns.

Proceedings. Chartridge Symposium on Real-Time Computing in Patient Management, 1975. Date not set. 28.50 (ISBN 0-901223-88-3, Pub. by Peregrinus England). Inst Elect Eng.

Proceedings. Chartridge Symposium on the Management of the Acutely Ill, 1976. Date not set. 29.50 (ISBN 0-901223-92-1, Pub. by Peregrinus England). Inst Elect Eng.

Proceedings, 5 vols. rev. ed. Colloquium of Microwave Communication, 5th, Budapest, 1970. Ed. by G. Bognar. LC 65-40139. 1974. Set. 75.00x (ISBN 963-05-0300-X). Intl Pubns Serv.

Proceedings. Colloquium on the Law of Outer Space - International Institute of Space Law of the International Astronautical Federation, 20th, 1977. Ed. by Mortimer D. Schwartz. v, 524p. 1978. pap. text ed. 32.50x (ISBN 0-8377-0439-1). Rothman.

Proceedings, 2 vols. Conference on Applied Physical Chemistry, 2nd, Veszprem, Hungary, 1971. Ed. by I. Buzas. LC 73-155062. (Illus.). 1500p. 1971. Set. 32.50x (ISBN 0-8002-1841-8). Intl Pubns Serv.

Proceedings. Conference on Computer in the Undergraduate Curricula, Second Annual, 1971. LC 79-165540. 1971. pap. 15.00 (ISBN 0-87451-084-8). U Pr of New Eng.

Proceedings. Conference on Space Science & Space Law. Ed. by Mortimer D. Schwartz. (Illus.). 176p. 1964. pap. text ed. 6.75x (ISBN 0-8377-1100-2). Rothman.

Proceedings. Cooley's Anemia Symposium, 4th et al. Ed. by Arthur Bank et al. LC 80-17575. (N.Y. Academy of Sciences Annals: Vol. 344). 1980. 79.00x (ISBN 0-89766-076-5); pap. write for info. NY Acad Sci.

Proceedings. Cranfield Fluidics Conference, 1st. 1965. 24.00. BHRA Fluid.

Proceedings. Cranfield Fluidics Conference, 6th. 1974. 45.00. BHRA Fluid.

Proceedings. Cranfield Fluidics Conference, 7th. 1977. 58.00 (ISBN 0-900983-50-7). BHRA Fluid.

Proceedings. Cshl Banbury Center Report 8 - Hormones & Breast Cancer et al. Ed. by Pentti K. Siiteri & Clifford W. Welsch. (Banbury Report Ser.: Vol. 8). 1981. 60.00 (ISBN 0-87969-207-3). Cold Spring Harbor.

Proceedings. Douglas McHenry International Symposium in Concrete & Concrete Structures. 1978. 28.95 (SP-55); 21.25. ACI.

Proceedings, 2 vols. Eighth International Conference on Fluid Sealing. Ed. by H. S. Stephens & N. G. Guy. (Illus.). 1979. pap. text ed. 70.00 (ISBN 0-900983-93-0, Dist. by Air Science Co.). BHRA Fluid.

Proceedings, 2 vols. European Conference on Mixing, 3rd. Ed. by H. S. Stephens & C. A. Stapleton. (European Conferences on Mixing Ser.). 500p. 1979. Set. PLB 73.00 (ISBN 0-906085-31-4, Dist. by Air Science Co.). BHRA Fluid.

Proceedings. European Conference on Psychosomatic Research, 12th July 1978. Ed. by H. Freyberger. (Psychotherapy & Psychosomatics: Vol. 32, No. 1-4). (Illus.). 324p. 1980. pap. 78.00 (ISBN 3-8055-3044-7). S Karger.

Proceedings. European Symposium On Medical Enzymology - 1st - Milan - 1960. Ed. by Nicola Dioguardi. 1962. 53.50 (ISBN 0-12-216950-6). Acad Pr.

Proceedings. Fifth Cranfield Fluidics Conference. 1972. text ed. 60.00 (ISBN 0-900983-24-8, Dist. by Air Science Co.). BHRA Fluid.

Proceedings, 2 vols. Fifth Fluid Power Symposium. Ed. by H. S. Stephens & C. A. Stapleton. (Illus.). 1979. Set. lib. bdg. 78.00 (ISBN 0-900983-96-5, Dist by Air Science Co.). BHRA Fluid.

Proceedings, 2 vols. Fifth International Conference on the Hydraulic Transport of Solids in Pipes. Ed. by H. S. Stephens & L. Gittins. (Illus.). 1979. Set. pap. text ed. 86.00 (ISBN 0-900983-82-5, Dist by Air Science Co.). BHRA Fluid.

Proceedings. Fifth International Conference on Fluid Sealing. 1971. text ed. 50.00 (ISBN 0-900983-12-4, Dist. by Air Science Co.). BHRA Fluid.

Proceedings. First European Conference on Mixing & Centrifugal Separation. 1975. text ed. 56.00 (ISBN 0-900983-39-6, Dist. by Air Science Co.). BHRA Fluid.

Proceedings. First Fluid Power Symposium. 1969. text ed. 29.00 (ISBN 0-900983-03-5, Dist. by Air Science Co.). BHRA Fluid.

Proceedings. First International Conference on Pressure Surges. 1973. text ed. 52.00 (ISBN 0-900983-25-6, Dist. by Air Science Co.). BHRA Fluid.

Proceedings. First International Conference on Drag Reduction. 1974. text ed. 52.00 (ISBN 0-900983-40-X, Dist. by Air Science Co.). BHRA Fluid.

Proceedings, 2 vols. First International Symposium on Wave & Tidal Energy. Ed. by H. S. Stephens. (Illus.). 1979. Set. pap. 78.00 (ISBN 0-906085-00-4, Dist. by Air Science Co.). BHRA Fluid.

Proceedings. First International Symposium on Dredging Technology. 1976. text ed. 65.00 (ISBN 0-900983-47-7, Dist. by Air Science Co.). BHRA Fluid.

Proceedings. First International Symposium on the Aerodynamics & Ventilation of Vehicle Tunnels. 1973. text ed. 52.00 (ISBN 0-900983-28-0, Dist. by Air Science Co.). BHRA Fluid.

Proceedings. Fluidized Combustion Conference, 1975. 1976. 47.50x (ISBN 0-8002-1847-7). Intl Pubns Serv.

Proceedings. Fourth Cranfield Fluidics Conference. 1970. text ed. 60.00 (ISBN 0-900983-08-6, Dist. by Air Science Co.). BHRA Fluid.

Proceedings. Fourth Fluid Power Symposium. 1975. text ed. 56.00 (ISBN 0-900983-45-0, Dist. by Air Science Co.). BHRA Fluid.

Proceedings. Fourth International Conference on the Pneumatic Transport of Solids in Pipes. Ed. by H. S. Stephens & C. A. Stapleton. (Illus.). 1979. pap. text ed. 71.00 (ISBN 0-900983-86-8, Dist by Air Science Co.). BHRA Fluid.

Proceedings, 2 vols. Fourth International Conference on Jet Cutting Technology. Ed. by H. S. Stephens. (Illus.). 1979. Set. pap. text ed. 68.00 (ISBN 0-900983-79-5, Dist. by Air Science Co.). BHRA Fluid.

Proceedings. Frinternational Symposium on X-Ray Optics & X-Ray Microanalysis - 3rd - Stanford - California - 1962. Ed. by Howard H. Pattee, Jr. et al. 1964. 58.50 (ISBN 0-12-547050-9). Acad Pr.

Proceedings. Heat Transfer & Fluid Mechanics Institute. Incl. 1958 Sessions. viii, 264p. pap. 12.50x (ISBN 0-8047-0422-8); 1959 Sessions. x, 242p. pap. 12.50x (ISBN 0-8047-0423-6); 1960 Sessions. Ed. by David M Mason et al. x, 260p. 12.50x (ISBN 0-8047-0424-4); 1961 Sessions. Ed. by Raymond C. Binder et al. xi, 236p. 12.50x (ISBN 0-8047-0425-2); 1962 Sessions. Ed. by F. Edward Ehlers et al. x, 294p. 12.50x (ISBN 0-8047-0426-0); 1963 Sessions. Ed. by Anatol Roshko et al. xii, 280p. 12.50x (ISBN 0-8047-0427-9); 1964 Sessions. Ed. by Warren H. Giedt & Salomon Levy. x, 275p. 12.50x (ISBN 0-8047-0428-7); 1965 Sessions. Ed. by Andrew F. Charwat et al. xii, 372p. 16.50x (ISBN 0-8047-0429-5); 1966 Sessions. Ed. by Michel A. Saad & James A. Miller. xii, 444p. 17.50x (ISBN 0-8047-0430-9); 1967 Sessions. Ed. by Paul A. Libby et al. x, 468p. 17.50x (ISBN 0-8047-0431-7); 1968 Sessions. Ed. by Ashley F. Emery & Creighton A. Depew. ix, 272p. 12.50x (ISBN 0-8047-0438-4); 1970 Sessions. Ed. by Turgut Sarpkaya. xii, 370p. 15.00x (ISBN 0-8047-0744-8); 1974 Sessions. Ed. by Lorin R. Davis & Robert E. Wilson. 17.50x (ISBN 0-8047-0865-7); 1976 Sessions. Ed. by Allan A. McKillop et al. 29.50x (ISBN 0-8047-0917-3); 1978 Sessions. Ed. by Clayton T. Crowe & William L. Grosshandler. 344p. text ed. 28.50x (ISBN 0-8047-1002-3); 1980 Sessions. Ed. by Melvin Gerstein & P. Roy Choudhury. text ed. 22.50x (ISBN 0-8047-1087-2). (Illus.). Stanford U Pr.

Proceedings. Inter-American Juridical Committee, Jul 25 - Aug 23 1972. (Inter-American Juridical Committee Ser). 102p. (Orig.). 1972. pap. 1.00 o.p. (ISBN 0-685-30409-4). OAS.

Proceedings. Internaional Numismatic Symposium, Warsaw & Budapest, 1976. Ed. by K. Niro-Sey & I. Gedai. (Illus.). 221p. 1980. 27.50x (ISBN 963-05-2055-9). Intl Pubns Serv.

Proceedings, 2 vols. Internal & External Protection of Pipes, 3rd International Conference. pap. 94.00 (ISBN 0-906085-18-7, Dist. by Air Science Co.). BHRA Fluid.

Proceedings. International Agricultural Machinery Workshop. 203p. 1978. pap. 16.00 (R036, IRRI). Unipub.

Proceedings. International Clean Air Congress, 2nd. Ed. by Harold M. Englund & W. T. Beery. 1971. 128.00 (ISBN 0-12-239450-X). Acad Pr.

Proceedings. International Codata Conference, 6th Biennial, Santa Flavia, Italy, May 22-25, 1978. Ed. by Bertrand Dreyfus. (Illus.). 400p. 1979. 145.00 (ISBN 0-08-023371-6). Pergamon.

Proceedings, 2 vols. International Computer Music Conference, 1978. Ed. by C. Roads. 1979. Vol. 1. pap. 10.00 (ISBN 0-8101-0600-0); Vol. 2. pap. 10.00 (ISBN 0-8101-0601-9). Northwestern U Pr.

Proceedings. International Conference on Computing Methods in Optimization Problems - 2nd San Remo, Italy - 1968. Ed. by A. V. Balakrishnan. LC 78-94162. (Lecture Notes in Operations Research & Mathematical Economics: Vol. 14). (Orig.). 1969. pap. 10.70 o.p. (ISBN 0-387-04637-2). Springer-Verlag.

Proceedings. International Conference on Drug Absorption, Edinburgh, 1979. Ed. by W. S. Nimmo & L. F. Prescott. 355p. 1980. text ed. 45.00 (ISBN 0-909337-30-6). ADIS Pr.

Proceedings. International Conference on Fluid Sealing, 6th. 1973. text ed. 52.00 (ISBN 0-900983-27-2, Dist. by Air Science Co.). BHRA Fluid.

Proceedings. International Conference on Fluid Sealing, 4th. 1969. 29.00 (ISBN 0-900983-04-3). BHRA Fluid.

Proceedings. International Conference on Fluid Sealing, 3rd. 1967. 47.00. BHRA Fluid.

Proceedings. International Conference on Fluid Sealing, 2nd. 1964. 45.00. BHRA Fluid.

Proceedings. International Conference on Fluid Sealing, 1st. 1961. 45.00. BHRA Fluid.

Proceedings. International Conference on Historical Linguistics, 3rd, Hamburg 22-26 August, 1977. (Current Issues in Linguistic Theory). 1980. text ed. 45.75x (ISBN 0-391-01653-9). Humanities.

Proceedings. International Conference on Hydraulics, Pneumatics & Fluidics in Control & Automation. 1977. text ed. 65.00 (ISBN 0-900983-53-1, Dist. by Air Science Co.). BHRA Fluid.

Proceedings. International Conference On Hyperbaric Medicine - 3rd - Durham - N. C. - 1965. Ed. by Ivan W. Brown & Barbara G. Cox. 1966. 16.00 (ISBN 0-309-01404-2). Natl Acad Pr.

Proceedings. International Conference on Internal & External Protection of Pipes, 1st. 1976. 60.00 (ISBN 0-900983-46-9). BHRA Fluid.

Proceedings. International Conference on Light Scattering in Solids, 3rd & M. Balkanski. 1976. 55.95 o.p. (ISBN 0-470-15034-3). Halsted Pr.

Proceedings, 2 vols. International Conference on Pressure Surges, 3rd. Ed. by J. A. Hansan & H. S. Stephens. 600p. (Orig.). 1980. PLB 99.00 (ISBN 0-906085-24-1, Dist. by Air Science Co.). BHRA Fluid.

Proceedings, 5 vols. International Conference on the Physics & Chemistry on Semiconductor Heterjunctions & Layer Structures, Budapest, 1970. Ed. by G. Szigeti. (Illus.). 1317p. 1970. pap. 82.50 o.p. (ISBN 0-685-27544-2). Adler.

Proceedings. International Conference on the Theory of Groups, 1969. Ed. by B. H. Neumann & L. G. Kovacs. 414p. 1969. 49.00 (ISBN 0-677-10780-3). Gordon.

Proceedings, 3 vols. International Conference on Thermal Analysis, 3rd, Davos, Switzerland, 23-28 August 1971. Ed. by H. G. Wiedemann. Incl. Vol. 1. Advances in Instrumentation. 65.00x (ISBN 3-7643-0636-X); Vol. 2. Inorganic Chemistry. 82.50x (ISBN 3-7643-0637-8); Vol. 3. Organic & Macromolecular Chemistry, Ceramics, Earth Sciences. 72.50x (ISBN 3-7643-0638-6). 1972. Intl Pubns Serv.

Proceedings. International Congress of Game Biologists, Thirteenth, Atlanta, Ga., March 11-15, 1977. Ed. by Tony J. Peterle. (Illus.). 538p. (Orig.). 1978. pap. 10.00 (ISBN 0-933564-04-X). Wildlife Soc.

Proceedings. International Congress of Mathematicians, 1978, Helsinki. 1980. 70.00 (ISBN 951-41-0352-1). Am Math.

Proceedings. International Congress of Protozoology, 5th. Ed. by S. H. Hutner. (Illus.). 222p. 1979. pap. text ed. 19.00 (ISBN 0-935868-00-3). Allen Pr.

Proceedings, Archivum, Vol. Xxvi. International Congress on Archives, 8th. Ed. by International Council on Archives. 207p. 1979. 35.00 (ISBN 0-89664-135-X, Pub. by K G Saur). Gale.

Proceedings. International Congress on Asian Pediatrics. Ed. by S. K. Bose. 31.50x o.p. (ISBN 0-210-26977-4). Asia.

Proceedings. International Deep-Water Rice Workshop, 1977. 239p. 1977. pap. 14.50 (R028, IRRI). Unipub.

Proceedings. International Gas Bearings Symposium, 5th. 1969. lib. bdg. 29.00. BHRA Fluid.

Proceedings. International Gas Bearings Symposium, 2nd. 1965. 26.00. BHRA Fluid.

Proceedings. International Gas Research Conference, 1st, 1980. LC 80-83454. 1016p. 1980. 43.50 (ISBN 0-86587-085-3) Gov Insts.

Proceedings. International Marine & Shipping Conference, 1969. (Illus.). 832p. 1970. 36.00 (ISBN 0-900976-93-4, Pub. by Inst Marine Eng). Intl Schol Bk Serv.

Proceedings. International Mine Ventilation Congress, 2nd. Ed. by Pierre Mousset-Jones. LC 80-52943. (Illus.). 864p. 1980. 34.00x (ISBN 0-89520-271-9). Soc Mining Eng.

Proceedings. International Organization of Citrus Virologists, 5th Conference. Ed. by W. C. Price. LC 59-63553. 1972. 11.50 (ISBN 0-8130-0327-X). U Presses Fla.

Proceedings. International Seaweed Symposium, 7th, Sappora, Japan, Aug. 1971. Ed. by Science Council of Japan. 607p. 1973. 53.95 (ISBN 0-470-77090-2). Halsted Pr.

Proceedings. International Summer School on Mathematical Systems Theory & Economics, Varenna, Italy, 1967. Ed. by H. W. Kuhn & G. P. Szegoe. LC 70-81409. (Lecture Notes in Operations Research and Mathematical Economics: Vols. 11 & 12). 1969. pap. 21.90 o.p. (ISBN 0-387-04635-6). Springer-Verlag.

Proceedings. International Symposium on Cooling Systems. 1975. pap. 34.00 (ISBN 0-900983-41-8, Dist. by Air Science Co.). BHRA Fluid.

Proceedings. International Symposium on Hydrotransport of Solids in Pipes, 4th. 1977. 60.00 (ISBN 0-900983-56-6). BHRA Fluid.

Proceedings. International Symposium on Hydrotransport of Solids in Pipes, 3rd. 1974. 50.00 (ISBN 0-900983-38-8). BHRA Fluid.

Proceedings. International Symposium on Malignant Lymphomas of the Nervous System. Ed. by K. Jellinger & F. Seitelberger. (Acta Neuropathologica Ser: Suppl. 6). (Illus.). 320p. 1975. pap. 49.60 o.p. (ISBN 0-387-07208-X). Springer-Verlag.

Proceedings. International Symposium on Pneumotransport of Solids in Pipes, 3rd. 1977. 60.00 (ISBN 0-900983-52-3). BHRA Fluid.

Proceedings. International Symposium on Pneumotransport of Solids in Pipes, 1st. 1972. 37.00 (ISBN 0-900983-15-9). BHRA Fluid.

Proceedings. International Symposium on Polymers in Concrete. 1978. 22.25 (SP-58); 17.50. ACI.

Proceedings. International Symposium on Quantum Biology & Quantum Pharmacology. (International Journal of Quantum Chemistry-Quantum Biology Symposium: No. 5). 472p. 1978. 40.50 (ISBN 0-471-05635-9). Wiley.

Proceedings. International Symposium on the Design & Operation of Siphons & Siphon Spillways. 1976. text ed. 52.00 (ISBN 0-900983-44-2, Dist. by Air Science Co.). BHRA Fluid.

Proceedings. International Symposium on the Use of Models in Fire Research - November 9-10, 1959. 1959. 6.00 o.p. (ISBN 0-309-00786-0). Natl Acad Pr.

Proceedings. International Symposium on Unsteady Flow in Open Channels. 1977. text ed. 68.00 (ISBN 0-900983-54-X, Dist. by Air Science Co.). BHRA Fluid.

Proceedings. International Symposium on Urban Storm Runoff, July 28-31, 1980. 1980. 33.50 (ISBN 0-89779-040-5). U of Ky OES Pubns.

Proceedings. International Technical Conference on Slurry Transportation, 2nd. Ed. by Charles W. Linderman. LC 77-81416. (Illus.). 152p. 1977. pap. 40.00 (ISBN 0-932066-02-X). Slurry Transport.

Proceedings. International Technical Conference on Slurry Transportation, 3rd. LC 78-52717. (Illus.). 224p. 1978. pap. 50.00 (ISBN 0-932066-03-8). Slurry Transport.

Proceedings. International Workshop on Ergonomic Aspects of Visual Display Terminals, Milan, March 1980. Ed. by Etienne Grandjean & E. Vigliani. (Illus.). 300p. 1980. 47.50x (ISBN 0-85066-211-7). Intl Pubns Serv.

Proceedings. Internatonal Deep-Water Rice Workshop, 1978. 300p. 1979. pap. 15.50 (R037, IRRI). Unipub.

Proceedings. Joint ISMAR-AMPERE International Conference on Magnetic Resonance. Ed. by J. Smidt. 1981. 60.00. Franklin Inst Pr.

Proceedings. P. O. Lowdin & Y. Ohrn. (International Journal of Quantum Chemistry-Quantum Chemistry Symposium: No. 12). 550p. 1978. 40.50 (ISBN 0-471-05633-2). Wiley.

Proceedings, 3 vols. Lunar & Planetary Science Conference, 9th, Houston, 1978. Compiled by Lunar & Planetary Institute, Houston, Texas. (Geochimica et Cosmochimicha Acta: Suppl. 10). 1979. Set. 245.00 (ISBN 0-08-022966-2). Pergamon.

Proceedings. Lunar & Planetary Science Conference, 10th, Houston, Texas, March 19-23, 1979. LC 79-22554. (Illus.). 3200p. 1980. 220.00 (ISBN 0-08-025128-5). Pergamon.

Proceedings. Lunar Science Conference, 8th, Houston, 1977. Compiled by Lunar Science Institute, Houston, Texas. (Lunar Science Ser.: No. 8). (Illus.). 1978. 255.00 (ISBN 0-08-022052-5). Pergamon.

Proceedings. Machine Tool & Design Research International Conference, 14th. Ed. by S. A. Tobias & S. A. Tobias. 1974. 114.95 (ISBN 0-470-49746-7). Halsted Pr.

Proceedings. Machine Tool Design & Research International Conference, 12th. Ed. by F. Koenigsberger & S. A. Tobias. LC 72-6276. 582p. 1972. 98.95 (ISBN 0-470-49745-9). Halsted Pr.

Proceedings. Machine Tool Design & Research International Conference 15th. Ed. by S. A. Tobias & F. Koenigsberger. LC 63-19240. 738p. 1975. 164.95 (ISBN 0-470-87532-1). Halsted Pr.

Proceedings. Membrane Processes for Industry, Symposium, May 19-20,1966. Ed. by Charles E. Feazel & Robert E. Lacey. LC 66-30620. (Illus.). 268p. 1966. pap. 5.00 (ISBN 0-686-27919-0). S Res Inst.

Proceedings. Luigi G. Napolitano & International Astronautical Congress, 27th, Anaheim, Ca., Oct. 1976. 1977. text ed. 64.00 (ISBN 0-08-021732-X). Pergamon.

Proceedings. Oil Shale Symposium, 11th. Ed. by James H. Gary. (Illus.). 389p. 1978. pap. 12.00 (ISBN 0-918062-03-9). Colo Sch Mines.

Proceedings. Princeton Conference on Cerebrovascular Disease, 11th., Mar. 1978. Ed. by Thomas R. Price & Erland Nelson. LC 77-84127. 1979. text ed. 30.00 (ISBN 0-89004-292-6). Raven.

Proceedings. Purdue University Industrial Waste Conference, 35th. Ed. by John M. Bell. 1981. text ed. 59.95 (ISBN 0-250-40363-3). Ann Arbor Science.

Proceedings. Report of the AFIPS Panel on Transborder Data Flow. Ed. by Rein Turn. LC 79-93002. (Transborder Data Flow: Concerns in Privacy Protection & Free Flow of Information: Vol. 1). (Illus.). xviii, 186p. 1979. pap. 15.00 (ISBN 0-88283-004-X). AFIPS Pr.

Proceedings. Rice Blast Workshop. 222p. 1979. pap. 18.50 (R008, IRRI). Unipub.

Proceedings. Seals in Fluid Power Symposium. 1973. pap. 29.00 (ISBN 0-900983-31-0, Dist. by Air Science Co.). BHRA Fluid.

Proceedings. Second Cranfield Fluidics Conference. 1967. text ed. 39.00 (ISBN 0-685-85166-4, Dist. by Air Science Co.). BHRA Fluid.

Proceedings. Second European Conference on Mixing. Ed. by H. S. Stephens & J. A. Clarke. 1978. pap. 68.00 (ISBN 0-900983-69-8, Dist. by Air Science Co.). BHRA Fluid.

Proceedings. Second Fluid Power Symposium. 1971. text ed. 47.00 (ISBN 0-900983-11-6, Dist. by Air Science Co.). BHRA Fluid.

Proceedings, 2 vols. Second International Conference on Dredging Technology. Ed. by H. S. Stephens. 1979. Set. pap. 71.00 (ISBN 0-900983-76-0, Dist. by Air Science Co). BHRA Fluid.

Proceedings. Second International Conference on the Internal & External Protection of Pipes. Ed. by H. S. Stephens & Jenny Clarke. 1978. pap. 68.00 (ISBN 0-900983-73-6, Dist. by Air Science Co.). BHRA Fluid.

Proceedings. Second International Conference on Pressure Surges. 1977. text ed. 65.00 (ISBN 0-900983-65-5, Dist. by Air Science Co.). BHRA Fluid.

Proceedings. Second International Conference on Drag Reduction. pap. 60.00 (ISBN 0-900983-71-X, Dist. by Air Science Co.). BHRA Fluid.

Proceedings, 2 vols. Second International Symposium on Wind Energy Systems. Ed. by H. S. Stephens & I. Fantom. (Illus.). 1979. Set. pap. text ed. 78.00 (ISBN 0-906085-03-9, Dist. by Air Science Co.). BHRA Fluid.

Proceedings. Second International Symposium on the Aerodynamics & Ventilation of Vehicle Tunnels. 1977. text ed. 68.00 (ISBN 0-900983-51-5, Dist. by Air Science Co.). BHRA Fluid.

Proceedings. Security Through Science & Engineering, Nineteen Eighty International Conference, September 23-26, 1980. 1980. 33.50 (ISBN 0-89779-042-1). U of Ky OES Pubns.

Proceedings. Seminar on Aacr-Two, Univ. of Nottingham, 1979. 1980. pap. 17.50x (ISBN 0-85365-593-6, Pub. by Lib Assn England). Oryx Pr.

Proceedings. Studies in Medieval Culture, Ii, Kalamazoo. 1966. 5.00 o.p. (ISBN 0-686-14883-5). Medieval Inst.

Proceedings. Studies in Medieval Culture, IIII. Ed. by John R. Sommerfeldt. 1970. pap. 5.00 (ISBN 0-686-14884-3). Medieval Inst.

Proceedings. Studies in Medieval Culture I,Kalamazoo. Ed. by John R. Sommerfeldt. 1964. 5.00 o.p. (ISBN 0-686-14882-7). Medieval Inst.

Proceedings. Studies in Medieval Culture, V. Ed. by John R. Sommerfeldt et al. 1975. pap. 5.00 (ISBN 0-686-14892-4). Medieval Inst.

Proceedings. Summer Workshop on Invariant Imbedding - University of Southern California - Jun-Aug, 1970. LC 79-170660. (Lecture Notes in Operations Research & Mathematical Systems: Vol. 52). (Illus.). 1971. pap. 10.70 o.p. (ISBN 0-387-05549-5). Springer-Verlag.

Proceedings. Syllabus for CME Credits, 130th, Toronto, Canada, 1977. 1977. 7.00 o.p. (ISBN 0-685-83184-1, 153-7). Am Psychiatric.

Proceedings. Sympoisum on Cropping Systems Research & Development for the Asian Rice Farmer. 454p. 1977. pap. 18.50 (R004, IRRI). Unipub.

Proceedings. Symposium of Commission V, ISP on the Biomedical & Bioengineering Applications of Photogrammetry, Washington, D.C., Sept. 1974. 5.00 o.p. (ISBN 0-686-21665-2); non-members o.p. 12.50 o.p. (ISBN 0-686-21666-0). ASP.

Proceedings. Symposium on Climate & Rice. 565p. 1976. pap. 37.50 (R025, IRRI). Unipub.

Proceedings. Symposium on Corrosion Fundamentals. Ed. by Anton Brasunas & E. E. Stansbury. LC 56-13073. (Illus.). 1956. 12.50x (ISBN 0-87049-016-8). U of Tenn Pr.

Proceedings. Symposium on Finite Groups, Urbana, Illinois, Nov. 24, 1967. Repr. of 1969 ed. 4.00 (ISBN 0-8218-0045-0, FIN). Am Math.

Proceedings. Symposium on Jet Pumps & Ejectors, 1st. 1972. 28.00. BHRA Fluid.

Proceedings. Symposium on Nucleic Acids, Chemistry, 4th, Kyoto, 1976. 156p. 16.00. Info Retrieval.

Proceedings. Symposium on Nucleic Acids Chemistry, 5th, Mishima, Japan, 1977. 190p. 12.00. Info Retrieval.

Proceedings. Symposium on Nucleic Acids Chemistry, 6th, Nagoya, Japan, 1978. 227p. 15.00. Info Retrieval.

Proceedings. Symposium on Nucleic Acids Chemistry, 7th, Okayama, Japan, 1979. 250p. 16.00. Info Retrieval.

Proceedings. Symposium on Psychophysiological Aspects of Space Flight, Brooks Air Force Base, Texas, 1960. Ed. by Bernard E. Flaherty. LC 60-15809. 1961. 22.50x (ISBN 0-231-02456-8). Columbia U Pr.

Proceedings. Symposium on Surface Mining Hydrology, Sedimentology, & Reclamataion, December 4-7, 1979. 1979. 33.50 (ISBN 0-89779-024-3). U of Ky OES Pubns.

Proceedings. Symposium on the Chemistry of Nucleic Acids Components, 3rd, Czechoslovakia, 1975. 183p. 15.00. Info Retrieval.

Proceedings. Symposium on the Chemistry of Nucleic Acids Components, 4th, Czechoslovakia, 1978. 250p. 14.00. Info Retrieval.

Proceedings. Symposium on the Granites of West Africa, Ivory Coast, Nigeria, Cameroon, 1965. 1968. 17.50 (ISBN 0-685-20791-9, U488, UNESCO). Unipub.

Proceedings. Symposium on the State of the Art in Communication, Point Mugu, California, October 1975. 15.00 (ISBN 0-87703-145-2). Soc Tech Comm.

Proceedings. Symposium On Underwater Physiology - 2nd - Feb. 25-26 - Washington D.C. - 1963. Ed. by Mine Advisory Committee. 1963. pap. 5.00 (ISBN 0-309-01181-7). Natl Acad Pr.

Proceedings. Symposium on Wind Energy, 1st. 1977. 65.00. BHRA Fluid.

Proceedings. Symposium on Wind Energy, 3rd. 1980. pap. 99.00 (ISBN 0-906085-47-0). BHRA Fluid.

Proceedings. Texas Symposium on Relativistic Astrophysics, 9th. Ed. by Judith J. Perry et al. LC 80-11614. (N.Y. Academy of Sciences Annals: Vol. 336). 599p. 1980. 105.00x (ISBN 0-89766-045-5). NY Acad Sci.

Proceedings. Third International Symposium on Dredging Technology. Ed. by H. S. Stephens. (Illus.). 446p. (Orig.). 1980. pap. write for info. (ISBN 0-906085-09-8). BHRA Fluid.

Proceedings. Uranium Seminar, Fourth. LC 80-70454. (Uranium Seminars Ser.). 1980. pap. 20.00x (ISBN 0-89520-280-8). Soc Mining Eng.

Proceedings. Ed. by Gerald Weissman et al. LC 78-55809. (Advances in Inflammation Research Ser.: Vol. 1). 1979. text ed. 67.00 (ISBN 0-89004-337-X). Raven.

Proceedings. Working Group Meeting on Energy Planning Program & Committee on Natural Resources, Fifth. (Energy Resources Development Ser.: No. 20). 151p. 1980. pap. 12.00 (ISBN 0-686-68966-6, UN79/2F11, UN). Unipub.

Proceedings. Workshop of the Phenomenon Known As 'El Nino' 284p. 1980. pap. 22.50 (ISBN 92-3-101509-5, U1019, UNESCO). Unipub.

Proceedings. Workshop on Chemical Aspects of Rice Grain Quality. 390p. 1979. pap. 20.50 (R027, IRRI). Unipub.

Proceedings. Workshop on the Genetic Conservation of Rice. 54p. 1978. pap. 7.50 (R034, IRRI). Unipub.

Proceedings. Workshop on the Interfaces Between Agriculture, Nutrition, & Food Science, 1977. 143p. 1979. pap. 7.25 (R087, IRRI). Unipub.

Proceedings. World Congress on Pain, 2nd, Montreal, Aug. 1978. Ed. by John J. Bonica et al. LC 79-87468. (Advances in Pain Research & Therapy Ser.: Vol. 3). 1979. text ed. 84.00 (ISBN 0-89004-270-5). Raven.

Proceedings. World Meteorological Congress, Eighth. 261p. 1980. pap. 30.00 (ISBN 92-63-10547-2, W472, WMO). Unipub.

Proceedings. World Petroleum Congress, 9th, Japan, 1975. Ed. by Applied Science Publishers Ltd. Incl. Vol. 1. Introduction; Vol. 2. Geology; Vol. 3. Exploration & Transportation; Vol. 4. Drilling & Production; Vol. 5. Processing & Storage; Vol. 6. Conservation & Safety; Vol. 7. Index. (Illus.). 1975. 745.00 set (ISBN 0-85334-670-4). Intl Ideas.

Proceedings, Vols. 1 & 2. Guangzhou Conference on Theoretical Particle Physics 1980. 1980. text ed. 89.50 (ISBN 0-442-20273-3, Pub. by Sci Pr China). Van Nos Reinhold.

Proceedings, Vols. 1 & 2. Symposium on Microdosimetry, Sixth, Brussels, Belgium, May 1978. Ed. by J. Booz & H. G. Ebert. (European Applied Research Reports Topics). 558p. 1978. lib. bdg. 48.75 ea. Vol. 1 (ISBN 0-906346-02-9). Vol. 2 (ISBN 0-906346-03-7). Harwood Academic.

Proceedings, Vol. 1. Studies in Medieval Culture,Iv 1. Ed. by John R. Sommerfeldt et al. 1974. pap. 5.00 (ISBN 0-686-14886-X). Medieval Inst.

Proceedings, Vol. 2. Studies in Medieval Culture, IV 2, Kalamazoo. Ed. by John R. Sommerfeldt et al. 1974. pap. 5.00 (ISBN 0-686-14888-6). Medieval Inst.

Proceedings, Vol. 3. Studies in Medieval Culture, Iv 3,Kalamazoo. Ed. by John R. Sommerfeldt et al. 1974. pap. 5.00 (ISBN 0-686-14890-8). Medieval Inst.

Proceedings, Vol. 4. International Academy of Oral Pathology. Ed. by L. R. Cahn. 1970. 49.50 (ISBN 0-677-62260-0). Gordon.

Proceedings, Vol. 8. Irving H. Leopold. Ed. by R. P. Burns. LC 66-22972. (Wiley Ser. in Clinical Opthalmology). 144p. 1976. 28.00 o.p. (ISBN 0-471-05151-9, Pub. by Wiley Medical). Wiley.

Proceedings, Vol. 8. Symposium on Ocular Therapy. Ed. by Irving H. Leopold & Robert P. Burns. LC 66-22972. 92p. 1976. 24.00 (ISBN 0-471-52771-8, Pub. by Wiley). Krieger.

Proceedings, Vol. 337. new ed. International Conference on Collective Phenomena, 3rd et al. Ed. by James S. Langer et al. LC 80-17323. (N.Y. Academy of Sciences Annals: Vol. 337). 39.00x (ISBN 0-89766-074-9); pap. write for info. (ISBN 0-89766-075-7). NY Acad Sci.

Proceedings & Addresses at the Freethinkers' Convention Held at Watkins, N. Y., 1878. LC 73-119051. (Civil Liberties in American History Ser). 1970. Repr. of 1878 ed. lib. bdg. 39.50 (ISBN 0-306-71937-1). Da Capo.

Proceedings & Debates of the Virginia State Convention of 1829-1830. LC 71-139729. (Law, Politics, & History Ser). 1971. Repr. of 1830 ed. lib. bdg. 75.00 (ISBN 0-306-70077-8). Da Capo.

Proceedings: Conference on Productivity Through Engineering, Pt. 3. 99p. 1977. 25.00 o.p. (ISBN 0-686-27577-2, 123-77). AAES.

Proceedings: Eleventh Lunar & Planetary Science Conference, Houston, Texas, March 17-21, 1980, 3 vols. Compiled by Lunar & Planetary Institute. (Geochimica & Cosmochimica Acta: Suppl. 14). 3000p. 1981. Set. 200.00 (ISBN 0-08-026314-3). Pergamon.

Proceedings: FEBS Meeting, 11th, 9 vols. Ed. by Per Schambye. (Illus.). 1978. Set. text ed. 295.00 (ISBN 0-08-021527-0). Pergamon.

Proceedings: Fifth International Bat Research Conference. Ed. by D. E. Wilson & A. L. Gardner. 434p. (Orig.). 1980. pap. 16.00 (ISBN 0-89672-083-7). Tex Tech Pr.

Proceedings, Fifth Session. Working Group Meeting on Energy Planning & Committee on Natural Resources. (Energy Resources Development Ser: No. 20). 151p. 1980. pap. 12.00 (UN79-2F11, UN). Unipub.

Proceedings: International Conference on Photoconductivity - 3rd - Stanford University - Aug. 12 1969. Ed. by Erik M. Pell. 1972. 82.00 (ISBN 0-08-016137-5). Pergamon.

Proceedings of a Workshop on Agricultural Potentiality Directed by Nutritional Needs. Ed. by Sandor Rajki. (Illus.). 238p. 1979. 25.00x (ISBN 963-05-1991-7). Intl Pubns Serv.

Proceedings of International Conference on Wind Effects on Buildings & Structures: Heathrow Nineteen Seventy-Five. Ed. by K. J. Eaton & K. J. Eaton. LC 75-2730. 650p. 1976. 97.50 (ISBN 0-521-20801-7). Cambridge U Pr.

Proceedings of Symposia in Pure Mathematics, Vol. 37. Ed. by Bruce Cooperstein & Geoffrey Mason. 1981. cancelled (ISBN 0-8218-1440-0). Am Math.

Proceedings of the American Academy & Institute of Arts & Letters. (Second Ser.: No. 31). 100p. 1981. 10.00 (ISBN 0-915974-25-8). Am Acad Inst Arts.

Proceedings of the Battle Conference on Anglo-Norman Studies II: 1979. Ed. by R. Allen Brown. (Illus.). 210p. 1980. 49.50x (ISBN 0-8476-3455-8). Rowman.

Proceedings of the Clean Energy Research Institute, 1st, Miami Beach, 1976. Ed. by T. Nejat Veziroglu. 1976. pap. text ed. 225.00 (ISBN 0-08-021561-0). Pergamon.

Proceedings of the Conference on Language & Language Behavior. Ed. by Eric M. Zale. LC 68-28144. 1968. 30.00x (ISBN 0-89197-906-9). Irvington.

Proceedings of the Eighth Annual International Bilingual Bicultural Education Conference. National Association for Bilingual Education. (Orig.). 1981. pap. write for info. (ISBN 0-89763-054-8). Natl Clearinghse Bilingual Ed.

Proceedings of the Eighth Hawaii Topical Conference in Particle Physics, 1979. Ed. by S. Pakvasa & V. S. Peterson. (Particle Physics Conference Proceedings). 1980. pap. text ed. 20.00x (ISBN 0-8248-0716-2). U Pr of Hawaii.

Proceedings of the Eighth International Conference on Numerical Taxonomy. Ed. by G. F. Estabrook. LC 75-31878. (Illus.). 1976. 31.95x (ISBN 0-7167-0555-9). W H Freeman.

Proceedings of the Eighth International Congress of Onomastic Sciences, Amsterdam, 1963. Ed. by D. P. Blok. (Janua Linguarum Series Major: No. 17). 1966. 135.30x (ISBN 90-2790-609-2). Mouton.

Proceedings of the Electoral Commission & of the Two Houses of Congress in Joint Meeting Relative to the Count of Electoral Votes Cast December 6, 1876, for the Presidential Term Commencing March 4, 1877. LC 69-11322. (Politics & Law Ser). 1970. Repr. of 1877 ed. lib. bdg. 85.00 (ISBN 0-306-71185-0). Da Capo.

Proceedings of the Eleventh International Conference on Underwater Education. Ed. by Cheri Boone. Date not set. pap. 17.00 (ISBN 0-916974-32-4); addendum to proceedings, 147 pp. incl. NAUI.

Proceedings of the Fifth International Congress of Aesthetics. Ed. by Jan Aler. 1968. pap. 205.90x (ISBN 90-2791-059-6). Mouton.

Proceedings of the First British-Soviet Geographical Seminar. Ed. by F. E. Hamilton. (Illus.). 152p. 1981. 28.60 (ISBN 0-08-025795-X). Pergamon.

Proceedings of the First International Congress for the Study of Child Language. Ed. by David Ingram et al. LC 80-7952. 668p. 1980. lib. bdg. 32.75 (ISBN 0-8191-1084-1). U Pr of Amer.

Proceedings of the First International Conference on Vehicle Mechanics, Detroit, 16-18 July, 1968. Ed. by H. K. Sachs. 735p. 1969. text ed. 80.00 (ISBN 90-265-0101-3, Pub. by Swets Pub Serv Holland). Swets North Am.

Proceedings of the First International UFO Congress. Curtis Fuller. 1980. pap. 2.75 (ISBN 0-446-95159-5). Warner Bks.

Proceedings of the Fourth Meeting of the French Colonial Historical Society. Ed. by Alf A. Heggoy & James J. Cooke. LC 79-63751. 1979. pap. text ed. 9.50 (ISBN 0-8191-0738-7). U Pr of Amer.

Proceedings of the Grisons in the Yeare 1618. LC 78-171760. (English Experience Ser.: No. 383). 94p. Repr. of 1619 ed. 14.00 (ISBN 90-221-0383-8). Walter J Johnson.

Proceedings of the International School of Nuclear Physics, Erice, 2-14 Sept. 1976. Ed. by D. Wilkinson. (Progress in Particle & Nuclear Physics Ser.: Vol. 1). 1979. 81.00 (ISBN 0-08-020327-2). Pergamon.

Proceedings of the International Symposium on Frontiers of Bioorganic Chemistry & Molcular Biology, Moscow & Tashkent, USSR, 1978: Proceedings of the International Symposium on Frontiers of Biorganic Chemistry & Molecular Biology, Moscow & Tashkent, USSR 1978. Ed. by S. N. Ananchenko & S. N. Ananchenko. (IUPAC Symposium Ser.). (Illus.). 435p. Date not set. 92.00 (ISBN 0-08-023967-6). Pergamon. Postponed.

Proceedings of the International Symposium on Stochastic Differential Equations, Kyoto, 1976. Ed. by Kiyosi Ito. LC 78-19655. 1978. 43.95 (ISBN 0-471-05375-9, Pub. by Wiley-Interscience). Wiley.

Proceedings of the Jakarta Workshop on Coastal Resources Managements. 106p. 1980. pap. 15.00 (ISBN 0-686-68813-9, TUNU100, UNU). Unipub.

Proceedings of the Ninth European Marine Biology Symposium, Oban 1974. Ed. by Harold Barhes. 1976. 55.00x (ISBN 0-900015-34-9). Taylor-Carlisle.

Proceedings of the Second International Conference on Vehicle Mechanics, Paris, 6-10 September, 1971. Ed. by H. K. Sachs & P. Rapin. 500p. 1973. text ed. 54.00 (ISBN 90-265-0166-8, Pub. by Swets Pub Serv Holland). Swets North Am.

Proceedings of the Second National Conference on Business Ethics. Ed. by W. Michael Hoffman. LC 79-64514. 1979. pap. text ed. 16.50 (ISBN 0-8191-0762-X). U Pr of Amer.

Proceedings of the Seventeenth International Machine, Tool, Design & Research Conference. S. A. Tobias & T. Koenigsbergen. 1978. 109.95 (ISBN 0-470-99076-7). Halsted Pr.

Proceedings of the Seventh International Congress on Archives, Moscow 1972. 388p. 1976. text ed. 36.50 (ISBN 3-7940-3774-X, Pub. by K G Saur). Shoe String.

Proceedings of the Seventh New England (Northeast) Bioengineering Conference: Held March 22-23, 1979, at Rensselaer Polytechnic Institute, Troy, New York. Lee E. Ostrander. LC 79-83927. (New England Bio-Engineering Conference Ser.: Vol. 7). (Illus.). 1979. 62.00 (ISBN 0-08-024634-6). Pergamon.

Proceedings of the Sixteenth Machine Tool Design & Research Conference. Ed. by T. Koenigsberger & S. A. Tobias. LC 76-5219. (International Machine Tool Design & Research Conference Ser.). 599p. 1976. text ed. 99.95 (ISBN 0-470-15100-5). Halsted Pr.

Proceedings of the Sixty-Eighth A.C.S.A. Annual Meeting. Ed. by John Neunier. 300p. 1981. pap. 17.50 (ISBN 0-8408-0506-3). Carrollton Pr.

Proceedings of the Sixty-Ninth Convention. International Association of Fish & Wildlife Agencies. Ed. by Ralph I. Blouch. (Orig.). 1980. 11.00 (ISBN 0-932108-04-0). IAFWA.

Proceedings of the Sixty-Seventh A.C.S.A. Annual Meeting. Ed. by Michael J. Bednar. 288p. 1980. 25.00 (ISBN 0-686-64816-1); pap. 17.50 (ISBN 0-686-64817-X). Carrollton Pr.

Proceedings of the Symposium of the International Society for Corneal Research. Ed. by J. Francois et al. (Documenta Ophthalmologica Proceedings Ser.: No. 20). 1979. pap. text ed. 47.40 (ISBN 90-6193-157-6, Dr. W. Junk Pub). Kluwer Boston.

Proceedings of the Texas Conference on Performatives, Presuppositions, & Implicatures. Ed. by Andy Rogers et al. LC 77-79322. 1977. pap. text ed. 9.95x o.p. (ISBN 0-87281-063-1). Ctr Appl Ling.

Proceedings of the Third General Conference, Vol. 3. I. P. R. A. 1970. pap. text ed. 59.00x (ISBN 90-232-0839-0). Humanities.

Proceedings of the Third International Conference on Vehicle System Dynamics, Blacksburg, VA, 12-15 August 1974. Ed. by H. K. Sachs. 324p. 1975. text ed. 54.00 (ISBN 90-265-0197-8, Pub. by Swets Pub Serv Holland). Swets North Am.

Proceedings of the Thirteenth International Machine Tool Design & Research Conference. Ed. by S. A. Tobias & F. Koenigsberger. LC 73-2955. 1973. 89.95 (ISBN 0-470-87529-1). Halsted Pr.

Proceedings of the Virgin Islands' Seminar on Unification Theology. Ed. by Darrol Bryant. LC 80-52594. (Conference Ser.: No. 6). (Illus.). xv, 323p. (Orig.). 1980. pap. text ed. 9.95 (ISBN 0-932894-06-2). Unif Theol Sem.

Proceedings of the Workshop on Biogas & Other Rural Energy Resources, Held at Suva, & the Roving Seminar on Rural Energy Development, Held at Bangkok, Manila, Tehran, & Jakarta. (Energy Resources Development Ser.: No.19-1979). 152p. 1979. pap. 10.00 (79-2F10, UN). Unipub.

Proceedings of the Workshop on Economic & Operational Requirements & Status of Large Scale Wind Systems. Ed. by Atlas Corporation. 447p. 1979. pap. 22.95 (ISBN 0-89934-022-9). Solar Energy Info.

Proceedings of Third International Symposium on Alcohol Fuel Technology. Ed. by Richard K. Pefley. 1000p. 1980. 79.95 (ISBN 0-686-65544-3); pap. 59.95 (ISBN 0-89934-020-2). Solar Energy Info.

Proceedings of Towing Tank Conference, 2 vols. Stuart Cohen. 1275p. 1981. Set. text ed. 88.00 (ISBN 0-250-40444-3). Ann Arbor Science.

Proceedings: Proceedings. Ed. by Elizabeth A. Hieb. 1978. spiral 8.75 (ISBN 0-89154-075-X). Intl Found Employ.

Proceedings: Proceedings. International Conference on Armenian Linguistics, 1st. LC 80-24203. 1980. 25.00 (ISBN 0-88206-044-9). Caravan Bks.

Proceedings: Special Volume Two. Caribbean Archives Conf., 2nd. (Archivum Ser.). 200p. 1980. pap. 23.00 (ISBN 0-89664-134-1). K G Saur.

Proceedings: State-Federal Geothermal Regulatory Interface Workshop, November 17-18, 1976, Asilomar, California. Ed. by Geothermal Resources Council. (Orig.). 1977. pap. 3.50 (ISBN 0-934412-73-1). Geothermal.

Proceedings: Symposium on Neuro-Opthalmology. New Orleans Academy of Opthalmology Symposium of 1975-76. LC 75-43983. (Illus.). 448p. 1976. text ed. 42.50 o.p. (ISBN 0-8016-3681-7). Mosby.

Proceedings: Textos Certificados De las Resoluciones y Otros Documentos, Vol. 1. Extraordinario De Sesiones, Primer Periodo, Washington, D. C., 1970. (General Assembly Ser.). (Fr., Span., Port.). pap. 2.00 (ISBN 0-8270-0880-5). OAS.

Proceedings: 30th Annual Conference Preprint of Paper's Summaries. new ed. Ed. by L. Jacobsen. (Illus.). 1977. pap. 12.00 (ISBN 0-89208-090-6). Soc Photo Sci & Eng.

Proces De l'Association Internationale Des Travailleurs. Premiere et Deuxieme Commissions Du Bureau De Paris. (Fr.). 1977. lib. bdg. 18.75x o.p. (ISBN 0-8287-0705-7); pap. text ed. 8.75x o.p. (ISBN 0-685-74934-7). Clearwater Pub.

Process Analysis & Simulation: Deterministic Systems. David M. Himmelblau. (Illus.). 333p. 1980. pap. text ed. 29.95 (ISBN 0-88408-132-X). Sterling Swift.

Process Analysis by Statistical Methods. David M. Himmelblau. (Illus.). 471p. 1981. pap. text ed. 29.95 (ISBN 0-88408-140-0). Sterling Swift.

Process & Action in Work with Groups: The Preconditions for Treatment & Growth. Ken Heap. 1978. text ed. 30.00 (ISBN 0-08-023023-7); pap. text ed. 11.25 (ISBN 0-08-023022-9). Pergamon.

Process & Divinity: The Hartshorne Festschrift. Ed. by William L. Reese & Eugene Freeman. LC 64-13547. 633p. 1964. 25.00 (ISBN 0-87548-054-3); pap. 8.95 o.p. (ISBN 0-87548-055-1). Open Court.

Process & Impact of Justice. Alan R. Coffey & Edward Eldefonso. (Criminal Justice Ser.). 1975. pap. text ed. 7.95x (ISBN 0-02-471750-9, 47175). Macmillan.

Process & Impact of the Juvenile Justice System. Edward Eldefonso & Alan Coffey. 1976. pap. 9.95x (ISBN 0-02-472490-4). Macmillan.

Process & Organization of Government Planning. John David Millett. LC 76-38753. (FDR & the Era of the New Deal Ser). 188p. 1972. Repr. of 1947 ed. lib. bdg. 22.50 (ISBN 0-306-70444-7). Da Capo.

Process Consultation: Its Role in Organization Development. Edgar H. Schein. LC 76-91149. (Organization Development Ser.). (Orig.). 1969. pap. text ed. 6.50 (ISBN 0-201-06733-1). A-W.

Process Control & Optimization Handbook. Ed. by Les A. Kane. (Illus.). 160p. (Orig.). 1980. pap. 15.95 (ISBN 0-87201-144-5). Gulf Pub.

Process Control Instrumentation Technology. Curtis D. Johnson. LC 76-26543. 1977. text ed. 21.95 (ISBN 0-471-44614-9). Wiley.

Process Design in Water Quality Engineering: New Concepts & Development. Ed. by Edward L. Thackston & W. W. Eckenfielder. (Illus.). 15.00 (ISBN 0-8363-0079-3). Jenkins.

Process Dynamics: Automatic Control of Steam Generation Plant. R. Dolezal & L. Varcop. (Illus.). 1970. 70.80x (ISBN 0-444-20042-8). Intl Ideas.

Process Engineering with Economic Objective. G. L. Wells. 1974. 18.95x (ISBN 0-249-44116-0). Intl Ideas.

Process Equipment Design: Vessel Design. Lloyd E. Brownell & Edwin H. Young. LC 59-5882. 1959. 45.00 (ISBN 0-471-11319-0, Pub by Wiley-Interscience). Wiley.

Process Flowsheeting. A. W. Westerberg et al. LC 78-51682. (Illus.). 1979. 29.50 (ISBN 0-521-22043-2). Cambridge U Pr.

Process Fluid Mechanics. M. Denn. 1980. 24.95 (ISBN 0-13-723163-6). P-H.

Process Heat Exchange. Chemical Engineering Magazine. (Chemical Engineering Book Ser.). (Illus.). 624p. 1980. 34.50 (ISBN 0-07-010742-4, P&RB). McGraw.

Process in Biomechanics. N. Akkas. (NATO Advaned Study Institute Ser.). 395p. 1979. 37.50x (ISBN 90-286-0479-0). Sijthoff & Noordhoff.

Process in Geomorphology. Ed. by Clifford Embleton & John Thornes. LC 79-18747. 436p. 1979. 47.95x (ISBN 0-470-26807-7); pap. 19.95x (ISBN 0-470-26808-5). Halsted Pr.

Process Instrumentation Manifolds: Their Selection & Application. P. E. Hewson. 350p. 1980. text ed. 35.00 (ISBN 0-87664-447-7). Instru Soc.

Process Instrumentation Primer. Norman Whitaker. 128p. 1980. 27.50 (ISBN 0-87814-128-6). Pennwell Pub.

Process Level Instrumentation & Control. Cheremisinoff. 200p. 1981. 29.75 (ISBN 0-8247-1212-9). Dekker.

Process of American Government: Cases & Problems. Bernard Feder. (Illus.). (gr. 9-12). 1972. text ed. 9.99 (ISBN 0-8107-2025-6, 9915); tchrs' guide 2.70 (ISBN 0-8107-2026-4, 9916); objectives, teaching techniques & evaluation procedures 2.70 (ISBN 0-8107-2041-8, 9917); tests 1.02 (ISBN 0-8107-2042-6, 9918). Bowmar-Noble.

Process of Becoming Ill. David Robinson. (Medicine, Illness & Society Ser). 1971. 18.00x (ISBN 0-7100-7096-9). Routledge & Kegan.

Process of Biology. Jeffrey J. Baker & Garland E. Allen. LC 73-93981. (Biology Ser). 1970. pap. 7.95 (ISBN 0-201-00372-4). A-W.

Process of Cognition. Arthur Blumenthal. (Illus.). 1977. ref. ed. 14.95 (ISBN 0-13-722983-6). P-H.

Process of Grant Proposal Development. Gerald V. Teague & Betty S. Heathington. LC 79-93120. (Fastback Ser.: No. 143). (Orig.). 1980. pap. 0.75 (ISBN 0-87367-143-0). Phi Delta Kappa.

Process of Group Communication. 2nd ed. Ronald Applbaum et al. LC 78-18501. 1979. text ed. 13.95 (ISBN 0-574-22710-5, 13-5710); instr's guide avail. (ISBN 0-574-22711-3, 13-5711). SRA.

Process of Human Development: A Holistic Approach. Clara Schuster & Shirley Ashburn. LC 79-91938. 1980. text ed. 19.95 (ISBN 0-316-77535-5). Little.

Process of Investigation: Concepts & Strategies for the Security Professional. Charles A. Sennewald. 255p. 1981. text ed. 21.95 (ISBN 0-409-95018-1). Butterworths.

Process of Learning Mathematics. L. R. Chapman. LC 71-178683. 405p. 1972. text ed. 51.00 (ISBN 0-08-016623-7); pap. text ed. 17.00 (ISBN 0-08-017357-8). Pergamon.

Process of Local Government Reform: 1966 - 1974. Bruce Wood. (New Local Government Ser.). 1976. text ed. 25.00x (ISBN 0-04-350052-8). Allen Unwin.

Process of Management: The Concepts, Behavior & Practice. 4th ed. William H. Newman. 1977. pap. 21.00 (ISBN 0-13-723429-5); study guide casebook 7.95 (ISBN 0-13-723411-2). P-H.

Process of Ongoing Human Evolution. Ed. by Gabriel Lasker. (Publications on Human Evolution Ser). 1960. 5.95x o.p. (ISBN 0-8143-1144-X). Wayne St U Pr.

Process of Parenting. Jane B. Brooks. (Illus.). 460p. (Orig.). 1981. write for info (ISBN 0-87484-474-6). Mayfield Pub.

Process of Patient Teaching in Nursing. 4th ed. Barbara K. Redman. LC 80-15310. (Illus.). 294p. 1980. pap. text ed. 11.95 (ISBN 0-8016-4100-4). Mosby.

Process of Political Domination in Ecuador. Agustin Cueva. Tr. by Danielle Salti from Span. 190p. 1981. 14.95 (ISBN 0-87855-338-X). Transaction Bks.

Process of Priority Formulation: U.S. Foreign Policy in the Indo-Pakistani War of 1971. Dan Haendel. LC 77-21372. 1978. lib. bdg. 32.50x (ISBN 0-89158-322-X). Westview.

Process of Recreation Programming: Theory & Technique. Patricia Farrell & Herberta M. Lundegren. LC 78-17100. 1978. text ed. 17.50 (ISBN 0-471-01709-4). Wiley.

Process of Revolution. George S. Pettee. LC 76-80581. 1971. Repr. 12.75 (ISBN 0-86527-159-3). Fertig.

Process of Rural Development in Latin America. T. Lynn Smith. LC 67-22199. (U of Fla. Social Sciences Monographs: No. 33). (Illus.). 1967. pap. 3.25 o.p. (ISBN 0-8130-0211-7). U Presses Fla.

Process of Rural Transformation: Eastern Europe, Latin America & Australia. Ed. by Ivan Volgyes & Richard E. Lonsdale. LC 79-10190. (Pergamon Policy Studies). 1979. 39.50 (ISBN 0-08-023110-1). Pergamon.

Process of Staff Development: Components for Change. 2nd ed. Helen M. Tobin & Pat S. Yoder. LC 78-31459. (Illus.). 1979. text ed. 17.95 (ISBN 0-8016-4996-X). Mosby.

Process of Technological Innovation. National Academy Of Engineering. LC 72-601240. (Illus., Orig.). 1969. pap. 4.75 (ISBN 0-309-01726-2). Natl Acad Pr.

Process One: A Multi-Media College Writing Program. George R. Bramer. 1976. pap. text ed. 10.95 (ISBN 0-675-08682-5); Set. cassettes & filmstrips 495.00 (ISBN 0-675-08683-3); 2-4 sets 300.00, 5-9 sets 250.00, 10 or more 195.00 (ISBN 0-686-67251-8). test 3.95 (ISBN 0-686-67253-4). Merrill.

Process Optimization with Applications in Metallurgy & Chemical Engineering. Willis H. Ray & Julian Szekely. LC 73-936. 400p. 1973. 39.00 (ISBN 0-471-71070-9, Pub. by Wiley-Interscience). Wiley.

Process, Performance & Pilgrimage. Victor Turner. 1979. text ed. 12.50x (ISBN 0-391-01929-5). Humanities.

Process Philosophy & Christian Thought. Delwin Brown et al. LC 74-127586. 1971. pap. 14.95 (ISBN 0-672-60799-9). Bobbs.

Process Philosophy & Christian Thought. Delwin Brown et al. LC 74-127586. 1971. 38.50x (ISBN 0-672-51529-6). Irvington.

Process Philosophy & Social Thought. Ed. by John B. Cobb, Jr. & W. Widick Schroeder. LC 80-70781. (Studies in Religion & Society). 250p. 1981. 19.95x (ISBN 0-913348-18-X). Ctr Sci Study.

Process Philosophy: Basic Writings. Ed. by Jack R. Sibley & Pete A. Gunter. LC 78-57668. 1978. pap. text ed. 16.00 (ISBN 0-8191-0531-7). U Pr of Amer.

Process Piping Systems. Ed. by David J. Deutsch & Chemical Engineering Magazine. LC 80-13774. (Chemical Engineering Ser.). 484p. 1980. 32.50 (ISBN 0-07-010706-8); pap. 27.50 (ISBN 0-07-606675-4). McGraw.

Process Synthesis. Dale F. Rudd et al. LC 73-3331. (International Ser. in Physical & Chemical Engineering). (Illus.). 320p. 1973. ref. ed. 25.95 (ISBN 0-13-723353-1). P-H.

Process Technology & Flowsheets. Chemical Engineering Magazine. LC 79-12117. (Chemical Engineering Bks). 384p. 1980. 24.95 (ISBN 0-07-010741-6, P&RB). McGraw.

Processed Meats. W. E. Kramlich et al. (Illus.). 1973. 29.50 (ISBN 0-87055-141-8). AVI.

Processes & Materials of Manufacture. 2nd ed. Roy A. Lindberg. 1977. text ed. 25.95x (ISBN 0-205-05414-5, 32544143); a. b. avail. (ISBN 0-205-05492-7, 3254143). Allyn.

Processes of Constitutional Decisionmaking: Cases & Materials. Paul Brest. 1375p. 1975. 27.50 (ISBN 0-316-10790-5); Suppl., 1980. pap. write for info. (ISBN 0-316-10791-3). Little.

Processes of Criminal Justice: Adjudication. 2nd ed. H. Richard Uviller. (American Casebook Ser.). 768p. 1979. pap. text ed. 14.95 (ISBN 0-8299-2064-1). West Pub.

Processes of Criminal Justice: Investigation & Adjudication. 2nd ed. H. Richard Uviller. LC 79-16743. (American Casebook Ser.). 1384p. 1979. text ed. 24.95 (ISBN 0-8299-2057-9). West Pub.

Processes of Criminal Justice: Investigation. 2nd ed. H. Richard Uviller. (American Casebook Ser.). 679p. 1979. pap. text ed. 13.95 (ISBN 0-8299-2065-X). West Pub.

Processes of Heredity. Bert W. Winterton. 304p. (Orig.). 1980. pap. 10.95 (ISBN 0-8403-2166-X). Kendall-Hunt.

Processes of Organic Evolution. 3rd ed. G. Ledyard Stebbins. (Illus.). 1977. pap. text ed. 11.95 (ISBN 0-13-723452-X). P-H.

Processes of the Earth's Surface. Susan Nuke. 96p. 1980. lab manual 6.95. Mountain Pr.

Processes of the World-System. Ed. by Terence K. Hopkins & Immanuel Wallerstein. LC 79-27385. (Political Economy of the World-System Annuals: Vol. 3). (Illus.). 320p. 1980. pap. 20.00x (ISBN 0-8039-1378-8); pap. 9.95 (ISBN 0-8039-1379-6). Sage.

Processing Equipment for Agricultural Products. 2nd ed. Carl W. Hall & Denny C. Davis. (Illus.). 1979. lib. bdg. 19.50 (ISBN 0-87055-270-8). AVI.

Processing of Crystalline Ceramics. Ed. by R. F. Davis et al. (Materials Science Research Ser.: Vol. 11). 664p. 1978. 49.50 (ISBN 0-306-40035-9, Plenum Pr). Plenum Pub.

Processing of Low-Grade Uranium Ores. 1967. pap. 14.00 (ISBN 92-0-041067-7, IAEA). Unipub.

Processing of Visible Language, Vol. 2. Ed. by Paul A. Kolers et al. 620p. 1980. 49.50 (ISBN 0-306-40576-8, Plenum Pr). Plenum Pub.

Processing Securities Transactions: Administrative Procedures of Brokerage Firms. H. V. Petrillo & C. L. Bullock. LC 73-89818. 260p. 1969. 23.95 (ISBN 0-8260-7145-7, 75801). Ronald Pr.

Procession of Friends. Daisy Newman. 1980. pap. 10.95 (ISBN 0-913408-59-X). Friends United.

Processor Design for the Efficient Implementation of APL. Charles R. Minter. LC 79-7305. (Outstanding Dissertations in the Computer Sciences Ser.: Vol. 11). 285p. 1980. lib. bdg. 28.00 (ISBN 0-8240-4421-5). Garland Pub.

Proclamation of Baha'u'llah. Baha'u'llah. LC 72-237435. 1967. 7.50 (ISBN 0-87743-064-0, 7-03-12); pap. 2.00 (ISBN 0-87743-065-9, 7-03-13). Baha'i.

Proclamations II, Chronological Series, 2 vols. Incl. No. 368. Proclamadion for the Marchauntes Adventurers. LC 74-171743. Repr. of 1559 ed (ISBN 90-221-0368-4); No. 369. By the Queene, Forbidding Unlicensed Plays. LC 78-171744. Repr. of 1559 ed (ISBN 90-221-0369-2); No. 370. A Proclamation Agaynst Breaking Monumentes of Antiquitie. LC 71-171745. Repr. of 1560 ed (ISBN 90-221-0370-6); No. 371. By the Queene, Forbidding Export of Armour to Russia. LC 75-171746. Repr. of 1561 ed (ISBN 90-221-0371-4); No. 372. This Is the Ordinance for the Quenes Swannes. LC 79-171747. Repr. of 1564 ed (ISBN 90-221-0371-4); No. 373. By the Queene, Against Ill-Treatment of "Informers". LC 72-171748. Repr. of 1566 ed (ISBN 90-221-0372-2); No. 374. By the Queene, Against the Earl of Northumberland. LC 76-171749. Repr. of 1569 ed (ISBN 90-221-0373-0); No. 375. By the Queene, a Proclamation Concerning Hattes & Cappes. LC 70-171750 (ISBN 90-221-0374-9); No. 376. By the Queene, for Discovering Authors of Libels. LC 74-171751. Repr. of 1576 ed (ISBN 90-221-0375-7); By the Queene, for Sowing Lands with Flax. LC 78-171752. (No. 377). Repr. of 1597 ed (ISBN 90-221-0376-5); No. 243. The King's Maiesties Declaration Concerning Lawfull Sports. LC 77-26398. Repr. of 1618 ed (ISBN 90-221-0377-3). (English Experience Ser.: Nos. 243, 368-377). 1970-71. Set. 21.00 (ISBN 90-221-0368-4). Walter J Johnson.

Proclamations of the Tudor Queens. F. A. Youngs. LC 75-30442. 304p. 1976. 46.50 (ISBN 0-521-21044-5). Cambridge U Pr.

Proclamations of Tudor Kings. R. M. Heinze. LC 27-22983. 320p. 1976. 49.50 (ISBN 0-521-20938-2). Cambridge U Pr.

Procopius. J. A. Evans. (World Authors Ser.: Greece: No. 170). lib. bdg. 10.95 (ISBN 0-8057-2722-1). Twayne.

Procopius. Procopius. LC 67-28144. 351p. 1967. text ed. 20.00x (ISBN 0-8290-0199-9). Irvington.

Procurement & Inventory Ordering Tables. Jerry Banks & Charles L. Hohenstein, Jr. LC 77-8663. 1978. pap. text ed. 14.50 (ISBN 0-08-021945-4). Pergamon.

Procurement Management: Strategy, Organization & Decision-Making. E. Raymond Corey. LC 78-5826. 1978. 19.95 (ISBN 0-8436-0759-9). CBI Pub.

Prodigal Women. Nancy Hale. 736p. 1981. pap. 3.50 (ISBN 0-380-53553-X, 53553). Avon.

Prodrome De la Flore Algologique Des Indes Neerlandaises et Partie Des Territoires De Borneo Etc. E. De Wildemann. 193p. 1978. lib. bdg. 55.00x (ISBN 3-87429-145-6). Lubrecht & Cramer.

Producers on Producing. Stephen Langley. LC 75-26817. (Illus.). 1976. 12.50x (ISBN 0-910482-68-3). Drama Bk.

Producers' Response to Changes in Prices & Marketing Policies. S. C. Gupta & A. Majid. 5.25x o.p. (ISBN 0-210-22628-5). Asia.

Producing Farm Crops. 2nd ed. L. V Boone et al. 1981. 16.65 o.p. (ISBN 0-8134-2151-9); text ed. 12.50x o.p. (ISBN 0-685-64715-3, 2151). Interstate.

Producing Farm Crops. 3rd ed. Ed. by L. V. Boone et al. 1981. 14.60 (ISBN 0-8134-2151-9); text ed. 10.95x. Interstate.

Producing, Financing, & Distributing Film. Donald C. Farber & Paul Baumgarten. LC 72-87054. 1973. 16.95 (ISBN 0-910482-31-4). Drama Bk.

Producing Hit Records. Dennis Lambert & Ronald Zalkind. LC 79-91505. (Illus.). 1980. 17.50 (ISBN 0-02-871950-6); pap. 9.95 (ISBN 0-02-871960-3). Schirmer Bks.

Producing Theatre: A Comprehensive Legal & Business Guide. Donald C. Farber. 384p. 1981. 17.95 (ISBN 0-89676-051-0). Drama Bk.

Producing Vegetable Crops. 2nd ed. Ware. 1975. 18.00 (ISBN 0-8134-2083-0). Thomson Pub CA.

Producing Vegetable Crops. 3rd ed. George W. Ware & J. P. McCollum. (Illus.). (gr. 9-12). 1980. 18.00 (ISBN 0-8134-2083-0); text ed. 13.50x (ISBN 0-686-60699-X). Interstate.

Producing Your Own Power: How to Make Nature's Energy Sources Work for You. Carol H. Stoner. LC 74-10765. (Illus.). 320p. 1974. 10.95 (ISBN 0-87857-088-8). Rodale Pr Inc.

Product Engineering Design Manual. Douglas C. Greenwood. (Illus.). 342p. 1981. Repr. text ed. write for info. (ISBN 0-89874-273-0). Krieger.

Product Innovation & Development. A. E. Berridge. 236p. 1977. text ed. 24.50x (ISBN 0-220-66325-4, Pub. by Busn Bks England). Renouf.

Product Labeling. Ed. by Louis Morris et al. LC 80-22728. (Banbury Report Ser.: Report 6). 325p. 1980. 45.00x (ISBN 0-87969-205-7). Cold Spring Harbor.

Product Liability: A Management Response. Irwin Gray et al. LC 75-1261. 256p. 1975. 14.95 (ISBN 0-8144-5373-2). Am Mgmt.

Product Liability for Supervisors & Managers. Michael M. Canavan. 1981. text ed. 15.95 (ISBN 0-8359-5630-X). Reston.

Product Liability Litigation. Gary J. Gordon. 200p. 1980. pap. 24.50 (ISBN 0-917126-20-3). Mason Pub.

Product Liability Portfolio. Lawrence Stessin. 1977. 39.95. Busn Res Pubns.

Product Management: Strategy & Organization. Edgar A. Pessemier. LC 77-2337. (Marketing Ser.). 1977. text ed. 24.95 (ISBN 0-471-68235-7). Wiley.

Product Planning: An Integrated Approach. Merlin Stone. LC 76-26335. 1976. 24.95 (ISBN 0-470-98915-7). Halsted Pr.

Product Planning Simplified. Philip Marvin. LC 74-188844. 240p. 1972. 14.50 o.p. (ISBN 0-8144-5299-X). Am Mgmt.

Product Policy: Cases & Concepts. Richard N. Cardozo. LC 78-67939. 1979. text ed. 17.95 (ISBN 0-201-00888-2). A-W.

Product Quality, Performance & Cost. National Academy of Engineering. LC 72-81092. (Illus.). 160p. 1972. pap. 8.75 (ISBN 0-309-02036-0). Natl Acad Pr.

Product Safety Management & Engineering. W. Hammer. 1980. 19.95 (ISBN 0-686-51706-7). P-H.

Production - Operations Management. Roger W. Schmenner. 480p. 1980. text ed. 17.95 (ISBN 0-574-19500-9, 13-2500); instr's. guide avail. (ISBN 0-574-19501-7, 13-2501). SRA.

Production & Distribution of Knowledge in the United States. Fritz Machlup et al. 415p. 1972. 20.00x o.p. (ISBN 0-691-08608-7); pap. 6.95 (ISBN 0-691-00356-4). Princeton U Pr.

Production & Hazards of a Hyperbaric Oxygen Environment: Proceedings. Ed. by G. S. Innes. 1970. 19.50 (ISBN 0-08-006767-0). Pergamon.

Production & Inventory Control: Principles & Techniques. G. Plossl & O. Wright. 1967. ref. ed. 21.95 (ISBN 0-13-725127-0). P-H.

Production & Inventory Control: Systems & Decisions. rev. ed. James H. Greene. 1974. text ed. 19.95 (ISBN 0-256-01431-0). Irwin.

Production & Inventory Management in the Computer Age. Oliver W. Wight. LC 74-7127. 300p. 1974. 18.95 (ISBN 0-8436-0732-7). CBI Pub.

Production & Operations Management. Norman Gaither. 784p. 1980. text ed. 21.95 (ISBN 0-03-042701-0). Dryden Pr.

Production & Operations Management. 4th ed. Richard A. Hopeman. (Marketing & Management Ser.). 608p. 1980. text ed. 19.95 (ISBN 0-675-08140-8); instructor's manual 3.95 (ISBN 0-686-63346-6). Merrill.

Production & Operations Management: A Life Cycle Approach. rev. ed. Richard B. Chase & Nicholas J. Aquilano. 1977. text ed. 20.95x (ISBN 0-256-01919-3). Irwin.

Production & Operations Management: A systems Concept. 2nd ed. Richard A. Johnson et al. 500p. 1974. text ed. 22.95 (ISBN 0-395-18029-5); instructor's manual 3.50 (ISBN 0-395-18028-7). HM.

Production & Operations Management: A Self-Correcting Approach. Ralph M. Stair, Jr. & Barry Render. 1980. pap. text ed. 13.95 (ISBN 0-205-06715-8, 086715-2). Allyn.

Production & Planning Applied to Building. 2nd ed. R. J. Hollins. 1971. 16.50x (ISBN 0-7121-4606-7). Intl Ideas.

Production & Properties of Staple-Fibre Yarns Made by Recently Developed Techniques. L. Hunter. 168p. 1978. 70.00x (ISBN 0-686-27733-3). State Mutual Bk.

Production & Staging of Plays. Conrad Carter et al. LC 63-10203. (Illus.). 216p. 1963. lib. bdg. 4.50 o.p. (ISBN 0-668-01051-7). Arco.

Production & Utilization of Radiation Vaccines Against Helminthic Diseases. (Technical Reports: No. 30). 1964. pap. 5.50 (ISBN 92-0-115164-0, IAEA). Unipub.

Production Conditions in Indian Agriculture. K. Bharadwaj. (Department of Applied Economics, Occasional Papers: No. 33). 175p. 1974. 25.50 (ISBN 0-521-08494-6); pap. 10.95 (ISBN 0-521-09862-9). Cambridge U Pr.

Production Ecology of Ants & Termites. Ed. by M. V. Brian. LC 76-54061. (International Biological Programme Ser.: No. 13). (Illus.). 1977. 72.50 (ISBN 0-521-21519-6). Cambridge U Pr.

Production Economics: Theory with Applications. John P. Doll & Frank Orazem. LC 76-41478. (Agricultural Economics Ser.). 1978. text ed. 21.50 (ISBN 0-88244-118-3). Grid Pub.

Production Engineering. Benjamin W. Niebel & Maurice S. Gjesdahl. LC 72-190969. (Illus.). 148p. 1975. 15.00 (ISBN 92-833-1003-9, APO57, APO). Unipub.

Production Engineering: Jig & Tool Design. 8th ed. E. J. Jones. 288p. 1973. 35.00x (ISBN 0-408-70308-3); pap. 25.00x (ISBN 0-408-00079-1). Transatlantic.

Production Handbook. 3rd ed. Ed. by Gordon B. Carson et al. (Illus.). 1470p. 1972. 45.95 (ISBN 0-8260-1820-3, 12602). Ronald Pr.

Production-Inventory Systems: Planning & Control. 3rd ed. Elwood S. Buffa & Jeffrey G. Miller. 1979. text ed. 20.95x (ISBN 0-256-02041-8). Irwin.

Production Management Handbook. B. H. Whalley. 512p. 1980. text ed. 49.25x (ISBN 0-566-02133-1, Pub. by Gower Pub Co England). Renouf.

Production Management Handbook. B. H. Whalley. 1980. text ed. 49.25x (ISBN 0-566-02133-1, Pub. by Gower Pub Co England). Renouf.

Production Manager's Handbook of Formulas & Tables. Lewis R. Zeyher. 1972. 27.95 o.p. (ISBN 0-13-724427-4). P-H.

Production of Commodities by Means of Commodities. P. Sraffa. (Illus.). 99p. 1975. pap. 10.95x (ISBN 0-521-09969-2). Cambridge U Pr.

Production-Operations Management. 7th ed. Franklin G. Moore & Thomas Hendrick. 1977. text ed. 17.50x o.p. (ISBN 0-256-01921-5). Irwin.

Production-Operations Management. 8th ed. Franklin G. Moore & Thomas Hendrick. 1980. 21.95x (ISBN 0-256-02286-0). Irwin.

Production Planning. John L. Burbridge. 427p. 1971. 29.50x (ISBN 0-8448-0182-8). Crane-Russak Co.

Production Planning & Control: An Introduction to Quantitative Methods. J. R. King. 1974. text ed. 42.00 (ISBN 0-08-017721-2); pap. text ed. 24.00 (ISBN 0-08-018983-0). Pergamon.

Production Planning & Information Systems. J. J. Verzijl. LC 76-7906. 1976. 29.95 (ISBN 0-470-90620-0). Halsted Pr.

Production, Pollution, Protection. W. B. Yapp & M. I. Smith. (Wykeham Science Ser.: No. 19). 1972. 9.95x (ISBN 0-8448-1121-1). Crane-Russak Co.

Production Relations, Class & Black Liberation: A Marxist Perspective in Afro-American Studies. Clarence J. Munford. (Philosophical Currents Ser. 24: No. 24). 1978. pap. text ed. 25.75x (ISBN 90-6032-107-3). Humanities.

Production Standards in Profit Planning. Spencer A. Tucker & Thomas H. Lennon. 256p. 1981. 19.95 (ISBN 0-444-00456-4, Thomond). Elsevier.

Production Techniques for Instructional Graphic Materials. C. Y. Oh. (Elementary Education Ser.). 1976. pap. text ed. 13.95 (ISBN 0-675-08462-8); instructor's manual 3.95 (ISBN 0-686-67618-1). Merrill.

Productions of Time. John Brunner. (Science Fiction Ser.). 1977. pap. 1.50 o.p. (ISBN 0-87997-329-3, UW1329). DAW Bks.

Productions Systems: Planning, Analysis, & Control. 2nd ed. J. L. Riggs. (Ser. in Management & Administration). 1976. 25.95 (ISBN 0-471-72186-7); tchrs. manual avail. (ISBN 0-471-01698-5). Wiley.

Productive Monopoly: The Effect of Railroad Control on New England Coastal Steamship Lines, 1870-1916. William L. Taylor. LC 70-111457. (Illus.). 323p. 1970. 15.00 (ISBN 0-87057-123-0, Pub. by Brown U Pr). Univ Pr of New England.

Productive Performance. Charles Lachenmeyer. (Analysis). 51p. (Orig.). 1980. pap. text ed. 14.95 (ISBN 0-938526-01-4). Inst Analysis.

Productive School: A Systems Analysis Approach to Educational Administration. J. Alan Thomas. LC 80-12531. 144p. 1980. Repr. of 1971 ed. lib. bdg. write for info. (ISBN 0-89874-164-5). Krieger.

Productive Society. Patrick E. Haggerty. 80p. 1974. 12.50x (ISBN 0-231-03864-X). Columbia U Pr.

Productivity Accounting. 3rd ed. Hiram S. Davis. 194p. 1980. pap. 15.00 (ISBN 0-89546-009-2). Indus Res Unit-Wharton.

Productivity & Creativity: A Social Dynamics Approach. Robert R. Blake & Jane S. Mouton. 143p. 1981. 9.95 (ISBN 0-8144-5692-8). Am Mgmt.

Productivity & Motivation: A Review of State & Local Government Initiatives. John Greiner & Harry Hatry. LC 80-53981. 1981. 18.00 (ISBN 0-87766-283-5, 29600). Urban Inst.

Productivity & Quality: Measurement As a Basis for Improvement. Everett E. Adam, Jr. & James C. Hershauer. (Illus.). 192p. 1981. text ed. 18.95 (ISBN 0-13-725002-9). P-H.

Productivity & Records Automation. Robert J. Kalthoff & Leonard S. Lee. (Illus.). 400p. 1981. text ed. 24.95 (ISBN 0-13-725234-X). P-H.

Productivity & Technical Change. W. E. Salter. (Cambridge Department of Applied Economics Monographs: No. 6). (Illus.). 1969. 35.50 (ISBN 0-521-06186-5); pap. 12.95x (ISBN 0-521-09568-9). Cambridge U Pr.

Productivity, Bargaining & Industrial Change. N. Stettner. 1969. 16.50 (ISBN 0-08-006756-5); pap. 7.75 (ISBN 0-08-006757-3). Pergamon.

Productivity Implications of Work & the Family. Patricia Voydanoff. Date not set. price not set. Work in Amer.

Productivity in General Merchandise Retailing. 1980. pap. 35.00 (G28680). Natl Ret Merch.

Productivity in Local Government. Frederick O. Hayes. LC 76-20400. 1977. 24.95 (ISBN 0-669-00883-4). Lexington Bks.

Productivity in Railroads: Proceedings of a Symposium Held at Princeton University, July, 1977. Ed. by Arnold D. Kerr & Alain L. Kornhauser. (Pergamon Policy Studies). 1980. 22.00 (ISBN 0-08-023871-8). Pergamon.

Productivity Measurement in Regulated Industries. Ed. by T. G. Cowing & R. E. Stevenson. (Economic Theory, Econometrics & Mathematical Economic Ser.). 1981. price not set (ISBN 0-12-194080-2). Acad Pr.

Productivity Measurements & Incentives. R. G. Norman & S. Bahiri. 20.00x (ISBN 0-408-70308-3). Transatlantic.

Productivity of World Ecosystems. International Biological Program, National Research Council. 1975. pap. 16.00 (ISBN 0-309-02317-3). Natl Acad Pr.

Productivity, People & Profits. Joe Ross. 150p. 1981. text ed. 17.95 (ISBN 0-8359-5473-0); pap. 10.95 (ISBN 0-8359-5472-2). Reston.

Productivity, Production Function & Technical Change. S. S. Mehta. 1980. text ed. 9.00x (ISBN 0-391-01830-2). Humanities.

Productivity: Prospects for Growth. Ed. by James M. Rosow. (Work in America Ser.). 288p. 1981. text ed. 19.95 (ISBN 0-442-29326-7). Van Nos Reinhold.

Productivity, Quality of Working Life & Labour-Management Relations. 23p. 1976. 2.75 (APO62, APO). Unipub.

Productivity, Technology, & Capital Economic Analysis, Managerial Strategies, & Government Policies. Bela Gold. LC 79-4749. 1979. 26.95 (ISBN 0-669-02957-2). Lexington Bks.

Products Liability & the Food Consumer. Reed Dickerson. LC 77-139130. 339p. 1972. Repr. of 1951 ed. lib. bdg. 27.50x (ISBN 0-8371-5746-3, DIPL). Greenwood.

Products Liability & the Reasonably Safe Product: A Guide for Management, Design & Marketing. Alvin S. Weinstein et al. LC 78-8749. 1978. 23.00 (ISBN 0-471-03904-7, Pub. by Wiley-Interscience). Wiley.

Products Liability in a Nutshell. 2nd ed. Dix Noel & Jerry J. Phillips. (Nutshell Ser.). 353p. 1981. pap. text ed. 6.95 (ISBN 0-8299-2121-4). West Pub.

Produits Tensoriels Topologiques et Espaces Nucleaires. Alexander Grothendieck. LC 52-42839. (Memoirs: No. 16). 1979. pap. 12.00 (ISBN 0-8218-1216-5, MEMO-16). Am Math.

Proensa: An Anthology of Troubador Poetry. Tr. by Paul Blackburn. LC 75-7466. 1978. 15.95x (ISBN 0-520-02985-2). U of Cal Pr.

Profane Culture. Paul E. Willis. 1978. 19.00x (ISBN 0-7100-8789-6). Routledge & Kegan.

Profectione Ludovici VII in Orienteni: The Journey of Louis the Seventh to the East. Odo of Deuil. Ed. & tr. by Virginia G. Berry. 1965. pap. 5.95x (ISBN 0-393-09662-9). Norton.

Professing Sociology: Studies in the Life Cycle of Social Science. abr. ed. Irving L. Horowitz. LC 75-15534. (Arcturus Books Paperbacks). 238p. 1976. pap. 6.95 (ISBN 0-8093-0741-3). S Ill U Pr.

Profession & Monopoly: A Study of Medicine in the United States & Great Britain. Jeffrey L. Berlant. 1975. 20.00x (ISBN 0-520-02734-5). U of Cal Pr.

Professional Accounting in 30 Countries. 1975. 38.50 o.p. (ISBN 0-685-58300-7). Am Inst CPA.

Professional Actor: From Audition to Performance. Tom Markus. LC 79-16668. 1980. 10.00 (ISBN 0-910482-91-8); pap. 8.95 (ISBN 0-89676-009-X). Drama Bk.

Professional Altruist: The Emergence of Social Work As a Career, 1880-1930. Roy Lubove. LC 65-12786. 1969. pap. text ed. 4.95x (ISBN 0-689-70130-6, 142). Atheneum.

Professional & Scientific Literature on Patient Education: A Guide to Information Sources. Ed. by Lawrence Green & Connie Kansler. (Health Affairs Information Guide Ser.: Vol. 5). 330p. 1980. 30.00 (ISBN 0-8103-1422-3). Gale.

Professional Applications in Typewriting. Farmer et al. 260p. 1977. text ed. 15.27 (ISBN 0-7715-0886-7); tchr's. manual 7.67 (ISBN 0-7715-0887-5); stationery & business forms 6.60 (ISBN 0-7715-0888-3); book of resource materials 44.60 (ISBN 0-7715-0833-6); typing facts & tips 3.00 ea. (ISBN 0-7715-0889-1); typing facts & tips, package of 10 21.33 (ISBN 0-7715-0896-4); certificate of proficiency (professional, 1 per student) free (ISBN 0-7715-0867-0); roll of honor for production efficiency (1 per classroom) free (ISBN 0-7715-0864-6). Forkner.

Professional Approach to Radiology Administration. Royce R. Osborn. (Illus.). 228p. 1980. 29.75 (ISBN 0-398-04097-4). C C Thomas.

Professional Approaches with Parents of Handicapped Children. Elizabeth J. Webster. 292p. 1976. 16.75 (ISBN 0-398-03521-0). C C Thomas.

Professional Army Officer in a Changing Society. Sam C. Sarkesian. LC 74-10917. 230p. 1974. 17.95 (ISBN 0-911012-62-1). Nelson-Hall.

Professional As Educator. Ed. by Arthur W. Foshay. LC 73-120602. 1970. pap. text ed. 6.00x (ISBN 0-8077-1378-3). Tchrs Coll.

Professional Blackjack. rev. ed. Stanford Wong. LC 80-82350. (Illus.). 240p. 1980. 19.95 (ISBN 0-935926-03-8). Pi Yee Pr.

Professional Broadcasting: A Brief Introduction. J. Bittner. 1981. pap. 12.95 (ISBN 0-13-725465-2). P-H.

Professional Burnout in the Human Services: Job Stress & the Loss of Commitment in the Novice. Cary Cherniss. LC 80-12136. 318p. 1980. 22.95 (ISBN 0-03-056912-5). Praeger.

Professional Chef. 5th ed. Culinary Institute of America. Ed. by LeRoj Folsom. 608p. Date not set. text ed. 29.95 (ISBN 0-8436-2201-6). CBI Pub. Postponed.

Professional Chef & the Recipe Cards. LeRoi A. Folsom. 1974. 44.95 (ISBN 0-8436-0586-3). CBI Pub.

Professional Chef's Art of Garde Manger. 2nd ed. Fredric H. Sonnenschmidt & Jean F. Nicolas. LC 72-92377. 1976. 22.95 (ISBN 0-8436-2067-6). CBI Pub.

Professional Chef's Baking Recipes. Jule Wilkinson & Joseph Amendola. (Illus.). 1974. pap. 8.95 (ISBN 0-8436-0526-X). CBI Pub.

Professional Chef's Book of Buffets. George K. Waldner & Klaus Mitterhauser. 1968. 22.95 (ISBN 0-8436-0505-7). CBI Pub.

Professional Chef's Knife. The Culinary Institute of America. LC 77-26689. (Illus.). 1978. pap. 8.95 (ISBN 0-8436-2125-7). CBI Pub.

Professional Chef's Soy Protein Recipe Ideas. Nancy Snider. Ed. by Jule Wilkinson. (Illus.). 80p. 1971. pap. 8.95 (ISBN 0-8436-0540-5). CBI Pub.

Professional Cooking & Baking. Mary F. Ray & Beda Dondi. (Illus.). 450p. 1981. text ed. 13.20 (ISBN 0-87002-328-4); write for info. tchr's guide (ISBN 0-87002-329-2); write for info. student guide (ISBN 0-87002-330-6). Bennett IL.

Professional Corporations 1978 Course Handbook. (Tax Law & Estate Planning Course Handbook Ser. 1977-78: Vol. 119). 1978. pap. 20.00 o.p. (ISBN 0-685-07706-3, J4-3449). PLI.

Professional Cosmetologist. 2nd ed. John Dalton. (Illus.). 1979. text ed. 14.95 (ISBN 0-8299-0186-8); pap. text ed. 11.50 (ISBN 0-8299-0231-7); study guide 8.50 (ISBN 0-8299-0280-5); cancelled (ISBN 0-686-52297-4); state board review questions 4.95 (ISBN 0-8299-0290-2); answer key 1.00 (ISBN 0-8299-0264-3). West Pub.

Professional Counseling: An Overview. Frank A. Nugent. LC 80-25726. 310p. 1981. text ed. 14.95 (ISBN 0-8185-0424-2). Brooks-Cole.

Professional Design Supplement to the MWPS Structures & Environment Handbook. 5th ed. Midwest Plan Service. LC 77-24229. (Illus.). 1978. pap. text ed. 9.50 (ISBN 0-89373-037-8, MWPS-17). Midwest Plan Serv.

Professional Diascotheque Management. Daniel A. Emenheiser. LC 80-20910. 256p. 1980. text ed. 16.95 (ISBN 0-8436-0768-8). CBI Pub.

Professional Dining Room Management. Carole King. (Ahrens Ser.). 160p. 1980. pap. 7.95 (ISBN 0-8104-9471-X). Hayden.

Professional Discotheque Management. Daniel A. Emenheiser. 1980. 15.95 o.p. (ISBN 0-8436-0768-8). CBI Pub.

Professional Dominance: The Social Structure of Medical Care. Eliot Freidson. LC 72-116538. 1970. 15.95x (ISBN 0-202-30203-2). Aldine Pub.

Professional Education of Teachers: A Humanistic Approach to Teacher Preparation. 2nd ed. Arthur W. Combs et al. 1974. pap. text ed. 10.95x (ISBN 0-205-04331-3, 2243318). Allyn.

Professional Education: Some New Directions. Carnegie Commission on Higher Education. Ed. by Edgar Schein. LC 76-38954. (Illus.). 176p. 1972. 10.95 o.p. (ISBN 0-07-010042-X, P&RB). McGraw.

Professional Ethics & Insignia. Jane Clapp. LC 74-10501. (Illus.). 1974. 32.50 (ISBN 0-8108-0735-1). Scarecrow.

Professional Fence. Carl B. Klockars. LC 74-483. 1976. pap. text ed. 6.95 (ISBN 0-02-917820-7). Free Pr.

Professional Food Preperation. 2nd ed. M. E. Terrell. 741p. 1979. 24.50 (ISBN 0-471-85202-3). Wiley.

Professional Guide for Families & Living with Children. Gerald R. Patterson. (Illus., Orig.). 1975. pap. text ed. 2.95 (ISBN 0-87822-160-3). Res Press.

Professional Guide to Drugs. (Illus.). 1150p. 1981. text ed. 17.95 (ISBN 0-916730-34-4). Intermed Comm.

Professional Guide to Real Estate Development. Gene Phillippo. LC 75-26106. (Illus.). 306p. 1976. 19.95 (ISBN 0-87094-111-9). Dow Jones-Irwin.

Professional Gunsmithing. Walter J. Howe. (Illus.). 518p. 1946. 24.95 (ISBN 0-8117-1375-X). Stackpole.

Professional Host. The Foodservice Editors of CBI. LC 80-15609. (Illus.). 496p. 1980. 24.95 (ISBN 0-8436-2154-0). CBI Pub.

Professional Housekeeper. Gina Tucker & Madelin S. Schneider. LC 75-29010. (Illus.). 240p. 1976. 23.95 (ISBN 0-8436-0591-X). CBI Pub.

Professional Houseparent. Eva E. Burmeister. LC 60-6548. 1960. 20.00x (ISBN 0-231-02370-7). Columbia U Pr.

Professional Hypnotism Manual: Introducting Physical & Emotional Suggestibility & Sexuality. rev. ed. 1978. pap. 12.50 (ISBN 0-686-57995-X). Borden.

Professional Income of Engineers-1980. 105p. 1980. 25.00 (ISBN 0-686-27581-0, 302-80). AAES.

Professional Industrial Photography. Derald Martin. (Illus.). 176p. 1980. 19.95 (ISBN 0-8174-4008-9). Amphoto.

Professional Liability Insurance & Psychiatric Malpractice. American Psychiatric Association Task Force. LC 77-94900. (Task Force Report: No. 13). 1978. pap. 6.00 o.p. (ISBN 0-685-55998-X). Am Psychiatric.

Professional Librarian's Reader in Library Automation & Technology. Knowledge Industry Publication Editors. LC 80-11636. (Professional Librarian Ser.). (Illus.). 256p. 1980. text ed. 24.50 (ISBN 0-914236-59-8); pap. text ed. 17.50 (ISBN 0-914236-57-1). Knowledge Indus.

Professional Life of Mr. Dibdin, Written by Himself, 4 vols. in 2. Charles Dibdin. LC 80-2272. 1981. Repr. of 1803 ed. Set. 150.00 (ISBN 0-404-18835-4). Vol. 1 (ISBN 0-404-18836-2). Vol. 2 (ISBN 0-404-18837-0). AMS Pr.

Professional Magic for Amateurs. Walter B. Gibson. (Illus.). 225p. 1974. pap. 3.50 (ISBN 0-486-23012-0). Dover.

Professional Managemant Via Telecommunications. Harry Newton. 1980. softcover 7.50 (ISBN 0-936648-03-1). Telecom Lib.

Professional Nursing: Foundations, Perspectives & Relationships. 9th ed. Lucille E. Notter & Eugenia K. Spalding. LC 76-2653. 1976. 16.95 o.p. (ISBN 0-397-54192-9); pap. 12.75 (ISBN 0-397-54182-1). Lippincott.

Professional Nursing: Foundations, Perspectives & Relationships. 8th ed. Eugenia K. Spalding & Lucille E. Notter. LC 76-109946. (Illus.). 1970. text ed. 10.75 o.p. (ISBN 0-397-54109-0). Lippincott.

Professional Obligations & Approaches to the Aged. Arthur N. Schwartz & Ivan N. Mensh. (Illus.). 392p. 1974. 22.50 (ISBN 0-398-02922-9). C C Thomas.

Professional Pattern Grading for Women's, Men's & Children's Apparel. Handford. (Illus.). 254p. 1980. spiral bdg. 14.95 (ISBN 0-686-65142-1). Burgess.

Professional Patternmaking for Designer's of Women's Wear. Jack Handford. LC 74-78635. (Illus.). 1977. spiral bdg. 14.95x (ISBN 0-916434-21-4). Plycon Pr.

Professional Photographer's Handbook. Larry L. Logan. LC 80-80056. (Illus.). 128p. (Orig.). 1980. pap. 14.95 (ISBN 0-9603856-0-6). Logan Design.

Professional Picture Framing for the Amateur. Barbara Wolf & Jack Wolf. LC 73-86764. (Illus.). 168p. 1974. pap. 4.95 (ISBN 0-8306-2674-3, 674). TAB Bks.

Professional Police-Human Relations Training. Arthur I. Siegel et al. (Illus.). 192p. 1970. 10.50 (ISBN 0-398-01753-0). C C Thomas.

Professional Practice of Design. Dorothy Goslett. 1978. 19.95 (ISBN 0-7134-1176-7, Pub. by Batsford England). David & Charles.

Professional Practitioner in Probation. Claude T. Mangrum, Jr. 288p. 1975. 16.75 (ISBN 0-398-03396-X). C C Thomas.

Professional Radio Broadcaster. John Hasling. (Illus.). Date not set. pap. text ed. 8.95 (ISBN 0-07-026992-0). McGraw.

Professional Real Estate Brokerage: A Guide for Real Estate Executives. Garfield R. Stock et al. LC 78-444. 1978. 11.95 o.p. (ISBN 0-87094-160-7). Dow Jones-Irwin.

Professional Reforming: Mobilization for Youth & the Failure of Social Science. Joseph H. Helfgot. 240p. 1981. 23.95 (ISBN 0-669-04100-9). Lexington Bks.

Professional Responsibility in a Nutshell. Robert H. Aronson & Donald T. Weckstein. LC 80-15007. (Nutshell Ser.). 448p. 1980. pap. text ed. 6.95 (ISBN 0-8299-2095-1). West Pub.

Professional Resume & Job Search Guide. Harold W. Dickhut. 272p. 1981. 5.95 (ISBN 0-13-725713-9, Spec); pap. 6.95 (ISBN 0-13-725705-8). P-H.

Professional Sales Representation. Frank Lebell. 208p. 1981. 19.95 (ISBN 0-89047-038-3). Herman Pub.

Professional Selling. B. Robert Anderson. (Illus.). 1977. text ed. 15.95 (ISBN 0-13-725937-9). P-H.

Professional Selling. B. Robert Anderson. (Illus.). 400p. 1981. text ed. 16.50 (ISBN 0-13-725960-3). P-H.

Professional Selling. rev. ed. David L. Kurtz et al. 1979. text ed. 16.95x (ISBN 0-256-02211-9). Business Pubns.

Professional Selling-Inside & Out. Gary A. Miller & C. Winston Borgen. LC 77-83518. 1979. pap. text ed. 8.80 (ISBN 0-8273-1638-0); instructor's guide 1.60 (ISBN 0-8273-1639-9). Delmar.

Professional Smithing. Donald Streeter. (Illus.). 144p. 1980. 19.95 (ISBN 0-684-16530-9, ScribT). Scribner.

Professional Soldier: A Social & Political Portrait. Morris Janowitz. LC 60-7090. 1960. 12.95 (ISBN 0-02-916170-3); pap. 6.95 (ISBN 0-02-916180-0). Free Pr.

Professional Stranger: An Informal Introduction to Ethnography. Michael H. Agar. LC 79-8870. (Studies in Anthropology). 1980. 12.50 (ISBN 0-12-043850-X). Acad Pr.

Professional Suicide. Donald W. Cole. 256p. 1980. 12.95 (ISBN 0-07-011697-0, P&RB). McGraw.

Professional Teacher's Handbook: A Guide for Improving Instruction in Today's Secondary School. Kenneth H. Hoover. 22.95x o.p. (ISBN 0-205-03813-1, 2238136). Allyn.

Professional Teacher's Handbook: A Guide for Improving Instruction in Today's Middle & Secondary Schools. 2nd abr. ed. Kenneth H. Hoover. 1976. text ed. 17.95x (ISBN 0-205-05582-6, 2255820). Allyn.

Professional Trading System. R. C. Allen. 1981. 20.00 (ISBN 0-910228-10-8). Best Bks.

Professional Training in Math. 1981. cancelled. Am Math.

Professional Training in Mathematics. rev. ed. M. K. Smith. 1979. Repr. of 1976 ed. 0.80 (ISBN 0-685-91809-2, PT). Am Math.

Professional Turnover: The Case of Nurses. James L. Price & Charles W. Mueller. (Health Systems Management Ser.). 218p. 1980. write for info. (ISBN 0-89335-124-5). Spectrum Pub.

Professional Union. J. E. Mortimer. 432p. 1980. text ed. 37.50x (ISBN 0-04-331076-1). Allen Unwin.

Professional Wine Reference. Frank E. Johnson. (Illus.). 354p. 1978. leather gold-gilded cover 19.95 (ISBN 0-9602566-1-X); pap. 8.95 (ISBN 0-9602566-0-1). Beverage Media.

Professional Writing for Nurses in Education, Practice & Research. Philip C. Kolin & Kolin. LC 79-29258. 1980. pap. text ed. 10.95 (ISBN 0-8016-2724-9). Mosby.

Professionalism & Public Interest. James W. Begun. (Health & Public Policy Ser.). 176p. 1981. text ed. 17.50x (ISBN 0-262-02156-0). MIT Pr.

Professionalizing Modern Medicine: Paris Surgeons & Medical Science & Institutions in the Eighteenth Century. Toby Gelfand. LC 79-8955. (Contributions in Medical History: No. 6). (Illus.). xviii, 271p. 1980. lib. bdg. 29.95 (ISBN 0-313-21488-3, GPM/). Greenwood.

Professionals & Paraprofessionals. Michael J. Austin. LC 77-26273. 295p. 1978. text ed. 22.95 (ISBN 0-87705-305-7). Human Sci Pr.

Professional's Business Guide for Proprietor & Partnerships. rev. ed. Luanna C. Blagrove. (Illus.). 185p. 1981. 29.95 (ISBN 0-9604466-5-6). Blagrove Pubns.

Professional's Guide to Publicity. Richard Weiner. LC 78-52626. 1978. 9.50 (ISBN 0-913046-36-1); pap. 6.50 o.p. (ISBN 0-913046-07-8). Public Relations.

Professionals Out of Work. Paula G. Leventman. LC 80-1645. (Illus.). 1981. 19.95 (ISBN 0-02-918800-8). Free Pr.

Professionals: Portraits of NFL Stars by America's Most Prominent Illustrators. Ray Didinger. 1980. 16.95 (ISBN 0-453-00391-5, H-391). NAL.

Professions & Professionalization. Ed. by John A. Jackson. LC 75-123346. (Sociological Studies: No. 3). 1970. 30.50 (ISBN 0-521-07982-9). Cambridge U Pr.

Professions & Their Prospects. Ed. by Eliot Freidson. LC 72-84048. 1977. pap. 9.95x (ISBN 0-8039-0937-3). Sage.

Professions for the People: The Politics of Skill. Ed. by Joel Gerstl & G. Jacobs. 1976. text ed. 11.95 (ISBN 0-470-29702-6); pap. 5.95 o.p. (ISBN 0-470-29703-4). Halsted Pr.

Professor. Charlotte Bronte. 1954. 10.50 (ISBN 0-460-00417-4, Evman); pap. 8.95 (ISBN 0-460-01417-X). Dutton.

Professor Dowell's Head. Alexander Beliaev. Tr. by Antonina W. Bouis. (Best of Soviet Science Fiction Ser.). 156p. 1981. pap. 2.95 (ISBN 0-02-016580-3, Collier). Macmillan.

Professor Googol Flying Time Machine & Atomic Space Capsule Math Primer. 3rd ed. Samuel W. Valenza, Jr. (Illus.). 196p. (gr. 7-12). 1974. 9.50 (ISBN 0-936918-00-4). Intergalactic NJ.

Professor Hoffmann's Modern Magic. Ed. by Richard Robinson. LC 77-78530. 1977. text ed. 11.95 o.p. (ISBN 0-8256-3073-8); pap. 6.95 o.p. (ISBN 0-8256-3084-3, 030073, Quick Fox). Music Sales.

Professor MMAA's Lecture. Stefan Themerson. LC 74-21585. 251p. 1975. 11.95 (ISBN 0-87951-029-3). Overlook Pr.

Professor Noah's Spaceship. Brian Wildsmith. (Illus.). 32p. (ps-3). 1980. 9.95 (ISBN 0-19-279741-7). Oxford U Pr.

Professor Oscar J. Goldrick & His Denver. Nolie Mumey. LC 59-11065. 1959. pap. 1.25 (ISBN 0-8040-0080-8). Swallow.

Professor Wormbog's Crazy Cut-Ups. Mercer Mayer. (Golden Book Ser.). (Illus.). 144p. (gr. 1-7). 1980. 3.95 (ISBN 0-307-15807-1, Golden Pr). Western Pub.

Professor's Daughter. Piers P. Read. 1980. pap. 2.25 (ISBN 0-380-49981-9, 49981). Avon.

Profile Canada: Social & Economic Projections. Gerald B. McCready. 1977. pap. 9.75x (ISBN 0-256-01703-4). Irwin.

Profile for a Christian Life Style: Titus. Gene Getz. pap. 2.95 (ISBN 0-310-25092-7). Zondervan.

Profile for Profitability: Using Cost Control & Profitability Analysis. Thomas S. Dudick. LC 72-4353. (Systems & Controls for Financial Management Ser.). 253p. 1972. 30.50 (ISBN 0-471-22362-X, Pub. by Wiley-Interscience). Wiley.

Profile Japan: A National Compendium of Facts, Figures & Essential Information. Serge Hays. 576p. 1980. cancelled (ISBN 0-87196-433-3). Facts on File.

Profile of a Citizen Soldier. John J. Maginnis. (Illus.). 254p. 1981. 9.95 (ISBN 0-89962-046-9). Todd & Honeywell.

Profile of Communism: A Fact-By-Fact Primer. rev. ed. Ed. by Moshe Decter. 1961. pap. 0.95 o.s.i. (ISBN 0-02-072820-4, Collier). Macmillan.

Profile of Higher Education in the South in 1985. 1977. 1.50 o.p. (ISBN 0-686-20626-6). S Regional Ed.

Profile of Indian Culture. K. K. Nair, pseud. (India Library Ser., Vol. 1). 202p. 1975. 8.95 (ISBN 0-88253-774-1). Ind-US Inc.

Profile of Mathematical Logic. Howard DeLong. (Intermediate Mathematics Geometry Topology Ser). 1970. text ed. 17.95 (ISBN 0-201-01499-8). A-W.

Profile of Selected Senior Citizen Programs. Wayne Lever. 72p. (Orig.). 1980. pap. text ed. 3.95 (ISBN 0-89536-458-1). CSS Pub.

Profile of the Residency-Trained Family Physician in the United States 1970-1979. Ed. by John P. Geyman. 72p. 1980. pap. 7.00x (ISBN 0-8385-7961-2). ACC.

Profile of Vachel Lindsay. John T. Flanagan. LC 79-130279. (Literary Profiles Ser.). 1970. pap. text ed. 2.95x (ISBN 0-675-09287-6). Merrill.

Profiles. Baron Wolman. LC 74-81290. (Illus.). 1974. deluxe ed. 15.00 signed, ltd., numbered (ISBN 0-916290-02-6); pap. 5.95 (ISBN 0-916290-01-8). Squarebooks.

Profiles & Portraits of American Presidents. Margaret Bassett. 1980. cancelled (ISBN 0-686-65651-2). McKay.

Profiles: Giants in Medicine. Frederick Eberson. (Illus.). 120p. (Orig.). 1980. pap. 5.95 (ISBN 0-934616-11-6). Valkyrie Pr.

Profiles in American Foreign Policy: Stimson, Kennan, Acheson, Dulles, Rusk, Kissinger, & Vance. Peter A. Poole. LC 80-5624. (Illus.). 54p. (Orig.). 1981. lib. bdg. 17.00 (ISBN 0-8191-1422-7); pap. text ed. 7.75 (ISBN 0-8191-1423-5). U Pr of Amer.

Profiles in Courage. John F. Kennedy. (Memorial ed.). 1964. pap. 2.50 (ISBN 0-06-080001-1, P1, PL). Har-Row.

Profiles in Human Development. Kaluger. LC 75-37505. (Illus.). 320p. 1976. pap. 8.50 (ISBN 0-8016-2607-2). Mosby.

Profiles in Innocence by Quentin K. Y. Huang: With an Introduction by Himself. J. Gareth Hitchcock. 64p. 1980. 8.00 o.p. (ISBN 0-682-49669-3). Exposition.

Profiles in Social Work. Mary Gottesfeld & Mary Pharis. LC 76-20697. 1977. text ed. 19.95 (ISBN 0-87705-296-4). Human Sci Pr.

Profiles of a Leader. Judson Cornwall. (Orig.). 1981. pap. 4.95 (ISBN 0-88270-503-2). Logos.

Profiles of American Colleges, Vol. 1. 12th ed. Barrons Educational College Division Staff. LC 80-21243. 1980. text ed. 23.95 (ISBN 0-8120-5407-5); pap. 9.95 (ISBN 0-8120-2201-7). Barron.

Profiles of American Colleges: Regional Editions-the Midwest. Barron's Educational Series Staff, College Division. LC 79-50110. (gr. 10-12). 1978. pap. 5.75 (ISBN 0-8120-2078-2). Barron.

Profiles of American Colleges: Regional Editions-the Northeast. rev. ed. Barron's Educational Series Staff, College Division. LC 79-50110. (gr. 10-12). 1979. pap. text ed. 5.75 (ISBN 0-8120-2075-8). Barron.

Profiles of Faith. Frank W. Lemons. 1971. pap. 2.25 (ISBN 0-87148-683-0). Pathway Pr.

Profiles of Northwest Plants: Food Uses, Medicinal Uses, & Legends. 2nd ed. Peggy Robinson. (Illus.). 168p. 1979. pap. 5.95 (ISBN 0-686-27923-9). P Robinson.

Profiles of PhD's in the Sciences. Office Of Scientific Personnel. 1965. pap. 3.75 (ISBN 0-309-01293-7). Natl Acad Pr.

Profiles of Protestant Saints. Howard V. Harper. LC 67-24071. 1968. 7.95 (ISBN 0-8303-0037-6). Fleet.

Profiles of Rural Poverty. International Labour Office, Geneva. (Illus.). 50p. (Orig.). 1979. pap. 4.30 (ISBN 9-22-102142-4). Intl Labour Office.

Profiles of the Future. Arthur C. Clarke. 1977. pap. 2.25 (ISBN 0-445-04061-0). Popular Lib.

Profiles of the Future: An Inquiry into the Limits of the Possible. rev. ed. Arthur C. Clarke. LC 72-6714. 288p. 1973. 10.95 o.s.i. (ISBN 0-06-010792-8, HarpT). Har-Row.

Profiles of the Presidents. Emerson R. West. LC 80-10455. 328p. 1980. 7.95 (ISBN 0-87747-800-7). Deseret Bk.

Profiles of Two Adult Homes & Their Communities: The Need to Bridge the Gap. 1980. 4.00. Comm Coun Great NY.

Profiles: People Who Are Helping to Change the World. Helen K. Hosier. 1977. 6.95 o.p. (ISBN 0-8015-6082-9). Dutton.

Profiling Fabrics: Properties, Performance, & Construction Techniques. Debbie A. Gioello. (Language of Fashion Ser.). (Illus.). 325p. 1980. text ed. 27.50 (ISBN 0-87005-259-4). Fairchild.

Profit Box System of Forecasting Stock Prices. Wilfred R. George. LC 76-15737. (Illus.). 1976. 19.95 o.p. (ISBN 0-87094-129-1). Dow Jones-Irwin.

Profit from Foodservice: A Q & A Approach. Pat Levings. LC 74-706. 160p. 1974. 11.95 (ISBN 0-8436-0584-7). CBI Pub.

Profit Measurement During Inflation: Accounting, Economic & Financial Aspects. Y. Goldschmidt & K. Admon. LC 77-4500. (Wiley Series in Operations Management). 1977. 29.95 (ISBN 0-471-01983-6, Pub. by Wiley-Interscience). Wiley.

Profit or People? The New Social Role of Money. James Robertson. (Ideas in Progress Ser.). 1978. 9.95 (ISBN 0-7145-0848-9, Pub. by M Boyars); pap. 4.95 (ISBN 0-7145-0773-3). Merrimack Bk Serv.

Profit Planning Handbook. B. H. Walley. 325p. 1978. text ed. 29.50x (ISBN 0-220-66342-4, Pub. by Busn Bks England). Renouf.

Profit Strategies for Business. Robert Rachlin. 144p. 1981. 12.95 (ISBN 0-13-726216-7, Spec); pap. 4.95 (ISBN 0-13-726208-6). P-H.

Profit Strategies for Business. Robert Rachlin. LC 79-88674. 1980. 14.95 (ISBN 0-938712-01-2). Marr Pubns.

Profitability Accounting: For Planning & Control. 2nd ed. R. Beyer & D. J. Trawicki. 403p. 1972. 29.95 (ISBN 0-471-06523-4). Wiley.

Profitability Accounting: For Planning & Control. 2nd ed. Robert Beyer & Donald J. Trawicki. (Illus.). 400p. 1972. 29.95 (ISBN 0-8260-1055-5, 06961). Ronald Pr.

Profitability Through Loss Control: Manual for Financial Institutions. Bill I. Ernstine & Jack A. Mack. 1977. pap. text ed. 8.95 o.p. (ISBN 0-87084-719-8). Anderson Pub Co.

Profitable Aeration of Waste Water. Ed. by H. S. Stephens & G. Priestley. (Illus.). 98p. (Orig.). 1980. pap. 45.00x (ISBN 0-906085-44-6). BHRA Fluid.

Profitable & Necessarie Booke of Observations. William Clowes. LC 73-171740. (English Experience Ser.: No. 366). 1971. Repr. of 1596 ed. 33.50 (ISBN 90-221-0366-8). Walter J Johnson.

Profitable Book...Treating of the Lawes of England. And Now Translated Out of French into English, Vol. 63. John Perkins. Ed. by David S. Berkowitz & Samuel E. Thorne. LC 77-86556. (Classics of English Legal History in the Modern Era Ser.). 1979. Repr. of 1827 ed. lib. bdg. 55.00 (ISBN 0-8240-3050-8). Garland Pub.

Profitable Catering. Bruce H. Axler. 1974. pap. 3.95 (ISBN 0-672-26118-9). Bobbs.

Profitable Food & Beverage Management: Planning. Eric F. Green et al. 1978. text ed. 17.95x (ISBN 0-8104-9480-9). Hayden.

Profitable Food & Beverage Management: Operations. Eric F. Green et al. 1978. text ed. 19.95 (ISBN 0-8104-9466-3). Hayden.

Profitable Garden Center Management. Louis M. Berninger. (Illus.). 1978. 14.95 (ISBN 0-8359-5632-6); instrs's manual avail. Reston.

Profitable Grain Trading. Ralph M. Ainsworth. LC 80-53316. 256p. 1980. Repr. of 1933 ed. text ed. 25.00 (ISBN 0-934380-04-X). Traders Pr.

Profitable Mail Order Marketing. Lawrence Cooklin. 1976. 18.95x (ISBN 0-434-90259-4). Intl Ideas.

Profitable Part-Time - Full-Time Freelancing. Clair F. Rees. LC 79-22724. 214p. 1980. 11.95 (ISBN 0-89879-012-3). Writers Digest.

Profitable Pasture Management. Roy A. Chessmore. LC 78-70056. 1979. 13.95 (ISBN 0-685-90887-9, 2056). Interstate.

Profitable Use of Excavation Equipment. Elmer R. Drevdahl. 14.95 (ISBN 0-89741-009-2); pap. 11.25 (ISBN 0-89741-009-2). Roadrunner Tech.

Profiting from the Word. A. W. Pink. 1977. pap. 2.45 (ISBN 0-85151-032-9). Banner of Truth.

Profits from Country Property: How to Select, Buy, Improve & Maintain Your Country Property. James H. Koch. (Illus.). 320p. 1980. 12.95 (ISBN 0-07-035248-8, P&RB). McGraw.

Profits from Real Estate Publicity. Roger Karvel. 225p. 1980. 21.95 (ISBN 0-88462-385-8). Real Estate Ed Co.

Profits, Power & Piety: An Inside Look at What Goes on Behind the Velvet Curtains of Christian Business. James Johnson. LC 72-83881. 1980. pap. 2.50 (ISBN 0-89081-240-3). Harvest Hse.

Profoundly Mentally Retarded. Charles C. Cleland. LC 79-1258. 1979. text ed. 17.95 (ISBN 0-13-729566-9). P-H.

Profundis. Richard Cowper. 1980. pap. write for info. (ISBN 0-671-83502-5). PB.

Progamming Standard Cobol. Winchung Chai & Henry Chai. 1976. 13.95 (ISBN 0-12-166550-X). Acad Pr.

Progess in Macrocyclic Chemistry, Vol. 2. Reed M. Izatt & James J. Christensen. (Progress in Macrocyclic Chemistry Ser.). 384p. 1981. 35.00 (ISBN 0-471-05178-0, Pub. by Wiley-Interscience). Wiley.

Progesterone Receptors in Normal & Neoplastic Tissues. Ed. by William L. McGuire et al. LC 77-72065. (Progress in Cancer Research & Therapy Ser.: Vol. 4). 1977. 31.50 (ISBN 0-89004-163-6). Raven.

Prognosis: Contemporary Outcomes of Disease. James F. Fries & George E. Ehrlich. (Illus.). 600p. 1980. 34.95 (ISBN 0-89303-005-8). Charles.

Prognostication Everlastinge of Righte Good Effecte: Lately Corrected & Augmented by Thomas Digges, His Sonne. Leonard Digges. LC 74-28846. (English Experience Ser.: No. 727). 1975. Repr. of 1576 ed. 9.50 (ISBN 90-221-0727-2). Walter J Johnson.

Program Analysis: The GSK Categorical Data Approach. Robert G. Lehnen & Ronald N. Forthofer. (Illus.). 225p. 1981. text ed. 25.00 (ISBN 0-534-97974-2). Lifetime Learn.

Program & Project Management in a Matrix Organization: A Case Study. Andre Delbecq & Alan Filley. (Wisconsin Business Monographs: No. 9). (Orig.). 1974. pap. 5.00 (ISBN 0-86603-001-8). Bureau Busn Res U Wis.

Program Budgeting. Stephen J. Knezevich. LC 72-5703. 1973. 17.90x (ISBN 0-8211-1014-4); text ed. 16.20x (ISBN 0-685-36206-X). McCutchan.

Program Decisions in Public Television. Natan Katzman. 72p. 1976. pap. 3.50 (Pub Telecomm). NAEB.

Program Development Process, Pt. 1: The Individual Programmer. Joel D. Aron. (IBM Systems Programming Ser.). (Illus.). 280p. 1974. text ed. 16.95 (ISBN 0-201-14451-4). A-W.

Program Evaluation in Social Research. Jonathan A. Morell. LC 78-11949. (Pergamon Series in General Psychology). 1980. 22.00 (ISBN 0-08-023360-0); pap. 9.95 (ISBN 0-08-023359-7). Pergamon.

Program Evaluation in the Health Fields, Vol. II. Ed. by Herbert C. Schulberg & Frank Baker. LC 78-102679. 1979. text ed. 29.95x (ISBN 0-87705-339-1). Human Sci Pr.

Program Evaluation in the Public Sector. Ed. by Albert C. Hyde & Jay Shafritz. LC 78-19742. (Praeger Special Studies). 325p. 1979. 29.95 (ISBN 0-03-042976-5). Praeger.

Program Evaluation Kit. rev. ed. Lynn L. Morris et al. LC 78-59613. (Illus.). 1080p. 1978. pap. 49.95 (ISBN 0-8039-1073-8). Sage.

Program Evaluation: Methods & Case Studies. Emile J. Posavac & Raymond G. Carey. (Illus.). 1980. text ed. 18.95 (ISBN 0-13-729665-7). P-H.

Program Flow Analysis: Theory & Application. Steven S. Muchnick & Neil D. Jones. (Software Ser.). (Illus.). 448p. 1981. 21.50 (ISBN 0-13-729681-9). P-H.

Program for Families of Children with Learning & Behavior Problems. Martin A. Kozloff. LC 78-26578. 1979. 28.95 (ISBN 0-471-04434-2, Pub. by Wiley-Interscience). Wiley.

Program for Renewed Partnersh8ip: A Report. Sloan Commission on Government & Higher Education. Ed. by Carl Kaysen. 1980. 18.50 (ISBN 0-88410-193-2). Ballinger Pub.

Program for Revision: A Practical Guide. David B. Jacobson. (Illus.). 352p. 1973. pap. text ed. 9.95 (ISBN 0-13-730671-7). P-H.

Program for Survival: Poems. Gibbons Ruark. LC 74-151089. 1971. pap. 3.95x (ISBN 0-8139-0325-4). U Pr of Va.

Program Guide for Infants & Toddlers with Neuromotor & Other Developmental Disabilities. Frances P. Connor et al. LC 77-28188. 1978. pap. 14.50x (ISBN 0-8077-2546-3). Tchrs Coll.

Program Housing Standards in the Experimental Housing Allowance Program: Analyzing Differences in the Demand & Supply Experiments. Joseph J. Valenza. (Institute Paper). pap. 4.00 (ISBN 0-87766-199-5, 19300). Urban Inst.

Program Innovation in Facilities for the Mentally Retarded. J. Thaw. 1981. 12.50 (ISBN 0-685-32569-5). Univ Park.

Program Issues in Developmental Disabilities: A Resource Manual for Surveyors & Reviewers. Ed. by James F. Gardner et al. LC 80-12555. (Illus.). 176p. (Orig.). 1980. pap. text ed. 12.95 (ISBN 0-933716-05-2). P H Brookes.

Program-Management Control Systems. Joseph A. Maciariello. LC 77-20030. (Systems & Controls for Financial Management Ser.). 1978. 29.50 (ISBN 0-471-01566-0, Pub. by Wiley-Interscience). Wiley.

Program Notes for the Singer's Repertoire. Berton Coffin & Werner Singer. LC 60-7265. 1962. 11.00 (ISBN 0-8108-0169-8). Scarecrow.

Program of Exercises for Management & Organizational Behavior. James A. Vaughn & Samuel D. Deep. 1975. pap. text ed. 6.95x (ISBN 0-02-479440-6); tchrs' manual free (ISBN 0-02-479450-3). Macmillan.

Program of Sequential Language Development: A Theoretical & Practical Guide for Remediation of Language, Reading & Learning Disorders. Harris M. Blumberg. (Illus.). 108p. 1975. 12.75 (ISBN 0-398-03320-X). C C Thomas.

Program of Studies on Socioeconomic Effects of Earthquake Predictions. Commission on Sociotechnical Systems, National Research Council. 1978. pap. text ed. 8.50x (ISBN 0-309-02789-6). Natl Acad Pr.

Program Style, Design, Efficiency, Debugging & Testing. 2nd ed. Dennis Van Tassel. (Illus.). 1978. ref. ed. 18.95 (ISBN 0-13-729947-8). P-H.

Program to Establish Speech Fluency. Donald E. Mowrer. 1979. pap. text ed. 5.95 (ISBN 0-675-08271-4); cassettes 60.00, 2 or more sets 40.00 (ISBN 0-675-08270-6). Merrill.

Program Your Heart for Health. Frank Murray. 368p. (Orig.). 1977. pap. 2.95 (ISBN 0-915962-20-9). Larchmont Bks.

Programa Interamericano de Formulacion y Evaluacion de Proyectos: (CETREDE) 1977. pap. 1.00 o.p. (ISBN 0-685-80051-2). OAS.

Programacion Fortran IV. Wilfred P. Rule. (Orig.). 1976. text ed. 7.20x (ISBN 0-06-316996-7, IntlDept). Har-Row.

Programas Del Dia De la Madre y Poesias. 62p. (Span.). 1980. pap. 1.10 (ISBN 0-311-07303-4). Casa Bautista.

Programas Para Dias Especiales Tomo I. Lopez A. Munoz. 107p. 1980. pap. 1.60 (ISBN 0-311-07005-1). Casa Bautista.

Programas Para Dias Especiales Tomo II. A. Lopez Munoz. 64p. 1980. Repr. of 1977 ed. pap. 1.60 (ISBN 0-311-07006-X). Casa Bautista.

Programas Para Reuniones Sociales y Banquetes. Ed. by Viola Campbell. (Illus.). 1979. pap. 1.20 (ISBN 0-311-11011-8). Casa Bautista.

Programed Introduction to Linguistics: Phonetics & Phonemics. Cynthia D. Buchanan. 1963. pap. text ed. 15.95x (ISBN 0-669-20453-6). Heath.

Programed Spelling Demons. George W. Feinstein. 240p. 1973. pap. text ed. 8.50 o.p. (ISBN 0-13-730135-9). P-H.

Programmable Pocket Calculators. Henry Mullish & Stephen Kochan. 264p. 1980. pap. 9.95 (ISBN 0-8104-5175-1). Hayden.

Programme of Industrial Activities Advisory Committee of Salaried Employees & Professional Workers, 8th Session, Geneva, 1981: The Effects of Technological & Structural Changes on the Employment & Working Conditions of Non-Manual Workers, Report II. International Labour Office. iv, 117p. (Orig.). 1980. pap. 8.55 (ISBN 92-2-102557-8). Intl Labour Office.

Programmed Approach to Good Spelling! Richard C. Baggett. 160p. 1981. pap. text ed. 6.95 (ISBN 0-13-729764-5). P-H.

Programmed Articulation Therapy: Time to Modify. Cynthia D. Psaltis & Sonja L. Spallato. 248p. 1973. pap. 12.50 (ISBN 0-398-02745-5). C C Thomas.

Programmed Astronomy: The Night Sky. Sullivan & Sullivan. 1972. pap. text ed. 9.00 incl. tchrs' manual & test (ISBN 0-8449-0504-6). Learning Line.

Programmed Astronomy: The Solar System. Sullivan & Sullivan. 1972. pap. text ed. 9.00 incl. tchrs' manual & test (ISBN 0-8449-0500-3). Learning Line.

Programmed Basic Chemistry for Allied Health Students. Danile Keily. LC 77-10774. (Illus.). 1978. pap. text ed. 12.95 (ISBN 0-8016-2637-4). Mosby.

Programmed Business Mathematics, Bk. 2. 4th, rev. ed. Harry Huffman. (Illus.). 256p. 1980. pap. text ed. 8.75 (ISBN 0-07-030902-7); test bklet 4.95 (ISBN 0-07-030905-1). McGraw.

Programmed Business Mathematics, Bk. 3. 4th rev. ed. Harry Huffman. (Illus.). 192p. 1980. pap. 8.70 (ISBN 0-07-030903-5, G). McGraw.

Programmed Case Studies in Geography. Gordon J. Fielding. 299p. 1974. pap. text ed. 8.50 scp (ISBN 0-06-042052-9, HarpC). Har-Row.

Programmed College Vocabulary Three Thousand Six Hundred. George W. Feinstein. 1979. pap. text ed. 9.50 (ISBN 0-13-729806-4). P-H.

Programmed Cost Accounting: A Participative Approach. Gerald E. Nichols. 1973. text ed. 18.95 (ISBN 0-256-01446-9). Irwin.

Programmed Course in Basic Algebra. William C. Beck & James R. Trier. (Mathematics Ser). 1971. 13.95 (ISBN 0-201-00445-3); 3.95 (ISBN 0-201-00446-1). A-W.

Programmed Environments Curriculum for the Handicapped. James Tawney et al. (Special Education Ser.). 1979. text ed. 21.95 (ISBN 0-675-08265-X); instructor's manual 3.95 (ISBN 0-686-67290-9). Merrill.

Programmed French Reading & Writing I. Eliane Burroughs. 1971. pap. text ed. 7.00 incl. tchrs' manual & test (ISBN 0-8449-1700-1). Learning Line.

Programmed French Reading & Writing II. Eliane Burroughs. 1964. pap. text ed. 7.00 incl. tchrs' manual & test (ISBN 0-8449-1704-4). Learning Line.

Programmed French Reading & Writing III. Eliane Burroughs. 1972. pap. text ed. 7.00 incl. tchrs' manual & test (ISBN 0-8449-1708-7). Learning Line.

Programmed Functional Anatomy. Glynn Leyshon. LC 73-22279. 1974. pap. text ed. 10.00 (ISBN 0-8016-2999-3). Mosby.

Programmed Guide to Tax Research. James E. Parker. 272p. 1979. pap. text ed. 9.95x (ISBN 0-534-00796-1). Wadsworth Pub.

Programmed Guide to the Dissection and Study of the Human Body. 2nd rev. ed. Frank H. Figge. (Prog. Bk.). 1968. 12.00 o.s.i. (ISBN 0-02-844630-5). Hafner.

Programmed Instruction in Arithmetic, Dosages, & Solutions. 4th ed. Dolores F. Saxton et al. LC 76-51283. 1977. pap. 7.00 (ISBN 0-8016-4329-5). Mosby.

Programmed Instruction: Radiation Therapy. Ed. by F. Pilapil & K. Studva. 55p. 1979. pap. 6.50 (ISBN 0-89352-099-3). Masson Pub.

Programmed Instruction: Understanding Cancer & Chemotherapy. Ed. by F. Pilapil & K. Studva. 80p. 1979. pap. 6.50 (ISBN 0-89352-081-0). Masson Pub.

Programmed Introduction to Critical Path Methods. Cambridge Consultants Training Ltd. 1975. pap. 6.25 (ISBN 0-08-014027-0). Pergamon.

Programmed Introduction to Microbiology. 2nd ed. Stewart M. Brooks. LC 72-88509. (Illus.). 120p. 1973. pap. text ed. 8.50 (ISBN 0-8016-0819-8). Mosby.

Programmed Introduction to PERT: Program Evaluation & Review Technique. Federal Electric Corporation. 1963. pap. 15.95 (ISBN 0-471-25680-3, Pub. by Wiley-Interscience). Wiley.

Programmed Introduction to the Game of Chess. M. W. Sullivan. 1972. text ed. 12.50 (ISBN 0-8449-1800-8). Learning Line.

Programmed Language & Speech Correction Through Perceptual Activities. Bernice E. Heasley & Jacqueline R. Grosklos. (Illus.). 136p. 1980. text ed. 11.50 spiral (lexotone) (ISBN 0-398-03956-9). C C Thomas.

Programmed Learning: A Bibliography of Programs & Presentation Devices. 4th ed. Carl H. Hendershot. LC 67-16988. (Incl. suppl. 1-6). 1971. 45.00 (ISBN 0-911832-04-1). Hendershot.

Programmed Learning: A Bibliography of Programs & Presentation Devices. 2nd ed. Compiled by Carl H. Hendershot. 1963. 15.00 (ISBN 0-911832-12-2). Hendershot.

Programmed Learning: A Bibliography of Programs & Presentation Devices. 3rd ed. Compiled by Carl H. Hendershot. LC 64-11824. (Illus.). 1965. 30.00 (ISBN 0-911832-11-4). Hendershot.

Programmed Learning Aid for Orientation to the Two-Year College. Richard W. Hostrop. 217p. 1970. lib. bdg. 5.95 o.p. (ISBN 0-256-01259-8, 22-0296-01). Learning Syst.

Programmed Learning & Individually Paced Instruction Bibliography. 5th ed. Compiled by Carl H. Hendershot. LC 73-77783. 1973. 45.00 (ISBN 0-911832-05-X); basic bibl. & suppls. 1-5 95.00 (ISBN 0-911832-14-9); basic bibl. & suppls. 1-4 o.p. 70.00 (ISBN 0-911832-07-6); basic bibl. & suppls. 1 & 2 o.p. 58.00 (ISBN 0-911832-06-8); suppl. 5 25.00 (ISBN 0-911832-13-0); suppl. 6 27.75 (ISBN 0-911832-06-8) (ISBN 0-911832-16-5). Hendershot.

Programmed Lessons for Young Language-Disabled Children: A Handbook for Therapists, Educators & Parents. Bernice E. Heasley & Jacqueline R. Grosklos. (Illus.). 172p. 1976. pap. text ed. 12.75 spiral (ISBN 0-398-03526-1). C C Thomas.

Programmed Mathematics of Drugs & Solutions: Nineteen Seventy-Nine Revision with Intravenous Rate Calculations & Mathematics Pretest. Mabel E. Weaver & Vera J. Koehler. LC 79-10790. 1979. pap. text ed. 4.95x (ISBN 0-397-54232-1). Lippincott.

Programmed Newswriting. John L. Griffith & Edward G. Weston. (Basic Skills in Journalism Ser.). (Illus.). 1978. pap. text ed. 6.95 (ISBN 0-13-730630-X). P-H.

Programmed Nutrition. 2nd ed. Helen A. Guthrie & Karen S. Braddock. (Illus.). 1978. pap. text ed. 12.95 (ISBN 0-8016-2003-1). Mosby.

Programmed Primer in Learning Disabilities. Jerome A. Kroth. (Illus.). 296p. 1974. 14.75 (ISBN 0-398-01055-2). C C Thomas.

Programmed Reading for Teachers. Robert M. Wilson et al. (Elementary Education Ser.: No. C22). 280p. 1980. pap. text ed. 10.95 (ISBN 0-675-08285-4). Merrill.

Programmed Reviews of Chemical Principles. 3rd ed. Jean D. Lassila et al. 1979. 9.95 (ISBN 0-8053-6027-1). Benjamin-Cummings.

Programmed Rudiments of Music. Robert Ottman & Frank Mainous. 1979. pap. 14.95 (ISBN 0-13-729962-1). P-H.

Programmed Study of Number Systems. Ruric E. Wheeler & Ed. R. Wheeler. (Contemporary Undergrad Math Ser). (Prog. Bk.). 1972. pap. text ed. 8.95 (ISBN 0-8185-0042-5). Brooks-Cole.

Programmed Text in Statistics. J. Hine & G. B. Wetherill. Incl. Bk. 1. Summarizing Data. 95p. pap. text ed. 10.95x o.p. (ISBN 0-412-13590-6); Bk. 3. The t-Test & Goodness of Fit. 53p. pap. text ed. 10.95x o.p. (ISBN 0-412-13740-2); Bk. 4. Tests on Variance & Regression. 69p. pap. text ed. 10.95x o.p. (ISBN 0-412-13750-X). (Orig.). 1975 (Pub. by Chapman & Hall). Methuen Inc.

Programmed Text in Statistics. J. Hine & G. B. Wetherill. Incl. Bk 1. Summarizing Data. 104p. pap. text ed. 8.95x o.p. (ISBN 0-470-40040-4); Bk. 2. Basic Theory. 116p. pap. text ed. o.p. (ISBN 0-470-40041-2); Bk 3. The T-Test & Goodness of Fit. 56p. pap. text ed. 7.50 o.p. (ISBN 0-470-40042-0); Bk. 4. Tests on Variance & Regression. 76p. pap. text ed. 8.95x o.p. (ISBN 0-686-10589-3). (Orig.). 1975. Halsted Pr.

Programmed Therapy for Stuttering in Children & Adults. Bruce P. Ryan. (Illus.). 200p. 1980. text ed. 12.50 (ISBN 0-398-03104-5); pap. text ed. 9.75 (ISBN 0-398-03100-2). C C Thomas.

Programmed Vocabulary. 3rd ed. James I. Brown. (The CPD Approach). 1980. pap. text ed. 8.95 (ISBN 0-13-729707-6). P-H.

Programmed Work Attack. 3rd ed. Robert M. Wilson & Marryanne Hall. 1979. text ed. 6.95 (ISBN 0-675-08286-2). Merrill.

Programmed Writing Skills. G. Feinstein. 1976. pap. 9.50 (ISBN 0-13-730523-0); instr. manual of tests 1.95 (ISBN 0-13-730515-X). P-H.

Programmer's Book of Rules. George Ledin, Jr. & Victor Ledin. LC 79-13746. 1979. pap. 9.95 (ISBN 0-534-97993-9). Lifetime Learn.

Programmer's Guide to COBOL. (Data Processing Ser.). 240p. 1980. text ed. 18.95 (ISBN 0-442-80040-1). Van Nos Reinhold.

Programmer's Guide to LISP. Ken Tracton. (Illus.). 1979. 10.95 (ISBN 0-8306-9761-6); pap. 6.95 (ISBN 0-8306-1045-6, 1045). TAB Bks.

Programmer's Guide to the IBM System-360. J. H. Bradley. 1969. 34.50 o.p. (ISBN 0-07-007063-6, P&RB). McGraw.

Programmes in Animation: Handbook for Animation Technicians. B. Salt. 1978. 150.00 (ISBN 0-08-023153-5). Pergamon.

Programming ALGOL. D. J. Malcome-Lawes. 1969. 13.75 (ISBN 0-08-006385-3); pap. 6.25 (ISBN 0-08-006384-5). Pergamon.

Programming: An Introduction to Computer Techniques. rev. 2nd ed. Ward D. Maurer. LC 70-188126. (Illus.). 1972. text ed. 23.95x (ISBN 0-8162-5453-2). Holden Day.

Programming & Interfacing the Sixty-Five-o-Two, with Experiments. Marvin L. De Jong. LC 79-67130. 1980. pap. 14.95 (ISBN 0-672-21651-5). Bobbs.

Programming & Ultilization of Research Reactors: Proceedings, 3 vols. International Atomic Energy Agency. Ed. by Sigvard Eklund. (International Atomic Energy Agency Symposia). 1962. Vol. 1. 17.00 (ISBN 0-12-572501-9); Vol. 2, 1963. 17.00 (ISBN 0-12-572502-7); Vol. 3. 17.00 (ISBN 0-12-572503-5). Acad Pr.

Programming Assembler Language. Peter Abel. (Illus.). 1979. text ed. 16.95 (ISBN 0-8359-5658-X); instrs'. manual avail. (ISBN 0-8359-5659-8). Reston.

Programming Business Applications in Fortran IV. Phillip T. May. LC 72-7634. 1973. pap. text ed. 14.25 (ISBN 0-395-14047-1, 3-34905); solutions man. pap. 1.50 (ISBN 0-395-17159-8, 3-34906). HM.

Programming Flowcharting for the Business Data Processing. Barry J. Passen. LC 77-25509. 1978. pap. text ed. 16.95 (ISBN 0-471-01410-9). Wiley.

Programming for a Digital Computer in the Fortran Language. Wilf. 1969. 6.50 (ISBN 0-201-08639-5). A-W.

Programming for Minicomputers. J. C. Cluley. LC 77-83270. (Computer Systems Engineering Ser.). 1978. 19.50x (ISBN 0-8448-1259-5). Crane-Russak Co.

Programming for Poets: A Gentle Introduction Using Pascal. Richard Conway et al. (Computer Science Ser.). 352p. 1980. pap. text ed. 11.95 (ISBN 0-87626-727-4). Winthrop.

Programming for Radio & Television. V. Jackson Smith. LC 80-5635. 141p. 1980. pap. text ed. 7.75 (ISBN 0-8191-1250-X). U Pr of Amer.

Programming FORTRAN Seventy-Seven. J. N. Hume & R. C. Holt. (Illus.). 1979. pap. text ed. 12.95 (ISBN 0-8359-5671-7). Reston.

Programming in BASIC. Tom Logsdon. LC 77-75505. 1977. pap. 9.95x (ISBN 0-88236-179-1). Anaheim Pub Co.

Programming in BASIC. Ralph M. Stair, Jr. 1979. pap. 11.50x (ISBN 0-256-02145-7). Irwin.

Programming in BASIC for Business. 2nd ed. Bruce Bosworth & Harry Nagel. 256p. 1981. text ed. 10.95 (ISBN 0-574-21325-2, 13-4325); instr's. guide avail. (ISBN 0-574-21326-0, 13-4326). SRA.

Programming in Basic-Plus. Jasper J. Sawatzky & Shu-Jen Chen. LC 80-27869. 336p. 1981. pap. 13.95 (ISBN 0-471-07729-1). Wiley.

Programming in BASIC with Applications. Tom Logsdon. LC 77-75504. 1977. pap. 10.95x (ISBN 0-88236-180-5). Anaheim Pub Co.

Programming in COBOL. G. T. Lancaster. 152p. 1972. pap. 11.25 (ISBN 0-08-016384-X). Pergamon.

Programming in FORTRAN. William F. Schallert & Carol R. Clark. LC 78-74039. 1979. pap. text ed. 13.95 (ISBN 0-201-06716-1). A-W.

Programming in Pascal. Peter Grogono. LC 77-90175. 1978. pap. text ed. 11.50 o.p. (ISBN 0-201-02473-X). A-W.

Programming in Pascal. rev. ed. Peter Grogono. LC 79-24640. 384p. 1980. pap. text ed. 13.95 (ISBN 0-201-02775-5). A W.

Programming Language One: A Structural Approach with PLC. Don Cassel. 1978. pap. 12.95 (ISBN 0-87909-650-0). Reston.

Programming Language Standardisation: Computer & Their Applications. I. D. Hill & B. L. Meek. LC 80-41092. 261p. 1980. 65.00 (ISBN 0-470-27077-2). Halsted Pr.

Programming Language Structure. Elliot I. Organick et al. (Computer Science & Applied Mathematics Ser.). 1978. text ed. 21.95 (ISBN 0-12-528260-5). Acad Pr.

Programming Languages. Ed. by F. Genuys. 1969. 54.50 (ISBN 0-12-279750-7). Acad Pr.

Programming Languages: Design & Implementation. Terence Pratt. (Illus.). 496p. 1975. 24.95 (ISBN 0-13-730432-3). P-H.

Programming Learning Disabilities. Robert E. Valett. 1969. text ed. 12.60 o.p. (ISBN 0-8224-5620-6). Pitman Learning.

Programming Methodology: Proceedings. Informatik Symposium, 4th, IBM Germany, Wildbad, Sept. 25-27, 1974. Ed. by C. E. Hackl. (Lecture Notes in Computer Science Ser.: Vol. 23). (Illus.). vi, 501p. 1975. pap. 20.40 o.p. (ISBN 0-387-07131-8). Springer-Verlag.

Programming Programmable Calculators. Harold S. Engelsohn. (Computer Programming Ser.). 1978. pap. 11.95 (ISBN 0-8104-5105-0). Hayden.

Programming Proverbs. Henry F. Ledgard. (Computer Programming Ser.). (Illus.). 144p. 1975. pap. text ed. 8.50x (ISBN 0-8104-5522-6). Hayden.

Programming Proverbs for FORTRAN Programmers. Henry F. Ledgard. LC 74-22074. (Computer Programming Ser.). (Illus.). 144p. (Orig.). 1975. pap. text ed. 8.35x (ISBN 0-8104-5820-9). Hayden.

Programming RPG II. Harice L. Seeds. LC 79-127669. 1971. pap. 17.50 (ISBN 0-471-77113-9). Wiley.

Programming Systems. Jeffrey D. Ullman. LC 75-374. (Illus.). 336p. 1976. text ed. 19.95 (ISBN 0-201-07654-3). A-W.

Programming Systems & Foreign Affairs Leadership: An Attempted Innovation. Frederick C. Mosher & John E. Harr. (Orig.). 1970. text ed. 9.95x (ISBN 0-19-501324-7); pap. text ed. 4.95x (ISBN 0-19-501325-5). Oxford U Pr.

Programming the IBM 1130. Joan Hughes. LC 69-16045. 1969. 24.95x (ISBN 0-471-42040-9). Wiley.

Programming the Network of Financial Intermediation. Sten Thore. 224p. 1983. pap. text ed. 14.00x (ISBN 82-00-05379-2). Universitet.

Programming the Z-Eight Thousand. Richard Mateosian. LC 80-80042. (C Ser.). (Illus.). 1980. pap. 15.95 (ISBN 0-89588-032-6). Sybex.

Programming Via Pascal. J. S. Rohl & H. J. Barrett. LC 79-17433. (Cambridge Computer Science Texts Ser.: No. 12). 300p. 1980. 38.50 (ISBN 0-521-22628-7); pap. 15.95 (ISBN 0-521-29583-1). Cambridge U Pr.

Programming with Ada: An Introduction by Means of Graduated Examples. P. Wegner. 1980. 13.95 (ISBN 0-13-730697-0). P-H.

Programs & Skits for Young Teens. Norma H. McPhee. 1978. pap. 2.50 (ISBN 0-8024-6892-6). Moody.

Programs for Advent & Christmas. Ed. by Vincie Alessi. 1978. pap. 3.75 (ISBN 0-8170-0808-X). Judson.

Programs for Digital Signal Processing. Ed. by Digital Signal Processing Committee. LC 79-89028. 1979. 35.95; tape version 50.00. Inst Electrical.

Programs for School Improvement: Cooperative Planning & Organization Development. Neale et al. 300p. 1980. text ed. 16.95 (ISBN 0-205-06950-9, 2369508). Allyn.

Programs in Aid of the Poor for the 1980's. Sar A. Levitan. LC 80-8093. (Policy Studies in Employment & Welfare: No. 1). (Illus.). 166p. 1980. text ed. 11.00 (ISBN 0-8018-2483-4); pap. text ed. 3.95 (ISBN 0-8018-2484-2). Johns Hopkins.

Programs in BASIC, a Lecture Notebook. 2nd ed. Bruce Bosworth. 1978. pap. text ed. 5.95 (ISBN 0-8403-1210-5). Kendall-Hunt.

Programs, Leaders, Consultants & Other Resources in Gifted & Talented Education. Frances A. Karnes & Herschel Peddicord, Jr. 360p. 1980. 29.75 (ISBN 0-398-04099-0). C C Thomas.

Programs of the Brain. J. Z. Young. (Illus.). 334p. 1981. pap. 6.95 (ISBN 0-19-286019-4, GB 641, GB). Oxford U Pr.

Progreso Del Peregrino. Juan Bunyan & L. P. Leavell. Tr. by Hiram F. Duffer, Jr. 1979. pap. 1.75 (ISBN 0-311-37006-3). Casa Bautista.

Progress: A Christian Doctrine? A. G. Woollard. 96p. 1973. pap. 1.95 o.p. (ISBN 0-8170-0576-5). Judson.

Progress & Its Problems: Towards a Theory of Scientific Growth. Larry Laudan. 1977. 15.75x (ISBN 0-520-03330-2); pap. 4.95 (ISBN 0-520-03721-9). U of Cal Pr.

Progress & Performance in the Primary Classroom. Maurice Galton & Brian Simon. 240p. 1980. 25.00 (ISBN 0-7100-0669-1); pap. 15.50 (ISBN 0-7100-0670-5). Routledge & Kegan.

Progress & Problems in Moral Education. Monica Taylor. (General Ser.). 239p. 1975. pap. text ed. 17.50x (ISBN 0-85633-069-8, NFER). Humanities.

Progress & Prosperity. Richard M. Wagner & Roy J. Wright. (Cincinnati Streetcars: No. 7). 1976. pap. 6.95 o.s.i. (ISBN 0-914196-16-2). Trolley Talk.

Progress & Regress in Philosophy: From Hume & Kant to Hegel & Fries, 2 vols. Leonard Nelson. Ed. by Julius Kraft. Tr. by Humphrey Palmer. Vol. 1, 1970. 17.50x o.p. (ISBN 0-631-12520-5, Pub. by Basil Blackwell); Vol. 2, 1971. 17.50x o.p. (ISBN 0-631-13850-1). Biblio Dist.

Progress & Survival: An Essay on the the Future of Mankind. Emile Benoit. Ed. by Jack B. Gohn. 144p. 1980. 17.95 (ISBN 0-03-056911-7). Praeger.

Progress & the Crisis of Man. Frank Yartz et al. LC 75-44451. 144p. 1976. 14.95 (ISBN 0-88229-165-3). Nelson-Hall.

Progress, Coexistence & Intellectual Freedom. Andrei D. Sakharov. 1968. 3.95 (ISBN 0-393-05362-8); pap. text ed. 3.95x (ISBN 0-393-09822-2, Norton C). Norton.

Progress in Allergy, Vol. 29. Ed. by H. Byron & B. H. Waksman. (Illus.). 250p. 1981. 90.00 (ISBN 3-8055-2434-X). S Karger.

Progress in Analytical Atomic Spectroscopy, 2 vols. C. L. Chakrabarti. (Illus.). 282p. 1980. 75.00 (ISBN 0-08-027126-X). Pergamon.

Progress in Anatomy, Vol. 1. Ed. by R. J. Harrison & R. L. Holmes. (Illus.). 250p. Date not set. price not set (ISBN 0-521-23603-7). Cambridge U Pr.

Progress in Animal Biometeorology: The Effects of Weather & Climate on Animals; Vol 1 Period 1963-1973, 2 pts. H. D. Johnson. Incl. Pt. 1. Effects of Temperature on Animals: Including Effects of Humidity, Radiation & Wind. 624p. 1976. text ed. 115.00 (ISBN 90-265-0196-X); Effect of Light, High Actitude, Noise, Electric, Magnetic & Electro-Magnetic Fields, Ionization, Gravity & Air Pollutions on Animals. 322p. 1976. text ed. 57.00 (ISBN 90-265-0235-4). (Progress in Biometeorology). 1976 (Pub. by Swets Pub Serv Holland). Swets North Am.

Progress in Arms Control? Readings from Scientific American. Bruce M. Russett. LC 78-31864. (Illus.). 1979. text ed. 18.95x (ISBN 0-7167-1060-9); pap. text ed. 9.95x (ISBN 0-7167-1061-7). W H Freeman.

Progress in Behavior Modification, Vol. 10. Ed. by Michel Hersen et al. 1980. 27.00 (ISBN 0-12-535610-2); 35.00 (ISBN 0-12-535692-7); microfiche ed. 19.00 (ISBN 0-12-535693-5). Acad Pr.

Progress in Behavior Modification, Vol. 11. Ed. by Michel Hersen et al. 1981. write for info. (ISBN 0-12-535611-0); lib. bdg. write for info. (ISBN 0-12-535694-3); price not set microfiche (ISBN 0-12-535695-1). Acad Pr.

Progress in Behavior Therapy with Delinquents. Jerome S. Stumphauzer. (Illus.). 408p. 1979. 33.75 (ISBN 0-398-03733-7); pap. 25.50 (ISBN 0-398-03738-8). C C Thomas.

Progress in Biophysics & Molecular Biology, Vol. 34. D. Noble. 1979. 62.50 (ISBN 0-08-024858-6). Pergamon.

Progress in Biophysics & Molecular Biology, Vol. 35. Ed. by D. Noble & T. L. Blundell. (Illus.). 206p. 1981. 62.50 (ISBN 0-08-027122-7). Pergamon.

Progress in Boron Chemistry, 3 vols. Ed. by H. Steinberg & A. L. McCloskey. LC 64-13501. Vol. 1, 1964. 62.00 (ISBN 0-08-010619-6); Vol. 2, 1970. 62.00 (ISBN 0-08-013079-8); Vol. 3, 1970. 62.00 (ISBN 0-08-013080-1). Pergamon.

Progress in Botany, Vol. 41. Ed. by H. Ellenberg et al. (Illus.). 1980. 70.30 o.p. (ISBN 0-387-09769-4). Springer-Verlag.

Progress in Botany, Vol. 42. Ed. by H. Ellenberg. 430p. 1981. 56.00 (ISBN 0-387-10430-5). Springer-Verlag.

Progress in Botany: Vol. 40. Ed. by H. Ellenberg et al. (Illus.). 1979. 77.70 o.p. (ISBN 0-387-09074-6). Springer-Verlag.

Progress in Cardiology, Vol. 9. Ed. by Paul N. Yu & John F. Goodwin. LC 77-157474. (Illus.). 193p. 1980. text ed. 15.00 (ISBN 0-8121-0728-4). Lea & Febiger.

Progress in Ceramic Science. J. E. Burke. 1961-1964. Vol. 3. 1964. 62.00 (ISBN 0-08-010026-0); Vol. 4. 1966. 62.00 (ISBN 0-08-011842-9). Pergamon.

Progress in Chemical Fibrinolysis & Thrombolysis, Vol. 1. Ed. by John F. Davidson et al. LC 75-14335. 425p. 1975. 36.00 (ISBN 0-89004-036-2). Raven.

Progress in Chemical Fibrinolysis & Thrombolysis, Vol. 2. Ed. by John F. Davidson. LC 75-14335. 1976. 19.00 (ISBN 0-89004-136-9). Raven.

Progress in Chemical Fibrinolysis & Thrombolysis, Vol. 3. Ed. by John F. Davidson et al. LC 75-14335. 1978. 56.00 (ISBN 0-89004-137-7). Raven.

Progress in Clinical Enzymology. Ed. by David M. Goldberg & Mario Werner. LC 80-80965. (Illus.). 304p. 1980. 45.00 (ISBN 0-89352-091-8). Masson Pub.

Progress in Clinical Pathology, Vol. 8. Ed. by Mario Stefanini & Ellis Benson. (Serial Publication Ser.). 1981. write for info. (ISBN 0-8089-1310-7). Grune.

Progress in Communication Sciences, Vol. 2. Ed. by Melvin J. Voigt & Brenda Dervin. 400p. 1980. text ed. 32.50 (ISBN 0-89391-060-0). Ablex Pub.

Progress in Crystal Growth, Vol. 2, Complete. Ed. by P. Pamplin. (Illus.). 404p. 1980. 112.50 (ISBN 0-08-026040-3). Pergamon.

Progress in Crystal Growth & Characterization, Vol. 1. Ed. by Dennis Elwell & Brian Pamplin. (Illus.). 248p. 1980. 112.50 (ISBN 0-08-026013-6). Pergamon.

Progress in Crystal Growth & Characterization, Vol. 1. Ed. by Brian R. Pamplin. 1977. Pt. 1 1977. pap. text ed. 21.00 (ISBN 0-08-021663-3); Pt. 2 1978. pap. text ed. 23.00 (ISBN 0-08-023050-4); Pt. 3 1978. pap. text ed. 23.00 (ISBN 0-08-023051-2); Pt. 4. pap. text ed. 17.75 (ISBN 0-08-023083-0). Pergamon.

Progress in Cybernetics & Systems Research, 5 vols. Ed. by Robert Trappl et al. Incl. Vol. 1. General Systems, Engineering Systems, Biocybernetics & Neural Systems. 24.50 (ISBN 0-470-88475-4); Vol. 2. Socio-Economic Systems, Cognition & Learning, Systems Education, Organization & Management. 24.50 (ISBN 0-470-88476-2); Vol. 3. General Systems Methodology, Fuzzy Mathematics & Fuzzy Systems, Biocybernetics & Theoretical Neurobiology. 40.00 (ISBN 0-470-26371-7); Vol. 4. Cybernetics of Cognition & Learning, Structure & Dynamics of Socioeconomic Systems, Health Care Systems, Engineering Systems Methodology. 40.00 (ISBN 0-470-99380-4); Vol. 5. Organization & Management, Organic Problem-Solving in Management System Approach in Urban & Regional Planning, Computer Performance, Control & Evaluation of Computer Linguistics. 50.00 (ISBN 0-470-26553-1). LC 75-6641. 1975-79. Halsted Pr.

Progress in Cybernetics & Systems Research, Vol. 6. Ed. by F. Pichler & R. Trappl. LC 75-6641. (Progress in Cybernetics & Systems Research Ser.). (Illus.). 500p. Date not set. text ed. 50.00 (ISBN 0-89116-194-5). Hemisphere Pub. Postponed.

Progress in Cybernetics & Systems Research, Vol. 7. F. Pichler & F. de P. Hanika. LC 75-6641. (Progress in Cybernetics & Systems Research Ser.). (Illus.). 393p. 1980. text ed. 50.00 (ISBN 0-89116-195-3). Hemisphere Pub.

Progress in Drug Abuse: Proceedings. Western Institute of Drug Problems Summer School, 3rd Annual & Paul H. Blachly. 336p. 1972. pap. 19.75 spiral o.p. (ISBN 0-398-02233-X). C C Thomas.

Progress in Drug Metabolism, Vols. 1-4. Ed. by J. W. Bridges & L. F. Chasseaud. Incl. Vol. 1. 1977. 46.00 (ISBN 0-471-10370-5); Vol. 2. 1977. 48.50 (ISBN 0-471-99442-1); Vol. 3. LC 75-19446. 1979. 52.95 (ISBN 0-471-99711-0); Vol. 4. LC 79-42723. 304p. 1980. 72.00 (ISBN 0-471-27702-9). Pub. by Wiley-Interscience). Wiley.

Progress in Drug Metabolism, Vol. 5. J. W. Bridges & L. F. Chasseaud. LC 80-40128. 384p. 1980. 72.00 (ISBN 0-471-27776-2, Pub. by Wiley-Interscience). Wiley.

Progress in Earthquake Prediction Research, Vol. 2. Vogel. 1980. write for info. (ISBN 0-9940013-4-7, Pub. by Vieweg & Sohn Germany). Heyden.

Progress in Energy & Combustion Science, Vol. 4. N. A. Chigier. 224p. 1980. 112.50 (ISBN 0-08-024257-X). Pergamon.

Progress in Energy & Combustion Science, Vol. 6, Pt. 2. Ed. by N. A. Chigier. 102p. 1980. pap. 24.50 (ISBN 0-08-026059-4). Pergamon.

Progress in Enzyme & Ion-Selective Electrodes. Ed. by D. W. Luebbers. (Illus.). 240p. 1981. pap. 34.30 (ISBN 0-387-10499-2). Springer-Verlag.

Progress in Experimental Personality Research. Ed. by B. Maher. Incl. Vol. 1. 1964. 32.50 (ISBN 0-12-541401-3); Vol. 2. 1965. 32.50 (ISBN 0-12-541402-1); Vol. 3. 1966. 32.50 (ISBN 0-12-541403-X); Vol. 4. 1968. 32.50 (ISBN 0-12-541404-8); Vol. 5. 1970. 32.50 (ISBN 0-12-541405-6); Vol. 6. 1972. 32.50 (ISBN 0-12-541406-4); Vol. 7. 1974. 32.50 (ISBN 0-12-541407-2). Acad Pr.

Progress in Flavour Research. Ed. by D. G. Land & H. E. Nursten. (Illus.). 1979. 57.00x (ISBN 0-85334-818-9). Intl Ideas.

Progress in Food & Nutrition Science, Vol. 2, No. 11-12. H. M. Sinclair. LC 75-7734. (Illus.). 70p. 1979. pap. 23.00 (ISBN 0-08-023758-4). Pergamon.

Progress in Glomerulonephritis. P. Kincaid-Smith et al. (Perspectives in Nephrology & Hypertension Ser.). 1979. 55.00 (ISBN 0-471-04424-5, Pub. by Wiley Med). Wiley.

Progress in High Temperature Physics & Chemistry, 5 vols. Ed. by C. A. Rouse. 1967-1973. Vols. 1 & 5. 62.00 ea.; Vol. 2-4. 58.00 ea. Vol. 1, 1967 (ISBN 0-08-012123-3). Vol. 2, 1968 (ISBN 0-08-012640-5). Vol. 3. 1969 (ISBN 0-08-013959-0). Vol. 4. 1971 (ISBN 0-08-016439-0). Vol. 5. 1973 (ISBN 0-08-017240-7). Pergamon.

Progress in Historical Geography. Ed. by Alan R. Baker. LC 72-75031. (Studies in Historical Geography). 1972. 15.95 (ISBN 0-471-04550-0). Halsted Pr.

Progress in Hormone Biochemistry & Pharmacology, Vol. 1. Ed. by Michael Briggs & Alan Corbin. (Endocrinology Ser.). (Illus.). 300p. 1980. 34.95 (ISBN 0-88831-076-5). Eden Med Res.

Progress in Human Biometeorology: The Effect of Weather & Climate on Man & His Living Environment, Period 1963 to 1970-75, Vol. 1. Solco W. Tromp. Incl. Pt. 1. Micro & Macroenvironments in the Atmosphere & Their Effects on Basic Physiological Mechanisms of Man. 726p. 1974. pap. text ed. 144.00 (ISBN 90-265-0167-6); Pt. 2. Pathological Biometeorology. 444p. 1977. pap. text ed. 86.50 (ISBN 90-265-0245-1); Pt. 3. Biometeorological Aspects of Plants, Trees & Animals in Human Life. 158p. 1972. pap. text ed. 31.50 (ISBN 90-265-0156-0). (Progress in Biometeorology Ser., Pub. by Swets Pub Serv Holland). Swets North Am.

Progress in Human Nutrition, Vol. 2. Ed. by Sheldon Margen. (Illus.). 1978. text ed. 23.50 (ISBN 0-87055-255-4). AVI.

Progress in Industrial Microbiology, Vol. 15. Ed. by M. J. Bull. 1979. 63.00 (ISBN 0-444-41815-6, North Holland). Elsevier.

Progress in Inorganic Chemistry. Stephen J. Lippard. LC 59-13035. (Progress in Inorganic Chemistry Ser.). Vol. 26, 1979. 38.50 (ISBN 0-471-04944-1, Pub. by Wiley-Interscience); Vol. 28, 1980. 54.00 (ISBN 0-471-08310-0). Wiley.

Progress in Inorganic Chemistry. Ed. by Stephen J. Lippard. (Progress in Inorganic Chemistry Ser.). Vol. 12, 1970. 38.50 o.p. (ISBN 0-471-54082-X); Vol. 15, 1972. 32.50 o.p. (ISBN 0-471-54085-4); Vol. 18, 1973. 45.50 o.p. (ISBN 0-471-54088-9); Vol. 20, 1976. 41.95 (ISBN 0-471-54090-0); Vol. 21, 1976. 33.50 (ISBN 0-471-54091-9); Vol. 22, 1976. 38.50 (ISBN 0-471-54092-7); Vol. 23, 1977. 40.50 (ISBN 0-471-02186-5); Vol. 24, 1978. 41.50 (ISBN 0-471-03874-1); Vol. 25, 1979. 33.95 (ISBN 0-471-04943-3). Wiley.

Progress in Linguistic Historiography: Papers from the International Conference on the History of the Language Sciences. Ed. by E. F. Koerner. (Studies in the History of Linguistics: No. 20). 400p. 1980. text ed. 51.50x (ISBN 90-272-4501-0). Humanities.

Progress in Linguistics: A Collection of Papers. Ed. by Manfred Bierwisch & Karl E. Heidolph. LC 78-123127. (Janua Linguarum Ser.: No. 43). 1970. text ed. 48.25x (ISBN 90-2790-723-4). Mouton.

Progress in Lipid Research, Vol. 17. Ed. by R. T. Holman. 396p. 1980. 68.75 (ISBN 0-08-023797-5). Pergamon.

Progress in Macrocyclic Chemistry, Vol. 2. Reed M. Izatt & James J. Christensen. 300p. 1981. 35.00 (ISBN 0-471-05178-0, Pub. by Wiley-Interscience). Wiley.

Progress in Material Science, Vol. 24. Ed. by J. W. Christian et al. (Illus.). 346p. 1980. 85.00 (ISBN 0-08-027107-3). Pergamon.

Progress in Materials Science, Vol. 23. Ed. by B. Chalmers. 280p. 1980. 85.00 (ISBN 0-08-024846-2). Pergamon.

Progress in Medical Genetics, Vol. 4. Ed. by Authur G. Steinberg et al. (Genetics of Gastrointestinal Disease Ser.). (Illus.). 320p. 1980. text ed. 39.50 (ISBN 0-7216-8604-4). Saunders.

Progress in Medical Terminology. Ed. by A. Manuila. (Illus.). vi, 118p. 1981. pap. 30.00 (ISBN 3-8055-2112-X). S Karger.

Progress in Medical Virology, Vol. 26. Ed. by J. L. Melnick. (Illus.). viii, 240p. 1980. 89.95 (ISBN 3-8055-0702-X). S Karger.

Progress in Mental Health Information Systems: Computer Applications. Ed. by Jeffrey L. Crawford et al. LC 73-17348. 384p. 1974. text ed. 25.00 o.p. (ISBN 0-88410-109-6). Ballinger Pub.

Progress in Molecular & Subcellular Biology, Vol. 7. Ed. by F. E. Hahn et al. (Illus.). 260p. 1980. 50.80 (ISBN 0-387-10150-0). Springer-Verlag.

Progress in Multiple Sclerosis: Research & Treatment. Ed. by Uri Leibowitz. 1973. 33.00 (ISBN 0-12-441350-1). Acad Pr.

Progress in Multiple Sclerosis Research. Ed. by H. J. Bauer. (Illus.). 630p. 1980. 46.60 (ISBN 0-387-09867-4). Springer-Verlag.

Progress in Neurobiology, Vol. 11. Ed. by G. A. Kerkut & J. W. Phillis. 1979. 103.00 (ISBN 0-08-024857-8). Pergamon.

Progress in Neurobiology, Vol. 12. G. A. Kerkut. (Illus.). 312p. 1980. pap. 103.00 (ISBN 0-08-024888-8). Pergamon.

Progress in Neurobiology, Vol. 13, Complete. Ed. by G. A. Kerkut. (Illus.). 440p. 1980. pap. 103.00 (ISBN 0-08-026039-X). Pergamon.

Progress in Neuropathology, Vol. IV. Ed. by Harry Zimmerman. (Vol 4). 1979. 41.00 (ISBN 0-89004-388-4). Raven.

Progress in NMR Spectroscopy, Vol. 12. J. W. Emsley. 288p. 1980. 87.50 (ISBN 0-08-024874-8). Pergamon.

Progress in NMR Spectroscopy: Vol. 11 Complete. Ed. by J. W. Emsley & L. H. Sutcliffe. LC 66-17931. 282p. 1978. 87.50 (ISBN 0-08-020325-6). Pergamon.

Progress in Nuclear Energy, 3 vols. Ed. by M. M. R. Williams. (Illus.). 252p. 1979. Set. 97.00 (ISBN 0-08-024875-6). Pergamon.

Progress in Nuclear Energy, Series 3. C. E. Stevenson et al. 1970. 97.00 (ISBN 0-08-013401-7). Pergamon.

Progress in Nuclear Energy, Vol. 3, No. 2. Ed. by M. M. Williams. (Illus.). 92p. 1979. pap. 39.00 (ISBN 0-08-024253-7). Pergamon.

Progress in Nuclear Energy, Vol. 3, No. 3. Ed. by M. M. Williams. 96p. 1979. pap. 39.00 (ISBN 0-08-024844-6). Pergamon.

Progress in Nuclear Energy: New Series. Ed. by M. M. Williams & R. Sher. (Illus.). 1977. Vol. 1, No. 1. pap. text ed. 27.00 (ISBN 0-08-022118-1); Vol. 1, Nos. 2-4. pap. text ed. o.p. (ISBN 0-685-81147-6); Vol. 2, No. 1. pap. text ed. 27.00 (ISBN 0-08-022710-4). Pergamon.

Progress in Nuclear Energy: The Role of the Boltzmann Transport Equation in Radiation Damage Calculations, Vol. 3, No. 1. M. M. Williams. LC 77-25743. (Progress in Nuclear Energy Ser.). (Illus.). 66p. 1979. pap. 39.00 (ISBN 0-08-024243-X). Pergamon.

Progress in Nuclear Physics, Vols. 2 & 5-9. Ed. by O. R. Frisch. Vol. 2. 1952. 81.00 (ISBN 0-08-013329-0); Vol. 5. 1956. 81.00 (ISBN 0-08-009043-5); Vol. 6. 1957. 81.00 (ISBN 0-08-009066-4); Vol. 7. 1959. 81.00 (ISBN 0-08-009186-5); Vol. 8. 1960. 81.00 (ISBN 0-08-009479-1); Vol. 9. 1963. 81.00 (ISBN 0-08-010063-5). Pergamon.

Progress in Nucleic Acid Research & Molecular Biology, Vol. 24. Ed. by Waldo E. Cohn. 1980. 32.50 (ISBN 0-12-540024-1); lib. ed. 42.50 (ISBN 0-12-540092-6); microfiche ed. 22.50 (ISBN 0-12-540093-4). Acad Pr.

Progress in Nucleic Acid Research & Molecular Biology, Vol. 25. Ed. by Waldo E. Cohn. (Serial Publication). 1981. 29.50 (ISBN 0-12-540025-X); lib. bdg. 38.50 (ISBN 0-12-540094-2); microfiche ed. 20.00 (ISBN 0-12-540095-0). Acad Pr.

Progress in Nucleic Acid Research & Molecular Biology: An International Series. Ed. by J. N. Davidson et al. Incl. Vol. 3. 1964. 48.00 (ISBN 0-12-540003-9); Vol. 4. 1965. 48.00 (ISBN 0-12-540004-7); Vol. 5. 1966. 48.00 (ISBN 0-12-540005-5); Vol. 6. 1967. 48.00 (ISBN 0-12-540006-3); Vol. 7. 1967. 48.00 (ISBN 0-12-540007-1); Vol. 8. 1968. 48.00 (ISBN 0-12-540008-X); Vol. 9. 1969. 48.00 (ISBN 0-12-540009-8); Vol. 10. 1970. 41.00 (ISBN 0-12-540010-1); Vol. 11. 1970. 51.00 (ISBN 0-12-540011-X); Vol. 12. 1972. 40.00 (ISBN 0-12-540012-8); Vol. 13. 1973. 44.50 (ISBN 0-12-540013-6); Vol. 20. 1977. 39.00 (ISBN 0-12-540020-9); lib. ed. 55.50 (ISBN 0-12-540084-5); microfiche 27.50 (ISBN 0-12-540085-3); Vol. 21. 1978. 28.00 (ISBN 0-12-540021-7); lib. ed. 35.00 (ISBN 0-12-540086-1); microfiche o. s. i. 21.00 (ISBN 0-12-540087-X); Vol. 22. 1979. 40.00 (ISBN 0-12-540022-5); lib ed. o. s. i. 54.50 (ISBN 0-12-540088-8); microfiche 29.00 (ISBN 0-12-540089-6). Acad Pr.

Progress in Nucleic Acid Research & Molecular Biology: DNA: Multiprotein Interactions, Vol. 26. Ed. by Waldo E. Cohn. (Serial Publication Ser.). 1981. write for info. (ISBN 0-12-540026-8); lib. ed. (ISBN 0-12-540095-0); microfiche ed. (ISBN 0-12-540096-9). Acad Pr.

Progress in Oceanography, Vols. 1 & 4-6. Ed. by M. Sears & Bruce Warren. LC 63-15353. text ed. 76.00 ea. Vol. 1 1963 (ISBN 0-08-010199-2). Vol. 4 1963 (ISBN 0-08-012124-1). Vol. 5 1968. (ISBN 0-08-012631-6). Vol. 6, 1974 (ISBN 0-08-017707-7). Pergamon.

Progress in Oceanography, Vol 7, Pt. 4: Observations of Rossby Waves Near Site D. R. O. Thompson. Ed. by Mary Swallow. LC 63-15353. 1977. pap. text ed. 8.75 (ISBN 0-685-86323-9). Pergamon.

Progress in Operations Research. R. L. Ackoff. LC 61-10415. (Operations Research Ser.: Vol. 1). 1961. 35.95 (ISBN 0-471-00330-1, Pub by Wiley-Interscience). Wiley.

Progress in Optical Communication. Ed. by P. J. Clarricoats. 1980. Repr. soft cover 35.00 (ISBN 0-906048-32-X). Inst Elect Eng.

Progress in Parasitology. P. C. Garnham. 1971. text ed. 12.50x (ISBN 0-485-26321-1, Athlone Pr). Humanities.

Progress in Particle & Nuclear Physics, Vol. 3. Ed. by Denys Wilkinson. 1980. 81.00 (ISBN 0-08-025020-3). Pergamon.

Progress in Particle & Nuclear Physics, Vol. 4. Ed. by Denys Wilkinson. (Illus.). 600p. 1980. 81.00 (ISBN 0-08-025039-4). Pergamon.

Progress in Penal Reform. Ed. by Louis Blom-Cooper. 296p. 1975. 36.00x (ISBN 0-19-825325-7). Oxford U Pr.

Progress in Pesticide Biochemistry, Vol. 1. D. H. Hutson & T. R. Roberts. 360p. 1981. 71.95 (ISBN 0-471-27920-X, Pub. by Wiley-Interscience). Wiley.

Progress in Physical Organic Chemistry, Vol. 12. Ed. by Robert W. Taft. LC 63-19364. 1976. 47.50 (ISBN 0-471-01738-8, Pub. by Wiley-Interscience). Wiley.

Progress in Phytochemistry, Vol. 6. Ed. by L. Reinhold et al. LC 68-24347. (Illus.). 1980. 87.50 (ISBN 0-08-024946-9). Pergamon.

Progress in Phytochemistry, Vol. 7. L. Reinhold et al. LC 68-24347. (Illus.). 410p. 1981. 87.50 (ISBN 0-08-026362-3). Pergamon.

Progress in Planning, Vol. 7. Ed. by D. R. Diamond & J. B. McLoughlin. (Illus.). 1979. 50.00 (ISBN 0-08-020333-7). Pergamon.

Progress in Planning, Vol. 9. Ed. by D. R. Diamond & J. B. McLoughlin. 300p. 1979. 50.00 (ISBN 0-08-025221-4). Pergamon.

Progress in Planning, Vol. 10. Ed. by D. R. Diamond & J. B. McLoughlin. (Illus.). 247p. 42.00 (ISBN 0-08-025788-7). Pergamon.

Progress in Planning, Vol. 11. Ed. by D. R. Diamond & J. B. McLoughlin. (Illus.). 280p. 1980. 50.00 (ISBN 0-08-025802-6). Pergamon.

Progress in Planning, Vol. 12. Ed. by D. R. Diamond & J. B. McLoughlin. 224p. 1980. 47.00 (ISBN 0-08-026100-0). Pergamon.

Progress in Policing: Essays on Change. Police Foundation. Ed. by Richard A. Staufenberger. 1980. prof. reference 19.50 (ISBN 0-88410-843-0). Ballinger Pub.

Progress in Polymer Science, Vol. 6. Ed. by V. Stannett & A. D. Jenkins. (Illus.). 266p. 1981. 35.00 (ISBN 0-08-020335-3). Pergamon.

Progress in Polymer Science, Japan, Vol. 5. Ed. by K. Imahori & S. Murahashi. LC 72-5794. 308p. 1973. 22.95 (ISBN 0-470-42661-6). Halsted Pr.

Progress in Polymer Science, Japan, Vol. 8. Ed. by K. Imahori & T. Higashimura. LC 72-7446. 244p. 1975. 38.95 (ISBN 0-470-65727-8). Halsted Pr.

Progress in Polymer Science, Japan, Vol. 7. Ed. by T. Otsu & M. Takayanagi. (Ser. of Progress in Polymer Science in Japan). 1974. 39.95 (ISBN 0-470-65725-1). Halsted Pr.

Progress in Powder Metallurgy: Proceedings, Vols. 34 & 35. National Powder Metallurgy Conferenes, Los Angeles & Cincinnati, 1978 & 1979. Ed. by W. Cebulak et al. (Illus., Orig.). 1980. pap. text ed. 56.00 (ISBN 0-918404-49-5). Metal Powder.

Progress in Protozoology. Ed. by J. Ludvik. (Illus.). 1964. 62.50 (ISBN 0-12-459450-6). Acad Pr.

Progress in Psychobiology & Physiological Psychology, Vol. 8. Ed. by James Sprague & Alan Epstein. LC 66-29640. 1979. 38.00 (ISBN 0-12-542108-7); lib. ed. 49.50 (ISBN 0-12-542178-8); microfiche 30.50 (ISBN 0-12-542179-6). Acad Pr.

Progress in Psychobiology & Physiological Psychology, Vol. 9. Ed. by James M. Sprague & Alan N. Epstein. 1980. 37.50 (ISBN 0-12-542109-5); lib. ed. 48.50 (ISBN 0-12-542180-X); microfiche 26.50 (ISBN 0-12-542181-8). Acad Pr.

Progress in Psychobiology: Readings from Scientific American. Intro. by Richard F. Thompson. LC 75-42362. (Illus.). 1976. text ed. 19.95x (ISBN 0-7167-0532-X); pap. text ed. 9.95x (ISBN 0-7167-0531-1). W H Freeman.

Progress in Reaction Kinetics: Vol. 9 Complete. Ed. by K. R. Jennings & R. B. Cundall. 368p. 1980. 76.00 (ISBN 0-08-020343-4). Pergamon.

Progress in Refrigeration Science & Technology, 4 vols. 1980. pap. 275.00 (ISBN 0-686-68835-X, IIR67, IIR). Unipub.

Progress in Refrigeration Science & Technology, 11th Conference, 3 Vols. International Institute of Refrigeration. 1965. Set. 180.00 (ISBN 0-08-011439-3). Pergamon.

Progress in Rehabilitation: A Review of Three Studies. M. L. Bowden et al. Ed. by C. Jones. LC 80-83417. (Illus.). 1981. 35.00 (ISBN 0-917478-35-5). Natl Inst Burn.

Progress in Resource Management & Environmental Planning. Timothy O'Riordan et al. LC 79-41729. Vol. 1, 1979. 44.50 (ISBN 0-471-27747-9, Pub. by Wiley-Interscience); Vol. 2, 1980, 272p. 49.00 (ISBN 0-471-27747-9). Wiley.

Progress in Solid State Chemistry, Vols. 1, 3 & 5-7. Ed. by H. Reiss et al. Vol. 1, 1964. text ed. 81.00 (ISBN 0-08-010246-8). Vol. 3. 1967. text ed. 81.00 (ISBN 0-08-011886-0). Vol. 5. 1971. text ed. 81.00 (ISBN 0-08-015846-3); Vol. 6. 1971. text ed. 81.00 (ISBN 0-08-016723-3); Vol. 7. 1972. text ed. 81.00 (ISBN 0-08-016916-3). Pergamon.

Progress in Solid State Chemistry, Vol. 12. Ed. by G. M. Rosenblatt. (Illus.). 332p. 1980. 81.00 (ISBN 0-08-022846-1). Pergamon.

Progress in Spanish: Grammar & Practice for the Second Year. 2nd ed. Ruth K. Crispin & John Crispin. 1978. 13.95x (ISBN 0-673-15147-6). Scott F.

Progress in Surgical Pathology, Vol. III. Fenoglio. 1981. 54.50 (ISBN 0-89352-122-1). Masson Pub.

Progress in Surgical Pathology, Vol. 1. Ed. by Cecilia M. Fenoglio & Marianne Wolff. LC 80-80334. (Illus.). 296p. 1980. 54.50 (ISBN 0-89352-087-X). Masson Pub.

Progress in Surgical Pathology, Vol. 2. Ed. by Cecilia M. Fenoglio & Marianne Wolff. LC 80-80334. (Illus.). 304p. 1980. 54.50 (ISBN 0-89352-090-X). Masson Pub.

Progress in the Chemistry of Organic Natural Products, Vols. 21-31. Ed. by W. Herz et al. Incl. Vol. 21. 1963. 56.70 (ISBN 0-387-80638-5); Vol. 22. 1964. 67.30 (ISBN 0-387-80678-4); Vol. 23. 1965. 70.30 (ISBN 0-387-80716-0); Vol. 24. 1966. 83.80 (ISBN 0-387-80757-8); Vol. 25. 1967. 57.90 (ISBN 0-387-80811-6); Vol. 26. 1968. 93.30 (ISBN 0-387-80864-7); Vol. 27. 1969. 83.80 (ISBN 0-387-80909-0); Vol. 28. 1970. 91.50 (ISBN 0-387-80975-9); Vol. 29. 1972. 106.80 (ISBN 0-387-81024-2); Vol. 30. 1973. 132.80 (ISBN 0-387-81062-5); Vol. 31. 1974. 136.30 (ISBN 0-387-81172-9). Springer-Verlag.

Progress in the Chemistry of Organic Natural Products, Vol. 38. Ed. by W. Herz et al. (Illus.). 450p. 1980. 115.10 (ISBN 0-387-81529-5). Springer-Verlag.

Progress in the Treatment of Parkinsonism. Ed. by D. B. Calne. LC 72-93317. (Advances in Neurology Ser.: Vol. 3). (Illus.). 340p. 1973. 31.50 (ISBN 0-911216-49-9). Raven.

Progress of Doctrine in the New Testament. Thomas Bernard. 1978. 9.00 (ISBN 0-686-12959-8). Klock & Klock.

Progress of Management: Process & Behavior in a Changing Environment. 3rd ed. Jerome E. Schnee et al. (Illus.). 1977. pap. text ed. 12.95 (ISBN 0-13-730622-9). P-H.

Progress of the World: In Arts, Agriculture, Century. Michael G. Mulhall. (Development of Industrial Society Ser.). 569p. 1980. Repr. 50.00x (ISBN 0-7165-1584-9, Pub. by Irish Academic Pr). Biblio Dist.

Progress Tests for the Developmentally Disabled: An Evaluation. John Doucette & Ruth Freedman. LC 79-55773. 1979. text ed. 27.50 (ISBN 0-89011-539-7). Abt Assoc.

Progress, War & Reaction: 1900-1933. Ed. by David R. Ross et al. LC 78-101951. (Structure of American History Ser: Vol. 5). 1970. pap. 4.95x (ISBN 0-88295-759-7). AHM Pub.

Progressed Horoscope. Alan Leo. 1978. pap. 6.95 (ISBN 0-685-62087-5). Weiser.

Progressions in Climbing. Chip Lee. (Illus.). 250p. 1981. pap. price not set (ISBN 0-910146-35-7). Appalach Mtn.

Progressive Audio-Lingual Drills in English. Francine Stieglitz. (gr. 9-12). 1970. pap. 4.50 (ISBN 0-88345-125-5); cassettes 125.00 (ISBN 0-685-65047-2). Regents Pub.

Progressive Cantonese Reader. Chiang. pap. 2.50x o.s.i. (ISBN 0-686-12049-3). Colton Bk.

Progressive Class Piano. Elmer Heerema. LC 79-25220. 1980. pap. 11.50 (ISBN 0-88284-106-8). Alfred Pub.

Progressive Dressage. Andre Jousseaume. Tr. by Jeanette Vigneron from Fr. pap. 8.75 (ISBN 0-85131-231-4). J A Allen.

Progressive Education: From Arcady to Academe: A History of the Progressive Education Association: 1919-1955. Patricia A. Graham. LC 67-26480. (Teachers College Studies in Education Ser.). 1967. text ed. 10.25x (ISBN 0-8077-1452-6). Tchrs Coll.

Progressive English Dictionary. 2nd ed. Ed. by A. S. Hornby & E. C. Parnwell. 352p. 1972. pap. 2.50x (ISBN 0-19-431120-1). Oxford U Pr.

Progressive Era & the Great War: 1896-1920. 2nd ed. Compiled by William M. Leary, Jr. & Arthur S. Link. LC 78-70030. (Goldentree Bibliographies in American History). 1978. pap. text ed. 12.95x (ISBN 0-88295-575-6). AHM Pub.

Progressive Era, 1901-1917. Ernest R. May. LC 63-8572. (Life History of the United States). (Illus.). (gr. 5 up). 1974. PLB 9.96 (ISBN 0-8094-0558-X, Pub. by Time-Life). Silver.

Progressive Exercises in Physics to Ordinary Level. 3rd ed. O. Wilson. 1971. pap. text ed. 3.95x o.p. (ISBN 0-435-67937-6). Heinemann Ed.

Progressive Farmer Country Living Recipes: 1980. Ed. by Progressive Farmer Food Staff & Ann Harvey. (Illus.). 128p. 1981. 9.95 (ISBN 0-8487-0514-9). Oxmoor Hse.

Progressive Grocer's Marketing Guidebook. Ed. by Lucy Tarzian. LC 68-126162. 1980. 149.00 (ISBN 0-911790-19-5). Prog Grocer.

Progressive Grocer's Marketing Guidebook. Ed. by Lucy Tarzian. LC 68-126162. 1981. 159.00 (ISBN 0-911790-20-9). Prog Grocer.

Progressive Historians. Richard Hofstadter. LC 68-23944. 1970. pap. 3.95 (ISBN 0-394-70591-2, Vin). Random.

Progressive Party in Canada. W. L. Morton. (Scholarly Reprint Ser.). 1980. Repr. 35.00x (ISBN 0-8020-7096-5). U of Toronto Pr.

Progressive Picture Compositions. Donn Byrne. 1975. pap. text ed. 2.00x (ISBN 0-582-52126-2); teacher's bk 3.00x (ISBN 0-582-52127-0); pictures-4 sets 28.00x (ISBN 0-582-52128-9). Longman.

Progressive Practice in Dentistry. E. Samson. 1956. 7.50 o.p. (ISBN 0-8022-1475-4). Philos Lib.

Progressive Reform: A Guide to Information Sources. Ed. by John D. Buenker & Nicholas C. Burckel. (American Government & History Information Guide Ser.: Vol. 8). 300p. 1981. 30.00 (ISBN 0-8103-1485-1). Gale.

Progressive Vitality & Dynamic Posture. D. Lawson-Wood & J. Lawson-Wood. 88p. 1977. 12.00x (ISBN 0-8464-1043-5). Beekman Pubs.

Progressive Weight Training. Jack R. Leighton. (Illus.). 1961. 14.95 (ISBN 0-8260-5375-0). Wiley.

Progressive Years: America Comes of Age. William O'Neill. LC 74-26163. 1975. 5.95 (ISBN 0-396-07197-X). Dodd.

Progressives. Ed. by Carl Resek. (Orig.). 1967. pap. 7.50 (ISBN 0-672-60084-6, AHSJ4). Bobbs.

Progressives & Prohibitionists: Texas Democrats in the Wilson Era. Lewis L. Gould. (Illus.). 380p. 1973. 17.95x (ISBN 0-292-76407-3); pap. 8.95x (ISBN 0-292-76428-6). U of Tex Pr.

Progressivism & Economic Growth: The Wisconsin Income Tax, 1911-1929. W. Elliot Brownlee, Jr. LC 74-80065. 1974. 13.50 (ISBN 0-8046-9091-X, Natl U). Kennikat.

Prohibition & Politics: Turbulent Decades in Tennessee, 1885-1920. Paul E. Isaac. LC 65-17347. 1965. 14.50x (ISBN 0-87049-059-1). U of Tenn Pr.

Prohibition: The Life of the Land. Sean D. Cashman. LC 80-1853. (Illus.). 1981. 15.95 (ISBN 0-02-905730-2). Free Pr.

Project Apollo: Man to the Moon. Tom Alexander. LC 63-17719. (Illus.). 1964. 8.95 o.p. (ISBN 0-06-000120-8, HarpT). Har-Row.

Project Appraisal & Policy Review. Timothy O'Riordan & W. R. Sewell. (Studies in Environmental Management & Resource Development). 320p. 1981. 35.75 (ISBN 0-471-27853-X, Pub. by Wiley-Interscience). Wiley.

Project Control by Critical Pathanalysis: A Basic Guide of CPA. C. W. Lowe. 258p. 1978. text ed. 30.75x (ISBN 0-220-67012-9, Pub. by Busn Bks England). Renouf.

Project Design & Recommendations for Watershed Reforestation & Fuelwood Development in Sri Lanka. William H. Bollinger et al. (Illus.). 122p. 1979. pap. 15.00 (ISBN 0-936130-03-2). Intl Sci Tech.

Project Engineering of Process Plants. H. F. Rase & M. H. Barrow. 1957. 39.00 (ISBN 0-471-70917-4, Pub. by Wiley-Interscience). Wiley.

Project Evaluation Methodologies & Techniques. (Illus.). 1978. pap. 9.25 (ISBN 92-3-101456-0, U845, UNESCO). Unipub.

Project Feasibility Analysis: A Guide to Profitable New Ventures. David S. Clifton, Jr. & David E. Fyffe. LC 76-51321. 1977. text ed. 26.95 (ISBN 0-471-01611-X, Pub. by Wiley-Interscience). Wiley.

Project Identification: The First Scientific Field Study of UFO Phenomena. Harley D. Rutledge. (Illus.). 1981. 12.95 (ISBN 0-13-730713-6); pap. 7.95 (ISBN 0-13-730705-5). P-H.

Project Independence Blueprint: Final Task Force Report, Solar Energy. Federal Energy Administration. 564p. Repr. of 1974 ed. 49.50 (ISBN 0-89934-062-8, V954-PP). Solar Energy Info.

Project Management: New Conceptions & Approaches, Proceedings. International Expert Seminar of the International Management Association. (Eng. & Ger.). 1979. pap. 25.00 o.p. (ISBN 0-89192-288-1, Pub. by Gottlieb Duttweiler Inst). Interbk Inc.

Project Manpower Management: Management Process in Construction Practice. S. D. Anderson & R. W. Woodhead. LC 80-22090. 350p. 1981. 32.95 (ISBN 0-471-95979-0, Pub. by Wiley-Interscience). Wiley.

Project Planning & Management: An Integrated Approach. Ed. by Louis J. Goodman & Ralph N. Love. LC 79-25990. (Pergamon Policy Studies). 312p. 1980. 33.00 (ISBN 0-08-024667-2); pap. 11.95 (ISBN 0-08-025962-6). Pergamon.

Project Planning by Network Techniques, Third International Congress, 3 vols. M. Ogander. LC 72-4802. 1972. Set. 94.95 (ISBN 0-470-65280-2). Halsted Pr.

Project Planning for Developing Economies. W. W. Shaner. LC 79-13225. (Praeger Special Studies Ser.). 256p. 1979. 25.95 (ISBN 0-03-051126-7). Praeger.

Project Sunlight. June Strong. LC 80-13011. (Orion Ser.). 1980. pap. 2.95 (ISBN 0-8127-0289-1). Southern Pub.

Project Technology Briefs. British Schools Council. (Project Technology Ser.). 1975. pap. text ed. 16.25x (ISBN 0-435-75898-5). Heinemann Ed.

Project Technology Handbook, Book 14: Simple Computer & Control Logic. Schools Council. (gr. 12). 1974. pap. text ed. 5.25x (ISBN 0-435-75913-2). Heinemann Ed.

Project Theory: Interpretations & Policy Relevance. Jack E. Vincent. LC 78-59172. 1978. pap. text ed. 11.25 (ISBN 0-8191-0551-1). U Pr of Amer.

Project Water Horse. Tim Dinsdale. (Illus.). 1975. 16.95 (ISBN 0-7100-8029-8); pap. 7.95 (ISBN 0-7100-8030-1). Routledge & Kegan.

Project Web. Barbara Rogers. LC 79-25673. 256p. 1980. 8.95 (ISBN 0-396-07795-1). Dodd.

Project Whirlwind: The History of a Pioneer Computer. Kent C. Redmond & Thomas M. Smith. (History of Computing Ser.). (Illus.). 1980. 21.00 (ISBN 0-932376-09-6). Digital Pr.

Project: You, a Manual of Rational Assertiveness Training. Claudine Paris & Bill Casey. LC 78-66974. 1974. 5.95 (ISBN 0-686-23447-2). Bridges Pr.

Projected Arab Court of Justice: A Study in Regional Jurisdiction with Specific Reference to the Muslim Law of Nations. Ezzeldin Foda. LC 79-2858. 258p. 1981. Repr. of 1957 ed. 22.50 (ISBN 0-8305-0031-6). Hyperion Conn.

Projected Pulp & Paper Mills in the World 1979-1989. 132p. 1980. pap. 7.25 (ISBN 92-5-100913-9, F1938, FAO). Unipub.

Projected Pulp & Paper Mills in the World, 1978-1988. 1979. pap. 8.50 (ISBN 92-5-100760-8, F1623, FAO). Unipub.

Projectile-Throwing Engines of the Ancients & Turkish & Other Oriental Bows of Mediaeval & Later Times. Ralph Payne-Gallwey. (Illus.). 70p. 1973. Repr. of 1907 ed. 12.50x o.p. (ISBN 0-87471-144-4). Rowman.

Projecting State & Local Populations. Donald B. Pittenger. LC 75-38694. 144p. 1975. 17.50 o.p. (ISBN 0-88410-356-0). Ballinger Pub.

Projection-Iterative Methods for Solution of Operator Equations. N. S. Kurpel. Ed. by R. G. Douglas. Tr. by Israel Program for Scientific Translations. LC 76-17114. (Translations of Mathematical Monographs). 1976. 24.80 (ISBN 0-8218-1596-2, MMONO-46). Am Math.

Projective Geometry & Algebraic Structures. R. J. Mihalek. 1972. text ed. 18.95 (ISBN 0-12-495550-9). Acad Pr.

Projective Geometry & Projective Metrics. Herbert Busemann & Paul J. Kelly. (Pure and Applied Mathematics Ser.: Vol. 3). 1953. 36.50 o.s.i. (ISBN 0-12-148356-8). Acad Pr.

Projective Geometry of N Dimensions. Otto Schreier & Emanuel Sperner. 11.95 (ISBN 0-8284-0126-8). Chelsea Pub.

Projective Planes. Frederick W. Stevenson. LC 72-156824. (Illus.). 1972. text ed. 26.95x (ISBN 0-7167-0443-9); teacher's manual avail. W H Freeman.

Projective Techniques & Cross-Cultural Research. Gardner Lindzey. LC 61-15951. (Century Psychology Ser.). 1976. 24.00x (ISBN 0-89197-361-3); pap. text ed. 10.95x (ISBN 0-89197-908-5). Irvington.

Projective Transformations. P. S. Modenov & A. S. Parkhomenko. 1966. 22.50 o.p. (ISBN 0-12-503102-5); pap. 9.00 o.p. (ISBN 0-12-503162-9). Acad Pr.

Projectometry. Johs. Sandven. 1975. text ed. 26.00 (ISBN 8-200-04844-6, Dist. by Columbia U Pr). Universitet.

Projects & Demonstrations in Astronomy. D. Tattersfield. LC 79-84264. 1979. 29.95x (ISBN 0-470-26715-1). Halsted Pr.

Projects for Preschoolers. Susan W. Allen & Karen H. Talbot. 72p. (Orig.). 1981. pap. 5.95 (ISBN 0-88290-161-3, 2048). Horizon Utah.

Projects for the Home. Ron Hildebrand. Ed. by Ortho Books Editorial Staff. LC 80-66343. (Illus.). 96p. (Orig.). 1981. pap. 4.95 (ISBN 0-917102-85-1, Ortho Bks). Chevron Chem.

Projects for the School Foundry. H. L. Pearson. (Illus.). 1970. 15.95x (ISBN 0-291-39673-9). Intl Ideas.

Projects in Biofeedback. George D. Fuller. (Orig.). 1980. pap. 9.95 (ISBN 0-686-27974-3). Biofeed Pr.

Projects in Electricity. Merle D. Collings. (gr. 9-12). 1941. pap. text ed. 5.00 (ISBN 0-685-04240-5). McKnight.

Projects in General Metalwork. M. J. Ruley. (gr. 9 up). 1969. text ed. 13.28 (ISBN 0-87345-135-X). McKnight.

Projects in History. Sheila Ferguson. 1970. 16.95 (ISBN 0-7134-2154-1, Pub. by Batsford England). David & Charles.

Projects in Oceanography. S. Simon. LC 75-190354. (Science at Work Ser). (gr. 5-8). 1972. 4.90 o.p. (ISBN 0-531-02580-2, C41). Watts.

Projects in Religious Education. Joan Tooke & Ken Russell. 1974. 16.95 (ISBN 0-7134-2840-6, Pub. by Batsford England). David & Charles.

Projects in Space Science. S. Simon. LC 70-171900. (Science at Work Ser). (gr. 5-8). 1971. 4.90 o.p. (ISBN 0-531-01997-7, O40). Watts.

Projects in Wood Furniture. rev. ed. J. Harvey Douglass. LC 67-21721. (Illus.). (gr. 7 up). 1967. text ed. 14.00 (ISBN 0-87345-027-2). McKnight.

Projects: Made in Philadelphia 4. Jeanne Silverthorne et al. LC 80-84522. (Illus.). 1979. pap. 4.00 (ISBN 0-88454-058-8). U of Pa Contemp Art.

Projects with Air. Seymour Simon. LC 74-26651. (Science at Work Ser.). (Illus.). 96p. (gr. 4-6). 1975. PLB 4.90 o.p. (ISBN 0-531-02807-0). Watts.

Projects with Plants. Seymour Simon. LC 73-5710. (Science at Work Ser). (Illus.). (gr. 4-6). 1973. PLB 4.90 o.p. (ISBN 0-531-02649-3). Watts.

Prolactin, Vol. 2. David F. Horrobin. (Annual Research Reviews Ser.). 1974. 19.20 (ISBN 0-85200-120-7). Eden Med Res.

Prolactin, Vol. 4. David F. Horrobin. (Annual Research Reviews Ser.). 1976. 24.00 (ISBN 0-904406-47-4). Eden Med Res.

Prolactin, Vol. 5. David F. Horrobin. LC 77-369577. (Annual Research Reviews Ser.). 1977. 24.00 (ISBN 0-88831-009-9). Eden Med Res.

Prolactin, Vol. 6. David F. Horrobin. (Annual Research Reviews Ser.). 1979. 21.60 (ISBN 0-88831-041-2). Eden Med Res.

Prolactin, Vol. 7. David F. Horrobin. LC 77-369577. (Annual Research Reviews Ser.). 126p. 1980. 18.00 (ISBN 0-88831-069-2). Eden Med Res.

Prolactin, Vol. 8. David F. Horrobin. (Annual Research Reviews Ser.). 152p. 1981. 24.00 (ISBN 0-88831-093-5). Eden Med Res.

Prolactin Responses to Neuroleptics. R. L. Oehman & R. A. Axelsson. (Journal of Neural Transmission Supplementum: Vol. 17). (Illus.). 75p. 1981. pap. 16.00 (ISBN 0-387-81605-4). Springer-Verlag.

Prolegomena for the Oxford Shakespeare: A Study in Editorial Method. R. B. McKerrow. 1939. 5.00x o.p. (ISBN 0-19-811685-3). Oxford U Pr.

Prolegomena to a Grammar of Basque. Terence Wilbur. (Current Issues in Linguistic Theory). 1980. text ed. 28.50x (ISBN 90-272-0909-X). Humanities.

Prolegomena to a Methodology: Reflections on Merleau-Ponty & Austin. David Fairchild. LC 78-58597. 1978. pap. text ed. 7.25 o.p. (ISBN 0-8191-0542-2). U Pr of Amer.

Prolegomena to a Theory of Language. rev. ed. Louis Hjelmslev. Tr. by Francis J. Whitfield. 1961. 15.00x (ISBN 0-299-02470-9). U of Wis Pr.

Prolegomena to All Future Metaeconomics. Paul F. Crosser. LC 72-13845. 240p. 1974. 10.00 (ISBN 0-87527-099-9). Fireside Bks.

Prolegomena to Any Future Metaphysics. rev. ed. Immanuel Kant. LC 51-10279. 1950. pap. 3.95 (ISBN 0-672-60187-7, LLA27). Bobbs.

Prolegomena to Servius 5-the Manuscripts. Charles E. Murgia. (Publications in Classical Studies: Vol. 2). 1975. pap. 14.50x (ISBN 0-520-09466-2). U of Cal Pr.

Prolegomena to the History of Ancient Israel. Julius Wellhausen. 9.00 (ISBN 0-8446-3147-7). Peter Smith.

Prolegomena to the Study of Greek Religion. Jane Harrison. 682p. 1981. text ed. 26.00x (ISBN 0-85036-262-8, Pub. by Merlin, England); pap. 13.25x. Humanities.

Prolegomenes D'ebn-Khaldoun, 3 vols. Quatremere. Arabic 40.00x (ISBN 0-685-77123-7). Intl Bk Ctr.

Proletarian Journey. Fred E. Beal. LC 70-146158. (Civil Liberties in American History Ser). 1971. Repr. of 1937 ed. lib. bdg. 39.50 (ISBN 0-306-70096-4). Da Capo.

Proletarian Revolution & the Renegade Kautsky. Vladimir I. Lenin. 1965. pap. 1.95 (ISBN 0-8351-0279-3). China Bks.

Proletarian Science: Marxism in Britain, 1917 to 1933. S. Macintyre. 1980. 27.50 (ISBN 0-521-50539-9). Cambridge U Pr.

Proletarian Writers of the Thirties. Ed. by David Madden. LC 78-16323. (Arcturus Books Paperbacks). 320p. 1979. pap. 8.95 (ISBN 0-8093-0895-9). S Ill U Pr.

Proliferation of Different Cell Types in the Brain. H. Korr. (Advances in Anatomy, Embryology & Cell Biology Ser.: Vol. 61). (Illus.). 80p. 1980. pap. 28.30 (ISBN 0-387-09899-2). Springer-Verlag.

Proliferation, Plutonium & Policy: Institutional & Technological Impediments to Nuclear Weapons Propogation. Alexander De Volpi. (Pergamon Policy Studies). (Illus.). 1979. 39.50 (ISBN 0-08-023872-6). Pergamon.

Prolific Pencil. Percy F. Rex. Ed. by Fredrika A. Burrows & Stephen W. Sullwold. LC 80-51482. (Illus.). 312p. 1980. 15.00 (ISBN 0-88492-037-2). W S Sullwold.

Prolific Tropical Sheep. (FAO Animal Production & Health Paper Ser.: No. 17). 124p. 1981. pap. 7.00 (ISBN 92-5-100845-0, F2107, FAO). Unipub.

Prologue to Conflict: The Crisis & Compromise of 1850. Holman Hamilton. LC 64-13999. 248p. 1964. 8.50x (ISBN 0-8131-1090-4). U Pr of Ky.

Prologue to Economic Understanding. Martin. 1966. pap. text ed. 4.95x (ISBN 0-675-09716-9). Merrill.

Prologue to Education. John N. Wales. 1979. 12.95 (ISBN 0-7100-0117-7). Routledge & Kegan.

Prologue to Independence: New Jersey in the Coming of the American Revolution. Larry R. Gerlach. 1976. 33.00 (ISBN 0-8135-0801-0). Rutgers U Pr.

Prologue to Love. Taylor Caldwell. 768p. 1980. pap. 2.95 (ISBN 0-553-14238-0). Bantam.

Prologue to Peron: Argentina in Depression & War, 1930-1943. Ed. by Mark Falcoff & Ronald Dolkart. LC 74-22961. 250p. 1976. 17.50x (ISBN 0-520-02874-0). U of Cal Pr.

Prologue to Philosophy. Hugh M. Curtler. LC 79-51465. 1979. pap. text ed. 6.40 o.p. (ISBN 0-8191-0750-6). U Pr of Amer.

Prologue to Population Geography. Wilbur Zelinsky. (Illus.). 1966. pap. 8.95 ref. ed. (ISBN 0-13-730788-8). P-H.

Prologue to Revolution: Sources & Documents on the Stamp Act Crisis, 1764-1766. Ed. by Edmund S. Morgan. (Documentary Problems in Early American History Ser.). 164p. 1972. pap. text ed. 3.95x (ISBN 0-393-09424-3). Norton.

Prologue to War: England & the United States, 1805-1812. Bradford Perkins. 1961. pap. 6.95x (ISBN 0-520-00996-7). U of Cal Pr.

Prolongevity. Albert Rosenfeld. 1977. pap. 2.50 (ISBN 0-380-01786-5, 35303, Discus). Avon.

Promenades: An Historian's Appreciation of Modern French Literature. Richard Cobb. 160p. 1980. 16.95x (ISBN 0-19-211758-0). Oxford U Pr.

Promenades. Litteraires & Grammaticales. Renee Waldinger & Gisele Corbiere-Gille. 1966. text ed. 11.95x (ISBN 0-669-28662-1); tapes. 6 reels o. p. 30.00 (ISBN 0-669-33977-6). Heath.

Promesas de Jesus. David Wilkerson. Orig. Title: Jesus Person Pocket Promise Book. 95p. (Span.). 1974. pap. 1.95 (ISBN 0-89922-027-4). Edit Caribe.

Prometheus Bound. Aeschylus. Tr. by Warren D. Anderson. (Orig.). 1963. pap. 2.95 (ISBN 0-672-60357-8, LLA143). Bobbs.

Prometheus Bound. Aeschylus. Ed. by William Arrowsmith. Tr. by James Scully & C. John Herington. (Greek Tragedy in New Translations Ser.). 112p. 1975. 10.95 (ISBN 0-19-501934-2). Oxford U Pr.

Prometheus Bound & Other Plays. Aeschylus. Tr. by Philip Vellacott. Incl. Suppliants; Seven Against Thebes; Persians. (Classics Ser.). (Orig.). 1961. pap. 2.75 (ISBN 0-14-044112-3). Penguin.

Prometheus Operation. Mark Elder. LC 80-14577. 312p. 1980. 11.95 (ISBN 0-07-019191-3, GB). McGraw.

Prometheus Question: A Moral and Theological Perspective on the Energy Crisis. Ed. by C. A. Cesaretti. 176p. 1980. pap. 3.95 (ISBN 0-8164-2285-0). Seabury.

Prometheus Unbound: An Interpretation. Carl H. Grabo. LC 68-19149. 1968. Repr. of 1935 ed. 7.50 (ISBN 0-87752-045-3). Gordian.

Prometheus Unbound & Hellas: An Approach to Shelley's Lyrical Dramas. John S. Flagg. (Salzburg Studies in English Literature, Romantic Reassessment: No. 14). 1972. pap. text ed. 25.00x (ISBN 0-391-01375-0). Humanities.

Prometiean Ethics: Living with Death, Competition, & Triage. Garrett Hardin. LC 79-56592. (Jesse & John Danz Lecture Ser.). 92p. 1980. 7.95 (ISBN 0-295-95717-4). U of Wash Pr.

Prominent Scientists: An Index to Collected Bibliographies. Paul Pelletier. 250p. 1980. 29.95 (ISBN 0-918212-41-3). Neal-Schuman.

Promiscuous Teenager. Daniel T. Gianturco & Harmon L. Smith. (Illus.). 128p. 1974. text ed. 12.75 (ISBN 0-398-03117-7). C C Thomas.

Promise & Fulfilment: Present to Professor S. H. Hooke, by the Society for O. T. Study. F. F. Bruce. 224p. 1963. text ed. 12.95x (ISBN 0-567-02055-X). Attic Pr.

Promise & Performance: Carter Builds a New Administration. Bruce Adams & Kathryn Kavanaugh-Baran. LC 78-24790. 224p. 1979. 21.00 (ISBN 0-669-02817-7). Lexington Bks.

Promise & Performance of American Democracy. 4th ed. Richard A. Watson. 500p. 1981. text ed. 12.95 (ISBN 0-471-07964-2). Wiley.

Promise & Performance of American Democracy: National Editon. 4th ed. Richard A. Watson & Michael R. Fitzgerald. 570p. 1981. text ed. 14.95 (ISBN 0-471-08380-1). Wiley.

Promise & Performance of American Democracy: State Edition. 4th ed. Richard A. Watson & Michael R. Fitzgerald. 650p. 1981. text ed. 16.95 (ISBN 0-471-08381-X). Wiley.

Promise at Midnight. Lilian Peake. (Harlequin Romances Ser.). 192p. 1981. pap. 1.25 (ISBN 0-373-02404-5, Pub. by Harlequin). PB.

Promise Kept. new ed. Kurth Sprague. (Illus.). 104p. 1975. 10.00 o.p. (ISBN 0-88426-043-7). Encino Pr.

Promise Me You'll Sing Mud. Ian Wallace. 1980. 13.95 (ISBN 0-7145-3500-1). Riverrun NY.

Promise of All Ages. rev., 3rd ed. George Townshend. 1972. 5.75 (ISBN 0-85398-044-6, 7-31-25, Pub. by G Ronald England); pap. 1.75 (ISBN 0-85398-006-3, 7-31-26, Pub. by George Ronald England). Baha'i.

Promise of Buber. Lowell D. Streiker. LC 69-16963. (Promise of Theology Ser). 1969. pap. 1.50 o.p. (ISBN 0-397-10089-2). Lippincott.

Promise of Bultmann. Norman Perrin. LC 78-19639. 112p. 1979. pap. 3.95 (ISBN 0-8006-1357-0, 1-1357). Fortress.

Promise of Cognitive Psychology. Richard E. Mayer. LC 80-39997. (Psychology Ser.). (Illus.). 1981. text ed. 10.95x (ISBN 0-7167-1275-X); pap. text ed. 5.95x (ISBN 0-7167-1276-8). W H Freeman.

Promise of Eden: The Canadian Expansionist Movement & the Idea of the West, 1856-1900. Doug Owram. 1980. 25.00x (ISBN 0-8020-5483-8); pap. 10.00 (ISBN 0-8020-6385-3). U of Toronto Pr.

Promise of Eurocommunism. Carl Marzani. 367p. (Orig.). 1980. 16.95 (ISBN 0-88208-110-1); pap. 8.95 (ISBN 0-88208-111-X). Lawrence Hill.

Promise of Happiness. F. Inglis. LC 80-49986. 250p. Date not set. 39.50 (ISBN 0-521-23142-6). Cambridge U Pr.

Promise of Love. Mary Renault. 1974. pap. 2.25 (ISBN 0-515-05147-0, A3422). Jove Pubns.

Promise of Love. Mary Renault. 382p. 1976. Repr. of 1939 ed. lib. bdg. 15.50x (ISBN 0-89244-079-1). Queens Hse.

Promise of Narrative Theology: Recovering the Gospel in the Church. George W. Stroup. LC 80-84654. 216p. (Orig.). 1981. pap. 8.50 (ISBN 0-8042-0683-X). John Knox.

Promise of Narrative Theology: Recovering the Gospel in the Church. George W. Stroup. LC 80-84654. pap. 8.50 (ISBN 0-8042-0683-X). John Knox.

Promise of Space. Arthur C. Clarke. LC 68-17042. (Illus.). 1968. 9.95 o.s.i. (ISBN 0-06-000931-4, HarpT). Har-Row.

Promise of the Coming Dark Age. L. S. Stavrianos. LC 76-8232. (Illus.). 1976. pap. text ed. 8.95x (ISBN 0-7167-0496-X). W H Freeman.

Promise to Keep. Lois A. Sunagel. (Orig.). 1980. pap. 1.95 (ISBN 0-532-23133-3). Manor Bks.

Promised Day Is Come. rev. ed. Shoghi Effendi. 1980. 10.00 (ISBN 0-87743-132-9, 7-08-17); pap. 5.00 (ISBN 0-87743-138-8, 7-08-18). Baha'i.

Promised Land. Abba Eban. LC 78-6241. (Illus.). 1978. 49.50 o.p. (ISBN 0-8407-4061-1). Nelson.

Promised Lands 2: Subdivisions in Florida's Wetlands, Vol. 2. Leslie Allan et al. LC 76-46735. (Promised Lands). (Illus.). 1977. pap. 20.00x o.p. (ISBN 0-918780-05-5). Inform.

Promises. Charlotte V. Allen. 1981. pap. 2.95 (ISBN 0-425-04843-8). Berkley Pub.

Promises from the Past. Donna Vitek. 192p. 1981. pap. 1.50 (ISBN 0-671-57066-8). S&S.

Promises of Jesus. LC 80-65437. (Illus.). 64p. 1980. 5.95 (ISBN 0-915684-69-1). Christian Herald.

Promises of the Good Life. S. Prakash Sethi. 1979. pap. 11.95 (ISBN 0-256-02230-5). Irwin.

Promises, Promises, Promises. Joel Nederhood. LC 79-18889. (Orig.). 1979. pap. text ed. 2.45 (ISBN 0-933140-09-6). Bd of Pubns CRC.

Promises to Keep: Carter's First 100 Days. Robert Shogan. LC 77-22818. 1977. 8.95 o.p. (ISBN 0-690-01497-X, TYC-T). T Y Crowell.

Promises to Keep: My Years in Public Life 1941-1969. Chester Bowles. LC 76-123917. (Illus.). 1971. 15.00 o.s.i. (ISBN 0-06-010421-X, HarpT). Har-Row.

Promises to Keep: Reading & Writing About Values. J. Dahlstrom & D. Ryel. 1977. pap. text ed. 10.95 (ISBN 0-13-731059-5). P-H.

Promises to Myself: Ziggy's Thirty-Day Ledger of I Owe Me's. Tom Wilson. (Alligator Bks). 1975. pap. 2.50 (ISBN 0-8362-0643-6). Andrews & McMeel.

Promises to the Fathers: Studies on the Patriarchal Narratives. Claus Westermann. Tr. by David E. Green from Ger. LC 79-7395. Orig. Title: Die Verheissungen an Die Vater. 208p. 1980. 12.95 (ISBN 0-8006-0580-2, 1-580). Fortress.

Promising Primate: Anthropological Specualtions on Human Evolution. Peter J. Wilson. 224p. write for info. Yale U Pr.

Promoted to Glory: The Apotheosis of George Washington. Patricia A. Anderson. (Illus.). 68p. (Orig.). 1980. pap. 8.75 (ISBN 0-87391-017-6). Smith Coll Mus Art.

Promoters & Politicians: The North-Shore Railways in the History of Quebec, 1854-1885. Brian J. Young. 1978. 17.50x (ISBN 0-8020-5377-7). U of Toronto Pr.

Promoting Competence in Clients: A New-Old Approach to Social Work Intervention. Ed. by Anthony N. Maluccio. LC 80-1056. (Illus.). 1981. 17.95 (ISBN 0-02-919830-5). Free Pr.

Promoting Competition in Regulated Markets. Ed. by Almarin Phillips. (Studies in the Regulation of Economic Activity). 397p. 1975. 15.95 (ISBN 0-8157-7052-9); pap. 6.95 (ISBN 0-8157-7051-0). Brookings.

Promoting Continuing Education Programs. Gayle A. Hendrickson. 80p. (Orig.). 1980. pap. 10.50 (ISBN 0-89964-169-5). CASE.

Promoting Health Through Public Policy. Nancy Milio. 320p. 1981. text ed. 25.00 (ISBN 0-8036-6177-0, 6177-0). Davis Co.

Promoting Innovation & Change in Organizations & Communities: A Planning Manual. J. Rothman et al. LC 75-19454. 1976. 14.95x o.p. (ISBN 0-471-73967-7). Wiley.

Promoting Moral Growth: From Piaget to Kohlberg. Richard H. Hersh et al. LC 78-19945. 256p. 1979. pap. text ed. write for info. Longman.

Promoting the Organization: A Guide to Low Budget Publicity. Jim Dudley. 1975. 16.95x (ISBN 0-7002-0259-5). Intl Ideas.

Promotion: Advertising, Publicity, Personal Selling, Sales Promotion. R. Stanley. (Illus.). 1977. text ed. 18.95 (ISBN 0-13-730770-5). P-H.

Promotion & Careers in Teaching. Sidney Hilsum & K. B. Start. (Research Reports Ser.). 312p. 1974. text ed. 22.00x (ISBN 0-85633-043-4, NFER). Humanities.

Promotion of Price Competition Where Sellers Are Few. Frank Kottke. LC 77-18328. (Illus.). 1978. 19.95 (ISBN 0-669-02094-X). Lexington Bks.

Promotion of the Development & Use of the Subsystem Concept of Building Construction. Building Research Advisory Board. LC 72-84109. 108p. 1972. pap. 3.75 (ISBN 0-309-02039-5). Natl Acad Pr.

Promotion of the Relationship Between Research & Industry in Mechanical Production. O. Kienzle et al. 1970. pap. 7.50 (ISBN 0-08-006607-0). Pergamon.

Promotion: Persuasive Communication in Marketing. rev ed. Rollie Tillman & C. A. Kirkpatrick. 1972. text ed. 16.50x o.p. (ISBN 0-256-00563-X). Irwin.

Promotion Planning Process: Sales Promotion Vs. Advertising. Roger A. Strang. (Praeger Special Studies Ser.). 144p. 1980. 18.95 (ISBN 0-03-049101-0). Praeger.

Promotion: Products, Servies & Ideas. William M. Kincaid. (Illus.). 360p. 1981. text ed. 19.95 (ISBN 0-675-08082-7); tchr's. manual avail. Merrill.

Promotional Strategy. 4th ed. James F. Engel et al. 1979. text ed. 19.95 (ISBN 0-256-02156-2). Irwin.

Promoton: Practices, Policies, & Affirmative Action. Elaine F. Gruenfeld. (Key Issues Ser.: No. 17). 1975. pap. 3.00 (ISBN 0-87546-222-7). NY Sch Indus Rel.

Prompt Fission Neutron Spectra. (Illus.). 176p. (Orig.). 1973. pap. 10.75 (ISBN 92-0-131172-9, IAEA). Unipub.

Proms. Ates Orga. LC 74-81007. (Illus.). 160p. 1974. 12.95 o.p. (ISBN 0-685-49929-4). David & Charles.

Pronoia and Paideusis: Studien Uber Origenes und Sein Verhaltnis Zum Platonismus. Hal Koch. LC 78-66597. (Ancient Philosophy Ser.). 347p. 1980. lib. bdg. 34.00 (ISBN 0-8240-9592-8). Garland Pub.

Pronouncing Borges. Gerald Locklin. 32p. 1977. pap. 2.00 (ISBN 0-935390-02-2). Wormwood Rev.

Pronouncing Dictionary of American English. 2nd ed. John S. Kenyon & Thomas A. Knott. 1953. 7.95 (ISBN 0-87779-047-7). Merriam.

Pronouncing Dictionary of English-Place Names. Klaus Forster. 308p. 1981. 30.00 (ISBN 0-7100-0756-6). Routledge & Kegan.

Pronouns & Determiners. Alice C. Pack. (Dyad Learning Program Ser.). 1977. pap. text ed. 6.50 bound with teacher's ed. (ISBN 0-88377-081-4); tchr's ed. avail. (ISBN 0-88377-082-2). Newbury Hse.

Pronunciation Contrasts in English. Don L. Nilsen & Alleen P. Nilsen. 1973. text ed. 4.50 o.p. (ISBN 0-88345-133-6, 17417); pap. text ed. 3.95 (ISBN 0-88345-134-4, 17416). Regents Pub.

Pronunciation Exercises in English. Elizabeth M. Clarey & Robert J. Dixson. (gr. 9 up). 1963. pap. text ed. 2.75 (ISBN 0-88345-135-2, 17418); with 3 records 18.00 (ISBN 0-685-02029-0). Regents Pub.

Pronunciation of American English. Arthur J. Bronstein. (Illus.). 1960. 14.95 (ISBN 0-13-730887-6). P-H.

Pronunciation of English in the Atlantic States: Based Upon the Collections of the Linguistic Atlas of the Eastern United States. Hans Kurath & Raven I. McDavid, Jr. LC 60-5671. (Illus.). 1961. 15.00 o.p. (ISBN 0-472-04541-5). U of Mich Pr.

Pronunciation of Ten Thousand Proper Names. Ed. by Mary S. Mackey & Maryette G. Mackey. 1979. Repr. of 1922 ed. 34.00 (ISBN 0-8103-4137-9). Gale.

Proof of the Gospel, 2 vols. in one. Eusebius. Ed. by W. J. Ferrar. (Twin Brooks Ser.). 568p. 1981. pap. 12.95 (ISBN 0-8010-3366-7). Baker Bk.

Proofs & Refutations. E. Lakatos. Ed. by J. Worrall. LC 75-32478. 160p. 1976. 32.50 (ISBN 0-521-21078-X); pap. 8.95 (ISBN 0-521-29038-4). Cambridge U Pr.

Proofs of a Conspiracy. John Robison. 1967. pap. 3.95 (ISBN 0-88279-121-4). Western Islands.

Proofs of Christianity. Charles Harris. LC 77-77215. (Radiant Life Ser.). 1977. pap. 1.50 (ISBN 0-88243-911-1, 02-0911); teacher's ed 2.50 (ISBN 0-88243-181-1, 320-181). Gospel Pub.

Propaganda for War. Horace C. Peterson. LC 68-15832. 1968. Repr. of 1939 ed. 16.00 (ISBN 0-8046-0365-0). Kennikat.

Propaganda Technique in World War One. Harold D. Lasswell. 1971. pap. 4.95 (ISBN 0-262-62018-9). MIT Pr.

Propaganda: The Art of Persuasion, World War II. Anthony Rhodes. Ed. by Victor Margolin. LC 75-17545. (Illus.). 300p. 1981. pap. 15.95 (ISBN 0-87754-078-0). Chelsea Hse.

Propagation. Alan Toogood. LC 80-6164. (Illus.). 336p. 1981. 13.95 (ISBN 0-8128-2772-4). Stein & Day.

Propagation Des Ondes. Jacques Hadamard. LC 52-9969. (Fr). 14.95 o.p. (ISBN 0-8284-0058-X). Chelsea Pub.

Propagation of Electromagnetic Waves in Plasmas. 2nd rev. ed. V. L. Ginzburg. 1971. 60.00 (ISBN 0-08-015569-3). Pergamon.

Propagation of Gamma Quanta in Matter. O. I. Leipunskii et al. 1965. 37.00 (ISBN 0-08-010553-X); pap. 22.00 (ISBN 0-08-013564-1). Pergamon.

Propagation of Waves. P. David & J. Voge. 1969. 37.00 (ISBN 0-08-012114-4). Pergamon.

Propane Conversion of Engines. rev. ed. Ross Smith. (Applied Technology Ser.). (Illus.). 76p. 1980. pap. 8.45 (ISBN 0-938260-01-4). Smith & Assoc.

Propane Conversion of Engines. rev. ed. Ross Smith. (Applied Technology Ser.). (Illus.). 76p. 1980. pap. 9.15. Ashford.

Propeller Island. Jules Verne. 1977. 7.95x o.s.i. (ISBN 0-8464-0769-8). Beekman Pubs.

Proper Place. Joan Lingard. LC 75-6591. (gr. 6 up). 1975. 7.95 o.p. (ISBN 0-525-66425-4). Elsevier-Nelson.

Proper Stations. Richard Faber. 1971. 6.95 o.p. (ISBN 0-571-09566-6, Pub. by Faber & Faber). Merrimack Bk Serv.

Proper Yacht. Arthur Beiser. 1966. 10.95 o.s.i. (ISBN 0-685-15800-4). Macmillan.

Proper Yacht. Arthur Beiser. LC 77-85406. (Illus.). 1978. 27.50 (ISBN 0-87742-096-3). Intl Marine.

Properties & Applications of Transistors. J. P. Vasseur. 1964. 32.00 (ISBN 0-08-010244-1); pap. 17.25 (ISBN 0-08-013647-8). Pergamon.

Properties & Management of Forest Soils. William L. Pritchett. LC 78-23196. 1979. text ed. 26.95 (ISBN 0-471-03718-4). Wiley.

Properties of Ceramic Raw Materials: In SI Units. 2nd ed. W. Ryan. 1978. text ed. 15.00 (ISBN 0-08-022113-0); pap. text ed. 5.75 (ISBN 0-08-022114-9). Pergamon.

Properties of Engineering Materials. R. A. Higgins. LC 77-22284. 448p. 1978. pap. 14.50 (ISBN 0-88275-575-7). Krieger.

Properties of Liquid & Solid Helium. John Wilks. (International Series of Monographs on Physics). 1967. 74.00x (ISBN 0-19-851245-7). Oxford U Pr.

Properties of Liquid Metals: Proceedings. International Conference, 2nd, Tokyo, 1972. Ed. by S. Takeuchi & S. Takeuchi. LC 73-1286. 640p. 1973. 46.95 (ISBN 0-470-84414-0). Halsted Pr.
Properties of Matter. B. H. Flowers & E. Mendoza. LC 70-11815. (Manchester Physics Ser.). 1970. 34.75 (ISBN 0-471-26497-0, Pub. by Wiley-Interscience). Wiley.
Properties of Nonmetallic Fluid Elements, Vol. III. Y. S. Touloukian & C. Y. Ho. (M-H-CINDAS Data Series on Material Properties). 224p. 1981. text ed. 33.50 (ISBN 0-07-065033-0). McGraw.
Properties of Nuclei. G. A. Jones. (Oxford Physics Ser.). (Illus.). 1976. 21.00x (ISBN 0-19-851828-5). Oxford U Pr.
Properties of Petroleum Fluids. William D. McCain, Jr. LC 73-78008. 325p. 1974. 27.00 (ISBN 0-87814-021-2). Pennwell Pub.
Properties of Polymers. R. Jenkins et al. (Advances in Polymer Sciences: Vol. 36). (Illus.). 150p. 1980. 40.20 (ISBN 0-387-10204-3). Springer-Verlag.
Properties of Reservoir Rocks: Core Analysis. R. Monicard. 204p. 1980. 24.95 (ISBN 0-87201-765-6). Gulf Pub.
Properties of Selected Ferrous Alloying Elements, Vol. III. Y. S. Touloukian & C. Y. Ho. (M-H-CINDAS Data Series on Material Properties). 288p. 1981. text ed. 33.50 (ISBN 0-07-065034-9). McGraw.
Propertius: A Critical Introduction. J. P. Sullivan. LC 75-10038. 224p. 1976. 23.95 (ISBN 0-521-20904-8). Cambridge U Pr.
Propertius: Classical Life & Letters. Margaret Hubbard. LC 75-11481. (Illus.). 182p. 1976. 10.00 o.p. (ISBN 0-684-14464-6, ScribT). Scribner.
Propertius: Elegies Book 1. Ed. by W. A. Camps. LC 77-82490. 1977. Bk. 1. 22.50 (ISBN 0-521-06000-1); Bk. 1. pap. 8.50 (ISBN 0-521-29210-7); Bk. 2. 22.50 (ISBN 0-521-06001-X); Bk. 3. 16.95 (ISBN 0-521-06002-8). Cambridge U Pr.
Property. Ed. by J. Roland Pennock & John W. Chapman. LC 79-55007. (Nomos XXII). 1980. 24.90x (ISBN 0-8147-6576-9). NYU Pr.
Property & Casuality Insurance Agent. Gary H. Snouffer. 224p. (Orig.). 1981. pap. 8.00 (ISBN 0-668-04308-3, 4308). Arco.
Property & Liability Insurance. 2nd ed. S. S. Huebner et al. (Risk & Insurance Ser.). 1976. 19.95 (ISBN 0-13-730960-0). P-H.
Property & Liability Insurance Handbook. Ed. by John D. Long & Davis W. Gregg. 1965. text ed. 16.95x o.p. (ISBN 0-256-00302-5). Irwin.
Property & Liability Insurance Investment Management. Samuel B. Jones. 1971. text ed. 7.95x o.p. (ISBN 0-256-00263-0). Irwin.
Property & Politics Eighteen-Seventy to Nineteen-Fourteen: Landownership, Law, Ideology & Urban Development in England. Avner Offer. LC 80-41010. (Illus.). 480p. Date not set. price not set (ISBN 0-521-22414-4). Cambridge U Pr.
Property & Riches in the Early Church: Aspects of a Social History of Early Christianity. Martin Hengel. Tr. by John Bowden from Ger. LC 75-305658. 104p. 1974. pap. 4.50 (ISBN 0-8006-1201-9, 1-1201). Fortress.
Property Boom: The Effects of Building Society Behaviour on House Prices. David G. Mayes. 146p. 1979. 30.50x (ISBN 0-85520-296-3, Pub by Martin Robertson England). Biblio Dist.
Property Library: An Annotated Bibliography Based on the Batchelder-McPharlin Collection at the University of New Mexico. Ed. by George B. Miller, Jr. et al. LC 80-23474. 200p. 1981. lib. bdg. 29.95 (ISBN 0-313-21359-3, HPL). Greenwood.
Property Management in Real Estate Investment Decision-Making. Jaffe. (Special Ser. in Real Estate & Urban Land Economics). (Illus.). 1979. 21.95 (ISBN 0-669-02453-8). Lexington Bks.
Property of. Alice Hoffman. 1977. 8.95 o.p. (ISBN 0-374-23828-6). FS&G.
Property of a Gentleman. Catherine Gaskin. 320p. 1975. pap. 1.75 o.p. (ISBN 0-449-22542-9, X2542, Crest). Fawcett.
Property, Paternalism, & Power: A Study of East Anglian Farmers. Howard Newby et al. LC 78-2030. (Illus.). 1979. Repr. 27.50 (ISBN 0-299-07870-1). U of Wis Pr.
Property, Power & Public Choice: An Inquiry into Law & Economics. A. Allan Schmid. LC 78-5930. (Praeger Special Studies). 1978. 24.95 (ISBN 0-03-042956-0). Praeger.
Property, Profits & Economic Justice. Virginia Held. 256p. 1979. pap. text ed. 8.95x (ISBN 0-534-00819-4). Wadsworth Pub.
Property Rights: Philosophic Foundations. Lawrence C. Becker. 1977. 17.00x (ISBN 0-7100-8679-2). Routledge & Kegan.
Property Rights: Philosophic Foundations. Lawrence C. Becker. 148p. 1980. pap. 5.95 (ISBN 0-7100-0606-3). Routledge & Kegan.
Property System Approach to the Electromagnetic Spectrum: A Legal-Economic-Engineering Study. Arthur S. De Vany et al. (Cato Paper Ser.: No. 10). 112p. 1980. pap. 4.00 (ISBN 0-932790-11-9). Cato Inst.
Property Tax & Alternative Local Taxes: An Economic Analysis. Larry D. Schroeder & David L. Sjoquist. LC 75-3751. (Special Studies). (Illus.). 128p. 1975. text ed. 22.95 (ISBN 0-275-07480-3). Praeger.
Property Tax & Its Administration: Proceedings. Committee On Taxation - Resources - And Economic Development Symposium - 1967. Ed. by Arthur D. Lynn, Jr. (Committee on Taxation, Resources & Economic Development Ser., No. 3). 1969. 20.00 (ISBN 0-299-05210-9); pap. 7.50x (ISBN 0-299-05214-1). U of Wis Pr.
Property Tax in New Mexico. Bruce W. Kimzey. 1977. pap. text ed. 7.50x (ISBN 0-8191-0131-1). U Pr of Amer.
Property Tax Preferences for Agricultural Land. Ed. by Neal A. Roberts. LC 79-52473. (Illus.). 140p. 1980. text ed. 18.00 (ISBN 0-916672-32-8). Allanheld.
Property Tax Reform. Ed. by George E. Peterson. 1973. pap. 4.95 (ISBN 0-87766-099-9, 49000). Urban Inst.
Property Tax Revolt: The Case of Proposition 13. Ed. by George Kaufman & Kenneth T. Rosen. (Real Estate & Urban Economics Ser.). 1981. price not set prof. - refer. (ISBN 0-88410-693-4). Ballinger Pub.
Property Taxation & the Finance of Education. Richard W. Lindholm. LC 73-2046. (TRED Ser.). 1974. 25.00x (ISBN 0-299-06440-9, 644). U of Wis Pr.
Property Taxation, USA: Proceedings. Ed. by Richard W. Lindholm. (Committee on Taxation, Resources and Economic Development Ser. No. 2). (Illus.). 1967. pap. 7.95 (ISBN 0-299-04544-7). U of Wis Pr.
Prophecies & Predictions: Everyone's Guide to the Coming Changes. rev. ed. Moira Timms. (Illus.). 288p. 1980. pap. 7.95 (ISBN 0-913300-55-1). Unity Pr.
Prophecies & Revelations About the Jesuits. 1.95 (ISBN 0-913452-27-0). Jesuit Bks.
Prophecies of Jeremiah. Hans C. von Orelli. 1977. 13.50 (ISBN 0-686-12974-1). Klock & Klock.
Prophecies of St. Malachy & St. Columbkille. 3rd ed. Peter Bander. 1979. pap. text ed. 6.00x (ISBN 0-901072-10-9). Humanities.
Prophecy & Ethics: Isaiah & the Ethical Traditions of Israel. Eryl Davies. (Journal for the Study of the Old Testament, Supplement Ser.: No. 16). 1980. 19.95x (ISBN 0-905774-26-4, Pub. by JSOT Pr England). Eisenbrauns.
Prophecy & History in Luke-Acts. David L. Tiede. LC 79-8897. 180p. 1980. 9.95 (ISBN 0-8006-0632-9, 1-632). Fortress.
Prophecy & Millenarianism. Ed. by Ann Williams. (Illus.). 1981. text ed. 60.00 (ISBN 0-582-36136-2). Longman.
Prophecy & Politics: Socialism, Nationalism, & the Russian Jews, 1862-1917. Jonathan Frankel. LC 80-14414. (Illus.). 816p. Date not set. price not set (ISBN 0-521-23028-4). Cambridge U Pr.
Prophecy: Essays Presented to Georg Fohrer on His Sixty-Fifth Birthday. Ed. by J. A. Emerton. (Beihefte zur Zeitschrift fur Die Alttest Amentliche Wissenschaft: No. 155). 240p. 1980. text ed. 61.50x (ISBN 3-11-007761-2). De Gruyter.
Prophecy in Ancient Israel. J. Lindblom. LC 63-907. 480p. 1962. 16.50 (ISBN 0-8006-0916-6, 1-916). Fortress.
Prophesying Peace: A Sequel to "Ancestral Voices". James Lees-Milne. 1978. 10.95 o.p. (ISBN 0-684-15646-6, ScribT). Scribner.
Prophet Against Prophet. Simon J. DeVries. pap. 7.95x (ISBN 0-8028-1743-2). Eerdmans.
Prophet & the Revolutionary: Arab Socialism in the Modern East. Stephen Goode. LC 75-6816. 160p. (gr. 7 up). 1975. PLB 6.90 (ISBN 0-531-02840-2). Watts.
Prophet Armed: Trotsky, 1879-1921. Isaac Deutscher. 1980. pap. 8.95 (ISBN 0-19-281064-2, GB 605, GB). Oxford U Pr.
Prophet in the Wilderness: The Works of Ezequiel Martinez Estrada. Peter G. Earle. (Texas Pan American Ser). 1971. 12.00 (ISBN 0-292-70107-1). U of Tex Pr.
Prophet of America: Emerson & the Problems of Today. Newton Dillaway. LC 80-2530. 1981. Repr. of 1936 ed. 44.50 (ISBN 0-404-19254-8). AMS Pr.
Prophet of Blood: The Story of the "Mormon Manson". Ben Bradlee, Jr. & Dale Van Atta. (Illus.). 384p. 1981. 12.95 (ISBN 0-399-12371-7). Putnam.
Prophet of Community: The Romantic Socialism of Gustav Landauer. Eugene Lunn. LC 70-186105. 1973. 25.00x (ISBN 0-520-02207-6). U of Cal Pr.
Prophet of Fire. John Creasey. 1978. 7.95 o.s.i. (ISBN 0-8027-5394-9). Walker & Co.
Prophet Outcast: Trotsky, 1929-1940. Isaac Deutscher. 1980. pap. 8.95 (ISBN 0-19-281066-9, GB 607, GB). Oxford U Pr.
Prophet Unarmed: Trotsky, 1921-1929. Isaac Deutscher. 1980. pap. 8.95 (ISBN 0-19-281065-0, GB 606, GB). Oxford U Pr.
Prophet Without Honor: Glenn H. Taylor & the Fight for American Liberalism. F. Ross Peterson. LC 72-91668. 1974. 13.50x (ISBN 0-8131-1286-9). U Pr of Ky.
Prophete. Giacomo Meyerbeer. Ed. by Philip Gossett & Charles Rosen. LC 76-49197. (Early Romantic Opera Ser.: Vol. 21). 1978. lib. bdg. 82.00 (ISBN 0-8240-2920-8). Garland Pub.
Prophetess. Janet Kidde. 1978. pap. 1.95 o.s.i. (ISBN 0-515-04456-3). Jove Pubns.
Prophetic Imagination. Walter Brueggemann. LC 78-54546. 128p. 1978. pap. 4.95 (ISBN 0-8006-1337-6, 1-1337). Fortress.
Prophetic Lectures on Daniel & Revelations. F. G. Smith. 260p. pap. 3.50. Faith Pub Hse.
Prophetic Melville. Rowland A. Sherrill. LC 78-20436. 227p. 1979. 17.00x (ISBN 0-8203-0455-7). U of Ga Pr.
Prophetic Milton. William Kerrigan. LC 74-6118. 1974. 13.95x (ISBN 0-8139-0512-5). U Pr of Va.
Prophetic Moment: An Essay on Spenser. Angus Fletcher. LC 73-130587. 1971. 15.00x (ISBN 0-226-25332-5). U. of Chicago Pr.
Prophetic of George Tyrrell. David Wells. LC 79-27097. (American Academy of Religion Monograph: No. 22). 12.00x (ISBN 0-89130-375-8, 01 00 22); pap. 7.50x (ISBN 0-89130-376-6). Scholars Pr CA.
Prophetic Words of Hosea: A Morphological Study. Martin J. Buss. (Beiheft 111 Zur Zeitschrift Fuer Die alttestamentliche Wissenschaft). 1969. 28.50x (ISBN 3-11-002579-5). De Gruyter.
Prophetic Writings of William Blake, 2 Vols. William Blake. Ed. by D. J. Sloss & J. P. Wallis. (Oxford English Texts Ser). (Illus.). 1926. Set. 74.00x set (ISBN 0-19-811801-5). Oxford U Pr.
Prophetical, Educational & Playing Cards. Mrs. John K. Van Rensselaer. LC 77-78249. (Illus.). 1971. Repr. of 1912 ed. 20.00 (ISBN 0-8103-3867-X). Gale.
Prophets & Kings. Ellen G. White. 752p. deluxe ed. 9.50 (ISBN 0-8163-0040-2, 16642-1); pap. 5.95 (ISBN 0-8163-0041-0, 16643-9). Pacific Pr Pub Assn.
Prophets & Millennialists: The Uses of Biblical Prophecy in England from the 1790s to the 1840s. W. H. Oliver. 1979. 17.95x (ISBN 0-19-647962-2). Oxford U Pr.
Prophets & the Powerless. James Limburg. LC 76-12397. 1976. pap. 3.95 (ISBN 0-8042-0156-0). John Knox.
Prophets in Babylon: Jews in the Arab World. Marion Woolfson. LC 80-670264. 304p. 1980. 38.00 (ISBN 0-571-11458-X, Pub. by Faber & Faber). Merrimack Bk Serv.
Prophet's Mantle in the Nation's Capital. George W. Buchanan. LC 78-59167. 1978. pap. text ed. 5.75 (ISBN 0-8191-0545-7). U Pr of Amer.
Prophets Now. Leslie F. Brandt. 1979. 7.50 (ISBN 0-570-03278-4, 15-2722). Concordia.
Prophets of Doom in an Age of Optimism. V. Kerry Inman. (Orig.). 1981. pap. 4.95 (ISBN 0-934688-02-8). Great Comm Pubns.
Prophets of Israel. William R. Smith. (Social Science Classics Ser.). 446p. 1982. 19.95 (ISBN 0-87855-318-5); text ed. 19.95 (ISBN 0-686-68059-6); pap. 7.95 (ISBN 0-87855-700-8); pap. text ed. 7.95 (ISBN 0-686-68060-X). Transaction Bks. Postponed.
Prophets of Prosperity. Paul K. Conkin. LC 79-3251. 352p. 1980. 25.00 (ISBN 0-253-30843-7). Ind U Pr.
Prophets on Main Street. rev. ed. J. Elliott Corbett. LC 77-79597. 1977. pap. 5.95 (ISBN 0-8042-0841-7). John Knox.
Prophets, Poets, Priests, & Kings: The Old Testament Story. F. Washington Jarvis. 288p. 1975. pap. 5.95 (ISBN 0-8164-2089-0). Crossroad NY.
Prophets with Honor. Alan Barth. 1974. 8.95 o.p. (ISBN 0-394-48557-2). Knopf.
Prophets with Honor: Great Dissenters in the Supreme Court. Alan Barth. 254p. Date not set. pap. 2.95 (ISBN 0-394-71571-3, Vin). Random.
Prophets Without Honor: A Background to Freud, Kafka, Einstein & Their World. Frederic V. Grunfeld. 1980. 5.95x (ISBN 0-07-025087-1). McGraw.
Prophylactic Approach to Hypertensive Disease: Symposium. Yukio Yamori et al. (Perspectives in Cardiovascular Research Ser.: Vol. 4). 1979. 58.50 (ISBN 0-89004-339-6). Raven.
Proportioning Concrete Mixes. 1974. pap. 21.25 (ISBN 0-685-85124-9, SP-46). ACI.
Proposals for Government Credit Allocation. Leland B. Yeager. 1977. pap. 2.75 (ISBN 0-8447-3281-8). Am Enterprise.
Proposals for the Improvement of Subchapter K. 1979. pap. 7.50. Am Inst CPA.
Proposals That Work: A Guide for Planning Research. Lawrence F. Locke & Waneen Wyrick-Spirduso. LC 76-4965. 1976. pap. 8.25x (ISBN 0-8077-2495-5). Tchrs Coll.
Proposed Amendments to the Constitution of the United States Introduced in Congress from Dec. 4, 1889 to July 2, 1926. U. S. Library of Congress Legislative Reference Service. Ed. by Charles C. Tansill. LC 75-35363. (U.S. Government Documents Program Ser.). 148p. 1976. Repr. of 1926 ed. lib. bdg. 13.75x (ISBN 0-8371-8606-4, USPA). Greenwood.
Proposed Fortification Policy for Cereal-Grain Products. National Research Council, Food & Nutrition Board. LC 74-10542. 44p. 1974. pap. 3.75 (ISBN 0-309-02232-0). Natl Acad Pr.
Proposed System for Food Safety Assessment: A Comprehensive Report on the Issues of Food Ingredient Testing. new ed. Ed. by Food Safety Council, Columbia, U. S. A. LC 78-40901. (Illus.). 1978. pap. text ed. 23.00 (ISBN 0-08-023752-5). Pergamon.
Proposition Fourteen: A Secessionist Remedy. Richard Cummings. LC 80-8917. 128p. 1981. pap. 5.95 postponed (ISBN 0-394-17890-4, Ever). Grove.
Proposition Fourteen: The Secessionist Remedy. Richard Cummings. LC 80-80357. 112p. 1980. 11.95 (ISBN 0-932966-09-8); pap. 5.95 (ISBN 0-932966-16-0). Permanent Pr.
Proposition Thirteen: A First Anniversary Assessment. (Lincoln Institute Monograph: No. 880-5). (Illus.). 1980. pap. text ed. 5.00. Lincoln Inst Land.
Proposition Thirteen & Land Use: A Case Study of Fiscal Limits in California. Jeffrey I. Chapman. LC 79-3749. 1981. 22.95x (ISBN 0-669-03471-1). Lexington Bks.
Propositional Logic. Jarrett Leplin. LC 79-63560. 1979. pap. text ed. 7.50 (ISBN 0-8191-0728-X). U Pr of Amer.
Proprietors of North Carolina. William S. Powell. (Illus.). 1968. pap. 1.00 (ISBN 0-86526-101-6). NC Archives.
Prosa De la Espana Moderna. Marvin Wasserman & Carol Wasserman. (gr. 11). 1972. pap. text ed. 5.17 (ISBN 0-87720-517-5). AMSCO Sch.
Prosateurs Francais XVIE Siecle. Frank Chambers. 1976. pap. 12.95x (ISBN 0-669-00016-7). Heath.
Proscribed Chinese Writing. 2nd ed. Ed. by Robert Tung. (Scandinavian Institute of Asian Studies Monographs: No. 21). (Illus.). 1979. pap. text ed. 13.00x (ISBN 0-7007-0090-0). Humanities.
Proscription Francaise En Suisse, 1871-1872. A. J. Claris. (Commune De Paris En 1871). (Fr.). 1976. lib. bdg. 15.00x o.p. (ISBN 0-8287-0201-2); pap. text ed. 5.00x o.p. (ISBN 0-685-74930-4). Clearwater Pub.
Prose Bowl. Barry N. Malzberg & Bill Pronzini. LC 80-2423. 192p. 1981. 9.95 (ISBN 0-385-17027-0). Doubleday.
Prose Classique. Ed. by M. Leroy Ellis. LC 65-14565. 1966. pap. text ed. 10.95 (ISBN 0-471-00151-1). Wiley.
Prose Edda of Snorri Sturluson: Tales from Norse Mythology. Snorri Sturluson. Tr. by Jean I. Young. 1964. pap. 3.95x (ISBN 0-520-01232-1, CAMPUS55). U of Cal Pr.
Prose Fiction of the Cuban Revolution. Seymour Menton. LC 75-5993. (Latin American Monographs: No. 37). 344p. 1975. 16.50x (ISBN 0-292-76421-9). U of Tex Pr.
Prose Fiction of Veniamin A. Kaverin. Hongor Oulanoff. 1976. soft cover 9.95 (ISBN 0-89357-032-X). Slavica.
Prose Fiction of W. B. Yeats: The Search for Those Simple Forms. Richard J. Finneran. (New Yeats Papers Ser.: Vol. 4). 1973. pap. text ed. 3.75x (ISBN 0-85105-217-7, Dolmen Pr). Humanities.
Prose Miscellanies. Thomas E. Watson. (Studies in Populism). 1980. lib. bdg. 69.95 (ISBN 0-686-68882-1). Revisionist Pr.
Prose of Mallarme. Judy Kravis. LC 75-22977. 272p. 1976. 42.00 (ISBN 0-521-20921-8). Cambridge U Pr.
Prose Pieces. Wytter Bynner. Ed. by James Kraft. LC 78-11441. 1979. 25.00 (ISBN 0-374-23833-2). FS&G.
Prose, Poetry, & Flows. James J. Carter. (Orig.). 1979. pap. 2.95 (ISBN 0-937004-01-4). Carter.
Prose Quotations from Socrates to Macauley. Samuel A. Allibone. LC 68-30642. 764p. 1973. Repr. of 1876 ed. 20.00 (ISBN 0-8103-3181-0). Gale.
Prose Salernitan Questions: An Anonymous Collection Dealing with Science & Medicine Written by an Englishman Circa 1200, with an Appendix of Ten Related Collections. Ed. by Brian Lawn. (British Academy: Auctores Britannici Medii Aevi: Vol. V). 1979. 89.00x (ISBN 0-19-725978-2). Oxford U Pr.
Prose Style for the Modern Writer. Robert Miles & Marc F. Bertonasco. 1977. pap. text ed. 8.95 (ISBN 0-13-731521-X). P-H.

Prose Style of John Jewel. David K. Weiser. (Salzburg Studies in English Literature, Elizabethan & Renaissance Studies: No. 9). 194p. 1973. pap. text ed. 25.00x (ISBN 0-391-01562-1). Humanities.
Prose Style of Samuel Taylor Coleridge. Lynn M. Grow. (Salzburg Studies in English Literature, Romantic Reassessment: No. 54). 161p. 1976. pap. text ed. 25.00x (ISBN 0-391-01395-5). Humanities.
Prose Works. Mary B. Eddy. new type ed. 35.00 (ISBN 0-686-00519-8); garnet new type ed. o.p. 60.00 (ISBN 0-686-00520-1); standard ed. 22.00 (ISBN 0-686-00521-X); new type bonded lea. ed. 47.00 (ISBN 0-686-00522-8). First Church.
Prose Works Eighteen Ninety-Two, 2 vols. Walt Whitman. Ed. by Floyd Stovall. Incl. Vol. 1. Specimen Days. 358p. 1963 (ISBN 0-8147-0442-5); Vol. 2. Collect & Other Prose. 445p. 1964 (ISBN 0-8147-0443-3). LC 60-15980. (Illus.). 25.00x ea. NYU Pr.
Prose Works of William Wordsworth, 3 vols. William Wordsworth. Ed. by W. J. Owen & Jane Worthington. (Oxford English Texts Ser.). 1355p. 1974. 125.00x (ISBN 0-19-812436-8). Oxford U Pr.
Prose Writings of Donald Lamont, 1874-1958. Ed. by Thomas M. Murchison. 1958. 15.00x (ISBN 0-7073-0038-X, Pub. by Scottish Academic Pr Scotland). Columbia U Pr.
Prose Writings of Robert Louis Stevenson: A Guide. Roger G. Swearingen. xxiii, 217p. 1980. 29.50 (ISBN 0-208-01826-3, Archon). Shoe String.
Prosecuting Crime in the Renaissance: England, Germany, France. John H. Langbein. LC 73-81670. (Studies in Legal History). 336p. 1974. text ed. 16.50x (ISBN 0-674-71675-2). Harvard U Pr.
Prosecution: The Decision to Charge a Suspect with a Crime. Frank W. Miller. 366p. 1970. pap. 6.95 (ISBN 0-316-57346-9). Little.
Prosecutor. Ed. by William F. McDonald. LC 79-14388. (Sage Criminal Justice System Annuals Ser.: Vol. 11). (Illus.). 279p. 1979. 20.00 (ISBN 0-8039-0815-6); pap. 9.95 (ISBN 0-8039-0816-4). Sage.
Prosecutor. James Mills. 256p. 1969. 5.95 (ISBN 0-374-23836-7). FS&G.
Prosim: A Production Management Simulation. P. S. Greenlaw & M. P. Hottenstein. 1969. pap. text ed. 11.50 scp (ISBN 0-685-88947-5, HarpC); instructor's manual avail. (ISBN 0-06-362455-9); scp 360 computer deck 35.95 (ISBN 0-685-88949-1); scp 700-7000 computer deck 18.50 (ISBN 0-685-88950-5). Har-Row.
Prosodic Systems & Intonation in English. D. Crystal. LC 69-13792. (Cambridge Studies in Linguisties: No. 1). (Illus.). 1969. 49.50 (ISBN 0-521-07387-1); pap. 15.50x (ISBN 0-521-29058-9). Cambridge U Pr.
Prosody Handbook. Karl J. Shapiro & R. Beum. 1965. text ed. 11.50 scp (ISBN 0-06-045960-3, HarpC). Har-Row.
Prosopography of the Later Roman Empire, Vol. 2, A.D. 395-527. Ed. by J. R. Martindale. LC 77-118859. (Illus.). 1980. 140.00 (ISBN 0-521-20159-4). Cambridge U Pr.
Prospect for Renewal: The Future of the Liberal Arts College. Ed. by Earl J. McGrath. LC 75-189040. (Higher Education Ser.). 1972. 11.95x o.p. (ISBN 0-87589-132-2). Jossey-Bass.
Prospect of a Drowning. Lee T. Pheng. (Writing in Asia Ser.). 1980. text ed. 3.50 (00245). Heinemann Ed.
Prospect of War: British Defence Policy Eighteen Forty-Seven to Nineteen Forty-Two. John Gooch. 150p. 1981. 25.00x (ISBN 0-7146-3128-0, F Cass Co). Biblio Dist.
Prospecting for Gold: From Dogtown to Virginia City, 1852-1864. Granville Stuart. Ed. by Paul C. Phillips. LC 77-7244. Orig. Title: Forty Years on the Frontier. (Illus.). 1977. 12.50x (ISBN 0-8032-0932-0); pap. 5.25 (ISBN 0-8032-5869-0, BB 647, Bison). U of Nebr Pr.
Prospective Issues in Infancy Research. Ed. by Kathleen Bloom. LC 80-17479. 208p. 1981. text ed. 19.95 (ISBN 0-89859-059-0). L Erlbaum Assocs.
Prospective Longitudinal Research in Europe: An Empirical Basis for the Primary Prevention of Psychosocial Disorders. Ed. by Sarnoff A. Mednick & Andre E. Baert. (Illus.). 450p. 1981. text ed. 99.50 (ISBN 0-19-261184-4). Oxford U Pr.
Prospective Rate Setting. William L. Dowling. LC 77-18700. 1977. text ed. 28.95 (ISBN 0-89443-028-9). Aspen Systems.
Prospectors' Manual. Arthur J. Burdick. (Illus.). 156p. pap. 7.50 (ISBN 0-8466-6018-0, SJU18). Shorey.
Prospects & Proposals: Lifetime Learning for Psychiatrists, 1972. H. T. Carmichael & S. A. Small. 148p. 1972. pap. 3.50 o.p. (ISBN 0-685-31188-0, 178). Am Psychiatric.
Prospects for Capital Formation & Capital Markets. Arnold W. Sametz. LC 76-55113. (Illus.). 1978. 15.95 (ISBN 0-669-01505-9). Lexington Bks.
Prospects for Change in Bibliographic Control. Ed. by Abraham Bookstein et al. (University of Chicago Studies in Library Science). 1977. lib. bdg. 10.00x (ISBN 0-226-06365-8). U of Chicago Pr.
Prospects for Growth: Changing Expectations for the Future. Ed. by Kenneth D. Wilson. LC 77-14567. (Praeger Special Studies). 1977. 24.95 (ISBN 0-03-041446-6); pap. 11.95 (ISBN 0-03-041441-5). Praeger.
Prospects for Metropolitan Water Management. Compiled by American Society of Civil Engineers. 256p. 1971. pap. text ed. 5.25 (ISBN 0-87262-026-3). Am Soc Civil Eng.
Prospects for Peace. Frank Barnaby. (Illus.). 105p. 1980. 21.50 (ISBN 0-08-027399-8); pap. 11.50 (ISBN 0-08-027398-X). Pergamon.
Prospects for Pragmatism. Ed. by D. H. Mellor. 270p. 1981. 29.50 (ISBN 0-521-22548-5). Cambridge U Pr.
Prospects for Rental Housing Production Under Rent: A Case Study of Washington, D.C. J. Thomas Black. (Research Report Ser.: No. 24). 1976. pap. 3.75 (ISBN 0-87420-561-1). Urban Land.
Prospects for Research & Development in Education. new ed. Ralph W. Tyler. LC 75-36111. 190p. 1978. 15.50x (ISBN 0-8211-1906-0); text ed. 14.00x (ISBN 0-685-61058-6). McCutchan.
Prospects of Industrial Civilisation. Bertrand Russell. 1959. text ed. 16.95x (ISBN 0-04-300013-4). Allen Unwin.
Prospects of Nuclear Power in Pakistan. (Technical Reports: No. 7). 1962. pap. 2.75 (ISBN 92-0-165062-0, IAEA). Unipub.
Prospects of Population Control: Evaluation of Contraception Activity. Kumudini Dandekar & Vaijayanti Bhate. 1951-1964. 12.00 (ISBN 0-8046-8802-8). Kennikat.
Prospects of the Soviet Power in the Nineteen Eighties. Ed. by Christoph Bertram. 126p. 1980. 19.50 (ISBN 0-208-01885-9, Archon). Shoe String.
Prospects of the World Food Supply. National Academy Of Sciences. 1966. pap. 1.50 (ISBN 0-685-17308-9). Natl Acad Pr.
Prospectus & Specimen of an Intended National Work by William & Robert Whistlecraft of Stowmarket. John H. Frere. Ed. by Donald H. Reiman. LC 75-31204. (Romantic Context Ser.: Poetry 1789-1830: Vol. 55). 1978. lib. bdg. 47.00 (ISBN 0-8240-2154-1). Garland Pub.
Prosper Merimee. Maxwell A. Smith. (World Authors Ser.: France: No. 249). lib. bdg. 10.95 (ISBN 0-8057-2612-8). Twayne.
Prosperity Amidst Crisis: Austria's Economic Policy & the Energy Crunch. Wilhelm Hankel. Tr. by Jean Steinberg. 234p. 1980. lib. bdg. 20.00x (ISBN 0-86531-101-3). Westview.
Prosperity Signs. Lynne Palmer. (Orig.). 1981. pap. 3.25 (ISBN 0-440-17144-X). Dell.
Prostacyclin. Ed. by John R. Vane & Sune Bergstrom. LC 78-601200. 1979. text ed. 46.50 (ISBN 0-89004-330-2). Raven.
Prostaglandin Abstracts: A Guide to the Literature, 1906-1970. Richard M. Sparks & Richard A. Shalita. Incl. Vol. 1. 497p. 1974 (ISBN 0-306-67011-9); Vol. 2. 451p. 1975 (ISBN 0-306-67012-7). LC 73-21780. 75.00 ea. IFI Plenum.
Prostaglandin Synthetase Inhibitors. Ed. by H. J. Robinson & J. R. Vane. LC 74-83454. 1974. 37.50 (ISBN 0-89004-011-7). Raven.
Prostaglandin Synthetase Inhibitors: New Clinical Applications Proceedings. Ed. by Peter Ramwell. LC 80-7797. (Prostaglandins & Related Lipids Ser.: Vol. 1). 410p. 1980. 34.00x (ISBN 0-8451-2100-6). A R Liss.
Prostaglandins & Cardiovascular Disease. Ed. by Ruth J. Hegyeli. (Atherosclerosis Reviews: Vol. 8). 220p. 1980. text ed. 25.00 (ISBN 0-89004-516-X). Raven.
Prostaglandins & Perinatal Medicine. Ed. by Flavio Coceani & Peter M. Olley. LC 77-17758. (Advances in Prostaglandin & Thromboxane Research Ser.: Vol. 4). 1978. 43.50 (ISBN 0-89004-216-0). Raven.
Prostaglandins & the Gut, Vol. 1. Alan Bennett. 14.40 (ISBN 0-904406-49-0). Eden Med Res.
Prostaglandins & Thromboxins: Proceedings of the Third International Symposium on Prostaglandins & Thromboxanes in the Cardiovascular System, Hale-Salle, GDR, 5-7 May 1980. Werner Forster et al. LC 80-41802. (Illus.). 500p. 1981. 80.00 (ISBN 0-08-027369-6). Pergamon.
Prostaglandins: Physiology, Pharmacology & Clinical Significance. David Horrobin. 1978. 21.60 (ISBN 0-88831-032-3). Eden Med Res.
Prostaglandins: Progress in Research. S. M. Karim. 372p. 1972. 18.95 (ISBN 0-471-45863-5). Wiley.
Prostaglandins, Prostacyclin, Thromboxanes Measurement. Ed. by J. M. Boeynaems & A. G. Herman. (Developments in Pharmacology Ser.: No. 1). (Illus.). 209p. 1981. PLB 34.00 (ISBN 90-247-2417-1, Pub. by Martinus Nijhoff). Kluwer Boston.
Prostanoids: Proceedings of the Third Congress of the Hungarian Pharmacological Society, Budapest, 1979. Ed. by Valeria Kecskemeti & J. Knoll. LC 80-41281. (Advances in Pharmacological Research & Practice Ser.: Vol. VI). 175p. 1981. 34.00 (ISBN 0-08-026391-7). Pergamon.
Prostatic Carcinoma: Biology & Diagnosis. Ed. by E. S. Hafez & E. Spring-Mills. (Clinics in Andrology: No. 6). (Illus.). 200p. 1981. PLB 68.50 (ISBN 0-686-28844-0). Kluwer Boston.
Prostatic Disease: Proceedings. American-European Symposium, Vienna, Nov. 3-5, 1975, Sponsored by Physicians Associated for Continuing Education, Johns Hopkins University, & the University of Vienna & the Univ. of Innesbruck. Ed. by H. Marberger et al. LC 75-42905. (Progress in Clinical & Biological Research Ser.: Vol. 6). 1976. 32.00x (ISBN 0-8451-0006-8). A R Liss.
Prostheses & Rehabilitation After Arm Amputation. Leonard F. Bender. (Illus.). 196p. 1974. text ed. 19.75 (ISBN 0-398-03094-4). C C Thomas.
Prosthetics & Contact Lens: Series 10PC - 79. James R. Critser, Jr. 1981. refer. - ring bdg. 60.00 (ISBN 0-686-69159-8). Lexington Data.
Prosthetics: Methods of Producing Facial & Body Restorations. Carl D. Clarke. (Illus.). 336p. 1965. 18.00 (ISBN 0-685-25471-2). Standard Arts.
Prosthodontic Treatment for Partially Edentulous Patients. George A. Zarb et al. 1978. text ed. 29.95 (ISBN 0-8016-5677-X). Mosby.
Prostitute. (Illus.). pap. 5.00 (ISBN 0-910550-78-6). Centurion Pr.
Prostitution & Drugs. Paul J. Goldstein. LC 78-24766. 208p. 1979. 19.95 (ISBN 0-669-02833-9). Lexington Bks.
Prostitution & Victorian Society. Judith R. Walkowitz. LC 79-21050. 368p. 1980. 22.00 (ISBN 0-521-22334-2). Cambridge U Pr.
Prostitution in the Modern World: Prostitution Ser. Gladys Hall. Ed. by Charles Winick. LC 78-60866. (Vol. 6). 200p. 1979. lib. bdg. 20.00 (ISBN 0-8240-9722-X). Garland Pub.
Protagoras. Plato. Ed. by Gregory Vlastos. Tr. by Benjamin Jowett & Martin Ostwald. LC 56-14580. 1956. pap. 3.50 (ISBN 0-672-60232-6, LLA59). Bobbs.
Protagoras. Plato. Ed. by James Adam & A. M. Adam. (Gr). text ed. 8.95x (ISBN 0-521-05962-3). Cambridge U Pr.
Protagoras & Meno. Plato. Tr. by W. K. Guthrie. Bd. with Meno. (Classics Ser.). 1957. pap. 2.50 (ISBN 0-14-044068-2). Penguin.
Protean Self: Dramatic Action in Contemporary Fiction. Alan Kennedy. 240p. 1974. 17.50 (ISBN 0-231-03922-0). Columbia U Pr.
Protect Your Company from A-Z. Arnold Naidich. 1976. 49.95. Busn Res Pubns.
Protect Your Home with a Declaration of Homestead. 3rd ed. Ralph E. Warner. (Illus.). 80p. 1978. pap. 4.95 (ISBN 0-917316-02-9). Nolo Pr.
Protect Your Home with a Declaration of Homestead. 5th ed. Ralph E. Warner et al. (Illus.). 80p. 1980. pap. 5.95 (ISBN 0-917316-31-2). Nolo Pr.
Protected by Angels. Don Dickerman. 1977. pap. 1.95 (ISBN 0-89728-054-7, 677228). Omega Pubns OR.
Protecting Buildings. S. A. Richardson. 1977. 14.95 (ISBN 0-7153-7321-8). David & Charles.
Protecting Individual Privacy in Evaluation Research. Committee on Federal Agency Evaluation Research, National Research Council. LC 75-18591. 133p. 1975. pap. 7.00 (ISBN 0-309-02406-4). Natl Acad Pr.
Protecting Our Environment. Ed. by Grant S. McClellan. LC 72-95636. (Reference Shelf Ser: Vol. 42, No. 1). 1970. 6.25 (ISBN 0-8242-0409-3). Wilson.
Protecting the Consumer: An Economic & Legal Analysis. Peter Smith & Dennis Swann. 286p. 1980. 36.00x (ISBN 0-85520-259-9, Pub. by Martin Robertson England); pap. 12.50x (ISBN 0-85520-258-0). Biblio Dist.
Protecting the Corporate Officer & Director from Liability 1979, Vol. 301. (Corporate Law & Practice Course Handbook Ser.1978-79). 1979. soft cover 20.00 (ISBN 0-685-47624-3, B4-5594). PLI.
Protecting the Pre-School Child. Ed. by Paul Gyorgy & Anne Burgess. 1965. 4.50 o.p. (ISBN 0-685-14254-X). Lippincott.
Protecting Your Collection: A Handbook, Survey, & Guide for the Security of Rare Books, Manuscripts, Archives, Works of Art, & the Circulating Library Collection. Slade R. Gandert. (Library & Archival Security Ser.: No. 4). 192p. 1981. text ed. 19.95 (ISBN 0-917724-78-X). Haworth Pr.
Protection Against Bombs & Incendiaries: For Business, Industrial & Educational Institutions. Earl A. Pike. (Illus.). 92p. 1973. 9.50 (ISBN 0-398-02517-7). C C Thomas.
Protection Against Depletion of Stratospheric Ozone by Chlorofluorocarbons. Committee on Impacts of Stratospheric Change et al. LC 79-57247. xvii, 392p. (Orig.). 1979. pap. text ed. 8.75 (ISBN 0-309-02947-3). Natl Acad Pr.
Protection Against Internally Generated Missles & Their Secondary Effects in Nuclear Power Plants. (Safety Ser.: No. 50-SG-D4). 43p. 1980. pap. 6.50 (ISBN 92-0-123880-0, ISP 552, IAEA). Unipub.
Protection & Development in Mexico. Adriann Tenkte & Robert B. Wallace. 1980. 35.00 (ISBN 0-312-65217-8). St Martin.
Protection & Prosperity: An Account of Tariff Legislation & Its Effect in Europe & America, 2 vols. George B. Curtiss. (Neglected American Economists Ser.). 1974. Set. lib. bdg. 76.00 (ISBN 0-8240-1032-9); lib. bdg. 50.00 ea. Garland Pub.
Protection for Wells & Suction Lines for Individual Water Supply Systems. Federal Housing Administration - Building Research Advisory Board. 1962. pap. 3.00 o.p. (ISBN 0-309-00826-3). Natl Acad Pr.
Protection of Assets Manual. T. J. Walsh & R. J. Healy. 1981. 212.00 (ISBN 0-930868-04-8). Merritt Co.
Protection of Ethnic Minorities: Comparative Perspectives. Ed. by Robert G. Wirsing. LC 80-25618. (Pergamon Policy Studies on International Politices Ser.). 350p. 1981. 39.50 (ISBN 0-08-025556-6). Pergamon.
Protection of Foreign Property: Draft Convention on the Protection of Foreign Property & Resolution of the Council of the OECD on the Draft Convention. Organization for Economic Cooperation & Development. 62p. 1967. 1.20 o.p. (ISBN 0-686-14795-2). OECD.
Protection of Minorities: Comparative Perspectives. Robert G. Wirsing. (Pergamon Policy Studies). 300p. Date not set. 39.51 (ISBN 0-08-025556-6). Pergamon.
Protection of Personal & Commercial Reputation. Robert M. Kunstadt. (IIC Studies in Industrial Property & Copyright Law: Vol. 3). 1980. pap. 36.30 (ISBN 0-89573-028-6). Verlag Chemie.
Protection of Vision in Children. Arnall Patz & Richard E. Hoover. (Illus.). 184p. 1969. text ed. 14.75 (ISBN 0-398-01456-6). C C Thomas.
Protection System & Related Features in Nuclear Power Plants. (Safety Ser.: No. 50-SG-D3). 55p. 1981. pap. 7.00 (ISBN 0-686-69442-2, ISP 551, IAEA). Unipub.
Protectionism or Industrial Adjustment. Ed. by G. H. Helleiner et al. (Atlantic Papers Ser.: No. 39). 72p. 1980. write for info. (ISBN 0-916672-79-4). Allanheld.
Protective & Carbonizing Atmospheres. R. Nemenyi. 1977. text ed. 48.01 (ISBN 0-08-019883-X). Pergamon.
Protective Coatings for Structural Steel in the Pulp & Paper Industry. Lawrence T. Coker & Robert S. Gaddis. (TAPPI PRESS Reports). 1980. pap. 44.95 (ISBN 0-89852-380-X, 01-01-R080). TAPPI.
Protective Groups in Organic Synthesis. Theodora W. Greene. LC 80-25348. 325p. 1981. 80.00 (ISBN 0-471-05764-9, Pub. by Wiley-Interscience). Wiley.
Protective Philosophy: A Discussion of the Principles of the American Protective System, As Embodied in the McKinley Bill. David H. Rice. (Neglected American Economists Ser.). 1974. lib. bdg. 50.00 (ISBN 0-8240-1024-8). Garland Pub.
Protective Relaying for Power Systems. S. H. Horowitz. 560p. 1980. 39.95 (ISBN 0-471-08968-0, Pub. by Wiley-Interscience); pap. 26.00 (ISBN 0-471-08967-2). Wiley.
Protector. Malcolm Braly. (Orig.). 1979. pap. 2.25 (ISBN 0-515-05178-0). Jove Pubns.
Protector. Larry Niven. 224p. (Orig.). 1981. pap. 2.25 (ISBN 0-345-29302-9, Del Rey). Ballantine.
Protector of the Faith: Cardinal Johannes De Turrecremata & the Defense of the Institutional Church. Thomas M. Izbicki. 1981. price not set (ISBN 0-8132-0558-1). Cath U Pr.
Protectorate & The Northumberland Conspiracy: Political Intrigue in the Reign of Edward VI. Daniel P. Brown. LC 80-65156. (European History: Ser. I-1001). (Illus.). 60p. (Orig.). (gr. 11-12). 1980. pap. 3.15 (ISBN 0-930860-02-0). Golden West Hist.
Protectors of the Wilderness: The First Forest Rangers. Teri Crawford. LC 78-14492. (Famous Firsts Ser.). (Illus.). 1978. lib. bdg. 7.35 (ISBN 0-686-51114-X). Silver.
Protege. Malcolm MacPherson. 256p. 1981. pap. 2.75 (ISBN 0-553-14706-4). Bantam.
Protein & Amino Acid Functions. Ed. by E. J. Bigwood. 536p. 1972. text ed. 130.00 (ISBN 0-08-016464-1). Pergamon.
Protein Biosynthesis: And Problems of Heredity, Development, & Aging. Zhores A. Medvedev. LC 66-28598. 584p. 1966. 49.50 (ISBN 0-306-30284-5, Plenum Pr). Plenum Pub.

Protein-Calorie Malnutrition. Ed. by Robert E. Olson. (Nutrition Foundation Monograph Ser). 1975. 48.00 (ISBN 0-12-526150-0). Acad Pr.
Protein, Calories & Development: Nutritional Variables in the Economics of Developing Nations. Bernard Schmitt. (Westview Special Studies in Society, Politics & Economics Development). 1979. lib. bdg. 24.50x (ISBN 0-89158-185-5). Westview.
Protein Deficiency & Pesticide Toxicity. Eldon M. Boyd. (Illus.). 480p. 1972. 42.50 (ISBN 0-398-02476-6). C C Thomas.
Protein Deposition in Animals. 29th ed. P. J. Buttery & D. B. Lindsay. LC 80-49869. (Nottingham Easter School Ser.). (Illus.). 320p. 1980. text ed. 64.95 (ISBN 0-408-10676-X). Butterworths.
Protein for Vegetarians. rev. ed. Gary Null. 1975. pap. 2.25 o.p. (ISBN 0-515-05692-8). Jove Pubns.
Protein Functionality in Foods. Ed. by John P. Cherry. (ACS Symposium Ser.: No. 147). 1981. price not set (ISBN 0-8412-0605-8). Am Chemical.
Protein Metabolism & Biological Functions. Ed. by C. Paul Bianchi & Russell Hilf. 1970. 18.50x o.p. (ISBN 0-8135-0617-4). Rutgers U. Pr.
Protein Methylation. Woon Ki Paik & Sangduk Kim. LC 79-19557. (Biochemistry: a Series of Monographs). 1980. 31.50 (ISBN 0-471-04867-4, Pub. by Wiley-Interscience). Wiley.
Protein Nutrition. Ed. by Henry Brown. (Illus.). 256p. 1974. 27.50 (ISBN 0-398-02897-4). C C Thomas.
Protein Nutrition & Free Amino Acid Patterns. James Leathem. 1968. 15.00x (ISBN 0-8135-0572-0). Rutgers U Pr.
Protein Phoporylation & Bio-Regulaion. Ed. by J. Gordon et al. (Illus.). x, 234p. 1980. 49.25 (ISBN 3-8055-1168-X). S Karger.
Protein Planner. Elizabeth S. Weiss & Rita P. Wolfson. 1974. pap. 1.00 o.s.i. (ISBN 0-515-03301-4, P3301). Jove Pubns.
Protein-Protein Interactions. Carl Frieden & Lawrence Nichol. 400p. 1981. 30.00 (ISBN 0-471-04979-4, Pub. by Wiley-Interscience). Wiley.
Protein Quality for Humans: Assessment & in Vitro Estimation. C. E. Bodwell & J. S. Adkins. (Illus.). 1981. lib. bdg. price not set (ISBN 0-87055-388-7). AVI.
Protein Resources & Technology. Ed. by Max Milner et al. (Illus.). 1978. text ed. 45.00 (ISBN 0-87055-249-X). AVI.
Protein Sequence Determination. L. R. Croft. LC 79-41488. 157p. 1980. 14.00 (ISBN 0-471-27710-X). Wiley.
Protein: Structure, Function & Industrial Applicatons. Ed. by E. Hofmann & E. Pfeil. (Federation of European Biochemical Society Ser.: Vol. 52). (Illus.). 1979. text ed. 60.00 (ISBN 0-08-023176-4). Pergamon.
Protein Supply-Demands: Changing Styles GA-049. 1981. 800.00 (ISBN 0-89336-287-5). BCC.
Protein Synthesis. M. A. Tribe et al. LC 76-2260. (Basic Biology Course Ser.: Bk. 9). (Illus.). 120p. 1976. 30.00 (ISBN 0-521-21092-5); pap. 10.95x (ISBN 0-521-21093-3). Cambridge U Pr.
Protein Transmission Through Living Membranes: Proceedings. Brambell Symposium 2nd, Wales, July 1978. Ed. by W. A. Hemmings. LC 79-15662. 1979. 88.00 (ISBN 0-444-80112-X, North Holland). Elsevier.
Proteinases & Tumor Invasion, Vol. 6. Ed. by Peter Strauli et al. (European Organization for Research on Treatment of Cancer (EORTC)). 227p. 1980. 22.50 (ISBN 0-89004-515-1). Raven.
Proteins, Vol. 1. 3rd ed. Hans Neurath & Robert L. Hill. 1975. 54.75 (ISBN 0-12-516301-0); by subscription 47.00 (ISBN 0-12-516301-0). Acad Pr.
Proteins: A Guide to Study by Physical & Chemical Methods. Rudolph Haschemeyer & Audrey H. Haschemeyer. LC 72-13134. 528p. 1973. 36.50 (ISBN 0-471-35850-9, Pub. by Wiley-Interscience). Wiley.
Proteins of Animal Cell Plasma Membranes, Vol. 1. Donald F. Wellach. 1978. 19.20 (ISBN 0-88831-011-0). Eden Med Res.
Proteins of the Nervous System. 2nd ed. Ed. by Ralph Bradshaw & Diana Schneider. 407p. 1980. 39.00 (ISBN 0-89004-327-2). Raven.
Proteins of the Nervous System. Ed. by Diana J. Schneider et al. LC 73-79287. 300p. 1973. 24.50 (ISBN 0-911216-54-5). Raven.
Proteins: Structure & Function, 2 bks. M. Funatsu et al. 1972. Vol. 1. 27.95 (ISBN 0-470-28770-5); Vol. 2. o.p. (ISBN 0-470-28771-3). Halsted Pr.
Protest & Punishment: The Story of the Social & Political Protesters Transported to Australia, 1788-1868. George Rude. 1978. 29.95x (ISBN 0-19-822430-3). Oxford U Pr.
Protest, Direct Action, Repression: Dissent in American Society from Colonial Times to the Present. Ed. by Dick Hoerder. 434p. 1977. text ed. 48.00 (ISBN 3-7940-7009-7, Pub. by K G Saur). Gale.
Protest from the Right. Robert A. Rosenstone. Ed. by Fred Krinsky & Joseph Boskin. (Insight Series: Studies in Contemporary Issues). 128p. 1968. pap. text ed. 4.95x (ISBN 0-02-477250-X, 47725). Macmillan.
Protest Makers: The British Nuclear Disarmament Movement 1958-1965, Twenty Years on. Richard Taylor & Colin Pritchard. (Illus.). 180p. 1980. 24.00 (ISBN 0-08-025211-7). Pergamon.
Protest Movements in America. Michael Useem. LC 74-34014. (Studies in Sociology Ser.). 68p. 1975. pap. text ed. 2.50 (ISBN 0-672-61356-5). Bobbs.
Protest Movements in Colonial East Africa-Aspects of Early African Response to European Rule. Robert Strayer et al. LC 73-85549. (Foreign & Comparative Studies-Eastern African Ser.: No.12). 96p. 1973. pap. 4.50x (ISBN 0-915984-09-1). Syracuse U Foreign Comp.
Protestant-Catholic-Jew: An Essay in American Religious Sociology. rev. ed. Will Herberg. LC 60-5931. 1955. pap. 2.50 (ISBN 0-385-09438-8, A195, Anch). Doubleday.
Protestant Church Music in America: A Short Survey of Men & Movements from 1564 to the Present. Robert Stevenson. (Illus.). 1970. pap. 2.95 o.p. (ISBN 0-393-00535-6, Norton Lib). Norton.
Protestant Dictionary: Containing Articles on the History, Doctrines, & Practices of the Christian Church. Ed. by Charles Wright & Charles Neil. LC 73-155436. 1971. Repr. of 1933 ed. 32.00 (ISBN 0-8103-3388-0). Gale.
Protestant Ethic & the Spirit of Capitalism. rev. ed. Max Weber. 1977. pap. 3.95 o.p. (ISBN 0-684-15502-8, SL756, ScribT). Scribner.
Protestant Tutor. Benjamin Harris. Ed. by Alison Lurie & Justin G. Schiller. Incl. New-England Primer, Enlarged. LC 75-32135. (Classics of Children's Literature 1621-1932 Ser.). PLB 38.00 (ISBN 0-8240-2252-1). Garland Pub.
Protestantism & the New South: North Carolina Baptists & Methodists in Political Crisis, 1894-1903. Frederick A. Bode. LC 75-1289. 300p. 1976. 10.95x (ISBN 0-8139-0597-4). U Pr of Va.
Protestation of the Generall Assemblie Made in the High Kirk, & at the Mercate Crosse of Glasgow. LC 79-26239. (English Experience Ser.: No. 343). 1971. Repr. of 1638 ed. 7.00 (ISBN 90-221-0525-3). Walter J Johnson.
Proteus: His Lies, His Truth. Robert M. Adams. 192p. 1973. 7.95x o.p. (ISBN 0-393-04353-3). Norton.
Protides of the Biological Fluids, Colloquium 28: Proceedings of the 28th Colloquium on Protides of the Biological Fluids, Brussels, 5-8 May 1980. LC 58-5908. (Illus.). 600p. 1980. 120.00 (ISBN 0-08-026370-4). Pergamon.
Protides of the Biological Fluids: Proceedings, Colloquium on Protides of the Biological Fluids, 25th. Dienstfrey. LC 58-5908. 1978. text ed. 150.00 (ISBN 0-08-021524-6). Pergamon.
Protides of the Biological Fluids: Prceedings, Colloquium on Protides of the Biological Fluids, 26th. Ed. by H. Peeters. LC 58-5908. (Illus.). 1978. text ed. 150.00 (ISBN 0-08-023182-9). Pergamon.
Protides of the Biological Fluids: Proceedings, Colloquium on Protides of the Biological Fluids, 24th. Ed. by H. Peeters. 1977. 150.00 (ISBN 0-08-020359-0). Pergamon.
Protides of the Biological Fluids: Proceedings. Colloquium on Protides of the Biological Fluids, 27th, Brussels, Apr. 30-May 3, 1979. Ed. by H. Peeters. LC 58-5908. (Illus.). 895p. 1980. 150.00 (ISBN 0-08-024933-7). Pergamon.
Proto Algonquians. Willard Walker. (Pdr Publications on North American Linguistic Prehistory Ser.: No.1). 18p. 1975. pap. text ed. 1.00x o.p. (ISBN 90-316-0058-X). Humanities.
Proto-Austronesian. 2nd ed. Otto C. Dahl. (Scandinavian Institute of Asian Studies Monograph: No. 15). 146p. (Orig.). 1977. pap. text ed. 11.00x (ISBN 0-7007-0064-1). Humanities.
Proto-Indo-European Syntax. Winfred P. Lehmann. LC 52-2570. 382p. 1974. 20.00x (ISBN 0-292-76419-7). U of Tex Pr.
Proto-Lolish. David Bradley. (Scandanavian Institute of Asian Studies Monograph: No. 39). (Orig.). 1980. pap. text ed. 18.00x (ISBN 0-7007-0128-1). Humanities.
Proto-Oceanic Palatals. Robert A. Blust. 1979. text ed. 15.00x (ISBN 0-8248-0684-0, Pub. by Polynesian Soc). U Pr of Hawaii.
Proto-Takanan Phonology. Victor Girard. (U. C. Publ. in Linguistics: Vol. 70). 1971. pap. 9.50x (ISBN 0-520-09369-0). U of Cal Pr.
Protocol of a Damnation: A Novel. Peter Berger. 250p. 1975. 7.95 (ISBN 0-8164-0280-9). Crossroad NY.
Protocols for Perinatal Practice. Rosanne H. Perez. (Illus.). 450p. 1981. text ed. 19.95 (ISBN 0-8016-3805-4). Mosby.
Protocols for Prehospital Emergency Care. Jean Abbott et al. (Illus.). 200p. 1980. softcover 11.95 (ISBN 0-683-01563-X). Williams & Wilkins.
Protocols Handbook for Nurse Practitioners. Billie J. Klaus. LC 79-14389. 1979. 13.95 (ISBN 0-471-05219-1, Pub. by Wiley-Medical). Wiley.
Protocols of the Meetings of the Learned Elders of Zion. Tr. by Victor E. Marsden from Russian. 1978. pap. 4.00x (ISBN 0-911038-42-6). Noontide.
Protoplasmic Streaming. N. Kamiya. (Protoplasmatologia: Vol. 8, Pt. 3a). (Illus.). 1959. pap. 57.90 o.p. (ISBN 0-387-80524-9). Springer-Verlag.
Protozoa. Albert Westphal. (Illus.). 1976. 35.00x (ISBN 0-216-90216-9). Intl Ideas.
Protozoa in Biological Research. Ed. by Gary N. Calkins & Francis M. Summers. (Illus.). 1964. Repr. of 1941 ed. 38.50 o.s.i. (ISBN 0-02-842460-3). Hafner.
Protozoa: Introduction to Protozoology. John N. Farmer. LC 80-10817. (Illus.). 1980. pap. text ed. 26.95 (ISBN 0-8016-1550-X). Mosby.
Protozoology. 2nd, rev. ed. K. G. Grell. LC 73-77394. (Illus.). vii, 554p. 1973. 26.20 (ISBN 0-387-06239-4). Springer-Verlag.
Protozoology. 5th ed. Richard R. Kudo. (Illus.). 1188p. 1977. 33.75 (ISBN 0-398-01058-7). C C Thomas.
Protracted Game: A Wei-Ch'i Interpretation of Maoist Revolutionary Strategy. Scott A. Boorman. LC 70-83039. 1969. 14.95 (ISBN 0-19-500490-6). Oxford U Pr.
Proud. Arthur Moore. (River of Fortune Ser.). 400p. (Orig.). 1980. pap. 2.50 (ISBN 0-89083-665-5). Zebra.
Proud & the Free. Howard Fast. 1977. pap. 1.75 o.p. (ISBN 0-449-30777-8, X777, Prem). Fawcett.
Proud Beggars. Albert Cossery. Tr. by Thomas Cushing from Fr. 230p. 1981. 14.00 (ISBN 0-87685-451-X); signed ed. 20.00 (ISBN 0-87685-452-8); pap. 6.50 (ISBN 0-87685-450-1). Black Sparrow.
Proud Flesh. James Purdy. 58p. 1981. limited signed ed. 40.00 (ISBN 0-935716-07-6). Lord John.
Proud Gun. Gordon D. Shirreffs. 1977. pap. 1.25 (ISBN 0-505-51197-5). Tower Bks.
Proud Hunter. Marianne Harvey. (Orig.). 1981. pap. 3.25 (ISBN 0-440-17098-2). Dell.
Proud Island. 2nd ed. Peadar O'Connell. 1975. 3.95 o.p. (ISBN 0-686-23687-4); pap. 3.95 o.p. (ISBN 0-905140-28-1). Irish Bk Ctr.
Proud Maiden, Tungak & the Sun. Adapted by & tr. by Mirra Ginsburg. LC 73-19060. (Illus.). 32p. (gr. k-2). 1974. 7.95 (ISBN 0-02-736260-4). Macmillan.
Proud Mexicans. Robert Decker & Esther T. Marquez. (Illus.). 250p. (gr. 7-12). 1976. pap. 5.25 (ISBN 0-88345-254-5). Regents Pub.
Proud Profession: Memoirs of a Wall Street Journal Reporter, Editor & Publisher. William F. Kerby. 200p. 1981. 12.95 (ISBN 0-87094-235-2). Dow Jones-Irwin.
Proud Tower. Barbara W. Tuchman. 1966. 16.95 (ISBN 0-02-620300-6). Macmillan.
Proud White Cat. Ruth Hurlimann. (Illus.). (ps-3). 1977. 8.25 (ISBN 0-688-22095-9); PLB 7.92 (ISBN 0-688-32095-3). Morrow.
Proudfoot's Way. Eleanor F. Lattimore. LC 77-20057. (Illus.). (gr. 2-5). 1978. 7.95 (ISBN 0-688-22145-9); PLB 7.63 (ISBN 0-688-32145-3). Morrow.
Proust Dictionary. Maxine A. Vogely. 765p. 1981. 50.00x (ISBN 0-87875-205-6). Whitston Pub.
Proust et le Texte Producteur. Ed. by John Erickson & Irene Pages. vi, 147p. (Orig., Fr & Eng.). 1980. pap. 7.95 (ISBN 0-88955-000-X). U of Guelph.
Proust et Peguy: Des Affinites Meconnues. Jacques Viard. 64p. 1972. pap. text ed. 5.00x (ISBN 0-485-16106-0, Athlone Pr). Humanities.
Proust: L'amour comme verite humaine et romanesque. new ed. Bernard Pluchart-Simon. (Collection themes et textes). 191p. (Orig., Fr.). 1975. pap. 6.75 (ISBN 2-03-035029-X, 2683). Larousse.
Proust Screenplay. Harold Pinter. LC 77-78081. 1977. pap. 3.95 (ISBN 0-394-17018-0, E690, Ever). Grove.
Proust's Additions, 2 vols. Alison Winton. Incl. Vol. 1. (ISBN 0-521-21610-9); Vol. 2. (ISBN 0-521-21611-7). LC 76-58869. 1977. 68.00 set (ISBN 0-521-21612-5). Cambridge U Pr.
Proust's "Recherche" A Psychoanalytic Interpretation. Randolph Splitter. 176p. 1981. 20.00 (ISBN 0-7100-0664-0). Routledge & Kegan.
Prout: The Alternative to Capitalism & Marxism. Ravi Batra. LC 80-67184. 221p. 1980. lib. bdg. 16.75 (ISBN 0-8191-1187-2); pap. text ed. 8.50 (ISBN 0-8191-1188-0). U Pr of Amer.
Provado Pelo Fogo. Tr. by Merrill Womach & Virginia Womach. (Portugese Bks.). (Port.). 1979. 1.25 (ISBN 0-8297-0842-1). Life Pubs Intl.
Provence. A. N. Brangham. (History, People & Places Ser.). (Illus.). 1978. 12.50 o.p. (ISBN 0-904978-15-X). Hippocrene Bks.
Provence & Pound. Peter Makin. LC 77-76186. 1979. 27.50x (ISBN 0-520-03488-0). U of Cal Pr.
Provence touristique. (Beautes de la France). (Illus.). 1978. 18.25 (ISBN 2-03-013925-4, 3156). Larousse.
Provenzalische Lautlehre: Mit Einer Karte. Carl L. Appel. LC 80-2165. (Provenzalische Chrestomathie Ser.). 1981. Repr. of 1918 ed. 30.00 (ISBN 0-404-19027-8). AMS Pr.
Proverbial Comparisons & Related Expressions in Spanish. Shirley L. Arora. (Publications in Folklore & Mythology Ser.: Vol.29). 1977. 20.00x (ISBN 0-520-09552-9). U of Cal Pr.
Proverbial Comparisons in Ricardo Palma's Tradiciones Peruanas. Shirley L. Arora. (U. C. Publ. in Folklore Studies: Vol. 16). 1966. pap. 11.00x (ISBN 0-520-09138-8). U of Cal Pr.
Proverbios: Reflexion de la Vida. Moises Chavez. 1976. pap. 2.75 (ISBN 0-311-46069-0, Edit Mundo). Casa Bautista.
Proverbs. Charles Bridges. (Geneva Commentaries Ser.). 1979. 14.95 (ISBN 0-85151-088-4). Banner of Truth.
Proverbs, Notes. H. A. Ironside. Date not set. 8.25 (ISBN 0-87213-382-6). Loizeaux.
Proverbs. C. H. Toy. LC 99-5903. (International Critical Commentary Ser.). 592p. Repr. of 1899 ed. text ed. 23.00x. Attic Pr.
Proverbs: A Selection. Ed. by Elvajean Hall. LC 73-10094. (Illustrated Editions). (Illus.). (gr. 7 up). 1970. PLB 3.90 o.p. (ISBN 0-531-01084-8). Watts.
Proverbs & Ecclesiastes. John J. Collins. LC 79-92067. (Knox Preaching Guides Ser.). 117p. (Orig., John Hayes series editor). 1980. pap. 4.50 (ISBN 0-8042-3218-0). John Knox.
Proverbs & Parables: God's Wisdom for Living. Dee Brestin. (Fisherman Bible Studyguides). 1975. saddle-stitch 1.95 (ISBN 0-87788-694-6). Shaw Pubs.
Proverbs for Easier Living. Jo Berry. LC 80-50540. 160p. 1980. pap. 4.95 (ISBN 0-8307-0748-4, 5413605). Regal.
Proverbs of Scotland. Alexander Hislop. LC 68-21774. 1968. Repr. of 1868 ed. 20.00 (ISBN 0-8103-3201-9). Gale.
Proverbs, Proverbial Expressions, & Popular Rhymes of Scotland. Ed. by Andrew Cheviot. LC 68-23144. 1969. Repr. of 1896 ed. 18.00 (ISBN 0-8103-3198-5). Gale.
Proverbs to Live by. Joshua S. Sperka. Bd. with Book of Proverbs. 246p. 1966. 4.95x (ISBN 0-8197-0183-1). Bloch.
Providence: A Pictorial History. Patrick T. Conley. Ed. by Donna R. Friedman. (Illus.). 205p. 1981. pap. price not set (ISBN 0-89865-128-X). Donning Co.
Providence in Colonial Times. Gertrude S. Kimball. LC 76-87452. (American Scene Ser.). (Illus.). 391p. 1972. Repr. of 1912 ed. lib. bdg. 49.50 (ISBN 0-306-71524-4). Da Capo.
Providence Island. Calder Willingham. LC 68-8088. 10.00 (ISBN 0-8149-0236-7). Vanguard.
Providence of Evil. P. T. Geach. LC 76-28005. 1977. 18.95 (ISBN 0-521-21477-7). Cambridge U Pr.
Providence Their Guide: The Story of the Long Range Desert Group 1940-1945. David L. Owen. (Elite Unit Ser.: No. 3). (Illus.). 238p. 1981. 19.95 (ISBN 0-89839-040-0). Battery Pr.
Providence: Ye Lost Towne at Severn in Maryland. James E. Moss. LC 76-5575. (Illus.). 1976. lib. bdg. 16.50x (ISBN 0-938420-14-3). Md Hist.
Providencia y Revolucion. Pedro Arana Q. 1.40 o.p. (ISBN 0-686-12563-0). Banner of Truth.
Providing Adequate Retirement Income: Pension Reform in the United States & Abroad. James Schulz et al. LC 74-82592. (Illus.). 350p. 1974. text ed. 20.00x (ISBN 0-87451-100-3). U Pr of New Eng.
Providing Early Mobility. LC 80-25062. (Nursing Photobook Ser.). (Illus.). 160p. 1980. text ed. 12.95 (ISBN 0-916730-27-1). InterMed Comm.
Providing for Leisure for the City Dweller: A Review of Needs & Processes with Guidelines for Charge. Martin Putterill & Cheree Bloch. (Illus.). 141p. 1978. pap. 16.00x (ISBN 0-8476-3113-3). Rowman.
Province Beyond the River: A Protestant's Days in a Trappist Monastery. W. P. Jones. 144p. (Orig.). 1981. pap. 5.95 (ISBN 0-8091-2363-0). Paulist Pr.
Province of Agra. Dharma Srivastava. 1979. text ed. 18.50x (ISBN 0-391-01814-0). Humanities.

Province of Rhetoric. 4th ed. Ed. by Joseph Schwartz & J. A. Rycenga. 1965. 11.95 (ISBN 0-8260-7955-5). Wiley.

Province of Sociology: Selected Profiles. William A. Pearman & Robert A. Rotz. LC 79-17996. 212p. 1981. text ed. 15.95 (ISBN 0-88229-434-2); pap. text ed. 8.95 (ISBN 0-88229-735-X). Nelson-Hall.

Provinces & Provincial Capitals of the World. Morris Fisher. 1967. 10.00 (ISBN 0-8108-0121-3). Scarecrow.

Provincial America, 1600-1763. Bradley Chapin. LC 65-11895. (Orig.). 1966. pap. text ed. 3.50 o.s.i. (ISBN 0-02-905320-X). Free Pr.

Provincial Cemetary of the Pyramid Age Naga-Ed-der, Pt. 3. George A. Reisner. (U. C. Publ. in Egyptain Archaeology: Vol. 6). 1932. 68.50x (ISBN 0-520-01060-4). U of Cal Pr.

Provincial Government of the Mughals, 1526-1658. 2nd ed. Paramatma Saran. (Illus.). 464p. 1973. lib. bdg. 12.95x (ISBN 0-210-22690-0). Asia.

Provincial Letters of Blaise Pascal with a Biographical Preface. 324p. 1980. Repr. lib. bdg. 20.00 (ISBN 0-89984-387-5). Century Bookbindery.

Provincial Militarism & the Chinese Republic: The Yunnan Army, Nineteen Hundred & Five to Nineteen Twenty-Five. Donald S. Sutton. (Michigan Studies on China). (Illus.). 384p. 1980. 18.50x (ISBN 0-472-08813-0). U of Mich Pr.

Provincial Mineral Policies: Newfoundland 1945-75. Michael J. Prince. 60p. (Orig.). 1977. pap. text ed. 3.50x (ISBN 0-686-63140-4, Pub. by Ctr Resource Stud Canada). Renouf.

Provincial Mineral Policies: Saskatchewan 1944-75. Ronald C. Murray. 65p. (Orig.). 1978. pap. text ed. 3.50x (ISBN 0-686-63139-0, Pub. by Ctr Resource Stud Canada). Renouf.

Provincial Politics & Indian Nationalism. G. Johnson. (South Asian Studies: No. 14). 300p. 1973. 29.95 (ISBN 0-521-20259-0). Cambridge U Pr.

Provincials. Eli Evans. LC 73-80747. 1976. pap. 7.95 (ISBN 0-689-70532-8, 221). Atheneum.

Proving Gun. Ray Hogan. LC 75-9224. 192p. 1975. 5.95 o.p. (ISBN 0-385-11177-0). Doubleday.

Proving Gun. Ray Hogan. 1980. lib. bdg. 10.95 (ISBN 0-8161-3172-4, Large Print Bks). G K Hall.

Provision for the Disabled. Eda Topliss. (Aspects of Social Policy Ser.). 1975. 14.00x o.p. (ISBN 0-631-16220-8, Pub. by Basil Blackwell England); pap. 6.50x o.p. (ISBN 0-631-16510-X). Biblio Dist.

Provision of Education in England & Wales. J. P. Parry. 1971. text ed. 27.50x (ISBN 0-04-371015-8). Allen Unwin.

Provisional Methodology for Soil Degradation Assessment. 94p. 1980. pap. 7.50 (ISBN 9-2510-0869-8, F1958, FAO). Unipub.

Provisional World List of Periodicals Dealing with Science & Technology Policies 1973. (Science Policy Studies & Documents Ser., No. 33). 112p. 1974. pap. 6.00 (ISBN 92-3-101189-8, U500, UNESCO). Unipub.

Provisions of Federal Law Held Unconstitutional by the Supreme Court of the United States. U. S. Library of Congress Legislative Reference Service. Ed. by Wilfred C. Gilbert. LC 75-35364. (U.S. Government Documents Program Ser.). 148p. 1976. Repr. of 1936 ed. lib. bdg. 13.75x (ISBN 0-8371-8605-6, USPF). Greenwood.

Provocateur. Rene-Victor Pilhes. Tr. by Denver Lindley & Helen Lindley. LC 76-5555. 1977. 10.00 o.s.i. (ISBN 0-06-013337-6, HarpT). Har-Row.

Provoked Wife. John Vanbrugh. Ed. by Curt A. Zimansky. LC 69-12337. (Regents Restoration Drama Ser). 1970. 9.50x (ISBN 0-8032-0374-8); pap. 2.65x (ISBN 0-8032-5373-7, BB 272, Bison). U of Nebr Pr.

Proximity Spaces. S. A. Naimpally & B. D. Warrack. LC 73-118858. (Tracts in Mathematics & Mathematical Physics: No. 59). 1971. 20.50 (ISBN 0-521-07935-7). Cambridge U Pr.

Proxy. Violette Newton. 4.50 o.p. (ISBN 0-685-48832-2). Nortex Pr.

Prudence. Jilly Cooper. 192p. 1981. pap. 1.95 (ISBN 0-449-24361-3, Crest). Fawcett.

Prune Orchard Management. David Ramos. (Illus.). 144p. (Orig.). Date not set. pap. text ed. price not set (ISBN 0-931876-45-1). AG Sci Pubns.

Pruning & Grafting. Oliver Allen. Ed. by Time-Life Books. (Encyclopedia of Gardening). (Illus.). 1979. 11.95 (ISBN 0-8094-2633-1). Time-Life.

Pruning & Grafting. James U. Crockett & Oliver E. Allen. (Time-Life Encyclopedia of Gardening Ser.). (Illus.). 1978. lib. bdg. 10.98 (ISBN 0-686-50001-6). Silver.

Pruning of Trees, Shrubs & Conifers. George E. Brown. 1977. 24.95 o.p. (ISBN 0-571-09853-3, Pub. by Faber & Faber); pap. 9.95 (ISBN 0-571-11084-3). Merrimack Bk Serv.

Pruning Simplified: A Complete Guide to Pruning Trees, Bushes, Hedges, Flowers, & House Plants. Lewis Hall. 1979. 12.95 (ISBN 0-87857-248-1). Rodale Pr Inc.

Pruning Simplified: A Complete Guide to Pruning Trees, Shrubs, Bushes, Hedges, Vines, Flowers, Garden Plants, Houseplants & Bonsai. Lewis Hill. Ed. by Roger B. Yepsen. (Illus.). 224p. 1981. pap. 9.95 (ISBN 0-87857-249-X). Rodale Pr Inc.

Pruning Word: The Parables of Flannery O'Connor. John R. May. LC 75-19878. 216p. 1976. text ed. 10.95x o.p. (ISBN 0-268-01518-X). U of Notre Dame Pr.

Prunings-Accruings. Richard Kostelanetz. 24p. 1978. pap. 25.00 signed & lettered. a-z (ISBN 0-932360-22-X). RK Edns.

Prussian Crusade. William Urban. LC 80-5647. 469p. 1980. lib. bdg. 24.00 (ISBN 0-8191-1278-X); pap. text ed. 15.50 (ISBN 0-8191-1279-8). U Pr of Amer.

Prussian Schoolteachers: Profession & Office, 1763-1848. Anthony J. La Vopa. LC 79-24873. 230p. 1980. 19.50x (ISBN 0-8078-1426-1). U of NC Pr.

Prytaneion: Its Function & Architectural Form. Stephen G. Miller. LC 76-24590. 1978. 20.00x (ISBN 0-520-03316-7). U of Cal Pr.

P.S. Write Soon. Colby Rodowsky. (gr. 5 up). 1978. PLB 7.90 s&l (ISBN 0-531-01474-6). Watts.

P.S. Write Soon. Colby Rodowsky. (YA) (gr. 7-12). 1980. pap. 1.50 (ISBN 0-440-97119-5, LFL). Dell.

PSA 1978: Symposia, Special Sessions & Invited Lectures, Vol. 2. Philosophy of Science Association, Biennial Meeting, 1978. Ed. by Peter D. Asqwith & Ian Hacking. 1981. write for info. (ISBN 0-917586-10-7); pap. write for info. (ISBN 0-917586-09-3). Philos Sci Assn.

PSA 1980, Vol. 1. Ed. by Peter D. Asquith & Ronald Giere. 315p. 1980. 9.50 (ISBN 0-917586-14-X); pap. 7.50 (ISBN 0-917586-13-1). Philos Sci Assn.

Psallite. Richard Patt. (Psallite Ser.: Series A). 1977. pap. 2.75 (ISBN 0-570-03764-6, 12-2698). Concordia.

Psallite-Series B. Richard Patt. 1978. pap. 2.75 (ISBN 0-570-03784-0, 12-2738). Concordia.

Psalm Eight from Voices of Children. G. A. Pottebaum. (Little People's Paperbacks Ser.). 1979. pap. 0.99 (ISBN 0-8164-2254-0). Crossroad NY.

Psalm Eighty-Four the Sparrow Finds a Home. G. A. Pottebaum. (Little People's Paperbacks Ser.). 1979. pap. 0.99 (ISBN 0-8164-2256-7). Crossroad NY.

Psalm Ninety-Eight Sing a New Song. G. A. Pottebaum. (Little People's Paperbacks Ser.). 1979. pap. 0.99 (ISBN 0-8164-2257-5). Crossroad NY.

Psalm One Hundred Fifty the Praise Parade. G. A. Pottebaum. (Little People's Paperback Ser.). 1979. pap. 0.99 (ISBN 0-8164-2258-3). Crossroad NY.

Psalm One Hundred Nineteen. Charles Bridges. 1977. 11.95 (ISBN 0-85151-176-7). Banner of Truth.

Psalm Singer's Amusement. William Billings. LC 73-5100. (Earlier American Music Ser.: Vol. 20). 104p. 1974. Repr. of 1781 ed. lib. bdg. 22.50 (ISBN 0-306-70587-7). Da Capo.

Psalm Twenty-Three. Haddon W. Robinson. (Illus., Orig.). 1968. pap. 1.95 (ISBN 0-8024-6935-3); pap. 2.95 large print (ISBN 0-8024-6934-5). Moody.

Psalm Twenty-Three My Shepherd Is the Lord. G. A. Pottebaum. (Little People's Paperbacks Ser.). 1979. pap. 0.99 (ISBN 0-8164-2255-9). Crossroad NY.

Psalms. C. A. Briggs & E. G. Briggs. LC 6-26084. (International Critical Commentary). 22.00x (ISBN 0-567-05011-4). Attic Pr.

Psalms. Ernesto Cardenal. 96p. (Span.). 1981. pap. 3.95 (ISBN 0-8245-0044-X). Crossroad NY.

Psalms. rev. ed. Arno C. Gaebelein. 1939. 6.75 (ISBN 0-87213-222-6). Loizeaux.

Psalms. Irving L. Jensen. (Bible Self-Study Ser). 1970. pap. 2.25 (ISBN 0-8024-1019-7). Moody.

Psalms. W. S. Plumer. (Geneva Commentaries Ser.). 1978. 26.95 (ISBN 0-85151-209-7). Banner of Truth.

Psalms, 3 vols. Date not set. 43.50 set (ISBN 0-86524-038-8). Klock & Klock.

Psalms: A Guide to Prayer & Praise. Ron Klug. (Fisherman Bible Study Guides). 1979. saddlestitched 1.95 (ISBN 0-87788-699-7). Shaw Pubs.

Psalms Around Us. Ed. by Countryside Press Editors. (Illus.). 96p. 1974. deluxe ed. 9.95 (ISBN 0-385-01087-7). Doubleday.

Psalms-Now. Leslie Brandt. LC 73-78108. 1973. 7.50 (ISBN 0-570-03230-X, 15-2125). Concordia.

Psalms of Comfort. Tr. by Leslie Brandt. (Psalms Now Gift Books). 1977. pap. 1.75 (ISBN 0-570-07452-5, 12-2686). Concordia.

Psalms of Joy. Tr. by Leslie Brandt. (Psalms Now Gift Books). 1977. pap. 1.75 (ISBN 0-570-07451-7, 12-2685). Concordia.

Psalms of Praise. Tr. by Leslie Brandt. (Psalms Now Gift Books). 1977. pap. 1.75 (ISBN 0-570-07453-3, 12-2687). Concordia.

Psalms of Strength. Leslie Brandt. (Psalms Now Gift Books). 1977. pap. 1.75 (ISBN 0-570-07450-9, 12-2684). Concordia.

Psalms of the Jerusalem Bible. Jones, Alexander (General Editor) 1970. pap. 2.95 (ISBN 0-385-02525-4, Im). Doubleday.

Psalms, Studies in the Hebrew Text. John J. Davis. pap. 8.00 o.p. (ISBN 0-88469-117-9). BMH Bks.

Psalms, Studies on Book One. H. A. Ironside. Date not set. 5.50 (ISBN 0-87213-383-4). Loizeaux.

Psalms to Live by. Ed. by J. Calvin Reid. Tr. by Kenneth N. Taylor. LC 72-86211. (Orig.). 1972. pap. 1.75 o.p. (ISBN 0-8307-0189-3, 50-071-00). Regal.

Psalter. 3.50 (ISBN 0-8164-0311-2). Crossroad NY.

PSAT (Preliminary Scholastic Aptitute Test) Jerry Bobrow & William A. Covino. Date not set. pap. text ed. cancelled. Cliffs.

Pschyotropic Drugs. Burrows & Norman. 528p. 1980. 68.00 (ISBN 0-8247-1009-6). Dekker.

Pseudo-Cleft Construction in English. F. R. Higgins. Ed. by Jorge Hankamer. LC 78-66547. (Outstanding Dissertations in Linguistics Ser.). 1979. lib. bdg. 44.00 (ISBN 0-8240-9683-5). Garland Pub.

Pseudo-Dionysius Aeropagite: The Divine Names & Mystical Theology. Tr. by John D. Jones. (Translation Ser.: No. 21). 320p. 24.95 (ISBN 0-87462-221-2). Marquette.

Pseudo-Epiphanius Testimony Book. Robert V. Hotchkiss. LC 74-15203. (Society of Biblical Literature. Texts & Translation-Early Christian Literature Ser.). 1974. pap. 4.50 (ISBN 0-88414-043-1, 060204). Scholars Pr Ca.

Pseudo-Hippocratic Tract & Greek Philosophy. J. Mansfeld. (Philosophy Texts & Studies: No. 20). 1970. text ed. 33.50x (ISBN 9-0232-0701-7). Humanities.

Pseudo-Plato, Axiochus. Jackson P. Hershbell. Tr. by Jackson P. Hershbell. LC 79-20127. (Society of Biblical Literature, Text & Translations: 21). Date not set. price not set (ISBN 0-89130-353-7, 060221); pap. price not set (ISBN 0-89130-354-5). Scholars Pr CA.

Pseudo-Riemannian Symmetric Spaces. Michel Cahen & Monique Parker. LC 79-27541. (Memoirs Ser.). 1980. 6.80 (ISBN 0-8218-2229-2, MEMO-229). Am Math.

Pseudo Science of B. F. Skinner. Tibor R. Machan. 1974. 9.95 o.p. (ISBN 0-87000-236-8). Arlington Hse.

Pseudo-Spin Method in Magnetism & Ferroelectricity. L. Novakovic. 200p. 1976. text ed. 34.00 (ISBN 0-08-018060-4). Pergamon.

Pseudodifferential Operators. Michael E. Taylor. LC 80-8580. (Princeton Mathematical Ser.: No. 34). 468p. 1981. 30.00x (ISBN 0-691-08282-0). Princeton U Pr.

Pseudomonas Aeruginosa: Ecological Aspects & Patient Colonization. Viola M. Young. LC 76-56919. 1977. 12.50 (ISBN 0-89004-149-0). Raven.

Pseudonyms & Nicknames Dictionary. Ed. by Jennifer Mossman. LC 80-13274. 700p. 1980. 55.00 (ISBN 0-8103-0549-6). Gale.

Pseudonyms of Authors. John E. Haynes. LC 68-30620. 1969. Repr. of 1882 ed. 18.00 (ISBN 0-8103-3142-X). Gale.

Pseudophakia: Current Trends & Concepts. Marvin L. Kwitko & Donald L. Praeger. (Illus.). 456p. 1980. lib. bdg. 50.00 (ISBN 0-683-04800-7). Williams & Wilkins.

Pseudophakos. new ed. Norman S. Jaffe et al. LC 77-27307. (Illus.). 1978. text ed. 44.50 (ISBN 0-8016-2401-0). Mosby.

Pseudoscience & Mental Ability: The Origins & Fallacies of the IQ Controversy. Jeffrey Blum. LC 77-81371. 1978. 13.95 o.p. (ISBN 0-85345-420-5, CL 4205). Natl Rail Hist Soc DC Chap.

Psi & Altered States of Consciousness: Proceedings. International Conference on Hypnosis, Drugs, Dreams, & Psi, France, 1967. Ed. by Roberto Cavanna & Montague Ullman. LC 68-8909. 1968. 7.00 (ISBN 0-912328-11-8). Parapsych Foun.

PSI & States of Awareness. Proceedings of the International Conference, Paris, France, 1977. Ed. by Betty Shapin & Lisette Coly. LC 78-50167. 1978. 14.00 (ISBN 0-912328-30-4). Parapsych Foun.

PSI & the Mind: An Information Processing Approach. H. J. Irwin. LC 79-20587. 1979. 10.00 (ISBN 0-8108-1258-4). Scarecrow.

PSI Factors in Creativity. Proceedings of an International Conference, France, 1969. Ed. by Allan Angoff & Betty Shapin. LC 71-140141. 1970. 7.00 (ISBN 0-912328-18-5). Parapsych Foun.

PSI Favorable States of Consciousness: Proceedings. International Conference on Methodology in Psi Research, France, 1968. Ed. by Roberto Cavanna. LC 75-97821. 1970. 8.00 (ISBN 0-912328-17-7). Parapsych Foun.

PSI Trek. Laile Bartlett. 300p. 1981. 12.95 (ISBN 0-07-003915-1, GB). McGraw.

Psicologia. David A. Statt. Ed. by Mei Mei A. Pulido & Jose C. Hernandez. Tr. by Jose G. Romero. 272p. 1980. pap. text ed. 6.00x (ISBN 0-06-316850-2, Pub. by HarLA Mexico). Har-Row.

Psicologia de Jesus y la Salud Mental. Raymond L. Cramer. Tr. by Carlos A. Vargas from Eng. LC 76-16438. 191p. (Orig., Span.). 1976. pap. 3.25 (ISBN 0-89922-074-6). Edit Caribe.

Psicologia General. B. Von Haller Gilmer. (Span.). 1975. 9.40 (ISBN 0-06-313150-1, IntlDept). Har-Row.

Psicologia Pastoral de la Iglesia. Jorge A. Leon. LC 77-43121. 192p. (Orig., Span.). 1978. pap. 4.95 (ISBN 0-89922-113-0). Edit Caribe.

Psicologia Pastoral para Todos los Cristianos. Jorge A. Leon. LC 76-43121. 181p. (Orig., Span.). 1976. pap. 4.95 (ISBN 0-89922-020-7). Edit Caribe.

Psicologia y el Ministerio Cristiano. James E. Giles. 1978. 2.50 (ISBN 0-311-42059-1). Casa Bautista.

Psicologia y Religion. J. W. Drakeford. 1980. pap. 8.95 (ISBN 0-311-46035-6, Edit Mundo). Casa Bautista.

Psience: A General Theory of Existence. J. W. Nicholas. LC 77-11135. pap. 3.95 (ISBN 0-915520-09-5). Ross-Erikson.

PSL Model Railroad Guide Five: Operating Your Layout. Michael Andress. (Illus.). 64p. 1981. pap. 9.95 (ISBN 0-85059-436-7). Aztex.

PSL Model Railroad Guide Six: Branchline Modelling. Michael Andress. (Illus.). 64p. 1981. pap. 9.95 (ISBN 0-85059-437-5). Aztex.

PSRO & the Law. John Blum. LC 77-70436. 1977. 24.95 (ISBN 0-912862-39-4). Aspen Systems.

PSRO Journal Articles. Morton N. Chalef. 1977. spiral bdg. 18.00 o.p. (ISBN 0-87488-792-5). Med Exam.

PSRO: Utilization & Audit in Patient Care. Sharon V. Davidson. LC 75-43980. (Illus.). 380p. 1976. 18.95 (ISBN 0-8016-1209-8). Mosby.

PSSC Physics. 4th ed. Uri Haber-Schaim et al. (gr. 11-12). 1976. text ed. 14.40 o.p. (ISBN 0-669-97451-X); tchr's res. bk. 14.40 o.p. (ISBN 0-669-97469-2); lab. guide 4.20 o.p. (ISBN 0-669-97477-3); other materials avail. write for info. o.p. (ISBN 0-685-67389-8). Heath.

Pssst Doggie. Ezra J. Keats. LC 72-8642. (Illus.). 32p. (ps-1). 1973. PLB 4.95 o.p. (ISBN 0-531-02598-5). Watts.

Psy Fi One: An Anthology of Psychology in Science Fiction. Ed. by Kenneth B. Melvin et al. 1977. pap. text ed. 5.95x (ISBN 0-394-30576-0). Random.

Psych City. Ed. by Robert Cohen et al. LC 72-11593. 348p. 1974. text ed. 21.00 (ISBN 0-08-017082-X); pap. text ed. 12.75 (ISBN 0-08-017083-8). Pergamon.

Psyche & Bible: Three Old Testament Themes. Rivkah S. Kluger. Ed. by James Hillman. 130p. (Orig.). 1973. pap. 7.50 (ISBN 0-88214-107-4). Spring Pubns.

Psyche & Symbol: A Selection from the Writings of C. G. Jung. Carl G. Jung. LC 58-6627. 1958. pap. 3.50 (ISBN 0-385-09349-7, A136, Anch). Doubleday.

Psyche: Lectures on Psychology & Philosophy. James F. Sheridan. LC 79-66579. 1979. pap. text ed. 8.75 (ISBN 0-8191-0843-X). U Pr of Amer.

Psyche; or, the Legend of Love. Mary Tighe. Ed. by Donald H. Reiman. LC 75-31268. (Romantic Context Ser.: Poetry 1789-1830: Vol. 114). 1978. Repr. of 1805 ed. lib. bdg. 47.00 (ISBN 0-8240-2214-9). Garland Pub.

Psychedelic Drugs Reconsidered. Lester Grinspoon & James B. Bakalar. 1981. pap. 7.95 (ISBN 0-465-06451-5). Basic.

Psychiatric Aftercare: Planning for Community Mental Health Service. Max Silverstein. LC 68-21550. 1968. 6.00 o.p. (ISBN 0-8122-7565-9). U of Pa Pr.

Psychiatric Aspects of Criminology. Seymour Halleck & Walter Bromberg. 88p. 1968. pap. 10.75 photocopy ed. spiral (ISBN 0-398-00761-6). C C Thomas.

Psychiatric Aspects of School Desegregation, Vol. 3. GAP Committee on Social Issues. LC 57-7606. (Report No. 37). 1957. pap. 2.00 (ISBN 0-87318-045-3). Adv Psychiatry.

Psychiatric Aspects of the Prevention of Nuclear War, Vol. 5. GAP Committee on Social Issues. LC 64-7800. (Report No. 57). 1964. pap. 4.00 (ISBN 0-87318-076-3). Adv Psychiatry.

Psychiatric Assessment by Speech & Hearing Behavior. Clyde L. Rousey. (Illus.). 392p. 1974. text ed. 26.75 (ISBN 0-398-03034-0). C C Thomas.

Psychiatric Community Mental Health Nursing Case Studies. Margery M. Chisholm et al. 1976. sprial bdg. 9.50 (ISBN 0-87488-391-1). Med Exam.

Psychiatric Diagnosis: A Review of Research. George Frank. LC 74-13884. 1975. text ed. 23.00 (ISBN 0-08-017712-3). Pergamon.

Psychiatric Dictionary. Ed. by Robert J. Campbell. 800p. 1981. 29.50 (ISBN 0-19-502817-1). Oxford U Pr.

Psychiatric Disorders of Children with Congenital Rubella. Ed. by Stella Chess et al. LC 71-173092. 1971. 12.50 o.p. (ISBN 0-87630-046-8). Brunner-Mazel.

Psychiatric Education & the Primary Physician. Robert J. Campbell. (Task Force Report: No. 2). 74p. 1970. pap. 5.00 (ISBN 0-685-24864-X, P241-0). Am Psychiatric.

Psychiatric Education: Prologue to the 1980's. Anne H. Rosenfeld. Ed. by Ewald W. Busse et al. 544p. 1976. 15.00 (ISBN 0-685-84651-2, P235-0). Am Psychiatric.

Psychiatric Emergencies & the General Hospital. Joint Committee of the American Psychiatric Association & the American Hospital Association. 1965. pap. 1.25 o.p. (ISBN 0-685-24846-1, 159). Am Psychiatric.

Psychiatric Emergency - a Study of Patterns of Service. R. M. Glasscote. 111p. 1966. pap. 3.50 (ISBN 0-685-24858-5, P179-0). Am Psychiatric.

Psychiatric Epidemiology & Mental Health Planning. Ed. by R. E. Monroe et al. 400p. 1967. pap. 5.00 (ISBN 0-685-24861-5, P022-0). Am Psychiatric.

Psychiatric Foundations of Medicine, 6 vols. Ed. by George Balis et al. (Illus.). 1978. text ed. 200.00x set (ISBN 0-409-95160-9). Butterworths.

Psychiatric Glossary. 5th ed. Ed. by American Psychiatric Assn. 1980. text ed. 9.95 (ISBN 0-316-03656-0). Little.

Psychiatric Glossary. 4th ed. 1975. pap. 3.00 o.p. (ISBN 0-685-52215-6). Am Psychiatric.

Psychiatric Guide to Iodine Trichloride Therapy. 4th ed. Doris S. Brown & Hillyer Senning. (Illus.). 1979. pap. text ed. 20.00 (ISBN 0-931918-02-2, D-3). Busn Psych.

Psychiatric Halfway House: A Case Study. Naomi Rothwell & Joan Doniger. 284p. 1966. pap. 11.00 spiral (ISBN 0-398-01615-1). C C Thomas.

Psychiatric Hospital Treatment for the Nineteen Eighties. Ira D. Glick & William A. Hargreaves. LC 77-26995. 1979. 18.95 (ISBN 0-669-01502-4). Lexington Bks.

Psychiatric Ideologies & Institutions. Anselm Strauss et al. 418p. 1981. 19.95 (ISBN 0-87855-361-4); pap. 7.95 (ISBN 0-87855-785-7). Transaction Bks.

Psychiatric Illness in Adolescence. M. T. Haslam. 1975. 21.95 (ISBN 0-407-00019-4). Butterworths.

Psychiatric-Mental Health Nursing. 3rd ed. Frances B. Arje et al. (Nursing Examination Review Book: Vol. 2). 1972. spiral bdg. 6.00 (ISBN 0-87488-502-7). Med Exam.

Psychiatric-Mental Health Nursing. 2nd. ed. Dorris B. Payne. Ed. by Patricia A. Clunn. LC 77-71852. (Nursing Outline Ser.). 1977. pap. 8.50 spiral bdg. (ISBN 0-87488-379-2). Med Exam.

Psychiatric-Mental Nursing Continuing Education Review. Dorothea R. Hays et al. 1973. spiral bdg. 9.50 (ISBN 0-87488-351-2). Med Exam.

Psychiatric Nurse As a Family Therapist. Ed. by Shirley Smoyak. LC 75-5813. 251p. 1975. 14.50 (ISBN 0-471-80770-2, Pub. by Wiley Medical). Wiley.

Psychiatric Nursing. 7th ed. Mary Topalis & Donna Aguilera. LC 77-13051. (Illus.). 1978. pap. text ed. 16.95 (ISBN 0-8016-3148-3). Mosby.

Psychiatric Nursing. Holly S. Wilson & Carol R. Kneisl. LC 78-7775. 1979. 22.95 (ISBN 0-201-08340-X, 08340, M&N Div); wkbk. 7.95 (ISBN 0-201-08342-6); instr's guide 3.95 (ISBN 0-685-94886-2, 08341). A-W.

Psychiatric Nursing: A Basic Manual. 5th ed. Annie L. Crawford & Virginia C. Kilander. LC 80-15880. 140p. 1980. pap. text ed. 7.25 (ISBN 0-8036-2112-4). Davis Co.

Psychiatric Nursing: A Basic Text. Patricia C. Pothier. 1980. pap. text ed. 12.95 (ISBN 0-316-71484-4). Little.

Psychiatric Nursing in the Hospital & the Community. 3rd ed. Ann W. Burgess & Aaron Lazare. (Illus.). 736p. 1981. text ed. 19.95 (ISBN 0-13-731927-4). P-H.

Psychiatric Nursing Objective Tests. M. Jalim. 128p. 1981. pap. 5.95 (ISBN 0-571-11582-9, Pub. by Faber & Faber). Merrimack Bk Serv.

Psychiatric Nursing: PreTest Self-Assessment & Review. Nancy Rozendal & Patricia Fallon. LC 78-50596. (Nursing: Pretest Self-Assessment & Review Ser.). 1978. pap. 6.95 (ISBN 0-07-051569-7). McGraw-Pretest.

Psychiatric Outpatient. Lynn Gillis & Stella Egert. 1973. text ed. 10.95x (ISBN 0-571-10202-6, Pub. by Faber & Faber). Merrimack Bk Serv.

Psychiatric Patient Records. 57p. 1971. 1.75 (ISBN 0-685-37532-3, P184-0). Am Psychiatric.

Psychiatric Presentation of Medical Illness: Somatopsychic Disorders. Ed. by Richard C. Hall. (Illus.). 428p. 1980. text ed. 35.00 (ISBN 0-89335-098-2). Spectrum Pub.

Psychiatric Problems in Opthalmology. Jerome T. Pearlman et al. (Illus.). 180p. 1977. 16.75 (ISBN 0-398-03596-2). C C Thomas.

Psychiatric Programming of People: Neo-Behavioral Orthomolecular Psychiatry. H. L. Newbold. 170p. 1972. 17.25 (ISBN 0-08-016791-8). Pergamon.

Psychiatric Records in Mental Health Care. Carole Siegel & Susan K. Fischer. (Illus.). 250p. (Orig.). 1981. 15.00 (ISBN 0-87630-241-X). Brunner Mazel.

Psychiatric Research & the Assessment of Change, Vol. 6. GAP Committee on Research. LC 62-2872. (Report No. 63). 1966. pap. 3.00 (ISBN 0-87318-088-7). Adv Psychiatry.

Psychiatric Research in Practice: Biobehavioral Themes. E. A. Serafetinides. (Seminars in Psychology Ser.). 1981. 24.50 (ISBN 0-8089-1316-6). Grune.

Psychiatric Research in Public Service. Ed. by R. M. Steinhilber & G. A. Ulett. 166p. 1962. pap. 3.00 (ISBN 0-685-24862-3, P015-0). Am Psychiatric.

Psychiatric Signs & Symptoms Due to Medical Problems. Sydney Walker, 3rd. 1967. 13.25 o.p. (ISBN 0-398-02008-6). C C Thomas.

Psychiatric Study of Jesus. Albert Schweitzer. 7.50 (ISBN 0-8446-2894-8). Peter Smith.

Psychiatric Study of Myths & Fairy Tales: Their Origins, Meaning & Usefulness. 2nd ed. Julius E. Heuscher. (Illus.). 440p. 1974. 21.50 (ISBN 0-398-02851-6). C C Thomas.

Psychiatric Treatment in the Community. C. K. Kanno & P. L. Scheidemandel. 1974. 4.00 (ISBN 0-685-55572-5, 207). Am Psychiatric.

Psychiatric Utilization Review: Principles & Objectives. 64p. 1968. pap. 2.25 o.p. (ISBN 0-685-65577-6, P207-0). Am Psychiatric.

Psychiatrist & Public Issues, Vol. 7. GAP Committee on International Relations. LC 62-2872. (Report No. 74). 1969. pap. 2.00 (ISBN 0-87318-103-4). Adv Psychiatry.

Psychiatrist & Public Welfare Agencies, Vol. 9. GAP Committee on Psychiatry & the Community. LC 75-37889. (Report no. 94). 1975. pap. 3.00 (ISBN 0-87318-131-X). Adv Psychiatry.

Psychiatrist As Psychohistorian. Ed. by American Psychiatric Association's Task Force on Psychohistory. (Task Force Reports: No. 11). 33p. 1976. 5.00 (ISBN 0-685-76790-6, P221-0). Am Psychiatric.

Psychiatrists & Their Patients: A National Study of Private Office Practice. Judd Marmor. 181p. 1975. pap. 9.00 (ISBN 0-685-63943-6, P210-0). Am Psychiatric.

Psychiatrists As Teachers in Schools of Social Work, Vol. 4. GAP Committee on Psychiatry & Community. (Report No. 53). 1962. pap. 2.00 (ISBN 0-87318-071-2). Adv Psychiatry.

Psychiatrists' Viewpoints on & Their Services to Religious Institutions & the Ministry. Ed. by American Psychiatric Association's Task Force on Religion & Psychiatry. (Task Force Reports: No. 10). 49p. 1975. 5.00 (ISBN 0-685-77445-7, P220-0). Am Psychiatric.

Psychiatry. 4th ed. Merrill T. Eaton et al. (Medical Outline Ser). 1981. 12.00 (ISBN 0-87488-621-X). Med Exam.

Psychiatry & Confidentiality: An Annotated Bibliography. APA Library. Ed. by Jean C. Jones. 51p. 1974. pap. 5.00 (ISBN 0-685-65578-4, P215-0). Am Psychiatric.

Psychiatry & Medical Education Two. Conference on Psychiatry & Medical Education, Atlanta, 1967. 1969. pap. 4.00 o.p. (ISBN 0-685-24857-7, 180). Am Psychiatric.

Psychiatry & Mysticism. Stanley R. Dean. LC 75-8771. (Illus.). 446p. 1975. 21.95 (ISBN 0-88229-189-0); pap. 12.95 (ISBN 0-88229-657-4). Nelson-Hall.

Psychiatry & Psychology in the Visual Arts & Aesthetics: A Bibliography. Ed. by Norman Kiell. 1965. 22.50x (ISBN 0-299-03500-X). U of Wis Pr.

Psychiatry & Religion. Ed. by Felix Marti-Ibanez. 1956. 3.00 o.p. (ISBN 0-910922-04-7). MD Pubns.

Psychiatry & the Criminal: A Guide to Psychiatric Examinations for the Criminal Courts. 3rd ed. John M. Macdonald. 524p. 1976. 37.75 (ISBN 0-398-03480-X). C C Thomas.

Psychiatry & the Dilemmas of Crime: A Study of Causes, Punishment & Treatment. Seymour L. Halleck. 1971. pap. 7.95x (ISBN 0-520-02059-6, CAL237). U of Cal Pr.

Psychiatry & the Pediatrician. Fred H. Stone. Ed. by John Apley. (Postgraduate Pediatrics Ser). 1976. 15.95 (ISBN 0-407-00074-7). Butterworths.

Psychiatry & the Public Health. G. R. Hargreaves. 1958. text ed. 3.75x (ISBN 0-485-26310-6, Athlone Pr). Humanities.

Psychiatry Continuing Education Review. 2nd. ed. Ed. by John C. Duffy & Lane A. Gerber. LC 79-91844. 1980. text ed. 13.75 (ISBN 0-87488-352-0). Med Exam.

Psychiatry for Social Workers. 2nd ed. Lawson G. Lowrey. LC 50-8887. 1950. 20.00x (ISBN 0-231-01768-5). Columbia U Pr.

Psychiatry for Social Workers. A. Munro & W. McCullough. LC 75-80842. 1970. 17.25 (ISBN 0-08-006366-7); pap. 9.75 (ISBN 0-08-006365-9). Pergamon.

Psychiatry for the House Officer. David A. Tomb. (House Officer Ser.). (Illus.). 231p. 1980. softcover 10.95 (ISBN 0-683-08336-8). Williams & Wilkins.

Psychiatry in Broad Perspective. Roy R. Grinker, Sr. LC 74-13012. 256p. 1975. deluxe ed. 22.95 (ISBN 0-87705-231-X). Human Sci Pr.

Psychiatry in Crisis. Ed. by Richard C. Hall. 1981. text ed. write for info. (ISBN 0-89335-133-4). Spectrum Pub.

Psychiatry in the Everyday Practice of Law. Martin Blinder. LC 72-95085. 305p. 1973. 40.00 (ISBN 0-686-05454-7). Lawyers Co-Op.

Psychiatry in the Practice of Medicine. Allen J. Enelow & Murray Wexler. 1966. 9.95x o.p. (ISBN 0-19-501127-9). Oxford U Pr.

Psychiatry-Law Dilemma. Elio Maggio. 1980. 13.95 (ISBN 0-533-04795-1). Vantage.

Psychiatry Observed: The Conflict Between Theory & Practice in a General Hospital Psychiatric Unit. Geoffrey Baruch & Andrew Treacher. 1978. pap. 14.95 (ISBN 0-7100-8876-0). Routledge & Kegan.

Psychiatry: PreTest Self-Assessment & Review. Ed. by J. Craig Nelson. LC 77-78729. (Clinical Sciences: PreTest Self-Assessment & Review Ser.). 1977. pap. 9.95 (ISBN 0-07-051604-9). McGraw-Pretest.

Psychiatry Specialty Board Review. 2nd ed. Marc A. Schuckit. Ed. by John P. Feighner. 1977. spiral bdg. 16.50 (ISBN 0-87488-312-1). Med Exam.

Psychiatry: What It Is, What It Does, a Book for Young People. Francine Klagsbrun. LC 75-79669. (Illus.). (gr. 7 up). 1969. PLB 3.90 o.p. (ISBN 0-531-01911-X). Watts.

Psychic & the Swamp Man. Kathleen M. Gordon. 1981. 12.95 (ISBN 0-670-58188-7). Viking Pr.

Psychic Archeology: Time Machine to the Past. Jeffrey Goodman. (YA) 1980. 2.50 (ISBN 0-425-05000-9). Berkley Pub.

Psychic Autobiography. Amanda T. Jones. Ed. by Annette K. Baxter. LC 79-8798. (Signal Lives Ser.). (Illus.). 1980. Repr. of 1910 ed. lib. bdg. 42.00x (ISBN 0-405-12845-2). Arno.

Psychic Breathing: Cosmic Vitality from the Air. Robert Crookall. 96p. (Orig.). 1980. pap. 4.95 o.s.i. (ISBN 0-85030-176-9). Newcastle Pub.

Psychic Development. Jean Porter. (Illus.). 1974. pap. 2.75 o.p. (ISBN 0-394-70939-X). Random.

Psychic Energy. M. Lietaert Peerbolte. 1979. 12.95 (ISBN 0-685-95695-4, Pub. by Servire BV Netherlands). Hunter Hse.

Psychic Energy: Its Source & Its Transformation. 2nd ed. M. Esther Harding. (Bollingen Ser.: Vol. 10). (Illus.). 520p. 1963. 25.00 (ISBN 0-691-09817-4); pap. 6.95 (ISBN 0-691-01790-5, 296). Princeton U Pr.

Psychic Experience: ESP Investigated. Sheila Ostrander & Lynn Schroeder. LC 77-79512. (gr. 5 up). 1977. 7.95 o.p. (ISBN 0-8069-3092-6); PLB 7.49 o.p. (ISBN 0-8069-3093-4). Sterling.

Psychic Healers of the Philippines. Joe Folz. 1981. pap. 2.95 (ISBN 0-88270-508-3). Logos.

Psychic Healing. Hans Holzer. (Orig.). 1979. pap. 2.25 (ISBN 0-532-23123-6). Manor Bks.

Psychic Is You. Kay Rhea & Maggie O'Leary. LC 79-53023. 168p. 1981. pap. 5.95 (ISBN 0-89087-311-9). Celestial Arts.

Psychic Manual. Duane Berry. 1978. pap. 1.95 (ISBN 0-686-01317-4). Cathedral of Knowledge.

Psychic Phenomena. Willard A. Heaps. LC 74-10266. 160p. 1975. 7.95 o.p. (ISBN 0-525-66418-1). Elsevier-Nelson.

Psychic Power of Pyramids. Bill Schul & Ed Pettit. 1978. pap. 3.95 (ISBN 0-449-90001-0, Columbine). Fawcett.

Psychic Roulette. G. E. Vandeman. 1973. pap. 3.95 (ISBN 0-8163-0136-0, 16693-4). Pacific Pr Pub Assn.

Psychic Side of American Dream. Robert W. Krajenke. 1976. pap. 2.00 o.p. (ISBN 0-87604-093-8). ARE Pr.

Psychic War in Men & Women. Helen Block Lewis. LC 74-21634. 321p. 1976. 12.00 (ISBN 0-8147-4960-7); pap. 6.00 (ISBN 0-8147-4982-8). NYU Pr.

Psychical Research & Spiritualism. Sanford E. Coates. (Illus.). 1980. deluxe ed. 49.75 (ISBN 0-89920-006-0). Am Classical Coll Pr.

Psychiology & Biomechanics of Cycling. I. E. Faria & P. R. Cavanagh. 179p. 1978. 14.95 (ISBN 0-471-25490-8). Wiley.

Psychitric, Psychologenic, & Somatopsychic Disorders Handbook. A. James Giannini. 1978. pap. 14.50 (ISBN 0-87488-596-5). Med Exam.

Psycho-Analytic Insight & Relationships: A Kleinian Approach. Isca Salzberger-Wittenberg. (Library of Social Work). 1970. cased 12.50 (ISBN 0-7100-6835-2). Routledge & Kegan.

Psycho-Analytic Insight & Relationships: A Kleinian Approach. Isca Salzberger-Wittenberg. (Library of Social Work). 1973. pap. 7.45 (ISBN 0-7100-7623-1). Routledge & Kegan.

Psycho-Chemical Warfare. A. Stanton Candlin. (Illus.). 1974. 14.95 o.p. (ISBN 0-87000-214-7). Arlington Hse.

Psycho-Cybernetics. Maxwell Maltz. pap. 2.95 (ISBN 0-671-43270-2). PB.

Psycho-Motor Behavior in Education & Sport: Selected Papers. Bryant J. Cratty. (Illus.). 190p. 1974. text ed. 18.50 (ISBN 0-398-03099-5). C C Thomas.

Psycho-Sales-Analysis: The New Art of Self-Taught Sales Success. Jack Huttig. LC 73-154979. (Illus.). 1971. 14.95 (ISBN 0-911012-09-5). Nelson-Hall.

Psycho-Social Aspects of a Severe Burn: a Review of the Literature: Supplement to International Bibliography on Burns 1979. Ed. by M. L. Bowden & I. Feller. C. A. Jones. LC 79-89259. 1979. pap. text ed. 16.00 (ISBN 0-917478-34-7). Natl Inst Burn.

Psycho-Yoga: The Practice of Mind Control. B. Edwin. 128p. (Orig.). 1980. pap. 4.95 o.s.i. (ISBN 0-7225-0543-4). Newcastle Pub.

Psychoacoustics. J. Donald Harris. LC 74-10512. (Studies in Communicative Disorders Ser). 1974. pap. text ed. 3.70 o.p. (ISBN 0-672-61332-8). Bobbs.

Psychoactive Drugs. Vincent J. D'Andrea. LC 76-24507. 1977. pap. 6.95 (ISBN 0-8465-1290-4). Benjamin-Cummings.

Psychoactive Drugs & Social Judgement: Theory & Research. Ed. by Kenneth R. Hammond. C. R. Joyce. LC 80-12506. 298p. 1980. Repr. of 1975 ed. lib. bdg. write for info. (ISBN 0-89874-171-8). Krieger.

Psychoanalysis: A Contemporary Appraisal. Ed. by Alan M. Jacobson & Dean X. Parmelee. 250p. 1981. 20.00 (ISBN 0-87630-269-X). Brunner-Mazel.

Psychoanalysis: Creativity & Literature. Ed. by Alan Roland. LC 77-26613. 1978. 22.50x (ISBN 0-231-04324-4). Columbia U Pr.

Psychoanalysis of Children. Melanie Klein. 396p. 1975. 17.50 o.s.i. (ISBN 0-440-06085-0, Sey Lawr). Delacorte.

Psychoanalysis of Culture. C. R. Badcock. 264p. 1980. 36.50x (ISBN 0-631-11701-6, Pub. by Basil Blackwell). Biblio Dist.

Psychoanalysis of Dreams. Angel Garma. LC 73-17741. 224p. (Orig.). 1974. 20.00x (ISBN 0-87668-118-6). Aronson.

Psychoanalysis, Psychiatry & Law. Jay Katz et al. LC 65-27757. 1967. text ed. 35.00 (ISBN 0-02-917200-4). Free Pr.

Psychoanalyst & the Artist. rev. ed. Daniel E. Schneider. 1978. pap. text ed. write for info. o.p. (ISBN 0-391-00889-7). Humanities.

Psychoanalytic Dialogues Two: The Clinical Experience & Its Setting. Robert Langs & Leo Stone. LC 79-64457. 1979. 30.00x (ISBN 0-87668-383-9). Aronson.

Psychoanalytic Psychotherapy. Ed. by George D. Goldman & Donald S. Milman. LC 77-79454. (Topics in Clinical Psychology: 3). 1978. pap. text ed. 7.50 (ISBN 0-201-02513-2). A-W.

Psychoanalytic Psychotherapy of the Borderline Patient. Arlene R. Wolberg. (Illus.). 350p. 1981. text ed. 30.00 (ISBN 0-86577-022-0). Thieme-Stratton.

Psychoanalytic Psychotherapy: Theory, Technique, Therapeutic Relationship & Treatability. Thomas J. Paolino, Jr. 350p. 1981. 20.00 (ISBN 0-87630-261-4). Brunner-Mazel.

Psychoanalytic Studies of the Personality. W. Ronald Fairbairn. 1966. Repr. of 1952 ed. 23.50x (ISBN 0-7100-1361-2). Routledge & Kegan.

Psychoanalytic Study of the Child, Vol. 35. Ed. by Albert J. Solnit et al. LC 80-5398. (Illus.). 544p. 1980. 27.50x (ISBN 0-300-02607-2). Yale U Pr.

Psychoanalytic Theory & Social Work Practice. Herbet S. Strean. Ed. by Francis J. Turner. LC 78-65223. (Treatment Approaches in the Human Services Ser.). 1979. text ed. 15.95 (ISBN 0-02-932220-0). Free Pr.

Psychoanalytic Theory of Defensive Processes. H. Sjoback. 1973. 14.95 (ISBN 0-470-79370-8). Halsted Pr.

Psychoanalytic Vision. Reuben Fine. LC 80-2154. 1981. 19.95 (ISBN 0-02-910270-7). Free Pr.

Psychobiological Vulnerabilities to Delinquency. Ed. by Dorothy O. Lewis. 1981. text ed. write for info. (ISBN 0-89335-136-9). Spectrum Pub.

Psychobiology of Affective Disorders. Ed. by J. Mendels. (Illus.). 192p. 1980. pap. 24.00 (ISBN 3-8055-1400-X). S Karger.

Psychobiology of Aggression & Violence. Luigi Valzelli. 265p. 1981. text ed. 24.00 (ISBN 0-89004-403-1). Raven.

Psychobiology of Cancer: Implications for a General Model of Health & Disease. Augustin De La Pena. 300p. 1981. 19.95x (ISBN 0-89789-004-3). J F Bergin.

Psychobiology of Consciousness. Ed. by Richard J. Davidson & Julian M. Davidson. 465p. 1980. 32.50 (ISBN 0-306-40138-X, Plenum Pr). Plenum Pub.

Psychobiology of the Depressive Disorders: Implications for the Effects of Stress. Ed. by Richard A. Depue. LC 79-51676. (Personality & Psychopathology Ser.). 1979. 32.00 (ISBN 0-12-211650-X). Acad Pr.

Psychodiagnostic Study of Children & Adolescents. Sidney L. Copel. 216p. 1967. pap. 14.75 photocopy ed. spiral (ISBN 0-398-00346-7). C C Thomas.

Psychodiagnostics & Personality Assessment: A Handbook. 2nd ed. Donald P. Ogdon. LC 66-29866. (Professional Handbook Ser.). 144p. 1977. pap. 9.75x (ISBN 0-87424-095-6). Western Psych.

Psychodrama. Adaline Starr. LC 76-49045. 1977. 18.95x (ISBN 0-88229-224-2); pap. 10.95x (ISBN 0-685-99103-2). Nelson-Hall.

Psychodrama. Lewis Yablonsky. 300p. Date not set. pap. text ed. 11.95 (ISBN 0-89876-016-X). Gardner Pr.

Psychodynamics of Patient Care. L. Schwartz & J. Schwartz. 448p. 1972. pap. 13.95 (ISBN 0-13-732578-9). P-H.

Psychodynamics of Race: Vicious & Benign Spirals. Rae Sherwood. 608p. 1980. text ed. 55.00x (ISBN 0-391-01804-3). Humanities.

Psychodynamics of the Emotionally Uncomfortable. David W. Shave. LC 79-50191. 489p. 1980. 27.75 (ISBN 0-87527-233-9). Green.

Psychoeducational Diagnosis of Exceptional Children. Milton V. Wisland. (Illus.). 408p. 1977. 19.75 (ISBN 0-398-02843-5). C C Thomas.

Psychoeducational Foundations of Learning Disabilities. D. Hallahan & W. Cruickshank. 1979. 8.95 (ISBN 0-13-734285-3). P-H.

Psychoeducational Treatment of Hyperactive Children. Robert E. Valett. 1974. text ed. 8.00 (ISBN 0-8224-5651-6); pap. 5.00 (ISBN 0-8224-5650-8). Pitman Learning.

Psychogenesis of Coronary Heart Disease: A Syllabus for Medical Researchers. Ed. by Albert Eglash. (Bibliographies in Psychosomatic Medicine Ser.: No. 1, Myocardial Infraction). (Illus.). 110p. (Orig.). 1980. lib. bdg. 20.00 (ISBN 0-935320-20-2). Quest Pr.

Psychogenic Biochemical Aspects of Cancer. Harold E. Simmons. 1979. pap. 9.95 (ISBN 0-87312-010-8). Gen Welfare.

Psycholinguistics. Joseph A. DeVito. LC 73-183112. (Studies in Communicative Disorders Ser). 36p. 1971. pap. 1.95 (ISBN 0-672-61277-1). Bobbs.

Psycholinguistics. 2nd ed. Dan I. Slobin. 1979. pap. text ed. 8.95x (ISBN 0-673-15140-9). Scott F.

Psycholinguistics: An Introduction to Research & Theory. H. Hoermann. Tr. by H. H. Stern. (Illus.). 1970. 25.20 o.p. (ISBN 0-387-05159-7); pap. 14.00 o.p. (ISBN 0-387-05665-3). Springer-Verlag.

Psycholinguistics: An Introduction to the Psychology of Language. Donald J. Foss & David T. Hakes. LC 77-27826. (Experimental Psychology Ser.). (Illus.). 1978. ref. 18.95 (ISBN 0-13-732446-4). P-H.

Psycholinguistics in Clinical Practice. Ed. by Michael A. Simpson. LC 79-11813. 450p. 1980. text ed. 24.50x (ISBN 0-8290-0091-7). Irvington.

Psycholinguistics: Introductory Perspectives. Joseph F. Kess. 1976. 16.95 (ISBN 0-12-405250-9). Acad Pr.

Psycholinguistics: Selected Papers. Ed. by Roger Brown. LC 73-95296. 1972. pap. text ed. 7.95 (ISBN 0-02-904840-0). Free Pr.

Psychological & Human Reproduction. James W. Selby et al. LC 80-1641. 1980. 19.95 (ISBN 0-02-928690-5). Free Pr.

Psychological & Medical Aspects of the Use of Nuclear Energy, Vol. 4. Group for the Advancement of Psychiatry. (Symposium No. 6). 1960. pap. 2.00 (ISBN 0-87318-059-3). Adv Psychiatry.

Psychological & Vocational Rehabilitation of the Youthful Delinquent. Ed. by Richard E. Hardy & John G. Cull. (American Lectures in Social Rehabilitation Psychology Ser.). (Illus.). 264p. 1974. 16.50 (ISBN 0-398-03154-1). C C Thomas.

Psychological Androgyny: Further Considerations. Ed. by Alexandra G. Kaplan. LC 79-1647. 1979. 7.95 (ISBN 0-87705-418-5). Human Sci Pr.

Psychological Approach to Abnormal Behaviour. 2nd ed. Leonard Ullmann & Leonard Krasner. LC 74-28271. 832p. 1975. text ed. 22.95 (ISBN 0-13-732545-2). P-H.

Psychological Approach to Fiction: Studies in Thackeray, Stendhal, George Eliot, Dostoevsky, & Conrad. Bernard J. Paris. LC 73-15239. 320p. 1974. 12.50x (ISBN 0-253-34650-9). Ind U Pr.

Psychological Approaches to Child Abuse. Ed. by Neil Frude. 200p. 1981. 19.50x (ISBN 0-8476-6925-4). Rowman.

Psychological Aspects of a First Pregnancy & Early Postnatal Adaptation. Pauline M. Shereshefsky & Leon J. Yarrow. LC 73-87877. 350p. 1973. 20.50 (ISBN 0-911216-65-0). Raven.

Psychological Aspects of Abortion. Ed. by David Mall & Walter F. Watts. 1979. 15.00 (ISBN 0-89093-298-0); pap. 5.00 (ISBN 0-89093-274-3). U Pubns Amer.

Psychological Aspects of Childhood Cancer. J. Kellerman. (Illus.). 336p. 1980. 32.50 (ISBN 0-398-03989-5). C C Thomas.

Psychological Aspects of Cystic Fibrosis. P. R. Patterson et al. 1973. 17.50x (ISBN 0-88238-702-2). Columbia U Pr.

Psychological Aspects of Gynecology & Obstetrics. Ed. by B. B. Wolman. 1978. 22.50 (ISBN 0-87489-009-8). Med Economics.

Psychological Aspects of Intensive Care Nursing. Ed. by Nathan Simon. 295p. 1980. text ed. 16.95 (ISBN 0-87619-663-6). R J Brady.

Psychological Aspects of Myocardial Infarction & Coronary Care. 2nd ed. W. Doyle Gentry & Redford B. Williams. LC 79-2554. (Illus.). 1979. pap. text ed. 12.95 (ISBN 0-8016-1796-0). Mosby.

Psychological Aspects of Myocardial Infarction & Coronary Care. W. Doyle Gentry & Redford B. Williams. LC 75-2461. 1975. pap. text ed. 7.50 o.p. (ISBN 0-8016-1799-5). Mosby.

Psychological Aspects of Physical Education & Sport. Ed. by J. E. Kane. 248p. 1975. pap. 7.75 (ISBN 0-7100-8299-1). Routledge & Kegan.

Psychological Aspects of Pregnancy, Birthing, & Bonding. Ed. by Barbara L. Blum. (New Directions in Psychotherapy Ser.: Vol. IV). 336p. 1980. 25.95 (ISBN 0-87705-210-7). Human Sci Pr.

Psychological Aspects of Pregnancy, Birthing, & Bonding. Ed. by Barbara L. Blum & Paul T. Olsen. (New Directions in Psychotheraphy Ser.: Vol. IV). 336p. 1980. 25.95 (ISBN 0-87705-210-7). Human Sci Pr.

Psychological Aspects of Stress. Harry S. Abram. 112p. 1970. pap. 11.75 photocopy ed. spiral (ISBN 0-398-00004-2). C C Thomas.

Psychological Aspects of the Aging Process with Sociological Implications. 2nd ed. Harold Geist. LC 80-13233. 174p. 1980. Repr. of 1968 ed. text ed. 11.50 (ISBN 0-89874-073-8). Krieger.

Psychological Assessment: A Conceptual Approach. Michael P. Maloney & Michael P. Ward. 450p. 1976. text ed. 16.95x (ISBN 0-19-502027-8). Oxford U Pr.

Psychological Assessment of Children. James O. Palmer. LC 70-101976. 1970. 28.95 (ISBN 0-471-65772-7). Wiley.

Psychological Assessment of Suicidal Risk. Ed. by Charles Neuringer. (Illus.). 256p. 1974. text ed. 16.50 (ISBN 0-398-03008-1). C C Thomas.

Psychological Basis of Handwriting Analysis: The Relationship of Handwriting to Personality & Psychopathology. David Lester. LC 79-23957. 192p. 1981. text ed. 18.95 (ISBN 0-88229-533-0). Nelson-Hall.

Psychological Care During Pregnancy & the Postpartum Period. W. Brown. 1979. 18.00 (ISBN 0-89004-371-X); pap. 11.00 (ISBN 0-686-66187-7). Raven.

Psychological Complexity & Preference: A Hedgehog Theory of Behavior. Edward L. Walker. LC 79-20291. 1980. text ed. 19.95 (ISBN 0-8185-0379-3). Brooks-Cole.

Psychological Consultation with a Police Department: A Demonstration of Cooperative Training in Mental Health. Philip A. Mann. 184p. 1973. text ed. 13.75 (ISBN 0-398-02695-5). C C Thomas.

Psychological Counseling in General Medical Practice. Allan Hodges. 1977. 14.95 (ISBN 0-669-01039-1). Lexington Bks.

Psychological Determinants of User Behavior: Proceedings. Report of Round Table, European Conference of Ministers of Transport on Transport Economics, 34th, Paris, May 6-7, 1976. 1977. 3.75 o.p. (ISBN 92-82-11041-9). OECD.

Psychological Development in Health & Disease. George L. Engel. LC 62-13582. 1962. 11.50 o.p. (ISBN 0-7216-3390-0). Saunders.

Psychological Development of the Child. 2nd ed. Langdon E. Longstreth. (Illus.). 1974. 20.50x (ISBN 0-8260-5526-5); instr's manual avail. (ISBN 0-471-07541-8). Wiley.

Psychological Development of the Child. 3rd ed. Paul Mussen. (Foundations of Modern Psychology). (Illus.). 1979. text ed. 12.95 (ISBN 0-13-732420-0); pap. text ed. 6.95 (ISBN 0-13-732412-X). P-H.

Psychological Dimensions of Social Interaction: Readings & Perspectives. Ed. by Darwyn E. Linder. LC 72-4707. 1973. pap. text ed. 9.95 (ISBN 0-201-04246-0). A-W.

Psychological Disturbance in Adolescence. Irving B. Weiner. (Personality Processes Ser.). 400p. 1970. 29.50 (ISBN 0-471-92568-3, Pub. by Wiley-Interscience). Wiley.

Psychological Effects of Motherhood: A Study of First Pregnancy. Myra Leifer. 22.95 (ISBN 0-03-055781-X); pap. 8.95 (ISBN 0-03-055776-3). Praeger.

Psychological Examination of Political Leaders. Ed. by Margaret G. Hermann & Thomas W. Milburn. LC 75-32366. 1977. 19.95 (ISBN 0-02-914590-2). Free Pr.

Psychological Experiment: A Practical Accomplishment. Harold B. Pepinsky & Michael J. Patton. LC 75-134829. 208p. 1971. 16.00 (ISBN 0-08-016515-X). Pergamon.

Psychological Experiments with Autistic Children. B. Hermelin & N. O'Connor. 1970. 27.00 (ISBN 0-08-016088-3). Pergamon.

Psychological Explanation: An Introduction to the Philosophy of Psychology. Jerry A Fodor. 1968. pap. text ed. 5.50 (ISBN 0-394-30663-5). Random.

Psychological Factors in Health Care: A Practitioner's Manual. Michael Jospe et al. Ed. by Barry D. Cohen. LC 77-11395. 496p. 1980. 29.95x (ISBN 0-669-02076-1). Lexington Bks.

Psychological Factors in Teaching Reading. Eldon Ekwall. LC 72-96688. 1973. text ed. 19.95 (ISBN 0-675-08965-4). Merrill.

Psychological Fitness: Twenty-One Days to Feeling Good. Richard Corriere & Joseph Hart. LC 78-14073. (Illus.). 1979. 9.95 o.p. (ISBN 0-15-175280-X). HarBraceJ.

Psychological Foundations of Attitudes. Anthony G. Greenwald et al. (Social Psychology Ser). 1968. text ed. 19.95 (ISBN 0-12-300750-X). Acad Pr.

Psychological Foundations of Criminal Justice: Contemporary Perpectives on Forensic Psychiartry & Psychology, Vol. 2. Ed. by Harold J. Vetter & Robert W. Rieber. LC 78-18781. (Illus.). 416p. 1980. 20.00x (ISBN 0-89444-025-X). John Jay Pr.

Psychological Foundations of Education: A Guide to Information Sources. Ed. by Charles A. Baatz & Olga K. Baatz. (Education Information Guide Ser.: Vol. 10). 350p. 1981. 30.00 (ISBN 0-8103-1467-3). Gale.

Psychological Foundations of Musical Behavior. Rudolf E. Radocy & J. David Boyle. (Illus.). 360p. 1979. text ed. 25.75 (ISBN 0-398-03841-4). C C Thomas.

Psychological Frontiers of Society. Abram Kardiner et al. 1945-1963. pap. 8.00x (ISBN 0-231-08548-6). Columbia U Pr.

Psychological Immortality: Using Your Mind to Extend Your Life. Jerry Gillies. 225p. 1981. 11.95 (ISBN 0-399-90103-5). Marek.

Psychological Inquiries: A Series of Essays Intended to Illustrate the Mutual Relations of the Physical Organization & the Mental Faculties. Benjamin Brodie. Bd. with On Animal Electricity. E. DuBois-Reymond. (Contributions to the History of Psychology Ser., Vol. VI, Pt. E). 1980. Repr. of 1854 ed. 30.00 (ISBN 0-89093-325-1). U Pubns Amer.

Psychological Interpretation of 'the Golden Ass of Apuleius' Marie-Louise Von Franz. Ed. by James Hillman. (Seminar Ser.). 188p. 1970. pap. text ed. 9.50 (ISBN 0-88214-103-1). Spring Pubns.

Psychological Medicine. 9th ed. Desmond Curran et al. 480p. 1980. pap. text ed. 21.50x (ISBN 0-443-02192-9). Churchill.

Psychological Methods of Testing Intelligence. William L. Stern. Tr. by G. M. Whipple from Ger. Bd. with Selected Essays. Alfred Binet et al. (Contributions to the History of Psychology Ser., Vol. IV, Pt. B: Psychometrics & Educational Psychology). 1978. Repr. of 1914 ed. 30.00 (ISBN 0-89093-164-X). U Pubns Amer.

Psychological Models in International Politics. Ed. by Lawrence S. Falkowski. (Special Studies in International Relations). 1979. lib. bdg. 26.50x (ISBN 0-89158-377-7); pap. text ed. 12.50x (ISBN 0-86531-043-2). Westview.

Psychological Needs & Political Behavior: A Theory of Personality & Political Efficacy. Stanley A. Renshon. LC 73-11735. 1974. 15.95 (ISBN 0-02-926320-4). Free Pr.

Psychological Origin & the Nature of Religion. James H. Leuba. 94p. 1980. Repr. of 1909 ed. lib. bdg. 12.50 (ISBN 0-8482-1622-9). Norwood Edns.

Psychological Problems: The Social Context. Ed. by Philip Feldman & Jim Orford. 360p. 1980. write for info. (ISBN 0-471-27741-X, Pub. by Wiley-Interscience). Wiley.

Psychological Readings for the Dental Profession. Ed. by Brenda L. Van Zoost. LC 75-15892. 180p. 1975. 17.95 (ISBN 0-88229-244-7). Nelson-Hall.

Psychological Reflections: A New Anthology of His Writings, 1905-1961. Carl G. Jung. Ed. by Jolande Jacobi & R. F. Hull. (Bollingen Ser.: Vol. 31). 332p. 1970. 18.00 (ISBN 0-691-09862-X); pap. 4.95 (ISBN 0-691-01786-7). Princeton U Pr.

Psychological Rehabilitation of the Amputee. Lawrence W. Friedmann. (Illus.). 176p. 1978. 18.50 (ISBN 0-398-03707-8). C C Thomas.

Psychological Report Writing. Norman Tallent. LC 75-33309. (Illus.). 272p. 1976. 19.95 (ISBN 0-13-732503-7). P-H.

Psychological Research. Benton J. Underwood. 1957. 15.95 (ISBN 0-13-732529-0). P-H.

Psychological Research: An Introduction. 4th ed. Arthur J. Bachrach. 205p. 1981. pap. text ed. 6.95 (ISBN 0-394-32288-6). Random.

Psychological Search for God. Roy V. Rowland. (Illus.). 1980. 34.75 (ISBN 0-89920-003-6). Am Inst Psych.

Psychological Services for Schools. Ed. by W. D. Wall. 1956. 7.00 (ISBN 0-685-36751-7, U501, UNESCO). Unipub.

Psychological Society. Martin L. Gross. 1978. 10.95 (ISBN 0-394-46233-5). Random.

Psychological Statistics. 4th ed. Quinn McNemar. 1969. 24.95 (ISBN 0-471-58708-7). Wiley.

Psychological Statistics, 7 vols. Herbert S. Terrace & Scott Parker. 1971. Set. 14.75 (ISBN 0-86589-014-5). Vol. 1, Units 1-3 (ISBN 0-86589-015-3). Vol. 2, Units 4,5 (ISBN 0-86589-016-1). Vol. 3, Units 6,7 (ISBN 0-86589-017-X). Vol. 4, Units 8,9 (ISBN 0-86589-018-8). Vol. 5, Units 10,11 (ISBN 0-86589-019-6). Vol. 6, Units 12,13 (ISBN 0-86589-020-X). Vol. 7, Units 14,15 (ISBN 0-86589-021-8). Individual Learn.

Psychological Statistics: A Case Approach. Carl Auerbach & Joseph L. Zinnes. text ed. 16.95 scp (ISBN 0-397-47376-1, HarpC); inst. manual free (ISBN 0-06-379301-6); scp student wkbk. 6.50 (ISBN 0-397-47398-2). Har-Row.

Psychological Stress in the Campus Community. Ed. by Bernard Bloom. LC 74-6184. (Community Psychology Ser: No. 3). 282p. 1975. text ed. 22.95 (ISBN 0-87705-145-3). Human Sci Pr.

Psychological Study of Literature: Limitations, Possibilities & Accomplishments. Martin S. Lindauer. LC 73-80499. 250p. 1974. 15.95 (ISBN 0-911012-74-5). Nelson-Hall.

Psychological Testing & Assessment. 3rd ed. Lewis R. Aiken, Jr. 1978. text ed. 18.95 (ISBN 0-205-06613-5, 7966148). Allyn.

Psychological Testing & Assessment. 2nd ed. Lewis R. Aiken, Jr. 368p. 1976. text ed. 15.95x o.p. (ISBN 0-205-04861-7). Allyn.

Psychological Testing & the Philosophy of Measurement. Donald L. Whaley. 58p. 1973. pap. text ed. 7.00 (ISBN 0-914474-02-2). F Fournies.

Psychological Testing in Personnel Assessment. K. M. Miller. LC 75-18451. 1976. 29.95 (ISBN 0-470-60392-5). Halsted Pr.

Psychological Testing of American Minorities: Issues & Consequences. Ronald J. Samuda. LC 74-26165. 232p. (Orig.). 1975. text ed. 12.95 scp (ISBN 0-06-045696-5, HarpC). Har-Row.

Psychological Testing of Children from Pre-School Through Adolescence: A Psychodynamic Approach. Miriam Siegel. 1981. write for info. (ISBN 0-8236-5615-2). Intl Univs Pr.

Psychological Theories & Human Learning: Kongor's Report. Guy R. Lefrancois. LC 76-164998. (Core Bks. in Psychology Ser.). 384p. 1971. text ed. 14.95 (ISBN 0-8185-0014-X); test items avail. (ISBN 0-685-23472-X). Brooks-Cole.

Psychological Theory & Educational Practice: Human Development, Learning & Assessment. H. S. McFarland. 1971. 20.00x (ISBN 0-7100-7009-8); pap. 8.95 (ISBN 0-7100-7010-1). Routledge & Kegan.

Psychological Theory of the Sexual Temptations. Vivian T. Birrell. 1979. deluxe ed. 43.15 (ISBN 0-930582-28-4). Gloucester Art.

Psychological Theory of the Voluptuous Woman. Bruce Daly. (Illus.). 1978. deluxe ed. 49.75 (ISBN 0-930582-18-7). Gloucester Art.

Psychological Thought from Pythagoras to Freud: An Informal Introduction. Gardner Murphy. LC 68-25371. (Orig.). 1968. pap. 3.65 o.p. (ISBN 0-15-674701-4, H068, Hbgr). HarBraceJ.

Psychologism & Psychoaesthetics: A Historical & Critical View of Their Relations. John Fizer. (Linguistic & Literary Studies in Eastern Europe Ser.: No. 6). 300p. 1980. text ed. 37.25x (ISBN 90-272-1506-5). Humanities.

Psychologistics. T. A. Waters. 1972. 8.95 o.p. (ISBN 0-394-46922-4). Random.

Psychologists, Vol. 2. Ed. by T. S. Krawiec. (Illus.). 350p. 1974. text ed. 12.95x (ISBN 0-19-501726-9); pap. text ed. 7.95x (ISBN 0-19-501725-0). Oxford U Pr.

Psychologists: What They Do & How They Came to Do It, Vol. 1. Ed. by T. S. Krawiec. (Illus.). 350p. 1972. text ed. 12.95x (ISBN 0-19-501568-1); pap. text ed. 7.95x (ISBN 0-19-501567-3). Oxford U Pr.

Psychology. J. Darley. 1981. 17.95 (ISBN 0-13-733154-1); pap. 5.95 (ISBN 0-13-733188-6). P-H.

Psychology. Henry Gleitman. (Illus.). 1981. 18.95x (ISBN 0-393-95102-2); study guide 7.95x (ISBN 0-393-95110-3). Norton.

Psychology. Guy R. Lefrancois. 672p. 1979. 19.95x (ISBN 0-534-00712-0); study guide 7.95x (ISBN 0-534-00844-5). Wadsworth Pub.

Psychology. Lester A. Lefton. 1979. text ed. 18.95 (ISBN 0-205-06421-3, 7964218); instr's man. o.p. avail. (ISBN 0-205-06422-1); study guide 7.95 (ISBN 0-205-06423-X, 7964234). Allyn.

Psychology. 2nd ed. Gardner Lindzey et al. LC 77-86622. (Illus.). 1978. 18.95x (ISBN 0-87901-089-4); study guide 6.95x (ISBN 0-87901-090-8). Worth.

Psychology. Elizabeth Loftus & Camille Wortman. 672p. 1981. text ed. 18.95 (ISBN 0-394-32428-5); wkbk. 6.95 (ISBN 0-394-32730-6). Knopf.

Psychology. Richard W. Malott & Donald L. Whaley. 1976. text ed. 24.50 scp o.p. (ISBN 0-06-168401-5, HarpC); test file avail. o.p. (ISBN 0-685-77067-2). Har-Row.

Psychology. Jack Rudman. (Undergraduate Program Field Test Ser.: UPFT-21). (Cloth bdg. avail. on request). pap. 9.95 (ISBN 0-8373-6021-8). Natl Learning.

Psychology. 3rd ed. Robert E. Silverman. (Illus.). 1978. text ed. 18.95 (ISBN 0-13-733022-7); pap. 6.95 study guide & wkbk. (ISBN 0-13-733048-0). P-H.

Psychology: A Brief Overview. Thomas K. Landauer. (Illus.). 416p. 1972. text ed. 16.95 o.p. (ISBN 0-07-036113-4, C); instructor's manual 2.95 o.p. (ISBN 0-07-036117-7); wkbk. & study guide 6.50 o.p. (ISBN 0-07-043625-8). McGraw.

Psychology: A Dynamic Science. Kurt Schlesinger et al. 740p. 1976. text ed. 15.95x (ISBN 0-697-06620-7); study guide 8.95x (ISBN 0-697-06621-5); instructor's manual 3.00 (ISBN 0-686-67227-5); test item file 10.00x (ISBN 0-697-06660-6). Wm C Brown.

Psychology: A Science in Conflict. Howard H. Kendler. (Illus.). 416p. 1981. text ed. 19.95x (ISBN 0-19-502900-3); pap. text ed. 9.95x (ISBN 0-19-502901-1). Oxford U Pr.

Psychology: A Scientific Study of Human Behavior. 5th ed. Lawrence S. Wrightsman et al. LC 78-59674. (Illus.). 1979. text ed. 17.95 (ISBN 0-8185-0280-0). Brooks-Cole.

Psychology: An Introduction. 4th ed. Jerome Kagan & Ernest Havemann. 647p. 1980. text ed. 16.95 (ISBN 0-15-572625-0, HC); instructor's manual avail.; write for info. study guide; test items avail. HarBraceJ.

Psychology: An Introduction. 3rd ed. C. Morris. 1979. 18.95 (ISBN 0-13-734194-6); study guide & wkbk. 6.95 (ISBN 0-13-734202-0); psi-unit mastery wkbk. 7.95 (ISBN 0-13-734269-1). P-H.

Psychology: An Introduction. 2nd ed. Paul Mussen & Mark Rosenzweig. 1976. text ed. 17.95x (ISBN 0-669-00497-9); instructor's manual free (ISBN 0-669-00521-5); study guide 5.95x (ISBN 0-669-00505-3); individualized prog. 5.95x (ISBN 0-669-00513-4); test item file to adopters free (ISBN 0-669-00539-8). Heath.

Psychology: An Introduction to a Behavioral Science. 4th ed. Henry C. Lindgren & Donn Byrne. LC 74-23293. 448p. 1975. text ed. 19.95 (ISBN 0-471-53603-2). Wiley.

Psychology: An Introduction to Human Behavior. 2nd ed. Morris K. Holland. 1978. text ed. 16.95x (ISBN 0-669-00994-6); inst. manual free (ISBN 0-669-00998-9); wkbk. 5.95x (ISBN 0-669-00995-4); indiv. prog. 6.95x (ISBN 0-669-00996-2); test item file to adopters free (ISBN 0-669-00997-0); tests for indiv. prog. free (ISBN 0-669-01161-4). Heath.

Psychology: An Orthodox Christian Perspective. Apostolos Makrakis. Ed. by Orthodox Christian Educational Society. Tr. by Denver Cummings from Hellenic. (Logos & Holy Spirit in the Unity of Christian Thought Ser.: Vol. 2). 151p. 1977. pap. 3.50x (ISBN 0-938366-05-X). Orthodox Chr.

Psychology: An Outline for the Intending Student. Ed. by John Cohen. (Outlines Ser). 1968. pap. 7.95 (ISBN 0-7100-2998-5). Routledge & Kegan.

Psychology & Behavior of Animals in Zoos & Circuses. H. Hediger. Tr. by Geoffrey Sircom. LC 68-55533. Orig. Title: Skizzen Zu Einer Tiorpsychologie Um und Im Zirkus. 1969. pap. text ed. 3.00 (ISBN 0-486-62218-5). Dover.

Psychology & Behavioral Medicine. S. J. Rachman & Clare Philips. LC 79-8589. (Illus.). 1980. 22.95 (ISBN 0-521-23178-7); pap. 6.95 (ISBN 0-521-29850-4). Cambridge U Pr.

Psychology & Common Sense. R. B. Joynson. 1974. 8.95x (ISBN 0-7100-7827-7); pap. 6.95 (ISBN 0-7100-7899-4). Routledge & Kegan.

Psychology & Community Change. Kenneth Heller & John Monahan. 1977. 17.50x (ISBN 0-256-01941-X). Dorsey.

Psychology & Counseling Careers. Rolland S. Parker. (Career Concise Guides Ser.). (gr. 7 up). 1977. PLB 6.45 (ISBN 0-531-01309-X). Watts.

Psychology & Education: A Science for Instruction. John R. Bergan & James A. Dunn. LC 75-14321 542p. 1976. text ed. 23.95 (ISBN 0-471-06910-8). Wiley.

Psychology & Education of Slow Learners. Roy I. Brown. 1978. pap. 6.50 (ISBN 0-7100-0046-4). Routledge & Kegan.

Psychology & Education of Slow Learners. Roy I. Brown. (Students Library of Education). 1976. 10.00x (ISBN 0-7100-8410-2). Routledge & Kegan.

Psychology & Education of the Gifted. 2nd ed. Ed. by W. B. Barbe & J. S. Renzulli. LC 75-14330. 1975. 15.95 o.p. (ISBN 0-470-04775-5). Halsted Pr.

Psychology & Education of the Gifted. 3rd ed. Ed. by Walter B. Barbe & Joseph S. Renzulli. 544p. 1981. text ed. 16.95x (ISBN 0-8290-0234-0). Irvington.

Psychology & Ethical Development. R. S. Peters. 1974. text ed. 25.00x o.p. (ISBN 0-04-150049-0); pap. text ed. 15.95x (ISBN 0-04-150050-4). Allen Unwin.

Psychology & Folk-Lore. Robert R. Marett. LC 74-10825. 275p. Repr. of 1920 ed. 18.00 (ISBN 0-8103-4045-3). Gale.

Psychology & Folklore. R. R. Marett. 284p. 1971. Repr. of 1920 ed. text ed. 14.75x (ISBN 9-0623-4028-8). Humanities.

Psychology & Human Experience. 2nd ed. John H. Brennecke & Robert G. Amick. 1978. pap. text ed. 9.95x (ISBN 0-02-471030-X); wkbk 5.95x (ISBN 0-02-471060-1); readings to accompany 6.95x (ISBN 0-02-471050-4). Macmillan.

Psychology & Instruction: A Practical Approach to Educational Psychology. Benjamin B. Lahey & Martha S. Johnson. 1978. pap. 12.95x (ISBN 0-673-15040-2). Scott F.

Psychology & Life. 10th ed. Philip G. Zimbardo. 1979. text ed. 18.95x (ISBN 0-673-15183-2). Scott F.

Psychology & Morals. J. A. Hadfield. 245p. 1980. Repr. of 1926 ed. lib. bdg. 30.00 (ISBN 0-8492-5282-2). R West.

Psychology & Personal Growth. 2nd ed. Arkoff. 1980. text ed. 13.95 (ISBN 0-205-06822-7, 7968221). Allyn.

Psychology & Personal Growth. Abe Arkoff. 480p. 1975. pap. text ed. 9.95x o.s.i. (ISBN 0-205-04682-7, 7946821); test items avail. o.s.i. (ISBN 0-205-04683-5). Allyn.

Psychology & Psychiatry in Courts & Corrections: Controversy & Change. Ellsworth A. Fersch. LC 80-11726. (Wiley Series on Personality Processes). 370p. 1980. 24.95 (ISBN 0-471-05604-9, Pub. by Wiley Interscience). Wiley.

Psychology & Psychiatry Today: A Marxist View. Joseph Nahem. 1981. 15.00 (ISBN 0-7178-0581-6); pap. 5.50 (ISBN 0-7178-0579-4). Intl Pub Co.

Psychology & Psychological Principles. James Ward. (Contributions to the History of Psychology Ser.: Vol. 8, Pt. a, Orientations). 1978. 30.00 (ISBN 0-89093-157-7). U Pubns Amer.

Psychology & the Language Learning Process. Aleksei A. Leontiev. LC 80-41819. 160p. 1981. 11.95 (ISBN 0-08-024601-X); pap. 5.95 (ISBN 0-08-024600-1). Pergamon.

Psychology & the Law. Gordon Bermant et al. LC 75-40628. 1976. 21.95 (ISBN 0-669-00452-9). Lexington Bks.

Psychology & the New Woman. Mary McHugh. (Choosing Careers & Life-Styles Ser.). 128p. (gr. 7 up). 1976. PLB 5.90 o.p. (ISBN 0-531-00348-5). Watts.

Psychology & the Philosophy of Science. Merle B. Turner. (Century Psychology Ser.). pap. text ed. 9.50x (ISBN 0-8290-0363-0). Irvington.

Psychology & the Stock Market. David N. Dreman. 1979. pap. 6.95 o.s.i. (ISBN 0-446-97071-9). Warner Bks.

Psychology & the Stock Market. new ed. David N. Dreman. LC 76-49986. 1977. 13.95 (ISBN 0-8144-5429-1). Am Mgmt.

Psychology & Theology. Gary R. Collins. 160p. (Orig.). 1981. pap. 5.95 (ISBN 0-687-34830-7). Abingdon.

Psychology & Theory. C. V. Adcock. LC 78-321163. 1976. pap. 6.50x (ISBN 0-7055-0553-7). Intl Pubns Serv.

Psychology & Women: In Transition. Jeanne E. Gullahorn. LC 78-16794. (In Transition Scripts Series in Personality & Social Psychology). 1979. 15.95 (ISBN 0-470-26459-4). Halsted Pr.

Psychology & You. David Dempsey & Philip G. Zimbardo. 1978. 16.95x (ISBN 0-673-15086-0). Scott F.

Psychology Applied to Industry. Marvin D. Dunnette & Wayne K. Kirchner. (Orig.). 1965. pap. 10.95 (ISBN 0-13-733253-X). P-H.

Psychology Applied to Life & Work. 6th ed. Harry W. Hepner. LC 78-11923. (Illus.). 1979. text ed. 17.95 (ISBN 0-13-732461-8). P-H.

Psychology Applied to Teaching. 3rd ed. Robert F. Biehler. LC 77-77665. (Illus.). 1978. pap. text ed. 16.95 (ISBN 0-395-25489-2); study guide & tching. handbook 7.30 (ISBN 0-395-25491-4); inst. manual 1.65 (ISBN 0-395-25490-6). HM.

Psychology Around the World. Ed. by Virginia S. Sexton & Henryk Misiak. LC 75-36017. 650p. 1976. text ed. 16.95x o.p. (ISBN 0-8185-0174-X). Brooks-Cole.

Psychology: Behavior in Perspective. 2nd ed. Arnold H. Buss. LC 77-11676. 1978. text ed. 19.95 (ISBN 0-471-12646-2); tchrs. manual avail. (ISBN 0-471-01726-4); tests avail. (ISBN 0-471-03774-5); study guide 6.95 (ISBN 0-471-03060-0). Wiley.

Psychology for a Changing World. 2nd ed. Idella M. Evans & Ron Murdoff. LC 77-13677. 1978. text ed. 18.95 (ISBN 0-471-24872-X); tchrs. manual avail. (ISBN 0-471-03754-0). Wiley.

Psychology for Architects. David Canter. LC 74-30415. 171p. 1975. 24.95 (ISBN 0-470-13460-7). Halsted Pr.

Psychology for Daily Living: Simple Guidance in Human Relations for Parents, Teachers, & Others. E. Rae Harcum. LC 79-1048. 1979. 14.95 (ISBN 0-88229-384-2); pap. 7.95x (ISBN 0-88229-696-5). Nelson-Hall.

Psychology for Future Education. Norman C. Dowsett. LC 80-51427. 1980. 11.95 (ISBN 0-533-04679-3). Vantage.

Psychology for Law Enforcement. Edward J. Green. LC 75-15634. 167p. 1976. text ed. 13.95 o.p. (ISBN 0-471-32474-4); pap. text ed. 9.95 (ISBN 0-471-32475-2). Wiley.

Psychology for Law Enforcement Officers. George J. Dudycha. (Police Science Ser). (Illus.). 416p. 1976. 16.75 (ISBN 0-398-00482-X). C C Thomas.

Psychology for Our Times: Readings. 2nd ed. Philip Zimbardo & Christina Maslach. 1977. pap. 7.95x (ISBN 0-673-15052-6). Scott F.

Psychology for Psychiatrists. C. G. Costello. 1966. 19.50 (ISBN 0-08-011729-5); pap. 10.50 (ISBN 0-08-011728-7). Pergamon.

Psychology for Teaching: A Bear Sometimes Faces the Front. 3rd ed. Guy R. Lefrancois. 1979. pap. text ed. 14.95x (ISBN 0-534-00602-7). Wadsworth Pub.

Psychology for the Classroom. J. Gibson. 1976. pap. text ed. 17.95 (ISBN 0-13-733287-4); study guide & wkbk. 4.95 (ISBN 0-13-733329-3). P-H.

Psychology for the Classroom. 2nd ed. Janice Gibson. (Illus.). 640p. 1981. pap. text ed. 17.95 (ISBN 0-13-733352-8). P-H.

Psychology for the Lawyer. Dwight G. McCarty. (Historical Foundations of Forensic Psychiatry & Psychology Ser.). Date not set. lib. bdg. 49.50 (ISBN 0-306-76068-1). Da Capo.

Psychology from an Empirical Standpoint. Franz Brentano. Ed. by Oskar Kraus & Linda L. McAlister. Tr. by Antos C. Rancurello et al from Ger. (International Library of Philosophy & Scientific Method). 520p. 1973. text ed. 32.50x (ISBN 0-391-00253-8). Humanities.

Psychology from the Standpoint of an Interbehaviorist. N. H. Pronko. LC 80-10247. 600p. 1980. text ed. 19.95 (ISBN 0-8185-0397-1). Brooks-Cole.

Psychology in Administration: Research Orientation Text with Integrated Readings. Timothy Costello & S. Zalkind. (Illus.). 1963. text ed. 19.95 (ISBN 0-13-732867-2). P-H.

Psychology in Contemporary China. L. B. Brown. 320p. 1981. 45.00 (ISBN 0-08-026063-2). Pergamon.

Psychology in Contemporary Sport: Guidelines for Coaches & Athletes. Bryant J. Cratty. (Illus.). 336p. 1973. ref. ed. 16.95 (ISBN 0-13-734079-6). P-H.

Psychology in Foreign Language Teaching. Steven H. McDonough. (Illus.). 176p. 1981. text ed. 25.00x (ISBN 0-04-418002-0, 2628-9); pap. text ed. 8.95x (ISBN 0-04-418003-9). Allen Unwin.

Psychology in Industrial Organizations. 4th ed. Norman R. Maier. LC 74-4797. 750p. 1973. text ed. 19.95 (ISBN 0-395-14046-3, 3-34269); instructor's manual pap. 2.50 (ISBN 0-395-15102-3, 3-34270). HM.

Psychology in Industrial Organizations. 3rd ed. Laurence Siegel & Irving M. Lane. 1974. text ed. 18.95x (ISBN 0-256-01563-5). Irwin.

Psychology in Progress: Readings from Scientific American. Intro. by Richard C. Atkinson. LC 74-23602. (Illus.). 1975. text ed. 19.95x (ISBN 0-7167-0517-6); pap. text ed. 9.95x (ISBN 0-7167-0516-8); test questions avail. (ISBN 0-685-99783-9). W H Freeman.

Psychology in Teaching Reading. 2nd ed. Emarld V. Dechant. 1977. text ed. 18.95 (ISBN 0-13-736686-8). P-H.

Psychology in the Classroom. rev., enl. ed. Rudolf Dreikurs. 1968. pap. text ed. 14.95 scp (ISBN 0-06-041756-0, HarpC). Har-Row.

Psychology in the Classroom: A Manual for Teachers. rev. & enl. ed. Rudolf Dreikurs. 1968. 8.95x o.p. (ISBN 0-06-031801-5, HarpT). Har-Row

Psychology in the Nursery School. Nelly Wolffheim. Tr. by Charles L. Hannam. LC 77-162630. 143p. 1972. Repr. of 1953 ed. lib. bdg. 16.00x (ISBN 0-8371-6197-5, WONS). Greenwood.

Psychology in the Vocational Rehabilitation of the Mentally Retarded. Murry Morgenstern & Harold Michal-Smith. 100p. 1973. text ed. 8.75 (ISBN 0-398-02696-3). C C Thomas.

Psychology: Looking at Ourselves. 2nd ed. James Geiwitz. (Illus.). 1980. 16.95 (ISBN 0-316-30706-8); instr's manual by P.S.Assocs. free (ISBN 0-316-30707-6); student guide by Syrdal-lasky 5.95 (ISBN 0-316-30710-6); test bank by P.S.Assocs. free (ISBN 0-316-30708-4). Little.

Psychology Made Simple. A. P. Sperling. 1957. pap. 3.50 (ISBN 0-385-01218-7, Made). Doubleday.

Psychology Misdirected. Seymour B. Sarason. LC 80-69283. 1981. 16.95 (ISBN 0-02-928100-8). Free Pr.

Psychology, Mon Amour: A Countertext. Klaus F. Riegel. LC 77-39422. (Illus.). 1978. pap. text ed. 9.50 (ISBN 0-395-25748-4). HM.

Psychology of a Musical Prodigy. G. Revesz. 180p. 1980. Repr. of 1925 ed. lib. bdg. 45.00 (ISBN 0-89987-715-X). Darby Bks.

Psychology of Adjustment. Irving Tucker. 489p. 1970. text ed. 18.95 (ISBN 0-12-702850-1). Acad Pr.

Psychology of Adjustment & Human Relationships. James F. Calhoun & Joan Acocella. 1978. text ed. 14.95x (ISBN 0-394-31203-1); wkbk. 5.95x (ISBN 0-394-32125-1). Random.

Psychology of Adjustment: Personal Growth in a Changing World. Warren E. Atwater. (Illus.). 1979. pap. 14.95 (ISBN 0-13-734830-4). P-H.

Psychology of Adolescence. 7th ed. Karl C. Garrison. 448p. 1975. 18.95 (ISBN 0-13-734996-3). P-H.

Psychology of Adolescence. 3rd ed. Dorothy Rogers. 1977. 18.95 (ISBN 0-13-734897-5). P-H.

Psychology of Aging. James E. Birren. 1964. text ed. 17.95 (ISBN 0-13-733428-1). P-H.

Psychology of Anomalous Experience: A Cognitive Approach. Graham Reed. 1972. text ed. 8.25x (ISBN 0-09-113240-1, Hutchinson U Lib). Humanities.

Psychology of Apartheid. Peter Lambley. LC 80-53595. 312p. 1981. lib. bdg. 16.50x (ISBN 0-8203-0548-0). U of Ga Pr.

Psychology of Apartheid: A Psychosocial Perspective on South Africa. Ed. by H. I. Van Der Spuy. LC 78-63064. 1978. pap. text ed. 7.50 (ISBN 0-8191-0610-0). U Pr of Amer.

Psychology of Aristotle: In Particular His Doctrine of the Active Intellect with an Appendix Concerning the Activity of Aristotle's God. Franz Brentano. Tr. by Rolf George. LC 75-17303. 1977. 16.75x (ISBN 0-520-03081-8). U of Cal Pr.

Psychology of Arithmetic. Edward L. Thorndike. 314p. 1980. Repr of 1922 ed. lib. bdg. 30.00 (ISBN 0-89760-890-9). Telegraph Bks.

Psychology of Behavior Exchange. Kenneth J. Gergen. Ed. by Charles A. Kiesler. (Topics in Social Psychology Ser). 1969. pap. text ed. 6.95 (ISBN 0-201-02350-4). A-W.

Psychology of Being Human: Brief Edition. Zick Rubin & Elton B. McNeil. 504p. 1979. pap. text ed. 15.50 scp (ISBN 0-06-044386-3, HarpC). Har-Row.

Psychology of Birds. Harold E. Burtt. 1967. 5.95 o.s.i. (ISBN 0-02-518550-0). Macmillan.

Psychology of Birth: Roots of Human Personality. Elizabeth Feher. 224p. 1981. 12.95 (ISBN 0-8264-0039-6). Continuum.
Psychology of Black Language. Jim Haskins & Hugh F. Butts. (College Outline Ser.). 112p. (Orig.). 1973. pap. 2.50 o.p. (ISBN 0-06-460142-0, 142, COS). Har-Row.
Psychology of Blindness. Donald D. Kirtley. LC 74-17155. 376p. 1974. 19.95 (ISBN 0-88229-178-5). Nelson-Hall.
Psychology of Buddhism. Ashok Kara. Date not set. pap. price not set (ISBN 0-89389-062-6). Himalayan Intl Inst.
Psychology of Children's Drawings: From the First Stroke to the Coloured Drawing. 2nd ed. Helga Eng. (International Library of Philosophy, Psychology & Scientific Method Ser). 1964. 22.50 (ISBN 0-7100-3096-7). Routledge & Kegan.
Psychology of Clothes. J. C. Flugel. (Illus.). 1969. Repr. text ed. 13.50x o.p. (ISBN 0-8236-5580-6). Intl Univs Pr.
Psychology of Coaching. Thomas Tutko & Jack Richards. 1971. text ed. 18.95 (ISBN 0-205-02904-3, 6229042). Allyn.
Psychology of College Success: A Dynamic Approach. Henry C. Lindgren. LC 79-25614. 158p. 1980. Repr. lib. bdg. 6.50 (ISBN 0-89874-035-5). Krieger.
Psychology of Color & Design. Deborah T. Sharpe. LC 73-91308. 184p. 1974. 14.95 (ISBN 0-88229-107-6). Nelson-Hall.
Psychology of Consciousness. Robert E. Ornstein. 1975. pap. 2.95 (ISBN 0-14-021679-0, Pelican). Penguin.
Psychology of Counseling. Clyde M. Narramore. 9.95 (ISBN 0-310-29930-6). Zondervan.
Psychology of Crime. David Abrahamsen. LC 59-13606. 1960. 18.50x (ISBN 0-231-02274-3). Columbia U Pr.
Psychology of Deafness. H. Hoemann. Date not set. cancelled (ISBN 0-685-32504-0). Univ Park.
Psychology of Deafness. Edna S. Levine. LC 60-7250. 1960. 20.00x (ISBN 0-231-02394-4). Columbia U Pr.
Psychology of Death, Dying & Bereavement. Richard Schulz. LC 77-83030. (Illus.). 1978. pap. text ed. 8.50 (ISBN 0-201-07328-5). A-W.
Psychology of Dress. Frank A. Parsons. LC 74-19187. (Illus.). 1975. Repr. of 1920 ed. 24.00 (ISBN 0-8103-4087-9). Gale.
Psychology of Driving: Factors of Traffic Enforcement. A. R. Lauer. (Illus.). 352p. 1972. 15.75 (ISBN 0-398-02337-9). C C Thomas.
Psychology of Education. Ed. by Donald H. Clark. LC 67-15144. 1967. pap. text ed. 4.50 o.s.i. (ISBN 0-02-905510-5). Free Pr.
Psychology of Education. 2nd ed. M. Ray Loree. 666p. 1970. 18.50 o.p. (ISBN 0-8260-5555-9); instr's manual avail. o.p. (ISBN 0-471-07539-6). Wiley.
Psychology of Effective Living. Norman E. Hankins & Roger C. Bailey. LC 79-19044. 1980. text ed. 15.95 (ISBN 0-8185-0360-2). Brooks-Cole.
Psychology of Efficient Thinking. Z. Pietrasinski. 1969. 27.00 (ISBN 0-08-012544-1). Pergamon.
Psychology of Enlightenment: Meditations on the Seven Energy Centers. Gurudev S. Chitrabhanu. LC 79-795. (Illus.). 1979. 6.95 (ISBN 0-396-07676-9). Dodd.
Psychology of Exceptional Children & Youth. 4th ed. W. Cruikshank. 1980. 20.95 (ISBN 0-13-733808-2). P-H.
Psychology of Fear: The Nightmare Formula of Edgar Allan Poe. David R. Saliba. LC 80-8267. 277p. 1980. lib. bdg. 18.50 (ISBN 0-8191-1269-0); pap. text ed. 10.25 (ISBN 0-8191-1270-4). U Pr of Amer.
Psychology of Freedom: Liberty & Love As a Way of Life. Peter R. Breggin. LC 80-7459. 242p. 1980. 12.95 (ISBN 0-87975-132-0). Prometheus Bks.
Psychology of Human Height. John S. Gillis. 200p. 1981. pap. 9.95 (ISBN 0-918296-15-3). Inst Personality & Ability.
Psychology of Imagination. Jean-Paul Sartre. 1980. pap. 4.95 (ISBN 0-8065-0305-X). Lyle Stuart.
Psychology of Individual & Group Differences. Lee Willerman. LC 78-9865. (Psychology Ser.). (Illus.). 1979. text ed. 18.95x (ISBN 0-7167-0292-4). W H Freeman.
Psychology of Individual Differences. Robert S. Ellis. 533p. 1980. Repr. of 1930 ed. lib. bdg. 45.00 (ISBN 0-89760-204-8). Telegraph Bks.
Psychology of Insanity. 5th ed. Bernard Hart. (Orig.). 1957. 23.50 (ISBN 0-521-05219-X). Cambridge U Pr.
Psychology of Intelligence. Jean Piaget. 1971. Repr. of 1950 ed. 16.95 (ISBN 0-7100-3136-X). Routledge & Kegan.
Psychology of Interpersonal Behaviour. Michael Argyle. lib. bdg. 9.50x o.p. (ISBN 0-88307-297-1). Gannon.
Psychology of Invention in the Mathematical Field. Jacques Hadamard. 1945. pap. text ed. 2.50 (ISBN 0-486-20107-4). Dover.
Psychology of Inventors & Money-Makers. F. W. Faussig. (Illus.). 103p. 1981. 43.25 (ISBN 0-89920-020-6). Am Inst Psych.
Psychology of Language & Learning. O. Hobart Mowrer. (Cognition & Language Ser.). (Illus.). 275p. 1980. 27.50 (ISBN 0-306-40371-4, Plenum Pr). Plenum Pub.
Psychology of Language & Thought: Essays on the Theory & History of Psycholinguistics. Ed. by Robert W. Rieber. (Applied Psycholinguistics & Communication Disorders Ser.). (Illus.). 280p. 1980. 27.50 (ISBN 0-306-40361-7, Plenum Pr). Plenum Pub.
Psychology of Learning: An Introduction for Students of Education. Gordon R. Cross. 1974. text ed. 29.00 (ISBN 0-08-018136-8); pap. text ed. 17.00 (ISBN 0-08-018135-X). Pergamon.
Psychology of Learning & Instruction: A Performance Based Course. new ed. Robert G. Packard. (Educational Psychology Ser.). 496p. 1975. pap. text ed. 14.95x (ISBN 0-675-08761-9); instructor's manual 3.95 (ISBN 0-686-67073-6). Merrill.
Psychology of Learning & Memory. Henry C. Ellis et al. LC 78-16292. (Illus.). 1979. text ed. 17.95 (ISBN 0-8185-0267-3). Brooks-Cole.
Psychology of Learning & Memory. Douglas L. Hintzman. LC 77-16295. (Psychology Ser.). (Illus.). 1978. text ed. 18.95x (ISBN 0-7167-0035-2). W H Freeman.
Psychology of Learning Applied to Teaching. 2nd ed. B. R. Bugelski. LC 79-149402. (Illus.). 1971. text ed. 13.95 (ISBN 0-672-60785-9). Bobbs.
Psychology of Learning: Readings. Ed. by William L. Mikulas. LC 77-8234. 1977. text ed. 23.95 (ISBN 0-88229-226-9); pap. 11.95 (ISBN 0-88229-519-5). Nelson-Hall.
Psychology of Left & Right. M. C. Corballis & I. L. Beale. LC 76-13233. 1976. text ed. 14.95 o.p. (ISBN 0-470-15104-8). Halsted Pr.
Psychology of Leisure Travel: Effective Marketing & Selling of Travel Services. Edward J. Mayo & Lance P. Jarvis. 448p. 1981. 9.95 (ISBN 0-8436-2204-0). CBI Pub.
Psychology of Mathematics for Instruction. Lauren B. Resnick & Wendy W. Ford. 368p. 1981. text ed. 24.95 (ISBN 0-89859-029-9). L Erlbaum Assocs.
Psychology of Misconduct, Vice, & Crime. Bernard Hollander. (Historical Foundations of Forensic Psychiatry & Psychology Ser.). 220p. 1980. Repr. lib. bdg. 25.00 (ISBN 0-306-76063-0). Da Capo.
Psychology of Motivation. Abraham K. Korman. (Experimental Psychology Ser). (Illus.). 288p. 1974. ref. ed. 18.95 (ISBN 0-13-733279-3). P-H.
Psychology of Motor Behavior & Sport 1980. Ed. by Daniel Landers & Glyn Roberts. 1981. text ed. 12.00x (ISBN 0-931250-19-6). Human Kinetics.
Psychology of Motor Behavior & Sport: 1979. Ed. by Claude Nadeau et al. LC 78-641529. (Illus.). 1980. text ed. 24.95x (ISBN 0-686-64327-5). Human Kinetics.
Psychology of Motor Learning. J. Oxendine. 1968. text ed. 17.95 (ISBN 0-13-736595-0). P-H.
Psychology of Murder: A Study in Criminal Psychology. Andreas Bjerre. Tr. by E. Classen from Swedish. (Historical Foundations of Forensic Psychiatry & Psychology Ser.). 164p. 1980. Repr. lib. bdg. 19.50 (ISBN 0-306-76067-3). Da Capo.
Psychology of Nirvana. Rune Johansson. 1969. text ed. 4.95x o.p. (ISBN 0-04-150026-1). Allen Unwin.
Psychology of Nonviolence. Leroy H. Pelton. LC 74-2156. 310p. 1975. text ed. 23.00 (ISBN 0-08-018099-X). Pergamon.
Psychology of Obesity: Dynamics & Treatment. Ed. by Norman Kiell. (Illus.). 480p. 1973. 19.75 (ISBN 0-398-02685-8). C C Thomas.
Psychology of Pain. Ed. by Richard A. Sternbach. LC 77-84554. 1978. 21.00 (ISBN 0-89004-278-0). Raven.
Psychology of Person Identification. Brian Clifford & Ray Bull. 1978. 22.50 (ISBN 0-7100-8867-1). Routledge & Kegan.
Psychology of Personal Development. 3rd ed. Henry C. Lindgren & Leonard W. Fisk, Jr. LC 75-34926. 1976. 19.95x (ISBN 0-471-53769-1). Wiley.
Psychology of Personality. English Bagby. 236p. 1980. Repr. of 1928 ed. lib. bdg. 35.00 (ISBN 0-8492-3590-1). R West.
Psychology of Personality. Jerry S. Wiggins et al. 1971. 20.95 (ISBN 0-201-08636-0); instr's manual 3.25 (ISBN 0-201-08637-9); test items 3.25 (ISBN 0-201-08638-7). A-W.
Psychology of Place. David Canter. LC 77-366169. (Illus.). 198p. 1977. 22.50x (ISBN 0-85139-532-5). Intl Pubns Serv.
Psychology of Politics. William F. Stone. LC 73-17647. (Illus.). 1974. 14.95 (ISBN 0-02-931690-1); pap. text ed. 8.95 (ISBN 0-02-931680-4). Free Pr.
Psychology of Pregnancy. Judith Ballou. LC 78-57242. 1978. 16.95 (ISBN 0-669-02377-9). Lexington Bks.
Psychology of Reading: Foundations of Instruction. Mildred C. Robeck & John A. Wilson. LC 73-13797. 600p. 1974. text ed. 23.95 (ISBN 0-471-72580-3). Wiley.
Psychology of Reasoning: Structure & Content. P. C. Wason & P. N. Johnson-Laird. LC 78-189160. 1972. 12.50 (ISBN 0-674-72126-8); pap. 3.95 (ISBN 0-674-72127-6). Harvard U Pr.
Psychology of Religion. G. E. Scobie. LC 74-21832. 189p. 1975. text ed. 16.95 (ISBN 0-470-76712-X); pap. text ed. 7.95 (ISBN 0-470-26689-9). Halsted Pr.
Psychology of Religion: A Guide to Information Sources. Ed. by Donald Capps et al. LC 73-17530. (Philosophy & Religion Information Guide Ser.: Vol. 1). vii, 380p. 1976. 30.00 (ISBN 0-8103-1356-1). Gale.
Psychology of Religious Mysticism. James H. Leuba. 1972. 22.50 (ISBN 0-7100-7317-8). Routledge & Kegan.
Psychology of Rigorous Humanism. Joseph F. Rychlak. LC 76-54838. 1977. 28.95 (ISBN 0-471-74796-3, Pub. by Wiley-Interscience). Wiley.
Psychology of Science. Abraham H. Maslow. 1966. 9.95 o.p. (ISBN 0-06-034145-9, HarpT). Har-Row.
Psychology of Second Language Learning. Ed. by Paul Pimsleur & Terence Quinn. (Illus.). 1971. 27.50 (ISBN 0-521-08236-6). Cambridge U Pr.
Psychology of Self-Determination. Edward L. Deci. LC 80-8373. 1980. 19.95 (ISBN 0-669-04045-2). Lexington Bks.
Psychology of Selling, 12 vols. Harold C. Cash & W. J. Crissy. Incl. Vol. 1. Point of View for Salesman; Vol. 2. Use of Appeals in Selling; Vol. 3. Motivation in Selling; Vol. 4. Personality & Sales Strategy; Vol. 5. Tactics for Conducting the Sales Call; Vol. 6. Salesman As a Self-Manager; Vol. 7. Communication in Selling; Vol. 8. Logic & Creativity in Selling; Vol. 9. Managing Sales Resistance; Vol. 10. Guiding Buying Behavior; Vol. 11. Selling in Depth; Vol. 12. Salesman's Role in Marketing. 4.00x ea. Personnel Dev.
Psychology of Sex Differences. Hilary M. Lips & Nina L. Colwill. (Illus.). 1978. 13.95 (ISBN 0-13-736561-6, Spec); pap. 5.95 (ISBN 0-13-736553-5). P-H.
Psychology of Sex Differences. Eleanor E. Maccoby & Carol N. Jacklin. LC 73-94488. 1974. 18.95x (ISBN 0-8047-0859-2); Vol. I: Text. pap. 7.50x (ISBN 0-8047-0974-2); Vol. II: Annotated Bibliography. pap. 4.95x (ISBN 0-8047-0975-0). Stanford U Pr.
Psychology of Sex Relations. Theodor Reik. LC 74-28525. 243p. 1975. Repr. of 1945 ed. lib. bdg. 21.00x (ISBN 0-8371-7916-5, RESR). Greenwood.
Psychology of Singing. Al Berkman. 1977. 10.00 (ISBN 0-934972-08-7). Melrose Pub Co.
Psychology of Social Situations: Selected Readings. Ed. by A. Furnham & M. Argyle. 350p. 1981. 40.00 (ISBN 0-08-024319-3); pap. 15.70 (ISBN 0-08-023719-3). Pergamon.
Psychology of Socialism. Gustave Le Bon. Repr. of 1965 ed. flexible cover 12.00 (ISBN 0-87034-025-5). Fraser Pub Co.
Psychology of Successful Weight Control. Mary C. Tyson & Robert Tyson. LC 73-84207. 192p. 1974. 11.95 (ISBN 0-88229-103-3). Nelson-Hall.
Psychology of Symbolic Activity. Howard R. Pollio. LC 72-1943. 1974. text ed. 20.95 (ISBN 0-201-05851-0). A-W.
Psychology of Teaching Methods: Seventy-Fifth Yearbook Part I. Ed. by N. L. Gage. LC 6-16938. (National Society for the Study of Education). 1976. lib. bdg. 13.00x o.s.i. (ISBN 0-226-60119-6). U of Chicago Pr.
Psychology of the Adolescent. Leta S. Hollingworth. 256p. 1980. Repr. lib. bdg. 30.00 (ISBN 0-89984-294-1). Century Bookbindery.
Psychology of the Arts. Hans Kreitler & Shulamith Kreitler. LC 70-185566. (Illus.). 1972. 18.75 (ISBN 0-8223-0269-1); pap. 9.75 (ISBN 0-8223-0437-6). Duke.
Psychology of the Learning Group. John McLeish et al. 1973. text ed. 9.00x (ISBN 0-09-114010-2, Hutchinson U Lib); pap. text ed. 4.75x (ISBN 0-09-114011-0). Humanities.
Psychology of the Psychic. David Marks & Richard Kammann. LC 80-7458. (Critiques of the Paranormal Ser.). 232p. 1980. 16.95 (ISBN 0-87975-121-5); pap. 8.95 (ISBN 0-87975-122-3). Prometheus Bks.
Psychology of the Soul. James H. Quitoriano. (Illus.). 1979. 37.50 (ISBN 0-89266-204-2). Am Classical Coll Pr.
Psychology of the TV Image. J. P. Baggaley et al. LC 79-92118. 1980. 21.95 (ISBN 0-03-046206-1). Praeger.
Psychology of the Youthful Offender. 2nd ed. Robert N. Walker. 164p. 1973. 14.75 (ISBN 0-398-02859-1). C C Thomas.
Psychology of Thinking. Lyle E. Bourne, Jr. et al. LC 79-135409. 1971. ref. ed. 19.95 (ISBN 0-13-736702-3). P-H.
Psychology of Tragic Drama. Patrick Roberts. 1975. 25.00x (ISBN 0-7100-8034-4). Routledge & Kegan.
Psychology of Transendence. Andrew Neher. (Transpersonal Ser.). (Illus.). 320p. 1980. text ed. 13.95 (ISBN 0-13-736652-3, Spec); pap. text ed. 6.95 (ISBN 0-13-736645-0). P-H.
Psychology of Union-Management Relations. Ross Stagner & Hjalmar Rosen. (Behavioral Science in Industry Ser). (Orig.). 1966. pap. text ed. 6.95 o.p. (ISBN 0-8185-0315-7). Brooks-Cole.
Psychology of Vision. Royal Society Discussion, March 7 & 8, 1979. Ed. by H. C. Longuet-Higgins & N. S. Sutherland. (Illus.). 218p. 1980. text ed. 61.00x (ISBN 0-85403-141-3, Pub. by Royal Soc London). Scholium Intl.
Psychology of Visual Illusion. J. O. Robinson. (Illus.). 288p. 1974. text ed. 10.75x (ISBN 0-09-112280-5, Hutchinson U Lib); pap. text ed. 5.50x (ISBN 0-09-112281-3). Humanities.
Psychology of Women: Selected Readings. Ed. by Juanita H. Williams. 1979. pap. text ed. 9.95x (ISBN 0-393-09068-X). Norton.
Psychology of Work Behavior. rev. ed. Frank J. Landy & Don A. Trumbo. 1980. text ed. 18.95x (ISBN 0-256-02324-7). Dorsey.
Psychology of Written Communication. Ed. by James Hartley. 1980. 32.50x (ISBN 0-89397-081-6). Nichols Pub.
Psychology on the Road: The Human Factor in Traffic Safety. David Shinar. LC 78-18219. 1978. text ed. 20.95 (ISBN 0-471-03997-7). Wiley.
Psychology Problem Solver. Research & Education Association Staff. LC 80-53174. (Illus.). 1056p. (Orig.). pap. text ed. 16.85x (ISBN 0-87891-523-0). Res & Educ.
Psychology, Religion & Healing. Leslie D. Weatherhead. (Series D). 1959. pap. 6.95 (ISBN 0-687-34885-4, Apex). Abingdon.
Psychology Survey, Vol. 1. Ed. by Brian Foss. (Psychology Yearbook Ser.). 1978. text ed. 17.95x (ISBN 0-04-150065-2); pap. text ed. 7.95x (ISBN 0-04-150066-0). Allen Unwin.
Psychology Survey, No. 3. Ed. by Malcolm Jeeves. 208p. (Orig.). 1980. text ed. 25.00x (ISBN 0-04-150073-3, 2311); pap. text ed. 11.50 (ISBN 0-04-150074-1, 2312). Allen Unwin.
Psychology: The Hybrid Science. 3rd ed. Frank B. McMahon. (Illus.). 1977. 18.95 (ISBN 0-13-732958-X); study guide & wkbk. 6.95 (ISBN 0-13-732966-0). P-H.
Psychology: The Leading Edge, Vol. 340. new ed. Ed. by Florence L. Denmark. (N.Y. Academy of Sciences Annals: Vol. 340). 114p. 1980. 20.00 (ISBN 0-89766-068-4); pap. write for info. (ISBN 0-89766-069-2). NY Acad Sci.
Psychology: Theoretical-Historical Perspectives. Ed. by Robert W. Rieber & Kurt Salzinger. LC 79-6790. 1980. 21.00 (ISBN 0-12-588265-3). Acad Pr.
Psychology Today. Emilio Servadio. LC 65-27637. 7.50 o.p. (ISBN 0-912326-16-6). Garrett-Helix.
Psychology Today: An Introduction. 4th ed. Communications Research Machines, Inc. 1979. text ed. 16.95x (ISBN 0-394-32066-2); wkbk. 6.95 (ISBN 0-394-32313-0). Random.
Psychology: Understanding Ourselves & Others. new ed. Norman Tallent & Charlotte I. Spungin. (Illus.). (gr. 11-12). 1977. text ed. 10.68 (ISBN 0-278-47332-6); tchr's guide 2.01 (ISBN 0-278-47334-2); tests 23.97 (ISBN 0-278-47336-9). ABC.
Psychomotor Continuum. Joyce Gardner & Ida La Fleur. (gr. k-2). 1977. 7.00x (ISBN 0-933892-09-8). Child Focus Co.
Psychomotor Epilepsy: A Polydimensional Study. Uros J. Jovanovic. (American Lectures in Living Chemistry Ser.). (Illus.). 544p. 1974. 42.75 (ISBN 0-398-02691-2). C C Thomas.
Psychonephrology One: Psychological Factors in Hemodialysis & Transplantation. Ed. by Norman B. Levy. 280p. 1981. 25.00 (ISBN 0-306-40586-5, Plenum Pr). Plenum Pub.
Psychoneuroendocrinology & Abnormal Behaviour. Ed. by J. Mendlewicz. (Advances in Biological Psychiatry: Vol. 5). (Illus.). vi, 130p. 1980. pap. 34.75 (ISBN 3-8055-0599-X). S Karger.
Psychoneuroendocrinology in Reproduction. Ed. by L. Zichella & P. Pancheri. (Developments in Endocrinology Ser.: Vol. 5). 602p. 1979. 59.50 (ISBN 0-444-80172-3, North Holland). Elsevier.
Psychoneuroimmunology. Ed. by Robert Ader. LC 80-265. (Behavioral Medicine Ser.). 1981. price not set (ISBN 0-12-043780-5). Acad Pr.
Psychopath Plague. Stephen G. Spruill. 1979. pap. 1.75 o.s.i. (ISBN 0-440-17230-6). Dell.
Psychopath Plague. Steven G. Spruill. LC 77-77661. 1978. 6.95 o.p. (ISBN 0-385-13147-X). Doubleday.

Psychopathic Disorders. Ed. by M. Craft. 1966. 12.10 o.p. (ISBN 0-08-011618-3); pap. 6.05 o.p. (ISBN 0-08-011617-5). Pergamon.

Psychopathological Disorders in Childhood: Theoretical Considerations & a Proposed Classification, Vol. 6. GAP Committee on Child Psychiatry. LC 62-2872. (Report No. 62). 1966. pap. 6.00 (ISBN 0-87318-087-9). Adv Psychiatry.

Psychopathological Disorders of Childhood. 2nd ed. Herbert C. Quay & John S. Werry. LC 78-24238. 1979. text ed. 22.95 (ISBN 0-471-04268-4). Wiley.

Psychopathological Researches. Boris Sidis. 329p. 1980. Repr. of 1902 ed. lib. bdg. 75.00 (ISBN 0-89984-411-1). Century Bookbindery.

Psychopathology & Brain Dysfunction. Ed. by Charles Shagass et al. LC 76-55487. (American Psychopathological Association Ser). 1977. 28.00 (ISBN 0-89004-120-2). Raven.

Psychopathology & Political Leadership, Vol. 16. R. S. Robins et al. LC 77-85747. 1977. lib. bdg. 17.50 o.p. (ISBN 0-930598-17-2); pap. text ed. 6.00 (ISBN 0-930598-16-4). Tulane Stud Pol.

Psychopathology: Experimental Models. Ed. by Jack D. Maser & Martin E. Seligman. LC 77-5032. (Psychology Ser.). (Illus.). 1977. text ed. 23.95x (ISBN 0-7167-0368-8); pap. text ed. 14.95x (ISBN 0-7167-0367-X). W H Freeman.

Psychopathology in the Aged. Ed. by Jonathan O. Cole & James E. Barrett. (American Psychopathology Association Ser.). 320p. 1980. text ed. 32.00 (ISBN 0-89004-406-6). Raven.

Psychopathology of Childhood. Jane W. Kessler. (Illus.). 1966. text ed. 19.95 (ISBN 0-13-736751-1). P-H.

Psychopathology of Childhood: A Clinical-Experimental Approach. Steven Schwartz & James H. Johnson. (Pergamon General Psychology Ser.). 400p. Date not set. 19.51 (ISBN 0-08-023885-8). Pergamon.

Psychopathology: The Science of Understanding Deviance. 2nd ed. James D. Page. (Illus.). 498p. 1975. 17.95x (ISBN 0-19-502293-9); instructor's manual avail., by Margaret & Herbert Rappaport (ISBN 0-19-502313-7). Oxford U Pr.

Psychopathy: Theory & Research. Robert D. Hare. LC 79-120704. (Foundations of Abnormal Psychology Ser). 1970. pap. text ed. 10.95 (ISBN 0-471-35147-4). Wiley.

Psychopedagogy: Psychological Theory & the Practice of Teaching. E. Stones. 490p. 1979. 21.95 (ISBN 0-416-71330-0, 2525); pap. 13.95 (ISBN 0-416-71340-8, 6420). Methuen Inc.

Psychopharmacologh for the Aged. Ed. by T. H. Ban. xii, 216p. 1980. softcover 23.50 (ISBN 3-8055-1204-X). S Karger.

Psychopharmacological Agents, 3 vols. Ed. by Maxwell Gordon. Incl. Vol. 1. 1964. 69.50 (ISBN 0-12-290550-4); Vol. 2. 1967. 69.50 (ISBN 0-12-290556-3); Vol. 3. 1974. 54.00 (ISBN 0-12-290558-X). (Medicinal Chemistry Ser.). Acad Pr.

Psychopharmacology: A Generation of Progress. Ed. by Morris A. Lipton et al. LC 77-83697. 1978. 69.50 (ISBN 0-89004-191-1). Raven.

Psychopharmacology & Psychotherapy: Synthesis or Antithesis? Norman Rosenzweig. LC 78-4088. 1978. text ed. 22.95 (ISBN 0-87705-354-5). Human Sci Pr.

Psychopharmacology & the Individual Patient. Ed. by J. R. Wittenborn et al. LC 71-116996. 1970. 19.00 (ISBN 0-911216-13-8). Raven.

Psychopharmacology Case Studies. David S. Janowsky et al. 1978. pap. 12.75 (ISBN 0-87488-052-1). Med Exam.

Psychopharmacology for Everyday Practice. T. A. Ban & M. H. Hollender. vi, 190p. 1981. pap. 19.75 (ISBN 3-8055-2241-X). S Karger.

Psychopharmacology in Family Practice. David Wheatley. (Illus.). 1973. 17.95x (ISBN 0-433-35680-4). Intl Ideas.

Psychopharmacology of Aggression. Ed. by Merton Sandler. 1979. 34.50 (ISBN 0-89004-392-2). Raven.

Psychopharmacology of Aging. Ed. by C. Eisdorfer & W. E. Faun. (Illus.). 327p. 1980. text ed. 40.00 (ISBN 0-89335-117-2). Spectrum Pub.

Psychopharmacology of Depression. Thomas A. Ban. (Illus.). 104p. 1980. pap. 14.00 (ISBN 3-8055-1154-X). S Karger.

Psychopharmacology of Hallucinogens. Ed. by R. C. Stillman & R. E. Willette. LC 78-14019. 1979. 40.00 (ISBN 0-08-021938-1). Pergamon.

Psychopharmacology of Thiothixene. Thomas A. Ban. LC 75-43191. 1978. 20.50 (ISBN 0-89004-108-3). Raven.

Psychopharmacology Update. Ed. by Jonathan O. Cole. LC 79-48064. 195p. 1980. 14.95 (ISBN 0-669-03695-1). Heath.

Psychophysical Analysis of Visual Space. J. C. Baird. 1970. text ed. 72.00 (ISBN 0-08-013876-4). Pergamon.

Psychophysical Elements in Parapsychological Traditions. A. Tanagras. LC 67-19168. (Parapsychological Monograph No. 7). 1967. pap. 4.00 (ISBN 0-912328-10-X). Parapsych Foun.

Psychophysical Physiological & Behavioral Studies in Hearing: Proceedings. International Symposium on Hearing, Fifth, Noordwijkerhout, the Netherlands, April 8-12, 1980. Ed. by G. Van den Brink & F. A. Bilsen. 480p. 1980. 42.50x (ISBN 90-286-0780-3). Sijthoff & Noordhoff.

Psychophysics and Physiology of Hearing. Ed. by E. F. Evans. 1978. 45.00 (ISBN 0-12-244050-1). Acad Pr.

Psychophysics: Introduction to Its Perceptual, Neutral & Social Prospects. S. S. Stevens. LC 74-13473. 1975. 30.95 (ISBN 0-471-82437-2, Pub. by Wiley-Interscience). Wiley.

Psychophysiological Aspects of Skin Disease, Vol. 8. F. A. Whitlock. LC 76-20942. (Illus.). 1976. 22.00 (ISBN 0-7216-9301-6). Saunders.

Psychophysiological Aspects of Spaceflight. Ed. by Bernard E. Flaherty. LC 60-15809. 1961. 22.50x (ISBN 0-231-02456-8). Columbia U Pr.

Psychophysiological Recording. Robert M. Stern et al. (Illus.). 256p. 1980. text ed. 14.95x (ISBN 0-19-502695-0); pap. text ed. 8.95x (ISBN 0-19-502696-9). Oxford U Pr.

Psychophysiology of Mental Illness. Malcolm Lader. (Social & Psychological Aspects of Medical Practice Ser.). 1975. 24.00x (ISBN 0-7100-8091-3). Routledge & Kegan.

Psychophysiology Today & Tomorrow: Proceedings of International Union of Physiological Sciences Conference on Psychophysiology, 1979. Ed. by N. P. Bechtereva. (Illus.). 270p. 1980. 60.00 (ISBN 0-08-025930-8). Pergamon.

Psychoses. Elton B. McNeil. (Lives in Disorder Ser). 1970. pap. 8.95 ref. ed. (ISBN 0-13-736413-X). P-H.

Psychosocial & Educational Aspects & Problems of Mental Retardation. Robert M. Allen & Arnold D. Cortazzo. 1970. pap. 14.75 photocopy ed. spiral (ISBN 0-398-00031-X). C C Thomas.

Psychosocial Aspects of Cancer. Ed. by Jerome Cohen et al. Orig. Title: Research Issues in Psychological Dimensions of Cancer. 300p. 1981. text ed. 25.00 (ISBN 0-89004-494-5). Raven.

Psychosocial Aspects of Cardiovascular Disease: The Life-Threatened Patient, the Family & the Staff. Ed. by James Reiffel et al. Austin H. Kutscher. LC 79-27765. (Foundation of Thanatology Ser.). (Illus.). 1980. 25.00x (ISBN 0-231-04354-6). Columbia U Pr.

Psychosocial Aspects of Drug Treatment for Hyperactivity. Ed. by Kenneth D. Gadow & Jan Loney. (AAAS Selected Symposium: No. 44). 460p. 1981. lib. bdg. 26.50x (ISBN 0-89158-834-5). Westview.

Psychosocial Aspects of Terminal Care. Ed. by Bernard Schoenberg et al. LC 73-184747. 385p. 1972. 22.50x (ISBN 0-231-03614-0). Columbia U Pr.

Psychosocial Needs of the Aged: A Health Care Perspective. rev. ed. Ed. by Eugene Seymour. LC 78-60818. 1978. pap. 5.00 (ISBN 0-88474-048-X). USC Andrus Geron.

Psychosocial Nursing Care of the Aged. Irene M. Burnside. (Illus.). 228p. 1972. pap. text ed. 8.95 o.p. (ISBN 0-07-009208-7, HP). McGraw.

Psychosocial Origins of Mental Retardation. Harold Simmons. 1980. pap. 5.95 (ISBN 0-87312-011-6). Gen Welfare.

Psychosocial Rehabilitation of the Blind. Alvin Roberts. 100p. 1973. 11.75 (ISBN 0-398-02834-6). C C Thomas.

Psychosocial Therapy: A Social Work Perspective. Ed. by Francis J. Turner. LC 77-90456. (Treatment Approaches in the Human Servics Ser.). 1978. text ed. 14.95 (ISBN 0-02-932720-2). Free Pr.

Psychosomatic Approach to Prevention of Disease: Proceedings. Annual Conference for Psychosomatic Research, 20th, London, Nov. 15-16, 1976. Ed. by M. Carruthers & R. Priest. 1978. pap. text ed. 22.00 (ISBN 0-08-022253-6). Pergamon.

Psychosomatic Disorders: A Behavioristic Interpretation. Sheldon J. Lachman. LC 78-37936. (Approaches to Behavior Pathology Ser.). 1972. pap. text ed. 10.95 (ISBN 0-471-51146-3). Wiley.

Psychosomatic Disorders in Childhood. Melitta Sperling. LC 76-22870. 1978. 25.00x (ISBN 0-87668-274-3). Aronson.

Psychosomatics & Pleasure: Proceedings of the Twenty-Third Annual Conference of the Society for Psychosomatic Research Held at the Royal College of Physicians, London, 19-20 November 1979. Ed. by C. Aitken. 88p. 1980. pap. 20.00 (ISBN 0-08-026797-1). Pergamon.

Psychosomatics in War & Peace: Proceedings. Society for Psychosomatic Research, 22nd, Royal College of Physicians, London, Nov. 27-28 1978. Ed. by P. Williams. 112p. 1980. pap. 22.00 (ISBN 0-08-026064-0). Pergamon.

Psychosurgery. E. Hitchcock et al. (Illus.). 456p. 1972. 33.75 (ISBN 0-398-02314-X). C C Thomas.

Psychosurgery & Society: A Symposium Organised by the Neuropsychiatric Institute, Sydney, Australia. Ed. by J. Sydney Smith & L. G. Kiloh. 37.00 (ISBN 0-08-021836-9). Pergamon.

Psychosurgery Debate: Scientific, Legal, & Ethical Perspectives. Ed. by Elliot S. Valenstein. LC 80-11187. (Psychology Ser.). (Illus.). 1980. text ed. 26.95x (ISBN 0-7167-1156-7); pap. text ed. 13.95x (ISBN 0-7167-1157-5). W H Freeman.

Psychotechnic Leagues. Poul Anderson. Ed. by Hank Stine. 450p. 1981. 20.00 (ISBN 0-89865-084-4, Starblaze); pap. 5.95 (ISBN 0-89865-083-6). Donning Co.

Psychotherapeutic Attraction. Arnold P. Goldstein. LC 79-119598. 260p. 1971. 15.25 (ISBN 0-08-016398-X). Pergamon.

Psychotherapeutic Treatment Approaches for the Aging. Ed. by Arthur M. Horton, Jr. 320p. 1981. 24.95 (ISBN 0-89789-007-8). J F Bergin.

Psychotherapeutics in Primary Care. Steven L. Dubovsky. 1981. price not set (ISBN 0-8089-1337-9). Grune.

Psychotherapy: An Eclectic Approach. Sol. L. Garfield. LC 79-17724. (Personality Processes Ser.). 1980. 22.95 (ISBN 0-471-04490-3, Pub. by Wiley-Interseience). Wiley.

Psychotherapy & National Health Insurance: Issues & Evidence. Thomas McGuire. 1981. price not set (ISBN 0-88410-711-6). Ballinger Pub.

Psychotherapy & Personality Change. Ed. by Carl R. Rogers & Rosalind F. Dymond. LC 54-11211, (Midway Reprint Ser.). 1978. pap. text ed. 20.00x (ISBN 0-226-72375-5). U of Chicago Pr.

Psychotherapy & Process: The Fundamentals of an Existential-Humanistic Approach. James F. Bugental. LC 77-83031. (Topics in Clinical Psychology). (Illus.). 1978. pap. text ed. 7.50 (ISBN 0-201-00333-3). A-W.

Psychotherapy & the Dual Research Tradition, Vol. 7. GAP Committee on Therapy. LC 62-2872. (Report No. 73). 1969. pap. 2.00 (ISBN 0-87318-102-6). Adv. Psychiatry.

Psychotherapy & the Role of the Environment. Harold Voth & Marjorie Orth. LC 72-13818. 368p. 1973. text ed. 24.95 (ISBN 0-87705-102-X). Human Sci Pr.

Psychotherapy & Training in Clinical Social Work. Ed. by Judith Mishne. LC 78-57616. (Clinical Social Work Ser.). 1978. 22.95x (ISBN 0-470-26387-3). Halsted Pr.

Psychotherapy: Approaches & Applications. Edward Lichtenstein. LC 79-25036. 1980. text ed. 14.95 (ISBN 0-8185-0381-5). Brooks-Cole.

Psychotherapy in Child Guidance. Gordon Hamilton. 1947. 15.00x (ISBN 0-231-01637-9). Columbia U Pr.

Psychotherapy Maze. Miriam Ehrenberg & Otto Ehrenberg. LC 77-71350. 1977. 8.95 o.p. (ISBN 0-03-016886-4); pap. 3.95 o.p. (ISBN 0-03-022881-6). HR&W.

Psychotherapy of Schizophrenia. Ed. by John S. Strauss et al. 300p. 1980. 27.50 (ISBN 0-306-40497-4). Plenum Pub.

Psychotherapy: The Hazardous Cure. Dorothy Tennov. LC 75-40755. 320p. 1976. pap. 3.50 (ISBN 0-385-11657-8, Anch). Doubleday.

Psychotherapy: The Private & Very Personal Viewpoints of Doctor & Patient. Harold E. McNeely & Norma Obele. LC 72-88581. 1973. 13.95 (ISBN 0-911012-35-4). Nelson-Hall.

Psychotherapy: What It's All About. Hendrik Ruitenbeek. 1976. pap. 1.95 o.p. (ISBN 0-380-00811-4, 30858). Avon.

Psychotherapy with Children. Clark E. Moustakas. 1973. pap. 1.65 o.p. (ISBN 0-345-23174-0, Walden). Ballantine.

Psychotomimetic Drugs. Ed. by Daniel H. Efron. LC 73-89388. (Illus.). 1970. 26.00 (ISBN 0-911216-07-3). Raven.

Psychotropic Agents Parti: Part I, Antipschotics & Antidepressants. Ed. by G. Stille. (Handbook of Experimental Pharmacology: Vol. 55, Pt. 1). (Illus.). 800p. 1980. 172.00 (ISBN 0-387-09858-5). Springer-Verlag.

Psychotropic Drugs & Related Compounds. 2nd ed. Earl Usdin & Daniel H. Efron. LC 79-42886. 780p. 1979. 41.00 (ISBN 0-08-025510-8). Pergamon.

Psychotropic Drugs in the Year 2000: Use by Normal Humans. Ed. by Wayne O. Evans & Nathan S. Kline. 192p. 1971. text ed. 14.50 (ISBN 0-398-02191-0). C C Thomas.

Psychrometric Tables & Charts. 2nd ed. O. T. Zimmerman & Irvin Lavine. 1964. 28.00 (ISBN 0-686-20570-7). Indus Res Serv.

Psycles: Using Your Circadian Rhythms to Control Accidents, Illness, & Psychological Problems. Dwight H. Bulkley. LC 80-692. 224p. 1981. 10.95 (ISBN 0-672-52651-4). Bobbs.

Psyclosis: The Circularity of Experience. Ralph Berger. LC 77-24398. (Biology Ser.). (Illus.). 1977. text ed. 17.95x (ISBN 0-7167-0018-2). W H Freeman.

PTL Devotional Guide. Jim Bakker et al. Ed. by Anton Marco. LC 80-81170. 370p. 1980. pap. 3.95 (ISBN 0-89221-077-X). New Leaf.

P.T.L.A. Frances G. Hunter. 1972. pap. 1.25 o.s.i. (ISBN 0-89129-074-5). Jove Pubns.

Ptolemaic Itanos & Hellenistic Crete. Stylianos Spyridakis. (U. C. Publ. in History: Vol. 82). 1970. pap. 7.00x (ISBN 0-520-09193-0). U of Cal Pr.

Ptolemaic Oinochoai & Portraits in Faience: Aspects of the Ruler-Cult. Dorothy B. Thompson. (Oxford Monographs on Classical Archeology). (Illus.). 252p. 1973. 79.00x (ISBN 0-19-813211-5). Oxford U Pr.

Ptolemaios und Porpayrios Uber Die Musik. Ingemar During. LC 78-20290. (Ancient Philosophy Ser.). 293p. 1980. lib. bdg. 28.50 (ISBN 0-8240-9599-5). Garland Pub.

Ptosis. 3rd ed. Crowell Beard. LC 80-21576. (Illus.). 276p. 1980. text ed. 44.50 (ISBN 0-8016-0532-6). Mosby.

Public Access Cable Television in the United States & Canada: With an Annotated Bibliography. Gilbert Gillespie. LC 75-15644. (Special Studies). 172p. 1975. text ed. 18.95 o.p. (ISBN 0-275-09980-6). Praeger.

Public Access to Library Automation: Proceedings. Clinic on Library Applications of Data Processing, 1980. Ed. by J. L. Divilbiss. 1981. 10.00 (ISBN 0-87845-065-3). U of Ill Lib Sci. Postponed.

Public Accountability & School System. A. W. Bacon. 1979. text ed. 15.70 (ISBN 0-06-318082-0, Pub. by Har-Row Ltd England). Har-Row.

Public Accounting Profession. Stanley C. Abraham. LC 77-7804. (Illus.). 1978. 19.95 (ISBN 0-669-01606-3). Lexington Bks.

Public Administration. 3rd ed. Paul C. Bartholomew. (Quality Paperback: No. 29). (Orig.). 1977. 3.95 (ISBN 0-8226-0029-3). Littlefield.

Public Administration. 6th ed. R. Presthus. 1975. text ed. 16.95x (ISBN 0-8260-7225-9). Wiley.

Public Administration & Legislatures: Experimentation & Exploration. John A. Worthley. LC 75-23150. 256p. 1976. 16.95 (ISBN 0-88229-233-1). Nelson-Hall.

Public Administration & Policy Analysis. R. A. Rhodes. 1979. text ed. 23.00x (ISBN 0-566-00239-6, Pub. by Gower Pub Co England). Renouf.

Public Administration & Public Policy. Ed. by H. George Frederickson & Charles Wise. LC 76-14280. (Policy Studies Organization Bk.). (Illus.). 1977. 19.95 (ISBN 0-669-00738-2). Lexington Bks.

Public Administration & the Department of Agriculture. John M. Gaus & Leon O. Wolcott. LC 75-8788. (FDR & the Era of the New Deal Ser.). 1975. Repr. of 1940 ed. lib. bdg. 45.00 (ISBN 0-306-70704-7). Da Capo.

Public Administration: Concepts & Cases. Richard Stillman. LC 75-31022. (Illus.). 384p. 1976. pap. text ed. 9.95 o.p. (ISBN 0-395-20606-5). HM.

Public Administration: Concepts & Cases. 2nd ed. Richard J. Stillman, II. LC 79-89817. (Illus.). 1980. text ed. 10.50 (ISBN 0-395-28634-4). HM.

Public Administration: Government in Action. Richardson & Baldwin. (Political Science Ser.). 1976. text ed. 15 50 o.p. (ISBN 0-675-08605-1); instructor's manual 3.95 o.p. (ISBN 0-686-67373-5). Merrill.

Public Administration in a Time of Turbulence. Ed. by Dwight Waldo. 1971. pap. text ed. 8.95 scp o.p. (ISBN 0-685-02949-2, HarpC). Har-Row.

Public Administration in American Society: A Guide to Information Sources. Ed. by John E. Rouse, Jr. (American Government & History Information Guice Ser.: Vol. 11). 300p. 1980. 30.00 (ISBN 0-8103-1424-X). Gale.

Public Administration in France. new ed. F. Ridley & J. Blondel. 1969. 25.00x (ISBN 0-7100-2037-6). Routledge & Kegan.

Public Administration of Economic Development. Irving Swerdlow. LC 74-9426. (Special Studies). (Illus.). 426p. 1975. text ed. 38.95 (ISBN 0-275-05730-5). Praeger.

Public Administration Ser.: Bibliographies, 2 vols. Hope L. Isaacs et al. (Public Administration Ser.: Bibliography: P-638). 304p. 1981. pap. 20.00. Vance Biblios.

Public Administration: The Execution of Public Policy. Don Allensworth. 250p. 1973. pap. text ed. 3.95 o.p. (ISBN 0-397-47272-2). Lippincott.

Public & Business Planning in the United States: A Bibliography. Ed. by Martha B. Lightwood. LC 79-165488. (Management Information Guide Ser.: No. 26). 1972. 30.00 (ISBN 0-8103-0826-6). Gale.
Public & Its Problems. John Dewey. LC 76-178242. 236p. 1954. pap. 4.95x (ISBN 0-8040-0254-1, 11). Swallow.
Public & Private. Humphrey Trevelyan. 208p. 1980. 27.00 (ISBN 0-241-10357-6, Pub. by Hamish Hamilton England). David & Charles.
Public & Private Enterprise in Mixed Economies. Ed. by Wolfgang Friedmann. LC 73-12406. 440p. 1974. 25.00x (ISBN 0-231-03776-7). Columbia U Pr.
Public & Private Morality. S. Hampshire. LC 78-2839. 1978. 20.95 (ISBN 0-521-22084-X); pap. 5.95x (ISBN 0-521-29352-9). Cambridge U Pr.
Public & Private Support for the Arts in New York City: A Review with Recommendations for Improvement in the 80's. Cultural Assistance Center. LC 80-65497. 160p. (Orig.). 1980. pap. 6.00 (Pub. by Cultural Assist). Pub Ctr Cult Res.
Public & the Police. William A. Belson. 1975. 4.80 o.p. (ISBN 0-06-318025-1, IntlDept). Har-Row.
Public & Urban Economics. Ed. by Ronald E. Grieson. LC 74-31877. 288p. 1976. 27.95 (ISBN 0-669-98400-0). Lexington Bks.
Public Assembly Facilities: Planning & Management. Don Jewell. LC 77-16524. 1978. 22.50 (ISBN 0-471-02437-6, Pub. by Wiley-Interscience). Wiley.
Public Assistance Data Book. Toby H. Campbell & Marc Bendick, Jr. (Institute Paper). 344p. 1977. pap. 10.00 (ISBN 0-87766-207-X, 20300). Urban Inst.
Public Assistance in France. Cindy Stevens. 94p. 1973. pap. text ed. 5.00x (ISBN 0-7135-1846-4, Pub. by Bedford England). Renouf.
Public Assistance to Industry: Protection & Subsidies in Britain & Germany. new ed. Ed. by W. M. Corden & Gerhard Fels. LC 76-19791. (Illus.). 1976. lib. bdg. 35.00x (ISBN 0-89158-632-6). Westview.
Public Broadcasting: The Role of the Federal Government, 1912-76. George H. Gibson. LC 77-24422. (Praeger Special Studies). 1977. 25.95 (ISBN 0-03-022831-X). Praeger.
Public Budgeting & Management. Alan W. Steiss. 1972. 16.95 (ISBN 0-669-82149-7). Lexington Bks.
Public Career of Sir Thomas More. J. A. Guy. LC 80-5391. 224p. 1980. 22.50x (ISBN 0-300-02546-7). Yale U Pr.
Public Choice. D. C. Mueller. LC 78-11197. (Surveys in Economic Literature). 1979. 35.50 (ISBN 0-521-22550-7); pap. 7.95x (ISBN 0-521-29548-3). Cambridge U Pr.
Public Church. Martin E. Marty. 192p. 1981. 10.95 (ISBN 0-8245-0019-9). Crossroad NY.
Public Communication in Business & the Professions. Jerry W. Koehler & John I. Sisco. 300p. 1981. text ed. 11.36 (ISBN 0-8299-0417-4). West Pub.
Public Communications. Pamela C. Leth & Steven A. Leth. Ed. by W. D. Brooks & R. A. Vogel. LC 76-44139. (Ser. in Speech Communication). 1977. pap. text ed. 5.95 (ISBN 0-8465-7604-X); instr's guide 3.95 (ISBN 0-8465-7607-4). Benjamin-Cummings.
Public Conference, Tahoe Nevada, Oct. 2-5, 1977: Proceedings. Ed. by James J. Neitzel. spiral bdg. 7.50 (ISBN 0-89154-074-1). Intl Found Employ.
Public Education Religion Studies: An Overview. Paul J. Will et al. Ed. by Mark Taylor. LC 80-12237. (Aids for the Study of Religion Ser.). 1981. write for info. (ISBN 0-89130-401-0); pap. write for info. (ISBN 0-89130-402-9). Scholars Pr CA.
Public Education System. Michael L. Berger. (American Government Ser). (Illus.). (gr. 7 up). 1977. lib. bdg. 6.90 s&l (ISBN 0-531-00399-X). Watts.
Public Employee Pension Funds: A Twentieth Century Fund Report. Robert Tilove. 384p. 1976. 22.50x (ISBN 0-231-04015-6). Columbia U Pr.
Public Employee Unionism: Structure, Growth, Policy. Jack Stieber. LC 73-1591. (Studies of Unionism in Government). 256p. 1973. 12.95 (ISBN 0-8157-8160-1); pap. 5.95 (ISBN 0-8157-8159-8). Brookings.
Public Employee Unions: A Study in the Crisis in Public Sector Labor Relations. Ed. by A. Lawrence Chickering. LC 76-25771. 1976. 19.95 (ISBN 0-669-00980-6). Lexington Bks.
Public Employees Conference, Sept. 12-15, San Francisco: Proceedings. Ed. by James J. Neitzel. 1977. spiral bdg 3.75 (ISBN 0-89154-055-5). Intl Found Employ.
Public Employees Conference, 1974: Proceedings. Ed. by James J. Neitzel. (Civil Service Pensions). 82p. 1975. spiral bdg 3.75 (ISBN 0-89154-035-0). Intl Found Employ.
Public Employees Conference 1975, Hollywood, Fla. Proceedings. Ed. by Jan Hatch. (Civil Service Pensions). 145p. 1976. spiral bdg 3.75 (ISBN 0-89154-044-X). Intl Found Employ.
Public Employment & Compensation in Canada: Myths & Realities. David K. Foot. 188p. 1978. pap. text ed. 10.95x (ISBN 0-409-88600-9, Pub. by Inst Res Pub Canada). Renouf.
Public Employment in Canada: Statistical Series. David K. Foot. 217p. 1979. pap. text ed. 15.00x (ISBN 0-409-88603-3, Pub. by Inst Res Pub Canada). Renouf.
Public Employment Service. Brian Showler. LC 76-8923. 1976. text ed. 13.00x (ISBN 0-582-48541-X); pap. text ed. 9.00x (ISBN 0-582-48542-8). Longman.
Public Enemy. Pat Martinelli. (Pal Paperbacks, - Pal Skills II Ser.). (Illus.). (gr. 5-12). 1980. pap. text ed. 1.25 (ISBN 0-8374-6811-6). Xerox Ed Pubns.
Public Enterprise & Economic Development. 2nd ed. A. H. Hanson. 1965. 25.00x (ISBN 0-7100-1490-2). Routledge & Kegan.
Public Enterprise: Economic Analysis of Theory & Practice. Ed. by William G. Shepherd. LC 75-41926. (Illus.). 256p. 1976. 18.95 (ISBN 0-669-00477-4). Lexington Bks.
Public Enterprise in Britain. V. V. Ramanadham. 176p. 1950. 22.50x (ISBN 0-7146-1245-6, F Cass Co). Biblio Dist.
Public Enterprise in Crisis: The Future of the Nationalised Industries. John Redwood. 211p. 1981. 19.50x (ISBN 0-631-12582-5, Pub. by Basil Blackwell England). Biblio Dist.
Public Entrance Doors. National Academy Of Sciences. 1961. pap. 6.00 (ISBN 0-309-00948-0). Natl Acad Pr.
Public Evaluation of Government Spending. G. Bruce Doern & Allan M. Maslove. 192p. 1979. pap. text ed. 10.95x (ISBN 0-920380-19-0, Pub. by Inst Res Pub Canada). Renouf.
Public Examinations in England, 1850-1900. John Roach. LC 71-123668. (Cambridge Texts & Studies in the History of Education). 1971. 37.50 (ISBN 0-521-07931-4). Cambridge U Pr.
Public Expenditure & Indian Development Policy Nineteen Sixty to Nineteen Seventy. F. J. Toye. LC 80-41011. 284p. Date not set. 39.50 (ISBN 0-521-23081-0). Cambridge U Pr.
Public Expenditure in Malaysia: Who Benefits & Why. Jacob P. Meerman. (World Bank Research Publications Ser.). (Illus.). 1979. 14.95x (ISBN 0-19-520096-9); pap. 6.95x (ISBN 0-19-520097-7). Oxford U Pr.
Public Expenditures & Social Policy in Australia. R. B. Scotten & Helen Ferber. Vol. 1. text ed. 28.50 (ISBN 0-582-71084-7); Vol. 2. text ed. 26.00 (ISBN 0-582-71086-3). Longman.
Public Expenditures: The Impact of Distribution on Income - the Ghana Case. Anthony K. Antwi. LC 78-63269. 1978. pap. text ed. 9.50 (ISBN 0-8191-0620-8). U Pr of Amer.
Public Finance. new ed. Ursula K. Hicks. (Cambridge Economic Handbook Ser). 1968. 10.95x (ISBN 0-521-08762-7). Cambridge U Pr.
Public Finance: An Introduction. Graham Hockley. (Illus.). 1979. 32.00 (ISBN 0-7100-0148-7); pap. 15.00 (ISBN 0-7100-0149-5). Routledge & Kegan.
Public Finance & Private Wealth: The Career of Sir Stephen Fox, 1627-1716. Christopher Clay. 1978. 45.00x (ISBN 0-19-822467-2). Oxford U Pr.
Public Finance in the Democratic Process. James M. Buchanan. 1967. 16.00x (ISBN 0-8078-1014-2). U of NC Pr.
Public Finance Information Sources. Ed. by Vera H. Knox. LC 64-16503. (Management Information Guide Ser.: No. 3). 1964. 30.00 (ISBN 0-8103-0803-7). Gale.
Public Finance, Planning & Economic Development: Essays in Honor of Ursula Hicks. Ed. by Wilfred L. David. LC 73-77734. (Illus.). 349p. 1980. 28.50x (ISBN 0-8290-0201-4). Irvington.
Public Finances: An Introductory Textbook. 4th ed. James M. Buchanan & Marilyn R. Flowers. 1975. text ed. 16.50x o.p. (ISBN 0-256-01633-X). Irwin.
Public Finances: An Introductory Textbook. 5th ed. James M. Buchanan & Marilyn R. Flowers. 1980. 18.95x (ISBN 0-256-02333-6). Irwin.
Public Financing of Voluntary Agency Foster Care Programs. Ruth M. Werner. LC 76-54383. (Orig.). 1976. pap. 3.95 (ISBN 0-87868-163-9). Child Welfare.
Public Fire Education: IFSTA 606. IFSTA Committee. Ed. by Connie Osterhout et al. LC 79-89165. (Illus., Orig.). 1979. pap. 7.00 (ISBN 0-87939-034-4). Intl Fire Serv.
Public Forum. Wallace V. Schmidt & Jo-Ann Graham. LC 78-23604. (Illus.). 1979. text ed. 10.95 (ISBN 0-88284-068-1). Alfred Pub.
Public Grazing Lands: Use & Misuse by Industry & Government. William Voigt, Jr. LC 75-42250. (Illus.). 365p. 1976. 25.00 (ISBN 0-8135-0819-3). Rutgers U Pr.
Public Guardianship & the Elderly. Winsor C. Schmidt et al. 300p. 1981. 19.00 (ISBN 0-88410-596-2). Ballinger Pub.
Public Health. Boy Scouts Of America. LC 19-600. (Illus.). 64p. (gr. 6-12). 1969. pap. 0.70x (ISBN 0-8395-3251-2, 3251). BSA.
Public Health: Administration & Practice. 6th. ed. John J. Hanlon. LC 74-8669. (Illus.). 1974. text ed. 22.50 o.p. (ISBN 0-8016-2045-7). Mosby.
Public Health: Administration & Practice. 7th ed. John J. Hanlon & George E. Pickett. LC 79-16132. (Illus.). 1979. text ed. 27.95 (ISBN 0-8016-2046-5). Mosby.
Public Health & Community Medicine. 3rd ed. L. E. Burton et al. (Illus.). 616p. 1980. softcover 29.95 (ISBN 0-683-01236-3). Williams & Wilkins.
Public Health & Preventive Medicine Continuing Education Review. Peter Isacson. 1980. pap. 15.00 (ISBN 0-87488-348-2). Med Exam.
Public Health & Preventive Medicine. 6th ed. Ed. by Raymond O. West. (Medical Examination Review Book Ser.: Vol .6). 1975. spiral bdg. 8.50 (ISBN 0-87488-106-4). Med Exam.
Public Health & the Law: Issues & Trends. L. L. Hogue. LC 80-15041. 427p. 1980. text ed. 29.95 (ISBN 0-89443-289-3). Aspen Systems.
Public Health & the Medical Profession in Renaissance Italy. C. M. Cipolla. LC 25-22984. (Illus.). 1976. 23.95 (ISBN 0-521-20959-5). Cambridge U Pr.
Public Health Engineering: Sewerage. 2nd ed. Ronald E. Bartlett. (Illus.). 1979. 31.00x (ISBN 0-85334-796-4). Intl Ideas.
Public Health Risks of Exposure to Asbestos. Commission of the European Communities. Ed. by R. L. Zielhuis. LC 76-51964. 1977. pap. text ed. 21.00 (ISBN 0-08-021580-7). Pergamon.
Public Higher Education in California. Ed. by Neil J. Smelser & Gabriel Almond. 1974. 24.95x (ISBN 0-520-02510-5). U of Cal Pr.
Public Housing & Urban Renewal: An Analysis of Federal-Local Relations. Richard D. Bingham. LC 74-19822. (Special Series). (Illus.). 282p. 1975. text ed. 27.95 (ISBN 0-275-05810-7). Praeger.
Public Housing for Australia. Paul R. Wilson. (Illus.). 1976. 10.95x (ISBN 0-7022-1363-2); pap. 7.90x (ISBN 0-7022-1363-2). U of Queensland Pr.
Public Housing in Europe & America. Ed. by J. S. Fuerst. LC 73-10890. 1974. 19.95 (ISBN 0-470-28515-X). Halsted Pr.
Public Image of Courts, Nineteen Seventy-Seven: General Public Data. Law Enforcement Assistance Administration. LC 79-91248. 1980. 16.00 (ISBN 0-89138-962-8). ICPSR.
Public Inquiries As an Instrument of Government. R. E. Wraith & G. B. Lamb. (Royal Institute of Public Administration). 1971. text ed. 42.50x (ISBN 0-04-351037-X). Allen Unwin.
Public Interest Law: An Economic & Institutional Analysis. Burton A. Weisbrod et al. 1978. 36.50x (ISBN 0-520-03355-8); pap. 9.50 (ISBN 0-520-03568-2). U of Cal Pr.
Public Interest Liberalism & the Crisis of Affluence: Reflections on Nader, Environmentalism, & the Politics of a Sustainable Society. Robert D. Holsworth. (Reference Bks.). 1980. lib. bdg. 17.50 (ISBN 0-8161-9032-1). G K Hall.
Public International Law of Money. M. R. Shuster. (Illus.). 359p. 1973. 32.00x (ISBN 0-19-825308-7). Oxford U Pr.
Public Involvement in Maritime Facility Development. Maritime Transportation Research Board, National Research Council. 1979. pap. text ed. 7.00 (ISBN 0-309-02868-X). Natl Acad Pr.
Public Knowledge: An Essay Concerning the Social Dimension of Science. John M. Ziman. 1968. 23.95 (ISBN 0-521-06894-0); pap. 7.95x (ISBN 0-521-09519-0). Cambridge U Pr.
Public Knowledge, Private Ignorance: Toward a Library & Information Policy. Patrick Wilson. LC 76-52327. (Contributions in Librarianship & Information Sciences: No. 10). 1977. lib. bdg. 15.00x (ISBN 0-8371-9485-7, WPN/). Greenwood.
Public Land Ownership. Ed. by Dalton Kehoe et al. LC 75-41925. 1976. 21.95 (ISBN 0-669-00486-3). Lexington Bks.
Public Land Surveys: History, Instructions, Methods. Lowell S. Stewart. 1976. Repr. of 1935 ed. 14.00 (ISBN 0-686-18867-5, 610). CARBEN Survey.
Public Lands of Texas, 1519-1970. Thomas L. Miller. LC 75-160500. (Illus.). 1972. 18.95 (ISBN 0-8061-0972-6); pap. 8.95 (ISBN 0-8061-1302-2). U of Okla Pr.
Public Lands: Studies in the History of the Public Domain. Ed. by Vernon Carstensen. 1963. pap. 9.95 (ISBN 0-299-02754-6). U of Wis Pr.
Public Law & Public Policy. Ed. by John A. Gardiner. LC 76-12851. (Special Studies). 1977. text ed. 24.95 o.p. (ISBN 0-275-23320-0); pap. 9.95 o.p. (ISBN 0-275-85750-6). Praeger.
Public Librarianship: A Reader. Jane R. Carter. 400p. 1981. lib. bdg. price not set (ISBN 0-87287-246-7). Libs Unl.
Public Libraries As Culture & Social Centers: The Origin of the Concept. David W. Davies. LC 74-8420. 1974. 9.00 (ISBN 0-8108-0738-6). Scarecrow.
Public Libraries in California, 1849-1878. R. E. Held. (U. C. Publ. in Librarianship: Vol. 4). 1963. pap. 8.00x (ISBN 0-520-09207-4). U of Cal Pr.
Public Libraries: Legislation, Administration, & Finance. B. J. Phillips et al. 1977. pap. text ed. 6.75x (ISBN 0-85365-750-5, Pub. by Lib Assn England). Oryx Pr.
Public Libraries of the Pacific Northwest. Ed. by Morton Kroll. LC 60-9873. (PNLA Library Development Project Reports, Ser.: Vol. 1). 461p. 1960. 9.50 (ISBN 0-295-73897-9). U of Wash Pr.
Public Library: Circumstances & Prospects: (Papers Presented at the 39th Annual Conference) W. Boyd Rayward. LC 78-19604. (University of Chicago Studies in Library Science). 1979. lib. bdg. 10.00x (ISBN 0-226-70585-4). U of Chicago Pr.
Public Library Government: Seven Case Studies. D. W. Koepp. (U. C. Publ. in Librarianship: Vol. 6). 1968. pap. 10.00x (ISBN 0-520-09209-0). U of Cal Pr.
Public Library in Perspective. Paul Sykes. 184p. 1979. 15.00 (ISBN 0-89664-401-4, Pub. by K G Saur). Shoe String.
Public Library in the Network Mode: A Preliminary Investigation. Genevieve Casey. (Illinois Regional Council Occasional Papers Ser.: No. 3). 51p. 1978. soft cover 7.50 (ISBN 0-917060-01-6). Ill Regional Lib Coun.
Public Library Operations & Services. 2nd rev. ed. C. G. Vishwanathan. 5.50x (ISBN 0-210-33927-6). Asia.
Public Library Service to Children: Foundation & Development. Harriet G. Long. LC 70-8592. 1970. 10.00 (ISBN 0-8108-0291-0). Scarecrow.
Public Library Trustee: Image & Performance on Funding. Ann E. Prentice. LC 73-1648. 1973. 10.00 (ISBN 0-8108-0597-9). Scarecrow.
Public Life in Renaissance Florence. Richard C. Trexler. LC 80-979. (Studies in Discontinuity). 1980. 45.00 (ISBN 0-12-699550-8). Acad Pr.
Public Life of Pierce Butler: South Carolina Statesman. Lewright B. Sikes. LC 78-66122. 1979. pap. text ed. 8.00 (ISBN 0-8191-0683-6). U Pr of Amer.
Public Management Systems. James L. Mercer & Edwin H. Koester. LC 77-16392. 1978. 24.95 (ISBN 0-8144-5456-9). Am Mgmt.
Public Management: Text & Cases. Joseph L. Bower & Charles J. Christenson. 1978. text ed. 19.95x (ISBN 0-256-02070-1). Irwin.
Public Men & Events, 2 vols. Nathan Sargent. LC 79-106496. (American Public Figures Ser). 1970. Repr. of 1875 ed. lib. bdg. 69.50 (ISBN 0-306-71873-1). Da Capo.
Public Men in & Out of Office. John Thomas Salter. LC 76-39131. (FDR & the Era of the New Deal Ser). (Illus.). 514p. 1972. Repr. of 1946 ed. lib. bdg. 49.50 (ISBN 0-306-70457-9). Da Capo.
Public Monument & Its Audience. Marianne Doezema & June Hargrove. LC 77-25428. (Themes in Art Ser.). (Illus.). 76p. 1977. pap. 4.95x (ISBN 0-910386-38-2, Pub. by Cleveland Mus Art). Ind U Pr.
Public Murders. Bill Granger. 288p. (Orig.). 1980. pap. 1.95 (ISBN 0-515-05130-6). Jove Pubns.
Public Officials & the Press. Delmer D. Dunn. (Political Science Ser). 1969. pap. 6.95 (ISBN 0-201-01565-X). A-W.
Public Opinion. 4th ed. Bernard C. Hennessy. LC 80-27733. 350p. (Orig.). 1981. pap. text ed. 12.95 (ISBN 0-8185-0449-8). Brooks-Cole.
Public Opinion. Robert E. Lane & David O. Sears. (Orig.). 1964. pap. 6.95 ref. ed. (ISBN 0-13-737809-2). P-H.
Public Opinion & Canadian Identity. Mildred A. Schwartz. 1967. 20.00x (ISBN 0-520-01156-2). U of Cal Pr.
Public Opinion & Popular Government. Robert Weissberg. (Illus.). 320p. 1976. pap. 10.95 (ISBN 0-13-737908-0). P-H.
Public Opinion & Propaganda. Daniel Katz et al. 1954. 28.00x (ISBN 0-03-005965-8); pap. text ed. 14.50x (ISBN 0-89197-909-3). Irvington.
Public Opinion & Public Policy. 3rd ed. Norman R. Luttbeg. LC 80-52446. 475p. 1981. pap. text ed. 11.95 (ISBN 0-87581-259-7). Peacock Pubs.
Public Opinion & the Military Establishment. Ed. by Charles C. Moskos, Jr. LC 70-151672. (Sage Research Progress Series on War, Revolution & Peacekeeping: Vol. 1). 1971. 20.00x o.p. (ISBN 0-8039-0115-1); pap. 9.95x (ISBN 0-8039-0116-X). Sage.

Public Opinion & the Steel Strike. Interchurch World Movement, Commission of Inquiry. LC 77-119052. (Civil Liberties in American History Ser). 1970. Repr. of 1921 ed. lib. bdg. 37.50 (ISBN 0-306-71938-X). Da Capo.
Public Opinion & the Teaching of History in the United States. Bessie L. Pierce. LC 71-107416. (Civil Liberties in American History Ser.). 1970. Repr. of 1926 ed. lib. bdg. 37.50 (ISBN 0-306-71883-9). Da Capo.
Public Opinion in European Socialist Systems. Walter D. Connor et al. LC 77-83471. (Praeger Special Studies). 1977. 21.95 (ISBN 0-03-040931-4). Praeger.
Public Opinion in the American Commonwealth. James Bryce. 1981. 18.95 (ISBN 0-87923-370-2); pap. 8.95 (ISBN 0-87923-371-0). Godine.
Public Opinion Polls. Michael Edison & Susan Heimann. LC 79-18542. (First Bks). (Illus.). 72p. (gr. 5-9). 1972. PLB 4.90 o.p. (ISBN 0-531-00764-2). Watts.
Public Papers of Governor Bert T. Combs, 1959-1963. Bert T. Combs. Ed. by George W. Robinson & Robert F. Sexton. LC 78-58103. (Public Papers of the Governors of Kentucky). 568p. 1980. 28.00x (ISBN 0-8131-0604-4). U Pr of Ky.
Public Papers of Governor Keen Johnson, Nineteen Thirty-Nine to Nineteen Forty-Three. Keene Johnson. Ed. by Robert F. Sexton. LC 79-57562. (The Public Papers of the Governors of Kentucky Ser.). 1981. 28.00x (ISBN 0-8131-0605-2). U Pr of Ky.
Public Papers of Governor Wendell H. Ford, Nineteen Seventy-One to Nineteen Seventy-Four. Wendell H. Ford. Ed. by W. Landis Jones. LC 77-73702. 1978. 28.00x o.p. (ISBN 0-8131-0602-8). U Pr of Ky.
Public Papers of the Secretaries General of the United Nations, Vol. 7, U Thant, 1965-1967. Ed. by Andrew W. Cordier & Max Harrelson. 1976. 30.00 (ISBN 0-231-04098-9). Columbia U Pr.
Public Papers of the Secretaries-General of the United Nations: Trygve Lie, 1946-1953, Vol. 1. Ed. by Andrew W. Cordier & Wilder Foote. LC 68-8873. 1969. 30.00x (ISBN 0-231-03137-8). Columbia U Pr.
Public Papers of the Secretaries-General of the United Nations: Dag Hammarskjold, 1953-1956, Vol. 2. Ed. by Andrew W. Cordier & Wilder Foote. LC 68-8873. 650p. 1972. 30.00x (ISBN 0-231-03633-7). Columbia U Pr.
Public Papers of the Secretaries General of the United Nations: Dag Hammarskjold, 1956-1957, Vol. 3. Ed. by Andrew W. Cordier & Wilder Foote. 784p. 1973. 30.00x (ISBN 0-231-03735-X). Columbia U Pr.
Public Papers of the Secretaries-General of the United Nations: Dag Hammarskjold, 1958-1960, Vol. 4. Ed. by Andrew W. Cordier & Wilder Foote. LC 68-8873. 736p. 1974. 30.00x (ISBN 0-231-03810-0). Columbia U Pr.
Public Participation in Britain. Anthony Barker. 192p. 1979. pap. text ed. 17.40x (ISBN 0-7199-1029-3, Pub. by Bedford England). Renouf.
Public Participation in Local School Districts. Ed. by Frank W. Lutz & Laurence Iannaccone. LC 77-260. (Politics of Education Ser.). 1978. 16.95- (ISBN 0-669-01466-4). Lexington Bks.
Public Pays - & Still Pays: A Study of Power Propaganda. rev. ed. Ernest Gruening. LC 64-16420. pap. 2.25 (ISBN 0-8149-0112-3). Vanguard.
Public Personnel & Administrative Behavior: Text & Cases. Peter Allan & Stephen Rosenberg. 200p. 1981. pap. text ed. 8.95 (ISBN 0-87872-287-4). Duxbury Pr.
Public Personnel Management: Readings, Cases & Contingency Plans. Ed. by Marvin J. Levine. 1979. pap. text ed. 11.95 (ISBN 0-89832-006-2). Brighton Pub Co.
Public Personnel Management: Readings in Contexts & Strategies. Ed. by Donald E. Klingner. (Illus.). 500p. (Orig.). 1981. write for info (ISBN 0-87484-517-3). Mayfield Pub.
Public Philosophy. Walter Lippmann. pap. 1.50 (ISBN 0-451-61866-1, MW1866, Ment). NAL.
Public Policies & Their Politics. Randall Ripley. 1967. 4.50x (ISBN 0-393-05337-7); pap. 3.95x (ISBN 0-393-09689-0, NortonC). Norton.
Public Policies for an Aging Population. Ed. by Elizabeth Markson & Gretchen Batra. LC 79-3249. (Boston University Ser. in Gerontology). 1980. 14.95 (ISBN 0-669-03398-7). Lexington Bks.
Public Policies Toward Business. 6th ed. William G. Shepherd & Wilcox Clair. 1979. 19.95x (ISBN 0-256-02183-X). Irwin.
Public Policies Toward Business: Readings & Cases. rev ed. Ed. by William G. Shepherd. 1979. pap. 11.95 (ISBN 0-256-02236-4). Irwin.
Public Policy Analysis: An Introduction. W. Dunn. 1981. pap. 18.50 (ISBN 0-13-737957-9). P-H.
Public Policy & Administration in the Soviet Union. Ed. by Gordon B. Smith. 240p. 1980. 23.95 (ISBN 0-03-057726-8); pap. 9.95 (ISBN 0-03-057727-6). Praeger.
Public Policy & Development Politics: The Politics of Technical Expertise in Africa. Mekki Mtewa. LC 79-48041. 364p. 1980. text ed. 20.75 (ISBN 0-8191-1003-5); pap. text ed. 12.00 (ISBN 0-8191-1004-3). U P of Amer.
Public Policy & Global Reality: Some Aspects of American Alliance Policy. Jayanta K. Ray. 1977. text ed. 15.00x (ISBN 0-391-01002-6). Humanities.
Public Policy & Private Higher Education. Ed. by David W. Breneman & D. Chester E. Finn. (Studies in Higher Education Policy). 1978. 18.95 (ISBN 0-8157-1066-6); pap. 8.95 (ISBN 0-8157-1065-8). Brookings.
Public Policy & the Arts. C. Richard Swaim & Kevin Mulcahy. (Special Studies in Public Policy & Public System Management). 300p. 1981. lib. bdg. 25.00x (ISBN 0-86531-115-3). Westview.
Public Policy & the Family: Wives & Mothers in the Labor Fource. Z. I. Giraldo. LC 80-7692. 240p. 1980. 22.95x (ISBN 0-669-03762-1). Lexington Bks.
Public Policy & the Tax System. G. A. Hughes & G. M. Heal. (Illus.). 224p. 1980. text ed. 29.50 (ISBN 0-04-336067-X, 2575). Allen Unwin.
Public Policy Aspects of Information Exchange in Canadian Mineral Exploration. Donald O. Downing & Brian W. Mackenzie. 60p. (Orig.). 1979. pap. text ed. 3.00x (ISBN 0-686-63138-2, Pub. by Ctr Resource Stud Canada). Renouf.
Public Policy Decision Making & Regulation. Douglas G. Hartle. 218p. 1979. pap. text ed. 12.95x (ISBN 0-920380-20-4, Pub. by Inst Res Pub Canada). Renouf.
Public Policy Evaluation. Ed. by Kenneth M. Dolbeare. LC 75-14631. (Sage Yearbooks in Politics & Public Policy: Vol. 2). 1975. 20.00x (ISBN 0-8039-0268-9); pap. 9.95x (ISBN 0-8039-0312-X). Sage.
Public Policy for the Black Community: Strategies & Perspectives. Ed. by Marguerite R. Barnett & James Hefner. LC 76-24466. (Illus.). 225p. 1976. pap. text ed. 7.95x (ISBN 0-88284-038-X). Alfred Pub.
Public Policy in a No-Party State: Spanish Planning & Budgeting in the Twilight of the Franquist Era. Richard Gunther. 1980. 18.50x (ISBN 0-520-03752-9). U of Cal Pr.
Public Policy: Issues, Analysis & Ideology. Ed. by Ellen F. Paul & Philip A. Russo, Jr. (Chatham House Ser. on Change in American Politics). 1981. pap. text ed. 8.95x (ISBN 0-934540-04-7). Chatham Hse Pubs.
Public Policy: Scope & Logic. Fred M. Frohock. LC 78-8382. 1979. 16.95 (ISBN 0-13-737932-3). P-H.
Public Policy Toward Disability. Monroe Berkowitz et al. LC 76-25081. (Illus.). 1976. 23.95 (ISBN 0-275-23290-5). Praeger.
Public Policy Toward General Aviation. Jeremy J. Warford. LC 70-161598. (Studies in the Regulation of Economic Activity). 1971. 10.95 (ISBN 0-8157-9226-3). Brookings.
Public Policymaking in America: Difficult Choices, Limited Solutions. Carl P. Chelf. 1981. text ed. write for info. (ISBN 0-8302-7376-X). Goodyear.
Public Prices for Public Products. Ed. by Selma J. Mushkin. Orig. Title: Property, Taxation, Housing & Urban Growth. 1972. 10.95 (ISBN 0-87766-010-7, 90010); pap. 6.50 (ISBN 0-87766-018-2, 90009). Urban Inst.
Public Prosecutor & Other Plays. Fritz Hochwalder. LC 78-8814. 1980. 16.50 (ISBN 0-8044-2391-1). Ungar.
Public Purchasing & Materials Management. Harry R. Page. LC 79-2039. 528p. 1980. 32.95x (ISBN 0-669-03059-7). Lexington Bks.
Public Purse: A Study in Canadian Democracy. Norman Ward. LC 62-5636. 1962. 22.50x o.p. (ISBN 0-8020-7058-2). U of Toronto Pr.
Public Recreation Administration. Jesse A. Reynolds & Marion Hormachea. (Illus.). 480p. 1976. 16.95x (ISBN 0-87909-662-4). Reston.
Public Regulation of Dangerous Products. Marshall S. Shapo. LC 80-13733. (University Casebook Ser.). 397p. 1980. write for info. (ISBN 0-88277-003-9). Foundation Pr.
Public Relations. Edward L. Bernays. 1977. 9.95 o.p. (ISBN 0-8061-0243-8); pap. 6.95 (ISBN 0-8061-1457-6). U of Okla Pr.
Public Relations. Frank Jefkins. 232p. 1980. pap. text ed. 11.95x (ISBN 0-7121-1698-2). Intl Ideas.
Public Relations & Fund Raising for Hospitals. H. P. Kurtz. (Illus.). 208p. 1980. 23.50 (ISBN 0-398-04082-6). C C Thomas.
Public Relations & Survey Research: Achieving Organizational Goals in a Communication Context. Edward J. Robinson. LC 77-79167. (Illus., Orig.). 1969. 28.50x (ISBN 0-89197-365-6); pap. text ed. 12.95x (ISBN 0-89197-366-4). Irvington.
Public Relations: Concepts & Practices. 2nd ed. Raymond Simon. LC 79-16160. (Grid Ser. in Advertising & Journalism). 1980. text ed. 19.50 (ISBN 0-88244-193-0). Grid Pub.
Public Relations for Art Education. 34p. pap. 3.50 (ISBN 0-686-11083-8). Natl Art Ed.
Public Relations for Libraries: Essays in Communications Techniques. Ed. by Allan Angoff. LC 72-776. (Contributions in Librarianship & Information Science: No. 5). 1973. lib. bdg. 17.50x (ISBN 0-8371-6060-X, ANP/). Greenwood.
Public Relations for Nursing Homes. John P. Bachner. (Illus.). 184p. 1974. text ed. 13.75 o.p. (ISBN 0-398-03111-8). C C Thomas.
Public Relations for Schools. Adolph Unruh & Robert A. Willier. LC 73-91798. 1974. pap. 5.95 (ISBN 0-8224-5750-4). Pitman Learning.
Public Relations in Health & Welfare. Ed. by Frances Schmidt & Harold M. Weiner. LC 66-19480. 1966. 20.00x (ISBN 0-231-02911-X). Columbia U Pr.
Public Relations in Local Government. Ed. by William H. Gilbert. LC 75-29400. (Municipal Management Ser.). 1975. text ed. 22.00 (ISBN 0-87326-012-0). Intl City Mgt.
Public Relations in the Emergency Department. Cyril T. Cameron. 126p. 1980. text ed. 14.95 (ISBN 0-87619-746-2). R J Brady.
Public Relations Information Sources. Ed. by Alice Norton. LC 77-137574. (Management Information Guide Ser.: No. 22). 1970. 30.00 (ISBN 0-8103-0822-3). Gale.
Public Relations Management: Cases & Simulations. 2nd ed. Raymond Simon. LC 76-47362. (Advertising & Journalism). 1977. pap. text ed. 9.95 (ISBN 0-88244-148-5). Grid Pub.
Public Relations Practices: Case Studies. Allen H. Center. (Illus.). 416p. 1975. 15.95 (ISBN 0-13-738682-6); pap. text ed. 12.95 (ISBN 0-13-738674-5). P-H.
Public Relations Practices: Case Studies. 2nd ed. Frank E. Walsh & Allen H. Center. (Illus.). 352p. 1981. pap. text ed. 12.95 (ISBN 0-13-738716-4). P-H.
Public Relations: Principles, Cases, & Problems. H. Frazier Moore & Bertrand R. Canfield. 1977. 18.95 (ISBN 0-256-01927-4). Irwin.
Public Relations, Promotions, & Fund-Raising for Athletic & Physical Education Programs. Robert T. Bronzan. LC 76-10950. 580p. 1977. text ed. 23.50 (ISBN 0-471-01540-7). Wiley.
Public Religious Services in the Hospital. S. Denton Bassett. (Illus.). 80p. 1976. 12.675 (ISBN 0-398-03563-6). C C Thomas.
Public Safety: A Growing Factor in Modern Design. National Academy Of Engineering. (Orig.). 1970. pap. 5.50 (ISBN 0-309-01752-1). Natl Acad Pr.
Public School & Academic Media Centers: A Guide to Information Sources. Ed. by Esther Dyer & Pam Berger. LC 74-11554. (Books, Publishing & Libraries Information Guide Ser.: Vol. 3). 350p. 1980. 30.00 (ISBN 0-8103-1286-7). Gale.
Public School & Finances. Mary F. Williams. LC 80-20771. (Education of the Public & the Public School Ser.). 64p. 1980. pap. 2.50 (ISBN 0-8298-0414-5). Pilgrim NY.
Public School & Moral Education. Henry C. Johnson, Jr. (Education of the Public & the Public School Ser.). 96p. (Orig.). 1981. pap. 3.95 (ISBN 0-8298-0420-X). Pilgrim NY.
Public School Monopoly: Education & State in American Society. Ed. by Robert Everhart. (Pacific Institute for Public Policy Research Ser.). 1981. price not set professional reference (ISBN 0-88410-383-8). Ballinger Pub.
Public School Word-Book. John S. Farmer. LC 68-17988. 1968. Repr. of 1900 ed. 15.00 (ISBN 0-8103-3280-9). Gale.
Public Schools: A Treatise on the Rights, Powers, Duties & Liabilities of School Boards, Officers & Teachers. Irwin Taylor. 411p. 1980. Repr. of 1893 ed. lib. bdg. 30.00x (ISBN 0-8377-1204-1). Rothman.
Public-Sector Bargaining: A Policy of Reappraisal. Myron Lieberman. LC 80-8426. 1980. 19.95 (ISBN 0-669-04110-6). Lexington Bks.
Public Sector Economics. C. V. Brown & P. M. Jackson. 452p. 1978. 48.50x (ISBN 0-85520-134-7, Pub by Martin Robertson England); pap. 21.95x (ISBN 0-85520-133-9). Biblio Dist.
Public Sector Investment Planning for Developing Countries. E. V. FitzGerald. 1978. text ed. 28.50x (ISBN 0-8419-5027-X). Holmes & Meier.
Public Service Commissions. Niru Hazarika. 1979. text ed. 9.00x (ISBN 0-391-01847-7). Humanities.
Public Service: The Human Side of Government. John W. Macy, Jr. LC 70-123950. 1971. 12.50 o.s.i. (ISBN 0-06-012769-4, HarpT). Har-Row.
Public Speaker's Treasure Chest. new, rev. ed. Herbert V. Prochnow. LC 75-25058. 1977. 15.95 (ISBN 0-06-013404-6, HarpT). Har-Row.
Public Speaking. Boy Scouts Of America. LC 19-600. (Illus.). 44p. (gr. 6-12). 1969. pap. 0.70x (ISBN 0-8395-3373-X, 3373). BSA.
Public Speaking. George Fluharty & Harold R. Ross. (Orig.). 1966. pap. 3.95 o.p. (ISBN 0-06-463207-5, 207, EH). Har-Row.
Public Speaking. 2nd ed. George W Fluharty & Harold R. Ross. (Illus.). 416p. (Orig.). 1981. pap. 5.95 (ISBN 0-06-463525-2, EH 525, EH). Har-Row.
Public Speaking. Gary Hunt. (Illus.). 386p. 1981. text ed. 12.95 (ISBN 0-13-738807-1). P-H.
Public Speaking: A Handbook for Christians. Duane Litfin. 400p. (Orig.). 1981. pap. 9.95 (ISBN 0-8010-5635-5). Baker Bk.
Public Speaking: A New Speech Book. Richard Heun & Linda Heun. (Illus.). 1979. pap. text ed. 11.50 (ISBN 0-8299-0239-2); instrs.' manual avail. (ISBN 0-8299-0488-3). West Pub.
Public Speaking Made Easy. R. C. Forman. (Speaker's & Toastmaster's Library). 1977. pap. 2.95 o.p. (ISBN 0-8010-3476-0). Baker Bk.
Public Speaking Today. Gordon I. Zimmerman. (Illus.). 1979. pap. text ed. 11.50 (ISBN 0-8299-0259-7); instrs.' manual avail. (ISBN 0-8299-0586-3). West Pub.
Public Spectales. Stephen Silverman. 1981. 9.95 (ISBN 0-525-18605-0). Dutton.
Public Technology: Key to Improved Government Productivity. Ed. by James L. Mercer & Ronald J. Philips 451p. 1981. 24.95 (ISBN 0-8144-5546-8). Am Mgmt.
Public Testimony on Public Schools. National Committee for Citizens in Education. LC 75-20297. 304p. 1975. 17.75x (ISBN 0-685-57430-X); text ed. 16.00x (ISBN 0-8211-1016-0). McCutchan.
Public Utilities & the National Power Policies. James C. Bonbright. LC 73-172007. (FDR & the Era of the New Deal Ser.). 1972. Repr. of 1940 ed. lib. bdg 14.50 (ISBN 0-306-70424-2). Da Capo.
Public Utilities Information Sources. Ed. by Florine E. Hunt. LC 65-24658. (Management Information Guide Ser.: No. 7). 1965. 30.00 (ISBN 0-8103-0807-X). Gale.
Public Utilities Law Anthology, Vol. 5. Ed. by Denis A. Cooper. LC 74-77644. (National Law Anthology Ser.). 1979. 59.95 (ISBN 0-914250-19-1). Intl Lib.
Public Utilities Law Anthology, 1980-1981, Vol. VI. Ed. by Denis A. Cowper. LC 74-77644. (National Law Anthology Ser.). 1981. text ed. 59.95. Intl Lib.
Public Utilities: Regulation, Management, & Ownership. Martin T. Farris & Roy J. Sampson. LC 72-85908. 420p. 1973. text ed. 20.95 (ISBN 0-395-13884-1). HM.
Public Utility Control in Massachusetts. Irston R. Barnes. 1930. 47.50x (ISBN 0-685-89774-5). Elliots Bks.
Public Utility Economics. Paul Garfield & W. Lovejoy. (Illus.). 1963. text ed. 21.95 (ISBN 0-13-739367-9). P-H.
Public Utility Rate Making in an Energy Conscious Environment. Werner Sichel. 1979. lib. bdg. 22.00x (ISBN 0-89158-180-4). Westview.
Public Utility Regulation of an Exhaustible Resource: The Case of Natural Gas. John C. Gault. LC 78-75016. (Outstanding Dissertations in Economics). 1980. lib. bdg. 31.00 (ISBN 0-8240-4051-1). Garland Pub.
Public Welfare Directory: 1980-1981. Ed. by Deborah Cunha. LC 41-4981. 1980. pap. 35.00x (ISBN 0-910106-11-8). Am Pub Welfare.
Public Welfare: Notes from Underground. Michael Greenblatt & Steven Richmond. 1979. text ed. 9.50 (ISBN 0-87073-767-8); pap. text ed. 5.95 (ISBN 0-686-66209-1). Schenkman.
Public Welfare Systems. J. W. LaPatra. (Illus.). 232p. 1975. 17.75 (ISBN 0-398-03469-9). C C Thomas.
Public Works & Society. Compiled by American Society of Civil Engineers. 256p. 1974. pap. text ed. 17.00 (ISBN 0-87262-064-6). Am Soc Civil Eng.
Public Works, Government Spending & Job Creation: The Job Opportunities Program. Robert Jerrett & Thomas A. Barocci. (Praeger Special Studies). 352p. 1979. 29.95 (ISBN 0-03-051336-7). Praeger.
Public Works: The Posters of Nathan Felde & Julius Friedman. Nathan Felde & Julius Friedman. (Illus.). 64p. pap. 14.95 (ISBN 0-937246-00-X). Chicago Review.
Publication Design Thirteen Plus Fourteen. new ed. Ed. by Liz Wilbur. (Illus.). 500p. 1980. 49.50 o.s.i. (ISBN 0-8038-5888-4, Visual Communication). Hastings.
Publication Design Twelve. Ed. by Liz Wilbur. Date not set. 24.95 o.p. (ISBN 0-8038-6756-5). Hastings.
Publication of Guiana's Plantation. LC 72-7836. (English Experience Ser.: No. 525). 24p. 1972. Repr. of 1632 ed. 6.00 (ISBN 90-221-0726-4). Walter J Johnson.
Publication, Teaching, & the Academic Reward Structure. Howard P. Tuckman. 1976. 16.95x (ISBN 0-669-00650-5). Lexington Bks.

Publicity & Public Relations Work Text. 4th ed. Raymond Simon. LC 78-50047. (Public Relations Ser.). 1978. pap. text ed. 10.95 (ISBN 0-88244-165-5). Grid Pub.

Publicity for Volunteer Groups: A Handbook. Virginia Bortin. 128p. 1981. 10.95 (ISBN 0-8027-0685-1); pap. 5.95 (ISBN 0-8027-7176-9). Walker & Co.

Publicity Manual. Kate Kelly. LC 79-55946. 166p. 1980. 29.95 (ISBN 0-9603740-1-9). Visibility Ent.

Public's Business: The Politics & Practices of Government Corporations. Annmarie H. Walsh. LC 77-15595. 456p. 1978. 23.00x (ISBN 0-262-23086-0); pap. 9.95 (ISBN 0-262-73055-3). MIT Pr.

Publiez Sa Justice. Tr. by Morris Williams. (French Bks.). (Fr.). 1979. 2.50 (ISBN 0-8297-0839-1). Life Pubs Intl.

Publish Your Own Handbound Books. Betty Doty. LC 80-67947. (Illus.). 127p. 1980. 8.95 (ISBN 0-930822-02-1); lib. bdg. 7.95 (ISBN 0-930822-03-X). Bookery.

Publish Your Own Hardbound Books. Betty Doty. 1981. 7.95. Green Hill.

Published Offical Sources of Financial Statistics. OECD. (Illus.). 132p. (Orig.). 1980. pap. 11.00x (ISBN 92-64-02095-0). OECD.

Publishers & Distributors of the United States: A Directory to Some 13,500 U. S. Publishers & Distributors Listing Editorial & Ordering Addresses & Including an ISBN Index. 2nd ed. 320p. 1980. 8.95 (ISBN 0-8352-1299-8). Bowker.

Publishers & Libraries: The Study of Scholarly & Research Journals. Bernard M. Fry & Herbert S. White. (Illus.). 1976. 18.95 (ISBN 0-669-00886-9). Lexington Bks.

Publishers Catalogs Annual 1980-81. Ed. by Deborah O'Hara. 30000p. 1981. 147.50 (ISBN 0-930466-19-5). Meckler Bks.

Publishers' International Directory. Ed. by Michael Zils. 798p. 1979. 140.00 (ISBN 0-89664-100-7, Pub. by K G Saur). Shoe String.

Publishing Agreements: A Book of Precedents. Charles Clark. 176p. 1980. text ed. 19.50x (ISBN 0-04-655015-1, 2481). Allen Unwin.

Publishing Careers: Books & Magazines. Charles P. May. (Career Concise Guides Ser.). (Illus.). (gr. 7 up). 1978. PLB 6.45 s&l (ISBN 0-531-01422-3). Watts.

Publishing in the Third World. Philip G. Altbach & Eva-Maria Rathgeber. LC 80-20146. 200p. 1980. 20.95 (ISBN 0-03-055931-6). Praeger.

Publishing Short-Run Books: How to Pasteup & Reproduce Books Instantly Using Your Copy Shop. new ed. Dan Poynter. LC 80-13614. (Illus.). 104p. (Orig.). 1980. pap. 6.95 (ISBN 0-915516-23-3). Para Pub.

Pubs & Pub Signs. Colourmaster. (Travel in England Ser.). (Illus.). 64p. 1975. 7.95 (ISBN 0-85933-105-9). Transatlantic.

Pubs of London. 1978. pap. 1.95 o.p. (ISBN 0-214-20346-8, 8017, Dist. by Arco). Barrie & Jenkins.

Pubs That Welcome Children. Jimmy Young. LC 79-56580. (Illus.). 96p. 1980. 5.95 (ISBN 0-7153-7965-8). David & Charles.

Puccini: The Man & His Music. William Weaver & Paul Hume. LC 77-6323. 1977. 8.95 o.p. (ISBN 0-525-18610-7). Dutton.

Pucciniosireae: Uredinales, Pucciniaceae. P. Buritica & J. F. Hennen. LC 79-27151. (Flora Neotropica Monograph: No. 24). (Illus.). 50p. 1980. pap. 7.75 (ISBN 0-89327-219-1). NY Botanical.

Puch Moped Owner Service-Repair: 1976-1977. Ed Scott. Ed. by Eric Jorgensen. (Illus.). pap. 6.00 (ISBN 0-89287-213-6, M437). Clymer Pubns.

Puckoon. 2nd ed. Spike Milligan. (Illus.). 1978. 9.95 (ISBN 0-7181-1271-7, Pub. by Michael Joseph). Merrimack Bk Serv.

PUD: A Better Way for the Suburbs. Maxwell C. Huntoon, Jr. LC 70-18755. (Special Report Ser.). (Illus.). 1971. pap. 9.75 (ISBN 0-87420-909-9). Urban Land.

Puddle Duck. Louis Ross. (Illus.). (ps-2). 1979. 1.95 (ISBN 0-525-69020-4, Gingerbread Bks); PLB 5.95 (ISBN 0-525-69021-2). Dutton.

Pudd'nhead Wilson. Mark Twain. (Classics Ser). (gr. 8 up). pap. 1.25 (ISBN 0-8049-0124-4, CL-124). Airmont.

Pudd'nhead Wilson & Those Extraordinary Twins. Samuel L. Clemens. Ed. by Sidney E. Berger. (Norton Critical Edition Ser.). 1980. text ed. 22.50 (ISBN 0-393-01337-5); pap. text ed. 5.95x (ISBN 0-393-95027-1). Norton.

Puebla: A Church Being Born. Gary McEoin & Nevita Riley. LC 79-91894. 160p. (Orig.). 1980. pap. 4.95 (ISBN 0-8091-2279-0). Paulist Pr.

Puebla Indians, Vol. Five: Findings of Fact, & Opinion. Indian Claims Commission. (American Indian Ethnohistory Ser: Indians of the Southwest). (Illus.). lib. bdg. 42.00 (ISBN 0-8240-0729-8). Garland Pub.

Pueblo, Hardscrabble, Greenhorn: The Upper Arkansas, 1832-1856. Janet Lecompte. LC 77-18616. (Illus.). 354p. 1981. pap. 7.95 (ISBN 0-8061-1723-0). U of Okla Pr.

Pueblo Indian Embroidery. H. P. Mera. LC 74-31607. (Illus.). 80p. 1975. 15.00 (ISBN 0-88307-512-1); pap. 4.95 (ISBN 0-88307-513-X). Gannon.

Pueblo Indians, Vol. 1. Incl. Anthropological Data Pertaining to the Taos Land Claim. Florence H. Ellis; Spanish & Mexican Land Policies & Grants in the Taos Pueblo Region, New Nexico. Harold H. Dunham; A Historical Study of Land Use Eastward of the Taos Indians' Pueblo Land Grant Prior to 1848. Harold H. Dunham; Findings of Fact, & Opinion. Indian Claims Commission. (American Indian Ethnohistory Ser: Indians of the Southwest). (Illus.). lib. bdg. 42.00 (ISBN 0-8240-0725-5). Garland Pub.

Pueblo Indians, Vol. 3. Incl. Anthropology of Laguna Pueblo Land Claims. Florence H. Ellis; Historical Treatise in Defense of the Pueblo of Acoma Land Claims. Ward A. Minge; Acoma Land Utilization. Robert L. Rands. (American Indian Ethnohistory Ser: Indians of the Southwest). (Illus.). lib. bdg. 42.00 (ISBN 0-8240-0727-1). Garland Pub.

Pueblo Indians, Vol. 4. Incl. History of the Laguna Pueblo Land Claims. Myra E. Jenkins; Laguna Land Utilization: an Ethnohistorical Report. Robert L. Rands. (American Indian Ethnohistory Ser: Indians of the Southwest). (Illus.). lib. bdg. 42.00 (ISBN 0-8240-0728-X). Garland Pub.

Pueblo Indians: Farmers of the Rio Grande. Sonia Bleeker. (Illus.). (gr. 3-6). 1955. PLB 6.67 (ISBN 0-688-31454-6). Morrow.

Pueblo Indians, Vol. Two: Archaeologic & Ethnologic Data: Acoma-Laguna Land Claims. Florence H. Ellis. (American Indian Ethnohistory Ser: Indians of the Southwest). (Illus.). lib. bdg. 42.00 (ISBN 0-8240-0726-3). Garland Pub.

Pueblo Population & Society: The Arroyo Hondo Skeletal & Mortuary Remains. Ann M. Palkovich & Douglas W. Schwartz. LC 80-5310. (Arroyo Hondo Archaeological Ser.: Vol. 3). (Illus.). 1981. pap. 6.25 (ISBN 0-933452-03-9). Schol Am Res.

Pueblos. Bertha P. Dutton. (Illus.). 112p. 1976. pap. text ed. 3.25 o.p. (ISBN 0-13-740159-0, Spec). P-H.

Puer Papers. James Hillman et al. (Dunquin Ser.). (Orig.). 1979. pap. 11.00 (ISBN 0-88214-310-7). Spring Pubns.

Puerto Rican Authors: A Biobibliographic Handbook. Marnesba Hill & Herbert B. Schleifer. LC 73-15604. 1974. 10.00 (ISBN 0-8108-0681-9). Scarecrow.

Puerto Rican Dishes. 3rd ed. B. Cabanillas. 1971. 9.75 (ISBN 0-8477-2776-9). Adler.

Puerto Rican Obituary. Pedro Pietri. LC 73-8058. 144p. 1974. 7.50 o.p. (ISBN 0-85345-300-4, CL-3004). Monthly Rev.

Puerto Rican Perspectives. Ed. by Edward Mapp. LC 73-20175. 1974. 10.00 (ISBN 0-8108-0691-6). Scarecrow.

Puerto Rican Women. Edna Acosta-Belen & Eli H. Christensen. LC 79-17638. (Praeger Special Studies Ser.). 186p. 1979. 20.95 (ISBN 0-03-052466-0). Praeger.

Puerto Ricans: A Documentary History. Ed. by Kal Wagenheim & Olga Jimenez de Wagenheim. 400p. 1975. pap. 3.50 o.p. (ISBN 0-385-08833-7, Anch). Doubleday.

Puerto Rico & the Puerto Ricans. Clifford A. Hauberg. (Immigrant Heritage of America Ser). 1974. lib. bdg. 12.95 (ISBN 0-8057-3259-4). Twayne.

Puerto Rico: Commonwealth or Colony? Roberta A. Johnson. LC 80-16879. 218p. 1980. 21.95 (ISBN 0-03-053576-X); text ed. 9.95 (ISBN 0-03-053581-6). Praeger.

Puerto Rico: Freedom & Power in the Caribbean. Gordon K. Lewis. LC 63-20065. 640p. 1975. Repr. of 1963 ed. 17.50 o.p. (ISBN 0-85345-316-0, CL-3160). Monthly Rev.

Puerto Rico in Pictures. Sterling Publishing Company Editors. LC 61-10399. (Visual Geography Ser). (gr. 6 up). PLB 4.99 (ISBN 0-8069-1015-1); pap. 2.95 (ISBN 0-8069-1014-3). Sterling.

Puerto Rico, Island Between Two Worlds. Lila Perl. LC 79-1130. (Illus.). (gr. 7-9). 1979. 9.50 (ISBN 0-688-22181-5); PLB 9.12 (ISBN 0-688-32181-X). Morrow.

Puerto Rico Plan: Environmental Protection Through Development Rights Transfer. John Costonis & Robert DeVoy. LC 75-15460. (Illus.). 90p. 1975. 9.00 (ISBN 0-87420-561-1). Urban Land.

Puerto Rico's Fighting Sixty-Fifth U. S. Infantry: From San Juan to Chorwan. W. W. Harris. LC 79-26889. (Illus.). 1980. 12.95 (ISBN 0-89141-056-2). Presidio Pr.

Puffball. Fay Weldon. LC 80-14585. 1980. 10.95 (ISBN 0-671-44809-9). Summit Bks.

Puffin, Bird of the Open Seas. Lynne Martin. LC 76-3486. (Illus.). (gr. 3-7). 1976. 7.25 (ISBN 0-688-22074-6); PLB 6.96 (ISBN 0-688-32074-0). Morrow.

Puffins, Come Back! Judi Friedman. LC 80-2786. (Illus.). 80p. (gr. 3-7). 1981. PLB 6.95 (ISBN 0-396-07940-7). Dodd.

Puget Sound Catechism: Compendium of Information. 28p. Repr. of 1889 ed. pap. 1.00 (ISBN 0-8466-0078-1, SJS78). Shorey.

Puget's Sound: A Narrative of Early Tacoma & the Southern Sound. Murray Morgan. LC 79-4844. (Illus.). 370p. 1979. 14.95 (ISBN 0-295-95680-1). U of Wash Pr.

Pugnacious Presidents: White House Warriors on Parade. Thomas A. Bailey. LC 80-1646. (Illus.). 1980. 17.95 (ISBN 0-02-901220-1). Free Pr.

Pugwash & the Ghost Ship. John Ryan. LC 68-23218. (Illus.) (gr. k-3). 1968. 8.95 (ISBN 0-87599-146-7). S G Phillips.

Pugwash in the Pacific. John Ryan. LC 73-929. (Illus.). 32p. (gr. k-3). 1973. 8.95 (ISBN 0-87599-199-8). S G Phillips.

Pulic Employees Conference, Dec. 5-8, 1979, Hollywood, Fla. Proceedings. Ed. by Mary E. Brennan. 160p. 1980. pap. 10.00 (ISBN 0-89154-126-8). Intl Found Employ.

Pulitzer Prize Editorials: America's Best Editorial Writing, 1917-1979. David Sloan. 182p. 1980. text ed. 10.50 (ISBN 0-8138-1490-1). Iowa St U Pr.

Pulitzer Prize Story. John Hohenberg. LC 59-7702. 1959. pap. 7.00x (ISBN 0-231-08663-6). Columbia U Pr.

Pulitzer Prizes. John Hohenberg. 1974. 20.00x (ISBN 0-231-03771-6). Columbia U Pr.

Pull Yourself Together. David Seabury. 1967. pap. 3.95 (ISBN 0-911336-14-1). Sci of Mind.

Pulled Thread Embroidery. Moyra McNeill. LC 70-185624. (Illus.). 207p. 1976. 9.95 (ISBN 0-8008-6562-6); pap. 5.95 (ISBN 0-8008-6563-4). Taplinger.

Pulling at Skirts of Liberty. Date not set. pap. 4.40 (ISBN 0-936112-06-9). Willyshe Pub. Postponed.

Pulling Our Own Strings: Feminist Humor & Satire. Ed. by Gloria Kaufman & Mary K. Blakely. LC 79-3382. 192p. 1980. 20.00 (ISBN 0-253-13034-4); pap. 7.95 (ISBN 0-253-20251-5). Ind U Pr.

Pullman: An Experiment in Industrial Order & Community Planning, 1880-1930. Stanley Buder. (Urban Life in America). 1967. pap. 4.95x (ISBN 0-19-500838-3). Oxford U Pr.

Pulmonary & Bronchial Circulations in Congenital Heart Disease. Colin M. Bloor & Averill A. Liebow. (Topics in Cardiovascular Disease Ser.). (Illus.). 284p. 1980. 32.50 (ISBN 0-306-40383-8, Plenum Pr). Plenum Pub.

Pulmonary Disease Review, Vol. 1. Roger C. Bone. 600p. 1980. 35.00 (ISBN 0-471-05736-3, Pub. by WileyMed). Wiley.

Pulmonary Diseases. 2nd ed. W. K. Morgan et al. (Medical Examination Review Book: Vol. 24). 1977. spiral bdg. 16.50 (ISBN 0-87488-143-9). Med Exam.

Pulmonary Embolism. Ed. by J. Widimsky. (Progress in Respiration Research: Vol. 13). (Illus.). viii, 192p. 1980. 87.00 (ISBN 3-8055-0487-X). S Karger.

Pulmonary Embolism. Walter G. Wolfe & David C. Sabiston, Jr. LC 79-66047. (Major Problems in Clinical Surgery Ser.: Vol. 25). (Illus.). 180p. 1980. text ed. 17.00 (ISBN 0-7216-9584-1). Saunders.

Pulp & Paper. Boy Scouts of America. LC 19-600. (Illus.). 40p. (gr. 6-12). 1974. pap. 0.70x (ISBN 0-8395-3343-8, 3343). BSA.

Pulp & Paper Capacities: Survey Nineteen Seventy-Eight to Nineteen Eighty-Three. 284p. 1979. pap. 15.50 (ISBN 92-5-000752-3, F1648, FAO) Unipub.

Pulp & Paper Capacities Survey, 1979-1984. 286p. 1980. pap. 15.25 (ISBN 92-5-000914-3, F1945, FAO). Unipub.

Pulp & Paper: Chemistry & Chemical Technology, 2 vols. 3rd ed. Ed. by James P. Casey. LC 79-13435. 1980. Vol. 1. 55.00 (ISBN 0-471-03175-5, Pub. by Wiley-Interscience); Vol. 2. 50.00 (ISBN 0-471-03176-3). Wiley.

Pulping & Paper-Making Properties of Fast Growing Plantation Wood Species, Vols. 1 & 2. (FAO Forestry Paper Ser.: No. 19). 1980. pap. 46.75 set (ISBN 0-686-68193-2, F1969, FAO); Vol. 1. 486 Pp. pap. 46.75 (ISBN 92-5-100865-5). Vol. 2, 400 Pp (ISBN 92-5-100866-3). Unipub.

Pulping Processes. Sven A. Rydholm. LC 65-18412. 1965. 80.00 (ISBN 0-471-74793-9, Pub. by Wiley-Interscience). Wiley.

Pulpit Commentary, 23 vols. H. D. Spence & T. S. Exell. Incl. Old Testament only, 14 Vols. 260.00 (ISBN 0-8028-8056-8, 2209); New Testament only, 8 Vols. 165.00 (ISBN 0-8028-8057-6, 2210). 1959. Repr. Set. 425.00 (ISBN 0-8028-8055-X, 2208). Eerdmans.

Pulpit of the American Revolution: Political Sermons of the Period of 1776. Ed. by John W. Thornton. LC 71-109611. (Era of the American Revolution Ser). 1970. Repr. of 1860 ed. lib. bdg. 45.00 (ISBN 0-306-71907-X). Da Capo.

Pulpwood Productions. 3rd ed. Ed. by Willard S. Bromley. LC 75-14771. (Illus.). 1976. text ed. 14.65 (ISBN 0-8134-1738-4, 1738); pap. text ed. 11.00x (ISBN 0-685-71184-6). Interstate.

Pulsars. Richard N. Manchester & Joseph H. Taylor. LC 77-4206. (Astronomy & Astrophysics Ser.). (Illus.). 1977. text ed. 29.95x (ISBN 0-7167-0358-0). W H Freeman.

Pulsars. F. G. Smith. LC 75-44569. (Cambridge Monographs on Physics). (Illus.). 1977. 39.50 (ISBN 0-521-21241-3). Cambridge U Pr.

Pulsating Stars. Ed. by B. V. Kukarkin. Tr. by R. R. Hardin from Rus. LC 75-17851. 320p. 1975. 54.95 (ISBN 0-470-51035-8). Halsted Pr.

Pulse. J. M. Henegan. 1980. 11.95 (ISBN 0-7145-3667-9); pap. 6.95 (ISBN 0-7145-3618-0). Riverrun NY.

Pulse & Logic Circuits. Richard L. Castellucis. LC 75-27995. 1976. pap. 6.00 (ISBN 0-8273-1134-6); instructor's guide 1.00 (ISBN 0-8273-1135-4). Delmar.

Pulse Circuits. Biswanath Chatterjee. 5.50x o.p. (ISBN 0-210-34015-0). Asia.

Pulse of Freedom: American Liberties-1920-1970. Alan Reitman. 1976. pap. 1.95 o.p. (ISBN 0-451-61484-4, MJ1484, Ment). NAL.

Pulsed Neutron Research, 2 vols. 1965. Vol 1. 33.75 (ISBN 92-0-030765-5, IAEA); Vol 2. 45.00 (ISBN 92-0-030865-1). Unipub.

Pulvinar-LP Complex. Irving S. Cooper et al. (Illus.). 312p. 1974. 29.50 (ISBN 0-398-02849-4). C C Thomas.

Pummeling, Falling, & Getting up--Sometimes. Gary Paulsen. LC 78-26997. (Sports on the Light Side Ser.). (Illus.). (gr. 4-6). 1979. PLB 9.65 (ISBN 0-8172-0195-5). Raintree Pubs.

Pump Users' Handbook. 2nd ed. F. Pollak. (Illus.). 208p. 1980. 19.95 (ISBN 0-87201-770-2). Gulf Pub.

Pump User's Handbook. 2nd ed. Ed. by Trade & Technical Press Ltd. (Illus.). 1979. 32.95x o.p. (ISBN 0-685-66962-9). Intl Ideas.

Pumped Storage. Compiled by American Society of Civil Engineers. 608p. 1975. pap. text ed. 19.00 (ISBN 0-87262-120-0). Am Soc Civil Eng.

Pumpernickle Tickle & Mean Green Cheese. Nancy Patz. (Illus.). (gr. k-3). 1978. 6.95 (ISBN 0-531-02492-X); PLB 7.90 (ISBN 0-531-02221-8). Watts.

Pumping & Collection of Wastewater. Metcalf & Eddy, Inc. & George Tchobanoglous. (Water Resources & Engineering Ser.). (Illus.). 400p. 1981. text ed. 28.95 (ISBN 0-07-041680-X, C); student's manual 4.95 (ISBN 0-07-041681-8). McGraw.

Pumping Data, Vol. 2. Ed. by Trade & Technical Press Ltd. 22.50x (ISBN 0-685-90215-3). Intl Ideas.

Pumping Data, Vol. 3. Ed. by Trade & Technical Press Ltd. 1969. 22.50x (ISBN 0-685-90214-5). Intl Ideas.

Pumping Mad. Mad Magazine Editors. (Mad Ser.: No. 56). (Illus.). 192p. (Orig.). 1981. pap. 1.75 (ISBN 0-446-94820-9). Warner Bks.

Pumping Manual. 6th ed. Ed. by Trade & Technical Press Ltd. (Illus.). 1979. 115.00x (ISBN 0-85461-081-2). Intl Ideas.

Pumping Stations for Water & Sewage. Ronald E. Bartlett. LC 73-22472. 150p. 1974. 24.95 (ISBN 0-470-05477-8). Halsted Pr.

Pumpkin Seed Point: Being Within the Hopi. Frank Waters. LC 76-75741. 175p. 1969. 8.50 (ISBN 0-8040-0255-X, SB); pap. 4.95 (ISBN 0-8040-0635-0). Swallow.

Pumpkin Shell. James Forman. 246p. (gr. 7 up). 1981. 9.95 (ISBN 0-374-36159-2). FS&G.

Pumpkin Smasher. Anita Benarde. LC 76-139792. (Illus.). 32p. (gr. k-3). 1972. 4.95 o.s.i. (ISBN 0-8027-6109-7); PLB 4.85 o.s.i. (ISBN 0-8027-6110-0). Walker & Co.

Pumps. 3rd ed. Harry L. Stewart. LC 77-75529. 1978. 10.95 (ISBN 0-672-23292-8). Audel.

Pumps Selection, Systems & Applications. R. H. Warring. (Illus.). 1969. 32.50x o.p. (ISBN 0-85461-039-1). Intl Ideas.

Pumps-the Developing Needs: Seventh Technical Conference of Thhe BPMA in Conjunction with BHRA. (Orig.). 1981. pap. 71.00 library ed. (ISBN 0-686-69310-8). BHRA Fluid.

Punch & Cookies Forever. Jack Weyland. LC 80-84566. 150p. 1981. 5.95 (ISBN 0-88290-173-7). Horizon Utah.

Punch & Judy Carry on. Gerald Rose & Elizabeth Rose. (Illus.). (ps-5). 1962. 6.95 (ISBN 0-571-05161-8, Pub. by Faber & Faber). Merrimack Bk Serv.

Punched-Card Data Processing. Harry W. Cadow. LC 72-95421. (Illus.). 344p. 1973. pap. text ed. 13.95 (ISBN 0-574-18485-6, 13-1485); instr's guide avail. (ISBN 0-574-18486-4, 13-1486). SRA.

Punctuate It Right. Harry Shaw. (Orig.). 1963. pap. 2.95 (ISBN 0-06-463255-5, EH 255, EH). Har-Row.

Punctuation. Philip Lutgendorf & Mary Jane Gray. LC 77-731014. (Illus.). (gr. 7-9). 1977. pap. text ed. 99.00 (ISBN 0-89290-120-9, A149-SAR). Soc for Visual.

Punctuation: Syllabus. 2nd ed. Theodore Yerian & Carl W. Salser. 1972. pap. text ed. 5.35 (ISBN 0-89420-020-8, 357498); cassette recordings 55.20 (ISBN 0-89420-178-6, 357500). Natl Book.

Punctuation Through Proofreading. Barbara Gregorich & Therese F. Waldowski. LC 78-730056. (Illus.). 1977. pap. text ed. 99.00 (ISBN 0-89290-124-1, A325). Soc for Visual.

Punctured Preconceptions: What North American Christians Think About the Church. Douglas W. Johnson & George W. Cornell. 128p. (Orig.). 1974. pap. 1.95 o.p. (ISBN 0-685-27369-5). Friend Pr.

Pungent Truths. B. T. Roberts. pap. 3.50 o.p. (ISBN 0-686-12903-2). Schmul Pub Co.

Punish Me with Kisses. William Bayer. 1980. 10.95 (ISBN 0-312-92664-2). Congdon & Lattes.

Punished with Love. Barbara Cartland. 160p. (Orig.). 1980. pap. 1.75 (ISBN 0-553-13910-X). Bantam.

Punishment. Gary C. Walters & Joan E. Grusec. LC 76-30920. (Psychology Ser.). (Illus.). 1977. text ed. 19.95x (ISBN 0-7167-0366-1); pap. text ed. 10.95x (ISBN 0-7167-0365-3). W H Freeman.

Punishment & Penal Discipline: Essays on the Prison & the Prisoner's Movement. Ed. by Tony Platt & Paul Takagi. LC 79-90275. (Vol. I). (Illus., Orig.). 1980. pap. 8.50 (ISBN 0-935206-00-0). Crime & Soc Justice.

Punishment & Rehabilitation. Jeffrie G. Murphy. 1973. pap. 7.95x (ISBN 0-534-00335-4). Wadsworth Pub.

Punishment & Responsibility: Essays in the Philosophy of Law. Herbert L. Hart. (Orig.). 1968. 14.95 (ISBN 0-19-500162-1); pap. 6.00x (ISBN 0-19-825181-5). Oxford U Pr.

Punishment, Danger & Stigma: The Morality of Criminal Justice. Nigel Walker. 206p. 1980. 22.50x (ISBN 0-389-20129-4). B&N.

Punishment: The Art of Punning. Harvey C. Gordon. 1980. pap. 2.95 (ISBN 0-446-97263-0). Warner Bks.

Punjab Disturbances, 1919-1920, 2 vols. Incl. Vol. 1. Indian Perspective. (ISBN 0-88386-915-2); Vol. 2. British Perspective (ISBN 0-88386-916-0). 1976. Repr. of 1920 ed. 12.00x ea. o.p. South Asia Bks.

Punjab Under the British Rule: 1849-1947. B. S. Nijjar. Incl. Vol. 1. 1849-1902. o.p.; Vol. 2. 1903-1926. 8.50x o.p.. LC 75-901549. 200p. 1974. South Asia Bks.

Punjabi Century, 1857-1947. Prakash Tandon. 1968. 18.50x (ISBN 0-520-01252-6); pap. 5.95 (ISBN 0-520-01253-4, CAL164). U of Cal Pr.

Punk Rock. Virginia Boston. (Large Format Ser.). (Illus.). 1978. pap. 7.95 o.p. (ISBN 0-14-004985-1). Penguin.

Punkin's First Halloween. Esther E. Reinecke. (Second Grade Bk.). (Illus.). (gr. 2-3). PLB 5.95 o.p. (ISBN 0-513-00395-9). Denison.

Puns & Poetry in Lucretius De Rerum Natura. Jane Snyder. 1980. text ed. 28.00 (ISBN 90-6032-124-3). Humanities.

Puns, Gags, Quips, & Riddles & Q's Are Weird O's. Roy Doty. (Illus.). (gr. 3-5). 1976. pap. 1.50 (ISBN 0-671-29909-3). PB.

Puntas de Partida: An Invitation to Spanish. Marty Knorre et al. Incl. Alice Arana & Oswaldo Arana. 224p. wkbk. 6.95; Maria S. Yates. 196p. lab manual 6.95 (ISBN 0-394-32630-X). 608p. 1981. text ed. 17.95 (ISBN 0-394-32618-0). Random.

Pupil. Keith M. Zinn. (Illus.). 152p. 1972. 14.95 (ISBN 0-398-02320-4). C C Thomas.

Pupil Rating Scale: Screening for Learning Disabilities. Helmer R. Myklebust. 1971. pap. 18.00 (ISBN 0-8089-0684-4); record forms, pkg. of 50 11.75 (ISBN 0-8089-0794-8); specimen set, 1 record form 11.75 (ISBN 0-8089-0752-2); computer scoring from, 50 scoring forms, 2 class header sheets, school report form 27.25 (ISBN 0-8089-0989-4). Grune.

Pupils Attitudes to Science: A Review of Research. M. B. Ormerod & D. Duckworth. (General Ser.). 160p. 1975. pap. text ed. 14.50x (ISBN 0-85633-077-9, NFER). Humanities.

Puppet Animation in the Cinema: History & Technique. L. Bruce Holman. LC 73-10523. (Illus.). 192p. 1975. 9.95 o.p. (ISBN 0-498-01385-5). A S Barnes.

Puppet Corner in Every Library. Nancy Renfro. (Illus.). 110p. 1977. pap. 8.95 (ISBN 0-931044-01-4). Renfro Studios.

Puppet-Making. Chester J. Alkema. LC 72-167668. (Little Craft Book Ser.). (Illus.). (gr. 4 up). 1971. 5.95 (ISBN 0-8069-5174-5); PLB 6.69 (ISBN 0-8069-5175-3). Sterling.

Puppet Masters. Robert A. Heinlein. 176p. (RL 7). Date not set. pap. 1.50 (ISBN 0-451-07339-8, W7339, Sig). NAL.

Puppet Parables for Children's Church. Catherine Weinaug. (Paperback Program Ser.). 88p. 1980. pap. 3.45 (ISBN 0-8010-9638-3). Baker Bk.

Puppet Party. Goldie T. Chernoff. LC 76-186171. 3.50 o.s.i. (ISBN 0-8027-6100-3). Walker & Co.

Puppet Show. Sharon Peters. (Illus.). 32p. (gr. k-2). 1980. PLB 2.96 (ISBN 0-89375-385-8); pap. 0.95 (ISBN 0-89375-286-X). Troll Assocs.

Puppet Shows to Make. Eric Hawkesworth. 1972. 4.95 o.p. (ISBN 0-571-09836-3, Pub. by Faber & Faber). Merrimack Bk Serv.

Puppet Theatre of Japan. A. C. Scott. LC 63-21179. (Illus.). 1973. pap. 4.95 (ISBN 0-8048-1116-4). C E Tuttle.

Puppeteer's Library Guide: A Bibliographic Index to the Literature of the World Puppet Theatre, Vol. 1, The Historical Background Of Puppetry & Its Related Fields. J. Frances Crothers. LC 71-149991. 1971. 20.50 (ISBN 0-8108-0319-4). Scarecrow.

Puppetry & Early Childhood Education: Preschool & Primary. Tamara Hunt & Nancy Renfro. Ed. by Ann W. Scwalb. (Puppetry in Education Ser.). (Illus.). 200p. (Orig.). Date not set. pap. 10.95 (ISBN 0-931044-04-9). Renfro Studios.

Puppetry & the Art of Story Creation. Nancy Renfro. (Puppetry in Education Ser.). (Illus.). 164p. (Orig.). 1979. pap. 10.95 (ISBN 0-931044-02-2). Renfro Studios.

Puppetry Library: An Annotated Bibliography Based on the Batchelder-McPharlin Collection at the University of New Mexico. Compiled by George B. Miller, Jr. et al. William E. Jr. Hannaford. LC 80-23474. 200p. 1981. lib. bdg. 29.95 (ISBN 0-313-21359-3, HPL/). Greenwood.

Puppets. Jan Bussell. Ed. by P. Pringle. LC 78-431256. (Pegasus Books: No. 16). 1968. 7.50x (ISBN 0-234-77154-2). Intl Pubns Serv.

Puppets. Jane Graver. (A Nice Place to Live Ser.). 1978. pap. 2.25 (ISBN 0-570-07757-5, 12-2716). Concordia.

Puppets. Barbara Snook. (gr. 4 up). 1966. 5.95 o.p. (ISBN 0-8231-3027-4). Branford.

Puppets & Puppetry. Peter Fraser. (Illus.). 168p. 1980. 24.00 (ISBN 0-7134-2073-1, Pub. by Batsford England). David & Charles.

Puppets for Bible Discovery. Ed. by Lynn Goree. LC 79-55016. (Bible Discovery Bks.). 1979. pap. 4.25 (ISBN 0-8344-0112-6). Sweet.

Puppies. Gabrielle Forbush. (Illus.). 2.95 (ISBN 0-87666-674-8, KW-023). TFH Pubns.

Puppies Need Love Too. Suzanne Taylor-Moore. 48p. 1980. pap. 3.50 (ISBN 0-686-28088-1). MTM Pub Co.

Puppy Book. Jan Pfloog. (Illus.). (ps-1). 1968. PLB 5.38 (ISBN 0-307-68946-8, Golden Pr). Western Pub.

Puppy Lost in Lapland. Peter Hallard. LC 74-151890. (Illus.). (gr. 3-7). 1971. 5.90 (ISBN 0-531-01998-5). Watts.

Puppy Love. Val C. Bagley. (Illus.). 96p. 1981. pap. 3.95 (ISBN 0-88290-158-3, 2043). Horizon Utah.

Puppy Who Wanted a Boy. Jane Thayer. (Illus.). (ps-3). 1958. PLB 7.44 (ISBN 0-688-31631-X). Morrow.

Puppy's One-Two-Three Book. Jim Kulas. (Illus.). (gr. k-1). 1978. PLB 5.38 (ISBN 0-307-68990-5, Golden Pr). Western Pub.

Pur-Sang Francais. Paola Ciechanowska. (Illus.). 18.35 (ISBN 0-85131-003-6, Dist. by Sporting Book Center). J A Allen.

Purcell. rev. ed. J. A. Westrup. (Master Musicians Ser.). (Illus.). 325p. 1980. 19.75 (ISBN 0-460-03177-5, Pub. by J M Dent England). Biblio Dist.

Purcell Papers with a Memoir by Alfred Perceval Graces. Joseph S. Le Fanu. (Nineteenth Century Fiction Ser.: Ireland: Vol. 58). 840p. 1979. lib. bdg. 46.00 (ISBN 0-8240-3507-0). Garland Pub.

Purchase of Alaska, March 30, 1867. Peter Sgroi. LC 74-26677. (Focus Bks). (Illus.). 72p. (gr. 7-9). 1975. PLB 4.90 o.p. (ISBN 0-531-01089-9). Watts.

Purchasing Agent: Medical. Jack Rudman. (Career Examination Ser.: C-2733). (Cloth bdg. avail. on request). 1980. pap. 10.00 (ISBN 0-8373-2733-4). Natl Learning.

Purchasing Agent: Printing. Jack Rudman. (Career Examination Ser.: C-2734). (Cloth bdg. avail. on request). 1980. pap. 10.00 (ISBN 0-8373-2734-2). Natl Learning.

Purchasing Agent's Guide to the Naked Salesman. Barry J. Hersker & Thomas F. Stroh. LC 75-17522. 1975. 15.95 (ISBN 0-8436-1308-4). CBI Pub.

Purchasing & Materials Management. 7th ed. Michael R. Leenders et al. 1980. 21.50x (ISBN 0-256-02374-3). Irwin.

Purchasing & Materials Management for Health Care Institutions. Dean S. Ammer. LC 74-11416. (Illus.). 1975. 16.95 (ISBN 0-669-95604-X). Lexington Bks.

Purchasing & Materials Management: Principles & Cases. 6th ed. Wilbur B. England et al. 1975. text ed. 18.95x o.p. (ISBN 0-256-01635-6). Irwin.

Purchasing & the Management of Materials. 5th ed. Gary L. Zenz. 600p. 1981. text ed. 21.95 (ISBN 0-471-06091-7); tchrs.' ed. avail. (ISBN 0-471-08935-4). Wiley.

Purchasing for the Health Care Facility. John H. Holmgren. (Illus.). 288p. 1975. 28.75 (ISBN 0-398-03399-4). C C Thomas.

Purchasing Handbook. 4th ed. National Association of Purchasing Management. Ed. by Paul V. Farrell. 1152p. Date not set. price not set (ISBN 0-07-045899-5, P&RB). McGraw. Postponed.

Purchasing Information Sources. Ed. by Douglas C. Basil et al. LC 75-7037. (Management Information Guide Ser.: No. 30). 380p. 1977. 30.00 (ISBN 0-8103-0830-4). Gale.

Purchasing Management: Materials in Motion. 4th ed. J. H. Westing et al. LC 75-38969. 624p. 1976. text ed. 26.50 (ISBN 0-471-93632-4). Wiley.

Purchasing Manager's Decision Handbook. Dennis A. Kudrna. LC 74-23120. 224p. 1975. 17.95 (ISBN 0-8436-1307-6). CBI Pub.

Purchasing-Marketing Interface: Text & Cases. J. Stevens & J. Grant. LC 75-9965. 1976. 19.95 (ISBN 0-470-82438-7). Halsted Pr.

Purchasing: Principles & Applications. 5th ed. Stuart F. Heinritz & Paul V. Farrell. (Business Management Ser). (Illus.). 1971. ref. ed. 18.95 (ISBN 0-13-742148-6). P-H.

Purdue Perceptual-Motor Survey. Eugene Roach & Newell Kephart. LC 66-14493. (To be used with The Slow Learner in the Classroom). 1966. pap. text ed. 13.95x spiral bdg. (ISBN 0-675-09797-5). Merrill.

Purdue Pharmacy: The First Century. Robert B. Eckles. LC 78-58059. (Illus.). 116p. 1979. 10.00 (ISBN 0-931682-01-0). Purdue Univ Bks.

Pure & Applied Math in People's Republic of China. Ed. by Anne Fitzgerald & Saunders M. Lane. LC 77-79329. (CSCPRC Report: No. 3). 1977. pap. 8.25 (ISBN 0-309-02609-1). Natl Acad Pr.

Pure & Applied Mathematics in the Peoples Republic of China. Committee on Scholarly Communications with the Peoples Republic of China National Research Council. 1977. pap. 12.00 (ISBN 0-686-25566-6, PB279 509); microfiche 3.50 (ISBN 0-686-25567-4). Natl Tech Info.

Pure & Simple. Marian Burro. 1979. pap. 3.50 (ISBN 0-425-04860-8). Berkley Pub.

Pure & the Impure. Colette. Tr. by Herma Briffault. 175p. 1967. 7.95 (ISBN 0-374-23920-7); pap. 4.95 (ISBN 0-374-50692-2). FS&G.

Pure Cultures of Algae: Their Preparation & Maintenance. E. G. Pringsheim. 1967. Repr. of 1946 ed. 5.95 o.s.i. (ISBN 0-02-850370-8). Hafner.

Pure Land Buddhist Painting. Joji Okazaki. Tr. by Elizabeth T. Grotenhuis from Jap. LC 76-9354. (Japanese Arts Library: Vol. 4). 1977. 16.95 (ISBN 0-87011-287-2). Kodansha.

Pure Magic. Elizabeth Coatsworth. LC 72-92435. (Illus.). 96p. (gr. 3-6). 1973. 7.95 (ISBN 0-02-721500-8, 72150). Macmillan.

Pure Magic! Henry Gross. LC 77-15069. (Illus.). 1978. 12.50 o.p. (ISBN 0-684-15338-6, SL 751, ScribT); pap. 6.95 o.p. (ISBN 0-684-15337-8, SL 751, ScribJ). Scribner.

Pure Mathematics, 2 vols. S. L. Parsonson. LC 70-100026. (Illus.). 1971. Vol. 1. text ed. 14.50x (ISBN 0-521-07683-8); Vol. 2. text ed. 16.95x (ISBN 0-521-08032-0). Cambridge U Pr.

Pure Mathematics, a University & College Course: Calculus. F. Gerrish. 1960. text ed. 28.95 (ISBN 0-521-05069-3). Cambridge U Pr.

Pure Mathematics at Advanced Level. L. Harwood Clarke. 1967. pap. text ed. 10.95x o.p. (ISBN 0-435-51179-3). Heinemann Ed.

Pure Pragmatics & Possible Worlds: The Early Essays of Wilfrid Sellars. Wilfrid Sellars. Ed. by Jeffrey Sicha. LC 78-65271. (Orig.). 1980. lib. bdg. 22.00 (ISBN 0-917930-26-6); pap. text ed. 8.50x (ISBN 0-917930-06-1). Ridgeview.

Pure Theory of International Trade & Distortions. Bharat R. Hazari. LC 78-9092. 1978. 27.95 (ISBN 0-470-26430-6). Halsted Pr.

Pure Theory of International Trade Under Uncertainty. R. N. Batra. LC 74-4820. 1975. text ed. 24.95 (ISBN 0-470-05687-8). Halsted Pr.

Pure Theory of Law. Hans Kelsen. Tr. by Max Knight from Ger. (Library Reprint Ser.: Vol. 94). 1978. 27.50x (ISBN 0-520-03692-1). U of Cal Pr.

Purgatory: Explained by the Lives & Legends of the Saints. F. X. Shouppe. LC 79-112489. 1973. pap. 6.50 (ISBN 0-89555-042-3, 143). TAN Bks Pubs.

Purification of Laboratory Chemicals. 2nd ed. D. D. Perrin et al. LC 79-41708. 580p. 1980. 72.00 (ISBN 0-08-022961-1). Pergamon.

Purifying the Faith: The Muhammadijah Movement in Indonesian Islam. James L. Peacock. LC 78-61992. 1978. 6.95 (ISBN 0-8053-7824-3). Benjamin-Cummings.

Purim. Molly Cone. LC 67-10071. (Holiday Ser.). (Illus.). (gr. k-3). 1967. PLB 7.89 (ISBN 0-690-65922-9, TYC-J). T Y Crowell.

Purim: A Joyous Holiday. Sophia N. Cedarbaum. (Illus.). (gr. k-2). 1960. 3.50 (ISBN 0-8074-0148-X, 301562). UAHC.

Purim Goat. Yuri Suhl. LC 79-6551. (Illus.). 64p. (gr. 2-6). 1980. 7.95 (ISBN 0-590-07658-2, Four Winds). Schol Bk Serv.

Purine Metabolism in Man III: Biochemical, Immunological, & Cancer Research, Pt. B. Ed. by A. Rapado et al. (Advances in Experimental Medicine & Biology Ser.: Vol. 122B). 482p. 1980. 45.00 (ISBN 0-306-40311-0, Plenum Pr). Plenum Pub.

Purine Metabolism in Man III: Clinical & Therapeutic Aspects, Pt. A. Ed. by A. Rapado et al. (Advances in Experimental Medicine & Biology Ser.: Vol. 122A). 466p. 1980. 45.00 (ISBN 0-306-40310-2, Plenum Pr). Plenum Pub.

Puritan Ethic & Woman Suffrage. Alan P. Grimes. LC 80-21799. xiii, 159p. 1980. Repr. of 1967 ed. lib. bdg. 19.50x (ISBN 0-313-22689-X, GRPE). Greenwood.

Puritan Hope. Iain H. Murray. 1975. pap. 5.45 (ISBN 0-686-12534-7). Banner of Truth.

Puritan in Voodoo-Land. Edna Taft. LC 73-174115. (Tower Bks). (Illus.). 1971. Repr. of 1938 ed. 20.00 (ISBN 0-8103-3919-6). Gale.

Puritan, Paranoid, Remissive: A Sociology of Modern Culture. John Carroll. 1977. 15.00 (ISBN 0-7100-8622-9). Routledge & Kegan.

Puritan Political Ideas 1558-1794. Ed. by Edmund S. Morgan. LC 65-22347. (Orig.). 1965. pap. 7.35 o.p. (ISBN 0-672-60042-0, AHS33). Bobbs.

Puritan Revolution & Education Thought: Background for Reform. Richard Greaves. 1970. 13.00 (ISBN 0-8135-0616-6). Rutgers U Pr.

Puritan Rhetoric: The Issue of Emotion in Religion. Eugene E. White. LC 76-181987. (Landmarks in Rhetoric & Public Address Ser.). 229p. 1972. 10.95x (ISBN 0-8093-0563-1). S Ill U Pr.

Puritan Sermon in America, 1630-1750, 4 vols. Ed. by Ronald A. Bosco. LC 78-114749. 1978. Repr. 200.00x set (ISBN 0-8201-1320-4). Schol Facsimiles.

Puritan Village: The Formation of a New England Town. Sumner C. Powell. LC 63-8862. (Illus.). 1963. 27.50x (ISBN 0-8195-3034-4, Pub. by Wesleyan U Pr); pap. 6.95 (ISBN 0-8195-6014-6). Columbia U Pr.

Puritan Way of Death: A Study in Religion, Culture & Social Change. David E. Stannard. LC 76-42647. (Illus.). 1977. 14.95x (ISBN 0-19-502226-2). Oxford U Pr.

Puritanism & the Wilderness: The Intellectual Significance of the New England Frontier, 1629-1700. Peter N. Carroll. LC 78-84673. 1969. 17.50x (ISBN 0-231-03253-6). Columbia U Pr.

Puritanism in America. Everett Emerson. (World Leaders Ser.: No. 71). 1977. lib. bdg. 9.95 (ISBN 0-8057-7692-3). Twayne.

Puritanism in North-West England: A Regional Study of the Diocese of Chester to 1642. R. C. Richardson. 214p. 1972. 15.00x (ISBN 0-87471-093-6). Rowman.

Puritans: A Sourcebook of Their Writings, 2 vols. Ed. by Perry Miller & Thomas H. Johnson. (Orig.). Vol. 1. pap. 5.95x (ISBN 0-06-131093-X, TB1093, Torch); Vol. 2. pap. 7.95x (ISBN 0-06-131094-8, TB1094, Torch). Har-Row.

Puritans Among the Indians: Accounts of Captivity & Redemption 1676-1724. Ed. by Alden T. Vaughan & Edward W. Clark. (John Harvard Library Ser.). (Illus.). 352p. 1981. text ed. 20.00 (ISBN 0-674-73901-9). Harvard U Pr.

Puritans & Music in England & New England: A Contribution to the Cultural History of 2 Nations. Percy A. Scholes. 1934. 34.50x (ISBN 0-19-816117-4). Oxford U Pr.

Puritans & Revolutionaries: Essays in Seventeenth-Century History Presented to Christopher Hill. Ed. by Donald Pennington & Keith Thomas. 1978. 45.00x (ISBN 0-19-822439-7). Oxford U Pr.

Purity & Danger: An Analysis of Concepts of Pollution & Taboo. Mary Douglas. 1978. pap. 7.95 (ISBN 0-7100-8827-2). Routledge & Kegan.

Purity & the Carnal Element in Love: The Story of a Concrete Case. Clarence T. Delfiore. (Intimate Life of Man Library). (Illus.). 111p. 1981. 39.75 (ISBN 0-89266-298-0). Am Classical Coll Pr.
Puro Mexicano. Ed. by J. Frank Dobie. LC 35-1517. (Texas Folklore Society Publication Ser.: No. 12). 272p. 1980. Repr. of 1935 ed. 7.95 (ISBN 0-87074-041-5). SMU Press.
Purple Bear. Nancy Reese. Ed. by Alton Jordan. (Elephant Ser.). (Illus.). (gr. k-3). 1975. PLB 3.50 (ISBN 0-89868-013-1, Read Res); pap. text ed. 1.75 (ISBN 0-89868-046-8). ARO Pub.
Purple-Braided People. Shree Devi. 8.00 (ISBN 0-89253-652-7); flexible cloth 4.80 (ISBN 0-89253-653-5). Ind-US Inc.
Purple Cloud. M. P. Shiel. lib. bdg. 14.95x (ISBN 0-89966-228-5). Buccaneer Bks.
Purple Dragon & Other Fantasies. L. Frank Baum. LC 76-44600. (Illus.). 1976. 8.50 (ISBN 0-934882-01-0). Fictioneer Bks.
Purple Eagle Mystery. Hal G. Evarts. LC 75-27704. 218p. (gr. 7-10). 1976. 6.95 (ISBN 0-684-16569-4, ScribJ). Scribner.
Purple Mouse. Elisabeth MacIntyre. LC 75-1318. 128p. (gr. 6 up). 1975. 6.95 o.p. (ISBN 0-525-66424-6). Elsevier-Nelson.
Purple Pages. Jeffrey Feinman. 1979. pap. 6.95 (ISBN 0-8015-6132-9, Hawthorn). Dutton.
Purple Passage: Life of Mrs Frank Leslie. Madeleine B. Stern. (Illus.). 1970. Repr. of 1953 ed. 11.95 (ISBN 0-8061-0271-3); pap. 5.95 (ISBN 0-8061-0939-4). U of Okla Pr.
Purple Violet Squish. David Wilkerson. (gr. 9 up). 1970. pap. 0.95 o.s.i. (ISBN 0-89129-179-2). Jove Pubns.
Purpose. Jim Wilson. 80p. pap. text ed. 3.25 (ISBN 0-227-67707-2). Attic Pr.
Purpose & Practice in Nursery Education. Lesley Webb. 1974. pap. 9.25x (ISBN 0-631-15240-7, Pub. by Basil Blackwell). Biblio Dist.
Purpose in Animal Behaviour. F. V. Smith. 1971. text ed. 7.75x (ISBN 0-09-109131-4, Hutchinson U Lib). Humanities.
Purpose of American Politics. rev. 2nd ed. Ed. by Hans J. Morgenthau. 384p. cancelled (ISBN 0-935764-05-4). Ark Hse NY.
Purpose of Authority? Lucius Annese. LC 78-72295. 1980. text ed. 10.00 (ISBN 0-933402-12-0); pap. text ed. 4.95 (ISBN 0-933402-00-7). Charisma Pr.
Purpose of Authority: A Drama. Lucius Annese. LC 79-57037. (Orig.). 1980. pap. write for info. (ISBN 0-933402-02-3). Charisma Pr.
Purpose of the Church & Its Ministry. H. Richard Niebuhr. LC 76-62925. (Orig.). 1977. pap. 4.95 (ISBN 0-06-066174-7, RD 211, HarpR). Har-Row.
Purposes & the Performance of Higher Education in the U. S. Approaching the Year 2000. Carnegie Commission on Higher Education. (Illus.). 125p. 1973. 5.50 o.p. (ISBN 0-07-010071-3, P&RB). McGraw.
Purposes of Art: An Introduction to the History & Appreciation of Art. 3rd ed. Albert E. Elsen. LC 77-171524. (Illus.). 488p. 1975. pap. text ed. 15.95x (ISBN 0-03-089708-4, HoltC). HR&W.
Purposes of Pentecost. Derek Prince. (Foundation Ser.: Bk. IV). 1965-66. pap. 2.50 (ISBN 0-934920-03-6). Derek Prince.
Purposive Behavior in Animals & Men. Edward C. Tolman. LC 67-20666. (Century Psychology Ser.). (Illus.). 1967. text ed. 28.50x (ISBN 0-89197-544-6); pap. text ed. 9.95x (ISBN 0-89197-545-4). Irvington.
Purser's Handbook. William E. Armstrong. LC 65-21748. (Illus.). 1966. 10.00x (ISBN 0-87033-086-1). Cornell Maritime.
Pursisniha: A Zoroastrian Catechism, 2 vols. Kaikhusroo M. Jamaspasa. LC 72-179885. 174p. 1971. Set. 42.50x (ISBN 3-447-01351-6). Intl Pubns Serv.
Pursuing Elegy: A Poem About Haiti. James Schevill. (Illus., Orig.). 1974. pap. 3.50 (ISBN 0-914278-01-0). Copper Beech.
Pursuing the American Dream. Ed. by Kenneth S. Knodt. 336p. 1976. pap. text ed. 9.50 (ISBN 0-13-742742-5). P-H.
Pursuit. J. D. Reed. 1981. pap. 2.75 (ISBN 0-440-17167-9). Dell.
Pursuit of a Dream. Janet S. Hermann. (Illus.). 288p. 1981. 17.50 (ISBN 0-19-502887-2). Oxford U Pr.
Pursuit of Competence in Social Work: Contemporary Issues in the Definition, Assessment, & Improvement of Effectiveness in the Human Services. Frank W. Clark et al. LC 79-83570. (Social & Behavioral Science Ser.). (Illus.). 1979. text ed. 16.95x (ISBN 0-87589-404-6). Jossey-Bass.
Pursuit of Death. Venjamin P. Kurtz. 339p. 1980. Repr. of 1933 ed. lib. bdg. 30.00 (ISBN 0-8495-3051-2). Arden Lib.
Pursuit of Equality in American History. J. R. Pole. LC 76-20020. (Jefferson Memorial Lecture Ser.). 1978. 18.50x (ISBN 0-520-03286-1); pap. 5.95 (ISBN 0-520-03947-5). U of Cal Pr.
Pursuit of Happiiness. Florence Littauer. LC 80-85333. 1981. pap. 4.95 (ISBN 0-89081-284-5). Harvest Hse.
Pursuit of Happiness. John Houston. 1981. pap. text ed. 7.95x (ISBN 0-673-15421-1). Scott F.
Pursuit of Happiness. Winston K. Pendleton. 1963. 3.95 o.p. (ISBN 0-8272-2922-4). Bethany Pr.
Pursuit of Happiness, & Other Sobering Thoughts. George F. Will. LC 77-6898. 1978. 10.95 o.s.i. (ISBN 0-06-014663-X, HarpT). Har-Row.
Pursuit of Holiness. Jerry Bridges. LC 78-18109. 1978. pap. 2.95 (ISBN 0-89109-430-X, 14308). NavPress.
Pursuit of Inequality. Philip Green. 1981. 14.95 (ISBN 0-394-50676-6). Pantheon.
Pursuit of Meaning: America - 1600-2000. Richard L. Rapson & Susan B. Rapson. 1977. pap. text ed. 11.25x (ISBN 0-8191-0175-3). U Pr of Amer.
Pursuit of Mental Health: For the Individual, the Community & the Nation. Melvin Herman & Lucy Freeman. LC 74-9774. 256p. 1974. 6.95 o.s.i. (ISBN 0-02-551190-4). Macmillan.
Pursuit of Nature. Alan Hodgkin et al. LC 76-58844. (Illus.). 1979. pap. 8.50 (ISBN 0-521-29617-X). Cambridge U Pr.
Pursuit of Nature. Alan Hodgkin et al. LC 76-58844. (Illus.). 1977. 35.50 (ISBN 0-521-21505-6). Cambridge U Pr.
Pursuit of Peace. Leonard W. Doob. LC 80-1201. 376p. 1981. lib. bdg. 29.95 (ISBN 0-313-22630-X, DPO/). Greenwood.
Pursuit of Pleasure: the Rococo Revival in French Romantic Art. Carol Duncan. LC 75-23789. (Outstanding Dissertations in the Fine Arts - 19th Century). (Illus.). 1976. lib. bdg. 31.00 (ISBN 0-8240-1985-7). Garland Pub.
Pursuit of the Presidency. Washington Post Staff Members. Ed. by Richard Harwood. Date not set. pap. 5.95 (ISBN 0-686-28876-9). Berkley Pub.
Pursuit of the Prodigal. Louis Auchincloss. 1971. pap. 0.95 o.p. (ISBN 0-380-01380-0, 06965). Avon.
Pursuivant of Arms; or, Heraldry Founded Upon Facts. James R. Planche. LC 72-10610. (Illus.). 299p. 1973. Repr. of 1874 ed. 15.00 (ISBN 0-8103-3171-3). Gale.
Push Pull, Empty Full: A Book of Opposites. Tana Hoban. LC 72-175597. (Illus.). (ps-2). 1972. 8.95 (ISBN 0-02-744810-X). Macmillan.
Pushcart Prize: Best of the Small Presses. Ed. by Bill Henderson. LC 75-40812. 1976. pap. 5.95 (ISBN 0-916366-01-4). Pushcart Pr.
Pushcart Prize II. Ed. by Bill Henderson. 1978. pap. 5.95 (ISBN 0-380-01895-0, 37275). Avon.
Pushcart Prize Six: Best of the Small Presses. Ed. by Bill Henderson. 1981. 19.50 (ISBN 0-916366-12-X). Pushcart Pr.
Pushcart Prize VI. Ed. by Bill Henderson. 600p. 1980. pap. 7.95 (ISBN 0-380-48827-2, 48827). Avon.
Pushkin. Ernest J. Simmons. 8.50 (ISBN 0-8446-0259-0). Peter Smith.
Puss in Boots. Rev. by M. Jean Craig. (gr. k-3). 1970. pap. 1.25 (ISBN 0-590-00395-X, Schol Pap); pap. 3.50 bk. & record (ISBN 0-590-04400-1). Schol Bk Serv.
Puss in Boots. Paul Galdone. LC 75-25505. (Illus.). 32p. (ps-4). 1976. 7.95 (ISBN 0-395-28808-8, Clarion). HM.
Puss in Boots. (Illus.). Arabic 2.50x (ISBN 0-685-82868-9). Intl Bk Ctr.
Puss-in-Boots (der Gestiefelte Kater) Ludwig Tieck. Ed. & tr. by Gerald Gillespie. LC 73-20869. (Edinburgh Bilingual Library Ser.: No. 8). 138p. 1974. 9.50x o.p. (ISBN 0-292-72702-X); pap. 3.45x o.p. (ISBN 0-292-72703-8). U of Tex Pr.
Pussy Willow. Margaret W. Brown. (Illus.). (ps-3). 1951. PLB 7.62 (ISBN 0-307-62448-X, Golden Pr). Western Pub.
Pussycat Tiger. Joan Bacon. (Illus.). 24p. (ps-4). 1972. PLB 5.00 (ISBN 0-307-60362-8, Golden Pr). Western Pub.
Pussycats Need Love, Too. George Booth. LC 80-17198. 128p. 1980. 8.95 (ISBN 0-396-07906-7). Dodd.
Pussywillow. Mama S. Rampa. 1976. pap. 2.50 (ISBN 0-685-72712-2). Weiser.
Put Down & Ripped off: The American Woman & the Beauty Cult. Nora S. Kinzer. LC 77-3619. 1977. 7.95 o.s.i. (ISBN 0-690-01243-8, TYC-T). T Y Crowell.
Put-Down Pro: Getting Along with Friends. Jack Canario. (Read on! - Write on! Ser.). (Illus.). 64p. (gr. 6-12). 1980. 2.85 (ISBN 0-915510-39-1). Janus Bks.
Put It in Writing. T. M. Brown & Robert Millar. 1968. pap. text ed. 3.50x o.p. (ISBN 0-435-10130-7). Heinemann Ed.
Put It in Writing: Writing Activities for Students of ESL. David Davidson & David Blot. (Illus.). 96p. (Orig.). 1981. pap. text ed. 3.95 (ISBN 0-88377-175-6). Newbury Hse.
Put-Offs & Come-Ons. A. H. Chapman. 1977. pap. 1.50 o.p. (ISBN 0-425-03382-1, Medallion). Berkley Pub.
Put Out the Light. Rae Foley. 1978. pap. 1.50 o.s.i. (ISBN 0-515-04493-8). Jove Pubns.
Put Them in Cages. Robert T. Smith. LC 72-89460. 32p. (gr. 5-12). 1973. PLB 4.95 (ISBN 0-87191-223-6). Creative Ed.
Put Your Foot in Your Mouth & Other Silly Sayings. James A. Cox. LC 80-12877. (Step-up Book: No. 31). (Illus.). 72p. (gr. 2-5). 1980. bds. 3.95 (ISBN 0-394-84503-X); PLB 3.99 (ISBN 0-394-94503-4). Random.
Put Your Kid in Show Biz. Lea B. Rapp. LC 80-54346. (Illus.). 160p. 1981. 12.95 (ISBN 0-8069-7040-5); lib. bdg. 11.69 (ISBN 0-8069-7041-3); pap. 6.95 (ISBN 0-8069-7508-3). Sterling.
Put Your Mother on the Ceiling: Children's Imagination Games. Richard De Mille. LC 67-23698. 192p. (gr. 1 up). 1981. Repr. of 1967 ed. 9.95 (ISBN 0-915520-39-7). Ross-Erikson.
Put Your Psychic Powers to Work: A Practical Guide to Parapsychology. Evelyn Monahan & Terry Bakken. LC 73-84208. 1973. 10.95 (ISBN 0-88229-132-7). Nelson-Hall.
Putter. Bob Rosburg. 160p. 1975. pap. 2.95 (ISBN 0-346-12356-9). Cornerstone.
Putting a Band Together. Ed. by Guitar Player Magazine. 1.95 (ISBN 0-8256-9509-0). Guitar Player.
Putting a Message Together. 2nd ed. Glen E. Mills. LC 78-179367. Orig. Title: Message Preparation: Analysis & Structure. 1972. pap. 3.95 (ISBN 0-672-61299-2, SC8). Bobbs.
Putting It All Together. Irene Kassorla. 224p. 1976. pap. 2.50 (ISBN 0-446-91802-4). Warner Bks.
Putting It All Together, A Consumer's Guide to Home Furnishings. Peggie Collins & Shirley Collins. LC 77-1885. (Illus.). 1977. 10.00 (ISBN 0-684-14883-8, ScribT); pap. 6.95 o.p. (ISBN 0-684-14884-6, ScribT). Scribner.
Putting It All Together: A Guide to Strategic Thinking. William E. Rothschild. LC 76-10535. (Illus.). 224p. 1976. 17.95 (ISBN 0-8144-5405-4). Am Mgmt.
Putting It All Together: Skills & Activities for the Elementary Child. Kitty K. Robinson & Ethel J. Greene. 1978. pap. text ed. 10.00x (ISBN 0-8191-0362-4). U Pr of Amer.
Putting It Up with Honey. Susan Geiskopf. LC 78-59871. 1979. pap. 6.95 (ISBN 0-930356-13-6). Quicksilver Prod.
Putting Participation into Practice. David Guest & Kenneth Knight. 1979. text ed. 26.50x (ISBN 0-566-02086-6, Pub. by Gower Pub Co England). Renouf.
Putting "Reality" Together: BBC News. Philip Schlesinger. LC 79-89074. (Communication & Society: Vol. 9). (Illus.). 1979. 22.00x (ISBN 0-8039-1357-5); pap. 12.50x (ISBN 0-8039-1358-3). Sage.
Putting up with Sherwood. Ellen Matthews. LC 80-17574. (Illus.). (gr. 3-5). 1980. PLB 9.95 (ISBN 0-664-32672-2). Westminster.
Putting up with Your Put Downs. Clark B. McCall. (Uplook Ser.). 1978. pap. 0.75 (ISBN 0-8163-0093-3, 16970-6). Pacific Pr Pub Assn.
Putting You in Creative Aerobic Dance: The Fun & Fitness of a Lifetime Sport Through Movement to Music. Colleen Kirby & Laura Roberts. Ed. by David Fritze. LC 80-84937. (Illus.). 150p. (Orig.). 1981. pap. write for info. Korakas-Roberts-Kirby.
Putt's Law & the Successful Technocrat. A. Putt. (Illus.). 124p. 1981. 8.00 (ISBN 0-682-49702-9). Exposition.
Putty. Keith Abbott. (Illus.). 1971. signed lettered A-Z o.p. 7.50 (ISBN 0-912652-32-2); pap. 3.50 (ISBN 0-912652-31-4). Blue Wind.
Puuc: An Architectural Survey of the Hill Country of Yucatan & North Casmpeche, Mexico, Memoirs, Vol. 19. H. E. Pollack. (Illus.). 612p. 1980. pap. 50.00 cancelled (ISBN 0-87365-693-8). Peabody Harvard.
Puzzle Blast. Fellows. (gr. 3-5). pap. 0.95 (ISBN 0-590-11894-3, Schol Pap). Schol Bk Serv.
Puzzle for Puppets. Patrick Quentin. 1979. pap. 2.25 (ISBN 0-380-48579-6, 48579). Avon.
Puzzle Forwantons. Patrick Quentin. 208p. 1980. pap. 2.25 (ISBN 0-380-49643-7, 49643). Avon.
Puzzle Fun. Gerard Mosler. (gr. 4-6). pap. 1.25 (ISBN 0-590-03203-8, Schol Pap). Schol Bk Serv.
Puzzle Panic. Donna L. Pape. (gr. 4-6). 1977. pap. 1.25 (ISBN 0-590-10314-8, Schol Pap). Schol Bk Serv.
Puzzle Power. Leonard F. Fellows. (gr. 4-6). 1976. pap. 1.25 (ISBN 0-590-10230-3, Schol Pap). Schol Bk Serv.
Puzzlers Gamebook. John Hall. (gr. 4 up). 1979. pap. 2.25 (ISBN 0-912300-50-7). Troubador Pr.
Puzzles. Dottie Rambo & Dave Huntsinger. (Creek Bank Kids Ser.: Vol. 6). (ps-8). 1979. 3.95 (ISBN 0-914850-76-8). Impact Tenn.
Puzzles. Walt Disney Productions. (Winnie-the-Pooh Hunny Pot Bk.). 24p. (ps-3). 1980. PLB 5.38 (ISBN 0-307-68872-0, Golden Pr). Western Pub.
Puzzles & Silly Riddles. Donna L. Pape et al. (gr. 4-6). 1974. pap. 1.25 (ISBN 0-590-06120-8, Schol Pap). Schol Bk Serv.
PVC Pipe-M23: American Water Works Association (AWWA Manuals) (Illus.). 96p. 1980. pap. text ed. 9.50 (ISBN 0-89867-241-4). Am Water Wks Assn.
Pygmalion. George B. Shaw. (gr. 9 up). 1973. pap. 2.25 (ISBN 0-671-43298-2). PB.
Pygmalion or Frankenstein? Alternative Schooling in American Education. John C. Carr et al. LC 76-2929. 1977. pap. text ed. 7.95 (ISBN 0-201-00898-X). A-W.
Pygmies: Africans of the Congo Forest. Sonia Bleeker. LC 68-25481. (Illus.). (gr. 3-6). 1968. PLB 6.67 (ISBN 0-688-31462-7). Morrow.
Pylgremage of the Sowle. Guillaume de Deguileville. Tr. by J. Lydgate. LC 74-28845. (English Experience Ser.: No. 726). 1975. Repr. of 1483 ed. 24.00 (ISBN 90-221-0740-X). Walter J Johnson.
Pylon. reissue ed. William Faulkner. 1965. 11.95 o.p. (ISBN 0-394-44156-7). Random.
Pynchon: The Voice of Ambiguity. Thomas H. Schaub. LC 80-11944. 175p. 1981. 13.50 (ISBN 0-252-00816-2). U of Ill Pr.
Pynchon's Fictions: Thomas Pynchon & the Literature of Information. John O. Stark. LC 79-28466. x, 183p. 1980. 13.95x (ISBN 0-8214-0419-9, 0419E). Ohio U Pr.
Pyne's Royal Residences. John Cornforth. (Folio Miniature Ser.). 1976. 4.95 (ISBN 0-7181-1476-0, Pub. by Michael Joseph). Merrimack Bk Serv.
Pyramid. John Hurd. 1977. 3.00 (ISBN 0-918116-05-8). Jawbone Pr.
Pyramid Builders. (MacDonald Educational Ser.). (Illus., Arabic.). 3.50 (ISBN 0-686-53082-9). Intl Bk Ctr.
Pyramid Power. Max Toth & Greg Nielsen. (Warner Destiny Bk.). (Orig.). 1976. pap. 2.25 o.s.i. (ISBN 0-446-82569-7). Warner Bks.
Pyramid Principle. David A. Womack. LC 76-46312. 1977. pap. 3.50 (ISBN 0-87123-462-9, 210462). Bethany Fell.
Pyramid Puzzles. Ed. by Malcolm Whyte. (Illus.). 40p. (Orig.). (gr. 1-12). 1979. pap. 2.25 (ISBN 0-89844-003-3). Troubador Pr.
Pyramiding in the Futures Market. Joseph R. Maxwell, Sr. (Illus.). Date not set. pap. 13.25 cancelled (ISBN 0-917832-17-5). Speer Bks.
Pyramids. John Weeks. (Introduction to the History of Mankind Ser.). (Illus.). 1971. 3.95 (ISBN 0-521-07240-9). Cambridge U Pr.
Pyramids of Life: Illuminations of Nature's Fearful Symmetry. John Reader & Harvey Croze. LC 76-50638. 1977. 12.95 o.p. (ISBN 0-397-01151-2). Lippincott.
Pyramids of Power: The Story of Roosevelt, Insull & the Utility Wars. Marion L. Ramsay. (FDR & the Era of the New Deal Ser.). (Illus.). 342p. 1975. Repr. of 1937 ed. lib. bdg. 32.50 (ISBN 0-306-70707-1). Da Capo.
Pyramids: Tombs for Eternity. Mildred M. Pace. LC 79-11999. (Illus.). 192p. (gr. 7-9). 1980. 7.95 (ISBN 0-07-048054-0, GB). McGraw.
Pyridine Nucleotide - Dependent Dehydrogenases. Ed. by Horst Sund. 513p. 1977. text ed. 97.00x (ISBN 3-11007-091-X). De Gruyter.
Pyrogenic Mineral Stability, Lower Member of the John Day Formation, Eastern Oregon. R. V. Fisher. (U. C. Publ. in Geological Sciences: Vol. 75). 1968. pap. 6.00x (ISBN 0-520-09178-7). U of Cal Pr.
Pyrotechnics. Joseph H. McLain. (Illus.). 225p. 1980. 24.50 (ISBN 0-89168-032-2). Franklin Inst.
Pyrrhon et le Scepticisme Grec. Leon Robin. LC 78-66561. (Ancient Philosophy Ser.). 264p. 1980. lib. bdg. 26.00 (ISBN 0-8240-9589-8). Garland Pub.
Pythagoras: A Life. Peter Gorman. 1978. 18.00 (ISBN 0-7100-0006-5). Routledge & Kegan.
Python. Joseph Fontenrose. 1959. 27.00x (ISBN 0-8196-0285-X). Biblo.
Python: A Study of Delphic Myth & Its Origins. Joseph Fontenrose. 637p. 1980. 30.00x (ISBN 0-520-04106-2); pap. 8.95 (ISBN 0-520-04091-0, CAL 449). U of Cal Pr.

Q

Q & A Auditing. LC 79-83863. 16.00 (ISBN 0-932788-07-6). Bradley CPA.
Q & A Law. Gary A. Laursen. LC 79-83862. 12.00 (ISBN 0-932788-09-2). Bradley CPA.
Q & A Practice. A. M. Partington & Frank Weinberg. LC 79-83860. 16.00 (ISBN 0-932788-06-8). Bradley CPA.
Q & A Theory. A. M. Partington. LC 79-83864. 12.00 (ISBN 0-932788-08-4). Bradley CPA.
Q-Baltimore & Ohio Railroad Q-Class Mikado Locomotives. Howard N. Barr & W. A. Barringer. LC 78-52708. (Illus.). 1978. 30.00 (ISBN 0-934118-15-9). Barnard Robert.

Q. Horatius Flaccus, 2 vols. 3rd ed. Richard Bentley. Ed. by Steele Commager. LC 77-24817. (Latin Poetry Ser.: Vol. 3). 1979. Repr. of 1869 ed. Set. lib. bdg. 73.00 (ISBN 0-8240-2952-6). Garland Pub.

Q Is for Duck. Mary Elting & Michael Folsom. (Illus.). 64p. (ps-1). 1980. 8.95 (ISBN 0-395-29437-1, Clarion); pap. 3.95 (ISBN 0-395-30062-2). HM.

Q M: An Introduction to Quantitative Methods for Business Applications. Roger D. Eck. 1979. text ed. 21.95x (ISBN 0-534-00625-6). Wadsworth Pub.

Qabalistic Tarot. Robert Wang. (Illus.). 320p. 1981. pap. 8.95 (ISBN 0-87728-520-9). Weiser.

Qhawala-li: Water Coming Down Place; "A History of Gualalal, Mendocino County, California. Annette W. Parks. LC 80-82462. (Illus.). 150p. 1981. 24.95 (ISBN 0-9605550-0-5); pap. 12.95 (ISBN 0-9605550-1-3). FreshCut.

Quack-Quack. Berta Hader & Elmer Hader. (Illus.). (gr. 1-3). 1961. 8.95 (ISBN 0-02-740250-9). Macmillan.

Quacks of Old London. C. J. Thompson. LC 75-89296. (Tower Bks). (Illus.). 1971. Repr. of 1929 ed. 20.00 (ISBN 0-8103-3212-4). Gale.

Quacky & Wacky. Ethel Barrett. (ps-1). 1978. pap. 6.95 book & cassette pac (ISBN 0-8307-0418-3, 5602505). Regal.

Quad Sound. Marvin Tepper. (Illus.). 128p. 1976. pap. 4.95 o.p. (ISBN 0-8104-5987-6). Hayden.

Quadratic Form Theory & Differential Equations. Ed. by John Gregory. LC 80-520. (Mathematics in Science & Engineering Ser.). 1981. 29.50 (ISBN 0-12-301450-6). Acad Pr.

Quadratic Forms & Matrices: An Introductory Approach. N. V. Yefimov. (Eng.). 1964. pap. 10.50 o.p. (ISBN 0-12-769956-2). Acad Pr.

Quadratic Functions & Equivalence. NAIS Task Force on Secondary Mathematics. (Occasional Papers Ser.: No. 3). (Illus.). 1979. pap. 3.25 (ISBN 0-934338-15-9). NAIS.

Quadrilingual Economics Dictionary. Ed. by Frits J. De Jong et al. 1981. lib. bdg. 48.00 (ISBN 90-247-2243-8, Pub. by Martinus Nijhoff). Kluwer Boston.

Quadrille. Marion Chesney. 224p. 1981. pap. 1.95 (ISBN 0-449-50174-4, Coventry). Fawcett.

Quadriplegia After Spinal Cord Injury: A Treatment Guide for Physical Therapists. Janet Duttarer & E. Edberg. LC 72-84793. 50p. 7.00x o.p. (ISBN 0-913590-03-7). C B Slack.

Quaestiones Alberti De Modis Significandi by Pseudo-Albertus Magnus. L. G. Kelly. (Studies in the History of Linguistics: No. 15). 1979. text ed. 37.25x (ISBN 0-391-01664-4). Humanities.

Quail in the Family. William J. Plummer. 128p. 1975. pap. 1.50 o.p. (ISBN 0-449-22568-2, Q2568, Crest). Fawcett.

Quaker Childhood. Helen T. Flexner. 1940. 27.50x o.p. (ISBN 0-686-51294-4). Elliots Bks.

Quaker Enterprises in Biscuits: Huntley & Palmers of Reading, 1822-1972. T. A. Corley. 1972. text ed. 10.50x (ISBN 0-09-111320-2). Humanities.

Quaker Profiles from the American West. Errol T. Elliot. LC 72-5126. 1972. pap. 2.95 (ISBN 0-913408-05-0). Friends United.

Quaker Testimonies & Economic Alternatives. Sevpryn Bruyn. LC 80-80915. 35p. pap. 1.25 (ISBN 0-87574-231-9). Pendle Hill.

Quakerism on the Eastern Shore. Kenneth Carroll. LC 70-112986. (Illus.). 1970. 12.50x (ISBN 0-938420-15-1). Md Hist.

Quakers in India. Marjorie Sykes. (Illus.). 176p. 1980. 12.95 (ISBN 0-04-275003-2, 2585). Allen Unwin.

Quakers in the Colonial Northeast. Arthur L. Worrall. LC 79-63086. 248p. 1980. text ed. 12.50 (ISBN 0-87451-174-7). U Pr of New Eng.

Qualified Products List & Sources. 60th ed. Ed. by Garnet Mills Liblich. 300p. 1981. lib. bdg. 65.00 perfect bdg (ISBN 0-912702-03-6). Global Eng.

Qualified Products List & Sources. 59th ed. Garnet M. Lieblich. Orig. Title: Military Specifications & Sources. 1980. 65.00x o.p. (ISBN 0-912702-01-X). Global Eng.

Qualified Student: A History of Selective College Admission in America. Harold Wechsler. LC 76-47692. 1977. 26.95 (ISBN 0-471-92441-5, Pub. by Wiley-Interscience). Wiley.

Qualifying Procedures for Health Visitors. Wendy Fader. (General Ser.). (Orig.). 1977. pap. text ed. 13.75x (ISBN 0-85633-111-2, NFER). Humanities.

Qualitative Analysis. Ray U. Brumblay. (Illus., Orig). 1964. pap. 3.95 (ISBN 0-06-460116-1, CO 116, COS). Har-Row.

Qualitative Analysis: Historical & Critical Essays. Paul F. Lazarsfeld. 1971. pap. text ed. 14.95x o.p. (ISBN 0-205-03221-4, 8132216). Allyn.

Qualitative Analysis of Flavor & Fragrance Volatiles by Glass Capillary Gas Chromtography. Walter Jennings & Takayuki Shibamoto. LC 79-26034. 1980. 39.00 (ISBN 0-12-384250-6). Acad Pr.

Qualitative Analysis of Physical Problems. Ed. by M. Gitterman & V. Halpern. LC 80-767. 1981. 24.50 (ISBN 0-12-285150-1). Acad Pr.

Qualitative & Quantitative Methods in Evaluation Research. Ed. by Thomas D. Cook & Charles S. Reichardt. LC 79-20962. (Sage Research Progress Ser. in Evaluation: Vol. 1). (Illus.). 1979. 12.95x (ISBN 0-8039-1300-1); pap. 6.50x (ISBN 0-8039-1301-X). Sage.

Qualitative Biomechanics. Ellen Kreighbaum. (Orig.). 1980. write for info. (ISBN 0-8087-1155-5). Burgess.

Qualitative Change in Human Geography. Ed. by S. S. Duncan. (Illus.). 127p. 1981. 29.00 (ISBN 0-08-025222-2). Pergamon.

Qualitative Evaluation Concepts & Cases in Curriculum Criticism. Ed. by George Willis. LC 77-23647. (Education Ser.). 1978. 21.50 (ISBN 0-8211-2257-6); text ed. 19.50 ten copies (ISBN 0-685-04974-4). McCutchan.

Qualitative Methods. Ed. by Robert B. Smith & Peter K. Manning. (Handbook of Social Science Methods Ser.: Vol. 1). (Illus.). 1981. text ed. 19.50x (ISBN 0-8290-0086-0). Irvington.

Qualitative Methods in Mathematical Analysis. L. E. El'sgol'c. LC 64-16170. (Translations of Mathematical Monographs: Vol. 12). 1980. Repr. of 1968 ed. 27.60 (ISBN 0-8218-1562-8, MMONO-12). Am Math.

Qualitative Theory of Second-Order Dynamic Systems. A. A. Andronov et al. LC 43-4704. 524p. 1973. 64.95 (ISBN 0-470-03195-6). Halsted Pr.

Quality & Accountability: A New Era in American Hospitals. Stanley A. Skillicorn. (Illus.). 143p. 1980. 14.00 (ISBN 0-917636-03-1). Edit Consult.

Quality & Equality: New Levels of Federal Responsibility for Higher Education. Carnegie Commission On Higher Education. 1969. text ed. 1.95 o.p. (ISBN 0-07-010002-0, P&RB). McGraw.

Quality & Equality: Revised Recommendations: New Levels of Federal Responsibility for Higher Education. Carnegie Commission On Higher Education. 1970. 1.95 o.p. (ISBN 0-07-010018-7, P&RB). McGraw.

Quality & Pleasure in Latin Poetry. Ed. by A. J. Woodman & D. West. 184p. 1975. 28.50 (ISBN 0-521-20532-8). Cambridge U Pr.

Quality & Quantity Assurance for Social Workers in Health Care: A Training Manual. Society for Hospital Social Work Directors of the American Hospital Association. LC 80-26488. (Illus.). 96p. (Orig.). 1980. manual 27.50 (ISBN 0-87258-325-2, 2100). Am Hospital.

Quality Assurance & Control in the Manufacture of Metal-Clad U02 Reactor Fuels. (Technical Reports Ser.: No. 173). (Illus.). 1976. pap. 6.00 (ISBN 92-0-155076-6, IAEA). Unipub.

Quality Assurance Auditing for Nuclear Power Plants. 23p. 1980. pap. 4.50 (ISBN 92-0-123380-9, ISP 560, IAEA). Unipub.

Quality Assurance for Computer Software. Robert Dunn & Richard Ullman. (Illus.). 1981. 19.50 (ISBN 0-07-018312-0, P&R&B). McGraw.

Quality Assurance for Safety in Nuclear Power Plants. (IAEA Safety Ser.: No. 50-C-QA). 33p. 1979. pap. 6.00 (ISBN 92-0-123678-6, ISP504, IAEA). Unipub.

Quality Assurance in Ambulatory Care. Paul B. Batalden & J. Paul O'Conner. LC 79-24700. 1980. text ed. 55.00 loose-leaf 3-ring binder (ISBN 0-89443-165-X). Aspen Systems.

Quality Assurance in Ceramic Industries. Ed. by V. D. Frechette et al. 1979. 39.50 (ISBN 0-306-40183-5, Plenum Pr). Plenum Pub.

Quality Assurance in Health Care. Ed. by Richard H. Egdahl & Paul M. Gertman. LC 76-15770. 1976. 28.95 (ISBN 0-912862-23-8). Aspen Systems.

Quality Assurance in Long Term Care. Thomas H. Ainsworth, Jr. LC 77-70432. 1977. 27.50 (ISBN 0-912862-40-8). Aspen Systems.

Quality Assurance in the Procurement of Items & Services for Nuclear Power Plants. (Safety Ser.: No. 50-SG-QA3). 1979. pap. 4.50 (ISBN 92-0-123679-4, ISP 533, IAEA). Unipub.

Quality Assurance Records System - a Safety Guide. (Safety Ser.: No. 50-SG-QA2). 1979. pap. 4.50 (ISBN 92-0-123579-8, ISP 532, IAEA). Unipub.

Quality Assurance Related to Offshore Activities. Norwegian Petroleum Society. 336p. 1980. 95.00x (ISBN 82-7270-009-3, Pub. by Norwegian Info Norway). State Mutual Bk.

Quality Brewing: A Guidebook for the Home Production of Fine Beers. Byron Burch. pap. 2.50 (ISBN 0-9604284-0-2). Joby Bks.

Quality Characteristics of Milled Rice Grown in Different Countries. (IRRI Research Paper Ser.: No. 48). 25p. 1981. pap. 5.00 (ISBN 0-686-69534-8, R 118, IRRI). Unipub.

Quality Circle Handbook. Donald L. Dewar. (Quality Circle Leader Manual & Instructional Guide, Quality Circle Member Manual). 640p. 1980. pap. 60.00 (ISBN 0-937670-03-0). Quality Circle.

Quality Circle Leader Manual & Instructional Guide. Donald L. Dewar. (Quality Circle Member Manual: Quality Circle Handbook). 248p. 1980. pap. 15.00 (ISBN 0-937670-02-2). Quality Circle.

Quality Circle Member Manual. Donald L. Dewar. (Quality Circle Handbook & Quality Circle Leader Manual & Instructional Guide Ser.). (Orig.). 1980. pap. 8.00 (ISBN 0-937670-01-4). Quality Circle.

Quality Circles: Questions & Answers to 100 Frequently Asked Questions. rev. ed. Donald L. Dewar. (Illus.). 1980. pap. 3.25 (ISBN 0-937670-00-6). Quality Circle.

Quality Control & Data Analysis of Binder-Ligand Assays: Radiommunoassay, Enzymeimmmunoassay, Flouroimmunoassay, a Programmed Text. Richard C. Rodgers. (Illus.). 1981. 36.00 (ISBN 0-930914-07-4). Sci Newsletters.

Quality Control & Industrial Statistics. 4th ed. Acheson J. Duncan. 1974. text ed. 22.95 (ISBN 0-256-01558-9). Irwin.

Quality Control & Reliability. N. L. Enrick. 1969. 25.95 (ISBN 0-87245-098-8). Textile Bk.

Quality Control & Reliability. 7th ed. N. L. Enrick. LC 76-54908. (Illus.). 1977. 16.00 (ISBN 0-8311-1115-1). Indus Pr.

Quality Control for Profit. Ronald H. Lester & Norbert Lloyd Enrick. LC 76-58534. (Illus.). 1977. 23.00 (ISBN 0-8311-1117-8). Indus Pr.

Quality Control for the Food Industry Vol. 1: Fundamentals. 3rd ed. Amihud Kramer & Bernard A. Twigg. (Illus.). 1970. text ed. 29.50 (ISBN 0-87055-072-1). AVI.

Quality Control for the Food Industry: Vol. 2, Applications. 3rd ed. Amihud Kramer & Bernard Twigg. (Illus.). 1973. text ed. 29.50 (ISBN 0-87055-127-2). AVI.

Quality Control in Analytical Chemistry. G. Kateman & F. W. Pijpers. (Chemical Analysis Ser.). 320p. 1981. 28.50 (ISBN 0-471-46020-6, Pub. by Wiley-Interscience). Wiley.

Quality Control in Clinical Chemistry. T. P. Whitehead. LC 76-44522. (Quality Control Methods in the Clinical Laboratory Ser). 1977. text ed. 26.95 (ISBN 0-471-94075-5, Pub. by Wiley Medical). Wiley.

Quality Control in Food Service. Marvin E. Thorner & Peter B. Manning. (Illus.). 1976. lib. bdg. 29.50 o.p. (ISBN 0-87055-195-7); pap. text ed. 17.50 (ISBN 0-87055-309-7). AVI.

Quality Control in Laboratory Medicine. John B. Henry & Joseph L. Giegel. LC 77-78559. (Illus.). 250p. 1977. 35.00 (ISBN 0-89352-008-X). Masson Pub.

Quality Control in Nuclear Medicine: Radiopharmaceuticals, Instrumentation & in-Vitro Assays. Ed. by Buck A. Rhodes. (Illus.). 1977. 44.50 o.p. (ISBN 0-8016-4115-2). Mosby.

Quality Control in the Pharmaceutical Industry, 3 vols. Ed. by Murray S. Cooper. Vol. 1, 1972. 39.00 (ISBN 0-12-187601-2); Vol. 2, 1972. 48.00 (ISBN 0-12-187602-0); Vol. 3, 1979. 32.50 (ISBN 0-12-187603-9). Acad Pr.

Quality Controlled Investing: Or How to Avoid the Pick & Pray Method. Frank R. Anderson. LC 78-7607. 1978. 19.95 (ISBN 0-471-04382-6, Pub. by Wiley-Interscience). Wiley.

Quality Day Care: A Handbook of Choices for Parents & Caregivers. Richard Endsley & Marilyn Bradbard. (Illus.). 256p. 1981. 13.95 (Spectrum); pap. 5.95. P-H.

Quality Educators, Ltd. Alain Diot. LC 77-73532. (gr. 1 up). 1977. pap. 1.95 (ISBN 0-8252-0478-X). Quist.

Quality Friendship. Gary Inrig. 192p. (Orig.). 1981. pap. 2.95 (ISBN 0-8024-2891-6). Moody.

Quality Health Care: The Role of Continuing Medical Education. Ed. by Richard H. Egdahl & Paul M. Gertman. LC 77-70434. 1977. 30.00 (ISBN 0-912862-37-8). Aspen Systems.

Quality in Urban Planning & Design. Roy Cresswell. 1979. pap. 35.95 (ISBN 0-408-00363-4). Butterworths.

Quality of Care Assessment & Assurance: An Annotated Bibliography with a Point of View. Norbert Hirschhorn et al. (Medical Bks.). 1979. lib. bdg. 15.95 (ISBN 0-8161-2123-0, Hall Medical). G K Hall.

Quality of Horticultural Products. V. D. Arthey. 1975. 21.95 (ISBN 0-470-03425-4). Halsted Pr.

Quality of Mercy. W. D. Howells. LC 78-20655. (Center for Editions of American Authors, a Selected Edition of W. D. Howells Ser.: Vol. 18). (Illus.). 472p. 1979. 20.00x (ISBN 0-253-35789-6). Ind U Pr.

Quality of Mercy: Amnesties & Traditional Chinese Justice. Brian E. McKnight. LC 80-26650. 224p. 1981. pap. 15.00x (ISBN 0-8248-0736-7). U Pr of Hawaii.

Quality of Mercy: An Autobiography. Mercedes McCambridge. 1981. 10.95 (ISBN 0-8129-0945-3). Times Bks.

Quality of Non Metropolitan Living: Evaluations, Behaviors, & Expectations of Northern Michigan Residents. Robert W. Marans & John D. Wellman. LC 70-69913. (Illus.). 352p. 1978. 17.00 (ISBN 0-87944-226-3); pap. 12.00 (ISBN 0-87944-225-5). U of Mich Soc Res.

Quality of Pig Meat: Progress of Food & Nutrition Science. Mogens Jul & Peter Zeuthen. (Vol. 4, No. 6). 80p. 1981. 20.00 (ISBN 0-08-026831-5). Pergamon.

Quality of Rural Living. Agricultural Board. LC 78-184629. 160p. 1971. pap. 3.75 (ISBN 0-309-01940-0). Natl Acad Pr.

Quality of School Life. Ed. by Joyce L. Epstein. LC 80-5350. 1980. write for info. (ISBN 0-669-03869-5). Lexington Bks.

Quality of the Environment. James L. McCamy. LC 72-80576. 1972. 12.95 (ISBN 0-02-920480-1). Free Pr.

Quality of Working Life: Cases & Commentary, Vol. 2. Ed. by Louis E. Davis & Albert B. Cherns. LC 74-24370. 1975. 19.95 (ISBN 0-02-907330-8); pap. text ed. 9.95 (ISBN 0-02-907340-5). Free Pr.

Quality of Working Life: Problems, Prospects & the State of the Art, Vol.1. Ed. by Louis E. Davis & Albert B. Cherns. LC 74-24369. 1975. 19.95 (ISBN 0-02-907390-1); pap. text ed. 9.95 (ISBN 0-02-907380-4). Free Pr.

Quality Patient Care & the Role of the Clinical Nurse Specialist. Ed. by Rachel Rotkovich. LC 76-5393. 1976. 18.50 (ISBN 0-471-74015-2, Pub. by Wiley Medical). Wiley.

Quality Patient Care Scale. Wandelt. (Illus.). 1974. pap. 7.95 (ISBN 0-685-78465-7). ACC.

Quality Quantity Cuisine, I. Harriet Johnston. LC 75-38975. 350p. 1976. 21.50 (ISBN 0-8436-2079-X). CBI Pub.

Quality Quantity Cuisine II. Harriet Johnston. LC 75-38975. 1976. 21.50 (ISBN 0-8436-2119-2). CBI Pub.

Quality System: A Sourcebook for Managers & Engineers. Frank Caplan. LC 80-969. 256p. 1980. 38.50 (ISBN 0-8019-6972-7). Chilton.

Quality System in Construction. Compiled by American Society of Civil Engineers. 224p. 1974. pap. text ed. 11.00 (ISBN 0-87262-073-5). Am Soc Civil Eng.

Quality Systems Management & Engineering. Frank Caplan. LC 80-969. 256p. Date not set. 38.50x o.p. (ISBN 0-8019-6972-7). Chilton.

Quality, Trending, & Management for the Eighties (QTM-80) Nancy Dixon et al. 236p. 1980. pap. 40.00 (ISBN 0-87258-345-7, 1377). Am Hospital.

Quanah: Leader of the Comanche. Julian May. LC 72-14173. 40p. (gr. 2-5). 1973. PLB 5.95 o.p. (ISBN 0-87191-227-9). Creative Ed.

Quantative Methods. 6th ed. Edward J. Gurry. LC 78-50970. 8.00 (ISBN 0-932788-03-3). Bradley CPA.

Quantification: A History of the Meaning of Measurement in the Natural & Social Sciences. Ed. by Harry Woolf. 1961. text ed. 28.50x (ISBN 0-672-60844-8); pap. text ed. 10.95x (ISBN 0-89197-913-1). Irvington.

Quantification & Psychology: Toward a 'new' History. Ed. by Harvey J. Graff & Paul Monaco. LC 79-3854. 526p. 1980. pap. text ed. 15.25 (ISBN 0-8191-0942-8). U Pr of Amer.

Quantification in History. William O. Aydelotte. LC 76-150517. (History Ser). 1971. pap. 5.95 (ISBN 0-201-00350-3). A-W.

Quantification in the History of Political Thought: Toward a Qualitative Approach. Robert Schware. LC 80-1704. (Contributions in Political Science Ser.: No. 55). 184p. 1981. lib. bdg. 25.00 (ISBN 0-313-22228-2, SPT/). Greenwood.

Quantification of Myocardial Ischemia. Kreuzer Heiss. (Advances in Clinical Cardiology: Vol. 1). 656p. 1980. pap. 36.00x (ISBN 0-933682-00-X). G Witzstrock Pub Hse.

Quantitative Acid-Base Physiology. Poul Kildeberg. (Illus.). 142p. 1981. 15.00. Igaku-Shoin.

Quantitative Aids for Management Decision Making. Colin Palmer. 1979. text ed. 21.50x (ISBN 0-566-00284-1, Pub. by Gower Pub Co England). Renouf.

Quantitative Analtical Chemistry. 4th ed. James S. Fritz & George H. Schenk, Jr. (Illus.). 1979. text ed. 23.95x (ISBN 0-205-06527-9, 6865275). Allyn.

Quantitative Analysis. 2nd ed. Ray U. Brumblay. (Orig.). 1972. pap. 4.50 (ISBN 0-06-460050-5, CO 50, COS). Har-Row.

Quantitative Analysis. 4th ed. R. A. Day, Jr. & Arthur L. Underwood. (Illus.). 1980. text ed. 23.95 (ISBN 0-13-746545-9); pap. 3.95 solutions manual (ISBN 0-13-746560-2); lab manual 9.95 (ISBN 0-13-746552-1). P-H.

Quantitative Analysis. 4th ed. W. C. Pierce et al. LC 58-7905. 1958. 23.95 (ISBN 0-471-68904-1). Wiley.

Quantitative Analysis for Business Decisions. 5th ed. Harold Bierman, Jr. et al. 1977. text ed. 19.95x (ISBN 0-256-01918-5). Irwin.

Quantitative Analysis for Public Policy. John K. Gohagan. (Quantitative Methods for Management). (Illus.). 1980. text ed. 25.00x (ISBN 0-07-023570-8); instructor's manual 8.95 (ISBN 0-07-023571-6); solutions manual 8.95 (ISBN 0-07-023571-6). McGraw.

Quantitative Analysis Methods for Substantive Analysts. Henry F. Defrancesco. LC 80-11355. 448p. 1981. Repr. of 1975 ed. lib. bdg. write for info. (ISBN 0-89874-139-4). Krieger.

Quantitative Analysis of Behavior, 4 vols. Michael Commons et al. 1980. write for info. (ISBN 0-88410-377-3). Ballinger Pub.

Quantitative Analysis of Behavior: Discriminative Properties of Reinforcement Schedules. Michael L. Commons & John A. Nevin. (General Psychology Ser.). Date not set. cancelled (ISBN 0-08-024642-7). Pergamon.

Quantitative Analysis of Organic Mixtures: Part 1, General Principles. T. S. Ma & Robert E. Lang. LC 78-23202. 1979. 28.95 (ISBN 0-471-55800-1, Pub. by Wiley-Interscience). Wiley.

Quantitative Analysis of Social Problems. Ed. by Edward R. Tufte. (Probability & Statistics Ser). 1970. text ed. 13.95 (ISBN 0-201-07610-1). A-W.

Quantitative Analytic Studies in Epilepsy. Ed. by Peter Kellaway & Ingemar S. Petersen. LC 76-22912. 1976. 48.00 (ISBN 0-89004-133-4). Raven.

Quantitative Analytical Chemistry. 3rd ed. James S. Fritz & George H. Schenk, Jr. (Illus.). 704p. 1974. text ed. 17.95x o.s.i. (ISBN 0-205-04464-6, 6942032); sol. manual 1.95x o.s.i. (ISBN 0-685-34568-8); answer bk. avail. o.s.i. (ISBN 0-685-34569-6). Allyn.

Quantitative Analytical Chemistry: Principles & Life Science Applications. George H. Schenk et al. 1977. text ed. 19.95 (ISBN 0-205-05700-4, 6857000); instr's manual o.p. free (ISBN 0-205-05701-2). Allyn.

Quantitative & Accounting Methods. B. Edwards. 192p. 1980. pap. text ed. 14.95x (ISBN 0-7121-1704-0). Intl Ideas.

Quantitative & Statistical Approaches to Geography: A Practical Manual. John A. Matthews. (Pergamon Oxford Geographies). Date not set. 19.21 (ISBN 0-686-66169-9); pap. price not set (ISBN 0-08-024295-2). Pergamon.

Quantitative Approach to Managerial Decisions. Leonard Hein. 1967. 17.95 o.p. (ISBN 0-13-746800-8). P-H.

Quantitative Approaches to Management. 4th ed. Richard I. Levin & Charles A. Kirkpatrick. (Illus.). 1978. text ed. 20.95 (ISBN 0-07-037423-6, C); instructor's manual 4.95 (ISBN 0-07-037424-4); student wkbk. 6.95 (ISBN 0-07-037434-1). McGraw.

Quantitative Approaches to Political Intelligence: The CIA Experience. Richards J. Heuer, Jr. (Westview Special Study). 1978. lib. bdg. 23.50x (ISBN 0-89158-096-4). Westview.

Quantitative Approximation. Ed. by R. A. DeVore & K. Scherer. LC 80-17554. 1980. 22.00 (ISBN 0-12-213650-0). Acad Pr.

Quantitative Aquatic Biological Indicators: Their Use to Monitor Trace Metal & Organochlorine Pollution. David J. Phillips. (Illus.). xii, 460p. 1980. 65.00x (ISBN 0-85334-884-7). Burgess-Intl Ideas.

Quantitative Aspects of Chemical Pharmacology. 256p. 1980. 80.00x (ISBN 0-85664-892-2, Pub. by Croom Helm England). State Mutual Bk.

Quantitative Aspects of Risk Assessment in Chemical Carcinogenesis. Ed. by J. Clemmensen. (Illus.). 350p. 1980. pap. 34.40 (ISBN 0-387-09584-5). Springer-Verlag.

Quantitative Aspects of Science & Technology. Aldridge. LC 67-22016. 1967. pap. text ed. 11.95x (ISBN 0-675-09699-5). Merrill.

Quantitative Chemical Analysis & Inorganic Preparations. 2nd ed. R. M. Caven. 1962. 19.95x (ISBN 0-686-63579-5). Intl Ideas.

Quantitative Concepts for Management Decision Making Without Algorithms. Gary D. Eppen & F. J. Gould. 1979. 21.95 (ISBN 0-13-746602-1). P-H.

Quantitative Decision-Making, Vol. 3. Albert J. Klee. Ed. by P. Aarne Vesilind. (Design & Management for Resource Recovery Ser.). 1980. 39.00 (ISBN 0-250-40313-7). Ann Arbor Science.

Quantitative Decision-Making for Business. Gilbert Gordon & Israel Pressman. LC 77-25831. (Illus.). 1978. ref. ed. 21.00 (ISBN 0-13-746701-X). P-H.

Quantitative Economic Policy & Planning: Theory & Models of Economic Control. new ed. Nicolas Spulber & Ira Horowitz. (Illus.). 550p. 1976. text ed. 18.95x (ISBN 0-393-09181-3). Norton.

Quantitative Economic Theory: A Synthetic Approach. Hans Brems. LC 77-17202. 514p. 1979. Repr. of 1968 ed. lib. bdg. 19.00 o.p. (ISBN 0-88275-646-X). Krieger.

Quantitative Genetics in Maize Breeding. Arnel R. Hallauer & J. B. Miranda, Jr. (Illus.). 1981. write for info. (ISBN 0-8138-1520-7). Iowa St U Pr.

Quantitative Geography in Britain: Retrospect & Prospect. Ed. by Neil Wrigley & Robert J. Bennett. 448p. 1981. price not set (ISBN 0-7100-0731-0). Routledge & Kegan.

Quantitative Industrial Hygiene. Harry J. Beaulieu & Roy M. Buchan. 1981. lib. bdg. 17.50 (ISBN 0-8240-7180-8). Garland Pub.

Quantitative International Politics. Ed. by J. D. Singer. LC 66-23083. 1968. 14.95 o.s.i. (ISBN 0-02-928940-8). Free Pr.

Quantitative Laboratory Experiments in General Chemistry. Francis Collier et al. LC 75-26087. (Illus.). 288p. 1976. pap. 10.50 (ISBN 0-395-18982-9). HM.

Quantitative Layer-by-Layer Perimetry: An Extented Analysis. Jay M. Enoch et al. (Current Ophthalmology Monographs). 1980. 29.50 (ISBN 0-8089-1282-8). Grune.

Quantitative Management Methods for Practicing Engineers. Scott Poage. LC 77-133267. 1970. 11.95 (ISBN 0-389-00531-2); pap. 9.95 (ISBN 0-8436-0334-8). CBI Pub.

Quantitative Measurements & Chemical Equilibria. Ernest H. Swift & Eliot A. Butler. LC 78-161009. (Chemistry Ser.). (Illus.). 1972. text ed. 31.95x (ISBN 0-7167-0170-7); tchrs' manual avail. W H Freeman.

Quantitative Methods for Administration. Colin E. Bell. 1977. 19.25x (ISBN 0-256-01875-8). Irwin.

Quantitative Methods for Business Decisions. Christopher K. McKenna. (Quantitative Methods for Management). (Illus.). 1980. text ed. 18.95 (ISBN 0-07-045351-9); instrs.' manual 4.95 (ISBN 0-07-045352-7). McGraw.

Quantitative Methods for Decision Making in Business. 3rd ed. Richard E. Trueman. LC 80-65810. 384p. 1981. text ed. 19.95 (ISBN 0-03-051356-1). Dryden Pr.

Quantitative Methods for Management. Ross H. Johnson & Paul R. Winn. LC 75-25239. (Illus.). 448p. 1976. text ed. 19.95 (ISBN 0-395-20633-2); inst. manual with solutions 2.00 (ISBN 0-395-20634-0). HM.

Quantitative Methods for Managerial Decisions. Kenneth S. Brown & Jack B. ReVelle. LC 76-10408. (Illus.). 1978. text ed. 17.95 (ISBN 0-201-06448-0). A-W.

Quantitative Methods in Construction Management & Design. J. F. Woodward. (Illus.). 1976. 27.50x (ISBN 0-333-17720-7); pap. text ed. 18.50x (ISBN 0-333-18602-8). Scholium Intl.

Quantitative Methods in Geography: An Introduction to Spatial Analysis. Peter J. Taylor. LC 75-26097. (Illus.). 384p. 1977. text ed. 19.95 (ISBN 0-395-18699-4). HM.

Quantitative Methods in Librarianship: Standards, Research, Management. Ed. by Irene B. Hoadley & Alice S. Clark. LC 73-149962. (Contributions in Librarianship & Information Science: No. 4). 256p. 1972. lib. bdg. 17.95 (ISBN 0-8371-6061-8, HOQ/). Greenwood.

Quantitative Methods in Management: Text & Cases. Paul A. Vatter et al. 1978. text ed. 20.95 (ISBN 0-256-02006-X). Irwin.

Quantitative Methods in Public Administration. Leonard D. Goodisman. LC 79-52724. 1979. pap. text ed. 12.25 (ISBN 0-8191-0782-4). U Pr of Amer.

Quantitative Models for Business Decisions. No Kyoon Kwak & Stephen A. DeLurgio. LC 78-27175. (Illus.). 1979. text ed. 19.95 (ISBN 0-87872-215-7). Duxbury Pr.

Quantitative Models of Commodity Markets. Ed. by Walter C. Labys. LC 74-13784. 400p. 1975. text ed. 25.00 o.p. (ISBN 0-88410-254-8). Ballinger Pub.

Quantitative Nuclear Cardiography. Ed. by Richard N. Pierson, Jr. et al. LC 74-201990. 304p. 1975. text ed. 37.50 o.p. (ISBN 0-471-68950-5, Pub. by Wiley Medical). Wiley.

Quantitative Practice of Anesthesia: Use of Closed Circuit. (Illus.). 220p. 1981. write for info. (5200-4). Williams & Wilkins.

Quantitative Problems in Biochemical Sciences. 2nd ed. Rex Montgomery & Charles A. Swenson. LC 75-42234. (Illus.). 1976. text ed. 10.95x (ISBN 0-7167-0178-2); answer bk. avail. W H Freeman.

Quantitative Problems in Biochemistry. 6th ed. E. A. Dawes. (Illus.). 340p. 1981. text ed. 32.00 (ISBN 0-582-44402-0). Longman.

Quantitative Problems in Physical & Chemical Biology: A Work Book. D. Siva Sankar. Date not set. price not set (ISBN 0-685-77285-3). PJD Pubns.

Quantitative Radiation Biology. K. G. Zimmer. Tr. by H. D. Griffith. (Illus.). 1961. 10.75 o.s.i. (ISBN 0-02-855800-6). Hafner.

Quantitative Scanning Electron Microscopy. Ed. by D. B. Holt et al. 1975. 79.00 (ISBN 0-12-353850-5). Acad Pr.

Quantitative Seismology: Theory & Methods, Vol. I. Keiiti Aki & Paul G. Richards. LC 79-17434. (Series of Books in Geology). (Illus.). 1980. text ed. 37.95x (ISBN 0-7167-1058-7). W H Freeman.

Quantitative Seismology: Theory & Methods, Vol. II. Keiiti Aki & Paul G. Richards. LC 79-17434. (Series of Books in Geology). (Illus.). 1980. text ed. 37.95x (ISBN 0-7167-1059-5). W H Freeman.

Quantitative Stereology. E. E. Underwood. 1970. 21.95 (ISBN 0-201-07650-0). A-W.

Quantitative Stratigraphic Correlation: Proceedings of the 6th Geochautauqua, Syracuse University, October 1977, Vol. 4, No. 3. Ed. by D. F. Merriam. (Illus.). 112p. 1979. pap. 41.25 (ISBN 0-08-023979-X). Pergamon.

Quantitative Techniques. C. R. Kothari. 1979. text ed. 18.95 (ISBN 0-7069-0642-X, Pub. by Vikas India). Advent Bk.

Quantitative Techniques for Business Decisions. Rodney D. Johnson & Bernard R. Siskin. (Illus.). 544p. 1976. 21.00 (ISBN 0-13-746990-X). P-H.

Quantitative Techniques for Hospital Planning & Control. John R. Griffith. LC 72-3550. (Illus.). 308p. 1972. 18.95 (ISBN 0-669-84087-4). Lexington Bks.

Quantitative Techniques for Management Decisions. Frank S. McLaughlin & Robert C. Pickhardt. LC 78-69586. (Illus.). 1978. text ed. 19.50 (ISBN 0-395-26669-6); inst. manual 2.90 (ISBN 0-395-26668-8). HM.

Quantities. Richard Howard. LC 62-18342. (Wesleyan Poetry Program: Vol. 16). (Orig.). 1962. 10.00x (ISBN 0-8195-2016-0, Pub. by Wesleyan U Pr); pap. 4.95 (ISBN 0-8195-1016-5). Columbia U Pr.

Quantitive Studies in Life Science. S. J. Poti. 250p. 1980. text ed. 25.00x (ISBN 0-7069-1247-0, Pub by Vikas India). Advent Bk.

Quantity Cooking. Thomas Mario. (Illus.). 1978. lib. bdg. 25.50 o.p. (ISBN 0-87055-236-8); pap. text ed. 16.00 (ISBN 0-87055-308-9). AVI.

Quantity Food Production. 3rd ed. Lendal H. Kotschevar. (Illus.). 1975. 33.60x (ISBN 0-85334-632-1). Intl Ideas.

Quantity Food Purchasing Guide. rev. ed. Francis N. Beau. 1974. pap. 9.95 spiral bdg. (ISBN 0-8436-2046-3). CBI Pub.

Quantity Food Sanitation. 3rd ed. Karla Longree. LC 80-11551. 1980. 27.50 (ISBN 0-471-06424-6, Pub. by Wiley Interscience). Wiley.

Quantity in Historical Phonology. K. Arnason. LC 79-41363. (Cambridge Studies in Linguistics: No. 30). (Illus.). 256p. 1980. 44.50 (ISBN 0-521-23040-3). Cambridge U Pr.

Quantity of Money. H. Visser. LC 75-4762. 294p. 1975. text ed. 18.95 (ISBN 0-470-90845-9). Halsted Pr.

Quantrell's Raiders. Frank Gruber. 1981. pap. 1.95 (ISBN 0-451-09735-1, J9735, Sig). NAL.

Quantrill & His Civil War Guerrillas. Carl W. Breiham. LC 59-8213. 174p. 1959. 6.95 (ISBN 0-8040-0256-8, SB). Swallow.

Quantum & Fermion Differential Geometry, Pt. A. Robert Hermann. (Interdisciplinary Mathematics Ser.: No. 16). 1977. 18.00 (ISBN 0-915692-22-8). Math Sci Pr.

Quantum Chemistry. Henry Eyring et al. 1944. 22.95 (ISBN 0-471-24981-5). Wiley.

Quantum Chemistry. 2nd ed. Ira N. Levine. 592p. 1974. text ed. 26.95 (ISBN 0-205-04305-4, 6843050). Allyn.

Quantum Chemistry: A Scientific Melting Pot. Per-Olov Lowdin et al. (International Journal of Quantum Chemistry Ser.: Vol. 12, Suppl.). 1978. 37.95 (ISBN 0-471-05248-5, Pub. by Wiley-Interscience). Wiley.

Quantum Chromodynamics. Ed. by William Frazer & Frank Henyey. LC 79-54969. (AIP Conference Ser.; Particles & Fields Sub-Ser.: No. 55; No. 18). (Illus.). 1979. lib. bdg. 20.50 (ISBN 0-88318-154-1). Am Inst Physics.

Quantum Chromodynamics: Proceedings. Ed. by J. L. Alonso & R. Tarrach. (Lecture Notes in Physics: Vol. 113). 306p. 1980. pap. 22.00 (ISBN 0-387-09731-7). Springer-Verlag.

Quantum Effects in Organic Chemistry. Peter Hedvig. 1975. 43.50 (ISBN 0-12-336450-7). Acad Pr.

Quantum Electrochemistry. J. O'M Backris & S. U. Khan. 480p. 1979. 49.50 (ISBN 0-306-31143-7, Plenum Pr). Plenum Pub.

Quantum Electrodynamics. J. Bialyniccy-Birula. LC 74-4473. 541p. 1975. text ed. 44.00 (ISBN 0-08-017188-5). Pergamon.

Quantum Electronics. 2nd ed. Amnon Yariv. LC 75-1392. 544p. 1975. text ed. 34.95 (ISBN 0-471-97176-6). Wiley.

Quantum Electronics-Vol. 2: Maser Amplifiers & Oscillators. V. M. Fain & Ya Khanin. 1969. 32.00 (ISBN 0-08-012238-8). Pergamon.

Quantum Field Theoretical Methods in Statistical Physics. A. A. Abrikosov et al. (Vol. 4). 1965. text ed. 16.25 o.p. (ISBN 0-08-010406-1); pap. text ed. 8.75 o.p. (ISBN 0-08-013470-X). Pergamon.

Quantum Field Theory, Vol. 1. A. Visconti. LC 66-18237. 1969. 37.00 (ISBN 0-08-011821-6). Pergamon.

Quantum Field Theory & Hydrodynamics. Ed. by D. V. Skobel'tsyn. LC 66-12629. (P. N. Lebedev Physics Institute Ser.: Vol. 29). 271p. 1967. 32.50 (ISBN 0-306-10768-6, Consultants). Plenum Pub.

Quantum Fields-Algebras, Processes. Ed. by L. Streit. (Illus.). 144p. 1981. 40.20 (ISBN 0-387-81607-0). Springer-Verlag.

Quantum Flavordynamics, Quantum Chromodynamics & Unified Theories. Ed. by K. T. Mahanthappa & James Randa. (NATO Advanced Study Institute Ser., Ser. B: Physics: Vol. 54). 505p. 1980. 59.50 (ISBN 0-306-40436-2, Plenum Pr). Plenum Pub.

Quantum Gods. Jeff Love. 1979. pap. 7.95 (ISBN 0-87728-476-8). Weiser.

Quantum Gravity: An Oxford Symposium. Ed. by C. J. Isham et al. (Illus.). 600p. 1975. 49.95x (ISBN 0-19-851943-5). Oxford U Pr.

Quantum Mechanical Three-Body Problem. E. W. Schmid & H. Ziegelmann. 222p. 1974. text ed. 40.00 (ISBN 0-08-018240-2). Pergamon.

Quantum Mechanics, 2 vols. Claude Cohen-Tannoudji et al. LC 76-5874. 1978. Vol. 1. 37.50 (ISBN 0-471-16432-1, Pub. by Wiley-Interscience); 34.50 (ISBN 0-471-16434-8); Vol. 1. pap. 21.95 (ISBN 0-471-16433-X); Vol. 2. pap. 20.50 (ISBN 0-471-16435-6). Wiley.

Quantum Mechanics. A. Messiah. Vol. 1, 1961. pap. 16.95x (ISBN 0-471-59766-X); Vol. 2 1962. pap. 14.95x (ISBN 0-471-59768-6). Halsted Pr.

Quantum Mechanics. John L. Powell & B. Crasemann. (Illus.). 1961. 24.95 (ISBN 0-201-05920-7). A-W.

Quantum Mechanics: A Physical World Picture. Antal Muller. LC 73-18062. 1974. text ed. 28.00 (ISBN 0-08-017936-3). Pergamon.

Quantum Mechanics: An Introduction. J. G. Taylor. (Unwin Studies in Physics & Applie Mathematics Ser.). 1970. text ed. 6.95x o.p. (ISBN 0-04-530014-3). Allen Unwin.

Quantum Mechanics for Applied Physics & Engineering. A. T. Fromhold. LC 80-19001. 1981. 34.50 (ISBN 0-12-269150-4). Acad Pr.

Quantum Mechanics in Chemistry. 3rd ed. Melvin Hanna. 1980. pap. text ed. 12.95 (ISBN 0-8053-3705-9, 33708); pap. text ed. 9.95 (33705). Benjamin-Cummings.

Quantum Mechanics in Hilbert Space. 2nd ed. Eduard Prugovecki. LC 80-534. (Pure & Applied Mathematics Ser.). 1981. write for info. (ISBN 0-12-566060-X). Acad Pr.

Quantum Mechanics of Molecular Rate Processes. Raphael D. Levine. 1969. 45.00x (ISBN 0-19-855343-9). Oxford U Pr.

Quantum Mechanics Primer: An Elementary Introduction to the Formal Theory of Non-Relativistic Quantum Mechanics. Daniel T. Gillespie. LC 74-3107. 137p. (Orig.). 1973. pap. text ed. 15.95 (ISBN 0-470-29912-6). Halsted Pr.

Quantum Mechanics: Principles & Applications. Marcelo Alonso & Henry Valk. LC 73-6504. 1973. pap. text ed. 15.95 (ISBN 0-201-00244-2). A-W.

Quantum Optics. Ed. by R. J. Glauber. (Italian Physical Society: Course 42). 1970. 67.00 (ISBN 0-12-368842-6). Acad Pr.

Quantum Pharmacology. Richards. 1977. text ed. 39.95 (ISBN 0-408-70919-7). Butterworths.

Quantum Physicists & an Introduction to Their Physics. William H. Cropper. 1970. pap. 6.95x (ISBN 0-19-500861-8). Oxford U Pr.

Quantum Physics. Rolf Winter. 1979. text ed. 23.95x (ISBN 0-534-00697-3). Wadsworth Pub.

Quantum Physics & Parapsychology: Proceedings. International Conference, Geneva, 1974. Ed. by Laura Oteri. LC 75-14867. 1975. 13.50 (ISBN 0-912328-26-6). Parapsych Foun.

Quantum Physics of Atoms, Molecules, Solids, Nuclei, & Particles. Robert Eisberg & Robert Resnick. LC 74-1195. 816p. 1974. text ed. 29.95 (ISBN 0-471-23464-8). Wiley.

Quantum Radiation of Radioactive Nuclides. new ed. N. G. Gusev & P. P. Dimitriev. 1979. text ed. 140.00 (ISBN 0-08-023058-X). Pergamon.

Quantum Radio Frequency Physics. L. D. Stepin. 1965. 17.50x (ISBN 0-262-19016-8). MIT Pr.

Quantum States of Atoms, Molecules, & Solids. M. A. Morrison et al. 204p. 1976. 28.95 (ISBN 0-13-747980-8). P-H.

Quantum Statistical Mechanics & Lie Group Harmonic Analysis, Pt. A. Norman Hurt & R. Hermann. (Lie Groups; History, Frontiers & Applications: Vol. X). 1980. text ed. 30.00x (ISBN 0-915692-30-9, QC174.8.H87). Math Sci Pr.

Quantum Theory. Ed. by D. R. Bates. Incl. Pt. 1. Elements. 1961. 51.50 o.p. (ISBN 0-12-081401-3); Pt. 2. Aggregates of Particles. 1961. 51.50 o.p. (ISBN 0-12-081402-1); Pt. 3. Radiation & High Energy Physics. 1961. 51.50 o.p. (ISBN 0-12-081403-X). Acad Pr.

Quantum Theory & Beyond: Essays & Discussions Arising from a Colloquium. Ed. by E. W. Bastin. LC 77-127237. (Illus.). 1971. 43.00 (ISBN 0-521-07956-X). Cambridge U Pr.

Quantum Theory of Chemical Reactions: Solvent Effect, Reaction Mechanisms, Photochemical Processes, Vol. 11. Ed. by Raymond Daudel et al. 340p. 1980. PLB 42.00 (ISBN 90-277-1182-8). Kluwer Boston.

Quantum Theory of Light. Rodney Loudon. (Illus.). 350p. 1973. 47.50 (ISBN 0-19-851130-2). Oxford U Pr.

Quantum Theory of Scattering Processes, Pt. 2. John E. Farina. LC 72-10162. 164p. 1973. text ed. 42.00 (ISBN 0-08-017047-1); pap. text ed. 19.50 (ISBN 0-08-018985-7). Pergamon.

Quantum Theory of Scattering Processes, Pt. 1: General Principles & Advanced Topics. John E. Farina. Ed. by R. McWeeny. LC 74-22357. 144p. 1976. text ed. 34.00 (ISBN 0-08-018130-9). Pergamon.

Quantum Theory of Solids. Charles Kittel. LC 63-20633. 1963. 29.95 (ISBN 0-471-49025-3). Wiley.

Quantum Theory of Solids. Rudolf E. Peierls. (International Series of Monographs on Physics). (Orig.). 1964. pap. 29.95x (ISBN 0-19-851240-6). Oxford U Pr.

Quarantine. Nicholas Hasluck. LC 78-14160. 1979. 8.95 o.p. (ISBN 0-03-044201-X). HR&W.

Quare Do's in Appalachia: Thirty Legends & Memorats of Eastern Kentucky. Berniece T. Hiser. LC 78-56593. 1978. pap. 6.00 (ISBN 0-933302-32-0). Pikeville Coll.

Quark Maneuver. Mike Jahn. (Orig.). 1977. pap. 1.50 o.p. (ISBN 0-685-75029-9, 345-25171-7-150). Ballantine.

Quarks & Leptons: Cargese Nineteen Seventy-Nine. Ed. by Maurice Levy et al. (NATO Advanced Study Institutes Ser. (Series B--Physics): Vol. 61). 760p. 1981. 75.00 (ISBN 0-306-40560-1, Plenum Pr). Plenum Pub.

Quarr Abbey & Its Lands, 1132-1631. S. F. Hockey. 1970. text ed. 12.00x (ISBN 0-7185-1087-9, Leicester). Humanities.

Quarrel of Witches. Margaret Storey. (Illus.). (ps-5). 1970. 7.95 o.p. (ISBN 0-571-09416-3, Pub. by Faber & Faber). Merrimack Bk Serv.

Quarrel Within: Art & Morality in Milton's Poetry. Lawrence Hyman. LC 76-189559. 1972. 11.00 (ISBN 0-8046-9018-9, Natl U). Kennikat.

Quarreling Kids: Stop the Fighting & Develop Loving Relationship Within the Family. Leah K. Acus. (Illus.). 192p. 1981. 10.95 (ISBN 0-13-748012-1, Spec); pap. 5.95 (ISBN 0-13-748004-0). P-H.

Quarry. Friedrich Durrenmatt. 1979. pap. 1.95 (ISBN 0-446-79909-2). Warner Bks.

Quarry: New Poems. Richard Eberhart. 1964. 9.95 (ISBN 0-19-500536-8). Oxford U Pr.

Quarrying, Opencast, & Alluvial Mining. John Sinclair. (Illus.). 1969. 59.60x (ISBN 0-444-20040-1). Intl Ideas.

Quarter Century of International Social Science: Internal Social Science Council. Ed. by Stein Rokkan. 1979. text ed. 56.25x (ISBN 0-391-01930-9). Humanities.

Quarter Horse Winner. Elizabeth Van Steenwyk. Ed. by Ann Fay. LC 79-28490. (Springboard Bk.). (Illus.). 64p. (gr. 3-7). 1980. 5.75g (ISBN 0-8075-6707-8). A Whitman.

Quarter-Midget Racing Is for Me. Mark Lerner. LC 81-41. (Sports for Me Bks.). (Illus.). (gr. 2-5). 1981. PLB 5.95 (ISBN 0-8225-1125-8). Lerner Pubns.

Quarterback Gamble. William C. Gault. LC 72-102743. (gr. 4 up). 1973. op o.p. (ISBN 0-525-37940-1, Anytime Bks); pap. 0.95 o.p. (ISBN 0-525-45015-7, Anytime Bks). Dutton.

Quarterbacks. Sam Masegawa. LC 74-23143. (Stars of the NFL Ser.). (gr. 4-12). 1975. PLB 7.95 (ISBN 0-87191-417-4). Creative Ed.

Quartered Questions & Queries. Monika Varma. 9.00 (ISBN 0-89253-747-7); flexible cloth 4.00 (ISBN 0-89253-748-5). Ind-US Inc.

Quarternary Stratigraphy of North America: Proceedings. Quarternary Stratigraphy Symposium, 1975. Ed. by W. C. Mahaney. 1976. 47.00 (ISBN 0-12-787045-8). Acad Pr.

Quartet. Jean Rhys. LC 77-138795. 1971. 8.95 o.s.i. (ISBN 0-06-013537-9, HarpT). Har-Row.

Quartet: A Book of Stories, Plays, Poems, & Critical Essays. 2nd ed. Ed. by Harold P. Simonson. 1973. pap. text ed. 14.50 scp o.p. (ISBN 0-06-046184-5, HarpC); instructor's manual free o.p. (ISBN 0-06-366185-3). Har-Row.

Quarto, Eighteen Ninety-Six to Ninety-Eight, 4 vols. in 2. Ed. by Peter Stansky. Rodney Shewan. (Aesthetic Movement & the Arts & Crafts Movement Ser.: Periodicals: Vol. 6). 1979. Set. lib. bdg. 53.00 each (ISBN 0-8240-3622-0). Garland Pub.

Quasars, Pulsars, & Black Holes: A Scientific Detective Story. Frederic Golden. LC 75-37646. (Illus.). 128p. 1976. 9.95 o.p. (ISBN 0-684-14501-4, ScribJ). Scribner.

Quasi-Ideals in Rings & Semi-Groups. Otto Steinfeld. LC 79-308570. (Illus.). 154p. 1978. 17.50x (ISBN 963-05-1696-9). Intl Pubns Serv.

Quasi-Stellar Objects. Geoffrey Burbidge & Margaret Burbidge. LC 67-17457. (Illus.). 1967. 18.95x (ISBN 0-7167-0321-1). W H Freeman.

Quasiconformal Mappings & Riemann Surfaces. Samuel L. Krushkal. LC 79-995. (Scripta Series in Mathematics). 1979. 27.95 (ISBN 0-470-26695-3). Halsted Pr.

Quaternary Geology. D. Q. Bowen. (Illus.). 224p. 1978. 39.00 (ISBN 0-08-020601-8); pap. 13.75 (ISBN 0-08-020409-0). Pergamon.

Quaternary History of the Irish Sea: Geological Journal Special Issue, No. 7. C. Kidson & M. J. Tooley. (Liverpool Geological Society & the Manchester Geological Association). 356p. 1980. 64.95 (ISBN 0-471-27754-1, Pub. by Wiley-Interscience). Wiley.

Quaternary of the United States. Ed. by Herbert E. Wright & D. G. Frey. (Illus.). 1965. 45.00x (ISBN 0-691-08021-6). Princeton U Pr.

Quaternary Plant Ecology: Fourteenth Symposium of the British Ecological Society, University of Cambridge 28-30 March 1972. Ed. by H. J. Birks. LC 73-10215. (British Ecological Society Symposia Ser.). 1974. 61.95 (ISBN 0-470-07534-1). Halsted Pr.

Quaternion: Stories, Poems, Plays, Essays. James M. Mellard. 1978. pap. 9.95x (ISBN 0-673-15102-6). Scott F.

Quayside Camera, 1845-1917. Basil Greenhill. LC 74-20469. (Illus.). 112p. 1975. 14.95x (ISBN 0-8195-4088-9, Pub. by Wesleyan U Pr). Columbia U Pr.

Que De las Drogas, el Ocultismo y la Astrologia? Lambert T. Dolphin. Tr. by Ana Maria Swenson. 1977. Repr. of 1972 ed. 1.45 (ISBN 0-311-46034-8). Casa Bautista.

Que divertido! Mary H. Jackson. (gr. 9-12). 1978. pap. text ed. 4.80 (ISBN 0-205-05881-7, 4258819). Allyn.

Que Nos Dice la Biblia. Henrietta C. Mears. Ed. by Esteban Marosi. Tr. by David Powell from Eng. 624p. (Span.). 1979. pap. text ed. 6.95 (ISBN 0-8297-0485-X). Vida Pubs.

Que Paso Con Estos Pecados? P. A. Deiros. 1979. pap. 1.95 (ISBN 0-311-42063-X). Casa Bautista.

Que Se Ponga De Pie el Verdadero Farsante! Tr. by Ethell Barrett. (Spanish Bks.). (Span.). 1978. 1.75 (ISBN 0-8297-0850-2). Life Pubs Intl.

Que Todos Debemos Saber Sobre la Homosexualidad. Jorge A. Leon. LC 76-19206. 136p. (Orig., Span.). 1976. pap. 2.95 (ISBN 0-89922-071-1). Edit Caribe.

Quebec & the Constitution: Nineteen Sixty to Nineteen Seventy Eight. Edward McWhinney. 1979. 15.00x o.p. (ISBN 0-8020-5456-0); pap. 5.95 (ISBN 0-8020-6364-0). U of Toronto Pr.

Queen & Her Court. Jerrold Packard. (Illus.). 256p. 1981. 12.50 (ISBN 0-684-16796-4, ScribT). Scribner.

Queen & Her Court: A Guide to the British Monarchy Today. Jerrold M. Packard. 256p. 1981. 14.95 (ISBN 0-684-16796-4, ScribT). Scribner.

Queen & I. Barbara J. Crane. (Crane Reading System-English Ser.). (Illus.). (gr. k-2). 1977. pap. text ed. 2.80 (ISBN 0-89075-093-9). Crane Pub Co.

Queen & Lord M. Jean Plaidy. 1978. pap. 1.75 o.p. (ISBN 0-449-23605-6, Crest). Fawcett.

Queen & Pawn Endings. Yuri Averbakh. 1976. 15.95 (ISBN 0-7134-3041-9). David & Charles.

Queen & Rosie Randall. Helen Oxenbury. LC 78-10375. (Illus.). (gr. k-3). 1979. 7.95 (ISBN 0-688-22171-8); PLB 7.63 (ISBN 0-688-32171-2). Morrow.

Queen Elizabeth & the Making of Policy, 1572-1588. Wallace T. MacCaffrey. LC 80-8564. 536p. 1981. 40.00x (ISBN 0-691-05324-3); pap. 15.00x (ISBN 0-691-10112-4). Princeton U Pr.

Queen Elizabeth & the Revolt of the Netherlands. Charles Wilson. LC 76-119009. 1970. 18.50x (ISBN 0-520-01744-7). U of Cal Pr.

Queen Elizabeth First: A Biography. J. E. Neale. 1957. pap. 3.95 (ISBN 0-385-09312-8, A105, Anch). Doubleday.

Queen Elizabeth in Drama & Related Studies. Frederick S. Boas. 212p. 1980. Repr. lib. bdg. 25.00 (ISBN 0-8492-3588-X). R West.

Queen Elizabeth Park & the Bloedel Conservatory. Daniel Murphy. Ed. by M. Campbell. (Illus.). 50p. (Orig.). 1981. pap. 4.95 (ISBN 0-88839-088-2). Hancock Hse.

Queen for a Day. Barbara Cohen. LC 80-28115. 160p. (gr. 5 up). 1981. 7.95 (ISBN 0-688-00437-7); PLB 7.63 (ISBN 0-688-00438-5). Morrow.

Queen Is Dead. Glenn Kezer. (Orig.). 1979. pap. 1.75 o.s.i. (ISBN 0-515-04856-9). Jove Pubns.

Queen Is in the Garbage. Lila Karp. LC 72-89665. 1969. 6.95 (ISBN 0-8149-0249-9). Vanguard.

Queen Juliana: The Richest Woman in the World. William Hoffman. Ed. by Carol Hill. LC 79-1827. 1979. 11.95 (ISBN 0-15-146531-2). HarBraceJ.

Queen of a Lonely Country. Megan Castell. 240p. 1980. pap. 2.25 (ISBN 0-671-82732-4). PB.

Queen of Cowtowns: Dodge City. Stanley Vestal. LC 51-11962. (Illus.). 1972. pap. 3.45 (ISBN 0-8032-5758-9, BB 551, Bison). U of Nebr Pr.

Queen of Eene. Jack Prelutsky. LC 77-17311. (Illus.). (gr. k-3). 1978. 7.95 (ISBN 0-688-80144-7); PLB 7.63 (ISBN 0-688-84144-9). Greenwillow.

Queen of Populists: The Story of Mary Elizabeth Lease. Richard Stiller. LC 78-94801. (Women of America Ser). (Illus.). (gr. 6-9). 1970. 6.95 o.p. (ISBN 0-690-66252-1, TYC-J). T Y Crowell.

Queen of Shaba: The Story of an African Leopard. Joy Adamson. LC 80-7931. (Helen & Kurt Wolff Bk). (Illus.). 256p. 1980. 14.95 (ISBN 0-15-175651-1). HarBraceJ.

Queen V. Rook Minor Piece Endings. Yuri Averbakh. 1978. 22.50 (ISBN 0-7134-0866-9, Pub. by Batsford England). David & Charles.

Queen Victoria. Cecil Woodman-Smith. 1974. pap. 1.75 o.s.i. (ISBN 0-440-17318-3). Dell.

Queen Victoria. Lesley Young. (Profiles Ser.). (Illus.). 64p. (gr. 3-6). 1981. 7.95 (ISBN 0-241-10480-7, Pub. by Hamish Hamilton England). David & Charles.

Queen Victoria's Jubillees Eighteen Eighty-Seven & Eighteen Ninety-Seven. Ed. by Caroline Chapman & Paul Roben. (Illus.). 1978. 15.95 o.p. (ISBN 0-670-58417-7, Debrett's Peerage, Ltd.). Viking Pr.

Queen Vs Louis Riel. Desmond Morton. LC 73-91562. (Social History of Canada Ser.). (Illus.). 1974. pap. 7.50 (ISBN 0-8020-6232-6). U of Toronto Pr.

Queen Who Flew. Ford Madox Ford. LC 65-23176. (Illus.). (gr. 4-6). 1965. 4.35 (ISBN 0-8076-0324-4). Braziller.

Queen Zix of Ix: The Story of the Magic Cloak. L. Frank Baum. (Illus.). 7.50 (ISBN 0-8446-0026-1). Peter Smith.

Queen's Gambit Declined. Sergiu Samarian. 1975. 18.95 (ISBN 0-7134-2865-1, Pub. by Batsford England). David & Charles.

Queen's Gambit Declined: Semi-Slav. T. D. Harding. (Illus.). 176p. 1981. pap. 18.50 (ISBN 0-7134-2448-6, Pub. by Batsford England). David & Charles.

Queen's Lady. Patricia Parkes. 504p. 1981. 12.95 (ISBN 0-312-66008-1). St Martin.

Queen's Necklace. (Classics Illus. Ser.). (Illus.). pap. 0.59 o.p. (ISBN 0-685-74105-2, 165). Guild Bks.

Queen's Peace. David Ascoli. (Origins & Development of the Metropolitan Police 1829-1979). (Illus.). 364p. 1980. 30.00 (ISBN 0-241-10296-0, Pub. by Hamish Hamilton England). David & Charles.

Queen's Play. Dorothy Dunnett. 1974. pap. 2.75 (ISBN 0-445-08496-0). Popular Lib.

Queen's Royal. John Quigley. 1978. pap. 2.25 o.p. (ISBN 0-449-23574-2, Crest). Fawcett.

Queer, the Quaint, the Quizzical. Francis H. Stauffer. LC 68-22052. 1968. Repr. of 1882 ed. 15.00 (ISBN 0-8103-3096-2). Gale.

Queer Things About Japan, to Which Is Added a Life of the Emperor of Japan. 4th ed. Douglas Sladen. LC 68-26607. (Illus.). 1968. Repr. of 1913 ed. 20.00 (ISBN 0-8103-3500-X). Gale.

Quellen der Hamburger Oper Sixteen Seventy Eight to Seventeen Thirty Eight. Walter Schultze. LC 80-2300. 1981. Repr. of 1938 ed. 25.50 (ISBN 0-404-18869-9). AMS Pr.

Quellenangaben bei Herodot: Studien zur Erzaehlkunst Herodots. Detlef Fehling. (Untersuchungen zur Antiken Literatur und Geschichte, 9). 198p. 1971. 25.90x (ISBN 3-11-003634-7). De Gruyter.

Quero Melhorar Meu Casamento. Tr. by Henry Brant & Phil Lamdrum. (Portuguese Bks.). 1979. 1.25 (ISBN 0-8297-0669-0). Life Pubs Intl.

Query Book. Gordon L. Burgett. LC 80-24144. (Illus.). 120p. (Orig.). 1981. pap. 7.95 (ISBN 0-9605078-0-9). Write to Sell.

Query Languages. J. Salter. 1980. write for info. (ISBN 0-85501-494-6). Heyden.

Quest. Ed. by David Bischoff. LC 76-44815. (Science Fiction Ser.). (Illus.). (gr. 3-6). 1977. PLB 7.75 (ISBN 0-8172-0527-6). Raintree Pubs.

Quest: An Autobiography. Leopold Infeld. viii, 361p. 1980. 14.95. Chelsea Pub.

Quest: An Autobiography. 2nd ed. Leopold Infeld. LC 79-55510. Orig. Title: Quest: the Evolution of a Scientist. 1979. text ed. 17.50 o.p. (ISBN 0-8284-0309-0). Chelsea Pub.

Quest at Glastonbury: A Biographical Study of Frederick Bligh Bond. William Kenawell. LC 65-18997. 1965. 8.50 o.p. (ISBN 0-912326-14-X). Garrett-Helix.

Quest for a Black Theology. Ed. by James J. Gardiner & J. Deotis Roberts. LC 76-151250. 128p. 1971. 6.95 (ISBN 0-8298-0196-0). Pilgrim NY.

Quest for a Sustainable Society. Ed. by James C. Coomer. LC 80-24158. (Pergamon Policy Studies on International Development). 230p. 1981. 24.01 (ISBN 0-08-027168-5). Pergamon.

Quest for an Image of the Brain. William H. Oldendorf. (Computerized Tomography in the Perspective of Past & Future Imaging Methods). 160p. 1980. text ed. 21.00 (ISBN 0-89004-429-5). Raven.

Quest for Barbel. William Howes. pap. 3.50x o.p. (ISBN 0-392-06529-0, SpS). Soccer.

Quest for Carp. Jack Hilton. (Illus.). 188p. 1972. 14.00 (ISBN 0-7207-0582-7). Transatlantic.

Quest for Christa T. Christa Wolf. 185p. 1970. 4.95 (ISBN 0-374-51534-4). FS&G.

Quest for Community. Robert A. Nisbet. 1962. pap. 5.95 (ISBN 0-19-500703-4, GB91, GB). Oxford U Pr.

Quest for Community: Social Aspects of Residential Growth. David C. Thorns. LC 75-16914. 1976. 19.95 (ISBN 0-470-86494-X). Halsted Pr.

Quest for Empire: The Political Kingdom of God & the Council of Fifty in Mormon History. Klaus J. Hansen. LC 74-8002. xxii, 237p. 1974. pap. 3.95 (ISBN 0-8032-5769-4, BB 591, Bison). U of Nebr Pr.

Quest for Eros: Browning & "Fifine". Samuel B. Southwell. LC 79-4945. 272p. 1980. 17.00x (ISBN 0-8131-1399-7). U Pr of Ky.

Quest for Excellence in Health Care Delivery. Ed. by Duncan Neuhauser. (Illus.). 180p. 1981. text ed. price not set (ISBN 0-914904-70-1). Health Admin Pr.

Quest for Extraterrestrial Life: A Book of Readings. Donald Goldsmith. LC 79-57423. (Illus.). 308p. 1980. 18.00 (ISBN 0-935702-08-3); pap. text ed. 12.00 (ISBN 0-935702-02-4). Univ Sci Bks.

Quest for General Education: Reflections on the Harvard Report. G. Ramanathan. 10.50x o.p. (ISBN 0-210-22539-4). Asia.

Quest for Maturity: A Study of William Wordsworth's "the Prelude". Penelope J. Stokes & Dorothea Steiner. (Salzburg Studies in English Literature, Romantic Reassessment: No. 44). 1974. pap. text ed. 25.00x (ISBN 0-391-01537-0). Humanities.

Quest for Meaning of Svami Vivekananda: A Study of Religious Change. George M. Williams. LC 74-10906. (Religious Quest Ser: Vol. 1). (Illus.). 158p. 1974. lib. bdg. 14.95x (ISBN 0-914914-02-2); pap. text ed. 5.50x (ISBN 0-914914-00-6). New Horizons.

Quest for National Efficiency: A Study in British Politics & Political Thought, 1899-1914. G. R. Searle. LC 75-126758. 1971. 20.00x (ISBN 0-520-01794-3). U of Cal Pr.

Quest for Noah's Ark. rev. ed. John W. Montgomery. LC 74-21993. (Illus.). 1972. pap. 3.95 (ISBN 0-87123-477-7, 200477). Bethany Fell.

Quest for Oil. W. G. Roberts. LC 76-54736. (Illus.). (gr. 9-12). 1977. 10.95 (ISBN 0-87599-225-0). S G Phillips.

Quest for Reality: An Anthology of the Short Poems in English. Ed. by Yvor Winters & Kenneth Fields. LC 78-75739. 199p. 1969. 10.00x o.p. (ISBN 0-8040-0257-6); pap. 4.95x (ISBN 0-8040-0258-4). Swallow.

Quest for Regional Cooperation: A Study of the New York Metropolitan Regional Council. Joan B. Aron. LC 69-16738. (California Studies in Urbanization & Environmental Design). 1969. 19.50x (ISBN 0-520-01505-3). U of Cal Pr.

Quest for Religious Maturity: The Obsessive-Compulsive Personality--Implications for Pastoral Counseling. Anne M. Dooley. LC 80-67255. 124p. (Orig.). 1981. lib. bdg. 16.00 (ISBN 0-8191-1442-1); pap. text ed. 7.50 (ISBN 0-8191-1443-X). U Pr of Amer.

Quest for Stability. Norman Nordhauser. Ed. by Frank Freidel. LC 78-62510. (Modern American History Ser.: Vol. 15). 1979. lib. bdg. 24.00 (ISBN 0-8240-3638-7). Garland Pub.

Quest for Survival & Growth: A Comparative Study of American, European, & Japanese Multinationals. Anant R. Negandhi. LC 78-71603. 1979. 29.95 (ISBN 0-03-046416-1). Praeger.

Quest for Tanelorn. Michael Moorcock. 1981. pap. 2.25 (ISBN 0-440-17193-8). Dell.

Quest for the Historical Israel. George W. Ramsey. LC 80-82188. 208p. (Orig.). 1981. pap. 12.50 (ISBN 0-8042-0187-0). John Knox.

Quest for the New Science: Language & Thought in Eighteenth-Century Science. Ed. by Karl J. Fink & James W. Marchand. LC 79-889. 110p. 1979. 7.95x (ISBN 0-8093-0917-3). S Ill U Pr.
Quest for Therapy in Lower Zaire. John M. Janzen. (Comparative Studies of Health Systems & Medical Care). 1978. 23.75x (ISBN 0-520-03295-0). U of Cal Pr.
Quest for Valid Economics. Howard B. Holroyd. 1981. 12.95 (ISBN 0-533-04830-3). Vantage.
Quest for Wilhelm Reich. Colin Wilson. LC 78-22774. 288p. 1981. 12.95 (ISBN 0-385-01845-2, Anchor Pr). Doubleday.
Quest for World Monetary System: Gold-Dollar System & It's Aftermath. Milton Gilbert. LC 80-17865. 255p. 1980. 19.95 (ISBN 0-471-07998-7, Pub. by Wiley-Interscience). Wiley.
Quest of a Hemisphere. Donzella C. Boyle. LC 71-113036. (Illus.). (gr. 7 up). 1970. PLB 15.00 (ISBN 0-88279-218-0). Western Islands.
Quest of Inquirie: Some Contexts of Tudor Literature. Howard C. Cole. LC 73-91621. 1973. 9.80 (ISBN 0-672-63583-6). Pegasus.
Quest of the Colonial. Robert Shackleton & Elizabeth Shackleton. LC 72-99075. (Illus.). 1970. Repr. of 1907 ed. 20.00 (ISBN 0-8103-3574-3). Gale.
Quest of the Dark Lady. Quinn Reade. 1976. pap. 1.25 (ISBN 0-505-51101-0). Tower Bks.
Quest of the Golden Stairs: A Mystery of Kinghood in Faerie. Arthur E. Waite. LC 80-19659. 176p. 1980. Repr. of 1974 ed. lib. bdg. 9.95x (ISBN 0-89370-628-0). Borgo Pr.
Quest: The Life of Elisabeth Kubler-Ross. Derek Gill. LC 78-19823. (Illus.). 1980. 11.95 (ISBN 0-06-011543-2, HarpT). Har-Row.
Questing Mind: Readings for Background & Comprehension. Ed. by Arthur Mullin. LC 68-22410. (Orig.). 1968. pap. 7.50 (ISBN 0-672-63095-8). Odyssey Pr.
Question & Answer Book About the Human Body. Ann McGovern. (Illus.). 1965. PLB 4.99 (ISBN 0-394-90780-9, BYR). Random.
Question in Search of an Answer: Learning Disability in Jewish Education. Roberta M. Greene. LC 8-18059. (Illus.). 262p. 1981. pap. 5.95 (ISBN 0-8074-0029-7). UAHC.
Question of Age: The Dorm & I. Kathryn Martin. 224p. 1981. price not set (ISBN 0-936988-01-0). Tompson & Rutter.
Question of Greek Independence: A Study of British Policy in the Near East, 1821-1833. C. W. Crawley. LC 74-144130. 272p. 1973. Repr. of 1930 ed. 16.00 (ISBN 0-86527-161-5). Fertig.
Question of Inheritance. Josephine Bell. 1981. 9.95 (ISBN 0-8027-5438-4). Walker & Co.
Question of Lay Analysis. Sigmund Freud. Ed. & tr. by James Strachey. (Standard ed.). 1969. pap. 3.95 (ISBN 0-393-00503-8, Norton Lib). Norton.
Question of Polish: The Antique Market in Australia. Terry Ingram. 176p. 1980. 27.95x (ISBN 0-00-216412-4, Pub. by W Collins Australia). Intl Schol Bk Serv.
Question of Quality? Roads to Assurance in Medical Care. Gordon McLachlan. (Nuffield Provincial Hospitals Trust Ser.). 1976. 34.00x (ISBN 0-19-721393-6). Oxford U Pr.
Question of Reality: A Novel of Poland. Kazimierz Brandys. Tr. by Isabel Barzun. 1980. 8.95 (ISBN 0-684-16599-6). Scribner.
Question of Religion. William Corlett & John Moore. LC 79-15140. (Questions Ser.). 1980. 8.95 (ISBN 0-87888-149-2). Bradbury Pr.
Question of Separatism: Quebec & the Struggle Over Sovereignty. Jane Jacobs. LC 80-5268. (Illus.). 160p. 1980. 8.95 (ISBN 0-394-50981-1). Random.
Question of Values. Martin Shepard. 1976. 7.95 o.p. (ISBN 0-8415-0449-0). Dutton.
Question Time. LC 55-12245. Vol. 1, 1955. pap. 10.00 (ISBN 0-8309-0180-9). Vol. 3, 1976 (ISBN 0-8309-0178-7). pap. 12.50. Herald Hse.
Question Whether a Jew, Born Within the British Dominions, Was, Before the Making of the Late Act of Parliament, a Person Capable by Law, to Purchase & Hold Lands to Him and His Heirs. Philip C. Webb & Joseph Grove. Ed. by David S. Berkowitz & Samuel E. Thorne. LC 77-86671. (Classics of English Legal History in the Modern Era Ser.: Vol. 48). 169p. 1979. lib. bdg. 40.00 (ISBN 0-8240-3097-4). Garland Pub.
Questioning Media Ethics. Ed. by Bernard Rubin. 1978. 25.95 (ISBN 0-03-046131-6); pap. 10.95 student ed. (ISBN 0-03-046126-X). Praeger.
Questioning: Skills for the Helping Process. Lynette Long et al. LC 80-24385. (Orig.). 1980. pap. text ed. 8.95 (ISBN 0-8185-0371-8). Brooks-Cole.
Questioning Strategies & Techniques. Francis P. Hunkins. (Illus.). 1972. text ed. 8.95x o.p. (ISBN 0-205-03406-3, 2234068). Allyn.
Questionnaire Design Handbook. Paul R. Lees-Haley. LC 80-82969. 150p. (Orig.). 1980. pap. 9.95 (ISBN 0-938124-00-5). Innova Assoc.
Questionnaires: Design & Use. Douglas R. Berdie & John F. Anderson. LC 74-4174. 1974. 10.00 (ISBN 0-8108-0719-X). Scarecrow.
Questions & Answers About Acne. John R. Reeves. LC 76-28514. (Illus.). (gr. 7 up). 1977. 6.95 (ISBN 0-13-748434-8). P-H.
Questions & Answers About Ants. Millicent E. Selsam. LC 67-25033. (Illus.). (gr. 2-5). 1967. 6.95 o.s.i. (ISBN 0-590-07054-1, Four Winds). Schol Bk Serv.
Questions & Answers About Horses. Millicent Selsam. LC 73-88073. (Illus.). 64p. (gr. k-3). 1974. 6.95 (ISBN 0-590-07352-4, Four Winds). Schol Bk Serv.
Questions & Answers About Love & Sex. Bride's Magazine Editors & Mary Calderone. 144p. (Orig.). 1980. pap. 1.95 (ISBN 0-380-52977-7, 52977). Avon.
Questions & Answers About Tape Recording. Herman Burstein. LC 73-89813. 1974. pap. 5.95 (ISBN 0-8306-2681-6, 681). TAB Bks.
Questions & Answers About Weather. M. Jean Craig. (gr. k-3). 1977. pap. 1.50 (ISBN 0-590-10414-4, Schol Pap). Schol Bk Serv.
Questions & Answers: First & Second Supplement to "Toward the Light". Ed. by Michael Agerskov. LC 79-9594. Orig. Title: Sporgsmaal Og Svar. 244p. 1979. pap. 6.95 (ISBN 87-87871-52-1). Toward the Light.
Questions & Answers for Electricians Examinations. 6th ed. Roland Palmquist. 1978. 8.95 (ISBN 0-672-23307-X). Audel.
Questions & Answers for Engineers & Firemen's Examinations. 3rd ed. Frank Graham & Kenneth Schank. 1979. 10.95 (ISBN 0-672-23327-4). Audel.
Questions & Answers for Plumbers Examinations. 2nd ed. Jules Oravetz. LC 73-85726. (Illus.). 1977. pap. 8.95 (ISBN 0-672-23285-5). Audel.
Questions & Answers in the Practice of Family Therapy. Ed. by Alan S. Gurman. 544p. 1981. 25.00 (ISBN 0-87630-246-0). Brunner-Mazel.
Questions & Answers on Contact Lens Practice. 2nd ed. Jack Hartstein. LC 73-4658. (Illus.). 1973. 21.50 o.p. (ISBN 0-8016-2088-0). Mosby.
Questions & Answers on Cutting Fuel Costs. W. Short et al. 104p. 1975. 11.00x (ISBN 0-86010-019-7, Pub. by Graham & Trotman England). State Mutual Bk.
Questions & Answers on Guru & Disciple. Herbert Guenther et al. (Illus.). 1978. pap. text ed. 3.00 (ISBN 0-931454-02-6). Timeless Bks.
Questions & Answers on Stuttering. Dominick A. Barbara. 112p. 1965. pap. 7.25 photocopy ed., spiral (ISBN 0-398-00088-3). C C Thomas.
Questions & Answers on the Rules of the Road. 3rd ed. J. R. Zaruba. (Illus.). 1979. pap. text ed. 7.50x (ISBN 0-87033-262-7). Cornell Maritime.
Questions & Answers on the Securities Markets: A Quick Review Guide to Preparing for Securities Examinations. Leo Loll, Jr. & Julian Buckley. 1968. 15.95 (ISBN 0-13-749374-6). P-H.
Questions & Answers to Help You Pass the Real Estate Exam. John Reilly & Paige Vitousek. 200p. (Orig.). 1981. pap. 13.95 (ISBN 0-88462-395-5). Real Estate Ed Co.
Questions & Answers to Help You Pass the Real Estate License Examination. John Reilly & Paige Vitousek. 200p. 1980. pap. cancelled (ISBN 0-695-81506-7). Real Estate Ed Co.
Questions & Politeness. Esther N. Goody. LC 77-6577. (Cambridge Papers in Social Anthropology Ser: No. 8). 1978. 32.50 (ISBN 0-521-21749-0); pap. 10.95x (ISBN 0-521-29250-6). Cambridge U Pr.
Questions & Problems in Auditing. F. Neuman. 1980. 9.20x (ISBN 0-87563-157-6). Stipes.
Questions Are the Answer. Wayne Robinson. LC 80-36780. 110p. 1980. pap. 5.95 (ISBN 0-8298-0409-9). Pilgrim NY.
Questions De Litterature. Jean Hytier. LC 68-4151. 1967. 20.00x (ISBN 0-231-03123-8). Columbia U Pr.
Questions Girls Ask. Marjorie Vetter & Laura Vitray. (gr. 7 up). 1959. PLB 5.50 o.p. (ISBN 0-525-37996-7). Dutton.
Questions in Physics. 3rd ed. J. G. Houston. 1971. pap. text ed. 5.50x o.p. (ISBN 0-435-67425-0). Heinemann Ed.
Questions of Form & Interpretation. Noam Chomsky. (PDR Press Publication on Philosophy of Language: No. 4). 1975. pap. 2.25x (ISBN 90-316-0005-9). Humanities.
Questions of Human Existence As Answered by Major World Religions, 6 bks. William Corlett & John Moore. Incl. Question of Religion (ISBN 0-87888-149-2); Christ Story (ISBN 0-87888-150-6); Hindu Sound (ISBN 0-87888-151-4); Judaic Law (ISBN 0-87888-152-2); Buddha Way (ISBN 0-87888-153-0); Islamic Space (ISBN 0-87888-154-9). (Illus.). 1979. 8.95 ea. Bradbury Pr.
Questions of King Melinda, 2 Vols, Vols. 35 & 36. Ed. by F. Max Mueller. Tr. by David & Oldenberg. (Sacred Books of the East Ser.). 15.00x ea.; Vol. 35. (ISBN 0-8426-1410-9); Vol. 36. (ISBN 0-8426-1411-7). Verry.
Questions on Geologic Principles. Eduard Reyer. Tr. by Allen Keller et al. LC 79-89374. (Microform Publication: No. 9). (Illus.). 1979. 4.00x (ISBN 0-8137-6009-7). Geol Soc.
Questions on Prophecy. Salem Kirban. 1979. pap. 2.95 (ISBN 0-8024-7055-6). Moody.
Queueing: Basic Theory & Application. Walter C. Giffen. LC 76-44996. (Industrial Engineering Ser.). 1978. text ed. 28.95 (ISBN 0-88244-133-7). Grid Pub.
Queueing Models for Computer Systems: With General Service Time Distributions. Annie W. Shum. LC 79-50229. (Outstanding Dissertations in the Computer Sciences Ser.: Vol. 19). 290p. 1980. lib. bdg. 28.00 (ISBN 0-8240-4404-5). Garland Pub.
Queueing Systems, 2 vols. Leonard Kleinrock. Incl. Vol. 1. Theory. 432p. 30.00 (ISBN 0-471-49110-1); Vol. 2. Computer Applications. 512p. 32.00 (ISBN 0-471-49111-X). LC 74-9846. 1975-76 (Pub. by Wiley-Interscience). Wiley.
Queueing Theory: A Solving Approach. Len Gorney. (Illus.). 300p. 1981. 20.00 (ISBN 0-89433-128-0). Petrocelli.
Quiche Mayas of Utatlan. Robert M. Carmack. LC 80-5241. (Civilization of the American Indian Ser.: No. 155). (Illus.). 400p. 1981. 24.95 (ISBN 0-8061-1546-7). U of Okla Pr.
Quichean Civilization: The Ethnohistoric, Ethnographic, & Archaelogical Sources. Robert M. Carmack. LC 70-149948. (Illus.). 1973. 25.75x (ISBN 0-520-01963-6). U of Cal Pr.
Quichean Linguistic Pre-History. Lyle Campbell. (Publications in Linguistics: Vol. 81). 1977. 11.50x (ISBN 0-520-09531-6). U of Cal Pr.
Quick & Easy Casseroles. Flo Price. 1976. pap. 1.50 (ISBN 0-89129-158-X). Jove Pubns.
Quick & Easy Cookbook. Robyn Supraner. LC 80-24021. (Illus.). 48p. (gr. 2-5). 1980. PLB 6.92 (ISBN 0-89375-438-2); pap. 1.75 (ISBN 0-89375-439-0). Troll Assocs.
Quick & Easy Exercises for Figure Beauty. Judy Smithdeal. pap. 2.00 (ISBN 0-87980-381-9). Wilshire.
Quick & Easy House Keeping! Rubie Saunders. LC 77-1078. (Concise Guides Ser.). (gr. 6-9). 1977. PLB 6.45 (ISBN 0-531-01277-8). Watts.
Quick & Easy Vegetarian Cookbook. Ruth A. Manners & William Manners. 288p. 1979. pap. 4.95 o.p. (ISBN 0-87131-303-0). M Evans.
Quick & the Deadly. Morgan Hill. (Orig.). 1981. pap. 1.95 (ISBN 0-440-17173-3). Dell.
Quick Arithmetic. Robert A. Carman & Marilyn J. Carman. LC 74-2476. (Wiley Self-Teaching Guides). 275p. 1974. pap. text ed. 6.95 (ISBN 0-471-13496-1). Wiley.
Quick As a Dodo. Ralph McInerny. LC 77-93301. (Illus.). 1978. 6.95 (ISBN 0-8149-0806-3). Vanguard.
Quick Badge. Martin Ryerson. 1981. pap. 1.95 (ISBN 0-8439-0863-7, Leisure Bks). Nordon Pubns.
Quick Change. Jay Cronley. LC 80-5450. (Illus.). 216p. 1981. 11.95 (ISBN 0-385-15180-2). Doubleday.
Quick-Easy Armour Cookbook. Armour & Company Kitchens. (Orig.). 5.95 (ISBN 0-87502-082-8). Benjamin Co.
Quick Fire Hombre. Nelson Nye. 1977. pap. 1.25 (ISBN 0-505-51177-0). Tower Bks.
Quick Graph: Collected Notes & Essays. Robert Creeley. Ed. by Donald Allen. LC 67-30650. (Writing Ser.: No. 22). 150p. (Orig.). 1970. 10.00 (ISBN 0-87704-010-9). Four Seasons Foun.
Quick Guide to the Wines of All the Americas. Robert Jay Misch. LC 76-23783. 1977. 4.95 o.p. (ISBN 0-385-06469-1). Doubleday.
Quick Job Hunting Map. Richard H. Bolles. (Orig.). 1976. pap. 1.25x (ISBN 0-913668-60-5). Ten Speed Pr.
Quick Job-Hunting Map: Advanced Version Trade. Richard N. Bolles. pap. 1.50 (ISBN 0-89815-008-6). Ten Speed Pr.
Quick Job-Hunting Map, Beginning Version. Richard Bolles. 1977. pap. 1.25x (ISBN 0-913668-59-1). Ten Speed Pr.
Quick Knife: Unnecessary Surgery U.S.A. Duane F. Stroman. (National University Publications). 1979. 15.00 (ISBN 0-8046-9226-2). Kennikat.
Quick Main Courses for Two. Margaret Happel. Ed. by B. Machtiger. (Savers Ser.). (Illus.). 128p. pap. cancelled (ISBN 0-88421-153-3). Butterick Pub.
Quick Medical Terminology. Genevieve L. Smith & Phyllis E. Davis. LC 72-4193. (Wiley Self-Teaching Guides Ser). 248p. 1972. 6.95 (ISBN 0-471-80198-4). Wiley.
Quick Neurological Screening Test. Harold Sterling et al. 1978. pap. 10.00 (ISBN 0-87879-185-X); 25 recording forms 5.00 (ISBN 0-685-85991-6). Acad Therapy.
Quick Red Fox. John D. Macdonald. LC 73-16074. 1974. 8.95 (ISBN 0-397-01015-X). Lippincott.
Quick Reference to Clinical Toxicology. Irwin B. Hanenson. 1980. pap. text ed. 14.00 (ISBN 0-397-50418-7). Lippincott.
Quick Simple Meals. Susan Graham. (Leisure Plan Bks). 1971. pap. 2.95 (ISBN 0-600-01354-5). Transatlantic.
Quick-Sketch: A New Technique in Interior Design Graphics. Richard W. Henton. 144p. 1980. pap. text ed. 8.95 (ISBN 0-8403-2233-X). Kendall-Hunt.
Quick Tennis: The Professional's Method for Quickness, Mobility, & Court Control--the Secret Ingredient in Winning Tennis. Henry Hines & Carol Morgenstern. LC 77-3402. 1977. pap. 4.95 o.p. (ISBN 0-525-04275-X). Dutton.
Quick Tips from the CBS Tennis Spot. Shep Campbell. (Illus.). 208p. (Orig.). 1981. pap. 6.95 (ISBN 0-914178-45-8, 42906-X). Tennis Mag.
Quick Tips from the Golf Spot. Nick Seitz. (Illus.). 208p. 1981. pap. 6.95 (ISBN 0-914178-43-1, 42903-5). Golf Digest Bks.
Quick Tips from the Tennis Spot. Shep Cambell. LC 80-84952. (Illus.). 208p. 1981. pap. 6.95 (ISBN 0-914178-45-8, 42906-X). Golf Digest Bks.
Quick to Fix Desserts. Eulalia C. Blair. LC 80-13124. (Foodservice Menu Planning Ser.). 1980. 16.50 (ISBN 0-8436-2183-4). CBI Pub.
Quickies for Singles. Fellowship Church, Baton Rouge, La, Members. Ed. by Gwen McKee. (Illus.). 80p. 1980. pap. 4.95 (ISBN 0-937552-03-8). Quail Ridge.
Quickpoint Book. Ed. by Susan Iglehart & Barbara Schweizer. LC 77-71371. (Illus.). 1977. 10.95 o.p. (ISBN 0-685-81541-2); pap. 5.95 o.p. (ISBN 0-03-016896-1). HR&W.
Quicksilver. Norman Hartley. 240p. (Orig.). 1980. pap. 2.50 (ISBN 0-380-51482-6, 51482). Avon.
Quicksilver Books: Aviation. Incl. Triangle of Fear. Elizabeth Van Steenwyk (ISBN 0-8372-3786-6); Emergency. P. M. Carr (ISBN 0-8372-3787-4); Operation Airdrop. Jessie R. Hull (ISBN 0-8372-3788-2); Ghost of Biplane Penny. Jane Clyapool (ISBN 0-8372-3789-0); Hijack at the Airport. Al Nussbaum (ISBN 0-8372-3790-4). (gr. 4-8). Date not set. pap. 0.99 ea.; tchr's pamphlet free; Set. 5 copies of ea. title 22.50 (ISBN 0-8372-3835-8). Bowmar-Noble.
Quicksilver Books: Cars & Cycles. Incl. Danger at the Racetrack. Jessie R. Hull (ISBN 0-8372-3776-9); Ghost Car of Apple Valley. James R. Hull (ISBN 0-8372-3777-7); Golden Lion. James McKimmey (ISBN 0-8372-3778-5); Wrecker Madness. Jane Claypool (ISBN 0-8372-3779-3); Champion. James McKimmey (ISBN 0-8372-3780-7). (Illus.). (gr. 4-8). Date not set. pap. 0.99 ea.; Set. 5 copies of ea. title 22.50 (ISBN 0-8372-3836-6). Bowmar-Noble.
Quicksilver Books: Crime Fighters. Incl. Deadly Fires. James McKimmey (ISBN 0-8372-3791-2); Hold-Up. Al Nussbaum (ISBN 0-8372-3792-0); Spy Eye's First Case. P. M. Carr (ISBN 0-8372-3793-9); Bicycle Rip-Off. Jessie R. Hull (ISBN 0-8372-3794-7); Seven Sisters. Jane Claypool (ISBN 0-8372-3795-5). (gr. 4-8). Date not set. pap. 0.99 ea. Bowmar-Noble.
Quicksilver Books: Dogs. Incl. Three-Dog Afternoon. Elizabeth Van Steenwyk (ISBN 0-8372-3771-8); Washed Out. Olive W. Burt (ISBN 0-8372-3773-4); Partridge Dog. Jim Kjelgaard (ISBN 0-8372-3772-6); Dog Named Benjie. Justin F. Denzel (ISBN 0-8372-3774-2); Mr. Bones. Dolly Cebulash (ISBN 0-8372-3775-0). (Illus.). (gr. 4-8). Date not set. pap. 0.99 ea.; tchr's pamphlet free (ISBN 0-8372-9056-2); Set. 5 copies of ea. title 22.50 (ISBN 0-8372-3834-X). Bowmar-Noble.
Quicksilver Books: Fads. Incl. Rainbow Roller. P. M. Carr (ISBN 0-8372-3781-5); Ghosts of Pilgrim Creek. Elizabeth Van Steenwyk (ISBN 0-8372-3782-3); Pasta Poodles. Eve Bunting (ISBN 0-8372-3783-1); Go Directly to Jail. P. M. Carr (ISBN 0-8372-3784-X); Marathon Madness. Jessie R. Hull (ISBN 0-8372-3785-8). (gr. 4-8). Date not set. pap. 0.99 ea. Bowmar-Noble.
Quicksilver Books: Horses. Incl. Bucky. Elizabeth Van Steenwyk (ISBN 0-8372-3766-1); Horse to Remember. Mel Cebulash (ISBN 0-8372-3767-X); Rebel Horse. Jim Kjelgaard (ISBN 0-8372-3768-8); King of the Mesa. Rutherford Montgomery (ISBN 0-8372-3769-6); Kid That Rode with Death. Bill Gulick (ISBN 0-8372-3770-X). (Illus.). (gr. 4-8). Date not set. pap. 0.99 ea.; tchr's pamphlet free (ISBN 0-8372-9055-4); Set. 5 copies of ea. title 22.50 (ISBN 0-8372-3833-1). Bowmar-Noble.
Quicksort. Robert Sedgewick. LC 79-50821. (Outstanding Dissertations in the Computer Sciences Ser.: Vol. 18). 350p. 1980. lib. bdg. 32.00 (ISBN 0-8240-4417-7). Garland Pub.

Quid: How to Make the Best Decisions of Your Life. James Jorgensen & Timothy Fautsko. LC 78-58623. 1978. 8.95 (ISBN 0-8027-0615-0); pap. 4.95 (ISBN 0-8027-7139-4). Walker & Co.

Quien Dice? Tr. by Fritz Ridenour. (Spanish Bks.). (Span.). 1978. 1.90 (ISBN 0-8297-0440-X). Life Pubs Intl.

Quien Movio la Piedra? Frank Morison. Tr. by Rhode Ward from Eng. LC 77-11752. 206p. (Orig., Span.). 1977. pap. 3.95 (ISBN 0-89922-100-9). Edit Caribe.

Quiero Mejorar Mi Matrimonio. Tr. by Henry Brant & Phil Landrum. (Spanish Bks.). (Span.). 1977. 1.90 (ISBN 0-8297-0778-6). Life Pubs Intl.

Quiet Desperation. Bill Weiner. 1980. 10.95 (ISBN 0-686-65059-X). Lyle Stuart.

Quiet Evening. Thacher Hurd. LC 78-2797. (Illus.). (gr. k-3). 1978. 6.95 (ISBN 0-688-80166-8); PLB 6.67 (ISBN 0-688-84166-X). Greenwillow.

Quiet Furies: Man & Disorder. E. McNeil. 1967. pap. text ed. 8.95 (ISBN 0-13-749770-9). P-H.

Quiet Healing Zone. Herbert L. Beierle. 1980. 10.00 (ISBN 0-686-23897-4). God Unltd U of Healing.

Quiet Killers II: Silencer Update. J. David Truby. (Illus.). 80p. (Orig.). 1979. pap. 6.00 (ISBN 0-87364-163-9). Paladin Ent.

Quiet Legend: Henry Aaron. F. M. Milverstedt. LC 75-19277. (Sports Profiles Ser.). (Illus.). 48p. (gr. 4-11). 1975. PLB 8.50 (ISBN 0-8172-0102-5). Raintree Pubs.

Quiet Man. rev. ed. Jean N. Dale & Willard D. Sheeler. (Reading & Exercise Ser.: No. 4). 1975. pap. 2.50 (ISBN 0-89285-053-1); cassette tapes 29.50 (ISBN 0-89285-071-X). ELS Intl.

Quiet Mind. White Eagle. 1972. 3.50 (ISBN 0-85487-009-1). De Vorss.

Quiet Miracle. Jo Montgomery. LC 62-10500. 1962. 6.00 o.p. (ISBN 0-8309-0251-1). Herald Hse.

Quiet Night: A Play for Christmas. Thomas J. Hatton. 24p. (Orig.). 1980. pap. text ed. 2.70 (ISBN 0-89536-438-7). CSS Pub.

Quiet Night of Fear. C. L. Grant. (Orig.). 1981. pap. 2.25 (ISBN 0-425-04844-6). Berkley Pub.

Quiet on Account of Dinosaur. Jane Thayer. (Illus.). (ps-3). 1964. PLB 7.44 (ISBN 0-688-31632-8). Morrow.

Quiet Place. Rose Blue. LC 69-1123. (Illus.). (gr. 4-6). 1969. PLB 4.33 o.p. (ISBN 0-531-01773-7). Watts.

Quiet, Please. James B. Cabell. 1952. 4.50 (ISBN 0-8130-0040-8). U Presses Fla.

Quiet River. P. M. Hubbard. LC 77-27709. 1978. 7.95 o.p. (ISBN 0-385-14244-7). Doubleday.

Quiet Therapies: Japanese Pathways to Personal Growth. David K. Reynolds. LC 80-17611. 144p. 1980. 8.95 (ISBN 0-8248-0690-5). U Pr of Hawaii.

Quiet Times. C. Griffith. 1979. 4.00 o.p. (ISBN 0-8062-1208-X). Carlton.

Quiet Violence. Sitakant Mahapatra. (Translated from Oriya). 6.75 (ISBN 0-89253-604-7); flexible cloth 4.80 (ISBN 0-89253-605-5). Ind-US Inc.

Quietly Crush the Lizard. Earle Hill. LC 79-155668. 1972. 6.95 (ISBN 0-8149-0698-2). Vanguard.

Quill. David Deihl. 1980. pap. 1.75 (ISBN 0-505-51472-9). Tower Bks.

Quiller Memorandum. Adam Hall. 1979. pap. 1.75 o.s.i. (ISBN 0-515-05211-6). Jove Pubns.

Quilp: The Old Curiosity Shop: Movie Edition. Charles Dickens. (Movie Edition Ser.). 320p. (RL 9). Date not set. pap. 1.25 (ISBN 0-451-06420-8, Y6420, Sig). NAL.

Quilt. Ted Pong. (Illus.). 87p. (Orig.). 1981. pap. 3.95. Pong.

Quilt Engagement Calendar 1982. Cyril I. Nelson. (Illus.). 114p. 1981. spiral 6.95 (ISBN 0-525-93179-1). Dutton.

Quilt Pattern Index. Linda Shogren. LC 79-63203. 50p. (Orig.). 1979. pap. 4.95 o.p. (ISBN 0-933758-06-5). L Shogren Quilt.

Quilted Tessellations: Designs from M. C. Escher. Kay Parker. (Illus.). 140p. 1981. 16.95 (ISBN 0-89594-045-0); pap. 9.95 (ISBN 0-89594-044-2). Crossing Pr.

Quilters - Women & Domestic Art. Patricia Cooper & Norma Bradley Buferd. LC 76-2765. 1977. 12.95 o.p. (ISBN 0-385-11685-3); pap. 6.95 (ISBN 0-385-12039-7). Doubleday.

Quilting. Betty Alfers. LC 78-55662. (Illus.). 1978. 14.95 o.p. (ISBN 0-672-52235-7). Bobbs.

Quilting. Averil Colby. 1979. pap. 17.95 (ISBN 0-7134-2665-9, Pub. by Batsford England). David & Charles.

Quilting & Patchwork. Sunset Editors. LC 72-92518. (Illus.). 80p. 1973. pap. 3.95 (ISBN 0-376-04663-5, Sunset Bks.). Sunset-Lane.

Quilting for Today. Moyra McNeill. (Illus.). 64p. 1976. 9.50 (ISBN 0-263-05601-5). Transatlantic.

Quilting in Squares. Katherine Fisher & Elizabeth Kay. LC 77-16137. (Illus.). 1978. 14.95 (ISBN 0-684-15501-X, ScribT). Scribner.

Quilting: Technique, Design & Application. Eirian Short. 1979. 24.00 (ISBN 0-7134-1540-1, Pub. by Batsford England). David & Charles.

Quiltmaker's Handbook. Michael James. LC 77-15592. (Creative Handcraft Ser.). (Illus.). 1978. 14.95 (ISBN 0-13-749416-5, Spec); pap. 7.95 (ISBN 0-13-749408-4, Spec). P-H.

Quiltmaking & Quiltmakers. Marilyn Lithgow. (Funk & W Bk.). 128p. 1974. pap. 4.50 o.s.i. (ISBN 0-308-10089-1, TYC-T). T Y Crowell.

Quilts in the Attic. Robbin Fleisher. LC 78-3597. (Illus.). (gr. k-3). 1978. 8.95 (ISBN 0-02-735420-2, 73542). Macmillan.

Quilts: Their Story & How to Make Them. Marie D. Webster. LC 75-174137. (Tower Bks). (Illus.). xviii, 178p. 1972. Repr. of 1915 ed. 18.00 (ISBN 0-8103-3111-X). Gale.

Quimble Wood. N. M. Bodecker. LC 80-24042. (Illus.). 32p. (ps-4). 1981. 9.95 (ISBN 0-689-50190-0, McElderry Bk). Atheneum.

Quimby's Science of Happiness. Erroll S. Collie. 119p. (Orig.). 1980. pap. 5.50 (ISBN 0-87516-410-2). De Vorss.

Quimica. Rod O'Connor. 1976. text ed. 12.00 (ISBN 0-06-316600-3, IntlDept). Har-Row.

Quimica Elemental. Glenn Miller. (Span.). 1978. pap. text ed. 6.80 (ISBN 0-06-315625-3, IntlDept). Har-Row.

Quimica General. Jesse H. Wood & Charles Keenan. (Span.). 1970. 8.00 (ISBN 0-06-317050-7, IntlDept). Har-Row.

Quince Cuentos De las Espanas. Doris K. Arjona & Carlos V. Arjona. LC 71-135971. 1971. pap. text ed. 5.95x (ISBN 0-684-41153-9, ScribC). Scribner.

Quinientas Ilustraciones. Compiled by Alfredo Lerin. 324p. (Span.). 1980. pap. 4.95 (ISBN 0-311-42037-0). Casa Bautista.

Quintescence of Irving Langmuir. A. Rosenfeld. 1966. 15.00 (ISBN 0-08-011049-5); pap. 7.50 (ISBN 0-08-011048-7). Pergamon.

Quintessence of Capitalism. Werner Sombart. 1967. 22.50 (ISBN 0-86527-162-3). Fertig.

Quintet: Five One-Act Plays. Sarah W. Miller. 1981. pap. 3.95 (ISBN 0-8054-7520-6). Broadman.

Quintet of Cuisines. Michael Field & Frances Field. (Foods of the World Ser). (Illus.). 1970. 14.95 (ISBN 0-8094-0048-0). Time-Life.

Quintet of Cuisines. Michael Field & Frances Field. LC 72-130359. (Foods of the World Ser.). (Illus.). (gr. 6 up). 1970. PLB 14.94 (ISBN 0-8094-0075-8, Pub. by Time-Life). Silver.

Quintets for Orchestra: Study Score. Lukas Foss. 60p. (Orig.). 1980. pap. 15.00 (ISBN 0-686-64720-3, PCB115). Fischer Inc NY.

Quintilian on Education. Ed. by William M. Smail. LC 66-13554. 1966. text ed. 8.75 (ISBN 0-8077-2173-5); pap. text ed. 4.00x (ISBN 0-8077-2170-0). Tchrs Coll.

Quips & Quirks. Clyde Watson. LC 75-4678. (Illus.). 64p. (gr. 3-7). 1975. 5.95 (ISBN 0-690-00733-7, TYC-J). T Y Crowell.

Quit India: The American Response in the Nineteen Forty-Two Struggle. M. S. Venkataramani & B. K. Shrivastava. 1979. 20.00x (ISBN 0-7069-0693-4, Pub. by Croom Helm Ltd. England). Biblio Dist.

Quit-Rent System in the American Colonies. Beverley W. Bond. 1919. 7.50 (ISBN 0-8446-1082-8). Peter Smith.

Quite Contrary: The Mary & Newt Stories. Stephen Dixon. LC 78-20202. 1979. 9.95 o.s.i. (ISBN 0-06-011072-4, HarpT). Har-Row.

Quite Early One Morning. Dylan Thomas. LC 54-12907. pap. 3.95 (ISBN 0-8112-0208-9, NDP90). New Directions.

Quite Man. Ed. by Jean N. Dale & Willard D. Sheeler. (Reading & Exercise Ser.). (gr. k-6). 1974. pap. text ed. 2.50x (ISBN 0-19-433622-0). Oxford U Pr.

Quitting: Knowing When to Leave. Dale A. Dauten. 216p. 1980. 12.95 (ISBN 0-8027-0660-6). Walker & Co.

Quiz Show Quiz Book. Frank W. Chinnock. 1977. pap. 1.25 o.p. (ISBN 0-425-03542-5, Medallion). Berkley Pub.

Quizzism & Its Key. Albert P. Southwick. LC 68-22051. 1970. Repr. of 1884 ed. 15.00 (ISBN 0-8103-3094-6). Gale.

Qumran Community: Its History & Scrolls. Charles T. Fritsch. 1973. Repr. of 1956 ed. 12.00x (ISBN 0-8196-0279-5). Biblo.

Qumran Text of Samuel & Josephus. Eugene C. Ulrich, Jr. LC 78-15254. (Harvard Semitic Museum. Harvard Semitic Monographs: No. 19). 1978. 10.50 (ISBN 0-89130-256-5, 040019). Scholars Pr Ca.

Quo Vadis? A Just Censure of Travell As It Is Commonly Undertaken by the Gentlemen of Our Nation. Joseph Hall. LC 74-28860. (English Experience Ser.: No. 740). 1975. Repr. of 1617 ed. 6.00 (ISBN 90-221-0165-7). Walter J Johnson.

Quorum of Cats. Ed. by Elizabeth Lee. 1976. 9.95 (ISBN 0-236-40019-3, Pub. by Paul Elek). Merrimack Bk Serv.

Quotable Quotations Book. Alec Lewis. 352p. 1981. pap. 5.95 (ISBN 0-346-12523-5). Cornerstone.

Quotable Quote Book. Alec Lewis. LC 78-22461. 1980. 12.95 (ISBN 0-690-01489-9, TYC-T). T Y Crowell.

Quotable Woman, 2 vols. Elaine Partrow. Incl. Vol. 1. Eighteen Hundred to Eighteen Ninety-Nine (ISBN 0-523-40859-5); Nineteen Hundred to the Present (ISBN 0-523-40874-9). (Orig.). 1980. pap. 3.95 ea.; pap. 7.90 boxed set (ISBN 0-686-65984-8). Pinnacle Bks.

Quotation Dictionary. Robin Hyman. 1965. 10.95 (ISBN 0-02-558060-4). Macmillan.

Quotations from Abraham Lincoln. Ralph Y. McGinnis. LC 77-24595. (Illus.). 1978. 15.95 (ISBN 0-88229-316-8); pap. 8.95 (ISBN 0-88229-507-1). Nelson-Hall.

Quotations in Black. Compiled by Anita King. LC 80-1794. (Illus.). 320p. 1981. lib. bdg. 25.00 (ISBN 0-313-22128-6, KQB/). Greenwood.

Quote It! Memorable Legal Quotations. Ed. by Eugene C. Gerhart. LC 78-83771. 1969. 30.00 (ISBN 0-87632-001-9). Boardman.

Quote Unquote. Lloyd Cory. 1977. text ed. 6.95 o.p. (ISBN 0-88207-810-0); pap. 4.95 (ISBN 0-88207-803-8). Victor Bks.

Quotoons: A Speakers Dictionary. O. A. Battista. 472p. 1981. 13.95 (ISBN 0-399-12573-6, Perigee); 5.95 (ISBN 0-399-50514-8). Putnam.

Quran. M. Baydun. (Arabic.). 25.00x (ISBN 0-686-63558-2). Intl Bk Ctr.

Quran. M. Baydun. (Arabic.). medium sized. 19.00x (ISBN 0-686-63559-0). Intl Bk Ctr.

Quran. M. Baydun. (Arabic.). with jacket. 10.95x (ISBN 0-686-63560-4). Intl Bk Ctr.

Quran. M. Baydun. (Arabic.). pocket sized. 4.95x (ISBN 0-686-63561-2). Intl Bk Ctr.

Quran. M. Baydun. (Arabic.). pap. 2.95x small pocket sized. (ISBN 0-686-63562-0). Intl Bk Ctr.

Qur'an, Vols. 6 & 9. Ed. by F. Max Mueller. Tr. by Winternitz. (Sacred Books of the East Ser.). 15.00x ea.; Vol. 6. (ISBN 0-8426-1412-5); Vol. 9. (ISBN 0-8426-1413-3). Verry.

Qur'an & Its Exegesis: Selected Texts with Classical & Modern Muslim Interpretations. Helmut Gatje. Ed. by Alford T. Welch. (Islamic World Ser). 1977. 26.50x (ISBN 0-520-02833-3). U of Cal Pr.

Qur'an As Scripture. Arthur Jeffery. LC 80-1924. 1981. Repr. of 1952 ed. 18.00 (ISBN 0-404-18970-9). AMS Pr.

Quranic Studies: Sources & Methods of Scriptural Interpretations, Vol. 31. J. Wansbrough. (London Oriental Ser). 1977. 55.00x (ISBN 0-19-713588-9). Oxford U Pr.

Qutr Al-Muhit: Concise Arabic-Arabic Dictionary, 2 vols. B. Bustani. Repr. of 1869 ed. 50.00 (ISBN 0-685-72056-X). Intl Bk Ctr.

Qwiktran. C. Kevin McCabe. LC 79-63962. 250p. 1979. pap. 12.95 (ISBN 0-918398-24-X). Dilithium Pr.

Qwint Systems, Inc. Z. Iwatsuki et al. 1976. 12.50 (ISBN 3-7682-1061-8). Qwint Systems.

R

R. A. Fisher: An Appreciation. Ed. by S. E. Fienberg & D. H. Hinkley. (Lecture Notes in Statistics: Vol. 1). 208p. 1980. pap. 14.00 (ISBN 0-387-90476-X). Springer-Verlag.

R. A. Fisher: The Life of a Scientist. Joan F. Box. LC 78-1668. (Probability & Mathematical Statistics Ser.). 1978. 28.95 (ISBN 0-471-09300-9, Pub. by Wiley-Interscience). Wiley.

R. Abraham B. Isaac Ha-Levi Tamakh Commentary on the Song of Songs. Leon Feldman. 1970. text ed. 14.75x (ISBN 90-232-0367-4). Humanities.

R & D Management: Methods Used by Federal Agencies. John G. Wirt et al. LC 74-27510. 288p. 1975. 15.00x o.p. (ISBN 0-669-97642-3). Lexington Bks.

R & D Under Uncertainty. Richard G. Richels. LC 78-74997. (Outstanding Dissertations on Energy Ser.). 1979. lib. bdg. 18.00 (ISBN 0-8240-3978-5). Garland Pub.

R & R Catolog & Guide to First Day Cover Collecting: 1980-1981 Edition. Intro. by Robert G. Driscoll. (Illus.). 112p. (Orig.). 1980. pap. 1.95 (ISBN 0-937458-05-8). Harris & Co.

R. C. M. P. & the Management of National Security. Richard French & Andre Beliveau. 77p. 1979. pap. text ed. 6.95x (ISBN 0-920380-18-2, Pub. by Inst Res Pub Canada). Renouf.

R C R A-Hazardous Waste Handbook. Thomas Watson et al. 850p. 1980. 65.00 (ISBN 0-86587-086-1). Gov Insts.

R. D. Blackmore. Max K. Sutton. (English Authors Ser.: No. 265). 1979. lib. bdg. 13.50 (ISBN 0-8057-6756-8). Twayne.

R. D. Mindlin & Applied Mechanics: A Collection of Studies in the Development of Applied Mechanics Dedicated to Prof. R. D. Mindlin by His Former Students. Ed. by George Herman. LC 73-22346. 1974. text ed. 46.00 (ISBN 0-08-017710-7). Pergamon.

R. E. Lee: An Abridgement. Douglas S. Freeman. (Illus.). 1961. lib. rep. ed. 30.00x (ISBN 0-684-15489-7, ScribT). Scribner.

R E T C Proceedings, 2 vols. Rapid Excavation & Tunneling Conference, 1979. Ed. by William A. Hustrulid & Alfred C. Maevis. LC 79-52280. (Illus.). 1819p. 1979. 55.00x (ISBN 0-89520-266-2). Soc Mining Eng.

R. G. Dun & Co., Eighteen Forty-One to Nineteen Hundred: The Development of Credit-Reporting in the Nineteenth Century. James D. Norris. LC 77-95359. (Contributions in Economics & Economic History: No. 20). (Illus.). 1978. lib. bdg. 18.95x (ISBN 0-313-20326-1, NDC/). Greenwood.

R. I. Watson's Selected Papers on the History of Psychology. Robert I. Watson. Ed. by Josef Brozek & Rand B. Evans. LC 76-11675. 409p. 1978. text ed. 25.00x (ISBN 0-87451-130-5). U Pr of New Eng.

R. L. Turner: Collected Papers 1912-1973. Ralph L. Turner. 432p. 1975. 35.00x (ISBN 0-19-713582-X). Oxford U Pr.

R-Master. Gordon R. Dickson. LC 73-13837. 1973. 6.95 o.p. (ISBN 0-397-00920-8). Lippincott.

R My Name Is Rosie. Cohen. (gr. 5). 1980. pap. 1.25 (ISBN 0-590-30331-7, Schol Pap). Schol Bk Serv.

R. O. Blechman: Behind the Lines. R. O. Blechman. LC 80-15191. (Illus.). 192p. 1980. 32.50 (ISBN 0-933920-07-5). Hudson Hills.

R. O. Buchanan & Economic Geography. M. J. Wise & E. M. Rawstron. (Advanced Edonoic Geography Ser.). 1973. lib. bdg. 20.00x (ISBN 0-7135-1766-2). Westview.

R. V. W. A Biography of Ralph Vaughan Williams. Ursula Vaughan Williams. (Illus.). 1964. 24.00x (ISBN 0-19-315411-0). Oxford U Pr.

RA Sixty-Eight Hundred ML: An M-Sixty Eight Hundred Relocatable Macro Assembler. Jack E. Hemenway. 184p. (Orig.). 1979. pap. 25.00 (ISBN 0-07-028056-8, BYTE Bks); instructor's manual 6.95 (ISBN 0-07-007036-9). McGraw.

Rabat: Urban Apartheid in Morocco. Janet L. Abu-Lughod. LC 80-7508. (Princeton Studies on the Near East). (Illus.). 400p. 1981. 30.00 (ISBN 0-691-05315-4); pap. 12.50 (ISBN 0-691-10098-5). Princeton U Pr.

Rabban Gamaliel II: The Legal Traditions. Shamai Kanter. LC 80-12229. (Brown Judaic Studies: No. 8). 15.00x (ISBN 0-89130-403-7, 14 00 08); pap. 10.50x (ISBN 0-89130-404-5). Scholars Pr CA.

Rabbi & the Twenty-Nine Witches. Marilyn Hirsh. LC 75-30710. (Illus.). 32p. (gr. k-3). 1981. PLB 7.95 (ISBN 0-8234-0270-3). Holiday.

Rabbi Tarfon: The Tradition, the Man & Early Rabbinic Judaism. Joel Gereboff. LC 78-15220. (Brown Judaic Studies: No. 7). 1979. 16.50 (ISBN 0-89130-257-3, 140007); pap. 12.00 (ISBN 0-89130-300-6). Scholars Pr Ca.

Rabbi: The American Experience. Murray Polner. LC 77-23123. 1977. 8.95 o.p. (ISBN 0-03-017716-2). HR&W.

Rabbinic Wisdom & Jewish Values. rev. ed. William B. Silverman. Orig. Title: Rabbinic Stories for Christian Ministers & Teachers. 1971. pap. 5.00 (ISBN 0-8074-0190-0, 383210). UAHC.

Rabbi's Wife. David Benedictus. 1977. pap. 1.75 o.p. (ISBN 0-449-23394-4, Crest). Fawcett.

Rabbit. John Burningham. LC 75-4566. (Illus.). (ps-1). 1975. 2.50 (ISBN 0-690-00906-2, TYC-J); PLB 4.89 (ISBN 0-690-00907-0). T Y Crowell.

Rabbit. Date not set. 4.95 (ISBN 0-8120-5381-8). Barron. Postponed.

Rabbit & His Friends. Richard Scarry. (Illus.). (ps-2). 1953. PLB 5.00 (ISBN 0-307-60169-2, Golden Pr). Western Pub.

Rabbit & Skunk & Spooks. Carla Stevens. (Illus.). (gr. 2-3). pap. 1.25 (ISBN 0-590-08087-3, Schol Pap); pap. 3.50 bk. & record (ISBN 0-590-20612-5). Schol Bk Serv.

Rabbit & Skunk & the Big Fight. Carla Stevens. (gr. k-3). 1976. pap. 1.25 (ISBN 0-590-01311-4, Schol Pap). Schol Bk Serv.

Rabbit & Skunk & the Scary Rock. Carla Stevens. (gr. k-3). 1970. pap. 1.25 (ISBN 0-590-00111-6, Schol Pap). Schol Bk Serv.

Rabbit Book. Christian Morgenstern. Tr. by Helga Barthold & John Theobald. (Illus.). 1980. text ed. 8.95 (ISBN 0-914676-43-1); pap. 5.95 (ISBN 0-914676-38-5). Green Tiger.

Rabbit Boy. Joan Tate. pap. text ed. 1.95x o.p. (ISBN 0-435-11877-3). Heinemann Ed.

Rabbit for Easter. Carol Carrick. LC 78-15647. (Illus.). (gr. 4-8). 1979. 7.50 (ISBN 0-688-80195-1); PLB 7.20 (ISBN 0-688-84195-3). Greenwillow.

Rabbit Has a Habit. Jane B. Moncure. LC 75-35608. (Illus.). (ps-3). 1976. 5.50 (ISBN 0-913778-35-4). Childs World.

Rabbit Hill. Robert Lawson. (Illus.). (gr. 4-6). 1944. PLB 8.95 (ISBN 0-670-58675-7). Viking Pr.

Rabbit Hill. Robert Lawson. (Illus.). (gr. 1-3). 1977. pap. 1.75 (ISBN 0-14-031010-X, Puffin). Penguin.

Rabbit Is Next. Gladys Leithauser & Lois Breitmeyer. (Young Reader Ser.). (Illus.). (gr. k-3). PLB 5.00 (ISBN 0-307-60173-0, Golden Pr). Western Pub.

Rabbit Keeping. G. R. Scott. LC 78-65764. 1979. 11.95 (ISBN 0-7153-7643-8). David & Charles.

Rabbit Pie. Gerald Rose. (Illus.). 32p. (gr. 5-8). 1980. 9.95 (ISBN 0-571-11480-6, Pub. by Faber & Faber). Merrimack Bk Serv.

Rabbit Raising. Boy Scouts Of America. LC 19-600. (Illus.). 32p. (gr. 6-12). 1974. pap. 0.70x (ISBN 0-8395-3375-6, 3375). BSA.

Rabbit Run. John Updike. 1978. pap. 2.50 (ISBN 0-449-24031-2, Crest). Fawcett.

Rabbit Scirocio, 1974-1980. Chilton's Automotive Editorial Dept. (Illus.). 1980. pap. 8.95 (ISBN 0-8019-6962-X). Chilton.

Rabbits. Fiona Henrie. (gr. 2-5). 1980. PLB 5.90 (ISBN 0-531-04122-0, G10). Watts.

Rabbits. Herbert S. Zim. (Illus.). (gr. 3-7). 1948. PLB 6.48 (ISBN 0-688-31566-6). Morrow.

Rabbit's Adventure. Betty R. Wright. (Young Reader Ser.). (Illus.). (gr. k-3). 1979. PLB 5.00 (ISBN 0-307-60164-1, Golden Pr). Western Pub.

Rabbits & Hares. Robert J. Whitehead. (First Bks.). (Illus.). 72p. (gr. 4-6). 1976. PLB 6.45 (ISBN 0-531-00338-8). Watts.

Rabbits & Other Small Mammals. LC 78-62754. (Wild, Wild World of Animals Ser.). (Illus.). 1978. lib. bdg. 11.97 (ISBN 0-686-51175-1). Silver.

Rabbits & Other Small Mammals. new ed. Time-Life Television Editors. (Wild, Wild World of Animals). (Illus.). 1979. 10.95 (ISBN 0-913948-22-5). Time-Life.

Rabbits & Redcoats. Robert N. Peck. (Illus.). 64p. (gr. 3-6). 1976. 6.95 o.s.i. (ISBN 0-8027-6241-7); PLB 6.85 o.s.i. (ISBN 0-8027-6242-5). Walker & Co.

Rabbits & Redcoats. Robert N. Peck. (N. H.-Vermont Historiettes). (Illus.). 64p. (gr. 3-4). 1976. pap. 0.95x (ISBN 0-915892-06-5). Regional Ctr Educ.

Rabble in Arms. Kenneth Roberts. 1977. pap. 1.95 o.p. (ISBN 0-449-30748-4, C748, Prem). Fawcett.

Rabboni. W. Phillip Keller. 1981. pap. 5.95 (ISBN 0-8007-5053-5). Revell.

Rabelais: A Critical Study in Prose Fiction. D. G. Coleman. LC 76-173822. 1971. 47.50 (ISBN 0-521-08125-4); pap. 10.50x (ISBN 0-521-29458-4). Cambridge U Pr.

Rabelais & Panurge: A Psychological Approach to Literary Character. Mary E. Ragland. 1976. pap. text ed. 20.00x (ISBN 90-6203-339-3). Humanities.

Rabies - The Facts. Ed. by Colin Kaplan. (Illus.). 1977. text ed. 11.95x (ISBN 0-19-264918-3). Oxford U Pr.

Rabies & Wildlife: A Biologist's Perspective. David W. MacDonald. (Illus.). 160p. 1980. text ed. 38.00x (ISBN 0-19-857567-X); pap. 11.95 (ISBN 0-19-857576-9). Oxford U Pr.

Rabin of Israel: A Biography. Robert Slater. (Illus.). 304p. 1977. 17.50x (ISBN 0-8476-3127-3). Rowman.

Rabindranath Tagore. Mary M. Lago. (World Authors Ser.: No. 402). 1976. lib. bdg. 12.50 (ISBN 0-8057-6242-6). Twayne.

Raccomandazione. Nat Scammacca. Ed. by Stanley H. Barkan. (Cross-Cultural Review Chapbook 1). 24p. (Ital. & Eng.). 1980. pap. 2.50 (ISBN 0-89304-800-3). Cross Cult.

Raccoon Family Pets. Leonore Brandt. pap. 2.50 (ISBN 0-87666-216-5, AP7500). TFH Pubns.

Race. Kare Holt. (YA) 1976. 8.95 o.s.i. (ISBN 0-440-07198-4, Sey Lawr). Delacorte.

Race Against Love. Sally Wentworth. (Harlequin Presents Ser.). 192p. (Orig.). 1981. pap. 1.50 (ISBN 0-373-10414-6, Pub. by Harlequin). PB.

Race Against Time: Human Relations & Politics in Kenya Before Independence. Richard Frost. (Illus.). 292p. 1978. 24.50x (ISBN 0-8476-3102-8). Rowman.

Race & Biology. Lesoie C. Dunn. 1965. pap. 2.50 (ISBN 92-3-100436-0, U505, UNESCO). Unipub.

Race & Class in Latin America. Ed. by Magnus Morner. (Institute for Latin American Studies). 1970. 17.50x (ISBN 0-231-03295-1); pap. 5.00x (ISBN 0-231-08661-X). Columbia U Pr.

Race & Class in the Southwest: A Theory of Racial Inequality. Mario Barrera. LC 78-62970. 261p. 1980. pap. text ed. 5.95 (ISBN 0-268-01601-1). U of Notre Dame Pr.

Race & Culture. Michel Leiris. 1965. pap. 2.50 (ISBN 92-3-100435-2, U506, UNESCO). Unipub.

Race & Culture. Robert E. Park. 1964. 8.95 o.s.i. (ISBN 0-02-923780-7); pap. text ed. 5.95 (ISBN 0-02-923790-4). Free Pr.

Race & Democratic Society. Franz Boas. LC 70-86641. 1969. Repr. of 1945 ed. 10.50x (ISBN 0-8196-0248-5). Biblo.

Race & Economics. Thomas Sowell. LC 74-19982. 1975. pap. text ed. 9.95x (ISBN 0-582-28015-X). Longman.

Race & Ethnic Relations. 4th ed. Brewton Berry & Henry L. Tischler. LC 77-78901. (Illus.). 1978. text ed. 19.50 (ISBN 0-395-25508-2); inst. manual 0.60 (ISBN 0-395-04188-0). HM.

Race & Ethnic Relations: The Social & Political Experience of Minority Groups. Reid Luhman & Stuart Gilman. 352p. 1980. pap. text ed. 12.95x (ISBN 0-534-00795-3). Wadsworth Pub.

Race & Ethnicity: South African & International Perspectives. Ed. by Hendrik Van der Merwe & Robert A. Schrire. 240p. 1981. pap. 12.95x (ISBN 0-8476-3651-8). Rowman.

Race & Industrial Conflict. M. Rimmer. Ed. by Hugh Clegg & George Bain. 1972. text ed. 4.95x o.p. (ISBN 0-435-85765-7). Heinemann Ed.

Race & Law in Britain & the U. S. Louis Claiborne. (Minority Rights Reports Ser.: No. 22). 1974. pap. 2.50 (ISBN 0-89192-108-7). Interbk Inc.

Race & Nationalism in Trinidad & Tobago. Selwyn Ryan. 1972. 25.00x (ISBN 0-8020-5256-8). U of Toronto Pr.

Race & Place: A Legal History of the Neighborhood School. Meyer Weinberg. 1968. pap. 3.60 (ISBN 0-912008-06-7). Integrated Ed Assoc.

Race & Radicalism: The NAACP & the Communist Party in Conflict. Wilson Record. 237p. 1966. pap. 3.95 (ISBN 0-8014-9035-9, CP35). Cornell U Pr.

Race & Residence: The Concentration & Dispersal of Immigrants in London. Trevor R. Lee. (Oxford Research Studies in Geography Ser). (Illus.). 1977. 29.95x (ISBN 0-19-823215-2). Oxford U Pr.

Race As News. 173p. (Orig.). 1974. pap. 9.25 (ISBN 92-3-101191-X, U508, UNESCO). Unipub.

Race Car Drivers School. Ed Radlauer & Dan Radlauer. LC 74-34061. (Schools for Action Ser). (Illus.). 48p. (gr. 3 up). 1975. PLB 6.90 o.p. (ISBN 0-531-02099-1). Watts.

Race, Change, & Urban Society. Ed. by Peter Orleans & William R. Ellis, Jr. LC 70-127992. (Urban Affairs Annual Reviews: Vol. 5). 1971. 25.00x (ISBN 0-8039-0009-0); pap. 9.95x (ISBN 0-8039-0354-5). Sage.

Race, Class & Politics in Colonial Mexico, 1610-1665. J. I. Israel. (Oxford Historical Monographs). 320p. 1975. text ed. 29.00x o.p. (ISBN 0-19-821860-5). Oxford U Pr.

Race, Class & Rebellion in the South Pacific. Ed. by A. Mamak & A. Ali. LC 78-74189. (Studies in Society: No. 4). 1979. text ed. 18.95x (ISBN 0-86861-009-7); pap. text ed. 8.50x (ISBN 0-86861-017-8). Allen Unwin.

Race, Colonialism & the City. John Rex. 324p. 1973. 25.00x (ISBN 0-7100-7412-3). Routledge & Kegan.

Race, Culture & Evolution: Essays in the History of Anthropology. George W. Stocking, Jr. LC 69-10279. (Illus.). 1968. 12.95 (ISBN 0-02-931530-1). Free Pr.

Race Differences--Twenty Years Later. Frank C. McGurk. 56p. (Orig.). 1978. pap. 2.00x (ISBN 0-911038-73-6, IAAEE). Noontide.

Race Differences in Intelligence. John C. Loehlin et al. LC 75-1081. (Psychology Ser.). (Illus.). 1975. text ed. 22.95x (ISBN 0-7167-0754-3); pap. text ed. 12.95x (ISBN 0-7167-0753-5). W H Freeman.

Race for Glory. Ed. by Thomas Mooney. (Pal Paperbacks Kit B Ser.). (Illus., Orig.). (gr. 7-12). 1973. pap. text ed. 1.25 (ISBN 0-8374-3521-8). Xerox Ed Pubns.

Race for Love. Faye Wildman. 192p. (Orig.). 1980. pap. 1.50 (ISBN 0-671-57048-X). S&S.

Race, IQ, & Jensen. James R. Flynn. 320p. 1980. 27.50 (ISBN 0-7100-0651-9). Routledge & Kegan.

Race Is Pace. Huey Mahl. (Gambler's Book Shelf). 64p. 1975. pap. 2.95 (ISBN 0-89650-550-2). Gamblers.

Race, Language & Culture. Franz Boas. 1966. pap. text ed. 6.95 o.s.i. (ISBN 0-02-904490-1). Free Pr.

Race Mixing in Public Schools. Charles V. Willie & Jerome Beker. LC 73-10947. (Special Studies in U.S. Economic, Social & Political Issues). 1973. 20.00x (ISBN 0-275-28812-9); pap. text ed. 8.95x (ISBN 0-89197-915-8). Irvington.

Race Mixture. Harry L. Shapiro. (Orig.). 1958. pap. 2.50 (ISBN 92-3-100416-6, U509, UNESCO). Unipub.

Race of the Century: Grundy & Bustino at Ascot. Christopher Hawkins. 1976. 10.95 o.p. (ISBN 0-04-796046-9). Allen Unwin.

Race, Poverty, & Youth: Can This Generation Build a Better America? Martin W. Sandler et al. (People Make a Nation Ser.). (gr. 7-12). 1971. pap. text ed. 5.20 (ISBN 0-205-03440-3, 7834403). Allyn.

Race, Propaganda & South Africa: The Manipulation of Western Opinion & Policies by the Forces of White Supremacy. John C. Laurence. 1981. text ed. 19.25 (ISBN 0-575-02691-X, Pub. by Gollancz England). Humanities.

Race Relations. 2nd ed. Harry H. Kitano. (Ser. in Sociology). (Illus.). 1980. text ed. 17.95 (ISBN 0-13-750091-2). P-H.

Race Relations & American Law. Jack Greenberg. LC 59-11179. 1959. 17.50x (ISBN 0-231-02313-8). Columbia U Pr.

Race Relations & Mental Health. Marie Jahoda. (Orig.). 1960. pap. 2.50 (ISBN 0-685-20792-7, U510, UNESCO). Unipub.

Race Relations at the Cape of Good Hope, Sixteen Fifty-Two to Seventeen Ninety-Five: A Bibliography. P. L. Scholtz et al. (Reference Bks.). 1981. lib. bdg. 27.50 (ISBN 0-8161-8500-X). G K Hall.

Race Relations in Colonial Trinidad Eighteen Seventy to Nineteen Hundred. Bridget Brereton. LC 78-72081. (Illus.). 1980. 41.50 (ISBN 0-521-22428-4). Cambridge U Pr.

Race Relations in the Urban South 1865-1890. Howard N. Rabinowitz. (Urban Life in America Ser.). (Illus.). 1978. 19.95x (ISBN 0-19-502283-1). Oxford U Pr.

Race, School & Community: A Survey of Research & Literature. Francine Taylor. (General Ser.). 200p. 1974. pap. text ed. 12.00x (ISBN 0-85633-033-7, NFER). Humanities.

Race, Science, & Society. Unesco. 368p. 1975. 15.00x (ISBN 0-231-03908-5); pap. 7.00x (ISBN 0-231-03910-7). Columbia U Pr.

Race, Sex, & Policy Problems. Ed. by Marian L. Palley & Michael B. Preston. (Policy Studies Organization Ser.). (Illus.). 1979. 22.95 (ISBN 0-669-01985-2). Lexington Bks.

Race to Win. Eve Cowen. (Sportellers Ser.). (Illus.). 64p. (gr. 5 up). 1981. PLB 7.95 (ISBN 0-516-02266-0). Childrens.

Race to Win. Roger Marshall. (Illus.). 1980. 15.95 (ISBN 0-393-03236-1). Norton.

Races: A Study of the Problems of Race Formation in Man. Carleton S. Coon et al. LC 80-24479. (American Lecture Ser.: No. 77). (Illus.). xiv, 153p. 1981. Repr. of 1950 ed. lib. bdg. 19.75x (ISBN 0-313-22878-7, CORA). Greenwood.

Races & Peoples of Europe. Bertil J. Lundman. Tr. by Donald A. Swan from German. (Illus.). 78p. 1977. pap. 2.00x (ISBN 0-911038-72-8). Noontide.

Races, Types & Ethnic Groups: The Problem of Human Variation. Stephen Molner. LC 74-23935. (Illus.). 224p. 1975. pap. 9.95 (ISBN 0-13-750240-0). P-H.

Racewalk to Fitness. Howard Jacobson. 1980. 11.95 (ISBN 0-686-62860-8, 24938). S&S.

Rachel. Mina Lewiton. (Illus.). (gr. 4-6). 1954. PLB 3.90 o.p. (ISBN 0-531-01908-X). Watts.

Rachel Crothers. Lois C. Gottlieb. (United States Authors Ser.: No. 332). 1979. lib. bdg. 12.50 (ISBN 0-8057-7222-7). Twayne.

Racial & Ethnic Relations. Joe R. Feagin. LC 77-27306. (P-H Ser. in Sociology). (Illus.). 1978. ref. 17.95 (ISBN 0-13-749887-X). P-H.

Racial & Ethnic Relations in America. McLemore. (Illus.). 1980. text ed. 16.95 (ISBN 0-205-06827-8, 816827X). Allyn.

Racial Conflict in Rhodesia: A Socio-Historical Study. Graham C. Kinloch. LC 78-64823. 1978. pap. text ed. 11.25 (ISBN 0-8191-0642-9). U Pr of Amer.

Racial Discrimination & Military Justice. Ronald W. Perry. LC 76-53541. (Special Studies). 1976. text ed. 20.95 (ISBN 0-275-24180-7). Praeger.

Racial Hybridity. Philip Jones. (Illus.). 241p. (Orig.). 1979. pap. 5.50x (ISBN 0-911038-77-9, Uriel Pubns). Noontide.

Racial Inequality: A Political-Economic Analysis. Michael Reich. LC 80-8573. 320p. 1981. 20.00x (ISBN 0-691-04227-6); pap. 6.95 (ISBN 0-691-00365-3). Princeton U Pr.

Racial Justice: Black Judges & Defendants in an Urban Trial Court. Thomas M. Uhlman. LC 78-19569. 144p. 1979. 15.50 (ISBN 0-669-02625-5). Lexington Bks.

Racial Prejudice in Imperial Rome. Adrian N. Sherwin-White. 1967. 19.95 (ISBN 0-521-06438-4). Cambridge U Pr.

Racial Prejudice, the Individual & Society. Christopher Bagley & Gajendra K. Verma. 1979. 19.95 (ISBN 0-566-00294-9, 03085-6, Pub. by Saxon Hse England). Lexington Bks.

Racial Problems in Hungary. R. W. Seton-Watson. 540p. 1973. Repr. of 1908 ed. 23.50 (ISBN 0-86527-163-1). Fertig.

Racial Segregation: Two Policy Views. Gary Orfield & William Taylor. LC 79-3166. (Illus.). 68p. 1979. pap. text ed. 3.95 (ISBN 0-916584-13-5). Ford Found.

Racial Strife in the U. S. Military: Toward the Elimination of Discrimination. Richard O. Hope. LC 79-65932. 144p. 1979. 21.95 (ISBN 0-03-046146-4). Praeger.

Racial Variations in Man: Proceedings. Royal Geographical Society, Symposium, London, 1974. Ed. by F. J. Ebling. LC 75-12803. 1976. 39.95 (ISBN 0-470-22955-1). Halsted Pr.

Racine: Five Plays. Jean Racine. Tr. & intro. by Kenneth Muir. Incl. Andromache; Britannicus; Berenice; Phaedra; Athaliah. 288p. (Orig.). 1969. pap. 7.95 (ISBN 0-8090-0717-7, Mermaid). Hill & Wang.

Racine: Or, the Triumph of Relevance. Odette De Mourgues. (Orig.). 1967. 34.50 (ISBN 0-521-06023-0); pap. 11.95x (ISBN 0-521-09428-3). Cambridge U Pr.

Racine's Phaedre. Tr. by Robert Lowell & Robert Lowell. 213p. 1961. pap. 4.95 (ISBN 0-374-50911-5, N403). FS&G.

Racing. (Library of Boating Ser.). (Illus.). 1976. 14.95 (ISBN 0-8094-2124-0). Time-Life.

Racing. Ed. by Time Life Books. LC 75-34791. (Library of Boating Ser.). (Illus.). (gr. 6 up). 1976. PLB 13.95 (ISBN 0-8094-2125-9, Pub. by Time-Life). Silver.

Racing Against the Odds: Robyn C. Smith. Fern Brown. LC 75-42320. (Sports Profiles Ser.). (Illus.). 48p. (gr. 4-11). 1976. PLB 8.50 (ISBN 0-8172-0118-1). Raintree Pubs.

Racing Car. (Activity Bks.). 1980. 2.95 (ISBN 0-8431-0671-9). Price Stern.

Racing Cars & Great Races. Frank Ross, Jr. LC 74-177329. (Illus.). 192p. (gr. 5-12). 1972. 8.25 o.p. (ISBN 0-688-41634-9); PLB 7.92 (ISBN 0-688-51634-3). Lothrop.

Racing Cars, 1898-1921. T. R. Nicholson. (Cars of the World in Color Ser.: No. 5). (Illus.). 1972. 3.95 o.s.i. (ISBN 0-02-589410-2). Macmillan.

Racing Driver's Manual. Frank Gardner. LC 73-93418. (Illus.). 1974. 8.50 o.p. (ISBN 0-668-03458-0). Arco.

Racing Maxims & Methods of Pittsburg Phil. Edward W. Cole. 1965. pap. 2.95 (ISBN 0-89650-506-5). Gamblers.

Racing Men of TV. new ed. Miles Napier. 1978. pap. 8.75 (ISBN 0-85131-301-9, Dist. by Sporting Book Center). J A Allen.

Racing on the Wind. E. Radlauer & R. S. Radlauer. LC 73-17055. (Sports Action Books). (Illus.). 48p. (gr. 3 up). 1974. PLB 5.90 o.p. (ISBN 0-531-02681-7). Watts.

Racing Planes & Air Races, Vol. 11. Reed Kinert. LC 67-16455. (Illus.). 96p. 1975. pap. 4.95 (ISBN 0-8168-7865-X). Aero.

Racing Planes & Air Races: Biennial 1979 to 1980, Vol. 14. Dusty Carter. LC 67-16455. (Illus.). 160p. 1981. pap. write for info. (ISBN 0-8168-7873-0). Aero.

Racing Round the Island. Bob Holliday. 5.95 (ISBN 0-7153-7205-X, Pub. by Batsford England). David & Charles.

Racing Techniques Explained. rev. ed. Conrad Gulcher. (Illus.). 1972. 7.50 (ISBN 0-8286-0062-7). De Graff.

Racing to Indy. Mike Kupper & Peter Sanders. LC 74-34462. (Venture Ser, a Reading Incentive Program). (Illus.). 80p. (gr. 7-12,RL 4.5-6.5). 1975. In Packs Of 5. text ed. 23.25 ea. pack (ISBN 0-8172-0212-9). Follett.

Racing to Win - Wood Brothers Style. Lyle K. Engel. LC 72-91065. (Illus.). 192p. (Orig.). 1974. 5.95 o.p. (ISBN 0-668-02886-6). Arco.

Racing Toward Judgement. David Wilkerson. (Orig.). pap. 1.50 (ISBN 0-89129-035-4). Jove Pubns.

Racing Without Tears. Caroline Ramsden. (Illus.). pap. 4.35 (ISBN 0-85131-004-4, Dist. by Sporting Book Center). J A Allen.

Racing Yachts. Time-Life Books Editors & A. B. Whipple. (Seafarers Ser.). (Illus.). 176p. 1981. 14.95 (ISBN 0-8094-2693-5). Time-Life.

Racism & Apartheid in Southern Africa: South Africa & Namibia. (Illus.). 156p. (Orig.). 1974. pap. 6.00 (ISBN 92-3-101199-5, U512, UNESCO). Unipub.

Racism & Inequality: The Policy Alternatives. Ed. by Harrell R. Rodgers, Jr. LC 75-15640. (Illus.). 1975. text ed. 12.00x (ISBN 0-7167-0796-9); pap. text ed. 4.50x (ISBN 0-7167-0795-0). W H Freeman.

Racism & Political Action in Britain. Ed. by Robert Miles & Annie Phizacklea. 1978. 23.50x (ISBN 0-7100-0035-9); pap. 10.00 (ISBN 0-7100-0036-7). Routledge & Kegan.

Racism & Reaction: A Profile of Handsworth. Peter Ratcliffe. (International Library of Sociology). 280p. 1981. price not set (ISBN 0-7100-0696-9). Routledge & Kegan.

Racism in American Education: A Model for Change. William E. Sedlacek & Glenwood C. Brooks, Jr. LC 76-6909. 236p. 1976. 17.95 (ISBN 0-88229-136-X); pap. 8.95 (ISBN 0-88229-585-3). Nelson-Hall.

Racism: Opposing Viewpoints. Ed. by Bruno Leone. (ISMS Ser.). (Illus.). (gr. 9-12). 1978. 8.95 (ISBN 0-912616-61-X); pap. 3.95 (ISBN 0-912616-60-1). Greenhaven.

Racist Reader: Analyzing Primary Source Readings by American Race Supremacists. Ed. by Gary E. McCuen. (Illus.). 1974. lib. bdg. 10.95 (ISBN 0-912616-33-4); pap. text ed. 4.95 (ISBN 0-912616-14-8). Greenhaven.

Racket & Paddle Games: A Guide to Information Sources. Ed. by David A. Peele. LC 80-23977. (Sports, Games & Pastimes Information Guide Ser., Part of the Gale Information Guide Library: Vol. 9). 300p. 1980. 30.00 (ISBN 0-8103-1480-0). Gale.

Racquetball. 3rd ed. Philip E. Alsen & Alan R. Witbeck. 112p. 1980. write for info. (ISBN 0-697-07172-3). Wm C Brown.

Racquetball. George S. Fichter. (First Bks.). (Illus.). (gr. 4 up). 1979. PLB 6.45 s&l (ISBN 0-531-04078-X). Watts.

Racquetball. John W. Reznik. LC 78-66320. 1979. 9.95 (ISBN 0-8069-4138-3); lib. bdg. 9.29 (ISBN 0-8069-4139-1). Sterling.

Racquetball for Women. Toni Hudson et al. pap. 3.00 (ISBN 0-87980-384-3). Wilshire.

Racquetball "For Women". 3rd ed. Joyce Weckstein. LC 75-39292. (Illus.). 1975. pap. 2.50 (ISBN 0-9600980-1-1, 9600980). J R Weckstein.

Racquetball: Paddle Ball Fundamentals. Ralph Wickstrom & Charles Larson. LC 78-172488. 96p. 1972. pap. text ed. 5.95 (ISBN 0-675-09173-X). Merrill.

Racquetball-Paddleball. 2nd ed. Philip E. Allsen & Alan R. Witbeck. (Physical Education Activities & Dance Ser). 1977. pap. text ed. 3.25 o.p. (ISBN 0-697-07073-5). Wm C Brown.

Radar & Electronic Navigation. 5th ed. G. J. Sonnenberg. LC 77-30476. 1978. 34.95 (ISBN 0-408-00272-7). Butterworths.

Radar Instruction Manual. 2nd ed. (Illus.). 120p. 1979. pap. text ed. 14.55 (ISBN 0-934114-26-9). Marine Educ.

Radar Precision & Resolution. G. J. Bird. LC 74-8158. 151p. 1974. 24.95 (ISBN 0-470-07380-2). Halsted Pr.

Radar Probing of the Auroral Plasma: Proceedings. EISCAT School. Ed. by Asgeir Brekke. 1977. pap. 36.00x (ISBN 82-00-02421-0, Dist. by Columbia U Pr). Universitet.

Radar Reflectivity of Land & Sea. Maurice W. Long. LC 75-13435. (Illus.). 400p. 1975. 26.95 (ISBN 0-669-00050-7). Lexington Bks.

Radar Signal Analysis. William S. Burdic. 1967. ref. ed. 21.95 (ISBN 0-13-750018-1). P-H.

Radar Target Detection: Handbook of Theory & Practice. Daniel P. Meyer & Herbert A. Mayer. (Electrical Science Series). 1973. 48.50 (ISBN 0-12-492850-1). Acad Pr.

Radha: Diary of a Woman's Search. Swami Sivananda Radha. Ed. by Margaret Gray & Swami Padmananda. LC 80-26470. (Illus.). 230p. (Orig.). 1981. pap. 7.95 (ISBN 0-931454-06-9). Timeless Bks.

Radhakrishnan & Integral Experience. J. G. Arapura. 6.25x o.p. (ISBN 0-210-33813-X). Asia.

Radhakrishnan on Hindu Moral Life & Action. Aloysius Michael. 1979. text ed. 14.50x (ISBN 0-391-01857-4). Humanities.

Radiance of the Inner Splendor. Lloyd J. Ogilvie. LC 80-51524. 144p. 1980. pap. text ed. 4.95x (ISBN 0-8358-0405-4). Upper Room.

Radiant Faith. Rudolph F. Norden. Ed. by Oscar E. Feucht. 1966. pap. 0.85 study guide (ISBN 0-570-03527-9, 14-1330); pap. 1.15 leader's manual (ISBN 0-570-03528-7, 14-1331). Concordia.

Radiant Universe: Electronic Images from Space. Michael Marten & John Chesterman. (Illus.). 128p. 1980. 17.95 (ISBN 0-02-580420-0). Macmillan.

Radiation & Aging. Ed. by Patricia J. Lindop & G. A. Sacher. 1966. pap. text ed. 18.95x (ISBN 0-685-83895-1). Intl Ideas.

Radiation & Quantum Physics. D. J. Ingram. (Oxford Physics Ser.). (Illus.). 112p. 1974. pap. text ed. 6.95x (ISBN 0-19-851814-5). Oxford U Pr.

Radiation & Radioisotopes Applied to Insects of Agricultural Importance. 1963. 18.75 (ISBN 92-0-010263-8, IAEA). Unipub.

Radiation & Radioisotopes for Industrial Microorganisms. 1971. pap. 19.50 (ISBN 92-0-010371-5, IAEA). Unipub.

Radiation & Scattering of Waves. Nathan Marcuvitz & L. B. Felsen. LC 78-167786. 1973. ref. ed. 38.00 (ISBN 0-13-750364-4). P-H.

Radiation & the Control of Immune Response. 1968. pap. 6.50 (ISBN 92-0-011168-8, IAEA). Unipub.

Radiation: Benefits-Dangers. Dinah Moche. (Impact Ser.). (Illus.). (gr. 7 up). 1979. PLB 6.90 s&l (ISBN 0-531-02860-7). Watts.

Radiation Biology in Cancer Research. Ed. by Rodney E. Meyn & H. R. Withers. (M. D. Anderson Symposia on Fundamental Cancer Research Ser.). 1980. text ed. 61.50 (ISBN 0-89004-402-3). Raven.

Radiation Chemistry, 2 Vols. Ed. by Edwin J. Hart. LC 68-55363. (Advances in Chemistry Ser: Nos. 81-82). 1968. Set. 78.00 (ISBN 0-8412-0619-8); No. 81. 45.25 (ISBN 0-8412-0082-3); No. 82. 41.50 (ISBN 0-8412-0083-1). Am Chemical.

Radiation Chemistry & Its Applications. (Technical Reports: No. 84). 1968. pap. 9.75 (ISBN 92-0-045068-7, IAEA). Unipub.

Radiation Chemistry of Carbohydrates. Ed. by N. K. Kochetkov et al. (Illus.). 1979. 50.00 (ISBN 0-08-022962-X). Pergamon.

Radiation Curing: A Discussion of Advantages, Features & Applications. Jim Lacey & Allen Keough. LC 80-52815. (Illus.). 89p. (Orig.). 1980. pap. text ed. 8.50 (ISBN 0-87263-060-9). SME.

Radiation Curing V: A Look to the 80's. Intro. by Ken Lawson. LC 80-52816. (Illus.). 544p. 1980. pap. text ed. 55.00 (ISBN 0-87263-059-5). SME.

Radiation Damage & Sulphydryl Compounds. 1969. pap. 10.75 (ISBN 92-0-011169-6, IAEA). Unipub.

Radiation Damage in Metals. Ed. by N. L. Peterson & S. D. Harkness. (TA 460.r23). 1976. 38.00 (ISBN 0-87170-055-7). ASM.

Radiation Damage in Reactor Materials - 1969, 2 vols. Vol. 1. pap. 29.50 (ISBN 92-0-030069-3, IAEA); Vol. 2. pap. 38.75 (ISBN 92-0-030169-X). Unipub.

Radiation Damage to the Nervous System: A Delayed Therapeutic Hazard. Harvey A. Gilbert & Robert A. Kagan. (Illus.). 225p. 1980. text ed. 27.00 (ISBN 0-89004-418-X). Raven.

Radiation Detection. W. H. Tait. LC 80-40240. 1980. text ed. 54.95 (ISBN 0-408-10645-X). Butterworths.

Radiation Engineering in the Academic Curriculum: Proceedings. Study Group Meeting, Haifa, Aug. 27-Sept. 4, 1973. (Illus.). 362p. 1975. pap. 26.75 (ISBN 92-0-161075-0, IAEA). Unipub.

Radiation for a Clean Environment: Proceedings. (Illus.). 672p. 1976. pap. 49.75 (ISBN 92-0-060075-1, IAEA). Unipub.

Radiation Gas Dynamics. Pai Shih-I. (Illus.). 1966. 31.90 o.p. (ISBN 0-387-80776-4). Springer-Verlag.

Radiation Heat Transfer: Augmented Edition. E. M. Sparrow & R. D. Cess. LC 77-24158. (McGraw-Hill Series in Thermal & Fluids Engineering). (Illus.). 1978. text ed. 25.95 (ISBN 0-07-059910-6, Hemisphere Pub. Corp.). McGraw.

Radiation Histopathology, 2 vols. George W. Casarett. Vol. 1, 160p. 52.95 (ISBN 0-8493-5357-2); Vol. 2, 176p. 52.95 (ISBN 0-8493-5358-0). CRC Pr.

Radiation Hydrodynamics. G. C. Pomraning. 304p. 1973. text ed. 50.00 (ISBN 0-08-016893-0). Pergamon.

Radiation in the Atmosphere. K. Ya Kondratyav. (International Geophysics Ser.: Vol. 12). 1969. 75.50 (ISBN 0-12-419050-2). Acad Pr.

Radiation-Induced Cancer. 1969. pap. 26.75 (ISBN 92-0-010269-7, IAEA). Unipub.

Radiation Oncology: Rationale, Technique, Results. 5th ed. William T. Moss et al. LC 79-14367. (Illus.). 1979. text ed. 49.50 (ISBN 0-8016-3556-X). Mosby.

Radiation Physics & Chemistry: Magat Memorial Issue, Vols. 2 & 3. Ed. by F. Kieffer. 300p. 1980. pap. 42.00 (ISBN 0-08-025069-6). Pergamon.

Radiation Physics & Chemistry of Polymers. F. A. Makhlis. Ed. by M. Weiss. Tr. by Thier from Rus. LC 74-13587. 287p. 1975. 44.95 (ISBN 0-470-56537-3). Halsted Pr.

Radiation Preservation of Food. 774p. (Orig.). 1972. pap. 50.50 (ISBN 92-0-010373-1, IAEA). Unipub.

Radiation Processing: Transactions of the First International Meeting on Radiation Processing, 2 vols. Ed. by Joseph Silverman & A. R. Van Dyken. LC 76-58383. 1977. Set. text ed. 165.00 (ISBN 0-08-021640-4). Pergamon.

Radiation Protection - Recommendations of the ICRP. International Commission on Radiological Protection. (ICRP Publication Ser.: No. 9). 1959. pap. 7.15 (ISBN 0-08-013160-3). Pergamon.

Radiation Protection--a Systematic Approach to Safety: Proceedings of the 5th Congress of the International Radiation Protection Society, March 1980, Jerusalem, 2 vols. Ed. by Eisenberg. (Illus.). 1055p. 1980. 215.00 (ISBN 0-08-025912-X). Pergamon.

Radiation Protection Measurement. H. Kiefer & R. Maushart. Tr. by Ralf Friese. LC 70-133884. 576p. 1972. text ed. 75.00 (ISBN 0-08-015838-2). Pergamon.

Radiation Protection Monitoring. 1969. pap. 35.00 (ISBN 92-0-020069-9, IAEA). Unipub.

Radiation Protection Nineteen Seventy-Nine. 909p. 1980. 130.00 (ISBN 3-7186-0047-1). Harwood Academic.

Radiation Protection Optimization--Present Experience & Methods: Proceedings of the European Scientific Seminar, Luxembourg, Oct. 1979. Ed. by H. Ebert et al. LC 80-41671. (Illus.). 330p. 1980. pap. 50.00 (ISBN 0-08-027291-6). Pergamon.

Radiation Protection Procedures. P. N. Krishnamoorthy & J. U. Ahmed. (Safety Ser.: No. 38). (Illus.). 198p. (Orig.). 1973. pap. 15.75 (ISBN 92-0-123373-6, IAEA). Unipub.

Radiation Protection: Proceedings of the First International Congress. Ed. by W. S. Snyder et al. LC 67-30114. 1968. 225.00 (ISBN 0-08-012413-5). Pergamon.

Radiation Protection Standards for Radioluminous Timepieces. (Safety Ser.: No. 23). 1967. pap. 3.25 (ISBN 92-0-123467-8, IAEA). Unipub.

Radiation Safety in Hot Facilities. (Proceedings Ser.: No. 238). (Illus., Orig.). 1970. pap. 41.75 (ISBN 92-0-020070-2, IAEA). Unipub.

Radiation Sensitivity of Toxins & Animal Poisons. (Illus., Orig.). 1970. pap. 6.50 (ISBN 92-0-111270-X, IAEA). Unipub.

Radiation Sensitizers: Their Use in the Clinical Management of Cancer, Vol. 5. Ed. by Luther W. Brady. LC 80-81987. (Cancer Management Series). (Illus.). 544p. 1980. 58.50 (ISBN 0-89352-112-4). Masson Pub.

Radiation Shielding & Dosimetry. A. Edward Profio. LC 78-15649. 1979. 36.50 (ISBN 0-471-04329-X, Pub. by Wiley-Interscience). Wiley.

Radiation Sterilisation of Plastic Medical Devices: Seminar Under the Auspices of the University of Lowell, Mass., March 1979. H. K. Mann. 128p. 1980. pap. 21.00 (ISBN 0-08-025067-X). Pergamon.

Radiation Techniques for Water-Use Efficiency Studies. (Technical Reports: No. 168). (Illus.). 127p. 1975. pap. 10.75 (ISBN 92-0-115075-X, IAEA). Unipub.

Radiation Therapy Mold Technology: Principles, Design & Applications. B. Watkins. (Illus.). 224p. 1981. 30.00 (ISBN 0-08-025373-3). Pergamon.

Radiation Therapy Technology Examination Review. John A. Stryker et al. LC 80-80369. 1980. pap. 14.00 (ISBN 0-87488-459-4). Med Exam.

Radiative Transfer & Interactions with Conduction & Convection. M. Necati Ozisik. LC 72-12824. 608p. 1973. 37.50 (ISBN 0-471-65722-0, Pub. by Wiley-Interscience). Wiley.

Radical Agriculture. Ed. by Richard Merrill. LC 76-23504. 1976. 17.50x (ISBN 0-8147-5414-7). NYU Pr.

Radical Alternatives to Prison & the Penal Lobby. Mick Ryan. LC 78-58895. 1975. 20.95 (ISBN 0-03-046351-3). Praeger.

Radical Approach to Job Enrichment. Lyle Yorks. LC 75-44481. 176p. 1976. 12.95 (ISBN 0-8144-5412-7). Am Mgmt.

Radical Brethren: Anabaptism & the English Reformation to 1558. Irvin B. Horst. (Bibliotheca Humanistica & Reformatorica: No. 2). 1972. text ed. 37.25x (ISBN 90-6004-292-1). Humanities.

Radical Criminology: The Coming Crises. Ed. by James A. Inciardi. LC 80-14408. (Sage Focus Editions: Vol. 23). (Illus.). 320p. 1980. 18.95 (ISBN 0-8039-1489-X); pap. 9.95 (ISBN 0-8039-1490-3). Sage.

Radical Currents in Contemporary Philosophy, Vol. II. David DeGrood. 1981. write for info. Fireside Bks.

Radical Discipleship. Stephen Bly. 128p. (Orig.). 1981. pap. 3.95 (ISBN 0-8024-8219-8). Moody.

Radical Dissent in Contemporary Israeli Politics: Cracks in the Wall. David Schnall. (Praeger Special Studies). 1978. 24.95 (ISBN 0-03-047096-X). Praeger.

Radical Education: A Critique of Freeschooling & Deschooling. Robin Barrow. LC 78-1972. 1978. 21.95 (ISBN 0-470-26329-6); pap. 11.95 (ISBN 0-470-26845-X). Halsted Pr.

Radical Enlightenment: Pantheists, Fremasons & Republicans. Margaret C. Jacob. (Early Modern Europe Today Ser.). (Illus.). 352p. 1981. text ed. 29.50x (ISBN 0-04-901029-8, 2595). Allen Unwin.

Radical Essays. B. P. Beckwith. 1981. 6.00 (ISBN 0-686-69571-2). Beckwith.

Radical Future of Liberal Feminism. Zillah R. Eisenstein. (Feminist Theory Ser.). (Illus.). 400p. 1980. text ed. 17.95 (ISBN 0-582-28205-5). Longman.

Radical Immigrant. Sally M. Miller. (Immigrant Heritage of America Ser.). 1974. lib. bdg. 9.95 (ISBN 0-8057-3266-7). Twayne.

Radical Issues in Criminology. Pat Carlen & Mike Collison. 212p. 1980. 24.50x (ISBN 0-389-20083-2). B&N.

Radical Journalist: Henry W. Massingham, 1860-1924. A. F. Havighurst. LC 73-83106. (Conference on British Studies Biographical Ser). 368p. 1974. 42.00 (ISBN 0-521-20355-4). Cambridge U Pr.

Radical Left & the Far Right: Fringe Groups Speak on the Problem of Race. rev. ed. Ed. by Gary McCuen & David L. Bender. (Opposing Viewpoints Ser.: Vol. 1). (Illus.). (gr. 9 up). 1973. lib. bdg. 10.60 o.p. (ISBN 0-912616-25-3); pap. text ed. 4.60 o.p. (ISBN 0-912616-07-5). Greenhaven.

Radical Life. Vera B. Weisbord. LC 76-28276. (Illus.). 352p. 1977. 15.00x (ISBN 0-253-34773-4). Ind U Pr.

Radical Monotheism in Western Culture. H. Richard Niebuhr. pap. 3.50x (ISBN 0-06-131491-9, TB1491, Torch). Har-Row.

Radical Nationalism in Cameroun: Social Origins of the U.P.C. Rebellion. Richard A. Joseph. 1977. 49.50x (ISBN 0-19-822706-X). Oxford U Pr.

Radical New Road to Wealth. rev. ed. A. David Silver. 1981. pap. 15.00 (ISBN 0-914306-53-7). Intl Wealth.

Radical Pragmatics. Ed. by Peter Cole. 1981. price not set (ISBN 0-12-179660-4). Acad Pr.

Radical Principles: Reflections of an Unreconstructed Democrat. Michael Walzer. LC 79-56371. 310p. 1980. 15.00 (ISBN 0-465-06824-3). Basic.

Radical Sophistication: Studies in Contemporary Jewish-American Novelists. Max F. Schulz. LC 69-15914. xvi, 224p. 1969. 12.00 o.s.i. (ISBN 0-8214-0045-2); pap. 5.50 (ISBN 0-8214-0106-8). Ohio U Pr.

Radical Vegetarianism: A Dialectic of Diet & Ethic. Mark Braunstein. 250p. (Orig.). 1980. 12.95 (ISBN 0-915572-52-4); pap. 6.95 (ISBN 0-915572-37-0). Panjandrum.

Radical Visions of the Future. Ed. by Seweryn Bialer & Sophia Sluzar. LC 76-39890. (Studies of the Research Institute on International Change, Columbia, University: Vol. 2). 1977. lib. bdg. 21.50x (ISBN 0-89158-131-6); lib. bdg. 60.00 3 vol. set. Westview.

Radical Wesley. Howard Snyder. LC 80-18197. 180p. (Orig.). 1980. pap. 5.25 (ISBN 0-87784-625-1). Inter-Varsity.

Radicalism & Reform: The Vrooman Family & American Social Thought, 1837-1937. Ross E. Paulson. LC 68-12970. 324p. 1968. 12.00x (ISBN 0-8131-1156-0). U Pr of Ky.

Radicalism & the Revolt Against Reason. Irving L. Horowitz. 1961. text ed. 8.75x (ISBN 0-391-02031-5). Humanities.

Radicalism & the Revolt Against Reason: The Social Theories of Georges Sorel. Irving L. Horowitz. LC 68-25562. (Arcturus Books Paperbacks). 287p. 1968. pap. 7.95 (ISBN 0-8093-0323-X). S Ill U Pr.

Radicals. D. C. Nonhebel & J. M. Tedder. LC 78-54721. (Cambridge Texts in Chemistry & Biochemistry Ser.). (Illus.). 1979. 38.50 (ISBN 0-521-22004-1); pap. 15.95x (ISBN 0-521-29332-4). Cambridge U Pr.

Radicals & Reactionaries: The Crisis of Conservatism in Wilhelmine Germany. Abraham J. Peck. LC 78-62921. (Illus.). 1978. pap. text ed. 12.00 (ISBN 0-8191-0601-1). U Pr of Amer.

Radicals in Social Work. Daphne Statham. (Radical Social Policy Ser.). 1978. 16.00 (ISBN 0-7100-8728-4); pap. 7.95 (ISBN 0-7100-8729-2). Routledge & Kegan.

Radicals of Rings. Ferenc Szasz. LC 79-40509. 1981. 34.50 (ISBN 0-471-27583-2, Pub. by Wiley-Interscience). Wiley.

Radigan Cares. Jeannette Eyerly. LC 71-11722. (gr. 7-9). 1970. 6.50 (ISBN 0-397-31151-6); PLB 8.79 (ISBN 0-397-31152-4). Lippincott.

Radigan Cares. Jeannette Eyerly. (YA) 1978. pap. 1.50 (ISBN 0-671-29914-X). PB.

Radio. Boy Scouts Of America. LC 19-600. (Illus.). 48p. (gr. 6-12). 1965. pap. 0.70x (ISBN 0-8395-3333-0, 3333). BSA.

Radio Advertising: How to Sell It & Write It. Sol Robinson. LC 76-162410. 1974. 12.95 o.p. (ISBN 0-8306-4565-9, 565). TAB Bks.

Radio Amateur Antenna Handbook. William I. Orr & Stuart D. Cowan. LC 78-53340. (Illus.). 190p. 1978. 6.95 (ISBN 0-933616-07-4). Radio Pubns.

Radio Amateur's Handbook: 1979 Edition. American Radio Relay League. LC 41-3345. 1978. 9.75 o.p. (ISBN 0-87259-156-5); pap. write for info. o.p. (ISBN 0-87259-056-9). Am Radio.

Radio Amateur's V. H. F. Manual. American Radio Relay League. LC 65-22343. 4.00 o.p. (ISBN 0-87259-553-6). Am Radio.

Radio & Line Transmission, Vol. 2. D. Roddy. 1972. 30.00 (ISBN 0-08-016289-4); pap. 12.75 (ISBN 0-08-016288-6). Pergamon.

Radio & Radar in Sail & Power Boats. Kenneth Wilkes. 120p. 1980. 15.00x (ISBN 0-245-53191-2, Pub. by Nautical England). State Mutual Bk.

Radio & Television. Stuart Hood. LC 75-19. (Profession Ser). 128p. 1975. 11.95 (ISBN 0-7153-6890-7). David & Charles.

Radio & Television: A Selected, Annotated Bibliography. William E. McCavitt. LC 77-28665. 1978. 12.00 (ISBN 0-8108-1113-8). Scarecrow.

Radio & Television: Readings in the Mass Media. Allen Kirschner & Linda Kirschner. LC 72-158975. 1971. pap. 8.50 (ISBN 0-672-73230-0). Odyssey Pr.

Radio Astronomy for Amateurs. Frank W. Hyde. (Illus.). 1963. 5.00 o.p. (ISBN 0-393-06331-3). Norton.

Radio Astrophysics: Nonthermal Processes in Galactic & Extragalactic Sources. A. G. Pacholczyk. LC 70-95657. (Astronomy & Astrophysics Ser.). (Illus.). 1970. text ed. 29.95x (ISBN 0-7167-0329-7). W H Freeman.

Radio Beasts. Ralph M. Farley. 1976. lib. bdg. 10.95x (ISBN 0-89968-030-5). Lightyear.

Radio Comedy. Arthur F. Wertheim. LC 78-10679. (Illus.). 1979. 19.95 (ISBN 0-19-502481-8). Oxford U Pr.

Radio Contrast Agents, 2 Vols. P. R. Knoefel. 1971. Set. 165.00 (ISBN 0-08-016144-8). Pergamon.

Radio Control Guide. 2nd ed. Norman Butcher. LC 77-359360. (Illus.). 250p. (Orig.). 1978. pap. 12.50x (ISBN 0-903676-07-9). Intl Pubns Serv.

Radio Control Handbook. 4th, rev. ed. Howard C. McEntee. (Illus.). 1979. pap. 11.95 (ISBN 0-8306-9772-1, 1093). TAB Bks.

Radio Control Manual: Systems, Circuits, Construction. 3rd ed. E. L. Safford, Jr. (Illus.). 1979. pap. 7.95 (ISBN 0-8306-1135-5, 1135). TAB Bks.

Radio Control Model Cars Manual. D. J. Laidlaw-Dickson. (Illus.). 128p. (Orig.). 1979. pap. 10.00x (ISBN 0-906958-00-8). Intl Pubns Serv.

Radio Control Soaring. rev. ed. Ed. by Dave Hughes. (Illus.). 270p. (Orig.). 1977. pap. 13.50x (ISBN 0-8002-2260-1). Intl Pubns Serv.

Radio Controlled Model Aircraft. Adrian Vale. (Illus.). 181p. (Orig.). 1979. pap. 10.50x (ISBN 0-905418-04-2). Intl Pubns Serv.

Radio-Diagnosis of Pleuro-Pulmonary Affections. J. Barjon. 1918. 47.50x (ISBN 0-685-89775-3). Elliots Bks.

Radio Dog. Anne Iglehardt. LC 79-1949. (Illus.). (ps-2). 1979. 1.95 (ISBN 0-525-69016-6, Gingerbread Bks); PLB 5.95 (ISBN 0-525-69017-4). Dutton.

Radio Emission of the Sun & Planets. V. V. Zheleznyakov. LC 75-76797. 1970. 115.00 (ISBN 0-08-013061-5). Pergamon.

Radio Experiments. Francis G. Rayer. LC 78-431666. (Pegasus Books: No. 20). (Illus.). 1968. 7.50x (ISBN 0-234-77182-8). Intl Pubns Serv.

Radio for Education & Development. Dean T. Jamison & Emile G. McAnany. LC 77-28472. (People & Communication Ser.: Vol. 4). 1978. 20.00x (ISBN 0-8039-0865-2); pap. 9.95x (ISBN 0-8039-0866-0). Sage.

Radio in the Television Age. Peter Fornatale & Joshua E. Mills. LC 79-67675. 1980. 12.95 (ISBN 0-87951-106-0). Overlook Pr.

Radio Journalism. Denise A. Bittner & John R. Bittner. LC 76-29048. (Speech Communication Ser.). (Illus.). 1977. pap. text ed. 12.95 (ISBN 0-13-750455-1). P-H.

Radio Logbook. Aviation Maintenance Publishers. 70p. 1974. pap. 3.95 (ISBN 0-89100-186-7, EA-ARL-1). Aviation Maintenance.

Radio Logbook. Aviation Maintenance Publishers. 70p. 1974. text ed. 4.95 (ISBN 0-89100-195-6, EA-ARL-2). Aviation Maintenance.

Radio Operator's License Q & A Manual. 9th, rev. ed. Milton Kaufman. 1979. 15.85 (ISBN 0-8104-0651-9); pap. 9.95 (ISBN 0-8104-0650-0). Hayden.

Radio Physics of the Sun: Proceedings. IUA Symposium, College Park, Md., Aug. 7-10, 1979. Ed. by T. E. Gergely & M. R. Kundu. (International Astronomical Union Symposium: No. 86). 472p. 1980. lib. bdg. 60.50 (ISBN 90-277-1120-8); pap. 28.95 (ISBN 90-277-1121-6). Kluwer Boston.

Radio Production Techniques. Jay Hoffer. LC 73-89814. 1974. 16.95 (ISBN 0-8306-3661-7, 661). TAB Bks.

Radio Soundtracks: A Reference Guide. Michael R. Pitts. LC 76-18888. 1976. 10.00 (ISBN 0-8108-0956-7). Scarecrow.

Radio Study Group Campaigns in the United Republic of Tanzania. (Experiments & Innovations in Education Ser: No. 15). (Illus.). 50p. 1976. pap. 2.50 (ISBN 92-3-101305-X, U517, UNESCO). Unipub.

Radio Systems for Technicians, No. 2. Danielson. 1981. text ed. price not set (ISBN 0-408-00561-0). Butterworth.

Radio: The Great Years. Derek Parker. LC 77-89378. 1977. 14.95 (ISBN 0-7153-7430-3). David & Charles.

Radio: The Psychology of an Art of Sound. Rudolf Arnheim. LC 73-164504. (Cinema Ser). 1972. Repr. of 1936 ed. lib. bdg. 29.50 (ISBN 0-306-70291-6). Da Capo.

Radio: Theory & Servicing. Clyde N. Herrick. (Illus.). 288p. 1975. 16.95 (ISBN 0-87909-697-7). Reston.

Radio Universe. 2nd ed. J. S. Hey. 256p. 1975. text ed. 28.00 (ISBN 0-08-018760-9); pap. text ed. 13.25 (ISBN 0-08-018761-7). Pergamon.

Radioactive Contamination of the Marine Environment. (Illus.). 786p. (Orig.). 1973. pap. 67.00 (ISBN 92-0-020073-7, ISP313, IAEA). Unipub.

Radioactive Dating. 1963. 16.25 (ISBN 92-0-030663-2, IAEA). Unipub.

Radioactive Dating & Methods of Low-Level Counting. 1967. pap. 41.75 (ISBN 92-0-030367-6, IAEA). Unipub.

Radioactive Isotopes in Biological Research. W. R. Hendee. LC 73-8966. 27.50 (ISBN 0-471-37043-6, Pub. by Wiley-Interscience). Wiley.

Radioactive Patient. Earl Van Roosenbeek & Luis Delclos. 1975. spiral bdg. 12.00 o.p. (ISBN 0-87488-966-9). Med Exam.

Radioactive Tracers in Chemistry & Industry. 2nd ed. P. Daudel. Tr. by U. Eisner from Fr. 210p. 1960. 27.00x (ISBN 0-85264-101-X, Pub. by Griffin England). State Mutual Bk.

Radioactive Tracers in Microbial Immunology. (Proceedings Ser.). (Illus.). 130p. (Orig.). 1973. pap. 8.25 (ISBN 92-0-111172-X, IAEA). Unipub.

Radioactive Waste Disposal into the Ground. (Safety Ser.: No. 15). 1965. pap. 5.00 (ISBN 92-0-123565-8, IAEA). Unipub.

Radioactive Waste Management & Disposal. Ed. by R. Simon & S. Orlowski. 703p. 1980. 82.00 (ISBN 3-7186-0056-0). Harwood Academic.

Radioactive Waste: Management & Regulation. Mason Willrich & Richard K. Lester. LC 77-80228. 1977. 17.95 (ISBN 0-02-934560-X). Free Pr.

Radioactive Wastes at the Hanford Reservation. Board on Mineral & Energy Resources. 1978. pap. 8.50 (ISBN 0-309-02745-4). Natl Acad Pr.

Radioactivity & Atomic Theory. Ed. by T. J. Trenn. LC 74-19168. 517p. 1975. 49.95 (ISBN 0-470-88520-3). Halsted Pr.

Radioactivity & Its Measurement. 2nd ed. Ed. by W. B. Mann & R. L. Ayres. (Illus.). 1980. 41.00 (ISBN 0-08-025028-9); pap. 14.50 (ISBN 0-08-025027-0). Pergamon.

Radioactivity in the Marine Environment. Committee On Oceanography. (Illus.). 1971. text ed. 15.75 o.p. (ISBN 0-309-01865-X). Natl Acad Pr.

Radioassay in Clinical Medicine. William T. Newton & Robert M. Donati. (Illus.). 200p. 1974. 16.50 (ISBN 0-398-03012-X). C C Thomas.

Radioastronomical Methods of Antenna Measurements. A. D. Kuzmin & A. E. Salomonovich. (Electrical Science Monographs). 1967. 27.50 (ISBN 0-12-431150-4). Acad Pr.

Radioastronomy: Extremes of the Universe. Carl E. Heiles. 375p. pap. text ed. 12.00x (ISBN 0-935702-06-7). Univ Sci Bks.

Radiobiological Applications of Neutron Irradiation. (Illus.). 263p. (Orig.). 1972. pap. 17.25 (ISBN 92-0-011172-6, IAEA). Unipub.

Radiobiological Equivalents of Chemical Pollutants. 115p. 1980. pap. 14.75 (ISBN 92-0-111180-0, ISP 544, IAEA). Unipub.

Radiobiological Factors in Manned Space Flight. Space Science Board. Ed. by Wright H. Langham. 1967. 8.75 (ISBN 0-309-01487-5). Natl Acad Pr.

Radiobiological Research & Radiotherapy, Vol. II. 1978. pap. 26.75 (ISBN 92-0-010477-0, ISP 441-2, IAEA). Unipub.

Radiobiological Research & Radiotherapy: Fractionation of Doses - Radiomodifiers Hyperthermia, Combine Radio & Chemotherapy, Vol. 1. (Illus.). 1978. pap. 48.25 (ISBN 92-0-010377-4, ISP 441-1, IAEA). Unipub.

Radiobiology Examination Review Book. Thongbliew Prempree et al. 1975. spiral bdg. 10.00 (ISBN 0-87488-487-X). Med Exam.

Radiocarbon Dating. Ed. by Rainer Berger & Hans E. Suess. 1980. 60.00x (ISBN 0-520-03680-8). U of Cal Pr.

Radiochemical Methods of Analysis, 2 vols. 1965. Vol 1. 18.75 (ISBN 92-0-030065-0, IAEA); Vol 2. 22.50 (ISBN 92-0-030165-7). Unipub.

Radiochemistry & the Discovery of Isotopes. Ed. by Alfred Romer. LC 74-91273. (Classics of Science Ser). (Orig., Fr. & Ger.). 1970. pap. text ed. 3.50 (ISBN 0-486-62507-9). Dover.

Radioecology. V. M. Klechkovskii et al. LC 73-4697. 371p. 1973. 51.95 (ISBN 0-470-49035-7). Halsted Pr.

Radioecology & Energy Resources: Proceedings. Symposium on Radioecology, Oregon State University, May 12-14, 1975. Ed. by C. E. Cushing, Jr. (Ecological Society of America Special Publications Ser.: No. 1). 1977. 42.00 (ISBN 0-12-786290-0). Acad Pr.

Radioelement Distribution & Heat Production in Precambrian Granitic Rocks, Southern Norway. P. G. Killeen & K. S. Heier. 1975. pap. 11.00x (ISBN 8-200-01463-0, Dist. by Columbia U Pr). Universitet.

Radiographic Anatomy. McInnes. (Illus.). 1975. 13.95 o.p. (ISBN 0-685-78464-9). ACC.

Radiographic Anatomy of the Chest & Abdomen: A Student's Handbook. D. Noreen Chesney & Muriel O. Chesney. (Blackwell Scientific Pubns.). (Illus.). 1976. 23.00 (ISBN 0-632-09440-0). Mosby.

Radiographic Evaluation of the Intensive Care Unit Patient. Lawrence R. Goodman & C. Putnam. LC 78-50186. 1981. write for info. (ISBN 0-87527-172-3). Green.

Radiographic Examination in Blunt Abdominal Trauma. James J. McCort. LC 66-18500. (Illus.). 1966. 10.50 o.p. (ISBN 0-7216-5905-5). Saunders.

Radiographic Fundamentals & Technique Guide. Jerry R. Eastman. (Illus.). 1979. pap. text ed. 12.50 (ISBN 0-8016-1493-7). Mosby.

Radiographic Interpretation for the Dentist. 3rd ed. S. N. Bhaskar. LC 74-14785. 1979. 34.50 (ISBN 0-8016-0690-X). Mosby.

Radiographic Positioning of Small Animals. Gerald D. Ryan. LC 80-26069. (Illus.). 147p. 1981. text ed. write for info. (ISBN 0-8121-0774-8). Lea & Febiger.

Radiographic Tumor Localizer. John C. Rathe. 196p. 1981. 15.00 (ISBN 0-87527-249-5). Green.

Radiography in Obstetrics. J. G. B. Russell & A. S. Fisher. 1975. 7.95 (ISBN 0-407-00009-7). Butterworths.

Radioimmunoassay & Related Procedures in Medicine. (Illus.). 471p. (Orig.). 1974. pap. 29.00 ea. (IAEA); Vol. 1. pap. (ISBN 92-0-010274-3); Vol. 2. pap. (ISBN 92-0-010374-X). Unipub.

Radioimmunoassay & Related Procedures in Medicine 1977, Vol. 1. 1978. pap. 63.25 (ISBN 92-0-010078-3, ISP469-1, IAEA). Unipub.

Radioimmunoassay & Related Procedures in Medicine 1977, Vol. 2. 1979. pap. 58.50 (ISBN 92-0-010178-X, ISP469-2, IAEA). Unipub.

Radioimmunoassay of Biologically Active Compounds. Charles W. Parker. (Illus.). 272p. 1976. pap. text ed. 22.95 (ISBN 0-13-750505-1). P-H.

Radioimmunoassay of Steroid Hormones. 2nd ed. Derek Gupta. (Illus.). 1980. 48.80 (ISBN 3-5272-5863-9). Verlag Chemie.

Radioisotope Instruments in Industry & Geophysics, 2 vols. 1966. Vol 1. pap. 26.75 (ISBN 92-0-060066-2, IAEA); Vol 2. pap. 22.50 (ISBN 92-0-060166-9). Unipub.

Radioisotope Lab Techniques. 4th ed. R. A. Faires & G. G. Boswell. LC 80-41045. 272p. 1980. text ed. 39.95 (ISBN 0-408-70940-5). Butterworths.

Radioisotope Production & Quality Control. (Technical Reports: No. 128). (Illus.). 968p. (Orig.). 1971. pap. 63.75 (ISBN 92-0-145171-7, IDC128, IAEA). Unipub.

Radioisotope Sample Measurement Techniques in Medicine & Biology. 1965. pap. 31.25 (ISBN 92-0-010165-8, IAEA). Unipub.

Radioisotope Techniques in the Study of Protein Metabolism. (Technical Reports: No. 45). 1965. pap. 10.75 (ISBN 92-0-115165-9, IAEA). Unipub.

Radioisotope Tracers in Industry & Geophysics. 1967. pap. 33.25 (ISBN 92-0-060067-0, IAEA). Unipub.

Radioisotope X-Ray Fluorescence Spectrometry. (Technical Reports: No. 115). (Illus., Orig.). 1970. pap. 6.00 (ISBN 92-0-165170-8, IAEA). Unipub.

Radioisotopes & Radiation. John H. Lawrence et al. LC 69-20423. (Illus.). 1969. pap. text ed. 3.00 (ISBN 0-486-62296-7). Dover.

Radioisotopes & Radiation in Dairy Science & Technology. 1966. pap. 12.00 (ISBN 92-0-010266-2, IAEA). Unipub.

Radioisotopes in Animal Nutrition & Physiology. 1965. pap. 20.00 (ISBN 92-0-010065-1, IAEA). Unipub.

Radioisotopes in Hydrology. 1963. 17.25 (ISBN 92-0-040063-9, IAEA). Unipub.

Radioisotopes in Radiodiagnosis. A. S. Bligh et al. 256p. 1975. 29.95 (ISBN 0-407-00036-4). Butterworths.

Radioisotopes in the Clinical Laboratory. Thomas D. Trainer et al. (Atlas Ser.). (Illus.). 1976. text & slides 70.00 (ISBN 0-89189-093-9, 15-8-01-00); microfiche ed. 22.00 (ISBN 0-89189-094-7, 17-8-001-00). Am Soc Clinical.

Radioisotopes in the Detection of Pesticide Residues. 1966. pap. 5.50 (ISBN 92-0-111166-5, IAEA). Unipub.

Radioisotopes in Tropical Medicine. 1962. 13.50 (ISBN 92-0-010062-7, IAEA). Unipub.

Radiolaria in Pelagic Sediments from the Indian & Atlantic Oceans. Catherine Nigrini. (Bulletin of the Scripps Institution of Oceanography: Vol. 11). 1967. pap. 8.00x (ISBN 0-520-09315-1). U of Cal Pr.

Radiologic Diagnosis of Polyps & Carcinoma of the Large Bowel. Masakazu Maruyama. LC 77-95452. (Illus.). 1978. 63.00 (ISBN 0-89640-025-5). Igaku-Shoin.

Radiologic Science for Technologists: Physics, Biology & Protection. Stewart Bushong. LC 74-20847. 1975. 17.95 o.p. (ISBN 0-8016-0915-1). Mosby.

Radiologic Science for Technologists: Physics, Biology & Protection. 2nd ed. Stewart C. Bushong. LC 80-19. (Illus.). 1980. 24.95 (ISBN 0-8016-0928-3). Mosby.

Radiologic Science Workbook & Laboratory Manual. 2nd ed. Stewart Bushong. (Illus.). 260p. 1980. pap. text ed. 11.95 (ISBN 0-8016-0927-5). Mosby.

Radiologic Technology Examination Review Book, Vol. 1. 4th ed. Ed. by William L. Leonard. 1979. pap. 9.50 (ISBN 0-87488-441-1). Med Exam.

Radiologic Transverse Anatomy of the Human Thorax, Abodomen, & Pelvis. Alvin C. Wyman et al. 1978. text ed. 45.00 (ISBN 0-316-96250-3). Little.

Radiological Anatomy. D. Nagy. 1966. 75.00 (ISBN 0-08-010675-7). Pergamon.

Radiological Evaluation of the Spinal Cord, 2 vols. Milosh Perovitch. 1981. Vol. 1, 240p. 64.95 (ISBN 0-8493-5041-7); Vol. 2, 192p. 52.95 (ISBN 0-8493-5043-3). CRC Pr.

Radiological Examination of the Lung & Mediastinum with the Aid of Posterior Oblique Tomography at an Angle of 55 Degrees. G. Favez & O. Soliman. (Illus., Eng., Fr. & Ger.). 1966. 16.25 o.s.i. (ISBN 0-02-844560-0). Hafner.

Radiological Physics Examination Review Book, Vol. 1. 2nd ed. Ed. by Colin G. Orton et al. 1978. spiral bdg. 13.50 (ISBN 0-87488-486-1). Med Exam.

Radiological Safety Aspects of the Operation of Electron Linear Accelerators. (Technical Reports Ser.: No. 188). 1979. pap. 40.75 (ISBN 92-0-125179-3, IDC188, IAEA). Unipub.

Radiological Safety Aspects of the Operation of Neutron Generators. R. F. Boggs. (Safety Ser.: No. 42). (Illus.). 1976. pap. 6.00 (ISBN 92-0-123076-1, ISP427, IAEA). Unipub.

Radiological Safety in Uranium & Thorium Mines & Mills. (Safety Ser: No. 43). 1976. pap. 9.75 (ISBN 92-0-123176-8, ISP449, IAEA). Unipub.

Radiological Significance & Management of Tritium, Carbon-14, Krypton-85, Iodine-129, Arising from the Nuclear Fuel Cycle. OECD-NEA. (Illus.). 222p. (Orig.). 1980. pap. text ed. 19.00x (ISBN 0-686-27701-5, 66-80-06-1) (ISBN 92-64-12083-1). OECD.

Radiological Surveillance of Airborne Contaminants in the Working Environment. (Safety Ser.: No. 49). 138p. 1980. pap. 18.25 (ISBN 92-0-623279-7, IDC 484, IAEA). Unipub.

Radiology. James R. Critser, Jr. 99p. 1980. 60.00 (ISBN 0-914428-68-3, 10R-79). Lexington Data.

Radiology. 2nd ed. Jerome H. Shapiro & Florencio A. Hipona. (Medical Examination Review Book: Vol. 17). 1972. spiral bdg. 16.50 (ISBN 0-87488-117-X). Med Exam.

Radiology & Injury in Sport. Bowerman. (Illus.). 1977. 28.50 (ISBN 0-8385-8250-8). ACC.

Radiology for Dental Auxiliaries. 2nd ed. Herbert H. Frommer. LC 77-15473. (Illus.). 1978. text ed. 14.50 (ISBN 0-8016-1706-5). Mosby.

Radiology in Primary Care. Ed. by Glenn V. Dalrymple & John E. Slayden. LC 74-28277. (Illus.). 330p. 1975. pap. text ed. 26.50 o.p. (ISBN 0-8016-1198-9). Mosby.

Radiology of Childhood Leukemia & Its Therapy. Nancy S. Rosenfield. (Illus.). 164p. 1981. 17.50 (ISBN 0-87527-173-1). Green.

Radiology of Emergency Medicine. 2nd ed. John H. Harris, Jr. & William H. Harris. (Illus.). 550p. 1981. write for info. (3883-4). Williams & Wilkins.

Radiology of Jaw Bone Masses in Adults & Children. Vivian J. Harris. (Illus.). 220p. 1981. 22.50 (ISBN 0-87527-212-6). Green. Postponed.

Radiology of Spinal Cord Injury. Leonid Calenoff. (Illus.). 500p. 1981. text ed. 42.50 (ISBN 0-8016-1114-8). Mosby.

Radiology of the Alimentary Tract in Infants & Children. Edward B. Singleton et al. LC 75-299. (Monograhs in Clinical Radiology: No. 10). (Illus.). 1977. text ed. 30.00 (ISBN 0-7216-8314-2). Saunders.

Radiology of the Ileocecal Area. Robert N. Berk & Elliot C. Lasser. LC 74-11684. (Monographs in Clinical Radiology: Vol. 5). (Illus.). 327p. 1975. text ed. 23.50 o.p. (ISBN 0-7216-1689-5). Saunders.

Radiology of the Liver. James G. McNulty. LC 77-75536. (Monographs in Clinical Radiology: 13). (Illus.). 1977. text ed. 32.00 (ISBN 0-7216-5969-1). Saunders.

Radiology of the Newborn & Young Infant. 2nd ed. Leonard E. Swischuk. (Illus.). 912p. 1980. 82.50 (ISBN 0-683-08053-9). Williams & Wilkins.

Radiology of the Orbit. G. A. Lloyd. (Monographs in Clinical Radiology: Vol. 7). (Illus.). 250p. 1975. text ed. 28.00 (ISBN 0-7216-5792-3). Saunders.

Radiology of the Pancreas & Duodenum. S. Boyd Eaton, Jr. & Joseph T. Ferrucci. LC 72-97909. (Monographs in Clinical Radiology: No. 3). (Illus.). 385p. 1973. text ed. 29.00 (ISBN 0-7216-3310-2). Saunders.

Radiology of the Postoperative Digestive Tract. Henri Nahum & Francois Fekete. Tr. by Alan E. Oestreich from Fr. LC 79-837338. (Illus.). 160p. 1979. 32.50 (ISBN 0-89352-027-6). Masson Pub.

Radiology of the Postoperative Hip. Matthew Freedman. LC 79-12411. 1979. 38.95 (ISBN 0-471-04416-4, Pub. by Wiley Medical). Wiley.

Radiology of the Sella Turcica. J. F. Bonneville et al. (Illus.). 262p. 1981. 116.80 (ISBN 0-387-10319-8). Springer-Verlag.

Radiology of the Skull & Brain: Anatomy & Pathology, Vol. III. Ed. by Thomas H. Newton & D. Gordon Potts. LC 78-173600. 1977. 60.00 (ISBN 0-8016-3648-5). Mosby.

Radiology of the Skull & Brain: Angiography, 4 pts, Vol. 2. Thomas H. Newton & D. Gordon Potts. LC 74-12407. 1974. text ed. 285.00 set (ISBN 0-8016-3647-7); text ed. 99.75 ea. part; Pt. 1. (ISBN 0-8016-3641-8); Pt. 2. (ISBN 0-8016-3642-6); Pt. 3. (ISBN 0-8016-3644-2); Pt. 4. (ISBN 0-8016-3649-3). Mosby.

Radiology of the Skull & Brain, Vol. 5: Technical Aspects of Computed Tomography. Thomas H. Newton. (Illus.). 616p. 1980. text ed. 79.50 (ISBN 0-8016-3662-0). Mosby.

Radiology of the Urinary System, 2 vols. Ed. by Milton Elkin. 1980. Set. text ed. 95.00 (ISBN 0-316-23275-0). Little.

Radiology of Trauma. Hermann Birzle et al. Tr. by Herbert Kaufmann. LC 76-20070. 1978. text ed. 69.00 (ISBN 0-7216-1703-4). Saunders.

Radiology of Trauma. Lee Rogers. (Illus.). Date not set. text ed. price not set (ISBN 0-443-08038-0). Churchill. Postponed.

Radiology of Tropical Disease with Epidemiological, Pathological & Clinical Correlation. Maurice M. Reeder & Philip E. Palmer. (Illus.). 1080p. 1981. lib. bdg. 110.00 (ISBN 0-683-07199-8). Williams & Wilkins.

Radiology of Vertebral Trauma. John A. Gehweiler et al. LC 78-65376. (Monograph in Clinical Radiology: No. 16). (Illus.). 496p. 1980. text ed. 39.00 (ISBN 0-7216-4065-6). Saunders.

Radiology Typists Handbook. Ed. by Norma B. Chernok. 150p. 1970. spiral bdg. 6.00 o.p. (ISBN 0-87488-981-2). Med Exam.

Radiomans Guide. 4th ed. Robert Middleton. LC 76-45882. (Illus.). 1977. 11.95 (ISBN 0-672-23259-6, 23259). Audel.

Radiometric Reporting Methods & Calibration in Uranium Exploration. (Technical Report Ser: NO. 174). (Illus.). 1976. pap. 5.50 (ISBN 92-0-145076-1, IAEA). Unipub.

Radiomographic Anatomic Atlas. H. Schmidt & K Morike. (Illus.). 1971. 27.50 o.s.i. (ISBN 0-02-851830-6). Hafner.

Radionics & the Subtle Anatomy of Man. David V. Tansley. 1980. 5.50 (ISBN 0-8464-1044-3). Beekman Pubs.

Radionics Interface with the Ether Fields. David V. Tansley. 112p. 1979. pap. text ed. 10.95x (ISBN 0-8464-1045-1). Beekman Pubs.

Radionuclide Release into the Environment: Assessment of Doses to Man. Ed. by F. D. Sowby. (International Commission on Radiological Protection Publications: No 29). (Illus.). pap. 18.25 (ISBN 0-08-022635-3). Pergamon.

Radionuclide Techniques in Medicine. Joan McAlister. LC 78-68348. (Techniques of Measurement in Medicine: No. 3). 1980. 41.50 (ISBN 0-521-22402-0); pap. 12.50x (ISBN 0-521-29474-6). Cambridge U Pr.

Radionuclide Tracer Techniques in Hematology. C. S. Bowring. 1981. text ed. price not set (ISBN 0-407-00183-2). Butterworth.

Radionuclides in Clinical Chemistry. Phillip L. Howard & Thomas D. Trainer. 1980. text ed. 22.50 (ISBN 0-316-37470-9). Little.

Radionuclides in Foods. 2nd rev. ed. Food & Nutrition Board. LC 62-60075. (Illus.). 104p. 1973. pap. 5.25 (ISBN 0-309-02113-8). Natl Acad Pr.

Radionuclides in Pharmacology, 2 Vols. Y. Cohen. 1971. Set. 160.00 (ISBN 0-08-016152-9). Pergamon.

Radiopharmaceuticals & Labelled Compounds, 2 vols. (Illus.). 847p. (Orig.). 1974. Vol. 1. pap. 40.25 (ISBN 92-0-040073-6, ISP344-1, IAEA); Vol. 2. pap. 26.25 (ISBN 92-0-040173-2, ISP344-2). Unipub.

Radiopharmaceuticals from Generator-Produced Radionuclides. 205p. 1971. pap. 12.00 (ISBN 92-0-111471-0, IAEA). Unipub.

Radiopharmaceuticals II: Proceedings. International Symposium on Radiopharmaceuticals, 2nd. Ed. by Sodd et al. LC 79-67730. (Illus.). 857p. (Orig.). 1979. pap. text ed. 42.50 (ISBN 0-932004-05-9). Soc Nuclear Med.

Radiopharmacy. Manuel Tubis & Walter Wolf. LC 75-28385. 911p. 1976. 68.50 (ISBN 0-471-89227-0, Pub. by Wiley-Interscience). Wiley.

Radio's Golden Years: The Encyclopedia of Radio Programs 1930-1960. Vincent Terrace. (Illus.). 288p. 1981. 15.00 (ISBN 0-498-02393-1). A S Barnes.

Radiosensitizers of Hypoxic Cells: Proceedings. A. Breccia & A. Breccia. 1979. 44.00 (ISBN 0-444-80124-3, Biomedical Pr). Elsevier.

Radiosterilization of Medical Products, Pharmaceuticals & Bioproducts. (Technical Reports: No. 72). 1967. pap. 5.00 (ISBN 92-0-115067-9, IAEA). Unipub.

Radiosterilization of Medical Products. (Eng., Fr., Rus. & Span.). 1967. pap. 30.50 (ISBN 92-0-010367-7, IAEA). Unipub.

Radiosterilization of Medical Products, 1974: Proceedings. Symposium on Ionizing Radiation for Sterilization of Medical Products & Biological Tissues, Bombay, Dec 9-13, 1974. (Illus.). 539p. 1975. pap. 48.25 (ISBN 92-0-010475-4, ISP383, IAEA). Unipub.

Radiotelephone Operator. Ed. by Richard A. Block. (Illus.). 70p. Date not set. pap. 9.00 (ISBN 0-934114-27-7). Marine Educ.

Radiotherapy in Modern Clinical Practice. H. F. Hope-Stone. 1976. text ed. 29.50 o.p. (ISBN 0-8016-8362-9). Mosby.

Radiotherapy Treatment Planning. Richard F. Mould. (Medical Physics Handbook: No. 7). 192p. 1981. 31.00 (ISBN 0-9960020-6-5, Pub. by a Hilger England). Heyden.

Radiotracer Methodology in the Biological Environmental & Physical Sciences. Chih H. Wang & David L. Willis. (Illus.). 512p. 1975. 25.95 (ISBN 0-13-752212-6). P-H.

Radiotracer Studies of Chemical Residues in Food & Agriculture. (Illus.). 166p. (Orig.). 1973. pap. 10.75 (ISBN 92-0-111272-6, IAEA). Unipub.

Radish River Caper. Ross Spencer. 144p. 1981. pap. 1.95 (ISBN 0-380-77248-5, 77248). Avon.

Radlauers Starting Line. Incl. Cats Book (ISBN 0-8372-2419-5); Wheels Book (ISBN 0-8372-2420-9); Racing (ISBN 0-8372-2421-7); Kickoff (ISBN 0-8372-2422-5). (Illus.). (gr. 1-3). 1976. pap. 2.52 ea; tchr's guide 1.83 (ISBN 0-8372-9145-3). Bowmar-Noble.

Radon in Uranium Mining: Proceedings. Panel, Washington D.C., Sept. 4-7, 1973. (Illus.). 173p. 1975. pap. 16.25 (ISBN 92-0-041075-8, ISP391, IAEA). Unipub.

Radulfus Niger "De Re Militari et Triplici Via Peregrinationis Ierosolimitane" (1187 88) Ed. by Ludwig Schmugge. (Beitraege Zur Geschichte und Quellenkunde des Mittelalters: Vol. 6). 1976. 72.25x (ISBN 3-11-006827-3). De Gruyter.

Radurization of Scampi, Shrimp & Cod. (Technical Reports: No. 124). (Illus., Orig.). 1971. pap. 6.00 (ISBN 92-0-115171-3, IAEA). Unipub.

Radziwills. T. Nawakowski. (Illus.). 352p. 1974. 12.50 o.p. (ISBN 0-440-07340-5, Sey Lawr). Delacorte.

Rafael Arevalo Martinez. Maria A. Salgado. (World Authors Ser.: No. 544). 1979. lib. bdg. 14.50 (ISBN 0-8057-6387-2). Twayne.

Rafael Dieste. Estelle Irizarry. (World Authors Ser.: No. 554). 1979. lib. bdg. 14.50 (ISBN 0-8057-6396-1). Twayne.

Rafael Ferrer: Enclosures. Rafael Ferrer & Stephen Prokopoff. (Illus.). 1971. 4.00 o.p. (ISBN 0-88454-008-1). U of Pa Contemp Art.

Raffles. Maurice Collis. 1970. 4.95 (ISBN 0-571-09227-6, Pub. by Faber & Faber). Merrimack Bk Serv.

Raffles. W. Hornung. 302p. 1980. lib. bdg. 14.50x (ISBN 0-89968-186-7). Lightyear.

Raffles Revisited: New Adventures of a Famous Gentleman Crook. Barry Perowne. LC 73-14321. (Illus.). 332p. 1974. 9.95 o.s.i. (ISBN 0-06-013314-7, HarpT). Har-Row.

Raffles: The Amateur Cracksman. Ernest W. Hornung. LC 75-38587. (Illus.). 1976. pap. 3.25 (ISBN 0-8032-5836-4, BB 616, Bison). U of Nebr Pr.

Rag Bag Clan. Richard Barth. 1979. pap. 1.95 (ISBN 0-380-46078-5, 46078). Avon.

Ragas of South India: A Catalogue of Scalar Material. Walter Kaufmann. LC 75-1941. (Oriental Ser.). 832p. 1976. 25.00x (ISBN 0-253-39508-9). Ind U Pr.

Ragazza Di Bube. Carlo Cassola. (Easy Readers, C). (Illus.). 1977. pap. text ed. 3.75 (ISBN 0-88436-284-1). EMC.

Rage Against Heaven. Fred M. Stewart. 1979. pap. 2.75 o.p. (ISBN 0-449-24037-1, Crest). Fawcett.

Rage Against Heaven. Fred M. Stewart. 1978. 10.95 o.p. (ISBN 0-670-58910-1). Viking Pr.

Rage of Angels. Sidney Sheldon. 1981. pap. 3.50 (ISBN 0-446-36007-4). Warner Bks.

Rage or Raillery: The Swift Manuscripts at the Huntington Library. Ed. by George P. Mayhew. LC 66-28200. 1967. 8.50 (ISBN 0-87328-029-6). Huntington Lib.

Ragged Edge of Science. L. Sprague De Camp. LC 79-92640. (Illus.). 254p. 1980. 16.00 (ISBN 0-913896-06-3). Owlswick Pr.

Ragged Plot. Richard Barth. 224p. 1981. 9.95 (ISBN 0-686-69089-3). Dial.

Raggedy Andy & the Jump-up Contest. Marjorie Schwaljie. (Tell-a-Tale Readers). (Illus.). (gr. k-3). 1978. PLB 4.77 (ISBN 0-307-68641-8, Whitman). Western Pub.

Raggedy Andy: The I Can Do It, You Can Do It Book. Norah Smaridge. (Illus.). (gr. k-2). 1973. 1.95 (ISBN 0-307-10494-X, Golden Pr); PLB 7.62 (ISBN 0-307-60494-2). Western Pub.

Raggedy Andy's Treasure Hunt. Marjory Schwalje. (Tell-a-Tale Readers). (Illus.). (gr. k-3). 1979. PLB 4.77 (ISBN 0-307-68420-2, Whitman). Western Pub.

Raggedy Ann: A Thank You, Please & I Love You Book. Nora Smaridge. (Illus.). (ps-1). 1970. 1.95 (ISBN 0-307-10487-7, Golden Pr); PLB 7.62 (ISBN 0-307-60487-X). Western Pub.

Raggedy Ann & Andy & the Five Birthday Parties in a Row. Eileen Daly. (Young Reader Ser.). (Illus.). (gr. k-3). 1979. PLB 5.00 (ISBN 0-307-60263-X, Golden Pr). Western Pub.

Raggedy Ann & Andy & the Rainy Day Circus. Barbara S. Hazen. (Illus.). (ps-1). 1973. PLB 5.00 (ISBN 0-307-60401-2, Golden Pr). Western Pub.

Raggedy Ann & Andy Book. Jan Sukus. (Illus.). (ps-1). 1973. PLB 5.38 (ISBN 0-307-68942-5, Golden Pr). Western Pub.

Raggedy Ann & Andy Go Flying. Mary Fulton. Tr. by Judith Hunt. 24p. (ps). 1.50 (ISBN 0-307-11986-6); PLB 6.08 (ISBN 0-307-61986-9). Western Pub.

Raggedy Ann & Andy: The Little Grey Kitten. Polly Curran. (Illus.). 24p. (ps-3). 1975. PLB 5.00 (ISBN 0-307-60139-0, Golden Pr). Western Pub.

Raggedy Ann & the Cookie Snatcher. Barbara Hazen. (Illus.). 24p. (ps-3). 1972. PLB 5.00 (ISBN 0-307-60262-1, Golden Pr). Western Pub.

Raggedy Ann & the Wonderful Witch. Johnny Gruelle. (Illus.). (gr. 1-4). 1977. 1.95 o.s.i. (ISBN 0-685-86227-5). Dell.

Raggedy Ann at the Carnival. Patricia Thackray. (Look-Look Ser.). (Illus.). 1977. PLB 5.38 (ISBN 0-307-61830-7, Golden Pr); pap. 0.95 (ISBN 0-307-11830-4). Western Pub.

Raggedy Ann Book. Janet Fulton. (Illus.). (ps-1). 1969. PLB 5.38 (ISBN 0-307-68951-4, Golden Pr). Western Pub.

Raggedy Ann's Cooking School. Marjorie Schwaljie. (Tell-a-Tale Readers). (Illus.). (gr. k-3). 1974. PLB 4.77 (ISBN 0-307-68498-9, Whitman). Western Pub.

Raging Bull. Jake LaMotta & Joseph Carter. 160p. 1980. pap. 2.25 (ISBN 0-553-13981-9). Bantam.

Raging Joys: Sublime Variations. Chandler Brossard. 1981. 12.50x (ISBN 0-916156-58-3); pap. 6.00x (ISBN 0-916156-57-5); signed & lettered ed. 25.00x (ISBN 0-916156-59-1). Cherry Valley.

Raging Moon. Chitra Pershad. 6.75 (ISBN 0-89253-716-7); flexible cloth 4.80 (ISBN 0-89253-717-5). Ind-US Inc.

Raging Talent. Jack Hoffenberg. 1972. pap. 1.95 o.p. (ISBN 0-380-00836-X, 31021). Avon.

Raging Winds of Heaven. June Shiplett. (Orig.). 1978. pap. 2.50 (ISBN 0-451-09439-5, E9439, Sig). NAL.

Rags. Patricia Scarry. (Illus.). (ps-3). 1970. PLB 5.00 (ISBN 0-307-60586-8, Golden Pr). Western Pub.

Rags to Righteousness. Gordon Hyde. LC 77-80684. (Dimension Ser.). 1978. pap. 5.95 (ISBN 0-8163-0296-0, 18031-5). Pacific Pr Pub Assn.

Ragtime. E. L. Doctorow. 384p. 1980. pap. 2.95 (ISBN 0-553-14128-7). Bantam.

Ragtime Rarities. Trebor J. Tichenor. LC 74-28941. (Illus.). 320p. (Orig.). 1975. pap. 7.95 (ISBN 0-486-23157-7). Dover.

Rahne. Susan Coon. 1979. pap. 1.95 (ISBN 0-380-75044-9, 75044). Avon.

Rahner Reader. Ed. by Gerald McCool. (Orig.). 1975. 13.50 (ISBN 0-8164-1173-5); pap. 6.95 (ISBN 0-8164-2107-2). Crossroad NY.

Raid on Harper's Ferry, October 17, 1859: A Brutal Skirmish Widens the Rift Between North & South. Robert N. Webb. LC 78-131151. (Focus Bks). (Illus.). (gr. 7 up). 1971. PLB 4.90 o.p. (ISBN 0-531-01020-1). Watts.

Raid on the Bremerton. Irv Eachus. 252p. 1980. 12.95 (ISBN 0-670-58912-8). Viking Pr.

Raid: The Untold Story of Patton's Secret Mission. Richard Baron et al. 288p. 1981. 12.95 (ISBN 0-399-12597-3). Putnam.

Raider. Jesse H. Ford. 1976. pap. 1.95 o.p. (ISBN 0-345-25214-4). Ballantine.

Raiders. Richard Garrett. 224p. 1980. 18.95 (ISBN 0-442-25873-9). Van Nos Reinhold.

Raiders Gold. J. D. Hardin. LC 80-85105. (J.D.Hardin Ser.). 256p. 1981. pap. 1.95 (ISBN 0-87216-861-1). Playboy Pbks.

Raiders of the Lost Ark: A Novelization Adapted from the Screenplay by Lawrence Kasden. Campbell Clark. 192p. 1981. pap. 2.50 (ISBN 0-345-29490-4). Ballantine.

Raiders of the Lost Ark Storybook. Les Martin. (Movie Storybooks Ser.). (Illus.). 64p. (gr. 5-9). 1981. PLB 6.99 (ISBN 0-394-94802-5); pap. 5.95 boards (ISBN 0-394-84802-0). Random.

Raider's Revenge. J. D. Hardin. LC 80-82851. (J. D. Hardin). 256p. (Orig.). 1981. pap. 1.95 (ISBN 0-87216-767-4). Playboy Pbks.

Rail Car, Locomotive & Trolley Builders: An All-Time Directory. Spencer Crump. 1980. write for info. (ISBN 0-87046-032-3). Trans-Anglo.

Rail Fences & Roosters. Hazel B. Girard & Marvin E. Girard. 1978. 6.00 (ISBN 0-8233-0276-8). Golden Quill.

Rail Rogues. Glebe Morgan. (Orig.). 1980. pap. 1.75 (ISBN 0-505-51490-7). Tower Bks.

Railfan's Guide to Colorado. Edgar H. Sibert. (Illus.). Date not set. pap. price not set o.s.i. (ISBN 0-87108-556-9). Pruett. Postponed.

Railroad Caboose. William F. Knapke & Freeman Hubbard. LC 67-28316. (Illus.). (gr. 10 up). 1968. 13.95 (ISBN 0-87095-011-8). Golden West.

Railroad Engineering, Vol. 1. William W. Hay. 1953. 28.50 (ISBN 0-471-36399-5). Wiley.

Railroad in the Clouds. 28.00. Chatham Pub CA.

Railroad Management. D. Daryl Wyckoff. LC 75-5237. 1976. 18.95x (ISBN 0-669-99770-6). Lexington Bks.

Railroad Scene. William D. Middleton. LC 69-20446. (Illus.). 1969. 15.95 (ISBN 0-87095-000-2). Golden West.

Railroad That Died at Sea: FEC's Key West Ext. Pat Parks. LC 68-54448. (Shortline Railroad Series). (Illus.). 1968. pap. 4.95 (ISBN 0-8289-0151-1). Greene.

Railroad That Ran by the Tide. Raymond J. Feagans. (Illus.). 146p. Date not set. Repr. of 1972 ed. 15.00 (ISBN 0-8310-7042-0). Howell-North.

Railroad Track; Theory & Practice: Material Properties, Cross Sections, Welding & Treatment. Ed. by Fritz Fastenrath. Tr. by Walter Grant from Ger. LC 80-5340. (Illus.). 1980. 65.00 (ISBN 0-8044-4231-2). Ungar.

Railroad: Trains & Train People. Miller Williams & James A. McPherson. 1976. 15.00 o.p. (ISBN 0-394-49857-7, BYR). Random.

Railroad: Trains & Train People. Miller Williams & James A. McPherson. 1976. pap. 7.95 (ISBN 0-394-73237-5). Random.

Railroaders. K. Wheeler. LC 73-84316. (Old West Ser). (Illus.). (gr. 5 up). 1973. kivar 12.96 (ISBN 0-8094-1467-8, Pub. by Time-Life). Silver.

Railroaders. Keith Wheeler. (Old West Ser.). (Illus.). 1973. 12.95 (ISBN 0-8094-1466-X). Time-Life.

Railroadiana Collector's Price Guide. Stanley L. Baker. (Illus.). 1977. pap. 4.95 o.p. (ISBN 0-8015-6219-8). Dutton.

Railroadiana: The Collectors Guide to Railroad Memorabilia. Charles Klamkin. LC 75-26977. (Funk & W Bk.). (Illus.). 1977. 10.95 o.s.i. (ISBN 0-308-10221-5, TYC-T); pap. 5.95 o.s.i. (ISBN 0-308-10319-X, TYC-T). T Y Crowell.

Railroading. Boy Scouts Of America. LC 19-600. (Illus.). 48p. (gr. 6-12). 1973. pap. 0.70x (ISBN 0-8395-3292-X, 3292). BSA.

Railroading West. 8.95 o.p. (ISBN 0-685-83379-8). Chatham Pub CA.

Railroads. Paul B. Cors. LC 74-31396. (Spare Time Guides Ser.: No. 8). 152p. 1975. lib. bdg. 10.00x o.p. (ISBN 0-87287-082-0). Libs Unl.

Railroads & the Granger Laws. George H. Miller. LC 75-138059. 1971. 25.00x (ISBN 0-299-05870-0). U of Wis Pr.

Railroads in the Woods. 15.00 (ISBN 0-685-83374-7). Chatham Pub CA.

Railroads, Lands & Politics: The Taxation of the Railroad Land Grants, 1864-1897. Leslie E. Decker. LC 64-11940. (Illus.). 435p. 1966. Repr. of 1964 ed. 20.00x (ISBN 0-87057-084-6, Pub. by Brown U Pr). Univ Pr of New England.

Railroads of Arizona, Vol. 1. David F. Myrick. (Illus.). 480p. Date not set. Repr. of 1975 ed. 30.00 (ISBN 0-8310-7117-6). Howell-North.

Railroads of Arizona, Vol. 2. David Myrick. LC 75-27787. (Illus.). 480p. 30.00 (ISBN 0-8310-7118-4). Howell-North.

Railroads of Nevada, Vol. 2. 20.00 o.p. (ISBN 0-685-83377-1). Chatham Pub CA.

Railroads One Hundred Years Ago. Abbott & Anon. (Sun Historical Ser.). (Illus.). 1980. 3.50 (ISBN 0-89540-048-0). Sun Pub.

Rails Across the Ranchos. Loren Nicholson. (Illus.). 160p. 1980. 18.95 (ISBN 0-913548-72-3, Valley Calif). Western Tanager.

Rails in the Mother Lode. 16.95 (ISBN 0-686-64900-1). Chatham Pub CA.

Rails in the North Woods. rev. ed. William Gore et al. 1978. Repr. of 1973 ed. 13.95 (ISBN 0-932052-16-9). North Country.

Rails North: The Story of the Railroads of Alaska & the Yukon. Howard Clifford. (Illus.). 176p. 1981. 19.95 (ISBN 0-87564-536-4). Superior Pub.

Rails of the Silver Gate. R. V. Dodge. LC 75-97231. (Illus.). 144p. 1975. 15.95 (ISBN 0-87095-019-3). Golden West.

Rails, Sagebrush & Pine. Mallory H. Ferrell. LC 67-28315. (Illus.). 1967. 15.95 (ISBN 0-87095-007-X). Golden West.

Rails That Climb. 24.95. Chatham Pub CA.

Railway Adventure. L. T. Rolt. 1977. 10.50 (ISBN 0-7153-7389-7). David & Charles.

Railway Antiques. James Mackay. (Orig.). 1980. pap. 8.95x (ISBN 0-8464-1046-X). Beekman Pubs.

Railway Archaeology. O. S. Nock. (Illus.). 160p. 1981. 35.95 (ISBN 0-85059-451-0). Aztex.

Railway Atlas of Ireland. S. Maxwell Hajducki. (Illus.). 1974. 14.95 (ISBN 0-7153-5167-2). David & Charles.

Railway History in Pictures: Chilterns & Cotswolds. R. Davies & M. D. Grant. 1977. 11.95 (ISBN 0-7153-7299-8). David & Charles.

Railway History in Pictures: The Stockton & Darlington Railway. K. Hoole. LC 74-81076. (Railway History in Pictures Ser). 1975. 11.95 (ISBN 0-7153-6770-6). David & Charles.

Railway in England & Wales, 1830-1914, Vol. 1: The System & Its Working. Jack Simmons. (Illus.). 1978. text ed. 31.25x (ISBN 0-7185-1146-8, Leicester). Humanities.

Railway in England & Wales, 1830-1914. Jack Simmons. Incl. Vol. 2. Town & Country. text ed. write for info. (ISBN 0-391-01168-5); Vol. 3. Mind & Eve. text ed. write for info. (ISBN 0-391-01169-3); Vol. 4. The Community. text ed. price not set (ISBN 0-391-01170-7). (Illus.). 1981. text ed. (ISBN 0-685-51832-9, Leicester). Humanities.

Railway Journeys. Ludovic Kennedy. LC 80-14520. (Illus.). 256p. 1980. cancelled (ISBN 0-89256-135-1). Rawson Wade.

Railway Modelling: An Introduction. W. A. Corkill. 1979. 14.95 (ISBN 0-7153-7571-7). David & Charles.

Railway Workers, Eighteen Forty to Nineteen Seventy. Frank McKenna. (Illus.). 288p. 1980. 30.00 (ISBN 0-571-11563-2, Pub. by Faber & Faber). Merrimack Bk Serv.

Railways Across the Andes. Edgar A. Haine. (Illus.). 250p. 1980. 34.95 (ISBN 0-87108-559-3). Pruett.

Railways & Geography. 2nd rev. ed. Andrew C. O'Dell & Peter S. Richards. 1971. pap. text ed. 6.25x (ISBN 0-09-106801-0, Hutchinson U Lib). Humanities.

Railways & the Copper Mines in Katanga. S. E. Katzenellenbogen. (Oxford Studies in African Affairs). (Illus.). 165p. 1973. 12.00x o.p. (ISBN 0-19-821676-9). Oxford U Pr.

Railways at the Zenith of Steam, 1920-1940. O. S. Nock. LC 71-115302. (Railways of the World in Color Ser.: Vol. 2). 1970. 8.95 (ISBN 0-02-589710-1). Macmillan.

Railways at Their Pre Eminence. O. S. Nock. (Railways of the World in Color Ser). (Illus.). 1971. 8.95 (ISBN 0-02-589720-9). Macmillan.

Railways at War. John Westwood. LC 80-25429. 224p. 1981. 17.50 (ISBN 0-8310-7138-9). Howell-North.

Railways in the Formative Years, 1851-1895. O. S. Nock. LC 72-12449. (Railways of the World in Color Ser.: Vol. 5). (Illus.). 80p. 1973. 8.95 (ISBN 0-02-589740-3). Macmillan.

Railways in the Years of Transition: 1940-1963. O. S. Nock. (Railways of the World in Color Ser.: Vol. 6). (Illus.). 170p. 1975. 5.95 o.s.i. (ISBN 0-02-589750-0). Macmillan.

Railways of New Zealand. David B. Leitch. 11.95 (ISBN 0-7153-5496-5). David & Charles.

Railways of Southern England Secondary & Branch Lines. Edwin Course. 1974. 22.50 o.p. (ISBN 0-7134-2835-X, Pub. by Batsford England). David & Charles.

Railways of the Modern Age Since 1963. O. S. Nock. LC 75-28489. (Macmillan Color Ser. Railways of the World in Color). (Illus.). 160p. 1976. 6.95 o.s.i. (ISBN 0-02-589760-8, 58976). Macmillan.

Railways of the Raj. Michael Satow & Ray Desmond. (Illus.). 120p. 1980. 29.95 (ISBN 0-8147-7816-X). NYU Pr.

Railways of Western Europe. O. S. Nock. (Illus.). 1978. 20.00 (ISBN 0-7136-1686-5). Transatlantic.

Railways Revived. P. J. Ransom. (Illus.). 1973. 7.95 (ISBN 0-571-09972-6, Pub. by Faber & Faber). Merrimack Bk Serv.

Railways Then & Now. Edwin Course. 1979. 24.00 (ISBN 0-7134-0533-3, Pub. by Batsford England). David & Charles.

Raimund & Vienna. Dorothy Prohaska. LC 70-116749. (Anglica Germanica Ser.: No. 2). (Illus.). 1971. 44.50 (ISBN 0-521-07789-3). Cambridge U Pr.

Rain. Robert Kalan. LC 77-25312. (Illus.). (gr. k-3). 1978. 7.95 (ISBN 0-688-80139-0); PLB 7.63 (ISBN 0-688-84139-2). Greenwillow.

Rain. Richard Latta. 1972. 12.00 o.p. (ISBN 0-685-67926-8). Windless Orchard.

Rain & Hail. Franklyn M. Branley. LC 63-12649. (Let's-Read-&-Find-Out Science Bk). (Illus.). (gr. k-3). 1963. 6.95 o.p. (ISBN 0-690-66844-9, TYC-J). T Y Crowell.

Rain Cloud. Mary Rayner. LC 79-3069. (Illus.). 32p. (ps-2). 1980. 8.95 (ISBN 0-689-30763-2). Atheneum.

Rain Drop Splash. Alvin R. Tresselt. (Illus.). (gr. k-3). 1946. PLB 8.16 (ISBN 0-688-51165-1). Lothrop.

Rain Forest. Armstrong Sperry. (Illus.). (gr. 7 up). 1947. 8.95 (ISBN 0-02-786230-5). Macmillan.

Rain Frog. LaRue Selman. Ed. by Alton Jordan. (Buppet Series). (Illus.). (gr. k-3). 1981. PLB 4.50 (ISBN 0-89868-091-3, Read Res); pap. text ed. 1.95 (ISBN 0-89868-102-2). ARO Pub.

Rain: I Can Read Underwater Bks. Alana Willoughby. Ed. by Alton Jordan. (gr. k-3). 1974. PLB 3.50 (ISBN 0-89868-003-4, Read Res); pap. text ed. 1.75 (ISBN 0-89868-036-0). ARO Pub.

Rain Lady. Faye Wildman. 192p. (Orig.). 1980. pap. 1.50 (ISBN 0-671-57029-3). S&S.

Rain of Wisdom. Chogyam Trungpa. Tr. by Nalanda Translation Committee. LC 80-51130. Orig. Title: Bka'-Rgyud Mgur-Mtsho. 400p. 1980. 17.50 (ISBN 0-394-51412-2); pap. 9.95 (ISBN 0-394-73972-8). Shambhala Pubns.

Rain on the Just: A Novel. Kathleen M. Morehouse. LC 79-18762. (Lost American Fiction Ser.). 333p. 1980. Repr. of 1936 ed. 13.95 (ISBN 0-8093-0945-9). S Ill U Pr.

Rain One Step Away. Melih C. Anday. Tr. by Talat Halman & Brian Swann. LC 80-68880. 1980. 7.50 (ISBN 0-686-62254-5). Charioteer.

Rain Through the Night. Buddladeva Bose. Tr. by Clinton B. Seely from Bengali. (Orient Paperbacks). 139p. 1974. pap. 1.80 (ISBN 0-88253-285-5). Ind-US Inc.

Rainbow. Nancy Lecourt. (Books I Can Read). 32p. (gr. 2). 1980. pap. 1.25 (ISBN 0-8127-0290-5). Southern Pub.

Rainbow & the Kings: A History of the Luba Empire to 1891. Thomas O. Reefe. 1981. 21.00x (ISBN 0-520-04140-2). U of Cal Pr.

Rainbow Annals. Grania Davis. 1980. pap. 1.95 (ISBN 0-686-69268-3, 76224). Avon.

Rainbow Book. Barbara Haislet. Ed. by Pat Blakely. (Illus.). (gr. 2-6). 1977. plastic comb bdg. 3.50 o.p. (ISBN 0-930408-00-4). Parkway Pr.

Rainbow Bridges. Peter Payack. 1978. pap. 1.00x (ISBN 0-686-07205-7). Samisdat.

Rainbow City & the Inner Earth People. Michael X. 1969. pap. 5.95 (ISBN 0-685-20200-3). Saucerian.

Rainbow Garden. Patricia M. St. John. (gr. 2-5). pap. 2.50 (ISBN 0-8024-0028-0). Moody.

Rainbow Generation: Over Fifty-Five & Living Forward. Carol V. Murdock & Kenneth Lawson. 176p. cancelled (ISBN 0-88421-098-7). Butterick Pub.

Rainbow in the Spray. Pamela Wynne. (Barbara Cartland's Library of Love: Vol. 13). 218p. 1980. 12.95x (ISBN 0-7156-1473-8, Pub. by Duckworth England). Biblio Dist.

Rainbow Jordan. Alice Childress. 160p. (gr. 7 up). 1981. 8.95 (ISBN 0-698-20531-6). Putnam.

Rainbow of My Own. Don Freeman. (Illus.). (gr. k-3). 1966. PLB 6.95 o.s.i. (ISBN 0-670-58928-4). Viking Pr.

Rainbow Rider. Jane Yolen. LC 73-19700. (Illus.). (ps-3). 1974. 8.79 (ISBN 0-690-00311-0, TYC-J). T Y Crowell.

Rainbow Route: An Illustrated History of the Silverton Railroad, the Silverton Northern Railroad & the Silverton, Gladstone & Northerly Railroad. Robert E. Sloan & Carl A. Skowronski. Ed. by Jackson C. Thode et al. (Illus.). 1975. 49.00 (ISBN 0-913582-12-3). Sundance.

Rainbow Season. Lisa Gregory. (Orig.). pap. 2.25 (ISBN 0-515-05350-3). Jove Pubns.

Rainbow: The Stormy Life of Judy Garland. Christofer Finch. 1978. pap. 1.95 o.p. (ISBN 0-345-28113-6). Ballantine.

Rainbow Trail. Zane Grey. 1980. pap. write for info. (ISBN 0-671-83540-8). PB.

Rainbows Annals. Grania Davis. 1980. pap. 1.95 (ISBN 0-380-76224-2, 76224). Avon.

Rainbows for the Fallen World. C. Seerveld. 1980. 14.95x (ISBN 0-919071-00-7); pap. 9.95x (ISBN 0-919071-01-5). Radix Bks.

Rainbows, Frost & Foggy Dew. Julian May. Ed. by Publication Associates. LC 73-156058. (Investigating the Earth Ser). (Illus.). (gr. 4-8). 1972. PLB 5.95 o.p. (ISBN 0-87191-066-7). Creative Ed.

Rainbows, Halos & Glories. Robert Greenler. LC 80-143722. (Illus.). 304p. 1980. 24.95 (ISBN 0-521-23605-3). Cambridge U Pr.

Rainbows. Halos, & Other Wonders. Kenneth Heuer. LC 77-16865. (gr. 5 up). 1978. 5.95 (ISBN 0-396-07557-6). Dodd.

Raincrow. Jane G. Rushing. 1978. pap. 1.95 (ISBN 0-380-41749-9, 41749). Avon.

Raindrop Has to Do Her Work. Ed. by Sarah Kennedy & John O. Simon. 72p. (Orig.). (gr. k-12). 1979. pap. text ed. 4.00 (ISBN 0-917744-29-2). Aldebaran Rev.

Raindrop Stories. Preston R. Bassett & Margaret F. Bartlett. LC 80-19036. (Illus.). 40p. (gr. k-3). 1981. 9.95 (ISBN 0-590-07628-0, Four Winds). Schol Bk Serv.

Rainer Maria Rilke. Arnold Bauer. Tr. by Ursula Lamm. LC 75-163151. (Modern Literature Ser.). 128p. 1972. 10.95 (ISBN 0-8044-2025-4). Ungar.

Rainer Maria Rilke's Gedichte an Die Nacht: An Essay in Interpretation. A. Stephens. LC 72-178284. (Anglica Germanica Ser.: No. 2). 288p. 1972. 47.00 (ISBN 0-521-08388-5). Cambridge U Pr.

Rainfed Lowland Rice As a Research Priority: An Economist's View. (IRRI Research Paper Ser.: No. 26). 50p. 1979. pap. 5.00 (R066, IRRI). Unipub.

Rainfed Lowland Rice: Selected Papers from the 1978 International Rice Research Conference. 341p. 1979. pap. 19.50 (R029, IRRI). Unipub.

Rainforest Children. Margaret Pittaway. (Illus.). 32p. (ps-3). 1980. 7.95 (ISBN 0-19-554238-X). Oxford U Pr.

Rainmakers: American "Pluviculture" to World War II. Clark C. Spence. LC 79-26022. xii, 181p. 1980. 15.95 (ISBN 0-8032-4117-8). U of Nebr Pr.

Rains of Eridan. H. M. Hoover. 1978. pap. 1.50 (ISBN 0-380-41871-1, 41871). Avon.

Raintree Illustrated Science Encyclopedia. LC 78-12093. (Illus.). (gr. 4-12). 1979. PLB 266.60 (ISBN 0-8172-1202-7). Raintree Pubs.

Rainy Day Surprises You Can Make. Robyn Supraner. LC 80-19858. (Illus.). 48p. (gr. 2-5). 1980. PLB 6.92 (ISBN 0-89375-428-5); pap. 1.75 (ISBN 0-89375-429-3). Troll Assocs.

Rainy Sunday. Eleanor Schick. LC 80-11596. (Easy-to-Read Ser.). (Illus.). 56p. (ps-3). 1981. PLB 5.99 (ISBN 0-8037-7369-2); pap. 2.50 (ISBN 0-8037-7371-4). Dial.

Raise & Show Guppies. Lou Wasserman. (Illus.). 1977. pap. 4.95 (ISBN 0-87666-453-2, PS-738). TFH Pubns.

Raise & Train Skunks. Charles Hume. pap. 2.50 (ISBN 0-87666-223-8, M527). TFH Pubns.

Raise Cash-Have Fun. Christine Fagg. 1969. 5.95 o.p. (ISBN 0-236-31121-2, Pub. by Paul Elek). Merrimack Bk Serv.

Raise Race Rays Raze: Essays Since 1965. Imamu A. Baraka, pseud. 1971. 10.00 (ISBN 0-685-77057-5). Univ Place.

Raise the Titanic! Clive Cussler. 384p. 1980. pap. 2.75 (ISBN 0-553-13880-4). Bantam.

Raise up off Me: A Portrait of Hampton Hawes. Hampton Hawes & Don Asher. 180p. 1979. pap. 5.95 (ISBN 0-686-68925-9). Da Capo.

Raising a Racket: Rosie Casals. Alida Thacher. LC 75-42036. (Sports Profiles Ser.). (gr. 4-11). 1976. PLB 8.50 (ISBN 0-8172-0132-7). Raintree Pubs.

Raising & Caring for Animals, a Handbook of Animal Husbandry & Veterinary Care. Guy Lockwood. LC 79-14025. 1979. pap. 8.95 (ISBN 0-684-16299-7). Scribner.

Raising Children with Love & Limits. Psyche Cattell. LC 77-187810. 232p. 1972. 12.95 (ISBN 0-911012-20-6). Nelson-Hall.

Raising Daisy Rothschild. Betty Leslie-Melville & Jock Leslie-Melville. (Illus.). 1979. pap. 1.95 o.s.i. (ISBN 0-446-89948-8). Warner Bks.

Raising God's Children. Anita Bryant & Bob Green. 1979. 6.95 o.p. (ISBN 0-8007-0878-4). Revell.

Raising Happy Healthy Children. Karen Olness. 1981. pap. 3.95 (ISBN 0-9602790-5-9). The Garden.

Raising International Capital: International Markets & the European Institutions. Charles R. Geisst. 176p. 1979. 20.95x (ISBN 0-566-00282-5, 03296-4, Pub. by Saxon Hse England). Lexington Bks.

Raising Money from Grants & Other Sources Success Kit. 2nd ed. Tyler G. Hicks. 496p. 1981. pap. 99.50 (ISBN 0-914306-45-6). Intl Wealth.

Raising of Lazarus. John Cornish. 1979. pap. 2.50 (ISBN 0-916786-36-6). St George Bk Serv.

Raising Other People's Kids: Successful Child-Rearing in the Restructured Family. Evelyn Felker. 160p. (Orig.). 1981. pap. 4.95 (ISBN 0-8028-1868-4). Eerdmans.

Raising Puppies for Pleasure & Profit. Elizabeth Schuler. Ed. by Dianne F. Harris. 1970. 8.95 (ISBN 0-02-607430-3). Macmillan.

Raising Rabbits. Ann Kanable. LC 77-23926. 1977. 8.95 (ISBN 0-87857-183-3); pap. 5.95 (ISBN 0-87857-314-3). Rodale Pr Inc.

Raising Small Animals for Fun & Profit. Paul Villiard. LC 72-79368. (Illus.). 1975. pap. 3.95 o.p. (ISBN 0-684-14366-6, SL602, ScribT). Scribner.

Raja Rao. C. D. Narasimaiah. (Indian Writers Ser.). 8.50 (ISBN 0-89253-511-3). Ind-US Inc.

Rajasthan: India's Enchanted Land. Ed. by Raghubir Singh. 1981. 27.50 (ISBN 0-500-54070-5). Thames Hudson.

Rakehell Dynasty: China Bride, No. 2. Michael W. Scott. 544p. 1981. pap. 2.75 (ISBN 0-446-95201-X). Warner Bks.

Rakes & Ruffians: The Underworld of Georgian Dublin. 3rd, rev. ed. John E. Walsh. 1979. Repr. of 1851 ed. 10.00x (ISBN 0-8476-6233-0). Rowman.

Rake's Reward. Madelaine Gibson. 176p. (Orig.). 1981. pap. 1.95 (ISBN 0-553-13191-5). Bantam.

Raku Pottery. Robert Piepenburg. (Illus.). 160p. 1976. pap. 9.95 (ISBN 0-02-011860-0, Collier). Macmillan.

Raku: Techniques for Contemporary Potters. Christopher Tyler & Richard Hirsch. (Illus.). 192p. 1975. 18.95 o.p. (ISBN 0-8230-4503-X). Watson-Guptill.

Ralegh's Lost Colony. David Durant. LC 80-65992. (Illus.). 320p. 1981. 12.95 (ISBN 0-689-11098-7). Atheneum.

Rallying. Richard L. Knudson. LC 80-17863. (Superwheels & Thrill Sports Bks.). (Illus.). 48p. (gr. 4 up). 1981. PLB 6.95g (ISBN 0-686-63304-0). Lerner Pubns.

Rallying Cries: Three Plays. Eric Bentley. LC 77-1973. 1977. o.s.i 10.00 o.p. (ISBN 0-915220-23-7); pap. 4.50 o.p. (ISBN 0-915220-24-5, 23034). New Republic.

Ralph Eugene Meatyard: An Aperture Monograph, V01.18. Ed. by James Baker Hall. LC 74-76879. (Illus.). 144p. 1974. 20.00 (ISBN 0-912334-61-4); pap. 12.50 (ISBN 0-912334-62-2). Aperture.

Ralph Fitch: Elizabethan in the Indies. Michael Edwardes. (Great Travellers Ser.). (Illus.). 1973. 6.95 o.p. (ISBN 0-571-10133-X, Pub. by Faber & Faber). Merrimack Bk Serv.

Ralph Gustafson. Wendy Keitner. (World Authors Ser.: No. 531). 1979. lib. bdg. 14.95 (ISBN 0-8057-6373-2). Twayne.

Ralph Linton. Adelin Linton & Charles Wagley. LC 76-174708. (Leaders of Modern Anthropology Ser). 1971. 15.00x (ISBN 0-231-03355-9); pap. 6.00x (ISBN 0-231-03398-2). Columbia U Pr.

Ralph Nader. James T. Olsen. LC 74-6421. (Personal Closeups Ser). 32p. 1974. 5.75 o.p. (ISBN 0-87191-355-0). Creative Ed.

Ralph Ogden & the Seven Mustangs. Ruth Goddard & J. Frank Dobie. LC 73-15099. 8.50 (ISBN 0-8363-0082-3). Jenkins.

Ralph Waldo Emerson. Oscar W. Firkins. LC 80-2532. 1981. Repr. of 1915 ed. 44.50 (ISBN 0-404-19258-0). AMS Pr.

Ralph Waldo Emerson. Oliver W. Holmes. LC 67-23884. 1967. Repr. of 1885 ed. 20.00 (ISBN 0-8103-3039-3). Gale.

Ralph Waldo Emerson. Oliver W. Holmes. LC 80-23687. (American Men & Women of Letters Ser.). 330p. 1981. pap. 5.95 (ISBN 0-87754-157-4). Chelsea Hse.

Ralph Waldo Emerson. Warren Staebler. (World Leaders Ser: No. 25). 1973. lib. bdg. 9.95 (ISBN 0-8057-3674-3). Twayne.

Ralph Waldo Emerson & the Critics: A Checklist of Criticism, 1900-1977. Jeanetta Boswell. LC 79-4670. (Author Bibliographies Ser.: No. 39). 1979. 10.00 (ISBN 0-8108-1211-8). Scarecrow.

Ralph Waldo Emerson in Deutschland: 1851-1932. Julius Simon. LC 80-2546. (Ger.). 1981. Repr. of 1936 ed. 25.50 (ISBN 0-404-19271-8). AMS Pr.

Ralphi Rhino. Lisl Weil. LC 73-92448. (Illus.). 32p. (ps-3). 1974. 4.95 o.s.i. (ISBN 0-8027-6176-3); PLB 4.85 o.s.i. (ISBN 0-8027-6177-1). Walker & Co.

Ram on the Rampage. Toller Cranston. 1977. pap. 4.95 o.s.i. (ISBN 0-685-76850-3). Vanguard.

Rama & the Bards: Epic Memory in the Ramayana. Robert Antoine. (Greybird Book). 114p. 1975. 12.00 (ISBN 0-88253-821-7); pap. 6.75 (ISBN 0-88253-822-5). Ind-US Inc.

Ramadan War. Nassan El Badri et al. 1978. 14.75 (ISBN 0-88254-460-8); pap. 6.95. Hippocrene Bks.

Ramakrishna & His Disciples. Christopher Isherwood. LC 65-17100. 384p. 1980. pap. 7.95 (ISBN 0-87481-037-X). Vedanta Pr.

Ramakrishna-Vedanta Wordbook: A Brief Dictionary of Hinduism. Ed. by Brahmacharini Usha. (Orig.). pap. 3.25 (ISBN 0-87481-017-5). Vedanta Pr.

Raman-IR Atlas of Organic Compounds. Ed. by B. Schrader & W. Meier. 1974-1976. Set. 467.70. Vol. 1,345p (ISBN 3-527-25539-7). Vol. 2,386p (ISBN 3-527-25541-9). Vol. 3,507p (ISBN 3-527-25542-7). Verlag Chemie.

Raman Spectra of Hydrocarbons: A Data Handbook. K. E. Sterin et al. LC 79-42704. 360p. 1980. 80.00 (ISBN 0-08-023596-4). Pergamon.
Raman Spectra of Molecules & Crystals. M. M. Suschinskii. LC 72-4139. 576p. 1969. 44.95 (ISBN 0-470-83630-X, Pub by Halsted Pr). Halsted Pr.
Ramana Maharshi. K. Swaminathan. (National Biography Ser.). 1979. pap. 2.25 o.p. (ISBN 0-89744-197-4). Auromere.
Ramayana. C. Rajagopalachari. 1979. pap. 3.95 (ISBN 0-89744-930-4). Auromere.
Ramayana of Valmiki, 3 vols. 3rd ed. Tr. by H. P. Shastri. 1976. Set. pap. 48.00 (ISBN 0-85424-016-0); Vol. 1. Vol. 2. (ISBN 0-85424-000-4); Vol. 3. (ISBN 0-85424-017-9). Orient Bk Dist.
Ramayana: The Story of Rama. Valmiki. LC 74-77601. (Illus.). 72p. (gr. 5-12). 1975. 8.50 (ISBN 0-88253-292-8); pap. 3.50 (ISBN 0-88253-291-X). Ind-US Inc.
Ramble Among the Musicians of Germany. 2nd ed. Edward Holmes. LC 68-16239. 1969. Repr. of 1828 ed. lib. bdg. 29.50 (ISBN 0-306-71086-2). Da Capo.
Ramblers' Ways. David Sharp. LC 79-56062. (Illus.). 192p. 1980. 19.95 (ISBN 0-7153-7972-0). David & Charles.
Rambles About Portsmouth, Vol. 1. Charles W. Brewster. LC 70-181350. 1971. Repr. 22.50x o.p. (ISBN 0-912274-12-3). NH Pub Co.
Rambles About Portsmouth, Vol. 2. Charles Brewster. LC 70-181350. 445p. 1972. Repr. 22.50x o.p. (ISBN 0-912274-21-2). NH Pub Co.
Rambles in Wonderland: Or up the Yellowstone & Among the Geysers & Other Curiosities of the National Park. Edwin J. Stanley. LC 75-7118. (Indian Captivities Ser.: Vol. 91). 1976. Repr. of 1878 ed. lib. bdg. 44.00 (ISBN 0-8240-1715-3). Garland Pub.
Rambling Rose. Calder Willingham. 1972. 6.95 o.p. (ISBN 0-440-07229-8). Delacorte.
Rambling Willie: The Horse That God Loved. Donald P. Evans & Philip S. Pikelny. LC 80-26884. (Illus.). 240p. 1981. 8.95 (ISBN 0-498-02542-X). A S Barnes.
Ramblings of a Sportsman-Naturalists "BB". (Illus.). 1980. 13.50 (ISBN 0-7181-1815-4, Pub. by Michael Joseph). Merrimack Bk Serv.
Rameau's Nephew & Other Works. Denis Diderot. Tr. by Jacques Barzun & Ralph Bowen. LC 55-9755. 1964. pap. 6.50 (ISBN 0-672-60440-X, LLA200). Bobbs.
Ramiro De Maeztu. Ricardo Landeira. (World Authors Ser.: No. 484). 1978. lib. bdg. 12.50 (ISBN 0-8057-6325-2). Twayne.
Ramon de la Cruz. John A. Moore. (World Authors Ser.: Spain: No. 179). lib. bdg. 10.95 (ISBN 0-8057-2252-1). Twayne.
Ramon De Mesonero Romanos. Richard A Curry. (World Authors Ser.: Spain: No. 385). 1976. lib. bdg. 12.50 (ISBN 0-8057-6226-4). Twayne.
Ramon del Valle-Inclan. Verity Smith. (World Authors Ser.: Spain: No. 160). lib. bdg. 10.95 (ISBN 0-8057-2924-0). Twayne.
Ramon J. Sender. Charles L. King. (World Authors Ser.: Spain: No. 307). 1974. lib. bdg. 12.50 (ISBN 0-8057-2815-5). Twayne.
Ramon J. Sender: An Annotated Bibliography, 1928-1974. Charles L. King. LC 76-9020. 301p. 1976. 14.50 (ISBN 0-8108-0933-8). Scarecrow.
Ramon Lull & Lullism in Fourteenth-Century France. J. N. Hillgarth. (Oxford-Warburg Ser.). 1971. 59.00x (ISBN 0-19-824348-0). Oxford U Pr.
Ramona. Helen H. Jackson. (Illus.). (gr. 6 up). 1939. Repr. of 1884 ed. 8.95 (ISBN 0-316-45467-2). Little.
Ramona. Helen H. Jackson. 1970. pap. 2.50 o.p. (ISBN 0-380-00383-X, 51680). Avon.
Ramona. Helen H. Jackson. 1976. lib. bdg. 20.10x (ISBN 0-89968-051-8). Lightyear.
Ramona & Her Father. Beverly Cleary. LC 77-1614. (gr. 3-7). 1977. 7.75 (ISBN 0-688-22114-9); PLB 7.44 (ISBN 0-688-32114-3). Morrow.
Ramona & Her Mother. Beverly Cleary. LC 79-10323. (Illus.). 192p. (gr. 4-6). 1979. 7.95 (ISBN 0-688-22195-5); PLB 7.63 (ISBN 0-688-32195-X). Morrow.
Ramona the Brave. Beverly Cleary. LC 74-164968. (Illus.). 192p. (gr. 3-7). 1975. 7.75 (ISBN 0-688-22015-0); PLB 7.44 (ISBN 0-688-32015-5). Morrow.
Ramona the Brave. Beverly Cleary. (gr. 4-6). 1977. pap. 1.50 (ISBN 0-590-10316-4, Schol Pap). Schol Bk Serv.
Ramona the Pest. Beverly Cleary. (Illus.). (gr. 3-7). 1968. 7.75 (ISBN 0-688-21721-4); PLB 7.44 (ISBN 0-688-31721-9). Morrow.
Ramona the Pest. Beverly Cleary. (gr. 4-6). 1976. pap. 1.50 (ISBN 0-590-04493-1, Schol Pap). Schol Bk Serv.
Ramos of Arunachal. M. M. Dhasmana. 1980. text ed. 16.50x (ISBN 0-391-01827-2). Humanities.
Rampa Story. T. Lobsang Rampa. pap. 2.50 (ISBN 0-685-91301-5). Weiser.
Rampage. Harry Whittington. 1978. pap. 1.95 o.p. (ISBN 0-449-14074-1, GM). Fawcett.
Ramparts We Guard. R. M. MacIver. 1952. 17.50x (ISBN 0-686-51296-0). Elliots Bks.
Ramsey Theory. Ronald Graham et al. LC 80-14110. (Wiley Interscience Ser. in Discrete Mathematics). 240p. 1980. 21.95 (ISBN 0-471-05997-8, Pub. by Wiley Interscience). Wiley.
Ranch & Modern Homes. Hiawatha T. Estes. (Illus.). 1981. 3.00 (ISBN 0-911008-19-5). H Estes.
Ranchers. Ogden Tanner. LC 77-85283. (Old West Ser.). (Illus.). 1977. lib. bdg. 12.96 (ISBN 0-686-51080-1). Silver.
Ranchers. Ed. by Time-Life Books & Time-Life Books. (Old West Ser.). (Illus.). 1978. 12.95 (ISBN 0-8094-1508-9). Time-Life.
Ranchers: A Book of Generations. Stan Steiner. LC 80-7646. (Illus.). 224p. 1980. 13.95 (ISBN 0-394-50193-4). Knopf.
Rancho Cucamonga & Dona Merced. new ed. Esther B. Black. LC 75-21294. (Illus.). 340p. 1975. 9.50 o.p. (ISBN 0-915158-09-4); pap. 7.50 o.p. (ISBN 0-915158-08-6). San Bernardino.
Rand McNally Economy Guide to Europe. Ed. by Peter Verstappen. LC 78-70555. 1981. pap. 7.95 (ISBN 0-528-84537-3). Rand.
Rand McNally Guide to France. Ed. by Peter Verstappen. LC 78-70557. 1981. pap. 6.95 (ISBN 0-528-84536-5). Rand.
Rand McNally Guide to Great Britain & Ireland. Ed. by Peter Verstappen. LC 78-70556. (Illus.). 1981. pap. 7.95 (ISBN 0-528-84535-7). Rand.
Rand McNally Recreational Vehicle Handbook. Connie B. Howes. LC 78-54622. (Illus.). 1979. pap. 2.95 o.s.i. (ISBN 0-528-84113-0). Rand.
Rand McNally Road Atlas: United States, Canada, Mexico. 1981. deluxe ed. 8.95 (ISBN 0-528-89205-3); pap. 5.95 (ISBN 0-528-89200-2); gift ed. 6.95 (ISBN 0-528-89203-7). Rand.
Rand McNally Road Atlas 1980. 1980. 4.95 o.p. (ISBN 0-528-89120-0). Rand.
Randall Jarrell. Sr. Bernetta Quinn. (United States Authors Ser.: No. 398). 1981. lib. bdg. 10.95 (ISBN 0-8057-7266-9). Twayne.
Randax Education Guide, 1979. 8th ed. Ed. by Stephen E. Marshall. 1979. pap. 5.75 o.p. (ISBN 0-914880-09-8). Educ Guide.
Randax Education Guide: 1981. 10th ed. 128p. 1981. pap. 7.95 (ISBN 0-914880-11-X). Educ Guide.
Randolph Bourne. James R. Vitelli. (United States Authors Ser.: No. 408). 1981. lib. bdg. 12.95 (ISBN 0-8057-7337-1). Twayne.
Randolph Caldecott. Henry Blackburn. LC 68-21757. 1969. Repr. of 1886 ed. 15.00 (ISBN 0-8103-3490-9). Gale.
Randolph Caldecott: Lord of the Nursery. Rodney K. Engen. (Illus.). 1977. 15.95 (ISBN 0-8467-0244-4, Oresko Bks); pap. 9.95 (ISBN 0-8467-0243-6). Hippocrene Bks.
Randolph Stow. Ray Willbanks. (World Authors Ser.: No. 472). 1978. lib. bdg. 12.50 (ISBN 0-8057-6313-9). Twayne.
Random Allocations. Valentin F. Kolchin et al. Tr. by A. V. Balakrishnan. (Scripta Ser. in Mathematics). 1978. 25.95 (ISBN 0-470-99394-4). Halsted Pr.
Random Data: Analysis & Measurement Procedures. Julius S. Bendat & Allan G. Piersol. LC 71-160211. (Illus.). 1971. 36.95 (ISBN 0-471-06470-X, Pub. by Wiley-Interscience). Wiley.
Random Differential Inequalities. G. S. Ladde & V. Laksmikantham. LC 80-521. (Mathematics in Science & Engineering Ser.). 1980. 30.00 (ISBN 0-12-432750-8). Acad Pr.
Random Factor. Linda J. LaRosa & Barry Tanenbaum. (Orig.). 1979. pap. 2.95 (ISBN 0-515-05166-7). Jove Pubns.
Random Factor. Linda J. LaRosa & Barry Tanenbaum. LC 77-82764. 1978. 8.95 o.p. (ISBN 0-385-13282-4). Doubleday.
Random Fields. C. Preston. (Lecture Notes in Mathematics: Vol. 534). 1976. soft cover 12.10 (ISBN 0-387-07852-5). Springer-Verlag.
Random Functions & Turbulence. S. Panchev. LC 70-124852. 1971. 67.00 (ISBN 0-08-015826-9). Pergamon.
Random House College Dictionary. 1975. 9.95 (ISBN 0-394-43500-1); thumb-indexed 10.95 (ISBN 0-394-43600-8); deluxe ed. 13.95 (ISBN 0-394-51192-1). Random.
Random House Dictionary. Ed. by Jess Stein. (Orig.). 1981. pap. 2.25 (ISBN 0-345-29096-8). Ballantine.
Random House Encyclopedia, 2 vols. 1978. Set. 71.50 (ISBN 0-87827-259-3). Ency Brit Ed.
Random House Guide to Writing. 2nd ed. Sandra Schor & Judith Fishman. 464p. 1981. pap. text ed. 10.95 (ISBN 0-394-32608-3). Random.
Random House Handbook. 2nd ed. Frederick Crews. 1977. pap. text ed. 9.50 o.p. (ISBN 0-394-31211-2). Random.
Random House Reader. Frederick Crews. 432p. 1981. pap. text ed. 8.95 (ISBN 0-394-32268-1). Random.
Random Killer. Hugh Pentacost. Date not set. pap. price not set (ISBN 0-440-17210-1). Dell.
Random Killer. Hugh Pentecost. LC 79-271. (Pierre Chambrun Mystery & Red Badge Novel of Suspense Ser.). 1979. 7.95 (ISBN 0-396-07654-8). Dodd.
Random Point Processes. Donald L. Snyder. LC 75-11556. 485p. 1975. 37.50 (ISBN 0-471-81021-5, Pub. by Wiley-Interscience). Wiley.
Random Possession. Mei-mei Berssenbrugge. LC 78-66087. 1979. pap. 5.95 (ISBN 0-918408-13-X). Reed & Cannon.
Random Processes & the Growth of Firms. Josef Steindl. 1965. 22.00 (ISBN 0-02-852950-2). Hafner.
Random Processes in Nuclear Reactors. M. M. Williams. LC 74-4066. 1974. text ed. 42.00 (ISBN 0-08-017920-7). Pergamon.
Random Processes, Pt. 1: Poisson & Jump Point Processes. A. Ephremides. LC 75-1287. (Benchmark Papers in Electrical Engineering & Computer Science Ser: No. 11). 352p. 1973. Vol. 1. 42.00 (ISBN 0-12-786431-8); Pt. 2,1975. 42.50 (ISBN 0-12-786432-6). Acad Pr.
Random Thoughts & Dialogues. Lo Guest. 1978. 5.95 o.p. (ISBN 0-533-03064-1). Vantage.
Random Variables & Probability Distribution. 3rd ed. Harald Cramer. (Cambridge Tracts in Mathematics & Mathematical Physics). 1970. 22.95 (ISBN 0-521-07685-4). Cambridge U Pr.
Random Vibration in Mechanical Systems. Stephen H. Crandall & W. D. Mark. 1963. 25.00 o.s.i. (ISBN 0-12-196750-6). Acad Pr.
Random Walk in Science: An Anthology. Robert L. Weber. LC 74-75874. (Illus.). 224p. 1974. 16.50x (ISBN 0-8448-0574-2). Crane-Russak Co.
Random Winds. Belva Plain. 1981. pap. 3.50 (ISBN 0-440-17158-X). Dell.
Randomization Texts. Ed. by E. Edgington. (Statistics, Textbooks & Monographs). 1980. 29.50 (ISBN 0-8247-6878-7). Dekker.
Randomized Trials in Cancer: A Critical Review by Sites. Ed. by Maurice J. Staquet. LC 77-17753. (European Organization for Research on Treatment of Cancer Monograph: Vol. 4). 1978. 45.00 (ISBN 0-89004-264-0). Raven.
Randy Roy Persnazznur. David B. Creps. (Orig.). 1980. pap. write for info.; pap. write for info. Great Basin.
Randy Visits the Doctor. Esther Lakritz. LC 61-5063. (Illus.). (ps). 1962. pap. 0.60 (ISBN 0-8054-4119-0); board 1.35 (ISBN 0-686-66386-1). Broadman.
Range Drifter. Thomas Thompson. 192p. 1981. pap. 1.95 (ISBN 0-553-14541-X). Bantam.
Range Rebel. Gordon D. Shirreffs. 1978. pap. 1.50 (ISBN 0-505-51226-2). Tower Bks.
Range Science: A Guide to Information Sources. Ed. by John F. Vallentine & Phillip L. Sims. (Natural World Information Guide Ser.: Vol. 2). 250p. 1980. 30.00 (ISBN 0-8103-1420-7). Gale.
Range Service (Gas, Electric, Microwave) Ed. by A. Ross Sabin. (Illus.). 253p. (gr. 11). 1979. 20.00 (ISBN 0-938336-06-1). Whirlpool.
Ranger, Vol. I. 2nd rev. ed. Theodore Enslin. 432p. 1980. 30.00 (ISBN 0-913028-79-7); pap. 12.95 (ISBN 0-913028-78-9). North Atlantic.
Ranger Battalion: American Rangers in World War Two. Milton Shapiro. LC 79-9548. (Illus.). 192p. (gr. 8-12). 1979. PLB 8.29 (ISBN 0-671-32928-6). Messner.
Ranger Escort West of the Pelos. Tom Lea. 3.00 o.p. (ISBN 0-292-77003-0). U of Tex Pr.
Ranger Handbook. U.S. Army Infantry School, Ft. Benning, Ga. (Illus.). 213p. 1977. pap. 8.00 (ISBN 0-87364-044-6). Paladin Ent.
Ranger Rick's Holiday Book. Ed. by Elizabeth G. Jones. LC 80-81621. (Illus.). 96p. (gr. 2-7). 1980. 8.95 (ISBN 0-912186-38-0). Natl Wildlife.
Ranger Volume II. Theodore Enslin. 256p. (Orig.). 1980. 25.00 (ISBN 0-913028-75-4); pap. 9.95 (ISBN 0-913028-74-6). North Atlantic.
Rangers & Pioneers of Texas. Andrew J. Sowell. (Illus.). 1964. Repr. of 1884 ed. 20.00 (ISBN 0-87266-029-X). Argosy.
Rank Among the Canaanite Gods: El, Baal, & the Raphaim. Conrad E. L'Heureux. LC 79-15582. (Harvard Semitic Monographs: No. 21). 1979. 10.50 (ISBN 0-89130-326-X, 040021). Scholars Pr Ca.
Rank & File. Hugh Jenkins. 181p. 1980. 25.00x (ISBN 0-7099-0331-6, Pub by Croom Helm Ltd England). Biblio Dist.
Rank & Religion in Tikopia. Raymond Firth. 1970. text ed. 35.00x (ISBN 0-04-200018-1). Allen Unwin.
Ransack. Mike Henson. LC 80-53807. (Illus.). 151p. (Orig.). 1980. pap. 3.00 (ISBN 0-931122-18-X). West End.
Ransom & Reunion: Through the Sanctuary. W. D. Frazee. LC 77-76135. (Horizon Ser.). 1977. pap. 4.50 (ISBN 0-8127-0138-0). Southern Pub.
Ransom Kidnapping in America, 1874-1974: The Creation of a Capital Crime. Ernest K. Alix. LC 78-1985. (Perspectives in Sociology Ser.). 256p. 1978. 15.00 (ISBN 0-8093-0849-5). S Ill U Pr.
Ransom Kidnapping in America, 1874-1974: The Creation of a Capital Crime. Ernest K. Alix. LC 78-1985. 256p. 1980. pap. 7.95 (ISBN 0-8093-0976-9). S Ill U Pr.
Ransom of Red Chief. O. Henry. (Creative's Classics Ser.). (Illus.). 40p. (gr. 4-9). 1980. PLB 6.95 (ISBN 0-87191-776-9). Creative Ed.
Ransom of Red Chief. Brian Kral. (Orig.). 1980. playscript 2.00 (ISBN 0-87602-227-1). Anchorage.
Ransom of Red Chief. O'Henry. Ed. by Walter Pauk & Raymond Harris. (Jamestown Classics Ser.). (Illus.). 40p. (Orig.). (gr. 6-12). 1979. pap. text ed. 1.60x (ISBN 0-89061-189-0, 405); tchrs. ed. 3.00 (ISBN 0-89061-191-2, 407). Jamestown Pubs.
Ransom Run. Martin Dibner. 1978. pap. 1.95 o.p. (ISBN 0-345-27172-6). Ballantine.
Ransom Town. Peter Alding. 1979. 7.95 o.s.i. (ISBN 0-8027-5409-0). Walker & Co.
Rantings of a Madman. Micheal Tankle. Date not set. 4.75 (ISBN 0-8062-1669-7). Carlton.
Raoul Walsh. Ed. by Phil Hardy. (EIFF Ser.). (Illus., Orig.). 1980. pap. 4.00 (ISBN 0-918432-25-1). NY Zoetrope.
Rapanui: Tradition & Survival on Easter Island. Grant McCall. LC 80-54833. 176p. 1981. text ed. 16.95x (ISBN 0-8248-0746-4). U Pr of Hawaii.
Rape & Woman's Identity. William B. Sanders. LC 80-13346. (Sage Library of Social Research: Vol. 106). (Illus.). 184p. 1980. 18.00x (ISBN 0-8039-1449-0); pap. 8.95x (ISBN 0-8039-1450-4). Sage.
Rape: Crisis & Recovery. Ann W. Burgess & Lynda L. Holmstrom. LC 79-51507. (Illus.). 350p. 1979. pap. 14.95 (ISBN 0-87619-433-1). R J Brady.
Rape Crisis Intervention Handbook: A Guide to Victim Care. Ed. by Sharon L. McCombie. (Illus.). 250p. 1980. 19.50 (ISBN 0-306-40401-X, Plenum Pr). Plenum Pub.
Rape File. Les Sussman & Sally Bordwell. 1981. 12.50 (ISBN 0-87754-094-2). Chelsea Hse.
Rape in Prison. Anthony M. Scacco, Jr. (Amer. Lectures in Behavioral Science & Law Ser.). 144p. 1975. 14.75 (ISBN 0-398-03314-5). C C Thomas.
Rape Intervention Resource Manual. Patrick Mills. (Illus.). 300p. 1977. 19.75 (ISBN 0-398-03594-6). C C Thomas.
Rape of Detroit. Argie W. Post. 50p. 1975. 4.00 o.p. (ISBN 0-682-48133-5). Exposition.
Rape of Tamar. Dan Jacobson. Ed. by Robert Markel. LC 78-119134. 1970. 5.95 o.s.i. (ISBN 0-02-558570-3). Macmillan.
Rape of the Lock. Alexander Pope. Ed. by John D. Hunt. LC 70-127574. (Casebook Ser). 1970. pap. text ed. 2.50 o.s.i. (ISBN 0-87695-045-4). Aurora Pubs.
Rape of the Lock & Its Illustrations 1714-1896. Robert Halsband. 176p. 1980. 29.95x (ISBN 0-19-812098-2). Oxford U Pr.
Rape of the Locks. Menander. Tr. by Gilbert Murray. 1942. pap. text ed. 3.95x (ISBN 0-04-882046-6). Allen Unwin.
Rape of the Nile: Tomb Robbers, Tourists, and Archaeologists in Egypt. Brian Fagan. LC 75-11857. (Illus.). 416p. 1975. 14.95 o.p. (ISBN 0-684-14235-X, ScribT). Scribner.
Rape: Offenders & Their Victims. John M. Macdonald. 352p. 1979. 21.75 (ISBN 0-398-01181-8). C C Thomas.
Rape: Preventing It; Coping with the Legal, Medical, & Emotional Aftermath. Janet Bode. (Impact Ser.). (gr. 7 up). 1979. PLB 6.90 s&l (ISBN 0-531-02289-7). Watts.
Rape Victim. Elaine Hilberman. 112p. 1976. 7.95 (ISBN 0-685-77446-5, P243-0, Basic); pap. 5.00 (ISBN 0-685-77447-3). Am Psychiatric.
Rape Victimology. LeRoy G. Schultz. 424p. 1975. 37.75 (ISBN 0-398-03183-5). C C Thomas.
Rape: What Woud You Do If...? Dianna D. Booher. 192p. (gr. 7 up). 1981. PLB price not set (ISBN 0-671-42201-4). Messner.
Raphael. James Beck. LC 73-12198. (Library of Great Painters). 1976. 35.00 (ISBN 0-8109-0432-2). Abrams.
Raphael. John Pope-Hennessy. LC 70-88138. (Wrightsman Lectures: Vol. 4). (Illus.). 1970. 20.00, uk (ISBN 0-8147-0476-X). NYU Pr.
Raphael of Urbino & His Father Giovanni Santi. Johann D. Passavant. Ed. by Sydney J. Freedberg. LC 77-25762. (Connoisseurship Criticism & Art History Ser.: Vol. 17). (Illus.). 1979. lib. bdg. 33.00 (ISBN 0-8240-3275-6). Garland Pub.
Raphael Soyer: Fifty Years of Printmaking, 1917-1967. Sylvan Cole, Jr. LC 67-29917. (Graphic Art Ser.). 1967. 27.50 (ISBN 0-306-70986-4). Da Capo.
Rapid Company Growth: How to Plan & Manage Small Company Expansion. A. C. Hazel & A. S. Reid. 166p. 1979. pap. 14.75x (ISBN 0-220-67025-0, Pub. by Busn Bks England). Renouf.

Rapid Excavation: Significance, Needs Opportunities. Division Of Engineering. (Orig.). 1968. pap. 3.75 (ISBN 0-309-01690-8). Natl Acad Pr.

Rapid Healing Foods. Ben Davis. LC 79-22770. 1980. 10.95 (ISBN 0-13-753137-0, Parker). P-H.

Rapid Inexpensive Tests for Determining Fracture Toughness. National Materials Advisory Board, National Research Council. LC 76-39632. 1976. pap. 8.25 (ISBN 0-309-02537-0). Natl Acad Pr.

Rapid Methods & Automation in Microbiology & Immunology: A Bibliography. 250p. 24.00 (ISBN 0-904147-07-X). Info Retrieval.

Rapid Methods for Measuring Radioactivity in the Environment. (Illus.). 967p. (Orig.). 1972. pap. 63.75 (ISBN 92-0-020371-X, ISP289, IAEA). Unipub.

Rapid Methods for the Analysis of Used Oils: Proceedings. French Institute of Petroleum, Paris, 1971 et al. (Illus.). 96p. 1973. text ed. 25.00x (ISBN 0-900645-10-5). Scholium Intl.

Rapid Perspective. Geoffrey Wickham. (gr. 10 up). 6.95 (ISBN 0-85458-050-6); pap. 3.75 (ISBN 0-85458-051-4). Transatlantic.

Rapid Population Growth & Macro Economic Development: The Philippines Case. Theodore K. Ruprecht. (Illus.). 1975. pap. text ed. 5.00 o.p. (ISBN 0-89249-004-7). Intl Development.

Rapid Reading Made Simple. John Waldman. 1958. pap. 3.50 (ISBN 0-385-01226-8, Made). Doubleday.

Rapid Review of English Grammar. 2nd ed. Jean Praninskas. (Illus.). 352p. 1975. pap. 10.95 (ISBN 0-13-753145-1). P-H.

Rapid Virus Diagnosis. 2nd ed. P. S. Gardner & J. McQuillan. LC 80-40239. (Illus.). 336p. 1980. text ed. 79.95 (ISBN 0-407-38441-3). Butterworths.

Rapid Writing Made Easy. Donna Hamlin. 1978. pap. 4.95 (ISBN 0-8119-0394-X). Fell.

Rapidly Quenched Metals--a Bibliography: 1973-1979. Compiled by C. Suryanarayana. 310p. 1980. 75.00 (ISBN 0-306-65194-7). IFI Plenum.

Rapids. Alan Sullivan. LC 74-163830. (Social History of Canada Ser.). 256p. 1972. pap. 4.50 (ISBN 0-8020-6148-6). U of Toronto Pr.

Rapping About Sex. Marshall L. Shearer & Marguerite R. Shearer. (Orig.). 1972. pap. 1.75 o.p. (ISBN 0-06-463319-5, 319, EH). Har-Row.

Rapport Pedagogique et Communication. 2nd ed. Ed. by Pierre Bourdieu et al. (Cahiers Du Centre De Sociologie Europeenne: No. 2). 1968. pap. 12.35x (ISBN 90-279-6254-5). Mouton.

Rapport Sur la Situation Des Droits De L'homme En Haiti. Ed. by OAS General Secretariat Inter-American Commission of Human Rights. (Human Rights Ser.). 76p. 1980. 5.00 (ISBN 0-8270-1098-2). OAS.

Rapture. Jeff Harlan. 1980. pap. 2.95. Maranatha Hse.

Raptures of Love. Jackson Reed. (Orig.). 1976. pap. 1.95 o.s.i. (ISBN 0-515-04082-7). Jove Pubns.

Rapunzel. Grimm Brothers. Ed. & illus. by Felix Hoffmann. LC 61-2865. (Illus.). (gr. k-3). 1961. 5.50 o.p. (ISBN 0-15-265656-1, HJ). HarBraceJ.

Rapunzel. (Illus.). Arabic 2.50x (ISBN 0-685-82869-7). Intl Bk Ctr.

Rapunzel. Judith Wolman. LC 78-74131. (Illus.). (gr. 2-5). Date not set. price not set (ISBN 0-89799-168-0); pap. price not set (ISBN 0-89799-167-2). Dandelion Pr. Postponed.

Rara Arithmetica & Arithmetical Books, 2 vols. in 1. 4th ed. David E. Smith & Augustus De Morgan. LC 74-113148. (Illus., Eng.). 1970. text ed. 29.50 (ISBN 0-8284-0192-6). Chelsea Pub.

Rare Afro-Americana: A Reconstruction of the Adger Library. Ed. by Wendy Hall. (Reference Book Ser.). 1981. 25.00 (ISBN 0-8161-8175-6). G K Hall.

Rare & Expensive Postcards: Book Two. Margaret Kaduck & John Kaduck. (Illus.). pap. 8.95 (ISBN 0-87069-267-4). Wallace-Homestead.

Rare & Undone Saints. Phyllis Demong. LC 80-16731. (Illus.). 96p. 1981. 4.95 (ISBN 0-8397-7071-5). Eriksson.

Rare & Unusual Animals. Nina Leen. (Illus.). 80p. (gr. 3-7). 1981. 8.95 (ISBN 0-03-057478-1). HR&W.

Rare Early Essays on Charles Dickens. Carmen J. Dello Buono. 207p. 1980. lib. bdg. 22.50 (ISBN 0-8482-0647-9). Norwood Edns.

Rare Early Essays on George Eliot. Dello Buono & Carmen Joseph. 211p. 1980. lib. bdg. 25.00 (ISBN 0-8482-3660-2). R West.

Rare Early Essays on George Eliot. Carmen J. Dello Buono. 202p. 1980. lib. bdg. 25.00 (ISBN 0-8482-3661-0). Norwood Edns.

Rare Early Essays on John Keats. Carmen J. Dello Buono. 208p. 1980. lib. bdg. 17.50 (ISBN 0-8482-3675-0). Norwood Edns.

Rare Early Essays on Percy Bysshe Shelley. Carmen J. Dello Buono. 220p. 1981. lib. bdg. 22.50 (ISBN 0-8482-3653-X). Norwood Edns.

Rare Early Essays on the Brontes. Dello Buono & Carmen Joseph. 218p. 1980. lib. bdg. 17.50 (ISBN 0-8482-0646-0). Norwood Edns.

Rare Early Essays on Walt Whitman. Carmen J. Dello Buono. 202p. 1980. lib. bdg. 17.50 (ISBN 0-8482-3699-8). Norwood Edns.

Rare Early Essays on William Shakespeare: Third Series. Carmen J. Dello Buno. 206p. 1980. lib. bdg. 17.50 (ISBN 0-8482-3651-3). Norwood Edns.

Rare Earths in Modern Science & Technology, Vol. 2. Ed. by G. J. McCarthy et al. 670p. 1980. 59.50 (ISBN 0-306-40347-1, Plenum Pr). Plenum Pub.

Rare Jewel of Christian Contentment. Jeremiah Burroughs. 1979. pap. 3.95 (ISBN 0-85151-091-4). Banner of Truth.

Rare Plant Conservation: Geographical Data Organization. Ed. by L. E. Morse & M. S. Henifin. 1981. pap. 25.00 (ISBN 0-89327-223-X). NY Botanical.

Rare Triumphs of Love & Fortune. Ed. by John I. Owen & Stephen Orgel. LC 78-66840. (Renaissance Drama Ser.). 1979. lib. bdg. 44.00 (ISBN 0-8240-9736-X). Garland Pub.

Rarer Action: Essays in Honor of Francis Fergusson. Ed. by Alan Cheuse & Richard Koffler. LC 70-127050. 1970. 23.00 (ISBN 0-8135-0670-0). Rutgers U Pr.

Rarities of the Musee Guimet. Intro. by Jeannine Auboyer. LC 74-81967. (Illus.). 124p. 1975. 19.50 (ISBN 0-87848-043-9). Asia Soc.

Rasbora. Martin Brittan. (Illus.). 1972. 9.95 (ISBN 0-87666-136-3, PS-681). TFH Pubns.

Rascal. Sterling North. (gr. 5 up). 1976. pap. 1.75 (ISBN 0-380-01518-8, 44800). Avon.

Rascals from Haskell's Gym. Betty Baker. (gr. 3-5). 1980. pap. 1.25 (ISBN 0-590-30231-0, Schol Pap). Schol Bk Serv.

Rash Resolve; or, the Untimely Disovery. Eliza Haywood. Bd. with Life & Adventures of the Lady Lucy. Penelope Aubin. LC 74-170561. (Foundations of the Novel Ser.: Vol. 43). lib. bdg. 50.00 (ISBN 0-8240-0555-4). Garland Pub.

Rashanyn Dark. William Tedford. (Timequest Ser.: No. 1). 1981. pap. 2.25 (ISBN 0-8439-0869-6, Leisure Bks). Nordon Pubns.

Rashi: His Life & Works. Maurice Liber. Tr. by Adele Szold from Fr. LC 70-136767. (Illus.). 1971. Repr. of 1906 ed. 12.50 (ISBN 0-87203-021-0). Hermon.

Rashomon. Akira Kurosawa. (Illus.). 1969. pap. 17.25 (ISBN 0-686-66133-8, ST00051). Grove.

Raspail, Scientist & Reformer. Dora B. Weiner. LC 68-19761. (Illus.). 1968. 20.00x (ISBN 0-231-03059-2). Columbia U Pr.

Rasputin & the Waning of the Russian Monarchy. Michel De Enden. 300p. (Orig.). 1980. pap. write for info. (ISBN 0-913124-46-X). Nordland Pub.

Rasputin: The Man Behind the Myth. Maria Rasputin & Patte Barham. (Illus.). 1978. pap. 2.95 (ISBN 0-446-93878-5). Warner Bks.

Rasputin: The Man Behind the Myth. Maria Rasputin & Patte Barrham. 328p. 1981. pap. 2.95. Warner Bks.

Rasskazy, 1921-1930. Mikhail Zoshchenko. (Rus.). 1980. pap. 5.00 (ISBN 0-88233-591-X). Ardis Pubs.

Rastafari: A Way of Life. Tracy Nicholas. LC 77-76285. (Illus.). 1979. pap. 7.95 (ISBN 0-385-11575-X, Anch). Doubleday.

Rat. J. Wells. 1966. pap. text ed. 6.50x o.p. (ISBN 0-435-60939-4). Heinemann Ed.

Rat-Catcher's Son & Other Stories. Carolyn London. (Children's Bks). (Illus.). 128p. (gr. 3-7). 1971. pap. 1.50 (ISBN 0-8024-1710-8). Moody.

Rat Is Dead & Ant Is Sad. Betty Baker. LC 78-1943. (I Can Read Bks.). (Illus.). 64p. (gr. k-3). 1981. 6.95 (ISBN 0-06-020346-3, HarpJ); PLB 7.89g (ISBN 0-06-020347-1). Har-Row.

Rat on Fire. George V. Higgins. LC 80-22713. 192p. 1981. 10.95 (ISBN 0-394-42409-3). Knopf.

Rate Bureaus & Antitrust Conflicts in Transportation Public Policy Issues. Grant M. Davis & Charles S. Sherwood. (Special Studies). (Illus.). 138p. 1975. text ed. 19.95 (ISBN 0-275-09880-X). Praeger.

Rate of Interest & Other Essays. Joan Robinson. LC 79-51867. 1981. Repr. of 1952 ed. 17.00 (ISBN 0-88355-959-5). Hyperion Conn.

Rate of Return Taxation of Minerals. 109p. (Orig.). 1977. pap. text ed. 5.00x (ISBN 0-88757-006-2, Pub. by Ctr Resource Stud Canada). Renouf.

Rates of Marchandizes, As They Are Set Down in the Booke of Rates. LC 72-227. (English Experience Ser.: No. 165). 1969. Repr. of 1609 ed. 14.00 (ISBN 90-221-0165-7). Walter J Johnson.

Rathbone Years: Masterpieces Acquired for the Museum of Fine Arts, Boston, 1955-1972 & for the St. Louis Art Museum, 1940-1955. Frwd. by Hanns Swarzenski. (Illus.). 1972. pap. 6.50 (ISBN 0-87846-067-5). Mus Fine Arts Boston.

Ratification of the Twenty-First Amendment to the Constitution of the United States. Everett S. Brown. LC 78-114757. (American Constitutional & Legal History Ser). 1970. Repr. of 1938 ed. 65.00 (ISBN 0-306-71928-2). Da Capo.

Ratio, Proporation & Percent. P. Driscoll et al. Ed. by K. West & D. Johnston. (Math Skills for Daily Living Ser.). (Illus.). 32p. (gr. 7-12). 1979. pap. text ed. 3.95x (ISBN 0-87453-094-6). Denoyer.

Rational & Social Foundations of Music. Max Weber. Tr. by Don Martindale et al. LC 56-12134. 198p. 1958. Repr. lib. bdg. 12.95x (ISBN 0-8093-0015-X). S Ill U Pr.

Rational & Social Foundations of Music. Max Weber. Tr. by Don Martindale et al. LC 56-12134. (Arcturus Books Paperbacks). 1969. pap. 6.95 (ISBN 0-8093-0355-8). S Ill U Pr.

Rational Decision-Making: Israel's Security Choices, 1967. Janice G. Stein & Raymond Tanter. LC 80-13589. 414p. 1980. 25.00 (ISBN 0-8142-0312-4). Ohio St U Pr.

Rational Economic Man. Martin I. Hollis & Edward J. Nell. (Illus.). 288p. 1975. 32.95x (ISBN 0-521-20408-9). Cambridge U Pr.

Rational Emotive Therapy in Practice. James A. Bard. LC 80-51923. 192p. 1980. pap. text ed. 8.95 (ISBN 0-87822-213-8, 2138). Res Press.

Rational Expectations & Econometric Practice. Ed. by Robert E. Lucas, Jr. & Thomas J. Sargent. 672p. 1981. 35.00x (ISBN 0-8166-0916-0); pap. 14.95x (ISBN 0-8166-0917-9). U of Minn Pr.

Rational Expectations & Monetary Policies. J. J. Sijben. LC 79-56565. 144p. 1980. 37.50x (ISBN 0-686-27288-9). Sijthoff & Noordhoff.

Rational Geraitrics. Ed. by J. Andrews & H. P. Von Hahn. (Illus.). vi, 194p. 1981. pap. 23.50 (ISBN 3-8055-1803-X). S Karger.

Rational Peasant: The Political Economy of Rural Society in Vietnam. Samuel Popkin. 1979. 16.50x (ISBN 0-520-03561-5); pap. 5.95x (ISBN 0-520-03954-8, CAMPUS NO. 236). U of Cal Pr.

Rational Sex Ethics. Ben N. Ard, Jr. LC 78-62739. 1978. pap. text ed. 7.75 (ISBN 0-8191-0592-9). U Pr of Amer.

Rationale of Judicial Evidence, Specially Applied to English Practice, 5 vols. Jeremy Bentham. Ed. by David Berkowitz & Samuel Thorne. LC 77-86645. (Classics of English Legal History in the Modern Era Ser.: Vol. 98). 1979. Set. lib. bdg. 225.00 (ISBN 0-8240-3085-0); lib. bdg. 55.00 ea. Garland Pub.

Rationalisierungsfalle. 123p. (Orig., Ger.). 1979. pap. text ed. 20.00 (ISBN 0-89192-297-0). Interbk Inc.

Rationalism & Revolution Sixteen Sixty to Eighteen Fifteen, Vol. II. Ed. by Thomas G. Barnes & Gerald D. Feldman. LC 79-66686. 1979. pap. text ed. 9.25 (ISBN 0-8191-0850-2). U Pr of Amer.

Rationalism in Greek Philosophy. George Boas. 504p. 1961. 25.00x o.p. (ISBN 0-8018-0079-X). Johns Hopkins.

Rationalismus der Weltbeherrschung. Wolfgang Schluchter. (Suhrkamp Taschenbuecher Wissenschaft). 336p. pap. text ed. 9.10 (ISBN 3-518-07922-0, Pub. by Insel Verlag Germany). Suhrkamp.

Rationalist Encyclopaedia: A Book of Reference on Religion, Philosophy, Ethics, & Science. Joseph McCabe. LC 79-164054. 1971. Repr. of 1948 ed. 26.00 (ISBN 0-8103-3754-1). Gale.

Rationalists: Theory & Design in the Modern Movement. Ed. by Dennis Sharp. Date not set. 32.50 (ISBN 0-8038-6219-6). Hastings.

Rationality. Ed. by Bryan R. Wilson. 1977. pap. 13.50x (ISBN 0-631-09900-X, Pub by Basil Blackwell). Biblio Dist.

Rationality: An Essay Towards an Analysis. Jonathan Bennett. (Studies in Philosophical Psychology). 1971. text ed. 4.50x (ISBN 0-7100-3841-0); pap. text ed. 3.50x (ISBN 0-391-00198-1). Humanities.

Rationality, Theory, & Experimentation in Ayurvedic Medicine. 35p. 1980. pap. 5.00 (ISBN 92-808-0106-6, TUNU097, UNU). Unipub.

Rationing Health Care. Michael Cooper. LC 74-32600. 150p. 1975. 19.95 (ISBN 0-470-17119-7). Halsted Pr.

Ratsel Vom Waldsee: Reader 2. Rita M. Walbruck. LC 80-22126. (Auf Heisser Spur Ser.). (gr. 9-12). 1981. pap. 1.95 (ISBN 0-88436-851-3). EMC.

Ratsmagic. Wayne Anderson & Christopher Logue. (Illus.). 1979. 7.95 o.p. (ISBN 0-670-58977-2, Studio). Viking Pr.

Rattlesnakes: Their Habits, Life Histories & Influence on Mankind, 2 vols. 2nd ed. Laurence M. Klauber. LC 56-5002. (Illus.). 1973. Boxed Set. 75.00 (ISBN 0-685-26757-1). Vol. 1 (ISBN 0-520-01775-7). Vol. 2 (ISBN 0-520-02286-6). U of Cal Pr.

Rattlesnakes: Their Habits, Life Histories, & Influence on Mankind. abr. ed. Laurence M. Klauber. (Illus.). 400p. 1981. 14.95 (ISBN 0-520-04038-4). U of Cal Pr.

Rauber. 2nd ed. Johann Schiller. Ed. by C. P. Magill & L. A. Willoughby. (Blackwell's German Text Ser.). 1974. pap. 4.50x o.p. (ISBN 0-631-01850-6, Pub. by Basil Blackwell). Biblio Dist.

Raum. Carl Sherrell. 1977. pap. 1.50 o.p. (ISBN 0-380-01646-X, 33043). Avon.

Rauschenberg. National Collection of Fine Arts. LC 76-58522. (Illus.). 216p. 1976. 27.50 (ISBN 0-87474-170-X); pap. 15.50 (ISBN 0-87474-171-8). Smithsonian.

Ravel: Man & Musican. Arbie Orenstein. LC 74-34022. (Illus.). 320p. 1975. 17.50x (ISBN 0-231-03902-6). Columbia U Pr.

Raveling of the Novel: Studies in Romantic Fiction from Walpole to Scott. rev. ed. Stephen Sandy. Ed. by Devendra P. Varma. LC 79-8476. (Gothic Studies & Dissertations Ser.). 1980. lib. bdg. 25.00x (ISBN 0-405-12660-3). Arno.

Raven. Shana Carrol. (Orig.). pap. 2.25 (ISBN 0-515-04439-3). Jove Pubns.

Raven & Other Fairy Tales. Joan B. Payne. LC 72-81379. (Illus.). (gr. k-3). 1969. PLB 3.72 o.s.i. (ISBN 0-8038-6310-1). Hastings.

Raven in Flight. Donald MacKenzie. 1981. pap. 1.95 (ISBN 0-425-04718-0). Berkley Pub.

Raven Rocks: A Woodland Rockshelter in Belmont County, Ohio. Olaf Prufer. Ed. by Mark F. Seeman. LC 80-84664. (Kent State Research Papers in Archaeology: No. 1). (Illus.). 104p. (Orig.). 1981. pap. 6.00x (ISBN 0-87338-254-4). Kent St U Pr.

Raven Settles a Score. Donald MacKenzie. 1981. pap. 1.95 (ISBN 0-425-04717-2). Berkley Pub.

Ravenburn. Laura Black. (Large Print Bks.). 1980. lib. bdg. 16.95 (ISBN 0-8161-3129-5). G K Hall.

Ravenna. Antonia Paolucci. (Scala Art Book). (Illus., Orig.). 1978. pap. 7.95 (ISBN 0-8467-0470-6, Pub. by Two Continents). Hippocrene Bks.

Raven's Story. Margaret E. Gant. LC 80-105389. (Illus.). 1979. 9.95 (ISBN 0-9603138-0-X). M E Gant.

Ravenscroft. Dorothy Eden. 1978. pap. 1.95 (ISBN 0-449-23760-5, Crest). Fawcett.

Ravenshoe. Henry Kingsley. Ed. by William H. Scheuerle. LC 67-12117. 1967. pap. 4.95x (ISBN 0-8032-5109-2, BB 365, Bison). U of Nebr Pr.

Ravenswood. Richard Ryan. (Orig.). 1974. pap. text ed. 3.25x (ISBN 0-85105-255-X, Dolmen Pr). Humanities.

Ravine Erosion in India. H. S. Sharma. (Illus.). 100p. 1980. text ed. 11.25x (ISBN 0-391-02142-7). Humanities.

Raving Mad. Mad Magazine Editors. (Mad Ser.). (Illus.). 192p. 1973. pap. 1.75 (ISBN 0-446-94382-7). Warner Bks.

Ravishers. Jeanne Duval. (Orig.). 1980. pap. 2.50 (ISBN 0-451-09523-5, E9523, Sig). NAL.

Ravishing Doctor. H. G. Gunther. (Gunther Ser.). pap. 1.95 (ISBN 0-515-05676-6). Jove Pubns.

Raw Hands & Bagging. Coco Gordon. (Illus.). 1978. pap. 2.50 (ISBN 0-931956-00-5). Water Mark.

Raw Honey. Marie Harris. LC 75-21787. 72p. 1975. pap. 4.95 (ISBN 0-914086-09-X). Alicejamesbooks.

Raw Materials & Foreign Policy. International Economic Studies Institute & Timothy W. Stanley. (Illus.). 1977. lib. bdg. 21.00x o.p. (ISBN 0-89158-340-8); pap. text ed. 11.50 o.p. (ISBN 0-89158-446-3). Westview.

Raw Notes: Documents & Scripts of the Performances: Stars, Moveyhouse, Massage, the Typewriter with annotations by the author. Claes Oldenburg. LC 73-83224. (Nova Scotia Ser). (Illus.). 544p. 1973. pap. 12.95, c (ISBN 0-919616-01-1). NYU Pr.

Raw Vegetable Juices. N. W. Walker. 1971. pap. 1.75 (ISBN 0-515-05330-9, V2570). Jove Pubns.

Rawhide Guns. rev. ed. Frank Bonham. (Orig.). 1981. pap. 1.95 (ISBN 0-425-04815-2). Berkley Pub.

Rawhide Range. Ernest Haycox. 192p. 1975. Repr. of 1952 ed. lib. bdg. 9.95 o.p. (ISBN 0-89190-975-3). Am Repr-Rivercity Pr.

Ray Bradbury. Wayne L. Johnson. LC 79-4825. (Recognitions Ser.). 1980. 10.95 (ISBN 0-8044-2426-8); pap. 4.95 (ISBN 0-8044-6318-2). Ungar.

Ray Bradbury Companion: A Life & Career History, Photolog, & Comprehensive Checklist of Writings, with Facsimiles from Ray Bradbury's Unpublished & Uncollected Works in All Media. Ed. by William F. Nolan. LC 74-10397. (Bruccoli Clark Book). (Illus.). 339p. 1974. 48.00 (ISBN 0-8103-0930-0). Gale.

Ray Charles. Sharon B. Mathis. LC 72-7552. (Biography Ser.). (Illus.). (gr. 1-5). 1973. 7.95 (ISBN 0-690-67065-6, TYC-J); PLB 6.89 o.p. (ISBN 0-690-67066-4). T Y Crowell.

Ray of Darkness. Margiad Evans. 1980. 11.50 (ISBN 0-7145-3727-6); pap. 4.95 (ISBN 0-7145-3607-5). Riverrun NY.

Ray Reardon's Fifty Best Trick Shots. Ray Reardon. LC 80-69348. (Illus.). 128p. 1980. 11.95 (ISBN 0-7153-7993-3). David & Charles.

Ray Stannard Baker: The Mind of a Progressive. Robert C. Bannister, Jr. Ed. by Frank Freidel. LC 78-66516. (The History of the United States Ser.: Vol. 1). 372p. 1979. lib. bdg. 28.00 (ISBN 0-8240-9711-4). Garland Pub.

Raymond Baxter's Farnborough Commentary. Raymond Baxter. (Illus.). 120p. 1980. 27.95 (ISBN 0-85059-434-0). Aztex.

Raymond Duchamp-Villon. George H. Hamilton & William C. Agee. 7.50 o.s.i. (ISBN 0-8027-0241-4); pap. 3.50 o.s.i. (ISBN 0-8027-7073-8). Walker & Co.

Raymond Fourth, Count of Toulouse. John Hill & Laurita Hill. LC 62-14120. 1962. 12.00x o.p. (ISBN 0-8156-0026-7). Syracuse U Pr.

Raymond Hood, Architect of Ideas. Walter H. Kilham, Jr. Date not set. 12.50 (ISBN 0-8038-0218-8). Hastings.

Raymond IV, Count of Toulouse. John H. Hill & Laurita L. Hill. LC 80-11116. (Illus.). viii, 177p. 1980. Repr. of 1962 ed. lib. bdg. 19.50x (ISBN 0-313-22362-9, HIRA). Greenwood.

Raymond Queneau. Jacques Guicharnaud. LC 65-26340. (Columbia Ser.: No. 14). (Orig.). 1965. pap. 2.00 (ISBN 0-231-02706-0, MW14). Columbia U Pr.

Raymond Roussel. Rayner Heppenstall. 1967. 16.50x (ISBN 0-520-00554-6). U of Cal Pr.

Rays from Sunshine. Cay Pruitt. 56p. 1980. 3.50 (ISBN 0-8059-2766-2). Dorrance.

Rays of Hope. D. O. Teasley. 95p. pap. 0.75. Faith Pub Hse.

Raza: The Mexican Americans. Stan Steiner. LC 77-83622. (Illus.). 1970. 12.50 o.p. (ISBN 0-06-014083-6, HarpT). Har-Row.

Razi: Modern Persian-English Dictionary. 20.00x o.p. (ISBN 0-686-09037-3). Colton Bk.

Razorback. Peter Brennan. 384p. (Orig.). 1981. pap. price not set (ISBN 0-515-05392-9). Jove Pubns.

RBP Pattern Resource Book. Ed. by Valerie Wilson. (Illus.). 1975. wire spiral 3.25 (ISBN 0-87227-016-5). Reg Baptist.

R.C.I.A. A Practical Approach to Christian Initiation. Rosalie Curtin et al. 136p. (Orig.). 1981. pap. 6.95. Wm C Brown.

RCT Mathematics: A Workbook. John Allasio et al. 168p. (gr. 9-12). 1980. pap. 5.95 (ISBN 0-937820-00-8); ans. key 1.00 (ISBN 0-937820-01-6). Westsea Pub.

RCT Writing: A Workbook. Rosalie Rafter & Cheri Alaia. 225p. (gr. 9-12). 1981. pap. 5.75 (ISBN 0-937820-10-5). Westsea Pub.

R.D. Laing: His Work & Its Relevance to Sociology. Martin Howarth-Williams. (Direct Editions Ser.). (Orig.). 1977. pap. 14.50 (ISBN 0-7100-8624-5). Routledge & Kegan.

Re-Action. Conn McAuliffe. LC 74-141218. (Illus.). 1971. pap. 5.95 o.p. (ISBN 0-87835-014-4). Boyd & Fraser.

Re-Educating the Delinquent. Samuel R. Slavson. 1961. pap. 1.50 o.s.i. (ISBN 0-02-078010-9, Collier). Macmillan.

Re-Entering: Successful Back-to-Work Strategies for Women Seeking a Fresh Start. Eleanor Berman. 192p. 1980. 8.95 (ISBN 0-517-53943-8). Crown.

Re-Entry. Paul Preuss. (Orig.). 1981. pap. 2.25 (ISBN 0-553-14834-6). Bantam.

Re-Entry into the Single Life. Jim Keelan. 1977. 5.00 (ISBN 0-686-18830-6, Pub. by Professional Writers Group). Comm Unltd.

Re-Entry Programs for Female Scientists. Alma E. Lantz et al. 1980. 21.95 (ISBN 0-03-055771-2). Praeger.

Re-Establishment of the Church of England, 1660-1663. I. M. Green. (Oxford Historical Monographs). 1978. 33.00x (ISBN 0-19-821867-2). Oxford U Pr.

Re-Interpretations: Seven Studies in Nineteenth Century German Literature. J. P. Stern. 370p. Date not set. price not set (ISBN 0-521-23983-4); pap. price not set (ISBN 0-521-28366-3). Cambridge U Pr.

Re-Organizing the National Health Service: A Case Study in Administrative Change. R. G. Brown. (Aspects of Social Policy Ser.). 232p. 1979. 24.50x (ISBN 0-631-18130-X, Pub. by Basil Blackwell). Biblio Dist.

Re-Thinking the Rapture. E. Schuyler English. 1954. pap. 2.25 (ISBN 0-87213-144-0). Loizeaux.

REACH. Hughes et al. (gr. 4-9). 1974. pap. text ed. 3.99 student's text (ISBN 0-87892-864-2); tchr's handbook 3.99 (ISBN 0-87892-870-7); tapes 159.60 (ISBN 0-87892-868-5). Economy Co.

Reach for Reading. rev. ed. Alice D. Lorenz. 128p. (gr. 4 up). 1981. write for info. wkbk. (ISBN 0-87895-904-1); write for info. manual with ans. key (ISBN 0-87895-905-X). Modern Curr.

Reach for the Sky. Paul Brickhill. 1954. 6.95 o.p. (ISBN 0-393-07376-9). Norton.

Reach for the Stars. Verna W. Sightler. (YA) 5.95 (ISBN 0-685-07456-0, Avalon). Bouregy.

Reach for Tomorrow. Verna Searle. (Orig.). 1980. pap. 4.95 (ISBN 0-88270-449-4). Logos.

Reach Out for a New Life. Robert H. Schuller. 1977. 9.95 (ISBN 0-8015-6247-3, Hawthorn). Dutton.

Reaching for Empire, 1890-1901. Bernard A. Weisberger. LC 63-8572. (Life History of the United States). (Illus.). (gr. 5 up). 1974. lib. bdg. 9.96 (ISBN 0-685-72982-6, Pub. by Time-Life). Silver.

Reaching for Rainbows: Resources for Creative Worship. Ann Weems. 1980. pap. write for info. (ISBN 0-664-24355-X). Westminster.

Reaching High: The Psychology of Spiritual Living. Marvin Gawryn. LC 80-24306. 200p. 1981. 11.95 (ISBN 0-938380-00-1); pap. 7.95 (ISBN 0-938380-01-X). Spiritual Renaissance.

Reaching Out. Alice Yardley. LC 72-95335. 112p. 1973. 3.25 o.p. (ISBN 0-590-07328-1, Citation). Schol Bk Serv.

Reaching Out: Advocacy for the Gifted & Talented. American Association for Gifted Children. Ed. by Abraham J. Tannenbaum. (Perspectives on Gifted & Talented Education Ser.). (Orig.). 1980. pap. text ed. 4.95x (ISBN 0-8077-2591-9). Tchrs Coll.

Reaching Out: Interpersonal Effectiveness & Self Actualization. David W. Johnson. (Illus.). 272p. 1972. ref. ed. 13.95 (ISBN 0-13-753277-6); pap. text ed. 10.95 ref. ed. (ISBN 0-13-753269-5). P-H.

Reaching Out: Interpersonal Effectiveness & Self-Actualization. 2nd ed. David W. Johnson. (Illus.). 320p. 1981. text ed. 14.95 (ISBN 0-13-753327-6); pap. text ed. 10.95 (ISBN 0-13-753319-5). P-H.

Reaching Out: Sensitivity & Order in Recent American Fiction by Women. Anne Z. Mickelson. LC 78-26164. 1979. lib. bdg. 12.00 (ISBN 0-8108-1194-4). Scarecrow.

Reaching Out: The Three Movements of Spiritual Life. Henri J. M. Nouwen. LC 74-9460. 120p. 1975. 7.95 (ISBN 0-385-03212-9). Doubleday.

Reaching Out with Love: Encounters with Troubled Youth. Jean M. Campbell. 144p. (Orig.). 1981. pap. 2.95 (ISBN 0-87239-453-0, 3652). Standard Pub.

Reaching People: The Structure of Neighborhood Services. Ed. by Daniel Thursz & Joseph L. Vigilante. LC 77-79869. (Social Service Delivery Systems: Vol. 3). (Illus.). 1978. 20.00 (ISBN 0-8039-0817-2); pap. 9.95 (ISBN 0-8039-0818-0). Sage.

Reaching: Poems by George P. Elliott. George P. Elliot. (Santa Susana Press Ser.). 1979. numbered 35.00 (ISBN 0-937048-21-6); lettered 60.00 (ISBN 0-937048-28-3). CSUN.

Reaching the Aged: Social Services in Forty-Four Countries. Ed. by Morton I. Teicher et al. LC 79-18525. (Social Service Delivery Systems: Vol. 4). 1979. 20.00x (ISBN 0-8039-1365-6); pap. 9.95x (ISBN 0-8039-1366-4). Sage.

Reaching the Disadvantaged Learner. Ed. by A. Harry Passow. LC 69-11364. 1970. text ed. 12.95x (ISBN 0-8077-1889-0); pap. text ed. 9.95x (ISBN 0-8077-1888-2). Tchrs Coll.

Reaching Toward the Heights. Richard Wurmbrand. 1977. pap. 5.95 (ISBN 0-310-35471-4). Zondervan.

Reaching Your Possibilities Through Commitment. Gerald W. Marshall. LC 80-53140. 128p. 1981. pap. 3.95 (ISBN 0-8307-0777-8, 5414407). Regal.

React & Interact: Situations for Communication. Donald R. Byrd & Isis C. Cabetas. (Illus.). 100p. (gr. 10-12). 1980. pap. text ed. 4.95 (ISBN 0-88345-412-2). Regents Pub.

Reaction Kinetic & Reactor Design. J. Butt. 1980. 26.95 (ISBN 0-13-753335-7). P-H.

Reaction Kinetics. James W. Beatty & Richard G. Scamehorn. 1978. pap. text ed. 9.25x (ISBN 0-8191-0376-4). U Pr of Amer.

Reaction Kinetics, 2 vols. K. J. Laidler. 1963. Vol. 1. text ed. 16.00 (ISBN 0-08-009834-7); Vol. 2. text ed. 13.75 (ISBN 0-08-009836-3); Vol. 1. pap. text ed. 7.75 (ISBN 0-08-009833-9); Vol. 2. pap. text ed. 6.25 (ISBN 0-08-009835-5). Pergamon.

Reaction Kinetics. M. J. Pilling. (Oxford Chemistry Ser). (Illus.). 144p. 1975. 24.95x (ISBN 0-19-855481-8). Oxford U Pr.

Reaction Kinetics in the Liquid Phase. S. G. Entelis & R. P. Tiger. Tr. by R. Kondor from Rus. LC 75-17857. 1976. 54.95 (ISBN 0-470-24330-9). Halsted Pr.

Reaction Mechanisms in Organic Analytical Chemistry. Kenneth A. Connors. LC 72-5845. 1973. 34.50 o.p. (ISBN 0-471-16845-9, Pub. by Wiley-Interscience). Wiley.

Reaction to Colonialism: A Prelude to the Politics of Independence in Northern Zambia, 1893-1939. Henry S. Meebelo. 1971. text ed. 9.00x (ISBN 0-7190-1028-4); pap. text ed. 4.75x (ISBN 0-7190-1029-2). Humanities.

Reaction to Conquest: Effects of Contact with Europeans on the Pondo of South Africa. abr. ed. Monica Hunter. (Illus.). 439p. 1979. pap. 14.00x (ISBN 0-8476-3112-5). Rowman.

Reactions to Ann Arbor: Vernacular Black English & Education. Ed. by Marcia F. Whiteman. 104p. (Orig.). 1980. pap. text ed. 5.95 (ISBN 0-87281-125-5). Ctr Appl Ling.

Reactions to Delinquency. William C. Smith. LC 78-70859. 1978. pap. text ed. 7.50 (ISBN 0-8191-0649-6). U Pr of Amer.

Reactive Intermediates, Vol. II. Maitland Jones & Robert A. Moss. (Serial Publication Ser.). 380p. 1981. 35.00 (ISBN 0-471-01875-9, Pub. by Wiley-Interscience). Wiley.

Reactive Intermediates, Vol. 1. Ed. by R. A. Abramovitch. (Illus.). 1980. 49.50 (ISBN 0-306-40220-3, Plenum Pr). Plenum Pub.

Reactive Intermediates in Organic Chemistry. Neil Isaacs. LC 73-8194. 560p. 1974. 60.25 (ISBN 0-471-42861-2, Pub. by Wiley-Interscience); pap. 24.75 (ISBN 0-471-42859-0, Pub. by Wiley-Interscience). Wiley.

Reactivity of Metal-Metal Bonds. Ed. by Malcolm Chisholm. (ACS Symposium Ser.: No. 155). 1981. price not set (ISBN 0-8412-0624-4). Am Chemical.

Reactor Burn-up Physics. (Illus.). 296p. (Orig.). 1973. pap. 18.75 (ISBN 92-0-051073-6, IAEA). Unipub.

Reactor Core Fuel Management. P. Silvennoinen. 250p. 1976. text ed. 42.00 (ISBN 0-08-019853-8); pap. text ed. 18.75 (ISBN 0-08-019852-X). Pergamon.

Reactor Noise - Smorn II: Proceedings of the 2nd Specialists' Meeting on Reactor Noise 1977. Ed. by M. M. Williams. 1978. pap. text ed. 182.00 (ISBN 0-686-68044-8). Pergamon.

Reactor Noise. an International Symposium: Special Multi Issue of Journal of Annals of Nuclear Energy. Ed. by M. M. Williams. 400p. 1976. pap. text ed. 55.00 (ISBN 0-08-019895-3). Pergamon.

Reactor Operation. J. Shaw. 1969. 25.00 (ISBN 0-08-013325-8); pap. 12.25 (ISBN 0-08-013324-X). Pergamon.

Reactor Physics in the Resonance & Thermal Regions, 2 vols. Ed. by Albert J. Goodjohn & Gerald C. Pomraning. Incl. Vol. 1. Neutron Thermalization. 450p (ISBN 0-262-07023-5); Vol. 2. Resonance Absorbtion. 450p (ISBN 0-262-07024-3). 1966. text ed. 30.00x ea. MIT Pr.

Reactor Physics Studies of H20 - D20 Moderated U02 Cores: A NORA Project Report. (Technical Reports: No. 67). 1966. pap. 4.50 (ISBN 92-0-155166-5, IAEA). Unipub.

Reactor Safeguards. C. R. Russell. 1962. 40.00 (ISBN 0-08-009706-5); pap. 15.00 (ISBN 0-08-013610-9). Pergamon.

Reactors & Reactions. Ed. by A. Fiechter. (Advances in Biochemical Engineering Ser.: Vol. 19). (Illus.). 250p. 1981. 57.90 (ISBN 0-387-10464-X). Springer-Verlag.

Reactors for University Research. Subcommittee on Nuclear Reactors. 1959. pap. 0.75 (ISBN 0-309-00075-0). Natl Acad Pr.

Read-a-Riddle, Pick-a-Joke. Audrey McKim & Dodie McKim. (Illus.). (gr. 2-3). 1975. pap. 1.25 (ISBN 0-590-09877-2, Schol Pap). Schol Bk Serv.

Read About the Policeman. Louis Slobodkin. LC 66-10582. (Read About Bks). (Illus.). (gr. k-3). 1966. PLB 4.47 o.p. (ISBN 0-531-01263-8). Watts.

Read About the Sanitation Man. Francine Klagsbrun. LC 71-171903. (Read About Bks). (Illus.). 72p. (gr. 4 up). 1972. PLB 4.47 o.p. (ISBN 0-531-01268-9). Watts.

Read & Do: Learning to Follow Written Directions. rev. & enl. ed. Katherine H. O'Connor. (Illus.). 51p. (gr. 1-2). 1973. wkbk 1.00 (ISBN 0-910812-09-8). Johnny Reads.

Read & Learn with Beth, the Traveler. Illus. by Jeff Zinggeler et al. (Read & Learn Ser.). (Illus.). 88p. (gr. 3-5). 1979. pap. 2.95 (ISBN 0-675-01056-X). Merrill.

Read & Recall: Passages for Advanced Reading Comprehension in English. Michael Berman. 1980. pap. 3.95 (ISBN 0-08-024531-5). Pergamon.

Read & Think Storybook Series, 15 bks. Sullivan Associates. Bks. 1-7. 6.56x (W); Bk. 8-15. 7.60x. tchrs. guide 9.20x (ISBN 0-686-60810-0). McGraw.

Read English. Piers Plowright. 1973. pap. text ed. 2.95x (ISBN 0-435-28705-2); tape 26.00x (ISBN 0-435-28706-0); cassette 22.00x (ISBN 0-435-28707-9). Heinemann Ed.

Read English, Book One. Royce & Zook. 80p. (Orig.). 1980. pap. text ed. 4.95 (ISBN 0-88499-675-1). Inst Mod Lang.

Read English, Book Two, Book 2. (Speak English Ser.). (Illus.). 64p. (Orig.). 1981. pap. 4.95 (ISBN 0-88499-676-X). Inst Mod Lang.

Read for Your Life: Two Successful Efforts to Help People Read & an Annotated List of Books That Made Them Want to. Julia R. Palmer. LC 73-14695. 1974. 18.50 (ISBN 0-8108-0654-1). Scarecrow.

Read It Right, & Remember What You Read. Samuel Smith. (Orig.). 1970. pap. 3.50 (ISBN 0-06-463306-3, EH 306, EH). Har-Row.

Read Me More Stories. Child Study Association Of America. LC 51-6972. (Illus.). (ps-1). 1951. 5.95 o.p. (ISBN 0-690-68690-0, TYC-J). T Y Crowell.

Read Right: Comprehension Power. J. E. Sparks & Carl E. Johnson. 1971. pap. text ed. 8.95x (ISBN 0-02-478390-0, 47839). Macmillan.

Read, Think & Answer. Gordon Green. 1969. tchrs ed. 2.50x (ISBN 0-19-432771-X). Oxford U Pr.

Read to Me Again. Child Study Association Of America. LC 60-11547. (Illus.). (ps-1). 1961. 7.95 (ISBN 0-690-68761-3, TYC-J). T Y Crowell.

Read-To-Me Storybook. Child Study Association Of America. LC 47-31488. (Illus.). (ps-1). 1947. 7.95 (ISBN 0-690-68832-6, TYC-J). T Y Crowell.

Read to Succeed. 2nd ed. Jane Bracy et al. (Illus.). 192p. 1980. pap. text ed. 9.95x (ISBN 0-07-007035-0); cassettes & tapes 60.00 (ISBN 0-07-007037-7); instructor's manual 6.95 (ISBN 0-07-007036-9). McGraw.

Read to Write. Halsey P. Taylor & Sheila F. Taylor. 1980. pap. text ed. 7.95x (ISBN 0-673-15388-6). Scott F.

Read Vietnamese. Nguyen-Dinh-Hoa. LC 66-18965. 189p. 1980. pap. 9.50 (ISBN 0-8048-1355-8). C E Tuttle.

Read Your Child's Thoughts: Pre-School Learning Piaget's Way. Sime. 1980. 13.95 (ISBN 0-500-01217-2). Thames Hudson.

Readability in the Classroom. Colin Harrison. LC 79-41794. (Illus.). 160p. 1980. 22.50 (ISBN 0-521-22712-7); pap. 7.95x (ISBN 0-521-29621-8). Cambridge U Pr.

Readable Maths & Statistics Book. Barry Edwards. (Illus.). 336p. (Orig.). 1980. text ed. 34.95x (ISBN 0-04-310007-4, 2550); pap. text ed. 13.50x (ISBN 0-04-310008-2, 2551). Allen Unwin.

Read'em & Weep: The Songs You Forgot to Remember. Sigmund Spaeth. (Music Reprint Ser.). 1979. Repr. of 1926 ed. lib. bdg. 22.50 (ISBN 0-306-79564-7). Da Capo.

Reader: An Introduction to Oral Interpretation. Donald N. Walters. LC 66-12939. (Orig.). 1966. pap. 2.65 o.p. (ISBN 0-672-63096-6). Odyssey Pr.

Reader & Shakespeare's Young Man Sonnets. Gerald Hammond. 247p. 1981. 22.50x (ISBN 0-389-20046-8). B&N.

Reader in Bureaucracy. Ed. by Robert K. Merton et al. 1965. pap. text ed. 10.95 (ISBN 0-02-921070-4). Free Pr.

Reader in Culture Change, 2 vols. Ed. by I. A. Brady & B. L. Isaac. Incl. Vol. 1. Theories. pap. text ed. 5.95 o.p. (ISBN 0-470-09533-4); Vol. 2. Case Studies. pap. text ed. 6.95 o.p. (ISBN 0-470-09534-2). 1975. Halsted Pr.

Reader in Library Administration. Ed. by Paul Wasserman. Mary Lee Bundy. LC 68-28324. (Reader Ser. in Library & Information Science: Vol. 1). 1969. 17.00 (ISBN 0-910972-16-8). IHS-PDS.

Reader in Library Communication. Ed. by Mary B. Cassata & Roger C. Palmer. LC 76-10123. (Reader in Librarianship & Information Science Ser.: Vol. 21). 1976. 20.00 o.s.i. (ISBN 0-910972-60-5). IHS-PDS.

Reader in Machine-Readable Social Data. Ed. by Howard D. White. LC 77-92432. (Readers Er. in Librarianship & Information Science: Vol. 24). 1978. lib. bdg. 21.00 (ISBN 0-910972-70-2). IHS-PDS.

Reader in Marxist Philosophy. Ed. by Howard Selsam & Harry Martel. LC 63-14262. (Orig.). 1963. 7.50 (ISBN 0-7178-0168-3); pap. 4.50 (ISBN 0-7178-0167-5). Intl Pub Co.

Reader in Planning Theory. Ed. by Andreas Faludi. 416p. 1973. text ed. 27.00 (ISBN 0-08-017066-8); pap. text ed. 10.75 (ISBN 0-08-017067-6). Pergamon.

Reader in Public Opinion & Mass Communication. 3rd ed. Ed. by Morris Janowitz & Paul Hirsch. LC 80-2444. 448p. 1981. pap. text ed. 10.95 (ISBN 0-02-916020-0). Free Pr.

Reader in the Dickens World. Susan R. Horton. LC 80-53031. 215p. 1981. 29.95 (ISBN 0-8229-1140-X). U of Pittsburgh Pr.

Reader in the History of the Eastern Slavic Languages: Russian, Belorussian, Ukranian. Ed. by George Y. Shevelov & Fred Holling. (Columbia Slavic Studies). 1958. pap. 6.00x (ISBN 0-231-02273-5). Columbia U Pr.

Reader in the Text: Essays on Audience & Interpretation. Ed. by Susan Suleiman & Inge Crosman. LC 79-27619. 1980. 30.00x (ISBN 0-691-06436-9); pap. 9.95 (ISBN 0-691-10096-9). Princeton U Pr.
Reader of Classical Urdu Poetry, 3 vols. Muhammad Abd-al-Rahman Barker. Incl. Vol. 1. pap. 10.00x (ISBN 0-87950-430-7); Vol. 2. pap. 10.00x (ISBN 0-87950-431-5); Vol. 3. pap. 10.00x (ISBN 0-87950-432-3). LC 77-73779. (Spoken Language Ser.). (Prog. Bk.). 1977. Set. pap. 24.00x (ISBN 0-87950-433-1); 6 dual track cassetes 75.00 (ISBN 0-87950-434-X); Set. incl. cassettes 95.00x (ISBN 0-87950-435-8). Spoken Lang Serv.
Reader on the Library Building. Ed. by Hal B. Schell. LC 73-93967. (Reader Ser in Librarianship & Information Science: Vol. 15). (Illus.). 1975. 22.00 (ISBN 0-910972-11-7). IHS-PDS.
Reader-Response Criticism: From Formalism to Post-Structuralism. Ed. by Jane P. Tompkins. LC 80-7966. 320p. 1981. text ed. 20.00x (ISBN 0-8018-2400-1); pap. text ed. 6.95x (ISBN 0-8018-2401-X). Johns Hopkins.
Reader, the Text, the Poem: The Transactional Theory of the Literary Work. Louise M. Rosenblatt. LC 78-16335. 214p. 1978. 11.95x (ISBN 0-8093-0883-5). S Ill U Pr.
Readers & Library Users. M. L. Ward. 1977. 8.25x (ISBN 0-85365-479-4, Pub. by Lib Assn England). Oryx Pr.
Reader's Choice: A Reading Skills Textbook for Students of English As a Second Language. E. Margaret Baudoin et al. 1977. pap. 7.50x (ISBN 0-472-08100-4). U of Mich Pr.
Reader's Digest Crafts & Hobbies. Reader's Digest. (Illus.). 1980. 19.95 (ISBN 0-89577-063-6, Pub. by Readers Digest Assoc). Norton.
Reader's Digest How to Write Better, Speak Better. 1972. 15.95 (ISBN 0-393-21433-8). Norton.
Reader's Digest Marvels & Mysteries of the World Around Us. (Illus.). 1973. 16.95 (ISBN 0-89577-012-1). Norton.
Reader's Digest Nineteen-Eighty One Almanac & Yearbook. 16th ed. Ed. by Reader's Digest. (Illus.). 1981. 6.95 (ISBN 0-89577-090-3, Pub. by Reader's Digest Assoc). Norton.
Reader's Digest of Books. enl. ed. Helen R. Keller. 1936. 9.95 o.s.i. (ISBN 0-02-561710-9). Macmillan.
Reader's Digest Secrets of Better Cooking. (Illus.). 1973. 14.95 (ISBN 0-89577-011-3). Norton.
Reader's Digest Stories Behind Everyday Things. Reader's Digest. (Illus.). 1980. 19.95 (ISBN 0-89577-068-7, Pub. by Readers Digest Assoc). Norton.
Reader's Digest Treasury of Best Loved Songs. 1972. 16.95 o.p. (ISBN 0-393-21432-X). Norton.
Readers Digest Wide World Atlas. LC 78-65321. (Illus.). 240p. 1979. 25.00 (ISBN 0-528-83110-0). Rand.
Reader's Digest You & the Law. 1971. 16.95 (ISBN 0-89577-038-5). Norton.
Reader's Encyclopedia of American Literature. Max J. Herzberg et al. LC 62-16546. (Illus.). 1962. 15.00 o.s.i. (ISBN 0-690-67341-8, TYC-T). T Y Crowell.
Reader's Encyclopedia of Shakespeare. Ed. by Oscar J. Campbell & Edward G. Quinn. LC 66-11946. (Illus.). 1966. 15.00 o.s.i. (ISBN 0-690-67412-0, TYC-T). T Y Crowell.
Reader's Eye: Studies in Didactic Literary Theory from Dante to Tasso. Robert L. Montgomery. 1979. 15.75x (ISBN 0-520-03700-6). U of Cal Pr.
Reader's Greek-English Lexicon of the New Testament. Sakae Kubo. 1975. text ed. 11.95 (ISBN 0-310-26920-2). Zondervan.
Reader's Guide to Alfred Bester. Carolyn Wendell. Ed. by Roger C. Schlobin. LC 80-19655. (Reader's Guide to Contemporary Science Fiction & Fantasy Authors Ser.: Vol. 6). (Illus., Orig.). 1980. pap. text ed. 3.95 (ISBN 0-916732-08-8). Starmont Hse.
Reader's Guide to Contemporary African Literature. 2nd, rev ed. Ed. by Hans Zell. 300p. 1981. text ed. 20.00x (ISBN 0-686-69153-9, Africana); pap. text ed. 10.00x (ISBN 0-8419-0640-8). Holmes & Meier.
Reader's Guide to D. H. Lawrence. Phillip Hobsbaum. 160p. 1981. 17.95 (ISBN 0-500-14023-5); pap. 9.95 (ISBN 0-500-15017-6). Thames Hudson.
Reader's Guide to Fifty American Poets. Peter Jones. (Reader's Guide Ser.). 386p. 1980. 16.50x (ISBN 0-389-20140-5). B&N.
Reader's Guide to Fifty British Plays: 1660-1900. John C. Thompson. (Reader's Guide Ser.). 448p. 1980. 16.50x (ISBN 0-389-20139-1). B&N.
Reader's Guide to Fifty British Poets: 1300-1900. Michael Schmidt. (Reader's Guide Ser.). 430p. 1980. 16.50x (ISBN 0-389-20137-5). B&N.
Reader's Guide to Fifty European Novels. Martin Seymour-Smith. (Reader's Guide Ser.). 528p. 1980. 20.75x (ISBN 0-389-20138-3). B&N.
Reader's Guide to Fifty Modern British Poets. Michael Schmidt. LC 79-53438. (Reader's Guide Ser.). 1979. 18.50x (ISBN 0-06-496110-9). B&N.
Reader's Guide to Frank Herbert. David M. Miller. Ed. by Roger C. Schlobin. LC 80-20880. (Reader's Guides to Contemporary Science Fiction & Fantasy Author Ser.: Vol. 5). (Illus., Orig.). 1980. pap. text ed. 3.95 (ISBN 0-916732-07-X). Starmont Hse.
Reader's Guide to Fritz Leiber. Jeff Frane. Ed. by Roger C. Scholbin. LC 80-22107. (Starmont Reader's Guides to Contemporary Science Fiction & Fantasy Authors Ser.: Vol. 8). (Illus.). 1980. pap. text ed. 3.95 (ISBN 0-916732-10-X). Starmont Hse.
Readers' Guide to James Joyce. William Tindall. 304p. 1959. pap. 5.95 (ISBN 0-374-50112-2). FS&G.
Reader's Guide to Joe Haldeman. Joan Gordon. Ed. by Roger C. Schlobin. LC 80-21388. (Reader's Guide to Contemporary Science Fiction & Fantasy Author Ser.: Vol. 4). (Illus., Orig.). 1980. pap. text ed. 3.95 (ISBN 0-916732-06-1). Starmont Hse.
Readers' Guide to Periodical Literature, 39 Vols. 1900-80. 62.00 ea. Wilson.
Reader's Guide to Philip Jose Farmer. Mary T. Brizzi. Ed. by Roger C. Schlobin. LC 79-17691. (Starmont Reader's Guides to Contemporary Science Fiction & Fantasy Authors Ser.: Vol. 3). (Illus., Orig.). 1980. pap. text ed. 3.95 (ISBN 0-916732-05-3). Starmont Hse.
Reader's Guide to Science Fiction. Baird Searles et al. 1979. pap. 2.95 (ISBN 0-380-46128-5, 46128). Avon.
Reader's Guide to the Great Religions. 2nd ed. Ed. by Charles J. Adams. LC 76-10496. 1977. 19.95 (ISBN 0-02-900240-0). Free Pr.
Reader's Guide to Theodore Sturgeon. Lana Diskin. Ed. by Roger C. Schlobin. LC 80-21423. (Reader's Guides to Contemporary Science Fiction & Fantasy Author Ser.: Vol. 7). (Illus., Orig.). 1980. pap. text ed. 3.95 (ISBN 0-916732-09-6). Starmont Hse.
Reader's Handbook: Famous Names in Fiction, Allusions, References, Proverbs, Plots, Stories, & Poems, 3 vols. E. Cobham Brewer. LC 71-134907. 1966. Repr. of 1899 ed. Set. 70.00 (ISBN 0-8103-0153-9). Gale.
Reader's Hebrew-English Lexicon of the Old Testament: (Genesis-Deuteronomy, Vol. 1. Ed. by Terry Armstrong et al. 1978. 9.95 (ISBN 0-310-37020-5). Zondervan.
Readers Theatre Comes to Church. Gordon C. Bennett. LC 72-1763. (Illus.). 128p. (Orig.). 1972. pap. 4.95 (ISBN 0-8042-1963-X). John Knox.
Readers Theatre Handbook: A Dramatic Approach to Literature. rev. ed. Leslie I. Coger & Melvin R. White. 1973. pap. 9.95x (ISBN 0-673-07859-0). Scott F.
Readiness for Kindergarten. James O. Massey. 1975. pap. 1.25 (ISBN 0-89106-014-6, 1281). Consulting Psychol.
Readiness for Religion. Ronald Goldman. 1970. pap. 3.95 (ISBN 0-8164-2060-2, SP70). Crossroad NY.
Readiness Transition: Level Two. Mabel O'Donnell et al. (Design for Reading). alphabet bk. 2.52 (ISBN 0-06-516322-2, SchDept); tchr's ed. 5.00 (ISBN 0-06-516421-0); readiness tests 14.28 (ISBN 0-06-516600-0); Alphabet cards 10.76 (ISBN 0-06-510503-6). Har-Row.
Reading. Richard L. Allington & Kathleen Krull. LC 80-16547. (Beginning to Learn About Ser.). (Illus.). 32p. (ps-2). 1980. PLB 9.65 (ISBN 0-8172-1322-8). Raintree Child.
Reading. Boys Scouts of America. LC 19-600. (Illus.). 32p. (gr. 6-12). 1974. pap. 0.70x (ISBN 0-8395-3393-4, 3393). BSA.
Reading: A Basic Guide for Parents & Teachers. Pamela McKeown. 170p. 1974. 16.00x (ISBN 0-7100-7418-2); pap. 4.95 (ISBN 0-7100-7424-7). Routledge & Kegan.
Reading a Novel. rev ed. Walter Allen. 1975. pap. text ed. 3.00x (ISBN 0-391-00529-4). Humanities.
Reading a Second Language. G. Truett Cates & Janet K. Swaffar. (Language in Education Ser.: No. 20). 1979. pap. 2.95 (ISBN 0-87281-106-9). Ctr Appl Ling.
Reading About Science, Skills & Concepts, 3 bks. Beth Atwood et al. Ed. by Joanne E. Kane. (Reading About Science, Skills & Concepts Ser.). (Illus.). (gr. 5-7). 1980. Bk. E, 144 Pgs. pap. text ed. 5.04x (ISBN 0-07-002425-1, W); Bk. F, 160 Pgs. pap. text ed. 5.28x (ISBN 0-07-002426-X); Bk. G, 160 Pgs. pap. text ed. 5.28x (ISBN 0-07-002427-8); tchrs. ed. 3.24 (ISBN 0-686-68698-5). McGraw.
Reading About Science, Skills & Concepts. John F. Mongillo et al. Ed. by Joanne E. Kane. (Reading About Science, Skills & Concepts Ser.). (Illus.). 128p. (gr. 4-6). 1980. Bk. C. pap. text ed. 4.84 (ISBN 0-07-002423-5, W); Bk. E. pap. text ed. 5.04 (ISBN 0-07-002425-1); Bk. F. pap. text ed. 5.28 (ISBN 0-07-002426-X); tchr's. guide 3.24 (ISBN 0-07-002428-6). McGraw.
Reading Activities for Child Involvement. 2nd ed. Evelyn B. Spache. 256p. 1976. pap. text ed. 9.40x (ISBN 0-205-04840-4). Allyn.
Reading Activities Handbook. Wilma H. Miller. 476p. 1980. pap. 15.95 (ISBN 0-03-051371-5). HR&W.
Reading Activities in Content Areas: An Ideabook for Middle & Secondary Schools. abr. ed. Dorothy Piercey. 1976. pap. text ed. 19.95x o.p. (ISBN 0-205-05510-9). Allyn.
Reading Aids for Every Class: Four Hundred Activities for Instruction & Enrichment. Ellen L. Thomas. 450p. 1980. text ed. 18.95 (ISBN 0-205-06955-X). Allyn.
Reading Aids Through the Grades: A Guide to Materials & 501 Activities for Individualizing Reading Instruction. 4th rev. ed. David Russell et al. LC 75-15639. 320p. 1981. pap. text ed. 11.50x (ISBN 0-8077-2609-5). Tchrs Coll.
Reading Aloud. 4th ed. Wayland M. Parrish. 1966. 13.95 o.p. (ISBN 0-8260-6995-9). Wiley.
Reading America. Eleanor M. Schneck. (Illus.). 288p. 1978. pap. text ed. 9.95 (ISBN 0-13-753293-8). P-H.
Reading: An ERIC Bibliography, 1970-1972. rev. ed. Educational Resources Information Center. LC 73-6203. 1973. 11.50 o.s.i. (ISBN 0-02-469340-5). Macmillan Info.
Reading & Dialect Differences. Walt Wolfram et al. (Dialects & Educational Equity Ser.: No. 4). pap. 2.50 (ISBN 0-87281-123-9). Ctr Appl Ling.
Reading & Evaluating Financial Reports. 1977. 24.95 (ISBN 0-935268-00-6). Xerox Learning.
Reading & Growing. Wilbert J. Levy. (gr. 7-10). 1975. pap. text ed. 5.42 (ISBN 0-87720-328-8). AMSCO Sch.
Reading & Its Difficulties: A Psychological Study. M. D. Vernon. LC 73-153013. 1971. 24.50 (ISBN 0-521-08217-X). Cambridge U Pr.
Reading & Learning Disabilities. 2nd ed. George Kaluger & Clifford Kolson. (Special Education Ser.). 1978. text ed. 18.50 (ISBN 0-675-08524-1). Merrill.
Reading & Learning from Text. Harry Singer & Dan Donlan. 543p. 1980. text ed. 15.95 (ISBN 0-316-79274-8). Little.
Reading & Learning in the Content Classroom: Diagnostic & Instructional Strategies. abr. ed. Thomas H. Estes & Joseph L. Vaughan, Jr. 1978. pap. text ed. 11.50 (ISBN 0-205-05986-4, 2359863). Allyn.
Reading & Loving. Leila Berg. 1976. 13.50 (ISBN 0-7100-8475-7); pap. 4.95 (ISBN 0-7100-8476-5). Routledge & Kegan.
Reading & Remedial Reading. A. E. Tansley. 1967. text ed. 9.25x (ISBN 0-7100-2169-0). Humanities.
Reading & Study Skills in the Secondary School. (NAIS Teacher Services Committee Occasional Papers Ser.). 1978. pap. 4.75 (ISBN 0-934338-19-1). NAIS.
Reading & the Gifted Child: A Guide for Teachers. Donald C. Cushenbery & Helen Howell. 186p. 1974. 16.50 (ISBN 0-398-03186-X). C C Thomas.
Reading & Thinking, 2 vols. A. J. Evans. 1979. pap. text ed. 8.25x set (ISBN 0-8077-2576-5). Tchrs Coll.
Reading & Thinking in English: Discourse in Action. Ed. by H. G. Widdowson. (Reading & Thinking in English Ser.). (Illus.). 128p. 1980. pap. 5.95 (ISBN 0-19-451357-2); 10.95 (ISBN 0-19-451358-0). Oxford U Pr.
Reading & Thinking in English: Exploring Functions. Ed. by H. G. Widdowson. (Reading & Thinking in English Ser.). (Illus.). 132p. 1979. pap. text ed. 5.95 o.p. (ISBN 0-19-451353-X); tchr's ed. 8.95 o.p. (ISBN 0-19-451354-8). Oxford U Pr.
Reading & Understanding Applied Statistics: A Self-Learning Approach. 2nd ed. Sidney M. Stahl & James D. Hennes. LC 79-29760. (Illus.). 1980. pap. text ed. 11.95 (ISBN 0-8016-4754-1). Mosby.
Reading & Word Skills. Raymond W. Hodges et al. Ed. by Barry M. Smith. LC 73-80232. (Basic Studies Program). (Illus.). 282p. 1973. pap. text ed. 11.25 (ISBN 0-913310-19-0). PAR Inc.
Reading & Word Study: For Students of English As a Second Language. Kenneth Croft. (Illus.). 1969. pap. text ed. 9.50 (ISBN 0-13-756742-1). P-H.
Reading & Writing About Language. Stephen Tollefson & Kim Davis. 1979. pap. text ed. 7.95x (ISBN 0-534-00617-5). Wadsworth Pub.
Reading Architectural Working Drawings. 2nd ed. E. Muller. 1981. 19.95 (ISBN 0-13-753939-8). P-H.
Reading Architectural Working Drawings. Edward J. Muller. (Illus.). 1971. pap. text ed. 19.95 (ISBN 0-13-753913-4). P-H.
Reading at Efficient Rates. 2nd ed. Alton L. Raygor & George B. Schick. (McGraw-Hill Basic Skills). (Illus.). 192p. 1980. pap. text ed. 9.95 (ISBN 0-07-044418-8, C). McGraw.
Reading Between the Lines: Drawing Correct Inferences. Walter Pauk. (Skill at a Time Ser). 64p. (gr. 9-12). 1975. pap. text ed. 2.40x (ISBN 0-89061-025-8). Jamestown Pubs.
Reading Blake's Poems. Zachery Leader. (Illus.). 256p. 1981. 27.50 (ISBN 0-7100-0635-7). Routledge & Kegan.
Reading Capital. Ben Fine & Lawrence Harris. 1979. 17.50x (ISBN 0-231-04792-4). Columbia U Pr.
Reading Castaneda: A Prologue to the Social Sciences. David Silverman. 1975. 15.00 (ISBN 0-7100-8145-6); pap. 7.95 (ISBN 0-7100-8146-4). Routledge & Kegan.
Reading Coleridge: Approaches & Applications. Ed. by Walter B. Crawford. LC 79-7616. 1979. 17.50x (ISBN 0-8014-1219-6). Cornell U Pr.
Reading Comprehension Mastery Kits, 6 bks. Donald C. Cushenbery & Ronald E. Meyer. Incl. Critiical Reading (ISBN 0-87628-701-1); Drawing Conclusions (ISBN 0-87628-698-8); Following Directions (ISBN 0-87628-699-6); Locating Hidden Meaning (ISBN 0-87628-700-3); Recognizing Main Ideas (ISBN 0-87628-697-X); Understanding Details (ISBN 0-87628-696-1). 1980. pap. 6.95x ea. Ctr Appl Res.
Reading Comprehension Skills. Jane Kahan & Gwendolyn Trotter. LC 78-730058. (Illus.). 1979. pap. text ed. 99.00 (ISBN 0-89290-104-7, A330-SATC). Soc for Visual.
Reading Comprehension: Workbook Lessons & Tests. rev. ed. Samuel F. Zimbal & Wilbert J. Levy. (gr. 7-10). 1969. text ed. 8.75 (ISBN 0-87720-363-6); pap. text ed. 4.42 (ISBN 0-87720-362-8); wkbk. 5.33 (ISBN 0-87720-323-7); tchrs' ed. 3.35 (ISBN 0-87720-324-5). AMSCO Sch.
Reading Construction Drawings: Trade Edition. Paul Wallach & Don Hepler. (Illus.). 320p. 1980. 18.95 (ISBN 0-07-067940-1, P&RB). McGraw.
Reading Difficulties: Their Analysis & Treatment. Jerry L. Milligan. 1981. pap. 7.50 (ISBN 0-87562-069-8). Spec Child.
Reading Difficulties: Their Diagnosis & Correction. 4th ed. Guy L. Bond et al. (Illus.). 1979. ref. 18.95 (ISBN 0-13-754978-4). P-H.
Reading Disabilities: Selections on Identification & Treatment. Harold Newman. LC 70-80026. 1969. pap. 11.95 (ISBN 0-672-63098-2). Odyssey Pr.
Reading Disability: Developmental Dyslexia. Lloyd J. Thompson. (Illus.). 228p. 1974. pap. text ed. 10.75 (ISBN 0-398-03123-1). C C Thomas.
Reading Drills. Edward B. Fry. (Illus.). 192p. (gr. 9 up). 1975. pap. text ed. 4.80x (ISBN 0-89061-039-8). Jamestown Pubs.
Reading English for Academic Study. Michael Long et al. Ed. by Douglas Potvin. (Illus.). 160p. (Orig.). 1980. pap. text ed. 6.95 (ISBN 0-88377-108-X). Newbury Hse.
Reading English Poetry. James G. Taaffe & John Lincks. LC 75-136271. 1971. pap. text ed. 4.50 o.s.i. (ISBN 0-02-932460-2). Free Pr.
Reading Faces. Leopold Bella & Samm S. Baker. LC 80-19235. (Illus.). 160p. 1981. 9.95 (ISBN 0-03-057869-8). HR&W.
Reading Faster & Understanding More Book III. Wanda Miller et al. (Illus.). 416p. 1981. pap. text ed. 12.95 (ISBN 0-87626-733-9). Winthrop.
Reading for Adults. Richard Lewis. (Illus.). 1977. Bk. 1. pap. text ed. 4.50x (ISBN 0-582-52790-2); Bk. 2. pap. text ed. 4.50x (ISBN 0-582-52791-0); Bk. 3. pap. text ed. 4.50x (ISBN 0-582-52792-9). Longman.
Reading for Facts. Walter Pauk & Josephine M. Wilson. 1978. pap. 8.95x (ISBN 0-582-28028-1). Longman.
Reading for Insight: A Perceptual Approach to College English. 2nd ed. J. Burl Hogins & Gerald A. Bryant. LC 73-7371. (Illus.). 416p. 1974. pap. text ed. 9.95 (ISBN 0-02-474880-3, 47488). Macmillan.
Reading for Insight: A Perceptual Approach to College English. J. Burl Hogins & Gerald A. Bryant, Jr. LC 70-101716. 1970. text ed. 6.95x o.p. (ISBN 0-02-474850-1, 47485). Glencoe.
Reading for Mathematics. Joyce Friedland & Irene Gross. 1977. pap. 2.25x (ISBN 0-88323-129-8, 218); tchrs answer key 3.00 (ISBN 0-88323-142-5, 231). Richards Pub.
Reading for Power & Flexibility. J. E. Sparks & C. E. Johnson. 1970. text ed. 6.95x (ISBN 0-02-478400-1, 47840). Macmillan.

Reading for Results. Laraine Flemming. LC 77-76422. (Illus.). 1978. pap. text ed. 9.75 (ISBN 0-395-25419-1); inst. manual 0.45 (ISBN 0-395-25430-2). HM.

Reading for Survival. Eileen Corcoran. 1978. pap. 2.25x (ISBN 0-88323-145-X, 234); tchr's. answer key free (ISBN 0-88323-151-4, 240). Richards Pub.

Reading for Young People: The Middle Atlantic. Ed. by Arabelle Pennypacker. LC 80-16021. 162p. 1980. pap. 8.00 (ISBN 0-8389-0295-2). ALA.

Reading: Foundations & Instructional Strategies. Pose M. Lamb & Richard D. Arnold. 1976. text ed. 15.95x o.p. (ISBN 0-534-00423-7). Wadsworth Pub.

Reading French in the Arts & Sciences. 3rd ed. Edward M. Stack. 265p. 1979. pap. text ed. 8.80 (ISBN 0-395-27505-9). HM.

Reading from Nursing Research. 92p. 1969. 3.00 o.p. (ISBN 0-686-11199-0, SP3). Am Journal Nurse.

Reading Fundamentals for Preschool and Primary Children. Robert L. Hillerich. (Elementary Education Ser.). 1977. pap. text ed. 9.95 (ISBN 0-675-08543-8). Merrill.

Reading Greek: Grammar, Vocabulary & Exercises. Joint Association of Classical Teachers. LC 77-91090. 1978. 10.95x (ISBN 0-521-21977-9). Cambridge U Pr.

Reading Guidance in a Media Age. Nancy Polette & Marjorie Hamlin. LC 75-26833. (Illus.). 1975. 12.00 (ISBN 0-8108-0873-0). Scarecrow.

Reading Improvement: A Complete Course for Increasing Speed and Comprehension. Barbara M. Klaeser. LC 76-49042. 384p. 1977. 16.95 (ISBN 0-88229-232-3); pap. 8.95 (ISBN 0-88229-406-7). Nelson-Hall.

Reading Improvement: Exercises for Students of English As a Second Language. David P. Harris. (Orig.). 1966. pap. text ed. 7.95 (ISBN 0-13-755058-8). P-H.

Reading Improvement in the Secondary School. Emerald Dechant. (Illus.). 448p. 1973. ref. ed. 18.95x (ISBN 0-13-755017-0). P-H.

Reading in American Schools: A Guide to Information Sources. Ed. by Maria E. Schantz & Joseph F. Brynner. LC 79-23770. (Education Information Guide Ser.: Vol. 5). 1980. 30.00 (ISBN 0-8103-1456-8). Gale.

Reading in English: For Students of ESL. 2nd ed. Dorothy Danielson et al. (Illus.). 1980. pap. text ed. 8.50 (ISBN 0-13-753442-6). P-H.

Reading in Humanistic Psychology. A. Sutich & M. Vich. LC 74-75206. 1969. 9.95 (ISBN 0-02-932280-4); pap. text ed. 8.95 (ISBN 0-02-932320-7). Free Pr.

Reading in the Applied Economics of Africa, 2 vols, Ed. by Edith J. Whethan & Jean I. Curie. Vol. 1, Micro-Economics. pap. 11.95x (ISBN 0-521-09437-2). Vol. 2, Macro-Economics. pap. 11.95x (ISBN 0-521-09438-0). Cambridge U Pr.

Reading in the Content Areas. Jane Kakn & Gwendolyn Trotter. LC 78-730059. (Illus.). 1978. pap. text ed. 99.00 (ISBN 0-89290-102-0, A328-SATC). Soc for Visual.

Reading in the Elementary School. 4th ed. Spache & Spache. 1977. text ed. 17.95 o.p. (ISBN 0-205-05784-5); student guide avail. o.p. (ISBN 0-205-05797-7). Allyn.

Reading in the Elementary Schools. 2nd ed. Jeannette Veatch. LC 78-14722. 628p. 1978. text ed. 19.95x (ISBN 0-471-06884-5). Wiley.

Reading in the Primary School. Geoffrey Roberts. (Students Library of Education). 1969. pap. text ed. 2.75x (ISBN 0-7100-6519-1). Humanities.

Reading Incentive Program Series: Spanish Edition. Ed Radlauer. Tr. by Ana Covarrubias from Eng. Incl. Carros Chistosos de Carreras de Arrastre. Orig. Title: Drag Racing - Funny Cars (ISBN 0-8372-0990-0); Carros Hechos a la Orden. Orig. Title: Custom Cars (ISBN 0-8372-0991-9); Los VW - Bugs. Orig. Title: VW - Bugs (ISBN 0-8372-0989-7). Orig. Title: Title Minibikes. (Illus., Span.). (gr. 3-12). 1973. pap. 2.85 ea.; multimedia kits with cassettes & filmstrips avail. Bowmar-Noble.

Reading Instruction for Today's Children. H. Robinson & N. Smith. 1980. 17.95 (ISBN 0-13-755157-6). P-H.

Reading Interpretation in Social Sciences, Natural Sciences, & Literature: Preparation & Review for the Reading Parts of the High School Equivalency Diploma Test. E. Guercio et al. LC 74-19739. (GED Preparation Ser.). 224p. (Orig.). 1975. lib. bdg. 7.00 (ISBN 0-668-03843-8); pap. 5.00 (ISBN 0-668-03690-7). Arco.

Reading John's Gospel Today. John Painter. LC 79-25332. (Biblical Foundations Ser.). Orig. Title: John: Witness & Theologian. 170p. 1980. pap. 5.95 (ISBN 0-8042-0522-1). John Knox.

Reading-Language Instruction: Innovative Practices. R. Ruddell. 1973. 19.95 (ISBN 0-13-753285-7). P-H.

Reading Nozick. Ed. by Jeffrey Paul. (Philosophy & Society Ser.). 1981. 25.00x (ISBN 0-8476-6279-9); pap. 10.95x (ISBN 0-8476-6280-2). Rowman.

Reading of Dante's Inferno. Wallace Fowlie. LC 80-19025. 248p. 1981. lib. bdg. 18.00 (ISBN 0-226-25887-4); pap. 6.50 (ISBN 0-226-25888-2). U of Chicago Pr.

Reading of Henry Green. A. Kingsley Weatherhead. LC 61-8767. 180p. 1961. 11.00 (ISBN 0-295-73902-9). U of Wash Pr.

Reading of Sir Gawain & the Green Knight. J. A. Burrow. 1978. pap. 7.95 (ISBN 0-7100-8695-4). Routledge & Kegan.

Reading of the Canterbury Tales. Trevor Whittock. (Orig.). 1969. 49.50 (ISBN 0-521-06795-2); pap. 11.95 (ISBN 0-521-09557-3). Cambridge U Pr.

Reading on the Statute of Uses. Sir Francis Bacon. Ed. by David S. Berkowitz & Samuel E. Thorne. LC 77-89249. (Classics of English Legal History in the Modern Era Ser.: Vol. 140). 1979. lib. bdg. 55.00 (ISBN 0-8240-3177-6). Garland Pub.

Reading Paul Today: A New Introduction to the Man & His Letters. Hubert Richards. LC 79-26287. (Biblical Foundations Ser.). (Illus.). 152p. 1980. pap. 4.95 (ISBN 0-8042-0374-1). John Knox.

Reading Power. James I. Brown. 1975. pap. 9.95x (ISBN 0-669-85571-5). Heath.

Reading Power. alternate ed. James I. Brown. 1978. pap. text ed. 9.95x (ISBN 0-669-00774-9). Heath.

Reading Power. Angelica Cass. Bk. 1. pap. 4.95 (ISBN 0-671-18720-1); Bk. 2. pap. 5.95 (ISBN 0-671-18721-X); Bk. 3. pap. 5.95 (ISBN 0-671-18722-8); Bk. 4. pap. 5.95 (ISBN 0-671-18723-6). Monarch Pr.

Reading Problems: A Multidisciplinary Perspective. Wayne Otto et al. LC 76-23987. (Illus.). 1977. text ed. 17.95 (ISBN 0-201-05513-9). A-W.

Reading Progress from Eight to Fifteen. Maxwell. 1977. pap. text ed. 18.75x (ISBN 0-85633-120-1, NFER). Humanities.

Reading Readiness, 4 bks. (gr. k-1). 1972. pap. text ed. 2.50 (ISBN 0-8449-3507-7); tchr's manual & placement exam avail. Learning Line.

Reading Readiness Readers, 6 bks. Sullivan Assoc. pap. text ed. 1.50 ea. (ISBN 0-8449-3701-0). Learning Line.

Reading Research: Advances in Theory & Practice, Vol. 2. Ed. by T. G. Waller & G. E. Mackinnon. (Serial Publication). 1981. price not set (ISBN 0-12-572302-4). Acad Pr.

Reading Seismograms: A Manual for the Interpretation of Earthquake Records. Ruth B. Simon. (Illus.). 200p. (Orig.). 1981. pap. text ed. 9.95 (ISBN 0-913232-81-5). W Kaufmann.

Reading Skills Activity Puzzles, 6 bks. Jerry J. Mallett. Incl. Brain-Twisters (ISBN 0-87628-738-0); Comprehension Challengers (ISBN 0-87628-735-6); Dynamite Decoding Puzzles (ISBN 0-87628-733-X); Puzzles for Super Sleuths (ISBN 0-87628-736-4); Thingumajigs for Thinking (ISBN 0-87628-737-2); Word Power (ISBN 0-87628-734-8). (gr. 2-6). 1980. pap. 6.95x ea. Ctr Appl Res.

Reading Skills for College Study. James F. Shepherd. LC 79-89520. (Illus.). 1979. pap. text ed. 9.50 (ISBN 0-395-28503-8); instrs.' manual 0.65 (ISBN 0-395-28504-6). HM.

Reading Skills for Law Students. Craig K. Mayfield. 199p. 1980. pap. 10.00 (ISBN 0-87215-313-4). Michie.

Reading Skills for Social Studies: Understanding Concepts, Level C. Dale I. Foreman & Sally Allen. (Skillbooster Ser.). 64p. (gr. 3). 1980. wkbk. 2.80 (ISBN 0-87895-351-5). Modern Curr.

Reading Skills for Social Studies: Understanding Concepts, Level E. Dale I. Foreman & Sally Allen. (Skillbooster Ser.). 64p. (gr. 5). 1981. wkbk. 2.80 (ISBN 0-87895-555-0). Modern Curr.

Reading Skills for Social Studies: Understanding Concepts, Level F. Dale I. Foreman & Sally Allen. (Skillbooster Ser.). 64p. (gr. 6). 1981. wkbk. 2.80 (ISBN 0-87895-657-3). Modern Curr.

Reading Skills for Social Studies: Understanding Concepts, Level D. Dale I. Foreman & Sally Allen. (Skillbooster Ser.). 64p. (gr. 4). 1980. wkbk. 2.80 (ISBN 0-87895-452-X). Modern Curr.

Reading Skills for Social Studies: Using Maps, Charts & Graphs, Level C. Dale I. Foreman & Sally Allen. (Skillbooster Ser.). 64p. (gr. 3). 1980. wkbk. 2.80 (ISBN 0-87895-350-7). Modern Curr.

Reading Skills for Social Studies: Using Maps, Charts & Graphs, Level D. Dale I. Foreman & Sally Allen. (Skillbooster Ser.). 64p. (gr. 4). 1980. wkbk. 2.80 (ISBN 0-87895-452-X). Modern Curr.

Reading Skills for Social Studies: Using Maps, Charts & Graphs, Level E. Dale I. Foreman & Sally Allen. (Skillbooster Ser.). 64p. (gr. 5). 1981. 2.80 (ISBN 0-87895-554-2). Modern Curr.

Reading Skills for Social Studies: Using Maps, Charts & Graphs, Level F. Dale I. Foreman & Sally Allen. (Skillbooster Ser.). 64p. (gr. 6). 1981. wkbk. 2.80 (ISBN 0-87895-656-5). Modern Curr.

Reading Skills for Successful Living. Irwin L. Joffe. 1979. pap. text ed. 8.95x (ISBN 0-534-00618-3). Wadsworth Pub.

Reading Skills Handbook. Harvey Wiener & Charles Bazerman. LC 77-74097. (Illus.). 1977. pap. text ed. 8.25 (ISBN 0-395-24556-7); inst. manual 0.45 (ISBN 0-395-24558-3). HM.

Reading, Spelling, Vocabulary, Pronunciation, 3 vols. Norman Lewis. Incl. Book 1. text ed. 8.75 (ISBN 0-87720-357-1); pap. text ed. 4.42 (ISBN 0-87720-356-3); tchr's ed 3.10 (ISBN 0-87720-315-6); wkbk 5.25 (ISBN 0-87720-314-8); Book 2. text ed. 8.75 (ISBN 0-87720-359-8); pap. text ed. 4.42 (ISBN 0-87720-358-X); tchr's ed. 3.10 (ISBN 0-87720-317-2); wkbk 5.25 (ISBN 0-87720-316-4); Book 3. text ed. 8.75 (ISBN 0-87720-361-X); pap. text ed. 4.42 (ISBN 0-87720-360-1); tchr's ed 3.10 (ISBN 0-87720-319-9); wkbk 5.25 (ISBN 0-87720-318-0). (RSVP Ser). (gr. 7-9). 1967. Amsco Sch.

Reading Standards of Children in Wales. T. R. Horton. (Illus.). 156p. 1973. pap. text ed. 11.25x (ISBN 0-85633-009-4, NFER). Humanities.

Reading Tests in the Classroom. Denis Vincent & Michael Cresswell. (General Ser.). 1976. pap. text ed. 15.25x (ISBN 0-85633-101-5, NFER). Humanities.

Reading the Bible with Understanding: A Guide for Beginners. John D. Trefzger. 1978. pap. 1.95 (ISBN 0-8272-3209-8). Bethany Pr.

Reading the Content Fields: English. Edward Spargo & Raymond Harris. (Content Skills Ser.-Middle Level). (Illus., Orig.). (gr. 6-8). 1978. pap. text ed. 2.40x (ISBN 0-89061-125-4, 551M). Jamestown Pubs.

Reading the Content Fields: English. Edward Spargo & Raymond Harris. (Content Skills Ser.-Advanced Level). (Orig.). (gr. 9-12). 1978. pap. text ed. 2.40x (ISBN 0-89061-135-1, 551-A). Jamestown Pubs.

Reading the Content Fields: Mathematics. Edward Spargo & Raymond Harris. (Content Skills Ser-Advanced Level). (Illus.). (gr. 9-12). 1978. pap. text ed. 2.40x (ISBN 0-89061-139-4, 553A). Jamestown Pubs.

Reading the Content Fields: Mathematics. Edward Spargo & Raymond Harris. (Content Skills Ser.-Middle Level). (Illus.). (gr. 6-8). 1978. pap. text ed. 2.40x (ISBN 0-89061-129-7, 553M). Jamestown Pubs.

Reading the Content Fields: Practical Arts. Edward Spargo & Raymond Harris. (Content Skills Ser.-Advanced Level). (Illus.). (gr. 9-12). 1978. pap. text ed. 2.40x (ISBN 0-89061-143-2, 555A). Jamestown Pubs.

Reading the Content Fields: Practical Arts. Edward Spargo & Raymond Harris. (Contents Skills Ser.-Middle Level). (Illus.). (gr. 6-8). 1978. pap. text ed. 2.40x (ISBN 0-89061-133-5, 555M). Jamestown Pubs.

Reading the Content Fields: Science. Edward Spargo & Raymond Harris. (Content Skills Ser.-Advanced Level). (Illus.). (gr. 9-12). 1978. pap. text ed. 2.40x (ISBN 0-89061-141-6, 554A). Jamestown Pubs.

Reading the Content Fields: Science. Edward Spargo & Raymond Harris. (Content Skills Ser.-Middle Level). (Illus.). (gr. 6-8). 1978. pap. text ed. 2.40x (ISBN 0-89061-131-9, 554M). Jamestown Pubs.

Reading the Content Fields: Social Studies. Edward Spargo & Raymond Harris. (Content Sskills Ser.-Middle Level). (Illus., Orig.). (gr. 6-8). 1978. pap. text ed. 2.40x (ISBN 0-89061-127-0, 552M). Jamestown Pubs.

Reading the Content Fields: Social Studies. Edward Spargo & Raymond Harris. (Content Skills Ser.-Advanced Level). (Illus., Orig.). (gr. 9-12). 1978. pap. text ed. 2.40x (ISBN 0-89061-137-8, 552A). Jamestown Pubs.

Reading the Landscape of America. rev. ed. May T. Watts. (Illus.). 288p. 1975. 12.95 o.s.i. (ISBN 0-02-624400-4). Macmillan.

Reading the New Testament. Ronald J. Wilkins. (To Live Is Christ Ser). 160p. 1978. pap. 3.80 extended study (ISBN 0-697-01672-2); pap. 3.00 short edition (ISBN 0-697-01673-0). Wm C Brown.

Reading the New Testament Today: An Introduction to the Study of the New Testament. Brian E. Beck. LC 78-14420. (Biblical Foundations Ser.). 1978. pap. 4.95 (ISBN 0-8042-0391-1). John Knox.

Reading the Past. Leonard Cottrell. (Illus.). (gr. 7-12). 1971. 5.95 o.s.i. (ISBN 0-02-724820-8, CCPr). Macmillan.

Reading: The Patterning of Complex Behaviour. 2nd ed. Marie M. Clay. 1980. pap. text ed. 11.95x (ISBN 0-686-64050-0, 00558). Heinemann Ed.

Reading the Rocks: A Layman's Guide to the Geologic Secrets of Canyons, Mesas & Buttes in the American Southwest. David A. Rahm. LC 74-78915. (Totebook). (Illus.). 192p. 1974. pap. 7.95 o.p. (ISBN 0-87156-103-4). Sierra.

Reading: The Teacher & the Learner. Sam V. Dauzat & Joann Dauzat. LC 80-19435. 518p. 1981. pap. text ed. 15.50 (ISBN 0-471-02668-9); tchr's manual 4.50 (ISBN 0-471-08582-0). Wiley.

Reading Through the Newspaper. Dorothy C. Davis. 1980. write for info. (ISBN 0-88252-108-X). Paladin Hse.

Reading to Learn: A Unit Approach. Charles Werner. LC 74-30264. 400p. 1975. pap. 12.95 (ISBN 0-87909-701-9); instrs'. manual avail. Reston.

Reading, Understanding & Writing About Short Stories. Harry Fenson & Hildreth Kritzer. LC 66-15498. (Orig.). 1966. pap. text ed. 8.95 (ISBN 0-02-910120-4). Free Pr.

Reading Vocabulary, 5 bks. Sullivan Assoc. pap. text ed. 2.75 ea. (ISBN 0-8449-4105-0); tchr's guide for bks. 1-4 avail. Learning Line.

Reading with Race Cars. Marne Isakson & Lonnie Bradley. (gr. k-3). 1981. 26.80 (ISBN 0-8027-9079-8). Walker & Co.

Reading with Your Child Through Age 5. rev. ed. Children's Book Committee. 44p. 1972. pap. 1.50 (ISBN 0-686-12288-7). Jewish Bd Family.

Reading Without Books. Julie Burns & Dorothy Swan. LC 78-72078. 1979. pap. 4.95 (ISBN 0-8224-5830-6). Pitman Learning.

Reading Without Nonsense. Frank Smith. LC 79-11078. 1979. pap. text ed. 7.50x (ISBN 0-8077-2567-6). Tchrs Coll.

Reading Workbook Four (Cowardly Lion's Book) Judith Conaway. (Funny Face Activity Bks.). (Illus.). 48p. (ps-1). 1981. pap. 1.95 saddle-stitched (ISBN 0-394-84695-8). Random.

Reading Workbook Three (Rascal Raccoon's Book) Judith Conaway. (Funny Face Activity Bks.). (Illus.). 48p. (ps-1). 1981. pap. 1.95 saddle stitched (ISBN 0-394-84440-8). Random.

Reading, 'Writing, & Reconstruction: The Education of Freedmen in the South, 1861-1870. Robert C. Morris. LC 80-25370. (Illus.). 1981. lib. bdg. price not set (ISBN 0-226-53928-8). U of Chicago Pr.

Reading, Writing & Rewriting. rev. ed. William T. Moynihan et al. LC 69-15533. 1969. pap. text ed. 4.75x o.p. (ISBN 0-397-47161-0). Lippincott.

Reading, Writing, & Rhetoric. 4th ed. James B. Hogins & Robert E. Yarber. LC 78-13940. 1979. pap. text ed. 9.95 (ISBN 0-574-22045-3, 13-5045); instr's guide avail. (ISBN 0-574-22046-1, 13-5046). SRA.

Reading, Writing & Speaking: Here & Now. Hudson & Weaver. (Illus.). 1980. pap. 2.95x (ISBN 0-88323-160-3, 248). Richards Pub.

Readings, 3 vols. Richard Doubleday. 1970. Vol. 1. pap. text ed. 3.95x ea. o.p. (ISBN 0-435-11235-X); Vol. 2. pap. text ed. (ISBN 0-435-11236-8); Vol. 3. pap. text ed. (ISBN 0-435-11237-6). Heinemann Ed.

Readings About Adolescent Literature. Ed. by Dennis Thomison. LC 79-9913. 1970. 10.00 (ISBN 0-8108-0282-1). Scarecrow.

Readings About Individual & Group Differences. Ed. by Lee Willerman & R. Gerald Turner. LC 78-13079. (Psychology Ser.). (Illus.). 1979. text ed. 17.95x (ISBN 0-7167-1015-3); pap. text ed. 8.95x (ISBN 0-7167-1014-5). W H Freeman.

Readings About the Social Animal. 2nd ed. Elliot Aronson. LC 76-22435. (Psychology Ser.). (Illus.). 1977. text ed. 18.75x o.p. (ISBN 0-7167-0380-7); pap. text ed. 7.75x o.p. (ISBN 0-7167-0379-3). W H Freeman.

Readings About the Social Animal. 3rd ed. Ed. by Elliot Aronson. LC 80-18208. (Psychology Ser.). (Illus.). 1981. text ed. 19.95x (ISBN 0-7167-1267-9); pap. text ed. 9.95x (ISBN 0-7167-1268-7). W H Freeman.

Readings & Cases in Auditing. rev. ed. Thomas D. Hubbard et al. LC 79-52071. 550p. (Orig.). 1980. pap. text ed. 10.95x (ISBN 0-931920-22-1). Dame Pubns.

Readings & Cases in Auditing, Vol. 1. Thomas D. Hubbard et al. LC 79-52071. (Illus.). 543p. (Orig.). 1979. pap. text ed. 10.95x o.p. (ISBN 0-931920-12-4). Dame Pubns.

Readings & Cases in Contemporary Labor Relations 1980. Kenneth A. Kovach. LC 80-1429. 359p. 1981. pap. text ed. 12.00 (ISBN 0-8191-1362-X). U Pr of Amer.

Readings & Cases in Personnel Management. Byars. 1979. 10.95 (ISBN 0-7216-2252-6). Dryden Pr.

Readings & Conversations: About the United States, Its People, Its History & Its Customs, 2 vols. rev. ed. English Language Services. 1976. text ed. 3.95 ea.; Vol. 1. (ISBN 0-87789-195-8); Vol. 2. (ISBN 0-87789-196-6); Set. cassette tapes 85.00 (ISBN 0-686-28557-3). Cassettes 1 (ISBN 0-87789-201-6). Cassettes 2 (ISBN 0-87789-202-4). Eng Language.

Readings, Cases, Materials in Canon Law: A Textbook for Ministerial Students. Jordan F. Hite et al. (Orig.). 1980. pap. text ed. 8.50 (ISBN 0-8146-1081-1). Liturgical Pr.

Readings for Nursing Research. Sydney D. Krampitz & Natalie Pavlovich. LC 80-18125. (Illus.). 285p. 1980. pap. text ed. 9.95 (ISBN 0-8016-2747-8). Mosby.

Readings for Organizational Communications. Phillip Lewis & John W. Williams. LC 79-19091. (Grid Ser. in Management). 1980. pap. text ed. 10.50 (ISBN 0-88244-200-7). Grid Pub.

Readings for Social Research. Theodore C. Wagenaar. 336p. 1980. pap. text ed. 10.95x (ISBN 0-534-00740-6). Wadsworth Pub.

Readings for the Group Insurance Specialty. Ed. by Life Office Management Association. (FLMI Insurance Education Program Ser.). (Orig.). 1980. pap. 3.75 (ISBN 0-915322-40-4). Loma.

Readings for the Information Systems Specialty. Ed. by Life Office Management Association. (FLMI Insurance Education Program Ser.). (Illus.). 186p. (Orig.). 1980. pap. text ed. 10.00x (ISBN 0-915322-39-0). Loma.

Readings for the Personnel Administration Specialty. Ed. by Life Office Management Association. (FLMI Insurance Education Program Ser.). 95p. (Orig.). 1980. pap. 6.00x (ISBN 0-915322-41-2). Loma.

Readings for Todays Writers. Steven H. Gale. LC 79-21312. 1980. pap. text ed. 9.95 (ISBN 0-471-05127-6); tchrs'. manual avail. (ISBN 0-471-07846-8). Wiley.

Readings from Futures. Ed. by R. Jones. 1980. pap. text ed. 40.00. Butterworths.

Readings from Left to Right. Victor E. Amend & Leo T. Hendrick. LC 77-93111. 1970. pap. text ed. 6.95 o.s.i. (ISBN 0-02-900610-4). Free Pr.

Readings in Abnormal Psychology. Goldstein & Baker. (Orig.). 1981. pap. text ed. 8.95 (ISBN 0-316-07830-1). Little.

Readings in Adult Psychology: Contemporary Perspectives. Ed. by Lawrence R. Allman & Dennis T. Jaffe. (Contemporary Perspectives Readers Ser.). 1977. pap. text ed. 10.50 scp (ISBN 0-06-047054-2, HarpC); inst. manual avail. (ISBN 0-685-77667-0). Har-Row.

Readings in Aging and Death: Contemporary Perspectives. Ed. by Steven H. Zarit. (Contemporary Perspectives Readers Ser.). 1977. pap. text ed. 9.50 scp (ISBN 0-06-047056-9, HarpC); instructor's manual avail. (ISBN 0-685-75417-0). Har-Row.

Readings in Agricultural Policy. Ed. by R. J. Hildreth. LC 68-12705. 1968. pap. 3.95x o.p. (ISBN 0-8032-5087-8, 380, Bison). U of Nebr Pr.

Readings in American History, 2 vols. 4th ed. Robert C. Cotner. LC 75-37038. (Illus.). 1976. Vol. 1. 9.75 (ISBN 0-395-17810-X); Vol. 2. pap. text ed. 9.75 (ISBN 0-395-17811-8). HM.

Readings in American Legal History. Ed. by M. Howe. LC 70-155924. (American Constitutional & Legal History Ser). 1971. Repr. of 1949 ed. lib. bdg. 49.50 (ISBN 0-306-70159-6). Da Capo.

Readings in Ancient History: From Gilgamesh to Diocletian. 2nd ed. Ed. by Nels Bailkey. 1977. pap. text ed. 8.95x (ISBN 0-669-00249-6). Heath.

Readings in Art History, 2 Vols. 2nd ed. Ed. by Harold Spencer. LC 76-7404. (Illus., Orig.). 1969. pap. text ed. 8.95x ea. (ScribC); Vol. 1 - Ancient Egypt Through The Middle Ages. pap. text ed. 9.95x (ISBN 0-684-14617-7, ScribC); Vol. 2 - The Renaissance To The Present. pap. text ed. (ISBN 0-684-14618-5, ScribC). Scribner.

Readings in Autism. rev. ed. (Special Education Ser.). (Illus.). 224p. pap. text ed. write for info. Spec Learn Corp.

Readings in Basic Management. 2nd ed. Hollingsworth. 1979. pap. 10.95 (ISBN 0-7216-4753-7). Dryden Pr.

Readings in Basic Marketing. rev. ed. Ed. by E. Jerome McCarthy et al. 1978. pap. text ed. 9.95 (ISBN 0-256-02050-7). Irwin.

Readings in Business. Ed. by Woodrow W. Baldwin & John T. O'Neill. LC 74-12552. (Illus.). 99p. 1973. pap. text ed. 6.20 (ISBN 0-913310-17-4). PAR Inc.

Readings in Business & Economic Research Management: Execution & Enterprise, Vol. 1. Association for University Business & Economic Research-AUBER. 1980. pap. 7.50 (ISBN 0-86603-000-X). Bureau Busn Res U Wis.

Readings in Business Communication. Richard B. Huseman et al. 1981. pap. text ed. 8.95 (ISBN 0-03-058206-7). Dryden Pr.

Readings in Business Cycle Theory. Compiled by American Economic Association Committee. LC 76-29403. (BCL Ser.). 736p. 1980. Repr. of 1951 ed. 33.50. AMS Pr.

Readings in Business Today. Barbara A. Pletcher. 1980. 6.95x (ISBN 0-256-02376-X). Irwin.

Readings in California Civilization: Interpretative Issues. Howard A. DeWitt. LC 80-83492. 240p. 1981. pap. text ed. 12.95 (ISBN 0-8403-2311-5). Kendall-Hunt.

Readings in Career Education. Hercules Kazanas. 1981. pap. text ed. 10.96 (ISBN 0-87002-308-X). Bennett IL.

Readings in Caribbean History & Economics: An Introduction to the Region. Roberta M. Delson. 300p. 1981. write for info. (ISBN 0-677-05280-4). Gordon.

Readings in Child & Adolescent Psychology. Paul H. Mussen et al. 280p. 1980. pap. text ed. 8.50 scp (ISBN 0-06-041888-5, HarpC). Har-Row.

Readings in Child & Adolescent Psychiatric Nursing. Ed. by Claire M. Fagin. LC 73-12565. 190p. 1974. pap. text ed. 8.95 o.p. (ISBN 0-8016-1536-4). Mosby.

Readings in Child Socialization. Kurt Danziger. 1970. 21.00 (ISBN 0-08-006882-0); pap. 9.75 (ISBN 0-08-006881-2). Pergamon.

Readings in Childhood Language Disorders. Ed. by Margaret Lahey. LC 77-21408. (Communications Disorders Ser.). 1978. text ed. 20.50 (ISBN 0-471-51167-6). Wiley.

Readings in Chinese Communist Documents. Ed. by Chi Wen-Shun. 1963. 20.00x o.p. (ISBN 0-520-00231-8). U of Cal Pr.

Readings in Chinese Communist Ideology. Ed. by Chi Wen-Shun. 1968. 24.50x (ISBN 0-520-00232-6). U of Cal Pr.

Readings in Community Organization Practice. 2nd ed. Ed. by Ralph M. Kramer & Harry Specht. (Illus.). 432p. 1975. pap. text ed. 14.95 (ISBN 0-13-755769-8). P-H.

Readings in Community Work. Ed. by David N. Thomas & Paul Henderson. 196p. 1981. text ed. 29.50x (ISBN 0-04-361045-5, 2650-1); pap. text ed. 14.95x (ISBN 0-04-361046-3). Allen Unwin.

Readings in Comparative Criminology. Ed. by Louise I. Shelley. LC 80-19533. (Science & International Affairs). 312p. 1981. 25.00x (ISBN 0-8093-0938-6). S Ill U Pr.

Readings in Consumer Behavior: Individuals, Groups & Organizations. Melanie Wallendorf & Gerald Zaltman. LC 78-13228. (Marketing Ser.). 1979. pap. text ed. 15.95x (ISBN 0-471-03021-X). Wiley.

Readings in Contemporary Transportation. Donald F. Wood & James C. Johnson. 256p. 1980. 11.95 (ISBN 0-87814-126-X). Pennwell Pub.

Readings in Cost & Managerial Accounting. Louis Geller & Jae K. Shim. 448p. 1980. pap. text ed. 9.95 (ISBN 0-8403-2266-6). Kendall-Hunt.

Readings in Cost Engineering, Vol. 1. Compiled by American Society of Civil Engineering. 732p. 1979. pap. text ed. 49.00 (ISBN 0-87262-147-2). Am Soc Civil Eng.

Readings in Creole Studies. I. F. Hancock. (Story-Scientia Linguistics Ser.: No. 2). 1980. text ed. 62.25x (ISBN 90-6439-163-7). Humanities.

Readings in Criminal Justice. Edward Eldefonso. LC 72-85758. (Criminal Justice Ser.). 512p. 1973. text ed. 7.95x (ISBN 0-02-474670-3). Macmillan.

Readings in Criminal Justice. Richter H. Moore, Jr. & Thomas C. Marks. LC 75-38727. 1976. pap. 10.95 (ISBN 0-672-61371-9). Bobbs.

Readings in Criminology & Penology. 2nd ed. David Dressler. LC 75-181783. 700p. 1972. 25.00x (ISBN 0-231-03429-6); pap. 12.00x (ISBN 0-231-08672-5). Columbia U Pr.

Readings in Democracy. Ed. by Aligarh Muslim University. 4.75x o.p. (ISBN 0-210-26982-0). Asia.

Readings in Early Development: For Occupational Physical Therapy Students. Ed. by Claire B. Kopp. (Illus.). 576p. 1971. 21.50 (ISBN 0-398-02333-6). C C Thomas.

Readings in Early English Language History. Ed. by Leonard H. Frey. LC 66-13894. (Orig.). 1966. pap. 4.50 (ISBN 0-672-63100-8). Odyssey Pr.

Readings in Economic Geography. Howard G. Roepke. LC 67-19451. 1967. 15.95 o.p. (ISBN 0-471-72971-X). Wiley.

Readings in Economics for China. C. F. Remer. LC 78-74358. (Modern Chinese Economy Ser.). 685p. 1980. lib. bdg. 77.00 (ISBN 0-8240-4278-6). Garland Pub.

Readings in Emotional & Behavioral Disorders. rev. ed. Ed. by Steve Imber. (Special Education Ser.). (Illus.). 224p. pap. text ed. 9.95 (ISBN 0-89568-294-X). Spec Learn Corp.

Readings in English, Bk. 2: Travel. Thoedore Gross. (gr. 9-12). 1981. pap. text ed. price not set (ISBN 0-88345-418-1, 18883). Regents Pub.

Readings in English: Careers, Bk 3. Marianthy McCarthy. 112p. (gr. 9-12). 1981. pap. text ed. price not set (ISBN 0-88345-425-4, 18884). Regents Pub.

Readings in English: Leisure. Andrew Jenkins-Murphy. (Readings in English Ser.). (gr. 9-12). 1981. pap. text ed. write for info. (ISBN 0-88345-417-3, 18882). Regents Pub.

Readings in English: The Arts, Bk 4. Lee Paradise. (Readings in English Ser.). 112p. (gr. 9-12). 1981. pap. text ed. price not set (ISBN 0-88345-426-2, 18885). Regents Pub.

Readings in English Transformational Grammar. Ed. by Roderick A. Jacobs & Peters S. Rosenbaum. LC 76-88102. 277p. Repr. of 1970 ed. text ed. 12.50x (ISBN 0-87840-187-3). Georgetown U Pr.

Readings in Ethical Theory. 2nd ed. Ed. by Wilfrid Sellars & John Hospers. 1970. text ed. 21.95 (ISBN 0-13-756007-9). P-H.

Readings in French Literature. Richard D. Kopp & Theodore P. Fraser. 1975. pap. text ed. 8.80 (ISBN 0-395-13638-5). HM.

Readings in Gerontology. 2nd ed. Ed. by Mollie Brown. LC 77-14088. (Illus.). 1978. pap. text ed. 8.00 (ISBN 0-8016-0734-5). Mosby.

Readings in Highest & Best Use. 224p. (Orig.). 1981. pap. 10.50 (ISBN 0-911780-51-3). Am Inst Real Estate Appraisers.

Readings in Hospital Risk Management. American Hospital Association. 64p. 1979. pap. 7.50 (ISBN 0-87258-284-1, 1360). Am Hospital.

Readings in Human Sexuality. Samuel Wilson et al. LC 75-4362. (Illus.). 252p. 1975. pap. text ed. 8.50 (ISBN 0-8299-0050-0). West Pub.

Readings in Human Sexuality: Contemporary Perspectives. 2nd ed. Ed. by Chad Gordon & Gayle Johnson. 1980. pap. text ed. 10.50 scp (ISBN 0-06-042399-4, HarpC); instructor's manual avail. (ISBN 0-685-60893-X). Har-Row.

Readings in Industrial Economics, 2 vols. Charles K. Rowley. LC 73-76642. 1973. Vol. 1. pap. 11.50x (ISBN 0-8448-0207-7); Vol. 2. pap. 11.50x (ISBN 0-8448-0208-5). Crane-Russak Co.

Readings in Industrial Sociology. Ed. by William A. Faunce. (Illus., Orig.). 1967. pap. text ed. 15.95 (ISBN 0-13-756577-1). P-H.

Readings in Intercultural Communication: Concepts & Courses, Vol. 2. Intro. by David S. Hoopes. LC 78-112304. pap. 5.50 o.p. (ISBN 0-933934-00-9). Intercult Pr.

Readings in Interpersonal & Organizational Communication. 3rd ed. Richard C. Huseman et al. 1977. text ed. 12.95 (ISBN 0-205-05900-7, 485777-1). Allyn.

Readings in Juvenile Delinquency. Gary F. Jensen & Dean G. Rojek. 448p. 1981. pap. text ed. 9.95 (ISBN 0-669-03763-X). Heath.

Readings in Kinship in Urban Society. C. C. Harris. 1970. 23.00 (ISBN 0-08-016039-5); pap. 12.75 (ISBN 0-08-016038-7). Pergamon.

Readings in Labor Economics & Labor Relations. 2nd ed. Lloyd G. Reynolds et al. (Illus.). 1978. pap. text ed. 11.95 (ISBN 0-13-761569-8). P-H.

Readings in Labor Economics & Labor Relations. 4th ed. Richard L. Rowan. 1980. pap. 11.95x (ISBN 0-256-02367-0). Irwin.

Readings in Labor Economics & Labor Relations. 3rd ed. Ed. by Richard L. Rowan. 1976. pap. text ed. 12.50x o.p. (ISBN 0-256-01829-4). Irwin.

Readings in Labour Economics. Ed. by J. E. King. (Illus.). 454p. 1980. text ed. 39.50x (ISBN 0-19-877132-0); pap. text ed. 13.95x (ISBN 0-19-877133-9). Oxford U Pr.

Readings in Language Development. Ed. by Lois Bloom. LC 77-10717. (Communications Disorders Ser.). 1978. text ed. 19.95 (ISBN 0-471-08221-X). Wiley.

Readings in Mainstreaming. rev. ed. Special Learning Corporation. Ed. by John M. Sullivan. (Special Education Ser.). (Illus.). 224p. 1981. pap. text ed. 9.95 (ISBN 0-89568-293-1). Spec Learn Corp.

Readings in Mammalian Cell Culture. rev. ed. Ed. by Robert Pollack. LC 75-15101. (Illus.). 884p. 1975. pap. text ed. 24.00 (ISBN 0-87969-116-6). Cold Spring Harbor.

Readings in Mammalian Cell Culture. 2nd ed. Ed. by Robert Pollack. 1981. pap. text ed. 26.00 (ISBN 0-686-69552-6). Cold Spring Harbor.

Readings in Management: Contingencies, Structure & Process. Henry L. Tosi. LC 76-5292. (Illus.). 1976. pap. text ed. 9.25 (ISBN 0-914292-07-2). Wiley.

Readings in Management Principles. Ed. by Life Office Management Association. (FLMI Insurance Education Program Ser.). 68p. (Orig.). 1980. pap. text ed. 5.00x (ISBN 0-915322-37-4). Loma.

Readings in Management Science. Ed. by Efraim Turban & N. Paul Loomba. 1976. pap. 10.95x (ISBN 0-256-01705-0). Business Pubns.

Readings in Managerial Economics. rev. ed. Thomas J. Coyne et al. 1977. pap. 9.95x (ISBN 0-256-01904-5). Business Pubns.

Readings in Managerial Economics. I. Ibrahim et al. LC 75-4618. 1976. text ed. 41.00 (ISBN 0-08-019605-5); pap. text ed. 18.00 (ISBN 0-08-019604-7). Pergamon.

Readings in Managerial Psychology. 3rd ed. Harold J. Leavitt & Louis R. Pondy. LC 79-21587. xii, 732p. 1980. lib. bdg. 25.00x (ISBN 0-226-46986-7); pap. text ed. 12.95x (ISBN 0-226-46987-5). U of Chicago Pr.

Readings in Managerial Psychology. 2nd ed. Ed. by Harold J. Leavitt & Louis R. Pondy. LC 64-15811. 1974. 17.50x o.s.i. (ISBN 0-226-46984-0); pap. 8.50x o.s.i. (ISBN 0-226-46985-9). U of Chicago Pr.

Readings in Marketing Management. Philip Kotler & Keith Cox. 1972. pap. text ed. 9.95 o.p. (ISBN 0-13-759241-8). P-H.

Readings in Marketing Strategy. Jean-Claude Larreche & Edward C. Strong. 1981. pap. text ed. 13.50x (ISBN 0-89426-030-8). Scientific Pr.

Readings in Materials Management. American Hospital Association. LC 73-87664. (Illus.). 100p. 1973. pap. 12.50 o.p. (ISBN 0-87258-136-5, 2510). Am Hospital.

Readings in Medical Sociology. Robert N. Wilson et al. 448p. Date not set. text ed. 12.95 (ISBN 0-669-03945-4). Heath. Postponed.

Readings in Mental Handicaps. rev. ed. Ed. by John Venn. (Special Education Ser.). (Illus.). 224p. pap. text ed. write for info. (ISBN 0-89568-195-1). Spec Learn Corp.

Readings in Missionary Anthropology II. 2nd rev. enl. ed. Ed. by William A. Smalley. LC 78-6009. (Applied Cultural Anthropology Ser.). 1978. pap. text ed. 12.95x (ISBN 0-87808-731-1). William Carey.

Readings in Money, National Income & Stabilization Policy. 4th ed. Ronald L. Teigen. 1978. pap. text ed. 13.95 (ISBN 0-256-02031-0). Irwin.

Readings in Moral Education. Ed. by Peter Scharf. 1978. pap. 9.95 (ISBN 0-03-021346-0). Winston Pr.

Readings in Moral Theology, No. 2: The Distinctiveness of Christian Ethics. Ed. by Charles E. Curran & Richard A. McCormick. 360p. 1980. pap. 8.95 (ISBN 0-8091-2303-7). Paulist Pr.

Readings in Oncology. Stacey B. Day et al. LC 80-80708. (Foundation Publication Ser.). (Illus.). 227p. (Orig.). pap. 12.00 (ISBN 0-934314-01-2). Intl Found Biosocial Dev.

Readings in Organizational Behavior & Human Performance. rev ed. William E. Scott & L. L. Cummings. 1973. pap. text ed. 13.95 (ISBN 0-256-01398-5). Irwin.

Readings in Organizational Behavior: Concepts and Applications. Jerry Gray & Frederick Starke. (Business Ser.). 1976. pap. text ed. 12.95 (ISBN 0-675-08522-5). Merrill.

Readings in Organizations: Behavior, Structure, Processes. 3rd ed. James L. Gibson et al. 1979. pap. 9.95x (ISBN 0-256-02247-X). Business Pubns.

Readings in Perception. Ed. by Peter A. Fried. 1974. pap. text ed. 8.95x o.p. (ISBN 0-669-89367-6). Heath.

Readings in Philosophical Analysis. Ed. by Herbert Feigl & Wilfrid Sellars. x, 593p. 1981. lib. bdg. 25.00 (ISBN 0-917930-29-0); pap. text ed. 12.50x (ISBN 0-917930-09-6). Ridgeview.

Readings in Philosophy. 3rd ed. John H. Randall, Jr. et al. 1972. pap. 5.95 (ISBN 0-06-460059-9, CO 59, COS). Har-Row.

Readings in Philosophy of Art & Aesthetics. M. Nahm. 1975. 19.95 (ISBN 0-13-760892-6). P-H.

Readings in Race & Ethnic Relations. Anthony H. Richmond. 350p. 1972. 27.00 (ISBN 0-08-016213-4); pap. 14.00 (ISBN 0-08-016212-6). Pergamon.

Readings in Real Estate Investment Analysis. 1977. pap. 10.50 (ISBN 0-911780-42-4). Am Inst Real Estate Appraisers.

Readings in Real Property Valuation Principles. 1977. pap. 10.50 (ISBN 0-911780-41-6). Am Inst Real Estate Appraisers.

Readings in Reference Group Theory & Research. Ed. by Herbert H. Hyman & Eleanor D. Singer. LC 68-10366. 1968. 17.95 (ISBN 0-02-915700-5). Free Pr.

Readings in Romance Linguistics. James M. Anderson & JoAnn Creore. (Illus.). 472p. (Orig.). 1972. pap. text ed. 38.25x (ISBN 90-2792-303-5). Mouton.

Readings in Russian Civilization, 3 vols. rev. ed. Ed. by Thomas Riha. Incl. Vol. 1. Russia Before Peter the Great, 900-1700. 8.75x (ISBN 0-226-71852-2); pap. 5.50 (ISBN 0-226-71853-0); Vol. 2. Imperial Russia, 1700-1917. o.s.i. (ISBN 0-226-71854-9); pap. 6.50 (ISBN 0-226-71855-7); Vol. 3. Soviet Russia, 1917-Present. 9.50x (ISBN 0-226-71856-5); pap. 8.00 (ISBN 0-226-71857-3). LC 69-14825. 1969. U of Chicago Pr.

Readings in Sex & Gender. Laurel W. Richardson. 416p. 1982. pap. text ed. 12.95 (ISBN 0-669-03370-7). Heath. Postponed.

Readings in Social Evolution & Development. Ed. by S. N. Eisenstadt. LC 78-96463. 1970. 25.00 (ISBN 0-08-006813-8); pap. 13.25 (ISBN 0-08-006812-X). Pergamon.

Readings in Social Geography. Ed. by Emrys Jones. (Illus.). 360p. 1975. pap. 8.95x (ISBN 0-19-874060-3). Oxford U Pr.

Readings in Social Problems: Contemporary Perspectives. 1977-1978 ed. Ed. by Peter Wickman. (Contemporary Perspective Readers Ser.). 1977. pap. text ed. 10.50 scp (ISBN 0-06-047053-4, HarpC); inst. manual free (ISBN 0-06-367163-8). Har-Row.

Readings in Social Psychology: A Symbolic Interaction Perspective. Jerry D. Cardwell. LC 73-77106. pap. 5.95x (ISBN 0-88295-202-1). AHM Pub.

Readings in Sociobiology. Ed. by T. H. Clutton-Brock & Paul H. Harvey. LC 77-22283. (Illus.). 1978. text ed. 23.95x (ISBN 0-7167-0191-X); pap. text ed. 11.95x (ISBN 0-7167-0190-1). W H Freeman.

Readings in Sociology: Contemporary Perspectives. 2nd ed. Phillip Whitten. 1979. pap. text ed. 9.50 scp (ISBN 0-06-045503-9, HarpC). Har-Row.

Readings in Teaching Business Subjects. Ed. by Louis C. Nanassy. LC 78-72079. 1979. pap. 16.00 (ISBN 0-8224-5828-4). Pitman Learning.

Readings in the Administration of Institutions for Delinquent Youth. William E. Amos & Raymond L. Manella. 228p. 1965. pap. 18.75 photovopy ed. spiral (ISBN 0-398-00041-7). C C Thomas.

Readings in the Appraisal of Special Purpose Properties. 280p. 1981. pap. 10.50 (ISBN 0-911780-52-1). Am Inst Real Estate Appraisers.

Readings in the Chinese Communist Cultural Revolution: A Manual for Students of the Chinese Language. Ed. by Chi Wen-Shun. LC 70-94988. (Center for Chinese Studies, UC Berkeley). 1971. 22.75x (ISBN 0-520-01593-2). U of Cal Pr.

Readings in the Concept & Measurement of Income. Ed. by R. H. Parker & G. C. Harcourt. LC 75-87137. (Illus.). 1969. 47.50 (ISBN 0-521-07463-0); pap. 15.95x (ISBN 0-521-09591-3). Cambridge U Pr.

Readings in the Income Approach to Real Property Valuation. 1977. pap. 10.50 (ISBN 0-911780-43-2). Am Inst Real Estate Appraisers.

Readings in the Philosophy of Language. Jay F. Rosenberg & Charles Travis. LC 70-132170. 1971. text ed. 19.95 (ISBN 0-13-759332-5). P-H.

Readings in the Philosophy of Religion: An Analytic Approach. Ed. by Baruch Brody. LC 73-20485. 608p. 1974. text ed. 19.95 (ISBN 0-13-759340-6). P-H.

Readings in the Philosophy of Science. Boruch Brody. LC 71-98091. (Philosophy Ser). 1970. text ed. 19.95 (ISBN 0-13-760702-4). P-H.

Readings in the Sociology of Migration. C. J. Jansen. LC 72-105954. 1970. 21.00 (ISBN 0-08-006915-0); pap. 11.25 (ISBN 0-08-006914-2). Pergamon.

Readings in the Sociology of Religion. Ed. by J. Brothers. 1967. 22.00 (ISBN 0-08-012186-1); text ed. 10.75 (ISBN 0-08-012187-X). Pergamon.

Readings in the Swedish Class Structure. Ed. by Richard Scase. 1976. text ed. 42.00 (ISBN 0-08-016663-6); pap. 16.25 (ISBN 0-08-020633-6). Pergamon.

Readings in the Theory of Educational Systems. Earl Hopper. 1971. text ed. 10.25x (ISBN 0-09-109230-2, Hutchinson U Lib). Humanities.

Readings in the Theory of Income Distribution. Compiled by American Economic Association Committee. LC 76-29414. (BCL II Ser.). 736p. 1980. Repr. of 1946 ed. 45.00 (ISBN 0-404-15332-1). AMS Pr.

Readings in Urban Geography. Ed. by Harold M. Mayer & Clyde F. Kohn. LC 59-11973. (Illus.). 1959. 12.50x (ISBN 0-226-51270-3). U of Chicago Pr.

Readings in Urban Sociology. Ed. by R. E. Pahl. 1968. text ed. 16.50 (ISBN 0-08-013303-7); pap. 7.75 (ISBN 0-08-013293-6). Pergamon.

Readings in Values Clarification. Howard Kirschenbaum & Sidney B. Simon. 1973. pap. 8.95 (ISBN 0-03-011936-7, 861). Winston Pr.

Readings in Wildlife Conservation. Ed. by James A. Bailey et al. LC 74-28405. (Illus.). 722p. (Orig.). 1974. pap. 9.00 (ISBN 0-933564-02-3). Wildlife Soc.

Readings on Concepts of Criminal Law. Ferguson. (Criminal Justice Ser.). 1975. pap. text ed. 12.95 (ISBN 0-8299-0619-3). West Pub.

Readings on Congress. Ed. by R. Wolfinger. 1971. pap. 9.95 o.p. (ISBN 0-13-761254-0). P-H.

Readings on Drug Education. American Foundation for Continuing Education at Syracuse University. Ed. by Michael V. Reagen. LC 72-7237. 1972. 10.00 (ISBN 0-8108-0548-0). Scarecrow.

Readings on Ethical & Social Issues in Biomedicine. Ed. by Richard W. Wertz. 320p. 1973. pap. 11.95 ref. ed. (ISBN 0-13-755884-8). P-H.

Readings on Fascism & National Socialism. University Of Colorado Department Of Philosophy. 112p. (Orig.). 1952. pap. 3.95x (ISBN 0-8040-0259-2, 3). Swallow.

Readings on Managing Hotels-Restaurants-Institutions. D. Sapienza et al. 1977. pap. text ed. 12.95x (ISBN 0-8104-9469-8); net instructor's manual 1.95 (ISBN 0-8104-9473-6). Hayden.

Readings on Mergers & Takeovers. J. M. Samuels. 1972. 39.95 (ISBN 0-236-17619-6, Pub. by Paul Elek). Merrimack Bk Serv.

Readings on Production Planning & Control. Ted C. Caubang. 178p. 1972. 11.75 (ISBN 92-833-1017-9, APO51, APO). Unipub.

Readings on Race. 2nd ed. Ed. by Stanley M. Garn. (Illus.). 1968. photocopy ed. spiral 24.75 (ISBN 0-398-00647-4). C C Thomas.

Readings on Religion: From Inside & Outside. Ed. by Robert S. Ellwood, Jr. 1978. pap. text ed. 12.95 (ISBN 0-13-760942-6). P-H.

Readings on Social Services in the Health Professions. Ed. by George B. Galinkin. 1976. pap. text ed. 9.50x (ISBN 0-8191-0083-8). U Pr of Amer.

Readings on State & Local Government. Irvin N. Gertzog. (Foundation of Modern Political Science Ser). 1970. pap. 10.95 ref. ed. (ISBN 0-13-761106-4). P-H.

Readings on the Multinational Corporation in Kenya. Ed. by Raphael Kaplinsky. 326p. 1978. text ed. 24.95x (ISBN 0-19-572446-1). Oxford U Pr.

Readings on the Research Process in Nursing. Fox. 1979. 16.50 (ISBN 0-8385-8266-4). ACC.

Readings on the Research Process in Nursing. D. J. Fox & I. Leeser. 232p. 1981. pap. 16.50 (ISBN 0-686-69604-2). ACC.

Readings on the Role of Education in Community & National Development in Problems in Education & Nation Building. Gale E. Jensen & William K. Medlin. 82p. 1969. pap. text ed. 3.50x o.p. (ISBN 0-89039-004-5). Ann Arbor Pubs.

Readings: Organizational Behavior. Altman. 1979. pap. text ed. 11.95. Dryden Pr.

Ready Always. Stanley Horton. LC 74-76802. (Radiant Life Ser). 1974. pap. 1.25 (ISBN 0-88243-575-2, 02-0575); teacher's ed 2.50 (ISBN 0-88243-182-X, 32-0182). Gospel Pub.

Ready Foods Systems for Health Care Facilities. Gordon A. Friesen International, Inc. LC 72-95360. 1973. 12.95 (ISBN 0-8436-0562-6). CBI Pub.

Ready for the Defense. Martin Garbus. 320p. 1971. write for info. FS&G.

Ready for the Tiger. Sam Ross. 1964. 3.95 o.p. (ISBN 0-374-24760-9). FS&G.

Ready, Get Set, Go! Sharon Peters. (Illus.). 32p. (gr. k-2). 1980. PLB 2.96 (ISBN 0-89375-386-6); pap. 0.95 (ISBN 0-89375-285-1). Troll Assocs.

Ready-Made Family. Antonia Forest. (Fanfares Ser.). (gr. 4 up). 1980. pap. 3.25 (ISBN 0-571-11494-6, Pub. by Faber & Faber). Merrimack Bk Serv.

Ready or Not. Richards Brock et al. 1977. 6.95 (ISBN 0-8027-0586-3); pap. 3.95 (ISBN 0-8027-7121-1). Walker & Co.

Ready Reference History of the English Bible. 6th ed. Ed. by M. T. Hills & E. J. Eisenhart. 1979. pap. 0.95 o.p. (ISBN 0-686-23172-4, 16228). United Bible.

Ready Sermon Outlines. Charles H. Spurgeon et al. (Sermon Outline Ser.). 1974. pap. 1.95 (ISBN 0-8010-7985-3). Baker Bk.

Ready, Set, Go: How to Give Your Children a Head Start Before They Go to School. Coleen K. Menlove. 1978. 10.95 (ISBN 0-13-762286-4, Spec); pap. 5.95 (ISBN 0-13-762278-3). P-H.

Ready to Hazard: A Biography of Commodore William Bainbridge, Seventeen Seventy-Two to Eighteen Thirty-Three. David F. Long. (Illus.). 400p. 1980. text ed. 20.00 (ISBN 0-8357-0579-X). Univ Microfilms.

Ready-to-Use Dollhouse Floor Coverings: Eight Full-Color Patterns to Decorate 8 Rooms. Munice Hendler. (Illus.). 1978. pap. 3.00 (ISBN 0-486-23666-8). Dover.

Ready-to-Use Floral Designs. Ed Sibbett. (Illus.). 64p. pap. 2.50 (ISBN 0-486-23976-4). Dover.

Ready-to-Use Marbelized Papers. Judith Saurman & Judith Pierce. 1979. pap. 3.50 (ISBN 0-486-23901-2). Dover.

Ready-to-Use Sale Announcements. David Gatti. (Dover Clip Art Pictorial Archive Ser.). (Illus.). 64p. (Orig.). 1980. pap. 2.50 (ISBN 0-486-24012-6). Dover.

Reaffirmation of Republicanism: Eisenhower & the Eighty-Third Congress. Gary W. Reichard. LC 75-1017. (Twentieth Century America Ser.). 320p. 1975. 18.50x (ISBN 0-87049-167-9). U of Tenn Pr.

Reagan. Hedrick Smith et al. 1981. 9.95. Macmillan.

Reagents for Organic Synthesis, Vol. 9. Mary Fieser et al. (Reagents for Organic Synthesis Ser.). 688p. 1981. 35.00 (ISBN 0-471-05631-6, Pub. by Wiley-Interscience). Wiley.

Real Analysis. Lang. 1976. 22.95 (ISBN 0-201-04179-0). A-W.

Real Analysis & Probability. Robert B. Ash. (Probability & Mathematical Statistics Ser.). 476p. 1972. 22.50 (ISBN 0-12-065201-3); solutions to problems 3.00 (ISBN 0-12-065240-4). Acad Pr.

Real Analytic Theory of Teichmueller Space. W. Abikoff. (Lecture Notes in Mathematics Ser.: Vol. 820). (Illus.). 144p. 1981. pap. 11.80 (ISBN 0-387-10237-X). Springer-Verlag.

Real Bread. Maggie Baylis & Coralie Castle. LC 80-21929. (Illus.). 240p. (Orig.). 1980. pap. 6.95 (ISBN 0-89286-179-7). One Hund One Prods.

Real Camelot: Paganism & the Arthurian Romances. John Darrah. 160p. 1981. 13.95 (ISBN 0-500-01250-4). Thames Hudson.

Real Centurions. Al Palmquist. 1979. 2.25 (ISBN 0-89728-014-8). Omega Pubns OR.

Real Estate. I. Edward Weich. (Orig.). 1967. pap. 3.95 (ISBN 0-06-460060-2, CO 60, COS). Har-Row.

Real Estate: A Woman's World. Mary Shern. 1979. 10.95 (ISBN 0-88462-373-4). Real Estate Ed Co.

Real Estate Accounting & Mathematics Handbook. Robert J. Wiley. LC 80-12990. (Real Estate for Professional Practitioners Ser.). 1980. 26.95 (ISBN 0-471-04812-7, Pub by Ronald Pr). Wiley.

Real Estate Acquisition Handbook: Money-Making Techniques for the Serious Investor. William T. Tappan. 1980. 16.95 (ISBN 0-13-762633-9, Spec); pap. 7.95 (ISBN 0-13-762625-8). P-H.

Real Estate Almanac. Robert D. Allen & Thomas E. Wolfe. LC 80-12417. (Real Estate for Professional Practitioners Ser.). 456p. 1980. 16.95 (ISBN 0-471-05854-8). Wiley.

Real Estate & Economics. Thomas Shafer. (Illus.). 320p. 1976. 15.95 (ISBN 0-87909-715-9). Reston.

Real Estate & Urban Development. rev ed. Halbert C. Smith et al. 1977. text ed. 19.50 (ISBN 0-256-01931-2). Irwin.

Real Estate & Urban Land Analysis. James R. Cooper & Karl L. Guntermann. LC 73-10397. (Special Ser. in Real Estate & Urban Land Economics). (Illus.). 544p. 1974. 32.95 (ISBN 0-669-90415-5). Lexington Bks.

Real Estate Appraisal & Investment. 2nd ed. Sanders A. Kahn & Frederick E. Case. LC 76-22316. 1977. 24.50 (ISBN 0-8260-4836-6, Pub. by Wiley-Hamilton). Wiley.

Real Estate Appraisal: Review & Outlook. Paul F. Wendt. LC 72-97939. 276p. 1974. 14.95x (ISBN 0-8203-0317-8). U of Ga Pr.

Real Estate Appraisal Terminology. 2nd ed. Ed. by Byrl N. Boyce. 1980. 14.50 (ISBN 0-88410-597-0). Ballinger Pub.

Real Estate Book: A Complete Guide to Acquiring, Financing, & Investing in a Home or Commercial Property. Robert L. Nessen. 272p. 1981. 12.95 (ISBN 0-686-69140-7). Little.

Real Estate Brokerage. Bruce Lindeman. 450p. 1981. text ed. 16.95 (ISBN 0-8359-6517-1); instr's. manual free (ISBN 0-8359-6518-X). Reston.

Real Estate Brokerage in the Eighties: Survival Among the Giants. Thomas W. Dooley. 1980. 10.95 (ISBN 0-88462-364-5). Real Estate Ed Co.

Real Estate Career Guide. William H. Pivar. LC 80-11544. 240p. 1980. lib. bdg. 11.95 (ISBN 0-668-04789-5); pap. 7.95 (ISBN 0-668-04970-7). Arco.

Real Estate Careers. Jim Haskins. (Career Concise Guides Ser.). (Illus.). (gr. 7 up). 1978. PLB 6.45 s&l (ISBN 0-531-01423-1). Watts.

Real Estate Development & Construction Financing 1980: Course Handbook. Charles Zalaznick. LC 80-80907. (Real Estate Law & Practice Course Handgook Ser.). 716p. 1980. pap. text ed. 25.00 (ISBN 0-686-68829-5, N4-4349). PLI.

Real Estate Dictionary No. 510. rev. ed. 192p. 1980. pap. 5.00 (ISBN 0-695-81526-1). Finan Pub.

Real Estate Education Company Real Estate Exam Manual. Douglas C. Smith & John T. Gibbons. (Orig.). 1980. pap. 14.95 (ISBN 0-88462-383-1). Real Estate Ed Co.

Real Estate Finance. William R. Beaton. (Illus.). 288p. 1975. 18.95 (ISBN 0-13-762708-4). P-H.

Real Estate Finance. Mary A. Hines. LC 77-13003. (Illus.). 1978. ref. 18.95 (ISBN 0-13-762724-6). P-H.

Real Estate Finance. 6th ed. Henry E. Hoagland et al. 1977. text ed. 18.95 (ISBN 0-256-01930-4). Irwin.

Real Estate Financial Reporting. Urban Land Institute Real Estate Financial Reporting & Steering Committees & Touche Ross & Company. LC 72-90085. (Special Report Ser.). 40p. 1972. pap. 4.75 (ISBN 0-87420-555-7). Urban Land.

Real Estate Financing. Frederick E. Case & John M. Clapp. LC 77-27938. 1978. text ed. 23.50 (ISBN 0-471-07248-6). Wiley.

Real Estate Fundamentals. Wade Gaddy & Robert Hart. 250p. (Orig.). 1981. pap. 13.95 (ISBN 0-88462-425-0). Real Estate Ed Co.

Real Estate Fundamentals. Mark L. Levine. LC 76-3508. 375p. 1976. text ed. 17.95 (ISBN 0-8299-0095-0); review manual 5.95 (ISBN 0-8299-0553-7); instrs.' manual avail. (ISBN 0-8299-0552-9). West Pub.

Real Estate in California. 11th ed. James B. Smith et al. LC 79-55422. (Illus.). 1980. 19.95 (ISBN 0-914504-08-8). General Educ.

Real Estate Information Sources. Ed. by Janice B. Babb & B. F. Dordick. LC 63-16246. (Management Information Guide Ser.: No. 1). 1963. 30.00 (ISBN 0-8103-0801-0). Gale.

Real Estate Investment. 2nd ed. W. R. Beaton & T. Robinson. 1977. text ed. 18.95 (ISBN 0-13-762971-0). P-H.

Real Estate Investment. Jay M. Kimmel. 1980. 9.95 (ISBN 0-346-12439-5). Cornerstone.

Real Estate Investment: Analysis & Strategy. Robert J. Wiley. LC 75-14950. 1976. 21.95 (ISBN 0-8260-9432-5). Ronald Pr.

Real Estate Investment & Finance. Sherman J. Maisel & Stephen E. Roulac. (Illus.). 1976. text ed. 20.50x (ISBN 0-07-039730-9, C); instr's manual 4.95 (ISBN 0-07-039731-7). McGraw.

Real Estate Investment for Profit Through Appreciation. Maury Seldin. 1980. text ed. 16.95 (ISBN 0-8359-6526-0). Reston.

Real Estate Investment for the Eighties: How to Build Financial Security in the Face of Inflation. Douglas M. Temple. (Illus.). 1981. 12.95 (ISBN 0-8092-7024-2). Contemp Bks.

Real Estate Investment Handbook. 1979. 12.50 o.p. (ISBN 0-685-67813-X). Porter.

Real Estate Investments. Herman Kelting. LC 78-6811. (Grid Series in Real Estate). 1980. 17.95 (ISBN 0-88244-171-X). Grid Pub.

Real Estate Investments: A Step by Step Guide. Charles McMullen. LC 80-20704. (Real Estate for Professional Practitioners Ser.). 156p. 1981. 19.95 (ISBN 0-471-08365-8, Pub. by Wiley-Interscience). Wiley.

Real Estate Investor & the Federal Income Tax. Gaylon E. Greer. LC 78-569. (Real Estate for Professional Practitioners Ser.). 1978. 26.50 (ISBN 0-471-01882-1, Pub. by Wiley-Interscience). Wiley.

Real Estate Investor's Tax & Profit Planner. Paul Lyons. 1981. pap. 12.95 (ISBN 0-8359-6529-5). Reston.

Real Estate Is Now...Investment Analysis & Exchange. 2nd ed. Danny Fogel & Randolph Howe. 256p. (Orig.). 1979. pap. text ed. 18.95 (ISBN 0-8403-2113-9). Kendall-Hunt.

Real Estate Law. 2nd ed. William L. Atteberry et al. LC 77-85043. (Real Estate-Business Law Ser.). 1978. text ed. 20.95 (ISBN 0-88244-161-2). Grid Pub.

Real Estate Law. 7th ed. Robert Kratovil & Raymond J. Werner. (P-H Ser. in Real Estate). (Illus.). 1979. 25.95 (ISBN 0-13-763268-1); text ed. 19.95 student ed. (ISBN 0-686-67336-0). P-H.

Real Estate Law. Donald R. Levi. (Illus.). 1980. text ed. 16.95 (ISBN 0-8359-6536-8). Reston.

Real Estate Law in California. 5th ed. Arthur G. Bowman & W. D. Milligan. 1978. ref. ed. 18.95 (ISBN 0-13-764043-9). P-H.

Real Estate Law of Texas. 7th, rev. ed. Harold F. Thurow. (Orig.). 1980. 12.95x (ISBN 0-914696-11-4); pap. 9.50x (ISBN 0-914696-12-2). Hemphill.

Real Estate License Examination: Salesman & Broker. 2nd ed. William Gladstone. LC 74-27434. 1976. pap. 6.00 o.p. (ISBN 0-668-03755-5). Arco.

Real Estate Limited Partnerships. Theodore S. Lynn et al. LC 77-11616. (Real Estate for Professional Practitioners Ser.). 1977. 31.50 (ISBN 0-471-55734-X, Pub. by Wiley-Interscience). Wiley.

Real Estate Math Made Easy. Tosh & Ordway. 1981. text ed. 15.95 (ISBN 0-8359-6556-2); instr's. manual free (ISBN 0-8359-6557-0). Reston.

Real Estate Math Using the Pocket Calculator-Computer. Fred R. Weber Co. 1979. pap. 8.95 (ISBN 0-8359-6554-6). Reston.

Real Estate Mathematics Study Manual & Reference Book. rev. ed. John R. Johnsich. (Illus.). 131p. 1980. pap. 9.95 (ISBN 0-914256-13-0). Real Estate Pub.

Real Estate Planning: Cases, Materials, Problems, Questions & Commentary on the Planning of Real Estate Transactions. 2nd ed. Norton L. Steuben. LC 80-17983. (University Casebook Ser.). 1264p. 1980. text ed. write for info. (ISBN 0-88277-013-6). Foundation Pr.

Real Estate Practicum. J. Ellis & B. Harwood. 1978. pap. 7.50 o.p. (ISBN 0-87909-750-7, 750). Reston.

Real Estate Primer. 35th ed. George R. Fessler & Ray D. Westcott. 298p. pap. 8.95 (ISBN 0-935810-00-5). Primer Pubs.

Real Estate Principles. Charles F. Floyd. 592p. 1981. text ed. 19.95 (ISBN 0-394-32263-0). Random.

Real Estate Principles & Practices. new ed. Ficek. 1976. text ed. 18.95 (ISBN 0-675-08585-3); instructor's manual 3.95 (ISBN 0-686-67318-2); transparencies 3.95 (ISBN 0-686-67319-0). Merrill.

Real Estate: Principles & Practices. 3rd ed. Karl G. Pearson & Michael P. Litka. LC 79-20017. (Real Estate Ser.). 1980. text ed. 19.95 (ISBN 0-88244-202-3). Grid Pub.

Real Estate Principles & Practices. 9th ed. Alfred A. Ring & Jerome Dasso. (Illus.). 752p. 1981. text ed. 21.00 (ISBN 0-13-765958-X). P-H.

Real Estate Principles in California. 4th ed. H. Davey & H. Mercer. 1981. 19.95. P-H.

Real Estate Principles in California. 3rd ed. Homer C. Davey & H. Glenn Mercer. 1976. 18.95 (ISBN 0-13-765693-9). P-H.

Real Estate Professional. rev. ed. William M. Shenkel. LC 78-52950. 1978. 14.95 (ISBN 0-87094-159-3). Dow Jones-Irwin.

Real Estate Professional's Design-a-Day 1980. Patricia Smith. 1979. text ed. 15.95 o.p. (ISBN 0-8359-6583-X); pap. text ed. 10.95 o.p. (ISBN 0-8359-6584-8). Reston.

Real Estate Professional's Design-a-Day: Nineteen Eighty Canadian Edition. Larry Ungerman. 1979. text ed. 18.95 o.p. (ISBN 0-8359-6585-6). Reston.

Real Estate Professionals Design-A-Day: 1981 Edition. Patricia Smith. 1980. 18.00 (ISBN 0-8359-6587-2). Reston.

Real Estate Profit Power: Managing Your Own Real Estate Office. Gerald Parks. 1981. text ed. 16.95 (ISBN 0-8359-6595-3); instr's manual free (ISBN 0-8359-6596-1). Reston.

Real Estate Resource Handbook. Ellis Harwood. (Illus.). 336p. 1980. pap. text ed. 7.95 (ISBN 0-8359-6564-3). Reston.

Real Estate Revolution! Who Will Survive. Thomas Ervin. 1980. 10.95 (ISBN 0-88462-387-4). Real Estate Ed Co.

Real Estate Riches Success Kit. 2nd ed. Tyler G. Hicks. 466p. 1981. pap. 99.50 (ISBN 0-914306-43-X). Intl Wealth.

Real Estate Taxes & Urban Housing. James Heilbrun. LC 66-20489. 1966. 15.00x (ISBN 0-231-02821-0). Columbia U Pr.

Real Estate Transactions: Cases & Materials on Land Transfer, Development & Finance. Paul Goldstein. LC 80-11638. (University Casebook Ser.). 842p. 1980. write for info. (ISBN 0-88277-005-5). Foundation Pr.

Real Estate Valuation Cost File, 1980: Square Foot & Cubic Foot Prices. William H. Edgerton & Albert J. Hlibok. 169p. 1980. pap. text ed. 29.95 (ISBN 0-442-25740-6). Van Nos Reinhold.

Real Evangelistic Preaching. Bailey E. Smith. 1981. 6.95 (ISBN 0-8054-6229-5). Broadman.

Real Flash Gordon. Katherine Leiner & Michael Arthur. LC 80-17779. (Old Friends Ser.). (Illus.). 80p. 1980. 6.95 (ISBN 0-916392-54-6). Oak Tree Pubns.

Real Food Cookbook. Ethel Renwick. 1978. spiral-bound kivar 8.95 (ISBN 0-310-31871-8). Zondervan.

Real Food: Simple, Sensuous & Splendid. Marian Tracy. pap. 5.95 (ISBN 0-14-046468-9). Penguin.

Real Ghosts. Daniel Cohen. LC 77-6502. (gr. 4-5). 1977. 5.95 (ISBN 0-396-07454-5). Dodd.

Real Ghosts. Daniel Cohen. (Illus.). (gr. 4 up). 1979. pap. 1.50 (ISBN 0-671-29908-5). PB.

Real History of the Rosicrucians. (Illus.). pap. 7.95 o.s.i. (ISBN 0-8334-1738-X). Steinerbks.

Real History of the Rosicrucians. Arthur E. Waite. (Illus.). 454p. 1975. pap. 7.95 o.s.i. (ISBN 0-8334-1738-X). Steinerbks.

Real Hole. Beverly Cleary. (Illus.). (ps-1). 1960. PLB 6.96 (ISBN 0-688-31655-7). Morrow.

Real Imagination: An Introduction to Poetry. Admont G. Clark. LC 70-190106. 480p. 1972. pap. text ed. 9.95 (ISBN 0-574-18560-7, 13-1560); instr's guide avail. (ISBN 0-574-18561-5, 13-1561). SRA.

Real Jesus. Garner T. Armstrong. 1978. pap. 2.25 (ISBN 0-380-40055-3, 40055). Avon.

Real-Life Adventures. Ed. by Mary Verdick. (Pal Paperbacks Kit B Ser.). (Illus., Orig.). (gr. 7-12). 1973. pap. text ed. 1.25 (ISBN 0-8374-3507-2). Xerox Ed Pubns.

Real-Life Contemporary Poems. Syneta E. King. 1981. 4.95 (ISBN 0-8062-1584-4). Carlton.

Real Life Mysteries. Linda Ruth. (gr. 2-3). 1977. pap. text ed. 2.95x (ISBN 0-933892-10-1). Child Focus Co.

Real Magnet Book. Mae Freeman. (gr. k-3). 1970. pap. 1.50 (ISBN 0-590-01660-1, Schol Pap). Schol Bk Serv.

Real Objects & Models. J. Steven Soulier. Ed. by James E. Duane. LC 80-21450. (Instructional Media Library: Vol. 12). (Illus.). 96p. 1981. 13.95 (ISBN 0-87778-172-9). Educ Tech Pubns.

Real Oscar. Peter Brown. (Illus.). 256p. 1981. 15.95 (ISBN 0-87000-498-0). Arlington Hse.

Real People. Alison Lurie. 1969. pap. 1.65 (ISBN 0-380-00227-2, 23747, Bard). Avon.

Real Personality. James Auld. 1981. 7.75 (ISBN 0-8062-1597-6). Carlton.

Real Presence. Richard Bausch. 1980. 9.95 (ISBN 0-8037-7779-5). Dial.

Real Property. Sara Davidson. 1981. pap. 2.95 (ISBN 0-671-41269-8). PB.

Real Race. Alfred T. Wilkins, Jr. & Joseph Dunn. LC 80-85152. (Illus.). 210p. 1981. 10.95 (ISBN 0-938694-04-9). Jordan & Co.

Real Readers & Human Teachers. Neila T. Pettit. 1974. 4.50x (ISBN 0-87543-119-4). Lucas.

Real Reason for Christmas: Letters to Children for the Twelve Nights of Christmas. Margaret Taliaferro. LC 76-55080. 1977. 6.95 (ISBN 0-385-12414-7). Doubleday.

Real Rewards of Real Estate. Venita VanCaspel. 1980. pap. 1.50 (ISBN 0-8359-6605-4). Reston.

Real Rhythm in English Poetry. Katherine M. Wilson. 171p. 1980. Repr. of 1929 ed. lib. bdg. 25.00 (ISBN 0-89987-860-1). Darby Bks.

Real Ringmaster. Austin Miles. Ed. by John Boneck & Cliff Dudley. LC 80-83458. 150p. 1980. 8.95 (ISBN 0-89221-079-6). New Leaf.

Real Science Riddles. Rose Wyler. (Illus.). (gr. 1-4). 1971. 5.95g (ISBN 0-8038-6320-9). Hastings.

Real Solids & Radiation. A. E. Hughes et al. LC 74-32348. (Wykeham Science Ser.: No. 35). 1975. 8.60x (ISBN 0-8448-1162-9). Crane-Russak Co.

Real Soviet Russia. David J. Dallin. 1947. 24.50x (ISBN 0-685-69807-6). Elliots Bks.

Real Stories from Baltimore County History. Isobel Davidson. LC 70-9245. (Illus.). x, 296p. Repr. of 1917 ed. 15.00 (ISBN 0-8103-5033-5). Gale.

Real Thing. Kurt Andersen. LC 78-22787. 192p. 1980. 8.95 (ISBN 0-385-14636-1). Doubleday.

Real Time BASIC for the TRS-Eighty. Don Inman et al. Date not set. pap. 9.95 (ISBN 0-918398-05-3). Dilithium Pr.

Real Time Method of Radar Plotting. 2nd ed. Max H. Carpenter & Wayne M. Waldo. (Illus.). 48p. 1981. pap. 8.00x (ISBN 0-87033-273-2). Cornell Maritime.

Real Time Programming Nineteen Seventy-Eight: Proceedings. IFAC-IFIP Workshop, Mariehamn-Aland, Finland, 1978. Ed. by B. Cronhjort. (IFAC Proceedings). (Illus.). 96p. 1979. 26.00 (ISBN 0-08-024492-0). Pergamon.

Real-Time Programming with Microcomputers. new ed. Ronald C. Turner. LC 77-80773. 1978. 18.95x (ISBN 0-669-01666-7). Lexington Bks.

Real Time Programming, 1980: Proceedings. IFAC - IFIP Workshop, Leibnitz, Austria, April 1980. Ed. by V. H. Haase. LC 80-49720. (IFAC Proceedings Ser.). 150p. 1980. 40.00 (ISBN 0-08-027305-X). Pergamon.

Real Tin Flower: Poems About the World at Nine. Aliki Barnstone. LC 68-22122. (Illus.). 1968. 7.95 (ISBN 0-02-708430-2, CCPr). Macmillan.

Real Tinsel. Bernard Rosenberg & Harry Silverstein. LC 73-112854. (Illus.). 436p. 1974. pap. 3.95 o.s.i. (ISBN 0-02-012550-X, Collier). Macmillan.

Real Tom Thumb. Helen R. Cross. LC 80-11447. (Illus.). 96p. (gr. 3-7). 1980. 8.95 (ISBN 0-590-07606-X, Four Winds). Schol Bk Serv.

Real Truth Concerning Apostolos Makrakis. Themistocles Livadeas & Minas Charitos. Ed. by Orthodox Christian Educational Society. Tr. by Denver Cummings from Hellenic. 230p. (Orig.). 1952. pap. 4.00x (ISBN 0-938366-30-0). Orthodox Chr.

Real War. Richard Nixon. 400p. 1981. pap. 3.50 (ISBN 0-446-96136-1). Warner Bks.

Real War. Richard Nixon. LC 79-28358. 320p. 1980. 12.50 (ISBN 0-446-51201-X). Warner Bks.

Real Word for the Real World. Don Deffner. (Preacher's Workshop Ser.). 48p. 1977. pap. 2.25 (ISBN 0-570-07402-9, 12-2674). Concordia.

Real World Measurement. Robert Rohm & John W. Shaw. LC 79-730249. (Illus.). 1979. pap. text ed. 99.00 (ISBN 0-89290-097-0, A513-SATC). Soc for Visual.

Real World of Ideology. Joe McCarney. (Philosophy Now Ser.). 1980. text ed. 32.50x (ISBN 0-391-01704-7); pap. text ed. 11.75x (ISBN 0-391-01705-5). Humanities.

Real World of the Small Business Owner. Richard Scase & Robert Goffee. 166p. 1980. 27.50x (ISBN 0-7099-0452-5, Pub. by Croom Helm Ltd England). Biblio Dist.

Realism: A Critique of Brentano & Meinong. Gustav Bergmann. (Orig.). 1967. 25.00x (ISBN 0-299-04330-4); pap. 9.95x (ISBN 0-299-04334-7). U of Wis Pr.

Realism, an Educational Philosophy of a Democratic Society. Catherine Palms. 1979. cancelled (ISBN 0-682-48937-9). Exposition.

Realism & Hope. Ronald H. Stone. 1977. pap. text ed. 8.75x (ISBN 0-8191-0128-1). U Pr of Amer.

Realism & Social Vision in Courbet & Proudhon. James H. Rubin. LC 80-17559. (Essays on the Arts: No. 10). (Illus.). 270p. 1980. 17.50x (ISBN 0-691-03960-7); pap. 8.95x (ISBN 0-691-00327-0). Princeton U Pr.

Realism & the Background of Phenomenology. Ed. by Roderick M. Chisholm. vii, 308p. 1981. lib. bdg. 22.00 (ISBN 0-917930-34-7); pap. text ed. 8.50x (ISBN 0-917930-14-2). Ridgeview.

Realism & the Explanation of Behavior. Merle B. Turner. (Century Psychology Ser.). 270p. 1980. text ed. 24.50x (ISBN 0-8290-0361-4); pap. text ed. 8.95x (ISBN 0-8290-0362-2). Irvington.

Realism & Tradition in Art, Eighteen Forty-Eight - Nineteen Hundred: Sources & Documents. Linda Nochlin. (Orig.). 1966. pap. 10.95 ref. ed. (ISBN 0-13-766584-9). P-H.

Realism in EEO. Harold P. Hayes. LC 79-2295. 1980. 27.95 (ISBN 0-471-05796-7, Pub. by Wiley-Interscience). Wiley.

Realism in Shakespeare's Romantic Comedies: "O Heavenly Mingle". Marvin Felheim & Philip Traci. LC 80-5580. 239p. 1980. lib. bdg. 17.55 (ISBN 0-8191-1282-8); pap. text ed. 9.75 (ISBN 0-8191-1283-6). U Pr of Amer.

Realism in the Application of ACI Standard 214-65. 1973. pap. 18.50 (ISBN 0-685-85114-1, SP-37) (ISBN 0-685-85115-X). ACI.

Realism Photo-Realism. John Arthur. LC 80-83113. (Illus.). 123p. 1980. 25.00 (ISBN 0-86659-002-1); pap. 16.50 (ISBN 0-86659-003-X). Philbrook.

Realistic Approach to Any Philosophy. Deborah Morea. 1981. pap. 7.95 (ISBN 0-9603022-2-0). Davida Pubns.

Realistic Imagination: English Fiction from Frankenstein to Lady Chatterley. George Levine. LC 80-17444. 1981. lib. bdg. 25.00x (ISBN 0-226-47550-6). U of Chicago Pr.

Realistic Movement in American Writing: 1865-1900. Ed. by Bruce R. McElderry, Jr. LC 65-19410. (Orig.). 1965. pap. 8.50 (ISBN 0-672-63104-0). Odyssey Pr.

Realities. M. Basilea Schlink. 128p. 1972. pap. 2.50 (ISBN 0-310-32602-8). Zondervan.

Realities & Illusions Eighteen Eighty-Six to Nineteen Thirty-Two. Raymond Moley. Ed. by Frank Freidel. LC 78-13887. (History of the United States 1876-1976: Vol. 13). 1980. lib. bdg. 20.00 (ISBN 0-8240-9692-4). Garland Pub.

Realities & Visions: Contributions to the Church's Mission Today. Ed. by Furman C. Stough & Urban T. Holmes, 3rd. 1976. pap. 3.95 (ISBN 0-8164-2130-7). Crossroad NY.

Realities of Free Trade. Duncan Burn & Barbara Epstein. 1972. text ed. 12.95x (ISBN 0-04-382016-6). Allen Unwin.

Realities of Literature. Ed. by Richard Dietrich. LC 70-136507. 1971. text ed. 16.50x long ed. (ISBN 0-471-00122-8); pap. text ed. 11.95 short ed. (ISBN 0-471-00123-6). Wiley.

Realities of Nursing Management: How to Cope. Florence McQuillan. LC 78-8298. 384p. 1978. text ed. 19.95 (ISBN 0-87618-991-5). R J Brady.

Realities of Nutrition. Ronald Deutsch. LC 76-23508. (Berkeley Series in Nutrition). (Illus.). 1976. 13.95 (ISBN 0-915950-07-3); pap. 9.95 (ISBN 0-915950-19-7). Bull Pub.

Realities of Planning. Ed. by Bernard Taylor & David Hussey. (Illus.). 224p. 1981. 36.00 (ISBN 0-08-022226-9). Pergamon.

Realities of Social Research. Jennifer Platt. LC 75-30275. 224p. 1976. 24.95 (ISBN 0-470-69119-0). Halsted Pr.

Reality. Larry Gianaris. LC 78-68900. 1980. 5.95 (ISBN 0-533-04184-8). Vantage.

Reality. Paul Weiss. LC 67-11699. 318p. 1967. lib. bdg. 11.95x (ISBN 0-8093-0243-8). S Ill U Pr.

Reality. Paul Weiss. LC 67-11699. (Arcturus Books Paperbacks). 318p. 1967. pap. 8.95 (ISBN 0-8093-0244-6). S Ill U Pr.

Reality & Career Planning: A Guide for Personal Growth. Nicholas W. Weiler. (Illus.). 224p. 1977. text ed. 13.95 (ISBN 0-201-08572-0); pap. text ed. 7.95 (ISBN 0-201-08570-4). A-W.

Reality & Fiction in Modern Japanese Literature. Noriko M. Lippit. LC 79-67859. 1980. 20.00 (ISBN 0-87332-137-5). M E Sharpe.

Reality and Other Writings. Richard H. James. 1977. 4.00 o.p. (ISBN 0-682-48917-4). Exposition.

Reality & Scientific Truth: Discussions with Einstein, Von Laue, & Planck. Ilse Rosenthal-Schneider. Ed. by Thomas Braun. (Illus.). 150p. 1981. 9.95 (ISBN 0-8143-1650-6). Wayne St U Pr.

Reality at Risk: A Defence of Realism in Philosophy & the Sciences. Roger Trigg. 216p. 1980. 26.50x (ISBN 0-389-20037-9). B&N.

Reality of Ethnomethodology. Hugh Mehan & Houston Wood. LC 75-1190. 259p. 1975. 21.50 (ISBN 0-471-59060-6, Pub. by Wiley-Interscience). Wiley.

Reality of Living Yoga. 212p. 1978. pap. 6.95x (ISBN 0-933740-01-8). Inst Self Dev.

Reality of Retirement: The Inner Experience of Becoming a Retired Person. Jules Z. Willing. 224p. 1981. 10.95 (ISBN 0-688-00298-6); pap. 6.95 (ISBN 0-688-00394-X). Morrow.

Reality Orientation: A Technique to Rehabilitate Elderly and Brain-Damaged Patients. rev. ed. 1975. 1.75 (ISBN 0-685-37534-X, P239-0); 10 or more copies 1.00 ea. (ISBN 0-685-37535-8). Am Psychiatric.

Reality Revealed: The Theory of Multidimensional Reality. Douglas Vogt & Gary Sultan. LC 77-88915. 460p. 1979. 12.95 (ISBN 0-930808-01-0). Ross-Erikson.

Reality Shock: Why Nurses Leave Nursing. Marlene Kramer. LC 73-22243. (Illus.). 1974. pap. text ed. 16.95 (ISBN 0-8016-2741-9). Mosby.

Realize What You Are: The Dynamics of Jain Meditation. Gurudev S. Chitrabhanu. Ed. by Leonard M. Marks. LC 78-9461. (Illus.). 1978. 7.95 (ISBN 0-396-07579-7). Dodd.

Realize Your Potential. Robert J. McKain, Jr. 1979. pap. 5.95 (ISBN 0-8144-7515-9). Am Mgmt.

Really Living. William Backus & Paul Malte. pap. 4.85 (ISBN 0-933350-04-X). Morse Pr.

Really, Marty! Bettilu D. Davies. 128p. (gr. 6-10). 1981. pap. 1.95 (ISBN 0-8024-9299-1). Moody.

Really Reading. Jean Greenlaw & Byron VanRoekel. (Design for Reading Ser). (Illus.). (gr. 1). 1972. pap. 3.60 (ISBN 0-06-516300-1, SchDept); tchrs. ed. 6.44 (ISBN 0-06-516400-8). Har-Row.

Realm of Algebra. Isaac Asimov. 1977. pap. 1.50 o.p. (ISBN 0-449-30804-9, Prem). Fawcett.

Realm of Numbers. Isaac Asimov. 1977. pap. 1.50 o.p. (ISBN 0-449-30805-7, Prem). Fawcett.

Realm of the Submarine. Paul Cohen. LC 69-12176. 1969. 5.95 o.s.i. (ISBN 0-685-15803-9). Macmillan.

Realm of the Terrestrial Planets. Zdenek Kopal. LC 79-40449. 223p. 1979. 22.95 (ISBN 0-470-26688-0). Halsted Pr.

Realms of the Self: Variations on a Theme in Modern Drama. Arthur Ganz. (Gotham Library). 256p. 1981. 17.95x (ISBN 0-8147-2979-7); pap. 8.95x (ISBN 0-8147-2980-0). NYU Pr.

Realtheism: A Religion & Bible for the Humanist Age. G. Merle Bergman. 160p. 1981. 10.95 (ISBN 0-938986-03-1); pap. 6.95 (ISBN 0-938986-04-X). Fellowship Pr.

Realtors' Liability. Levine. LC 79-4133. (Real Estate for Professional Practitioners Ser.). 1979. 23.95 (ISBN 0-471-05208-6, Pub. by Ronald). Wiley.

Reanaway Country. new ed. Mary Sutliff. LC 79-66697. (Illus., Orig.). 1980. pap. 4.95 (ISBN 0-913140-39-2). Signpost Bk Pub.

Reap in Tears. Jack Hoffenberg. 1969. pap. 1.95 (ISBN 0-380-00477-1, 26401). Avon.

Reap the Wind. Elizabeth Bright. (Orig.). 1981. pap. write for info. (ISBN 0-671-41782-7). PB.

Reaping. Bernard Taylor. 236p. 1981. 9.95 (ISBN 0-312-66528-8). St Martin.

Reaping the Whirlwind: A Christian Interpretation of History. Langdon Gilkey. 1977. 17.50 (ISBN 0-8164-0308-2). Crossroad NY.

Reapportionment in the 1970s. Ed. by Nelson W. Polsby. LC 73-142046. (Institute of Governmental Studies, UC Berkely). 1971. 21.50x (ISBN 0-520-01885-0). U of Cal Pr.

Reappraisal of Marxian Economics. Murray Wolfson. LC 66-14790. 1966. 17.50x (ISBN 0-231-02880-6). Columbia U Pr.

Reappraisals of Rousseau: Studies in Honour of R. A. Leigh. Ed. by Simon Harvey et al. 312p. 1980. 27.50x (ISBN 0-389-20067-0). B&N.

Rear Admiral John Rodgers: 1812-1882. Robert E. Johnson. LC 79-6110. (Navies & Men Ser.). (Illus.). 1980. Repr. of 1967 ed. lib. bdg. 35.00x (ISBN 0-405-13039-2). Arno.

Reason & Analysis. 2nd ed. Brand Blanshard. LC 62-9576. (Paul Carus Lectures Ser.). 505p. 1962. 22.50 (ISBN 0-87548-104-3); pap. 8.95 o.p. (ISBN 0-87548-112-4). Open Court.

Reason & Argument. P. T. Geach. LC 76-19961. 1977. pap. 4.95x (ISBN 0-520-03289-6). U of Cal Pr.

Reason & Commitment. R. Trigg. LC 72-89806. 192p. 1973. 23.95 (ISBN 0-521-20119-5); pap. 6.95x (ISBN 0-521-09784-3). Cambridge U Pr.

Reason & Morality. Alan Gewirth. 416p. 1981. pap. 9.95x (ISBN 0-226-28876-5). U of Chicago Pr.

Reason & Morality. Alan Gewirth. pap. 9.95 (ISBN 0-226-28876-5). U of Chicago Pr.

Reason & Religion: An Introduction to the Philosophy of Religion. Rem B. Edwards. LC 78-66278. 1979. pap. text ed. 11.25 (ISBN 0-8191-0690-9). U Pr of Amer.

Reason & Responsibility. 4th ed. Joel Feinberg. 1978. text ed. 17.95x (ISBN 0-8221-0209-9). Dickenson.

Reason & Responsibility. 5th ed. Joel Feinberg. 640p. 1980. text ed. 17.95x (ISBN 0-534-00924-7). Wadsworth Pub.

Reason & Revelation in the Middle Ages. Etienne Gilson. pap. text ed. 4.95x (ISBN 0-684-15026-3, ScribC). Scribner.

Reason & Rhetoric: The Intellectual Foundations of Twentieth Century Liberal Educational Policy. Walter Feinberg. LC 74-16009. 304p. 1975. text ed. 21.95 (ISBN 0-471-25697-8). Wiley.

Reason & Sensuality: Studies & Notes, Vol. 2. John Lydgate. Ed. by Ernst Sieper. (Early English Text Society Ser.). 1903. 9.95x (ISBN 0-19-722534-9). Oxford U Pr.

Reason & Society. Alexander Murray. 1978. 49.50x (ISBN 0-19-822540-7). Oxford U Pr.

Reason & Teaching. Israel Scheffler. LC 72-86641. 1973. pap. text ed. 8.95 (ISBN 0-672-61253-4). Bobbs.

Reason & Virtue: A Study in the Ethics of Richard Price. Antonio S. Cua. LC 66-10868. xv, 196p. 1966. 12.00x (ISBN 0-8214-0014-2). Ohio U Pr.

Reason Awake: Science for Man. Rene J. Dubos. LC 70-111327. 1970. 16.00x (ISBN 0-231-03181-5); pap. 5.00 (ISBN 0-231-08629-6). Columbia U Pr.

Reason Enough. Clark Pinnock. LC 79-3632. (Orig.). 1980. pap. 3.50 (ISBN 0-87784-623-5). Inter-Varsity.

Reason, Experience & the Moral Life. Benjamin S. Llamzon. LC 78-58444. 1978. pap. text ed. 10.25 (ISBN 0-8191-0534-1). U Pr of Amer.

Reason for Hope. Lane T. Dennis. 1976. 5.95 o.p. (ISBN 0-8007-0772-9). Revell.

Reason for Rivalry. Helen Tucker. (Regency Romance Ser). 1979. pap. 1.75 o.p. (ISBN 0-449-24139-4, Crest). Fawcett.

Reason I'm Not Quite Finished Tying My Shoes. Martha W. Hickman. LC 80-22237. 32p. (gr. k-3). 1981. 8.95g (ISBN 0-687-35595-8). Abingdon.

Reason in Ethics. Stephen Toulmin. 1950-1960. 35.00 (ISBN 0-521-06643-3); pap. 8.95x (ISBN 0-521-09116-0, 116). Cambridge U Pr.

Reason in History: A General Introduction to the Philosophy of History. Georg W. Hegel. Tr. by Robert S. Hartman. LC 53-4476. 1953. pap. 3.95 (ISBN 0-672-60200-8, LLA35). Bobbs.

Reason, Rule & Revolt in English Classicism. Francis Gallaway. 384p. 1966. pap. 5.75x (ISBN 0-8131-0105-0). U Pr of Ky.

Reason to Read. Ed. by George Sullivan. 120p. 1976. pap. 3.00 (ISBN 0-89492-000-6). Interbk Inc.

Reason Why. Elinor Glyn. (Barbara Cartland's Library of Love: Vol. 6). 246p. 1979. 12.95x (ISBN 0-7156-1382-0, Pub. by Duckworth England). Biblio Dist.

Reason Why. Robert A. Laidlaw. 48p. 1975. pap. 0.95 (ISBN 0-310-27112-6). Zondervan.

Reason Why the Closet-Man Is Never Sad. Russell Edson. LC 76-55942. (Wesleyan Poetry Program: Vol. 84). 1977. 10.00x (ISBN 0-8195-2084-5, Pub. by Wesleyan U Pr); pap. 4.95 (ISBN 0-8195-1084-X). Columbia U Pr.

Reasonable Belief: An Outline of the Christian Faith. Anthony Hanson & Richard Hanson. 300p. 1981. 24.95 (ISBN 0-19-213235-0). Oxford U Pr.

Reasonable Man: Trollope's Legal Fictions. Coral Lansbury. LC 80-8560. 260p. 1981. 16.50x (ISBN 0-691-06457-1). Princeton U Pr.

Reasonableness of Christianity. 311p. Repr. of 1927 ed. text ed. 4.95. Attic Pr.

Reasoned Argument in Social Science: Linking Research to Policy Ser. Eugene J. Meehan. LC 80-1198. (Illus.). 248p. 1981. lib. bdg. 27.50 (ISBN 0-313-22481-1, MRE). Greenwood.

Reasoning Ability of Mildly Retarded Learners. Herbert Goldstein & Marjorie T. Goldstein. LC 80-65500. 80p. (Orig.). 1980. pap. 6.25 (ISBN 0-86586-102-1). Coun Exc Child.

Reasoning & the Explanation of Action. David Milligan. 1980. text ed. 42.50x (ISBN 0-391-01802-7). Humanities.

Reasons & Faiths. Ninian Smart. 1958. text ed. 15.75x (ISBN 0-7100-3155-6). Humanities.

Reasons for Going It on Foot. William P. Root. LC 80-69369. Orig. Title: Wheel Turning on the Hub of the Sun. 80p. 1981. 10.00 (ISBN 0-689-11138-X); pap. 5.95 (ISBN 0-689-11164-9). Atheneum.

Reasons for Hope. W. H. Carroll et al. 203p. (Orig.). 1978. pap. 5.95 (ISBN 0-931888-01-8, Chris. Coll. Pr.). Christendom Pubns.

Reasons for Jewish Customs & Traditions. Abraham I. Sperling. Tr. by Abraham Matts. LC 68-31711. 1975. 10.00x (ISBN 0-8197-0184-X); pap. 6.95x (ISBN 0-8197-0008-8). Bloch.

Reasons of State. Shashi Tharoor. 250p. 1981. text ed. 17.50x (ISBN 0-7069-1275-6, Pub by Vikas India). Advent Bk.

Reasons of the Heart. John S. Dunne. 1978. 7.95 o.s.i. (ISBN 0-02-533950-8). Macmillan.

Reasons Why Place Names in Arizona Are So Named. Charles H. Newton. 48p. pap. 1.95 (ISBN 0-915030-25-X). Tecolote Pr.

Reassessing & Developing Management Skills: Perception, Vol. 1. Cabot Jaffee. 204p. 1981. 3-ring special binder 19.95 (ISBN 0-8436-0791-2). CBI Pub.

Reassessment of British Aid Policy: 1951-1970, Vol. 3. D. J. Morgan. (Official History of Colonial Development Ser.). 1980. text ed. cancelled (ISBN 0-391-01686-5). Humanities.

Reassessment of Inactivated Poliomyelitis Vaccine. Ed. by W. Hennessen & A. L. Van Wezel. (Developmentsin Biological Standardization Ser.: Vol. 47). (Illus.). 1981. soft cover 45.00 (ISBN 3-8055-1820-X). S Karger.

Reassessment of the Concept of Criminality: An Analysis of Criminal Behavior in Terms of Individual & Current Environment: the Application of a Stochastic Model. Eggert Petersen. LC 76-51327. 1977. 36.95 (ISBN 0-470-99034-1). Halsted Pr.

Rebecca. Daphne Du Maurier. 1948. 9.95 (ISBN 0-385-04380-5). Doubleday.

Rebecca. Daphne Du Maurier. 1971. pap. 2.50 (ISBN 0-380-00917-X, 48603). Avon.

Rebecca Notebook & Other Memories. Daphne Du Maurier. LC 80-652. 288p. 1980. 12.50 (ISBN 0-385-15885-8). Doubleday.

Rebecca of Sunnybrook Farm. Kate D. Wiggin. LC 75-32202. (Classics of Children's Literature, 1621-1932: Vol. 63). (Illus.). 1976. Repr. of 1902 ed. PLB 38.00 (ISBN 0-8240-2312-9). Garland Pub.

Rebecca of Sunnybrook Farm. Wiggins. (gr. 4-6). 1973. pap. 1.25 (ISBN 0-590-04487-7, Schol Pap). Schol Bk Serv.

Rebecca's World. Terry Nation. Tr. by Larry Learmonth. LC 76-39725. (Illus.). 114p. (gr. 3-5). 1977. 7.95 (ISBN 0-8149-0779-2). Vanguard.

Rebel America. Lillian Symes. LC 76-172100. (Civil Liberties in American History Ser.). 408p. 1972. Repr. of 1934 ed. lib. bdg. 37.50 (ISBN 0-306-70226-6). Da Capo.

Rebel & Statesman: The Vladimir Jabotinsky Story-the Early Years. Joseph E. Schechtman. (Return to Zion Ser.). (Illus.). 467p. 1980. Repr. of 1956 ed. lib. bdg. 27.50x (ISBN 0-87991-143-3). Porcupine Pr.

Rebel Guns. A. A. Baker. 192p. (YA) 1975. 5.95 (ISBN 0-685-52653-4, Avalon). Bouregy.

Rebel: His Moment & His Motives. J. Cole & F. Schepman. 1971. pap. 8.95 (ISBN 0-13-767368-X). P-H.

Rebel in Love. Veronica Howard. (Orig.). 1981. pap. 1.50 (ISBN 0-440-17423-6). Dell.

Rebel Jew. Henry Marshh. 160p. 1980. 19.50x (ISBN 0-7050-0078-8, Pub. by Skilton & Shaw England). State Mutual Bk.

Rebel Jew: Paul of Tarsus. Henry Marsh. 1980. cancelled (ISBN 0-7050-0078-8). Attic Pr.

Rebel Leadership: Commitment & Charisma in the Revolutionary Process. James V. Downton, Jr. LC 72-77283. 1973. 19.95 (ISBN 0-02-907560-2). Free Pr.

Rebel of Antares. Dray Prescot. (Science Fiction Ser.). 1980. pap. 1.95 (ISBN 0-87997-582-2, UJ1582). DAW Bks.

Rebel on a Rock. Nina Bawden. (gr. 7-12). 1980. pap. 1.50 (ISBN 0-440-97423-2, LFL). Dell.

Rebel Pride. Sylvia F. Sommerfield. 512p. (Orig.). 1980. pap. 2.75 (ISBN 0-89083-691-4). Zebra.

Rebel Prince. Henry W. Coray. (Spire Bks.). 1975. pap. 1.50 o.p. (ISBN 0-8007-8225-9). Revell.

Rebel Raider: A Biography of Admiral Semmes. Evangeline Davis & Burke Davis. (Illus.). (gr. 7-9). 1966. 4.95 o.p. (ISBN 0-397-30910-4). Lippincott.

Rebel Slave. Nancy Kelton. LC 76-46446. (When They Were Young Ser.). (Illus.). (gr. k-3). 1977. PLB 7.95 (ISBN 0-8172-0450-4). Raintree Pubs.

Rebel Yell. Leslie Ernenwein. 1979. pap. 1.25 (ISBN 0-505-51358-7). Tower Bks.

Rebelion De los Negros. Jose Sanchez-Boudy. LC 79-56654. (Coleccion Teatro Ser.). 78p. (Orig., Span.). Date not set. pap. 5.95 (ISBN 0-89729-247-2). Ediciones.

Rebellion & Democracy in Meiji Japan: A Study of Commoners in the Popular Rights Movement. Roger W. Bowen. 450p. 1980. 25.00x (ISBN 0-520-03665-4). U of Cal Pr.

Rebellion in India, 1857. F. W. Rawding. (Cambridge Introduction to the History of Mankind Ser.). (Illus.). (gr. 4-5). 1977. pap. 3.95 (ISBN 0-521-20683-9). Cambridge U Pr.

Rebellion Town: Williamsburg, 1776. Theodore Taylor. LC 73-10187. (Illus.). (gr. 5-9). 1973. 8.95 (ISBN 0-690-00019-7, TYC-J). T Y Crowell.

Rebellions in Canada. Morton & Desmond Morton. (gr. 6-10). 1980. PLB 6.90 (ISBN 0-531-00449-X). Watts.

Rebellious Century: 1830-1930. Charles Tilly et al. LC 74-16802. 1975. 18.50 (ISBN 0-674-74955-3). Harvard U Pr.

Rebellious Prophets: A Study of Messianic Movements in Indian Religions. Stephen Fuchs. 1965. 8.95x (ISBN 0-210-27136-1). Asia.

Rebellious Ranger: Rip Ford & the Old Southwest. W. J. Hughes. (Illus.). 300p. 1964. pap. 6.95 o.p. (ISBN 0-8061-1084-8). U of Okla Pr.

Rebellious Rebecca. Mary Ranger. (Starlight Ser.). (Illus.). (gr. 5-8). 1977. pap. 2.25 (ISBN 0-570-03612-7, 39-1100). Concordia.

Rebellious Thought of Albert Camus. V. John Bachman. LC 77-73998. 1979. 7.00 o.p. (ISBN 0-89430-008-3). Morgan-Pacific.

Rebels, No. 2. John Jakes. (Kent Family Chronicle). (Orig.). 1979. pap. 2.95 (ISBN 0-515-05894-7). Jove Pubns.

Rebels Against War: The American Peace Movement 1941-1960. Lawrence S. Wittner. LC 69-19464. (Contemporary American History Ser.: No. 1). 1969. 22.50x (ISBN 0-231-03220-X); pap. 6.00 o.p. (ISBN 0-231-08641-5). Columbia U Pr.

Rebels & Bureaucrats: China's December 9ers. John Israel & Donald Klein. LC 74-18757. 1976. 21.50x (ISBN 0-520-02861-9). U of Cal Pr.

Rebels & Democrats. E. P. Douglass. LC 77-160853. (Era of the American Revolution Ser.). 368p. 1971. Repr. of 1955 ed. 35.00 (ISBN 0-306-70402-1). Da Capo.

Rebels & Revolutionaries in North China, 1845-1945. Elizabeth J. Perry. LC 79-65179. (Illus.). xvi, 324p. 1980. 25.00x (ISBN 0-8047-1055-4). Stanford U Pr.

Rebels & Victims: The Fiction of Richard Wright & Bernard Malamud. Evelyn Avery. (National Univ. Pubns. Literary Criticism Ser.). 1979. 10.00 (ISBN 0-8046-9234-3). Kennikat.

Rebel's Rapture. Pamela Windsor. 1979. pap. 1.95 o.p. (ISBN 0-425-04129-8). Berkley Pub.

Rebels Under Sail: The American Navy During the Revolution. William M. Fowler, Jr. LC 75-38556. (Encore Edition). (Illus.). 384p. 1976. 6.95 o.p. (ISBN 0-684-15406-4, ScribT). Scribner.

Rebirth & Destiny of Israel. David Ben-Gurion. (Return to Zion Ser.). 539p. 1980. Repr. of 1954 ed. lib. bdg. 35.00x (ISBN 0-87991-139-5). Porcupine Pr.

Rebirth of a Nation: Wales 1880-1980. Kenneth O. Morgan. (History of Wales Ser.: Vol. VI). 1981. 25.00 (ISBN 0-19-821736-6). Oxford U Pr.

Rebirth of Images: The Making of Saint John's Apocalypse. Austin Farrar. 7.50 (ISBN 0-8446-0617-0). Peter Smith.

Rebirth of Norway's Peasantry: Folk Leader Hans Nielsen Hauge. Magnus Nodtuedt. 305p. 1965. octavo 5.95. Holmes.

Rebirth of the Mexican Petroleum Industry: Developmental Directions & Policy Implications. Edward J. Williams. LC 79-1546. 240p. 1979. 20.95 (ISBN 0-669-02908-4). Lexington Bks.

Rebound to Better Health: Includes Trampolining. Albert E. Carter. 59p. 1977. pap. 2.95 (ISBN 0-938302-10-8). NIRH.

Rebounding Aerobics. Morton Walker. Ed. by Frank Angelo. LC 80-83600. (Illus.). 240p. (Orig.). 1980. pap. 6.95 (ISBN 0-938302-19-1). NIRH.

Rebuilding Grain Reserves: Toward an International System. Philip H. Trezise. 1976. pap. 3.95 (ISBN 0-8157-8529-1). Brookings.

Rebuilding the Christian Commonwealth: New England Congregationalists & Foreign Missions, 1800-1830. John A. Andrew, III. LC 75-38214. 1976. 17.00x (ISBN 0-8131-1333-4). U Pr of Ky.

Rebuilding: When Your Relationship Ends. Bruce Fisher. LC 79-24440. 1981. pap. 5.95 (ISBN 0-915166-30-5). Impact Pubs Cal.

Recall & Recognition. J. Brown. LC 75-8770. 1976. 43.75 (ISBN 0-471-11229-1, Pub. by Wiley-Interscience). Wiley.

Recall the Poppies. Marjorie Bryant. (Illus.). 1979. pap. 6.00 o.p. (ISBN 0-931832-14-4). No Dead Lines.

Recapitulated Fall: A Comparative Study in Medieval Literature. Brian O. Murdoch. LC 73-91188. (Amsterdamer Publikationen Zur Sprache und Literatur: No. 11). 207p. (Orig.). 1974. pap. text ed. 20.00x (ISBN 90-6203-021-1). Humanities.

Recapitulation. Wallace Stegner. 1980. pap. 2.50 o.p. (ISBN 0-449-24263-3, Crest). Fawcett.

Receivers. Jay H. Smith. LC 74-23400. (Stars of the NFL Ser.). (gr. 4-12). 1975. PLB 7.95 (ISBN 0-87191-418-2). Creative Ed.

Receiving, Marking & Merchandise Handling. 1981. pap. 16.25 (ISBN 0-685-74623-2, SM86376). Natl Ret Merch.

Receiving Woman: Studies Inthe; Psychology & Theology Jof the Feminine0. Ann B. Ulanov. LC 80-26813. 1981. pap. 9.95 (ISBN 0-664-24360-6). Westminster.

Recent Advances in Addictions Research: Selected Proceedings from the Taos International Conference on Treatment of Addictive Disorders Held in the University of New Mexico 1979. Ed. by William Miller. 100p. 1980. 24.50 (ISBN 0-08-025771-2). Pergamon.

Recent Advances in Animal Nutrition. Ed. by W. Haresign. LC 80-41606. (Studies in the Agricultural & Food Sciences). (Illus.). 256p. 1980. text ed. 38.25 (ISBN 0-408-71013-6). Butterworths.

Recent Advances in Aquaculture. Ed. by James F. Muir & Ronald J. Roberts. 320p. 1980. 50.00x (Pub. by Croom Helm England). State Mutual Bk.

Recent Advances in Aquatic Mycology. E. B. Gareth Jones. LC 74-27179. 1976. 64.95 (ISBN 0-470-29176-1). Halsted Pr.

Recent Advances in Canadian Neuropsychopharmacology. Ed. by P. Grof. 132p. 1981. pap. 30.00 (ISBN 3-8055-1459-X). S Karger.

Recent Advances in Cancer Research: Cell Biology, Molecular Biology & Tumor Virology. Ed. by Robert C. Gallo. (Uniscience Ser.). 1977. Vol. 1, 280p. 64.95 (ISBN 0-8493-5138-3); Vol. 2, 240p. 59.95 (ISBN 0-8493-5139-1). CRC Pr.

Recent Advances in Cancer Treatment. Ed. by H. J. Tagnon & M. Staquet. LC 77-5277. (European Organization for Research & Treatment of Cancer (EORTC): Vol. 3). 1977. 32.00 (ISBN 0-89004-192-X). Raven.

Recent Advances in Cardiology, Vol. 8. John Hamer & Derek J. Rowlands. (Recent Advances Ser.). (Illus.). 360p. 1980. lib. bdg. 50.00 (ISBN 0-443-01995-9). Churchill.

Recent Advances in Cardiology, No. 8. Ed. by Rowlands & Humern. (R-A in Cardiology Ser.). (Illus.). 1981. text ed. price not set. Churchill.

Recent Advances in Clinical Immunology, No. 2. Ed. by R. A. Thompson. (Recent Advances Ser.). (Illus.). 361p. 1980. text ed. 49.00x (ISBN 0-443-01963-0). Churchill.

Recent Advances in Clinical Oncology: Proceedings of a Conference Held in Williamsburg, Va., Feb.-March 1977. Ed. by Tapan A. Hazra & Michael C. Beachley. LC 78-14907. (Progress in Clinical & Biological Research: Vol. 25). (Illus.). 1978. 19.00x (ISBN 0-8451-0025-4). A R Liss.

Recent Advances in Clinical Pharmacology, No. 2. Ed. by Paul Turner & David G. Shand. (Recent Advances Ser.). (Illus.). 178p. 1981. lib. bdg. 40.00 (ISBN 0-443-02183-X). Churchill.

Recent Advances in Clinical Virology. Gueh-Djen Hsiung. 128p. 1981. 19.95 (ISBN 0-03-059013-2); pap. 8.95 (ISBN 0-03-059014-0). Praeger.

Recent Advances in Clinical Virology, No. 2. Ed. by A. P. Waterson. (Illus.). 178p. 1980. text ed. 40.00 (ISBN 0-443-02094-9). Churchill.

Recent Advances in Dermatology, No. 5. Ed. by Arthur Rook & J. A. Savin. (Recent Advances Ser.). (Illus.). 325p. 1980. text ed. 45.00x (ISBN 0-443-01958-4). Churchill.

Recent Advances in Diagnostic Ultrasound. Ed. by Elias Rand. (Illus.). 160p. 1971. 15.50 (ISBN 0-398-02386-7). C C Thomas.

Recent Advances in Gastroenterology, No. 4. Ed. by Ian A. Bouchier. (Illus.). 352p. 1980. text ed. 39.50x (ISBN 0-443-01748-4). Churchill.

Recent Advances in Geomathematics: An International Symposium. Ed. by D. F. Merriam. 1978. text ed. 45.00 (ISBN 0-08-022095-9). Pergamon.

Recent Advances in Histopathology. 10th ed. Neville Woolf & P. P. Anthony. (Illus.). 1979. pap. text ed. 32.00 (ISBN 0-443-01783-2). Churchill.

Recent Advances in Lifeline Earthquake Engineering in Japan. Ed. by H. Shibata & T. Ariman. (PVP: No. 43). 158p. 1980. 24.00 (H00170). ASME.

Recent Advances in Liquid - Liquid Extraction. C. Hanson. 1971. 65.00 o.p. (ISBN 0-08-015682-7). Pergamon.

Recent Advances in Microcirculatory Research. Ed. by P. Gaehtgens. (Bibliotheca Anatomica Ser.: No. 20). (Illus.). xiv, 746p. 1980. soft cover 149.25 (ISBN 3-8055-2272-X). S Karger.

Recent Advances in Neuropsychopharmacology: Selected Papers from the 12th Congress of the Collegium Internationale Neuro-Psychopharmacologicum Goteborg, Sweden, 22-26 June, 1980. Ed. by B. Angrist et al. (Illus.). 422p. 1981. 110.00 (ISBN 0-08-026382-8). Pergamon.

Recent Advances in Orthopaedic Surgery in Infancy & Childhood. Association of Bone & Joint Surgeons. Ed. by Marshall R. Urist. (Clinical Orthopaedics Ser, Vol. 14). 1959. 15.00 (ISBN 0-685-14257-4). Lippincott.

Recent Advances in Paediatrics, No. 6. David Hull. (Recent Advances Ser.). (Illus.). 300p. 1981. lib. bdg. 42.50 (ISBN 0-443-02208-9). Churchill.

Recent Advances in Pediatric Nephrology. Ed. by J. F. Pascual & P. L. Calcagno. (Contributions to Nephrology Ser.: Vol. 27). (Illus.). vi, 150p. 1981. pap. 54.00 (ISBN 3-8055-1851-X). S Karger.

Recent Advances in Perinatal Pathology & Physiology: Ultra Sound in Biomedicine Research Ser, Vol. 4. D. N. White. (Research Studies Press Ser.). 264p. 1981. 54.00 (ISBN 0-471-27925-0, Pub. by Wiley-Interscience). Wiley.

Recent Advances in Phytochemistry: Structure, Biogenesis, Distribution. Phytochemical Society of North American Symposium. Ed. by V. C. Runeckles & T. J. Mabry. 1974. Vol. 7. 37.00 (ISBN 0-12-612407-8); Vol. 8. 37.00 (ISBN 0-12-612408-6). Acad Pr.

Recent Advances in Phytochemistry: Vol. 9, Phytochemistry in Disease & Medicine. Ed. by V. C. Runeckles. LC 67-26242. 299p. 1975. 32.50 (ISBN 0-306-34709-1, Plenum Pr). Plenum Pub.

Recent Advances in Reproduction & Regulation of Fertility: Proceedings. Symposium, New Delhi, October 1978. Ed. by G. P. Talwar. 1979. 73.25 (ISBN 0-444-80123-5, North Holland). Elsevier.

Recent Advances in Researches on Filariasis & Schistosomiasis in Japan. Ed. by Manabu Sasa. (Illus.). 1970. 39.50 (ISBN 0-8391-0032-9). Univ Park.

Recent Advances in Respiratory Medicine, No. 2. Ed. by D. C. Flenley. (Recent Advances Ser.). (Illus.). 272p. 1981. lib. bdg. 42.25 (ISBN 0-443-02012-4). Churchill.

Recent Advances in Rheumatology, Pt. Two: Clinical Features & Treatment. Watson W. Buchanan & Carson W. Dick. LC 75-22434. (Recent Advances Ser.). (Illus.). 240p. 1976. text ed. 30.00x (ISBN 0-443-01362-4). Churchill.

Recent Advances in Sexually Transmitted Diseases, No. 2. Ed. by Harris. 1981. text ed. 45.00 (ISBN 0-443-01817-0). Churchill.

Recent Advances in Steroid Biochemistry, Vols. 2-3. Ed. by J. R. Pasqualini. LC 75-4332. Vol. 2, 312p., 1975. pap. text ed. 55.00 (ISBN 0-08-019709-4); Vol. 3, 1977. pap. text ed. 50.00 (ISBN 0-08-021307-3). Pergamon.

Recent Advances in Surgery, No. 10. Ed. by Selwyn Taylor. (Illus.). 352p. 1980. text ed. 27.50 (ISBN 0-443-01966-5). Churchill.

Recent Advances in the Analytical Chemistry of the Noble Metals. F. E. Beamish & J. C. Van Loon. LC 77-166010. 527p. 1972. text ed. 105.00 (ISBN 0-08-016751-9). Pergamon.

Recent Advances in the Developmental Biology of Central Nervous System Malformations. Ed. by Ntinos C. Myrianthopoulos & Daniel Bergsma. LC 79-4947. (Alan R. Liss Ser.: Vol. 15, No. 3). 1979. 16.00 (ISBN 0-8451-1026-8). March of Dimes.

Recent Advances in the Diagnosis & Treatment of Pituitary Tumors. Ed. by John A. Linfoot. LC 78-64817. 1979. text ed. 44.50 (ISBN 0-89004-365-5). Raven.

Recent Advances in the Field of Crystallization & Fusion of Polymers. J. P. Mercier & R. Legras. (Journal of Polymer Science Symposia). 1977. 14.95 (ISBN 0-471-04425-3, Pub. by Wiley-Interscience). Wiley.

Recent Advances of Avian Endocrinology: Proceedings of a Satellite Symposium of the 28th International Congress of Physiological Sciences, Budapest, Hungary, 1980. Ed. by G. Pethes et al. LC 80-42007. (Advances in Physiological Sciences: Vol. 33). (Illus.). 450p. 1981. 50.00 (ISBN 0-08-027355-6). Pergamon.

Recent Advances of the Chronobiology of Allergy & Immunology: Symposium on Chronobiology in Allergy & Immunology, Israel, 1979. Ed. by M. H. Smolensky & A. Reinberg. LC 80-41028. (Illus.). 350p. 1980. 50.00 (ISBN 0-08-025891-3). Pergamon.

Recent Advances on Pain: Pathophysiology & Clinical Aspects. Ed. by John J. Bonica et al. (Illus.). 352p. 1974. 32.50 (ISBN 0-398-02964-4). C C Thomas.

Recent Advances on the Lacrimal System. Yamaguchi. Date not set. 47.50 (ISBN 0-89352-140-X). Masson Pub.

Recent Advences in Biological Nitrogen Fixation. Ed. by N. S. Subba Rao. 500p. 1980. text ed. 38.95x (ISBN 0-8419-5825-4). Holmes & Meier.

Recent American History, 2 vols. Ralph F. De Bedts. 1973. Vol. 1. pap. text ed. 11.50x (ISBN 0-686-66959-2); Vol. 2. (ISBN 0-256-01414-0); pap. text ed. (ISBN 0-256-01510-4). Dorsey.

Recent Analytical Developments in the Petroleum Industry. Ed. by D. R. Hodges. LC 74-23137. 337p. 1974. 44.95 (ISBN 0-470-40208-3). Halsted Pr.

Recent Archaeological Excavations in Europe. Ed. by Rupert Bruce-Mitford. 1975. 35.00x o.p. (ISBN 0-7100-7963-X). Routledge & Kegan.

Recent Conservative Political Thought: American Perspectives. Russell G. Fryer. LC 78-68568. 1979. pap. text ed. 11.75 (ISBN 0-8191-0694-1). U Pr of Amer.

Recent Contributions to Geochemistry & Analytical Chemistry. Ed. by A. I. Tugarinov. Tr. by D. Slutzkin from Rus. LC 74-8165. 694p. 1976. 79.95 (ISBN 0-470-89228-5). Halsted Pr.

Recent Developements in Research on Nitrogen Fertilizers for Rice. (IRRI Research Paper Ser.: No. 49). 11p. 1981. pap. 5.00 (ISBN 0-686-69535-6, R 119, IRRI). Unipub.

Recent Developments in Classical Wave Scattering: Focus on the T-Matrix Approach. International Symposium on Recent Developments in Classical Wave Scattering, Ohio State Univ., Columbus, 1979. Ed. by V. V. Varadan & V. K. Varadan. (Illus.). 670p. 1980. 70.00 (ISBN 0-08-025096-3). Pergamon.

Recent Developments in High-Energy Physics. Ed. by Behram Kursunoglu et al. (Studies in the Natural Sciences Ser.: Vol. 17). 320p. 1980. 39.50 (ISBN 0-306-40565-2, Plenum Pr). Plenum Pub.

Recent Developments in Regional Science. R. Funck. (Karlsruhe Papers in Regional Science). 153p. 1980. pap. text ed. 10.00x (ISBN 0-85086-034-2, Pub. by Pion). Methuen Inc.

Recent Developments in Separation Science, 5 vols. Ed. by Norman N. Li. LC 72-88417. (Uniscience Ser.). Vol. 1. 54.95 (ISBN 0-8493-5029-8); Vol. 2, 1972, 292p. 59.95 (ISBN 0-8493-5030-1); Vol. 3A, 1977, 224p. 55.95 (ISBN 0-8493-5481-1); Vol. 3B, 1977, 200p. 49.95 (ISBN 0-8493-5482-X); Vol. 4, 1978, 248p. 58.95 (ISBN 0-8493-5483-8). CRC Pr.

Recent Developments in the Design & Construction of Piles. Institute of Civil of Engineers. 380p. 1980. 80.00x (ISBN 0-7277-0082-0, Pub. by Telford England). State Mutual Bk.

Recent Developments in Vision Research. Armed Forces - NRC Committee On Vision. 1965. pap. 5.00 (ISBN 0-309-01272-4). Natl Acad Pr.

Recent Economic Changes. D. A. Wells. LC 69-16654. (American Scene Ser.). 1970. Repr. of 1889 ed. lib. bdg. 49.50 (ISBN 0-306-71143-5). Da Capo.

Recent Education from Local Sources. Malcolm Seabourne. 1967. text ed. 5.50x (ISBN 0-7100-4204-3); pap. text ed. 3.00x (ISBN 0-7100-4208-6). Humanities.

Recent Ideals of American Art. George W. Sheldon. LC 75-28882. (Art Experience in Late 19th Century America Ser.: Vol. 16). (Illus.). 1976. Repr. of 1890 ed. lib. bdg. 87.00 (ISBN 0-8240-2240-8). Garland Pub.

Recent Issues in World Developement: A Collection of Survey Articles. Paul Streeten. (Illus.). 450p. 1981. 115.00 (ISBN 0-08-026812-9). Pergamon.

Recent Mammals of the World: A Synopsis of Families. Ed. by Sydney Anderson & J. Knox Jones, Jr. (Illus.). 1967. 24.95 (ISBN 0-8260-0440-7, Pub. by Wiley-Interscience). Wiley.

Recent Mollusks Gulf Coast. C. J. Maury. 1971. Repr. 5.00 (ISBN 0-87710-361-5). Paleo Res.

Recent Music & Musicians As Described in the Diaries & Correspondence of Ignatz Moscheles. Ignatz Moscheles. LC 73-125057. (Music Ser). 1970. Repr. of 1873 ed. lib. bdg. 32.50 (ISBN 0-306-70022-0). Da Capo.

Recent Orientations of Regional Analysis in French Geography. Ed. by E. Juillard. 1976. pap. text ed. 28.00 (ISBN 0-08-019970-4). Pergamon.

Recent Progress in Cell Biology: Leukocytes & Platelets. Ed. by O. N. Ulutin. (Bibliotheca Haematologica: No. 45). (Illus.). 1978. pap. 56.50 (ISBN 3-8055-2897-3). S Karger.

Recent Progress in Combinatorics: Proceedings. Ed. by W. T. Tutte. 1969. 48.50 (ISBN 0-12-705150-3). Acad Pr.

Recent Progress in Hormone Research, Vol. 37. Ed. by Roy Greep. (Serial Publication). 1981. price not set (ISBN 0-12-571137-9). Acad Pr.

Recent Progress in Hormone Research: Proceedings. Laurentian Hormone Conferences. Ed. by Gregory Pincus. Incl. Vols. 1-5. 1947-50. Set (ISBN 0-685-30520-1). Vol. 1. 47.50 (ISBN 0-12-571101-8); Vol. 2. 47.50 (ISBN 0-12-571102-6); Vol. 3. 48.50 (ISBN 0-12-571103-4); Vol. 4. 48.50 (ISBN 0-12-571104-2); Vol. 5. 48.50 (ISBN 0-12-571105-0); Vols. 6-11. 1951-55. 48.50 ea.; Vol. 6. o.s.i (ISBN 0-12-571106-9). Vol. 7 (ISBN 0-12-571107-7). Vol. 8 (ISBN 0-12-571108-5). Vol. 9 (ISBN 0-12-571109-3). Vol. 10 (ISBN 0-12-571110-7). Vol. 11 (ISBN 0-12-571111-5); Vol. 12. 1956. 48.50 (ISBN 0-12-571112-3); Vol. 13. 1957. 48.50 (ISBN 0-12-571113-1); Vols. 14-15. 1958-59. 48.50 ea. Vol. 14 (ISBN 0-12-571114-X). Vol. 15 (ISBN 0-12-571115-8); Vol. 16. 1960. 48.50 (ISBN 0-12-571116-6); Vols. 17-18. 1961-62. 48.50 ea. Vol. 17 (ISBN 0-12-571117-4). Vol. 18 (ISBN 0-12-571118-2); Vol. 19. 1963. 54.00 (ISBN 0-12-571119-0); Vol. 20. 1964. 54.00 (ISBN 0-12-571120-4); Vol. 21. 1965. 54.00 (ISBN 0-12-571121-2); Vol. 22. 1966. 54.00 (ISBN 0-12-571122-0); Vol. 23. 1967. 61.00 (ISBN 0-12-571123-9); Vol. 24. Ed. by E. B. Astwood. 1968. 61.00 (ISBN 0-12-571124-7); Vol. 25. 1969. 61.00 (ISBN 0-12-571125-5); Vols. 26-27. 1970-71. 61.00 ea. Vol. 26 (ISBN 0-12-571126-3). Vol. 27 (ISBN 0-12-571127-1); Vol. 28. 1972. 58.00 (ISBN 0-12-571128-X); Vol. 29. 1973. 61.00 (ISBN 0-12-571129-8); Vol. 32. Ed. by Roy O. Greep. 1976. 61.00 (ISBN 0-12-571132-8); Vol. 33. Ed. by Roy O. Greep. 1977. 52.50 (ISBN 0-12-571133-6); Vol. 34. Ed. by Roy O. Greep. 1978. 51.50 (ISBN 0-12-571134-4). Acad Pr.

Recent Progress in Surface & Membrane Science. Ed. by J. F. Danielli et al. Incl. Vol. 4. 1971. 53.50 (ISBN 0-12-571804-7); Vol. 5. 1972. 53.50 (ISBN 0-12-571805-5); Vol. 6. 1973. 53.50 (ISBN 0-12-571806-3); Vol. 7. 1973. 153.50 (ISBN 0-12-571807-1); Vol. 8. 1974. 53.50 (ISBN 0-12-571808-X); Vol. 9. 1975. 53.50 (ISBN 0-12-571809-8); lib ed. 68.00 (ISBN 0-12-571874-8); microfiche 38.50 (ISBN 0-12-571875-6); Vol. 10. 1976. 53.50 (ISBN 0-12-571810-1); Vol. 11. 1976. 53.50 (ISBN 0-12-571811-X); lib. ed 68.00 (ISBN 0-12-571878-0); microfiche 38.50 (ISBN 0-12-571879-9). Orig. Title: Progress in Surface & Membrane Science. Acad Pr.

Recent Research on Ben Jonson. Renu Juneja et al. (Salzburg Studies in English Literature, Jacobean Drama Studies: No.76). 1978. pap. text ed. 25.00x (ISBN 0-391-01441-2). Humanities.

Recent Research on Schizophrenia. Ed. by P. Solomon & B. C. Glueck. 1964. pap. 4.00 o.p. (ISBN 0-685-24874-7, 019). Am Psychiatric.

Recent Results in Peptide Hormone & Androgenic Steroid Research. Ed. by F. A. Laszlo. (Illus.). 325p. 1979. 30.00x (ISBN 963-05-2292-6). Intl Pubns Serv.

Recent Results in Stochastic Programming: Proceedings. Ed. by P. Kall & A. Prekopa. (Lecture Notes in Economics & Mathematical Systems: Vol. 179). (Illus.). 256p. 1980. pap. 19.00 (ISBN 0-387-10013-X). Springer-Verlag.

Recent Sediments of Southeast Texas-A Field Guide to the Brazos Alluvial & Deltaic Plains & the Galveston Barrier Island Complex. H. A. Bernard et al. 132p. 1970. Repr. 5.00 (GB 11). Bur Econ Geology.

Recent Student Flows in Higher Education. Ignace Hecquet et al. 189p. (Orig.). 1976. pap. text ed. 5.00 (ISBN 0-89192-313-6). Interbk Inc.

Recent Studies in Britain Based on the Work of Jean Piaget: 1970 Report of 1960 Edition. E. A. Lunzer. 1970. pap. text ed. 5.00x (ISBN 0-85633-024-8, NFER). Humanities.

Recent Studies on Rice Tungro Disease at IRRI. (IRRI Research Paper Ser.: No. 1). 11p. 1976. pap. 5.00 (R041, IRRI). Unipub.

Recent Trends & Concepts in Geography, 3 vols. Ed. by R. B. Mandal & V. N. Sinha. Incl. Vol. 1. 1980 (ISBN 0-391-01820-5); Vol. 2. 1980 (ISBN 0-391-01821-3); Vol. 3. 1980 (ISBN 0-391-01822-1). text ed. 27.75x ea. Humanities.

Recent Trends in Monopoly in Great Britain. G. Walshe. (Illus.). 132p. 1974. 16.95x (ISBN 0-521-09863-7). Cambridge U Pr.

Recent Trends in the Cooperative Movement in India. R. B. Tyagi. 15.50x o.p. (ISBN 0-210-22596-3). Asia.

Reception of Classical German Literature in England, 1760-1860: A Documentary History from Contemporary Periodicals, 10 vols. Ed. & intro. by John Boening. Incl. Vol. 1. General Introduction & Reviews from 1760 to 1813 (ISBN 0-8240-0990-8); Vol. 2. Reviews from 1813 to 1835 (ISBN 0-8240-0991-6); Vol. 3. Reviews from 1835 to 1860 (ISBN 0-8240-0992-4); Vol. 4. Authors from Bodmer to Klopstock (ISBN 0-8240-0993-2); Vol. 5. Authors from Lavater to Novalis (ISBN 0-8240-0994-0); Vol. 6. The Reception of Early German Romantics: Richter, the Brothers Schlegel, Tieck & Hoffmann (ISBN 0-8240-0995-9); Vol. 7. General Critical Articles on Goethe & Reviews Which Discuss Goethe & Schiller Together, Arranged in Order of Appearance (ISBN 0-8240-0996-7); Vol. 8. Reviews of Werther, Goethe's Early Works, His Poems & Faust (ISBN 0-8240-0997-5); Vol. 9. The Works of Goethe's Midcareer, Wilhelm Meister & Such Works As Dichtung und Wahrheit, Etc (ISBN 0-8240-0998-3); Vol. 10. The English Reception of Specific Works of Schiller, from the Early Plays to the Historical Works (ISBN 0-8240-0999-1). 1977. Set. lib. bdg. 110.00 each. Garland Pub.

Reception of Scott's Poetry by His Correspondents, 2 vols. J. H. Alexander. (SSEL Romantic Reassessment Ser.: No. 84). (Orig.). 1979. pap. text ed. 25.00x ea. Humanities.

Reception of Unconventional Science by the Scientific Community. Ed. by Seymour H. Mauskopf. 1979. lib. bdg. 17.00x (ISBN 0-89158-297-5). Westview.

Receptor Binding Studies in Adrenergic Pharmacology. Lewis T. Williams & Robert J. Lefkowitz. LC 78-3011. 1978. 19.50 (ISBN 0-89004-164-4). Raven.

Receptors & Hormone Action, Vol. 1. Ed. by B. W. O'Malley & L. Birnbaumer. 1978. 49.00 (ISBN 0-12-526301-5); by subscription 42.25 (ISBN 0-685-79544-6). Acad Pr.

Receptors & Human Disease. Melvin Blecher & Robert S. Barr. (Illus.). 350p. 1981. write for info. (0609-6). Williams & Wilkins.

Receptors for Neurotransmitters & Peptide Hormones. Ed. by Giancarlo Pepeu et al. (Advances in Biological Psychopharmacology Ser.: Vol. 21). 1980. text ed. 56.00 (ISBN 0-89004-408-2). Raven.

Recetas Norteamericanas En Ingles Y Espanol. 168p. 1980. 5.95 (ISBN 0-686-27595-0). Lang Svcs CA.

Rechargable Batteries: Advances Since 1977. Ed. by Robert W. Graham. LC 80-13152. (Energy Technology Review Ser. No. 55; Chemical Technology Review Ser. No.160). 452p. 1980. 54.00 (ISBN 0-8155-0802-6). Noyes.

Recherche de Dieu, Livre Premier. Tr. by Robert Roch from Eng. (Fr.). 1978. pap. 10.00 (ISBN 0-87604-111-X). ARE Pr.

Recherches Philosophiques Sur le Droit De Propriete Considere Dans la Nature, Pour Servir De Premier Chapitre a la Theorie Des Loix De M. Linguet, Par un Jeune Philosophe. Jean-Pierre Brissot. (Fr.). 1977. lib. bdg. 21.25x o.p. (ISBN 0-8287-0143-1); pap. text ed. 11.25x o.p. (ISBN 0-685-74932-0). Clearwater Pub.

Recherches Sur la Population Des Generalities D'auvergne, De Lyon, De Rouen et De Queleques Provinces et Villes Du Royaume. Messance. (Principal French Demographic Works of the 18th Century Ser.). (Fr.). 1976. lib. bdg. 60.00x o.p. (ISBN 0-8287-0609-3); pap. text ed. 50.00x o.p. (ISBN 0-685-71503-5). Clearwater Pub.

Recherches Sur le Surreslisme, No. 2. Ed. by F. Drijkoningen. 1978. 19.25x (ISBN 0-391-02035-8). Humanities.

Recherches sur les Ceramiaceae de la Mediterranee. Genevieve Feldmann-Mazoyer. 1977. pap. text ed. 88.00x (ISBN 3-87429-120-0). Lubrecht & Cramer.

Recherches Sur les Conditions De la Connaissance Essai D'une Theoretique Pure. Gaston Berger. Ed. by Maurice Natanson. LC 78-66755. (Phenomenology Ser.: Vol. 1). 194p. 1979. lib. bdg. 20.00 (ISBN 0-8240-9569-3). Garland Pub.

Recherches Sur les Cours Laiques Du Xe Au XIIIe Siecle. Yvonne Bongert. LC 80-1996. 1981. Repr. of 1949 ed. 34.00 (ISBN 0-404-18554-1). AMS Pr.

Recipes & Reminiscences of New Orleans. Illus. by Emery Clark. (Illus.). 237p. (Orig.). 1971. pap. 6.95 (ISBN 0-9604718-0-4). Old Ursuline.

Recipes for Busy People. Ed. by Sylvia Schur. (Orig.). 1980. pap. 2.50 (ISBN 0-446-91542-4). Warner Bks.

Recipes for Healthier Childern. rev. ed. Edith Redman. 1977. pap. 4.95 o.s.i. (ISBN 0-7715-9329-5). Vanguard.

Recipes for Healthier Families. Edith Redmen. 208p. 1976. 9.95 o.s.i. (ISBN 0-7715-9940-4). Vanguard.

Recipes for Life. Ann Wigmore. Ed. by Betsy Kimball. (Illus.). 181p. pap. text ed. 7.95. Hippocrates.

Recipes for Runners: A Complete Nutrition Guide for Runners. Craig Whitley. (Illus.). 272p. 1981. cancelled (ISBN 0-913276-34-0). Stone Wall Pr.

Recipes from a Brooklyn Childhood. Sidney Gross & Sue Gross. 1979. pap. write for info. cancelled (ISBN 0-917234-14-6). Kitchen Harvest.

Recipes from a Country Kitchen. Marika H. Tenison. 1979. 14.95x (ISBN 0-8464-0063-4). Beekman Pubs.

Recipes from an Old Farmhouse. Alison Uttley. (Illus., Orig.). 1973. pap. 3.95 (ISBN 0-571-10178-X, Pub. by Faber & Faber). Merrimack Bk Serv.

Reciprocity & the Position of Women: Anthropological Papers. J. Van Baal. 128p. 1976. pap. text ed. 9.25x (ISBN 90-232-1320-3). Humanities.

Recit fantastique: La Poetique de l'incertain. new ed. Irene Bessiere. (Collection Themes et Textes). 256p. (Orig., Fr.). 1974. pap. 6.75 (ISBN 2-03-035023-0, 2674). Larousse.

Recitation & Interpretation of the Qur'an. M. A. Quasem. 121p. 1980. 9.95x (ISBN 0-89955-206-4, Pub. by M A Quasem Malaysia); pap. 6.95x (ISBN 0-89955-207-2). Intl Schol Bk Serv.

Recits de Resurrection des Morts dans le Nouveau Testament. G. Rochais. LC 79-41615. (Society for New Testament Studies Monographs). 240p. (Fr.). Date not set. price not set (ISBN 0-521-22381-4). Cambridge U Pr.

Reckless Era. James M. Bryant. 1968. pap. 5.50 (ISBN 0-686-27961-1). J M Bryant.

Reckless Homicide: Ford's Pinto Trial. Lee P. Strobel. (Illus.). 220p. 1980. 4.95 (ISBN 0-89708-022-X). And Bks.

Reckless Masquerade. Rachelle Edwards. 1977. pap. 1.50 o.p. (ISBN 0-449-23302-2, Crest). Fawcett.

Reckoning with Slavery: Critical Essays in the Quantitative History of American Negro Slavery. Paul A. David et al. LC 75-38098. 352p. 1976. 19.95 (ISBN 0-19-502034-0); pap. text ed. 5.95x (ISBN 0-19-502033-2). Oxford U Pr.

Reclaiming Functional Communication. L. K. Lovestedt. 1980. pap. 19.75 spiral (ISBN 0-398-03994-1). C C Thomas.

Reclaiming the West: The Coal Industry & Surface Mined Lands. Daniel P. Wiener. LC 80-81777. 1980. pap. 75.00 (ISBN 0-918780-16-0). Inform.

Reclassification of the Sphecinae, with a Revision of the Nearctic Species of the Tribes Sceliphronini & Sphecini (Hymenoptera, Sphecidae) R. M. Bohart & A. S. Menke. (U. C. Publ. in Entomology: Vol. 30.2). 1963. pap. 6.50x (ISBN 0-520-09098-5). U of Cal Pr.

Recognition & Evaluation of Uraniferous Areas. (Illus.). 1977. pap. 34.25 (ISBN 92-0-041077-4, ISP450, IAEA). Unipub.

Recognition of Health Hazards in Industry: A Review of Materials & Processes. William A. Burgess. 372p. 1981. 28.00 (ISBN 0-471-06339-8, Pub. by Wiley-Interscience). Wiley.

Recognition of Henry David Thoreau: Selected Criticism Since 1848. Ed. by Wendell Glick. LC 69-15845. 1969. 9.50 o.p. (ISBN 0-472-37200-9). U of Mich Pr.

Recognizable Patterns of Human Deformation: Identification & Management of Mechanical Effects on Morphogenesis. David W. Smith. (Illus.). 240p. 1981. text ed. write for info. (ISBN 0-7216-8401-7). Saunders.

Recognizing Points of View: Whose Mind; Where's He Standing? Walter Pauk. (Skill at a Time Ser). 64p. (gr. 9-12). 1975. pap. text ed. 2.40x (ISBN 0-89061-028-2). Jamestown Pubs.

Recognizing Tone: Advanced Level. James A. Giroux & Glenn R. Williston. Ed. by Edward Spargo. (Comprehension Skills Ser). (Illus.). (gr. 9-12). 1974. pap. text ed. 2.40x (ISBN 0-89061-017-7). Jamestown Pubs.

Recognizing Tone: Middle Level. Glenn R. Williston. (Comprehension Skill Ser.). (Illus.). 64p. (gr. 6-8). 1976. pap. text ed. 2.40x (ISBN 0-89061-069-X, CB6M). Jamestown Pubs.

Recognizing Traits of Character: How Does the Author Build His Characters? Walter Pauk. (Skill at a Time Ser). 64p. (gr. 9-12). 1975. pap. text ed. 2.40x (ISBN 0-89061-027-4). Jamestown Pubs.

Recoil. Brian Garfield. 1978. pap. 1.95 o.p. (ISBN 0-449-23552-1, Crest). Fawcett.

Recollections & Essays. Leo Tolstoy. Tr. by Aylmer Maude. (World's Classics Ser). 10.95 (ISBN 0-19-250459-2). Oxford U Pr.

Recollections & Opinions of an Old Pioneer. Peter H. Burnett. LC 76-87661. (American Scene Ser.). 1969. Repr. of 1880 ed. lib. bdg. 45.00 (ISBN 0-306-71765-4). Da Capo.

Recollections & Reflections. James R. Planche. (Music Reprint, 1978 Ser.). (Illus.). 1978. Repr. of 1901 ed. lib. bdg. 42.50 (ISBN 0-306-79501-9). Da Capo.

Recollections of a Civil War Quartermaster. William G. Le Duc. LC 63-64537. 167p. 1963. 3.75 (ISBN 0-685-47098-9). Minn Hist.

Recollections of a Lifetime, or Men & Things I Have Seen. Samuel G. Goodrich. LC 67-23886. 1967. Repr. of 1857 ed. 20.00 (ISBN 0-8103-3041-5). Gale.

Recollections of Alexander H. Stephens: His Diary Kept When a Prisoner at Fort Warren, Boston Harbor, 1865. Ed. by Myrta L. Avary. LC 76-124914. (American Public Figures Ser). 1971. Repr. of 1910 ed. lib. bdg. 55.00 (ISBN 0-306-71984-3). Da Capo.

Recollections of an Egyptologist. Dows Dunham. (Illus.). 1972. pap. 3.25 (ISBN 0-87846-082-9). Mus Fine Arts Boston.

Recollections of an Irish Rebel. J. Devoy. 508p. 1969. Repr. of 1929 ed. 25.00x (ISBN 0-7165-0045-0, Pub. by Irish Academic Pr Ireland). Biblio Dist.

Recollections of an Old Musician. Thomas Ryan. (Music Reprint Ser.). 1979. Repr. of 1899 ed. lib. bdg. 29.50 (ISBN 0-306-79521-3). Da Capo.

Recollections of Baron Gros's Embassy to China & Japan in 1857 to 1858. Marquis De Moges. 1972. Repr. of 1860 ed. 30.00x (ISBN 0-686-28318-X, Pub. by Irish Academic Pr). Biblio Dist.

Recollections of Charley Russell. Frank B. Linderman. Ed. by H. G. Merriam. LC 63-18074. 148p. 1963. 9.95 (ISBN 0-8061-0582-8). U of Okla Pr.

Recollections of Fenians & Fenianism, 2 vols. in 1. John O'Leary. 248p. 1968. Repr. of 1896 ed. 20.00x (ISBN 0-7165-0606-8, Pub. by Irish Academic Pr Ireland). Biblio Dist.

Recollections of Gustav Mahler. Natalie Bauer-Lechner. Ed. by P. Franklin. Tr. by D. Newlin from Ger. LC 80-834. (Illus.). 241p. 1980. 22.50 (ISBN 0-521-23572-3). Cambridge U Pr.

Recollections of Ninety-Two Years 1824-1916. Elizabeth A. Meriwether. (Illus.). 262p. 1958. 8.50x o.p. (ISBN 0-87402-011-5). U of Tenn Pr.

Recollections of Rubens. Jakob Burckhardt. Ed. by Sydney J. Freedberg. LC 77-18674. (Connoisseurship Criticism & Art History Ser.: Vol. 4). 374p. 1979. lib. bdg. 33.00 (ISBN 0-8240-3261-6). Garland Pub.

Recollections of Seventy Years. Franklin B. Sanborn. LC 67-23889. 1967. Repr. of 1909 ed. 24.00 (ISBN 0-8103-3045-8). Gale.

Recollections of the Last Ten Years in the Valley of the Mississippi. 2nd ed. Timothy Flint. LC 68-24891. (American Scene Ser). 1968. Repr. of 1826 ed. lib. bdg. 39.50 (ISBN 0-306-71136-2). Da Capo.

Recollections of the Powys Brothers. Ed. by Belinda Humfrey. 1980. text ed. 26.00x (ISBN 0-7206-0547-4). Humanities.

Recollections of Woodrow Wilson. Winthrop M. Daniels. 1944. 17.50x (ISBN 0-685-89776-1). Elliots Bks.

Recombinant DNA: A Scrapbook Edited by James D. Watson & John Tooze. Ed. by James D. Watson & John Tooze. (Illus.). 1981. text ed. price not set (ISBN 0-7167-1292-X). W H Freeman.

Recombinant DNA & Genetic Experimentation: Proceedings. Conference on Recombinant DNA, Committee on Genetic Experimentation (COGENE) & the Royal Society of London, Wye College, Kent, UK, April, 1979. Ed. by Joan Morgan & W. J. Whelan. LC 79-40962. (Illus.). 334p. 1979. 61.00 (ISBN 0-08-024427-0). Pergamon.

Recombinant DNA Battle. David A. Jackson & Stephen P. Stitch. 1979. text ed. 25.95 (ISBN 0-13-767442-2). P-H.

Recombinant DNA: Readings from Scientific American. Intro. by David Freifelder. LC 77-29159. (Illus.). 1978. pap. text ed. 8.95x (ISBN 0-7167-0092-1). W H Freeman.

Recombinant Molecules: Impact on Science & Society. Ed. by Roland F. Beers, Jr. & Edward G. Bassett. LC 77-5276. (Miles International Symposium Ser: 10th). 1977. 49.00 (ISBN 0-89004-131-8). Raven.

Recommendation Concerning Fire Safety Requirements for Cargo Ships. 25p. 1976. 7.00 (IMCO). Unipub.

Recommendation on Basic Principles & Operational Guidance Relating to Navigational Watchkeeping. 12p. 1974. pap. 7.75 (ISBN 92-801-1032-2, IMCO 62, IMCO). Unipub.

Recommendations Concerning Reservoirs. 1967. pap. 2.50 (ISBN 92-3-100664-9, U520, UNESCO). Unipub.

Recommendations de la Comision Internationale de Protection Radiologique. Ed. by A. Duchene & H. Jammet. (ICRP Publicaton Ser.: No. 26). 63p. 1980. pap. 15.75 (ISBN 0-08-025529-9). Pergamon.

Recommendations for Chilled Storage of Perishable Produce. 148p. 1980. pap. 11.00 (ISBN 0-686-60076-2, IIR 63, IIR). Unipub.

Recommendations for Symbolism & Nomenclature for Mass Spectroscopy. new ed. Ed. by J. H. Beynon. 1978. pap. text ed. 6.60 o.p. (ISBN 0-08-022368-0). Pergamon.

Recommendations for the Presentation of Infrared Absorption Spectra in Data Collections-A: Condensed Phases. Ed. by D. E. Becker. 1978. pap. text ed. 10.00 (ISBN 0-08-022376-1). Pergamon.

Recommendations: Manual on Early Medical Treatment of Possible Radiation Injury. (IAEA Safety Ser.: No. 47). 1979. pap. 14.00 (ISBN 92-0-123278-0, ISP506, IAEA). Unipub.

Recommendations on International Effluent Standards & Guidelines for Performance Tests for Sewage Treatment Plants. 9p. 1977. 5.50 (IMCO). Unipub.

Recommendations on International Performance & Test Specifications for Oily-Water Separating Equipment & Oil Content Meters. 36p. 1978. 8.25 (IMCO). Unipub.

Recommendations on Statistics of International Migration. (Statistical Papers Ser. M: No. 58). 73p. 1979. pap. 6.00 (ISBN 0-686-68967-4, UN79/17/18, UN). Unipub.

Recommendations on the Safe Use of Pesticides in Ships. 14p. 1973. 5.50 (IMCO). Unipub.

Recommended Dietary Allowances. 9th ed. Dietary Allowances Comm. & Food & Nutrition Board. (Illus.). 1980. pap. 6.00 (ISBN 0-686-64858-7). Natl Acad Pr.

Recommended Dietary Allowances. 8th ed. Dietary Allowances Committee & Food & Nutrition Board. LC 74-5170. (Illus.). 136p. 1974. pap. 4.25 o.p. (ISBN 0-309-02216-9). Natl Acad Pr.

Recommended Dietary Allowances: Ninth Edition. 1980. 6.00 (ISBN 0-309-02941-4). Natl Acad Pr.

Recommended Instrumentation for Uranium & Thorium Exploration. (Technical Reports Ser., No. 158). 104p. (Orig.). 1974. pap. 10.00 (ISBN 92-0-145074-5, IAEA). Unipub.

Recommended International Code of Hygienic Practice for Molluscan Shellfish. 22p. 1980. pap. 5.25 (ISBN 92-5-100893-0, F1949, FAO). Unipub.

Recommended International Code of Practice for Shrimps or Prawns. 1980. pap. 5.25 (ISBN 92-5-100915-5, F1950, FAO). Unipub.

Recommended International Code of Practice for the Processing & Handling of Quick Frozen Foods: Appendix One Method for Checking Product Temperature. 8p. 1980. pap. 3.00 (ISBN 92-5-100697-0, F1426, FAO). Unipub.

Recommended International Standard for Cocoa Powder (Cocoas) & Dry Sugar Mixtures. 8p. 1980. pap. 3.00 (ISBN 9-25100-852-3, F1915, FAO). Unipub.

Recommended International Standard for Quick Frozen Blueberries. 11p. 1980. pap. 3.00 (ISBN 9-25100-803-5, F1916, FAO). Unipub.

Recommended Methods for Meausurment of Pest Resistance to Pesticides. (FAO Plant Production & Protection Paper: No. 21). 136p. 1981. pap. 7.25 (ISBN 92-5-100883-3, F2079, FAO). Unipub.

Recommended Methods for Purification of Solvents. Ed. by J. F. Coetzee. (International Union of Pure & Applied Chemistry). 1979. pap. text ed. 14.51 (ISBN 0-08-022370-2). Pergamon.

Recommended Model Provisions for a Preservation Ordinance. Stephen N. Dennis. 151p. (Orig.). 1980. pap. text ed. 7.95 (ISBN 0-89133-090-9). Preservation Pr.

Recommended Procedures for Measuring Productivity of Plankton Standing Stock & Related Ocean Properties. Committee On Oceanography. (Orig.). 1970. pap. 4.00 (ISBN 0-309-01760-2). Natl Acad Pr.

Reconciliation: A Study of Paul's Theology. Ralph Martin, Ed. by Peter Toon. LC 80-16340. (New Foundations Theological Library). 272p. 1981. 18.50 (ISBN 0-8042-3709-3); pap. 11.95 (ISBN 0-8042-3729-8). John Knox.

Reconciliation & Liberation: Challenging a One-Dimensional View of Salvation. Jan M. Lochman. LC 80-24060. 160p. (Orig.). 1980. pap. 6.95 (ISBN 0-8006-1340-6, 1-1340). Fortress.

Reconciliation & the New Age. Ralph H. Elliott. LC 72-9568. 128p. (Orig.). 1973. pap. 2.95 o.p. (ISBN 0-8170-0586-2). Judson.

Reconciliation in the Church. Leonce Hamelin. Tr. by Matthew J. O'Connell from Fr. Orig. Title: La Reconciliation en Eglise. 125p. 1981. pap. text ed. 5.50 (ISBN 0-8146-1215-6). Liturgical Pr.

Reconciliation Primer. John Gerstner. Date not set. pap. 1.95 (ISBN 0-88469-143-8). BMH Bks.

Reconditioning the Bicycle. (Illus.). 96p. 1980. pap. 2.95 (ISBN 0-87857-285-6). Rodale Pr Inc.

Reconnaissance Geology of the State of Baja California. R. Gordon Gastil et al. LC 74-83806. (Memoir: No. 140). (Illus.). 1975. 25.00x (ISBN 0-8137-1140-1); pap. 21.00x (ISBN 0-685-56041-4). Geol Soc.

Reconquest of Mexico: An Amiable Journey in Persuit of Cortes. Matthew Bruccoli. LC 74-76440. 1974. 8.95 (ISBN 0-8149-0742-3). Vanguard.

Reconquest of Spain. Derek W. Lomax. LC 77-3030. (Illus.). 1978. text ed. 19.50x (ISBN 0-582-50209-8). Longman.

Reconstituted Family: A Study of Remarried Couples & Their Children. Lucile Duberman. LC 75-8840. 185p. 1975. 16.95 (ISBN 0-88229-168-8). Nelson-Hall.

Reconstructing African Culture History. Ed. by Creighton Gabel & Norman R. Bennett. LC 67-25932. (Pub. by Boston U Pr). 1967. 9.50x (ISBN 0-8419-8704-1, Africana). Holmes & Meier.

Reconstructing Aphra: A Social Biography of Aphra Behn. Angeline Goreau. (Illus.). 339p. 1980. 14.95 (ISBN 0-8037-7478-8). Dial.

Reconstructing Psychological Practice. Ian McPherson & Andrew Sutton. 192p. 1981. 26.00x (ISBN 0-7099-0419-3, Pub. by Croom Helm LTD England). Biblio Dist.

Reconstructing the Past. Alan Sorrell. Ed. by Mark Sorrell. (Illus.). 168p. 1981. 19.50x (ISBN 0-389-20196-0). B&N.

Reconstructing the Past. Alan Sorrell. Ed. by Mark Sorrell. LC 79-56473. (Illus.). 168p. 1980. 24.00 (ISBN 0-7134-1588-6, Pub. by Batsford England). David & Charles.

Reconstructiom of the New York Democracy, 1861-1874. Jerome Mushkat. LC 79-16826. 328p. 1981. 25.00 (ISBN 0-8386-3002-2). Fairleigh Dickinson.

Reconstruction & Rehabilitation of the Burned Patient. Ed. by Irving Feller & William C. Grabb. LC 78-61362. (Illus.). 1979. text ed. 98.00 (ISBN 0-917478-50-9); text ed. 208.00 genuine leather bdg. (ISBN 0-917478-51-7). Natl Inst Burn.

Reconstruction & the Constitution, 1866-1876. John W. Burgess. LC 70-99479. (American Constitutional & Legal History Ser.: Americana Ser). 1970. Repr. of 1902 ed. lib. bdg. 35.00 (ISBN 0-306-71849-9). Da Capo.

Reconstruction Following Disaster. J. Eugene Haas et al. LC 77-23176. (Mit Press Environmental Studies Ser). 1977. text ed. 23.00x (ISBN 0-262-08094-X). MIT Pr.

Reconstruction in Indian Territory. M. Thomas Bailey. LC 77-189551. 1972. 13.50 (ISBN 0-8046-9022-7). Kennikat.

Reconstruction in Mississippi. James W. Garner. LC 12-1798. 1968. pap. text ed. 7.95x (ISBN 0-8071-0137-0). La State U Pr.

Reconstruction of the Elliott Wave Principle, 2 vols. rev. & enl. ed. R. N. Elliott. (Institute for Economic & Financial Research Ser). (Illus.). 97p. 1975. Set. 145.00 (ISBN 0-913314-63-3). Am Classical Coll Pr.

Reconstruction of the Head & Neck. Malcolm A. Lesavoy. (Illus.). 350p. 1981. write for info. (ISBN 0-683-04949-6). Williams & Wilkins.

Reconstruction of the Hogen-Heiji Monogatari Emaki. Penelope E. Mason. LC 76-23639. (Outstanding Dissertations in the Fine Arts). (Illus.). 1977. Repr. of 1970 ed. lib. bdg. 48.50 (ISBN 0-685-76431-1). Garland Pub.

Reconstruction of the New York Democracy, 1861-1874. Jerome Mushkat. LC 78-16826. 328p. 1981. 25.00 (ISBN 0-8386-3002-2, 3002). Fairleigh Dickinson.

Reconstruction: 1865-1877. Robert W. Johannsen. LC 74-91691. (Orig.). 1970. pap. text ed. 4.95 (ISBN 0-02-916540-7). Free Pr.

Reconstructive & Plastic Surgery of the Eyelids. Frank P. English & Warren A. Keats. (Illus.). 112p. 1975. 16.75 (ISBN 0-398-03386-2). C C Thomas.

Record & Tape Reviews Index, 1971. Antoinette Maleady. LC 72-3355. 1972. 10.00 (ISBN 0-8108-0522-7). Scarecrow.

Record & Tape Reviews Index, 1972. Antoinette Maleady. LC 72-3355. 1973. 16.50 (ISBN 0-8108-0672-X). Scarecrow.

Record & Tape Reviews Index, 1973. Antoinette Maleady. LC 72-3355. 1974. 24.00 (ISBN 0-8108-0720-3). Scarecrow.

Record & Tape Reviews Index, 1974. Antoinette Maleady. LC 72-3355. 580p. 1975. 22.50 (ISBN 0-8108-0817-X). Scarecrow.

Record Breakers. Maury Allen. LC 68-31402. (Illus.). 1968. 5.95 o.p. (ISBN 0-13-767426-0). P-H.

Record Houses of 1980. Architectural Record Magazine. (Architectural Record Bks.). 128p. 1980. pap. 5.95 (ISBN 0-07-002333-6). McGraw.

Record Keeping for Business: Syllabus. Marvin W. Hempel. 1977. pap. text ed. 8.75 (ISBN 0-89420-018-6, 359090); cassette recordings 138.60 (ISBN 0-89420-180-8, 359000). Natl Book.

Record Keeping for Personal Finance: Syllabus. Marvin W. Hempel. 1976. pap. text ed. 7.95 (ISBN 0-89420-005-4, 358080); cassette recordings 123.25 (ISBN 0-89420-181-6, 358000). Natl Book.

Record of a Friendship: The Correspondence of Wilhelm Reich and A.S. Neill. Ed. by Beverley Placzek. 1981. 15.95 (ISBN 0-374-24807-9). FS&G.

Record of European Armour & Arms Through Seven Centuries, 5 vols. Guy F. Laking. LC 79-8365. (Illus.). Repr. 295.00 set (ISBN 0-404-18344-1). AMS Pr.

Record of Geologic Time: A Vicarious Trip. D. Nations. (McGraw-Hill Concepts in Introductory Geology). (Illus.). 80p. 1975. text ed. 7.95x (ISBN 0-07-012326-8, C); slides 50.00 (ISBN 0-07-074427-0). McGraw.

Recording: Guidelines for Social Workers. Suanna J. Wilson. LC 79-7636. 241p. 1980. 19.95 (ISBN 0-02-935940-6). Free Pr.

Recording in Social Work. Noel Timms. (Library of Social Work). 1972. 12.50 (ISBN 0-7100-7288-0); pap. 6.95 (ISBN 0-7100-7289-9). Routledge & Kegan.

Recording: Working Guidelines for Social Workers. Suanna J. Wilson. LC 79-7636. 1980. 19.95 (ISBN 0-02-935940-6); pap. text ed. 9.95 (ISBN 0-02-935810-8). Free Pr.

Records & Record Searching. Walter Rye. LC 68-30663. 1969. Repr. of 1897 ed. 20.00 (ISBN 0-8103-3133-0). Gale.

Records & Recording Classical Guide 1978. Ed. by Ates Orga. 1978. pap. 5.95 (ISBN 0-8467-0450-1, Pub. by Two Continents). Hippocrene Bks.

Records, Notes, Reports Connected with the Removal to Germany in the Year 1945. The Hungarian Historical Research Society. LC 77-95243. 120p. 1980. pap. 6.50 (ISBN 0-935484-07-8). Universe Pub Co.

Records of California Men in the War of the Rebellion: 1861-1867. Compiled by Richard Orton. LC 78-23517. 1979. Repr. of 1890 ed. 64.00 (ISBN 0-8103-3347-3). Gale.

Records of Colonial Gloucester County, Virginia. Polly C. Mason. (Illus.). 146p. (Repr. of 1946-1948 eds.). 30.00x o.p. (ISBN 0-685-65079-0). Va Bk.

Records of Federal Officials: A Selection of Materials from the National Study Commission on Records & Documents of Federal Officials. Ed. by Anna K. Nelson. LC 78-9907. (History of the United States 1876-1976 Ser.: Vol. 15). 1979. lib. bdg. 38.00 (ISBN 0-8240-3672-7). Garland Pub.

Records of Han Administration, 2 Vols. Michael Loewe. (University of Cambridge Oriental Pubns.). 1967. Vol. 1. 47.00 (ISBN 0-521-05586-5); Vol. 2. 79.00 (ISBN 0-521-05587-3). Cambridge U Pr.

Records of Salem Witchcraft, Copied from the Original Documents, 2 Vols. LC 78-75274. (American History, Politics & Law Ser). 1969. lib. bdg. 39.50 (ISBN 0-306-71309-8). Da Capo.

Records of Selected Players, 1979. USTA Public Relations Office. 1980. 6.00 (ISBN 0-938822-08-X). USTA.

Records of the Columbia Historical Society of Washington D.C. Ed. by Francis C. Rosenberger. Incl. 1957-1959. (Illus.). 1961. 15.00x (ISBN 0-8139-0493-5); 1960-1962. (Illus.). 1963. 15.00x (ISBN 0-8139-0494-3); 1963-1965. (Illus.). 1966. 15.00x (ISBN 0-8139-0495-1); 1966-1968. (Illus.). 1969. 15.00x (ISBN 0-8139-0496-X); 1969-1970. LC 1-17677. (Illus.). 1971. 20.00x (ISBN 0-8139-0497-8); 1971-1972. 1973. 20.00x (ISBN 0-8139-0501-X); 1973-74. 1976. 20.00x (ISBN 0-685-38490-X). LC 73-84160. U Pr of Va.

Records of the Columbia Historical Society of Washington D. C, Vol. 50. Ed. by Francis C. Rosenberger. (Illus.). 550p. 1980. 20.00x (ISBN 0-8139-0866-3). U Pr of Va.

Records of the General Conference Twentieth Session: Proceedings, Vol. 3. 1157p. 1980. pap. 37.50 (ISBN 9-2300-1776-0, U1038, UNESCO). Unipub.

Records of the Grand Historian of China, 2 vols. Tr. by Burton Watson. Incl. Vol. 1. Early Years of the Han Dynasty, 209 to 141 B.C. o.p. (ISBN 0-231-08933-3); Vol. 2. Age of Emperor Wu, 140 to c. 100 B.C (ISBN 0-231-08934-1). LC 60-13348. (Records of Civilization: Sources & Studies: No. 6). (Illus.). 1961. 22.50x ea. Columbia U Pr.

Records of the Historian. Tr. by Burton Watson from Chinese. LC 70-89860. (Translations from the Oriental Classics). Orig. Title: Chapters from the Shih Chi of Ssu-Ma Ch'ien. 1970. pap. text ed. 8.50x (ISBN 0-231-03321-4). Columbia U Pr.

Records of Women: With Other Poems. Felicia D. Hemans. Ed. by Donald H. Reiman. LC 75-31218. (Romantic Context Ser.: Poetry 1789-1930 Ser.). 1978. lib. bdg. 47.00 (ISBN 0-8240-2168-1). Garland Pub.

Recortable Pouch: What's Happening? 1980. 950.00 (ISBN 0-89336-268-9, P-060). BCC.

Recovery from Alcoholism: A Social Treatment Model. R. G. O'Briant et al. 112p. 1973. 10.50 (ISBN 0-398-02830-3). C C Thomas.

Recovery in Aphasics. Ed. by Yvan Lebrun & Richard Hoops. (Neurolinguistics Ser.: Vol. 4). 270p. 1976. text ed. 34.50 (ISBN 90-265-0228-1, Pub. by Swets Pub Serv Holland). Swets North Am.

Recovery of American Cities. Paul R. Porter. LC 75-39090. (Illus.). 192p. 1976. 8.95 (ISBN 0-8467-0152-9, Pub. by Two Continents). Hippocrene Bks.

Recovery of Culture. Henry B. Stevens. 1963. 5.95 o.p. (ISBN 0-686-00957-6). Wellington.

Recovery of Culture. Henry B. Stevens. 1980. text ed. 4.75 o.p. (ISBN 0-8464-1047-8). Beekman Pubs.

Recovery of Freedom. Paul Johnson. 232p. 1980. 19.95x (ISBN 0-631-12562-0, Pub. by Basil Blackwell England). Biblio Dist.

Recovery of Spirit in Higher Education. Myron B. Bloy, Jr. et al. Ed. by Robert Rankin. 1980. 14.95 (ISBN 0-8164-0469-0). Seabury.

Recovery of the Sacred. James Hitchcock. LC 73-17899. 1974. 6.95 (ISBN 0-8164-1150-6). Crossroad NY.

Recovery of Uranium. (Illus., Orig.). 1971. pap. 33.75 (ISBN 92-0-040071-X, ISP262, IAEA). Unipub.

Recovery Problem in the United States. Harold G. Moulton et al. LC 73-176337. (FDR & the Era of the New Deal Ser.). (Illus.). Repr. lib. bdg. 65.00 (ISBN 0-306-70421-8). Da Capo.

Recreacion Cristiana. Viola D. Campbell. (Illus.). 160p. (Span.). 1980. pap. 3.60 (ISBN 0-311-11037-1). Casa Bautista.

Recreation: A Medical Viewpoint. Paul Haun. LC 65-12572. (Orig.). 1965. pap. text ed. 4.50x (ISBN 0-8077-1503-4). Tchrs Coll.

Recreation & Aesthetics. George S. Tolley & Roger J. Vaughan. (Environmental Policy Ser.: Vol. V). 1980. write for info. (ISBN 0-88410-628-4). Ballinger Pub.

Recreation & Leisure: The Changing Scene. 3rd ed. Reynolds E. Carlson et al. 1979. text ed. 17.95x (ISBN 0-534-00585-3). Wadsworth Pub.

Recreation & Outdoor Life Directory. Ed. by Paul Wasserman & Steven R. Wasserman. LC 79-4594. 500p. 1979. 68.00 (ISBN 0-8103-0315-9). Gale.

Recreation & Special Populations. 2nd ed. Stein & Sessoms. 430p. 1977. text ed. 16.95 (ISBN 0-205-05690-3, 845690-9). Allyn.

Recreation Areas, Their Design & Equipment. 2nd ed. George D. Butler. (Illus.). 1958. 18.95 (ISBN 0-8260-1625-1). Wiley.

Recreation for the Elderly: A Leadership Theory & Source Book. Eleanor B. Wapner. (Illus.). 192p. 1981. 16.50 (ISBN 0-89962-052-3). Todd & Honeywell.

Recreation for the Handicapped. Valerie V. Hunt. 1955. text ed. 15.95 (ISBN 0-13-767640-9). P-H.

Recreation for Today's Society. Charles A. Bucher & Richard D. Bucher. (Illus.). 224p. 1974. 12.95 (ISBN 0-13-768721-4). P-H.

Recreation in America. Ed. by Pauline Madow. (Reference Shelf Ser: Vol. 37, No. 2). 1965. 6.25 (ISBN 0-8242-0085-3). Wilson.

Recreation in Total Rehabilitation. Josephine Rathbone & Carol Lucas. 424p. 1970. lexofone 13.50 (ISBN 0-398-01555-4). C C Thomas.

Recreation Leader's Handbook. 0.75 o.p. (ISBN 0-87421-078-X). Utah St U Pr.

Recreation Planning & Development. Compiled by American Society of Civil Engineers. 784p. 1980. pap. text ed. 56.50 (ISBN 0-87262-200-2). Am Soc Civil Eng.

Recreation: The Profession. Joseph E. Curtis. LC 78-31266. (Illus.). 1979. pap. text ed. 13.95 (ISBN 0-8016-1183-0). Mosby.

Recreational Activity Development for the Aging in Homes, Hospitals, & Nursing Homes. Carol Lucas. (Illus.). 68p. 1978. pap. 5.75 (ISBN 0-398-03058-8). C C Thomas.

Recreational Areas. Ed. by Time-Life Books Editors. (Home Repair & Improvement Ser.). (Illus.). 1980. 10.95 (ISBN 0-686-59879-2). Time-Life.

Recreational Jazz Dance. 2nd ed. Ann I. Czompo. Ed. by Andor Czompo. LC 79-26223. (Illus.). 1979. pap. text ed. 9.95 (ISBN 0-935496-00-9). AC Pubns.

Recreational Service for the Aging. Jay S. Shivers & Hollis F. Fait. LC 80-360. (Illus.). 324p. 1980. text ed. 16.50 (ISBN 0-8121-0713-6). Lea & Febiger.

Recreational Vehicle Maintenance. Tim Lockwood. Ed. by Jeff Robinson. (Illus.). 232p. 1973. pap. text ed. 8.95 (ISBN 0-89287-081-8, X930). Clymer Pubns.

Recruiting & Selecting Salesmen. John Lidstone. 1979. text ed. 28.50x (ISBN 0-566-02153-6, Pub. by Gower Pub Co England). Renouf.

Recruiting & Training Volunteers. Paul Ilsley & John A. Niemi. (Adult Education Association Professional Development Ser.). (Illus.). 176p. 1980. text ed. 12.95x (ISBN 0-07-000556-7, C). McGraw.

Recruiting Minority Students. NAIS Admission & Minority Affairs Committees. 1979. pap. 3.25 (ISBN 0-934338-41-8). NAIS.

Recruiting Officer. George Farquhar. Ed. by Michael Shugrue. LC 65-15341. (Regents Restoration Drama Ser). 1965. 8.95x (ISBN 0-8032-0358-6); pap. 2.35x (ISBN 0-8032-5357-5, BB 253, Bison). U of Nebr Pr.

Recruitment & Parent Stock in Fishes. David H. Cushing. (Washington Sea Grant). 197p. 1973. pap. 10.50 (ISBN 0-295-95311-X). U of Wash Pr.

Recruitment & Training of the Research Psychiatrist, Vol. 6. GAP Committee on Psychopathology. LC 62-2872. (Report No. 65). 1967. pap. 2.00 (ISBN 0-87318-090-9). Adv Psychiatry.

Recrystallization & Grain Growth in Metals. P. Cotterill & P. R. Mould. LC 75-33874. 1976. 34.95 (ISBN 0-470-17527-3). Halsted Pr.

Rector & the Doctor's Family, 1863. Margaret O. Oliphant. Ed. by Robert L. Wolff. LC 75-1543. (Victorian Fiction Ser). 1975. lib. bdg. 66.00 (ISBN 0-8240-1613-0). Garland Pub.

Recueil De Chansons Pieuses Du XIIIe Siecle. Edward G. Jarnstrom. LC 80-2162. 1981. Repr. of 1910 ed. 29.50 (ISBN 0-404-19024-3). AMS Pr.

Recueils, 4 vols. Societe Jean Bodin Pour L'histoire Comparative Des Institutions. Incl. Vol. 1. Liens De Vassalite et les Immunities (ISBN 0-404-18596-7); Vol. 2. Servage (ISBN 0-404-18597-5); Vol. 3. Tenure (ISBN 0-404-18598-3); Vol. 4. Domaine (ISBN 0-404-18599-1). LC 80-2205. 1981. 139.50 set (ISBN 0-404-18595-9); 35.00 ea. AMS Pr.

Recurrence & Discrete Dynamic Systems. I. Gumowski & C. Mira. (Lecture Notes in Mathematics: Vol. 809). (Illus.). 272p. 1980. pap. 16.80 (ISBN 0-387-10017-2). Springer-Verlag.

Recurrence in Ergodic Theory & Combinatorial Number Theory. H. Furstenberg. LC 80-7518. (Rice University, Dept. of Mathematics, M. B. Porter Lectures). 228p. 1981. 19.50 (ISBN 0-691-08269-3). Princeton U Pr.

Recurrent Education: Denmark. 1976. 2.50 o.p. (ISBN 92-64-11536-6). OECD.

Recurring Library Issues: A Reader. Ed. by Caroline M. Coughlin. LC 79-14966. 543p. 1979. 19.00 (ISBN 0-8108-1227-4). Scarecrow.

Recurring Miracle. Ed. by Derick R. Marsh. 208p. 1980. pap. 14.00x (ISBN 0-424-00085-7, Pub. by Sydney U Pr Australia). Intl Schol Bk Serv.

Recursion on the Countable Functionals. D. Normann. (Lecture Notes in Mathematics: Vol. 811). 191p. 1980. pap. 11.80 (ISBN 0-387-10019-9). Springer-Verlag.

Recursion-Theoretic Hierarchies. P. G. Hinman. (Perspectives in Mathematical Logic). 1977. 46.20 (ISBN 0-387-07904-1). Springer-Verlag.

Recursion Theory: Its Generalisations & Applications; Proceedings. Logic Colloquim '79 Leeds, August 1979 et al. Ed. by F. R. Drake & S. S Wainer. (London Mathematical Society Lecture Notes Ser.: No. 45). 300p. 1980. pap. 24.50 (ISBN 0-521-23543-X). Cambridge U Pr.

Recursive Function Theory: Proceedings, Vol. 5. Symposia in Pure Mathematics-New York-1961. Ed. by J. Dekker. LC 50-1183. 1979. Repr. of 1962 ed. with corrections 20.80 (ISBN 0-8218-1405-2, PSPUM-5). Am Math.

Recycled Buildings: A Bibliography of Adaptive Use Literature Since Nineteen Seventy. Margaret T. Will. (Architecture Ser.: Bibliography A-154). 71p. 1979. pap. 7.50 (ISBN 0-686-26957-8). Vance Biblios.

Recycled for Living. Earl G. Lee. LC 72-94753. 128p. (Orig.). 1973. pap. 1.65 o.p. (ISBN 0-8307-0217-2, 50-091-03). Regal.

Recycling & Disposal of Solid Waste. M. E. Henstock. LC 75-4235. 223p. 1975. pap. 34.00 (ISBN 0-08-019685-3). Pergamon.

Recycling & Repairing, Nineteen Twelve to Nineteen Forty Eight. Compiled by Keith W. Daniels. (Illus.). 290p. (Orig.). 1978. pap. 7.95 (ISBN 0-937468-00-2). Lost Data.

Recycling of Nickel Alloys & Stainless Steel Scrap. 7.50 o.p. (ISBN 0-686-23294-1). Natl Recycling.

Recycling Resources. Laurence Pringle. LC 72-81062. (Illus.). 128p. (gr. 7 up). 1974. 5.95g o.s.i. (ISBN 0-02-775310-7). Macmillan.

Recycling: Reusing Our World's Solid Wastes. James Hahn & Lynn Hahn. LC 73-4372. (First Bks.). (gr. 5 up). 1973. PLB 4.90 o.p. (ISBN 0-531-00805-3). Watts.

Recycling the Past: Popular Uses of American History. Ed. by Leila Zenderland. LC 77-20306. 1978. 15.00 o.p. (ISBN 0-8122-7740-6); pap. 5.95x (ISBN 0-8122-1095-6). U of Pa Pr.

Recycling the Prague Linguistic Circle. Ed. & tr. by Marta K. Johnson. (Linguistica Extranea Ser.: Studia 6). 103p. 1978. pap. 5.50 (ISBN 0-89720-010-1). Karoma.

Recycling Waste. Paul I. Smith. 1976. text ed. 22.50x (ISBN 0-87936-011-9). Scholium Intl.

Recyclopedia. Robin Simons. (Illus.). (gr. 3-7). 1976. 9.95 (ISBN 0-395-24390-4). HM.

Recyclopedia. Robin Simons. (gr. 1 up). 1976. pap. 5.95 (ISBN 0-395-24380-7, Sandpiper). HM.

Red Acre's Titan. Jane Seligson. 8.75 (ISBN 0-8062-1687-5). Carlton.

Red & Black: An Annotated Text with Critical Essays. Stendhal. Ed. by Robert M. Adams. (Norton Critical Editions Ser.). 1969. pap. 7.95x (ISBN 0-393-09821-4, NortonC). Norton.

Red & the Black. Stendhal. Tr. by Lloyd C. Parks. (Orig.). 1970. pap. 1.95 (ISBN 0-451-51398-3, CJ1398, Sig Classics). NAL.

Red & the Black. Stendhal. Ed. by Charles Tergie. 1961. pap. 0.95 o.s.i. (ISBN 0-02-054080-9, Collier). Macmillan.

Red Apache Sun. Robert E. Mills. (Kansan Ser.: No. 3). 1981. pap. 1.95 (ISBN 0-8439-0877-7, Leisure Bks). Nordon Pubns.

Red Are the Embers. Gua N. Gordon. 1980. 8.50 (ISBN 0-8233-0317-9). Golden Quill.

Red Badge of Courage. Stephen Crane. (Literature Ser). (gr. 7-12). 1969. pap. text ed. 3.42 (ISBN 0-87720-712-7). AMSCO Sch.

Red Badge of Courage. Stephen Crane. Ed. by Van A. Bradley. LC 76-76032. (First Edition American Classics in Fascimile Ser., No. 1). 1969. 8.50 o.p. (ISBN 0-8303-0075-9). Fleet.

Red Badge of Courage. Stephen Crane. (gr. 9 up). 1962. 3.95g o.s.i. (ISBN 0-02-724910-7). Macmillan.

Red Badge of Courage. Stephen Crane. (Keith Jennison Large Type Bks). (gr. 6 up). PLB 7.95 o.p. (ISBN 0-531-00270-5). Watts.

Red Badge of Courage. Stephen Crane. (gr. 7-12). 1972. pap. 1.25 (ISBN 0-590-02117-6, Schol Pap). Schol Bk Serv.

Red Badge of Courage. rev. ed. Stephen Crane. Ed. by Robert J. Dixson. (American Classics Ser.: Bk. 10). (gr. 9 up). 1974. pap. text ed. 2.75 (ISBN 0-88345-206-5); cassettes 40.00 (ISBN 0-685-38931-6, 18129); tapes 35.00 (ISBN 0-685-38932-4). Regents Pub.

Red Badge of Courage. Stephen Crane. (Childrens Illustrated Classics Ser). (Illus.). 1971. 9.00x o.p. (ISBN 0-460-05090-7, Pub. by J. M. Dent England). Biblio Dist.

Red Badge of Courage. Stephen Crane. LC 69-13318. (Merrill Standard Ser). 1975. 6.00 (ISBN 0-910294-29-1); pap. 4.00 (ISBN 0-910294-30-5). Brown Bk.

Red Badge of Courage, with Reader's Guide. Stephen Crane. (AMSCO Literature Program). (gr. 9-12). 1971. pap. text ed. 4.17 (ISBN 0-87720-811-5); tchrs. ed. 2.70 (ISBN 0-87720-911-1). AMSCO Sch.

Red Baron. Manfred Von Richthofen. Ed. by Stanley M. Ulanoff. Tr. by Peter Kilduff from Ger. LC 80-68107. (Illus.). 241p. 1980. Repr. 12.95 (ISBN 0-8168-7925-7). Aero.

Red, Black & Green. A. Pinkney. LC 75-22550. 256p. 1976. 29.95 (ISBN 0-521-20887-4); pap. 6.95 (ISBN 0-521-29459-2). Cambridge U Pr.

Red Blood at White River. Ed Will. (Orig.). 1980. pap. 1.75 (ISBN 0-532-23143-0). Manor Bks.

Red Blood Cell, 2 vols. 2nd ed. Ed. by Douglas N. Surgenor. Vol. 1, 1974. 64.50 (ISBN 0-12-677201-0); Vol. 2, 1975. 65.50 (ISBN 0-12-677202-9); Set. 106.00. Acad Pr.

Red Book of Fruit Jars, No. 3. Alice Creswick. (Illus.). 1978. pap. 11.95 (ISBN 0-89145-076-9). Collector Bks.

Red Book of Marine Engineering Questions & Answers, Vol. 1: Third & Second Assistant Engineers. 3rd ed. William B. Paterson. LC 76-153141. (Illus.). 1971. pap. 9.00x (ISBN 0-87033-088-8). Cornell Maritime.

Red Book of Marine Engineering Questions & Answers, Vol. 2: First Assistant & Chief Engineer. 2nd ed. William B. Paterson. LC 65-13. (Illus.). 1973. pap. 9.00x (ISBN 0-87033-089-6). Cornell Maritime.

Red Book on Transportation of Hazardous Materials. Lawrence W. Bierlein. LC 76-44394. 1977. 80.00 (ISBN 0-8436-1407-2). CBI Pub.

Red Box. Rex Stout. pap. 1.75 (ISBN 0-515-05117-9). Jove Pubns.

Red Carnelian. Phyllis A. Whitney. (Orig.). 1974. pap. 1.75 o.s.i. (ISBN 0-446-84670-8). Warner Bks.

Red Carpet. Rex Parkin. (Illus.). (gr. k-3). 1967. 8.95g (ISBN 0-02-770020-8). Macmillan.

Red Carpet for the Shah. Peter Ritner. LC 75-15806. 224p. 1975. 6.95 o.p. (ISBN 0-688-02957-4). Morrow.

Red Cedar Scroll. Robert Schuler. 1980. pap. 3.00 (ISBN 0-930600-14-2). Uzzano Pr.

Red Cell: Production, Metabolism, Destruction, Normal & Abnormal. rev. ed. John W. Harris & Robert Kellermeyer. LC 77-130344. (Commonwealth Fund Publications Ser). 1970. 25.00x (ISBN 0-674-75101-9); pap. 8.95x (ISBN 0-674-75102-7). Harvard U Pr.

Red Cell Structure & Its Breakdown. E. P. Ponder. (Protoplasmatologia: Vol. 10, Pt. 2). (Illus.). 1955. pap. 34.90 o.p. (ISBN 0-387-80388-2). Springer-Verlag.
Red Centre: The Landscape and People of Outback Australia. Keith Willey & Robin Smith. (Illus.). 106p. 1976. 12.00 (ISBN 0-584-97049-8). Transatlantic.
Red Chiefs & White Challengers. J. Jay Myers. (gr. 7-12). 1972. pap. 1.25 o.s.i. (ISBN 0-671-48125-8). WSP.
Red Children in White America. Ann H. Beuf. LC 76-49737. 168p. 1977. 10.95x (ISBN 0-8122-7719-8). U of Pa Pr.
Red China in Prophecy. Gordon Lindsay. (Prophecy Ser.). 1.25 (ISBN 0-89985-059-6). Christ Nations.
Red Cloud & the Sioux Problem. James C. Olson. LC 65-10048. (Illus.). xii, 375p. 1965. 15.00x (ISBN 0-8032-0136-2); pap. 5.50 (ISBN 0-8032-5817-8, BB 602, Bison). U of Nebr Pr.
Red Coal. Gerald Stern. 96p. 1981. 10.95 (ISBN 0-686-69058-3); pap. 5.95 (ISBN 0-686-69059-1). HM.
Red Cross, Black Eagle: A Biography of Albania's American School. Joan F. Kontos. (East European Monographs: No. 75). 240p. 1981. text ed. 17.00x (ISBN 0-914710-69-9). East Eur Quarterly.
Red Crossbills of Colorado. Afred M. Bailey et al. (Museum Pictorial: No. 9). 1953. pap. 1.10 o.p. (ISBN 0-916278-38-7). Denver Mus Natl Hist.
Red Crow, Warrior Chief. Hugh A. Dempsey. LC 80-51872. (Illus.). viii, 247p. 1980. 16.95 (ISBN 0-8032-1657-2). U of Nebr Pr.
Red Deer. Brian Staines. (Mammal Society Ser.). (Illus.). 50p. 1980. 6.95 (ISBN 0-7137-0898-0, Pub. by Blandford Pr England). Sterling.
Red Door. Edith R. Locke. LC 65-20821. (Illus.). (gr. k-3). 1965. 4.50 (ISBN 0-8149-0353-3). Vanguard.
Red Eagles of the Northwest: The Story of Chief Joseph & His People. Francis Haines. LC 76-43728. (Illus.). 376p. 1980. Repr. of 1939 ed. 32.50 (ISBN 0-404-15569-3). AMS Pr.
Red Embers. Dorothy Lyons. LC 48-8369. (Illus.). (gr. 7-9). 4.50 o.p. (ISBN 0-15-266014-3, HJ). HarBraceJ.
Red Fairy Book. Andrew Lang. (gr. 6-8). 7.00 (ISBN 0-8446-0756-8). Peter Smith.
Red-Figured Vases of Apulia, Vol. I. A. D. Trendall & A. Cambitoglou. (Monographs on Classical Archaeology). (Illus.). 1978. 79.00 (ISBN 0-19-813218-2). Oxford U Pr.
Red Fog Over America. William G. Carr. 1978. pap. 4.00x (ISBN 0-911038-30-2). Noontide.
Red for Danger. new ed. L. T. Rolt. LC 76-28618. (Illus.). 16.95 (ISBN 0-7153-4009-3). David & Charles.
Red Fox. H. G. Lloyd. (Illus.). 320p. 1980. 45.00 (ISBN 0-7134-1190-2, Pub. by Batsford England). David & Charles.
Red Fox & His Canoe. Nathaniel Benchley. (gr. k-3). 1969. pap. 0.95 o.p. (ISBN 0-590-08089-X, Schol Pap); pap. 2.95 bk. & record o.p. (ISBN 0-590-20794-6). Schol Bk Serv.
Red Fox: Symposium on Behavior & Ecology. Ed. by E. Zimen. (Biogeographica Ser.: Vol. 18). 286p. 1980. lib. bdg. 73.50 (ISBN 0-686-28665-0, Pub. by Dr. W. Junk). Kluwer Boston.
Red Fury. George G. Gilman. (Edge Ser.: No. 33). 160p. 1980. pap. 1.75 (ISBN 0-523-41315-7). Pinnacle Bks.
Red Ghost. Steven Otfinoski. Ed. by Mary Verdick. (Beginning Pal Paperbacks Ser.). (Illus., Orig.). (gr. 7-12). 1977. pap. text ed. 1.25 (ISBN 0-8374-3466-1). Xerox Ed Pubns.
Red Giants & White Dwarfs. Robert Jastrow. 1980. pap. 7.95 (ISBN 0-446-97349-1). Warner Bks.
Red Gods. Donald Lindquist. 1981. 11.95 (ISBN 0-440-07349-9). Delacorte.
Red Gold: The Conquest of the Brazilian Indians, 1500-1760. John Hemming. LC 77-22863. 1978. 20.00 (ISBN 0-674-75107-8). Harvard U Pr.
Red-Haired Brat. Joanna Dessau. 1979. 7.95 o.p. (ISBN 0-312-66720-5). St Martin.
Red-Headed League. Arthur Conan Doyle. Ed. by Walter Pauk & Raymond Harris. (Classics Ser). (Illus.). (gr. 6-12). 1976. pap. text ed. 2.40x (ISBN 0-89061-060-6, 541); tchrs. ed. 3.00 (ISBN 0-89061-061-4, 543). Jamestown Pubs.
Red Heroin. Jerry Pournelle. Date not set. pap. 1.95 o.p. (ISBN 0-425-04195-6). Berkley Pub.
Red Horse Hill. Stephen W. Meader. LC 30-23594. (Illus.). (gr. 6 up). 6.95 o.p. (ISBN 0-15-266193-X, HJ). HarBraceJ.
Red Jasmine. Inglis Fletcher. 320p. 1976. Repr. of 1932 ed. lib. bdg. 14.95x (ISBN 0-89244-012-0). Queens Hse.
Red Lamp of Incest: What the Taboo Can Tell Us About Who We Are & How We Got That Way. Robin Fox. (Illus.). 288p. 1980. 12.95 (ISBN 0-525-18943-2). Dutton.
Red Land, Black Land: Daily Life in Ancient Egypt. Barbara Mertz. LC 78-9552. (Illus.). 1978. 12.95 (ISBN 0-396-07575-4); pap. 7.95 (ISBN 0-396-07640-8). Dodd.
Red Man in the New World Drama. Jennings C. Wise & Vine Deloria, Jr. 1971. 12.95 (ISBN 0-02-630550-X). Macmillan.
Red Man's America: A History of Indians in the United States. rev. ed. Ruth M. Underhill. LC 79-171345. 398p. 1971. pap. 7.95 (ISBN 0-226-84165-0, P437, Phoen). U of Chicago Pr.
Red Mutiny. John Wingate. LC 77-14717. 1978. 7.95 o.p. (ISBN 0-312-66661-6). St Martin.
Red Nails. Robert E. Howard. 1979. 2.25 (ISBN 0-425-04360-6). Berkley Pub.
Red Notebook of Charles Darwin. Ed. by Sandra Herbert. LC 78-74215. (Illus.). 1980. 19.50x (ISBN 0-8014-1226-9). Cornell U Pr.
Red Over Black: Black Slavery Among the Cherokee Indians. R. Halliburton, Jr. LC 76-15329. (Illus.). 1977. lib. bdg. 17.95 (ISBN 0-8371-9034-7, HAR/). Greenwood.
Red Power on the Rio Grande: The Native American Revolution of 1680. Franklin Folsom. LC 72-85581. 160p. (gr. 7-9). 1973. 5.95 o.p. (ISBN 0-695-80374-3, T0374); lib. ed. 5.97 o.p. (ISBN 0-695-40374-5, L0374). Follett.
Red, Red Rose. Tess Oliver. 192p. (Orig.). 1980. pap. 1.50 (ISBN 0-671-57014-5). S&S.
Red River Controversy. C. A. Welborn. 6.95 (ISBN 0-685-48787-3). Nortex Pr.
Red River: Paul Bunyan's Own Lumber Company & Its Railroads. Robert M. Hanft. LC 79-53190. (Illus.). 304p. 32.50 (ISBN 0-9602894-5-3). CSU Ctr Busn Econ.
Red River Settlement. Alexander Ross. Repr. 12.50 o.p. (ISBN 0-87018-055-X). Ross.
Red Rock Over the River. Patricia Beatty. LC 72-5883. 256p. (gr. 7-9). 1973. PLB 8.40 (ISBN 0-688-30065-0). Morrow.
Red Room Riddle. Scott Corbett. 1978. pap. 1.25 o.s.i. (ISBN 0-440-47524-4). Dell.
Red Rose. Margot Tracey. (Illus.). 1978. 17.95 (ISBN 0-7153-7440-0). David & Charles.
Red Rover. James F. Cooper. 1976. lib. bdg. 16.95x (ISBN 0-89968-158-1). Lightyear.
Red Rowan Berry. Frances Murray. 1978. pap. 1.95 o.p. (ISBN 0-345-25956-4). Ballantine.
Red Saint. Warwick Deeping. 1976. lib. bdg. 16.75x (ISBN 0-89968-024-0). Lightyear.
Red Sea. Francine Jacobs. (Illus.). (gr. 4-6). 1978. 6.95 (ISBN 0-688-22150-5); PLB 6.67 (ISBN 0-688-32150-X). Morrow.
Red Shift. Alan Garner. LC 73-584. 256p. (gr. 10 up). 1973. 5.95g o.s.i. (ISBN 0-02-735870-4). Macmillan.
Red Shoes Ballet & the Tales of Hoffman, Vol. 14. Monk Gibbon. Ed. by Bruce S. Kupelnick. LC 76-52106. (Classics of Film Literature Ser.). 1978. lib. bdg. 39.00 (ISBN 0-8240-2878-3). Garland Pub.
Red Sky at Morning. Richard Bradford. LC 68-11272. 1968. 10.95 (ISBN 0-397-00549-0). Lippincott.
Red Snow: Story of the Alaska Gray Wolf. James Greiner. LC 77-82943. 240p. 1980. 10.95 (ISBN 0-385-13169-0). Doubleday.
Red Son Rising. Adele Arnold. LC 74-17283. (Illus.). (gr. 5 up). 1974. 6.95 (ISBN 0-87518-077-9). Dillon.
Red Spies in the U. S. George Carpozi, Jr. (Illus.). 256p. 1973. 8.95 o.p. (ISBN 0-87000-223-6). Arlington Hse.
Red Squirrel. Andrew Tittensor. (Mammal Society Ser.). (Illus.). 50p. 1980. 6.95 (ISBN 0-7137-0902-2, Pub. by Blandford Pr England). Sterling.
Red Sun Setting: The Battle of the Philippine Sea. William T. Y'Blood. 208p. 1981. 18.95 (ISBN 0-87021-532-9). Naval Inst Pr.
Red-Tailed Hawk Named Bucket. Gaird Wallig. LC 76-57546. (Illus.). 224p. 1980. 9.95 (ISBN 0-89087-276-7). Celestial Arts.
Red Tape: Its Origins, Uses & Abuses. Herbert Kaufman. 1977. 9.95 (ISBN 0-8157-4842-6); pap. 3.95 (ISBN 0-8157-4841-8). Brookings.
Red Threads. Rex Stout. 1979. pap. 1.75 o.s.i. (ISBN 0-515-05280-9). Jove Pubns.
Red Tower. Lucile V. Stevens. (YA) 5.95 (ISBN 0-685-07457-9, Avalon). Bouregy.
Red Towers of Granada. Geoffrey Trease. LC 67-18646. (Illus.). (gr. 6-10). 6.95 (ISBN 0-8149-0424-6). Vanguard.
Red Trailer Mystery. (Trixie Belden Mystery Stories Ser.). (gr. 4 up). 1977. PLB 5.52 (ISBN 0-307-61525-1, Golden Pr); pap. 1.25 (ISBN 0-307-21525-3). Western Pub.
Red Trains Remembered. Robert S. Ford. Ed. by Mac Sebree. LC 80-81976. (Interurbans Special Ser.: 75). 120p. 1980. 16.95 (ISBN 0-916374-44-0). Interurban.
Red Wagons & Billy Goats. Eunice Soper. 1980. pap. 2.25 (ISBN 0-8280-0054-9, 18125-5). Review & Herald.
Red, White, & Black: The Peoples of Early America. Gary B. Nash. (Illus.). 320p. 1974. pap. text ed. 10.95 (ISBN 0-13-769802-X). P-H.
Red Years: European Socialism Versus Bolshevism, 1919-1921. Albert S. Lindemann. LC 73-80834. 1975. 23.75x (ISBN 0-520-02511-3). U of Cal Pr.
Redactional Style in the Marcan Gospel. E. J. Pryke. LC 76-52184. (Society for New Testament Studies Monographs). 1978. 37.00 (ISBN 0-521-21430-0). Cambridge U Pr.
Redating the Exodus & Conquest. John J. Bimson. (JSOT Supplement Ser.: No. 5). 351p. 1978. text ed. o.p. (ISBN 0-905774-10-8, Pub. by JSOT Pr England); pap. text ed. 23.95x (ISBN 0-905774-03-5, Pub. by JSOT Pr England). Eisenbrauns.
Redbook Report on Female Sexuality. Carol Tavris & Susan Sadd. 1977. 8.95 o.p. (ISBN 0-440-07560-2). Delacorte.
Redbook Wise Woman's Diet: All-Time Favorite Recipes. Redbook Magazine. Ed. by Ruth Pomeroy. (Illus.). 176p. 1980. 14.95 (ISBN 0-88421-161-4). Butterick Pub.
Redbook's Guide to Buying Your First Home. Ruth Pomeroy. 1980. 11.95 (ISBN 0-686-60933-6, 24716); pap. 4.95 (ISBN 0-686-60934-4, 25385). S&S.
Redbook's the Young Mothers. Ed. by Barbara Belford. (Orig.). 1977. pap. 1.95 o.s.i. (ISBN 0-446-89381-1). Warner Bks.
Redburn: His First Voyage. Herman Melville. 1957. pap. 2.95 (ISBN 0-385-09321-7, A118, Anch). Doubleday.
Redcoat in Boston. Ann Finlayson. LC 75-150364. (gr. 7-12). 1971. 5.95 o.p. (ISBN 0-7232-6089-3). Warne.
Redd Foxx, B. S. (Before Sanford) Joe X. Price. LC 77-75839. (Illus.). 1979. 8.95 o.p. (ISBN 0-8092-7856-1). Contemp Bks.
Redeemed Captive, Returning to Zion. John Williams. LC 75-7024. (Indian Captivities Ser.: Vol. 5). 1976. Repr. of 1707 ed. lib. bdg. 44.00 (ISBN 0-8240-1629-7). Garland Pub.
Redeemer Nation: The Idea of America's Millenial Role. Ernest L. Tuveson. LC 68-14009. 1968. 10.00x o.s.i. (ISBN 0-226-81919-1). U of Chicago Pr.
Redefining Government's Role in the Market System. Committee for Economic Development. (CED Statement on National Policy Ser.). 1979. lib. bdg. 6.50 (ISBN 0-87186-768-0); pap. 5.00 (ISBN 0-87186-068-6). Comm Econ Dev.
Redefining Rigor: Ideology & Statistics in Political Inquiry. Philip L. Beardsley. (Sage Library of Social Research: Vol. 104). (Illus.). 199p. 1980. 18.00x (ISBN 0-8039-1472-5); pap. 8.95x (ISBN 0-8039-1473-3). Sage.
Redefining the Discipline of Adult Education. Robert D. Boyd et al. LC 80-8006. (Higher Education Ser.). 1980. text ed. 15.95x (ISBN 0-87589-482-8). Jossey-Bass.
Redefining the Enviorment. Jerome Abarbanel. (Key Issues Ser.: No. 9). 1972. pap. 2.00 (ISBN 0-87546-200-6). NY Sch Indus Rel.
Redemption of Howard Gray. C. W. Naylor. 72p. pap. 0.50. Faith Pub Hse.
Redemption of Man. T. B. Kilpatrick. (Short Course Ser.). 163p. 1920. text ed. 2.95 (ISBN 0-567-08320-9). Attic Pr.
Redemption Truths. Robert Anderson. LC 80-16161. (Sir Robert Anderson Library). Orig. Title: For Us Men. 192p. 1980. pap. 3.50 (ISBN 0-8254-2131-4). Kregel.
Redemptive History & Biblical Interpretation. Geerhardus Vos. Ed. by Richard B. Gaffin, Jr. 584p. 1981. 17.50 (ISBN 0-8010-9286-8). Baker Bk.
Redemptive History & Biblical Interpretation: The Shorter Writings of Geerhardus Vos. Ed. by Richard B. Gaffin, Jr. 1980. 17.50 (ISBN 0-87552-270-X). Presby & Reformed.
Redesigning the Future: A Systems Approach to Societal Problems. Russell L. Ackoff. LC 74-10627. 320p. 1974. 17.95 (ISBN 0-471-00296-8, Pub. by. Wiley-Interscience). Wiley.
Redhouse English-Turkish Dictionary. 1974. 30.00x (ISBN 0-686-16859-3). Intl Learn Syst.
Redigging the Wells. Monroe E. Hawley. 1976. 6.95 (ISBN 0-89137-513-9); pap. 4.95 (ISBN 0-89137-512-0). Quality Pubns.
Rediscoverers: Major Writers in the Portuguese Literature of National Regeneration. Ronald W. Sousa. LC 80-21453. (Illus.). 208p. 1981. 17.50x (ISBN 0-271-00300-6). Pa St U Pr.
Rediscoveries in Art: Taste, Fashion & Collecting in England & France. Francis Haskell. (Wrightsman Lecture Ser.). (Illus.). 1980. pap. 14.95 o.p. (ISBN 0-8014-9187-8). Cornell U Pr.
Rediscovering Astronomy. Eugene F. Provenzo, Jr. & Asterie B. Provenzo. LC 80-17210. (Young Inventor's Ser.). (Illus.). 128p. 1980. 8.95 (ISBN 0-916392-61-9). Oak Tree Pubns.
Rediscovering Photography. Eugene F. Provenzo & Asterie B. Provenzo. LC 80-17769. (Young Inventor's Ser.). 128p. 1980. 8.95 (ISBN 0-916392-55-4). Oak Tree Pubns.
Rediscovering the Angels & Natives of Eternity. 6th ed. Flower A. Newhouse. (Illus.). 8.50 (ISBN 0-910378-02-9). Christward.
Rediscovering the Traditions of Israel: The Development of the Tradition-Historical Research of the Old Testament, with Special Consideration of Scandinavian Contributions. Douglas A. Knight. LC 75-6868. (Society of Biblical Literature. Dissertation Ser.). 1975. pap. 9.00 (ISBN 0-89130-235-2, 060109). Scholars Pr Ca.
Rediscovery of Christ. Norma A. McKinley. (Illus.). 1980. deluxe ed. 49.75 (ISBN 0-89266-224-7). Am Classical Coll Pr.
Rediscovery of the Business Cycle. Paul A. Volcker. LC 78-19850. 1978. 12.95 (ISBN 0-02-933430-6). Free Pr.
Rediscovery of the New World. (Eng. & Span.). 1972. pap. 1.00 Eng. ed. (ISBN 0-8270-4545-X); pap. 1.00 Span. ed. (ISBN 0-8270-4550-6). OAS.
Redistribution of Accessory Elements in Mining & Mineral Processing: Coal & Oil Shale, Pt. I. Board on Mineral & Energy Resources. 1979. pap. 9.25 (ISBN 0-309-02897-3). Natl Acad Pr.
Redistribution of Accessory Elements in Mining & Mineral Processing: Uranium, Phosphate, & Alumina, Pt. II. Board on Mineral & Energy Resources. 1979. pap. 12.25 (ISBN 0-309-02899-X). Natl Acad Pr.
Redistribution Through Public Choice. Harold M. Hochman & George E. Peterson. 1974. 20.00x (ISBN 0-231-03775-9). Columbia U Pr.
Redistribution Through the Financial System: The Grants Economics of Money & Credit. Ed. by Kenneth E. Boulding & Thomas F. Wilson. LC 78-18017. 1978. 32.95 (ISBN 0-03-045341-0). Praeger.
Redistributive Effects of Government Programmes: The Chilean Case. A. Foxley et al. (Illus.). 1979. 32.00 (ISBN 0-08-023130-6). Pergamon.
Redneck Mothers, Good Ol' Girls & Other Southern Belles. Sharon McKern. 1979. 10.95 o.p. (ISBN 0-670-59249-8). Viking Pr.
Redneck Poacher's Son. Luke Wallin. 224p. (gr. 7 up). 1981. 8.95 (ISBN 0-87888-174-3). Bradbury Pr.
Redoing America. Edmund Faltermayer. 1969. pap. 1.95 o.s.i. (ISBN 0-02-073170-1, Collier). Macmillan.
Redon, Seurat, & the Symbolists. (Illus.). 1975. Repr. 5.95 o.p. (ISBN 0-88308-012-5). Lamplight Pub.
Redoute Roses. Frank Anderson. (Abbeville Library of Art Ser.). (Illus.). 112p. 1981. pap. 4.95 (ISBN 0-89659-096-8). Abbeville Pr.
Redox Indicators: Characteristics & Applications. Ed. by Adam Hulanicki & Stanislaw Glab. 1978. pap. text ed. 10.00 (ISBN 0-08-022383-4). Pergamon.
Reduce Your Tax Bite. Ed. by Henry Myers. LC 79-21653. (Orig.). 1980. pap. 5.95 (ISBN 0-87128-583-5, Pub. by Dow Jones). Dow Jones-Irwin.
Reduced Dose Mammography. Wende W. Logan & E. Phillip Muntz. LC 79-63202. (Illus.). 576p. 1979. 41.25 (ISBN 0-89352-060-8). Masson Pub.
Reduced Fare & Fare-Free Urban Transit Services: Some Case Studies. Michael A. Kemp. 37p. 1974. pap. 2.50 o.p. (ISBN 0-87766-122-7, 79000). Urban Inst.
Reducing Delinquency. Gregory R. Falkin. (Illus.). 240p. 1979. 21.95 (ISBN 0-669-02318-3). Lexington Bks.
Reducing Global Inequities. W. Howard Wriggins & Gunnar Adler-Karlsson. (Nineteen Eighties Project (Council on Foreign Relations)). 1978. text ed. 10.95 o.p. (ISBN 0-07-071925-X, P&RB); pap. text ed. 5.95 o.p. (ISBN 0-07-071926-8). McGraw.
Reducing Made Easy: The Elments of Microfilm. James H. Mann. LC 76-25335. 12.00 (ISBN 0-87716-069-4). Moore Pub Co.
Redward Edward Papers. Avram Davidson. LC 74-27578. 1978. 7.95 o.p. (ISBN 0-385-02058-9). Doubleday.
Redwoods Are the Tallest Trees in the World. David A. Adler. LC 77-4713. (Let's-Read-and-Find-Out Science Bk). (Illus.). (gr. k-3). 1978. PLB 7.89 (ISBN 0-690-01368-X, TYC-J). T Y Crowell.
Reed's Nautical Almanac & Coast Pilot, 1980. (Illus.). 1979. pap. 14.95 (ISBN 0-910990-45-X). Hearst Bks.
Reef. lib. rep. ed. Edith Wharton. LC 65-21879. 1970. 17.50x (ISBN 0-684-15557-5, ScribT). Scribner.
Reefs of Space. Frederik Pohl & Jack Williamson. 1973. pap. 1.25 o.p. (ISBN 0-345-23448-0). Ballantine.
Reel Change: A Guide to Social Issue Films. Ed. by Patricia Peyton. LC 79-54657. (Film Fund Ser.). (Illus., Orig.). 1980. pap. 6.95. NY Zoetrope.
Reel People. (Orig.). 1979. pap. 15.00x o.p. (ISBN 0-87314-078-8). Peter Glenn.
Reeling. Pauline Kael. 1977. pap. 2.95 o.s.i. (ISBN 0-446-83420-3). Warner Bks.

Rees Howells: Intercessor. Norman P. Grubb. 1964-1967. 4.95 o.p. (ISBN 0-87508-220-3); pap. 3.95 (ISBN 0-87508-219-X). Chr Lit.

Reese Chronological Bible. Compiled by Edward Reese. 1649p. 1980. Repr. of 1977 ed. 24.95 (ISBN 0-87123-115-8, 230115). Bethany Fell.

Reevaluating Spillway Adequacy of Existing Dams. Compiled by American Society of Civil Engineers. 64p. 1975. pap. text ed. 9.50 (ISBN 0-87262-119-7). Am Soc Civil Eng.

Reference & Generality: An Examination of Some Medieval & Modern Theories. 3rd ed. Peter T. Geach. LC 80-10977. (Contempory Philosophy Ser.). 256p. 1980. 19.50x (ISBN 0-8014-1315-X). Cornell U Pr.

Reference & Information Services: A Reader. William A. Katz & Andrea Tarr. LC 77-20698. 1978. 15.00 (ISBN 0-8108-1091-3). Scarecrow.

Reference As the Promotion of Free Inquiry. Louis Shores. LC 76-6150. 189p. 1976. lib. bdg. 11.50x o.p. (ISBN 0-87287-156-8). Libs Unl.

Reference Book for World Traders, 1971. LC 61-10661. 85.00 (ISBN 0-87514-000-9). Croner.

Reference Book of Department Personnel. 1980. 2.50 (ISBN 0-686-21010-7). AASHTO.

Reference Book of English Words & Phrases for Foreign Science Students. R. F. Price. 1976. text ed. 18.75 (ISBN 0-08-011750-3); pap. text ed. 6.50 (ISBN 0-08-020381-7). Pergamon.

Reference Books for Elementary & Junior High School Libraries. 2nd ed. Carolyn S. Peterson. LC 75-8537. 321p. 1975. 12.00 (ISBN 0-8108-0816-1). Scarecrow.

Reference Books for Small & Medium-Sized Libraries. 3rd ed. American Library Association Reference & Adult Services Division. LC 79-13004. 1979. pap. 9.00 (ISBN 0-8389-3227-4). ALA.

Reference Books in Paperback: An Annotated Guide. 2nd ed. Ed. by Bohdan S. Wynar. LC 76-44238. 1976. PLB 18.50x (ISBN 0-87287-166-5). Libs Unl.

Reference Electrodes: Theory & Practice. Ed. by David G. Ives & George J. Janz. 1969. pap. 33.00 (ISBN 0-12-376856-X). Acad Pr.

Reference Grammar for Students of English. Reg A. Close. (Illus.). 384p. 1975. pap. text ed. 9.00x (ISBN 0-582-52277-3). Longman.

Reference Groups & the Theory of Revolution. John Urry. (International Library of Sociology). 256p. 1973. 20.00x (ISBN 0-7100-7541-3). Routledge & Kegan.

Reference Guide to American Science Fiction Films: Vol. II, 1930-1950. A. W. Strickland. 400p. 1980. pap. text ed. write for info. (ISBN 0-89917-269-5). TIS Inc.

Reference Guide to American Science Fiction Films: 1951-1979, Vol. III. A. W. Strickland. 400p. 1980. pap. write for info. (ISBN 0-89917-270-9). TIS Inc.

Reference Guide to Georgia Legal History & Legal Research. Leah F. Chanin. 175p. 1980. 20.00 (ISBN 0-87215-315-0). Michie.

Reference Guide to Handbooks & Annuals. rev. ed. J. William Pfeiffer & John E. Jones. LC 75-14661. 150p. 1981. pap. 9.50 (ISBN 0-88390-069-6). Univ Assocs.

Reference Guide to the Study of Public Opinion. Harwood L. Childs. LC 73-12777. Repr. of 1934 ed. 18.00 (ISBN 0-8103-3704-5). Gale.

Reference Guie to the American Film Noir: 1940-1958. Robert Ottoson. LC 80-23176. 290p. 1981. 15.00 (ISBN 0-8108-1363-7). Scarecrow.

Reference Handbook: Basic Science Concepts & Applications. American Water Works Association. (General References Ser.). (Illus.). 756p. 1980. text ed. 18.50 (ISBN 0-89867-202-3). Am Water Wks Assn.

Reference Handbook of Grammar & Usage. Porter G. Perrin. (Derived from Writer's guide & Index to English). 1972. 7.95 (ISBN 0-688-00061-4). Morrow.

Reference Materials & Periodicals in Economics: An International List, Agriculture. Emma L. Fundaburk. LC 78-142232. 1971. 21.00 (ISBN 0-8108-0349-6). Scarecrow.

Reference Materials & Periodicals in Economics: An International List, Major Manufacturing Industries - Automotive, Chemical, Iron & Steel, Petrole. Emma L. Fundaburk. LC 78-142232. 1972. 23.50 (ISBN 0-8108-0453-0). Scarecrow.

Reference Materials on Mexican Americans: An Annotated Bibliography. Richard D. Woods. LC 76-10663. 197p. 1976. 10.00 (ISBN 0-8108-0963-X). Scarecrow.

Reference Methods for Marine Radioactivity Studies. (Technical Reports: No. 118). (Illus., Orig.). 1970. pap. 16.25 (ISBN 92-0-125470-9, IAEA). Unipub.

Reference Methods for Marine Radioactivity Studies II. (Technical Reports Ser: No. 169). (Illus.). 239p. 1975. pap. 18.25 (ISBN 92-0-125275-7, IAEA). Unipub.

Reference Resources: A Systematic Approach. James M. Doyle & George H. Grimes. LC 76-7080. 1976. 12.00 (ISBN 0-8108-0928-1). Scarecrow.

Reference Seismic Grond Motions in Nuclear Safety Assessments. OECD-NEA. (Illus.). 171p. (Orig.). 1980. pap. text ed. 16.00x (ISBN 92-64-12100-5). OECD.

Reference Service. Donald Davidson. 1980. text ed. 19.00 (ISBN 0-89664-423-5, Pub. by K G Saur). Shoe String.

Reference Service. 2nd rev. ed. Krishan Kumar. 390p. 1980. text ed. 18.95 (ISBN 0-7069-0637-3, Pub. by Vikas India). Advent Bk.

Reference Service: An Annotated Bibliographic Guide. Marjorie E. Murfin & Lubomyr R. Wynar. LC 76-54879. 1977. lib. bdg. 18.50x (ISBN 0-87287-132-0). Libs Unl.

Reference Services: A Guide to Information Sources. Evelyn Greenberg. LC 74-11553. (Books, Publishing & Libraries Information Guide Ser.). 30.00 (ISBN 0-8103-1285-9). Gale.

Reference Sources in English & American Literature: An Annotated Bibliography. Robert C. Schweik & Dieter Riesner. 1977. 12.95x (ISBN 0-393-04484-X); pap. 7.95x (ISBN 0-393-09104-X). Norton.

Reference Sources Nineteen Eighty. Ed. by S. Balachandran & M. Balachandran. 1981. 65.00 (ISBN 0-87650-127-7). Pierian.

Reference Sources, 1980. Ed. by S. Balachdran & M. Balachdran. 1981. 65.00 (ISBN 0-87650-127-7). Pierian.

Reference Work in the Humanities. Edmund F. SantaVicca. LC 80-18783. 173p. 1980. 10.00 (ISBN 0-8108-1342-4). Scarecrow.

Referendum in America. Ellis P. Oberholtzer. LC 70-153370. (American Constitutional & Legal History Ser). 1971. Repr. of 1912 ed. lib. bdg. 49.50 (ISBN 0-306-70149-9). Da Capo.

Referring the Psychiatric Patient: A Guide for the Physician. Larry R. Kimsey & Jean L. Roberts. (American Lectures in Clinical Psychiatry Ser.). 100p. 1973. text ed. 9.50 (ISBN 0-398-02725-0). C C Thomas.

Refinement of Character. Ali Miskawayh. Tr. by Constantine Zurayk. 1977. pap. 14.00x (ISBN 0-8156-6051-0, Am U Beirut). Syracuse U Pr.

Reflected Glory in a Bottle: Chinese Snuff Bottle Portraits. Emily B. Curtis. (Illus.). 128p. 1980. 25.00 (ISBN 0-9605096-0-7). Soho Bodhi.

Reflecting Pond. Lianne Cordes. 1980. pap. 6.95 (ISBN 0-89486-121-2). Hazelden.

Reflection on the Atomic Bomb: The Previously Uncollected Writings of Gertrude Stein, Vol. 1. Gertrude Stein. Ed. by Robert B. Haas. 100p. (Orig.). 1975. 14.00 (ISBN 0-87685-166-9); pap. 5.00 (ISBN 0-87685-167-7). Black Sparrow.

Reflection on the Holocaust. Irene G. Shur & Franklin H. Littell. Ed. by Richard D. Lambert. LC 80-66618. (Annals of the American Academy of Political & Social Science: No. 450). 250p. 1980. 5.50x (ISBN 0-87761-252-8); pap. text ed. 7.00x (ISBN 0-87761-253-6). Am Acad Pol Soc Sci.

Reflection Seismology. 2nd ed. Kenneth H. Waters. 350p. 1981. 34.95 (ISBN 0-471-08224-4, Pub. by Wiley-Interscience). Wiley.

Reflection, Time & the Novel. Angel Medina. (International Library of Phenomenology & Moral Sciences). 1979. 20.00x (ISBN 0-7100-0273-4). Routledge & Kegan.

Reflections: An Anthology. Wichita Falls Poetry Society. 3.95 o.p. (ISBN 0-685-48828-4). Nortex Pr.

Reflections: Anthology. Women's Aglow Editors. 216p. 1979. pap. 6.95 (ISBN 0-930756-48-7, 4230-AD1). Women's Aglow.

Reflections from a Village. Frank Swinnerton. 1979. 19.95 (ISBN 0-241-89998-2, Pub. by Hamish Hamilton England). David & Charles.

Reflections in a Quiet Pool: The Prints of David Milne. Rosemarie L. Tovell. (National Gallery of Canada Ser.). (Illus.). 256p. 1981. lib. bdg. 45.00x (ISBN 0-88884-461-1, 56494-0, Pub. by Natl Mus Canada). U of Chicago Pr.

Reflections of a Nuclear War & the Energy Shortage. Peter J. Peloquin. 64p. 1980. pap. 2.95 (ISBN 0-936448-00-8). Peloquin Pubns.

Reflections of a Rock Star. Ian Hunter. LC 75-45514. (Illus.). 196p. (Orig.). 1976. pap. 3.95 o.p. (ISBN 0-8256-3905-0, Quick Fox). Music Sales.

Reflections of Mind: Western Psychology Meets Tibetan Buddhism. Tarthang Tulku. LC 75-5254. (Illus.). 1975. 12.95 (ISBN 0-913546-15-1); pap. 5.95 o.p. (ISBN 0-913546-14-3). Dharma Pub.

Reflections of My Spirit. Rita Burton. LC 76-24042. 1977. pap. 2.95 o.p. (ISBN 0-89221-024-9). New Leaf.

Reflections of the Self. Swami Muktananda. LC 80-50391. (Illus., Orig.). 1980. pap. 5.95 (ISBN 0-914602-50-0). SYDA Found.

Reflections on Behaviorism & Society. B. F. Skinner. (Century Psychology Ser.). (Illus.). 1978. ref. 17.95 (ISBN 0-13-770057-1). P-H.

Reflections on Black Psychology. Ed. by William D. Smith et al. LC 79-63256. 1979. pap. text ed. 15.25 (ISBN 0-8191-0722-0). U Pr of Amer.

Reflections on Equestrian Art. Nuno Oliveira. Tr. by Phyllis Fields from Portuguese. (Illus.). 12.25 (ISBN 0-85131-257-8, Dist. by Sporting Book Center). J A Allen.

Reflections on Field & Stream. Lord Home. (Illus.). 112p. 1980. 12.50 (ISBN 0-316-37196-3). Little.

Reflections on Fieldwork in Morocco. Paul Rabinow. (Quantum Ser.). 1977. 14.50x (ISBN 0-520-03450-3); pap. 4.95x (ISBN 0-520-03529-1). U of Cal Pr.

Reflections on Life Long Education & the School. (UIE Monographs: No. 3). 1976. pap. 2.50 (ISBN 92-820-1006-6, U541, UNESCO). Unipub.

Reflections on Muscle. Andrew Huxley. LC 79-5480. (Illus.). 120p. 1980. 15.95x (ISBN 0-691-08255-3). Princeton U Pr.

Reflections on Revival. Charles Finney. LC 78-26527. 1979. pap. 3.95 (ISBN 0-87123-157-3, 210157). Bethany Fell.

Reflections on Senghor. Chikeho M. Mbabuike. 140p. 1981. 12.95 (ISBN 0-88254-504-3). Hippocrene Bks.

Reflections on the Brazilian Counterrevolution. Florestan Fernandes. Pref. by Warren Dean. Tr. by Michel Vale from Portuguese. LC 80-5456. 200p. 1981. 25.00 (ISBN 0-87332-177-4). M E Sharpe.

Reflections on the Decline of Science in England & on Some of Its Causes. C. Babbage. 256p. 1971. Repr. of 1830 ed. 25.00x (ISBN 0-7165-1578-4, Pub. by Irish Academic Pr Ireland). Biblio Dist.

Reflections on the English Progressive. Magnus Ljung. (Gothenberg Studies in English: 46). 166p. 1981. pap. text ed. 19.75x (ISBN 91-7346-080-X, Pub. by Acta Univertatis, Sweden). Humanities.

Reflections on the Failure of Socialism. Max Eastman. LC 55-7352. 128p. 1981. pap. 4.95 (ISBN 0-8159-6707-1). Devin.

Reflections on the Hero As Quixote. Alexander Welsh. LC 80-8584. 256p. 1981. 15.00x (ISBN 0-691-06465-2). Princeton U Pr.

Reflections on the Mathematics Experience. Ed. by Marshall Gordon. LC 79-83694. (Educational Ser.). 1979. text ed. cancelled (ISBN 0-8211-0614-7). McCutchan.

Reflections on the Organ Stoplist: Theory & Practice from the Organ Workshop. Hans G. Klais. Tr. by Homer D. Blanchard from Ger. (Illus.). 1975. 17.50 o.s.i. (ISBN 0-930112-00-8). Praestant.

Reflections on the Path. Herbert B. Puryear. (Illus.). 183p. (Orig.). 1979. pap. 3.95 (ISBN 0-87604-113-6). ARE Pr.

Reflections on the Present Condition of the Female Sex: With Suggestions for Its Improvement. Priscilla Wakefield. Ed. by Gina Luria. (Feminist Controversy in England, 1788-1810 Ser.). 1974. lib. bdg. 50.00 (ISBN 0-8240-0882-0). Garland Pub.

Reflections on the Revolution in France & Other Essays. Edmund Burke. 1953. 5.00x o.p. (ISBN 0-460-00460-3, Evman); pap. 2.75 o.p. o.p. (ISBN 0-460-01460-9). Dutton.

Reflections on the Revolution in France. Edmund Burke. Ed. by Thomas H. Mahoney. 1955. pap. 6.95 (ISBN 0-672-60213-X, LLA46). Bobbs.

Reflections on the Revolution in France: 1968. Charles Posner. 6.75 (ISBN 0-8446-0852-1). Peter Smith.

Reflections on the Role of Liberal Education. Association of American Colleges. 1964. 3.00 o.p. (ISBN 0-685-26072-0). ACE.

Reflections on the Stage & Mr. Collyer's Defence of the Short View. John Oldmixon. LC 73-170447. (English Stage Ser.: Vol. 33). lib. bdg. 50.00 (ISBN 0-8240-0616-X). Garland Pub.

Reflections on the Tantras. Sudhakar Chattopadhyaya. 1978. 7.50 (ISBN 0-89684-028-X, Pub. by Motilal Banarsidass India). Orient Bk Dist.

Reflections on Things at Hand: The Neo-Cunfucian Anthology. Tr. by Wing Tstit Chan. LC 65-22548. (Records of Civilization Sources Studies). xli, 441p. 1967. 27.50x (ISBN 0-231-02819-9). Columbia U Pr.

Reflex. Dick Francis. 288p. 1981. 11.95 (ISBN 0-399-12598-1). Putnam.

Reflex Activity of the Spinal Cord. R. S. Creed et al. (Illus.). 210p. 1972. 24.95x (ISBN 0-19-857355-3). Oxford U Pr.

Reflex Control of Posture & Movement: Proceedings. IBRO Symposium, Italy, September 1978. Ed. by R. Granit & O. Pompeiano. (Progress in Brain Research Ser.: Vol. 50). 1980. 122.00 (ISBN 0-444-80099-9, North Holland). Elsevier.

Reflex Testing Methods for Evaluating C. N. S. Development. 2nd ed. Mary R. Fiorentino. (American Lecture Orthopaedic Surgery). (Illus.). 72p. 1979. 11.75 (ISBN 0-398-02584-3). C C Thomas.

Reflexions on Poetry & Poetics. Howard Nemerov. LC 74-185396. 1972. 17.50 (ISBN 0-8135-0727-8). Rutgers U Pr.

Reflexions Sur l'Opera. Toussaint Remond De Saint-Mard. LC 80-2294. 1981. Repr. of 1741 ed. 18.50 (ISBN 0-404-18863-X). AMS Pr.

Reflexive Universe: Evolution of Consciousness. Arthur M. Young. 1976. 15.95 o.s.i. (ISBN 0-440-05925-9, Sey Lawr); pap. 6.95 (ISBN 0-440-05924-0). Delacorte.

Reflexology for Good Health. Anna Kaye & Don C. Mathan. pap. 3.00 (ISBN 0-87980-383-5). Wilshire.

Reflux & Renal Scarring. P. G. Ransley & R. A. Ridson. 1980. 15.00x (Pub. by Brit Inst Radiology). State Mutual Bk.

Reflux Nephropathy. Ed. by John C. Hodson & Priscilla Kincaid-Smith. LC 79-84477. (Illus.). 366p. 1979. text ed. 43.50 (ISBN 0-89352-044-6). Masson Pub.

Reform & Development of Higher Education: A European Symposium. Lloyd James et al. (Council of Europe Ser.). 1978. pap. text ed. 27.00x (ISBN 0-85633-152-X, NFER). Humanities.

Reform & Reformation: England & the Continent c.1380-c.1750. Ed. by Derek Baker. (Studies in Church History: Subsidia 2). (Illus.). 1979. 36.00x (ISBN 0-631-19270-0, Pub. by Basil Blackwell England). Biblio Dist.

Reform & Reformation: England, 1509-1558. G. R. Elton. LC 77-6464. (Harvard Paperback Ser.: No. 146, The New History of England). 1979. 18.50x (ISBN 0-674-75245-7); pap. 7.95x (ISBN 0-674-75248-1). Harvard U Pr.

Reform & Regulation of Long Term Care. Ed. by Valerie LaPorte & Jeffrey Rubin. LC 79-9761. 230p. 1979. 22.95 (ISBN 0-03-049341-2). Praeger.

Reform & Regulations: American Politics, 1900-1916. Lewis L. Gould. LC 77-21058. (Critical Episodes in American Policy Ser.). 1978. pap. text ed. 7.95 (ISBN 0-471-31914-7). Wiley.

Reform & Renewal, Thomas Cromwell & the Common Weal. Geoffrey R. Elton. (Wiles Lectures, 1972). 230p. 1973. 29.50 (ISBN 0-521-20054-7); pap. 7.95x (ISBN 0-521-09809-2). Cambridge U Pr.

Reform & Resistance in the International Order. Ian Clark. LC 79-54017. 1980. 29.50 (ISBN 0-521-22998-7); pap. 8.95 (ISBN 0-521-29763-X). Cambridge U Pr.

Reform & Revolution in China: The 1911 Revolution in Hunan & Hubei. Joseph W. Esherick. 1976. 20.00x (ISBN 0-520-03084-2). U of Cal Pr.

Reform & Revolution in Mainz, 1743-1803. T. C. Blanning. (Studies in Early Modern History). 384p. 1974. 41.95 (ISBN 0-521-20418-6). Cambridge U Pr.

Reform & Revolution: Transformation of Hungary's Agriculture 1945-1970. Ferenc Donath. Tr. by Gisela Vizmathy-Susits. (Illus.). 489p. (Orig.). 1980. pap. 10.00x (ISBN 963-13-0911-8). Intl Pubns Serv.

Reform Bill of 1832. George Woodbridge. LC 78-107301. (AHM Europe Since 1500 Ser.). (Orig.). 1970. pap. 5.95x (ISBN 0-88295-772-4). AHM Pub.

Reform in Corrections: Problems & Issues. Ed. by Harry E. Allen & Nancy J. Beran. LC 76-12840. (Special Studies). 1977. text ed. 16.95 o.p. (ISBN 0-275-24270-6). Praeger.

Reform in Oaxaca, 1856-76: A Microhistory of the Liberal Revolution. Charles R. Berry. LC 80-15378. (Illus.). xx, 282p. 1981. 20.00x (ISBN 0-8032-1158-9). U of Nebr Pr.

Reform in Soviet Politics: The Lessons of Recent Policies on Land & Water. Thane Gustafson. LC 80-24286. (Illus.). 224p. Date not set. price not set (ISBN 0-521-23377-1). Cambridge U Pr.

Reform Judaism - Then & Now. Sylvan D. Schwartzman. (Illus.). (gr. 10). 1971. text ed. 7.50 (ISBN 0-8074-0191-9, 161900). UAHC.

Reform Judaism in the Making. Schwartzman. 1959. 7.50 (ISBN 0-8074-0192-7, 183542). UAHC.

Reform of Medical Education. National Academy Of Sciences. 1970. 8.75 (ISBN 0-309-01757-2). Natl Acad Pr.

Reform of the Fallen World: The Virtuous Prince in Jonsonian Tragedy & Comedy. William D. Wolf. (Salzburg Studies in English Literature, Jacobean Drama Studies: No. 27). 1973. pap. text ed. 25.00x (ISBN 0-391-01575-3). Humanities.

Reform of Undergraduate Education. Arthur E. Levine & John R. Weingart. LC 73-7154. (Higher Education Ser). 176p. 1973. 11.95x o.p. (ISBN 0-87589-186-1). Jossey-Bass.

Reform on Campus: Changing Students, Changing Academic Programs. Carnegie Commission on Higher Education. LC 72-4783. 160p. 1972. 4.50 o.p. (ISBN 0-07-010052-7, P&RB). McGraw.

Reform, Reaction & Resources: The 3 Rs of Educational Planning. Miriam E. David. (General Ser.). 1977. pap. text ed. 25.50x (ISBN 0-85633-127-9, NFER). Humanities.

Reformatio Perennis: Essays on Calvin & the Reformation in Honor of Ford Lewis Battles. Ed. by Brian Gerrish. (Pittsburgh Theological Monograph Ser.: No. 32). 1981. pap. 12.95 (ISBN 0-915138-41-7). Pickwick.

Reformation. Peter Klassen. LC 79-54030. (Problems in Civilization Ser.). (Orig.). 1980. pap. text ed. 3.95x (ISBN 0-88273-408-3). Forum Pr MO.

Reformation. T. M. Lindsay. (Handbooks for Bible Classes). 224p. 1977. text ed. 8.95. Attic Pr.

Reformation. Edith Simon. LC 66-22782. (Great Ages of Man). (Illus.). (gr. 6 up). 1966. PLB 11.97 (ISBN 0-8094-0370-6, Pub. by Time-Life). Silver.

Reformation. Edith Simon. (Great Ages of Man Ser). (Illus.). 1966. 12.95 (ISBN 0-8094-0348-X); lib. bdg. avail. (ISBN 0-685-20549-5). Time-Life.

Reformation & Resistance in Tudor Lancashire. C. Haigh. LC 73-88308. (Illus.). 416p. 1974. 42.95 (ISBN 0-521-20367-8). Cambridge U Pr.

Reformation Europe: Age of Reform & Revolution. De Lamar Jensen. 480p. 1981. pap. text ed. 10.95 (ISBN 0-669-03626-9). Heath.

Reformation in England, 2 vols. Merle D'Aubigne. 1977. Vol. 1. 14.95 (ISBN 0-85151-059-0); Vol. 2. 14.95 (ISBN 0-85151-094-9). Set. 27.95. Banner of Truth.

Reformation in England. Frederick M. Powicke. (Oxford Paperbacks Ser). 1961. pap. 3.95x (ISBN 0-19-285001-6). Oxford U Pr.

Reformation of Images: Destruction of Art in England, 1530-1665. John R. Phillips. 1974. 20.00x (ISBN 0-520-02424-9). U of Cal Pr.

Reformation of the Sixteenth Century in Its Relation to Modern Thought & Knowledge. Charles Beard. LC 80-12915. xxviii, 450p. 1980. Repr. of 1962 ed. lib. bdg. 33.50x (ISBN 0-313-22410-2, BERF). Greenwood.

Reformation Parliament Fifteen Twenty-Nine - Fifteen Thirty-Six. S. E. Lehmberg. LC 70-85723. (Illus., Orig.). 1970. 35.50 (ISBN 0-521-07655-2). Cambridge U Pr.

Reformation Principle & Practice: Essays in Honour of A. G. Dickens. Ed. by Peter N. Brooks. 256p. 1980. 40.00x (ISBN 0-85967-579-3, Pub. by Scolar Pr England). Biblio Dist.

Reformatory Education. Henry Barnard. 361p. 1980. Repr. of 1857 ed. lib. bdg. 20.00 (ISBN 0-8492-3589-8). R West.

Reform'd Coquet. Mary Davys. Bd. with Familiar Letters Betwixt a Gentleman & a Lady; Mercenary Lover: or the Unfortunate Heiresses. Eliza Haywood. LC 72-170558. (Foundations of the Novel Ser.: Vol. 42). lib. bdg. 50.00 (ISBN 0-8240-0553-8). Garland Pub.

Reformed & Catholic: Selected Theological Writings of Phillip Schaff. Ed. by Charles Yrigoyen. Jr. & George H Bricker. LC 79-17391. (Pittsburgh Original Texts & Translations Ser: No. 4). 1979. pap. text ed. 12.95 (ISBN 0-915138-40-9). Pickwick.

Reformed Dogmatics. Herman Hoeksema. LC 66-24047. 1966. 12.95 (ISBN 0-8254-2806-8). Kregel.

Reformed Local Government System. 4th ed. Peter G. Richards. (New Local Government Ser.). 192p. 1980. pap. text ed. 8.95 (ISBN 0-04-352090-1, 2491). Allen Unwin.

Reformed Pastor. Richard Baxter. 1979. pap. 3.95 (ISBN 0-85151-191-0). Banner of Truth.

Reformers & the Theology of Reformation. William Cunningham. 1979. 15.95 (ISBN 0-85151-013-2). Banner of Truth.

Reforming Corrections for Juvenile Offenders. Yitzhak Bakal & Howard W. Polsky. LC 73-11680. 1979. 17.95 (ISBN 0-669-90209-8). Lexington Bks.

Reforming Government: Winning Strategies Against Waste, Corruption, & Mismanagement. Daniel L. Feldman. LC 80-24963. 225p. 1981. 11.95 (ISBN 0-688-03729-1). Morrow.

Reforming Regulation: Processes & Problems. Lawrence J. White. (Illus.). 240p. 1981. text ed. 13.95 (ISBN 0-13-770115-2); pap. text ed. 8.95 (ISBN 0-13-770107-1). P-H.

Reforming School Finance. Robert D. Reischauer et al. (Studies in Social Economics). 1973. 11.95 (ISBN 0-8157-7396-X); pap. 4.95 (ISBN 0-8157-7395-1). Brookings.

Reforming Schools: Problems in Program Implementation & Evaluation. Wendy P. Abt et al. LC 80-23339. (Contemporary Evaluation Research Ser.: Vol. 4). (Illus.). 200p. 1981. 20.00 (ISBN 0-8039-1459-8); pap. 9.95 (ISBN 0-8039-1460-1). Sage.

Reforming the Long-Term-Care System: Financial & Organizational Options. Ed. by James J. Callahan, Jr. & Stanley S. Wallack. LC 80-8366. (University Health Policy Consortium Ser.). 272p. 1981. 24.95x (ISBN 0-669-04040-1). Lexington Bks.

Reforms & Restraints in Modern French Education. W. R. Fraser. (World Education Ser). 1971. 16.50 (ISBN 0-7100-7174-4). Routledge & Kegan.

Reforms of Tax Systems: Proceedings. International Institute of Public Finance, 35th Congress, 1979. Ed. by Karl W. Roskamp. 1981. 30.00 (ISBN 0-686-64651-7). Wayne St U Pr.

Refraction & Clinical Optics. Aran Safir. (Illus.). 565p. 1980. text ed. 37.50 (ISBN 0-06-142318-1, Harper Medical). Har-Row.

Refractions: Essays in Comparative Literature. Harry Levin. 1968. pap. 5.95 (ISBN 0-19-500771-9, GB). Oxford U Pr.

Refractories. 4th ed. Frederick H. Norton. 1968. text ed. 37.50 o.p. (ISBN 0-07-047538-5, P&RB). McGraw.

Refractory Anemia. Lawrence Kass & Bertram Schnitzer. (Illus.). 160p. 1975. 32.75 (ISBN 0-398-03341-2). C C Thomas.

Refractory Concrete. 1978. 22.25 (SP-57); 17.25. ACI.

Refractory Materials. G. B. Rothenberg. LC 76-17943. (Chemical Technology Review: No. 76). (Illus.). 1977. 39.00 o.p. (ISBN 0-8155-0635-X). Noyes.

Refractory Materials: Developments Since 1977. Ed. by J. I. Duffy. LC 80-21945. (Chemical Technology Review: No. 178). (Illus.). 367p. 1981. 42.00 (ISBN 0-8155-0827-1). Noyes.

Reframing the Constitution: An Imperative for Modern America. Leland D. Baldwin. LC 78-187927. (Illus.). 145p. 1972. text ed. 16.50 (ISBN 0-87436-082-X); pap. text ed. 2.50 (ISBN 0-87436-083-8). ABC-Clio.

Refresher Mathematics. rev. ed. Edwin I. Stein. (gr. 7-12). 1974. text ed. 13.56 (ISBN 0-205-04306-2, 5643066); tchrs'. guide 5.12 (ISBN 0-205-04307-0, 5643074). Allyn.

Refresher Mathematics. Edwin I. Stein. (gr. 7-12). 1980. text ed. 13.56 (ISBN 0-205-06160-5, 5661609); tchrs'. guide 5.12 (ISBN 0-205-06161-3, 5661617). Allyn.

Refrigeration. G. H. Reed. LC 74-15129. (Illus.). 1969. 8.95 (ISBN 0-8306-0295-X); pap. 4.95 (ISBN 0-8306-9295-9, 295). TAB Bks.

Refrigeration, Pt. I. Ed. by A. Ross Sabin. (Illus.). 144p. (gr. 11). 1974. 20.00 (ISBN 0-938336-01-0). Whirlpool.

Refrigeration, Pt. II. Ed. by A. Ross Sabin. (Illus.). 203p. (gr. 11). 1974. 20.00 (ISBN 0-938336-02-9). Whirlpool.

Refrigeration: A Practical Manual for Apprentices. 3rd ed. G. H. Reed. (Illus.). 1974. pap. text ed. 12.40x (ISBN 0-85334-605-4). Intl Ideas.

Refrigeration: A Practical Manual for Mechanics. G. H. Reed. (Illus.). 1972. 26.00x (ISBN 0-85334-531-7, Pub. by Applied Science). Burgess-Intl Ideas.

Refrigeration & Thermometry Below One Kelvin. D. S. Betts. LC 75-34695. (Illus.). 304p. 1976. 29.50x (ISBN 0-8448-0853-9). Crane-Russak Co.

Refrigeration at Sea. 2nd ed. R. Munton & J. R. Stott. (Illus.). 1978. text ed. 51.30x (ISBN 0-85334-766-2, Pub. by Applied Science). Burgess-Intl Ideas.

Refrigeration: Home & Commercial. Roland Palmquist. LC 77-71583. 1977. 12.95 (ISBN 0-672-23286-3). Audel.

Refrigeration Licenses: (Contractor-Journeyman-Operator) Unlimited. Clayton H. Carrico. 1980. text ed. 25.00x (ISBN 0-912524-20-0). Busn News.

Refrigeration Processes: A Practical Handbook on the Physical Properties of Refrigerants & Their Applications. M. H. Meacock. (International Series in Heating, Ventilation & Refrigeration: Vol. 12). 1979. 41.00 (ISBN 0-08-024211-1); pap. 18.75 (ISBN 0-08-024234-0). Pergamon.

Refrigeration Servicing. Paul F. Goliber. LC 75-6064. 112p. 1976. pap. 4.80 (ISBN 0-8273-1005-6). Delmar.

Refrigeration Technician's Pocketbook. Meredith. 1981. text ed. price not set (ISBN 0-408-00545-9). Butterworth.

Refugee in the Postwar World. Jacques Vernant. 1953. 42.50x o.p. (ISBN 0-685-69880-7). Elliots Bks.

Refugee Question in Mid-Victorian Politics. Bernard Porter. LC 78-73947. (Illus.). 1980. 41.50 (ISBN 0-521-22638-4). Cambridge U Pr.

Refugees: a Problem of Our Time: The Work of the United Nations High Commissioner for Refugees; 1951-1972, 2 vols. Louise W. Holborn. LC 74-19471. (Illus.). 1975. Set. 55.00 (ISBN 0-8108-0746-7). Scarecrow.

Refugees: A Tale of Two Continents. Arthur Conan Doyle. 8.95 (ISBN 0-685-20618-1). Transatlantic.

Refugees: Viewpoints, Case Studies & Theoretical Considerations on the Care & Management of Refugees. F. Souza. (Illus.). 136p. 1980. 19.25 (ISBN 0-08-025460-8). Pergamon.

Refugio Secreto. Tr. by Corrie Ten Boom. (Spanish Bks.). (Span.). 1978. 1.95 (ISBN 0-8297-0593-7). Life Pubs Intl.

Refugium Botanicum or Figurs & Descriptions from Living Specimens of Little Known or New Plants of Botanical Interest, Vol. II. Illus. by W. H. Fitch. (Orchid Ser.). (Illus.). 1980. Repr. text ed. 27.50 (ISBN 0-930576-19-5). E M Coleman Ent.

Refunding of International Debt. Henry J. Bittermann. LC 72-93542. 234p. 1973. 14.75 (ISBN 0-8223-0280-2). Duke.

Refuse Recycling & Recovery: A Review of the State of the Art. John R. Holmes. 168p. 1981. 38.00 (ISBN 0-471-27902-1, Pub. by Wiley-Interscience); pap. 14.00 (ISBN 0-471-27903-X). Wiley.

Refusenik: Trapped in the Soviet Union. Mark Y. Azbel. Ed. by Grace P. Forbes. (Illus.). 528p. 1981. 17.95 (ISBN 0-395-30226-9). HM.

Refutation of Machiavelli's Prince or Anti-Machiavel. Frederick Of Prussia. Tr. by Paul Sonnino. LC 80-15801. viii, 173p. 1981. 13.95x (ISBN 0-8214-0559-4); pap. 5.95 (ISBN 0-8214-0598-5). Ohio U Pr.

Regalo. Cynthia Walcott. Tr. by Baha'i Publishing Committee. LC 76-5502. (Illus.). (gr. 1-5). 1976. 7.00 (ISBN 0-87743-106-X, 7-93-68); with cassette narration 12.00 (ISBN 0-87743-109-4, 7-93-67). Baha'i.

Regard Contemplatif Chez Valery et Mallarme. Ludmilla M. Wills. (Orig., Fr.). 1976. pap. text ed. 14.50x (ISBN 90-620-3407-1). Humanities.

Regarding Wave. Gary Snyder. LC 72-122107. 1970. 6.00 (ISBN 0-8112-0386-7); pap. 4.95 (ISBN 0-8112-0196-1, NDP306). New Directions.

Regatta. Douglas Wallop. 1981. 12.95 (ISBN 0-393-01364-2). Norton.

Regency Charade. Elizabeth Mansfield. 224p. 1981. pap. 2.25 (ISBN 0-425-04835-7). Berkley Pub.

Regency Furniture, Eighteen Hundred to Eighteen Thirty. 2nd ed. Clifford Musgrave. 1970. 26.00 o.p. (ISBN 0-571-04694-0, Pub. by Faber & Faber). Merrimack Bk Serv.

Regency Galatea. Elizabeth Mansfield. 1981. pap. 2.25 (ISBN 0-425-04739-3). Berkley Pub.

Regency Pageant. Paul H. Emden. 295p. 1980. Repr. of 1936 ed. lib. bdg. 35.00 (ISBN 0-89987-204-2). Darby Bks.

Regeneration Through Violence: The Mythology of the American Frontier, 1600-1860. Richard S. Slotkin. LC 72-3725. 670p. (Orig.). 1973. 27.50x (ISBN 0-8195-4055-2, Pub. by Wesleyan U Pr); pap. 8.95 (ISBN 0-8195-6034-0). Columbia U Pr.

Regents English Workbooks, 3 Bks. Robert J. Dixson. (gr. 6 up). 1956-1969. pap. text ed. 2.95 ea.; Bk. 1. pap. text ed. (ISBN 0-88345-139-5, 17420); Bk. 2. pap. text ed. (ISBN 0-88345-140-9, 17421); Bk. 3. pap. text ed. (ISBN 0-88345-141-7, 17742); answer key 1.25 (ISBN 0-685-19803-0). Regents Pub.

Regesta Regum Anglo-Normannorum, 1066 to 1135, 2 vols. Ed. by Henry W. David & R. J. Whitwell. LC 80-2220. 1981. Repr. of 1956 ed. Set. 135.00 (ISBN 0-686-69546-1); 67.50 ea. AMS Pr.

Reggae Bloodlines. Stephen Davis & Peter Simon. LC 76-42428. 1977. pap. 8.95 (ISBN 0-385-12330-2, Anch). Doubleday.

Reggie Jackson. Gary Libman. (Sports Superstars Ser.). (Illus.). (gr. 3-9). 1979. PLB 5.95 (ISBN 0-87191-724-6); pap. 2.95 (ISBN 0-89812-162-0). Creative Ed.

Reggie Jackson: Yankee Superstar. Dick O'Connor. (gr. 4-6). 1978. pap. 1.25 (ISBN 0-590-05396-5, Schol Pap). Schol Bk Serv.

Regime Feodal De l'Italie Normande. Claude Cahen. LC 80-1995. 1981. Repr. of 1923 ed. 22.00 (ISBN 0-404-18555-X). AMS Pr.

Regimes for the Ocean, Outer Space, & Weather. Seyom Brown et al. 1977. 14.95 (ISBN 0-8157-1156-5); pap. 5.95 (ISBN 0-8157-1155-7). Brookings.

Regimes, Movements, & Ideologies: A Comparative Introduction to Political Science. Mark N. Hagopian. LC 77-7718. (Illus.). 1978. pap. 13.50x (ISBN 0-582-28044-3); instructor's manual free (ISBN 0-582-28055-9). Longman.

Regina, the German Captive, or, True Piety Among the Lowly. Reuben Weiser. LC 75-7093. (Indian Captivities Ser.: Vol. 69). 1977. Repr. of 1856 ed. lib. bdg. 44.00 (ISBN 0-8240-1693-9). Garland Pub.

Regina's Song. Sharleen C. Cohen. (Orig.). 1980. pap. 2.50 o.s.i. (ISBN 0-440-17414-7). Dell.

Regiomontanus: On Triangles. Tr. by Barnabas Hughes. (Illus.). 1967. 25.00x (ISBN 0-299-04210-3). U of Wis Pr.

Region Building in the Pacific. Ed. by Gavin Boyd. (Pergamon Policy Studies). 400p. Date not set. price not set (ISBN 0-08-025985-5). Pergamon.

Region of Revolt: Focus on Southeast Asia. M. Osborne. LC 75-133332. 1970. 11.50 (ISBN 0-08-017533-3). Pergamon.

Regional Accounts. Regina B. Armstrong. LC 79-3659. 256p. 1980. 18.50x (ISBN 0-253-17965-3). Ind U Pr.

Regional Analysis, 2 vols. Ed. by Carol A. Smith. (Studies in Anthropology). 1976. 31.00 ea. Vol. 1 (ISBN 0-12-652101-8). Vol. 2 (ISBN 0-12-652102-6). Set. 49.00 (ISBN 0-686-57828-7). Acad Pr.

Regional & Interregional Intersectoral Flow Analysis: The Method & an Application to the Tennessee Economy. Tong H. Lee et al. LC 72-187360. 168p. 1973. 10.50x (ISBN 0-87049-139-3). U of Tenn Pr.

Regional & Interregional Social Accounting. Stan Czamanski. LC 73-9857. (Regional Science Monograph Ser.). (Illus.). 192p. 1973. 19.95 (ISBN 0-669-90563-1). Lexington Bks.

Regional & Rural Development: Essays in Theory & Practice. P. J. Drudy. (Illus.). 1976. text ed. 11.00x (ISBN 0-905193-02-4). Humanities.

Regional Anesthesia of the Oral Cavity. 1st ed. J. Theodore Jastak & John A. Yagiela. (Illus.). 200p. 1981. text ed. 20.00 (ISBN 0-8016-2434-7). Mosby.

Regional Block: A Handbook for Use in the Clinical Practice of Medicine & Surgery. 4th ed. Daniel C. Moore. (Illus.). 1979. 23.75 (ISBN 0-398-01337-3). C C Thomas.

Regional Blocks for Nurse Anesthetists. P. A. Roberts. (Illus.). 128p. 1978. 11.75 (ISBN 0-398-03808-2). C C Thomas.

Regional Co-Operation in the Development of Coarse Grains, Pulses, Roots & Tuber (CGPRT) Crops in Asia & the Pacific. 242p. 1979. pap. 14.00 (ISBN 0-686-61477-1, UN78-2F7, UN). Unipub.

Regional Decline of a National Party: Liberals on the Prairies. David E. Smith. (Canadian Government Ser.). 184p. 1981. 14.00x (ISBN 0-8020-2421-1); pap. 6.50 (ISBN 0-8020-6430-2). U of Toronto Pr.

Regional Demographic Development. Ed. by John Hobcraft & Philip Rees. (Illus.). 287p. 1977. 36.00x (ISBN 0-7099-0245-X, Pub. by Croom Helm Ltd England). Biblio Dist.

Regional Development in Britain. 2nd ed. Gerald Manners et al. LC 79-42901. 1980. 49.50 (ISBN 0-471-27636-7, Pub. by Wiley-Interscience). Wiley.

Regional Development in Western Europe. Hugh D. Clout. 432p. 1981. 16.50 (ISBN 0-471-27846-7, Pub. by Wiley-Interscience); pap. 7.50 (ISBN 0-471-27845-9). Wiley.

Regional Development Policy & Planning in Spain. Harry W. Richardson. (Illus.). 264p. 1975. 24.95 (ISBN 0-347-01091-1, 99440-5, Pub. by Saxon Hse). Lexington Bks.

Regional Dictionary of Chicano Slang. Librado K. Vasquez & Maria E. Vasquez. 111p. 1975. 13.50 (ISBN 0-8363-0083-1). Jenkins.

Regional Disparities in Educational Development: A Controversial Issue. 257p. 1981. pap. 18.75 (ISBN 92-803-1085-2, U1048, UNESCO). Unipub.

Regional Disparities in Educational Development: Diagnosis & Policies for Reduction. 409p. 1981. pap. 18.75 (ISBN 92-803-1086-0, U1049, UNESCO). Unipub.

Regional Disparity & Economic Development in the European Community. W. Molle et al. LC 79-91668. 428p. 1980. text ed. 37.50 (ISBN 0-916672-50-6). Allanheld.

Regional Diversity of Political Values: Idaho Political Culture. Robert H. Blank. LC 78-62742. 1978. pap. text ed. 8.75 (ISBN 0-8191-0590-2). U Pr of Amer.

Regional Economic Analysis for Practitioners: An Introduction to Common Descriptive Methods. rev. ed. Avrom Bendavid. LC 73-22260. (Special Studies). (Illus.). 1974. text ed. 17.95 o.p. (ISBN 0-275-08450-7); pap. text ed. 11.95 (ISBN 0-275-88820-7). Praeger.

Regional Economic Policy & Its Analysis. Harvey Armstrong & Jim Taylor. 352p. 1978. 43.50x (ISBN 0-86003-015-6, Pub. by Allan Pubs England); pap. 21.75x (ISBN 0-86003-116-0). State Mutual Bk.

Regional Economics. D. L. McKee et al. LC 70-94625. 1970. pap. text ed. 7.25 o.s.i. (ISBN 0-02-920530-1). Free Pr.

Regional Factors in National Planning & Development. United States, National Resources Committee. LC 72-174478. (FDR & the Era of the New Deal Ser). 223p. 1975. Repr. of 1935 ed. lib. bdg. 25.00 (ISBN 0-306-70387-4). Da Capo.

Regional French Cookery. Kenneth Toye. (Illus.). 1979. 13.50 (ISBN 0-7153-6327-1). David & Charles.

Regional Geography. Roger Minshull. 168p. 1967. text ed. 4.50x (ISBN 0-09-082772-4, Hutchinson U Pr); pap. text ed. 2.00x (ISBN 0-09-082773-2). Humanities.

Regional Geography of Anglo-America. 5th ed. C. Langdon White et al. (Illus.). 1979. text ed. 20.95 (ISBN 0-13-770883-1). P-H.

Regional Government & Political Integration in Southwest China, 1949-1954: A Case Study. Dorothy J. Solinger. LC 75-22662. 1977. 27.50x (ISBN 0-520-03104-0). U of Cal Pr.

Regional Growth & Decline in the United States: The Rise of the Sunbelt & the Decline of the Northeast. Bernard L. Weinstein & Robert E. Firestine. LC 77-25447. (Praeger Special Studies). 1978. 22.50 (ISBN 0-275-23950-0). Praeger.
Regional Growth & Unemployment in the United Kingdom. R. J. Dixon & A. P. Thirlwall. 1975. text ed. 35.00x (ISBN 0-8419-5010-5). Holmes & Meier.
Regional Growth Theory. H. W. Richardson. LC 73-5749. 264p. 1973. 27.95 (ISBN 0-470-71952-4). Halsted Pr.
Regional History of the Railway of Great Britain, Vol. 5. D. I. Gordon. 1976. 19.95 (ISBN 0-7153-7431-1). David & Charles.
Regional History of the Railways of Great Britain: Greater London, Vol. 3. H. P. White. (Illus.). 1971. 19.95 (ISBN 0-7153-5337-3). David & Charles.
Regional History of the Railways of Great Britain: South & West Yorkshire, Vol. 8. David Joy. LC 74-20464. (Illus.). 288p. 1975. 19.95 (ISBN 0-7153-6883-4). David & Charles.
Regional History of the Railways of Great Britain: Southern England, Vol. 2. H. P. White. (Regional History of the Railways of Great Britain Ser.). (Illus.). 1974. 16.95 (ISBN 0-7153-4070-0). David & Charles.
Regional History of the Railways of Great Britain: Scotland, the Lowland & the Borders, Vol. 6. John Thomas. (Illus.). 288p. 1971. 19.95 (ISBN 0-7153-5408-6). David & Charles.
Regional History of the Railways of Great Britain: South Wales, Vol. 12, Vol. 12. D. S. Barrie. LC 80-67609. (Illus.). 1980. 30.00 (ISBN 0-7153-7970-4). David & Charles.
Regional History of the Railways of Great Britain: The East Midlands, Vol. 9. Robin Leleux. LC 76-8786. (Regional Railway History Ser). (Illus.). 1976. 19.95 (ISBN 0-7153-7165-7). David & Charles.
Regional History of the Railways of Great Britain: The North East, Vol. 4. K. Hoole. (Illus.). 240p. 1974. 18.95 o.p. (ISBN 0-7153-6439-1). David & Charles.
Regional History of the Railways of Great Britain: The North West, Vol. 10. G. O. Holt. 1978. 19.95 (ISBN 0-7153-7521-0). David & Charles.
Regional History of the Railways of Great Britain: The West Country, Vol. 1. 4th ed. David Thomas. 15.95 o.p. (ISBN 0-7153-6208-9). David & Charles.
Regional History of the Railways of Great Britain: The West Midlands, Vol. 7. Rex Christiansen. 1973. 19.95 (ISBN 0-7153-6093-0). David & Charles.
Regional History of the Railways of Great Britain: Vol. Eleven-North & Mid Wales. Peter E. Baughan. LC 79-56255. (Illus.). 208p. 1980. 24.00 (ISBN 0-7153-7850-3). David & Charles.
Regional History of the Railways of Great Britian: Volume I, The West Country. David St. John Thomas. LC 80-70296. (Illus.). 256p. 1981. 28.00 (ISBN 0-7153-8152-0). David & Charles.
Regional Impact of Monetary Policy in the United States. Randall J. Miller. LC 78-59750. (Illus.). 1978. 19.95 (ISBN 0-669-02373-6). Lexington Bks.
Regional Impacts of Federal Fiscal Policy. Thanos Catsambas. LC 77-12282. 1978. 16.95 (ISBN 0-669-01953-4). Lexington Bks.
Regional Imperative: The Administration of U. S. Policy Towards the South Asian States Under Presidents Johnson & Nixon. Lloyd Rudolph & Susanne Rudolph. 1980. text ed. 16.50x (ISBN 0-391-02178-8). Humanities.
Regional Inequality & Development: A Case Study of Kenya. Arne Bigsten. 200p. 1980. text ed. 44.00x (ISBN 0-566-00382-1, Pub. by Gower Pub Co England). Renouf.
Regional Integration & National Policy Development. Royce Q. Shaw. 1978. lib. bdg. 24.50 o.p. (ISBN 0-89158-278-9). Westview.
Regional Italian Cooking: From the Alps to the Mediterranean. Wilma R. La Sasso. (Illus.). 268p. 1975. 5.95 o.s.i. (ISBN 0-02-568400-0). Macmillan.
Regional Landscape Analysis. Paul Anderson. LC 80-6837. 1980. pap. 19.50 (ISBN 0-918436-11-7). Environ Des VA.
Regional Landscapes of the United States & Canada. Stephen S. Birdsall & John W. Florin. LC 77-28103. 1978. text ed. 20.95 (ISBN 0-471-07397-0). Wiley.
Regional Language in France. Ed. by Andree Tabouret-Keller. (International Journal of the Sociology of Language: No. 25). 1980. pap. text ed. 21.00x (ISBN 90-279-3068-6). Mouton.
Regional Model of Residential Construction. Kenneth Rosen. 220p. Date not set. 18.00 (ISBN 0-88410-618-7). Ballinger Pub.
Regional Nuclear Fuel Cycle Centres, 2 vols. Incl. Vol. 1. Summary 1977 Report of the IAEA Study Project. pap. 15.00 (ISBN 92-0-159177-2, ISP445-1); Vol. 2. Basic Studies 1977 Report of the IAEA Study Project. pap. 32.25 (ISBN 92-0-159277-9). (Illus.). 1977 (IAEA). Unipub.
Regional Planning: A Comprehensive View. J. Alden & R. Morgan. LC 74-12635. 1974. 24.95 (ISBN 0-470-02053-9). Halsted Pr.
Regional Planning & Location of Industry. 3rd ed. Derek Lee. (Studies in the British Economy). 1980. pap. text ed. 6.50 (ISBN 0-435-84577-2). Heinemann Ed.
Regional Planning & Nation Development. Ed. by R. P. Misra et al. 1979. 34.00x (ISBN 0-7069-0555-5, Pub. by Croom Helm Ltd. England). Biblio Dist.
Regional Planning Process. Ed. by David Gillingwater & D. A. Hart. 1978. 22.95 (ISBN 0-347-01130-6, 00412-X, Pub. by Saxon Hse). Lexington Bks.
Regional Policy: A European Approach. Norbert Vanhove & Leo H. Klaassen. LC 79-55648. 540p. 1980. text ed. 39.95 (ISBN 0-916672-49-2). Allanheld.
Regional Policy: Past Experience & New Directions. Duncan Maclennan & John B. Parr. 334p. 1979. 41.95x (ISBN 0-85520-217-3, Pub by Martin Robertson England); pap. 17.25x (ISBN 0-85520-216-5, Pub. by Martin Robertson England). Biblio Dist.
Regional Refresher Courses in Anesthesiology, Vol. 1. American Society of Anesthesiologists & American College of Anesthesiology. 1973. 10.00 (ISBN 0-685-34605-6). Lippincott.
Regional Statistics: A Guide to Information Sources. Ed. by M. Balachandran. LC 80-14260. (Economics Information Guide Ser.: Vol. 13). 230p. 1980. 30.00 (ISBN 0-8103-1463-0). Gale.
Regional Unemployment Differences in Great Britain. P. D. Cheshire. Bd. with Interregional Migration Models & Their Application to Great Britain. R. Weeden. LC 73-86048. (National Institute of Economic & Social Research - Regional Studies: No. 2). (Illus.). 200p. 1973. 13.95 (ISBN 0-521-20376-7). Cambridge U Pr.
Regional Variations in Britain: Studies in Economic & Social Geography. B. E. Coats & E. M. Tawstron. 1972. 40.00 (ISBN 0-7134-2103-7, Pub. by Batsford England). David & Charles.
Regional Vocabulary of Texas. 2nd ed. E. Bagby Atwood. LC 62-9784. (Illus.). 1969. pap. 6.95 (ISBN 0-292-77008-1). U of Tex Pr.
Regional Wage Variations in Britain 1850-1914. E. H. Hunt. (Illus.). 398p. 1973. 23.50x o.p. (ISBN 0-19-828262-1). Oxford U Pr.
Regionalism & National Unity in Nepal. Frederick H. Gaige. LC 74-30520. 1975. 21.50x (ISBN 0-520-02728-0). U of Cal Pr.
Regionalism & the New World Order: A Strategy for Progress. Ed. by Ervin Laszlo. 375p. Date not set. 45.01 (ISBN 0-08-026318-6). Pergamon.
Regionalism in America. Ed. by Merrill Jensen. 1965. pap. 9.95 (ISBN 0-299-00794-4). U of Wis Pr.
Regionalization of Personal Health Services. rev. ed. Ed. by E. W. Saward. 1976. text ed. 15.00 o.p. (ISBN 0-88202-067-6); pap. text ed. 6.95 o.p. (ISBN 0-686-67234-8). N Watson.
Regionalization of Water Management: A Revolution in England & Wales. Daniel A. Okun. (Illus.). 1977. 62.10x (ISBN 0-85334-738-7, Pub. by Applied Science). Burgess-Intl Ideas.
Regions of Tommorrow: Towards the Open City. Maurice Ash. LC 70-85676. (Illus.). 1969. 5.95x (ISBN 0-8052-3221-4). Schocken.
Regis Debray & the Latin American Revolution. Ed. by Leo Huberman & Paul M. Sweezy. LC 68-8077. 5.00 o.p. (ISBN 0-85345-077-3, CL-0773). Monthly Rev.
Register of Development Research Projects in Asia. OECD. (Liason Bulletin Ser.). 350p. (Orig.). 1980. pap. text ed. 17.50x (ISBN 92-64-02096-9, 40-80-01-3). OECD.
Register of Educational Research in the United Kingdom, 1973-76, Vol. 1. National Foundation for Educational Research in England & Wales. (General Ser.). 450p. (Orig.). 1976. pap. text ed. 45.00x (ISBN 0-85633-117-1, NFER). Humanities.
Register of Educational Research in the UK: 1976-1977, Vol. 2. National Foundation for Educational Research in England & Wales. (General Ser.). 1978. pap. text ed. 49.50x (ISBN 0-85633-145-7, NFER). Humanities.
Register of Eighteenth Century Bibliographies & References: A Chronological Quarter-Century Survey Relating to English Literature, Booksellers, Newspapers, Periodicals, Printing & Publishing, Aesthetics, Art & Music, Economics, History & Science, a Preliminary Contribution. Francesco Cordasco. LC 76-4182. 1968. Repr. of 1950 ed. 15.00 (ISBN 0-8103-3521-2). Gale.
Register of New Fruit & Nut Varieties. 2nd rev. & enl. ed. Reid M. Brooks & Harold P. Olmo. LC 76-100017. 512p. 1972. 23.75x (ISBN 0-520-01638-6). U of Cal Pr.
Register of Research in the United Kingdom: 1977-78, Vol. 3. National Foundation for Educational Research in England & Wales. (Orig.). 1979. pap. text ed. 77.00x (ISBN 0-85633-187-2). Humanities.
Register of Research: Investigation in Adult Education. ERIC & Adult Education Association of the U. S. A. 1968 2.30 (ISBN 0-685-85633-X); 1970 6.90 (ISBN 0-685-85634-8). Adult Ed.
Register of United States Breweries: 1876 to 1976: an Alphabetical Index, Vol. 2. Manfred Friedrich & Donald Bull. LC 76-23150. 1976. pap. 10.95 (ISBN 0-9601190-2-7). D Bull.
Register of United States Breweries: 1876-1976, Vol. 1. Manfred Friedrich & D. Bull. LC 76-23156. 1976. pap. 10.95 (ISBN 0-9601190-1-9). D Bull.
Registered As Disabled. Sally Sainsbury. 205p. 1970. pap. text ed. 6.25x (ISBN 0-7135-1619-4, Pub. by Bedford England). Renouf.
Registry of Mass Spectral Data, 4 vols. Ed. by E. Stenhagen et al. LC 74-910. 3200p. 1974. Set. 450.00 (ISBN 0-471-82115-2, Pub. by Wiley-Interscience). Wiley.
Reglamento de las construcciones de concreto reforzado: Aci 318-71 y commentarios. (Sp.). 1975. 28.00 (ISBN 0-685-85085-4, 318-71S) (ISBN 0-685-85086-2). ACI.
Reglas Parlamentarias. H. F. Kerfoot. Tr. by Jose M. Sanchez. 1980. Repr. of 1978 ed. 1.50 (ISBN 0-311-11012-6). Casa Bautista.
Regnal Formulas in Byzantine Egypt. Roger S. Bagnall & K. A. Worp. LC 79-1316. (Supplements to the Bulletin of American Society of Papyrologists). 1979. pap. 9.00 (ISBN 0-89130-280-8, 311102). Scholars Pr Ca.
Regression Analysis by Example. Samprit Chatterjee & Bertram Price. LC 77-24510. (Probability & Mathematical Statistics Ser.: Applied Probability Section). 1977. 21.95 (ISBN 0-471-01521-0, Pub. by Wiley-Interscience). Wiley.
Regression Diagnostics: Identifying Influential Data & Sources of Collinearity. David A. Belsley et al. LC 79-19876. (Ser. in Probability & Mathematical Statistics: Applied Probability & Statistics). 1980. 21.95 (ISBN 0-471-05856-4, Pub. by Wiley-Interscience). Wiley.
Regressive Therapy: Therapeutic Regression in Schizophrenic Children, Adolescents & Young Adults. Richard H. Cox & Truman G. Ezua. LC 73-84135. 1974. 10.00 o.p. (ISBN 0-87630-081-6). Brunner-Mazel.
Regrets: Choix de poemes. Jaochim De Bellay. (Documentation thematique). (Illus., Fr.). 1975. pap. 2.95 (ISBN 0-685-64173-2). Larousse.
Regular Polytopes. H. S. Coxeter. (Illus.). 321p. 1973. pap. 5.50 (ISBN 0-486-61480-8). Dover.
Regulars. Stephen Lewis. (Orig.). 1980. pap. 2.50 (ISBN 0-8439-0735-5, Leisure Bks). Nordon Pubns.
Regulated Industries. Paul W. Macavoy. 1979. 11.95 (ISBN 0-393-01280-8); pap. 4.95x (ISBN 0-393-95094-8). Norton.
Regulating America, Regulating Sweden: A Comparative Study of Occupational Safety & Health Regulations. Steven Kelman. 320p. 1981. text ed. 19.95x (ISBN 0-262-11076-8). MIT Pr.
Regulating Business: Law & Consumer Agencies. Ross Cranston. (Oxford Socio-Legal Studies Ser.). 1979. text ed. 27.50x (ISBN 0-333-23890-7). Humanities.
Regulating Competition in Oil: Government Intervention in the U.S. Refining Industry, 1948-1975. E. Anthony Copp. LC 76-19795. (Texas A&M University Economics Ser.: No. 1). 304p. 1976. 22.50x (ISBN 0-89096-014-3). Tex A&M Univ Pr.
Regulating Pesticides. Committee on Prototype Explicit Analysis for Pesticides. xiii, 288p. 1980. pap. text ed. 11.00 (ISBN 0-309-02946-5). Natl Acad Pr.
Regulating Sensitive Lands. Jon A. Kusler. 256p. 1980. 25.00 (ISBN 0-88410-095-2). Ballinger Pub.
Regulation & Expansion of Health Facilities. Eleanore Rothenberg. LC 76-7381. (Special Studies). (Illus.). 130p. 1976. text ed. 22.95 (ISBN 0-275-23080-5). Praeger.
Regulation & the Quality of Dental Care. Peter Milgrom. LC 78-1922. 1978. text ed. 28.00 (ISBN 0-89443-034-3). Aspen Systems.
Regulation, Economics, & the Law. Bernard H. Siegan. LC 77-11398. 144p. 1979. 15.95 (ISBN 0-669-02091-5). Lexington Bks.
Regulation, Federalism, and Interstate Commerce. Edmund W. Kitch. Ed. by A. Dan Tarlock. LC 80-23166. 176p. 1981. lib. bdg. 20.00 (ISBN 0-89946-065-8). Oelgeschlager.
Regulation, Market Prices, & Process Innovation: The Case of the Ammonia Industry. Edward Greenberg et al. (Westview Replica Edition). 1979. lib. bdg. 25.50x (ISBN 0-89158-381-5). Westview.
Regulation of Broadcasting: Law & Policy Towards Radio, Television & Cable Communications. Douglas H. Ginsburg. LC 78-11973. (American Casebook Ser.). 741p. 1978. text ed. 20.95 (ISBN 0-8299-2017-X). West Pub.
Regulation of Businessmen: Social Conditions of Government Economic Control. Robert Lane. LC 66-14606. 1966. Repr. of 1954 ed. 13.50 (ISBN 0-208-00515-3, Archon). Shoe String.
Regulation of Cell Membrane Activities in Plants. Arnold E. Menze. 1977. 39.00 (ISBN 0-7204-0615-3, North-Holland). Elsevier.
Regulation of Commerce Under the Federal Constitution. Thomas H. Calvert. (Studies in Constitutional Law). xiv, 380p. 1981. Repr. of 1907 ed. lib. bdg. 32.50x (ISBN 0-8377-0429-4). Rothman.
Regulation of Direct Broadcasting from Satellites: The UN Involvement. Benno Signitzer. LC 76-14372. (Special Studies). (Illus.). 175p. 1976. text ed. 23.50 (ISBN 0-275-56800-8). Praeger.
Regulation of Fishing Effort. (FAO Fisheries Technical Paper: No. 197). 82p. 1981. pap. 6.00 (ISBN 92-5-100947-3, F2067, FAO). Unipub.
Regulation of Forward Markets. Waman R. Natu. 8.95x (ISBN 0-210-34069-X). Asia.
Regulation of Male Fertility. Ed. by G. R. Cunningham et al. (Clinics in Andrology Ser.: No. 5). (Illus.). 245p. 1981. PLB 68.50 (ISBN 90-247-2373-6, Pub. by Martinus Nijhoff). Kluwer Boston.
Regulation of Medical Care: Is the Price Too High? John Goodman. LC 80-25397. (Cato Public Policy Research Monograph: No. 3). (Orig.). 1980. pap. 5.00 (ISBN 0-932790-23-2). Cato Inst.
Regulation of Money Managers, 4 vols. Tamar Frankel. 1980. Vol. 1. (ISBN 0-316-29191-9); Vol. 2. text ed. (ISBN 0-316-29192-7); text ed. write for info. (ISBN 0-316-29193-5); Vol. 4. text ed. 50.00 ea. (ISBN 0-316-29194-3); 195.00 set (ISBN 0-316-29190-0). Little.
Regulation of Muscle Contraction: Excitation-Contraction Coupling. Ed. by Alan D. Grinnell et al. (UCLA Forum in Medical Sciences: Vol. 22). 1981. price not set (ISBN 0-12-303780-8). Acad Pr.
Regulation of Rail & Trucking Industries. Ann F. Friedlaender & Richard H. Spady. 512p. 1980. text ed. 30.00x (ISBN 0-262-06072-8). MIT Pr.
Regulation of Scientific Inquiry: Societal Concerns with Research. Ed. by Keith M. Wulff. (AAAS Selected Symposium: No. 37). 1979. lib. bdg. 22.50x (ISBN 0-89158-492-7). Westview.
Regulation of Secondary Product & Plant Hormone Metabolism: Proceedings. FEBS Meeting, 12th, Dresden, 1978. Ed. by M. Luckner & K. Schreiber. (Federation of European Biochemical Society Ser.: Vol. 55). (Illus.). 1979. 60.00 (ISBN 0-08-023179-9). Pergamon.
Regulation, Service Quality, & Market Performance: A Model of Airline Rivalry. John C. Panzar. LC 78-75053. (Outstanding Dissertations in Economics Ser.). 1979. lib. bdg. 16.00 (ISBN 0-8240-4131-3). Garland Pub.
Regulations for Aircraft Maintenance. rev. ed. Compiled by Samuel W. Merrill. 1975. pap. 8.75 (ISBN 0-685-69727-4). Intermtn Air.
Regulations for Safe Transport or Radioactive Materials: Advisory Material. (Safety Ser.: No. 37). 190p. (Orig.). 1974. pap. 14.50 (ISBN 92-0-123273-X, ISP324, IAEA). Unipub.
Regulations for the Safe Transport of Radioactive Materials. amended ed. (Safety Ser.: No. 6). 171p. 1980. pap. 22.75 (ISBN 92-0-623179-0, ISP-517, IAEA). Unipub.
Regulations for the Safe Transport of Radioactive Materials: Notes on Certain Aspects of the Regulations. (Safety Ser.: No. 7). 1961. pap. 4.50 (ISBN 92-0-123361-2, ISP32, IAEA). Unipub.
Regulations Made Easy for Commercial Pilots. Richard Doberstein. (Illus.). Date not set. pap. 4.95x (Pub. by Simplified). Aviation.
Regulations Made Easy for Instrument Pilots. Richard Doberstein. (Illus.). Date not set. pap. 4.95x (Pub. by Simplified). Aviation.
Regulations Made Easy for Private Pilots. Richard Doberstein. (Illus.). Date not set. pap. 4.95x (Pub. by Simplified). Aviation.
Regulators. William Degenhard. 600p. Repr. of 1943 ed. 22.50 (ISBN 0-933256-22-1). Second Chance.

Regulatory & Paperwork Maze. Laurie H. Hutzler. Incl. A Guide for Association Executives. pap. (ISBN 0-937542-03-2); A Guide for Government Personnel. pap. (ISBN 0-937542-04-0); A Guide for Small Business. pap. (ISBN 0-937542-02-4). (Illus.). 1980. pap. 10.00 ea. Legal Mgmt Serv.

Regulatory & Paperwork Maze: A Guide for Small Business, New 1981 "Reagan" Edition. 2nd ed. Laurie H. Hutzler. (Illus.). 1981. pap. 15.00 (ISBN 0-937542-06-7). Legal Mgmt Serv.

Regulatory Functions of Interferons. new ed. Ed. by Jan Vilcek et al. LC 80-25207. (Vol. 350). 641p. 1980. 124.00 (ISBN 0-89766-089-7). NY Acad Sci.

Regulatory Functions of Interferons, Vol. 350. Ed. by Jan Vilcek et al. LC 80-25207. 641p. 1980. 124.00x (ISBN 0-89766-089-7); pap. write for info. (ISBN 0-89766-090-0). NY Acad Sci.

Regulatory Functions of the Cns - Sybsystems: Proceedings of the 28th International Congress of Physiological Sciences, Budapest, 1980. J. Szentagothai et al. LC 80-41884. (Advances in Physiological Sciences: Vol. 2). (Illus.). 293p. 1981. 35.00 (ISBN 0-08-027371-8). Pergamon.

Regulatory Functions of the CNS- Motion & Organization Principles: Proceedings of the 28th International Congress of Physiological Sciences, Budapest, 1980. J. Szentagothai et al. LC 80-41885. (Advances in Physiological Sciences: Vol. 1). (Illus.). 300p. 1981. 35.00 (ISBN 0-08-026814-5). Pergamon.

Regulatory Genetics of the Immune System. Ed. by Eli Sercarz. 1977. 38.00 (ISBN 0-12-637160-1). Acad Pr.

Regulatory Politics & Electric Utilities. Douglas D. Anderson. 200p. 1981. 19.95 (ISBN 0-86569-058-8). Auburn Hse.

Regulatory Reform in Air Cargo Transportation. Lucille S. Keyes. 1980. pap. 4.25 (ISBN 0-8447-3371-7). Am Enterprise.

Regulatory Reform of Telecommunications: A Selected Bibliography. Felix Chin. (Public Administration Ser.: Bibliography P-521). 50p. 1980. pap. 5.50. Vance Biblios.

Regulatory T Lymphocytes. Ed. by Benvenuto Pernis & Henry J. Vogel. (P & S Biomedical Science Ser.). 1980. 47.50 (ISBN 0-12-551860-9). Acad Pr.

Rehabbing for Profit. Jerry C. Davis. (Illus.). 224p. 1981. 17.50 (ISBN 0-07-015695-6, P&RB). McGraw.

Rehabilitating People with Disabilities into the Mainstream of Society. Allen D. Spiegel & Simon Podair. LC 80-16497. (Illus.). 350p. 1981. 28.00 (ISBN 0-8155-0839-5). Noyes.

Rehabilitating the Mentally Ill in the Community: A Study of Psychosocial Rehabilitation Centers. R. M. Glasscote et al. 214p. 1971. 7.50 (ISBN 0-685-24869-0, P-157-0). Am Psychiatric.

Rehabilitation Administrative Procedures for Extended Care Facilities. Roslyn Davidson. (Illus.). 116p. 1973. pap. 11.75 spiral (ISBN 0-398-02611-4). C C Thomas.

Rehabilitation & Handicapped Literature, 1950-1978: A Bibliographic Guide to the Microfiche Collection. 1980. text ed. write for info. (ISBN 0-667-00614-1). Microfilming Corp.

Rehabilitation & the Retarded Offender. Philip L. Browning. (Illus.). 360p. 1976. 22.50 (ISBN 0-398-03481-8). C C Thomas.

Rehabilitation Engineering Sourcebook Supplement. Institute for Information Studies. Ed. by Carolyn Vash et al. LC 79-24747. (Illus.). 85p. 1981. pap. write for info. (ISBN 0-935294-05-8). Inst Info Stud.

Rehabilitation Environment. Carroll M. Brodsky& Robert T. Platt. LC 77-26370. 1978. 16.95 (ISBN 0-669-02168-7). Lexington Bks.

Rehabilitation Facility Approaches in Severe Disabilities. Ed. by John G. Cull & Richard E. Hardy. (American Lectures in Social & Rehabilitation Psychology Ser.). (Illus.). 352p. 1975. 26.75 (ISBN 0-398-03324-2). C C Thomas.

Rehabilitation in Ischemic Heart Disease. Ed. by William P. Blocker, Jr. & David Cardus. 624p. 1981. text ed. 80.00 (ISBN 0-89335-096-6). Spectrum Pub.

Rehabilitation Management of Rheumatic Conditions. George E. Ehrlich. (Rehabilitation Medicine Library Ser.). (Illus.). 336p. 1980. 34.95 (ISBN 0-683-02791-3). Williams & Wilkins.

Rehabilitation Medicine. 2nd ed. P. J. Nichols. LC 79-42891. 1980. text ed. 39.95 (ISBN 0-407-00175-1). Butterworths.

Rehabilitation Medicine. 4th ed. Ed. by Howard A. Rusk. LC 76-30550. (Illus.). 1977. 44.50 (ISBN 0-8016-4213-2). Mosby.

Rehabilitation Medicine & Psychiatry. Jack Meislin. (Illus.). 564p. 1976. 32.75 (ISBN 0-398-03432-X). C C Thomas.

Rehabilitation Medicine Services. Laurence P. Ince. (Illus.). 592p. 1974. 32.50 (ISBN 0-398-02852-4). C C Thomas.

Rehabilitation of Criminal Offenders: Problems & Prospects. Committee on Research on Law Enforcement & Criminal Justice. 1979. pap. 13.75 (ISBN 0-309-02895-7). Natl Acad Pr.

Rehabilitation of Say's Law. W. H. Hutt. LC 74-82499. xiii, 150p. 1974. 10.95x (ISBN 0-8214-0164-5). Ohio U Pr.

Rehabilitation of the Aged. Ed. by T. Franklin Williams. 1981. price not set (ISBN 0-89004-417-1, 471). Raven.

Rehabilitation of the Coronary Patient. Nanette K. Wenger & H. K. Hellerstein. LC 78-12531. 1978. 28.00 (ISBN 0-471-93369-4, Pub. by Wiley Medical). Wiley.

Rehabilitation of the Drug Abuser with Delinquent Behavior. Ed. by Richard E. Hardy & John G. Cull. (Amer. Lec. in Social & Rehabilitation Psychology). 208p. 1974. 14.75 (ISBN 0-398-02823-0). C C Thomas.

Rehabilitation of the Drunken Driver: A Corrective Course in Phoenix, Arizona for Persons Convicted of Driving Under the Influence of Alcohol. Ernest I. Stewart & James L. Malfetti. LC 73-137738. 1970. pap. 7.00x (ISBN 0-8077-1801-7). Tchrs Coll.

Rehabilitation of the Facially Disfigured. J. J. Longacre. (Illus.). 144p. 1973. 21.50 (ISBN 0-398-02597-5). C C Thomas.

Rehabilitation of the Hand. James M. Hunter et al. LC 78-59659. 1978. text ed. 74.50 (ISBN 0-8016-2317-0). Mosby.

Rehabilitation of the Hand. 3rd ed. C. B. W. Parry. 1973. Repr. of 1977 ed. 49.95 (ISBN 0-407-38501-0). Butterworths.

Rehabilitation of the Hand. 4th rev. ed. C. B. Wynn-Parry. LC 80-41761. (Illus.). 1981. text ed. price not set (ISBN 0-407-38502-9). Butterworths.

Rehabilitation of the Severely Disabled-1: Evaluation of a Disabled Living Unit. E. A. Goble et al. 268p. 1971. 15.95 (ISBN 0-407-38510-X). Butterworths.

Rehabilitation of the Severely Mentally Retarded Trainable Child. Edna Earle Heyward. 1978. 10.00 o.p. (ISBN 0-682-49044-X). Exposition.

Rehabilitation of the Urban Disadvantaged. Ed. by John G. Cull & Richard E. Hardy. (Amer. Lec. Social & Rehabilitation Psychology Ser.). 232p. 1973. 19.75 (ISBN 0-398-02795-1). C C Thomas.

Rehabilitation Oncology. J. Herbert Dietz. 224p. 1981. 24.50 (ISBN 0-471-08414-X, Pub. by Wiley Med). Wiley.

Rehabilitation Practices with the Physically Disabled. James Garrett & Edna Levine. 500p. 1973. text ed. 25.00x (ISBN 0-231-03523-3). Columbia U Pr.

Rehabilitation Techniques in Severe Disability: Case Studies. Ed. by John G. Cull & Richard E. Hardy. (American Lectures in Social & Rehabilitation Psychology Ser.). 256p. 1974. text ed. 22.75 (ISBN 0-398-02963-6). C C Thomas.

Rehabilitative Nursing Case Studies. Ed. by Kathryn L. Riffle. 1979. pap. 9.50 (ISBN 0-87488-035-1). Med Exam.

Rehabiltation Oncology. J. Dietz. LC 80-22911. 1981. write for info. (ISBN 0-471-08414-X). Wiley.

Rehearsal for Disaster: The Boom & Collapse of 1919-1920. John D. Hicks. LC 61-12136. 1961. 4.00 (ISBN 0-8130-0110-2). U Presses Fla.

Rehearsal for Republicanism: Free Soil & the Politics of Antislavery. John Mayfield. (National University Publications, Political Science Ser.). 1980. 17.50 (ISBN 0-8046-9253-X). Kennikat.

Rehearsal: The Principles & Practice of Acting for the Stage. 5th ed. Miriam A. Franklin. (Illus.). 256p. 1972. pap. 14.95 ref. ed. (ISBN 0-13-771592-7). P-H.

Rehearsal's Off. George Booth. LC 78-41380. (Illus.). 1976. 7.95 (ISBN 0-396-07389-1). Dodd.

Reich & Nation: The Holy Roman Empire As Idea & Reality, 1763-1806. John G. Gagliardo. LC 79-2170. 416p. 1980. 25.00x (ISBN 0-253-16773-6). Ind U Pr.

Reichenbachia Found in the United States West of the Continental Divide (Coleoptera: Pselaphidae) A. A. Grigarick & R. O. Schuster. (U. C. Publ. in Entomology: Vol. 47). 1967. pap. 6.00x (ISBN 0-520-09119-1). U of Cal Pr.

Reichstag Fire, February, 1933: Hitler Utilizes Arson to Extend His Dictatorship. Henry Gilfond. LC 78-8182. (World Focus Bks.). (Illus.). 96p. 1973. PLB 4.90 o.p. (ISBN 0-531-02168-8). Watts.

Reichswehr & Politics: Nineteen Eighteen to Nineteen Thirty-Three. F. L. Carsten. 1974. pap. 6.95x (ISBN 0-520-02492-3). U of Cal Pr.

Reichswehr & Politics: Nineteen Eighteen to Nineteen Thirty-Three. Franz L. Carsten. 1966. 36.00x (ISBN 0-19-821457-X). Oxford U Pr.

Reid's Branson Instruction to Juries, 7 Vols. 3rd ed. Set. with 1980 suppl. 175.00 (ISBN 0-672-84048-0, Bobbs-Merrill Law); 1980 suppl. 60.00 (ISBN 0-672-84285-8). Michie.

Reign of Elizabeth, Fifteen Fifty-Eight to Sixteen Three. 2nd ed. J. B. Black. (Oxford History of England Ser.). 1959. 33.00x (ISBN 0-19-821701-3). Oxford U Pr.

Reign of Ets: The Corporation That Makes up Minds. Allan Nairn & Associates. LC 80-107761. (Ralph Nader Report on the Educational Testing Service). 554p. (Orig.). 1980. pap. 30.00 (ISBN 0-936486-00-7). R Nader.

Reign of George Third, Seventeen Sixty to Eighteen Fifteen. J. Steven Watson. (Oxford History of England Ser.). 1960. 33.00x (ISBN 0-19-821713-7). Oxford U Pr.

Reign of Patti. Herman Klein. LC 77-17874. (Music Reprint Ser.: 1978). (Illus.). 1978. Repr. of 1920 ed. lib. bdg. 35.00 (ISBN 0-306-77530-1). Da Capo.

Reign of Philip the Fair. Joseph R. Strayer. LC 79-3232. 1980. 35.00 (ISBN 0-691-05302-2); pap. 13.50 (ISBN 0-691-10089-6). Princeton U Pr.

Reign of Relativity. Viscount Haldane. 434p. 1981. Repr. lib. bdg. 35.00 (ISBN 0-8495-2354-0). Arden Lib.

Reign of the Madman: The Birdcatcher. Walter J. Schenck, Jr. LC 80-81523. (Illus.). 1980. 14.95 (ISBN 0-936978-01-5); pap. 6.95 (ISBN 0-936978-00-7). Schenck Pubns.

Reign of Wonder. T. Tanner. LC 76-62589. 1977. pap. 11.50x (ISBN 0-521-29198-4). Cambridge U Pr.

Reigning Passions. Kathrin Perutz. LC 77-20701. 1978. 10.00 o.p. (ISBN 0-397-01247-0). Lippincott.

Reigning with Christ. F. J. Huegel. 1969. pap. 1.50 (ISBN 0-87123-480-7, 200480). Bethany Fell.

Reincarnation. Swami Abhedananda. 3.95 o.p. (ISBN 0-87481-604-1). Vedanta Pr.

Reincarnation. 11th ed. Annie Besant. 1975. 2.50 (ISBN 0-8356-7019-8). Theos Pub Hse.

Reincarnation & Christianity. Robert A. Morey. 64p. 1980. pap. 1.95 (ISBN 0-87123-493-9, 210493). Bethany Fell.

Reincarnation & Immortality. Rudolf Steiner. LC 79-3592. (Harper Library of Spiritual Wisdom). 208p. 1980. pap. 5.95 (ISBN 0-06-067571-3, RD 404). Har-Row.

Reincarnation & the Soul in the Parables of Jesus. William David & Margaret Gibson. 80p. 1980. pap. 3.95 (ISBN 0-87516-412-9). De Vorss.

Reincarnation, Edgar Cayce & the Bible. Phillip J. Swihart. LC 75-5186. 64p. 1975. pap. 1.95 o.p. (ISBN 0-87784-416-X). Inter-Varsity.

Reincarnation, Key to Immortality. Marcia Moore & Mark Douglas. LC 67-19603. 1968. 10.00 (ISBN 0-912240-02-4). Arcane Pubns.

Reincarnation of Bridgett. Joseph F. Coscia. 160p. 1981. 6.00 (ISBN 0-682-49699-5). Exposition.

Reincarnation of Robert Macready. Robert Macready. 336p. (Orig.). 1981. pap. 2.75 (ISBN 0-89083-703-1). Zebra.

Reincarnation: The Best Short Stories of Cunninghame Graham. R. Cunninghame Graham. LC 79-28208. 160p. 1980. 8.95 (ISBN 0-89919-004-9). Ticknor & Fields.

Reincarnation Through the Zodiac. Joan Hodgson. LC 79-444. (Illus.). 1979. pap. 4.95 (ISBN 0-916360-11-3). CRCS Pubns NV.

Reindeer Trail. Berta Hader & Elmer Hader. (Illus.). (gr. 1-3). 1959. 4.95g o.s.i. (ISBN 0-02-740560-5). Macmillan.

Reinforced & Prestressed Concrete. F. K. Kong & R. H. Evans. 1975. text ed. 29.95x (ISBN 0-17-761040-9). Intl Ideas.

Reinforced & Prestressed Microconcrete Models. Ed. by F. K. Garas & G. S. T. Armer. (Illus.). 400p. 1980. text ed. 55.00 cased (ISBN 0-86095-880-9). Longman.

Reinforced Cement Concrete: A Textbook for Polytechnic Students. H. K. Rao. pap. 5.00x (ISBN 0-210-34062-2). Asia.

Reinforced Concrete. George Wynne. 1981. text ed. 19.95 (ISBN 0-8359-6638-0); instrs'. manual avail. (ISBN 0-8359-6639-9). Reston.

Reinforced Concrete Chimneys & Towers. Geoffrey M. Pinfold. (C & CA Viewpoint Publication Ser.). (Illus.). 1976. text ed. 21.50 (ISBN 0-7210-0993-X). Scholium Intl.

Reinforced Concrete Columns. 1975. pap. 23.25 (ISBN 0-685-85132-X, SP-50) (ISBN 0-685-85133-8). ACI.

Reinforced Concrete Design. 3rd ed. George E. Large & T. Y. Chen. LC 69-14677. (Illus.). 1969. 27.95 (ISBN 0-8260-5225-8). Wiley.

Reinforced Concrete Design Handbook: Working Stress Method. 3rd ed. 1965. pap. 21.25 (ISBN 0-685-85089-7, SP-3) (ISBN 0-685-85090-0). ACI.

Reinforced Concrete Detailer's Manual. Brian Boughton. 1979. pap. text ed. 16.25x (ISBN 0-258-97128-2, Pub. by Granada England). Renouf.

Reinforced Concrete Engineering, Vol. 1. Boris Bresler. LC 73-19862. 576p. 1974. 35.00 (ISBN 0-471-10279-2, Pub. by Wiley-Interscience). Wiley.

Reinforced Concrete Floor Slabs-Research & Design. Compiled by American Society of Civil Engineers. 224p. 1978. pap. text ed. 15.00 (ISBN 0-87262-136-7). Am Soc Civil Eng.

Reinforced Concrete Fundamentals. 4th ed. Phil M. Ferguson. LC 78-21555. 1979. text ed. 29.95 (ISBN 0-471-01459-1); solutions manual (ISBN 0-471-05000-8). Wiley.

Reinforced Concrete Fundamentals: SI Version. 4th ed. Phil M. Ferguson. 736p. 1981. text ed. 28.95 (ISBN 0-471-05897-1). Wiley.

Reinforced Concrete Slabs. R. Park & W. L. Gamble. LC 80-10229. 1980. 40.00 (ISBN 0-471-65915-0, Pub. by Wiley-Interscience). Wiley.

Reinforced Concrete Structures in Seismic Zones. 1977. 25.00 (SP-53). ACC.

Reinforced Concrete Structures in Seismic Zones: SP-53. Ed. by Neil M. Hawkins & Denis Mitchell. LC 77-74267. 1977. 25.00 (ISBN 0-685-87990-9) (ISBN 0-685-87991-7). ACI.

Reinforced Concrete Structures Subjected to Wind & Earthquake Forces. 1980. 32.95 (SP-63). ACI.

Reinforced Masonry Design. R. Schneider & W. Dickey. 1980. 36.00 (ISBN 0-13-771733-4). P-H.

Reinforced Plastics, P-002r. 1979. 750.00 (ISBN 0-89336-136-4). BCC.

Reinforced Plastics: Theory & Practice. 2nd ed. M. W. Gaylord. LC 74-9842. 213p. 1974. 17.95 o.p. (ISBN 0-8436-1210-X). CBI Pub.

Reinforced Thermoplastics. W. V. Titow & B. J. Lenham. LC 75-16335. 295p. 1975. 39.95 (ISBN 0-470-87518-6). Halsted Pr.

Reinforcement Schedules & Multioperant Analysis. Ed. by Travis Thompson & John G. Grabowski. LC 76-182306. (Illus.). 1972. 19.95 (ISBN 0-13-771709-1). P-H.

Reinforcing Home Activities: Program for Articulation Improvement. Agnes Beveridge-Wavering & Mavis Seibert-Shook. 1981. pap. 7.50 (ISBN 0-8134-2158-6, 2158). Interstate.

Reinhard Heydrich. Gunther Deschner. LC 80-6263. 376p. 1981. 16.95 (ISBN 0-8128-2809-7). Stein & Day.

Reinhold Visuals Study Guide. John Lidstone & Stanley Lewis. 160p. 1980. pap. 8.95 (ISBN 0-442-25399-0). Van Nos Reinhold.

Reinmars Women: A Study of the Womans Song of Reinmar der Alte. William E. Jackson. (German Language & Literature Monographs: No. 9). 300p. 1980. text ed. 37.25x (ISBN 90-272-4002-7). Humanities.

Reintegrating the Offender: Assessing the Impact of Community Corrections. John Hylton. LC 80-5730. 334p. 1981. lib. bdg. 20.75 (ISBN 0-8191-1387-5); pap. text ed. 11.75 (ISBN 0-8191-1388-3). U Pr of Amer.

Reinventing Anarchy: What Are Anarchists Thinking These Days? Howard J. Ehrlich et al. (Illus.). 1979. pap. 15.00 (ISBN 0-7100-0128-2). Routledge & Kegan.

Reinventing Womanhood. Carolyn Heilbrun. 248p. 1981. pap. 4.95 (ISBN 0-393-00997-1). Norton.

Reister's Desire: The Origin of Reisterstown... with a Genealigical History of the Reister Family. Lillian B. Marks. LC 75-18893. (Illus.). 1976. 15.00 (ISBN 0-938420-16-X). Md Hist.

Rejected Essays, & Other Matters. new ed. Roberta Kalechofsky. LC 80-83108. 256p. 1980. pap. 5.00 (ISBN 0-916288-08-0). Micah Pubns.

Rejoicing Heart. Joyce M. Smith. 1979. pap. 1.75 (ISBN 0-8423-5418-2). Tyndale.

Rejuvenation: Dr. Ann Wigmore's Complete Diet & Health Program. Stephen Blauer. 197p. pap. 4.95. Hippocrates.

Rejuvenation Through Yoga. Goldie Lipson. 1978. pap. 1.50 o.s.i. (ISBN 0-515-04480-6). Jove Pubns.

Rekindled Flame. Elizabeth Ashton. (Harlequin Romances Ser.). 192p. 1980. pap. 1.25 (ISBN 0-373-02347-2, Pub. by Harlequin). PB.

Relapse. John Vanbrugh. Ed. by Curt A. Zimansky. LC 70-107279. (Regents Restoration Drama Ser). 1970. 9.95x (ISBN 0-8032-0376-4); pap. 2.75x (ISBN 0-8032-5375-3, BB 274, Bison). U of Nebr Pr.

Relating. Michele McCarty. 128p. (Orig.). (gr. 11-12). 1979. pap. text ed. 4.00 (ISBN 0-697-01710-9); tchr's manual 5.00 (ISBN 0-697-01711-7). Wm C Brown.

Relating Environment to Mental Health & Illness: The Ecopsychiatric Base. Ed. by Jay T. Shurley. (Task Force Reports: 16). 58p. 1979. pap. 5.00 (ISBN 0-685-95864-7, P147-0). Am Psychiatric.

Relating the Arts. Gingrich. write for info. (ISBN 0-87628-216-8). Ctr Appl Res.

Relation of Angioid Streaks to Systemic Disease. David Paton. (Amer. Lec. Living Chemistry Ser). (Illus.). 96p. 1972. 11.50 (ISBN 0-398-02375-1). C C Thomas.

Relation of Hormones to Development: Proceedings, Vol. 10. Cold Spring Harbor Symposia On Quantitative Biology. Repr. of 1942 ed. 22.00 (ISBN 0-384-50250-4). Johnson Repr.

Relation of Religion & Health. Paul Tillich. 150p. 1981. 15.00 (ISBN 0-913028-81-9); pap. 5.95 (ISBN 0-686-69475-9). North Atlantic.

Relation of Religion to Civil Government in the United States. Isaac J. Cornelison. LC 75-107409. (Civil Liberties in American History Ser). 1970. Repr. of 1895 ed. lib. bdg. 35.00 (ISBN 0-306-71890-1). Da Capo.

Relation of Seneca False Face Masks to Seneca & Ontario Archeology. Zena P. Mathews. LC 77-94707. (Outstanding Dissertations in the Fine Arts Ser.). 1978. lib. bdg. 36.00x (ISBN 0-8240-3239-X). Garland Pub.

Relation of Some Yeares Travaile Begunne Anno 1626, into Afrique & the Greater Asia. Sir Thomas Herbert. LC 76-25706. (English Experience Ser.: No. 349). 1971. Repr. of 1634 ed. 42.00 (ISBN 90-221-0349-8). Walter J Johnson.

Relation of the Expongnable Attempt & Conquest of the Ylande of Tercera. Alvaro De Bacan. LC 76-57352. (English Experience Ser.: No. 772). 1977. Repr. of 1584 ed. lib. bdg. 6.00 (ISBN 90-221-0772-8). Walter J Johnson.

Relation of the Judiciary to the Constitution. W. M. Meigs. LC 73-124896. (American Constitutional & Legal History Ser). 1971. Repr. of 1919 ed. lib. bdg. 29.50 (ISBN 0-306-71988-6). Da Capo.

Relation of the Quakers to the American Revolution. Arthur J. Mekeel. LC 79-66173. 1979. pap. text ed. 12.50 (ISBN 0-8191-0792-1). U Pr of Amer.

Relation of Theory to Practice in Psychotherapy. Ed. by Leonard D. Eron & Robert Callahan. LC 69-13705. 1969. 29.50x (ISBN 0-202-26017-8). Irvington.

Relation or Journall of the Beginning of the English Plantation at Plimoth. LC 74-80210. (English Experience Ser.: No. 683). 1974. Repr. of 1622 ed. 8.00 (ISBN 90-221-0683-7). Walter J Johnson.

Relational Data Base Management System. A. T. Hutt. 208p. 1979. 27.00 (ISBN 0-471-27612-X, Pub. by Wiley-Interscience). Wiley.

Relations Between Combinatorics & Other Parts of Mathematics. Ed. by D. K. Ray-Chaudhuri. LC 78-25979. (Proceedings of Symposia in Pure Mathematics: Vol. 34). 1980. Repr. of 1979 ed. 16.00 (ISBN 0-8218-1434-6). Am Math.

Relations Between Combinatorics, & Other Parts of Mathematics: Proceedings of Symposia in Pure Mathematics, Vol. 34. Ed. by D. K. Ray-Chaudhuri. 1979. write for info. o.p. (ISBN 0-8218-1434-6). Am Math.

Relations Between Structure & Function in the Prokaryotic Cell. Ed. by R. Y. Stanier & H. J. Rogers. LC 77-21093. (Society for General Microbiology Symposium: No. 28). (Illus.). 1978. 65.00 (ISBN 0-521-21909-4). Cambridge U Pr.

Relations in Public. Erving Goffman. 390p. 1972. pap. 7.95x (ISBN 0-06-131957-0, TB 1957, Torch). Har-Row.

Relations of Indian, Greek, & Christian Thought in Antiquity. Kenneth R. Stunkel. LC 79-63750. 1979. pap. text ed. 9.00 (ISBN 0-8191-0737-9). U Pr of Amer.

Relationship Between Engine Oil Viscosity & Engine Performance, Pts. V & VI. Society of Automotive Engineers. 1980. 18.00. Soc Auto Engineers.

Relationship of Magnesium to Disease in Domestic Animals & in Humans. Jerry K. Aikawa. (Illus.). 160p. 1971. 16.75 (ISBN 0-398-02215-1). C C Thomas.

Relationship of Painting & Literature: A Guide to Information Sources. Ed. by Eugene L. Huddleston & Douglas A. Noverr. LC 78-53436. (American Studies Information Guide Ser.: Vol. 4). 1978. 30.00 (ISBN 0-8103-1394-4). Gale.

Relationship of Renaissance Concepts of Honour to Shakespeare's Problem Plays. Alice Shalvi. (Salzburg Studies in English Literature, Jacobean Drama Studies: No.7). 1972. pap. text ed. 25.00x (ISBN 0-391-01519-2). Humanities.

Relationship of Verbal & Non-Verbal Communication. Ed. by Mary R. Key. (Contributions to the Sociology of Language: No. 25). 1980. text ed. 41.25x (ISBN 90-279-7878-6); pap. text ed. 12.50x (ISBN 90-279-7637-6). Mouton.

Relationships. Berman. 1978. pap. 8.95 (ISBN 0-8015-6269-4, Hawthorn). Dutton.

Relationships & Life Cycles: Modern Dimensions of Astrology. Stephen Arroyo. LC 79-53979. 1979. pap. 6.95 (ISBN 0-916360-12-1). CRCS Pubns NV.

Relationships Between Doctors & Patients. Alan Davis. 1978. 17.95 (ISBN 0-566-00200-0, 01896-X, Pub. by Saxon Hse England). Lexington Bks.

Relationships in Adolescence. John C. Coleman. 1974. 22.50x (ISBN 0-7100-7868-4). Routledge & Kegan.

Relationships of the Protoceratid Artiodactyls, & Description of a New Genus. R. A. Stirton. (U. C. Publ. in Geological Sciences: Vol. 72). 1967. pap. 6.00x (ISBN 0-520-09175-2). U of Cal Pr.

Relative Deprivation & Social Justice. W. G. Runciman. (Reports of the Institute of Community Studies). 1980. Repr. pap. 35.00 (ISBN 0-7100-3923-9). Routledge & Kegan.

Relativism in Contemporary Christian Ethics. Millard J. Erickson. 1974. pap. 3.95 (ISBN 0-8010-3315-2). Baker Bk.

Relativistic Cosmology: An Introduction. J. Heidmann. (Illus.). 168p. 1980. pap. 24.80 (ISBN 0-387-10138-1). Springer-Verlag.

Relativistic Point Dynamics. H. Arzelies. LC 72-142173. 416p. 1972. text ed. 60.00 (ISBN 0-08-015842-0). Pergamon.

Relativity & Common Sense: A New Approach to Einstein. Hermann Bondi. (Illus.). 177p. 1980. pap. 3.00 (ISBN 0-486-24021-5). Dover.

Relativity & High Energy Physics. W. G. Rosser & R. K. McCulloch. (Wykeham Science Ser.: No. 7). 1969. 9.95x (ISBN 0-8448-1109-2). Crane-Russak Co.

Relativity: The Theory & Its Philosophy. Roger B. Angel. (Foundations & Philosophy of Science & Technology Ser.). (Illus.). 320p. 1980. 48.00 (ISBN 0-08-025197-8); pap. 21.00 (ISBN 0-08-025196-X). Pergamon.

Relativity Theory & Astrophysics: Relativity & Cosmology. Ed. by J. Ehlers. LC 62-21481. (Lectures in Applied Mathematics Ser.: Vol. 8). 1979. Repr. of 1972 ed. 17.60 (ISBN 0-8218-1108-8, LAM-8). Am Math.

Relax & Stretch. Ruth B. Simon. 1974. 7.95 o.s.i. (ISBN 0-8027-0410-7). Walker & Co.

Relaxation & (Re-, or) De-Sensitization Training, Set-RD. rev. ed. Russell E. Mason. 1975. pap. 50.00x (ISBN 0-89533-006-7); tape-1a, t-1, t-2, t-5a, t-6, t-9, relaxation training, clinical application 1979 & hierarchy incl. F I Comm.

Relaxation Book: An Illustrated Self-Help Program. Gerald Rosen. (Psychology Today Book Club). (Illus.). 1978. 10.95 (ISBN 0-13-772210-9, Spec); pap. 4.95 (ISBN 0-13-772202-8, Spec). P-H.

Relaxation Phenomena in Polymers. Ed. by G. M. Bartenev & Y. V. Zelenev. LC 74-13015. 349p. 1974. 49.95 (ISBN 0-470-05429-8). Halsted Pr.

Relaxation Response. Herbert Benson. LC 75-14309. (Illus.). 128p. 1975. 5.95 o.p. (ISBN 0-688-02955-8). Morrow.

Relearning the Alphabet. Denise Levertov. LC 72-103373. 1970. 6.00 (ISBN 0-8112-0303-4); pap. 3.95 (ISBN 0-8112-0085-X, NDP290). New Directions.

Release from Isolation: How to Find Friendship, Love, & Happiness. J. S. Martindale. LC 79-162932. 1971. 11.95 (ISBN 0-911012-08-7). Nelson-Hall.

Release from Your Problems. David Seabury. 1966. pap. 3.95 (ISBN 0-911336-15-X). Sci of Mind.

Release of Catecholamines from Adrenergic Neurons. new ed. Ed. by David M. Paton. 1978. text ed. 60.00 (ISBN 0-08-021536-X); pap. text ed. 29.00 (ISBN 0-08-023755-X). Pergamon.

Release the Sun. rev. ed. William Sears. LC 60-8220. 1960. 10.00 (ISBN 0-87743-027-6, 7-31-27); pap. 5.00 (ISBN 0-87743-003-9, 7-31-28). Baha'i.

Release Your Brakes! James W. Newman. 1978. pap. 2.95 (ISBN 0-446-93889-0). Warner Bks.

Release Your Cosmic Powers. Michael X. 1969. pap. 5.95 (ISBN 0-685-20201-1). Saucerian.

Releasing Test Scores. William J. Banach et al. 1976. pap. text ed. 5.75 o.p. (ISBN 0-87545-006-7). Natl Sch Pr.

Relentless Gun. Giles A. Lutz. 144p. 1981. pap. 1.75 (ISBN 0-449-13996-4, GM). Fawcett.

Relentless Storm. Claire Lorrimer. 224p. 1981. pap. 2.25 (ISBN 0-553-13658-5). Bantam.

Relevance & the Social Studies: A Conceptual Analysis. Robert F. Madgic. LC 73-77590. 1973. pap. 3.60 (ISBN 0-8224-5840-3). Pitman Learning.

Relevance of Apocalyptic. 3rd ed. H. H. Rowley. LC 64-12221. 240p. pap. text ed. 7.95 (ISBN 0-87921-061-3). Attic Pr.

Relevance of History. Gordon Connell-Smith & Howell A. Lloyd. 1972. text ed. 6.95x o.p. (ISBN 0-435-32805-0). Heinemann Ed.

Relevance of Liberalism. Zbigniew Brzezinski. LC 77-8202. (Studies of the Research Institute on International Change, Columbia University: Vol. 2). 1978. lib. bdg. 22.50x (ISBN 0-89158-134-0). Westview.

Relevance of Parasitology to Human Welfare Today. Ed. by Angela E. Taylor & Ralph Muller. (Symposia of the British Society for Parasitology: Vol. 16). (Illus.). 1978. pap. 19.75 (ISBN 0-632-00422-3, Blackwell). Mosby.

Relevance of School Learning Experience to Performance in Industry. Ed. by Elizabeth Orna. 1977. 22.95x (ISBN 0-85083-339-6). Intl Ideas.

Relevance of Sociology. Ed. by Jack D. Douglas. (Orig.). 1970. 10.95 (ISBN 0-13-773093-4). P-H.

Relevance of the Prophets. rev. ed. R. B. Scott. 1969. 9.95 (ISBN 0-02-608780-4); pap. 2.95 (ISBN 0-02-089270-5). Macmillan.

Relevant Mathematics. George N. Stone & Lawrence W. Becker. Incl. Algebra I. (gr. 9). 1970 (ISBN 0-88334-024-0); Geometry. (gr. 10). 1971 (ISBN 0-88334-043-7); Advanced Algebra & Trigonometry. (gr. 11-12). 1971 (ISBN 0-88334-044-5). pap. text ed. 5.75 ea. Ind Sch Pr.

Relevant Rhetoric. Irving J. Rein. 1969. pap. text ed. 7.95 (ISBN 0-02-926140-6). Free Pr.

Relevant War Against Poverty: A Study of Community Action Programs & Observable Social Change. Kenneth B. Clark & Jeannette Hopkins. LC 72-88633. 1969. 10.00 o.s.i. (ISBN 0-06-010798-7, HarpT). Har-Row.

Relevent Problems for Chemical Principles. 3rd ed. Ian S. Butler & Arthur E. Grosse. 1979. text ed. 10.95 (ISBN 0-8053-1587-X). Benjamin-Cummings.

Reliability & Risk Analysis: Methods & Nuclear Power Applications. Norman J. McCormick. 1981. write for info. (ISBN 0-12-482360-2). Acad Pr.

Reliability & Validity Assessment. Edward G. Carmines & Richard A. Zeller. LC 79-67629. (Quantitative Applications in the Social Sciences: No. 17). (Illus.). 1979. pap. 3.50x (ISBN 0-8039-1371-0). Sage.

Reliability, Availability & Maintainability: RAM. Joseph W. Foster, 3rd et al. 300p. 1981. 39.95 (ISBN 0-930206-05-3). M-a Pr.

Reliability Engineering. Arinc Research Corporation. 1964. ref. ed. 29.95 (ISBN 0-13-773127-2). P-H.

Reliability Engineering & Risk Assessment. E. Henley. 1980. 39.00 (ISBN 0-13-772251-6). P-H.

Reliability Evaluation of Some Fault-Tolerant Computer Architectures. S. Osaki & T. Nishio. (Lecture Notes in Computer Science Ser.: Vol. 97). 129p. 1981. pap. 9.80 (ISBN 0-387-10274-4). Springer-Verlag.

Reliability Handbook. William G. Ireson. 1966. 49.50 o.p. (ISBN 0-07-032040-3, P&RB). McGraw.

Reliability in Engineering Design. K. C. Kapur & L. K. Lamberson. LC 76-1304. 1977. text ed. 30.95 (ISBN 0-471-51191-9). Wiley.

Reliability, Maintainability, and Availability Assessment. Mitchell O. Locks. (Illus.). 1973. 15.95x o.p. (ISBN 0-8104-9204-0, Spartan). Hayden.

Reliability: Management, Methods & Mathematics. 2nd rev. ed. David K. Lloyd & Myron Lipow. LC 77-80554. 1977. Repr. of 1962 ed. 17.50 (ISBN 0-9601504-1-2). Lloyd & Lipow.

Reliability of Nuclear Power Plants. (Illus.). 751p. 1976. pap. 49.25 (ISBN 92-0-050075-7, IAEA). Unipub.

Reliability Problems of Reactor Pressure Components, Vol. 1. 1978. pap. 49.25 (ISBN 92-0-050078-1, ISP 467-1, IAEA). Unipub.

Reliability Technology. A. E. Green & A. J. Bourne. LC 73-161691. 400p. 1972. 79.25 (ISBN 0-471-32480-9, Pub. by Wiley-Interscience). Wiley.

Reliable Knowledge. J. M. Ziman. LC 78-3792. (Illus.). 1979. 23.95 (ISBN 0-521-22087-4). Cambridge U Pr.

Relics of Ancient Exegesis. D. W. Gooding. LC 74-19523. (Society for Old Testament Studies Monograph No. 4). 100p. 1976. 28.50 (ISBN 0-521-20700-2). Cambridge U Pr.

Religio Medici & Other Works. Thomas Browne. Ed. by Leonard C. Martin. 1964. 37.50x (ISBN 0-19-811429-X). Oxford U Pr.

Religion. Desmond Painter & John Shepard. Ed. by Malcolm Yapp & Margaret Killinger. (World History Ser.). (Illus.). 32p. (gr. 10). 1980. lib. bdg. 5.95 (ISBN 0-89908-145-2); pap. text ed. 1.95 (ISBN 0-89908-120-7). Greenhaven.

Religion, 3 vols. (British Parliamentary Papers Ser.). 1971. Set. 189.00x (ISBN 0-7165-1498-2, Pub. by Irish Academic Pr Ireland). Biblio Dist.

Religion Among the Primitives. William J. Goode. 1951. 10.95 o.s.i. (ISBN 0-02-912410-7); pap. text ed. 3.50 o.s.i. (ISBN 0-02-912420-4). Free Pr.

Religion: An Anthropological View. Anthony F. Wallace. 1966. text ed. 10.95x (ISBN 0-394-30543-4). Random.

Religion & Culture. Sarvepalli Radhakrishnan. 176p. 1971. pap. 2.40 (ISBN 0-88253-074-7). Ind-US Inc.

Religion & Culture of Israel: Selected Issues. Frank E. Eakin. 1977. pap. 10.50 (ISBN 0-8191-0208-3). U Pr of Amer.

Religion & Doubt: Toward a Faith of Your Own. Richard Creel. 1977. 10.50 o.p. (ISBN 0-13-771949-3); pap. 7.95 (ISBN 0-13-771931-0). P-H.

Religion & Education Under the Constitution. James Milton O'Neill. LC 72-171389. (Civil Liberties in American History Ser). 338p. 1972. Repr. of 1949 ed. lib. bdg. 35.00 (ISBN 0-306-70228-2). Da Capo.

Religion & Fertility: Arab Christian-Muslim Differentials. Joseph Chamie. LC 80-19787. (ASA Rose Monograph Ser.). (Illus.). 176p. Date not set. price not set (ISBN 0-521-23677-0); pap. price not set (ISBN 0-521-28147-4). Cambridge U Pr.

Religion & Healing in Mandari. Jean Buxton. (Illus.). 446p. 1973. 45.00x (ISBN 0-19-823174-1). Oxford U Pr.

Religion & Human Experience. Andrew Panzarella. LC 73-87024. 1974. pap. 3.30x (ISBN 0-88489-058-9); tchr's ed 2.60x (ISBN 0-88489-080-5). St Marys.

Religion & Human Purpose. William Horosz. LC 73-176179. 500p. Date not set. 16.50 (ISBN 0-87527-109-X). Green. Postponed.

Religion & Humanism. Ed. by Derek Baker. (Studies in Church History: Vol. 17). 500p. 1981. 36.00x (ISBN 0-631-18050-8, Pub. by Basil Blackwell). Biblio Dist.

Religion & Learning at Yale: Church of Christ in the College & University, 1757-1957. Ralph H. Gabriel. 1958. 27.50x (ISBN 0-685-69820-3). Elliots Bks.

Religion & Legitimation of Power in Sri Lanka. Ed. by Bardwell L. Smith. LC 77-7449. 1978. pap. 7.95 (ISBN 0-89012-008-0). Anima Pubns.

Religion & Legitimation of Power in Thailand, Laos & Burma. Ed. by Bardwell L. Smith. LC 77-7444. 1978. pap. 7.95 (ISBN 0-89012-009-9). Anima Pubns.

Religion & Modernization in the Soviet Union. Dennis J. Dunn. LC 77-86372. 1978. lib. bdg. 28.50x (ISBN 0-89158-241-X). Westview.

Religion & Nationalism in Southeast Asia: Burma, Indonesia, & the Philippines. Fred R. Von Der Mehden. (Illus.). 1963. pap. 6.95 (ISBN 0-299-02944-1). U of Wis Pr.

Religion & Personality in the Spiral of Life. David Belgum. LC 79-66478. 1979. pap. text ed. 11.50 (ISBN 0-8191-0832-4). U Pr of Amer.

Religion & Philosophy: Collected Papers. Fritz Marti. LC 78-68801. 1979. pap. text ed. 9.50 (ISBN 0-8191-0702-6). U Pr of Amer.

Religion & Political Culture in Kano. John N. Paden. LC 74-153548. 1973. 27.50x (ISBN 0-520-02020-0). U of Cal Pr.

Religion & Politics in Burma. Donald E. Smith. 1965. 20.00 (ISBN 0-691-03054-5). Princeton U Pr.

Religion & Politics in the Middle East. Ed. by Michael Curtis. 300p. 1981. lib. bdg. 24.00x (ISBN 0-86531-065-3). Westview.

Religion & Politics in Tibet. Bina R. Burman. 1979. 14.00x (ISBN 0-7069-0801-5, Pub. by Croom Helm Ltd. England). Biblio Dist.

Religion & Politics: The Intentions of the Athors of the First Amendment. Michael J. Malbin. 1978. pap. 3.25 (ISBN 0-8447-3302-4). Am Enterprise.

Religion & Public Doctrine in Modern England. M. Cowling. (Cambridge Studies in the History & Theory of Politics). 498p. 1981. 49.50 (ISBN 0-521-23289-9). Cambridge U Pr.

Religion & Rational Choice. Shivesh C. Thakur. (Library of Philosophy & Religion Ser.). 176p. 1981. 32.50x (ISBN 0-389-20047-6). B&N.

Religion & Reality. James H. Tuckwell. LC 77-118552. 1971. Repr. of 1915 ed. 13.00 (ISBN 0-8046-1177-7). Kennikat.

Religion & Respectability: Sunday Schools & English Working Class Culture, 1780-1850. Thomas W. Laqueur. LC 74-29728. 1976. 27.50x (ISBN 0-300-01859-2). Yale U Pr.

Religion & Rituals Among Muslims in India. Ed. by Imtiaz Ahmad. 1981. 14.00x (ISBN 0-685-74912-6). South Asia Bks.

Religion & Rural Society: South Lindsey, 1825-1875. James Obelkevich. (Illus.). 1976. 42.00x (ISBN 0-19-822426-5). Oxford U Pr.

Religion & Science Examine God. Parker L. Johnstone. LC 80-83297. 212p. 1980. 7.95 (ISBN 0-917802-04-7). Theoscience Found.

Religion & Self-Acceptance: A Study of the Relationship Between Belief in God & the Desire to Know. John F. Haught. LC 80-5872. 195p. 1980. lib. bdg. 17.00 (ISBN 0-8191-1296-8); pap. text ed. 8.75 (ISBN 0-8191-1297-6). U Pr of Amer.

Religion & Sexuality: Three American Communal Experiments of the Nineteenth Century. Lawrence Foster. 400p. 1981. 19.95 (ISBN 0-19-502794-9). Oxford U Pr.

Religion & Social Change in Southern Africa: Anthropological Essays in Honour of Monica Wilson. M. G. Whisson & Martin West. 1977. text ed. 18.00x (ISBN 0-949968-44-7). Verry.

Religion & Social Class: The Disruption. A. Allan Maclaren. (Scottish Ser.). 1974. 22.00 (ISBN 0-7100-7789-0). Routledge & Kegan.

Religion & Society in Industrial England. Alan D. Gilbert. (Themes in British Social History Ser.). (Illus.). 260p. 1976. pap. text ed. 12.95x (ISBN 0-582-48323-9). Longman.

Religion & Society in Interaction: The Sociology of Religion. Ronald L. Johnstone. 368p. 1975. text ed. 17.95 (ISBN 0-13-773085-3). P-H.

Religion & State in Iran, Seventeen Eighty-Five to Nineteen Six: The Role of the 'Ulama in the Qajar Period. Hamid Algar. LC 72-79959. (Near Eastern Center, UCLA). 1969. 18.50x (ISBN 0-520-01384-0). U of Cal Pr.

Religion & the Artifice of Jacobean & Caroline Drama. Peter F. Mullany. (Salzburg Studies in English Literature: Jacobean Drama Studies: No. 41). 1977. pap. text ed. 25.00x (ISBN 0-391-01486-2). Humanities.

Religion & the Constitution. Paul G. Kauper. LC 64-7898. (Edward Douglass White Lectures). 1964. 8.95 (ISBN 0-8071-0546-5); pap. text ed. 3.95x (ISBN 0-8071-0114-1). La State U Pr.

Religion & the Decline of Magic. Keith Thomas. LC 74-141707. 1971. pap. text ed. 13.95x (ISBN 0-684-14542-1, ScribC). Scribner.

Religion & the Human Image. Mark C. Taylor et al. (Illus.). 1977. pap. text ed. 10.95x (ISBN 0-13-773424-7). P-H.

Religion & the Life of Man. Bernard Phillips. Ed. by O'Hyun Park. LC 77-74731. 1977. pap. 3.75 o.p. (ISBN 0-87707-181-0). CSA Pr.

Religion & the Modern Mind. Walter T. Stace. LC 52-7471. 1960. pap. 3.50 o.p. (ISBN 0-397-00142-8, KB21, Key). Lippincott.

Religion & the Modern Mind. Walter T. Stace. LC 80-24093. 285p. 1980. Repr. of 1952 ed. lib. bdg. 22.50x (ISBN 0-313-22662-8, STRM). Greenwood.

Religion & the Public Order, 3 Vols. Ed. by Donald A. Giannella. LC 64-17164. 1964-66. Vol. 1. 10.00x o.s.i. (ISBN 0-226-29046-8); Vol. 2. 9.50x o.s.i. (ISBN 0-226-29047-6); Vol. 3. 11.00x o.s.i. (ISBN 0-226-29048-4). U of Chicago Pr.

Religion & the Transformation of Society: A Study in Social Change in Africa. Monica Wilson. LC 73-134622. (Scott Holland Memorial Lecturers of 1969 Ser). (Illus.). 1971. 19.95 (ISBN 0-521-07991-8). Cambridge U Pr.

Religion & Western Culture: Selected Issues. Frank E. Eakin. 1977. 10.75 (ISBN 0-8191-0256-3). U Pr of Amer.

Religion & World History: A Selection from the Works of Christopher Dawson. Ed. by James Oliver & Christina Scott. LC 74-33612. 480p. 1975. pap. 2.45 (ISBN 0-385-09551-1, Im). Doubleday.

Religion As Anxiety & Tranquillity: An Essay in Comparative Phenomenology of the Spirit. J. G. Arapura. (Religion & Reason Ser.: No. 5). 1973. 21.20x (ISBN 90-2797-180-3). Mouton.

Religion Cristiana En Su Expresion Doctrinal. Edgar Y. Mullins. Tr. by Sara A. Hale. Orig. Title: Christian Religion in Its Doctrinal Expression. 522p. 1980. pap. 8.95 (ISBN 0-311-09042-7). Casa Bautista.

Religion, Cults & the Law. A. Burstein. 1980. 5.95 (ISBN 0-379-11133-0). Oceana.

Religion for a Dislocated Generation. Barbara Hargrove. 144p. 1981. 9.95 (ISBN 0-8170-0891-8). Judson.

Religion for Mankind. Horace Holley. 1956. 8.95 (ISBN 0-87743-028-4, 7-31-29); pap. 2.95 (ISBN 0-85398-000-4, 7-31-30, Pub. by George Ronald England). Baha'i.

Religion from Tolstoy to Camus: Basic Writings on Religious Truth & Morals. Ed. by Walter Kaufmann. pap. 8.95x (ISBN 0-06-130123-X, TB123, Torch). Har-Row.

Religion in America. 2nd ed. Winthrop S. Hudson. 1973. pap. text ed. 9.95x (ISBN 0-684-13873-5, ScribC). Scribner.

Religion in America: A Critical Abridgment. Robert Baird. 7.50 (ISBN 0-8446-0471-2). Peter Smith.

Religion in American History: Interpretive Essays. John F. Wilson & John M. Mulder. 448p. 1978. text ed. 14.95 (ISBN 0-13-771998-1); pap. text ed. 11.95 (ISBN 0-13-771980-9). P-H.

Religion in American Life. Compiled by Nelson R. Burr. LC 70-136219. (Goldentree Bibliographies in American History Ser.). (Orig.). 1971. pap. 6.95x (ISBN 0-88295-506-3). AHM Pub.

Religion in American Public Law. David Fellman. LC 65-17006. 1965. 9.50x (ISBN 0-8419-8714-9, Pub. by Boston U Pr). Holmes & Meier.

Religion in American Society: The Effective Presence. John Wilson. LC 77-16808. 1978. ref. ed. 17.95 (ISBN 0-13-773259-7). P-H.

Religion in China. Richard C. Bush. Ed. by Donald K. Swearer. (Major World Religion Ser.). pap. 3.95 (ISBN 0-913592-98-6). Argus Comm.

Religion in Colonial America. William W. Sweet. LC 65-17183. 1965. Repr. of 1942 ed. 27.50x (ISBN 0-8154-0226-0). Cooper Sq.

Religion in Contemporary Society. Chalfant. 1981. 14.95 (ISBN 0-88284-126-2). Alfred Pub.

Religion in England, Fifteen Fifty-Eight to Sixteen Sixty-Two. H. G. Alexander. 233p. 1968. 4.00x o.p. (ISBN 0-87471-292-0). Rowman.

Religion in Japanese History. Joseph M. Kitagawa. LC 65-23669. 1966. 25.00x (ISBN 0-231-02834-2). Columbia U Pr.

Religion in North America. Ronald J. Wilkins. (To Live Is Christ Ser.). 208p. 1979. pap. text ed. 4.10 (ISBN 0-697-01701-X). Wm C Brown.

Religion in Overalls. William Johnsson. LC 77-22464. (Anvil Ser.). 1977. pap. 7.95 (ISBN 0-8127-0143-7). Southern Pub.

Religion in the Eighteenth Century. Ed. by John Browning & Richard Morton. LC 79-17715. (Eighteenth Century Ser.). 145p. 1979. lib. bdg. 20.00 (ISBN 0-8240-4005-8). Garland Pub.

Religion in the Middle East, 2 Vols. Arthur J. Arberry. LC 68-21187. (Illus.). 1969. Set. 88.00 (ISBN 0-521-07400-2); 54.00 ea.; Vol. 1. (ISBN 0-521-20543-3); Vol. 2. (ISBN 0-521-20544-1). Cambridge U Pr.

Religion in the New Netherland, 1623-1664. Frederick K. Zwierlein. LC 72-120851. (Civil Liberties in American History Ser). 1970. Repr. of 1910 ed. lib. bdg. 35.00 (ISBN 0-306-71960-6). Da Capo.

Religion in Twentieth Century America. Herbert W. Schneider. LC 52-8219. (Library of Congress Ser. in American Civilization). (Illus.). 1952. 10.00x (ISBN 0-674-75700-9). Harvard U Pr.

Religion In Wood: A Book of Shaker Furniture. Edward D. Andrews & Faith Andrews. LC 66-12722. (Illus.). 128p. 1966. 7.95x (ISBN 0-253-17360-4). Ind U Pr.

Religion, Nationalism & Chinese Students: The Anti-Christian Movement of 1922-1927. Ka-Che Yip. (Studies on East Asia). (Illus.). 133p. 1980. pap. 7.50 (ISBN 0-914584-15-4). West Wash Univ.

Religion, Nationalism & Economic Action Critical Questions on Durkheim & Weber. Matthews Schoffeleers & Daniel Meijers. 1978. pap. text ed. 9.25x (ISBN 90-232-1614-8). Humanities.

Religion? No! Good Living? Yes! George W. Lugg. LC 80-51444. 128p. (Orig.). 1980. pap. 3.95x (ISBN 0-935834-03-6). Rainbow-Betty.

Religion of China. Max Weber. 1951. 8.95 o.s.i. (ISBN 0-02-934440-9); pap. text ed. 5.95 o.s.i. (ISBN 0-02-934450-6). Free Pr.

Religion of Love. Swami Vivekananda. 114p. pap. 1.95 (ISBN 0-87481-129-5). Vedanta Pr.

Religion of Nature Delineated. William Wollaston. Ed. by Rene Wellek. LC 75-11267. (British Philosophers & Theologians of the 17th & 18th Centuries Ser.). 1978. Repr. of 1722 ed. lib. bdg. 42.00 (ISBN 0-8240-1816-8). Garland Pub.

Religion of the Chinese. Jan J. Groot. LC 79-2824. 230p. 1981. Repr. of 1910 ed. 19.50 (ISBN 0-8305-0004-9). Hyperion Conn.

Religion of the Heart: Anglican Evangelicalism & the Nineteenth-Century Novel. Elisabeth Jay. 1979. write for info. (ISBN 0-19-812092-3). Oxford U Pr.

Religion of the Hindus: Interpreted by Hindus. Ed. by Kenneth W. Morgan. 1953. 21.50 (ISBN 0-8260-6260-1). Wiley.

Religion of the Rigveda. H. D. Griswold. 1971. 7.50 (ISBN 0-89684-305-X). Orient Bk Dist.

Religion of the Sikhs. Gopal Singh. 1971. 5.50x (ISBN 0-210-22296-4). Asia.

Religion, Philosophy & Psychical Research. C. D. Broad. (International Library of Psychology, Philosophy & Scientific Method Ser.). 1969. Repr. of 1953 ed. text ed. 10.00x (ISBN 0-391-00441-7). Humanities.

Religion, Politics & Social Change in the Third World. Donald E. Smith. LC 73-143516. 1971. 12.95 (ISBN 0-02-929490-8); pap. text ed. 6.95 (ISBN 0-02-929460-6). Free Pr.

Religion Southern Style: Southern Baptists & Society in Histoical Pspective. Norman A. Yance. LC 78-61185. (Special Studies Ser.: No. 4). 1978. 3.95 (ISBN 0-932180-03-5). Assn Baptist Profs.

Religion, the State & the School. John M. Swomley, Jr. LC 68-21040. 1968. 6.60 o.p. (ISBN 0-672-53584-X); pap. 5.50 (ISBN 0-672-63584-4). Bobbs.

Religion, Truth & Language-Games. Patrick Sherry. LC 75-41579. (Library of Philosophy & Religion Ser.). 234p. 1977. text ed. 18.50x (ISBN 0-06-496236-9). B&N.

Religion Without Explanation. D. Z. Phillips. 1976. 18.50x (ISBN 0-631-17100-2, Pub. by Basil Blackwell). Biblio Dist.

Religiones Vivas. Roberto E. Hume. Tr. by Manuel Beltroy from Eng. Orig. Title: Living Religions of the World. 320p. (Span.). 1980. pap. 4.50 (ISBN 0-311-05758-6, Edit Mundo). Casa Bautista.

Religions East & West. Larry Kettelkamp. (Illus.). 128p. (gr. 5-9). 1972. PLB 6.96 (ISBN 0-688-31926-2). Morrow.

Religions in America. Ed. by Herbert L. Marx. (Reference Shelf Ser.). 1977. 6.25 (ISBN 0-8242-0608-8). Wilson.

Religions in Japan. Ed. by William K. Bunce. LC 59-9234. 216p. 1981. pap. 5.25 (ISBN 0-8048-0500-8). C E Tuttle.

Religions in Modern India, Vol. 5. Ed. by Giri Raj Gupta. 368p. 1981. text ed. 27.50x (ISBN 0-7069-0793-0, Pub. by Vikas India). Advent Bk.

Religions of Man. Huston Smith. pap. 4.95 (ISBN 0-06-090043-1, CN43, CN). Har-Row.

Religions of Mongolia. Walther Heissig. Tr. by Geoffrey Samuel from Ger. 1980. 17.50x (ISBN 0-520-03857-6). U of Cal Pr.

Religions of Old Korea: New York, 1932. Charles A. Clark. LC 78-74297. (Oriental Religions Ser.: Vol. 14). 295p. 1981. lib. bdg. 33.00 (ISBN 0-8240-3916-5). Garland Pub.

Religions of the American Indians. Ake Hultkrantz. (Hermeneutics--Studies in the History of Religions: Vol. 7). 1979. 14.95 (ISBN 0-520-02653-5); pap. 5.95 (ISBN 0-520-04239-5, CAL 463). U of Cal Pr.

Religions of the Roman Empire. John Ferguson. LC 71-110992. (Aspects of Greek & Roman Life Ser). (Illus.). 1970. 19.50x (ISBN 0-8014-0567-X). Cornell U Pr.

Religions of the World. Gerald L. Berry. (Orig.). 1956. pap. 2.50 (ISBN 0-06-463224-5, EH 224, EH). Har-Row.

Religions of the World. D. E. Hardin. (Liberal Studies Ser.). 1966. pap. text ed. 2.50x o.p. (ISBN 0-435-46531-7). Heinemann Ed.

Religions of the World, 2 Vols. Hardon, John A., S.J. (YA) 1968. Vol. 1. pap. 1.45 (ISBN 0-385-01570-4, D241B). Vol. 2 (D241B). Doubleday.

Religions of the World. Lewis M. Hopfe. 1976. pap. 8.95x (ISBN 0-02-474810-2). Macmillan.

Religions of the World. S. Vernon McCasland et al. (Illus.). 1969. 13.95 (ISBN 0-394-30384-9). Random.

Religions of the World. rev. ed. Ronald J. Wilkins. (To Live Is Christ Ser.). 240p. 1979. pap. 4.25 (ISBN 0-697-01715-X). Wm C Brown.

Religions of the World Made Simple. rev. ed. John Lewis. 1958. pap. 3.50 (ISBN 0-385-02276-X, Made). Doubleday.

Religious & Political History & Thought in the Byzantine Empire. Paul J. Alexander. 360p. 1980. 60.00x (ISBN 0-86078-016-3, Pub. by Variorum England). State Mutual Bk.

Religious & Spiritual Groups in Modern America. Robert S. Ellwood, Jr. 352p. 1973. pap. 10.95 (ISBN 0-13-773309-7). P-H.

Religious Archives: An Introduction. August R. Suelflow. LC 80-17159. (SAA Basic Archival Manual Ser.). 1980. pap. text ed. 7.00 (ISBN 0-931828-20-1). Soc Am Archivists.

Religious Assortative Mariage in the United States. Robert A. Johnson. LC 80-978. (Studies in Population). 1980. 25.00 (ISBN 0-12-386580-8). Acad Pr.

Religious Bibliographies in Serial Literature: A Guide. Michael J. Walsh et al. LC 81-312. 224p. 1981. lib. bdg. 35.00 (ISBN 0-313-22987-2, WRB/). Greenwood.

Religious Body. Catherine Aird. 176p. 1980. pap. 1.95 (ISBN 0-553-13951-7). Bantam.

Religious Body: Design for a New Reformation. Gabriel Moran. 1974. 8.95 (ISBN 0-8164-1176-X). Crossroad NY.

Religious Books & Serials in Print, 1980-1981. LC 78-63633. 1500p. 1980. 42.00 (ISBN 0-8352-1306-4). Bowker.

Religious Ceremonies & Customs of the Parsees: Bombay, 1922. Jivanji J. Modi. LC 78-74280. (Oriental Religions Ser.: Vol. 7). 563p. 1980. lib. bdg. 60.50 (ISBN 0-8240-3913-0). Garland Pub.

Religious Change in Zambia: Exploratory Studies. Wim M. J. Van Binsbergen. (Monographs from the African Studies Centre, Leiden). (Illus.). 416p. 1981. price not set (ISBN 0-7103-0000-X). Routledge & Kegan.

Religious Concerns in Contemporary Education. Philip H. Phenix. LC 59-11329. 1959. 5.75x (ISBN 0-8077-1905-6). Tchrs Coll.

Religious Conversion & Personal Identity. V. Bailey Gillespie. LC 79-15605. 264p. (Orig.). 1979. pap. 8.95 (ISBN 0-89135-018-7). Religious Educ.

Religious Currents in the Nineteenth Century. Vilhelm Gronbech. Tr. by P. M. Mitchell & W. D. Paden. LC 72-11829. (Arcturus Bks. Paperbacks). 206p. 1973. lib. bdg. 7.00x (ISBN 0-8093-0629-8); pap. 2.45 (ISBN 0-8093-0630-1). S Ill U Pr.

Religious Dimension in Hispanic Los Angeles: A Protestant Case Study. Clifton L. Holland. LC 74-5123. 542p. (Orig.). 1974. pap. 10.95 (ISBN 0-87808-309-X). William Carey Lib.

Religious Drama, Vol. 1: Five Plays. Ed. by Marvin Halverson. 8.00 (ISBN 0-8446-2792-5). Peter Smith.

Religious Drama, Vol. 2: 21 Medieval Mystery & Morality Plays. Ed. by E. Martin Browne. 8.00 (ISBN 0-8446-2793-3). Peter Smith.

Religious Drama, Vol. 3. Ed. by Marvin Halverson. 8.00 (ISBN 0-8446-2794-1). Peter Smith.

Religious Education & Religious Understanding: An Introduction to the Philosophy of Religious Education. Raymond Holley. 1978. 19.50x (ISBN 0-7100-8995-3). Routledge & Kegan.

Religious Education in a Psychological Key. John H. Peatling. 380p. (Orig.). 1981. pap. price not set (ISBN 0-89135-027-6). Religious Educ.

Religious Education in German Schools: An Historical Approach. Ernst C. Helmreich. LC 59-11509. 1959. 17.50x (ISBN 0-674-75850-1). Harvard U Pr.

Religious Education of Preschool Children. Lucie W. Barber. 190p. (Orig.). 1981. pap. write for info. (ISBN 0-89135-026-8). Religious Educ.

Religious Education of Preschool Children. Lucie W. Barber. LC 80-27623. 190p. (Orig.). 1981. pap. price not set (ISBN 0-89135-026-8). Religious Educ.

Religious Education of the Deaf. Ed. by J. Van Eijndhoven. (Modern Approaches to the Diagnosis & Instruction of Multi-Handicapped Children Ser.: Vol. 11). 168p. 1973. text ed. 20.25 (ISBN 90-237-4111-0, Pub. by Swets Pub. Ser Holland). Swets North Am.

Religious Education Press, Inc. Samuel Johnson. 323p. 1979. Repr. of 1888 ed. lib. bdg. 32.50 (ISBN 0-8482-1396-3). Norwood Edns.

Religious Element in Life. Dennis Ryan. LC 77-18568. 1978. pap. text ed. 7.50x (ISBN 0-8191-0405-1). U Pr of Amer.

Religious Experience & Scientific Method. Henry N. Wieman. 387p. 1971. Repr. of 1927 ed. lib. bdg. 11.95x (ISBN 0-8093-0537-2). S Ill U Pr.

Religious Experience & Scientific Method. Henry N. Wieman. (Arcturus Books Paperbacks). 387p. 1971. pap. 9.95 (ISBN 0-8093-0530-5). S Ill U Pr.

Religious Experience: Its Nature & Function in the Human Psyche. Walter H. Clark et al. (Illus.). 168p. 1973. 11.75 (ISBN 0-398-02550-9). C C Thomas.

Religious Experience of the Roman People: From the Earliest Times to the Age of Augustus. William W. Fowler. LC 71-145870. 1971. Repr. of 1911 ed. lib. bdg. 37.50x (ISBN 0-8154-0372-0). Cooper Sq.

Religious Faith & Twentieth Century Man. F. C. Happold. 192p. 1981. 6.95 (ISBN 0-8245-0046-6). Crossroad NY.

Religious Formation of the Adolescent. E. F. O'Doherty. LC 73-12969. 109p. 1973. pap. 2.95 o.p. (ISBN 0-8189-0280-9). Alba.

Religious Guide to Europe. Daniel M. Madden. 384p. 1975. pap. 4.95 o.s.i. (ISBN 0-02-097950-9, Collier). Macmillan.

Religious History of the American People, 2 vols. S. E. Ahlstrom. LC 75-22362. (Illus.). 720p. 1975. pap. 3.50 ea. (Im); Vol. 1. pap. (ISBN 0-385-11164-9); Vol. 2. pap. (ISBN 0-385-11165-7). Doubleday.

Religious Humanism & the Victorian Novel: George Eliot, Walter Pater, & Samuel Butler. U. C. Knoepflmacher. 1970. 18.00 o.p. (ISBN 0-691-06112-2); pap. 3.95 o.p. (ISBN 0-691-01295-4, 187). Princeton U Pr.

Religious Humanism in America: Dietrich, Reese & Potter. Mason Olds. 1977. 10.00 (ISBN 0-8191-0267-9). U Pr of Amer.

Religious Language of Nicholas of Cusa. James E. Biechler. LC 75-23096. (American Academy of Religion. Dissertation Ser.). 1975. pap. 7.50 (ISBN 0-89130-021-X, 010108). Scholars Pr Ca.

Religious Liberty: An Inquiry. M. Searle Bates. LC 77-166096. (Civil Liberties in American History Ser.). 1972. Repr. of 1945 ed. lib. bdg. 39.50 (ISBN 0-306-70235-5). Da Capo.

Religious Life in Ancient Egypt. W. M. Petrie. LC 72-78238. (Illus.). 1972. Repr. of 1924 ed. lib. bdg. 22.50x (ISBN 0-8154-0422-0). Cooper Sq.

Religious Life of Ancient Rome. Jesse B. Carter. 270p. 1972. Repr. of 1911 ed. lib. bdg. 26.50x (ISBN 0-8154-0429-8). Cooper Sq.

Religious Life of Man: Guide to Basic Literature. Leszek M. Karpinski. LC 77-19338. 1978. 19.50 (ISBN 0-8108-1110-3). Scarecrow.

Religious Life Today. Karl Rahner. 1976. 5.95 (ISBN 0-8164-0323-6). Crossroad NY.

Religious Ministry in a Transcendentless Culture. Ronald B. Mayers. LC 79-3424. 1980. pap. text ed. 8.50 (ISBN 0-8191-0889-8). U Pr of Amer.

Religious Minorities in the Soviet Union. Michael Bourdoux. (Minority Rights Group: No. 1). 1975. pap. 2.50 (ISBN 0-89192-091-9). Interbk Inc.

Religious Motivation: Biographical & Sociological Problems for the Church Historian. Derek Baker. (Studies in Church History: Vol. 15). 1978. 36.00x (ISBN 0-631-19250-6, Pub. by Basil Blackwell England). Biblio Dist.

Religious Observances in Tibet: Patterns & Functions. Robert B. Ekvall. LC 64-23423. 1964. 12.50x o.s.i. (ISBN 0-226-20078-7). U of Chicago Pr.

Religious Orders in England. David Knowles. Incl. Vol. 1. The Old Orders. 1948. 47.50 (ISBN 0-521-05480-X); pap. 14.50 (ISBN 0-521-29566-1); Vol. 2. End of the Middle Ages. 1955. 53.50 (ISBN 0-521-05481-8); pap. 15.50 (ISBN 0-521-29567-X). Cambridge U Pr.

Religious Orders in England: The Tudor Age, Vol. 3. David Knowles. LC 78-73953. 1979. 59.50 (ISBN 0-521-05482-6); pap. 19.50 (ISBN 0-521-29568-8). Cambridge U Pr.

Religious Origins of the American Revolution. Page Smith. LC 76-13157. (American Academy of Religion, Aids for the Study of Religion). 1976. pap. 7.50 (ISBN 0-89130-121-6, 010303). Scholars Pr Ca.

Religious Philosophy of William James. Robert J. Vanden Burgt. LC 80-22936. 176p. 1981. text ed. 16.95 (ISBN 0-88229-594-2); pap. text ed. 8.95 (ISBN 0-88229-767-8). Nelson-Hall.

Religious Plays That Click. Al Bryant. 1954. pap. 2.95 (ISBN 0-310-22101-3). Zondervan.

Religious Practices of Primitive Peoples. Norman P. Mayfair. (Illus.). 139p. 1980. deluxe ed. 47.75 (ISBN 0-89266-241-7). Am Classical Coll.

Religious Publishing & Communications. Judith S. Duke. (Communications Library). 235p. 1980. 24.95x (ISBN 0-914236-61-X). Knowledge Indus.

Religious Quest of the Graeco-Roman World: A Study in the Historical Background of Early Christianity. Samuel Angus. LC 66-30791. 1929. 15.00x (ISBN 0-8196-0196-9). Biblo.

Religious Reason: The Rational & Moral Basis of Religious Belief. Ronald M. Green. 1978. text ed. 13.95 (ISBN 0-19-502388-9); pap. text ed. 4.50 (ISBN 0-19-502389-7). Oxford U Pr.

Religious School Board: A Manual. Louis Lister & Rebecca Lister. 1978. pap. 5.00 (ISBN 0-8074-0014-9, 243870). UAHC.

Religious Significance of Atheism. Alasdair MacIntyre & Paul Ricoeur. LC 68-28398. (Bampton Lectures in America Ser.: No. 18). 1969. 12.50x (ISBN 0-231-03139-4). Columbia U Pr.

Religious Sublime: Christian Poetry & Critical Tradition in Eighteenth-Century England. David B. Morris. LC 70-190534. 272p. 1972. 12.00x (ISBN 0-8131-1270-2). U Pr of Ky.

Religious Syncretism in Antiquity. Ed. by Birger A. Pearson. LC 75-29421. (American Academy of Religion-University of California Institute of Religious Studies). 225p. 1975. pap. 7.50 (ISBN 0-89130-037-6, 010401). Scholars Pr Ca.

Religious Systems & Psychotherapy. Ed. by Richard H. Cox. 520p. 1973. text ed. 29.75 (ISBN 0-398-02753-6). C C Thomas.

Religious Thinking from Childhood to Adolescence. Ronald Goldman. 1968. pap. text ed. 3.95 (ISBN 0-8164-2061-0, SP53). Crossroad NY.

Religious Thought in India. T. N. Sharma. 1980. 11.00x (ISBN 0-8364-0619-2, Pub. by Ramneek). South Asia Bks.

Religious Thought in the Nineteenth Century. Bernard M. Reardon. (Orig.). 1966. 49.50 (ISBN 0-521-06049-4); pap. 12.50x (ISBN 0-521-09386-4). Cambridge U Pr.

Religious Thought of Samuel Taylor Coleridge. David Pym. 1979. text ed. 12.50x (ISBN 0-901072-65-6). Humanities.

Religious Trends in English Poetry, 6 vols. Hoxie N. Fairchild. Incl. Vol. 1. Protestantism & the Cult of Sentiment: 1700-1740 (ISBN 0-231-08821-3); Vol. 2. Religious Sentimentalism in the Age of Johnson: 1740-1780. 1942 (ISBN 0-231-08822-1); Vol. 3. Romantic Faith: 1780-1830. 1949 (ISBN 0-231-08823-X); Vol. 4. Christianity & Romanticism in the Victorian Era: 1830-1880. 1957 (ISBN 0-231-08824-8); Vol. 5. Gods of a Changing Poetry: 1880-1920. 1962 (ISBN 0-231-08825-6); Vol. 6. Valley of Dry Bones: 1920-1965. 1968 (ISBN 0-231-08826-4). LC 39-12839. 25.00x ea. Columbia U Pr.

Religious Values & Development. Ed. by Kenneth P. Jameson & Charles K. Wilber. (Illus.). 154p. 1981. 34.50 (ISBN 0-08-026107-8). Pergamon.

Religious Writers Marketplace. William H. Gentz & Elaine W. Colvin. 221p. 1980. 12.95 (ISBN 0-89471-132-6); lib. bdg. 19.80 (ISBN 0-89471-106-7). Running Pr.

Religiousness in Yoga: Lectures on Theory & Practice. T. K. Desikachar. Ed. by Mary L. Skelton & J. R. Carter. LC 79-9643. (Illus.). 314p. 1980. text ed. 19.00 (ISBN 0-8191-0966-5); pap. text ed. 10.50 (ISBN 0-8191-0967-3). U Pr of Amer.

Reliques of Ancient English Poetry, 3 Vols. Thomas Percy. Ed. by Henry B. Wheatley. 1966. pap. text ed. 4.00 ea.; Vol. 1. pap. text ed. o.p. (ISBN 0-486-21611-X); Vol. 2. pap. text ed. (ISBN 0-486-21612-8); Vol. 3. pap. text ed. (ISBN 0-486-21613-6). Dover.

Reliques of Irish Poetry, 1789. Ed. by Charlotte Brooke. Bd. with Memoir of Miss Brooke, 1816. A. C. Seymour. LC 76-133327. 544p. 1970. 54.00x (ISBN 0-8201-1082-5). Schol Facsimiles.

Reliquiae Baldwinianae. William Darlington. (Classica Botanica Americana Ser: Suppl. 2). 1968. Repr. of 1843 ed. 19.25 o.s.i. (ISBN 0-02-843650-4). Hafner.

Reliquiae Juveniles: Miscellaneous Thoughts in Prose & Verse. Isaac Watts. LC 68-17018. 1968. Repr. of 1734 ed. 38.00x (ISBN 0-8201-1049-3). Schol Facsimiles.

Relish for Eternity: The Process of Divinization in the Poetry of John Clare. Gregory D. Crossan. (Salzburg Studies in English Literature, Romantic Reassessment: No. 53). 291p. 1976. pap. text ed. 25.00x (ISBN 0-391-01354-8). Humanities.

Re'lize Whut Ahm Talkin Bout? Stephen D. Chennault. 7.95 (ISBN 0-912216-24-7). Green Hill.

Reloading for Shotgunners. Ed. by Robert S. Anderson. LC 81-65119. (Illus.). 224p. 1981. pap. 7.95 (ISBN 0-910676-25-9, 2606). DBI.

Reluctant Doctor. Jean B. Moliere. Tr. by W. Hannan. (Orig.). 1963. pap. 2.25x (ISBN 0-87830-535-1). Theatre Arts.

Reluctant Dragon. Kenneth Grahame. (Illus.). 58p. (gr. 3-6). 1953. 5.95 (ISBN 0-8234-0093-X). Holiday.

Reluctant Duke. Marilyn Lowery. (Orig.). 1981. pap. 1.50 (ISBN 0-440-17234-9). Dell.

Reluctant Goddess. Oleda Baker. 480p. (Orig.). 1981. pap. 2.75 (ISBN 0-515-05869-6). Jove Pubns.

Reluctant Guru. R. K. Narayan. 173p. 1975. pap. 2.50 (ISBN 0-88253-729-6). Ind-US Inc.

Reluctant Hangman & Other Stories of Crime. Grant Allan. Ed. by Tom Schantz & Enid Schantz. (Illus.). 56p. 1975. pap. 4.50 o.p. (ISBN 0-915230-00-3). Rue Morgue.

Reluctant Heiress. Lisabet Norcross. 1978. pap. 1.50 o.s.i. (ISBN 0-515-04463-6). Jove Pubns.

Reluctant Militants. B. C. Roberts et al. 1972. text ed. 15.75x o.p. (ISBN 0-435-85780-0). Heinemann Ed.

Reluctant Partnership. Elizabeth Ashton. (Harlequin Romance Ser.). (Orig.). 1980. pap. 1.25 o.p. (ISBN 0-373-02324-3, Pub. by Harlequin). PB.

Reluctant Princess: A Legend of Love in Siam. Ed. by Mom D. Paribatra. LC 63-8716. (Illus.). (gr. 9 up). 5.00 o.p. (ISBN 0-8048-0501-6). C E Tuttle.

Reluctant Rebel. Fola Oyewole. 210p. 1975. 10.75x o.p. (ISBN 0-8476-1234-1). Rowman.

Reluctant Suitor. Megan Daniel. (Orig.). 1981. pap. 1.95 (ISBN 0-451-09671-1, J9671, Sig). NAL.

Reluctant Weekend Gardener. Carlo Wallach. (Illus.). 200p. 1974. 7.95 o.s.i. (ISBN 0-02-623150-6). Macmillan.

Reluctant Wizard. Neil K. Newell. (Orig.). 1980. pap. 1.95 (ISBN 0-532-23315-8). Manor Bks.

Remains of Henry White, with an Account of His Life. Robert Southey. Ed. by Donald H. Reiman. LC 75-31271. (Romantic Context Ser.: Poetry 1789-1830). 1978. lib. bdg. 47.00 (ISBN 0-8240-2217-3). Garland Pub.

Remaking Cities. Alison Ravetz. 375p. 1980. 37.50x (ISBN 0-85664-293-2, Pub. by Croom Helm Ltd England). Biblio Dist.

Remarkable Birth of Planet Earth. new ed. Henry M. Morris. 112p. 1972. pap. 1.50 (ISBN 0-87123-485-8, 200485). Bethany Fell.

Remarkable Miracles. G. C. Bevington. LC 73-85242. 209p. 1974. pap. text ed. 2.50 o.p. (ISBN 0-88270-063-4). Logos.

Remarkable Names of Real People. John Train. (Illus.). 1977. 5.95 (ISBN 0-517-53130-5). Potter.

Remarkable Occurrences. John Train. (Illus.). 1978. 5.95 (ISBN 0-517-53505-X, Dist. by Crown). Potter.

Remarkable Providences. Ed. by John Demos. LC 74-160130. (American Culture Ser). 1972. 8.95 (ISBN 0-8076-0617-0); pap. 7.95 (ISBN 0-8076-0616-2). Braziller.

Remarkable Return of Winston Potter Crisply. Eve Rice. LC 77-28101. (gr. 5-9). 1978. 7.95 (ISBN 0-688-80145-5); PLB 7.63 (ISBN 0-688-84145-7). Greenwillow.

Remarkable Trials of All Countries; Particularly of the United States, Great Britain, Ireland & France: With Notes & Speeches of Counsel. Containing Thrilling Narratives of Fact from the Court-Room, Also Historical Reminiscences of Wonderful Events. Thomas Dunphy & Thomas J. Cummins. 464p. 1981. Repr. of 1867 ed. lib. bdg. 35.00x (ISBN 0-8377-0512-6). Rothman.

Remarkable Words: With Astonishing Origins, Remarkable Ser. John Train. (Clarkson N. Potter Bks.). 1980. 5.95 (ISBN 0-517-54185-8). Crown.

Remarkable Writing Machine. Carol H. Behrman. (Illus.). 64p. (gr. 3-5). 1981. PLB 6.97 (ISBN 0-686-69297-7). Messner.

Remarks on Colour. Ludwig Wittgenstein. Ed. by G. E. Anscombe. Tr. by Linda L. McAlister & Margarete Schattle. 1978. 14.50x (ISBN 0-520-03357-4); pap. 2.95 (ISBN 0-520-03727-8, CAL 406). U of Cal Pr.

Remarks on Mr. Rowes Tragedy of Lady Jane Grey & All His Other Plays. Charles Gildon. LC 74-7279. (English Stage Ser.). lib. bdg. 50.00 (ISBN 0-685-41744-1). Garland Pub.

Remarks on the Philosophy of Psychology, Vol. 1. Ludwig Wittgenstein. Ed. by G. E. Anscombe & G. H. Von Wright. LC 80-52781. 408p. 1980. lib. bdg. 35.00x (ISBN 0-226-90433-4). U of Chicago Pr.

Remarks on the Philosophy of Psychology, Vol. 2. Ludwig Wittgenstein. Ed. by G. H. Von Wright & Heikki Nyman. Tr. by C. G. Luckhardt & A. E. Aue. LC 80-52781. 1980. lib. bdg. 27.50x (ISBN 0-226-90434-2). U of Chicago Pr.

Remarks on the Theory of Prime Ends. H. D. Ursell & L. C. Young. LC 52-42839. (Memoirs: No. 3). 1978. pap. 4.40 (ISBN 0-8218-1203-3, MEMO-3). Am Math.

Remarks Upon Alchemy & the Alchemists. Ethan A. Hitchcock. LC 79-8614. Repr. of 1857 ed. 30.00 (ISBN 0-404-18478-2). AMS Pr.

Rembrandt. Bob Haak. (Illus.). 1981. pap. 2.95 (ISBN 0-8120-2103-7). Barron.

Rembrandt. Ludwig Munnz & B. Haak. (Library of Great Painters Ser). 1966. 35.00 (ISBN 0-8109-0437-3). Abrams.

Rembrandt. (Artists Ser.). (Illus.). 1976. pap. 5.95 (ISBN 0-8120-0764-6). Barron.

Rembrandt. Gladys Schmitt. 1961. 12.95 o.p. (ISBN 0-394-44252-0). Random.

Rembrandt. Leonard Slatkes. LC 79-57583. (Abbeville Library of Art Ser.: No. 7). (Illus.). 112p. 1980. pap. 4.95 (ISBN 0-89659-134-4). Abbeville Pr.

Rembrandt & the Italian Renaissance. Kenneth Clark. LC 66-13550. (Illus.). 1966. 19.95 (ISBN 0-8147-0080-2). NYU Pr.

Rembrandt Decisions. Anne V. Badgley. LC 79-13159. 1979. 8.95 (ISBN 0-396-07622-X). Dodd.

Rembrandt: Experimental Etcher. (Illus.). 1969. pap. 5.00 (ISBN 0-87846-034-9). Mus Fine Arts Boston.

Rembrandt: His Life, His Work, His Times. Bob Haal. 125.00 (ISBN 0-8109-4750-1). Abrams.

Rembrandt of the Comic Strip. Rick Marschall. 1981. 6.95 (ISBN 0-918348-04-8). Green Hill.

Rembrandt Panel. large print ed. Oliver Banks. LC 80-27955. 1981. Repr. of 1980 ed. 11.95 (ISBN 0-89621-264-5). Thorndike Pr.

Rembrandt: The Etchings. Rembrandt Van Rijn. LC 77-87012. (Illus.). 1977. 29.95 (ISBN 0-8467-0411-0, Pub. by Two Continents); pap. 13.95 (ISBN 0-8467-0414-5). Hippocrene Bks.

Remede a Tout, Ou Constitution Invulnerable De la Felicite Publique. Francois-Joseph Lange. (Fr.). 1977. lib. bdg. 23.75x o.p. (ISBN 0-8287-0507-0); pap. text ed. 13.75x o.p. (ISBN 0-685-77004-4). Clearwater Pub.

Remedial Drama. Sue Jennings. LC 74-77191. 1978. pap. 5.85 (ISBN 0-87830-563-7). Theatre Arts.

Remedial Education. Olive Sampson. (Special Needs in Education Ser.). 1975. 11.50x (ISBN 0-7100-8141-3); pap. 6.00 (ISBN 0-7100-8142-1). Routledge & Kegan.

Remedial Treatment of Buildings. Barry Richardson. (Construction Press Ser.). (Illus.). 236p. 1981. 42.00 (ISBN 0-904406-74-1). Longman.

Remediating Reading Disabilities: Simple Things That Work. J. E. Cook & Elsie C. Earlley. LC 79-20412. 1979. text ed. 27.00 (ISBN 0-89443-154-4). Aspen Systems.

Remediation of Learning Disabilities: A Handbook of Psychoeducational Resource Programs. 2nd ed. Robert E. Valett. LC 67-26847. 1974. 3-ring bdg. 19.50 (ISBN 0-8224-5850-0). Pitman Learning.

Remedies for Positive Living. Henry Causly. 1981. 4.75 (ISBN 0-8062-1690-5). Carlton.

Remember Me? Ed. by Mary Verdick. (Pal Paperbacks - Pal Skills Ser.). (Illus., Orig.). (gr. 7-12). 1978. pap. text ed. 1.25 (ISBN 0-8374-6709-8). Xerox Ed Pubns.

Remember Me to Tom. 2nd ed. Edwina D. Williams & Lucy Freeman. 336p. 1980. pap. 5.95 (ISBN 0-86629-006-0). Sunrise MO.

Remember Me When This You See. Ed. by Lillian Morrison. LC 60-11536. (Illus.). (gr. 4 up). 1961. 8.95 (ISBN 0-690-69613-2, TYC-J). T Y Crowell.

Remember Ruben. Mongo Beti, pseud. 350p. (Orig.). 1981. 14.00x (ISBN 0-89410-240-0); pap. 7.00x (ISBN 0-89410-241-9). Three Continents.

Remember the Alamo. Amelia Barr. 329p. 1980. Repr. of 1880 ed. lib. bdg. 11.95x (ISBN 0-89968-215-4). Lightyear.

Remember the Days: A Short History of the Jewish American. Milton Meltzer. LC 74-5531. 128p. 1974. 4.95 (ISBN 0-385-05946-9, Zenith); pap. 2.50 (ISBN 0-385-07676-2). Doubleday.

Remember to Remember. Jeanne Savage. 1981. 7.95 (ISBN 0-533-04462-6). Vantage.

Remember When-Trolley Wires Spanned the Country: Bullentin-119. Ed. by Norman Carlson & Arthur Peterson. LC 78-74495. (Illus.). 1980. 30.00 (ISBN 0-915348-20-9). Central Electric.

Remembered Death. Agatha Christie. 1980. pap. write for info. (ISBN 0-671-83442-8). PB.

Remembered Earth: An Anthology of Contemporary Native American Literature. Ed. by Geary Hobson. (Illus.). 1978. pap. text ed. 6.95 o.p. (ISBN 0-918434-03-3). Red Earth.

Remembered Gate: Origins of American Feminism - the Woman & the City 1800-1860. Barbara Berg. (Urban Life in America Ser.). 1978. 16.95x (ISBN 0-19-502280-7). Oxford U Pr.

Remembered Village. M. N. Srinivas. 1977. 21.50x (ISBN 0-520-02997-6); pap. 6.95 (ISBN 0-520-03948-3). U of Cal Pr.

Remembering. Bruce Gilbert. LC 80-54370. 96p. 1981. 3.95 (ISBN 0-87159-139-1). Unity Bks.

Remembering: A Study in Experimental & Social Psychology. Frederic C. Bartlett. 1932. 35.00 (ISBN 0-521-04114-7); pap. 9.95x (ISBN 0-521-09441-0). Cambridge U Pr.

Remembering Garden. Rosanne Sanders. (Clarkson N. Potter Bks.). (Illus.). 1980. 17.95 (ISBN 0-517-54169-6). Crown.

Remembering People: The Key to Success. Harry Lorayne. 1976. pap. 2.25 o.s.i. (ISBN 0-446-82922-6). Warner Bks.

Remembering Poets. Donald Hall. LC 76-47266. (Illus.). 1978. 10.95 o.s.i. (ISBN 0-06-011723-0, HarpT). Har-Row.

Remembering: The University of Utah. Ed. by Elizabeth Haglund. (Illus.). 250p. 1981. 25.00 (ISBN 0-87480-191-5). U of Utah Pr.

Remembering Who We Are. Barbara Deming. LC 80-66371. 224p. (Orig.). 1980. pap. cancelled (ISBN 0-9603628-1-9). Frog in Well.

Remembrance & Pantomime. Derek Walcott. 176p. 1980. 15.00 (ISBN 0-374-24912-1); pap. 6.95 (ISBN 0-374-51569-7). FS&G.

Remington Warm-up Studies for Trombone. Donald Hunsberger. LC 80-67541. (Illus.). 1980. 8.95 (ISBN 0-918194-10-5). Accura.

Remington's Pharmaceutical Sciences. 16th ed. 1980. 55.00 (ISBN 0-912734-02-7). Mack Pub.

Reminiscences & Memorials of Men of the Revolution. Artemas B. Muzzey. LC 70-142542. 1971. Repr. of 1883 ed. 26.00 (ISBN 0-8103-3629-4). Gale.

Reminiscences & Souvenirs of the Assassination of Abraham Lincoln. J. E. Buckingham, Sr. LC 80-128964. (Illus.). 89p. 22.50 (ISBN 0-686-28744-4); pap. 17.50 (ISBN 0-686-28745-2). J L Barbour.

Reminiscences (Mainly Personal) of William Graham Sumner. Albert G. Keller. 1933. 32.50x (ISBN 0-686-51300-2). Elliots Bks.

Reminiscences of a Portrait Painter. G. P. A. Healy. LC 78-96439. (Library of American Art Ser). (Illus.). 1970. Repr. of 1894 ed. lib. bdg. 29.50 (ISBN 0-306-71829-4). Da Capo.

Reminiscences of a Ranchman. Edgar B. Bronson. LC 62-8407. xvi, 370p. 1962. 15.00x (ISBN 0-8032-0886-3); pap. 4.50 (ISBN 0-8032-5023-1, BB 127, Bison). U of Nebr Pr.

Reminiscences of a Small County Lawyer. Archibald M. Matthews. 1981. 5.75 (ISBN 0-8062-1689-1). Carlton.

Reminiscences of a Stock Operator. Edwin Lefevre. 1980. Repr. of 1923 ed. flexible cover 12.00 (ISBN 0-87034-058-1). Fraser Pub Co.
Reminiscences of Augustus Saint-Gaudens, 2 vols. Ed. by Homer Saint-Gaudens & H. Barbara Weinberg. LC 75-28890. (Art Experience in Late 19th Century America Ser.: Vol. 23). (Illus.). 1976. Repr. of 1913 ed. Set. lib. bdg. 72.50 (ISBN 0-8240-2247-5). Garland Pub.
Reminiscences of Confederate Service. Francis W. Dawson. Ed. by Bell I. Wiley. LC 79-26720. (Library of Southern Civilization). 220p. 1980. 14.95x (ISBN 0-8071-0689-5). La State U Pr.
Reminiscences of Emerson: An AMS Anthology. LC 80-2543. 1981. 57.50 (ISBN 0-404-19268-8). AMS Pr.
Reminiscences of Lenin. N. K. Krupskaya. LC 67-27253. (Illus.). 1970. 7.50 (ISBN 0-7178-0253-1); pap. 4.95 (ISBN 0-7178-0254-X). Intl Pub Co.
Reminiscences of Literary London from 1779 - 1853. Thomas Rees. LC 68-24476. 1969. Repr. of 1896 ed. 15.00 (ISBN 0-8103-3888-2). Gale.
Reminiscences of Los Alamos: 1943-1945. Ed. by Lawrence Badash & H. P. Broida. (Studies in the History of Modern Science: No. 5). 180p. 1980. lib. bdg. 26.50 (ISBN 90-277-1097-X); pap. 9.95 (ISBN 90-277-1098-8). Kluwer Boston.
Reminiscences of Manchester Fifty Years Ago. J. T. Slugg. (Development of Industrial Society Ser.). 355p. 1980. Repr. 24.00x (ISBN 0-7165-1771-X, Pub. by Irish Academic Pr). Biblio Dist.
Reminiscences of Michael Kelly of the King's Theatre & Theatre Royal Drury Lane 2 Vols. 2nd ed. Michael Kelly. LC 68-16243. (Music Ser). 1968. Repr. of 1826 ed. lib. bdg. 45.00 (ISBN 0-306-71094-3). Da Capo.
Reminiscences of My Father, Peter A. Stolypin: An Annotated Translation from the Russian. Maria P. Von Bock. Tr. by Margaret Patoski from Rus. LC 75-16442. 1970. 10.00 (ISBN 0-8108-0331-3). Scarecrow.
Reminiscences of My Life. Charles Santley. LC 80-2297. 1981. Repr. of 1909 ed. 37.50 (ISBN 0-404-18865-6). AMS Pr.
Reminiscences of My Life in the Highlands, 1884: Containing Notices of the Changes in the Country During the Present Century, Vol. 2. Joseph Mitchell. 288p. 1971. 11.00 (ISBN 0-7153-5300-4). David & Charles.
Reminiscences of My Youth. Maxim Gorki. 334p. 1980. Repr. of 1924 ed. lib. bdg. 25.00 (ISBN 0-8492-4961-9). R West.
Reminiscences of Tolstoy. Ed. by Kalpana Sahni. 144p. 1981. text ed. 10.00 (ISBN 0-391-02021-8). Humanities.
Remnants of Every Day Life. Bobby Pizzi. 1979. 6.95 (ISBN 0-533-04529-0). Vantage.
Remnants of Glory. Teresa L. Miller. LC 80-52413. 352p. 1981. 12.95 (ISBN 0-87223-657-9). Seaview Bks.
Remodel, Don't Move: Make Your Home Fit Your Lifestyle. William Hague. LC 80-498. (Illus.). 256p. 1981. 14.95 (ISBN 0-385-15910-2). Doubleday.
Remodeling: A Bibliography of Periodical Articles. Mary Vance. (Architecture Ser.: Bibliography A-295). 68p. 1980. pap. 7.50. Vance Biblios.
Remodeling Your Bathroom. LC 79-91444. (Popular Science Skill Bks.). (Orig.). 1980. pap. 4.95 (ISBN 0-06-090780-0, CN 780, CN). Har-Row.
Remodeling Your Kitchen & Building Your Own Cabinets. Virginia Habeeb & Ralph Treves. LC 79-33571. (Popular Science Skill Bks.). (Orig.). 1980. pap. 4.95 (ISBN 0-06-090781-9, CN 781, CN). Har-Row.
Remodeling Your Kitchen or Bathroom. Walter G. Salm. LC 68-2130. (Illus.). 1967. Repr. of 1967 ed. lib. bdg. 3.50 o.p. (ISBN 0-668-01781-3). Arco.
Remodelling Rooms. Richard Day. LC 68-54468. (Illus.). 1977. 4.95 (ISBN 0-668-01814-3); pap. 2.50 o. p. (ISBN 0-668-04073-4). Arco.
Remote Sensing & Ecosystem Management. D. M. Lavigne et al. (Norsk Polarinstitutt Skrifter: Vol. 166). (Illus.). 51p. 1980. pap. text ed. 5.00x. Universitet.
Remote Sensing & Image Interpretation. Thomas M. Lillesand & Ralph W. Kiefer. LC 78-27846. 1979. text ed. 27.95 (ISBN 0-471-02609-3). Wiley.
Remote-Sensing Applications for Mineral Exploration. Ed. by W. L. Smith. 1977. 62.00 (ISBN 0-12-787477-1). Acad Pr.
Remote Sensing of Atmospheres & Oceans. Ed. by Adarsh Deepak. LC 80-18881. 1980. 45.00 (ISBN 0-12-208460-8). Acad Pr.
Remote Sensing of Earth Resources: A Guide to Information Sources. Ed. by M. Leonard Bryan. LC 79-22792. (Geography & Travel Information Guide Ser.: Vol. 1). (Illus.). 1979. 30.00 (ISBN 0-8103-1413-4). Gale.
Remote Sensing of Environment. Ed. by Joseph Lintz, Jr. & David S. Simonett. LC 76-47661. (Illus.). 1976. text ed. 35.50 (ISBN 0-201-04245-2, Adv Bk Prog). A-W.
Remote Sensing: Principles & Interpretation. Floyd F. Sabins, Jr. LC 77-27595. (Earth Sciences Ser.). (Illus.). 1978. text ed. 31.95x (ISBN 0-7167-0023-9). W H Freeman.
Remote Sensing with Special Reference to Agriculture & Forestry. Agricultural Board-Division of Biology & Agriculture. LC 77-600961. (Illus.). 1970. 13.75 o.p. (ISBN 0-309-01723-8). Natl Acad Pr.
Remote Sounding of the Atmosphere from Space: Proceedings of the 21st Plenary Meeting, Innsbruck, Austria, 1978. Committee on Space Research. Ed. by H. J. Bolle. (Illus.). 1979. 63.00 (ISBN 0-08-023419-4). Pergamon.
Removable Closure of the Interdental Space. Arnold Gaerny. (Illus.). 196p. 1972. 52.50. Quint Pub Co.
Removable Partial Prosthodontics. Ernest L. Miller. 21.00 o.p. (ISBN 0-683-05989-0). Williams & Wilkins.
Removable Partial Prosthodontics. 2nd ed. Ernest L. Miller & Joseph E. Grasso. 440p. 1981. write for info. (5990-4). Williams & Wilkins.
Removal & Return: The Socio-Economic Effects of the War on Japanese Americans. Leonard Broom & Ruth Riemer. (California Library Reprint). 1974. 20.00x (ISBN 0-520-02522-9). U of Cal Pr.
Removal of the Choctaw Indians. Arthur H. DeRosier, Jr. LC 70-111044. (Illus.). 1970. 12.50 (ISBN 0-87049-113-X). U of Tenn Pr.
Removing Roadblocks in Reading. new ed. Katherine H. O'Connor. LC 72-96305. (Illus.). 200p. 1976. text ed. 12.95 (ISBN 0-910812-10-1); pap. text ed. 8.75 (ISBN 0-910812-11-X). Johnny Reads.
Removing Taxes on Knowledge. 1969. pap. 2.50 (ISBN 92-3-100746-7, U545, UNESCO). Unipub.
Remy de Gourmont. Paul E. Jacob. 176p. 1980. Repr. of 1931 ed. lib. bdg. 25.00 (ISBN 0-89984-260-7). Century Bookbindery.
Renaat Braem Architect. Francois Strauven. (Archives d'Architecture Moderne). 150p. (Orig., Fr. & Eng.). 1980. write for info. (ISBN 0-8150-0922-4). Wittenborn.
Renagade No. Four: Death Hunter. Ramsay Thorne. (Orig.). 1980. pap. 1.95 (ISBN 0-446-90902-5). Warner Bks.
Renagade No. Three: Fear Merchant. Ramsay Thorne. (Orig.). 1980. pap. 1.95 (ISBN 0-446-90761-8). Warner Bks.
Renaissance. John R. Hale. LC 65-28051. (Great Ages of Man). (Illus., Fr.). (gr. 6 up). 1965. PLB 11.97 (ISBN 0-8094-0366-8, Pub. by Time-Life). Silver.
Renaissance. Rosa M. Letts. (Cambridge Introduction to the History of Art Ser.: No. 3). (Illus.). 100p. Date not set. 19.95 (ISBN 0-521-23394-1); pap. 6.95 (ISBN 0-521-29957-8). Cambridge U Pr.
Renaissance: A Reconsideration of the Theories & Interpretations of the Age. Symposium on the Renaissance, University of Wisconsin, 1959. Ed. by Tinsley Helton. LC 80-21869. xiii, 160p. 1980. Repr. of 1961 ed. lib. bdg. 19.50x (ISBN 0-313-22797-7, SYRE). Greenwood.
Renaissance & English Humanism. Douglas Bush. LC 40-11006. 1939. pap. 3.50 (ISBN 0-8020-6008-0). U of Toronto Pr.
Renaissance & Reformation. Bard Thompson. (Texts & Studies in Religion, Vol. 11). (Orig.). 1981. soft cover 24.95x (ISBN 0-88946-915-6). E Mellen.
Renaissance & Renascences in Western Art. Erwin Panofsky. (Icon Edition). (Illus.). 380p. 1972. pap. 7.95 (ISBN 0-06-430026-9, IN-26, HarpT). Har-Row.
Renaissance & Renewal in Christian History. Derek Baker. (Studies in Church History: Vol. 14). 1977. 36.00x (ISBN 0-631-17780-9, Pub. by Basil Blackwell). Biblio Dist.
Renaissance Architecture. Roger T. Smith. (Illus.). 1979. 61.75 (ISBN 0-930582-46-2). Gloucester Art.
Renaissance Architeture. Peter Murray. LC 70-149850. (History of World Architecture). (Illus.). 1971. 45.00 (ISBN 0-8109-1000-4). Abrams.
Renaissance Bronzes: From Ohio Collections. William D. Wixom. LC 75-30966. (Illus.). 196p. 1975. pap. 15.00x (ISBN 0-910386-24-2, Pub. by Cleveland Mus Art). Ind U Pr.
Renaissance Chaucer. Alice S. Miskimin. LC 74-79174. 328p. 1975. 18.50x o.p. (ISBN 0-300-01768-5). Yale U Pr.
Renaissance Cookbook, Vol. 1. William Edwards et al. (Illus.). 184p. 1980. 5.95 (ISBN 0-938054-01-5); pap. 3.25 (ISBN 0-938054-00-7). Tri-B Pubns.
Renaissance Discovery of Classical Antiquity. Roberto Weiss. 1969. text ed. 18.25x (ISBN 0-631-11690-7). Humanities.
Renaissance Drama. Intro. by Derek Traversi. 128p. 1981. pap. 5.95 (ISBN 0-312-67160-1). St Martin.
Renaissance Entertainment: Festivities for the Marriage of Cosimo I, Duke of Florence, in 1539. Ed. by Andrew C. Minor & M. Bonner Mitchell. LC 68-11348. (Illus.). 1968. 15.00x (ISBN 0-8262-8522-8). U of Mo Pr.
Renaissance Europe: Age of Recovery & Reconciliation. De Lamar Jensen. 416p. 1980. pap. text ed. 10.95 (ISBN 0-669-51722-4). Heath.
Renaissance Europe: The Individual & Society, 1480-1520. J. R. Hale. (Library Reprint Ser.). 1978. 18.50x (ISBN 0-520-03470-8, CAMPUS 194); pap. 5.50x (ISBN 0-520-03471-6). U of Cal Pr.
Renaissance Fancies & Studies: Being a Sequel to Euphorion. Vernon Lee. LC 76-20099. (Decadent Consciousness Ser.: Vol. 19). 1977. Repr. of 1895 ed. lib. bdg. 38.00 (ISBN 0-8240-2767-1). Garland Pub.
Renaissance Florence. Gene A. Brucker. (New Dimensions in History-Historical Cities Ser.). 306p. 1969. pap. text ed. 9.95 (ISBN 0-471-11371-9). Wiley.
Renaissance Imagination: Essays & Lectures. P. J. Gordon. Ed. by Stephen Orgel. LC 74-81432. 1976. 33.75x (ISBN 0-520-02817-1). U of Cal Pr.
Renaissance Italy. Powell. (Warwick Press Ser.). (gr. 5 up). 1980. PLB 6.90 (ISBN 0-531-09164-3, B34). Watts.
Renaissance Letters: Revelations of a World Reborn. Ed. by Robert J. Clements & Lorna Levant. LC 75-21806. 469p. 1976. 20.00x o.p. (ISBN 0-8147-1362-9); pap. 9.50x (ISBN 0-8147-1363-7). NYU Pr.
Renaissance Likeness: Art & Culture in Raphael's Julius II. Loren Partridge & Randolph Starn. (Quantum Ser.). (Illus.). 1980. 16.95x (ISBN 0-520-03901-7). U of Cal Pr.
Renaissance Man. Agnes Heller. Tr. by Richard E. Allen. 1978. 45.00x (ISBN 0-7100-8881-7). Routledge & Kegan.
Renaissance Man. Agnes Heller. LC 80-6192. 490p. 1981. pap. 9.95 (ISBN 0-8052-0674-4). Schocken.
Renaissance Man & Creative Thinking: A History of Concepts of Harmony 1400-1700. Dorothy Koenigsberger. LC 78-956. 1979. text ed. 27.50x (ISBN 0-391-00851-X). Humanities.
Renaissance Miniature Painters & Classical Imagery. Armstrong. 1980. write for info. (ISBN 0-905203-24-0, Pub. by H Miller England). Heyden.
Renaissance New Testament, 20 vols. Randolph O. Yaeger. Incl. Vol. 1 (ISBN 0-88289-957-0); Vol. 2 (ISBN 0-88289-657-1); Vol. 3 (ISBN 0-88289-357-2); Vol. 4 (ISBN 0-88289-857-4); Vol. 5 (ISBN 0-88289-257-6); Vol. 6 (ISBN 0-88289-757-8). 3360p. 1980. each 19.95. Pelican.
Renaissance New Testament, Vol. 7. Ed. by Randolph O. Yeager. 1981. 19.95 (ISBN 0-88289-457-9). Pelican.
Renaissance of Islam: Art of the Mamluks. Esin Atil. LC 80-607866. (Illus.). 256p. (Orig.). 1981. 47.50 (ISBN 0-87474-214-5); pap. 19.95 (ISBN 0-87474-213-7). Smithsonian.
Renaissance of the Twelfth Century. Charles Haskins. pap. 5.95 o.p. (ISBN 0-452-00456-X, F456, Mer). NAL.
Renaissance of the Twelfth Century. Charles H. Haskins. x, 437p. 1971. 18.50x (ISBN 0-674-76077-8); pap. 5.95 (ISBN 0-674-76075-1). Harvard U Pr.
Renaissance, Reformation, & Absolutism Fourteen Hundred to Sixteen Sixty, Vol. I. Ed. by Thomas G. Barnes & Gerald D. Feldman. LC 79-66685. 1979. pap. text ed. 9.25 (ISBN 0-8191-0847-2). U Pr of Amer.
Renaissance, Reformation, & Absolutism: 1450 to 1650. 2nd ed. Ed. by Norman F. Cantor & Michael S. Werthman. LC 72-76355. (AHM Structure of European History Ser.: Vol. 3). 319p. 1972. pap. text ed. 5.95x (ISBN 0-88295-712-0). AHM Pub.
Renaissance, Reformation & the Outer World, 1450-1660. M. L. Bush. (History of Europe Ser.). 1967. text ed. 6.50x o.p. (ISBN 0-7137-0452-7). Humanities.
Renaissance Rhetoric: A Short Title Catalogue. James J. Murphy. LC 80-8501. 400p. 1981. lib. bdg. 50.00 (ISBN 0-8240-9487-5). Garland Pub.
Renaissance Rome: A Portrait of a Society, 1500-1559. Peter Partner. 1977. 22.75x (ISBN 0-520-03026-5); pap. 6.95 (ISBN 0-520-03945-9). U of Cal Pr.
Renaissance Sculpture in Spain. Manuel Gomez-Moreno. Tr. by Bernard Bevan from Span. LC 76-116354. (Illus.). 1971. Repr. of 1931 ed. buckram 40.00 (ISBN 0-87817-042-1). Hacker.
Renaissance Self-Fashioning: More to Shakespeare. Stephen Greenblatt. LC 80-13837. 272p. 1980. 20.00 (ISBN 0-226-30653-4). U of Chicago Pr.
Renaissance Singer. Ed. by Thomas Dunn. LC 75-20077. 1976. 7.00 (ISBN 0-911318-10-0). E C Schirmer.
Renaissance Theatre Costume. Stella M. Newton. (Illus.). 1975. 29.95 (ISBN 0-87830-108-9). Theatre Arts.
Renaissance Thought & Its Sources. Paul O. Kristeller. Ed. by Michael Mooney. LC 79-15521. 1979. 27.50x (ISBN 0-231-04512-3). Columbia U Pr.
Renaissance Thought & Its Sources. Paul O. Kristeller. Ed. by Michael Mooney. 352p. 1981. Repr. 9.50 (ISBN 0-231-04513-1). Columbia U Pr.
Renal & Electrolyte Disorders. Robert W. Schrier. LC 75-30300. 1976. text ed. 18.50 o.p. (ISBN 0-316-77475-8). Little.
Renal & Electrolyte Disorders. 2nd ed. Ed. by Robert W. Schrier. 500p. 1980. text ed. 22.95 (ISBN 0-316-77476-6). Little.
Renal Biopsy Pathology with Diagnostic & Therapeutic Implications. Benjamin H. Spargo et al. 1979. 42.50 (ISBN 0-471-03119-4, Pub. by Wiley-Interscience). Wiley.
Renal Cortical Necrosis. F. A. Laszlo. (Contributions to Nephrology Ser.: Vol. 28). (Illus.). vi, 210p. 1981. pap. 45.00 (ISBN 3-8055-2109-X). S Karger.
Renal Failure. Ed. by Jose Strauss. 1978. lib. bdg. 37.50 (ISBN 0-8240-7011-9). Garland Pub.
Renal Failure Diet Manual Utilizing the Food Exchange System. Mary E. Spitzer et al. 132p. 1976. pap. 11.75 (ISBN 0-398-03466-4). C C Thomas.
Renal Function Tests. Cristobal G. Duarte. (Laboratory Medicine Ser.). 1980. text ed. 27.50 (ISBN 0-316-19398-4). Little.
Renal, Genitourinary, & Breast Pathology & Pathophysiology Case Studies. Richert E. Goyette. 1976. spiral bdg 12.00 o.p. (ISBN 0-87488-077-7). Med Exam.
Renal Microvascular Disease. Joseph J. Bookstein & Richard L. Clark. 1980. text ed. 42.50 (ISBN 0-316-10237-7). Little.
Renal Nursing. 2nd ed. Robert Uldall. (Blackwell Scientific Pubns.). 1977. 16.00 (ISBN 0-632-00086-4). Mosby.
Renal Papilla and Hypertension. Ed. by Anil K. Mandal & Sven-Olof Bohman. (Illus.). 230p. 1980. 27.50 (ISBN 0-306-40506-7, Plenum Med Bk). Plenum Pub.
Renal Pathology. E. M. Darmady & A. McIver. LC 79-42838. (Postgraduate Pathology Ser.). 560p. 1980. 99.95 (ISBN 0-407-00119-0). Butterworths.
Renal Pathophysiology. 2nd ed. Alexander Leaf & Ramzi Cotran. (Illus.). 448p. 1980. text ed. 18.95x (ISBN 0-19-502688-8); pap. text ed. 11.95x (ISBN 0-19-502689-6). Oxford U Pr.
Renal Pathophysiology - Recent Advances. Ed. by Alexander Leaf et al. 1980. text ed. 35.50 (ISBN 0-89004-399-X). Raven.
Renal Physiology. Arthur J. Vander. (Illus.). 192p. (Orig.). 1975. pap. text ed. 7.95 o.p. (ISBN 0-07-066957-0, C). McGraw.
Renal Physiology: Principles & Functions. Esmail Koushanpour. LC 75-12489. (Illus.). 1976. pap. 13.50 o.p. (ISBN 0-7216-5493-2). Saunders.
Renal Problems: A Critical Care Nursing Focus. Mary Jackle & Claire Rasmussen. LC 79-9498. (Illus.). 356p. 1979. pap. text ed. 16.95 (ISBN 0-87619-408-0). R J Brady.
Renal Prostaglandins, Vol. 1. Ed. by James B. Lee. (Annual Research Reviews Ser.). 1979. 28.80 (ISBN 0-88831-037-4). Eden Med Res.
Renal Transplantation. Ed. by Satya N. Chatterjee. 1980. 26.50 (ISBN 0-89004-308-6). Raven.
Renal Transplantation Case Studies. Robert J. Corry & John S. Thompson. 1977. spiral bdg. 14.00 (ISBN 0-87488-015-7). Med Exam.
Renal Transplantation: Theory & Practice. 2nd ed. Jean Hamburger et al. (Illus.). 375p. 1981. write for info. (3872-9). Williams & Wilkins.
Renal Transplantaton - A Nursing Perspective. Bonnie L. Sachs. 1977. spiral bdg. 9.50 (ISBN 0-87488-358-X). Med Exam.
Renal Tubular Dysfunction. Vardaman M. Buckalew & Micahel A. Moore. LC 79-92915. (Discussions in Patient Management Ser.). 1980. pap. 13.50 (ISBN 0-87488-889-1). Med Exam.
Renascent Africa. Nnamdi Azikiwe. (Africana Modern Library: No. 6). 1968. Repr. of 1937 ed. text ed. 11.75x (ISBN 0-7146-1744-X). Humanities.
Rendering of God in the Old Testament, No. 10. Dale Patrick. Ed. by Walter Brueggemann & John R. Donahue. LC 80-2389. (Overtures to Biblical Theology Ser.). 176p. (Orig.). 1981. pap. 8.95 (ISBN 0-8006-1533-6, 1-1533). Fortress.
Renderings of Stefanos: Book I, Science & Technology. Stefan Grunwald. LC 79-10680. 1980. pap. 4.95 (ISBN 0-915442-91-4, Unilaw). Donning Co.

Rendez-Vous en France. Sten-Gunnar Hellstrom et al. 1972. pap. text ed. 4.25 (ISBN 0-912022-28-0); exercise bk 3.50 (ISBN 0-912022-29-9). EMC.

Rendezvous. Evelyn Anthony. 1977. pap. 1.95 o.p. (ISBN 0-425-03573-5, Medallion). Berkley Pub.

Rendezvous - South Atlantic. Douglas Reeman. pap. 2.25 (ISBN 0-515-05717-7). Jove Pubns.

Rendezvous at the Hallows. Juanita T. Osborne. 192p. (YA) 1975. 5.95 (ISBN 0-685-50529-4, Avalon). Bouregy.

Rendezvous with Destiny. Leonard Rapport & Arthur Northwood, Jr. (Illus.). 1977. 14.00 (ISBN 0-686-26296-4). One Hund First Air.

Rene Char. Mary Ann Caws. (World Authors Ser.: No. 428). 1977. lib. bdg. 12.50 (ISBN 0-8057-6268-X). Twayne.

Rene Clair. Celia McGerr. (Theater Arts Ser.). 1980. lib. bdg. 12.95 (ISBN 0-8057-9262-7). Twayne.

Rene Magritte. Rene Passeron. (Filipacchi Art Bks). (Illus.). 96p. 1981. 25.00 (ISBN 2-8501-8098-X); pap. 9.95 (ISBN 2-8501-8099-8). Hippocrene Bks.

Rene Magritte. Schneede. 1981. pap. 3.50 (ISBN 0-8120-2187-8). Barron.

Rene Marques. Eleanor J. Martin. (World Authors Ser.: No. 516). 1979. lib. bdg. 14.50 (ISBN 0-8057-6357-0). Twayne.

Rene Wellek. Martin Bucco. (United States Authors Ser.: No. 410). 1981. lib. bdg. 12.95 (ISBN 0-8057-7339-8). Twayne.

Renegade. J. T. Edson. (J. T. Edson Ser.). 1978. pap. 1.50 o.p. (ISBN 0-425-03845-9, Medallion). Berkley Pub.

Renegade No. Eight: Over the Andes to Hell. Ramsay Thorne. 192p. (Orig.). 1981. pap. 1.95 (ISBN 0-446-90549-6). Warner Bks.

Renegade No. Five: Macumba Killer. Ramsay Thorne. 224p. (Orig.). 1980. pap. 1.95 (ISBN 0-446-90234-9). Warner Bks.

Renegade No. One. Ramsay Thorne. (Orig.). 1979. pap. 1.95 (ISBN 0-446-90976-9). Warner Bks.

Renegade No. Seven: Death in High Places. Ramsay Thorne. 192p. (Orig.). 1981. pap. 1.95 (ISBN 0-446-90548-8). Warner Bks.

Renegade No. Six: Panama Gunner. Ramsay Thorne. 256p. (Orig.). 1980. pap. 1.95 (ISBN 0-446-90235-7). Warner Bks.

Renegade No. Two: Blood Runner. Ramsay Thorne. (Orig.). 1979. pap. 1.75 (ISBN 0-446-94231-6). Warner Bks.

Renegade Ramrod. Leslie Ernenwein. 1976. pap. 0.95 o.p. (ISBN 0-685-64016-7, LB345, Leisure Bks). Nordon Pubns.

Renegade Riders. Donald McGregor. (Orig.). 1980. pap. 1.75 (ISBN 0-505-51549-0). Tower Bks.

Renegade Sheriff. W. C. Tuttle. (YA) 1972. 4.95 o.p. (ISBN 0-685-26711-3, Avalon). Bouregy.

Renegotiations in International Business Transactions: The Process of Dispute-Resolution Between Multinational Investors & Host Societies. William A. Stoever. LC 79-4727. 1981. 27.95 (ISBN 0-669-03057-0). Lexington Bks.

Renew Your Life Through Yoga. Indra Devi. (Illus.). 256p. 1972. pap. 1.95 o.s.i. (ISBN 0-446-89515-6). Warner Bks.

Renewable Energy Prospects: Proceedings. Conference on Non-Fossil Fuel & Non-Nuclear Fuel Energy Strategies, Honolulu, USS, January 1979. Ed. by W. Bach et al. 340p. 1980. 57.50 (ISBN 0-08-024252-9). Pergamon.

Renewable Energy Resources & Rural Applications in the Developing World. Ed. by Norman L. Brown. (AAAS Selected Symposium Ser: No. 6). (Illus.). 1978. lib. bdg. 20.00x (ISBN 0-89158-433-1). Westview.

Renewable Natural Resources: A Management Handbook for the Eighties. Ed. by Dennis L. Little et al. (Special Studies in Natural Resources & Energy Management). 375p. (Orig.). 1981. lib. bdg. 19.50x (ISBN 0-89158-665-2). Westview.

Renewable Resource Management for Forestry & Agriculture. Ed. by James S. Bethel & Martin A. Massengale. LC 78-25994. (Geo. S. Long Publication Ser.). 136p. 1979. 10.00 (ISBN 0-295-95624-0). U of Wash Pr.

Renewable Resource Utilization for Development. Robert P. Morgan & Larry J. Icerman. (PPS on International Development Ser.). 325p. 1981. 35.00 (ISBN 0-08-026338-0). Pergamon.

Renewable Resources for Industrial Materials. Board on Agriculture and Renewable Resources, National Research Council. LC 76-44604. 1976. pap. 8.25 (ISBN 0-309-02528-1). Natl Acad Pr.

Renewal from Within. Lee H. Bristol, Jr. 1978. 1.00 (ISBN 0-686-28790-8). Forward Movement.

Renewal in Song: No. 2. Carol Perkins. pap. 3.95 (ISBN 0-88270-333-1). Logos.

Renewal of American Catholicism. David J. O'Brien. 320p. 1972. 11.95 (ISBN 0-19-501601-7). Oxford U Pr.

Renewal of Buddhism in China: Chu-Hung & the Late Ming Synthesis. Chun-fang Yu. LC 79-28073. (Buddhist Studies). (Illus.). 1980. 25.00x (ISBN 0-231-04972-2). Columbia U Pr.

Renewal of Civilization. rev. ed. David Hofman. 1969. 2.95 (ISBN 0-87743-009-8, 7-31-31); pap. 1.50 o.s.i. (ISBN 0-87743-057-8, 7-31-32). Baha'i.

Renewed Day by Day. Aiden W. Tozer. LC 80-69301. 380p. pap. 6.95 (ISBN 0-87509-292-6). Chr Pubns.

Renewed Day by Day: Three Hundred & Sixty Five Daily Devotions. A. W. Tozer. 1981. 12.95 (ISBN 0-8010-8861-5). Baker Bk.

Renewed Mind. Larry Cristenson. LC 74-12770. 144p. (Orig.). 1974. pap. 3.50 (ISBN 0-87123-487-4, 210487). Bethany Fell.

Renewing Higher Education from Within: A Guide for Campus Change Teams. Walter W. Sikes et al. LC 74-9113. (Higher Education Ser.). 1974. 12.95x o.p. (ISBN 0-87589-239-6). Jossey-Bass.

Renewing the Earth: Catholic Documents on Peace, Justice & Liberation. Ed. by David J. O'Brien & Thomas A. Shannon. LC 76-52008. 1977. pap. 3.95 (ISBN 0-385-12954-8, Im). Doubleday.

Renewing Urban Teaching. L. F. Claydon. LC 73-77266. (Illus.). 180p. 1974. 23.50 (ISBN 0-521-20268-X); pap. 9.95x (ISBN 0-521-09844-0). Cambridge U Pr.

Renin. Suzanne Oparil et al. Ed. by D. F. Horrobin. (Annual Research Reviews Ser.: Vol. 5). 368p. 1980. 38.00 (ISBN 0-88831-092-7). Eden Med Res.

Renin, Vol. 1. Suzanne Oparil. 1977. 26.40 (ISBN 0-88831-000-5). Eden Med Res.

Renin, Vol. 2. Suzanne Oparil & Richard Katholi. Ed. by D. Horrobin. 1978. 28.80 (ISBN 0-88831-014-5). Eden Med Res.

Renin-Angiotensin System. Ed. by J. Alan Johnson & Ralph R. Anderson. (Advances in Experimental Medicine & Biology Ser.: Vol. 130). 315p. 1980. 37.50 (ISBN 0-306-40469-9, Plenum Pr). Plenum Pub.

Renoir. Anthea Callen. LC 77-10354. (Oresko Art Book). (Illus.). 1978. 15.95 (ISBN 0-8467-0377-7, Pub. by Two Continents); pap. 9.95 (ISBN 0-8467-0378-5). Hippocrene Bks.

Renoir. Walter Pach. (Library of Great Painters Ser). (Illus.). 1950. 35.00 (ISBN 0-8109-0446-2). Abrams.

Renoir. (Masters of Art Ser.). (Illus.). 1979. pap. 3.95 (ISBN 0-8120-2153-3). Barron.

Renoir: The Man, the Painter, & His World. Lawrence Hanson. 1972. 14.95x o.p. (ISBN 0-8464-0789-2). Beekman Pubs.

Renovating the Victorian House: A Guide for Aficionados of Old Houses. Katherine Rusk. (Illus.). 250p. (Orig.). 1981. pap. 8.95 (ISBN 0-89286-187-8). One Hurd One Prods.

Renovation & Re-Use of Waste Waters. Ed. by Frank M. D'Itri. 1978. text ed. 33.21 o.p. (ISBN 0-08-021774-5). Pergamon.

Renovator's Primer. Meryl Bennett & Jeffrey Bennett. LC 77-87470. (Illus.). 1978. pap. 6.95 o.p. (ISBN 0-8069-8618-2, 034700). Sterling.

Rent a Wife. Rachel Lindsay. (Harlequin Presents Ser.). 192p. 1980. pap. 1.50 (ISBN 0-373-10375-1, Pub. by Harlequin). PB.

Rent Control: A Case for. Herbert L. Selesnick. LC 75-312990. 1976. 15.95 (ISBN 0-669-00338-7). Lexington Bks.

Rent Control: A Source Book. Ed. by John I. Gilderbloom. 314p. (Orig.). 1981. pap. 9.95 (ISBN 0-938806-00-9). Foun Natl Prog.

Rent Control: The Perennial Folly. Charles Baird. LC 80-16317. (Cato Public Policy Research Cato Monograph: No. 2). 110p. (Orig.). 1980. pap. 5.00 (ISBN 0-932790-22-4). Cato Inst.

Rent Stabilization & Control Laws in N. Y. Jeffrey H. Gallet et al. (Supplemented annually). 25.00 (ISBN 0-87526-082-9). Gould.

Rents of Council Houses. R. A. Parker. 90p. 1967. pap. text ed. 5.00x (Pub. by Bedford England). Renouf.

Reoperative Gastrointestinal Surgery. 2nd ed. Thomas T. White & R. Cameron Harrison. 1979. text ed. 38.50 (ISBN 0-316-93604-9). Little.

Reorganization of British Local Government. John Dearlove. LC 78-18092. 1979. 39.95 (ISBN 0-521-22341-5); pap. 10.95 (ISBN 0-521-29456-8). Cambridge U Pr.

Reorganization of Secondary Education. Phillip H. James. 145p. 1980. pap. text ed. 19.25x (ISBN 0-85633-214-3, NFER). Humanities.

Reorganization of the Federal Judiciary, 6 vols. in 3. United States Senate Committee on the Judiciary, 75th Congress, 1st Session. LC 73-124924. (American Constitutional & Legal History Ser.). 1970. Repr. of 1937 ed. lib. bdg. 175.00 (ISBN 0-306-71991-6). Da Capo.

Reorganizing State Government: The Executive Branch. James L. Garnett. (Westview Special Studies in Public Policy & Public Systems Management). (Illus.). 320p. 1980. lib. bdg. 25.00x (ISBN 0-89158-835-3). Westview.

Reorientation of African Beliefs: A Prime Necessity. Fred Bowman. 1981. 4.95 (ISBN 0-8062-1566-6). Carlton.

Repair & Remodeling Cost Data Nineteen Eighty. Robert S. Godfrey. 325p. 1980. pap. 32.00 (ISBN 0-911950-28-1). Means.

Repair & Remodeling Cost Data, 1981. 2nd ed. Robert S. Godfrey. 325p. 1981. pap. 32.00 (ISBN 0-911950-34-6). Means.

Repair & Strengthening of Old Steel Truss Bridges. Compiled by American Society of Civil Engineers. 144p. 1979. pap. text ed. 14.00 (ISBN 0-87262-194-4). Am Soc Civil Eng.

Repair of Wooden Boats. John Lewis. 1977. 14.95 (ISBN 0-7153-7378-1). David & Charles.

Repairing Furniture. Editors of Time-Life Books. (Home Repair & Improvement). (Illus.). 128p. 1981. 10.95 (ISBN 0-8094-2438-X). Time-Life.

Repairing Watch Cases: Schwanatus & Fenimore 1909. 1981. pap. 4.00 (ISBN 0-915706-14-8). Am Reprints.

Repairman of Cyclops. John Brunner. 1981. pap. 2.25 (ISBN 0-87997-638-1, UE1638). DAW Bks.

Reparation in World Politics: France & European Economic Diplomacy, 1916-1923. Marc Trachtenberg. LC 79-26898. 1980. 25.00x (ISBN 0-231-04786-X). Columbia U Pr.

Repaso. rev. ed. Ed. by Donald D. Walsh & Harlan Sturm. (Sp). 1971. text ed. 9.95x (ISBN 0-393-09955-5, NortonC). Norton.

Repaso Oral. Francesca Colecchia. 1967. text ed. 9.95x o.p. (ISBN 0-669-31419-6); tapes. 5 reels o.p. 25.00 o.p. (ISBN 0-669-34140-1). Heath.

Repent & Believe. Derek Prince. (Foundation Ser.: Bk. II). 1965-66. pap. 1.75 (ISBN 0-934920-01-X, B-11). Derek Prince.

Repentance. John Colquhoun. pap. 1.95 o.p. (ISBN 0-686-12536-3). Banner of Truth.

Repentance - the Joy-Filled Life. M. Basilea Schlink. pap. 1.95 (ISBN 0-310-32612-5). Zondervan.

Repentance & Twentieth-Century Man. C. John Miller. (Orig.). 1980. pap. 1.95 (ISBN 0-87508-334-X). Chr Lit.

Repertoire De la Cuisine. Louis Saulnier. 239p. 1970. text ed. 14.95x thumb indexed (ISBN 0-685-04746-6). Radio City.

Repertoire De la Cuisine. Louis Saulnier. 1976. text ed. 9.95 (ISBN 0-8120-5108-4); text ed. 14.95 deluxe ed. (ISBN 0-8120-5109-2). Barron.

Repertoire for the Solo Voice: A Fully Annotated Guide to Works for the Solo Voice Published in Modern Editions and Covering Material from the 13th Century to the Present, Vols. 1&2. Noni Espina. LC 76-30441. 1977. 50.00 (ISBN 0-8108-0943-5). Scarecrow.

Repertorium der Griechischen Christlichen Papyri, Pt.1: Biblische Papyri, Altes Testament, Neues Testament, Varia, Apokryphen. Ed. by Kurt Aland. (Patristische Texte und Studien, Vol. 18). 473p. 1976. 93.00x (ISBN 3-11-004674-1). De Gruyter.

Repetitions: Poetry by Judge-Bruce Wright. LC 80-53692. 1980. 8.95 (ISBN 0-89388-207-0); pap. 5.95 (ISBN 0-89388-208-9). Okpaku Communications.

Replacement Cost Accounting. Lawrence Revsine. (Contemporary Topics in Accounting Ser). (Illus.). 224p. (Ref. ed). 1973. pap. 9.95 (ISBN 0-13-773630-4). P-H.

Replacement Parts Guide: 1980. Ed. by Henry Kinney. 1980. pap. write for info. (ISBN 0-934890-02-1). Hoffman Pubns.

Reply of the Orthodox Church to Roman Catholic Overtures on Reunion. Anthimos. 1977. pap. 1.00 (ISBN 0-913026-15-8). St Nectarios.

Report About & from America: Given from First-Hand Observation in the Years 1848 &1849. (Mississippi Valley Collection Bulletin, No. 3). 84p. 1970. pap. 5.95 (ISBN 0-87870-080-3). Memphis St Univ.

Report After Action: The Story of the 103rd Infantry Division. Ralph Mueller & Jerry Turk. (Divisional Ser.: No. 1). (Illus.). 1978. pap. 15.00 o.p. (ISBN 0-89839-010-9). Battery Pr.

Report from a Chinese Village. Jan Myrdal. (Illus.). 1981. pap. 6.95 (ISBN 0-394-74802-6). Pantheon.

Report from Engine Company Eighty Two. Dennis E. Smith. LC 71-154259. 1972. 5.95 o.p. (ISBN 0-8415-0138-6). Dutton.

Report from Red China. Harrison Forman. LC 74-28417. (China in the 20th Century Ser). (Illus.). iv, 250p. 1975. Repr. of 1945 ed. lib. bdg. 22.50 (ISBN 0-306-70676-8). Da Capo.

Report from the Secret Committee on Joint Stock Banks, 20 August 1836. Great Britain, Parliament, House of Commons, Secret Committee on Joint Stock Banks. LC 70-363560. 1981. Repr. of 1836 ed. lib. bdg. 25.00x (ISBN 0-678-05228-X). Kelley.

Report from the Select Committee on Public Libraries, 23 July 1849. Great Britain, Parliament, House of Commons, Select Committee on Public Libraries. LC 74-366370. 1981. Repr. of 1849 ed. lib. bdg. 27.50x (ISBN 0-678-05231-X). Kelley.

Report from the Select Committee on the Health of Towns. Great Britain, Parliament, House of Commons, Select Committee on the Health of Towns. LC 68-111978. 1981. Repr. of 1840 ed. lib. bdg. 25.00x (ISBN 0-678-05230-1). Kelley.

Report from the Select Committee to Whom the Several Petitions Complaining of the Distressed State of the Agriculture in the United Kingdom Were Referred, 18 June 1821. Great Britain, Parliament, House of Commons. LC 68-112457. 1981. Repr. of 1821 ed. lib. bdg. 35.00x (ISBN 0-678-05227-1). Kelley.

Report of a Committee of Citizens of Boston & Vicinity, Opposed to a Further Increase of Duties on Importations. Henry Lee. Bd. with An Examination of the Report, & Review of the Report. (Neglected American Economists Ser.). 1974. lib. bdg. 50.00 (ISBN 0-8240-1004-3). Garland Pub.

Report of a Rice Cold Tolerance Workshop. 139p. 1979. pap. 16.00 (R001, IRRI). Unipub.

Report of Captaine Ward & Danseker, Pirates. Andrew Barker. LC 68-54615. (English Experience Ser.: No. 21). 56p. 1968. Repr. of 1609 ed. 8.00 (ISBN 90-221-0021-9). Walter J Johnson.

Report of the ACMRR Working Party on the Scientific Basis of Determining Management Measures. (FAO Fisheries Report Ser.: No. 236). 149p. 1980. pap. 10.50 (ISBN 92-5-100938-4, F2051, FAO). Unipub.

Report of the Ad Hoc Advisory Committee Meeting on the Programme on the Use & Management of Natural Resources. 14p. 1979. pap. 5.00 (ISBN 0-686-61492-5, TUNU 002, UNU). Unipub.

Report of the Ad Hoc Consultation of Aquaculture Research. (FAO Fisheries Report Ser.: No. 238). 26p. 1980. pap. 6.00 (ISBN 92-5-100949-X, F2038, FAO). Unipub.

Report of the Alcohol Fuels Policy Review. U. S. Department of Energy. 119p. 1979. pap. 10.95 (ISBN 0-89934-024-5). Solar Energy Info.

Report of the Case of Edward Prigg Against the Commonwealth of Pennsylvania. Edward Prigg. LC 70-111587. Repr. of 1842 ed. 11.75x (ISBN 0-8371-4613-5). Negro U Pr.

Report of the Commission on Government Security. United States, Commission on Government Security. LC 79-152788. (Civil Liberties in American History Ser). 1971. Repr. of 1957 ed. lib. bdg. 75.00 (ISBN 0-306-70146-4). Da Capo.

Report of the Conference of FAO: 20th Session, 1979. 234p. 1980. pap. 20.25 (ISBN 92-5-100892-2, F-1904, FAO). Unipub.

Report of the Council of FAO: 76th Session. 91p. 1980. pap. 7.50 (ISBN 92-5-100871-X, F-1910, FAO). Unipub.

Report of the Council of FAO: 77th Session. 35p. 1980. pap. 7.50 (ISBN 92-5-100889-2, F1909, FAO). Unipub.

Report of the Debates: Proceedings. Peace Convention - Washington D.C. - Feb 1861. Ed. by L. E. Chittenden. (Law Politics & History Ser). 1971. Repr. of 1864 ed. lib. bdg. 59.50 (ISBN 0-306-70190-1). Da Capo.

Report of the Decision of the Supreme Court of the United States & the Opinions of Judges Thereof, in the Case of Dred Scott vs John F. A. Sanford. facsimile ed. LC 69-11323. (Law, Politics & History Ser.). 240p. 1970. Repr. of 1857 ed. lib. bdg. 25.00 (ISBN 0-306-71183-4). Da Capo.

Report of the EIFAC, IUNS & ICES Working Group on the Standardization of Methodology in Fish Nutrition Research. (EIFAC Technical Paper Ser.: No. 36). 24p. 1980. pap. 6.75 (ISBN 92-5-100918-X, F2048, FAO). Unipub.

Report of the EIFAC Workshop on Mass Rearing of Fry & Fingerlings of Freshwater Fishes. (EIFAC Technical Paper: No. 35). 23p. 1980. pap. 6.00 (ISBN 92-5-100829-9, F 1874, FAO). Unipub.

Report of the Eighth Session of FAO Advisory Committee on Forestry Education. 47p. 1980. pap. 7.50 (ISBN 92-5-100480-3, F1968, FAO). Unipub.

Report of the Eleventh Session of the Committee on Improvement on National Statistics (COINS) (IASI Ser). (Span. & Eng.). 1975. 3.00 ea. o.p. OAS.

Report of the FAO Expert Consultation on Fish Technology in Africa. (FAO Fisheries Report Ser.: No. 237). 18p. 1981. pap. 6.00 (ISBN 92-5-100981-3, F2101, FAO). Unipub.

Report of the Fifteenth FAO Regional Conference for Asia & the Pacific. 97p. 1981. pap. 6.00 (ISBN 92-5-100963-5, F2084, FAO). Unipub.

Report of the Fifteenth Session of the Intergovernmental Group on Hard Fibres to the Committee on Commodity Problems. 1980. pap. 6.00 (ISBN 92-5-100905-8, F1951, FAO). Unipub.

Report of the Fifteenth Session of the Intergovernmental Group on Jute Kenaf & Allied Fibres to the CCP. 18p. 1980. pap. 7.50 (ISBN 92-5-100863-9, F1908, FAO). Unipub.

Report of the First Session of the Joint Scientific Committee. 140p. 1980. pap. 25.00 (W474, WMO). Unipub.

Report of the First Session of the Working Party on Acoustic Methods for Fish Detection & Abundance Estimation of the General Fisheries Council for the Mediterranean. General Fisheries Council for the Mediterranean. (FAO Fisheries Report: No. 231). 27p. 1980. pap. 6.00 (ISBN 92-5-100928-7, F2039, FAO). Unipub.

Report of the Government Consultation on the International Plant Protection Convention. 50p. 1977. pap. 6.00 (ISBN 92-5-100355-6, F1983, FAO). Unipub.

Report of the Indo-Pacific Fishery Commision Working Party on Aquaculture & Environment. 16p. 1981. pap. 6.00 (ISBN 92-5-100962-7, F2074, FAO). Unipub.

Report of the International Narcotics Board for 1979. 39p. 1980. pap. 5.00 (ISBN 0-686-68968-2, UN80/XI/2, UN). Unipub.

Report of the Joint Committee on the Investigation of the Pearl Harbor Attack. United States, 79th Congress, 2nd Session. LC 74-166954. (FDR & the Era of the New Deal Ser.). (Illus.). 1972. Repr. of 1946 ed. lib. bdg. 49.50 (ISBN 0-306-70331-9). Da Capo.

Report of the Kingdome of Congo, Gathered by P. Pigafetta. Duarte Lopes. Tr. by A. Hartwell. LC 75-25675. (English Experience Ser.: No. 260). 1970. Repr. of 1597 ed. 35.00 (ISBN 90-221-0260-2). Walter J Johnson.

Report of the Mayor's Committee on Cultural Policy, October 15, 1974. LC 74-20048. 100p. 1974. pap. 2.00x (ISBN 0-89062-014-8, Pub. by Mayor's Comm Cultural). Pub Ctr Cult Res.

Report of the Seventh Session of the Intergovernmental Group on Bananas. 17p. 1981. pap. 6.00 (ISBN 92-5-100950-3, F2091, FAO). Unipub.

Report of the Sixth FAO-SIDA Training Course on Seed Technology. 26p. 1976. pap. 6.00 (F1985, FAO). Unipub.

Report of the Sixth Joint Meeting of the Indian Ocean Fishery Commission, Committee on Management of Indian Ocean Tuna. Indian Ocean Fishery Commission. 18p. 1980. pap. 6.00 (ISBN 92-5-100939-2, F2045, FAO). Unipub.

Report of the Sixth Session of the Fishery Committee for the Eastern Central Atlantic (CECAF) (FAO Fisheries Report: No. 229). 70p. 1980. pap. 6.00 (ISBN 92-5-100900-7, F1952, FAO). Unipub.

Report of the Sixth Session of the Indian Ocean Fishery Commission. (FAO Fisheries Report: No. 234). 35p. 1981. pap. 6.00 (ISBN 92-5-100930-9, F2088, FAO). Unipub.

Report of the Special Committee on the Federal Loyalty Security Program. The Association of the Bar of the City of New York. LC 74-6494. (Civil Liberties in American History Ser.). 301p. 1974. Repr. of 1956 ed. lib. bdg. 32.50 (ISBN 0-306-70596-6). Da Capo.

Report of the Symposium on Prevention of Marine Pollution from Ships: Acapulco-1976. 90p. 1976. 12.50 (IMCO). Unipub.

Report of the Technical Consultation on the Assessment & Management of the Black Sea Turbot (GFCM) Working Party on Resource Evaluation & Fishery Statistics. 23p. 1980. pap. 7.50 (ISBN 92-5-100879-5, F1964, FAO). Unipub.

Report of the Thirs Session of the Committee on Resource Managment of the General Fisheries Council for the Mediterranean. (FAO Fisheries Report: No. 240). 20p. 1981. pap. 6.00 (ISBN 92-5-100966-X, F2087, FAO). Unipub.

Report of the Thirteenth Session Codex Alimentarius Commission. 103p. 1981. pap. 6.00 (ISBN 92-5-100912-0, F2071, FAO). Unipub.

Report of the Trial of Castner Hanway for Treason. Castner Hanway. LC 70-107508. Repr. of 1852 ed. 15.75x (ISBN 0-8371-3779-9). Negro U Pr.

Report of the Trial of James H. Peck. Arthur Joseph Stansbury. LC 70-38789. (Law, Politics & History Ser). 592p. 1972. Repr. of 1833 ed. lib. bdg. 59.50 (ISBN 0-306-70443-9). Da Capo.

Report of the Twentieth Session of the Intergovernmental Group on Grains to the Committee on Commodity Problems. 30p. 1980. pap. 6.00 (ISBN 92-5-100919-8, F1953, FAO). Unipub.

Report of the Twenty-Third Session of the Intergovernmental Group on Rice to the Committee on Commodity Problems. Intergovernmental Group on Rice. 29p. 1980. pap. 6.00 (ISBN 92-5-100926-0, F2043, FAO). Unipub.

Report of the United Nations University Expert Group on Human & Social Development. 36p. 1980. pap. 5.00 (ISBN 92-808-0145-7, TUNU082, UNU). Unipub.

Report on a Collection of Mammals from Eastern New Guinea, Including Species Keys for Fourteen Genera. W. Z. Lidicker, Jr. & A. C. Ziegler. (U. C. Publ. in Zoology: Vol. 87). 1968. pap. 6.50x (ISBN 0-520-09344-5). U of Cal Pr.

Report on a Negotiation: Helsinki-Geneva-Helsinki Nineteen Seventy-Two to Nineteen Seventy-Five. Ed. by Luigi V. Ferraris. Tr. by Marie-Claire Barber from Italian. (Collections De Relations Internationales Ser.). 439p. 1980. 46.00x (ISBN 9-0286-0779-X). Sijthoff & Noordhoff.

Report on a Plan for San Francisco: A Facsimile Reprint of the 1906 Plan. facsimile ed. Daniel H. Burnham & Edward H. Bennett. LC 77-182132. (Illus.). 217p. 1972. Repr. of 1905 ed. 25.00x o.p. (ISBN 0-686-02407-9). Urban Bks.

Report on a Tour of Exploration of the Antiquities of Kapilavastu, Tarai of Nepal During February & March 1899. Purna C. Mukherji. (Illus.). 1969. 13.00x o.p. (ISBN 0-8426-0004-3). Verry.

Report on a Visit to Sikhim & the Thibetan Border. E. Ware Edgar. (Illus.). 1970. Repr. of 1874 ed. 8.50x o.p. (ISBN 0-685-19340-3). Paragon.

Report on American Manuscripts in the Royal Institution of Great Britain, 4 vols. Great Britain Historical Manuscripts Commission. Ed. by George Billias. LC 72-8703. (American Revolutionary Ser.). 1979. Repr. of 1909 ed. Set. lib. bdg. 94.00x (ISBN 0-8398-0801-1). Irvington.

Report on Chinese-English Mathematical Dictionaries. S. H. Gould. 1969. 1.00 o.p. (ISBN 0-686-67535-5, CED). Am Math.

Report on Economic Conditions of the South. U. S. Emergency Council. LC 70-172009. 1972. Repr. lib. bdg. 12.50 (ISBN 0-306-70438-2). Da Capo.

Report on Highway & Bridge Surveys. Compiled by American Society of Civil Engineers. (Manual & Report on Engineering Practice Ser.: No. 44). 160p. 1962. pap. text ed. 7.50 (ISBN 0-87262-219-3). Am Soc Civil Eng.

Report on Japan to the Secret Committee of the English East India Company. Sir Stanford Raffles. Ed. by M. Paske-Smith. (Records of Asian History). (Illus.). 1971. text ed. 13.00x (ISBN 0-7007-0003-X). Humanities.

Report on Pipeline Location. Compiled by American Society of Civil Engineers. (Manual & Report on Engineering Practice Ser.: No. 46). 88p. 1965. pap. text ed. 8.50 (ISBN 0-87262-040-9). Am Soc Civil Eng.

Report on Planet Three & Other Speculations. Arthur C. Clarke. 1973. pap. 1.50 (ISBN 0-451-07864-0, W7864, Sig). NAL.

Report on Probability. Brian Aldiss. 144p. 1980. pap. 1.95 (ISBN 0-380-52498-8, 52498). Avon.

Report on Professional Salaries in New York State Museums. M. J. Gladstone. 48p. 1972. pap. 3.00x (ISBN 0-89062-020-2, Pub. by NYS Assn Mus). Pub Ctr Cult Res.

Report on Small Craft Harbors. Compiled by American Society of Civil Engineers. (Manual & Report on Engineering Practice Ser.: No. 50). 148p. 1969. pap. 10.00 (ISBN 0-87262-224-X). Am Soc Civil Eng.

Report on Social Security for Canada. Leonard Marsh. LC 74-82286. (Social History of Canada Ser.). 1975. 17.50x o.p. (ISBN 0-8020-2168-9); pap. 6.50 o.p. (ISBN 0-8020-6250-4). U of Toronto Pr.

Report on Special Committee on Audit Committee. 1978. pap. 1.50. Am Inst CPA.

Report on the Agro-Ecological Zones Project: Methodology & Results for Africa. (World Soil Resources Report: No. 48). 185p. 1980. pap. 11.00 (ISBN 92-5-100589-3, F 1873, FAO). Unipub.

Report on the Agro-Ecological Zones Project: Vol. 2 Results for Southwest Asia. (World Soil Resources Report: No. 48-2). 34p. 1980. pap. 6.00 (ISBN 92-5-100694-6, F 1872, FAO). Unipub.

Report on the Fourteenth Session of the Intergovernmental Group on Oilseeds, Oils & Fats. Intergovernmental Group on Oilseeds, Oils & Fats. 14p. 1980. pap. 6.00 (ISBN 92-5-100937-6, F2044, FAO): Unipub.

Report on the Fourth Session of the Cooperative Programme of Research on Aquaculture of the General Fisheries Council for the Mediterranean. (FAO Fisheries Report: No. 232). 32p. 1981. pap. 6.00 (ISBN 92-5-100927-9, F2068, FAO). Unipub.

Report on the Iban. 2nd ed. Derek Freeman. (Monographs on Sooial Anthropology Ser: No. 41). (Illus.). 1970. text ed. 26.25x (ISBN 0-391-00113-2, Athlone Pr). Humanities.

Report on the International Conference on New Musical Notation Organized by the Index of New Musical Notation (New York) & the Seminar of Musicology (Ghent) Ed. by Herman Sabbe et al. 120p. 1975. pap. text ed. 25.50 (ISBN 90-265-0221-4, Pub. by Swets Pub Serv Holland). Swets North Am.

Report on the Programming Language PLZ-SYS. T. Snoock et al. (Illus.). 1979. pap. 3.50 (ISBN 0-387-90374-7). Springer-Verlag.

Report on the Second FAO-UNFPA Expert Consultation on Land Resources for Populations of the Future. 369p. 1981. pap. 20.25 (ISBN 92-5-100925-2, F2073, FAO). Unipub.

Report on the Situation of Human Rights in Haiti. OAS General Secretariat Inter-American Commission of Human Rights. (Human Rights Ser.). 81p. 1980. lib. bdg. 5.00 (ISBN 0-8270-1094-X). OAS.

Report on the Situation of Human Rights in Argentina. OAS General Secretariat Inter-American Commission of Human Rights. (Human Rights Ser.). 266p. (Orig.). 1980. 12.00 (ISBN 0-8270-1099-0). OAS.

Report on the Situation of Human Rights in Paraguay-Informe Sobre la Situacion De los Derechos Humanos En Paraguay. (Eng. & Span.). 1978. pap. 3.00 Eng. ed. (ISBN 0-8270-2595-5); pap. 3.00 Span. ed. (ISBN 0-8270-2565-3). OAS.

Report on the Situation of Human Rights in Uruguay-Informe Sobre la Situacion De los Derechos Humanos En Uruguay. 1978. Eng. & Span eds. 3.00 ea. (ISBN 0-685-67897-0); Eng. Ed. pap. 3.00 Span. ed. (ISBN 0-8270-2570-X). Span Ed (ISBN 0-8270-2570-X). OAS.

Report on the Steel Strike of 1919. Interchurch World Movement. LC 73-139200. (Civil Liberties in American History Ser). (Illus.). 1971. Repr. of 1920 ed. lib. bdg. 29.50 (ISBN 0-306-70081-6). Da Capo.

Report on the Theory of Numbers. Henry J. Smith. LC 64-8080. 1966. 14.95 (ISBN 0-8284-0186-1). Chelsea Pub.

Report on Trade Conditions in China. Harry Burrill & Raymond F. Crist. LC 78-74353. (Modern Chinese Economy Ser.). 130p. 1980. lib. bdg. 16.50 (ISBN 0-8240-4265-4). Garland Pub.

Report on United States Catholic Schools, 1972-73. 98p. 1973. 2.00. Natl Cath Educ.

Report on United States Catholic Schools 1971-72. 67p. 1972. 2.00. Natl Cath Educ.

Report on United States Catholic Schools, 1970-71. 54p. 1971. 2.00. Natl Cath Educ.

Report: Presented to Parliament by Command of Her Majesty, Sept, 1953. Great Britain, Royal Commission on Capital Punishment, 1949-1953. LC 79-25707. 505p. 1980. Repr. of 1953 ed. lib. bdg. 35.00x (ISBN 0-313-22121-9, GBCP). Greenwood.

Report Upon the Colorado River of the West. Joseph C. Ives. LC 69-18459. (American Scene Ser). (Illus.). 1969. Repr. of 1861 ed. lib. bdg. 45.00 (ISBN 0-685-19443-4). Da Capo.

Report Writing. 4th ed. Harold F. Graves & L. Hoffman. 1965. text ed. 12.95 (ISBN 0-13-773671-1). P-H.

Report Writing for Business. 5th ed. Raymond V. Lesikar. 1977. text ed. 17.25x (ISBN 0-256-01900-2). Irwin.

Report Writing for Management. William J. Gallagher. (Orig.). 1969. pap. 8.95 (ISBN 0-201-02256-7). A-W.

Report Writing in Special Education. Norman Tallent. (Illus.). 1980. text ed. 17.95 (ISBN 0-13-773606-1). P-H.

Reporte of a Discourse Concerning Supreme Power in Affaires of Religion. John Hayward. LC 79-84116. (English Experience Ser.: No. 935). 64p. 1979. Repr. of 1606 ed. lib. bdg. 8.00 (ISBN 90-221-0935-6). Walter J Johnson.

Reporters & Officials: The Organization & Politics of New Making. Leon V. Sigal. LC 72-7014. (Illus.). 256p. 1973. 17.95 (ISBN 0-669-85035-7). Lexington Bks.

Reporting. Lillian Ross. 442p. 1981. 12.94 (ISBN 0-396-07948-2); pap. 8.95 (ISBN 0-396-07949-0). Dodd.

Reporting Agriculture Through Newspapers, Magazines, Radio, Television. 2nd ed. William Ward. 402p. 1959. 15.00 (ISBN 0-8014-0441-X). Cornell U Pr.

Reporting on Business & the Economy. Ed. by Louis Kohlmeier et al. 336p. 1981. text ed. 14.95 (ISBN 0-13-773879-X). P-H.

Reporting on Comparative Financial Statements. (Statements on Standards for Accounting & Review Services Ser.: No. 2). 1979. pap. 1.50. Am Inst CPA.

Reporting System for Hospital Social Work. Society for Hospital Social Work Directors of the American Hospital Association. LC 78-5696. 1978. pap. 8.75 (ISBN 0-87258-237-X, 1562). Am Hospital.

Reporting Technical Information. 3rd ed. Kenneth W. Houp & Thomas E. Pearsall. 1977. pap. text ed. 9.95 (ISBN 0-02-475430-7). Macmillan.

Reportorie of Records at Westminster. A. Agard. LC 72-225. (English Experience Ser.: No. 291). 1971. Repr. of 1631 ed. 22.00 (ISBN 90-221-0291-2). Walter J Johnson.

Reports, 19 vols. U. S. Industrial Commission, Washington, D. C., 1900-1902. LC 73-103309. (Illus.). 1900-02. Repr. lib. bdg. 500.00x (ISBN 0-8371-9920-4, RIC). Greenwood.

REPORTS--Programme Commissions Administrative Commission Legal Committee, Vol. 2. 242p. pap. 11.50 (ISBN 92-3-101756-X, U 966, UNESCO). Unipub.

Reports by Management: Conclusions & Recommendations of the AICPA Special Advisory Committee. 1979. pap. 1.50. Am Inst CPA.

Reports of Cases Decided by Chief Justice Chase in the Circuit Court of the United States for the Fourth Circuit: 1865-1869. facsimile ed. Bradley T. Johnson. LC 75-75292. (American Constitutional & Legal History Ser.). 1972. Repr. of 1876 ed. lib. bdg. 59.50 (ISBN 0-306-71291-1). Da Capo.

Reports of Cases in the Vice Admiralty of the Province of New York & in the Courts of Admiralty of the State of New York, 1715-1788. Charles M. Hough. (Yale Historical Pubs., Manuscripts & Edited Texts Ser.: No. VIII). 1925. 65.00x (ISBN 0-685-89777-X). Elliots Bks.

Reports of the Ayacucho Archaeological-Botanical Project. Incl. First Annual Report of the Ayacucho Project. R. MacNeish. 1969. 3.00; Second Annual Repoert of the Ayacucho Project. R. MacNeish et al. 1970. 3.00. 3.00 (ISBN 0-686-22138-9). Peabody Found.

Reports of the Cambridge Anthropological Expedition to Torres Straits, 6 vols. Ed. by A. C. Haddon. Incl. General Ethnography. Repr. of 1935 ed. 33.00 (ISBN 0-685-27602-3); Physiology & Psychology. Repr. of 1901 ed. 19.00 (ISBN 0-685-27603-1); Linguistics. S. H. Ray. Repr. of 1907 ed. 29.00 (ISBN 0-685-27604-X); Arts & Crafts. Repr. of 1912 ed. Vols. 4-6. 33.00 ea.; Sociology, Magic & Religion of the Western Islanders. Repr. of 1904 ed. 33.00 (ISBN 0-685-27606-6); Sociology, Magic & Religion of the Eastern Islanders. Repr. of 1908 ed. 26.00 (ISBN 0-685-27607-4). (Landmarks in Anthropology Ser). 2242p. Set. 196.00 (ISBN 0-686-57612-8). Johnson Repr.

Reports of the FAO-Norway Training Course on Logging Operations. 110p. 1980. pap. 6.50 (ISBN 0-686-68194-0, F1937, FAO). Unipub.

Reports of the Proceedings & Debates. New York Constitutional Convention, 1821. LC 72-133168. (Law, Politics & History Ser.). 1970. Repr. of 1821 ed. lib. bdg. 65.00 (ISBN 0-306-70069-7). Da Capo.

Reports of the Trials of Colonel Aaron Burr, 2 Vols. Aaron Burr. LC 69-11321. (Law, Politics & History Ser). 1969. Repr. of 1808 ed. 69.50 (ISBN 0-306-71182-6). Da Capo.

Reports on Selected Topics in Telecommunications. Committee On Telecommunications. (Orig.). 1969. pap. 5.75 (ISBN 0-309-01751-3). Natl Acad Pr.

Reports on Taxation One. Nicholas Kaldor. LC 78-31926. (Collected Economic Essays Ser.: Vol. 7). 1980. text ed. 39.50x (ISBN 0-8419-0296-8). Holmes & Meier.

Reports on Taxation Two. Nicholas Kaldor. LC 78-31926. (Collected Economics Essays Ser.: Vol. 8). 1980. text ed. 39.50x (ISBN 0-8419-0297-6). Holmes & Meier.

Representation & Administrative Tribunals. Anne Frost & Coral Howard. (Direct Editions Ser). (Orig.). 1977. pap. 10.00 (ISBN 0-7100-8701-2). Routledge & Kegan.

Representation & Architecture. Ed. by Omar Akin. 300p. 1981. pap. 19.50 o.p. (ISBN 0-8408-0506-3). Carrollton Pr.

Representation & Presidential Primaries: The Democratic Party in the Post-Reform Era. James I. Langle. LC 80-1791. (Contributions in Political Science Ser.: No. 57). (Illus.). 192p. 1981. lib. bdg. 25.00 (ISBN 0-313-22482-X, LEP/). Greenwood.

Representation & the Imagination: Beckett, Kafka, Nabokov, & Schoenberg. Daniel Albright. LC 80-26975. (Chicago Originals Ser.). 256p. 1981. lib. bdg. 20.00x (ISBN 0-226-01252-2). U of Chicago Pr.

Representation, Comprehension & Communication of Sets: The Role of Number. 32p. 1980. pap. 5.00 (ISBN 92-808-0133-3, TUNU-055, UNU). Unipub.

Representation in the Juvenile Court. Richard Anderson. (Direct Editions Ser.). (Orig.). 1978. pap. 10.00 (ISBN 0-7100-8578-8). Routledge & Kegan.

Representation of Meaning in Memory. Walter Kintsch. LC 74-17331. (Experimental Psychology Ser). 275p. 1974. 14.95 o.p. (ISBN 0-470-48074-2). Halsted Pr.

Representation of Witnesses Before Federal Grand Juries. National Lawyers Guild. LC 76-20443. 1976. looseleaf with 1979 rev. pages 55.00 (ISBN 0-87632-107-4). Boardman.

Representation Problem for Frechet Surfaces. J. W. Youngs. LC 52-42839. (Memoirs: No. 8). 1980. pap. 9.20 (ISBN 0-8218-1208-4, MEMO-8). Am Math.

Representation Theory I. Ed. by V. Dlab & P. Gabriel. (Lecture Notes in Mathematics Ser.: Vol. 831). 373p. 1981. pap. 22.00 (ISBN 0-387-10263-9). Springer-Verlag.

Representation Theory II. Ed. by V. Dlab & P. Gabriel. (Lecture Notes in Mathematics: Vol. 832). 673p. 1981. pap. 40.20 (ISBN 0-387-10264-7). Springer-Verlag.

Representation Theory of Finite Groups & Associative Algebras. Charles W. Curtis & Irving Reiner. LC 62-16994. (Pure & Applied Mathematics Ser). 1962. 48.50 (ISBN 0-470-18975-4, Pub. by Wiley-Interscience). Wiley.

Representation Theory of Finite Groups & Orders. Irving Reiner & Charles W. Curtis. (Pure & Applied Mathematics: Texts, Monographs & Tracts). 900p. 1981. 60.00 (ISBN 0-471-18994-4, Pub. by Wiley-Interscience). Wiley.

Representation Theory of Lie Groups. M. F. Atiyah et al. LC 78-73820. (London Mathematical Society Lecture Note: No. 34). 1980. pap. 29.50x (ISBN 0-521-22636-8). Cambridge U Pr.

Representations of Finite Chevalley Groups. B. Srinivasan. (Lecture Notes in Mathematics: Vol. 764). 177p. 1980. pap. text ed. 11.80 (ISBN 0-387-09716-3). Springer-Verlag.

Representations: Philosophical Essays on the Foundations of Cognitive Science. Jerry A. Fodor. (Illus.). 368p. 1980. text ed. cancelled (ISBN 0-89706-011-3). Bradford Bks.

Representations: Philosophical Essays on the Foundations of Cognitive Science. Jerry A. Fodor. LC 81-24313. (Illus.). 384p. 1981. text ed. 20.00 (ISBN 0-89706-011-3). Bradford Bks.

Representative American Speeches. Incl. 1966-1967. Ed. by Lester Thonssen. 197p. 1969. o.p. (ISBN 0-8242-0098-5); 1968-1969. 200p. 1969 (ISBN 0-8242-0109-4); 1969-1970. 1970 (ISBN 0-8242-0412-3); 1970-1971. Ed. by Waldo W. Braden. 200p. 1971 (ISBN 0-8242-0449-2); 1971-1972. 200p. 1972 (ISBN 0-8242-0467-0); 1972-1973. 1973 (ISBN 0-8242-0507-3); 1973-1974. 1974 (ISBN 0-8242-0524-3); 1974-1975. 1975 (ISBN 0-8242-0572-3); 1975-1976. 1976 (ISBN 0-8242-0598-7); 1976-1977. 1977 (ISBN 0-8242-0606-1); 1977-78. 1978 (ISBN 0-8242-0625-8); 1978-1979. 1979 (ISBN 0-8242-0634-7). (Reference Shelf Ser). 6.25 ea. Wilson.

Representative Americans: The Colonists, Vol. I. Norman K. Risjord. (Representative Americans Ser.). 272p. 1980. pap. text ed. 6.95 (ISBN 0-669-02831-2). Heath.

Representative Bureaucracy. Samuel Krislov. LC 73-21814. (Foundations of Public Administration Ser.). (Illus.). 160p. 1974. pap. text ed. 7.95 (ISBN 0-13-773747-5). P-H.

Representative French Poetry. rev. ed. Ed. by Victor E. Graham. LC 67-55719. 1965. 3.50x o.p. (ISBN 0-8020-1338-4). U of Toronto Pr.

Representative Government in Early Modern France. J. Russell Major. LC 79-14711. (Illus.). 800p. 1980. text ed. 45.00x (ISBN 0-300-02300-6). Yale U Pr.

Representative Man: Ralph Waldo Emerson in His Time. Joel Porte. (Illus.). 1979. 17.50x (ISBN 0-19-502436-2). Oxford U Pr.

Representative of the People? D. Hirst. LC 75-9283. 320p. 1975. 35.50 (ISBN 0-521-20810-6). Cambridge U Pr.

Representative Opinions of Mr. Justice Holmes. Oliver W. Holmes, Jr. Compiled by Alfred Lief. LC 76-156194. 319p. 1972. Repr. of 1931 ed. lib. bdg. 22.50x (ISBN 0-8371-6143-6, HORO). Greenwood.

Representative Works. Jackson Mac Low. Ed. by Jerome Rothenberg. (New Wilderness Poetics Ser.). 1981. 16.00 (ISBN 0-915520-35-4); special limited ed. 25.00 (ISBN 0-915520-36-2); pap. 7.95 (ISBN 0-915520-34-6). Ross-Erikson.

Representative Works of Contemporary American Artists. Alfred Trumble. Ed. by H. Barbara Weinberg. LC 75-28879. (Art Experience in Late 19th Century America Ser.: Vol. 13). (Illus.). 1976. Repr. of 1887 ed. lib. bdg. 72.50 (ISBN 0-8240-2237-8). Garland Pub.

Representing Professional Athletes & Teams 1980. Martin E. Blackman & Phillip R. Hochberg. LC 80-81911. (Real Estate Law & Practice Course Handbook Ser.). 699p. 1980. pap. text ed. 25.00 (ISBN 0-686-68830-9, G4-3678). PLI.

Representing Publicly Traded Corporations, 1980, 2 vols. Ed. by Klaus Eppler & Thomas Gilroy. LC 80-83000. (Nineteen-Eighty to Nineteen Eighty-One Corporate Law & Practice Course Handbook Ser.). 1925p. 1980. pap. text ed. 40.00 (ISBN 0-686-69171-7, B6-6555). PLI.

Representing Publicly Traded Corporations 1980, 2 vols. (Corporate Law & Practice Course Handbook Series 1980-81: Vols. 349 & 350). 1980. pap. 40.00 set (ISBN 0-685-90313-3, B6-6563). PLI.

Representing Super Doll. Richard Peck. 192p. (gr. 7 up). 1974. 6.95 o.p. (ISBN 0-670-59492-X). Viking Pr.

Representing the Consumer Interest: Mayors, Political Parties, & Interest Groups in Bureaucratic Politics. Ardith Maney. LC 78-66417. 1978. pap. text ed. 12.50 (ISBN 0-8191-0427-2). U Pr of Amer.

Representing the Professional Athlete, Nineteen Seventy-Eight. Martin E. Blackman. LC 78-58673. (Patents, Copyrights, Trademarks, & Literary Property Course Handbook Ser.: 1978-1979). 1978. pap. text ed. 20.00 o.p. (ISBN 0-686-59560-2, G4-3641). PLI.

Repression & Repressive Violence. Mario Hoefnagels. (Publications of the Ppolemological Centre of the Free University of Brussels: Vol. 7). 200p. 1977. pap. text ed. 20.50 (ISBN 90-265-0256-7, Pub. by Swets Pub Serv Holland). Swets North Am.

Repression of Heresy in Medieval Germany. Richard Kieckhefer. LC 78-65112. (Middle Ages Ser.). 1979. 14.00x (ISBN 0-8122-7758-9). U of Pa Pr.

Reprint of Status of the Safety Professional. cancelled (ISBN 0-686-21676-8). ASSE.

Reprints of Selected Articles on the Analysis of Pesticides by Chromatographic Methods. Ed. by Malcom C. Bowman. 1977. 25.00 (ISBN 0-912474-08-4). PolyScience.

Reprise. John G. Boucher & Andre O. Hurtgen. (Orig.). (gr. 10-12). 1975. text ed. 15.12 (ISBN 0-205-04171-X, 3641716); tchrs'. guide 5.12 (ISBN 0-205-04172-8, 3641724); wkbk. 5.60 (ISBN 0-205-04173-6, 3641732); cassettes 296.00 (ISBN 0-205-04174-4, 3641740); dup. masters 38.00 (ISBN 0-205-05404-8, 3654044). Allyn.

Reprocessing & Disposal of Waste Petroeum Oils. L. Y. Hess. LC 79-20213. (Pollution Technology Review No. 64; Chemical Technology Review: No. 140). (Illus.). 1980. 42.00 (ISBN 0-8155-0775-5). Noyes.

Reproduced by Permission of the Author. Sammy Tippit. 144p. 1979. pap. 2.50 (ISBN 0-88207-579-9). Victor Bks.

Reproducible Skills & Concept Ideas: Reading Activities for Child Involvement. new ed. Evelyn B. Spache. 1978. text ed. 18.95 (ISBN 0-205-06557-0). Allyn.

Reproducing Furniture in Miniature. Ann K. Pipe. LC 75-32981. (Illus.). 224p. 1976. 15.00 o.p. (ISBN 0-8092-8294-1); pap. 5.95 o.p. (ISBN 0-8092-8072-8). Contemp Bks.

Reproducing Period Furniture & Accessories in Miniature. Virginia Merrill & Susan M. Richardson. Ed. by Brant Aymar. 1981. 25.00 (ISBN 0-517-53816-4). Crown.

Reproduction. Jack Cohen. 1977. 14.95 (ISBN 0-408-70798-4). Butterworths.

Reproduction. Stanley L. Weinberg & Herbert J. Stoltze. (Action Biology Ser.). (gr. 9-12). 1974. pap. text ed. 3.20 (ISBN 0-205-04142-6, 6741428). Allyn.

Reproduction & Development: Proceedings of the 28th International Congress of Physiological Sciences, Budapest, 1980. Ed. by B. Flerko et al. LC 80-41877. (Advances in Physiological Sciences: Vol. 15). (Illus.). 200p. 1981. 25.00 (ISBN 0-08-027336-X). Pergamon.

Reproduction in Farm Animals. 4th ed. Ed. by E. S. Hafez. LC 80-10489. (Illus.). 627p. 1980. text ed. 31.00 (ISBN 0-8121-0697-0). Lea & Febiger.

Reproduction in the Pig. Paul Hughes & Mike Varley. LC 80-40241. 254p. 1980. text ed. 39.95 (ISBN 0-408-70946-4); pap. text ed. 23.95 (ISBN 0-408-70921-9). Butterworths.

Reproduction: Molecular, Subcellular & Cellular. Society For The Study Of Developmental Biology - 24th Symposium. Ed. by M. Locke. 1966. 43.50 (ISBN 0-12-454174-7). Acad Pr.

Reproduction of Colour in Photography, Printing & Television. 3rd ed. R. W. Hunt. LC 76-6096. 1976. 19.95 (ISBN 0-470-15085-8). Halsted Pr.

Reproduction of Sound in High Fidelity & Stereo Phonographs. Edgar Villchur. (Illus.). 1966. pap. text ed. 2.00 (ISBN 0-486-21515-6). Dover.

Reproduction, Sex, & Preparation for Marriage. 2nd ed. Lawrence Crawley et al. (Illus.). 256p. 1973. pap. 10.95 (ISBN 0-13-773937-0). P-H.

Reproductive & Fat Cycles in Caribbean Anolis Lizards. Paul Licht & George Gorman. (U. C. Publ. in Zoology: Vol. 95). 1971. pap. 7.00x (ISBN 0-520-09374-7). U of Cal Pr.

Reproductive Biology of the Great Apes: Comparative & Biomedical Perspectives. Ed. by Charles E. Graham. 1981. write for info. (ISBN 0-12-295020-8). Acad Pr.

Reproductive Physiology of Mammals & Birds: The Comparative Physiology of Domestic & Laboratory Animals & Man. 3rd ed. A. V. Nalbandov. LC 75-25890. (Animal Science Ser.). (Illus.). 1976. 24.95x (ISBN 0-7167-0843-4). W H Freeman.

Reproductive System: Disease, Diagnosis, Treatment. W. Roberts. (Clinical Monographs Ser.). (Illus.). 1974. pap. 7.95 (ISBN 0-87618-062-4). R J Brady.

Reprographic Management Handbook. 2nd ed. Frederick C. Crix. 332p. 1979. text ed. 30.75x (ISBN 0-220-67010-2, Pub. by Busn Bks England). Renouf.

Reptile Mania. Ed Radlauer & Ruth Radlauer. LC 80-21575. (Mania Bks). (Illus.). 32p. (gr. k-5). 1981. PLB 7.95g (ISBN 0-516-07785-6, Elk Grove Bks). Childrens.

Reptile Study. Boy Scouts Of America. LC 19-600. (Illus.). 64p. (gr. 6-12). 1972. pap. 0.70x (ISBN 0-8395-3342-X, 3342). BSA.

Reptiles. Archie Carr. LC 63-12781. (Life Nature Library). (Illus.). (gr. 5 up). 1963. PLB 8.97 o.p. (ISBN 0-8094-0623-3, Pub. by Time-Life). Silver.

Reptiles. Archie Carr. (Young Readers Library). (Illus.). 1977. lib. bdg. 7.98 (ISBN 0-686-51093-3). Silver.

Reptiles. Susan Harris. (Easy-Read Fact Books Ser.). (gr. 2-4). 1978. PLB 6.90 (ISBN 0-531-01335-9). Watts.

Reptiles & Amphibians. Susan DeTreville & Stan DeTreville. (Illus.). 32p. (Orig.). 1981. pap. 3.50 (ISBN 0-89844-025-4). Troubador Pr.

Reptiles & Amphibians. (Wild, Wild World of Animals Ser.). 1976. 10.95 (ISBN 0-913948-06-3). Time-Life.

Reptiles & Amphibians. LC 76-4658. (Illus.). (gr. 5 up). 1976. lib. bdg. 11.97 (ISBN 0-685-73293-2, Pub. by Time-Life Television). Silver.

Reptiles & Amphibians in Color. Hans Hvass. (European Ecology Ser.). (Illus.). 1972. 9.95 (ISBN 0-7137-0743-7, Pub by Blandford Pr England). Sterling.

Reptiles & Amphibians in the Service of Man. Wilfred T. Neill. LC 73-8745. (Biological Science Ser). 1974. pap. 5.95 (ISBN 0-672-53687-0). Pegasus.

Reptiles & Amphibians of Alabama. Robert H. Mount. (Illus.). 354p. 1975. pap. 9.95 (ISBN 0-8173-0054-6, Pub. by Ag Experiment). U of Ala Pr.

Reptiles & Amphibians of the American Southwest. M. M. Heymann. LC 74-81405. (Illus.). Date not set. pap. 6.95 (ISBN 0-9603270-1-0). Doubleshoe.

Reptiles & How They Reproduce. Dorothy H. Patent. LC 77-3817. (Illus.). (gr. 5-7). 1977. 8.95 (ISBN 0-8234-0310-6). Holiday.

Reptiles of Northern & Central Europe. Don Street. 1979. 38.00 (ISBN 0-7134-1374-3, Pub. by Batsford England). David & Charles.

Reptiles of Oklahoma. R. G. Webb. LC 69-16716. (Stovall Museum Publication Ser.: No. 2). (Illus.). 1975. pap. 8.95 (ISBN 0-8061-0896-7). U of Okla Pr.

Reptiles We Know. Julian May. LC 73-4908. (Illus.). (gr. 2-4). 1973. PLB 5.95 o.p. (ISBN 0-87191-245-7). Creative Ed.

Reptilia & Batrachia. John Anderson. (Zoology of Egypt: No. 1). (Illus.). 1965. Repr. of 1898 ed. 150.00 (ISBN 3-7682-0240-2). Lubrecht & Cramer.

Republic, 2 Vols. rev. ed. Plato. Ed. by James Adam. (Gr.). Vol. 1, Bks. 1-5. text ed. 56.00x (ISBN 0-521-05963-1); Vol. 2, Bks. 6-10. text ed. 66.00x (ISBN 0-521-05964-X). Cambridge U Pr.

Republic. Plato. Tr. by A. D. Lindsay. 1957. pap. 5.95 (ISBN 0-525-47004-2). Dutton.

Republic & Other Works. Plato. Tr. by Benjamin Jowett. Incl. Symposiums; Parmenides; Euthyphro; Apology; Crito; Phaedo. pap. 4.95 (ISBN 0-385-09497-3, C12, Anch). Doubleday.

Republic & the School: Horace Mann on the Education of Free Men. 7th ed. Ed. by Lawrence A. Cremin. LC 57-9102. (Orig.). 1957. pap. text ed. 3.50x (ISBN 0-8077-1206-X). Tchrs Coll.

Republic F-Eighty-Four: From Lead Sled to Super Hawg. Rhodes Arnold. (Illus.). 128p. 1981. pap. 9.95 (ISBN 0-89404-054-5). Aztex.

Republic F-84: From "Lead Sled" to "Super Hawg". Arnold Rhodes. (Illus.). 128p. 1981. pap. 9.95 (ISBN 0-89404-054-5). Aztex.

Republic of Armenia, Vol. 1: the First Year, 1918-1919. Richard G. Hovannisian. LC 72-129613. (Illus.). 1971. 24.50x (ISBN 0-520-01984-9). U of Cal Pr.

Republic of Austria, Nineteen Eighteen to Nineteen Thirty-Four: A Study in the Failure of Democratic Government. Mary Proudfoot. LC 79-2291. 1981. Repr. of 1946 ed. 16.50 (ISBN 0-88355-967-6). Hyperion Conn.

Republic of Liberia, Liberia Supreme Court Records. 35.00 ea. Vol. 24, March Term 1975 To October Term 1975 (ISBN 0-8014-1197-1). Vol. 25, March Term 1976 To October Term 1976 (ISBN 0-8014-1272-2). Cornell U Pr.

Republic of Zaire. Robin McKown. LC 72-1873. (First Bks). (Illus.). 96p. (gr. 4-6). 1972. PLB 4.47 o.p. (ISBN 0-531-00770-7). Watts.

Republic P-Forty-Seven Thunderbolt. Ernest R. McDowell. Ed. & illus. by Richard Ward. LC 75-86566. (Arco-Aircam Aviation Ser., No. 2). (Illus., Orig.). 1968. pap. 2.95 o.p. (ISBN 0-668-02095-4). Arco.

Republic Studios: Between Poverty Row & the Majors. Richard M. Hurst. LC 79-19844. 1979. 14.50 (ISBN 0-8108-1254-1). Scarecrow.

Republican Chaos: Campaigns from Truman Through Nixon. Joseph Miller. (Illus.). 1980. 9.00 (ISBN 0-912472-24-3). Miller Bks.

Republican Command, Eighteen Ninety-Seven to Nineteen Thirteen. Horace S. Merrill & Marion G. Merrill. LC 76-147852. (Illus.). 376p. 1971. 17.00x (ISBN 0-8131-1245-1). U Pr of Ky.

Republican Era, 1869-1901. Leonard D. White. 1958. 9.95 (ISBN 0-02-626860-4). Macmillan.

Republican Foreign Policy, 1921-1933. L. Ethan Ellis. LC 68-20886. (Illus.). 1968. 25.00 (ISBN 0-8135-0574-7). Rutgers U Pr.

Republican Germany. Hugh Quigley & R. T. Clark. LC 67-24592. (Illus.). 1968. Repr. of 1928 ed. 16.50 (ISBN 0-86527-166-6). Fertig.

Republican Heyday: Republicanism Through the McKinley Years. Clarence A. Stern. 1962. pap. 1.25 (ISBN 0-9600116-2-5). Stern.

Republican Iraq: A Study in Iraqi Politics Since the Revolution of 1958. Majid Khadduri. LC 80-1923. 1981. Repr. of 1969 ed. 37.00 (ISBN 0-404-18973-3). AMS Pr.

Republican or, a Series of Essays on the Principles & Policy of Free States. William C. Jarvis. Ed. by Michael Hudson. (Neglected American Economists Ser.). 1974. lib. bdg. 50.00 (ISBN 0-8240-1001-9). Garland Pub.

Republican Party: A History. William S. Myers. (Government & Political Science Ser). 1968. Repr. of 1928 ed. 25.50 (ISBN 0-384-40741-2); with Democratic Party by Kent 46.00 (ISBN 0-685-13576-4). Johnson Repr.

Republican Party & Black America: From McKinley to Hoover, 1896-1933. Richard B. Sherman. LC 72-96714. 1973. 12.95x (ISBN 0-8139-0467-6). U Pr of Va.

Republican Portugal: A Political History, 1910-1926. Douglas L. Wheeler. LC 77-15059. (Illus.). 1978. 20.00 (ISBN 0-299-07450-1). U of Wis Pr.

Republican Protestantism in Aztlan. E. C. Orozco. 261p. 1980. 22.00 (ISBN 0-686-28883-1); pap. 11.00 (ISBN 0-686-28884-X). Petereins Pr.

Republican Rome, the Army & the Allies. Emilio Gabba. Tr. by P. J. Cuff. 1977. 30.00x (ISBN 0-520-03259-4). U. of Cal Pr.

Republicans & Federalists in Pennsylvania: 1790-1801. Harry M. Tinkcom. LC 50-9356. (Orig.). 1950. pap. 5.00 (ISBN 0-911124-24-1). Pa Hist & Mus.

Republicans & Labor, 1919-1929. Robert H. Zieger. LC 77-80087. 320p. 1969. 14.50x (ISBN 0-8131-1180-3). U Pr of Ky.

Republic's Private Navy: The American Privateering Business As Practiced by Baltimore During the War of 1812. Jerome R. Garitee. LC 76-41487. (American Maritime Library: Vol. 8). (Illus.). 356p. 1977. 17.50 (ISBN 0-8195-5004-3); limited ed. 35.00 (ISBN 0-8195-5005-1). Mystic Seaport.

Republique des Philsophes du Histoire des Ajaoiens. Fontenelle. (Fr.). 1977. Repr. of 1768 ed. lib. bdg. 27.50x o.p. (ISBN 0-8287-0352-3). Clearwater Pub.

Reputation of the American Businessman. Sigmund Diamond. 6.75 (ISBN 0-8446-0581-6). Peter Smith.

Reputations Live on: An Early Malay Autobiography. Amin Sweeney. 150p. 1980. 20.00x (ISBN 0-520-04073-2). U of Cal Pr.

Request Presented to the King of Spayn by the Inhabitants of the Lowe Countreyes, Protesting That They Will Live According to the Reformation of the Gospell. LC 71-26044. (English Experience Ser.: No. 266). 1970. Repr. of 1578 ed. 7.00 (ISBN 90-221-0266-1). Walter J Johnson.

Requiem for a People: The Rogue Indians & the Frontiersmen. Stephen D. Beckham. LC 79-145497. (Civilization of the American Indian Ser.: Vol. 108). (Illus.). 1971. 9.95 (ISBN 0-8061-0942-4); pap. 4.95 (ISBN 0-8061-1036-8). U of Okla Pr.

Requiem for Heurtebise: Homage to Jean Cocteau. David L. Fisher. 1974. pap. 1.00 (ISBN 0-686-18853-5); signed ed. 2.00 (ISBN 0-686-18854-3). Man-Root.

Requiem for the Card Catalog: Management Issues in Automated Cataloging. Ed. by Daniel Gore et al. LC 78-7129. (New Directions in Librarianship: No. 2). 1979. lib. bdg. 18.95 (ISBN 0-313-20608-2, GMI/). Greenwood.

Requiem por un Campesino. Sender. (Easy Reader, C). pap. 3.75 (ISBN 0-88436-055-5, SPA201052). EMC.

Requiem: The Decline & Demise of Mayor Daley & His Era. Len O'Connor. 1978. pap. 3.95 o.p. (ISBN 0-8092-7409-4). Contemp Bks.

Requiems & Other Celebrations. William Parham. LC 80-53538. 80p. (Orig.). 1981. pap. 4.75 (ISBN 0-938264-01-X). Veritas.

Requirements for Certification: Of Teachers, Counselors, Librarians, Administrators for Elementary Schools, Secondary Schools, Junior Colleges, 1981-82. 45th ed. Elizabeth H. Woellner. (Illus.). 240p. 1981. lib. bdg. price not set (ISBN 0-226-90466-0, A43-1905). U of Chicago Pr.

Requirements for the Irradiaton of Food on a Commercial Scale: Proceedings. Panel, Vienna, March 18-22, 1974. (Illus.). 216p. 1975. pap. 16.75 (ISBN 92-0-111275-0, IAEA). Unipub.

Reruns. Sabina Thorne. LC 80-52008. 228p. 1981. 11.95 (ISBN 0-670-59526-8). Viking Pr.

Res Gestae Divi Augusti. Augustus. Ed. by P. A. Brunt & J. M. Moore. 1967. pap. 6.95x (ISBN 0-19-831772-7). Oxford U Pr.

Rescue. Dennis McGee. 1981. 8.95 (ISBN 0-533-04792-7). Vantage.

Rescue: A Handbook of Classroom Ideas to Motivate the Teaching of Remedial Reading. (Spice Ser). 1979. 6.50 (ISBN 0-89273-108-7). Educ Serv.

Rescue & Home Care of Native Wildlife. Rosemary K. Collett & Charlie Briggs. 1976. pap. 5.95 (ISBN 0-8015-6292-9, Hawthorn). Dutton.

Rescue Chopper. Ruth Hallman. LC 80-15593. (Hiway Bk.). 1980. 8.95 (ISBN 0-664-32667-6). Westminster.

Rescue Duplicating Master: Remedial Reading. (Spice Ser.). 1975. 5.95 (ISBN 0-89273-509-0). Educ Serv.

Rescue Emergency Care. K. C. Easton. (Illus.). 1977. 29.95x (ISBN 0-433-08000-0). Intl Ideas.

Rescue for Brownie. Thomas B. Leekley. LC 59-15202. (gr. 4-8). 3.95 (ISBN 0-8149-0350-9). Vanguard.

Rescue from Disaster: The Story of the RFD Group. Harold Nockolds. LC 80-66422. (Illus.). 224p. (Orig.). 1980. 32.00 (ISBN 0-7153-7969-0). David & Charles.

Rescue Mission. John Ball. LC 66-13854. 1966. 8.95 o.s.i. (ISBN 0-06-010196-2, HarpT). Har-Row.

Rescue of the Eighteen Fifty-Six Handcraft Companies. Rebecca Cornwall & Leonard J. Arrington. (Charles Redd Monographs in Western History: No. 11). (Illus.). 64p. 1981. pap. text ed. 4.95 (ISBN 0-8425-1941-6). Brigham.

Rescue of the Sun & Other Tales from the Far North. Edythe W. Newell. LC 76-91741. (Folklore Ser). (Illus.). (gr. 3 up). 1970. 5.95g o.p. (ISBN 0-8075-6948-8). A Whitman.

Rescue the Dead. David Ignatow. LC 68-16005. (Wesleyan Poetry Program: Vol. 37). (Orig.). 1968. pap. text ed. 10.00x (ISBN 0-8195-2037-3, Pub. by Wesleyan U Pr). Columbia U Pr.

Rescue: True Stories of Heroism. L. B. Taylor, Jr. (Illus.). (gr. 5 up). 1978. PLB 6.90 s&l (ISBN 0-531-02223-4). Watts.

Rescued! America's Endangered Wildlife on the Comeback Trail. Olive W. Burt. LC 80-10638. (Illus.). 128p. (gr. 4-6). 1980. PLB 7.79 (ISBN 0-671-32984-7). Messner.

Rescued by Love. Joan Vincent. (Orig.). 1981. pap. 1.50 (ISBN 0-440-17433-3). Dell.

Research: A National Resource, 3 vols. in 1. U. S. National Resources Committee. Ed. by I. Bernard Cohen. LC 79-7985. (Three Centuries of Science in America Ser.). (Illus.). 1980. Repr. of 1941 ed. lib. bdg. 78.00x (ISBN 0-405-12567-4). Arno.

Research About Nineteenth-Century Children & Books: Portrait Studies. Ed. by Selma K. Richardson. (Monograph: No. 17). (Illus.). 1980. pap. 8.00 (ISBN 0-87845-055-6). U of Ill Lib Sci.

Research Advances in Alcohol & Drug Problems, 3 vols. Ed. by Robert J. Gibbins et al. LC 73-18088. 384p. 1974-76. Vol. 1. 45.95 (ISBN 0-471-29737-2); Vol. 2. 47.95 (ISBN 0-471-29738-0); Vol. 3. 51.95 (ISBN 0-471-29736-4, Pub. by Wiley-Medical). Wiley.

Research Advances in Alcohol & Drug Problems: Volume 5, Drug Problems in Women. Ed. by Kalant. 730p. 1980. 55.00 (ISBN 0-306-40394-3, Plenum Pr). Plenum Pub.

Research & American Industrial Development. Harold Vagtborg. LC 75-14439. 1976. text ed. 57.00 (ISBN 0-08-019791-4). Pergamon.

Research & Clinical Applications of the Bender-Gesalt Test. Alexander Tolor & Gary Brannigan. (Illus.). 224p. 1980. 22.50 (ISBN 0-398-04088-5). C C Thomas.

Research & Development Abroad by U. S. Multinationals. Robert Ronstadt. LC 77-10672. (Praeger Special Studies). 1977. 21.95 (ISBN 0-03-022661-9). Praeger.

Research & Development & the Prospects for International Security. Frederick Seitz & Rodney W. Nichols. LC 73-90816. 88p. 1974. 6.50x (ISBN 0-8448-0261-1); pap. 2.75x (ISBN 0-8448-0262-X). Crane-Russak Co.

Research & Development in U.S. Manufacturing. Albert N. Link. 124p. 1981. 18.95 (ISBN 0-03-057677-6). Praeger.

Research & Experiment in Stuttering, H. R. Beech & F. Fransella. 1968. 34.00 (ISBN 0-08-012539-5). Pergamon.

Research & Health of Americans. Stephen P. Strickland. LC 77-25779. (Illus.). 1978. 17.95x (ISBN 0-669-02165-2). Lexington Bks.

Research & Public Health. John Charles. 1961. text ed. 3.00x (ISBN 0-485-26312-2, Athlone Pr). Humanities.

Research & Reform in Teacher Education. William Taylor. (Council of Europe: European Trend Reports on Educational Research: No. 4). (Illus.). 1978. pap. text ed. 22.00x (ISBN 0-85633-140-6, NFER). Humanities.

Research & Report Writing in the Behavioral Sciences: Psychiatry, Psychology, Sociology, Educational Psychology, Cultural Anthropology, Managerial Psychology. Robert L. Noland. 108p. 1970. pap. 10.75 (ISBN 0-398-01406-X). C C Thomas.

Research & Technology As Economic Activities. Green & Morphet. (Sicon Bks.). 1977. 3.95 (ISBN 0-408-71300-3). Butterworths.

Research & the Library: A Student Guide to Basic Techniques. Alan L. Whipple. 120p. (Orig.). (gr. 8-11). 1974. pap. text ed. 2.95x (ISBN 0-88334-062-3). Ind Sch Pr.

Research & Theory in Current Archeology. Charles L. Redman. LC 73-6717. 384p. 1973. pap. text ed. 17.50 (ISBN 0-471-71291-4, Pub. by Wiley-Interscience). Wiley.

Research & Theory in Current Archeology. Ed. by Charles L. Redman. 400p. 1980. Repr. of 1973 ed. lib. bdg. write for info. (ISBN 0-89874-226-9). Krieger.

Research Applications of Nuclear Pulsed Systems. 1967. pap. 12.00 (ISBN 92-0-151067-5, IAEA). Unipub.

Research Conference on Shear Strength of Cohesive Soils. Compiled by American Society of Civil Engineers. 1174p. 1966. pap. text ed. 37.50 (ISBN 0-87262-004-2). Am Soc Civil Eng.

Research Design in Speech Pathology & Audiology: Asking & Answering Questions. Frank H. Silverman. (Illus.). 1977. text ed. 19.95 (ISBN 0-13-774117-0). P-H.

Research Directions in Computer Control of Urban Traffic Systems. Compiled by American Society of Civil Engineers. 400p. 1979. pap. text ed. 20.00 (ISBN 0-87262-179-0). Am Soc Civil Eng.

Research Excellence Through the Year 2000. Committee on Continuity in Academic Research Performance. LC 79-67784. xiv, 241p. 1979. pap. 9.00 (ISBN 0-309-02938-4). Natl Acad Pr.

Research for Social Welfare: Six Case Studies in Cyprus. L. G. Moseley. 143p. 1979. pap. text ed. 9.90x (ISBN 0-7199-0948-1, Pub. by Bedford England). Renouf.

Research Frontiers in Fertility Regulation. Gerald I. Zatuchni et al. (Illus.). 416p. 1981. text ed. write for info. (ISBN 0-06-142902-3, Harper Medical). Har-Row.

Research Games: An Approach to the Study of Decision Processes. K. C. Bowen. (ORASA Text Ser.: No. 3). 1978. pap. 19.95 (ISBN 0-470-26535-3). Halsted Pr.

Research Guide to Argentine Literature. David W. Foster & Virginia R. Foster. LC 70-9731. 1970. 10.00 (ISBN 0-8108-0298-8). Scarecrow.

Research Highlights for 1977. 122p. Date not set. pap. 18.50 (R127, IRRI). Unipub.

Research Highlights for 1978. 118p. 1979. pap. 21.50 (R 126, IRRI). Unipub.

Research in Clinical Psychology: Effective Coping Through Data Collection. Leonard P. Ullmann. (Pergamon General Psychology Ser.). 325p. Date not set. write for info. (ISBN 0-08-025945-6); pap. write for info. (ISBN 0-08-025944-8). Pergamon.

Research in Culture Learning: Language & Conceptual Studies. Ed. by Michael P. Hamnett. Richard W. Brislin. LC 80-21761. 195p. 1980. pap. 10.00x (ISBN 0-8248-0738-3). U Pr of Hawaii.

Research in Education. 4th ed. John. Best. (Illus.). 400p. 1981. text ed. 18.95 (ISBN 0-13-774026-3). P-H.

Research in Education. 3rd ed. John W. Best. (Illus.). 1977. text ed. 18.95 (ISBN 0-13-774018-2). P-H.

Research in Forest Economics & Forest Policy. Ed. by Marion Clawson. LC 77-81676. (Research for the Future Research Paper Ser: No. 3). 1977. pap. text ed. 8.95x o.p. (ISBN 0-8018-2033-2). Johns Hopkins.

Research in General Practice. J. G. Howie. 193p. 1979. 30.00x (ISBN 0-85664-506-0, Pub. by Croom Helm Ltd England). Biblio Dist.

Research in Mathematics Education. Ed. by Richard Shumway. National Council of Teachers of Mathematics. 1980. 27.00 (ISBN 0-87353-163-9). NCTM.

Research in Mexican History: Topics, Methodology, Sources, & a Practical Guide to Field Research. Ed. by Richard E. Greenleaf & Michael C. Meyer. LC 72-86020. (Illus.). xiv, 226p. 1973. pap. 3.75x (ISBN 0-8032-5773-2, BB 516, Bison). U of Nebr Pr.

Research in Music Behavior: Modifying Music Behavior in the Classroom. Ed. by Clifford K. Madsen et al. LC 74-13632. 1975. text ed. 16.50x (ISBN 0-8077-2436-X). Tchrs Coll.

Research in Nursing. Carolyn F. Waltz & R. Barker Bausell. LC 80-18669. (Illus.). 350p. 1981. 13.95 (ISBN 0-686-65103-0). Davis Co.

Research in Optical Spectroscopy: Present Status & Prospects. Division Of Physical Sciences. (Orig.). 1968. pap. 3.25 o.p. (ISBN 0-309-01699-1). Natl Acad Pr.

Research in Parapsychology 1972: Abstracts & Papers from the 15th Annual Convention of the Parapsychological Association, 1972. Parapsychological Association. Ed. by W. G. Roll et al. LC 66-28580. 1973. 11.00 (ISBN 0-8108-0666-5). Scarecrow.

Research in Parapsychology 1973: Abstracts & Papers from the 16th Annual Convention of the Parapsychological Association, 1973. Parapsychological Association. Ed. by W. G. Roll et al. LC 66-28580. 1974. 11.00 (ISBN 0-8108-0708-4). Scarecrow.

Research in Parapsychology 1974: Abstracts & Papers from the 17th Annual Convention of the Parapsychological Association, 1974. Parapsychological Association. Ed. by J. D. Morris & W. G. Roll. LC 66-28580. 272p. 1975. 11.00 (ISBN 0-8108-0850-1). Scarecrow.

Research in Parapsychology 1975: Abstracts & Papers from the 18th Annual Convention of the Parapsychological Association, 1975. Parapsychological Association. Ed. by J. D. Morris et al. LC 66-28580. 277p. 1976. 11.00 (ISBN 0-8108-0895-1). Scarecrow.

Research in Parapsychology 1976: Abstracts & Papers from the 19th Annual Convention of the Parapsychological Association, 1976. Parapsychological Association. Ed. by J. D. Morris et al. LC 66-28580. 1977. 11.00 (ISBN 0-8108-1080-8). Scarecrow.

Research in Parapsychology 1977: Abstracts & Papers from the 20th Annual Convention of the Parapsychological Association, 1977. Parapsychological Association. Ed. by William G. Roll. LC 66-28580. 1978. lib. bdg. 11.00 (ISBN 0-8108-1131-6). Scarecrow.

Research in Parapsychology 1978. Parapsychological Association. Ed. by William G. Roll. LC 66-28580. 1979. 11.00 (ISBN 0-8108-1195-2). Scarecrow.

Research in Parapsychology 1979: Abstracts & Papers from the Twenty-Second Annual Convention of the Parapsychological Association. Ed. by William G. Roll. LC 66-2858. 238p. 1980. 12.00 (ISBN 0-8108-1327-0). Scarecrow.

Research in Phenomenology, Vol. 9. John Sallis. (Orig.). 1979. pap. text ed. 10.00x (ISBN 0-391-01297-5). Humanities.

Research in Protozoology, Vol. 4. Ed. by T. T. Chen. 1972. 64.00 (ISBN 0-08-016437-4). Pergamon.

Research in Science Education in Europe: Report of a Cooperative Study & a European Contact Workshop Organised by the Council of Europe & the Institute for Science Education, FRG (Kiel) Ed. by Karl Frey et al. 394p. 1977. pap. text ed. 25.50 (ISBN 90-265-0266-4, Pub. by Swets Serv Pub Holland). Swets North Am.

Research in Science Education: 1938-1947. Ed. by Robert W. Boenig. LC 69-12581. 1969. text ed. 12.75x (ISBN 0-8077-1093-8). Tchrs Coll.

Research in Science Education 1948 Through 1952. Ed. by J. Nathan Swift. LC 69-12580. (Illus.). 1969. text ed. 12.75x (ISBN 0-8077-2238-3). Tchrs Coll.

Research in Science Education: 1953 Through 1957. Elizabeth P. Lawlor. LC 70-112927. 1970. text ed. 12.75x (ISBN 0-8077-1669-3). Tchrs Coll.

Research in Second Language Acquisition: Selected Papers of the Los Angeles Second Language Acquisition Research Forum. Ed. by Robin C. Scarcella & Stephen D. Krashen. (Issues in Second Language Research Ser.). 1981. pap. 13.95 (ISBN 0-88377-143-8). Newbury Hse.

Research in Solid State Sciences: Opportunities & Relevance to National Needs. Division Of Physical Sciences. LC 8-61848. 1968. pap. 4.75 (ISBN 0-309-01600-2). Natl Acad Pr.

Research in Speech Communication. Raymond Tucker et al. (Ser. in Speech Communication). (Illus.). 352p. 1981. text ed. 18.95 (ISBN 0-13-774273-8). P-H.

Research in Teacher Education: A Symposium. Ed. by B. Othanel Smith. LC 73-138471. (Illus.). 1971. ref. ed. 12.95 (ISBN 0-13-774455-2). P-H.

Research in the Chemical Industry: The Environment, Objectives & Strategy. A. Baines et al. (Illus.). 1969. 33.60x (ISBN 0-444-20035-5, Pub. by Applied Science). Burgess-Intl Ideas.

Research in the Social Services: A Five-Year Review. Ed. by Henry S. Maas et al. LC 75-139833. 232p. (Orig.). 1971. pap. 8.00x (ISBN 0-87101-616-8, CBO-616-C). Natl Assn Soc Wkrs.

Research in Transportation: Legal-Legislative & Economic Sources & Procedures. Ed. by Kenneth U. Flood. LC 72-118792. (Management Information Guides Ser.: No. 20). 1970. 30.00 (ISBN 0-8103-0820-7). Gale.

Research in Zoos & Aquariums. Institute of Laboratory Animal Resources. 1975. pap. 10.00 (ISBN 0-309-02319-X). Natl Acad Pr.

Research Index of NAEB Journals, 1957 to 1979. Robert K. Avery et al. 169p. 1980. pap. 13.50. NAEB.

Research into Classroom Processes: Recent Developments & Next Steps. Ed. by Ian Westbury & Arno A. Bellack. LC 70-170131. 280p. 1971. text ed. 14.25x (ISBN 0-8077-2327-4). Tchrs Coll.

Research into Personal Development: Educational & Vocational Choice. Ed. by Anders Duner. 192p. 1978. pap. text ed. 16.00 (ISBN 90-265-0284-2, Pub. by Swets Serv Pub Holland). Swets North Am.

Research into Rheumatoid Arthritis & Allied Diseases. Ed. by D. C. Dumonde & R. N. Maini. Date not set. 34.50 o.p. (ISBN 0-8391-1180-0). Univ Park.

Research Inventory of the Mexican Collection of Colonial Parish Registers. David Robinson. (Finding Aids to the Microfilmed Manuscript Collection of the Genealogical Society of Utah). 350p. (Orig.). 1981. pap. 15.00 (ISBN 0-87480-181-8). U of Utah Pr.

Research: Its Role in Development. Marcia K. McGill. 1978. pap. 2.50 (ISBN 0-934338-34-5). NAIS.

Research Libraries & Technology. Herman H. Fussler. 1974. 10.00x (ISBN 0-226-27558-2). U of Chicago Pr.

Research Methodology & Its Application to Nursing. Yvonne M. Williamson. 360p. 1981. 13.95 (ISBN 0-471-03313-8, Pub. by Wiley Med). Wiley.

Research Methodology in Accounting. Ed. by Robert R. Sterling. LC 72-77235. 1972. text ed. 10.00 (ISBN 0-914348-13-2). Scholars Bk.

Research Methods. R. Dominowski. 1980. 18.95 (ISBN 0-13-774315-7). P-H.

Research Methods for Community Health & Welfare: An Introduction. Karl E. Bauman. 160p. 1980. 13.95x (ISBN 0-19-502698-5); pap. 7.95x (ISBN 0-19-502699-3). Oxford U Pr.

Research Methods for Counselors: Practical Approaches in Field Settings. Ed. by Leo Goldman. LC 77-10950. (Counseling & Human Development Ser.). 1978. text ed. 21.95 (ISBN 0-471-02339-6). Wiley.

Research Methods for Needs Assessment. John M. Nickens et al. LC 80-5126. 98p. 1980. pap. text ed. 6.75 (ISBN 0-8191-1047-7). U Pr of Amer.

Research Methods for Nurses. Winona B. Ackerman & Paul R. Lohnes. (Illus.). 304p. 1981. text ed. 16.95x (ISBN 0-07-000182-0, HP). McGraw.

Research Methods for Oral Health Professionals: An Introduction. Michele L. Darby & Denise M. Bowen. LC 79-18208. 1979. pap. text ed. 13.95 (ISBN 0-8016-1207-1). Mosby.

Research Methods in Librarianship: Techniques & Interpretation. Ed. by Charles H. Busha & Stephen P. Harter. LC 79-8864. (Library & Information Science Ser.). 432p. 1980. tchrs' ed. 19.50 (ISBN 0-12-147550-6). Acad Pr.

Research Methods in Marine Biology. Ed. by Carl Schlieper. LC 72-6089. (Biology Ser.). (Illus.). 300p. 1972. 16.00 (ISBN 0-295-95234-2). U of Wash Pr.

Research Methods in Mass Communication. Guido H. Stempel, III & Bruce H. Westley. (Illus.). 480p. 1981. text ed. 19.95 (ISBN 0-13-774240-1). P-H.

Research Methods in Plant Ecology. G. S. Puri et al. 1968. 12.50x (ISBN 0-210-26925-1). Asia.

Research Methods in Psychopathology. T. Millon & H. I. Diessenhaus. (Approaches to Behavior Pathology Ser.). 1972. pap. 10.95x (ISBN 0-471-60626-X). Wiley.

Research Methods: Statistical Concepts & Research Practicum. John H. Behling. 1977. pap. text ed. 6.00x (ISBN 0-8191-0084-6). U Pr of Amer.

Research Monograph, 27 vols. United States Works Progress Administration. (FDR & the Era of the New Deal Ser.). 1971. lib. bdg. 345.00 (ISBN 0-306-70359-9). Da Capo.

Research Odyssey: Developing & Testing a Community Theory. George Hillary. 158p. 1981. 15.95 (ISBN 0-87855-400-9); text ed. 15.95 (ISBN 0-686-68061-8). Transaction Bks.

Research on Deviance. Jack D. Douglas. 320p. 1972. pap. text ed. 4.95x o.p. (ISBN 0-394-31154-X, RanC). Random.

Research on Multiple Sclerosis. C. W. Adams. (Amer. Lec. Living Chemistry Ser.). (Illus.). 192p. 1972. 18.75 (ISBN 0-398-02214-3). C C Thomas.

Research on Service Delivery to Battered Women & Crime Victims. 1980. 3.00. Comm Coun Great NY.

Research on Steroids, Vol. 4. C. Conti et al. 1971. 50.00 (ISBN 0-08-017573-2). Pergamon.

Research on Teaching: Concepts, Findings & Implications. Ed. by Penelope L. Peterson & Herbert J. Walberg. LC 78-62102. (Education Ser.). 1979. 15.50 (ISBN 0-8211-1518-9); text ed. 14.00 in ten or more copies (ISBN 0-685-63681-X). McCutchan.

Research Paper. Barbara Gregorich & Therese F. Waldowski. LC 78-730060. (Illus.). 1977. pap. text ed. 99.00 (ISBN 0-89290-124-1, A323). Soc for Visual.

Research Paper Workbook. Ellen Strenski & Madge Manfred. (English & Humanities Ser.). (Illus.). 283p. (Orig.). pap. text ed. 7.95x (ISBN 0-582-28203-9). Longman.

Research Papers. 5th ed. William Coyle. LC 79-14110. 1980. pap. 5.95 (ISBN 0-672-61500-2). Bobbs.

Research Perspectives on the Transition from School to Work: Report of a European Contact Workshop Organised by the Institute of Education (ECF) Under the Auspices of the Commission of the European Communities, Bruges, July 1977. Ed. by Guy Neave. 144p. 1978. pap. text ed. 12.75 (ISBN 90-265-0278-8, Pub. by Swets Pub Serv Holland). Swets North Am.

Research Priorities for Crime Reduction Efforts. Henry Ruth. (Institute Paper). 140p. 1977. pap. 3.50 (ISBN 0-87766-183-9, 17200). Urban Inst.

Research Priorities in Tropical Biology. Committee on Research Priorities in Tropical Biology. xii, 116p. 1980. pap. text ed. 8.25 (ISBN 0-309-03043-9). Natl Acad Pr.

Research Process in Nursing. Particia Dempsey & Arthur Dempsey. 1980. 13.95 (ISBN 0-442-20884-7). D Van Nostrand.

Research Processes in Physical Education, Recreation & Health. David H. Clarke & H. Harrison Clarke. (Physical Education Ser). 1970. text ed. 17.95 (ISBN 0-13-774463-3). P-H.

Research Programs in the Medical Sciences. Ed. by Jaques Cattell Press. 816p. 1980. 79.95 (ISBN 0-8352-1293-9). Bowker.

Research Reactor Utilization. (Technical Reports: No. 71). 1967. pap. 5.00 (ISBN 92-0-155067-7, IAEA). Unipub.

Research Review Nineteen Sixty-Six to Nineteen Eighty: Adolescent Problems. Fred Streit. 71p. 1980. pap. 15.00. Essence Pubns.

Research Standards & Methods for Social Workers. rev. ed. Harris K. Goldstein. LC 70-84001. 1980. pap. 12.50x (ISBN 0-87655-551-2). Whitehall Co.

Research Strategies in Psychotherapy. Edward S. Bordin. LC 74-11272. (Personality Processes Ser). 272p. 1974. 24.95 (ISBN 0-471-08885-4, Pub. by Wiley-Interscience). Wiley.

Research Techniques for Program Planning, Monitoring & Evaluation. Irwin Epstein & Tony Tripodi. LC 76-51825. 1977. 15.00x (ISBN 0-231-03944-1). Columbia U Pr.

Research, Technological Change & Economic Analysis. Ed. by Bela Gold. LC 76-50496. (Illus.). 1977. 21.95 (ISBN 0-669-01286-6). Lexington Bks.

Research to Practice in Mental Retardation: IASSMD Proceedings, 3 vols. Ed. by P. Mittler. 1977. Vol. 1. 29.50 (ISBN 0-8391-1122-3); Vol. 2. 29.50 (ISBN 0-8391-1123-1); Vol. 3. 29.50 (ISBN 0-8391-1124-X). Univ Park.

Research Utilization Inventory: A Survey of Current Research of Social & Health Agencies in New York City. 1976. pap. 6.00 (ISBN 0-86671-033-7). Comm Coun Great NY.

Research with Recombinant DNA. Academy Forum. 1977. pap. text ed. 8.50 (ISBN 0-309-02641-5). Natl Acad Pr.

Researcher's Guide to Iron Ore: An Annotated Bibliography on the Economic Geography of Iron Ore. Fillmore C. Earney. LC 74-76986. 1974. lib. bdg. 50.00 (ISBN 0-87287-095-2). Libs Unl.

Researcher's Guide to Statistics: Glossary & Decision Map. Terry C. Wilson. LC 78-56267. 1978. pap. text ed. 7.25 (ISBN 0-8191-0519-8). U Pr of Amer.

Researcher's Guide to Washington: Fifth Edition. Ed. by Micheal Glennon. LC 77-95197. 1981. pap. 45.00 (ISBN 0-686-26089-9). Wash Res.

Researches into the Laws of Chemical Affinity. 2nd ed. Claude-Louis Berthollet. LC 65-23404. 1966. Repr. of 1809 ed. 22.50 (ISBN 0-306-70914-7). Da Capo.

Researches on Living Pteridophytes in India, Burma & Ceylon. Nira P. Chowdhury. (Illus.). 1971. text ed. 6.95x (ISBN 0-210-22349-9). Asia.

Researches on Waring's Problem. L. E. Dickson. 257p. 1935. 13.75 o.p. (ISBN 0-87279-474-1, 464). Carnegie Inst.

Researching & Writing in History. F. N. McCoy. 1974. 11.95x (ISBN 0-520-02447-8); pap. 3.95 (ISBN 0-520-02621-7). U of Cal Pr.

Researching Science Information. Peter Fenner. 250p. (Orig.). 1981. pap. 7.95 (ISBN 0-86576-010-1). W Kaufmann.

Researching the Old House. Ed. by Greater Portland Landmarks Research Committee. (Illus.). 70p. 1980. price not set o.p. (ISBN 0-9600612-9-0). Greater Portland.

Reserves & Resources of Uranium in the United States: Mineral Resources & the Environment Supplementary Report. Committee on Mineral Resources & Environment, National Research Council. ix, 236p. 1975. pap. 7.00 (ISBN 0-309-02423-4). Natl Acad Pr.

Reservoir Engineering Aspects of Fractured Formations. L. H. Reiss. 200p. (Orig.). 1981. pap. text ed. 14.95 (ISBN 0-87201-303-0). Gulf Pub.

Reservoir Flood Standards. Institute of Civil Engineers, UK. 1980. pap. 20.00x (ISBN 0-7277-0023-5, Pub. by Telford England). State Mutual Bk.

Resettlement. Arthur J. Demarest. 166p. 1970. 6.50x (ISBN 0-911038-75-2, New Voices). Noontide.

Resettling America: Energy, Ecology, & Community. Gary Coates. (Illus.). 400p. 1981. pap. 10.95 (ISBN 0-931790-06-9). Brick Hse Pub.

Resettling Retarded Adults in a Managed Community. Arnold Birenbaum & Samuel Seiffer. LC 75-19765. (Special Studies). 150p. 1976. text ed. 24.95 (ISBN 0-275-55520-8). Praeger.

Reshaping Ambulatory Care Programs: Report & Recommendations of a Conference on Ambulatory Care. American Hospital Association. LC 73-86670. (Illus.). 68p. 1973. pap. 8.75 o.p. (ISBN 0-87258-133-0, 3615). Am Hospital.

Reshaping of French Democracy. Gordon Wright. LC 68-9654. 1970. Repr. of 1948 ed. 15.00 (ISBN 0-86527-167-4). Fertig.

Reshith Binah: A Hebrew Primer. Sidney M. Fish. 1976. pap. 2.50x (ISBN 0-8197-0035-5). Bloch.

Residence of Twenty-One Years in the Sandwich Islands: A Civil, Religious, & Political History. rev. 3rd ed. Hiram Bingham. LC 77-83041. 1981. 27.50 (ISBN 0-8048-1252-7). C E Tuttle.

Resident Witch. Marian T. Place. (Illus.). (gr. 2-5). 1974. pap. 1.75 (ISBN 0-380-00852-1, 51425, Camelot). Avon.

Residential Building Sewers. Building Research Advisory Board - Federal Housing Administration. 1960. pap. 3.00 o.p. (ISBN 0-309-00787-9). Natl Acad Pr.

Residential Care for the Mentally Retarded. E. Stephen. 64p. 1970. pap. 6.25 (ISBN 0-08-016106-5). Pergamon.

Residential Community. Howard Jones. (Library of Social Work). 1979. 17.00x (ISBN 0-7100-0122-3); pap. 8.95 (ISBN 0-7100-0123-1). Routledge & Kegan.

Residential Condominiums: A Guide to Analysis & Appraisal. Robert W. Dombal. 1976. pap. 10.00 (ISBN 0-911780-37-8). Am Inst Real Estate Appraisers.

Residential Cost Manual 1981: New Construction, Remodeling, & Valuation. Coert Engelsman. 347p. 1980. pap. text ed. 29.95 (ISBN 0-442-12224-1). Van Nos Reinhold.

Residential Crowding in Urban America. Mark Baldassare. LC 77-83102. 1979. 13.95x (ISBN 0-520-03563-1). U of Cal Pr.

Residential Designs: How to Get the Most for Your Housing Dollar. Ed. by David E. Link. LC 73-76442. 1972. 15.95 o.p. (ISBN 0-8436-0116-7). CBI Pub.

Residential Development Handbook. W. P. O'Mara et al. LC 77-930497. (Community Builders Handbook Ser.). (Illus.). 350p. 1978. 34.00 (ISBN 0-87420-580-8). Urban Land.

Residential Districts. Jorg C. Kirchenmann & Christian Muschalek. (Illus.). 192p. 1980. 32.50 (ISBN 0-8230-7491-9). Watson-Guptill.

Residential Education. W. R. Fraser. LC 68-24064. 1968. 25.00 (ISBN 0-08-012909-9); pap. 12.75 (ISBN 0-08-012908-0). Pergamon.

Residential Energy Conservation. Office of Technology Assessment, Congress of the United States. LC 79-55053. 342p. 1980. text ed. 15.00 (ISBN 0-916672-38-7). Allanheld.

Residential Erosion & Sediment Control. Compiled by American Society of Civil Engineers. 64p. 1978. pap. text ed. 10.00 (ISBN 0-87262-133-2). Am Soc Civil Eng.

Residential Marinas & Yachting Amenities. Derek Head. (Marinas Ser.: No. 3). (Illus.). 84p. (Orig.). 1980. pap. text ed. 15.00 (ISBN 0-7210-1135-7, Pub. by C & CA London). Scholium Intl.

Residential Mobility & Public Policy. Ed. by W. A. V. Clark & Eric G. Moore. LC 80-12624. (Urban Affairs Annual Reviews: Vol. 19). (Illus.). 320p. 1980. 20.00 (ISBN 0-8039-1447-4); pap. 9.95 (ISBN 0-8039-1448-2). Sage.

Residential Psychiatric Treatment of Children. Ed. by Philip Barker. LC 74-7208. 354p. 1974. 33.50 (ISBN 0-470-04910-3). Halsted Pr.

Residential Real Estate Appraisal: An Introduction to Real Estate Appraising. George H. Miller & Kenneth W. Gidbeau. (Illus.). 1980. text ed. 18.95 (ISBN 0-13-774521-4). P-H.

Residential Real Estate Practice. F. Peter Wigginton. LC 78-832. 1978. text ed. 18.95 (ISBN 0-672-97102-X). Bobbs.

Residential Roof Framing. Alonzo Wass & Saunders. (Illus.). 268p. 1980. text ed. 16.95 (ISBN 0-8359-6655-0). Reston.

Residential Storm Water Management. Compiled by American Society of Civil Engineers. 64p. 1976. pap. text ed. 7.50 (ISBN 0-87262-160-X). Am Soc Civil Eng.

Residential Streets. Compiled by American Society of Civil Engineers. 48p. 1974. pap. text ed. 7.50 (ISBN 0-87262-159-6). Am Soc Civil Eng.

Residential Treatment of Emotionally Disturbed Children. Ed. by George H. Weber & Bernard J. Haberlein. LC 78-189948. (Child Care Ser). 350p. 1973. text ed. 24.95 (ISBN 0-87705-067-8). Human Sci Pr.

Residential Wiring. Rex Miller. (Illus.). 300p. 1981. text ed. 10.64 (ISBN 0-87002-331-4); price not set student guide (ISBN 0-87002-332-2). Bennett IL.

Residential Work with the Elderly. C. Brearley. (Library of Social Work Ser.). 1977. 13.50x (ISBN 0-7100-8587-7); pap. 7.95 (ISBN 0-7100-8588-5). Routledge & Kegan.

Residential Zoning & Equal Housing Opportunities: A Case Study in Black Jack, Missouri. Ronald F. Kirby et al. 34p. 1972. pap. 2.00 o.p. (ISBN 0-87766-075-1, 19000). Urban Inst.

Residuation Theory. T. S. Blyth & M. F. Janowitz. LC 77-142177. 380p. 1972. text ed. 60.00 (ISBN 0-08-016408-0). Pergamon.

Residue Reviews, Vol. 74. (Illus.). 150p. 1980. 26.80 (ISBN 0-387-90503-0). Springer-Verlag.

Residue Reviews, Vol. 75. Ed. by F. A. Gunther. (Illus.). 189p. 1981. 29.80 (ISBN 0-387-90534-0). Springer-Verlag.

Residue Reviews, Vol. 76. Ed. by F. A. Gunther. (Illus.). 218p. 1981. 29.80 (ISBN 0-387-90535-9). Springer-Verlag.

Residue Reviews, Vol. 79. Ed. by F. A. Gunther. (Illus.). 280p. 1981. 39.80 (ISBN 0-387-90539-1). Springer-Verlag.

Residues of Carbofuran Applied As a Systematic Insecticide in Irrigated Wetland Rice: Implications for Insect Control. (IRRI Research Paper Ser.: No. 17). 28p. 1978. pap. 5.00 (R057, IRRI). Unipub.

Resignation of Nixon: A Discredited President Gives up the Highest Office. Ed. by Robin McKown. LC 75-8538. (Focus Bks). (Illus.). 72p. (gr. 7 up). 1975. PLB 6.45 (ISBN 0-531-01092-9). Watts.

Resins for Aerospace. Ed. by Clayton A. May. LC 80-15342. (ACS Symposium Ser.: No. 132). 1980. 48.00 (ISBN 0-8412-0567-1). Am Chemical.

Resistance. R. Miller. (World War II Ser.). (Illus.). 1979. lib. bdg. 14.94 (ISBN 0-8094-2523-8); kivar bdg. 9.93 (ISBN 0-8094-2524-6). Silver.

Resistance & Caribbean Literature. Selwyn R. Cudjoe. LC 76-25616. xii, 319p. 1981. 16.95x (ISBN 0-8214-0353-2); pap. 8.95x (ISBN 0-8214-0573-X). Ohio U Pr.

Resistance & Deformation of Solid Media. Daniel Rosenthal. LC 72-10583. 372p. 1975. text ed. 23.00 (ISBN 0-08-017100-1). Pergamon.

Resistance & Revolution in China: The Communists & the Second United Front. Tetsuya Kataoka. LC 73-84386. (Illus.). 1974. 25.00x (ISBN 0-520-02553-9). U of Cal Pr.

Resistance in Vichy France. H. R. Kedward. (Illus.). 1978. 29.95x (ISBN 0-19-822529-6). Oxford U Pr.

Resistance of Pseudomonas Aeruginosa. M. Brown. 335p. 1975. 60.50 (ISBN 0-471-11210-0). Wiley.

Resistance of Pseudomonas Aeruginosa. R. W. Brown. LC 74-30224. 335p. 1975. 60.50 o.p. (ISBN 0-471-11210-0, Pub. by Wiley-Interscience). Wiley.

Resistances & Interventions. Robert Langs. LC 80-69667. 460p. 1981. 30.00 (ISBN 0-87668-433-9). Aronson.

Resisted Revolution: Urban America & the Industrialization of Agriculture, 1900-1930. David B. Danbom. 1979. text ed. 10.95 (ISBN 0-8138-0945-2). Iowa St U Pr.

Resisting Reader: A Feminist Approach to American Fiction. Judith Fetterley. LC 78-3242. 224p. 1978. 12.50x (ISBN 0-253-31078-4). Ind U Pr.

Resoluciones De la Junta De Personal De Puerto Rico, Vols. 1, 3 & 4. Compiled by Irma Garcia de Serrano. (Illus., Sp.). 1980. Set. write for info. (ISBN 0-8477-2218-X). Vol. I (ISBN 0-8477-2221-X). Vol. II (ISBN 0-8477-2223-6). Vol. III. Vol. IV (ISBN 0-8477-2224-4). U of PR Pr.

Resolutions & Decisions of the Communist Party of the Soviet Union: 1898-1964, 4 vols. Ed. by Robert H. McNeal. Incl. Vol. 1. Russian Social Democratic Labour Party, 1898-October 1917. Ed. by Ralph C. Elwood; Vol. 2. Early Soviet Period, 1917-1929. Ed. by Richard Gregor; Vol. 3. Stalin Years, 1929-1953. Ed. by Robert H. McNeil; Vol. 4. Khrushchev Years, 1953-1964. Ed. by Grey Hodnett. LC 74-81931. 1974. Set. 95.00x (ISBN 0-8020-2157-3); 25.00 ea. U of Toronto Pr.

Resolves, a Duple Century. 3rd ed. Owen Feltham. LC 74-28853. (English Experience Ser.: No. 734). 1975. Repr. of 1628 ed. 35.00 (ISBN 90-221-0734-5). Walter J Johnson.

Resolving Church Conflicts: A Case Study Approach for Local Congregations. Douglass Lewis. LC 80-8347. 192p. (Orig.). 1981. pap. 6.95 (ISBN 0-06-065244-6, HarpR). Har-Row.

Resolving Classroom Conflict. Craig Pearson. LC 74-16805. (Learning Handbooks Ser.). 1974. pap. 3.95 (ISBN 0-8224-1910-6). Pitman Learning.

Resolving Nationality Conflicts: The Role of Public Opinion Research. Ed. by W. Phillips Davison & Leon Gordenker. LC 80-15128. 245p. 1980. 23.95 (ISBN 0-03-056229-5). Praeger.

Resolving the Housing Crisis. Ed. by M. Bruce Johnson. (Pacific Institute on Public Policy Research Ser.). 1981. price not set professional reference (ISBN 0-88410-381-1). Ballinger Pub.

Resolving Treatment Impasses. Saretsky. 1981. 19.95x (ISBN 0-87705-088-0). Human Sci Pr.

Resortes. Harlan Wade. Tr. by Mamie M. Contreras from Eng. LC 78-26852. (Book About Ser.). Orig. Title: Springs. (Illus., Sp.). (gr. k-3). 1979. PLB 7.30 (ISBN 0-8172-1480-1). Raintree Pubs.

Resorts. Harlan Wade. Tr. by Claude Potvin & Rose-Ella Potvin. (Book About Ser.). Orig. Title: Springs. (Illus., Fr.). (gr. k-3). 1979. PLB 7.30 (ISBN 0-8172-1455-0). Raintree Pubs.

Resource Allocation & Cost Benefit Analysis. R. Thomas. (Studies in the British Economy). Date not set. pap. text ed. write for info. (ISBN 0-435-84561-6). Heinemann Ed.

Resource Based Learning in Post-Compulsory Education. Pat Noble. 200p. 1980. 25.00x (ISBN 0-89397-091-3). Nichols Pub.

Resource Book for Teaching Reading in the Content Areas. Pauline Hodges. 96p. 1980. pap. text ed. 6.95 (ISBN 0-8403-2263-1). Kendall-Hunt.

Resource Book for the Kindergarten Teacher. Walter B. Barbe. (Illus.). 1980. 34.95 (ISBN 0-88309-103-8). Zaner-Bloser.

Resource Book for the Teaching of Astronomy & Instructor's Manual for Ivan King's Text, "The Universe Unfolding". Andrew Fraknoi. 1977. pap. text ed. 6.95x (ISBN 0-7167-0288-6). W H Freeman.

Resource Book on Aging. Ed. by M. A. Suseelan. 112p. (Orig.). 1981. pap. 8.95 (ISBN 0-8298-0447-1). Pilgrim NY.

Resource Conservation & Recovery Act: A Compliance Analysis. Ed. by Thomas F. Sullivan. LC 78-78342. 162p. 1978. pap. text ed. 22.50 (ISBN 0-86587-077-2). Gov Insts.

Resource Directory on Rural America. Ed. by Donald A. Gall. 51p. (Orig.). 1981. pap. 4.95 (ISBN 0-8298-0446-3). Pilgrim NY.

Resource Guide for Adult Religious Education. rev. 2nd ed. Ed. by Clarence Thomson. 208p. soft cover, perfect bdg. 9.95 (ISBN 0-934134-10-3). Natl Cath Reporter.

Resource Guide for Mainstreaming. E. Haglund & V. L. Stevens. (Illus.). 192p. 1980. 14.75 (ISBN 0-398-04003-6). C C Thomas.

Resource Management & Environmental Uncertainty: Lessons from Coastal Upwelling Fisheries. Ed. by Micheal H. Glantz & J. Dana Thompson. LC 80-16645. (Advances in Environmental Science & Technology Ser.). 550p. 36.50 (ISBN 0-471-05984-6, Pub. by Wiley-Interscience). Wiley.

Resource Manual for a Living Revolution. Virginia Coover et al. 351p. 1977. pap. 5.00 (ISBN 0-86571-008-2). Movement New Soc.

Resource Materials. Ed. by Thomas A. McClure & Deward S. Lipinsky. (Handbook of Biosolar Resources Ser.: Vol. 2). 560p. 1981. 69.95 (ISBN 0-8493-3473-X). CRC Pr.

Resource Materials: Domsetic Taxation of Hard Minerals. 254p. 1980. pap. 30.00 (T159). ALI-ABA.

Resource Recovery & Recycling. A. F. Barton. LC 78-13601. (Environmental Science & Technology Ser.). 1979. 32.00 (ISBN 0-471-02773-1, Pub. by Wiley-Interscience). Wiley.

Resource Recovery from Municipal Solid Wastes: Mineral Resources & the Environment Supplementary Report. Committee on Mineral Resources & the Environment, National Research Council. 432p. 1975. pap. 9.25 (ISBN 0-309-02422-6). Natl Acad Pr.

Resource Recovery Planning & Management. Gillean Robert Clark. 1981. text ed. 24.00 (ISBN 0-250-40298-X). Ann Arbor Science.

Resource Room: An Educational Asset for Children with Special Needs. Margaret F. Hawisher & Mary L. Calhoun. (Special Education Ser.). 1978. pap. text ed. 9.95x (ISBN 0-675-08354-0); instructor's manual 3.95 (ISBN 0-686-67987-3). Merrill.

Resource Sharing of Libraries in Developing Countries. Ed. by H. D. Vervliet. (IFLA Publications: No. 14). 286p. 1979. 19.00 (ISBN 0-89664-114-7, Pub. by K G Saur). Shoe String.

Resource Structure of Agriculture: An Economic Analysis. K. Cowling et al. LC 70-114570. 1970. 23.00 (ISBN 0-08-015585-5). Pergamon.

Resource Teacher: A Guide to Effective Practices. J. Lee Wiederholt et al. 1978. pap. text ed. 10.95 (ISBN 0-205-05970-8); ring binder 29.95 (ISBN 0-205-05971-6). Allyn.

Resource Teaching: A Mainstreaming Simulation. Sandra B. Cohen. 1978. pap. text ed. 4.95 (ISBN 0-675-08351-6); 125.00, 4 cassettes 4 filmstrips (ISBN 0-675-08444-X); 2-5 sets 75.00, 6 or more sets 60.00 (ISBN 0-686-67988-1). cards 3.95 (ISBN 0-686-67990-3). Merrill.

Resourceful Alternatives: Teaching Through Media. Pamela Hanson. 1981. pap. write for info. (ISBN 0-914562-07-X). Merriam Eddy.

Resources & Development in the Indian Ocean Region. Ed. by Alex Kerr. 256p. 1981. lib. bdg. 26.50x (ISBN 0-86531-123-4). Westview.

Resources & Development: Natural Resource Policies & Economic Development in an Interdependent World. Ed. by Peter Dorner & Mahmoud A. El-Shafie. 516p. 1980. 20.00 (ISBN 0-299-08250-4). U of Wis Pr.

Resources, Environment & Economics: Applications of the Materials-Energy Balance Principle. Robert U. Ayres. LC 77-20049. 1978. 34.00 (ISBN 0-471-02627-1, Pub. by Wiley-Interscience). Wiley.

Resources: For Child Placement & Other Human Services. Armand Lauffer. LC 78-26352. (Sage Human Service Guides: Vol. 6). 1979. pap. 8.00x (ISBN 0-8039-1218-8). Sage.

Resources for Christian Leaders. rev. ed. 1980. pap. 3.00 (ISBN 0-912552-16-6). MARC.

Resources for Education. John Sheehan & John Valzey. 1974. pap. text ed. 9.50x (ISBN 0-04-370022-5). Allen Unwin.

Resources for Educational Research & Development. Vernon Ward. (Research Reports). 160p. 1973. pap. text ed. 14.50x (ISBN 0-85633-026-4, NFER). Humanities.

Resources for South Asian Area Studies in the United States. Ed. by Richard D. Lambert. LC 62-11263. 1962. 9.00x o.p. (ISBN 0-8122-7362-1). U of Pa Pr.

Resources for Writing for Publication in Education. Sidney B. Katz et al. 1980. pap. text ed. 6.50x (ISBN 0-8077-2579-X). Tchrs Coll.

Resources in Bilingual Education: A Preliminary Guide to Government Agency Programs of Interest to Minority Language Groups. National Clearinghouse for Bilingual Education. 1978. pap. 3.50 o.p. (ISBN 0-89763-010-6). Natl Clearinghse Bilingual Ed.

Resources of American Music History: A Directory of Source Materials from Colonial Times to World War II. Ed. by D. W. Krummel et al. LC 80-14873. (Music in American Life Ser.). 500p. 1981. lib. bdg. 44.95 (ISBN 0-252-00828-6). U of Ill Pr.

Resources of Kind: Genre-Theory in the Renaissance. Rosalie Colie. 1974. 15.00x (ISBN 0-520-02397-8). U of Cal Pr.

Resources of New Mexico. The Territorial Bureau of Immigration. LC 73-80703. 76p. 1973. Repr. of 1881 ed. 9.50 (ISBN 0-88307-504-0); pap. 1.25 (ISBN 0-88307-503-2). Gannon.

Respect for Acting. Uta Hagen & Haskel Frankel. LC 72-2328. 256p. 1973. 9.95 (ISBN 0-02-547390-5). Macmillan.

Respect for Life: The Traditional Upbringing of American Indian Children. Ed. by Sylvester M. Morey & Olivia L. Gilliam. LC 80-83371. (Illus.). 202p. 1980. pap. text ed. 4.95 (ISBN 0-913098-34-5). Myrin Institute.

Respectable Army: The War for Independence & America's Military Origins, 1763-1783. James K. Martin & Mark Lender. LC 77-86040. (American History Ser.). Date not set. pap. 4.95 (ISBN 0-88295-775-9). AHM Pub.

Respectable Minority: The Democratic Party in the Civil War Era, 1860-1868. Joel H. Silbey. 1977. 12.95 (ISBN 0-393-05648-1); pap. 4.95x (ISBN 0-393-09087-6). Norton.

Respecting Children: Social Work with Young People. Margaret Crompton. LC 80-5820. (Illus.). 246p. 1980. 20.00 (ISBN 0-8039-1544-6); pap. 9.95 (ISBN 0-8039-1545-4). Sage.

Respective Roles of State & Local Governments in Land Policy & Taxation. Ed. by George Lefcoe. (Lincoln Institute Monograph: No. 80-7). 271p. 1980. write for info. Lincoln Inst Land.

Respiration: Proceedings of the 28th International Congress of Physiological Sciences, Budapest 1980. Ed. by I. Hutas & L. A. Debreczeni. (Advances in Physiological Sciences: Vol. 10). (Illus.). 665p. 1981. 70.00 (ISBN 0-08-026823-4). Pergamon.

Respirators & Protective Clothing. E. C. Hyatt & J. M. White. (Safety Ser.: No. 22). 1967. pap. 5.00 (ISBN 92-0-123367-1, IAEA). Unipub.

Respiratory Allergy. Ed. by G. Melillo et al. 214p. 26.50. Masson Pub.

Respiratory Care. H. H. Bendixen et al. LC 65-27642. (Illus.). 1965. 22.50 o.p. (ISBN 0-8016-0605-5). Mosby.

Respiratory Care Case Studies, Vol. 1. 2nd ed. Thomas J. DeKornfeld & Jay S. Finch. 1976. spiral bdg. 12.75 (ISBN 0-87488-019-X). Med Exam.

Respiratory Diseases. 3rd ed. John Crofton & Andrew Douglas. (Illus.). 912p. 1980. 85.00 (ISBN 0-632-00577-7, Blackwell). Mosby.

Respiratory Dysfunction in Neurologic Disease. Ed. by William J. Weiner. LC 80-68262. (Illus.). 344p. 1980. monograph 32.50 (ISBN 0-87993-152-3). Futura Pub.

Respiratory Emergencies. Elaine Shibel & Kenneth M. Moser. LC 77-8139. (Illus.). 1977. pap. text ed. 24.50 (ISBN 0-8016-4583-2). Mosby.

Respiratory Function of the Lung & Its Control. Fred S. Grodins & Stanley M. Yamashiro. (Illus.). 1978. text ed. 13.50 (ISBN 0-02-348190-0); pap. text ed. 9.95 (ISBN 0-02-348120-X). Macmillan.

Respiratory Intensive Care Nursing. 2nd ed. Beth Israel Hospital, Boston. 1979. spiral bdg. 12.95 (ISBN 0-316-09237-1). Little.

Respiratory Nursing Continuing Education Review. Marilyn K. Chrisman. 1976. spiral bdg. 9.50 (ISBN 0-87488-396-2). Med Exam.

Respiratory Pharmacology, 3 vols. Ed. by J. G. Widdicombe. (International Encyclopedia of Pharmacology & Therapeutics: Section 104). Date not set. Set. 135.00 (ISBN 0-08-022673-6). Pergamon.

Respiratory Physical Therapy & Pulmonary Care. Ulla Ingwersen. LC 76-27094. 1976. 20.95 (ISBN 0-471-02473-2, Pub. by Wiley Medical). Wiley.

Respiratory Physiology. Allan Mines. (Raven Press Ser. in Physiology). 180p. 1981. 12.50 (ISBN 0-89004-634-4). Raven.

Respiratory System, Vol. 7. Illus. by Frank Netter. (Medical Illustrations Ser.). (Illus.). 1979. 47.00x (ISBN 0-914168-09-6). C I B A Pharm.

Respiratory System Basic Sciences. Thomas P. Lim. 1972. spiral bdg. 7.00 o.p. (ISBN 0-87488-213-3). Med Exam.

Respiratory System: Disease, Diagnosis, Treatment. H. S. Zarren. (Clinical Monographs Ser.). (Illus.). 1973. pap. 7.95 (ISBN 0-87618-056-X). R J Brady.

Respiratory Therapist Manual. Stanley Pincus. LC 74-79838. (Allied Health Ser). 1975. pap. 7.05 (ISBN 0-672-61389-1). Bobbs.

Respiratory Therapy: Basics for Nursing & Allied Health Professions. Dennis W. Glover & Margaret M. Glover. LC 78-6500. (Illus.). 1978. pap. 10.50 (ISBN 0-8016-1863-0). Mosby.

Respiratory Therapy Equipment. 2nd ed. Steven P. McPherson. (Illus.). 514p. 1980. text ed. 24.95 (ISBN 0-8016-3313-3). Mosby.

Respiratory Therapy Examination Review Book, Vol. 1. 3rd ed. Vincent D. Kracum. 1975. spiral bdg. 9.50 (ISBN 0-87488-471-3). Med Exam.

Respiratory Therapy Examination Review Book, Vol. 2. 2nd ed. Thomas J. Dekornfeld et al. Orig. Title: Inhalation Therapy Examination Review Book, Vol. 2. 1974. spiral bdg. 9.50 (ISBN 0-87488-344-X). Med Exam.

Respiratory Therapy in Critical Care. Hugh S. Mathewson. LC 76-13633. (Illus., Orig.). 1976. pap. 10.00 (ISBN 0-8016-3158-0). Mosby.

Respiratory Tract Fluid. Eldon M. Boyd. (Illus.). 336p. 1972. 29.75 (ISBN 0-398-02239-9). C C Thomas.

Responding to Casualties of Ships Bearing Hazardous Cargoes. Marine Board. 1979. pap. 8.25 (ISBN 0-309-02935-X). Natl Acad Pr.

Responding to Drinking Problems. Stan Shaw et al. 272p. 1980. 40.00x (ISBN 0-85664-525-7, Pub. by Croom Helm England). State Mutual Bk.

Responding to the Terrorist Threat: Security & Crisis Management. Ed. by Richard H. Shultz, Jr. & Stephen Sloan. (Policy Studies). 1981. 27.50 (ISBN 0-08-025106-4). Pergamon.

Response to Meprobamate-A Predictive Analysis. J. R. Wittenborn. LC 70-107228. 1970. 13.50 (ISBN 0-911216-11-1). Raven.

Responses of Fish to Environmental Changes. Walter Chavin. (Illus.). 472p. 1973. text ed. 36.75 (ISBN 0-398-02743-9). C C Thomas.

Responses of the Presidents to Charges of Misconduct. C. Vann Woodward. 1974. 10.00 o.p. (ISBN 0-440-05923-2). Delacorte.

Responses to Children's Literature: Proceedings. Fourth Symposium of the International Research Society for Children's Literature, Held at the University of Exeter, September 9-12, 1978 & Geoff Fox. 150p. 1980. text ed. 17.80 (ISBN 0-89664-949-0). K G Saur.

Responses to Crime: An Introduction to Swedish Criminal Law & Administration. Alvar Nelson. Tr. by Jerome L. Getz from Swedish. (New York University Criminal Law Education & Research Center Monograph: No. 6). vi, 90p. 1972. pap. text ed. 8.50x (ISBN 0-8377-0900-8). Rothman.

Responsibilities to Future Generations: Environmental Ethics. Ed. by Ernest Partridge. 275p. (Orig.). 1981. 17.95 (ISBN 0-87975-153-3); pap. text ed. 8.95 (ISBN 0-87975-142-8). Prometheus Bks.

Responsibility. Jonathan Glover. (International Library of Philosophy and Scientific Method). 1970. text ed. 23.25x (ISBN 0-391-00097-7). Humanities.

Responsibility & Culture. L. P. Jacks. 1924. 19.50x (ISBN 0-685-89778-8). Elliots Bks.

Responsibility & Liability of Public & Private Interests on Dams. Compiled by American Society of Civil Engineers. 216p. 1976. pap. text ed. 12.00 (ISBN 0-87262-167-7). Am Soc Civil Eng.

Responsibility for Evil in the Theodicy of IV Ezra. Alden Thompson. LC 76-40915. (Society of Biblical Literature. Dissertation Ser.). 1977. pap. 9.00 (ISBN 0-89130-091-0, 060129). Scholars Pr Ca.

Responsibility in Business: Issues & Problems. Blair J. Kolasa. LC 72-170645. 1972. pap. text ed. 9.95 (ISBN 0-13-773739-4). P-H.

Responsibility in Mass Communication. 3rd ed. William L. Rivers et al. LC 79-3400. 320p. 1980. 14.95 (ISBN 0-06-013594-8, HarpT). Har-Row.

Responsibility in Mental Disease. Henry Maudsley. Bd. with Treatise on Insanity. (Contributions to the History of Psychology Ser., Vol. III, Pt. C: Medical Psychology). 1978. Repr. of 1876 ed. 30.00 (ISBN 0-89093-167-4). U Pubns Amer.

Responsibility: Selected Readings. Joel Feinberg & Hyman Gross. 1975. pap. text ed. 9.95x (ISBN 0-8221-0171-8). Dickenson.

Responsible & Effective Communication. Wayne N. Thompson. LC 77-77006. (Illus.). 1978. text ed. 13.50 (ISBN 0-395-25075-7); inst. manual 0.55 (ISBN 0-395-25076-5). HM.

Responsible God: A Study of the Christian Philosophy of H. Richard Niebuhr. Donald E. Fadner. LC 75-29373. (American Academy of Religion. Dissertation Ser.). 1975. pap. 7.50 (ISBN 0-89130-041-4, 010113). Scholars Pr Ca.

Responsible Government in Ontario. Fred F. Schindeler. LC 70-390334. 1969. pap. 6.00 (ISBN 0-8020-6189-3). U of Toronto Pr.

Responsible Society. Stephen B. Roman & Eugen Loebl. LC 77-9155. 1978. 6.95 (ISBN 0-8467-0360-2, Pub. by Two Continents). Hippocrene Bks.

Responsive Arts. Judy Nagle. 1980. pap. 15.95 (ISBN 0-88284-101-7). Alfred Pub.

Responsive Capitalism: Case Studies in Corporate Social Conduct. Earl A. Molander. (Management Ser.). (Illus.). 432p. 1980. text ed. 10.00x (ISBN 0-07-042658-9, C); pap. text ed. 5.95 (ISBN 0-07-042659-7); instructor's manual 4.95 (ISBN 0-07-042659-7). McGraw.

Responsive Chord. Tony Schwartz. LC 73-81420. 192p. 1974. pap. 2.95 (ISBN 0-385-08895-7, Anch). Doubleday.

Responsive Curriculum Development: Theory & Action. Glenys G. Unruh. LC 74-24476. (Illus.). 250p. 1975. 17.50x (ISBN 0-8211-2002-6); text ed. 15.75x (ISBN 0-685-51462-5). McCutchan.

Respublica Lacedaemoniorum Ascribed to Xenophon. K. M. T. Chrimes. 119p. 1948. 24.00x (ISBN 0-7190-1207-4, Pub. by Manchester U Pr England). State Mutual Bk.

Respuesta a la Alabanza. Tr. by David Wilkerson. (Spanish Bks.). (Span.). 1979. 1.80 (ISBN 0-8297-0446-9). Life Pubs Intl.

Ressurection of Life. John Brown. 1978. 13.25 (ISBN 0-686-12962-8). Klock & Klock.

Rest & Be Thankful. Helen MacInnes. 1978. pap. 2.25 (ISBN 0-449-23621-8, Crest). Fawcett.

Rest Days, the Christian Sunday, the Jewish Sabbath & Their Historical & Anthropological Prototypes. Hutton Webster. LC 68-58165. 1968. Repr. of 1916 ed. 24.00 (ISBN 0-8103-3342-2). Gale.

Rest Is Silence & Other Stories. Warren Beck. LC 63-12585. 132p. (Orig.). 1963. pap. 3.95 (ISBN 0-8040-0261-4, 46). Swallow.

Rest of the Week. Kenneth J. Roberts. LC 73-87984. 1975. pap. 2.95 (ISBN 0-87973-549-X). Our Sunday Visitor.

Rest Principle: A Neurophysiological Theory of Behavior. John D. Sinclair. LC 80-17396. 240p. 1981. text ed. 16.50 (ISBN 0-89859-065-5). L Erlbaum Assocs.

Restaining the Wicked: The Incapacitation of the Dangerous Criminal. Stephen VanDine et al. (Illus.). 1979. 15.95 (ISBN 0-669-01774-4). Lexington Bks.

Restaurant & Food Store Surveys, 1979: Evaluating the Potential for a Small Business Information System in Wisconsin. William A. Strang. (Wisconsin Economy Studies: No. 18). (Orig.). 1979. pap. 5.00 (ISBN 0-86603-007-7). Bureau Busn Res U Wis.

Restaurant & Food Store Surveys 1979: Evaluating the Potential for a Small Business Information System in Wisconsin: Evaluating the Potential for a Small Business Information System in Wisconsin. William A. Strang. (Wisconsin Economy Studies: No. 18). (Illus.). 101p. 1979. 5.00 (ISBN 0-86603-007-7). U Wis Grad Sch Bush.

Restaurants (Architecture) G. Aloi. (Illus.). 1972. 50.00 (ISBN 0-685-25486-0). Heinman.

Restitution in Criminal Justice: A Critical Assessment of Sanctions. Ed. by Joe Hudson & Burt Galaway. LC 76-43614. 1977. 18.95 (ISBN 0-669-00991-1). Lexington Bks.

Restitution of Decayed Intelligence: In Antiquities, Concerning the...English Nation. by the Studie & Travaile of R. Verstagen. Dedicated Unto the Kings Most Excellent Majestie. Richard Rowlands. LC 79-84134. (English Experience Ser.: No. 952). 380p. 1979. Repr. of 1605 ed. lib. bdg. 35.00 (ISBN 90-221-0952-6). Walter J Johnson.

Restless Caribbean: Changing Patterns of International Relations. Ed. by Richard Millett & W. Marvin Will. LC 78-19764. 1979. 24.95 (ISBN 0-03-041806-2). Praeger.

Restless Centuries: Student Study Guide. Kenneth R. Bain & James L. Gormly. (Orig.). 1979. pap. 4.25 (ISBN 0-8087-4029-6). Burgess.

Restless Frontier. Duncan MacNeil. 1980. 8.95 (ISBN 0-312-67782-0). St Martin.

Restless House. Emile Zola. 1971. 13.95 (ISBN 0-236-30967-6, Pub. by Paul Elek). Merrimack Bk Serv.

Restless River. Jerry E. Mueller. LC 74-80107. 1975. 8.00 o.p. (ISBN 0-87404-050-7); pap. 5.00 o.p. (ISBN 0-685-56283-2). Tex Western.

Restless Spirit: The Story of Robert Frost. Natalie S. Bober. LC 80-23930. (Illus.). 224p. (gr. 6 up). 1981. PLB 10.95 (ISBN 0-689-30801-9). Atheneum.

Restless Universe: An Introduction to Astronomy. Harry L. Shipman. LC 77-78584. (Illus.). 1978. text ed. 20.50 (ISBN 0-395-25392-6); inst. manual 0.45 (ISBN 0-395-25393-4). HM.

Restless Wanderers: Shakespeare & the Pattern of Romance. John Dean. (Orig.). 1979. text ed. 25.00x (ISBN 0-391-01708-X). Humanities.

Reston Home Owners Association: A Case Study in New Community Management. Karl J. Ingebritsen. Ed. by Dianne Ader-Brin. 1977. pap. text ed. 11.50 (ISBN 0-912104-26-0). Inst Real Estate.

Restoration Adaptations. Ed. by Edward A. Langhans. LC 78-66611. (Eighteenth Century English Drama Ser.). 1980. lib. bdg. 50.00 (ISBN 0-8240-3575-5). Garland Pub.

Restoration & Eighteenth Century Drama. Intro. by Arthur Scouten. 160p. 1981. pap. 5.95 (ISBN 0-312-67787-1). St Martin.

Restoration & Eighteenth-Century Poetry 1660-1780. Eric Rothstein. (Routledge Histort of English Poetry Ser.). 350p. 1981. price not set (ISBN 0-7100-0660-8). Routledge & Kegan.

Restoration Comedies. Ed. by Dennis Davison. (Oxford Paperbacks Ser). 1970. pap. 5.95x (ISBN 0-19-281063-4). Oxford U Pr.

Restoration England, 1660-1689. William L. Sachse. (Conference on British Studies, Bibliographical Handbks). 1971. 17.50 (ISBN 0-521-08171-8). Cambridge U Pr.

Restoration Literature: Poetry & Prose, 1660-1700. Cecil A. Moore. 1981. 38.50x (ISBN 0-89197-383-4); pap. text ed. 18.50x (ISBN 0-89197-919-0). Irvington.

Restoration of the Han Dynasty, 2 vols. in 1. Hans Bielenstein. (Perspectives in Asian History Ser.: No. 8). 161p. Repr. of 1954 ed. lib. bdg. 37.50x (ISBN 0-87991-479-3). Porcupine Pr.

Restoration of the Land. A. D. Bradshaw & M. J. Chadwick. (Blackwell Ecology Ser.: Vol. 6). 1980. 27.50 (ISBN 0-520-03961-0). U of Cal Pr.

Restoration of the 'Nereid Monument' at Xanthos. Carla Gottlieb. (Illus.). 340p. 1980. 30.00 (ISBN 0-9604420-0-6); pap. 25.00 (ISBN 0-686-28889-0). Boian Bks.

Restoration of the Smack Emma C. Berry. Willits D. Ansel. LC 72-95937. (Illus.). 94p. 1973. pap. 7.00 (ISBN 0-913372-08-0). Mystic Seaport.

Restoration: Our Philosophy Through Inspired Poems. Ed. by Rosa M. Williams. LC 79-66586. 1980. 6.50x (ISBN 0-9602366-1-9); pap. 4.50x (ISBN 0-686-65878-7). Sooty-Face.

Restoration Plays. Ed. by Edmund Gosse. 1953. 6.00x (ISBN 0-460-00604-5, Evman); pap. 4.95 (ISBN 0-460-01604-0). Dutton.

Restoration Promptbooks. Edward A. Langhans. LC 80-15626. 704p. 1981. price not set (ISBN 0-8093-0855-X). S Ill U Pr.

Restoration Studies, Nineteen Eighty. Ed. by Maurice L. Draper. 1980. pap. 12.00 (ISBN 0-8309-0292-9). Herald Hse.

Restorative Dental Materials. 6th ed. Robert G. Craig. LC 80-12105. (Illus.). 1980. pap. text ed. 23.95 (ISBN 0-8016-3866-6). Mosby.

Restorative Nursing in a General Hospital. H. Ruth Schickedanz & Pamela D. Mayhall. (Illus.). 232p. 1975. 19.75 (ISBN 0-398-03312-9); pap. 14.75 (ISBN 0-398-03313-7). C C Thomas.

Restorative Techniques for Individual Teeth. Ed. by Lloyd Baum. LC 80-81989. (Masson Monographs in Dentistry: Vol. 2). (Illus.). 224p. 1980. 29.50 (ISBN 0-89352-113-2). Masson Pub.

Restored: Anthology. 152p. 1979. pap. 3.95 (ISBN 0-930756-34-7, 4230-RE). Women's Aglow.

Restoree. Anne McCaffrey. (Del Rey Bk.). 1977. pap. 2.25 o.p. (ISBN 0-345-29179-4, 345-25744-8-150). Ballantine.

Restoring Furniture. Kenneth Davis & Thom Henvey. LC 77-11401. (Illus.). 1978. 16.95 o.p. (ISBN 0-668-04545-0, 4545). Arco.

Restoring Old Houses. Nigel Hutchins. 240p. 1980. 29.95 (ISBN 0-442-29625-8). Van Nos Reinhold.

Restoring Shakespeare: A Critical Analysis of the Misreadings in Shakespeare's Works. Leon Kellner. LC 78-77027. (Illus.). 1969. Repr. of 1925 ed. 9.50x (ISBN 0-8196-0244-2). Biblo.

Restoring the American Dream. Ringer. 1981. pap. 2.95 (ISBN 0-449-24314-1). Fawcett.

Restoring the Victorian House. John Bracken & Linda Stone. (Illus.). 192p. 1981. pap. 8.95 (ISBN 0-87701-222-9). Chronicle Bks.

Restoring Vintage Boats. John Lewis. LC 75-4329. (Illus.). 192p. 1975. 22.50 (ISBN 0-87742-054-8). Intl Marine.

Restraints on War: Studies in the Limitation of Armed Conflict. Ed. by Michael Howard. 1979. 24.00x (ISBN 0-19-822545-8). Oxford U Pr.

Restricting Handguns: The Liberal Sceptics Speak Out. Dan B. Kates. 9.95 (ISBN 0-88427-033-5). Green Hill.

Restrictions on Business Mobility: Political Rhetoric & Economic Reality. Richared B. McKenzie. 1979. pap. 4.25 (ISBN 0-8447-3338-5). Am Enterprise.

Restructuring Federal Medicaid Controls & Incentives. John Holahan et al. (Medicaid Cost Containment Ser.). 96p. 1977. pap. 2.00 (ISBN 0-87766-198-7, 18100). Urban Inst.

Restructuring of Social & Political Theory. Richard J. Bernstein. LC 76-12544. 1978. pap. 7.95x (ISBN 0-8122-7742-2). U of Pa Pr.

Restyling Your Wardrobe. Ed. by Time Life Books. LC 76-37283. (Art of Sewing). (Illus.). (gr. 6 up). 1976. 11.97 (ISBN 0-8094-1767-7, Pub. by Time-Life). Silver.

Resultances: Poems by Frank Manley. Frank Manley. LC 80-14241. 64p. 1981. text ed. 10.00x (ISBN 0-8262-0312-4). U of Mo Pr.

Results from Norwegian Antartic Research, Nineteen Seventy Four to Nineteen Seventy Seven. Tore Gjelsvik. (Norsk Polarinstitutt Skrifter: Vol. 169). (Illus.). 117p. 1980. pap. text ed. 7.50x (ISBN 82-90307-03-9). Universitet.

Results in Neurochemistry, Neuroendocrinology, Neurophysiology & Behavior, Neuropharmacology, Neuropathology, Cybernetics. Lissak. 1976. 19.50 (ISBN 0-9960007-2-0, Pub. by Kaido Hungary). Heyden.

Results in Neuroendocrinology, Neurochemistry & Sleep Research. Ed. by K. Lissak. LC 76-379912. (Recent Developments of Neurobiology in Hungary: Vol. VII). (Illus.). 190p. 1978. 20.00x (ISBN 963-05-1587-3). Intl Pubns Serv.

Results of Treatment in Cerebral Palsy. James M. Wolf. 344p. 1969. pap. 26.25 spiral (ISBN 0-398-02104-X). C C Thomas.

Results-Oriented Management: How to Effectively Get Things Done. C. E. Watson. 1981. pap. write for info. (ISBN 0-201-08355-8). A-W.

Resume Builder. John J. Komar. 120p. 1980. pap. 4.95 (ISBN 0-695-81437-0). Follett.

Resume Manual for the Military: A Complete Job-Hunting Guide for Present & Future Veterans. Caroline S. De Prez & Richard J. De Prez. LC 80-68132. (Illus.). 177p. (Orig.). 1980. pap. 10.95 (ISBN 0-9604728-0-0). Alfa Sierra.

Resume of a Theory of Language. Louis Hjelmslev. Tr. by Francis J. Whitfield. 1976. 25.00x (ISBN 0-299-07040-9). U of Wis Pr.

Resume Writing: A Comprehensive How-to-Do-It Guide. 2nd ed. Ed. by Burdette E. Bostwick. LC 80-18100. 256p. 1980. 12.95 (ISBN 0-471-08067-5, Pub. by Wiley-Interscience). Wiley.

Resumes for Better Jobs. Stanley Strand & Edward C. Gruber. pap. 3.95 (ISBN 0-671-18708-2). Monarch Pr.

Resumes That Get Jobs. Resume Service Staff. LC 75-24504. (Orig.). 1976. lib. bdg. 7.00 (ISBN 0-668-03935-3); pap. 3.95 (ISBN 0-668-03909-4). Arco.

Resurgence of Class Conflict in Western Europe Since 1968. Ed. by Colin Crouch & Alessandro Pizzorno. 349p. 1980. pap. text ed. cancelled (ISBN 0-8419-0647-5). Holmes & Meier.

Resurgent Republicanism: The Handiwork of Hanna. Clarence A. Stern. 1963. pap. 1.25 (ISBN 0-9600116-3-3). Stern.

Resurging Plastics Pipe Industry P-043. BCC Staff. (Illus.). 1980. 750.00 (ISBN 0-89336-165-8). BCC.

Resurrection. Margoe Jane. 1976. 4.00 (ISBN 0-686-14638-7). Margoe Jane.

Resurrection According to Matthew, Mark, & Luke. Norman Perrin. LC 76-47913. 96p. (Orig.). 1977. pap. 3.50 (ISBN 0-8006-1248-5, 1-1248). Fortress.

Resurrection Factor. Josh McDowell. 180p. (Orig.). 1981. 8.95 (ISBN 0-918956-71-4, Dist. by Here's Life Publishers Inc.); pap. 4.95 (ISBN 0-918956-72-2). Campus Crusade.

Resurrection Is Not a Fairy Tale. George Nutting. 1981. 5.75 (ISBN 0-8062-1649-2). Carlton.

Resurrection Life & Power. Samuel L. Brengle. 1978. Repr. of 1925 ed. 3.25 (ISBN 0-86544-005-0). Salvation Army.

Resurrection of Christ. H. C. Moule & J. Orr. Date not set. 16.95 (ISBN 0-86524-062-0). Klock & Klock.

Resurrection of Jesus Christ. J. M. Shaw. 223p. 1920. text ed. 4.95. Attic Pr.

Resurrection of the Dead. Derek Prince. (Foundation Ser.: Bk. VI). 1965-66. pap. 1.75 (ISBN 0-934920-05-2, B-15). Derek Prince.

Resurrection of the Word. Carlo Suares. LC 74-75098. 1975. 8.95 o.p. (ISBN 0-394-49520-9). Random.

Resurrection Two. Bo Grady. 80p. 1981. 5.50 (ISBN 0-682-49698-7). Exposition.

Resuscitation & Life Support in Disasters: Relief of Pain & Suffering in Disaster Situations. Ed. by R. Frey & P. Safer. (Disaster Medicine Ser.: Vol. 2). (Illus.). 320p. 1980. pap. 49.60 (ISBN 0-387-09044-4). Springer-Verlag.

Retablos. Kieth Wilson. (Illus.). 32p. (Orig.). 1980. pap. 3.00 (ISBN 0-88235-042-0). San Marcos.

Retail Accounting & Financial Control. 4th ed. Louis C. Moscarello et al. LC 76-24550. 1976. 32.50 (ISBN 0-8260-6402-7). Ronald Pr.

Retail Advertising & Sales Promotion. Charles M. Edwards, Jr. & Carl R. Lebowitz. (Illus.). 576p. 1981. text ed. 19.95 (ISBN 0-13-775098-6); pap. 17.95 (ISBN 0-13-775080-3). P-H.

Retail Banking in the Electronic Age: The Law & Economics of Electronic Funds Transfer. William F. Baxter et al. LC 76-28594. (Illus.). 208p. 1977. text ed. 18.50 (ISBN 0-916672-06-9). Allanheld.

Retail Fast Foods, GA-038: Business Opportunities. Ed. by Business Communications Co. 1980. 675.00 (ISBN 0-89336-236-0). BCC.

Retail Floral Shop Management. H. Mitchell. 1982. text ed. 16.95 (ISBN 0-8359-6676-3); instr's. manual free (ISBN 0-8359-6677-1). Reston.

Retail Florist Business. 3rd ed. Peter B. Pfahl. LC 76-50302. (Illus.). 1977. 16.65 (ISBN 0-8134-1898-4); text ed. 12.50x (ISBN 0-685-85669-0). Interstate.

Retail Fruit Species: Your Shopper's Guide to Their Best Varieties. 2nd ed. Jordan Levenson. LC 79-369. (Illus.). 1980. pap. 9.87x (ISBN 0-914442-06-6). Levenson Pr.

Retail Geography. John A. Dawson. 175p. 1980. 29.95 (ISBN 0-470-27014-4, Pub. by Hlasted Pr). Wiley.

Retail Location & Retail Planning in Britain. Clifford M. Guy. 208p. 1980. text ed. 30.00x (ISBN 0-566-00270-1, Pub. by Gower Pub Co England). Renouf.

Retail Management. 2nd ed. R. A. Marquardt et al. LC 78-56199. 1979. text ed. 20.95 (ISBN 0-03-043686-9). Dryden Pr.

Retail Management: A Marketing Channels Approach. Roger A. Dickinson. 1974. 16.95x o.p. (ISBN 0-534-00318-4). Wadsworth Pub.

Retail Management Cases. D. L. Thompson & D. J. Dalrymple. LC 69-18525. 1969. pap. text ed. 7.95 (ISBN 0-02-932500-5). Free Pr.

Retail Marketing. Bert Rosenbloom. 470p. 1981. text ed. 20.95 (ISBN 0-394-32191-X). Random.

Retail Merchandise Management. John W. Wingate et al. LC 73-168617. (Illus.). 1972. ref. ed. 18.95 (ISBN 0-13-778753-7). P-H.

Retail Merchandising: Principles & Applications. Ralph D. Shipp. LC 75-31040. (Illus.). 352p. 1976. text ed. 17.75 (ISBN 0-395-20271-X); inst. manual 1.75 (ISBN 0-395-20270-1). HM.

Retail Revolution: Market Transformation, Investment, & Labor in the Modern Department Store. Barry Bluestone et al. LC 80-26036. (Illus.). 192p. 1980. 19.95 (ISBN 0-86569-052-9). Auburn Hse.

Retail Store Credit Card Use in New York. new ed. Robert P. Shay & William C. Dunkelberg. (Studies in Consumer Credit, No. 4). 100p. 1975. pap. 6.00x (ISBN 0-231-03964-6). Columbia U Pr.

Retail Strategy & Structure. 2nd ed. David J. Rachman. (Illus.). 496p. 1975. 18.95 (ISBN 0-13-780478-4). P-H.

Retail Trade Developments in Great Britain. 4th ed. A. Buckley & C. Swain. 1979. text ed. 82.25x (ISBN 0-566-02152-8, Pub. by Gower Pub Co England). Renouf.

Retailer's Basic Accounting Handbook: A Manual Retail Accounting System. Harry F. Landsburg et al. 80p. 1980. 15.00 (C15080). Natl Ret Merch.

Retailer's Guide to Managing Communications Expenses. Robert W. Snouffer. Date not set. cancelled (ISBN 0-686-25107-5). Telecom Lib.

Retailer's Guide to Understanding Leases. Nordahl L. Brue. 200p. 1980. 26.00 (C6580). Natl Ret Merch.

Retailing. Patrick J. O'Connor. LC 79-54049. (Marketing Distribution Ser.). 352p. 1981. pap. 9.20 (ISBN 0-8273-1777-8); instr's. guide 1.45 (ISBN 0-8273-1778-6). Delmar.

Retailing: An Economic View. D. J. Dalrymple. LC 69-11840. 1969. text ed. 12.95 (ISBN 0-02-906970-X). Free Pr.

Retailing: Challenge & Opportunity. Robert F. Hartley. 1975. text ed. 16.50 o.p. (ISBN 0-395-17073-7); instructor's manual 1.75 o.p. (ISBN 0-395-18787-7). HM.

Retailing: Challenge & Opportunity. 2nd ed. Robert F. Hartley. LC 79-88102. 1980. text ed. 18.95 (ISBN 0-395-28185-7); instructor's manual 2.00 (ISBN 0-395-28186-5). HM.

Retailing in England During the Industrial Revolution. David Alexander. 1970. text ed. 28.75x (ISBN 0-485-11116-0, Athlone Pr). Humanities.

Retailing Management. 4th ed. W. R. Davidson et al. 1975. 24.50 (ISBN 0-8260-2423-8); instructors' manual avail. (ISBN 0-471-07457-8). Wiley.

Retailing Principles & Practices. 7th ed. Warren G. Meyer et al. LC 80-24885. (Illus.). 560p. (gr. 11-12). text ed. 13.48 (ISBN 0-07-041693-1, G). McGraw.

Retailing Principles & Practices. 5th ed. G. H. Richert et al. 1968. text ed. 13.96x (ISBN 0-07-052321-5, G); tchrs. manual & key 4.50x (ISBN 0-07-052323-1); Set. problems 4.96x (ISBN 0-07-052320-7); Set. projects 4.96x (ISBN 0-07-052322-3); tests 2.96x (ISBN 0-07-052324-X). McGraw.

Retained Austenite & Its Measurement by X-Ray Diffraction. Society of Automotive Engineers. 1980. 8.50 (ISBN 0-89883-224-1). Soc Auto Engineers.

Retaining Concepts & Organizing Facts: Advanced Level. James A. Giroux & Glenn R. Williston. (Comprehension Skills Ser). (Illus.). (gr. 9-12). 1974. pap. text ed. 2.40x (ISBN 0-89061-019-3). Jamestown Pubs.

Retaining Concepts & Organizing Facts: Middle Level. Glenn R. Williston. (Comprehension Skills Ser.). (Illus.). 64p. (gr. 6-8). 1976. pap. text ed. 2.40x (ISBN 0-89061-071-1, CB8M). Jamestown Pubs.

Retarded Adult in the Community. Elias Katz. (Illus.). 292p. 1977. 17.50 (ISBN 0-398-00981-3). C C Thomas.

Retarded Child: Answers to Questions Parents Ask. Arthur A. Attwell & D. A. Clabby. LC 72-182924. 139p. 1975. pap. 7.95x (ISBN 0-87424-120-0). Western Psych.

Rethinking Anthropology. E. R. Leach. (Monographs on Social Anthropology Ser: No. 22). 1971. text ed. 15.75x (ISBN 0-391-02078-1, Athlone Pr); pap. text ed. 9.50x (ISBN 0-391-00146-9). Humanities.

Rethinking Australia's Defence. Ross Babbage. (Illus.). 312p. 1981. text ed. 30.25x (ISBN 0-7022-1486-8). U of Queensland Pr.

Rethinking Curriculum Studies. Martin Lawn. 224p. 27.95 (ISBN 0-470-27097-7). Halsted Pr.

Rethinking Curriculum Studies: A Radical Approach. Martin Lawn. 224p. 1981. 27.95 (ISBN 0-470-27097-7). Halsted Pr.

Rethinking Economic Development. Robert D'A. Shaw. (Development Papers: No. 8). 58p. 1972. pap. 1.00 (ISBN 0-686-28680-4). Overseas Dev Council.

Rethinking Educational Equality. Andrew Kopan & Herbert Walberg. LC 73-20856. 1974. 15.25x (ISBN 0-8211-0012-2); text ed. 13.75x (ISBN 0-685-42637-8). McCutchan.

Rethinking Modernization. Ed. by John J. Poggie, Jr. & Robert N. Lynch. LC 72-826. 352p. 1974. lib. bdg. 17.95x (ISBN 0-8371-6394-3, POM/). Greenwood.

Rethinking Sociology: A Critique of Contemporary Theory. Irving Zeitlin. (Sociology Ser.). 300p. 1973. 17.95 (ISBN 0-13-778654-9). P-H.

Rethinking Symbolism. D. Sperber. Tr. by A. L. Morton from Fr. LC 75-18433. (Studies in Social Anthropology: No. 11). 164p. 1975. 19.95 (ISBN 0-521-20834-3); pap. 6.95x (ISBN 0-521-09967-6). Cambridge U Pr.

Rethinking Urban Education: A Sourcebook of Contemporary Issues. Ed. by Herbert J. Walberg. Andrew T. Kopan. LC 72-83962. (Higher Education Ser.). 1972. 15.95x o.p. (ISBN 0-87589-140-3). Jossey-Bass.

Reticular Formation. Ed. by J. Allan Hobson & Mary A. Brazier. (International Brain Research Organization Monograph: Vol. 6). 1979. text ed. 53.50 (ISBN 0-89004-379-5). Raven.

Reticuloendothalial System--a Comprehensive Treatise: Morphology, Vol. 1. Ed. by Ian Carr & W. T. Daems. (Illus.). 771p. 1980. 49.50 (ISBN 0-686-62966-3, Plenum Pr). Plenum Pub.

Reticuloendothelial System. John Rebuck et al. LC 79-23857. (International Academy of Pathology Monograph). 342p. 1980. Repr. 21.50 (ISBN 0-89874-101-7). Krieger.

Reticuloendothelial System: A Comprehensive Treatise, 2 vols. Ed. by Anthony J. Sbarra & Robert Strauss. Incl. Vol. 1. Morphology. Ed. by Ian Carr & W. T. Daems. 700p. 49.50 (ISBN 0-306-40291-2); Vol. 2. Ed. by Anthony J. Sbarra & Robert Strauss. 560p. 45.00 (ISBN 0-306-40292-0). 1980 (Plenum Pr). Plenum Pub.

Retief & the Rebels. Keith Laumer. 1980. pap. write for info. (ISBN 0-671-81866-X). PB.

Retina: Morphology, Function, & Clinical Characteristics. Ed. by Bradley R. Straatsma et al. (UCLA Forum in Medical Sciences: No. 8). (Illus.). 1969. 57.50x (ISBN 0-520-01533-9). U of Cal Pr.

Retinal Detachment Diagnosis & Treatment. William E. Benson. (Illus.). 208p. 1980. text ed. 27.50 (ISBN 0-06-140410-1, Harper Medical). Har-Row.

Retired Man's Way to Riches. Don P. Smith. 330p. 1980. pap. 15.00 (ISBN 0-937514-10-1, New Era). World Merch Import.

Retirement Edens. Peter Dickinson. 1981. 14.95 (ISBN 0-525-93173-2); pap. 8.95 (ISBN 0-525-93174-0). Dutton.

Retirement Policy in an Aging Society. Ed. by Robert L. Clark. LC 79-56502. (Illus.). vii, 215p. 1980. 16.75 (ISBN 0-8223-0441-4). Duke.

Retirement Systems for Public Employees. Thomas Bleakney. 1972. text ed. 9.75x (ISBN 0-256-01407-8). Irwin.

Retorno. Tr. by John W. White. (Portugese Bks.). (Port.). 1979. 1.40 (ISBN 0-8297-0684-4). Life Pubs Intl.

Retraining & Tradition. Kenneth Hall & Isobel Miller. 1975. text ed. 21.00x (ISBN 0-04-658215-0). Allen Unwin.

Retraining the Unemployed. Ed. by Gerald G. Somers. 1968. 29.50x (ISBN 0-299-04820-9). U of Wis Pr.

Retransformation of the School: The Emergence of Contemporary Alternative Schools in the United States. Daniel L. Duke. LC 77-25257. 1978. 16.95 (ISBN 0-88229-294-3); pap. 8.95 (ISBN 0-88229-606-X). Nelson-Hall.

Retratos Contemporaneos. Fernando Alegria. 247p. 1979. pap. text ed. 7.95 (ISBN 0-15-576680-5, HC). HarBraceJ.

Retreat from China: British Policy in the Far East, 1937-1941. Nicholas Clifford. (China in the 20th Century Ser.). 1976. Repr. of 1967 ed. lib. bdg. 22.50 (ISBN 0-306-70757-8). Da Capo.

Retreat from Sanity: The Structure of Emerging Psychosis. Malcolm B. Bowers, Jr. LC 73-20296. 248p. 1974. 19.95 (ISBN 0-87705-134-8). Human Sci Pr.

Retreat into Eternity. Amar Jyoti. LC 80-54236. (Illus.). 128p. (Orig.). 1980. pap. 10.95 (ISBN 0-933572-03-4). Truth Consciousness.

Retreat to the Ghetto: The End of a Dream? Thomas L. Blair. 263p. 1977. 10.00 o.p. (ISBN 0-8090-8078-8); pap. 5.95 (ISBN 0-8090-0127-6). Hill & Wang.

Retreat with Stillwell. Jack Belden. (China in the 20th Century Ser). (Illus.). 368p. 1975. Repr. of 1943 ed. lib. bdg. 22.50 (ISBN 0-306-70734-9). Da Capo.

Retreats: Away-to-Pray Weekends. Perry Garfinkel. (Illus.). 1977. 0.25 (ISBN 0-89570-140-5). Claretian Pubns.

Retrieval from Limbo: The Intermediary Group Treatment of Inaccessible Children. Ganter et al. LC 67-14602. 117p. 1967. pap. 2.40 o.p. (ISBN 0-87868-026-8, CW-23). Child Welfare.

Retriever Owner's Encyclopedia. Gwen Broadley. 1968. 9.95 (ISBN 0-7207-0172-4, Pub. by Michael Joseph). Merrimack Bk Serv.

Retriever Training. Susan Scales. LC 76-40806. (Illus.). 1977. 14.95 (ISBN 0-7153-7246-7). David & Charles.

Retrospective Exhibition of Gustave Dore. Ed. by Theodore Reff. (Modern Art in Paris 1855 to 1900 Ser.). 221p. 1981. lib. bdg. 44.00 (ISBN 0-8240-4746-X). Garland Pub.

Retrospective Exhibitions of Ernest Meissonier. Ed. by Theodore Reff. (Modern Art in Paris 1855 to 1900 Ser.). 353p. 1981. lib. bdg. 44.00 (ISBN 0-8240-4747-8). Garland Pub.

Retrospective Index to Theses of Great Britain & Ireland: Vol 1, Social Sciences & Humanities. new ed. Ed. by Roger R. Bilboul. 1975. text ed. 168.75 o.p. (ISBN 0-903450-03-8). ABC-Clio.

Retrospective Voting in American National Electiona. Morris P. Fiorina. LC 80-24454. (Illus.). 288p. 1981. text ed. 35.00x (ISBN 0-300-02557-2); pap. 9.95 (ISBN 0-300-02703-6). Yale U Pr.

Return Engagement. Diana Dixon. 192p. (Orig.). 1980. pap. 1.50 (ISBN 0-671-57030-7). S&S.

Return from the River Kwai. Joan Blair & Clay Blair, Jr. 320p. 1981. pap. 2.75 (ISBN 0-345-29007-0). Ballantine.

Return from the Stars. Stanislaw Lem. Tr. by Barbara Marszal & Frank Simpson. LC 79-3358. (Helen & Kurt Wolff Bk.). 312p. 1980. 9.95 (ISBN 0-15-177082-4). HarBraceJ.

Return from Tomorrow. George G. Ritchie, Jr. 1978. 6.95 (ISBN 0-912376-23-6). Chosen Bks Pub.

Return from Witchmountain. Alexander Key. (gr. 5-7). 1978. pap. 1.75 (ISBN 0-671-56073-5). PB.

Return of Arthur Conan Doyle. Grace Cooke & Ivan Cooke. (Illus.). 1963. 12.00; pap. 6.50 o.p. De Vorss.

Return of Dr. Fu Manchu. Sax Rohmer. 1976. lib. bdg. 13.95x (ISBN 0-89968-141-7). Lightyear.

Return of Eden: Five Essays on Milton's Epics. Northrop Frye. 1975. 10.00x (ISBN 0-8020-1353-8); pap. 4.50 (ISBN 0-8020-6281-4). U of Toronto Pr.

Return of Philip Latinovicz. Miroslav Krleza. LC 67-29443. 1968. 8.95 (ISBN 0-8149-0136-0). Vanguard.

Return of Sherlock Holmes. Arthur Conan Doyle. (gr. 10 up). pap. 1.95 (ISBN 0-425-04871-3, Medallion). Berkley Pub.

Return of Skull-Face. Robert E. Howard & Richard Lupoff. LC 77-89158. 1977. 9.95 (ISBN 0-913960-17-9). Fax Collect.

Return of the Birds: Selected Nature Essays of John Burroughs, Vol. 1. John Burroughs. Ed. by Frank Bergon. (Literature of the American Wilderness). 320p. 1981. pap. 4.45 (ISBN 0-87905-081-0). Peregrine Smith.

Return of the Eagle. Nancy Dorer & Frances Dorer. (Orig.). 1979. pap. 1.95 (ISBN 0-532-23267-4). Manor Bks.

Return of the Great Brain. John D. Fitzgerald. (gr. 3-5). 1975. pap. 1.50 (ISBN 0-440-45941-9, YB). Dell.

Return of the Moose. Daniel M. Pinkwater. LC 78-22434. (Illus.). (gr. 5 up). 1979. 6.95 (ISBN 0-396-07674-2). Dodd.

Return of the Native. Thomas Hardy. Ed. by James Gindin. (Critical Ed. Ser). 1969. 7.00 (ISBN 0-393-04300-2); pap. 6.95 (ISBN 0-393-09791-9). Norton.

Return of the Native. Thomas Hardy. (Classics Ser). (gr. 10 up). 1964. pap. 1.95 (ISBN 0-8049-0038-8, CL-38). Airmont.

Return of the Native. Thomas Hardy. (Literature Ser). (gr. 9-12). 1969. pap. text ed. 3.58 (ISBN 0-87720-713-5). AMSCO Sch.

Return of the Native. Thomas Hardy. pap. 1.75. Bantam.

Return of the Native. Karl Meyer. (Orig.). 1980. pap. 1.75 (ISBN 0-532-23184-8). Manor Bks.

Return of the Native with Reader's Guide. Thomas Hardy. (AMSCO Literature Program). (gr. 10-12). 1970. pap. 4.17 (ISBN 0-87720-807-7); with model ans. s.p. 2.70 (ISBN 0-87720-907-3). AMSCO Sch.

Return of the Pink Panther. Frank Waldman. (Orig.). 1977. pap. 1.50 o.p. (ISBN 0-685-75032-9, 345-25123-1-150). Ballantine.

Return of the Plague: British Society & the Cholera 1831-32. Michael Durey. 1979. text ed. 39.00x (ISBN 0-391-01038-7). Humanities.

Return of the Shaman. Gene Fowler. Ed. by A. D. Winans. (Illus.). 64p. (Orig.). 1981. pap. 4.00 (ISBN 0-915016-29-X). Second Coming.

Return of the Star of Bethlehem. Kenneth Boa & William Proctor. LC 79-8548. 216p. 1980. 8.95 (ISBN 0-385-15454-2, Galilee). Doubleday.

Return of the Texan. Burt Arthur. 1975. pap. 0.95 o.p. (ISBN 0-685-61048-9, LB321, Leisure Bks). Nordon Pubns.

Return of the Twelves. Pauline Clark. (Children's Literature Ser.). 1981. PLB 9.95 (ISBN 0-8398-2718-0). Gregg.

Return of the Whistler. Blossom Elfman. 160p. 1981. 8.95 (ISBN 0-686-69060-5). HM.

Return on Investment: Strategies for Profit. Robert Rachlin. LC 75-44668. 1976. 14.95 (ISBN 0-938712-00-4). Marr Pubns.

Return to Arcady. Adelaide N. Baker. LC 73-80849. (Illus.). 192p. 1973. 8.95 o.p. (ISBN 0-88208-018-0). Lawrence Hill.

Return to Barton. W. E. Ross. (YA) 1978. 5.95 (ISBN 0-685-86411-1, Avalon). Bouregy.

Return to Black River Camp. Daniel Weber. (Illus.). 60p. (Orig.). 1980. pap. 5.00 (ISBN 0-934996-11-3). Am Stud Pr.

Return to Earth. H. M. Hoover. 144p. 1981. pap. 1.95 (ISBN 0-380-54486-5). Avon.

Return to Elkhorne. Lester W. Merha. (YA) 1977. 4.95 o.p. (ISBN 0-685-73813-2, Avalon). Bouregy.

Return to Fort Yavapa. Al Cody. (YA) 1975. 5.95 (ISBN 0-685-52990-8, Avalon). Bouregy.

Return to Lanmore. Sheila Douglas. (Harlequin Presents Ser.). (Orig.). 1980. pap. text ed. 1.25 o.p. (ISBN 0-373-02336-7, Pub. by Harlequin). PB.

Return to Meaningfulness. Robert Powell. LC 80-54613. 180p. 1981. pap. text ed. 7.95 (ISBN 0-932238-07-6). Word Shop.

Return to Night. Mary Renault. 1974. pap. 1.50 o.s.i. (ISBN 0-515-03337-5, A3337). Jove Pubns.

Return to Night. Mary Renault. 303p. 1976. Repr. of 1947 ed. lib. bdg. 13.95x (ISBN 0-89244-082-1). Queens Hse.

Return to Oasis. Ed. by Victor Selwyn et al. 256p. 1980. 25.00x (ISBN 0-85683-047-X, Pub by Shepheard-Walwyn England). State Mutual Bk.

Return to Paradise. James A. Michener. 416p. 1978. pap. 2.75 (ISBN 0-449-23831-8, Crest). Fawcett.

Return to Red Castle. Dorothy M. Keddington. 200p. 1981. 6.95 (ISBN 0-913420-93-X). Olympus Pub Co.

Return to Sender. Sandy Hutson. (Orig.). 1981. price not set (ISBN 0-451-09808-0, Signet Bks). NAL.

Return to Sender. Raymond Mungo. 1975. 3.95 (ISBN 0-685-59658-3, Pub. by Montana Bks). Madrona Pubs.

Return to South Town. Lorenz Graham. LC 75-33712. (gr. 7 up). 1976. 8.95 (ISBN 0-690-01081-8, TYC-J). T Y Crowell.

Return to Steam: Steam Tours on British Rail from Nineteen Sixty-Nine. David Eatwell & John H. Cooper-Smith. 1978. 19.95 (ISBN 0-7134-0864-2, Pub. by Batsford England). David & Charles.

Return to Taos: A Sketchbook of Roadside Americana. Eric Sloane. LC 60-14499. (Funk & W Bk.). (Illus.). 1969. 11.95 o.s.i. (ISBN 0-308-70099-6, TYC-T). T Y Crowell.

Return to the Gate. William Corlett. LC 76-57889. 1977. 6.95 (ISBN 0-87888-112-3). Bradbury Pr.

Return to the Philippines. Rafael Steinberg. (World War II Ser.). (Illus.). 1979. lib. bdg. 14.94 (ISBN 0-686-51052-6). Silver.

Return to the Planet of the Apes, No.2. William Arrow. (Orig.). 1976. pap. 1.50 o.p. (ISBN 0-345-25167-9). Ballantine.

Return to the Planet of the Apes: Man, the Hunted Animal, No.3. William Arrow. (YA) 1976. pap. 1.50 o.p. (ISBN 0-345-25211-X). Ballantine.

Return to the Punjab. Prakash Tandon. 300p. 1981. 18.50x (ISBN 0-520-01759-5). U of Cal Pr.

Return to the Shadows. Robert Serumaga. (African Writers Ser.). 1969. pap. text ed. 4.95x (ISBN 0-435-90054-4). Heinemann Ed.

Return to the Source: Selected Speeches of Amilcar Cabral. Amilcar Cabral. Ed. by Africa Information Service. LC 74-7788. (Illus.). 128p. 1974. 7.50 o.p. (ISBN 0-85345-345-4, CL-3454); pap. 2.95 (ISBN 0-85345-347-0, PB3470). Monthly Rev.

Return to Vision. 2nd ed. Ed. by Richard L. Cherry et al. Robert J. Conley & Bernard A. Hirsch. 432p. 1975. pap. text ed. 9.95 (ISBN 0-395-17836-3); instructors' manual 1.00x (ISBN 0-395-17869-X). HM.

Return to Windhaven. Marie De Jourlet. (Windhaven). 1978. pap. 2.50 (ISBN 0-523-40348-8). Pinnacle Bks.

Return to Yesterday. Ford Madox Ford. 1972. 12.95 (ISBN 0-87140-563-6); pap. 4.45 (ISBN 0-87140-071-5). Liveright.

Return to...The Joys of Parenthood: Tots to Teens Training for Family Unity. Emily S. Owen. LC 77-89860. 1980. 12.95 (ISBN 0-86533-002-6, Pub. by New World Comm.). Amber Crest.

Returned Captive: A Poem, Repr. Of 1787 Ed. Bd. with John Graham's Address to the Master & Worthy Family of His House; Shewing His Suffering Among the Indians of West Florida. Repr. of 1787 ed; New Travels to the Westward, or Unknown Parts of America. (Repr. of 1788 & 1797 eds.); Remarkable Adventures of Jackson Johonnet, of Massachusetts...Containing an Account of His Captivity, Sufferings & Escape from Kickapoo Indians. (Repr. of 1793 & 1816 eds.). LC 75-7039. (Indian Captivities Ser.: Vol. 18). 1976. lib. bdg. 44.00 (ISBN 0-8240-1642-4). Garland Pub.

Returning Home: Tao-Chi's Album of Landscapes and Flowers. Tr. by Fong Wen from Chinese. Intro. by Wen Fong. LC 76-15911. (Illus.). 92p. 1976. slipcase 25.00 (ISBN 0-8076-0827-0). Braziller.

Returning to a Dream. William L. Sieller. 1979. 6.50 (ISBN 0-8233-0308-X). Golden Quill.

Returning to Eden: Animal Rights & Human Responsibility. Michael W. Fox. LC 79-56281. 300p. 1980. 13.95 (ISBN 0-670-12722-1). Viking Pr.

Returning Women Students in Higher Education: Defining Policy Issues. Carol K. Tittle & Elenor R. Denker. LC 80-13993. 224p. 1980. 21.95 (ISBN 0-03-050656-5). Praeger.

Reuben Dario: A Selective Classified & Annotated Bibliography. Hensley C. Woodbridge. LC 74-30490. 1975. 12.00 (ISBN 0-8108-0790-4). Scarecrow.

Reunion: A Self Portrait of the Group Theatre (1976) Ed. by Helen K. Chinoy. 77p. Repr. 4.00. Am Theatre Assoc.

Reunion: A Self Portrait of the Group Theatre. Ed. by Helen K. Chinoy. 77p. 1976. Repr. 4.00; AA members 3.00. Am Theatre Assoc.

Reunion & Dark Pony: Two Plays. David Mamet. LC 79-2319. 1979. pap. 2.95 (ISBN 0-394-17459-3, E728, Ever). Grove.

Reunion of Christendom: A Survey of Present Position. James Marchant. 329p. 1980. Repr. of 1929 ed. lib. bdg. 30.00 (ISBN 0-8495-3771-1). Arden Lib.

Reunion: Tools for Transformation. rev. ed. Marcus Allen et al. (Illus.). 1978. pap. 4.95 (ISBN 0-931432-01-4). Whatever Pub.

Reunion Without Compromise: The South & Reconstruction, 1865-1868. M. Perman. LC 72-86418. (Illus.). 384p. 1973. 37.95 (ISBN 0-521-20044-X); pap. 11.95x (ISBN 0-521-09779-7). Cambridge U Pr.

Reuven Rubin. Sarah Wilkinson. LC 72-166215. (Contemporary Art & Artists Ser.). (Illus.). 252p. 1974. 65.00 o.p. (ISBN 0-8109-0463-2); ltd. ed. signed 500.00 o.p. (ISBN 0-686-67060-4). Abrams.

Rev. A. A. Lindsley. E. P. Hill. 6p. Repr. of 1902 ed. pap. 0.50 (ISBN 0-8466-0059-5, SJS59). Shorey.

Rev. Dr. John Walker's Report on the Hebrides of 1764 to 1771. Margaret M. McKay. 263p. 1980. text ed. 39.00x (ISBN 0-85976-043-X). Humanities.

Rev. Sun Myung Moon. Chong Sun Kim. LC 78-52115. 1978. pap. text ed. 7.75 (ISBN 0-8191-0494-9). U Pr of Amer.

Revealed Preference of Government. Keith Basu. LC 78-67300. 1980. 24.95 (ISBN 0-521-22489-6). Cambridge U Pr.

Revel. Junior League of Shreveport, Inc. LC 79-89035. (Illus.). 416p. 1980. 8.95 (ISBN 0-9602246-1-0); stacon 5.37 (ISBN 0-686-58146-6). Jr League Shreveport.

Revelation. G. R. Beasley-Murray. Ed. by Matthew Black. (New Century Bible Commentary Ser.). 352p. (Orig.). 1981. pap. 7.95 (ISBN 0-8028-1885-4). Eerdmans.

Revelation. Ed. by G. R. Beasley-Murray. (New Century Bible Ser.). 1974. 13.95 o.p. (ISBN 0-551-00533-5). Attic Pr.

Revelation, Vol. I. R. H. Charles. LC 21-5413. (International Critical Commentary Ser.). 568p. 1920. text ed. 22.00x (ISBN 0-567-05038-6). Attic Pr.

Revelation, Vol. II. R. H. Charles. LC 21-5413. (International Critical Commentary Ser.). 506p. 1920. text ed. 22.00x (ISBN 0-567-05039-4). Attic Pr.

Revelation. H. A. Ironside. Date not set. 6.75 (ISBN 0-87213-384-2); 0.15, chart only (ISBN 0-87213-385-0). Loizeaux.

Revelation. Irving L. Jensen. (Bible Self-Study Ser.). 124p. (Orig.). 1971. pap. 2.25 (ISBN 0-8024-1066-9). Moody.

Revelation. Lehman Strauss. LC 64-8641. Orig. Title: Book of the Revelation. 6.75 (ISBN 0-87213-825-9). Loizeaux.

Revelation: An Exposition of the First Eleven Chapters. James B. Ramsey. (Geneva Commentary Ser.). 1977. 14.95 (ISBN 0-85151-256-9). Banner of Truth.

Revelation: An Expositional Commentary. Donald G. Barnhouse. 1971. 12.95 (ISBN 0-310-20490-9). Zondervan.

Revelation & Experience. Ed. by Edward Schillebeeck & B. Van Iersel. (Concilium Ser.: Vol. 113). 1979. pap. 4.95 (ISBN 0-8164-2609-0). Crossroad NY.

Revelation & Reason in Advaita Vedanta. K. S. Murty. 1974. Repr. 9.95 (ISBN 0-8426-0662-9). Orient Bk Dist.

Revelation and Reason in Islam. Arthur J. Arberry. LC 80-1936. 1981. Repr. of 1957 ed. 20.00 (ISBN 0-404-18952-0). AMS Pr.

Revelation Art: All Things New. Cliff McReynolds. (Illus., Orig.). 1980. pap. 10.95 (ISBN 0-917556-04-6). Pomegranate Calif.

Revelation: Drama of the Ages. Herbert Lockyer. LC 80-80639. 475p. 1980. pap. 6.95 (ISBN 0-89081-247-0). Harvest Hse.

Revelation Explained. F. G. Smith. 464p. 5.50. Faith Pub Hse.

Revelation of Baha'u'llah: Adrianople, 1863-1868, Vol. II. Adib Taherzadeh. (Illus.). 1977. 15.95 (ISBN 0-85398-070-5, 7-31-92, Pub. by George Ronald England); pap. 8.95 (7-31-93, Pub. by George Ronald England). Bahai.

Revelation of Baha'u'llah: Baghdad 1853-1863, Vol. I. Adib Taherzadeh. (Illus.). 1974. 14.95 (ISBN 0-85398-052-7, 7-31-90, Pub. by George Ronald England); pap. 7.95 (ISBN 0-85398-057-8, 7-31-91). Baha'i.

Revelation of Israel's Messiah: The Seven Churches, Vol. 1. Gordon J. Walstrom. 1980. 11.95 (ISBN 0-533-04581-9). Vantage.

Revelation of Law in Scripture. Patrick Fairbairn. Date not set. 15.95 (ISBN 0-88469-135-7). BMH Bks.

Revelation of Treasure Hid--Concerning Freedom, Concerning the Motherland, Concerning Justice, Apostolical Canons Respecting Baptism. Apostolos Makrakis. Ed. by Orthodox Christian Educational Society. Tr. by Denver Cummings from Hellenic. 80p. (Orig.). 1952. pap. 1.00x (ISBN 0-938366-23-8). Orthodox Chr.

Revelation: The Divine Fire. Brad Steiger. 1981. pap. 2.50 (ISBN 0-425-04615-X). Berkley Pub.

Revelation, the Future Foretold. Keith L. Brooks. (Teach Yourself the Bible Ser). 1962. pap. 1.75 (ISBN 0-8024-7308-3). Moody.

Revelation: The Last Book in the Bible. Luther Poellot. LC 61-18228. 1976. lib. bdg. 8.25 (ISBN 0-8100-0048-2, 15N0355); pap. 5.25 (ISBN 0-8100-0049-0, 15N0356). Northwest Pub.

Revelation-The Last Book of the Bible. Edwin A. Schick. LC 76-62602. 80p. (Orig.). 1977. pap. 2.75 (ISBN 0-8006-1253-1, 1-1253). Fortress.

Revelation Theology. Avery Dulles. 1969. 6.95 (ISBN 0-8164-1112-3). Crossroad NY.

Revelation to John. J. W. Roberts. Ed. by Everett Ferguson. LC 73-20857. (Living Word New Testament Commentary Ser.: Vol. 19). 1974. 7.95 (ISBN 0-8344-0074-X). Sweet.

Revelations. Phyllis Naylor. 1981. pap. 2.95 o.s.i. (ISBN 0-440-16923-2). Dell.

Revelations. Phyllis Naylor. 1980. 10.95 (ISBN 0-312-67928-9). St Martin.

Revelations: Forerunner of Christ. Herbert H. Ogletree. 1977. 6.50 o.p. (ISBN 0-682-48934-4). Exposition.

Revelations of an Army Nurse. Catherine Hagarty. 1981. 6.75 (ISBN 0-8062-1591-7). Carlton.

Revelations One: Noah's Flood Was a Result of Nuclear War. Kostis Kandias. (Illus.). 256p. 1981. 10.00 (ISBN 0-682-49672-3). Exposition.

Revenant: A Song-Cycle for Hedli Anderson. Louis MacNeice. 1975. text ed. 19.50x (ISBN 0-391-01597-4). Humanities.

Revenge at Blue Valley. W. G. Schreiber. (YA) 1978. 5.95 (ISBN 0-685-86412-X, Avalon). Bouregy.

Revenge Motive in Websterian Tragedy. Melvin Seiden. (Salzburg Studies in English Literature, Jacobean Drama Studies: No.15). 1973. pap. text ed. 25.00x (ISBN 0-391-01517-6). Humanities.

Revenge of Bussy D'Ambois by George Chapman. Robert J. Lordi. (Salzburg Studies in English Literature, Jacobean Drama Studies: No. 75). (Illus.). 1977. pap. text ed. 25.00x (ISBN 0-391-01463-3). Humanities.

Revenge of Dracula. Peter Tremayne. 1981. pap. 2.50 (ISBN 0-440-17374-4). Dell.

Revenger's Comedy. Derwent May. 191p. 1981. 10.95 (ISBN 0-7011-2461-X, Pub. by Chatto-Bodley-Jonathan). Merrimack Bk Serv.

Revenger's Madness: A Study of Revenge Tragedy Motifs. Charles A. Hallett & Elaine S. Hallett. LC 80-13893. xii, 349p. 1981. 21.50x (ISBN 0-8032-2309-9). U of Nebr Pr.

Revenger's Tragedy. Cyril Tourneur. Ed. by Lawrence J. Ross. LC 66-12744. (Regents Renaissance Drama Ser). 1966. 8.95x (ISBN 0-8032-0283-0); pap. 2.75x (ISBN 0-8032-5284-6, BB 218, Bison). U of Nebr Pr.

Revenue & Taxation of the Chinese Empire. Joseph Edkins. LC 78-74331. (Modern Chinese Economy Ser.). 240p. 1980. lib. bdg. 26.00 (ISBN 0-8240-4252-2). Garland Pub.

Revenue Patterns in U. S. Cities & Suburbs: A Comparative Analysis. Susan A. MacManus. LC 77-27499. (Praeger Special Studies). 1978. 25.95 (ISBN 0-03-022846-8). Praeger.

Revenue Sharing & the Planning Process: Shifting the Locus of Responsibility for Domestic Problem Solving. Advisory Committee to the Dept of Housing & Urban Development. LC 74-6418. 108p. 1974. pap. 6.25 (ISBN 0-309-02214-2). Natl Acad Pr.

Revenue Sharing Renewal. John T. Marlin. (COMP Papers Ser.). 52p. pap. 7.50 (ISBN 0-916450-36-8). Coun on Municipal.

Revenue Statistics of OECD Member Countries, 1965-1974. Organization for Economic Cooperation & Development. 1976. 10.00 o.p. (ISBN 92-64-01563-9). OECD.

Revenue Systems of Asean Countries. Mukul G. Asher. 76p. 1980. pap. 5.00 (ISBN 0-8214-0546-2). Swallow.

Reverdy-Braque, No. 135-136. (Maeght Gallery: Derriere le Miroir Ser.). (Fr.). 1977. pap. 19.95 (ISBN 0-8120-0916-9). Barron.

Reverence for Wood. Eric Sloane. LC 65-25668. (Funk & W Bk.). (Illus.). 12.95 (ISBN 0-308-70048-1, 710220, TYC-T). T Y Crowell.

Reverence for Wood. Eric Sloane. 1975. pap. 2.95 o.p. (ISBN 0-345-24492-3). Ballantine.

Reverie; or, a Flight to the Paradise of Fools, 1763, 2 vols. in 1. Charles Johnstone. LC 74-16307. (Novel in England, 1700-1775 Ser). 1974. lib. bdg. 50.00 (ISBN 0-8240-1162-7). Garland Pub.

Reversals. Anne Stevenson. LC 73-82545. (Wesleyan Poetry Program: Vol. 47). 1969. 10.00x (ISBN 0-8195-2047-0, Pub. by Wesleyan U Pr); pap. 4.95x (ISBN 0-8195-1047-5). Columbia U Pr.

Reverse Acronyms, Initialisms, & Abbreviations Dictionary. 7th ed. Ed. by Ellen T. Crowley. (Acronyms, Initialisms & Abbreviations Dictionary: Vol. 3). 1500p. 1980. 74.00 (ISBN 0-8103-0506-2). Gale.

Reverse Dictionary of Urdu. Donald Becker. 1980. 38.00x (ISBN 0-8364-0656-7, Pub. by Manohaar India). South Asia Bks.

Reverse Discrimination Controversy: A Moral & Legal Analysis. Robert K. Fullinwider. (Philosophy & Society Ser.). 300p. 1980. 22.50x (ISBN 0-8476-6273-X); pap. 9.95x (ISBN 0-8476-6901-7). Rowman.

Reverse the Charges: How to Save Dollars on Your Phone Bill. Joseph W. Waz, Jr. 1980. pap. 3.50 (ISBN 0-9603466-5-1). NCCB.

Review - Nineteen Seventy Nine Session of the Congress: Nineteen Seventy-Nine Session of the Congress. 1980. pap. 3.75 (ISBN 0-8447-0228-5). Am Enterprise.

Review & Assessment in Family Practice. Ernest Y. Yen. 288p. 1980. pap. 12.95x (ISBN 0-8385-2539-3). ACC.

Review & Reduction of Real Property Assessments in New York. 2nd ed. Harry O. Lee & Wilford A. LeForestier. LC 77-14270. 1978. 45.00 (ISBN 0-87632-214-3); 1979 supplement incl. (ISBN 0-685-99204-7). Boardman.

Review-Coastal Ecosystems, Nineteen Eighty. (UNEP Report Ser.: No. 4). 65p. 1980. pap. 7.50 (UNEP 033, UNEP). Unipub.

Review-Island Ecosystems. (UNEP Report Ser.: No. 3). 34p. 1980. pap. 6.00 (UNEP 032, UNEP). Unipub.

Review Latin Grammar. John K. Colby. (gr. 8-10). 1971. pap. text ed. 2.75x (ISBN 0-88334-034-8). Ind Sch Pr.

Review-Mountain Ecosystems, Nineteen Eighty. (UNEP Report Ser.: No. 2). 38p. 1980. pap. 6.00 (UNEP 031, UNEP). Unipub.

Review: Nineteen Seventy-Eight Session of the Congress. 1979. pap. 3.75 (ISBN 0-8447-0215-3). Am Enterprise.

Review: Nineteen Seventy-Six Session of the Congress. 1977. pap. 2.00 (ISBN 0-8447-0183-1). Am Enterprise.

Review of Agricultural Policies in OECD Member Countries, 1979. Organization for Economic Cooperation & Development. (Agricultural Policy Reports Ser.). (Illus.). 116p. (Orig.). 1980. pap. text ed. 12.00x (ISBN 0-686-27336-2, 51 80 04 1). OECD.

Review of Agricultural Policies in OECD Member Countries, 1978. 141p. 1979. 12.00 (ISBN 92-64-11988-4). OECD.

Review of Allied Health Education, No. 1. Ed. by Joseph Hamburg. LC 74-7876. (Illus.). 244p. 1974. 9.00x (ISBN 0-8131-1322-9). U Pr of Ky.

Review of Allied Health Education, No. 3. Ed. by Joseph Hamburg. LC 74-7876. 167p. 1979. 9.00x (ISBN 0-8131-1367-9). U Pr of Ky.

Review of Basic Sciences & Clinical Dentistry, 2 vols. Ed. by Jack E. Wells et al. Incl. Vol. 1. Basic Science. 262p. text ed. 27.50 (ISBN 0-06-142657-1); Vol. 2. Clinical Dentistry. 466p. text ed. 42.50 (ISBN 0-06-142658-X). (Illus.). 1400p. 1980. text ed. write for info. (Harper Medical). Har-Row.

Review of Child Development Research, 9 chapters, Vol. 3. Betty E. Caldwell & Henry N. Ricciuti. Incl. Chap. 1. Development of Infant-Mother Attachment. pap. 30.00x ea, in packets of 10 (ISBN 0-226-09055-8); Chap. 2. Control of Aggression. pap. 20.00x ea, in packets of 10 (ISBN 0-226-09046-9); Chap. 3. Children in Fatherless Families. pap. 25.00x ea., in packets of 10 (ISBN 0-226-09047-7); Chap. 4. Social Class & Child Development. pap. 15.00x ea., in packets of 10 (ISBN 0-226-09048-5); Chap. 5. Operant Behavior Modification. pap. 15.00x ea., in packets of 10 (ISBN 0-226-09049-3); Chap. 7. Programs for Disadvantaged Parents. pap. 20.00 ea, in packets of 10 (ISBN 0-226-09051-5); Chap. 8. Adoption: A Policy Perspective. pap. 15.00x ea., in packets of 10 (ISBN 0-226-09052-3); Chap. 9. Child & the Law. pap. 15.00x ea., in packets of 10 (ISBN 0-226-09053-1). 1975. pap. 20.00x (ISBN 0-226-09045-0). U of Chicago Pr.

Review of Child Development Research, 9 chapters, Vol. 5. Ed. by E. Mavis Hetherington. Incl. Chap. 1. Your Ancients Revisited: A History of Child Development. Robert S. Sears. 80p. pap. 2.50x (ISBN 0-226-33154-7); Chap. 2. Ecological Psychology & Children. Paul V. Gump. 64p. pap. 2.25x (ISBN 0-226-33156-3); Chap. 3. Children's Cooperation & Helping Behaviors. James H. Bryan. 64p. 2.25x (ISBN 0-226-33157-1); Chap. 4. Impact of Television on Children & Youth. Aletha H. Stein & Lynette K. Friedrich. 80p. pap. 3.00x (ISBN 0-226-33159-8); Chap. 5. Development of Social Cognition. Carolyn U. Shantz. 72p. pap. 3.25x (ISBN 0-226-33160-1); Chap. 6. Children's Attention: The Development of Selectivity. Anne D. Pick et al. 72p. pap. 2.25x (ISBN 0-226-33162-8); Chap. 7. Problems & Prospects in the Study of Learning Disabilities. Joseph Torgeson. 64p. pap. 2.25x (ISBN 0-226-33163-6); Chap. 9. Interdisciplinary Analysis. Ross D. Parke & Candace W. Collmer. 88p. pap. 3.25x (ISBN 0-226-33165-2). LC 64-20472. (Review of Child Development Research Ser). 608p. 1976. PLB 20.00x (ISBN 0-226-33155-5); pap. in indiv. chapters avail. (ISBN 0-685-63976-2). U of Chicago Pr.

Review of Clinical Laboratory Methods: A Key Word Index System. Kanai Lai Mukherjee. LC 79-15463. (Illus.). 1979. pap. text ed. 13.95 (ISBN 0-8016-3589-6). Mosby.

Review of Dental Assisting. Betty A. Ladley & Shirley A. Wilson. LC 79-18921. 1979. pap. text ed. 10.95 (ISBN 0-8016-2806-7). Mosby.

Review of Dental Assisting. Hazel O. Torres & Lois E. Mazzucchi. (Illus.). 350p. 1980. write for info. (ISBN 0-7216-8883-7). Saunders.

Review of Dentistry: Questions & Answers. 7th ed. Maynard K. Hine & Ralph W. Phillips. LC 78-15590. 1979. pap. text ed. 19.95 (ISBN 0-8016-2197-6). Mosby.

Review of Diaphragm Walls. Institute of Civil Engineers. 158p. 1980. 35.00x (ISBN 0-7277-0045-6, Pub. by Telford England). State Mutual Bk.

Review of Economic Theory. Edwin Cannan. Repr. of 1929 ed. 25.00x (ISBN 0-678-05040-6). Kelley.

Review of Economic Theory. 2nd ed. Ed. by Edwin Cannan. 448p. 1964. 30.00x (ISBN 0-7146-1211-1, F Cass Co). Biblio Dist.

Review of Fisheries in OECD Member Countries Nineteen Seventy-Nine. OECD. (Illus.). 253p. (Orig.). 1980. pap. 12.00 (ISBN 92-64-12103-X). OECD.

Review of Hemodialysis for Nurses and Dialysis Personnel. 2nd ed. C. F. Gutch & Martha H. Stoner. LC 75-4637. (Illus.). 1975. pap. 12.50 o.p. (ISBN 0-8016-1993-9). Mosby.

Review of Leadership in Nursing. 2nd ed. Laura M. Douglass. LC 76-41258. 1977. pap. text ed. 9.95 (ISBN 0-8016-1442-2). Mosby.

Review of Maritime Transport, 1977. 60p. 1979. pap. 7.00 (ISBN 0-686-68969-0, 79/2D7, UN). Unipub.

Review of Maternal & Child Nursing. Janice L. Goerzen & Peggy L. Chinn. LC 74-20973. 1975. text ed. 9.00 (ISBN 0-8016-1852-5). Mosby.

Review of Mathematics, for Beginning Science & Engineering Students. Festus L. Minnear & Ruby M. Grimes. LC 60-5903. (Illus.). 1960. pap. text ed. 6.75x o.p. (ISBN 0-7167-0404-8). W H Freeman.

Review of Medical Histology. Jacques Poirier & Jean-Louis R. Dumas. Tr. by Ursula Taube. LC 76-28944. (Illus.). 1977. pap. text ed. 10.95 (ISBN 0-7216-7273-6). Saunders.

Review of Medical Pharmacology. 7th, rev. ed. Frederick H. Meyers et al. LC 80-82744. (Illus.). 747p. 1980. lexotone cover 17.50 (ISBN 0-87041-153-5). Lange.

Review of Medical Terminology. Mary E. Kinn. 1980. 7.50. Thieme Stratton.

Review of Pathology. John S. Meyer. LC 74-8558. 1974. pap. 13.95 o.p. (ISBN 0-8016-3420-2). Mosby.

Review of Pediatric Nursing. 2nd ed. Florence B. Roberts. LC 77-14579. 1978. pap. text ed. 9.50 (ISBN 0-8016-4133-0). Mosby.

Review of Pediatrics. Richard D. Krugman. 400p. Date not set. text ed. 10.95 (ISBN 0-7216-5549-1). Saunders. Postponed.

Review of Personality & Social Psychology: No. 1. Ed. by Ladd Wheeler. (Illus.). 352p. 1980. 20.00 (ISBN 0-8039-1457-1). Sage.

Review of Personality & Social Psychology: No. 1. Ed. by Ladd Wheeler. (Illus.). 352p. 1980. pap. 9.95 (ISBN 0-8039-1458-X). Sage.

Review of Pharmacology in Nursing. 2nd ed. Betty S. Bergersen & Jurate A. Sakalys. LC 78-5717. 1978. pap. text ed. 11.00 (ISBN 0-8016-0624-1). Mosby.

Review of Psychiatric Nursing. Donna C. Aguilera. LC 76-40460. 1977. pap. text ed. 8.50 (ISBN 0-8016-0090-1). Mosby.

Review of Published Research on the Relationship of Some Personality Variables to ESP Scoring Level. Gordon L. Mangan. (Parapsychological Monographs, No. 1). 1958. pap. 2.00 (ISBN 0-912328-03-7). Parapsych Foun.

Review of Refraction. Jack Hartstein. (Comprehensive Review Ser). (Illus.). 1971. 17.50 o.p. (ISBN 0-8016-2091-0). Mosby.

Review of Research in Education, Four, 1976. Ed. by Lee Shulman. LC 72-89719. 1977. text ed. 15.00 o.p. (ISBN 0-87581-214-7). Peacock Pubs.

Review of Security & the State Nineteen Seventy-Nine. 2nd ed. State Research. 154p. 1980. 27.50x (ISBN 0-905290-04-6). Nichols Pub.

Review of Short Haul Passenger Transportation. Committee on Transportation, Assembly of Engineering, Natl. Research Council. 1976. pap. 6.25 (ISBN 0-309-02445-5). Natl Acad Pr.

Review of Silvrian Brachiopods from Gotland. Michael G. Bassett & Leonard R. Cocks. (Fossils & Strata Ser: No. 3). 1974. 10.50x (ISBN 8-200-09349-2, Dist. by Columbia U Pr). Universitet.

Review of the Macropodid Genus Sthenurus. R. H. Tedford. (U. C. Publ. in Geological Sciences: Vol. 57). 1966. pap. 6.50x (ISBN 0-520-09158-2). U of Cal Pr.

Review of the North American Eocene & Oligocene Apatemyidae (Mammalia: Insectivora) Robert M. West. (Special Publications: No. 3). (Illus.). 42p. 1973. pap. 2.00 (ISBN 0-89672-028-4). Tex Tech Pr.

Review of the North American Leptoconops (Diptera: Ceratopogonidae) Willis W. Wirth & William R. Atchley. (Graduate Studies: No. 5). (Illus., Orig.). 1973. pap. 3.00 (ISBN 0-89672-012-8). Tex Tech Pr.

Review of the Primates, 3 vols. Daniel G. Elliot. LC 78-72714. Repr. of 1913 ed. Set. 225.00 (ISBN 0-404-18284-4). Vol. 1 (ISBN 0-404-18285-2). Vol. 2 (ISBN 0-404-18286-0). Vol. 3 (ISBN 0-404-18287-9). AMS Pr.

Review of the Subfamily Cylleniinae with a World Revision of the Genus Thevenemyia Bigot (Eclimus Acut.) (Diptera: Bombyliidae) Jack C. Hall. (U. C. Publ. in Entomology: Vol. 56). 1969. pap. 7.00x (ISBN 0-520-09129-9). U of Cal Pr.

Review of the Swedish KBS-II Plan for Disposal of Spent Nuclear Fuel. Committee on Radioactive Waste Management. Ed. by Subcommittee for Review of the KBS-II Plan. LC 80-80362. xiii, 91p. 1980. pap. text ed. 7.75 (ISBN 0-309-03036-6). Natl Acad Pr.

Review of the World Resources of Mesopelagic Fish. (FAO Fish Tech Paper: No. 193). 151p. 1981. pap. 8.50 (ISBN 92-5-100924-4, F2074, FAO). Unipub.

Review Outlines & Materials for Business Law & CPA Law Review. William T. Schantz & Janice E. Jackson. LC 80-13096. 997p. 1980. pap. text ed. write for info. (ISBN 0-8299-2071-4). West Pub.

Review Papers: International Solar-Terrestrial Physics Symposium, Sao-Paolo, June, 1974. Ed. by S. A. Bowhill. 212p. 1976. pap. 55.00 (ISBN 0-08-019959-3). Pergamon.

Review Series. 1974. 1970-74 eds. 2.00 ea. o.p. Interbk Inc.

Review Text in American History. Irving L. Gordon. (Illus., Orig.). (gr. 10-12). 1968. pap. text ed. 6.75 (ISBN 0-87720-606-6). AMSCO Sch.

Review Text in Biology. Mark A. Hall & Milton S. Lesser. (Illus., Orig.). (gr. 10-12). 1966. pap. text ed. 5.67 (ISBN 0-87720-051-3). AMSCO Sch.

Review Text in Chemistry. Maxwell Gelender. (Illus., Orig.). (gr. 10-12). 1964. pap. text ed. 5.67 (ISBN 0-87720-104-8). AMSCO Sch.

Review Text in Earth Science, Intermediate Level. Constantine Constant. (Orig.). (gr. 7-9). 1971. pap. text ed. 6.08 (ISBN 0-87720-152-8). AMSCO Sch.

Review Text in French First Year. 2nd ed. Eli Blume. (Illus., Orig.). (gr. 7-12). 1967. pap. text ed. 4.83 (ISBN 0-87720-451-9). AMSCO Sch.

Review Text in French Three Years. Eli Blume. (Illus., Orig.). (gr. 7-12). 1963. pap. text ed. 4.92 o.p. (ISBN 0-87720-457-8). AMSCO Sch.

Review Text in French Three Years. 2nd ed. Eli Blume. (Orig.). (gr. 11-12). 1980. pap. text ed. 6.33 (ISBN 0-87720-471-3). AMSCO Sch.

Review Text in French Two Years. 2nd ed. Eli Blume. (Illus., Orig.). (gr. 7-12). 1966. pap. text ed. 5.33 (ISBN 0-87720-454-3). AMSCO Sch.

Review Text in General Science. 2nd ed. J. Albert Mould & Saul L. Geffner. (gr. 10-12). 1974. pap. text ed. 5.92 (ISBN 0-87720-001-7). AMSCO Sch.

Review Text in German, First Year. Harry Reinert. (Orig.). (gr. 10-12). 1971. pap. text ed. 5.33 (ISBN 0-87720-581-7). AMSCO Sch.

Review Text in Health. Bro. Patricius & Sr. Carmel Crifer. (30 Line Drawings, Index, 336p). (gr. 7-12). 1962. pap. text ed. 5.58 (ISBN 0-87720-161-7). AMSCO Sch.

Review Text in Latin First Year. 2nd ed. Charles I. Freundlich. (Illus., Orig.). (gr. 7-12). 1966. pap. text ed. 5.33 (ISBN 0-87720-551-5). AMSCO Sch.

Review Text in Latin Three & Four Years. Charles I. Freundlich. (Orig.). (gr. 7-12). 1967. pap. text ed. 6.42 (ISBN 0-87720-558-2). AMSCO Sch.

Review Text in Latin Two Years. Charles I. Freundlich. (gr. 7-12). 1966. pap. text ed. 5.75 (ISBN 0-87720-555-8). AMSCO Sch.

Review Text in Physical Science: Intermediate Level. Jules Weisler. (gr. 7-10). 1970. pap. text ed. 6.17 (ISBN 0-87720-007-6). AMSCO Sch.

Review Text in Physics. Walter L. Ahner & Harold G. Kastan. (Illus., Orig.). (gr. 10-12). 1966. pap. text ed. 5.67 (ISBN 0-87720-171-4). AMSCO Sch.

Review Text in Preliminary Mathematics. Isidore Dressler. (Illus.). (gr. 7-9). 1962. text ed. 9.83 (ISBN 0-87720-203-6); pap. text ed. 6.25 (ISBN 0-87720-202-8). AMSCO Sch.

Review Text in Spanish First Year. 2nd ed. Robert J. Nassi & Bernard Bernstein. (Illus., Orig.). (gr. 7-12). 1972. pap. text ed. 5.33 (ISBN 0-87720-500-0). AMSCO Sch.

Review Text in Spanish Three Years. Robert J. Nassi et al. (Illus., Orig.). (gr. 7-12). 1965. pap. text ed. 5.33 (ISBN 0-87720-508-6). AMSCO Sch.

Review Text in Spanish Two Years. 2nd ed. Robert J. Nassi & Bernard Bernstein. (Illus., Orig.). (gr. 7-12). 1969. pap. text ed. 5.33 (ISBN 0-87720-505-1). AMSCO Sch.

Review Text in United States History. rev. ed. Paul M. Roberts. (Illus., Orig.). (gr. 7-9). 1967. pap. text ed. 6.75 (ISBN 0-87720-601-5). AMSCO Sch.

Review Text in World History. rev. ed. Irving L. Gordon. (Illus., Orig.). (gr. 10-12). 1968. pap. text ed. 6.75 (ISBN 0-87720-604-X). AMSCO Sch.

Review-Tropical Woodlands & Forest Ecosystems, Nineteen Eighty. (UNEP Report Ser.: No. 4). 84p. 1980. pap. 9.00 (UNEP 030, UNEP). Unipub.

Review: Vol. 2. Ed. by James O. Hoge & James L. West. 1981. 20.00x (ISBN 0-8139-0865-5). U Pr of Va.

Review-1970 Session of the Congress & Index of AEI, Publications. U. S. Congress, 92nd. (Legislative Analysis Ser.: No. 1). 1971. pap. 2.00 o.p. (ISBN 0-8447-0125-4). Am Enterprise.

Reviewing English Preliminary. Joseph Bellafiore. (gr. 7-12). 1958. pap. text ed. 4.33 (ISBN 0-87720-305-9). AMSCO Sch.

Reviewing German Grammar & Building Vocabulary. Roselinde Konrad. 1977. pap. text ed. 10.95 scp o.p. (ISBN 0-06-043752-9, HarpC); instructor's manual avail. o.p. (ISBN 0-06-363700-6). Har-Row.

Reviewing Reference Books: An Evaluation of the Effectiveness of Selected Announcement, Review & Index Media in Their Coverage of Reference Books. Alma A. Covey. LC 70-182831. 142p. 1972. lib. bdg. 10.00 (ISBN 0-8108-0456-5). Scarecrow.

Reviews in Engineering Geology, Vol. 4: Geology in the Siting of Nuclear Power Plants. Ed. by Allen W. Hatheway & Cole R. McClure. LC 62-51690. (Illus.). 1979. 41.00x (ISBN 0-8137-4104-1). Geol Soc.

Reviews in Graph Theory, 4 vols. Ed. by William G. Brown. 1980. Set. 200.00 (ISBN 0-8218-0214-3); Vol. 1. 68.00 (ISBN 0-8218-0210-0); Vol. 2. 68.00 (ISBN 0-8218-0211-9); Vol. 3. 68.00 (ISBN 0-8218-0212-7); Vol. 4. 40.00 (ISBN 0-8218-0213-5). Am Math.

Reviews in Perinatal Medicine, Vol. 2. Ed. by Emile M. Scarpelli & Ermelando V. Cosmi. LC 77-74616. 1978. 34.50 (ISBN 0-89004-195-4). Raven.

Reviews in Perinatal Medicine, Vol. 3. Ed. by Emile M. Scarpelli & Ermelando V. Cosmi. LC 77-74616. 1979. text ed. 45.50 (ISBN 0-89004-249-7). Raven.

Reviews in Perinatal Medicine, Vol. 4. Ed. by Emilie Scarpelli & Ermelando Cosmi. 550p. 1981. 39.00 (ISBN 0-89004-364-7). Raven.

Reviews of Diagnosis: Oral Medicine, Radiology & Treatment Planning. Wood. LC 79-15358. 1979. pap. 15.95 (ISBN 0-8016-5614-1). Mosby.

Reviews of National Science Policy: United States. Organisation for Economic Co-Operation & Development. Ed. by I. Bernard Cohen. LC 79-7979. (Three Centuries of Science in America Ser.). 1980. Repr. of 1968 ed. lib. bdg. 44.00x (ISBN 0-405-12561-5). Arno.

Reviews of Neuroscience, Vol. 1. Ed. by Seymour Ehrenpreis & Irwin J. Kopin. LC 74-80538. 1974. 34.50 (ISBN 0-911216-84-7). Raven.

Reviews of Neuroscience, Vol. 2. Ed. by Seymour Ehrenpreis & Irwin J. Kopin. LC 74-80538. 1976. 27.00 (ISBN 0-89004-105-9). Raven.

Reviews of Neuroscience, Vol. 3. Ed. by Seymour Ehrenpreis & Irwin J. Kopin. LC 74-80538. 1978. 24.50 (ISBN 0-89004-168-7). Raven.

Reviews of Neuroscience, Vol. 4. Ed. by Diana S. Schneider. 1979. text ed. 20.50 (ISBN 0-89004-282-9). Raven.

Reviews of Physiology, Biochemistry & Pharmacology, Vol. 77. Ed. by R. H. Adrian et al. LC 74-3674. (Illus.). 1977. 61.10 (ISBN 0-387-07963-7). Springer-Verlag.

Reviews of Physiology Biochemistry & Pharmacology, Vol. 87. (Illus.). 250p. 1980. 51.90 (ISBN 0-387-09944-1). Springer-Verlag.

Reviews of Physiology, Biochemistry, & Pharmacology, Vol. 88. R. H. Adrian. (Illus.). 280p. 1981. 52.00 (ISBN 0-387-10408-9). Springer-Verlag.

Reviews of Physiology, Biochemistry & Pharmacology, Vol. 89. Ed. by R. H. Adrian. (Illus.). 260p. 1981. 54.30 (ISBN 0-387-10495-X). Springer-Verlag.

Reviews of Plasma Physics, Vol. 8. Ed. by M. A. Leontovich. 425p. 1980. 42.50 (ISBN 0-306-17068-X, Consultants Bureau). Plenum Pub.

Reviews of Research in Science Education Series, 6 vols. Francis D. Curtis. 1971. Set. 57.75x (ISBN 0-8077-2433-5). Tchrs Coll.

Reviews of the World Situation: 1949-50. Ed. by Richard D. Challener. (Legislative Origins of American Foreign Policy Ser.: Vol. 8). 1979. lib. bdg. 55.00 (ISBN 0-8240-3037-0). Garland Pub.

Revised Chapter Six of the Anglo-American Cataloging Rules. Gertrude Koh. pap. 1.00 (ISBN 0-686-24157-6). CHCUS Inc.

Revised Compleat Sinatra. new, rev. ed. Albert I. Lonstein & Vito Marino. LC 79-88307. (Illus.). 702p. 1980. 49.95 (ISBN 0-87990-000-8). Lonstein Pubns.

Revised Financial Reporting Model for Municipalities. John C. Burton. (Government Auditing Ser.). 1980. pap. 6.00. Coun on Municipal.

Revised Medieval Latin Word-List from British & Irish Sources. Ed. by Ronald E. Latham. (British Academy Ser.). 1965. 49.00x (ISBN 0-19-725891-3). Oxford U Pr.

Revised Shapley-Ames Catalog of Bright Galaxies. Allan Sandage & G. A. Tammann. 1981. 29.00 (ISBN 0-87279-646-9). Carnegie Inst.

Revised Techniques of Ballroom Dancing. 9th ed. Alex Moore. 108p. 1980. pap. text ed. 12.50x (ISBN 0-392-07521-0, LTB). Soccer.

Revised Token Test. M. McNeil. 1978. 17.95 (ISBN 0-8391-1289-0); manual/score sheets 11.95 (ISBN 0-8391-1262-9). Univ Park.

Revising Prose. Richard A. Lanham. 1979. pap. text ed. 3.95x (ISBN 0-684-15987-2, ScribC). Scribner.

Revision & Amendment of State Constitutions. W. F. Dodd. LC 73-120854. (American Constitutional & Legal History Ser). 1970. Repr. of 1910 ed. lib. bdg. 35.00 (ISBN 0-306-71959-2). Da Capo.

Revision Book in Ordinary Level Physics. 3rd ed. M. Nelkon. 1973. pap. text ed. 5.95x o.p. (ISBN 0-435-67661-X). Heinemann Ed.

Revision Chemistry. M. A. Cowd & P. J. Miller. LC 79-41164. 1980. text ed. 8.95 (ISBN 0-408-10607-7). Butterworths.

Revision Notes in Advanced Level Chemistry: Organic Chemistry. A. Holderness. 1975. pap. text ed. 7.50x o.p. (ISBN 0-435-65433-0). Heinemann Ed.

Revision Notes in Physics, 2 bks. 4th ed. M. Nelkon. Incl. Bk. 1. Mechanics, Electricity, Atomic Physics. 1979. pap. text ed. 3.50x o.p. (ISBN 0-435-68640-2); Bk. 2. Optics, Waves, Sound, Heat, Properties of Matter. 1977. pap. text ed. 6.50x o.p. (ISBN 0-435-68658-5). Heinemann Ed.

Revision Notes on Building Measurement. Saunt. 1981. text ed. price not set. Butterworth.

Revision of Actium Casey & Actiastes Casey (Coleoptera: Pselaphidae) Albert A. Grigarick & Robert O. Schuster. (U. C. Publ. in Entomology: Vol. 67). 1971. pap. 6.00x (ISBN 0-520-09398-4). U of Cal Pr.

Revision of North American Bees of the Subgenus Cnemidandrena. Barry J. Donovan. (Publ. in Entomolgy Ser: Vol. 81). pap. 7.75x (ISBN 0-520-09566-9). U of Cal Pr.

Revision of North American Trichodes (Herbst) (Coleoptera: Cleridae) David E. Foster. (Special Publications: No. 11). (Illus.). 1976. 4.00 (ISBN 0-89672-037-3). Tex Tech Pr.

Revision of the Flea Genus Thrassis Jordan 1933 (Siphonaptera: Ceratophyllidae) With Observations on Ecology & Relationship to Plague. Harold E. Stark. (U. C. Pub. in Entomology: Vol. 53). 1970. pap. 9.00x (ISBN 0-520-09126-4). U of Cal Pr.

Revision of the Genus Bowlesia Ruiz & Pav (Umbelliferae-Hydrocotyloideae) & Its Relatives. Mildred E. Mathias & Lincoln Constance. (U. C. Publ. in Botany: Vol. 38). 1965. pap. 6.00x (ISBN 0-520-09010-1). U of Cal Pr.

Revision of the Genus Clausocalanus (Copepoda: Calanoida) with Remarks on Distributional Patterns in Diagnostic Characters. B. Frost & A. Fleminger. (Bulletin of the Scripps Institution of Oceanography: Vol. 12). 1968. pap. 10.00x (ISBN 0-520-09317-8). U of Cal Pr.

Revision of the Genus Pelidnota of America North of Panama (Coleopera-Scarabaeidae, Rutelinae) Alan R. Hardy. (Publications in Entomology: Vol. 78). 1975. pap. 9.00x (ISBN 0-520-09529-4). U of Cal Pr.

Revision of the Genus Pseudopanurgus of North America (Hymenoptera: Apoidea) P. H. Timberlake. (U. C.Publications in Entomology: Vol. 72). 1973. pap. 7.50x (ISBN 0-520-09475-1). U of Cal Pr.

Revision of the Genus Rhodocybe Maire: Agaricales. T. J. Baroni. (Nova Hedwigia Beiheft). (Illus.). 300p. 1981. lib. bdg. 60.00x (ISBN 3-7682-5467-4). Lubrecht & Cramer.

Revision of the Genus Thrips Linnaeus in the New World with a Catalogue of the World Species (Thysanoptera: Thripidae) A. G. Gentile & S. F. Bailey. (U. C. Publ. in Entomology: Vol. 51). 1968. pap. 8.00x (ISBN 0-520-09124-8). U of Cal Pr.

Revision of the Genus Zethus Fabricius in the Western Hemisphere (Hymenoptera: Eumenidae) R. M. Bohart & L. A. Stange. (U. C. Publ. in Entomology: Vol. 40). 1965. pap. 9.00x (ISBN 0-520-09112-4). U of Cal Pr.

Revision of the Labyrinthodont Family Capitosauridae & a Description of Parotosaurus Peabodyi N. Sp. from the Wupatki Member of the Moenkopi Formation of Northern Arizona. S. P. Welles & John Cosgriff. (U. C. Publ. in Geological Sciences: Vol. 54). 1965. pap. 7.50x (ISBN 0-520-09155-8). U of Cal Pr.

Revision of the Male Wasps of the Genus Brachycistis in America North of Mexico (Hymenoptera: Tiphiidae) M. S. Wasbauer. (U. C. Publ. in Entomology: Vol. 43). 1966. pap. 7.50x (ISBN 0-520-09115-9). U of Cal Pr.

Revision of the Marine Nematodes of the Superfamily Draconematoidea Filipjev. M. W. Allen & Ella M. Noffsinger. (Publications in Zoology Ser.: Vol. 109). 1978. 8.75x (ISBN 0-520-09583-9). U of Cal Pr.

Revision of the New World Species of Ricinus (Mallophaga) Occuring on Passeriformes (Aves) Bernard C. Nelson. (U. C. Publ. in Entomology: Vol. 68). 1973. pap. 10.50x (ISBN 0-520-09412-3). U of Cal Pr.

Revision of the Stigonematacaea: With a Summary of the Classification of Blue-Green Algae. F. Drouet. (Nova Hedwigia Beiheft: No. 66). (Illus.). 300p. 1981. lib. bdg. 60.00x (ISBN 3-7682-5466-6). Lubrecht & Cramer.

Revision Questions & Worked Examples in "H" Grade Chemistry. A. W. Mackaill & J. A. Maclean. 1975. pap. text ed. 3.75x o.p. (ISBN 0-435-65561-2). Heinemann Ed.

Revisional Study of the Bees of the Genus Perdita F. Smith, with Special Reference to the Fauna of the Pacific Coast (Hymenoptera, Apoidea) P. H. Timberlake. Incl. Pt. IV. (U. C. Publ. in Entomology: Vol. 17.1). 1960. pap. 7.00x (ISBN 0-520-09076-4); Pt. V. (U. C. Publ. in Entomology: Vol. 28.1). 1962. pap. 7.00x (ISBN 0-520-09094-2); Pt. VII (Including Index to Pts. I to VII) (U. C. Publ. in Entomology: Vol. 49). 1968. pap. 10.00x (ISBN 0-520-09121-3). U of Cal Pr.

Revisional Study of the Masarid Wasps (Hymenoptera, Vespoidea) O. W. Richards. (Illus.). 294p. 1962. 24.00x (ISBN 0-565-00697-5, Pub. by Brit Mus Nat Hist England). Sabbot-Natural Hist Bks.

Revisionism: A Key to Peace & Other Essays, 3 essays. Harry E. Barnes. LC 80-15902. (Cato Paper Ser.: No. 12). Orig. Title: Revisionism: a Key to Peace & the Historical Blackout & How 1984 Trends Threaten American Peace, Freedom, & Prosperity. 200p. 1980. pap. 4.00 (ISBN 0-932790-18-6). Cato Inst.

Revisionist. Douglas Crase. 96p. 1981. 10.95 (ISBN 0-316-16062-8); pap. 5.95 (ISBN 0-316-16060-1). Little.

Revisiting Blassingame's "The Slave Community" The Scholar's Respond. Ed. by Al-Tony Gilmore. LC 77-84765. (Contributions in Afro-American & African Studies: No. 37). 1978. lib. bdg. 17.50 (ISBN 0-8371-9879-8, GJB/). Greenwood.

Revista a los Examenes De Cosmetologia Que Hace la Junta Estatal (State Board Review Examinations in Cosmetology) Anthony B. Colletti. 1976. pap. 6.00 (ISBN 0-912126-12-4, 1271-00). Keystone Pubns.

Revista Interamericana De Bibliografia: (Inter-American Review of Bibliography) OAS General Secretariat. (Vol. XXX, No. 3). 116p. (Engl. & Span.). 1980. pap. text ed. 2.00. OAS.

Revisting Wertheimer's Seminars, 2 vols. Abraham S. Luchins & Edith H. Luchins. Incl. Vol. 1. Value, Social Influence, & Power (ISBN 0-8387-1227-4); Vol. 2. Problems in Social Psychology (ISBN 0-8387-1570-2). LC 72-3525. 1978. Set. 65.00 (ISBN 0-8387-1570-2); 32.50 ea. Bucknell U Pr.

Revitalizing America. Ronald E. Muller. 1980. 13.95 (ISBN 0-671-24889-8). S&S.

Revitalizing Cities. Ed. by Herrington J. Bryce. (Urban Round Table Ser.: No.2). (Illus.). 320p. 1979. 24.95 (ISBN 0-669-02846-0). Lexington Bks.

Revitalizing Educational Psychology: Readings in Method & Substance. Ed. by William E. Roweton. LC 76-20603. 384p. 1976. 18.95 (ISBN 0-88229-195-5). Nelson-Hall.

Revival Addresses. R. A. Torrey. 282p. 1974. Repr. of 1903 ed. 10.50 (ISBN 0-227-67808-7). Attic Pr.

Revival in Tin Town. Effie M. Williams. 84p. pap. 0.75. Faith Pub Hse.

Revival of American Socialism: Selected Papers of the Socialist Scholars Conference. Ed. by George Fischer. 1971. 17.95 (ISBN 0-19-501412-X). Oxford U Pr.

Revival of Civic Learning: A Rationale for Citizenship Education in American Schools. R. Freeman Butts. LC 80-81870. (Foundation Monograph Ser.). 170p. (Orig.). 1980. pap. 6.00 (ISBN 0-87367-423-5). Phi Delta Kappa.

Revival Praying. Leonard Ravenhill. 1962. pap. 3.50 (ISBN 0-87123-482-3, 210482). Bethany Fell.

Revivalism & Social Reform: American Protestantism on the Eve of the Civil War. Timothy Smith. LC 80-8114. Orig. Title: Revialism & Social Reform in Mid-Nineteenth Century America. 272p. 1980. pap. text ed. 5.95x (ISBN 0-8018-2477-X). Johns Hopkins.

Revivals, Awakening, & Reform: An Essay on Religion & Social Change in America, 1607 to 1977. William G. McLoughlin. LC 77-27830. xvi, 240p. 1980. pap. 5.95 (ISBN 0-226-56092-9, P891, Phoen). U of Chicago Pr.

Revivals, Awakenings, & Reform. William G. McLoughlin. LC 77-27830. 1978. 15.00x (ISBN 0-226-56091-0). U of Chicago Pr.

Revolt. Menachem Begin. (Illus.). 1977. Repr. 12.95 o.p. (ISBN 0-8402-1370-0). Nash Pub.

Revolt Against Chivalry: Jessie Daniel Ames & the Women's Campaign Against Lynching. Jacquelyn D. Hall. 1979. 17.50 (ISBN 0-231-04040-7). Columbia U Pr.

Revolt from the Centre. Niels I. Meyer et al. Tr. by Christine Hauch. LC 79-56838. (Open Forum Ser.). 192p. 1980. 14.00 (ISBN 0-7145-2701-7, Pub. by M Boyars). Merrimack Bk Serv.

Revolt of the Hereros. Jon M. Bridgeman. (Perspectives on Southern Africa Ser.). 200p. 1980. 12.50 (ISBN 0-520-04113-5). U of Cal Pr.

Revolt of the Perverts: Gay Short Stories. Daniel Curzon. 1978. pap. 4.50 (ISBN 0-930650-01-8). D Brown Bks.

Revolt of the Provinces: Conservatives & Radicals in the English Civil War, 1630-1650. J. S. Morrill. (Historical Problems: Studies & Documents). 1976. pap. text ed. 8.95x o.p. (ISBN 0-04-942159-X). Allen Unwin.

Revolt of the Widows: The Social World of the Apocryphal Acts. Stevan L. Davies. LC 80-11331. 160p. 1980. 10.95x (ISBN 0-8093-0958-0). S Ill U Pr.

Revolucion En las Matematicas Escolares: Segunda Fase. (Serie De Matematica: No. 13). (Span.). 1971. pap. 1.25 o.p. (ISBN 0-8270-6290-7). OAS.

Revolution & After. Gordon Lindsay. (Old Testament Ser.). 1.25 (ISBN 0-89985-152-5). Christ Nations.

Revolution & Chinese Foreign Policy: Peking's Support for Wars of National Liberation. Peter Van Ness. (Center for Chinese Studies UC Berkeley). 1970. 20.00x (ISBN 0-520-01583-5); pap. 6.95x (ISBN 0-520-02055-3, CAMPUS63). U of Cal Pr.

Revolution & Class Struggle: A Reader in Marxist Politics. Ed. by Robin Blackburn. LC 77-1640. 1978. text ed. 24.75x (ISBN 0-391-00712-2). Humanities.

Revolution & Cosmopolitanism: The Western Stage & the Chinese Stages. Joseph R. Levenson. LC 73-121188. (Illus.). 1971. 13.75x (ISBN 0-520-01737-4). U of Cal Pr.

Revolution & Counter-Revolution in Hungary. Oscar Jaszi. LC 68-9595. 1969. Repr. of 1924 ed. 15.50 (ISBN 0-86527-168-2). Fertig.

Revolution & History: Origins of Marxist Historiography in China, 1919-1937. Arif Dirlik. LC 77-80469. 1978. 23.75x (ISBN 0-520-03541-0). U of Cal Pr.

Revolution & Improvement, 1775-1848. John Roberts. LC 75-17288. 1976. 28.50x (ISBN 0-520-03076-1). U of Cal Pr.

Revolution & Power Politics in Yoruvaland 1840-1893: Ibadan Expansion & the Rise of Ekitparapo. S. A. Akintoye. (Ibadan History Ser). 1971. text ed. 11.00x o.p. (ISBN 0-391-00168-X). Humanities.

Revolution & Reaction in Cuba, 1933-1960: A Political Sociology from Machado to Castro. Samuel Farber. LC 76-7190. 1976. 20.00x (ISBN 0-8195-4099-4, Pub. by Wesleyan U Pr). Columbia U Pr.

Revolution & Reality: Essays on the Origin of the Soviet System. Bertram D. Wolfe. LC 80-16178. (Illus.). 422p. 1981. 19.00x (ISBN 0-8078-1453-9); pap. 11.00x (ISBN 0-8078-4073-4). U of NC Pr.

Revolution & Repetition: Marx-Hugo-Balzac. Jeffrey Mehlman. (Quantum Ser.). 1977. 11.95x (ISBN 0-520-03111-3); pap. 2.45 (ISBN 0-520-03531-3). U of Cal Pr.

Revolution & the Rebirth of Inequality: Stratification in Post-Revolutionary Bolivia. Jonathan Kelley & Herbert S. Klein. 1980. 14.95 (ISBN 0-520-04072-4). U of Cal Pr.

Revolution & the Transformation of Societies: A Comparative Study of Civilizations. S. N. Eisenstadt. LC 77-5203. 1978. 17.95 (ISBN 0-02-909390-2). Free Pr.

Revolution & Tradition in Tientsin, 1949-1952. Kenneth G. Lieberthal. LC 79-64215. 1980. 18.50x (ISBN 0-8047-1044-9). Stanford U Pr.

Revolution at Queretaro: The Mexican Constitutional Convention of 1916-1917. E. V. Niemeyer, Jr. LC 73-20203. (Latin American Monographs: No. 33). (Illus.). 326p. 1974. 14.95 (ISBN 0-292-77005-7). U of Tex Pr.

Revolution Francaise et l'abolition Del'Esclavage, 12 vols. 2200p. (Fr.). 1976. Set. lib. bdg. 390.00x o.p. (ISBN 0-8287-0723-5); Set. pap. text ed. 310.00x o.p. (ISBN 0-685-64323-9). Clearwater Pub.

Revolution Francaise et L'emancipation Des Juifs, 8 vols. Ed. by Leon Centner. 1900p. (Fr.). 1976. Set. lib. bdg. 195.00 o.p. (ISBN 0-8287-0724-3); Set. pap. text ed. 135.00 o.p. (ISBN 0-685-64325-5). Clearwater Pub.

Revolution from Rosinante. Alexis A. Gilliland. 192p. (Orig.). 1981. pap. 2.25 (Del Rey). Ballantine.

Revolution in British Management Education. Mildred Wheatcroft. 1971. 12.00x o.p. (ISBN 0-8464-0795-7). Beekman Pubs.

Revolution in Central Europe, 1918-1919. F. L. Carsten. LC 78-165225. 1972. 25.00x (ISBN 0-520-02084-7). U of Cal Pr.

Revolution in German Theatre, Nineteen Hundred to Nineteen Thirty-Three. Michael Patterson. (Illus.). 226p. 1981. price not set (ISBN 0-7100-0659-4). Routledge & Kegan.

Revolution in Guinea: Selected Texts. Amilcar Cabral. Ed. & tr. by Richard Handyside. LC 73-124084. 144p. 1970. 4.95 o.p. (ISBN 0-85345-144-3, CL-1443); pap. 3.95 (ISBN 0-85345-222-9, PB-2229). Monthly Rev.

Revolution in Judaea: Jesus & the Jewish Resistance. Hyam Maccoby. LC 80-16752. 256p. 1980. 9.95 (ISBN 0-8008-6784-X). Taplinger.

Revolution in Learning: The Years from Birth to Six. Maya Pines. LC 66-10657. 1967. 10.00 o.s.i. (ISBN 0-06-034866-6, HarpT). Har-Row.

Revolution in Miniature. E. Braun & S. Macdonald. LC 77-82489. (Illus.). 1978. 29.95 (ISBN 0-521-21815-2). Cambridge U Pr.

Revolution in Perspective: Essays on the Hungarian Soviet Republic. Ed. by Andrew C. Janos & William B. Slottman. LC 74-138510. 1971. 21.50x (ISBN 0-520-01920-2). U of Cal Pr.

Revolution in Psychiatry: The New Understanding of Man. Ernest Becker. LC 64-11213. 1974. pap. 3.95 (ISBN 0-02-902130-8). Free Pr.

Revolution in Tanner's Lane, 1887. William H. White. Ed. by Robert L. Wolff. Bd. with Miriam's Schooling, Eighteen Ninety. LC 75-1515. (Victorian Fiction Ser.). 1975. lib. bdg. 66.00 (ISBN 0-8240-1588-6). Garland Pub.

Revolution in the New York Party System: 1840-1860. Mark L. Berger. LC 72-89990. 1973. 11.00 (ISBN 0-8046-9030-8, Natl U). Kennikat.

Revolution in Warfare. Basil H. Liddell Hart. LC 79-22632. 1980. Repr. of 1947 ed. lib. bdg. 16.75x (ISBN 0-313-22173-1, LHRW). Greenwood.

Revolution Is Not a Dinner Party: A Feast of Images of the Maoist Transformation of China. Richard H. Solomon. LC 74-25123. 1978. 6.95 o.p. (ISBN 0-385-09926-6, Anch). Doubleday.

Revolution Island. Julian Fane. 352p. 1980. 17.95 (ISBN 0-241-10319-3, Pub. by Hamish Hamilton England). David & Charles.

Revolution of Eighteen Forty Eight-Forty Nine: Articles from the Neue Rheinische Zeitung. Karl Marx & Frederick Engels. LC 77-188755. 240p. 1973. 7.50 (ISBN 0-7178-0339-2); pap. 2.25 o.p. (ISBN 0-7178-0340-6). Intl Pub Co.

Revolution of Love. K. Neill Foster. 96p. 1973. pap. 0.95 (ISBN 0-87123-486-6, 200486). Bethany Fell.

Revolution of Things. Miron Bialoszewski. Tr. by Bogdan Czaykowski & Andrzej Busza. LC 74-81212. 1974. 7.50 (ISBN 0-685-41660-7). Charioteer.

Revolution on the Pampas: A Social History of Argentine Wheat. James R. Scobie. (Latin American Monograph: No. 1). 1964. 9.95 (ISBN 0-292-73352-6). U of Tex Pr.

Revolution Reform & Social Justice: Studies in the Theory & Practice of Marxism. Sidney Hook. LC 74-21610. 307p. 1975. uKE 15.00x (ISBN 0-8147-3368-9); pap. 7.00x uke (ISBN 0-8147-3400-6). NYU Pr.

Revolution That Wasn't: A Contemporary Assessment of 1776. Ed. by Richard M. Fulton. (National University Publication, American Studies). 1981. 19.50 (ISBN 0-8046-9259-9). Kennikat.

Revolution, the Constitution & America's Third Century, 2 vols. American Academy of Political & Social Science. 1980. 35.00x (ISBN 0-8122-7763-5). U of Pa Pr.

Revolution Through Ballot: India, January - March 1977. Anirudha Gupta. 1977. 8.00x o.p. (ISBN 0-8364-0460-2). South Asia Bks.

Revolutionaries in Modern Britain. Peter Shipley. 256p. 1976. 16.95 (ISBN 0-370-11311-X). Transatlantic.

Revolutionaries in Modern Britain. Peter Shipley. 1979. 12.95 (ISBN 0-370-11311-X, Pub. by Chatto Bodley Jonathan). Merrimack Bk Serv.

Revolutionaries Without Revolution. Andre Thirion. LC 74-9859. (Illus.). 512p. 1975. 15.95 o.s.i. (ISBN 0-02-617400-6, 61740). Macmillan.

Revolutionary. Hans Koningsberger. 212p. 1967. 4.95 (ISBN 0-374-24984-9). FS&G.

Revolutionary Age of Andrew Jackson. Robert V. Remini. 1977. pap. 1.50 (ISBN 0-380-01753-9, 34652). Avon.

Revolutionary & Imperial France: 1750-1815. Ernest J. Knapton. LC 76-181037. 150p. 1972. 6.95 o.p. (ISBN 0-684-12718-0, ScribT). Scribner.

Revolutionary & Napoleonic Era. J. H. Rose. 387p. 1980. Repr. of 1894 ed. lib. bdg. 40.00 (ISBN 0-89760-737-6). Telegraph Bks.

Revolutionary Breakthroughs & National Development: The Case of Romania, 1944-1965. Kenneth Jowitt. 1971. 25.00x (ISBN 0-520-01762-5). U of Cal Pr.

Revolutionary Continuity: Marxist Leadership in the U. S., 1848-1917. 1981. 20.00 (ISBN 0-913460-85-0); pap. 5.45 (ISBN 0-913460-84-2). Monad Pr.

Revolutionary Corporations: Engines of Plenty, Engines of Growth, Engines of Change. John D. Glover. LC 80-66021. 350p. 1980. 35.00 (ISBN 0-87094-217-4). Dow Jones-Irwin.

Revolutionary Cuba. Terence Cannon. LC 77-26587. (Illus.). 368p. (gr. 9 up). 1980. 16.95 (ISBN 0-690-01307-8, TYC-J). T Y Crowell.

Revolutionary Diplomacy: Chinese Foreign Policy & the United Front Doctrine. J. D. Armstrong. 259p. 1981. 21.00x (ISBN 0-520-03251-9, CAMPUS 268); pap. 5.95x (ISBN 0-520-04273-5). U of Cal Pr.

Revolutionary Empire. Angus Calder. 1981. 35.00 (ISBN 0-525-19080-5). Dutton.

Revolutionary Enigma: A Re-Appraisal of General Philip Schuyler of New York. Martin H. Bush. LC 78-8329. (Empire State Historical Publications Ser). 1969. 12.95 (ISBN 0-8046-8080-9). Friedman.

Revolutionary Histories: Contemporary Narratives of the American Revolution. Lester H. Cohen. LC 80-11243. 1980. 15.00x (ISBN 0-8014-1277-3). Cornell U Pr.

Revolutionary Humanism & Historicism in Modern Italy. Edmund D. Jacobitti. LC 80-5393. 240p. 1981. text ed. 18.00x (ISBN 0-300-02479-7). Yale U Pr.

Revolutionary Journal of Baron Ludwig Von Closen, 1780-1783. Ludwig Von Closen. Ed. by Evelyn M. Acomb. (Institute of Early American History & Culture Ser.). 1958. 19.50x (ISBN 0-8078-0745-1). U of NC Pr.

Revolutionary Justice: A Study of the Organization, Personnel & Procedure of the Paris Tribunal 1793-1795. James Godfrey. (Perspectives in Europen History Ser.: No. 42). vi, 166p. 1981. Repr. of 1951 ed. lib. bdg. 15.00x (ISBN 0-87991-640-0). Porcupine Pr.

Revolutionary Law & Order: Politics & Social Change in the USSR. Peter H. Juviler. LC 76-12832. 1976. 17.95 (ISBN 0-02-916800-7). Free Pr.

Revolutionary Medicine, Seventeen Hundred to Eighteen Hundred. C. Keith M. D. Wilbur. LC 80-82790. (Illus.). 96p. (Orig.). 1980. pap. 8.95 (ISBN 0-87106-041-8). Globe Pequot.

Revolutionary Origins of Modern Japan. Thomas M. Huber. LC 79-64214. (Illus.). 288p. 1981. 18.50x (ISBN 0-8047-1048-1). Stanford U Pr.

Revolutionary Path. Kwame Nkrumah. LC 73-78905. 1973. 12.50 (ISBN 0-7178-0400-3); pap. 4.95 (ISBN 0-7178-0401-1). Intl Pub Co.

Revolutionary Pressures in Africa. Claude Ake. 112p. 1978. 12.95 (Pub. by Zed Pr); pap. 6.95 (ISBN 0-905762-15-0). Lawrence Hill.

Revolutionary Syndicalism & French Labor. Peter N. Stearns. 1971. 13.00 (ISBN 0-8135-0688-3). Rutgers U Pr.

Revolutionary Syndicalism in France. F. F. Ridley. LC 73-123663. 1971. 38.50 (ISBN 0-521-07907-1). Cambridge U Pr.

Revolutionary Terrorism: The FLN in Algeria, 1954-1962. Martha C. Hutchinson. LC 78-59130. (Publications 196 Ser.). 1978. 10.95 (ISBN 0-8179-6961-6). Hoover Inst Pr.

Revolutionary Thought from Marx to Mao, 10 vols. 1977. Set. pap. 8.95 (ISBN 0-8351-0310-2). China Bks.

Revolutionary Thought in the Twentieth Century. Ben Turok. 360p. (Orig.). 1980. 18.95 (ISBN 0-905762-42-8, Pub. by Zed Pr); pap. 8.95 (ISBN 0-905762-43-6). Lawrence Hill.

Revolutionary Violence: The Theories. Anthony Burton. LC 77-83808. 1978. 14.00x (ISBN 0-8448-1262-5). Crane-Russak Co.

Revolutionary Virginia: The Road to Independence, Clash of Arms & the Fourth Convention, 1775-1776, a Documentary Record, Vol. V. Compiled by Robert L. Scribner & Brent Tarter. LC 72-96023. 1980. 30.00x (ISBN 0-8139-0806-X). U Pr of Va.

Revolutionary Virginia, the Road to Independence, Vol. 4: The Committee of Safety & the Balance of Forces, 1775 a Documentary Record. Compiled by Robert L. Scriber & Brent Tarter. LC 72-96023. 1978. 25.00x (ISBN 0-8139-0748-9). U Pr of Va.

Revolutionary War & Issachar Bates. John S. Williams. 1960. 1.00 (ISBN 0-937942-02-2). Shaker Mus.

Revolutionary War Journals of Henry Dearborn, 1775-1783. Ed. by Lloyd A. Brown & Howard H. Peckham. LC 74-146143. (Era of the American Revolution Ser). 1971. Repr. of 1939 ed. lib. bdg. 29.50 (ISBN 0-306-70107-3). Da Capo.

Revolutionary War: Western Response. Ed. by David S. Sullivan & Martin J. Sattler. LC 73-171976. 1971. 20.00x (ISBN 0-231-03564-0); pap. 5.00x (ISBN 0-231-08664-4). Columbia U Pr.

Revolutionary Years: West Africa Since Eighteen Hundred. J. B. Webster & A. A. Boahen. (Growth of African Civilization Ser.). (Illus.). 1981. pap. text ed. 5.95 (ISBN 0-582-60332-3). Longman.

Revolutions & Reconstructions in the Philosophy of Science. Mary Hesse. LC 80-7819. 224p. 1980. 22.50x (ISBN 0-253-33381-4). Ind U Pr.

Revolutions & Revolutionaries. A. J. Raylor. LC 80-66006. 1980. 12.95 (ISBN 0-689-11069-3). Atheneum.

Revolutions Du XIXe Siecle: 1830-1834. 1116.00 o.p. (ISBN 0-8287-0725-1). Clearwater Pub.

Revolutions in Spanish America: The Independence Movements of 1808-1825. Albert Prago. (gr. 8 up). 1970. 5.95g o.s.i. (ISBN 0-02-775110-4). Macmillan.

Revolving College Doors: The Causes & Consequences of Dropping Out, Stopping Out & Transferring. Robert Cope & William Hannah. LC 75-16472. 190p. 1975. 20.95 (ISBN 0-471-17124-7, Pub. by Wiley-Interscience). Wiley.

Revue Blanche, No. 158-159. (Maeght Gallery: Derriere le Miroir Ser.). (Fr.). 1977. pap. 19.95 o.p. (ISBN 0-8120-0900-2). Barron.

Revue De la Musique Dramatique En France. Felix Crozet. Bd. with Supplement a la Revue De la Musique Dramatique En France. LC 80-2270. 1981. 48.50 (ISBN 0-404-18833-8). AMS Pr.

Reward System in British & American Science. Jerry Gaston. LC 77-17404. (Science, Culture & Society Ser.). 1978. 24.50 (ISBN 0-471-29293-1, Pub. by Wiley-Interscience). Wiley.

Reward Worth Having. Jay Williams. LC 76-56135. (Illus.). 32p. (gr. k-3). 1977. 6.95 (ISBN 0-590-07342-7, Four Winds). Schol Bk Serv.

Rewards of Public Service: Compensating Top Federal Officials. Ed. by Robert W. Hartman & Arnold R. Weber. 1980. 14.95 (ISBN 0-8157-3494-8); pap. 5.95 (ISBN 0-8157-3493-X). Brookings.

Rewinding Small Motors. 3rd ed. Daniel H. Braymer & A. C. Roe. LC 80-29580. 432p. 1981. Repr. of 1949 ed. lib. bdg. price not set (ISBN 0-89874-291-9). Krieger.

Rewriting Nursing History. Ed. by Celia Davies. 226p. 1981. 23.50x (ISBN 0-389-20153-7). B&N.

Rewyll of Seynt Sauioure, Vol. 1. James Hogg. (Salzburg Studien zur Anglistik und Amerikanistik). 1980. pap. text ed. 31.25x (ISBN 0-391-01195-2). Humanities.

Rewyll of Seynt Sauioure & Other Middle English Brigittine Legislative, Vol. 2. James Hogg. (Salzburger Studien Zur Anglistik und Amerikanistik: No. 6). 1978. pap. text ed. 38.75x (ISBN 0-391-01415-3). Humanities.

Rex: An Autobiography. Rex Harrison. 1975. 7.95 o.p. (ISBN 0-688-02881-0). Morrow.

Rex Ingram: Master of the Silent Cinema. Liam O'Leary. (Illus.). 224p. 1980. 28.50. B&N.

Rex Stout: A Primary & Secondary Bibliography. Guy Townsend et al. LC 80-8507. 210p. 1980. lib. bdg. 30.00. Garland Pub.

Rey Mas Maravilloso. Dave Hill. Tr. by Ronald Ross from Eng. (Libros Arco). (Illus.). 32p. (Span.). (gr. 1-3). 1972. pap. 0.95 o.s.i. (ISBN 0-89922-046-0). Edit Caribe.

Reynard the Fox: A Study of the Fox in Medieval Enlish Art. Kenneth Varty. 1967. text ed. 25.00x (ISBN 0-391-01055-7, Leicester). Humanities.

Reynolds. David Manning. (Oresko-Jupiter Art Bks). (Illus.). 96p. 1981. 17.95 (ISBN 0-933516-85-1, Pub. by Oresko-Jupiter England). Hippocrene Bks.

Reynolds Campaign on Powder River. Jesse W. Vaughn. (Illus.). 239p. 1961. 12.50 o.p. (ISBN 0-8061-0511-9). U of Okla Pr.

Reynoldsburg Book of Lists. Cornelia M. Parkinson. (Orig.). 1981. pap. text ed. 7.50 (ISBN 0-938404-03-2). Hist Tales.

Rhapsody in Blue of Mickey Klein. Ben Herman. 144p. (gr. 7 up). 1981. 8.95 (ISBN 0-916144-68-2). Stemmer Hse.

Rhapsody of Words. Ivor Brown. 1972. 5.95 (ISBN 0-370-00333-0). Transatlantic.

Rheological Techniques. R. W. Whorlow. LC 79-40992. (Physics in Medicine & Biology Ser.). 447p. 1980. 89.95x (ISBN 0-470-26736-4). Halsted Pr.

Rheology & Texture in Food Quality. Ed. by J. M. DeMan et al. (Illus.). 1976. lib. bdg. 48.00 (ISBN 0-87055-197-3); pap. text ed. 26.00 (ISBN 0-87055-295-3). AVI.

Rheology of Biological Systems. Henry L. Gabelnick & Mitchell Litt. (Illus.). 320p. 1973. 24.50 (ISBN 0-398-02589-4). C C Thomas.

Rheology of Blood & Synovial Fluids. Horst Chmiel & Eckehard Walitza. 184p. 1981. 42.00 (ISBN 0-471-27858-0, Pub. by Wiley-Interscience). Wiley.

Rheology of Lubricants. Ed. by T. C. Davenport. LC 72-13462. (Illus.). 148p. 1973. 15.95 o.p. (ISBN 0-470-19672-6). Halsted Pr.

Rheology of Polymers. G. V. Vinogradov & A. Y. Malkin. (Illus.). 468p. 1981. 58.00 (ISBN 0-387-09778-3). Springer-Verlag.

Rheology of the Circulation. R. L. Whitmore. LC 68-18535. 232p. 1968. 32.00 (ISBN 0-08-012661-8). Pergamon.

Rheology: Theory & Applications, 5 Vols. Ed. by Frederick R. Eirich. 1956-1969. Vol. 1. 1956. 68.50 (ISBN 0-12-234301-8); Vol. 2. 1958. 61.75 (ISBN 0-12-234302-6); Vol. 3. 1959. 61.75 (ISBN 0-12-234303-4); Vol. 4. 1967. 68.50 (ISBN 0-12-234304-2); Vol. 5. 1970. 68.50 (ISBN 0-12-234305-0). Acad Pr.

Rheometry: Industrial Applications. Kenneth Walters. 432p. 1981. write for info. (ISBN 0-471-27878-5, Pub. by Wiley-Interscience). Wiley.

Rhesos. Euripides. Tr. by Richard E. Braun from Greek. (Greek Tragedy in New Translations). 1978. 10.95 (ISBN 0-19-502049-9). Oxford U Pr.

Rhesus. Euripides. Tr. by Gilbert Murray. 1913. pap. text ed. 3.95x (ISBN 0-04-882040-7). Allen Unwin.

Rhetores Latini Minores. Ed. by C. Halm. (Classical Studies Ser.). (Lat.). Repr. of 1853 ed. lib. bdg. 29.50x (ISBN 0-697-00038-9). Irvington.

Rhetoric: a Tradition in Transition. Ed. by Walter R. Fisher. 315p. 1974. 12.50x (ISBN 0-87013-188-5). Mich St U Pr.

Rhetoric & Composition: A Sourcebook for Teachers. Richard L. Graves. (English Language Ser). 1976. pap. text ed. 9.50x (ISBN 0-8104-5984-1). Hayden.

Rhetoric & Truth in France: Descartes to Diderot. Peter France. 1972. 24.95x (ISBN 0-19-815709-6). Oxford U Pr.

Rhetoric in a Modern Mode, with Selected Readings. 3rd ed. James K. Bell & Adrian Cohn. 1976. pap. text ed. 9.95 (ISBN 0-02-470600-0). Macmillan.

Rhetoric in Effective Communication. Mary H. Manoni & Elizabeth L. O'Donnell. LC 78-730061. (Illus.). 1977. pap. text ed. 99.00 (ISBN 0-89290-122-5, A321). Soc for Visual.

Rhetoric in Spenser's Poetry. Herbert D. Rix. 88p. 1980. Repr. of 1940 ed. lib. bdg. 15.00 (ISBN 0-89987-712-5). Darby Bks.

Rhetoric in the Middle Ages: A History of Rhetorical Theory from Saint Augustine to the Renaissance. James J. Murphy. 1981. pap. 7.95x (ISBN 0-520-04406-1, CAMPUS 277). U of Cal Pr.

Rhetoric in the Middle Ages, A.D. 400-1500, the Renaissance. James J. Murphy. 1974. 23.75x (ISBN 0-520-02439-7). U of Cal Pr.

Rhetoric of Aristotle with a Commentary, 3 vols. E. M. Cope. Ed. by J. E. Sandys. (Classical Studies Ser.). (Gr. & Eng.). Repr. of 1877 ed. Set. lib. bdg. 76.00x (ISBN 0-89197-922-0); Vol. 1. lib. bdg. 29.00x (ISBN 0-697-00033-8); Vol. 2. lib. bdg. 27.00x (ISBN 0-697-00034-6); Vol. 3. lib. bdg. 32.00x (ISBN 0-697-00035-4). Irvington.

Rhetoric of Irony. Wayne C. Booth. LC 73-87298. xviii, 292p. 1975. 14.00x (ISBN 0-226-06552-9); pap. 5.95 (ISBN 0-226-06553-7, P641). U of Chicago Pr.

Rhetoric of Love in Lyly's Euthues & His England & Sidney's Arcadia (1590) James E. O'Hara, Jr. (Salzburg Studies in English Literature, Elizabethan & Renaissance Studies: No. 76). (Orig.). 1978. pap. text ed. 25.00x (ISBN 0-391-01243-6). Humanities.

Rhetoric of Motives. Kenneth Burke. LC 69-16742. 1969. 16.50x (ISBN 0-520-01545-2); pap. 6.95x (ISBN 0-520-01546-0, CAL178). U of Cal Pr.

Rhetoric of Pascal. Patricia Topliss. 1966. text ed. 18.75x (ISBN 0-7185-1062-3, Leicester). Humanities.

Rhetoric of Protest & Reform, 1878-1898. Ed. by Paul H. Boase. LC 80-11631. 354p. 1980. 16.95x (ISBN 0-8214-0421-0, 0421E). Ohio U Pr.

Rhetoric of Renaissance Poetry. Ed. by Thomas O. Sloan & Raymond B. Waddington. LC 73-80824. 1974. 16.95x (ISBN 0-520-02501-6). U of Cal Pr.

Rhetoric of Television. Ronald Primeau. LC 78-2492. (English & Humanities Ser.). 1978. pap. text ed. 9.95x (ISBN 0-582-28058-3). Longman.

Rhetoric of the Contemporary Lyric. Jonathan Holden. LC 79-3383. 160p. 1980. 12.95x (ISBN 0-253-15667-X). Ind U Pr.

Rhetoric of the People: Is There Any Better or Equal Hope in the World? Ed. by Harold Barrett. 335p. (Orig.). 1974. pap. text ed. 16.75x (ISBN 90-6203-001-7). Humanities.

Rhetoric of the Speaker: Speeches & Criticism. Ed. by Haig A. Bosmajian. (Uses of English Ser.). 1967. pap. text ed. 2.95x o.p. (ISBN 0-669-20982-1). Heath.

Rhetoric: Principles & Usage. 2nd ed. Richard E. Hughes & P. A. Duhamel. 1967. text ed. 12.95 (ISBN 0-13-780718-X). P-H.

Rhetoric Three: The Rhetoric Section from Rhetoric in a Modern Mode. 3rd ed. James K. Bell & Adrian Cohn. 1976. pap. text ed. 4.95 (ISBN 0-02-470620-5). Macmillan.

Rhetorical Criticism: A Study in Method. Edwin Black. LC 77-91050. 1978. 15.00 (ISBN 0-299-07550-8); pap. text ed. 6.95 (ISBN 0-299-07554-0). U of Wis Pr.

Rhetorical Form of Carlyle's Sartor Resartus. Gerry H. Brookes. LC 71-185974. 208p. 1972. 17.00x (ISBN 0-520-02213-0). U of Cal Pr.

Rhetorical Patterns: An Anthology of Contemporary Essays. John P. Ferre & Steven E. Pauley. (Illus.). 208p. 1981. pap. text ed. 6.95 (ISBN 0-675-08023-1). Merrill.

Rhetorical Perspectives on Communication and Mass Madia. Richard J Jensen et al. 176p. 1980. pap. text ed. 9.95 (ISBN 0-8403-1902-9). Kendall-Hunt.

Rhetorique generale. Jacques Dubois et al. (Langue et langage). (Fr). 1970. pap. 12.25 (ISBN 0-685-14067-9, 3638). Larousse.

Rheumatic Disease. M. H. Weisman. 1981. text ed. price not set (ISBN 0-443-08100-X). Churchill.

Rheumatic Disorders in Childhood. Barbara M. Ansell. LC 80-40275. (Postgraduate Paediatrics Ser.). (Illus.). 344p. 1980. text ed. 66.95 (ISBN 0-407-00186-7). Butterworths.

Rheumatic Fever. 2nd ed. Milton Markowitz & Leon Gordis. LC 72-82808. (Major Problems in Clinical Pediatrics Ser.: Vol. 2). (Illus.). 309p. 1972. 13.50 (ISBN 0-7216-6091-6). Saunders.

Rheumatism in Populations. J. S. Lawrence. (Illus.). 1977. 70.00x (ISBN 0-433-19070-1). Intl Ideas.

Rheumatoid Arthritis. Ralph C. Williams, Jr. LC 74-4594. (Major Problems in Internal Medicine Ser.: Vol. 4). (Illus.). 255p. 1974. text ed. 14.50 (ISBN 0-7216-9417-9). Saunders.

Rheumatoid Arthritis & Related Conditions, Vol. 1. G. S. Panayi. (Annual Research Reviews Ser.). 1977. 14.40 (ISBN 0-88831-003-X). Eden Med Res.

Rheumatoid Arthritis & Related Conditions, Vol. 2. G. S. Panayi. LC 78-317911. (Annual Research Reviews Ser.). 1978. 19.20 (ISBN 0-88831-022-6). Eden Med Res.

Rheumatoid Arthritis: It Roughs up All the Edges. M. Ross. 4.50 o.p. (ISBN 0-8062-1220-9). Carlton.

Rheumatology. Ed. by Rodney Bluestone. (UCLA Postgraduate Medicine Ser.). 1980. 30.00 (ISBN 0-89289-375-3). HM Prof Med Div.

Rheumatology. Robert E. Pieroni & William P. Beetham, Jr. (Medical Examination Review Book: Vol. 31). 1974. spiral bdg. 16.50 (ISBN 0-87488-144-7). Med Exam.

Rheumatology. Edward E. Rosenbaum. (New Directions in Therapy Ser.). 1980. pap. 15.50 (ISBN 0-87488-683-X). Med Exam.

Rheumatology Continuing Education Review. Anthony Bohan. 1980. spiral bdg. 14.00 (ISBN 0-87488-333-4). Med Exam.

Rheumetic Disease. Michael Weisman. (Illus.). 288p. 1981. lib. bdg. 25.00 (ISBN 0-443-08100-X). Churchill.

Rhind Mathematical Papyrus. National Council of Teachers of Mathematics. 1979. Repr. 15.00 (ISBN 0-87353-133-7). NCTM.

Rhine. Car Hills. LC 78-62989. (Rivers of the World Ser.). (Illus.). 1978. lib. bdg. 7.95 (ISBN 0-686-50006-7). Silver.

Rhineland: Winter in a Missouri Rivertown. Ed. by Donna Holman. (Illus.). 191p. (Orig.). 1979. pap. text ed. 8.00 (ISBN 0-930552-02-4). Tech Ed Serv.

Rhinelander Center. Barbara Harrison. 464p. (Orig.). 1981. pap. 2.75 (ISBN 0-89083-704-X). Zebra.

Rhinestone As Big As the Ritz. Alan Coren. LC 79-83524. 1979. 8.95 o.p. (ISBN 0-312-68091-0). St Martin.

Rhinoceros in the Classroom. R. Murray Schafer. 1975. pap. 5.00 (ISBN 0-900938-44-7, 50-26922). Eur-Am Music.

Rhinoceros Success. Scott Alexander. LC 80-51648. (Illus.). 123p. (Orig.). (gr. 7 up). 1980. pap. 4.95 (ISBN 0-937382-00-0). Rhinos Pr.

Rhizoctonia Solani: Biology & Pathology. Ed. by J. R. Parmeter. LC 69-16510. (Illus.). 1970. 30.00x (ISBN 0-520-01497-9). U of Cal Pr.

Rhizome & the Flower: The Perennial Philosophy--Yeats & Jung. James Olney. 1980. 23.50x (ISBN 0-520-03748-0). U of Cal Pr.

Rhoads' West. Fred Rhoads. LC 72-86327. (Illus.). 124p. 1972. 6.95 o.p. (ISBN 0-87358-102-4). Northland.

Rhode Island. 23.00 (ISBN 0-89770-115-1). Curriculum Info Ctr.

Rhode Island: A Guide to the Smallest State. Federal Writers' Project. 500p. 1937. Repr. 45.00 (ISBN 0-403-02188-X). Somerset Pub.

Rhode Island: A History. William G. McLoughlin. (States and the Nation Ser.). (Illus.). 1978. 12.95 (ISBN 0-393-05675-9). Norton.

Rhode Island & the Union, 1774-1795. Irwin H. Polishook. (Studies in History Ser.: No. 5). 1969. 12.95x o.s.i. (ISBN 0-8101-0003-7). Northwestern U Pr.

Rhode Island Architecture. 2nd ed. Henry-Russell Hitchcock. LC 68-27725. (Architecture & Decorative Art Ser.: Vol. 19). (Illus.). 1968. Repr. of 1939 ed. lib. bdg. 29.50 (ISBN 0-306-71037-4). Da Capo.

Rhode Island Atlas. Marion I. Wright & Robert J. Sullivan. (Illus.). 192p. (Orig., Contains considerable text). 1981. pap. write for info. (ISBN 0-917012-19-4). RI Pubns Soc.

Rhode Island Campaign of 1778: Inauspicious Dawn of Alliance. Paul F. Dearden. LC 78-68920. (Illus.). 1980. 6.95 (ISBN 0-917012-17-8). RI Pubns Soc.

Rhode Island Chronology & Factbook, Vol. 39. R. I. Vexler. 1978. 8.50 (ISBN 0-379-16164-8). Oceana.

Rhode Island Colony. Clifford L. Alderman. LC 69-10461. (Forge of Freedom Ser). (Illus.). (gr. 5 up). 1969. 8.95 o.s.i. (ISBN 0-02-700250-0, CCPr). Macmillan.

Rhode Island in the Continental Congress, 1765-1790. W. R. Staples. LC 71-153373. (Era of the American Revolution Ser.). 726p. 1972. Repr. of 1870 ed. lib. bdg. 65.00 (ISBN 0-306-70203-7). Da Capo.

Rhode Island: In Words & Pictures. Dennis Fradin. LC 80-22669. (Young People's Stories of Our States Ser.). (Illus.). 48p. (gr. 2-5). 1981. PLB 8.65g (ISBN 0-516-03939-3, Time Line). Childrens.

Rhode Island Politics & the American Revolution, 1760-1776. David S. Lovejoy. LC 58-10478. (Brown University Studies: No. 23). (Illus.). 256p. 1969. Repr. of 1958 ed. 10.00 (ISBN 0-87057-053-6, Pub. by Brown U Pr). Univ Pr of New England.

Rhode Island State Industrial Directory, 1980-81. State Industrial Directories Corp. 1979. pap. 20.00 (ISBN 0-89910-019-8). State Indus Dir.

Rhode Islanders Record the Revolution: The Journals of William Humphrey & Zuriel Waterman. Nathaniel N. Shipton & David Swain. LC 78-68840. (Rhode Island Revolutionary Heritage Ser.: Vol. 4). (Illus.). 125p. 1981. 10.95 (ISBN 0-917012-03-8). RI Pubns Soc.

Rhode Island's Coastal Natural Areas: Priorities for Protection & Management. George L. Seavey. (Marine Technical Report Ser.: No. 43). 1975. pap. 2.00 (ISBN 0-938412-13-2). URI MAS.

Rhodes. Brian Dicks. (Islands Ser.). 1974. 14.95 (ISBN 0-7153-6571-1). David & Charles.

Rhodes, the Tswana, & the British: Colonialism, Collaboration, & Conflict in the Bechuanaland Protectorate, 1885-1899. Paul Maylam. LC 79-8582. (Contributions in Comparative Colonial Studies: No. 4). (Illus.). x, 245p. 1980. lib. bdg. 29.25 (ISBN 0-313-20885-9, MTB/). Greenwood.

Rhodesia - The Problem. D. Smith. 1969. text ed. 14.50 (ISBN 0-08-007094-9). Pergamon.

Rhodesia Alone. Ed. by James E. Dornan et al. 1977. pap. 10.00 (ISBN 0-685-85741-7). Coun Am Affairs.

Rhodesia & the U. N. Ed. by Avrahm Mezerik. 1966. 15.00 (ISBN 0-685-40642-3, 89). Intl Review.

Rhodesia, the Problem. D. Smith. 1969. Repr. 14.50 (ISBN 0-08-007094-9). Pergamon.

Rhodesia: The Struggle for a Birthright. Eshmael Mlambo. 1972. pap. text ed. 9.50x (ISBN 0-900966-72-6). Humanities.

Rhodesia: The Struggle for Freedom. Leonard Kapungu. LC 74-76966. 160p. 1974. 5.95x o.p. (ISBN 0-88344-435-6). Orbis Bks.

Rhodesia-Zimbabwe. Oliver Pollak & Karen Pollak. (World Bibliographical Ser.: No. 4). 197p. 1979. 25.25 (ISBN 0-903450-14-3). ABC-Clio.

Rhododencrons & Azaleas. Judith Berrisford. (Illus.). 1973. 17.95 (ISBN 0-571-04798-X, Pub. by Faber & Faber). Merrimack Bk Serv.

Rhododendrons in America. 2nd ed. Ted Van Veen. LC 77-104390. (Illus.). 1980. pap. 25.00 (ISBN 0-8323-0374-7). Binford.

Rhubarb Cookbook. Pamela G. Wubben. LC 79-66754. (Illus.). 65p. 1979. 4.95 (ISBN 0-935442-00-6). One Percent.

Rhyme & Punishment: Random & Not So Academic Graffiti. S. Santhi. (Indian Poetry Ser.). 80p. 1975. 6.00 (ISBN 0-89253-015-4). Ind-US Inc.

Rhyme & Reason. Fred S. Baylis. 1978. 4.00 o.p. (ISBN 0-682-49040-7). Exposition.

Rhyme? & Reason? Lewis Carroll. LC 75-32188. (Classics of Children's Literature, 1621-1932: Vol. 51). (Illus.). 1976. Repr. of 1883 ed. PLB 38.00 (ISBN 0-8240-2300-5). Garland Pub.

Rhymers' Lexicon. 2nd. ed. Andrew Loring. LC 78-156926. 1971. Repr. of 1905 ed. 26.00 (ISBN 0-8103-3341-4). Gale.

Rhymes & Runes of the Toad. Susan F. Schaeffer. Ed. by Sebastian Fleuret. LC 75-15927. (Illus.). 72p. 1975. 6.95 o.s.i. (ISBN 0-02-607040-5). Macmillan.

Rhymes O' a Driftin' Cowboy. Chuck Haas. LC 75-110942. 1970. 7.50 o.p. (ISBN 0-87358-048-6). Northland.

Rhymes Without Reason. Silas H. Shoemaker. 59p. 1980. 3.95 (ISBN 0-8059-2744-1). Dorrance.

Rhyming Cockney Slang. (Illus.). 1978. pap. cancelled o.p. (ISBN 0-902920-04-9, Abson Bks). Bradt Ent.

Rhyming Rainbow. Cicely M. Barker. (Cicely Mary Barker Storybks). (Illus.). (gr. k-4). 1977. 3.95 (ISBN 0-8467-0259-2, Pub. by Two Continents). Hippocrene Bks.

Rhyming Reporter. Rosalee G. Porter. LC 80-68921. 178p. (Orig.). 1981. pap. 5.95x (ISBN 0-935774-00-9). Elgen Pub Co.

Rhyolite - Death Valley's Ghost City of Golden Dreams. 8th ed. Harold O. Weight & Lucile Weight. 1978. pap. 1.50 o.p. (ISBN 0-912714-04-2). Calico Pr.

Rhyolite-Death Valley's Ghost City of Golden Dreams. 9th ed. Harold O. Weight & Lucile Weight. 1980. pap. 1.95. Calico Pr.

Rhythm: An Annotated Bibliography. Steven D. Winick. LC 74-14582. 1974. 10.00 (ISBN 0-8108-0767-X). Scarecrow.

Rhythm & Blues Records: An Encyclopedic Discography Nineteen Forty-Three to Seventy-Five. Ed. by Cliff Martin & Frank Scott. (Ethnic Music Ser.: Vol. 1). Date not set. pap. 19.95 (ISBN 0-936518-05-7). Nighthawk Pr.

Rhythm Band Book. Ruth Etkin. LC 78-57886. (Illus.). (gr. 2 up). 1978. 8.95 (ISBN 0-8069-4570-2); PLB 8.29 (ISBN 0-8069-4571-0). Sterling.

Rhythm in Drama. Kathleen George. LC 79-24432. 1980. 9.95 (ISBN 0-8229-3416-7); pap. 4.95 (ISBN 0-8229-5316-1). U of Pittsburgh Pr.

Rhythm in the Novel. E. K. Brown. LC 77-14165. 1978. 8.50x (ISBN 0-8032-1150-3); pap. 2.25x (ISBN 0-8032-6050-4, BB 667, Bison). U of Nebr Pr.

Rhythm of God: A Philosophy of Worship. Geddes MacGregor. LC 74-13598. 1974. 5.95 (ISBN 0-8164-1174-3). Crossroad NY.

Rhythm of the Zodiac & the Wisdom Dinner. Eric V. Moore. LC 80-51680. (Illus.). 80p. (Orig.). 1980. pap. 4.00 (ISBN 0-937236-00-4, 4W). Sonrise Prods.

Rhythmic Phenomena in Plants. B. M. Sweeney. (Experimental Botany Monographs, Vol. 3). 1969. 24.50 (ISBN 0-12-679050-7). Acad Pr.

Rhythmic Sightsinging. Walter L. Wehner. LC 78-66281. 1979. pap. text ed. 7.50 (ISBN 0-8191-0687-9). U Pr of Amer.

Rhythmic Thoughts. James E. Acree. Date not set. 5.95 (ISBN 0-533-04855-9). Vantage.

Rhythms. Michael French. 1981. pap. 2.75 (ISBN 0-425-05023-8). Berkley Pub.

Rhythms, Music & Instruments to Make. John Hawkinson & Martha Faulhaber. LC 70-91737. (Activity Bks. - Music Involvement Ser.: No. 2). (Illus.). (gr. 3 up). 1970. 6.50g (ISBN 0-8075-6958-5). A Whitman.

Rhythms of a Himalayan Village. Hugh R. Downs. LC 79-2983. (Illus.). 240p. (Orig.). 1980. pap. 9.95 (ISBN 0-06-250240-9). Har-Row.

Rhythms of Vision. Lawrence Blair. 1977. pap. 2.50 o.s.i. (ISBN 0-446-81232-3). Warner Bks.

Rhythms of Western Art. John P. Sedgwick. LC 73-170648. (Illus.). 1972. 14.50 (ISBN 0-8108-0449-2). Scarecrow.

Rhythms to Reading, 12 bks. new ed. Lucille Wood. Incl. Autumn (ISBN 0-8372-0622-7); Camping in the Mountains (ISBN 0-8372-0618-9); December Holidays (ISBN 0-8372-0620-0); Easter Lady (ISBN 0-8372-0623-5); February Holidays (ISBN 0-8372-0613-8); Halloween (ISBN 0-8372-0621-9); Harbor & the Sea (ISBN 0-8372-0617-0); Spring Secret (ISBN 0-8372-0615-4); Springtime Walk (ISBN 0-8372-0614-6); A Summer Day on the Farm (ISBN 0-8372-0616-2); Winter Days (ISBN 0-8372-0612-X); Zoo & the Circus (ISBN 0-8372-0619-7). (ps-3). 1973. text ed. 6.60 ea.; text ed. 15.96 picture songbk. (ISBN 0-8372-0743-6); lp records 8.49 ea.; cassettes 8.97 ea. of bks, records & songbook in bkshelf container 189.00 set, cassette ed. (ISBN 0-8372-0959-5); filmstrip sets, with spirit masters, cassettes, & tchr's guide avail. (ISBN 0-685-29087-5). Bowmar-Noble.

Rib Section. Carol Benjamin. (Orig.). 1981. pap. 4.95 (ISBN 0-88270-498-2). Logos.

Ribbin', Jivin', & Playin' the Dozens: The Unrecognized Dilemma of Inner-City Schools. Herbert L. Foster. LC 74-7393. 304p. 1974. text ed. 16.50 o.s.i. (ISBN 0-88410-150-9); pap. 9.95 (ISBN 0-88410-163-0). Ballinger Pub.

Ribbons in Her Hair. Luci Walker. Date not set. pap. 1.75 (ISBN 0-345-29278-2). Ballantine.

Ribonucleic Acids. Ed. by P. R. Stewart & D. S. Letham. LC 73-76335. (Illus.). xv, 268p. 1973. 26.20 o.p. (ISBN 0-387-06190-8). Springer-Verlag.

Ribsy. Beverly Cleary. (Illus.). (gr. 3-7). 1964. 7.75 (ISBN 0-688-21662-5); PLB 7.44 (ISBN 0-688-31662-X). Morrow.

Ribsy. Beverly Cleary. (gr. 3-5). 1975. pap. 1.75 o.s.i. (ISBN 0-671-56090-5). Archway.

Ricardo Guiraldes: Don Segundo Sombra. Ed. by P. R. Beardsell. 252p. 1973. text ed. 8.65 (ISBN 0-08-017009-9); pap. text ed. 8.30 (ISBN 0-08-017010-2). Pergamon.

Ricardo Palma: Tradiciones Peruanas. Ed. by P. Francis. LC 72-92110. 1970. 5.40 (ISBN 0-08-006665-8); pap. 4.30 (ISBN 0-08-006666-6). Pergamon.

Ricasoli & the Risorgimento in Tuscany. William K. Hancock. LC 68-9603. 1969. Repr. of 1926 ed. 16.50 (ISBN 0-86527-171-2). Fertig.

Ricciardo E Zoraide, 2 vols. Gioachino Rossini. Ed. by Phillip Gossett & Charles Rosen. LC 76-49184. (Early Romantic Opera Ser.: No. 10). 1980. Set. lib. bdg. 82.00 (ISBN 0-8240-2909-7). Garland Pub.

Rice & Man: Agricultural Ecology in Southeast Asia. Lucien M. Hanks. LC 78-169512. (Worlds of Man Ser). 1972. text ed. 11.00x (ISBN 0-88295-606-X); pap. text ed. 5.75x (ISBN 0-88295-607-8). AHM Pub.

Rice Bowl Pet. Patricia M. Martin. LC 62-7744. (Illus.). (gr. k-3). 1962. PLB 8.79 (ISBN 0-690-69969-7, TYC-J). T Y Crowell.

Rice Breeders in Asia: A Ten Country Survey of Their Backgrounds, Attitudes & Use of Genetic Materials. (IRRI Research Paper Ser.: No. 13). 18p. 1978. pap. 5.00 (R053, IRRI). Unipub.

Rice Breeding. 738p. 1972. pap. 43.00 (R030, IRRI). Unipub.

Rice Breeding with Induced Mutations. (Technical Reports: No. 86). 1968. pap. 8.25 (ISBN 92-0-115068-7, IAEA). Unipub.

Rice Breeding with Induced Mutations - 2. (Technical Reports: No. 102). (Illus.). 124p. (Orig.). 1970. pap. 8.25 (ISBN 92-0-115070-9, IAEA). Unipub.

Rice Breeding with Induced Mutations - 3. (Technical Reports: No. 131). (Illus.). 198p. (Orig.). 1972. pap. 12.00 (ISBN 92-0-115271-X, IAEA). Unipub.

Rice Cookery. Uncle Ben's Inc. LC 77-93278. 1977. pap. 5.95 (ISBN 0-912656-78-6). H P Bks.

Rice Cooking. Robin Howe. 276p. 1973. 10.00 (ISBN 0-233-96364-2). Transatlantic.

Rice Cultivation for the Million. Seizo Matsushima. 350p. 1980. 35.00x (ISBN 0-89955-203-X, Pub. by JSSP Japan). Intl Schol Bk Serv.

Rice Fertilization. (Technical Reports: No. 108). (Illus., Orig.). 1970. pap. 10.75 (ISBN 92-0-115270-1, IAEA). Unipub.

Rice Improvement. 186p. 1979. pap. 19.50 (R033, IRRI). Unipub.

Rice Improvement in China & Other Asian Countries. 307p. 1980. pap. 19.50 (ISBN 0-686-69537-2, R 116, IRRI). Unipub.

Rice in the Tropics: A Guide to Development of National Programs. Robert F. Chandler, Jr. (IADS Development-Oriented Literature Ser.). 1979. lib. bdg. 22.00x (ISBN 0-89158-361-0). Westview.

Rice in the Tropics: A Guide to the Development of National Programs. 256p. 1979. pap. 19.50 (R019, IRRI). Unipub.

Rice in West Africa: Policy & Economics. Scott R. Pearson & J. Dirck Stryker. LC 80-50906. (Illus.). 472p. 1981. 39.00x (ISBN 0-8047-1095-3). Stanford U Pr.
Rice Leaf Folder: Mass Rearing & a Proposal for Screening for Varietal Resistance in the Greenhouse. (IRRI Research Paper Ser.: No. 27). 17p. 1979. pap. 5.00 (R067, IRRI). Unipub.
Rice Milling Equipment Operation & Maintenance. (Agricultural Services Bulletin: No. 22). 95p. 1974. pap. 6.00 (F1972, FAO). Unipub.
Rice: Production & Utilization. Bor S. Luh. (Illus.). 1980. lib. bdg. 49.50 (ISBN 0-87055-332-1). AVI.
Rice Production Manual. 382p. 1970. pap. 21.50 (R018, IRRI). Unipub.
Rice Ragged Stunt Disease in the Phillipines. (IRRI Research Paper Ser.: No. 16). 25p. 1978. pap. 5.00 (R056, IRRI). Unipub.
Rice Research & Production in China: An IRRI Team's View. 119p. 1978. pap. 7.50 (R016, IRRI). Unipub.
Rice, Science & Man: Papers Presented at the Tenth Anniversary Celebration of the International Rice Research Institute. 163p. 1975. pap. 8.00 (R017, IRRI). Unipub.
Rice: Soil, Water, Land. 185p. 1978. pap. 18.50 (R015, IRRI). Unipub.
Rice Virus Diseases. 142p. 1972. pap. 4.00 (R014, IRRI). Unipub.
Ricercar A 3 for 3 Contrabasses. Robert Erickson. (U. C. Publ. in Contemporary Music: Vol. 5). 1975. pap. 10.00x (ISBN 0-520-09357-7). U of Cal Pr.
Rich & Other Atrocities. Charlotte Curtis. LC 76-5121. (Illus.). 1976. 12.95 o.s.i. (ISBN 0-06-010931-9, HarpT). Har-Row.
Rich & the Lonely. G. Christopher Morgan. LC 80-27486. 256p. 1981. 10.95 (ISBN 0-8253-0043-6). Beaufort Bks NY.
Rich & the Pore. Henry Parker. LC 77-7419. (English Experience Ser.: No. 882). 1977. Repr. of 1493 ed. lib. bdg. 69.00 (ISBN 90-221-0882-1). Walter J Johnson.
Rich Christian in the Church of the Early Empire: Contradictions & Accomodations. L. Wm. Countryman. (Texts & Studies in Religion: Vol. 7). 1980. soft cover 24.95x (ISBN 0-88946-970-9). E Mellen.
Rich Feast: Encountering the Bible from Genesis to Revelation. Chad Walsh. LC 80-8356. 192p. 1981. 9.95 (ISBN 0-06-069249-9, HarpR, HarpR). Har-Row.
Rich Friends. Jacqueline Briskin. 468p. 1976. 8.95 o.p. (ISBN 0-440-07367-7). Delacorte.
Rich Man & Lazarus. Brownlow North. 1979. pap. 2.45 (ISBN 0-85151-121-X). Banner of Truth.
Rich Man, Poor Man. Herman P. Miller. LC 75-127609. (Apollo Eds.). (Illus.). 1971. pap. 3.95 o.s.i. (ISBN 0-8152-0289-X, A289-G, TYC-T). T Y Crowell.
Rich Nations & the Poor Nations. Barbara Ward. 1962. pap. 4.95 (ISBN 0-393-00746-4, Norton Lib). Norton.
Rich, the Poor - & the Bible. rev. ed. Conrad Boerma. Tr. by John Bowden from Dutch. LC 80-15337. 1980. write for info. (ISBN 0-664-24349-5). Westminster.
Rich Uncle from Fiji. M. P. Adams. (Gambler's Book Shelf). (Illus.). 1977. pap. 2.95 (ISBN 0-911996-82-6). Gamblers.
Rich World, Poor World. Geoffrey Lean. 1979. text ed. 17.95x (ISBN 0-04-309010-9); pap. 13.50 (ISBN 0-04-309012-5). Allen Unwin.
Richard A. Sol Yurick. LC 80-66497. 1981. 11.95 (ISBN 0-87795-272-8). Arbor Hse.
Richard Aldington. Richard E. Smith. (English Authors Ser.: No. 222). 1977. lib. bdg. 12.50 (ISBN 0-8057-6691-X). Twayne.
Richard Alsop "A Hartford Wit". Karl P. Harrington. LC 69-17788. 1969. 12.00x (ISBN 0-8195-4000-5, Pub. by Wesleyan U Pr). Columbia U Pr.
Richard Baker's Music Guide. Richard Baker. LC 79-52366. (Illus.). 144p. 1980. 11.95 (ISBN 0-7153-7782-5). David & Charles.
Richard Brauer: Collected Papers, 3 vols. Richard Brauer. Ed. by Warren Wong & Paul Fong. 888p. 1980. Vol. 1. text ed. 55.00x (ISBN 0-262-02135-8); Vol. 2. text ed. 55.00x (ISBN 0-262-02148-X); Vol. 3. text ed. 55.00x (ISBN 0-262-02149-8). MIT Pr.
Richard Brinsley Sheridan. Jack D. Durant. LC 75-1094. (English Authors Ser.: No. 183). 1975. lib. bdg. 12.50 (ISBN 0-8057-6650-2). Twayne.
Richard Brinsley Sheridan: A Reference Guide. Jack D. Durant. (Reference Books Ser.). 1981. lib. bdg. 30.00 (ISBN 0-8161-8146-2). G K Hall.
Richard Carvel. Winston Churchill. (Illus.). 1914. 12.95 (ISBN 0-02-525660-2). Macmillan.
Richard Cumberland. Richard Dircks. LC 76-28361. (English Authors Ser.: No. 196). 1976. lib. bdg. 12.50 (ISBN 0-8057-6654-5). Twayne.
Richard Dadd: The Rock & Castle of Seclusion. David Greysmith. LC 74-2648. (Illus.). 192p. 1975. 17.95 o.s.i. (ISBN 0-02-545600-8). Macmillan.
Richard Dawson & Family Feud. Mary Ann Norbom. (Illus., Orig.). 1981. pap. 1.95 (ISBN 0-451-09773-4, J9773, Sig). NAL.
Richard Deacon's Microwave Cookery. Richard Deacon. LC 73-93782. (Illus.). 160p. 1977. 7.95 o.p. (ISBN 0-912656-74-3); pap. 5.95 (ISBN 0-912656-73-5). H P Bks.
Richard Harding Davis. Scott C. Osborn & Robert Phillips. (United States Authors Ser.: No. 289). 1978. lib. bdg. 12.50 (ISBN 0-8057-7192-1). Twayne.
Richard Harris Barham. William G. Lane. 1967. 11.00 (ISBN 0-8262-0070-2). U of Mo Pr.
Richard Henry Dana, 2 Vols. Charles F. Adams. LC 67-23883. 1968. Repr. of 1890 ed. 20.00 (ISBN 0-8103-3038-5). Gale.
Richard Henry Dana. Robert L. Gale. LC 68-24301. (U. S. Authors Ser.: No. 143). 1969. lib. bdg. 10.95 (ISBN 0-8057-0184-2). Twayne.
Richard Hovey. William R. Linneman. (U. S. Authors Ser.: No. 263). 1976. lib. bdg. 10.95 (ISBN 0-8057-7162-X). Twayne.
Richard III. William Shakespeare. 1968. pap. text ed. 3.95 (ISBN 0-471-00550-9). Wiley.
Richard III: The Making of a Legend. Roxane C. Murph. LC 77-4021. 1977. 10.00 (ISBN 0-8108-1034-4). Scarecrow.
Richard Jefferies. Edward Thomas. Ed. by Roland Gant. 1978. 12.95 (ISBN 0-571-11236-6, Pub. by Faber & Faber); pap. 7.95 (ISBN 0-571-11237-4). Merrimack Bk Serv.
Richard Lindner. Hilton Kramer. LC 74-78458. (Illus.). 256p. 1975. 42.50 (ISBN 0-8212-0513-7, 743224). NYGS.
Richard Lion Heart. James A. Brundage. LC 73-1361. (Illus.). 288p. 1974. 10.00 (ISBN 0-684-13802-6, ScribT). Scribner.
Richard M. Nixon, Communism & China. Fu-Mei C. Wu. LC 78-69834. 1978. pap. text ed. 9.50 (ISBN 0-8191-0578-3). U Pr of Amer.
Richard Malcolm Johnston. Bert Hitchcock. (United States Authors Ser.: No. 314). 1978. 12.50 (ISBN 0-8057-7238-3). Twayne.
Richard Mather of Dorchester. B. R. Burg. LC 75-41987. 224p. 1976. 17.00x (ISBN 0-8131-1343-1). U Pr of Ky.
Richard Mulcaster's Positions. Ed. by Richard Demolen. LC 77-168389. 1970. text ed. 9.75 (ISBN 0-8077-1238-8). Tchrs Coll.
Richard Murphy: Poet of Two Traditions. Ed. by Maurice Harmon. (Interdisciplinary Studies). (Illus.). 1978. text ed. 13.75x (ISBN 0-905473-17-5). Humanities.
Richard Neutra. Esther McCoy. LC 60-13309. (Masters of World Architecture Ser.). (Illus.). 1960. 7.95 o.s.i. (ISBN 0-8076-0132-2); pap. 3.95 o.s.i. (ISBN 0-8076-0229-9). Braziller.
Richard Norman Shaw. Andrew Saint. LC 75-43333. (Studies in British Art Ser.). 1976. 55.00x (ISBN 0-300-01955-6). Yale U Pr.
Richard Olney & His Public Service. Henry James. LC 70-87445. (American Scene Ser). (Illus.). 1971. Repr. of 1923 ed. lib. bdg. 32.50 (ISBN 0-306-71516-3). Da Capo.
Richard Palmer Blackmur. Gerald Pannick. (United States Authors Ser.: No. 409). 1981. lib. bdg. 12.95 (ISBN 0-8057-7338-X). Twayne.
Richard Petty. Thomas Braun. LC 75-37887. (Sports Superstars Ser.). (Illus.). (gr. 3-9). 1976. PLB 5.50 o.p. (ISBN 0-87191-500-6). Creative Ed.
Richard R. Niebuhr on Christ & Religion: The Four-Stage Development of His Thought. Patrick Primeaux. (Toronto Studies in Theology: Vol. 4). 1981. soft cover 19.95x (ISBN 0-88946-973-3). E Mellen.
Richard Scarry's Best Mother Goose Ever. Illus. by Richard Scarry. (Illus.). (ps-1). 1970. 5.95 (ISBN 0-307-15578-1, Golden Pr); PLB 12.23 (ISBN 0-307-65578-4). Western Pub.
Richard Scarry's Best Word Book Ever. Richard Scarry. (Illus.). (ps-3). 1963. 4.95 (ISBN 0-307-15510-2, Golden Pr); PLB 12.23 (ISBN 0-307-65510-5). Western Pub.
Richard Scarry's Busy Busy World. Richard Scarry. (Illus.). (gr. k-5). 5.95 (ISBN 0-307-15511-0, Golden Pr); PLB 12.23 (ISBN 0-307-65539-3). Western Pub.
Richard Scarry's Cars & Trucks & Things That Go. Richard Scarry. 1974. 4.95 (ISBN 0-307-15785-7, Golden Pr); PLB 12.23 (ISBN 0-307-65785-X). Western Pub.
Richard Scarry's Color Book. Richard Scarry. LC 75-36465. (Illus.). 14p. (ps-1). 1976. 2.95 (ISBN 0-394-83237-X, BYR). Random.
Richard Scarry's Lowly Worm Word Book. Richard Scarry. LC 80-53103. (Chunky Bks.). (Illus.). 28p. (ps). 1981. pap. 2.50 board (ISBN 0-686-69031-1). Random.
Richard Scarry's Nicky Goes to the Doctor. Richard Scarry. (Look-Look Bks.). (gr. k-1). 1978. PLB 5.38 (ISBN 0-307-61842-0, Golden Pr); pap. 0.95 (ISBN 0-307-11842-8). Western Pub.
Richard Scarry's Peasant Pig & the Terrible Dragon. Richard Scarry. LC 80-5086. (Illus.). 48p. (ps-3). 1980. bds. 4.95 (ISBN 0-394-84567-6); PLB 5.99 (ISBN 0-394-94567-0). Random.
Richard Scarry's Toy Book. Richard Scarry. (Illus.). (ps-3). 1978. pap. 3.95 (ISBN 0-394-83962-5, BYR). Random.
Richard Second. William Shakespeare. Ed. by Arthur Quiller-Couch et al. (New Shakespeare Ser). 23.95 (ISBN 0-521-07552-1); pap. 4.50x (ISBN 0-521-09495-X). Cambridge U Pr.
Richard Second. William Shakespeare. Ed. by Matthew W. Black. (Shakespeare Ser.). (YA) (gr. 9 up). 1957. pap. 2.25 (ISBN 0-14-071406-5, Pelican). Penguin.
Richard Stanihurst the Dubliner Fifteen Forty-Seven-Sixteen Eighteen. Colm Lennon. 200p. 1981. 27.50x (Pub. by Irish Academic Pr Ireland). Biblio Dist.
Richard Strauss & Romain Rolland: Correspondence, Diary, & Essays. Ed. by Rollo Myers. 1968. 20.00x (ISBN 0-520-00913-4). U of Cal Pr.
Richard Strauss: The Staging of His Operas & Ballets. Rudolf Hartmann. (Illus.). 226p. 1981. 39.95 (ISBN 0-19-520251-1). Oxford U Pr.
Richard Third. William Shakespeare. Ed. by Arthur Quiller-Couch et al. LC 68-133495. (New Shakespeare Ser). 1968. 23.95 (ISBN 0-521-07553-X); pap. 4.50x (ISBN 0-521-09496-8). Cambridge U Pr.
Richard Third & His Early Historians 1483-1535. Alison Hanham. 236p. 1975. 33.00x (ISBN 0-19-822434-6). Oxford U Pr.
Richard Upjohn, Architect & Churchman. Everard M. Upjohn. LC 68-26119. (Architecture & Decorative Art Ser). (Illus.). 1968. Repr. of 1939 ed. lib. bdg. 25.00 (ISBN 0-306-71043-9). Da Capo.
Richard Wagner. Robert Raphael. (World Authors Ser.: Germany: No. 77). lib. bdg. 10.95 (ISBN 0-8057-2976-3). Twayne.
Richard Wagner & His World. Charles Osborne. LC 76-56892. (Encore Edition). (Illus.). 1977. 3.95 (ISBN 0-684-16915-0, ScribT). Scribner.
Richard Wagner: Lohengrin. Ed. by Michael Von Soden. (Insel Taschenbuecher: No. 445). (Illus.). 257p. 1980. pap. text ed. 5.85 (ISBN 3-458-32145-4, Pub. by Insel Verlag Germany). Suhrkamp.
Richard Wagner: Parsifal. Lucy Beckett. (Cambridge Opera Handbooks Ser.). (Illus.). 220p. Date not set. price not set (ISBN 0-521-22825-5); pap. price not set (ISBN 0-521-29662-5). Cambridge U Pr.
Richard Wagner: Patriot & Politician. Frank B. Josserand. LC 80-5638. 351p. (Orig.). 1981. lib. bdg. 20.50 (ISBN 0-8191-1418-9); pap. text ed. 11.75 (ISBN 0-8191-1419-7). U Pr of Amer.
Richard Wagner's Music Dramas. Carl Dahlhaus. Tr. by Mary Whittall. LC 78-68359. 1979. 14.95 (ISBN 0-521-22397-0). Cambridge U Pr.
Richard Whytford: A Dayly Exercyse of Dethe. Ed. by James Hogg. (Salzburg Institute for English Literature: Elizabethan Studies: No. 89: Pt. 5). (Orig.). 1979. pap. text ed. 25.00x (ISBN 0-391-01709-8). Humanities.
Richard Whytford's the Pype or Tonne of the Lyfe of Perfection, Vol. 2, Pt. 1. James Hogg. (Elizabethen Studies: No. 89). (Orig.). 1979. pap. text ed. 25.00x (ISBN 0-391-01693-8). Humanities.
Richard Whytford's the Pype or Tonne of the Lyfe of Perfection, Vol. 3, Pt. 2. James Hogg. (Elizabethan Studies: No. 89). (Orig.). 1979. pap. text ed. 25.00x (ISBN 0-391-01692-X). Humanities.
Richard Whytford's the Pype or Tonne of the Lyfe of Perfection, Vol. 4, Pt. 3. James Hogg. (Elizabethan & Renaissance Studies: No. 89). 1979. pap. text ed. 25.00 (ISBN 0-391-01689-X). Humanities.
Richard Wright. David Bakish. LC 71-190353. (Modern Literature Ser.). 121p. 1973. 10.95 (ISBN 0-8044-2015-7). Ungar.
Richard Wright: Ordeal of a Native Son. Addison Gayle. LC 77-12854. (Illus.). 1980. 14.95 (ISBN 0-385-08877-9, Anchor Pr). Doubleday.
Richard Wright Reader. Richard Wright. Ed. by Ellen Wright & Michel Fabre. LC 77-76690. (Illus.). 1978. 15.95 o.s.i. (ISBN 0-06-014737-7, HarpT); pap. 7.95 (ISBN 0-06-014736-9, TD-292, HarpT). Har-Row.
Richard Wright's Hero: The Faces of a Rebel-Victim. Katherine Fishburn. LC 76-51787. 1977. 11.00 (ISBN 0-8108-1013-1). Scarecrow.
Richard Yates: Civil War Governor. Ed. by John H. Krenkel. LC 65-16499. 1966. text ed. 8.95x (ISBN 0-8134-0821-0, 821). Interstate.
Richardson the Novelist: The Psychological Patters. Gerald Levin. (Costerus New Ser.: No. 9). 1978. pap. text ed. 17.25x (ISBN 90-6203-410-1). Humanities.
Richardsoniana, 25 vols. Incl. Vol. 1. lib. bdg. (ISBN 0-8240-1304-2); Vol. 2. lib. bdg. (ISBN 0-8240-1305-0); Vol. 3. lib. bdg. (ISBN 0-8240-1306-9); Vol. 4 & 5. lib. bdg. (ISBN 0-8240-1307-7); Vol. 6. lib. bdg. (ISBN 0-8240-1308-5); Vol. 7. lib. bdg. (ISBN 0-8240-1309-3); Vol. 8. lib. bdg. (ISBN 0-8240-1310-7); Vol. 9. lib. bdg. (ISBN 0-8240-1311-5); Vol. 10. lib. bdg. (ISBN 0-8240-1312-3); Vol. 11. lib. bdg. (ISBN 0-8240-1313-1); Vol. 12. lib. bdg. (ISBN 0-8240-1314-X); Vol. 13. lib. bdg. (ISBN 0-8240-1315-8); Vol. 14. lib. bdg. (ISBN 0-8240-1316-6); Vol. 15. lib. bdg. (ISBN 0-8240-1317-4); Vols. 16-19. Set. lib. bdg. 152.00 (ISBN 0-8240-1318-2); lib. bdg.; Vols. 20 & 21. Set. lib. bdg. 76.00 (ISBN 0-8240-1319-0); lib. bdg.; Vols. 22-25. Set. lib. bdg. 152.00 (ISBN 0-8240-1320-4); lib. bdg.. (Life & Times of Seven Major British Writers Ser). 1974. lib. bdg. 47.00 ea. Garland Pub.
Richardus Tertius. Thomas Legge. Ed. by Robert J. Lordi & Stephen Orgel. LC 78-66843. (Renaissance Drama Ser.). 1979. lib. bdg. 50.00 (ISBN 0-8240-9741-6). Garland Pub.
Richer Dust: Echoes from an Edwardian Album. Colin Gordon. 1979. 15.00 o.s.i. (ISBN 0-397-01350-7). Lippincott.
Richer Living. Ernest Holmes & Raymond C. Barker. 366p. 1973. pap. 7.95 (ISBN 0-911336-48-6). Sci of Mind.
Riches & Poverty: London Nineteen Six. L. C. Chiozza Money. LC 79-56955. (English Working Class Ser.). 1980. lib. bdg. 30.00. Garland Pub.
Riches of His Grace. Robert Menzies. 175p. Repr. of 1956 ed. 7.95 (ISBN 0-227-67583-5). Attic Pr.
Riches Within Your Reach: The Law of the Higher Potential. Robert Collier. 9.95 (ISBN 0-912576-00-6). R Collier.
Richest Girl in the World. Nona Coxhead. 1979. pap. 2.50 o.s.i. (ISBN 0-515-05080-6). Jove Pubns.
Richest Lady in Town. Joyce Landorf. 1979. pap. 2.25 (ISBN 0-310-27142-8). Zondervan.
Richest Man in Babylon. George S. Clason. 1955. 8.95 (ISBN 0-8015-6360-7, Hawthorn); pap. 3.50 (ISBN 0-8015-6366-6, Hawthorn). Dutton.
Richest Poor Folks. Leland F. Cooley. LC 77-1267. 1977. 10.00 o.p. (ISBN 0-312-68225-5). St Martin.
Richie. Thomas Thompson. 1981. pap. 2.50 (ISBN 0-440-17401-5). Dell.
Richlands. Agnes S. Turnbull. 240p. 1976. pap. 1.50 o.p. (ISBN 0-449-22844-4, Q2844, Crest). Fawcett.
Richleighs of Tantamount. Barbara Willard. LC 67-16229. (Illus.). (gr. 6-8). 1966. 5.50 o.p. (ISBN 0-15-266750-4, HJ). HarBraceJ.
Richmond After the War, Eighteen Sixty-Five to Eighteen Ninety. Michael B. Chesson. (Illus.). 1981. write for info. (ISBN 0-88490-085-1); pap. write for info. (ISBN 0-88490-086-X). VA State Lib.
Richmond Redeemed: The Seige at Petersburg. Richard J. Sommers & Frank E. Vandiver. LC 79-7844. (Illus.). 648p. 1981. 22.50 (ISBN 0-385-15626-X). Doubleday.
Richmond School Decision. Merhige. LC 72-83394. pap. 6.00 (ISBN 0-912008-02-4). Integrated Ed Assoc.
Richmond: The Story of a City. Virginius Dabney. LC 73-9150. 1976. 12.95 (ISBN 0-385-02046-5, Pub. by Doubleday). U Pr of Va.
Richmond, Vol. 1: The Flame. Elizabeth Fritch. 480p. (Orig.). 1980. pap. 2.75 (ISBN 0-89083-654-X). Zebra.
Richmond Volume 2: The Fire. Elizabeth Fritch. 1980. pap. 2.75 (ISBN 0-89083-679-5, Kable News Co). Zebra.
Richter und Sein Henker. Friedrich Durrenmatt. Ed. by William Gillis & J. J. Neumaier. 1964. pap. text ed. 6.95 (ISBN 0-395-04499-5). HM.
Rick Barry. Robert Armstrong. (Sports Superstars Ser.). (Illus.). (gr. 3-9). 1977. PLB 5.95 (ISBN 0-87191-539-1); pap. 2.95 (ISBN 0-89812-185-X). Creative Ed.
Rico Lebrun Drawings. Rico Lebrun. 1961. 21.50x (ISBN 0-520-00717-4). U of Cal Pr.
Rico's Cat. Dana Brookins. LC 76-8841. (Illus.). (gr. 3-6). 1976. 6.95 (ISBN 0-395-28850-9, Clarion). HM.
Riddle. Dan Sherman. 1978. pap. 1.95 o.p. (ISBN 0-449-23765-6, Crest). Fawcett.
Riddle Ages. Ann Bishop. Ed. by Caroline Rubin. LC 77-12828. (Riddle Bk.). (Illus.). (gr. 1-4). 1977. 5.75g (ISBN 0-8075-6965-8). A Whitman.
Riddle Book. Roy McKie. LC 77-85237. (Picturebacks Ser.). (ps-2). 1978. PLB 4.99 (ISBN 0-394-93732-5, BYR); pap. 1.25 (ISBN 0-394-83732-0). Random.
Riddle Calendar, 1980. Jane Sarnoff & Reynold Ruffins. (Illus.). (gr. 1 up). 1979. 4.95 o.p. (ISBN 0-684-16209-1, ScribT). Scribner.
Riddle Giggles. Helen Hoke. LC 74-26364. (Illus.). 48p. (gr. k-4). 1975. PLB 4.90 o.p. (ISBN 0-531-02096-7). Watts.

Riddle-Iculous Rid-Alphabet Book. Ann Bishop. LC 78-150799. (Riddle Bk.). (Illus.). (gr. 2-4). 1971. 5.75g (ISBN 0-8075-6970-4). A Whitman.
Riddle of Raven Hollow. Mary F. Shura. (gr. 4-6). 1976. pap. 1.25 (ISBN 0-590-03568-1, Schol Pap). Schol Bk Serv.
Riddle of the Black Knight & Other Stories from the Middle Ages Based on the Gesta Romanorum. Thomas B. Leekley. LC 57-12262. (Illus.). (gr. 3-7). 1957. 6.95 (ISBN 0-8149-0347-9). Vanguard.
Riddle of the Drum, A Tale from Tizapan, Mexico. Retold by Verna Aardema. LC 78-23791. (Illus.). 32p. (gr. k-3). 1979. 8.95 (ISBN 0-590-07489-X, Four Winds). Schol Bk Serv.
Riddle of the Future. Andrew MacKenzie. (RL 10). 1978. pap. 1.75 o.p. (ISBN 0-451-08096-3, E8096, Sig). NAL.
Riddle of the Universe. William M. Smart. LC 68-25830. (Illus.). 1968. 9.95 (ISBN 0-471-79914-9). Halsted Pr.
Riddle of Violence. Kenneth Kaunda. LC 80-8348. 192p. 1981. 9.95 (ISBN 0-06-250450-9, HarpR, HarpR). Har-Row.
Riddle Pot. William Wiesner. 128p. (ps-2). 1977. PLB 5.95 (ISBN 0-525-38285-2); pap. 1.50 o.p. (ISBN 0-525-45033-5). Dutton.
Riddle Raddle, Fiddle Faddle. Ann Bishop. LC 68-22189. (Riddle Bk.). (Illus.). (gr. 2-4). 1966. 5.75g (ISBN 0-8075-6974-7). A Whitman.
Riddle Red Riddle Book. Ann Bishop. LC 72-79549. (Riddle Bk.). (Illus.). (gr. 2-5). 1969. 5.75g (ISBN 0-8075-6979-8). A Whitman.
Riddle Riot. Mike Thaler. (gr. 4-6). 1976. pap. 0.95 (ISBN 0-590-03594-0, Schol Pap). Schol Bk Serv.
Riddles. Illus. by Robert Alley. (Look Look Bks). (Illus.). 24p. (ps-3). 1981. pap. 1.25 (ISBN 0-307-11860-6, Golden Pr). Western Pub.
Riddles & Jokes & Foolish Facts. Duncan Emrich. (gr. 4-6). 1976. pap. 1.25 (ISBN 0-590-04281-5, Schol Pap). Schol Bk Serv.
Riddles in the British Landscape. Richard Muir. (Illus.). 200p. 1981. 17.95 (ISBN 0-500-24108-2). Thames Hudson.
Riddles of Consciousness. Gopi Krishna. 160p. 1977. pap. 3.95 o.s.i. (ISBN 0-8334-1779-7). Multimedia.
Riddles of Finnegans Wake. Patrick A. McCarthy. LC 79-24075. 184p. 1980. 16.50 (ISBN 0-8386-3005-7). Fairleigh Dickinson.
Riddles of the Stone Age. Jean M. McMann. LC 79-67658. (Illus.). 160p. 1980. 16.95 (ISBN 0-500-05033-3). Thames Hudson.
Riddles, Riddles from A to Z. Carl Memlimg. (ps-3). 1962. PLB 5.00 (ISBN 0-307-60940-5, Golden Pr). Western Pub.
Riddles, Riddles, Riddles. Joseph Leeming. 1979. pap. 1.75 (ISBN 0-449-14014-8, GM). Fawcett.
Riddles, Riddles, Riddles. Ed. by Joseph Leeming. (Terrific Triple Titles Ser). (gr. 4-6). 1953. PLB 7.90 (ISBN 0-531-01777-X). Watts.
Riddley Walker. Russell Hoban. 1981. 12.95 (ISBN 0-671-42147-6). Summit Bks.
Ride a Cock-Horse. Illus. by Mervyn Peake. LC 75-509235. (Illus.). (ps-2). 1979. 7.95 (ISBN 0-7011-5015-7, Pub. by Chatto Bodley Jonathan); pap. 2.95 (ISBN 0-7011-1945-4, Pub. by Chatto Bodley Jonathan). Merrimack Bk Serv.
Ride a Cock Horse. Elma Williams. 1972. 8.95 (ISBN 0-7181-0930-9). Transatlantic.
Ride a Crooked Trail. Burt Arthur & Budd Arthur. 1979. pap. 1.25 (ISBN 0-505-51389-7). Tower Bks.
Ride a Proud Horse. Barbara Morgenroth. LC 77-21111. (gr. 6-9). 1978. 8.95 (ISBN 0-689-30624-5). Atheneum.
Ride a Tall Horse. Lewis B. Patten. 1981. pap. price not set (ISBN 0-451-09816-1, Signet Bks). NAL.
Ride American. Louis Taylor. LC 63-10624. (Illus.). 1963. 9.95 o.s.i. (ISBN 0-06-006720-9, HarpT). Har-Row.
Ride, & Stay Alive. Pedr Davis & Mike McCarthy. Ed. by Jeff Robinson. (Illus.). 128p. 1973. pap. text ed. 4.95 (ISBN 0-89287-024-9, X910). Clymer Pubns.
Ride East, Ride West. Anne Powers. 1978. pap. 1.95 (ISBN 0-505-51300-5). Tower Bks.
Ride into Danger. Wayne D. Overholser. 144p. (Orig.). 1980. pap. 1.75 (ISBN 0-553-13575-9). Bantam.
Ride into Danger. Henry Treece. LC 59-12203. (Illus.). (gr. 7-10). 1959. 9.95 (ISBN 0-87599-113-0). S G Phillips.
Ride on Tumbleweeds! Tom K. Ryan. 1978. pap. 1.25 o.p. (ISBN 0-449-14040-7, GM). Fawcett.
Ride Out the Storm. Aleen Malcom. (Orig.). Date not set. pap. 3.25 (ISBN 0-440-17399-X). Dell.
Ride, Slocum, Ride. Jake Logan. LC 75-14619. (John Slocum Ser.: No. 2). 192p. 1975. pap. 1.50 (ISBN 0-87216-679-1, B16281). Playboy Pbks.
Ride the Blue Riband. Rosalind Laker. 1978. pap. 1.95 o.p. (ISBN 0-451-08252-4, J8252, Sig). NAL.
Ride the Blue Riband. Rosalind Laker. LC 76-29791. 1977. 7.95 o.p. (ISBN 0-385-12416-3). Doubleday.
Ride the Golden Tiger. new ed. Jonathan Black. LC 75-30828. 312p. 1976. 8.95 o.p. (ISBN 0-688-03001-7). Morrow.
Ride the Thunder. Janet Dailey. pap. 2.75 (ISBN 0-686-68324-2). PB.
Ride the Wild Country. Wade Hamilton. 1977. pap. 1.50 (ISBN 0-505-51205-X). Tower Bks.
Ride the Wild Storm. Marjorie Reynolds. LC 69-11305. (Illus.). (gr. 4-6). 1969. 4.95g o.s.i. (ISBN 0-02-776040-5). Macmillan.
Ride the Wild Trail. Max Brand. 1981. pap. 1.75 (ISBN 0-671-41556-5). PB.
Ride to Blizzard. Archie Joscelyn. 256p. (YA) 1973. 5.95 (ISBN 0-685-30372-1, Avalon). Bouregy.
Ride to Hell. Ben Thompson. 1978. pap. 1.50 (ISBN 0-505-51287-4). Tower Bks.
Ride Western: A Complete Guide to Western Horsemanship. Louis Taylor. LC 68-15998. (Illus.). 1968. 10.95 o.p. (ISBN 0-06-006696-2, HarpT). Har-Row.
Ride When You're Ready. Evelyn Bolton. LC 74-9763. (Evelyn Bolton's Horse Stories Ser). (Illus.). 32p. (gr. 3-7). 1974. PLB 5.95 (ISBN 0-87191-373-9); pap. 2.95 (ISBN 0-89812-130-2). Creative Ed.
Ride, Willy Ride. new ed. Carl Memling. LC 78-85950. (Beginning-to-Read Bks). (Illus.). (gr. 1-3). 1970. 2.50 o.p. (ISBN 0-695-80087-6); PLB 3.39 o.p. (ISBN 0-695-40087-8); pap. 1.50 o.p. (ISBN 0-695-30087-3). Follett.
Rideau Waterway. rev. ed. Robert F. Legget. LC 56-1252. (Illus.). 1972. pap. 6.95 (ISBN 0-8020-6156-7). U of Toronto Pr.
Rider of High Mesa. Ernest Haycox. 128p. 1975. Repr. of 1956 ed. lib. bdg. 9.95 o.p. (ISBN 0-89190-980-X). Am Repr-Rivercity Pr.
Rider Tarot Deck. Arthur E. Waite. 8.00 (ISBN 0-685-47282-5). Weiser.
Rider's Handbook. Diana Tuke. (Illus.). pap. 4.55 (ISBN 0-85131-258-6). J A Allen.
Riders of Judgment. Frederick Manfred. (Western Fiction Ser.). 1980. lib. bdg. 15.95 (ISBN 0-8398-2593-5). Gregg.
Riders of the Storm. Hester Burton. LC 73-4404. (Illus.). 256p. (gr. 5 up). 1973. 7.95 o.p. (ISBN 0-690-70074-1, TYC-J). T Y Crowell.
Riders to the Sea. John M. Synge. 60p. 1970. 40.00x (ISBN 0-7165-1410-9, Pub. by Irish Academic Pr Ireland). Biblio Dist.
Rides & Races. Robert B. Ruddell et al. (Pathfinder - Allyn & Bacon Reading Program: Level 6). (gr. 1). 1978. pap. text ed. 3.28 (ISBN 0-205-05111-1, 5451116); tchr's ed. 8.80 (ISBN 0-205-05127-8, 5451272); 3.28. Allyn.
Ridge Runner. Gerald Averill. LC 79-14339. (Illus.). 1979. lib. bdg. 10.50 o.p. (ISBN 0-89621-031-6); pap. 4.95 (ISBN 0-89621-030-8). Thorndike Pr.
Ridgely Torrence. John M. Clum. (U. S. Authors Ser.: No. 212). lib. bdg. 10.95 (ISBN 0-8057-0740-9). Twayne.
Riding High. Hank Madison. 1979. pap. 1.50 (ISBN 0-505-51430-3). Tower Bks.
Riding High: Bicycling for Young People. Ross R. Olney. LC 80-28566. (Illus.). 192p. (gr. 5 up). 1981. 8.95 (ISBN 0-688-41979-8); PLB 8.59 (ISBN 0-688-51979-2). Morrow.
Riding on a Blue Note: Jazz & American Pop. Gary Giddins. 275p. 1981. 16.95 (ISBN 0-19-502835-X). Oxford U Pr.
Riding Rainbows. Robert B. Ruddell et al. (Pathfinder - Allyn & Bacon Reading Program: Level 12). (gr. 3). 1978. text ed. 8.20 (ISBN 0-205-05147-2, 5451477); tchr's ed. 12.20 (ISBN 0-205-05148-0, 5451485); 3.60. Allyn.
Riding Side Saddle. Janet MacDonald & Valerie Francis. (Pelham Horsemaster Ser.). (Illus.). 1979. 14.00 (ISBN 0-7207-1100-2). Transatlantic.
Riding Teacher: A Basic Guide to Correct Methods of Classical Instruction. Alois Podhajsky. LC 72-84937. 240p. 1973. 7.95 o.p. (ISBN 0-385-02540-8). Doubleday.
Riding the Dirt. Bob Sanford. 1973. 10.95 (ISBN 0-87880-012-3). Norton.
Riding the Midnight River: Selected Poems of Pritish Nandy. Pritish Nandy. (Indian Poetry Ser.). 144p. 1975. 9.00 (ISBN 0-89253-013-8). Ind-US Inc.
Riding the Pony Express. Clyde R. Bulla. LC 48-8051. (Illus.). (gr. 2-5). 1948. PLB 7.89 (ISBN 0-690-70111-X, TYC-J). T Y Crowell.
Riding the Storm 1956-1959. Harold Macmillan. LC 79-156535. (Illus.). 1971. 20.00 o.p. (ISBN 0-06-012744-9, HarpT). Har-Row.
Riding the Wind. George T. Montague. 1977. pap. 1.25 (ISBN 0-89129-256-X). Jove Pubns.
Riding Through the Downers, Hassles, Snags & Funks. Ari Kiev. 96p. 1980. 7.95 (ISBN 0-525-93138-4). Dutton.
Riding to Hounds. British Horse Society & Pony Club. 1976. pap. 1.95 (ISBN 0-8120-0756-5). Barron.
Riding Tough. Jim Busbee. 1981. pap. price not set (Leisure Bks). Nordon Pubns.
Riel Rebellions: A Cartographic History. Ed. by William A. Oppen. LC 79-94166. (Illus.). 1980. pap. 15.00x (ISBN 0-8020-6427-2). U of Toronto Pr.
Riemann Surfaces & Related Topics: Proceedings of the 1978 Stony Brook Conference. Ed. by I. Kra & B. Maskit. 1980 (ISBN 0-691-08264-2). pap. 9.50 (ISBN 0-691-08267-7). Princeton U Pr.
Riemann Surfaces & Related Topics: Proceedings of the 1978 Stony Brook Conference. Ed. by I. Kra & B. Maskit. LC 79-27923. (Annals of Mathematics Studies: No.97). 400p. 1981. 25.00x (ISBN 0-691-08264-2); pap. 9.50x (ISBN 0-691-08267-7). Princeton U Pr.
Riemann-Type Integral That Includes Lebesgue-Stieltjes, Bochner & Stochastic Integrals. E. J. McShane. LC 52-42839. (Memoirs: No. 88). 1979. pap. 6.00 (ISBN 0-8218-1288-2, MEMO-88). Am Math.
Rietz Master Food Guide. Norman W. Desrosier. (Illus.). 1978. pap. text ed. 19.00 (ISBN 0-87055-246-5). AVI.
Riff, Remember. Lynn Hall. (gr. 3-7). 1975. pap. 0.95 o.s.i. (ISBN 0-380-00186-1, 21899, Camelot). Avon.
Rifka Bangs the Teakettle. Chaya Burstein. LC 79-91068. (Illus.). (gr. 4-6). 1970. 4.95 o.p. (ISBN 0-15-266944-2, HJ). HarBraceJ.
Rifle & Shotgun Shooting. Boy Scouts Of America. LC 19-600. (Illus.). 80p. (gr. 6-12). 1967. pap. 0.70x (ISBN 0-8395-3311-X, 3311). BSA.
Rifles of Colonial America, 2 vols. George Shumway. Incl. Vol. 1. 352p (ISBN 0-87387-079-4); Vol. 2. 318p (ISBN 0-87387-082-4). (Congrifle Ser.). (Illus.). 352p. 1980. casebound ea. 49.50 (ISBN 0-686-65023-9). Shumway.
Rift Valley Fever. Ed. by N. Goldblum et al. (Contributions to Epidemiology & Biostatistics Ser.: Vol. 3). (Illus.). 200p. 1981. pap. 60.00 (ISBN 3-8055-1770-X). S Karger.
Rift Zones of the World Oceans. Ed. by A. P. Vinogradov & G. B. Udintsev. Tr. by N. Kaner from Rus. LC 75-16178. 503p. 1975. 69.95 (ISBN 0-470-90838-6). Halsted Pr.
Riga Interzonals 1979. A. J. Miles & Spearman. 1979. 9.95 (ISBN 0-7134-3429-5, Pub. by Batsford England). David & Charles.
Rigadoon. Louis-Ferdinand Celine. 273p. 1974. 8.95 o.p. (ISBN 0-440-07364-2, Sey Lawr). Delacorte.
Right & Wrong: A Philosophical Dialogue Between Father & Son. Paul Weiss & Jonathan Weiss. LC 73-12702. (Arcturus Books Paperbacks). 222p. 1974. pap. 5.95 (ISBN 0-8093-0658-1). S Ill U Pr.
Right Angles: Paper-Folding Geometry. Jo Phillips. LC 72-171007. (Young Math Ser.). (Illus.). (gr. 1-4). 1972. 6.95 o.p. (ISBN 0-690-60916-7, TYC-J); PLB 7.89 (ISBN 0-690-60917-5). T Y Crowell.
Right Dog for You. Daniel Tortora. 1980. 12.95 (ISBN 0-686-62850-0, 24221). S&S.
Right Down Your Alley: The Complete Book of Bowling. Vesma Grinfelds & Bonnie Hultstrand. LC 80-82071. (Illus.). 208p. (Orig.). 1980. pap. text ed. 4.95 (ISBN 0-918438-58-6). Leisure Pr.
Right from the Start: Meeting the Challenges of Mothering Your Unborn & Newborn Baby. Gail S. Brewer & Janice P. Greene. Ed. by Charlie Gerras. (Illus.). 256p. (Orig.). 1981. pap. 11.95 (ISBN 0-87857-273-2). Rodale Pr Inc.
Right Living in a World Gone Wrong. David A. Hubbard. 128p. (Orig.). 1981. pap. 3.25 (ISBN 0-87784-470-4). Inter Varsity.
Right of Assembly & Association. Glenn Abernathy. 300p. 1981. pap. text ed. 7.95 (ISBN 0-87249-410-1). U of SC Pr.
Right of Privacy: A Symposium. R. G. Dixon et al. LC 75-147833. (Symposia on Law & Society Ser). 1971. Repr. of 1965 ed. lib. bdg. 17.50 (ISBN 0-306-70114-6). Da Capo.
Right of the Community to a Priest, Concilium 133. Ed. by Edward Schillebeeckx & Johann B. Metz. (New Concilium 1980). 128p. 1980. pap. 5.95 (ISBN 0-8164-4766-7). Crossroad NY.
Right of the People: An Introduction to American Politics. Herbert Hirsch. LC 79-47987. 531p. 1980. text ed. 22.50 (ISBN 0-8191-0990-8); pap. text ed. 12.75 (ISBN 0-8191-0991-6). U Pr of Amer.
Right of Way. Gilbert Parker. 1976. lib. bdg. 16.25x (ISBN 0-89968-079-8). Lightyear.
Right on Dellums. Robert Fitch. LC 70-161311. (Illus.). (gr. 4-8). 1972. PLB 6.95 (ISBN 0-87191-079-9). Creative Ed.
Right on: From Blues to Soul in Black America. Michael Haralambos. (Roots of Jazz Ser.). 1979. Repr. of 1974 ed. 19.50 (ISBN 0-306-79531-0). Da Capo.
Right Opposition: The Lovestoneites & the International Communist Opposition of the 1930's. Robert J. Alexander. LC 80-1705. (Contributions in Political Science: No. 54). 312p. 1981. lib. bdg. 32.50 (ISBN 0-313-22070-0, AOP/). Greenwood.
Right Opposition: The Lovestoneities & the International Communist Opposition of the 1930's. Robert J. Alexander. LC 80-1711. (Contributions in Political Science Ser.: No. 54). 320p. 1981. lib. bdg. 32.50 (AOP/). Greenwood.
Right or Wrong. rev. 14th ed. T. B. Maston & William M. Pinson, Jr. LC 75-143282. (gr. 8 up). 1971. 5.50 (ISBN 0-8054-6101-9); pap. 2.50 (ISBN 0-686-66307-1). Broadman.
Right People in the Right Jobs. John Finnigan. 1973. 14.00x (ISBN 0-8464-0797-3). Beekman Pubs.
Right Side of the Hedge. Christopher Chapman. LC 77-89372. 1977. 8.95 (ISBN 0-7153-7342-0). David & Charles.
Right Stuff. Tom Wolfe. 384p. 1980. pap. 3.50 (ISBN 0-553-13828-6). Bantam.
Right to Abortion: A Psychiatric View. Group for the Advancement of Psychiatry. 1970. 5.95 o.p. (ISBN 0-684-10200-5, ScribT). Scribner.
Right to Abortion: a Psychiatric View, Vol. 7. GAP Committee on Psychiatry & Law. LC 62-2872. (Report No. 75). 1969. pap. 2.00 (ISBN 0-87318-104-2). Adv Psychiatry.
Right to Be Different. Nicholas Kittrie. 1973. pap. 4.50 o.p. (ISBN 0-14-021538-7, Pelican). Penguin.
Right to Be Intelligent. Luis A. Machado. 85p. 1980. 12.75 (ISBN 0-08-025781-X). Pergamon.
Right to Die. Milton D. Heifetz & Charles Mangel. pap. 1.95 o.p. (ISBN 0-425-03151-9). Berkley Pub.
Right to Die. William May & Richard Westley. (Catholic Perspectives Ser.). 112p. 1980. pap. 3.95 (ISBN 0-88347-115-9). Thomas More.
Right to Die: Decision & Decision Makers. Group for the Advancement of Psychiatry. LC 73-17780. 90p. 1974. 15.00x (ISBN 0-87668-127-5). Aronson.
Right to Health As a Human Right: Colloquim 1978 of the Hague Academy of International Law. Ed. by R. J. Dupuy. 513p. 1980. 40.00x (ISBN 90-286-1028-6). Sijthoff & Noordhoff.
Right to Health: The Problem of Access to Primary Medical Care. Charles Lewis et al. LC 76-18129. (Health, Medicine, & Society Ser.). 416p. 1976. 27.95 (ISBN 0-471-01494-X, Pub. by Wiley-Interscience). Wiley.
Right to Hunt. James B. Whisker. 156p. 1981. 7.95 (ISBN 0-88427-042-4, Dist. by Caroline Hse). North River.
Right to Know- a Review of Advice Services in Rural Areas. National Council of Social Service. 71p. 1978. pap. text ed. 1.90x (ISBN 0-7199-0954-6, Pub. by Bedford England). Renouf.
Right to Know: Censorship in America. Robert A. Liston. LC 73-1266. 192p. (gr. 7 up). 1973. PLB 5.90 o.p. (ISBN 0-531-02612-4). Watts.
Right to Love. Jennifer A. Lawson. 64p. 1980. 5.00 (ISBN 0-682-49651-0). Exposition.
Right to Participate: Inmate Involvement in Prison Administration. J. E. Baker. LC 74-7071. 1974. 10.00 (ISBN 0-8108-0727-0). Scarecrow.
Right to Privacy. Ed. by Grant S. McClellan. (Reference Shelf Ser.). 1976. 6.25 (ISBN 0-8242-0595-2). Wilson.
Right to Property: A Theme in American History. Marcus Cunliffe. (Sir George Watson Lectures Ser). 1974. pap. text ed. 1.50x (ISBN 0-7185-1129-8, Leicester). Humanities.
Right to Remarry. Dwight H. Small. 1977. pap. 1.75 o.p. (ISBN 0-8007-8272-0, Spire). Revell.
Right to Self-Determination. 86p. 1979. pap. 8.00 (79-14-5, UN). Unipub.
Right to Self-Determination: Implementation of United Nations Resolutions. Ed. by Hector G. Espiell. 1980. 8.00 (E.79.XIV5). UN.
Right to Strike in Public Employment. Antone Aboud & Grace S Aboud. (Key Issues Ser.: No. 15). 1974. pap. 2.00 (ISBN 0-87546-201-4). NY Sch Indus Rel.
Right Versus Privilege: The Open Admissions Experiment at the City University of New York. David E. Lavin et al. LC 80-69571. (Illus.). 1981. 24.95 (ISBN 0-02-918080-5). Free Pr.
Right Way to a Good Job. F. J. Taylor. 174p. 1979. pap. 9.75x (ISBN 0-220-66364-5, Pub. by Busn Bks England). Renouf.
Righteousness in Matthew & His World of Thought. Benno Przybylski. LC 79-41371. (Society for New Testament Studies Monographs: No. 41). 240p. 1981. 24.50 (ISBN 0-521-22566-3). Cambridge U Pr.
Righteousness in the Septuagint of Isaiah: A Contextual Study. John W. Olley. LC 78-3425. (Society of Biblical Literature, Septuagint & Cognate Studies: No. 8). 1979. 12.00 (ISBN 0-89130-226-3); pap. 7.50 (ISBN 0-89130-365-0). Scholars Pr Ca.

Rightly Dividing the Word of Truth. C. I. Scofield. 72p. (Orig.). 1974. pap. 1.95 (ISBN 0-310-32662-1, 6364P). Zondervan.

Rights & Persons. A. I. Melden. 1978. 20.00x (ISBN 0-520-03528-3); pap. 5.95 (ISBN 0-520-03839-8). U of Cal Pr.

Rights & Responsibilities in Modern Medicine: The Second Volume in a Series on Ethics, Humanism, & Medicine. Ed. by Marc D. Basson. (Progress in Clinical & Biological Research: Vol. 50). 250p. 1980. write for info. A R Liss.

Rights & Wrongs: Women's Struggle for Legal Equality. Susan C. Nicholas et al. (Women's Lives-Women's Work Ser). (Illus.). 1979. pap. 3.95 (ISBN 0-912670-58-4, Co-Pub. by McGraw). Feminist Pr.

Rights in Conflict: Report of the Twentieth Century Fund Task Force on Justice, Publicity & the First Amendment. Twentieth Century Fund, Inc. LC 75-43831. 1976. text ed. 6.95 o.p. (ISBN 0-07-065625-8, P&RB); pap. text ed. 3.95 o.p. (ISBN 0-07-065626-6). McGraw.

Rights, Justice & the Bounds of Liberty: Essays in Social Philosophy. Joel Feinberg. LC 79-48024. (Princeton Series of Collected Essays). 1980. 20.00x (ISBN 0-691-07254-X); pap. 4.95 (ISBN 0-691-02012-4). Princeton U Pr.

Rights of Adolescents in the Mental Health System. John P. Wilson. LC 77-4542. 1978. 24.95 (ISBN 0-669-01485-0). Lexington Bks.

Rights of Infants. Margaret A. Ribble. 128p. 1973. pap. 1.25 (ISBN 0-451-07735-0, Y7735, Sig). NAL.

Rights of Infants: Early Psychological Needs & Their Satisfaction. 2nd ed. Margaretha A. Ribble. LC 65-24832. 1965. 15.00x (ISBN 0-231-02849-0). Columbia U Pr.

Rights of Juvenile: The Juvenile Justice System. Samuel M. Davis. 1980. 45.00 (ISBN 0-87632-104-X). Boardman.

Rights of Labor. Bengt Abrahamsson & Anders Brostrom. LC 80-16233. 301p. 25.00 (ISBN 0-8039-1477-6). Sage.

Rights of Lawyers & Clients. Stephen Gillers. 1978. pap. 1.95 (ISBN 0-380-42382-0, 42382, Discus). Avon.

Rights of Man Today. Louis Henkin. LC 78-6722. 1978. lib. bdg. 17.50x (ISBN 0-89158-174-X). Westview.

Rights of Mental Patients. Bruce J. Ennis & Richard D. Emery. 1972. pap. 2.50 (ISBN 0-380-01859-4, 36574, Discus). Avon.

Rights of Parents. Alan Sussman & Martin Guggenheim. 288p. (Orig.). 1980. pap. 2.50 (ISBN 0-380-76729-5, 76729). Avon.

Rights of Parents in the Education of Their Children. Schimmel & Fischer. LC 77-90016. 1977. pap. text ed. 4.95 (ISBN 0-934460-05-1). NCCE.

Rights of Prisoners. David Rudovsky et al. 1972. pap. 1.50 (ISBN 0-380-01387-8, 35436, Discus). Avon.

Rights of Racial Minorities. E. Richard Larson & Laughlin McDonald. 1979. pap. 1.95 (ISBN 0-380-75077-5, 75077, Discus). Avon.

Rights of the Imprisoned, Cases, Materials, & Directions. Singer & Statsky. 1265p. 1974. 24.00 (ISBN 0-672-81874-4, Bobbs-Merrill Law); 1979 suppl 7.50 (ISBN 0-672-84049-9). Michie.

Rights of the People: The Major Decisions of the Warren Court. Walter Goodman & Elaine Goodman. LC 79-157926. (gr. 7 up). 1971. 4.95 (ISBN 0-374-36279-3). FS&G.

Rights of the Students & the Responsibilities of the Schools. Christian M. Samuel. (Illus.). 1980. deluxe ed. 39.75 (ISBN 0-89266-222-0). Am Classical Coll Pr.

Rights of Women: A Comparative Study in History & Legislation. Moisei A. Ostrogorskii. Repr. of 1893 ed. lib. bdg. 16.00x (ISBN 0-87991-960-4). Porcupine Pr.

Rights We Have. rev. ed. Osmond K. Fraenkel. 256p. 1974. 6.95 o.s.i. (ISBN 0-690-00585-7, TYC-T). T Y Crowell.

Rigid Chain Polymers: Synthesis & Properties. G. C. Berry & C. E. Sroog. (Journal of Polymer Science Symposium Ser.: No. 65). 226p. 1979. 20.50 (ISBN 0-471-05802-5). Wiley.

Rigoletto. F. M. Piave. Ed. by E. J. Dent. 1939. 2.50 o.p. (ISBN 0-19-313314-8). Oxford U Pr.

Riley's Flute Melodies, 2vols. in 1. Edward Riley. Ed. & intro. by H. Wiley Hitchcock. LC 72-14213. (Earlier American Music Ser.: Vol. 18). 200p. 1973. Repr. of 1816 ed. lib. bdg. 17.50 (ISBN 0-306-70565-6). Da Capo.

Rilke, Europe, & the English-Speaking World. Eudo C. Mason. 1961. 43.50 (ISBN 0-521-05687-X). Cambridge U Pr.

Rilke on Love & Other Difficulties: Translations & Considerations of Rainer Maria Rilke. Ravier M. Rilke. Ed. by John Mood. 121p. 1975. 7.50 (ISBN 0-393-04390-8); pap. 5.95 (ISBN 0-393-04404-1). Norton.

Rilke, Valery & Yeats: The Domain of the Self. Priscilla W. Shaw. 1964. 16.00 (ISBN 0-8135-0454-6). Rutgers U Pr.

Rim of Space. A. Bertram Chandler. 192p. 1981. 12.95 (ISBN 0-8052-8090-1, Pub. by Allison & Busby England). Schocken.

Rim of the Tub. Elizabeth A. Scott. 1970. 5.95 o.p. (ISBN 0-688-02392-4). Morrow.

Rim to Rim: History of Will Hamblen. Eutha Hamblen. 3.95 o.p. (ISBN 0-685-48812-8). Nortex Pr.

Rimas del Pesebre. Luis Salem. LC 77-82265. 86p. (Orig., Span.). (gr. 4 up). 1978. pap. 1.50 (ISBN 0-89922-118-1). Edit Caribe.

Rimas, Leyendas & Narraciones. G. Becquer. (Span). 4.50x o.s.i. (ISBN 0-686-00884-7). Colton Bk.

Rimbaud. C. A. Hackett. LC 80-40455. (Major European Authors Ser.). 250p. Date not set. price not set; pap. price not set (ISBN 0-521-29756-7). Cambridge U Pr.

Rime of the Ancient Mariner. Samuel T. Coleridge. (Illus.). 1979. 8.50 (ISBN 0-7011-2277-3, Pub. by Chatto Bodley Jonathan). Merrimack Bk Serv.

Rimers of Eldritch & Other Plays. Lanford Wilson. Incl. The Rimers of Eldritch; This Is the Rill Speaking; Wandering; Days Ahead; The Madness of Lady Bright. 122p. (Orig.). 1967. pap. 3.95 (ISBN 0-8090-1214-6, New Mermaid). Hill & Wang.

Rimmonim Bells: Ten Generations of the Behrman, Drucker, Hahn, Stockler & Sztynberg Families Plus Ten Related Lines. Richard J. Alperin. LC 80-65119. (Illus.). 249p. 1980. 39.95x (ISBN 0-9603932-0-X). Junius Inc.

Rimrock Renegade. Lee Floren. 1978. pap. 1.25 (ISBN 0-505-51247-5). Tower Bks.

Rimrock Vengeance. Al Cody. 1981. pap. 1.75 (ISBN 0-8439-0879-3, Leisure Bks). Nordon Pubns.

Rinconete & Cortadillo. Miguel de Cervantes. pap. 2.00 (ISBN 0-8283-1453-5, IPL). Branden.

Rinehart Lifts. R. R. Knudson. LC 80-66825. 192p. (gr. 4 up). 1980. 8.95 (ISBN 0-374-36294-7). FS&G.

Ring. Danielle Steel. 1980. 10.95 (ISBN 0-440-07622-6). Delacorte.

Ring Culture. Frank W. Allerton. (Illus.). 1972. 9.95 (ISBN 0-571-04751-3, Pub. by Faber & Faber). Merrimack Bk Serv.

Ring-Disc Electrodes. W. J. Albery & M. L. Hitchman. (Oxford Science Research Papers Ser). (Illus.). 1971. pap. 29.00x (ISBN 0-19-855349-8). Oxford U Pr.

Ring for a Fortune. Lilian Peake. (Harlequin Presents Ser.). 192p. 1980. pap. 1.50 (ISBN 0-373-10384-0, Pub. by Harlequin). PB.

Ring Lardner. Elizabeth Evans. LC 79-4829. (Modern Literature Ser.). 1980. 10.95 (ISBN 0-8044-2185-4). Ungar.

Ring Lardner. Walton R. Patrick. (U. S. Authors Ser.: No. 32). lib. bdg. 10.95 (ISBN 0-8057-0440-X). Twayne.

Ring Lardner & the Portrait of Folly. Maxwell Geismar. LC 77-175105. (Twentieth-Century American Writers Ser). (gr. 6-9). 1972. 7.95 (ISBN 0-690-70234-5, TYC-J). T Y Crowell.

Ring Lardner Reader. Ring Lardner. Ed. by Maxwell Geismar. 1963. 25.00x (ISBN 0-684-15365-3, ScribT). Scribner.

Ring of Dancers: Images of Faroese Culture. Jonathan Wylie & David Margolin. 1980. text ed. 19.95x (ISBN 0-8122-7783-X). U of Pa Pr.

Ring of Endless Light. Madeleine L'Engle. LC 79-27679. 356p. (gr. 4 up). 1980. 9.95 (ISBN 0-374-36299-8). FS&G.

Ring of Fire. David Ritchie. LC 80-69391. 1981. 12.95 (ISBN 0-689-11150-9). Atheneum.

Ring of Fire. David Ritchie. LC 80-69391. (Illus.). 296p. 1981. 12.95 (ISBN 0-689-11150-9). Atheneum.

Ring of Hades. Dorothy Higgins. LC 79-77795. (Illus.). 160p. (gr. 3-7). 1969. 5.95 o.s.i. (ISBN 0-8193-0297-X, Four Winds); PLB 5.41 o.s.i. (ISBN 0-8193-0298-8). Schol Bk Serv.

Ring of the Nibelung. (Illus.). 204p. 1980. 32.50 (ISBN 0-500-01241-5). Thames Hudson.

Ring of the Nibelung. Richard Wagner. Tr. by Andrew Porter. 1976. 26.95 (ISBN 0-393-02192-0, N867, Norton Lib); pap. 5.95 (ISBN 0-393-00867-3). Norton.

Ring of Words. Ivor Brown. 1972. 5.95 (ISBN 0-370-00426-4). Transatlantic.

Ring on My Finger. Joan Tate. (gr. 7 up). 1977. pap. 1.25 (ISBN 0-590-10318-0, Schol Pap). Schol Bk Serv.

Ring Out! A Book of Bells. Jane Yolen. LC 74-4043. (gr. 4-7). 1974. 6.95 (ISBN 0-395-28886-X, Clarion). HM.

Ring the Doorbell with Your Elbow: A Cookbook of "Portables". rev. ed. Wilma M. McCartney. LC 80-84349. (Illus.). 136p. 1981. pap. 6.95 (ISBN 0-933050-07-0). New Eng Pr VT.

Ring Theory, Antwerp Nineteen-Eighty: Prooceedings. Ed. by F. Van Oystaeyen. (Lecture Notes in Mathematics Ser.: Vol. 825). 209p. 1981. pap. 14.00 (ISBN 0-387-10246-9). Springer-Verlag.

Ring Twice to Enter. Mark Ashley. 320p. (Orig.). 1980. pap. 2.50 (ISBN 0-441-72703-4). Charter Bks.

Ringed Castle. Dorothy Dunnett. 640p. 1981. pap. 2.75 (ISBN 0-445-08495-2). Popular Lib.

Ringling Brothers. Molly Cone. LC 70-132295. (Biography Ser). (Illus.). (gr. 2-5). 1971. 7.95 (ISBN 0-690-70287-6, TYC-J); PLB 7.89 (ISBN 0-690-70288-4). T Y Crowell.

Ringmaster. Darryl Ponicsan. 1978. 8.95 o.p. (ISBN 0-440-07579-3). Delacorte.

Rings Around Your Mind: How to Program Your Mind to Control Stress, Fear, & Self-Destructive Behavior Patterns. Michael C. Giammatteo. (Illus.). 1976. pap. text ed. 10.00 (ISBN 0-918428-08-4). Sylvan Inst.

Rings of Continuous Functions. L. Gillman & M. Jerison. LC 60-14787. xi, 300p. 1975. 11.50 o.p. (ISBN 0-387-90120-5). Springer-Verlag.

Ringworld. Larry Niven. 352p. (Orig.). 1981. pap. 2.50 (ISBN 0-345-29301-0, Del Rey). Ballantine.

Ringworld Engineers. Larry Niven. 368p. 1981. pap. 2.50 (ISBN 0-345-26009-0, Del Rey). Ballantine.

Rio. Douglas Botting. (Great Cities Ser.). (Illus.). 1978. lib. bdg. 14.94 (ISBN 0-686-51006-2). Silver.

Rio De Janeiro. Douglas Botting. Ed. by Time-Life Books. (Great Cities Ser). 1978. 14.95 (ISBN 0-8094-2294-8). Time-Life.

Rio De Janeiro Interzonals 1979. A. J. Miles. 1979. 9.95 (ISBN 0-7134-3427-9, Pub. by Batsford England). David & Charles.

Rio Grande. 25.00. Chatham Pub CA.

Rio Grande... to the Pacific! Robert LeMassena. (Illus.). 416p. 35.00 (ISBN 0-913582-10-7). Sundance.

Rio Grande Glory Days. Gilbert Lathrop. LC 76-45760. (Illus.). 356p. 1976. 14.95 (ISBN 0-87095-056-8). Golden West.

Rio Grande Pictorial. Dell McCoy & Russell Collman. (Illus.). 216p. 30.00 (ISBN 0-913582-02-6). Sundance.

Rio Grande...to the Pacific. Robert A. Le Massena. Ed. by Russ Collman. (Illus.). 1974. 35.00 (ISBN 0-913582-10-7). Sundance.

Rio Renegade. Leslie Erenwein. 1975. pap. 0.95 o.p. (ISBN 0-685-54125-8, LB296NK, Leisure Bks). Nordon Pubns.

Rio Report: Reshaping the International Order: a Report to the Club of Rome Coordinator. Jan Tinbergen. 1977. pap. 2.50 (ISBN 0-451-07708-3, E7708, Sig). NAL.

RIO: Reshaping the International Order. Jan Tinbergen. LC 76-6556. 1976. 10.00 (ISBN 0-525-19250-6); pap. 4.95 o.p. (ISBN 0-525-04340-3). Dutton.

Rios De Agua Viva. Ruth Paxson. 1979. pap. 1.60 (ISBN 0-311-46065-8). Casa Bautista.

Rios De Tinta: Historia y Ministerio De la Casa Bautista De Publicaciones. Tomas Hill. Tr. by Josie Smith from Eng. Orig. Title: Rivers of Ink. 64p. 1980. pap. 1.25 (ISBN 0-311-29009-4). Casa Bautista.

Riot Control. Anthony Deane-Drummond. LC 75-7555. 158p. 1975. 14.00x (ISBN 0-8448-0711-7). Crane-Russak Co.

Riot Control: Materiel & Techniques. 4th rev. ed. Rex Applegate. (Illus.). 320p. 1981. 15.95 (ISBN 0-8117-1489-6). Paladin Ent.

Riots, Revolts, & Insurrections. Raymond M. Momboisse. (Illus.). 544p. 1977. 17.50 (ISBN 0-398-01326-8). C C Thomas.

Riots, U. S. A. rev. ed. Willard A. Heaps. LC 69-13444. (gr. 8-12). 1970. 6.95 (ISBN 0-395-28907-6, Clarion). HM.

Rip-Off. Carter Brown. 1979. pap. 1.50 (ISBN 0-505-51425-7). Tower Bks.

Rip-off: How to Spot It, How to Avoid It. Peter Maiken. 1979. 12.95 o.p. (ISBN 0-8362-6203-4); pap. 5.95 o.p. (ISBN 0-8362-6204-2). Andrews & McMeel.

Rip off Mad. Mad Magazine Editors. (Mad Ser.). (Illus.). 1973. pap. 1.50 (ISBN 0-446-88739-0). Warner Bks.

Rip off the Big Game: The Exploitation of Sports by the Power Elite. Paul Hoch. LC 72-76230. 200p. 1972. pap. 2.50 o.p. (ISBN 0-385-04960-9, Anch). Doubleday.

Rip Van Winkle. George Bristow. (Early American Music Ser.: No. 25). 297p. 1980. 39.50. Da Capo.

Rip Van Winkle. Sanford Friedman. LC 80-66016. 1980. 12.95 (ISBN 0-689-11099-5). Atheneum.

Rip Van Winkle. W. Irving. (Peter Possum Paperbacks Ser). 1967. pap. 0.95 o.p. (ISBN 0-531-05127-7). Watts.

Rip Van Winkle & the Legend of Sleepy Hollow. Washington Irving. (gr. 4-6). 4.95g o.s.i. (ISBN 0-02-747390-2). Macmillan.

Rip Van Winkle Goes to the Play. Brander Matthews. LC 67-27625. 1967. Repr. of 1926 ed. 12.00 (ISBN 0-8046-0303-0). Kennikat.

Ripley's Giant Book of "Believe It or Not". Robert L. Ripley. (Illus.). 256p. (Orig.). 1976. pap. 8.95 (ISBN 0-446-97686-5). Warner Bks.

Risalat at-Tawabic Wa Z-Zawabi (the Treatise of Familiar Spirits - Demons) by Abu a Mir Ibn Shuhaid Al-Ashja I, Al-Andalusi. Ed. & tr. by James T. Monroe. (U. C. Publ. in Near Eastern Studies: Vol. 15). 1971. pap. 8.00x (ISBN 0-520-09382-8). U of Cal Pr.

Risby. Beverly Cleary. (Illus.). (gr. 3-5). 1975. pap. 1.75 (ISBN 0-671-56090-5). PB.

Rise & Decline of a Dialect: A Study in the Revival of Modern Hebrew. Aaron Bar-Adon. LC 74-80121. (Janua Linguarum, Ser. Practica: No. 197). 116p. (Orig.). 1975. pap. text ed. 28.25x (ISBN 90-2793-206-9). Mouton.

Rise & Development of Western Civilization, Pt. 1: Beginnings to 1500. 2nd ed. John Stipp et al. LC 72-2661. (Illus.). 640p. 1972. pap. text ed. 16.95x (ISBN 0-471-82601-4). Wiley.

Rise & Development of Western Civilization, Pt. 3: 1815 to Present. 2nd ed. John Stipp et al. LC 72-2661. (Illus.). 416p. 1972. pap. text ed. 12.95x o.p. (ISBN 0-471-82609-X). Wiley.

Rise & Expansion of the British Dominion in India. Alfred Lyall. LC 67-24585. 1968. Repr. of 1894 ed. 15.50 (ISBN 0-86527-172-0). Fertig.

Rise & Fall & Rise of Modern Dance. Don McDonagh. (RL 7). 1971. pap. 1.25 o.p. (ISBN 0-451-61117-9, MY1117, Ment). NAL.

Rise & Fall & Rise of Modern Dance. Don McDonagh. 1970. 7.95 (ISBN 0-87690-013-9). Dutton.

Rise & Fall of a Teen-Age Wacko. Mary Anderson. LC 80-12396. 180p. (gr. 5-9). 1980. 8.95 (ISBN 0-689-30767-5). Atheneum.

Rise & Fall of British Naval Mastery. Paul Kennedy. LC 75-34942. (Illus.). 405p. 1976. 15.00 o.p. (ISBN 0-684-14609-6, ScribT). Scribner.

Rise & Fall of Civilization. Shepard B. Clough. 1951. pap. 7.50x (ISBN 0-231-08521-4, 21). Columbia U Pr.

Rise & Fall of Economic Growth. H. W. Arndt. 1978. text ed. 16.00 (ISBN 0-582-71214-9); pap. text ed. 10.95 (ISBN 0-582-71213-0). Longman.

Rise & Fall of Freedom of Contract. Patrick S. Atiyah. 804p. 1979. 59.00 (ISBN 0-19-825342-7). Oxford U Pr.

Rise & Fall of Jim Crow: The Long Struggle Against the Supreme Court's Separate-But-Equal Ruling. Frank B. Latham. LC 70-80897. (Focus Bks). (gr. 7 up). 1969. PLB 4.47 o.p. (ISBN 0-531-01011-2); pap. 0.95 o.p. (ISBN 0-531-02335-4). Watts.

Rise & Fall of Nazi Germany. T. L. Jarman. LC 56-9548. 388p. 1956. 15.00x, usa (ISBN 0-8147-0217-1). NYU Pr.

Rise & Fall of Scottish Industry: Seventeen Seven to Nineteen Thirty-Nine. R. H. Campbell. 217p. 1980. text ed. 32.50x (ISBN 0-85976-054-5). Humanities.

Rise & Fall of Slavery in America. Louis Filler. ix, 165p. 1980. lib. bdg. 9.95x (ISBN 0-89198-122-5); pap. text ed. 5.95x (ISBN 0-89198-123-3). Ozer.

Rise & Fall of South African Peasantry. Colin Bundy. (Perspectives on Southern Africa Ser.: No. 28). 1979. 22.50x (ISBN 0-520-03754-5). U of Cal Pr.

Rise & Fall of Superwoman. Carole Sheron. LC 79-26704. (Orion Ser.). 96p. 1980. pap. 2.50 (ISBN 0-8127-1270-6). Southern Pub.

Rise & Fall of the Choctaw Republic. 2nd ed. Angie Debo. LC 69-7973. (Civilization of the American Indian Ser.: No. 6). (Illus.). 1934. pap. 5.95 (ISBN 0-8061-1247-6). U of Okla Pr.

Rise & Fall of the Confederate Government. abr. ed. Jefferson Davis. 11.50 (ISBN 0-8446-0074-1). Peter Smith.

Rise & Fall of the East India Company: A Sociological Appraisal. Ramkrishna Mukherjee. LC 73-90082. (Illus.). 464p. 1974. 15.00x o.p. (ISBN 0-85345-315-2, CL-3152); pap. 6.50 (ISBN 0-85345-407-8). Monthly Rev.

Rise & Fall of the Horror Film. David Soren. 1977. perfect bdg. 5.50x (ISBN 0-87543-136-4). Lucas.

Rise & Fall of the League of Nations. George Scott. LC 73-20179. (Illus.). 432p. 1974. 9.95 o.s.i. (ISBN 0-02-608630-1). Macmillan.

Rise & Fall of the People's Century: Henry A. Wallace & American Liberalism, 1941-1948. Norman D. Markowitz. LC 72-86508. (Illus.). 1973. 8.95 o.s.i. (ISBN 0-02-920090-3). Free Pr.

Rise & Fall of the Peruvian Military Radicals 1968-1976. G. D. Philip. (Univ. of London Institute of Latin American Studies Monographs: No. 9). 1978. text ed. 31.25x (ISBN 0-485-17709-9, Athlone Pr). Humanities.

Rise & Fall of the Third Reich. William Shirer. 1981. price not set (ISBN 0-671-42813-6, Touchstone). S&S.

Rise & Fall of the Well Made Play. John R. Taylor. LC 67-25684. 1967. pap. 1.95 o.p. (ISBN 0-8090-0546-8, Drama). Hill & Wang.

Rise, & Fight Again. Charles B. Flood. LC 76-29619. (Illus.). 1976. 12.95 (ISBN 0-396-07356-5). Dodd.
Rise & Growth of American Politics. 2nd ed. Henry J. Ford. LC 67-23377. (Law, Politics, & History Ser). 1967. Repr. of 1898 ed. lib. bdg. 25.00 (ISBN 0-306-70946-5). Da Capo.
Rise & Progress of Religion in the Soul. Philip Doddridge. (Summit Bks). 1977. pap. 2.95 (ISBN 0-8010-2875-2). Baker Bk.
Rise & Progress of the English Constitution, 2 vols. Jea L. De Lolme. Ed. by David S. Berkowitz & Samuel E. Thorne. LC 77-86589. (Classics of English Legal History in the Modern Era Ser.: Vol. 20). 1322p. 1979. lib. bdg. 80.00 (ISBN 0-8240-3069-9). Garland Pub.
Rise & Progress of the English Constitution, Vol. 82. Jean L. De Lolme. Ed. by David Berkowitz & Samuel Thorne. LC 77-86589. (Classics of English Legal History in the Modern Era). 1979. Repr. of 1838 ed. lib. bdg. 55.00 (ISBN 0-8240-3069-9). Garland Pub.
Rise & Progress of the Present Taste in Planting Packs, Pleasure Grounds, Gardens, Etc. facsimile ed. Intro. by John Harris. 1970. 15.50 o.s.i. (ISBN 0-85362-104-7, Oriel). Routledge & Kegan.
Rise of a Central Authority for English Education. A. S. Bishop. LC 70-128634. (Cambridge Texts & Studies in the History of Education). (Illus.). 1971. 34.50 (ISBN 0-521-08023-1). Cambridge U Pr.
Rise of African Nationalism in South Africa: The African National Congress, 1912-1952. Peter Walshe. (Perspectives on Southern Africa: No. 3). 1971. 29.50x (ISBN 0-520-01810-9). U of Cal Pr.
Rise of Afrikanerdom: Power, Apartheid, & the Afrikaner Civil Religion. T. Dunbar Moodie. LC 72-85512. (Perspectives on Southern Africa Ser). 1975. 19.50x (ISBN 0-520-02310-2); pap. 5.95 (ISBN 0-520-03943-2). U of Cal Pr.
Rise of American Naval Power, Seventeen Seventy-Six to Nineteen Eighteen. Harold Sprout & Margaret Sprout. LC 79-93093. 420p. 1980. 14.95x (ISBN 0-87021-534-5). Naval Inst Pr.
Rise of American Political Parties. Fred Cook. LC 77-161834. (First Bks). (Illus.). (gr. 7 up). 1971. PLB 4.90 o.p. (ISBN 0-531-00741-3). Watts.
Rise of Anthropological Theory: A History of Theories of Culture. Marvin Harris. LC 68-17392. 1968. scp 22.95 (ISBN 0-690-70322-8, HarpC). Har-Row.
Rise of Civilization: From Early Farmers to Urban Society in the Ancient Near East. Charles L. Redman. LC 78-1493. (Illus.). 1978. text ed. 24.95x (ISBN 0-7167-0056-5); pap. text ed. 14.95x (ISBN 0-7167-0055-7). W H Freeman.
Rise of Communist China. Schools Council History 13-16 Project. (Modern World Problems Ser.). (Illus.). 1979. lib. bdg. 9.95 (ISBN 0-912616-70-9); pap. text ed. 4.45 (ISBN 0-912616-69-5). Greenhaven.
Rise of Cotton Mills in the South. 2nd ed. Broadus Mitchell. LC 68-8128. (American Scene Ser). 1968. Repr. of 1921 ed. lib. bdg. 27.50 (ISBN 0-306-71141-9). Da Capo.
Rise of David Levinsky. Abraham Cahan. 7.50 (ISBN 0-8446-1794-6). Peter Smith.
Rise of English Opera. Eric W. White. LC 78-87683. (Music Ser.). (Illus.). 374p. 1972. Repr. of 1951 ed. lib. bdg. 27.50 (ISBN 0-306-71709-3). Da Capo.
Rise of Facism. 2nd ed. F. L. Corsten. 1980. 18.50 (ISBN 0-520-04307-3). U of Cal Pr.
Rise of Free Trade Imperialism. Bernard Semmel. LC 71-112473. 1970. 41.50 (ISBN 0-521-07725-7). Cambridge U Pr.
Rise of German Industrial Power, 1834-1914. W. O. Henderson. LC 75-17293. 1976. 22.50x (ISBN 0-520-03073-7); pap. 5.95x (ISBN 0-520-03120-2). U of Cal Pr.
Rise of Indonesian Communism. Ruth J. McVey. 1965. 24.50x o.p. (ISBN 0-8014-0287-5). Cornell U Pr.
Rise of Modern Japan. Peter Duus. LC 75-33416. (Illus.). 304p. 1976. text ed. 13.50 (ISBN 0-395-20665-0). HM.
Rise of Modern Mythology, Sixteen Eighty to Eighteen Sixty. Burton Feldman & Robert D. Richardson. LC 71-135005. (Midland Bks.: No. 188). 592p. 1972. 15.00x (ISBN 0-253-35012-3); pap. 5.95x (ISBN 0-253-20188-8). Ind U Pr.
Rise of Parti Quebecois 1967-1976. John Saywell. 1977. pap. 5.95 (ISBN 0-8020-6317-9). U of Toronto Pr.
Rise of Party in England: The Rockingham Whigs, 1760-1782. Frank O'Gorman. 1975. text ed. 32.50x o.p. (ISBN 0-04-942135-2). Allen Unwin.
Rise of Pennsylvania Protectionsim. Malcolm R. Eiselen. (Neglected American Economists Ser.). 1974. lib. bdg. 50.00 (ISBN 0-8240-1035-3). Garland Pub.
Rise of Professionalism: A Sociological Analysis. Magali S. Larson. 1977. 20.00x (ISBN 0-520-02938-0); pap. 7.50x (ISBN 0-520-03950-5). U of Cal Pr.
Rise of Puritanism. William Halier. LC 57-10117. 479p. 1972. pap. 8.50x (ISBN 0-8122-1048-4, Pa Paperbks). U of Pa Pr.
Rise of Reform Judaism: A Sourcebook of Its European Origins. W. Gunther Plaut. Incl. Growth of Reform Judaism: American & European Sources to 1948. 1965. 1963. 10.00 (ISBN 0-8074-0089-0, 382770, Pub. by World Union). UAHC.
Rise of Religious Education Among Negro Baptists. James D. Tyms. LC 79-66419. 1979. pap. text ed. 13.00 (ISBN 0-8191-0827-8). U Pr of Amer.
Rise of Religious Liberty in America: A History. Sanford H. Cobb. LC 68-27517. 541p. 1968. Repr. of 1902 ed. 32.50x (ISBN 0-8154-0051-9). Cooper Sq.
Rise of Romance. Eugene Vinaver. 1971. 12.95 (ISBN 0-19-501446-4). Oxford U Pr.
Rise of Romantic Opera. E. J. Dent. Ed. by W. Dean. LC 76-14029. (Illus.). 1976. 32.95 (ISBN 0-521-21337-1); pap. 8.50x (ISBN 0-521-29659-5). Cambridge U Pr.
Rise of Rome. Jacques Heurgon. LC 70-126762. 1973. 21.50x (ISBN 0-520-01795-1). U of Cal Pr.
Rise of Ronald Reagan. Bill Boyarsky. (Illus.). 1981. Repr. of 1964 ed. price not set. Random.
Rise of Russia. Robert Wallace. (Great Ages of Man Ser). (Illus.). 1967. 12.95 (ISBN 0-8094-0353-6); lib. bdg. avail. (ISBN 0-685-04843-8). Time-Life.
Rise of Scientific Philosophy. Hans Reichenbach. 1951. 17.95x (ISBN 0-520-01053-1); pap. 4.95 (ISBN 0-520-01055-8, CAL3). U of Cal Pr.
Rise of Silas Lapham. W. D. Howells. LC 70-92321. (Selected Edition of W.D. Howells: Center for Editions of American Authors: Vol. 12). 434p. 1971. 17.50x (ISBN 0-253-35016-6). Ind U Pr.
Rise of Silas Lapham. William D. Howells. (Literature Ser). (gr. 10-12). 1970. pap. text ed. 3.67 (ISBN 0-87720-737-2). AMSCO Sch.
Rise of Silas Lapham. William D. Howells. (RL 9). pap. 1.95 (ISBN 0-451-51400-9, CJ1400, Sig Classics). NAL.
Rise of Silas Lapham. rev. ed. William D. Howells. Ed. by Robert J. Dixson. (American Classics Ser.: No. 8). 1974. pap. text ed. 2.75 (ISBN 0-88345-204-9, 18127); cassettes 40.00 (ISBN 0-685-38925-1); tapes 40.00 (ISBN 0-685-38926-X). Regents Pub.
Rise of Social Democracy in Russia. J. L. Keep. 1963. 29.95x (ISBN 0-19-827147-6). Oxford U Pr.
Rise of Systems Theory: An Ideological Analysis. Robert Lilienfeld. LC 77-12609. 1978. 26.95 (ISBN 0-471-53533-8, Pub. by Wiley-Inerscience). Wiley.
Rise of Teamster Power in the West. Donald Garnel. 1971. 25.00x (ISBN 0-520-01733-1). U of Cal Pr.
Rise of the American Electrochemicals Industry, 1880-1910: Studies in the American Technological Environment. Martha M. Trescott. LC 80-23469. (Contributions in Economics & Economic History Ser.: No. 38). (Illus.). 424p. 1981. lib. bdg. 45.00 (ISBN 0-313-20766-6, TRI/). Greenwood.
Rise of the American Film: A Critical History with an Essay "Experimental Cinema in America 1921-1947". Lewis Jacobs. LC 68-25845. (Illus.). 1968. text ed. 21.50 (ISBN 0-8077-1556-5); pap. 14.95x (ISBN 0-8077-1555-7). Tchrs Coll.
Rise of the Arts on the American Campus. Carnegie Commission on Higher Education. Ed. by Jack Morrison. LC 72-10456. (Illus.). 244p. 1973. 12.50 o.p. (ISBN 0-07-010055-1, P&RB). McGraw.
Rise of the Celts. Henri H. Hubert. LC 66-23521. (Illus.). 1934. 15.00x (ISBN 0-8196-0183-7). Biblo.
Rise of the Cults. rev. ed. Walter Martin. 138p. 1980. pap. 3.95 (ISBN 0-88449-044-0). Vision Hse.
Rise of the English Shipping Industry in the 17th & 18th Centuries. Ralph Davis. 427p. 1972. Repr. of 1962 ed. 17.50x (ISBN 0-87471-314-5). Rowman.
Rise of the Gulag: Intellectual Origins of Leninism. Alain Besancon. 272p. 1980. 19.50 (ISBN 0-8264-0014-0). Continuum.
Rise of the Imams of Sanaa. Arthur S. Tritton. LC 79-2887. 144p. 1981. Repr. of 1925 ed. 15.00 (ISBN 0-8305-0053-7). Hyperion Conn.
Rise of the Israelite Monarchy: The Growth & Development of I Samuel 7-15. Bruce C. Birch. LC 76-20680. (Society of Biblical Literature. Dissertation Ser.). 1976. pap. 7.50 (ISBN 0-89130-112-7, 060127). Scholars Pr Ca.
Rise of the London Money Market 1640-1826. W. R. Bisschop. LC 67-31557. Repr. of 1910 ed. 25.00x (ISBN 0-678-05027-9). Kelley.
Rise of the Modern Woman. LC 78-56350. (Problems in Civilization Ser). (Orig.). 1978. pap. text ed. 3.95x (ISBN 0-88273-404-0). Forum Pr MO.
Rise of the Monophysite Movement: Chapters in the History of the Church in the Fifth & Sixth Centuries. W. H. Frend. LC 72-75302. (Illus.). 400p. 1972. 69.50 (ISBN 0-521-08130-0). Cambridge U Pr.
Rise of the New Model Army. Mark A. Kishlansky. LC 79-4285. 1979. 21.50 (ISBN 0-521-22751-8). Cambridge U Pr.
Rise of the Peking Opera 1770-1870: Social Aspects of the Theatre in Manchu China. Colin P. Mackerras. (Illus.). 290p. 1972. 34.95x (ISBN 0-19-815137-3). Oxford U Pr.
Rise of the Raj. Peggy Woodford. (Illus.). 1978. text ed. 22.25x (ISBN 0-391-00867-6). Humanities.
Rise of the Russian Novel: Studies in the Russian Novel from Eugene Onegin to War & Peace. R. Freeborn. LC 75-190417. 250p. 1973. 49.50 (ISBN 0-521-08588-8); pap. 12.95x (ISBN 0-521-09738-X). Cambridge U Pr.
Rise of the Unmeltable Ethnics. Michael Novak. LC 70-185143. 1972. 7.95 o.s.i. (ISBN 0-02-590780-8). Macmillan.
Rise of the Vice-Presidency. Irving G. Williams. 5.00 (ISBN 0-8183-0204-6). Pub Aff Pr.
Rise of the West: A History of the Human Community. William H. McNeill. LC 63-13067. 1970. pap. 9.95 (ISBN 0-226-56144-5, P385, Phoen). U of Chicago Pr.
Rise of the West, 1754-1830. Francis S. Philbrick. LC 65-21377. (New American Nation Ser.). 1965. 15.00x o.s.i. (ISBN 0-06-013330-9, HarpT). Har-Row.
Rise of the Western World: A New Economic History. D. C. North & R. P. Thomas. LC 73-77258. (Illus.). 192p. 1973. 23.95 (ISBN 0-521-20171-3); pap. 6.95x (ISBN 0-521-29099-6). Cambridge U Pr.
Rise of Theodore Roosevelt. Edmund Morris. 1980. pap. 8.95 (ISBN 0-345-28707-X). Ballantine.
Rise of World Anthropology. L. P. Vidyarthi. 180p. 1979. text ed. 9.00x (ISBN 0-391-01784-5). Humanities.
Rise to Follow: An Autobiography. Albert Spalding. LC 77-5563. (Music Reprint Ser.). 1977. Repr. of 1943 ed. lib. bdg. 27.50 (ISBN 0-306-77421-6). Da Capo.
Rise up & Remember. Barbara Nauer. LC 76-54011. 120p. 1977. pap. 2.95 o.p. (ISBN 0-385-12955-6). Doubleday.
Rise with the Wind. A. C. Marin. 1978. pap. 1.75 o.p. (ISBN 0-523-40455-7, Dist. by Independent News Co.). Pinnacle Bks.
Risen Christ & the Eucharistic World. Gustave Martelet. 1977. 10.95 (ISBN 0-8164-0316-3). Crossroad NY.
Rising Above Decline. Betsy Wachtel & Brian Powers. Ed. by Nancy Seymour. 198p. (Orig.). 1979. pap. 4.50 (ISBN 0-917754-14-X). Inst Responsive.
Rising Cost of Hospital Care. Martin S. Feldstein. LC 72-171922. (Illus.). 88p. 1971. pap. text ed. 7.50 (ISBN 0-87815-004-8). Info Resources.
Rising Glory of America, 1760-1820. Ed. by Gordon S. Wood. LC 75-151798. (American Culture Ser). (Illus.). 1971. 8.95 o.s.i. (ISBN 0-8076-0611-1); pap. 4.95 (ISBN 0-8076-0610-3). Braziller.
Rising Higher. Robert S. Nathan. 312p. 1981. 11.95 (ISBN 0-686-69091-5). Dial.
Rising Star. Brenda Treet. 192p. 1981. pap. 1.50 (ISBN 0-671-57056-0). S&S.
Rising Sun. A. Zich. LC 76-52547. (World War II Ser.). (Illus.). (gr. 6 up). 1977. 14.94 (ISBN 0-8094-2463-0, Pub. by Time-Life). Silver.
Rising Sun. Ed. by Arthor Zich. (World War II Ser.). 1977. 12.95 (ISBN 0-8094-2462-2). Time-Life.
Rising Tide. Mabel E. Allan. LC 77-14653. (gr. 4-7). 1978. 6.95 o.s.i. (ISBN 0-8027-6317-0). Walker & Co.
Rising Tide. Richard F. Pourade. LC 67-11865. (Historic Birthplace of California Ser.: Vol. 6). (Illus.). 267p. 1967. 14.50 (ISBN 0-913938-06-8). Copley Bks.
Rising Tides: Twentieth Century American Women Poets. Ed. by Laura Chester & Sharon Barba. (Orig.). 1973. pap. 2.50 o.s.i. (ISBN 0-671-48753-1). WSP.
Rising Trout. rev., 2nd ed. Charles K. Fox. LC 77-92364. 1978. 11.95 (ISBN 0-8015-6394-1, Hawthorn); pap. 6.95 (ISBN 0-8015-6395-X, Hawthorn). Dutton.
Risk & Failure Analysis for Improved Performance & Reliability. Ed. by John J. Burke & Volker Weiss. (Sagamore Army Materials Research Conference Ser.: Vol. 24). 365p. 1980. 42.50 (ISBN 0-306-40446-X, Plenum Pr). Plenum Pub.
Risk & Insurance. 4th ed. James L. Athearn. (Illus.). 550p. 1981. text ed. 15.96 (ISBN 0-8299-0298-8). West Pub.
Risk & Insurance. 2nd ed. Herbert S. Denenberg et al. 1974. 18.95 (ISBN 0-13-781294-9). P-H.
Risk & Prevention of Arterial Lipidoses. P. Schwandt. 1981. 27.50 (ISBN 0-87527-232-0). Green.
Risk & Response. James E. Post. (Illus.). 1976. 21.50 (ISBN 0-669-00645-9). Lexington Bks.
Risk & Uncertainty As Factors in Crop Improvement Research. (IRRI Research Paper Ser.: No. 15). 19p. 1978. pap. 5.00 (R055, IRRI). Unipub.
Risk & Uncertainty in Accounting & Finance. Ed. by John P. Dickinson. LC 74-3917. 239p. 1975. 21.95x o.p. (ISBN 0-347-01042-3, 93468-2, Pub. by Saxon Hse). Lexington Bks.
Risk Assessment of Environmental Hazard: Scope Report 8. Robert W. Kates. LC 77-12909. (Scientific Committee on Problems of the Environment). 1978. 15.75 (ISBN 0-471-99582-7, Pub. by Wiley-Interscience). Wiley.
Risk Assessment of N-Nitroso Compounds for Human Health: Oncology. Dietrich Schmaehl. (Oncology Journal: Vol. 37). (Illus.). 120p. 1980. pap. 36.75 (ISBN 3-8055-1137-X). S Karger.
Risk-Benefit Analysis. Richard Wilson & Edmond Crouch. Date not set. price not set (ISBN 0-88410-667-5). Ballinger Pub.
Risk Business: British Industrial Design Innovation. Michael Blakstad. 1979. 10.00x (ISBN 0-85072-098-2). Nichols Pub.
Risk, Communication, & Decision Making in Genetic Counseling. Ed. by Charles J. Epstein. LC 79-5120. (Alan R. Liss Ser.: Vol. 15, No. 5c). 1979. 36.00 (ISBN 0-8451-1030-6). March of Dimes.
Risk, Communication, & Decision Making in Genetic Counseling: Proceedings, Annual Review of Birth Defects, 1978, Pt. C. Birth Defects Converence, 1978, San Francisco. Ed. by Charles J. Epstein et al. LC 79-5120. (Birth Defects: Original Article Ser.: Vol. XV, No. 5C). 1979. 36.00x (ISBN 0-8451-1030-6). A R Liss.
Risk Evaluation for Protection of the Public in Radiation Accidents. (Safety Ser.: No. 21). 1967. pap. 5.00 (ISBN 92-0-123267-5, IAEA). Unipub.
Risk in Business Decision. P. G. Moore. LC 72-11307. 365p. 1972. 26.95x (ISBN 0-470-61440-4). Halsted Pr.
Risk Management & Insurance. 4th ed. C. Arthur Williams, Jr. & Richard M. Heins. (Insurance Ser.). (Illus.). 672p. 1980. text ed. 19.95 (ISBN 0-07-070564-X, C); instructor's manual 5.95 (ISBN 0-07-070565-8). McGraw.
Risk Management: Concepts & Applications. Robert I. Mehr & Bob A. Hedges. 1974. text ed. 18.50 (ISBN 0-256-01614-3). Irwin.
Risk Management for Hospitals: A Practical Approach. Bernard L. Brown. LC 78-31925. 1979. text ed. 28.00 (ISBN 0-89443-090-4). Aspen Systems.
Risk Management Manual. Matthew Lenz, Jr. 225p. 1971. 122.00, incl. supplemental service o.p. (ISBN 0-88245-011-5). Merritt Co.
Risk Management Manual. Matthew Lenz, Jr. 1981. 188.00 (ISBN 0-930868-02-1). Merritt Co.
Risk of Love. W. H. Vanstone. 1978. 8.95 (ISBN 0-19-520053-5). Oxford U Pr.
Risk-Taking Behavior: Concepts, Methods, & Applications to Smoking & Drug Abuse. Ed. by Richard E. Carney. (Illus.). 224p. 1971. 19.75 (ISBN 0-398-00287-8). C C Thomas.
Risk Theory: The Stochastic Basis of Insurance. 2nd ed. R. E. Beard et al. LC 77-1637. 195p. 1977. text ed. 17.95x o.p. (ISBN 0-412-15100-6, Pub. by Chapman & Hall). Methuen Inc.
Risk Theory: The Stochastic Basis of Insurance. 2nd ed. R. E. Beard et al. LC 77-1637. 1977. 13.95 o.p. (ISBN 0-470-99119-4). Halsted Pr.
Risking Intimacy: Daring to Be Close, Loving, Committed. Barbara Fast. (YA) 1978. 8.95 o.p. (ISBN 0-399-11978-7, Dist. by Putnam). Berkley Pub.
Risks in the Practice of Modern Obstetrics, Vol. 2. Silvio Aladjem et al. LC 75-22148. (Illus.). 426p. 1975. 37.50 o.p. (ISBN 0-8016-0099-5). Mosby.
Rita Davenport's Sourdough Cookery. new ed. Rita Davenport. LC 77-71168. (Illus.). 1977. 6.95 o.p. (ISBN 0-912656-64-6); pap. 4.95 o.p. (ISBN 0-912656-63-8). H P Bks.
Ritchie Perry Promotion, a Hard Man to Kill, No. 2. Ritchie Perry. (Super Secret Agent Thrillers Ser.: No. 2). 1981. pap. 2.25 (ISBN 0-345-29056-9). Ballantine.
Ritchie Perry Promotion, the Fall Guy, No. 1. Ritchie Perry. (Super Secret Agent Thrillers Ser.: No. 2). 1981. pap. 2.25 (ISBN 0-345-29055-0). Ballantine.
Rites & Symbols of Initiation: The Mysteries of Birth & Rebirth. Mircea Eliade. 8.50 (ISBN 0-8446-2027-0). Peter Smith.
Rites for a Plebian Statue. Pritish Nandy. 8.00 (ISBN 0-89253-654-3); flexible cloth 4.80 (ISBN 0-89253-655-1). Ind-US Inc.
Rites of Passage. William Golding. 278p. 1980. 10.95 (ISBN 0-374-25086-3). FS&G.

Rites of Passage in a Student Culture. Thomas A. Leemon. LC 72-81190. 1972. pap. text ed. 7.50x (ISBN 0-8077-1673-1). Tchrs Coll.

Ritual & Drama: The Mediaeval Theater. Francis Edwards. (Illus.). 1976. pap. text ed. 11.00x (ISBN 0-7188-2180-7). Intl Ideas.

Ritual Book of Magic. Compiled by Clifford Bias. 160p. 1981. pap. 6.95 (ISBN 0-87728-532-2). Weiser.

Ritual Cosmos: The Sanctification of Life in African Religions. Evan M. Zuesse. LC 79-13454. x, 256p. 1980. 18.00x (ISBN 0-8214-0398-2). Ohio U Pr.

Ritual Dinners in Early Historic Sardis. C. H. Greenewalt, Jr. (Publications in Classical Studies: Vol. 17). 1978. pap. 11.50x (ISBN 0-520-09563-4). U of Cal Pr.

Ritual Humor in Highland Chiapas. Victoria R. Bricker. LC 73-6501. (Texas Pan American Ser). (Illus.). 257p. 1973. 15.00x (ISBN 0-292-77004-9). U of Tex Pr.

Ritual Lament in Greek Tradition. Margaret Alexiou. LC 72-97879. (Illus.). 216p. 1974. 34.00 (ISBN 0-521-20226-4). Cambridge U Pr.

Ritual Magic. E. M. Butler. LC 78-73949. 1979. 36.00 (ISBN 0-521-22563-9); pap. 9.95 (ISBN 0-521-29553-X). Cambridge U Pr.

Ritual Magic. E. M. Butler. LC 80-19324. 329p. 1980. Repr. of 1971 ed. lib. bdg. 10.95x (ISBN 0-89370-601-9). Borgo Pr.

Ritual of Battle: Krishna in the Mahabharata. Alf Hiltebeitel. LC 75-18496. 1975. 25.00x (ISBN 0-8014-0970-5). Cornell U Pr.

Ritual of the Bacabs. Tr. by Ralph L. Roys. (Civilization of the American Indian Ser.: No. 77). 1965. 10.95 o.p. (ISBN 0-8061-0662-X). U of Okla Pr.

Ritual of the Hearth. R. Sickler. 1973. pap. 3.95 o.s.i. (ISBN 0-02-010350-6, Collier). Macmillan.

Ritual: Psychoanalytic Studies. Theodor Reik. LC 73-2645. (Illus.). 367p. 1975. Repr. of 1946 ed. lib. bdg. 25.25x (ISBN 0-8371-6814-7, RERI). Greenwood.

Rituals & Magic for Perfect Living. Rita Norling. 1974. 7.95 o.p. (ISBN 0-13-781328-7). P-H.

Rituals of the Kandyan State. H. L. Seneviratne. LC 77-80842. (Studies in Social Anthropology: No. 22). (Illus.). 1978. 27.50 (ISBN 0-521-21736-9). Cambridge U Pr.

Ritz & Other Plays. Terrence McNally. LC 76-17603. (Illus.). 1976. 9.95 (ISBN 0-396-07315-8). Dodd.

Rivages de la Mediterranee. (Illus.). 1978. text ed. 18.95x (ISBN 2-03-013904-1, 3183). Larousse.

Rivages de l'Atlantique. (Beautes de la France). (Illus.). 1978. 24.25x (ISBN 2-03-013909-2, 3188). Larousse.

Rival Queens. Nathaniel Lee. Ed. by P. F. Vernon. LC 72-91330. (Regents Restoration Drama Ser). 1970. 7.95x (ISBN 0-8032-0375-6); pap. 1.65x (ISBN 0-8032-5374-5, BB 273, Bison). U of Nebr Pr.

Rivals & Tracy's Ambition. Gerald Griffin. (Nineteenth Century Fiction Ser.: Ireland: Vol. 29). 976p. 1979. lib. bdg. 46.00 (ISBN 0-8240-3478-3). Garland Pub.

Rivals of D.W. Griffith: Alternate Auteurs, 1913 to 1918. Richard Koszarski et al. (Illus.). 58p. (Orig.). 1980. pap. 4.95 (ISBN 0-918432-32-4). Ny Zoetrope.

Rivals on Ice. Elizabeth Van Steenwyk. Ed. by Kathy Pacini. LC 78-31102. (Springboard Bk.). (Illus.). 64p. (gr. 3-7). 1979. 5.75g (ISBN 0-8075-7071-0). A Whitman.

River & I. John G. Neihardt. LC 68-13650. (Illus.). 1968. pap. 4.95 (ISBN 0-8032-5144-0, BB 378, Bison). U of Nebr Pr.

River Basin. D. I. Smith & P. Stopp. LC 77-85688. (Topics in Geography Ser.). (Illus.). 1979. 17.95 (ISBN 0-521-21900-0); pap. 7.95x (ISBN 0-521-29307-3). Cambridge U Pr.

River Camping: Touring by Canoe, Raft, Dory, & Kayak. Verne Hauser. (Soltice Press Bk.). (Illus.). 1981. pap. 9.95 (ISBN 0-8037-7256-4). Dial.

River Congo: The Discovery, Exploration, & Exploitation of the World's Most Dramatic River. Peter Forbath. 1979. pap. 7.95 o.p. (ISBN 0-525-47573-7). Dutton.

River Devils. large print ed. Carter Vaughan. LC 80-28166. 1981. Repr. of 1969 ed. 10.95 (ISBN 0-89621-266-1). Thorndike Pr.

River Ecology. B. A. Whitton. LC 75-10884. 735p. 1975. 57.50x (ISBN 0-520-03016-8). U of Cal Pr.

River Morphology. Ed. by Stanley A. Schumm. LC 72-78310. (Benchmark Papers in Geology Ser.). 1972. pap. 32.00 (ISBN 0-12-787440-2). Acad Pr.

River, No More: The Colorado River & the West. Philip L. Fradkin. LC 80-2713. (Illus.). 384p. 1981. 15.95 (ISBN 0-394-41579-5). Knopf.

River Notes: The Dance of the Herons. Barry H. Lopez. 96p. 1980. pap. 2.25 (ISBN 0-380-52514-3, 52514). Avon.

River of Miracles. G. R. Schoepfer. Ed. by Virginia B. Schoepfer. (Illus.). (gr. 1-11). 1978. pap. text ed. 2.75 (ISBN 0-931436-01-X, Children's Books). G R Schoepfer.

River of No Return. Cort Conley & John Carrey. LC 78-52373. 1978. pap. 10.95 (ISBN 0-9603566-2-2). Backeddy Bks.

River of the Long Water. Alma Hetherington. LC 79-92112. (Illus.). 1980. 17.95 (ISBN 0-913122-09-2). Mickler Hse.

River People. Lee D. Willoughby. 1981. pap. 2.75 (ISBN 0-440-07248-4). Dell.

River Place. Doug Baker. 176p. 1980. pap. 7.95 (ISBN 0-917304-57-8, Pub. by Timber Pr). Intl Schol Bk Serv.

River Plains & Sea Coasts. Richard J. Russell. 1967. 19.50x (ISBN 0-520-01107-4). U of Cal Pr.

River Plants. S. M. Haslam. LC 76-46857. (Illus.). 1978. 90.00 (ISBN 0-521-21493-9); pap. 22.95x (ISBN 0-521-29172-0). Cambridge U Pr.

River Pollution Control. Ed. by M. J. Stiff. 300p. 1980. 99.95x (ISBN 0-470-27004-7). Halsted Pr.

River Runners: A Tale of Hardship & Bravery. James Houston. LC 79-14337. (Illus.). (gr. 7 up). 1979. 8.95 (ISBN 0-689-50151-X, McElderry Bk). Atheneum.

River Through Time: The Course of Western Civilization. C. Warren Hollister et al. LC 74-14972. 576p. 1975. pap. 14.95x (ISBN 0-471-40695-3). Wiley.

River Vegetation: Its Identification, Assessment & Management; a Field Guide to the Macrophytic Vegetation of British Watercourses. S. M. Haslam & P. A. Wolseley. 96p. Date not set. text ed. price not set (ISBN 0-521-23186-8); pap. text ed. price not set (ISBN 0-521-23187-6). Cambridge U Pr.

River World & Other Explorations. Berton Roueche. LC 78-4738. 1978. 9.95 o.s.i. (ISBN 0-06-013686-3, HarpT). Har-Row.

Riverbank Publications, 3 vols. William F. Friedman. (Cryptographic Ser.). 1979. 16.80 ea. Vol. 1 (ISBN 0-89412-032-8). Vol. 2 (ISBN 0-89412-033-6). Vol. 3 (ISBN 0-89412-034-4). Aegean Park Pr.

Riverbend Casebook. Bruce A. Shuman. 1981. lib. bdg. 14.95x (ISBN 0-912700-57-2). Oryx Pr.

Rivergate House. large print ed. Elissa Grandower. LC 80-29028. 1981. Repr. of 1980 ed. 11.95 (ISBN 0-89621-268-8). Thorndike Pr.

Rivergate House. Elissa Grandower. LC 79-6036. 288p. 1980. 10.95 (ISBN 0-385-15420-8). Doubleday.

Rivermen. Paul O'Neil. (Old West Ser.). (Illus.). 240p. 1975. 12.95 (ISBN 0-8094-1496-1). Time-Life.

Rivermen. Paul O'Neil. LC 75-7193. (Old West). (Illus.). (gr. 5 up). 1975. kivar 12.96 (ISBN 0-8094-1498-8, Pub. by Time-Life). Silver.

Riverrun. Felicia Andrews. (Orig.). 1979. pap. 2.50 (ISBN 0-515-04545-4). Jove Pubns.

Rivers. Delia Goetz. (Illus.). (gr. 3-7). 1969. PLB 6.48 (ISBN 0-688-31480-5). Morrow.

Rivers. Sam Hunter. (Abrams-Meridian Modern Painters Ser). (Illus.). pap. 3.95 o.p. (ISBN 0-452-00357-1, FM357, Mer). NAL.

Rivers. Ronald Russell. 1978. 14.95 (ISBN 0-7153-7473-7). David & Charles.

Rivers & Lakes. Eckart Pott. (Illus.). 144p. 1981. pap. 5.95 (ISBN 0-7011-2544-6, Pub. by Chatto-Bodley-Jonathan). Merrimack Bk Serv.

Rivers of Eros. Cyrus Colter. LC 73-189191. 219p. 1972. 9.95 (ISBN 0-8040-0563-X). Swallow.

Rivers of Florida. H. S. Marks & Gene B. Riggs. 4.95 (ISBN 0-915536-00-5). H S Marks.

Rivers of Glory. F. Van Wyck Mason. pap. 1.95 o.p. (ISBN 0-425-03177-2). Berkley Pub.

Rivers of Living Water. Ruth Paxson. pap. 1.50 (ISBN 0-8024-7367-9). Moody.

Rivers of Norway. T. Sylte. (Illus.). 1966. 15.00x (ISBN 82-09-00841-2, N447). Vanous.

Rivers of Time. Jean B. Hudson. 1978. pap. 1.95 (ISBN 0-380-40444-3, 40444). Avon.

Rivers Seventy-Six. Compiled by American Society of Civil Engineers. 1824p. 1976. pap. text ed. 72.50 (ISBN 0-87262-164-2). Am Soc Civil Eng.

Riverside. Morty Sklar. (Outstanding Author Ser.: No. 1). 13p. 1974. pap. 2.25 (ISBN 0-930370-00-7). Spirit That Moves.

Riverside Reader. Joseph Trimmer & Maxine Hairston. LC 80-82759. 544p. 1981. pap. text ed. 7.95 (ISBN 0-395-28940-8); instr's manual 0.75. HM.

Riverside Shakespeare. William Shakespeare. Ed. by G. Blakemore Evans et al. 1728p. 1974. text ed. 22.50 (ISBN 0-395-04402-2). HM.

Riverwitch. Felicia Andrews. (Orig.). 1979. pap. 2.75 (ISBN 0-515-05861-0). Jove Pubns.

Riverwood. Jane Corby. 1975. pap. 1.25 o.p. (ISBN 0-685-61049-7, LB317, Leisure Bks). Nordon Pubns.

Riverworld & Other Stories. Philip J. Farmer. (Science Fiction Ser.). 1981. lib. bdg. 15.95 (ISBN 0-8398-2618-4). Gregg.

Riverworld War: The Suppressed Fiction of Philip Jose Farmer. Philip J. Farmer. 112p. 1980. pap. 6.95 o.p. (ISBN 0-933180-13-6). Ellis Pr.

Riviera Puzzle: An Inspector Damiot Mystery. Vincent McConner. 228p. 1981. 10.95 (ISBN 0-02-582930-0). Macmillan.

Rivulins of the Old World. Joegen Scheel. 14.95 (ISBN 0-87666-137-1, PS660). TFH Pubns.

R.K. Narayan. P. S. Sundaram. (Indian Writers Ser.). 1973. 8.50 (ISBN 0-89253-510-5). Ind-US Inc.

RN: The Memoirs of Richard Nixon, 2 vols. Richard Nixon. (Illus.). 1979. pap. 2.95 ea. Vol. 1, 736p (ISBN 0-446-93259-0). Vol. 3, 728p (ISBN 0-446-93260-4). Warner Bks.

Road. Nagib Mahfouz. pap. 5.50 arabic (ISBN 0-685-82870-0). Intl Bk Ctr.

Road & Track Illustrated Auto Dictionary. John Dinkel. (Illus.). 96p. 1981. pap. 3.95 (ISBN 0-393-00028-1). Norton.

Road Back. 2nd ed. Macaba. 200p. (Orig.). 1979. pap. 9.75 (ISBN 0-911038-89-2). Noontide.

Road Block to Moscow. Nick Savoca & Dick Schneider. (Illus.). 160p. 1974. 4.95 o.p. (ISBN 0-8007-0658-7); pap. 2.95 o.p. (ISBN 0-8007-0659-5). Revell.

Road Building Materials in Texas. J. P. Nash et al. (Illus.). 159p. 1918. 0.50 (BULL 1839). Bur Econ Geology.

Road East: America's New Discovery of Eastern Wisdom. Harrison Pope, Jr. LC 73-16887. 256p. 1974. pap. 3.45 o.p. (ISBN 0-8070-1127-4, BP476). Beacon Pr.

Road from Home: The Story of an Armenian Childhood. David Kherdian. LC 78-72511. (gr. 7 up). 1979. 9.50 (ISBN 0-688-80205-2); PLB 9.12 (ISBN 0-688-84205-4). Greenwillow.

Road from Runnymede: Magna Carta & Constitutionalism in America. A. D. Howard. LC 68-15941. (Virginia Legal Studies Series). (Illus.). 492p. 1968. 20.00x (ISBN 0-8139-0122-7). U Pr of Va.

Road Goes Ever on: A Song Cycle. 72p. (Music by Donald Swann; poetry by J. R. R. tolkien). 1975. pap. 4.95 o.p. (ISBN 0-345-24733-7). Ballantine.

Road Home: Sketches of Rural Canada. B. Swarbrick. 1976. 19.95 o.p. (ISBN 0-13-781559-X). P-H.

Road Lighting. W. J. Van Bommel & J. B. DeBoer. (Philips Technical Library). (Illus.). 363p. 1980. text ed. 69.50x (ISBN 0-333-30679-1). Scholium Intl.

Road Not Taken: The Editorial Opinions of Frederick C. Thorne. Ed. by T. S. Krawiec. 1981. pap. 11.95 (ISBN 0-88422-013-3). Clinical Psych.

Road Notes. LC 80-53814. 1981. pap. 6.95 (ISBN 0-528-84546-2). Rand.

Road of Azrael. Robert E. Howard. 192p. 1980. pap. 2.25 (ISBN 0-553-13326-8). Bantam.

Road of Inquiry: C. S. Pierce's Pragmatic Realism. Peter Skagestad. LC 80-25278. 296p. 1981. 20.00x (ISBN 0-231-05004-6). Columbia U Pr.

Road of Science & the Ways to God. Stanley L. Jaki. LC 77-21667. viii, 478p. 1980. pap. 8.95 (ISBN 0-226-39145-0, P897). U of Chicago Pr.

Road of the Intellectuals to Class Power: A Sociological Study of the Role of the Intelligentsi in Socialism. George Konrad & Ivan Szelenyi. Tr. by Andrew Arato & Richard E. Allen. LC 77-92547. 1979. 10.00 o.p. (ISBN 0-685-94990-7). HarBraceJ.

Road of the Sea Horse. Poul Anderson. (Last Viking Ser.: No. 2). 400p. (Orig.). 1980. pap. 2.50 (ISBN 0-89083-610-8). Zebra.

Road Passenger Transport & Road Goods Transport. Denys Munby & A. H. Watson. Ed. by W. F. Manunder. LC 77-30558. 1978. text ed. 37.00 (ISBN 0-08-022449-0). Pergamon.

Road Pricing & Transit Improvement Program in Berkeley, California: A Preliminary Analysis. Melvyn Cheslow. (Institute Paper). 73p. 1978. pap. 5.00 (ISBN 0-87766-233-9, 22300). Urban Inst.

Road Safety at Night. (Road Research Ser.). 112p. 1980. 10.00 (ISBN 92-64-12069-6). OECD.

Road to Confrontation: American Policy Toward China & Korea, 1947 - 1950. William W. Stueck, Jr. LC 80-11818. (Illus.). 337p. 1981. 22.00x (ISBN 0-8078-1445-8); pap. 10.00x (ISBN 0-8078-4080-7). U of NC Pr.

Road to Exile: Indonesian Nationalist Movement. John Ingleson. 1979. text ed. 28.95x o.p. (ISBN 0-686-65416-1); pap. text ed. 12.50x (ISBN 0-686-65417-X, 00130). Heinemann Ed.

Road to Fort Sumter. LeRoy Hayman. LC 71-171004. (Illus.). (gr. 5-8). 1972. 8.95 (ISBN 0-690-70566-2, TYC-J). T Y Crowell.

Road to Gdansk: Eastern Europe on the Move. Daniel Singer. LC 80-39914. 288p. 1981. 15.00 (ISBN 0-85345-567-8). Monthly Rev.

Road to Glory: A Screenplay. Joel Sayre & William Faulkner. Ed. by Matthew J. Bruccoli. (Illus.). 168p. 1981. price not set (ISBN 0-8093-0995-5); pap. price not set (ISBN 0-8093-0996-3). S Ill U Pr.

Road to Haworth. John Cannon. (Illus.). 176p. 1981. 10.95 (ISBN 0-670-60079-2). Viking Pr.

Road to Infinity. Isaac Asimov. 256p. 1981. pap. 2.75 (ISBN 0-380-54155-6, 54155). Avon.

Road to Infoterm. Ed. by Eugene Wuster. (Infoterm Ser.: Vol. 1). 144p. 1974. pap. text ed. 25.00 (ISBN 3-7940-5501-2, Pub. by K G Saur). K G Saur.

Road to Jerusalem. Walter Laquer. 1968. 6.95 o.s.i. (ISBN 0-02-568360-8). Macmillan.

Road to Mecca. Muhammad Asad. LC 80-1937. 1981. Repr. of 1954 ed. 42.00 (ISBN 0-404-18953-9). AMS Pr.

Road to Megiddo. Philip Singer. LC 77-94858. 1978. softcover 7.00 (ISBN 0-89430-025-3). Morgan-Pacific.

Road to Miklagard. Henry Treece. LC 57-12280. (Illus.). (gr. 6-10). 1957. 9.95 (ISBN 0-87599-118-1). S G Phillips.

Road to Music. Nicolas Slonimsky. (Music Reprint Ser.). 1979. Repr. of 1966 ed. lib. bdg. 17.95 (ISBN 0-306-79566-3). Da Capo.

Road to Number One: A Personal Chronicle of Penn State Football with a Foreword by Head Coach Joseph V. Paterno. Ridge Riley. LC 75-40740. 1977. 5.95 o.p. (ISBN 0-385-11397-8). Doubleday.

Road to Nuremberg. Bradley Smith. LC 80-68174. 336p. 1980. 13.95 (ISBN 0-465-07056-6). Basic.

Road to Passchendaele: The Flanders Offensive of 1917: a Study in Inevitability. John Terraine. (Illus.). xxiv, 365p. 1977. 27.50. Shoe String.

Road to Pearl Harbor: The Coming of the War Between the United States & Japan. Herbert Feis. 1950. 20.00x (ISBN 0-691-05632-3); pap. 5.95 (ISBN 0-691-01061-7). Princeton U Pr.

Road to Ramadan. Mohamed Heikal. 1976. pap. 1.95 o.p. (ISBN 0-345-25351-5). Ballantine.

Road to Resistance: An Autobiography. George Millar. (Illus.). 432p. 1980. 13.95 (ISBN 0-316-57143-1). Little.

Road to Ruin. Thomas Holcroft. Ed. by Ruth I. Aldrich. LC 68-18245. 1968. 8.95x (ISBN 0-8032-0074-9); pap. 1.65x o.p. (ISBN 0-8032-5090-8). U of Nebr Pr.

Road to Rydal Mount: A Survey of William Wordsworth's Reading. Ronald B. Hearn. (Salzburg Studies in English Literature, Romantic Reassessment: No. 6). 1973. pap. text ed. 25.00x (ISBN 0-391-01403-X). Humanities.

Road to San Jancinto. L. L. Foreman. 1977. pap. 1.25 (ISBN 0-505-51117-7). Tower Bks.

Road to Spindletop: Economic Change in Texas, 1875-1901. John S. Spratt. (Texas History Paperbacks Ser: No. 5). 1970. pap. 6.95 (ISBN 0-292-70030-X). U of Tex Pr.

Road to Stalingrad. John Erickson. LC 74-24657. (Illus.). 604p. 1975. 25.00 o.p. (ISBN 0-06-011141-0, HarpT). Har-Row.

Road to the Bazaar. Ruskin Bond. (gr. 2-6). 1980. PLB 6.90 (ISBN 0-531-04181-6). Watts.

Road to the Isles: Travellers in the Hebrides, 1770-1914. Derek Cooper. 1979. 18.00 (ISBN 0-7100-0256-4). Routledge & Kegan.

Road to the Village: Case Studies in African Community Development. Ed. by James R. Sheffield. 152p. 1974. pap. 1.50 o.p. (ISBN 0-89192-075-7, Pub by African-American Institute). Interbk Inc.

Road to Total Freedom. Roy Wallis. LC 76-27273. 1977. 15.00x (ISBN 0-231-04200-0). Columbia U Pr.

Road to Understanding. Eleanor H. Porter. 1976. lib. bdg. 16.75x (ISBN 0-89968-108-5). Lightyear.

Road to War: America, 1914-1917. Walter Millis. LC 68-9614. 1970. Repr. 27.50 (ISBN 0-86527-173-9). Fertig.

Road to Winesburg: A Mosaic of the Imaginative Life of Sherwood Anderson. William A. Sutton. LC 73-181997. (Illus.). 1972. 20.50 (ISBN 0-8108-0312-7). Scarecrow.

Road to World War II: A Documentary History. Ed. by Keith Eubank. LC 74-179768. 1973. pap. 9.95x (ISBN 0-88295-734-1). AHM Pub.

Road to Zimbabwe: The Political Economy of Settler Colonialism, National Liberation & Foreign Intervention. C. Munhamu Botsio Utete. LC 78-57669. 1978. pap. text ed. 9.00 (ISBN 0-8191-0536-8). U Pr of Amer.

Road Traffic Noise. A. Alexandre et al. LC 75-14297. 219p. 1975. 32.95 (ISBN 0-470-02160-8). Halsted Pr.

Road Transport Management. R. G. Bassett. 1975. 19.95x (ISBN 0-434-90097-4). Intl Ideas.

Road User Charges-Some Practical Considerations. Ronald F. Kirby. 17p. 1974. pap. 1.50 o.p. (ISBN 0-87766-115-4, 66000). Urban Inst.

Road Vehicle Aerodynamics. A. J. Scibor-Rylski. LC 74-26859. 213p. 1975. 34.95 (ISBN 0-470-75920-8); pap. 18.95x (ISBN 0-470-26655-4). Halsted Pr.

Road West: Saga of the Thirty Fifth Parallel. Bertha S. Dodge. LC 79-21051. (Illus.). 222p. 1980. 15.95 (ISBN 0-8263-0526-1). U of NM Pr.

Roadblock to Moscow. Nick Savoca & Dick Schneider. LC 77-89445. 1977. pap. 1.95 (ISBN 0-87123-489-0, 200489). Bethany Fell.

Roadmap for Seekers of the Journey into Self. Diane K. Pike. (Illus., Orig.). 1981. pap. price not set (ISBN 0-916192-17-2). L P Pubns.

Roadrunner. Naomi John. LC 80-10213. (Illus.). 32p. (gr. k-3). 1980. PLB 8.95 (ISBN 0-525-38485-5). Dutton.

Roads & Trails of Olympic National Park. 2nd ed. Frederick Leissler. (Illus.). 114p. 1976. pap. 6.95 (ISBN 0-295-95533-3). U of Wash Pr.

Roads & Trails of Olympic National Park. 4th rev. ed. Frederick Leissler. LC 57-3575. (Illus.). 114p. 1981. pap. 6.95 (ISBN 0-295-95819-7). U of Wash Pr.

Roads to Extinction: Essays on the Holocaust. Ed. by Ada J. Friedman. 616p. 1980. 27.50 (ISBN 0-8276-0170-0, 446). Jewish Pubn.

Roads to Recovery. Richard Anderson. 1974. pap. 1.50 (ISBN 0-570-03175-3, 12-2578). Concordia.

Roadside Geology of Texas. Robert A. Sheldon. (Illus.). 180p. 1980. pap. 6.95. Corona Pub.

Roadside Picnic & Tale of the Troika. Arkady Strugatsky & Boris Strugatsky. Tr. by Antonina W. Bouis. 1977. 10.95 (ISBN 0-02-615170-7, 61517). Macmillan.

Roadside Trees & Shrubs of Oklahoma. Doyle McCoy. LC 80-5944. (Illus.). 180p. (Orig.). 1981. pap. 9.95 (ISBN 0-8061-1556-4). U of Okla Pr.

Roadside Wild Fruits of Oklahoma. Doyle McCoy. LC 79-6705. (Illus.). 96p. (Orig.). 1980. pap. 8.95 (ISBN 0-8061-1626-9). U of Okla Pr.

Roadway Maintenance, E-027. Ed. by Business Communications. 1981. 725.00 (ISBN 0-89336-224-7). BCC.

Roadways & Airport Pavements. 1975. pap. 20.75 (ISBN 0-685-85134-6, SP-51) (ISBN 0-685-85135-4). ACI.

Roadwork: A Novel of the First Energy Crisis. Richard Bachman. (Orig.). 1981. pap. 2.25 (ISBN 0-451-09668-1, Sig). NAL.

Roaring Fork Valley: An Illustrated Chronicle. 3rd ed. Len Shoemaker. Ed. by Russ Collman. (Illus.). 1979. 27.00 (ISBN 0-913582-06-9). Sundance.

Roaring Fork Valley: An Illustrated Chronicle. Len Shoemaker. (Illus.). 216p. 27.00 (ISBN 0-913582-06-9). Sundance.

Roaring Twenties: An Album of Early Motor Racing. Cyril. (Illus.). 128p. 1980. 17.50 (ISBN 0-7137-0967-7, Pub. by Blandford Pr England). Sterling.

Rob Roy. Walter Scott. 1973. 11.50x (ISBN 0-460-00142-6, Evman); pap. 5.50 (ISBN 0-460-01142-1). Dutton.

Robber! a Robber! Franz Brandenberg. LC 75-26999. (Illus.). 32p. (gr. k-3). 1976. 7.25 (ISBN 0-688-80027-0); PLB 7.92 (ISBN 0-688-84027-2). Greenwillow.

Robber Baroness. William K. Clarke. LC 78-21417. 1979. 2.95 (ISBN 0-312-68549-1). St Martin.

Robber Noblemen. Joyce Pettigrew. 1975. 24.00 (ISBN 0-7100-7999-0). Routledge & Kegan.

Robber's Cook. 1st ed. David Hoag. 50p. 1973. pap. 1.95x o.p. (ISBN 0-686-05510-1). SF Arts & Letters.

Robbie & the Stolen Minibike. VaDonna Leaf. LC 77-78849. (Robbie Ser.). (gr. 4-9). 1978. pap. 2.95 (ISBN 0-88419-127-3). Creation Hse.

Robby on Ice. Laurence Swinburne. LC 72-75124. (Mystery & Adventure Ser.). (gr. 2-4). 1973. PLB 6.75 (ISBN 0-87191-099-3). Creative Ed.

Robert A. Heinlein: America As Science Fiction. H. Bruce Franklin. (Science Fiction Writers Ser.: No. Gb 610). (Illus.). 250p. 1980. 18.95 (ISBN 0-19-502746-9, GB); pap. 4.95 (ISBN 0-19-502747-7). Oxford U Pr.

Robert & Elizabeth Barrett Browning: An Annotated Bibliography, 1951-1970. William S. Peterson. LC 74-24915. (Illus.). 1974. 26.50x (ISBN 0-685-27180-3, Pub. by Browning Inst). Pub Ctr Cult Res.

Robert Anderson. Thomas P. Adler. (United States Authors Ser: No. 300). 1978. lib. bdg. 12.50 (ISBN 0-8057-7204-9). Twayne.

Robert Bage. Peter Faulkner. (English Authors Ser.: No. 249). 1979. lib. bdg. 11.95 (ISBN 0-8057-6739-8). Twayne.

Robert Baillie & the Second Scots Reformation. F. N. McCoy. 1974. 20.00x (ISBN 0-520-02385-4). U of Cal Pr.

Robert Benchley. Norris W. Yates. LC 68-24296. (U. S. Authors Ser.: No. 138). 1968. lib. bdg. 10.95 (ISBN 0-8057-0048-X). Twayne.

Robert Benjamin & the Disappearing Act. Jeanette Grise. LC 80-19519. (Illus.). (gr. 3-5). 1980. 8.95 (ISBN 0-664-32673-0). Westminster.

Robert Bloomfield (Seventeen Sixty-Six to Eighteen Twenty-Three) Rural Tales, Ballads & Songs. Robert Bloomfield. Ed. by Donald H. Reiman. LC 75-31161. (Romantic Context Ser.: Poetry 1789-1830). 1977. lib. bdg. 47.00 (ISBN 0-8240-2115-0). Garland Pub.

Robert Bloomfield: Wild Flowers; or, Pastoral & Local Poetry. 1806. Robert Bloomfield. Ed. by Donald H. Reiman. LC 75-31162. (Romantic Context Ser.: Poetry 1789-1830). 1977. lib. bdg. 47.00 (ISBN 0-8240-2116-9). Garland Pub.

Robert Browning. Robert B. Pearsall. (English Authors Ser.: No. 168). 1974. lib. bdg. 9.95 (ISBN 0-8057-1065-5). Twayne.

Robert Browning: A Shelley Promethean. Paul A. Cundiff. LC 77-77039. 1977. 12.95 o.p. (ISBN 0-912760-49-4); pap. 9.95 o.p. (ISBN 0-685-81416-5). Valkyrie Pr.

Robert Browning & Other Victorian Theatre Vol. 2: Acting Versions of Strafford, a Blot on the Scutcheon & Colombe's Birthday. James Hogg. (Salzburger Studien Zur Anglistik und Amerikanistik: No. 4). 1977. pap. text ed. 34.75x (ISBN 0-391-01414-5). Humanities.

Robert Browning, the Poems, Vol. I. Ed. by John Pettigrew. LC 80-53976. 1218p. 1981. text ed. 35.00x (ISBN 0-300-02675-7); pap. 12.95 (ISBN 0-300-02683-8). Yale U Pr.

Robert Browning, the Poems, Vol. II. Ed. by John Pettigrew. LC 80-53976. 1156p. 1981. text ed. 35.00x (ISBN 0-300-02676-5); pap. 12.95 (ISBN 0-300-02684-6). Yale U Pr.

Robert Browning: The Ring & the Book. Richard D. Altick. LC 80-53977. 707p. 1981. text ed. 30.00x (ISBN 0-300-02677-3); pap. 7.95. Yale U Pr.

Robert Browning's Theory of the Poet, 1833-1841. Charles L. Rivers. (Salzburg Studies in English Literature, Romantic Reassessment Ser.: No. 58). (Orig.). 1976. pap. text ed. 25.00x (ISBN 0-391-01507-9). Humanities.

Robert Bruce & the Community of the Realm of Scotland. G. W. S. Barrow. 1965. 23.50x (ISBN 0-520-00083-8). U of Cal Pr.

Robert Burns: The Critical Heritage. Ed. by Donald A. Low. (Critical Heritage Ser.). 1974. 38.00 (ISBN 0-7100-7797-1). Routledge & Kegan.

Robert Cavelier De la Salle. William J. Jacobs. LC 75-8598. (Visual Biography Ser). 64p. (gr. 4-6). 1975. PLB 4.90 o.p. (ISBN 0-531-02843-7). Watts.

Robert Charles Dallas. Robert C. Dallas. Ed. by Donald H. Reiman. LC 75-31192. (Romantic Context Ser.: Poetry 1789-1830). 1977. lib. bdg. 47.00 (ISBN 0-8240-2143-6). Garland Pub.

Robert Collier Letter Book. 6th ed. Robert Collier. 1950. 14.95 o.p. (ISBN 0-13-781500-X). P-H.

Robert Collier Letter Book. Robert Collier. 14.95 o.p. (ISBN 0-13-781500-X). R Collier.

Robert Coover. Richard Anderson. (United States Authors Ser.: No. 300). 1981. lib. bdg. 11.95 (ISBN 0-8057-7330-4). Twayne.

Robert Creeley. Arthur L. Ford. (United States Authors Ser.: No. 310). 1978. lib. bdg. 10.95 (ISBN 0-8057-7220-0). Twayne.

Robert D. FitzGerald. A. Grove Day. (World Authors Ser.: Australia: No. 286). 1974. lib. bdg. 10.95 (ISBN 0-8057-2311-0). Twayne.

Robert de Blois' Floris et Lyriope. Paul Barrette. (U. C. Publications in Modern Philology, Vol. 92). 1968. pap. 9.50x (ISBN 0-520-09287-2). U of Cal Pr.

Robert E. Lee. Matthew G. Grant. LC 73-18078. 1974. PLB 5.95 (ISBN 0-87191-302-X). Creative Ed.

Robert Elsmere. Mrs. Humphrey Ward. Ed. by Clyde De L. Ryals. LC 67-12116. 1967. pap. 2.85x (ISBN 0-8032-5210-2, BB 348, Bison). U of Nebr Pr.

Robert Elsmere. Mary A. Ward. Ed. by Robert L. Wolff. LC 75-1534. (Victorian Fiction Ser.). 1975. Repr. of 1888 ed. lib. bdg. 66.00 (ISBN 0-8240-1606-8). Garland Pub.

Robert Falconer. George MacDonald. Ed. by Robert L. Wolff. LC 75-1510. (Victorian Fiction Ser.). 1975. Repr. of 1868 ed. lib. bdg. 66.00 (ISBN 0-8240-1584-3). Garland Pub.

Robert Feke, Colonial Portrait Painter. Henry W. Foote. LC 72-75357. (Library of American Art Ser). 1969. Repr. of 1950 ed. lib. bdg. 29.50 (ISBN 0-306-71319-5). Da Capo.

Robert Finigan's Guide to Discriminating Dining in San Francisco. Robert Finigan. (Illus.). 192p. (Orig.). 1981. pap. 6.95 (ISBN 0-89141-123-2). Presidio Pr.

Robert Frost. Elaine Barry. LC 72-79942. (Modern Literature Ser.). 1973. 10.95 (ISBN 0-8044-2016-5). Ungar.

Robert Frost. Philip L. Gerber. (U. S. Authors Ser.: No. 107). 1966. lib. bdg. 9.95 (ISBN 0-8057-0296-2). Twayne.

Robert Frost: A Bibliography, 1913-1974. Frank Lentricchia & Melissa C. Lentricchia. LC 75-44093. (Author Bibliographies Ser.: No. 25). 1976. 11.00 (ISBN 0-8108-0896-X). Scarecrow.

Robert Frost & Sidney Cox: Forty Years of Friendship. William R. Evans. 310p. 1981. 15.00 (ISBN 0-87451-195-X). U Pr of New Eng.

Robert Frost Country. Betsy Melvin & Tom Melvin. LC 76-2806. (Illus.). 1977. 17.95 (ISBN 0-385-12180-6). Doubleday.

Robert Frost: Farm-Poultryman--the Story of Robert Frost's Carreer As a Breeder & Fancier of Hens. Robert Frost. Ed. by Lawrance Thompson & Edward C. Lathem. LC 64-638. 116p. 1981. pap. 5.00 (ISBN 0-87451-202-6). U Pr of New Eng.

Robert Frost on Writing. Elaine Barry. 1974. 14.00 (ISBN 0-8135-0692-1); pap. 3.95 (ISBN 0-8135-0789-8). Rutgers U Pr.

Robert Frost Speaks. Daniel Smyth. 158p. 18.95x (ISBN 0-8290-0203-0). Irvington.

Robert Frost: The Early Years, 1894-1915. Ed. by L. Thompson. LC 66-20523. 1966. 12.50 o.p. (ISBN 0-03-059770-6). HR&W.

Robert Frost: The Later Years, 1938-1963. R. H. Winnick & Lawrence Thompson. 1977. 17.95 o.p. (ISBN 0-686-67554-1). HR&W.

Robert Frost: The Years of Triumph, 1915-1938. Ed. by L. Thompson. LC 66-20523. 1970. 15.00 o.p. (ISBN 0-03-084530-0). HR&W.

Robert Frost's Imagery & the Poetic Consciousness. Dennis Vail. (Graduate Studies: No. 12). (Orig.). 1976. pap. 4.00 (ISBN 0-89672-022-5). Tex Tech Pr.

Robert Frost's Poetic Style. T. R. S. Sharma. 1980. text ed. write for info. (ISBN 0-391-01794-2). Humanities.

Robert Fulton: Pioneer of Undersea Warfare. Wallace S. Hutcheon, Jr. 192p. 1981. 15.95 (ISBN 0-87021-547-7). Naval Inst Pr.

Robert Garnier & the Themes of Political Tragedy. Gillian Jondorf. LC 69-11027. 1969. 36.00 (ISBN 0-521-07386-3). Cambridge U Pr.

Robert Gordy: Paintings & Drawings. Gene Baro. (Illus.). 1981. pap. price not set (ISBN 0-89494-011-2). New Orleans Mus Art.

Robert Graves. George Stade. LC 67-16890. (Columbia: No. 25). (Orig.). 1967. pap. 2.00 (ISBN 0-231-02907-1, MW25). Columbia U Pr.

Robert Greene Criticism: A Comprehensive Bibliography. Tetsumaro Hayashi. LC 79-142235. (Author Bibliographies Ser.: No. 6). 1971. 10.00 (ISBN 0-8108-0340-2). Scarecrow.

Robert Grosseteste & the Origins of Experimental Science, 1100-1700. Alistair C. Crombie. 1955. 49.00x (ISBN 0-19-824189-5). Oxford U Pr.

Robert Grosseteste: Scholar & Bishop. Ed. by D. A. Callus. 1955. 22.50x (ISBN 0-19-821387-5). Oxford U Pr.

Robert H. Lowie, Ethnologist: A Personal Record. Robert H. Lowie. (Illus.). 1959. 22.75x (ISBN 0-520-00775-1). U of Cal Pr.

Robert Harley & the Press. J. A. Downie. LC 78-67810. 1979. 33.50 (ISBN 0-521-22187-0). Cambridge U Pr.

Robert Henryson. Robert L. Kindrick. (English Authors Ser.: No. 274). 1979. 14.50 (ISBN 0-8057-6758-4). Twayne.

Robert Koch: Father of Bacteriology. David C. Knight. (Biography Ser). (Illus.). (gr. 7 up). 1961. PLB 5.90 o.p. (ISBN 0-531-00891-6). Watts.

Robert Lansing & American Neutrality, 1914-1917. Daniel M. Smith. LC 79-126610. (American Scene: Comments & Commentators Ser.). (Illus.). 254p. 1972. Repr. of 1958 ed. lib. bdg. 25.00 (ISBN 0-306-70057-3). Da Capo.

Robert le Diable, 2 vols. Giacomo Meyerbeer. Ed. by Phillip Gossett & Charles Rosen. LC 76-49194. (Early Romantic Opera Ser.: No. 19). 1980. Set. lib. bdg. 82.00 (ISBN 0-8240-2918-6). Garland Pub.

Robert Leroy Platzman Memorial. H. Hering. 428p. 1976. pap. text ed. 71.00 (ISBN 0-08-019957-7). Pergamon.

Robert Louis Stevenson. Irving S. Saposnik. (English Authors Ser.: No. 167). 168p. 1974. lib. bdg. 10.95 (ISBN 0-8057-1517-7). Twayne.

Robert Louis Stevenson: A Critical Celebration. Ed. by Jenni Calder. (Illus.). 104p. 1981. 15.00x (ISBN 0-389-20145-6). B&N.

Robert Louis Stevenson: A Life Study. Jenni Calder. (Illus.). 296p. 1980. 19.95 (ISBN 0-19-520210-4). Oxford U Pr.

Robert Louis Stevenson, a Teller of Tales. Eulalie O. Grover. LC 71-164308. x, 265p. (YA) 1975. Repr. of 1940 ed. 20.00 (ISBN 0-8103-4080-1). Gale.

Robert Louis Stevenson: The Critical Heritage. Paul Maixner. (Critical Heritage Ser.). 1981. write for info. (ISBN 0-7100-0505-9). Routledge & Kegan.

Robert Lowe & Education. D. W. Sylvester. LC 73-82446. (Cambridge Texts & Studies in the History of Education: No. 15). 260p. 1974. 29.50 (ISBN 0-521-20310-4). Cambridge U Pr.

Robert Lowell. 2nd ed. Richard J. Fein. (United States Authors Ser.: No. 176). 1979. lib. bdg. 9.95 (ISBN 0-8057-7279-0). Twayne.

Robert Lowell's Poems: A Selection. Ed. by Jonathan Raban. Robert Lowell. 1974. 9.95 (ISBN 0-571-10594-7, Pub. by Faber & Faber); pap. 5.95 (ISBN 0-571-10182-8). Merrimack Bk Serv.

Robert Lowery: Radical & Chartist. Robert Lowery. Ed. by Brian Harrison & Patrica Hollis. LC 80-472644. (Illus.). 283p. 1979. 35.00x (ISBN 0-905118-31-6). Intl Pubns Serv.

Robert Lowie. Robert F. Murphy. LC 72-1969. (Leaders of Modern Anthropology Ser). (Illus.). 200p. 1972. 15.00x (ISBN 0-231-03375-3); pap. 6.00x (ISBN 0-231-03397-4). Columbia U Pr.

Robert Lowth. Brian Hepworth. (English Authors Ser.: No. 224). 1978. lib. bdg. 12.50 (ISBN 0-8057-6695-2). Twayne.

Robert M. LaFollette, 2 vols. B. C. LaFollette & F. LaFollette. 1971. Repr. of 1953 ed. 38.50 o.s.i. (ISBN 0-02-848290-5). Hafner.

Robert Marion la Follette. Fred Greenbaum. LC 74-26675. (World Leaders Ser: No. 44). 1975. lib. bdg. 12.50 (ISBN 0-8057-3057-5). Twayne.

Robert Morris. Michael Compton & David Sylvester. (Tate Gallery Art Ser.). (Illus.). 1977. 4.50 (ISBN 0-8120-5143-2). Barron.

Robert Morton: The Collected Works. Robert Morton. Ed. by Allan Atlas. (Masters & Monuments of the Renaissance Ser.: Vol. 2). xxxvi, 105p. 1981. 30.00x (ISBN 0-8450-7302-8). Broude.

Robert Motherwell. 2nd, rev. ed. H. H. Arnason. (Illus.). 252p. 1980. 65.00 o.p. (ISBN 0-686-62702-4, 0289-3). Abrams.

Robert Musil, Master of the Hoveny Life. Frederick G. Peters. LC 78-5158. 1978. 17.50x (ISBN 0-231-04476-3). Columbia U Pr.

Robert Oppenheimer: Letters & Recollections. Ed. by Alice K. Smith & Charles Weiner. LC 80-10106. 1980. 20.00 (ISBN 0-674-52833-6). Harvard U Pr.

Robert Owen. Karen C. Altfest. (World Leaders Ser.: No. 60). 1977. lib. bdg. 12.50 (ISBN 0-8057-7711-3). Twayne.

Robert Owen on Education. Ed. by Harold Silver. LC 69-10432. (Cambridge Texts & Studies in Education). 1969. 27.50 (ISBN 0-521-07353-7). Cambridge U Pr.

Robert Penn Warren. Charles H. Bohner. (U. S. Authors Ser.: No. 69). 1964. lib. bdg. 9.95 (ISBN 0-8057-0772-7). Twayne.

Robert Pinget: Plays, 2 vols. Robert Pinget. Tr. by Barbara Bray & Samuel Beckett. pap. 4.95 ea.; Vol. I. (ISBN 0-7145-0474-2); Vol. II. (ISBN 0-7145-0036-4). Riverrun NY.

Robert Pinget: Three Plays, Vol. 2. Robert Pinget. 192p. 1968. 5.00 (ISBN 0-8090-7631-4). Hill & Wang.

Robert R. Church Family of Memphis: Guide to the Papers with Selected Facsimiles of Documents & Photographs. Ed. by Pamela Palmer. LC 79-124374. (Mississippi Valley Collection Bulletin: No. 10). (Illus.). 87p. 1979. 12.95x (ISBN 0-87870-059-5); pap. 8.95x (ISBN 0-87870-060-9). Memphis St Univ.

Robert Redford. David Paige. (Stars of Stage & Screen Ser.). (Illus.). (gr. 4-12). 1977. PLB 5.50 o.p. (ISBN 0-87191-554-5). Creative Ed.

Robert Redford: The Superstar Nobody Knows. David Hanna. (Illus., Orig.). 1975. pap. 1.50 o.p. (ISBN 0-685-54126-6, LB291, Leisure Bks). Nordon Pubns.

Robert Robinson: American Illustator. Q. David Bowers & Christine Bowers. (Illus.). 68p. 1981. pap. 9.95 (ISBN 0-911572-19-8). Vestal.

Robert Schuller's Life Changers. Ed. by Robert A. Schuller. 1981. 7.95 (ISBN 0-8007-1182-3). Revell.

Robert Schumann: The Man & His Music. Ed. by Alan Walker. 1978. pap. 11.95 o.p. (ISBN 0-214-20340-9, 8027, Dist. by Arco). Barrie & Jenkins.

Robert Service: A Biography. Carl F. Klinck. LC 76-22706. (Illus.). 1977. 8.95 (ISBN 0-396-07391-3). Dodd.

Robert Silverberg Omnibus: Downward to Earth, the Man in the Maze, & Nightwings. Robert Silverberg. LC 80-8232. 540p. 1981. 14.95 (ISBN 0-06-014047-X, HarpT). Har-Row.

Robert Smith Surtees. Bonnie R. Neumann. (English Authors Ser.: No. 220). 1978. 12.50 (ISBN 0-8057-6722-3). Twayne.

Robert Southey. Ernest Bernhardt-Kabisch. (English Authors Ser.: No. 223). 1977. lib. bdg. 10.95 (ISBN 0-8057-6692-8). Twayne.

Robert Southey: The Critical Heritage. Ed. by Lionel Madden. (Critical Heritage Ser). 1972. 38.50x (ISBN 0-7100-7375-5). Routledge & Kegan.

Robert Stewart Hyer, the Man I Knew. Ray H. Brown. (Illus.). 1957. 8.00 (ISBN 0-685-05005-X). A Jones.

Robert W. Johnson Jr., 77th Birthday Celebration. Association of Bone & Joint Surgeons. Ed. by Marshall R. Urist & Anthony F. De Palma. (Clinical Orthopaedics & Related Research Ser. No. 56). (Illus.). 15.00 (ISBN 0-685-24742-2). Lippincott.

Robert Walser: Leben und Werk in Daten und Bildern. Ed. by Peter Mamm. (Insel Taschenbuecher: No. 264). (Illus.). 317p. (Orig.). 1980. pap. text ed. 10.40 (ISBN 3-458-31964-6, Pub. by Insel Verlag Germany). Suhrkamp.

Robert Winchelsey & the Crown, 1294-1313. J. H. Denton. (Cambridge Studies in Medieval Life & Thought: No. 14). 1980. 42.50 (ISBN 0-521-22963-4). Cambridge U Pr.

Robert Y. Hayne & His Times. Theodore D. Jervey. LC 73-104330. (American Scene Ser). (Illus.). 1970. Repr. of 1909 ed. lib. bdg. 49.50 (ISBN 0-306-71870-7). Da Capo.

Robert Zakanitch. Janet Kardon. (Illus.). 1980. pap. 10.00 (ISBN 0-88454-025-1). U of Pa Contemp Art.

Roberta Flack. Charles Morse & Ann Morse. LC 74-13938. (Rock'n Pop Stars Ser.). (Illus.). 32p. (gr. 3-6). 1974. PLB 5.95 (ISBN 0-87191-396-8); pap. 2.75 o. p. (ISBN 0-89812-105-1). Creative Ed.

Roberto Arlt y la Rebelion Alienada. Beatriz Pastor. LC 80-70560. 135p. (Span.). 1980. pap. write for info. (ISBN 0-935318-05-4). Edins Hispamerica.

Roberto Clemente. Kenneth Rudeen. LC 73-12794. (Biography Ser.). (Illus.). (gr. 1-5). 1974. PLB 7.89 (ISBN 0-690-00322-6, TYC-J). T Y Crowell.

Robert's Dinner for Six. Robert Dickson. LC 78-64486. 1978. 5.00 (ISBN 0-937684-05-8). Tradd St Pr.

Robert's Rules of Order. H. M. Robert. (Spire Bk). 1967. pap. 1.95 (ISBN 0-8007-8038-8). Revell.

Robert's Rules of Order. Henry M. Robert. Ed. by Rachel Vixman. (YA) (gr. 9-12). 1967. pap. 1.95 (ISBN 0-515-05366-X). Jove Pubns.

Robert's Rules of Order Newly Revised. Henry M. Robert et al. 1970. 10.95x (ISBN 0-673-05714-3); lea. 24.95x (ISBN 0-673-07675-X). Scott F.

Robert's Rules of Order Revised. Henry M. Robert. 1971. pap. 3.95 (ISBN 0-688-05306-8). Morrow.

Robespierre & the French Revolution. James M. Thompson. 1962. pap. 1.95 o.s.i. (ISBN 0-02-037840-8, Collier). Macmillan.

Robespierre Serial. Nicholas Luard. 1976. pap. 1.75 o.p. (ISBN 0-345-24902-X). Ballantine.

Robin Hood & His Merrie Men. Illus. by Derick Bown. LC 78-4201. (Raintree's Illustrated Classics). (Illus.). (gr. 5-8). 1978. PLB 9.65 (ISBN 0-8393-6201-3). Raintree Child.

Robin Hood: Disney Classic. 1976. pap. 1.50 o.s.i. (ISBN 0-515-04167-X). Jove Pubns.

Robin Hood of Sherwood Forest. Ed. by Anne McGovern. LC 68-11066. (Hero Tales Ser). (Illus.). (gr. 3-6). 1968. 8.95 (ISBN 0-690-70607-3, TYC-J). T Y Crowell.

Robin Hood Tradition in the English Renaissance. Malcolm A. Nelson. (Salzburg Studies in English Literature, Elizabethan & Renaissance Studies: No. 14). 269p. 1973. pap. text ed. 25.00x (ISBN 0-391-01491-9). Humanities.

Robin Ray's Music Quiz. Robin Ray. 1978. 13.50 (ISBN 0-7134-1492-8, Pub. by Batsford England). David & Charles.

Robin Williams: Jr. Bio. Mary E. Moore. Ed. by Kathy O'Hehir. (Junior Bio Ser.). (Illus.). 1980. pap. 1.95 (ISBN 0-448-17128-7, Tempo). G&D.

Robina. E. V. Timms. 1977. pap. 1.50 o.s.i. (ISBN 0-515-04399-0). Jove Pubns.

Robins Fly North, Robins Fly South. John Kaufmann. LC 70-109907. (Illus.). (gr. 2-5). 1970. PLB 7.89 (ISBN 0-690-70643-X, TYC-J). T Y Crowell.

Robinson Crusoe. Daniel Defoe. (Literature Ser). (gr. 7-12). 1970. pap. text ed. 3.58 (ISBN 0-87720-736-4). AMSCO Sch.

Robinson Crusoe. Daniel Defoe. (Illus.). (gr. 7 up). 1962. 3.95 o.s.i. (ISBN 0-02-726460-2); PLB 4.24 o.s.i. (ISBN 0-02-726470-X). Macmillan.

Robinson Crusoe. Daniel Defoe. (Keith Jennison Large Type Bks). (gr. 4-6). PLB 7.95 o.p. (ISBN 0-531-00273-X). Watts.

Robinson Crusoe. Daniel Defoe. (gr. 7-12). 1973. pap. 0.95 o.p. (ISBN 0-590-01357-2, Schol Pap). Schol Bk Serv.

Robinson Crusoe. Daniel Defoe. Ed. by Michael Shinagel. (Critical Editions Ser.). 399p. 1975. pap. text ed. 4.95x (ISBN 0-393-09231-3). Norton.

Robinson Crusoe. Daniel Defoe. (Span.). 7.95 (ISBN 84-241-5636-6). E Torres & Sons.

Robinson Crusoe. Daniel Defoe. LC 78-3384. (Raintree's Illustrated Classics). (Illus.). (gr. 5-8). 1978. PLB 9.65 (ISBN 0-8393-6212-9). Raintree Child.

Robinson Crusoe & Other Writings. Daniel Defoe. Ed. by James Sutherland. LC 77-77300. (Gotham Library). 416p. 1977. 12.00x (ISBN 0-8147-7784-8); pap. 7.00x (ISBN 0-8147-7785-6). NYU Pr.

Robinson Crusoe: My Journals & Sketchbooks. Robinson Crusoe. LC 74-2240. 80p. (gr. 3-7). 1974. 6.95 (ISBN 0-15-267836-0, HJ). HarBraceJ.

Robinson Jeffers. Frederic I. Carpenter. (U. S. Authors Ser.: No. 22). lib. bdg. 10.95 (ISBN 0-8057-0412-4). Twayne.

Robinson Jeffers: Poet of Inhumanism. Arthur B. Coffin. LC 74-121767. 1971. 25.00 (ISBN 0-299-05840-9). U of Wis Pr.

Robot Explorers. Kenneth Gatland. LC 72-78611. 1972. 5.95 o.s.i. (ISBN 0-02-542870-5). Macmillan.

Robot in the Closet. Ron Goulart. 1981. pap. 1.75 (ISBN 0-87997-626-8, UE1626, Daw Bks). NAL.

Robot People. Eve Bunting. (Science Fiction Ser.). (Illus.). (gr. 3-9). 1978. PLB 5.95 (ISBN 0-87191-622-3); pap. 2.95 (ISBN 0-89812-051-9). Creative Ed.

Robotics in Practice. Joseph F. Engelberger. 1981. 39.95 (ISBN 0-8144-5645-6). Am Mgmt.

Robots. Art Kleiner. LC 80-11681. (Look Inside Ser.). (Illus.). 48p. (gr. 4-12). 1981. PLB 10.25 (ISBN 0-8172-1401-1). Raintree Child.

Robots. H. Zimmerman. 1979. pap. 7.95 (ISBN 0-931064-12-0). Starlog Pr.

Robots. Howard Zimmerman. LC 79-63382. 1979. pap. 7.95 (ISBN 0-931064-12-0). Starlog.

Robots A Two Z. Thomas H. Metos. LC 80-21004. (Illus.). 80p. (gr. 4 up). 1980. PLB 7.79 (ISBN 0-671-34027-1). Messner.

Robots & Manipulator Systems, 2 pts. E. Heer. LC 77-73105. 1977. Pt. 1. pap. text ed. 29.50 (ISBN 0-08-021727-3); Pt. 2. pap. text ed. 29.50 (ISBN 0-08-022681-7). Pergamon.

Robots, Men & Minds. Ludwig Von Bertalanffy. LC 67-27524. 1969. pap. 4.95 o.p. (ISBN 0-8076-0428-3). Braziller.

Robots on Your Doorstep: A Book About Thinking Machines. Nels Winklessless & Iben Browning. LC 78-50710. 1978. pap. 7.95 (ISBN 0-89661-000-4). Robotics Pr.

Robust Estimates of Location: Survey & Advances. J. W. Tukey et al. LC 72-39019. 376p. 1972. 12.50 o.p. (ISBN 0-691-08113-1); pap. 8.50x (ISBN 0-691-08116-6). Princeton U Pr.

Robust Statistics. Peter J. Huber. LC 80-18627. (Wiley Ser. on Probability & Math Statistics). 300p. 1981. 22.95 (ISBN 0-471-41805-6, Pub. by Wiley-Interscience). Wiley.

Rocannon's World. Ursula K. LeGuin. Ed. by Lester Del Rey. LC 75-419. (Library of Science Fiction). 1975. lib. bdg. 17.50 (ISBN 0-8240-1424-3). Garland Pub.

Rochester: The Critical Heritage. Ed. by David Farley-Hills. 1972. 34.00x (ISBN 0-7100-7157-4). Routledge & Kegan.

Rochford Book of Flowering Pot Plants. 2nd ed. Richard Gorer & Thomas Rochford. (Illus.). 1974. 9.95 (ISBN 0-571-04853-6, Pub. by Faber & Faber). Merrimack Bk Serv.

Rochford's House-Plants for Everyone. Richard Gorer & Thomas Rochford. (Illus., Orig.). 1978. pap. 4.95 (ISBN 0-571-08827-9, Pub. by Faber & Faber). Merrimack Bk Serv.

Rock. Bob Larson. 1980. pap. write for info. (ISBN 0-8423-5685-1). Tyndale.

Rock & Me Immediately. A. Christine Straayer. LC 79-84578. (Illus.). (ps-5). 1981. pap. 5.00 (ISBN 0-934816-05-0). Metis Pr Inc.

Rock & Mineral Analysis. Wesley M. Johnson & John A. Maxwell. 584p. 1981. 40.00 (ISBN 0-471-02743-X, Pub. by Wiley-Interscience). Wiley.

Rock & Mineral Analysis. John A. Maxwell. LC 68-29396. (Chemical Analysis Ser: Vol. 27). 1968. 45.00 (ISBN 0-471-57900-9, Pub. by Wiley-Interscience). Wiley.

Rock & Mineral Resources of East Texas. W. L. Fisher. (Illus.). 439p. 1965. 5.00 (RI 54). Bur Econ Geology.

Rock & Water Gardens. James U. Crockett & Ogden Tanner. (Time-Life Encyclopedia of Gardening Ser.). (Illus.). 1979. lib. bdg. 10.98 (ISBN 0-8094-2626-9); kivar bdg. 8.95 (ISBN 0-8094-2627-7). Silver.

Rock Art in New Mexico. Polly Schaafsma. LC 75-5496. (Illus.). 209p. 1975. pap. 10.95 o.p. (ISBN 0-8263-0372-2). U of NM Pr.

Rock Art of the American Indian. Campbell Grant. (Illus.). 192p. 1981. pap. 9.95 (ISBN 0-89646-060-6). Outbooks.

Rock Art of Utah. Polly Schaafsma. Ed. by Emily Flint. LC 72-173663. (Papers of the Peabody Museum Ser.: Vol.65). (Illus.). 1976. pap. 15.00 (ISBN 0-87365-186-3). Peabody Harvard.

Rock Band: Big Men in a Great Big Town. Carolyn Meyer. LC 80-13349. 168p. (gr. 9 up). 1980. 8.95 (ISBN 0-689-50181-1, McElderry Bk). Atheneum.

Rock Bolting: A Practical Handbook Describing All Aspects of Rock Bolts & Their Application in Rock Engineering. Norwegian Institute of Rock Schach Blasting Techniques. 1979. 13.75 (ISBN 0-08-022503-9). Pergamon.

Rock Carving in Norway. Anders Hagen. (Tanum of Norway Tokens Ser). (Illus.). pap. 8.00x o.p. (ISBN 82-518-0004-8, N442). Vanous.

Rock Characterization, Testing & Monitoring: ISRM Suggested Methods. Ed. by E. T. Brown. LC 80-49711. 200p. 1981. 40.00 (ISBN 0-08-027308-4); pap. 20.00 (ISBN 0-08-027309-2). Pergamon.

Rock Drawings, 2 pts. Pontus Hellstrom & Hans Langballe. Ed. by Torgny Save-Soderbergh. (Scandinavian Joint Expedition to Sudanese Nubia). (Illus.). 1970. Set. text ed. 55.00x (ISBN 0-8419-8800-5). Holmes & Meier.

Rock Engineering for Foundations & Slopes. Compiled by American Society of Civil Engineers. 728p. 1976. pap. text ed. 27.50 (ISBN 0-87262-082-4). Am Soc Civil Eng.

Rock Fever, No. 4. Ellen Rabinowich. (Hi Lo Ser.). 96p. (gr. 6 up). 1981. pap. 1.50 (ISBN 0-553-14621-1). Bantam.

Rock-Forming Minerals, Vol. 2A. 2nd ed. W. A. Deer et al. LC 78-40451. 1979. 59.95x (ISBN 0-470-26455-1). Halsted Pr.

Rock Gardening. 1.95 (ISBN 0-686-21121-9). Bklyn Botanic.

Rock Gardens. Wilhelm Schacht. (Illus.). 190p. Repr. 17.50 (ISBN 0-87663-354-8, Pica Pr). Universe.

Rock Guitarists, Vol II. Ed. by Editors of Guitar Player Magazine. LC 77-87210. (Illus.). 222p. 1977. 6.95 (ISBN 0-8256-9506-6). Guitar Player.

Rock Guitarists, Vol. I. Ed. by Guitar Player Magazine. LC 74-25845. (Illus.). 176p. (Orig.). 1975. pap. 6.95 (ISBN 0-8256-9505-8). Guitar Player.

Rock Hunter's Guide. Russell P. MacFall. LC 78-22457. (Illus.). 1980. 12.95 (ISBN 0-690-01812-6, TYC-T). T Y Crowell.

Rock Is My Home: Structures in Stone. Werner Blaser. (Illus.). 224p. (Eng., Fr. & Ger.). 1976. text ed. 15.00 (ISBN 0-89192-299-7). Interbk Inc.

Rock Mechanics. CISM (International Center for Mechanical Sciences) Dept. of Mechanics of Solids. Ed. by L. Mueller. (CISM Pubns. Ser.: Vol. 165). (Illus.). v, 390p. 1975. pap. 34.30 o.p. (ISBN 0-387-81301-2). Springer-Verlag.

Rock Mechanics & Engineering. 2nd ed. C. Jaeger. LC 77-85700. (Illus.). 1979. 90.00 (ISBN 0-521-21898-5). Cambridge U Pr.

Rock Mechanics & the Design of Structures in Rock. Leonard Obert & W. L. Duvall. LC 66-26753. 650p. 1967. 49.95 (ISBN 0-471-65235-0, Pub. by Wiley-Interscience). Wiley.

Rock-Mechanics Research in the U. S. Division Of Earth Sciences. (Illus.). 1966. pap. 4.25 (ISBN 0-309-01466-2). Natl Acad Pr.

Rock Music. Brian Van Der Horst. LC 73-4959. (First Bks.). (gr. 5 up). 1973. PLB 4.90 o.p. (ISBN 0-531-00789-8). Watts.

Rock Music Scrapbook. Lin Oliver. LC 79-3336. (Illus.). (gr. 5 up). 1980. 8.95 o.p. (ISBN 0-397-31856-1); PLB 8.79 o.p. (ISBN 0-397-31905-3). Lippincott.

Rock Music Source Book. Bob Macken et al. LC 78-1196. 648p. (Orig.). 1980. pap. 9.95 (ISBN 0-385-14139-4, Anch). Doubleday.

Rock 'n' Roll Is Here to Pay: The History & Politics of the Music Industry. Reebee Garofalo & Steve Chapple. LC 77-10488. 1978. 17.95 (ISBN 0-88229-395-8); pap. 10.95 (ISBN 0-88229-437-7). Nelson-Hall.

Rock on: The Illustrated Encyclopedia of Rock 'n Roll: the Solid Gold Years. Norm N. Nite. LC 74-12247. (Illus.). 448p. 1974. 16.95 (ISBN 0-690-00583-0, TYC-T). T Y Crowell.

Rock One Hundred. 2nd ed. Jim Quirin & Barry Cohen. LC 76-12441. (Illus.). 1976. Set. pap. text ed. 5.00 (ISBN 0-917190-01-7); pap. 0.75 ea. Suppl., 1976 (ISBN 0-917190-03-3). Suppl., 1977 (ISBN 0-917190-03-3). Suppl., 1978 (ISBN 0-917190-05-X). Suppl., 1979 (ISBN 0-917190-06-8). Chartmasters.

Rock Point Experience: A Longitudinal Study of a Navajo School Program (Saad Naaki Bee Na'nitin) Paul Rosier & Wayne Holm. LC 80-19695. (Bilingual Education Ser.: No. 8). 95p. (Orig.). 1980. pap. text ed. 6.50 (ISBN 0-87281-119-0). Ctr Appl Ling.

Rock Quarry Book. Michael Kehoe. LC 80-28165. (Illus.). 32p. (gr. k-3). 1981. PLB 5.95 (ISBN 0-87614-142-4). Carolrhoda Bks.

Rock Revolution: What's Happening in Today's Music. Arnold Shaw. LC 69-11109. (Illus.). (gr. 8 up). 1969. 9.95 (ISBN 0-02-782400-4, CCPr). Macmillan.

Rock Shelters of the Perigord: Geological Stratigraphy & Archaeological Succession. Henri Laville et al. LC 80-511. (Studies in Archaeology). 1980. 29.50 (ISBN 0-12-438750-0). Acad Pr.

Rock Springs: Sodom & Gomorrah in America. Timothy S. Lowry. LC 80-29293. (Illus.). 224p. 1981. 11.95 (ISBN 0-8253-0044-4). Beaufort Bks NY.

Rock Stars. Ditlea. (gr. 7-12). 1980. pap. 1.25 (ISBN 0-590-31206-5, Schol Pap). Schol Bk Serv.

Rock Stars: People at the Top of the Charts. Andrew David. (Illus.). 96p. 1979. 4.98 (ISBN 0-89196-076-7, Domus Bks). EPWP.

Rock Strata & the Bible Record. Paul Zimmermann. LC 78-111692. 1970. 7.50 (ISBN 0-570-03206-7, 15-2103). Concordia.

Rock Talk. Barbara Rowes. (YA) (gr. 7-12). 1977. pap. 1.25 (ISBN 0-590-10417-9, Schol Pap). Schol Bk Serv.

Rock, Time, & Landforms. Jerome Wyckoff. LC 66-10662. (Illus.). 1966. 13.50 o.s.i. (ISBN 0-06-072110-3, HarpT). Har-Row.

Rock v. Minor Piece Endings. Yuri Averbakh. 1978. 18.95 (ISBN 0-7134-0868-5, Pub. by Batsford England). David & Charles.

Rockaby & Other Works. Samuel Beckett. LC 80-8916. 128p. 1981. 12.50 (ISBN 0-394-51953-1, Ever); pap. 4.95 (ISBN 0-394-17924-2). Grove.

Rockabye Baby: Lullabies from Many Nations & Peoples. Compiled by Carl Miller. (gr. k-8). 1975. pap. 3.50 (ISBN 0-935738-04-5, 5035). US Comm Unicef.

Rockbound: A Novel. Frank P. Day. LC 73-81763. (Literature of Canada Ser.). 1973. pap. 6.95 (ISBN 0-8020-6200-8). U of Toronto Pr.

Rockefeller Center. Carol Krinsky. (Illus.). 1978. 19.95 (ISBN 0-19-502317-X). Oxford U Pr.

Rocket Propulsion Elements: An Introduction to the Engineering of Rockets. 4th ed. George A. Sutton & Donald M. Ross. LC 75-29197. 592p. 1976. 37.50 (ISBN 0-471-83836-5, Pub. by Wiley-Interscience). Wiley.

Rocket Team. Frederick I. Ordway & Mitchell R. Sharpe. LC 78-3313. (Illus.). 1979. 14.95 (ISBN 0-690-01656-5, TYC-T). T Y Crowell.

Rocket to the Moon. Brooks Frederick, pseud. (Redbird Ser). 118p. 1975. 15.00 (ISBN 0-88253-616-8); pap. text ed. 4.80 (ISBN 0-88253-615-X). Ind-US Inc.

Rockets & Satellites. rev. ed. Franklyn M. Branley. LC 73-101923. (Let's-Read-&-Find-Out Science Bk). (Illus.). (gr. k-3). 1970. 6.95 o.p. (ISBN 0-690-70820-3, TYC-J). T Y Crowell.

Rockets & Space Travel. Kenneth Gatland. LC 78-64661. (Fact Finders Ser.). (Illus.). 1979. lib. bdg. 3.96 (ISBN 0-686-51130-1). Silver.

Rockets Don't Go to Chicago, Andy. Jane Thayer. (Illus.). (ps-3). 1967. 6.95 (ISBN 0-688-21660-9). Morrow.

Rockhound's Manual. Gordon Fay. (Illus.). 300p. (Orig.). 1973. pap. 4.95 (ISBN 0-06-463323-3, EH 323, EH). Har-Row.

Rockhound's Manual. Gordon S. Fay. LC 72-79661. (Illus.). 278p. (YA) 1972. 10.95 o.p. (ISBN 0-06-011218-2, HarpT). Har-Row.

Rockies. rev. ed. David Lavender. LC 75-6345. (Regions of America Ser.). (Illus.). 448p. (YA) 1975. 13.95 o.p. (ISBN 0-06-012522-5, HarpT). Har-Row.

Rockin' Fifties. Arnold Shaw. (Illus.). 256p. 1974. 13.50 (ISBN 0-8015-6432-8, Hawthorn); pap. 4.95 (ISBN 0-8015-6434-4, Hawthorn). Dutton.

Rockin' Steady: A Guide to Basketball & Cool. Walt Frazier & Ira Berkow. LC 73-20933. (Illus.). 160p. 1974. 3.50 o.p. (ISBN 0-13-782235-9). P-H.

Rocking Horse. Lalitha Venkateswaran. (Redbird Ser). 1975. 8.00 (ISBN 0-88253-618-4); pap. text ed. 4.80 (ISBN 0-88253-617-6). Ind-US Inc.

Rocking Horse Secret. Rumer Godden. (gr. 4-6). 1979. pap. 1.25 (ISBN 0-590-03168-6, Schol Pap). Schol Bk Serv.

Rockrose. Menke Katz. 4.50 (ISBN 0-912292-10-5). The Smith.

Rocks All Around Us. Anne T. White. (gr. 3-6). 1959. 2.95 o.p. (ISBN 0-394-80109-1, BYR). Random.

Rocks & Fossils. Rhoda Ritter. (Easy-Read Fact Book Ser.). (Illus.). 48p. (gr. 2-4). 1977. PLB 4.47 o.p. (ISBN 0-531-00358-2). Watts.

Rocks & Minerals. Robin Kerrod. (Modern Knowledge Library). (Illus.). (gr. 5 up). 1978. 3.95 o.p. (ISBN 0-531-09083-3); PLB 5.90 o.p. (ISBN 0-531-09058-2). Watts.

Rocks & Minerals. Lou W. Page. (Illus.). (gr. 2-9). 1962. lib. ed. 2.97 o.p. (ISBN 0-695-47774-9). Follett.

Rocks & Minerals. Richard M. Pearl. (Orig.). 1969. pap. 2.75 (ISBN 0-06-463260-1, EH 260, EH). Har-Row.

Rocks & Minerals. B. Simpson. 1966. 23.00 (ISBN 0-08-011744-9); pap. 9.00 (ISBN 0-08-011743-0). Pergamon.

Rocks & Minerals. Charles Sorrell. (Golden Field Guide Ser). (Illus.). 280p. 1974. 7.95 (ISBN 0-307-47005-9, Golden Pr); pap. 4.95 (ISBN 0-307-13661-2). Western Pub.

Rocks & Minerals. 2nd rev. ed. Janet Watson. (Introducing Geology Ser.). (Illus.). pap. text ed. 4.95x (ISBN 0-04-551031-8). Allen Unwin.

Rocks & Minerals of the Western United States. Elsie Hanauer. LC 73-144. (Illus.). 224p. 1976. 12.00 o.p. (ISBN 0-498-01273-5). A S Barnes.

Rocks & Rock Minerals. Richard V. Dietrich & Brian J. Skinner. LC 79-1211. 1979. text ed. 14.95 (ISBN 0-471-02934-3). Wiley.

Rocks & Shoals: Order & Discipline in the Old Navy, 1800-1861. James E. Valle. LC 79-91914. (Illus.). 408p. 1980. 18.95 (ISBN 0-87021-538-8). Naval Inst Pr.

Rocks, Relics & Biblical Reliability. Clifford A. Wilson. (Probe Ser.). 1977. pap. 4.95 (ISBN 0-310-35701-2). Zondervan.

Rockstore Seventy-Seven: Proceedings of the First International Symposium on Storage in Excavated Rock Caverns, Stockholm, Sweden, Sept. 5-8 1977, 3 vols. Ed. by Magnus Bergman. LC 77-30591. 1978. Set. text ed. 375.00 (ISBN 0-08-022407-5). Pergamon.

Rocky Horror Picture Show Book. Bill Henkin. LC 79-63619. (Illus., Orig.). 1979. pap. 8.95 (ISBN 0-8015-6436-0, Hawthorn). Dutton.

Rocky Mount: A Pictorial History. Bugs Barringer et al. LC 77-8620. (Illus.). 1977. 14.95 (ISBN 0-915442-31-0). Donning Co.

Rocky Mountain Mining Camps: The Urban Frontier. Duane A. Smith. LC 67-24522. (Illus.). xii, 304p. 1974. pap. 3.50 (ISBN 0-8032-5792-9, BB 582, Bison). U of Nebr Pr.

Rocky Mountain National Park Hiking Trails-Including Indian Peaks. Kent Dannen & Donna Dannen. LC 77-25701. (Illus.). 288p. 1978. lib. bdg. 10.25 o.p. (ISBN 0-914788-06-X). East Woods.

Rocky Mountain Railroad Album: Stream & Steel Cross the Great Divide. W. H. Jackson. (Illus.). 79p. 195.00 (ISBN 0-913582-14-X). Sundance.

Rocky Mountain Wild Flowers. A. E. Porsild. (Illus.). 1974. pap. 7.95 (ISBN 0-660-00073-3, 56495-9, Pub. by Natl Gallery Canada). U of Chicago Pr.

Rocky Shore. John M. Kingsbury. LC 71-122758. (Illus.). 1970. 5.95 (ISBN 0-85699-015-9). Chatham Pr.

Rococo to Revolution: Major Trends in Eighteenth-Century Painting. Michael Levey. (World of Art Ser.). (Illus.). 1966. pap. 9.95 (ISBN 0-19-519960-X). Oxford U Pr.

Rococo to Romanticism: Art & Architecture 1700-1850. LC 76-14072. (Garland Library of the History of Art). 1976. lib. bdg. 50.00 (ISBN 0-8240-2420-6). Garland Pub.

Rod-&-Reel Trouble. Bobbi Katz. LC 74-3314. (Springboard Sports Ser.). (Illus.). 64p. (gr. 3-5). 1974. 5.75g (ISBN 0-8075-7097-4). A Whitman.

Rod in Hand. C. V. Hancock. 9.95x (ISBN 0-392-06434-0, SpS). Soccer.

Rod Stewart: A Biography. Paul Nelson. LC 80-8063. (Illus.). 160p. 1980. pap. 8.95 cancelled (ISBN 0-394-17745-2, E 770, BC). Grove.

Rod VS the M&M's. Reuben Hilde. (Dimension Ser.). 1976. pap. 5.95 (ISBN 0-8163-0221-9, 18340-0). Pacific Pr Pub Assn.

Rodale Herb Book: How to Use, Grow & Buy Nature's Miracle Plants. Ed. by William Hylton. LC 73-18902. (Illus.). 658p. 1974. 13.95 (ISBN 0-87857-076-4); deluxe ed. 15.95 (ISBN 0-87857-196-5). Rodale Pr Inc.

Rodale Plans Insulating Window Shade. Ray Wolf. (Illus.). 86p. 1980. 14.95 (ISBN 0-87857-311-9). Rodale Pr Inc.

Rodale Plans: Solar Food Dryer. Jim Hoffman. Ed. by Ray Wolf. (Illus.). 64p. (Orig.). 1981. pap. 12.95 (ISBN 0-87857-333-X). Rodale Pr Inc.

Rodale Plans Solar Growing Frame. Ed. by Ray Wolf. (Illus.). 80p. 1980. pap. 14.95 (ISBN 0-87857-305-4). Rodale Pr Inc.

Rodale's Color Handbook of Garden Insects. Anna Carr & William Olkowski. (Illus.). 1979. 12.95 (ISBN 0-87857-250-3). Rodale Pr Inc.

Rodale's Encyclopedia of Indoor Gardening. Ed. by Anne M. Halpin. (Illus.). 912p. 1980. 29.95 (ISBN 0-87857-319-4). Rodale Pr Inc.

Rodale's Soups & Salads Cookbook & Kitchen Album. Ed. by Charles Gerras. (Illus.). 352p. 1981. 14.95 (ISBN 0-87857-332-1). Rodale Pr Inc.

Rodenticides Analyses, Specifications Formulations for Use in Public Health & Agriculture. (FAO Plant Production & Protection Paper: No. 16). 81p. 1980. pap. 6.00 (ISBN 92-5-100798-5, F1867, FAO). Unipub.

Rodeo. Douglas K. Hall. 1976. pap. 7.95 o.p. (ISBN 0-345-24877-5). Ballantine.

Rodeo. Paul Perry. LC 78-68562. (Illus.). 144p. 1980. pap. cancelled (ISBN 0-89037-224-1). Anderson World.

Rodeo Drive. Barney Leason. 416p. (Orig.). 1981. pap. 2.95 (ISBN 0-523-41031-X). Pinnacle Bks.

Rodeo Riders. Vella Munn. LC 80-81792. (Illus.). 96p. (gr. 4-9). 1981. PLB 6.59 (ISBN 0-8178-0013-1). Harvey.

Roderick Hudson. Henry James. 1981. pap. 3.95 (ISBN 0-14-002982-6). Penguin.

Roderick Random. Tobias G. Smollett. 1958. 11.50x (ISBN 0-460-00790-4, Evman); pap. 2.95 (ISBN 0-460-01790-X). Dutton.

Rodin. Rainer M. Rilke. Tr. by Robert Firmage from Ger. (Illus.). 1979. pap. 9.95 (ISBN 0-87905-044-6). Peregrine Smith.

Rodin Graphics: A Catalogue Raisonne of Drypoints & Book Illustrations. Victoria Thorson. LC 75-16941. (Illus.). 1977. pap. 4.95 (ISBN 0-88401-007-4, Pub. by Fine Arts Mus). C E Tuttle.

Rodin on Art. 2nd ed. Rodin. LC 70-132323. (Illus.). 304p. 1981. pap. 7.95 (ISBN 0-8180-0114-3). Horizon.

Rodney & Lucinda's Amazing Race. John Stadler. (Illus.). 32p. (ps-2). 1981. 8.95 (ISBN 0-87888-179-4). Bradbury Pr.

Rodney Peppe's Moving Toys. Rodney Peppe. (Illus.). 128p. 1981. 14.95 (ISBN 0-8069-5422-1); lib. bdg. 13.29 (ISBN 0-8069-5423-X); pap. 6.95 (ISBN 0-8069-5424-8). Sterling.

Rodney Peppe's Puzzle Book. Illus. by Rodney Peppe. 1977. 7.95 o.p. (ISBN 0-670-60261-2). Viking Pr.

Rodney Rabbit Builds a House. Porter Productions. (Rodney Rabbit Build-up Board Ser.). (Illus.). 18p. (ps-1). 1980. bds. 2.95 (ISBN 0-675-01021-7). Merrill.

Roehenstart: A Late Stuart Pretender. George Sherburn. LC 60-8402. 1960. 7.50x o.s.i. (ISBN 0-226-75294-1). U of Chicago Pr.

Roemer Healthcare Systems & Comparative Manpower Policies. Roemer. Date not set. price not set (ISBN 0-8247-1389-3). Dekker.

Roemerzimmer. Winnig. (Easy Reader, A). pap. 2.90 (ISBN 0-88436-041-5, GEA110053). EMC.

Roemischen Inschriften von Tarraco. Geza Alfoeldy. (Madrider Forschungen Ser.: Vol. 10). (Ger.). 1975. text & plate volume 188.25x (ISBN 3-11-004403-X). De Gruyter.

Roentgen Diagnosis of Diseases of the Bone. Jack Edeiken. (Golden's Diagnostic Radiology Ser.: Section No. 6). (Illus.). 1752p. 1981. price not set (2744-1). Williams & Wilkins.

Roentgen Examinations in Acute Abdominal Diseases. 3rd ed. J. Frimann-Dahl. (Illus.). 632p. 1974. text ed. 49.50 (ISBN 0-398-02939-3). C C Thomas.

Roentgenographic Diagnosis of Diseases of the Thoracic Aorta. Steven H. Cornell. (Illus.). 292p. 1973. 29.50 (ISBN 0-398-02687-4). C C Thomas.

Roe's Laboratory Guide in Chemistry. 7th ed. Laughlin. (Illus.). 1976. pap. text ed. 8.50 (ISBN 0-8016-1473-2). Mosby.

Roger B. Taney: Jacksonian Jurist. Charles W. Smith. LC 72-8802. (American Constitutional & Legal History Ser.). 252p. 1973. Repr. of 1936 ed. lib. bdg. 27.50 (ISBN 0-685-30417-5). Da Capo.

Roger, Bishop of Worcestor Eleven Sixty Four to Eleven Seventy Nine: An English Bishop of the Age of Becket. Mary G. Cheney. (Oxford Historical Monographs). (Illus.). 320p. 1980. 49.50 (ISBN 0-19-821879-6). Oxford U Pr.

Roger Boyle: First Earl of Orrery. Kathleen M. Lynch. LC 65-17438. (Illus.). 1965. 15.00x (ISBN 0-87049-060-5). U of Tenn Pr.

Roger Brown. Mitchell D. Kahan. LC 80-24063. (Illus.). 96p. (Orig.). 1980. pap. 10.00 (ISBN 0-89280-042-9). Montgomery Mus.

Roger Caras Pet Book. Roger Caras. 1977. 7.95 o.p. (ISBN 0-03-017506-2). HR&W.

Roger Fry & the Beginnings of Formalist Art Criticism. Jacqueline V. Falkenheim. Ed. by Donald B. Kuspit. (Studies in Fine Arts: Criticism). 186p. 1980. 23.95 (ISBN 0-8357-1086-6, Pub. by UMI Res Pr). Univ Microfilms.

Roger, Karl, Rick, & Shane Are Friends of Mine. Charles Stetler. 1980. 2.00 (ISBN 0-917554-16-7). Maelstrom.

Roger of Salisbury, Viceroy of England. Edward J. Kealey. (Illus.). 350p. 1972. 22.75x (ISBN 0-520-01985-7). U of Cal Pr.

Roger Planchon: Director & Playwright. Yvette Daoust. (Illus.). 200p. Date not set. 44.95 (ISBN 0-521-23414-X). Cambridge U Pr.

Roger Sherman: Signer & Statesman. R. S. Boardman. LC 75-168671. (Era of the American Revolution Ser.). 396p. 1972. Repr. of 1938 ed. lib. bdg. 37.50 (ISBN 0-306-70412-9). Da Capo.

Roger Staubach: Time Enough to Win. Roger Staubach & Frank Luksa. 256p. 1980. 9.95 (ISBN 0-8499-0274-6). Word Bks.

Roger' Upside-Down Day. Betty R. Wright. (Tell-a-Tale Reader). 32p. (ps-3). 1980. PLB 4.77 (ISBN 0-307-68481-4, Golden Pr). Western Pub.

Roger Verge's Cuisine of the South of France. Roger Verge. (Illus.). 1980. 14.95 (ISBN 0-688-03684-8). Morrow.

Roger Was a Razor Fish & Other Poems. Compiled by Jill Bennett. LC 80-17166. (Illus.). 48p. (gr. 2-6). 1981. 7.95 (ISBN 0-688-41986-0). Morrow.

Roger Williams. William J. Jacobs. LC 74-12280. (Visual Biography Ser). (Illus.). (gr. 4-6). 1975. PLB 4.90 o.p. (ISBN 0-531-02784-8). Watts.

Roger Zelazny. Carl Yoke. LC 80-19170. (Starmont Reader's Guide Ser.: No. 2). 111p. 1980. Repr. of 1979 ed. lib. bdg. 9.95x (ISBN 0-89370-033-9). Borgo Pr.

Roget's International Thesaurus. 4th ed. Peter M. Roget. LC 62-12806. 1977. 11.50 (ISBN 0-690-00010-3, TYC-T); thumb indexed 12.95 (ISBN 0-690-00011-1). T Y Crowell.

Roget's University Thesaurus. Peter M. Roget. Ed. by C. O. Mawson. (Apollo Eds.). (YA) (gr. 9-12). pap. 6.95 (ISBN 0-8152-0062-5, A62, TYC-T). T Y Crowell.

Rogue. Janet Dailey. (Orig.). 1980. pap. 2.75 (ISBN 0-671-82843-6). PB.

Rogue Black. Raymond Giles. 208p. 1978. pap. 2.25 (ISBN 0-449-13809-7, GM). Fawcett.

Rogue Bull. Robert Duffield. 320p. 1980. 20.95x (ISBN 0-00-216423-X, Pub. by W Collins Australia); pap. 8.95x (ISBN 0-00-634515-8). Intl Schol Bk Serv.

Rogue Eagle. James McClure. 1978. pap. 1.75 (ISBN 0-380-42267-0, 42267). Avon.

Rogue Eagle. James McClure. LC 76-9211. 256p. 1976. 8.95 o.p. (ISBN 0-06-012949-2, HarpT). Har-Row.

Rogue I Remember. Wallace L. Ohrt. LC 79-17166. (Illus.). 128p. 1979. pap. 6.95 (ISBN 0-916890-94-5). Mountaineers.

Rogue of Gor. John Norman. 1981. pap. 2.50 (ISBN 0-87997-602-0, UE1602). Daw Bks.

Rogue Planet. Dan Dare. (Illus.). 112p. 1980. pap. 9.95 (ISBN 0-8256-9553-8, Quick Fox). Music Sales.

Rogue Roman. Lance Horner. 1978. pap. 2.25 (ISBN 0-449-13968-9, GM). Fawcett.

Rogue Sergeant. Lawrence Cortesi. 1979. pap. 1.75 (ISBN 0-505-51352-8). Tower Bks.

Rogue Sheriff. James Wyckoff. 1977. pap. 1.25 o.s.i. (ISBN 0-440-14138-9). Dell.

Rogue Star. Frederik Pohl & Jack Williamson. 1973. pap. 1.25 o.p. (ISBN 0-345-23450-2). Ballantine.

Rogues' Covenant. Sylvia Thorpe. 1976. pap. 1.50 o.p. (ISBN 0-449-23041-4, Crest). Fawcett.

Rogues' Gallery. R. D. Wormald & G. M. Lyne. (Lat). 1939. text ed. 7.95x (ISBN 0-521-06869-X). Cambridge U Pr.

Rogues in the Gallery: The Modern Plague of Art Thefts. Hugh McLeave. 1981. 14.95 (ISBN 0-87923-378-8). Godine.

Rohan Master. Intro. by Millard Meiss. LC 73-77880. (Illus.). 248p. 1973. slipcase 65.00 (ISBN 0-8076-0690-1). Braziller.

Rohstoffe Des Pflanzenreichs, 7 pts. 5th ed. J. Von Wiesner & C. Von Regel. Incl. Pt. 1. Tanning Materials (Gerbstoffe) H. Endres et al. (Eng. & Ger.). 1962. 40.00 (ISBN 3-7682-0111-2); Pt. 2. Antibiotiques (Antibiotica) G. Hagemann. (Fr.). 1964. 48.00 (ISBN 3-7682-0170-8); Pt. 3. Organic Acids. G. C. Whitting. 1964. 34.00 (ISBN 3-7682-0244-5); Pt. 4. Insecticides. A. J. Fuell. 1965. 40.00 (ISBN 3-7682-0259-3); Pt. 5. Glykoside. L. Zechner. 1966. 40.00 (ISBN 3-7682-0298-4); Pt. 6. Staerke. E. Samecl & M. Bling. (Illus.). 1966. 40.00 (ISBN 3-7682-0186-4); Pt. 7. Aetherische Oele. K. Bournot & M. Weber. (Illus.). 1968. 40.00 (ISBN 3-7682-0562-2). Lubrecht & Cramer.

ROI: Practical Theory & Innovative Application. rev. & enl. ed. Robert A. Peters. 1979. 23.95 (ISBN 0-8144-5496-8). Am Mgmt.

Roi se meurt. Eugene Ionesco. (Documentation thematique). (Illus., Fr.). pap. 2.95 (ISBN 0-685-14068-7, 245). Larousse.

Rokudan: A Tale of Love in Six Movements. Pat Burch. LC 80-29375. 192p. 1981. 8.95 (ISBN 0-8008-6818-8). Taplinger.

Roland Barthes: A Conservative Estimate. Philip Thody. LC 77-5918. 1977. text ed. 23.25x (ISBN 0-391-00730-0). Humanities.

Role & Status of Women in the Soviet Union. Donald Brown et al. LC 68-27326. 1968. text ed. 8.75x (ISBN 0-8077-1128-4); pap. 5.75x (ISBN 0-8077-2466-1). Tchrs Coll.

Role Conflict & the Teacher. Gerald R. Grace. (International Library of Sociology). 1972. 14.00x (ISBN 0-7100-7353-4). Routledge & Kegan.

Role Models & Readers: A Sociological Analysis. Martin J. Croghan & Penelope P. Croghan. LC 79-5430. 1980. pap. 9.00 (ISBN 0-8191-0879-0). U Pr of Amer.

Role of Additives in Plastics. Leno Mascia. LC 73-14098. 172p. 1974. 17.95 (ISBN 0-470-57410-0). Halsted Pr.

Role of Agrometeorology in Agricultural Development & Investment Projects. (WMO Technical Note Ser.: No. 168). 85p. 1980. pap. 10.00 (ISBN 92-63-10536-7, W 462, WMO). Unipub.

Role of Airfreight in Physical Distribution: Including Two Cases by J. D. Steele. H. T. Lewis & J. W. Culliton. 1970. Repr. of 1956 ed. 18.50 (ISBN 0-08-018744-7). Pergamon.

Role of American Intelligence Organizations. George Wittman. (Reference Shelf Ser.). 1976. 6.25 (ISBN 0-8242-0599-5). Wilson.

Role of Anxiety in English Tragedy, 1580-1642. Charlotte N. Clay. (Salzburg Studies in English Literature, Jacobean Drama Studies: No. 23). 1974. pap. text ed. 25.00x (ISBN 0-391-01343-2). Humanities.

Role of Cassava in the Etiology of Endemic Goitre & Cretinism. 182p. 1980. pap. 10.00 (ISBN 0-686-62998-1, IDRC-136, IDRC). Unipub.

Role of Citrus in Health & Disease. Willard A Krehl. LC 76-4502. 1976. 6.50 (ISBN 0-8130-0532-9); pap. 2.95 o.p. (ISBN 0-8130-0571-X). U Presses Fla.

Role of Commissions in Policy Making. Ed. by Richard Chapman. 1973. pap. text ed. 9.50x o.p. (ISBN 0-04-350043-9). Allen Unwin.

Role of Computers in Radiotherapy. 1968. pap. 10.75 (ISBN 92-0-111668-3, IAEA). Unipub.

Role of Consciousness in the Physical World. R. G. Jahn. (AAAS Selected Symposium: No. 57). 136p. 1981. lib. bdg. 15.00x (ISBN 0-89158-955-4). Westview.

Role of Culture Collections in the Era of Molecular Biology: Proceedings of the 50th Anniversary Symposium of the American Type, Culture Collection. Ed. by Rita R. Colwell. LC 76-4273. (American Type Culture Collection Ser.). 1976. 12.00 (ISBN 0-914826-08-5). Am Soc Microbio.

Role of Cyclic AMP in Cell Function. Ed. by P. Greengard & E. Costa. LC 73-84113. (Advances in Biochemical Psychopharmacology Ser.: Vol. 3). 1970. 24.50 (ISBN 0-911216-15-4). Raven.

Role of Immunological Factors in Infectious, Allergic, & Autoimmune Processes. Ed. by Roland F. Beers, Jr. & Edward G. Bassett. LC 75-25109. (Miles International Symposium Ser: No. 8). 1976. 45.00 (ISBN 0-89004-073-7). Raven.

Role of Interest Groups in the European Community. Emil Kirchner & Konrad Schwaiger. 1979. text ed. 22.25x (ISBN 0-566-00257-4, Pub. by Gower Pub Co England). Renouf.

Role of Labor in African Nation-Building. Ed. by Willard A. Beling. 15.00 (ISBN 0-685-37307-X). Univ Place.

Role of Laboratory Teaching in University Courses. Ed. by A. R. Cole et al. 1979. text ed. 15.00 (ISBN 0-08-023914-5). Pergamon.

Role of Libraries in the Growth of Knowledge. Ed. by Don R. Swanson. LC 79-5467. 1980. lib. bdg. 10.00x (ISBN 0-226-78468-1). U of Chicago Pr.

Role of Medroxyprogesterone in Endocrine-Related Tumors. Ed. by Stefano Iacobelli & A. Dimarco. (Progress in Cancer Research & Therapy Ser.: Vol. 15). 168p. 1980. text ed. 15.00 (ISBN 0-89004-512-7). Raven.

Role of Multinational Companies in Latin America: A Case Study in Mexico. Remy Montavon et al. 124p. 1980. 27.50 (ISBN 0-03-057973-2). Praeger.

Role of Nitrogen in Intensive Grassland Production. 171p. 1981. pap. 30.00 (ISBN 90-220-0734-0, PDC 214, Pudoc). Unipub.

Role of Peptides in Neuronal Function. Ed. by J. Barker & T. Smith. 1980. 95.00 (ISBN 0-8247-6926-0). Dekker.

Role of Perception in Science. Charles N. Martin. 1963. text ed. 4.50x (ISBN 0-391-02039-0). Humanities.

Role of Prescriptivism in American Linguistics, 1820-1970. Glendon F. Drake. (Studies in the History of Linguistics: No. 13). 1977. text ed. 23.00x (ISBN 90-27209-54-5). Humanities.

Role of Private Placements in Corporate Finance. Eli Shapiro & Charles R. Wolff. 1972. text ed. 12.50 (ISBN 0-87584-099-X). Harvard U Pr.

Role of Psychosocial Factors in the Pathogenesis of Coronary Heart Disease, 1980. Ed. by A. Appels & P. Falger. (Journal: Psychotherapy & Psychosomatics: Vol. 34, No. 2-3). (Illus.). iv, 160p. 1981. pap. price not set (ISBN 3-8055-2286-X). S Karger.

Role of Terrestrial & Aquatic Organisms in Decomposition Processes. Ed. by J. M. Anderson & A. MacFadden. LC 76-9830. (British Ecological Society Symposia Ser.). 474p. 1977. 38.95 (ISBN 0-470-15105-6). Halsted Pr.

Role of the Augsburg Confession: Catholic & Lutheran Views. Ed. by Joseph A. Burgess. LC 79-7373. 224p. 1980. 13.95 (ISBN 0-8006-0549-7, 1-549). Fortress.

Role of the Bomber. Ronald W. Clark. LC 77-11570. (Illus.). 1978. 15.95 o.p. (ISBN 0-690-01720-0, TYC-T). T Y Crowell.

Role of the Bomber. Ronald W. Clark. (Illus.). 1980. 14.95 (ISBN 0-690-01720-0). Quality Bks IL.

Role of the Brain. Ronald Bailey. (Human Behavior Ser.). (Illus.). 176p. 1975. 9.95 (ISBN 0-8094-1920-3); lib. bdg. avail. (ISBN 0-685-53584-3). Time-Life.

Role of the Brain. Ronald Bailey. LC 75-939. (Human Behavior). (Illus.). (gr. 6 up). 1975. PLB 9.99 o.p. (ISBN 0-8094-1921-1, Pub. by Time-Life). Silver.

Role of the British Press in the 1976 Presidential Election. George Osborn. 64p. 1981. 10.00 (ISBN 0-682-49667-7). Exposition.

Role of the Chief Executive. James Lines. 172p. 1978. text ed. 24.50x (ISBN 0-220-66355-6, Pub. by Busn Bks England). Renouf.

Role of the Congressman. Roger H. Davidson. LC 68-27986. 1969. 18.50x (ISBN 0-672-53587-4). Irvington.

Role of the Family in the Rehabilitation of the Physically Disabled. P. Power. 1980. 19.95 (ISBN 0-8391-1549-0). Univ Park.

Role of the Father in Child Development. Michael E. Lamb. LC 76-21778. (Personality Processes Ser.). 1976. 23.50 (ISBN 0-471-51172-2, Pub. by Wiley-Interscience). Wiley.

Role of the Lawyer in the European Communities. Andre M. Donner. LC 68-17735. (Julius Rosenthal Memorial Lectures Ser.: 1968). 1968. 7.95x o.s.i. (ISBN 0-8101-0032-0). Northwestern U Pr.

Role of the Library in an Electronic Society: Proceedings. Library Applications of Data Processing Clinic, 1979. Ed. by F. W. Lancaster. LC 79-19449. 200p. 1980. 9.00 (ISBN 0-87845-053-X). U of Ill Lib Sci.

Role of the Major Histocompatibility Complex in Immunobiology. Martin E. Dorf. LC 80-772. 525p. 1981. lib. bdg. 47.50 (ISBN 0-8240-7129-8). Garland Pub.

Role of the Military in Underdeveloped Countries: Papers of a Conference Sponsored by the Rand Corp. at Santa Monica, Calif. in August 1959. Ed. by John J. Johnson. LC 80-25808. viii, 423p. 1981. Repr. of 1967 ed. lib. bdg. 39.75x (ISBN 0-313-22784-5, JORM). Greenwood.

Role of the Military in Underdeveloped Countries: Papers of a Conference Sponsored by the Rand Corp. at Santa Monica, Calif. in August 1959. Ed. by John J. Johnson. LC 80-25808. viii, 423p. 1981. Repr. of 1962 ed. lib. bdg. 39.75x (ISBN 0-313-22784-5, JORM). Greenwood.

Role of the Pupil. Barbara Calvert. (Students Library of Education Ser.). 1975. 12.00 (ISBN 0-7100-8065-4); pap. 6.00 (ISBN 0-7100-8066-2). Routledge & Kegan.

Role of the Supreme Court in American Government & Politics 1835-1864. Charles G. Haines. LC 73-604. (American Constitutional & Legal History Ser.). 544p. 1973. Repr. of 1957 ed. lib. bdg. 49.50 (ISBN 0-306-70566-4). Da Capo.

Role of the Supreme Court in American Government & Politics 1795-1835. Charles G. Haines. LC 73-604. (American Constitutional & Legal History Ser.). 698p. 1973. Repr. of 1944 ed. lib. bdg. 69.50 (ISBN 0-306-70571-0). Da Capo.

Role of the Supreme Court in American Government. Archibald Cox. 128p. 1976. 10.95x (ISBN 0-19-827411-4). Oxford U Pr.

Role of the Supreme Court in American Government. x1976 ed. Archibald Cox. LC 75-29958. 1977. pap. 2.95 (ISBN 0-19-519909-X, 482, GB). Oxford U Pr.

Role of the Teacher. Eric Hoyle. (Students Library of Education). 1969. text ed. 6.75x (ISBN 0-7100-6435-7); pap. text ed. 2.75x (ISBN 0-7100-6436-5). Humanities.

Role of the Teacher in the Nursery School. Joan E. Cass. 97p. 1975. 12.75 (ISBN 0-08-018282-8); pap. text ed. 7.00 (ISBN 0-08-018281-X). Pergamon.

Role of the United Nations in the Maintenance of World Peace. C. Setalvad. 1968. 3.50x o.p. (ISBN 0-210-22686-2). Asia.

Role of the Yankee in the Old South. Fletcher Green. LC 68-54086. (Mercer University Lamar Lecture Ser: No. 11). 156p. 1972. 9.95x (ISBN 0-8203-0233-3). U of Ga Pr.

Role of Top Management in the Control of Inventory. George W. Plossl & W. Evert Welch. (Illus.). 1978. 16.95 (ISBN 0-8359-6697-6). Reston.

Role of U. S. Multinationals in East-West Trade. Martin Schnitzer. LC 78-19794. (Praeger Special Studies Ser.). 168p. 1980. 19.95 (ISBN 0-03-043026-7). Praeger.

Role of Vincent Van Gogh's Copies in the Development of His Art. Charles Chetham. LC 75-23788. (Outstanding Dissertations in the Fine Arts - 19th Century). (Illus.). 1976. lib. bdg. 41.00 (ISBN 0-8240-1984-9). Garland Pub.

Role of Violence in History & the Metaphysics of War. Wilfred T. Russell. (Illus.). 1979. deluxe ed. 47.50 (ISBN 0-930008-42-1). Inst Econ Pol.

Role of Vitamin B-Six in Neurobiology. Ed. by M. Ebadi & E. Costa. LC 73-84113. (Advances in Biochemical Psychopharmacology Ser.: Vol. 4). (Illus.). 1972. 24.50 (ISBN 0-911216-18-9). Raven.

Role-Play Technique: A Handbook for Management & Leadership Practice. Norman R. F. Maier et al. LC 74-30943. Orig. Title: Supervisory & Executive Development. 290p. 1975. pap. 14.50 (ISBN 0-88390-104-8). Univ Assocs.

Role Playing: A Practical Manual for Group Facilitators. Malcolm E. Shaw et al. LC 79-67712. 202p. 1980. pap. 15.50 (ISBN 0-88390-156-0). Univ Assocs.

Role Playing for Managers. J. Towers. 1975. text ed. 34.00 (ISBN 0-08-017827-8); pap. text ed. 20.00 (ISBN 0-08-018984-9). Pergamon.

Role-Playing for Social Values: Decision-Making in the Social Studies. Fannie R. Shaftel & G. Shaftel. (Illus.). 1967. pap. text ed. 17.95 (ISBN 0-13-782938-8). P-H.

Role Theory: Concepts & Research. B. J. Biddle & E. J. Thomas. 468p. 1979. Repr. of 1966 ed. lib. bdg. 21.00 (ISBN 0-88275-817-9). Krieger.

Role Theory: Perspectives for the Health Professions. Ed. by Margaret E. Hardy. (Illus.). 1978. pap. 16.50 (ISBN 0-8385-8471-3). ACC.

Role Transitions in Later Life. Linda K. George. LC 79-25239. (Social Gerontology Ser.). (Orig.). 1980. pap. text ed. 6.95 (ISBN 0-8185-0382-3). Brooks-Cole.

Roles & Relationships. Ralph Ruddock. (Library of Social Work). 1970. pap. text ed. 7.75x (ISBN 0-7100-6634-1). Humanities.

Roles in the Liturgical Assembly. Von Allmen et al. Tr. by Matthew J. O'Connell from Fr. (Orig.). 1981. pap. 12.50 (ISBN 0-916134-44-X). Pueblo Pub Co.

Roles of the Police in Urban Society: Conflicts & Consequences. Norman L. Weiner. LC 76-14958. 1976. pap. text ed. 3.95 (ISBN 0-672-61365-4). Bobbs.

Rolf Hochhuth. Rainer Taeni. (Modern German Authors: No. 5). 1977. text ed. 9.25x (ISBN 0-85496-057-0). Humanities.

Rolf Hochhuth. Margaret E. Ward. (World Authors Ser.: No. 463). 1977. lib. bdg. 11.95 (ISBN 0-8057-6300-7). Twayne.

Roll Call. William Cohen. 1981. 14.95 (ISBN 0-671-25142-2). S&S.

Roll Call 1979. Congressional Quarterly Inc. (Roll Call Ser.). 1980. pap. text ed. 12.00 (ISBN 0-87187-191-2). Congr Quarterly.

Roll, Jordan, Roll: The World the Slaves Made. Eugene D. Genovese. 1976. pap. 8.95 (ISBN 0-394-71652-3, Vin). Random.

Roll Over! A Counting Song Book. Merle Peek. (Illus.). 32p. (ps-2). 1981. 8.95 (ISBN 0-395-29438-X, Clarion). HM.

Roll Your Own: The Complete Guide to Living in a Truck, Bus, Van, or Camper. Jody R. Pallidini & Beverly Dubin. (Illus.). 192p. 1974. pap. 3.95 o.s.i. (ISBN 0-02-081050-4, Collier). Macmillan.

Roller Babies. Connie Cantu & Peter Steinberg. LC 80-14071. (Illus.). 1980. pap. 7.95 (ISBN 0-13-782409-2). P-H.

Roller Coaster Fever. John Waldrop. LC 79-63380. 1979. pap. 6.95 (ISBN 0-931064-08-2). Starlog.

Roller Disco Dancing: The Basic Steps on Wheels. Kerry Kollmar & Melody Mason. LC 79-63091. (Illus.). 1979. pap. 3.95 o.p. (ISBN 0-8069-8858-4). Sterling.

Roller Fever. Konner. (gr. 7-12). 1980. pap. 1.50 (ISBN 0-590-30029-6, Schol Pap). Schol Bk Serv.

Roller Skating. D. J. Herda. (First Bks.). (Illus.). (gr. 4 up). 1979. PLB 6.45 s&l (ISBN 0-531-02262-5). Watts.

Roller Skating. Jerolyn Nentl. Ed. by Howard Schroeder. LC 80-10475. (Funseekers Ser.). (Illus.). (gr. 3-5). 1980. lib. bdg. 5.95 (ISBN 0-89686-072-8); pap. 2.95 (ISBN 0-89686-076-0). Crestwood Hse.

Roller Skating: A Beginner'sguide. I. G. Edwards. (Illus.). (gr. 5-7). 1979. pap. 1.95 (ISBN 0-671-43292-3). PB.

Roller Skating Book. LaVada Weir. LC 79-19653. (Illus.). 128p. (gr. 4 up). 1979. PLB 8.29 (ISBN 0-671-33048-9). Messner.

Roller Skating Is for Me. Tom Moran. (Sports for Me Bks.). (Illus.). (gr. 2-5). 1981. PLB 5.95 (ISBN 0-8225-1097-9). Lerner Pubns.

Roller Skating: The Sport of a Lifetime. Carol A. Waugh & Judith L. Larsen. (Illus.). 1979. 9.95 (ISBN 0-02-062446-8, Collier); pap. 3.95 (ISBN 0-02-029950-8, Collier). Macmillan.

Rollicking Shore. E. R. Karr. 1960. 7.95 (ISBN 0-8392-1093-0). Astor-Honor.

Rollin' on: A Wheelchair Guide to U. S. Cities. Maxine H. Atwater. LC 78-15289. (Illus.). 1978. 9.95 (ISBN 0-396-07548-7). Dodd.

Rolling Bearing Analysis. Tedric A. Harris. LC 66-25221. 1966. 59.50 (ISBN 0-471-35265-9, Pub. by Wiley-Interscience). Wiley.

Rolling Bearings. T. S. Nisbet. (Engineering Design Guides Ser.). (Illus.). 1974. pap. 12.50x (ISBN 0-19-859135-7). Oxford U Pr.

Rolling Stone Illustrated History of Rock & Roll. Rolling Stone Press. 1976. pap. 10.95 o.p. (ISBN 0-394-73238-3). Random.

Rolling Stone Illustrated History of Rock & Roll, 1950-1980. rev. & updated ed. Rolling Stone Press. Ed. by Jim Miller. (Illus.). 1980. 20.00 (ISBN 0-394-51322-3); pap. 10.95 (ISBN 0-394-73938-8). Random.

Rolling Stone Interviews, No. 1. Rolling Stone Editors. 464p. 1973. pap. 1.75 o.s.i. (ISBN 0-446-59866-6). Warner Bks.

Rolling Stone Visits Saturday Night Live. Rolling Stone Press. LC 79-5123. (Illus.). 1979. pap. 8.95 o.p. (ISBN 0-385-15674-X, Dolp). Doubleday.

Rolling Thunder: The Coming Earth Changes. Joey R. Jochmans. (Illus.). 240p. (Orig.). 1980. pap. 7.50 (ISBN 0-89540-058-8). Sun Pub.

Rolling Years. Agnes S. Turnbull. 1953. 12.95 (ISBN 0-02-620730-3). Macmillan.

Rolls on the Rocks: The History of Rolls-Royce. Robert Gray. (Illus.). 96p. 1971. 4.95 o.p. (ISBN 0-900193-01-8, Pub. by Compton Pr England). Motorbooks Intl.

Rolls-Royce Alpine Compendium: 1913-1973. Ed. by Christopher Leefe. (Illus.). 164p. 1973. 12.95 o.p. (ISBN 0-85184-005-1, Pub. by Transport Bkman England). Motorbooks Intl.

Rolls-Royce Silver Shadow. John Bolster. (AutoHistory Ser.). (Illus.). 1979. 12.95 (ISBN 0-85045-324-0, Pub. by Osprey Pubns. England). Motorbooks Intl.

Rom: Europe's Gypsies. Grattan Puxon. (Minority Rights Group: No. 14). 1973. pap. 2.50 (ISBN 0-89192-113-3). Interbk Inc.

Roman Architecture. J. B. Ward-Perkins. LC 75-29475. (Illus.). 1977. 45.00 (ISBN 0-8109-1022-5). Abrams.

Roman Army. Peter Hodge. (Aspects of Roman Life). (Illus.). 1978. pap. text ed. 2.95x (ISBN 0-582-31414-3). Longman.

Roman Army. J. Wilkes. (Introduction to the History of Mankind Ser). (Illus.). (gr. 4 up). 1973. 3.95 (ISBN 0-521-07243-3). Cambridge U Pr.

Roman Army from Caesar to Trajan. Michael Simkins. LC 74-76629. (Men-at-Arms Ser). (Illus.). 40p. (Orig.). 1974. pap. 7.95 o.p. (ISBN 0-88254-229-X). Hippocrene Bks.

Roman Art: A Modern Survey of the Art of Ancient Rome. George M. Hanfmann. (Illus.). 250p. 1975. pap. text ed. 8.95x (ISBN 0-393-09222-4). Norton.

Roman Art & Architecture. Mortimer Wheeler. (World of Art Ser.). (Illus.). 1964. pap. 9.95 (ISBN 0-19-519921-9). Oxford U Pr.

Roman Bath Discovered. Barry Cunliffe. (Illus.). 1971. 25.00 (ISBN 0-7100-6826-3). Routledge & Kegan.

Roman Britain. Aileen Fox. (Illus.). (gr. 7 up). 1968. 7.50 (ISBN 0-8023-1143-1). Dufour.

Roman Britain. Peter Lane. (Visual Sources Ser.). (Illus.). 96p. (gr. 7 up). 1980. text ed. 14.95 (ISBN 0-7134-3354-X, Pub. by Batsford England). David & Charles.

Roman Britain & the English Settlements. 2nd ed. Robin G. Collingwood & J. N. Myres. (Oxford History of England Ser.). (Illus.). 1937. 34.50 (ISBN 0-19-821703-X). Oxford U Pr.

Roman Candle. Glen Chase. (Cherry Delight Ser.). (Orig.). 1975. pap. 1.25 o.p. (ISBN 0-685-54127-4, LB2932K, Leisure Bks). Nordon Pubns.

Roman Catholic Church. John L. McKenzie. 1971. pap. 3.95 (ISBN 0-385-02944-6, Im). Doubleday.

Roman Catholic Hierarchy. Thomas E. Watson. (Studies in Populism). 1980. lib. bdg. 69.95 (ISBN 0-686-68883-X). Revisionist Pr.

Roman Citizenship. 2nd ed. A. N. Sherwin-White. 496p. 1980. pap. 24.95x (ISBN 0-19-814847-X). Oxford U Pr.

Roman Civil Law: Ueber As Aeltere Roemische Klagenrecht, Vol. 1 Of 2 Vol. Set. Friedrich Julius Stahl. LC 77-74020. 1977. pap. text ed. 5.75 limited ed. o.p. (ISBN 0-918288-04-5). Slavia Lib.

Roman Coins. J. P. Kent. LC 77-77534. (Illus.). 1978. 60.00 o.p. (ISBN 0-8109-1584-7). Abrams.

Roman Curia & the Communion of Churches. Ed. by Peter Huizing & Knut Walf. (New Concilium: Vol. 127). 120p. (Orig.). 1980. pap. 4.95 (ISBN 0-8164-2042-4). Crossroad NY.

Roman de Renart. (Documentation thematique). (Illus., Fr.). pap. 2.95 (ISBN 0-685-14069-5, 282). Larousse.

Roman Drama: Nine Plays of Terence, Plautus & Seneca. Tr. by Frank O. Copley. LC 64-66074. (YA) (gr. 11 up). 1965. pap. 7.95 (ISBN 0-672-60455-8, LLA209). Bobbs.

Roman Economy: Studies in Ancient Economic & Administrative History. A. H. Jones. Ed. by P. A. Brunt. 450p. 1974. 27.50x o.p. (ISBN 0-87471-194-0). Rowman.

Roman Elegists' Attitude Towards Women. Saara Lilja. Ed. by Steele Commager. LC 77-70836. (Latin Poetry Ser.: Vol. 25). 1979. Repr. of 1965 ed. lib. bdg. 31.00 (ISBN 0-8240-2974-7). Garland Pub.

Roman Frontiers of Britain. David Wilson. 1967. 3.95x o.p. (ISBN 0-435-32966-9). Heinemann Ed.

Roman Group Portraiture: The Funerary Reliefs of the Late Republic & Early Empire. Diana E. Kleiner. LC 76-23634. (Outstanding Dissertations in the Fine Arts - 2nd Series - Ancient). (Illus.). 1977. Repr. lib. bdg. 63.00 (ISBN 0-8240-2703-5). Garland Pub.

Roman History from Coins. Michael Grant. (Illus.). 1968. pap. 5.95 (ISBN 0-521-09549-2). Cambridge U Pr.

Roman House. Peter Hodge. (Aspects of Roman Life Ser.). (Illus.). 1976. pap. text ed. 2.95x (ISBN 0-582-20300-7). Longman.

Roman Imperial Coins in the Hunter Coin Cabinet, University of Glasgow: Pertinax to Aemilian, Vol. 3. Anne S. Robertson. (Illus.). 1977. 98.00x (ISBN 0-19-713306-1). Oxford U Pr.

Roman Imperialism in the Late Republic. 2nd ed. E. Badian. 1969. 8.50x (ISBN 0-8014-0024-4); pap. 2.45 (ISBN 0-8014-9109-6, CP109). Cornell U Pr.

Roman Invasion of Britain. Graham Webster. (Illus.). 224p. 1980. 14.00x (ISBN 0-389-20107-3). B&N.

Roman Jakobson: Echoes of His Scholarship. Ed. by Daniel Armstrong & C. H. Schooneveld. 1977. pap. text ed. 68.50x (ISBN 90-316-0147-0). Humanities.

Roman Jakobson's Science of Language. Linda R. Waugh. (PDR Press Publications on Roman Jakobson: No. 2). (Orig.). 1977. pap. text ed. 10.25x (ISBN 90-316-0112-8). Humanities.

Roman Law. L. B. Curzon. 240p. 1974. pap. 9.95x (ISBN 0-7121-1853-5, Pub. by Macdonald & Evans England). Intl Ideas.

Roman Law: An Historical Introduction. Hans J. Wolff. 1976. pap. 5.95x (ISBN 0-8061-1296-4). U of Okla Pr.

Roman Life in the Days of Cicero. Alfred J. Church. LC 61-24994. (gr. 7-11). 9.50x (ISBN 0-8196-0105-5). Biblo.

Roman Literature & Society. R. M. Ogilvie. 1980. text ed. 19.50x (ISBN 0-391-01679-2). Humanities.

Roman Literature & Society. R. M. Ogilvie. 303p. 1980. 23.50x (ISBN 0-389-20069-7). B&N.

Roman London. Peter Marsden. (Illus.). 224p. 1981. 19.95 (ISBN 0-500-25073-1). Thames Hudson.

Roman Medallions. 2nd enl. ed. Mary Comstock & Cornelius Vermeule. (Illus.). 1975. Repr. of 1962 ed. 5.00 (ISBN 0-87846-177-9). Mus Fine Arts Boston.

Roman Mind at Work. Paul MacKendrick. LC 80-13022. (ANVIL Ser.). 192p. 1980. pap. text ed. 4.95 (ISBN 0-89874-200-5). Krieger.

Roman Novel. P. G. Walsh. LC 78-98700. 1970. 34.00 (ISBN 0-521-07658-7). Cambridge U Pr.

Roman Numerals. David A. Adler. LC 77-2270. (Young Math Ser.). (Illus.). (gr. 1-4). 1977. PLB 7.89 (ISBN 0-690-01302-7, TYC-J). T Y Crowell.

Roman Papers, 2 vols. Ronald Syme. Ed. by E. Badian. (Illus.). 948p. 1976. 95.00x (ISBN 0-19-814367-2). Oxford U Pr.

Roman Poetry & Prose. Eberhard C. Kennedy. 1957. text ed. 7.50x (ISBN 0-521-05880-5). Cambridge U Pr.

Roman Poetry from the Republic to the Silver Age. Tr. by Dorothea Wender from Latin. LC 79-28219. 160p. 1980. 9.95x (ISBN 0-8093-0963-7). S Ill U Pr.

Roman Poets of the Augustan Age. William Y. Sellar. Incl. Bk. 1. Horace & the Elegiac Poets. Memoir by Andrew Lang. LC 65-23488. (Illus.). xviii, 362p. Repr. of 1892 ed. o.p. (ISBN 0-8196-0165-9); Bk. 2. Virgil. 3rd ed. LC 65-23489. xiv, 423p. Repr. of 1908 ed. 15.00x (ISBN 0-8196-0162-4). Biblo.

Roman Polanski: A Biography. Thomas Kiernan. LC 80-997. (Illus.). 1980. 12.95 (ISBN 0-394-51396-7, GP835). Grove.

Roman Portraits: Aspects of Self & Society. K. Patricia Erhart et al. (Illus.). 108p. (Orig.). 1980. pap. 7.75. J P Getty Mus.

Roman Questions of Plutarchus. Plutarchus. Tr. by H. J. Rose. 1924. 15.00x (ISBN 0-8196-0284-1). Biblo.

Roman Realities. Finley Hooper. LC 78-15237. (Illus.). (YA) 1978. 15.00x (ISBN 0-8143-1593-3); pap. 7.50x (ISBN 0-8143-1594-1). Wayne St U Pr.

Roman Republic. Michael Crawford. (Fontana History of the Ancient World Ser.). 1978. text ed. 24.75x (ISBN 0-391-00832-3). Humanities.

Roman Republican Coinage. Michael Crawford. LC 77-164450. (Illus.). 750p. 1975. 190.00 (ISBN 0-521-07492-4). Cambridge U Pr.

Roman Revolution. Ronald Syme. (Oxford Paperbacks Ser). 1939. pap. 11.95x (ISBN 0-19-881001-6). Oxford U Pr.

Roman Roads. Raymond Chevallier. LC 74-82845. 1976. 36.50x (ISBN 0-520-02834-1). U of Cal Pr.

Roman Roads of Europe. Nigel Sitwell. (Illus.). 240p. 1981. 35.00 (ISBN 0-312-69080-0). St Martin.

Roman Rulers & Rebels. Gordon P. Stillman. (gr. 8-11). 1972. pap. text ed. 4.50x (ISBN 0-88334-048-8). Ind Sch Pr.

Roman Social Relations, 50 B. C to A. D. 284. Ramsay MacMullen. LC 73-86909. 317p. 1981. pap. 4.95x (ISBN 0-300-02702-8). Yale U Pr.

Roman Sonnets of Giuseppe Gioacchino Belli. Giuseppe G. Belli. Tr. & intro. by Harold Norse. LC 73-79284. (Perivale Translation Ser.: No. 1). 54p. 1974. pap. 3.75 (ISBN 0-912288-06-X). Perivale Pr.

Roman Spirit in Religion, Thought & Art. Albert Grenier. Tr. by M. R. Dobie. LC 76-118639. (Illus.). 1970. Repr. of 1926 ed. lib. bdg. 29.50x (ISBN 0-8154-0330-5). Cooper Sq.

Roman Sport & Entertainment. D. Buchanan. (Aspects of Roman Life). (Illus.). 1976. pap. text ed. 2.95x (ISBN 0-582-31415-1). Longman.

Roman Stamp: Frame & Facade in Some Forms of Neo-Classicism. Robert M. Adams. (Illus.). 1974. 20.00x (ISBN 0-520-02345-5); pap. 6.95 (ISBN 0-520-03715-4). U. of Cal Pr.

Roman Times. (Picture Panorama of British History Ser.). 1977. pap. 4.95 (ISBN 0-263-06238-4). Transatlantic.

Roman Towns. Peter Hodge. (Aspects of Roman Life). (Illus.). 1977. pap. text ed. 2.95x (ISBN 0-582-20301-5). Longman.

Roman Towns in Britain. Alan Sorrell. 1976. 17.95 (ISBN 0-7134-3237-3). David & Charles.

Roman Trade & Travel. Peter Hodge. (Aspects of Roman Life Ser). (Illus.). 1978. pap. text ed. 2.95x (ISBN 0-582-31413-5). Longman.

Roman Villa: A Historical Introduction. John Percival. 1976. 28.50x (ISBN 0-520-03233-0). U of Cal Pr.

Roman Voting Assemblies: From the Hannibalic War to the Dictatorship of Caesar. Lily R. Taylor. LC 66-17025. (Jerome Lecture Ser). (Illus.). 1966. 7.50 o.p. (ISBN 0-472-04906-2). U of Mich Pr.

Roman World. Victor Chapot. 449p. 1980. Repr. of 1928 ed. lib. bdg. 50.00 (ISBN 0-89760-118-1). Telegraph Bks.

Roman World. Paul Titley. (Let's Make History Ser.). (Orig.). 1980. pap. 3.50 (ISBN 0-263-06336-4). Transatlantic.

Roman Years of Margaret Fuller. Joseph J. Deiss. (Illus.). 352p. 1976. pap. 4.95 o.s.i. (ISBN 0-690-01017-6, TYC-T). T Y Crowell.

Romance Along the Bayou. new ed. Sallie L. Bell. 192p. (Orig.). 1974. pap. 2.25 (ISBN 0-310-21022-4). Zondervan.

Romance & Tragedy: A Study of the Classic & Romantic Elements in the Great Tragedies of European Literature. Prosser H. Frye. LC 61-10518. (Landmark Edns.). xiv, 372p. 1980. 21.00x (ISBN 0-8032-1955-5). U. of Nebr Pr.

Romance in America. Joel Porte. LC 69-17795. 1972. 9.00x (ISBN 0-8195-6024-3, Pub. by Wesleyan U Pr England). Columbia U Pr.

Romance in Italy. Mabel E. Allan. LC 62-11214. (gr. 8-11). 5.95 (ISBN 0-8149-0257-X). Vanguard.

Romance in the Headlines. Mary A. Taylor. Bd. with Bon Voyage, My Darling. 1980. pap. 1.95 (ISBN 0-451-09175-2, J9175, Sig). NAL.

Romance Languages. W. D. Elcock. (Great Language Ser.). 1975. text ed. 45.50x (ISBN 0-571-06152-4). Humanities.

Romance Languages: A Linguistic Introduction. R. Posner. 7.75 (ISBN 0-8446-0853-X). Peter Smith.

Romance of Alexander the Great. Tr. by Albert M. Wolohojian from Armenian. LC 74-84593. (Records of Civilization Ser: No. 82). 1969. 17.50x (ISBN 0-231-03297-8). Columbia U Pr.

Romance of American Transportation. rev. ed. Franklin M. Reck. LC 62-18235. (Illus.). (gr. 5 up). 1962. 7.95 o.p. (ISBN 0-690-71033-X, TYC-J). T Y Crowell.

Romance of Atlantis. Taylor Caldwell & Jess Stearn. LC 74-17399. 320p. 1975. 7.95 o.p. (ISBN 0-688-00334-6). Morrow.

Romance of Atlantis. Taylor Caldwell & Jess Stearn. 272p. 1978. pap. 2.25 (ISBN 0-449-23787-7, Crest). Fawcett.

Romance of Casco Bay. Edward R. Snow. LC 75-29352. (Illus.). 1975. 7.95 (ISBN 0-396-07214-3). Dodd.

Romance of Chivalry. A. R. Moncrieff. (Newcastle Mythology Library: Vol. 2). Orig. Title: Romance & Legend of Chivalry. (Illus.). 439p. 1976. pap. 4.95 (ISBN 0-87877-038-0, M-38). Newcastle Pub.

Romance of Chivalry. A. R. Moncrieff. LC 80-23872. (Newcastle Mythology Library: Vol. 2). 439p. 1980. Repr. of 1976 ed. lib. bdg. 11.95x (ISBN 0-89370-638-8). Borgo Pr.

Romance of Greeting Cards: An Historical Account of the Origin, Evolution, & Development. Ernest D. Chase. LC 76-159914. (Tower Bks). (Illus.). 1971. Repr. of 1926 ed. 26.00 (ISBN 0-8103-3903-X). Gale.

Romance of Healing. Rustom J. Vakil. 6.95x o.p. (ISBN 0-210-33941-1). Asia.

Romance of London. John Timbs. LC 68-22058. 1968. Repr. of 1865 ed. 38.00 (ISBN 0-8103-3498-4). Gale.

Romance of Sorcery. Sax Rohmer. 1973. Repr. of 1914 ed. 18.00 (ISBN 0-685-70657-5). Gale.

Romance of Symbolism & It's Relation to Church Ornament & Architecture. Sidney Heath. LC 70-174054. (Illus.). 1976. Repr. of 1909 ed. 18.00 (ISBN 0-8103-4302-9). Gale.

Romance of the Hebrew Language. William H. Saulex. 243p. Date not set. Repr. of 1913 ed. lib. bdg. 25.00 (ISBN 0-8482-6303-0). Norwood Edns.

Romance of the London Directory. Charles W. Bardsley. LC 72-78115. 1971. Repr. of 1879 ed. 18.00 (ISBN 0-8103-3782-7). Gale.

Romance of the Piano. Eric Blom. LC 69-15608. (Music Ser). (Illus.). 1969. Repr. of 1928 ed. 19.50 (ISBN 0-306-71060-9). Da Capo.

Romance of the Rose. Guillaume De Lorris & Jean De Meun. Tr. by Harry W. Robbins. 1962. pap. 6.50 (ISBN 0-525-47090-5). Dutton.

Romance of the Shoe. Thomas Wright. LC 68-26624. 1968. Repr. of 1922 ed. 22.00 (ISBN 0-8103-3543-3). Gale.

Romance of the Western Chamber. S. I. Hsiung. LC 68-22412. (Translations from the Oriental Classics Series). (Illus.). 1968. 20.00x (ISBN 0-231-02996-9); pap. 7.50x (ISBN 0-231-08615-6). Columbia U Pr.

Romance of Tristan: A Poem of the Twelfth Century, Vol. 1 & 2. Beroul. Ed. by Alfred Ewert. 1977. Vol. 1. pap. 8.00x o.p. (ISBN 0-631-02510-3, Pub. by Basil Blackwell); Vol. 2. pap. 9.00x o.p. (ISBN 0-631-12770-4, Pub. by Basil Blackwell). Biblio Dist.

Romance of Tristan & Iseult. Joseph Bedier. 1965. pap. 1.65 (ISBN 0-394-70271-9, Vin, V271). Random.

Romance of Two Worlds. Marie Corelli. Ed. by Robert L. Wolff. LC 75-484. (Victorian Fiction Ser.). 1975. Repr. of 1886 ed. lib. bdg. 66.00 (ISBN 0-8240-1561-4). Garland Pub.

Romancero Biblico. Luis D. Salem. 144p. (Orig., Spanish.). 1980. pap. 3.50 (ISBN 0-89922-203-X). Edit Caribe.

Romances Sans Paroles. Verlaine. Ed. by D. Hillery. (French Poets Ser.). 110p. 1976. text ed. 11.25x (ISBN 0-485-14712-2, Athlone Pr); pap. text ed. 8.75x (ISBN 0-485-12712-1, Athlone Pr). Humanities.

Romanesque. Ralph McInerny. LC 77-6891. 1978. 8.95 o.s.i. (ISBN 0-06-012966-2, HarpT). Har-Row.

Romanesque Architecture. H. Erich Kubach. LC 73-21549. (History of World Architecture Ser.). 1975. 45.00 (ISBN 0-8109-1024-1). Abrams.

Romanesque Sculpture from the Cathedral of Saint-Etienne, Toulouse. Linda Seidel. LC 76-23646. (Outstanding Dissertations in the Fine Arts). (Illus.). 1977. Repr. of 1965 ed. lib. bdg. 52.00 (ISBN 0-8240-2729-9). Garland Pub.

Romani. Cyril E. Robinson. 1941. text ed. 5.25x (ISBN 0-521-06108-3). Cambridge U Pr.

Romania: A Profile. Lawrence S. Graham. (Nations of Contemporary Eastern Europe Ser.). 128p. 1981. lib. bdg. 16.50x (ISBN 0-89158-925-2). Westview.

Romania in the Nineteen Eighties. Ed. by Daniel N. Nelson. (Westview Special Studies on the Soviet Union & Eastern Europe). 250p. 1981. lib. bdg. 22.50x (ISBN 0-86531-027-0). Westview.

Romanian-English Dictionary & Grammar for the Mathematical Sciences. Ed. by S. H. Gould & P. E. Obreanu. 60p. (Eng & Romanian.). 1979. Repr. of 1969 ed. 6.00 (ISBN 0-8218-0038-8, ROMA). Am Math.

Romanian-Finnish Seminar on Complex Analysis. Ed. by C. A. Cazacu et al. (Lecture Notes in Mathematics: Vol. 743). 713p. 1980. pap. 33.00 (ISBN 0-387-09550-0). Springer-Verlag.

Romanian Icons Painted on Glass. Cornel Irimie & Marcela Focsa. (Illus.). 1971. 75.00x (ISBN 0-393-04309-6). Norton.

Romanian Policy Since 1965: The Political & Military Limits of Autonomy. Aurel Braun. LC 78-9516. (Praeger Special Studies). 1978. 25.95 (ISBN 0-03-043471-8). Praeger.

Romanians in America & Canada: A Guide to Information Sources. Ed. by Vladimir Wertsman. LC 80-191. (Gale Information Guide Library, Ethnic Information Guide Ser.: Vol. 5). 175p. 1980. 30.00 (ISBN 0-8103-1417-7). Gale.

Romano-British Bibliography: 55B.C.-449A.D, Vol. 1 & 2. Wilfrid Bonser. 1977. Set. 225.00x (ISBN 0-631-08380-4, Pub. by Basil Blackwell). Biblic Dist.

Romanov Ransom. Anne A. Thompson. 1978. pap. 1.95 o.s.i. (ISBN 0-685-54632-2, 04723-6). Jove Pubns.

Romans, Vol.i. C. E. Cranfield. (International Critical Commentary Ser.). 480p. Repr. of 1980 ed. text ed. 24.00x (ISBN 0-567-05040-8). Attic Pr.

Romans, Vol. Ii. C. E. Cranfield. (International Critical Commentary Ser.). 448p. Repr. of 1979 ed. text ed. 28.50x (ISBN 0-567-05041-6). Attic Pr.

Romans. Joan Forman & Harry Strongman. LC 77-86188. (Peoples of the Past Ser.). (Illus.). 1977. lib. bdg. 7.95 (ISBN 0-686-51160-3). Silver.

Romans. Martin H. Franzmann. LC 68-19990. (Concordia Commentary Ser). 1968. 10.95 (ISBN 0-570-06284-5, 15-2061). Concordia.

Romans. Charles Hodge. (Geneva Commentaries Ser.). 1975. 11.95 (ISBN 0-85151-213-5). Banner of Truth.

Romans. H. A. Ironside. Date not set. 4.95 (ISBN 0-87213-386-9). Loizeaux.

Romans. Eugene H. Maly. Ed. by Wilfrid Harrington & Donald Senior. (New Testament Message Ser.: Vol. 9). 160p. 1980. 9.00 (ISBN 0-89453-132-8); pap. 4.95 (ISBN 0-89453-197-2). M Glazier.

Romans. 5th ed. W. Sanday & A. C. Headlam. (International Critical Commentary Ser.). 568p. Repr. of 1977 ed. 23.00x (ISBN 0-567-05026-2). Attic Pr.

Romans. Geoffrey Wilson. 254p. 1977. pap. 4.25 (ISBN 0-85151-238-0). Banner of Truth.

Romans, Vol. 1. William Hendriksen. 336p. 1980. 14.95 (ISBN 0-8010-4236-4). Baker Bk.

Romans: An Access Guide. Robert Karris. 128p. (Orig.). 1981. pap. 4.95 (ISBN 0-8215-5926-5). Sadlier.

Romans & Barbarians. Department of Classical Art. 1977. 35.00 o.p. (ISBN 0-87846-110-8); pap. 12.00 o.p. (ISBN 0-87846-178-7). Mus Fine Arts Boston.

Romans & Their Gods in the Age of Augustus. R. M. Ogilvie. (Ancient Culture & Society Ser). (Illus.). 1970. 5.00x (ISBN 0-393-05399-7); pap. 4.95 (ISBN 0-393-00543-7). Norton.

Romans: Assurance, Vol. 2. D. Martyn Lloyd-Jones. 272p. 1972. 10.95 (ISBN 0-310-27890-2). Zondervan.

Romans: Christianity on Trial. Carolyn Nystrom. (Young Fisherman Bible Studyguides). (Illus.). 124p. 1980. tchr's ed 4.95 (ISBN 0-87788-899-X); student wkbk. 3.95 (ISBN 0-87788-898-1). Shaw Pubs.

Romans de Tristan et Iseut: Introduction a une lecture plurielle. new ed. F. Barteau. (Collection L). 288p. (Orig., Fr.). 1972. pap. 19.95 (ISBN 2-03-036007-4). Larousse.

Romans: Justification by Faith. William MacDonald. (Orig.). 1981. pap. 6.50 (ISBN 0-937396-36-2). Walterick Pubs.

Romans: Made Righteous by Faith. Gladys Hunt. (Fisherman Bible Studyguide Ser.). 94p. (Orig.). 1981. saddle stitch 2.25 (ISBN 0-87788-733-0). Shaw Pubs.

Romans Realized. Don DeWelt. LC 72-1068. (Bible Study Textbook Ser.). (Illus.). 1959. 11.50 (ISBN 0-89900-037-1). College Pr Pub.

Romans: The Gospel for All. Keith L. Brooks. (Teach Yourself the Bible Ser). 1962. pap. 1.75 (ISBN 0-8024-7372-5). Moody.

Romans, the Gospel of God's Grace. Alva J. McClain. 8.95 (ISBN 0-88469-080-6). BMH Bks.

Romans: The Law-Chapter 7: 1 to 8: 4, 6 vols. D. Martyn Lloyd-Jones. 368p. 1974. 11.95 (ISBN 0-310-27910-0); Six-volume Set. text ed. 65.70 (ISBN 0-310-27948-8, 10575). Zondervan.

Romans: The New Man, Vol. 3. D. Martyn Lloyd-Jones. 1973. text ed. 11.95 (ISBN 0-310-27900-3). Zondervan.

Romans Verse by Verse. William R. Newell. 1938. 12.95 (ISBN 0-8024-7385-7). Moody.

Roman's World. Frank G. Moore. LC 65-23486. (Illus.). 502p. (gr. 7 up). 1936. 15.00x (ISBN 0-8196-0155-1). Biblo.

Romantic Age in Prose. Ed. by A. W. Bellringer & C. B. Jones. (Costerus Ser.: Vol. XXIX). 159p. 1981. pap. text ed. 28.50x (Pub. by Radopi, Holland). Humanities.

Romantic Approach to Don Quixote. A. Close. LC 76-57097. 1978. 47.50 (ISBN 0-521-21490-4). Cambridge U Pr.

Romantic Art. William Vaughan. LC 77-76818. (World of Art Ser.). 1978. 17.95 (ISBN 0-19-519984-7); pap. 9.95 (ISBN 0-19-519981-2). Oxford U Pr.

Romantic Ballet as Seen by Theophile Gautier. Theophile Gautier. LC 79-7764. (Dance Ser.). (Illus.). 1980. Repr. of 1932 ed. lib. bdg. 14.00x (ISBN 0-8369-9292-X). Arno.

Romantic Ballet in England: Its Development, Fulfillment & Decline. 2nd ed. Ivor Guest. LC 77-172138. (Illus.). 176p. 1972. 20.00x (ISBN 0-8195-4050-1, Pub. by Wesleyan U Pr). Columbia U Pr.

Romantic Criticism of Shakespearean Drama. John Crawford. (Salzberg Studies in English Literature: Romantic Reassessment Ser.: No. 79). 1978. pap. text ed. 25.00x (ISBN 0-391-01352-1). Humanities.

Romantic Education. Patricia Hampl. 320p. 1981. 11.95 (ISBN 0-395-29697-8). HM.

Romantic Egoists: A Pictorial Autobiography from the Albums of Scott & Zelda Fitzgerald. F. Scott Fitzgerald. Compiled by Scottie F. Smith et al. (Illus.). 1977. Encore Edition. 14.95 (ISBN 0-684-14973-7, ScribT). Scribner.

Romantic England. Peter Quennell. LC 78-119142. (Illus.). 1970. 11.95 o.s.i. (ISBN 0-02-600100-4). Macmillan.

Romantic Exiles. Edward H. Carr. 392p. 1981. pap. 8.95 (ISBN 0-262-53040-6). MIT Pr.

Romantic Frenchman. Mary A. Gibbs. 208p. 1976. pap. 1.25 o.p. (ISBN 0-449-22869-X, P2869, Crest). Fawcett.

Romantic Imagination. C. Maurice Bowra. (Oxford Paperbook Bks). 1961. pap. 8.95x (ISBN 0-19-281006-5). Oxford U Pr.

Romantic Indian: Sentimental Views from Nineteenth-Century American Literature, 4 vols. LC 80-19248. 1980. write for info. (ISBN 0-8201-1356-5). Schol Facsimiles.

Romantic Landscape Vision: Constable & Wordsworth. Karl Kroeber. LC 74-5905. 176p. 1975. 17.50x (ISBN 0-299-06710-6). U of Wis Pr.

Romantic Movement. Alan Menhennet. (Literary History of Germany Ser.: Vol. 6). 276p. 1981. 28.50x (ISBN 0-389-20104-9). B&N.

Romantic Movement: A Selective & Critical Bibliography for Nineteen Seventy-Nine. Compiled by David V. Erdman et al. LC 80-8494. 350p. 1980. lib. bdg. 35.00 (ISBN 0-8240-9512-X). Garland Pub.

Romantic Narrative Art. Karl Kroeber. (Illus.). 1960. pap. 7.50x (ISBN 0-299-02244-7). U of Wis Pr.

Romantic Nationalism & Liberalism: Joachim Lelewel & the Polish National Idea. Joan S. Skurnowicz. (East European Monographs: No. 83). 224p. 1981. text ed. 16.00x (ISBN 0-914710-77-X). East Eur Quarterly.

Romantic New Orleans. Deirdre Stanforth. (Large Format Ser). (Illus.). 1979. pap. 7.95 o.p. (ISBN 0-14-005058-2). Penguin.

Romantic Opera & Literary Form. Peter Conrad. (Quantum Ser.). 1977. 14.00 (ISBN 0-520-03258-6). U. of Cal Pr.

Romantic Orpheus: Profiles of Clemens Brentano. John F. Fetzer. 1974. 21.50x (ISBN 0-520-02312-9). U. of Cal Pr.

Romantic Period. Intro. by Kenneth Muir. 140p. 1981. pap. 5.95 (ISBN 0-312-69174-2). St Martin.

Romantic Quest and Modern Query: A History of the Modern Theater. Tom F. Driver. LC 80-5756. 510p. 1980. lib. bdg. 18.50 (ISBN 0-8191-1217-8); pap. text ed. 10.00 (ISBN 0-8191-1218-6). U Pr of Amer.

Romantic Reassessmeent: Studies in Nineteenth Century Literature. Ed. by James Hogg. (Salzberg Studies in English Literature: 87-2). 144p. 1981. pap. text ed. 25.00x (ISBN 0-391-02245-8, Pub. by Salzburg, Austria). Humanities.

Romantic Revolt. Charles E. Vaughn. 507p. 1980. Repr. of 1907 ed. lib. bdg. 40.00 (ISBN 0-8495-5527-2). Arden Lib.

Romantic Triangle: Schleiermacher & Early German Romanticism. Jack Forstman. LC 76-55709. (American Academy of Religion. Dissertation Ser.). 1977. pap. 7.50 (ISBN 0-89130-124-0, 010013). Scholars Pr Ca.

Romanticism: A Structural Analysis. David Morse. 252p. 1981. 29.50x (ISBN 0-389-20165-0). B&N.

Romanticism & Consciousness. Ed. by Harold Bloom. (Orig.). 1970. pap. text ed. 7.95x (ISBN 0-393-09954-7, NortonC). Norton.

Romanticism and Religion. Stephen Prickett. LC 75-2254. 320p. 1976. 44.50 (ISBN 0-521-21072-0). Cambridge U Pr.

Romanticism & the Forms of Ruin: Wordsworth, Coleridge & Modalities of Fragmentation. Thomas McFarland. LC 80-7546. 432p. 1981. 30.00 (ISBN 0-691-06437-7); pap. 9.50 (ISBN 0-691-10108-6). Princeton U Pr.

Romanticism in Perspective. 2nd ed. Lilian R. Furst. 1979. text ed. 13.00x (ISBN 0-391-00003-9). Humanities.

Romanticism, Modernism, Postmodernism: Vol. 25, No. 2. Ed. by Harry Garvin. LC 79-50103. (Bucknell Review Ser.). 192p. 1980. 12.00 (ISBN 0-8387-5004-4). Bucknell U Pr.

Romanticism Reconsidered. Ed. by Northrop Frye. LC 63-18020. (English Institute). 1963. 12.50x (ISBN 0-231-02671-4); pap. 5.00x (ISBN 0-231-08589-3, 89). Columbia U Pr.

Romanticism: The Culture of the Nineteenth Century. Ed. by Morse Peckham. LC 65-23181. (Cultures of Mankind Ser). (Illus.). 1965. 6.95 o.s.i. (ISBN 0-8076-0314-7). Braziller.

Romantics Reviewed: A Collection in Depth of Periodical Reviews (1793-1830, 11 vols. Ed. & intro. by Donald H. Reiman. Incl. Vols. I & II. Pt. A. lib. bdg. 93.00 each (ISBN 0-8240-0509-0); Vols. I To V. Pt. B. lib. bdg. 375.00 5 vol. set (ISBN 0-8240-0510-4); Vols. I & II. Pt. C. lib. bdg. 93.00 each 2 vol. set (ISBN 0-8240-0511-2); Vols. I & II. Bibliography of Literary Reviews in British Periodicals 1798-1820. Ed. by William S. Ward. lib. bdg. 60.00 ea.. Set. lib. bdg. 740.00 (ISBN 0-8240-0512-0); lib. bdg. 93.00 ea. vols. comprising pts. a,b, & c. Garland Pub.

Romantics Third Voice: A Study of the Dramatic Works of the English Romantic Poets. Pratyush Purkayastha. (Salzburg Studies in English Literature, Poetic Drama & Poetic Theory: No. 41). 1978. pap. text ed. 25.00x (ISBN 0-391-01505-2). Humanities.

Romantics to Rodin: French Nineteenth-Century Sculpture from North American Collections. Peter Fusco et al. LC 79-27101. (Illus.). 1980. pap. 11.95 (ISBN 0-87587-091-0). LA Co Art Mus.

Romantik Hotels & Restaurants. Romantik Hotels. 160p. 1981. 4.98 (ISBN 0-912944-66-8). Berkshire Traveller.

Romantische Poesie. Raimund Belgardt. (Ger). 1970. text ed. 40.00x (ISBN 90-2791-248-3). Mouton.

Romantisme anglais: Le Defi des vulnerables. new ed. Paul Rozenberg. (Collection L). 287p. (Orig., Fr.). 1973. pap. 13.95 (ISBN 2-03-036010-4). Larousse.

Romany Passions. Alexandra Ellis. 1978. pap. 1.95 o.p. (ISBN 0-425-03672-3, Medallion). Berkley Pub.

Romany Remedies & Recipes. Gipsy Petulengro. LC 80-20035. 126p. 1980. Repr. of 1972 ed. lib. bdg. 9.95x (ISBN 0-89370-616-7). Borgo Pr.

Romaunt of the Rose & Le Roman de la Rose. Ronald Sutherland. LC 68-14794. (Eng. & Fr.). 1968. 17.50x (ISBN 0-520-01243-7). U of Cal Pr.

Rome. Russell Chamberlain. (Great Cities Ser.). (Illus.). 1976. 14.95 (ISBN 0-8094-2258-1). Time-Life.

Rome. Russell Chamberlain. (The Great Cities Ser.). (Illus.). (gr. 6 up). 1976. PLB 14.94 (ISBN 0-8094-2259-X, Pub by Time-Life). Silver.

Rome. Anthony Pereira. (Illus.). 1975. 12.50 o.p. (ISBN 0-8038-6334-9). Hastings.

Rome. Mikhail I. Rostovtzeff. Ed. by Elias J. Bickerman. Tr. by J. D. Duff. 1960. pap. 5.95x (ISBN 0-19-500224-5). Oxford U Pr.

Rome. David Willey. LC 80-50997. (Rand McNally Pocket Guide Ser.). (Illus.). 1980. pap. 3.95 (ISBN 0-528-84309-5). Rand.

Rome & Canterbury: From Henry VIII to the 1970's with an American Epilogue by Arthur A. Vogel. Bernard Pawley. 1975. 13.50 (ISBN 0-8164-1178-6). Crossroad NY.

Rome & Romans According to Shakespeare. Michael Platt. (Salzburg Studies in English Literature, Jacobean Drama Studies: No. 51). 295p. (Orig.). 1976. pap. text ed. 25.00x (ISBN 0-391-01498-6). Humanities.

Rome & the Counter-Reformation in Scandinavia. Oskar Garstein. 630p. 1980. 40.00x (ISBN 82-00-06165-5). Universitet.

Rome, England, the United States & the Forces for the Decline & the Death of the Empires. Peter H. Wright. (Science of Man Library Bk.). 1978. deluxe ed. 43.65 (ISBN 0-930008-14-6). Inst Econ Pol.

Rome in the Augustan Age. Henry T. Rowell. (Centers of Civilization Ser: No. 5). 1971. pap. 4.95x (ISBN 0-8061-0956-4). U of Okla Pr.

Rome of the Twelve Tables: Persons & Property. Alan Watson. LC 75-3481. 235p. 1975. 18.00 (ISBN 0-691-03548-2). Princeton U Pr.

Romeo & Juliet. William Shakespeare. (Illus.). (gr. 7 up). 1970. pap. 1.25 (ISBN 0-590-02921-5, Schol Pap). Schol Bk Serv.

Romeo & Juliet. William Shakespeare. Ed. by Arthur Quiller-Couch et al. (New Shakespeare Ser). 1969. 23.95 (ISBN 0-521-07554-8); pap. 4.50x (ISBN 0-521-09497-6). Cambridge U Pr.

Romeo & Juliet. Robert K. Turner, Jr. & George W. Williams. 1970. pap. 4.95x (ISBN 0-673-07519-2). Scott F.

Romeo & Juliet: A Study Text. John R. Nickelsen. LC 79-26683. (Illus.). 1980. pap. text ed. 5.25 (ISBN 0-684-16497-3, SSP 46, ScribC). Scribner.

Romeo & Juliet, with Reader's Guide. Shakespeare. (Orig.). (gr. 10-12). 1974. pap. text ed. 4.92 (ISBN 0-87720-821-2); tchr's ed. s.p. 3.15 (ISBN 0-87720-921-9). AMSCO Sch.

Rommel: A Narrative & Pictorial History. Richard D. Law & Craig W. Luther. (Illus.). 368p. 1980. 17.95 (ISBN 0-912138-20-3). Bender Pub CA.

Rommel Plot. John Tarrant. LC 77-5731. 1977. 8.95 o.p. (ISBN 0-397-01235-7). Lippincott.

Rommel, the Desert Fox. Desmond Young. LC 51-9112. (Illus.). 1951. lib. bdg. 9.87 o.p. (ISBN 0-06-014776-8, HarpT). Har-Row.

Rommel's Desert War: The Life & Death of the Afrika Korps. Samual W. Mitcham, Jr. LC 80-6153. 228p. 1981. 13.95 (ISBN 0-8128-2784-8). Stein & Day.

Romney, Hythe & Dymchurch Railway. W. J. Davies. (Railway History Ser). (Illus.). 184p. 1975. 14.95 (ISBN 0-7153-6827-3). David & Charles.

Rompecabezas y actividades espanoles. Iris H. Myers. (gr. 7-12). 1976. dup. masters 28.00 (ISBN 0-205-05458-7, 4254589). Allyn.

Ronald Brunlees McKerrow: A Selection of His Essays. Compiled by J. Philip Immroth. LC 73-19882. (Great Bibliographers Ser.: No. 1). (Illus.). 1974. 10.00 (ISBN 0-8108-0690-8). Scarecrow.

Ronald Duncan: Verse Dramatist & Poet Interviewed. William B. Wahl. (Salzburg Studies in English Literature, Poetic Drama, & Poetic Theory: No. 20). 171p. 1973. pap. text ed. 25.00x (ISBN 0-391-01551-6). Humanities.

Ronald Firbank. Jocelyn Brooke. Incl. John Betjeman. Jocelyn Brook. pap. 2.95 (ISBN 0-8277-6153-8). British Bk Ctr.

Ronald Firbank. Edward M. Potoker. LC 76-92032. (Columbia Essays on Modern Writers Ser.: No. 43). 1970. pap. 2.00 (ISBN 0-231-03168-8, MW43). Columbia U Pr.

Ronald Firbank-Memoirs & Critiques: Memoir by I. Kyrle Fletcher Included. Ed. by Mervyn Horder. 228p. 1977. 28.00x (ISBN 0-7156-0763-4, Pub. by Duckworth England). Biblio Dist.

Ronald Reagan. Frank Van Der Linden. 288p. 1981. 10.95 (ISBN 0-686-69236-5). Morrow.

Ronald Reagan's Call to Action. Ronald Reagan & Charles Hobbs. (Illus.). 176p. 1976. pap. 1.75 o.s.i. (ISBN 0-446-84233-8). Warner Bks.

Ronnie & Rosey. Judie Angell. (YA) 1979. pap. 1.50 (ISBN 0-440-97491-7, LFL). Dell.

Ronnie & Rosey. Judie Angell. LC 77-75362. (gr. 6-9). 1977. 8.95 (ISBN 0-87888-124-7). Bradbury Pr.

Ronnie & the Chief's Son. Elizabeth Coatsworth. (Illus.). (gr. 4-6). 1962. 6.95 (ISBN 0-02-721600-4). Macmillan.

Ronsard's Ordered Chaos: Visions of Flux & Stability in the Poetry of Pierre de Ronsard. Malcolm Quainton. 252p. 1980. 25.00x (ISBN 0-389-20023-9). B&N.

Roof Framing. H. H. Siegele. LC 74-25285. (Drake Home Craftsman Ser.). (Illus.). 176p. 1975. 7.95 o.p. (ISBN 0-8069-8624-7). Sterling.

Roof Slates & Other Poems of Pierre Reverdy. Ed. by Mary Ann Caws & Patricia Terry. LC 80-26806. (Illus.). 340p. 1981. 17.95x (ISBN 0-930350-09-X). NE U Pr.

Roofing & Siding. Sunset Editors. LC 80-53487. (Illus.). 112p. (Orig.). 1981. pap. 4.95 (ISBN 0-376-01490-3, Sunset Bks). Sunset-Lane.

Roofs & Siding. (Home Repair & Improvement Ser.). (Illus.). 1978. lib. bdg. 11.97 (ISBN 0-686-51039-9). Silver.

Roofs & Siding. Time-Life Editors. (Home Repair & Improvement Ser.). 1977. 10.95 (ISBN 0-8094-2390-1). Time-Life.

Roofs & Siding: A Practical Guide. Don Geary. (Illus.). 1978. 10.95 (ISBN 0-87909-752-3). Reston.

Roofs of Gold: Poems to Read Aloud. Padraic Colum. (gr. 7 up). 1964. 5.95g o.s.i. (ISBN 0-02-722920-3). Macmillan.

Rooftops. Tom Lewis. 300p. 1981. 11.95 (ISBN 0-87131-345-6). M Evans.

Rooftops: A Novel. Tom Lewis. Ed. by Fred Graver. 300p. 1981. 10.95 (ISBN 0-87131-345-6). M Evans.

Rook Endings. Levenfish & Smuslov. pap. 10.95 (ISBN 0-7134-0449-3, Pub. by Batsford England). David & Charles.

Rookie Running Back. Cliff Hankins. LC 68-57466. (gr. 7 up). 6.95 (ISBN 0-8149-0313-4). Vanguard.

Rookies. Ed Walton. LC 80-5892. 288p. 1981. 14.95 (ISBN 0-8128-2778-3). Stein & Day.

Room. Ruth Holland. LC 73-6240. 192p. (gr. 5-9). 1973. 5.95 o.s.i. (ISBN 0-440-07541-6). Delacorte.

Room Acoustics. H. Kuttruff. LC 73-16149. (Illus.). 298p. 1973. 43.95 (ISBN 0-470-51105-2). Halsted Pr.

Room Acoustics. 2nd ed. K. H. Kuttruff. (Illus.). 1979. 49.20x (ISBN 0-85334-813-8, Pub. by Applied Science). Burgess-Intl Ideas.

Room & Situation: The Political Economy of Land-Use Policy. James C. Hite. LC 79-11691. 1979. 19.95 (ISBN 0-88229-479-2); pap. 10.95 (ISBN 0-88229-700-7). Nelson-Hall.

Room Care for Hotels & Motels. Bruce H. Axler. 1974. pap. 3.95 (ISBN 0-672-96125-3). Bobbs.

Room for Cathy. Catherine Woolley. (Illus.). (gr. 3-7). 1956. PLB 7.92 (ISBN 0-688-31687-5). Morrow.

Room for Me & a Mountain Lion: Poetry of Open Space. Ed. by Nancy Larrick. LC 73-87710. (Illus.). 192p. (gr. 5 up). 1974. 7.95 (ISBN 0-87131-124-0). M Evans.

Room for Wonder: Indian Painting During the British Period, 1760 to 1880. Stuart C. Welsh. LC 78-50093. (Illus.). 192p. 1981. pap. 14.95 (ISBN 0-917418-60-3). Agrinde Pubns. Postponed.

Room of Delight. Oldřich Otypka. LC 73-22598. (Illus.). 288p. 1976. 15.00 o.p. (ISBN 0-498-01467-3). A S Barnes.

Room Outside: A New Approach to Garden Design. John Brookes. (Large Format Ser.). (Illus.). 1979. pap. 6.95 o.p. (ISBN 0-14-005077-9). Penguin.

Room to Breathe. David Clewell. LC 76-42865. 1976. pap. 4.00 (ISBN 0-915316-29-3); signed ltd. ed. 10.00x (ISBN 0-915316-30-7). Pentagram.

Room to Grow. Sylvia Gappa & Deirdre Glenn. LC 80-81681. (Learning Handbooks Ser.). 1981. pap. 5.95 (ISBN 0-8224-5875-6). Pitman Learning.

Room to Grow: A Study of Parent-Child Relationships. Carroll Davis. LC 66-6602. 1966. 10.00 o.p. (ISBN 0-8020-5173-1). U of Toronto Pr.

Room with a View. E. M. Forster. Ed. by Oliver Stallybrass. (Abinger Edition of E. M. Forster Ser.). 1978. text ed. 24.50x (ISBN 0-8419-5804-1). Holmes & Meier.

Room with Dark Mirrors. Velda Johnston. 1976. pap. 1.50 o.p. (ISBN 0-451-07143-3, W7143, Sig). NAL.

Roomful of Hovings & Other Profiles. John McPhee. LC 68-23746. 250p. 1969. 9.95 (ISBN 0-374-25208-4); pap. 4.95 (ISBN 0-374-51501-8). FS&G.

Roommate. Jacqueline Wein. 1980. pap. 2.25 (ISBN 0-451-09160-4, E9160, Sig). NAL.

Room's Dictionary of Confusibles. Adrian Room. 1979. 16.00 (ISBN 0-7100-0120-7). Routledge & Kegan.

Rooms for Rent. Margaret Mahy. LC 72-2882. (Illus.). (gr. k-3). 1974. PLB 4.90 o.p. (ISBN 0-531-02590-X). Watts.

Roosevelt. Edmund O'Connor. Ed. by Malcolm Yapp & Margaret Killingray. (World History Ser.). (Illus.). 32p. (gr. 10). 1980. lib. bdg. 5.95 (ISBN 0-89908-125-8); pap. text ed. 1.95 (ISBN 0-89908-100-2). Greenhaven.

Roosevelt After Inauguration. William S. Burroughs. LC 79-21111. 1979. pap. 0.50 (ISBN 0-87286-115-5). City Lights.

Roosevelt File. Michael Rawcliffe. (Illus.). 96p. (gr. 9-12). 1980. 14.95 (ISBN 0-7134-1921-0, Pub. by Batsford England). David & Charles.

Roosevelt: From Munich to Pearl Harbor. Basil Rauch. LC 74-34446. (FDR & the Era of the New Deal Ser). 527p. 1975. Repr. of 1967 ed. lib. bdg. 39.50 (ISBN 0-306-70739-X). Da Capo.

Roosevelt, Gandhi, Churchill. M. S. Venkataramani & B. K. Shrivastava. 300p. 1980. text ed. 18.50 (ISBN 0-391-01971-6). Humanities.

Roosevelt Leadership Nineteen Thirty Three to Nineteen Fourty Five. E. E. Robinson. LC 75-146154. (American Scene Ser.). 1972. Repr. of 1955 ed. lib. bdg. 42.50 (ISBN 0-306-70202-9). Da Capo.

Roosevelt Revolution, First Phase. Ernest K. Lindley. LC 74-637. (FDR & the Era of the New Deal Ser.). 328p. 1974. Repr. of 1933 ed. lib. bdg. 32.50 (ISBN 0-306-70651-2). Da Capo.

Roosevelts: A Family in Turmoil. Lillian R. Parks & Frances S. Leighton. (Illus.). 300p. 1981. 12.50 (ISBN 0-13-783043-2). P-H.

Roosevelt's Farmer: Claude R. Wickard in the New Deal. Dean Albertson. LC 74-23430. (Fdr & the Era of the New Deal Ser.). 1975. Repr. of 1961 ed. lib. bdg. 39.50 (ISBN 0-306-70702-0). Da Capo.

Roosevelt's Image Brokers: Poets, Playwrights & the Use of the Lincoln Symbol. Alfred H. Jones. LC 74-77651. 129p. 1974. 12.95 (ISBN 0-8046-9079-0, Natl U). Kennikat.

Roosevelt's Revolution: The First Year-a Personal Perspective. Rexford G. Tugwell. 1977. 14.95 o.s.i. (ISBN 0-02-620370-7, 62037). Macmillan.

Roosevelt's Road to Russia. George N. Crocker. LC 74-26540. (Fdr & the Era of the New Deal Ser.). (Illus.). xvii, 312p. 1975. Repr. of 1959 ed. lib. bdg. 32.50 (ISBN 0-306-70714-4). Da Capo.

Rooster Brother. Nonny Hogrogian. LC 73-8090. (Illus.). 32p. (gr. 1-4). 1974. 5.95g o.s.i. (ISBN 0-02-743990-9). Macmillan.

Rooster Crows. Maud Petersham & Miska Petersham. (Illus.). (gr. k-1). 1945. 10.95g (ISBN 0-02-773100-6). Macmillan.

Rooster Who Set Out to See the World. Eric Carle. LC 78-171902. (Illus.). 32p. (gr. k-3). 1972. PLB 5.95 o.p. (ISBN 0-531-02042-8). Watts.

Rooster Who Understood Japanese. Yoshiko Uchida. LC 76-13450. (Illus.). 32p. (gr. 1-3). 1976. reinforced bdg. 6.95 (ISBN 0-684-14672-X, ScribJ). Scribner.

Roosters, Rhymes, & Railroad Tracks. George D. Hendricks. 200p. 1980. pap. 6.95 (ISBN 0-87074-177-2). SMU Press.

Root Activity Patterns of Some Tree Crops. (Technical Reports Ser.: No. 170). 154p. 1976. pap. 12.00 (ISBN 92-0-115175-6, IAEA). Unipub.

Root Cellaring the Simple no-Processing Way to Store Fruits & Vegetables. Mike Bubel & Nancy Bubel. (Illus.). 320p. 1979. 12.95 (ISBN 0-87857-277-5). Rodale Pr Inc.

Root Diseases & Soil-Borne Pathogens. Ed. by T. A. Toussoun et al. LC 73-84531. (Illus.). 1970. 38.50x (ISBN 0-520-01582-7). U of Cal Pr.

Root of Bitterness: Documents of the Social History of American Women. Ed. by Nancy Cott. 1972. pap. 8.50 (ISBN 0-525-47328-9). Dutton.

Rootabaga Stories, Repr. Of 1922 Ed. Carl Sandburg. Incl. Rootabaga Pigeons. Repr. of 1923 ed. LC 75-32204. (Classics of Children's Literature, 1621-1932: Vol. 65). (Illus.). 1976. PLB 38.00 (ISBN 0-8240-2314-5). Garland Pub.

Roots & Branches: Ancestry for Australians. Errol Lea-Scarlett. 256p. 1980. pap. 6.95x (ISBN 0-00-216415-9, Pub. by W Collins Australia). Intl Schol Bk Serv.

Roots & Branches: Current Directions in Slave Studies. Michael Craton. LC 79-22464. 304p. 1980. 41.00 (ISBN 0-08-025367-9). Pergamon.

Roots & Reaches of United Nations Actions & Decisions. Moses Moskowitz. LC 80-51741. 220p. 1980. 28.50x (ISBN 90-286-0140-6). Sijthoff & Noordhoff.

Roots & Sky: Poetry from the Plays of Christopher Fry. Ed. by Charles E. Wadsworth & Jean G. Wadsworth. (Illus., Ltd. ed. 220 copies). special bdg. 250.00 (ISBN 0-930954-17-3); limited ed. 200 copies avail. (ISBN 0-930954-17-3). Tidal Pr.

Roots Are Food Finders. Franklyn M. Branley. LC 74-23924. (Let's Read & Find Out Bk). (Illus.). 40p. (gr. k-3). 1975. PLB 7.89 (ISBN 0-690-00703-5, TYC-J). T Y Crowell.

Roots: Family Histories of Familiar Words. Peter Davies. (Illus.). 224p. Date not set. 15.95 (ISBN 0-07-015449-X, P&RB). McGraw.

Roots of a Radical. John A. Robinson. 176p. 1981. 9.95 (ISBN 0-8245-0028-8). Crossroad NY.

Roots of American Civilization: A History of American Colonial Life. 2nd ed. Curtis P. Nettels. LC 63-8707. (Illus.). 1963. 34.50x (ISBN 0-89197-386-9); pap. text ed. 18.50x (ISBN 0-89197-925-5). Irvington.

Roots of Appeasement. Martin Gilbert. pap. 3.50 o.p. (ISBN 0-452-25024-2, Z5024, Plume). NAL.

Roots of Black Nationalism. Rodney Carlisle. (National University Publications Ser. in American Studies). 1975. 11.50 (ISBN 0-8046-9098-7, Natl U). Kennikat.

Roots of Caring, Sharing, & Helping: The Development of Prosocial Behavior in Children. Paul Mussen & Nancy Eisenberg-Berg. LC 77-22750. (Psychology Ser.). (Illus.). 1977. text ed. 16.95x (ISBN 0-7167-0045-X); pap. text ed. 7.95x (ISBN 0-7167-0044-1). W H Freeman.

Roots of Consciousness. enl. ed. David C. McClelland. (Illus.). 1981. text ed. 18.50x (ISBN 0-8290-0124-7). Irvington.

Roots of Contemporary American Architecture. Lewis Mumford. LC 75-171490. 1972. pap. text ed. 6.00 (ISBN 0-486-22072-9). Dover.

Roots of Crime: What You Need to Know About Crime & What You Can Do About It. Eda LeShan. LC 80-69999. 192p. (gr. 7 up). 1981. 8.95 (ISBN 0-590-07532-2, Four Winds). Schol Bk Serv.

Roots of Disunity: A Look at Canadian Political Culture. David Bell & Lorne Tepperman. 262p. 1980. pap. 10.00x (ISBN 0-7710-1196-2). NYU Pr.

Roots of Evil: A Social History of Crime & Punishment. Christopher Hibbert. LC 77-18940. 1978. Repr. of 1963 ed. lib. bdg. 32.75x (ISBN 0-313-20198-6, HIRE). Greenwood.

Roots of Human Behavior: An Introduction to the Psychobiology of Early Development. Myron Hofer. LC 80-28377. (Psychology Ser.). (Illus.). 1981. text ed. price not set (ISBN 0-7167-1277-6); pap. text ed. price not set (ISBN 0-7167-1278-4). W H Freeman.

Roots of Indian Art. S. P. Gupta. (Illus.). Date not set. 102.50 (ISBN 0-391-02172-9). Humanities.

Roots of Individuality: A Survey of Human Behavior Genetics. Linda K. Dixon & Ronald C. Johnson. LC 79-26601. 1980. pap. text ed. 9.95 (ISBN 0-8185-0376-9). Brooks-Cole.

Roots of Isolationism: Congressional Voting & Presidential Leadership in Foreign Policy. Leroy N. Rieselbach. (Orig.). 1966. 9.50 (ISBN 0-672-51169-X); pap. 4.35 o.p. (ISBN 0-672-60770-0). Bobbs.

Roots of Love: Helping Your Child Learn to Love in the First Three Years of Life. Helene S. Arnstein. LC 74-17674. 240p. 1975. 8.95 o.p. (ISBN 0-672-51845-7). Bobbs.

Roots of Nationalism: Studies in Northern Europe. Rosalind Mitchison. 175p. 1980. text ed. 31.25x (ISBN 0-85976-058-8). Humanities.

Roots of Oppression: The American Indian Question. Steve Talbot. (Orig.). 1981. 14.00 (ISBN 0-7178-0591-3); pap. 4.75 (ISBN 0-7178-0583-2). Intl Pub Co.

Roots of Psychotherapy. Carl A. Whitaker & Thomas P. Malone. LC 80-24437. (Brunner Mazel Classics in Psychoanalysis & Psychotherapy: No. 9). 272p. 1981. Repr. 17.50 (ISBN 0-87630-265-7). Brunner-Mazel.

Roots of Reading: A Study of Twelve Infant Schools in Deprived Areas. Brian Cane & Jane Smithers. Ed. by Gabriel Chanan. (General Ser.). 1971. pap. text ed. 5.75x (ISBN 0-901225-74-6, NFER). Humanities.

Roots of Renewal in Myth & Madness: The Meaning of Psychotic Episodes. John W. Perry. LC 76-19500. (Social & Behavioral Science Ser.). 1976. 14.95x (ISBN 0-87589-297-3). Jossey-Bass.

Roots of Resistance: Land Tenure in New Mexico, Sixteen Eighty to Nineteen Eighty. Roxanne D. Ortiz. LC 80-18935. 202p. (Orig.). 1980. 14.95 (ISBN 0-89551-050-2); pap. 9.95 (ISBN 0-89551-050-2). UCLA Chicano Stud.

Roots of Rural Poverty in Central & Southern Africa. Ed. by Robin Palmer & Neil Parsons. (Campus Ser.: No. 199). 1978. 22.75x (ISBN 0-520-03318-3); pap. 7.95x (ISBN 0-520-03505-4). U of Cal Pr.

Roots of Success. Cynthia Pincus et al. LC 80-18462. 1980. 8.95 (ISBN 0-13-783258-3). P-H.

Roots of the American Indian. Edward P. Kellogg. LC 79-91921. 1980. text ed. 14.95 (ISBN 0-9603914-0-1). EHUD.

Roots of the American Working Class: The Industrialization of Crafts in Newark, 1800-1860. Susan E. Hirsch. LC 78-51784. (Illus.). 1978. 15.00 (ISBN 0-8122-7747-3). U of Pa Pr.

Roots of the Bill of Rights: An Illustrated Sourcebook of American Freedom, 5 vols. rev. ed. Bernard Schwartz. LC 80-22931. (Illus.). 1500p. 1981. Set. pap. 64.95 (ISBN 0-87754-207-4). Chelsea Hse.

Roots of the Blues: An African Search. Samuel Charters. 160p. 1981. 15.00 (ISBN 0-7145-2705-X). Merrimack Bk Serv.

Roots of the Mountains: Wherein Is Told Somewhat of the Lives of the Men of Burgdale, Their Friends, Their Neighbours, Their Foeman & Their Fellows in Arms. William Morris. Ed. by R. Reginald & Douglas Menville. LC 80-19676. (Newcastle Forgotten Fantasy Library Ser.: Vol. 19). 424p. 1980. Repr. of 1979 ed. lib. bdg. 11.95x (ISBN 0-89370-518-7). Borgo Pr.

Roots of Totalitarianism: Fascism, National Socialism, and Communism. J. Lucien Radel. 1975. text ed. 19.50x (ISBN 0-8448-0374-X); pap. text ed. 9.50x (ISBN 0-8448-0600-5). Crane-Russak Co.

Roots of Tragedy: The United States & the Struggle for Asia, 1945-1953. Lisle A. Rose. LC 75-35354. (Contributions in American History: No. 48). 352p. 1976. lib. bdg. 18.50 (ISBN 0-8371-8592-0, RRT/). Greenwood.

Roots of Two Black Marine Sergeant Majors. Jesse J. Johnson. LC 78-55171. (Illus.). 1978. 10.00 (ISBN 0-915044-13-7); pap. 2.25 (ISBN 0-915044-14-5). Carver Pub.

Roots of Western Cultures: Pagan, Secular & Christian Options. Herman Dooyeweerd. 1979. 12.95 (ISBN 0-88906-104-1). Radix Bks.

Roots Out of Dry Ground. Reuben J. Swanson. 1979. 8.50 (ISBN 0-915948-06-0); pap. 6.50 (ISBN 0-686-57420-6). Western NC Pr.

Roots, Verb Forms & Primary Derivatives of the Sanskrit Language. William D. Whitney. (American Oriental Ser.: Vol. 30). 1945. 9.00x (ISBN 0-686-00014-5). Am Orient Soc.

Rope Dances. David Porush. LC 78-68135. 8.95 o.p. (ISBN 0-914590-50-2); pap. 3.95 o.p. (ISBN 0-914590-51-0). Braziller.

Rope in the Jungle. Gary Jennings. LC 76-14466. (gr. 5-7). 1976. 7.95 o.p. (ISBN 0-397-31267-9). Lippincott.

Rope of God. James T. Siegel. (Library Reprint Ser.: Vol. 96). 1978. 18.50x (ISBN 0-520-03714-6). U of Cal Pr.

Rope of Moka. Andrew Strathern. 26.95 (ISBN 0-521-07987-X); pap. 10.95x (ISBN 0-521-09957-9). Cambridge U Pr.

Rope the Wild Wind. Lee Floren. (Orig.). 1979. pap. 1.75 (ISBN 0-532-23149-X). Manor Bks.

Ropes, Knots & Slings for Climbers. rev. ed. Walt Wheelock. (Illus.). 1967. wrappers 1.50 (ISBN 0-910856-00-1). La Siesta.

Roquefort Gang. Sandy Clifford. (gr. 2-6). 1981. 5.95 (ISBN 0-395-29521-1). HM.

Rorschach: A Comprehensive System. John E. Exner. (Personality Processes Ser.: Current Research & Advanced Interpretation: Vol 2). 1978. 41.00 (ISBN 0-471-04166-1, Pub. by Wiley-Interscience). Wiley.

Rorschach: A Comprehensive System. John Exner, Jr. LC 74-8888. (Personality Processes Ser: Vol. 1). 512p. 1974. 41.00 (ISBN 0-471-24964-5, Pub. by Wiley-Interscience). Wiley.

Rory Story. Bill Binzen. LC 73-9011. 32p. (gr. 1-3). 1974. 4.95 o.p. (ISBN 0-385-09332-2). Doubleday.

Rosa Bonheur: A Life & a Legend. Dore Ashton & Denise B Hare. LC 80-36749. (Illus.). 192p. 1981. 20.00 (ISBN 0-670-60813-0). Viking Pr.

Rosa Parks. Eloise Greenfield. LC 72-83782. (Biography Ser.). (Illus.). (gr. 1-5). 1973. 7.95 (ISBN 0-690-71210-3, TYC-J); PLB 7.89 (ISBN 0-690-71211-1). T Y Crowell.

Rosalia De Castro. Kathleen K. Hill. (World Authors Ser.: No. 446). lib. bdg. 12.50 (ISBN 0-8057-6282-5). Twayne.

Rosalynn. Howard Norton. 1977. pap. 2.95 o.p. (ISBN 0-88270-260-2). Logos.

Rosario Biblico. Christianica Ctr. (Illus.). 1980. 4.50 (ISBN 0-911346-04-X). Christianica.

Rosary in Action. John S. Johnson. LC 54-8388. 1977. pap. 4.00 (ISBN 0-89555-023-7, 185). TAN Bks Pubs.

Rosary Murders. William Kienzle. 1979. 9.95 o.p. (ISBN 0-8362-6101-1). Andrews & McMeel.

Roscher & Knies: The Logical Problems of Historical Economics. Max Weber. Tr. & intro. by Guy Oakes. LC 75-6315. 1975. 14.95 (ISBN 0-02-934050-0). Free Pr.

Rose & Her Bath. Sarah Garland. (Illus.). (ps-5). 1970. 6.95 (ISBN 0-571-08728-0, Pub. by Faber & Faber); pap. 2.45 (ISBN 0-571-11017-7). Merrimack Bk Serv.

Rose & the Ring. William M. Thackeray. (Illus.). 1947. 30.00 (ISBN 0-87598-006-6). Pierpont Morgan.

Rose & the Thorn. Nancy L. Harvey. (Illus.). 288p. 1975. 13.95 (ISBN 0-02-548550-4). Macmillan.

Rose-Bloom at My Fingertips. Rose Orlich. 80p. 1981. 6.95. Adams Minn.

Rose Bowl. Julian May. LC 76-8459. (Sports Classics Ser.). (Illus.). (gr. 4-12). 1976. PLB 8.95 o.p. (ISBN 0-87191-521-9). Creative Ed.

Rose by Any Other Name. David Zaslow. (Illus.). 96p. (Orig.). Date not set. pap. 5.00 (ISBN 0-89411-002-0). Onset Pubns.

Rose Colored Glasses: Melanie Adjusts to Poor Vision. Linda Leggett & Linda Andrews. LC 79-12501. 1979. 8.95 (ISBN 0-87705-408-8). Human Sci Pr.

Rose Garden. Richard A. Matera. LC 79-56881. 79p. 1981. 4.95 (ISBN 0-533-04551-7). Vantage.

Rose Growing for Everyone. E. B. Le Grice. (Illus.). 1969. 7.95 o.p. (ISBN 0-571-08682-9, Pub. by Faber & Faber). Merrimack Bk Serv.

Rose in Bloom. Louisa M. Alcott. (gr. 7 up). 1876. 9.95 (ISBN 0-316-03098-8). Little.

Rose in the Heart. Edna O'Brien. 1980. pap. 2.75 (ISBN 0-380-50021-3, 50021). Avon.

Rose Kennedy. Patricia M. Eldred. LC 75-1119. (Creative Education Closeup Bks.). (Illus.). 32p. (gr. 3-6). 1975. PLB 5.95 (ISBN 0-87191-423-9). Creative Ed.

Rose Kennedy: No Time for Tears. Carol B. Church. Ed. by David L. Bender & Gary E. Mc Cuen. (Focus on Famous Women Ser.). (Illus.). (gr. 3-9). 1976. 6.95 (ISBN 0-912616-44-X); read-along cassette 9.95 (ISBN 0-89908-243-2). Greenhaven.

Rose of Dutcher's Coolly. Hamlin Garland. Ed. by Donald Pizer. LC 79-82509. 1970. pap. 3.95 (ISBN 0-8032-5071-1, BB 506, Bison). U of Nebr Pr.

Rose of Flesh. Jan Wolkers. Tr. by John Scott. LC 67-12383. 1963. 4.50 o.p. (ISBN 0-8076-0403-8). Braziller.

Rose of Honor. H. A. Covington. 207p. 1980. 8.95 (ISBN 0-8059-2735-2). Dorrance.

Rose Recipes from Olden Times. Eleanour S. Rohde. (Illus.). 95p. 1973. pap. 2.00 (ISBN 0-486-22957-2). Dover.

Rose, the Bath & the Merboy. Sarah Garland. (Illus.). (ps-5). 6.95 (ISBN 0-571-09581-X, Pub. by Faber & Faber). Merrimack Bk Serv.

Rose Wilder Lane: Her Story. Rose W. Lane & Roger L. MacBride. LC 77-12072. 238p. 1980. pap. 6.95 (ISBN 0-8128-6077-2). Stein & Day.

Rose Windows. Painton Cowen. LC 78-23286. (Illus.). 1979. 22.50 (ISBN 0-87701-121-4, Prism Edition). Chronicle Bks.

Rosegarden & Labyrinth: A Study in Art Education. Seonaid M. Robertson. (Illus.). 1963. 16.95x (ISBN 0-7100-2046-5). Routledge & Kegan.

Rosemary Tree. Elizabeth Goudge. 1976. pap. 1.75 o.s.i. (ISBN 0-515-04147-5). Jove Pubns.

Rosenzweig Picture-Frustration (P-F) Study--Basic Manual. Saul Rosenzweig. LC 77-95428. 1978. 8.00 (ISBN 0-930172-02-7); pap. 3.50 o.p. (ISBN 0-685-06633-9). Rana Hse.

Roses. James U. Crockett. (Encycloedia of Gardening Ser). (Illus.). 1971. 11.95 (ISBN 0-8094-1085-0); lib. bdg. avail. (ISBN 0-685-04844-6). Time-Life.

Roses. James U. Crockett. LC 78-140420. (Time-Life Encyclopedia of Gardening). (Illus.). (gr. 6 up). 1971. lib. bdg. 11.97 (ISBN 0-8094-1086-9, Pub. by Time-Life). Silver.

Roses. Richard Ray & Michael MacCaskey. (Gardening Ser.). (Orig.). 1981. pap. 7.95 (ISBN 0-89586-079-1). H P Bks.

Roses for Every Garden. F. C. Witchell. (Leisure Plan Bks). 1971. pap. 2.95 (ISBN 0-600-44178-4). Transatlantic.

Roses: How to Grow. rev. ed. Sunset Editors. LC 79-90334. (Illus.). 96p. 1980. pap. 3.95 (ISBN 0-376-03655-9). Sunset-Lane.

Roses in December: Edwardian Recollections. Amy S. Fraser. (Illus.). 1981. price not set (ISBN 0-7100-0823-6). Routledge & Kegan.

Roses Out of Reach. Marjorie Vernon. (Aston Hall Romances Ser.). 192p. (Orig.). 1981. pap. 1.75 (ISBN 0-523-41127-8). Pinnacle Bks.

Roses Under Glass. 78p. 1980. pap. 9.95 (ISBN 0-901361-36-4, Pub. by Grower Bks England). Intl Schol Bk Serv.

Rosewell Garland of Virginia. Claude O. Lanciano, Jr. (Illus.). 1978. 12.50 (ISBN 0-9603558-3-9). Lands End Bks.

Rosibelle Lee Wildcat Tennessee. Raymond Andrews. (Illus.). 1980. 9.95 (ISBN 0-8037-8336-1). Dial.

Rosicrucian Enlightenment. Frances A. Yates. (Illus.). 286p. 1972. 22.50 (ISBN 0-7100-7380-1). Routledge & Kegan.

Rosie's Walk. Pat Hutchins. (Illus.). (gr. k-2). 1968. 8.95 (ISBN 0-02-745850-4). Macmillan.

Rosita. Tom C. Patten & Robert Carpenter. (Illus.). 1975. 4.95 o.p. (ISBN 0-88415-795-4). Pacesetter Pr.

Ross MacDonald. Jerry Speir. LC 78-4297. (Recognitions Ser.). 1978. 10.95 (ISBN 0-8044-2824-7); pap. 4.95 (ISBN 0-8044-6871-0). Ungar.

Ross Peterson: A New Edgar Cayce. Allen Spraggett. 1978. pap. 2.25 (ISBN 0-515-04579-9). Jove Pubns.

Rossetti. John Nicoll. LC 75-23267. (Illus.). 176p. 1976. 22.95 o.s.i. (ISBN 0-02-589340-8, 58934). Macmillan.

Rossetti & the Fair Lady. David Sonstroem. LC 70-105506. (Illus.). 1970. 17.50x (ISBN 0-8195-4019-6, Pub. by Wesleyan U Pr). Columbia U Pr.

Rosshalde. Hermann Hesse. (Suhrkamp Taschenbuecher: No. 312). 192p. 1980. pap. text ed. 3.90 (ISBN 0-686-64718-1, Pub. by Insel Verlag Germany). Suhrkamp.

Roster of Revolutionary Soldiers & Patriots in Alabama. Louise Julich. (Alabama Society Daughters of the American Revolution). 1979. 25.00 (ISBN 0-88428-045-4). Parchment Pr.

Roswell Heritage. Mary F. Ford. (YA) 1968. 4.95 o.p. (ISBN 0-685-07458-7, Avalon). Bouregy.

Roswell Incident. Charles Berlitz & William L. Moore. 1980. 10.00 (ISBN 0-686-69014-1). G&D.

Rosy Crucifixion. Henry Miller. Incl. Sexus; Plexus; Nexus. LC 80-8064. 1600p. 1980. box set 11.95 (ISBN 0-394-17774-6, B 449, BC). Grove.

Rosy Crucifixion: Sexus, Plexus, & Nexus, 3 vols. boxed set. Henry Miller. LC 80-8064. 1600p. 1980. 10.95 (ISBN 0-394-17774-6). Grove.

Rota Veneris. Boncompagno da Signa. Ed. by Josef Purkart. LC 74-18250. 128p. 1975. Repr. of 1474 ed. lib. bdg. 20.00x (ISBN 0-8201-1137-6). Schol Facsimiles.

Rotating Electrical Equipment Testing, 2 vols. Ed. by R. L. Caton et al. (Engineering Craftsmen: No. G22). (Illus.). 1969. Set. spiral bdg. 41.50x (ISBN 0-85083-072-9). Intl Ideas.

Rotating Electrical Equipment Winding & Building, 2 vols. Ed. by R. T. Anderson et al. (Engineering Craftsmen: No. G2). (Illus.). 1969. Set. spiral bdg. 46.95x (ISBN 0-85083-030-3). Intl Ideas.

Rotation of the Earth. W. H. Munk. LC 73-130911. (Monographs in Mechanics & Applied Mathematics). (Illus.). 323p. 1975. 29.95 (ISBN 0-521-20778-9). Cambridge U Pr.

Rotatoria. Ed. by H. J. Dumont & J. Green. (Developments in Hydrobiology Ser.: No. 1). 268p. 1980. lib. bdg. 79.00 (ISBN 90-6193-754-X, Pub. by Dr. W. Junk). Kluwer Boston.

Rote Kapelle: The CIA's History of Soviet Intelligence & Espionage Networks in Western Europe, 1936-1945. CIA. Ed. by Paul Kesaris. 1979. 29.50 (ISBN 0-89093-203-4). U Pubns Amer.

Rote Liste, 1980. (Illus., Ger.). 1980. 35.00x (ISBN 3-87193-055-5). Intl Pubns Serv.

Rothmans Book of Sporting Records 1979. Graham Edge & Keith Walmsley. 1979. 17.95 o.s.i. (ISBN 0-8464-0801-5). Beekman Pubs.

Rothschild Buildings: Life in an East End Tenement Block 1887-1920. Jerry White. (History Workshop Ser.). 1980. 30.00 (ISBN 0-7100-0429-X); pap. 15.00 (ISBN 0-686-65998-8). Routledge & Kegan.

Rothschilds. Frederic Morton. 1977. pap. 1.75 o.p. (ISBN 0-449-23242-5, Crest). Fawcett.

Rotondo on Racing Pigeons. Ed. by Joe Rotondo. (Illus.). 330p. 1981. 35.00. North Am Fal Hunt.

Rottenteeth. Jan Needle. (Illus.). (gr. k-3). 1980. 8.95 (ISBN 0-233-97205-6). Andre Deutsch.

Rotterdam in Drawings: Rotterdam Getekend. P. Ratsma. (Illus.). 1979. 35.00x (ISBN 90-247-2261-6). Heinman.

Rouault. Waldemar George & Genevieve Nouaille-Rouault. (Artists Ser.). (Illus.). 1976. pap. 5.95 (ISBN 0-8120-0713-1). Barron.

Roue. Harlan Wade. Tr. by Claude Potvin & Rose-Ella Potvin. (Book About Ser.). Orig. Title: Wheel. (Illus., Fr.). (gr. k-3). 1979. PLB 7.30 (ISBN 0-8172-1457-7). Raintree Pubs.

Rouge et le noir de Stendhal: Le Roman possible. new ed. G. Mouillaud. (Collection themes et textes). 240p. (Orig., Fr.). 1973. pap. 6.75 (ISBN 2-03-035014-1, 2658). Larousse.

Rough & the Righteous. Ardis Walker. (Illus.). 1971. 14.00 (ISBN 0-685-59752-0). Acoma Bks.

Rough Country. Lee Floren. 1976. pap. 0.95 o.p. (ISBN 0-685-69149-7, LB362NK, Leisure Bks). Nordon Pubns.

Rough Justice. Ernest Haycox. 177p. 1975. Repr. of 1950 ed. lib. bdg. 9.95 o.p. (ISBN 0-89190-978-8). Am Repr-Rivercity Pr.

Rough Justice. LC 79-50482. (Mary Elizabeth Braddon Ser.: Vol. 12). 1980. Repr. of 1898 ed. lib. bdg. 38.00 (ISBN 0-8240-4361-8). Garland Pub.

Rough Rapids Ahead. Aleda Renken. LC 74-38. (Haley Adventure Bks.). (Illus.). 96p. (gr. 3-7). 1974. pap. 2.50 (ISBN 0-570-03605-4, 39-1027). Concordia.

Rough Road. Margaret M. MacPherson. LC 65-21701. (Illus.). (gr. 7-9). 1966. 4.75 o.p. (ISBN 0-15-269147-2, HJ). HarBraceJ.

Rough Shooting. 3rd ed. Roderick Willett & Gurney A. Grattan. (Illus.). 1975. 15.95 o.p. (ISBN 0-571-04850-1, Pub. by Faber & Faber). Merrimack Bk Serv.

Rough Strife. Lynne S. Schwartz. LC 80-85111. 240p. 1981. pap. 2.75 (ISBN 0-87216-846-8). Playboy Pbks.

Rough Times. Ed. by Jerome Agel. (Orig.). 1973. pap. 1.65 o.p. (ISBN 0-345-23059-0). Ballantine.

Rough Weather. Iris Bromige. (Aston Hall Romances Ser.). 192p. (Orig.). 1981. pap. 1.75 (ISBN 0-523-41133-2). Pinnacle Bks.

Roughing It Easy. Dian Thomas. (Illus.). 248p. 1976. pap. 2.75 (ISBN 0-446-95662-7). Warner Bks.

Roughing It Easy, Two. Dian Thomas. (Illus.). 224p. (Orig.). 1978. pap. 2.75 (ISBN 0-446-95843-3). Warner Bks.

Roulette by the Dozens. Allan Ackerman. (System Check Ser.). 1978. pap. 2.95 (ISBN 0-89650-885-4). Gamblers.

Roulette by the Numbers. Huey Mahl. (System Check Ser.). 1978. pap. 2.95 (ISBN 0-89650-888-9). Gamblers.

Roulette Rouge et Noir. Allan Ackerman. (System Check Ser.). 1978. pap. 2.95 (ISBN 0-89650-894-3). Gamblers.

Round About a Pound a Week: London, Ninetee Thirteen. M. S. Pember-Reeves. LC 79-56968. (English Working Class Ser.). 1980. lib. bdg. 25.00 (ISBN 0-8240-0119-2). Garland Pub.

Round About the City: Stories You Can Read to Yourself. Child Study Association Of America. LC 66-10055. (Illus.). (gr. k-5). 1966. 7.95 (ISBN 0-690-71317-7, TYC-J); PLB 7.89 (ISBN 0-690-71318-5). T Y Crowell.

Round Garden: Plans for a Small Intensive Vegetable Garden for Year Round Production in the Tropics. Franklin W. Martin & Ruth Ruberte. (Studies in Tropical Agriculture). 1980. lib. bdg. 59.95 (ISBN 0-8490-3073-0). Gordon Pr.

Round River: From the Journals of Aldo Leopold. Ed. by Luna B. Leopold. (Illus.). 188p. 1972. pap. 3.95 (ISBN 0-19-501563-0, 372, GB). Oxford U Pr.

Round Sultan & the Straight Answer. Barbara K. Walker. LC 71-117559. (Illus.). (gr. k-3). 1970. 5.95 o.s.i. (ISBN 0-8193-0400-X, Four Winds). Schol Bk Serv.

Round the Clock. James Lees-Milne. 1978. 7.95 o.p. (ISBN 0-684-15882-5, ScribT). Scribner.

Round the Italian Coast. Philip Bristow. 256p. 1980. 15.00x (ISBN 0-245-52648-X, Pub. by Nautical England). State Mutual Bk.

Round Trip Space Ship. Louis Slobodkin. LC 68-11007. (gr. 3-7). 1968. 4.95g o.s.i. (ISBN 0-686-66486-8). Macmillan.

Rounders. Max Evans. (Western Fiction Ser.). 1980. lib. bdg. 10.95 (ISBN 0-8398-2686-9). Gregg.

Rounding Third: Professional Baseball in Washington. Brian Price et al. (Commentaries on the National Pastime Ser.). (Illus., Orig.). 1979. pap. 1.25 o.s.i. (ISBN 0-89133-083-6). Preservation Pr.

Rounds About Rounds. Compiled by Jane Yolen. (Illus.). (gr. 4-6). 1977. PLB 9.90 (ISBN 0-531-00125-3). Watts.

Roundtable Justice: Case Studies in Conflict Resolution. Ed. by Robert B. Goldmann. (Westview Special Studies in Peace, Conflict, & Conflict Resolution). 231p. 1980. lib. bdg. 24.50x (ISBN 0-89158-962-7); pap. text ed. 9.00x (ISBN 0-86531-139-0). Westview.

Roundup: A Nebraska Reader. Ed. by Virginia Faulkner. LC 57-8597. (Illus.). 1975. pap. 4.95 (ISBN 0-8032-5807-0, BB 593, Bison). U of Nebr Pr.

Rous Roll. John Rous. (Illus.). 144p. 1980. text ed. 31.50x (ISBN 0-904387-43-7). Humanities.

Rouse the Demon. Carolyn Weston. 1976. 6.95 o.p. (ISBN 0-394-40703-2). Random.

Rousseau. (Artists Ser.). (Illus.). 1977. pap. 5.95 (ISBN 0-8120-0715-8). Barron.

Rousseau & Representation. Richard Fralin. LC 78-15903. 1979. 17.50x (ISBN 0-231-04474-7). Columbia U Pr.

Rousseau & the French Revolution 1762-91. Joan McDonald. (Univ. of London Historical Studies: No. 17). 1965. text ed. 20.75x (ISBN 0-485-13117-X, Athlone Pr). Humanities.

Rousseau in England: The Context for Shelley's Critique of the Enlightenment. Edward Duffy. 1979. 14.00x (ISBN 0-520-03695-6). U of Cal Pr.

Rousseau on the Education of Women. Helen E. Misenheimer. LC 80-5857. 109p. 1981. lib. bdg. 15.75 (ISBN 0-8191-1404-9); pap. text ed. 7.50 (ISBN 0-8191-1405-7). U Pr of Amer.

Rousseau: Solitude et Communaute. Bronislaw Baczko. Tr. by Claire Brendhel-Lamhout. (Civilisation et Societes: No. 30). 1974. pap. 35.90x (ISBN 90-2797-505-1). Mouton.

Rousseau's Emile. William H. Payne. 363p. 1980. Repr. of 1911 ed. lib. bdg. 35.00 (ISBN 0-89987-659-5). Darby Bks.

Rousseau's Political Philosophy: An Exposition & Interpretation. Ramon M. Lemos. LC 74-18584. 344p. 1977. 18.00x (ISBN 0-8203-0388-7). U of Ga Pr.

Route Across the Rocky Mountains. Overton Johnson. Ed. by William H. Winter. LC 77-87648. (American Scene Ser). (Illus.). 200p. 1972. Repr. of 1932 ed. lib. bdg. 25.00 (ISBN 0-306-71780-8). Da Capo.

Route of the Warbonnets. Joe McMillan. LC 77-81470. (Illus.). 1977. 22.95 (ISBN 0-934228-01-9). McMillan Pubns.

Route One. Agnes Sanford. LC 74-25139. 1976. pap. 3.95 o.p. (ISBN 0-88270-155-X). Logos.

Routes & Rocks in the Mt. Challenger Quadrangle. R. W. Tabor & D. F. Crowder. LC 68-9291. (Illus.). 47p. (Orig.). pap. 2.95 o.p. (ISBN 0-916890-14-7). Mountaineers.

Routes from the Onion's Dark. 2nd ed. John Judson. (Orig.). 1978. pap. 3.00x (ISBN 0-685-69451-8); ltd. signed ed. 7.50x (ISBN 0-685-69452-6). Pentagram.

Rover. Aphra Behn. Ed. by Frederick M. Link. LC 66-20828. (Regents Restoration Drama Ser). 1967. 8.95x (ISBN 0-8032-0350-0); pap. 3.95x (ISBN 0-8032-5350-8, BB 260, Bison). U of Nebr Pr.

Rowan County: A Brief History. James S. Brawley. (Illus.). 1977. pap. 2.00 (ISBN 0-86526-129-6). NC Archives.

Rowan County, N. C., Abstrcts of Deeds: Vol. 2, 1763 to 1774. 197p. 1972. softcover 17.50 (ISBN 0-918470-07-2). J W Linn.

Rowena Country. A. E. Skinner. 11.95 (ISBN 0-685-48806-3). Nortex Pr.

Rowing. Boy Scouts Of America. LC 19-600. (Illus.). 44p. (gr. 6-12). 1964. pap. 0.70x (ISBN 0-8395-3392-6, 3392). BSA.

Rowing Toward Eden. Ted Morgan. 256p. 1981. 10.95 (ISBN 0-395-29714-1). HM.

Rowland Hilder: Artist & Illustrator. John Lewis. (Illus.). 1979. 29.95 o.p. (ISBN 0-214-20425-1, 8059, Dist. by Arco). Barrie & Jenkins.

Roxy's Ski Guide to New England. Roxy Rothafel. LC 78-61682. (Illus.). 192p. 1978. lib. bdg. 9.25 o.p. (ISBN 0-914788-08-6). East Woods.

Roy Acuff: The Smoky Mountain Boy. Elizabeth Schlappi. Ed. by James Calhoun. LC 77-11649. (Illus.). 1978. 13.95 (ISBN 0-88289-144-8). Pelican.

Roy Campbell. John Povey. (World Authors Ser.: No. 439). 1977. lib. bdg. 12.50 (ISBN 0-8057-6277-9). Twayne.

Roy Campbell: A Descriptive & Annotated Bibliography. D. S. Parsons. LC 79-7930. (Illus.). 250p. 1980. 20.00cancelled o.p. (ISBN 0-8240-9526-X). Garland Pub.

Roy Fuller. Allan E. Austin. (English Authors Ser.: No. 253). 1979. lib. bdg. 12.95 (ISBN 0-8057-6743-6). Twayne.

Roy Lichtenstein Ceramic Sculpture. Constance W. Glenn. (Illus.). 64p. (Orig.). 1977. pap. 8.00 (ISBN 0-936270-05-5). Art Mus Gall.

Roy Lichtenstein Drawings & Prints. Illus. by Roy Lichtenstein. LC 73-90344. (Illus.). 276p. 1981. pap. 19.95 (ISBN 0-87754-203-1). Chelsea Hse.

Roy Lichtenstein: 1970-1980. Jack Cowart. LC 80-28348. (Illus.). 192p. 1981. 35.00 (ISBN 0-933920-14-8); pap. 16.00 (ISBN 0-933920-15-6). Hudson Hills.

Roy Wood Sellars. W. Preston Warren. LC 74-30132. (World Leaders Ser: No. 45). 1975. lib. bdg. 9.95 (ISBN 0-8057-3719-7). Twayne.

Royal & Ancient. F. Ward-Thomas. (Illus.). 200p. 1980. 14.95x (ISBN 0-7073-0260-9, Pub. by Scottish Academic Pr Scotland). Columbia U Pr.

Royal Ballet: The First Fifty Years. Alexander Bland. LC 80-2403. (Illus.). 288p. 1981. 35.00 (ISBN 0-385-17043-2). Doubleday.

Royal Book of Ballet. Shirley Goulden. LC 64-16319. (Illus.). (gr. 5 up). 1964. 7.95 (ISBN 0-695-90040-4). Follett.

Royal Britain. Automobile Association - British Tourist Authority. (Illus.). 1979. pap. 9.95 (ISBN 0-09-128200-4, Pub. by B T a). Merrimack Bk Serv.

Royal Canadian Academy, Eighteen Hundred to Nineteen Thirteen. Charles C. Hill. (Illus.). 225p. 1980. write for info. (ISBN 0-88884-429-8, 56496-7, Pub. by Natl Mus Canada). U of Chicago Pr.

Royal Canadian Academy of Arts: Exhibitions & Members, 1880-1979. Ed. by Evelyn McMann. 356p. 1981. 60.00x (ISBN 0-8020-2366-5). U of Toronto Pr.

Royal Captives: A Fragment of Secret History, 4 vols. Ann Yearsley. Ed. by Gina Luria. (Feminist Controversy in England, 1788-1810 Ser.). 1974. Set. lib. bdg. write for info. (ISBN 0-8240-0892-8); lib. bdg. 50.00 ea. Garland Pub.

Royal Cemeteries of Kush, 5 vols. Dows Dunham. Incl. Vol. 1. Kurru. 1950. 25.00 (ISBN 0-685-72186-8); Vol. 2. Nuri. 1955. 35.00 (ISBN 0-87846-040-3); Vol. 3. Decorated Chapels of the Meroitic Pyramids at Meroe & Barkal. Suzanne E. Chapman. 1952. 30.00 (ISBN 0-87846-041-1); Vol. 4. Royal Tombs at Meroe & Barkal. 1957. 35.00 (ISBN 0-87846-043-8); Vol. 5. West & South Cemeteries of Meroe. 1963. 35.00 (ISBN 0-87846-043-8). (Illus.). Mus Fine Arts Boston.

Royal Champion: The Story of Steeplechasing's First Lady. Bill Curling. (Illus.). 272p. 1981. 29.95 (ISBN 0-7181-1930-4). Merrimack Bk Serv.

Royal Charles. Antonia Fraser. 1980. pap. 8.95 (ISBN 0-440-56960-5, Delta). Dell.

Royal Confinements. Jack Dewhurst. 198p. 1981. 12.95 (ISBN 0-312-69466-0). St Martin.

Royal Dirk. John Beatty & Patricia Beatty. (gr. 7 up). 1966. 8.75 o.p. (ISBN 0-688-21431-2). Morrow.

Royal Forests of Medieval England. Charles R. Young. LC 78-65109. (Middle Ages Ser.). (Illus.). 1979. 15.00x (ISBN 0-8122-7760-0). U of Pa Pr.

Royal Government in Colonial Brazil: With Special Reference to the Administration of the Marquis of Lavradio, Viceroy, 1769-1779. Dauril Alden. (Illus.). 1968. 32.50x (ISBN 0-520-00008-0). U of Cal Pr.

Royal House of Windsor. Elizabeth Longford. 1974. 15.00 o.p. (ISBN 0-394-47906-8). Knopf.

Royal Journey to London. Emily V. Warinner. LC 75-28654. 1975. pap. 2.95 (ISBN 0-914916-11-4). Topgallant.

Royal Navy & the Siege of Bilbao. Sir James Cable. LC 78-73238. (Illus.). 1980. 21.50 (ISBN 0-521-22516-7). Cambridge U Pr.

Royal Opposition: The British Generals in the American Revolution. Clifford L. Alderman. LC 73-119122. (Illus.). (gr. 7-12). 1970. 7.95 (ISBN 0-02-700240-3, CCPr). Macmillan.

Royal Pavilion Brighton. Martyn Goff. (Folio Miniature Ser.). 1976. 4.95 (ISBN 0-7181-1477-9, Pub. by Michael Joseph). Merrimack Bk Serv.

Royal Road. Stephan H. Hoeller. LC 75-4244. (Illus.). 119p. (Orig.). 1975. pap. 4.75 (ISBN 0-8356-0465-9, Quest). Theos Pub Hse.

Royal Road of the Inca! Victor W. Von Hagen. 1976. 29.95 o.p. (ISBN 0-86033-009-5). Gordon-Cremonesi.

Royal Road to Card Magic. Jean Hugard & Frederick Braue. 1949. 9.50 (ISBN 0-571-11399-0, Pub. by Faber & Faber). Merrimack Bk Serv.

Royal Scots & Patriots of the LMS. O. S. Nock. 1978. 14.95 (ISBN 0-7153-7480-X). David & Charles.

Royal Shakespeare Company, Nineteen Eighty. Royal Shakespeare Company. 124p. 1980. pap. text ed. 8.95x (ISBN 0-904844-33-1, Pub. by TQ & Royal Shakespeare England). Advent Bk.

Royal Victorians: King Edward VII His Family & Friends. Christopher Hibbert. LC 75-46507. (Illus.). 1976. 12.95 o.p. (ISBN 0-397-01111-3). Lippincott.

Royal Worcester Porcelain from 1862 to the Present Day. Henry Sandon. 1979. 29.95 o.p. (ISBN 0-214-20106-6, 8070, Dist. by Arco). Barrie & Jenkins.

Royall Tyler. Ada Carson & Herbert Carson. (United States Authors Ser.: No. 344). 1979. lib. bdg. 13.50 (ISBN 0-8057-7281-2). Twayne.

Royces Voyage Down Under: A Journey of the Mind. Frank M. Oppenheim. LC 79-4007. 136p. 1980. 11.50 (ISBN 0-8131-1394-6). U Pr of Ky.

Royo County. Robert Roper. 1979. pap. 1.95 o.p. (ISBN 0-449-23971-3, Crest). Fawcett.

RPG: Language & Techniques. M. Kushner & C. Zucker. LC 73-8644. 1974. pap. 20.95 (ISBN 0-471-51117-X). Wiley.

RPG-Two Programming. Edward Essick. 304p. 1981. pap. text ed. 14.95 (ISBN 0-574-21315-5, 13-4315); instr's. guide avail. (ISBN 0-574-21316-3, 13-4316). SRA.

RPG Two with Business Applications. Stanley Myers. (Illus.). 544p. 1980. text ed. 19.95 (ISBN 0-8359-6303-9). Reston.

RSV Handy Concordance. 192p. 1972. pap. 3.95 (ISBN 0-310-32391-6). Zondervan.

RSV Interlinear Greek, New Testament. Alfred Marshall. 17.95 (ISBN 0-310-20410-0). Zondervan.

RSVP Cycles. Lawrence Halprin. 1970. 15.00 o.s.i. (ISBN 0-8076-0557-3); pap. 6.95 o.s.i. (ISBN 0-8076-0628-6). Braziller.

RSVP for College English Power, Bk. 1. Norman Lewis. 1977. wkbk 6.92 (ISBN 0-87720-953-7). Amsco Sch.

RSVP for College English Power, Bk. 2. Norman Lewis. 1978. wkbk. 6.33 (ISBN 0-87720-959-6). AMSCO Sch.

RSVP for College English Power, Bk. 3. Norman Lewis. 1979. 6.33 (ISBN 0-87720-960-X). AMSCO Sch.

RSVP: The Houghton Mifflin Reading, Study, & Vocabulary Program. James F. Shepherd. LC 80-82698. (Illus.). 352p. 1981. pap. text ed. 8.50 (ISBN 0-395-29342-1); instr's manual avail. (ISBN 0-395-29343-X). HM.

RSVP: The Houghton Mifflin Reading, Study, & Vocabulary Program. James F. Shepherd. (Illus.). 352p. 1981. pap. text ed. 8.50 (ISBN 0-395-29342-1); write for info. instr's manual (ISBN 0-395-29343-X). HM.

RSVP with Etymology, Bk. I. Norman Lewis. (Orig.). (gr. 7-9). 1981. pap. text ed. price not set (ISBN 0-87720-395-4). AMSCO Sch.

Rub Book. James E. Seidelman & Grace Mintonye. (Illus.). (gr. k-3). 1968. 3.50g o.s.i. (ISBN 0-02-781590-0, CCPr). Macmillan.

Rub of Cultures in Modern Turkey: Literary View of Education. Frank A. Stone. (Uralic & Altaic Ser.: No. 123). 184p. 1973. pap. text ed. 42.50x (ISBN 0-686-27757-0). Mouton.

Rubaiyat. Omar Khayyam. Tr. by Edward Fitzgerald. LC 64-20696. 1964. 6.95 o.p. (ISBN 0-690-71388-6). T Y Crowell.

Rubaiyat of Omar Khayaam. Tr. by Edward Fitzgerald. (Illus.). 7.95 (ISBN 0-385-00146-0); pap. 2.50 (ISBN 0-385-09499-X). Doubleday.

Rubaiyat of Omar Khayyam. Omar Khayyam. Tr. by Edward Fitzgerald. (Illus.). 1930. pap. 2.50 (ISBN 0-385-09499-X, C28, Dolp). Doubleday.

Rubaiyat of Omar Khayyam. Omar Khayyam. Tr. by Edward Fitzgerald. (Illus.). pap. 2.00 (ISBN 0-8283-1452-7, 12, IPL). Branden.

Rubber Band. Rex Stout. 1979. pap. 1.75 o.s.i. (ISBN 0-515-04867-4). Jove Pubns.

Rubber Bands, Baseballs & Doughnuts: A Book About Topology. Robert Froman. LC 74-158690. (Young Math Ser). (Illus.). (gr. 1-4). 1972. 7.95 (ISBN 0-690-71353-3, TYC-J); PLB 7.89 (ISBN 0-690-71354-1). T Y Crowell.

Rubber Springs Design. E. F. Gobel. Ed. & tr. by A. M. Brichta. LC 74-9997. 211p. 1974. 39.95 (ISBN 0-470-30855-9). Halsted Pr.

Rubber, Tea & Cacao with Special Sections on Coffee, Spices & Tobacco. W. A. Maclaren. 1980. lib. bdg. 75.00 (ISBN 0-8490-3110-9). Gordon Pr.

Rube Goldberg: His Life & Work. Peter C. Marzio. LC 73-4108. (Illus.). 336p. 1973. 12.50 o.s.i. (ISBN 0-06-012830-5, HarpT). Har-Row.

Rube Goldberg Vs. the Machine Age. Reuben Goldberg. LC 68-31688. (Illus.). 1968. 12.95 (ISBN 0-8038-6305-5). Hastings.

Rubel on Karl Marx: Five Essays. Maximilien Rubel. Ed. by Joseph O'Malley & Keith Algozin. LC 80-21734. 272p. Date not set. price not set (ISBN 0-521-23839-0); pap. price not set (ISBN 0-521-28251-9). Cambridge U Pr.

Rubella: Proceedings. Ed. by Herman Friedman & James E. Prier. (American Lectures in Clinical Microbiology Ser). (Illus.). 164p. 1973. 14.75 (ISBN 0-398-02650-5). C C Thomas.

Rubens. Frans Baudouin. LC 77-82339. (Illus.). 1977. 60.00 o.p. (ISBN 0-8109-1586-3). Abrams.

Rubens. (Artists Ser.). (Illus.). 1977. pap. 5.95 (ISBN 0-8120-0714-X). Barron.

Rubens & the Counter Reformation: Studies in His Religious Paintings Between 1609 & 1620. Thomas L. Glen. LC 76-23621. (Outstanding Dissertations in the Fine Arts Ser.). 1977. lib. bdg. 56.00x (ISBN 0-685-38855-7). Garland Pub.

Rubens: Drawings & Sketches. John Rowlands. (Illus.). 1978. 17.50 o.p. (ISBN 0-684-15649-0, ScribT). Scribner.

Rubik's Cube. David Singmaster. 64p. 1981. pap. 5.95 (ISBN 0-89490-043-9). Enslow Pubs.

Ruby! Amy Aitken. LC 78-21283. (Illus.). (gr. k-2). 1979. 8.95 (ISBN 0-87888-144-1). Bradbury Pr.

Ruby Cover Up. Seth Kantor. 1980. pap. 2.95 (ISBN 0-89083-680-9, Kable News Co). Zebra.

Ruby Red. William P. Fox. LC 75-146686. 1971. 6.95 o.s.i. (ISBN 0-397-00710-8). Lippincott.

Ruby Sweetwater & the Ringo Kid. Sheldon Bart. LC 80-14683. 384p. 1980. 11.95 (ISBN 0-07-003872-4, GB). McGraw.

Ruby the Donkey: A Winter Story. 119p. Date not set. lib. bdg. 3.95 (ISBN 0-07-010321-6). McGraw.

Rudder. Agapius et al. Ed. by Orthodox Christian Educational Society & Apostolos Makrakis. Tr. by Denver Cummings from Hellenic. Orig. Title: Pedalion. 1097p. 1957. 15.00x (ISBN 0-938366-00-9). Orthodox Chr.

Rude & Barbarous Kingdom: Russia in the Accounts of Sixteenth-Century English Voyagers. Ed. by Lloyd E. Berry & Robert O. Crummey. LC 68-16059. (Illus.). 416p. 1972. 25.00 (ISBN 0-299-04760-1, 476); pap. 9.95x (ISBN 0-299-04764-4). U of Wis Pr.

Rudelstein Affair. Michael Marsh. LC 80-29323. 1981. 9.95 (ISBN 0-918056-02-0). Ariadne Pr.

Rudens. abr. ed. Plautus. Ed. by W. A. Sonnenschein. 1901. 12.95x (ISBN 0-19-872093-9). Oxford U Pr.

Ruderal Vegetation Along Some California Roadsides. Robert E. Frenkel. (California Library Reprint Ser.: No. 92). 1978. Repr. of 1970 ed. 13.75x (ISBN 0-520-03589-5). U of Cal Pr.

Rudiments of Militarie Dicipline. LC 70-25967. (English Experience Ser.: No. 105). 14p. 1969. Repr. of 1638 ed. 7.00 (ISBN 90-221-0105-3). Walter J Johnson.

Rudiments of Music. Robert W. Ottman & Frank D. Mainous. 1970. pap. text ed. 14.95 (ISBN 0-13-783662-7). P-H.

Rudiments of Music: A Detailed Study in Music Essentials. Jeannette Cass. (Illus., Orig.). 1956. pap. text ed. 14.95 (ISBN 0-13-783654-6). P-H.

Rudolf Bahro: Critical Responses. Ed. by Ulf Wolter. Tr. by Michel Vale from Ger., Fr., Ital. LC 80-5453. 1980. 22.50 (ISBN 0-87332-159-6). M E Sharpe.

Rudolf Bultmann. Ian Henderson. Ed. by D. E. Nineham & E. H. Robertson. LC 66-11071. (Makers of Contemporary Theology Ser). 1966. pap. 3.45 (ISBN 0-8042-0698-8). John Knox.

Rudolf Steiner: Herald of a New Epoch. Stewart C. Easton. LC 80-67026. (Illus.). 1980. pap. 9.95 (ISBN 0-910142-93-9). Anthroposophic.

Rudolph Diesel: Pioneer in the Age of Power. W. Robert Nitske & Charles M. Wilson. (Illus.). 318p. (Orig.). 1965. pap. 7.95 (ISBN 0-8061-1164-X). U of Okla Pr.

Rudolph Focke & the Theory of the Classified Catalog. Gordon Stevenson. (Occasional Papers: No. 145). 1980. pap. 3.00. U of Ill Lib Sci.

Rudolph the Red-Nosed Reindeer. (gr. 2-4). 1975. 1.95 (ISBN 0-307-10849-X, Golden Pr); PLB 7.62 (ISBN 0-307-60849-2). Western Pub.

Rudolph the Red-Nosed Reindeer & Rudolph Shines Again. Robert L. May. LC 64-21581. (Illus.). 1964. 5.95 o.p. (ISBN 0-695-87780-1). Follett.

Rudyard Kipling. Lord Birkenhead. 1978. 15.00 (ISBN 0-394-50315-5). Random.

Rudyard Kipling: Creative Adventurer. Seon Manley. LC 65-10230. (Illus.). (gr. 7 up). 7.95 (ISBN 0-8149-0360-6). Vanguard.

Rudyard Kipling's India. K. Bhaskara Rao. 1975. pap. 4.95x (ISBN 0-8061-1243-3). U of Okla Pr.

Rudyard Kipling's Verse. Rudyard Kipling. LC 40-29931. 1940. 12.95 (ISBN 0-385-04407-0). Doubleday.

Rue & Grace: Poems. Cathleen Quirk. 64p. 1981. 7.95 (ISBN 0-89594-054-X); pap. 3.95 (ISBN 0-89594-055-8). Crossing Pr.

Rueckfahrt. E. Y. Meyer. (Suhrkamp Taschenbuecher: 578). 448p. (Ger.). 1980. pap. text ed. 6.50 (ISBN 3-518-37078-2, Pub. by Insel Verlag Germany). Suhrkamp.

Rueda. Harlan Wade. Tr. by Mamie M. Contreras from Eng. LC 78-26747. (Book About Ser.). Orig. Title: Wheel. (Illus., Sp.). (gr. k-3). 1979. PLB 7.30 (ISBN 0-8172-1482-8). Raintree Pubs.

Ruelle-Araki Transfer Operator in Classical Statistical Mechanics. D. H. Mayer. (Lecture Notes in Physics: Vol. 123). 154p. 1980. pap. 12.00 (ISBN 0-387-09990-5). Springer-Verlag.

Ruffles & Drums. Betty Cavanna. LC 75-9630. (Illus.). (gr. 7-9). 1975. 7.75 (ISBN 0-688-22035-5); PLB 7.44 (ISBN 0-688-32035-X). Morrow.

Rufino Tamayo: Fifty Years of His Painting. Intro. by James B. Lynch, Jr. LC 78-10760. (Illus.). 90p. 1981. 15.00 (ISBN 0-295-95816-2, Pub. by Phillips); pap. 7.50 (ISBN 0-295-95822-7). U of Wash Pr.

Rufus Porter Rediscovered. Jean Lipman. (Illus.). 224p. 1980. 16.95 (ISBN 0-517-54115-7). Potter.

Rufus, Red Rufus. Patricia Beatty. LC 74-26981. (Illus.). 192p. (gr. 7 up). 1975. 8.25 (ISBN 0-688-22021-5); PLB 7.92 (ISBN 0-688-32021-X). Morrow.

Rug Before My Time: Memoirs of Pecker the Cat. Pecker The Cat. (Illus.). 32p. 1981. pap. 1.18 (ISBN 0-9604894-1-X). Borf Bks.

Rug Book: How to Make All Kinds of Rugs. Lillian M. Quirke. (Creative Handcrafts Ser.). (Illus.). 1980. 16.95 (ISBN 0-13-783704-6, Spec); pap. 8.95 (ISBN 0-13-783712-7). P-H.

Rug Hooking & Rag Tapestries. Ann Wiseman. 1981. pap. 7.95 (ISBN 0-442-20658-5). Van Nos Reinhold.

Rugby. F. N. Creek & Don Rutherford. (Teach Yourself Ser.). 1975. pap. 5.50 (ISBN 0-679-10374-0). McKay.

Rugby Sevens. Mike Williams. 1975. 8.95 o.p. (ISBN 0-571-10523-8, Pub. by Faber & Faber); pap. 5.50 (ISBN 0-571-10679-X). Merrimack Bk Serv.

Rugby Union. John Dawes. (Pelham Pictorial Sports Instruction Ser). (Illus.). 1977. 10.95 (ISBN 0-7207-0792-7). Transatlantic.

Rugged Heart. E. K. Vande Vere. LC 79-9291. (Horizon Ser.). 1979. pap. 4.50 (ISBN 0-8127-0241-7). Southern Pub.

Rugs & Wall Hangings. Maggie Lane. LC 76-10177. (Illus.). 160p. 1976. 14.95 o.p. (ISBN 0-684-14670-3, ScribT). Scribner.

Rugs As an Investment. Parviz Nemati. (Illus.). 212p. Date not set. 60.00 (ISBN 0-937266-01-9). Agate Pr.

Rugs to Riches: An Insider's Guide to Oriental Rugs. Caroline Bosly. (Illus.). 1980. 15.95 (ISBN 0-394-50039-3). Pantheon.

Rugweaving: Technique & Design. Brian Knight. (Illus.). 1981. 22.50 (ISBN 0-7134-2582-2, Pub. by Batsford England). David & Charles.

Ruined Cottage & the Pedlar. William Wordsworth. Ed. by James Butler. LC 78-58066. (Cornell Wordsworth Ser.). (Illus.). 1978. 38.00x (ISBN 0-8014-1153-X). Cornell U Pr.

Ruined Eden of the Present: Hawthorne, Melville, & Poe. Ed. by G. R. Thompson & Virgil L. Lokke. LC 80-80816. (Illus.). 320p. (Critical essays in honor of darrel abel). 1981. 15.75 (ISBN 0-911198-60-1). Purdue.

Ruins in a Landscape. Stuart Piggott. 1976. 12.00x (ISBN 0-85224-303-0, Pub. by Edinburgh U Pr Scotland); pap. 6.95 (ISBN 0-85224-311-1). Columbia U Pr.

Ruins of Altar De Sacrificios, Department of Peten, Guatemala: An Introduction. Gordon R. Willey & A. Ledyard Smith. LC 74-82521. (Peabody Museum Papers: Vol. 62, No. 1). 1969. pap. 10.00 (ISBN 0-87365-177-4). Peabody Harvard.

Ruins of Rome: A Guide to the Classical Antiquities. C. Wade Meade. LC 80-81128. (Illus.). 1980. 16.95 (ISBN 0-936638-00-1); pap. 10.95 (ISBN 0-936638-01-X). Palatine Pubns.

Ruins of the Morning. S. C. Saha. 8.00 (ISBN 0-89253-729-9); flexible cloth 4.00 (ISBN 0-89253-730-2). Ind-US Inc.

Ruins of Time: Four & a Half Centuries of Conquest & Discovery Among the Maya. David Adamson. (Illus.). 1975. 12.50 o.p. (ISBN 0-04-972008-2, 2262). Allen Unwin.

Ruka: (Roman O Palache) Yuz Aleshkovsky. 400p. (Rus.). 1980. pap. 16.50 (ISBN 0-89830-015-0). Russica Pubs.

Rule for a New Brother. H. Van Der Looy. 1976. pap. 1.95 (ISBN 0-87243-065-0). Templegate.

Rule of Law: Albert Venn Dicey, Victorian Jurist. Richard A. Cosgrove. LC 79-18027. (Studies in Legal History Ser.). 340p. 1980. 19.50x (ISBN 0-8078-1410-5). U of NC Pr.

Rule of Law in the United States: A Survey. 1962. pap. 3.75 o.p. (ISBN 0-89192-122-2, Pub. by Int'l Commission of Jurists). Interbk Inc.

Rule of Saint Benedict. Saint Benedict. Tr. by Cardinal Gasquet. LC 66-30730. (Medieval Library). Repr. of 1926 ed. 15.00x (ISBN 0-8154-0022-5). Cooper Sq.

Rule of St. Benedict. Tr. by Anthony C. Meisel & M. L. Del Mastro. LC 74-33611. 120p. 1975. pap. 2.45 (ISBN 0-385-00948-8, Im). Doubleday.

Rule of Saint Benedict RB 1980: In Latin and English with Notes. Ed. by Timothy Fry et al. 650p. 1981. 21.95 (ISBN 0-8146-1211-3); pap. 16.95 (ISBN 0-8146-1220-2). Liturgical Pr.

Rule of Taize. Roger Schutz. LC 74-10118. 1974. pap. 2.95 (ISBN 0-8164-2564-7). Crossroad NY.

Rule, Protest, Identity: Aspects of Modern South Asia. Ed. by Peter Robb & David Taylor. (Collected Papers on South Asia: No. 1). 1978. text ed. 11.75x (ISBN 0-391-00866-8). Humanities.

Ruled by the Spirit. Basilea Schlink. 1970. pap. 1.95 (ISBN 0-87123-483-1, 200483). Bethany Fell.

Ruler of the Nativity. Alexander Volguine. LC 74-90427. (French Astrology Ser.). 1973. 6.95 (ISBN 0-88231-076-3). ASI Pubs Inc.

Ruler's Imperative: Strategies for Political Survival in Asia & Africa. W. Howard Wriggins. LC 73-90431. (Southern Asian Institute Publications Ser.). 1969. 17.50x (ISBN 0-231-03314-1). Columbia U Pr.

Rulers of the City. Thomas Fleming. 1980. pap. 2.25 (ISBN 0-446-82612-X). Warner Bks.

Rules - Who Needs Them? Ethel Barrett. LC 73-90623. (Orig.). (gr. 4-8). 1974. pap. 1.95 (ISBN 0-8307-0282-2, 54-070-01). Regal.

Rules & Conflicts: An Introduction to Political Life & Its Study. A. Lee Brown. (Illus.). 384p. 1981. pap. text ed. 9.95 (ISBN 0-13-783738-0). P-H.

Rules & Lore of Baseball. Richard Marazzi. LC 79-3895. 224p. 1980. 12.95 (ISBN 0-8128-2715-5); pap. 7.95 (ISBN 0-8128-6058-6). Stein & Day.

Rules & Regulations for State and Local Law Enforcement Agencies. Robert C. Wadman & Don Svet. 108p. 1975. pap. 7.75 (ISBN 0-398-03366-8). C C Thomas.

Rules & Resolutions, Nineteen Eighty. Ed. by Paul A. Wellington. LC 74-84765. 1980. 7.50 (ISBN 0-8309-0136-1). Herald Hse.

Rules & the Game: Democratic National Convention Delegate Selection in Iowa & Wisconsin. Steven E. Schier. LC 79-5495. 1980. text ed. 24.00 (ISBN 0-8191-0891-X); pap. text ed. 15.00 (ISBN 0-8191-0892-8). U Pr of Amer.

Rules for Raising Kids. Robert I. Lesowitz. (Illus.). 200p. 1974. pap. 9.50 (ISBN 0-398-03146-0). C C Thomas.

Rules of Disorder. Peter Marsh et al. (Social Worlds of Childhood Ser.). (Illus.). 1978. 14.00x (ISBN 0-7100-8747-0). Routledge & Kegan.

Rules of Evidence. George T. Felkenes. LC 73-11824. 224p. 1974. pap. 9.20 (ISBN 0-8273-1425-6); instructor's guide 1.60 (ISBN 0-8273-0426-9). Delmar.

Rules of Law on Technical Data. 1971. 7.00 (ISBN 0-686-27831-3). M & A Products.

Rules of Marriage. Sheila Bishop. (Regency Romance Ser.). 1978. pap. 1.75 o.p. (ISBN 0-449-23819-9, Crest). Fawcett.

Rules of Printed English. Herbert Rels. 1980. 25.00x (ISBN 0-232-51038-5, Pub. by Darton-Longman-Todd England). State Mutual Bk.

Rules of Sociological Method. 8th ed. Emile Durkheim. 1950. 10.95 (ISBN 0-02-908490-3); pap. text ed. 5.95 (ISBN 0-02-908500-4). Free Pr.

Rules of the U. S. Bankruptcy Court for the Eastern District of Virginia. Ed. by Michie Staff. 156p. 1980. pap. text ed. 15.00 (ISBN 0-87215-328-2). Michie.

Rules of the U.S. Courts in New York. rev. ed. Ed. by A. Daniel Fusaro. LC 78-83771. 1978. with 1979 rev. pages 35.00 (ISBN 0-87632-070-1). Boardman.

Ruling Class. Gaetano Mosca. Ed. by Arthur Livingston. Tr. by Hannah D. Kahn from Italian. LC 80-17230. xli, 514p. 1980. Repr. of 1939 ed. lib. bdg. 37.50x (ISBN 0-313-22617-2, MORU). Greenwood.

Ruling Class in Italy Before 1900. Vilfredo Pareto. LC 73-20130. 143p. 1975. Repr. of 1950 ed. 14.00 (ISBN 0-86527-176-3). Fertig.

Ruling Illusions: Philosophy & the Social Order. Anthony Skillen. 1978. text ed. 22.25x (ISBN 0-391-00770-X); pap. text ed. 9.25x (ISBN 0-391-00775-0). Humanities.

Rum Pum Pum. Maggie Duff. LC 77-12389. (ps-3). 1978. 8.95 (ISBN 0-02-732950-X, 73295). Macmillan.

Rum, Religion, & Votes: Nineteen Twenty-Eight Re-Examined. Ruth C. Silva. LC 80-24997. ix, 76p. 1981. Repr. of 1962 ed. lib. bdg. 22.50x (ISBN 0-313-22768-3, SIRR). Greenwood.

Rum, Religion, & Votes: Nineteen Twenty-Eight Re-Examined. Ruth C. Silva. LC 80-24997. 85p. 1981. Repr. of 1962 ed. lib. bdg. 22.50 (ISBN 0-313-22768-3, SIRR). Greenwood.

Rum, Slaves & Molasses: The Story of New England's Triangular Trade. Clifford L. Alderman. LC 70-188772. (gr. 5-8). 1972. 4.95g o.s.i. (ISBN 0-02-700230-6, CCPr). Macmillan.

Rumanian-English Dictionary. Serban Andronescu. 15.00 (ISBN 0-685-20189-9); thumb indexed o.p. 11.50 (ISBN 0-685-20190-2). Saphrograph.

Rumanian-English, English-Rumanian Pocket Dictionary, 2 vols. 1978. Set. pap. 6.50 o.p. (ISBN 0-685-85951-7). Heinman.

Rumble Seat Pony. Clarence W. Anderson. LC 71-127466. (Illus.). (gr. k-3). 1971. 7.95 (ISBN 0-02-705490-X). Macmillan.

Rumer Godden. Hassell A. Simpson. (English Authors Ser.: No. 151). 1973. lib. bdg. 10.95 (ISBN 0-8057-1219-4). Twayne.

Rumi: Mystical Poems: Poems 201-400. Jalal Al-Din Rumi. Tr. by A. J. Arberry. (Bibliotheca Persica: Persian Heritage Ser.: No. 23). 1979. lib. bdg. 22.50x (ISBN 0-89158-477-3). Westview.

Rumi: Poet & Mystics 1207-1273. Ed. by Reynold A. Nicholson. (Ethical & Religious Classics of East & West Ser: No. 1). 1950. text ed. 8.75x o.p. (ISBN 0-04-891021-X). Humanities.

Ruminants: Cattle, Sheep & Goats, Guidelines for Breeding, Care & Management of Laboratory Animals. Institute of Laboratory Animal Resources. (Illus.). 76p. 1974. pap. 5.50 (ISBN 0-309-02149-9). Natl Acad Pr.

Rummy Kid Goes Home & Other Stories of the Southwest. Ross Santee. (Illus.). 1965. 6.95 (ISBN 0-8038-6306-3). Hastings.

Rumors of Peace. Ella Leffland. 1980. pap. 2.50 (ISBN 0-445-04587-6). Popular Lib.

Rumour of the Flesh & Soul. Modhusudan Sanyal. (Writers Workshop Redbird Ser.). 1975. 8.00 (ISBN 0-88253-620-6); pap. text ed. 4.00 (ISBN 0-88253-619-2). Ind-US Inc.

Rumours. Seamus Deane. 1977. pap. text ed. 6.25x (ISBN 0-85105-320-3, Dolmen Pr). Humanities.

Rump Parliament, 1648-1653. B. Worden. LC 73-77264. 500p. 1974. 41.95 (ISBN 0-521-20205-1); pap. 14.95 (ISBN 0-521-29213-1). Cambridge U Pr.

Rumpelstiltskin. Ed. & illus. by Jacqueline Ayer. LC 67-20165. (gr. k-3). 7.50 (ISBN 0-15-269525-7, HJ). HarBraceJ.

Rumpelstiltskin. Grimm Brothers. LC 74-2139. (Illus.). 48p. (gr. k-3). 1974. 3.95g o.s.i. (ISBN 0-590-07393-1, Four Winds). Schol Bk Serv.

Rumpelstiltskin. Ed McBain. (Matthew Hope Mystery Ser.). 1981. 12.95 (ISBN 0-670-61059-3). Viking Pr.

Rumpelstiltskin. Ed. by Matt H. Newman. (Children's Stories Bk). (Illus.). 18p. (ps). 1980. pap. 22.00 ten bks & one cass. (ISBN 0-89290-086-5, BC15-3). Soc for Visual.

Rumpelstiltskin. (Illus.). Arabic 2.50x (ISBN 0-685-82871-9). Intl Bk Ctr.

Rumptydoolers. Ester Wier. LC 64-16260. (Illus.). (gr. 4-7). 5.95 (ISBN 0-8149-0439-4). Vanguard.

Run-a-Day Logbook. Charles Holbrook & Linda Holbrook. Ed. by Vicki Groninger. (Illus.). 420p. (Orig.). 1980. pap. 8.95 (ISBN 0-9604998-0-6). DCT Ent.

Run Away Home. Paula Roberts. (Orig.). 1980. pap. 1.75 (ISBN 0-505-51484-2). Tower Bks.

Run Baby Run. Nicky Cruz & Jamie Buckingham. (gr. 9-12). 1969. pap. 2.25 (ISBN 0-515-05562-X). Jove Pubns.

Run Baby Run: The Story of a Gang-Lord Turned Crusader. Nicky Cruz. LC 68-23446. 240p. 1968. pap. 2.95 (ISBN 0-912106-58-1). Logos.

Run, Billy, Run. Matt Christopher. 156p. (gr. 3-6). 1980. 7.95 (ISBN 0-316-14020-1). Little.

Run, Come See Jerusalem. Richard C. Meredith. 256p. (Orig.). 1976. pap. 1.50 o.p. (ISBN 0-345-25066-4). Ballantine.

Run, Computer, Run: The Mythology of Educational Innovation. G. Oettinger. 1971. pap. 1.95 o.s.i. (ISBN 0-02-015040-7, Collier). Macmillan.

Run, Don't Walk. Harriet M. Savitz. 1980. pap. 1.50 (ISBN 0-451-09421-2, W9421, Sig). NAL.

Run, Ellen, Run. Elaine F. Wells. (YA) 1978. 5.95 (ISBN 0-685-37348-X, Avalon). Bouregy.

Run for Cover. John Welcome. 1972. pap. 0.95 o.p. (ISBN 0-06-087027-3, HW). Har-Row.

Run for the Elbertas. James Still. LC 80-51019. 160p. 1980. 12.50 (ISBN 0-8131-1414-4); pap. 5.50 (ISBN 0-8131-0151-4). U Pr of Ky.

Run for Your Life. Mollen, Art, Dr. LC 77-78517. 1978. pap. 4.95 (ISBN 0-385-13257-3, Dolp). Doubleday.

Run for Your Life. Kin Platt. LC 77-3172. (Triumph Bks.). (Illus.). (gr. 4up). 1977. PLB 6.90 (ISBN 0-531-01327-8). Watts.

Run from a Scarecrow. Irene B. Brown. (Midwestern Memories Ser.). (Illus.). (gr. 5-9). 1978. 5.95 (ISBN 0-570-07806-7, 39-1001); pap. 3.50 (ISBN 0-570-07801-6, 39-1011). Concordia.

Run from Danger. Jo Stewart. LC 80-26611. (Prime Time Adventures Ser.). (Illus.). 64p. (gr. 4 up). 1981. PLB 7.95 (ISBN 0-516-02109-5). Childrens.

Run Me a River. Janice H. Giles. 1976. pap. 1.75 (ISBN 0-380-00875-0, 31427). Avon.

Run River. Joan Didion. 1961. 9.95 (ISBN 0-8392-1094-9). Astor-Honor.

Run, Run Fast. George Sullivan. LC 78-22502. (Illus.). 64p. (gr. 4 up). 1980. 8.95 (ISBN 0-690-03969-7, TYC-J); PLB 8.79 (ISBN 0-690-03970-0). T Y Crowell.

Run Sara Run. Anne Worboys. 288p. 1981. 10.95 (ISBN 0-684-16818-9). Scribner.

Run the Cat Roads: A True Story of Bank Robbers in the Thirties. L. L. Edge. LC 80-25930. 1981. 12.50 (ISBN 0-934878-01-3). Dembner Bks.

Run-Through. John Houseman. 1981. pap. 6.95 (ISBN 0-671-41391-0, Touchstone Bks). S&S.

Run, Westy, Run. Gudrun Alcock. LC 66-14612. (Illus.). (gr. 4-7). 1966. PLB 7.44 o.p. (ISBN 0-688-51058-2). Lothrop.

Run with the Ring. Kathryn Vinson. LC 65-22747. (gr. 7 up). 1965. 5.50 o.p. (ISBN 0-15-269793-4, HJ). HarBraceJ.

Run Your Car on Sunshine: Using Solar Energy for a Solar Powered Car. James N. Blake. LC 80-82734. (Illus.). 64p. 1981. lib. bdg. 12.95 (ISBN 0-915216-64-7); pap. 4.95 (ISBN 0-915216-65-5). Love Street.

Run Your Life by the Stars? William J. Petersen. 1977. pap. 1.50 o.p. (ISBN 0-88207-506-3). Victor Bks.

Run Your Own Retail Store: From Raising the Money to Counting the Profits. Irving Burstinger. (Illus.). 304p. 1981. 19.95 (ISBN 0-13-784017-9, Spec); pap. 12.95 (ISBN 0-13-784009-8). P-H.

Run Your Own Store: From Raising the Money to Counting the Profits. Irving Burnstiner. (Illus.). 304p. 1981. 19.95 (ISBN 0-13-784017-9, Spectrum); pap. 12.95 (ISBN 0-13-784009-8). P-H.

Runaway. Ed. by Mary Verdick. (Pal Paperbacks Kit A Ser.). (Illus., Orig.). (gr. 7-12). 1976. pap. text ed. 1.25 (ISBN 0-8374-3486-6). Xerox Ed Pubns.

Runaway Bride. Jane A. Hodge. 1978. pap. 1.75 o.p. (ISBN 0-449-23591-2, Crest). Fawcett.

Runaway Church: Post-Conciliar Growth or Decline. Peter Hebblethwaite. 250p. 1976. 8.95 (ISBN 0-8164-0291-4). Crossroad NY.

Runaway Flying Horse. Paul J. Bonzon. LC 76-2525. (Illus.). 40p. (gr. k-4). 1976. 5.95 o.s.i. (ISBN 0-8193-0875-7, Four Winds); PLB 5.41 o.s.i. (ISBN 0-8193-0876-5). Schol Bk Serv.

Runaway Heart. Norma E. Koenig. (Orig.). (gr. 4-6). 1981. pap. 4.95 (ISBN 0-377-00112-0). Friend Pr.

Runaway Jonah & Other Tales. Jan Wahl. LC 68-12084. (ps-3). 1968. 3.95g o.s.i. (ISBN 0-02-792340-1). Macmillan.

Runaway Marie Louise. Natalie S. Carlson. LC 77-9448. (Illus.). 32p. (gr. k-3). 1977. 9.95 (ISBN 0-684-15045-X). Scribner.

Runaway Molly Midnight, the Artist's Cat. S. Nadja Maril. LC 80-17097. (Illus.). 40p. (gr. k up). 1980. 9.95 (ISBN 0-916144-62-3); pap. 5.95 (ISBN 0-916144-63-1). Stemmer Hse.

Runaway Ralph. Beverly Cleary. (Illus.). (gr. 3-7). 1970. 7.95 (ISBN 0-688-21701-X); PLB 7.63 (ISBN 0-688-31701-4). Morrow.

Runaway Ralph. Beverly Cleary. (gr. k-6). 1981. pap. 1.75 (ISBN 0-440-47519-8, YB). Dell.

Runaway Ralph. Beverly Cleary. (gr. 3-5). 1974. pap. 1.50 o.p. (ISBN 0-671-56017-4). Archway.

Runaway Universe. Paul Davies. LC 78-2128. (Illus.). 1978. 11.95 o.s.i. (ISBN 0-06-010971-8, HarpT). Har-Row.

Runaway Voyage. Betty Cavanna. (gr. 7-9). 1978. PLB 7.63 (ISBN 0-688-32152-6). Morrow.

Runaway World. Michael Green. LC 74-78819. (Orig.). 1969. pap. 2.25 o.p. (ISBN 0-87784-688-X). Inter-Varsity.

Runaways. Victor Canning. (gr. 4-7). 1976. pap. 1.50 (ISBN 0-590-10231-1, Schol Pap). Schol Bk Serv.

Runaways. John R. Townsend. Ed. by David Fickling. (Australian Bibliographies Ser.). 96p. (Orig.). 1979. pap. text ed. 2.24x (ISBN 0-19-424211-0). Oxford U Pr.

Runaway's Chance. Brenda Knight. 1973. 6.50 (ISBN 0-571-10208-5, Pub. by Faber & Faber). Merrimack Bk Serv.

Runaway's Diary. Marilyn Harris. (gr. 7-9). 1974. pap. 1.75 (ISBN 0-671-41304-X). Archway.

Runaways, Illegal Aliens in Their Own Land: Implications for Service. Dorothy Miller. LC 79-11682. (Praeger Special Studies Ser.). 224p. 1980. 22.95 (ISBN 0-03-051051-1). Praeger.

Rundown. James Magnuson. 1979. pap. 1.75 o.s.i. (ISBN 0-515-04725-2). Jove Pubns.

Rune. Karl Kempton. (Illus.). 100p. 1981. 50.00 (ISBN 0-686-69461-9). Porter.

Runes: An Introduction. Ralph W. V. Elliott. LC 80-26090. (Illus.). xvi, 124p. 1981. Repr. of 1959 ed. lib. bdg. 21.00x (ISBN 0-313-22870-1, ELRU). Greenwood.

Runic Records of the Norsemen in America. O. G. Landsverk. (Library of Scandinavian Literature). 1974. lib. bdg. 20.00x (ISBN 0-8057-5457-1). Irvington.

Runnaway's Diary. Marilyn Harris. (YA) (gr. 7-9). 1974. pap. 1.75 (ISBN 0-671-41304-X). PB.

Runner of the Mountain Tops: The Life of Louis Agassiz. Mabel L. Robinson. LC 73-167139. 1971. Repr. of 1939 ed. 18.00 (ISBN 0-8103-3806-8). Gale.

Runner Stumbles. Milan Stitt. 1979. pap. 2.25 (ISBN 0-380-44719-3, 44719, Bard). Avon.

Runner-up. Mike Neigoff. LC 75-1089. (Pilot Book Ser.). (Illus.). (gr. 4-8). 1975. 6.95g (ISBN 0-8075-7181-4). A Whitman.

Runners & Walkers. John Cumming. (Illus.). 196p. 1981. pap. 9.95 (ISBN 0-89526-889-2). Regnery-Gateway.

Runner's Book. Raymond Bridge. LC 78-18747. (Encore Editions). (Illus.). 1978. pap. 1.45 o.p. (ISBN 0-684-16698-4, ScribT). Scribner.

Runners: How the Champions Train, Race & Persevered--a Success Formula for All Runners. The Runner Magazine. (Orig.). 1979. pap. 2.75 (ISBN 0-515-05857-2). Jove Pubns.

Runner's Repair Manual. Murray Weisenfeld. 192p. 1981. pap. 4.95 (ISBN 0-312-69597-7). St Martin.

Runner's World Natural Foods Cookbook. Pamela Hannan. LC 80-23973. 88p. (Orig.). 1981. pap. 11.95 (ISBN 0-89037-208-X). Anderson World.

Running. Leonore Fleischer. (Orig.). 1979. pap. 2.25 (ISBN 0-515-05114-4). Jove Pubns.

Running a Home. Joan Storey. (Illus.). 1968. 5.95 (ISBN 0-571-08443-5, Pub. by Faber & Faber). Merrimack Bk Serv.

Running Against the Wind. Lewis C. Warden. 1981. 9.75 (ISBN 0-8158-0401-6). Chris Mass.

Running an Effective Sales Office. Patrick Forsyth. 160p. 1980. text ed. 37.25x (ISBN 0-566-02185-4, Pub. by Gower Pub Co England). Renouf.

Running & Maintenance of the Marine Diesel Engine. John Lamb. 722p. 1977. 57.95x (ISBN 0-85264-105-2, Pub. by Griffin England). State Mutual Bk.

Running Away. Charlotte V. Allen. (Orig.). 1977. pap. 1.75 o.p. (ISBN 0-451-07740-7, E7740, Sig). NAL.

Running Away from Home: A Guide to Running Trails in 32 Cities Across America. David Colker. (Orig.). 1979. pap. 2.50 (ISBN 0-515-05398-8). Jove Pubns.

Running Back. Steve Heidenreich & Dave Dorr. 1979. 11.95 (ISBN 0-8015-6494-8, Hawthorn). Dutton.

Running Backs. C. A. Morse. LC 74-23176. (Stars of the NFL Ser.). (gr. 4-12). 1975. PLB 7.95 (ISBN 0-87191-416-6). Creative Ed.

Running Blind. Desmond Bagley. LC 71-135711. 1971. 5.95 o.p. (ISBN 0-385-06551-5). Doubleday.

Running Conventions, Conferences & Meetings. Robert W. Lord. 400p. 1981. 21.95 (ISBN 0-8144-5643-X). Am Mgmt.

Running Fence Project: Christo. Werner Spies. LC 77-13109. (Illus.). 1978. pap. 9.95 o.p. (ISBN 0-8109-2080-8). Abrams.

Running Foot Doctor. Steven Subotnick. LC 77-73653. (Illus.). 144p. 1977. pap. 3.95 (ISBN 0-89037-117-2); handbk. 6.95 (ISBN 0-89037-116-4). Anderson World.

Running for the Exit. H. W. Wright. (Illus., Orig.). 1981. pap. 6.95 (ISBN 0-89407-035-5). Strawberry Hill.

Running Free. Richard Rodes. LC 74-7514. (Illus.). 64p. (Orig.). 1974. pap. 3.00 o.p. (ISBN 0-8170-0637-0). Judson.

Running Harder. Donald Honig. (Target Bks.). (Illus.). 48p. (gr. 3 up). 1976. PLB 6.45 (ISBN 0-531-01184-4). Watts.

Running Healthy: A Guide to Cardiovascular Fitness. Sidney Alexander. LC 80-12387. (Illus.). 1980. 12.95 (ISBN 0-8289-0387-5). Greene.

Running Home. Michael Spino. 1978. pap. 2.25 o.p. (ISBN 0-425-04005-4, Dist. by Putnam). Berkley Pub.

Running in Circles. Achim Broger. Tr. by Patricia Crampton from Germ. (gr. 7 up). 1977. 8.25 (ISBN 0-688-22119-X); PLB 7.92 (ISBN 0-688-32119-4). Morrow.

Running, Jumping, & Throwing - If You Can. Gary Paulsen. LC 77-27479. (Sports on the Light Side Ser.). (Illus.). (gr. 3-6). 1978. PLB 9.65 (ISBN 0-8172-1160-8). Raintree Pubs.

Running on Empty: New Poems. Robert Phillips. LC 80-2429. 72p. 1981. 8.95 (ISBN 0-385-17304-0); pap. 4.95 (ISBN 0-385-17305-9). Doubleday.

Running Out of Time. Elizabeth Levy. LC 79-28064. (Capers Ser.). (Illus.). 128p. (gr. 3-6). 1980. PLB 4.99 (ISBN 0-394-94422-4); pap. 1.95 (ISBN 0-394-84422-X). Knopf.

Running Rugby. Ray French. (Illus.). 80p. 1980. 13.95 (ISBN 0-571-11597-7, Pub. by Faber & Faber); pap. 5.95 (ISBN 0-571-11600-0, Pub. by Faber & Faber). Merrimack Bk Serv.

Running Scared. Thomas Dygard. LC 76-56862. (gr. 7 up). 1977. 7.25 (ISBN 0-688-22103-3); PLB 6.96 (ISBN 0-688-32103-8). Morrow.

Running Scared. Gregory McDonald. 1977. pap. 1.95 o.p. (ISBN 0-380-00924-2, 42481). Avon.

Running Shoe Book. Peter Cavanagh. LC 80-20365. (Illus.). 400p. 1980. pap. 11.95 (ISBN 0-89037-182-2). Anderson World.

Running the Twin Cities. Gretchen Kreuter. (Illus.). 95p. 1980. pap. 3.95 (ISBN 0-931714-08-7). Nodin Pr.

Running Through the Wall: A Guide for the Serious Runner. Raymond Bridge. (Illus.). 220p. 1980. pap. 7.95 (ISBN 0-8037-7609-8). Dial.

Running to Keep Fit. Brian Mitchell. 96p. 1980. pap. 2.95 o.p. (ISBN 0-679-12428-4). McKay.

Running Together: The Family Book of Jogging. Robert Hoffman & Jed Cantlay. LC 79-92135. (West Point Sports Fitness Ser.: Vol. 5). (Illus.). 1980. pap. text ed. 4.95 (ISBN 0-918438-18-7). Leisure Pr.

Running, Walking & Jumping: The Science of Locomotion. A. I. Dagg & A. James. LC 77-15301. (Wykeham Science Ser.: No. 42). 1977. 14.95x (ISBN 0-8448-1169-6). Crane-Russak Co.

Running Wild the Next Industrial Revolution. Adam Osborne. (Orig.). 1979. pap. 3.95 (ISBN 0-931988-28-4). Osborne-McGraw.

Runs Far, Son of the Chichimecs. Alice M. Wesche. (gr. 3-7). 1981. pap. 5.95 (ISBN 0-89013-133-3). Museum NM Pr.

Runt. Elizabeth Levy. (Orig.). (gr. k-6). 1981. pap. 1.95 (ISBN 0-440-47538-4, YB). Dell.

Runway to Death. Macartney Filgate. Orig. Title: Bravo Charley. 154p. 1980. 9.95 (ISBN 0-8027-5428-7). Walker & Co.

Ruodlieb. 2nd rev. facsim. ed. LC 67-6905. 1967. 100.00 o.p. (ISBN 0-916760-02-2). Medieval Latin.

Rupert Brooke: The Man & Poet. R. B. Pearsall. 174p. (Orig.). 1975. pap. text ed. 14.25x (ISBN 90-6203-437-3). Humanities.

Rupert of Hentzau (Sequel to Prisoner of Zenda) Anthony Hope. lib. bdg. 14.95x (ISBN 0-89966-227-7). Buccaneer Bks.

Rural Access Roads Programme: Apropriate Technology in Kenya. J. J. De Veen. Ed. by International Labour Office, Geneva. (Illus.). 175p. (Orig.). 1980. pap. 11.40 (ISBN 92-2-102204-8). Intl Labour Office.

Rural Africa. A. T. Grove & F. Klein. LC 77-82496. (Topics in Geography Ser.). (Illus.). 1979. 22.50 (ISBN 0-521-21825-X); pap. 6.95x (ISBN 0-521-29282-4). Cambridge U Pr.

Rural America. Ed. by Morrow Wilson & Suzanne Fremon. (Reference Shelf Ser.). 1976. 6.25 (ISBN 0-8242-0597-9). Wilson.

Rural & Appalachian Health. Ed. by Robert L. Nolan & Jerome L. Schwartz. 272p. 1973. 16.75 (ISBN 0-398-02605-X). C C Thomas.

Rural & Small Town Planning. Ed. by Judith Getzels et al. LC 79-93345. (Illus.). 326p. (Orig.). 1980. pap. 12.95 (ISBN 0-918286-19-0). Planners Pr.

Rural Architecture of Scotland. Alexander Fenton & Bruce Walker. (Illus.). 1980. text ed. 34.50x (ISBN 0-85976-020-0). Humanities.

Rural Asia: Challenge & Opportunity. Asian Development Bank. LC 77-25907. (Praeger Special Studies Ser.). 1978. 34.95 (ISBN 0-03-042601-4). Praeger.

Rural Banks for Rural Development. Charan D. Wadhva. 1980. 16.00x (ISBN 0-8364-0642-7, Pub. by Macmillan India). South Asia Bks.

Rural Biology. C. D. Bingham. 1965. pap. text ed. 5.50x o.p. (ISBN 0-435-59090-1). Heinemann Ed.

Rural Change & Public Policy: Eastern Europe, Latin America & Australia. Ed. by William P. Avery et al. (Pergamon Policy Studies). 1980. 39.00 (ISBN 0-08-023109-8). Pergamon.

Rural Communes in China - Organizational Problems. Gargi Dutt. (Indian School of International Studies Series). 1968. 5.25x o.p. (ISBN 0-210-22704-4). Asia.

Rural Communities: A Social Geography. G. J. Lewis. LC 78-74090. (Modern Geography Ser.). 1979. 28.00 (ISBN 0-7153-7768-X). David & Charles.

Rural Communities in Advanced Industrial Society: Development & Developers. Ted K. Bradshaw & Edward J. Blakely. LC 78-19736. 1979. 21.95 (ISBN 0-03-041626-4). Praeger.

Rural Communities: Inter-Cooperation & Development. Ed. by Yehuda H. Landau et al. LC 75-19779. (Special Studies). (Illus.). 175p. 1976. text ed. 22.95 (ISBN 0-275-55700-6). Praeger.

Rural Community Studies in Europe: Trends, Selected & Annotated Bibliographies, Analyses, Vol. I. Ed. by Jean-Louis Durand-Drouhin & Lili-Marie Szwengrub. LC 80-41523. (Publications of the Vienna Centre Ser.). (Illus.). 342p. 1981. 70.50 (ISBN 0-08-021384-7). Pergamon.

Rural Community: Webster City, Iowa. (gr. 2). 1974. pap. text ed. 5.40 (ISBN 0-205-03890-5, 8038902); tchrs. guide 12.00 (ISBN 0-205-03884-0, 8038848). Allyn.

Rural-Craftsmen & Their Work. E. Fischer & H. Shah. 20.00 (ISBN 0-88253-403-3). Ind-US Inc.

Rural Crime: Integrating Research & Prevention. Ed. by Timothy J. Carter et al. 1981. text ed. 25.00 (ISBN 0-86598-023-3). Allanheld.

Rural Deprivation & Planning. J. Martin Shaw. 207p. 1980. 14.75x (ISBN 0-86094-020-9, Pub. by GEO Abstracts England); pap. 12.01x (ISBN 0-86094-019-5, Pub. by GEO Abstracts England). State Mutual Bk.

Rural Development Administration: A Kenyan Experience. Walter O. Oyugi. 192p. 1981. text ed. 20.00x (ISBN 0-7069-1131-8, Pub. by Vikas India). Advent Bk.

Rural Development & the Changing Countries of the World, Bks. 1 & 2. Ed. by P. Manniche & J. F. Porter. LC 65-14224. 1970. 34.00 (ISBN 0-08-011155-6). Pergamon.

Rural Development & Urban Bound Migration in Mexico. Arthur Silvers & Pierre R. Crosson. LC 80-8024. (Resources for the Future Research Ser.: Paper R-17). (Illus.). 160p. (Orig.). 1980. pap. text ed. 6.95x (ISBN 0-8018-2493-1). Johns Hopkins.

Rural Development in Costa Rica. 112p. 1977. pap. 4.50 (ISBN 0-89192-194-X). Interbk Inc.

Rural Development in Pakistan. Ed. by Richard A. Stanford. LC 77-88663. (Illus.). 180p. 1980. pap. 7.95 (ISBN 0-686-60269-2). Carolina Acad Pr.

Rural Economy & Society in the Duchy of Cornwall, 1300-1500. John Hatcher. LC 74-105495. (Illus.). 1970. 44.50 (ISBN 0-521-07660-9). Cambridge U Pr.

Rural Education in Urbanized Nations: Issues & Innovations. Ed. by Jonathan P. Sher. (Special Studies in Education). 425p. 1981. lib. bdg. 27.50x (ISBN 0-89158-964-3). Westview.

Rural Electrification & Development: Social & Economic Impact in Costa Rica & Columbia. John Saunders et al. 1978. lib. bdg. 22.50x (ISBN 0-89158-274-6). Westview.

Rural Energy Systems in the Humid Tropics. 56p. 1980. pap. 8.50 (ISBN 92-808-0093-0, TUNU088, UNU). Unipub.

Rural England, Ten Eighty-Six to Eleven Thirty-Five: A Study of Social & Agrarian Conditions. Reginald V. Lennard. LC 80-2222. 1981. Repr. of 1959 ed. 49.50 (ISBN 0-404-18767-6). AMS Pr.

Rural Essays. Andrew J. Downing. Ed. by George W. Curtis. LC 69-13713. (Architecture & Decorative Art Ser). 640p. 1974. Repr. of 1854 ed. lib. bdg. 39.50 (ISBN 0-306-71035-8). Da Capo.

Rural Families on Relief. C. C. Zimmerman & N. L. Whetten. LC 70-165606. (FDR & the Era of the New Deal Ser.). 1971. Repr. of 1938 ed. lib. bdg. 17.50 (ISBN 0-306-70349-1). Da Capo.

Rural Geography. Hugh D. Clout. 1972. 18.00 (ISBN 0-08-017041-2); pap. 9.95 (ISBN 0-08-017042-0). Pergamon.

Rural Health Development in Tanzania: A Case-Study of Medical Sociology in a Developing Country. G. M. Van Etten. (Studies of Developing Countries: No. 18). (Illus.). 1976. pap. text ed. 17.00x (ISBN 90-232-1378-5). Humanities.

Rural Housing. Alwyn Jones. 76p. 1975. pap. text ed. 5.00x (ISBN 0-7135-1887-1, Pub. by Bedford England). Renouf.

Rural Human Services: A Book of Readings. Ed. by H. Wayne Johnson. LC 79-91102. 228p. 1980. pap. text ed. 7.95 (ISBN 0-87581-248-1). Peacock Pubs.

Rural Life in Canada. John MacDougall. LC 72-75735. (Social History of Canada Ser.). 216p. 1973. pap. 5.50 (ISBN 0-8020-6145-1). U of Toronto Pr.

Rural Life of England. William Howitt. 615p. Repr. of 1844 ed. 31.00x (ISBN 0-686-28330-9, Pub. by Irish Academic Pr). Biblio Dist.

Rural Migration in the United States. C. E. Lively & Conrad Taeuber. LC 71-165601. (FDR & the Era of the New Deal Ser.). 1971. Repr. of 1939 ed. pap. 19.50 (ISBN 0-306-70351-3). Da Capo.

Rural Route, No. 2. Richard E. McMullen. LC 79-15513. (Poems for People Ser.). (Orig.). 1979. pap. cancelled (ISBN 0-914908-32-4). Street Fiction.

Rural Self-Government in Metropolitan Calcutta. Mohit Bhattacharya. 1965. 4.50x o.p. (ISBN 0-210-22662-5). Asia.

Rural Settlement & Land Use: An Essay in Location. Michael Chisholm. 1966. text ed. 16.25x (ISBN 0-09-063001-7, Hutchinson U Lib). Humanities.

Rural Small-Scale Industry in the People's Republic of China. Ed. by Dwight Perkins. LC 76-20015. 1977. 20.00x (ISBN 0-520-03284-5). U of Cal Pr.

Rural Small-Scale Industry in the People's Republic of China. Ed. by Dwight Perkins. 1981. pap. 7.95 (ISBN 0-520-04401-0, CAL 499). U of Cal Pr.

Rural Society & Environment in America. Carlson & Lassey. (Agricultural Science Ser.). (Illus.). 448p. 1981. text ed. 15.95x (ISBN 0-07-009959-6, C). McGraw.

Rural Sociology of the Advanced Societies: Critical Perspectives. Ed. by Frederick H. Buttel & Howard Newby. LC 79-5177. 538p. 1980. text ed. 20.50 (ISBN 0-916672-30-1); pap. text ed. 9.50 (ISBN 0-916672-34-4). Allanheld.

Rural U.S.A. Persistence & Change. Ed. by Thomas R. Ford. (Illus.). 1978. text ed. 10.95 (ISBN 0-8138-1345-X). Iowa St U Pr.

Rural Women: Unequal Partners in Development, a WEP Study. Martha F. Loutfi. Ed. by Intl Labour Office. (Illus.). iii, 81p. 1980. pap. 7.15 (ISBN 92-2-102389-3). Intl Labour Office.

Rural World: Social Change in the English Counryside 1780-1850. Pamela Horn. 1981. 25.00 (ISBN 0-312-69606-X). St Martin.

Rural Youth: Education, Occupation & Social Outlook. P. M. Shingi et al. 1980. 10.00x (ISBN 0-8364-0663-X, Pub. by Abhinav India). South Asia Bks.

Rural Youth on Relief. Bruce L. Melvin. LC 78-165686. (FDR & the Era of the New Deal Ser). 1971. Repr. of 1937 ed. lib. bdg. 15.00 (ISBN 0-306-70343-2). Da Capo.

Rush. Ed. by Neil Fuller. (Australian Theatre Workshop Ser.). 1975. pap. text ed. 5.95x (ISBN 0-686-65418-8, 00537). Heinemann Ed.

Rush Hour of the Gods. H. Neill McFarland. 1967. 9.95 (ISBN 0-02-583200-X). Macmillan.

Rush to the Alps. Paul P. Bernard. (Eastern European Monographs: No. 37). 1978. 15.00x (ISBN 0-914710-30-3, Dist. by Columbia U Pr). East Eur Quarterly.

Rushes. John Rechy. LC 79-2302. 288p. 1981. pap. 3.50 (ISBN 0-394-17883-1, BC). Grove.

Rusi & Brassey's Defence Yearbook, 1977-78. Ed. by Royal United Services Institute for Defense Studies. LC 75-29923. 1978. lib. bdg. 37.50x (ISBN 0-89158-823-X). Westview.

Rusi & Brassey's Defence Yearbook: 1978/79. 89th ed. LC 75-641843. 1979. 27.50x (ISBN 0-8448-1366-4). Crane-Russak Co.

Rusi & Brassey's Defense Yearbook, 1975-76. 86th ed. 372p. 1976. 36.50x (ISBN 0-89158-524-9). Westview.

Rusi & Brassey's Defense Yearbook 1976-77, Vol. 87. Ed. by R. G. Bidwell. LC 76-29923. (Defense Publications Ser.). 1977. lib. bdg. 36.00x (ISBN 0-89158-630-X). Westview.

RUSI Brassey's Defence Yearbook: 1981. 91st ed. Ed. by Royal United Services Institute for Defence Studies. 376p. 1980. 45.00 (ISBN 0-08-027006-9). Pergamon.

Ruskin & Turner. Luke Herrmann. 1968. 17.95 o.p. (ISBN 0-571-08497-4, Pub. by Faber & Faber). Merrimack Bk Serv.

Ruskin College: A Challenge to Adult & Labor Education. Al Nash. 1981. pap. price not set (ISBN 0-87546-084-4). NY Sch Indus Rel.

Ruskin on Architecture: His Thought & Influence. Kristine O. Garrigan. LC 73-2045. 368p. 1973. 19.50x (ISBN 0-299-06460-3). U of Wis Pr.

Ruskins & the Grays. Mary Lutyens. LC 73-86125. (Illus.). 296p. Date not set. 10.00 (ISBN 0-8149-0737-7). Vanguard. Postponed.

Ruskins in Normandy: A Tour in 1848 with Murrays Handbook. J. G. Links. LC 78-134669. (Illus.). Date not set. 6.95 (ISBN 0-8149-0689-3). Vanguard. Postponed.

Rusky -- Poetry & Prose Vignettes. James H. Weidner. LC 80-68817. 104p. (Orig.). 1980. pap. 5.95 (ISBN 0-9701-7619-X). Foris Pubns.

Russell. Mark Sainsbury. (Arguments of the Philosophers Ser.). 1979. 36.00x (ISBN 0-7100-0155-X). Routledge & Kegan.

Russell Lee: Photographer. F. Jack Hurley. LC 78-61494. 1979. o.p. (ISBN 0-87100-151-9, 2151); pap. 15.95 (ISBN 0-87100-150-0, 2150). Morgan.

Russia. Robert G. Kaiser. (gr. 10 up). 1980. pap. 3.95 (ISBN 0-671-43285-0). PB.

Russia, 2 vols. Incl. Horizon History of Russia. Ian Grey. LC 76-117351. 404p; Vol. 2. Horizon Book of the Arts of Russia. Horizon Magazine Editors. LC 70-117352. 383p. (Illus.). 1970. Boxed Set. 45.00 (ISBN 0-8281-0102-7, Dist. by Scribner). Am Heritage.

Russia - U. S. S. R. Anthony Thompson. (World Bibliographical Ser.: No. 6). 287p. 1979. 34.75 (ISBN 0-903450-18-6). ABC-Clio.

Russia & Orthodoxy: Essays in Honor of Georges Florovsky. Vol. One: Georges Florovsky: Russian Intellectual & Orthodox Churchman. Ed. by Andrew Blane. (Slavistic Printings & Reprintings Ser.: No. 260-1). 1979. 65.80. Mouton.

Russia & Postwar Europe. David J. Dallin. 1943. 24.50x (ISBN 0-685-69808-4). Elliots Bks.

Russia & the Allies Nineteen Seventeen to Nineteen Twenty, Vol. I: The Allies & the Russian Collapse; March 1917-1918. Michael Kettle. (Illus.). 300p. 1981. 27.50x (ISBN 0-8166-0981-0). U of Minn Pr.

Russia & the Balkans: Inter-Balkan Rivalries & Russian Foreign Policy 1908-1914. Andrew Rossos. 320p. 1981. 35.00x (ISBN 0-8020-5516-8). U of Toronto Pr.

Russia & the Cholera, Eighteen Twenty-Three to Eighteen Thirty-Two. Roderick E. McGrew. (Illus.). 1965. 20.00 (ISBN 0-299-03710-X). U of Wis Pr.

Russia & the Communist Countries. J. A. Naik. 1980. text ed. 49.25x (ISBN 0-391-01792-6). Humanities.

Russia & the Outbreak of the Seven Years' War. Herbert H. Kaplan. 1968. 17.50x (ISBN 0-520-00623-2). U of Cal Pr.

Russia & the United States. Kolai V. Sivachev & Nikolai N. Yakovlev. Tr. by Olga A. Titelbaum. LC 78-10554. xvi, 303p. 1980. pap. 5.95 (ISBN 0-226-76150-9, P902, Phoen). U of Chicago Pr.

Russia & the West Under Lenin & Stalin. George F. Kennan. pap. 2.25 (ISBN 0-451-61861-0, ME1861, Ment). NAL.

Russia & the Western World. J. A. Naik. 227p. 1980. text ed. 25.00x (ISBN 0-391-01745-4). Humanities.

Russia Besieged. Nicholas Bethell. LC 77-77799. (World War II Ser.). (Illus.). (gr. 6 up). 1977. PLB 14.94 (ISBN 0-8094-2471-1, Pub. by Time-Life). Silver.

Russia Besieged. Nicholas Bethell. Ed. by Time-Life Books. (World War II Ser.). 1977. 12.95 (ISBN 0-8094-2470-3). Time-Life.

Russia: By a Recent Traveler. Charles H. Pearson. (Russia Through European Eyes Ser). 1971. Repr. of 1859 ed. lib. bdg. 39.50 (ISBN 0-306-77030-X). Da Capo.

Russia in Original Photographs: 1860-1920. Marvin Lyons. LC 77-73931. (Illus.). 1978. 20.00 o.p. (ISBN 0-684-15274-6, ScribT). Scribner.

Russia in Pictures. Sterling Publishing Company Editors. LC 66-25201. (Visual Geography Ser.). (Illus., Orig.). (gr. 6 up). 1966. PLB 4.99 (ISBN 0-8069-1073-9); pap. 2.95 (ISBN 0-8069-1072-0). Sterling.

Russia in Revolution. E. M. Halliday & Cyril E. Black. LC 67-26349. (Horizon Caravel Books). (Illus.). 153p. (gr. 6 up). 1967. 9.95 (ISBN 0-8281-0393-3, J032-0); PLB 12.89 (ISBN 0-06-020123-1, Dist. by Har-Row). Am Heritage.

Russia in Revolution. Peter Lee & Graham Bearman. 1974. pap. text ed. 6.95x (ISBN 0-435-31176-X). Heinemann Ed.

Russia in the Age of Catherine the Great. Isabel De Madariaga. LC 80-21993. (Illus.). 728p. 1981. 40.00x (ISBN 0-300-02515-7). Yale U Pr.

Russia in the Far East. Leo Pasvolsky. LC 79-2918. 181p. 1981. Repr. of 1922 ed. 17.50 (ISBN 0-8305-0087-1). Hyperion Conn.

Russia in the Reign of Aleksej Mixajlovic: Text & Commentary. Grigorij Kotosixin. Ed. by A. E. Pennington. (Illus.). 740p. 1980. 165.00x (ISBN 0-19-815639-1). Oxford U Pr.

Russia Nineteen Hundred Seventeen. George Katkov. (Illus.). 240p. 1980. text ed. 22.50 (ISBN 0-582-49101-0). Longman.

Russia of the Tsars & Poets. Sergius A. Wilde. LC 76-12944. 1976. pap. 4.95 o.p. (ISBN 0-8158-0342-7). Chris Mass.

Russia of War & Peace. Alan Palmer. LC 72-89539. (Illus.). 1973. 10.00 o.s.i. (ISBN 0-02-594600-5). Macmillan.

Russia on Canvas: Ilya Repin. Fan Parker & Stephen J. Parker. LC 79-20577. (Illus.). 196p. 1980. 27.50x (ISBN 0-271-00252-2). Pa St U Pr.

Russia: Regional Study. Hyman Kublin. (World Regional Studies). (Orig.). (gr. 7 up). 1970. pap. 6.60 (ISBN 0-395-17718-9, 2-31056). HM.

Russia: Selected Readings. Hyman Kublin. (World Regional Studies). (Orig.). (gr. 7 up). 1969. pap. 6.60 (ISBN 0-395-17715-4, 2-31062). HM.

Russia Since 1801: The Making of a New Society. Edward C. Thaden. LC 71-144333. (Illus.). 1971. text ed. 23.95x (ISBN 0-471-85510-3). Wiley.

Russia, the Soviet Union & Eastern Europe: A Survey of Holdings at the Hoover Institution on War, Revolution & Peace. Joseph D. Dwyer. LC 78-70888. (Survey Ser.: No. 6). 245p. 1980. 18.95 (ISBN 0-8179-5011-7). Hoover Inst Pr.

Russia Under Catherine the Great, 2 vols. Paul Dukes. 1978. 24.00 set (ISBN 0-89250-104-9); Vol. 1. 12.00 ea. (ISBN 0-89250-106-5). Vol. 2 (ISBN 0-89250-105-7). pap. 0.00 set o. p. (ISBN 0-89250-107-3). Orient Res Partners.

Russian. (Harper Phrase Books for the the Traveler Ser.). (Orig.). 1977. pap. 1.00 (ISBN 0-8467-0314-9, Pub. by Two Continents). Hippocrene Bks.

Russian - Chinese - English Glossary of Education. C. T. Hu & Beatrice Beach. LC 73-108419. 1970. text ed. 9.25x (ISBN 0-8077-1529-8). Tchrs Coll.

Russian: A Complete Elementary Course. Peter Rudy et al. 1970. 15.95x (ISBN 0-393-09871-0, NortonC); text & tape set o.p. 90.00 (ISBN 0-686-66509-0); tapes for duplication by school free (ISBN 0-393-99126-1). Norton.

Russian Adventure. Burton K. Janes. 1980. 5.95 (ISBN 0-533-04479-0). Vantage.

Russian Alphabet & Phonetics. Leon Stilman. LC 51-4951. (Columbia Slavic Studies). (gr. 9 up). 1951. pap. 6.00x (ISBN 0-231-09922-3). Columbia U Pr.

Russian-America, Statistical & Ethnographical Information. Ferdinand P. Wrangell. Ed. by Richard A. Pierce. Tr. by Mary Sadouski from Ger. (Materials for the Study of Alaska History: No. 15). (Illus.). 1980. 16.50 (ISBN 0-919642-79-9). Limestone Pr.

Russian American Social Mobility: An Analysis of the Achievement Syndrome. Barry V. Johnston. LC 80-65609. 145p. 1981. perfect bdg. 10.95 (ISBN 0-86548-041-9). Century Twenty One.

Russian Anarchists. Paul Avrich. LC 80-21590. (Studies of the Russian Institute, Columbia University). (Illus.). vii, 303p. 1980. Repr. of 1967 ed. lib. bdg. 28.50x (ISBN 0-313-22571-0, AVRA). Greenwood.

Russian Army in World War One. Ward Rutherford. 1975. 15.95 o.p. (ISBN 0-86033-002-8). Gordon-Cremonesi.

Russian Artist. Tobia Frankel. (Russia Old & New Ser.). (Illus.). 224p. 1972. 5.95 o.s.i. (ISBN 0-02-540650-7). Macmillan.

Russian Autocracy in Crisis, 1878-1882. Peter A. Zaionchkovsky. 1979. 26.50 (ISBN 0-87569-031-9). Academic Intl.

Russian Autocracy Under Alexander III. P. A. Zaionchkovsky. Ed. & tr. by David R. Jones. (Russian Series: Vol. 22). 1976. 21.50 (ISBN 0-87569-067-X). Academic Intl.

Russian Beauty & Other Stories. Vladimir Nabokov. Tr. by Dmitri Nabokov & Simon Karlinsky. LC 72-10094. 224p. 1974. pap. 4.95 (ISBN 0-07-045711-5, SP). McGraw.

Russian Communist Party & the Sovietization of Ukraine: A Study in the Communist Doctrine of the Self-Determination of Nations. Jurij Borys. LC 79-2895. 374p. 1981. Repr. of 1960 ed. 29.50 (ISBN 0-8305-0063-4). Hyperion Conn.

Russian Composers & Musicians: A Biographical Dictionary. Ed. by Alexandria Vodorsky-Shiraeff. LC 71-76422. (Music Ser.). 1969. Repr. of 1940 ed. lib. bdg. 19.50 (ISBN 0-306-71321-7). Da Capo.

Russian Cooking. Helen Papashvily & George Papashvily. (Foods of the World Ser). (Illus.). 1969. 14.95 (ISBN 0-8094-0043-X). Time-Life.

Russian Cooking. Helen Papashvily & George Papashvily. LC 78-103302. (Foods of the World Ser). (Illus.). (gr. 6 up). 1969. PLB 14.94 (ISBN 0-8094-0070-7, Pub. by Time-Life). Silver.

Russian Course. Alexander Lipson. Date not set. price not set (ISBN 0-89357-040-0). Slavica.

Russian Cultural Renaissance: A Critical Anthology of Russian Emigre Literature Before Nineteen Thirty Nine. Tamira Pachmuss. LC 80-20670. 416p. 1981. 29.50x (ISBN 0-87049-296-9); pap. 9.95x (ISBN 0-87049-306-X). U of Tenn Pr. Postponed.

Russian Dialogues. Alexander Blum. 1968. 15.00 (ISBN 0-08-012519-0); pap. 7.00 (ISBN 0-08-012518-2). Pergamon.

Russian Dictionary of... (a, e, i, ya) Tel' Words. Charles Parsons. (Orig.). 1980. pap. 5.00x o.p. (ISBN 0-917564-08-1). Translation Research.

Russian Economic History: A Guide to Information Sources. Ed. by Daniel R. Kazmer & Vera Kazmer. LC 73-17588. (Economics Information Guide Ser: Vol. 4). 550p. 1977. 30.00 (ISBN 0-8103-1304-9). Gale.

Russian Empire: A Portrait in Photographs. Chloe Obolensky & Max Hayward. LC 78-21800. 1979. 20.00 (ISBN 0-394-41029-7). Random.

Russian Empire & Soviet Union: A Guide to Manuscripts & Archival Materials in the United States. John H. Brown & Steven A. Grant. (Supplement). 1981. lib. bdg. 75.00 (ISBN 0-8161-1300-9). G K Hall.

Russian Empire: Its People, Institutions & Resources, 2 vols. Baron Von Haxthausen. (Russia Through European Eyes Ser.). 1968. Repr. of 1856 ed. Set. lib. bdg. 85.00 (ISBN 0-306-77024-5). Da Capo.

Russian Empire, 1801-1917. Hugh Seton-Watson. (Oxford History of Modern Europe Ser). 1967. 45.00x (ISBN 0-19-822103-7). Oxford U Pr.

Russian-English - English-Russian Glossary of Statistical Terms. new ed. Sanuel Kotz. 1973. 13.75 o.s.i. (ISBN 0-02-848030-9, 84803). Hafner.

Russian-English Chemical & Polytechnical Dictionary. 3rd ed. Ludmilla I. Callaham. LC 75-5982. 852p. 1975. 51.95 (ISBN 0-471-12998-4, Pub. by Wiley-Interscience). Wiley.

Russian-English Dictionary. rev. ed. Ed. by A. I. Smirnitsky. 1973. 19.95 o.p. (ISBN 0-525-19520-3). Dutton.

Russian-English Dictionary of...(a,e,i,ya) tel' Words. Charles Parsons. (Orig.). 1980. pap. 5.00x (ISBN 0-917564-08-1). Translation Research.

Russian-English Dictionary of Modern Terms in Aeronautics & Rocketry. M. M. Konarski. 1962. 82.00 (ISBN 0-08-009658-1). Pergamon.

Russian-English Dictionary of Surnames: Important Names from Science & Technology. James F. Shipp. xvi, 317p. (Orig.). 1981. pap. 30.00x (ISBN 0-917564-10-3). Translation Research.

Russian-English Dictionary of the Mathematical Sciences. A. J. Lohwater. LC 61-15685. 267p. (Eng. & Rus.). 1979. Repr. of 1974 ed. 7.60 (ISBN 0-8218-0036-1, RED). Am Math.

Russian-English Dictionary of...OCTB Words. Parsons. 1978. 10.00 o.p. (ISBN 0-686-64130-2). Translation Research.

Russian-English, English-Russian Dictionary. S. G. Zaimovsky. pap. 6.00 (ISBN 0-685-20192-9, 069-0). Saphrograph.

Russian-English Index to Scientific Apparatus Nomenclature. James F. Shipp. (Orig.). 1977. pap. 10.00x o.p. (ISBN 0-917564-03-0). Translation Research.

Russian-English Mathematical Dictionary. L. M. Milne-Thomson. (Mathematical Research Center Pubns., No. 7). 1962. 40.00x (ISBN 0-299-02600-0). U of Wis Pr.

Russian-English Polytechnical Dictionary. Ed. by B. Kuznetsov. LC 80-41193. 900p. 1981. 100.00 (ISBN 0-08-023609-X). Pergamon.

Russian-English Scientific & Technical Dictionary, 2 vols. M. H. Alford & V. L. Alford. LC 73-88348. 1970. Set. 87.00 (ISBN 0-08-012227-2). Pergamon.

Russian-English Vocabulary with Grammatical Sketch. Ed. by Gabrielle Rainich & A. H. Kuipers. 66p. 1980. Repr. of 1972 ed. with corrections 5.20 (ISBN 0-8218-0037-X, REV). Am Math.

Russian Facists: Tragedy & Farce in Exile, 1925-1945. John J. Stephan. LC 77-11804. (Illus.). 1978. 15.00 o.s.i. (ISBN 0-06-014099-2, HarpT). Har-Row.

Russian Fairy Tales. Aleksandr Afanas'Ev. LC 44-37884. (gr. 6 up). 1976. pap. 6.95 (ISBN 0-394-73090-9). Pantheon.

Russian Farewell. Leonard E. Fisher. LC 80-342. (Illus.). 144p. (gr. 5 up). 1980. 9.95 (ISBN 0-590-07525-X, Four Winds). Schol Bk Serv.

Russian Folk Tales: Illustrated by Ivan Bilibin. Compiled By Alexander Afanasyev. Tr. by Robert Chandler from Russian. LC 80-50746. (Illus.). 80p. 1980. 14.95 (ISBN 0-394-51353-3). Shambhala Pubns.

Russian Folk-Tales with Introduction & Notes. Leonard A. Magnus. LC 74-6486. 1974. Repr. of 1916 ed. 20.00 (ISBN 0-8103-3654-5). Gale.

Russian Folklore. Yury M. Sokolov. Tr. by Catherine R. Smith. LC 79-134444. (Illus.). 1971. Repr. of 1966 ed. 30.00 (ISBN 0-8103-5020-3). Gale.

Russian for Beginners. Charles Duff & Dmitri Makaroff. 1962. pap. 3.95 (ISBN 0-06-463287-3, EH 287, EH). Har-Row.

Russian Formalism: History-Doctrine. 2nd ed. Victor Erlich. (Slavistic Printings & Reprintings Ser: No. 4). 1965. text ed. 34.75x (ISBN 90-2790-450-2). Mouton.

Russian Formalist Criticism: Four Essays. Tr. by Lee T. Lemon & Marion J. Reis. LC 65-21899. (Regents Critics Ser). 1965. 9.50x (ISBN 0-8032-0460-4); pap. 3.50x (ISBN 0-8032-5460-1, BB 405, Bison). U of Nebr Pr.

Russian Futurism: A History. Vladimir Markov. (Illus.). 1968. 22.75x o.p. (ISBN 0-520-00811-1). U of Cal Pr.

Russian Grammar. Boris O. Unbegaun. 1957. 19.50x (ISBN 0-19-815611-1). Oxford U Pr.

Russian Historical Grammar. W. K. Matthews. (London East European: No. 1). 1960. text ed. 26.25x (ISBN 0-485-17509-6, Athlone Pr). Humanities.

Russian History Atlas. Martin Gilbert. LC 72-80174. (Illus.), 160p. 1972. 12.95 (ISBN 0-02-543320-2). Macmillan.

Russian Imperialism: From Ivan the Great to the Revolution. Ed. by Taras Hunczak. (Illus.). 415p. 1974. 27.50 (ISBN 0-8135-0737-5). Rutgers U Pr.

Russian Influence on English Education. W. H. Armytage. (Students Library of Education). 1969. text ed. 7.25x (ISBN 0-7100-6492-6). Humanities.

Russian Institutions & Culture up to Peter the Great. Marc Szeftel. 374p. 1980. 60.00x (ISBN 0-902089-80-3, Pub. by Variorum England). State Mutual Bk.

Russian Intonation. B. V. Bratus. LC 78-82443. 149p. 1972. text ed. 28.00 (ISBN 0-08-012535-2). Pergamon.

Russian Jew Under Tsars & Soviets. rev. ed. Salo W. Baron. 480p. 1976. 14.95 o.s.i. (ISBN 0-02-507300-1). Macmillan.

Russian Landed Gentry & the Peasant Emancipation of 1861. Terence Emmons. LC 68-29654. 1968. 41.95 (ISBN 0-521-07340-5). Cambridge U Pr.

Russian Language: A Brief History. G. O. Vinokur. Ed. by J. Forsyth. LC 70-127238. (Illus.). 1971. 28.50 (ISBN 0-521-07944-6). Cambridge U Pr.

Russian Language Since the Revolution. Bernard Comrie & Gerald Stone. 1978. 36.00x (ISBN 0-19-815648-0). Oxford U Pr.

Russian Letters of Direction. Staretz Macarius. LC 75-1064. 115p. 1975. pap. 3.95 (ISBN 0-913836-23-0). St Vladimirs.

Russian Lexicology. N. M. Shanskii. 1969. 14.50 (ISBN 0-08-012842-4). Pergamon.

Russian Literature: An Introduction. Robert Lord. LC 79-63625. 1980. 9.95 (ISBN 0-8008-6940-0). Taplinger.

Russian Mystics. Sergius Bolshakoff. (Cistercian Studies: No. 26). Orig. Title: I Mistici Russi. 303p. 1981. pap. 6.95 (ISBN 0-87907-926-6). Cistercian Pubns.

Russian Neo-Realism: An Anthology (the "Znanie" School of Writers) Ed. by Nicholas Luker. (Illus.). 1981. 20.00 (ISBN 0-88233-421-2); pap. 7.50 (ISBN 0-88233-422-0). Ardis Pubs.

Russian New Right: Right-Wing Ideologies in the Contemporary USSR. Alexander Yanov. Tr. by Stephen P. Dunn from Rus. LC 78-620020. (Research Ser: No. 35). 1978. pap. 4.50x (ISBN 0-87725-135-5). U of Cal Intl St.

Russian Orders, Decorations & Medals. 2nd ed. R. Werlich. (Illus.). 1981. 36.00 (ISBN 0-685-90818-6). Quaker.

Russian Peasant. Howard P. Kennard. LC 77-87519. (Anthro. Ser.). (Illus.). 336p. 1980. Repr. of 1908 ed. 28.50 (ISBN 0-404-16607-5). AMS Pr.

Russian Peasant Organisation Before Collectivisation. D. J. Male. LC 70-123662. (Soviet & East European Studies). 1971. 33.50 (ISBN 0-521-07884-9). Cambridge U Pr.

Russian Philosophe, Alexander Radischev, Seventeen Forty-Nine to Eighteen Hundred Two. Allen McConnell. LC 79-2911. 228p. 1981. Repr. of 1964 ed. 21.00 (ISBN 0-8305-0080-4). Hyperion Conn.

Russian Pronunciation Illustrated. Dennis Ward & G. Him. 1966. text ed. 9.95x (ISBN 0-521-06738-3). Cambridge U Pr.

Russian Prose Composition: Annotated Passages for Translation into Russian. F. M. Borras & R. F. Christian. 1964. 4.50 o.p. (ISBN 0-19-815618-9); pap. 11.95x (ISBN 0-19-815646-4). Oxford U Pr.

Russian Readings in Popular Science. Gordon H. Fairbanks et al. LC 63-8805. (gr. 9 up). 1963. 15.00x (ISBN 0-231-02566-1). Columbia U Pr.

Russian Revolution. Nicolas Berdyaev. 1961. pap. 1.75 o.p. (ISBN 0-472-06055-4, 55, AA). U of Mich Pr.

Russian Revolution. Ed. by Daniel Brower. LC 78-67917. (Problems in Civilization Ser.). (Orig.). 1979. pap. text ed. 3.95x (ISBN 0-88273-406-7). Forum Pr MO.

Russian Revolution. Anthony Cash. (Jackdaw Ser: No. 42). (Illus.). 1968. 5.95 o.s.i. (ISBN 0-670-61366-5, Grossman). Viking Pr.

Russian Revolution. David Killingray. Ed. by Malcolm Yapp et al. (World History Ser.). (Illus.). (gr. 10). 1980. Repr. of 1977 ed. lib. bdg. 5.95 (ISBN 0-89908-138-X); pap. text ed. 1.95 (ISBN 0-89908-113-4). Greenhaven.

Russian Revolution, Vol. 1. Paul N. Miliukov. (Russian Ser.: Vol. 44, Pt. 1). 18.50 (ISBN 0-87569-027-0). Academic Intl.

Russian Revolution, & Leninism or Marxism? Rosa Luxemburg. LC 80-24374. (Ann Arbor Ser. for the Study of Communism & Marxism). 109p. 1981. Repr. of 1961 ed. lib. bdg. 18.75x (ISBN 0-313-22429-3, LURR). Greenwood.

Russian Revolution in Nineteen Hundred Five. Tania S. Toplitsky. 164p. 1981. 13.50 (ISBN 0-682-49720-7). Exposition.

Russian Revolution in Switzerland, 1914-1917. Alfred E. Senn. LC 76-143766. 1971. 25.00x (ISBN 0-299-05941-3). U of Wis Pr.

Russian Revolution: The Overthrow of Tzarism & the Triumph of the Soviets. abr. ed. Leon Trotsky. LC 59-6990. 1959. pap. 3.50 (ISBN 0-385-09398-5, A170, Anch). Doubleday.

Russian Revolution: Why Did the Bolsheviks Win? Robert H. McNeal. 62p. 1959. pap. 1.50 o.p. (ISBN 0-03-009145-4). Krieger.

Russian Revolutionary Art. John Milner. (Oresko-Jupiter Art Bks). (Illus.). 96p. 1980. 17.95 (ISBN 0-905368-22-3, Pub. by Oresko-Jupiter England). Hippocrene Bks.

Russian Revolutionary Intelligentsia. Philip Pomper. LC 75-107303. (AHM Europe Since 1500 Ser.). 1970. pap. 5.95x (ISBN 0-88295-749-X). AHM Pub.

Russian Rockefellers: The Saga of the Nobel Family & the Russian Oil Industry. Robert W. Tolf. (Publications Ser.: No. 158). (Illus.). 1976. 14.95 (ISBN 0-8179-6581-5). Hoover Inst Pr.
Russian Romanticism: Studies in the Poetic Codes. Ed. by Nils A. Nilsson. (Stockholm Studies in Russian Literature: No. 10). 226p. 1980. pap. 29.50x (ISBN 91-22-00281-2). Humanities.
Russian Root List with a Sketch of Russian Word Formation. Charles E. Gribble. 1981. soft cover 3.95 (ISBN 0-89357-052-4). Slavica.
Russian Science Grammar. A. G. Waring. 1967. 16.50 (ISBN 0-08-011342-7); pap. 7.75 (ISBN 0-08-011341-9). Pergamon.
Russian Scientific Reader. E. J. Warne. (Rus). 1967. pap. 2.95x (ISBN 0-393-09712-9, NortonC). Norton.
Russian Scientist. Albert Parry. Ed. by Jules Koslow. LC 72-92454. (Russia Old & New Series). (Illus.). 192p. 1973. 5.95 o.s.i. (ISBN 0-02-594820-2). Macmillan.
Russian Short Stories. Tr. by Rochelle Townsend. 1979. 8.95x (ISBN 0-460-00758-0, Evman); pap. 3.75 o.p. (ISBN 0-460-01758-6). Dutton.
Russian Social Democracy: The Menshevik Movement-A Bibliography. A. M. Bourguina. LC 68-21035. (Bibliographical Ser.: No. 36). (Rus). 1968. 10.00 (ISBN 0-8179-2361-6). Hoover Inst Pr.
Russian Surnames. Boris O. Unbegan. 452p. 1972. 37.50x (ISBN 0-19-815635-9). Oxford U Pr.
Russian Syntax: Aspects of Modern Russian Syntax & Vocabulary. 2nd ed. F. M. Borras. 1971. 27.50x (ISBN 0-19-815634-0); pap. 22.50x (ISBN 0-19-872029-7). Oxford U Pr.
Russian Tales. Nadezhda Harley. LC 69-12163. (Illus., Rus.). 1969. text ed. 3.95x (ISBN 0-521-07357-X). Cambridge U Pr.
Russian Tales of Fabulous Beasts & Marvels. Lee Wyndham. LC 76-77797. (Illus.). 96p. (gr. 4 up). 1969. 5.95 o.s.i. (ISBN 0-8193-0303-8, Four Winds); PLB 5.41 o.s.i. (ISBN 0-8193-0304-6). Schol Bk Serv.
Russian Themes. Ed. by Miriam Kochan & Lionel Kochan. LC 67-106641. (Selections from History Today Ser.: No. 3). (Illus.). 1967. 5.00 (ISBN 0-685-09196-1); pap. 3.95 (ISBN 0-685-09197-X). Dufour.
Russian Themes. Mihajlo Mihajlov. LC 68-20172. 373p. 1968. 6.95 (ISBN 0-374-25292-0); pap. 2.45 o.p. (ISBN 0-374-50700-7). FS&G.
Russian Verbs of Motion. Leon Stilman. LC 51-7695. (Columbia Slavic Studies). 1951. pap. 6.00x (ISBN 0-231-09931-2). Columbia U Pr.
Russian Versification: The Theories of Trediakovsky, Lomonosov & Kantemir. Ed. by Rimvydas Silbajoris. LC 67-13777. (Russian Institute Occasional Papers Ser.). 1968. 15.00x (ISBN 0-231-03011-8). Columbia U Pr.
Russians As People. Wright Miller. 1961. pap. 2.95 o.p. (ISBN 0-525-47085-9). Dutton.
Russians at Port Jackson. Glen Barratt. 1980. text ed. write for info. (ISBN 0-391-02165-6); pap. text ed. write for info. (ISBN 0-391-02166-4). Humanities.
Russians: How They Live & Work. W. H. Parker. LC 72-93295. 179p. 1973. text ed. 8.95 (ISBN 0-03-029581-5, HoltC). HR&W.
Russians in America. Nancy Eubank. LC 72-3589. (In America Bks.). (Illus.). 96p. (gr. 5-11). 1973. PLB 5.95 o.p. (ISBN 0-8225-0226-7). Lerner Pubns.
Russians in America. Nancy Eubank. LC 72-3598. (In America Bks.). (Illus.). 96p. (gr. 5-11). 1979. PLB 5.95. Lerner Pubns.
Russia's Failed Revolutions: From the Decembrists to the Dissidents. Adam B. Ulam. LC 80-50534. 432p. 1981. 18.95 (ISBN 0-465-07152-X). Basic.
Russia's Hawaiian Adventure, 1815-1817. Richard A. Pierce. (Materials for the Study of Alaska History Ser.: No. 8). (Illus.). 1976. 10.00x (ISBN 0-919642-68-3); pap. 5.50x (ISBN 0-919642-69-1). Limestone Pr.
Russia's Road to the Cold War. Vojtech Mastny. 1979. 20.00 (ISBN 0-231-04360-0). Columbia U Pr.
Russia's Road to the Cold War: Diplomacy, Strategy, & the Politics of Communism, 1941-1945. Vojtech Mastny. 384p. 1980. pap. 8.50x (ISBN 0-231-04361-9). Columbia U Pr.
Russie. new ed. Ed. by Daniel Moreau. (Collection monde et voyages). (Illus.). 159p. (Fr.). 1973. 21.00 (ISBN 2-03-053112-X, 3902). Larousse.
Russification in the Baltic Provinces & Finland, 1855-1914. Ed. by E. C. Thaden. LC 80-7557. 1980. 40.00 (ISBN 0-691-05314-6); pap. 17.50 (ISBN 0-691-10103-5). Princeton U Pr.
Russkaia Literaturnaia Parodiia. (Rus.). 1981. pap. 6.50 (ISBN 0-88233-604-5). Ardis Pubs.
Russkie Perezvony: An Album of Soviet Russian Recordings. Alexander Blum. LC 71-136569. 155p. 1972. 21.00 (ISBN 0-08-006878-2). Pergamon.
Russkij Narodnyj Stix V Literaturnyx Imitacijax. M. L. Gasparov. (PDR Press Publications on Russian Poetics Ser.). (Orig., Russian.). 1976. pap. text ed. 4.50x (ISBN 90-316-0013-X). Humanities.
Russo-American Relations, 1815-1867. Benjamin P. Thomas. LC 70-87709. (American History, Politics & Law Ser). 1969. Repr. of 1930 ed. lib. bdg. 22.50 (ISBN 0-306-71681-X). Da Capo.
Russo-Chinese Diplomacy. Ken S. Weigh. LC 79-2845. 382p. 1981. Repr. of 1928 ed. 29.50 (ISBN 0-8305-0021-9). Hyperion Conn.
Russo-Chinese Empire. Alexander Ular. (Studies in Chinese History & Civilization). 334p. 1977. Repr. of 1904 ed. 24.00 (ISBN 0-89093-086-4). U Pubns Amer.
Russo-Japanese Conflict: It Causes & Issues. K. Asakawa. (Illus.). 399p. 1972. Repr. of 1904 ed. 31.00x (ISBN 0-7165-2048-6, Pub. by Irish Academic Pr Ireland). Biblio Dist.
Rust. R. C. Calif. (Orig.). 1980. pap. 1.95 (ISBN 0-532-23198-8). Manor Bks.
Rust. Conrad Hilberry. LC 73-92903. 61p. 1974. 6.95 (ISBN 0-8214-0153-X). Ohio U Pr.
Rusted Laughter. Vijay N. Shankar. (Writers Workshop Redbird Ser.). 1975. 6.75 (ISBN 0-88253-622-2); pap. text ed. 4.00 (ISBN 0-88253-621-4). Ind-US Inc.
Rustic Speech & Folklore. Elizabeth M. Wright. LC 68-18011. 1968. Repr. of 1913 ed. 18.00 (ISBN 0-8103-3294-9). Gale.
Rustle of Spring: An Edwardian Childhood in London's East End. Clare Cameron. 288p. 1980. 19.75x (ISBN 0-7050-0074-5, Pub. by Skilton & Shaw England). State Mutual Bk.
Rustlers of Beacon Creek. Max Brand. 1976. pap. 1.75 (ISBN 0-446-94541-2). Warner Bks.
Rusty Colt of the Cross L. Gene Tuttle. 192p. (YA) 1975. 5.95 (ISBN 0-685-51771-3, Avalon). Bouregy.
Rusty Rings a Bell. Franklyn M. Branley & Eleanor K. Vaughan. LC 57-7492. (Illus.). (gr. k-3). 1957. 3.95 o.p. (ISBN 0-690-71601-X, TYC-J); PLB 5.79 (ISBN 0-690-71602-8). T Y Crowell.
Rut. Gordon Stowell. Tr. by S. D. de Lerin from English. (Libros Pescaditos Sobre Personajes Biblicos). (Illus.). 1980. pap. 0.40 (ISBN 0-311-38513-3, Edit Mundo). Casa Bautista.
Ruth. Ethel Barrett. LC 80-52961. (Great Heroes of the Bible Ser.). 128p. (gr. 3-9). 1980. pap. 1.95 (ISBN 0-8307-0764-6, 5810418). Regal.
Ruth. Elizabeth C. Gaskell. Ed. by Robert L. Wolff. LC 75-1507. (Victorian Fiction Ser.). 1975. Repr. of 1853 ed. lib. bdg. 66.00 (ISBN 0-8240-1581-9). Garland Pub.
Ruth Benedict. Margaret Mead. (Illus.). 1974. 15.00x (ISBN 0-231-03519-5); pap. 6.00x (ISBN 0-231-03520-9). Columbia U Pr.
Ruth Prawer Jhabvala. new,enlarged ed. Vasant A. Shahane. (Indian Writers Ser.: Vol. 11). 1981. 12.00 (ISBN 0-89253-074-X). Ind-US Inc.
Ruth: Romance of Redemption. Martin R. De Haan. 4.95 (ISBN 0-310-23451-4). Zondervan.
Ruth, The Gleaner, & the Boy Samuel. Gordon Lindsay. (Old Testament Ser.). 1.25 (ISBN 0-89985-137-1). Christ Nations.
Ruthless Gun. Ted Lewellen. 160p. 1981. pap. 1.75 (ISBN 0-449-12796-6, GM). Fawcett.
Rutland. Ed. by Frank Thorn. (Domesday Book Ser.). (Illus.). 52p. (From a draft translation prepared by Celia Parker). 1980. 15.00x (ISBN 0-8476-3260-1). Rowman.
Rutland Road. rev. ed. Jim Shaugnessy. LC 80-19534. (Illus.). 370p. 1980. 20.00 (ISBN 0-8310-7128-1). Howell-North.
Rutland Street: The Story of an Educational Experiment for Disadvantaged Children in Dublin. Seamas Holland. (Illus.). 1979. 17.75 (ISBN 0-685-97185-6). Pergamon.
Ruxton of the Rockies. George F. Ruxton. Ed. by LeRoy R. Hafen. (Illus.). 1980. 15.95 (ISBN 0-8061-1591-2); pap. 7.95 (ISBN 0-8061-1603-X). U of Okla Pr.
Ruxton of the Rockies. George F. Ruxton. Ed. by LeRoy R. Hafen. (American Exploration & Travel Ser.: Vol. 13). (Illus.). 326p. 1979. pap. 7.95 (ISBN 0-8061-1603-X). U of Okla Pr.
Ruy Lopez: Breyer System. L. S. Blackstock. 1976. 15.95 (ISBN 0-7134-3124-5, Pub. by Batsford England); pap. 12.50 (ISBN 0-7134-3142-3). David & Charles.
Ruy Lopez: Winning Chess with IP-K4. L. W. Barden. 11.25 (ISBN 0-08-013006-2); pap. 5.75 (ISBN 0-08-009997-1). Pergamon.
RV Buyer's Guide. 1980. pap. 2.95 (ISBN 0-685-87265-3). Woodall.
Rwala Bedouin Today. William Lancaster. (Changing Cultures Ser.). (Illus.). 192p. Date not set. price not set (ISBN 0-521-23877-3); pap. price not set (ISBN 0-521-28275-6). Cambridge U Pr.
Rx for Hilarity. Abraham Unger. 1980. pap. 1.50 (ISBN 0-505-51468-0). Tower Bks.
Rx for Learning Disability. Emmett C. Velten, Jr. & Carlene Sampson. LC 77-8595. 1978. 13.95 (ISBN 0-88229-330-3); pap. 7.95 (ISBN 0-88229-559-4). Nelson-Hall.
Rx for Small Business Success: Accounting, Planning, & Recordkeeping Techniques for a Healthy Bottom Line. Jeffrey Slater. (Illus.). 256p. 1981. 18.95 (Spec); pap. 12.95 (ISBN 0-13-785006-9). P-H.
Rx for Us-a Revitalized Constitution: Increased Democracy. Kenneth E. Hoffman. LC 78-66119. 1979. pap. text ed. 8.75 (ISBN 0-8191-0686-0). U Pr of Amer.
Rx: Spiritist As Needed; a Study of a Puerto Rican Community Mental Health Resource. Alan Harwood. LC 76-54841. (Contemporary Religious Movements). 1977. 25.95 (ISBN 0-471-35828-2, Pub. by Wiley-Interscience). Wiley.
Ryder. Djuna Barnes. 1979. 10.95 (ISBN 0-312-69640-X). St Martin.
Ryerson Genealogy: Genealogy & History of the Knickerbocker Families of Ryerson, Ryerse, Ryerss, Also Adriane & Martense Families All Descendants of Martin & Adriane Reyersz (Reyerszen) of Amsterdam, Holland. Albert W. Ryerson. Ed. by Alfred L. Holman. 85.00x (ISBN 0-685-88555-0). Elliots Bks.
Ryme & Thought. Mary A. Bailes. 48p. (Orig.). 1981. pap. 2.95 (ISBN 0-938468-00-6). Marcella.
Ryme Index to the Manuscript Texts of Chaucer's Minor Poems. Walter W. Skeat. 1887. 40.00 (ISBN 0-8274-3318-2). R West.

S

S a, Nineteen Seventy-Six: Symposia, Vol. 2. Philosophy of Science Biennial Meeting, 1976. Ed. by Peter D. Asquith & Frederick Suppe. LC 76-27152. 1977. 9.75 (ISBN 0-917586-04-2); pap. 6.25 (ISBN 0-917586-03-4). Philos Sci Assn.
S. E. Britaines Busse: Or Herring-Fishing Ship, with the States Proclamation Annexed Unto the Same, As Concerning Herring-Fishing. LC 74-80211. (English Experience Ser.: No. 690). 1974. Repr. of 1615 ed. 5.00 (ISBN 90-221-0690-X). Walter J Johnson.
S E V E N. John D. MacDonald. 1979. pap. 1.75 o.p. (ISBN 0-449-14126-8, GM). Fawcett.
S. I. Units: An Introduction. B. Chiswell & E. C. Grigg. LC 74-139498. 1971. pap. 5.95 o.p. (ISBN 0-471-15588-8, Pub. by Wiley-Interscience). Wiley.
S. M. Eisenstein. Jacques Charriere. 1974. pap. 8.95 o.p. (ISBN 0-525-47371-8). Dutton.
S. N. Behrman. Kenneth T. Reed. LC 75-2085. (U. S. Authors Ser.: No. 256). 152p. 1975. lib. bdg. 10.95 (ISBN 0-8057-7154-9). Twayne.
S. O. P. H. I. A. Pierre Boulle. LC 59-12392. 1959. 8.95 (ISBN 0-8149-0067-4). Vanguard.
S. O. S. An Exposition of the Song of Solomon. Max Sidders. 1981. 5.95 (ISBN 0-533-04640-8). Vantage.
S-One Hundred Bus Handbook. Dave Bursky. 280p. 1980. pap. 14.50 (ISBN 0-8104-0897-X). Hayden.
S. R. Ranganathan: Papers Given at Memorial Meeting in January, 1973. Ed. by E. Dudley. 1974. pap. 5.50x (ISBN 0-85365-197-3, Pub. by Lib Assn England). Oryx Pr.
S S T A Bibliography. rev. ed. 63p. 1975. 3.50; ATA members 2.50. Am Theatre Assoc.
S. T. O. P. Smoking. Barbara H. Hanson. 100p. (Orig.). 1981. 9.95 (ISBN 0-934400-14-8). Landmark Bks.
S. T. P. A Journey Through America with the Rolling Stones. Robert Greenfield. LC 73-16346. 352p. 1974. pap. 3.95 o.p. (ISBN 0-8415-0323-0). Dutton.
S. W. A. T. Team Manual. Robert P. Cappel. (Illus.). 150p. 1979. pap. 10.00 (ISBN 0-87364-169-8). Paladin Ent.
S. Y. Agnon. Harold Fisch. LC 74-76126. (Modern Literature Ser.). 124p. 1975. 10.95 (ISBN 0-8044-2197-8). Ungar.
S-Z. Roland Barthes. Tr. by Richard Miller. 271p. 1974. 8.95 (ISBN 0-8090-8375-2); pap. 5.95 (ISBN 0-8090-1377-0). Hill & Wang.
Saab Service Repair Handbook 95, 96, 99, & Sonett 1967-1979. Ray Hoy. Ed. by Jeff Robinson. (Illus.). 1976. pap. 10.95 (ISBN 0-89287-121-0, A185). Clymer Pubns.
Saab: The Innovator. Mark Chatterton. (Illus.). 192p. 1980. 25.00 (ISBN 0-7153-7945-3). David & Charles.
Sabbath: A Day of Delight. Sophia N. Cedarbaum. (Illus.). (gr. k-2). 1960. 3.50 o.p. (ISBN 0-685-20757-9, 301582). UAHC.
Sabbath, a Kit. Herbert A. Greenberg & Barbara Greenberg. 1971. boxed 11.00 (ISBN 0-8074-0149-8, 101075). UAHC.
Sabbath & the Lord's Day. H. M. Riggle. 160p. pap. 1.50. Faith Pub Hse.
Sabbath in Puritan New England. Alice M. Earle. LC 68-17961. 1968. Repr. of 1891 ed. 15.00 (ISBN 0-8103-3430-5). Gale.
Sabbath-Law of R. Meir. Robert Goldenberg. LC 78-14370. (Brown University. Brown Judaic Studies: No. 6). 1978. pap. 9.00 (ISBN 0-89130-249-2, 140006). Scholars Pr Ca.
Sabbath of the New Testament. Patrick O'Sullivan. (Illus.). 52p. 1981. pap. 2.50 (ISBN 0-933464-12-6). D M Battle Pubns.
Sabbatical in Japan. Akhtar Qamber. 1976. 8.00 (ISBN 0-89253-819-8); flexible cloth 4.00 (ISBN 0-89253-820-1). Ind-US Inc.
Saber-Toothed Tiger & Other Ice-Age Mammals. Joanna Cole. (Illus.). (gr. 1-5). 1977. 8.25 (ISBN 0-688-22120-3); PLB 7.92 (ISBN 0-688-32120-8). Morrow.
Sabers in the Wind. Duane Schultz. 448p. 1981. pap. 2.50 (ISBN 0-449-14380-5, GM). Fawcett.
Sabian Book: Letters of Insight. Marc E. Jones. LC 73-76920. 1973. 13.50 o.p. (ISBN 0-87878-013-0, Sabian). Great Eastern.
Sabian Manual. Marc E. Jones. LC 57-11471. 1957. 10.50 o.p. (ISBN 0-87878-010-6, Sabian). Great Eastern.
Sabian Symbols in Astrology. Marc E. Jones. LC 72-91460. 1972. 13.50 o.p. (ISBN 0-87878-009-2, Sabian). Great Eastern.
Sabine. Nicolas Freeling. LC 74-15871. (Harper Novel of Suspense). 1978. 7.95 o.p. (ISBN 0-06-011356-1, HarpT). Har-Row.
Sable. Harlan Wade. Tr. by Claude Potvin & Rose-Ella Potvin. (Book About Ser.). Orig. Title: Sand. (Illus., Fr.). (gr. k-3). 1979. PLB 7.30 (ISBN 0-8172-1451-8). Raintree Pubs.
Sable & Gold. Jack Canon. 288p. (Orig.). 1981. pap. 2.50 (ISBN 0-523-41105-7). Pinnacle Bks.
Sable Island. Bruce Armstrong. LC 80-2745. (Illus.). 256p. 1981. 19.95 (ISBN 0-385-13113-5). Doubleday.
Sable Moon. Nancy Springer. 1981. pap. 2.50 (ISBN 0-671-83157-7). PB.
Sabotage: A Study in Industrial Conflict. Geoff Brown. 1977. 26.00x o.p. (ISBN 0-8476-2321-1). Rowman.
Sabrina. Madeleine Polland. 1978. 9.95 (ISBN 0-440-07893-8). Delacorte.
Sac & Fox Indians. William T. Hagan. LC 58-6851. (Civilization of the American Indian Ser.: Vol. 48). (Illus.). 320p. 1958. 14.95 (ISBN 0-8061-0397-3). U of Okla Pr.
Sac, Fox & Iowa Indians, Vol. 1. Zachary Gussow et al. Ed. by David A. Horr. (American Indian Ethnohistory Ser.). 1978. lib. bdg. 42.00 (ISBN 0-8240-0789-1). Garland Pub.
Sac, Fox & Iowa Indians, Vol. 2: Indians of E. Missouri, W. Illinois & S. Wisconsin, from the Proto-Historic Period to 1804. David B. Stout. (American Indian Ethnohistory Ser: North Central & Northeastern Indians). (Illus.). lib. bdg. 42.00 (ISBN 0-8240-0790-5). Garland Pub.
Sac, Fox & Iowa Indians, Vol. 3: Findings of Fact, & Opinion. Indian Claims Commission. (American Indian Ethnohistory Ser: North Central & Northeastern Indians). (Illus.). lib. bdg. 42.00 (ISBN 0-8240-0791-3). Garland Pub.
Sacajawea. Olive Burt. LC 78-1572. (Visual Biography Ser.). (Illus.). (gr. 6 up). 1978. PLB 6.90 s&l (ISBN 0-531-00975-0). Watts.
Sachem. Donald C. Porter. 352p. 1981. pap. 2.95 (ISBN 0-553-13681-X). Bantam.
Sachs Engine Service-Repair Handbook: 100 & 125cc, All Years. Mike Bishop. Ed. by Jeff Robinson. (Illus.). 144p. 1974. pap. text ed. 9.95 (ISBN 0-89287-025-7, M427). Clymer Pubns.
Sack of Rome. E. R. Chamberlin. (Illus.). 1980. 25.00 (ISBN 0-7134-1645-9, Pub. by Batsford England). David & Charles.
Sack Time. Dik Browne. Ed. by Wendy Wallace. (Hagar the Horrible Ser.: No. 6). 128p. (gr. 2 up). 1981. pap. 1.50 (ISBN 0-448-12623-0, Tempo). G&D.
Sackcloth & Ashes: Liturgical Reflections for Lenten Weekdays. James A. Griffin. LC 74-44463. 1976. pap. 2.50 (ISBN 0-8189-0336-8). Alba.
Sacral Kingship in Ancient Israel. rev. ed. Aubrey R. Johnson. 1967. 18.00 (ISBN 0-7083-0344-7). Verry.
Sacrament. Peter Gzowski. LC 80-51208. 1980. 9.95 (ISBN 0-689-11114-2). Atheneum.
Sacramental & Occasional Homilies. David Q. Liptak. LC 80-29287. 96p. (Orig.). 1981. pap. 4.95 (ISBN 0-8189-0406-2). Alba.
Sacramental Reconciliation. Ed. by Edward Schillebeeckx. LC 76-129760. (Concilium Ser.: Religion in the Seventies: Vol. 61). 1971. pap. 4.95 (ISBN 0-8164-2517-5). Crossroad NY.
Sacramento Region: Planning, Growth & Development, A Bibliographic Guide. Eileen Heaser & Les Kong. (Public Administration Ser.: Bibliographies: P-673). 61p. 1981. 9.00. Vance Biblios.
Sacraments. Maureen Curley. (Children of the Kingdom Activities Ser.). (gr. 4-7). 1975. 7.95 (ISBN 0-686-13691-8). Pflaum Pr.

Sacraments & You. Michael Pennock. (Illus.). 272p. (gr. 10-12). 1981. pap. 3.95 (ISBN 0-87793-221-2); teachers ed. 2.25 (ISBN 0-87793-222-0). Ave Maria.

Sacraments in a World of Change. Joseph M. Champlin. LC 73-83347. (Know Your Faith Ser.). 144p. (Orig.). 1973. pap. 1.65 (ISBN 0-87793-085-6). Ave Maria.

Sacraments: Readings in Contemporary Theology. Ed. by Michael J. Taylor. LC 80-9534. 274p. (Orig.). 1981. pap. 7.95 (ISBN 0-8189-0406-2). Alba.

Sacred & Profane. Margaret Maitland. 1978. pap. 1.75 (ISBN 0-505-51241-6). Tower Bks.

Sacred Books of China, Vols. 3, 16, 27, 28, 39, & 40. Ed. by F. Max Mueller. Tr. by Palmer. (Sacred Books of the East Ser.). 15.00x ea.; Vol. 3. (ISBN 0-8426-1414-1); Vol. 16. (ISBN 0-8426-1415-X); Vol. 27. (ISBN 0-8426-1416-8); Vol. 28. (ISBN 0-8426-1417-6); Vol. 39. (ISBN 0-8426-1418-4); Vol. 40. (ISBN 0-8426-1419-2). Verry.

Sacred Books of the East, 50 Vols. Ed. by F. Max Mueller. Set. 700.00x (ISBN 0-8426-1420-6); 12.00x ea. Verry.

Sacred Books of the East, 50 vols. Ed. by Max Muller. 1977-1980. Repr. of 1975 ed. 11.50 ea. Orient Bk Dist.

Sacred Books of the East: Index Volume, Vol. 50. Ed. by F. M. Mueller. 1979. 15.00 (ISBN 0-8426-1603-9). Verry.

Sacred Bridge. Eric Werner. (Music Reprint Ser.). 1979. Repr. of 1959 ed. lib. bdg. 42.50 (ISBN 0-306-79581-7). Da Capo.

Sacred Calligraphy of the East. John Stevens. LC 80-53446. (Illus.). 176p. (Orig.). 1981. pap. 9.95 (ISBN 0-394-74832-8). Shambhala Pubn.

Sacred Complex in Hindu Gaya. 2nd ed. L. P. Vidyarthi. 264p. 1980. pap. text ed. 11.25x (ISBN 0-391-02214-8). Humanities.

Sacred Complex of Kashi. L. P. Vidyarthi. 1979. text ed. 17.50x (ISBN 0-391-01856-6). Humanities.

Sacred Cows. J. A. Walter. 224p. 1980. pap. 5.95 (ISBN 0-310-42421-6). Zondervan.

Sacred Cows Are Dying: Exploding the Myths We Try to Live by. Art Greer. LC 77-70123. 1978. 6.95 (ISBN 0-8015-6509-X, Hawthorn). Dutton.

Sacred Cows, Sacred Places: Origins & Survivals of Animal Homes in India. Deryck O. Lodrick. (Illus.). 350p. 1981. 20.00x (ISBN 0-520-04109-7). U of Cal Pr.

Sacred Harp: A Tradition & Its Music. Buell E. Cobb, Jr. LC 76-12680. 248p. 1978. 12.50x (ISBN 0-8203-0426-3). U of Ga Pr.

Sacred Heart of Christmas. Flower A. Newhouse. Ed. by Athene Bengtson. LC 78-74956. (Illus.). 1978. pap. 5.00 (ISBN 0-910378-14-2). Christward.

Sacred Journeys: Conversion & Commitment to Divine Light Mission. James V. Downton, Jr. LC 79-546. (Illus.). 1979. 15.00 (ISBN 0-231-04198-5). Columbia U Pr.

Sacred Keeper: A Biography of Patrick Kavanagh. Peter Kavanagh. (Illus.). 404p. 1980. text ed. 21.00x (ISBN 0-904984-48-6). Humanities.

Sacred Kural. 2nd. ed. Ed. & tr. by H. A. Popley. Orig. Title: Tamil Veda of Tiruvalluvar. 159p. pap. 2.80 (ISBN 0-88253-386-X). Ind-US Inc.

Sacred Laws of the Aryas, Vols. 2 & 14. Ed. by F. Max Mueller. Tr. by Buhler. (Sacred Books of the East Ser.). 15.00x ea.; Vol. 2. (ISBN 0-8426-1421-4); Vol. 14. (ISBN 0-8426-1422-2). Verry.

Sacred Meadows: A Structural Analysis of Religious Symbolism in an East African Town. Abdul H. El-Zein. LC 73-91310. (Studies in African Religion). 1974. text ed. 19.95x o.s.i. (ISBN 0-8101-0443-1). Northwestern U Pr.

Sacred Narcotic Plants of the New World Indians: An Anthology of Texts from the 16th Century to Date. Hedwig Schleiffer. (Orig.). 1974. pap. 6.50 o.s.i. (ISBN 0-02-851780-6). Hafner.

Sacred Pipe: Black Elk's Account of the Seven Rites of Oglala Sioux. Ed. by Joseph E. Brown. (Civilization of the American Indian Ser.: No. 36). (Illus.). 1953. 9.95 (ISBN 0-8061-0272-1). U of Okla Pr.

Sacred Pipe: Black Elk's Account of the Seven Rites of the Oglala Sioux. Ed. by Joseph E. Brown. (Metaphysical Library Ser.). 1971. pap. 3.25 (ISBN 0-14-003346-7). Penguin.

Sacred Places: Religious Architecture of the 18th & 19th Centuries in British Columbia. Barry Downs. (Illus.). 160p. 1980. 29.95 (ISBN 0-295-95774-3, Pub. by Douglas & McIntyre Canada). U of Wash Pr.

Sacred Science: The King of Pharaonic Theocracy. R. A. Schwaller De Lubicz. Tr. by A. Vandenbroeck & G. Vandenbroeck. (Illus.). 1981. 12.95 (ISBN 0-89281-007-6). Inner Tradit.

Sacred Words: A Study of Navajo Religion & Prayer. Sam D. Gill. LC 80-659. (Contributions in Intercultural & Comparative Studies: No. 4). (Illus.). 272p. 1981. lib. bdg. 29.95 (ISBN 0-313-22165-0, GSW/). Greenwood.

Sacrifice. Pamela Ferguson. 1981. 13.95 (ISBN 0-689-11035-9). Atheneum.

Sacrifice. Marvin Moore. LC 78-21712. (Flame Ser.). 1979. pap. 0.95 (ISBN 0-8127-0214-X). Southern Pub.

Sacrifice. Ed. by Robert Vitarelli. (Pal Paperbacks Kit A Ser.). (Illus., Orig.). (gr. 7-12). 1973. pap. text ed. 1.25 (ISBN 0-8374-3485-8). Xerox Ed Pubns.

Sacrifice Play. John Ballem. 256p. 1981. pap. 2.25 (ISBN 0-449-14381-3, GM). Fawcett.

Sacrifices in the Sicilian. D. N. Levy. (Batsford Chess Ser.). 196p. 1981. 19.95 (ISBN 0-7134-2596-2, Pub. by Batsford England); pap. 10.95 (ISBN 0-7134-2597-0). David & Charles.

Sad. Sylvia R. Tester. (What Does It Mean Ser.). (Illus.). 1980. 7.35g (ISBN 0-516-06448-7). Childrens.

Sa'd B. Mansur Ibn Kammuna's Examination of the Inquiries into the Three Faiths. Moshe Perlmann. (U. C. Publ. in Near Eastern Studies: Vol. 6). 1967. pap. 8.00x (ISBN 0-520-09299-6). U of Cal Pr.

Sad Sontag Plays His Hunch. Wilbur C. Tuttle. 1976. lib. bdg. 10.95x (ISBN 0-89968-129-8). Lightyear.

Sad Story of the Little Bluebird & the Hungry Cat. Edna M. Preston. (gr. k-3). 1977. pap. 0.95 o.p. (ISBN 0-590-10276-1, Schol Pap). Schol Bk Serv.

Sad Variety. Nicholas Blake. LC 64-18086. 1979. pap. 2.25 (ISBN 0-06-080495-5, P 495, PL). Har-Row.

Sadat's Realistic Peace Initiative. William Y. Kosman. Date not set. 8.95 (ISBN 0-533-04614-9). Vantage.

Saddharma-Pundarika or the Lotus of the True Law, Vol. 21. Ed. by F. Max Mueller. Tr. by Davids & Oldenberg. (Sacred Books of the East Ser.). 15.00x (ISBN 0-8426-1423-0). Verry.

Saddle Bag & Spinning Wheel. George P. Cuttino. LC 80-83663. 330p. 1981. 18.95x (ISBN 0-86554-004-7). Mercer Univ Pr.

Saddle Bow Slim. Nelson Nye. 1979. pap. 1.25 (ISBN 0-505-51378-1). Tower Bks.

Saddle by Starlight. Luke Short. 176p. 1981. pap. 1.95 (ISBN 0-553-14531-2). Bantam.

Saddlery. E. H. Edwards. (Illus.). Date not set. 12.25 (ISBN 0-85131-151-2, Dist. by Sporting Book Center). J A Allen.

Saddlery & Harness Making. Paul N. Hasluck. (Illus.). 12.25 (ISBN 0-85131-148-2, Dist. by Sporting Book Center). J A Allen.

Saddles. Russel H. Beatie. LC 79-6708. (Illus.). 375p. 1980. 35.00 (ISBN 0-8061-1584-X). U of Okla Pr.

Saddles & Spurs: The Pony Express Saga. Raymond W. Settle & Mary L. Settle. LC 55-10776. x, 217p. 1972. pap. 2.95 (ISBN 0-8032-5765-1, BB 556, Bison). U of Nebr Pr.

Sadeian Woman: And the Ideaology of Pornography. Angela Carter. LC 78-20412. 1980. pap. 3.50 (ISBN 0-06-090768-1, CN 768, CN). Har-Row.

Sadhana. Swami Mutananda. 1976. pap. 7.95 (ISBN 0-914602-63-2). SYDA Found.

Sadhana. Swami Sivananda. 1978. 15.95 (ISBN 0-89684-345-9); pap. 11.50 (ISBN 0-89684-311-4). Orient Bk Dist.

Sadhana in Sri Aurobindo's Yoga. M. P. Pandit. LC 78-59851. 1978. pap. 3.95 (ISBN 0-89744-000-5, Pub. by Atmaniketan Ashram). Auromere.

Sadie Shapiro, Matchmaker. Robert K. Smith. 192p. 1981. pap. 2.50 (ISBN 0-449-24406-7, Crest). Fawcett.

Sadie Shapiro's Knitting Book. Robert K. Smith. 224p. 1975. pap. 1.25 o.p. (ISBN 0-449-22318-3, P2318-125, Crest). Fawcett.

Sadist. (Ryker Ser). 1975. pap. 1.25 o.p. (ISBN 0-685-59192-1, LB309ZK, Leisure Bks). Nordon Pubns.

Sadistic Statistics: An Introduction to Statistics for the Behavioral Sciences. Gideon Horowitz. 1979. pap. text ed. 9.95 (ISBN 0-89529-091-X). Avery Pub.

Sadness. Donald Barthelme. 183p. 1972. 7.95 o.p. (ISBN 0-374-25333-1). FS&G.

Sadness. Donald Barthleme. 1980. pap. write for info. (ISBN 0-671-83204-2). PB.

Sadr al-Din Shirazi & His Transcendent Theosophy. Seyyed H. Nasr. LC 78-62006. 1979. 9.50 (ISBN 0-87773-734-7). Great Eastern.

Saducismus Triumphatus: Or, Full & Plain Evidence Concerning Witches & Apparitions. Joseph Glanvill. LC 66-60009. 1966. Repr. of 1689 ed. 65.00x (ISBN 0-8201-1021-3). Schol Facsimiles.

Saeculomastix. Incl. Sacred Leisure. Francis Hodgson. Ed. by Donald H. Reiman. Repr. of 1820 ed. LC 75-31224. (Romantic Context Ser.: Poetry 1789-1830). 1978. Repr. of 1819 ed. lib. bdg. 47.00 (ISBN 0-8240-2174-6). Garland Pub.

Saeculum: History & Society in the Theology of St Augustine. R. A. Markus. LC 71-87136. 1970. 42.00 (ISBN 0-521-07621-8). Cambridge U Pr.

Safari: A Saga of the African Blue. Martin Johnson. LC 72-170251. (Tower Bks). (Illus.). x, 294p. 1972. Repr. of 1928 ed. 18.00 (ISBN 0-8103-3934-X). Gale.

Safari En Cote d'Ivoire. R. J. Cazziol. (Illus.). 40p. 1974. pap. 2.25x (ISBN 0-521-20434-8). Cambridge U Pr.

Safe & Efficient Plant Operation & Maintenance. Chemical Engineering Magazine. LC 80-14762. (Chemical Engineering Ser.). 400p. 1980. 29.50 (ISBN 0-07-010707-6); pap. 24.50. McGraw.

Safe Central Venous Nutrition: Guidelines for Prevention & Management of Complications. Mohamad H. Parsa et al. 280p. 1974. pap. 22.25 spiral (ISBN 0-398-02785-4). C C Thomas.

Safe Drinking Water; Current & Future Problems: Proceedings of a Natonal Conference in Washngton D. C. Ed. by Clifford S. Russell. LC 78-19840. pap. 12.00x (ISBN 0-8018-2181-9). Johns Hopkins.

Safe Food Guide. Barbara Le Duc. 1979. pap. 1.95 (ISBN 0-345-28424-0). Ballantine.

Safe Handling of Chemical Carcinogens, Mutagens Teratogens & Highly Toxic Substances. Ed. by Douglas B. Walters. LC 79-88922. 1980. Vol. 1. 33.95 (ISBN 0-250-40303-X); Vol. 2. 33.95 (ISBN 0-250-40354-4). Ann Arbor Science.

Safe Handling of Plutonium. (Safety Ser.: No. 39). (Illus.). 134p. (Orig.). 1974. pap. 11.25 (ISBN 92-0-123473-2, ISP358, IAEA). Unipub.

Safe Handling of Radionuclides. (Safety Ser.: No. 1). 91p. (Orig.). 1973. pap. 8.25 (ISBN 92-0-123073-7, ISP319, IAEA). Unipub.

Safe Operation of Critical Assemblies & Research Reactors, 1971. (Safety Ser.: No. 35). (Orig.). 1971. pap. 12.50 (ISBN 92-0-123071-0, ISP225, IAEA). Unipub.

Safe Operation of Nuclear Power Plants. (Safety Ser.: No. 31). (Orig.). 1969. pap. 9.25 (ISBN 92-0-123169-5, IAEA). Unipub.

SAFE: Security Audit & Field Evaluation for Computer Facilities & Information Systems. Leonard I. Krauss. 308p. 1981. 29.95 (ISBN 0-8144-5526-3). Am Mgmt.

Safe Use of Radioactive Tracers in Industrial Processes. (Safety Ser.: No. 40). 54p. (Orig.). 1974. pap. 3.75 (ISBN 92-0-123074-5, ISP369, IAEA). Unipub.

Safe Water: A Factbook on the SDWA for Noncommunity Water Systems. American Water Works Association. (Illus.). 52p. 1980. pap. 1.50 (ISBN 0-89867-224-4). Am Water Wks Assn.

Safe Within Yourself: A Woman's Guide to Rape Prevention & Self-Defense. Doris Kaufman et al. LC 79-566334. (Illus.). 1980. pap. 7.95 (ISBN 0-916818-05-5). Visage Pr.

Safed & Keturah. William E. Barton. LC 69-19473. 1969. pap. 2.45 (ISBN 0-8042-3425-6). John Knox.

Safed the Sage: Selections from Wit & Wisdom of Safed the Sage. William E. Barton. LC 65-13377. 1965. pap. 2.45 (ISBN 0-8042-3424-8). John Knox.

Safeguarding Nuclear Materials, Vol. II: Proceedings. Symposium, Vienna, 20-24 October, 1975. (Illus., Orig.). 1976. pap. 64.75 (ISBN 92-0-070176-0, ISP408-2, IAEA). Unipub.

Safeguarding Nuclear Materials, Vol. 1: Proceedings. (Illus.). 1976. pap. 58.50 (ISBN 92-0-070076-4, ISP408-1, IAEA). Unipub.

Safeguarding the Hospital's Assets. 2nd ed. LC 78-67106. (Illus.). 1978. 9.00 (ISBN 0-930228-09-X). Hospital Finan.

Safeguarding the Land. Gloria Skurzynski. LC 80-8805. (Illus.). 192p. (gr. 7-12). 1981. pap. 3.95 (ISBN 0-15-269957-0, VoyB). HarBraceJ.

Safeguarding the Land. Gloria Skurzynski. LC 80-8805. (Illus.). 192p. (gr. 7 up). 1981. 9.95 (ISBN 0-15-269956-2, HJ). HarBraceJ.

Safeguards Techniques, 2 Vols. (Illus., Orig.). 1970. Vol. 1. pap. 43.00 (ISBN 92-0-070270-8, ISP260-1, IAEA); Vol. 2. pap. 35.00 (ISBN 92-0-070370-4, ISP260-2). Unipub.

Safety. Boy Scouts Of America. LC 19-600. (Illus.). 48p. (gr. 6-12). 1971. pap. 0.70x (ISBN 0-8395-3347-0, 3347). BSA.

Safety. Virginia Parkinson. (Pointers for Little Persons Ser.). (Illus.). (ps-2). 1963. PLB 5.99 (ISBN 0-8178-5062-7). Harvey.

Safety & Health & the Working Environment: International Labour Conference, 1981, 67th Session. International Labour Office. 68p. (Orig.). 1980. pap. 8.55 (ISBN 92-2-102407-5). Intl Labour Office.

Safety & Reliability of Metal Structures. Compiled by American Society of Civil Engineers. 464p. 1972. pap. text ed. 12.75 (ISBN 0-87262-042-5). Am Soc Civil Eng.

Safety & Seamanship. John Chamier. (Illus.). 1979. 13.95 (ISBN 0-229-11501-2, ScribT). Scribner.

Safety & Seamanship. John Chamier. 1979. 14.95x (ISBN 0-8464-0067-7). Beekman Pubs.

Safety Aspects of the Design & Equipment of Hot Laboratories. (Safety Ser.: No. 30). 1969. pap. 6.00 (ISBN 92-0-123069-9, IAEA). Unipub.

Safety Assurance Systems. Ed. by W. Johnson. (Occupational Safety & Health Ser.). 1980. 35.00 (ISBN 0-8247-6897-3). Dekker.

Safety Can Be Fun. rev. ed. Munro Leaf. LC 61-14579. (Illus.). (gr. k-3). 1961. 7.89 (ISBN 0-397-31593-7). Lippincott.

Safety: Concepts & Instruction. 2nd ed. Alton L. Thygerson. (Illus.). 160p. 1976. pap. text ed. 7.95 (ISBN 0-13-785733-0). P-H.

Safety Considerations in the Use of Ports & Approaches by Nuclear Merchant Ships. (Safety Ser.: No. 27). 1968. pap. 2.75 (ISBN 92-0-123168-7, IAEA). Unipub.

Safety for Carpenters & Woodworkers. Gaspar Lewis. LC 80-66859. (Carpentry-Cabinetmaking Ser.). 1981. pap. text ed. 4.40 (ISBN 0-8273-1869-3); instructor's guide 0.85 (ISBN 0-8273-1870-7). Delmar.

Safety for Masons. Richard T. Kreh. LC 78-53663. 1979. pap. text ed. 3.60 (ISBN 0-8273-1668-2); instructor's guide 0.75 (ISBN 0-8273-1669-0). Delmar.

Safety for Sheet Metal Workers. C. J. Zinngrabe & F. W. Schumacher. LC 76-49325. (gr. 9-12). 1977. pap. 3.80 (ISBN 0-8273-1614-3); tchr's guide 0.75 (ISBN 0-8273-1615-1). Delmar.

Safety for Welders. Larry Jeffus. LC 78-73579. (Metalworking Ser.). (gr. 8). 1980. pap. text ed. 3.20 (ISBN 0-8273-1684-4); instructor's guide 1.50 (ISBN 0-8273-1685-2). Delmar.

Safety Functions & Component Classification from BWR, PWR & PTR. (Safety Ser.: No. 50-SG-D1). 55p. 1980. pap. 8.50 (ISBN 92-0-123979-3, IDC 542, IAEA). Unipub.

Safety, Health & Welfare in the Printing Industry. M. C. Fairley. 1969. pap. 5.75 (ISBN 0-08-013033-X). Pergamon.

Safety in Nuclear Power Plant Operation, Including Commissioning & Decommissioning. (IAEA Safety Ser.: No. 50-C-O). 35p. 1979. pap. 6.00 (ISBN 92-0-123578-X, ISP503, IAEA). Unipub.

Safety in Nuclear Power Plant Siting. (IAEA Safety Ser.: No. 50-C-S). 37p. 1979. pap. 6.00 (ISBN 92-0-123378-7, ISP510, IAEA). Unipub.

Safety in Process Plant Design. G. L. Wells. 276p. 1980. 59.95x (ISBN 0-470-26907-3). Halsted Pr.

Safety in Sewers & at Sewage Works. Institute of Civil Engineers, UK. 64p. 1980. pap. 12.00x (ISBN 0-901948-12-8, Pub. by Telford England). State Mutual Bk.

Safety in the Elementary Science Classroom. 1978. pap. 2.00 (ISBN 0-87355-011-0). Natl Sci Tchrs.

Safety in the Secondary Science Classroom. 1978. pap. 4.00 (ISBN 0-87355-011-0). Natl Sci Tchrs.

Safety in Wells & Boreholes. Institute of Civil Engineers, UK. 1980. pap. 12.00x (ISBN 0-901948-57-8, Pub. by Telford England). State Mutual Bk.

Safety Management. 3rd ed. John V. Grimaldi & Rollin H. Simonds. 1975. 19.95 (ISBN 0-256-01564-3). Irwin.

Safety Match. Ian Hay. (Barbara Cartland's Library of Love: Vol. 4). 181p. 1979. 12.95x (ISBN 0-7156-1380-4, Pub. by Duckworth England). Biblio Dist.

Safety of Computer Control Systems: Proceedings of the IFAC Workshop, Stuttgart, Federal Republic of Germany, 16-18 May 1979. Ed. by R. Lauber. (Illus.). 230p. 1980. 52.00 (ISBN 0-08-024453-X). Pergamon.

Safety of Foods. 2nd ed. Horace D. Graham. (Illus.). 1980. lib. bdg. 49.00 (ISBN 0-87055-337-2). AVI.

Safety of Medicines: Evaluation & Prediction. P. I. Folb. (Illus.). 120p. 1980. pap. 12.90 (ISBN 0-387-10143-8). Springer-Verlag.

Safety of Small Dams. Compiled by American Society of Civil Engineers. 472p. 1975. pap. text ed. 23.00 (ISBN 0-87262-112-X). Am Soc Civil Eng.

Safety on Construction Sites. Thomas Telford Ltd. Editorial Staff. 122p. 1980. 75.00x (Pub. by Telford England). State Mutual Bk.

Safety on the Road. Ed. by Grant S. McClellan. (Reference Shelf Ser: Vol. 38, No. 1). 1966. 6.25 (ISBN 0-8242-0089-6). Wilson.

Safety on Wheels. Boyer. LC 73-87802. (Safety Ser). (Illus.). (gr. k-5). 1974. prebound 7.99 (ISBN 0-87783-133-5); pap. 2.75 deluxe ed. (ISBN 0-87783-134-3); cassette 5.95 (ISBN 0-685-42417-0). Oddo.

Safety Plays in Bridge. Terence Reese & Roger Trezel. LC 76-13613. 64p. 1976. pap. 3.95 (ISBN 0-8119-0395-8). Fell.
Safety Resource List. (Orig.). 1980. pap. write for info. (ISBN 0-89514-029-2). Am Voc Assn.
Safety Training for the Supervisor. 3rd ed. James E. Gardner. LC 78-52505. 1979. pap. text ed. 8.95 (ISBN 0-201-03090-X). A-W.
Safety Training Methods. Jack B. ReVelle. LC 80-16601. 300p. 1980. 24.95 (ISBN 0-471-07761-5, Pub. by Wiley-Interscience). Wiley.
Safety with Lasers & Other Optical Sources: A Comprehensive Handbook. David Sliney & Myron Wolbarsht. 1060p. 1980. 49.50 (ISBN 0-306-40434-6, Plenum Pr). Plenum Pub.
Saffron Robe. T. Lobsang Rampa. 1974. pap. 2.50 (ISBN 0-685-70567-6). Weiser.
Saffron Robe: The Dramatic & Intense Life of Renowned Christian Mystic, Sadhu Sundar Singh. Janey Lynch-Watson. 1977. pap. 1.75 o.p. (ISBN 0-310-28452-X). Zondervan.
Safire's Washington. William Safire. 416p. 1980. 15.00 (ISBN 0-8129-0919-4). Times Bks.
Safiri the Singer: East African Tales. Eleanor B. Heady. LC 76-161551. (Illus.). 96p. (gr. 2-4). 1972. 5.95 o.p. (ISBN 0-695-80244-5); PLB 5.97 o.p. (ISBN 0-695-40244-7). Follett.
Saga of a Mud Road Doctor. C. Curtis Allen. (Illus.). 132p. 1975. 7.95 (ISBN 0-89015-099-0). Nortex Pr.
Saga of a Wayward Sailor. Tristan Jones. 1979. 9.95 o.p. (ISBN 0-8362-6303-0). Andrews & McMeel.
Saga of a Wayward Sailor. Tristan Jones. 272p. (Orig.). 1980. pap. 2.75 (ISBN 0-380-52985-8, 52985). Avon.
Saga of a Whitetail Deer. Lillian Brady. LC 77-77113. (Illus.). 182p. 1980. 12.50 (ISBN 0-86533-004-2). Amber Crest.
Saga of an American Jewish Family Since the Revolution: A History of the Family of Jonas Phillips. Samuel Rezneck. LC 79-6725. 1980. text ed. 17.75 (ISBN 0-8191-0939-8); pap. text ed. 9.50 (ISBN 0-8191-0940-1). U Pr of Amer.
Saga of Ben Holladay. Ellis Lucia. 1959. 9.95 (ISBN 0-8038-6641-0). Hastings.
Saga of Cimba. Richard Maury. 1973. 7.50 (ISBN 0-8286-0063-5). De Graff.
Saga of Coe Ridge: A Study in Oral History. William L. Montell. LC 74-77846. (Illus.). 1970. 13.50x (ISBN 0-87049-096-6). U of Tenn Pr.
Saga of Denny McCune. Burt Arthur & Budd Arthur. 1979. pap. 1.25 (ISBN 0-505-51397-8). Tower Bks.
Saga of Felix Senac: Being the Legend & Biography of a Confederate Agent in Europe. Regina Rapier. (Illus.). 216p. 1972. 10.00x (ISBN 0-9600584-2-7). R C Rapier.
Saga of Gisli the Outlaw. Tr. by George Johnston. LC 67-207. (Illus.). 1963. pap. 5.50 (ISBN 0-8020-6219-9). U of Toronto Pr.
Saga of Hugh Glass: Pirate, Pawnee, & Mountain Man. John M. Myers. LC 75-38613. viii, 237p. 1976. 14.50x (ISBN 0-8032-0867-7); pap. 3.25 (ISBN 0-8032-5834-8, BB 614, Bison). U of Nebr Pr.
Saga of Iron Mining in Michigan's Upper Peninsula. Burton H. Boyum. 1977. pap. 3.75 (ISBN 0-938746-03-0). Marquette Cnty Hist.
Saga of Smokey Stover. Clark G. Reynolds. LC 78-64485. 1978. 6.00 (ISBN 0-937684-06-6). Tradd St Pr.
Saga of the Colt Six Shooter: And the Famous Men Who Used It. George Virgines. LC 69-10772. (gr. 9 up). 1969. 7.95 (ISBN 0-8119-0148-3). Fell.
Saga of the Fist. John V. Grombach. LC 75-20594. 1977. 19.95 (ISBN 0-498-01681-1). A S Barnes.
Saga of the Phenwick Women: Letitia, the Dreamer, Vol. 35. Kathryn Kimbrough. 1981. pap. 2.25 (ISBN 0-445-04638-4). Popular Lib.
Saga of the Superfortress: The Dramatic Story of the B-29 & the Twentieth Air Force. Steven Birdsall. LC 78-22303. (Illus.). 352p. 1980. 19.95 (ISBN 0-385-13668-4). Doubleday.
Saga of the Volsungs. Tr. by George K. Anderson. LC 80-65685. 200p. 1981. 18.00 (ISBN 0-87413-172-3). U Delaware Pr.
Saga of Tristram & Isond. Tr. & intro. by Paul Schach. LC 73-76351. (Illus.). xxiv, 148p. 1973. 9.50x (ISBN 0-8032-0832-4); pap. 2.25x (ISBN 0-8032-5847-X, BB 608, Bison). U of Nebr Pr.
Sagbare und das Unsagbare: Studien Zur Neueren Franzoesischen Hermeneutik. Manfred Frank. (Suhrkamp Taschenbuecher Wissenschaft: 317). 224p. (Orig., Ger.). 1980. pap. text ed. 7.15 (ISBN 3-518-07917-4, Pub. by Insel Verlag Germany). Suhrkamp.
Sage International Yearbook of Foreign Policy Studies, Vol. 1. Ed. by Patrick J. McGowan. LC 72-98039. 1973. 20.00x (ISBN 0-8039-0202-6). Sage.
Sage International Yearbook of Foreign Policy Studies, Vol. 2. Ed. by Patrick J. McGowan. LC 72-98039. 1974. 20.00x (ISBN 0-8039-0471-1); pap. 9.95x (ISBN 0-8039-0496-7). Sage.
Sage International Yearbook of Foreign Policy Studies, Vol. 3. Ed. by Patrick J. McGowan. LC 72-98039. 1975. 20.00x (ISBN 0-8039-0323-5); pap. 9.95x (ISBN 0-8039-0324-3). Sage.
Sage of Kanchi. Ed. by T. M. P. Mahadevan. 93p. 1975. lib. bdg. 6.25 (ISBN 0-89253-018-9). Ind-US Inc.
Sagebrush Country. Don Jackson. (American Wilderness Ser). (Illus.). 184p. 1975. 12.95 (ISBN 0-8094-1217-9). Time-Life.
Sagebrush Country. Donald Jackson. LC 74-32622. (American Wilderness Ser.). (Illus.). 184p. (gr. 6 up). 1975. lib. bdg. 11.97 (ISBN 0-8094-1218-7). Silver.
Sages & Schoolmen. Arland Ussher. 1965. 6.25 (ISBN 0-8023-1139-3). Dufour.
Sagesse. Paul Verlaine. Ed. by Charles Chadwick. (Athlone French Poets Ser.). 1973. text ed. 16.25x (ISBN 0-485-14704-1, Athlone Pr); pap. text ed. 4.50x (ISBN 0-485-12704-0, Athlone Pr). Humanities.
Saggy, Baggy Elephant. Kathryn Jackson & Byron Jackson. (Illus.). (ps-1). 1975. PLB 5.38 (ISBN 0-307-68908-5, Golden Pr). Western Pub.
Sagittarius. Julia Parker. (Pocket Guide to Astrology Ser.). (Orig.). 1980. pap. write for info. (ISBN 0-671-25556-8, Fireside). S&S.
Sagittarius. Paula Taylor. (Sun Signs Ser.). (Illus.). (gr. 4 up). 1978. PLB 5.95 (ISBN 0-87191-649-5); pap. 2.95 (ISBN 0-89812-079-9). Creative Ed.
Sagittarius in Warsaw. Richard Lourie. LC 73-83036. 192p. 1973. 7.95 (ISBN 0-8149-0729-6). Vanguard.
Sag's Auf Deutsch: A First Book for German Conversation. C. R. Goedsche. (Illus., Ger.). (gr. 10 up). 1979. text ed. 21.00x o.p. (ISBN 0-89197-387-7); pap. text ed. 6.95x (ISBN 0-8290-0026-7). Irvington.
Sahaidak: Virshi, 1922-1924. Iurii Darahan. LC 75-546612. (Ukrai.). 1965. pap. 2.75 (ISBN 0-918884-16-0). Slavia Lib.
Sahara. Jeremy Swift. (World's Wild Places Ser.). (Illus.). 184p. 1975. 12.95 (ISBN 0-8094-2015-5). Time-Life.
Sahara & Sudan: Bornu, Kanem, Borku, Ennedi, Vol. II. Gustav Nachtigal. Tr. by Allan G. Fisher & Humphrey J. Fisher. (Illus.). 1980. text ed. 60.00x (ISBN 0-8419-5752-5). Holmes & Meier.
Sahara & Sudan, Vol. IV: Wadai & Darfur. Gustav Nachtigal. 1971. 38.75x (ISBN 0-520-01789-7). U of Cal Pr.
Sahara Handbook. Simon Glen & Jan Glen. (Illus.). 316p. (Orig.). 1980. pap. 19.95 (ISBN 0-903909-10-3, Roger Lascelles). Bradt Ent.
Sahityakantakodhara. T. Venkatacharya. 96p. 1980. text ed. 10.50 (ISBN 0-8426-1650-0). Verry.
Sahtain: Middle East Cookbook. 10.00 (ISBN 0-686-63567-1). Intl Bk Ctr.
Sai Baba, the Saint of Shirdi. Mani Sahukar. LC 75-29273. 1977. 3.95 o.p. (ISBN 0-913922-11-0). Dawn Horse Pr.
Sai Karate Weapon of Self-Defense. Fumio Demura. LC 74-83597. (Ser. 115). (Illus.). 1974. pap. text ed. 6.95 (ISBN 0-89750-010-5). Ohara Pubns.
Sai Krishna Lila. William J. Jackson. LC 80-67137. 1980. pap. 3.60 (ISBN 0-9600958-7-X). Birth Day.
Saikaku's the Japanese Family Storehouse. Ed. by G. W. Sargent. (University of Cambridge Oriental Pubns.). 1959. 48.00 (ISBN 0-521-06182-2). Cambridge U Pr.
Saikei: Living Landscapes in Miniature. Toshio Kawamoto. LC 67-26311. (Illus.). 132p. 1980. pap. 8.95 (ISBN 0-87011-418-2). Kodansha.
Sail Before Sunset. Earl Hinz. (Illus.). 244p. 1979. 12.95 (ISBN 0-679-51350-7). Western Marine Ent.
Sail Ho. James Bisset & P. R. Stephensen. LC 58-5447. (Illus.). 1958. 14.95 (ISBN 0-87599-015-0). S G Phillips.
Sail Racer. Jack Knights. (Illus.). 235p. 1974. 15.00 (ISBN 0-229-98674-9). Transatlantic.
Sailboarding: A Beginner's Guide to Boardboat Sailing. A. H. Drummond, Jr. LC 73-83627. 160p. (gr. 5-9). 1974. 4.95 o.p. (ISBN 0-385-08670-9). Doubleday.
Sailboat Auxiliary Engine Maintenance: Atomic, Chrysler, Ford, Perkins, Pisces, Volvo-Penta, Westerbeke, Yanmar. Brick Price. Ed. by Jeff Robinson. (Illus.). 144p. 1975. pap. text ed. 9.00 o.p. (ISBN 0-89287-079-6). Clymer Pubns.
Sailboat: Barco De Vela, Bk. 3. Edward B. Fry. Tr. by Monica Gunning. (Storybooks for Beginners Ser.). (Illus.). 15p. (Eng. & Span.). 1980. pap. 12.50 set (ISBN 0-89061-214-5). Jamestown Pubs.
Sailboat in the Wind: Barco De Vela En el Viento, Bk. 4. Edward B. Fry. Tr. by Monica Gunning. (Storybooks for Beginners Ser.). (Illus.). 15p. (Eng. & Span.). (gr. 1). 1980. pap. 12.50 (ISBN 0-89061-215-3). Jamestown Pubs.
Sailboat Maintenance. (Illus.). 336p. 9.00 o.p. (ISBN 0-686-62675-3, B600). Western Marine Ent.
Sailboat Racing. Claire Jones. LC 80-12846. (Superwheels & Thrill Sports Bks.). (Illus.). (YA) (gr. 4 up). 1981. PLB 6.95g (ISBN 0-8225-0434-0). Lerner Pubns.
Sailfish: Swashbuckler of the Open Seas. Jim B. Tinsley. LC 64-7908. 1964. deluxe ed. 16.50 (ISBN 0-8130-0328-8). U Presses Fla.
Sailing. Henry Beard & Roy McKie. LC 80-54621. (Illus.). 96p. 1981. 8.95 (ISBN 0-89480-158-9); pap. 4.95 (ISBN 0-89480-144-9). Workman Pub.
Sailing. Tom Crichton. LC 68-1556. (Pegasus Books: No. 4). 1965. 7.50x (ISBN 0-234-77848-2). Intl Pubns Serv.
Sailing. Roland Denk. (Illus.). 140p. 1981. 12.95 (ISBN 0-8069-9144-5, Pub. by EP Publishing England). Sterling.
Sailing. Robin Knox-Johnston. (International Library). (Illus.). 128p. (gr. 7 up). 1976. PLB 6.90 o.p. (ISBN 0-531-02125-4). Watts.
Sailing Alone Around the World. Joshua Slocum. (Illus.). 1956. pap. 3.50 (ISBN 0-486-20326-3). Dover.
Sailing & Seamanship. 3rd ed. United States Coast Guard Auxiliary. LC 76-29794. (Illus.). 1980. pap. text ed. 7.50 (ISBN 0-930028-02-3). US Coast Guard.
Sailing Cruiser. W. M. Nixon. LC 77-28372. (Illus.). 1978. 12.95 (ISBN 0-396-07573-8). Dodd.
Sailing Drifters. Edward March. 1977. 38.00 (ISBN 0-7153-4679-2). David & Charles.
Sailing Encyclopedia. Ed. by Michael Rickey & Donald M. Street. (Illus.). 1980. 29.95 (ISBN 0-690-01922-X). Lippincott.
Sailing for Beginners. rev. ed. Moulton M. Faraham. (Illus.). 272p. 1981. 14.95 (ISBN 0-02-537140-1). Macmillan.
Sailing from Start to Finish. Yves-Louis Pinaud. 1979. 19.95 (ISBN 0-229-11548-9, Scribner-T). Scribner.
Sailing Is for Me. Tom Vandervoort. (Sports for Me Bks.). (Illus.). (gr. 2-5). 1981. PLB 5.95 (ISBN 0-8225-1128-2). Lerner Pubns.
Sailing Pilots of the Bristol Channel. Stuckey. 1977. 14.95 (ISBN 0-7153-7373-0). David & Charles.
Sailing Round Ireland. Wallace Clark. 1976. 22.50 (ISBN 0-7134-3133-4, Pub. by Batsford England). David & Charles.
Sailing Ships. 2nd ed. Bjorn Landstrom. LC 78-1011. 1978. 8.95 o.p. (ISBN 0-385-14408-3). Doubleday.
Sailing Technique. Harold A. Calahan. (Illus.). 1950. 12.95 (ISBN 0-02-520670-2). Macmillan.
Sailing the Bay. Kimball Livingston. (Illus.). 128p. (Orig.). 1981. pap. 5.95 (ISBN 0-87701-180-X). Chronicle Bks.
Sailing to an Island. Richard Murphy. 1968. pap. 4.95 (ISBN 0-571-08354-4, Pub. by Faber & Faber). Merrimack Bk Serv.
Sailing Trawlers. Edward March. 1977. 38.00 (ISBN 0-7153-4711-X). David & Charles.
Sailing with Children. Conrad Dixon & Edward Sevious. 1969. text ed. 3.00x o.p. (ISBN 0-685-09503-7). Humanities.
Sailing with Dr. Summers. James P. Pettegrove. Date not set. 6.95 (ISBN 0-533-04668-8). Vantage.
Sailing with Paul. H. A. Ironside. Date not set. pap. 1.25 (ISBN 0-87213-387-7). Loizeaux.
Sailing Yacht Design. Douglas Phillips-Birt. (Illus.). 1979. 32.50 (ISBN 0-229-11563-2, ScribT). Scribner.
Sailing Yacht Design: An Appreciation of a Fine Art. Robert G. Henry & Richards T. Miller. LC 65-18207. (Illus.). 1965. 6.00 (ISBN 0-87033-093-4). Cornell Maritime.
Sailmaking. rev ed. William Schmit. LC 76-21094. (Illus.). 136p. 1976. Repr. 10.95 (ISBN 0-8069-8634-4); PLB 9.29 (ISBN 0-8069-8635-2). Sterling.
Sailor from Gibraltar. Marguerite Duras. 1980. pap. 6.95 (ISBN 0-7145-0511-0). Riverrun NY.
Sailor's Admiral: A Biography of William F. Halsey. James M. Merrill. LC 76-8880. (Illus.). 1976. 9.95 o.s.i. (ISBN 0-690-01163-6, TYC-T). T Y Crowell.
Sailors Snug Harbor Eighteen Hundred & One to Nineteen Seventy-Six. Barnett Shepard. LC 79-16979. (Illus.). 105p. (Orig.). 1979. 11.95 (ISBN 0-9604254-1-1); pap. 7.95 (ISBN 0-9604254-0-3). Snug Harbor NY.
Sailor's World. Arthur Beiser. 1972. 19.95 o.p. (ISBN 0-394-46852-X, Co-Pub. by Ridge Pr). Random.
Sailplanes & Soaring. James E. Mrazek. (Illus.). pap. 2.95 o.p. (ISBN 0-8015-6512-X). Dutton.
Sails. rev. ed. Jeremy Howard-Williams. LC 68-19075. (Illus.). 1972. 15.00 (ISBN 0-8286-0054-6). De Graff.
Sails of Hope: The Secret Mission of Christopher Columbus. Simon Wiesenthal. Tr. by Richard Winston & Clara Winston. LC 73-2126. (Illus.). 256p. 1973. 5.95 o.s.i. (ISBN 0-02-628400-6). Macmillan.
Sainsbury's Woodturning Projects for Dining. John Sainsbury. LC 80-54347. (Illus.). 160p. 1981. 14.95 (ISBN 0-8069-5436-1). Sterling.
Saint. Conrad F. Meyer. Tr. by E. F. Hauch from Ger. 1976. Repr. of 1930 ed. 12.00 (ISBN 0-86527-298-0). Fertig.
Saint. Conrad F. Meyer. Tr. by W. F. Twaddell. LC 77-7038. 129p. 1977. 7.50 (ISBN 0-87057-149-4, Pub. by Brown U Pr). Univ Pr of New England.
Saint & Sufi in Modern Egypt: An Essay in the Sociology of Religion. Michael Gilsenan. (Monographs in Social Anthropology). (Illus.). 258p. 1973. 22.50x (ISBN 0-19-823181-4). Oxford U Pr.
Saint & the People Importers. Leslie Charteris. (Saint Ser.). 1979. pap. 1.95 (ISBN 0-441-74900-3). Charter Bks.
Saint & the Sinner. Susie R. Wrentz. LC 79-66397. 1980. 7.95 (ISBN 0-533-04389-1). Vantage.
Saint & the Sizzling Saboteur. Leslie Charteris. (Saint Ser.). 160p. 1981. pap. 2.25 (ISBN 0-441-74908-9). Charter Bks.
Saint & the Skeptics: Joan of Arc in the Work of Mark Twain, Anatole France, & Bernard Shaw. William Searle. LC 75-26709. 178p. 1976. text ed. 12.50x (ISBN 0-8143-1541-0). Wayne St U Pr.
St. Anselm & His Biographer. Richard W. Southern. 58.00 (ISBN 0-521-06532-1). Cambridge U Pr.
St. Antholin's; or, Old Churches & New: A Tale for the Times, 1841. Francis E. Paget. Ed. by Robert L. Wolff. Bd. with Milford Malvoisin; or, Pews & Pew-Holders, 1842. LC 75-469. (Victorian Fiction Ser.). 1975. lib. bdg. 66.00 (ISBN 0-8240-1547-9). Garland Pub.
St. Augustine, Faith, Hope & Charity. Ed. by J. Wuasten & J. Plumpe. Tr. by Louis A. Arand. (Ancient Christian Writers Ser.: No. 3). 165p. 1947. 8.95 (ISBN 0-8091-0045-2). Paulist Pr.
St. Augustine, Sermons for Christmas & Epiphany. St. Augustine. Ed. by J. Quasten & J. Plumpe. Tr. by Thomas Lawler. (Ancient Christian Writers Ser.: No. 15). 250p. 1952. 10.95 (ISBN 0-8091-0137-8). Paulist Pr.
St. Augustine: The Greatness of the Soul, Vol. 9. St. Augustine. Ed. by J. Quasten & J. Plumpe. Tr. by Joseph M. Colleran. (Ancient Christian Writers Ser.: No. 9). 255p. 1950. 11.95 (ISBN 0-8091-0060-6). Paulist Pr.
Saint Augustine's Early Theory of Man, A. D. 386-391. Robert J. O'Connell. LC 68-21981. 1968. text ed. 16.50x (ISBN 0-674-78520-7, Belknap Pr). Harvard U Pr.
St. Augustine's Pigeon: The Selected Stories. Evan S. Connell. Ed. by Gus Blaisdell. 288p. 1980. 12.50 (ISBN 0-86547-013-8). N Point Pr.
Saint Basil on the Value of Greek Literature. N. G. Wilson. (Illus.). 75p. 1975. 17.95x (ISBN 0-7156-0872-X, Pub. by Duckworth England). Biblio Dist.
St. Basil the Great on the Holy Spirit. Tr. by David Anderson from Greek. LC 80-25502. 1980. pap. 3.95 (ISBN 0-913836-74-5). St Vladimirs.
Saint Benedict. Ed. by Pieter Dom Batlelier. (Illus.). 450p. 125.00 (ISBN 0-933516-19-3). Alpine Fine Arts.
St. Benedict: Blessed by God. Guy-Marie Oury. Tr. by John A. Otto from Fr. LC 80-13253. Orig. Title: Ce que croyait Benoit. (Orig.). 1980. pap. text ed. 4.50 (ISBN 0-8146-1181-8). Liturgical Pr.
St. Catherine of Siena. Alice Curtayne. LC 80-53745. 1980. pap. write for info. (ISBN 0-89555-162-4). Tan Bks Pubs.
St. Catherine of Siena. Igino Giordani. LC 75-1624. 1975. 5.95 o.s.i. (ISBN 0-8198-0493-2). Dghtrs St Paul.
Saint Clair Papers: The Life & Public Services of Arthur St. Clair, with His Correspondence & Other Papers, 2 Vols. William H. Smith. LC 79-119058. (Illus.). 1970. Repr. of 1882 ed. lib. bdg. 95.00. Da Capo.
St. Clair Summer. Marvin Werlin & Mark Werlin. 1981. 13.95 (ISBN 0-453-00395-8, H395). NAL.
St. Croix Boyhood. Ralph L. Henry. LC 72-84771. (Illus.). 107p. 1972. 4.95 (ISBN 0-685-26839-X). Minn Hist.
St. Elmo. Augusta Evans. 440p. 1980. Repr. of 1896 ed. lib. bdg. 17.25x (ISBN 0-89968-210-3). Lightyear.
Saint Erkenwald. new ed. Ed. by Clifford Peterson. LC 76-53197. (Haney Foundation Ser). 1977. 10.00x (ISBN 0-8122-7723-6). U of Pa Pr.
Saint Errant. Leslie Charteris. (Saint Ser.). 224p. 1981. pap. 2.25 (ISBN 0-441-74888-0). Charter Bks.

Saint for Your Name: Saints for Boys. Albert J. Nevins. LC 79-92504. (Illus.). 120p. (YA) (gr. 7 up). 1980. 7.95 (ISBN 0-87973-330-6, 330); pap. 4.95 (ISBN 0-87973-320-9, 320). Our Sunday Visitor.

Saint for Your Name: Saints for Girls. Albert J. Nevins. LC 79-92502. (Illus.). 104p. (YA) (gr. 7 up). 1980. 7.95 (ISBN 0-87973-331-4, 331); pap. 4.95 (ISBN 0-87973-321-7, 321). Our Sunday Visitor.

St. Francis Effect. Zach Hughes. pap. 1.75 o.p. (ISBN 0-425-03111-X). Berkley Pub.

St. Francis, Nature Mystic: The Derivation & Significance of the Nature Stories in the Franciscan Legend. Edward A. Armstrong. 1963. 20.00x (ISBN 0-520-01966-0); pap. 5.95 (ISBN 0-520-03040-0). U of Cal Pr.

Saint Francis of Assisi. G. K. Chesterton. LC 57-1230. 1957. pap. 1.95 (ISBN 0-385-02900-4, D50, Im). Doubleday.

Saint Francis of Assisi. Lawrence S. Cunningham. LC 76-14219. (World Authors Ser: No. 409). 1976. lib. bdg. 12.50 (ISBN 0-8057-6249-3). Twayne.

St. Francis of Assisi. Tomie De Paola. (Illus.). 48p. (ps). 1981. PLB 10.95 (ISBN 0-8234-0435-8). Holiday.

Saint Francis of Assisi. Johannes Jorgensen. pap. 2.95 (ISBN 0-385-02875-X, D22, Im). Doubleday.

Saint Francis of Assisi. Douglas Liversidge. LC 68-10187. (Biography Ser). (Map). (gr. 7 up). 1968. PLB 5.90 o.p. (ISBN 0-531-00922-X). Watts.

Saint Francis of Assisi: A Great Life in Brief. E. M. Almedingen. (YA) 1967. 5.99 o.p. (ISBN 0-394-44429-9). Knopf.

St. Francis of Paola: God's Miracle Worker Supreme. Gino J. Simi & Mario M. Segreti. LC 77-78097. 1977. pap. 3.00 (ISBN 0-89555-065-2, 200). TAN Bks Pubs.

Saint Gall Passion Play. Larry E. West. 1976. 11.50 o.s.i. (ISBN 0-686-23383-2). Classical Folia.

Saint Gemma, the Passion Flower. Bardi. 3.50 o.s.i. (ISBN 0-8198-0136-4). Dghtrs St Paul.

Saint Genet: Actor & Martyr. Jean-Paul Sartre. 8.50 o.s.i. (ISBN 0-8076-0243-4). Braziller.

St. Godwin: A Tale of the Sixteenth, Seventeenth, & Eighteenth Centuries, by Count Reginald De St. Leon. Edward Du Bois. Ed. by Gina Luria. (Feminist Controversy in England, 1788-1810 Ser.). 1974. lib. bdg. 50.00 (ISBN 0-8240-0853-7). Garland Pub.

St. Ignatius's Own Story. Tr. by William Young. 1980. Repr. 3.95 (ISBN 0-8294-0359-0). Loyola.

St. Ives Album. Andrew Lanyon. 72p. 1980. 10.00x (ISBN 0-906720-00-1, Pub. by Hodge England). State Mutual Bk.

Saint James. J. H. Ropes. LC 16-6543. (International Critical Commentary Ser.). 336p. Repr. of 1916 ed. 17.50x (ISBN 0-567-05035-1). Attic Pr.

Saint Joan. George B. Shaw. Ed. by Stanley Weintraub. LC 76-134308. 1971. pap. 7.50 (ISBN 0-672-61091-4). Bobbs.

Saint Joan, a Screenplay. Bernard Shaw. Ed. by Bernard F. Dukore. LC 68-11039. (Illus.). 224p. 1968. 9.95 (ISBN 0-295-97885-6); pap. 2.45 (ISBN 0-295-95072-2, WP56). U of Wash Pr.

Saint John, 2 vols. J. H. Bernard. LC 29-17737. (International Critical Commentary Ser.). Repr. of 1928 ed. Vol. 1, 480p. 22.00x (ISBN 0-567-05024-6); Vol. 2, 456p. 22.00x (ISBN 0-567-05025-4). Attic Pr.

St. John: Chapters 1-8, Vol. I. G. Reith. (Handbooks for Bible Classes Ser.). 197p. Repr. of 1889 ed. text ed. 7.50 (ISBN 0-567-08114-1). Attic Pr.

St. John: Chapters 8-21, Vol. II. G. Reith. (Handbooks for Bible Classes). 178p. Repr. of 1889 ed. text ed. 7.50 (ISBN 0-567-08115-X). Attic Pr.

St. John of the Cross: His Life & Poetry. G. Brenan. Tr. by Lynda Nicholson. LC 72-83577. (Illus.). 224p. 1973. 38.50 (ISBN 0-521-20006-7); pap. 8.95x (ISBN 0-521-09953-6). Cambridge U Pr.

Saint-John Perse. Rene Galand. (World Authors Ser.: France: No. 244). lib. bdg. 10.95 (ISBN 0-8057-2690-X). Twayne.

Saint-John Perse. Roger Little. (Athlone French Poets Ser.). 1973. text ed. 16.25x (ISBN 0-485-14602-9, Athlone Pr); pap. text ed. 8.75x (ISBN 0-485-12202-2, Athlone Pr). Humanities.

Saint Judas. James Wright. LC 59-12481. (Wesleyan Poetry Program: Vol. 4). (Orig.). 1959. 10.00x (ISBN 0-8195-2004-7, Pub. by Wesleyan U Pr). Columbia U Pr.

St. Leon: A Tale of the Sixteenth Century, 4 vols. William Godwin. (Feminist Controversy in England, 1788-1810 Ser.). 1974. Set. lib. bdg. 152.00 (ISBN 0-8240-0862-6); lib. bdg. 50.00 ea. Garland Pub.

St. Louis-A History. Primm. (Western Urban History Ser.). (Illus.). 1981. 16.95 (ISBN 0-87108-546-1). Pruett.

St. Louis & the Arch. Joel Meyerowitz. 112p. 1981. pap. 29.95 (ISBN 0-8212-1105-6). NYGS.

Saint Louis in 1884. William H. Bishop. Ed. by William R. Jones. (Illus.). 24p. 1977. Repr. of 1884 ed. pap. 2.50 (ISBN 0-89646-024-X). Outbooks.

St. Louis to Me. Howard F. Baer. 1978. 10.95 (ISBN 0-86629-005-2). Sunrise MO.

St. Luke. 5th ed. Alfred Plummer. (International Critical Commentary Ser.). 688p. Repr. of 1901 ed. text ed. 23.00x (ISBN 0-567-05023-8). Attic Pr.

St. Margaret Mary Alacoque. Leon Cristiani. 1976. 5.00 (ISBN 0-8198-0456-8); pap. 4.00 o.s.i. (ISBN 0-8198-0457-6). Dghtrs St Paul.

Saint Mark. E. P. Gould. LC 25-17683. (International Critical Commentary Ser.). 376p. 1896. text ed. 20.00x (ISBN 0-567-05022-X). Attic Pr.

Saint Mark. D. E. Nineham. LC 77-81621. (Westminster Pelican Commentaries Ser.). 1978. 12.95 (ISBN 0-664-21344-8). Westminster.

St. Matthew. 3rd ed. W. C. Allen. (International Critical Commentary Ser.). 456p. Repr. of 1907 ed. text ed. 20.00x. Attic Pr.

St. Matthew's Earthquake: Judgement & Discipleship in the Gospel of Matthew. Paul Hinnebusch. 154p. (Orig.). 1980. pap. 3.95 (ISBN 0-89283-093-X). Servant.

St. Mick. Jack Challenge. 270p. 1981. 13.95 (ISBN 0-915520-41-9); pap. 6.95 (ISBN 0-915520-41-9). Ross-Erikson.

St. Nicholas Book. Martin Greif. LC 76-5089. (Illus.). 60p. 1976. 5.95 o.s.i. (ISBN 0-87663-234-7). Universe.

Saint-Nicholas Liturgy & Its Literary Relationship (10th-12th Centuries) Charles W. Jones. (U. C. Publ. in English Studies: Vol. 27). 1963. pap. 7.00x (ISBN 0-520-09068-3). U of Cal Pr.

Saint of the Wilderness. Jess Carr. LC 74-77781. 441p. 1974. 8.95 (ISBN 0-89227-008-X); pap. 4.95 (ISBN 0-89227-026-8). Commonwealth Pr.

Saint on the Spanish Main. Leslie Charteris. (Saint Ser.). 224p. 1981. pap. 2.25 (ISBN 0-441-74889-9). Charter Bks.

Saint Overboard. Leslie Charteris. 1976. Repr. of 1936 ed. lib. bdg. 12.85 (ISBN 0-89190-381-X). Am Repr-Rivercity Pr.

Saint Overboard. Leslie Charteris. (The Saint Ser.). 288p. 1981. pap. 2.25 (ISBN 0-441-74895-3). Charter Bks.

St. Patrick & Irish Christianity. T. Corfe. LC 73-75862. (Introduction to the History of Mankind Ser.). 48p. 1973. 3.95 (ISBN 0-521-20228-0). Cambridge U Pr.

St. Patrick for Ireland by James Shirley. Ed. by John P. Turner, Jr. & Stephen Orgel. LC 78-66857. (Renaissance Drama Ser.). 1979. lib. bdg. 28.00 (ISBN 0-8240-9729-7). Garland Pub.

St. Patrick: His Writings & Muirchu's Life. Ed. by A. B. Hood. (History from the Sources Ser.). 101p. 1978. 12.50x (ISBN 0-8476-6080-X). Rowman.

Saint Patrick's Day. Bob Reese. Ed. by Alton Jordan. (Holidays Ser.). (Illus.). (gr. k-3). 1977. PLB 3.50 (ISBN 0-89868-030-1, Read Res); pap. text ed. 1.75 (ISBN 0-89868-063-8). ARO Pub.

Saint Paul, Apostle & Martyr. Igino Giordani. 1941. 7.00 o.s.i. (ISBN 0-8198-0138-0); pap. 6.00 o.s.i. (ISBN 0-8198-0139-9). Dghtrs St Paul.

St. Paul, Oregon, Eighteen Thirty to Eighteen Ninety. Harvey J. McKay. LC 80-69228. (Illus.). 1980. 15.00 (ISBN 0-8323-0384-4). Binford.

Saint Paul's Epistle to the Ephesians. Brooke F. Westcott. 1978. 9.75 (ISBN 0-686-12958-X). Klock & Klock.

St. Pauls Within-the-Walls: Rome, a History. Judith Millon. 1981. 8.95 (ISBN 0-87233-058-3). Bauhan.

Saint Peter & Saint Jude, 2 vols. Charles Bigg. LC 2-12311. (International Critical Commentary Ser.). 376p. Repr. of 1978 ed. Vol. 1, 534p. 20.00x (ISBN 0-567-05036-X); Vol. 2, 580p. 22.00x (ISBN 0-567-05012-2). Attic Pr.

Saint-Simon & Saint-Simonism: A Chapter in the History of Socialism in France. Arthur J. Booth. 202p. 1970. Repr. of 1871 ed. text ed. 34.25x (ISBN 90-6090-161-4). Humanities.

Saint-Simonian Religion in Germany. E. M. Butler. 1968. Repr. of 1926 ed. 21.00 (ISBN 0-86527-177-1). Fertig.

Saint Simonian's Mill & Carlyle: A Preface to Modern Thought. Richard Pankhurst. 1957. text ed. 4.75x (ISBN 0-391-02042-0). Humanities.

St. Simons: Enchanted Island. Barbara S. Hull. LC 80-80048. (Illus.). 136p. 1980. 7.95 (ISBN 0-87797-049-1). Cherokee.

Saint Sophia in Istanbul: An Architectural Survey, Installment I. Robert L. Van Nice. LC 65-29029. (Illus.). 1966. 80.00 o.p. (ISBN 0-88402-015-0, Ctr Byzantine). Dumbarton Oaks.

St. Stephen's Green or the Generous Lovers. Ed. by Christopher Murray. (Dolmen Texts Ser.: No. 6). (Illus.). 112p. 1980. text ed. 15.00x (ISBN 0-85105-367-X, Dolmen Pr). Humanities.

St. Teresa of Avila. Carmelite Sisters. (gr. 4-8). 0.75 o.s.i. (ISBN 0-8198-0224-7). Dghtrs St Paul.

Saint Theresa, the Little Flower. Sr. Gesualda Of The Holy Spirit. (Illus.). 1960. 4.95 o.s.i. (ISBN 0-8198-0142-9). Dghtrs St Paul.

St. Therese of Lisieux: Her Last Conversations. Tr. by John Clarke from Fr. LC 76-27207. (Illus.). 1977. pap. 6.95x (ISBN 0-9600876-3-X). ICS Pubns.

Saint Thomas: poems. Tram Combs. LC 65-14050. (Wesleyan Poetry Program: Vol. 25). (Orig.). 1965. 10.00x (ISBN 0-8195-2025-X, Pub. by Wesleyan U Pr); pap. 4.95 (ISBN 0-8195-1025-4). Columbia U Pr.

Saint Under Stress. Norval F. Pease. LC 70-88927. (Dimension Ser.). 1980. pap. 5.95 (ISBN 0-8163-0384-3, 19129-6). Pacific Pr Pub Assn.

Saint Valentine's Day. Clyde R. Bulla. LC 65-11643. (Holiday Ser.). (Illus.). (gr. 1-3). 1965. PLB 7.89 (ISBN 0-690-71744-X, TYC-J). T Y Crowell.

St. Wilfrid at Hexham. Ed. by D. P. Kirby. 1974. 22.00 (ISBN 0-85362-155-1, Oriel). Routledge & Kegan.

Saint with a Gun: The Unlawful American Private Eye. William Ruehlmann. LC 74-11490. 155p. 1974. 12.00 (ISBN 0-8147-7355-9). NYU Pr.

Sainte Vierge: Etudes Archeologiques et Iconographiques, 2 vols. C. Rohault De Fleury. (Illus., Fr.). 1981. Repr. of 1878 ed. Set. 325.00x (ISBN 0-89241-154-6). Caratzas Bros.

Saints. Jean Pedrick. (Chapbook Ser.: No. 1). 40p. (Orig.). 1980. pap. 4.95 (ISBN 0-937672-00-9). Rowan Tree.

Saints. Edith Simon. 1968. 4.50 o.s.i. (ISBN 0-440-07585-8). Delacorte.

Saints: Adventures in Courage. Mary O'Neill. LC 63-17278. (Illus.). (gr. 4-7). 1963. 7.95 o.p. (ISBN 0-385-04970-6). Doubleday.

Saints & Festivals of the Christian Church. Harold P. Brewster. LC 73-159869. (Illus.). xiv, 558p. 1975. Repr. of 1904 ed. 24.00 (ISBN 0-8103-3992-7). Gale.

Saints & Fireworks, Religion & Politics in Rural Malta. Jeremy Boissevain. (Monographs on Social Anthropology Ser: No. 30). 1969. pap. text ed. 3.25x (ISBN 0-391-00756-4, Athlone Pr). Humanities.

Saints & Heroes Speak. Robert J. Fox. LC 77-70206. 1977. pap. 7.95 o.p. (ISBN 0-87973-640-2). Our Sunday Visitor.

Saints & Householders: A Study of Hindu Ritual & Myth Among the Kangra Rajputs. J. Gabriel Campbell. (Illus.). 11.50x (ISBN 0-685-89506-8). Himalaya Hse.

Saints & Politicians. D. B. O'Brien. LC 74-82221. (African Studies: No. 15). (Illus.). 224p. 1975. 24.95 (ISBN 0-521-20572-7). Cambridge U Pr.

Saints & the Union: Utah Territory During the Civil War. E. B. Long. LC 80-16775. (Illus.). 292p. 1981. 17.95 (ISBN 0-252-00821-9). U of Ill Pr.

Saints & Their Emblems. Maurice Drake & Wilfred Drake. LC 68-18021. xiv, 235p. 1972. Repr. of 1916 ed. 25.00 (ISBN 0-8103-3032-6). Gale.

Saints Are People: Church History Through the Saints. Alfred McBride. 144p. (Orig.). 1981. pap. 4.00 (ISBN 0-697-01783-4). Wm C Brown.

Saints Book. Catherine Dooley. 64p. (Orig.). (gr. k-3). 1981. pap. 2.95 (ISBN 0-8091-6547-3). Paulist Pr.

Saints Go Marching in. Robert F. Holtzclaw. LC 78-71499. (Illus.). 216p. 1980. 12.50 (ISBN 0-933144-00-8). Keeble Pr.

Saints' Harmony. Ed. by Mark H. Forscutt. (Heritage Reprint Ser.). 566p. 1974. Repr. of 1889 ed. 19.95 o.p. (ISBN 0-8309-0120-5). Herald Hse.

Saints in Art. Clara E. Clement. LC 77-89303. 1976. Repr. of 1899 ed. 17.00 (ISBN 0-8103-3030-X). Gale.

Saints in Art. Margaret E. Tabor. LC 68-18031. (Illus.). 1969. Repr. of 1908 ed. 15.00 (ISBN 0-8103-3076-8). Gale.

Saints of Gwynedd. Molly Miller. (Studies in Celtic History). 132p. 1979. 19.50x (ISBN 0-8476-6186-5). Rowman.

Saints of Sage & Saddle: Folklore Among the Mormons. Austin Fife & Alta Fife. 375p. 1981. pap. 15.00 (ISBN 0-87480-180-X). U of Utah Pr.

Saints of the Cauvery Delta. R. Krishnamurthy. 1979. text ed. 10.00x (ISBN 0-391-01844-2). Humanities.

Saints, Sinners, & Christian History. James S. Packer. (Orig.). 1980. pap. 6.25 (ISBN 0-9604090-0-9). Paladium Pr.

Sakharov Speaks. Andrei D. Sakharou. Intro. by Harrison E. Salisbury. 1974. pap. 1.65 (ISBN 0-394-71302-8, Vin). Random.

Sakkara: A Guide to the Necropolis of Sakkara & the Site of Memphis. Jill Kamil. LC 77-27546. (Illus.). 1978. pap. text ed. 7.50x (ISBN 0-582-78069-1). Longman.

Sakshi Gopal: A Witness for the Wedding. Illus. by Tom Foley. (Illus.). 16p. (gr. 1-4). 1981. pap. 2.95 (ISBN 0-89647-010-5). Bala Bks.

Saktas, an Introductory & Comparative Study: Calcutta & London, Nineteen Thirty-Three. Ernest A. Payne. LC 78-74270. (Oriental Religions Ser.: Vol. 8). (Illus.). 167p. 1980. lib. bdg. 22.00 (ISBN 0-8240-3905-X). Garland Pub.

Sakti & Sakta. John Woodroffe. 16.95 (ISBN 0-89744-116-8, Pub. by Ganesh & Co. India). Auromere.

Salad a Day. Ruth Moorman & Lalla Williams. (Illus.). 80p. 1980. pap. 4.95 (ISBN 0-937552-02-X). Quail Ridge.

Salad Bar Syndrome. Albert J. Pollard. 1981. 6.95 (ISBN 0-533-04573-8). Vantage.

Salad Preparation. Ser-Vo-Tel Institute. (Foodservice Career Education Ser.). 1975. pap. 4.95 (ISBN 0-8436-2019-6). CBI Pub.

Saladin: Politics of Holy War. M. Lyons & D. Jackson. LC 79-13078. (Cambridge University Oriental Publications Ser.). (Illus.). 400p. Date not set. price not set (ISBN 0-521-22358-X). Cambridge U Pr.

Salads. Fuhrmann. 1981. 8.95 (ISBN 0-8120-5398-2). Barron.

Salads. Time-Life Books Editors. (Good Cook Ser.). (Illus.). 176p. 1980. 12.95 (ISBN 0-8094-2879-2). Time-Life.

Salads & Salad Dressings for Food Service Menu Planning. Ed. by Eulalia Blair. LC 73-89528. (Foodservice Menu Planning Ser.). 1974. 16.50 (ISBN 0-8436-0576-6). CBI Pub.

Salads from Beginning to Endive. Kraft Kitchens. (Orig.). pap. 5.95 (ISBN 0-87502-073-9). Benjamin Co.

Salamander. Morris West. 1981. pap. 2.95 (ISBN 0-671-42432-7). PB.

Salamander Migration & Other Poems. Cary Waterman. LC 79-24291. (Pitt Poetry Ser.). 1980. 9.95 (ISBN 0-8229-3415-9); pap. 4.50 (ISBN 0-8229-5315-3). U of Pittsburgh Pr.

Salamanders. Charlene W. Billings. LC 80-21838. (Skylight Bk.). (Illus.). 48p. (gr. 2-5). 1981. PLB 5.95 (ISBN 0-396-07913-X). Dodd.

Salar the Salmon. Henry Williamson. (Illus., Orig.). 1973. pap. 6.95 (ISBN 0-571-04811-0, Pub. by Faber & Faber). Merrimack Bk Serv.

Salaries & Related Matters in the Service Department 1980. Steven Langer. 1980. pap. 60.00 (ISBN 0-916506-38-X). Abbott Langer Assocs.

Salaries & Related Matters in the Service Department, 1981. Ed. by Steven Langer. 1981. pap. 85.00 (ISBN 0-686-69467-8). Abbott Langer Assocs.

Salaries & Related Personnel Practices in Voluntary Social & Health Agencies in New York City. 1974. pap. 5.00 - bulletin 1, 2 & 3 (ISBN 0-86671-018-3). Comm Coun Great NY.

Salaries of Engineering Technicians & Technologists. 112p. 1979. 75.00 (ISBN 0-686-27582-9, 304-79). AAES.

Salaries of Engineers in Education - 1980. Date not set. 15.00 (307-80). AAES.

Salary Equity: Detecting Sex Bias in Salaries Among College & University Professors. Thomas R. Pezzullo & Barbara E. Brittingham. LC 78-24634. 1979. 17.95 (ISBN 0-669-02770-7). Lexington Bks.

Salary Ranges of Personnel Employed in State Mental Hospitals & Community Mental Health Centers-1970. Charles K. Kanno & Patricia L. Scheidemandel. pap. 5.00 (ISBN 0-685-24871-2, P156-0). Am Psychiatric.

Salary Study 1981. 1981. pap. text ed. 5.75 (ISBN 0-87868-203-1). Child Welfare.

Sale-Leasebacks: Economics, Tax Aspects, & Lease Terms Course Handbook. (Real Estate Law & Practice Course Handbook Ser.,1977-78: Vol. 148). 1978. pap. 20.00 o.p. (ISBN 0-685-59710-5, N4-4316). PLI.

Salekov Kill. Guy Richards. 256p. (Orig.). 1981. pap. 2.50 (ISBN 0-449-14405-4, GM). Fawcett.

Salem: A Pictorial History. Harry Stein. (Illus.). 205p. 1981. pap. price not set (ISBN 0-89865-125-5). Donning Co.

Salem Chapel. Margaret W. Oliphant. Ed. by Robert L. Wolff. LC 75-1508. (Victorian Fiction Ser.). 1975. Repr. of 1863 ed. lib. bdg. 66.00 (ISBN 0-8240-1582-7). Garland Pub.

Salem, Massachusetts, 1626-1683: A Covenant Community. Richard P. Gildrie. LC 74-20841. (Illus.). 1975. 9.95x (ISBN 0-8139-0532-X). U Pr of Va.

Salem Witchcraft Papers: Verbatim Transcripts, 3 vols. Ed. by Paul Boyer & Stephen Nissenbaum. 1977. lib. bdg. 125.00 (ISBN 0-306-70655-5). Da Capo.

Salem Witchcraft Trials: Have You Made No Contract with the Devil? Alice Dickinson. LC 73-12085. (Focus Bks). (Illus.). 72p. (gr. 7 up). 1974. PLB 4.90 o.p. (ISBN 0-531-01049-X). Watts.

Salem's Daughter. Maggie Osborne. (Orig.). 1981. pap. 2.75 (ISBN 0-451-09602-9, E9602, Sig). NAL.

Salem's Lot. Stephen King. LC 73-22804. 1975. 11.95 (ISBN 0-385-00751-5). Doubleday.

Salem's Lot: TV Edition. Stephen King. (Illus.). (RL 10). 1979. pap. 2.75 (ISBN 0-451-09231-7, E9231, Sig). NAL.

Salerno Ivories: Ars Sacra from Medieval Amalfi. Robert P. Bergman. LC 79-22616. 1980. 37.50x (ISBN 0-674-78528-2). Harvard U Pr.

Sales & Sales Management. 2nd ed. P. Allen. (Illus.). 288p. 1979. pap. 12.95x (ISBN 0-7121-1962-0, Pub. by Macdonald & Evans England). Intl Ideas.

Sales Force Management. Kenneth R. Davis & Frederick E. Webster, Jr. LC 68-12886. (Illus.). 1968. 24.95 (ISBN 0-8260-2525-0, 22271). Wiley.

Sales Horizons. 3rd ed. Kenneth B. Haas & Enos C. Perry. (gr. 9-12). text ed. 10.96 o.p. (ISBN 0-685-04697-4, 78769-7); 3.68 o.p. (ISBN 0-685-04698-2, 78771-3); chapter tests 1.52 o.p. (ISBN 0-685-04699-0); tchrs' guide to text, wkbk. & tests s.p. 2.32 o.p. (ISBN 0-685-04700-8, 78770-5). P-H.

Sales in a Nutshell. 2nd ed. John M. Stockton. LC 80-25579. (Nutshell Ser.). 358p. 1980. pap. text ed. write for info. (ISBN 0-8299-2116-8). West Pub.

Sales Management. Edward W. Cundiff et al. (Illus.). 656p. 1981. text ed. 20.95 (ISBN 0-13-788059-6). P-H.

Sales Management. Charles M. Futrell. LC 80-65796. 528p. 1981. text ed. 17.95 (ISBN 0-03-049276-9). Dryden Pr.

Sales Management. Robert F. Hartley. LC 78-69614. (Illus.). 1979. text ed. 18.95 (ISBN 0-395-26511-8); inst. manual 1.10 (ISBN 0-395-26512-6); test bank 1.25 (ISBN 0-395-29301-4). HM.

Sales Management: A Review of the Current Literature. Danny N. Bellenger & Robert L Berl. (Research Monograph: No. 89). 1981. spiral bdg. 10.00 (ISBN 0-88406-147-7). GA St U Busn Pub.

Sales Management: Decisions, Policies & Cases. 3rd ed. R. R. Still et al. (Illus.). 544p. 1976. 21.00 (ISBN 0-13-788042-1). P-H.

Sales Management Game. Boone & Kurtz. (Orig.). 1978. pap. 10.95 (ISBN 0-686-28581-6). Pennwell Pub.

Sales Manager's Guide to Selection & Control of Export Agents. Colin MacMillan & Sydney Paulden. LC 68-58695. 1969. 14.95 (ISBN 0-8436-0900-1). CBI Pub.

Sales Negotiation Strategies: Building the Win-Win Customer Relationship. Mack Hanan et al. LC 76-44021. 1977. 11.95 (ISBN 0-8144-5431-3). Am Mgmt.

Sales of Securities by Corporate Insiders: The Impact of the 140 Series. 2nd ed. Robert L. Frome & Victor M. Rosenzweig. 1975. 20.00 o.p. (ISBN 0-685-85359-4, B1-1216). PLI.

Sales Promotion Handbook. Ed. by Tony Dakin. 450p. 1974. 25.00 o.p. (ISBN 0-7161-0097-5). Herman Pub.

Sales Promotion: Its Place in Marketing Strategy. 2nd ed. Peter Spillard. 1976. 27.50x o.p. (ISBN 0-8464-0811-2). Beekman Pubs.

Sales Situation Elements. General Electric Marketing Consulting Services. 1973. 55.00 (ISBN 0-932078-02-8). GE Tech Prom & Train.

Sales Tax Strategies of Wisconsin Businesses. Percy Werner. Ed. by M. Fischer-Williams. LC 80-65336. 94p. (Orig.). 1980. pap. 12.75 (ISBN 0-936400-01-3). Gearhart-Edwards.

Salesman in the Field. 108p. 1980. pap. 9.50 (ISBN 92-2-102308-7, ILO149, ILO). Unipub.

Salesman in the Field: Conditions of Work & Employment of Commercial Travellers & Representatives. Michael Bell. Ed. by International Labour Office, Geneva. viii, 108p. (Orig.). 1980. pap. 8.55 (ISBN 92-2-102308-7). Intl Labour Office.

Salesman Performance Appraisal: A National Study. Ferdinand F. Fournies. 1975. 25.00 (ISBN 0-917472-01-2). F Fournies.

Salesmanship. Boy Scouts Of America. LC 19-600. (Illus.). 32p. (gr. 6-12). 1971. pap. 0.70x (ISBN 0-8395-3351-9, 3351). BSA.

Salesmanship. S. A. Williams. (Teach Yourself Ser.). 1974. pap. 2.95 o.p. (ISBN 0-679-10485-2). McKay.

Salesmanship: A Contemporary Approach. Paul Preston & Ralph Nelson. 1981. 15.95 (ISBN 0-8359-6933-9); instr's manual free. Reston.

Salesmanship: Modern Principles & Practices. U. Grant Marsh. LC 74-160524. (Illus.). 1972. 15.95x (ISBN 0-13-789453-8). P-H.

Salesperson's Legal Guide. Steven M. Sack & Howard J. Steinberg. LC 80-22647. 144p. 1981. 12.95 (ISBN 0-13-788190-8); pap. 5.95 (ISBN 0-13-788182-7). P-H.

Saleswoman: A Guide to Career Success. Barbara Fletcher. (gr. 12). 1980. pap. 2.50 (ISBN 0-671-82895-9). PB.

Salinity in Irrigation & Water Resources. Yaron. 448p. 1981. 49.75 (ISBN 0-8247-6741-1). Dekker.

Saliva & Salivation: Proceedings of a Satellite Symposium to the 28th International Congress of Physiological Held at Szekesfehervar, Hungary, 1980. Ed. by T. Zelles. LC 80-41878. (Advances in Physiological Sciences: Vol. 28). (Illus.). 500p. 1981. 60.00 (ISBN 0-08-027349-1). Pergamon.

Saliva Tree. Brian Aldiss. (Science Fiction Ser.). 1981. lib. bdg. 16.95 (ISBN 0-8398-2566-8). Gregg.

Salivary Gland Tumors. Ed. by Ludwika Sikorowa et al. LC 80-14975. 200p. 1981. 9.50 (ISBN 0-08-025557-4). Pergamon.

Salle of the Mississippi. Ronald Syme. (Illus.). (gr. 7 up). 1953. PLB 6.50 o.p. (ISBN 0-688-21591-2). Morrow.

Sallinka & the Golden Bird. A. Scholey. 1979. 6.95 (ISBN 0-13-789487-2). P-H.

Sally & Joe. Bob Sang. 288p. (Orig.). 1981. pap. 2.75 (ISBN 0-932844-04-9). R H Sang & Son.

Sally-Ann in the Snow. Petronella Breinburg. (Illus.). 1979. 6.50 (ISBN 0-370-01809-5, Pub. by Chatto Bodley Jonathan). Merrimack Bk Serv.

Sally-Ann's Umbrella. Petronella Breinburg. (Illus.). 1979. 6.95 (ISBN 0-370-10752-7, Pub. by Chatto Bodley Jonathan). Merrimack Bk Serv.

Sally Can't See. Palle Petersen. LC 77-628. (Illus.). (gr. k-4). 1977. PLB 5.79 o.p. (ISBN 0-381-90058-4, JD-J). John Day.

Sally Hemings. Barbara Chase-Riboud. 1980. pap. 2.75 (ISBN 0-380-48686-5, 48686). Avon.

Sally's Secret. Shirley Hughes. 32p. (ps-1). 1980. 6.50 (ISBN 0-370-02010-3, Pub. Chatto Bodley Jonathan). Merrimack Bk Serv.

Sally's Secret. Bernice Myers. (gr. k-3). 1977. pap. 1.25 (ISBN 0-590-10418-7, Schol Pap). Schol Bk Serv.

Salmon. Paula Z. Hogan. LC 78-21178. (Life Cycles Ser.). (Illus.). (gr. k-3). 1979. PLB 9.95 (ISBN 0-8172-1255-8). Raintree Pubs.

Salmon & Sea Trout. Ed. by Kenneth Mansfield. 1979. 4.50 o.p. (ISBN 0-214-66837-1, ADON 8088-4, Dist by Arco). Barrie & Jenkins.

Salmon & Trout Farming in Norway. 1978. 24.75 (ISBN 0-85238-093-3, FN 75, FN). Unipub.

Salmon, Beavers & Sea Otters. Jacques-Yves Cousteau. (Illus.). 1980. 19.95 o.p. (ISBN 0-8227-8031-3). Petersen Pub.

Salmon Fisheries of Scotland. (Illus.). 1978. pap. 8.00 (ISBN 0-85238-091-7, FN67, FN). Unipub.

Salmon Flies: Their Character, Style, & Dressing. Poul Jorgensen. LC 78-17941. (Illus.). 192p. 1978. 19.95 (ISBN 0-8117-1426-8). Stackpole.

Salmon P. Chase. Albert B. Hart. LC 80-21705. (American Statesmen Ser.). 470p. 1981. pap. 6.95 (ISBN 0-87754-191-4). Chelsea Hse.

Salmonid Ecosystems of the North Pacific. Ed. by William J. McNeil & Daniel C. Himsworth. LC 80-17800. (Illus.). 348p. pap. 15.00 (ISBN 0-87071-335-3); pap. text ed. 15.00 (ISBN 0-686-68208-4). Oreg St U Pr.

Salo Wittmayer Baron Jubilee Volume: On the Occasion of His Eightieth Birthday, 3 vols. new ed. Ed. by Saul Lieberman & Arthur Hyman. LC 74-82633. 1533p. 1975. 90.00x set (ISBN 0-685-51945-7); Vol. 1. (ISBN 0-231-03911-5); Vol. 2. (ISBN 0-231-03912-3); Vol. 3. (ISBN 0-231-03913-1). Columbia U Pr.

Salome. Oscar Wilde. 1962. pap. 2.50 (ISBN 0-8283-1466-7, 65). Branden.

Salomon Gessner. J. Hibberd. LC 76-7139. (Anglica Germanica Ser.: No. 2). (Illus.). 1977. 33.00 (ISBN 0-521-21234-0). Cambridge U Pr.

Salons of the "Independants", 1884 to 1891. Ed. by Theodore Reff. (Modern Art in Paris 1855 to 1900 Ser.). 253p. 1981. lib. bdg. 44.00 (ISBN 0-8240-4709-5). Garland Pub.

Salons of the "Independants", 1892 to 1895. Ed. by Theodore Reff. (Modern Art in Paris 1855 to 1900 Ser.). 320p. 1981. lib. bdg. 44.00 (ISBN 0-8240-4710-9). Garland Pub.

Salons of the "Independants", 1896 to 1900. Ed. by Theodore Reff. (Modern Art in Paris 1855 to 1900 Ser.). 280p. 1981. lib. bdg. 44.00 (ISBN 0-8240-4711-7). Garland Pub.

Salons of the "Nationale", 1890. Ed. by Theodore Reff. (Modern Art in Paris 1855 to 1900 Ser.). (Illus.). 256p. 1981. lib. bdg. 44.00 (ISBN 0-8240-4712-5). Garland Pub.

Salons of the "Nationale", 1891. Ed. by Theodore Reff. (Modern Art in Paris 1855 to 1900 Ser.). (Illus.). 302p. 1981. lib. bdg. 44.00 (ISBN 0-8240-4713-3). Garland Pub.

Salons of the "Nationale", 1892. Ed. by Theodore Reff. (Modern Art in Paris 1855 to 1900 Ser.). (Illus.). 294p. 1981. lib. bdg. 44.00 (ISBN 0-8240-4714-1). Garland Pub.

Salons of the "Nationale", 1893. Ed. by Theodore Reff. (Modern Art in Paris 1855 to 1900 Ser.). (Illus.). 275p. 1981. lib. bdg. 44.00 (ISBN 0-8240-4715-X). Garland Pub.

Salons of the "Nationale", 1894. Ed. by Theodore Reff. (Modern Art in Paris 1855 to 1900 Ser.). (Illus.). 254p. 1981. lib. bdg. 44.00 (ISBN 0-8240-4716-8). Garland Pub.

Salons of the "Nationale", 1895. Ed. by Theodore Reff. (Modern Art in Paris 1855 to 1900 Ser.). (Illus.). 288p. 1981. lib. bdg. 44.00 (ISBN 0-8240-4717-6). Garland Pub.

Salons of the "Nationale", 1896. Ed. by Theodore Reff. (Modern Art in Paris 1855 to 1900 Ser.). (Illus.). 263p. 1981. lib. bdg. 44.00 (ISBN 0-8240-4718-4). Garland Pub.

Salons of the "Nationale", 1897. Ed. by Theodore Reff. (Modern Art in Paris 1855 to 1900 Ser.). (Illus.). 291p. 1981. lib. bdg. 44.00 (ISBN 0-8240-4719-2). Garland Pub.

Salons of the "Nationale", 1898. Ed. by Theodore Reff. (Modern Art in Paris 1855 to 1900 Ser.). (Illus.). 259p. 1981. lib. bdg. 44.00 (ISBN 0-8240-4720-6). Garland Pub.

Salons of the "Nationale", 1899. Ed. by Theodore Reff. (Modern Art in Paris 1855 to 1900 Ser.). (Illus.). 256p. 1981. lib. bdg. 44.00 (ISBN 0-8240-4721-4). Garland Pub.

Salons of the "Refuses". Ed. by Theodore Reff. (Modern Art in Paris 1855 to 1900 Ser.). 133p. 1981. lib. bdg. 44.00 (ISBN 0-8240-4722-2). Garland Pub.

Saloon Society. Bill Manville. 192p. 1980. pap. 2.25 (ISBN 0-515-05490-9). Jove Pubns.

Saloons of the American West. Robert L. Brown. (Illus.). 144p. 16.50 (ISBN 0-913582-24-7). Sundance.

Salt. George Cecil. (Easy-Read Fact Bks.). (Illus.). 48p. (gr. 2-4). 1976. PLB 4.47 o.p. (ISBN 0-531-00359-0). Watts.

Salt. Augusta Goldin. LC 65-18696. (Let's-Read-&-Find-Out Science Bk). (Illus.). (gr. k-3). 1966. PLB 7.89 (ISBN 0-690-71815-2, TYC-J). T Y Crowell.

Salt Book. Pamela Wood. LC 76-53419. 480p. 1977. pap. 5.95 (ISBN 0-385-11423-0, Anchor Pr); pap. 5.95 (ISBN 0-385-11423-0, Anch). Doubleday.

Salt Cycle. E. Radlauer & R. S. Radlauer. LC 72-7113. (Sports Action Bks.). (Illus.). 48p. (gr. 3 up). 1973. PLB 5.20 o.p. (ISBN 0-531-02585-3). Watts.

Salt Doll: A Novel on India. Shouri Daniels. 1977. 6.50x o.p. (ISBN 0-8364-0055-0). South Asia Bks.

Salt Dome Utilization & Environmental Considerations: Proceedings of a Symposium. Ed. by Joseph D. Martinez. 1977. pap. 17.50x (ISBN 0-8071-0380-2). La State U Pr.

Salt from the Psalter. Mary F. Owens. LC 80-67147. 1981. pap. 4.50 (ISBN 0-8054-1218-2). Broadman.

Salt Glands in Birds & Reptiles. M. Peaker & J. L. Linzell. LC 74-12966. (Physiological Society Monographs: No. 32). (Illus.). 296p. 1975. 53.50 (ISBN 0-521-20629-4). Cambridge U Pr.

SALT Handbook: Key Documents & Issues, 1972-1979. Ed. by Roger Labrie. 1979. pap. 12.25 (ISBN 0-8447-3316-4). Am Enterprise.

Salt II & U. S.-Soviet Strategic Forces. Jacquelyn K. Davis et al. LC 79-2713. (Special Reports Ser.). 1979. 5.00 (ISBN 0-89549-016-1). Inst Foreign Policy Anal.

Salt or the Education of Griffith Adams: A Novel. Charles G. Norris. (Lost American Fiction Ser.). 400p. 1981. Repr. of 1918 ed. price not set (ISBN 0-8093-1011-2). S Ill U Pr.

Salt River Times. William Mayne. LC 80-20806. 160p. (gr. 5-7). 1981. 7.95 (ISBN 0-688-80311-3). Greenwillow.

Salt-Sea Mastodon: A Reading of Moby-Dick. Robert Zoellner. 1973. 17.50x (ISBN 0-520-02339-0). U of Cal Pr.

SALT: The Moscow Agreements & Beyond. Mason Willrich & John B. Rhinelander. LC 73-10698. (Illus.). 1975. pap. text ed. 7.95 (ISBN 0-02-935470-6). Free Pr.

Salt Two: Boatbuilding, Sailmaking, Island People, River Driving, Bean Hold Beans, Wooden Paddles, & More Yankee Doings. Ed. by Pamela Wood. LC 80-553. (Illus.). 448p. 1980. 14.95 (ISBN 0-385-14346-X, Anchor Pr); pap. 7.95. Doubleday.

Salt-Water Fisherman's Bible. Erwin A. Bauer. LC 62-14182. pap. 3.50 (ISBN 0-385-02337-5). Doubleday.

Salt Water Flies: Popular Patterns & How to Tie Them. Herman Kessler & Kenneth Bay. LC 72-6109. (Illus.). 1972. 8.95 o.s.i. (ISBN 0-397-00939-9). Lippincott.

Salt-Water Fly-Fishing Handbook. Sam Nix. LC 71-180095. 168p. 1973. 3.95 o.p. (ISBN 0-385-04033-4). Doubleday.

Salt-water Palaces. Maldwin Drummond. 1980. 16.95 (ISBN 0-670-61636-2). Viking Pr.

Salt-Water Poems & Ballads. John Masefield. (gr. 7 up). 1953. 4.95 o.s.i. (ISBN 0-02-581000-6); pap. 1.25 (ISBN 0-02-069930-1). Macmillan.

Salt-Water Tropical Fish in Your Home. Gail Campbell. LC 76-1175. (Illus.). 160p. (YA) 1976. 10.95 (ISBN 0-8069-3730-0); PLB 9.29 (ISBN 0-8069-3731-9). Sterling.

Salted Lemons. Doris B. Smith. LC 80-66250. 240p. (gr. 3-7). 1980. 9.95 (ISBN 0-590-07666-3, Four Winds). Schol Bk Serv.

Salted Peanuts: Eighteen Hundred Little Known Facts. E. C. McKenzie. (Direction Bks). 1976. pap. 3.95 large print ed. (ISBN 0-8010-5914-3); pap. 1.25 (ISBN 0-8010-5914-3). Baker Bk.

Saltwater Game Fishing. Joe Brooks. (Illus.). 1968. 15.95 o.p. (ISBN 0-06-070547-7, HarpT). Har-Row.

Salty Christians. Hans-Ruedi Weber. 1963. pap. 0.75 (ISBN 0-8164-2062-9). Crossroad NY.

Salus: Low Cost Rural Health Care & Health Manpower Training, Vol. 6. 157p. 1980. pap. 10.00 (ISBN 0-88936-249-1, IDRC153, IDRC). Unipub.

Salut Du Peuple, Journal De la Science Sociale. Constantin Pecqueur. 236p. (Fr.). 1977. lib. bdg. 32.50x o.p. (ISBN 0-8287-0673-5); pap. text ed. 22.50x o.p. (ISBN 0-685-75618-1). Clearwater Pub.

Salute. Clarence W. Anderson. (Illus.). (gr. 2-4). 1967. 3.95g o.s.i. (ISBN 0-02-705270-2). Macmillan.

Salute to Courage. Ed. by Dennis P. Ryan. 1979. 19.95 (ISBN 0-231-04230-2). Columbia U Pr.

Salvage. Dorothy S. Thomas. 1975. Repr. of 1952 ed. 24.75x (ISBN 0-520-02915-1). U of Cal Pr.

Salvage & Overhaul Practices: FSTA, 104. 6th ed. Ed. by Jerry Laughlin & Connie Osterhout. LC 79-84252. 1979. pap. text ed. 7.00 (ISBN 0-87939-030-1). Intl Fire Serv.

Salvation. Lewis S. Chafer. 160p. 1972. pap. 3.95 (ISBN 0-310-22351-2). Zondervan.

Salvation. H. D. McDonald. (Foundations for Faith). 4.95 (ISBN 0-89107-225-X). Good News.

Salvation & Behavior. W. Graham Scroggie. LC 80-8075. (W. Graham Scroggie Library). 104p. 1981. pap. 2.50 (ISBN 0-8254-3735-0). Kregel.

Salvation Behind Bars. Roger Elwood. 1977. pap. 1.50 (ISBN 0-505-51142-8). Tower Bks.

Salvation by Faith & Your Will. Morris L. Venden. LC 78-7597. (Horizon Ser.). 1978. pap. 4.50 (ISBN 0-8127-0190-9). Southern Pub.

Salvation: God's Amazing Plan. Millard J. Erickson. 1978. pap. 3.95 (ISBN 0-88207-772-4). Victor Bks.

Salvation in the Slums: Evangelical Social Welfare Work, 1865-1920. Norris Magnuson. LC 76-54890. (No. 10). 1977. 14.50 (ISBN 0-8108-1001-8). Scarecrow.

Salvation Is a Necessary Evil. Joseph S. Russo. Bd. with Science of Human Existence. LC 74-11822. 1981. pap. 5.95 (ISBN 0-932742-01-7). World Action.

Salvation Merchants. Janelle Viglini. 1975. 7.50 o.p. (ISBN 0-685-53334-4, 0-911156-13-8). Porter.

Salvation, Present, Perfect, Now or Never. D. S. Warner. 63p. pap. 0.40; pap. 1.00 3 copies. Faith Pub Hse.

Salvation Tomorrow. Stephen Neill. 1976. pap. 3.95 o.p. (ISBN 0-687-36799-9). Abingdon.

Salzburg Studies in English Literature & the Critics: Review of Don Juan Criticism, 1900 to 1973. James Hogg & Charles J. Clancy. (Salzburg Studies in English Literature, Romantic Reassessment: No. 40). 1974. pap. text ed. 25.00x (ISBN 0-391-01413-7). Humanities.

Sam & Emma. Donald Nelsen. LC 72-136998. (Illus.). (gr. k-3). 1971. 5.95 o.s.i. (ISBN 0-8193-0467-0, Four Winds); PLB 5.41 o.s.i. (ISBN 0-8193-0468-9). Schol Bk Serv.

Sam & His Cart. Arthur Honeyman. LC 80-36714. (Illus.). 64p. (gr. 2-6). 1980. Repr. of 1977 ed. 6.95 (ISBN 0-88436-793-2). EMC.

Sam & Violet Are Twins. Nicole Rubel. 32p. (gr. 1-3). 1981. pap. 1.95 (ISBN 0-380-76919-0, Camelot). Avon.

Sam & Violet Go Camping. Nicole Rubel. 32p. (gr. 1-3). 1981. pap. 1.95 (ISBN 0-380-76927-1, Camelot). Avon.

Sam Bass. Wayne Gard. LC 36-17302. (Illus.). x, 262p. 1969. 10.50x (ISBN 0-8032-0868-5); pap. 3.65 (ISBN 0-8032-5068-1, BB 391, Bison). U of Nebr Pr.

Sam Casanova. Max Catto. 1977. pap. 1.75 o.p. (ISBN 0-451-07790-3, E7790, Sig). NAL.

Sam Diego, a Coloring Adventure in San Diego, California. Barbara Plunkett. (Illus.). (ps). 1977. pap. 1.25 (ISBN 0-914488-14-7). Rand-Tofua.

Sam Grilli's Complete Guide to Lake Erie Walleye. Sam Grilli. (Illus.). 160p. (gr. 4-12). 1980. 5.95 (ISBN 0-9604304-0-7); pap. 5.95 (ISBN 0-686-64677-0). Sport Fishing.
Sam Higginbottom of Allahabad. Gary R. Hess. LC 67-17631. 1967. 7.95x (ISBN 0-8139-0118-9). U Pr of Va.
Sam Houston. Matthew G. Grant. LC 73-18080. 1974. PLB 5.95 (ISBN 0-87191-299-6). Creative Ed.
Sam Houston. Herman Toepperwein. pap. 1.50 (ISBN 0-910722-09-9). Highland Pr.
Sam Houston & the Senate. John F. Kennedy. Ed. by Larry Smitherman. LC 79-14422. 12.50 (ISBN 0-8363-0087-4). Jenkins.
Sam Houston: The Great Designer. Llerena B. Friend. LC 54-13252. (Illus.). 1954. pap. 7.95x (ISBN 0-292-78422-8). U of Tex Pr.
Sam Houston's Texas. Sue Flanagan. LC 64-22338. (Illus.). 214p. 1973. 20.00 (ISBN 0-292-73363-1). U of Tex Pr.
Sam Peckinpah. Douglas McKinney. (Theatrical Arts Ser.). 1979. lib. bdg. 10.95 (ISBN 0-8057-9264-3). Twayne.
Sam Slick. Thomas C. Haliburton. Ed. by Ray P. Baker. 420p. 1981. Repr. of 1923 ed. lib. bdg. 45.00 (ISBN 0-8495-2373-7). Arden Lib.
Sam Who Never Forgets. Eve Rice. LC 76-30370. (ps-3). 1977. 7.95 (ISBN 0-688-80088-2); PLB 7.63 (ISBN 0-688-84088-4). Greenwillow.
Samain. Meg E. Atkins. pap. 1.50 o.p. (ISBN 0-345-26006-6). Ballantine.
Samaki: The Story of an Otter in Africa. Joseph A. Davis. 1979. 10.95 o.p. (ISBN 0-525-19601-3). Dutton.
Samarkand Dawn. Graham Diamond. LC 80-82850. 256p. (Orig.). 1981. pap. 2.25 (ISBN 0-87216-781-X). Playboy Pbks.
Sambo Sahib: The Story of Little Black Sambo. Elizabeth Hay & Helen Bannerman. (Illus.). 196p. 1981. 16.50x (ISBN 0-389-20151-0). B&N.
Samizdat Register. Ed. by Roy A. Medvedev. 1977. pap. 24.95 (ISBN 0-393-05652-X); pap. write for info. (ISBN 0-393-09081-7). Norton.
Samizdat Reigister Two. Ed. by Roy Medvedev. 1981. 19.95 (ISBN 0-393-01419-3). Norton.
Samkhya-Sutras of Pancasikha & the Samkhyatattvalcka. Hariharananda Aranya. 1977. 9.50 (ISBN 0-89684-313-0, Pub. by Motilal Banarsidass India); pap. 6.50 (ISBN 0-89684-346-7). Orient Bk Dist.
Sammy & the Cat Party. Ron Van Der Meer & Atie Van Der Meer. (Illus.). 32p. 1980. 8.95 (ISBN 0-241-10141-7, Pub. by Hamish Hamilton England). David & Charles.
Sammy Miller on Trials. Sammy Miller. (Illus.). 1971. 5.95 (ISBN 0-87880-002-6). Norton.
Sammy Skunk. Ron Reese. Ed. by Alton Jordan. (I Can Read Underwater Bks). (Illus.). (gr. k-3). 1974. PLB 3.50 (ISBN 0-89868-009-3, Read Res); pap. text ed. 1.75 (ISBN 0-89868-042-5). ARO Pub.
Sammy Skunk Plays the Clown. LaRue Selman. Ed. by Alton Jordan. (Buppet Series). (Illus.). (gr. k-3). 1981. PLB 4.50 (ISBN 0-89868-097-2, Read Res); pap. text ed. 1.95 (ISBN 0-89868-108-1). ARO Pub.
Samnium & the Samnites. E. T. Salmon. 1967. 49.50 (ISBN 0-521-06185-7). Cambridge U Pr.
Samoa in Colour. James Siers. (Illus.). 1970. 11.95 o.p. (ISBN 0-589-00455-7, Dist. by C E Tuttle). Reed.
Samoa: Yesterday, Today & Tommorow. Napoleone A. Tuiteleleapaga. 160p. 1980. 9.95 (ISBN 0-89962-018-3). Todd & Honeywell.
Samoan Tangle: A Study in Anglo-German-American Relations 1878-1900. Paul M. Kennedy. 325p. 1974. 30.00x (ISBN 0-686-28320-1, Pub. by Irish Academic Pr). Biblio Dist.
Samoe Glavnoe. Nikolai Evreinov. (Rus.). 1980. 13.00 (ISBN 0-88233-700-9); pap. 4.50 (ISBN 0-88233-701-7). Ardis Pubs.
Samothrace Excavations: Conducted by the Institute of Fine Arts of New York University, 4 vols. Ed. by Karl Lehmann & P. W. Lehmann. Incl. Vol. 1. Ancient Literary Sources. Ed. & tr. by Naphtali Lewis. 1958. 20.00x (ISBN 0-691-09820-4); Vol. 2, Pt. 1. Inscriptions on Stone. P. M. Fraser. 1960. 25.00x (ISBN 0-691-09821-2); Vol. 2, Pt. 2. Inscriptions on Ceramics & Minor Objects. Karl Lehmann. 1960. 25.00x (ISBN 0-691-09822-0); Vol. 3. Hieron. P. Lehmann. 1969. 3 vols. boxed set 70.00 (ISBN 0-691-09823-9); Vol. 4, Pt. 1. Hall of Votive Gifts. Karl Lehmann. 1962. 25.00x (ISBN 0-691-09824-7); Vol. 4, Pt. 2. Altar Court. Karl Lehmann & Denys Spittle. 1964. 30.00x (ISBN 0-691-09825-5). (Bollingen Ser.: Vol. 60). Princeton U Pr.
Samoyeds. Joyce Reynaud. (Illus.). 128p. 1980. 2.95 (ISBN 0-87666-680-2, KW-072). TFH Pubns.
Sample Cataloguing Forms: Illustrations of Solutions to Problems of Description (with Particular Reference to Chapters 1-13 of the Anglo-American Cataloguing Rules, Second Edition) 3rd ed. Robert B. Slocum. LC 80-21507. (Illus.). 121p. 1980. 11.00 (ISBN 0-8108-1364-5). Scarecrow.
Sample Design in Business Research. William E. Deming. LC 60-6451. (Probability & Mathematical Statistics Ser.). 1960. 39.95 (ISBN 0-471-20724-1, Pub. by Wiley-Interscience). Wiley.
Sample Survey Methods & Theory, 2 Vols. M. H. Hansen et al. LC 53-8112. 1953. Vol. 1: Methods & Applications. 35.95 (ISBN 0-471-34914-3); Vol. 2: Theory. 33.50 (ISBN 0-471-34947-X, Pub. by Wiley-Interscience). Wiley.
Sampler on Sampling. Bill Williams. LC 77-23839. (Probability & Mathematical Statistics Ser.). 1978. 19.95 (ISBN 0-471-03036-8, Pub. by Wiley-Interscience). Wiley.
Sampling for Health Professionals. Paul S. Levy & Stanley Lemeshow. LC 80-14733. 320p. 1980. pap. text ed. 22.95 solutions manual (ISBN 0-534-97986-6). Lifetime Learn.
Sampling Inspection Tables: Single & Double Sampling. 2nd ed. Harold F. Dodge & Harry G. Romig. LC 59-6763. (Ser. in Probability & Mathematical Statistics). (Illus.). 1959. 32.95 (ISBN 0-471-21747-6, Pub. by Wiley-Interscience). Wiley.
Sampling Methods for Censuses & Surveys. 3rd, rev. ed. Frank Yates. 1965. 20.75 o.s.i. (ISBN 0-02-855500-7). Hafner.
Sampling Representations & Approximations for Certain Functions & Stochastic Processes. Muhammad K. Habib. 100p. 1980. pap. 3.15 (1260). U of NC Pr.
Sampling Systems for Process Analyzers. Cornish et al. 1981. write for info. Butterworths.
Sam's First Fish. Leonard Shortall. (Illus.). (ps-3). 1962. PLB 7.44 (ISBN 0-688-31658-1). Morrow.
Sam's World. Sam Cornish. 1978. 7.95 o.p. (ISBN 0-916276-03-1). Decatur Hse.
Samson Agonistes. John Milton. Ed. by F. T. Prince. 1957. pap. 5.95x (ISBN 0-19-831910-X). Oxford U Pr.
Samson, Last of the California Grizzlies. Robert M. McClung. (Illus.). 96p. (gr. 3-7). 1973. PLB 6.25 o.p. (ISBN 0-688-21935-7); PLB 6.48 (ISBN 0-688-31935-1). Morrow.
Samson Strike. Tony Williamson. 256p. 1981. pap. 2.50 (ISBN 0-445-04643-0). Popular Lib.
Samuel Adams. James K. Hosmer. LC 80-23753. (American Statesmen Ser.). 445p. 1980. pap. 6.95 (ISBN 0-87754-195-7). Chelsea Hse.
Samuel Beckett. Ed. by Lawrence Graver & Raymond Federman. (Critical Heritage Ser.). 1979. 27.00x (ISBN 0-7100-8948-1). Routledge & Kegan.
Samuel Beckett. John Pilling. 1976. 18.00 (ISBN 0-7100-8323-8). Routledge & Kegan.
Samuel Beckett. William Y. Tindall. LC 64-22640. (Columbia Essays on Modern Writers Ser.: No. 4). (Orig.). 1964. pap. 2.00 (ISBN 0-231-02659-5, MW4). Columbia U Pr.
Samuel Beckett & the Pessimistic Tradition. Steven Rosen. LC 76-2506. 1976. 17.00 (ISBN 0-8135-0809-6). Rutgers U Pr.
Samuel Beckett: The Comic Gamut. Ruby Cohn. 1962. 18.00 (ISBN 0-8135-0402-3). Rutgers U Pr.
Samuel Butler. George R. Wasserman. (English Author Ser.: No. 193). 1976. lib. bdg. 10.95 (ISBN 0-8057-6667-7). Twayne.
Samuel Butler, Hudibras: Parts 1 & 2, & Selected Other Writings. Samuel Butler. Ed. by John Wilders & Hugh De Quehen. 1973. pap. 11.50x (ISBN 0-19-871067-4). Oxford U Pr.
Samuel Coleridge-Taylor: Anglo-Black Composer, 1875-1912. William Tortolano. LC 76-57172. (Illus.). 1977. 10.00 (ISBN 0-8108-1010-7). Scarecrow.
Samuel Cooper: 1609-1672. Daphne Foskett. 1974. 25.00 (ISBN 0-571-10346-4, Pub. by Faber & Faber). Merrimack Bk Serv.
Samuel Davies: Apostle of Dissent in Colonial Virginia. George W. Pilcher. LC 77-134737. 1971. 13.50x (ISBN 0-87049-121-0). U of Tenn Pr.
Samuel De Champlain. William J. Jacobs. LC 73-14554. (Visual Biography Ser). (Illus.). 64p. (gr. 4-5). 1974. PLB 4.90 o.p. (ISBN 0-531-01275-1). Watts.
Samuel E. Dyke Collection of Kentucky Pistols. Frank Klay. 30p. 1980. 2.00 (ISBN 0-88227-004-4). Gun Room.
Samuel F.B. Morse: His Letters & Journals, 2 vols. Ed. by Edward L. Morse. 440p. 1980. Repr. of 1914 ed. lib. bdg. 65.00 (ISBN 0-89984-331-X). Century Bookbindery.
Samuel George Washington Jones Snake. George M. Hay. (Illus.). 32p. (gr. 1-4). 1980. 8.95 (ISBN 0-938490-00-1). Abbincott.
Samuel Goldwyn Presents. Alvin H. Marill. LC 75-20598. (Illus.). 352p. 1976. 19.95 o.p. (ISBN 0-498-01658-7). A S Barnes.
Samuel Hopkins & the New Divinity Movement: Calvinism, the Congregational Ministry, & Reform in New England Between the Great Awakenings. Joseph Conforti. 240p. (Orig.). 1981. pap. 12.95 (ISBN 0-8028-1871-4). Eerdmans.
Samuel Johnson. Donald Greene. (English Authors Ser.: No. 95). lib. bdg. 10.95 (ISBN 0-8057-1296-8). Twayne.
Samuel Johnson - Book Reviewer in the Literary Magazine: Or Universal Review 1756-1758. Donald D. Eddy. LC 78-53000. 170p. 1979. lib. bdg. 17.00 (ISBN 0-8240-3425-2). Garland Pub.
Samuel Johnson: A Critical Study. J. P. Hardy. 1979. 22.00x (ISBN 0-7100-0291-2). Routledge & Kegan.
Samuel Johnson: A Layman's Religion. Maurice J. Quinlan. (Illus.). 1964. 20.00x (ISBN 0-299-03030-X). U of Wis Pr.
Samuel Johnson & the New Science. Richard B. Schwartz. 1971. 20.00x (ISBN 0-299-06010-1). U of Wis Pr.
Samuel Johnson: Selected Poetry & Prose. Ed. by Frank Brady & W. K. Wimsatt. 1978. 30.00x (ISBN 0-520-02929-1); pap. 6.95 (ISBN 0-520-03552-6). U of Cal Pr.
Samuel Johnson's Literary Criticism. Samuel Johnson. Ed. by R. D. Stock. LC 73-91398. (Regents Critics Ser). xvi, 286p. 1974. 12.50x (ISBN 0-8032-0469-8); pap. 3.50x (ISBN 0-8032-5467-9, BB 415, Bison). U of Nebr Pr.
Samuel One & Two. Ralph D. Gehrke. (Concordia Commentary Ser). 1968. 10.95 (ISBN 0-570-06280-2, 15-2029). Concordia.
Samuel Palmer: A Biography. Raymond Lister. 1974. 17.95 (ISBN 0-571-09732-4, Pub. by Faber & Faber). Merrimack Bk Serv.
Samuel Pepys. Arthur Ponsonby. 160p. 1980. Repr. of 1928 ed. lib. bdg. 20.00 (ISBN 0-89760-706-6). Telegraph Bks.
Samuel Pepys Esq. Richard Barber. LC 70-123622. (Illus.). 1970. 11.95 (ISBN 0-520-01763-3). U of Cal Pr.
Samuel Pepys' Penny Merriments. Roger Thompson. LC 76-50544. 1977. 18.00x (ISBN 0-231-04280-9); pap. 6.95 (ISBN 0-231-04281-7). Columbia U Pr.
Samuel Pepys's Spanish Plays. Edward M. Wilson & Don W. Cruickshank. 160p. 1981. 74.00 (ISBN 0-19-721793-1). Oxford U Pr.
Samuel Phelps & Sadler's Wells Theatre. Shirley S. Allen. LC 72-120259. (Illus.). 1971. 20.00x (ISBN 0-8195-4029-3, Pub. by Wesleyan U Pr). Columbia U Pr.
Samuel Richardson. Austin Dobson. LC 67-23877. 1968. Repr. of 1902 ed. 15.00 (ISBN 0-8103-3055-5). Gale.
Samuel Richardson: An Annotated Bibliography of Critical Studies. Richard Hannaford. LC 79-7916. (Garland Reference Library of Humanities). 450p. 1980. lib. bdg. 40.00 (ISBN 0-8240-9531-6). Garland Pub.
Samuel Seabury, 1729-1796: A Study in the High Church Tradition. Bruce E. Steiner. LC 78-181686. (Illus.). xiii, 508p. 1971. 17.50x (ISBN 0-8214-0098-3). Ohio U Pr.
Samuel Sewall & the World He Lived in. N. H. Chamberlain. 319p. 1980. Repr. of 1897 ed. lib. bdg. 30.00 (ISBN 0-89987-110-0). Darby Bks.
Samuel Taylor Coleridge. Virginia L. Radley. (English Authors Ser.: No. 36). 1966. lib. bdg. 9.95 (ISBN 0-8057-1100-7). Twayne.
Samuel Taylor Coleridge: A Selective Bibliography of Criticism, 1935-1977. Ed. by Jefferson D. Caskey & Melinda M. Stapp. LC 78-57765. 1978. lib. bdg. 17.95 (ISBN 0-313-20564-7, CCO/). Greenwood.
Samuel, The Prophet. Gordon Lindsay. (Old Testament Ser.). 1.25 (ISBN 0-89985-138-X). Christ Nations.
Samurai -- a Military History. Stephen Turnbull. LC 76-50595. 1977. 22.95 (ISBN 0-02-620540-8, 62054). Macmillan.
Samurai Sword: A Handbook. John M. Yumoto. LC 58-7497. (Illus.). 1958. 11.00 (ISBN 0-8048-0509-1). C E Tuttle.
San Antonio in the Eighteenth Century. 2nd ed. San Antonio Bicentennial Heritage Committee. (Illus.). 154p. 1976. pap. 7.95 (ISBN 0-933164-22-X). U of Tex Inst Tex Culture.
San Antonio River. Fritz Toepperwein & Emilie Toepperwein. 1977. pap. 1.50 (ISBN 0-910722-11-0). Highland Pr.
San Bernardino of Siena & Sant Antonino of Florence. Raymond De Roover. (Kress Library of Business & Economics: No. 9). (Illus.). 1967. pap. 5.00x (ISBN 0-678-09913-8, Baker Lib). Kelley.
San-Ch'u: Its Technique & Imagery. Wayne Schlepp. 1970. 15.00x (ISBN 0-299-05540-X). U of Wis Pr.
San Cristobal de las Casas, Chiapas: City & Area Guide. 3rd ed. Mike Shawcross. (Illus.). 74p. 1980. pap. 4.95 (ISBN 0-933982-16-X). Bradt Ent.
San Diego: California's Cornerstone. Iris W. Engstrand. Ed. by Ellen S. Blakey & Larry P. Silvey. LC 80-66336. (American Portrait Ser.). (Illus.). 224p. 1980. 24.95 (ISBN 0-932986-09-9). Continent Herit.
San Diego Chargers. Julian May. (NFL Today Ser.). (gr. 4-8). 1980. PLB 6.45 (ISBN 0-87191-733-5); pap. 2.95 (ISBN 0-89812-236-8). Creative Ed.
San Diego County Indians As Farmers & Wage Earners. Teo Couro. pap. 1.00 (ISBN 0-686-69102-4). Acoma Bks.
San Diego Disco & Dance Guide: Guide to San Diego's Dance Spots. Diane DesRoches. LC 80-51178. (Disco & Dance Directories Ser.). 60p. (Orig.). 1981. pap. 2.50 (ISBN 0-936854-00-6). Word Factory.
San Elizario. Eugene Porter. (Illus.). 14.95 (ISBN 0-8363-0117-X); special ed 125.00 (ISBN 0-685-83963-X). Jenkins.
San Francisco. Federal Writers' Project. 538p. 1940. Repr. 45.00 (ISBN 0-403-02205-3). Somerset Pub.
San Francisco. C. Moorhouse. (Great Cities Ser.). (Illus.). 1979. lib. bdg. 14.94 (ISBN 0-686-51010-0). Silver.
San Francisco. Geoffrey Moorhouse. Ed. by Time-Life Books. (Great Cities). (Illus.). 1979. 14.95 (ISBN 0-8094-2347-2). Time-Life.
San Francisco: A Screenplay. Anita Loos. LC 78-9034. (Screenplay Library). (Illus.). 212p. 1979. 10.00 (ISBN 0-8093-0876-2); pap. 6.95 (ISBN 0-8093-0877-0). S Ill U Pr.
San Francisco Affordable Feasts, Vol. 1. R. B. Read. LC 77-74627. (California Living Book). (Illus.). 1977. pap. 3.95 (ISBN 0-89395-001-7). Cal Living Bks.
San Francisco Bay Area People's Yellow Pages. 4th ed. Donnis Mary et al. Ed. by Diane Sampson & Jan Zobel. (Illus., Orig.). 1975. pap. 3.50 o.p. (ISBN 0-686-20765-3). SF Bay Area.
San Francisco Bay Area People's Yellow Pages. 5th ed. Ed. by Jan Zobel. (Illus.). 1981. pap. 4.95. SF Bay Area.
San Francisco Begins, Seventeen Seventy-Six. Parker L. Johnstone. (gr. 4-5). 1979. 7.95 (ISBN 0-912748-01-X). Mission Dolores.
San Francisco: Cool, Gray City of Love. Jean Porter & Leonard Cahn. 1981. 19.95 (ISBN 0-525-93180-5, Hawthorn); pap. 10.95 (ISBN 0-525-47663-6). Dutton.
San Francisco Earthquake. Gordon Thomas & Max M. Witts. pap. 2.95 (ISBN 0-8128-7028-X). Stein & Day.
San Francisco, Eighteen Forty-Six to Eighteen Fifty-Six: From Hamlet to City. Roger W. Lotchin. (Urban Life in America Ser.). (Illus.). 340p. 1974. 17.95 (ISBN 0-19-501749-8). Oxford U Pr.
San Francisco Forty Nine'ers. Julian May. (NFL Today). (Illus.). (gr. 3-6). 1977. PLB 6.45 (ISBN 0-87191-599-5); pap. 2.95 (ISBN 0-686-67474-X). Creative Ed.
San Francisco Insider's Guide: A Unique Guide to Bay Area Restaurants, Bars, Best Bets, Bargains, Sex & Sensuality, & More... John K. Bailey. 224p. 1980. pap. 4.95 (ISBN 0-936816-00-7). Non Stop Bks.
San Francisco Nineteen Thirty-Nine. Seymour Snaer. 1980. pap. 9.95 (ISBN 0-9602462-5-8). Working Pr CA.
San Francisco Scavengers: Dirty Work & the Pride of Ownership. Stewart E. Perry. 1978. 12.95 (ISBN 0-520-03518-6). U of Cal Pr.
San Francisco Scenes. Greg Frazier. (City Scenes Ser.). (Illus.). 32p. 1972. pap. 3.50 (ISBN 0-912300-29-9, 29-9). Troubador Pr.
San Francisco, the Way It Was Then & Now. Phyllis Zauner & Lou Zauner. (Western Mini-Histories Ser.). (Illus.). 64p. (Orig.). 1980. pap. 3.00 (ISBN 0-936914-04-1). Zanel Pubns.
San Francisco: Walks & Tours in the Golden Gate City. Randolph Delehanty. (Illus.). 340p. 1980. pap. 9.95 (ISBN 0-8037-7651-9). Dial.
San Jose: California's First City. Donald O. DeMers, Jr. & Edwin A. Beilharz. Ed. by Ellen S. Blakey & Larry P. Silvey. LC 80-66340. (American Portrait Ser.). (Illus.). 223p. 1980. 24.95 (ISBN 0-932986-13-7). Continent Herit.
San Juan Bautista: Gateway to Spanish Texas. Robert S. Weddle. (Illus.). 1968. 17.95 (ISBN 0-292-73306-2). U of Tex Pr.
San Juan Island: Coastal Place Names & Cartographic Nomenclature. Bryce Wood. LC 80-17728. (Sponsor Ser.). 280p. (Orig.). 1980. pap. 20.75 (ISBN 0-8357-0526-9, SS-00132). Univ Microfilms.
San Miguel at the Turn of the Century. Leo L. Stanley. (Illus.). 1976. pap. 3.95 o.p. (ISBN 0-913548-33-2, Valley Calif). Western Tanager.
San Min Chu I: The Three Principles of the People. Sun Yat-sen. Ed. by L. T. Chen. Tr. by Frank W. Price from Chinese. LC 75-1033. (China in the 20th Century Ser.). xvi, 514p. 1975. Repr. of 1927 ed. lib. bdg. 45.00 (ISBN 0-306-70698-9). Da Capo.
San Patricio. Jeanne Williams. 1980. pap. write for info. (ISBN 0-671-82732-4). PB.

Sanado De Cancer. Tr. by Jill Lawson. (Spanish Bks.). 1979. 1.40 (ISBN 0-8297-0532-5). Life Pubs Intl.

Sanchez & Other Stories. Richard Dokey. (Regional Ser.). 125p. (Orig.). 1981. pap. 4.75 (ISBN 0-933906-14-5). Gusto Pr.

Sanctification. J. W. Byers. 96p. 0.75. Faith Pub Hse.

Sanctifying Life, Time & Space: An Introduction to Liturgical Study. Marion J. Hatchett. 1976. 8.95 (ISBN 0-8164-0290-6). Crossroad NY.

Sanctions & Social Deviance: The Question of Deterrence. Charles R. Tittle. LC 79-24397. 368p. 1980. 27.95 (ISBN 0-03-052156-4). Praeger.

Sanctions for Evil: Sources of Social Destructiveness. Nevitt Sanford & Craig Comstock. LC 79-129769. (Social & Behavioral Science Ser.). 1971. 17.95x o.p. (ISBN 0-87589-077-6). Jossey-Bass.

Sanctius' Theory of Language: A Contribution to the History of Renaissance Linguistics. Manuel Breva-Claramonte. (Studies in the History of Linguistics). 1980. text ed. 42.75x (ISBN 0-391-01673-3). Humanities.

Sanctuary for Lent, Nineteen Eighty. Maxie D. Dunnam. (Creative Leadership Ser.). 1980. per 100 20.00 o.p. (ISBN 0-687-36842-1). Abingdon.

Sanctuary for Lent, Nineteen Eighty-One. Maxie D. Dunnam. (Orig.). 1981. pap. 20.00 per 100 (ISBN 0-687-36843-X). Abingdon.

Sand. rev. ed. Harlan Wade. LC 78-20971. (Book About Ser.). (Illus.). (gr. k-3). 1979. PLB 7.30 (ISBN 0-8172-1526-3). Raintree Pubs.

Sand & Sandstone. F. J. Pettijohn et al. LC 79-168605. 1972. 31.10 o.p. (ISBN 0-387-05528-2); pap. 19.80 (ISBN 0-387-90071-3). Springer-Verlag.

Sand Castle. Ronald Wegen. LC 75-30707. (gr. k-3). 1977. 6.25 (ISBN 0-688-80033-5); PLB 6.00 (ISBN 0-688-84033-7). Greenwillow.

Sand Castles. Frank Camper. (Orig.). 1980. pap. 2.25 (ISBN 0-532-23132-5). Manor Bks.

Sand County Almanac, & Sketches Here & There. Aldo Leopold. (Illus.). 1949. pap. 4.95 (ISBN 0-19-500777-8, GB). Oxford U Pr.

Sand County Almanac: With Other Essays on Conservation from Round River. Aldo Leopold. (Illus.). 1966. 15.95 (ISBN 0-19-500619-4). Oxford U Pr.

Sand Design for Aquariums and Terrariums. Agnes P. Miller. (Illus.). 1975. pap. 0.50 (ISBN 0-87666-625-X, P-901). TFH Pubns.

Sand Dollar Shuffle. Nell Nale. (Kindergarten Keys Ser). (Illus.). 1975. pap. text ed. 2.49 (ISBN 0-87892-658-5); tchr's manual 2.49 (ISBN 0-87892-659-3). Economy Co.

Sand in Her Shoes. Mildred Lawrence. LC 49-10407. (Illus.). (gr. 4-7). 1949. 4.95 o.p. (ISBN 0-15-270129-X, HJ). HarBraceJ.

Sand in My Shoes. Marion McNeil. 1980. 6.95 (ISBN 0-89962-004-3). Todd & Honeywell.

Sand in the Bag & Other Stories of Ohio, Indiana & Illinois. Moritz A. Jagendorf. LC 52-11125. (Illus.). (gr. 4-9). 7.95 (ISBN 0-8149-0332-0). Vanguard.

Sand Painting for Aquariums & Terrariums. Herbert R. Axelrod. (Illus.). 128p. 1975. pap. 1.00 (ISBN 0-87666-626-8, P-902). TFH Pubns.

Sand Pebbles. Richard McKenna. LC 62-15726. 1963. 11.95 o.p. (ISBN 0-06-012910-7, HarpT). Har-Row.

Sand Pilot of Morecambe Bay. Cedric Robinson. LC 79-56054. (Illus.). 168p. 1980. 14.95 (ISBN 0-7153-7915-1). David & Charles.

Sand Rivers. Peter Matthiessen. LC 80-36703. (Illus.). 240p. 1981. 19.95 (ISBN 0-670-61696-6, Studio). Viking Pr.

Sand, the Sea, & Me. Ed. by M. Jean Craig. (Illus.). 32p. (gr. k-3). 1972. PLB 4.50 o.s.i. (ISBN 0-8027-6107-0); reinforced bdg. 4.41 o.s.i. (ISBN 0-8027-6108-9). Walker & Co.

Sand Tiger Shark. Carol Carrick. LC 76-40206. (gr. 1-5). 1977. 6.95 (ISBN 0-395-28779-0, Clarion). HM.

Sandaled Foot. David Craig. (Cleveland Poets Ser.: No. 27). 60p. (Orig.). 1980. pap. 3.50 (ISBN 0-914946-25-0). Cleveland St Univ Poetry Ctr.

Sandalwood Tree. Margaret Chatterjee. 4.80 (ISBN 0-89253-457-5); flexible cloth 4.00 (ISBN 0-89253-458-3). Ind-US Inc.

Sandcastles. Joseph Allen et al. LC 80-1648. (Illus.). 164p. 1981. pap. 8.95 (ISBN 0-385-15931-5, Dolp). Doubleday.

Sandcastles & Cucumber Ships Last Forever. LC 78-74555. 48p. (Orig.). 2.95 (ISBN 0-916872-06-8). Delafield Pr.

Sandhi: The Theoretical, Phonetic, & Historical Bases of Word-Junction in Sanskrit. W. Sidney Allen. (Janua Linguarum Ser. Minor: No. 17). 1972. pap. text ed. 18.80x (ISBN 90-2792-360-4). Mouton.

Sandler Inquiry. Noel Hynd. 1979. pap. 2.50 o.s.i. (ISBN 0-440-17958-0). Dell.

Sandman Who Lost His Sand. Nancy Moore & Edward Leight. LC 59-7769. (Illus.). (ps-3). 5.95 (ISBN 0-8149-0371-1). Vanguard.

Sandor Petofi. Eniko M. Basa. (World Author Ser.: No. 587). 1980. lib. bdg. 13.50 (ISBN 0-8057-6429-1). Twayne.

Sandpail Book. Dick Martin. (Illus.). 24p. (ps-4). 1977. Repr. of 1964 ed. PLB 5.38 (ISBN 0-307-68920-4, Golden Pr). Western Pub.

Sandra Street & Other Stories. Michael Anthony. (Heinemann Secondary Readers Ser.). 1973. pap. text ed. 2.95x (ISBN 0-435-92512-1). Heinemann Ed.

Sandro Iz Chegema: Sandro from Chegem. Fazil Iskander. 1979. 20.00 (ISBN 0-88233-392-5); pap. 10.00 o.p. (ISBN 0-88233-394-1). Ardis Pubs.

Sands of Mars. Arthur C. Clark. (RL 7). pap. 1.75 (ISBN 0-451-08176-5, E8176, Sig). NAL.

Sands of Time. Ann Owen. 192p. (Orig.). 1980. pap. 1.50 (ISBN 0-671-57041-2). S&S.

Sandsong. Alex Cord. 224p. 1976. pap. 1.75 o.s.i. (ISBN 0-446-59772-4). Warner Bks.

Sandstone Depositional Models for Exploration for Fossil Fuels. George D. Klein. (Illus.). 1975. pap. 12.00 (ISBN 0-89469-083-3, CEPCO). Burgess.

Sandstone of Time. Louise Wall. LC 79-93208. (Illus.). 104p. (Orig.). 1980. 8.95x (ISBN 0-935834-01-X). Rainbow-Betty.

Sandstorm. Anne Mather. (Harlequin Presents Ser.). 192p. 1980. pap. 1.50 (ISBN 0-373-10382-4, Pub. by Harlequin). PB.

Sandtiquity. Connie Simo et al. LC 78-20696. (Illus.). 1980. 10.95 (ISBN 0-8008-6989-3); pap. 4.95 (ISBN 0-8008-6990-7). Taplinger.

Sandwich Courses: An Integated Education? Alan G. Smithers. (Orig.). 1976. pap. text ed. 13.75x (ISBN 0-85633-088-4, NFER). Humanities.

Sandwich Preparation. Ser-Vo-Tel Institute. (Foodservice Career Education Ser.). 1975. pap. 4.95 (ISBN 0-8436-2015-3). CBI Pub.

Sandwichery: Recipes, Riddles & Funny Facts About Food. Patricia Stubis. LC 74-12294. (Illus.). 56p. (gr. k-3). 1975. 5.95 o.s.i. (ISBN 0-685-53688-2, Four Winds); PLB 5.41 o.s.i. (ISBN 0-8193-0780-7). Schol Bk Serv.

Sandy Calder & His Magical Mobiles. Jean Lipman & Margaret Aspinwall. (Illus.). (ps up). 1981. 15.00 (ISBN 0-933920-17-2); pap. 7.00 (ISBN 0-933920-18-0). Hudson Hills.

Sandy Lesburg's One Hundred Great Restaurants of America. Sandy Lesburg. Ed. by Herbert Michaelman. 1981. 12.95 (ISBN 0-517-53988-8, Michaelman Books). Crown.

Sandy, the Talking Cat. Esther M. Newhall. (Illus.). 1977. 5.00 o.p. (ISBN 0-682-48932-8). Exposition.

Sane Living in a Mad World. Robert Rodale. pap. 1.25 (ISBN 0-451-05385-0, Y5385, Sig). NAL.

Sane Positivist: A Biography of Edward L. Thorndike. Geraldine Joncich. LC 68-27542. (Illus.). 1968. 32.50x (ISBN 0-8195-3093-X, Pub. by Wesleyan U Pr). Columbia U Pr.

Sane Society. Erich Fromm. 320p. 1977. pap. 2.50 (ISBN 0-449-30821-9, Prem). Fawcett.

Sanford Robinson Gifford (1823-1880) Ila Weiss. LC 76-23655. (Outstanding Dissertations in the Fine Arts - American). (Illus.). 1977. Repr. of 1968 ed. lib. bdg. 80.00 (ISBN 0-8240-2737-X). Garland Pub.

Sang Branch Settlers: Folksongs & Tales of a Kentucky Mountain Family. Leonard Roberts. LC 74-3357. (American Folklore Society Memoir Ser.: No. 61). (Illus.). 534p. 1974. 17.50x o.p. (ISBN 0-292-77510-5). U of Tex Pr.

Sang Branch Settlers: Tales & Songs of an Eastern Kentucky Family. Leonard Roberts. text ed. 12.00 (ISBN 0-933302-05-3); pap. text ed. 7.95 (ISBN 0-933302-06-1). Pikeville Coll.

Sangers' Pioneer Texas Merchants. Leon J. Rosenberg. LC 78-62426. (Illus.). 1978. 12.95 (ISBN 0-87611-037-5). Tex St Hist Assn.

Sanitarian's Handbook: Theory & Administrative Practice for Environmental Health. Ben Freedman. 1977. 69.50 (ISBN 0-930234-02-2). Peerless.

Sanitary Landfill, Manual 39. Compiled by American Society of Civil Engineers. (ASCE Manual & Report on Engineering Practice Ser.: No. 39). 92p. looseleaf binder 27.50 (ISBN 0-87262-215-0). Am Soc Civil Eng.

Sanitation Details in SI Metric, 2 vols. (Illus.). 1977. 27.50x set, spiral binding (ISBN 0-686-65560-5). Vol. 1 (ISBN 0-7198-2610-1). Vol. 2. Intl Ideas.

Sanitation for Food Service Workers. 2nd ed. Treva M. Richardson. LC 74-23606. 1974. pap. 10.95 (ISBN 0-8436-0582-0). tchr's guide 1.95 (ISBN 0-8436-2049-8). CBI Pub.

Sanitation, Safety, & Maintenance Management. Bruce H. Axler. 1974. 13.25 o.p. (ISBN 0-672-96106-7); tchrs' manual 5.00 o.p. (ISBN 0-672-96108-3); wkbk 6.45 o.p. (ISBN 0-672-96107-5). Bobbs.

Sanitation Strategy for a Lakefront Metropolis: The Case of Chicago. Louis P. Cain. LC 76-14711. 161p. 1979. 15.00 (ISBN 0-87580-064-5). N Ill U Pr.

Sanity in the Summertime. Linda Dillow & Claudia Arp. 224p. 1981. 8.95 (ISBN 0-8407-5237-7); pap. 4.95 (ISBN 0-8407-5754-9). Nelson.

Sanity Inspector. Alan Coren. 176p. 1975. 6.95 o.p. (ISBN 0-312-69930-1). St Martin.

Sanjo. Evelyn W. Mayerson. (gr. 10 up). 1980. pap. write for info. (ISBN 0-671-83397-9). PB.

Sankaracharya. T. M. Mahadevan. (Orig.). 1979. pap. 2.50 (ISBN 0-89744-204-0). Auromere.

Sankey Still Sings. Charles Ludwig. (Christian Biography Ser.). 176p. 1981. pap. 2.95 (ISBN 0-8010-5601-2). Baker Bk.

Sankhyana Srauta Sutra. W. Caland. Tr. by L. Chandra. 483p. 1980. text ed. 45.00x (ISBN 0-8426-1646-2). Verry.

Sanskrit Drama in Performance. Rachel Baumer & James R. Brandon. 1981. 27.50 (ISBN 0-8248-0688-3). U Pr of Hawaii.

Sanskrit Drama in Performance. Rachel Baumer & James R. Brandon. (Illus.). 352p. 1981. text ed. 27.50x (ISBN 0-8248-0688-3). U Pr of Hawaii.

Sanskrit-English Dictionary. Monier-Williams. 1973. 37.00x (ISBN 0-8364-0464-5). South Asia Bks.

Sanskrit-English Dictionary. rev. ed. Monier Monier-Williams et al. 1899. 89.00x (ISBN 0-19-864308-X). Oxford U Pr.

Sanskrit Grammar for Students. 3rd ed. Arthur A. MacDonnell. 1927. 16.50x (ISBN 0-19-815415-1). Oxford U Pr.

Sanskrit Love Lyrics. Tr. by P. Lal from Sanskrit. 31p. 1973. 6.75 (ISBN 0-88253-265-0); flexible bdg. 4.80 (ISBN 0-89253-525-3). Ind-US Inc.

Sanskrit Primer. Edward D. Perry. LC 36-19814. 1959. 15.00x (ISBN 0-231-00858-9). Columbia U Pr.

Sanskrit Primer. 4th. ed. Edward D. Perry. 1978. 6.95 (ISBN 0-89684-026-3, Pub. by Motilal Banarsidass India); pap. text ed. 4.95 (ISBN 0-89684-027-1). Orient Bk Dist.

Santa Barbara County "California's Wonderful Corner". Walter A. Tomkins. 1974. 4.50x (ISBN 0-686-17214-0). Sandollar Pr.

Santa Biblia Dios Habla Hoy. 1504p. 1980. write for info. (Edit Mundo). Casa Bautista.

Santa Casa di Loreto: Problems in Cinquecento Sculpture. Kathleen W. Garris. LC 76-23653. (Outstanding Dissertations in the Fine Arts Ser.). 1977. lib. bdg. 133.00x (ISBN 0-8240-2735-3). Garland Pub.

Santa Cruz: The Early Years. Leon Rowland. Ed. by Michael S. Gant. (Illus.). 260p. 1980. cancelled (ISBN 0-934136-03-3, Paper Vision); pap. 7.95 (ISBN 0-934136-04-1). Western Tanager.

Santa Fe Guide. Waite Thompson & Richard M. Gottleib. Ed. by Gerald Hausman. LC 80-18575. (Illus.). 64p. (Orig.). 1980. pap. 4.50 (ISBN 0-913270-89-X). Sunstone Pr.

Santa Fe Passage. Clay Fisher. 176p. 1981. pap. 1.95 (ISBN 0-553-14540-1). Bantam.

Santa Fe: Steel Rails Through California. Donald Duke & Stan Kistler. LC 63-23869. (Illus.). 1963. 18.95 (ISBN 0-87095-009-6). Golden West.

Santa Fe: The Autobiography of a Southwestern Town. Oliver La Farge & Arthur N. Morgan. (Illus.). 1959. 14.95 o.p. (ISBN 0-8061-0434-1). U. of Okla Pr.

Santa Fe Trail. Samuel H. Adams. (Landmark Ser.: No. 13). (Illus.). (gr. 4-6). 1951. PLB 5.99 (ISBN 0-394-90313-7, BYR). Random.

Santa Fe Trail. Robert L. Duffus. LC 30-26894. (Zia Bks). (Illus.). 283p. 1972. pap. 7.95 (ISBN 0-8263-0235-1). U of NM Pr.

Santa Rat. Betty Baker. LC 79-24904. (Illus.). 64p. (gr. 3-5). 1980. 7.95 (ISBN 0-688-80262-1); PLB 7.63 (ISBN 0-688-84262-3). Greenwillow.

Santa Spreads Love Through God. Salli L. Marzetti. (Illus.). 1980. 4.50 (ISBN 0-533-03800-6). Vantage.

Santaberry & the Snard. Joel Schick & Alice Schick. LC 78-23796. (Lippincott I-Like-to-Read Books). (Illus.). (gr. k-2). 1979. 6.95 (ISBN 0-397-31824-3). Lippincott.

Santanic Condition. David Thoreau. LC 80-66499. 1981. 10.95 (ISBN 0-87795-274-4). Arbor Hse.

Santaroga Barrier. Frank Herbert. LC 77-49. (YA) 1977. 1.95 (ISBN 0-425-04334-7, Dist. by Putnam). Berkley Pub.

Santa's Christmas Tree. Beverly Weiler. LC 79-54318. (Once-Upon-a-Time Book). (Illus.). 64p. (gr. k-5). 1980. 7.95g (ISBN 0-9604572-0-8). Great Western.

Santa's Crash-Bang Christmas. Steven Kroll. LC 77-3025. (Illus.). (gr. k-3). 1977. reinforced bdg. 8.95 (ISBN 0-8234-0302-5). Holiday.

Santa's Problem. Myra J. Jordan & Roy E. Grant. (Illus.). 30p. (Orig.). (ps-1). 1980. pap. 4.50 (ISBN 0-914562-08-8). Merriam-Eddy.

Santayana: An Examination of His Philosophy. Timothy Sprigge. (Arguments of the Philosophers Ser). 1974. 19.00x (ISBN 0-7100-7721-1). Routledge & Kegan.

Santayana: The Later Years. Daniel Cory. LC 63-19573. 7.50 o.s.i. (ISBN 0-8076-0246-9). Braziller.

Santha Rama Rau. S. K. Desai. (Indian Writers Ser.: Vol. Xiil). 1977. 8.50 (ISBN 0-89253-451-6). Ind-US Inc.

Santhana: One Man's Road to the East. Borna Bebek. 224p. 1981. 11.95 (ISBN 0-370-30260-5, Pub. by Chatto-Bodley-Jonathan). Merrimack Bk Serv.

Santiago Alvarez. Ed. by Michael Chanan. (BFI Dossier Ser.: No. 2). 71p. (Orig.). 1980. pap. 7.50 (ISBN 0-918432-35-9). NY Zoetrope.

Santiago Campaign Eighteen Ninety-Eight. Joseph Wheeler. LC 70-137930. 1970. Repr. of 1898 ed. 15.00 o.p. (ISBN 0-8046-1492-X). Kennikat.

Santiago Vidaurri & the Southern Confederacy. Ronnie C. Tyler. LC 73-186709. 1973. 8.00 (ISBN 0-87611-029-4). Tex St Hist Assn.

Santiago's Sword: Chatino Peasant Religion & Economics. James B. Greenberg. 250p. 1981. 16.95x (ISBN 0-520-04135-6). U of Cal Pr.

Santification & Liberation: Liberation Theologies in Light of the Wesleyan Tradition. Ed. by Theodore H. Runyon. LC 80-20287. 1981. 6.95 (ISBN 0-687-36810-3). Abingdon.

Sanusi of Cyrenaica. Edward E. Evans-Pritchard. 1949. 27.00x (ISBN 0-19-823107-5). Oxford U Pr.

Sapphire Legacy. large type ed. Rachel C. Payes. pap. 1.25 o.p. (ISBN 0-425-03185-3). Berkley Pub.

Sapphire Planet. Url Lanham. LC 77-13160. 1978. 20.00x (ISBN 0-231-03956-5). Columbia U Pr.

Sappho: A Play in Verse. Lawrence Durrell. 1967. pap. 4.95 (ISBN 0-571-08161-4, Pub. by Faber & Faber). Merrimack Bk Serv.

Sappho by the Sea: An Illustrated Guide to the Hamptons. Mary A. McCarthy. LC 76-21830. (Illus.). 98p. 1980. Repr. of 1976 ed. 7.95 (ISBN 0-87754-252-X). Chelsea Hse.

Saqt Al Zand (the Spark from the Flint) Abu Ala Al Ma'Arri. Tr. by Arthur Wormhoudt. (Arab Translation Ser.: No. 2). 125p. 1972. pap. 6.50 (ISBN 0-916358-52-6). Wormhoudt.

Sara & the Door. Virginia A. Jensen. LC 76-28987. (Illus.). (gr. k-1). 1977. 5.95 (ISBN 0-201-03446-8, 3446, A-W Childrens). A-W.

Sara & the Pinch. Carla Stevens. (Illus.). 48p. (gr. k-3). 1980. 6.95 (ISBN 0-395-29435-5, Clarion). HM.

Sara & the Winter Gift. Miriam E. Mason. (Illus.). (gr. 2-4). 1968. 4.50g o.s.i. (ISBN 0-02-763060-9). Macmillan.

Sara Dane. Catherine Gaskin. 1978. pap. 1.95 o.p. (ISBN 0-449-23528-9, Crest). Fawcett.

Sara Somebody. Florence Slobodkin & Louis Slobodkin. LC 75-103162. (Illus.). (gr. 7 up). 1969. 5.95 (ISBN 0-8149-0663-X). Vanguard.

Sarah & the Darnley Boys. Margaret Epp. 120p. (gr. 6-12). 1981. pap. 2.25 (ISBN 0-88207-490-3). Victor Bks.

Sarah & the Magic Twenty-Fifth. Margret Epp. (gr. 3-7). 1977. pap. 1.95 (ISBN 0-88207-477-6). Victor Bks.

Sarah Bernhardt. William Emboden. (Illus.). 176p. 1975. 12.95 o.s.i. (ISBN 0-02-535470-1). Macmillan.

Sarah-Christina: A Girl of Old Portland. Ruth Slade. Ed. by Constance Hunting. (gr. 4-8). 1981. pap. text ed. 5.95 (ISBN 0-913006-19-X). Puckerbrush.

Sarah Dunes, Weird Person. Lois I. Fisher. LC 80-2780. 176p. (gr. 5 up). 1981. PLB 7.95 (ISBN 0-396-07929-6). Dodd.

Sarah, in Passing. Eithne Strong. 72p. (Orig.). 1974. pap. text ed. 4.50x (ISBN 0-85105-267-3, Dolmen Pr). Humanities.

Sarah O. Jewett: Letters. rev. & enl. ed. Sarah O. Jewett. Ed. by Richard Cary. 1967. 7.50 o.p. (ISBN 0-910394-06-7). Colby.

Sarah Orne Jewett. Josephine L. Donovan. LC 80-5334. (Modern Literature Ser.). 160p. 1980. 10.95 (ISBN 0-8044-2137-4). Ungar.

Sarah Whitcher's Story. 2nd ed. Elizabeth Yates. (Illus.). 93p. (gr. 4-8). 1979. pap. 2.65x (ISBN 0-915892-11-1). Regional Ctr Educ.

Sarah Winnemucca. Doris Kloss. LC 81-390. (Story of an American Indian Ser.). (Illus.). (gr. 5 up). 1981. PLB 6.95 (ISBN 0-87518-178-3). Dillon.

Sara's Giant & the Upside-Down House. John Cunliffe. (Illus.). (ps-2). 1980. 8.95 (ISBN 0-233-97202-1). Andre Deutsch.

Saratoga Trunk. Edna Ferber. LC 41-24504. 1951. 5.95 o.p. (ISBN 0-385-04902-1). Doubleday.

Sarcoidosis: A Clinical Approach. Om P. Sharma. (Illus.). 248p. 1975. 23.75 (ISBN 0-398-03303-X). C C Thomas.

Sarcoplasmic Reticulum: With Special Reference to Transport & Energy Transduction. Leopoldo & De Meis. (Transport in the Life Sciences Ser.). 150p. 1981. 25.00 (ISBN 0-471-05025-3, Pub. by Wiley-Interscience). Wiley.

Sardinia. Virginia Waite. 1977. 22.50 (ISBN 0-7134-0039-0, Pub. by Batsford England). David & Charles.

Sardis in the Age of Croesus. John G. Pedley. (Centers of Civilization Ser: No. 24). (Illus.). 1968. 4.95x o.p. (ISBN 0-8061-0786-3). U of Okla Pr.

Sargasso. Edwin Corley. 1981. pap. price not set o.p. (ISBN 0-440-17575-5). Dell.

Sargasso Sea: An Ocean Desert. Francine Jacobs. LC 74-30376. (Illus.). 96p. (gr. 3-7). 1975. PLB 6.48 o.p. (ISBN 0-688-32029-5). Morrow.

Sark. Ken Hawkes. 1977. 7.50 (ISBN 0-7153-7335-8). David & Charles.

Sarnia. Hilary Ford. 256p. 1975. pap. 1.50 o.p. (ISBN 0-345-24551-2). Ballantine.

Sarojini Naidu: A Biography. Padmini Sengupta. (Illus.). 1966. 10.00 o.p. (ISBN 0-210-27023-3). Asia.

Sartor Resartus. Thomas Carlyle. Incl. On Heroes & Hero Worship. 1954. 11.50x (ISBN 0-460-00278-3, Evman); pap. 2.95 (ISBN 0-460-01278-9, Evman). Dutton.

Sartor Resartus: The Life & Opinions of Herr Teufelsdrockh. Thomas Carlyle. Ed. by C. F. Harrold. 1937. 8.95 (ISBN 0-672-63200-4). Odyssey Pr.

Sartre. Hazel Barnes. LC 72-13764. 1973. 6.95 o.s.i. (ISBN 0-397-00750-7). Lippincott.

Sartre. M. Cransten. 1978. cancelled (ISBN 0-685-54459-1). Chips.

Sartre & Marxism. Pietro Chiodi. Tr. by Kate Soper from It. (European Philosophy & the Human Sciences Ser.). 1976. text ed. 26.25x (ISBN 0-391-00590-1); pap. text ed. 10.50x (ISBN 0-391-00886-2). Humanities.

Sartre: Romantic Realist. Iris Murdoch. 78p. 1980. Repr. of 1953 ed. 15.00x (ISBN 0-06-495034-4). B&N.

Sarvodaya: A Political & Economic Study. Adi H. Doctor. 1968. 7.25x (ISBN 0-210-22653-6). Asia.

SAS. LC 79-83865. 7.00 (ISBN 0-932788-10-6). Bradley CPA.

SAS Applications Guide, 1980. Ed. by SAS Institute Inc. (Illus.). 204p. (Orig.). 1980. pap. 9.95. SAS Inst.

SAS-ETS User's Guide, 1980. Ed. by Sas Institute Inc. 342p. 1980. pap. 14.95. Sas Inst.

SAS-GRAPH User's Guide, 1980 Edition. SAS Institute Inc. (Illus.). 72p. (Orig.). 1980. pap. 9.95 o.s.i. (ISBN 0-686-62125-5). SAS Inst.

SAS Programmer's Guide, Nineteen Eighty-One Edition. Ed. by SAS Institute Inc. (SAS Programmer's Guide). 208p. (Orig.). 1980. pap. 9.95. SAS Inst.

SAS Programmer's Guide, 1979 Edition. 1979. pap. 9.95 o.s.i. (ISBN 0-917382-02-1). SAS Inst.

SAS User's Guide Nineteen Seventy-Nine Edition. LC 78-71108. (Illus.). 494p. 1979. pap. 9.95 (ISBN 0-685-91472-0). SAS Inst.

SAS Views: Statistics, 1980 Edition. Ed. by SAS Institute Inc. 322p. 1980. pap. 40.00 (ISBN 0-686-62786-5). SAS Inst.

Sas Views, 1980 Edition. Ed. by SAS Institute Inc. 424p. 1980. pap. 40.00 (ISBN 0-686-62785-7). SAS Inst.

Sasquatch. Don Hunter & Rene Dahinden. 208p. (RL 9). Date not set. pap. 1.95 (ISBN 0-451-09186-8, J9186, Sig). NAL.

Sassafras. Mary Vann Hunter. 288p. Date not set. pap. 2.50 (ISBN 0-523-41476-5). Pinnacle Bks.

Sassy. Claudette Williams. 1977. pap. 1.50 o.p. (ISBN 0-449-23371-5, Crest). Fawcett.

SAT (Scholastic Apitute Test) Jerry Bobrow & William A. Covino. Date not set. pap. text ed. cancelled. Cliffs.

Sata Anda Solto. Tr. by Nicky Cruz. (Portugese Bks.). (Port.). 1979. 1.30 (ISBN 0-8297-0686-0). Life Pubs Intl.

Satan Black & Cargo Unknown. Kenneth Robeson. (Doc Savage Ser.: Nos. 97 & 98). 224p. 1980. pap. 1.95 (ISBN 0-553-13421-3). Bantam.

Satan Cast Out. Frederick Leahy. 1975. pap. 4.45 (ISBN 0-85151-234-8). Banner of Truth.

Satan Is Alive & Well on Planet Earth. large print ed. Hal Lindsey & C. C. Carlson. 1974. kivar 4.95 o.p. (ISBN 0-310-27797-3). Zondervan.

Satan Trap: Dangers of the Occult. Ed. by Martin Ebon. LC 75-14816. 288p. 1976. 7.95 o.p. (ISBN 0-385-07941-9). Doubleday.

Satana Anda Suelto. Tr. by Nicky Cruz. (Spanish Bks.). (Span.). 1978. 1.90 (ISBN 0-8297-0595-3). Life Pubs Intl.

Satanic Bible. Anton S. La Vey. 1969. pap. 2.75 (ISBN 0-380-01539-0, 53207). Avon.

Satanic Cult. Gerhard Zacharias. Tr. by Christine Trollope. (Illus.). 208p. (Ger.). 1980. 22.50x (ISBN 0-04-133008-0, 2370). Allen Unwin.

Satanic Mill. Otfried Preussler. Tr. by Anthea Bell from Ger. 240p. (gr. 7 up). 1973. 7.95g (ISBN 0-02-775170-8). Macmillan.

Satanic Rituals. Anton S. LaVey. (Orig.). 1972. pap. 2.75 (ISBN 0-380-01392-4, 76877). Avon.

Satan's Devices. Kurt E. Koch. LC 78-5066. 1978. pap. 7.95 o.p. (ISBN 0-8254-3024-0). Kregel.

Satan's Invisible World Discovered. George Sinclair. LC 68-17017. 1969. Repr. of 1685 ed. 31.00x (ISBN 0-8201-1068-X). Schol Facsimiles.

Satan's Mistress. Rachel C. Payes. LC 80-81632. 352p. (Orig.). 1981. pap. 2.75 (ISBN 0-87216-726-7). Playboy Pbks.

Satan's Power: A Deviant Psychotherapy Cult. William S. Bainbridge. LC 77-80466. 1978. 18.50x (ISBN 0-520-03546-1). U of Cal Pr.

Satanstoe. James F. Cooper. LC 62-9515. 1962. pap. 4.50x (ISBN 0-8032-5036-3, BB 138, Bison). U of Nebr Pr.

Satapatha-Brahmana, Vols. 12, 26, 41, 43 & 44. Ed. by F. Max Mueller. Tr. by Eggeling. (Sacred Books of the East Ser.). 15.00x ea.; Vol. 12. (ISBN 0-8426-1424-9); Vol. 26. (ISBN 0-8426-1425-7); Vol. 41. (ISBN 0-8426-1426-5); Vol. 43. (ISBN 0-8426-1427-3); Vol. 44. (ISBN 0-8426-1428-1). Verry.

Satellite Cells of the Sensory Canglia. E. Pannese. (Advances in Antomy, Embryology & Cell Biology Ser.: Vol. 65). (Illus.). 98p. 1981. pap. 33.00 (ISBN 0-387-10219-1). Springer-Verlag.

Satellite Communications. 4.75 o.p. (ISBN 0-87259-302-9). Am Radio.

Satellite Communications. Ed. by H. L. Van Trees. LC 78-65704. 1979. 42.95 (ISBN 0-87942-121-5). Inst Electrical.

Satellite State: Problems in the History of the 17th & 18th Centuries. Ed. by Stale Dyrvik et al. 1979. pap. 18.00x (ISBN 8-2000-5283-4, Dist. by Columbia U. Pr.). Universitet.

Satin Principle. Roy Masters. LC 78-78158. 1978. pap. 6.50 (ISBN 0-933900-05-8). Foun Human Under.

Satin Slipper or the Worst Is Not the Surest. Paul Claudel. 1931. 42.50x (ISBN 0-686-51305-3). Elliots Bks.

Satire: An Anthology. Ed. by Ashley Brown & John L. Kimmey. 1978. pap. 8.50 scp (ISBN 0-690-01524-0, HarpC). Har-Row.

Satire, Burlesque, Protest & Ridicule 1. Ed. by Walter H. Rubsamen. (Ballad Opera Ser.). 1974. lib. bdg. 50.00 (ISBN 0-8240-0904-5). Garland Pub.

Satire, Burlesque, Protest, & Ridicule 2. Ed. by Walter H. Rubsamen. (Ballad Opera Ser.). 1974. lib. bdg. 50.00 (ISBN 0-8240-0905-3). Garland Pub.

Satire: From Aesop to Buchwald. Ed. by Frederick T. Kiley & Jack M. Shuttleworth. LC 70-134892. 1971. pap. 7.50 (ISBN 0-672-63110-5). Odyssey Pr.

Satire in Jacobean Tragedy. Joseph H. Stodder. (Salzburg Studies in English Literature, Jacobean Drama Studies: No. 35). 186p. 1974. pap. text ed. 25.00x (ISBN 0-391-01535-4). Humanities.

Satires. Juvenal. Ed. by James D. Duff. (Pitt Ser). 1971. text ed. 16.95x (ISBN 0-521-07370-7). Cambridge U Pr.

Satires Against Man: The Poems of Rochester. Dustin H. Griffin. 1974. 18.50x (ISBN 0-520-02394-3). U of Cal Pr.

Satires & Epistles. Horace. Tr. by Smith P. Bovie. LC 59-16413. 1959. pap. 6.50 (ISBN 0-226-06777-7, P39, Phoen). U of Chicago Pr.

Satires of Ludovico Ariosto: A Renaissance Autobiography. Tr. by Peter Desa Wiggins. LC 74-80810. xiv, 187p. 1976. 12.95x (ISBN 0-8214-0171-8). Ohio U Pr.

Satiric Catharsis in Shakespeare: A Theory of Dramatic Structure. Alice L. Birney. 1973. 18.50x (ISBN 0-520-02214-9). U of Cal Pr.

Satiric Poems of John Trumbull: The Progress of Dulness & M'Fingal. Ed. by Edwin T. Bowden. LC 61-15829. 1971. Repr. of 1962 ed. 12.50x (ISBN 0-292-73366-6). U of Tex Pr.

Satow's Guide to Diplomatic Practice. 5th ed. Ed. by Lord Gore-Booth. LC 77-12580. 1979. text ed. 36.00x (ISBN 0-582-50109-1). Longman.

Satrianum: The Archaeological Investigations Conducted by Brown University in 1966 & 1967. R. Ross Holloway. LC 76-91654. (Illus.). 150p. 1970. 25.00x (ISBN 0-87057-118-4, Pub. by Brown U Pr). Univ Pr of New England.

Satsang with Baba, 2 vols. Swami Muktananda. LC 76-1384. Vol. 1 1974. pap. 5.95 (ISBN 0-914602-30-6); Vol. 2 1976. pap. 5.95 (ISBN 0-914602-31-4). SYDA Found.

Satsang with Baba, Vol. 4. Swami Muktananda. (Illus.). 319p. 1978. pap. text ed. 5.95 (ISBN 0-914602-32-2). SYDA Found.

Satsuma: An Illustrated Guide. Sandra Andacht. 1978. softbound 7.95 o.p. (ISBN 0-87069-227-5). Wallace-Homestead.

Satsuma Rebellion: An Episode of Modern Japanese History. Augustus H. Mounsey. (Studies in Japanese History & Civilization). 1979p. Repr. of 1879 ed. 24.00 (ISBN 0-89093-259-X). U Pubns Amer.

Saturae with Juvenal's Saturae. Persius & Juvenal. Ed. by W. V. Clausen. (Oxford Classical Texts Ser). 1959. 14.95x (ISBN 0-19-814640-X). Oxford U Pr.

Saturated Model Theory. G. E. Sacks. (Mathematics Lecture Series: No. 52). 1972. pap. text ed. 12.50 (ISBN 0-8053-8381-6, Adv Bk Prog). Benjamin Cummings.

Saturday Evening Post: All American Cookbook. Charlotte Turgeon & Frederic A. Birmingham. LC 75-32275. (Illus.). 320p. 1976. 9.95 o.p. (ISBN 0-8407-4054-9). Nelson.

Saturday Evening Post Animal Book. LC 78-5308. (Illus.). 1978. 9.95 (ISBN 0-89387-019-6). Sat Eve Post.

Saturday Evening Post Automobile Book. LC 78-9002. (Illus.). 1977. 12.95 (ISBN 0-89387-012-9). Sat Eve Post.

Saturday Evening Post Book of the Sea & Ships. LC 78-61519. (Illus.). 1978. 11.95 (ISBN 0-89387-023-4). Sat Eve Post.

Saturday Evening Post Christmas Book. 3rd ed. LC 76-24034. (Illus.). 1978. 11.95 (ISBN 0-89387-001-3). Sat Eve Post.

Saturday Evening Post Christmas Stories. LC 80-67058. (Illus.). 1980. 11.95 (ISBN 0-89387-046-3). Sat Eve Post.

Saturday Evening Post Dried Foods Cookbook. E. F. Raigan. LC 80-67060. (Illus.). 1980. pap. 5.95 (ISBN 0-89387-041-2). Sat Eve Post.

Saturday Evening Post Family Album. LC 80-67059. (Illus.). 1980. 15.95 (ISBN 0-89387-047-1). Sat Eve Post.

Saturday Evening Post Family Cookbook: Collectors Edition. LC 74-18928. (Illus.). 1979. pap. 5.95 (ISBN 0-89387-030-7). Sat Eve Post.

Saturday Evening Post Fiber & Bran Better Health Cookbook. Cory SerVaas et al. LC 77-7804. (Illus.). 1977. 12.95 (ISBN 0-89387-008-0). Sat Eve Post.

Saturday Evening Post Fiber & Bran Better Health Cookbook. Cory SerVaas et al. LC 80-67052. (Illus.). 1977. pap. 6.50 (ISBN 0-89387-048-X). Sat Eve Post.

Saturday Evening Post I Can Cook Children's Cookbook. LC 80-67055. (Illus., Orig.). (gr. 1 up). 1980. 7.95 (ISBN 0-89387-049-8). Sat Eve Post.

Saturday Evening Post Movie Book. LC 77-85389. (Illus.). 1977. 10.95 (ISBN 0-89387-013-7); pap. 7.95 (ISBN 0-89387-013-7). Sat Eve Post.

Saturday Evening Post Norman Rockwell Book. LC 77-12286. (Illus.). 1977. 11.95 (ISBN 0-89387-007-2). Sat Eve Post.

Saturday Evening Post Reflections of a Decade, 1901-1910. LC 80-67053. (Illus.). 1980. 13.95 (ISBN 0-89387-044-7). Sat Eve Post.

Saturday Evening Post Saga of the American West. LC 80-67057. (Illus.). 1980. 13.95 (ISBN 0-89387-043-9). Sat Eve Post.

Saturday Evening Post Small-Batch Canning & Freezing Cookbook. Charlotte Turgeon. LC 78-53040. (Illus.). 1978. 8.95 (ISBN 0-89387-020-X); pap. 4.95 (ISBN 0-89387-020-X). Sat Eve Post.

Saturday Evening Post Time to Entertain Cookbook. Charlotte Turgeon & Charles Turgeon. LC 78-73386. 1978. 9.95 (ISBN 0-89387-025-0). Sat Eve Post.

Saturday Morning Gardener: A Guide to Once-a-Week Maintenance. rev. ed. Donald Wyman. LC 73-11833. (Illus.). 256p. 1974. pap. 2.95 o.s.i. (ISBN 0-02-063950-3, Collier). Macmillan.

Saturday Morning TV. Gary Grossman. (Orig.). 1981. pap. 9.95 (ISBN 0-440-52397-4, Delta). Dell. Postponed.

Saturday Night at Daisy's. Jeff Cohn. LC 77-92055. 1978. 8.95 o.p. (ISBN 0-15-179412-X). HarBraceJ.

Saturday Night at Gilley's. Bob Claypool. LC 80-8061. (Illus.). 1980. pap. 8.95 (ISBN 0-394-17727-4, E758, Delilah-Ever). Grove.

Saturday Night Knife & Gun Club. B. P. Reiter. LC 76-51437. 1977. 8.95 o.p. (ISBN 0-397-01141-5). Lippincott.

Saturday Night Live. Ed. by Anne Beatts & John Head. (Illus.). 1977. pap. 7.95 (ISBN 0-380-01801-2, 51342). Avon.

Saturday Night, Sunday Morning. Nicholas B. Christoff. LC 77-7830. 1978. 7.95 o.p. (ISBN 0-06-061380-7, HarpR). Har-Row.

Saturday Night, Sunday Morning: Singles of the Church. Nicholas B. Christoff. LC 77-7841. 160p. 1980. pap. 4.95 (ISBN 0-06-061381-5, RD 341, HarpR). Har-Row.

Saturday or Sunday? Letter to a Sunday-Keeping Minister. Don E. Casebolt. LC 78-8672. (Flame Ser.). 1978. pap. 0.95 (ISBN 0-8127-0182-8). Southern Pub.

Saturday with Daddy. Alex Cervantes & E. DeMichael Cervantes. LC 78-73527. (Illus.). (gr. k-4). Date not set. pap. price not set (ISBN 0-89799-079-X); pap. text ed. price not set (ISBN 0-89799-161-3). Dandelion Pr. Postponed.

Saturday's Children: One Fighting Season with Texas College Football. Giles Tippette. 288p. 1973. 6.95 o.s.i. (ISBN 0-02-619060-5). Macmillan.

Satyagraha & the State. K. Santhanam. 2.75x o.p. (ISBN 0-210-33743-5). Asia.

Satyagraha in South Africa. M. K. Gandhi. Tr. by V. G. Desai. 1980. 8.00 (ISBN 0-934676-15-1). Greenlf Bks.

Satyagraha: M. K. Gandhi in South Africa, 1893-1914. Constance De Jong & Philip Glass. (Illus., Orig.). 1980. pap. 5.00 (ISBN 0-918746-04-3). Standard Edns.

Satyajit Ray's Art. Feroze R. Walla. 132p. 1980. 15.00 (ISBN 0-89684-260-6, Pub. by Clarion India). Orient Bk Dist.

Satyr. Linda C. Gray. LC 81-80085. 224p. (Orig.). 1981. pap. 2.50 (ISBN 0-87216-849-2). Playboy Pbks.

Satyr. Susan Hartman. Ed. by Stanley H. Barkan. (Cross-Cultural Review Chapbook 7). 16p. 1980. pap. 2.00 (ISBN 0-89304-806-2). Cross Cult.

Satyricon. Petronius. Tr. by William Arrowsmith from Lat. LC 59-6026. 1959. 24.00x (ISBN 0-472-72935-7). Irvington.

Satzstellung des Finiten Verbs im Tocharischen. Stefan Zimmer. (Janua Linguarum, Ser. Practica: No. 238). 108p. 1976. pap. text ed. 26.25x (ISBN 90-279-3461-4). Mouton.

Sauce It! Making Sauces, Purees & Gravies from Fruits & Vegetables. Marjorie Blanchard. (Illus.). 160p. (Orig.). 1980. pap. 5.95 (ISBN 0-88266-149-3). Garden Way Pub.

Saudi Arabia. Frank A. Clements. (World Bibliographical Ser.: No. 5). 197p. 1979. 25.25 (ISBN 0-903450-15-1). ABC-Clio.

Saudi Arabia. H. Philby. (Arab Background Ser.). 18.00x (ISBN 0-685-72057-8). Intl Bk Ctr.

Saudi Arabia. Geraldine Wood. (First Bks). (Illus.). (gr. 4-6). 1978. PLB 6.45 s&l (ISBN 0-531-02234-X). Watts.

Saudi Arabia & Its Place in the World. (Illus.). cased 45.00. Three Continents.

Saudi Arabia & the Economic & Political Control of the World. Harry M. Hallam. 1979. 55.80 (ISBN 0-930008-44-8). Inst Econ Pol.

Saudi Arabia in Pictures. rev. ed. Sterling Publishing Company Editors. LC 72-95213. (Visual Geography Ser.). (Illus.). 64p. (Orig.). (gr. 6 up). 1978. PLB 4.99 (ISBN 0-8069-1169-7); pap. 2.95 (ISBN 0-8069-1168-9). Sterling.

Saudi Arabian Economy. Ramon Knauerhase. LC 75-8407. (Special Studies). (Illus.). 390p. 1975. text ed. 37.50 (ISBN 0-275-09000-0). Praeger.

Saudi Decision-Making Body: The House of Al-Saud. Enver M. Koury. LC 77-90773. 96p. 1978. pap. 5.00 (ISBN 0-934484-12-0). Inst Mid East & North Africa.

Saugethiere des schweizerischen Eocaens. Hans G. Stehlin. LC 78-72723. Repr. of 1912 ed. 67.50 (ISBN 0-404-18300-X). AMS Pr.

Saul & Jonathan. Gordon Lindsay. (Old Testament Ser.). 1.25 (ISBN 0-89985-140-1). Christ Nations.

Saul & Selected Poems. Charles Heavysege. LC 76-17038. (Literature of Canada Ser.). 1976. pap. 7.95 (ISBN 0-8020-6262-8). U of Toronto Pr.

Saul Bellow. Robert R. Dutton. (U. S. Authors Ser.: No. 181). lib. bdg. 12.50 (ISBN 0-8057-0044-7). Twayne.

Saul Bellow. Brigitte Scheer-Schaezler. LC 70-178167. (Modern Literature Ser.). 128p. 1972. 10.95 (ISBN 0-8044-2765-8). Ungar.

Saul Bellow, Drumlin Woodchuck. Mark Harris. LC 80-14390. 192p. 1980. 9.95 (ISBN 0-8203-0529-4). U of Ga Pr.

Saul, Israel's First King. Gordon Lindsay. (Old Testament Ser.). 1.25 (ISBN 0-89985-139-8). Christ Nations.

Saunders Tests for Self-Evaluation of Nursing Competence. rev. ed. Dee A. Gillies & Irene B. Alyn. 1980. text ed. write for info. (ISBN 0-7216-4157-1). Saunders.

Sausage & Small Goods Production: Practical Handbook on the Manufacture of Sausages & Other Meat-Based Products. 6th ed. Frank Gerrard. (Illus.). 1976. 19.95x (ISBN 0-7198-2587-3). Intl Ideas.

Sausage Products Technology. E. Karmas. LC 76-47276. (Food Technology Review Ser.: No. 39). (Illus.). 1977. 39.00 o.p. (ISBN 0-8155-0646-5). Noyes.

Sausalito. Sam Dodson. 1978. pap. 1.95 o.p. (ISBN 0-449-13940-9, GM). Fawcett.

Sauternes: A Study of the Great Sweet Wines of Bordeaux. Jeffrey Benson & Alastair MacKenzie. (Illus.). 172p. 1979. 26.00 (ISBN 0-85667-062-6, Pub. by Sotheby Parke Bernet England). Biblio Dist.

Sauve Qui Peut. Lawrence Durrell. (Illus.). 82p. 1980. 4.95 (ISBN 0-571-09224-1, Pub by Faber & Faber). Merrimack Bk Serv.

Savage. Frances C. Kerns. 576p. (Orig.). 1981. pap. 2.75 (ISBN 0-446-95603-1). Warner Bks.

Savage. Peter McCurtin. (Sundance Ser.: No. 28). 1979. pap. 1.75 (ISBN 0-8439-0678-2, Leisure Bks). Nordon Pubns.

Savage & Beautiful Country. Alan McGlashan. LC 66-66707. 1979. 7.95 o.p. (ISBN 0-7011-0922-X, Pub. by Chatto Bodley Jonathan). Merrimack Bk Serv.

Savage Barbarism. Translated from the Spanish Publication of March 1790. in: "Connecticut Centinel," Vol. XXXII, Tues., Nov. 12, 1805, P. 4, Repr. Of 1805. Ed. by Wilcomb E. Washburn. Bd. with Narrative of the Captivity of Joseph Bartlett Among the French & Indians. Repr. of 1807 ed; Horrid Murder. By the Indians. Extract of a Letter from a Gentleman in Augustine to His Friend in Virginia. in: "The New-Jersey & Pennsylvania Almanac for the Year 1808". Repr. of 1808 ed; Narrative of the Captivity of Isaac Webster. Repr. of 1808 ed; Narrative of the Life, Occurences, Vicissitudes & Present Situation of K. White. Repr. of 1809 ed. (Narratives of North American Indian Captivities Ser.). 1979. lib. bdg. 44.00 (ISBN 0-8240-1651-3). Garland Pub.

Savage Comedy Since King Ubu: A Tangent to "The Absurd". Kenneth S. White. 1977. pap. text ed. 6.75x (ISBN 0-8191-0152-4). U Pr of Amer.

Savage Comedy: Structure of Humor. Ed. by Kenneth S. White. 1978. pap. text ed. 11.75x (ISBN 90-6203-310-5). Humanities.

Savage Day. Jack Higgins. 1979. pap. 1.75 o.p. (ISBN 0-449-23982-9, Crest). Fawcett.

Savage Destiny. Suzanne Hay. 1979. pap. 2.25 (ISBN 0-515-04891-7). Jove Pubns.

Savage Embrace. Jessica Howard. (Orig.). 1978. pap. 2.25 o.s.i. (ISBN 0-446-82322-8). Warner Bks.

Savage Empire. Jean Lorrah. LC 80-83592. 224p. (Orig.). 1981. pap. 2.25 (ISBN 0-87216-794-1). Playboy Pbks.

Savage God: A Study of Suicide. A. Alvarez. 1972. 7.95 o.p. (ISBN 0-394-47451-1). Random.

Savage in Literature. Brian V. Street. (International Library of Anthropology). 1975. 21.00 (ISBN 0-7100-8110-3). Routledge & Kegan.

Savage in Silk. Donna C. Zide. (Orig.). 1978. pap. 2.50 (ISBN 0-446-81878-X). Warner Bks.

Savage Journey. Allen W. Eckert. LC 79-13646. 1979. 9.95 (ISBN 0-316-20876-0). Little.

Savage Kingdom. Zane Grey. 1978. pap. 1.50 (ISBN 0-505-51293-9). Tower Bks.

Savage Messiah. H. S. Ede. 1972. 6.95 (ISBN 0-87690-081-3). Dutton.

Savage Passage. Gardner Fox. 1978. pap. 1.95 (ISBN 0-505-51270-X). Tower Bks.

Savage Passion. Barbara A. Cooper. 400p. (Orig.). 1981. pap. 2.50 (ISBN 0-89083-707-4). Zebra.

Savage Sam. Fred Gipson. (gr. 1-5). 1976. pap. 1.95 (ISBN 0-06-080377-0, P377, PL). Har-Row.

Savage Scene: The Life & Times of James Kirker, Frontier King. William C. McGaw. (Illus.). 288p. 1972. 9.95 (ISBN 0-8038-6712-3). Hastings.

Savage Season. Mayo L. Gray. 1978. pap. 1.95 o.p. (ISBN 0-449-14036-9, GM). Fawcett.

Savage Surrender. Charlotte Lamb. (Harlequin Presents Ser.). 192p. 1980. pap. 1.50 (ISBN 0-373-10401-4, Pub. by Harlequin). PB.

Savage Surrender. Natasha Peters. 1977. pap. 2.50 (ISBN 0-441-75156-3). Ace Bks.

Savage Survivor: 300 Million Years of the Shark. Dale Copps. (gr. 7 up). 1976. 5.95 o.p. (ISBN 0-685-78821-0, Dist. by Westwind Pr); lib. ed. 5.97 o.p. (ISBN 0-695-40663-9). Follett.

Savage Women. Mike Curtis. 1976. pap. 1.50 o.p. (ISBN 0-685-72353-4, LB379DK, Leisure Bks). Nordon Pubns.

Savages. Christopher Hampton. 1974. 8.50 (ISBN 0-571-10437-1, Pub. by Faber & Faber); pap. 4.95 (ISBN 0-571-10348-0). Merrimack Bk Serv.

Savages & Naturals: Black Portraits by White Writers in Modern American Literature. John Cooley. Date not set. 12.00 (ISBN 0-87413-167-7). U Delaware Pr. Postponed.

Savages & Scientists: The Smithsonian Institution & the Development of American Anthropology, 1846-1910. Charles M. Hinsley, Jr. (Illus.). 225p. 1980. text ed. 15.00x (ISBN 0-87474-518-7). Smithsonian.

Savages & Scientists: The Smithsonian Institution & the Development of American Anthropology 1846-1910. Curtis M. Hinsley, Jr. (Illus.). 326p. 1981. text ed. 17.50x (ISBN 0-87474-518-7). Smithsonian.

Savages & Shakespeare Wallah. James Ivory. 1973. pap. 3.95 (ISBN 0-394-17799-1, E604, Ever). Grove.

Savagism & Civility. Bernard Sheehan. LC 79-18189. 1980. 35.50 (ISBN 0-521-22927-8); pap. 7.50 (ISBN 0-521-29723-0). Cambridge U Pr.

Savannah Blue. William Harrison. 288p. 1981. 12.50 (ISBN 0-399-90081-0). Marek.

Savannah Duels & Duellists: 1733-1877. Thomas Gamble. LC 74-2325. (Illus.). 322p. 1974. Repr. of 1923 ed. 18.00 (ISBN 0-87152-169-5). Reprint.

Savannah Game. Dan E. Jones. LC 80-68111. (Illus.). 106p. (Orig.). (gr. 5 up). 1980. pap. 9.95 (ISBN 0-9604808-0-3). Halfrubber.

Save It, Invest It & Retire: The Updated Guide to Carefree Retirement. Donald I. Rogers. (Illus.). 224p. 1973. 7.95 o.p. (ISBN 0-87000-202-3). Arlington Hse.

Save Johanna. F. P. Pascal. 254p. 1981. 10.95 (ISBN 0-688-00448-2). Morrow.

Save Me the Waltz. Zelda Fitzgerald. LC 32-30021. (Arcturus Books Paperbacks). 224p. 1967. pap. 6.95 (ISBN 0-8093-0255-1). S Ill U Pr.

Save Money Buying Meat, Poultry, & Fish. Reggie Leipsic. (Illus.). 200p. (Orig.). 1981. pap. 6.95 (ISBN 0-89141-113-5). Presidio Pr.

Save-Money Home Fix-It Guide. (Illus.). 1973. pap. 2.98x o.p. (ISBN 0-912542-02-0). Nature Bks Pubs.

Save Queen of Sheba. Louise Moeri. LC 80-23019. (gr. 4-7). 1981. PLB 8.95 (ISBN 0-525-33202-2). Dutton.

Save Sirrushany! (Also Agotha, Princess Gwyn & All the Fearsome Beasts) Betty Baker. LC 77-20137. (gr. 5-9). 1978. 8.95 (ISBN 0-02-708230-X, 70823). Macmillan.

Save That Energy. Robert Gardner. (Illus.). 192p. (gr. 8-12). 1981. PLB price not set (ISBN 0-671-34066-2). Messner.

Save the Inch! Aron Breslow. 1981. 2.00 (ISBN 0-918430-02-X). Happy History.

Save the Last Dance for Me. Judi Miller. 1981. pap. 2.75 (ISBN 0-671-83650-1). PB.

Save-Your-Life Defense Handbook. Matthew Braun. (Illus.). 1977. 10.00x (ISBN 0-8159-5711-4); pap. 7.95x (ISBN 0-8159-5712-2). Devin.

Save Your Marriage. Barry R. Berkey. LC 75-45338. 224p. 1976. 15.95 (ISBN 0-88229-235-8). Nelson-Hall.

Save Your Stomach. Lawrence Galton. 1978. pap. 2.25 o.s.i. (ISBN 0-515-04485-7). Jove Pubns.

Saved by a Broken Pole & Other Stories. Compiled by Joyce K. Ellis. 75p. (Orig.). (gr. 2-6). 1980. pap. 1.75 (ISBN 0-89323-007-3). BMA Pr.

Saved by Grace...for Service. Robert L. Sumner. 1979. 8.95 (ISBN 0-87398-797-7, Pub. by Bibl Evang Pr). Sword of Lord.

Saving America's Cities. Ed. by Evelyn Geller. (Reference Shelf Ser.). 1979. 6.25 (ISBN 0-8242-0631-2). Wilson.

Saving & Spending. Jeffrey Mark. 1980. lib. bdg. 59.95 (ISBN 0-8490-3083-8). Gordon Pr.

Saving Graces. Rhoda Tagliacozzo. LC 79-16343. 1979. 10.95 (ISBN 0-312-69988-3). St Martin.

Saving Lake Superior. Wendy W. Adamson. LC 74-17351. (Story of Environmental Action Ser.). (Illus.). (gr. 7 up). 1974. PLB 7.95 (ISBN 0-87518-083-3). Dillon.

Saving Life of Christ. W. I. Thomas. 1961. pap. 2.50 (ISBN 0-310-33262-1). Zondervan.

Saving Our Wildlife. J. J. McCoy. (Surveyor Bks). (Illus.). (gr. 7-12). 1970. 5.95 o.s.i. (ISBN 0-02-765420-6, CCPr). Macmillan.

Saving Social Security. Robert Schuettinger. 1977. pap. 10.00 (ISBN 0-685-79966-2). Coun Am Affairs.

Saving the Big-Deal Baby. Louise Armstrong. LC 79-22838. (Illus.). (gr. 7 up). 1980. PLB 7.95 (ISBN 0-525-38805-2, Skinny Book); pap. 2.50 (ISBN 0-525-45050-5, Skinny Book). Dutton.

Saving the Channel Ports. W. D. Joynt. (Illus.). 233p. 1976. 19.95 (ISBN 0-85885-202-0). David & Charles.

Saving the Queen. William F. Buckley, Jr. 1977. pap. 2.25 o.p. (ISBN 0-446-89164-9). Warner Bks.

Saving the Texts: Literature-Derrida-Philosophy. Geoffrey H. Hartman. LC 80-21748. (Illus.). 190p. 1981. text ed. 12.95x (ISBN 0-8018-2452-4). Johns Hopkins.

Saving the Tiger. Guy Montfort. LC 80-5363. 120p. 1981. 16.95 (ISBN 0-670-61999-X, Studio). Viking Pr.

Savior. Marvin Werlin & Mark Werlin. 1980. pap. 2.75 (ISBN 0-440-17748-0). Dell.

Savior of the World. Michael Wilcock. Ed. by J. A. Motyer & John R. Stott. LC 79-2720. (Bible Speaks Today Ser.). (Orig.). 1979. pap. 4.75 (ISBN 0-87784-599-9). Inter-Varsity.

Saviour God: Comparative Studies in the Concept of Salvation Presented to Edwin Oliver James. Ed. by Samuel G. Brandon. LC 80-14924. xxii, 242p. 1980. Repr. of 1963 ed. lib. bdg. 22.50x (ISBN 0-313-22416-1, BRSG). Greenwood.

Savitri: A Legend & a Symbol. Sri Aurobindo. 1978. lib. bdg. 20.00 (ISBN 0-89744-954-1); Two-Vol. Set. lib. bdg. 17.00 (ISBN 0-89744-953-3). Auromere.

Savoring Mexico: A Travel Cookbook. Sharon Cadwallader. (McGraw-Hill Paperbacks Ser.). (Illus.). 160p. (Orig.). 1980. 10.95 (ISBN 0-07-009532-9, GB); pap. 6.95 (ISBN 0-07-009531-0). McGraw.

Savoring the Sabbath. Janet Watkins. LC 80-83865. 80p. (Orig.). 1980. pap. 4.95 (ISBN 0-88290-165-6, 1058). Horizon Utah.

Savory Pie. Anna T. Callen. Ed. by Marion Behrman. 288p. 1981. 15.95 (ISBN 0-517-54380-X). Crown.

Savory Wild Mushroom. rev. ed. Margaret McKenny. Ed. by Daniel E. Stuntz. LC 78-160288. (Illus.). 296p. 1971. 15.95 (ISBN 0-295-95155-9); pap. 8.95 (ISBN 0-295-95156-7). U of Wash Pr.

Savoury & Sweet Dishes for Two. Caroline Hastie. 1978. pap. text ed. 4.50 o.p. (ISBN 0-435-42510-2). Heinemann Ed.

Saw, Hammer & Paint: Woodworking & Finishing for Beginners. Carolyn Meyer. (Illus.). 128p. (gr. 7 up). 1973. 7.25 o.p. (ISBN 0-688-20069-9); PLB 6.96 o.p. (ISBN 0-688-30069-3). Morrow.

Sawtooth National Recreation Area. Luther Linkhart. Ed. by Thomas Winnett. LC 79-57594. (Illus., Orig.). 1981. pap. 9.95 (ISBN 0-911824-96-0). Wilderness.

Sawyer's Turbomachinery Maintenance Handbook, 3 vols. Ed. by John W. Sawyer & Kurt Hallberg. LC 80-63559. (Illus.). 1060p. 1981. Set. 115.50 (ISBN 0-937506-03-6). Busn Journals.

Sawyer's Turbomachinery Maintenance Handbook: Gas Turbines - Turbocompressors. Ed. by John W. Sawyer & Kurt Hallberg. LC 80-52103. (Illus.). 375p. 1980. 38.50 (ISBN 0-937506-01-X). Busn Journals.

Sawyer's Turbomachinery Maintenance Handbook: Steam Turbines - Power Recovery Turbines. Ed. by John W. Sawyer & Kurt Hallberg. LC 80-52104. (Illus.). 350p. 1981. 38.50 (ISBN 0-937506-00-1). Busn Journals.

Sawyer's Turbomachinery Maintenance Handbook, Vol. III: Support Services & Equipment. Ed. by John W. Sawyer & Kurt Hallberg. LC 80-53539. (Illus.). 340p. 1981. 38.00 (ISBN 0-937506-02-8). Busn Journals.

Saxe Gallante; or, the Amorous Adventures & Intrigues of Frederick-Augustus 2. Karl L. Pollnitz. LC 78-170589. (Foundations of the Novel Ser.: Vol. 59). 1972. lib. bdg. 50.00 (ISBN 0-8240-0571-6). Garland Pub.

Saxo Grammaticus: History of the Danes, Vol. II. Ed. by Hilda E. Davidson. Tr. by Peter Fisher. (Illus.). 209p. 1980. 35.00x (ISBN 0-8476-6938-6). Rowman.

Saxo Grammaticus: The History of the Danes, Vol. 1-Englist Text. Ed. by Hilda Davidson. Tr. by Peter Fisher. 297p. 1979. 36.50x (ISBN 0-8476-6221-7). Rowman.

Saxon Age: Commentaries of an Era. A. F. Scott. (Illus.). 182p. 1979. 20.00x (ISBN 0-85664-905-8, Pub. by Croom Helm Ltd England). Biblio Dist.

Saxon & Norman Kings. Christopher Brook. 1978. 28.00 (ISBN 0-7134-1534-7, Pub. by Batsford England). David & Charles.

Saxon & Norman Times. (Picture Panorama of British History Ser.). 1977. pap. 4.95 (ISBN 0-263-06239-2). Transatlantic.

Saxon England. John Hamilton & Alan Sorrell. (Illus.). (gr. 6-9). 1968. 7.50 (ISBN 0-8023-1149-0). Dufour.

Saxon Garters. Janelle Viglini. 1975. 7.50 o.p. (ISBN 0-685-52659-3, 0-911156-14-5). Porter.

Saxon House. George E. Burcaw. LC 79-65600. (GEM Books Ser.). (Illus.). 122p. (Orig.). 1980. pap. 7.95 (ISBN 0-89301-065-0). U Pr of Idaho.

Saxon Kings. Richard Humble. (Illus.). 223p. 1980. 17.00x (ISBN 0-297-77784-X, Pub. by Weidenfeld & Nicolson England). Biblio Dist.

Saxon Shore. D. E. Johnston. 92p. 1980. pap. 20.95x (ISBN 0-900312-43-2, Pub. by Coun Brit Arch England). Intl Schol Bk.

Say Cheesecake - & Smile. Elvira Monroe. 220p. 1981. pap. 5.95 (ISBN 0-933174-11-X). Wide World.

Say Hello to Yesterday. Sally Wentworth. (Harlequin Presents Ser.). 192p. 1981. pap. 1.50 (ISBN 0-373-10426-X, Pub. by Harlequin). PB.

Say It Again: Dorothy Uris's Personal Collection of Quotes & Anecdotes. Dorothy Uris. 1979. 12.50 o.p. (ISBN 0-87690-308-1). Dutton.

Say It in Hindi. Veena T. Oldenburg. (Say It Ser.). 192p. (Orig.). Date not set. pap. 2.00 (ISBN 0-486-23959-4). Dover.

Say It My Way. Willard Espy. 220p. 1981. pap. 4.95 (ISBN 0-14-005733-1). Penguin.

Say It with Hands. Louie J. Fant, Jr. (Illus.). 1964. 5.50 (ISBN 0-913072-02-8). Natl Assn Deaf.

Say It with Love. Howard G. Hendricks. 143p. 1972. pap. 3.95 (ISBN 0-88207-050-9). Victor Bks.

Say It with Words. Charles W. Ferguson. LC 59-8085. 1969. pap. 3.25x (ISBN 0-8032-5058-4, BB 395, Bison). U of Nebr Pr.

Say Pardon. David Ignatow. LC 61-6973. (Wesleyan Poetry Program: Vol. 10). (Orig.). 1961. 10.00x (ISBN 0-8195-2010-1, Pub. by Wesleyan U Pr); pap. 2.45 o.p. (ISBN 0-8195-1010-6). Columbia U Pr.

Say What You Mean: The Paragraph, Bk 2. John Gehlmann & Philip Eisman. LC 66-19065. 1968. 5.85 o.p. (ISBN 0-672-73231-9). Odyssey Pr.

Say What You Mean: The Sentence, Bk 1. John Gehlmann & Philip Eisman. LC 66-19065. 1967. 6.50 (ISBN 0-672-73232-7). Odyssey Pr.

Say Yes! Paula Morgan. 144p. pap. 2.25 (ISBN 0-523-41408-0). Pinnacle Bks.

Saybrook at the Mouth of the Connecticut River: The First One Hundred Years. Gilman C. Gates. 1935. 42.50x (ISBN 0-685-89040-6). Elliots Bks.

Sayer's Manual of Classification. A. Maltby. (Grafton Books on Library Science). 1977. lib. bdg. 26.50x (ISBN 0-233-96603-X). Westview.

Saying & Meaning in Puerto Rico: Some Problems in the Ethnography of Discourse. Marshall Morris. (Language & Communication Library: Vol. 1). 186p. 1980. 19.50 (ISBN 0-08-025822-0). Pergamon.

Saying Is Believing: Developing Credential Speeches. James E. Jones. 1979. pap. text ed. 10.95 (ISBN 0-8403-2076-0). Kendall-Hunt.

Sayings of Confucius. Confucius. Tr. by James R. Ware. (Orig.). pap. 1.50 (ISBN 0-451-61885-8, MW1885, Ment). NAL.

Sayings of Doctor Johnson. Samuel Johnson. (Little Treasury Ser). 1969. 1.75 o.p. (ISBN 0-212-99827-7). Dufour.

Sayings of Jesus: A Pocket Guide. Bryce D. Bartruff. 1976. pap. 1.95 (ISBN 0-87123-461-0, 200461). Bethany Fell.

Sayings of Jesus in the Pseudo-Clementine Homilies. Leslie L. Kline. LC 75-1645. (Society of Biblical Literature. Dissertation Ser.). ix, 198p. 1975. pap. 7.50 (ISBN 0-89130-060-0, 060114). Scholars Pr Ca.

Sayings of the Desert Fathers. Tr. by Benedicta Ward. (Cistercian Studies Ser.: No. 59). 1975. pap. 4.00 o.p. (ISBN 0-87907-959-2). Cistercian Pubns.

Sayings of the Seventies. Ed. by Colin Cross. 1980. 8.95 (ISBN 0-7153-7938-0). David & Charles.

Sayings of the Week. Ed. by Valerie Ferguson. 1978. 8.95 (ISBN 0-7153-7600-4). David & Charles.

Sayles' & Strauss' Behavioral Stategies for Managers. Leonard Sayles & George Strauss. 304p. 1980. text ed. 17.95 (ISBN 0-13-791459-8). P-H.

Sayles Complex: A Late Milling Stone Horizon Assemblage from Cajon Pass, California, & the Ecological Implications of Its Scraper Planes. Makoto Kowta. (U. C. Publ. in Anthropology: Vol. 6). 1969. pap. 6.50x (ISBN 0-520-09005-5). U of Cal Pr.

Saynday's People: The Kiowa Indians & the Stories They Told. Alice Marriott. LC 63-10928. (Illus.). 1963. pap. 2.45 (ISBN 0-8032-5125-4, BB 174, Bison). U of Nebr Pr.

Sayonara. James A. Michener. 1978. pap. 2.50 (ISBN 0-449-23857-1, Crest). Fawcett.

Sayonara Streetcar. Ralph Forty. Ed. by Mac Sebree. (Special Ser.: No. 70). 1978. pap. 8.00 (ISBN 0-916374-33-5). Interurban.

Says I, Says He. Ron Hutchinson. (Phoenix Theatre Ser.). pap. 2.95 (ISBN 0-912262-69-9). Proscenium.

Says Who?--Authority & Old Adam. Otis Dunbar Richardson. 1978. 7.00 o.p. (ISBN 0-682-49010-5). Exposition.

Sayyid Jamal Ad-Din "Al-Afghani" A Political Biography. Nikki R. Keddie. LC 74-159671. (Near Eastern Center, UCLA). 520p. 1972. 30.00x (ISBN 0-520-01986-5). U of Cal Pr.

Scale Full of Fish: And Other Turnabouts. Naomi Bossom. LC 78-13293. (gr. k-3). 1979. 7.50 (ISBN 0-688-80203-6); PLB 7.20 (ISBN 0-688-84203-8). Greenwillow.

Scale Model Aircraft from Vac-Form Kits. Hugh Markham. (Illus.). 48p. (Orig.). 1978. pap. 5.00x (ISBN 0-905418-34-4). Intl Pubns Serv.

Scale Model Aircraft in Wood. V. J. Woodason. (Illus.). 64p. (Orig.). 1978. pap. 5.00x (ISBN 0-905418-27-1). Intl Pubns Serv.

Scales for Rating Behavioral Characteristics of Superior Students. Joseph S. Renzulli et al. 1977. pap. 5.95 (ISBN 0-936386-00-2). Creative Learning.

Scales of Justice. Ngaio Marsh. 256p. 1980. pap. 1.95 (ISBN 0-515-05436-4). Jove Pubns.

Scaling Concepts in Polymer Physics. Pierre-Gilles De Gennes. LC 78-21314. 1979. 42.50x (ISBN 0-8014-1203-X). Cornell U Pr.

Scaling in Two-Phase Flows. Ed. by P. Saha & N. M. Farukhi. (HTD: Vol. 14). 53p. 1980. 12.00 (G00187). ASME.

Scallops & the Diver-Fisherman. 1980. 42.25x (ISBN 0-686-64738-6, Pub. by Fishing News England). State Mutual Bk.

Scalphunters. Ed Friend. 1970. pap. 0.60 o.p. (ISBN 0-685-88321-3, R2351, GM). Fawcett.

Scaly Wings: A Book About Moths & Their Caterpillars. Ross E. Hutchins. LC 78-131257. (Finding-Out Book). (Illus.). 64p. (gr. 2-3). 1971. PLB 6.45 o.s.i. (ISBN 0-8193-0440-9). Enslow Pubs.

Scandal & Reform: Controlling Police Corruption. Lawrence W. Sherman. LC 77-79236. 1978. 17.50x (ISBN 0-520-03523-2). U of Cal Pr.

Scandal of Christianity. Emil Brunner. LC 65-12729. 1965. pap. 3.95 (ISBN 0-8042-0708-9). John Knox.
Scandal of '51: How the Gamblers Almost Killed College Basketball. Charles Rosen. LC 77-215355. (Illus.). 1978. 10.00 o.p. (ISBN 0-03-040701-X). HR&W.
Scandal Sensation & Social Democracy. A. Hall. LC 76-46856. 1977. 32.95 (ISBN 0-521-21531-5). Cambridge U Pr.
Scandalous Affair. Clarissa Ross. 1977. pap. 1.50 (ISBN 0-505-51213-0). Tower Bks.
Scandalous Saint. John C. Hagee. 1974. pap. 1.25 o.p. (ISBN 0-88368-056-4). Whitaker Hse.
Scandalous Woman & Other Stories. Edna O'Brien. 144p. 1976. pap. 1.75 o.p. (ISBN 0-345-24805-8). Ballantine.
Scandanavian Charted Designs. Lindberg Press. (Illus.). 1979. pap. 1.75 (ISBN 0-486-23787-7). Dover.
Scandinavia. W. R. Mead & Wendy Hall. (Nations & Peoples Library). 1972. 8.50x o.s.i. (ISBN 0-8027-2125-7). Walker & Co.
Scandinavia on Twenty-Five Dollars a Day, 1981-82. 336p. 1981. pap. 5.95 (ISBN 0-671-43031-9). Frommer-Pasmantier.
Scandinavian. Holloway Staff. (Harper Phrase Books for the Traveler Ser.). (Orig.). 1977. pap. 1.00 o.p. (ISBN 0-8467-0315-7, Pub. by Two Continents). Hippocrene Bks.
Scandinavian England: Collected Papers. Frederick T. Wainwright. Ed. by H. P. Finberg. 387p. 1975. 27.50x (ISBN 0-87471-783-3). Rowman.
Scandinavian Folk-Lore. William A. Craigie. LC 74-78129. 1970. Repr. of 1896 ed. 26.00 (ISBN 0-8103-3587-5). Gale.
Scandinavian Kingdom of Dublin. Charles Haliday. 300p. 1980. Repr. of 1884 ed. 15.00 (ISBN 0-7165-0052-3, Pub. by Irish Academic Pr Ireland). Biblio Dist.
Scandinavian Kings in the British Isles, 850-880. Alfred P. Smyth. (Oxford Historical Monographs). 1978. 42.00x (ISBN 0-19-821865-6). Oxford U Pr.
Scandinavian Knitting Designs. Pauline Chatterton. LC 76-27879. (Encore Edition). (Illus.). 1977. 5.95 (ISBN 0-684-16538-4, ScribT). Scribner.
Scandinavian Option Opportunities & Opportunity Costs in Postwar Scandinavian Foreign Politics. Barbara G. Haskel. 1976. pap. 19.50x (ISBN 8-200-01561-0, Dist. by Columbia U Pr). Universitet.
Scandinavian Psychoanalytic Review. Ed. by Bo Larsson. 1978. pap. 18.00x (ISBN 82-00-05174-9, Dist. by Columbia U Pr). Universitet.
Scandinavian Studies in Criminology, Vol. 5. Ed. by Nils Christie. 125p. 1980. cancelled (ISBN 0-85520-095-2, Pub. by Martin Robertson England). Biblio Dist.
Scandinavian York & Dublin, No. 2. Alfred P. Smyth. 1980. pap. text ed. 15.00x (ISBN 0-391-01049-2). Humanities.
Scandinavie, new ed. Ed. by Daniel Moreau. (Collecion monde et voyages). 159p. (Fr.). 1973. 21.00 (ISBN 2-03-053116-2, 5164). Larousse.
Scanlon of the Sub Service. Dan Senseney. LC 63-11210. (gr. 6-9). 5.95 o.p. (ISBN 0-385-05149-2). Doubleday.
Scanning Electron Microscope. C. W. Oatley. LC 70-190413. (Physics Monographs). (Illus.). 200p. 1972. 32.95 (ISBN 0-521-08531-4). Cambridge U Pr.
Scanning Electron Microscope Study of Green Plants. John N. Lott. LC 75-33863. (Illus.). 192p. 1976. text ed. 14.95 o.p. (ISBN 0-8016-3033-9); pap. text ed. 8.25 o.p. (ISBN 0-8016-3034-7). Mosby.
Scanning Electron Microscopy of Human Reproduction. Ed. by E. S. Hafez. LC 77-85087. (Perspectives in Human Reproduction Ser.: Vol. 4). (Illus.). 1978. 38.00 (ISBN 0-250-40181-9). Ann Arbor Science.
Scanning Electron Microscopy 1980, No. II. R. P. Becker & O. Johari. LC 72-626068. (Illus.). xiv, 658p. 50.00 (ISBN 0-931288-12-6). Scanning Electron.
Scanning Electron Microscopy 1980, Pt. I. Om Johari. LC 72-626068. (Illus.). xvi, 608p. 1980. 50.00 (ISBN 0-931288-11-8). Scanning Electron.
Scanning Electron Microscopy 1980, No. III. Ed. by Om Johari & R. P. Becker. LC 72-62608. (Illus.). xx, 670p. 50.00 (ISBN 0-931288-13-4). Scanning Electron.
Scanning the Land, Poems in North Dakota. Richard Lyons. 157p. 1970. 11.75 (ISBN 0-911042-23-7). N Dak Inst.
Scapegoat: Ritual & Literature. Ed. by John B. Vickery & J'nan M Sellery. LC 70-166472. (Myth & Dramatic Form Ser). (Orig.). 1972. pap. text ed. 8.50 (ISBN 0-395-11256-7, 3-57680). HM.
Scar Tissue-Its Use & Abuse: The Surgical Correction of Deformation Due to Hypertrophic Scar & the Prevention of Its Formation. J. J. Longacre. (Illus.). 192p. 1972. 25.75 (ISBN 0-398-02343-3). C C Thomas.
Scarab for Luck. Enid L. Meadowcroft. LC 63-18417. (Illus.). (gr. 3-7). 1964. 7.95 o.p. (ISBN 0-690-72027-0, TYC-J). T Y Crowell.
Scarborough House. Sharon Salvato. 1977. pap. 1.95 o.p. (ISBN 0-685-75033-7, 345-25168-7-195). Ballantine.
Scarcity & Opportunity in an Indian Village. James M. Freeman. LC 76-4423. (Kiste-Ogan Social Change Ser.). 1976. pap. text ed. 6.95 (ISBN 0-8465-2115-6). Benjamin-Cummings.
Scarcity, Choice, & Public Policy in Middle Africa. Donald Rothchild & Robert L. Curry, Jr. LC 76-50255. 1978. 20.00x (ISBN 0-520-03378-7); pap. 6.95x (ISBN 0-520-03534-8). U of Cal Pr.
Scarcity, Energy and Economic Progress. Ferdinand E. Banks. LC 77-4630. 1977. 21.00 (ISBN 0-669-01781-7). Lexington Bks.
Scarecrow. Floyd Collins. LC 79-19491. 1980. pap. 3.95 (ISBN 0-918518-06-7). St Luke TN.
Scared Straight: Fear in the Deterrence of Delinquency. Sidney Langer. LC 80-5859. 141p. 1981. lib. bdg. 15.50 (ISBN 0-8191-1494-4); pap. text ed. 6.75 (ISBN 0-8191-1495-2). U Pr of Amer.
Scaredy Cat. Phyllis Krasilovsky. (gr. k-2). 1959. 6.95g (ISBN 0-685-15889-6). Macmillan.
Scarlet Kisses. Stephanie Blake. LC 81-80079. 368p. (Orig.). 1981. pap. 2.95 (ISBN 0-87216-847-6). Playboy Pbks.
Scarlet Letter. Nathaniel Hawthorne. Ed. by B. Rajan & A. G. George. Bd. with Life of Hawthorne. Henry James. 7.95x (ISBN 0-210-26920-0). Asia.
Scarlet Letter. Nathaniel Hawthorne. (Enriched Classics Ser.). (gr. 9 up). 1972. pap. 2.25 (ISBN 0-671-42142-5, RE). WSP.
Scarlet Letter. Nathaniel Hawthorne. (gr. 7 up). 1972. pap. 1.50 (ISBN 0-590-09075-5, Schol Pap). Schol Bk Serv.
Scarlet Letter. Nathaniel Hawthorne. (Literature Ser). (gr. 9-12). 1969. pap. text ed. 3.67 (ISBN 0-87720-714-3). AMSCO Sch.
Scarlet Letter. Nathaniel Hawthorne. LC 69-13317. (Merrill Standard Ser). 1975. 6.00 (ISBN 0-910294-31-3); pap. 4.00 (ISBN 0-910294-32-1). Brown Bk.
Scarlet Letter. 2nd ed. Nathaniel Hawthorne. Ed. by Sculley Bradley et al. (Norton Critical Edition Ser.). 1978. 12.95 (ISBN 0-393-04495-5); pap. 3.95x (ISBN 0-393-09073-6). Norton.
Scarlet Letter. Nathaniel Hawthorne. LC 79-52171. (Illus.). 1979. 15.00x (ISBN 0-913870-93-5). Abaris Bks.
Scarlet Letter: A Romance. Nathaniel Hawthorne. Ed. by Larzer Ziff. LC 62-21260. 1963. pap. 4.50 (ISBN 0-672-60966-5, LL1). Bobbs.
Scarlet Letter with Reader's Guide. Nathaniel Hawthorne. (AMSCO Literature Program). (gr. 10-12). 1970. pap. text ed. 4.42 (ISBN 0-87720-808-5); tchr's ed. s.p. 2.85 (ISBN 0-87720-908-1). AMSCO Sch.
Scarlet Letters. Ellery Queen. Bd. with Glass Village. 1981. pap. 2.25 (ISBN 0-451-09675-4, E9675, Sig). NAL.
Scarlet Net. Louise Louis. (Illus.). 68p. 1972. text ed. 7.50. Pen-Art.
Scarlet Pimpernel. Emmuska Orczy. (gr. 7 up). 1964. 3.95 o.s.i. (ISBN 0-02-768630-2). Macmillan.
Scarlet Pimpernel. Emmuska Orczy. 1976. lib. bdg. 15.75x (ISBN 0-89968-072-0). Lightyear.
Scarlet Ruse. John D. MacDonald. (Travis McGee Ser.). 1978. pap. 2.25 o.p. (ISBN 0-449-13952-2, GM). Fawcett.
Scarlet Ruse. John D. MacDonald. 320p. 1981. pap. 2.50 (ISBN 0-449-13952-2, GM). Fawcett.
Scarne on Cards. John Scarne. 1973. pap. 2.25 (ISBN 0-451-08559-0, E8559, Sig). NAL.
Scarne on Dice. rev. ed. John Scarne. LC 62-7251. (Illus.). 1974. 12.95 o.p. (ISBN 0-8117-1516-7). Stackpole.
Scarred. Bruce Lowery. LC 61-15476. 1961. 6.95 (ISBN 0-8149-0147-6). Vanguard.
Scarrons Novels. Paul Scarron. Tr. by John Davies. LC 80-2497. 1981. Repr. of 1694 ed. 69.50 (ISBN 0-404-19133-9). AMS Pr.
Scary Bears. Lea A. Stuart. 1981. 4.95 (ISBN 0-8062-1714-6). Carlton.
Scat Cat Finds a Friend. June Ciancio. (Make-a-Bk). (Illus.). 32p. (Orig.). (ps-6). 1975. pap. 1.95 (ISBN 0-8467-0047-6, Pub. by Two Continents). Hippocrene Bks.
Scatology in Modern Drama. Sidney Shrager. 128p. 1981. text ed. 20.00x (ISBN 0-8290-0261-8). Irvington.
Scattered on: Omens & Curses. Martin J. Rosenblum. LC 74-33057. (Illus.). 80p. (Orig.). 1975. pap. 5.00x (ISBN 0-915316-04-8). Pentagram.
Scattering of Light by Crystals. William Hayes & Rodney Loudon. LC 78-9008. 1978. 35.95 (ISBN 0-471-03191-7, Pub. by Wiley-Interscience). Wiley.
Scattering Theory. John R. Taylor. LC 75-37938. 536p. 1972. 26.95 (ISBN 0-471-84900-6). Wiley.
Scattering Theory of Waves & Particles. Roger G. Newton. 1966. text ed. 29.95 o.p. (ISBN 0-07-046409-X, C). McGraw.
Scavengers. Olive L. Earle. LC 72-3799. (Illus.). 64p. (gr. 3-7). 1973. PLB 6.00 o.p. (ISBN 0-688-31933-5). Morrow.
Scavenger's Son. Thakazhi S. Pillai. Tr. by R. E. Asher from Malayalam. 143p. 1975. pap. 2.50 (ISBN 0-89253-025-1). Ind-US Inc.
Scenarios. Ed. by Richard Kostelanetz. LC 80-68155. (Illus.). 1981. pap. 16.00 (ISBN 0-686-69411-2). Assembling Pr.
Scene Design: A Guide to the Stage. Henning Nelms. LC 74-25249. (Illus.). 96p. 1975. pap. 3.50 (ISBN 0-486-23153-4). Dover.
Scenery: Model Railway Guide 4. Michael Andress. 64p. 1980. pap. 9.95 (ISBN 0-85059-401-4). Aztex.
Scenery of the Plains, Mountains & Mines. Franklin Langworthy. LC 76-87645. (American Scene Ser). (Illus.). 292p. 1972. Repr. of 1932 ed. lib. bdg. 32.50 (ISBN 0-306-71785-9). Da Capo.
Scenes & Characters of the Middle Ages. Edward L. Cutts. LC 67-27866. (Social History Reference Ser.). (Illus.). 1968. Repr. of 1872 ed. 22.00 (ISBN 0-8103-3257-4). Gale.
Scenes for the Actor. Robert Westrom. 76p. (Orig.). 1979. pap. 2.95 (ISBN 0-938230-03-4). Westrom.
Scenes from a Marriage. David Barker. 40p. 1979. pap. 2.00 (ISBN 0-935390-04-9). Wormwood Rev.
Scenes from a Receding Past. Aidan Higgins. 1979. 9.95 (ISBN 0-7145-3556-7); pap. 5.95 (ISBN 0-7145-3753-5). Riverrun NY.
Scenes from American Life: Contemporary Short Fiction. Joyce C. Oates. 256p. 1972. pap. text ed. 6.95 (ISBN 0-394-31683-5). Random.
Scenes from Childhood. Mary B. Sharon. (Illus.). (ps up). 1978. PLB 8.95 o.p. (ISBN 0-525-38820-6). Dutton.
Scenes from Greek Drama. Bruno Snell. (Sather Classical Lectures: No. 34). 1964. 18.50x (ISBN 0-520-01191-0). U of Cal Pr.
Scenes from the Birds. Aristophanes. Ed. by Wilfred H. Oldaker. (Gr). 1926. text ed. 6.50x (ISBN 0-521-04047-7). Cambridge U Pr.
Scenes from the Nineteenth-Century Stage in Advertising Woodcuts. Ed. by Stanley Appelbaum. (Pictorial Archive Ser.). (Illus.). 176p. 1977. pap. 6.00 (ISBN 0-486-23434-7). Dover.
Scenes of Clerical Life. George Eliot. Ed. by Robert L. Wolff. LC 75-491. (Victorian Fiction Ser.). 1975. Repr. of 1858 ed. lib. bdg. 66.00 (ISBN 0-8240-1567-3). Garland Pub.
Scenes of Life at the Capital. Philip Whalen. LC 72-163756. 74p. (Orig.). 1971. 7.00 (ISBN 0-912516-10-0); pap. 2.50 (ISBN 0-912516-00-3). Grey Fox.
Scenes of the Stanislaus. Jeanette Maino & Dena Boer. 1979. 7.95 o.p. (ISBN 0-914330-25-X). Pioneer Pub Co.
Scenic Route. Fleur Adcock. 1974. pap. 4.95x (ISBN 0-19-211843-9). Oxford U Pr.
Scenic Wonders of America. 1973. 17.95 (ISBN 0-393-21412-5, Pub. by Reader's Digest). Norton.
Scenographic Imagination. Darwin R. Payne. (Illus.). 1981. price not set (ISBN 0-8093-1009-0); pap. price not set (ISBN 0-8093-1010-4). S Ill U Pr.
Scent of Apples: A Collection of Stories. Bienvenido N. Santos. LC 79-4857. 250p. 1979. 12.95 (ISBN 0-295-95683-6); pap. 6.95 (ISBN 0-295-95695-X). U of Wash Pr.
Scent of Cloves. Norah Lofts. 256p. 1981. pap. 2.50 o.p. (ISBN 0-449-22977-7, Crest). Fawcett.
Scent of Fear. Margaret Yorke. 224p. 1981. 9.95 (ISBN 0-312-70048-2). St Martin.
Scented Garden. Eleanour S. Rohde. LC 70-175781. 1974. Repr. of 1931 ed. 22.00 (ISBN 0-8103-3874-2). Gale.
Scented Gardens for the Blind. Janet Frame. LC 64-10786. 1964. 4.50 o.s.i. (ISBN 0-8076-0268-X). Braziller.
Scepter of Egypt: A Background for the Study of Egyptian Antiquities in the Metropolitan Museum of Art. William C. Hayes. Incl. Vol. 1. From the Earliest Times to the End of the Middle Kingdom. 25.00 (ISBN 0-87099-072-1); pap. 18.50 (ISBN 0-686-60651-5); Vol. 2. Hyksos Period & the New Kingdom (1675-1080 B.C.) 16.95 o.p. (ISBN 0-87099-074-8); pap. 18.50 (ISBN 0-87099-191-4). LC 52-7286. (Illus.). 1959. Metro Mus Art.
Sceptical Chymist. Robert Boyle. 1964. 5.00x o.p. (ISBN 0-460-00559-6, Evman). Dutton.
Sceptical Essays. Bertrand Russell. (Unwin Paperbacks). 1960. text ed. 9.50x o.p. (ISBN 0-04-104001-5); pap. 4.50 (ISBN 0-04-104003-1). Allen Unwin.
Sceptical Feminist: A Philosophical Enquiry. Janet R. Richards. 320p. 1980. 32.00 (ISBN 0-7100-0673-X). Routledge & Kegan.
Sceptical Nutritionist. Michael A. Weiner. 256p. 1981. 9.95 (ISBN 0-02-625620-7). Macmillan.
Sceptical Vision of Moliere: A Study in Paradox. Robert McBride. LC 76-7847. 1977. text ed. 23.50x (ISBN 0-06-494676-2). B&N.
Scepticism. Arne Naess. LC 68-22775. (International Library of Philosophy & Scientific Method). 1968. text ed. 11.25x (ISBN 0-7100-3639-6). Humanities.
Scepticism: A Critical Reappraisal. Nicholas Rescher. 265p. 1980. 30.00x (ISBN 0-8476-6240-3). Rowman.
Scepticism & Animal Faith: Introduction to a System of Philosophy. George Santayana. 1955. pap. text ed. 5.00 (ISBN 0-486-20236-4). Dover.
Scepticism & Poetry: An Essay on the Poetic Imagination. David G. James. LC 80-21749. 274p. 1980. Repr. of 1960 ed. lib. bdg. 25.00x (ISBN 0-313-22840-X, JASP). Greenwood.
Sceptre: A Computer Program for Circuit & System Analysis. James C. Bowers & Stephen Sedore. (Illus.). 1971. ref. ed. 22.95 o.p. (ISBN 0-13-791590-X). P-H.
Schaum's Outline of Accounting I. 2nd ed. James A. Cashin & Joel J. Lerner. (Schaum's Outline Ser.). 1980. pap. 5.95 (ISBN 0-07-010251-1). McGraw.
Schaum's Outline of Accounting II. 2nd ed. James A. Cashin & Joel J. Lerner. (Schaum's Outline Ser.). 288p. 1980. pap. 5.95 (ISBN 0-07-010252-X, SP). McGraw.
Schaum's Outline of Basic Circuit Analysis. John O'Malley. (Schaum's Outline Ser.). 400p. 1981. pap. 6.95 (ISBN 0-07-047820-1). McGraw.
Schaum's Outline of Electric Machines & Electromechanics. Syed A. Nasar. (Schaum's Outline Ser.). (Illus.). 208p. 1981. pap. 6.95 (ISBN 0-07-045886-3, SP). McGraw.
Schaum's Outline of French Grammar. Mary Coffman. (Schaum's Outline Ser.). 288p. 1980. pap. 4.95 (ISBN 0-07-011553-2, SP). McGraw.
Schaum's Outline of Italian Grammar. 2nd ed. Joseph Germano & Conrad Schmitt. (Schaum's Outline Ser.). 288p. 1981. pap. 4.95 (ISBN 0-07-023031-5, SP). McGraw.
Schaum's Outline of Mathematics for Electricity & Electronics. Arthur Beiser. (Schaum's Outline Ser.). (Illus.). 208p. 1980. pap. 4.95 (ISBN 0-07-004378-7, SP). McGraw.
Schaum's Outline of Psychology of Learning. Arno Wittig. (Schaum's Outline Ser.). (Illus.). 1980. pap. 6.95 (ISBN 0-07-071192-5). McGraw.
Schaum's Outline of Space Structural Analysis. Jan J. Tuma & M. N. Reddy. (Illus.). 272p. 1981. pap. 8.95 (ISBN 0-07-065432-8). McGraw.
Schedule-Induced Behavior, Vol. 1. W. P. Christian et al. LC 77-307775. 1977. 14.40 (ISBN 0-904406-52-0). Eden Med Res.
Schedule of Postgraduate Courses in United Kingdom Universities, 1979-1980. 16th ed. Association of Commonwealth Universities. LC 75-644246. 109p. 1979. pap. 7.50x (ISBN 0-85143-061-9). Intl Pubns Serv.
Schedules of Reinforcement. C. Ferster & B. Skinner. 1957. 23.00 (ISBN 0-13-792309-0). P-H.
Scherz und Ernst: A German Intermediate Oral Reader. Ed. by Kenneth E. Keeton. LC 67-15832. (Orig., Ger.). 1967. pap. text ed. 5.95x (ISBN 0-89197-389-3). Irvington.
Scherzo. Johan W. Vis. Date not set. 8.95 (ISBN 0-533-04811-7). Vantage.
Schiller: Dramatic Writer: a Study of Style in the Plays. H. G. Garland. 1969. 29.95x (ISBN 0-19-815387-2). Oxford U Pr.
Schillers Junge Idealisten. Rolf N. Linn. (U. C. Publ. in Modern Philology: Vol. 106). 1973. 8.00 (ISBN 0-520-09429-8). U of Cal Pr.
Schillinger System of Musical Composition. Joseph Schillinger. LC 77-21709. (Music Reprint Ser.). 1977. Reprnt Vol. 1. lib. bdg. 85.00 (ISBN 0-306-77521-2); Vol. 2. lib. bdg. 37.50 (ISBN 0-306-77522-0). Set. lib. bdg. 75.00 (ISBN 0-306-77552-2). Da Capo.
Schindler. David Gebbard. (Illus.). 240p. 1980. pap. 9.95 (ISBN 0-87905-077-2). Peregrine Smith.
Schirmer Pronouncing Pocket Manual of Musical Terms. 4th ed. Theodore Baker. LC 77-5236. 1978. pap. 3.50 (ISBN 0-02-870250-6). Schirmer Bks.
Schirmer Scores: A Repertory of Western Music. Jocelyn Godwin. LC 75-557. 1975. pap. text ed. 12.95 o.s.i. (ISBN 0-02-870700-1). Schirmer Bks.
Schistosoma Mansoni: The Parasite Surface in Relation to Host Immunity. Diane J. McLaren. (Tropical Medicine Research Studies Ser.). 1981. write for info. (ISBN 0-471-27869-6, Pub. by Wiley-Interscience). Wiley.
Schiwetz Legacy: An Artist's Tribute to Texas, 1910-1971. E. M. Schiwetz. (Illus.). 152p. 1972. 29.95 (ISBN 0-292-77502-4). U of Tex Pr.

Schizoid World of Jean-Paul Sartre & R. D. Laing. Douglas Kirsner. LC 76-44197. 1977. text ed. 23.50x (ISBN 0-391-00677-0). Humanities.

Schizophernia: A Bibliography of Books in English. 146p. 1981. lib. bdg. 22.50 (ISBN 0-8482-7064-9). Norwood Edns.

Schizophrenia. John M. Neale & Thomas F. Oltmanns. LC 80-10169. 1980. text ed. 23.95 (ISBN 0-471-63086-1). Wiley.

Schizophrenia: A Developmental Analysis. Sidney J. Blatt & Cynthia Wild. 1976. 25.00 (ISBN 0-12-105050-5). Acad Pr.

Schizophrenia & Genetics. Irving I. Gottesman & James Shields. (Personality & Psychopathology Ser.: Vol. 13). 1972. 39.00 (ISBN 0-12-293450-4). Acad Pr.

Schizophrenia As a Human Process. Harry S. Sullivan. 400p. 1974. pap. 6.95 (ISBN 0-393-00721-9, Norton Lib). Norton.

Schizophrenia: Behavioral Aspects. Kurt Salzinger. LC 73-1276. (Approaches to Behavior Pathology Ser.). 192p. 1973. pap. text ed. 11.50x (ISBN 0-471-75090-5). Wiley.

Schizophrenia: Medical Diagnosis or Moral Verdict? Theodore R. Sarbin & James C. Mancuso. (Pergamon General Psychology Ser.). 25.00 (ISBN 0-08-024613-3); pap. 9.50 (ISBN 0-08-024612-5). Pergamon.

Schizophrenia: Symptoms, Causes, Treatments. Kayla F. Bernheim & Richard R. J. Lewine. 1979. 14.95 (ISBN 0-393-01174-7); pap. 6.95 (ISBN 0-393-09017-5). Norton.

Schizophrenia 75. J. Jorstad & E. Ugelstad. 1976. text ed. 31.00x (ISBN 8-200-02372-9, Dist. by Columbia U Pr). Universitet.

Schizophrenias: Yours & Mine. Carl C. Pfeiffer et al. 1970. pap. 2.50 (ISBN 0-515-05835-1). Jove Pubns.

Schizophrenics in the Community: An Experimental Study in the Prevention of Hospitalization. Benjamin Pasamanick et al. LC 66-25455. (Illus.). 1967. 24.00x (ISBN 0-89197-390-7); pap. text ed. 6.95x (ISBN 0-89197-391-5). Irvington.

Schlerman in the Kitchen. Gene Schlerman. 240p. 1980. 12.95 (ISBN 0-914842-56-0). Madrona Pubs.

Schlieren Methods. L. A. Vasil'Ev. 1968. 36.95 (ISBN 0-470-90335-X). Halsted Pr.

Schlumberger, The History of a Technique. Louis Allaud & Maurice H. Martin. LC 77-23566. 1977. 34.95 (ISBN 0-471-01667-5, Pub. by Wiley-Interscience). Wiley.

Schlumpf Obsession. Denis Jenkinson & Peter Verstappen. LC 78-50878. 1978. 8.95 (ISBN 0-385-14409-1). Doubleday.

Schoenberg. Anthony Payne. (Oxford Studies of Composers). 1968. pap. 7.95x (ISBN 0-19-314116-7). Oxford U Pr.

Schoenberg & His School: The Contemporary Stage of the Language of Music. Rene Leibowitz. Tr. by Dika Newlin from Fr. LC 75-115338. (Music Ser). 1970. Repr. of 1949 ed. lib. bdg. 27.50 (ISBN 0-306-71930-4). Da Capo.

Schoene 27. September. Thomas Brasch. 100p. (Ger.). 1980. pap. 6.50 (ISBN 3-518-02264-4, Pub. by Insel Verlag Germany). Suhrkamp.

Scholae Academicae: Some Account of Studies at English Universities in the 18th Century. Christopher Wordsworth. LC 79-93271. Repr. of 1877 ed. 22.50x (ISBN 0-678-05085-6). Kelley.

Scholar Collects: Selections from the Anthony Morris Clark Bequest. Ed. by Ulrich W. Hiesinger & Ann Percy. LC 80-82234. (Illus.). 171p. (Orig.). 1980. pap. 14.95 (ISBN 0-87633-036-7). Phila Mus Art.

Scholar Revolutionary: Eoin Macneil 1867-1945, & the Making of the New Ireland. F. X Martin & Byrne. (Illus.). 320p. 1973. 20.00x (ISBN 0-7165-0577-0, Pub. by Irish Academic Pr Ireland). Biblio Dist.

Scholars. Wu Ching-Tsu. silk 14.95 (ISBN 0-8351-0316-1). China Bks.

Scholars & Gypsies: An Autobiography. Walter Starkie. (Illus.). 1963. 20.00 (ISBN 0-520-01205-4). U of Cal Pr.

Scholars, Dollars, & Bureaucrats. Chester E. Finn, Jr. LC 78-13363. (Studies in Higher Education Policy). 1978. 14.95 (ISBN 0-8157-2828-X); pap. 5.95 (ISBN 0-8157-2827-1). Brookings.

Scholars' Guide to Washington D. C. Film & Video Collections. Bonnie Rowan. (Scholars' Guide to Washington D. C. Ser.: No. 6). 282p. 1980. text ed. 25.00x (ISBN 0-87474-818-6); pap. text ed. 8.95x (ISBN 0-87474-819-4). Smithsonian.

Scholars' Guide to Washington, D.C. for East Asian Studies. Hong N. Kim. LC 79-17344. (Scholars' Guide to Washington, D.C. Ser.: No. 3). 413p. 1979. text ed. 19.95x (ISBN 0-87474-582-9); pap. text ed. 8.95x (ISBN 0-87474-581-0). Smithsonian.

Scholars on Parade. D. A. Lockmiller. 1969. 6.95 o.s.i. (ISBN 0-02-573960-3). Macmillan.

Scholars, Saints & Sufis: Muslim Religious Institutions Since 1500. Ed. by Nikki R. Keddie. LC 77-153546. (Near Eastern Center, UCLA). 350p. 1972. 25.00 o.p. (ISBN 0-520-02027-8); pap. 7.95x (ISBN 0-520-03644-1). U of Cal Pr.

Scholarship. Boy Scouts Of America. LC 19-600. (Illus.). 64p. (gr. 6-12). 1970. pap. 0.70x (ISBN 0-8395-3384-5, 3384). BSA.

Scholarship Physics. 4th ed. M. Nelkon. 1971. text ed. 12.95x o.p. (ISBN 0-435-68646-1). Heinemann Ed.

Scholarships Guide for Commonwealth Postgraduate Students, 1980-82. 4th ed. Association of Commonwealth Universities. 326p. (Orig.). 1979. pap. 13.50x (ISBN 0-85143-062-7). Intl Pubns Serv.

Scholastic Aptitude Test Preparation Guide. Jerry Bobrow & William A. Covino. (Cliffs Test Preparation Ser.). (Illus.). (gr. 11-12). 1979. pap. 3.50 wkbk. (ISBN 0-8220-2000-9). Cliffs.

Scholastic Aptitude Test (SAT) Ed. by Gabriel F. Freedman et al. LC 80-88. 512p. 1981. lib. bdg. 12.00 (ISBN 0-668-04916-2, 4916). Arco.

Scholastic Aptitude Test (SAT) Ed. by Brigitte Saunders et al. LC 80-88. 512p. (Orig.). 1980. lib. bdg. 12.00 (ISBN 0-668-04916-2, 4916); pap. 6.95 (ISBN 0-668-04920-0, 4920-0). Arco.

Scholastic Culture of the Middle Ages: 1000-1300. John W. Baldwin. LC 70-120060. (Civilization & Society Ser). 192p. 1971. pap. 5.95x (ISBN 0-669-62059-9). Heath.

Scholastic Dictionary. 1.95 (ISBN 0-8049-2001-X, D1). Airmont.

Scholastic Philosophy. Jack Rudman. (Undergraduate Program Field Test Ser.: UPFT-22). (Cloth bdg. avail. on request). pap. 9.95 (ISBN 0-8373-6022-6). Natl Learning.

Scholasticism in the Modern World. Ed. by George F. McLean. (Proceedings of the American Catholic Philosophical Association: Vol. 40). 1966. pap. 8.00 o.p. (ISBN 0-918090-00-8). Am Cath Philo.

Scholemaster: Or, Plaine & Perfite Way of Teachyng Children the Latin Tong. Roger Ascham. LC 68-54609. (English Experience Ser.: No. 15). 134p. 1968. Repr. of 1570 ed. 14.00 (ISBN 90-221-0015-4). Walter J Johnson.

School. John Burningham. LC 75-4611. (Illus.). (ps-1). 1975. 2.50 (ISBN 0-690-00902-X, TYC-J); PLB 4.89 (ISBN 0-690-00903-8). T Y Crowell.

School-Age Mothers: Problems, Programs & Policy. Lorraine V. Klerman & James F. Jekel. 256p. (Orig.). 1973. 6.00 o.p. (ISBN 0-208-01412-8, Linnet); pap. 2.95 (ISBN 0-208-01413-6, Linnet). Shoe String.

School & After: A European Symposium. W. B. Dockrell et al. (General Ser.). 1978. pap. text ed. 27.00x (ISBN 0-85633-169-4, NFER). Humanities.

School & College: Studies of Post-Sixteen Education. R. King. 1976. 16.95x (ISBN 0-7100-8359-9); pap. 9.50 (ISBN 0-7100-8360-2). Routledge & Kegan.

School & Community. C. Lindsay. 1970. pap. 7.00 (ISBN 0-08-016043-3). Pergamon.

School & Community, Vol. II. OECD. (Illus.). 129p. 1980. pap. 8.00x (ISBN 92-64-12082-3, 96-80-01-1). OECD.

School & Community Relations. 2nd ed. L. W. Kindred et al. LC 75-9699. (Illus.). 368p. 1976. 18.95 (ISBN 0-13-792259-0). P-H.

School & Community Relations: A Book of Readings. Calvin L. Doss. 1976. pap. text ed. 6.75x (ISBN 0-8191-0030-7). U Pr of Amer.

School & Community Theater Management: A Handbook for Survival. new ed. Lawrence Stern. 1979. text ed. 18.95 (ISBN 0-205-06174-5). Allyn.

School & Home. Elizabeth J. Goodacre. 1970. pap. text ed. 5.00x (ISBN 0-391-02083-8, NFER). Humanities.

School & the Social Order. Frank Musgrove. LC 79-40738. 1980. 34.00 (ISBN 0-471-27651-0, Pub. by Wiley-Interscience); pap. 15.00 (ISBN 0-471-27653-7, Pub. by Wiley-Interscience). Wiley.

School Architecture. E. R. Robson. Ed. & intro. by Malcolm Seaborne. (Victorian Library). (Illus.). 440p. 1972. Repr. of 1874 ed. text ed. 15.50x (ISBN 0-391-00251-1, Leicester). Humanities.

School As a Center of Inquiry. Robert J. Schaefer. (John Dewey Society Lectureship Ser.). 1967. 10.00x o.s.i. (ISBN 0-06-035814-9, HarpT). Har-Row.

School at Ash Green. W. C. Chalk. 1971. pap. text ed. 2.50x o.p. (ISBN 0-435-11192-2). Heinemann Ed.

School at Home. Theodore E. Wade, Jr. et al. 186p. 1980. pap. 5.95 (ISBN 0-930192-09-5). Gazelle Pubns.

School at Home, Teach Your Own Child. Ingeborg U. Kendall. 1981. 6.95 (ISBN 0-914704-03-6). Intl Ctr Environment.

School Based Management: New Fad or New Force. 1981. pap. 0.50 (ISBN 0-934460-09-4). NCCE. Postponed.

School Behind Bars: A Descriptive Overview of Correctional Education in the American. Ed. by Michael V. Reagen & Donald M. Stoughton. LC 75-40001. 1976. 15.00 (ISBN 0-8108-0891-9). Scarecrow.

School Board Meeting. Ed. by Robert Olds. 1970. pap. text ed. 4.75 o.p. (ISBN 0-685-04603-6, 411-3131). Natl Sch Pr.

School Can Wait. Raymond S. Moore et al. LC 78-19198. 1979. 12.95 o.p. (ISBN 0-8425-1283-7); pap. 7.95 (ISBN 0-8425-1314-0). Brigham.

School Climate. Edgar A. Kelley. Ed. by Thomas F. Koerner. 80p. (Orig.). 1981. pap. text ed. 4.00 (ISBN 0-88210-115-3). Natl Assn Principals.

School Community Interaction. Richard Saxe. LC 74-13595. 288p. 1975. 17.50x (ISBN 0-685-52301-2); text ed. 15.75x (ISBN 0-685-52302-0). McCutchan.

School Consultation: Readings about Preventive Techniques for Pupil Personnel Workers. Joel Meyers et al. (Illus.). 368p. 1977. pap. 16.75 (ISBN 0-398-03485-0). C C Thomas.

School Desegregation: Outcomes for Children. Nancy H. St. John. LC 74-18492. 192p. 1975. 20.95 o.p. (ISBN 0-471-82633-2, Pub. by Wiley-Interscience). Wiley.

School Desegregation: Past, Present, & Future. Ed. by Walter G. Stephan & Joe R. Feagin. (Perspectives in Social Psychology Ser.). (Illus.). 370p. 1980. 21.50 (ISBN 0-306-40378-1, Plenum Pr). Plenum Pub.

School Desegregation Policy. new ed. Everett F. Cataldo et al. LC 77-6080. (Politics of Education Ser.). (Illus.). 1978. 14.95 (ISBN 0-669-01536-9). Lexington Bks.

School Education of Girls. 180p. 1981. pap. 10.50 (ISBN 92-3-101782-9, U1058, UNESCO). Unipub.

School Evaluation: Politics & Process. Ed. by Ernest R. House. LC 72-91622. 370p. 1973. 17.90x (ISBN 0-8211-0750-X); text ed. 16.20x (ISBN 0-685-28806-4). McCutchan.

School, Family, & Neighborhood. Eugene Litwak & Henry Meyer. 400p. 1974. 17.50x (ISBN 0-231-03354-0). Columbia U Pr.

School Finance Policies & Practices: The Nineteen-Eighties: Decade of Conflict. Ed. by James W. Guthrie. 312p. 1981. 22.50 (ISBN 0-88410-195-9). Ballinger Pub.

School Finance: The Economics & Politics of Public Education. Walter I. Garms et al. (Illus.). 1978. text ed. 18.95 (ISBN 0-13-793315-0). P-H.

School Food Action Packet. new ed. CSPI Staff. (Illus.). 1977. 1.50 o.p. (ISBN 0-89329-009-2). Ctr Sci Public.

School Foodservice. Dorothy Van Egmond. 1974. text ed. 34.00 o.p. (ISBN 0-87055-160-4). AVI.

School Foodservice. Dorothy Van Egmond-Pannell. (Illus.). 1981. pap. text ed. 17.00 (ISBN 0-87055-378-X). AVI.

School for Saints, Repr. Of 1897 Ed. Pearl M. Craigie. Ed. by Robert L. Wolff. Bd. with Robert Orange. Repr. of 1900 ed. LC 75-463. (Victorian Fiction Ser.). 1975. lib. bdg. 66.00 (ISBN 0-8240-1541-X). Garland Pub.

School for Sillies. Jay Williams. LC 71-77785. (gr. k-3). 1969. 5.95 o.s.i. (ISBN 0-8193-0305-4, Four Winds); PLB 5.41 o.s.i. (ISBN 0-8193-0306-2). Schol Bk Serv.

School for Soldiers: West Point & the Profession of Arms. Joseph Ellis & Robert Moore. LC 74-79638. (Illus.). 303p. 1976. pap. 5.95 (ISBN 0-19-502022-7, 454, GB). Oxford U Pr.

School for Tomorrow. Jack R. Frymier. LC 72-10647. 286p. 1973. 17.50x (ISBN 0-8211-0505-1); text ed. 15.75x (ISBN 0-685-28804-8). McCutchan.

School for Wives-Robert-Genevieve or the Unfinished Confidence. Andre Gide. Tr. by Dorothy Bussy from Fr. LC 79-23993. 1980. Repr. of 1929 ed. lib. bdg. 10.00x (ISBN 0-8376-0454-0). Bentley.

School Grounds: Some Ecological Enquiries. Peter Jenkins. Ed. by D. F. Wright. 1973. pap. text ed. 3.95x o.p. (ISBN 0-435-59450-8). Heinemann Ed.

School Guidance Systems: Objectives, Functions, Evaluation, & Change. Merville C. Shaw. LC 72-5248. 400p. 1973. text ed. 16.75 o.p. (ISBN 0-395-14058-7); instructor's manual. pap. 2.65 o.p. (ISBN 0-395-14059-5). HM.

School Health in America. 2nd ed. 1979. pap. 1.00 (ISBN 0-917160-12-6). Am Sch Health.

School Health in America. write for info o.p. (ISBN 0-917160-00-2). Am Sch Health.

School Health Practice. 6th ed. C. L. Anderson & William H. Creswell, Jr. LC 75-37562. (Illus.). 480p. 1976. 13.95 o.p. (ISBN 0-8016-0215-7). Mosby.

School Health Practice. 7th ed. Carl L. Anderson & William H. Creswell, Jr. LC 79-27664. (Illus.). 1980. text ed. 16.95 (ISBN 0-8016-0216-5). Mosby.

School Health Problems. G. R. Knotts & J. P. McGovern. (Illus.). 352p. 1976. 26.75 (ISBN 0-398-03220-3). C C Thomas.

School in Contemporary Society. David A. Goslin. 1965. 7.95x o.p. (ISBN 0-673-05538-8); pap. 4.95x o.p. (ISBN 0-673-05535-3). Scott F.

School in Question: A Comparative Study of School & Its Future in Western Societies. Torstein Husen. (Illus.). 1979. 22.00x (ISBN 0-19-874085-9); pap. 11.95x (ISBN 0-19-874086-7). Oxford U Pr.

School in Society: Studies in the Sociology of Education. Ed. by Sam D. Sieber & David E. Wilder. LC 72-80079. (Illus.). 1973. text ed. 14.95 (ISBN 0-02-928680-8). Free Pr.

School Law. Kern Alexander. LC 79-24471. 939p. 1980. text ed. 18.95 (ISBN 0-8299-2078-1). West Pub.

School Leadership Today: Strategies for the Educator. new ed. L. Craig Wilson. 1978. text ed. 18.95 (ISBN 0-205-06019-6). Allyn.

School Librarian As Educator. Lillian B. Wehmeyer. LC 76-41303. 250p. 1976. lib. bdg. 17.50x (ISBN 0-87287-165-7). Libs Unl.

School Libraries: International Developments. Jean E. Lowrie. LC 72-3440. 1972. 10.00 (ISBN 0-8108-0505-7). Scarecrow.

School Libraries Worth Their Keep: A Philosophy Plus Tricks. Carolyn C. Leopold. LC 72-7497. (Illus.). 1972. 13.50 (ISBN 0-8108-0503-0). Scarecrow.

School Library. Lawrence J. Babin. 1981. pap. 1.95 (ISBN 0-912492-17-1). Pyquag.

School Library and Media Center Acquisitions Policies & Procedures. Ed. by Mary M. Taylor. 1981. lib. bdg. 17.50 (ISBN 0-912700-70-X). Oryx Pr.

School Library Media Center. 2nd ed. Emanuel T. Prostano & Joyce S. Prostano. LC 76-30402. (Library Science Text Ser). (Illus.). 1977. lib. bdg. 15.00x (ISBN 0-87287-137-1). Libs Unl.

School Library Resource Centre. Margaret Allan. (Illus.). 192p. 1974. 18.00x o.p. (ISBN 0-8464-0815-5). Beekman Pubs.

School Library Volunteer. Lillian B. Wehmeyer. LC 75-12586. (Illus.). 128p. 1975. lib. bdg. 10.00x (ISBN 0-87287-110-X). Libs Unl.

School Life & Organizational Psychology. American Psychological Association. (Human Behavior Curriculum Project Ser.). 64p. (Orig.). 1981. pap. text ed. 3.95x (ISBN 0-8077-2617-6). Tchrs Coll.

School Managers: Power & Conflict in American Public Education. Donald J. McCarty & Charles E. Ramsey. LC 70-105975. (Illus.). 281p. 1971. lib. bdg. 16.95 (ISBN 0-8371-3299-1, MSM/). Greenwood.

School Music Administrator & Supervisor: Catalysts for Change in Music Education. Robert H. Klotman. LC 72-6635. (Illus.). 256p. 1973. ref. ed. 13.95 (ISBN 0-13-793711-3). P-H.

School Newspaper: How It Works, How to Write for It. Nanci A. Lyman. LC 73-6803. (First Bks.). (gr. 7 up). 1973. PLB 4.90 o.p. (ISBN 0-531-00810-X). Watts.

School Nursing: A Framework for Practice. Susan J. Wold. (Illus.). 530p. 1981. pap. text ed. 15.95 (ISBN 0-8016-5611-7). Mosby.

School Nursing in Transition. Doris S. Bryan. LC 73-11115. 1973. text ed. 11.95 o.p. (ISBN 0-8016-0840-6). Mosby.

School of Heroes. Murshed Garmo. (Arabic.). pap. 12.00x. Intl Bk Ctr.

School of Obedience. Andrew Murray. pap. 1.50 (ISBN 0-8024-7627-9). Moody.

School of Paris: Paintings from the Florene May Schoenbrorn & Samuel A. Marx Collection. James T. Soby. LC 65-25727. (Illus.). 56p. 1965. pap. 7.95 (ISBN 0-87070-575-X). Museum Mod Art.

School of Practical Composition, 3 vols. Carl Czerny. (Music Reprint Ser.). 1979. Repr. of 1848 ed. Set. lib. bdg. 75.00 (ISBN 0-306-79595-7). Da Capo.

School of Shakespeare. D. L. Frost. LC 68-11283. 1968. 49.50 (ISBN 0-521-05044-8). Cambridge U Pr.

School Organisation & Pupil Involvement: A Study of Secondary Schools. Ronald King. (International Library of Sociology). (Illus.). 266p. 1973. 22.50 (ISBN 0-7100-7610-X). Routledge & Kegan.

School Organization for the Mentally Retarded: Basic Guides. 2nd ed. S. E. Jackson & G. R. Taylor. (Illus.). 160p. 1973. 13.75 (ISBN 0-398-02742-0). C C Thomas.

School: Pass at Your Own Risk. Arthur Daigon & Richard A. Dempsey. (Illus.). 228p. 1973. pap. text ed. 10.95 (ISBN 0-13-793877-2). P-H.

School Personnel Systems. Claude W. Fawcett. LC 78-57240. (Illus.). write for info. (ISBN 0-669-02375-2). Lexington Bks.

School Play: A Complete Handbook. Peter Griffith. (Illus.). 168p. 1981. 14.95 (ISBN 0-7134-3541-0, Pub. by Batsford England). David & Charles.

School Power: Implications of an Intervention Project. James P. Comer. LC 80-757. 1980. 14.95 (ISBN 0-02-906550-X). Free Pr.

School Programs for Disruptive Adolescents. D. Safer. 1981. 22.95 (ISBN 0-685-32554-7). Univ Park.

School Programs in Speech-Language: Organization & Management. Elizabeth Neidecker. (Illus.). 1980. text ed. 17.95 (ISBN 0-13-794321-0). P-H.

School Projects in Natural History. Ed. by Devon Trust for Nature Conservation. 1972. pap. text ed. 6.50x o.p. (ISBN 0-435-59920-8). Heinemann Ed.

School Psychology. Jack I. Bardon & Virginia C. Bennett. LC 73-11419. (Foundations of Modern Psychology Ser). (Illus.). 224p. 1973. pap. text ed. 7.95 (ISBN 0-13-794412-8). P-H.

School Psychology & Early Childhood Education. Walter Hodges et al. LC 68-52341. 1977. pap. 6.95 (ISBN 0-87705-326-X). Human Sci Pr.

School Psychology & Program Evaluation. Ed. by J. Gary Hoover & Charles A. Maher. 1979. pap. 6.95x (ISBN 0-87705-387-1). Human Sci Pr.

School Publications: A Guidebook. Ross & Sellmeyer. 11.95x o.p. (ISBN 0-205-04195-7, 5141958). Allyn.

School Readiness Project. Wincenty Okon & Barbara Wilgocka-Okon. (Experiments & Innovations in Education Ser.). 53p. (Orig.). 1973. pap. 2.50 (ISBN 92-3-101065-4, U568, UNESCO). Unipub.

School Reading Program: A Handbook for Teachers, Supervisors, & Specialists. Richard J. Smith et al. LC 77-77993. (Illus.). 1978. text ed. 17.95 (ISBN 0-395-25452-3). HM.

School Reading Teacher. Beverly Stuhlman. (Teachers Education Ser.: No. 4). Date not set. pap. cancelled (ISBN 0-934402-08-6). BYLS Pr.

School Renewal Through Staff Development. Judith Schiffer. 1980. pap. 11.95x (ISBN 0-8077-2582-X). Tchrs Coll.

School Resources, Social Class, & Student Achievement. R. D. Noonan. LC 76-7957. (IEA Monograph Studies: No. 5). 1976. pap. 14.95 (ISBN 0-470-15091-2). Halsted Pr.

School Science for Tomorrow's Citizens. M. Bassey. 1963. pap. 4.20 (ISBN 0-08-009797-9). Pergamon.

School Science Laboratories: A Handbook of Design, Management & Organisation. W. F. Archenhold et al. 303p. 1980. 35.00x (ISBN 0-7195-3436-4, Pub. by Murray Pubs England). State Mutual Bk.

School Secretary. David R. Turner. LC 66-20315. (Orig.). 1971. pap. 4.00 o.p. (ISBN 0-668-00117-8). Arco.

School Segregation Cases: Brown Vs. Board of Education of Topeka & Others. Janet Stevenson. LC 73-5722. (Focus Bks.). (gr. 7-12). 1973. PLB 4.90 o.p. (ISBN 0-531-01046-5). Watts.

School Segregation in Malmo, Sweden. Harold Swedner. LC 70-158358. 1971. 2.35 (ISBN 0-912008-08-3). Integrated Ed Assoc.

School Social Work & the Law. Intro. by Betty Deshler. LC 80-83075. (Conference Proceedings Ser.). 192p. (Orig.). pap. text ed. 7.50 (ISBN 0-87101-088-7, CBP-088-C). Natl Assn Soc Wkrs.

School Social Work & the Law. LC 80-83075. (NASW Conference Proceedings Ser.). 192p. 1980. pap. text ed. 7.50x (ISBN 0-87101-088-7, CBP-088-C). Natl Assn Soc Wkrs.

School Spirit. Tom McHale. 1977. pap. 1.75 o.p. (ISBN 0-345-25760-X). Ballantine.

School Stress & Anxiety. Beeman N. Phillips. LC 77-21658. 1978. 16.95 (ISBN 0-87705-324-3). Human Sci Pr.

School Strikes in Prussian Poland, 1901 to 1907: The Struggle Over Bilingual Education. John J. Kulczycki. (East Eropean Monographs: No. 82). 320p. 1981. 21.00x (ISBN 0-914710-76-1). East Eur Quarterly.

School Survival Guide. Trager. (gr. 7-12). Date not set. pap. cancelled (ISBN 0-590-30915-3, Schol Pap). Schol Bk Serv.

School Systems & Student Achievement. Wilbur Brookover. LC 79-10758. 1979. 25.95 (ISBN 0-03-052721-X). Praeger.

School Teacher in England & the United States. R. K. Kelsall & H. M. Kelsall. 1969. 22.00 (ISBN 0-08-006519-8); pap. 11.25 (ISBN 0-08-006518-X). Pergamon.

School Vandalism: Cause & Cure. Robert B. Williams & Joseph L. Venturini. LC 80-69230. 130p. 1981. perfect bdg. 9.50 (ISBN 0-86548-060-5). Century Twenty One.

School Vandalism: Strategies for Prevention. Michael D. Casserly et al. LC 80-8118. 1980. 17.95 (ISBN 0-669-03956-X). Lexington Bks.

School, Work, & Career 17-Year-Olds in Australia. Trevor Williams et al. (Australian Council for Educational Research Monograph: No. 6). 167p. 1980. pap. text ed. 22.50 (ISBN 0-85563-206-2). Verry.

Schooldays in Imperial Japan: A Study in the Culture of a Student Elite. Donald T. Roden. (Illus.). 300p. 1980. 24.50x (ISBN 0-520-03910-6). U of Cal Pr.

Schoole of Musicke, Wherein Is Taught the Perfect Method of True Fingering of the Lute, Pandora, Orpharion & Viol da Gamba. Thomas Robinson. LC 73-6122. (English Experience Ser.: No. 589). 1973. Repr. of 1603 ed. 16.00 (ISBN 90-221-0589-X). Walter J Johnson.

Schoole (Sic) of Abuse. Stephen Gosson. Bd. with Reply to Gosson's Schoole of Abuse. Thomas Lodge. (English Stage Ser.: Vol. 2). lib. bdg. 50.00 (ISBN 0-8240-0585-6). Garland Pub.

Schooled to Order: A Social History of Public Schooling in the United States. David Nasaw. 316p. 1981. pap. 5.95 (ISBN 0-19-502892-9, GB 626, OPB). Oxford U Pr.

Schoolhouse Mystery. Gertrude C. Warner. LC 65-23889. (Boxcar Children Mysteries-Pilot Bk.). (Illus.). 128p. (gr. 3-7). 1965. 6.95g (ISBN 0-8075-7262-4). A Whitman.

Schooling, Academic Performance & Occupational Attainment in a Non-Industrialized Society. Stephen P. Heyneman & Janice K. Currie. LC 79-63564. 1979. pap. text ed. 8.00 (ISBN 0-8191-0729-8). U Pr of Amer.

Schooling & Innovation: The Rhetoric & the Reality. Angela E. Fraley. 288p. 1981. text ed. write for info. (ISBN 0-9605520-0-6). Gibson Pubs.

Schooling & the Rights of Children. Ed. by Vernon F. Haubrich & Michael W. Apple. LC 74-24477. 200p. 1975. 16.00x (ISBN 0-8211-0755-0); text ed. 14.50x (ISBN 0-685-51464-1). McCutchan.

Schooling by the Natural Method. Rolf Becher. (Illus.). 8.75 (ISBN 0-85131-105-9, Dist. by Sporting Book Center). J A Allen.

Schooling for the New Slavery: Black Industrial Education, 1868-1915. Donald Spivey. LC 77-87974. (Contributions in Afro-American & African Studies.: No. 38). 1978. lib. bdg. 16.95x (ISBN 0-313-20051-3, SSN/). Greenwood.

Schooling of the Western Horse. Richard Young. (Illus.). 15.75 (ISBN 0-85131-182-2). J A Allen.

Schoolmaking: An Alternative in Teacher Education. Carolyn L. Ellner & B. J. Barnes. LC 77-2679. 1977. 19.95 (ISBN 0-669-01626-8). Lexington Bks.

Schoolmasters. Leonard E. Fisher. LC 67-18896. (Colonial Americans Ser). (Illus.). (gr. 4-6). 1967. PLB 4.47 o.p. (ISBN 0-531-01034-1). Watts.

Schools & School Days in Riverdale, Kingsbridge, Spuyten Duyvil: New York City. William A. Tieck. LC 77-149738. (Illus.). 1971. 19.50x (ISBN 0-9600398-1-3). W A Tieck.

Schools & Schooling in England & Wales (1800-1977) A Documentary History. Michael Hyndman. 1978. 16.95 o.p. (ISBN 0-06-318077-4, IntlDept); pap. text ed. 11.90 (ISBN 0-06-318078-2, IntlDept). Har-Row.

Schools & Social Work. Margaret Robinson. 1978. 21.00x (ISBN 0-7100-0004-9); pap. 12.50 (ISBN 0-7100-0005-7). Routledge & Kegan.

Schools Are Where You Find Them. Jean Speiser. LC 70-135278. (Illus.). (gr. 2-4). 1971. PLB 9.89 (ISBN 0-381-99701-4, A67700, JD-J). John Day.

Schools, Conflict & Change. Ed. by Mike M. Milstein. LC 79-30327. 1980. 19.95x (ISBN 0-8077-2571-4). Tchrs Coll.

Schools in Transition. Kenneth A. Tye & Jerrold M. Novotney. (I-D-E-A Reports on Schooling). 288p. 1975. 9.95 o.p. (ISBN 0-07-065690-8, P&RB). McGraw.

Schools of Hellas. Ed. by Kenneth J. Freeman. LC 73-7994. (Illus.). 1969. text ed. 10.50 (ISBN 0-8077-1391-0); pap. text ed. 5.25x (ISBN 0-8077-1390-2). Tchrs Coll.

Schools of Linguistics. Geoffrey Sampson. LC 80-81140. 272p. 1980. 23.50x (ISBN 0-8047-1084-8). Stanford U Pr.

Schools of Thought. Mary Warnock. 1977. 13.95 o.p. (ISBN 0-571-10963-2, Pub. by Faber & Faber); pap. 7.95 (ISBN 0-571-11161-0). Merrimack Bk Serv.

Schools, Scholars & Society. rev. ed. Jean D. Grambs. LC 77-12417. 1978. pap. 10.95 (ISBN 0-13-793802-0). P-H.

Schools, the Courts & the Public Interest. John C. Hogan. LC 73-1005. (Politics of Education Ser.). 320p. 1974. 17.95 (ISBN 0-669-86892-2). Lexington Bks.

Schools Where Parents Make a Difference. Ed. by Don Davies. 163p. (Orig.). 1976. pap. text ed. 3.95 (ISBN 0-917754-00-X). Inst Responsive.

Schools Without Counselors: Guidance Practices for Teachers. William B. Stafford. LC 73-90567. 1974. 16.95 (ISBN 0-911012-52-4). Nelson-Hall.

Schools Without Failure. William Glasser. 256p. 1975. pap. 2.50 (ISBN 0-06-080349-5, P349, PL). Har-Row.

Schoolteacher: A Sociological Study. Dan C. Lortie. LC 74-11428. 1977. 6.95 (ISBN 0-226-49351-2); pap. 4.95 (ISBN 0-226-49354-7, P748, Phoen). U of Chicago Pr.

Schoolwide Secondary Reading Program: Here's How. Burt Liebert & Marjorie Liebert. LC 78-10904. 1979. text ed. 18.95x (ISBN 0-471-03549-1). Wiley.

Schoolworlds 1976. Ed. by Donald Bigelow. LC 76-15293. 1976. 17.50x (ISBN 0-8211-0130-7); text ed. 15.65x ea. 10 or more copies. McCutchan.

Schooners. Basil Greenhill. LC 79-91086. (Illus.). 168p. 1980. 24.95 (ISBN 0-87021-960-X). Naval Inst Pr.

Schopenhauer: His Philosophical Achievement. Ed. by Michael Fox. 276p. 1980. 28.50x (ISBN 0-389-20097-2). B&N.

Schottky Groups & Mumford Curves. L. Gerritzen & M. Van Der Put. (Lecture Notes in Mathematics: Vol. 817). 317p. 1980. pap. 19.50 (ISBN 0-387-10229-9). Springer-Verlag.

Schubert. John Reed. (Great Composer Ser). (Illus.). 1978. 9.50 o.p. (ISBN 0-571-10327-8, Pub. by Faber & Faber). Merrimack Bk Serv.

Schubert: A Critical Biography. Maurice J. Brown. LC 77-4160. (Music Reprint Ser., 1977). (Illus.). 1977. Repr. of 1958 ed. lib. bdg. 29.50 (ISBN 0-306-77409-7). Da Capo.

Schubert: A Documentary Biography. Otto E. Deutsch. Tr. by Eric Blom. LC 77-5499. (Music Reprint Ser.). (Illus.). 1977. Repr. of 1946 ed. lib. bdg. 57.50 (ISBN 0-306-77420-8). Da Capo.

Schubert: His Life & Times. Peggy Woodford. LC 78-53223. (Life & Times of the Composer Ser.). (Illus.). 1978. 16.95 (ISBN 0-8467-0489-7, Pub. by Two Continents); pap. 5.95 (ISBN 0-8467-0462-5). Hippocrene Bks.

Schubert, His Life & Times. expanded ed. Peggy Woodford. (Illus.). 192p. Repr. of 1978 ed. 19.95 (ISBN 0-87666-640-3). Paganiniana Pubns.

Schubert Song Cycles: With Thoughts on Performance. Gerald Moore. 240p. 1979. 22.50 (ISBN 0-241-89082-9, Pub. by Hamish Hamilton England). David & Charles.

Schubert Symphony in B Minor (Unfinished) Franz Schubert. Ed. by Martin Chusid. 1971. 7.95x (ISBN 0-393-02170-X); pap. 4.95x (ISBN 0-393-09731-5). Norton.

Schubert's Song Technique. Ernest G. Porter. (Student's Music Library Ser). (Illus.). 1959. bds. 10.95 (ISBN 0-234-77457-6). Dufour.

Schubert's Songs. Richard Capell. LC 77-5524. (Music Reprint Ser.). 1977. Repr. of 1928 ed. lib. bdg. 25.00 (ISBN 0-306-77422-4). Da Capo.

Schulschwierigkeiten bei Kindern. A. Hundsalz & B. Fachinger. (Psycholgische Praxis Ser.: Vol. 53). (Illus.). 1980. pap. 21.95 (ISBN 3-8055-0148-X). S Karger.

Schulz. J. P. Donleavy. 1980. pap. 6.95 o.p. (ISBN 0-440-58378-0, Delta). Dell.

Schumacher Lectures. Ed. by Satish Kumar. LC 80-8408. 288p. (Orig.). 1981. pap. 4.95 (ISBN 0-06-090843-2, CN 843, CN). Har-Row.

Schumann. rev. ed. Joan Chissell. (Master Musicians Ser.). (Illus.). 1981. cancelled (ISBN 0-460-03170-8, Pub. by J. M. Dent England). Biblio Dist.

Schumann. Alan Walker. (Great Composers Ser.). (Illus.). 1976. 9.95 (ISBN 0-571-10269-7, Pub. by Faber & Faber). Merrimack Bk Serv.

Schumann As Critic. Leon B. Plantinga. LC 76-7599. (Music Reprint Ser.). 1976. Repr. of 1967 ed. pap. 27.50 (ISBN 0-306-70785-3). Da Capo.

Schumann Orchestral Music. Hans Gal. LC 79-52145. (BBC Music Guides Ser.: No. 40). (Illus.). 64p. (Orig.). 1980. pap. 2.95 (ISBN 0-295-95696-8). U of Wash Pr.

Schumann Resonances in the Earth Ionosphere Cavity. P. V. Bliokh et al. Ed. by D. Llanwyn Jones. Tr. by S. Chomer. (Iee Electromagnetic Waves Ser.). (Illus.). 176p. 1980. softcover 62.00 (ISBN 0-906048-33-8, Pub. by Peregrinus London). Inst Elect Eng.

Schwarze Spinne. Jeremias Gotthelf. Ed. by H. M. Waidson. 1976. pap. 9.95x (ISBN 0-631-01620-1, Pub. by Basil Blackwell). Biblio Dist.

Schweizerische Gesellschaft Fuer Dermatologie und Venerologie, 61. Jahresversammlung, Lausanne, Oktober 1979. Ed. by R. Schuppli. (Illus.). viii, 68p. 1981. pap. 6.75 (ISBN 3-8055-2353-X). S Karger.

Schweizerische Gesellschaft Fuer Gynaekologie Bericht Ueber Die Jahresversammlung, St. Gallen. June 1980. Ed. by E. Dreher. (Journal: Gynaekologische Rundschau: Vol. 20, No. 1). (Illus.). iv, 144p. 1980. pap. write for info. (ISBN 3-8055-2126-X). S Karger.

Schweizerische Gesellschaft fuer Gynaekologie, Bericht ueber die Jahresversammlung, Montreux, Juni 1979. Ed. by E. Dreher. (Journal: Gynaekologische Rundschau: Vol. 19, Suppl. 2). 1980. pap. 19.75 (ISBN 3-8055-0456-X). S Karger.

Science Against Crime. Stuart Kind & Michael Overman. LC 76-178896. 160p. 1972. PLB 7.95 o.p. (ISBN 0-385-09293-8). Doubleday.

Science & Agricultural Development. Ed. by Lawrence Busch. 220p. 1981. text ed. 28.00 (ISBN 0-86598-022-5). Allanheld.

Science & Art Dental Ceramics, Vol. 1. John McLean. (Illus.). 334p. 1979. 42.00 (ISBN 0-931386-04-7). Quint Pub Co.

Science & Art of Dental Ceramics, Vol. II. John McLean. (Illus.). 496p. 1978. 120.00 (ISBN 0-931386-11-X). Quint Pub Co.

Science & Behavior: An Introduction to the Methods of Research. 2nd ed. John M. Neale & Robert M. Liebert. (Ser. in Social Learning Theory). (Illus.). 1980. text ed. 17.95 (ISBN 0-13-795195-7). P-H.

Science & Building: Structural & Environmental Design in the Nineteenth & Twentieth Centuries. Henry J. Cowan. LC 77-7297. 1978. 30.00 (ISBN 0-471-02738-3, Pub. by Wiley-Interscience). Wiley.

Science & Civilisation in China: Vol. 5, Pt. 4, Spagyrical Discovery & Invention: Apparatus, Theories & Gifts. J. Needham. 1980. 105.00 (ISBN 0-521-08573-X). Cambridge U Pr.

Science & Civilization in China, 5 vols. Joseph Needham. Incl. Vol. 1. Introductory Orientations. 1954. 50.00 (ISBN 0-521-05799-X); Vol. 2. History of Scientific Thought. 85.00 (ISBN 0-521-05800-7); Vol. 3. Mathematics & the Sciences of the Heavens & the Earth. 125.00 (ISBN 0-521-05801-5); Vol. 4. Physics & Physical Technology, 3 pts; Pt. 1. Physics. 1962. 65.00 (ISBN 0-521-05802-3); Pt. 2. Mechanical Engineering. 105.00 (ISBN 0-521-05803-1); Pt. 3. Engineering & Nautics. 1970. 125.00 (ISBN 0-521-07060-0); Pt. 4. Spagyrical Discovery & Invention. 500p. 105.00 (ISBN 0-521-08573-X). Cambridge U Pr.

Science & Creation in the Middle Ages: Henry of Langenstein (d. 1397) on Genesis. Nicholas H. Steneck. LC 75-19881. 256p. 1976. text ed. 14.95x (ISBN 0-268-01672-0); pap. write for info. (ISBN 0-268-01691-7). U of Notre Dame Pr.

Science & E. S. P. Ed. by J. R. Smythies. (International Library of Philosophy & Scientific Method Ser.). 1967. text ed. 15.50x (ISBN 0-7100-3638-8). Humanities.

Science & Engineering Literature: A Guide to Reference Sources. 2nd ed. H. R. Malinowsky et al. LC 76-17794. (Library Science Text Ser.). 1976. 18.50x (ISBN 0-87287-098-7). Libs Unl.

Science & Engineering Literature: A Guide to Reference Sources. 3rd ed. H. Robert Malinowsky & Jeanne M. Richardson. (Library Science Text Ser.). 380p. 1980. lib. bdg. 22.50 (ISBN 0-87287-230-0); pap. text ed. 14.50 (ISBN 0-87287-245-9). Libs Unl.

Science & Epilepsy: Neuroscience Gains in Epilepsy Research. Ed. by James L. O'Leary & Sidney Goldring. LC 75-21860. 303p. 1976. 26.00 (ISBN 0-89004-072-9). Raven.

Science & Ethical Responsibility. Ed. by Sanford A. Lakoff. 1980. pap. text ed. 17.50 (ISBN 0-201-03993-1). A-W.

Science & Human Values. enl. ed. Jacob Bronowski. pap. 3.50 (ISBN 0-06-090468-2, CN468, CN). Har-Row.

Science & Immortality: The Eloges of the Paris Academy of Sciences (1699-1791) Charles B. Paul. 250p. 1980. 19.50x (ISBN 0-520-03986-6). U of Cal Pr.

Science & Its Critics. John Passmore. (Mason Welch Gross Lecture Ser). 1978. 9.00 (ISBN 0-8135-0852-5). Rutgers U Pr.

Science & Metaphysics: Variations on Kantian Themes. Wilfrid Sellars. LC 68-12258. (International Library of Philosophy & Scientific Method). 1968. text ed. 21.00x (ISBN 0-7100-3501-2). Humanities.

Science & Morality in Medicine: A Survey of Medical Educators. Earl R. Babbie. LC 71-92674. 1970. 19.50x (ISBN 0-520-01559-2). U of Cal Pr.

Science & Our Troubled Conscience. J. Robert Nelson. LC 80-8045. 192p. (Orig.). 1980. pap. 6.95 (ISBN 0-8006-1398-8, 1-1398). Fortress.

Science & Patterns of Child Care. Elizabeth M. Lomax et al. LC 78-4972. (Psychology Ser.). 1978. text ed. 15.95x (ISBN 0-7167-0296-7); pap. text ed. 8.95x (ISBN 0-7167-0295-9). W H Freeman.

Science & Polity in France at the End of the Old Regime. Charles C. Gillispie. LC 80-7521. (Illus.). 472p. 1980. 40.00x (ISBN 0-691-08233-2). Princeton U Pr.

Science & Practice of Welding. 7th ed. Arthur C. Davies. LC 77-71408. (Illus.). 1977. 23.95x (ISBN 0-521-21557-9). Cambridge U Pr.

Science and Religion-Convergence or Collision. R. H. Twining. pap. 2.50 (ISBN 0-686-12939-3). Pyramid Iowa.

Science & Religion in America, 1800-1860. Herbert Hovenkamp. LC 78-53332. 1978. 18.00x (ISBN 0-8122-7748-1). U of Pa Pr.

Science & Religion: Toward a More Useful Dialogue, Vol. 1. Wilford Hess. 1979. perfect bdg. 7.95 (ISBN 0-88252-089-X). Paladin Hse.

Science & Sanity: An Introduction to Non-Aristotelian Systems & General Semantics. 4th ed. Alfred Korzybski. LC 58-6260. 806p. 1958. 19.50x (ISBN 0-937298-01-8). Inst Gen Semantics.

Science & Social Action. Stephen Bodington. 192p. 1980. 14.00x (ISBN 0-85031-270-1, Pub. by Allison & Busby England); pap. 7.95 (ISBN 0-85031-349-X, Pub. by Allison & Busby England). Schocken.

Science & Social Structure: A Festschrift for Robert K. Merton. LC 80-13464. (N.Y. Academy of Sciences Transactions: Vol. 39). 173p. 1980. 15.00x (ISBN 0-89766-043-9). NY Acad Sci.

Science & Social Welfare in the Age of Newton. George N. Clark. 1949. 19.50x (ISBN 0-19-822326-9). Oxford U Pr.

Science & Socialist Construction in China. Xu Liangying & Fan Dianian. Ed. by Pierre M. Perrolle. Tr. by John C. Hsu from Chinese. 250p. 25.00 (ISBN 0-87332-189-8). M E Sharpe.

Science & Societal Issues: A Guide for Science Teachers. Charles R. Barman et al. (Illus.). 152p. 1981. pap. text ed. 9.00 (ISBN 0-8138-0485-X). Iowa St U Pr.

Science & Society in Ancient India. Debiprasad Chattopadhyaya. (Philosophical Currents Ser.: No. 22). 1978. text ed. 34.25x (ISBN 90-6032-098-0). Humanities.

Science & Society in Restoration England. Michael Hunter. LC 80-41071. 224p. Date not set. 37.50 (ISBN 0-521-22866-2); pap. 12.95 (ISBN 0-521-29685-4). Cambridge U Pr.

Science & Society, 1600-1900. Ed. by Peter Mathias. (Illus.). 176p. 1972. 23.95 (ISBN 0-521-08375-3). Cambridge U Pr.

Science & Starvation. D. J. Hughes. 1969. 14.50 (ISBN 0-08-012327-9); pap. 10.75 (ISBN 0-08-012326-0). Pergamon.

Science & Subjectivity. Israel Scheffler. LC 67-27839. (Orig.). 1967. pap. 4.95 (ISBN 0-672-60724-7). Bobbs.

Science & Technical Libraries of the Seventies: A Guide to Information Sources. Ed. by Ellis Mount. (Books, Publishing & Libraries Information Guide Ser.: Vol. 4). 300p. 1980. 30.00 (ISBN 0-8103-1483-5). Gale.

Science & Technology & the Future, 2 pts. Ed. by Hans Bucholz & Wolfgang Gmelin. 1439p. 1979. pap. text ed. 58.00 (ISBN 0-686-65493-5, Pub. by K G Saur). Shoe String.

Science & Technology for Development: A Review of Schools of Thought on Science, Technology, Development, & Technical Change. (STPI Module Ser.: No. 1). 55p. 1980. pap. 5.00 (ISBN 0-88936-215-7, IDRCTS18, IDRC). Unipub.

Science & Technology for Development Series: Planning in the Stpi Countries. 1979. pap. 8.50 (ISBN 0-88936-182-7, IDRC133, IDRC). Unipub.

Science & Technology for Development Series: Technology Policy & Industrialization in the People's Republic of China. 1979. pap. 8.50 (ISBN 0-88936-210-6, IDRC130, IDRC). Unipub.

Science & Technology for Development: The Role of U. S. Universities. Robert P. Morgan et al. (Policy Studies). (Illus.). 1979. 47.00 (ISBN 0-08-025107-2). Pergamon.

Science & Technology in a Changing International Order: The United Nations Conference on Science & Technology for Development. Ed. by Volker Ritterberger. (Special Studies in Social, Political, & Economic Development). 200p. 1981. lib. bdg. 25.00x (ISBN 0-86531-146-3). Westview.

Science & Technology in China. Rudi Volti. (Special Studies on China & East Asia). 350p. 1981. lib. bdg. 25.00x (ISBN 0-89158-951-1). Westview.

Science & Technology in Economic Growth: Proceedings of a Conference Held by the International Economic Association at St. Anton, Austria. Ed. by B. R. Williams. LC 72-14227. (International Economic Association Ser.). 1973. 26.95 (ISBN 0-470-94679-2). Halsted Pr.

Science & Technology in Providence, 1760-1914: An Essay in the History of Brown University in the Metropolitan Community. Donald Fleming. (Illus.). 54p. 1952. pap. 3.00 (ISBN 0-87057-031-5, Pub. by Brown U Pr). Univ Pr of New England.

Science & Technology of Aerosol Packaging. Ed. by John J. Sciarra & Leonard Stoller. 736p. 1974. 62.50 (ISBN 0-471-76693-3, Pub. by Wiley-Interscience). Wiley.

Science & Technology of Rare Earth Materials. Ed. by E. C. Subbarao & W. E. Wallace. 1980. 29.00 (ISBN 0-12-675640-6). Acad Pr.

Science & Technology Policies Information Exchange System (SPINES) Feasibility Study. (Science Policy Studies & Documents Ser., No. 33). (Illus.). 115p. (Orig.). 1974. pap. 6.00 (ISBN 92-3-101185-5, U571, UNESCO). Unipub.

Science & Technology Policies: Yesterday, Today & Tomorrow. Ed. by Gabor Strasser & Eugene Simons. LC 73-17229. 1973. text ed. 18.50 o.p. (ISBN 0-88410-013-8). Ballinger Pub.

Science & Technology Policy. Joseph Haberer. LC 77-70081. (Policy Studies Organization Book Ser.). (Illus.). 1977. 21.95 (ISBN 0-669-01374-9). Lexington Bks.

Science & the Bible in Lutheran Theology: From Luther to the Missouri Synod. William J. Hausmann. LC 78-52287. 1978. pap. text ed. 8.75x o.p. (ISBN 0-8191-0482-5). U Pr of Amer.

Science & the Bible...Can We Believe Both? Larry Richards. 32p. 1973. pap. 0.69 o.p. (ISBN 0-88207-372-9). Victor Bks.

Science & the Christian Experiment. A. R. Peacocke. 224p. 1971. 13.00x (ISBN 0-19-213953-3); pap. 6.95x (ISBN 0-19-213956-8). Oxford U Pr.

Science & the Concept of Race. Ed. by Margaret Mead et al. LC 68-19754. 1969. 15.00x (ISBN 0-231-03101-7); pap. 5.00x (ISBN 0-231-08594-X). Columbia U Pr.

Science & the Media. Peter Farago. (Science & Engineering Policy Ser.). 1976. 17.95x (ISBN 0-19-858324-9). Oxford U Pr.

Science and the Paranormal. George D. Abell & Barry Singer. (Illus.). 320p. 1981. 12.95 (ISBN 0-684-16655-0, ScribT). Scribner.

Science & the Question of Human Equality. Ed. by Margaret S. Collins et al. (AAAS Selected Symposium: No. 58). 180p. 1981. lib. bdg. 16.00x (ISBN 0-89158-952-X). Westview.

Science & the Renaissance, 2 vols. William P. Wightman. Incl. Vol. 1. Introduction to the Study of the Emergence of the Sciences in the Sixteenth Century; Vol. 2. Annotated Bibliography of the Sixteenth Century Books Relating to the Sciences in the Library of the University of Aberdeen. (Books Relating to the Sciences in the Library of Aberdeen). 1962. Set. 27.25 o.s.i. (ISBN 0-02-854830-2). Hafner.

Science & the Second Renaissance of Europe. A. Danzin. 1978. pap. text ed. 25.00 (ISBN 0-08-022442-3). Pergamon.

Science & the Social Order. Bernard Barber. LC 78-1569. 228p. 1978. Repr. of 1952 ed. lib. bdg. 22.25x (ISBN 0-313-20356-3, BASSO). Greenwood.

Science & the Spook. George Owen & Victor Sims. LC 71-88054. (Illus.). 1970. 4.50 o.p. (ISBN 0-912326-26-3). Garrett-Helix.

Science & the Supernatural. John Taylor. 1980. 10.95 (ISBN 0-525-19790-7). Dutton.

Science & the Supernatural: A Scientific Overview of the Occult. Aaron E. Klein. LC 76-42339. (gr. 7-9). 1979. 7.95a (ISBN 0-385-12036-2); PLB (ISBN 0-385-12037-0). Doubleday.

Science & Values. Joseph Grunfeld. 210p. 1980. text ed. 23.00x (ISBN 90-6032-018-2). Humanities.

Science & Wonders of the Atmosphere. Stanley D. Gedzelman. LC 79-23835. 1980. text ed. 22.95 (ISBN 0-471-02972-6); avail. tchrs' manual (ISBN 0-471-08013-6). Wiley.

Science Anxiety: Fear of Science & How to Overcome It. Jeffry Mallow. 256p. 1981. 9.95 (ISBN 0-444-00457-2, Thomond). Elsevier.

Science Arabe & Son Role Dans l'Evolution Scientifique Mondiale. Aldo Mieli. (Medieval Studies Reprint Ser.). (Fr.). Repr. of 1938 ed. lib. bdg. 29.50x (ISBN 0-697-00044-3). Irvington.

Science As a Human Endeavor. George F. Kneller. LC 77-19167. 1978. 17.50x (ISBN 0-231-04206-X). Columbia U Pr.

Science As Behavior: Sociological Approaches to the Sciences. Ed. by Eike Gebhardt. 320p. 1981. 24.50 (ISBN 0-8264-0015-9); pap. 12.95 (ISBN 0-8264-0024-8). Continuum.

Science at the Ballgame. Thomas G. Aylesworth. (gr. 4). 1977. 5.95 o.s.i. (ISBN 0-8027-6279-4); PLB 5.85 o.s.i. (ISBN 0-8027-6280-8). Walker & Co.

Science at the White House: A Political Liability. Edward J. Burger, Jr. LC 80-81425. 208p. 1981. text ed. 14.95x (ISBN 0-8018-2433-8). Johns Hopkins.

Science Between Culture & Counter Culture. C. I. Dessaur. 128p. 1975. pap. text ed. 12.25x (ISBN 90-255-9813-7). Humanities.

Science Book of Volcanoes. Patricia Lauber. (Illus.). (gr. 4-6). 1972. pap. 1.25 (ISBN 0-590-02560-0, Schol Pap). Schol Bk Serv.

Science Can Be Fun. Munro Leaf. LC 58-10135. (Illus.). (gr. k-3). 1958. 4.50 o.p. (ISBN 0-397-30431-5); PLB 4.82 o.p. (ISBN 0-397-30430-7). Lippincott.

Science Career Exploration for Women. Walter S. Smith & Kala M. Stroup. 1978. pap. 2.50 (ISBN 0-87355-010-2). Natl Sci Tchrs.

Science, Chance & Providence. Donald M. McKay. (Riddell Memorial Lectures Ser.). (Illus.). 78p. 1978. text ed. 13.95x. Oxford U Pr.

Science, Class & Society: On the Formation of Sociology & Historical Materialism. Goran Therborn. 461p. 1980. pap. 9.50 (ISBN 0-86091-724-X, Pub. by NLB). Schocken.

Science Committee. Scientific Personnel Office. Ed. by Carole W. Parsons. (Illus.). 1972. pap. 5.25 (ISBN 0-309-02031-X). Natl Acad Pr.

Science Cookbook. Julia B. Waxter. LC 79-57431. 1981. pap. 6.95 (ISBN 0-8224-6292-3). Pitman Learning.

Science Data. 4th ed. J. N. Friend. 120p. 1960. 10.00x (ISBN 0-85264-090-0, Pub. by Griffin England). State Mutual Bk.

Science, Democracy, and Islam: And Other Essays. Kabir Humayun. LC 80-2195. 1981. Repr. of 1955 ed. 20.00 (ISBN 0-404-18967-9). AMS Pr.

Science Development: An Evaluation Study. National Board on Graduate Education. 1975. pap. 8.00 (ISBN 0-309-02329-7). Natl Acad Pr.

Science Dictionary of the Animal World. Michael Chinery. LC 68-17109. (gr. 9 up). 1969. PLB 4.95 o.p. (ISBN 0-531-01784-2). Watts.

Science Dictionary of the Plant World. Michael Chinery. LC 68-17110. (gr. 9 up). 1969. PLB 4.95 o.p. (ISBN 0-531-01785-0). Watts.

Science Education in Eleven Countries: An Empirical Study. Ed. by L. C. Comber & J. P. Keeves. LC 73-8048. (International Studies in Evaluation Ser: Vol. 1). 403p. 1973. pap. 14.95 (ISBN 0-470-16682-7). Halsted Pr.

Science, Engineering, & the City. National Academy Of Engineering. 1967. pap. 5.75 (ISBN 0-309-01498-0). Natl Acad Pr.

Science Experiences for the Early Childhood Years. 2nd ed. Harlan. (Early Childhood Education Ser.: No. C24). 256p. 1980. pap. text ed. 10.95 (ISBN 0-675-08155-6). Merrill.

Science Experiments & Amusements for Children. Charles Vivian. LC 67-28142. Orig. Title: Science Games for Children, Il. (ps-6). 1967. pap. 2.50 (ISBN 0-486-21856-2). Dover.

Science Experiments You Can Eat. Vicki Cobb. LC 71-151474. (Illus.). (gr. 7 up). 1972. 7.95 (ISBN 0-397-31179-6); pap. 4.95 (ISBN 0-397-31253-9, LSC-14). Lippincott.

Science Fair Project Index: Nineteen Sixty to Nineteen Seventy-Two. Ed. by Janet Y. Stoffer. LC 74-30269. 1975. 30.00 (ISBN 0-8108-0783-1). Scarecrow.

Science, Faith & Man. Ed. by W. Warren Wagar. LC 68-27382. (Documentary History of Western Civilization Ser). 1968. 15.00x o.s.i. (ISBN 0-8027-2020-X). Walker & Co.

Science Fiction Aliens. Ed Naha. Ed. by Jon-Michael Reed & Howard Zimmerman. (Illus.). (gr. 3 up). 1977. pap. 7.95 (ISBN 0-931064-01-5). Starlog.

Science Fiction & Fantasy Annual, Vol. 1. Neil Barron & R. Reginald. LC 80-392. (Borgo Reference Library). 1980. lib. bdg. 11.95x cancelled (ISBN 0-89370-141-6); pap. 5.95 cancelled (ISBN 0-89370-241-2). Borgo Pr.

Science Fiction & Fantasy Literature: A Checklist from 1700 to 1974...with Contemporary Science Fiction Authors II, 2 vols. Ed. by Robert Reginald. LC 76-46130. 1979. 85.00 set (ISBN 0-8103-1051-1). Gale.

Science Fiction & Fantasy Reference Guide: An Annotated History of Critical & Biographical Works. L. W. Currey & R. Reginald. LC 80-22715. (Borgo Reference Library: Vol. 4). 64p. (Orig.). 1981. lib. bdg. 8.95x (ISBN 0-89370-145-9); pap. text ed. 2.95x (ISBN 0-89370-245-5). Borgo Pr.

Science Fiction & Fantasy Statistics. R. Reginald & Dan Lewis. LC 80-10690. (Borgo Reference Library: Vol. 3). 64p. 1981. lib. bdg. 8.95x (ISBN 0-89370-804-6); pap. 2.95x (ISBN 0-89370-904-2). Borgo Pr.

Science Fiction Book Review Index 1923-1973. Ed. by H. W. Hall. LC 74-29085. 1975. 70.00 (ISBN 0-8103-1054-6). Gale.

Science Fiction Books Published in Britain, 1972 & 1973. Gerald Bishop. LC 80-20590. 64p. 1980. Repr. of 1975 ed. lib. bdg. 9.95 (ISBN 0-89370-086-X). Borgo Pr.

Science Fiction Books Publishing in Britain: 1974 to 1978. Gerald Bishop. LC 80-20576. 82p. 1980. Repr. of 1979 ed. lib. bdg. 15.95x (ISBN 0-89370-087-8). Borgo Pr.

Science Fiction Film Awards. Donald A. Reed & Patrick Pattison. 1981. lib. bdg. 14.95 (ISBN 0-912076-39-9); pap. 9.95 (ISBN 0-686-65799-3). Ese Calif.

Science Fiction Film: Focus on. W. Johnson. 1972. pap. 2.95 (ISBN 0-13-795161-2). P-H.

Science Fiction Hall of Fame, Vol. 1. Ed. by R. Silverberg. 1971. pap. 2.50 (ISBN 0-380-00795-9, 44933). Avon.

Science Fiction Handbook, Revised. L. Sprague De Camp & Catherine C. De Camp. LC 75-21796. 1975. 8.50 o.p. (ISBN 0-913896-03-9). Owlswick Pr.

Science Fiction: History-Science-Vision. Robert Scholes & Eric Rabkin. 1977. pap. 4.95 (ISBN 0-19-502174-6, 498, GB). Oxford U Pr.

Science Fiction in the Thirties. Damon Knight. 1977. pap. 4.95 (ISBN 0-380-00904-8, 31708). Avon.

Science Fiction: Masters of Today. Arthur Liebman. 140p. 1981. lib. bdg. 7.97 (ISBN 0-8239-0537-3). Rosen Pr.

Science Fiction Mazes. Vladimir Koziakin. 128p. (gr. 4 up). pap. 1.50 (ISBN 0-448-17259-3, Tempo). G&D.

Science Fiction of H. G. Wells. Frank McConnell. (Science Fiction Writers Ser.). (Illus.). 250p. 1981. 18.95 (ISBN 0-19-502811-2). Oxford U Pr.

Science Fiction of H. G. Wells. Frank McConnell. (Science Fiction Writers Ser.: No. 622). (Illus.). 250p. 1981. pap. 4.95 (ISBN 0-19-502812-0, GB). Oxford U Pr.

Science Fiction of H. G. Wells: A Concise Guide. LC 80-65231. 60p. 1980. pap. 2.25 (ISBN 0-9602738-1-6). Auriga.

Science Fiction of the Fifties. Martin Greenberg & Joseph Olander. 1979. pap. 4.95 (ISBN 0-380-46409-8, 46409). Avon.

Science Fiction of the Forties. Ed. by Frederick Puhl. 1978. pap. 4.95 (ISBN 0-380-40097-9, 40097). Avon.

Science Fiction Origins. Ed. by William Fl Nolan & Martin H. Greenberg. 1980. 2.25 (ISBN 0-445-04626-0). Popular Lib.

Science-Fiction Price Guide. R. Reginald & L. W. Currey. (Borgo Reference Library: Vol. 7). 256p. (Orig.). 1981. lib. bdg. 29.95x (ISBN 0-89370-150-5); pap. text ed. 19.95 (ISBN 0-89370-250-1). Borgo Pr.

Science Fiction Puzzle Tales. Martin Gardner. Ed. by Nancy Novograd. (Illus.). 128p. 1981. 10.95 (ISBN 0-517-54380-X); pap. 4.95 (ISBN 0-517-54381-8). Potter.

Science Fiction Tales: Invaders, Creatures, & Alien Worlds. Ed. by Roger Elwood. (Illus.). (gr. 5-9). 1973. pap. 2.50 (ISBN 0-528-87028-9). Rand.

Science Fiction Thinking Machines. Ed. by Groff Conklin. LC 54-6995. 1954. 8.95 (ISBN 0-8149-0040-2). Vanguard.

Science Fiction Toys & Models, Vol. I. Stephen Sansweet. 1980. pap. 3.95 (ISBN 0-931064-27-9). O'Quinn Studio.

Science-Fiction Voices, No. 4: Interviews with Science-Fiction Authors. Jeffrey M. Elliot. LC 80-22580. (Milford Series: Popular Writers of Today: Vol. 33). 64p. (Orig.). 1981. lib. bdg. 8.95x (ISBN 0-89370-148-3); pap. text ed. 2.95x (ISBN 0-89370-248-X). Borgo Pr.

Science Fiction Voices, No. 5: Interviews with Science-Fiction Writers. Darrell Schweitzer. (Milford Series: Popular Writers of Today: Vol. 35). 64p. 1981. lib. bdg. 8.95 (ISBN 0-89370-151-3); pap. text ed. 2.95x (ISBN 0-89370-251-X). Borgo Pr.

Science Fiction Writer's Workshop: An Introduction to Fiction Mechanics, Vol. 1. Barry B. Longyear. 168p. 1980. pap. 5.95 (ISBN 0-913896-18-7). Owlswick Pr.

Science Fiction's Greatest Monsters. Daniel Cohen. LC 80-1087. (High Interest-Low Vocabulary Ser.). (Illus.). (gr. 4-9). 1980. 5.95g (ISBN 0-396-07859-1). Dodd.

Science for All Seasons. Sheila K. Blackwelder. (Human Science Ser.). (Illus.). 272p. 1980. 11.95 (ISBN 0-13-795286-4, Spec); pap. 5.95 (ISBN 0-13-795278-3). P-H.

Science for Chemical Process Operators. C. A. Colman-Porter. 1972. pap. 7.24 (ISBN 0-08-015725-4). Pergamon.

Science for Children: A Book for Teachers. Willard Jacobson & Abby Bergman. (Illus.). 1980. text ed. 18.95 (ISBN 0-13-794784-4). P-H.

Science for Hairdressing Students. 2nd ed. C. M. Lee & J. K. Inglis. 1972. text ed. 16.50 (ISBN 0-08-016665-2); pap. text ed. 7.75 (ISBN 0-08-016666-0). Pergamon.

Science for Physical Geographers. Donald Davidson. LC 78-11957. 1978. 16.95 (ISBN 0-470-26556-6). Halsted Pr.

Science for Textile Designers. J. M. Woodhouse. 1975. 14.95 o.p. (ISBN 0-236-31047-X, Pub. by Paul Elek); pap. 9.95x (ISBN 0-236-31048-8). Merrimack Bk Serv.

Science for the Seventies, 2 bks. A. J. Mee et al. pap. text ed. 4.95x ea.; Bk. 1. pap. text ed. (ISBN 0-435-57574-0); Bk. 2. pap. text ed. (ISBN 0-435-57576-7); Bk. 1. tchrs'. ed. 7.95x (ISBN 0-435-57575-9); Bk. 2. tchrs'. ed. 9.95 (ISBN 0-435-57577-5). Heinemann Ed.

Science from Toys: Stages 1 & 2 & Background. Don Radford. LC 77-83000. (Science 5-13 Ser.). (Illus.). 1977. pap. text ed. 9.30 (ISBN 0-356-04006-2). Raintree Child.

Science from Water Play. John Bird. LC 77-82984. (Teaching Primary Science Ser.). (Illus.). 1977. pap. text ed. 6.95 (ISBN 0-356-05071-8). Raintree Child.

Science from Wood. Dorothy Diamond. LC 77-82981. (Teaching Primary Science Ser.). (Illus.). 1977. pap. text ed. 6.95 (ISBN 0-356-05073-4). Raintree Child.

Science Fun Every Day in Every Way, a Total Environment Calendar. Amy Benham & Doris Ensminger. (Illus.). 1977. pap. 9.50 (ISBN 0-87355-017-X). Natl Sci Tchrs.

Science Game: An Introduction to Research in the Behavorial Sciences. 2nd ed. Neil M. Agnew & S. W. Pike. (P-H Ser. in Experimental Psychology). (Illus.). 1978. pap. 10.95 (ISBN 0-13-795336-4). P-H.

Science, God & the 80's. Harold Sala. 160p. (Orig.). 1980. pap. 2.25 (ISBN 0-89081-255-1). Harvest Hse.

Science Ideology & Development-Three Essays on Development Theory. Archie Mafeje. 1978. pap. text ed. 9.50x (ISBN 0-8419-9731-4). Holmes & Meier.

Science, Ideology, & World View: Essays in the History of Evolutionary Ideas. John C. Greene. 1981. 14.00 (ISBN 0-520-04217-4); pap. 4.95 (ISBN 0-520-04218-2). U of Cal Pr.

Science in a Renaissance Society. W. P. Wightman. 1972. text ed. 8.00x (ISBN 0-09-111650-3, Hutchinson U Lib); pap. text ed. 3.50x (ISBN 0-09-111651-1). Humanities.

Science in America, Historical Selections. John C. Burnham. 1971. text ed. 3.50 (ISBN 0-03-085288-9). N Watson.

Science in Contemporary China. Ed. by Leo A. Orleans. LC 79-65178. 640p. 1980. 35.00x (ISBN 0-8047-1078-3). Stanford U Pr.

Science in Culture: A Study of Values & Institutions. Ivan T. Sanderson. LC 79-57289. 1980. 10.95 (ISBN 0-89754-007-7); pap. 3.50 (ISBN 0-89754-006-9). Dan River Pr.

Science in France in the Revolutionary Era. Ed. by Maruice P. Crosland & Thomas Bugge. 1969. 15.00x o.p. (ISBN 0-262-03029-2). MIT Pr.

Science in the Bible. Jean S. Morton. 1978. pap. 14.95 (ISBN 0-8024-7629-5). Moody.

Science in the Elementary School: Content & Methods. John G. Navarra & Joseph Zafforoni. LC 74-83046. (Elementary Education Ser). 640p. 1975. text ed. 18.95 (ISBN 0-675-08772-4). Merrill.

Science in the Middle Ages. Ed. by David C. Lindberg. LC 78-5367. (Chicago History of Science & Medicine). 1980. pap. 9.95 (ISBN 0-226-48233-2, P870, Phoen). U of Chicago Pr.

Science in the World Around Us. William C. Vergara. LC 72-79699. (Illus.). 288p. 1973. 10.95 o.s.i. (ISBN 0-06-014766-0, HarpT). Har-Row.

Science Investigations for Elementary School Teachers. Kenneth D. George et al. 1973. pap. text ed. 4.95x (ISBN 0-669-83154-9). Heath.

Science: Its Method & Outlook. 4.00x o.p. (ISBN 0-210-27058-6). Asia.

Science Library, 6 vols. Set. 49.00 (ISBN 0-448-35030-0). Ency Brit Ed.

Science Magic Tricks: Over 50 Fun Tricks That Mystify & Dazzle. Nathan Shalit. LC 79-18645. (Illus.). 128p. (gr. 4-7). 1981. 8.95 (ISBN 0-03-047116-8); pap. 3.95 (ISBN 0-03-059269-0). HR&W.

Science, Models & Toys: Stage 3. Don Radford. LC 77-82998. (Science 5-13 Ser.). (Illus.). 1977. pap. text ed. 9.30 (ISBN 0-356-04351-7). Raintree Child.

Science, Numbers, & I. Isaac Asimov. LC 68-14207. 1968. 5.50 o.p. (ISBN 0-385-01908-4). Doubleday.

Science of Classification: Finding Order Among Living & Nonliving Objects. Martin J. Gutrick. (gr. 4 up). 1980. PLB 6.45 (ISBN 0-531-04160-3). Watts.

Science of Color. Committee on Colorimetry of the Optical Society of America. LC 52-7039. (Illus.). 340p. 1963. 20.00x (ISBN 0-9600380-1-9). Optical Soc.

Science of Design. G. L. Glegg. (Illus.). 112p. 1973. 16.95 (ISBN 0-521-20327-9). Cambridge U Pr.

Science of Education. J. F. Herbart. Bd. with Education of Man. (Contributions to the History of Psychology Ser.). 1978. Repr. of 1902 ed. 30.00 (ISBN 0-89093-161-5). U Pubns Amer.

Science of Engineering Materials. 2nd ed. Charles O. Smith. (Illus.). 1977. text ed. 25.95 (ISBN 0-13-794990-1). P-H.

Science of Engineering Materials. C. R. Tottle. 1966. pap. text ed. 8.95x o.p. (ISBN 0-435-71785-5). Heinemann Ed.

Science of Fairy Tales: An Inquiry into Fairy Mythology. Edwin S. Hartland. LC 68-31149. 1968. Repr. of 1891 ed. 22.00 (ISBN 0-8103-3464-X). Gale.

Science of Food: An Introduction to Food Science, Nutrition & Microbiology. 2nd ed. P. M. Gaman & K. B. Sherrington. (Illus.). 224p. 1980. 30.00 (ISBN 0-08-025896-4); pap. 12.50 (ISBN 0-08-025895-6). Pergamon.

Science of Food an Introduction to Food Science, Nutrition & Microbiology. Pamela D. Gaman & Kathleen B. Shernington. LC 76-27697. 1977. text ed. 32.00 (ISBN 0-08-019948-8); pap. text ed. 12.50 (ISBN 0-08-019947-X). Pergamon.

Science of Food & Cooking. 3rd ed. Allan Cameron. (Illus.). 1973. pap. 13.95x (ISBN 0-7131-1791-5) Intl Ideas.

Science of Genetics. 4th ed. George W. Burns. (Illus.). 1979. text ed. 18.95 (ISBN 0-02-317140-5). Macmillan.

Science of Genetics. W. Hexter & H. T. Yost. (Illus.). 592p. 1976. 21.95 (ISBN 0-13-794750-X). P-H.

Science of Health. W. Guild et al. 1969. 16.95 (ISBN 0-13-794818-2). P-H.

Science of Herbal Medicine. John Heinerman. pap. 15.95 (ISBN 0-89557-044-0). Bi World Indus.

Science of Hi-Fidelity. Kenneth W. Johnson & Willard C. Walker. LC 77-79557. (Illus.). 1981. pap. text ed. 16.95 (ISBN 0-8403-2297-6). Kendall-Hunt.

Science of Hockey. 2nd ed. Horst Wein. Tr. by David Belchamber. (Illus.). 22.00 (ISBN 0-7207-1149-5). Transatlantic.

Science of Homeopathy. George Vithoulkas. 1980. 9.50 (ISBN 0-394-17560-3, E746, Ever). Grove.

Science of Housekeeping. 2nd ed. Gina Tucker. 1973. pap. 10.95 (ISBN 0-8436-0577-4). CBI Pub.

Science of Human Progress. Robin Holliday. 112p. 1981. 21.00 (ISBN 0-19-854711-0). Oxford U Pr.

Science of Judo. Anthony P. Harrington. (Illus.). 6.95 o.s.i. (ISBN 0-87523-143-8). Emerson.

Science of Life: Contributions of Biology to Human Welfare. Ed. by K. D. Fisher & A. U. Nixon. LC 77-957. 358p. 1977. softcover 7.50 (ISBN 0-306-20025-2, Rosetta). Plenum Pub.

Science of Life: With Affirmations of Jesus Christ. Robert A. Smith. 1970. 2.25 (ISBN 0-912128-07-0). Pubns Living.

Science of Living. Alfred Adler. LC 69-12246. 1969. pap. 2.50 o.p. (ISBN 0-385-07139-6, A667, Anch) Doubleday.

Science of Mantras: A Manual of Happiness & Prosperity. Kailash Vajpeyi. 128p. 1980. 13.50 (ISBN 0-391-02213-X). Humanities.

Science of Medicine. Guilio Bedeschi. LC 74-12752. (International Library). 128p. (gr. 7 up). 1975. PLB 6.90 o.p. (ISBN 0-531-02122-X). Watts.

Science of Meditation. Rohit Mehta. 1978. 7.50 (ISBN 0-89684-007-7, Pub. by Motilal Banarsidass India); pap. 4.50 (ISBN 0-89684-008-5). Orient Bk Dist.

Science of Mind Hymnal. Thomas L. McClellan. 7.50 o.p. (ISBN 0-87516-343-2). De Vorss.

Science of Philosophy. F. H. George. 1981. price not set (ISBN 0-677-05550-1). Gordon.

Science of Photography. 3rd ed. Harry Baines. LC 73-19208. 1967. 17.95 (ISBN 0-471-04340-0). Halsted Pr.

Science of Popular Voice: Voice Production for the Pop Singer. Al Berkman. 1979. 12.95 (ISBN 0-934972-09-5). Melrose Pub Co.

Science of Psi: ESP & PK. Nash. 308p. 1978. 19.75 (ISBN 0-398-03803-1). C C Thomas.

Science of Religion. William S. Hatcher. (Etudes Baha'i Studies Ser: Vol. 2). 1977. pap. 2.95 (ISBN 0-87743-124-8, 7-32-55). Baha'i.

Science of Revolution: Fundamentals of Marxism-Leninism, Mao Tse Tung Thought & the Line of the Revolutionary Communist Party, Usa. Victor Wild. 352p. (Orig.). 1981. 17.95 (ISBN 0-89851-035-X); pap. 5.95 (ISBN 0-89851-036-8). RCP Pubns.

Science of Scientific Writing. Judson Monroe et al. LC 76-46822. 1976. pap. text ed. 5.95 (ISBN 0-8403-1645-3). Kendall-Hunt.

Science of Self Realization. Swami Bhaktivedanta. (Illus.). 1977. 9.95 (ISBN 0-89213-101-2). Bhaktivedanta.

Science of Social Issues. Bruce Stewart. 1971. 10.00 (ISBN 0-8108-0410-7). Scarecrow.

Science of Society, 4 vols. Wm. G. Sumner & A. G. Keller. 1927. 50.00x ea.; 200.00x set (ISBN 0-685-69873-4). Elliots Bks.

Science of Sound: Musical, Electronic, Environmental. Thomas D. Rossing. LC 80-12028. (Chemistry Ser.). (Illus.). 512p. 1981. text ed. price not set (ISBN 0-201-06505-3). A-W.

Science of Swimming. James Counsilman. 1968. ref. ed. 17.95 (ISBN 0-13-795385-2). P-H.

Science of Two, Four, Five-T & Associated Phenoxy Herbicides. Rodney W. Bovey & Alvin L. Young. 1980. 37.50 (ISBN 0-471-05134-9, Pub. by Wiley-Interscience). Wiley.

Science of Violin Playing. 2nd ed. Raphael Bronstein. 288p. 1980. 20.00 (ISBN 0-87666-601-2, Z-10). Paganiniana Pubns.

Science of Vocal Pedagogy: Theory & Application. D. Ralph Appelman. LC 67-10107. (Illus.). 448p. 1967. 19.50x (ISBN 0-253-35110-3); of 3 tapes 15.00 set (ISBN 0-253-35115-4); Tape 1. tapes 15.00 (ISBN 0-253-35112-X); Tape 2. tapes 15.00 (ISBN 0-253-35113-8); Tape 3. tapes 5.95 (ISBN 0-253-35114-6). Ind U Pr.

Science, Perception & Reality. Wilfred Sellars. (International Library of Philosophy & Scientific Method). 1963. text ed. 24.75x (ISBN 0-7100-3619-1). Humanities.

Science, Philosophy & Culture. K. Satchidananda Murty et al. 12.50x (ISBN 0-210-22678-1). Asia.

Science, Politics & Controversy: Civilian Nuclear Power in the United States, 1946-1974. Steven L. Del Sesto. LC 79-5227. (Westview Special Studies in Science, Technology & Public Policy). 1979. lib. bdg. 23.00x (ISBN 0-89158-566-4). Westview.

Science Principles. University of Missouri - Home Economics Resource Units. text ed. 2.75x spiral bdg. (ISBN 0-87543-027-9). Lucas.

Science Projects & Experiments, 4 bks. Eric J. Barker & W. F. Millard. Incl. Materials & Elements (ISBN 0-668-01498-9); Nature & Engergy (ISBN 0-668-01500-4); Five Senses (ISBN 0-668-01497-0); Machines & Energy (ISBN 0-668-01499-7). (YA) 1964. 4.50 ea. o.p. Arco.

Science Projects for the Intermediate Grades. Maxine S. Schneider. LC 70-132146. (Illus.). 1971. pap. 4.50 (ISBN 0-8224-6310-5). Pitman Learning.

Science Projects That Make Sense. A. Harris Stone. LC 72-113737. (Illus.). (gr. 3-5). 1971. PLB 6.95 o.p. (ISBN 0-525-38825-7). Dutton.

Science Projects with Eggs. David Webster. LC 76-15015. 72p. (gr. 4-6). 1976. PLB 6.45 (ISBN 0-531-01212-3). Watts.

Science Projects You Can Do. George K. Stone. Orig. Title: One Hundred One Science Projects. (Illus.). (gr. 7-9). 1963. PLB 6.95 (ISBN 0-13-795377-1); pap. 1.95 (ISBN 0-13-795328-3). P-H.

Science Puzzle Pictures. Hy Ruchlis. (Illus.). 8p. (Orig.). (gr. 4-8). 1972. pap. 4.00 set of twenty, with Tchr's Manual o.p. (ISBN 0-87594-048-X, 1300). Book-Lab.

Science Puzzles. Jerome Williams & Lelia Williams. (Illus.). (gr. 4-6). 1979. PLB 6.90 s&l (ISBN 0-531-02876-3). Watts.

Science, Revolution & Discontinuity. John Krige. (Harvester Studies in Philosophy: No. 10). 220p. Date not set. text ed. 30.00x (ISBN 0-391-02094-3). Humanities.

Science, Scientists & Public Policy. D. Schooler. LC 70-122274. 1971. 8.95 o.s.i. (ISBN 0-02-928000-1); pap. text ed. 4.50 o.s.i. (ISBN 0-02-928010-9). Free Pr.

Science Secrets. Robyn Supraner. LC 80-23794. (Illus.). 48p. (gr. 2-5). 1980. PLB 6.92 (ISBN 0-89375-426-9); pap. 1.75 (ISBN 0-89375-427-7). Troll Assocs.

Science, Sin & Scholarship: The Politics of Reverend Moon & the Unification Church. Ed. by Irving L. Horowitz. 312p. 1980. 12.50 (ISBN 0-262-08100-8); pap. 6.95 (ISBN 0-262-58042-X). MIT Pr.

Science: Some Sociological Perspectives. Nicholas Mullins. LC 72-12826. (Studies in Sociology Ser.). 42p. 1973. pap. text ed. 2.50 (ISBN 0-672-61205-4). Bobbs.

Science Speaks. Peter W. Stoner. 1958. pap. 1.50 (ISBN 0-8024-7630-9). Moody.

Science, Students, & Schools: A Guide for the Middle & Secondary Teacher. Ronald D. Simpson & Norman D. Anderson. LC 80-23124. 400p. 1981. text ed. 16.95 (ISBN 0-471-02477-5). Wiley.

Science Teaching. Joan Solomon. 224p. 1981. 25.00x (ISBN 0-7099-2304-X, Pub. by Croom Helm Ltd England). Biblio Dist.

Science, Technology & China's Drive for Modernization. Richard P. Suttmeier. LC 79-88587. (Publication: No. 223). 133p. 1980. pap. 6.95 (ISBN 0-8179-7232-3). Hoover Inst Pr.

Science, Technology & Economic Development: A Historical & Comparative Study. Ed. by William Beranek & Gustav Ranis. LC 78-5660. 1978. 32.95 (ISBN 0-03-041801-1). Praeger.

Science, Technology & Economic Growth in the Developing Countries. Ed. by G. E. Skorov. 1978. text ed. 27.00 (ISBN 0-08-022223-4). Pergamon.

Science, Technology, & Freedom. Willis H. Truitt & T. W. Solomons. 432p. 1974. pap. text ed. 9.75 (ISBN 0-395-17685-9). HM.

Science Technology & Global Problems--Views from the Developing World. Ed. by S. Radhakrishna. (Illus.). 1980. 45.00 (ISBN 0-08-024489-0). Pergamon.

Science, Technology & Global Problems; Issues of Development: Towards a New Role for Science & Technology. International Symposium on Science & Technology for Development, Singapore, 1979. Ed. by Maurice Goldsmith & Alexander King. LC 79-40879. (Illus.). 200p. 1979. 48.00 (ISBN 0-08-024691-5). Pergamon.

Science, Technology & Global Problems: Proceedings of the Symposium on the Role of Science & Technology in Solving Global Problems, Tallinn, USSR, Jan 1979. Ed. by J. Gvishiani. LC 79-40546. 1979. 82.00 (ISBN 0-08-024469-6). Pergamon.

Science, Technology & Global Problems: Science & Technology in Development Planning. International Symposium on Science & Technology for Development, Mexico City, 1979. Ed. by Victor L. Urquidi. LC 79-40912. 200p. 1979. 41.00 (ISBN 0-08-025227-3). Pergamon.

Science, Technology & Global Problems: The United Nations Advisory Committee on the Application of Science & Technology to Development. Office for Science & Technology. 62p. 1979. 16.00 (ISBN 0-08-025131-5). Pergamon.

Science, Technology & Society--Needs, Challenges & Limitations: Proceedings. International Colloquium on Science, Technology & Society, Vienna, 1979. Ed. by Klaus-Heinrich Standke. (Pergamon Policy Studies on International Development). 656p. 1980. 100.00 (ISBN 0-08-025947-2). Pergamon.

Science, Technology & Society in Seventeenth Century England. R. Merton. LC 79-82308. 1970. 19.50 (ISBN 0-86527-178-X). Fertig.

Science, Technology & Society in Seventeenth Century England. Robert K. Merton. 1978. pap. text ed. 6.95x (ISBN 0-685-41725-5). Humanities.

Science, Technology & the Future: Soviet Scientists Analysis of the Problems of & Prospects for the Development of Science & Technology & Their Role in Society. Ed. by E. P. Velikhov et al. LC 79-40113. (Illus.). 1980. 36.00 (ISBN 0-08-024743-1). Pergamon.

Science, Technology & the Human Prospect. Ed. by Chauncey Starr & Philip C. Ritterbush. (Pergamon Policy Studies). 1980. 66.00 (ISBN 0-08-024650-8); leather bdg. 350.00 (ISBN 0-685-97190-2) (ISBN 0-08-024652-4). Pergamon.

Science, Technology & the Labor Process. Les Levidow & Bob Young. (Marxist Studies: Vol. 1). 1980. pap. text ed. write for info. (ISBN 0-906336-20-1); pap. text ed. write for info. (ISBN 0-906336-21-X). Humanities.

Science Technology & the Modern Industrial State. Pavitt & Worboye. (Sicon Bks.). 1977. pap. 3.95 (ISBN 0-408-71299-6). Butterworths.

Science: The Glorious Entertainment. Jacques Barzun. LC 62-14520. 1964. 8.95 o.s.i. (ISBN 0-06-010240-3, HarpT). Har-Row.

Science Tricks & Puzzles. Alan Ward. 1977. 14.95 (ISBN 0-7134-0285-7, Pub. by Batsford England). David & Charles.

Science Update: 1977 Issue. Ed. by Thomas C. Aylesworth & Stanley Klein. pap. 29.95 o.p. (ISBN 0-685-42982-2, 9365/77). Gaylord Prof Pubns.

Science Within Art. Lynette I. Rhodes. LC 79-93193. (Illus.). 72p. 1980. pap. 7.95x (ISBN 0-910386-57-9, Pub. by Cleveland Mus Art). Ind U Pr.

Science Year, the World Book Science Annual. World Book-Childcraft International. LC 65-21776. (Illus.). 432p. (gr. 7-12). 1980. PLB 11.95 (ISBN 0-7166-0581-3); text ed. 10.95 (ISBN 0-686-27566-7). World Bk Childcraft.

Sciences & the Humanities: Conflict & Reconciliation. W. T. Jones. 1965. 15.75x (ISBN 0-520-00610-0); pap. 2.25 (ISBN 0-520-00611-9, CAL144). U of Cal Pr.

Sciences & Theology in the Twentiety Century. A. R. Peacocke. (Oxford International Symposia). 320p. 1981. price not set (ISBN 0-85362-188-8). Routledge & Kegan.

Sciences of the Artificial. 2nd, rev. ed. Herbert Simon. 192p. 1981. text ed. 15.00 (ISBN 0-262-19193-8); pap. 4.95 (ISBN 0-262-69073-X). MIT Pr.

Sciences, the Humanities, & the Technological Threat. Ed. by R. Niblett. LC 74-11838. 1975. 18.95 (ISBN 0-470-63655-6). Halsted Pr.

Science,Technology & Development: Political Economy of Technical Advance in Underdeveloped Countries. Ed. by Charles Cooper. 204p. 1973. 27.50x (ISBN 0-7146-2999-5, F Cass Co). Biblio Dist.

Sciencing: An Involvement Approach to Elementary Science Methods. Sandra G. Cain & Jack M. Evans. 1979. 12.95 (ISBN 0-675-08364-8); instructor's manual 3.95 (ISBN 0-685-96162-1). Merrill.

Scientific Aids in Hospital Diagnosis. Ed. by J. P. Nicholson. 288p. 1976. 35.00 (ISBN 0-306-30938-6, Plenum Pr). Plenum Pub.

Scientific American Resource Library: Readings in Psychology, 3 vols. Scientific American Editors. LC 73-80078. (Illus.). 1973. lib. bdg. 60.00x set (ISBN 0-7167-0990-2). W H Freeman.
Scientific American Resource Library: Readings in the Earth Sciences, 3 vols. Scientific American Editors. (Illus.). 1973. Set. lib. bdg. 60.00x (ISBN 0-7167-0988-0). W H Freeman.
Scientific American Resource Library: Readings in the Life Sciences, 3 vols, Vols. 8-10. Scientific American Editors. 1967-1973. Set. 60.00x set (ISBN 0-7167-0989-9). W H Freeman.
Scientific American Resource Library: Readings in the Social Sciences, 2 vols. Scientific American Editors. LC 78-8722. (Illus.). 1973. lib. bdg. 40.00x set (ISBN 0-7167-0992-9). W H Freeman.
Scientific Analysis for Programmable Calculators. H. R. Meck. (Illus.). 160p. 1981. 13.95 (ISBN 0-13-796417-X, Spec); pap. 6.95 (ISBN 0-13-796409-9). P-H.
Scientific & Technical Communication: A Pressing National Problem & Recommendations for Its Solution. Committee On Scientific And Technical Communication. LC 76-601241. (Illus., Orig.). 1969. pap. 8.25 o.p. (ISBN 0-309-01707-6). Natl Acad Pr.
Scientific & Technical Series: A Select Bibliography. Emanuel B. Ocran. LC 72-10880. 1973. 20.50 (ISBN 0-8108-0566-9). Scarecrow.
Scientific & Technical Translation. Isadore Pinchuck. LC 77-4933. 1977. lib. bdg. 23.50 o.p. (ISBN 0-89158-737-3). Westview.
Scientific Approach to Women's Gymnastics. Darlene Schmidt. (Brighton Ser. in Health & Physical Education). 1980. text ed. 12.95x (ISBN 0-89832-011-9). Brighton Pub Co.
Scientific Aspects of Acupuncture. Felix Mann. 1978. 21.00x (ISBN 0-433-20309-9). Intl Ideas.
Scientific Aspects of Dental Materials. J. A. Von Fraunhofer. 1975. 49.95 (ISBN 0-407-00001-1). Butterworths.
Scientific Aspects of Sports Training. Ed. by Albert W. Taylor. (Illus.). 344p. 1975. text ed. 28.50 (ISBN 0-398-03028-6). C C Thomas.
Scientific Ballooning: Proceedings of a Symposium of the 21st Plenary Meeting of the Committee on Space Research, Innsbruck, Austria, May 29-June 10 1978. Ed. by W. Riedler. LC 78-41182. (Illus.). 226p. 63.00 (ISBN 0-08-023420-8). Pergamon.
Scientific Basis of Air Conditioning. Ken-Ichi Kimura. (Illus.). 1977. 46.70x (ISBN 0-85334-732-8, Pub. by Applied Science). Burgess-Intl Ideas.
Scientific Basis of Flocculation. Ed. by K. J. Ives. 375p. 1978. 36.00x (ISBN 90-286-0758-7). Sijthoff & Noordhoff.
Scientific Basis of Joint Replacement. Ed. by S. A. Swanson & M. A. Freeman. LC 76-51524. 1977. 26.95 (ISBN 0-471-03012-0, Pub. by Wiley Medical). Wiley.
Scientific Basis of Medicine: Annual Reviews. British Postgraduate Medical Federation. Incl. 1966. text ed. 6.50x (ISBN 0-685-37476-9); 1967, 1968 & 1970. text ed. 8.25x ea.; 1973. text ed. 13.50x (ISBN 0-685-37478-5). Athlone Pr). Humanities.
Scientific Basis of Social Work. Maurice J. Karpf. 424p. 1981. Repr. of 1931 ed. lib. bdg. 35.00 (ISBN 0-8495-3049-0). Arden Lib.
Scientific Basis of the Art of Teaching. N. L. Gage. LC 78-6250. 1978. pap. text ed. 6.50x (ISBN 0-8077-2537-4). Tchrs Coll.
Scientific Books, Libraries, & Collectors. 3rd ed. J. L. Thorton & R. I. Tully. 1971. 31.00x (ISBN 0-85365-424-7, Pub. by Lib Assn England); suppl. 1978 15.50x (ISBN 0-85365-920-6). Oryx Pr.
Scientific Bowling. rev. ed. Don R. Sebolt & William E. McCubbin. (Illus.). 1976. pap. text ed. 2.95 o.p. (ISBN 0-8403-0685-7). Kendall-Hunt.
Scientific Communication Among Rice Breeders in 10 Asian Nations. (IRRI Research Paper Ser.: No. 12). 15p. 1978. pap. 5.00 (R052, IRRI). Unipub.
Scientific Conscience: Reflections on the Modern Biologist & Humanism. Catherine Roberts. LC 67-11553. (Orig.). 1967. pap. 1.95 o.s.i. (ISBN 0-8076-0410-0). Braziller.
Scientific Considerations in Monitoring & Evaluating Toxicological Research. Ed. by E. J. Gralla. LC 80-21367. (CIIT Ser.). (Illus.). 221p. 1980. 24.50 (ISBN 0-89116-209-7). Hemisphere Pub.
Scientific Diet Management for Business Executives: How to Eat All You Want & Still Lose One Pound a Day. John M. Murry. (International Council for Excellence in Management Library). (Illus.). 99p. 1980. plastic spiral bdg. 29.95 (ISBN 0-89266-246-8). Am Classical Coll Pr.
Scientific Discovery: Case Studies. Ed. by Thomas Nickles. (Boston Studies in the Philosophy of Science: No. 60). 386p. 1980. lib. bdg. 36.50 (ISBN 90-277-1092-9); pap. 15.95 (ISBN 90-277-1093-7). Kluwer Boston.
Scientific Elite: Nobel Laureates in the United States. Harriet Zuckerman. LC 76-26444. (Illus.). 1977. 14.95 (ISBN 0-02-935760-8); pap. text ed. 7.95 (ISBN 0-02-935880-9). Free Pr.
Scientific Explanation. Nicholas Rescher. LC 71-80675. 1970. 12.95 (ISBN 0-02-926330-1). Free Pr.
Scientific Exploration of the South Pacific. Committee On Oceanography. LC 72-603750. (Orig.). 1970. 11.50 (ISBN 0-309-01755-6). Natl Acad Pr.
Scientific Foundation of Man's Intimate Existence. Charles S. Sprague. (Illus.). 1980. deluxe ed. 37.45 (ISBN 0-89266-235-2). Am Classical Coll Pr.
Scientific Foundations of Gastroenterology. Wilfred Sircus & Adam N. Smith. LC 80-5260. (Illus.). 650p. 1980. 90.00 (ISBN 0-7216-8319-3). Saunders.
Scientific Guide to Peaceful Living. Betty Y. Ho. LC 77-142457. (Illus., Orig.). 1973. pap. 7.50 (ISBN 0-9600148-2-9). Juvenescent.
Scientific Ideas of G.K. Gilbert. Ed. by Ellis L. Yochelson. LC 80-67676. (Special Paper Ser.: No. 183). (Illus., Orig.). 1980. pap. write for info. (ISBN 0-8137-2183-0). Geol Soc.
Scientific Image. B. C. VanFrassen. (Clarendon Library of Logic & Philosophy Ser.). 248p. 1980. text ed. 45.00x (ISBN 0-19-824424-X). Oxford U Pr.
Scientific Images & Their Social Uses. Iain Cameron. (Science in a Social Context Ser.). 1979. pap. text ed. 3.95 (ISBN 0-408-71309-7). Butterworths.
Scientific Imagination. G. Holton. LC 76-47196. (Illus.). 1978. 39.95 (ISBN 0-521-21700-8); pap. 10.95 (ISBN 0-521-29237-9). Cambridge U Pr.
Scientific Inference. 3rd ed. Harold Jeffreys. LC 71-179159. (Illus.). 280p. 1973. 42.50 (ISBN 0-521-08446-6). Cambridge U Pr.
Scientific Information Systems & the Principle of Selectivity. William Goffman & Kenneth Warren. 20.95 (ISBN 0-03-056081-0). Praeger.
Scientific Informer. Robert J. Ferguson, Jr. (Illus.). 248p. 1971. 16.50 (ISBN 0-398-00558-3). C C Thomas.
Scientific Insights into Yoruba Traditional Medicine. James I. Durodola. (Traditional Healing Ser.). 1981. 27.50 (ISBN 0-932426-17-4). Trado-Medic.
Scientific Instruments of the Seventeenth & Eighteenth Centuries. Maurice Daumas. Ed. & tr. by Mary Holbrook. LC 77-112019. (Illus.). 1972. text ed. 39.75x (ISBN 0-7134-0727-1). Humanities.
Scientific Investigator. Richard O. Arther (Illus.). 248p. 1976. pap. 18.75 photocopy edition, spiral (ISBN 0-398-00055-7). C C Thomas.
Scientific Journal: Editorial Policies & Practices. Lois DeBakey. LC 76-6046. 1976. text ed. 12.50 (ISBN 0-8016-1223-3). Mosby.
Scientific Karatedo: Spiritual Development of Individuality in Mind and Body. Masayuki Hisatake. (Illus.). 256p. 1976. 25.00 (ISBN 0-87040-362-1). Japan Pubns.
Scientific Knowledge & Its Social Problems. J. R. Ravetz. 1971. 42.00x (ISBN 0-19-827213-8). Oxford U Pr.
Scientific Knowledge & Sociological Theory. Barry Barnes. (Monographs in Social Theory). 1974. 16.50 (ISBN 0-7100-7961-3); pap. 8.95 (ISBN 0-7100-7962-1). Routledge & Kegan.
Scientific Management of Library Operations. Richard M. Dougherty & Fred. J. Heinritz. LC 66-13741. 1966. 10.00 (ISBN 0-8108-0132-9). Scarecrow.
Scientific Management: The Essential Knowledge Which Everyone, but Absolutely Everyone Ought to Possess of the Main Guiding Principles Which Intelligent Men Follow in the Management of Their Business & Personal Affairs. Thomas Alden. (Essential Knowledge Ser.). 1978. plastic spiral bdg. 28.45 (ISBN 0-89266-120-8). Am Classical Coll Pr.
Scientific Method: Optimizing Applied Research Decisions. R. L. Ackoff. LC 62-10914. 1962. 27.50 (ISBN 0-471-00297-6). Wiley.
Scientific Methods in Medieval Archaeology. Ed. by Rainer Berger. LC 75-99771. (UCLA Center for Medieval & Renaissance Studies). (Illus.). 1971. 36.50x (ISBN 0-520-01626-2). U of Cal Pr.
Scientific Papers, 2 vols. J. Willard Gibbs. Set. 16.00 (ISBN 0-8446-2127-7). Peter Smith.
Scientific Papers, 4 vols. Geoffrey I. Taylor. Ed. by G. K. Batchelor. Incl. Vol. 1. Mechanics of Solids. 90.00 (ISBN 0-521-06608-5); Vol. 2. Meteorology, Oceanography & Turbulent Flow. 1960. 90.00 (ISBN 0-521-06609-3); Vol. 3. Aerodynamics & the Mechanics of Projectiles & Explosions. 1963. 90.00 (ISBN 0-521-06610-7); Vol. 4. Mechanics of Fluids: Miscellaneous Topics. (Illus.). 1971. 90.00 (ISBN 0-521-07995-0). Cambridge U Pr.
Scientific Papers: Physiology-Medicine-Surgery. Ed. by Charles W. Eliot. LC 75-95626. (Illus.). Repr. of 1910 ed. 15.00x (ISBN 0-678-03757-4). Kelley.
Scientific Principles & Methods of Strength Fitness. 2nd ed. John P. O'Shea. LC 75-18158. (Physical Education Ser.). (Illus.). 208p. 1976. pap. text ed. 9.50 (ISBN 0-201-05517-1). A-W.
Scientific Principles in Nursing. 8th ed. Dorothy Elhart et al. LC 77-23961. (Illus.). 1978. pap. text ed. 15.95 (ISBN 0-8016-1953-X). Mosby.
Scientific Productivity. Ed. by F. Andrews. LC 78-21978. (Illus.). 1979. 29.95 (ISBN 0-521-22586-8). Cambridge U Pr.
Scientific Productivity: The Effectiveness of Research Groups in Six Countries. 469p. 1980. 34.50 (ISBN 0-521-22586-8, UM42, UNESCO). Unipub.
Scientific Proof of the Existence of God Will Soon Be Announced by the White House. Da Free John. 1980. pap. 12.95 (ISBN 0-913922-48-X). Dawn Horse Pr.
Scientific Proof of the Existence of God Will Soon Be Announced by the White House. Da Free John. LC 80-81175. 1980. pap. 12.95 (ISBN 0-913922-48-X). Dawn Horse Pr.
Scientific Proof of the Existence of Reincarnation & Transmigration. Richard Van Den Tak. (Illus.). 1980. 16.50 (ISBN 0-89962-015-9). Todd & Honeywell.
Scientific Quotations: The Harvest of a Quiet Eye. Alan L. Mackay. Ed. by Maurice Ebison. LC 76-48396. 1977. 22.50x (ISBN 0-8448-1050-9). Crane-Russak Co.
Scientific Rationality: Studies in the Foundations of Science & Ethics. Ed. by Risto Hilpinen. (Philosophical Studies in Philosophy: No. 21). 247p. 1980. lib. bdg. 44.75 (ISBN 90-277-1112-7, Pub. by D. Reidel). Kluwer Boston.
Scientific Realism & the Plasticity of Mind. P. M. Churchland. LC 78-73240. (Cambridge Studies in Philosophy). (Illus.). 1979. 22.50 (ISBN 0-521-22632-5). Cambridge U Pr.
Scientific Revolution. Peter Amey. Ed. by Malcolm Yapp et al. (World History Ser.). (Illus.). (gr. 10). 1980. lib. bdg. 5.95 (ISBN 0-89908-132-0); pap. text ed. 1.95 (ISBN 0-89908-107-X). Greenhaven.
Scientific Russian Reader. Ed. by Nina Syniawska. LC 61-7717. 1961. 15.00x (ISBN 0-231-02453-3). Columbia U Pr.
Scientific Sailboat Racing. rev. ed. Ted Wells & Lowry Lamb. LC 79-13553. 1979. 10.95 (ISBN 0-396-07690-4). Dodd.
Scientific Sampling for Statistical Quality Control. William C. Guenther. LC 77-72042. (Griffin Statistical Monographs: No. 37). 1977. 16.25 (ISBN 0-02-845560-6). Macmillan.
Scientific Study of Marihuana. Ed. by Ernest L. Abel. LC 76-4508. 288p. 1976. 18.95 (ISBN 0-88229-144-0). Nelson-Hall.
Scientific, Technological & Institutional Aspects of Water Resource Policy. Yacov Y. Haimes. (AAAS Selected Symposium: No. 49). 125p. 1980. lib. bdg. 15.00x (ISBN 0-89158-842-6). Westview.
Scientific-Technological Change & the Role of Women in Development. Ed. by Davidson Nicol & Pamela D'Onofrio-Flores. (Special Studies in Social, Political, & Economic Development). 200p. 1981. lib. bdg. 25.00x (ISBN 0-86531-145-5). Westview.
Scientific Technology & Social Change: Readings from Scientific American. Intro. by Gene I. Rochlin. LC 74-3282. (Illus.). 1974. text ed. 19.95x (ISBN 0-7167-0501-X); pap. text ed. 9.95x (ISBN 0-7167-0500-1). W H Freeman.
Scientific Thought Nineteen Hundred to Nineteen Sixty: A Selective Survey. Ed. by R. Harre. 1969. 24.95x (ISBN 0-19-858125-4); pap. 12.50x (ISBN 0-19-858126-2). Oxford U Pr.
Scientific Use of Man's Imagination. John Tyndall. (Illus.). 181p. 1977. 43.15 (ISBN 0-89266-037-6). Am Classical Coll Pr.
Scientific Work of Rene Descartes. J. F. Scott. LC 76-40683. 1976. 19.50x (ISBN 0-8448-1030-4). Crane-Russak Co.
Scientism in Chinese Thought, 1900-1950. D. W. Kwok. LC 73-162297. 231p. 1972. Repr. of 1965 ed. 12.00x (ISBN 0-8196-0275-2). Biblo.
Scientist. Henry Margenau & David Bergamini. LC 64-8795. (Life Science Library). (Illus.). (gr. 5 up). 1964. PLB 8.97 o.p. (ISBN 0-8094-0466-4, Pub. by Time-Life). Silver.
Scientist. Robert S. Morison. 1964. 4.95 o.s.i. (ISBN 0-02-586980-9). Macmillan.
Scientist: A Novel Autobiography. John C. Lilly. LC 78-3545. (Illus.). 1978. 10.00 o.p. (ISBN 0-397-01274-8). Lippincott.
Scientist As Editor: Guidelines for Editors of Books & Journals. Maeve O'Connor. LC 78-60428. 218p. 1979. 14.50 (ISBN 0-471-04932-8, Pub. by Wiley Medical). Wiley.
Scientist As Subject: The Psychological Imperative. Michael J. Mahoney. LC 76-5878. 192p. 1976. 16.50 (ISBN 0-88410-505-9); pap. text ed. 6.95 (ISBN 0-88410-514-8). Ballinger Pub.
Scientist in American Life: The Essays & Lectures of Joseph Henry. Arthur P. Molella et al. LC 80-19367. (Illus.). 145p. 1981. pap. 6.95 (ISBN 0-87474-641-8). Smithsonian.
Scientists & World Order: The Uses of Technical Knowledge in International Organizations. Ernst B. Haas et al. 1978. 23.75x (ISBN 0-520-03341-8). U of Cal Pr.
Scientists As Writers. Ed. by James Harrison. 1965. 16.00x o.p. (ISBN 0-262-08022-2); pap. 4.95x (ISBN 0-262-58004-7, 32). MIT Pr.
Scientists at Work: The Creative Process of Scientific Research. Ed. by John N. Wilford. LC 78-18256. (Illus.). 1979. 9.95 (ISBN 0-396-07603-3). Dodd.
Scientists Confront Scientists Who Confront Velikovsky. 2nd ed. Velikovsky et al. Ed. by Lewis M. Greenberg et al. (Illus., Orig.). pap. 5.00 (ISBN 0-917994-06-X). Kronos Pr.
Scientists Face to Face. Ed. by Istvan Kardos. (Illus.). 400p. (Orig.). 1978. pap. 5.00x (ISBN 963-13-0373-X). Intl Pubns Serv.
Scientists in Whitehall. P. Gummett. 1980. text ed. 38.00x (ISBN 0-7190-0791-7). Humanities.
Scientists Must Write: A Guide to Better Writing for Scientists, Engineers & Students. Robert Barrass. LC 77-18561. 176p. 1978. text ed. 9.95x o.p. (ISBN 0-412-15440-4, Pub. by Chapman & Hall); pap. 8.50x o.p. (ISBN 0-412-15430-7). Methuen Inc.
Scientists Must Write: A Guide to Better Writing for Scientists, Engineers & Students. Robert Barrass. LC 77-18561. 1978. 9.95 o.p. (ISBN 0-470-99388-X). Halsted Pr.
Scipione Africano. Francesco Cavalli. Ed. by Howard M. Brown. LC 76-20963. (Italian Opera 1640-1770 Ser.). 1978. lib. bdg. 70.00 (ISBN 0-8240-2604-7). Garland Pub.
Sclera & Systemic Disorders. Peter G. Watson & Brian L. Hazleman. LC 76-26776. (Major Problems in Ophthalmology Ser.: Vol. 2). (Illus.). 1976. text ed. 24.00 (ISBN 0-7216-9134-X). Saunders.
Scoliosis. Ed. by Gordon Robin. 1973. 21.50 (ISBN 0-12-589850-9). Acad Pr.
Scoliosis & Allied Deformities of the Spine. Ed. by H. Leon Brooks. 1981. write for info. (ISBN 0-88416-270-2). PSG Pub.
Scoliosis & Muscle. P. A. Zorab. (Clinics in Developmental Medicine Ser., Research Monographs: Vol. 4A). 220p. 1974. 26.00 o.p. (ISBN 0-685-59047-X). Lippincott.
Scoliosis & Neurological Disease. Gordon C. Robin. LC 75-19283. 1975. 36.95 (ISBN 0-470-72795-0). Halsted Pr.
Scoliosis & Other Spinal Deformities. John H. Moe et al. LC 76-50153. (Illus.). 1978. text ed. 49.00 (ISBN 0-7216-6427-X). Saunders.
Scope & Authority of the Bible. James Barr. LC 80-21394. 1981. pap. 7.95 (ISBN 0-664-24361-4). Westminster.
Scope & Methods of Political Science: An Introduction to the Methodology of Political Inquiry. 3rd. rev. ed. Alan C. Isaak. 1980. pap. text ed. 10.95x (ISBN 0-256-02375-1). Dorsey.
Scope for Railway Transport in Urban Areas: Scope for Railway Transport in Urban Areas. ECMT for OCED. (ECMT Round Table Ser.: No. 47). (Illus.). 375p. (Orig.). 1980. pap. 20.00x (ISBN 92-821-1063-X, 75-80-06-1). OECD.
Scope of American Linguistics. Ed. by Roberg Austerlitz. 1977. text ed. 10.25x (ISBN 90-316-0003-2). Humanities.
Scope of Astrological Prediction. Marc E. Jones. LC 69-19863. 1973. 16.50 o.p. (ISBN 0-87878-012-2, Sabian). Great Eastern.
Scope of Fiction. Cleanth Brooks & Robert P. Warren. 1960. text ed. 11.95 (ISBN 0-13-796656-3). P-H.
Scope of Local Initiative: A Study of Cheshire County Council 1961-1974. J. M. Lee et al. 208p. 1974. 30.50x (ISBN 0-85520-059-6, Pub by Martin Robertson England). Biblio Dist.
Scope of Philosophy: An Introductory Study-Book. F. W. Garforth. 1971. text ed. 8.75x (ISBN 0-391-00186-8); pap. text ed. 5.00x (ISBN 0-391-00187-6). Humanities.
Scope of Political Theology. Ed. by Alistair Kee. 1978. pap. text ed. 9.00x o.s.i. (ISBN 0-685-99193-8). Allenson.
Scope of Public Sector Bargaining. Walter J Gershenfeld et al. LC 76-53904. 1977. 18.95 (ISBN 0-669-01298-X). Lexington Bks.
Scope of Rhetoric: A Handbook for Composition & Literature. James E. Robinson. 1970. pap. 5.95x (ISBN 0-673-05246-X). Scott F.

Scope of Satire. Charles Sanders. 1971. pap. 5.95x o.p. (ISBN 0-673-05887-5). Scott F.
Scope of Total Architecture. Walter Gropius. 1962. pap. 1.25 o.s.i. (ISBN 0-02-000500-8, Collier). Macmillan.
Scope of Understanding in Sociology. Werner Pelz. 1974. 22.50x (ISBN 0-7100-7854-4); pap. 10.00 (ISBN 0-7100-8009-3). Routledge & Kegan.
Scopes Trial. Mary Lee Settle. LC 73-181449. (Illus.). 128p. (gr. 7 up). 1972. PLB 5.88 o.p. (ISBN 0-531-02027-4). Watts.
Score Better at Skeet. Fred Missildine & Nick Karas. (Illus.). 1972. 7.95 (ISBN 0-87691-049-5); pap. 5.95 (ISBN 0-87691-050-9). Winchester Pr.
Score Better at Trap. Fred Missildine & Nicholas Karas. (Illus.). 1970. 7.95 (ISBN 0-87691-025-8); pap. 5.95 (ISBN 0-87691-153-X). Winchester Pr.
Score for Lovers Made Men, a Masque by Ben Jonson. Ben Jonson. Ed. by Andrew J. Sabol. LC 63-8400. 93p. 1963. pap. 5.00 (ISBN 0-87057-073-0, Pub. by Brown U Pr). Univ Pr of New England.
Scorecard. Aronson. 1979. Set Of 5. pap. 6.95 (ISBN 0-7216-1409-4). Dryden Pr.
Scores: An Anthology of New Music. Commentary by Roger Johnson. LC 80-53302. (Illus.). 450p. 1981. pap. text ed. 12.95 (ISBN 0-02-871190-4). Schirmer Bks.
Scoring: The Shots. Paul J. Deegan. LC 76-12423. (Sports Instruction Ser.). (Illus.). (gr. 3-9). 1976. PLB 5.95 (ISBN 0-87191-526-X); pap. 2.95 (ISBN 0-686-67438-3). Creative Ed.
Scornful Simkin. L Lorenz. 1980. pap. 8.95 (ISBN 0-13-796664-4). P-H.
Scornfyl Lady. Francis Beaumont & John Fletcher. LC 73-38152. (English Experience Ser.: No. 432). 70p. 1972. Repr. of 1616 ed. 9.50 (ISBN 90-221-0432-X). Walter J Johnson.
Scorpio. Paula Harris. (Sun Signs). (Illus.). (gr. 4-12). 1978. PLB 5.95 (ISBN 0-87191-648-7); pap. 2.95 (ISBN 0-89812-078-0). Creative Ed.
Scorpio. Julia Parker. (Pocket Guide to Astrology Ser.). (Orig.). 1980. pap. write for info. (ISBN 0-671-25550-9, Fireside). S&S.
Scorpio Letter. Victor Canning. 272p. 1981. pap. 2.25 (ISBN 0-441-75519-4). Charter Bks.
Scorpio Letters. Victor Canning. 1964. 5.95 o.p. (ISBN 0-688-02436-X). Morrow.
Scorpion. Michael R. Linaker. 1981. pap. 1.95 (ISBN 0-451-09606-1, J9606, Sig). NAL.
Scorpion. Peter McCurtin. (Sundance Ser.: No. 32). 1980. pap. 1.75 (ISBN 0-8439-0756-8, Leisure Bks). Nordon Pubns.
Scorpion: A Good Bad Horse. Will James. LC 36-23527. (Illus.). vi, 312p. 1975. pap. 5.95 (ISBN 0-8032-5822-4, BB 604, Bison). U of Nebr Pr.
Scorpion East. Jerrold Margulas. 1981. 12.95 (ISBN 0-87223-653-6). Seaview Bks.
Scorpion Sanction. Gordon Pape & Tony Aspler. LC 79-56262. 372p. 1980. 13.95 (ISBN 0-670-19965-6). Viking Pr.
Scorpion Signal. Adam Hall. LC 80-85103. 288p. 1981. pap. 2.95 (ISBN 0-87216-831-X). Playboy Pbks.
Scorpiones: Arachnida I, Vol. 3. G. Levy & P. Amitai. (Fauna Palestina Ser.). (Illus.). 132p. 1981. text ed. 25.00x (ISBN 0-87474-606-X). Smithsonian.
Scorpions of Medical Importance. Hugh L. Keegan. LC 80-16419. (Illus.). 1980. 22.50 (ISBN 0-87805-124-4). U Pr of Miss.
Scotch. G. S. Botterill & T. D. Harding. 1977. 16.95 (ISBN 0-7134-0224-5, Pub. by Batsford England). David & Charles.
Scotch Rogue: The Life and Actions of Donald MacDonald, a Highland Scot. LC 80-2491. 1981. Repr. of 1784 ed. 39.50 (ISBN 0-404-19125-8). AMS Pr.
Scotch Twins. Lucy F. Perkins. (Twin Ser). (Illus.). (gr. 3-5). 1969. Repr. PLB 4.85 o.s.i. (ISBN 0-8027-6062-7). Walker & Co.
Scotland. Nigel Tranter. LC 68-1791. (Pegasus Books: No. 2). 1964. 7.50x (ISBN 0-234-77793-1). Intl Pubns Serv.
Scotland: An Archaeological Guide. Euan MacKie. LC 74-32286. (Illus.). 1975. 15.00 o.p. (ISBN 0-8155-5034-0, NP). Noyes.
Scotland: An Archaeological Guide. Euan W. Mackie. (Illus., Orig.). 1975. pap. 7.95 o.p. (ISBN 0-571-10735-4, Pub. by Faber & Faber). Merrimack Bk Serv.
Scotland; Archaeology & Early History. Anna Ritchie & Graham Ritchie. (Ancient People & Places Ser.). (Illus.). 192p. 1981. 19.95 (ISBN 0-500-02100-7). Thames Hudson.
Scotland: Bed & Breakfast. rev. ed. 184p. 1980. pap. 3.95 o.p. (ISBN 0-85419-138-0, Pub. by B T A). Merrimack Bk Serv.
Scotland: Bed & Breakfast. rev. ed. Scottish Tourist Board. (Illus.). 252p. 1981. pap. price not set (ISBN 0-85419-170-4, Pub. by Auto Assn-British Tourist Authority England). Merrimack Bk Serv.
Scotland for the Motorist. Automobile Association - British Tourist Authority. 1979. pap. 2.50 o.p. (ISBN 0-686-24008-1, Pub. by B T A). Merrimack Bk Serv.
Scotland Forever Home: An Introduction to the Homeland for American & Other Scots. Geddes MacGregor. LC 79-24066. 284p. 1980. 9.95 (ISBN 0-396-07804-4). Dodd.
Scotland from the Air. Ann Glen & Michael Williams. 1975. pap. text ed. 7.95x o.p. (ISBN 0-435-34363-7). Heinemann Ed.
Scotland from the Earliest Times to 1603. 3rd ed. W. Croft Dickinson. Ed. by Archibald A. Duncan. (Illus.). 1977. text ed. 36.00x (ISBN 0-19-822453-2). Oxford U Pr.
Scotland: Hotels & Guesthouses. rev. ed. 304p. 1980. pap. 3.95 o.p. (ISBN 0-85419-137-2, Pub. by B T A). Merrimack Bk Serv.
Scotland: Hotels & Guesthouses. rev. ed. Scottish Tourist Board. (Illus.). 328p. 1981. pap. price not set (ISBN 0-85419-169-0, Pub. by Auto Assn-British Tourist Authority England). Merrimack Bk Serv.
Scotland in Colour. Alastair I. Dunnett. 1977. 13.50 (ISBN 0-7134-0019-6, Pub. by Batsford England). David & Charles.
Scotland in Pictures. rev. ed. Sterling Publishing Company Editors. LC 62-18638. (Visual Geography Ser). (Illus., Orig.). (gr. 6 up). 1978. PLB 4.99 (ISBN 0-8069-1051-8); pap. 2.95 (ISBN 0-8069-1050-X). Sterling.
Scotland Nineteen Eighty: The Economics of Self-Government. Ed. by Donald Mackay. 1979. text ed. 18.25x (ISBN 0-905470-03-6). Humanities.
Scotland: Shaping of a Nation. rev. ed. Gordon Donaldson. 272p. 1980. 25.00 (ISBN 0-7153-7975-5). David & Charles.
Scotland's Voice in International Affairs. Ed. by Clive Archer & John Main. 160p. 1980. 19.95x (ISBN 0-7735-0512-1). McGill-Queens U Pr.
Scots. Clifford Hanley. 240p. 1980. 12.50 (ISBN 0-8129-0946-1). Times Bks.
Scots Quair: A Trilogy of Sunset Song, Cloud Howe, & Grey Granite. Lewis G. Gibbon. LC 77-75288. 1977. 10.95 (ISBN 0-8052-3661-9). Schocken.
Scotsman in Buckskin: Sir William Drummond Stewart & the Rocky Mountain Fur Trade. Mae R. Porter & Odessa Davenport. Date not set. 9.50 (ISBN 0-8038-6648-8). Hastings.
Scott. Angus Calder & Jenni Calder. (Literary Critiques Ser). (Illus.). 1970. lib. bdg. 4.95 o.p. (ISBN 0-668-02354-6). Arco.
Scott & Ernest: The Authority of Failure & the Authority of Success. Matthew Bruccoli. LC 79-26848. 192p. 1980. pap. 7.95 (ISBN 0-8093-0977-7). S Ill U Pr.
Scott Brown's Diseases of the Ear, Nose, & Throat. 4th ed. Ed. by John Ballantyne & John Groves. Incl. Vol. 1. Ear, Nose & Throat Diseases. 115.00 (ISBN 0-407-00147-6); Vol. 2. The Ear. 145.00 (ISBN 0-407-00148-4); Vol. 3. The Nose. 69.95 (ISBN 0-407-00149-2); Vol. 4. The Throat. 99.95 (ISBN 0-407-00150-6). LC 79-41008. (Illus.). 1979. Set. text ed. 400.00 (ISBN 0-407-00143-3). Butterworths.
Scott Fitzgerald. Andrew Turnbull. LC 62-9315. 1975. 4.95 o.p. (ISBN 0-684-14661-4, ScribT). Scribner.
Scott, Foresman Advanced Dictionary. Ed. by Clarence L. Barnhart. 1978. 15.95 (ISBN 0-385-14852-6). Doubleday.
Scott, Foresman Beginning Dictionary. Ed. by Clarence L. Barnhart. 12.95 (ISBN 0-385-13330-8). Doubleday.
Scott, Foresman Intermediate Dictionary. Ed. by Clarence L. Barnhart. 1978. 15.95 (ISBN 0-385-14853-4). Doubleday.
Scott, Foresman Robert's Rules of Order. rev. ed. William J. Evans. 1980. 17.95x (ISBN 0-673-15472-6). Scott F.
Scott Free. Scott Ross et al. 1976. 5.95 o.p. (ISBN 0-912376-15-5). Chosen Bks Pub.
Scott Joplin & the Ragtime Years. Mark Evans. LC 75-38362. 1976. 5.95 (ISBN 0-396-07308-5). Dodd.
Scott Joplin: The Man Who Made Ragtime. James Haskins. LC 76-50768. (Illus.). 264p. (Orig.). 1980. pap. 6.95 (ISBN 0-686-64767-X). Stein & Day.
Scott Nearing: Apostle of American Radicalism. Stephen J. Whitfield. 1974. 15.00x (ISBN 0-231-03816-X). Columbia U Pr.
Scott on Himself. David Hewitt. 288p. 1981. 15.00x (ISBN 0-7073-0283-8, Pub. by Scottish Academic Pr Scotland). Columbia U Pr.
Scott: The Critical Heritage. Ed. by John O. Hayden. 1970. 38.50x (ISBN 0-7100-6724-0). Routledge & Kegan.
Scottish Ballad Book. Ed. by David Buchan. 244p. 1973. 16.00 (ISBN 0-7100-7566-9). Routledge & Kegan.
Scottish Ballad Operas, One: Pastoral Comedies. Ed. by Walter H. Rubsamen. (Ballad Opera Ser.). 1974. lib. bdg. 50.00 (ISBN 0-8240-0923-1). Garland Pub.
Scottish Ballad Operas, Three: Farce & Satire. Ed. by Walter H. Rubsamen. (Ballad Opera Ser.). 1974. lib. bdg. 50.00 (ISBN 0-8240-0925-8). Garland Pub.
Scottish Ballad Operas, Two: History & Politics. Ed. by Walter H. Rubsamen. (Ballad Opera Ser.). 1974. lib. bdg. 50.00 (ISBN 0-8240-0924-X). Garland Pub.
Scottish Capital on the American Credit Frontier. W. G. Kerr. LC 75-16575. (Illus.). xviii, 246p. 1976. 13.00 (ISBN 0-87611-035-9). Tex St Hist Assn.
Scottish Capitalism. Dickson. 1980. text ed. 24.75x (ISBN 0-85315-482-1). Humanities.
Scottish Church Attitudes to Sex, Marriage & the Family 1850-1914. Kenneth M. Boyd. 410p. 1980. text ed. 47.00x (ISBN 0-85976-056-1). Humanities.
Scottish Clans & Their Tartans. (Illus.). Repr. 6.95 (ISBN 0-7179-4504-9). Transatlantic.
Scottish Educational System. 2nd rev. ed. S. Leslie Hunter. 296p. 1972. text ed. 17.25 (ISBN 0-08-016667-9); pap. text ed. 7.75 (ISBN 0-08-016668-7). Pergamon.
Scottish Enlightenment & the American College Ideal. Douglas Sloan. LC 75-132938. 1971. text ed. 12.75x (ISBN 0-8077-2168-9). Tchrs Coll.
Scottish Folk Tales. Ruth Ratcliff. (Illus.). 1977. 10.00 (ISBN 0-584-62393-3). Transatlantic.
Scottish Government Year Book, 1978. Ed. by Henry M. Drucker & Michael G. Clarke. 208p. 1978. 22.50x (ISBN 0-87471-878-3). Rowman.
Scottish Lighthouses. William Munro. (Illus.). 240p. 1980. 22.50 (ISBN 0-906191-32-7, Pub. by Thule Pr England). Intl Schol Bk Serv.
Scottish Linen Industry in the Eighteenth Century. Alastair Durie. (Illus.). 1979. text ed. 31.25x (ISBN 0-685-94719-X). Humanities.
Scottish Metrical Psalter (1650) A Revision. Nichol Grieve. 183p. pap. text ed. 2.95 (ISBN 0-567-02127-0). Attic Pr.
Scottish Mountain Climbs. Donald Bennet. (Illus.). 192p. 1980. 30.00 (ISBN 0-7134-1048-5, Pub. by Batsford England). David & Charles.
Scottish Novel: From Smollett to Spark. Francis R. Hart. LC 77-20680. 1978. 20.00x (ISBN 0-674-79584-9). Harvard U Pr.
Scottish Painters. David Irwin & Francina Irwin. 1975. 78.00 (ISBN 0-571-08822-8, Pub. by Faber & Faber). Merrimack Bk Serv.
Scottish Painting: 1837-1939. William Hardie. 1977. 35.00 (ISBN 0-02-548110-X). Macmillan.
Scottish Philosophy, Biographical, Expository, Critical, from Hutcheson to Hamilton. James McCosh. LC 75-3266. (A. P. (Philo. in Amer)). 496p. 1980. Repr. of 1875 ed. 33.50 (ISBN 0-404-59255-4). AMS Pr.
Scottish Place-Names. W. F. Nicoliasen. 1976. 19.95 (ISBN 0-7134-3253-5). David & Charles.
Scottish Political System. 2nd ed. J. G. Kellas. LC 75-2733. (Illus.). 1975. 33.95 (ISBN 0-521-20864-5); pap. 10.95x (ISBN 0-521-09972-2). Cambridge U Pr.
Scottish Population History: From the Seventeenth Century to the 1930s. Michael W. Flinn. LC 76-11060. (Illus.). 1978. 68.00 (ISBN 0-521-21173-5). Cambridge U Pr.
Scottish Prose, Fifteen Fifty-Seventeen Hundred. Ed. by Ronald Jack. (Scottish Library Ser). 220p. 1971. text ed. 13.00x (ISBN 0-7145-0798-9). Humanities.
Scottish Proverbs. Andrew Henderson. LC 70-75962. 1969. Repr. of 1881 ed. 18.00 (ISBN 0-8103-3894-7). Gale.
Scottish Railway Book. John Thomas. 1977. 9.95 o.p. (ISBN 0-685-74791-3). David & Charles.
Scottish Reformation. G. Donaldson. 42.00 (ISBN 0-521-08675-2). Cambridge U Pr.
Scottish Rural Society in the Sixteenth Century. M. H. Sanderson. 1980. text ed. 27.75x (ISBN 0-85976-027-8). Humanities.
Scottish Sail: A Forgotten Era. Robert Simper. LC 74-81055. 1974. 8.95 (ISBN 0-7153-6703-X). David & Charles.
Scottish Sixth. Andrew McPherson & Guy Neave. (General Ser.). 170p. 1976. pap. text ed. 13.25x (ISBN 0-85633-093-0, NFER). Humanities.
Scottish Sketches of R. B. Cunningham Graham. John Walker. (Illus.). 232p. 1981. 13.50x (ISBN 0-7073-0288-9, Pub. by Scottish Academic Pr Scotland). Columbia U Pr.
Scottish Tartans. (Illus.). 6.95 (ISBN 0-7179-4504-9). Transatlantic.
Scottish Terrier. D. A. Caspersz. LC 76-11027. (Illus.). 1976. bds. 2.25 o.p. (ISBN 0-668-03975-2). Arco.
Scottish Theology: In Relation to Church History. John MacLeod. 1974. 8.95 (ISBN 0-85151-193-7). Banner of Truth.
Scottish Vernacular Literature: A Succinct History. 3rd. ed. Thomas F. Henderson. LC 70-75473. 1969. Repr. of 1910 ed. 22.00 (ISBN 0-8103-3884-X). Gale.
Scottish Visitors: A Story About 'Abdu'l-Baha in Britain. Anthony A. Lee. (Stories About 'abdu'l-Baha Ser.). (Illus.). 24p. (Orig.). (gr. k-5). 1981. pap. 2.50 (ISBN 0-933770-05-7). Kalimat.
Scottish Weapons & Fortifications, Eleven Hundred-Eighteen Hundred. Ed. by David Caldwell. (Illus.). 1980. text ed. 34.50x (ISBN 0-85976-047-2). Humanities.
Scott's Fingerprint Mechanics. Robert D. Olsen, Sr. (Illus.). 480p. 1978. 32.75 (ISBN 0-398-03730-2). C C Thomas.
Scottsboro: A Tragedy of the American South. Dan T. Carter. LC 79-1090. 1979. 24.95x (ISBN 0-8071-0568-6); pap. 7.95 (ISBN 0-8071-0498-1). La State U Pr.
Scourge. Thomas L. Dunne. 1979. pap. 2.50 o.p. (ISBN 0-345-28063-6). Ballantine.
Scourge of Scapa Flow. J. Farragut Jones. (Orig.). 1981. pap. 2.75 (ISBN 0-440-17701-4). Dell.
Scourge of Secrecy: A/Personal Testimony & Appeal. Richard Harger. LC 80-50239. 218p. 1980. pap. 6.80 (ISBN 0-936472-00-6). Gordy Pr.
Scout & Ranger. James Pike. LC 74-39282. (American Scene Ser). (Illus.). 164p. 1972. Repr. of 1932 ed. lib. bdg. 19.50 (ISBN 0-306-70458-7). Da Capo.
Scout of Santa Fe. June A. Elmer. (Illus.). 1981. 8.95 (ISBN 0-8062-1677-8). Carlton.
Scout Songbook. Boy Scouts Of America. 128p. (gr. 6-12). 1972. pap. 0.90x (ISBN 0-8395-3224-5, 3224). BSA.
Scouting & Patrolling. Rex Applegate. (Illus.). 135p. 1980. 15.95 (ISBN 0-87364-184-1). Paladin Ent.
Scouting for the Mentally Retarded. Boys Scouts Of America. (Illus.). 1967. pap. 0.95x (ISBN 0-8395-3058-7). BSA.
Scouting for the Physically Handicapped. Boy Scouts Of America. 96p. 1971. pap. 2.00x (ISBN 0-8395-3039-0, 3039). BSA.
Scoutmaster's Handbook. Boy Scouts Of America. (Illus.). 384p. 1972. flexible bdg 3.45x (ISBN 0-8395-6504-6, 6504). BSA.
Scouts. Keith Wheeler. (Old West Ser.). (Illus.). 1978. 12.95 (ISBN 0-8094-2304-9). Time-Life.
Scouts. Keith Wheeler. LC 78-1364. (Old West Ser.). (Illus.). 1978. lib. bdg. 12.96 (ISBN 0-686-51081-X). Silver.
Scouts of Stonewall. Joseph Altsheler. 1976. lib. bdg. 15.80x (ISBN 0-89968-004-6). Lightyear.
Scrabble Grams. Judd Haubrick. Ed. by Harriet Bell. 96p. 1981. pap. 2.95 (ISBN 0-517-54271-4, Harmony). Crown.
Scrabble Trade Mark Crossword Games Scorebook. Ed. by Running Press. 128p. (Orig.). 1980. lib. bdg. 12.90 (ISBN 0-89471-104-0); pap. 3.95 (ISBN 0-89471-105-9). Running Pr.
Scramble Cycle. E. Radlauer & R. S. Radlauer. LC 72-151887. (Sports Action Bks). (Illus.). (gr. 3 up). 1971. 5.90 o.p. (ISBN 0-531-01999-3). Watts.
Scramble for Southern Africa: 1877-1895. D. M. Schreuder. LC 78-58800. (Cambridge Commonwealth Ser.). 1980. 29.50 (ISBN 0-521-20279-5). Cambridge U Pr.
Scrambled Eggs Super! Dr. Seuss. LC 53-5013. (Dr. Seuss Paperback Classics Ser.). (Illus.). 64p. (gr. k-3). 1980. pap. 2.95 (ISBN 0-394-84544-7). Random.
Scrambles Amongst the Alps in the Years Eighteen Sixty to Eighteen Sixty-Nine. Edward Whymper. (Illus.). 176p. 1981. pap. 5.95 (ISBN 0-89815-043-4). Ten Speed Pr.
Scrambling: Zig-Zagging Your Way to the Top. Elwood N. Chapman. 192p. 1981. 8.95 (ISBN 0-87477-129-3). J P Tarcher.
Scrap Book. James Scully. LC 77-89528. 1977. pap. 3.50 (ISBN 0-917488-03-2). Ziesing Bros.
Scrap Screen. Alice Buchan. (Illus.). 1979. 24.00 (ISBN 0-241-10223-5, Pub. by Hamish Hamilton England). David & Charles.
Scrapbook of Katherine Mansfield. Katherine Mansfield. LC 74-16042. 288p. 1975. Repr. of 1939 ed. 22.50 (ISBN 0-86527-299-9). Fertig.
Scratch Papers. Theodore L. Harris et al. (Keys to Reading Ser.). (Illus.). (gr. 5). 1975. pap. text ed. 2.97 (ISBN 0-87892-452-3); tchr's ed. 2.97 (ISBN 0-87892-453-1); duplicating masters 15.51 (ISBN 0-87892-050-1). Economy Co.
Scream Along with Me. Alfred Hitchcock. 1981. pap. 2.25 (ISBN 0-440-13633-4). Dell.
Scream Away. Andrea Harris. LC 78-62017. 1979. pap. 1.50 o.p. (ISBN 0-87216-510-8). Playboy Pbks.
Screed. Jack Saunders. LC 80-53288. 250p. 1981. 12.95x (ISBN 0-912824-23-9); pap. 5.95 (ISBN 0-912824-24-7). Vagabond Pr.
Screen Greats: Bogart. M. Samuels. 1980. pap. 2.95 (ISBN 0-931064-31-7). O'Quinn Studio.
Screen Greats: Hollywood Nostalgia. M. Samuels. 1980. pap. 2.00 (ISBN 0-931064-30-9). O'Quinn Studio.
Screen Greats: Monroe. M. Samuels. 1980. pap. 2.95 (ISBN 0-931064-32-5). O'Quinn Studio.

Screen Image of Youth: Movies About Children & Adolescents. Ruth M. Goldstein & Edith Zornow. LC 80-14053. (Illus.). xxi, 363p. 1980. 20.00 (ISBN 0-8108-1316-5). Scarecrow.

Screen Reader One: Cinema, Ideology, Politics. Intro. by John Ellis. (Screen Ser.). 1977. pap. 15.00 (ISBN 0-900676-07-8). NY Zoetrope.

Screen World, 10 vols. 1949, 1951-1959. Daniel Blum. LC 70-84068. (Illus.). 1969. Set. 165.00x (ISBN 0-8196-0255-8); 18.00x ea. Biblo.

Screening Methods in Pharmacology, Vol. 2. Robert A. Turner & Peter Hebborn. 1971. 43.00 o.p. (ISBN 0-12-704252-0). Acad Pr.

Screening Rice for Tolerance to Mineral Stresses. (IRRI Research Paper Ser.: No. 6). 20p. 1977. pap. 5.00 (R046, IRRI). Unipub.

Screenplay for "Three Comrades" by Erich Maria Remarque. F. Scott Fitzgerald. Ed. by Matthew J. Bruccoli. LC 77-28077. (Screenplay Library). (Illus.). 303p. 1978. 10.00 (ISBN 0-8093-0854-1); pap. 7.95 (ISBN 0-8093-0853-3). S Ill U Pr.

Screenplays. Werner Herzog. Tr. by Alan Greenberg from Ger. 208p. 1980. 10.95 (ISBN 0-934378-02-9); pap. 5.95 (ISBN 0-934378-03-7). Tanam Pr.

Screens. Jean Genet. Tr. by Bernard Frechtman from Fr. 1962. pap. 4.95 (ISBN 0-394-17245-0, E374, Ever). Grove.

Screenwriter: The Life & Times of Nunnally Johnson. Tom Stempel. LC 78-75339. (Illus.). 1980. 12.00 (ISBN 0-498-02362-1). A S Barnes.

Screenwriter's Handbook: What to Write, How to Write It, Where to Sell It. Constance Nash & Virginia Oakey. LC 77-76031. 1978. 10.95 o.p. (ISBN 0-06-013162-4, HarpT). Har-Row.

Screw-Retained Dental Prostheses. Shimegi Matsuo. 140p. 1981. 42.00 (ISBN 0-931386-35-7). Quint Pub Co.

Screwtape Letters. C. S. Lewis. LC 80-18591. (Illus.). 136p. 1980. Repr. of 1979 ed. 9.95 (ISBN 0-8006-0650-7, 1-650). Fortress.

Scriabin. Alfred J. Swan. LC 75-76423. (Music Ser). 1969. Repr. of 1928 ed. lib. bdg. 16.50 (ISBN 0-306-71322-5). Da Capo.

Scribble-Foolers. Bernard Hamber. LC 79-92052. 175p. (Orig.). 1980. pap. 6.75 (ISBN 0-9604896-8-1). BH Ent.

Scribe: A Handbook of Classroom Ideas to Motivate the Teaching of Handwriting. (Spice Ser.). 1976. 6.50 (ISBN 0-89273-122-2). Educ Serv.

Scribes & Scholars: A Guide to the Transmission of Greek & Latin Literature. 2nd ed. L. D. Reynolds & N. G. Wilson. (Illus.). 266p. 1974. pap. text ed. 11.50x (ISBN 0-19-814372-9). Oxford U Pr.

Scribner Anthology for Young People. Ed. by Anne Diven. LC 76-48217. 192p. (gr. 2 up). 1976. reinforced bdg. 8.95 (ISBN 0-684-14757-2, ScribT). Scribner.

Scrimshaw: A Traditional Folk Art, a Contemporary Craft. Leslie Linsley. (Illus.). 1979. pap. 6.95 (ISBN 0-8015-6609-6, Hawthorn). Dutton.

Scrimshaw at Mystic Seaport. Edouard A. Stackpole. 1958. 5.95 (ISBN 0-8286-0048-1). De Graff.

Script Continuity & the Production Secretary. Avril J. Rowlands. (Media Manuals Ser.). Date not set. pap. 6.95 o.p. (ISBN 0-8038-6737-9). Hastings.

Scripta Numaria Romana. R. A. Carson & C. M. Kraay. 1979. 60.00 (ISBN 0-686-63876-X, Pub. by Spink & Son England). S J Durst.

Scripted Drama. A. England. 260p. Date not set. price not set (ISBN 0-521-23235-X). Cambridge U Pr.

Scripting for Video & Audiovisual Media. Dwight Swain. 1981. 22.95 (ISBN 0-240-51075-5). Focal Pr.

Scripts for the Pageant. James Merrill. LC 79-55588. 1980. 12.95 (ISBN 0-689-11053-7); pap. 8.95 (ISBN 0-689-11065-0). Atheneum.

Scripts of Ancient Northwest Semitic Seals. Larry G. Herr. LC 78-18933. (Harvard Semitic Museum. Harvard Semitic Monographs: No. 18). (Illus.). 1978. 9.00 (ISBN 0-89130-237-9, 040018). Scholars Pr Ca.

Scripts People Live. Claude M. Steiner. 1974. 8.95 (ISBN 0-394-49267-6, GP7480). Grove.

Scriptural Light on Speaking in Tongues. Wesley Bouterse. 1980. pap. 0.85 (ISBN 0-86544-010-7). Salvation Army.

Scriptural Refutation of the Pope's Primacy. Apostolos Makrakis. Tr. by Denver Cummings from Hellenic. 171p. (Orig.). 1952. pap. 2.00x (ISBN 0-938366-40-8). Orthodox Chr.

Scriptural Rosary. Christianica Center. LC 64-66463. (Illus.). 1961. 4.50 (ISBN 0-911346-01-5). Christianica.

Scripture of Golden Eternity. new ed. Jack Kerouac. 45p. 1970. pap. 4.00 (ISBN 0-87091-049-3). Corinth Bks.

Scripture of the Lotus Blossom of the Fine Dharma. Tr. by Leon Hurvitz from Chin & Sanskrit. LC 75-45381. 1976. 20.00x (ISBN 0-231-03789-9); pap. 10.00x (ISBN 0-231-03920-4). Columbia U Pr.

Scripture, Tradition, Interpretation. Ward Gasque & William Lasor. 12.95 o.p. (ISBN 0-8028-3507-4). Eerdmans.

Scripture Twisting: Twenty Ways the Cults Misread the Bible. James W. Sire. LC 80-19309. 216p. (Orig.). 1980. pap. 4.95 (ISBN 0-87784-611-1). Inter-Varsity.

Scripture Unbroken. Lester Kuyper. 1978. pap. 6.95 o.p. (ISBN 0-8028-1734-3). Eerdmans.

Scripture Word Search. Wenonah S. Deffner. (Quiz & Puzzle Bks.). 1980. pap. 2.45 (ISBN 0-8010-2897-3). Baker Bk.

Scriptures of the World; a Compilation of 1,603 Languages in Which at Least One Book of the Bible Has Been Published. 6th ed. Ed. by American Bible Society. (Illus.). 1976. pap. 2.00 o.p. (ISBN 0-686-16537-3, 17602). United Bible.

Scriptures of the World; a Compilation of 1,659 Languages in Which at Least One Book of the Bible Has Been Published. 7th ed. Ed. by Elizabeth J. Eisenhart. (Illus.). 1978. pap. 2.00 o.p. (ISBN 0-686-24936-4). United Bible.

Scrooge. Elaine Donaldson. LC 71-127561. (Illus.). (gr. 3-10). 1970. pap. 1.95 o.s.i. (ISBN 0-87695-118-3). Aurora Pubs.

Scroogie. Tug McGraw & Mike Witte. (Orig.). 1976. pap. 0.95 o.p. (ISBN 0-451-06961-7, Q6961, Sig). NAL.

Scrub Dog of Alaska. Walt Morey. (gr. 4 up). 1971. PLB 8.95 (ISBN 0-525-38908-3). Dutton.

Scrub Fire. Ann De Roo. LC 80-12267. 120p. (gr. 4-7). 1980. 7.95 (ISBN 0-689-30775-6). Atheneum.

Scruffy. Jack Stonely. 1981. Repr. pap. 1.95 (ISBN 0-671-41304-X). Archway.

Scruples. Judith Krantz. 1979. pap. 3.50 (ISBN 0-446-96743-2). Warner Bks.

Scryptics. Shirl Solomon. (Orig.). 1977. pap. 1.75 o.p. (ISBN 0-451-07555-2, E7555, Sig). NAL.

SCSS: A User's Guide to the SCSS Conversational System. Nie et al. (Illus.). 592p. 1980. text ed. 22.95 (ISBN 0-07-046538-X, C); pap. text ed. 14.95 (ISBN 0-07-046533-9). McGraw.

Scuba Diver's Guide to Underwater Ventures. Judy G. May. LC 73-9949. (Illus.). 192p. 1973. pap. 3.95 o.p. (ISBN 0-8117-2017-9). Stackpole.

Scuba Handbook for Humans. 2nd ed. Scott Ascher & William Shadburne. LC 75-3832. (Illus.). 1977. pap. text ed. 6.95 (ISBN 0-8403-1126-5). Kendall-Hunt.

Scuba Safe & Simple. J. Reseck, Jr. 1975. 8.95 o.p. (ISBN 0-13-796714-4); pap. 4.95 (ISBN 0-13-796680-6). P-H.

Scuffy the Tugboat. Gertrude Crampton. (Illus.). 24p. (ps-2). 1973. 1.95 (ISBN 0-307-10490-7, Golden Pr); PLB 7.62 (ISBN 0-307-60490-X); 4.57 (ISBN 0-307-60633-3, Golden Pr). Western Pub.

Scuffy the Tugboat. Tibor Gergely. (Illus.). (ps-1). 1972. PLB 5.38 (ISBN 0-307-68928-X, Golden Pr). Western Pub.

Sculpting with Cement: Direct Modeling in a Permanent Medium. Lynn Olson. (Illus.). 106p. (Orig.). (gr. 11-12). 1981. pap. price not set (ISBN 0-9605678-0-1). Steelstone.

Sculptor Giovanni Bologna. James Holderbaum. LC 76-23626. (Outstanding Dissertations in the Fine Arts Ser.). 1978. lib. bdg. 56.00x (ISBN 0-8240-2696-9). Garland Pub.

Sculptor Jules Dalou: Studies in His Style & Imagery. John M. Hunisak. LC 76-23629. (Outstanding Dissertations in the Fine Arts - 19th Century). (Illus.). 1977. Repr. of 1976 ed. lib. bdg. 60.00 (ISBN 0-8240-2699-3). Garland Pub.

Sculpture. Boy Scouts Of America. LC 19-600. (Illus.). 24p. (gr. 6-12). 1969. pap. 0.70x (ISBN 0-8395-3322-5, 3322). BSA.

Sculpture & Drawing of Charles Umlauf. Gibson A. Danes. (Illus.). 128p. Date not set. 25.00 (ISBN 0-292-77561-X). U of Tex Pr.

Sculpture & Enlivened Space: Aesthetics & History. F. David Martin. LC 79-4006. 344p. Date not set. 23.50x (ISBN 0-8131-1386-5). U Pr of Ky. Postponed.

Sculpture in Paper. rev. ed. Ralph Fabri. (Illus.). 1976. pap. 6.95 o.p. (ISBN 0-8230-4699-0). Watson-Guptill.

Sculpture in Stone: The Greek, Roman & Etruscan Collections of the Museum of Fine Arts Boston. Mary B. Comstock & Cornelius C. Vermeule. LC 76-40711. (Illus.). 1978. 35.00 (ISBN 0-87846-103-5, Pub. by Mus Fine Arts Boston); pap. 15.00 (ISBN 0-686-68049-9). C E Tuttle.

Sculpture Index: Sculpture of Europe & the Contemporary Middle East, Vol. 1. Jane Clapp. LC 79-9538. 1970. 35.00 o.p. (ISBN 0-8108-0249-X). Scarecrow.

Sculpture Index: Sculpture of the Americas, the Orient, Africa, the Pacific Area & the Classical World, Vol. 2. Jane Clapp. LC 79-9538. 1970. 45.00 (ISBN 0-8108-0311-9). Scarecrow.

Sculpture of a City: Philadelphia's Treasures in Bronze & Stone. Fairmount Park Art Association. LC 74-79214. (Illus.). 1974. 25.00 o.s.i. (ISBN 0-8027-0459-X). Walker & Co.

Sculpture of Gaston Lachaise. Kramer et al. LC 67-17017. (Illus., Orig.). 1967. 15.00x (ISBN 0-87130-016-8); pap. 9.00x (ISBN 0-87130-017-6). Eakins.

Sculpture of Isidore Konti, 1862-1939. LC 74-33142. (Illus.). 128p. 1974. pap. 8.00 (ISBN 0-89062-016-4, Pub. by Hudson River Mus). Pub Ctr Cult Res.

Sculpture of Jose De Creeft. Jules Campos. LC 72-16688. (Illus.). 238p. 1972. lib. bdg. 45.00 (ISBN 0-306-70562-1); lib. bdg. 30.00 (ISBN 0-306-70294-0). Da Capo.

Sculpture of Life. Ernest Borek. LC 73-6831. (Illus.). 192p. 1973. 17.50x (ISBN 0-231-03425-3); pap. 4.00x (ISBN 0-231-08334-3). Columbia U Pr.

Sculpture of Vincenzo Danti. David Summers. LC 77-94718. (Outstanding Dissertations in the Fine Arts Ser.). (Illus.). 641p. 1980. lib. bdg. 60.50 (ISBN 0-8240-3252-7). Garland Pub.

Sculpture: Principles & Practice. Louis Slobodkin. (Illus.). 256p. 1973. pap. 6.00 (ISBN 0-486-22960-2). Dover.

Sculpture: Tools, Materials, & Techniques. Wilbert Verhelst. (Illus.). 304p. 1973. ref. ed. 20.95 (ISBN 0-13-796615-6). P-H.

Sculptures from the David Daniels Collection. The Minneapolis Institute of Arts. (Illus.). 1979. 15.00. Minneapolis Inst Arts.

Scuttle, the Stowaway Mouse. Jean C. Soule & Nancy J. Soule. LC 68-21083. (Illus.). (gr. k-3). 1969. 5.95 o.s.i. (ISBN 0-8193-0253-8, Four Winds); PLB 5.41 o.s.i. (ISBN 0-8193-0254-6). Schol Bk Serv.

Scuttle Watch. Marion C. Ryder. LC 79-91988. (Illus.). 286p. (gr. 4-12). 1979. pap. 4.95 (ISBN 0-88492-034-8). W S Sullwold.

Scythe Book: Mowing Hay, Cutting Weeds, & Harvesting Small Grains with Hand Tools. David Tresemer. LC 80-70277. (Illus.). 112p. (Orig.). 1981. pap. 5.95 (ISBN 0-938670-00-X). By Hand & Foot.

Scythians & Greeks. Ellis H. Minns. LC 65-15248. (Illus.). 1913. 50.00x (ISBN 0-8196-0277-9). Biblo.

Se Encontraron Con Jesus. Marilyn Kunz & Catherine Schell. Tr. by Jose R. Velez from Eng. LC 76-1299. (Encuentros Biblicos). 55p. (Orig., Span.). 1976. pap. 1.25 (ISBN 0-89922-065-7). Edit Caribe.

Se Eu Posso, Tu Podes. Tr. by Joyce Landorf. (Portuguese Bks.). 1979. 1.30 (ISBN 0-8297-0769-7). Life Pubs Intl.

Se Habla Espanol. John A. Crow. 1979. text ed. 16.95 scp (ISBN 0-06-041434-0, HarpC); scp tapes 229.00 (ISBN 0-06-047489-0); inst. manual free (ISBN 0-06-361450-2); scp student wkbk. 7.50 (ISBN 0-06-041435-9). Har-Row.

Sea. Leonard Engel. LC 61-15324. (Life Nature Library). (Illus.). (gr. 5 up). 1969. 8.97 o.p. (ISBN 0-8094-0613-6, Pub. by Time-Life). Silver.

Sea. Leonard Engel. (Young Readers Library). (Illus.). 1977. lib. bdg. 7.95 (ISBN 0-686-51094-1). Silver.

Sea. Robert C. Miller. (Illus.). 1966. 20.00 o.p. (ISBN 0-394-44400-0). Random.

Sea: A Select Bibliography on the Legal, Political, Economic & Technological Aspects, 1978-1979. 46p. 1980. pap. 5.00 (ISBN 0-686-68970-4, UN80/16, UN). Unipub.

Sea Against Hunger. new, rev. ed. C. P. Idyll. LC 77-2655. (Apollo Eds.). (Illus.). 1978. pap. 6.95 o.s.i. (ISBN 0-8152-0422-1, A-422, TYC-T). T Y Crowell.

Sea Anchor. E. A. Whitehead. (Orig.). 1975. pap. 4.95 (ISBN 0-571-10640-4, Pub. by Faber & Faber). Merrimack Bk Serv.

Sea & Cedar: How the Northwest Coast Indians Lived. Lois McConkey. (Illus.). 1973. paper-Over-boards 6.95 (ISBN 0-88894-158-7, Pub. by Douglas & McIntyre). Madrona Pubs.

Sea Angling for Beginners. Alan Young. (Angler's Library). 1978. 4.50 o.p. (ISBN 0-257-65229-9, 8003, Dist. by Arco). Barrie & Jenkins.

Sea Angling: Modern Methods, Baits & Tackle. Alan Young. (Angler's Library). 1978. 4.50 o.p. (ISBN 0-257-65228-0, 8004, Dist. by Arco). Barrie & Jenkins.

Sea Around Us. Rachel L. Carson. 1954. pap. 2.25 (ISBN 0-451-61873-4, ME1873, Ment). NAL.

Sea Battles: A Reference Guide. Michael Sanderson. LC 74-21917. (Illus.). 216p. 1975. 14.95x (ISBN 0-8195-4080-3, Pub. by Wesleyan U Pr). Columbia U Pr.

Sea Battles in Miniature. Paul Hague. 160p. 1980. 29.95 o.p. (ISBN 0-85059-414-6). Aztex.

Sea Canoeing. 2nd ed. Derek Hutchinson. (Illus.). 204p. 1980. 24.00 (ISBN 0-7136-2005-6). Transatlantic.

Sea Change. Dorothy Pitkin. (gr. 7-11). 1964. PLB 5.69 o.p. (ISBN 0-394-91592-5). Pantheon.

Sea-Change: An Anthology of Short Stories. Ralph E. West. 228p. (Orig.). (gr. 11-12). 1980. pap. text ed. 4.50x (ISBN 0-88334-126-3). Ind Sch Pr.

Sea Disasters. Walter Brown & Norman Anderson. LC 80-27156. (Illus.). 112p. (gr. 4-7). 1981. PLB 7.95 (ISBN 0-201-09154-2, 9154, A-W Childrens). A-W.

Sea Disasters & Inland Catastrophes. Edward R. Snow. LC 80-23876. (Illus.). 288p. 1980. 9.95 (ISBN 0-396-07908-3). Dodd.

Sea Dogs. Neville Williams. LC 75-10503. (Illus.). 280p. 1975. 15.00 o.s.i. (ISBN 0-02-629120-7). Macmillan.

Sea Exploring Manual. Boy Scouts Of America. LC 66-19112. 456p. (gr. 6-12). 1966. flexible bdg. 5.95x (ISBN 0-8395-3229-6, 3229). BSA.

Sea Fever. K. M. Peyton. 1980. pap. 1.50 (ISBN 0-448-17129-5, Tempo). G&D.

Sea Fever. Anthony Trew. 229p. 1981. 10.95 (ISBN 0-312-70813-0). St Martin.

Sea Fiction Guide. Myron J. Smith, Jr. & Robert C. Weller. LC 76-7590. 1976. 12.00 (ISBN 0-8108-0929-X). Scarecrow.

Sea File. Jack D. Scott. 288p. 1981. 10.95 (ISBN 0-07-056110-9, GB). McGraw.

Sea Fishing. Harvey Torbett. 10.00x (ISBN 0-392-06546-0, SpS). Soccer.

Sea Frog, City Frog. Dorothy O. Van Woerkom. (Illus.). 48p. (gr. 1-4). 1975. 7.95 (ISBN 0-02-791300-7, 79130). Macmillan.

Sea-Green Horse: A Collection of Short Stories. Ed. by Barbara Howes & Gregory J. Smith. LC 73-89589. (gr. 7-12). 1970. 5.95g o.s.i. (ISBN 0-02-744610-7). Macmillan.

Sea Gypsy. Fern Michaels. 192p. (Orig.). 1980. pap. 1.50 (ISBN 0-671-57015-3). S&S.

Sea Has Wings. Franklin Russell. 1973. 10.00 (ISBN 0-87690-097-X). Dutton.

Sea Horses in Your Home. 1969. pap. 2.00 (ISBN 0-87666-114-2, M537). TFH Pubns.

Sea Hunters: Indians of the Northwestern Coast. Sonia Bleeker. (Illus.). (gr. 3-6). 1951. PLB 6.67 (ISBN 0-688-31451-1). Morrow.

Sea: Ideas & Observations on Progress in the Study of the Seas, Vol. 5, Marine Chemistry. Ed. by Edward D. Goldberg. LC 62-18366. 896p. 1974. 65.00 (ISBN 0-471-31090-5, Pub. by Wiley-Interscience). Wiley.

Sea; Ideas & Observations on Progress in the Study on the Seas, Vol. 6: Marine Modeling. Ed. by Edward D. Goldberg et al. LC 62-18366. 992p. 1977. 69.95 (ISBN 0-471-31091-3, Pub. by Wiley-Interscience). Wiley.

Sea Islands of the South. Bill Gleasner & Diana Gleasner. LC 79-24730. (Illus.). 176p. 1980. lib. bdg. 12.25 o.p. (ISBN 0-914788-21-3). East Woods.

Sea Kayaking: A Manual for Long-Distance Touring. John Dowd. (Illus.). 300p. 1981. 10.00 (ISBN 0-295-95807-3). U of Wash Pr.

Sea King's Daughter. Barbara Michaels. LC 75-28200. 1975. 7.95 (ISBN 0-396-07208-9). Dodd.

Sea Language Comes Ashore. Joanna C. Colcord. LC 45-966. 1945. pap. 5.00 (ISBN 0-87033-095-0). Cornell Maritime.

Sea-Level Changes: North-West England During the Flandrian Stage. M. J. Tooley. (Research Studies in Geography Ser.). (Illus.). 1979. 39.50x (ISBN 0-19-823228-4). Oxford U Pr.

Sea Lightning. Linda Harrel. (Harlequin Romances Ser.). (Orig.). 1980. pap. text ed. 1.25 o.p. (ISBN 0-373-02337-5, Pub. by Harlequin). PB.

Sea Magic & Other Stories of Enchantment. Rosemary Harris. 192p. (gr. 7 up). 1974. 8.95 (ISBN 0-02-742650-5). Macmillan.

Sea Mammals & Reptiles of the Pacific Coast. Vinson Brown. (Illus.). 1976. 10.95 o.s.i. (ISBN 0-02-517310-3). Macmillan.

Sea-Mans Practice. Richard Norwood. LC 74-28877. (English Experience Ser.: No. 755). 1975. Repr. of 1637 ed. 13.00 (ISBN 90-221-0755-8). Walter J Johnson.

Sea Mice. Ruth Tomalin. (Illus.). 1962. 6.95 (ISBN 0-571-05213-4, Pub. by Faber & Faber). Merrimack Bk Serv.

Sea Microbes. John M. Sieburth. (Illus.). 1979. text ed. 59.95x (ISBN 0-19-502419-2). Oxford U Pr.

Sea Monsters of Long Ago. Millicent E. Selsam. LC 78-5385. (Illus.). 32p. (gr. k-3). 1978. 6.95 (ISBN 0-590-07567-5, Four Winds). Schol Bk Serv.

Sea Monsters of Long Ago. Millicent E. Selsam. (gr. k-3). 1977. pap. 1.95 (ISBN 0-590-10419-5, Schol Pap). Schol Bk Serv.

Sea of Cortez: A Leisurely Journal of Travel & Research. John Steinbeck & Edward F. Ricketts. (Illus.). 640p. Repr. of 1941 ed. 22.50 o.s.i. (ISBN 0-911858-08-3). Appel.

Sea of Process. Alexander Steinmetz. 1975. 5.00 o.p. (ISBN 0-87482-043-X). Wake-Brook.

Sea of Sadness. Alma Guadalupe. 64p. 1981. 5.95 (ISBN 0-89962-041-8). Todd & Honeywell.

Sea of the Bear. M. A. Ransom & Eloise K. Engle. LC 79-6122. (Navies & Men Ser.). (Illus.). 1980. Repr. of 1964 ed. lib. bdg. 19.00x (ISBN 0-405-13076-7). Arno.

Sea on Fire. Rory Brennan. (Orig.). 1980. pap. text ed. 8.00x (ISBN 0-85105-308-4, Dolmen Pr). Humanities.

Sea Power & Influence: Iold Issues & New Challenges. Ed. by Jonathan Alford. LC 80-67840. (Adelphi Library: Vol. 2). 224p. 1981. text ed. 31.50 (ISBN 0-916672-72-7). Allanheld.

Sea Power & the Law of the Sea. Mark W. Janis. LC 76-11973. (Lexington Books Studies of Marine Affairs). (Illus.). 1976. 15.95 (ISBN 0-669-00717-X). Lexington Bks.

Sea Power in the 1970's. Ed. by George Quester. LC 73-88666. 1975. 15.00 (ISBN 0-8046-7088-9). Kennikat.

Sea Power of the State. S. G. Gorshkov. (Illus.). 1979. text ed. 39.00 (ISBN 0-685-93645-7). Pergamon.

Sea Power of the State. Sergei Gorshkov. Tr. by Alan Crozey from Rus. LC 77-88875. 1979. 18.95 o.s.i. (ISBN 0-87021-961-8). Naval Inst Pr.

Sea Run. Mary L. Shields. LC 80-52406. 352p. 1981. 11.95 (ISBN 0-87223-665-X). Seaview Bks.

Sea Shells of Sri Lanka: Including Forms Scattered Throughout the Indian & Pacific Oceans. Parakrama Kirtisinghe. LC 77-72607. (Illus.). 1978. 12.50 (ISBN 0-8048-1189-X). C E Tuttle.

Sea, Ships, & Sailors. Ed. by William Cole. (Illus.). 1967. 4.95 o.p. (ISBN 0-670-62642-2). Viking Pr.

Sea-Slug Gastropods. Wesley M. Farmer. (Illus.). 177p. (Orig.). 1980. pap. 10.00 (ISBN 0-937772-00-3). Farmer Ent.

Sea Star. Robert M. McClung. LC 75-2247. (Illus.). 48p. (gr. k-3). 1975. PLB 6.96 (ISBN 0-688-32034-1). Morrow.

Sea Stars & Their Kin. Herbert S. Zim & Lucretia Krantz. LC 75-17633. (Illus.). 64p. (gr. 3-7). 1976. PLB 6.96 (ISBN 0-688-32053-8) (ISBN 0-688-22053-3). Morrow.

Sea Survival. Dougal Robertson. 9.95 (ISBN 0-236-31089-5, Pub. by Paul Elek). Merrimack Bk Serv.

Sea Traders. Maitland Edey. LC 73-92665. (Emergence of Man Ser.). (gr. 6 up). 1974. PLB 9.63 o.p. (ISBN 0-8094-1317-5, Pub. by Time-Life). Silver.

Sea Traders. Maitland A. Edey. (Emergence of Man Ser.). (Illus.). 1974. 9.95 (ISBN 0-8094-1316-7); lib. bdg. avail. (ISBN 0-685-48125-5). Time-Life.

Sea Treasure. Elisabeth Barr. LC 80-82847. 208p. (Orig.). 1981. pap. 1.95 (ISBN 0-87216-780-1). Playboy Pbks.

Sea Trial. Frank De Felitta. 288p. 1980. pap. 4.95 (ISBN 0-380-76042-8, 76042). Avon.

Sea Turtles. Francine Jacobs. LC 74-187717. (Illus.). 64p. (gr. 3-7). 1972. PLB 6.00 o.p. (ISBN 0-688-31937-8). Morrow.

Sea Vegetable Gelatin Cookbook. Judith Cooper Madlener. (Illus., Orig.). 1981. pap. 7.95 (ISBN 0-912800-76-3). Woodbridge Pr.

Sea View Hotel. James Stevenson. LC 78-2749. (Illus.). (gr. k-3). 1978. 7.95 (ISBN 0-688-80168-4); PLB 7.63 (ISBN 0-688-84168-6). Greenwillow.

Sea: Vol. 1 Physical Oceanography. 2nd ed. M. N. Hill. 880p. 1981. Repr. of 1962 ed. lib. bdg. write for info. (ISBN 0-89874-097-5). Krieger. Postponed.

Sea: Vol. 2, Composition of Sea Water. Ed. by M. N. Hill. 570p. 1981. Repr. of 1963 ed. lib. bdg. write for info. (ISBN 0-89874-098-3). Krieger. Postponed.

Sea: Vol. 3 the Earth Beneath the Sea; History. Ed. by M. N. Hill. LC 80-248. 980p. 1981. Repr. of 1963 ed. lib. bdg. write for info. (ISBN 0-89874-099-1). Krieger.

Sea Warfare, 1939-1945. John Creswell. (Illus.). 1967. 20.00x (ISBN 0-520-00277-6). U of Cal Pr.

Sea Watch. Beverly Keller. LC 80-70000. 128p. (gr. 3-7). 1981. 7.95 (ISBN 0-590-07703-1, Four Winds). Schol Bk Serv.

Sea Wolf. Jack London. 351p. Repr. of 1904 ed. lib. bdg. 14.30x (ISBN 0-89190-657-6). Am Repr-Rivercity Pr.

Sea Wolves. Wolfgang Frank. 224p. 1981. pap. 2.50 (ISBN 0-345-29504-8). Ballantine.

Seacoast Life: An Ecological Guide. Judith Spitsbergen. LC 80-15282. (Illus.). 1980. 5.95 (ISBN 0-917134-03-6). NC Natl Hist.

Seacook. R. T. Heppel. 1979. 12.95x (ISBN 0-8464-0066-9). Beekman Pubs.

Seademons. Lawrence Yep. LC 77-3809. 1977. 8.95 o.p. (ISBN 0-06-014771-7, HarpT). Har-Row.

Seadon Fortune. Leonard St. Clair. 1979. pap. 2.25 o.p. (ISBN 0-425-03865-3). Berkley Pub.

Seafarer & Community. Ed. by Peter H. Fricke. 164p. 1973. bds. 17.50x (ISBN 0-87471-197-5). Rowman.

Seafaring in Colonial Massachusetts. Ed. by Philip Chadwich & Foster Smith. LC 80-51256. (Illus.). xvii, 240p. 1981. 25.00x (ISBN 0-8139-0897-3, Colonial Soc MA). U Pr of Va.

Seafishing Yarns. Zane Grey. 276p. Repr. lib. bdg. 12.15x (ISBN 0-89190-766-1). Am Repr-Rivercity Pr.

Seafood Cook Book. 3rd ed. Sunset Editors. LC 80-53482. (Illus.). 128p. 1981. pap. 4.95 (ISBN 0-376-02586-7, Sunset Bks). Sunset-Lane.

Seafood Cook Book. 5th ed. Sunset Editors. LC 80-53482. (Illus.). 128p. 1981. pap. 4.95 (ISBN 0-376-02586-7, Sunset Books). Sunset-Lane.

Seafood Fishing for Amateur & Professional. R. C. O'Farrell. (Illus.). 196p. 10.00 (ISBN 0-85238-097-6, FN). Unipub.

Seagull. Yashar Kemal. 1981. 11.95 (ISBN 0-394-51856-X). Pantheon.

Seagull Wind. John W. Cobb, III. LC 80-80556. (Illus.). 64p. (Orig.). 1980. pap. 4.95x (ISBN 0-9602968-0-8). Cobb Ent.

Seal Family. Anne LaBastille. Ed. by Russell Bourne & Natalie Rifkin. LC 73-91356. (Ranger Rick's Best Friends Ser.: No. 2). (Illus.). 32p. (gr. 1-6). 1974. 2.50 o.p. (ISBN 0-912186-09-7). Natl Wildlife.

Seal Morning. Rowena Farre. (gr. 7-9). 1972. pap. 0.95 o.p. (ISBN 0-590-02215-6, Schol Pap). Schol Bk Serv.

Seal of Jai. Elisabeth B. Booz. (Illus.). (gr. 4-6). 1968. 4.50g o.s.i. (ISBN 0-02-711760-X). Macmillan.

Seal Secret. Aidan Chambers. LC 80-8456. 128p. (gr. 5 up). 1981. 8.95 (ISBN 0-06-021258-6, HarpJ); PLB 8.79g (ISBN 0-06-021259-4). Har-Row.

Seal-Singing. Rosemary Harris. (Illus.). (gr. 7 up). 1971. 8.95 o.s.i. (ISBN 0-02-742680-7). Macmillan.

Seal-Singing. Rosemary Harris. LC 75-155265. 288p. (gr. 7 up). 1974. pap. 1.25 o.s.i. (ISBN 0-02-043550-9, 04355, Collier). Macmillan.

Seal Song. Brian Davies. (Large Format Ser). (Illus.). 1979. pap. 5.95 o.p. (ISBN 0-14-004740-9). Penguin.

Sealing Mechanisms of Flexible Packings. White & Denny. 1947. 16.00. BHRA Fluid.

Seals. Robert Burton. LC 79-13701. (New Biology Ser.). (Illus.). (gr. 4 up). 1980. 7.95 (ISBN 0-07-009285-0). McGraw.

Seals. Alice Fields. (gr. 2-4). 1980. PLB 6.45 (ISBN 0-531-03242-6). Watts.

Seals, Sea Lions, & Walruses. Ellen Rabinowich. (gr. 4 up). 1980. PLB 6.90 (ISBN 0-531-04106-9). Watts.

Sealyham Terriers. Frida J. Chenuz. Ed. by W. G. Foyle. (Foyle Handbks). (Illus.). 1973. 3.95 (ISBN 0-685-55795-2). Palmetto Pub.

Seaman's Friend. Richard Dana. LC 79-4623. 1979. Repr. of 1841 ed. lib. bdg. 25.00x (ISBN 0-8201-1330-1). Schol Facsimiles.

Seaman's Guide to the Rule of the Road. LC 75-6241. (Illus.). 9.95 (ISBN 0-87021-873-5). Naval Inst Pr.

Seamanship. (Library of Boating Ser.). (Illus.). 176p. 1975. 14.95 (ISBN 0-8094-2108-9). Time-Life.

Seamanship: A Handbook for Oceanographers. Carvel H. Blair. LC 76-56349. (Illus.). 1977. 9.00x (ISBN 0-87033-228-7). Cornell Maritime.

Seamanship for New Skippers. George H. Ludins. (Illus.). 1980. pap. 5.95 (ISBN 0-916224-54-6). Banyan Bks.

Seamanship: Fundamentals for the Deck Officer. 2nd ed. S. E. Kyriss & D. O. Dodge. LC 80-81089. (Fundamentals of Naval Science: Vol. 2). 272p. 1981. text ed. 16.95 (ISBN 0-87021-613-9). Naval Inst Pr.

Seamless Web. Stanley Burnshaw. LC 71-97603. 1970. 6.50 (ISBN 0-8076-0535-2); pap. 4.95 (ISBN 0-8076-0534-4). Braziller.

Seamy Side of Government: Essays on Punishment & Coercion. H. Keith Quincy. LC 78-78400. 1979. pap. text ed. 7.50 (ISBN 0-8191-0707-7). U Pr of Amer.

Sean Mooney's Practical Guide to Running a Pub. Sean Mooney & George Green. LC 78-27436. 1979. 14.95 (ISBN 0-88229-400-8); pap. 8.95 (ISBN 0-88229-681-7). Nelson-Hall.

Sean O'Casey. Hugh Hunt. (Gillis Irish Lives Ser.). 153p. 1980. 20.00 (ISBN 0-7171-1080-X, Pub. by Gill & Macmillan Ireland); pap. 6.50 (ISBN 0-7171-1034-6). Irish Bk Ctr.

Sean O'Casey. James R. Scrimgeour. (English Authors Ser.: No. 245). 1978. 12.50 (ISBN 0-8057-6735-5). Twayne.

Sean O'Casey & His World. David Krause. LC 76-7182. (Encore Edition). (Illus.). 128p. 1976. 3.95 (ISBN 0-684-16547-3, ScribT). Scribner.

Sean O'Casey: Centenary Essays. Ed. by David Krause & Robert G. Lowery. (Irish Literary Studies 7). 257p. 1981. 24.75x (ISBN 0-389-20096-4). B&N.

Sean O'Casey: From Times Past by Brooks Atkinson. Brooks Atkinson. Ed. by Robert G. Lowery. 1980. 26.50x (ISBN 0-389-20180-4). B&N.

Sean O'Casey: Politics & Art. C. Desmond Greaves. 1980. text ed. 18.25x (ISBN 0-391-01023-9). Humanities.

Sean O'Casey: The Man & His World. rev. ed. David Krause. LC 74-11129. 416p. 1975. 8.95 o.s.i. (ISBN 0-02-566640-1, 50664). Macmillan.

Seance. Isaac B. Singer. 256p. 1981. pap. 2.75 (ISBN 0-449-24364-8, Crest). Fawcett.

Seaplanes. H. R. Palmer. LC 65-16861. 52p. 1980. 4.95 (ISBN 0-8168-5649-4). Aero.

Seaplanes. Henry R. Palmer, Jr. LC 65-16861. (Famous Aircraft Ser). (Illus.). 1965. pap. 4.95 o.p. (ISBN 0-668-01293-5). Arco.

Seaport: Architecture & Townscape of Liverpool. F. Quentin Hughes. 16.00 (ISBN 0-685-20625-4). Transatlantic.

Seaport City: New York 1775. Floyd Shumway. LC 75-3940. 1975. pap. 1.95 o.s.i. (ISBN 0-913344-20-6). Interbk Inc.

Seaport in Virginia: George Washington's Alexandria. rev. ed. Gay M. Moore. LC 73-188711. 274p. 1972. Repr. 12.95 (ISBN 0-8139-0183-9). U Pr of Va.

Seaports: Ships, Piers, & People. Paul Scotti. LC 80-21655. (Illus.). 64p. (gr. 4-6). 1980. PLB 7.29 (ISBN 0-671-34032-8). Messner.

Search-a-Picture Puzzles. Tony Tallarico. Ed. by Meg Schneider. (Puzzlebacks Ser.). 64p. (gr. 3-7). 1981. pap. 1.25 (ISBN 0-671-42656-7, Wanderer). S&S.

Search & Destroy. Robin Moore. 352p. 1980. pap. 2.50 (ISBN 0-441-75691-3). Charter Bks.

Search & Rescue: The Story of the Coast Guard Service. Nancy Martin. LC 74-81053. (David & Charles Children's Bks). (Illus.). 80p. (gr. 3-8). 1975. 5.95 (ISBN 0-7153-6501-0). David & Charles.

Search & Screening: General Principles with Historical Applications. Bernard O. Koopman. LC 79-16909. (Illus.). 400p. 1980. 50.00 (ISBN 0-08-023136-5); pap. 21.00 (ISBN 0-08-023135-7). Pergamon.

Search & Seizure Checklists. Michele G. Hermann. LC 79-9734. 1979. pap. 11.50 spiral (ISBN 0-87632-110-4). Boardman.

Search for a Judicial Philosophy: Mr. Justice Roberts & the Constitutional Revolution of 1937. Charles A. Leonard. LC 77-139358. (National University Publications). 1971. 15.00 (ISBN 0-8046-9009-X). Kennikat.

Search for a Scientific Profession: Library Science Education in the U.S. & Canada. L. Houser & Alvin M. Schrader. LC 77-17563. 1978. 10.00 (ISBN 0-8108-1062-X). Scarecrow.

Search for a Soul: Taylor Caldwell's Psychic Lives. Jess Stearn. 1978. pap. 2.25 (ISBN 0-449-23437-1, Crest). Fawcett.

Search for Acceptance: The Adolescent & Self-Esteem. Janet Kizziar & Judy Hagedorn. LC 78-11491. 1979. 13.95 (ISBN 0-88229-369-9); pap. 6.95 (ISBN 0-88229-648-5). Nelson-Hall.

Search for Accounting Principles. Reed K. Storey. LC 77-81833. 1977. Repr. of 1964 ed. text ed. 10.00 (ISBN 0-914348-20-5). Scholars Bk.

Search for Air Safety. Stephen Barlay. (Illus.). 1970. 7.95 o.p. (ISBN 0-688-02441-6). Morrow.

Search for Alexander: An Exhibition. Ed. by Nicholas M. Yalouris & Katerina Rhomiopoulou. 1980. 22.50 (ISBN 0-8212-1108-0, 779105); pap. 12.95 (ISBN 0-8212-1117-X, 779113). NYGS.

Search for an Eternal Norm: As Represented by Three Classics. Louis J. Halle. LC 80-5793. 220p. 1981. lib. bdg. 18.75 (ISBN 0-8191-1444-8); pap. text ed. 9.75 (ISBN 0-8191-1445-6). U Pr of Amer.

Search for Anna Fisher. Florence Fisher. 224p. 1981. pap. 2.50 (ISBN 0-449-23473-8, Crest). Fawcett.

Search for Authenticity in Modern Japanese Literature. H. Yamanouchi. LC 77-84815. 1978. 29.95 (ISBN 0-521-21856-X). Cambridge U Pr.

Search for Authenticity in Modern Japanese Literature. H. Yamanouchi. LC 77-84815. 214p. 1980. pap. 10.95 (ISBN 0-521-29974-8). Cambridge U Pr.

Search for Black Identity. Robert V. Behr. (gr. 10-12). 1970. pap. text ed. 3.50x o.p. (ISBN 0-88334-023-2); tchrs' manual avail. o.p. (ISBN 0-685-39241-4). Ind Sch Pr.

Search for Bridey Murphy. rev. ed. Morey Bernstein. LC 65-17244. 1965. 7.95 o.p. (ISBN 0-385-06621-X). Doubleday.

Search for Criminal Man. Ysabel Rennie. LC 77-3109. (Dangerous Offenders Project Ser.). 1978. 21.95 (ISBN 0-669-01480-X). Lexington Bks.

Search for Delicious. Natalie Babbitt. (gr. 3-7). 1974. pap. 1.50 o.s.i. (ISBN 0-380-01541-2, 42085, Camelot). Avon.

Search for Enchantment. Shirley F. Sanders. (YA) 1978. 5.95 (ISBN 0-685-86142-2, Avalon). Bouregy.

Search for Environmental Ethics: An Initial Bibliography. Compiled By Mary Anglemyer et al. LC 80-15026. 119p. (Orig.). 1980. text ed. 8.95x (ISBN 0-87474-212-9). Smithsonian.

Search for Extraterrestrial Intelligence. National Aeronautics & Space Administration. (Illus.). 190p. 1980. pap. 3.00 (ISBN 0-486-23890-3). Dover.

Search for God. rev. ed. Marchette Chute. 1949. 10.00 o.p. (ISBN 0-525-19842-3). Dutton.

Search for Goodbye-to-Rains. Paul McHugh. LC 79-28565. 192p. 1980. pap. 7.50 (ISBN 0-933280-07-6). Island CA.

Search for Gravity Waves. P. C. Davies. (Illus.). 160p. 1980. 13.95 (ISBN 0-521-23197-3). Cambridge U Pr.

Search for Happiness, Futility or Fulfillment. Batsell Barrett Baxter & Dan Harless. (Direction Bks). 1977. pap. 1.95 o.p. (ISBN 0-8010-0707-0). Baker Bk.

Search for Home. Sashthi Brata. 152p. 1975. pap. 2.50 (ISBN 0-88253-771-7). Ind-US Inc.

Search for Identity. Ed. by Arnold T. Olson. LC 80-66030. 160p. 1980. 8.95 (ISBN 0-911802-46-0). Free Church Pubns.

Search for Inner Peace. Habel Verghese. pap. 1.95 (ISBN 0-89728-055-5, 665278). Omega Pubns OR.

Search for JFK. Clay Blair, Jr. 1977. pap. 2.25 o.p. (ISBN 0-425-03354-6, Medallion). Berkley Pub.

Search for JFK. Clay Blair, Jr. & Joan Blair. LC 76-8257. (Illus.). (YA) 1976. 12.95 o.p. (ISBN 0-399-11418-1). Berkley Pub.

Search for Justice: Neighborhood Courts in Allende's Chile. Jack Spence. 1979. lib. bdg. 22.50x (ISBN 0-89158-279-7). Westview.

Search for King Arthur. Christopher Hibbert & Charles Thomas. LC 77-91594. (Horizon Caravel Bks). (Illus.). 153p. (gr. 6 up). 1969. 9.95 (ISBN 0-06-022313-8, Dist. by Har-Row); PLB 12.89 (ISBN 0-06-022314-6, Dist. by Har-Row). Am Heritage.

Search for Life Beyond Earth. Dinah Moche. (Impact Bks.). (Illus.). (gr. 7 up). 1978. lib. bdg. 6.90 (ISBN 0-531-02204-8). Watts.

Search for Life in the Universe. D. Goldsmith & T. Owen. 1980. pap. 12.95 (ISBN 0-8053-3325-8). A-W.

Search for Lost America: The Mysteries of the Stone Ruins. Salvatore M. Trento. LC 77-91180. 1978. 10.95 (ISBN 0-8092-7852-9). Contemp Bks.

Search for Love & Achievement: Marriage & the Family in a Changing World. 2nd ed. David S. Shapiro & Elaine S. Shapiro. 1980. pap. text ed. 10.95x (ISBN 0-917974-48-4). Waveland Pr.

Search for Meaning in Love, Sex, & Marriage. rev. ed. Hugo Hurst. LC 75-9961. 232p. (gr. 11-12). 1975. pap. text ed. 4.60x (ISBN 0-88489-063-5); tchr's ed. 2.60x (ISBN 0-88489-119-4). St. Marys.

Search for National Integration in Africa. David R. Smock & Kwamina Bentsi-Enchill. LC 74-33090. 1976. 19.95 (ISBN 0-02-929560-2). Free Pr.

Search for New Arts. Charles Biederman. LC 79-90835. 1979. 20.00 (ISBN 0-935476-01-6); pap. 15.00 (ISBN 0-686-64371-2). Art History.

Search for Order in the Physical Universe. Clifford Swartz & Theodore Goldfarb. LC 73-19743. (Illus.). 1974. text ed. 22.95x (ISBN 0-7167-0345-9). W H Freeman.

Search for Organic Reaction Pathways. Peter Sykes. LC 72-4192. 247p. 1972. 13.95 (ISBN 0-470-84130-3). Halsted Pr.

Search for Peace & Justice: Reflections of Michael Scott. A. Paul Hare & Herbert H. Blumberg. (Illus.). 255p. 1980. 19.50x. Rowman.

Search for Personal Freedom, Vol. 1. 6th ed. Neal M. Cross et al. 500p. 1981. pap. write for info. (ISBN 0-697-03121-7). Vol. 2 (ISBN 0-697-03122-5). Wm C Brown.

Search for Power: The Weaker Sex in Seventeenth Century New England. Lyle Koehler. LC 80-16666. 570p. 1980. 25.00 (ISBN 0-252-00808-1). U of Ill Pr.

Search for Self: An Introduction to Personal Social Adjustment. Joseph Simons. 1980. pap. text ed. 12.95 (ISBN 0-669-02570-4); inst. manual cancelled (ISBN 0-669-02571-2). Heath.

Search for Sex. (Illus.). pap. 5.00 (ISBN 0-910550-79-4). Centurion Pr.

Search for Significance. Donald Lombardi. LC 75-17676. (Illus.). 144p. 1975. 10.95 (ISBN 0-88229-109-2). Nelson-Hall.

Search for Structure: Selected Essays in Science, Art & History. Cyril S. Smith. (Illus.). 480p. 1981. 30.00 (ISBN 0-262-19191-1). MIT Pr.

Search for the Cause of Multiple Sclerosis & Other Chronic Diseases of the Central Nervous System. Ed. by A. Boese. (Illus.). 516p. (Orig.). pap. text ed. 55.00 (ISBN 3-527-25875-2). Verlag Chemie.

Search for the Maya. Victor W. Von Hagen. 1978. pap. 8.50 (ISBN 0-86033-064-8). Gordon-Cremonesi.

Search for the Northwest Passage. George M. Thomson. LC 75-15814. (Illus.). 288p. 1975. 12.95 o.s.i. (ISBN 0-02-617750-1, 61775). Macmillan.

Search for the Past: An Introduction to Paleontology. 2nd ed. James R. Beerbower. LC 68-18060. (Illus.). 1968. ref. ed. 22.95 (ISBN 0-13-797316-0). P-H.

Search for the Peking Man. Christopher G. Janus & William Brashler. (Illus.). 208p. 1975. 11.95 o.s.i. (ISBN 0-02-558990-3). Macmillan.

Search for the Perfect Swing. Alastair Cochran & John Stobbs. LC 68-9441. (Illus.). 1968. 19.95 o.s.i. (ISBN 0-397-00552-0). Lippincott.

Search for the Real Self: Humanistic Psychology & Literature. Jack Heitner. LC 78-62174. 1978. pap. text ed. 8.75 (ISBN 0-8191-0474-4). U Pr of Amer.

Search for the Soul. Milbourne Christopher. LC 78-3298. 1979. 10.95 (ISBN 0-690-01760-X, TYC-T). T Y Crowell.

Search for the Twelve Apostles. William McBirnie. 1973. pap. 1.25 o.s.i. (ISBN 0-515-02902-5). Jove Pubns.

Search for Truth. Natasha Rawson. 100p. 1981. write for info. (Pub. by the Linolean Press). Larksdale.

Search for Two Bad Mice. Eleanor Clymer. LC 80-12789. (Illus.). 80p. (gr. 2-5). 1980. 7.95 (ISBN 0-689-30771-3). Atheneum.

Search for World Order: Studies by Students & Colleagues of Quincy Wright. Ed. by Albert Lepawsky et al. LC 75-147119. (Orig.). 1971. 38.50x (ISBN 0-89197-479-2). Irvington.

Search in Secret Egypt. Paul Brunton. LC 78-16641. 1980. pap. 4.50 (ISBN 0-87728-060-6). Weiser.

Search in Secret India. Paul Brunton. (Illus.). 1981. pap. 4.50 (ISBN 0-87728-061-4). Weiser.

Search in the Shadows. Paulette Warren. (Caliban Ser.). pap. 1.25 o.p. (ISBN 0-425-03113-6). Berkley Pub.

Search Is on. Earl Hubbard. 1969. pap. 2.00 o.p. (ISBN 0-89192-081-1). Interbk Inc.

Search: Journey on the Inner Path. Jean Sulzberger. LC 78-4430. 1979. 10.00 o.p. (ISBN 0-685-66357-4, HarpR); pap. 5.95 (ISBN 0-06-067765-1, RD 271, HarpR). Har-Row.

Search Manual. Archie A. Silver & Rosa A. Hagin. LC 75-43437. 112p. (Orig.). 1975. pap. text ed. 11.80 (ISBN 0-8027-9035-6). Walker Educ.

Search on Mount St. Helens. Jeffry W. Doran. Ed. by George Pica. (Illus.). 96p. (Orig.). pap. 7.95 (ISBN 0-938700-00-6). Imagesmith.

Search: The Continuing Story of the Tracker. Tom Brown, Jr. & William Owen. LC 80-20588. 1980. 10.95 (ISBN 0-13-796953-8). P-H.

Search the Scriptures. rev. ed. Ed. by Alan M. Stibbs. 7.95 (ISBN 0-87784-856-4). Inter-Varsity.

Search the Scriptures: Modern Medicine & Biblical Personages. 3rd enl. ed. Robert B. Greenblatt. LC 76-50054. 1977. 10.50 o.p. (ISBN 0-397-59060-1). Lippincott.

Search the Silence: Poems of Self-Discovery. Betsy Ryan. (Illus.). (gr. 10-12). 1975. pap. 1.25 (ISBN 0-590-09828-4, Schol Pap). Schol Bk Serv.

Search Theory & Applications. Ed. by K. Brian Haley & Lawrence D. Stone. (NATO Conference Ser. (Series II--Systems Science): Vol. 8). 260p. 1980. 35.00 (ISBN 0-306-40562-8, Plenum Pr). Plenum Pub.

Search to Find Happiness. Patsy Janousek. 1981. 5.95 (ISBN 0-8062-1613-1). Carlton.

Searchers. Alan LeMay. (Western Fiction Ser.). 1978. lib. bdg. 9.95 (ISBN 0-8398-2464-5). Gregg.

Searchers. Gustaf Stromberg. 1967. pap. 6.50 (ISBN 0-911336-16-8). Sci of Mind.

Searcher's Manual. George Lowy. 1965. 10.00 (ISBN 0-208-00789-X); pap. 6.50 (ISBN 0-686-68498-2). Shoe String.

Searches & Seizures, Arrests & Confessions. 2nd ed. William E. Ringel. LC 70-186243. 550p. 1979. 50.00 (ISBN 0-87632-079-5). Boardman.

Searching for a Better Way. Monroe E. Hawley. 1980. pap. write for info. (ISBN 0-89137-525-2). Quality Pubns.

Searching for Atlantis. Ashley Saunders. 32p. 1980. 2.95 (ISBN 0-8059-2741-7). Dorrance.

Searching for Shona. Anderson. (gr. 3-5). Date not set. pap. cancelled (ISBN 0-590-30313-9, Schol Pap). Schol Bk Serv.

Searching for Structure. rev. ed. John A. Sonquist et al. LC 73-620236. 236p. 1974. cloth 10.00 (ISBN 0-87944-110-0); pap. 6.50 (ISBN 0-87944-109-7). U of Mich Soc Res.

Searching for Truth. Mark E. Temme. 96p. 1978. 3.95 (ISBN 0-8059-2601-1). Dorrance.

Searching for Your Ancestors: The How & Why of Geneaology. 5th ed. Gilbert H. Doane & James B. Bell. 1980. 10.95 (ISBN 0-8166-0934-9). U of Minn Pr.

Searching the Prophets for Values. Balfour Brickner. 1981. 6.95 (ISBN 0-8074-0047-5). UAHC.

Searching Writing. Ken Macrorie. 352p. 1980. pap. 8.95x (ISBN 0-8104-6037-8). Hayden.

Searching Years. Lee Bryan. 1981. pap. 2.25 (ISBN 0-8439-0871-8, Leisure Bks). Nordon Pubns.

Searchlight. rev. ed. Roger E. Van Harn. 84p. 1980. pap. 1.95 (ISBN 0-933140-16-9). Bd of Pubns CRC.

Searing. John Coyne. 1981. pap. 2.75 (ISBN 0-425-04924-8). Berkley Pub.

Searoom Handbook with Radar Anti-Collision Tables. E. S. Quilter. LC 76-240. 1976. 15.00x (ISBN 0-87033-221-X). Cornell Maritime.

Seas & the Oceans in Color. C. F. Hickling & Peter Lancaster Brown. LC 73-18511. (Color Ser). (Illus.). 192p. 1974. 9.95 (ISBN 0-02-551380-X). Macmillan.

Sea's Harvest: The Story of Aquaculture. Joseph E. Brown. LC 75-9646. (Illus.). 96p. (gr. 5 up). 1975. PLB 5.95 (ISBN 0-396-07153-8). Dodd.

Seasalt & Your Life. Jacques De Langre. LC 80-84990. (Illus.). 128p. (Orig.). 1980. 8.00 (ISBN 0-916508-08-0). Happiness Pr.

Seashell Collector's Handbook & Identifier. Sonja J. Murray. LC 73-93592. (Illus.). 240p. 1975. 8.95 o.p. (ISBN 0-8069-3064-0); lib. bdg. 8.29 o.p. (ISBN 0-8069-3065-9). Sterling.

Seashells of the S. E. Coast. Julius Gordon & Townsend E. Weeks. Ed. by Margaret Campbell. (Illus.). 50p. (Orig.). 1981. pap. 4.95 (ISBN 0-88839-080-7). Hancock Hse.

Seashore. H. Angel. 1975. pap. 5.00 o.p. (ISBN 0-85242-403-5, Pub. by Fountain). Morgan.

Seashore. David Lambert. (Modern Knowledge Library). (Illus.). (gr. 5 up). 1978. 3.95 o.p. (ISBN 0-685-86307-7); PLB 5.90 s&l o.p. (ISBN 0-531-09061-2). Watts.

Seashore. Nancy Scott. LC 68-2032. (Pegasus Books: No. 3). (Illus.). 1965. 7.50x (ISBN 0-234-77837-7). Intl Pubns Serv.

Seashore Animals of the Pacific Coast. Myrtle E. Johnson & H. J. Snook. (Illus.). 12.50 (ISBN 0-8446-2336-9). Peter Smith.

Seashore Life in Color. Gwynne Vevers. (European Ecology Ser.). (Illus.). 1969. 9.95 (ISBN 0-7137-0012-2, Pub by Blandford Pr England). Sterling.

Seaside Piers. Simon Adamson. 1977. 16.95 o.p. (ISBN 0-7134-0242-3, Pub. by Batsford England). David & Charles.

Season at Brighton. Alice C. Ley. 192p. (Orig.). 1976. pap. 1.50 (ISBN 0-345-28577-8). Ballantine.

Season in Hell. Percy Knauth. LC 74-1826. 124p. 1975. 7.95 o.p. (ISBN 0-06-012421-0, HarpT). Har-Row.

Season in Hell. Arthur Rimbaud. Tr. by Louise Varese. Bd. with Drunken Boat. LC 61-14900. (Eng. & Fr.). pap. 2.95 (ISBN 0-8112-0185-6, NDP97). New Directions.

Season in Hell. Arthur Rimbaud. Tr. by Enid R. Peschel. Bd. with Illuminations. (Illus., Engl. & Fre.). 1974. pap. 4.95 (ISBN 0-19-501760-9, 403, GB). Oxford U Pr.

Season of Assasins. Geoffrey Wagner. 1980. pap. 1.75 (ISBN 0-505-51457-5). Tower Bks.

Season of Birds: A Norfolk Diary, Nineteen Eleven. James Vincent. (Illus.). 160p. 1980. 14.95 (ISBN 0-89479-068-4). A & W Pubs.

Season of Birth: Its Relation to Human Abilities. Ellsworth Huntington. 1938. 27.50 (ISBN 0-686-51307-X). Elliots Bks.

Season of Danger. Rosemary Gatenby. 1977. pap. 1.50 o.s.i. (ISBN 0-515-04429-6). Jove Pubns.

Season of Delight. Joanne Greenberg. LC 80-20421. 240p. 1981. 11.95 (ISBN 0-03-057627-X). HR&W.

Season of Discovery. Gloria Goldreich. LC 76-40482. (gr. 6-12). 1977. 6.95 o.p. (ISBN 0-525-66523-4). Elsevier-Nelson.

Season of Migration to the North. Tayeb Salih. Tr. by Denys Johnson-Davies from Arabic. 168p. 1978. 9.00 (ISBN 0-89410-198-6); pap. 5.00 (ISBN 0-89410-199-4). Three Continents.

Season of Surprises. Rebecca Ashley. (Orig.). 1981. pap. 1.50 (ISBN 0-440-18281-6). Dell.

Season of the Elk. Dean Krakel, II. LC 75-42982. (Illus.). 128p. 1980. 20.00 (ISBN 0-913504-28-9); pap. 12.95 (ISBN 0-913504-29-7). Lowell Pr.

Season of the Heart. Clare Barroll. 1978. pap. 1.95 o.p. (ISBN 0-345-25902-5). Ballantine.

Season of the Owl. Miles Wolff, Jr. LC 80-51607. 192p. 1980. 10.95 (ISBN 0-8128-2744-9). Stein & Day.

Season of Vengeance. W. W. Southard. 192p. 1981. pap. 1.95 (ISBN 0-553-14741-2). Bantam.

Season of Voting: Japanese Elections of 1976 & 1977. Ed. by Herbert Passm. 1979. pap. 6.25 (ISBN 0-8447-3343-1). Am Enterprise.

Season on the Earth: Selected Poems of Nirala. Tr. by David Rubin. LC 76-40026. 1977. 15.00x (ISBN 0-231-04160-8); pap. 6.00x (ISBN 0-231-04161-6). Columbia U Pr.

Season to Be Born. Suzanne Arms & John Arms. 1973. pap. 4.50 o.p. (ISBN 0-06-090323-6, CN323, CN). Har-Row.

Season with the Savior: Meditations on Mark. Edward R. Sims. 1979. 6.95 (ISBN 0-8164-0413-5); pap. 3.95 (ISBN 0-8164-2195-1). Crossroad NY.

Seasonal Kindergarten Units. Mary P. Baumer. 1972. pap. 5.95 o.p. (ISBN 0-8224-6330-X). Pitman Learning.

Seasonal Parties for Convalescents. Agnes P. Schaller & Analee Kinney. 1981. write for info (ISBN 0-398-04452-X). C C Thomas.

Seasonal Patterns of Hospital Activity. P. Joseph Phillip & Stephen J. Dombrosk. LC 79-1752. 160p. 1979. 15.95 (ISBN 0-669-02926-2). Lexington Bks.

Seasonal Reproduction in Higher Vertebrates. Ed. by R. J. Reiter & B. K. Follett. (Progress in Reproductive Biology Ser.: Vol. 5). (Illus.). 1980. 93.00 (ISBN 3-8055-0246-X). S Karger.

Seasoned Authors for a New Season: The Search for Standards in Popular Writing. Louis Filler. LC 79-90128. 1980. 15.95 (ISBN 0-87972-143-X). Bowling Green.

Seasoning Cookbook. Jule Wilkinson. LC 80-14412. (Illus.). 208p. 1980. spiral bd. 16.95 (ISBN 0-8436-2188-5). CBI Pub.

Seasonings for Sermons. Phillip H. Barnhart. 88p. (Orig.). 1980. pap. text ed. 5.50 (ISBN 0-89536-451-4). CSS Pub.

Seasons. Hal Borland. LC 73-5988. (Illus.). 1973. 14.95 o.s.i. (ISBN 0-397-00996-8). Lippincott.

Seasons. (Golden Photo Board Bks.). (Illus.). 12p. (ps). 1980. 1.50 (ISBN 0-307-06075-6, Golden Pr). Western Pub.

Seasons. Brian Wildsmith. (Illus.). 24p. (ps-3). 1981. 5.95 (ISBN 0-19-279730-1). Oxford U Pr.

Seasons Change. Helen Cannon. 320p. 1981. pap. 2.50 (ISBN 0-380-77164-0, 77164). Avon.

Season's Edge. Edith Hodgkinson. 1980. pap. 2.00 (ISBN 0-914610-22-8). Hanging Loose.

Seasons of Death. M. K. Wren. (Crime Club Ser.). 192p. 1981. 9.95 (ISBN 0-385-17413-6). Doubleday.

Seasons of Inspiration. Compiled by Clinton T. Howell. LC 74-14556. (Illus.). 160p. 1974. gift ed. 8.95 o.p. (ISBN 0-8407-5050-1). Nelson.

Seasons of Life. Paul Tournier. Tr. by John S. Gilmour. LC 63-8709. 1963. 4.25 (ISBN 0-8042-2160-X). John Knox.

Seasons of Life. Paul Tournier. 1976. pap. 1.25 (ISBN 0-89129-170-9). Jove Pubns.

Seasons of Life. Paul Tournier. Tr. by John S. Gilmour. LC 63-8709. 1976. pap. 1.25 (ISBN 0-8042-3651-8). John Knox.

Seasons of Love. Genevieve Dormann. 1960. 4.50 o.s.i. (ISBN 0-8076-0120-9). Braziller.

Seasons of Rebellion: Protest & Radicalism in Recent America. Ed. by Joseph Boskin & Robert A. Rosenstone. LC 79-9678. 349p. 1980. text ed. 19.25 (ISBN 0-8191-0976-2); pap. text ed. 10.50 (ISBN 0-8191-0977-0). U Pr of Amer.

Seasons of the Owl. Miles Wolff, Jr. LC 80-51788. 256p. 1981. cancelled (ISBN 0-8128-2750-3). Stein & Day.

Seasons of the Ram. Maurice Pons. Tr. by Frances Frenaye. LC 76-28052. 1977. 7.95 o.p. (ISBN 0-312-70822-X). St Martin.

Seasons of the Self. Max Coots. LC 71-158676. (Illus.). 1971. 3.50 (ISBN 0-687-37140-6). Unitarian.

Seat of Empire. Carl Bridenbaugh. LC 58-13522. (Williamsburg in America Ser: Vol. I). (Illus.). 1958. 3.95 o.p. (ISBN 0-910412-51-0). Williamsburg.

Seat Weaving. C. Perry. 1917. pap. 3.80 (ISBN 0-87002-015-3). Bennett IL.

Seatramps: Five Years of Ocean Life. Sheila Martin. (Illus.). 1978. 12.95 (ISBN 0-236-40090-8, Pub by Paul Elek). Merrimack Bk Serv.

Seats & Causes of Disease Investigated by Anatomy, 3 vols. John B. Morgagni. Tr. by Benjamin Alexander. LC 60-13365. (History of Medicine Ser.). 1980. Repr. of 1960 ed. Set. monograph 85.00 (ISBN 0-87993-148-5). Futura Pub.

Seats of the Mighty. Gilbert Parker. 1976. lib. bdg. 16.75x (ISBN 0-89968-077-1). Lightyear.

Seattle. Photos by David Barnes. LC 80-60. (Illus.). 80p. 1980. 22.50 (ISBN 0-914718-51-7); pap. 12.95 (ISBN 0-914718-50-9). Pacific Search.

Seattle: A Pictorial History. Lane Morgan & Murray C. Morgan. (Illus.). 205p. 1981. pap. price not set (ISBN 0-89865-091-7). Donning Co.

Seattle Book: The Weekly's Guide to Seattle. Ed. by David Brewster & Rebecca Earnest. (Illus.). 1978. pap. 4.95 (ISBN 0-914842-27-7). Madrona Pubs.

Seattle Discovered. Bob Peterson. LC 76-41333. (Illus.). 1976. pap. 8.95 (ISBN 0-914842-13-7). Madrona Pubs.

Seattle Epicure. Ed. by Elliott Wolf. (Epicure Ser.). 160p. (Orig.). 1979. pap. 4.95 (ISBN 0-89716-026-6). Peanut Butter.

Seattle Seahawks. Jim Rothaus. (NFL Today Ser.). (gr. 3-12). 1980. PLB 6.45 (ISBN 0-87191-795-5); pap. 2.95 (ISBN 0-89812-247-3). Creative Ed.

Seaward Margin of Belize Barrier & Atoll Reefs. N. P. James & R. N. Ginsburg. (Special Publication of the International Association of Sedimentologist Ser.: No. 3). 191p. 1980. pap. 29.95x (ISBN 0-470-26928-6). Halsted Pr.

Seawater & Desalting, Vol. 1. A. E. Delyannis & E. E. Delyannis. 180p. 1980. 34.90 (ISBN 0-387-10206-X). Springer-Verlag.

Seawater Aquariums: The Captive Environment. Stephen Spotte. LC 79-11038. 1979. 27.50 (ISBN 0-471-05665-0, Pub. by Wiley-Interscience). Wiley.

Seawater Corrosion Data. Dechema: the West German National Scientific Society. (Chemical Engineering Book Ser.). 160p. 1981. 57.50 (ISBN 0-07-016207-7). McGraw.

Seaweed in Agriculture & Horticulture. 3rd ed. W. A. Stephenson. Ed. by Bargyla & Gylver Rateaver. LC 74-12812. (Conservation Gardening & Farming Ser: Ser. C). 1974. pap. 7.00 (ISBN 0-9600698-3-6). Rateavers.

Seba Smith. Milton Rickels & Patricia Rickels. (U.S. Authors Ser.: No. 283). 1977. lib. bdg. 10.95 (ISBN 0-8057-7185-9). Twayne.

Sebastiano Del Piombo. Michael Hirst. (Studies in the History of Art & Architecture). (Illus.). 288p. 1981. 98.00 (ISBN 0-19-817308-3). Oxford U Pr.

Sebastopol. Leo Tolstoi. 1961. pap. 4.50 (ISBN 0-472-06058-9, 58, AA). U of Mich Pr.

Sebei Law. Walter Goldschmidt. 1967. 19.50x (ISBN 0-520-00489-2). U of Cal Pr.

SEC Accounting. J. W. Buckley et al. 1980. text ed. 20.95 (ISBN 0-471-01861-9); tchrs' manual (ISBN 0-471-07778-X). Wiley.

SEC Accounting Practice & Procedure. 3rd ed. Louis H. Rappaport. 1260p. 1972. 42.50 (ISBN 0-8260-7325-5, 77831). Ronald Pr.

SEC & the Public Interest. Susan Phillips & Richard Zecher. (Illus.). 184p. 1981. text ed. 19.95x (ISBN 0-262-16080-3). MIT Pr.

Seceders. J. H. Philpot. pap. 2.25 (ISBN 0-686-12539-8). Banner of Truth.

Secession & Restoration of Louisiana. Willie M. Caskey. LC 78-75302. (American Scene Ser). (Illus.). 1970. Repr. of 1938 ed. lib. bdg. 32.50 (ISBN 0-306-71263-6). Da Capo.

Secession Movement in South Carolina, 1847-1852. P. M. Hamer. LC 75-124883. (American Scene Ser). 1971. Repr. of 1918 ed. lib. bdg. 17.50 (ISBN 0-306-71036-6). Da Capo.

Seclusion Room. Fredric Neuman. 1979. pap. 1.95 o.p. (ISBN 0-449-24152-1, Crest). Fawcett.

Second Abstract of British Historical Statistics. B. R. Mitchell & H. G. Jones. LC 72-128502. (Department of Applied Economics Monographs: No. 18). (Illus.). 1971. 45.00 (ISBN 0-521-08001-0). Cambridge U Pr.

Second Adler Book of Puzzles & Riddles. Peggy Adler. LC 63-15912. (Illus.). (gr. 3-6). 1963. PLB 7.89 (ISBN 0-381-99946-7, A68801, JD-J). John Day.

Second & Third Blast of Retrait from Plaies & Theaters. Anthony Mundy. LC 77-170405. (English Stage Ser.: Vol. 4). lib. bdg. 45.00 (ISBN 0-8240-0587-2). Garland Pub.

Second Anglo-Saxon Reader: Archaic & Dialectal. 2nd ed. Henry Sweet. 1978. text ed. 19.95x (ISBN 0-19-811170-3); pap. 14.50 (ISBN 0-19-811176-2). Oxford U Pr.

Second Athenian League: Empire or Free Alliance. Jack Cargill. 325p. 1981. 17.50x (ISBN 0-520-04069-4). U of Cal Pr.

Second Avenue Rag. Allan Knee. (Phoenix Theatre Ser.). pap. 2.95 (ISBN 0-912262-71-0). Proscenium.

Second Barnhart Dictionary of New English. Clarence L. Barnhart et al. LC 79-6815. 1980. 19.95 (ISBN 0-06-010154-7, HarpT). Har-Row.

Second Barrel. Eric Sloane. (Funk & W Bk.). (Illus.). 1969. 10.95 o.s.i. (ISBN 0-308-70100-3, TYC-T). T Y Crowell.

Second Battle of New Orleans: A History of the Vieux Carre Riverfront Expressway Controversy. Richard O. Baumbach, Jr. & William E. Borah. (Illus.). 1980. 27.50 (ISBN 0-8173-4840-9); pap. 12.95 (ISBN 0-8173-4841-7). U of Ala Pr.

Second Body. Sue Payer. 1979. pap. 1.95 (ISBN 0-505-51381-1). Tower Bks.

Second Book of Chess Strategy. G. M. Lisitsyn & Bernard Cafferty. 1978. pap. 8.95 (ISBN 0-7134-1425-1, Pub. by Batsford England). David & Charles.

Second Book of Chess Strategy. G. M. Lisitsyn & B. Caffery. (Chess Player Ser.). (Illus.). 1978. pap. 3.95 o.p. (ISBN 0-900928-83-2). Hippocrene Bks.

Second Book of Kings. F. W. Farrar. Date not set. 16.75 (ISBN 0-86524-036-1). Klock & Klock.

Second Book of Modern Lace Knitting. rev. ed. Marianne Kinzel. LC 72-86064. (Illus.). 128p. 1973. pap. 4.00 (ISBN 0-486-22905-X). Dover.

Second Book of Operas, Their Histories, Their Plots & Their Music. Henry E. Krehbiel. LC 80-2280. 1981. Repr. of 1917 ed. 36.50 (ISBN 0-404-18852-4). AMS Pr.

Second Book of Samuel. William G. Blaikie. 1978. 13.50 (ISBN 0-686-12947-4). Klock & Klock.

Second Centering Book: More Awareness Activites for Children, Parents, & Teachers. G. Hendricks & T. Roberts. 1977. 11.95 (ISBN 0-13-797332-2, Spec); pap. 5.95 (ISBN 0-13-797324-1, Spec). P-H.

Second Century of the English Parliament. Goronwy Edwards. 1978. 22.50x (ISBN 0-19-822479-6). Oxford U Pr.

Second Chance. Hayden A. Duggan. LC 77-15814. (Illus.). 1978. 18.95 (ISBN 0-669-02060-5). Lexington Bks.

Second Chance. Alan Sillitoe. 1981. 12.95 (ISBN 0-671-42761-X). S&S.

Second Chance. David Van Wade & Sarah Van Wade. LC 75-20899. 1975. 5.95 (ISBN 0-88270-137-1); pap. 4.95 (ISBN 0-88270-138-X). Logos.

Second Chance: Blueprints for Life Change. Herbert B. Livesey. LC 77-8571. 1977. 8.95 o.p. (ISBN 0-397-01223-3). Lippincott.

Second Chinese Revolution. K. S. Karol. Tr. by Mervyn Jones. 1975. 12.95 o.p. (ISBN 0-8090-8516-X). Hill & Wang.

Second City Politics: Democratic Processes & Decision-Making in Birmingham. Kenneth Newton. (Illus.). 1976. pap. 22.50x (ISBN 0-19-827197-2). Oxford U Pr.

Second Class FCC Encyclopedia: Complete Study Guide to the Commercial Radio Telephone Exam. Ken Sessions. LC 74-75219. 602p. 1975. pap. 12.95 (ISBN 0-8306-4652-3, 652). TAB Bks.

Second Class Radiotelephone License Handbook. 6th ed. Edward M. Noll. LC 80-51713. (Illus.). 1980. pap. 12.50 (ISBN 0-672-21722-8). SAMS.

Second Coming. Walker Percy. 368p. 1980. 12.95 (ISBN 0-374-25674-8); signed, limited ed. 60.00 (ISBN 0-374-25675-6). FS&G.

Second Coming of Christ Is Now. Lafayette Robinson. LC 80-83601. (Illus.). 160p. Date not set. pap. price not set (ISBN 0-8187-0041-6). Harlo Pr.

Second Coming: Popular Millenarianism 1780-1850. John F. Harrison. 1979. 21.00 (ISBN 0-8135-0879-7). Rutgers U Pr.

Second Confession. Rex Stout. 208p. 1980. pap. 1.95 (ISBN 0-553-14448-0). Bantam.

Second Corinthians. Francis T. Fallon. (New Testament Message Ser.). 9.95 (ISBN 0-89453-134-4); pap. 4.95 (ISBN 0-89453-199-9). M Glazier.

Second Corinthians. Irving Jensen. (Bible Self-Study Ser). (Illus.). 108p. 1972. pap. 2.25 (ISBN 0-8024-1047-2). Moody.

Second Corinthians. Geoffrey Wilson. 1979. pap. 3.95 (ISBN 0-85151-295-X). Banner of Truth.

Second Corinthians: Keys to Triumphant Living. Edgar C. James. (Teach Yourself the Bible Ser). 1964. pap. 1.75 (ISBN 0-8024-7680-5). Moody.

Second Courante of Newes from the East India in Two Letters. LC 74-28849. (English Experience Ser.: No. 730). 1975. Repr. of 1622 ed. 3.50 (ISBN 90-221-0730-2). Walter J Johnson.

Second Course in Calculus. Harley Flanders & Justin J. Price. 1974. text ed. 19.95 (ISBN 0-12-259662-5); instrs' manual 3.00 (ISBN 0-12-259663-3). Acad Pr.

Second Course in Fundamentals of Mathematics. Edwin I. Stein. (gr. 7-12). 1978. text ed. 14.20 (ISBN 0-205-05538-9, 5655382); tchr's guide 2.40 (ISBN 0-205-05539-7, 5655390). Allyn.

Second Course in Mathematical Analysis. J. C. Burkhill & H. Burkhill. LC 69-16278. (Illus.). 1970. text ed. 35.50x (ISBN 0-521-07519-X). Cambridge U Pr.

Second Course in Stochastic Processes. Samuel Karlin & Howard M. Taylor. LC 80-533. 1980. 35.00 (ISBN 0-12-398650-8). Acad Pr.

Second Crossword Puzzle Book. Leslie Hill & P. R. Popkin. 62p. 1969. pap. text ed. 2.95x (ISBN 0-19-432552-0). Oxford U Pr.

Second Cup of Coffee. Jean Shaw. 192p. (Orig.). 1981. pap. 2.95 (ISBN 0-310-43542-0). Zondervan.

Second Day: Reflections on Remarriage. Robert F. Capon. LC 80-15750. 160p. 1980. 8.95 (ISBN 0-688-03680-5). Morrow.

Second Defence of the Short View of the English Stage. Jeremy Collier. LC 76-170445. (English Stage Ser.: Vol. 34). lib. bdg. 50.00 (ISBN 0-8240-0617-8). Garland Pub.

Second Deluge. Garrett P. Serviss. 1976. lib. bdg. 12.95x (ISBN 0-89968-172-7). Lightyear.

Second Diesel Spotter's Guide. Jerry A. Pinkepank. LC 66-22894. (Illus.). 459p. 1973. 12.75 (ISBN 0-89024-025-6); pap. 10.95 (ISBN 0-89024-026-4). Kalmbach.

Second Digest of Investigations in the Teaching of Science. Francis D. Curtis. LC 74-153694. 1971. Repr. of 1931 ed. text ed. 12.75x (ISBN 0-8077-1225-6). Tchrs Coll.

Second Elizabethan Journal. Ed. by G. B. Harrison. 1974. 32.50x (ISBN 0-7100-7882-X). Routledge & Kegan.

Second Empire, Eighteen Fifty-Two to Eighteen Seventy: Art in France Under Napoleon III. Philadelphia Museum of Art & Detroit Institute of Arts, Grand Palais, Paris. LC 78-60516. (Illus.). 1978. 18.95x (ISBN 0-8143-1630-1, Pub. by Phila Mus Art). Wayne St U Pr.

Second Empire Opera. T. J. Walsh. 1981. 35.00 (ISBN 0-7145-3659-8). Riverrun NY.

Second Empire Revisited: A Study in French Historiography. Stuart L. Campbell. LC 77-20247. 1978. 17.00 (ISBN 0-8135-0856-8). Rutgers U Pr.

Second European Congress on Information Systems & Networks. 231p. 1975. text ed. 21.50 (ISBN 3-7940-5164-5). K G Saur.

Second Federalist: Congress Creates a Government. Ed. by Charles S. Hyneman & George W. Carey. LC 66-27380. (Orig.). 1966. pap. text ed. 6.95x (ISBN 0-89197-510-1). Irvington.

Second Fly-Tyer's Almanac. Robert H. Boyle & Dave Whitlock. (Illus.). 1978. 14.95 o.s.i. (ISBN 0-397-01286-1). Lippincott.

Second Foundation. Isaac Asimov. 1976. pap. 1.95 (ISBN 0-380-00823-8, 45351). Avon.

Second Front. D. Botting. Ed. by Time-Life Books. (World War II). (Illus.). 1979. 12.95 (ISBN 0-8094-2498-3). Time-Life.

Second Front. Douglas Botting. LC 78-3405. (World War II Ser.). (Illus.). 1978. lib. bdg. 13.95 (ISBN 0-686-51050-X). Silver.

Second Game. Charles De Vet & Katherine MacLean. (Science Fiction Ser.). 1981. pap. 2.25 (ISBN 0-87997-620-9, UE1620). DAW Bks.

Second Generation. Howard Fast. 1979. pap. 3.25 (ISBN 0-440-17915-7). Dell.

Second Generation. B. A. Pauw. (Xhosa in Town Ser.). 261p. 1973. pap. 15.95x (ISBN 0-19-570028-7). Oxford U Pr.

Second Growth. Dale Hobson. (Illus.). 36p. (Orig.). 1980. pap. 3.00 (ISBN 0-918092-09-4). Tamarack Edns.

Second Handshake. Will Fowler. (Illus.). 1980. 12.50 (ISBN 0-8184-0287-3). Lyle Stuart.

Second Homes: Curse or Blessing. Ed. by J. T. Coppock. 1977. text ed. 23.00 (ISBN 0-08-021371-5); pap. text ed. 8.50 (ISBN 0-08-021370-7). Pergamon.

Second Industrial Revolution. Russell Ackoff. 1978. 0.75 (ISBN 0-686-28791-6). Forward Movement.

Second International Directory of Private Presses (Letterpresses) Directory of Private Presses & Letterpress Printers & Publishers. Ed. by Budd Westreich. (Illus.). 132p. (Orig.). 1980. 18.00 (ISBN 0-686-27375-3); pap. 10.00 (ISBN 0-936300-01-9). Pr Arden Park.

Second International Symposium on Desmid Research Lake Itasca, Minnesota 1976: Proceedings. Ed. by P. Biebel. (Beiheft Zur Nova Hedwigia 56 Ser.). 1981. lib. bdg. 60.00 (ISBN 3-7682-5456-9). Lubrecht & Cramer.

Second International Waterbone Transportation Conference. Compiled by American Society of Civil Engineers. 780p. 1978. pap. text ed. 42.00 (ISBN 0-87262-099-9). Am Soc Civil Eng.

Second International 1889-1914. 2nd ed. James Joll. 1975. 21.50x (ISBN 0-7100-7966-4). Routledge & Kean.

Second Isaiah Introduction, Translation & Commentary to Chapters 15-55. Christopher R. North. 1964. 22.95x (ISBN 0-19-826154-3). Oxford U Pr.

Second Kings with Chronicles. rev. ed. Ed. by Irving L. Jensen. (Bible Self-Study Ser). (Illus., Orig.). 1968. pap. 2.25 (ISBN 0-8024-1012-X). Moody.

Second LACUS Forum: Proceedings. Linguistic Association of Canada & the U.S. Ed. by Peter A. Reich. pap. text ed. 10.95 (ISBN 0-685-69722-3). Hornbeam Pr.

Second Lady Cameron. Frieda Thomsen. 1977. pap. 1.50 (ISBN 0-505-51204-1). Tower Bks.

Second-Language Acquisition & Foreign Language Teaching. Ed. by Rosario C. Gingras. LC 78-74014. 1978. pap. text ed. 7.25x (ISBN 0-87281-090-9). Ctr Appl Ling.

Second Language Acquisition & Second Language Learning. Stephen Krashen. (Language Teaching Methodology Ser.). 176p. 1981. pap. 9.95 (ISBN 0-08-025338-5). Pergamon.

Second Latin. Cora C. Scanlon & Charles L. Scanlon. LC 48-748. 1976. pap. 6.00 (ISBN 0-89555-003-2). TAN Bks Pubs.

Second Law of Thermodynamics. Ed. by Joseph Kestin. (Benchmark Papers on Energy: Vol. 5). 1976. 43.00 (ISBN 0-12-786839-9). Acad Pr.

Second Letter of Paul to the Corinthians. James Thompson. Ed. by Everett Ferguson. (Living Word New Testament Commentary Ser.: Vol. 9). 1970. 7.95 (ISBN 0-8344-0054-5). Sweet.

Second-Level Basic Electronics. U. S. Navy (Bureau of Naval Personnel) Orig. Title: Basic Electronics Vol. 2. (Illus.). 352p. 1971. pap. text ed. 4.50 (ISBN 0-486-22841-X). Dover.

Second Level Nursing: Study Modules. Venner Farley. LC 80-70482. (Associate Degree Nursing Ser.). (Illus.). 272p. (Orig.). 1981. pap. text ed. price not set (ISBN 0-8273-1876-6); price not set instr's. guide (ISBN 0-8273-1877-4). Delmar.

Second Long Walk: The Navajo-Hopi Land Dispute. Jerry Kammer. 1980. 14.95 (ISBN 0-8263-0549-0). U of NM Pr.

Second Look: The Nonprofit Arts & Cultural Industry of New York State 1975-76. National Research Center of the Arts, Inc. 308p. 1978. pap. 8.50x (ISBN 0-89062-097-0, Pub. by NY Found Arts). Pub Ctr Cult Res.

Second Man. Edward Grierson. LC 80-8411. 320p. 1981. pap. 2.25 (ISBN 0-06-080528-5, P 528, PL). Har-Row.

Second Man in U. S. Maria Roeschl & Ernst Lehrs. 1978. pap. 7.95 (ISBN 0-904822-07-9, Pub by Henry Goulden, Ltd.). St George Bk Serv.

Second Nature. Grodon Glasco. 432p. (Orig.). 1980. pap. cancelled (ISBN 0-446-83954-X). Warner Bks.

Second Opinion. Isadore Rosenfeld. 1981. 14.95 (ISBN 0-686-68757-4, Linden). S&S.

Second Part of the Anatomie of Abuses. Philip Stubbes. LC 71-170409. (English Stage Ser.: Vol. 8). lib. bdg. 50.00 (ISBN 0-8240-0591-0). Garland Pub.

Second Passive Solar Catalog. David A. Bainbridge. (Illus.). 110p. (Orig.). 1980. pap. 11.95 (ISBN 0-933490-02-X). Passive Solar.

Second Progress Report & Recommendations. Television Research Committee. (Orig.). 1970. pap. text ed. 5.25x (ISBN 0-7185-1090-9, Leicester). Humanities.

Second Quarter Century of American Racing. Date not set. 27.25 (ISBN 0-936032-08-1). Thoroughbred Own & Breed.

Second Quilter's Companion. Dolores A. Hinson. LC 80-17912. (Illus.). 288p. 1980. 12.95 (ISBN 0-668-04924-3, 4924-3). Arco.

Second Quiltmaker's Handbook. Michael James. (Creative Handcrafts Ser.). 208p. 1981. 24.95 (ISBN 0-13-797795-6, Spec); pap. 10.95 (ISBN 0-13-797787-5). P-H.

Second "R". William Harpin. (Unwin Education Bks.: No. 31). text ed. 17.95x (ISBN 0-04-372018-8); pap. text ed. 8.95x (ISBN 0-04-372019-6). Allen Unwin.

Second Report of the Commissioners Appointed to Inquire into the Truck System (Shetland), 1892. Intro. by Hans Smith. 1980. pap. 10.95x (ISBN 0-906191-06-8, Pub. by Thule Pr England). Intl Schol Bk Serv.

Second Season: Life, Love & Sex in the Middle Years. Fuchs, Estelle, Ph.D. LC 77-70897. 1977. 3.95 (ISBN 0-385-09761-1, Anchor Pr). Doubleday.

Second Set of Madrigales to 3. 4. 5. & 6. Parts Apt Both for Voyals & Voyces. John Wilbye. LC 73-6171. (English Experience Ser.: No. 633). 1973. Repr. of 1609 ed. 27.00 (ISBN 90-221-0633-0). Walter J Johnson.

Second Sight. Cecilia Bartholomew. 1981. pap. 2.75 (ISBN 0-425-04798-9). Berkley Pub.

Second Sight. David Williams. 1979. pap. 1.75 o.s.i. (ISBN 0-515-04708-2). Jove Pubns.

Second Sight of Jennifer Hamilton. Sally Emerson. LC 80-1722. 312p. 1981. 11.95 (ISBN 0-385-15815-7). Doubleday.

Second Skin. 2nd ed. Marilyn J. Horn. 1975. text ed. 19.50 (ISBN 0-395-18552-1); instructor's manual pap. 2.00 (ISBN 0-395-18780-X). HM.

Second Skin: An Interdisciplinary Study of Clothing. 3rd ed. Marilyn J. Horn & Lois M. Gurel. LC 80-81918. (Illus.). 480p. 1981. text ed. write for info. (ISBN 0-395-28974-2); instr's. manual 1.60 (ISBN 0-395-28963-7). HM.

Second Song. Clarissa Start. 232p. (Orig.). 1980. pap. 5.95 (ISBN 0-86629-013-3). Sunrise MO.

Second Sourcebook for Science Supervisors. rev. ed. Ed. by Mary Harbeck. 1976. pap. 3.50 (ISBN 0-87355-004-8). Natl Sci Tchrs.

Second Special Conference Issue: Sixth International Conference on Social Science & Medicine, Amsterdam 1979. Ed. by Peter J. McEwan. 80p. 1980. pap. 14.40 (ISBN 0-08-026763-7). Pergamon.

Second Spring: U. S. Catholicism in the 1980s. Charles A. Fracchia. LC 79-3599. 208p. 1980. 9.95 (ISBN 0-06-063012-4, HarpR, HarpR). Har-Row.

Second Stage. Betty Friedan. 320p. 1981. 12.95 (ISBN 0-671-41034-2). Summit Bks.

Second Stage Lensman. E. E. Smith. 1973. pap. 1.50 o.s.i. (ISBN 0-515-03172-0, V3172). Jove Pubns.

Second Start. Paul Salsini. LC 79-92442. 168p. (Orig.). 1980. pap. 4.95 (ISBN 0-87973-525-2, 525). Our Sunday Visitor.

Second Stories. Gloria Frym. LC 79-9390. (Illus.). 1980. pap. 7.95 (ISBN 0-87701-152-4). Chronicle Bks.

Second Sunrise. Francesca Greer. 284p. (Orig.). 1981. pap. 2.50 (ISBN 0-446-91214-X). Warner Bks.

Second Tale of a Tub, or, the History of Robert Powel the Puppet-Show-Man. Sir Thomas Burnet & George Duckett. Ed. by Michael Shugrue. LC 71-170539. (Foundations of the Novel Ser: Vol. 26). iv, 219p. 1973. Repr. of 1715 ed. lib. bdg. 50.00 (ISBN 0-8240-0538-4). Garland Pub.

Second Thoughts on the Dead Sea Scrolls. Ed. by Frederick F. Bruce. 1956. pap. 4.95 (ISBN 0-8028-1026-8). Eerdmans.

Second Time Around. Hugh McLeave. 1981. 9.95 (ISBN 0-8027-5439-2). Walker & Co.

Second Time Around: An Honest Widow Reveals Her Intimate & Humorous Experiences in the Dating & Mating Game. Otty Lippi. LC 80-27189. 1981. 12.95 (ISBN 0-934878-03-X). Dembner Bks.

Second Time Is Better. Bill Adler & Gary Wagner. LC 78-70091. 1979. pap. 1.95 o.p. (ISBN 0-87216-515-9). Playboy Pbks.

Second Tomorrow. Ann Hampson. 192p. (Orig.). 1980. pap. 1.50 (ISBN 0-671-57016-1). S&S.

Second Tomorrow. Anne Hampson. (Silhouette Ser.: No. 16). pap. 1.50 (ISBN 0-686-68325-0). PB.

Second Touch. Keith Miller. 1976. pap. 1.75 (ISBN 0-89129-133-4). Jove Pubns.

Second Treasure Chest of Tales. Paul Stroyer. (Illus.). 1960. 8.95 (ISBN 0-8392-3032-X). Astor-Honor.

Second Treatise of Government. John Locke. Ed. by Thomas P. Peardon. LC 52-14648. (gr. 11 up). 1952. pap. 3.95 (ISBN 0-672-60193-1, LLA31). Bobbs.

Second Treatise of Government. John Locke. Ed. by C. B. Macpherson. (Philosophical Classsics Ser.). 138p. 1980. lib. bdg. 12.50 (ISBN 0-915144-93-X); pap. text ed. 2.75 (ISBN 0-915144-86-7). Hackett Pub.

Second Tree from the Corner. E. B. White. LC 53-11864. 1954. 12.95 o.p. (ISBN 0-06-014590-0, HarpT). Har-Row.

Second Trimester Abortion. Ed. by Gary S. Berger et al. 456p. 1981. text ed. 29.50 (ISBN 0-88416-256-7). PSG Pub.

Second Try: Labour & the EEC. U. Kitzinger. 1969. 25.00 (ISBN 0-08-012961-7); pap. 13.25 (ISBN 0-08-012960-9). Pergamon.

Second Vendee: The Continuity of Counter-Revolution in the Department of the Gard 1789-1815. Gwynne Lewis. (Illus.). 1978. 37.50x (ISBN 0-19-822544-X). Oxford U Pr.

Second Vespers. Ralph McInerny. LC 79-56379. (Father Dowling Mystery Ser.). 256p. 1980. 9.95 (ISBN 0-8149-0837-3). Vanguard.

Second Vespers. large print ed. Ralph McInerny. 1981. Repr. of 1980 ed. 10.95 (ISBN 0-89621-272-6). Thorndike Pr.

Second Vienna School. Luigi Rognoni. Tr. by Robert Mann. (Illus.). 420p. 1980. lib. bdg. 27.50 (ISBN 0-7145-3528-1). Riverrun NY.

Second Virial Coefficients of Pure Gases & Mixtures: A Critical Compilation. J. H. Dymond & E. B. Smith. (Oxford Science Research Papers Ser.). (Illus.). 534p. 1980. pap. text ed. 69.00x (ISBN 0-19-855361-7). Oxford U Pr.

Second Workbook in Spanish. Ivor A. Richards et al. pap. 0.75 o.s.i. (ISBN 0-671-46897-9). WSP.

Second Writers Workshop Literary Reader: An Anthology. Ed. by P. Lal. 72p. 1975. 15.00 (ISBN 0-88253-624-9); pap. text ed. 6.75 (ISBN 0-88253-623-0). Ind-US Inc.

Second Year Latin. rev. ed. Charles Jenney, Jr. et al. (gr. 7-12). 1979. text ed. 14.80 (ISBN 0-205-06182-6, 3961826); 4.96 (ISBN 0-205-02488-2, 3924882); tchrs'. guide 3.60 (ISBN 0-205-02489-0, 3924890); tests 3.60 (ISBN 0-205-02490-4, 3924904); tchrs'. ed. 3.60 (ISBN 0-205-02491-2, 3924912). Allyn.

Second Year Nurse: Nancy Kimball at City Hospital. Carli Laklan. LC 67-10052. (gr. 5-9). 1967. 5.95 o.p. (ISBN 0-385-06288-5). Doubleday.

Secondary Analysis of Sample Surveys: Principles, Procedures & Potentialities. Herbert H. Hyman. LC 72-251. 347p. 1972. 18.50 (ISBN 0-471-42605-9, Pub. by Wiley). Krieger.

Secondary Batteries-Recent Advances. R. W. Graham. LC 77-94228. (Chemical Technology Review 106; Energy Technology Review 26). (Illus.). 1978. 42.00 o.p. (ISBN 0-8155-0696-1). Noyes.

Secondary Curriculum for a Changing World. Frank L. Steeves & Fenwick W. English. 1978. text ed. 15.95 (ISBN 0-675-08424-5); instructor's manual 3.95 (ISBN 0-686-67991-1). Merrill.

Secondary Diabetes: The Spectrum of the Diabetics Syndromes. Ed. by Stephen Podolsky & M. Viswanathan. 1980. 52.00 (ISBN 0-89004-372-8). Raven.

Secondary Education & the Formation of an Elite: The Impact of Education on Gwembe District, Zambia. Thayer Scudder & Elizabeth Colson. (Studies in Anthropology). 1980. 24.50 (ISBN 0-12-634280-6). Acad Pr.

Secondary Education: School & Community. William Van Til. LC 77-76861. (Illus.). 1978. text ed. 16.75 (ISBN 0-395-25751-4); inst. manual 0.50 (ISBN 0-395-25764-6). HM.

Secondary Metabolism. J. Mann. (Chemistry Ser.). (Illus.). 1978. text ed. 29.00 (ISBN 0-19-855506-7). Oxford U Pr.

Secondary Principal's Handbook: A Guide to Executive Action. Larry W. Hughes & Gerald C. Ubben. 350p. 1980. text ed. 18.95 (ISBN 0-205-06875-8). Allyn.

Secondary Reading Inventory. Jerry L. Johns. 100p. (gr. 7 up). 1981. write for info. wire coil (ISBN 0-697-06058-6). Wm C Brown.

Secondary (Reciprocal) Trigonometric Ratios: Unit 4. Rudolph A. Zimmer. 49p. 1980. pap. text ed. 4.50 (ISBN 0-8403-2277-1). Kendall-Hunt.

Secondary School Administration: A Management Approach. 2nd ed. Ed. by M. G. Hughes. LC 74-4453. 1974. text ed. 16.50 (ISBN 0-08-018010-8); pap. text ed. 8.50 (ISBN 0-08-018011-6). Pergamon.

Secondary School Curriculum Improvement: Challenges, Humanism, Accountability. 2nd ed. J. Lloyd Trump & Delmas F. Miller. 1973. text ed. 13.95x o.s.i. (ISBN 0-205-03733-X, 2237334). Allyn.

Secondary School Curriculum Improvement: Meeting Challenges of the Times. 3rd ed. J. Lloyd Trump & Delmas F. Miller. 1979. pap. text ed. 11.95 (ISBN 0-205-06600-3, 2366002). Allyn.

Secondary School Graduation: University Entrance Qualification in Socialist Countries. new ed. Wolfgang Mitter. LC 77-30471. 1978. text ed. 23.00 (ISBN 0-08-022237-4); pap. text ed. 15.00 (ISBN 0-08-022238-2). Pergamon.

Secondary School Principal: Manager & Supervisor. Charles L. Wood et al. 1978. text ed. 18.95 (ISBN 0-205-06165-6, 2361655). Allyn.

Secondary School Reading: Process-Program-Procedure. Walter R. Hill. 1978. text ed. 17.95 (ISBN 0-205-06129-X, 2361299). Allyn.

Secondary Schools for American Youth. L. A. Williams. 529p. 1980. Repr. of 1944 ed. lib. bdg. 25.00 (ISBN 0-89984-524-X). Century Bookbindery.

Secondary Social Studies Introduction, Curriculum, Evaluation. John U. Michaelis & J. Nelson. (Illus.). 1980. text ed. 17.95 (ISBN 0-13-797753-0). P-H.

Secondary Spread of Cancer. Ed. by R. W. Baldwin. 1978. 35.00 (ISBN 0-12-076850-X). Acad Pr.

Secondary Teacher's Day. S. Hilsum & C. R. Strong. (Research Report). (Illus.). 1978. pap. text ed. 25.50x (ISBN 0-85633-139-2, NFER). Humanities.

Secondary Teaching Methods. Kenneth T. Henson. 384p. 1980. text ed. 14.95 (ISBN 0-669-03316-2). Heath.

Secrecy: A Cross-Cultural Perspective. Ed. by Stanton K. Tefft. LC 79-25454. 400p. 1980. text ed. 19.95x (ISBN 0-87705-442-8); pap. text ed. 9.95x (ISBN 0-87705-443-6). Human Sci Pr.

Secrecy, or the Ruin on the Rock, 3 vols. Eliza Fenwick. Ed. by Gina Luria. (Feminist Controversy in England 1788-1810 Ser.). 1974. Set. lib. bdg. 50.00 ea. (ISBN 0-8240-0859-6); lib. bdg. 45.00 ea. Garland Pub.

Secret. Elizabeth Clarke. 1972. 6.50 (ISBN 0-571-09981-5, Pub. by Faber & Faber). Merrimack Bk Serv.

Secret Adversary. Agatha Christie. 224p. 1981. pap. 2.25 (ISBN 0-553-13777-8). Bantam.

Secret Affair. Lilian Peake. (Harlequin Presents Ser.). 192p. (Orig.). 1981. pap. 1.50 (ISBN 0-373-10407-3, Pub. by Harlequin). PB.

Secret Agent. Joseph Conrad. 1953. pap. 2.95 (ISBN 0-385-09352-7, A8, Anch). Doubleday.

Secret Agent. Joseph Conrad. lib. bdg. 12.95x (ISBN 0-89966-058-4). Buccaneer Bks.

Secret Agent Nine. Alex Raymond & Dashiell Hammett. Ed. by Woody Gelman. LC 76-19616. (Illus.). 176p. 1976. pap. 8.95 (ISBN 0-686-65518-4). Nostalgia Pr.

Secret & Secure: Privacy, Cryptography & Secure Communication. C. C. Pierce. LC 77-73804. (Illus.). 1977. pap. 3.25 o.s.i. (ISBN 0-9601564-1-0). C C Pierce.

Secret & Secure: Privacy, Cryptography & Secure Communication. rev. ed. Clayton C. Pierce. LC 77-73804. (Illus.). 1979. cancelled (ISBN 0-9601564-2-9); pap. 5.95 (ISBN 0-9601564-3-7). C C Pierce.

Secret Art of Ian Miller. Ian Miller. (Illus.). 96p. 1980. pap. 9.95 (ISBN 0-8256-9551-1, Quick Fox). Music Sales.

Secret Birthday Message. Eric Carle. LC 75-168726. (Illus.). (ps-3). 1972. 8.95 (ISBN 0-690-72347-4, TYC-J); PLB 6.85 (ISBN 0-690-72348-2). T Y Crowell.

Secret Chambers & Hiding-Places. rev. ed. 3rd ed. Allan Fea. LC 79-155739. 1971. Repr. of 1901 ed. 20.00 (ISBN 0-8103-3385-6). Gale.

Secret Codes. Helen J. Fletcher. (gr. 1-3). 1980. PLB 7.90 (ISBN 0-531-04146-8). Watts.

Secret Country. Janet Bord & Colin Bord. 1978. pap. 2.50 o.s.i. (ISBN 0-446-81648-5). Warner Bks.

Secret Country of C. S. Lewis. Anne Arnott. (YA) 1975. 4.95 o.p. (ISBN 0-8028-3468-X). Eerdmans.

Secret Cross of Lorraine. Thea J. Brow. (gr. 5-8). 1981. 8.95 (ISBN 0-395-30344-3). HM.

Secret Doctrine, 2 vols. facsimile of 1888 ed. Helena P. Blavatsky. LC 74-76603. 1977. Repr. of 1888 ed. Set. 17.00 (ISBN 0-911500-00-6); Set. softcover 12.50 (ISBN 0-911500-01-4). Theos U Pr.

Secret Doctrine: The Synthesis of Science, Religion, & Philosophy, 2 vols. in 1. Helena P. Blavatsky. xci, 1474p. 1925. Repr. of 1888 ed. 14.00 (ISBN 0-938998-00-5). Theosophy.

Secret Dream. Muriel F. Blackwell. (gr. 6-8). 1981. 7.95 (ISBN 0-8054-4804-7). Broadman.

Secret Eden: Africa's Enchanted Wilderness. Eric Robins. (Illus.). 128p. 1981. 27.00 (ISBN 0-241-10423-8, Pub. by Hamish Hamilton England). David & Charles.

Secret Emily. Carol K. Scism. (Illus.). (gr. 4-6). 1975. pap. 0.95 o.p. (ISBN 0-590-09944-2, Schol Pap). Schol Bk Serv.

Secret Factory. W. C. Chalk. pap. text ed. 2.95x o.p. (ISBN 0-435-11221-X). Heinemann Ed.

Secret Fallout: Low-Level Radiation from Hiroshima to Three-Mile Island. rev. ed. Ernest Sternglass. (McGraw-Hill Paperbacks Ser.). 300p. (Orig.). 1981. pap. 5.95 (ISBN 0-07-061242-0, GB). McGraw.

Secret Fear, No. 23. Barbara Cartland. 1977. pap. 1.50 o.s.i. (ISBN 0-515-04461-X). Jove Pubns.

Secret Fighting Arts of the World. John F. Gilbey. LC 63-7910. (Illus.). 1963. bds. 9.75 (ISBN 0-8048-0515-6). C E Tuttle.

Secret File on John Birch. James Hefley & Marti Hefley. 1980. pap. 4.95 (ISBN 0-8423-5862-5). Tyndale.

Secret for Grandmother's Birthday. Franz Brandenberg. LC 75-10606. (Illus.). 32p. (ps-3). 1975. 7.92 (ISBN 0-688-84012-4). Greenwillow.

Secret Friend. Marilyn Sachs. LC 77-25606. (gr. 4-7). 1978. 7.95a (ISBN 0-385-13569-6); PLB (ISBN 0-385-13570-X). Doubleday.

Secret Friends. Doris Rust. (Illus.). (ps-5). 1962. 3.95 o.p. (ISBN 0-571-05182-0, Pub. by Faber & Faber). Merrimack Bk Serv.

Secret Garden. Frances H. Burnett. LC 78-2914. (Raintree's Illustrated Classics). (Illus.). (gr. 5-8). 1978. PLB 9.65 (ISBN 0-8393-6204-8). Raintree Child.

Secret Hiding-Places the Origins, Histories & Descriptions of English Secret Hiding-Places Used by Priests, Cavaliers, Jacobites & Smugglers. Granville Squiers. LC 70-157499. (Tower Bks). (Illus.). 1971. Repr. of 1934 ed. 20.00 (ISBN 0-8103-3920-X). Gale.

Secret History. Procopius. (Penguin Classics). 1980. pap. 3.95 (ISBN 0-14-044182-4). Penguin.

Secret History of Queen Zarah & the Zarazians. Mary D. Manley. LC 79-170514. (Foundations of the Novel Ser.: Vol. 10). lib. bdg. 50.00 (ISBN 0-8240-0522-8). Garland Pub.

Secret History of the English Occupation of Egypt. Wilfred S. Blunt. 1967. 18.50 (ISBN 0-86527-179-8). Fertig.

Secret History of the Present Intrigues of the Court of Caramania. Eliza Haywood. LC 71-170571. (Foundations of the Novel Ser.: Vol. 50). lib. bdg. 50.00 (ISBN 0-8240-0562-7). Garland Pub.

Secret Horse. Marion Holland. (gr. 4-6). 1976. pap. 1.50 (ISBN 0-590-03845-1, Schol Pap). Schol Bk Serv.

Secret in Miranda's Closet. Sheila Greenwald. (gr. 4-6). 1978. pap. 0.95 o.p. (ISBN 0-590-11895-1, Schol Pap). Schol Bk Serv.

Secret in the Garden. Winifred B. Newman. (Illus.). 32p. (Orig.). (gr. k-5). 1980. 5.00 (ISBN 0-87743-151-5); pap. 2.50 (ISBN 0-87743-159-0). Baha'i.

Secret Isaac. Jerome Charyn. 240p. 1980. pap. 2.75 (ISBN 0-380-47126-4, 47126). Avon.

Secret Island. S. E. Moore. LC 77-7331. (Illus.). 224p. (gr. 5 up). 1977. 8.95 (ISBN 0-590-07479-2, Four Winds). Schol Bk Serv.

Secret Journal & Other Writings. Pierre Drieu La Rochelle. Tr. by Alastair Hamilton from Fr. 1974. 13.25 (ISBN 0-86527-300-6). Fertig.

Secret Language of Animals, Communication by Pheromones. Francine Jacobs. LC 75-42409. (gr. 4-6). 1976. 6.25 (ISBN 0-688-22071-1); PLB 6.00 (ISBN 0-688-32071-6). Morrow.

Secret Language of Your Child. David Lewis. pap. 2.75 (ISBN 0-425-04547-1). Berkley Pub.

Secret Life of Animals: Pioneering Discoveries in Animal Behavior. Lorus Milne et al. LC 75-10073. 200p. 1975. 29.95 o.p. (ISBN 0-525-19932-2). Dutton.

Secret Life of Harold the Bird Watcher. Hila Colman. LC 77-11559. (Illus.). (gr. 3-6). 1978. 5.95 (ISBN 0-690-01306-X, TYC-J); PLB 7.89 (ISBN 0-690-03830-5). T y Crowell.

Secret Life of Mother Wonderful. Myra Chanin. LC 80-22904. 192p. 1980. 9.95 (ISBN 0-8253-0021-5). Beaufort Bks NY.

Secret Life of Plants. Peter Tompkins & Christopher Bird. LC 72-9160. (Illus.). 416p. 1973. 12.95 o.s.i. (ISBN 0-06-014326-6, HarpT). Har-Row.

Secret Life of the Unborn Child. Thomas Verny & John Kelly. 256p. 1981. 12.95 (ISBN 0-671-25312-3). Summit Bks.

Secret Life of the Underwater Champ. Joy Cowley. LC 80-15651. (Capers Ser.). (Illus.). 128p. (gr. 5 up). 1981. pap. 4.99 (ISBN 0-686-68782-5); pap. 1.95 (ISBN 0-394-84563-3). Knopf.

Secret Lives. Evans Chigounis. LC 74-185195. (Wesleyan Poetry Program: Vol. 60). 80p. (Orig.). 1972. 10.00x (ISBN 0-8195-2060-8, Pub. by Wesleyan U Pr); pap. 4.95 (ISBN 0-8195-1060-2). Columbia U Pr.

Secret Lives of Fishes. rev. ed. Bernard L. Gordon. (Illus.). 306p. 1980. pap. text ed. 7.95 (ISBN 0-910258-12-0). Book & Tackle.

Secret Lore of Magic. Ed. by Sayed I. Shah. 1965. Repr. of 1957 ed. text ed. 11.50x (ISBN 0-584-10250-X). Humanities.

Secret Love Story of Napoleon & Madame Walewska. Roger P. Wyndham. (Essential Knowledge Library Bk). 1979. plastic spiral bdg. 24.00 (ISBN 0-89266-169-0). Am Classical Coll Pr.

Secret Lovers. Charles McCarry. 1978. pap. 1.95 o.p. (ISBN 0-449-23549-1, Crest). Fawcett.

Secret Loving Shadows. Meg E. Atkins. 1977. pap. 1.75 o.p. (ISBN 0-685-75034-5, 345-25301-9-175). Ballantine.

Secret Memoirs & Manners of Several Persons of Quality of Both Sexes from the New Atalantis. Mary D. Manley. LC 74-170520. (Foundations of the Novel Ser.: Vol. 15). lib. bdg. 50.00 (ISBN 0-8240-0527-9). Garland Pub.

Secret Memoirs of Lord Byron. Christopher Nicole. 1978. 10.95 o.p. (ISBN 0-397-01290-X). Lippincott.

Secret Neighbors: Wildlife in a City Lot. Mary Adrian. (Illus.). (gr. 2-5). 1972. 5.95g (ISBN 0-8038-6708-5). Hastings.

Secret of Apache Canyon. Richard Telfair. 1978. pap. 1.25 o.p. (ISBN 0-449-13985-9, GM). Fawcett.

Secret of Beaver Valley. Robert B. Goodman & Robert A. Spicer. LC 73-77781. (Illus.). (gr. 1-7). 1963. 5.95 (ISBN 0-89610-017-0). Island Her.

Secret of Believing Prayer. Andrew Murray. 96p. 1980. pap. 2.50 (ISBN 0-87123-528-5, 210528). Bethany Fell.

Secret of Bourke's Mansion. Carolyn Moyer. (YA) 1977. 4.95 o.p. (ISBN 0-685-75642-4, Avalon). Bouregy.

Secret of Childhood. Maria Montessori. 1972. pap. 1.50 o.p. (ISBN 0-345-22554-6). Ballantine.

Secret of Communion with God. Matthew Henry. LC 79-93431. (Shepperd Classics Ser.). 144p. 1981. pap. 5.95 (ISBN 0-87983-245-2). Keats.

Secret of Crete. Hans G. Wunderlich. Tr. by Richard Winston. LC 74-12403. (Illus.). 320p. 1974. 8.95 o.p. (ISBN 0-02-631600-5). Macmillan.

Secret of Divine Civilization. 2nd ed. Abdu'l-Baha. Tr. by Marzieh Gail. LC 56-12427. 1970. 9.00 (ISBN 0-87743-008-X, 7-06-06). Baha'i.

Secret of Effective Prayer. Helen S. Shoemaker. 1976. pap. 1.75 (ISBN 0-89129-211-X). Jove Pubns.

Secret of Grandfather's Diary. Milton Lomask. (Illus.). (gr. 4-6). 1968. pap. 1.25 (ISBN 0-671-29797-X). PB.

Secret of Guidance. F. B. Meyer. LC 77-93177. 1978. pap. 1.95 (ISBN 0-87123-501-3, 200501). Bethany Fell.

Secret of Guidance. Frederick B. Meyer. pap. 1.50 (ISBN 0-8024-7682-1, 33-32, MG). Moody.

Secret of Harpen's Landing. Sally T. Smith. (YA) 1978. 5.95 (ISBN 0-685-86414-6, Avalon). Bouregy.

Secret of Hell's Kitchen: A Parable for Young People. Eric De Saussure. (Illus.). 112p. 1980. 8.95 (ISBN 0-8164-0460-7). Seabury.

Secret of Humor. Leonard Feinberg. 1978. pap. text ed. 23.00 (ISBN 90-6203-370-9). Humanities.

Secret of Life. Roy Masters. LC 77-9148. 1972. pap. 6.50 (ISBN 0-933900-02-3). Foun Human Under.

Secret of Madame Doll. Frances Cavanah. LC 65-26160. (Illus.). (gr. 4-7). 1965. 6.95 (ISBN 0-8149-0288-X). Vanguard.

Secret of Married Love. Anna B. Mow. 1976. pap. 1.50 (ISBN 0-89129-190-3). Jove Pubns.

Secret of MI6. Lou Smith. LC 80-83570. 240p. 1981. pap. 2.50 (ISBN 0-87216-800-X). Playboy Pbks.

Secret of Salvation. E. E. Byrum. 264p. pap. 2.50. Faith Pub Hse.

Secret of San Felipe. Peter Buck. (Mercenary Ser.: No. 2). (Orig.). 1981. pap. 1.95 (ISBN 0-451-09894-3, J9894, Sig). NAL.

Secret of Spirit Mountain. Helen K. Olson. LC 80-1014. (Illus.). (gr. 5 up). 1980. 6.95g (ISBN 0-396-07856-7). Dodd.

Secret of Stalingrad. Walter Kerr. LC 79-52759. (World War II Ser.). 272p. 1981. pap. 2.25 (ISBN 0-87216-569-8). Playboy Pbks.

Secret of Stone House Farm. Miriam Young. LC 63-15405. (Illus.). (gr. 5-7). 1966. pap. 0.60 o.p. (ISBN 0-15-679994-4, AVB48, VoyB). HarBraceJ.

Secret of Telfair Inn. Idella Bodie. LC 79-177909. (Illus.). 112p. (gr. 5-9). 1971. 3.95 o.p. (ISBN 0-87844-015-1). Sandlapper Store.

Secret of the Ages. Robert Collier. pocketbook ed. 4.00 (ISBN 0-912576-06-5); deluxe ed. 9.95 (ISBN 0-912576-07-3). R Collier.

Secret of the Andes. Ann N. Clark. (Illus.). (gr. 4-8). 1952. 8.95 (ISBN 0-670-62975-8). Viking Pr.

Secret of the Forest. (Sharazad Stories Ser.). (Illus., Arabic.). pap. 3.50 (ISBN 0-685-99206-3). Intl Bk Ctr.

Secret of the Mansion. (Trixie Belden Mystery Stories Ser.). (gr. 4 up). 1977. PLB 5.52 (ISBN 0-307-61524-3, Golden Pr); pap. 1.25 (ISBN 0-307-21524-5). Western Pub.

Secret of the Marauder Satellite. Ted White. 1978. pap. 1.75 o.p. (ISBN 0-425-03888-2, Dist. by Putnam). Berkley Pub.

Secret of the Mouse Gray Room. Tibor Varady. Tr. by Alan Duff. 1981. pap. 4.95 (ISBN 0-7145-3843-4). Riverrun NY.

Secret of the Old Bridge. Philip Weidling. (gr. 6-8). 1975. 4.95 o.p. (ISBN 0-87482-044-8). Wake-Brook.

Secret of the Old Church. Dave Holland. LC 39-1109. (Bro-Kee Ser.). (gr. 5-10). 1978. pap. 3.50 (ISBN 0-570-07763-X, 39-1109). Concordia.

Secret of the Porcelain Cats. Lila S. McGinnis. Ed. by Kathy Pacini. LC 78-15225. (Pilot Bks). (Illus.). (gr. 3-8). 1978. 6.95g (ISBN 0-8075-7288-8). A Whitman.

Secret of the Rosewood Box. Helen F. Orton. LC 37-28568. (Illus.). (gr. 4-6). 1937. 8.95 (ISBN 0-397-31596-1). Lippincott.

Secret of the Sea Legacy. Emily Raimondi. LC 73-83033. 192p. (gr. 5-8). 1974. 6.95 (ISBN 0-8149-0725-3). Vanguard.

Secret of the Seven Crows. Wylly F. St. John. (Illus.). (gr. 3-5). 1975. pap. 1.75 (ISBN 0-380-00433-X, 51763, Camelot). Avon.

Secret of the Sierra Madre: The Man Who Was B. Traven. Will Wyatt. LC 79-8570. (Illus.). 384p. 1980. 14.95 (ISBN 0-385-15600-6). Doubleday.

Secret of the Undersea Bell. John S. Douglas. LC 51-13649. (gr. 9 up). 1951. 5.95 (ISBN 0-396-03322-9). Dodd.

Secret of the Unseen Treasure. (Trixie Belden Mystery Stories Ser.). (gr. 4 up). 1977. PLB 5.52 (ISBN 0-307-61590-1, Golden Pr); pap. 1.25 (ISBN 0-307-21590-3). Western Pub.

Secret of the Witch's Stairway. (Meg Bks.). (gr. 3 up). 1978. pap. 1.25 (ISBN 0-307-21528-8, Golden Pr). Western Pub.

Secret of Thundermyer House. Ruth Burnett. (YA) 1976. 4.95 o.p. (ISBN 0-685-68912-3). Bouregy.

Secret Petrarch. Edmund J. Mills. 219p. 1980. Repr. lib. bdg. 45.00 (ISBN 0-89984-336-0). Century Bookbindery.

Secret Places. Beverley Brodsky. LC 77-16391. (Illus.). (gr. 1-3). 1979. 9.95 (ISBN 0-397-31790-5). Lippincott.

Secret Places. Robert DeMaria. (Orig.). 1980. pap. 2.25 (ISBN 0-515-05160-8). Jove Pubns.

Secret Places & Other Essays. Alison Uttley. 1972. 8.50 (ISBN 0-571-09924-6, Pub. by Faber & Faber). Merrimack Bk Serv.

Secret Raft. Hazel Krantz. LC 65-17372. (Illus.). (gr. 5-8). 1965. 6.95 (ISBN 0-8149-0343-6). Vanguard.

Secret Record: Modern Erotic Literature. Michael Perkins. LC 76-18832. 1976. 7.95 o.p. (ISBN 0-688-03121-8); pap. 4.50 (ISBN 0-688-08121-5). Morrow.

Secret Report on the Cuban Revolution. Carlos A. Montaner. Tr. by Eduardo Zayas-Bazan from Span. LC 79-66693. 292p. (Orig.). 1981. 14.95 (ISBN 0-87855-300-2); pap. 6.95 (ISBN 0-87855-720-2). Transaction Bks.

Secret Revelations of Tibetan Thangkas. Detlef-Ingo Lauf. (Illus.). 1979. 40.00 (ISBN 3-591-08025-X, Pub. by Aurum Verlag Germany). Hunter Hse.

Secret River. Marjorie K. Rawlings. (Illus.). (gr. 1-4). 1955. pap. 0.95 o.p. (ISBN 0-684-12636-2, SBF8, ScribT). Scribner.

Secret Sam Marlow: The Further Adventures of the Man with Bogart's Face. Andrew J. Fenady. 1979. 9.95 (ISBN 0-8092-5989-3). Contemp Bks.

Secret Selves. Judie Angell. LC 79-12710. (gr. 5-7). 1979. 8.95 (ISBN 0-87888-158-1). Bradbury Pr.

Secret Soldier: The Story of Deborah Sampson. Ann McGovern. LC 75-15819. (Illus.). 64p. (gr. 1-5). 1975. 5.95 (ISBN 0-590-07432-6, Four Winds). Schol Bk Serv.

Secret Strength of Depression. Frederic Flach. LC 74-3097. 1974. 7.95 o.s.i. (ISBN 0-397-01031-1). Lippincott.

Secret Summer of L. E. B. Barbara B. Wallace. LC 73-93557. (Illus.). 192p. (gr. 3-6). 1974. 5.95 o.p. (ISBN 0-695-80481-2); lib. bdg. 5.97 o.p. (ISBN 0-695-40481-4). Follett.

Secret Temple. Robert Wang. 1980. 15.00 (ISBN 0-87728-490-3); pap. 7.95 (ISBN 0-87728-518-7). Weiser.

Secret Truth About Fat People. Don Schwerdtfeger. LC 80-82369. (Illus.). 204p. Date not set. 11.95 (ISBN 0-8119-0409-1, Pegasus Rex). Fell.

Secret Valley. Clyde R. Bulla. LC 49-10917. (Illus.). (gr. 2-5). 1949. PLB 7.95 o.p. (ISBN 0-690-72383-0, TYC-J). T Y Crowell.

Secret War. Francis Russell. (World War II). 208p. 1980. 12.95 (ISBN 0-8094-2546-7). Time-Life.

Secret War of Captain Johnny Mitchell. Johnny Mitchell. LC 76-2963. 103p. 1976. 5.95 (ISBN 0-685-66076-1). Pacesetter Pr.

Secret War Report of the O.S.S. Ed. by Anthony C. Brown. pap. 1.95 o.p. (ISBN 0-425-03253-1). Berkley Pub.

Secret Wars: A Guide to Sources in English: Vol. 1, Intelligence, Propaganda & Psychological Warfare, Resistance Movements & Secret Operations, 1939-1945. Myron J. Smith, Jr. Ed. by Richard D. Burns. (War-Peace Bibliography Ser.: No. 12). 250p. 1980. 34.50 (ISBN 0-87436-271-7). ABC-Clio.

Secret Wars: A Guide to Sources in English: Vol. 2, Intelligence, Propaganda & Psychological Warfare, Covert Operations, 1945-1980. Myron J. Smith, Jr. Ed. by Richard D. Burns. (War-Peace Bibliography Ser.: No. 13). 375p. 1981. 47.00 (ISBN 0-87436-303-9). ABC Clio.

Secret Wars: A Guide to Sources in English: Vol. 3, International Terrorism, 1968 to 1980. Myron J. Smith, Jr. Ed. by Richard D. Burns. (War-Peace Bibliography Ser.: No. 14). 237p. 1980. 33.75 (ISBN 0-87436-304-7). ABC-Clio.

Secret Woman. Victoria Holt. 352p. 1981. pap. 2.50 (ISBN 0-449-23283-2, Crest). Fawcett.

Secret World of the Baby. Beth Day & H. M. Liley. (gr. 5 up). 1968. 3.95 o.p. (ISBN 0-394-81555-6). Random.

Secret Worldian Epos. Zeylmans. 1980. pap. 2.25. St George Bk Serv.

Secret Writing-Codes & Messages. Eugene Baker. (Junior Detective Bks.). (Illus.). 1980. 7.35g (ISBN 0-516-06473-8). Childrens.

Secreta Secretorum. Aristotle. Tr. by Robert Copland. LC 71-26095. (English Experience Ser.: No. 220). 72p. Repr. of 1528 ed. 11.50 (ISBN 90-221-0220-3). Walter J Johnson.

Secretarial & Administrative Practice. 3rd ed. L. Hall. (Illus.). 304p. 1978. pap. 10.95 (ISBN 0-7121-1958-2, Pub. by Macdonald & Evans England). Intl Ideas.

Secretarial Dental Assistant. Mary A. Douglas. LC 75-19522. 1976. pap. 9.20 (ISBN 0-8273-0349-1); instructor's guide 1.60 (ISBN 0-8273-0350-5). Delmar.

Secretarial Dental Assistant. Mary A. Douglas. 304p. 1981. text ed. 14.95 (ISBN 0-442-21860-5). Van Nos Reinhold.

Secretarial English. Donald A. Sheff. (gr. 9-12). 1964. pap. text ed. 4.25 (ISBN 0-88345-144-1, 17512). Regents Pub.

Secretarial Specialist. Alfred C. Pascale. LC 73-34193. (Illus.). 216p. 1968. pap. text ed. 11.25 (ISBN 0-913310-02-6). PAR Inc.

Secretariat. Pamela Barclay. LC 74-11378. (Sports Superstars Ser.). (Illus.). 32p. (gr. 3-6). 1974. PLB 5.95 (ISBN 0-87191-377-1); pap. 2.95 (ISBN 0-89812-189-2). Creative Ed.

Secretariat of the United Nations. Sydney D. Bailey. LC 78-2880. (Carnegie Endowment for International Studies: No. 11). 1978. Repr. of 1964 ed. lib. bdg. 15.17x (ISBN 0-313-20338-5, BASU). Greenwood.

Secretary of Defense. Douglas Kinnard. LC 80-5178. 256p. 1981. 19.50 (ISBN 0-8131-1434-9). U Pr of Ky.

Secretary's Manual. James H. Stroman. (Orig.). 1968. pap. 1.50 o.p. (ISBN 0-451-08976-6, W8976, Sig). NAL.

Secretary's Reference Guide. Blanche Ettinger. 1978. 5.00 o.p. (ISBN 0-89529-030-8). Avery Pub.

Secrete Correspondences of the Leaders of Governments in the Year Nineteen Forty-Four & Earlier Years. The Hungarian Historical Research Society. LC 80-65046. Orig. Title: Allamvezetok Titkos Levelei Az 1944 Ev Elotti Es Az 1944 Evbol. 110p. 1980. pap. 7.95 (ISBN 0-935484-04-3). Universe Pub Co.

Secretes of Alexis of Piemount. Alessio. Tr. by W. Warde from Fr. LC 74-28825. (English Experience Ser.: No. 707). 1975. Repr. of 1558 ed. 21.00 (ISBN 90-221-0707-8). Walter J Johnson.

Secretin, Cholecystokinin - Pancreozymin & Gastrin. Ed. by T. E. Jorpes & V. Mutt. (Handbook of Experimental Pharmacology: Vol. 34). (Illus.). 350p. 1973. 106.20 (ISBN 0-387-05952-0). Springer-Verlag.

Secreto de la Felicidad. Billy Graham. Orig. Title: The Secret of Happiness. 192p. (Span.). Date not set. pap. price not set (ISBN 0-311-04352-6). Casa Bautista.

Secreto De la Vida Cristiana. J. C. Ryle. 3.50 (ISBN 0-686-12553-3). Banner of Truth.

Secretory Diarrhea. American Physiological Society et al. (American Physiological Society Clinical Physiology Ser.). (Illus.). 700p. 1980. lib. bdg. 30.00 (ISBN 0-683-03201-1). Williams & Wilkins.

Secrets. Michael Smith. 238p. 1981. 10.95 (ISBN 0-312-70913-7). St Martin.

Secrets. Paul Tournier. Tr. by J. Embry. LC 65-13442. 1965. 4.25 (ISBN 0-8042-2165-0). John Knox.

Secrets. Paul Tournier. LC 65-13442. 1976. pap. 1.25 (ISBN 0-8042-3655-0). John Knox.

Secrets. Paul Tournier. 1976. pap. 1.25 (ISBN 0-89129-169-5). Jove Pubns.

Secrets & Surprises. Wayman & Plum. (gr. k-8). 1977. 7.95 (ISBN 0-916456-13-7, GA70). Good Apple.

Secrets for Staying Slim. Lelord Kordel. 208p. 1972. pap. 2.25 (ISBN 0-451-09220-1, E9220, Sig). NAL.

Secrets Not Shared. Aimee Martel. 1981. pap. 2.25 (ISBN 0-8439-0874-2, Leisure Bks). Nordon Pubns.

Secrets of a Corporate Headhunter. John Wareham. LC 79-55603. 1980. 10.95 (ISBN 0-689-11059-6). Atheneum.

Secrets of a Salt Marsh. John Snow. 64p. (Orig.). (gr. 4-10). pap. 5.95 (ISBN 0-930096-09-6). G Gannett.

Secrets of Alkazar: A Book of Magic. Allan Z. Kronzek. LC 80-11436. (Illus.). 128p. (gr. 7 up). 1980. 9.95 (ISBN 0-590-07425-3, Four Winds). Schol Bk Serv.

Secrets of Baitfishing. D. W. Bennett. Ed. by M. Campbell. (North East Fishing Ser.). (Illus.). 128p. 1981. pap. 4.95 (ISBN 0-88839-087-4). Hancock Hse.

Secrets of Blue Fishing. D. W. Bennett. Ed. by M. Campbell. (North East Fishing Ser.). (Illus.). 50p. (Orig.). 1981. pap. 3.95 (ISBN 0-88839-086-6). Hancock Hse.

Secrets of Chinese Karate. Ed Parker. (Funk & W Bk.). (Illus.). 1968. pap. 2.95 (ISBN 0-308-90041-3, F23, TYC-T). T Y Crowell.

Secrets of Chinese Karate. Edmund K. Parker. 1963. 8.95 (ISBN 0-13-797852-9); pap. 5.95 (ISBN 0-13-797845-6). P-H.

Secrets of Eskimo Skin Sewing. Edna Wilder. LC 76-3783. (Illus., Orig.). 1976. pap. 6.95 (ISBN 0-88240-026-6). Alaska Northwest.

Secrets of Graceful Living. Boye De Mente. 1980. pap. 4.95 (ISBN 0-914778-22-6). Phoenix Bks.

Secrets of Green Thumb Gardening. Charles W. Knight. LC 64-17301. (gr. 9 up). 1964. 6.95 (ISBN 0-8119-0154-8). Fell.

Secrets of Health & Beauty. Linda Clark. 1979. pap. 1.95 (ISBN 0-515-05077-6). Jove Pubns.

Secrets of Hidden Creek. Wylly F. St. John. 1976. pap. 1.75 (ISBN 0-380-00746-0, 51359, Camelot). Avon.

Secrets of Higher Contact. Michael X. 1969. pap. 5.95 (ISBN 0-685-20202-X). Saucerian.

Secrets of Houdini. J. C. Cannell. LC 74-10523. (Illus.). 1974. Repr. of 1931 ed. 24.00 (ISBN 0-8103-3725-8). Gale.

Secrets of Life Extension. John A. Mann. LC 80-15479. 180p. 1980. pap. 7.95 (ISBN 0-915904-47-0). And-Or Pr.

Secrets of Life Extension. John A. Mann. (Illus.). 256p. (Orig.). 1980. 12.95 (ISBN 0-936602-06-6). Harbor Pub CA.

Secrets of Mind Power. Harry Lorayne. LC 61-9267. 242p. 1961. 9.95 (ISBN 0-8119-0156-4). Fell.

Secrets of Our National Literature: Chapters in the History of the Anonymous & Pseudonymous Writings of Our Countrymen. William P. Courtney. LC 68-21761. 1968. Repr. of 1908 ed. 20.00 (ISBN 0-8103-3140-3). Gale.

Secrets of Our Spaceship Moon. Don Wilson. 1979. pap. 1.95 o.s.i. (ISBN 0-440-17847-9). Dell.

Secrets of Photographing Women. Peter Gowland. Ed. by Herbert Michelman. (Illus.). 224p. 1981. 12.95 (ISBN 0-517-54180-7, Michelman Books). Crown.

Secrets of Prayer Joy. Jeanne Hill. 64p. 1981. pap. 2.95 (ISBN 0-8170-0910-8). Judson.

Secrets of Spirulina. Ed. by C. Hills. LC 80-22087. 1980. 6.95 (ISBN 0-916438-38-4). Univ of Trees.

Secrets of Stage Hypnotism. Leonidas. LC 80-19741. 149p. 1980. Repr. of 1975 ed. lib. bdg. 9.95x (ISBN 0-89370-629-9). Borgo Pr.

Secrets of Striped Bass Fishing. D. W. Bennett. (N. E. Fishing Ser.). (Illus.). 70p. (Orig.). 1981. pap. 6.95 (ISBN 0-88839-103-X). Hancock Hse.

Secrets of the Aura. Beverly C. Jaegers. 3.00 (ISBN 0-89861-014-1). Esoteric Pubns.

Secrets of the Bermuda Triangle. Alan Landsburg. (Orig.). 1978. pap. 1.95 (ISBN 0-446-89626-8). Warner Bks.

Secrets of the Fascist Era: How Uncle Sam Obtained Some of the Top-Level Documents of Mussolini's Period. Howard M. Smyth. LC 74-31340. (Illus.). 336p. 1979. pap. 9.95 (ISBN 0-8093-0924-6). S Ill U Pr.

Secrets of the Great Magicians. Carrie Carmichael. LC 77-13297. (Myth, Magic & Superstition Ser.). (Illus.). (gr. 4-5). 1977. PLB 9.65 (ISBN 0-8172-1031-8). Raintree Pubs.

Secrets of the Gypsies. Pierre Derlon. 1977. pap. 1.75 o.p. (ISBN 0-345-25405-8). Ballantine.

Secrets of the Heart. Pearl S. Buck. LC 76-6550. (John Day Bk.). 1976. 9.95 (ISBN 0-381-98287-4, TYC-T). T Y Crowell.

Secrets of the Inner World. Sri Chinmoy. (Illus.). 54p. (Orig.). 1980. pap. 2.00 (ISBN 0-88497-499-5). Aum Pubns.

Secrets of the Lost Races. Rene Noorbergen. (Illus.). 1978. pap. 4.50 (ISBN 0-06-464025-6, CO 32, BN). Har-Row.

Secrets of the Lotus: Studies in Buddhist Meditation. Donald K. Swearer. Ed. by C. Alexandre. 1971. 6.95 o.s.i. (ISBN 0-02-615590-7); pap. 1.95 o.s.i. (ISBN 0-02-089610-7). Macmillan.

Secrets of the Past. Ed. by Reader's Digest Editors. (Orig.). 1980. pap. 2.50 (ISBN 0-425-04551-X). Berkley Pub.

Secrets of the Research Paper: An Easy Guide to Success. William Russo. 1980. pap. 1.95 (ISBN 0-931660-03-3). R Oman Pubns.

Secrets of the Samurai: A Survey of the Martial Arts of Feudal Japan. O. Ratti & A. Westbrook. LC 72-91551. 1973. 35.00 (ISBN 0-8048-0917-8). C E Tuttle.

Secrets of the SS. Glenn B. Infield. LC 80-5434. 304p. 1981. 14.95 (ISBN 0-8128-2790-2). Stein & Day.

Secrets of the Venus's Fly Trap. Jerome Wexler. LC 80-2775. (Illus.). 64p. (gr. 2-5). 1981. PLB 6.95 (ISBN 0-396-07941-5). Dodd.

Secrets of the World's Best-Selling Writer: The Storytelling Techniques of Erle Stanley Gardner. Francis L. Fugate & Roberta B. Fugate. LC 80-82544. (Illus.). 352p. 1980. 12.95 (ISBN 0-688-03701-1). Morrow.

Secrets of Tutankhamen. Leonard Cottrell. (Illus.). 1978. pap. 3.95 (ISBN 0-8467-0456-0, Pub. by Two Continents). Hippocrene Bks.

Secrets of Tut's Tomb & the Pyramids. Stephanie A. Reiff. LC 77-22770. (Great Unsolved Mysteries Ser.). (Illus.). (gr. 4-5). 1977. PLB 9.65 (ISBN 0-8172-1051-2). Raintree Pubs.

Secrets of Washington Journalists. Steve Weinberg. 1981. 12.50 (ISBN 0-87491-424-8). Acropolis.

Secrets of Winning Bridge. Jeff Rubens. 241p. 1981. pap. 4.00 (ISBN 0-486-24076-2). Dover.

Secrets, Signs, Signals & Codes. Shari Lewis. LC 79-3837. (Kids-Only Club Bks.). (Illus.). 96p. (gr. 3-6). 1980. 6.95 (ISBN 0-03-049711-6); pap. 3.95 (ISBN 0-03-049716-7). HR&W.

Sectarianism: Analyses of Religious & Non-Religious Sects. Ed. by Roy Wallis. LC 75-9715. 1975. 18.95 (ISBN 0-470-91910-8). Halsted Pr.

Sectarianism & Religious Persecution in China: A Page in the History of Religions, 2 vols. J. J. De Groot. 872p. 1972. Repr. of 1903 ed. 55.00x (ISBN 0-7165-2035-4, Pub. by Irish Academic Pr Ireland). Biblio Dist.

Section C-3, Personnel Administration & Volunteer Service. rev. ed. (Self-Study & Evaluation Guide Ser.). xii, 48p. 1980. pap. 1.50 (ISBN 0-912948-71-X). NACASBVH.

Section D-20, Curriculum Planning & Evaluation. rev. ed. (Self-Study & Evaluation Guide Ser.). 1979. pap. 1.50 (ISBN 0-912948-51-5). NACASBVH.

Section D-9, Low Vision Services. National Accreditation Council. (Self-Study & Evaluation Guide). 1981. 1.50. NACASBVH.

Section Headings for the New Testament. Ed. by R. G. Bratcher. 1961. pap. 0.85 (ISBN 0-8267-0001-2, 08505). United Bible.

Sectional Crisis & Northern Methodism: A Study in Piety, Political Ethics & Civil Religion. Donald G. Jones. LC 78-9978. 1979. lib. bdg. 16.50 (ISBN 0-8108-1175-8). Scarecrow.

Sectionalism & Representation in South Carolina. W. A. Schaper. LC 68-31582. (American Scene Ser). (Illus.). 1968. Repr. of 1901 ed. lib. bdg. 25.00 (ISBN 0-306-71158-3). Da Capo.

Sectionalism, Politics & American Diplomacy. Edward W. Chester. LC 74-30418. 1975. 15.00 (ISBN 0-8108-0787-4). Scarecrow.

Sectionalsim in American Politics, 1774-1787. Joseph L. Davis. LC 76-11310. 1977. 22.50 (ISBN 0-299-07020-4). U of Wis Pr.

Sectoral Clash & Industrialization in Latin America. Dale Story. LC 80-28553. (Latin American Foreign & Comparative Studies Program: No. 2). 1981. pap. text ed. 6.00x (ISBN 0-915984-93-8). Syracuse U Foreign Comp.

Sectoral Study of Transnational Enterprises in Latin America: The Banana Industry. Organization of American States. 1978. pap. text ed. 5.00 (ISBN 0-8270-3305-2). Span. Ed (ISBN 0-8270-3310-9). OAS.

Secular Education & the Logic of Religion: Heslington Lectures, University of York, 1966. Ninian Smart. 1969. text ed. 5.00x (ISBN 0-571-08284-X). Humanities.

Secular Humanist Declaration. Ed. by Paul Kurtz. 40p. 81. pap. 1.95 (ISBN 0-87975-149-5). Prometheus Bks.

Secular Relevance of the Church. Gayraud S. Wilmore. (Orig.). 1962. pap. 1.25 o.s.i. (ISBN 0-664-24410-6). Westminster.

Secular Ritual. Ed. by Sally F. Moore & Barbara G. Meyerhoff. 1977. text ed. 37.00x (ISBN 90-232-1457-9). Humanities.

Secular Sanctity. Edward M. Hays. LC 80-80872. 112p. (Orig.). 1980. pap. 3.50 (ISBN 0-8091-2314-2). Paulist Pr.

Secularist Heresy. Harry Blamires. 160p. 1980. pap. 4.95 (ISBN 0-89283-095-6). Servant.

Secularization of the European Mind in the Nineteenth Century. O. Chadwick. LC 77-88670. (Gifford Lectures in the University of Edinburgh Ser.: 1973-1974). 278p. 1976. 33.50 (ISBN 0-521-20892-0); pap. 9.95x (ISBN 0-521-29317-0). Cambridge U Pr.

Secure the Shadow: Lachlan McLean, Colorado Mining Photographer. Duane A. Smith & Hank Wieler. LC 80-10693. (Illus.). 100p. 1980. 13.50 (ISBN 0-918062-09-8). Colo Sch Mines.

Secured Creditors & Lessors Under the Bankrupted (Reform Act 1980) (Commercial Law & Practice Course Handbook Ser., 1980-81: Vol. 240). 1980. pap. 25.00 (ISBN 0-685-86098-1, A4-3087). PLI.

Securing an Executive Position in the Sunbelt. C. J. Basehore & Carter H. Marantette. 57p. (Orig.). 1980. pap. 5.95 (ISBN 0-939148-00-5). Exec West.

Securing Open Space for Urban America: Conservation Easements. William H. Whyte, Jr. (Illus.). 1959. pap. 4.75 (ISBN 0-87420-036-9). Urban Land.

Securing the Seas: The Soviet Naval Challenge & Western Alliance Options. Paul H. Nitz et al. (Illus.). 1979. lib. bdg. 29.50x (ISBN 0-89158-359-9); pap. text ed. 14.50x (ISBN 0-89158-360-2). Westview.

Securing U. S. Energy Supplies: The Private Sector As an Instrument of Public Policy. William G. Prast. LC 79-2978. 1981. 15.95x (ISBN 0-669-03305-7). Lexington Bks.

Securities Activities of Commercial Banks. Ed. by Arnold Sametz. LC 80-8339. 1981. write for info. (ISBN 0-669-04031-2). Lexington Bks.

Securities & Commodities Enforcement: Criminal Prosecutions & Civil Injunctions. Howard M. Friedman. LC 79-9685. 1981. price not set (ISBN 0-669-03617-X). Lexington Bks.

Securities & Federal Corporate Law, 3 vols. Harold Bloomenthal. LC 72-90956. 1972. Set. looseleaf with 1979 rev. pages 215.00 (ISBN 0-87632-086-8). Boardman.

Securities, Exchanges & the SEC. Ed. by Poyntz Tyler. (Reference Shelf Ser: Vol. 37, No. 3). 1965. 6.25 (ISBN 0-8242-0086-1). Wilson.

Securities Filings: Review & Update. (Corporate Law & Practice Course Handbook Series 1978-79: Vol. 288). 1978. pap. 20.00 (ISBN 0-685-90305-2, B4-5581). PLI.

Securities Law Handbook, 1979. Harold S. Bloomenthal. 1979. pap. 11.75 (ISBN 0-87632-273-9). Boardman.

Securities Law in Perspective. Harold S. Bloomenthal. 1977. pap. text ed. 6.95 (ISBN 0-316-09988-0). Little.

Securities Law Review Annual. Ed. by Harold S. Bloomenthal. Incl. 1976 (ISBN 0-87632-177-5); 1977 (ISBN 0-87632-178-3); 1978 (ISBN 0-87632-179-1). LC 72-96215. 47.50 ea. Boardman.

Securities Law Review: Annual. 3rd ed. Incl. 1969. Ed. by R. Alan Stotsenburg (ISBN 0-87632-041-8); 1970. Ed. by Ernest L. Folk (ISBN 0-87632-043-4); 1971. Ed. by Ernest L. Folk (ISBN 0-87632-046-9); 1972. Ed. by Ernest L. Folk (ISBN 0-87632-080-9); 1973. Ed. by Ernest L. Folk (ISBN 0-87632-092-2); 1974. Ed. by Ernest L. Folk (ISBN 0-87632-175-9); 1975. Ed. by Ernest L. Folk (ISBN 0-87632-176-7); 1978. Ed. by Harold S. Bloomenthal. 47.50 (ISBN 0-87632-179-1). 1969-1977, per. volume 42.50. Boardman.

Securities Regulation, 6 vols. 2nd ed. Louis Loss. Incl. 1969 Supplement, 3 vols. 2053p. 1969. 260.00 (ISBN 0-316-53320-3). 2199p. 1961. Little.

Securities Regulation Forms - Compliance-Practice, 3 vols. Ronald M. Shapiro et al. LC 75-17451. 1975. with 1979 suppl. 165.00 (ISBN 0-87632-194-5). Boardman.

Securities Regulation Series, 10 vols. Incl. Vol. 1. An Introduction. John T. Marlin & Peter F. Rousmaniere. 36p; Vol. 2. Certain Legal Considerations. Chadbourne et al. 129p. (Vols. 1 & 2 bound together) (ISBN 0-916450-09-0); Vol. 3. Self Regulation: Is It Working? Peter F. Rousmaniere. 148p (ISBN 0-916450-10-4); Vol. 4. Summary of Publications & Hearings. Chadbourne et al. 264p; Vol. 5. Federal Legislative Background. Chadbourne et al; Vol. 6. Four Legal Memoranda. Chadbourne et al. (Vols. 5 & 6 bound together, 122p.) (ISBN 0-916450-13-9); Vol. 7. Municipal Disclosure Standards Sourcebook. Kay Anderson. 199p (ISBN 0-916450-18-X); Vol. 8. State Laws. Chadbourne et al. 204p (ISBN 0-916450-19-8); State Level Disclosure Guidelines. Peter F. Rousmaniere. 233p (ISBN 0-916450-20-1); Vol. 10. Way Back: Toward Accountability in America's Cities. Peter F. Rousmaniere. 231p (ISBN 0-916450-21-X). 1977-80. Set. 300.00. Coun on Municipal.

Securities Regulation: Student Edition. 2nd ed. Louis Loss. 1234p. 1961. 20.00 (ISBN 0-316-53313-0). Little.

Security Against Sickness. Isidore Sydney Falk. LC 79-38822. (FDR & the Era of the New Deal Ser). 424p. 1972. Repr. of 1936 ed. lib. bdg. 37.50 (ISBN 0-306-70447-1). Da Capo.

Security Analysis & Portfolio Management. 2nd ed. Henry A. Latane et al. 1975. 24.95 (ISBN 0-8260-5256-8). Wiley.

Security & Crime Prevention. c ed. Robert L. O'Block. (Illus.). 378p. 1981. pap. text ed. 13.95 (ISBN 0-8016-3738-4). Mosby.

Security & Privacy in Computer Systems. L. J. Hoffman. LC 73-6744. 1973. 35.50 (ISBN 0-471-40611-2, Pub. by Wiley-Interscience). Wiley.

Security for Hotels, Motels, & Restaurants. Bruce H. Axler. 1974. pap. 3.95 (ISBN 0-672-96123-7). Bobbs.

Security in the Nuclear Age: Developing U.S. Strategic Arms Policy. Jerome H. Kahan. 351p. 1975. 16.95 (ISBN 0-8157-4818-3); pap. 7.95 (ISBN 0-8157-4817-5). Brookings.

Security Interests in Personal Property, 2 Vols. Grant Gilmore. 1508p. 1965. 75.00 (ISBN 0-316-31374-2). Little.

Security Investments. David L. Scott. (Illus.). 1981. 17.95x (ISBN 0-8476-6971-8). Rowman.

Security Investments. David L. Scott. (Littlefield, Adams Quality Paperbacks: No. 352). (Illus., Orig.). 1981. pap. 7.95 (ISBN 0-8226-0352-7). Littlefield.

Security Management Systems. Henry S. Ursic & LeRoy E. Pagano. (Illus.). 384p. 1974. text ed. 29.75 photocopy ed. spiral (ISBN 0-398-02972-5). C C Thomas.

Security Manual. Eric Oliver & John Wilson. 1979. text ed. 8.00x (ISBN 0-566-02116-1, Pub. by Gower Pub Co England). Renouf.

Security Manual. 3rd ed. Ed. by Eric Oliver & John Wilson. (Illus.). 1976. 7.50 o.s.i. (ISBN 0-8464-0831-7). Beekman Pubs.

Security of China. Arthur Huck. LC 72-113406. 1970. 15.00x (ISBN 0-231-03410-5); pap. 5.00x (ISBN 0-231-08636-9). Columbia U Pr.

Security of Salvation. Richard C. Nies. LC 78-17523. (Waymark Ser.). 1978. pap. 1.25 (ISBN 0-8127-0187-9). Southern Pub.

Security Problems in a Modern Society. Ed. by Sheryl Strauss. (Illus.). 314p. 1980. text ed. 9.95 (ISBN 0-409-95079-3). Butterworths.

Security Regulations in Hong Kong, Nineteen Seventy-Two to Nineteen Seventy-Seven. M. F. Higgins. 192p. 1978. 25.00x (ISBN 90-286-0948-2). Sijthoff & Noordhoff.

Security Risk Management: A Practitioners Guide to Building Security. The Mosler Anti-Crime Bureau. Ed. by Robert Rosberg. (Illus.). 192p. 1980. 10.95 (ISBN 0-916752-42-9). Dorison Hse.

Security Subjects: An Officer's Guide to Plant Protection. Thomas W. Wathen. (Illus.). 1972. pap. 6.50 o.p. (ISBN 0-398-02492-8). C C Thomas.

Security Supervision: A Handbook for Supervisors & Managers. Eugene Finneran. 300p. 1981. text ed. 19.95 (ISBN 0-409-95025-4). Butterworths.

Security Through Science & Engineering: Proceedings. Third International Conference. Ed. by R. William De Vore & J. S. Jackson. LC 80-83300. (Illus.). 1980. pap. 33.50 (ISBN 0-89779-042-1, UKYBU122); 4.50 (ISBN 0-89779-043-X). OES Pubns.

Security Work & Relief Policies. United States National Resources Planning Board. LC 72-2385. (FDR & the Era of the New Deal Ser.). 640p. 1973. Repr. of 1942 ed. lib. bdg. 65.00 (ISBN 0-306-70520-6). Da Capo.

Securtiy: Checklist for Computer Center Self-Audits. Peter S. Browne. LC 79-56012. (Illus.). 189p. 1979. pap. 35.00 (ISBN 0-88283-024-4). AFIPS Pr.

Sed Llenos del Espiritu Santo. rev. ed. John R. Stott. Tr. by David A. Cook from Eng. LC 77-162. 112p. (Orig., Span.). 1977. pap. 2.50 (ISBN 0-89922-084-3). Edit Caribe.

Sedation. Harold L. Hamburg. (Illus.). 198p. 1980. pap. 16.00 (ISBN 0-931386-07-1). Quint Pub Co.

Sedation, Local & General Anesthesia in Dentistry. 3rd ed. Niels B. Jorgensen & Jess Hayden. LC 79-20549. (Illus.). 299p. 1980. text ed. 27.50 (ISBN 0-8121-0684-9). Lea & Febiger.

Sedges: Cyperus to Scleria. Robert H. Mohlenbrock. LC 76-15267. (Illustrated Flora of Illinois Ser.). (Illus.). 208p. 1976. 22.95x (ISBN 0-8093-0604-2). S Ill U Pr.

Sedimentary Petrology & History of the Haymond Formation (Pennsylvanian), Marathon Basin, Texas. E. F. McBride. 101p. 1966. 2.50 (RI 57). Bur Econ Geology.

Sedimentary Petrology: The Origin of Sediments & Sedimentary Rocks, Part III. W. V. Engelhardt et al. Tr. by William D. Johns. LC 67-28575. 1977. 64.95 (ISBN 0-470-99142-9). Halsted Pr.

Sedimentation Engineering. Compiled by American Society of Civil Engineering. (Manual & Report on Engineering Practice Ser.: No. 54). 768p. 1975. text ed. 32.50 (ISBN 0-87262-001-8). Am Soc Civil Eng.

Sedimentation of Oblique-Slip Mobile Zones. Ed. by P. F. Ballance & H. G. Reading. (International Association of Sedimentologists & the Societ As Internationalis Limnological Symposium). 265p. 1980. pap. 37.50x (ISBN 0-470-26927-8). Halsted Pr.

Sediments & Sedimentary Rocks, Vol. 2, Pt. 1. Hans Fuchtbauer & G. Muller. LC 67-28575. (Sedimentary Petrology Ser.). (Illus.). 1974. 64.95 (ISBN 0-471-28500-5). Halsted Pr.

Seducers. Martin Shepard. 218p. 1981. Repr. of 1976 ed. 11.95 (ISBN 0-932966-12-8). Permanent Pr.

Seduction. Charlotte Lamb. (Harlequin Presents Ser.). 192p. 1981. pap. 1.50 (ISBN 0-373-10428-6, Pub. by Harlequin). PB.

Seduction & Betrayal: Women & Literature. Elizabeth Hardwick. 1974. 6.95 o.p. (ISBN 0-394-49069-X). Random.

Seduction of Lady Mattson. Dell McLaren. 1977. pap. 1.50 (ISBN 0-505-51179-7). Tower Bks.

Seduction of the Minotaur. Anais Nin. LC 61-17529. (Orig.). 1961. pap. 5.95 (ISBN 0-8040-0268-1, 28). Swallow.

Sedum of North America North of the Mexican Plateau. Ed. by Robert T. Clausen. LC 75-6084. (Illus.). 784p. 1975. 80.00x (ISBN 0-8014-0950-0). Comstock.

See America First--on Film. 1978. pap. 2.25 (ISBN 0-918734-24-X). Reymont.

See America Free. Mary VanMeer. Ed. by Leo VanMeer. LC 80-53384. (Illus.). 725p. (Orig.). 1981. pap. 6.95 (ISBN 0-937826-00-6). VanMeer Pubns.

See Dave Run. Jeannette Eyerly. (YA) (gr. 7-9). 1979. pap. 1.75 (ISBN 0-671-56031-X). PB.

See His Banners Go. Joanne Marxhausen. (Illus.). 32p. 1975. pap. 2.75 (ISBN 0-570-03702-6, 12-2604). Concordia.

See How the Winds Blows. Bob Slosser. 1980. pap. 4.95 (ISBN 0-88270-398-6). Logos.

See Inside a Galleon. Jonathan Rutland. (See Inside Bks.). (Illus.). (gr. 4-6). 1978. PLB 5.90 s&l o.p. (ISBN 0-531-09062-0). Watts.

See Inside a Roman Town. Jonathan Rutland. (See Inside Bks.). (Illus.). (gr. 4-6). 1978. PLB 5.90 s&l o.p. (ISBN 0-531-09063-9). Watts.

See Inside a Submarine. Rutland. (gr. 5 up). 1980. PLB 6.90 (ISBN 0-531-09172-4, G16). Watts.

See Inside an Airport. Joseph Rutland. (See Inside Bks.). (Illus.). (gr. 5 up). 1978. PLB 6.90 s&l (ISBN 0-531-09065-5). Watts.

See Inside an Aztec Town. Cottie Burland. (gr. 5 up). 1980. PLB 6.90 (ISBN 0-531-09173-2, G18). Watts.

See Inside an Egyptian Town. R. J. Unstead. LC 77-85159. (See Inside Bks.). (Illus.). (gr. 4-6). 1978. PLB 5.90 s&l o.p. (ISBN 0-531-09068-X). Watts.

See It Again, Sam. Carter Brown. 1979. pap. 1.50 (ISBN 0-505-51415-X). Tower Bks.

See It & Say It in French. Margarita Madrigal & Collette Dulac. (Orig.). pap. 1.75 (ISBN 0-451-08941-3, E8941, Sig). NAL.

See It & Say It in Italian. Margarita Madrigal & Giuseppina Salvadori. (Orig.). pap. 1.75 (ISBN 0-451-09399-2, E9399, Sig). NAL.

See My Garden Grow. Jane B. Moncure. LC 76-4512. (Illus.). (ps-3). 1976. 5.95 (ISBN 0-913778-38-9). Childs World.

See, Say & Write, Bk. 1. Norman Lewis. (Orig.). (gr. 6-8). 1973. 6.17 (ISBN 0-87720-346-6). AMSCO Sch.

See, Say & Write, Bk. 2. Norman Lewis. (Orig.). (gr. 7-9). 1973. 6.17 (ISBN 0-87720-348-2). AMSCO Sch.

See So That We May See: Performances & Interpretations of Traditional Tales from Tanzania. Peter Seitel. LC 79-3036. 320p. 1980. 32.50x (ISBN 0-253-15917-2); pap. 12.50x (ISBN 0-253-20242-6). Ind U Pr.

See the Kid Run. Bob Ottum. 272p. 1981. pap. 2.75 (ISBN 0-446-95123-4). Warner Bks.

See the Moon: A Glow-in-the-Dark Book. Robert Kraus. LC 80-51361. (Windmill Board Bks.). (Illus.). 8p. (ps). 1980. 3.95 (ISBN 0-671-41206-X, Pub. by Windmill). S&S.

See the Woman. Dallas Barnes. 1974. pap. 1.50 o.p. (ISBN 0-451-07768-7, W7768, Sig). NAL.

See You in Yasukuni. Gerald Hanley. 1978. pap. 1.50 (ISBN 0-505-51294-7). Tower Bks.

Seed Identification Manual. Alexander C. Martin & William D. Barkely. 1973. 22.75x (ISBN 0-520-00814-6). U of Cal Pr.

Seed Legislation. (Legislative Study: No. 16). 122p. 1981. pap. 6.75 (ISBN 92-5-100832-9, F2083, FAO). Unipub.

Seed Money: The Guggenheim Story. Milton Lomask. 1964. 6.50 o.p. (ISBN 0-374-25741-8). FS&G.

Seed of Evil. Petrina Crawford. 1976. pap. 1.25 o.p. (ISBN 0-685-73459-5, LB410, Leisure Bks). Nordon Pubns.

Seed Production. Ed. by Paul Hebblethwaite & J. Ivins. LC 80-40012. (Studies in the Agricultural & Food Sciences). 1980. text ed. 99.95 (ISBN 0-408-10621-2). Butterworths.

Seed Protein Improvement by Nuclear Techniques. (Panel Proceedings Ser). 1978. pap. 48.25 (ISBN 92-0-111078-2, ISP 479, IAEA). Unipub.

Seed Protein Improvement in Cereals & Grain Legumes, 2 vols. 1979. pap. 48.25 (ISBN 92-0-010079-1, ISP496-1, IAEA); pap. 53.50 (ISBN 92-0-010179-8, ISP496-2, IAEA). Unipub.

Seed Proteins Symposium. George E. Inglett. (Illus.). 1972. text ed. 28.00 (ISBN 0-87055-117-5). AVI.

Seed-Time & Harvest; or, During My Apprenticeship. Fritz Reuter. 292p. 1976. Repr. of 1871 ed. 15.00 (ISBN 0-86527-301-4). Fertig.

Seed to Civilization: The Story of Food. 2nd ed. Charles B. Heiser, Jr. LC 80-18208. (Illus.). 1981. text ed. 19.95x (ISBN 0-7167-1264-4); pap. text ed. 9.95x (ISBN 0-7167-1265-2). W H Freeman.

Seed to Civilization: The Story of Man's Food. Charles B. Heiser, Jr. LC 73-2949. (Biology Ser.). (Illus.). 1973. pap. text ed. 9.95x (ISBN 0-7167-0594-X). W H Freeman.

Seedling Stars. James Blish. 160p. 1972. pap. 1.25 (ISBN 0-451-06977-3, Y6977, Sig). NAL.

Seeds & Seedlings. Dorothy Diamond. LC 77-82986. (Teaching Primary Science Ser.). (Illus.). 1977. pap. text ed. 6.95 (ISBN 0-356-05072-6). Raintree Child.

Seeds & Their Uses. C. M. Duffus & J. C. Slaughter. LC 80-40283. 176p. 1980. 34.00 (ISBN 0-471-27799-1, Pub. by Wiley-Interscience); pap. write for info. (ISBN 0-471-27798-3). Wiley.

Seeds by Wind & Water. Helene J. Jordan. LC 62-12820. (Let's-Read-&-Find-Out Science Bk). (Illus.). (gr. k-3). 1962. bds. 7.95 (ISBN 0-690-72452-7, TYC-J); PLB 7.89 (ISBN 0-690-72453-5). T Y Crowell.

Seeds in the Passes: Special Issue 25 - The Smith. Robert Summers. pap. 1.00 o.p. (ISBN 0-685-78411-8). The Smith.

Seeds of Conflict. Charles DeLoach. LC 73-92247. 1974. 4.95 o.p. (ISBN 0-88270-077-4); pap. 2.95 o.p. (ISBN 0-88270-076-6). Logos.

Seeds of Dicotyledons, 2 vols. E. J. H. Corner. LC 74-14434. (Illus.). 860p. 1976. Vol. 1. 79.00 (ISBN 0-521-20688-X); Vol. 2. 115.00 (ISBN 0-521-20687-1). Cambridge U Pr.

Seeds of Discord: New Mexico in the Aftermath of the American Conquest, 1846-1861. Alvin Sunseri. LC 78-24315. 1979. 15.95 (ISBN 0-88229-141-6). Nelson-Hall.

Seeds of Discovery. W. E. B. Beveridge. (Illus.). 1981. 12.95 (ISBN 0-393-01444-4). Norton.

Seeds of Famine: Ecological Destruction & the Development Dilemma in the West African Sahel. Richard Franke & Barbara Chasin. LC 79-52471. 284p. 1980. text ed. 19.50 (ISBN 0-916672-26-3). Allanheld.

Seeds of Liberation. Ed. by Paul Goodman. 1962. 7.50 o.s.i. (ISBN 0-8076-0291-4). Braziller.

Seeds of Mideast Crisis: The United States Diplomatic Role in the Middle East During World War II. Thomas A. Bryson. LC 80-15896. 224p. 1981. lib. bdg. 15.95x (ISBN 0-89950-019-6). McFarland & Co.

Seeds of Plenty, Seeds of Want: A Critical Analysis of the Green Revolution. Andrew Pearse. 280p. 1980. 22.50 (ISBN 0-19-877150-9). Oxford U Pr.

Seeds of Progess. Leonard E. Read. 128p. 1980. 3.00 (ISBN 0-910614-65-2); pap. 1.00 (ISBN 0-910614-66-0). Foun Econ Ed.

Seeds of Rebellion. Chet Cunningham. (Patriots Bicentennial Ser.). 1977. pap. 1.75 (ISBN 0-505-51129-0). Tower Bks.

Seedtime & Harvest: A Popular Study of the Period Between the Testaments. Henry Voogd. 1977. pap. text ed. 9.50x (ISBN 0-8191-0169-9). U Pr of Amer.

Seefahrts-Worterbuch: Dictionary of Nautical Terms. 2nd ed. Werner Dietel. LC 66-56741. (Ger. Eng.). 1964. 32.00x (ISBN 3-7637-0028-5). Intl Pubns Serv.

Seeing. William P. McGivern. (Orig.). 1980. pap. 2.50 (ISBN 0-505-51493-1). Tower Bks.

Seeing & Being: The Plight of the Participant-Observer in Emerson, Jones, Adams, Faulkner. Carolyn Porter. 400p. 1981. 22.50x (ISBN 0-8195-5054-X). Wesleyan U Pr.

Seeing & Describing: Selected Descriptive Writing. Ed. by Lawrence S. Hall. (Uses of English Ser.). 1966. pap. text ed. 2.95x o.p. (ISBN 0-669-21006-4). Heath.

Seeing & Knowing. Fred I. Dretske. pap. write for info. (ISBN 0-226-16245-1). U of Chicago Pr.

Seeing Britain on a Budget. British Tourist Authority. (Illus.). 1981. pap. write for info. (ISBN 0-906318-07-6, Pub. by Auto Assn-British Tourist Authority England). Merrimack Bk Serv.

Seeing Circle: A Parable for Children Over & Under 21. Jim Ballard. LC 75-25393. (Mandala Ser. in Education). 1975. pap. 2.50 (ISBN 0-916250-07-5). Irvington.

Seeing Hand: A Treasury of Great Master Drawings. Colin Eisler. LC 74-1804. (Illus.). 224p. 1975. 37.50 o.s.i. (ISBN 0-06-011143-7, HarpT). Har-Row.

Seeing Is Not Believing. Gyles Brandreth. LC 79-91401. (Illus.). 96p. (gr. 3-12). 1980. 5.95 (ISBN 0-8069-4615-6); PLB 6.69 (ISBN 0-8069-4615-6). Sterling.

Seeing Is Perceiving. Julia Atkinson. 312p. 1978. pap. 5.00 (ISBN 0-931040-02-7). Independence Unltd.

Seeing Red. Robert J. Wolff. LC 67-24052. (Illus.). (gr. 1-5). 1967. reinforced bdg. 5.95 o.p. (ISBN 0-684-12826-8, ScribJ). Scribner.

Seeing Stick. Jane Yolen. LC 75-6946. (Illus.). (gr. k up). 1977. 8.95 (ISBN 0-690-00455-9, TYC-J); PLB 8.79 (ISBN 0-690-00596-2). T Y Crowell.

Seeing the Earth from Space. rev. ed. Irving Adler. LC 61-18218. (Illus.). (gr. 6 up). 1961. 4.95 o.p. (ISBN 0-381-99985-8, A69000, JD-J). John Day.

Seeing the Insane: A Cultural History of Psychiatric Illustration. Sander L. Gilman. (Illus.). 500p. 1981. 50.00 (ISBN 0-87630-233-9). Brunner-Mazel.

Seeing the Real Amsterdam. Eddy Debuer & Henriette Debuer. Date not set. pap. 7.95 (ISBN 0-8120-2243-2). Barron. Postponed.

Seeing the Real London. Barish & Schla. Date not set. pap. 7.95 (ISBN 0-8120-2241-6). Barron. Postponed.

Seeing the Real Moscow. Kuballa. Date not set. pap. 7.95 (ISBN 0-8120-2180-0). Barron. Postponed.

Seeing the Real New York. Amin & Mayor. 1981. pap. 7.95 (ISBN 0-8120-2242-4). Barron.

Seeing the Real Paris. Von Kardoff & Sittl. 1981. pap. 7.95 (ISBN 0-8120-2179-7). Barron.

Seeing the Real San Francisco. Gerdes. 1981. pap. 7.95 (ISBN 0-8120-2244-0). Barron.

Seeing Things. Charlotte Painter. 1976. 8.95 o.p. (ISBN 0-394-49739-2). Random.

Seeing Things. Charlotte Painter. 1981. pap. 6.95 (ISBN 0-932654-02-9). Context Pubns.

Seeing Things: A Book of Poems. Robert Froman. LC 73-18494. 64p. (gr. 5-9). 1974. 7.95 (ISBN 0-690-00291-2, TYC-J). T Y Crowell.

Seeing Through Clothes. Anne Hollander. 528p. 1980. pap. 8.95 (ISBN 0-380-48777-2, 48777-2). Avon.

Seeing with the Native Eye: Contibutions to the Study of Native American Religion. Ed. by Walter H. Capps. LC 76-9980. 1976. pap. 4.95x (ISBN 0-06-061312-2, RD-177, HarpR). Har-Row.

Seekers. John DeCenzo. LC 76-5073. (Destiny Ser.). 1977. pap. 4.95 (ISBN 0-8163-0285-5). Pacific Pr Pub Assn.

Seekers. Steven Griffin. 1978. 4.95 (ISBN 0-533-03321-7). Vantage.

Seekers, No. 3. John Jakes. (Kent Family Chronicles). (Orig.). 1979. pap. 2.75 (ISBN 0-515-05712-6). Jove Pubns.

Seeking a Faith for a New Age. Henry N. Wieman. Ed. by Cedric L. Hepler. LC 74-34052. 1975. 15.00 (ISBN 0-8108-0795-5). Scarecrow.

Seeking & Finding. Robert A. Smith. 1974. 1.75 (ISBN 0-912128-08-9). Pubns Living.

Seeking Sword. Jaan Kangilaski. 352p. (Orig.). 1981. pap. 2.25 (ISBN 0-345-29073-9, Del Rey). Ballantine.

Seeking the Competitive Dollar: College Management in the Seventies. John W. Leslie. 1971. pap. 3.00 (ISBN 0-89964-033-8). CASE.

Seeking the Elephant, Eighteen Forty-Nine: James Mason Hutchings' Journal of His Overland Trek to California. James M. Hutchings. Ed. by Shirley Sargent. LC 80-67777. (American Trail Ser.: No. XII). (Illus.). 210p. 1981. 30.00 (ISBN 0-87062-136-X). A H Clark.

Seeking Wisdom. N. Sri Ram. 1969. 3.50 (ISBN 0-8356-7194-1). Theos Pub Hse.

Seems Like Yesterday. Ann Buchwald & Art Buchwald. 1981. pap. 2.75 (ISBN 0-425-04833-0). Berkley Pub.

Seen Any Cats? Frank Modell. LC 79-11607. (Illus.). (gr. k-3). 1979. 6.95 (ISBN 0-688-80229-X); PLB 6.67 (ISBN 0-688-84229-1). Greenwillow.

Seer, the Saviour, & the Saved. rev. ed. James D. Strauss. (Bible Study Textbook Ser.). (Illus.). 1972. 13.50 (ISBN 0-89900-048-7). College Pr Pub.

Seetee. Jack Williamson. 1979. pap. 1.95 (ISBN 0-515-05150-0). Jove Pubns.

Segmented Society: An Introduction to the Meaning of America. Robert H. Wiebe. 1975. 12.95 (ISBN 0-19-501839-7). Oxford U Pr.

Segovia: An Autobiography of the Years 1893-1920. Andres Segovia. (Illus.). 1976. 14.95 (ISBN 0-02-609080-5, 60908). Macmillan.

Segregated Sabbaths: Richard Allen & the Rise of Independent Black Churches, 1760-1840. Carol V. George. 225p. 1973. 11.95 (ISBN 0-19-501678-5); pap. 3.95x (ISBN 0-19-501677-7). Oxford U Pr.

Segregation Era, Eighteen Sixty Three to Nineteen Fifty Four. Ed. by Allen Weinstein & Frank O. Gatell. (gr. 9-12). 1970. 4.95x (ISBN 0-19-500657-7); pap. 4.50x (ISBN 0-19-501099-X). Oxford U Pr.

Segregation in Residential Areas. Social Science Panel of the Advisory Committee to HUD. LC 72-85593. 256p. 1973. pap. 7.25 (ISBN 0-309-02042-5). Natl Acad Pr.

Segregationist Violence & Civil Rights Movements in Tuscaloosa. Anthony J. Blasi. LC 79-3714. 1980. text ed. 14.50 (ISBN 0-8191-0913-4); pap. text ed. 9.00 (ISBN 0-8191-0914-2). U Pr of Amer.

Segu Tukulor Empire. B. O. Oloruntimehin. (Ibadan History Ser.). (Illus.). 357p. 1972. text ed. 14.00x (ISBN 0-391-00206-6). Humanities.

Seguy's Decorative Butterflies & Insects in Full Color. E. A. Seguy. LC 77-83361. (Illus., Orig.). 1977. pap. 6.00 (ISBN 0-486-23552-1). Dover.

Seidman's Legislative History of Excess Profit Tax Laws: 1917-1946. J. Seidman. 1959. 15.00. P-H.

Seidman's Legislative History of Federal Income & Excess Profits Tax Laws: 1939-1953, 2 vols. J. Seidman. 1959. 50.00 (ISBN 0-13-799742-6). P-H.

Seidman's Legislative History of Federal Income Tax Laws: 1851-1938. J. Seidman. 25.00 (ISBN 0-13-799767-1). P-H.

Seige of Gibraltar, 1779-1783. T. H. McGuffie. (Illus.). 1965. 6.95 (ISBN 0-8023-1074-5). Dufour.

Seige of Malta Rediscovered. Donald E. Sultana. 1977. 17.50x (ISBN 0-7073-0131-9, Pub. by Scottish Academic Pr Scotland). Columbia U Pr.

Seige of Savannah: Era of the American Revolution Ser. Franklin B. Hough. LC 77-165683. 187p. 1974. Repr. of 1866 ed. lib. bdg. 20.00 (ISBN 0-306-70619-9). Da Capo.

Seiko. Olga Abrahams. Orig. Title: The Spiders Thread. 1973. pap. 1.25 (ISBN 0-85363-112-3). OMF Bks.

Seine Net: Its Origin, Evolution & Use. David Thomson. 12.00 (FN). Unipub.

Seismic Analysis & Testing of Nuclear Power Plants. (Safety Ser.: No. 50-SG-S2). 59p. 1979. pap. 9.00 (ISBN 0-686-65378-5, ISP 545, IAEA). Unipub.

Seismic Applications of Homomorphic Signal Processing. J. Tribolet. 1979. 29.00 (ISBN 0-13-779801-6). P-H.

Seismic Design for the Professional Engineering Examination. Michael R. Lindeburg. LC 80-81796. (Engineering Review Manual Ser.). (Illus.). 104p. 1980. pap. 9.50 (ISBN 0-932276-20-2). Prof Engine.

Seismology: Responsibilities & Requirements of a Growing Science. Committee on Seismology-Division of Earth Sciences. Incl. Part 1. Summary & Recommendations. o.p.; Part 2. Problems & Prospects. o.p. (ISBN 0-309-01738-6). LC 70-602511. (Illus., Orig.). 1969. Set. pap. 6.75 (ISBN 0-686-66876-6). Natl Acad Pr.

Seize the Day. Saul Bellow. 1977. pap. 1.75 (ISBN 0-380-01649-4, 33076). Avon.

Seizure. Charles L. Mee, Jr. 1979. pap. 2.25 (ISBN 0-515-05424-0). Jove Pubns.

Seizure Disorders: A Pharmacological Approach to Treatment. B. Joseph Wilder & Joseph Bruni. 1981. text ed. price not set (ISBN 0-89004-539-9). Raven.

Seizure of Territory, the Stimson Doctrine & Related Principles in Legal Theory & Diplomatic Practice. Robert Langer. Repr. of 1947 ed. lib. bdg. 18.75x (ISBN 0-8371-0907-8, LASD). Greenwood.

Sejour En France. Pierre Christin et al. LC 73-1317. (Illus.). 1975. pap. 6.95x o.p. (ISBN 0-684-14019-5, ScribC). Scribner.

Sekai Dai-Hyakka Jitten - World Encyclopedia, 33 vols. new ed. (Japanese.). 1972. 1720.00, incl. 2 vol. atlas (ISBN 0-8277-3101-9). Maxwell Sci Intl.

Selchie's Seed. Shulamith Oppenheim. LC 74-22854. (Illus.). 96p. (gr. 4-6). 1975. 7.95 o.p. (ISBN 0-87888-076-3). Bradbury Pr.

Seleccion de Romances. (Span.). 7.95 (ISBN 84-241-5619-6). E Torres & Sons.

Select Architecture. Robert Morris. LC 72-87427. (Architecture & Decorative Art Ser.). 102p. 1973. Repr. of 1757 ed. lib. bdg. 25.00 (ISBN 0-306-71573-2). Da Capo.

Select Bibliography on Economic Development: With Annotations. John P. Powelson. (Special Studies in Social, Political & Economic Development). 1979. lib. bdg. 29.50x (ISBN 0-89158-497-8). Westview.

Select Discourses. John Smith. LC 79-15690. 1979. Repr. of 1660 ed. 58.00x (ISBN 0-8201-1335-2). Schol Facsimiles.

Select Discourses. John Smith. Ed. by Rene Wellek. LC 75-11252. (British Philosophers & Theologians of the 17th & 18th Centuries Ser.). 1978. Repr. of 1660 ed. lib. bdg. 42.00 (ISBN 0-8240-1803-6). Garland Pub.

Select Documents on Japanese Foreign Policy, 1853-1868. Tr. by W. G. Beasley. 1955. 27.50x (ISBN 0-19-713508-0). Oxford U Pr.

Select Historical Documents of the Middle Ages. Ed. by Ernest F. Henderson. LC 65-15247. 1892. 10.50x (ISBN 0-8196-0149-7). Biblo.

Select Letters, 2 vols. Cicero. Ed. by W. W. How. Vol. 1. 1925 Text. 14.95x (ISBN 0-19-814403-2); Vol. 2. 1926 Notes. 24.00x (ISBN 0-19-814404-0). Oxford U Pr.

Select List of British Parliamentary Papers 1833-1899. P. Ford & G. Ford. 188p. 1969. Repr. of 1953 ed. 20.00x (ISBN 0-7165-0574-6, Pub. by Irish Academic Pr Ireland). Biblio Dist.

Select List of British Parliamentary Papers 1955-1964. P. Ford et al. 128p. 1970. 17.00x (ISBN 0-7165-0884-2, Pub. by Irish Academic Pr Ireland). Biblio Dist.

Select List of Reports of Inquiries of the Irish Dail & Senate: Fifty Years of Policy Making, 1922-72. P. Ford & G. Ford. 64p. 1974. 15.00x (ISBN 0-7165-2254-3, Pub. by Irish Academic Pr Ireland). Biblio Dist.

Selectarum Stirpium Americanarum Historia. Nicolaus J. Jacquin. 1971. Repr. of 1763 ed. 77.00 o.s.i. (ISBN 0-02-847130-X). Hafner.

Selected Abstracts on Structural Applications of Plastics. Compiled by American Society of Civil Engineers. (Manual & Report on Engineering Practices Ser.: No. 47). 80p. 1967. pap. text ed. 4.00 (ISBN 0-87262-221-5). Am Soc Civil Eng.

Selected & Annotated Bibliography of Economic Literature in the Arabic Countries of the Middle East, 2 vols. Vol. 1, 1938-1952. pap. 8.00x (ISBN 0-8156-6020-0, Am U Beirut); Vol. 2, 1953-1965. pap. 12.00x (ISBN 0-8156-6021-9). Syracuse U Pr.

Selected & Collected Poems. Bill Knott. LC 77-3473. 1977. 10.00 (ISBN 0-915342-17-0); pap. 4.00 (ISBN 0-915342-16-2). SUN.

Selected & New Poems: 1950-1980. Vassar Miller. 1980. write for info.; pap. write for info. Latitudes Pr.

Selected Annotated Bibliography for Teaching English to Speakers of Vietnamese. Compiled by Barbara Robson & Kenton Sutherland. LC 75-24859. (Vietnamese Refugee Education Ser.: No. 4). 1975. pap. text ed. 2.50x (ISBN 0-87281-046-1). Ctr Appl Ling.

Selected Annotated Bibliography of Works on Western European Building Conservation, Housing, & Inner Cities. Robin E. Datel. (Architecture Ser.: Bibliography: A-396). 51p. 1980. pap. 7.50. Vance Biblios.

Selected Annotated Bibliography on Breast Feeding 1970-1977. Food & Nutrition Board, National Research Council. 1978. pap. text ed. 6.50 (ISBN 0-309-02796-9). Natl Acad Pr.

Selected Annotated Bibliography on New Town Planning & Development. Melville C. Branch & Eliane G. Mazza. (Architecture Ser.: Bibliography a-216). 133p. 1980. pap. 14.00. Vance Biblios.

Selected Antitrust Cases: Landmark Decisions. 6th ed. Irwin M. Stelzer. 1981. pap. text ed. 12.95x (ISBN 0-256-02339-5). Irwin.

Selected Articles by Harry Gunnison Brown: The Case for Land Value Taxation. Harry G. Brown. 320p. 1980. 12.50x (ISBN 0-911312-50-1). Schalkenbach.

Selected Bibliography of American Constitutional History. Ed. by Stephen M. Millett. LC 75-8677. 116p. 1975. 4.50 (ISBN 0-87436-204-0). ABC-Clio.

Selected Bibliography of German Literature in English Translation, 1956-1960: A Second Supplement to Bayard Quincy Morgan's - A Critical Bibliography of German Literature in English Translation. Murray F. Smith. LC 76-157727. 1972. 14.50 (ISBN 0-8108-0411-5). Scarecrow.

Selected Bibliography of Minnesota Government, Politics, & Public Finance Since 1900. G. Theodore Mitau. (Studies in Minn. Govt. & Politics). 94p. 1960. pap. 2.50 (ISBN 0-685-47099-7). Minn Hist.

Selected Bibliography of Natal Maps. C. E. Merrett. 1979. lib. bdg. 42.50 (ISBN 0-8161-8276-0). G K Hall.

Selected Bibliography of Socio-Economic Development of Japan: Part B Sixteen Hundred to Nineteen Forty. 156p. 1980. pap. 5.00 (ISBN 92-808-0199-6, TUNU094, UNU). Unipub.

Selected Bibliography of Special Education. I. Ignacy Goldberg. LC 67-19388. (Orig.). 1967. pap. 3.25x (ISBN 0-8077-1434-8). Tchrs Coll.

Selected Bibliography on Pelagic Fish Egg & Larva Surveys. (FAO Fisheries Circular: No. 706). 97p. 1980. pap. 6.00 (ISBN 0-686-68187-8, F2023, FAO). Unipub.

Selected Bibliography on Political Economy of Iran. Ali-Akbar Mahdi. (Public Administration Ser.: Bibliography P-598). 104p. 1980. pap. 15.25. Vance Biblios.

Selected Botanical Papers. Irving W. Knobloch. (Illus.). 1963. pap. text ed. 11.95 (ISBN 0-13-800300-9). P-H.

Selected Case Studies in American History, 2 vols. new ed. William E. Gardner et al. (gr. 8-12). 1975. Vol. 1. pap. text ed. 5.40 (ISBN 0-205-04902-8, 7849028); Vol. 2. pap. text ed. 5.20 (ISBN 0-205-03771-2, 7837712); Tchrs.' Guide. Vol. 1. 2.40 (ISBN 0-205-02165-4, 7821654); Tchrs.' Guide. Vol. 2. 2.40 (ISBN 0-205-03772-0, 7837720). Allyn.

Selected Cases in Fashion Marketing, 2 vols. 3rd ed. Nathan Axelrod. 1968. pap. 11.00 ea.; Vol. 1. pap. (ISBN 0-672-96037-0); Vol. 2. pap. (ISBN 0-672-96038-9). Bobbs.

Selected Cases on the Law of Shoplifting. Sherman E. Fein & Arthur M. Maskell. 92p. 1975. 11.50 (ISBN 0-398-03354-4); pap. 8.50 (ISBN 0-398-03355-2). C C Thomas.

Selected Community Hospital Indicators: 1977 Data. American Hospital Association. LC 79-665. (Illus.). 1979. pap. 7.50 o.p. (ISBN 0-87258-275-2, 1893). Am Hospital.

Selected Community Hospital Indicators: 1976 Data. American Hospital Association. LC 78-22110. (Illus.). 1978. pap. 6.25 o.p. (ISBN 0-87258-232-9, 1892). Am Hospital.

Selected Contributions to Marketing Thought: An Annotated Bibliography. Larry M. Robinson & Roy D. Adler. (Research Monographs: No. 91). 150p. 1981. pap. 9.95 (ISBN 0-88406-142-6). Ga St U Busn Pub.

Selected Correspondence of Michael Faraday, 2 Vols. Leslie P. Williams. LC 77-138377. (Illus.). 1971. Set. 150.00 (ISBN 0-521-07475-4). Cambridge U Pr.

Selected Critical Writings, 2 Vols. George Santayana. Ed. by Norman Henfrey. (Orig.). 1968. Vol. 1. 42.00 (ISBN 0-521-07103-8); Vol. 2. 35.50 o.p. (ISBN 0-521-07104-6); Vol. 1. pap. 13.95 (ISBN 0-521-09463-1); Vol. 2. pap. 10.50 (ISBN 0-521-09464-X). Cambridge U Pr.

Selected Directory of Business Contacts in the Arab World. 1978. 20.00 o.s.i. (ISBN 0-916400-04-2). Inter-Crescent.

Selected Documents from the Aligarh Archives. Ed. by Yusuf Husain. 1967. 10.00x o.p. (ISBN 0-210-98101-6). Asia.

Selected Documents of the International Petroleum Industry: Saudi Arabia, pre-1966. 1976. 23.50x (ISBN 0-8002-0005-5). Intl Pubns Serv.

Selected Documents of the International Petroleum Industry: Socialist Peoples, Libyan Arab Jamahiriya & Quatar, Pre-1966. LC 79-311061. 1977. 23.50x (ISBN 0-8002-0006-3). Intl Pubns Serv.

Selected Documents of the International Petroleum Industry: 1967. Ed. by Nameer A. Jawdat. 1968. 32.50x (ISBN 0-8002-0003-9). Intl Pubns Serv.

Selected Documents of the International Petroleum Industry: 1974. 1976. 23.50x (ISBN 0-8002-0004-7). Intl Pubns Serv.

Selected Documents on International Environmental Law. British Institute of International & Comparative Law. 1977. 15.00 (ISBN 0-379-00348-1). Oceana.

Selected Drawings by Chinese Children. 1979. 3.95 (ISBN 0-8351-0666-7). China Bks.

Selected Drawings of Claude Lorrain. Marco Chiarini. (Illus.). 188p. 1969. 125.00x o.p. (ISBN 0-271-00077-5). Pa Hist & Mus.

Selected Economic Essays & Addresses. Sir Arnold Plant. Ed. by Arthur Seldon. 260p. 1974. 26.00 (ISBN 0-7100-7935-4). Routledge & Kegan.

Selected English Letters: Fifteen to Nineteen Centuries. anthology ed. 460p. 1980. Repr. of 1913 ed. lib. bdg. 12.50 (ISBN 0-8495-1060-0). Arden Lib.

Selected English Letters: Fifteenth to Nineteenth Centuries. M. Duckitt & H. Wragg. 599p. 1981. Repr. of 1941 ed. lib. bdg. 20.00 (ISBN 0-89987-158-5). Darby Bks.

Selected Essays. Hugo Von Hofmannsthal. Ed. by Mary E. Gilbert. (Blackwell's German Text Ser.). 1955. pap. 5.00x o.p. (ISBN 0-631-01600-7, Pub. by Basil Blackwell). Biblio Dist.

Selected Essays. G. Hough. LC 77-85692. 1978. 32.50 (ISBN 0-521-21901-9). Cambridge U Pr.

Selected Essays from the Tatler, the Spectator, & the Guardian. Joseph Addison & Richard Steele. Ed. by Daniel McDonald. LC 73-179472. (Library of Literature Ser: No. 15). 1973. pap. 5.95 (ISBN 0-672-60990-8). Bobbs.

Selected Essays in Chinese Economic Development. Ed. by Ramon H. Myers. LC 78-74360. (Modern Chinese Economy Ser.). 251p. 1980. 33.00 (ISBN 0-8240-4277-8). Garland Pub.

Selected Essays of Fredrik Barth: Process & Form in Social Life. Fredrik Barth. (International Library of Anthropology). 1981. 35.00 (ISBN 0-7100-0720-5). Routledge & Kegan.

Selected Essays of Lou Andreas-Salome. Lou Andreas-Salome. Ed. by Rudolph Binion. 500p. (Orig.). 1981. price not set (ISBN 0-937406-15-5); pap. price not set (ISBN 0-937406-14-7); price not set limited ed. (ISBN 0-937406-16-3). Logbridge-Rhodes.

Selected Essays on Employment & Growth. Richard Kahn. LC 78-187079. 240p. 1972. 35.50 (ISBN 0-521-08493-8). Cambridge U Pr.

Selected Essays on Rhetoric. Thomas De Quincey. Ed. by Frederick Burwick. LC 67-21038. (Landmarks in Rhetoric & Public Address Ser.). 329p. 1967. 11.95x (ISBN 0-8093-0262-4). S Ill U Pr.

Selected Essays on the Economic Growth of the Socialist & Mixed Economy, Vol. 2. Michael Kalecki. LC 73-179162. (Illus.). 188p. 1972. 29.50 (ISBN 0-521-08447-4). Cambridge U Pr.

Selected Exercises from Microbes in Action: A Laboratory Manual of Microbiology. 2nd ed. Harry W. Seeley, Jr. & Paul J. Van Demark. (Illus.). 1972. lab manual 8.95x (ISBN 0-7167-0690-3); teacher's manual avail. W H Freeman.

Selected Exercises from Microbes in Action: A Laboratory Manual of Microbiology. 3rd ed. Harry W. Seeley, Jr & Paul J. VanDemark. (Illus.). 1981. price not set (ISBN 0-7167-1260-1). W H Freeman.

Selected Exercises in Galactic Astronomy. I. Atanasijevic. LC 73-159652. (Astrophysics & Space Science Library: Vol. 26). (Illus.). 156p. 1972. 12.80 o.p. (ISBN 0-387-91087-5). Springer-Verlag.

Selected Exercises Upon Geological Maps. John Platt. 1974. pap. text ed. 3.25x (ISBN 0-04-550021-5). Allen Unwin.

Selected Experiments in Organic Chemistry. 2nd ed. George K. Helmkamp & Harry Johnson, Jr. (Illus.). 1968. lab manual 9.95x (ISBN 0-7167-0138-3); teacher's manual avail. (ISBN 0-685-00895-9); indiv. experiments 0.50 ea. W H Freeman.

Selected Flowers of Evil. rev. ed. Charles Baudelaire. Ed. by Marthiel Mathews & Jackson Mathews. LC 58-9276. (Eng & Fr). 1946. pap. 2.95 (ISBN 0-8112-0006-X, NDP71). New Directions.

Selected Free Materials for Classroom Teachers. 6th ed. Ruth H. Aubrey. LC 77-90627. 1978. pap. 5.50 (ISBN 0-8224-6560-4). Pitman Learning.

Selected Games from the Carlsbad International Chess Tournament 1929. Aron Nimzovich. Tr. by Jim Marfia from Rus. 143p. (Orig.). 1981. pap. price not set (ISBN 0-486-24115-7). Dover.

Selected Games Nineteen Sixty-Seven to Nineteen Seventy. M. M. Botvinnik. Tr. by K. P. Neat. (Pergamon Russian Chess Ser.). (Illus.). 150p. 1981. 29.00 (ISBN 0-08-024124-7); pap. 13.95 (ISBN 0-08-024123-9). Pergamon.

Selected Games: 1967-1970. M. M. Botvinnik. LC 80-40181. (Pergamon Russian Chess Ser.). (Illus.). 318p. 1981. 29.00 (ISBN 0-08-024124-7); pap. 13.95 (ISBN 0-08-024123-9). Pergamon.

Selected German Ballads. Ed. by George A. Scherer. (Heath Visible Vocabulary German Ser). 1951. pap. text ed. 1.95x o.p. (ISBN 0-669-29728-3). Heath.

Selected Guide to Anthropological Bibliographies. Ed. by Yvonne M. Damien & Margo L. Smith. 1981. write for info. (ISBN 0-913178-63-2). Redgrave Pub Co.

Selected Handicrafts from the Collections of the Palace Museum. (Illus.). 1974. 35.00 (ISBN 0-8351-0320-X). China Bks.

Selected Highland Folktales. R. Macdonald Robertson. 1977. 11.95 (ISBN 0-7153-7436-2). David & Charles.

Selected Histochemical & Histopathological Methods. Samuel W. Thompson. (Illus.). 1680p. 1974. text ed. 90.50 (ISBN 0-398-03132-0). C C Thomas.

Selected Historical Essays. Frederic W. Maitland. Ed. by H. M. Cam. 1957. 41.50 (ISBN 0-521-05659-4). Cambridge U Pr.

Selected Issues in Health Policies in Africa & Latin America. Ed. by T. Bossert & D. Dunlop. 82p. 1981. 17.50 (ISBN 0-08-024723-7). Pergamon.

Selected Issues in Mathematics Education. Ed. by Mary M. Lindquist. LC 80-82903. 250p. 1981. write for info (ISBN 0-8211-1114-0); text ed. write for info. McCutchan.

Selected Later Poems of Marie Luise Kaschnitz. Mary L. Kaschnitz. LC 80-7537. (Lockert Library of Poetry Translation). 128p. 1980. 9.95 (ISBN 0-691-06442-3); pap. 4.95 (ISBN 0-691-01374-8). Princeton U Pr.

Selected Legal Documents of the People's Republic of China. Ed. by Joseph E. Wang. LC 76-5167. (Studies in Chinese Government & Law). 564p. 1979. 32.50 (ISBN 0-89093-067-8). U Pubns Amer.

Selected Legal Documents of the People's Republic of China: Volume II. Ed. by Joseph E. Wang. LC 76-5167. (Studies in Chinese Government & Law). 564p. 1979. 32.50 (ISBN 0-89093-241-7). U Pubns Amer.

Selected Letters of Gordon Holmes. Gordon Holmes. Ed. by C. G. Phillips. (Illus.). 500p. 1979. text ed. 53.00 (ISBN 0-19-920105-6). Oxford U Pr.

Selected Letters of John Keats. Ed. by Robert Park. pap. 1.95 (ISBN 0-451-50697-9, CJ697, Sig Classics). NAL.

Selected Letters of Oscar Wilde. Oscar Wilde. Ed. by Rupert Hart-Davis. 1979. 19.95 (ISBN 0-19-212205-3). Oxford U Pr.

Selected Letters of Voltaire. Ed. by Richard A. Brooks. LC 72-96429. 349p. 1973. 18.50x (ISBN 0-8147-0972-9). NYU Pr.

Selected Letters of W. D. Howells, Vol. III. Ed. by Robert C. Leitz et al. (Critical Editions Program Ser.). 1980. lib. bdg. 27.50 (ISBN 0-8057-8529-9). Twayne.

Selected Letters of W. D. Howells: 1852-1872, Vol. 1. W. D. Howells. Ed. by George Arms et al. (Critical Editions Programs Ser.). 1979. lib. bdg. 30.00 (ISBN 0-8057-8527-2). Twayne.

Selected Letters of W. D. Howells, 1892-1901, Vol. 4. Ed. by Thomas Wortham et al. (Critical Editions Program Ser.). 1981. lib. bdg. 30.00 (ISBN 0-8057-8530-2). Twayne.

Selected Literary Criticism. Ed. by Morris Shapira. 374p. 1981. pap. 7.95 o.p. (ISBN 0-8180-1130-0). Horizon.

Selected Literary Criticism of Edwin Muir. Ed. by Andrew Noble. (Barnes & Noble Critical Studies). 208p. 1981. 27.50x (ISBN 0-389-20202-9). B&N.

Selected Literary Essays. Clive S. Lewis. Ed. by Walter Hooper. LC 74-85724. 1969. 42.00 (ISBN 0-521-07441-X); pap. 8.95 (ISBN 0-521-29680-3). Cambridge U Pr.

Selected Love Poems. Michael J. Phillips. 120p. 1980. 18.50 (ISBN 0-915144-87-5); pap. 6.95 (ISBN 0-915144-88-3). Hackett Pub.

Selected Lower-Limb Anomalies. Committee On Prosthetics Research And Development. LC 76-611159. 1971. pap. text ed. 3.50 (ISBN 0-309-01915-X). Natl Acad Pr.

Selected Lyrics: Nineteen Fifty to Nineteen Eighty. Jerry Leiber. 1981. 12.95 (ISBN 0-89396-015-2); pap. 5.95 (ISBN 0-89396-016-0). Urizen Bks.

Selected Mark Twain-Howells Letters. Mark Twain & William D. Howells. Ed. by Frederick Anderson et al. LC 67-13251. 1968. pap. 5.95 (ISBN 0-689-70004-0, 114). Atheneum.

Selected Mathematicae Papers of Axel Thue. Ed. by Trygve Nagell et al. 1977. 40.00x (ISBN 82-00-01649-8, Dist. by Columbia U Pr). Universitet.

Selected Messages, Vol. III. Ellen G. White. 1980. Christian Home Library Ed. 5.95 (ISBN 0-8280-0055-7, 19275-7); Shield Ser. Ed. 4.50 (ISBN 0-8280-0056-5, 19276-5); Special Ed. pap. 2.95 (ISBN 0-8280-0057-3, 19277-3). Review & Herald.

Selected Messages, 3 vols. Ellen G. White. 1980. Set. pap. 7.95 (ISBN 0-8280-0059-X, 19269-0). Review & Herald.

Selected Methods for the Small Clinical Chemistry Laboratory. Ed. by Willard R. Faulkner & Samuel Meites. LC 80-66528. (Selected Methods of Clinical Chemistry Ser.: Vol. 9). 450p. 1981. 31.95 (ISBN 0-915274-13-2). Am Assn Clinical Chem.

Selected Methods in Cellular Immunology. Ed. by Barbara B. Mishell & Stanley M. Shiigi. LC 79-19990. (Illus.). 1980. text ed. 31.95x (ISBN 0-7167-1106-0). W H Freeman.

Selected Military Writings, 1928-1949. Mao Tse-Tung. 1967-1968. 6.95 (ISBN 0-8351-0321-8); red plastic 3.95 (ISBN 0-8351-0323-4); pap. 4.95 (ISBN 0-8351-0322-6). China Bks.

Selected Numerical Methods & Computer Programs for Chemical Engineers. Huan-Yang Chang & Ira Earl Over. 235p. (Orig.). 1981. pap. text ed. 11.95 (ISBN 0-88408-131-1). Sterling Swift.

Selected Paintings & Sculptures from the Yale University Art Gallery. Intro. by Andrew C. Ritchie. LC 76-179475. (University Ser.: No. 2). (Illus.). 380p. 1972. 25.00x o.p. (ISBN 0-300-01562-3). Yale U Pr.

Selected Paintings of Cheng Shan-Shi. Cheng Shan-Hse. 220p. 1980. 39.95 (ISBN 0-89955-140-8, Pub. by Art Bk Co Taiwan). Intl Schol Bk Serv.

Selected Paintings of the Historical Gallery, Budapest. Gyorgy Rozsa. Tr. by Lili Halapy from Hungarian. LC 78-369118. (Treasures of the Hungarian National Museum Ser.). (Illus.). 1977. 13.50x (ISBN 963-13-0081-1). Intl Pubns Serv.

Selected Papers. Solomon Lefschetz. LC 73-113137. 1971. text ed. 27.50 (ISBN 0-8284-0234-5). Chelsea Pub.

Selected Papers. M. Morse. (Illus.). 710p. 1981. 35.00 (ISBN 0-387-90532-4). Springer-Verlag.

Selected Papers, Vol. 3. International Congress on Child Abuse & Neglect, 2nd, London, 1978. Ed. by C. H. Kempe et al. 1100p. 1980. 125.00 (ISBN 0-08-023430-5). Pergamon.

Selected Papers by Alfred M. Freudenthal. Compiled by American Society of Civil Engineers. 816p. 1981. pap. text ed. 54.00 (ISBN 0-87262-263-0). Am Soc Civil Eng.

Selected Papers in Digital Signal Processing II. Digital Signal Processing Committee (IEEE) (IEEE Press Selected Reprint Ser.). 582p. 1976. 21.95 (ISBN 0-471-01519-9). Wiley.

Selected Papers in Digital Signal Processing, II. Ed. by Digital Signal Processing Committee. LC 75-22925. 1976. 21.95 (ISBN 0-87942-059-6). Inst Electrical.

Selected Papers in Digital Signal Processing. LC 75-22925. (IEEE Press Selected Reprint Ser.). 582p. 1976. 21.95 (ISBN 0-471-01519-9, Pub. by Wiley-Interscience). Wiley.

Selected Papers in Inhalation Therapy. Ed. by Thomas J. DeKornfeld. 416p. 1971. spiral bdg. 12.00 o.p. (ISBN 0-87488-523-X). Med Exam.

Selected Papers in Respiratory Therapy. 2nd ed. Ed. by Thomas J. Dekornfeld. 1979. pap. 24.00 (ISBN 0-87488-525-6). Med Exam.

Selected Papers in Structural Linguistics. Bohumil Trnka. (Janua Linguarum, Ser. Major: No. 88). 1980. text ed. 37.50x (ISBN 90-279-3148-8). Mouton.

Selected Papers of E. S. Pearson. 327p. 1966. 25.00x (ISBN 0-85264-705-0, Pub. by Griffin England). State Mutual Bk.

Selected Papers of Homer Cummings. Ed. by Carl B. Swisher. LC 79-168392. (FDR & the Era of the New Deal Ser.). (Illus.). 1972. Repr. of 1939 ed. lib. bdg. 32.50 (ISBN 0-306-70329-7). Da Capo.

Selected Papers of Jerzy Neyman & E. S. Pearson, 3 vols. Jerzy Neyman & E. S. Pearson. Incl. Vol. 1. The Selected Papers of E. S. Pearson. 1966. 17.00 o.p. (ISBN 0-520-00990-8); Vol. 2. Joint Statistical Papers. 1967. 25.00x (ISBN 0-520-00991-6); Vol. 3. A Selection of Early Statistical Papers of J. Neyman. 1967. 28.50x (ISBN 0-520-00992-4). U of Cal Pr.

Selected Papers of Richard von Mises, 2 vols. Ed. by P. Frank et al. (Illus.). Vol. 1 (Geometry, Mechanics, Analysis) 19.60 o.p. (ISBN 0-8218-0043-4, VM-1); Vol. 1, 1963. 17.20 o.p. (ISBN 0-8218-0044-2, VM-2). Am Math.

Selected Papers of the Commission on Education for Health Administration, Vol. 2. Commission on Education for Health Administration. LC 74-17537. 350p. 1975. 12.50 (ISBN 0-914904-05-1). Health Admin Pr.

Selected Papers on Human Factors in the Design & Use of Control Systems. Ed. by H. Wallace Sinaiko. (Illus., Orig.). 1961. pap. text ed. 6.00 (ISBN 0-486-60140-4). Dover.

Selected Papers on New Techniques for Energy Conversion. Ed. by Sumner N. Levine. pap. text ed. 6.00 (ISBN 0-486-60037-8). Dover.

Selected Papers on Nuclear Pharmacy. 1976. 12.00 (ISBN 0-917330-07-2). Am Pharm Assn.

Selected Papers on Philosophy. William James. 1917. 5.00x o.p. (ISBN 0-460-00739-4, Evman). Dutton.

Selected Papers on Physical Processes in Ionized Plasmas. Ed. by Donald H. Menzel. (Orig.). 1962. pap. text ed. 5.00 (ISBN 0-486-60060-2). Dover.

Selected Papers on Quantum Electrodynamics. Ed. by Julian Schwinger. 1958. pap. text ed. 6.00 (ISBN 0-486-60444-6). Dover.

Selected Papers on the Subfossil Lemurs of Madagascar: 1934-1956. Charles Lamberton. LC 78-72726. 1980. 67.50 (ISBN 0-404-18297-6). AMS Pr.

Selected Philisophical Works. Vissarion G. Belinskii. LC 79-2893. li, 552p. 1981. Repr. of 1948 ed. 37.50 (ISBN 0-8305-0061-8). Hyperion Conn.

Selected Philosophical Essays. Nikolai G. Chernyshevskii. LC 79-2896. 610p. 1981. Repr. of 1953 ed. 37.50 (ISBN 0-8305-0064-2). Hyperion Conn.

Selected Philosophical Essays. Nikolai A. Dobroliubov. Tr. by J. Finberg. LC 79-2899. 659p. 1981. Repr. of 1956 ed. 42.50 (ISBN 0-8305-0070-7). Hyperion Conn.

Selected Philosophical, Social, & Political Essays. Dimitri I. Pisarev. Tr. by R. Dixon & J. Katzer. LC 79-2919. (Illus.). 711p. 1981. Repr. of 1958 ed. 45.00 (ISBN 0-8305-0089-8). Hyperion Conn.

Selected Piano Music. Clara Schumann. (Music Reprint Ser.). 1979. Repr. of 1846 ed. lib. bdg. 18.95 (ISBN 0-306-79554-X). Da Capo.

Selected Plays. Francis Beaumont & John Fletcher. 1953. 6.00x o.p. (ISBN 0-460-00506-5, Evman). Dutton.

Selected Plays. Frank O'Hara. LC 78-9658. 1978. 14.95 (ISBN 0-916190-08-0); pap. 6.00 (ISBN 0-916190-09-9). Full Court NY.

Selected Plays. John Webster & John Ford. 1953. 6.00x (ISBN 0-460-00899-4, Evman); pap. 3.50 (ISBN 0-460-01899-X). Dutton.

Selected Plays: Bernard Shaw. Bernard Shaw. 900p. 1981. 19.95 (ISBN 0-396-07905-9). Dodd.

Selected Plays of Philip Massinger. Ed. by C. Gibson. LC 77-80835. (Plays by Renaissance & Restoration Dramatists Ser.). 1978. 47.50 (ISBN 0-521-21728-8); pap. 10.50x (ISBN 0-521-29243-3). Cambridge U Pr.

Selected Plays of Thomas Middleton. Ed. by D. L. Frost. LC 77-23339. (Plays by Renaissance & Restoration Dramatists Ser.). 1978. 47.50 (ISBN 0-521-21698-2); 11.50x (ISBN 0-521-29236-0). Cambridge U Pr.

Selected Poems. Mirella Aquila. 64p. (Orig.). 1981. pap. 5.00 (ISBN 0-682-49666-9). Exposition.

Selected Poems. W. H. Auden. Ed. by Edward Mendelson. LC 78-55719. 1979. pap. 5.95 (ISBN 0-394-72506-9, V-506, Vin). Random.

Selected Poems. William Blake. Ed. by Stanley Gardner. 1973. pap. 3.75 (ISBN 0-340-08199-6). Dufour.

Selected Poems. Alain Bosquet. Tr. by Samuel Beckett et al from Fr. & Eng. LC 71-181687. 189p. 1972. 10.00 (ISBN 0-8214-0111-4); pap. 5.95 (ISBN 0-8214-0112-2). Ohio U Pr.

Selected Poems. George G. Byron. (World's Classics Ser.). 5.95 o.p. (ISBN 0-19-250180-1). Oxford U Pr.

Selected Poems. John Clare. Ed. by S. W. Hibble. 1965. 6.00x (ISBN 0-460-00563-4, Evman); pap. 7.95 (ISBN 0-460-01563-X). Dutton.

Selected Poems. Walter De La Mare. 1973. pap. 5.95 (ISBN 0-571-10401-0, Pub. by Faber & Faber). Merrimack Bk Serv.

Selected Poems. Pierre De Ronsard. Ed. by Christine M. Scollen. 192p. 1974. text ed. 13.00x (ISBN 0-485-13807-7, Athlone Pr); pap. text ed. 6.25x (ISBN 0-485-12807-1, Athlone Pr). Humanities.

Selected Poems. Bishnu Dey. Ed. by Samir Dasgupta. (Writers Workshop Saffronbird Ser). 1975. 12.00 (ISBN 0-88253-626-5); pap. text ed. 4.80 (ISBN 0-88253-625-7). Ind-US Inc.

Selected Poems. T. S. Eliot. LC 67-23064. (gr. 7-12). 1967. pap. 1.75 (ISBN 0-15-680647-9, HPL21, HPL). HarBraceJ.

Selected Poems. Lincoln Fitzell. 88p. 1955. 4.95 (ISBN 0-8040-0269-X). Swallow.

Selected Poems. M. Ghose. 8.00 (ISBN 0-89253-546-6); flexible cloth 4.00 (ISBN 0-89253-547-4). Ind-US Inc.

Selected Poems. Thom Gunn & Ted Hughes. 1962. pap. 3.95 (ISBN 0-571-05019-0, Pub. by Faber & Faber). Merrimack Bk Serv.

Selected Poems. Daryl Hine. LC 80-68135. 144p. 1981. 10.95 (ISBN 0-689-11117-7); pap. 6.95 (ISBN 0-689-11118-5). Atheneum.

Selected Poems. Donald Justice. LC 79-52416. 1979. 10.95 (ISBN 0-689-11016-2); pap. 6.95 (ISBN 0-689-11020-0). Atheneum.

Selected Poems. Henriqueta Lisboa. 119p. 1980. Repr. of 1978 ed. lib. bdg. 20.00 (ISBN 0-8414-5761-1). Folcroft.

Selected Poems. Federico Garcia Lorca. Ed. by Donald M. Allen. LC 54-9872. (Span. & Eng., Cloth 1955; pap 1968). pap. 3.95 (ISBN 0-8112-0091-4, NDP114). New Directions.

Selected Poems. Louis MacNeice. Ed. by Auden. (Orig.). 1964. pap. 5.95 (ISBN 0-571-06089-7, Pub. by Faber & Faber). Merrimack Bk Serv.

Selected Poems. John Masefield. 1978. 14.95 (ISBN 0-02-581010-3). Macmillan.

Selected Poems. Czeslaw Milosz. LC 73-6424. 144p. 1973. 8.95 (ISBN 0-8264-0049-3). Continuum.

Selected Poems. rev. ed. Czeslaw Milosz. LC 80-21470. 129p. 1981. pap. 8.95 (ISBN 0-912946-76-8). Ecco Pr.

Selected Poems. Bob Moates. 3.50 o.p. (ISBN 0-685-48831-4). Nortex Pr.

Selected Poems. Howard Moss. LC 70-139321. 1971. pap. 3.95 (ISBN 0-689-10561-4). Atheneum.

Selected Poems. Edwin Muir. 1965. pap. 4.95 (ISBN 0-571-06342-X, Pub. by Faber & Faber). Merrimack Bk Serv.

Selected Poems. Norman Nicholson. 1966. pap. 4.95 (ISBN 0-571-06733-6, Pub. by Faber & Faber). Merrimack Bk Serv.

Selected Poems. Frank O'Hara. Ed. by Donald Allen. 1974. pap. 4.95 (ISBN 0-394-71973-5, V-973, Vin). Random.

Selected Poems. Janos Pilinszky. Tr. by Ted Hughes & Janos Csokits. LC 76-52273. 1977. 8.95 (ISBN 0-89255-017-1); pap. 4.95 (ISBN 0-89255-018-X). Persea Bks.

Selected Poems. Ezra Pound. LC 57-8603. 1957. pap. 2.95 (ISBN 0-8112-0162-7, NDP66). New Directions.

Selected Poems. Raymond Queneau. Tr. by Teo Savory. LC 69-13017. (French Ser). (Eng. & Fr., Fr). 1970. 10.00 (ISBN 0-87775-084-X); pap. 4.00 (ISBN 0-87775-084-X). Unicorn Pr.

Selected Poems. Siegfried Sassoon. 1968. pap. 4.95 (ISBN 0-571-08540-7, Pub. by Faber & Faber). Merrimack Bk Serv.

Selected Poems. Phillip Sidney. Ed. by Katherine Duncan-Jones. 1973. pap. 8.95x (ISBN 0-19-871053-4). Oxford U Pr.

Selected Poems. Christopher Smart. Ed. by Marcus Walsh. (Fyfield Ser.). 150p. (Orig.). 1979. pap. 3.95 (ISBN 0-85635-307-8, Pub. by New Pr England). Persea Bks.

Selected Poems. Stephan Spender. 1965. pap. 4.95 (ISBN 0-571-06358-6, Pub. by Faber & Faber). Merrimack Bk Serv.

Selected Poems. Stephen Spender. 1964. pap. 6.95 (ISBN 0-394-40445-9). Random.

Selected Poems. Wallace Stevens. 1965. pap. 5.95 (ISBN 0-571-06384-5, Pub. by Faber & Faber). Merrimack Bk Serv.

Selected Poems. Mark Strand. 1980. 10.95 (ISBN 0-689-11088-X); pap. 6.95 (ISBN 0-689-11089-8). Atheneum.

Selected Poems. Algernon C. Swinburne. LC 80-19421. 339p. 1980. Repr. of 1951 ed. lib. bdg. 29.75x (ISBN 0-313-22649-0, SWSP). Greenwood.

Selected Poems. Tomas Transtromer. Tr. by Robin Fulton from Swed. 1981. 15.00x (ISBN 0-88233-462-X); pap. 5.00x (ISBN 0-88233-463-8). Ardis Pubs.

Selected Poems. William Wordsworth. 12.95 (ISBN 0-19-250189-5, WC 189). Oxford U Pr.

Selected Poems & Prose of John Clare. John Clare. Ed. by Eric Robinson & Geoffrey Summerfield. (Illus.). 1967. 14.95x (ISBN 0-19-212164-2); pap. 8.95 (ISBN 0-19-281232-7). Oxford U Pr.

Selected Poems from Moods. Theodore Dreiser. Ed. by Robert Palmer Saalbach. 1969. 7.50 o.p. (ISBN 0-682-46914-9, University). Exposition.

Selected Poems from the Divani Shamsi Tabriz. Ed. by Reynold A. Nicholson. LC 77-1340. 1977. pap. text ed. 47.50 (ISBN 0-521-21646-X); pap. 15.95x (ISBN 0-521-29217-4). Cambridge U Pr.

Selected Poems, Nineteen Fifty to Nineteen Seventy-Five. Thom Gunn. 1979. 12.95 (ISBN 0-374-25865-1). FS&G.

Selected Poems, Nineteen Sixty-Three to Nineteen Eighty. Michael Longley. LC 80-52997. 54p. pap. 5.50 (ISBN 0-916390-14-4). Wake Forest.

Selected Poems of Antonio Machado. Antonio Machado. Tr. by Betty Craig. LC 78-57504. 1978. 11.95x (ISBN 0-8071-0456-6). La State U Pr.
Selected Poems of Barnabe Googe. Barnabe Googe. Ed. by Alan Stephens. LC 80-29155. (Books of the Renaissance Ser.). 60p. 1981. Repr. of 1961 ed. lib. bdg. 17.50x (ISBN 0-313-22830-2, GOSEP). Greenwood.
Selected Poems of Cesar Vallejo. Cesar Vallejo. Tr. by H. R. Hays from Sp. 122p. 1981. 13.50 (ISBN 0-937584-01-0); pap. 6.95 (ISBN 0-937584-02-9). Sachem Pr.
Selected Poems of Christina Rossetti. Christina Rossetti. Ed. by Marya Zaturenska. LC 77-95183. 1970. pap. 9.95 (ISBN 0-02-633400-3). Macmillan.
Selected Poems of Jaime Torres Bodet. Jaime T. Bodet. Tr. by Sonja Karsen. LC 64-10832. 160p. (Fr. & Eng.). 1964. 7.50x o.p. (ISBN 0-253-17890-8). Ind U Pr.
Selected Poems of Leopold Sedar Senghor. Ed. by F. A. Irele. LC 76-16919. 1977. 23.95 (ISBN 0-521-21339-8); pap. 8.50x (ISBN 0-521-29111-9). Cambridge U Pr.
Selected Poems of Luis Cernuda. Luis Cernuda. Tr. by Reginald Gibbons from Span. LC 75-3767. 1976. 14.95x (ISBN 0-520-02984-4). U of Cal Pr.
Selected Poems of Rainer Maria Rilke: A Translation from the German & Commentary. Rainer M. Rilke. Tr. by Robert Bly. LC 78-2114. (Ger.). 1981. pap. 5.95 (ISBN 0-06-090727-4, CN). Har-Row.
Selected Poems of Rainer Maria Rilke: A Translation from the German & Commentary. Rainer M. Rilke. Tr. by Robert Bly from Ger. LC 78-2114. 192p. 1981. 13.95 (ISBN 0-06-010432-5, CN727, HarpT); pap. 5.95. Har-Row.
Selected Poems of Rosemary Thomas. Rosemary Thomas. LC 67-25189. 161p. 1968. text ec. 17.95x (ISBN 0-8290-0204-9). Irvington.
Selected Poems of S. T. Coleridge. Ed. by James Reeves. (Poetry Bookshelf). 1959. pap. text ed. 6.50x (ISBN 0-435-15021-9). Heinemann Ed.
Selected Poems of Thomas Hardy. Ed. by James Reeves & Robert Gittings. (Poetry Bookself Ser.). 1981. 11.50x (ISBN 0-389-20080-8). B&N.
Selected Poems of Thomas Hood. Thomas Hood. Ed. by John Clubbe. LC 72-95924. 1970. 18.50x (ISBN 0-674-79915-1). Harvard U Pr.
Selected Poems of W. H. Auden. 2nd ed. W. H. Auden. Date not set. pap. 2.45 (ISBN 0-394-71102-5, Vin). Random.
Selected Poems of Walther Von der Vogelweide. 4th, new & rev. ed. Ed. by Margaret F. Richey & Hugh Sacker. (Blackwell's German Text Ser.). 1967. pap. 4.50x o.p. (ISBN 0-631-01820-4, Pub. by Basil Blackwell). Biblio Dist.
Selected Poems: 1958 to 1980. Gilbert Sorrentino. 225p. (Orig.). 1981. 14.00 (ISBN 0-87685-502-8); pap. 7.50 (ISBN 0-87685-501-X); signed ed. 20.00 (ISBN 0-87685-503-6). Black Sparrow.
Selected Poetry & Critical Prose. Charles G. Roberts. Ed. by W. J. Keith. LC 73-91558. (Literature of Canada Ser.). 1974. pap. 5.95 (ISBN 0-8020-6206-7). U of Toronto Pr.
Selected Poetry & Prose of John T. Napier. John T. Napier. Ed. by David Rubin. 73p. pap. 1.00. Pikeville Coll.
Selected Poetry of William Blake. Ed. by David V. Erdman. pap. 2.95 (ISBN 0-451-51373-8, CE1373, Sig Classics). NAL.
Selected Political Speeches. Cicero. Tr. by Michael Grant. (Classics Ser). 1977. pap. 2.95 (ISBN 0-14-044214-6). Penguin.
Selected Political Writings. Rosa Luxemburg. Ed. by Dick Howard. LC 75-142991. 1971. 11.50 o.p. (ISBN 0-85345-142-7, CL-1427); pap. 6.95 (ISBN 0-85345-197-4, PB-1974). Monthly Rev.
Selected Power Reactor Projects in Canada & the United States of America. (Technical Reports: No. 36). 1964. pap. 3.25 (ISBN 92-0-155264-5, IAEA). Unipub.
Selected Prayers by Robert Louis Stevenson. Robert L. Stevenson. (Illus.). 1980. Repr. of 1904 ed. 29.75 (ISBN 0-89901-004-0). Found Class Reprints.
Selected Problems in Yavapai Syntax: The Verde Valley Dialect. Martha B. Kendall. LC 75-25118. (American Indian Linguistics Ser.). 1976. lib. bdg. 42.00 (ISBN 0-8240-1969-5). Garland Pub.
Selected Problems of State Administration. Stanley T. Gabis. 1979. write for info. (ISBN 0-87543-151-8). Lucas.
Selected Prose & Poetry. Walter Raleigh. Ed. by Agnes M. Latham. 1965. text ed. 3.00x (ISBN 0-485-61005-1, Athlone Pr). Humanities.
Selected Prose of N. M. Karamzin. N. M. Karamzin. Tr. by Henry M. Nebel, Jr. (Publications of 18th Cent. Russ. Lit. Ser). 1969. 10.95x o.s.i. (ISBN 0-8101-0021-5). Northwestern U Pr.
Selected Prose of Robert Frost. Robert Frost. Ed. by Hyde Cox & Edward C. Lathem. LC 66-10268. 1968. pap. 1.95 o.s.i. (ISBN 0-02-051000-4, Collier). Macmillan.
Selected Prose of T. S. Eliot. Ed. by Frank Kermode. 320p. 1975. 10.95x (ISBN 0-15-180702-7, Co-Pub by FS&G); pap. 5.50 (ISBN 0-15-680654-1). HarBraceJ.
Selected Readings. Noam Chomsky. Ed. by J. P. Allen & Paul Van Buren. (Language & Learning Ser). 1971. text ed. 16.95x (ISBN 0-19-437046-1). Oxford U Pr.
Selected Readings. Mao Tse-Tung. 504p. 1971. 6.95 (ISBN 0-8351-0324-2). China Bks.
Selected Readings in Chemical Kinetics. Ed. by M. Back & K. J. Laidler. 1967. text ed. 19.50 (ISBN 0-08-012344-9); pap. text ed. 12.75 (ISBN 0-08-012343-0). Pergamon.
Selected Readings in Chromatography. R. J. Magee. (Selected Readings in Analytical Chemistry). (Illus.). 1970. pap. 6.00 o.p. (ISBN 0-08-015851-X). Pergamon.
Selected Readings in Movement Education. Robert Sweeney. LC 78-116865. (Health & Physical Education Ser). 1970. pap. 9.50 (ISBN 0-201-07387-0). A-W.
Selected Readings in Quantitative Urban Analysis. Samuel J. Bernstein & W. Giles Mellon. LC 77-30458. 1978. text ed. 34.00 (ISBN 0-08-019593-8); pap. text ed. 22.00 (ISBN 0-08-019592-X). Pergamon.
Selected Readings in Traditional Healing. Philip Singer & Elizabeth M. Titus. (Traditional Healing Ser.: Vol. 2). 1980. text ed. 15.75x (ISBN 0-932426-01-8); pap. text ed. 10.00x (ISBN 0-932426-05-0). Trado-Medic.
Selected Readings on International Payoffs. Yerachmiel Kugel & Gladys Gruenberg. LC 76-48404. 1977. 19.95 (ISBN 0-669-01458-3). Lexington Bks.
Selected Receipts of a Van Rensselaer Family: 1785-1835. Jane C. Kellar & Ellen Miller. LC 77-85726. (Illus.). 110p. 1976. pap. 6.00 (ISBN 0-89062-026-1, Pub. by Historic Cherry). Pub Ctr Cult Res.
Selected Recipes from Ivy Award Winners. Ed. by Jule Wilkinson. 272p. 1976. 16.95 (ISBN 0-8436-2069-2). CBI Pub.
Selected References in Medical Anthropology. Keith V. Bletzer. (Public Administration Ser.: Bibliography P-551). 59p. 1980. pap. 6.50. Vance Biblios.
Selected Science Fiction & Fantasy Stories. Jack London. LC 76-52712. (Illus.). 1979. 8.50 (ISBN 0-934882-03-7). Fictioneer Bks.
Selected Short Stories. Wolfgang Borchert. Ed. by A. W. Hornsey. 1964. 3.35 (ISBN 0-08-010714-1); pap. 3.00 (ISBN 0-08-010713-3). Pergamon.
Selected Speeches & Statements of General of the Army George C. Marshall. George C. Marshall. Ed. by H. A. DeWeerd. LC 72-10365. (FDR & the Era of the New Deal Ser.). 1973. Repr. of 1945 ed. lib. bdg. 29.50 (ISBN 0-306-70556-7). Da Capo.
Selected Speeches & Writings. A. N. Kosygin. LC 80-41077. 352p. 1981. 100.00 (ISBN 0-08-023610-3). Pergamon.
Selected Speeches & Writings. Boris N. Ponomarev. LC 80-40182. 384p. Date not set. 47.50 (ISBN 0-08-023606-5). Pergamon.
Selected Speeches & Writings on Foreign Affairs. Leonid I. Brezhnev. LC 78-40614. 1978. text ed. 45.00 (ISBN 0-08-023569-7). Pergamon.
Selected Standards & Policy Statements of Special Interest to Women Workers Adopted Under the Auspices of the ILO. 132p. 1980. pap. 8.00 (ISBN 92-2-102441-5, ILO150, ILO). Unipub.
Selected Stories. G. K. Chesterton. Ed. by Kingsley Amis. 1972. 9.95 (ISBN 0-571-09914-9, Pub. by Faber & Faber). Merrimack Bk Serv.
Selected Stories. 3rd ed. Lu Hsun. 1972. 6.95 (ISBN 0-8351-0326-9); pap. 4.95 (ISBN 0-8351-0327-7). China Bks.
Selected Stories, Reminiscences, & Essays. Mikhail Osorgin. Tr. by Donald Fiene from Rus. 300p. 1981. 15.00 (ISBN 0-88233-445-X). Ardis Pubs.
Selected Studies of Archean Gneisses & Lower Proterozoic Rocks: Southern Canadian Shield. Ed. by G. B. Morey & Gilbert N. Hanson. LC 80-67113. (Special Paper Ser.: No. 182). (Illus., Orig.). 1980. pap. write for info. (ISBN 0-8137-2182-2). Geol Soc.
Selected Studies on Energy: Background Papers for Energy: the Next Twenty Years. Ed. by Hans Landsberg. LC 79-24800. 1980. 35.00 (ISBN 0-88410-093-6). Ballinger Pub.
Selected Topics in Algebraic Geometry, 2 Vols in 1. 2nd ed. Virgil Snyder et al. LC 78-113149. 1970. text ed. 13.95 (ISBN 0-8284-0189-6). Chelsea Pub.
Selected Topics in Environmental Biology. Ed. by B. Bhatia et al. 530p. 1980. 47.50x (ISBN 0-89955-317-6, Pub. by Interprint India). Intl Schol Bk Serv.
Selected Topics in Exercise Cardiology & Rehabilitation. Ed. by A. Raineri et al. (Ettore Majorana International Science Ser.--Life Sciences: Vol. 4). 285p. 1981. pap. 35.00 (ISBN 0-306-40566-0, Plenum Pr). Plenum Pub.
Selected Topics in Nuclear Theory. 1963. 19.25 (ISBN 92-0-030563-6, IAEA). Unipub.
Selected Topics in Number Theory. H. Gupta. 1980. 55.00x (ISBN 0-85626-177-7, Pub. by Abacus Pr). Intl Schol Bk Serv.
Selected Topics in Radiation Dosimetry. 1961. 21.50 (ISBN 92-0-030061-8, IAEA). Unipub.
Selected Topics in Venous Disorders: Pathophysiology & Treatment. D. E. Strandness & Brian L. Thiele. LC 80-69527. (Illus.). 1981. 29.50 (ISBN 0-87993-154-X). Futura Pub.
Selected Tracts, 3 vols. Joseph Galloway. LC 70-166326. (Era of the American Revolution Ser.). 1974. lib. bdg. 125.00 (ISBN 0-306-70222-3). Da Capo.
Selected Treatises. St. Cyprian. (Fathers of the Church Ser.: Vol. 36). 18.50 (ISBN 0-8132-0036-9). Cath U Pr.
Selected Water Problems in Islands & Coastal Waters: Proceedings, Malta, 1978. United Nations Economic Commission for Europe, Committee on Water Problems. (ECE Seminars & Symposia). (Illus.). 92.00 (ISBN 0-08-024447-5). Pergamon.
Selected W.H.O. Documents Relating to Traditional Healing. Philip Singer & Elizabeth A. Titus. (Traditional Healing Ser.: Vol. 3). 1981. text ed. 19.50x (ISBN 0-932426-02-6); pap. text ed. 10.00x (ISBN 0-932426-06-9). Trado-Medic.
Selected Works, 1-vol. ed. V. I. Lenin. LC 75-175177. 800p. 1971. pap. 5.75 (ISBN 0-7178-0300-7). Intl Pub Co.
Selected Works, 4 vols. Mao Tse-Tung. Incl. Vol. 1. 1924-37. 1965 (ISBN 0-8351-0328-5); Vol. 2. 1937-41. 1965 (ISBN 0-8351-0330-7); Vol. 3. 1941-45. 1965 (ISBN 0-8351-0332-3) (ISBN 0-8351-0333-1); Vol. 4. 1945-49. 1961 (ISBN 0-8351-0334-X) (ISBN 0-8351-0335-8). 7.95 ea.; pap. 5.95 ea. China Bks.
Selected Works in Organic Chemistry. A. N. Nesmeyanov. 1964. 105.00 (ISBN 0-08-010158-5). Pergamon.
Selected Works of Djuna Barnes. Djuna Barnes. 1980. 12.95 (ISBN 0-374-25936-4). FS&G.
Selected Works of Eighteenth Century French Art in the Collections of the Art Institute of Chicago. Ed. by John W. Keefe & Susan Wise. LC 76-410. (Illus.). 219p. (Orig.). 1976. pap. 12.50 (ISBN 0-86559-019-2). Art Inst Chi.
Selected Works of Giuseppe Peano. Giuseppe Peano. Tr. by Hubert C. Kennedy. LC 70-185719. 272p. 1973. 15.00x o.p. (ISBN 0-8020-5267-3). U of Toronto Pr.
Selected Works of Mao Tse-Tung, 5 vols. Mao Tse-Tung. LC 77-30658. 1977. Set. text ed. 60.00 (ISBN 0-08-022262-5); text ed. 15.00 (ISBN 0-686-68045-6). Vol. I (ISBN 0-08-022980-8). Vol. II (ISBN 0-08-022981-6). Vol. III (ISBN 0-08-022982-4). Vol. IV (ISBN 0-08-022983-2). Vol. V (ISBN 0-08-022984-0). Pergamon.
Selected Works of Mao Tse-Tung, Vol. 5. Mao Tse Tung. 1977. 7.95 (ISBN 0-8351-0336-6); pap. 5.95 (ISBN 0-8351-0337-4). China Bks.
Selected Works of Marx & Engels. Karl Marx & Frederick Engels. (Orig.). 1968. pap. 5.75 (ISBN 0-7178-0184-5). Intl Pub Co.
Selected Works of Peter A. Boodberg. Peter A. Boodberg. Ed. by Alvin P. Cohen. LC 76-24580. 1979. 22.75x (ISBN 0-520-03314-0). U of Cal Pr.
Selected Works: The Agony of Christianity & Essays on Faith, Vol. 5. Miguel De Unamuno. Ed. by Anthony Kerrigan & Martin Nozick. Tr. by Anthony Kerrigan from Span. LC 67-22341. (Bollingen Ser.: Vol. 85). 300p. 1974. 16.00 (ISBN 0-691-09933-2). Princeton U Pr.
Selected Works: The Cleveland Museum of Art. Cleveland Museum of Art Staff. LC 66-21226. (Illus.). 252p. 1966. slipcased 12.50x (ISBN 0-910386-12-9, Pub. by Cleveland Mus Art). Ind U Pr.
Selected Works: Tragic Sense of Life, Vol. 4. Miguel De Unamuno. Ed. by Anthony Kerrigan. (Bollingen Ser.: Vol. 85). 1968. 25.00x (ISBN 0-691-09860-3); pap. 6.95 (ISBN 0-691-01820-0). Princeton U Pr.
Selected Works, Vol. II: Poetry. Rainer M. Rilke. Tr. by J. B. Leishman from Ger. LC 60-8714. 17.95 (ISBN 0-8112-0379-4). New Directions.
Selected Writings. Ed. by Russell Kahl. LC 73-8385. 1973. 9.95 (ISBN 0-8195-4039-0, Pub. by Wesleyan U Pr); pap. 5.95 (ISBN 0-913372-10-2). Columbia U Pr.
Selected Writings. Ulrich Zwingli. Tr. by Samuel M. Jackson from Ger. LC 72-80383. (Sources of Medieval History Ser.). (Eng.). 1972. 12.50x o.p. (ISBN 0-8122-7670-1); pap. 3.95x (ISBN 0-8122-1049-2, Pa Paperbks). U of Pa Pr.
Selected Writings: George Herbert Mead. Ed. by Andrew J. Reck. LC 80-27248. lxxii, 416p. 1981. 24.00x (ISBN 0-226-51672-5); pap. 10.95 (ISBN 0-226-51671-7). U of Chicago Pr.
Selected Writings of Baha'u'llah. Baha'U'Llah. LC 79-15136. 1979. Repr. of 1975 ed. 9.00 (ISBN 0-87743-133-7, 7-03-24). Baha'i.
Selected Writings of Baha'u'llah. rev. ed. Baha'u'llah. 1975. pap. 1.50 (ISBN 0-87743-077-2, 7-03-23). Baha'i.
Selected Writings of Caroline Norton. Caroline S. Norton. LC 78-18828. 1978. 85.00x (ISBN 0-8201-1312-3). Schol Facsimiles.
Selected Writings of Edward Sapir in Language, Culture, & Personality. Edward Sapir. Ed. by David G. Mandelbaum. 1949. 30.00x (ISBN 0-520-01115-5). U of Cal Pr.
Selected Writings of Fulke Greville. Fulke Greville. Ed. by Rees. (Athlone Renaissance Library). 1973. text ed. 23.50x (ISBN 0-485-13603-1, Athlone Pr); pap. text ed. 13.00x (ISBN 0-686-66967-3). Humanities.
Selected Writings of Jonathan Edwards. Jonathan Edwards. Ed. by Harold P. Simonson. LC 78-115064. (Milestones of Thought Ser.). 1970. pap. 3.75 (ISBN 0-8044-6132-5). Ungar.
Selected Writings of Russell H. Fitzgibbon. Russell H. Fitzgibbon. Date not set. text ed. price not set (ISBN 0-87918-039-0). ASU Lat Am St.
Selected Writings of St. Thomas Aquinas. St. Thomas Aquinas. Tr. by Robert P. Goodwin. Incl. Principles of Nature; On Being & Essence; On the Virtues in General; On Free Choice. LC 65-26529. (Orig.). 1965. pap. 2.95 (ISBN 0-672-60469-8, LLA217). Bobbs.
Selected Writings of Shoghi Effendi. rev. ed. Shoghi Effendi. 1975. pap. 1.50 (ISBN 0-87743-079-9, 7-08-43). Baha'i.
Selected Writings of Teresa of Avila. Sheila M. Green. 4.50 o.p. (ISBN 0-685-58944-7). Vantage.
Selecting & Training First-Line Supervisors. Donald L. Kirkpatrick et al. 396p. 1980. 69.50 (ISBN 0-85013-114-6). Dartnell Corp.
Selecting, Developing & Retaining Women Executives: A Corporate Strategy for the Eighties. Helen J. McLane. 256p. 1980. 14.95 (ISBN 0-442-20165-6). Van Nos Reinhold.
Selecting Educational Equipment & Materials for School & Home. rev. ed. ACEI Committee et al. Ed. by Monroe D. Cohen. LC 75-35900. (Illus.). 96p. (Orig.). 1976. 4.00x (ISBN 0-87173-010-3). ACEI.
Selecting Foster Parents: The Ideal & the Reality. Martin Wolins. LC 63-19855. 1964. 17.50x (ISBN 0-231-02514-9). Columbia U Pr.
Selecting Instructional Media: A Guide to Audiovisual & Other Instructional Media Lists. 2nd ed. Mary R. Sive. LC 77-27278. 1978. lib. bdg. 18.50x (ISBN 0-87287-181-9). Libs Unl.
Selecting Materials for Instruction: Issues & Policies. Marda Woodbury. LC 79-18400. (Illus.). 1979. lib. bdg. 22.50 (ISBN 0-87287-197-5). Libs Unl.
Selecting Materials for Instruction: Media & the Curriculum. Marda Woodbury. LC 79-18400. (Illus.). 1980. lib. bdg. 22.50 (ISBN 0-87287-212-2). Libs Unl.
Selecting Materials for Instruction: Subject Areas & Implementation. Marda Woodbury. LC 79-18400. (Illus.). 1980. lib. bdg. 22.50x (ISBN 0-87287-213-0). Libs Unl.
Selecting Materials for Libraries. 2nd ed. Robert N. Broodus. 1981. write for info. (ISBN 0-8242-0510-3). Wilson.
Selecting Materials for Process Equipment. Chemical Engineering Magazine. (Chemical Engineering Ser.). 280p. 1980. 24.50 (ISBN 0-07-010692-4). McGraw.
Selection & Employment of Management Consultants for Health Care. American Hospital Association of the Hospital Management Systems Society. LC 78-4971. (Illus.). 64p. 1978. pap. 12.00 (ISBN 0-87258-233-7, 1062). Am Hospital.
Selection & Evaluation of Teachers. Dale Bolton. LC 72-10648. 260p. 1973. 16.00x (ISBN 0-8211-0123-4); text ed. 14.50x (ISBN 0-685-28805-6). McCutchan.
Selection & Use of Thermoplastics. P. C. Powell. (Engineering Design Guides Ser.). (Illus.). 1977. pap. 4.50x o.p. (ISBN 0-19-859156-X). Oxford U Pr.
Selection-Election, 1980. Robert S. Hirschfield. 264p. 1981. text ed. price not set. Aldine Pub.
Selection from Andrew Lang's Fairy Tales. Andrew Lang. Ed. by Alice Dickinson. (Keith Jennison Large Type Bks). (Illus.). (gr. 4-7). 1971. 8.95 o.p. (ISBN 0-531-00316-7). Watts.
Selection from His Writings. Fred Froebel. Ed. by Irene M. Lilley. (Cambridge Texts & Studies in Education). 22.50 (ISBN 0-521-05043-X). Cambridge U Pr.
Selection Interviewing for Managers. Thomas L. Moffatt. LC 78-9302. (Continuing Management Education Ser.). 1979. text ed. 13.95 scp (ISBN 0-06-044573-4, HarpC). Har-Row.

Selection of Ancient Chinese Bronzes. 1975. 15.00 (ISBN 0-8351-0340-4). China Bks.

Selection of Archaeological Finds from the People's Republic of China. 1976. 15.00 (ISBN 0-8351-0511-3). China Bks.

Selection of Data Communications Equiptment. E. Nichols & S. Jocelyn. (Illus.). 239p. (Orig.). 1979. pap. 37.50x (ISBN 0-85012-217-1). Intl Pubns Serv.

Selection of Design. Gordon L. Glegg. LC 72-80591. (Illus.). 96p. 1972. 14.50 (ISBN 0-521-08686-8). Cambridge U Pr.

Selection of Etchings by John Sloan. Ed. by Robert F. Bussabarger & Frank Stack. LC 67-22228. (Illus.). 1967. pap. 10.00x o.p. (ISBN 0-8262-0059-1). U of Mo Pr.

Selection of Folk Dances, Vol. 1-5. J. R. Richardson. Repr. Vol. 1. 1965. pap. 3.00 (ISBN 0-685-77384-1); Vol. 2. 1966. pap. 3.80 (ISBN 0-08-010842-3); Vol. 3. 1966. pap. 3.80 (ISBN 0-08-011926-3); Vol. 4. 1971. pap. 3.80 (ISBN 0-08-016190-1); Vol. 5. 1978. pap. 3.80 (ISBN 0-08-021589-0). Pergamon.

Selection of Greek Historical Inscriptions to the End of the 5th Century, B. C. Ed. by Russell Meiggs & David Lewis. 1969. 34.00x (ISBN 0-19-814266-8). Oxford U Pr.

Selection of Historic American Papers on Concrete: 1876-1926. 1976. 23.25 (ISBN 0-685-85765-4, SP-52) (ISBN 0-685-85766-2). ACI.

Selection of Japan's Emergency Legislation. Tr. by William J. Sebald. (Studies in Japanese Law & Government). 177p. 1979. Repr. of 1937 ed. 16.00 (ISBN 0-89093-219-0). U Pubns Amer.

Selection of Papers from Info II, 3 vols. Ed. by D. G. Lainiotis & N. S. Tzannes. 1980. lib. bdg. 47.50 ea. Vol. 1, 530p (ISBN 90-277-1140-2). Vol. 2, 600p (ISBN 90-277-1129-1). Vol. 3, 530p (ISBN 90-277-1143-7). Kluwer Boston.

Selection, of Some of the Most Interesting Narratives, of Outrages, Committed by the Indians, in Their Wars, with the White People, 2 vols. Archibald Loudon. LC 75-7052. (Indian Captivities Ser.: Vols. 29 & 30). 1977. Repr. of 1811 ed. Vol. 1. lib. bdg. 44.00 (ISBN 0-8240-1653-X); Vol. 2. lib. bdg. 44.00 (ISBN 0-8240-1654-8). Garland Pub.

Selection of Treatment for Alcoholics. Ed. by E. Mansell Pattison. LC 79-620007. (NIAAA-RUCAS Alcoholism Treatment Ser.: No. 1). 1981. pap. 10.00 (ISBN 0-911290-47-8). Rutgers Ctr Alcohol.

Selections. Martial & Pliny. Ed. by E. C. Kennedy. text ed. 5.75x (ISBN 0-521-05683-7). Cambridge U Pr.

Selections. Plautus. Ed. by K. M. Westaway. text ed. 4.25x (ISBN 0-521-07197-6). Cambridge U Pr.

Selections for Developing English Language Skills. rev. ed. Mary Finocchiaro & Violet H. Lavenda. 230p. (gr. 6 up). 1973. pap. 4.75 (ISBN 0-88345-195-6, 18078); cassettes 25.00 (ISBN 0-685-38987-1); ans. key 1.00 (ISBN 0-686-66893-6). Regents Pub.

Selections from "A Line on Texas". abr. ed. Norman Baxter. (Illus.). 128p. 1980. pap. 6.95 (ISBN 0-88415-429-7). Gulf Pub.

Selections from Catullus Handbook. Ed. by R. O. Lyne. (Cambridge Latin Texts Ser.). 96p. 1975. pap. text ed. 5.50x (ISBN 0-521-20490-9). Cambridge U Pr.

Selections from Cicero: Orations, Philosophical Writings & Letters. Cicero. Tr. by Joseph Pearl. LC 68-17258. 1968. pap. text ed. 2.95 (ISBN 0-8120-0301-2). Barron.

Selections from Contemporary Portugese Poetry. Jean Longland. 1966. 3.50 (ISBN 0-8178-3782-5). Hispanic Soc.

Selections from Early Greek Philosophy. 4th ed. Ed. by Milton C. Nahm. (Orig.). 1964. pap. text ed. 10.95 (ISBN 0-13-800508-7). P-H.

Selections from Eclogues Georgics & Aeneid: Selections from Eclogues,Georgics & Aeneid. Jackson W. Knight. (Roman World Ser.). 1970. pap. text ed. 3.95x (ISBN 0-04-873001-7). Allen Unwin.

Selections from English Wycliffite Writings. Ed. by Anne Hudson. LC 77-1506. 1978. 38.50 (ISBN 0-521-21667-2). Cambridge U Pr.

Selections from Homer's Iliad. Homer. Ed. by Allen R. Benner. (Gr.). 1976. Repr. of 1931 ed. text ed. 16.95x (ISBN 0-89197-636-1). Irvington.

Selections from Italian Poetry. A. Michael DeLuca & William Giuliano. LC 66-10394. (Illus.). 128p. (gr. 9 up). 1966. PLB 5.29 (ISBN 0-8178-3792-2). Harvey.

Selections from Les Amours jaunes. Tristan Corbiere. Tr. by C. F. MacIntyre. (Fr & Eng). 1954. 15.00x (ISBN 0-520-00270-9). U of Cal Pr.

Selections from Medieval Philosophers, 2 vols. Ed. by R. McKeon. 1971. pap. 2.95 ea. (ScribT). Vol. 1, O.p (ISBN 0-684-12552-8, SL309, ScribT). Vol. 2 (ISBN 0-684-12553-6, SL310). Scribner.

Selections from Records of the Historian. Szuma Chien. 1979. pap. 6.95 (ISBN 0-8351-0618-7). China Bks.

Selections from Science & Sanity. Ed. by G. E. Janssen. 1972. Repr. of 1948 ed. 8.00x (ISBN 0-937298-02-6). Inst Gen Semantics.

Selections from Tacitus Annals II-III, Germanicus & Piso. Ed. by D. C. Chandler. (Latin Texts Ser.). (Illus., Orig.). 1980. pap. 3.95 (ISBN 0-521-22650-3). Cambridge U Pr.

Selections from the Autobiography of Madam Guyon. Madame Guyon. Ed. by Warner A. Hutchinson. Tr. by Thomas T. Allen from Fr. LC 80-82324. (Shepherd Classic Ser.). 1980. pap. 5.95 (ISBN 0-87983-234-7). Keats.

Selections from the Black Brown Book. 2nd ed. Ed. by Edward Spargo. (College Reading Skills Ser). (Illus.). 176p. (gr. 12 up). 1974. pap. text ed. 4.80x (ISBN 0-89061-001-0). Jamestown Pubs.

Selections from the Black Olive Book. 2nd ed. Ed. by Edward Spargo. (College Reading Skills Ser). (Illus.). 176p. (gr. 12 up). 1974. pap. text ed. 4.80x (ISBN 0-89061-000-2). Jamestown Pubs.

Selections from the Black Purple Book. 2nd ed. Ed. by Edward Spargo. (College Reading Skills Ser). (Illus.). 176p. (gr. 12 up). 1974. pap. text ed. 4.80x (ISBN 0-89061-002-9). Jamestown Pubs.

Selections from the Correspondence of Theodore Roosevelt & Henry Cabot Lodge, 1884-1918, 2 Vols. Ed. by H. C. Lodge & C. F. Redmond. LC 72-146156. (American Public Figures Ser). 1971. Repr. of 1925 ed. Set. lib. bdg. 95.00 (ISBN 0-306-70129-4). Da Capo.

Selections from the Critical Writings of Edgar Allan Poe. Ed. by Frederick C. Prescott. 425p. 1981. Repr. of 1909 ed. 15.00 (ISBN 0-87752-182-4). Gordian.

Selections from the Gutter: Portraits from the Jazz Record. Ed. by Art Hodes & Chadwick Hansen. LC 75-7193. 1977. 15.95x (ISBN 0-520-02999-2); pap. 5.95 (ISBN 0-520-03719-7). U of Cal Pr.

Selections from the Letters of Abdu'l-Baha. 309p. (Persian.). 1980. 10.00 (ISBN 0-87743-157-4, 7-89-46); pap. 5.00 (ISBN 0-87743-158-2, 7-89-47). Baha'i.

Selections from the Permanent Collection of the Springfield Art Museum. Edgar A. Albin et al. Ed. by William C. Landwehr. LC 80-53333. 100p. (Orig.). 1980. pap. text ed. 9.95 (ISBN 0-934306-03-6). Springfield.

Selections from the Poetical Literature of the West. Ed. by William D. Gallagher. LC 68-29083. 1968. Repr. of 1841 ed. 29.00x (ISBN 0-8201-1019-1). Schol Facsimiles.

Selections from the Poetry of Bassar. Ed. by A. F. Beeston. LC 77-928. 1977. 28.50 (ISBN 0-521-21664-8); pap. 7.95x (ISBN 0-521-29223-9). Cambridge U Pr.

Selections from the Quran. Tr. by Arthur Wormhoudt from Classical Arabic. (Arab Translation Ser.: No. 51). 175p. 1981. pap. 6.50x (ISBN 0-916358-03-8). Wormhoudt.

Selections from the Smuts Papers, 4 vols. J. C. Smuts. Ed. by William K. Hancock & Jean Van Der Poel. Vol. 1, 1886-1902. 85.50 (ISBN 0-521-05190-8); Vol. 2, From 1902-1910. 85.50 (ISBN 0-521-05191-6); Vol. 3, From 1910-1918. 85.50 (ISBN 0-521-05192-4); Vol. 4, From 1918-1919. 85.50 (ISBN 0-521-05193-2); Vol. 5. from 1945-1950 94.00 (ISBN 0-521-08604-3); Vol. 5, From 1919-1943. 93.50 (ISBN 0-521-08602-7); Vol. 6, From 1934-1945. 94.00 (ISBN 0-521-08603-5). Cambridge U Pr.

Selections from the Upanishads & The Tao Te King. Tr. by Charles Johnston & Lionel Giles. 142p. 1951. Repr. of 1897 ed. 3.00 (ISBN 0-938998-15-3). Cunningham Pr.

Selections from the Works of Thomas Paine. Thomas Paine. Ed. by A. W. Peach. 378p. 1980. Repr. lib. bdg. 30.00 (ISBN 0-8495-4385-1). Arden Lib.

Selections from the Writings of Abdu'l-Baha. Abdu'l-Baha. Tr. by Shoghi Effendi & Marzieh Gail. 1978. 10.00 (ISBN 0-85398-081-0, 7-06-25); pap. 5.00 (ISBN 0-85398-084-5, 7-06-26). Baha'i.

Selections from the Writings of the Bab. The Bab. LC 79-670141. 1976. 7.50 (ISBN 0-85398-066-7, 7-05-50). Bahai.

Selections from William Caxton. William Caxton. Ed. by N. F. Blake. (Clarendon Medieval & Tudor Ser.). 1973. 13.00x o.p. (ISBN 0-19-871081-X). Oxford U Pr.

Selections in Two Keys. K. Srinivasan. 10.00 (ISBN 0-89253-548-2). Ind-US Inc.

Selective Genocide in Burundi. Rene Lemarchand & David Martin. (Minority Rights Group: No. 20). 1974. pap. 2.50 (ISBN 0-89192-106-0). Interbk Inc.

Selective Music Bibliography from the Period 1663-1763. James Pruett & Lee Rigsby. (Illus.). 1962. pap. 1.00 (ISBN 0-86526-109-1). NC Archives.

Selective Mutism: Implications for Research & Treatment. Thomas R. Kratochwill. LC 80-18631. 224p. 1981. profess. & reference 19.95 (ISBN 0-89859-064-7). L Erlbaum Assocs.

Selective Reading. rev. ed. Barry M. Smith & Edward Spargo. LC 73-9349. (Powereading Program Ser., Bk. 4). 54p. 1974. pap. text ed. 3.95 (ISBN 0-913310-01-8). PAR Inc.

Selective Toxicity: The Physico-Chemical Basis of Theory. 6th ed. Adrien Albert. LC 78-15491. 662p. 1979. text ed. 39.95x (ISBN 0-412-15650-4, Pub. by Chapman & Hall). Methuen Inc.

Selective Toxicity: The Physico-Chemical Basis of Theory. 6th ed. Adrien Albert. LC 78-15491. 1979. 42.50 (ISBN 0-470-26482-9). Halsted Pr.

Selenium. Committee on Medical and Biologic Effects of Environmental Pollutants, National Research Council. LC 76-40687. (Medical and Biologic Effects of Environmental Pollutants Ser). 1976. pap. 10.25 (ISBN 0-309-02503-6). Natl Acad Pr.

Selenium As Food & As Medicine. Richard A. Passwater. LC 80-82325. 200p. 1981. 10.95 (ISBN 0-87983-237-1); pap. 2.95 (ISBN 0-87983-229-0). Keats.

Selenium in Biology & Medicine: Second International Symposium. J. E. Spallholz et al. (Illus.). 1981. lib. bdg. 45.00 (ISBN 0-87055-379-8). AVI.

Selenium in Nutrition. Committee On Animal Nutrition. LC 74-172093. 1971. pap. 3.75 (ISBN 0-309-01926-5). Natl Acad Pr.

Seleucid Army. B. Bar-Kochva. (Cambridge Classical Studies Ser.). 1976. 26.50 (ISBN 0-521-20667-7). Cambridge U Pr.

Self-Adjoint Operators. W. G. Faris. (Lecture Notes in Mathematics Ser.: Vol. 433). vii, 115p. 1975. pap. 9.50 (ISBN 0-387-07030-3). Springer-Verlag.

Self-Analysis. Karen Horney. 1942 6.50 (ISBN 0-393-01025-2); pap. 3.95, 1968 (ISBN 0-393-00134-2). Norton.

Self Analysis: The Book About Life. James J. Carter. (Illus., Orig.). 1979. pap. 4.95 (ISBN 0-937004-00-6). Carter.

Self & Cinema. Marsha Kinder & Beverle Houston. 1980. pap. 7.90 (ISBN 0-913178-62-4). Redgrave Pub Co.

Self & Non-Self in Early Buddhism. Joacquin Perez-Ramon. (Religon & Society Ser.: No. 17). 1980. 47.00x (ISBN 90-279-7987-1). Mouton.

Self & Not Self: Cellular Immunology, Bk. 1. F. Macfarlane Burnet. (Illus.). 1969. 32.50 (ISBN 0-521-07521-1); pap. 14.50x (ISBN 0-521-09558-1, 558). Cambridge U Pr.

Self & Society: A Symbolic Interactionist Social Psychology. John P. Hewitt. 312p. 1976. text ed. 11.95x o.s.i. (ISBN 0-205-05471-4); pap. text ed. 6.95x o.s.i. (ISBN 0-685-63061-7). Allyn.

Self & Society in Aristophanes. Dana F. Sutton. LC 80-5235. 125p. 1980. lib. bdg. 15.50 (ISBN 0-8191-1067-1); pap. text ed. 7.50 (ISBN 0-8191-1068-X). U Pr of Amer.

Self & Society in Ming Thought. Ed. by William T. De Bary. LC 78-101229. (Studies in Oriental Culture Ser). 1969. 27.50x (ISBN 0-231-03271-4); pap. 12.50x (ISBN 0-231-08313-0). Columbia U Pr.

Self & World. Eli Siegel. LC 75-44647. 1981. pap. price not set (ISBN 0-910492-27-1); text ed. price not set (ISBN 0-910492-28-X). Definition. Postponed.

Self-Anointed: Love & Terror in My Father's House. Gladis L. Depree. LC 77-3746. 1978. 9.95 o.s.i. (ISBN 0-06-011058-9, HarpT). Har-Row.

Self-Assertion for Women. rev. ed. Paméla E. Butler. LC 80-8904. (Illus.). 320p. (Orig.). 1981. pap. 7.95 (ISBN 0-06-250121-6, HarpR). Har-Row.

Self-Assessment of Current Kmowledge in Geriatric Nursing. Laurie M. Gunter & Joanne E. Ryan. 1976. spiral bdg. 9.50 (ISBN 0-87488-295-8). Med Exam.

Self-Assessment of Current Knowledge in Oncology. John F. Foley. 1975. spiral bdg. 14.00 (ISBN 0-87488-284-2). Med Exam.

Self-Assessment of Current Knowledge in Allergy. Claude A. Frazier. 1976. spiral bdg. 14.00 (ISBN 0-87488-296-6). Med Exam.

Self-Assessment of Current Knowledge in Neurology. 3rd ed. Ed. by Armin F. Haerer. LC 80-81657. 1980. spiral bdg. 17.00 (ISBN 0-87488-254-0). Med Exam.

Self-Assessment of Current Knowledge in Urology. 2nd ed. Stephen M. Lazarus. 1974. spiral bdg. 12.00 o.s.i. (ISBN 0-87488-251-6). Med Exam.

Self-Assessment of Current Knowledge in Pharmacy. Fotios M. Plakogiannis & Anthony J. Cutie. 1976. spiral bdg. 9.50 (ISBN 0-87488-272-9). Med Exam.

Self-Assessment of Current Knowledge in Surgery. Ed. by M. D. Ram. LC 80-18730. 1980. pap. 16.50 (ISBN 0-87488-223-0). Med Exam.

Self-Assessment of Current Knowledge in Pathology. 3rd ed. Morton J. Robinson. 1977. spiral bdg. 14.00 (ISBN 0-87488-253-2). Med Exam.

Self-Assessment of Current Knowledge in Psychosis. Ed. by Brent G. Waters & Mary B. Jurek. LC 80-18729. 1980. pap. 18.00 (ISBN 0-87488-233-8). Med Exam.

Self-Assessment of Current Knowledge for the Nurse Anesthetist. 2nd ed. Alice R. Bakutis. 1976. spiral bdg. 9.50 (ISBN 0-87488-715-1). Med Exam.

Self-Assessment of Current Knowledge for the Operating Room Technician. 2nd ed. Margaret A. Burns & Lois E. Morrissy. 1976. pap. 9.50 (ISBN 0-87488-474-8). Med Exam.

Self-Assessment of Current Knowledge in Anesthesiology. 2nd. ed. David L. Trickey. 1980. pap. 14.75 (ISBN 0-87488-245-1). Med Exam.

Self-Assessment of Current Knowledge in Blood Banking. Joseph B. Dudley. 1974. spiral bdg. 8.50 o.s.i. (ISBN 0-87488-289-3). Med Exam.

Self-Assessment of Current Knowledge in Child & Adolescent Psychiatry. 2nd. ed. G. Pirooz Sholevar. LC 80-18727. 1980. pap. 15.00 (ISBN 0-87488-287-7). Med Exam.

Self-Assessment of Current Knowledge in Clinical Biochemistry. 2nd ed. Marge A. Brewster. 1976. 9.50 (ISBN 0-87488-266-4). Med Exam.

Self-Assessment of Current Knowledge in Cardiovascular Disease. Robert A. O'Rourke & John Ross, Jr. 1973. spiral bdg. 14.00 (ISBN 0-87488-275-3). Med Exam.

Self-Assessment of Current Knowledge in Clinical Endocrinology, Metabolism & Diabetes. Kay F. McFarland & Edwin D. Bransome, Jr. 1975. spiral bdg. 12.00 o.s.i. (ISBN 0-87488-297-4). Med Exam.

Self-Assessment of Current Knowledge in Community Health Nursing. Carl O. Helvie. 1975. spiral bdg. 9.50 (ISBN 0-87488-285-0). Med Exam.

Self-Assessment of Current Knowledge in Child Health Nursing. Charlene McKaig et al. 1975. spiral bdg. 8.00 o.p. (ISBN 0-87488-292-3). Med Exam.

Self-Assessment of Current Knowledge in Cardiopulmonary Nursing. Sue B. Foster. 1975. spiral bdg. 9.50 (ISBN 0-87488-288-5). Med Exam.

Self-Assessment of Current Knowledge in Clinical Pharmacy. 2nd ed. Ed. by Philip P. Gerbino. 1978. pap. 9.50 (ISBN 0-87488-281-8). Med Exam.

Self-Assessment of Current Knowledge in Cardiothoracic Surgery. 2nd. ed. Ed. by G. Frank Tyers. LC 79-92911. 1980. pap. 18.00 (ISBN 0-87488-276-1). Med Exam.

Self-Assessment of Current Knowledge in Diagnostic Radiology. 2nd. ed. Ed. by Theodore E. Keats. LC 80-81734. 1980. pap. 16.50 (ISBN 0-87488-278-8). Med Exam.

Self-Assessment of Current Knowledge in Forensic & Organic Psychiatry. Selwyn M. Smith & Erwin K. Koranyi. 1978. spiral bdg. 15.00 (ISBN 0-87488-235-4). Med Exam.

Self-Assessment of Current Knowledge in Family Practice. 2nd ed. Ed. by Marvin Don et al. 1976. pap. 14.50 (ISBN 0-87488-261-3). Med Exam.

Self-Assessment of Current Knowledge in Gynecologic Nursing & Women's Health Care. Patricia G. Dean. LC 79-92917. 1980. pap. 9.50 (ISBN 0-87488-268-0). Med Exam.

Self-Assessment of Current Knowledge in General Surgery. 2nd ed. Lester F. Williams. 1974. spiral bdg. 12.00 o.p. (ISBN 0-87488-250-8). Med Exam.

Self-Assessment of Current Knowledge in General Surgical Nursing. Bonnie G. Steele. 1978. spiral bdg. 9.50 (ISBN 0-87488-290-7). Med Exam.

Self-Assessment of Current Knowledge in Hematology, Part One: Textbook Review. 2nd ed. Samir K. Ballas. 1977. 15.00 (ISBN 0-87488-248-6). Med Exam.

Self-Assessment of Current Knowledge in Hematology, Part 2: Literature Review. Ed. by Frances S. Morrison et al. 1975. spiral bdg. 13.00 (ISBN 0-87488-283-4). Med Exam.

Self-Assessment of Current Knowledge in Infertility & Gynecologic Endocrinology. B. Norman Barwin et al. 1979. spiral bdg. 14.50 (ISBN 0-87488-231-1). Med Exam.

Self-Assessment of Current Knowledge in Intensive Care Nursing. Phyllis S. Turner. 1980. pap. 9.75 (ISBN 0-87488-227-3). Med Exam.

Self-Assessment of Current Knowledge in Infectious Diseases. 2nd ed. Richard V. McCloskey. 1974. spiral bdg. 14.00 (ISBN 0-87488-263-X). Med Exam.

Self-Assessment of Current Knowledge in Internal Medicine. 4th ed. Ed. by James W. Holsinger. LC 79-91971. 1980. pap. 16.50 (ISBN 0-87488-257-5). Med Exam.

Self-Assessment of Current Knowledge in Mental Health Nursing. Doris Stoltzfus. 1979. spiral bdg. 9.50 (ISBN 0-87488-264-8). Med Exam.

Self-Assessment of Current Knowledge in Maternity Nursing. Carol L. Miller et al. 1975. spiral bdg. 8.00 o.p. (ISBN 0-87488-299-0). Med Exam.
Self-Assessment of Current Knowledge in Medical Technology-Hematology. Arthur Simmons. 1974. spiral bdg. 8.50 o.p. (ISBN 0-87488-273-7). Med Exam.
Self-Assessment of Current Knowledge in Nephrology. 2nd ed. Ed. by Arthur V. Williams, Jr. et al. 1976. 14.00 (ISBN 0-87488-280-X). Med Exam.
Self-Assessment of Current Knowledge in Neurology & Neurosurgical Nursing. Judy Strayer & Lois A. Ahlborn. 1976. spiral bdg. 8.00 o.p. (ISBN 0-87488-243-5). Med Exam.
Self-Assessment of Current Knowledge in Neonatology & Perinatal Medicine. Fereydun Mansubi. 1976. spiral bdg. 14.50 (ISBN 0-87488-240-0). Med Exam.
Self-Assessment of Current Knowledge in Neurological Surgery. James H. Salmon & Donald H. Pearson. 1976. spiral bdg. 14.50 (ISBN 0-87488-247-8). Med Exam.
Self-Assessment of Current Knowledge in Orthodontics. Donald T. Rosenbloom. 1976. spiral bdg. 13.50 o.p. (ISBN 0-87488-244-3). Med Exam.
Self-Assessment of Current Knowledge in Otolaryngology. 2nd ed. Ed. by George I. Uhde. 1976. spiral bdg. 14.50 (ISBN 0-87488-270-2). Med Exam.
Self-Assessment of Current Knowledge in Ophthalmology. Timothy Van Scott & Sidney J. Weiss. 1977. spiral bdg. 16.50 (ISBN 0-87488-255-9). Med Exam.
Self-Assessment of Current Knowledge in Obstetrics & Gynecology. 3rd ed. David Charles. LC 79-91970. 1980. pap. 16.50 (ISBN 0-87488-260-5). Med Exam.
Self-Assessment of Current Knowledge in Orthopedic & Rehabilitative Nursing. Rosemary Czaplinski et al. 1979. pap. 9.50 (ISBN 0-87488-230-3). Med Exam.
Self-Assessment of Current Knowledge in Oncology Nursing. Rosemary Y. Wang & Ann M. Kelley. 1979. spiral bdg. 10.50 (ISBN 0-87488-236-2). Med Exam.
Self-Assessment of Current Knowledge in Occupational Therapy. Elizabeth A. Moyer. 1976. spiral bdg. 9.50 (ISBN 0-87488-249-4). Med Exam.
Self-Assessment of Current Knowledge in Pediatrics. 2nd ed. David S. Smith. 1974. spiral bdg. 14.00 (ISBN 0-87488-256-7). Med Exam.
Self-Assessment of Current Knowledge in Psychiatry. 4th ed. Ed. by John A. Talbott. 1980. pap. price not set o.p. (ISBN 0-685-48747-4). Med Exam.
Self-Assessment of Current Knowledge in Pediatric Allergy. Edward J. O'Connell et al. LC 79-91200. 1980. pap. 18.00 (ISBN 0-87488-238-9). Med Exam.
Self-Assessment of Current Knowledge in Pediatric Cardiology. Moshe Steier. 1977. spiral bdg. 15.00 (ISBN 0-87488-241-9). Med Exam.
Self-Assessment of Current Knowledge in Pulmonary Diseases. Ed. by Nicholas Gross. 1973. spiral bdg. 12.00 o.s.i. (ISBN 0-87488-271-0). Med Exam.
Self-Assessment of Current Knowledge in Pediatric Hematology & Oncology. Thomas E. Williams. 1974. 15.00 (ISBN 0-87488-277-X). Med Exam.
Self-Assessment of Current Knowledge in Peripheral Vascular Disorders. David I. Abramson & M. Beth Casey. 1980. pap. 18.00 (ISBN 0-87488-291-5). Med Exam.
Self-Assessment of Current Knowledge in Rheumatology. 2nd ed. Robert E. Pieroni. 1976. spiral bdg. 13.00 o.s.i. (ISBN 0-87488-258-3). Med Exam.
Self-Assessment of Current Knowledge in Radiologic Technology. 2nd ed. Richard C. Kebart et al. 1979. pap. 9.50 (ISBN 0-87488-274-5). Med Exam.
Self Assessment of Current Knowledge in Surgery for Family Physicians. Warner F. Bowers. 1972. spiral bdg. 12.00 o.p. (ISBN 0-87488-259-1). Med Exam.
Self-Assessment of Current Knowledge in Therapeutic Radiology. 2nd ed. Ned B. Hornback. 1979. spiral bdg. 16.50 (ISBN 0-87488-286-9). Med Exam.
Self-Assessment of Knowledge in Orthopedic Surgery. Curtis V. Spear. LC 80-80368. 1980. pap. 16.50 (ISBN 0-87488-229-X). Med Exam.
Self-Awareness Through Huna- Hawaii's Ancient Wisdom. Erika S. Nau. Ed. by Stefan Grunwald. (Orig.). 1981. pap. write for info. (ISBN 0-89865-099-2, Unilaw). Donning Co.
Self-Care in Health. John D. Williamson & Kate Danaher. 1978. lib. bdg. 22.50 (ISBN 0-85664-484-6). N Watson.
Self-Catering in Britain. rev. ed. 240p. 1980. pap. 7.95 o.p. (ISBN 0-86145-009-4, Pub. by B T A). Merrimack Bk Serv.
Self Concept: Advances in Theory & Research. Ed. by Mervin D. Lynch et al. 1981. write for info. (ISBN 0-88410-376-5). Ballinger Pub.
Self-Concept & School Achievement. William W. Purkey, Sr. 1970. pap. text ed. 7.95 (ISBN 0-13-803163-0). P-H.
Self Concept in Psychology & Education. J. B. Thomas. (Bibliographies Ser). 28p. (Orig.). 1973. pap. text ed. 3.75x (ISBN 0-85633-019-1, NFER). Humanities.
Self Concept: Theory, Measurement, Development & Behaviour. R. B. Burns. (Illus.). 1979. pap. text ed. 12.95 (ISBN 0-582-48951-2). Longman.
Self-Consciousness & Social Anxiety. Arnold H. Buss. LC 79-20890. (Psychology Ser.). (Illus.). 1980. text ed. 16.95x (ISBN 0-7167-1158-3); pap. text ed. 8.95x (ISBN 0-7167-1159-1). W H Freeman.
Self-Consistent Fields in Atoms. Norman H. March. 1975. text ed. 27.00 (ISBN 0-08-017819-7); pap. text ed. 14.50 (ISBN 0-08-017820-0). Pergamon.
Self-Contained Celestial Navigation with H.O. 208. John Letcher. LC 76-8782. (Illus.). 1977. 17.50 (ISBN 0-87742-082-3). Intl Marine.
Self-Control: A Novel, 2 vols. Mary Brunton. Ed. by Gina Luria. (Feminist Controversy in England, 1788-1810 Ser.). 1974. Set. lib. bdg. 50.00 ea. (ISBN 0-8240-0852-9). Garland Pub.
Self-Correcting Approach to Managerial Finance: Theory & Techniques. Dennis J. O'Connor & Alberto T. Bueso. (Illus.). 320p. 1981. pap. text ed. 9.95 (ISBN 0-13-803189-4). P-H.
Self-Correcting Problems in Finance. 3rd ed. Roland I. Robinson & Robert W. Johnson. 272p. 1976. pap. text ed. 12.95 (ISBN 0-205-05444-7, 0854441). Allyn.
Self-Correcting Problems in Statistics. Whitmore et al. text ed. 12.95 (ISBN 0-205-02617-6, 1626175). Allyn.
Self Creation. George Weinberg. 1978. pap. 2.50 (ISBN 0-380-43521-7, 43521). Avon.
Self Creation. George Weinberg. LC 77-10375. 1978. 8.95 o.p. (ISBN 0-312-71232-4). St Martin.
Self-Defeated Man: Personal Identity & Beyond. Xavier Rubert De Ventos. 192p. (Orig.). 1975. pap. 2.95 o.p. (ISBN 0-06-090354-6, CN354, CN). Har-Row.
Self-Defense: A Basic Course. Bruce Tegner. LC 79-13556. (Illus.). 1979. 5.95 (ISBN 0-87407-517-3); kivar 3.95 (ISBN 0-87407-031-7). Thor.
Self-Defense & Assault Prevention for Girls & Women. Tegner & McGrath. 1980. pap. 2.95 (ISBN 0-87407-026-0). Thor.
Self-Defense for Boys & Men: A Physical Education Course. rev. ed. Bruce Tegner. LC 72-13186. (Illus., Orig.). (YA) (gr. 9 up). 1969. 4.95 o.p. (ISBN 0-87407-506-8). Thor.
Self-Defense Karate. Sihak H. Cho. LC 71-84824. (Illus.). 1969. 7.95 (ISBN 0-87396-005-X); pap. 3.95 (ISBN 0-87396-006-8). Stravon.
Self-Defense Nerve Centers & Pressure Points for Karate, Jujitsu & Atemi-Waza. rev. enlarged ed. Bruce Tegner. LC 78-18169. (Illus.). 1978. 5.95 (ISBN 0-87407-519-X, T-29); pap. 2.95. Thor.
Self-Destruct: Dismantling America's Internal Security. Robert Morris. 1979. 12.95 o.p. (ISBN 0-87000-437-9). Arlington Hse.
Self-Destructive Behavior. Albert R. Roberts. (Illus.). 232p. 1975. 22.75 (ISBN 0-398-03290-4). C C Thomas.
Self Determination in Social Work: A Collection of Essays on Self-Determination & Related Concepts. F. E. McDermott. (International Library of Welfare & Philosophy). 1975. 17.50x (ISBN 0-7100-7980-X); pap. 8.95 (ISBN 0-7100-7981-8). Routledge & Kegan.
Self-Determination: National, Regional, & Global Dimensions. Ed. by Yonah Alexander & Robert A. Friedlander. (Special Studies in National & International Terrorism). 1980. lib. bdg. 27.50x (ISBN 0-89158-090-5). Westview.
Self Directed Behavior: Self-Modification for Personal Adjustment. 3rd ed. David L. Watson & Roland G. Tharp. LC 80-24411. 300p. 1981. text ed. 10.95 (ISBN 0-8185-0443-9). Brooks-Cole.
Self-Directed Systemic Desensitization. Wes W. Wenrich et al. LC 76-9019. (Illus.). 95p. (Orig.). 1980. pap. 7.00 (ISBN 0-917472-05-5). F Fournies.
Self-Directing Guide to the Study of Child Psychology. Gerald Levin. LC 72-92046. (Statistics Ser.). (Illus., Orig.). 1973. pap. text ed. 10.95 o.p. (ISBN 0-8185-0076-X); instructor's manual avail. o.p. (ISBN 0-685-28534-0). Brooks-Cole.
Self-Direction & Adjustment. Norman Fenton. 121p. 1980. Repr. of 1926 ed. lib. bdg. 22.50 (ISBN 0-89760-225-0). Telegraph Bks.
Self Discovery & Social Awareness. Everett Ostrovsky. LC 73-17333. 320p. 1974. pap. text ed. 12.95x o.p. (ISBN 0-471-65716-6). Wiley.
Self-Discovery Through Self-Expression: Use of Art in Psychotherapy with Children & Adolescents. Mala Betensky. (Illus.). 384p. 1973. 34.75 (ISBN 0-398-02574-6). C C Thomas.
Self-Education-Self Assessment in Thoracic Surgery. Coordinating Committee for Continuing Education in Thoracic Surgery. 208p. 1980. pap. text ed. 100.00 (ISBN 0-8403-2331-X). Kendall-Hunt.
Self Embodiment of God. Thomas J. Altizer. LC 76-62952. 1977. 6.95 o.p. (ISBN 0-06-060160-4, HarpR). Har-Row.
Self Esteem in the Classroom. Verne Faust. LC 79-65212. 1980. 13.95 (ISBN 0-934162-02-6). Thomas Paine Pr.
Self: Explorations in Personal Growth. Ed. by Clark E. Moustakas. 1956. 9.95x o.p. (ISBN 0-06-034530-6, HarpT). Har-Row.
Self-Fulfilling Prophecies: Social, Psychological, & Physiological Effects of Expectancies. Russell A. Jones. 1977. 14.95 o.p. (ISBN 0-470-99301-4). Halsted Pr.
Self-Governing Dominion: California, 1849-1860. William H. Ellison. (Library Reprint Ser.: Vol. 95). 1978. 18.50x (ISBN 0-520-03713-8). U of Cal Pr.
Self-Governing Socialism: A Reader, 2 vols. Ed. by Branko Horvat et al. Incl. Vol. 1. 491p. text ed. 25.50 (ISBN 0-87332-050-6); pap. 10.95 (ISBN 0-87332-060-3); Vol. 2. 329p. text ed. 22.50 (ISBN 0-87332-061-1); pap. 9.95 (ISBN 0-87332-062-X). LC 73-92805. 1975. Set (ISBN 0-87332-048-4). M E Sharpe.
Self-Guiding Society. Warren Breed. LC 75-128472. 1971. 8.95 (ISBN 0-02-904640-8); pap. text ed. 4.95 (ISBN 0-02-904650-5). Free Pr.
Self-Help. Samuel Smiles. 1959. 15.00 (ISBN 0-7195-1294-8). Transatlantic.
Self-Help & Health: Mutual Aid for Modern Problems. David Robinson & Stuart Henry. 164p. 1977. 21.95x (ISBN 0-85520-167-3, Pub. by Martin Robertson England). Biblio Dist.
Self-Help & Health: Mutual Aid for Modern Problems. David Robinson & Stuart Henry. 1977. pap. 12.50x (ISBN 0-85520-317-X, Pub by Martin Robertson England). Biblio Dist.
Self-Help Guide to Divorce, Children & Welfare. 2nd rev. ed. Penelope Jahn & Charles Campbell. 116p. 1979. pap. 4.95 (ISBN 0-88784-075-2, Pub. by Hse Anansi Pr Canada). U of Toronto Pr.
Self Help Handbook. B. Hafen et al. 1980. 14.95 (ISBN 0-13-803304-8); pap. 7.95 (ISBN 0-13-803296-3). P-H.
Self-Hypnosis: A Conditioned - Response Technique. Laurence Sparks. pap. 4.00 (ISBN 0-87980-139-5). Wilshire.
Self Hypnosis Explained. Gilbert Oakley. 1978. pap. 4.95 (ISBN 0-8119-0396-6). Fell.
Self-Hypnosis: Its Theory, Technique & Application. Melvin Powers. pap. 3.00 (ISBN 0-87980-138-7). Wilshire.
Self in Education. J. R. Thomas. 114p. 1981. pap. text ed. 18.00x (ISBN 0-85633-212-7, NFER). Humanities.
Self in Social Work. John Shaw. (Library of Social Work). 1974. 12.50x (ISBN 0-7100-7920-6); pap. 6.95 (ISBN 0-7100-7921-4). Routledge & Kegan.
Self in Transformation: Psychoanalysis, Philosophy & the Life of the Spirit. Herbert Fingarette. LC 63-12846. 1977. pap. text ed. 6.95x (ISBN 0-06-131177-4, TB1177, Torch). Har-Row.
Self-Instruction for IFSTA 200: Essentials of Fire Fighting, SI-200. 1st ed. IFSTA Committee & Lorrin Walker. Ed. by Gene Carlson & Charles Orton. LC 77-75408. (Illus.). 204p. (Orig.). 1980. pap. text ed. 7.00 (ISBN 0-87939-042-5). Intl Fire Serv.
Self-Instructional Guide to Federal Income Taxation, 1973 Edition. Albert J. Schneider. (Illus.). 400p. 1973. pap. text ed. 6.95 o.p. (ISBN 0-13-803510-5). P-H.
Self-Instructional Program in Educational Psychology. Norman T. Bell et al. 1970. pap. 4.95x o.p. (ISBN 0-673-05859-X). Scott F.
Self Instructional Workbook for Emergency Care. 2nd ed. J. Bergeron. (Illus.). 1978. pap. 7.95 (ISBN 0-87618-996-6). R J Brady.
Self-Interest (L'Interesse) Nicolo Secchi. Ed. by Helen A. Kaufman. Tr. by William Reymes. LC 53-13162. (Illus.). 136p. 1953. pap. 4.00 (ISBN 0-295-73930-4). U of Wash Pr.
Self-Knowledge: Sankara's "Atmabodha". Tr. by Swami Nikhilananda. LC 50-36440. 248p. with notes 6.00 (ISBN 0-911206-11-6). Ramakrishna.
Self Liberation. L. A. Amman. 1981. pap. 6.95 (ISBN 0-87728-511-X). Weiser.
Self-Love. Robert H. Schuller. (Spire Bks). 1975. pap. 2.50 (ISBN 0-8007-8195-3). Revell.
Self-Love. Robert H. Schuller. (Orig.). pap. 1.95 (ISBN 0-515-05829-7). Jove Pubns.
Self Love: The Dynamic Force of Success. Robert H. Schuller. 1969. 6.95 (ISBN 0-8015-6714-9, Hawthorn); pap. 3.50 (ISBN 0-8015-6720-3, Hawthorn). Dutton.
Self-Made Man in America. Irvin G. Wyllie. 1966. pap. text ed. 7.95 (ISBN 0-02-935670-9). Free Pr.
Self-Made Man in Meija Japanese Thought: From Samurai to Salary Man. Earl H. Kinmonth. (Illus.). 400p. 1981. 22.50x (ISBN 0-520-04159-3). U of Cal Pr.
Self-Made Olympian. Ron Daws. LC 75-20960. (Illus.). 158p. 1977. pap. 3.95 (ISBN 0-89037-103-2); handbk. 5.95 (ISBN 0-89037-104-0). Anderson World.
Self-Made Snowman. Fernando Krahn. LC 74-551. (gr. 1-3). 1974. PLB 7.89 (ISBN 0-397-31472-8). Lippincott.
Self-Management & Behavior Change: From Theory to Practice. Ed. by Paul Karoly & Frederick H. Kanfer. (Pergamon General Psychology Ser.). 400p. Date not set. price not set (ISBN 0-08-025987-1); pap. price not set (ISBN 0-08-025986-3). Pergamon.
Self-Management: New Dimensions to Democracy. Ichak Adizes & Elisabeth M. Borgese. 162p. Repr. of 1975 ed. pap. text ed. 6.95x (ISBN 0-87436-202-4). Irvington.
Self-Management: New Dimensions to Democracy. Ed. by Ichak Adizes & Elisabeth M. Borgese. LC 74-34220. (Studies in International & Comparative Politics: No. 7). 162p. 1975. text ed. 13.00 (ISBN 0-87436-202-4); pap. text ed. 4.60 (ISBN 0-87436-203-2). ABC-Clio.
Self-Mastery. David Seabury. Ed. by Willis Kinnear. 96p. (Orig.). 1974. pap. 3.95 (ISBN 0-911336-58-3). Sci of Mind.
Self-Mutilation. Robert R. Ross & Hugh B. McKay. (Illus.). 1979. 21.00 (ISBN 0-669-02116-4). Lexington Bks.
Self-Mutilation of an Aged Apple Woman. Laurel Speer. LC 79-22664. 1980. pap. 4.95 (ISBN 0-914974-21-1). Holmgangers.
Self-Organization & Dissipative Structures: Applications in the Physical & Social Sciences. Ed. by William C. Schieve & Peter M. Allen. (Illus.). 472p. 1981. text ed. 50.00x (ISBN 0-292-70354-6). U of Tex Pr.
Self-Organizing Universe: Scientific & Human Implications of the Emerging Paradigm of Evolution. Erich Jantsch. (Systems Science & World Order Library). (Illus.). 1980. text ed. 52.00 (ISBN 0-08-024312-6); pap. text ed. 16.00 (ISBN 0-08-024311-8). Pergamon.
Self-Pacing Biology Experiences. James L. Kelly & Alan R. Orr. (Illus.). 1980. 11.50 (ISBN 0-8138-1725-0). Iowa St U Pr.
Self-Perception: The Psychology of Personal Awareness. Chris L. Kleinke. LC 78-1370. (Psychology Ser.). (Illus.). 1978. pap. text ed. 8.95x (ISBN 0-7167-0062-X). W H Freeman.
Self-Portrait. Gene Tierney & Mickey Hershowitz. 1980. pap. 2.75 (ISBN 0-425-04485-8). Berkley Pub.
Self Portrait: An Autobiographical Discourse. 2nd ed. Patrick Kavanagh. 32p. 1975. pap. text ed. 2.25x (ISBN 0-85105-275-4, Dolmen Pr). Humanities.
Self Portrait: Book People Picture Themselves. Burt Britton. 1976. 12.50 o.p. (ISBN 0-394-49648-5); pap. 6.95 (ISBN 0-394-73104-2). Random.
Self-Portrait of a Hero: The Letters of Jonathan Netanyahu (1963-1976) Compiled by Benjamin Netanyahu & Iddo Netanyahu. 1981. 12.95 (ISBN 0-394-51376-2). Random.
Self Portrait of the Artist As a Man: Sean O'Casey's Letters. David Krause. 40p. 1968. pap. text ed. 2.50x (ISBN 0-85105-127-8, Dolmen Pr). Humanities.
Self-Portrait: Trina Schart Hyman. Trina S. Hyman. LC 80-26662. (Self-Portrait Collection Ser.). (Illus.). 32p. (gr. 1-9). 1981. PLB 8.95 (ISBN 0-201-09308-1, A-W Childrens). A-W.
Self-Portraits in Autographs. Rudolf S. Hearns. 1981. 7.95 (ISBN 0-8062-1550-X). Carlton.
Self-Programming Self-Hypnosis. Cline Clark. (Orig.). 1980. pap. text ed. 17.95 (ISBN 0-937798-00-2). Packard Pub.
Self-Propelled in the Southern Sierra, Vol. 1. J. C. Jenkins. Ed. by Thomas Winnett. LC 74-27689. (Illus., Orig.). 1978. pap. 9.95 (ISBN 0-911824-39-1). Wilderness.
Self-Propelled in the Southern Sierra, Vol. 2. J. C. Jenkins. Ed. by Thomas Winnett. (Illus., Orig.). 1979. pap. 9.95 (ISBN 0-911824-77-4). Wilderness.
Self-Protection at Close Quarters & Beyond. Evan S. Baltazzi. (Illus.). 50.00 (ISBN 0-918948-03-7). Evanel.
Self: Psychological & Philosophical Issues. Ed. by Theodore Mischel. 1977. 23.50x o.p. (ISBN 0-87471-969-0). Rowman.
Self: Psychological & Philosophical Issues. Ed. by Theodore Mischel. 359p. 1977. pap. 12.00x (ISBN 0-8476-6946-7). Rowman.

Self Psychotherapy, Vol. 1. Albert V. Steinkirchner. LC 75-760. 159p. 1974. 9.95 (ISBN 0-915352-00-1); pap. 4.95 (ISBN 0-915352-01-X). Aquin Pub.

Self-Publishing Manual: How to Write, Print & Sell Your Own Book. 2nd ed. Dan Poynter. LC 79-712. (Illus.). 1980. 14.95 (ISBN 0-915516-22-5); pap. 9.95 (ISBN 0-915516-21-7). Para Pub.

Self Relaxation: Comfort in Times of Tension. Harley D. Christiansen. (Illus.). 96p. (Orig.). 1981. pap. 8.95 (ISBN 0-915456-02-8). P Juul Pr.

Self-Reliance. Gene Dekovic. LC 75-12544. (Funk & W Bk.). (Illus.). 96p. 1975. 9.95 o.s.i. (ISBN 0-308-10203-7, TYC-T); pap. 3.95 o.s.i. (ISBN 0-308-10204-5, TYC-T). T Y Crowell.

Self-Reliance & Social Security, 1870-1917. Hace S. Tishler. LC 79-139361. (National University Publications). 1971. 13.50 (ISBN 0-8046-9012-X). Kennikat.

Self-Renewal: The Individual & the Innovative Society. John W. Gardner. 1964. pap. 1.75 o.p. (ISBN 0-06-090054-7, CN54, CN). Har-Row.

Self-Revelation Through Relationships. Ronald Levy. LC 73-167896. 1972. 7.95 (ISBN 0-13-803569-5). P-H.

Self, Society, & Womankind: The Dialectic of Liberation. Kathy E. Ferguson. LC 79-6831. (Contributions in Women's Studies: No. 17). xii, 200p. 1980. lib. bdg. 22.95 (ISBN 0-313-22245-2, FSS/). Greenwood.

Self Study & Evaluation Guide for Day School Programs for Visually Handicapped Pupils: A Guide for Program Improvement. Geraldine T. Scholl. LC 80-68282. 128p. 1980. pap. 14.50 (ISBN 0-86586-111-0). Coun Exc Child.

Self Study Bible Course. Derek Prince. 1969. pap. 3.95 (ISBN 0-934920-08-7, B-90). Derek Prince.

Self-Study Data Forms. AAG Consulting Panel, 1974. pap. 1.00 (ISBN 0-89291-142-5). Assn Am Geographers.

Self-Study Guide for Nutrition & Diet Therapy. 2nd ed. Sue R. Williams. 1978. pap. text ed. 8.50 (ISBN 0-8016-5573-0). Mosby.

Self-Study Processes: A Guide for Postsecondary Institutions. H. R. Kells. 132p. 1980. 15.00 (ISBN 0-8268-1442-5). ACE.

Self-Study Processes: A Guide for Postsecondary Institutions. H. R. Kells. 1980. 15.00 o.p. (ISBN 0-686-65234-7). ACE.

Self-Sufficiency for Children. Mary Norwak. (Illus.). 96p. (gr. 8 up). 1981. 10.95 (ISBN 0-7207-1095-2). Merrimack Bk Serv.

Self-Sufficient Gardener: A Complete Guide to Growing & Preserving All Your Own Food. John Seymour. LC 78-19223. 1979. pap. write for info (ISBN 0-385-14671-X, Dolp). Doubleday.

Self-Sufficient House. Frank Coffed. LC 80-13434. (Illus.). 1981. 16.95 (ISBN 0-03-053611-1); pap. 8.95 (ISBN 0-686-69126-1). HR&W.

Self-Sufficient Pottery. Judy Cunningham-Smith & Mollie Herbert. LC 79-53741. (Illus.). 1979. 14.95 (ISBN 0-7153-7674-8). David & Charles.

Self-Suggestion & Its Influence on the Human Organism. A. S. Romen. Ed. by A. S. Lewis & V. Forsky. (Illus.). 220p. 1980. 20.00 (ISBN 0-87332-195-2). M E Sharpe.

Self Teaching Guide to Physical Examination. D. W. Beaven et al. 1976. pap. 9.95x (ISBN 0-433-01770-8). Intl Ideas.

Self-Teaching Process in Higher Education. P. J. Hills. LC 75-44716. 1976. 15.95 (ISBN 0-470-15024-6). Halsted Pr.

Self-Teaching Tests in Arithmetic for Nurses. 10th. ed. Ruth W. McHenry. LC 80-10859. (Illus.). 1980. pap. text ed. 8.95 (ISBN 0-8016-2505-X). Mosby.

Self Therapy. Muriel Schiffman. LC 73-75227. 176p. (Orig.). 1980. pap. 3.95 (ISBN 0-914640-01-1, Pub. by Self Therapy Pr). Wingbow Pr.

Self-Understanding: An Introduction to Transactional Analysis. David Sheinkin. 86p. 1973. pap. text ed. 4.00x (ISBN 0-89039-061-4); instructor's guide 1.50x (ISBN 0-89039-062-2). Ann Arbor Pubs.

Self-Working Card Tricks: Seventy-Two Foolproof Card Miracles for the Amateur Magician. Karl Fulves. (Illus.). 113p. (Orig.). 1976. pap. 2.00 (ISBN 0-486-23334-0). Dover.

Self-Working Table Magic: Ninety-Seven Foolproof Tricks with Everyday Objects. Karl Fulves. (Illus.). 128p. (Orig.). 1981. pap. price not set (ISBN 0-486-24116-5). Dover.

Selfish Gene. Richard Dawkins. 1976. 12.95 (ISBN 0-19-857519-X). Oxford U Pr.

Selfish Gene. Richard Dawkins. LC 76-29168. 1978. pap. 3.95 (ISBN 0-19-520000-4, GB500, GB). Oxford U Pr.

Selig Perlman's Lectures on Capitalism & Socialism. A. L. Owen. LC 74-27312. 264p. 1976. 17.50 (ISBN 0-299-06780-7). U of Wis Pr.

Sell Your Way to Success. David M. Brownstone. 224p. 1981. 12.95 (ISBN 0-471-09257-6); pap. 7.95 (ISBN 0-471-09242-8). Wiley.

Sell Your Way to Success. 6th ed. Alfred Tack. 256p. 1978. pap. 13.50x (ISBN 0-220-66366-1, Pub. by Busn Bks England). Renouf.

Selling. James F. Robeson et al. 1978. text ed. 16.50 (ISBN 0-256-01967-3). Irwin.

Selling in Agribusiness. Larry Miller. Ed. by Jasper S. Lee. (Career Preparation for Agriculture-Agribusiness Ser.). (Illus.). 1979. pap. text ed. 5.80x (ISBN 0-07-041962-0, G); activity guide 3.60x (ISBN 0-07-041963-9); tchr's manual & key 2.75x (ISBN 0-07-041964-7). McGraw.

Selling Lucky. Art Fettig. LC 77-89820. (Illus.). 1977. 7.95 (ISBN 0-9601334-1-0). Growth Unltd.

Selling of You: A Practical Guide to Job Hunting. new ed. Gerald W. Montgomery. 103p. 1980. 12.95 (ISBN 0-937096-01-6); pap. 9.95 (ISBN 0-937096-00-8). Montgomery Comm.

Selling: Principles & Methods. 6th ed. Carlton A. Pederson & Milburn D. Wright. 1976. text ed. 17.95 (ISBN 0-256-01646-1). Irwin.

Selling Principles & Practices. 5th ed. John Ernest & Richard Ashmun. LC 79-17748. (Illus.). 1980. text ed. 11.84 (ISBN 0-07-019620-6); student activity guide 5.32 (ISBN 0-07-019621-4); tchrs. manual & key 3.95 (ISBN 0-07-019622-2). McGraw.

Selling Real Estate by Mortgage Equity Analysis. Irvin E. Johnson. LC 74-15543. (Special Ser. in Real Estate & Urban Land Economics). (Illus.). 352p. 1976. 18.95 (ISBN 0-669-95588-4). Lexington Bks.

Selling Strategy for Getting Orders. Michael Gross. LC 73-80141. 196p. 1974. pap. 1.50 o.p. (ISBN 0-668-03322-3). Arc Bks.

Selling the People's Cadillac: The Edsel & Corporate Responsibility. Jan G. Deutsch. LC 75-37292. 300p. 1976. 25.00x (ISBN 0-300-01950-5); pap. 9.95x (ISBN 0-300-02014-7). Yale U Pr.

Selling: The Personal Force in Marketing. W. J. Crissy et al. LC 76-45848. (Marketing Ser.). 1977. text ed. 21.95 (ISBN 0-471-18757-7). Wiley.

Selling the Solar Home: California Edition. Yvonne Howell & Harry Miller. 93p. 1981. pap. 10.00 (ISBN 0-89934-081-4). Solar Energy Info.

Selling Your City: A Primer for Government Officials on Communicating with the Investment Community. Peter F. K Rousmaniere et al. 70p. 1978. pap. 8.00 (ISBN 0-916450-22-8). Coun on Municipal.

Selling Your Graphic Design & Illustration. Tad Crawford & Arie Kopelman. 272p. 1981. 13.95 (ISBN 0-312-71252-9). St Martin.

Selling Your Handcrafts. William E. Garrison. LC 74-16304. (Creative Crafts Series). 1974. 10.95 (ISBN 0-8019-6042-8); pap. 6.95 (ISBN 0-8019-6043-6). Chilton.

Sell's British Aviation. 30th ed. LC 57-22102. 1977. 15.00x o.p. (ISBN 0-85499-882-9). Intl Pubns Serv.

Sell's British Exporters 1980. LC 75-640255. (Illus.). 230p. (Orig.). 1980. pap. 32.50x (ISBN 0-85499-547-1). Intl Pubns Serv.

Sell's Directory of Products & Services 1980, 2 vols. 95th ed. LC 73-640793. (Orig., Vol. 1, 452pp. Vol. 2, 479 pp.). 1980. Set. pap. 42.50x (ISBN 0-85499-527-7). Intl Pubns Serv.

Selves of Quinte. Marcel Moreau. LC 65-14604. 1965. 5.00 o.s.i. (ISBN 0-8076-0298-1). Braziller.

Selye's Guide to Stress Research, Vol. 1. (Van Nostrand Reinhold Stress Research & Management Ser.). 368p. 1980. text ed. 22.50 (ISBN 0-442-27483-1). Van Nos Reinhold.

Selznick Players. Ronald L. Bowers. LC 74-9278. (Illus.). 288p. 1976. 17.50 o.p. (ISBN 0-498-01375-8). A S Barnes.

Semantic & Pragmatic Language Disorders: Assessment & Remediation. Ellyn Lucas. 250p. 1980. text ed. 21.95 (ISBN 0-89443-327-X). Aspen Systems.

Semantic Problems of Translated Subject Headings. Gertrude Soonja Lee Koh. 1979. write for info. (ISBN 0-686-25169-5). CHCUS Inc.

Semantico-Syntax. Frans Liefrink. (Linguistics Library Ser). 192p. 1974. text ed. 15.95x (ISBN 0-582-55035-1). Longman.

Semantics: A New Outline. F. R. Palmer. LC 75-9089. (Illus.). 160p. 1976. 23.50 (ISBN 0-521-20927-7); pap. 7.95x (ISBN 0-521-09999-4). Cambridge U Pr.

Semantics: An Interdisciplinary Reader in Philosophy, Linguistics & Psychology. D. D. Steinberg & L. A. Jakobovits. LC 78-123675. (Illus.). 1971. 49.50 (ISBN 0-521-07822-9); pap. 14.95x (ISBN 0-521-20499-2). Cambridge U Pr.

Semantics & Language Analysis. Robert L. Benjamin. LC 77-75141. (Speech Communication Ser). 1970. pap. 3.35 o.p. (ISBN 0-672-61085-X, SC15). Bobbs.

Semantics & Philosophy. Ed. by Milton K. Munitz & Peter K. Unger. LC 74-15427. 291p. 1974. 18.00x (ISBN 0-8147-5366-3); pap. 7.00x (ISBN 0-8147-5376-0). NYU Pr.

Semantics-Directed Compiler Generation: Proceedings. Ed. by N. D. Jones. (Lecture Notes in Computer Science Ser.: Vol. 94). 489p. 1981. pap. 27.00 (ISBN 0-387-10250-7). Springer-Verlag.

Semantics for a Question-Answering System. William A. Woods. LC 79-50824. (Outstanding Dissertations in the Computer Sciences Ser.: Vol. 27). 1980. lib. bdg. 31.00 (ISBN 0-8240-4419-3). Garland Pub.

Semantics of Biblical Language. James Barr. 1961. 27.50x (ISBN 0-19-826607-3). Oxford U Pr.

Semantics of Coordination. Ewald Lang & William L. Taylor. (Studies in Language Companion Ser.: 9). 350p. Date not set. text ed. 54.25x (ISBN 90-272-3008-0). Humanities.

Semantics of Scope in English. Anthony S. Kroch. Ed. by Jorge Hankamer. LC 78-66559. (Outstanding Dissertations in Linguistics Ser.). 1979. lib. bdg. 30.00 (ISBN 0-8240-9681-9). Garland Pub.

Semantics of the Modal Auxiliaries in Contemporary German. Lowell Bouma. (Janua Linguarum Ser. Practica: No. 146). 1973. pap. text ed. 28.25x (ISBN 90-279-2390-6). Mouton.

Semantics One. J. Lyons. LC 76-40838. (Illus.). 1977. 42.50 (ISBN 0-521-21473-4); pap. 11.95x (ISBN 0-521-29165-8). Cambridge U Pr.

Semantics: Theories of Meaning in Generative Grammer. J. A. Fodor. 1977. text ed. 18.50 scp o.p. (ISBN 0-690-00866-X, HarpC). Har-Row.

Semantics: Theories of Meaning in Generative Grammar. Janet D. Fodor. (Language & Thought Ser.). 240p. 1980. pap. 7.95 (ISBN 0-674-80134-2). Harvard U Pr.

Semantics Two. J. Lyons. LC 76-40838. (Illus.). 1977. 49.50 (ISBN 0-521-21560-9); pap. 13.95x (ISBN 0-521-29186-0). Cambridge U Pr.

Semantische Relationen im Text und im System. Erhard Agricola. (Janua Linguarum, Ser. Minor: No. 113). 1972. pap. text ed. 22.50x (ISBN 90-279-1977-1). Mouton.

Semasia: Beitrage Zue Germanischromanischen Sorachforschung, Band IV. Robert Anderson. 1977. pap. text ed. 23.00x (ISBN 0-391-02045-5). Humanities.

Semasia: Beitrage Zur Germanisch-Romanischen Sprachforschung, Band 1. Ed. by Robert Anderson et al. (Orig., Ger.). 1974. pap. text ed. 15.00x (ISBN 0-391-02046-3). Humanities.

Semasia: Beitrage Zur Germanisch-Romanischen Sprachforschung, Band 2. Ed. by Robert Anderson et al. (Orig., Ger.). 1975. pap. text ed. 40.00x (ISBN 0-391-02045-5). Humanities.

Semasia: Beitrage zur Germanisch-Romanischen Sprachforschung, Band 5. Ed. by Robert Anderson. (Orig.). 1980. pap. text ed. 19.50x (ISBN 0-391-02047-1). Humanities.

Semi-Aquatic & Aquatic Hemiptera of California (Herteroptera: Hemiptera) Ed. by Arnold Menke. (California Insect Survey Ser.: Vol. 21). 1979. pap. 19.50x (ISBN 0-520-09592-8). U of Cal Pr.

Semi-Conductor C-029: Crystals, Junctions, Dopants. 1981. 850.00 (ISBN 0-89336-251-4). BCC.

Semi-Constructs of the Secretaire De Registre. Carl D. Clark & Loris Essary. 1980. pap. 2.00 signed ed. (ISBN 0-918406-07-2). Future Pr.

Semi-Professions and Their Organization. Amitai Etzioni. LC 69-10481. 1969. 13.95 o.s.i. (ISBN 0-02-909600-6). Free Pr.

Semiannual Report: A Kentucky Energy Resource Utilization Program. Ed. by R. William De Vore. 1978. pap. text ed. 5.00 (ISBN 0-89779-004-9); microfiche 1.50 (ISBN 0-89779-005-7). OES Pubns.

Semiconductor Circuit Elements. T. D. Towers & Sol Libes. (Illus.). (gr. 10 up). 1977. pap. 8.35 (ISBN 0-8104-0859-7). Hayden.

Semiconductor Electronics. Paul Ankrum. LC 76-135025. (Illus.). 1971. 26.95 (ISBN 0-13-806257-9). P-H.

Semiconductor Electronics Design. Fred K. Manasse. LC 76-13638. (Illus.). 1977. text ed. 26.95 (ISBN 0-13-806273-0). P-H.

Semiconductor Fundamentals. R. F. Coughlin & F. F. Driscoll. (Illus.). 336p. 1976. 18.95 (ISBN 0-13-806406-7). P-H.

Semiconductor General Purpose Replacements. 2nd ed. The Howard W. Sams Engineering Staff. LC 78-64982. 1979. pap. 14.95 o.p. (ISBN 0-672-21576-4). Sams.

Semiconductor General Purpose Replacements. 3rd ed. Howard W. Sams Engineering Staff. 1980. pap. 17.95 (ISBN 0-672-21730-9). Sams.

Semiconductor Heterojunctions. B. L. Sharma & R. K. Purohit. LC 73-18449. 1974. text ed. 45.00 (ISBN 0-08-017747-6). Pergamon.

Semiconductor Injection Lasers. J. K. Butler. LC 79-91615. 400p. 1980. 36.95 (ISBN 0-471-08156-6, Pub. by Wiley Interscience); pap. 24.00 (ISBN 0-471-08157-4). Wiley.

Semiconductor Injection Lasers. Ed. by J. K. Butler. LC 79-91615. 1980. 36.95 (ISBN 0-87942-129-0). Inst Electrical.

Semiconductor Logic & Switching Circuits. 2nd ed. Samuel Oppenheimer. LC 72-92573. 1973. text ed. 19.95x (ISBN 0-675-09016-4); instructor's manual 3.95 (ISBN 0-686-66490-6). Merrill.

Semiconductor Memories. Ed. by J. Eimbinder. LC 72-148501. 1971. 20.95 o.p. (ISBN 0-471-23460-5, Pub. by Wiley-Interscience). Wiley.

Semiconductor Memories. Ed. by David A. Hodges. LC 72-86206. 1972. 8.95 o.p. (ISBN 0-87942-013-8). Inst Electrical.

Semiconductor Nuclear-Particle Detectors & Circuits. National Academy Of Sciences Division Of Physical Sciences. 1969. 26.00 (ISBN 0-309-01593-6). Natl Acad Pr.

Semiconductor Optoelectronics: Proceedings. Ed. by Marian A. Herman. 1981. 44.00 (ISBN 0-471-27589-1, Pub. by Wiley-Interscience). Wiley.

Semiconductor Plasma Instabilities. Hans L. Hartnagel. 1969. text ed. 14.95x o.p. (ISBN 0-435-69390-5). Heinemann Ed.

Semiconductor Power Devices: Physics of Operation & Fabrication Technology. Sorab K. Ghandhi. LC 77-8019. 1977. 26.95 (ISBN 0-471-02999-8, Pub by Wiley-Interscience). Wiley.

Semiconductores. (Serie de Fisica: No. 6). (Span.). 1970. pap. 1.00 o.p. (ISBN 0-8270-6170-6). OAS.

Semiconductors. 2nd ed. OAS General Secretariat Department of Scientific & Technological Affairs. (Serie De Fisica (Monograph on Physics): No. 6). 63p. 1980. Repr. text ed. 2.00 (ISBN 0-8270-1068-0). OAS.

Semiconductors. 2nd ed. R. A. Smith. LC 77-82515. 1978. 86.50 (ISBN 0-521-21824-1); pap. 25.95x (ISBN 0-521-29314-6). Cambridge U Pr.

Semiconductors & Semimetals. Ed. by R. K. Willardson & A. C. Beer. Incl. Vol. 1. Physics of III-V Compounds. 1967. 52.75 (ISBN 0-12-752101-1); Vol. 2. Physics of III-V Compounds. 1966. 52.75 (ISBN 0-12-752102-X); Vol. 3. Optical Properties of III-V Compounds. 1967. 52.75 (ISBN 0-12-752103-8); Vol. 4. Physics of III-V Compounds. 1968. 52.75 (ISBN 0-12-752104-6); Vol. 5. Infrared Detectors. 1970. 52.75 (ISBN 0-12-752105-4); Vol. 6. Injection Phenomena. 1970. 52.75 (ISBN 0-12-752106-2); Vol. 7A. Semiconductor Applications & Devices. 1971. 52.75 (ISBN 0-12-752107-0); Vol. 7B. Applications & Devices. 1971. 52.75 (ISBN 0-12-752147-X); Vol. 8. Techniques for Studying Semiconducting Materials. 1971. 52.75 (ISBN 0-12-752108-9); Vol. 9. Modulation Techniques. 1972. 52.75 (ISBN 0-12-752109-7); Vol. 10. 1975. 52.75 (ISBN 0-12-752110-0); Vol. 11. 1976. 52.75 (ISBN 0-685-23206-9); Vol. 12. 1977. 50.50 (ISBN 0-12-752112-7). Acad Pr.

Semiconductors & Semimetals: Cadmium Telluride. Ed. by R. K. Willardson et al. 1978. Vol. 13. 28.00 (ISBN 0-12-752113-5); Vol. 14. 1979. 32.00 (ISBN 0-12-752114-3). Acad Pr.

Semiconductors & Semimetals: Contacts, Junctions, Emitters, Vol. 15. Ed. by Robert Willardson & A. C. Beer. 1981. price not set (ISBN 0-12-752115-1). Acad Pr.

Semigroups. Ed. by T. E. Hall et al. LC 80-23748. 1980. 18.00 (ISBN 0-12-319450-4). Acad Pr.

Semilia De Zanahoria (Carrot Seed) (ps-3). pap. 1.50 (ISBN 0-590-05417-1, Schol Pap). Schol Bk Serv.

Semimicro Qualitative Analysis. 3rd ed. Alfred B. Garrett et al. 1966. pap. 16.95 (ISBN 0-471-00192-9). Wiley.

Semimicro Qualitative Organic Analysis. 3rd ed. Nicholas D. Cheronis et al. LC 80-461. (Systematic Identification of Organic Compounds). 1072p. 1981. Repr. of 1965 ed. lib. bdg. write for info. (ISBN 0-89874-124-6). Krieger.

Seminal Cases & Contemporary Commentaries: England. Ed. by Daniel N. Robinson. (Contributions to the History of Psychology Ser.: Insanity & Jurisprudence). 1980. 30.00 (ISBN 0-89093-331-6). U Pubns Amer.

Seminal Cases & Contemporary Commentaries: The United States. Ed. by Daniel N. Robinson. (Insanity & Jurisprudence). 1980. 30.00 (ISBN 0-89093-330-8). U Pubns Amer.

Seminal Research Papers. D. A. Spalding et al. (Contributions to the History of Psycholgy Ser.: No. 11, Pt. A Orientations). 1978. Repr. of 1873 ed. 30.00 (ISBN 0-89093-160-7). U Pubns Amer.

Seminar on AACR2. Ed. by G. Rae. 1980. pap. 17.50 (ISBN 0-85365-563-4, Pub. by Lib Assn England). Oryx Pr.

Seminar on Energy Policy: The Carter Proposals. 1979. pap. 3.25 (ISBN 0-8447-3355-5). Am Enterprise.
Seminar on Haematology & Oncology. Ed. by H. Ekert. (Journal: Paediatrician: Vol. 9, No. 2). (Illus.). 88p. 1980. softcover 19.75 (ISBN 3-8055-1302-X). S Karger.
Seminaries & Psychology. 70p. 1978. 2.95. Natl Cath Educ.
Seminario sobre Prioridades para el Desarrollo Cientifico & Tecnologico de Paraguay. (Studies on Scientific & Technological Development: No. 29). 1977. pap. text ed. 3.00 (ISBN 0-8270-6005-X). OAS.
Seminars in Nephrology. Ed. by E. Lovell Becker. LC 76-28438. (Perspectives in Nephrology & Hypertension Ser.). 1976. 25.00 o.p. (ISBN 0-471-01804-X, Pub. by Wiley Medical). Wiley.
Seminole Chief (Billy Bowlegs) Or the Captives of Kissimmee, Repr. Of 1865 Ed. Hazelton. Bd. with Old Rube, the Hunter: Or the Crow Captive. a Tale of the Great Plains. Hamilton Holmes. Repr. of 1866 ed. LC 75-7105. (Indian Captivities Ser.: Vol. 80). 1976. lib. bdg. 44.00 (ISBN 0-8240-1704-8). Garland Pub.
Seminole Indians. Sonia Bleeker. (Illus.). (gr. 3-6). 1954. PLB 6.67 (ISBN 0-688-31455-4). Morrow.
Seminole Music. Frances Densmore. LC 72-1878. (Music Ser.). (Illus.). 276p. 1972. Repr. of 1956 ed. lib. bdg. 19.50 (ISBN 0-306-70506-0). Da Capo.
Seminoles. Edwin C. McReynolds. (Civilization of the American Indian Ser.: No. 47). (Illus.). 1957. 15.95 o.p. (ISBN 0-8061-0382-5); pap. 7.95 (ISBN 0-8061-1255-7). U of Okla Pr.
Semiochemicals: Their Role in Pest Control. Ed. by Donald A. Nordlund et al. 400p. 1981. 27.50 (ISBN 0-471-05803-3, Pub. by Wiley-Interscience). Wiley.
Semiologies Des Litteraires. G. Mounin. (Casal Bequest Lecture Ser). 1977. text ed. 3.75x (ISBN 0-485-16107-9, Athlone Pr). Humanities.
Semiology. Pierre Guiraud. 1975. 12.00x (ISBN 0-7100-8005-0); pap. 6.95 (ISBN 0-7100-8011-5). Routledge & Kegan.
Semiotic Themes. Ed. by Richard T. De George. (University of Kansas Humanistic Studies: No. 53). (Illus.). 284p. 1981. pap. 12.00 (ISBN 0-686-28731-2). U of KS Pubns.
Semiotics & Dialects: Ideology & the Text. Ed. by Peter V. Zima. (Linguistic & Literary Studies in Eastern Europe Ser.: No. 5). 400p. 1980. text ed. 45.75x (ISBN 90-272-1505-7). Humanities.
Semiotics of Culture. Ed. by Irene P. Winner & Jean Rmiker-Sebeok. (Approaches to Semiotics: No. 53). 1979. text ed. 51.75x (ISBN 90-279-7988-X). Mouton.
Semiotics of Films. Ed. by Achim Eschlach & Wendelin Rader. 203p. 1978. 26.00 (ISBN 0-89664-080-9, Pub. by K G Saur). Gale.
Semiotics of the Built Environment: An Introduction to Architectonic Analysis. Donald Preziosi. LC 78-20404. (Advances in Semiotics Ser.). (Illus.). 128p. 1979. 15.00x (ISBN 0-253-17638-7). Ind U Pr.
Semiotics Reader: The Manipulation of Signs & Symbols in Culture. Ed. by Marshal Blonsky. Date not set. 17.50 (ISBN 0-89396-008-X); pap. 7.95 (ISBN 0-89396-009-8). Urizen Bks.
Semiramide. Gioachino Rossini. Ed. by Philip Gossett & Charles Rosen. LC 76-49188. (Early Romantic Opera Ser.: Vol. 13). 1978. lib. bdg. 82.00 (ISBN 0-8240-2912-7). Garland Pub.
Semisynthetic Proteins. R. E. Offord. LC 79-40521. 235p. 1980. 58.95 (ISBN 0-471-27615-4, Pub. by Wiley-Interscience). Wiley.
Semitic Interference in Marcan Syntax. Elliott C. Maloney. LC 80-13016. (Society of Biblical Literature Dissertation Ser.: No. 51). 15.00x (06 01 51); pap. 10.50x (ISBN 0-89130-406-1). Scholars Pr CA.
Semitic Writing: From Pictograph to Alphabet. 3rd ed. Godfrey Driver. (Schweich Lectures). (Illus.). 1976. 47.50x (ISBN 0-19-725917-0). Oxford U Pr.
Semo: A Dolphin's Search for Christ. Sara G. Harrell. (Illus.). (gr. 5-7). 1977. 5.95 (ISBN 0-570-03458-2, 56-1292); pap. 2.50 (ISBN 0-570-03459-0, 56-1293). Concordia.
Semper Fidelis: The History of the United States Marine Corps. Allan R. Millett. LC 80-1059. (Macmillan Wars of the United States Ser.). (Illus.). 1980. 29.95 (ISBN 0-02-921590-0). Free Pr.
Senate & the Versailles Mandate System. Rayford W. Logan. LC 74-14357. 112p. 1975. Repr. of 1945 ed. lib. bdg. 11.75x (ISBN 0-8371-7798-7, LOVM). Greenwood.
Senate & Treaties, 1789-1817. Ralston Hayden. LC 73-127295. (Law, Politics, & History Ser). 1970. Repr. of 1920 ed. lib. bdg. 27.50 (ISBN 0-306-71164-8). Da Capo.
Senate Establishment. Joseph S. Clark et al. (Orig.). 1963. pap. 1.50 o.p. (ISBN 0-8090-0067-9, AmCen). Hill & Wang.
Senate Journal, 1943-1945. Allen Drury. LC 76-38824. (FDR & the Era of the New Deal Ser.). 1972. Repr. of 1963 ed. lib. bdg. 45.00 (ISBN 0-306-70448-X). Da Capo.
Senate Nobody Knows. Bernard Asbell. LC 80-8928. 480p. 1981. pap. text ed. 6.95x (ISBN 0-8018-2620-9). Johns Hopkins.
Senator Joe McCarthy. David M. Oshinsky. LC 77-18474. 1981. 12.95 (ISBN 0-02-923490-5). Free Pr.
Senator William J. Stone & the Politics of Compromise. Ruth Towne. (National University Publications, Political Science Ser). 1979. 15.00 (ISBN 0-8046-9232-7). Kennikat.
Send in the Lions. Eric Clark. LC 80-69371. 1981. 9.95 (ISBN 0-689-11125-8). Atheneum.
Send My Roots Rain: A Study of Religious Experience in the Poetry of Gerard Manley Hopkins. Donald Walhout. LC 80-23549. 210p. 1981. 14.95x (ISBN 0-8214-0565-9). Ohio U Pr.
Sendai. William Woolfolk. 288p. 1981. pap. 2.75 (ISBN 0-445-04628-7). Popular Lib.
Senderos De Navidad. Juan R. Picasso. 1980. pap. 0.65 (ISBN 0-311-08218-1). Casa Bautista.
Sending. Geoffrey Household. 192p. 1981. pap. 2.95 (ISBN 0-14-005780-3). Penguin.
Seneca. Ed. by C. D. Costa. (Greek & Latin Studies Ser.). 252p. 1974. 20.00x (ISBN 0-7100-7900-1). Routledge & Kegan.
Seneca: Agamemnon. Ed. by J. R. Tarrant. LC 76-15668. (Cambridge Classical Texts & Commentaries Ser.: No. 18). (Illus.). 1977. 59.00 (ISBN 0-521-20807-6). Cambridge U Pr.
Seneca Garden. Geri Guidetti. (Illus.). 26p. (Orig.). (gr. 2-8). 1981. pap. 3.95 (ISBN 0-938928-00-7). KMG Pubns OR.
Seneca, the Philosopher & His Modern Message. Richard M. Gummere. LC 63-10274. (Our Debt to Greece & Rome Ser). 145p. 1963. Repr. of 1930 ed. 15.00x (ISBN 0-8154-0098-5). Cooper Sq.
Seneca's Apocolocyntosis, New York, Nineteen Hundred & Two. Allan P. Ball. Ed. by Steele Commager. LC 77-70769. (Latin Poetry Ser.). 1979. lib. bdg. 27.50 (ISBN 0-8240-2951-8). Garland Pub.
Senegal. Sheldon Gellar. (Nations of Contemporary Africa Ser.). 128p. 1981. lib. bdg. 16.50x (ISBN 0-89158-837-X). Westview.
Senescence in Plants. Kenneth V. Thimann. 288p. 1980. 69.95 (ISBN 0-8493-5803-5). CRC Pr.
Sengai, the Zen Master. Daisetz T. Suzuki. LC 68-25738. (Illus.). 1971. 15.00 o.p. (ISBN 0-8212-0319-3). NYGS.
Senhor, Faze-Me Chorar. Tr. by Cookie Rodriguez. (Portugese Bks.). (Port.). 1979. 1.50 (ISBN 0-8297-0690-9). Life Pubs Intl.
Senior Adult Theatre: The American Theatre Association Handbook. Ed. by Roger Cornish & C. Robert Kase. LC 80-23485. (Illus.). 96p. 1981. 8.95x (ISBN 0-271-00275-1); pap. text ed. 5.95x (ISBN 0-271-00275-1). Pa St U Pr.
Senior Engineering Inspector. Jack Rudman. (Career Examination Ser.: C-2808). (Cloth bdg. avail. on request). 1980. pap. 12.00 (ISBN 0-8373-2808-X). Natl Learning.
Senior Forestry Technician. Jack Rudman. (Career Examination Ser.: C-2715). (Cloth bdg. avail. on request). 1980. pap. 12.00 (ISBN 0-8373-2715-6). Natl Learning.
Senior Golf. Robert O'Byrne. 1977. 10.95 (ISBN 0-87691-231-5). Winchester Pr.
Senior Hi Artist. Henry J. Filson. (Draw-Sketch Practice Ser.). (Illus.). 44p. 1978. plastic bdg. 3.75 (ISBN 0-918554-02-0). Old Violin.
Senior High School Library Catalog: 1980 Supplement to the 11th Ed. 1980. 50.00 (ISBN 0-8242-0619-3). Wilson.
Senior Medical Services Specialist. Jack Rudman. (Career Examination Ser.: C-2747). (Cloth bdg. avail. on request). 1980. pap. 14.00 (ISBN 0-8373-2747-4). Natl Learning.
Senior Micrographics Technician. Jack Rudman. (Career Examination Ser.: C-2762). (Cloth bdg. avail. on request). 1980. pap. 12.00 (ISBN 0-8373-2762-8). Natl Learning.
Senior Multiple Residence Inspector. Jack Rudman. (Career Examination Ser.: C-2843). (Cloth bdg. avail. on request). 1980. pap. 12.00 (ISBN 0-8373-2843-8). Natl Learning.
Senior Prom. Rosamond Du Jardin. (gr. 7-10). pap. 0.95 o.p. (ISBN 0-425-03534-4, Highland). Berkley Pub.
Senior Prom. Rosamond Du Jardin. (gr. 4-9). 1957. 9.89 (ISBN 0-397-30388-2). Lippincott.
Senior Research Assistant. Jack Rudman. (Career Examination Ser.: C-2717). (Cloth bdg. avail. on request). 1980. pap. 14.00 (ISBN 0-8373-2717-2). Natl Learning.
Senior Title Searcher. Jack Rudman. (Career Examination Ser.: C-2086). (Cloth bdg. avail. on request). 1977. write for info. (ISBN 0-8373-2086-0). Natl Learning.
Senior Zoning Inspector. Jack Rudman. (Career Examination Ser.: C-2856). (Cloth bdg. avail. on request). 1980. pap. 12.00 (ISBN 0-8373-2856-X). Natl Learning.
Senor, Hazme Llorar. Tr. by Cookie Rodriguez. (Spanish Bks.). (Span.). 1978. 1.95 (ISBN 0-8297-0597-X). Life Pubs Intl.
Senor Presidente. Miguel Asturias. Tr. by Frances Partridge from Span. LC 64-10908. 1975. pap. text ed. 4.95x (ISBN 0-689-70521-2, 211). Atheneum.
Sens-Plastique. 2nd, rev. ed. Malcolm De Chazal. Ed. by Irving Weiss. LC 79-25078. 163p. (Orig.). 1980. pap. 6.00 (ISBN 0-915342-29-4). SUN.
Sensacion de Ser Alguien. Maurice Wagner. Tr. by David A. Cook from Eng. LC 77-16714. 300p. (Orig., Span.). 1977. pap. 4.95 (ISBN 0-89922-104-1). Edit Caribe.
Sensation & Perception. Stanley Coren et al. 439p. 1979. 19.95 (ISBN 0-12-188550-X). Acad Pr.
Sensation & Perception. E. Bruce Goldstein. 512p. 1980. text ed. 22.95x (ISBN 0-534-00760-0). Wadsworth Pub.
Sensation & Perception: An Integrated Approach. H. R. Schiffman. LC 76-185. 1976. text ed. 23.95 (ISBN 0-471-76091-9). Wiley.
Sensation & Perception in the History of Experimental Psychology. Edwin G. Boring. (Century Psychology Ser). 1977. 34.50x (ISBN 0-89197-491-1); pap. text ed. 19.50x (ISBN 0-89197-933-6). Irvington.
Sensation of Being Somebody. Maurice Wagner. 256p. 1975. 9.95 (ISBN 0-310-33970-7). Zondervan.
Sense & Nonsense About Prayer. Lehman Strauss. 1976. pap. 1.50 (ISBN 0-8024-7701-1). Moody.
Sense & Nonsense of Weld Defects. 2nd ed. Helmut Thielsch. (Monticello Bks). 56p. 1981. soft cover 5.00 (ISBN 0-686-28905-6). Jefferson Pubns.
Sense & Sense Development. rev. ed. R. A. Waldron. (Andre Deutsch Language Library). 1979. 35.50x (ISBN 0-233-95948-3). Westview.
Sense & Sensibility. Jane Austen. (Literature Ser). (gr. 10-12). 1970. pap. text ed. 3.58 (ISBN 0-87720-738-0). AMSCO Sch.
Sense & Sensibility. Jane Austen. (Zodiac Press Ser). 1978. 10.95 (ISBN 0-7011-1237-9, Pub. by Chatto Bodley Jonathan). Merrimack Bk Serv.
Sense & Sensibility. Jane Austen. 544p. 1981. Repr. lib. bdg. 19.95x (ISBN 0-89966-287-0). Buccaneer Bks.
Sense of Beauty. George Santayana. 1896. pap. text ed. 2.50 (ISBN 0-486-20238-0). Dover.
Sense of Biblical Narrative: Three Structural Analyses in the Old Testament. David Jobling. (JSOT Supplement Ser.: No. 7). 104p. 1978. text ed. 25.95x (ISBN 0-905774-06-X, Pub. by JSOT Pr England); pap. text ed. 12.95x (ISBN 0-905774-12-4, Pub. by JSOT Pr England). Eisenbrauns.
Sense of Detachment. John Osborne. 1973. 5.95 o.p. (ISBN 0-571-10211-5, Pub. by Faber & Faber). Merrimack Bk Serv.
Sense of Form in Art. Heinrich Woelfflin. LC 57-12877. (Illus., Orig.). pap. 4.95 (ISBN 0-8284-0153-5). Chelsea Pub.
Sense of History in Greek & Shakespearean Drama. Tom F. Driver. LC 59-15146. 1960. pap. 6.00x (ISBN 0-231-08576-1). Columbia U Pr.
Sense of Honor. James Webb. LC 80-25852. 81. 10.95 (ISBN 0-13-806646-9). P-H.
Sense of Injustice. Edmond Cahn. 7.50 (ISBN 0-8446-1795-4). Peter Smith.
Sense of Life, a Sense of Sin. Kennedy, Eugene C., M.M. 200p. 1976. pap. 1.95 (ISBN 0-385-12070-2, Im). Doubleday.
Sense of Mission: Guidance from the Gospel of John. Albert C. Winn. 1981. pap. price not set (ISBN 0-664-24365-7). Westminster.
Sense of Movement. Thom Gunn. 1968. pap. 3.95 (ISBN 0-571-08530-X, Pub. by Faber & Faber). Merrimack Bk Serv.
Sense of Sentences. Wilbert J. Levy. (Orig.). (gr. 9-12). 1976. wkbk 5.67 (ISBN 0-87720-336-9). AMSCO Sch.
Sense of Shadow. Kate Wilhelm. 1981. 9.95 (ISBN 0-686-69061-3). HM.
Sense of Sociology. rev. ed. Lee Braude. LC 79-20785. 160p. 1981. Repr. of 1974 ed. write for info. (ISBN 0-89874-016-9). Krieger.
Sense of Story: Essays on Contemporary Writers for Children. John R. Townsend. 216p. 1973. pap. 6.50 (ISBN 0-87675-276-8). Horn Bk.
Sense of the Cosmos: The Encounter of Modern Science & Ancient Truth. Jacob Needleman. 1977. pap. 4.50 (ISBN 0-525-47446-3). Dutton.
Sense of the Sixties. Edward G. Quinn & Paul J. Dolan. LC 68-12834. (Orig.). 1968. pap. text ed. 7.95 (ISBN 0-02-925560-0). Free Pr.
Sense of Well Being in America: Recent Patterns & Trends. Angus Campbell. 256p. 1980. 14.95 (ISBN 0-07-009683-X). McGraw.
Sense of Where You Are. John McPhee. 1978. 9.95 o.p. (ISBN 0-374-26093-1); pap. 4.95 (ISBN 0-374-51485-2). FS&G.
Sense of Wonder. Edgar J. Saxon. 64p. 1980. pap. 3.25x (ISBN 0-8464-1048-6). Beekman Pubs.
Sense Relaxation Below Your Mind. Bernard Gunther. 1968. 6.95 o.s.i. (ISBN 0-02-546600-3). Macmillan.
Sense, Understanding & Reason: A Digest of Kant's First Critique. Narayanrao A. Nikam. 1966. 4.00 o.p. (ISBN 0-210-22654-4). Asia.
Sensei & His People: The Building of a Japanese Commune. Yoshie Sugihara & David W. Plath. LC 69-15427. 1969. 18.50x (ISBN 0-520-01449-9). U of Cal Pr.
Senses & Sensitivity. Alice Yardley. LC 72-95335. 144p. 1973. 3.25 o.p. (ISBN 0-590-07329-X, Citation). Schol Bk Serv.
Senses & the Intellect. Alexander Bain. (Contributions to the History of Psychology Ser.: No. 4, Pt. A Orientations). 1978. Repr. of 1855 ed. 30.00 (ISBN 0-89093-153-4). U Pubns Amer.
Senses Considered As Perceptual Systems. James J. Gibson. LC 66-7132. 1966. text ed. 29.95 (ISBN 0-395-04494-4). HM.
Senses of Animals. E. T. Burtt & A. Pringle. LC 73-77794. (Wykeham Science Ser.: No. 26). 1974. 9.95x (ISBN 0-8448-1153-X). Crane-Russak Co.
Senses: Seeing, Hearing, Tasting, Touching & Smelling. John M. Scott. LC 75-2189. (Finding-Out Books for Science & Social Studies, Grades 1-4). (Illus.). 64p. (gr. 2-4). 1975. PLB 5.41 o.p. (ISBN 0-8193-0821-8). Enslow Pubs.
Sensible Talk About Cancer: A Physician's Program for Prevention. Siegfried Heyden & Elen S. Pittillo. 128p. (Orig.). 1981. pap. 3.95 (ISBN 0-8326-2247-8, 7440). Delair.
Sensibly Thin. Stanley H. Title & Charles M. Klein. LC 78-27039. 1979. 11.95 (ISBN 0-88229-446-6); pap. 6.95 (ISBN 0-88229-665-5). Nelson-Hall.
Sensitivity in the Foreign Language Classroom. Ed. by James W. Dodge. Incl. Individualization of Instruction. Ronald L. Gougher; Interraction in the Foreign Language Class. Gertrude Moskowitz; Teaching Spanish to the Native Spanish Speaker. Herman LaFontaine. 142p. 1973. pap. 7.95x (ISBN 0-915432-73-0). NE Conf Teach Foreign.
Sensitivity Methods in Control Theory. Ed. by L. Radanovic. 1966. 28.00 (ISBN 0-08-011827-5); pap. 14.50 (ISBN 0-08-013784-9). Pergamon.
Sensitivity Training for Educators: An Evaluation. J. L. Khanna & Prabha Khanna. 1981. 7.95 (ISBN 0-533-04031-0). Vantage.
Sensorineural Hearing Loss, Vertigo & Tinnitus: International Symposium. Michael M. Paparella et al. 232p. 1981. write for info. (6750-8). Williams & Wilkins.
Sensors for Automotive Systems. Society of Automotive Engineers. 1980. 18.00 (ISBN 0-89883-229-2). Soc Auto Engineers.
Sensory Aids for the Hearing Impaired. Ed. by H. Levitt et al. LC 76-28875. 1980. 46.95 (ISBN 0-87942-133-9). Inst Electrical.
Sensory Aids of the Hearing Impaired. Levitt. LC 76-28875. 640p. 1980. 46.95 (ISBN 0-471-08436-0, Pub. by Wiley-Interscience); pap. 30.50 (ISBN 0-471-08437-9). Wiley.
Sensory & Noetic Consciousness (Psychology from an Empirical Standpoint III) Franz Brentano. Tr. by Margaret Schattle & Linda L. McAlister. 1980. text ed. 20.75x (ISBN 0-391-01175-8). Humanities.
Sensory Assessment of Water Quality. B. C. Zoeteman. (Pergamon Series on Environmental Science: Vol. 2). (Illus.). 160p. 1980. 33.00 (ISBN 0-08-023848-3). Pergamon.
Sensory Awareness: The Study of Living As Experience. Charles V. Brooks. LC 73-7432. (Esalen Books). (Illus.). 320p. 1974. 12.95 o.p. (ISBN 0-670-63391-7). Viking Pr.
Sensory Changes in the Elderly. Francis B. Colavita. (Illus.). 152p. 1978. 14.50 (ISBN 0-398-03829-5). C C Thomas.
Sensory Coding in the Mammalian Nervous System. George Somjen. LC 75-31519. 286p. 1975. softcover 7.95 (ISBN 0-306-20020-1, Rosetta). Plenum Pub.
Sensory Deprivation: Fifteen Years of Research. Ed. by John P. Zubek. LC 69-12143. (Century Psychology Ser.). (Illus.). 1969. 26.50x (ISBN 0-89197-400-8); pap. text ed. 8.95x (ISBN 0-89197-401-6). Irvington.
Sensory Functions: Proceedings of the 28th International Congress of Physiological Sciences, Budapest, 1980. Ed. by E. Grastyan & P. Molnar. LC 80-41852. (Advances in Physiological Sciences). (Illus.). 350p. 1981. 40.00 (ISBN 0-08-027337-8). Pergamon.
Sensory Integration & Learning Disorders. A. Jean Ayres. LC 72-91446. 294p. 1973. 15.50x (ISBN 0-87424-303-3). Western Psych.
Sensory Integration & the Child. A. Jean Ayres. LC 79-66987. 191p. 1979. pap. text ed. 8.95 (ISBN 0-87424-158-8). Western Psych.

Sensory Integration in Children: Evoked Potentials & Intersensory Functions in Pediatrics & Psychology. Thorne Shipley. (Illus.). 176p. 1980. 15.75 (ISBN 0-398-03869-4). C C Thomas.

Sensory Isolation & Personality Change. Mark Kammerman. (Illus.). 324p. 1977. 17.50 (ISBN 0-398-03581-4). C C Thomas.

Sensory-Motor Dysfunction & Therapy in Infancy & Early Childhood. Delmont Morrison et al. (Illus.). 288p. 1978. 17.50 (ISBN 0-398-03766-3). C C Thomas.

Sensory Physiology & Structure of Molecules. (Structure & Bonding Ser.: Vol. 114). (Illus.). 146p. 1980. 36.80 (ISBN 0-387-09958-1). Springer-Verlag.

Sensory Processes at the Neuronal & Behavioral Levels. Ed. by G. V. Gersuni. 1971. 46.50 (ISBN 0-12-281350-2). Acad Pr.

Sensory Processing, Perception, & Behavior. Robert B. Livingston. LC 76-19854. 1978. soft cover 10.50 (ISBN 0-89004-134-2). Raven.

Sensory Properties of Food. Ed. by G. G. Birch et al. (Illus.). 1977. 49.70x (ISBN 0-85334-744-1). Burgess-Intl Ideas.

Sensory Saltation: Metastability in the Perceptual World. Frank A. Geldard. LC 75-22269. 133p. 1975. 10.00 (ISBN 0-470-29571-6). Halsted Pr.

Sensory Systems & Communication in the Elderly. Ed. by J. Mark Ordy & Ken Brizzee. LC 79-65426. (Aging Ser.: Vol. 10). 1979. text ed. 32.00 (ISBN 0-89004-235-7). Raven.

Sensual Drugs. H. B. Jones & Helen C. Jones. LC 76-8154. (Illus.). 1977. 29.50 (ISBN 0-521-21247-2); pap. 7.95 (ISBN 0-521-29077-5). Cambridge U Pr.

Sensual Gospel. Michael T. Darkow. Date not set. 8.95 (ISBN 0-533-04774-9). Vantage.

Sensuous Couple. 2nd ed. Robert Chartham. 192p. 1981. pap. 2.50 (ISBN 0-345-29543-9); 12 copy counter display 30.00 (ISBN 0-345-29543-9). Ballantine.

Sensuous Dirty Old Man. Dr. A., pseud. pap. 1.50 (ISBN 0-451-07199-9, W7199, Sig). NAL.

Sentence. Pauline Smolin & Philip T. Clayton. 1977. pap. text ed. 5.95x (ISBN 0-669-00783-8). Heath.

Sentence Analysis in Modern Malay. Martha B. Lewis. LC 69-10062. 1969. 54.00 (ISBN 0-521-05554-7). Cambridge U Pr.

Sentence Combination: Writing & Combining Standard English Sentences, Bk. II. Alice Pack & Lynn Henrichsen. 1980. pap. 4.95 (ISBN 0-88377-174-8). Newbury Hse.

Sentence Combination: Writing & Combining Standard English Sentences, Bk. II. Alice C. Pack & Lynn Henrichsen. 128p. (Orig.). 1981. pap. text ed. 5.95 (ISBN 0-88377-174-8). Newbury Hse.

Sentence Combing & Paragraph Building. William Strong. (Illus.). 320p. 1981. pap. text ed. 8.95 (ISBN 0-394-31264-3). Random.

Sentence Combining in Second Language Construction. T. Cooper et al. (Language in Education Ser.: No. 31). 1980. pap. text ed. 7.95 (ISBN 0-87281-130-1). Ctr Appl Ling.

Sentence Composing Eleven. Don Killgallon. 152p. (gr. 10-12). 1979. pap. text ed. 5.20x (ISBN 0-8104-6123-4); teacher's guide 1.75 (ISBN 0-8104-6121-8). Hayden.

Sentence Composing Ten. Don Killgallon. 160p. (gr. 10-12). 1980. pap. 5.20x (ISBN 0-8104-6122-6); tchr's. guide 1.75 (ISBN 0-8104-6121-8). Hayden.

Sentence Composing Twelve. Don Killgallon. 160p. (gr. 10-12). 1979. pap. 5.20x (ISBN 0-8104-6124-2); 1.75 (ISBN 0-8104-6121-8). Hayden.

Sentence Composition. Wilbert J. Levy. (Orig.). 1976. wkbk 5.67 (ISBN 0-87720-950-2). AMSCO Sch.

Sentence: How It Works. John Almquist. 1977. pap. text ed. 4.25x (ISBN 0-88334-100-X). Ind Sch Pr.

Sentence in Biblical Hebrew. Francis I. Andersen. (Janua Linguarum, Ser. Practica: No. 231). 209p. 1974. pap. text ed. 34.10x (ISBN 90-2792-673-5). Mouton.

Sentence in Written English: A Syntactic Study Based on an Analysis of Scientific Texts. Rodney D. Huddleston. LC 76-139714. (Cambridge Studies in Linguistics). 1971. 49.50 (ISBN 0-521-08062-2). Cambridge U Pr.

Sentence Mastery. 2nd ed. Jack S. Romine. 1966. text ed. 8.95 (ISBN 0-13-806695-7). P-H.

Sentence Mastery: A & B. Edgar H. Schuster. Ed. by Hester E. Weeden. (Sentence Mastery Ser.). (Illus.). 160p. (gr. 7). 1980. A. 3.96 (ISBN 0-07-055621-0, W); B. 3.96 (ISBN 0-07-055622-9). McGraw.

Sentence Mastery B: Pupil's Edition. Edgar H. Schuster. (Sentence Mastery Ser.). (Illus.). 160p. (gr. 8). 1980. 3.96 (ISBN 0-07-055622-9, W). McGraw.

Sentence Structure. Philip Lutgendorf & Mary Jane Gray. LC 77-730353. (Illus.). (gr. 7-9). 1977. pap. text ed. 95.00 (ISBN 0-89290-119-5, A144). Soc for Visual.

Sentence Writing. William Klink. LC 80-5805. (Illus.). 141p. (Orig.). 1981. pap. text ed. 7.50 (ISBN 0-8191-1430-8). U Pr of Amer.

Sentencecraft. Sheila Y. Graham. (Illus.). 128p. 1976. pap. text ed. 6.95 (ISBN 0-13-806224-2). P-H.

Sentenced to Life: Reflections on Politics, Education, & Law. John P. Roche. LC 73-13361. 450p. 1974. 12.95 o.s.i. (ISBN 0-02-604350-5). Macmillan.

Sentences. Howard Nemerov. LC 80-17702. 76p. 1980. 8.95 (ISBN 0-226-57260-9). U of Chicago Pr.

Sentences & Other Systems: A Language & Learning Curriculum for Hearing-Impaired Children. Peter M. Blackwell et al. 1978. 11.75 (ISBN 0-88200-118-3). Bell Assn Deaf.

Sentences, Paragraphs, & Short Essays. Anthony Winkler & Jo Ray McCuen. 256p. 1980. pap. text ed. 8.95 (ISBN 0-574-22060-7, 13-5060); instr's. guide avail. (ISBN 0-574-22061-5, 13-5061). SRA.

Sentencing. Ed. by Hyman Gross & Andrew Von Hirsch. 416p. 1981. text ed. 19.95x (ISBN 0-19-502763-9); pap. text ed. 9.95x (ISBN 0-19-502764-7). Oxford U Pr.

Sentencing Councils in the Federal Courts: An Evaluation. Charles D. Phillips. LC 79-3784. 128p. 1980. 19.95x (ISBN 0-669-03514-9). Lexington Bks.

Sentencing: Process & Purpose. Gerhard O. Mueller. (Criminal Law Education & Research Center Ser.). 228p. 1977. 19.75 (ISBN 0-398-03591-1). C C Thomas.

Sentics: The Touch of Emotions. Clynes, Manfred, Dr. LC 74-17608. 1978. pap. 3.95 (ISBN 0-385-08622-9, Anch). Doubleday.

Sentience. Wallace I. Matson. LC 75-3774. 160p. 1976. 13.75x (ISBN 0-520-02987-9). U of Cal Pr.

Sentimens sur la Distinction Des Manieres de Peinture, des Sein et Graeure. Abraham Bosse. (Documents of Art & Architectural History Series 2: Vol. 5). 142p. (Fr.). 1981. Repr. of 1649 ed. 27.50x (ISBN 0-89371-205-1). Broude Intl Edns.

Sentimental Education. Tr. by Gustave Flaubert. pap. 1.50 o.p. (ISBN 0-451-50579-4, CW579, Sig Classics). NAL.

Sentimental Education: Stories. Joyce C. Oates. 192p. 1981. 12.95 (ISBN 0-525-19950-0). Dutton.

Sentimental Journey Through France & Italy by Mr. Yorick. rev. ed. Laurence Sterne. Ed. by Gardner D. Stout, Jr. (Illus.). 1967. 22.75x (ISBN 0-520-01228-3). U of Cal Pr.

Sentimental Revolution: French Writers of 1690-1740. Geoffroy Atkinson. Ed. by Abraham C. Keller. LC 64-18424. 200p. 1966. 10.50 (ISBN 0-295-74024-8). U of Wash Pr.

Sentiments & Activities. George C. Homans. LC 62-10590. 1962. 9.95 o.s.i. (ISBN 0-02-914890-1). Free Pr.

Sentinel. Emerson Daggett. 12p. (Orig.). 1981. pap. 2.00 (ISBN 0-932942-01-6). Pacific NW Labor.

Sentinels. Peter Carter. 200p. (gr. 7 up). 1980. 10.95 (ISBN 0-19-271438-4). Oxford U Pr.

Separate Life. S. A. Padmanab. 9.00 (ISBN 0-89253-712-4); flexible cloth 4.80 (ISBN 0-89253-713-2). Ind-US Inc.

Separate Peace. John Knowles. (gr. 9 up). 1960. 11.95 (ISBN 0-02-564840-3); large print ed. 6.95 (ISBN 0-02-489390-0). Macmillan.

Separate, Unequal, but More Autonomous. Ward Morehouse. (Working Papers in the World Order Models Project Ser.). 50p. (Orig.). 1981. pap. 1.50 (ISBN 0-686-28913-7). Transaction Bks.

Separates That Travel. Editors of Time-Life Books. LC 75-21824. (Art of Sewing). (Illus.). (gr. 6 up). 1975. PLB 11.97 (ISBN 0-8094-1759-6, Pub. by Time-Life). Silver.

Separation & Suffering: Hindu & Christian Views of Love. Dorothy Perkins. (Orig.). 1980. pap. 3.00 (ISBN 0-9604742-0-X). D J Perkins.

Separation-Individuation Theory & Clinical Practice. Joyce Edward et al. 324p. 1981. text ed. 22.95 (ISBN 0-89876-018-6). Gardner Pr.

Separation Methods in Biochemistry. 2nd ed. C. J. Morris & P. Morris. LC 73-9380. 1976. 92.95x (ISBN 0-470-61579-6). Halsted Pr.

Separation Methods in Chemical Analysis. James M. Miller. LC 74-13781. 320p. 1975. 26.00 (ISBN 0-471-60490-9, Pub. by Wiley-Interscience). Wiley.

Separation of Cells & Subcellular Elements. Ed. by H. Peeters. (Illus.). 1979. 22.00 (ISBN 0-08-024957-4). Pergamon.

Separation of Church & State in the United States. Alvin W. Johnson & Frank H. Yost. Repr. of 1948 ed. lib. bdg. 15.75x (ISBN 0-8371-2436-0, JOCS). Greenwood.

Separation of Church & State in Virginia. Hamilton J. Eckenrode. LC 75-122164. (Civil Liberties in American History Ser). 1971. Repr. of 1910 ed. lib. bdg. 17.50 (ISBN 0-306-71969-X). Da Capo.

Separation Processes. 2nd ed. C. Judson King. (Chemical Engineering Ser.). (Illus.). 1979. text ed. 28.95 (ISBN 0-07-034612-7); solutions manual 8.50 (ISBN 0-07-034613-5). McGraw.

Separation, Storage & Disposal of Krypton-85. (Technical Reports Ser.: No. 199). 66p. 1980. pap. 9.75 (ISBN 92-0-125180-7, IDC199, IAEA). Unipub.

Separation Techniques I: Liquid-Liquid Systems. Chemical Engineering Magazine. (Chemical Engineering Book Ser.). 384p. 1980. 29.50 (ISBN 0-07-010711-4). McGraw.

Separation Techniques II: Gas-Liquid-Solid Systems. Chemical Engineering Magazine. (Chemical Engineering Book Ser.). 400p. 1980. 29.50 (ISBN 0-07-010717-3). McGraw.

Separations by Centrifugal Phenomena. Arnold Weissberger & Hsien-Wen Hsu. (Techniques of Chemistry Ser.: Vol. 16). 400p. 49.50 (ISBN 0-471-05564-6, Pub. by Wiley-Interscience). Wiley.

Sepastian Agente Secreto. James L. Johnson. Tr. by Francisco Lievano. 1977. pap. 2.50 (ISBN 0-311-37021-7). Casa Bautista.

Sept Histoires on Sapsag: Racontees Par Nazam Met et Suivies De Quelques Remarques Sur la Parler Du Conteur. Rieks Smeets. (PDR Press Publication on North Caucasian Languages Ser.: No. 2). 1976. pap. text ed. 10.25x (ISBN 9-0316-0105-5). Humanities.

September Champions: The Story of America's Air Racing Pioneers. Robert Hull. (Illus.). 224p. 1979. 21.95 (ISBN 0-8117-1519-1); pap. 14.95 (ISBN 0-8117-2096-9). Stackpole.

September, September. Shelby Foote. 1979. pap. 2.25 o.p. (ISBN 0-345-26027-9). Ballantine.

September Storm. Harriette S. Abels. (Prime Time Adventures Ser.). (Illus.). 64p. (gr. 4 up). PLB 7.95 (ISBN 0-516-02110-9). Childrens.

Septemlingual Dictionary of the Names of European Animals, 2 vols. Ed. by Laszlo Gozmany. 2228p. 1979. Set. 200.00x (ISBN 963-05-1381-1). Intl Pubns Serv.

Septic Tank Practices. Peter Warshall. LC 77-76288. 1979. pap. 3.95 (ISBN 0-385-12764-2, Anch). Doubleday.

Septimus Fry or How Mrs Fry Had the Cleverest Baby in the World. Bill Gillham. LC 80-65661. (Illus.). 32p. (ps-3). 1980. 8.95 (ISBN 0-233-97253-6). Andre Deutsch.

Septuagint & Apocrypha in Greek & English. 1390p. 1972. 39.95 (ISBN 0-310-20430-5). Zondervan.

Septuagint Translation of Jeremiah & Baruch: A Discussion of an Early Revision of the IXX of Jeremiah 29-52 & Baruch 1: 1-3: 8. Emanual Tov. LC 75-43872. (Harvard Semitic Monographs). 1976. 9.00 (ISBN 0-89130-070-8, 040008). Scholars Pr Ca.

Septuaginta, 2 vols. Ed. by A. Rahlfs. 1965. Repr. of 1935 ed. 30.35 (ISBN 3-438-05120-6, 56400). United Bible.

Septuagintal Lexicography. Robert A. Kraft. LC 75-15894. (Society of Biblical Literature. Septuagint & Cognate Studies). 1975. pap. 7.50 (ISBN 0-89130-008-2, 060401). Scholars Pr Ca.

Sequel to Bretton Woods: A Proposal to Reform the World Monetary System. Lawrence B. Krause. 50p. 1971. pap. 2.95 (ISBN 0-8157-5035-8). Brookings.

Sequels. 6th ed. Ed. by Frank M. Gardner. 1974. 39.00 o.p. (ISBN 0-934598-75-4). Am Lib Pub Co.

Sequence. Elinor Glyn. (Barbara Cartland's Library of Love: Vol. 17). 213p. 1980. 12.95x (ISBN 0-7156-1477-0, Pub. by Duckworth England). Biblio Dist.

Sequence Dancing. Michael Gwynne. 17.95x (ISBN 0-392-06935-0, LTB). Soccer.

Sequence Transformations & Their Applications. Jet Wimp. LC 80-68564. (Mathematics in Science & Engineering Ser.). 1981. price not set (ISBN 0-12-757940-0). Acad Pr.

Sequences. Frederick Palmer. 1973. pap. text ed. 13.50x o.p. (ISBN 0-435-10685-6). Heinemann Ed.

Sequential Analysis. Abraham Wald. LC 73-85900. 1973. pap. text ed. 4.00 (ISBN 0-486-61579-0). Dover.

Sequential Curriculum for the Severely & Profoundly Mentally Retarded-Multi-Handicapped. Ellen M. Kissinger. 216p. 1981. pap. 22.75 spiral (ISBN 0-398-04145-8). C C Thomas.

Sequential Machines & Automata Theory. Taylor L. Booth. 608p. 1981. Repr. of 1967 ed. text ed. price not set (ISBN 0-89874-269-2). Krieger.

Sequential Medical Trials. 2nd ed. P. Armitage. LC 75-2211. 194p. 1975. 25.95 (ISBN 0-470-03323-1). Halsted Pr.

Sequential Methods in Statistics. 2nd ed. G. B. Wetherill. LC 74-16164. 240p. 1975. text ed. 12.95 o.p. (ISBN 0-470-93709-2). Halsted Pr.

Sequential Nonparametrics: Invariance Principles & Statistical Inference. P. K. Sen. (Probability & Mathematical Statistics Ser.). 350p. 1981. 30.00 (ISBN 0-471-06013-5, Pub. by Wiley-Interscience). Wiley.

Sequential Novels of C.P. Snow: A Study of the Themes of Power & Morality. S. N. Sinha. 242p. 1979. text ed. 15.00 (ISBN 0-8426-1655-1). Verry.

Sequential Sourcebook for Elementary School Music. 2nd ed. Laura Hochheimer. 1980. pap. 12.95 (ISBN 0-918812-12-7). Magnamusic.

Sequential Statistical Analysis of Hypothesis Testing, Point & Interval Estimation, & Decision Theory. Zakkula Govindarajulu. LC 80-68287. (American Sciences Press Ser. in Mathematical & Management Sciences: Vol. 5). 1981. text ed. write for info. (ISBN 0-935950-02-8). Am Sciences Pr.

Sequoia-Kings Canyon: The Story Behind the Scenery. William C. Tweed. Ed. by Gweneth R. DenDooven. LC 79-87571. (Illus.). 7.95 (ISBN 0-916122-66-2); pap. 3.50 (ISBN 0-916122-65-4). K C Pubns.

Sequoyah. Grant Foreman. (Civilization of the American Indian Ser.: No. 16). (Illus.). 1938. pap. 2.95 (ISBN 0-8061-1056-2). U of Okla Pr.

Seraphim's Seraphim: The Life of Pelagia Ivanovna Serebrenikova, Fool for Christ's Sake of the Seraphim-Diveyevo Convent. Tr. by Holy Transfiguration Monastery. LC 79-90720. (Illus.). 184p. (Orig.). 1980. pap. 4.50 (ISBN 0-913026-08-5). St Nectarios.

Seraphina. Mary K. Harris. 1960. 6.50 (ISBN 0-571-07012-4, Pub. by Faber & Faber). Merrimack Bk Serv.

Seraphina. Jean Merrill. 224p. (Orig.). 1980. pap. 1.75 (ISBN 0-449-50124-8, Coventry). Fawcett.

Seraphita. Honore De Balzac. LC 76-12203. 188p. 1976. pap. 2.50 (ISBN 0-8336-1757-5). Steinerbks.

Seras Lo Que Quieras Ser. Tr. by Robert Schuller. (Spanish Bks.). (Span.). 1978. 1.90 (ISBN 0-8297-0514-7). Life Pubs Intl.

Serbia, Nikola Pasic & Yugoslavia. Alex N. Dragnich. 1974. 19.00 (ISBN 0-8135-0773-1). Rutgers U Pr.

Serbo-Croatian. (Teach Yourself Ser.). pap. 2.95 (ISBN 0-679-10195-0). McKay.

Serbo-Croatian Prose & Verse. Ed. by Vera Javarek. 1958. text ed. 13.25x (ISBN 0-485-17506-1, Athlone Pr). Humanities.

Serbocroatian-English Dictionary. Ed. by Morton Benson. LC 79-146959. 1971. text ed. 35.00x (ISBN 0-8122-7636-1). U of Pa Pr.

Serebriannyi Golub' Andrei Belyi. (Rus.). 1980. pap. 6.50 (ISBN 0-88233-398-4). Ardis Pubs.

Serendipity in St. Helena. I. Shine. 1970. 34.00 (ISBN 0-08-012794-0). Pergamon.

Serengeti: Dynamics of an Ecosystem. A. R. Sinclair & M. Norton-Griffiths. LC 79-10146. (Illus.). 384p. 1979. lib. bdg. 32.00x (ISBN 0-226-76028-6). U of Chicago Pr.

Serengeti Lion: A Study of Predator-Prey Relations. George B. Schaller. LC 78-180043. (Wildlife Behavior & Ecology Ser.). (Illus.). 472p. 1976. pap. 12.95 (ISBN 0-226-73640-7, P661, Phoen). U of Chicago Pr.

Serf, Seigneur & Sovereign: An Agrarian Reform in Eighteenth-Century Bohemia. William E. Wright. LC 66-29653. 1966. 8.95x (ISBN 0-8166-0411-8). U of Minn Pr.

Serfs, Peasants, & Socialists: A Former Serf Village in the Republic of Guinea. William Derman. LC 78-117148. 1973. 21.50x (ISBN 0-520-01728-5). U of Cal Pr.

Sergeant Back Again. Charles Coleman. LC 80-7061. 352p. 1980. 10.95 (ISBN 0-06-010864-9, HarpT). Har-Row.

Sergeant Finney's Family. Carol Farley. LC 78-79667. (Illus.). (gr. 4-6). 1969. PLB 4.90 o.p. (ISBN 0-531-01915-2). Watts.

Sergeant Series, No. 4. Gordon Davis. 192p. (Orig.). 1981. pap. 2.25 (ISBN 0-553-14708-0). Bantam.

Sergei Nechaev. Philip Pomper. (Illus.). 1979. 19.50 (ISBN 0-8135-0867-3). Rutgers U Pr.

Sergei Rachmaninoff: A Lifetime in Music. Sergei Bertensson & Jay Leyda. LC 55-10065. (Illus.). 1956. 17.50x (ISBN 0-8147-0044-6). NYU Pr.

Sergey Esenin. Constantin V. Ponomareff. (World Authors Ser.: No. 478). 1978. lib. bdg. 12.50 (ISBN 0-8057-6319-8). Twayne.

Serial Bibliographies for Medieval Studies. Ed. by Richard H. Rouse. LC 68-31637. (UCLA Center for Medieval & Renaissance Studies). 1969. 17.50x (ISBN 0-520-01456-1). U of Cal Pr.

Serial Compositon & Atonality: An Introduction to the Music of Schoenberg, Berg, & Webern. 5th ed. George Perle. 1981. 16.50x (ISBN 0-520-04365-0). U of Cal Pr.

Serial Discussions of the Human Brain. Carlton G. Smith. (Illus.). 100p. 1981. text ed. price not set (ISBN 0-8067-1811-0). Urban & S.

Serial Literature of Entomology: A Descriptive Study. Ed. by Hammack. 1970. 3.35 (ISBN 0-686-18866-7). Entomol Soc.

Serial Music: A Classified Bibliography of Writings on 12 Tone & Electronic Music. Ann Basart. LC 75-45460. 151p. 1976. Repr. of 1961 ed. lib. bdg. 16.50x (ISBN 0-8371-8753-2, BASM). Greenwood.

Serial Publications. 3rd ed. Andrew D. Osborn. LC 80-11686. 486p. 1980. 20.00 (ISBN 0-8389-0299-5). ALA.

Serial Publications Containing Medical Classics. 2nd ed. Lee Ash. 1979. 22.50 (ISBN 0-9603990-0-3). Antiquarium.

Serials. 2nd, rev. & enl. ed. Raymond W. Stedman. (Suspense & Drama by Installment). 574p. 1980. pap. 9.95 (ISBN 0-8061-1695-1). U of Okla Pr.

Serials Automation in the United States: A Bibliographic History. Gary M. Pitkin. LC 76-18116. 1976. 10.00 (ISBN 0-8108-0955-9). Scarecrow.

Serials for Libraries. Compiled by Joan K. Marshall. LC 78-31144. 494p. 1979. lib. bdg. 52.50 (ISBN 0-87436-280-6). ABC-Clio.

Series in Mathematics Modules: Six Modules. Leon J. Ablon et al. Incl. Module 1. Operations on Numbers. 2nd ed. 4.95 (ISBN 0-8465-0240-2); Module 1A. Arithmetic. 2nd ed. 3.95 (ISBN 0-8465-6713-X); Module 2. Operations on Numbers. 2nd ed. 4.95 (ISBN 0-8465-0241-0); Module 3. Linear Equations & Lines. 2nd ed. 4.95 (ISBN 0-8465-0242-9); Module 4. Factoring & Operations on Algebraic Functions. 2nd ed. 4.95 (ISBN 0-8465-0243-7); Module 5. Quadratic Equations & Curves. 2nd ed. 4.95 (ISBN 0-8465-0244-5); Module 6. Basic Trigonometry. 2nd ed. 3.75 (ISBN 0-8465-0260-7); Module M. Medical Dosage Calculations. 2nd ed. 6.95 (ISBN 0-8053-7570-8). LC 72-94408. 1973. instr's guide 3.95 (ISBN 0-8465-0245-3). Benjamin-Cummings.

Series of Elementary Exercises Upon Geological Maps. John Platt. 1974. pap. text ed. 3.25x (ISBN 0-04-550019-3). Allen Unwin.

Series of Lectures on Social Justice. C. E. Coughlin. LC 71-173652. (FDR & the Era of the New Deal). 242p. 1972. Repr. of 1935 ed. lib. bdg. 27.50 (ISBN 0-306-70373-4). Da Capo.

Series of Old American Songs. Ed. by S. Foster Damon. 1936. boxed set 6.00 (ISBN 0-87057-014-5, Pub. by Brown U Pr). Univ Pr of New England.

Series of Plays: In Which It Is Attempted to Delineate the Strongest Passions of the Mind, 3 vols. Joanna Baillie. LC 75-31145. (Romantic Context: Poetry 1789-1830 Ser.: Vol. 2). 1977. Repr. of 1812 ed. Set. lib. bdg. 47.00 ea. (ISBN 0-8240-2101-0). Garland Pub.

Serigraphy: Silk Screen Techniques for the Artist. Kenneth W. Auvil. (Illus., Orig.). 1965. 9.95 (ISBN 0-13-807164-0). P-H.

Serindia, 5 vols. Aurel Stein. (Illus.). 500p. 1981. 75.00 ea. (Pub. by Motilal Banarsidass); Set. 350.00 (ISBN 0-686-69377-9); Vol. 1. (ISBN 0-89581-504-4); Vol. 2. (ISBN 0-89581-505-2); Vol. 3. (ISBN 0-89581-506-0); Vol. 4. (ISBN 0-89581-507-9); Vol. 5. (ISBN 0-89581-508-7). Lancaster-Miller.

Serious & Tragic Elements in the Comedy of Thomas Dekker. Peggy F. Shirley. (Salzburg Studies in English Literature, Jacobean Drama Studies: No. 50). 132p. 1975. pap. text ed. 25.00x (ISBN 0-391-01522-2). Humanities.

Serious Reflections on the Scandalous Abuse & Effects of the Stage. Arthur Bedford. Bd. with Second Advertisement Concerning the Profaneness of the Play-House; Sermon Preached in the Parish-Church of St. Butolph's Algate, in the City of London: Occasioned by the Erecting of a Play-House in the Neighborhood. (English Stage Ser.: Vol. 41). lib. bdg. 50.00 (ISBN 0-8240-0624-0). Garland Pub.

Serious Remonstrance in Behalf of the Christian Religion Against English Play-Houses. Arthur Bedfrod. LC 79-170478. (English Stage Ser.: Vol. 42). lib. bdg. 50.00 (ISBN 0-8240-0625-9). Garland Pub.

Seriously Handicapping Orthodontic Conditions. Assembly of Life Sciences, National Research Council. LC 76-16344. 1976. pap. 5.25 (ISBN 0-309-02501-X). Natl Acad Pr.

Sermon As God's Word: Theologies for Preaching. Robert W. Duke. LC 80-18094. (Abingdon Preacher's Library). 128p. (Orig.). 1980. pap. 4.95 (ISBN 0-687-37520-7). Abingdon.

Sermon As Part of the Liturgy. Paul Bosch. (Preacher's Workshop Ser.). 48p. 1977. pap. 2.25 (ISBN 0-570-07405-3, 12-2677). Concordia.

Sermon by the Sea. Ernest Holmes. 1967. pap. 2.50 o.p. (ISBN 0-911336-17-6). Sci of Mind.

Sermon Charts & Outlines, 3 vols. W. E. Skipper. spiral bdg. 2.95 ea. (ISBN 0-685-70356-8). Vol. 1 (ISBN 0-89315-253-6). Vol. 2 (ISBN 0-89315-254-4). Vol. 3 (ISBN 0-89315-255-2). Lambert Bk.

Sermon Del Monte, Vol. 1. D. M. Lloyd-Jones. 1978. 3.95 (ISBN 0-686-12554-1). Banner of Truth.

Sermon Is More Than Words. Eldon Weisheit. (Preacher's Workshop Ser.). 48p. 1977. pap. 2.25 (ISBN 0-570-07407-X, 12-2679). Concordia.

Sermon of Repentance. John Bradford. LC 74-28835. (English Experience Ser.: No. 716). 1975. Repr. of 1553 ed. 6.00 (ISBN 90-221-0716-7). Walter J Johnson.

Sermon on the Mount. James M. Boice. LC 72-83882. 256p. 1972. 14.95 (ISBN 0-310-21510-2). Zondervan.

Sermon on the Mount. James M. Boice. 328p. (Orig.). 1981. pap. 7.95 (ISBN 0-310-21511-0). Zondervan.

Sermon on the Mount. William D. Davies. (Orig.). 1966. pap. 6.50x (ISBN 0-521-09384-8, 384). Cambridge U Pr.

Sermon on the Mount. Clarence Jordan. 1970. pap. 2.50 (ISBN 0-8170-0501-3). Judson.

Sermon on the Mount: A History of Interpretation & Bibliography. Warren S. Kissinger. LC 75-29031. (ATLA Bibliography Ser.: No. 3). 1975. 15.00 (ISBN 0-8108-0843-9). Scarecrow.

Sermon on the Mount for to-Day. T. H. Wright. 298p. Repr. of 1927 ed. 4.95 (ISBN 0-567-02296-X). Attic Pr.

Sermon on the Mountain. Carol Gonsalves. (Arch Bk. Supplement Ser.). 1981. pap. 0.79 (ISBN 0-570-06149-0, 59-1304). Concordia.

Sermon Outlines for Evangelism. H. Lee Mason. (Sermon Outline Ser.). (Orig.). 1981. pap. 1.45 (ISBN 0-8010-6120-2). Baker Bk.

Sermon Outlines for Funerals. C. W. Keiningham. (Sermon Outline Ser.). (Orig.). 1981. pap. 1.45 (ISBN 0-8010-5427-3). Baker Bk.

Sermon Outlines from Acts. Croft M. Pentz. (Sermon Outline Ser.). 1978. pap. 1.95 (ISBN 0-8010-7039-2). Baker Bk.

Sermon Outlines on Christian Service. Eric W. Hayden. (Sermon Outline Ser.). 64p. (Orig.). 1980. pap. 1.95 (ISBN 0-8010-4239-9). Baker Bk.

Sermon Outlines on Paul & His Message. James H. Bolick. (Dollar Sermon Library). 1976. pap. 1.00 o.p. (ISBN 0-8010-0658-9). Baker Bk.

Sermon Outlines on the Person & Work of Christ. George W. Lockaby. 1981. pap. 2.25 (ISBN 0-8054-2238-2). Broadman.

Sermones Para Dias Especiales. Adolfo Robleto. (Tomo II). 1979. 2.25 (ISBN 0-311-07011-6). Casa Bautista.

Sermones Para Dias Especiales. Adolfo Robleto. 1980. Repr. of 1978 ed. 1.95 (ISBN 0-311-07009-4). Casa Bautista.

Sermons. Lancelot Andrewes. Ed. by G. M. Story. 1967. 22.00x o.p. (ISBN 0-19-811467-2). Oxford U Pr.

Sermons for Revival Preaching. James H. Bolick. (Pocket Pulpit Library Ser). pap. 1.45 (ISBN 0-8010-0551-5). Baker Bk.

Sermons for Special Occasions. 1981. pap. 4.95 (ISBN 0-570-03825-1, 12-2790). Concordia.

Sermons from Early America. 2nd ed. 1974. 6.00 (ISBN 0-686-10023-9). Pbbc Pr.

Sermons from Hell: Help for the Distressed. Ed. by Ward A. Knights, Jr. LC 75-4830. 192p. (Orig.). 1975. pap. 1.25 (ISBN 0-8272-3414-7). Bethany Pr.

Sermons from the Bible. Robert A. Smith. 1981. pap. 3.00 (ISBN 0-912128-21-6). Pubns Living.

Sermons in Candles. C. H. Spurgeon. 3.95 (ISBN 0-686-09093-4). Pilgrim Pubns.

Sermons of R. M. M'Cheyne. R. M. M'Cheyne. pap. 1.95 o.p. (ISBN 0-686-12540-1). Banner of Truth.

Sermons of the Liturgical Seasons. St. Augustine. (Fathers of the Church Ser.: Vol. 38). 23.00 (ISBN 0-8132-0038-5). Cath U Pr.

Sermons on Ephesians. John Calvin. 1979. 16.95 (ISBN 0-85151-170-8). Banner of Truth.

Sermons on Evangelism. Hyman Apperlman. (Pocket Pulpit Library). 96p. 1981. pap. 1.95 (ISBN 0-8010-0068-8). Baker Bk.

Sermons on Isaiah's Prophecy of the Death & Passion of Christ. John Calvin. Tr. by T. H. Parker. write for info. (ISBN 0-227-67427-8). Attic Pr.

Sermons on Subjects of the Day. John H. Newman. 1968. 10.50 o.p. (ISBN 0-87061-020-1). Chr Classics.

Sermons on the Major Holy Days of the Orthodox Church. A. M. Coniaris. 1978. pap. 4.95 (ISBN 0-937032-03-4). Light & Life Pub Co MN.

Sermons on to Eighty. St. Caesarius Of Arls. (Fathers of the Church Ser.: Vol. 31). 20.00 (ISBN 0-8132-0031-8). Cath U Pr.

Sermons Preached on Various Occasions. John H. Newman. 1968. 10.50 o.p. (ISBN 0-87061-021-X). Chr Classics.

Sermons to the Natural Man. W. G. Shedd. 1977. 11.95 (ISBN 0-85151-260-7). Banner of Truth.

Serology, Immunology & Blood Banking. Ed. by Harriet B. Williams. (Functional Mdical Laboratory Manual). (Illus.). 1978. pap. text ed. 10.00 (ISBN 0-87055-266-X). AVI.

Serotonin, New Vistas: Biochemistry & Behavioral & Clinical Studies. Ed. by E. Costa et al. LC 73-91166. (Advances in Biochemical Psychopharmacology Ser.: Vol. 11). 446p. 1974. 31.50 (ISBN 0-911216-69-3). Raven.

Serotonin, New Vistas: Histochemistry & Pharmacology. Ed. by E. Costa et al. LC 73-91165. (Advances in Biochemical Psychopharmacology Ser.: Vol. 10). 345p. 1974. 31.50 (ISBN 0-911216-68-5). Raven.

Serotonin Transmission & Behavior. Ed. by Barry L. Jacobs & Alan Gelperin. 430p. 1981. text ed. 45.00x (ISBN 0-686-69226-8). MIT Pr.

Serpent. Jane Gaskell. LC 76-62771. 1977. 8.95 o.p. (ISBN 0-312-71312-6). St Martin.

Serpent for a Dove: The Suppression of the American Indian. Noel Grisham. (Illus.). 168p. 7.50 (ISBN 0-8363-0089-0). Jenkins.

Serpent Is Shut Out from Paradise: A Revaluation of Romantic Love in Shelley. Seraphia De Ville Leyda (Salzburg Studies in English Literature, Romantic Reassessment: No. 4). 1972. pap. text ed. 25.00x (ISBN 0-391-01459-5). Humanities.

Serpentine. Thomas Thompson. 1981. pap. 3.50 (ISBN 0-440-17611-5). Dell.

Serpentine Track. Carl Malone. LC 79-90666. 1980. 9.95 (ISBN 0-533-04459-6). Vantage.

Serpent's Coil. Farley Mowat. 1976. pap. 1.75 o.p. (ISBN 0-345-25029-X). Ballantine.

Serpent's Egg: A Collection of Literature & Art. LC 79-84549. 1979. pap. 10.00 (ISBN 0-931350-02-6). Moonlight Pubns.

Sert: Mediterranean Architecture. Maria L. Borras. LC 75-9108. (Illus.). 1975. 19.50 o.p. (ISBN 0-8212-0675-3). NYGS.

Serum Protein Abnormalities: Diagnostic & Clinical Aspects. Ed. by Stephan E. Ritzmann & Jerry C. Daniels. (Series in Laboratory Medicine). (Illus.). 440p. 1975. 32.50 (ISBN 0-316-74754-8). Little.

Serum Proteins in Clinical Medicine. T. M. Ward. 1981. text ed. price not set (ISBN 0-407-00161-1). Butterworth.

Serun Cholesterol Levels of Persons Aged 4-74 Years by Socioeconomic Characteristics United States, 1971-74. Ed. by Audrey Shipp. (Series 11: No. 217). 1979. pap. text ed. 1.75 (ISBN 0-8406-0180-8). Natl Ctr Health Stats.

Servant & Son: Jesus in Parable & Gospel. J. Ramsey Michaels. LC 80-8465. 1981. pap. 8.95 (ISBN 0-8042-0409-8). John Knox.

Servant Story (Mark) Leader's Guide. Mabeth Clem. (New Horizons Bible Study Ser.). 48p. 1980. pap. 1.75 (ISBN 0-89367-050-2). Light & Life.

Servant Story (Mark) Study Guide. Robert Q. Bailey. (New Horizons Bible Study Ser.). 64p. 1980. pap. 2.25 (ISBN 0-89367-049-9). Light & Life.

Servants of All. LeRoy F. Harlow. (Illus.). 384p. 1981. 19.95 (ISBN 0-8425-1892-4). Brigham.

Servants of Power. Loren Baritz. LC 73-17924. 273p. 1974. Repr. of 1960 ed. lib. bdg. 19.75x (ISBN 0-8371-7275-6, BASP). Greenwood.

Servants of the Spring. Ernst Kreidolf. (Illus.). 1979. 9.95 (ISBN 0-914676-11-3); pap. write for info (ISBN 0-914676-19-9). Green Tiger.

Service Industries: Strategy, Structure & Financial Performance. Derek F. Channon. 1978. text ed. 53.75x (ISBN 0-8419-5032-6). Holmes & Meier.

Service of All the Dead. Collin Dexter. 1980. 9.95 (ISBN 0-312-71316-9). St Martin.

Service Project Ideas. Sandra Ziegler. (Ideas Ser.). (Illus.). 1977. pap. text ed. 1.75 (ISBN 0-87239-122-1, 7962). Standard Pub.

Service Station Operation & Management. N. Fritz. 1968. text ed. 7.96 o.p. (ISBN 0-07-022475-7, G). McGraw.

Service to Children in Their Own Homes: Its Nature & Outcome. Edmund A. Sherman et al. LC 72-92326. 1973. pap. text ed. 2.25 o.p. (ISBN 0-87868-106-X). Child Welfare.

Services & Environmental Engineering. 2nd ed. Building Research Establishment. (BRE Digests Volumes). (Illus.). 1977. text ed. 20.00x (ISBN 0-904406-44-X). Longman.

Services for Children & Their Families. T. Stroud. 1973. 32.00 (ISBN 0-08-016604-0); pap. 17.00 (ISBN 0-08-016605-9). Pergamon.

Services for the Chemical Industry. J. Davidson Pratt & T. F. West. 1968. 21.00 (ISBN 0-08-012665-0); pap. 10.50 (ISBN 0-08-012664-2). Pergamon.

Services for the Mentally Handicapped in Britain. Nigel Malin et al. 266p. 1980. boards 30.00x (ISBN 0-85664-869-8, Pub. by Croom Helm Ltd England). Biblio Dist.

Services on & off the Motorways. Jimmy Young. 1978. 5.95 (ISBN 0-7153-7609-8). David & Charles.

Servicing Sony TV for 1974-1975, Vol. 1. Stan Prentiss. LC 75-17001. (Illus.). 1975. pap. 12.95 (ISBN 0-672-21223-4, 21223). Sams.

Servicing the New Modular Color TV Receivers, Vol. 1. Stan Prentiss. LC 73-78195. (Schematic Servicing Manual Ser). (Illus.). 178p. 1973. leatherette o.p. 9.95 (ISBN 0-8306-3662-5); pap. 6.95 (ISBN 0-8306-2662-X, 662). TAB Bks.

Serving & Surviving As a Human Service Worker. J. Robert Russo. LC 80-18016. 170p. (Orig.). 1980. pap. text ed. 7.95 (ISBN 0-8185-0383-1). Brooks-Cole.

Serving God Always. Arnold G. Kuntz. 1966. pap. text ed. 2.15 (ISBN 0-570-06645-X, 22-2014); pap. 4.85 manual (ISBN 0-570-06646-8, 22-2015). Concordia.

Serving Our Generation: Evangelical Strategies for the Eighties. Ed. by Waldron Scott. 281p. (Orig.). 1980. pap. 5.95 o.s.i. (ISBN 0-936444-03-7). World Evang Fellow.

Serving Physically Disabled People: An Information Handbook for All Libraries. Ruth A. Velleman. LC 79-17082. 382p. 1979. 17.50 (ISBN 0-8352-1167-3). Bowker.

Serving Successful Salads: A Merchandising Cookbook. Helen M. Albert. LC 75-33339. 250p. 1975. 16.50 (ISBN 0-8436-2068-4). CBI Pub.

Serving the Federal Evaluation Market: Strategic Alternatives for Managers & Evaluators. Richard E. Schmidt et al. (Institute Paper). 93p. 1976. pap. 4.50 o.p. (ISBN 0-685-99532-1, 17400). Urban Inst.

Serving the Few: Corporate Capitalism & the Bias of Government Policy. E. S. Greenberg. 1974. pap. 8.95x (ISBN 0-471-32487-6). Wiley.

Servomechanisms. L. J. Bulliet. 1967. text ed. 16.95 (ISBN 0-201-00725-8). A-W.

Servomechanisms: Devices & Fundamentals. Miller. 1977. text ed. 17.95 (ISBN 0-87909-760-4); instrs'. manual avail. Reston.

Sesame & Lillies. John Ruskin. 1919. 2.95 o.p. (ISBN 0-04-824008-7). Allen Unwin.

Sesame Street Birthday Book. (Wipe off Bks.). 9p. (ps). Date not set. 2.39 (ISBN 0-307-01855-5, Golden Pr). Western Pub.

Sesame Street Book of People & Things. Ed. by Children's TV Workshop. (Illus.). (gr. k-2). 1971. pap. 0.75 (ISBN 0-451-04502-5, Q4502, Sig). NAL.

Sesame Street Do-It-Yourself Alphabet Book. Illus. by Richard Brown. (Golden Play & Learn Ser.). 14p. (ps). Date not set. pap. 2.95 (ISBN 0-307-13647-7, Golden Pr). Western Pub.

Sesame Street Storybook. Sesame Street. (Illus.). (ps-4). 1971. 4.95 (ISBN 0-394-82332-X, BYR); PLB 5.99 (ISBN 0-394-92332-4). Random.

Sesame Street Storytime Play Set. Date not set. boxed set 5.50 (ISBN 0-307-13647-7, Golden Pr). Western Pub.

Sesame Street What's Inside? Illus. by Tom Leigh. (Touch & Feel Bk.). (Illus.). 18p. (ps). Date not set. 3.95 (ISBN 0-307-12153-4, Golden Pr). Western Pub.

Session d'athenes Nineteen Seventy-Nine. Ed. by Institut De Droit International. (Institut de Droit international Annuaire: Vol. 58, Tome II). vii, 260p. 1980. 141.50 (ISBN 3-8055-3076-5). S Karger.

Session D'Athens Nineteen Seventy-Nine: Travaux Preparatoires, 2 vols. Ed. by Institut de Droit international. 600p. 1980. Set. 320.00 (ISBN 3-8055-0070-X). S Karger.

Session One: Self-Awareness & the Counselor Within. Charles E. Skirvin. LC 78-72500. 124p. 1979. pap. 4.95 (ISBN 0-8059-2578-3). Dorrance.

Sestra Moia Zhizn' Boris Pasternak. 1976. 11.00 o.p. (ISBN 0-88233-231-7); pap. 3.50 o.p. (ISBN 0-88233-232-5). Ardis Pubs.

Set Free. Betty Tapscott. 1978. pap. 3.50 (ISBN 0-917726-24-3). Hunter Bks.

Set, H.E.S.T-a: Humanistic Endeavor & Surgent Train-Ascendance. Russell E. Mason. 1975. pap. 3.00 (ISBN 0-89533-028-8). F I Comm.

Set of ABC Books, 2 bks. J. M. Stifle. 1981. pap. 5.25 (ISBN 0-570-04055-8, 56-1716). Concordia.

Set the Stars Alight. Denise Robins. 1978. pap. 1.75 (ISBN 0-380-42424-X, 42424). Avon.

Set the Stars on Fire. Sally Wentworth. (Harlequin Presents Ser.). 192p. 1980 (ISBN 0-373-10389-1, Pub. by Harlequin). pap. 1.50 (ISBN 0-686-68314-5). PB.

Set Theory. 2nd ed. Felix Hausdorff. LC 57-8493. 14.95 (ISBN 0-8284-0119-5). Chelsea Pub.

Set Theory. Charles C. Pinter. LC 77-131203. (Mathematics Ser). 1971. text ed. 15.95 (ISBN 0-201-05827-8). A-W.

Set Theory & Logic. Robert R. Stoll. 474p. 1979. pap. 6.50 (ISBN 0-486-63829-4). Dover.

Set Topology. 2nd ed. R. Vaidyanathaswamy. LC 60-8968. 12.95 (ISBN 0-8284-0139-X). Chelsea Pub.

Set Your Course. Gerald P. Cosgrave. 1978. pap. text ed. 4.00x (ISBN 0-8077-8063-4, Pub. by Guid Ctr U of Toronto). Tchrs Coll.

Seth Bullock: Frontier Marshall. Kenneth C. Kellar. LC 72-92726. 191p. 1972. 4.95 (ISBN 0-87970-126-9). North Plains.

Seth Low: The Patrician As Social Reformer; the Patrician As Social Architect--a Biography. Gerald Kurland. LC 76-125816. 415p. 1971. text ed. 24.50x (ISBN 0-8290-0205-7). Irvington.

Seth Speaks. Jane Roberts. LC 78-38925. (Illus.). 552p. 1972. 9.95 (ISBN 0-13-807206-X); pap. 5.95 (ISBN 0-13-807222-1). P-H.

Seth Thomas Clock Company, 1879. 1977. pap. 5.95 (ISBN 0-915706-04-0). Am Reprints.

Sets & Groups. J. A. Green. (Library of Mathematics). 1971. pap. 5.00 (ISBN 0-7100-4356-2). Routledge & Kegan.

Sets & Logic. Samuel C. Hanna et al. 1971. pap. text ed. 10.50 (ISBN 0-256-00230-4). Irwin.

Sets & Numbers. S. Swierczkowski. (Library of Mathematics). 1972. pap. 5.00 (ISBN 0-7100-7137-X). Routledge & Kegan.

Sets & Relations in Phonology: An Axiomatic Approach to the Description of Speech. J. W. Mulder. 1968. 13.75x o.p. (ISBN 0-19-811932-1). Oxford U Pr.

Sette Racconti. Moravia. (Easy Reader, C). pap. 3.75 (ISBN 0-88436-060-1, ITA301051). EMC.

Settecento Musicale in Europa. Antonio Capri. LC 77-5523. (Music Reprint Ser). 1977. Repr. of 1936 ed. lib. bdg. 35.00 (ISBN 0-306-77413-5). Da Capo.

Setting Conditions for Creative Teaching in the Elementary School. James A. Smith. 1966. 9.95x o.p. (ISBN 0-205-00132-7, 2201321). Allyn.

Setting Free the Bears. John Irving. LC 68-28537. 1968. 8.95 o.p. (ISBN 0-394-44496-5). Random.

Setting Municipal Priorities, Nineteen Eighty-One. Ed. by Charles Brecher & Raymond D. Horton. LC 80-67392. 212p. 1981. text ed. 25.00 (ISBN 0-86598-010-1). Allanheld.

Setting Municipal Priorities, Nineteen Eighty. Ed. by Raymond D. Horton & Charles Brecher. LC 79-88261. 224p. 1979. text ed. 24.00 (ISBN 0-916672-37-9). Allanheld.

Setting Municipal Priorities, 1980. Ed. by Raymond D. Horton & Charles Brecher. LC 79-88261. 224p. Date not set. price not set o.s.i. Allanheld & Schram.

Setting National Priorities: A the Next Ten Years. Ed. by Henry Owen & Charles L. Schultze. 325p. 1976. 18.95 (ISBN 0-8157-6764-1); pap. 8.95 (ISBN 0-8157-6763-3). Brookings.

Setting National Priorities: B the 1971 Budget. Charles L. Schultze et al. 1970. 11.95 (ISBN 0-8157-7750-7); pap. 4.95 (ISBN 0-8157-7749-3). Brookings.

Setting National Priorities: C the 1972 Budget. Charles L. Schultze et al. 1971. 14.95 (ISBN 0-8157-7756-6); pap. 5.95 (ISBN 0-8157-7755-8). Brookings.

Setting National Priorities: D the 1973 Budget. Charles L. Schultze et al. 350p. 1972. 14.95 (ISBN 0-8157-7758-2); pap. 5.95 (ISBN 0-8157-7757-4). Brookings.

Setting National Priorities: E the 1974 Budget. Edward R. Fried et al. LC 73-1076. 446p. 1973. 14.95 (ISBN 0-8157-2934-0); pap. 5.95 (ISBN 0-8157-2933-2). Brookings.

Setting National Priorities: F the 1975 Budget. Barry M. E. Blechman et al. LC 74-282. 1974. 11.95 (ISBN 0-8157-0994-3); pap. 4.95 (ISBN 0-8157-0993-5). Brookings.

Setting National Priorities: G the 1976 Budget. Barry M. F. Blechman et al. 200p. 1975. 11.95 (ISBN 0-8157-0992-7); pap. 4.95 (ISBN 0-8157-0991-9). Brookings.

Setting National Priorities: H the 1978 Budget. Joseph A. E. Pechman. 1977. 14.95 (ISBN 0-8157-6980-6); pap. 5.95 (ISBN 0-8157-6979-2). Brookings.

Setting National Priorities: K Agenda for the 1980s. Ed. by Joseph A. Pechman. 1980. 18.95 (ISBN 0-8157-6988-1); pap. 9.95 (ISBN 0-8157-6987-3). Brookings.

Setting of the Sermon on the Mount. William D. Davies. 1964. 64.00 (ISBN 0-521-04797-8); pap. 16.95x (ISBN 0-521-29124-0). Cambridge U Pr.

Setting the World on Fire. Angus Wilson. 312p. 1980. 12.95 (ISBN 0-670-63502-2). Viking Pr.

Settled Out of Court. 2nd ed. H. L. Ross. 1980. 14.95 (ISBN 0-686-65269-X); pap. 7.95 class lots of twenty or more (ISBN 0-202-30296-2). Aldine Pub.

Settlement & Unsettlement in Early America: The Crisis of Political Legitimacy Before the Revolution. Kenneth A. Lockridge. LC 80-25658. (Illus.). 96p. Date not set. price not set (ISBN 0-521-23707-6). Cambridge U Pr.

Settlement of Structures. British Geotechnical Society. LC 74-9514. 730p. 1975. 71.95 o.p. (ISBN 0-470-10476-7). Halsted Pr.

Settlement Systems in Sparsely Populated Regions: The United States & Australia. Ed. by Richard E. Lonsdale & John H. Holmes. LC 80-27278. (Pergamon Policy Studies on Urban Affairs; Comparative Rural Transformation Ser.). (Illus.). 360p. 1981. 40.00 (ISBN 0-08-023111-X). Pergamon.

Settlement Systems in Sparsely Populated Regions: The United States & Australia. Ed. by Richard E. Lonsdale & John H. Holmes. (Pergamon Policy Studies, Comparative Rural Transofrmation). 200p. Date not set. 40.01 (ISBN 0-08-023111-X). Pergamon.

Settlements to Society, 1607-1763: A Documentary History of Colonial America. Ed. by Jack P. Greene. 400p. 1975. pap. 5.95x (ISBN 0-393-09232-1). Norton.

Settler Mac & the Charmed Quarter-Section. Mrs. Hal Russell. 159p. 1956. 4.95 (ISBN 0-8040-0271-1, SB). Swallow.

Settlers. William S. Long. (Orig.). 1980. pap. 2.95 o.s.i. (ISBN 0-440-15923-7). Dell.

Settlers & Strangers: Native Americans of the Desert Southwest & History As They Saw It. Betty Baker. LC 77-4925. (Illus.). (gr. 3-6). 1977. 8.95 (ISBN 0-02-708220-2, 70822). Macmillan.

Settlers in Canada. Marryat. 1956. 5.00x o.p. (ISBN 0-460-00370-4, Evman). Dutton.

Settling America: The Ethnic Expression of Fourteen Contemporary Poets. Ed. by David Kherdian. LC 73-19066. 144p. (gr. 7 up). 1974. 8.95 (ISBN 0-02-750240-6). Macmillan.

Settling the Desert. Ed. by Louis Berkofsky et al. 272p. 1981. write for info. (ISBN 0-677-16280-4). Gordon.

Settling the Facts. Pamela J. Utz. LC 77-9119. 1978. 18.95x (ISBN 0-669-01673-X). Lexington Bks.

Seu Futuro Esta Nas Maos De Deus. 1980. pap. 1.30 (ISBN 0-686-69354-X). Vida Pubs.

Seu Obstinado Amor. Tr. by Joyce Landorf. (Portuguese Bks.). 1979. 1.35 (ISBN 0-8297-0691-7). Life Pubs Intl.

Seurat. Pierre Courthion. LC 68-13066. (Library of Great Painters Ser.). (Illus.). 1968. 35.00 (ISBN 0-8109-0474-8). Abrams.

Seurat. John Russell. (World of Art Ser.). (Illus.). 1965. pap. 9.95 (ISBN 0-19-519954-5). Oxford U Pr.

Seven Against Odds: Shapers of Our Democratic Heritage. Samuel Steinberg. Date not set. 7.95 (ISBN 0-533-04639-4). Vantage.

Seven Against Thebes. Aeschylus. Tr. by Gilbert Murray. 1935. pap. text ed. 3.95x (ISBN 0-04-882015-6). Allen Unwin.

Seven Against Thebes. Ed. by Leo Kaiser. Henry D. Thoreau. LC 80-2522. (Emerson Society Quarterly No. Seventeen Nineteen Fifty Nine,1-30). 1981. Repr. of 1959 ed. 14.00 (ISBN 0-404-19070-7). AMS Pr.

Seven Against Thebes: Greek Tragedy Ser. Aeschylus. Tr. by Anthony Hecht & Helen Bacon. (The Greek Tragedy in New Translations Ser.). 80p. 1973. 10.95 (ISBN 0-19-501732-3). Oxford U Pr.

Seven Ages of Man: A Survey of Human Development. Ed. by Robert R. Sears & S. Shirley Feldman. LC 73-12029. 145p. 1973. 8.95 o.p. (ISBN 0-913232-07-6); pap. 5.50 (ISBN 0-913232-06-8). W Kaufmann.

Seven Alone. Honore Morrow. (gr. 7-12). 1977. pap. 1.50 (ISBN 0-590-10291-5, Schol Pap). Schol Bk Serv.

Seven Altars of Dusarra. Lawrence Watt-Evans. 240p. 1981. pap. 2.50 (ISBN 0-345-29264-2, Del Rey). Ballantine.

Seven & Nine Years Among the Camanches & Apaches: An Autobiography. Ediwn Eastman. LC 75-7115. (Indian Captivities Ser.: Vol. 88). 1977. Repr. of 1873 ed. lib. bdg. 44.00 (ISBN 0-8240-1712-9). Garland Pub.

Seven at One Blow. Freya Littledale. (gr. k-3). 1977. pap. 1.50 (ISBN 0-590-10319-9, Schol Pap); pap. 3.50 bk. & record (ISBN 0-590-20600-1). Schol Bk Serv.

Seven Baths for Naaman. Carol Greene. (I Can Read a Bible Story Ser.: No. 2). (Illus.). 48p. (gr. 2-4). 1977. 4.95 (ISBN 0-570-07321-9, 56-1512); pap. 1.95 (ISBN 0-570-07315-4, 56-1412). Concordia.

Seven Bears. Roberts. (gr. 3-5). pap. 1.25 (ISBN 0-590-05413-9, Schol Pap). Schol Bk Serv.

Seven Beginnings. Walker Knight & Ken Touchton. LC 75-44496. (Human Torch Ser.: 2nd). (Illus.). 1976. 5.95 (ISBN 0-937170-17-8). Home Mission.

Seven Card Stud: The Waiting Game. George Percy. (Gambler's Book Shelf). 1979. pap. 2.95 (ISBN 0-89650-903-6). Gamblers.

Seven Caves: Archaeological Explorations in the Middle East. Carleton S. Coon. LC 80-24503. (Illus.). xx, 354p. 1981. Repr. of 1957 ed. lib. bdg. 31.50x (ISBN 0-313-22824-8, COSCA). Greenwood.

Seven Centuries of Art. Time-Life Books Editors. (Library of Art). (Illus.). 200p. 1970. 15.95 (ISBN 0-8094-0259-9). Time-Life.

Seven Centuries of the Problem of Church & State. Frank Gavin. 1938. 11.50 (ISBN 0-86527-180-1). Fertig.

Seven Centuries of Verse: English & American. 3rd & rev ed. Ed. by Arthur J. Smith. 1967. text ed. 9.95x o.p. (ISBN 0-684-41441-4, ScribC). Scribner.

Seven Chinese Stories. T. J. Sheridan. (Oxford Progressive English Readers Ser.). (Illus.). 1975. pap. 2.95x (ISBN 0-19-638230-0). Oxford U Pr.

Seven Chocolate Sins. Ruth Moorman & Lalla Williams. (Illus.). 80p. 1979. pap. 4.95 (ISBN 0-937552-01-1). Quail Ridge.

Seven Comedies by Marivaux. Pierre De Marivaux. Ed. by Oscar Mandel & Adrienne Mandel. LC 68-16386. 1979. Repr. of 1968 ed. 26.50x (ISBN 0-686-60850-X). Irvington.

Seven Cycles: Public Rituals. Mary B. Edelson. (Illus.). 64p. (Orig.). 1980. pap. 10.00x (ISBN 0-9604650-0-6). Edelson.

Seven Dada Manifestos. Tristan Tzara. Tr. by Barbara Wright. 1979. 8.95 (ISBN 0-7145-3557-5); pap. 4.95. Riverrun NY.

Seven Daughters. Thelma P. Hope. (Americana Ser.). 150p. (Orig.). 1981. pap. 6.90 (ISBN 0-686-69154-7). Gusto Pr.

Seven Day Mystery. John H. Tiner. (Voyager Ser.). 176p. (Orig.). (gr. 6-10). 1981. pap. 2.95 (ISBN 0-8010-8856-9). Baker Bk.

Seven Days to a Brand-New Me. Ellen Conford. 96p. (gr. 5 up). 1981. 7.95 (ISBN 0-316-15311-7). Little.

Seven Deadly Sins. Stanford Lyman. 1978. text ed. 15.95x (ISBN 0-312-71324-X); pap. text ed. 8.95x (ISBN 0-312-71325-8). St Martin.

Seven Deadly Sins of Science Fiction. Ed. by Isaac Asimov et al. 1980. pap. 2.50 (ISBN 0-449-24349-4, Crest). Fawcett.

Seven Deadly Sins Today. Henry Fairlie. LC 78-3646. (Illus.). 1978. 10.00 o.p. (ISBN 0-915220-41-5). New Republic.

Seven Decades of Progress: History of G. E. Engine Group. 238p. 1980. 24.95 (ISBN 0-8168-8355-6). Aero.

Seven Decades of Rural Social Work: From Country Life Commission to Rural Caucus. Emilia E. Martinez-Brawley. 275p. 1981. 21.95 (ISBN 0-03-058027-7). Praeger.

Seven Epistles of Love. William Van Zant. 1981. 5.95 (ISBN 0-8062-1719-7). Carlton.

Seven Expressionist Plays. 1980. pap. 6.95 (ISBN 0-7145-0521-8). Riverrun NY.

Seven Fallen Pillars. Jon Kimche. LC 76-6848. (Middle East in the 20th Century). 1976. Repr. of 1950 ed. lib. bdg. 39.50 (ISBN 0-306-70820-5). Da Capo.

Seven Famous Trials in History. Robin McKown. LC 63-13800. (Illus.). (gr. 7 up). 1963. 7.95 (ISBN 0-8149-0367-3). Vanguard.

Seven for the People: Public Interest Groups at Work. Zena Collier. LC 79-136. 192p. (gr. 7 up). 1979. PLB 8.29 (ISBN 0-671-32926-X). Messner.

Seven for the Sea. W. Towrie Cutt. LC 73-93556. 96p. (gr. 3-6). 1974. 4.95 o.p. (ISBN 0-695-80480-4); lib. bdg. 4.98 o.p. (ISBN 0-695-40480-6). Follett.

Seven Golds: Mark Spitz' Own Story. Mark Spitz & Mickey Herskowitz. LC 80-1694. (Illus.). 256p. 1981. 10.95 (ISBN 0-385-12135-0). Doubleday.

Seven Great Bibles: The Sacred Scriptures of Hinduism, Buddhism, Zoroastrianism, Confucianism, (Taoism), Mohammedanism, Judism & Christianity. Alfred W. Martin. LC 74-11849. 277p. 1975. Repr. of 1930 ed. lib. bdg. 25.00x (ISBN 0-8154-0495-6). Cooper Sq.

Seven Great Detective Stories. Ed. by William H. Larson. (gr. 3 up). 1979. pap. 1.25 (ISBN 0-307-21627-6, Golden Pr). Western Pub.

Seven Human Temperaments. 6th ed. Geoffrey Hodson. 1977. 3.25 (ISBN 0-8356-7222-0). Theos Pub Hse.

Seven Hundred MB Atlas for the Northern Hemisphere: Five-Day Mean Heights, Standard Deviations, & Changes. Eberhard W. Wahl & James F. Lahey. LC 69-5. 1969. plastic comb. bdg. 50.00x (ISBN 0-299-05383-0). U of Wis Pr.

Seven in a Bed. Ruth A. Sonneborn. LC 68-27564. (Illus.). (gr. k-2). 1968. PLB 3.95 o.p. (ISBN 0-670-63507-3). Viking Pr.

Seven in One Blow. Friere Wright & Michael Foreman. (Pictureback Ser.). (Illus.). 32p. (ps-3). 1981. PLB 4.99 (ISBN 0-394-93805-4); pap. 1.25 (ISBN 0-686-68750-7). Random.

Seven Interpretive Essays on Peruvian Reality. Jose C. Mariategui. Tr. by Marjory Urquidi. LC 73-156346. (Texas Pan American Ser.). xxxvi, 302p. 1971. pap. 5.95 (ISBN 0-292-70115-2); pap. 5.95 (ISBN 0-292-77517-2). U of Tex Pr.

Seven Japanese Tales. Junichiro Tanizaki. Tr. by Howard Hibbett from Jap. (Perigee Japanese Library). 320p. 1981. pap. 5.95 (ISBN 0-399-50523-7, Perigee). Putnam.

Seven Keys to Baldpate. Earl D. Biggers. (Charlie Chan Mysteries Ser.). 1976. Repr. of 1917 ed. lib. bdg. 17.15x (ISBN 0-89966-076-2). Buccaneer Bks.

Seven Keys to Colour Healing. Roland Hunt. 124p. 1971. 7.25x (ISBN 0-8464-1063-X). Beekman Pubs.

Seven Keys to Maximum Communication. Paul A. Cedar. 1980. pap. 2.95 (ISBN 0-8423-5875-7). Tyndale.

Seven Keys to Triumphant Christian Living. Gordon Lindsay. 1.25 (ISBN 0-89985-006-5). Christ Nations.

Seven Kings of England. Geoffrey Trease. LC 55-7892. (gr. 6 up). 1955. 7.95 (ISBN 0-8149-0431-9). Vanguard.

Seven Lamps of Architecture. John Ruskin. 210p. 1961. pap. 5.95 (ISBN 0-374-50188-2, N215). FS&G.

Seven Last Years. Carol Balizet. 368p. 1980. pap. 2.75 (ISBN 0-553-14136-8). Bantam.

Seven Laws of Teaching. 3rd ed. John M. Gregory. 1976. 6.00 (ISBN 0-8010-3652-6). PBBC Pr.

Seven Lean Years. Thomas Jackson Woofter & Ellen E. Winston. LC 79-39479. (FDR & the Era of the New Deal Ser). 1972. Repr. of 1939 ed. lib. bdg. 20.00 (ISBN 0-306-70463-3). Da Capo.

Seven Little Rabbits. Becker. (gr. k-3). 1977. pap. 1.50 (ISBN 0-590-04429-X); pap. 3.50 bk. & record (ISBN 0-590-20620-6). Schol Bk Serv.

Seven Little Rabbits. John Becker. LC 72-86974. (Illus.). 4.95 o.p. (ISBN 0-8027-6129-1); PLB 5.85 (ISBN 0-8027-6130-5). Walker & Co.

Seven Minutes Past Midnight. Walter Winward. 1980. 12.95 (ISBN 0-671-24932-0). S&S.

Seven Modern American Novelists: An Introduction. Ed. by William V. O'Connor. LC 64-18175. (Library on American Writers: No. 1). 1964. 15.00x (ISBN 0-8166-0327-8). U of Minn Pr.

Seven of Swords. R. E. Harrington. 1977. pap. 1.95 o.p. (ISBN 0-685-78261-1, 40-069-1). Pinnacle Bks.

Seven-Pillared Relationship. Richard J. Hamersma & Robert A. Mark. LC 79-20450. 192p. 1981. 13.95 (ISBN 0-88229-443-1). Nelson-Hall.

Seven-Place Natural Trigonometrical Functions. Howard C. Ives & P. Kissam. 1929. 19.50 (ISBN 0-471-43098-6, Pub. by Wiley-Interscience). Wiley.

Seven Plays from American Literature. rev. ed. Adapted by George P. McCallum. 1971. pap. 2.95 (ISBN 0-87789-062-5); cassette tapes 39.50 (ISBN 0-87789-126-5). Eng Language.

Seven Plays of the Sea. Eugene O'Neill. 199p. Date not set. pap. 2.95 (ISBN 0-394-71856-9, Vin). Random.

Seven Principles of Poetry. Anne Hamilton. 8.95 (ISBN 0-87116-029-3). Writer.

Seven Psychologies. Edna Heidbreder. (Orig.). 1963. pap. 12.95 (ISBN 0-13-807354-6). P-H.

Seven Queens of England. Geoffrey Trease. LC 53-6900. (gr. 6 up). 5.95 (ISBN 0-8149-0430-0). Vanguard.

Seven Ravens. Brothers Grimm. Tr. by Elizabeth D. Crawford from Ger. LC 80-25365. (Illus.). 24p. (gr. k-3). 1981. 8.95 (ISBN 0-688-00371-0); PLB 8.59 (ISBN 0-688-00372-9). Morrow.

Seven Ravens. Ed. by Felix Hoffman. LC 63-2506. (Illus.). (gr. k-3). 1963. 6.95 (ISBN 0-15-272920-8, HJ). HarBraceJ.

Seven Red Sundays. Ramon J. Sender. 1961. pap. 0.95 o.s.i. (ISBN 0-02-024870-9, Collier). Macmillan.

Seven Sayings of Our Saviour on the Cross. Arthur W. Pink. (Summit Bks). 1977. pap. 2.45 (ISBN 0-8010-7015-5). Baker Bk.

Seven Seas World Stamp Album. Ed. by Larry Grossman. (Illus.). 1979. 7.95 (ISBN 0-686-64403-4). Grossman Stamp.

Seven Silly Stories. Jenny Taylor & Terry Ingleby. Incl. Fox & Stork; Brer Rabbit & the Honey Pot; Noisy Neville; Mr. Stupid; Foolish Tortoise; Well Diggers; Miller & His Donkey. (gr. k-4). 1976. pap. text ed. 15.60 set (ISBN 0-8372-2222-2). Bowmar-Noble.

Seven Simple Sermons on the Savior's Last Words. W. Herschel Ford. pap. 3.95 (ISBN 0-310-24621-0). Zondervan.

Seven Simple Sermons on the Second Coming. W. Herschel Ford. pap. 3.95 (ISBN 0-310-24631-8). Zondervan.

Seven Sixes Are Forty-Three. Kiran Nagarkar. Tr. by Shubha Slee from Marathi. (Asian & Pacific Writing Ser.: No. 14). 213p. 1981. text ed. 15.75 (ISBN 0-7022-1503-1); pap. 8.50 (ISBN 0-7022-1502-3). U of Queensland Pr.

Seven Sovereign Queens. Geoffrey Trease. LC 71-89662. (Illus.). (gr. 7 up). 1969. 7.95 (ISBN 0-8149-0660-5). Vanguard.

Seven Spells to Sunday. Andre Norton & Phyllis Miller. (gr. 4-7). 1980. pap. write for info. (ISBN 0-671-56086-7). PB.

Seven Stages. Geoffrey Trease. LC 65-26138. (Illus.). (gr. 7-9). 1965. 7.95 (ISBN 0-8149-0425-4). Vanguard.

Seven Steeples. Margaret K. Henrichsen. LC 78-26203. 1978. lib. bdg. 11.50 o.p. (ISBN 0-89621-023-5); pap. 4.95x (ISBN 0-89621-022-7). Thorndike Pr.

Seven Steps Along the Way. F. Dale Simpson. 1981. pap. write for info. (ISBN 0-89137-527-9). Quality Pubns.

Seven Steps on How to Become a Mystic & Enjoy the Most Exhilirating Pleasure Available to Man on This Earth. Gilbert J. Malfitano. (Illus.). 1979. deluxe ed. 37.50 (ISBN 0-930582-37-3). Gloucester Art.

Seven Storey Mountain. Thomas Merton. LC 78-7109. 1978. pap. 5.95 (ISBN 0-15-680679-7, Harv). HarBraceJ.

Seven Stories. James Hall. Ed. by Mary Burtschi. LC 75-23549. 1975. 5.00 (ISBN 0-9601642-1-9). Little Brick Hse.

Seven Stories. James Hall. Ed. by Mary Burtschi. 1981. 5.95. Little Brick Hse.

Seven Stories by Hans Christian Andersen. Eric Carle. LC 78-2302. (Illus.). (gr. k-3). 1978. 5.95 (ISBN 0-531-02919-0); PLB 7.90 s&l (ISBN 0-531-02493-8). Watts.

Seven Stories from Spanish America. Ed. by G. Brotherston & M. V. Llosa. 1968. 5.40 (ISBN 0-08-012676-6); pap. 4.10 (ISBN 0-08-012675-8). Pergamon.

Seven Stranded Coal Towns: A Study of an American Depressed Area. Malcolm Brown & John N. Webb. LC 76-165680. (FDR & the Era of the New Deal Ser). 1971. Repr. of 1941 ed. lib. bdg. 19.50 (ISBN 0-306-70355-6). Da Capo.

Seven Symphonies. Carlo D'Ordonez. Ed. by Peter Brown & Barry S. Brook. LC 79-12057. (Symphony 1720-1840, Ser. B: Vol. IV). 255p. 1980. lib. bdg. 60.00 (ISBN 0-8240-3800-2). Garland Pub.

Seven Theories of Human Nature. Leslie Stevenson. 1974. text ed. 8.95 (ISBN 0-19-875033-1); pap. text ed. 3.95x (ISBN 0-19-875034-X). Oxford U Pr.

Seven Tribes of Central Africa. Ed. by Elizabeth Colson & Max Gluckman. (Rhodes Livingston Institute Publications). 1968. text ed. 9.25x o.p. (ISBN 0-7190-1014-4). Humanities.

Seven True Dog Stories. Margaret Davidson. (gr. 2-4). 1977. 6.95 (ISBN 0-8038-6738-7). Hastings.

Seven True Elephant Stories. Barbara Williams. (Illus.). (gr. 3-6). 1977. 6.95 (ISBN 0-8038-6746-8). Hastings.

Seven True Horse Stories. Margaret Davidson. (Illus.). (gr. 2-5). 1979. 6.95g (ISBN 0-8038-6760-3). Hastings.

Seven-Twenty-Seven Scrapbook. Len Morgan & Terry Morgan. LC 78-72164. 1978. 12.00 (ISBN 0-8168-8344-0); pap. 7.95 (ISBN 0-8168-8349-1). Aero.

Seven Unusual Business Careers: Guaranteed Maximal Profit Potential for the Intelligent College Graduate & the Daring Businessman. C. M. Flumiani. LC 76-115460. (Illus.). 90p. 1974. 37.50 (ISBN 0-913314-47-1). Am Classical Coll Pr.

Seven Valleys & the Four Valleys. 3rd rev. ed. Baha'U'llah. Tr. by Marzieh Gail. LC 77-23326. 1978. 4.00 (ISBN 0-87743-113-2, 7-03-15); pap. 2.50 (ISBN 0-87743-114-0, 7-03-16). Baha'i.

Seven Veils Over Consciousness. C. Jinarajadasa. 2.50 (ISBN 0-8356-7231-X). Theos Pub Hse.

Seven Ways to Collect Plants. Joan E. Rahn. LC 77-21181. (gr. 4-6). 1978. 6.95 (ISBN 0-689-30640-7). Atheneum.

Seven Who Shaped Our Destiny: The Founding Fathers As Revolutionaries. Richard B. Morris. LC 73-4111. (Illus.). 348p. (YA) 1973. 11.95 o.s.i. (ISBN 0-06-013078-4, HarpT). Har-Row.

Seven Wonders of New Jersey--& Then Some. Thomas C. Murray & Valerie Barnes. (Illus.). 128p. 1980. 7.95 o.p. (ISBN 0-89490-016-1). Enslow Pubs.

Seven Wonders of New Jersey--& Then Some. Thomas C. Murray & Valerie Barnes. LC 80-16424. (Illus.). 128p. 1981. pap. 6.95 (ISBN 0-89490-017-X). Enslow Pubs.

Seven Wonders of the Ancient World. Robert Silverberg. LC 70-95298. (Illus.). (gr. 6-9). 1970. 8.95 (ISBN 0-02-782650-3, CCPr). Macmillan.

Seven Words: The Words of Jesus on the Cross Reveal the Heart of the Christian Faith. Clovis G. Chappell. (Procket Pulpit Library). 80p. 1976. pap. 1.75 (ISBN 0-8010-2387-4). Baker Bk.

Seven Years from Home. Rose Blue. LC 75-42105. (Values in Fiction Ser.). (Illus.). (gr. 5 up). 1976. 7.75 (ISBN 0-8172-0076-2). Raintree Pubs.

Seven Years in Russia & Siberia, 1914-1921. Roman Dyboski. Tr. by Marion M. Coleman from Polish. LC 79-137001. (Illus., Orig.). 1971. pap. 5.00 (ISBN 0-910366-09-8). Alliance Coll.

Seven Years Old in the Home Environment. John Newson & Elizabeth Newson. LC 75-17184. 1976. 35.95 (ISBN 0-470-63585-1). Halsted Pr.

Seventeen Guide to Knowing Yourself. Daniel A. Sugarman & Rolaine Hochstein. (gr. 7-12). 1968. 9.95 (ISBN 0-02-615300-9). Macmillan.

Seventeen Interviews: Film Stars & Superstars. Edwin Miller. (Illus.). (gr. 7 up). 1970. 6.95 o.s.i. (ISBN 0-02-584830-5). Macmillan.

Seventeen Lectures on the Study of Medieval & Modern History. William Stubbs. 1967. 15.00 (ISBN 0-86527-219-0). Fertig.

Seventeen More Poems. Roshen Alkazi. (Writers Workshop Redbird Ser.). 1975. 8.00 (ISBN 0-88253-628-1); pap. text ed. 4.00 (ISBN 0-88253-627-3). Ind-US Inc.

Seventeen Plays: Sophocles to Baraka. Bernard F. Dukore. 1976. scp 10.95 (ISBN 0-690-00846-5, HarpC). Har-Row.

Seventeen Poems. Roshen Alkazi. 8.00 (ISBN 0-89253-549-0). Ind-US Inc.

Seventeen Seventy-Six: Or, the War of Independence. Benson J. Lossing. LC 74-99070. (Illus.). 1970. Repr. of 1847 ed. 20.00 (ISBN 0-8103-3584-0). Gale.

Seventeen Seventy-Six: Year of Independence. Genevieve Foster. LC 75-106531. (Illus.). (gr. 2-6). 1970. 4.50 (ISBN 0-684-20822-9, ScribJ). Scribner.

Seventeenth & Eighteenth Century Art: Baroque Painting, Sculpture & Architecture. Julius Held & Donald Posner. Ed. by H. Janson. (Illus.). 492p. 1972. text ed. 21.95 (ISBN 0-13-807339-2). P-H.

Seventeenth Century. 2nd ed. George Clark. 1961. pap. 5.95 (ISBN 0-19-500227-X, GB). Oxford U Pr.

Seventeenth Century. Ed. by Andrew Lossky. LC 67-10426. (Orig.). 1967. pap. text ed. 7.95 (ISBN 0-02-919400-8). Free Pr.

Seventeenth Century. Madeleine Mainstone. LC 80-40039. (Cambridge History of Art Ser.: No. 4). (Illus.). 100p. Date not set. 19.95 (ISBN 0-521-22162-5); pap. 6.95 (ISBN 0-521-29376-6). Cambridge U Pr.

Seventeenth-Century American Poetry. Ed. by Harrison T. Meserole. LC 68-29435. (Stuart Editions). 1968. 22.50x (ISBN 0-8147-0301-1). NYU Pr.

Seventeenth Century Art in Flanders & Holland. LC 76-14071. (Garland Library of the History of Art). 1976. lib. bdg. 50.00 (ISBN 0-8240-2419-2). Garland Pub.

Seventeenth Century Art in Italy, France, & Spain. LC 76-14070. (Garland Library of the History of Art). 1976. lib. bdg. 50.00 (ISBN 0-8240-2418-4). Garland Pub.

Seventeenth Century Background: Studies in the Thought of the Age in Relation to Poetry & Religion. Basil Willey. LC 34-21849. 1942. 20.00x (ISBN 0-231-01395-7). Columbia U Pr.

Seventeenth-Century Economic Documents. Ed. by Joan Thirsk & J. P. Cooper. 1972. 33.00x (ISBN 0-19-828256-7). Oxford U Pr.

Seventeenth-Century England: A Changing Culture, Modern Studies, Vol. 2. Ed. by W. R. Owens. 1981. 28.50x (ISBN 0-389-20169-3). B&N.

Seventeenth-Century England: A Changing Culture, Primary Sources, Vol. 1. Ed. by Ann Hughes. 1981. 28.50x (ISBN 0-389-20168-5). B&N.

Seventeenth Century Europe. D. H. Pennington. (General History of Europe Ser.). (Illus.). 1972. pap. text ed. 10.95x (ISBN 0-582-48312-3). Longman.

Seventeenth-Century French Drama: The Background. John Lough. (Illus.). 1979. 14.95x (ISBN 0-19-815756-8). Oxford U Pr.

Seventeenth Century Imagery: Essays on Uses of Figurative Language from Donne to Farquhar. Ed. by Earl Miner. LC 76-132417. (Seventeenth & Eighteenth Centuries Studies Group, UCLA: No. 1). 1971. 18.50x (ISBN 0-520-01825-7). U of Cal Pr.

Seventeenth Century North America: French & Spanish Accounts. Carl O. Sauer. (New World Writing Ser.). (Illus.). 1977. 19.95 (ISBN 0-913666-23-8); pap. 9.95 (ISBN 0-913666-22-X). Turtle Isl Foun.

Seventeenth Century Resolve: A Historical Anthology of a Literary Form. John L. Lievsay. LC 79-4004. 224p. 1980. 15.50x (ISBN 0-8131-1393-8). U Pr of Ky.

Seventeenth-Century View of European Libraries: Lomeier's De Bibliothecis Chapter X. Tr. by J. W. Montgomery. (U. C. Publ. in Librarianship: Vol. 3). 1962. pap. 7.50x (ISBN 0-520-09206-6). U of Cal Pr.

Seventeenth Report to the Fellows of the Pierpont Morgan Library: 1972-1974. Ed. & pref. by Charles Ryskamp. (Illus.). 1976. 25.00 (ISBN 0-87598-064-3). Pierpont Morgan.

Seventeenth Stair. Barbara Paul. 1976. pap. 1.75 o.p. (ISBN 0-345-25200-4). Ballantine.

Seventh Cousin. Florence Laughlin. (Illus.). (gr. 4-6). 1966. 3.95g o.s.i. (ISBN 0-02-754540-7). Macmillan.

Seventh Earl of Shaftesbury. Grace Irwin. 1976. 6.95 (ISBN 0-8028-6058-3). Eerdmans.

Seventh Escape. Jan Doward. LC 68-54399. (Destiny Ser.). 1979. pap. 4.95 (ISBN 0-8163-0385-1, 19295-5). Pacific Pr Pub Assn.

Seventh Level. William Nicholson. 1980. pap. 2.75 (ISBN 0-451-09479-4, E9479, Sig). NAL.

Seventh Power. James Mills. 1977. pap. 1.95 o.s.i. (ISBN 0-515-04415-6). Jove Pubns.

Seventh Sense. Harrison R. Thompson. (Orig.). 1979. pap. 2.25 (ISBN 0-532-23275-5). Manor Bks.

Seventh Station: A Father Dowling Mystery. Ralph McInerny. LC 77-77417. 1977. 7.95 (ISBN 0-8149-0787-3). Vanguard.

Seventh Suitor. Laura Matthews. 208p. (Orig.). 1979. pap. 1.75 (ISBN 0-446-94340-1). Warner Bks.

Seventh Symposium on Microdosimetry. Ed. by H. G. Ebert. 550p. 1980. 82.50 (ISBN 3-7186-0049-8). Harwood Academic.

Seventh Trumpet. Mark Link. 1978. 6.95 (ISBN 0-89505-014-5). Argus Comm.

Seventies No. 1: An Anthology of Leaping Poetry. Ed. by Robert Bly. pap. 1.50 (ISBN 0-685-31525-8). Eighties Pr.

Seventies: The Decade That Changed the Future. Christopher Booker. LC 80-5389. 350p. 1980. 16.95 (ISBN 0-8128-2757-0). Stein & Day.

Seventy Billion in the Black: America's Black Consumers. Parke D. Gibson. 1978. 12.95 (ISBN 0-02-543160-9). Macmillan.

Seventy-First Came...to Gunskirchen Lager. Fred R. Crawford. LC 79-51047. (Witness to the Holocaust: No. 1). (Illus.). 1979. pap. 1.00 (ISBN 0-89937-027-6). Ctr Res Soc Chg.

Seventy-Five Years of Texas History: The Texas State Historical Association, 1897-1972. Dorman H. Winfrey. 38p. (YA) 1975. 17.50 (ISBN 0-8363-0131-5). Jenkins.

Seventy Nine Squares. Malcolm Bosse. (YA) (gr. 7-12). pap. 1.95 (ISBN 0-440-98901-9, LE). Dell.

Seventy Poems. Lindley W. Hubbell. LC 65-16528. 96p. 1965. 6.95 (ISBN 0-8040-0272-X). Swallow.

Seventy Seven. R. Rabindranath Menon. (Writers Workshop Redbird Ser.). 78p. 1975. 14.00 (ISBN 0-88253-630-3); pap. text ed. 4.80 (ISBN 0-88253-629-X). Ind-US Inc.

Seventy-Seven Dynamic Ideas for Teaching the Bible to Children. Patsy Campbell et al. (Ideas Ser.). (Illus.). 1977. pap. text ed. 1.50 o.p. (ISBN 0-87239-130-2, 7966). Standard Pub.

Seventy-Seven Ways of Involving Youth in the Church. Richard Bimler. (Illus.). 1976. pap. 4.50 (ISBN 0-570-03737-9, 12-2641). Concordia.

Seventy-Six - Seventy-Seven Directory of Educational Resources of New York City's Museums, Zoos & Botanical Gardens. 188p. 1976. pap. 5.00 (ISBN 0-89062-038-5, Pub. by Museums Collaborative). Pub Ctr Cult Res.

Seventy-Six Hours: The Invasion of Tirawa. Eric Hammel & John Lane. 1980. pap. 2.25 (ISBN 0-686-59463-0). Tower Bks.

Seventy-Six: One World & the Cantos of Ezra Pound. Forrest Read. LC 80-15892. (Illus.). 475p. 1981. 25.00x (ISBN 0-8078-1455-5); pap. 14.00x (ISBN 0-8078-4076-9). U of NC Pr.

Seventy Times Seven. Robert Hoyer. LC 75-30668. 112p. 1976. pap. 3.25 o.p. (ISBN 0-687-38199-1). Abingdon.

Seventy-Two Hours at the Crap Table. new ed. B. Mickelson. (Gamblers Book Shelf). (Illus.). 64p. (Orig.). 1972. pap. 2.95 (ISBN 0-89650-529-4). Gamblers.

Seventy Years, 1852-1922. Augusta Gregory. Ed. by Colin Smythe. (Illus.). 608p. 1976. 15.00 o.s.i. (ISBN 0-02-545550-8). Macmillan.

Several More Lives to Live: Thoreau's Political Reputation in America. Michael Meyer. LC 76-56622. (Contributions in American Studies: No. 29). 1977. lib. bdg. 16.95 (ISBN 0-8371-9477-6, MES/). Greenwood.

Severe Disabilities: Social & Rehabilitation Approaches. Ed. by Richard E. Hardy & John G. Cull. (American Lectures in Social & Rehabilitation Psychology Ser.). 336p. 1974. 19.75 (ISBN 0-398-02943-1). C C Thomas.

Severe Mercy. Sheldon Vanauken. LC 77-6161. 1977. 12.95 (ISBN 0-06-068821-1, HarpR). Har-Row.

Severe Storms: Predicion, Detection & Warning. Ed. by Committee on Atmospheric Sciences. LC 77-77588. (Illus.). 1977. pap. text ed. 6.50 (ISBN 0-309-02613-X). Natl Acad Pr.

Severed Head. Iris Murdoch. 1976. pap. 2.50 (ISBN 0-14-002003-9). Penguin.

Severely & Profoundly Handicapped: Programs, Methods & Materials. Glen Van Etten & Claudia Arkell. LC 79-28841. 1980. pap. text ed. 19.95 (ISBN 0-8016-5215-4). Mosby.

Severely Motorically Impaired Student: A Handbook for the Classroom Teacher. Harriet Healy & Susan Stainback. (Illus.). 90p. 1980. 11.75 (ISBN 0-398-04050-8); pap. 7.50 (ISBN 0-398-04061-3). C C Thomas.

Severely Retarded Children: Wider Horizons. D'Amelio. LC 74-147053. text ed. 9.95x (ISBN 0-675-09220-5). Merrill.

Severity Weighting of Data on Accidents Involving Consumer Products. (Document Ser.). 68p. 1979. 4.50 (ISBN 92-64-11980-9). OECD.

Severn Basin: Regional Archaeology. K. S. Painter. 1967. 3.95x o.p. (ISBN 0-435-32962-6). Heinemann Ed.

Severus Scroll & 1Q1SA. Jonathan P. Siegel. LC 75-28372. (Society of Biblical Literature, Masoretic Studies). 1975. pap. 7.50 (ISBN 0-89130-028-7, 060502). Scholars Pr Ca.

Sevinc Malaysia. Carlson. LC 75-13846. (The Washington Papers: No. 25). 1975. 3.50x (ISBN 0-8039-0563-7). Sage.

Sew a Beautiful Wedding. Karen Dillon & Gail Brown. 1980. pap. 4.95 (ISBN 0-935278-05-2). Palmer-Pletsch.

Sew Big...a Fashion Guide for the Fuller Figure. Marilyn Thelen. 1980. pap. 4.95 (ISBN 0-935278-04-4). Palmer-Pletsch.

Sew-Fit Manual. Ruth Oblander et al. Ed. by Judy Plum. LC 77-84538. (Illus.). 1978. 24.00 (ISBN 0-933956-03-7); tchrs. ed 19.20. Sew-Fit.

Sew-It-Yourself Decorating Book: Manual Making Home Furnishings. Ed. by Yvonne Deutch. LC 77-7456. (Illus.). 1978. 14.95 o.s.i. (ISBN 0-690-01660-3, TYC-T). T Y Crowell.

Sew, Recycle, & Save: Practical Solutions to the Challenges of the 80's. Dian D. Hymer. (Urban Life Ser.). (Illus.). 96p. (Orig.). 1981. pap. 4.95 (ISBN 0-87701-179-6). Chronicle Bks.

Sew Something Special. (Illus.). 96p. 1977. pap. 1.75 (ISBN 0-918178-10-X). Simplicity.

Sewage Treatment in Hot Climates. Duncan Mara. LC 75-23421. 240p. 1976. 30.25 (ISBN 0-471-56784-1, Pub. by Wiley-Interscience). Wiley.

Sewell's Dog's Medical Dictionary. Robert C. White. 1976. cased 14.00 (ISBN 0-7100-8365-3); pap. 6.95 (ISBN 0-7100-8366-1). Routledge & Kegan.

Sewerage & Sewage Treatment. 8th ed. Harold E. Babbitt & E. R. Baumann. LC 58-13453. (Illus.). 1958. 33.95 o.p. (ISBN 0-471-03927-6). Wiley.

Sewing Dictionary. Judy A. Meyer. LC 77-84579. (Illus.). 1979. cloth 12.00 (ISBN 0-498-02306-0); pap. 5.95 (ISBN 0-498-02306-0). A S Barnes.

Sewing for Fashion Design. Nurie Relis & Gail Strauss. (Illus.). 1978. ref. 13.95 (ISBN 0-87909-755-8). Reston.

Sewing Fundamentals. 2nd ed. Constance Warch. LC 79-88755. (Illus.). 1979. pap. 14.95x spiral bdg. (ISBN 0-916434-32-X). Plycon Pr.

Sewing Hints for Men. A. J. Abrams & Sondra R. Albert. 96p. 1980. 9.95 (ISBN 0-442-26782-7). Van Nos Reinhold.

Sewing Magic. Barbara Hellyer. Ed. by Nancy L. Zieman & Paula W. Buttel. LC 79-92573. (Illus.). 56p. 1979. pap. 3.80 (ISBN 0-933956-04-5); 3.04. Sew-Fit.

Sewing with Scraps. Phyllis Guth & Georgeanna Goff. (Illus.). (YA) (gr. 10 up). 1977. 8.95 (ISBN 0-8306-7878-6); pap. 5.95 (ISBN 0-8306-6878-0, 878). TAB Bks.

Sewing with the New Knits: Techniques for Today's New Fabrics. Phyllis Schwebke & Margery Dorfmeister. LC 72-11675. (Illus.). 480p. 1974. 14.95 o.s.i. (ISBN 0-02-607780-9). Macmillan.

Sewing Without Pins. Ruth Oblander. LC 76-53269. 1977. 3.80 (ISBN 0-933956-01-0); tchrs ed. 3.04 (ISBN 0-686-23591-6). Sew-Fit.

Sewing Without Tears. Violet Wilson. LC 78-38767. (Encore Edition). (Illus.). 1972. 3.95 o.p. (ISBN 0-684-15471-4, ScribT). Scribner.

Sex. J. G. Bennett. 128p. 1981. pap. 5.95 (ISBN 0-87728-533-0). Weiser.

Sex -- Our Myth Theology? Harlan C. Musser. 196p. 1981. pap. 7.95 (ISBN 0-8059-2768-9). Dorrance.

Sex: A User's Manual. The Diagram Group. (Illus.). 196p. 1981. 14.95 (ISBN 0-399-12574-4, Perigee); pap. 6.95 (ISBN 0-399-50517-2). Putnam.

Sex After 40. (Illus.). pap. 5.00 (ISBN 0-910550-80-8). Centurion Pr.

Sex Aids. (Illus.). 4.95 (ISBN 0-910550-81-6). Centurion Pr.

Sex & Birth Control: A Guide for the Young. rev. ed. E. J. Lieberman & Ellen Peck. LC 79-7094. (Illus.). 304p. 1981. 10.95 (ISBN 0-690-01837-1, HarpT). Har-Row.

Sex & Class in Latin America. new ed. Ed. by June Nash & Helen I. Safa. (Illus.). 352p. 1980. lib. bdg. 19.95x (ISBN 0-89789-002-7); pap. text ed. 9.95x (ISBN 0-89789-003-5). J F Bergin.

Sex & Disease in a Mountain Community. Paul Hockings. 1980. 14.00x (ISBN 0-8364-0625-7, Pub. by Vikas). South Asia Bks.

Sex & Ecstasy. (Illus.). 4.95 (ISBN 0-910550-82-4). Centurion Pr.

Sex & Emotion. (Illus.). pap. 5.00 (ISBN 0-910550-83-2). Centurion Pr.

Sex & Loving Touch. (Illus.). pap. 5.00 (ISBN 0-910550-84-0). Centurion Pr.

Sex & Marriage in England Today: A Study of the Views & Experience of the Under 45's. Geoffrey Gorer. 318p. 1971. text ed. 10.00x (ISBN 0-391-00236-8). Humanities.

Sex & Personality. Lewis M. Terman & Catherine C. Miles. 600p. 1980. Repr. of 1936 ed. lib. bdg. 50.00 (ISBN 0-89987-811-3). Darby Bks.

Sex & Rage. Eve Babitz. 208p. 1981. pap. 2.50 (ISBN 0-380-53009-0, 53009). Avon.

Sex & Repression in Savage Society. Bronislaw Malinowski. 1955. pap. 3.95 o.p. (ISBN 0-452-00405-5, F405, Mer). NAL.

Sex & Self Improvement. (Illus.). pap. 5.00 (ISBN 0-910550-85-9). Centurion Pr.

Sex & Sensibility: Ideal & Erotic Love from Milton to Mozart. Jean H. Hagstrum. LC 79-20657. (Illus.). 1980. text ed. 25.00 (ISBN 0-226-31289-5). U of Chicago Pr.

Sex & Sensuality. (Illus.). 4.95 (ISBN 0-910550-86-7). Centurion Pr.

Sex & Status. Doris Jonas & David Jonas. LC 74-23275. 214p. (Orig.). 1980. pap. 6.95 (ISBN 0-8128-6069-1). Stein & Day.

Sex and the Aging Heart. Scheingold & Wagner. 1975. pap. 1.50 (ISBN 0-515-03663-3). Jove Pubns.

Sex & the College Student, Vol. 6. GAP Committee on the College Student. LC 65-28363. (Report No. 60). 1965. pap. 2.00 (ISBN 0-87318-085-2). Adv Psychiatry.

Sex & the Media. Ed. by Veronica Elias & James Elias. (Pergamon Policy Studies). 200p. Date not set. 20.01 (ISBN 0-08-025984-7). Pergamon.

Sex & the Mentally Handicapped. Michael Craft & Ann Craft. 1978. 12.50x (ISBN 0-7100-8847-7). Routledge & Kegan.

Sex & the Outer Planets. Barbara Watters. 1971. 4.95 o.s.i. (ISBN 0-912356-03-0). Arcane Pubns.

Sex & the Singing Girl. Al Berkman. 1975. 12.50 (ISBN 0-934972-03-6). Melrose Pub Co.

Sex & the Single Cell. Dolores E. Keller. LC 71-175220. (Science & Society Ser). 1972. pap. 4.50 (ISBN 0-672-63593-3). Pegasus.

Sex & the Single Teen. Jim Smith. 31p. 1972. pap. 0.69 o.p. (ISBN 0-88207-365-6). Victor Bks.

Sex & the Spiritual Path. Herbert B. Puryear. 225p. (Orig.). 1980. pap. 5.95 (ISBN 0-87604-129-2). ARE Pr.

Sex & the Supernatural. Benjamin Walker. 128p. 1973. pap. 1.25 o.p. (ISBN 0-06-087043-5, HW). Har-Row.

Sex & the Swinging Girl. (Illus.). pap. 5.00 (ISBN 0-910550-87-5). Centurion Pr.

Sex & the Young Teen-Ager. Eleanor Kay. LC 73-5861. (Career Concise Guides Ser.). (gr. 7-12). 1973. PLB 4.90 o.p. (ISBN 0-531-02641-8). Watts.

Sex & V. D. Derek Llewellyn-Jones. 1975. 8.95 (ISBN 0-571-10482-7, Pub. by Faber & Faber); pap. 3.50 (ISBN 0-571-10483-5). Merrimack Bk Serv.

Sex-Based Discrimination, Release 1. H. Taubenfeld. 1980. 35.00. Oceana.

Sex Before Twenty: New Answers for Young People. rev. ed. Helen Southard. 1971. 6.95 o.p. (ISBN 0-525-20099-1). Dutton.

Sex Begins in the Kitchen. Kevin Leman. LC 80-54004. 144p. 1981. text ed. 7.95 (ISBN 0-8307-0787-5). Regal.

Sex Beliefs & Practices in a Navaho Community with Comparative Material from Other Navaho Areas. Flora L. Bailey. LC 52-8354. (Papers: Vol. 40, No. 2). 1950. pap. 10.00 (ISBN 0-87365-118-9). Peabody Harvard.

Sex Bias in Education. Margaret B. Sutherland. (Theory & Practice in Education Ser.: Vol. 2). 208p. 1981. 25.00x (ISBN 0-631-10851-3, Pub. by Basil Blackwell England); pap. 12.50x (ISBN 0-631-12617-1). Biblio Dist.

Sex Bias in School Leadership. Jacqueline P. Clement. LC 75-3712. 1975. 2.70 (ISBN 0-685-52790-5). Integrated Ed Assoc.

Sex Book for Those Who Think They Know It All. Charles L. Pelton. Ed. by Sheryl Klinkel. (Illus.). 227p. 1980. lib. bdg. 24.95 (ISBN 0-931470-03-X); pap. 14.95 (ISBN 0-931470-04-8). C L Pelton.

Sex, Career & Family. Michael P. Fogarty et al. LC 70-158823. 1970. 20.00x (ISBN 0-8039-0121-6); pap. 9.95x (ISBN 0-8039-0348-0). Sage.

Sex Change: The Achievement of Gender Identity by Feminized Transsexuals. Thomas Kando. 172p. 1973. 10.75 (ISBN 0-398-02731-5). C C Thomas.

Sex Chromosome Aneuploidy: Prospective Studies on Children. Ed. by Arthur Robinson et al. LC 78-13921. (Alan R. Liss Ser.: Vol. 15, No. 1). 1979. 32.00 (ISBN 0-8451-1024-1). March of Dimes.

Sex Clinic. Linda Dubreuil. 1975. pap. 1.50 o.p. (ISBN 0-685-59193-X, LB307DK, Leisure Bks). Nordon Pubns.

Sex Communes Today. (Illus.). pap. 5.00 (ISBN 0-910550-88-3). Centurion Pr.

Sex Differences. Ed. by Michael Teitelbaum. LC 75-6172. 240p. 1976. pap. 2.95 (ISBN 0-385-00826-0, Anch). Doubleday.

Sex Differences in Human Communication. Barbara Eakins & R. Gene Eakins. LC 77-77660. (Illus.). 1978. pap. text ed. 7.75 (ISBN 0-395-25510-4). HM.

Sex Differentiation, Hermaphroditism & Intersexuality in Vertebrates Including Man. N. G. Lepori. (Illus.). 372p. 1980. text ed. 49.50x (ISBN 88-212-0747-1, Pub. by Piccin Italy). J K Burgess.

Sex, Discrimination, & the Division of Labor. Ed. by Cynthia B. Lloyd. LC 74-32175. 432p. 1975. 25.00x (ISBN 0-231-03750-3); pap. 10.00x (ISBN 0-231-03751-1). Columbia U Pr.

Sex Discrimination in Career Counseling & Education. Michele Harway & Helen S. Astin. LC 77-7829. (Praeger Special Studies). 1977. 23.95 (ISBN 0-03-021826-8). Praeger.

Sex Doesn't Count When... Sara Parriott. LC 79-66310. (Illus.). 96p. 1979. pap. 2.95 (ISBN 0-87477-113-7). J P Tarcher.

Sex Drive. (Illus.). softcover 5.00 (ISBN 0-910550-89-1). Centurion Pr.

Sex Education & Counseling of Special Groups. W. R. Johnson. 224p. 1975. 16.75 (ISBN 0-398-03197-5). C C Thomas.

Sex Education & the New Morality. Eisenberg et al. 1967. pap. 1.95 (ISBN 0-686-12286-0). Jewish Bd Family.

Sex Education & the Public Schools. Lawrence J. Haims. LC 73-1014. 112p. 1973. 15.95 (ISBN 0-669-86793-4). Lexington Bks.

Sex Education: Attitudes & Research. Ed. by Anthony Pugliese. 1978. pap. 9.50 o.p. (ISBN 0-686-00912-6, D-114). Essence Pubns.

Sex-Education Controversy. James W. Hottois & Neal Milner. LC 72-469. (Politics of Education Ser.). 1975. 18.95 (ISBN 0-669-83634-6). Lexington Bks.

Sex Education for Physically Handicapped Youth. C. Edmund Hopper & William A. Allen. (Illus.). 154p. 1980. pap. text ed. 9.75 (ISBN 0-398-03935-6). C C Thomas.

Sex Education in School & Society. D. M. Dallas. (Exploring Education Ser.). 104p. (Orig.). 1972. pap. text ed. 5.00x (ISBN 0-901225-91-6, NFER). Humanities.

Sex Education Notebook. (Illus.). 59p. (Orig.). 1981. pap. 7.00 (ISBN 0-686-28927-7). Mor Mac.

Sex Education on Film: A Guide to Visual Aids & Programs. Laura J. Singer & Judith Buskin. LC 75-154694. 1971. pap. 5.25x (ISBN 0-8077-2160-3). Tchrs Coll.

Sex Education: Syllabus. Lester A. Kirkendall & Ruth F. Osborne. 1971. pap. text ed. 4.65 (ISBN 0-89420-087-9, 216786); cassette recordings 82.60 (ISBN 0-89420-184-0, 180800). Natl Book.

Sex Energy: The Sexual Force in Man & Animals. Robert S. De Ropp. 1969. 6.95 o.p. (ISBN 0-440-07818-0, Sey Lawr). Delacorte.

Sex Fact & Fancy. (Illus.). 4.95 (ISBN 0-910550-90-5). Centurion Pr.

Sex Factor & the Management of Schools. Neal Gross & Anne E. Trask. LC 75-34337. 304p. 1976. 24.95 (ISBN 0-471-32800-6, Pub. by Wiley-Interscience). Wiley.

Sex Fantasies. (Illus.). pap. 5.00 (ISBN 0-910550-91-3). Centurion Pr.

Sex, Fertility & Birth Control. Isadore Rossman. (Illus.). 1967. 9.95 (ISBN 0-87396-022-X). Stravon.

Sex for Sale. (Illus.). 4.95 (ISBN 0-910550-92-1). Centurion Pr.

Sex, Hormones & Behaviour. CIBA Foundation. (CIBA Foundation Symposium: No. 62). 1979. 41.00 (ISBN 0-444-90045-4). Elsevier.

Sex-If I Didn't I'd Cry. Jess Lair. LC 77-27678. 1979. pap. 5.95 (ISBN 0-385-13391-X). Doubleday.

Sex: If I Didn't Laugh, I'd Cry. Jess Lair. 1980. pap. 2.50 (ISBN 0-449-24336-2, Crest). Fawcett.

Sex in a Medieval Europe. Vern Bullough & James Brundage. (New Concepts in Human Sexuality Ser.). 250p. 1981. text ed. 17.95 (ISBN 0-87975-141-X); pap. text ed. 9.95 (ISBN 0-87975-151-7). Prometheus Bks.

Sex in Groups. J. N. Galena. 1974. pap. 1.25 o.p. (ISBN 0-685-51414-5, LB221ZK, Leisure Bks). Nordon Pubns.

Sex in History. Reay Tannahill. LC 79-15053. 480p. 1981. pap. 8.95 (ISBN 0-8128-6115-9). Stein & Day.

Sex in History. G. Rattray Taylor. LC 76-139982. 1954. 12.50 (ISBN 0-8149-0220-0). Vanguard.

Sex in Literature, Vol. 2. John Atkins. 1980. 15.95 (ISBN 0-7145-0919-1); pap. 6.95 (ISBN 0-7145-1138-2). Riverrun NY.

Sex in Literature, Vol. 3. John Atkins. 1981. 25.00 (ISBN 0-7145-3668-7). Riverrun NY.

Sex in Music. (Illus.). 4.95 (ISBN 0-910550-93-X). Centurion Pr.

Sex in Our Schools. (Illus.). 4.95 (ISBN 0-910550-94-8). Centurion Pr.

Sex in Society: Perspectives on Stratification. Joyce M. Nielsen. 1978. pap. 7.95x (ISBN 0-534-00573-X). Wadsworth Pub.

Sex in the Garden. Tom Riker. LC 76-4135. (Illus.). 192p. 1976. 9.95 o.p. (ISBN 0-688-03063-7). Morrow.

Sex in the Light of Reincarnation & Freedom. Alan Howard. 1980. pap. 4.95 (ISBN 0-916786-48-X). St George Bk Serv.

Sex in the Middle Ages. Ed. by Vern Bullough & James Brundage. LC 80-85227. (New Concepts in Human Sexuality Ser.). 250p. 1980. 17.95 (ISBN 0-87975-141-X); pap. 9.95 (ISBN 0-87975-151-7). Prometheus Bks.

Sex in the U.S.S.R. Mikhail Stern. 384p. 1981. 12.95 (ISBN 0-8129-0942-9). Times Bks.

Sex Is a Parent Affair. Letha Scanzoni. LC 72-77114. 1973. pap. 3.50 o.p. (ISBN 0-8307-0160-5, 54-065-01). Regal.

Sex Is for Giving. John Webster. (Illus.). 1968. 5.95 (ISBN 0-910550-12-3). Elysium.

Sex Is Not to Lose Sleep Over. Dick Jewett. LC 78-70729. (Redwood Ser.). 1979. pap. 3.95 (ISBN 0-8163-0246-4). Pacific Pr Pub Assn.

Sex Joke Book. Max Brodnick. (Illus., Orig.). 1975. pap. 1.25 o.p. (ISBN 0-685-52937-1, LB264ZK, Leisure Bks). Nordon Pubns.

Sex Jokes & Male Chauvinism. George Fine. (Illus.). 192p. 1981. 9.95 (ISBN 0-8065-0753-5). Citadel Pr.

Sex, Liquor, Tobacco and Candy Are Bad for You. Dick Sutphen. LC 73-186725. 96p. 1972. pap. 2.25 o.p. (ISBN 0-911842-10-1). Valley Sun.

Sex Magazines in the Library Collection: Serials Librarian Monographic Supplement to Vol. 4. Ed. by Peter Gellatly. LC 80-15011. 1981. text ed. 14.95 (ISBN 0-917724-16-X). Haworth Pr.

Sex: Male-Gender: Masculine. John W. Petras. LC 74-32335. 265p. 1975. pap. text ed. 7.95x (ISBN 0-88284-019-3). Alfred Pub.

Sex Marchers. Ed. by Jefferson Poland. 1968. 5.95 (ISBN 0-910550-13-1). Elysium.

Sex, Motivation & the Criminal Offender. Robert H. Morneau, Jr. & Robert R. Rockwell. (Illus.). 416p. 1980. text ed. 29.75 (ISBN 0-398-03933-X). C C Thomas.

Sex Over Lightly. Gerry Blumenfeld & Harold Blumenfeld. 1976. pap. 1.25 o.p. (ISBN 0-685-72355-0, LB381ZK, Leisure Bks). Nordon Pubns.

Sex-Pol: Essays 1929-1934. Wilhelm Reich. Ed. by Lee Baxandall. LC 72-2735. 1972. pap. 2.45 (ISBN 0-394-71791-0, V-791, Vin). Random.

Sex Problems & the Wife. (Illus.). pap. 5.00 (ISBN 0-910550-95-6). Centurion Pr.

Sex Profession. Patricia Schiller. 252p. 1981. pap. 8.00 (ISBN 0-88416-340-7). PSG Pub.

Sex Profession: What Sex Therapy Can Do. Patricia Schiller. 250p. (Orig.). 1980. 11.00 (ISBN 0-937532-00-2); pap. 8.00 (ISBN 0-937532-01-0). Chilmark Hse.

Sex-Role Cycle: Socialization from Infancy to Old Age. Ed. by Florence Howe & John A. Rothermich. (Women's Lives - Women's Work Ser.). 192p. (Orig.). 1980. pap. text ed. 4.23. Webster-McGraw.

Sex-Role Cycle: Socialization from Infancy to Old Age. Nancy Romer. (Women's Lives - Women's Work Ser.). (Illus.). 190p. (Orig.). (gr. 11-12). 1981. pap. 5.95 (ISBN 0-912670-69-X). Feminist Pr.

Sex-Role Issues in Mental Health. Kay F. Schaffer. LC 79-53872. (Clinical & Professional Psychology Ser.). 1980. pap. text ed. 7.95 (ISBN 0-201-06762-5). A-W.

Sex-Role Psychology. Frank Wesley & Claire Wesley. LC 77-1308. 1977. text ed. 22.95 (ISBN 0-87705-307-3); pap. 8.95 (ISBN 0-87705-357-X). Human Sci Pr.

Sex Role Stereotypes: Traditions & Alternatives. Susan Basow. LC 80-19086. 320p. (Orig.). 1980. pap. text ed. 10.95 (ISBN 0-8185-0394-7). Brooks-Cole.

Sex Roles & Human Behavior. Kay R. Schaffer. (Psychology Ser.). 448p. 1981. text ed. 14.95 (ISBN 0-87626-807-6). Winthrop.

Sex Roles & Personal Awareness. Barbara L. Forisha. 1978. pap. text ed. 9.95x (ISBN 0-673-15307-X). Scott F.

Sex Roles & Social Policy: A Complex Social Science Equation. Ed. by Jean Lipman-Blumen & Jessie Bernard. LC 77-90858. (Sage Studies in International Sociology: Vol. 14). 1979. 18.00x (ISBN 0-8039-9870-8); pap. 9.95x (ISBN 0-8039-9871-6). Sage.

Sex Roles in Law & Society: Cases & Materials. Leo Kanowitz. LC 72-94656. 720p. 1973. 20.00x o.p. (ISBN 0-8263-0254-8); pap. 9.95x (ISBN 0-8263-0326-9). U of NM Pr.

Sex Roles in Literature. Mary Beth Pringle & Anne Stericker. (English & Humanities Ser.). 1980. pap. text ed. 9.95 (ISBN 0-582-28103-2). Longman.

Sex Roles, Life Styles & Childbearing: Changing Patterns in Marriage & the Family. John H. Scanzoni. LC 74-28939. (Illus.). 1975. 17.95 (ISBN 0-02-927720-5). Free Pr.

Sex Roles: Origins, Influences & Implications for Women. Ed. by Cannie S. Adamec. 1980. 17.95 (ISBN 0-920792-00-6). EPWP.

Sex Roles, Sex Inequality, & Sex Role Development. Jean Stockard & Miriam M. Johnson. (Illus.). 1980. pap. text ed. 13.95 (ISBN 0-13-807560-3). P-H.

Sex Roles, Women's Work, & Marital Conflict. John Scanzoni. LC 78-58981. (Illus.). 1978. 17.95 (ISBN 0-669-02400-7). Lexington Bks.

Sex, Satan, & Jesus. Richard Hoque. LC 73-86668. 4.95 (ISBN 0-8054-5319-9); pap. 3.50 (ISBN 0-8054-5320-2). Broadman.

Sex Self Taught: A Home - Study Course for Underachievers. Don R. King. LC 77-5909. 1977. 14.95 (ISBN 0-88229-386-9); pap. 7.95 (ISBN 0-88229-490-3). Nelson-Hall.

Sex, Sexuality, & You: A Handbook for Growing Christians. Nancy H. Cooney. 100p. (Orig.). 1980. pap. text ed. 3.50 (ISBN 0-697-01741-9); tchr's resource guide 0.75 (ISBN 0-697-01742-7). Wm C Brown.

Sex Signs. Judith Bennett. 384p. 1981. pap. 7.95 (ISBN 0-312-71339-8). St Martin.

Sex, Sin & Salvation. Roy Masters. LC 77-78040. 267p. 1977. pap. 6.50 (ISBN 0-933900-06-6). Foun Human Under.

Sex, Sisterhood, & Self-Delusion: What Happened to Women's Magazines? Mary L. Coakley. 1980. 10.95 o.p. (ISBN 0-87000-452-2). Arlington Hse.

Sex Slavery. Stephen Barlay. 1977. pap. 1.75 o.p. (ISBN 0-685-79746-5). Ballantine.

Sex Songs. Jocelyn Hollis. LC 78-75357. (Contemporary American Traditional Poetry Ser.: Vol. 1, No. 4). 60p. 1980. pap. cancelled (ISBN 0-933486-00-6). Am Poetry Pr.

Sex: Telling It Straight. Eric W. Johnson. LC 79-124545. 1979. 8.95 (ISBN 0-397-01323-X). Lippincott.

Sex Wars: Free Adaptations of Ibsen & Strindberg. Charles Marowitz. 192p. 1981. 15.00. (Pub. by M Boyars); pap. 8.95 (ISBN 0-7145-2722-X). Merrimack Bk Serv.

Sex, with Love: A Guide for Young People. Eleanor Hamilton. LC 77-75442. (Illus.). (gr. 7-10). 1978. 10.95 (ISBN 0-8070-2580-1); pap. 4.50 (ISBN 0-8070-2581-X, BP653). Beacon Pr.

Sex Without Love: A Philosophical Exploration. Russell Vannoy. LC 79-57534. 226p. 1980. text ed. 14.95 (ISBN 0-87975-128-2); pap. text ed. 7.95 (ISBN 0-87975-129-0). Prometheus Bks.

Sex Without Men. (Illus.). 4.95 (ISBN 0-910550-96-4). Centurion Pr.

Sexism & the Law: Male Beliefs & Legal Bias in Britain & the United States. Albie Sachs & Joan H. Wilson. LC 78-63402. 1979. 15.95 (ISBN 0-02-927640-3). Free Pr.

Sexism: Scientific Debates. Ed. by Clarice S. Stoll. LC 72-11077. 1973. pap. text ed. 5.50 (ISBN 0-201-07308-0). A-W.

Sexism: The Male Monopoly on History & Thought. Marielouise Janssen-Jurreit. Tr. by Verne Moberg from Ger. 384p. 1981. 19.95 (ISBN 0-374-26167-9). FS&G.

Sexist Language: A Modern Philosophical Analysis. Ed. by Vetterling-Braggin & Mary. (Littlefield, Adams Quality Paperbacks Ser.: No. 353). 1981. pap. 7.95 (ISBN 0-8226-0353-5). Littlefield.

Sexist Language: A Modern Philosophical Analysis. Ed. by Mary Vetterling-Braggin. 1981. 22.50x (ISBN 0-8476-6293-4). Rowman.

Sexo y Juventud. Luis Palau. 83p. (Orig., Span.). (YA) 1974. pap. 1.95 (ISBN 0-89922-032-0). Edit Caribe.

Sexpionage. David Lewis. 1977. pap. 1.75 o.p. (ISBN 0-345-25714-6). Ballantine.

Sextette: Translations from the French Symbolists. Tr. by Dorothy Martin. LC 80-10539. (Symbolists Ser.). 112p. 1980. Repr. of 1928 ed. 18.50 (ISBN 0-404-16331-9). AMS Pr.

Sexto Curso de Derecho Internationsl Organizado Por el Comite Juridico Interamericano: Julio-Agosto de 1979, Conferencias e Informes. OAS General Secretariat, Dept. of Publications. 630p. (Span.). 1979. pap. text ed. 25.00 (ISBN 0-8270-1144-X). OAS.

Sexual Abuse: Clinical Problems & Practical Approaches. Jean M. Goodwin. 1981. write for info. (ISBN 0-88416-326-1). PSG Pub.

Sexual Abuse of Children: Implications from the Sexual Trauma Treatment Program of Connecticut-Special Report of Two Research Utilization Workshops. 1979. 3.00. Comm Coun Great NY.

Sexual Acupuncture. Frank Z. Warren & Walter I. Fischman. 1978. 14.95 o.p. (ISBN 0-525-20118-1); pap. 7.95 o.p. (ISBN 0-525-04435-3). Dutton.

Sexual & Asexual Pursuit. Herbert Hoffmann. (Occasional Papers Ser.: No. 34). 1977. pap. text ed. 8.00x (ISBN 0-391-01111-1). Humanities.

Sexual Anxiety: A Study of Male Impotence. Eric Carlton. 197p. 1980. 22.50x. B&N.

Sexual Arena & Women's Liberation. Edward J. Bardon. LC 77-23937. 1978. 15.95 (ISBN 0-88229-219-6); pap. 7.95 (ISBN 0-88229-558-6). Nelson-Hall.

Sexual Arousal Techniques. (Illus.). pap. 5.00 (ISBN 0-910550-97-2). Centurion Pr.

Sexual Assault. Ed. by Marcia J. Walker & Stanley L. Brodsky. 1978. pap. text ed. 6.95x o.p. (ISBN 0-669-01645-4). Heath.

Sexual Assault of Children & Adolescents. Ann W. Burgess et al. LC 77-10217. 1978. 22.95 (ISBN 0-669-01890-2); pap. 9.95 (ISBN 0-669-01892-9). Lexington Bks.

Sexual Assault: The Victim & the Rapist. Marcia J. Walker & Stanley L. Brodsky. LC 75-24560. (Illus.). 208p. 1976. 18.95 (ISBN 0-669-00196-1). Lexington Bks.

Sexual Attraction. Mark Cook & R. McHenry. 1978. text ed. 21.00 (ISBN 0-08-022231-5); pap. text ed. 8.25 (ISBN 0-08-022230-7). Pergamon.

Sexual Barrier: Legal, Medical, Economic & Social Aspects of Sex Discrimination. Marija M. Hughes. LC 77-83214. 1977. 60.00 (ISBN 0-912560-04-5). Hughes Pr.

Sexual Behavior: Pharmacology & Biochemistry. Ed. by M. Sandler & G. L. Gessa. LC 74-14478. 364p. 1975. 34.50 (ISBN 0-89004-005-2). Raven.

Sexual Behaviour in Canada: Patterns & Problems. Benjamin Schlesinger. 1977. pap. 6.95 (ISBN 0-8020-6314-4). U of Toronto Pr.

Sexual Bond. Francois Duyckaerts. 1970. 6.95 o.p. (ISBN 0-440-07847-4). Delacorte.

Sexual Celibate. Don Goergen. 256p. 1975. 8.95 (ISBN 0-8164-0268-X). Crossroad NY.

Sexual Celibate. Donald Goergen. 1979. pap. 3.95 (ISBN 0-385-14902-6, Im). Doubleday.

Sexual Choices: An Introduction to Human Sexuality. Nass et al. (Illus.). 550p. 1981. text ed. 17.95 (ISBN 0-87872-285-8). Duxbury Pr.

Sexual Counseling. Eugene Kennedy. LC 76-30875. 1977. 9.95 o.p. (ISBN 0-8164-9312-X). Continuum.

Sexual Counseling for Ostomates: A Resource Book for Health Care Professionals. Ellen A. Shipes & Sally T. Lehr. (Illus.). 118p. 1980. text ed. 8.50 lexotone (ISBN 0-398-03950-X). C C Thomas.

Sexual Dimensions of the Celibate Life. William Kraft. 1979. 12.95 o.p. (ISBN 0-8362-3908-3). Andrews & McMeel.

Sexual Endocrinology: Proceedings of the Fondation pour la recherche en endocrinologie sexuelle et la reproduction humaine. Ed. by R. Vokaer & G. De Bock. 252p. 1975. text ed. 44.00 (ISBN 0-08-018170-8). Pergamon.

Sexual Experience Between Men & Boys. Parker Rossman. 1976. 10.95 o.p. (ISBN 0-8096-1911-3, Assn Pr). Follett.

Sexual Freedom & Venereal Disease. R. S. Morton. (Contemporary Issues Ser: No. 5). 1971. text ed. 17.00x (ISBN 0-7206-0411-7). Humanities.

Sexual Identity: Implications for Mental Health. Ronald A. LaTorre. LC 78-26442. 1979. 16.95 (ISBN 0-88229-360-5). Nelson-Hall.

Sexual Identity: Sex Roles & Social Change. Betty Yorburg. LC 80-22489. 240p. 1981. Repr. text ed. 8.50 (ISBN 0-89874-265-X). Krieger.

Sexual Interactions in Eukaryotic Microbes. Ed. by D. H. O'Day & P. A. Horgen. LC 80-39593. (Cell Biology Ser.). 1981. 45.00 (ISBN 0-12-524160-7). Acad Pr.

Sexual Intimacy. Andrew M. Greeley. 199p. 1975. pap. 3.95 (ISBN 0-8164-2591-4). Crossroad NY.

Sexual Joy in Marriage. Michael Clark & Dorothy Clark. (Illus.). 256p. (Orig.). 1980. pap. 7.95 (ISBN 0-523-41137-5). Pinnacle Bks.

Sexual Joy in Marriage. Michael Clarke & Dorothy Clarke. pap. 6.95 o.p. (ISBN 0-523-41137-5). Pinnacle Bks.

Sexual Key to the Tarot. Theodor Laurence. 1973. pap. 1.50 (ISBN 0-451-07581-1, W7581, Sig). NAL.

Sexual Labyrinth of Nikolai Gogol. Simon Karlinsky. 1976. 15.00x (ISBN 0-674-80281-0). Harvard U Pr.

Sexual Life in Ancient China. Robert H. Van Gulik. 1974. Repr. of 1961 ed. text ed. 54.75x (ISBN 0-685-12486-X). Humanities.

Sexual Maladjustment & Disease: An Introduction to Modern Venereology. Gavin Hart. LC 76-29073. 1977. 18.95 (ISBN 0-88229-325-7). Nelson-Hall.

Sexual, Marital, & Familial Relations. R. H. Woody & J. D. Woody. (Illus.). 312p. 1973. 16.50 (ISBN 0-398-02803-6). C C Thomas.

Sexual Maturity: Physiological & Clinical Parameters. Ed. by E. S. Hafez & J. J. Peluso. LC 76-22248. (Perspectives in Human Reproduction: Vol. 3). 1976. 24.00 (ISBN 0-250-40112-6). Ann Arbor Science.

Sexual Medicine & Counseling in Office Practice. Dennis J. Munjack & L. Jerome Oziel. 1980. text ed. 15.95 (ISBN 0-316-58940-3). Little.

Sexual Obsession. (Illus.). softcover 5.00 (ISBN 0-910550-98-0). Centurion Pr.

Sexual Pleasure Enhancement Program. The G-Jo Institute. 1980. pap. 4.50 (ISBN 0-916878-12-0). Falkynor Bks.

Sexual Preferences. Sandra Kahn & Jean Davis. 256p. 1981. 9.95 (ISBN 0-312-71351-7). St Martin.

Sexual Profile of Men in Power. Barbara Bess et al. 1978. pap. 2.50 (ISBN 0-446-81484-9). Warner Bks.

Sexual Release: Orgasm. (Illus.). 4.95 (ISBN 0-910550-99-9). Centurion Pr.

Sexual Revolution: Traditional Mores Versus New Values. Ed. by David L. Bender & Gary E. McCuen. (Opposing Viewpoints Ser.: Vol. 7). (Illus.). (gr. 9 up). 1972. lib. bdg. 8.95 (ISBN 0-912616-31-8); pap. 3.95 (ISBN 0-912616-12-1). Greenhaven.

Sexual Rights for People Who Happen to Be Handicapped. Sol Gordon. 1979. 1.00 (ISBN 0-937540-03-X, HPP-10). Human Policy Pr.

Sexual Sabotage: How to Enjoy Sex Inspite of Physical & Emotional Problems. Sherwin A. Kaufman. 256p. 1981. 13.95 (ISBN 0-02-560740-5). Macmillan.

Sexual Solution. Michael Castleman. 1981. 11.95 (ISBN 0-671-24688-7). S&S.

Sexual Stratification: A Cross-Cultural View. Ed. by Alice Schlegel. LC 77-2742. 1977. 22.50x (ISBN 0-231-04214-0); pap. 10.00x (ISBN 0-231-04215-9). Columbia U Pr.

Sexual Superstars. R. T. Larkin. 1976. pap. 1.75 o.p. (ISBN 0-685-69155-1, LB363KK, Leisure Bks). Nordon Pubns.

Sexual Tour of the Deep South. Rosemary Daniell. LC 74-15473. 112p. 1975. 6.95 o.p. (ISBN 0-03-013726-8); pap. 3.95 o.p. (ISBN 0-685-93059-9). HR&W.

Sexual Understanding Before Marriage. Herbert J. Miles. 224p. 1972. pap. 2.95 (ISBN 0-310-29212-3). Zondervan.

Sexual Unfolding: Sexual Development & Sex Therapies in Late Adolescence. Lorna J. Sarrel & Philip M. Sarrel. 1979. text ed. 15.95 (ISBN 0-316-77100-7). Little.

Sexual Variations: Fetishism, Sadomasochism & Transvestism. Glenn Wilson & Chris Gosselin. 1981. 12.95 (ISBN 0-671-24624-0). S&S.

Sexual Victimology of Youth. LeRoy G. Schultz. (Illus.). 432p. 1980. text ed. 19.75 (ISBN 0-398-03925-9). C C Thomas.

Sexuality & Aging. rev. ed. Robert L. Solnick. LC 78-51932. 1978. pap. 5.50 (ISBN 0-88474-023-4). USC Andrus Geron.

Sexuality & Homosexuality: A New View. Arno Karlen. 1971. 15.00 o.p. (ISBN 0-393-01087-2). Norton.

Sexuality: Guidelines for Teenagers. Arvis J. Olsen. 80p. (Orig.). 1981. pap. 1.95 (ISBN 0-8010-6674-3). Baker Bk.

Sexuality in Contemporary Catholicism. Ed. by Franz Bockle & Jean-Marie Pohier. (Concilium Ser.: Religion in the Seventies: Vol. 100). 1977. pap. 4.95 (ISBN 0-8164-2097-1). Crossroad NY.

Sexuality, Law, & the Developmentally Disabled Person: Legal & Clinical Aspects of Marriage, Parenthood, & Sterilization. Sarah F. Haavik & Karl A. Menninger, 2nd. 210p. (Orig.). 1981. pap. text ed. 13.95 (ISBN 0-933716-21-4). P H Brookes.

Sexuality of Jesus. William E. Phipps. LC 74-126282. 1979. pap. 3.95 o.p. (ISBN 0-06-066562-9, RD141, HarpR). Har-Row.

Sexually Abused Children & Their Families. Patricia B. Mrazek & C. H. Kempe. 300p. 1981. 72.01 (ISBN 0-08-026796-3). Pergamon.

Sexually Exciting Female. (Illus.). 4.95 (ISBN 0-910550-74-3). Centurion Pr.

Sexually Fulfilled Man. Rachel Copelan. 1973. pap. 1.50 (ISBN 0-451-05675-2, W5675, Sig). NAL.

Sexually Fulfilled Woman. Rachel Coplan. 1973. pap. 1.50 (ISBN 0-451-05676-0, W5676, Sig). NAL.

Sexually Superior Male. (Illus.). 4.95 (ISBN 0-910550-73-5). Centurion Pr.

Sexually Transmitted Diseases. Leslie Nicholas. (Illus.). 264p. 1973. 19.75 (ISBN 0-398-02697-1). C C Thomas.

Sexually Transmitted Diseases. Robert C. Noble. LC 78-71163. (Discussions in Patient Management Ser.). 1979. pap. 9.50 (ISBN 0-87488-881-6). Med Exam.

Sexually Transmitted Diseases: The Facts. David Barlow. (Illus.). 1979. text ed. 11.95x (ISBN 0-19-261157-7). Oxford U Pr.

Sexually Victimized Children. David Finkelhor. LC 79-7104. 1981. pap. text ed. 7.95 (ISBN 0-02-910400-9). Free Pr.

Seymour Britchky's New Revised Guide to the Restaurants of New York: An Irreverent Appraisal of the Best, Most Interesting, Most Famous, Most Underated or Worst Restaurants in New York City. Seymour Britchky. 1976. pap. 5.95 o.p. (ISBN 0-394-73222-7). Random.

Seymour Britchky's Restaurants of New York, 1977-1978. Seymour Britchky. (Illus.). 1977. pap. 5.95 o.p. (ISBN 0-394-73414-9). Random.

Seymour the Prince. Sue Alexander. LC 78-31406. (I Am Reading Bks.). (Illus.). (gr. 2-4). 1979. 4.95 (ISBN 0-394-84141-7); PLB 5.99 (ISBN 0-394-94141-1). Pantheon.

SF Authors' Choice: 4. Ed. by Harry Harrison. 192p. (YA) 1974. 5.95 o.p. (ISBN 0-399-11188-3, Dist. by Putnam). Berkley Pub.

SF in Dimension. 2nd ed. Alexei Panshin & Cory Panshin. LC 80-68572. 1980. pap. 6.00 (ISBN 0-911682-24-4). Advent.

SF Published in Nineteen Seventy-Five. Joanne Burger. LC 71-10701. 64p. 1980. Repr. of 1976 ed. lib. bdg. 9.95x (ISBN 0-89370-053-3). Borgo Pr.

SF Published in Nineteen Seventy-Four. Joanne Burger. LC 71-10701. 64p. 1980. Repr. of 1975 ed. lib. bdg. 9.95x (ISBN 0-89370-052-5). Borgo Pr.

SF Published in Nineteen Seventy-Seven. Joanne Burger. LC 71-10701. 64p. 1980. Repr. of 1979 ed. lib. bdg. 9.95x (ISBN 0-89370-055-X). Borgo Pr.

SF Published in Nineteen Seventy-Six. Joanne Burger. LC 71-10701. 64p. 1980. Repr. of 1977 ed. lib. bdg. 9.95x (ISBN 0-89370-054-1). Borgo Pr.

SF Published in Nineteen Seventy-Three. Joanne Burger. LC 71-10701. 64p. 1980. Repr. of 1974 ed. lib. bdg. 9.95x (ISBN 0-89370-051-7). Borgo Pr.

SF Published in Nineteen Seventy-Two. Joanne Burger. LC 71-10701. 64p. 1980. Repr. of 1973 ed. lib. bdg. 9.95x (ISBN 0-89370-050-9). Borgo Pr.

SF Yearbook. David Gerrold. LC 79-63463. 1979. pap. 4.95 (ISBN 0-931064-10-4). Starlog.

SFBRI: Science Fiction Book Review Index, 10 vols. H. W. Hall. Incl. Vol. 1. 1970 (ISBN 0-89370-066-5); Vol. 2. 1971 (ISBN 0-89370-067-3); Vol. 3. 1972 (ISBN 0-89370-068-1); Vol. 4. 1973 (ISBN 0-89370-069-X); Vol. 5. 1974 (ISBN 0-89370-070-3); Vol. 6. 1975 (ISBN 0-89370-071-1); Vol. 7. 1976 (ISBN 0-89370-072-X); Vol. 8. 1977 (ISBN 0-89370-073-8); Vol. 9. 1978 (ISBN 0-89370-074-6); Vol. 12. 1979 (ISBN 0-89370-075-4). LC 72-625320. 64p. Vols. 1-9. lib. bdg. 11.95x ea.; Vol. 12. lib. bdg. 12.95x. Borgo Pr.

SFBRI: Science Fiction Book Review Index, Vol. 11, 1980. H. W. Hall. LC 72-625320. 54p. (Orig.). 1981. pap. text ed. 5.00 (ISBN 0-935064-06-0). H W Hall.

SFBRI: Science Fiction Book Review Index, Vol. 5: 1974. H. W. Hall. LC 72-625320. 1975. 5.00 (ISBN 0-935064-00-1). H W Hall.

SFBRI: Science Fiction Book Review Index, Vol. 7: 1976. H. W. Hall. LC 72-625320. 1977. 5.00 (ISBN 0-935064-02-8). H W Hall.

SFBRI: Science Fiction Book Review Index, Vol. 9: 1978. Ed. by H. W. Hall. LC 72-625320. 1979. pap. 4.50 (ISBN 0-935064-04-4). H W Hall.

SFBRI: 1975. H. W. Hall. LC 72-625320. 1976. 5.00 (ISBN 0-935064-01-X). H W Hall.

SG Elementary Statistics for Business. Johnson & Swanson. (Illus.). 1980. write for info. Duxbury Pr.

SG Understanding Statistics. Beaver & Beaver. 1980. pap. text ed. write for info. (ISBN 0-87872-241-6). Duxbury Pr.

Shabbat Can Be. Audrey F. Marcus & Raymond A. Zwerin. Ed. by Daniel B. Syme. (Illus.). (gr. k-3). 1979. pap. text ed. 5.00 (ISBN 0-8074-0023-8, 102560); tchrs'. guide 3.00 (ISBN 0-8074-0024-6, 208025). UAHC.

Shackleton's Boat Journey. F. A. Worsley. 1978. pap. 1.95 o.s.i. (ISBN 0-515-04486-5). Jove Pubns.

Shaddai. Kenneth E. Hagin. 1980. pap. 1.25 (ISBN 0-89276-401-5). Hagin Ministries.

Shade Book. rev. ed. Judy Lindahl. (Illus.). 128p. pap. 4.95 (ISBN 0-9603032-2-7). Lindahl.

Shade Gardens. James U. Crockett & Oliver E. Allen. (Time-Life Encyclopedia of Gardening Ser.). (Illus.). 1979. lib. bdg. 11.97 (ISBN 0-8094-2646-3); kivar bdg. 8.95 (ISBN 0-8094-2647-1). Silver.

Shades. Betty Brock. (gr. 3-5). 1973. pap. 1.25 o.s.i. (ISBN 0-380-01545-5, 27888, Camelot). Avon.

Shades of Blue. Nellie L. Bryant. 1981. 4.50 (ISBN 0-8062-1705-7). Carlton.

Shades of Brown: New Perspectives on School Desegregation. Ed. by Derrick Bell. LC 80-21877. 1980. text ed. 12.95x (ISBN 0-8077-2595-1). Tchrs Coll.

Shades of Green. Shree Devi. (Writers Workshop Redbird Ser). 1975. 8.00 (ISBN 0-88253-632-X); pap. text ed. 4.00 (ISBN 0-88253-631-1). Ind-US Inc.

Shades of Grey. Mark Denning. (Orig.). 1976. pap. 1.25 o.s.i. (ISBN 0-515-03891-1). Jove Pubns.

Shades of Heathcliffe & Death of Captain Doughty. John Spurling. 1978. 10.95 (ISBN 0-7145-2517-0, Pub. by M Boyars); pap. 5.95 (ISBN 0-7145-2518-9). Merrimack Bk Serv.

Shades of Jade. Val Colebrook. LC 80-52170. (Illus.). 52p. (Orig.). 1980. pap. 3.50 (ISBN 0-932384-11-0). Tashmoo.

Shadow. Benito P. Galdos. Tr. by Karen O. Austin from Sp. LC 80-10549. Orig. Title: Sombra. 65p. 1980. 7.95 (ISBN 0-8214-0553-5, 0553E). Ohio U Pr.

Shadow & Evil in Fairytales. M-L Von Franz. Ed. by James Hillman. (Seminar Ser., No. 9). 250p. 1973. pap. 12.50 (ISBN 0-88214-109-0). Spring Pubns.

Shadow & Flowers. W. Scarfe. 8.00 (ISBN 0-89253-733-7). Ind-US Inc.

Shadow & Substance. P. Donizetti. 1967. 15.00 (ISBN 0-08-012182-9); pap. 11.25 (ISBN 0-08-012181-0). Pergamon.

Shadow & Substance. John P. Roche. 1969. pap. 2.95 o.s.i. (ISBN 0-02-074650-4, Collier). Macmillan.

Shadow & Sun. Mary Carroll. 192p. (Orig.). pap. 1.50 (ISBN 0-671-57002-1). S&S.

Shadow & the Fear. Jane Corby. 1977. pap. 1.50 (ISBN 0-505-51174-6). Tower Bks.

Shadow Bear. Joan Harlow. LC 80-7507. (Illus.). 32p. (gr. 3). 1981. 7.95a (ISBN 0-385-15066-0); PLB (ISBN 0-385-15067-9). Doubleday.

Shadow Book. Beatrice S. De Regniers & Isabel Gordon. LC 60-10244. (Illus.). (gr. k-3). 1960. 5.95 o.p. (ISBN 0-15-272991-7, HJ). HarBraceJ.

Shadow Box. Michael Cristofer. 1977. pap. 2.25 (ISBN 0-380-01865-9, 46839, Bard). Avon.

Shadow Box. George Plimpton. LC 77-4275. (Illus.). (YA) 1977. 9.95 o.p. (ISBN 0-399-11995-7, Dist. by Putnam). Berkley Pub.

Shadow Cabinet in British Politics. D. R. Turner. 1969. text ed. 6.00x (ISBN 0-7100-6489-6). Humanities.

Shadow from Ladakh. Bhabani Bhattacharya. 359p. 1969. pap. 3.00 (ISBN 0-88253-018-6). Ind-US Inc.

Shadow Geometry. Daphne H. Trivett. LC 72-7561. (Young Math Ser.). (Illus.). (gr. 1-4). 1974. PLB 6.89 o.p. (ISBN 0-690-73057-8, TYC-J). T Y Crowell.

Shadow Guests. Joan Aiken. LC 80-65830. 160p. (gr. 5 up). 1980. 7.95 (ISBN 0-440-07746-X). Delacorte.

Shadow Guns. Dan James. (YA) 1972. 5.95 (ISBN 0-685-24999-9, Avalon). Bouregy.

Shadow Hawk. Andre Norton. 1979. pap. 1.95 o.p. (ISBN 0-449-24186-6, Crest). Fawcett.

Shadow Land: Selected Poems. Johannes Bobrowski. Tr. by Ruth Mead & Matthew Mead. (Poetry in Europe: No. 1). 1966. 4.95 o.p. (ISBN 0-8040-0273-8). Swallow.

Shadow Like a Leopard. Myron Levoy. LC 79-2812. 192p. (YA) (gr. 7 up). 1981. 8.95 (ISBN 0-06-023816-X, HarpJ); PLB 8.79g (ISBN 0-06-023817-8). Har-Row.

Shadow Man: A Documentary Life of Dashiell Hammett. Richard Layman. 300p. 1981. 14.95 (ISBN 0-15-181459-7). HarBraceJ.

Shadow of a Bull. Maria Wojciechowska. (Illus.). (gr. 5 up). 1972. pap. 2.95 (ISBN 0-689-70298-1, Aladdin). Atheneum.

Shadow of a Dream & An Imperative Duty. W. D. Howells. LC 71-79475. (Selected Edition of W. D. Howells: Center for Editions of American Authors: Vol. 17). 272p. 1969. 15.00x (ISBN 0-253-35190-1). Ind U Pr.

Shadow of a Lady. Jane A. Hodge. 1977. pap. 1.75 o.p. (ISBN 0-449-23117-8, Crest). Fawcett.

Shadow of Alpha. C. L. Grant. pap. 1.25 o.p. (ISBN 0-425-03143-8). Berkley Pub.

Shadow of an Eagle. Sue Peters. (Harlequin Romances Ser.). 192p. 1980. pap. 1.25 (ISBN 0-373-02351-0, Pub. by Harlequin). PB.

Shadow of Apollo. Anne Hampson. 192p. 1981. pap. 1.50 (ISBN 0-671-57064-1). S&S.

Shadow of Death. Thomas C. Callahan & Freda Turner. LC 80-50008. (Illus.). 192p. 1980. 9.95 (ISBN 0-936354-01-1). Val-Hse Pub.

Shadow of Desire. Sara Craven. (Harlequin Presents Ser.). 192p. 1980. pap. 1.50 (ISBN 0-373-10398-0, Pub. by Harlequin). PB.

Shadow of Dolores. Georgia M. Shewmake. (YA) 1978. 5.95 (ISBN 0-685-86413-8, Avalon). Bouregy.

Shadow of Eternity: The Poetry of Herbert, Vaughan, & Traherne. Sharon C. Seelig. LC 80-51018. 1981. price not set (ISBN 0-8131-1444-6). U Pr of Ky.

Shadow of His Hand. Kenneth C. Hendricks. (Orig.). 1967. kivar 3.95 o.p. (ISBN 0-8272-3402-3). Bethany Pr.

Shadow of His Hand. Norris L. Wogen. LC 74-21059. 1974. pap. 2.25 (ISBN 0-87123-533-1, 210533). Bethany Fell.

Shadow of Love. Sondra Stanford. 192p. (Orig.). 1980. pap. 1.50 (ISBN 0-671-57025-0). S&S.

Shadow of Reddoch's Landing. Melissa Lee. 1976. pap. 1.25 o.p. (ISBN 0-685-74576-7, LB424ZK, Leisure Bks). Nordon Pubns.

Shadow of Sequoyah: Social Documents of the Cherokees, 1862-1964. Jack F. Kilpatrick & Anna G. Kilpatrick. LC 65-24205. 1965. 7.95 (ISBN 0-8061-0677-8); pap. 3.50 (ISBN 0-8061-1274-3, CAI81). U of Okla Pr.

Shadow of Slavery: Peonage in the South, 1901-1969. Pete Daniel. LC 70-174779. (Illus.). 222p. 1973. pap. 3.95x (ISBN 0-19-519742-9, GB396). Oxford U Pr.

Shadow of Suspicion, No. 7. Emile Loring. 208p. 1981. pap. 1.95 (ISBN 0-553-14296-8). Bantam.

Shadow of the Almighty: The Life & Testament of Jim Elliot. Elizabeth Elliot. LC 58-10365. 1979. pap. 4.95 (ISBN 0-06-062211-3, RD 305, HarpR). Har-Row.

Shadow of the Big Horn. E. E. Halleran. 160p. 1981. pap. text ed. 1.75 (ISBN 0-345-29430-0). Ballantine.

Shadow of the Butte. Thomas Thompson. 144p. (Orig.). 1981. pap. 1.75 (ISBN 0-553-14747-1). Bantam.

Shadow of the Crescent: The Renaissance Image of the Turk, 1453-1517. Robert Schwoebel. 1979. text ed. 42.75x (ISBN 90-6004-169-0). Humanities.

Shadow of the Hawk & Other Stories. Marie De France. Ed. by James Reeves. LC 76-28949. (gr. 3-9). 1977. 7.95 (ISBN 0-395-28820-7, Clarion). HM.

Shadow of the Hunter: Stories of Eskimo Life. Richard K. Nelson. LC 80-11091. 272p. 1980. lib. bdg. 12.50 (ISBN 0-226-57179-3). U of Chicago Pr.

Shadow of the Land - a Study of British Policy & Racial Conflict in New Zealand 1832-1852. Ian Wards. (Illus.). 1968. 10.50x o.p. (ISBN 0-8426-1586-5). Verry.

Shadow of the Lynx. Victoria Holt. LC 72-144273. 1971. 11.95 (ISBN 0-385-05427-0). Doubleday.

Shadow of the Lynx. Victoria Holt. 320p. 1981. pap. 2.50 (ISBN 0-449-23278-6, Crest). Fawcett.

Shadow of the Moon. M. M. Kaye. 816p. 1980. pap. 3.95 (ISBN 0-553-13752-2). Bantam.

Shadow of the Needle. Lois A. Sunagel. (YA) 1976. 5.95 (ISBN 0-685-69052-0, Avalon). Bouregy.

Shadow of the Parthenon: Studies in Ancient History & Literature. Peter Green. LC 72-87205. 1973. 17.50x (ISBN 0-520-02322-6). U of Cal Pr.

Shadow of the Past. Robert Sorensen. Ed. by Richard Uhlich. (Bluejeans Paperback Ser.). (Illus., Orig.). (gr. 7-12). 1978. pap. text ed. 1.25 (ISBN 0-8374-5003-9). Xerox Ed Pubns.

Shadow of the Rock. Patricia Wright. 384p. 1979. pap. 2.50 (ISBN 0-380-49064-1, 49064). Avon.

Shadow of the Rope. Ray Gaulden. 1979. pap. 1.50 (ISBN 0-505-51439-7). Tower Bks.

Shadow of the Sun. Sylvia Pell. 384p. 1981. pap. 2.50 (ISBN 0-380-50658-0, 50658). Avon.

Shadow of the Swan. M. K. Wren. 1981. pap. text ed. 2.75 (ISBN 0-425-04747-4). Berkley Pub.

Shadow of the Torturer. Gene Wolfe. 1981. pap. 2.50 (ISBN 0-671-82825-8). PB.

Shadow of Thunder. Max Evans. LC 69-20469. 78p. 1969. 6.50 (ISBN 0-8040-0274-6). Swallow.

Shadow of Vesuvius-Pompeii A. D. Seventy-Nine. Raleigh Trevelyan. (Illus.). 1976. 9.95 o.p. (ISBN 0-7181-1557-0, Pub. by Michael Joseph). Merrimack Bk Serv.

Shadow on the House. Florence Stevenson. 1975. pap. 1.25 o.p. (ISBN 0-451-06520-4, Y6520, Sig). NAL.

Shadow on the Plains. Alice W. Greve. 1944. 6.50 o.p. (ISBN 0-8323-0113-2). Binford.

Shadow on the Sun. Rosemary Harris. LC 73-120716. (gr. 7 up). 1970. 5.95 o.s.i. (ISBN 0-02-742690-4). Macmillan.

Shadow Over Beauclaire. Sylva Miles. 192p. (YA) 1975. 5.95 (ISBN 0-685-51237-1, Avalon). Bouregy.

Shadow Over the Garden. 1976. pap. 1.25 o.p. (ISBN 0-685-73460-9, LB402, Leisure Bks). Nordon Pubns.

Shadow Over the Promised Land: Slavery, Race, & Violence in Melville's America. Carolyn L. Karcher. LC 79-14861. 1980. text ed. 25.00x (ISBN 0-8071-0565-1); pap. 8.95x (ISBN 0-8071-0595-3). La State U Pr.

Shadow Over Wyndham Hall. Juanita T. Osborne. 192p. (YA) 1976. 5.95 (ISBN 0-685-66478-3, Avalon). Bouregy.

Shadow Play. Michele Spence. (Orig.). 1981. pap. 2.75 (ISBN 0-440-17655-7). Dell.

Shadow Puppet Book. Janet Lynch-Watson. LC 79-65069. (Illus.). (gr. 3 up). 1979. 9.95 (ISBN 0-8069-7030-8); PLB 9.29 (ISBN 0-8069-7031-6). Sterling.

Shadow Scrapbook. Walter Gibson. LC 78-22277. (Orig.). 1979. pap. 8.95 (ISBN 0-15-681475-7, Harv). HarBraceJ.

Shadow Spy. Nicholas Luard. 1980. pap. 2.25 (ISBN 0-345-28789-4). Ballantine.

Shadow Valley. Barry Cord. 1978. pap. 1.25 (ISBN 0-505-51329-3). Tower Bks.

Shadow Wife. Dorothy Eden. 1978. pap. 1.95 (ISBN 0-449-23699-4, Crest). Fawcett.

Shadow Work. Ivan Illich. 160p. 1981. 15.00 (ISBN 0-7145-2710-6, Pub. by M. Boyars); pap. 5.95 (ISBN 0-7145-2711-4). Merrimack Bk Serv.

Shadowboxer. Mark A. Calde. 1977. pap. 1.75 o.p. (ISBN 0-345-25802-9). Ballantine.

Shadowed Reunion. Lillian Cheatham. 1981. pap. 1.50 (ISBN 0-440-18247-6). Dell.

Shadowers. Donald Hamilton. 144p. 1980. pap. 1.95 (ISBN 0-449-14006-7, GM). Fawcett.

Shadowinnower. Agueda Pizarro. Tr. by Barbara S. Miller from Sp. LC 79-12561. 1979. 12.50x (ISBN 0-231-04828-9); pap. 4.95 (ISBN 0-231-04829-7). Columbia U Pr.

Shadowland. William Arnold. 1979. pap. 2.25 (ISBN 0-515-05124-1). Jove Pubns.

Shadows Fall Across the Little Horn: Custer's Last Stand. Joseph G. Masters. 62p. 1951. 20.00. South Pass Pr.

Shadows from the Past. Dorothy Daniels. (Orig.). 1975. pap. 1.75 o.s.i. (ISBN 0-446-84808-5). Warner Bks.

Shadows in the Stillness: Early Man on the Rainy River. Marx Swanholm. LC 77-180501. (Minn Historic Sites Pamphlet Ser.: No. 16). 28p. 1978. pap. 1.50 (ISBN 0-87351-123-9). Minn Hist.

Shadows in the Sun. R. Rabindranath Menon. 1976. 8.00 (ISBN 0-89253-813-9); flexible cloth 4.80 (ISBN 0-89253-814-7). Ind-US Inc.

Shadows of Chaos. rev. ed. Don P. Smith. 1981. pap. 5.00 (ISBN 0-937514-09-8). World Merch Import.

Shadows of Fieldcrest Manor. Casey Stephens. 224p. (Orig.). 1980. pap. 1.95 (ISBN 0-89083-698-1). Zebra.

Shadows of Forgotten Ancestors. Mykhailo Kotsiubynsky. Tr. by Marco Carynnk from Ukrainian. (Ukrainian Classics in Transiation Ser.: No. 4). 215p. 1981. lib. bdg. 9.50 (ISBN 0-87287-205-X, Ukrainian Acad Pr). Libs Unl.

Shadows of Good Things, or the Gospel in Type. R. R. Byrum. (Illus.). 144p. pap. 1.50. Faith Pub Hse.

Shadows of Heaven: Religion & Fantasy in the Writing of C. S. Lewis, Charles Williams & J. R. R. Tolkien. Gunnar Urang. LC 73-153998. 208p. 1971. 7.95 (ISBN 0-8298-0197-9). Pilgrim NY.

Shadows of Imagination: The Fantasies of C. S. Lewis, J. R. R. Tolkien, & Charles Williams. 2nd ed. Ed. by Mark R. Hillegas. LC 78-13983. (Crosscurrents Modern Critiques Ser.). 210p. 1979. 12.95 (ISBN 0-8093-0897-5). S Ill U Pr.

Shadows of Imagination: The Fantasies of C. S. Lewis, J. R. R. Tolkien, & Charles Williams. 2nd ed. Ed. by Mark R. Hillegas. LC 78-13983. (Arcturus Books Paperbacks). 210p. 1979. pap. 6.95 (ISBN 0-8093-0908-4). S Ill U Pr.

Shadows of Jeremy Pimm. Betsy Haynes. LC 80-28920. 160p. (gr. 6 up). 1981. 7.95 (ISBN 0-8253-0045-2). Beaufort Bks NY.

Shadows of Passion. Patricia Gallagher. 1976. pap. 1.75 (ISBN 0-380-00928-5, 31906). Avon.

Shadows of the Heart. Florence Hurd. 400p. 1980. pap. 2.50 (ISBN 0-380-76406-7, 76406). Avon.

Shadows of the Sun: The Diaries of Harry Crosby. Harry Crosby. Ed. by Edward Germain. 300p. (Orig.). 1977. 14.00 (ISBN 0-87685-304-1); pap. 7.50 (ISBN 0-87685-303-3). Black Sparrow.

Shadows on the Grass. Isak Dinesen. 160p. 1961. pap. 1.95 (ISBN 0-394-71062-2, Vin). Random.

Shadows on the Moon. Nancy Fairweather. 1978. pap. 1.50 (ISBN 0-505-51234-3). Tower Bks.

Shadows on the Tor. Susan Brand. 1978. pap. 1.50 o.s.i. (ISBN 0-515-04630-2). Jove Pubns.

Shadows on the Wall. Phyllis R. Naylor. LC 80-12967. (gr. 6 up). 1980. 8.95 (ISBN 0-689-30785-3). Atheneum.

Shadows Over Silver Sands. large type ed. Margaret Pemberton. pap. 1.25 o.p. (ISBN 0-425-03049-0). Berkley Pub.

Shadows Over the Land. J. J. McCoy. LC 77-111212. (gr. 5 up). 1970. 6.50 o.p. (ISBN 0-8164-3061-6, Clarion). HM.

Shadowy Heroes: Irish Literature of the 1890's. Wayne E. Hall. LC 80-21383. (Irish Studies). (Illus.). 1980. 20.00x (ISBN 0-8156-2231-7). Syracuse U Pr.

Shadrach. Meindert DeJong. LC 53-5250. (Illus.). 192p. (gr. 3-6). 1980. pap. 1.95 (ISBN 0-06-440115-4, Trophy). Har-Row.

Shafer's Medical-Surgical Nursing. 7th ed. Wilma J. Phipps et al. LC 79-27334. (Illus.). 1014p. 1980. text ed. 25.95 (ISBN 0-8016-3934-4). Mosby.

Shaft of Sunlight. Philip Mason. (Illus.). 1978. 12.50 o.p. (ISBN 0-684-15920-1, ScribT). Scribner.

Shaftsbury, Rousseau & Kant: An Introduction to the Conflict Between Aesthetic & Moral Values in Modern Thought. John A. Bernstein. LC 78-75190. 192p. 1980. write for info. (ISBN 0-8386-2351-4). Fairleigh Dickinson.

Shags Has a Dream. Gyo Fujikawa. LC 80-3352. (Gyo Fujikawa Ser.). (Illus.). (gr. k-3). 1981. 3.95 (ISBN 0-448-11749-5); PLB 9.30 (ISBN 0-448-13653-8). G&D.

Shah 'Abbas & the Arts of Isfahan. Anthony Welch. LC 73-76938. (Illus.). 152p. 1973. 19.95 (ISBN 0-87848-041-2). Asia Soc.

Shahhat: An Egyptian. Richard Critchfield. 1978. 12.95 (ISBN 0-8156-2202-3); pap. 6.96 o.p. (ISBN 0-8156-0151-4). Syracuse U Pr.

Shahhat: An Egyptian. Richard Critchfield. 1979. pap. 3.50 (ISBN 0-380-48405-6, 48405, Discus). Avon.

Shaitan. Max Ehrlich. LC 80-66498. 320p. Date not set. 12.95 (ISBN 0-87795-273-6). Arbor Hse.

Shaka Zulu. E. A. Ritter. 408p. (RL 10). 1973. pap. 1.95 o.p. (ISBN 0-451-61231-0, MJ1231, Ment). NAL.

Shake Hands with the Dragon. Carl Glick. LC 75-162513. 334p. 1971. Repr. of 1941 ed. 20.00 (ISBN 0-8103-3765-7). Gale.

Shake up Your Faith. C. William Nichols. 1978. pap. 2.95 (ISBN 0-8272-3416-3). Bethany Pr.

Shaker Adventure. Marguerite F. Melcher. 1975. pap. 7.50 o.p. (ISBN 0-686-11180-X). Shaker Mus.

Shaker Adventure. Marguerite F. Melcher. 1980. pap. 6.00 (ISBN 0-937942-08-1). Shaker Mus.

Shaker Furniture: The Craftmanship of an American Communal Sect. Edward D. Andrews & F. Andrews. (Illus.). 9.00 (ISBN 0-8446-1537-4). Peter Smith.

Shaker House Peoms. Lyn Lishfin. 1976. 3.95 (ISBN 0-915298-02-3). Sagarin Pr.

Shaker Reader. Ed. by Milton R. Rose & Emily M. Rose. LC 77-70773. (Antiques Magazine Library). (Illus.). 1977. 12.95x (ISBN 0-87663-297-5, Main Street); pap. 7.95 (ISBN 0-87663-969-4). Universe.

Shaker Religious Concept. John S. Williams. (Illus.). 1959. 1.25 (ISBN 0-937942-04-9). Shaker Mus.

Shaker Seed Industry. Margaret F. Sommer. (Illus., Orig.). 1972. lib. bdg. 6.50 (ISBN 0-937942-05-7); pap. text ed. 3.00 (ISBN 0-937942-06-5). Shaker Mus.

Shakers: A Brief Summary. John S. Williams. 1977. 1.00 (ISBN 0-937942-07-3). Shaker Mus.

Shakespeare. Compiled by David Bevington. LC 76-5220. (Goldentree Bibliographies in Language & Literature). 1978. text ed. 17.95x (ISBN 0-88295-556-X); pap. text ed. 12.95x (ISBN 0-88295-555-1). AHM Pub.

Shakespeare - the Tragedies: A Collection of Critical Essays. Clifford Leech. LC 65-17295. (Midway Reprint Ser.). xxxii, 256p. 1975. pap. 11.00x (ISBN 0-226-47018-0). U of Chicago Pr.

Shakespeare & Burbage: The Sound of Shakespeare As Devised to Suit the Voice & Talents of His Principal Player. Martin Holmes. 209p. 1978. 19.50x (ISBN 0-8476-6070-2). Rowman.

Shakespeare & Commun Sense. Edwin R. Hunter. 1954. 4.00 o.p. (ISBN 0-8158-0119-X). Chris Mass.

Shakespeare & His Players. Martin Holmes. LC 72-2773. (Illus.). 1979. pap. 3.95 o.p. (ISBN 0-684-15971-6). Scribner.

Shakespeare & His Theater. Gerald E. Bentley. LC 64-11350. (Landmark Eds.). viii, 128p. 1964. 11.50x (ISBN 0-8032-0220-2). U of Nebr Pr.

Shakespeare & His World. F. E. Halliday. (And His-Her World Ser.). (Illus.). 1980. Encore Edition. 4.95 (ISBN 0-684-16898-7, ScribT). Scribner.

Shakespeare & Music. Edward W. Naylor. LC 65-16244. (Music Ser). 1965. Repr. of 1931 ed. lib. bdg. 18.50 (ISBN 0-306-70908-2). Da Capo.

Shakespeare & Our World. Alwin Thaler. LC 66-11626. 1966. 12.50x (ISBN 0-87049-063-X). U of Tenn Pr.

Shakespeare & the Allegory of Evil: The History of a Metaphor in Relation to His Major Villains. Bernard Spivack. LC 57-12758. 1958. 25.00x (ISBN 0-231-01912-2). Columbia U Pr.

Shakespeare & the Bawdy Court of Stratford. E. R. Brinkworth. (Illus.). 184p. 1972. 16.50x (ISBN 0-87471-642-X). Rowman.

Shakespeare & the Comedy of Forgiveness. Robert G. Hunter. LC 65-15096. 1965. 17.50x (ISBN 0-231-02757-5). Columbia U Pr.

Shakespeare & the Common Understanding. Norman Rabkin. LC 67-19237. (Orig.). 1967. 8.95 o.s.i. (ISBN 0-02-925660-7); pap. 2.95 (ISBN 0-02-925650-X). Free Pr.

Shakespeare & the Courtly Aesthetic. Gary Schmidgall. (Illus.). 344p. 1981. 22.50x (ISBN 0-520-04130-5). U of Cal Pr.

Shakespeare & the Critics. A. L. French. LC 75-183221. 224p. 1972. 42.00 (ISBN 0-521-08470-9). Cambridge U Pr.

Shakespeare & the Critics' Debate. Raymond Powell. 167p. 1980. 19.50x (ISBN 0-8476-6227-6). Rowman.

Shakespeare & the Greek Romance: A Study of Origins. Carol Gesner. LC 70-11509. 232p. 1970. 11.00x (ISBN 0-8131-1220-6). U Pr of Ky.

Shakespeare & the Idea of the Play. Anne Barton. LC 76-58419. 1977. Repr. of 1962 ed. lib. bdg. 17.00x (ISBN 0-8371-9446-6, BASI). Greenwood.

Shakespeare & the Mystery of God's Judgments. Robert G. Hunter. LC 75-11449. 208p. 1976. 12.50x (ISBN 0-8203-0388-7). U of Ga Pr.

Shakespeare & the Nature of Women. Juliet Dusinberre. LC 75-3514. 1979. Repr. of 1975 ed. 23.50x (ISBN 0-06-491842-4). B&N.

Shakespeare & the Outer Mystery. Robert H. West. LC 68-56300. 216p. 1968. 10.00x (ISBN 0-8131-1166-8). U Pr of Ky.

Shakespeare & the Problem of Meaning. Norman Rabkin. LC 80-18538. 1981. lib. bdg. 16.00x (ISBN 0-226-70177-8). U of Chicago Pr.

Shakespeare & the Revolution of the Times: Perspectives & Commentaries. Harry Levin. 1978. pap. 5.95 (ISBN 0-19-502362-5, GB528, GB). Oxford U Pr.

Shakespeare & the Solitary Man. Janette Dillon. 191p. 1981. 23.50x (ISBN 0-8476-6254-3). Rowman.

Shakespeare & the Story: Aspects of the Creation. Joan Rees. 1978. text ed. 31.25x (ISBN 0-485-11179-9, Athlone Pr). Humanities.

Shakespeare & the Students. D. J. Enright. 1979. pap. 6.95 (ISBN 0-7011-1568-8, Pub. by Chatto Bodley Jonathan). Merrimack Bk Serv.

Shakespeare & the Traditions of Comedy. L. G. Salingar. LC 73-91617. 368p. 1974. 60.00 (ISBN 0-521-20384-8); pap. 12.95x (ISBN 0-521-29113-5). Cambridge U Pr.

Shakespeare & the Tragic Theme. Arthur H. Fairchild. 145p. 1980. Repr. of 1944 ed. lib. bdg. 25.00 (ISBN 0-89987-258-1). Darby Bks.

Shakespeare & the "Two Noble Kinsmen". Paul D. Bertram. 1965. 21.00 (ISBN 0-8135-0499-6). Rutgers U Pr.

Shakespeare & Tragedy. John Bayley. 224p. 1981. price not set (ISBN 0-7100-0632-2); pap. price not set (ISBN 0-7100-0607-1). Routledge & Kegan.

Shakespeare by Hilliard. Leslie Hotson. 1977. 18.50x (ISBN 0-520-03313-2). U of Cal Pr.

Shakespeare Companion. Gareth Lloyd Evans & Barbara Lloyd Evans. (Encore Edition). (Illus.). 1978. 5.95 (ISBN 0-684-16908-8, ScribT). Scribner.

Shakespeare: Contemporary Critical Approaches: Bucknel Review, Spring 1979. Ed. by Harry R. Garvin. LC 79-50103. 192p. 1980. 12.00 (ISBN 0-8387-2376-4). Bucknell U Pr.

Shakespeare Criticism, 1935-1960. Ed. by Anne B. Ridler. (Oxford Paperbacks Ser). 1970. pap. 4.95x o.p. (ISBN 0-19-281082-0). Oxford U Pr.

Shakespeare Explained. Forrest S. Hunt. 191p. 1980. Repr. of 1915 ed. lib. bdg. 25.00 (ISBN 0-8495-3255-8). Arden Lib.

Shakespeare: From the Dark Comedies to the Last Plays. R. A. Foakes. 1971. 19.00x (ISBN 0-7100-6963-4). Routledge & Kegan.

Shakespeare Garden: With Numerous Illustrations from Photographs & Reproductions of Old Wood Cuts. Esther Singleton. LC 74-8203. 1974. Repr. of 1922 ed. 22.00 (ISBN 0-8103-4048-8). Gale.

Shakespeare Glossary. 2nd rev ed. Charles T. Onions. 1919. pap. 10.95 (ISBN 0-19-871094-1). Oxford U Pr.

Shakespeare, His Ethical Teaching. Harold Ford. 112p. 1980. Repr. lib. bdg. 30.00 (ISBN 0-89987-257-3). Century Bookbindery.

Shakespeare in the Theatre. R. David. LC 77-82494. (Illus.). 1978. 22.50 (ISBN 0-521-21833-0). Cambridge U Pr.

Shakespeare, Jonson, Moliere: The Comic Contract. Nicholas Grene. 246p. 1980. 26.50x (ISBN 0-389-20093-X). B&N.

Shakespeare Lexicon & Quotation Dictionary, 2 vols. Alexander Schmidt. 8.95 ea. Vol. 1 (ISBN 0-486-22726-X). Vol. 2 (ISBN 0-486-22727-8). Dover.

Shakespeare Music. Edward W. Naylor. LC 75-171080. 68p. 1973. Repr. of 1927 ed. lib. bdg. 14.95 (ISBN 0-306-70275-4). Da Capo.

Shakespeare Nineteen Seventy-One: Proceedings. World Shakespeare Congress, Vancouver, August 1971. Ed. by Clifford Leech & John M. Margeson. LC 72-86265. 1972. 15.00x o.p. (ISBN 0-8020-1906-4); pap. 5.95 o.p. (ISBN 0-8020-6259-8). U of Toronto Pr.

Shakespeare of London. Marchette Chute. 1950. 8.95 o.p. (ISBN 0-525-20182-3); pap. 4.95 (ISBN 0-525-47001-8). Dutton.

Shakespeare on Silent Film. Robert H. Ball. LC 68-14014. (Illus.). 1968. 3.10 (ISBN 0-87830-116-X). Theatre Arts.

Shakespeare Play As Poem. S. Viswanathan. LC 79-41618. 250p. 1980. 29.50 (ISBN 0-521-22547-7). Cambridge U Pr.

Shakespeare Revolution. J. L. Styan. LC 76-3043. (Illus.). 1977. 26.50 (ISBN 0-521-21193-X). Cambridge U Pr.

Shakespeare: Select Bibliographical Guides. Ed. by Sidney W. Wells. 384p. 1974. text ed. 18.95x (ISBN 0-19-871026-7); pap. text ed. 9.95x (ISBN 0-19-871032-1). Oxford U Pr.

Shakespeare: Seven Tragedies: the Dramatist's Manipulation of Response. E. A. Honigmann. LC 79-54988. 1978. 23.50x (ISBN 0-06-492965-5); pap. 11.50x (ISBN 0-06-492967-1). B&N.

Shakespeare Sonnet Order: Poems & Groups. Brents Stirling. 1968. 17.50x (ISBN 0-520-01221-6, CAMPUS 240); pap. 5.95x (ISBN 0-520-03958-0). U of Cal Pr.

Shakespeare Studies: Historical & Comparative in Method. Edgar E. Stoll. 502p. 1980. lib. bdg. 50.00 (ISBN 0-89984-410-3). Century Bookbindery.

Shakespeare Survey, Vols. 1-18, 25 & 28-31. Ed. by K. Muir. Incl. Vols. 1-18. Ed. by Allardyce Nicoll; Vol. 25. Shakespeare's Problem Plays. 200p. 1972 (ISBN 0-521-08528-4); Vol. 28. 200p. 1975 (ISBN 0-521-20837-8); Vol. 29. 1976 (ISBN 0-521-21227-8); Vol. 30. 1977 (ISBN 0-521-21636-2); Vol. 31. 1979 (ISBN 0-521-22011-4). LC 49-1639. 32.50 ea.. Cambridge U Pr.

Shakespeare Survey: King Lear, No. 33. Ed. by K. Muir. LC 49-1639. (Shakespeare Surveys Ser.). (Illus.). 230p. Date not set. 39.50 (ISBN 0-521-23249-X). Cambridge U Pr.

Shakespeare: the Critical Heritage. Brian Vickers. Incl. Vol. 1. 1623-1692. 38.00x (ISBN 0-7100-7716-5); Vol. 2. 1693-1733. 40.00x (ISBN 0-7100-7807-2); Vol. 3. 1733-1752. 38.50x (ISBN 0-7100-7990-7); Vol. 4. 1753-1765. 1976. 41.00x (ISBN 0-7100-8297-5). (Critical Heritage Ser). 1974. Routledge & Kegan.

Shakespeare: The Critical Heritage, 1765-1774, Vol. 5. Ed. by Brian Vickers. (Critical Heritage Ser). 1979. 38.50 (ISBN 0-7100-8788-8). Routledge & Kegan.

Shakespeare, the Dark Comedies to the Last Plays: From Satire to Celebration. R. A. Foakes. LC 70-146536. 200p. 1971. 9.95x (ISBN 0-8139-0327-0). U Pr of Va.

Shakespeare: The Histories: A Collection of Critical Essays. Ed. by Eugene M. Waith. 1965. pap. 2.95 (ISBN 0-13-807701-0, Spec). P-H.

Shakespeare: The Poet in His World. Muriel C. Bradbrook. 272p. 1980. pap. 5.95 (ISBN 0-231-04649-9). Columbia U Pr.

Shakespeare: The Tempest. Ed. by D. J. Palmer. (Casebook Ser.). 1970. 2.50 o.s.i. (ISBN 0-87695-053-5). Aurora Pubs.

Shakespeare: The Writer & His Work. Stanley Wells. (Illus.). 1979. 8.95 (ISBN 0-684-15983-X, ScribT); pap. 1.95 encore ed. (ISBN 0-684-16932-0, ScribT). Scribner.

Shakespeare Vignettes: Adaptations for Acting. Albert Johnson. LC 79-88273. 1970. 7.95 o.p. (ISBN 0-498-06768-8). A S Barnes.

Shakespeare Workbook, 2 vols. Bertram Joseph. 1980. pap. 10.45 ea. Vol. 1 Tragedies (ISBN 0-87830-566-1). Vol. 2 Comedies & Histories (ISBN 0-87830-571-8). Theatre Arts.

Shakespeare 1564-1964: A Collection of Modern Essays by Various Hands. Ed. by Edward A. Bloom. LC 64-17777. 226p. 1967. Repr. of 1964 ed. 10.00x (ISBN 0-87057-083-8, Pub. by Brown U Pr). Univ Pr of New England.

Shakespearean Comedy: Theories & Traditions. Ed. by Maurice Charney. LC 79-52616. (New York Literary Forum). 320p. 1980. lib. bdg. 22.50x (ISBN 0-931196-07-8). NY Lit Forum.

Shakespearean Imagination: A Critical Introduction. Norman N. Holland. LC 63-15685. (Midland Bks.: No. 114). (Illus.). 1968. pap. 3.95x o.p. (ISBN 0-253-20114-4). Ind U Pr.

Shakespearean Moment & Its Place in the Poetry of the Seventeenth Century. Patrick Cruttwell. LC 55-541. 262p. 1955. 20.00x (ISBN 0-231-02082-1). Columbia U Pr.

Shakespearean Prompt-Books of the Seventeenth Century. Ed. by G. Blakemore Evans. Incl. Vol. 3, Pt. 1. The Comedy of Errors; Vol. 3, Pt. 2. A Midsummer Night's Dream; Vol. 4. Hamlet. o.p.; Vol. 5, Pt. 1 & 2. Smock Alley Macbeth. LC 60-2680. vol. 1 & 2 o.p. (ISBN 0-685-26270-7); pap. 15.00x boxed set vol. 3 pt. 1 & 2 (ISBN 0-8139-0216-9); Vol. 4. pap. o.p.; Vol. 5. pap. 25.00x boxed set pt. 1 & 2 (ISBN 0-8139-0301-7). U Pr of Va.

Shakespearean Stage, Fifteen Seventy-Four - Sixteen Forty-Two. Andrew Gurr. LC 72-116747. (Illus.). 1970. 36.00 (ISBN 0-521-07816-4); pap. 8.95x (ISBN 0-521-09632-4). Cambridge U Pr.

Shakespearean Stage, 1574-1642. 2nd ed. A. Gurr. LC 80-40085. (Illus.). 220p. 1981. 49.50 (ISBN 0-521-23029-2); pap. 12.95 (ISBN 0-521-29772-9). Cambridge U Pr.

Shakespearean Tragedy. Andrew C. Bradley. 1977. pap. 1.95 o.p. (ISBN 0-449-30817-0, Prem). Fawcett.

Shakespeare's Anonymous Editors: Scribe & Compositor in the Folio Text of "2 Henry IV". Eleanor Prosser. LC 79-66179. (Illus.). xiv, 219p. 1981. 18.50x (ISBN 0-8047-1033-3). Stanford U Pr.

Shakespeare's Art from a Comparative Perspective: Proceedings. Comparative Literature Symposium, No. 12. Ed. by Wendell M. Aycock. (Proceedings of the Comparative Literature Symposium). (Illus.). 197p. (Orig.). 1981. pap. write for info. (ISBN 0-89672-081-0). Tex Tech Pr.

Shakespeare's Audience. Alfred Harbage. LC 41-26970. 1941. pap. 6.00x (ISBN 0-231-08513-3, 13). Columbia U Pr.

Shakespeare's Bones. Clement M. Ingleby. 48p. 1980. Repr. of 1883 ed. lib. bdg. 10.00 (ISBN 0-89987-400-2). Darby Bks.

Shakespeare's Comedies. Jack A. Vaughn. LC 79-48080. (World Dramatists Ser.). (Illus.). 190p. 1980. 10.95 (ISBN 0-8044-2938-3). Ungar.

Shakespeare's Comedies of Play. J. Dennis Huston. LC 80-21366. 150p. 1981. text ed. 15.00x (ISBN 0-231-05142-5). Columbia U Pr.

Shakespeare's Complete Works. William Shakespeare. 1230p. 34.50 (ISBN 0-686-68309-9). Porter.

Shakespeare's Development & Problem Comedies: Turn & Counter-Turn. Richard P. Wheeler. 275p. 1981. 18.50x (ISBN 0-520-03902-5). U of Cal Pr.

Shakespeare's Division of Experience. Marilyn French. LC 80-23147. 384p. 1981. 15.95 (ISBN 0-671-44865-X). Summit Bks.

Shakespeare's Doctrine of Nature: A Study of King Lear. John F. Danby. (Orig.). 1961. pap. 5.50 (ISBN 0-686-24621-7, Pub. by Faber & Faber). Merrimack Bk Serv.

Shakespeare's Dramatic Language. Madeleine Doran. LC 75-32072. 240p. 1976. 19.50 (ISBN 0-299-07010-7). U of Wis Pr.

Shakespeare's Dramatic Style. John R. Brown. 1970. 7.95x o.p. (ISBN 0-435-18081-9); pap. text ed. 2.95x (ISBN 0-435-18082-7). Heinemann Ed.

Shakespeare's Early Tragedies. Ed. by K. Muir. LC 49-1639. (Shakespeare Survey Ser.: No. 27). (Illus.). 200p. 1974. 32.50 (ISBN 0-521-20468-2). Cambridge U Pr.

Shakespeare's England: An Account of the Life & Manners of His Age, 2 Vols. Ed. by Walter Raleigh et al. (Illus.). 1916. 59.00x (ISBN 0-19-821252-6). Oxford U Pr.

Shakespeare's Festive Comedy. C. L. Barber. 1972. 16.50x (ISBN 0-691-06043-6); pap. 4.95 (ISBN 0-691-01304-7, 271). Princeton U Pr.

Shakespeare's Garden: Being a Compendium of Quotations & References from the Bard to All Manner of Flower, Tree, Bush, Vine & Herb. J. Harvey Bloom. LC 78-77000. (Tower Bks). (Illus.). 1971. Repr. of 1903 ed. 22.00 (ISBN 0-8103-3916-1). Gale.

Shakespeare's Globe Playhouse: A Modern Reconstruction. Irwin Smith. LC 56-6150. (Encore Edition). (Illus.). 1979. pap. 4.95 (ISBN 0-684-16926-6, ScribT). Scribner.

Shakespeare's Imagery. Caroline Spurgeon. 1952. 54.00 (ISBN 0-521-06538-0); pap. 9.95x (ISBN 0-521-09258-2). Cambridge U Pr.

Shakespeare's Images of Pregnancy. Elizabeth Sacks. 1980. 16.95 (ISBN 0-312-71595-1). St Martin.

Shakespeare's Jacobean Tragedies. K. Muir. LC 72-97884. (Shakespeare Survey Ser.: No. 26). (Illus.). 200p. 1973. 32.50 (ISBN 0-521-20216-7). Cambridge U Pr.

Shakespeare's Last Plays. Frances A. Yates. 1975. 15.00 (ISBN 0-7100-8100-6). Routledge & Kegan.

Shakespeare's Late Plays: Essays in Honor of Charles Crow. Ed. by Richard C. Tobias & Paul G. Zolbrod. LC 74-27704. xiv, 235p. 1974. 14.00x (ISBN 0-8214-0178-5). Ohio U Pr.

Shakespeare's Lives. Samuel Schoenbaum. LC 74-118290. 1970. 27.50 (ISBN 0-19-501243-7). Oxford U Pr.

Shakespeare's "Love's Labor's Won". T. W. Baldwin. LC 56-9515. 54p. 1957. 5.00x (ISBN 0-8093-0010-9). S Ill U Pr.

Shakespeare's Military World. Paul A. Jorgensen. (California Library Reprint). 1974. 24.50x (ISBN 0-520-02519-9). U of Cal Pr.

Shakespeare's Othello: The Study & the Stage, 1604-1904. Gino J. Matteo. (Salzburg Studies in English Literature, Poetic Drama & Poetic Theory: No. 11). 286p. 1974. pap. text ed. 25.00x (ISBN 0-391-01476-5). Humanities.

Shakespeare's Pagan World: The Roman Tragedies. J. L. Simmons. LC 73-80126. 1973. 10.95x (ISBN 0-8139-0488-9). U Pr of Va.

Shakespeare's Planet. Clifford D. Simak. LC 75-43651. (YA) 1976. 6.95 o.p. (ISBN 0-399-11729-6, Dist. by Putnam). Berkley Pub.

Shakespeare's Political Plays. H. M. Richmond. 7.50 (ISBN 0-8446-2804-2). Peter Smith.

Shakespeare's Professional Skills. Nevill Coghill. 1964. 42.00 (ISBN 0-521-04681-5). Cambridge U Pr.

Shakespeare's Proverbial Language: An Index. R. W. Dent. 378p. 1981. 24.50x (ISBN 0-520-03894-0). U of Cal Pr.

Shakespeare's Revision of King Lear. Steven Urkowitz. LC 79-3234. (Princeton Lectures in Literature Ser.). 1980. 13.50x (ISBN 0-691-06432-6). Princeton U Pr.

Shakespeare's Romances: A Study of Some Ways of the Imagination. Hallett Smith. LC 72-79314. 1972. 10.00 (ISBN 0-87328-052-0); pap. 3.50 (ISBN 0-87328-053-9). Huntington Lib.

Shakespeare's Sonnets: A Record of Twentieth Century Criticism. Tetsumaro Hayashi. LC 77-184764. 1972. 10.00 (ISBN 0-8108-0462-X). Scarecrow.

Shakespeare's Sonnets: Self, Love & Art. Philip Martin. LC 73-189593. 160p. 1972. 26.50 (ISBN 0-521-08525-X). Cambridge U Pr.

Shakespeare's Stagecraft. J. L. Styan. (Illus.). 1967. 42.00 (ISBN 0-521-06902-5); pap. 8.95 (ISBN 0-521-09435-6). Cambridge U Pr.

Shakespeare's "The Pheonix & Turtle" A Survey of Scholarship. Richard A. Underwood. (Salzburg Studies in English Literature, Elizabethan & Renaissance Studies: No. 15). 366p. 1974. pap. text ed. 25.00x (ISBN 0-391-01549-4). Humanities.

Shakespeare's Tragic Practice. Bertrand Evans. 1980. 29.95x (ISBN 0-19-812094-X). Oxford U Pr.

Shakespeare's Use of Music: A Study of the Music & Its Performance in the Original Production of Seven Comedies. John H. Long. LC 77-5643. (Music Reprint Ser.). 1977. Repr. of 1955 ed. lib. bdg. 22.50 (ISBN 0-306-77423-2). Da Capo.

Shakespeare's Use of Music: The Final Comedies. John H. Long. LC 77-5644. (Music Reprint Ser.). 1977. Repr. of 1961 ed. lib. bdg. 22.50 (ISBN 0-306-77424-0). Da Capo.

Shakespeare's Women. Angela Pitt. (Illus.). 224p. 1981. 16.50x (ISBN 0-389-20122-7). B&N.

Shakespeare's Works & Elizabethan Pronunciation. Fausto Cercignani. 448p. 1981. 74.00 (ISBN 0-19-811937-2). Oxford U Pr.

Shakespearian & Other Studies. Frank P. Wilson. Ed. by Helen Gardner. 1969. 26.00x (ISBN 0-19-811677-2). Oxford U Pr.

Shakespearian Comedy. Ed. by Malcolm Bradbury & David Palmer. (Stratford-Upon-Aon Studies: No. 14). 247p. 1972. pap. text ed. 11.50x (ISBN 0-8419-5820-3). Holmes & Meier.

Shakespearian Costume. 2nd rev. ed. F. M. Kelly. Ed. by A. Mansfield. LC 76-123629. (Illus.). 1970. 14.95 o.s.i. (ISBN 0-87830-117-8). Theatre Arts.

Shaking of the Foundations. Paul Tillich. 1948. pap. 3.95 (ISBN 0-684-71910-X, SL 684, ScribT). Scribner.

Shaking the Money Tree: New Growth Opportunities in Common Stocks. Winthrop Knowlton & John L. Furth. LC 76-156529. 192p. 1972. 7.50 o.s.i. (ISBN 0-06-012441-5, HarpT). Har-Row.

Shaking the Pumpkin: Traditional Poetry of the Indian North Americas. Ed. by Jerome Rothenberg. LC 74-171317. 1972. pap. 4.95 (ISBN 0-385-01296-9, Anch). Doubleday.

Shalako. Louis L'Amour. 176p. (Orig.). 1980. pap. 1.95 (ISBN 0-553-14013-2). Bantam.

Shall We Gather at the River. James Wright. LC 68-27545. (Wesleyan Poetry Program: Vol. 43). 1968. 10.00x (ISBN 0-8195-2043-8, Pub. by Wesleyan U Pr); pap. 4.95 (ISBN 0-8195-1043-2). Columbia U Pr.

Shallow Grass. Tom Horn. 1968. 5.95 o.s.i. (ISBN 0-02-554100-5). Macmillan.

Shallow Lakes: Contributions to Their Limnology. Ed. by M. Dokulil et al. (Developmrnts in Hydrobiology Ser.: No. 3). 218p. 1981. PLB 59.50 (ISBN 0-686-28842-4, Pub. by W. Junk). Kluwer Boston.

Shallow Land Burial of Low-Level Radioactively Contaminated Solid Waste. Commission on Natural Resources, National Research Council. LC 76-56928. 1976. pap. 7.00 (ISBN 0-309-02535-4). Natl Acad Pr.

Shallow-Water Gammaridean Ampphipoda of New England. E. L. Bousfield. LC 72-4636. (Illus.). 1973. 35.00x (ISBN 0-8014-0726-5). Comstock.

Shallow Waters: A Year of Cape Cod's Pleasant Bay. Bill Sargent. (Illus.). 144p. 1981. 17.95 (ISBN 0-395-29481-9). HM.

Shallows of Night. Eric V. Lustbader. 1979. pap. cancelled o.s.i. (ISBN 0-515-04715-5). Jove Pubns.

Shallows of Night. Eric Van Lustbader. LC 77-12884. 1978. 7.95 o.p. (ISBN 0-385-12968-8). Doubleday.

Shallows of Night. Eric Van Lustbader. 1980. pap. 2.50 (ISBN 0-425-04453-X). Berkley Pub.

Shalom, My Love. Ida Hills. (Orig.). 1981. pap. 1.50 (ISBN 0-440-17928-9). Dell.

Shalom: Peace. Haring, Bernard, C.Ss.R. LC 75-78750. pap. 1.95 o.p. (ISBN 0-385-07971-0, D264, Im). Doubleday.

Shamanism in Western North America. Willard Z. Park. LC 74-12553. 166p. 1975. Repr. of 1938 ed. lib. bdg. 16.50x (ISBN 0-8154-0497-2). Cooper Sq.

Shaman's Daughter. Nan Salerno & Rosamund Vanderburgh. 1981. pap. 3.25 (ISBN 0-440-17863-0). Dell.

Shaman's Doorway. Stephen Larsen. 1977. pap. 4.95 (ISBN 0-06-090547-6, CN 547, CN). Har-Row.

Shambaa Kingdom: A History. Steven Feierman. LC 72-7985. 224p. 1974. 20.00x (ISBN 0-299-06360-7). U of Wis Pr.

Shambala: The Constitution of a Traditional State. Edgar V. Winans. (Illus.). 1962. 20.00x (ISBN 0-520-01348-4). U of Cal Pr.

Shame the Devil. Phillip Appleman. Ed. by Herbert Michaelman. 160p. 1981. 10.00 (ISBN 0-517-54286-2, Michaelman Books). Crown.

Shame: The Power of Caring. Gershen Kaufman. LC 80-17090. 160p. 1980. text ed. 13.25x (ISBN 0-87073-651-5); pap. text ed. 6.95x (ISBN 0-87073-652-3). Schenkman.

Shameless. Jim Gustafson. 1979. pap. 4.00 (ISBN 0-686-28245-0). Tombouctou.

Shameless Hussy: Selected Prose & Poetry. Alta. LC 80-15551. (Crossing Press Feminist Ser.). 1980. 10.95 (ISBN 0-89594-035-3); pap. 5.95 (ISBN 0-89594-036-1). Crossing Pr.

Shameless Nude. E. Lange et al. (Illus.). 12.50 (ISBN 0-910550-14-X). Elysium.

Shamra, the Camera: A Story & Coloring Book for Children. T. Jane Spoto. (Illus.). 1981. 4.95 (ISBN 0-533-04739-0). Vantage.

Shamrocks, Harps, and Shillelaghs: The Story of the St. Patrick's Day Symbols. Edna Barth. LC 77-369. (gr. 3-6). 1977. 8.95 (ISBN 0-395-28845-2, Clarion). HM.

Shand's Handbook of Orthopaedic Surgery. 9th ed. H. Robert Brashear & R. Beverly Raney. LC 78-65. 1978. text ed. 29.95 (ISBN 0-8016-4082-2). Mosby.

Shane. Jack Schaefer. (Literature Ser.). (gr. 9-12). 1949. pap. text ed. 3.58 (ISBN 0-87720-757-7). AMSCO Sch.

Shane. Jack Schaefer. (Illus.). (gr. 7 up). 1954. 9.95 (ISBN 0-395-07090-2). HM.

Shane Comes to Dublin. Patricia Lynch. LC 58-5902. (Illus.). (gr. 4-7). 1958. 8.95 (ISBN 0-87599-070-3). S G Phillips.

Shanghai. Christopher Howe. LC 79-41616. (Contemporary China Institute Publications). (Illus.). 456p. Date not set. 69.50 (ISBN 0-521-23198-1). Cambridge U Pr.

Shanghai. Barth J. Sussman. (Orig.). 1981. pap. 2.75 (ISBN 0-451-09563-4, E9563, Sig). NAL.

Shanghai Pierce: A Fair Likeness. Chris Emmett. (Illus.). 326p. 1953. 14.95 o.p. (ISBN 0-8061-1125-9); pap. 6.95 (ISBN 0-8061-1151-8). U of Okla Pr.

Shanghai's Old-Style Bangles. Andrea L. McElderry. (Michigan Papers in Chinese Studies Ser: No. 25). 1976. pap. 4.00 (ISBN 0-89264-025-1). U of Mich Ctr Chinese.

Shank's Mare. Ikku Jippensha. LC 60-14370. (Illus.). 1960. pap. 8.25 (ISBN 0-8048-0524-5). C E Tuttle.

Shannon. Patricia Gallagher. 1976. pap. 1.50 (ISBN 0-380-00918-8, 31807). Avon.

Shantung Compound. Langdon Gilkey. LC 75-9312. 272p. 1975. pap. 4.95x (ISBN 0-06-063112-0, RD101, HarpR). Har-Row.

Shantung Question: A Study in Diplomacy & World Politics. Ge-Zay Wood. (Studies in Chinese History Civilization). 1977. 21.50 (ISBN 0-89093-089-9). U Pubns Amer.

Shaolin Chin Na. Yang Ywing-Ming. LC 80-53546. (Illus.). 144p. (Orig.). 1980. pap. 6.95 (ISBN 0-86568-012-4). Unique Pubns.

Shaolin Fighting. Douglas L. Wong. LC 76-55613. (Illus.). 1975. pap. 4.95 (ISBN 0-86568-031-0). Unique Pubns.

Shaolin Long Fist. Yang Jwing-Ming. (Illus.). 250p. (Orig.). 1981. pap. 7.95 (ISBN 0-86568-020-5). Unique Pubns.

Shape It & Bake It: Quick & Simple Ideas for Children from Frozen Bread Dough. Sylvia Ogren. LC 79-23923. (Doing & Learning Bks.). (Illus.). 128p. (gr. 5 up). 1981. PLB 7.95 (ISBN 0-87518-193-7). Dillon.
Shape of American Education. Geraldine J. Clifford. (Illus.). 288p. 1975. 16.95 (ISBN 0-13-807891-2). P-H.
Shape of Fiction. 2nd ed. Alan H. Casty. 448p. 1975. pap. text ed. 9.95x (ISBN 0-669-91066-X); instructor's manual free (ISBN 0-669-91074-0). Heath.
Shape of Fiction: British & American Short Stories. 2nd ed. Leo Hamalian & Frederick R. Karl. LC 77-5839. 1978. pap. text ed. 10.95x (ISBN 0-07-025699-3, C). McGraw.
Shape of Fiction: British & American Short Stories. Ed. by Leo Hamalian & F. R. Karl. 1967. pap. text ed. 7.95 o.p. (ISBN 0-07-025697-7, C). McGraw.
Shape of Further Things. Brian W. Aldiss. 1970. 7.50 (ISBN 0-571-09472-4, Pub. by Faber & Faber). Merrimack Bk Serv.
Shape of German Romanticism. Marshall Brown. LC 79-14313. 1979. 15.00x (ISBN 0-8014-1228-5). Cornell U Pr.
Shape of Paradox: An Essay on Waiting for Godot. Bert O. States. (Quantum Bk.). 1978. 11.95x (ISBN 0-520-03549-6); pap. 2.65 (ISBN 0-520-03572-0). U of Cal Pr.
Shape of Sacred Space: Four Biblical Studies. Robert L. Cohn. Ed. by Conrad Cherry. LC 80-11086. (Studies in Religion: No. 23). 12.00x (ISBN 0-89130-383-9, 01 00 23); pap. 7.50x (ISBN 0-89130-384-7). Scholars Pr CA.
Shape of Space. G. Nerlich. 260p. 1976. 33.95 (ISBN 0-521-21101-8). Cambridge U Pr.
Shape of the Church to Come. Karl Rahner. 1974. 6.95 (ISBN 0-8164-1181-6). Crossroad NY.
Shape of the Past. John W. Montgomery. LC 75-26651. 400p. 1975. pap. 5.95 (ISBN 0-87123-535-8, 210535). Bethany Fell.
Shape Shifters: Fantasy & Science Fiction Tales About Humans Who Can Change Their Shapes. Compiled by Jane Yolen. LC 77-13646. (gr. 6 up). 1978. 8.95 (ISBN 0-395-28933-5, Clarion). HM.
Shape up! Donald P. Loren. LC 79-88437. 73p. 1980. 11.00x (ISBN 0-87021-626-0). Naval Inst Pr.
Shape up for Soccer. Pete Broccoletti & Rich Hunter. (Illus.). 256p. 1981. 14.95 (ISBN 0-89651-750-0); wirebd. 9.95 (ISBN 0-89651-751-9). Icarus.
Shape up for Super Sex. Mary A. Crenshaw & Nicholas Kounovsky. 1977. 8.95 o.s.i. (ISBN 0-440-07931-4). Delacorte.
Shape Up with Baby: Exercise Games for the New Parent & Child. Ann Fienup-Riordan. LC 80-82128. (Illus., Orig.). 1980. pap. 5.95 (ISBN 0-937604-04-6). Pennypress.
Shape up Your Bust in Ten Minutes a Day: "Anita & Franco Columbu's Shape up in Minutes-a-Day Program". Anita Columbu & Franco Columbo. (Anita & Franco Columbu's Shape up in Minutes-a-Day Program). (Illus., Orig.). 1980. pap. 1.95 (ISBN 0-8092-7074-9); 48-copy sorted prepack 93.60 (ISBN 0-686-65599-0). Contemp Bks.
Shape Your Swing the Modern Way. new ed. Byron Nelson & Larry Dennis. LC 76-264. (Illus.). 1979. pap. 5.95 o.p. (ISBN 0-914178-25-3, 24920). Golf Digest.
Shaped Canvas: Constructing, Stretching, Painting. Bruce Bowman. LC 76-1183. (Illus.). 64p. (YA) 1976. 6.95 o.p. (ISBN 0-8069-5360-8); PLB 6.69 o.p. (ISBN 0-8069-5361-6). Sterling.
Shapedown: Weight Management Program for Adolescents. Laurel Mellin. LC 80-67385. (Illus.). 186p. (Orig.). (gr. 7-12). 1980. tchr's ed. 10.00 (ISBN 0-935902-02-3); wkbk. 10.00 (ISBN 0-935902-01-5). Balboa Pub.
Shapes. Richard L. Allington. LC 79-19852. (Beginning to Learn About Ser.). (Illus.). (gr. k-2). 1979. PLB 9.65 (ISBN 0-8172-1277-9). Raintree Pubs.
Shapes. Jeanne Bendick. LC 68-11889. (Science Experiences Ser.). (Illus.). (gr. 4-6). 1968. PLB 4.90 o.p. (ISBN 0-531-01433-9); pap. 1.25 o.p. (ISBN 0-531-02322-2). Watts.
Shapes. John J. Reiss. LC 73-76545. (Illus.). 32p. (ps-2). 1974. 8.95 (ISBN 0-87888-053-4). Bradbury Pr.
Shapes. Gillian Youldon. (Picture Play Ser.). (Illus.). (ps-2). 1979. 3.50 (ISBN 0-531-02389-3); PLB 5.45 s&l (ISBN 0-531-00441-4). Watts.
Shapes & Colors, No. 2. (Shapes & Colors Ser.). 1980. 1.95 o.p. (ISBN 0-686-65206-1). Price Stern.
Shapes & People. Geoffrey Grigson. LC 76-11954. (gr. 9 up). 7.95 (ISBN 0-8149-0662-1). Vanguard.
Shapes & Stories: A Book About Pictures. Geoffrey Grigson. LC 65-25262. (Illus.). (gr. 5 up). 7.95 (ISBN 0-8149-0311-8). Vanguard.
Shapes & Things. Illus. by Tana Hoban. (Illus.). (ps-3). 1970. 8.95 (ISBN 0-02-744060-5). Macmillan.
Shapes, Animals & Special Creatures. Geoffrey Grigson. LC 72-77789. (Illus.). (gr. 5 up). Date not set. 6.95 (ISBN 0-8149-0717-2). Vanguard. Postponed.
Shapes in the Fire: London Eighteen Ninety-Five. M. P. Shiel. Ed. by Ian Fletcher & John Stokes. LC 76-20072. (Decadent Consciousness Ser.). 1977. lib. bdg. 38.00 (ISBN 0-8240-2771-X). Garland Pub.
Shapes of Change. Marcia B. Siegel. 400p. 1981. pap. 3.95 (ISBN 0-380-53892-X, 53892, Discus). Avon.
Shapes of Midnight. Joseph P. Brennan. 1980. pap. 2.25 o.p. (ISBN 0-425-04567-6). Berkley Pub.
Shapes of Time. Peter Munz. LC 77-2459. 1977. lib. bdg. 20.00x (ISBN 0-8195-5017-5, Pub. by Wesleyan U Pr). Columbia U Pr.
Shapes, Space, & Symmetry. Alan Holden. LC 71-158459. (Illus.). 1971. 17.50x (ISBN 0-231-03549-7); pap. 7.50 (ISBN 0-231-08323-8). Columbia U Pr.
Shaping Accelerated Development & International Changes. 45p. 1980. pap. 3.00 (ISBN 0-686-68971-2, UN80/2A4, UN). Unipub.
Shaping an Urban World: Planning in the Twentieth Century. Ed. by Gordon E. Cherry. LC 80-17276. 1980. 27.50 (ISBN 0-312-71618-4). St Martin.
Shaping Forces in Music: An Inquiry into the Nature of Harmony, Melody, Counterpoint, Form. Ernst Toch. 1977. pap. text ed. 3.50 (ISBN 0-486-23346-4). Dover.
Shaping Library Collections for the Eighties. Ed. by Peter Spyers-Duran & Thomas Mann, Jr. 1981. lib. bdg. 18.50 (ISBN 0-912700-58-0). Oryx Pr.
Shaping of a Man of Faith. Ben E. Ferguson. 1979. pap. 1.95 (ISBN 0-88207-516-0). Victor Bks.
Shaping of America. John Warwick Montgomery. LC 76-15682. 1976. 6.95 (ISBN 0-87123-227-8, 230227). Bethany Fell.
Shaping of American Graduate Education: Daniel Coit Gilman & the Protean Ph. D. Francesco Cordasco. 164p. 1973. Repr. of 1959 ed. 10.00x o.p. (ISBN 0-87471-161-4). Rowman.
Shaping of Cambridge Botany. S. M. Walters. (Illus.). 128p. Date not set. price not set (ISBN 0-521-23795-5). Cambridge U Pr.
Shaping of Chinese Foreign Policy. Greg O'Leary. LC 80-10231. 320p. 1980. 25.00 (ISBN 0-312-71620-6). St Martin.
Shaping of Peace, Vol. I: Canada & the Search for World Order 1943-57. John W. Holmes. 1979. 25.00 (ISBN 0-8020-5461-7). U of Toronto Pr.
Shaping of Personality: Conflict, Choice & Growth. Frank Barron. 1979. text ed. 19.50 scp (ISBN 0-06-040504-X, HarpC). Har-Row.
Shaping of Tess of the D'Urbervilles. J. T. Laird. (Illus.). 202p. 1975. 29.95x o.p. (ISBN 0-19-812060-5). Oxford U Pr.
Shaping of the American Tradition. Louis M. Hacker. LC 47-1257. 1947. 37.50x (ISBN 0-231-01574-7). Columbia U Pr.
Shaping of the Earth. William F. Smith. (Illus.). 128p. 1981. 7.00 (ISBN 0-682-49715-0). Exposition.
Shaping of the Foundations: Being at Home in the Transcendental Method. Philip McShane. 9.50 (ISBN 0-8191-0209-1). U Pr of Amer.
Shaping of the Point: Pittsburgh's Renaissance Park. Robert C. Alberts. LC 79-26885. (Illus.). 264p. 1981. 12.95 (ISBN 0-8229-3422-1). U of Pittsburgh Pr.
Shaping of the Swedish Health System. Ed. by Arnold J. Heidenheimer & Nile Elvander. LC 80-12410. 256p. 1980. write for info. (ISBN 0-312-71627-3). St Martin.
Shaping of Urban Society: A History of City Forms & Functions. 2nd ed. Janet Roebuck. LC 73-18205. (Illus.). 288p. 1974. 8.95 o.p. (ISBN 0-684-13644-9, ScribC); pap. text ed. 4.95x o.p. (ISBN 0-684-13700-3, ScribC). Scribner.
Shaping Room. Michael Bradley. LC 77-16877. (gr. 5 up). 1978. 5.95 (ISBN 0-396-07540-1). Dodd.
Shaping Sentences & Paragraphs: A Systematic Approach to Sentence & Paragraph Construction. Fred Brengelman. 128p. 1980. pap. 6.95 (ISBN 0-8403-2292-5). Kendall-Hunt.
Shaping the American Educational State: 1900 to the Present. Ed. by Clarence J. Karier. LC 74-4647. (Urgent Issues in American Society Ser). (Illus.). 1975. 10.95 o.s.i. (ISBN 0-02-917040-0); pap. text ed. 7.95 (ISBN 0-02-917030-3). Free Pr.
Shaping the Coming Age of Religious Life. Lawrence Cada et al. 1979. 10.95x (ISBN 0-8164-0425-9); pap. 4.50x (ISBN 0-8164-2207-9). Crossroad NY.
Shaping the Congregation. Robert L. Wilson. LC 80-22228. (Into Our Third Century Ser.). 144p. (Orig.). 1981. pap. 3.95 (ISBN 0-687-38334-X). Abingdon.
Shaping the Defense Civilian Work Force: Economics, Politics, & National Security. Martin Binkin. LC 78-14897. (Studies in Defense Policy). 1978. pap. 3.95 (ISBN 0-8157-0967-6). Brookings.
Shaping the Education of Slow Learners. W. K. Brennan. (Special Needs in Education Ser.). 1974. 9.50 (ISBN 0-7100-7984-2); pap. 4.50 (ISBN 0-7100-7985-0). Routledge & Kegan.
Shaping the Future: Resources for the Post-Modern World. Frederick Ferre. LC 75-36755. 192p. 1976. 7.95 o.p. (ISBN 0-06-062371-3, HarpR). Har-Row.
Shaping the New Social Work. Alfred J. Kahn. LC 73-4189. (Social Work & Social Issues Ser). 224p. 1973. 17.50x (ISBN 0-231-03605-1); pap. 6.00x (ISBN 0-231-08356-4). Columbia U Pr.
Shaping up: How to Reduce Your Sags & Bulges & Reshape Any Area of Your Body in One Month. Sidney Filson. 1980. 9.95 (ISBN 0-316-28215-4). Little.
Shaping up: The Complete Guide to a Customized Fitness Program. George Mazzei. (Orig.). 1981. pap. 7.95 (ISBN 0-345-29471-8). Ballantine.
Sharad: Camel Driver for the Kings. Russell Q. Chilcote. 1978. pap. 1.25x (ISBN 0-8358-0379-1). Upper Room.
Share Your Faith with a Muslim. Charles R. Marsh. 1975. pap. 2.25 (ISBN 0-8024-7900-6). Moody.
Shared Decision-Making. Frank F. Maple. LC 77-12109. (Sage Human Service Guides Ser.: Vol. 4). 1977. pap. 6.00x (ISBN 0-8039-0883-0). Sage.
Shared Experiences in Human Communication. Stewart L. Tubbs & Robert M. Carter. 1978. pap. text ed. 10.75x (ISBN 0-8104-6089-0). Hayden.
Shared Fate. H. David Kirk. LC 64-13232. 1964. 12.95 (ISBN 0-02-917340-X). Free Pr.
Shared Hospital Computer Services Evaluation. Computer Information Services, Chicago Hospital Council. 165p. 1975. 15.00 (ISBN 0-686-68578-4, 14912). Hospital Finan.
Shared Houses, Shared Lives: The New Extended Families. Eric Raimy. LC 78-65366. 1979. 10.00 o.p. (ISBN 0-312-90859-8); pap. 4.95 o.p. (ISBN 0-312-90860-1). St Martin.
Shared Intimacies: Women's Sexual Experiences. Lonnie Barbach & Linda Levine. LC 80-917. 384p. 1980. 12.95 (ISBN 0-385-17177-3, Anchor Pr). Doubleday.
Shares of Fletcher, Field & Massinger in Twelve Plays of the Beaumont & Fletcher Canon, 2 vols. Bertha Hensman. (Salzburg Studies in English Literature, Jacobean Drama Studies: No.6). 1974. Set. pap. text ed. 50.25x (ISBN 0-391-01406-4). Humanities.
Sharing God's Love with Others. Molly M. Wyatt. 1979. pap. 3.50 (ISBN 0-570-07795-8, 56-1333). Concordia.
Sharing Intimacy: What We Reveal to Others & Why. Alan L. Chaikin & Valerian J. Derlega. 1975. 12.95 (ISBN 0-13-807867-X, Spec); pap. 3.45 (ISBN 0-13-807859-9). P-H.
Sharing Is Fun. Beverly Amstutz. 22p. (ps-6). 1979. pap. 2.25 (ISBN 0-937836-00-1). Precious Res.
Sharing Literature with Children: A Thematic Anthology. Ed. by Francelia Butler. (English & Humanities Ser.). 1977. 22.50 (ISBN 0-679-30328-6, Pub. by McKay); pap. 12.95x (ISBN 0-582-28114-8); instr's manual free. Longman.
Sharing of Scripture. Clarence Roberts et al. LC 78-61724. 1978. pap. 2.95 (ISBN 0-8091-2141-7). Paulist Pr.
Sharing Possessions: Mandate & Symbol of Faith, No. 9. Luke T. Johnson. Ed. by Walter Brueggemann & John R. Donahue. LC 80-2390. (Overtures to Biblical Theology Ser.). 176p. (Orig.). 1981. pap. 8.95 (ISBN 0-8006-1534-4, 1-1534). Fortress.
Sharing Responsibility for Patient Safety. American Hospital Association et al. 1979. 5.75 (ISBN 0-87258-248-5, 1152). Am Hospital.
Sharing the Children. Nora Harlow. 1976. pap. 2.95 o.p. (ISBN 0-06-090512-3, CN512, CN). Har-Row.
Sharing the Christian Message: A Program Manual for Volunteer Catechists, 11th & 12th Grade. Thomas Zanzig. (Illus.). (gr. 11-12). 1979. pap. 38.00 (ISBN 0-88489-110-0); spiritmasters 9.95 (ISBN 0-88489-130-5). St Marys.
Sharing the Christian Message: A Program Manual for Volunteer Catechists, Tenth Grade. Thomas Zanzig. 1977. pap. 9.95 (ISBN 0-88489-089-9); duplicating masters 4.95 (ISBN 0-88489-129-1). St Marys.
Sharing the Christian Message: A Program Manual for Volunteer Catechist, Ninth Grade. Thomas Zanzig. 1977. pap. 9.95 (ISBN 0-88489-086-4); duplicating masters 4.95 (ISBN 0-88489-128-3). St Mary's.
Sharing the Sun, Vols. 1-10. Ed. by K. W. Boer. Incl. Vol. 1. International & US Programs Solar Flux. pap. text ed. 33.00 (ISBN 0-08-021686-2); Vol. 2. Solar Collectors. pap. text ed. 33.00 (ISBN 0-08-021687-0); Vol. 3. Solar Heating & Cooling Buildings. pap. text ed. 33.00 (ISBN 0-08-021688-9); Vol. 4. Solar System, Simulation, Design. pap. text ed. 38.50 (ISBN 0-08-021689-7); Vol. 5. Solar Thermal & Ocean Thermal. pap. text ed. 44.00 (ISBN 0-08-021690-0); Vol. 6. Photovoltaics & Materials. pap. text ed. 33.00 (ISBN 0-08-021691-9); Vol. 7. Agriculture, Biomass, Wind, New Developments. pap. text ed. 33.00 (ISBN 0-08-021692-7); Vol. 8. Storage, Water Heater, Data Communication, Education. pap. text ed. 33.00 (ISBN 0-08-021693-5); Vol. 9. Socio - Economics & Cultural. pap. text ed. 27.50 (ISBN 0-08-021694-3); Vol. 10. Business & Commercial Implications. pap. text ed. 22.00 (ISBN 0-08-021695-1). 1976. Set. pap. text ed. 350.00 (ISBN 0-08-021696-X). Pergamon.
Sharing the Vision: The Church Teaching Series Reader. Ed. by Ruth G. Cheney. 112p. (Orig.). 1980. pap. 3.95 (ISBN 0-8164-2044-0). Crossroad NY.
Sharing the Work: An Analysis of the Issues of Worksharing & Jobsharing. Noah Meltz et al. 100p. 1981. 7.50 (ISBN 0-8020-2383-5). U of Toronto Pr.
Sharing the World's Resources. Oscar Schachter. LC 76-28422. 1977. 12.50x (ISBN 0-231-04110-1). Columbia U Pr.
Shark. Jacques-Yves Cousteau & Philippe Cousteau. (Undersea Discoveries of Jacques-Yves Cousteau). (Illus.). 1978. pap. 8.95 (ISBN 0-89104-112-5). A & W Pubs.
Shark. Zane Grey. Ed. by Loren Grey. 1978. pap. 1.50 (ISBN 0-505-51265-3). Tower Bks.
Shark Attack. H. David Baldridge. (Orig.). 1975. pap. 1.95 (ISBN 0-425-03988-9, Medallion). Berkley Pub.
Shark Attack & Treatment of Victims in Southern African Waters. Tim Wallett. 1980. 25.00x (Pub. by Bailey & Swinton South Africa). State Mutual Bk.
Shark Gourmet Seafood of the Future. Eddy Hovey. Ed. by George Sharp. LC 80-52109. (Illus.). 111p. pap. 6.95 (ISBN 0-937496-00-6). Sea Harvest.
Shark Lady: True Adventures of Eugenie Clark. Ann McGovern. LC 78-22126. (Illus.). 96p. (gr. 1-5). 1979. 7.95 (ISBN 0-590-07604-3, Four Winds). Schol Bk Serv.
Shark Wanted! Dead or Alive. Hal Scharp & Mary Scharp. LC 75-29700. (Illus.). 256p. 1976. 12.00 o.p. (ISBN 0-498-01832-6). A S Barnes.
Sharks. Rhoda Blumberg. (First Bks.). (Illus.). 72p. (gr. 4 up). 1976. PLB 6.45 (ISBN 0-531-00846-0). Watts.
Sharks. Rhoda Blumberg. 1980. pap. 1.75 (ISBN 0-380-49247-4, 49247, Camelot). Avon.
Sharks. Robert F. Burgess. LC 75-107669. (gr. 4-9). 1971. PLB 5.95 (ISBN 0-385-04795-9). Doubleday.
Sharks. Ann McGovern. LC 76-17122. (Illus.). 48p. (gr. k-3). 1976. 7.95 (ISBN 0-590-07468-7, Four Winds). Schol Bk Serv.
Sharks. Sarah R. Riedman. (Easy-Read Fact Bks.). (Illus.). (gr. 2-4). 1977. PLB 6.45 (ISBN 0-531-01314-6). Watts.
Sharks. Herbert S. Zim. (Illus.). (gr. 4-6). 1966. PLB 6.00 (ISBN 0-688-26810-2). Morrow.
Sharks & Other Dangerous Sea Creatures. Idaz Greenberg & Jerry Greenberg. (Illus.). 1981. saddlestiched 4.95 (ISBN 0-913008-09-5). Seahawk Pr.
Sharks & Troubled Waters. Margaret Harris. LC 77-10760. (Myth, Magic & Superstition Ser.). (Illus.). (gr. 4-5). 1977. PLB 9.65 (ISBN 0-8172-1041-5). Raintree Pubs.
Sharky's Machine. William Diehl. 1979. pap. 2.50 o.s.i. (ISBN 0-440-18292-1). Dell.
Sharp End. John Ellis. 1980. 17.95 (ISBN 0-684-16728-X, ScribT). Scribner.
Sharp Focus Watercolor Painting: Techniques for Hot-Pressed Surfaces. Georg Shook & Gary Witt. 144p. 1981. 21.95 (ISBN 0-8230-4794-6). Watson-Guptill.
Sharp Lookout: Nature Essays of John Burroughs, Vol. II. John Burroughs. Ed. by Frank Bergone. (Literature of the American Wilderness). 320p. 1981. pap. 4.45 (ISBN 0-87905-082-9). Peregrine Smith.
Sharp Rise in Crime. John Creasey. 1979. 7.95 o.p. (ISBN 0-684-14921-4, ScribT). Scribner.
Sharpe's Eagle. Bernard Cornwell. LC 80-54081. 264p. 1981. 12.95 (ISBN 0-670-63944-3). Viking Pr.
Sharples. Katherine M. Knox. LC 70-87456. (Library of American Art Ser.). 133p. 1972. Repr. of 1930 ed. lib. bdg. 35.00 (ISBN 0-306-71529-5). Da Capo.

Sharp's Firearms. Frank Sellers. LC 77-71186. 358p. 1978. 34.95 (ISBN 0-917714-12-1). Beinfeld Pub.

Shattered Chain. Marion Z. Bradley. (Science Fiction Ser.). 1976. pap. 2.25 (ISBN 0-87997-327-7, UE1566). DAW Bks.

Shattered Spectrum: A Survey of Contemporary Theology. Lonnie D. Kliever. LC 80-82184. 276p. (Orig.). 1981. pap. 9.95 (ISBN 0-8042-0707-0). John Knox.

Shaun Cassidy. Craig Schumacher. (Rock 'n Pop Stars Ser.). (Illus.). (gr. 4-12). 1979. PLB 5.95 (ISBN 0-87191-717-3); pap. 2.95 (ISBN 0-89812-097-7). Creative Ed.

Shaw. John S. Collis. LC 70-160748. 1971. Repr. of 1925 ed. 12.00 o.p. (ISBN 0-8046-1561-6). Kennikat.

Shaw en el mundo Hispanico. Asela Rodriguez-Seda de Laguna. LC 79-22415. (Coleccion Mente y Palabra). 142p. (Sp.). 1980. 6.25 (ISBN 0-8477-0564-1); pap. 5.00 (ISBN 0-8477-0565-X). U of PR Pr.

Shaw: The Critical Heritage. Ed. by T. F. Evans. (Critical Heritage Ser.). 1976. 36.00x (ISBN 0-7100-8280-0). Routledge & Kegan.

Shawnee: The Ceremonialism of a Native American Tribe & Its Cultural Background. James H. Howard. LC 80-23752. (Illus.). xvi, 434p. 1981. 24.95 (ISBN 0-8214-0417-2); pap. 11.95 (ISBN 0-8214-0614-0). Ohio U Pr.

Shawn's Red Bike. Petronella Breinburg. LC 73-40362. (Illus.). 32p. (gr. k-3). 1976. 5.95 (ISBN 0-685-63197-4, TYC-J); PLB 7.89 o.p. (ISBN 0-690-01115-6). T Y Crowell.

Shaw's Champions: G. B. S. & Prize Fighting from Cashel Byron to Gene Tunney. Benny Green. (Illus.). 1978. 19.95 (ISBN 0-241-89735-1, Pub. by Hamish Hamilton England). David & Charles.

Shaw's Fortune: The Picture Story of a Colonial Plantation. Edwin Tunis. LC 75-29640. (Illus.). 64p. (gr. 2-6). 1976. 12.95 (ISBN 0-690-01066-4, TYC-J). T Y Crowell.

Shaw's Music: The Complete Musical Criticism, 3 vols. Ed. by Dan H. Laurence. LC 80-1113. 1981. Boxed Set. 150.00 (ISBN 0-686-69572-0). Vol. 1 (ISBN 0-396-07960-1). Vol. 2 (ISBN 0-396-07961-X). Vol. 3 (ISBN 0-396-07962-8). Dodd.

Shaw's Plays: Man & Superman Notes & Caesar & Cleopatra Notes. James K. Lowers. 1964. pap. 1.95 (ISBN 0-8220-0808-4). Cliffs.

Shay Agnon's World of Mystery & Allegory: An Analysis of Iddo & 'Aynam. Israel Rosenberg. 143p. 1978. 5.95 (ISBN 0-8059-2538-4). Dorrance.

Shaykh Al-Damanhuri Against the Churches of Cairo (1739) Ed. by Moshe Perlmann. (Publications in Near Eastern Studies: Vol. 19). 1975. pap. 11.50x (ISBN 0-520-09513-8). U of Cal Pr.

Shay's Rebellion 1786-87: Americans Take up Arms Against an Unjust Law. Monroe Stearns. LC 68-17705. (Focus Bks). (Illus.). (gr. 7 up). 1968. PLB 4.47 o.p. (ISBN 0-531-01003-1). Watts.

She. H. Rider Haggard. 1976. Repr. of 1887 ed. lib. bdg. 12.95 (ISBN 0-89190-705-X). Am Repr-Rivercity Pr.

She & Allan. H. Rider Haggard. Ed. by R. Reginald & Douglas Menville. LC 80-19461. (Newcastle Forgotten Fantasy Library Ser.: Vol. 6). 303p. 1980. Repr. of 1977 ed. lib. bdg. 10.95x (ISBN 0-89370-505-5). Borgo Pr.

She Come Bringing Me That Little Baby Girl. Eloise Greenfield. LC 74-8104. (gr. k-3). 1974. 8.79 (ISBN 0-397-31586-4). Lippincott.

She Hath Done What She Could. Jane McWhorter. 1973. 3.75 (ISBN 0-89137-405-1). Quality Pubns.

She Said Yes. Rosa Maria Arenas. 26p. 1980. pap. 3.00 (ISBN 0-931598-09-5). Fallen Angel.

She Shall Be Called Woman. rev. ed. Frances Vander Velde. LC 57-13178. (Illus.). 1971. pap. 4.95 (ISBN 0-8254-3950-7). Kregel.

She Stoops to Conquer. Oliver Goldsmith. Ed. by Vincent F. Hopper & Gerald B. Lahey. (Illus.). (gr. 9 up). 1958. pap. text ed. 2.50 (ISBN 0-8120-0158-3). Barron.

She Stoops to Conquer. Oliver Goldsmith. Ed. by Katherine G. Balderston. LC 51-6755. (Crofts Classics Ser.). 1951. pap. text ed. 2.75x (ISBN 0-88295-039-8). AHM Pub.

She Wanted to Read: The Story of Mary Bethune. Ella K. Carruth. (Illus.). (gr. 3-5). 1969. pap. 1.25 (ISBN 0-671-29861-5). PB.

She Wanted to Read: The Story of Mary McLeod Bethune. Ella K. Carruth. (gr. 3-5). 1969. pap. 1.25 o.s.i. (ISBN 0-671-29861-5). Archway.

She Was There: Stories of Pioneering Women Journalists. Jean Collins. LC 80-36769. (Illus.). 192p. (gr. 7 up). 1980. PLB 8.79 (ISBN 0-671-33082-9). Messner.

She Who Was King. Wendy Lozano. 384p. 1980. pap. 2.50 (ISBN 0-345-28638-3). Ballantine.

She Would If She Could. George Etherege. Ed. by Charlene M. Taylor. LC 76-128913. (Regents Restoration Drama Ser). xxx, 132p. 1971. pap. 3.50x (ISBN 0-8032-6700-2, BB 281, Bison). U of Nebr Pr.

Sheaf of Japanese Papers: In Tribute to Heinz Kaempfer on His Seventy-Fifth Birthday. Ed. by Matthi Forrer et al. 1980. 20.00x (ISBN 90-70265-71-0). Humanities.

Sheaf Theory. B. R. Tennison. LC 74-31791. (London Mathematical Society Lecture Note Ser.: No. 20). 120p. 1976. pap. 16.95 (ISBN 0-521-20784-3). Cambridge U Pr.

Shear Zones in Rocks: Papers Presented at the International Conference Held at the University of Barcelona, May 1979. J. Carreras et al. 200p. 1980. pap. 40.00 (ISBN 0-08-026244-9). Pergamon.

Shearer Furniture Designs. R. Fastnedge. 1966. 8.95 (ISBN 0-685-52092-7). Transatlantic.

Shearer's Manual of Human Dissection. 6th ed. Charles E. Tobin & John J. Jacobs. (Illus.). 352p. 1981. pap. text ed. 16.95 (ISBN 0-07-064926-X). McGraw.

Sheba: A Story of Girlhood. Mrs. Desmond Humphreys. Ed. by Robert L. Wolff. LC 75-1535. (Victorian Fiction Ser.). 1975. lib. bdg. 66.00 (ISBN 0-8240-1607-6). Garland Pub.

Shedmaster to Railway Inspectorate. Christian H. Hewison. LC 80-68694. (Illus.). 192p. 1981. 19.95 (ISBN 0-7153-8074-5). David & Charles.

Sheep & Sheep Hunting. Jack O'Connor. 1974. 12.95 (ISBN 0-87691-145-9). Winchester Pr.

Sheep & Wool Science. 4th ed. M. Eugene Ensminger. LC 73-79612. (gr. 9-12). 1970. text ed. 23.35 (ISBN 0-8134-1113-0); pap. text ed. 17.50x (ISBN 0-685-03921-8). Interstate.

Sheep Book. Carmen Goodyear. 26p. (ps-1). 1972. pap. 2.75 (ISBN 0-914996-02-9). Lollipop Power.

Sheep Dog: Its Work & Training. Tim Longton & Edward Hart. (Illus.). 128p. 1976. 12.95 (ISBN 0-7153-7149-5). David & Charles.

Sheep Look up. John Brunner. 192p. 1981. pap. 2.95 (ISBN 0-345-27503-9, Del Rey). Ballantine.

Sheep of the World in Color. Kenneth Ponting. (Illus.). 132p. 1980. 14.95 (ISBN 0-7137-0941-3, Pub. by Blandford Pr England). Sterling.

Sheep Production. John B. Owen. (Illus.). 436p. 1976. text ed. 18.50 (ISBN 0-8121-0748-9). Lea & Febiger.

Sheep Production: Science into Practice. Andrew W. Speedy. (Longman Handbooks in Agriculture Ser.). (Illus.). 208p. (Orig.). 1980. pap. text ed. 16.95 (ISBN 0-582-45582-0). Longman.

Sheepdogs: My Faithful Friends. Eric Halsall. (Illus.). 216p. 1980. 35.95 (ISBN 0-85059-431-6). Aztex.

Sheepherders. Michael Mathers. (Illus.). 1975. 4.95 (ISBN 0-395-20723-1, Pub. by Montana Bks). Madrona Pubs.

Sheet Magic: Games, Toys & Gifts from Old Sheets. Peggy Parish. (Illus.). (gr. 4-6). 1971. 6.95g (ISBN 0-02-769870-X). Macmillan.

Sheet Metal Blueprint Reading: For the Building Trades. Zinngrabe. LC 79-2748. 1980. 10.00 (ISBN 0-8273-1352-7); instructor's guide 1.65 (ISBN 0-8273-1353-5). Delmar.

Sheet Metal Fabrication. W. Watkins. (Illus.). 1971. pap. text ed. 22.30x (ISBN 0-444-20124-6, Pub. by Applied Science). Burgess-Intl Ideas.

Sheet Metal Forming Proceedings. (Illus.). 362p. 1978. 65.00x (ISBN 0-86108-012-2). Intl Pubns Serv.

Sheet Metal Hand Processes. C. J. Zinngrabe & F. W. Schumacher. LC 73-2159. 1974. 7.40 (ISBN 0-8273-0220-7); instructor's guide 1.50 (ISBN 0-8273-0221-5). Delmar.

Sheet Metal Industries Yearbook 1979. LC 65-79511. pap. 27.50x (ISBN 0-86108-042-4). Intl Pubns Serv.

Sheet Metal Machine Processes. C. J. Zinngrabe & F. W. Schumacher. LC 73-2160. 1975. pap. text ed. 7.40 (ISBN 0-8273-0222-3); instructor's guide 1.60 (ISBN 0-8273-0223-1). Delmar.

Sheet-Metal Pattern Drafting & Shop Problems. rev. ed. J. S. Daugherty & R. E. Powell. 196p. 1975. pap. text ed. 11.96 (ISBN 0-87002-155-9). Bennett IL.

Sheet Metal Technology. 2nd ed. Richard S. Budzik. 1981. 13.95 (ISBN 0-672-97360-X); instr's. guide 3.33 (ISBN 0-672-97361-8); students manual 6.55 (ISBN 0-672-97362-6). Bobbs.

Sheet Metalwork. R. E. Smith. pap. 5.00 (ISBN 0-87345-111-2). McKnight.

Sheik. Maggie Davis. 1978. pap. 1.95 o.p. (ISBN 0-449-23554-8, Crest). Fawcett.

Sheik. E. M. Hull. (Barbara Cartland's Library of Love: Vol. 1). 216p. 1980. 12.95x (ISBN 0-7156-1377-4, Pub. by Duckworth England). Biblio Dist.

Shelburne Essays, 11 vols. Ed. by Paul E. More. Incl. Vol. 1. 1904. 253p. (ISBN 0-685-22556-9); Vol. 2. 1905. 253p. (ISBN 0-685-22557-7); Vol. 3. 1906. 265p. (ISBN 0-685-22558-5); Vol. 4. 1906. 286p. (ISBN 0-685-22559-3); Vol. 5. 1908. 216p. (ISBN 0-685-22560-7); Vol. 6. Studies in Religious Dualism, 1909. 355p. (ISBN 0-685-22561-5); Vol. 7. 1910. 272p. (ISBN 0-685-22562-3); Vol. 8. Drift of Romanticism, 1913. 316p. (ISBN 0-685-22563-1); Vol. 9. Aristocracy & Justice, 1915. 253p. (ISBN 0-685-22564-X); Vol. 10. With the Wits, 1919. 323p. (ISBN 0-685-22565-8); Vol. 11. A New England Group & Others, 1921. 300p. (ISBN 0-685-22566-6). LC 67-17764. 1967. Repr. of 1921 ed. 8.00 ea.; Set. 85.00 (ISBN 0-87753-028-9). Phaeton.

Shelburne Farms: The History of an Agricultural Estate. Ed. by William C. Lipke. (Illus.). 79p. (Orig.). 1979. pap. 7.50 (ISBN 0-87451-990-X). U Pr of New Eng.

Sheldon's Lunch. Bruce Lemerise. LC 80-10449. (Illus.). 48p. (ps-3). 1980. 4.95 (ISBN 0-8193-1025-5); PLB 5.95 (ISBN 0-8193-1026-3). Parents.

Sheldon's Retail & Phelon's Resident Byers Book. 97th ed. Ed. by Phelon, Sheldon, & Masar, Inc. 1981. pap. 70.00 (ISBN 0-686-28951-X). P S & M Inc.

Sheldrake. Date not set. 4.95 (ISBN 0-8120-5380-X). Barron. Postponed.

Shelf Book: Complete Do-It-Yourself Systems for Building Shelves in Living Rooms, Kitchens, Closets, Basements, Garages, Etc. Jon M. Zegel. LC 77-12366. (Illus.). 1977. lib. bdg. 12.90 (ISBN 0-89471-001-X); pap. 5.95 (ISBN 0-89471-000-1). Running Pr.

Shelf Classification Research. Richard Hyman. (Occasional Papers: No. 146). 1980. pap. 3.00. U of Ill Lib Sci.

She'll Be Comin' 'round the Mountain. Robert Quackenbush. LC 73-2943. (Illus.). 40p. (gr. k-2). 1973. 8.95 (ISBN 0-397-31480-9). Lippincott.

Shell Book of Country Parks. Mary Waugh. LC 80-68695. (Illus.). 224p. 1981. 19.95 (ISBN 0-7153-7963-1). David & Charles.

Shell Book of Practical & Decorative Ropework. Eric C. Fry & Peter Wilson. (Illus.). 1979. 12.95 (ISBN 0-7153-7615-2). David & Charles.

Shell Book of the Home in Britain: Decoration, Design & Construction of Vernacula Interiors, 1500-1850. James Ayres. (Shell Book Ser.). (Illus.). 240p. 1981. 25.00 (ISBN 0-571-11625-6, Pub. by Faber & Faber). Merrimack Bk Serv.

Shell Craft. Elizabeth D. Logan. LC 74-2018. (Illus.). 224p. 1974. 14.95 o.p. (ISBN 0-684-13863-8, ScribT). Scribner.

Shell Craft. Glen Pownall. (New Crafts Books Ser.). 72p. 1980. 7.50 (ISBN 0-85467-021-1, Pub. by Viking Sevenseas New Zealand). Intl Schol Bk Serv.

Shell Designs. Christine Haragan. 1980. 9.95x (ISBN 0-85936-137-3, Pub. by Midas Bks England). Intl Schol Bk Serv.

Shell: Five Hundred Million Years of Inspired Design. Hugh Stix & Marguerite Stix. LC 68-12922. (Illus.). 1968. 45.00 (ISBN 0-8109-0475-6); pap. 8.95 (ISBN 0-8109-2098-0). Abrams.

Shell Makers: Introducing Mollusks. Alan Solem. LC 73-20315. 304p. 1974. 16.95 (ISBN 0-471-81210-2, Pub. by Wiley-Interscience). Wiley.

Shell Weekend Guide to London & the South East. Ed. by Robert Nicholson. (Illus.). 1979. 15.00 o.p. (ISBN 0-905522-12-5, ADON 8111-2, Pub. by R Nicholson). Barrie & Jenkins.

Shelley Also Known As Shirley. Shelley Winters. 512p. 1981. pap. 3.50 (ISBN 0-345-29506-4). Ballantine.

Shelley: An Essay. Adolphus A. Jack. LC 70-113337. 1970. Repr. of 1904 ed. 11.00 (ISBN 0-8046-1022-3). Kennikat.

Shelley, an Essay. Adolphus A. Jack. 127p. 1980. Repr. of 1904 ed. lib. bdg. 15.00 (ISBN 0-8492-1368-1). R West.

Shelley & the Concept of Humanity: A Study of His Moral Vision. James Brazell. (Salzburg Studies in English Literature, Romantic Reassessment: No. 7). 1972. pap. text ed. 25.00x (ISBN 0-391-01331-9). Humanities.

Shelley & the Dramatic Form. Sheila U. Singh. (Salzburg Studies in English Literature, Romantic Reassessment: No. 1). 1972. pap. text ed. 25.00x (ISBN 0-391-01527-3). Humanities.

Shelley & the New Criticism: The Anatomy of a Critical Misvaluation. Wilfrid C. Barton. (Salzburg Studies in English Literature, Romantic Reassessment: No. 5). 228p. 1973. pap. text ed. 25.00x (ISBN 0-391-01314-9). Humanities.

Shelley in the Twentieth Century: A Study of the Development of Shelley Criticism in England & America, 1916-71. Nancy Fogarty. (Salzburg Studies in English Literature, Romantic Reassessment: No. 56). 179p. 1976. pap. text ed. 25.00x (ISBN 0-391-01377-7). Humanities.

Shelley-Moore Debate (Baptism, Sprinkling or Immersion) pap. 3.95 (ISBN 0-89315-256-0). Lambert Bk.

Shelley: Selected Poetry, Prose & Letters. Ed. by A S Glover. 1978. 11.95 (ISBN 0-370-00516-3, Pub. by Chatto Bodley Jonathan). Merrimack Bk Serv.

Shelley: The Critical Heritage. Ed. by James E. Barcus. (Critical Heritage Ser.). 1975. 38.00x (ISBN 0-7100-8148-0). Routledge & Kegan.

Shelley: The Golden Years. Kenneth N. Cameron. LC 73-80566. 1974. text ed. 22.50x (ISBN 0-674-80605-0). Harvard U Pr.

Shelley's Critical Prose. Percy B. Shelley. Ed. by B. R. McElderry, Jr. LC 66-19856. (Regents Critics Ser). 1967. 9.95x (ISBN 0-8032-0461-2); pap. 2.95x (ISBN 0-8032-5462-8, BB 407, Bison). U of Nebr Pr.

Shelley's Knowledge & Use of Natural History. Lloyd N. Jeffrey. (Salzburg Studies: Romantic Reassessment Ser.: No. 48). 1976. pap. text ed. 25.00x (ISBN 0-391-01436-6). Humanities.

Shelley's Poetic Thoughts. Richard Cronin. 1981. 22.50 (ISBN 0-312-71664-8). St Martin.

Shelley's Poetry & Prose. Percy Shelley. Ed. by Donald H. Reiman. LC 76-26929. (Norton Critical Editions). 1977. 15.95 (ISBN 0-393-04436-X); pap. text ed. 10.95x (ISBN 0-393-09164-3). Norton.

Shelley's Polar Paradise: A Reading of Prometheus Unbound. William H. Hildebrand. (Salzburg Studies in English Literature, Romantic Reassessment: No.18). 1974. pap. text ed. 25.00x (ISBN 0-391-01409-9). Humanities.

Shelley's "Prometheus Unbound" A Variorum Edition. Ed. by Lawrence J. Zillman. LC 59-9913. (Illus.). 812p. 1959. 17.50 (ISBN 0-295-73931-2). U of Wash Pr.

Shelley's the Revolt of Islam. James L. Ruff. (Salzburg Studies in English Literature, Romantic Reassessment: No.10). 1972. pap. text ed. 25.00x (ISBN 0-391-01512-5). Humanities.

Shellfish Cookery. Jane Chekenian & Monica Meyer. (Illus.). 1971. 12.50 o.s.i. (ISBN 0-02-524610-0). Macmillan.

Shells Are Skeletons. Joan B. Victor. LC 75-23258. (Let's Read & Find Out Science Book Ser.). (Illus.). (gr. k-3). 1977. 7.89 (ISBN 0-690-01038-9, TYC-J). T Y Crowell.

Shells in Color. Kjell B. Sandved & R. Tucker Abbott. (Illus.). 1976. pap. 4.95 o.p. (ISBN 0-14-004237-7). Penguin.

Shells on Stamps of the World. Kohman Y. Arakawa. (Illus.). 234p. (Jap.). 1979. 15.95 (ISBN 0-915826-07-0). Am Malacologists.

Shells: Treasures from the Sea. James A. Cox. LC 79-7520. (Illus.). 1979. 19.95 o.p. (ISBN 0-88332-118-1). Larousse.

Shellsort & Sorting Networks. Vaughan R. Pratt. LC 79-50559. (Outstanding Dissertations in the Computer Sciences). 1980. lib. bdg. 11.00 (ISBN 0-8240-4406-1). Garland Pub.

Shelly--Alastor & Other Poems, Prometheus Unbound with Other Poems,Adonais. Ed. by P. H. Butter. (Illus.). 368p. 1980. pap. 13.95x (ISBN 0-7121-0145-4). Intl Ideas.

Shelter. Ed. by Lloyd Kahn, Jr. LC 73-5415. (Illus.). 1973. 20.00 (ISBN 0-394-48829-6); pap. 6.00 (ISBN 0-394-70991-8). Random.

Shelter - Need & Response: Housing, Land & Settlement Policies in Seventeen Third World Nations. Jorge E. Hardoy & David Satterthwaite. 1981. price not set (ISBN 0-471-27919-6, Pub. by Wiley-Interscience). Wiley.

Shelter & Society. Ed. by Paul Oliver. 1978. pap. 7.95 o.p. (ISBN 0-214-20200-3, 8009, Dist. by Arco). Barrie & Jenkins.

Shelter & Subsidies: Who Benefits from Federal Housing Policies? Henry J. Aaron. (Studies in Social Economics). 200p. 1972. 11.95 (ISBN 0-8157-0018-0); pap. 4.95 (ISBN 0-8157-0017-2). Brookings.

Shelter for the Poor: The Case of Poona. Meera Bapat. (Progress in Planning Ser.: Vol. 15, Pt. 3). 85p. 1981. pap. 13.50 (ISBN 0-08-026811-0). Pergamon.

Shelter from the Wind. Marion D. Bauer. LC 75-28184. 128p. (gr. 5-12). 1976. 6.95 (ISBN 0-395-28890-8, Clarion). HM.

Shelter II. Ed. by Lloyd Kahn. (Illus.). 224p. (Orig.). 1978. 15.00 (ISBN 0-394-50219-1); pap. 9.50 (ISBN 0-394-73611-7). Shelter Pubns.

Shelter in Africa. Ed. by Paul Oliver. 1978. 8.50 o.p. (ISBN 0-214-20205-4, 8010, Dist. by Arco). Barrie & Jenkins.

Shelter on Blue Barns Road. C. S. Adler. LC 80-24715. (Illus.). 144p. (gr. 5-9). 1981. PLB 8.95 (ISBN 0-02-700280-2). Macmillan.

Shelter, Sign & Symbol. Ed. by Paul Oliver. LC 77-77089. (Illus.). 1980. pap. 9.95 (ISBN 0-87951-112-5). Overlook Pr.

Shelter: The Cave Re-Examined. Don Fabun. 1971. pap. text ed. 2.50x (ISBN 0-02-475390-4, 47539). Macmillan.

Sheltered at the Edge. Jean Pumphrey. 1981. 4.95. Solo Pr.

Sheltering Battered Women: A National Study & Service Guide. Albert R. Roberts. LC 80-19827. (Focus on Women Ser.: No. 3). 228p. 1980. text ed. 22.95 (ISBN 0-8261-2690-1); pap. text ed. 15.95 (ISBN 0-8261-2691-X). Springer Pub.

Sheltering Branch. Marzieh Gail. 1959. 4.75 (ISBN 0-87743-058-6, 7-31-33, Pub. by George Ronald England). Baha'i.

Shemya Island. Herbert N. Cook. 63p. 1980. 3.95 (ISBN 0-8059-2461-2). Dorrance.

Shen Ts'Ung-Wen. Hua-ling Nieh. (World Authors Ser.: China: No. 237). lib. bdg. 10.95 (ISBN 0-8057-2818-X). Twayne.

Shen Tzu Fragments. P. M. Thompson. (London Oriental Ser.). (Illus.). 1979. 125.00x (ISBN 0-19-713579-X). Oxford U Pr.

Shenandoah: The Story Behind the Scenery. Hugh Crandall. Ed. by Gweneth R. DenDooven. LC 74-30797. (Illus.). 1975. 7.95 (ISBN 0-916122-40-9); pap. 2.50 (ISBN 0-916122-15-8). K C Pubns.

Shenandoah Valley Pioneers & Their Descendants. Thomas K. Cartmell. LC 64-1062. (Illus.). 572p. Repr. of 1909 ed. 32.50 (ISBN 0-686-63647-3). Va Bk.

Shenandoah Vestiges: What the Mountain People Left Behind. Jack Reder & Carolyn Reeder. LC 80-81761. 72p. 1980. pap. 3.75 (ISBN 0-915746-14-X). Potomac Appalach.

Shenandoah Vestiges: What the Mountain People Left Behind. Jack Reeder & Carolyn Reeder. LC 80-81761. 72p. (Orig.). 1980. pap. 3.75 (ISBN 0-915746-14-X). Potomac Appalach.

Shepard's Handbook of Wine Cocktails & Non-Alcoholic Drinks: A Guide for Foodservice & Bar Managers. John S. Shepard. (Foodservice Guides Ser.). 1981. 20.00 (ISBN 0-89047-031-6); spiral bdg. 20.00 (ISBN 0-89047-032-4). Herman Pub.

Shepard's Wine & Liquor Pricing Guide. John S. Shepard. (Foodservice Guides Ser.). 1981. spiral bdg. 15.00 (ISBN 0-89047-034-0). Herman Pub.

Shepherd. Helga Aichinger. LC 67-18394. (Illus.). (gr. k-3). 1967. 8.95 (ISBN 0-690-73021-7, TYC-J). T Y Crowell.

Shepherd Boy of Bethlehem. Lucy Diamond. (Ladybird Ser). (Illus.). 1954. bds. 1.49 (ISBN 0-87508-858-9). Chr Lit.

Shepherd Kings. Peter Danielson. 448p. (Orig.). 1981. pap. 2.95 (ISBN 0-553-14653-X). Bantam.

Shepherd Looks at the Good Shepherd & His Sheep. Philip Keller. 1979. 7.95 (ISBN 0-310-26800-1); large print kivar 4.95 (ISBN 0-310-26807-9). Zondervan.

Shepherd of Jerusalem. Dov P. Elkins. LC 75-39436. (Illus.). (gr. 8-12). 1976. 6.95 (ISBN 0-88400-045-1). Shengold.

Shepherd of My Soul. 1981. 4.95 (ISBN 0-8198-6801-9); pap. 3.50 (ISBN 0-8198-6802-7). Dghtrs St Paul.

Shepherd Psalm. Ron Hembree. (Direction Bks). 64p. 1981. pap. text ed. 1.75 (ISBN 0-8010-4249-6). Baker Bk.

Shepherd Under Christ. Armin W. Schuetze & Irwin J. Habezk. LC 74-81794. 1974. text ed. 12.00 (ISBN 0-8100-0046-6, 15N0351). Northwest Pub.

Shepherd Watches, a Shepherd Sings. Louis Irigaray & Theodore Taylor. LC 76-50772. 1977. 8.95 o.p. (ISBN 0-385-11652-7). Doubleday.

Shepherding God's Flock. one vol. ed. Jay E. Adams. 1979. pap. 8.95 (ISBN 0-87552-058-8). Presby & Reformed.

Shepherd's Historical Atlas. 9th rev. ed. William R. Shepherd. (Illus.). (gr. 7 up). 1976. 28.50x (ISBN 0-06-013846-7). B&N.

Shepherd's Historical Atlas. 9th ed. William R. Shepherd. (Illus.). 368p. (YA) 1973. Repr. of 1964 ed. 22.50x (ISBN 0-06-013846-7, HarpT). Har-Row.

Shepherds of the Delectable Mountains: The Story of the Washington County Mission. Moira Mathieson. 1979. 2.00 (ISBN 0-686-28792-4). Forward Movement.

Shepherd's Year. Denis Thorpe & Alan Dunn. LC 78-74075. 1979. 11.95 (ISBN 0-7153-7762-0). David & Charles.

Sheraton Furniture Design. Ralph Edwards. (Illus.). 1974. pap. 6.95 (ISBN 0-85458-909-0). Transatlantic.

Sherborne; or, the House at the Four Ways, 1875. Edward H. Dering. Ed. by Robert L. Wolff. LC 75-457. (Victorian Fiction Ser.). 1975. lib. bdg. 66.00 (ISBN 0-8240-1536-3). Garland Pub.

Sheridan le Fanu & Victorian Ireland. W. J. McCormack. (Illus.). 334p. 1980. text ed. 36.00x (ISBN 0-19-812629-8). Oxford U Pr.

Sheridan: Six Plays. Richard B. Sheridan. Ed. & intro. by Louis Kronenberger. Incl. The Rivals; St. Patrick's Day; The Duenna; A Trip to Scarborough; The School for Scandal; The Critic. 359p. (Orig.). 1957. pap. 4.95 (ISBN 0-8090-0705-3, Mermaid). Hill & Wang.

Sheridan: The Track of a Comet. Madeline Bingham. 1972. text ed. 17.95x o.p. (ISBN 0-04-928024-4); pap. 7.50 o.p. (ISBN 0-04-928036-8). Allen Unwin.

Sheriff of Singing River. Al Cody. 1981. pap. 1.75 (ISBN 0-8439-0862-9, Leisure Bks). Nordon Pubns.

Sherington: Fiefs & Fields of a Buckinghamshire Village. A. C. Chibnall. 1966. 57.50 (ISBN 0-521-04637-8). Cambridge U Pr.

Sherlock Bones: Tracer of Missing Pets. John Keane. 1979. 8.95 o.s.i. (ISBN 0-397-01335-3). Lippincott.

Sherlock Hemlock: Great Twiddlebug Mystery. Sesame Street. (Tell-a-Tale Readers). (Illus.). (gr. k-3). 1972. PLB 4.77 (ISBN 0-307-68564-0, Whitman). Western Pub.

Sherlock Holmes. Sir Arthur C. Doyle. (Young Fiction & Classics). pap. 1.25 (ISBN 0-307-12215-8, Golden Pr). Western Pub.

Sherlock Holmes. (Deluxe Illustrated Classics Ser.). 1977. 3.50 (ISBN 0-307-12215-8, Golden Pr). Western Pub.

Sherlock Holmes & the Sacred Sword. Frank Thomas. 256p. (Orig.). 1980. pap. 2.50 o.p. (ISBN 0-523-41013-1). Pinnacle Bks.

Sherlock Holmes Cookbook. Sean Wright & John Farrell. LC 75-10547. (Illus.). 1975. 8.95 o.p. (ISBN 0-8473-1003-5). Sterling.

Sherlock Holmes in Dallas. Edmund Aubrey. LC 80-15980. 240p. 1980. 9.95 (ISBN 0-396-07904-0). Dodd.

Sherlock Holmes in New York. D. R. Bensen. (Orig.). 1976. pap. 1.50 o.p. (ISBN 0-345-25571-2). Ballantine.

Sherlock Holmes Puzzle Book. Dale Copps. (Illus.). 160p. 1980. pap. 3.95 (ISBN 0-385-14839-9, Dolp). Doubleday.

Sherlock Holmes Reference Guide. William D. Goodrich. LC 80-67701. (Sherlock Holmes Reference Ser.). Date not set. price not set (ISBN 0-934468-06-0). Gaslight.

Sherlock Holmes: Selected Stories. Arthur Conan Doyle. 12.95 (ISBN 0-19-250528-9, WC528). Oxford U Pr.

Sherlock Holmes' War of the Worlds. Manley W. Wellman & Wade Wellman. 208p. (Orig.). 1975. pap. 1.25 o.s.i. (ISBN 0-446-76982-7). Warner Bks.

Sherman Day: Artist, Engineer & Forty Niner. Murphy D. Smith. 30.00 (ISBN 0-89453-152-2). M Glazier.

Sherman Letters. 2nd ed. Ed. by Rachel S. Thorndike. LC 68-8693. (American Scene Ser.). 1969. Repr. of 1894 ed. lib. bdg. 39.50 (ISBN 0-306-71175-3). Da Capo.

Shermans: A Sketch of Family History & a Genealogical Record, 1570-1890 with Some Account of Families Intermarried. Roger Sherman. 1946. pap. 24.50x (ISBN 0-685-89781-8). Elliots Bks.

Sherman's March. Richard Wheeler. LC 78-3321. (Illus.). 1978. 11.95 o.p. (ISBN 0-690-01746-4, TYC-T). T Y Crowell.

Sherpa Architecture. 1979. pap. 7.00 (ISBN 92-3-201612-5, U887, UNESCO). Unipub.

Sherry: The Noble Wine. Manuel M. Gonzalez Gordon. LC 73-151683. (Illus.). 237p. 1972. 15.00 (ISBN 0-304-93472-0). Intl Pubns Serv.

Sherwood Anderson. Rex Burbank. (U. S. Authors Ser.: No. 65). 1964. lib. bdg. 10.95 (ISBN 0-8057-0020-X). Twayne.

Sherwood Anderson. Welford D. Taylor. LC 77-6948. (Modern Literature Ser.). 1977. 10.95 (ISBN 0-8044-2861-1). Ungar.

Sherwood Anderson: A Selective, Annotated Bibliography. Douglas Rogers. LC 75-45225. (Author Bibliographies Ser.: No. 26). 163p. 1976. 10.00 (ISBN 0-8108-0900-1). Scarecrow.

Sherwood Bonner (Catherine McDowell) William L. Frank. LC 76-6900. (U. S. Authors Ser.: No. 267). 1976. lib. bdg. 10.95 (ISBN 0-8057-7169-7). Twayne.

Sheryl. Ralph Hayes. 1980. pap. 2.25 (ISBN 0-505-51452-4). Tower Bks.

She's a Good Skate, Charlie Brown. Charles M. Schulz. LC 80-20285. (Charlie Brown TV Special). (Illus.). 48p. 1981. PLB 4.99 (ISBN 0-394-94495-X); pap. 4.95 boards (ISBN 0-394-84495-5). Random.

She's Gone. E. S. Caldwell. LC 75-43158. (Radiant Life Ser). 128p. (Orig.). 1976. pap. 1.95 (ISBN 0-88243-893-X, 020893); teacher's ed 2.50 (ISBN 0-88243-167-6, 32-0167). Gospel Pub.

She's Not My Real Mother. Judith Vigna. Ed. by Ann Fay. LC 80-19073. (Concept Bks.). (Illus.). 32p. (gr. k-3). 1980. 6.95g (ISBN 0-8075-7340-X). A Whitman.

Shestov Anthology. Ed. by Bernard Martin. LC 74-81453. xvii, 328p. 1970. 15.00x (ISBN 0-8214-0070-3). Ohio U Pr.

Shetland. new, rev. ed. James R. Nicholson. LC 79-52367. (Illus.). 1979. 17.95 (ISBN 0-7153-7808-2). David & Charles.

Shetland Dictionary. John Graham. 144p. 1980. 13.95x (ISBN 0-906191-33-5, Pub. by Thule Pr England). Intl Schol Bk Serv.

Shetland Sheepdogs. Beverly Pisano & Mark Taynton. 125p. 1979. 2.95 (ISBN 0-87666-685-3, KW-079). TFH Pubns.

Shetland Sheepdogs. rev. ed. Mark Taynton. (Illus.). 128p. 1974. pap. 2.95 o.p. (ISBN 0-87666-387-0, HS1085). TFH Pubns.

Shetland's Living Landscape. David Spence. 160p. 1980. 17.95x (ISBN 0-906191-14-9, Pub. by Thule Pr England). Intl Schol Bk Serv.

Shevchenko & the Critics, Eighteen Sixty-One to Nineteen Seventy-Eight. Ed. by G. S. Luckyj. 1981. 30.00x (ISBN 0-8020-2346-0); pap. 8.50 (ISBN 0-8020-6377-2). U of Toronto Pr.

Shiatsu: Japanese Finger-Pressure Therapy. Tokujiro Namikoshi. LC 68-19983. (Illus.). 84p. 1972. pap. 6.95 (ISBN 0-87040-169-6). Japan Pubns.

Shiatsu Therapy: Its Theory & Practice. Toru Namikoshi. (Illus.). 1977. pap. 7.95 (ISBN 0-87040-270-6). Japan Pubns.

Shiatzu: Japanese Finger Pressure for Energy. Yukiko Irwin & James Wagenvoord. (Illus.). 240p. 1976. 9.50 o.p. (ISBN 0-397-01054-0); pap. 7.95 (ISBN 0-397-01107-5). Lippincott.

Shibumi. Trevanian. 448p. 1980. Repr. of 1979 ed. pap. 2.95 (ISBN 0-345-28585-9). Ballantine.

Shiel in Diverse Hands: A Series of Essays. Moskowitz et al. Date not set. price not set. Reynolds Morse.

Shield of Achilles. W. H. Auden. 1955. 6.95 o.p. (ISBN 0-394-40446-7). Random.

Shift Work. Paul E. Mott et al. LC 65-11466. (Illus.). 1965. 8.50x o.p. (ISBN 0-472-08675-8). U of Mich Pr.

Shifting Cultivation in Southeastern Asia. J. E. Spencer. (California Library Reprint Ser.). 1978. 20.00x (ISBN 0-520-03517-8). U of Cal Pr.

Shifting Skies. Ed. by Rita S. Mathur. 192p. 1980. text ed. 17.95 (ISBN 0-7069-1271-3, Pub by Vikas India). Advent Bk.

Shi'ite Religion: A History of Islam in Persia & Irak. Dwight M. Donaldson. LC 80-1933. 45.00 (ISBN 0-404-18959-8). AMS Pr.

Shikar. Jamshed Butt. 1967. pap. 2.35 (ISBN 0-88253-128-X). Ind-US Inc.

Shikimate Pathway. E. Haslam. LC 73-18377. 316p. 1974. 43.95 (ISBN 0-470-35882-3). Halsted Pr.

Shin Buddhism. D. T. Suzuki. 3.95 o.p. (ISBN 0-685-47281-7). Weiser.

Shindano-Swahili Essays & Other Stories. Alice Grant et al. (Foreign & Comparative Studies-African Special Publications Ser.: No.6). 55p. 1971. pap. 2.50x. Syracuse U Foreign Comp.

Shine on Bright & Dangerous Object. Laurie Colwin. 1979. pap. 2.95 (ISBN 0-345-28415-1). Ballantine.

Shingle Style & the Stick Style: Architectural Theory & Design from Richardson to the Origins of Wright. rev. ed. Vincent Scully. (Publications in the History of Art Ser.: No. 20). (Illus.). 1971. 25.00x (ISBN 0-300-01434-1); pap. 10.95 (ISBN 0-300-01519-4). Yale U Pr.

Shingle Style Today, or the Historian's Revenge. Vincent Scully, Jr. LC 74-79058. (Illus.). 112p. 1974. 12.50 (ISBN 0-8076-0759-2); pap. 5.95 (ISBN 0-8076-0760-6). Braziller.

Shingu: A Japanese Fishing Community. Arne Kalland. (Scandanavian Institute of Asian Studies Monograph: No. 44). (Orig.). 1980. pap. text ed. 12.50x (ISBN 0-7007-0136-2). Humanities.

Shinichi Suzuki: The Man & His Philosophy. Evelyn Hermann. LC 80-67542. 1980. write for info (ISBN 0-918194-07-5). Accura.

Shining. King. 1980. pap. 2.75 o.p. (ISBN 0-451-09216-3, Sig). NAL.

Shining. Stephen King. (RL 6). 1978. pap. 2.95 o.p. (ISBN 0-451-07872-1, E7872, Sig). NAL.

Shining Clarity: God & Man in the Works of Robinson Jeffers. Marlan Beilke. LC 77-70786. 1978. separate ed. 100.00x (ISBN 0-918466-01-6); separate ed. 100.00x (ISBN 0-918466-01-6). Quintessence.

Shining Clarity: God & Man in the Works of Robinson Jeffers. rev. ed. Marlan Beilke. (Illus., Orig.). 1980. pap. write for info o.p. (ISBN 0-918466-05-9). Quintessence.

Shining Day. Frank Ross. LC 80-69394. 1981. 12.95 (ISBN 0-689-11111-8). Atheneum.

Shining Examples: Model Projects Using Renewable Resources. Ed. by Anita Gunn & Kathleen Courrier. LC 80-67831. (Illus.). 210p. 1980. 6.95 (ISBN 0-937446-00-9). Ctr Renewable.

Shining Levels: The Story of a Man Who Went Back to Nature. John Wyatt. LC 74-9642. 1974. 6.95 o.p. (ISBN 0-397-01037-0). Lippincott.

Shining Searchlights. Walter B. Barbe et al. (Design for Reading Ser). (Illus.). (gr. 7). 1972. text ed. 13.28 (ISBN 0-06-516010-X, SchDept); tchrs' manual 13.80 (ISBN 0-06-516208-0). Har-Row.

Shining Stranger. rev. ed. Preston Harold. LC 73-19480. 1974. 9.50 (ISBN 0-396-06931-2, Pub. by Wayfarer Pr); pap. 6.00 (ISBN 0-396-06932-0, Pub. by Wayfarer Pr.). Dodd.

Shining Stranger. Herald. 3.95 (ISBN 0-916438-29-5). Univ of Trees.

Shining Sword. Charles G. Coleman. LC 56-31266. 1956. pap. 1.75 (ISBN 0-87213-086-X). Loizeaux.

Shining Trumpets: A History of Jazz. rev. 2nd ed. Rudi Blesh. LC 75-31664. (Roots of Jazz Ser). (Illus.). xxxii, 412p. 1975. lib. bdg. 27.50 (ISBN 0-306-70658-X); pap. 7.95 (ISBN 0-306-80029-2). Da Capo.

Shinkansen High-Speed Rail Network of Japan: Procceedings of a IIASA Conference, June 27-30 1977. Ed. by A. Straszak & R. Tuch. (IIASA Proceedings Ser.: Vol. 7). 1980. 130.00 (ISBN 0-08-024444-0). Pergamon.

Shinners' Spring Flora of the Dallas-Ft. Worth Area. 2nd rev. ed. Lloyd H. Shinners. Ed. by William F. Mahler. Orig. Title: Spring Flora of the Dallas-Ft. Worth Area. (Illus.). 1972. pap. 8.50x (ISBN 0-934786-01-1). G Davis.

Shino & Oribe Ceramics. Ryoichi Fujioka. Tr. by Samuel C. Morse from Jap. LC 76-9357. (Japanese Arts Library: Vol. 1). 1977. 16.95 (ISBN 0-87011-284-8). Kodansha.

Shinto: Japan's Spiritual Roots. Stuart D. Picken & Edwin O. Reischauer. LC 79-91520. (Illus.). 80p. 1980. 17.50 (ISBN 0-87011-410-7). Kodansha.

Ship & Aircraft Fairing & Development: For Draftsman & Loftsmen & Sheet Metal Workers. S. S. Rabl. (Illus.). 1941. pap. 6.00x spiral bdg. (ISBN 0-87033-096-9). Cornell Maritime.

Ship Design & Construction. 3rd ed. Ed. by Robert Taggart. (Illus.). 748p. 1980. 60.00 (ISBN 0-9603048-0-0). Soc Naval Arch.

Ship Handling in Narrow Channels. 3rd ed. C. J. Plummer. LC 78-15384. (Illus.). 1966. pap. 7.00x (ISBN 0-87033-247-3). Cornell Maritime.

Ship in a Storm on the Way to Tarsish. Norma Farber. LC 77-23288. (Illus.). (ps-3). 1977. 8.25 (ISBN 0-688-80096-3); PLB 7.92 (ISBN 0-688-84096-5). Greenwillow.

Ship Models & How to Build Them. Harvey Weiss. LC 72-7562. (Illus.). (gr. 5-9). 1973. 10.95 (ISBN 0-690-73270-8, TYC-J). T Y Crowell.

Ship Must Die. Douglas Reeman. 256p. 1981. pap. 2.50 (ISBN 0-515-05954-4). Jove Pubns.

Ship of Bells. George Hitchcock. (Illus.). 1968. pap. 1.50 o.p. (ISBN 0-87711-022-0). Kayak.

Ship of Sulaiman. Tr. by John O'Kane from Persian. LC 70-186605. (Persian Heritage Ser). 250p. 1972. 17.50x (ISBN 0-231-03654-X). Columbia U Pr.

Ship Stability for Masters & Mates. 3rd ed. D. R. Derrett. 1977. 20.00 o.p. (ISBN 0-540-01403-6). Heinman.

Ship That Flew. Hilda Lewis. LC 58-5903. (Illus.). (gr. 3-7). 1958. 9.95 (ISBN 0-87599-067-3). S G Phillips.

Shipbuilders. Leonard E. Fisher. LC 72-150733. (Colonial Americans Ser). (Illus.). (gr. 5 up). 1971. PLB 4.90 o.p. (ISBN 0-531-01043-0). Watts.

Shipmaster's Handbook on Ship's Business. Ben Martin. LC 68-20976. 1969. 12.00x (ISBN 0-87033-098-5). Cornell Maritime.

Shipping & Craft in Silhouette. Charles G. Davis. LC 70-162509. (Tower Bks). (Illus.). 221p. 1972. Repr. of 1929 ed. 18.00 (ISBN 0-8103-3945-5). Gale.

Shipping, Maritime Trade & the Economic Development of Colonial America. J. F. Shepherd & G. Walton. LC 76-176256. (Illus.). 350p. 1972. 29.95 (ISBN 0-521-08409-1). Cambridge U Pr.

Shipping Out. Mariam G. Sherar. LC 72-78239. 1973. pap. 6.00x (ISBN 0-87033-173-6). Cornell Maritime.

Shipping Situation Between New York City & Philadelphia: A Survey of the Factors Causing the Growth of Motor Truck Transportation for the Purpose of Presenting Specifications to Be Met in Coordinating Rail & Motor Truck Transportation for Intercity Service. Russell Talbot. 1931. pap. 27.50x (ISBN 0-685-89782-6). Elliots Bks.

Shipping Terms & Abbreviations: Maritime-Insurance-International Trade. W. G. Woollam. LC 62-22181. 1963. 5.00x (ISBN 0-87033-107-8). Cornell Maritime.

Shipping Two Thousand: The Evolution of Maritime Trade in the Next 10 to 25 Years: An International Conference Held Under the Auspices of the British Shipper's Council, London Hilton-June 19th & 20th, 1979. British Shippers' Council. 124p. 1979. 85.00x (ISBN 0-7099-0212-3, Pub. by Croom Helm Ltd England). Biblio Dist.

Ships. Edward V. Lewis & Robert O'Brien. LC 65-28353. (Life Science Library). (Illus.). (gr. 5 up). 1970. PLB 8.97 o.p. (ISBN 0-8094-0472-9, Pub. by Time-Life). Silver.

Ships. Jonathan Rutland. LC 76-15007. (Modern Knowledge Library). (Illus.). 48p. (gr. 5 up). 1976. 3.95 (ISBN 0-531-02447-4); PLB 6.90 (ISBN 0-685-67488-6). Watts.

Ships & Aircraft of the U. S. Fleet: 1950, 1958, & 1965 Editions, 3 vols. James C. Fahey. LC 76-15840. (Illus.). 192p. 1980. soft bdg. slipcased 11.95 (ISBN 0-87021-647-3). Naval Inst Pr.

Ships & Aircraft of the U. S. Fleet. 12th ed. Norman Polmar. 416p. 1981. 24.95 (ISBN 0-87021-643-0). Naval Inst Pr.

Ships & Men of the Great Lakes. Dwight Boyer. LC 77-5901. (Illus.). 1977. 8.95 (ISBN 0-396-07446-4). Dodd.

Ships & Narrow Gauge Rails: The Story of the Pacific Coast Company. Gerald M. Best. (Illus.). 155p. Date not set. Repr. of 1964 ed. 15.00 (ISBN 0-8310-7042-0). Howell-North.

Ships & the River. David Canright. 32p. (gr. 5 up). 1975. pap. 2.00 o.s.i. (ISBN 0-913344-22-2). Interbk Inc.

Ship's Cook Ginger. Edward Ardizzone. LC 78-7518. (Illus.). (gr. 1-4). 1978. 8.95 (ISBN 0-02-705680-5, 70568). Macmillan.

Ships: From Noah's Ark to Nuclear Submarine. Frank Knight. LC 70-124418. (Illus.). (gr. 5-8). 1971. 4.95 o.s.i. (ISBN 0-02-750890-0, CCPr). Macmillan.

Ships of British Oak: The Rise & Decline of Wooden Shipbuilding in Hampshire. A. J. Holland. (Illus.). 192p. 1972. 5.95 o.p. (ISBN 0-7153-5344-6). David & Charles.

Ship's Routing. 4th ed. 150p. 1978. 55.00 (IMCO). Unipub.

Shipton Quebec Canada Eighteen Twenty Five Census. Jay M. Hobrook. LC 76-364055. 1976. pap. 7.50 (ISBN 0-931248-07-8). Holbrook Res.

Shipwrecks & Sea Monsters of California's Central Coast. Randall A. Reinstedt. LC 76-350548. (Illus.). 1975. pap. 5.95 (ISBN 0-933818-02-5). Ghost Town.

Shipwrecks of Great Britain & Ireland. Richard Larn. LC 80-68898. (Illus.). 1981. 24.00 (ISBN 0-7153-7491-5). David & Charles.

Shipwrecks of North Wales. Ivor W. Jones. (Regional Shipwreck Ser.). (Illus.). 1973. pap. 8.95 (ISBN 0-7153-5787-5). David & Charles.

Shipwrecks of the Lakes. Dana T. Bowen. 1952. 9.50 (ISBN 0-685-11636-0). Freshwater.

Shipwrecks off the New Jersey Coast. Walter Krotee & Richard Krotee. (Illus.). cancelled o.s.i. (ISBN 0-913352-07-1). Mariners Boston.

Shiraz: Persian City of Saints & Poets. A. J. Arberry. (Centers of Civilization Ser.: No. 2). 1960. 5.95 o.p. (ISBN 0-8061-0461-9). U of Okla Pr.

Shirley: A Tale. Charlotte Bronte. (World's Classics Ser.). 14.95 (ISBN 0-19-250014-7). Oxford U Pr.

Shirley Jackson. Lenemaja Friedman. LC 74-31244. (U. S. Authors Ser.: No. 253). 1975. lib. bdg. 9.95 (ISBN 0-8057-0402-7). Twayne.

Shirley Jackson. Ed. by Lenemaja Friedman. LC 74-31244. (Twayne's U. S. Authors Ser.). 182p. 1975. pap. text ed. 4.95 (ISBN 0-672-61507-X). Bobbs.

Shirley Letters. Louise Clappe. LC 77-141468. (Illus.). 1970. pap. 4.95 (ISBN 0-87905-004-7). Peregrine Smith.

Shirley Temple Scrapbook. Loraine Burdick. LC 74-31298. (Illus.). 1975. 12.95 o.p. (ISBN 0-8246-0195-5). Jonathan David.

Shirley Temple's Dolls & Related Delights. rev. ed. Loraine Burdick. 1977. pap. 5.50x o.p. (ISBN 0-87588-102-5). Hobby Hse.

Shirley's Twentieth Century Lovers' Guide. Grace Shirley. 160p. (Orig.). 1981. pap. 2.50 (ISBN 0-523-40868-4). Pinnacle Bks.

Shirlick Holmes & the Case of the Wandering Wardrobe. Jane Yolen. (Illus.). 80p. (gr. 9-12). 1981. 7.95 (ISBN 0-698-20498-0). Coward.

Shirt Sleeve Approach to Long Range Planning for the Smaller Growing Corporation. R. Linneman. 1980. 15.95 (ISBN 0-13-808972-8). P-H.

Shirt-Sleeves Management. James F. Evered. 273p. 1981. 12.95 (ISBN 0-8144-5636-7). Am Mgmt.

Shishi Embroidery: Traditional Mirrorwork of India, Pakistan & Afghanistan. Nancy D. Gross & Frank Fontana. (Illus.). 80p. (Orig.). Date not set. pap. price not set (ISBN 0-486-24043-6). Dover.

Shito-Ryu Karate. Fumio Demura. LC 74-169720. (Ser. 110). (Illus.). 1971. pap. text ed. 5.95 (ISBN 0-89750-005-9). Ohara Pubns.

Shiva Descending. Gregory Benford & William Rotsler. 400p. 1979. pap. 2.50 (ISBN 0-380-75168-2, 75168). Avon.

Shivapur: A South Indian Village. K. Ishwaran. (International Library of Sociology & Social Reconstruction). (Illus.). 1968. text ed. 9.00x (ISBN 0-7100-3499-7). Humanities.

Shivering Sands. Victoria Holt. 1978. pap. 1.95 o.p. (ISBN 0-449-23282-4, Crest). Fawcett.

Shivering Sands. Victoria Holt. 288p. 1981. pap. 2.50 (ISBN 0-449-23282-4, Crest). Fawcett.

Shmueli Family, 2 bks. Incl. Bk. 1. Cartoon Adventure. 6.00x (ISBN 0-685-55046-X, 405310); Bk. 2. More Cartoon Adventures. 6.00x (ISBN 0-685-55047-8, 405311). 1975. UAHC.

Shoal of Fishes. Ando Hiroshige. LC 80-5170. 1980. 16.95 (ISBN 0-670-37262-5, Studio). Viking Pr.

Shoal of Time. Gavan Daws. (Illus.). 1968. 9.95 o.s.i. (ISBN 0-02-530070-9). Macmillan.

Shock. G. Tomas Shires et al. LC 73-85076. (Major Problems in Clinical Surgery Ser.: Vol. 13). (Illus.). 175p. 1973. text ed. 14.00 (ISBN 0-7216-8250-2). Saunders.

Shock: A Clinicopathologic Correlation. Vincent J. McGovern & David J. Tiller. LC 79-87539. (Illus.). 192p. 1980. 27.00 (ISBN 0-89352-073-X). Masson Pub.

Shock I. Richard Matheson. 1979. pap. 1.75 o.p. (ISBN 0-425-04095-X). Berkley Pub.

Shock of the New: Art & the Century of Change. Robert Hughes. 423p. 1981. pap. text ed. 15.95 (ISBN 0-394-32800-0). Knopf.

Shock of the New: The Life & Death of Modern Art. Robert Hughes. LC 80-7631. (Illus.). 400p. 1981. 29.95 (ISBN 0-394-51378-9). Knopf.

Shock, Physiological Surgery & George Washington Crile: Medical Innovation in the Progressive Era. Peter C. English. LC 79-8579. (Contributions in Medical History: No. 5). xi, 271p. 1980. lib. bdg. 25.00 (ISBN 0-313-21490-5, EMI/). Greenwood.

Shock Syndrome: Mechanisms & Manifestations; Nursing Assessment Intervention & Evaluation. Martha Thompson. (Illus.). 1978. 7.95 (ISBN 0-201-07660-8, M&N Div). A-W.

Shock Tube & Shock Wave Research: Proceedings of the Eleventh International Symposium on Shock Tubes & Waves. Ed. by Boye Ahlborn et al. LC 77-20168. (Illus.). 670p. 1978. 45.00 (ISBN 0-295-95582-1). U of Wash Pr.

Shock Two. Richard Matheson. 1979. pap. 1.95 o.p. (ISBN 0-425-04158-1). Berkley Pub.

Shock Waves. Richard Matheson. 1979. pap. 1.95 o.p. (ISBN 0-425-04218-9). Berkley Pub.

Shocktrauma. Jon Franklin & Alan Doelp. 256p. 1981. pap. 2.95 (ISBN 0-449-24387-7, Crest). Fawcett.

Shockwave Rider. John Brunner. LC 74-1877. 304p. (YA) 1975. 8.95 o.p. (ISBN 0-06-010559-3, HarpT). Har-Row.

Shoe Leather Treatment. Bill Thomas & S. L. Stebel. 1980. 10.00 o.p. (ISBN 0-312-90861-X). St Martin.

Shoe Leather Treatment... Bill Thomas & Sid Stebel. LC 79-56300. (Illus.). 1979. 11.95 (ISBN 0-312-90861-X). J P Tarcher.

Shoe Show: British Shoes Since Seventeen Ninety. Ed. by Ken Baynes & Kate Baynes. 96p. 1979. 20.00x (ISBN 0-903798-37-9, Pub. by Jolly & Barber England). State Mutual Bk.

Shoe: Willie Shoemaker's Illustrated Book of Racing. Willie Shoemaker & Daniel G. Smith. LC 76-46368. (Illus.). 208p. 1976. 14.95 o.p. (ISBN 0-528-81845-7). Rand.

Shoemaker & the Elves. Brothers Grimm. (Illus.). 32p. (gr. k-3). Repr. of 1960 ed. pap. 2.95 (ISBN 0-689-70480-1, A-107, Aladdin). Atheneum.

Shoemakers. Leonard E. Fisher. LC 67-10296. (Colonial Americans Ser). (Illus.). (gr. 4-6). 1967. PLB 5.90 o.p. (ISBN 0-531-01035-X). Watts.

Shoeshine Girl. Buila. (gr. 3-5). pap. 1.25 (ISBN 0-590-11897-8, Schol Pap). Schol Bk Serv.

Shoghi Effendi: Recollections. Ugo Giachery. (Illus.). 1973. 9.95 (ISBN 0-85398-050-0, 7-31-65, Pub. by George Ronald England). Baha'i.

Shogun. James Clavell. LC 74-77840. 1975. 19.95 (ISBN 0-689-10565-7). Atheneum.

Shogun. James Clavell. 1980. pap. 3.50 (ISBN 0-440-17800-2). Dell.

Shoji Hamada: A Potter's Way & Work. Susan Peterson. LC 74-77957. (Illus.). 240p. 1974. 22.50 (ISBN 0-87011-228-7). Kodansha.

Shojin Cooking: The Buddhist Vegeterian Cook Book. Keizo Kobayashi. Tr. by D. Ooka from Japanese. (Illus.). 1977. 7.95 o.p. (ISBN 0-89346-013-3). Heian Intl.

Sholom Aleichem. Joseph Butwin & Frances Butwin. (World Authors Ser.: No. 460). 1977. lib. bdg. 10.95 (ISBN 0-8057-6297-3). Twayne.

Shona & Zimbabwe Nine Hundred to Eighteen Fifty: An Outline of Shona History. D. N. Beach. LC 80-14116. 424p. 1980. text ed. 45.00x (ISBN 0-8419-0624-6, Africana). Holmes & Meier.

Shona Praise Poetry. Ed. by Aaron C. Hodza & George Fortune. (Oxford Library of African Literature). (Illus.). 1979. 49.50x (ISBN 0-19-815144-6). Oxford U Pr.

Shoot Apex & Leaf Growth. R. F. Williams. (Illus.). 280p. 1975. 35.50 (ISBN 0-521-20453-4). Cambridge U Pr.

Shoot-Out at Dawn--An Arizona Tragedy. John Whitlach. Ed. by Boye De Mente. (Illus.). 176p. (Orig.). 1980. pap. 6.95 (ISBN 0-914778-37-4). Phoenix Bks.

Shoot! (Si Gira) The Notebooks of Serafino Gubbio, Cinematograph Operator. Luigi Pirandello. Tr. by C. K. Moncrieff from It. LC 74-12380. 334p. 1975. Repr. of 1926 ed. 17.50 (ISBN 0-86527-302-2). Fertig.

Shoot the Works. Judith Glashow et al. (Illus.). 128p. 1980. 14.95 (ISBN 0-87165-058-4); pap. 7.95 (ISBN 0-87165-059-2). Ziff-Davis Pub.

Shooter, Fighter, Wild Horse Rider. David Johnson. LC 79-90843. (Illus.). 72p. (Orig.). 1981. pap. 4.95 (ISBN 0-935342-05-2). Jalapeno Pr.

Shooter's Bible 1981, No. 72. 35th ed. Ed. by Robert F. Scott. 576p. 1980. pap. 9.95 (ISBN 0-695-81450-8). Stoeger Pub Co.

Shooter's Workbench. John A. Mosher. (Illus.). 1977. 12.95 (ISBN 0-87691-199-8). Winchester Pr.

Shootin' Mad. Sergio Aragones. (Mad Ser.). (Illus., Orig.). 1979. pap. 1.75 (ISBN 0-446-94397-5). Warner Bks.

Shooting - Why We Miss: Questions & Answers on the Successful Use of the Shotgun. Macdonald Hastings. 1977. 6.95 o.p. (ISBN 0-679-50720-5); pap. 3.95 o.p. (ISBN 0-679-50721-3). McKay.

Shooting: A Complete Guide for Beginners. John Marchington. (Illus.). 1972. 12.95 (ISBN 0-571-09868-1, Pub. by Faber & Faber). Merrimack Bk Serv.

Shooting of Dan McGrew & Other Favorite Poems. Robert Service. LC 80-16040. 1980. pap. 3.95 (ISBN 0-396-07897-4). Dodd.

Shooting Party. Isabele Colgate. 192p. 1981. 11.95 (ISBN 0-670-64064-6). Viking Pr.

Shooting Scripts. Adam Cornford. (Illus.). 1979. 25.00 (ISBN 0-686-28250-7); pap. 10.00 (ISBN 0-686-28251-5). Black Stone.

Shooting Star, T-Bird & Starfire: A Famous Lockheed Family. Rhodes Arnold. (Illus.). 128p. 1981. pap. 12.95 (ISBN 0-89404-035-9). Aztex.

Shooting the Executive Rapids: The First Year in a New Assignment. John Arnold. Ed. by William R. Newton. (Illus.). 288p. 1981. price not set (ISBN 0-07-002312-3, P&RB). McGraw.

Shootist. Glendon Swarthout. LC 74-17772. 192p. 1975. 6.95 o.p. (ISBN 0-385-06099-8). Doubleday.

Shop & Laboratory Instructor's Handbook: A Guide to Improving Education. new ed. Albert J. Pautler, Jr. 1978. text ed. 17.95 o.p. (ISBN 0-205-05841-8). Allyn.

Shop Management. Frederick W. Taylor. 207p. 1980. Repr. of 1911 ed. lib. bdg. 30.00 (ISBN 0-8495-5200-1). Arden Lib.

Shop Stewards in Action: The Organization of Workplace Conflict & Accomodation. Eric Batstone et al. 1977. 20.00x o.p. (ISBN 0-631-17260-2, Pub. by Basil Blackwell); pap. 11.50x (ISBN 0-631-16690-4). Biblio Dist.

Shopkeeper's Millennium: Society & Revivals in Rochester, N. Y. 1815 to 1837. Paul E. Johnson. 1979. 10.95 (ISBN 0-8090-8654-9, AmCen); pap. 5.95 (ISBN 0-8090-0136-5). Hill & Wang.

Shoplifter. Richard H. Smithies. 1968. 4.95 o.s.i. (ISBN 0-8180-0601-3). Horizon.

Shoplifting. L. B. Taylor, Jr. (gr. 7 up). 1979. PLB 7.90 s&l (ISBN 0-531-02877-1). Watts.

Shoplifting & Shrinkage Protection for Stores. Loren E. Edwards. (Illus.). 272p. 1976. 15.75 (ISBN 0-398-00498-6). C C Thomas.

Shopper's Guide to Mexico: What, Where & How to Buy. rev. ed. James Norman & Margaret Fox Schmidt. LC 72-85363. 280p. 1973. pap. 2.50 (ISBN 0-385-02055-4, Dolp). Doubleday.

Shopping Bag Ladies. Ann M. Rosseau. (Illus.). 244p. 1981. 16.95 (ISBN 0-8298-0413-7). Pilgrim NY.

Shopping Basket. John Burningham. LC 80-7987. (Illus.). 32p. (ps-2). 1980. 9.95 (ISBN 0-690-04082-2, TYC-J); PLB 9.79 (ISBN 0-690-04083-0). T Y Crowell.

Shopping Book. Jan Sukus & William Dugan. (Illus.). (ps-1). 1972. PLB 5.38 (ISBN 0-307-68923-9, Golden Pr). Western Pub.

Shopping Center Development Handbook. ULI Commercial & Office Development Council. Ed. by Frank H. Spink, Jr. LC 77-79326. (Community Builders' Handbook Ser.). 1976. 29.00 (ISBN 0-87420-576-X). Urban Land.

Shopping Center Zoning. J. Ross McKeever. LC 73-88224. (Illus.). 73p. 1973. pap. 9.75 (ISBN 0-87420-069-5). Urban Land.

Shopping Centers, Nineteen Eighty-Eight: Answers for the Next Decade. Intro. by Albert Sussman. LC 79-84514. 1979. pap. text ed. 27.00 (ISBN 0-913598-07-0). Intl Coun Shop.

Shops & Markets. Stephanie Thompson. LC 78-64655. (Fact Finders Ser.). (Illus.). 1979. lib. bdg. 3.96 (ISBN 0-686-51131-X). Silver.

Shops & Markets. Paul White. (Junior Reference Ser.). (Illus.). 64p. (gr. 7 up). 1971. 7.95 (ISBN 0-7136-1155-3). Dufour.

Shoptalk. Mayerson. 1979. 13.95 (ISBN 0-7216-6207-2). Dryden Pr.

Shopwell Dairy Lovers' Cookbook. 6.95 (ISBN 0-916752-10-0). Green Hill.

Shopwork on the Farm. 2nd ed. Mack M. Jones. (Test Ed.). 1955. text ed. 17.32x (ISBN 0-07-032868-4, W); text-films o.p. (ISBN 0-685-14477-1). McGraw.

Shore of Pearls: Hainan Island in Early Times. Edward H. Schafer. LC 78-94990. (Illus.). 1970. 18.50x (ISBN 0-520-01592-4). U of Cal Pr.

Shore Wildflowers of California, Oregon, & Washington. Philip A. Munz. (Illus., Orig.). 1965. 6.50x o.p. (ISBN 0-520-00902-9); pap. 4.95 (ISBN 0-520-00903-7). U of Cal Pr.

Shorebirds & Predators: Birds of the Pacific Northwest, Part 1. John Rodgers. (Illus.). 1974. 10.00 (ISBN 0-88894-067-X, Pub. by Douglas & McIntyre). Madrona Pubs.

Shoreline & Sextant: Practical Coastline Navigation. John P. Budlong. 224p. 1980. pap. text ed. 9.95 (ISBN 0-442-21928-8). Van Nos Reinhold.

Shorelines Management: The Washington Experience. Ed. by Roger Leed. (Washington Sea Grant Ser.). 184p. 1973. pap. 6.50 (ISBN 0-295-95309-8). U of Wash Pr.

Shoremen: An Anthology of Eastern Shore Prose & Verse. Harold D. Jopp & R. H. Ingersoll. LC 74-7497. 1974. pap. 6.00 (ISBN 0-87033-186-8, Pub. by Tidewater). Cornell Maritime.

Short Account of Early Muslim Architecture. Creswell. 1968. 15.00x (ISBN 0-685-77130-X). Intl Bk Ctr.

Short Account of the History of Mathematics. W. W. Ball. LC 60-3187. 1960. lib. bdg. 13.50x (ISBN 0-88307-009-X). Gannon.

Short & Long. Elizabeth Gregory. (Illus.). 1981. 6.95 (ISBN 0-933184-09-3); pap. 4.95 (ISBN 0-933184-10-7). Flame Intl.

Short & Tall. Richard Scarry. (Golden Look-Look Bks.). (Illus.). (ps-1). 1976. PLB 5.38 (ISBN 0-307-61827-7, Golden Pr); pap. 0.95 (ISBN 0-307-11827-4). Western Pub.

Short Audit Case: The Valley Publishing Company. 3rd ed. Ben Barr & Robert L. Grinaker. 1976. text ed. 11.95x o.p. (ISBN 0-256-01629-1). Irwin.

Short Audit Case: The Valley Publishing Company. 4th ed. Ben Barr & Robert L. Grinaker. 1980. pap. 13.95x (ISBN 0-256-02327-1). Irwin.

Short Bengali-English, English-Bengali Dictionary. 3rd ed. Jack A. Dabbs. LC 78-149931. 1971. 4.00 o.s.i. (ISBN 0-911494-01-4). Dabbs.

Short Bible Reference System. Ed. by R. G. Bratcher. 1961. soft cover 2.85 (ISBN 0-686-14410-4, 08506). United Bible.

Short Bike Rides in Rhode Island. Howard Stone. LC 78-73547. (Illus.). 224p. (Orig.). pap. 4.95 (ISBN 0-87106-021-3). Globe Pequot.

Short Biography. Leonid I. Brezhnev. LC 77-30493. 1978. text ed. 15.00 (ISBN 0-08-022266-8); pap. text ed. 5.00 o.p. (ISBN 0-08-022265-X). Pergamon.

Short Calculus. 3rd ed. Daniel Saltz. 1980. text ed. 17.95 (ISBN 0-87620-820-0); answers to even-numbered problems free (ISBN 0-8302-8201-7). Goodyear.

Short Cases in Industrial Management. K. G. Lockyer & W. McEwan-Young. 1972. text ed. 14.75x (ISBN 0-7002-0177-7). Intl Ideas.

Short Cases in Marketing Management. K. J. Blois & D. W. Cowell. 1973. text ed. 16.50x (ISBN 0-7002-0207-2). Intl Ideas.

Short Course in Biochemistry. Albert L. Lehninger. LC 72-93199. (Illus.). 400p. 1973. text ed. 21.95x (ISBN 0-87901-024-X). Worth.

Short Course in Calculus. Bodh R. Gulati. LC 79-67409. 560p. 1981. text ed. 17.95 (ISBN 0-03-047466-3). Dryden Pr.

Short Course in Cloud Physics. 2nd ed. R. R. Rogers. 1979. 37.00 (ISBN 0-08-023040-7); pap. text ed. 17.50 (ISBN 0-08-023041-5). Pergamon.

Short Course in Cloud Physics. R. R. Rogers et al. Ed. by D. Ter Haar & J. W. Blaker. 224p. 1975. text ed. 19.80 o.p. (ISBN 0-08-019694-2). Pergamon.

Short Course in Foundation Engineering. Simons & Menzies. 1977. 19.95 (ISBN 0-408-00295-6). Butterworths.

Short Course in General Relativity. J. Foster & J. D. Nightingale. (Illus.). 1979. pap. text ed. 14.95 (ISBN 0-582-44194-3). Longman.

Short Course in PL-I PL-C. Ann L. Clark & Steven L. Mandell. (Series in Data Processing & Information Systems). 1978. pap. text ed. 9.95 (ISBN 0-8299-0219-8); instrs.' manual avail. (ISBN 0-8299-0465-4). West Pub.

Short Course in Sheet Metal Shop Theory. Richard S. Budzik. 128p. 1980. 12.50 o.p. (ISBN 0-912914-05-X). Prakken.

Short Course in Sheet Metal Shop Theory. 128p. 1980. 12.50 (ISBN 0-912914-05-X). Practical Pubns.

Short Course in Spoken English. Ronald Mackin. 1975. pap. 4.95 (ISBN 0-87789-137-0); cassettes 50.00 (ISBN 0-87789-140-0). Eng Language.

Short Course in Spoken English. Ronald Mackin & Marcia Evans. 150p. 1975. pap. text ed. 4.95x (ISBN 0-19-453062-0). Oxford U Pr.

Short-Cut Recipes. Ed. by Better Homes & Gardens Books Editors. (Illus.). 96p. 1981. 4.95 (ISBN 0-696-00655-3). Meredith Corp.

Short Cuts for Busy Dressmakers. Ann Ladbury. (Illus.). 144p. 1980. 24.00 (ISBN 0-7134-1811-7, Pub. by Batsford England); pap. 11.95 (ISBN 0-7134-1812-5). David & Charles.

Short Dictionary of Furniture. John Gloag. 1976. pap. 14.95 (ISBN 0-04-749009-8). Allen Unwin.

Short Discourse of the Three Kindes of Peppers in Common Use. Walter Bailey. LC 77-38145. (English Experience Ser.: No. 425). 48p. Repr. of 1588 ed. 7.00 (ISBN 90-221-0425-7). Walter J Johnson.

Short Economic History of Modern Japan. C. G. Allen. 272p. 1980. 19.95 (ISBN 0-312-71771-7). St Martin.

Short English Workbook. David E. Fear & Gerald J. Schiffhorst. 1979. pap. text ed. 4.95x (ISBN 0-673-15161-1). Scott F.

Short Fiction: A Critical Collection. 2nd ed. James R. Frakes & Isadore Traschen. LC 69-11382. 1968. pap. text ed. 9.95 (ISBN 0-13-809178-1). P-H.

Short Fiction of Edgar Allan Poe: An Annotated Edition. Edgar A. Poe. Ed. by Stuart Levine & Susan Levine. LC 74-12377. (LL Ser: No. 40). (Illus.). 672p. 1975. 14.95 o.p. (ISBN 0-672-51462-1); pap. text ed. 14.95 (ISBN 0-672-61032-9). Bobbs.

Short Fiction of Norman Mailer. Norman Mailer. LC 79-20189. 285p. 1980. Repr. of 1967 ed. 15.95 (ISBN 0-86527-303-0). Fertig.

Short Forms of the MMPI. Thomas R. Faschingbauer & Charles S. Newmark. LC 77-6934. 1978. 18.95 (ISBN 0-669-01641-1). Lexington Bks.

Short Guide to the High Plains, For Ed Dorn. Tom Clark. Ed. by Jeffrey Miller. 1981. signed limited ed. 15.00 (ISBN 0-932274-18-8); pap. 3.50 (ISBN 0-932274-17-X). Cadmus Eds.

Short Hikes & Strolls in Glacier National Park. Dick Nelson & Sharon Nelson. (Illus.). 48p. (Orig.). (gr. 7-12). 1978. pap. 2.95 (ISBN 0-915030-23-3). Tecolote Pr.

Short History of Africa. rev. ed. Roland Oliver & J. D. Fage. LC 63-11304. 1962. 15.00x (ISBN 0-8147-0329-1). NYU Pr.

Short History of Ale. Jimmy Young. LC 79-52373. (Illus.). 1979. 7.50 (ISBN 0-7153-7839-2). David & Charles.

Short History of American Law Enforcement. William J. Bopp & Donald O. Schultz. (Illus.). 192p. 1977. pap. 8.75 (ISBN 0-398-02479-0). C C Thomas.

Short History of American Poetry. Donald B. Stauffer. LC 69-13347. 1974. pap. 6.95 o.p. (ISBN 0-525-47318-1). Dutton.

Short History of American Rowing. Thomas Mendenhall. (Illus., Orig.). 1980. 14.95 (ISBN 0-89182-019-1); pap. 7.95 (ISBN 0-89182-026-4). Charles River Bks.

Short History of Anatomy & Physiology: From the Greeks to Harvey. Charles Singer. Orig. Title: Evolution of Anatomy. (Illus.). 1957. pap. text ed. 4.50 (ISBN 0-486-20389-1). Dover.

Short History of Biology. Isaac Asimov. LC 80-15464. (American Museum Science Bks.). (Illus.). ix, 189p. 1980. Repr. of 1964 ed. lib. bdg. 17.25x (ISBN 0-313-22583-4, ASSB). Greenwood.

Short History of Botany in the United States. Ed. by Joseph Ewan. 1969. 8.95 (ISBN 0-02-844360-8). Hafner.

Short History of Chess. Henry Davidson. 1968. 6.95 o.p. (ISBN 0-679-13035-7). McKay.

Short History of China. Hilda Hookham. 1972. pap. 2.50 (ISBN 0-451-61871-8, ME1871, Ment). NAL.

Short History of Chinese Philosophy. abr. ed. Yu-Lan Fung. Ed. by Derk Bedde. Orig. Title: History of Chinese Philosophy. 1966. pap. text ed. 5.95 (ISBN 0-02-910980-9). Free Pr.

Short History of Christianity. Ed. by Archibald G. Baker. LC 40-34185. 1940. 10.00x (ISBN 0-226-03529-8); pap. 7.50x (ISBN 0-226-03530-1). U of Chicago Pr.

Short History of Economic Progress. Y. S. Brenner. LC 68-21447. (Illus.). 1969. 24.00x (ISBN 0-678-05014-7). Kelley.

Short History of England. Reginald J. White. (Illus.). 1967. 38.50 (ISBN 0-521-06784-7); pap. 10.50x (ISBN 0-521-09439-9). Cambridge U Pr.

Short History of English Poetry. G. S. Fraser. 250p. 1981. 23.50x (ISBN 0-389-20174-X); pap. 9.95x (ISBN 0-389-20175-8). B&N.

Short History of France from Early Times to 1972. 2nd ed. J. H. Jackson. (Illus.). 260p. 1974. 34.95 (ISBN 0-521-20485-2); pap. 8.95x (ISBN 0-521-09864-5). Cambridge U Pr.

Short History of French Literature. I. C. Thimann. 1967. 15.00 (ISBN 0-08-012011-3); pap. 7.00 (ISBN 0-08-012010-5). Pergamon.

Short History of Germany: Eighteen Fifteen - Nineteen Forty-Five. Ernest J. Passant. 1962. 32.95 (ISBN 0-521-05915-1); pap. 8.95x (ISBN 0-521-09173-X). Cambridge U Pr.

Short History of Glass. Chloe Zerwick. (Illus.). 95p. 1981. pap. price not set (ISBN 0-486-24158-0). Dover.

Short History of Glass. Chloe Zerwick. LC 79-57251. (Illus.). 96p. 1980. pap. 5.00 (ISBN 0-87290-072-X). Corning.

Short History of Greek Mathematics. James Gow. LC 68-21639. 1968. 11.95 (ISBN 0-8284-0218-3). Chelsea Pub.

Short History of Ireland. 6th ed. James C. Beckett. 1975. 17.50x (ISBN 0-391-02079-X, Hutchinson U Lib); pap. text ed. 8.25x (ISBN 0-391-02080-3). Humanities.

Short History of Ireland. Martin Wallace. 1974. 10.95 (ISBN 0-7153-6306-9). David & Charles.

Short History of Italy. H. Hearder & Daniel P. Waley. (Illus.). 1963. pap. 9.95 (ISBN 0-521-09394-5, 394). Cambridge U Pr.

Short History of Latin America. Benjamin Keen & Mark Wasserman. 1979. pap. text ed. 13.50 (ISBN 0-395-27838-4). HM.

Short History of Marriage: Marriage Rites, Customs, & Folklore in Many Countries in All Ages. Ethel L. Urlin. LC 69-16071. 1969. Repr. of 1913 ed. 20.00 (ISBN 0-8103-3569-7). Gale.

Short History of Mexico. rev. ed. J. Patrick McHenry. LC 75-107354. 1970. pap. 1.95 (ISBN 0-385-02391-X, C363, Dolp). Doubleday.

Short History of Mexico. rev. ed. Selden Rodman. LC 80-6151. 264p. 1981. 14.95 (ISBN 0-8128-2808-9). Stein & Day.

Short History of Modern Greece. R. Clogg. LC 78-72083. (Illus.). 1979. 29.95 (ISBN 0-521-22479-9); pap. 9.95 (ISBN 0-521-29517-3). Cambridge U Pr.

Short History of North Africa. Jane S. Nickerson. LC 68-54233. 1961. 9.00x (ISBN 0-8196-0219-1). Biblo.

Short History of Opera. 2nd ed. Donald J. Grout. LC 64-11043. (gr. 9 up). 1965. text ed. 20.00x (ISBN 0-231-02422-3). Columbia U Pr.

Short History of Painting in America. Edgar P. Richardson. (Orig.). 1963. pap. 10.95 scp (ISBN 0-690-73377-1, HarpC); pap. text ed. 6.50 o.p. (ISBN 0-686-68500-8). Har-Row.

Short History of Roman Law: Being the First Part of His "Manuel Elementaire De Droit Romain.". Paul F. Girard. Tr. by A. H. Lefrox & J. H. Cameron. LC 79-1603. 1981. Repr. of 1906 ed. 18.50 (ISBN 0-88355-906-4). Hyperion Conn.

Short History of Russia. Richard D. Charques. 1958. pap. 3.95 o.p. (ISBN 0-525-47015-8). Dutton.

Short History of Scientific Ideas to 1900. Charles Singer. 1959. pap. 9.95x (ISBN 0-19-881049-0). Oxford U Pr.

Short History of Sierra Leone. new ed. Christopher Fyfe. (Illus.). 1979. pap. text ed. 5.50 (ISBN 0-582-60358-7). Longman.

Short History of Sierra Leone. Christopher Fyfe. (Illus., Orig.). 1962. pap. text ed. 3.25x (ISBN 0-582-60251-3). Humanities.

Short History of South Africa. Davis. 1979. pap. 5.95 (ISBN 0-582-60349-8). Longman.

Short History of Spanish Literature: Revised & Updated Edition. James R. Stamm. LC 78-53803. (Gotham Library). 1979. 16.00x (ISBN 0-8147-7791-0); pap. 7.00x (ISBN 0-8147-7792-9). NYU Pr.

Short History of Spanish Music. Ann Livermore. 262p. 1972. 40.50x (ISBN 0-7156-0634-4, Pub. by Duckworth England); pap. 13.50x (ISBN 0-7156-0886-X). Biblio Dist.

Short History of the American Nation. 2nd, abr. ed. John A. Garraty. (Illus.). 1977. pap. text ed. 14.95 scp o.p. (ISBN 0-06-042266-1, HarpC); instructor's manual avail. o.p. (ISBN 0-685-71546-9); scp student's review manual 6.50 o.p. (ISBN 0-06-044708-7). Har-Row.

Short History of the American Teilhard Association. Winifred McCulloch. 1979. pap. 2.00 (ISBN 0-89012-013-7). Anima Pubns.

Short History of the Art of Distillation from the Beginnings up to the Death of Cellier Blumenthal. Robert J. Forbes. LC 79-8608. Repr. of 1948 ed. 37.50 (ISBN 0-404-18470-7). AMS Pr.

Short History of the Camera. John Wade. 1978. pap. 13.95 o.p. (ISBN 0-85242-632-1, Pub. by Fountain). Morgan.

Short History of the Camera. John Wade. LC 79-670346. (Illus., Orig.). 1979. pap. text ed. 12.50x (ISBN 0-85242-640-2). Intl Pubns Serv.

Short History of the Egyptian People. Ernest A. Budge. 280p. 1980. lib. bdg. 30.00 (ISBN 0-8482-0148-5). Norwood Edns.

Short History of the English People, 2 Vols. John R. Green. 1960. Vol. 1. 21.00x (ISBN 0-460-00727-0, Evman); Vol. 2. 5.00x (ISBN 0-460-00728-9). Dutton.

Short History of the Episcopal Church. George Hodges. 1967. 1.10 (ISBN 0-686-28793-2). Forward Movement.

Short History of the French Revolution, 1789-1799. Albert Soboul. Tr. by Geoffrey Symcox. (Cal Ser.: No. 360). 1977. 18.50x (ISBN 0-520-02855-4); pap. 4.25x (ISBN 0-520-03419-8). U of Cal Pr.

Short History of the Gout & the Rheumatic Diseases. W. S. C. Copeman. 1964. 20.00x (ISBN 0-520-00267-9). U of Cal Pr.

Short History of the Hebrews: From the Patriarchs to Herod the Great. B. K. Rattey. (Illus.). 1976. pap. 6.95x (ISBN 0-19-832121-X). Oxford U Pr.

Short History of the Hungarian Communist Party. Mikos Molnar. LC 77-27898. (Special Studies on the Soviet Union & Eastern Europe Ser.). 1978. lib. bdg. 21.00 o.p. (ISBN 0-89158-332-7). Westview.

Short History of the International Economy Since 1850. 3rd ed. William Ashworth. 1976. text ed. 20.00x (ISBN 0-582-44060-2); pap. text ed. 12.95x (ISBN 0-582-44061-0). Longman.

Short History of the Mail Service. Carl H. Scheele. LC 69-12675. (Illus.). 250p. 1970. 8.95x o.p. (ISBN 0-87474-090-8). Smithsonian.

Short History of the Movies. 2nd ed. Gerald Mast. LC 75-14302. 1975. pap. 10.50 o.p. (ISBN 0-672-63719-7). Pegasus.

Short History of the Movies. Gerald Mast. LC 80-18024. (Illus.). 516p. 1980. pap. text ed. 13.95 (ISBN 0-672-61521-5). Bobbs.

Short History of the Printed Word. Warren Chappell. LC 72-127091. (Illus.). 1970. 12.50 o.p. (ISBN 0-394-44534-1). Knopf.

Short History of the Printed Word. Warren Chappell. LC 79-90409. (Nonpareil Bks.). (Illus.). 288p. 1980. pap. 9.95 (ISBN 0-87923-312-5). Godine.

Short History of the Twelve Buddhist Sects. Tr. by Bunyiu Nanjio from Japanese. (Studies in Japanese History & Civilization). 1979. Repr. of 1886 ed. 19.75 (ISBN 0-89093-252-2). U Pubns Amer.

Short History of the Vietnam War. Ed. by Allan R. Millett. LC 77-23623. (Midland Bks: No. 210). 224p. 1978. 12.50x (ISBN 0-253-35215-0); pap. 3.95x (ISBN 0-253-20210-8). Ind U Pr.

Short History of the Western Liturgy. Theodor Klauser. Tr. by John Halliburton from Ger. 1979. text ed. 14.95x (ISBN 0-19-213224-5); pap. text ed. 6.95x (ISBN 0-19-213223-7). Oxford U Pr.

Short History of Wales: Welsh Life & Customs. A. H. Dodd. 1977. pap. 11.95 (ISBN 0-7134-1466-9, Pub. by Batsford England). David & Charles.

Short History of Warfare. David H. Zook, Jr. & Robin Higham. LC 65-28533. (Illus.). 12.50 o.p. (ISBN 0-685-59133-6, H-587). Hippocrene Bks.

Short History of Western Music. Arthur Jacobs. 16.95 (ISBN 0-7153-5743-3). David & Charles.

Short History of World War I. James L. Stokesbury. LC 80-22206. (Illus.). 352p. 1981. 13.95 (ISBN 0-688-00128-9). Morrow.

Short History of World War I. James L. Stokesbury. LC 80-22207. (Illus.). 352p. 1981. pap. 7.95 (ISBN 0-688-00129-7, Quill). Morrow.

Short History of World War Two, 1939-1945. Peter Young. (Apollo Eds.). (Illus.). pap. 5.50 (ISBN 0-8152-0181-8, A181, TYC-T). T Y Crowell.

Short History of Yugoslavia. Ed. by Stephen Clissold et al. LC 66-20181. (Illus.). 1968. 32.95 (ISBN 0-521-04676-9); pap. 11.95x (ISBN 0-521-09531-X, 531). Cambridge U Pr.

Short Index to the Bible. Ed. by R. G. Bratcher & J. A. Thompson. 1973. pap. 1.15 (ISBN 0-8267-0007-1, 03519). United Bible.

Short Introduction to English Usage. J. J. Lamberts. 400p. 1981. Repr. lib. bdg. write for info. (ISBN 0-89874-328-1). Krieger.

Short Introduction to Modern Growth Theory. Ching-yao Haieh et al. LC 78-61916. 1978. pap. text ed. 9.00 (ISBN 0-8191-0628-3). U Pr of Amer.

Short Introduction to the History & Politics of South-East Asia. Richard Allen. (Illus.). 316p. 1968. 14.95 (ISBN 0-19-500815-4). Oxford U Pr.

Short Italian Dictionary, 2 vol. in 1. Ed. by A. Hoare. 59.50 (ISBN 0-521-05279-3). Cambridge U Pr.

Short Life. Thomas B. Allen. LC 77-11979. (YA) 1978. 9.95 o.p. (ISBN 0-399-11966-3). Berkley Pub.

Short Life: A Novel. Aharon Megged. Tr. by Miriam Arad from Hebrew. LC 80-13001. Orig. Title: Ha-Hayim ha-Ketsarim. 288p. 1980. 10.95 (ISBN 0-8008-7180-4). Taplinger.

Short Life of Charles Dickens with Selections from His Letters. Charles H. Jones. 260p. 1980. Repr. of 1900 ed. lib. bdg. 30.00 (ISBN 0-8414-5406-X). Folcroft.

Short Model Essays. Ann M. Taylor. (Orig.). 1981. pap. text ed. 6.95 (ISBN 0-316-83358-4); tchrs'. manual free (ISBN 0-316-83359-2). Little.

Short of Merger: Countywide Police Resource Pooling. George D. Eastman & Samuel G. Chapman. LC 75-36013. (Illus.). 1976. 17.95 (ISBN 0-669-00373-5). Lexington Bks.

Short Old French Dictionary for Students. Ed. by Kenneth Urwin. 108p. 1972. pap. 7.50x (ISBN 0-631-07970-X, Pub. by Basil Blackwell). Biblio Dist.

Short Plays. Anton Chekhov. Tr. by Ronald Hingley. 1969. pap. 2.95x o.p. (ISBN 0-19-281057-X, OPB). Oxford U Pr.

Short Reference Grammar of Iraqi Arabic. Wallace M. Erwin. (Richard Slade Harrell Arabic Ser). 392p. 1963. pap. 8.50 (ISBN 0-87840-002-8); Set. 2 cassettes 10.50 (ISBN 0-87840-013-3); write for info. five-inch reel set (ISBN 0-87840-018-4). Georgetown U Pr.

Short Reference Grammar of Moroccan Arabic. Richard S. Harrell. (Richard Slade Harrell Arabic Ser.). 263p. 1962. pap. 8.50 (ISBN 0-87840-006-0); one cassette 5.00 (ISBN 0-87840-016-8); write for info. five-inch reel (ISBN 0-87840-017-6). Georgetown U Pr.

Short-Run Economic Outlook for Higher Education. Carol Frances. 64p. 1980. 7.95 (ISBN 0-8268-1395-X). ACE.

Short Sentimental Journey & Other Stories. Italo Svevo. 1967. 17.50x (ISBN 0-520-01244-5). U of Cal Pr.

Short Short Stories. Norvin Pallas. (Newbury Hse Readers Ser.: Stage 4 - Intermediate Level). (Illus.). (gr. 7-12). 1981. pap. text ed. 2.80 (ISBN 0-88377-198-5). Newbury Hse.

Short Short Stories, 5 vols. Sullivan Assoc. pap. text ed. 3.75 ea. Learning Line.

Short Sketch of the Life of Mr. Lent Munson: Alexander Viets Criswold. Ed. by Wilcomb E. Washburn. Incl. Narrative of the Captivity & Sufferings of Mr. Ebenezer Fletcher of Newipswich. (Repr. of 1798; 2nd ed., repr. of 1813; 4th ed., enl., repr. of 1827); Surprizing Account of the Captivity of Miss Hannah Willis... to Which Is Added an Affecting History, of the Dreadful Distresses of Frederic Manheim's Family. Repr. of 1799 ed; Narrative of the Singular Adventures & Captivity of Mr. Thomas Barry, Among the Monsipi Indians, in the Unexplored Regions of North America. Repr. of 1800 ed. (Narratives of North American Indian Captivities Ser.: Vol. 24). 1980. lib. bdg. 44.00 (ISBN 0-8240-1648-3). Garland Pub.

Short Stories. Guy De Maupassant. 1956. 6.00x (ISBN 0-460-00907-9, Evman); pap. 8.95 (ISBN 0-460-01907-4). Dutton.

Short Stories of Edith Wharton, 1910-1937. Edith Wharton. 1975. lib. rep. ed. 30.00x (ISBN 0-684-14420-4, ScribT). Scribner.

Short Stories of Ernest Hemingway. Ernest Hemingway. 1938. lib. rep. ed. 25.00x (ISBN 0-684-15155-3, ScribT); pap. 5.95 (ISBN 0-684-71806-5, SL141, ScribT). Scribner.

Short Stories of Ernest Hemingway: Critical Essays. Ed. by Jackson J. Benson. LC 74-75815. xv, 375p. 1975. 14.75 (ISBN 0-8223-0320-5); pap. 7.75 (ISBN 0-8223-0386-8). Duke.

Short Stories of Grace Livingston Hill. Grace L. Hill. Ed. by J. E. Clauss. 1976. lib. bdg. 8.20 (ISBN 0-89190-101-9). Am Repr-Rivercity Pr.

Short Stories of Padriac Pearse. Ed. by Desmond Malguire. 117p. (Dual language Irish & Eng.). 1968. pap. 4.25 (ISBN 0-85342-117-X). Irish Bk Ctr.

Short Stories on Film. Carol A. Emmens. LC 78-13488. 1978. lib. bdg. 25.00x (ISBN 0-87287-146-0). Libs Unl.

Short Story: A Contemporary Looking Glass. Elliott L. Smith & Andrew W. Hart. 678p. 1981. pap. text ed. 9.95 (ISBN 0-394-32529-X). Random.

Short Story & the Oral Tradition. Paul Sherr. LC 70-101314. 1970. pap. text ed. 6.95x o.p. (ISBN 0-87835-002-0). Boyd & Fraser.

Short Story Index: Collections Indexed 1900-1978. 1979. 25.00 (ISBN 0-8242-0643-6). Wilson.

Short Story Reader. 3rd ed. Berkley & Saundra Gould. pap. 5.95 (ISBN 0-672-73292-0). Bobbs.

Short Story Theories. Ed. by Charles E. May. LC 75-36982. xiv, 251p. 1976. 13.00x (ISBN 0-8214-0189-0); pap. 5.95x (ISBN 0-8214-0221-8). Ohio U Pr.

Short Story Writing. Charls R. Barrett. 257p. 1981. Repr. lib. bdg. 30.00 (ISBN 0-8495-0465-1). Arden Lib.

Short Syntax of New Testament Greek. 5th ed. Henry P. Nunn. 1931. text ed. 7.50x (ISBN 0-521-09941-2). Cambridge U Pr.

Short-Term Approaches to Psychotheraphy, Vol. 3. Ed. by Henry Grayson. LC 78-27605. (New Directions in Psychotherapy). 1979. 22.95 (ISBN 0-87705-345-6). Human Sci Pr.

Short-Term Changes in Neural Activity & Behaviour. Ed. by G. Horn & R. A. Hinde. LC 71-121367. (Illus.). 1970. 92.00 (ISBN 0-521-07942-X). Cambridge U Pr.

Short-Term Contracts in Social Work. Joan M. Hutten. (Library of Social Work Ser.). 1977. 15.00x (ISBN 0-7100-8584-2); pap. 7.95 (ISBN 0-7100-8585-0). Routledge & Kegan.

Short-Term Dynamic Therapy. Ed. by H. Davanloo. LC 80-67986. 1980. 30.00 (ISBN 0-87668-418-5). Aronson.

Short-Term Economic Reports: Colombia, Vol. 1. 2nd ed. OAS General Secretariat. (Short Term Economic Reports Ser.). 77p. 1980. pap. text ed. 5.00 (ISBN 0-8270-1261-6). OAS.

Short-Term Economic Reports, Vol. IV: Brazil-Relatorios Economicos De Curto Prazo, Brazil. (Eng. & Portuguese.). 1978. pap. 2.00 Eng. ed. (ISBN 0-8270-3675-2); pap. 2.00 Port. ed. (ISBN 0-8270-3615-9). OAS.

Short-Term Economic Reports, Vol. V: Venezuela-Informes Economicos De Corto Plazo, Venezuela. (Eng. & Span.). 1978. pap. 2.00 Eng. ed. (ISBN 0-8270-3595-0); pap. 2.00 Span. ed. (ISBN 0-8270-3625-6). OAS.

Short Textbook Ear Nose & Throat. 2nd ed. R. Pracy et al. (Illus.). 1975. pap. 7.00 o.p. (ISBN 0-397-58151-3). Lippincott.

Short Textbook of Kidney Disease. Adrian P. Douglas & David Kerr. (Illus.). 1968. 12.00 o.p. (ISBN 0-397-58081-9). Lippincott.

Short Textbook of Medicine. 5th ed. J. C. Houston et al. (Illus., Orig.). 1975. pap. 14.75 o.p. (ISBN 0-397-58159-9). Lippincott.

Short Textbook of Medicine. 6th ed. J. C. Houston et al. (Illus., Orig.). 1980. pap. 14.75 (ISBN 0-397-58266-8). Lippincott.

Short Time to Live. Mervyn Jones. 294p. 1981. 12.95 (ISBN 0-312-72221-4). St Martin.

Short-Title Catalogue of Books Printed on the Continent of Europe, Fifteen Hundred to Sixteen Hundred, in Aberdeen University Library. Compiled by H. J. Drummond. 326p. 1979. text ed. 65.00x (ISBN 0-19-714106-4). Oxford U Pr.

Short Title Catalogue of French Books 1601-1700 in the Library of the British Museum. V. F. Goldsmith. 1973. 90.00 (ISBN 0-7129-0575-8, Dist. by Shoe String). Dawson Pub.

Short Treatise of Geometrie. John Babington. LC 76-25837. (English Experience Ser.: No. 296). 200p. Repr. of 1635 ed. 35.00 (ISBN 90-221-0296-3). Walter J Johnson.

Short Treatise of the Laws of England. Walter Mantell et al. Ed. by David S. Berkowitz & Samuel E. Thorne. LC 77-86578. (Classics of English Legal History in the Modern Era Ser.: Vol. 17). 351p. 1979. lib. bdg. 40.00 (ISBN 0-8240-3066-4). Garland Pub.

Short Unit on General Semantics. Louis E. Glorfeld. LC 69-17339. 125p. 1969. pap. text ed. 3.95x (ISBN 0-02-474210-4, 47421). Macmillan.

Short View of the Immorality, & Profaneness of the English Stage. Jeremy Collier. LC 70-170438. (English Stage Ser.: Vol. 22). lib. bdg. 50.00 (ISBN 0-8240-0605-4). Garland Pub.

Short Vindication of the Relapse & the Provok'd Wife. Sir John Vanbrugh. LC 75-170442. (English Stage Ser.: Vol. 28). lib. bdg. 50.00 (ISBN 0-8240-0611-9). Garland Pub.

Short Vowels. Virginia Polish. (Starting off with Phonics Ser.: Bk. 5). (Illus.). (gr. k). 1980. pap. text ed. 2.12 (ISBN 0-87895-055-9); tchrs. ed. 2.00 (ISBN 0-87895-065-6). Modern Curr.

Short Walk. Alice Childress. 336p. 1981. pap. 3.50 (ISBN 0-380-54239-0, 54239, Bard). Avon.

Short Walk in the Hindu Kush. Ed. by Eric Newby. 1981. pap. 4.95 (ISBN 0-14-002663-0). Penguin.

Short Walks Along the Maine Coast. Ruth Sadlier & Paul Sadlier. LC 76-51125. (Illus.). 1977. pap. 3.50 (ISBN 0-87106-077-9). Globe Pequot.

Short Walks on Cape Cod. Ruth Sadlier & Paul Sadlier. LC 75-34252. (Illus.). 896p. 1976. pap. 4.95 (ISBN 0-87106-066-3). Globe Pequot.

Short-War Illusion: German Policy, Strategy & Domestic Affairs, August-December 1914. Lancelot L. Farrar, Jr. LC 72-95267. (Twentieth Century Ser.: No. 7). (Illus.). 207p. 1973. text ed. 5.95 (ISBN 0-87436-118-4); pap. text ed. 2.50 (ISBN 0-87436-119-2). ABC-Clio.

Short Way to Lower Scoring. Paul Runyan & Dick Aultman. LC 79-52549. (Illus.). 175p. 1980. 13.50 (ISBN 0-914178-27-X, 24921-5). Golf Digest.

Shortchanged: Minorities & Women in Banking. Ed. by Rodney Alexander & Elizabeth Sapery. LC 73-79033. 190p. 1973. 15.00 (ISBN 0-8046-7066-8); pap. 7.95 (ISBN 0-8046-7067-6). Kennikat.

Shortcut Cooking. rev. ed. Charlotte Erickson. (Illus.). 1981. pap. 6.95 (ISBN 0-8092-5887-0). Contemp Bks.

Shortcut Gourmet Cookbook. Leo Kuhle & Debbie Monroe. (Illus., Orig.). 1981. pap. 6.95 (ISBN 0-933474-20-2, Gabriel Bks). Minn Scholarly.

Shortcut to Devil's Claw. William O. Turner. (Orig.). 1977. pap. 1.25 o.p. (ISBN 0-425-03410-0). Berkley Pub.

Shortcuts to Elegance. Editors of Time-Life Books. LC 73-91757. (Art of Sewing). (Illus.). (gr. 6 up). 1974. PLB 11.97 (ISBN 0-8094-1711-1, Pub. by Time-Life). Silver.

Shorte & Briefe Narration of the Two Navigations to Newe Fraunce. Jacques Cartier. Tr. by J. Florio. LC 73-6110. (English Experience Ser.: No. 718). 1975. Repr. of 1580 ed. 8.00 (ISBN 90-221-0718-3). Walter J Johnson.

Shortened CPA Law Review. 4th ed. George C. Thompson & Gerald P. Brady. 1977. 19.95x (ISBN 0-534-00496-2). Wadsworth Pub.

Shortened CPA Law Review. George C. Thompson & Gerald P. Brady. (Business Ser.). 560p. 1980. text ed. 17.95x (ISBN 0-686-69155-5). Kent Pub Co.

Shorter Cambridge Medieval History, 2 vols. C. W. Previte-Orton. Incl. Vol. 1. The Later Roman Empire to the Twelfth Century. (Illus.). 644p (ISBN 0-521-20962-5). pap. (ISBN 0-521-09976-5); Vol. 2. The Twelfth Century to the Renaissance. (Illus.). 558p. pap. (ISBN 0-521-09977-3). (Medieval History Ser). 1975. 53.95 ea.; pap. 15.95 ea. Cambridge U Pr.

Shorter Cambridge Medieval History, 2 vols. Ed. by C. W. Previte-Orton. Set. 89.50 (ISBN 0-521-05993-3); Set. pap. 27.95 (ISBN 0-521-08758-9). Cambridge U Pr.

Shorter Catechism: A Study Manual, 2 vols. G. I. Williamson. Vol. 1. pap. 3.75 (ISBN 0-87552-539-3); Vol. 2. pap. 3.75 (ISBN 0-87552-540-7). Presby & Reformed.

Shorter Catechism Explained from Scripture. Thomas Vincent. (Puritan Paperbacks). 282p. (Orig.). 1980. pap. 3.95 (ISBN 0-85151-314-X). Banner of Truth.

Shorter Catechism with Scripture Proofs. Westminster Assembly. Date not set. 0.75 (ISBN 0-686-28948-X). Banner of Truth.

Shorter Encyclopedia of Islam. Ed. by H. A. Gibb & J. H. Kramers. (Illus.). 1957. 45.00x (ISBN 0-8014-0150-X). Cornell U Pr.

Shorter Life of Christ. Donald Guthrie. LC 71-120039. (Contemporary Evangelical Perspectives Ser). 1970. kivar 4.95 (ISBN 0-310-25441-8). Zondervan.

Shorter Novels of Herman Melville. Ed. by Raymond Weaver. 1977. pap. 2.50 (ISBN 0-449-30798-0, Prem). Fawcett.

Shorter Poems & Songs from the Plays & Masques. William Davenant. Ed. by A. M. Gibbs. 568p. 1972. 39.00x (ISBN 0-19-812434-1). Oxford U Pr.

Shorter Science & Civilisation in China, Vol. 1. C. A. Ronan. LC 77-82513. (Illus.). 1978. 29.95 (ISBN 0-521-21821-7). Cambridge U Pr.

Shorter Science & Civilization in China, Vol. 1. Colin A. Ronan & J. Needham. LC 77-82513. (Illus.). 337p. 1980. pap. 12.95 (ISBN 0-521-29286-7). Cambridge U Pr.

Shorter Works for Pianoforte Solo. Franz Schubert. 199p. 1970. pap. 6.50 (ISBN 0-486-22648-4). Dover.

Shorterhand Dictionary of Common Words. G. A. Reid & Evelina Thompson. Ed. by M. Angus. 1974. pap. 5.10 (ISBN 0-8224-4154-3). Pitman Learning.

Shorthand. John C. Evans. 1963. pap. 2.95 (ISBN 0-06-463225-3, EH 225, EH). Har-Row.

Shorthand Guide to Legal Terminology. 1981 ed. 700p. 1978. 12.00 (ISBN 0-87526-211-2). Gould.

Shorthand in Four Days. rev. ed. Benjamin Friedlander. LC 52-3478. 24p. 1974. pap. 2.98 o.p. (ISBN 0-917520-02-5). Fineline.

Shortwave Listener's Handbook. rev., 2nd ed. Norman Fallon. (Illus., Orig.). 1976. pap. 5.95 (ISBN 0-8104-5044-5). Hayden.

Shortwave Listerner's Guide. 8th ed. H. Charles Woodruff. LC 79-67132. 1980. pap. 5.95 (ISBN 0-672-21655-8). Bobbs.

Shosha. Isaac B. Singer. 1979. pap. 2.95 (ISBN 0-449-23997-7, Crest). Fawcett.

Shoshone Indians. Incl. The Gosiute Indians. Carling Malouf; The Shoshones in the Rocky Mt. Area. Ake Hultkrantz; The Indians in Yellowstone Park. Ake Hultkrantz; Findings of Fact, & Opinion. Indian Claims Commission. (American Indian Ethnohistory Ser: California & Basin Plateau Indians). (Illus.). lib. bdg. 42.00 (ISBN 0-8240-0735-2). Garland Pub.

Shoshoni Indians of Inyo County, California. Charles N. Irwin. (Ballena Press Publications in Archaeology, Ethnology & History: No. 15). (Illus.). 114p. (Orig.). 1980. pap. 6.95 (ISBN 0-87919-090-6). Ballena Pr.

Shoshonis: Sentinels of the Rockies. Virginia C. Trenholm & Maurine Carley. (Civilization of the American Indian Ser: No. 74). (Illus.). 1964. pap. 8.95 (ISBN 0-8061-1055-4). U of Okla Pr.

Shostakovich Symphonies. Hugh Ottaway. LC 77-82651. (BBC Music Guides: No. 39). (Illus.). 64p. (Orig.). 1978. pap. 2.95 (ISBN 0-295-95573-2). U of Wash Pr.

Shostakovitch. Norman Kay. (Oxford Studies of Composers Ser). 72p. 1972. pap. 6.95x (ISBN 0-19-315422-6). Oxford U Pr.

Shot History of Aviation. Keith Woodmansee. LC 65-14328. 1965. 4.95 o.p. (ISBN 0-8168-8400-5); pap. 4.95 o.p. (ISBN 0-8168-8404-8). Aero.

Shot in the Ass with Pesos: A Collection of Frontier Tales. Budge Ruffner. (Illus.). 112p. (Orig.). 1979. pap. 4.95 (ISBN 0-918080-11-8). Treasure Chest.

Shotcrete for Ground Support: Proceedings, SP-54. Engineering Foundation Conference on Shotcrete, 1976. 1977. 29.00 (ISBN 0-685-87992-5) (ISBN 0-685-87993-3). ACI.

Shotgun & the Shooter. Percy Stanbury & G. L. Carlisle. 1978. 11.95 o.p. (ISBN 0-214-66874-6, 8029, Dist. by Arco). Barrie & Jenkins.

Shotgun Digest. 2nd ed. Jack Lewis & Jack Mitchell. 288p. 1980. pap. 8.95 (ISBN 0-910676-13-5). DBI.

Shotgun Gap. W. F. Bragg. 1981. pap. 1.75 (ISBN 0-8439-0895-5, Leisure Bks). Nordon Pubns.

Shotgun Marksmanship. Percy Stanbury & G. L. Carlisle. 1978. 11.95 o.p. (ISBN 0-214-20065-5, 8030, Dist. by Arco). Barrie & Jenkins.

Shotgun Marshal. Wade Everett. 1981. pap. 1.75 (ISBN 0-345-29434-3). Ballantine.

Shotguns & Cartridges for Game & Clays. 3rd ed. Gough Thomas. (Illus.). 254p. 1976. 25.00 (ISBN 0-7136-1583-4). Transatlantic.

Shots at Whitetails. rev. ed. Lawrence R. Koller. LC 78-98642. (Illus.). 1970. 12.50 o.p. (ISBN 0-394-44526-0). Knopf.

Should Anyone Say Forever on Making, Keeping & Breaking Commitments. Haughey, John C., S.J. LC 74-12690. 1977. pap. 2.45 (ISBN 0-385-13261-1, Im). Doubleday.

Should Christians Smoke? Gordon Lindsay. 1.00 o.p. (ISBN 0-89985-009-X). Christ Nations.

Should Government Encourage Homeownership? Raymond J. Struyk. (Institute Paper). 85p. 1977. pap. 5.50 (ISBN 0-87766-192-8, 18700). Urban Inst.

Should We Limit Science & Technology. Ed. by L. Steg. 1976. pap. text ed. 16.25 (ISBN 0-08-019981-X). Pergamon.

Should We Stop Teaching Art? C. R. Ashbee. Ed. by Peter Stansky & Rodney Shewan. LC 76-17774. (Aesthetic Movement & the Arts & Crafts Movement Ser.). 1978. Repr. of 1911 ed. lib. bdg. 44.00x (ISBN 0-8240-2478-8). Garland Pub.

Shoulder Lesions. 3rd ed. H. F. Moseley. 1969. 57.00x o.p. (ISBN 0-443-00634-2). Churchill.

Shoulder Pain. 2nd ed. Rene Cailliet. 1981. 9.95 (ISBN 0-8036-1613-9). Davis Co.

Shoulder Reconstruction. C. S. Neer. (Illus.). 1981. text ed. write for info. Churchill.

Shout Against the Wind. Mary Ray. (Faber Fanfares Ser.). (Illus.). 176p. (Orig.). (gr. 4-9). 1980. pap. 3.25 (ISBN 0-571-11489-X, Pub. by Faber & Faber). Merrimack Bk Serv.

Shout at the Devil. Wilbur Smith. LC 77-87166. 1978. Repr. of 1968 ed. lib. bdg. 12.50x (ISBN 0-8376-0421-4). Bentley.

Shout in the Street. Roger W. Thomas. Ed. by Orrin Root. LC 76-47988. 1977. pap. 1.95 o.p. (ISBN 0-87239-124-8, 40041). Standard Pub.

Shout It from the Housetops: The Story of the Founder of the Christian Broadcasting Network. Pat Robertson & Jamie Buckingham. LC 72-76591. 248p. 1972. pap. 2.95 (ISBN 0-88270-097-9). Logos.

Shouting Signpainters: A Literary & Political Account of Quebec Revolutionary Nationalism. Malcolm Reid. LC 75-158922. 320p. 1972. 8.95 o.p. (ISBN 0-85345-154-0, CL-1540); pap. 3.95 (ISBN 0-85345-283-0, PB-2830). Monthly Rev.

Show & Tell. Patricia Relf. (Sesame Street Early Bird Bks). (Illus.). 32p. (ps). 1981. 3.50 (ISBN 0-307-11606-9, Golden Pr). Western Pub.

Show Jumper. Dorian Williams. LC 70-101235. (Illus.). 1968. pap. 1.95 o.p. (ISBN 0-668-02817-3). Arco.

Show Me the Way. Coye F. Riley. 1981. 4.74 (ISBN 0-8062-1588-7). Carlton.

Show of Force. Charles D. Taylor. 384p. 1981. pap. 2.95 (ISBN 0-441-76197-6). Charter Bks.

Show of Force. Charles D. Taylor. 1980. 11.95 (ISBN 0-312-72314-8). St Martin.

Show of Hands: Say It in Sign Language. Mary Beth Sullivan & Linda Bourke. LC 80-15997. (Illus.). 96p. (gr. 4-8). 1980. PLB 6.95 (ISBN 0-201-07456-7, 7456, A-W Childrens). A-W.

Show People. Kenneth Tynan. 1981. pap. 2.95 (ISBN 0-425-04750-4). Berkley Pub.

Show Racer. Douglas McClary. (Illus.). 1976. 11.95 (ISBN 0-571-10761-3, Pub. by Faber & Faber). Merrimack Bk Serv.

Show Your Own Dog. Virginia Nichols. 1970. 9.95 (ISBN 0-87666-661-6, PS607). TFH Pubns.

Showdown. Errol Flynn. 1976. Repr. of 1946 ed. lib. bdg. 16.95x (ISBN 0-89966-094-0). Buccaneer Bks.

Showdown at Eureka. James Wesley. (YA) 1978. 5.954 (ISBN 0-685-85782-4, Avalon). Bouregy.

Showdown at the MB Ranch. James Wesley. 192p. (YA) 1976. 5.95 (ISBN 0-685-66575-5, Avalon). Bouregy.

Showdown: Western Gunfighters in Moments of Truth. Herman Toepperwein. LC 74-84581. (Illus.). 101p. 1974. 8.95 (ISBN 0-89052-013-5). Madrona Pr.

Showers of Sunlight. Donna Vitek. 192p. (Orig.). 1980. pap. 1.50 (ISBN 0-671-57047-1). S&S.

Showing Livestock. Edward Hart. LC 78-74086. 1979. 14.95 (ISBN 0-7153-7537-7). David & Charles.

Showing Your Dog. Leslie Perrins. (Foyle's Handbks). (Illus.). 1973. 3.95 (ISBN 0-685-55790-1). Palmetto Pub.

Showing Your Dog. Leslie Perrins. LC 76-11724. (Illus.). 1976. bds. 2.25 o.p. (ISBN 0-668-03977-9). Arco.

Showmanship in the Dining Room. Bruce H. Axler. 1974. pap. 3.95 (ISBN 0-672-96117-2). Bobbs.

Shree Rudram: Namakam & Chamakam. Illus. by SYDA Foundation. (Illus., Orig.). 1978. pap. 3.50 (ISBN 0-914602-64-0). SYDA Found.

Shrewsbury, Vermont: Our Town As It Was. Dawn Hance. LC 80-69447. 328p. 1980. 20.00 (ISBN 0-914960-28-8). Academy Bks.

Shrieks at Midnight: Macabre Poems, Eerie & Humorous. Ed. by Sara Brewton & John E. Brewton. LC 69-11824. (Illus.). (gr. 4 up). 1969. 8.95 (ISBN 0-690-73518-9, TYC-J). T Y Crowell.

Shrikant. Saratchandra Chattopadhyaya. 168p. 1969. pap. 2.50 (ISBN 0-88253-028-3). Ind-US Inc.

Shrimp & Anemone. L. P. Hartley. 1963. pap. 2.95 (ISBN 0-571-07061-2, Pub. by Faber & Faber). Merrimack Bk Serv.

Shrimp & Prawn Farming in the Western Hemisphere: State of the Art Review & Status Assessment. Ed. by Joe A. Hanson & Harold L. Goodwin. 1977. 29.00 (ISBN 0-12-786626-4). Acad Pr.

Shrimpers Woman. Patti Beckman. 192p. 1981. pap. 1.50 (ISBN 0-671-57054-4). S&S.

Shrimps of the Pacific Coast of Canada. 280p. 1981. 32.50 (ISBN 0-660-10177-7, SSC 148, SSC). Unipub.

Shringar: The Golden Book of Indian Hair Styles. Earl Cumine. (Illus.). 1975. pap. 2.50 English, Urdu, & Tamil (ISBN 0-88253-454-8). Ind-US Inc.

Shrinkage & Creep in Concrete. ACI Committee 209. (Bibliography: No. 10). 1972. pap. 26.25 (ISBN 0-685-85150-8, B-10) (ISBN 0-685-85151-6). ACI.

Shrinking of Treehorn. Florence P. Heide. (gr. k-3). 1979. pap. 1.75 (ISBN 0-440-47684-4, YB). Dell.

Shrinking Perimeter: Unionism & Labor Relations in the Manufacturing Sector. Ed. by Hervey A. Juris & Myron Roomkin. LC 79-1864. 240p. 1980. 22.95 (ISBN 0-669-02939-4). Lexington Bks.

Shrinking Political Arena: Participation & Ethnicity in African Politics, with a Case of Uganda. Nelson Kasfir. LC 73-85790. 320p. 1976. 33.75x (ISBN 0-520-02576-8). U of Cal Pr.

Shrinking Pond. Juanita T. Osborne. 192p. (YA) 1974. 5.95 (ISBN 0-685-39179-5, Avalon). Bouregy.

Shropshire Lad. A. E. Housman. 100p. 1981. Repr. lib. bdg. 9.95x (ISBN 0-89966-285-4). Buccaneer Bks.

Shroud of Turin: The Burial Cloth of Jesus Christ. Ian Wilson. LC 79-1942. (Illus.). 1979. pap. 4.50 (ISBN 0-385-15042-3, Im). Doubleday.

Shrouded Walls. Susan Howatch. 1978. pap. 2.25 (ISBN 0-449-23385-5, Crest). Fawcett.

Shrouded Walls of Boranga. Mike Sirota. (Ro-Lan Ser.: No. 2). 304p. (Orig.). 1980. pap. 1.95 (ISBN 0-89083-677-9). Zebra.

Shrubs & Vines for Southern Landscapes. Bill Adams. LC 76-15455. (Illus.). 1979. pap. 3.95 (ISBN 0-88415-804-7). Pacesetter Pr.

Shrubs for All Seasons. Ann Bonar. (Leisure Plan Books in Color). pap. 2.95 (ISBN 0-600-44175-X). Transatlantic.

Shrunken Planets. Robert Louthan. LC 79-54883. 64p. 1980. pap. 4.95 (ISBN 0-914086-28-6). Alicejamesbooks.

Shtetl & Other Yiddish Novellas. Ruth R. Wisse. LC 73-10252. (Library of Jewish Studies). 368p. 1973. 6.95x o.p. (ISBN 0-87441-201-3). Behrman.

Shtetl Book. Diane K. Roskies & David G Roskies. pap. 8.95x (ISBN 0-685-56215-8). Ktav.

Shtetl Finder. Chester G. Cohen. 1980. pap. 8.25. Periday.

Shubert: A Musical Portrait. Alfred Einstein. (Music Ser.). ix, 343p. 1981. Repr. of 1951 ed. lib. bdg. 27.50 (ISBN 0-306-76083-5). Da Capo.

Shudder Pulps. Robert Kenneth Jones. LC 74-82614. 1975. 11.95 (ISBN 0-913960-04-7). Fax Collect.

Shudders. Ed. by Ross R. Olney. (gr. 3 up). 1979. pap. 1.25 (ISBN 0-307-21617-9, Golden Pr). Western Pub.

Shufflebrain. Paul Pietsch. (Illus.). 288p. 1981. 10.95 (ISBN 0-395-29480-0). HM.

Shula: Code Name the Pearl. Aviezier Golan & Danny Pinkas. 1981. pap. 3.50 (ISBN 0-440-17805-3). Dell.

Shulamith. Meera Mahadevan. (Indian Novel Ser.). 208p. 1976. 8.50 (ISBN 0-89253-047-2). Ind-US Inc.

Shuster Mission & the Persian Constitutional Revolution. Robert A. McDaniel. LC 72-96696. (Studies in Middle Eastern History: No. 1). 1974. 25.00x (ISBN 0-88297-004-6). Bibliotheca.

Shuttered Room & Other Tales of Horror. H. P. Lovecraft. 1974. pap. 1.50 o.p. (ISBN 0-345-24302-1). Ballantine.

Shuttered Window. Elizabeth Levy. (Orig.). (gr. k-6). 1981. pap. 1.95 (ISBN 0-440-47980-0, YB). Dell.

Shuttle. Robert M. Powers. LC 79-652. (Illus.). 256p. 1979. 16.95 o.p. (ISBN 0-8117-1686-4); pap. 12.95 (ISBN 0-8117-2112-4). Stackpole.

Shuttle-Craft Book of American Hand-Weaving. rev. ed. Mary M. Atwater. (Illus.). 1951. 16.95 (ISBN 0-02-504380-3). Macmillan.

Shuttle Down. Lee Corey. 224p. (Orig.). 1981. pap. 2.25 (ISBN 0-345-29262-6, Del Rey). Ballantine.

Shuttle: The World's First Spaceship. Robert M. Powers. 1980. pap. 2.75 (ISBN 0-446-95331-8). Warner Bks.

Shuttlecock Action. Ballard J. Moore & Thomas E. Henderson. (Illus.). 1977. pap. text ed. 4.50 (ISBN 0-8403-1773-5). Kendall-Hunt.

Shu'Ubiyya in Al'Andalus: The Risala of Ibn Garcia & Five Refutations. James T. Monroe. (U. C. Publ. in Near Eastern Studies: Vol. 13). 1970. pap. 7.50x (ISBN 0-520-09307-0). U of Cal Pr.

Shy Leopardess: The Neustrian Cycle, Bk. 3. Leslie Barringer. Ed. by R. Reginald & Douglas Menville. LC 80-19240. (Newcastle Forgotten Fantasy Library Ser.: Vol. 13). 392p. 1980. Repr. of 1977 ed. lib. bdg. 11.95x (ISBN 0-89370-512-8). Borgo Pr.

Shy Ones. Lynn Hall. (YA) (gr. 9-12). 1977. pap. 1.50 (ISBN 0-380-45310-X, 45310, Camelot). Avon.

Shy Stegosaurus of Cricket Creek. Evelyn S. Lampman. LC 55-9233. (gr. 3-7). 1955. 6.95 o.p. (ISBN 0-385-07490-5). Doubleday.

Shylock & Shakespeare. Abraham Morevski. LC 67-19382. 112p. 1967. 3.95 (ISBN 0-87529-056-6). Fireside Bks.

Shyness. Philip Zimbardo. 1978. pap. 2.25 (ISBN 0-515-04587-X). Jove Pubns.

Shyp of Folys of the Worlde. Sebastian Brant. Tr. by Alexander Barcley. LC 74-25743. (English Experience Ser.: No. 229). 1970. Repr. of 1509 ed. 76.00 (ISBN 90-221-0229-7). Walter J Johnson.

SI Metric Handbook. Feirer. 1977. text ed. 25.00 (ISBN 0-87002-908-8). Bennett IL.

SI Metric Handbook. John Feirer. (Illus.). 1977. 27.50 (ISBN 0-87002-908-8, ScribT). Scribner.

Si Units for Nursing. J. Glenn. 1981. pap. text ed. 5.15 (ISBN 0-06-318180-0, Pub. by Har-Row Ltd England). Har-Row.

Si Yo Puedo, Tu Tambien. (Spanish Bks.). 1977. 1.50 (ISBN 0-8297-0599-6). Life Pubs Intl.

Siam Directory, 1979-80. 24th ed. LC 48-11053. 1979. 40.00x (ISBN 0-8002-2329-2). Intl Pubns Serv.

Siamese Cat. Phyllis Lauder. (Illus.). 1979. 9.95 o.p. (ISBN 0-684-16078-1, ScribT). Scribner.

Siamese Cat. Phyllis Lauder. 1978. 19.95 (ISBN 0-7134-1733-1, Pub. by Batsford England). David & Charles.

Siamese Cats. Louise B. Van Der Meid. (Orig.). pap. 2.00 (ISBN 0-87666-183-5, M509). TFH Pubns.

Siamese Fighting Fish. Myron Gordon & Herbert R. Axelrod. pap. 2.00 (ISBN 0-87666-145-2, M536). TFH Pubns.

Siamese White. Maurice Collis. (Orig.). 1965. pap. 4.95 (ISBN 0-571-06511-2, Pub. by Faber & Faber). Merrimack Bk Serv.

Sibelius, Vol. 1. Erik Tawaststjerna. LC 75-13147. 330p. 1976. 38.50x (ISBN 0-520-03014-1). U of Cal Pr.

Siberia. Emil Lengyel. LC 73-14873. (First Bks). (Illus.). 72p. (gr. 5-8). 1974. PLB 4.90 o.p. (ISBN 0-531-00821-5). Watts.

Siberia: The Land Beyond the Mountains. Leonid Shinkarev. 352p. 1973. 7.95 o.s.i. (ISBN 0-02-610520-9). Macmillan.

Siberian Huskies. Beverly Pisano. (Illus.). 128p. 1979. 2.95 (ISBN 0-87666-677-2, KW-068). TFH Pubns.

Sibylline Oracles of Egyptian Judaism. John J. Collins. LC 74-81099. (Society of Biblical Literature. Dissertation Ser.). 1975. pap. 7.50 (ISBN 0-89130-260-3, 060113). Scholars Pr Ca.

Sibyl's Dream. Mary Helen. 1980. deluxe ed. 14.95 autographed (ISBN 0-912492-18-X). Pyquag.

Sicher's Oral Anatomy. 7th ed. E. Lloyd DuBrul. LC 80-15943. (Illus.). 578p. 1980. text ed. 27.95 (ISBN 0-8016-4605-7). Mosby.

Sicilian. T. D. Harding & P. R. Markland. 1975. pap. 13.50 (ISBN 0-7134-3209-8, Pub. by Batsford England). David & Charles.

Sicilian Accelerated Dragons. David Levy. 1975. 17.50 (ISBN 0-7134-3031-1, Pub. by Batsford England). David & Charles.

Sicilian Antigruppo. Ed. by Stanley H. Barkan & Saverio A. Scammacca. (Illus.). 30p. Date not set. 5.00 (ISBN 0-89304-008-8). Cross Cult.

Sicilian Defence, Bk. 1. S. Gligoric & V. Sokolov. 1970. pap. 10.50 (ISBN 0-08-017276-8). Pergamon.

Sicilian Defence Series 8: Lines with B-QN5. L. M. Pickett. (Chess Player Ser.). 1977. pap. 5.95 o.p. (ISBN 0-900928-85-9, H-1193). Hippocrene Bks.

Sicilian Dragon. David Levy. 1976. 19.95 (ISBN 0-7134-2931-3, Pub. by Batsford England). David & Charles.

Sicilian Dragon: Classical & Levenfish Variations. D. N. Levy. 96p. 1981. pap. 11.95 (ISBN 0-7134-2744-2, Pub. by Batsford England). David & Charles.

Sicilian Dragon: Yugoslav Attack. Tony Miles & Erik Moskow. 1979. 18.95 (ISBN 0-7134-2029-4, Pub. by Batsford England); pap. 13.50 (ISBN 0-7134-2030-8). David & Charles.

Sicilian: Lasker-Pelikan. Robert Wade et al. 1978. 15.95 (ISBN 0-7134-1634-3, Pub. by Batsford England). David & Charles.

Sicilian: Najdorf. Michael Stean. 1976. pap. 10.95 o.p. (ISBN 0-7134-0099-4). David & Charles.

Sicilian Richter-Rauzer. T. D. Harding & P. R. Markland. 1975. 18.95 (ISBN 0-7134-3209-8, Pub. by Batsford England). David & Charles.

Sicilian Scheveningen. C. W. Pritchett. 1977. 21.50 (ISBN 0-7134-0087-0, Pub. by Batsford England). David & Charles.

Sicilian Slaughter. Don Pendleton. (Executioner Ser. No. 16). pap. 1.95 (ISBN 0-523-40752-1). Pinnacle Bks.

Sicilian Sozin. T. D. Harding et al. 1974. 18.95 (ISBN 0-7134-2848-1, Pub. by Batsford England). David & Charles.

Sicilian Story, 1820; Mirandola 1821: Proctor Bryan Waller. Ed. by Donald H. Reiman & Donald H. Reiman. LC 75-31247. (Romantic Context: Poetry 1789-1830 Ser.). 1977. lib. bdg. 47.00 (ISBN 0-8240-2195-9). Garland Pub.

Sicilian Summer. Elizabeth Ashton. (Harlequin Romances Ser.). 192p. 1981. pap. 1.25 (ISBN 0-373-02401-0, Pub. by Harlequin). PB.

Sicilian Vespers. Steven Runciman. 1958. 35.50 (ISBN 0-521-06167-9). Cambridge U Pr.

Sicilian 2c3. Murray Chandler. (Algebraic Chess Openings Ser.). (Illus.). 96p. 1981. pap. 11.50 (ISBN 0-7134-1933-4, Pub. by Batsford England). David & Charles.

Sicily. G. C. Skipper. (World at War Ser.). (Illus.). 48p. (gr. 3-8). PLB 7.95 (ISBN 0-516-04792-2). Childrens.

Sicily & the Greeks: Studies in the Interrelationship between the Indigenous Populations & the Greek Colonists. Erik Sjoeqvist. LC 79-163625. (Jerome Lecture Ser: No. 9). (Illus.). 1972. 10.00x o.p. (ISBN 0-472-08795-9). U of Mich Pr.

Sicily Enough. Claire Rabe. LC 76-28246. 73p. 1980. pap. 3.75 (ISBN 0-88496-070-6). Ross-Erikson.

Sick Book: Questions & Answers About Hiccups & Mumps, Sneezes & Bumps & Other Things That Go Wrong with Us. Marie Winn. LC 75-34470. (Illus.). 160p. (gr. 2-6). 1976. 9.95 (ISBN 0-590-07259-5, Four Winds). Schol Bk Serv.

Sick Cities. M. Gordon. 1963. 6.95 o.s.i. (ISBN 0-02-544730-0). Macmillan.

Sickle Cell Anemia. Cerami & Washington. LC 72-93681. 1973. 8.95 (ISBN 0-89388-068-X). Okpaku Communications.

Sickness & Health: A Novel. Colin Douglas. LC 80-28316. 200p. 1981. 8.95 (ISBN 0-8008-7178-2). Taplinger.

Sickness & Health in America: Readings in the History of Medicine & Public Health. Ed. by Judith W. Leavitt & Ronald L. Numbers. LC 78-53288. 1978. 27.50 (ISBN 0-299-07620-2); pap. 10.95 (ISBN 0-299-07624-5). U of Wis Pr.

Sickness Behavior & the Sick Role. Andrew C. Twaddle. 1981. pap. text ed. 7.95 (ISBN 0-87073-886-0). Schenkman.

Sickness Unto Death: A Christian Psychological Exposition for Upbuilding & Awakening. Soren Kierkegaard. Tr. by Howard V. Hong & Edna H. Hong. LC 79-3218. (Kierkegaard's Writings Ser.: Vol. XIX). 1980. 16.50x (ISBN 0-691-07247-7). Princeton U Pr.

Siddha Meditation. Swami Muktananda. pap. 2.95 (ISBN 0-914602-22-5). SYDA Found.

Siddur: Sabbath Eve Service. Nosson Scherman. 1980. 8.95 (ISBN 0-686-68764-7); pap. 5.95 (ISBN 0-686-68765-5). Mesorah Pubns.

Side by Each. Willie S. Ethridge. LC 73-83034. 192p. 1973. 7.95 (ISBN 0-8149-0733-4). Vanguard.

Side by Side: English Grammar Through Guided Conversations, Bk. I. Steven J. Molinsky & Bill Bliss. 1980. pap. text ed. 7.95 (ISBN 0-13-809848-4); tapes 129.95 (ISBN 0-13-809830-1). P-H.

Side Effects. Mel Silverstein & Karen Silverstein. LC 77-92231. 1978. 7.95 o.p. (ISBN 0-385-13632-3). Doubleday.

Side Effects of Estrogen Drug Therapy: Contraception & Menopause. Harold Simmons. 1979. pap. 4.95 (ISBN 0-87312-007-8). Gen Welfare.

Side Glimpses from the Colonial Meeting House. William R. Bliss. LC 70-140410. 1970. Repr. of 1894 ed. 18.00 (ISBN 0-8103-3594-8). Gale.

Side-Lights on English Society: Sketches from Life, Social & Satirical. rev ed. E. C. Murray. LC 75-83371. (Illus.). xii, 436p. 1969. Repr. of 1885 ed. 20.00 (ISBN 0-8103-3285-X). Gale.

Sidelights of Colorado. Al Look. 1967. 4.95 (ISBN 0-87315-073-2). Golden Bell.

Sidelights on Elizabethan Drama. D. H. Sykes. 1967. Repr. of 1924 ed. text ed. 10.00x (ISBN 0-391-02050-1). Humanities.

Sidereality. Ella Blanche. (Illus.). 240p. (Orig.). 1980. pap. 6.00 (ISBN 0-9601542-4-8). Ivy Hill.

Sides of Fortune, Nineteen Fourty-Five to Nineteen Fifty-Five. Harold Macmillan. LC 78-83609. (Illus.). 1969. 20.00 o.p. (ISBN 0-06-012746-5, HarpT). Har-Row.

Sideshow. rev. ed. William Shawcross. 1981. price not set (ISBN 0-671-25414-6, Touchstone). S&S.

Sidetracked Home Executives: From Pigpen to Paradise. Pam Brace & Peggy Jones. LC 79-56324. (Illus.). 1979. pap. 5.95 (ISBN 0-8323-0355-0); 10.95 o.p. (ISBN 0-8323-0349-6). Binford.

Sidewalk Games. Lani Van Ryzin. LC 77-28327. (Games & Activities Ser.). (Illus.). (gr. k-3). 1978. PLB 9.30 (ISBN 0-8172-1166-7). Raintree Pubs.

Sidewalk Prayers. Orlando L. Tibbetts. LC 71-139501. 1971. pap. 1.95 o.p. (ISBN 0-8170-0489-0). Judson.

Sidewalk Psalms... & Some from Country Lanes. Wilma Burton. LC 79-92015. 119p. 1980. 6.95 (ISBN 0-89107-165-2). Good News.

Sidewinder. J. T. Edson. 1979. pap. 1.75 o.p. (ISBN 0-425-04416-5). Berkley Pub.

Sidlatches Are Coming. M. T. Brown. (Illus.). 1980. pap. 9.95 o.p. (ISBN 0-930490-29-0). Future Shop.

Sidmouth Letters. Jane Gardam. LC 80-23940. 163p. 1980. 8.95 (ISBN 0-688-00134-3). Morrow.

Sidney Howard. Sidney H. White. (United States Authors Ser.: No. 288). 1977. lib. bdg. 12.50 (ISBN 0-8057-7191-3). Twayne.

Sidney Poitier. David Paige. (Stars of Stage & Screen Ser.). (Illus.). (gr. 4-12). 1977. PLB 5.95 (ISBN 0-87191-556-1). Creative Ed.

Sidney Sime: Master of the Mysterious. Simon Heneage & Henry Ford. 1980. pap. 8.95 (ISBN 0-500-27154-2). Thames Hudson.

Sidney's Arcadian Poems. John A. Galm (Salzburg Studies in English Literature,Elizabethan & Renaissance Studies: No. 1). 229p. 1973. pap. text ed. 25.00x (ISBN 0-391-01379-3). Humanities.

Sieben Zwerge Scheewittchens. Bertold Loffler. (Insel Taschbuecher Fuer Kinder: It 489). 40p. (Ger.). pap. text ed. 4.55 (ISBN 3-458-32189-6, Pub. by Insel Verlag Germany). Suhrkamp.

Siege. Thurman Petty, Jr. (Orion Ser.). 144p. (gr. 7-10). 1980. pap. write for info. (ISBN 0-8127-0302-2). Southern Pub.

Siege De Corinthe. Gioachino Rossini. Ed. by Phillip Gossett & Charles Rosen. LC 76-49189. (Early Romantic Opera Ser.: No. 14). 1980. lib. bdg. 82.00 (ISBN 0-8240-2913-5). Garland Pub.

Siege in Peking: China Against the World. William A. Martin. (Illus.). 190p. 1972. Repr. of 1900 ed. 25.00x (ISBN 0-686-28322-8, Pub. by Irish Academic Pr). Biblio Dist.

Siege in the Sun. Dorothy Eden. 1979. pap. 2.25 (ISBN 0-449-23884-9, Crest). Fawcett.

Siege of Atlanta, 1864. Samuel Carter, 3rd. 1976. pap. 1.95 o.p. (ISBN 0-345-24424-9). Ballantine.

Siege of Calais. Claudine Tencin. Ed. by Michael F. Shugrue. (Flowering of the Novel, 1740-1775 Ser). 1974. Repr. of 1740 ed. lib. bdg. 50.00 (ISBN 0-8240-1101-5). Garland Pub.

Siege of Krishnapur. J. G. Farrell. LC 74-1228. 352p. 1974. 7.95 o.p. (ISBN 0-15-182323-5). HarBraceJ.

Siege of Silent Henry. Lynn Hall. LC 72-2789. 160p. (gr. 7 up). 1972. 4.95 o.p. (ISBN 0-695-80041-8). Follett.

Siege of the Alcazar, July-September, 1936: Facism Defeats Democracy in the Spanish Civil War. Robert C. Goldston. LC 75-188689. (World Focus Bks.). (Illus.). 72p. (gr. 7-12). 1972. PLB 6.45 (ISBN 0-531-02164-5). Watts.

Siege of Valencia...the Last Constantine & Other Poems. 1823. Felicia D. Hemans. Ed. by Donald H. Reiman. LC 75-31216. (Romantic Context Ser.: Poetry 1789-1830). 1978. lib. bdg. 47.00 (ISBN 0-8240-2166-5). Garland Pub.

Siege of Vicksburg. Richard Wheeler. LC 77-14258. (Illus.). 1978. 12.95 o.p. (ISBN 0-690-01427-9, TYC-T). T Y Crowell.

Siege Warfare: The Fortress in the Early Modern World, 1494-1660. Christopher Duffy. (Illus.). 1979. 30.00x (ISBN 0-7100-8871-X). Routledge & Kegan.

Siegfried Lenz. Brian Murdoch & Malcolm Read. (Modern German Authors Ser.: No. 6). 1978. text ed. 10.50x (ISBN 0-85496-068-6). Humanities.

Siena Baptistry Font: A Study of an Early Renaissance Collaborative Program, 1416-1434. John T. Paoletti. LC 78-74374. (Fine Arts Dissertations, Fourth Ser.). (Illus.). 1980. lib. bdg. 33.00 (ISBN 0-8240-3961-0). Garland Pub.

Sienese Painter Paolo Di Giovanni Fei (c.1345-1411) Michael Mallory. LC 75-23802. (Outstanding Dissertations in the Fine Arts - 15th Century). (Illus.). 1976. lib. bdg. 41.00 (ISBN 0-8240-1997-0). Garland Pub.

Sierra Album: A Pictorial History. Paul C. Johnson. LC 73-144276. 1971. 4.95 o.p. (ISBN 0-385-04832-7). Doubleday.

Sierra Big Trees. abr. ed. John Muir. Ed. by William R. Jones. (Illus.). 80p. 1981. pap. 3.95 (ISBN 0-89646-069-X). Outbooks.

Sierra Club Naturalist's Guide to the Piedmont. Michael A. Godfrey. LC 79-22328. (Naturalists Guide Ser.). (Illus.). 1980. 19.95 (ISBN 0-87156-268-5); pap. 9.95 (ISBN 0-87156-269-3). Sierra.

Sierra Club Naturalist's Guide to the Deserts of the Southwest. Peggy Larson & Lane Larson. LC 76-24835. (Naturalist's Guide Ser). (Illus.). 1977. pap. 5.95 (ISBN 0-87156-186-7). Sierra.

Sierra Club Naturalist's Guide to the North Atlantic Coast. Michael Berrill & Deborah Berrill. (Sierra Club Naturalist's Guides). (Illus.). 512p. (Orig.). 1981. 24.95 (ISBN 0-87156-242-1); pap. 10.95 (ISBN 0-87156-243-X). Sierra.

Sierra Club Naturlist's Guide to the North Woods of Michigan, Wisconsin, & Minnesota. Glenda Daniel & Jerry Sullivan. (Naturalist's Guide Ser.). (Illus.). 384p. 1981. 24.95 (ISBN 0-87156-248-0); pap. 9.95 (ISBN 0-87156-277-4). Sierra.

Sierra Flower Finder: A Guide to Sierra Nevada Wildflowers. Glenn Keator. (Illus.). 1980. pap. 3.00 (ISBN 0-912550-09-0). Nature Study.

Sierra Madre. D. Jackson & Peter Wood. (American Wilderness Ser.). (Illus.). 184p. 1975. 12.95 (ISBN 0-8094-1342-6). Time-Life.

Sierra Madre. D. D. Jackson & P. Wood. LC 75-21613. (American Wilderness). (Illus.). (gr. 6 up). 1975. PLB 11.97 (ISBN 0-8094-1339-6, Pub. by Time-Life). Silver.

Sierra North. 3rd ed. Thomas Winnett. LC 75-38175. (Trail Guide Ser). (Illus., Orig.). 1976. pap. 8.95 (ISBN 0-911824-46-4). Wilderness.

Sierra Railroad: A Portfolio. Lowell Amrine. Ed. by Bill Amrine. (Illus.). 32p. 1980. pap. 6.95 (ISBN 0-936616-01-6). Galliard Pr.

Siete Necesidades Basicas Del Nino. John M. Drescher. 160p. (Span.). 1981. pap. write for info. (ISBN 0-311-46085-2). Casa Bautista.

Sieve Methods. H. Halberstam & H. E. Richert. 1975. 52.00 (ISBN 0-12-318250-6). Acad Pr.

Sight & Sound: A Manual of Aural Musicianship, 2 vols. L. Kreter. 1976. Vol. 1. pap. 12.95 (ISBN 0-13-809905-7); Vol. 2. pap. 13.50 (ISBN 0-13-809913-8); Recording Vols. 1 & 2. 150.00 (ISBN 0-13-809921-9). P-H.

Sight & Sound: The Sensible & Sensitive Use of Audio-Visual Aids. Ed. by Mills F. Edgerton, Jr. 1969. pap. 7.95x (ISBN 0-915432-69-2). NE Conf Teach.

Sight Reading for the Pop Singer. Al Berkman. 1969. 4.50 (ISBN 0-934972-05-2). Melrose Pub Co.

Sight-Singing Manual. 3rd ed. Allen I. McHose & Ruth N. Tibbs. 1957. 10.95 (ISBN 0-13-809707-0). P-H.

Sight, Sound, & Sense. Thomas A. Sebeok. LC 77-21520. (Advances in Semiotics Ser.). 320p. 1978. 17.50x (ISBN 0-253-35230-4). Ind U Pr.

Sights & Sounds: The Very Special Senses. Charles E. Kupchella. LC 75-1446. 1975. pap. text ed. 6.95 (ISBN 0-672-63695-6). Bobbs.

Sights of Seattle: Downtown. Earl D. Layman. (Illus.). 96p. (Orig.). 1981. pap. 6.95 (ISBN 0-914842-59-5). Madrona Pubs.

Sightseer's London. (Illus.). 1979. pap. 1.95 o.p. (ISBN 0-905522-20-6, ADON 8102-3, Pub. by Nickolson). Barrie & Jenkins.

Sigmet Active. Thomas Page. 288p. 1980. pap. 2.25 (ISBN 0-441-76330-8). Charter Bks.

Sigmond. Jonathan Shebar & Sharon Shebar. (gr. 3-6). 1981. write for info. (ISBN 0-671-34003-4). Messner.

Sigmund Freud. Giovanni Costigan. 1965. 5.95 o.s.i. (ISBN 0-02-528450-9). Macmillan.

Sigmund Freud. Gerald Levin. LC 74-31135. (World Authors Ser.: Austria: No. 357). 1975. lib. bdg. 12.50 (ISBN 0-8057-2330-7). Twayne.

Sigmund Freud. Richard Wollheim. 316p. Date not set. pap. price not set (ISBN 0-521-28385-X). Cambridge U Pr.

Sigmund Freud & the Jewish Mystical Tradition. David Bakan. 1975. pap. 4.95 o.p. (ISBN 0-8070-2963-7, BP510). Beacon Pr.

Sigmund Freud's Dreams. Alexander Grinstein. LC 79-2485. 475p. 1980. text ed. 22.50x (ISBN 0-8236-6074-5). Intl Univs Pr.

Sign & Subject: Semiotic & Psychoanalytic Investigations into Poetry. Daniel Laferriere. (Studies in Semiotics Ser.: No. 14). (Orig.). 1978. pap. text ed. 11.50x (ISBN 9-0316-0138-1). Humanities.

Sign Book. William Dugan. (Illus.). 24p. (gr. k-1). 1976. PLB 5.38 (ISBN 0-307-68974-3, Golden Pr). Western Pub.

Sign for Cain. F. Wertham. 1966. 12.95 (ISBN 0-02-625970-2). Macmillan.

Sign Here: A Contracting Book for Children & Their Parents. 2nd ed. Jill C. Dardig & William L. Heward. LC 76-18757. (Illus.). 166p. 1981. pap. 10.00 (ISBN 0-917472-04-7); leader's manual 3.00 (ISBN 0-914474-27-8). F Fournies.

Sign in Music & Literature. Ed. by Wendy Steiner. (Illus.). 264p. 1981. text ed. 25.00x (ISBN 0-292-77563-6). U of Tex Pr.

Sign in the Straw. Richard C. Hoefler. 128p. (Orig.). 1980. pap. text ed. 6.25 (ISBN 0-89536-465-4). CSS Pub.

Sign Language & Language Acquisition in Man & Ape. Ed. by Fred C. Peng. (AAAS Selected Symposium Ser.: No. 15). (Illus.). 1978. lib. bdg. 19.50x (ISBN 0-89158-445-5). Westview.

Sign Language & the Deaf Community: Essays in Honor of William Stokoe. Charlotte Baker & Robbin Battison. (Illus.). 267p. 1981. text ed. 12.00 (ISBN 0-913072-37-0); pap. text ed. 8.00 (ISBN 0-913072-36-2). Natl Assn Deaf.

Sign Language Evaluation Manual for Evaluators. Richard D. Dirst. 51p. 1980. pap. text ed. 3.50 (ISBN 0-9602220-3-0). RIFD.

Sign Language for Everyone: A Basic Course in Communication with the Deaf. John R. Rice. LC 77-14592. 1978. 9.95 (ISBN 0-8407-9002-3). Nelson.

Sign Language Structure. rev. ed. William C. Stokoe. 1978. pap. text ed. 4.00x (ISBN 0-932130-03-8). Linstok Pr.

Sign of Contradiction. Karol Wojtyla. 1979. 8.95 (ISBN 0-8164-0433-X). Crossroad NY.

Sign of Contradiction. Karol Wojtyla. 1980. pap. 3.95 (ISBN 0-8164-2048-3). Crossroad NY.

Sign of Dawn. abr. ed. James Wylie. LC 80-52009. (Illus.). 372p. 1981. 14.95 (ISBN 0-670-64462-5). Viking Pr.

Sign of Jonas. Thomas Merton. pap. 3.95 (ISBN 0-385-07898-6, Im). Doubleday.

Sign of the Chrysanthemum. Katherine Paterson. (Illus.). (gr. 6 up). 1980. pap. 1.75 (ISBN 0-380-49288-1, 49288, Camelot). Avon.

Sign of the Fish. Peter Quennell. (Illus.). 255p. 1980. Repr. of 1960 ed. lib. bdg. 30.00 (ISBN 0-8492-2209-5). R West.

Sign of the Four. Arthur C. Doyle. lib. bdg. 13.95x (ISBN 0-89966-230-7). Buccaneer Bks.

Sign of the Kingdom. Lesslie Newbigin. 48p. (Orig.). 1981. pap. 1.95 (ISBN 0-8028-1878-1). Eerdmans.

Sign of the Owl. Deborah Chester. LC 80-69998. 256p. (gr. 5-9). 1981. 9.95 (ISBN 0-590-07729-5, Four Winds). Schol Bk Serv.

Sign of the Prayer Shawl. (Nick Carter Ser.). 1978. pap. 1.75 (ISBN 0-441-76355-3). Charter Bks.

Sign of the Scorpion. LC 73-111002. 224p. 1981. pap. 2.95 (ISBN 0-394-17894-7, BC). Grove.

Sign User's Guide. R. J. Claus & K. E. Claus. (Illus.). 1978. 7.50 (ISBN 0-686-27783-X). Signs of Times.

Signage Communication Standards. Mick Blackistone & Charles McLendon. (Illus.). 192p. 1982. 24.95 (ISBN 0-07-005740-0, P&RB). McGraw.

Signal - Close Action. Alexander Kent. pap. 2.25 (ISBN 0-515-05719-3). Jove Pubns.

Signaling. Boy Scouts Of America. LC 19-600. (Illus.). 32p. (gr. 6-12). 1974. pap. 0.70x (ISBN 0-8395-3237-7, 3237). BSA.

Signals. F. R. Connor. (Introductory Topics in Electronics & Telecommunications Ser.). (Illus.). 1972. pap. text ed. 11.00x (ISBN 0-7131-3262-0). Intl Ideas.

Signals & Linear Systems. 2nd ed. Robert A. Gabel & Richard A. Roberts. LC 80-14811. 480p. 1980. text ed. 29.95 (ISBN 0-471-04958-1). Wiley.

Signals in Linear Circuits. Jose B. Cruz & M. E. Van Valkenburg. 480p. 1974. text ed. 24.95 (ISBN 0-395-16971-2); lab. manual 6.50 (ISBN 0-395-17838-X). HM.

Signature of All Things. Jacob Boehme. 1968. 12.95 (ISBN 0-227-67733-1). Attic Pr.

Signe Zodiacal Du Scorpion Dans les Traditions Occidentales De L'antiquite Grego-Latine a la Renaissance. Luigi Aurigemma. (Civilisations et Societes.: No. 54). (Illus.). 1976. text ed. 47.05x (ISBN 90-2797-573-6). Mouton.

Signed & Spoken Language: Biological Constraints on Linguistic Form. Ed. by U. Bellugi & M. Studdert-Kennedy. (Dahlem Workshop Reports, Life Science Research Report Ser.: No. 19). (Illus.). 379p. (Orig.). 1980. pap. 35.70 (ISBN 0-89573-034-0). Verlag Chemie.

Signed English Dictionary. Harry Bornstein. Tr. by Ralph Miller. (Signed English Ser.). (Illus.). 300p. 1975. 17.50 (ISBN 0-913580-46-5). Gallaudet Coll.

Signed Numbers, Linear Functions, Surface Area Blocks. NAIS Task Force on Secondary Mathematics. (Occasional Papers Ser.: No. 1). (Illus.). 21p. 1977. pap. 3.25 (ISBN 0-934338-13-2). NAIS.

Signet Book of Coffee & Tea. Peter Quimme. 1976. pap. 1.75 o.p. (ISBN 0-451-07149-2, E7149, Sig). NAL.

Signet Book of World Winners. Judith Norback. 1980. pap. 2.95 (ISBN 0-451-09585-5, E9585, Sig). NAL.

Signet Classic Book of Restoration Drama. Ronald Berman. 1980. pap. 3.95 (ISBN 0-451-51402-5, CE1402, Sig Cl). NAL.

Signet Ring. Adora Sheridan. 1979. pap. 1.75 o.p. (ISBN 0-345-27785-6). Ballantine.

Significance of Children's Play. Joan E. Cass. 1977. 14.95 (ISBN 0-7134-0689-5, Pub. by Batsford England). David & Charles.

Significance of Mineralogy in the Development of Flow Sheets for Processing Uranium Ores. (Technical Reports Ser.: No. 196). 267p. 1980. pap. 33.75 (ISBN 92-0-145080-X, IDC 196, IAEA). Unipub.

Significance of Silence. Arnold T. Olson. 200p. 1980. write for info. Free Church Pubns.

Significance Tests. Evelyn Caulcott. (Applied Statistics Ser). 1973. 16.00x (ISBN 0-7100-7406-9); pap. 8.00 (ISBN 0-7100-8385-8). Routledge & Kegan.

Significance: The Struggle We Share. 2nd ed. John H. Brennecke & Robert G. Amick. 1975. pap. text ed. 7.95x (ISBN 0-02-471020-2, 47102). Macmillan.

Significant Decisions of the Supreme Court: 1978-1979 Term. Bruce E. Fein. 1980. pap. 6.25 (ISBN 0-8447-3387-3). Am Enterprise.

Significant Influence People: A Sip of Discipline & Encouragement. Joseph C. Rotter et al. LC 80-69233. 110p. 1981. perfect bdg. 8.95 (ISBN 0-86548-055-9). Century Twenty One.

Significant References in Psychiatry & Mental Health. Ed. by B. Greenberg. 1979. lib. bdg. 25.00 o.p. (ISBN 0-89495-004-5). ISI Pr.

Significant State Appellate Decisions. National Judicial College. (Ser. 1850). 1980. pap. 7.50 (ISBN 0-686-08770-4). Natl Judicial Coll.

Significant Writings on Life & Man. Alighar Muslim University. 1963. 4.00x o.p. (ISBN 0-210-26967-7). Asia.

Signifying Animal. Ed. by Irmengard Rauch & Gerald F. Carr. LC 79-3624. (Advances in Semiotics). 384p. 1980. 24.95x (ISBN 0-253-18496-7). Ind U Pr.

Signing Exact English: 1980 Edition. Gerilee Gustason et al. (Illus.). xix, 460p. (gr. k-12). 1980. 21.00 (ISBN 0-916708-02-0); pap. 16.00 (ISBN 0-916708-03-9). Modern Signs.

Signpost to Love, No. 131. Barbara Cartland. 144p. (Orig.). 1981. pap. 1.75 (ISBN 0-553-14360-3). Bantam.

Signposts. Roger Hecht. LC 74-112873. 56p. 1973. 7.95 (ISBN 0-8040-0277-0); pap. 4.25 (ISBN 0-8040-0639-3). Swallow.

Signposts for the Future. Hans Kung. LC 77-75387. 1978. 7.95 o.p. (ISBN 0-385-13151-8). Doubleday.

Signposts to Homoeopathic Remedies. Noel Puddephatt. 1980. text ed. 4.50 o.p. (ISBN 0-8464-1049-4). Beekman Pubs.

Signs & Seasons. John Burroughs. (Nature Library Ser.). 300p. 1981. pap. 5.95 (ISBN 0-06-090840-8, CN 840, CN). Har-Row.

Signs & Symbols in Chaucer's Poetry. John P. Hermann & John J. Burke, Jr. 272p. 1981. 16.75 (ISBN 0-8173-0038-4); pap. 8.95 (ISBN 0-8173-0042-2). U of Ala Pr.

Signs & Symbols in Christian Art. George Ferguson. (Illus.). 1959. 18.95 (ISBN 0-19-501168-6). Oxford U Pr.

Signs & Symbols of the Sun. Elizabeth S. Helfman. LC 73-20121. (Illus.). (gr. 4-7). 1974. 8.95 (ISBN 0-395-28860-6, Clarion). HM.

Signs & Symptoms of Chemical Exposure. J. Bradford Block. 164p. 1980. text ed. 12.75 lexotone (ISBN 0-398-03958-5). C C Thomas.

Signs of Celebration. Edie Lauckner. 1978. 2.25 (ISBN 0-570-03770-0, 12-2706). Concordia.

Signs of His Coming. Arthur E. Bloomfield. LC 57-8724. 1962. pap. 3.95 (ISBN 0-87123-513-7, 210513). Bethany Fell.

Signs of Life. Sumner L. Elliott. LC 80-21914. 288p. 1981. 11.95 (ISBN 0-89919-022-7). Ticknor & Fields.

Signs of Our Times: Theological Essays on Art in the Twentieth Century. George S. Heyer, Jr. 1980. 15.95 (ISBN 0-8028-3543-0). Eerdmans.

Signs of Spring. Laurel Lee. 128p. 1981. pap. 2.25 (ISBN 0-553-14342-5). Bantam.

Signs of the Apostles. Walter Chantry. 1979. pap. 3.45 (ISBN 0-85151-175-9). Banner of Truth.

Signs of the Hidden. Tiefenbrun. 1980. pap. text ed. 28.50x (ISBN 9-0040-3778-0). Humanities.

Signs of the Times Articles, Vol. 1. E. G. White. 1976. 26.00 (ISBN 0-8163-0220-0, 05391-8). Pacific Pr Pub Assn.

Signs of the Times Articles, Vol. 2. E. G. White. 1977. 26.00 (ISBN 0-8163-0166-2, 05392-6). Pacific Pr Pub Assn.

Signs of the Times Articles, Vol. 3. E. G. White. 1977. 26.00 (ISBN 0-8163-0167-0, 05393-4). Pacific Pr Pub Assn.

Signs, Symbols & Architecture. Geoffrey Broadbent et al. LC 78-13557. 1980. 54.25 (ISBN 0-471-99718-8, Pub. by Wiley-Interscience). Wiley.

Sikh Portraits by European Artists. F. S. Aijazuddin. (Illus.). 160p. 1979. 40.00x (ISBN 0-85667-059-6, Pub. by Sotheby Parke Bernet England). Biblio Dist.

Sikh Studies: Comparative Perspectives of a Changing Tradition. Ed. by Mark Juergensmeyer & Gerald Barrier. 1980. 16.00 (ISBN 0-89581-100-6). Lancaster-Miller.

Sikhs in England: The Development of a Migrant Community. Arthur W. Helweg. (Illus.). 190p. 1979. text ed. 10.95x (ISBN 0-19-561150-0). Oxford U Pr.

Sikhs: Their Religious Beliefs & Practices. W. Owen Cole & Piara S. Sambhi. (Library of Religious Beliefs & Practices). 1978. 22.50 (ISBN 0-7100-8842-6); pap. 9.00 (ISBN 0-7100-8843-4). Routledge & Kegan.

Silas & the Black Mare. Cecil Bodker. Tr. by Sheila La Farge. LC 77-86303. (gr. 5-9). 1978. 7.95 (ISBN 0-440-07921-7, Sey Lawr); PLB 7.45 (ISBN 0-440-07922-5). Delacorte.

Silas Crockett. Mary E. Chase. 1943. 10.95 (ISBN 0-02-524450-7). Macmillan.

Silas Marner. George Eliot. (Zodiac Press Ser.). 1979. 9.95 (ISBN 0-7011-1247-6, Pub. by Chatto Bodley Jonathan). Merrimack Bk Serv.

Silas Marner. George Eliot. (Literature Ser). (gr. 9-12). 1969. pap. text ed. 3.42 (ISBN 0-87720-715-1). AMSCO Sch.

Silas Marner (with Reader's Guide) George Eliot. (Amsco Literature Program). (gr. 10-12). 1971. pap. text ed. 4.17 (ISBN 0-87720-814-X); tchr's ed. 2.70 (ISBN 0-87720-914-6). AMSCO Sch.

Silence. Lily Lerner & S. L. Stuart. 1980. 10.95 (ISBN 0-8184-0306-3). Lyle Stuart.

Silence & Other Stories. Krishna B. Vaid. (Writers Workshop Greenbird Ser.). 94p. 1975. 14.00 (ISBN 0-88253-634-6); pap. text ed. 4.80 (ISBN 0-88253-633-8). Ind-US Inc.

Silence at Yorktown. William R. McHale. 1976. pap. 1.25 o.p. (ISBN 0-685-69512-3, LB372ZK, Leisure Bks). Nordon Pubns.

Silence in Eden. Jerry Potter. LC 77-18639. 1978. 9.95 o.s.i. (ISBN 0-690-01742-1, TYC-T). T Y Crowell.

Silence in the Snowy Fields. Robert Bly. LC 62-18340. (Wesleyan Poetry Program: Vol. 15). (Orig.). 1962. 10.00x (ISBN 0-8195-2015-2, Pub. by Wesleyan U Pr); pap. 4.95 (ISBN 0-8195-1015-7). Columbia U Pr.

Silence Is Not Golden - It's Yellow. Tom Anderson. LC 73-176510. 1973. 7.00 (ISBN 0-88279-227-X). Western Islands.

Silence: Lectures & Writings. John Cage. LC 61-14238. 1961. 15.00x o.p. (ISBN 0-8195-3021-2, Pub. by Wesleyan U Pr); pap. 7.95 (ISBN 0-8195-6028-6). Columbia U Pr.

Silence Observed. Michael Iunes. 160p. 1975. pap. 1.25 o.p. (ISBN 0-345-24627-6). Ballantine.

Silence of Love: Twentieth-Century Korean Poetry. Ed. by Peter H. Lee. LC 80-21999. 368p. 1980. text ed. 17.95x (ISBN 0-8248-0711-1); pap. 8.95 (ISBN 0-8248-0732-4). U Pr of Hawaii.

Silence of the North. Olive A. Fredrickson & Ben East. 224p. 1981. pap. 2.50 (ISBN 0-446-81559-4). Warner Bks.

Silence Over Dunkerque. John R. Tunis. (Illus.). (gr. 7 up). 1962. PLB 8.40 (ISBN 0-688-31760-X). Morrow.

Silence Speaks--from the Chalkboard of Baba Hari Dass. Baba Hari Dasss et al. LC 76-53902. (Illus.). 224p. (Orig.). 1977. pap. 4.95 (ISBN 0-918100-01-1). SRI Rama.

Silencers: Patterns & Principles, Vol. 2. American Machines & Foundry Co. (Illus.). 202p. 1972. pap. 9.95 (ISBN 0-87364-018-7). Paladin Ent.

Silences. Vijay Munshi. (Redbird Book Ser). 24p. 1975. 8.00 (ISBN 0-88253-846-2); pap. text ed. 4.80 (ISBN 0-88253-715-6). Ind-US Inc.

Silent Bells. William MacKellar. LC 78-7744. (Illus.). (gr. 4 up). 1978. 5.95 (ISBN 0-396-07618-1). Dodd.

Silent Children: A Parent's Guide to the Prevention of Child Abuse. Linda T. Sanford. LC 79-6284. 312p. 1980. 12.95 (ISBN 0-385-15142-X, Anchor Pr). Doubleday.

Silent Cry. Kenzaburo Oe. Tr. by John Bester from Japanese. LC 74-77961. Orig. Title: Man'en Gannen No Football. 274p. 1974. 10.00x (ISBN 0-87011-232-5). Kodansha.

Silent Death: Shadow No. 22. Maxwell Grant. 1978. pap. 1.25 o.s.i. (ISBN 0-515-04281-1). Jove Pubns.

Silent "E's" from Outer Space. Byron Preiss. (Electric Company Ser.). (Illus.). (gr. 1-5). 1973. PLB 5.38 (ISBN 0-307-64821-4, Golden Pr). Western Pub.

Silent Halls of Ashenden. Dorothy Daniels. (Orig.). 1973. pap. 1.75 o.s.i. (ISBN 0-446-84659-7). Warner Bks.

Silent in Court. Susanne Dell. 64p. 1971. pap. text ed. 5.00x (ISBN 0-7135-1576-7, Pub. by Bedford England). Renouf.

Silent Intruder: Surviving the Radiation Age. Charles Panati & Michael Hudson. 224p. 1981. 9.95 (ISBN 0-686-69062-1). HM.

Silent Language. Edward T. Hall. LC 72-97265. 240p. 1973. pap. 3.50 (ISBN 0-385-05549-8, Anch). Doubleday.

Silent Life. Thomas Merton. 178p. 1975. pap. 4.50 (ISBN 0-374-51281-7). FS&G.

Silent Majority: Families of Emotionally Healthy College Students. William A. Westley & Nathan B. Epstein. LC 77-75937. (Higher Education Ser). 1969. 11.95x o.p. (ISBN 0-87589-039-3). Jossey-Bass.

Silent Messages. Albert Mehrabian. 1971. pap. 8.95x (ISBN 0-534-00059-2). Wadsworth Pub.

Silent Messages: Implicit Communication of Emotions & Attitudes. 2nd ed. Albert Mehrabian. 208p. 1980. pap. text ed. 8.95x (ISBN 0-534-00910-7). Wadsworth Pub.

Silent Misery-Why Marriages Fail. G. G. Griffin. (American Lecture in Social & Rehabilitation Psychology). 296p. 1974. 13.75 (ISBN 0-398-03214-9); pap. 8.75 (ISBN 0-398-03237-8). C C Thomas.

Silent Movie. Mel Brooks. 1976. pap. 1.75 o.p. (ISBN 0-345-23918-0). Ballantine.

Silent One. Cowley. LC 80-21853. (Illus.). (gr. 4-6). 1981. 8.95 (ISBN 0-394-84761-X); PLB 7.99 (ISBN 0-394-94761-4). Knopf.

Silent Partners. Albert Kovetz. 400p. (Orig.). 1980. pap. 2.50 (ISBN 0-89083-688-4). Zebra.

Silent People. Walter Macken. 1962. Repr. 10.95 (ISBN 0-02-578000-X). Macmillan.

Silent Places. Stewart E. White. 1976. lib. bdg. 14.25x (ISBN 0-89968-123-9). Lightyear.

Silent Pulse. George Leonard. 208p. 1981. pap. 2.95 (ISBN 0-553-14368-9). Bantam.

Silent Revolution: The Effects of Westernization on Aboriginal Religion. Erich Kolig. (Illus.). 240p. 1981. text ed. 18.50x (ISBN 0-89727-020-7). Inst Study Hum.

Silent Sage. Ken Reed. LC 74-27531. (Illus.). 1974. 6.95 (ISBN 0-914794-00-0); pap. 3.95 (ISBN 0-685-53189-9). Wisdom Garden.

Silent Salesman. 2nd ed. 156p. 1973. text ed. 19.50x (ISBN 0-220-66203-7, Pub. by Busn Bks England). Renouf.

Silent Seasons. Ed. by Russell Chatham. 1978. 11.95 o.p. (ISBN 0-525-20456-3). Dutton.

Silent Sound: The World of Ultrasonics. David C. Knight. LC 80-19118. (Illus.). 96p. (gr. 4-6). 1980. 6.95 (ISBN 0-688-22244-7); PLB 6.67 (ISBN 0-688-32244-1). Morrow.

Silent Storm. Marion Brown & Ruth Crone. (gr. 6-8). 1963. 7.95 o.p. (ISBN 0-687-38453-2). Abingdon.

Silent Tarn. Hannah Closs. 1962. 10.00 o.s.i. (ISBN 0-8149-0038-0). Vanguard.

Silent Thunder. Bernard Palmer. LC 74-21363. 96p. (gr. 6-10). 1975. pap. 1.50 (ISBN 0-87123-531-5, 200531). Bethany Fell.

Silent Tragedy: Child Abuse in the Community. Peter DeCourcy & Judith DeCourcy. LC 72-95493. 231p. 1973. pap. 14.50 (ISBN 0-88284-005-3). Alfred Pub.

Silent Victory. Carmen McBride. LC 73-84602. 11.95 (ISBN 0-911012-03-6). Nelson-Hall.

Silent Voices. Jared Angira. (African Writers Ser.). 1972. pap. text ed. 1.95x (ISBN 0-435-90111-7). Heinemann Ed.

Silent Warriors. S. Tadmor. Ed. by Raphael Rothstein. (Illus.). 1969. 5.95 o.s.i. (ISBN 0-02-615910-4). Macmillan.

Silent Witness. Susan Yankowitz. 1976. 7.95 o.p. (ISBN 0-394-49943-3). Knopf.

Silent World. Jacques-Yves Cousteau & Frederic Dumas. LC 52-5431. 1953. 15.00 o.s.i. (ISBN 0-06-010890-8, HarpT). Har-Row.

Silents to Sound: A History of the Movies. Juliet P. Schoen. LC 76-16092. (Illus.). 192p. (gr. 7 up). 1976. 7.95 (ISBN 0-590-07337-0, Four Winds). Schol Bk Serv.

Silhouette De la France: A First Reader in French Civilization. Charles W. Lovy. LC 67-10548. (Fr). 1967. pap. 8.95x o.p. (ISBN 0-471-00346-8). Wiley.

Silicate Glass Technology Methods. C. L. Babcock. LC 76-30716. (Pure & Applied Optics Ser). 1977. 38.95 (ISBN 0-471-03965-9, Pub. by Wiley-Interscience). Wiley.

Silicate Science: A Treatise, 5 vols. Ed. by Wilhelm Eitel. Incl. Vol. 1. Silicate Structures. 1964 (ISBN 0-12-236301-9); Vol. 2. Glasses, Enamels, Slags. 1965 (ISBN 0-12-236302-7); Vol. 3. Dry Silicate Systems. 1965 (ISBN 0-12-236303-5); Vol. 4. Hydrothermal Silical Systems. 1966 (ISBN 0-12-236304-3); Vol. 5. Ceramics & Hydraulic Binders. 1966 (ISBN 0-12-236305-1). 67.25 ea.; by subscription 57.50 ea. Acad Pr.

Silicon Carbide-1968. H. K. Henisch & R. Roy. 1969. 28.00 (ISBN 0-08-006768-9). Pergamon.

Silicon Chips: The Magical Mineral in Your Telephone, Calculator, Toys, Automobile, Hospital, Air Conditioning, Factory, Furnace, Sewing Machine, & Countless Other Future Inventions. C. D. Renmore. LC 80-24153. (Illus.). 160p. 1980. 8.95 (ISBN 0-8253-0022-3). Beaufort Bks NY.

Silicon Semiconductor Data. H. F. Wolf. 1969. 105.00 (ISBN 0-08-013019-4). Pergamon.

Silicones, 2 vols. M. W. Ranney. Incl. Vol. 1. Rubber, Electrical Molding Resins & Functional Fluids (ISBN 0-8155-0665-1); Vol. 2. Coatings, Printing Inks, Cellular Plastics, Textiles & Consumer Products (ISBN 0-8155-0669-4). LC 77-77019. (Chemical Technology Review Ser.: Vols. 91-92). (Illus.). 1977. 39.00 ea. Noyes.

Silk & Saber. Aola Vandergriff. 512p. (Orig.). 1981. pap. 2.75 (ISBN 0-446-85584-7). Warner Bks.

Silk & Steel. Stephen Alter. 327p. 1980. 11.95 (ISBN 0-374-26411-2). FS&G.

Silk Road: Fabrics from the Han to the T'ang Dynasty. (Illus.). 1972. silk bdg. 25.00 (ISBN 0-8351-0348-X). China Bks.

Silk Screen Printing. rev. ed. James Eisenberg & Francis J. Kafka. (Illus.). (gr. 9 up). 1957. pap. 5.00 (ISBN 0-87345-205-4). McKnight.

Silk-Screen Printing for Artists & Craftsmen. Mathilda V. Schwalbach & James A. Schwalbach. (Illus.). 150p. Date not set. pap. write for info. (ISBN 0-486-24046-0). Dover.

Silken Bond. Flora Kidd. (Harlequin Presents Ser.). 192p. 1980. pap. 1.50 (ISBN 0-373-10379-4, Pub. by Harlequin). PB.

Silken Eyes. Francoise Sagan. Tr. by Joanna Kilmartin from French. 1977. 6.95 o.s.i. (ISBN 0-440-08308-7, E Friede). Delacorte.

Silken Net. Rachelle Edwards. (Regency Love Story Ser.). 1979. pap. 1.75 o.p. (ISBN 0-449-24233-1, Crest). Fawcett.

Silken Secret. Geoffrey Trease. LC 54-11525. (gr. 6 up). 1954. 6.95 (ISBN 0-8149-0432-7). Vanguard.

Silken Trap. Charlotte Lamb. (Harlequin Presents Ser.). 192p. 1980. pap. 1.50 (ISBN 0-373-10374-3, Pub. by Harlequin). PB.

Silkscreening. Maria Termini. LC 77-10719. (Creative Handcraft Ser.). (Illus.). 1978. 15.95 (ISBN 0-13-809996-0, Spec); pap. 6.95 (ISBN 0-13-809988-X, Spec). P-H.

Silkworms & Science: The Story of Silk. Elizabeth K. Cooper. (Illus.). (gr. 5-9). 1961. 4.95 o.p. (ISBN 0-15-274241-7, HJ). HarBraceJ.

Silky! Leo Rosten. 240p. 1980. pap. 2.25 (ISBN 0-553-13547-3). Bantam.

Silky Terrier. Betty Young. (Illus.). 1970. pap. 2.00 (ISBN 0-87666-393-5, DS1044). TFH Pubns.

Silla de Plata. C. S. Lewis. Tr. by Julio Orozco from Eng. (Cronicas de Narnia Ser.). 251p. (Orig., Span.). (gr. 4 up). 1979. pap. 2.95 (ISBN 0-89922-137-8). Edit Caribe.

Silly Animal Jokes & Riddles. Seymour Simon. 64p. (gr. 1-3). 7.95 (ISBN 0-07-057397-2). McGraw.

Silly Egg. Nancy Reese. Ed. by Alton Jordan. (Illus.). (gr. k-3). 1974. PLB 3.50 (ISBN 0-89868-004-2, Read Res); pap. text ed. 1.75 (ISBN 0-89868-037-9). ARO Pub.

Silly Mysteries. John Petersen. (Illus.). (gr. k-3). 1976. pap. 1.25 o.p. (ISBN 0-590-10151-X, Schol Pap). Schol Bk Serv.

Silly Old Uncle Feedle. Postgate & Firmin. 1975. 3.95 (ISBN 0-7207-0783-8, Pub. by Michael Joseph). Merrimack Bk Serv.

Silly Putty & Other Children's Sermons. William E. Parsons, Jr. LC 73-3451. 112p. 1978. pap. 3.95 (ISBN 0-687-38464-8). Abingdon.

Silly Song Book. C. Keller. 1980. pap. 1.95 (ISBN 0-13-809954-5). P-H.

Silly Story. Mercer Mayer. LC 80-16784. (Illus.). 48p. (ps-3). 1980. Repr. of 1972 ed. 7.95 (ISBN 0-590-07778-3, Four Winds). Schol Bk Serv.

Silurian & Devonian Graptolites of Central Nevada. W. B. Berry & M. A. Murphy. (Publications in Geological Sciences: Vol. 110). 1975. pap. 12.50x (ISBN 0-520-09515-4). U of Cal Pr.

Silurian Chitinozoa from Gotland. Sven Laufeld. (Fossils & Strata Ser: No. 5). 1974. pap. 25.00x (ISBN 8-200-09358-1, Dist. by Columbia U Pr). Universitet.

Silurian-Lower Devonian Conodont Sequence in the Roberts Mountains Formation of Central Nevada. Gilbert Klapper & M. A. Murphy. (Publications in Geological Sciences: Vol. 3). 1975. pap. 10.00x (ISBN 0-520-09517-0). U of Cal Pr.

Silva Mind Control Method. Jose Silva & Philip Miele. 1978. pap. 2.95 (ISBN 0-671-43343-1). PB.

Silvabamba. Dan D'Amelio. (Pacesetters Ser.). (Illus.). 64p. (gr. 4 up). 1978. PLB 7.95 (ISBN 0-516-02158-3). Childrens.

Silver: An Analysis of Factors Affecting Its Price. 2nd ed. Y. S. Leong. (Brookings Institution Reprint Ser). Repr. of 1934 ed. lib. bdg. 28.00x (ISBN 0-697-00162-8). Irvington.

Silver: An Instructional Guide to the Silversmith's Art. Reul O. Redinger. (Illus.). 144p. 1980. 14.95 (ISBN 0-13-810218-X, Spec); pap. 6.95 (ISBN 0-13-810200-7). P-H.

Silver Azide, Cyanide, Cyanamides, Cyanate, Selenocyanate & Thiocyanate: Solubilities of Solids. M. Salomon. (Solubility Data Ser.: Vol. 3). 1979. 100.00 o.p. (ISBN 0-08-022353-2). Pergamon.

Silver Bird: A Tale for Those Who Dream. Joyce S. Petschek. LC 80-70049. (Illus.). 192p. 1981. pap. 8.95 (ISBN 0-89087-318-6). Celestial Arts.

Silver Bridge. Gray Barker. 1970. 9.95 o.p. (ISBN 0-685-20203-8). Saucerian.

Silver Bullet: The Martini in American Civilization. Lowell Edmunds. LC 80-1196. (Contributions in American Studies: No. 52). (Illus.). 160p. 1981. lib. bdg. 19.95 (ISBN 0-313-22225-8, ESB/). Greenwood.

Silver Bulls. Paul Sarnoff. (Illus.). 265p. 1980. 12.95 (ISBN 0-87000-480-8). Arlington Hse.

Silver Castle. Erica Quest. LC 77-26527. 1978. 7.95 o.p. (ISBN 0-385-14172-6). Doubleday.

Silver Chair. C. S. Lewis. (Illus.). (gr. 4-6). 1953. 8.95 (ISBN 0-02-758770-3). Macmillan.

Silver Chanter: Traditional Scottish Tales & Legends. Wendy Wood. LC 80-670272. (Illus.). 108p. (gr. 4-7). 1980. 10.95 (ISBN 0-7011-2448-2, Pub. by Chatto Bodley Jonathan). Merrimack Bk Serv.

Silver Christmas Ornaments: A Collector's Guide. Clara J. Scroggins. LC 79-15323. (Illus.). 208p. 1980. 25.00 (ISBN 0-498-02385-0). A S Barnes.

Silver Christmas Tree. Pat Hutchins. LC 73-19052. (Illus.). 32p. (gr. k-3). 1974. 6.95 o.s.i. (ISBN 0-02-745920-9). Macmillan.

Silver City. David Norman. (Frontier Rakers: No. 4). (Orig.). 1980. pap. 2.75 (ISBN 0-89083-681-7, Kable News Co). Zebra.

Silver City. Leland Wilson. 96p. (Orig.). 1980. pap. 3.95 (ISBN 0-87178-790-3). Brethren.

Silver Coinage of Massachusetts. Sydney P. Noe. LC 72-77024. 300p. 1974. Repr. 35.00x (ISBN 0-88000-005-8). Quarterman.

Silver Collector's Glossary & a List of Early American Silversmiths & Their Marks. Hollis French. LC 67-27454. (Architecture & Decorative Art Ser). 1967. lib. bdg. 17.50 (ISBN 0-306-70969-4). Da Capo.

Silver Dust & Spanish Wine: A History of Mexico. Joan Olson & Gene Olson. LC 80-51869. (Illus.). 336p. (Orig.). (gr. 9 up). 1980. pap. text ed. 6.97x (ISBN 0-913366-06-4). Windyridge.

Silver Gilt. Netta Muskett. 1978. pap. 1.75 o.s.i. (ISBN 0-515-04538-1). Jove Pubns.

Silver: Its History & Romance. Benjamin White. LC 71-174144. (Illus.). xxviii, 325p. 1972. Repr. of 1920 ed. 24.00 (ISBN 0-8103-3930-7). Gale.

Silver Jasmine. Janet L. Roberts. (Orig.). 1980. pap. 2.50 (ISBN 0-446-81998-0). Warner Bks.

Silver Lobby: A Guide to Advocacy for Older Persons. Clinton W. Hess & Paul A. Kerschner. LC 78-61804. 1978. pap. 2.50 (ISBN 0-88474-075-7). USC Andrus Geron.

Silver Mace. Maud Petersham & Miska Petersham. (gr. 4-6). 1964. 4.75g o.s.i. (ISBN 0-02-773660-1). Macmillan.

Silver Masking of Transparencies with Three-Aim-Point Control. 1980. pap. 4.00 (ISBN 0-87985-259-3, Q-7A). Eastman Kodak.

Silver Mistress. Peter O'Donnell. (Modesty Blaise Ser.). (Illus.). 256p. 1980. 9.95 (ISBN 0-915822-51-2). Archival Pr.

Silver Mistress. Brad Spear. 1981. pap. 2.25 (ISBN 0-440-07940-3). Dell.

Silver Nightingale. Sylvia Thorpe. 224p. 1977. pap. 1.50 o.p. (ISBN 0-449-23379-0, Crest). Fawcett.

Silver Pilgrimage. M. Anantanarayanan. (Indian Novels Ser.). 160p. 1976. pap. 2.75 (ISBN 0-89253-022-7). Ind-US Inc.

Silver Poets of the Sixteenth Century. Ed. by Gerald Bullett. 1955. 12.95x (ISBN 0-460-00985-0, Evman); pap. 4.95 (ISBN 0-460-01985-6). Dutton.

Silver Queen: The Fabulous Story of Baby Doe Tabor. Caroline Bancroft. pap. 2.75 (ISBN 0-933472-21-8). Johnson Colo.

Silver Revolution & the New Monetary Order of the World. John D. Radigan. (Illus.). 129p. 1981. 49.85 (ISBN 0-89266-283-2). Am Classical Coll Pr.

Silver Spooner. Darcy O'Brien. 1981. 13.95 (ISBN 0-671-25264-X). S&S.

Silver Spurs. R. Knigge. LC 75-10111. 1973. 4.25 (ISBN 0-915614-01-4); incl. record 5.95 (ISBN 0-685-57207-2). Knollwood Pub.

Silver Spurs. Charles A. Seltzer. 277p. 1975. Repr. of 1935 ed. lib. bdg. 12.25 (ISBN 0-88411-109-1). Amereon Ltd.

Silver Streak. Jim Rogers. 1976. pap. 1.75 o.p. (ISBN 0-345-25458-9). Ballantine.

Silver Sun. Nancy Springer. (gr. 10-12). 1980. pap. write for info. (ISBN 0-671-83496-7). PB.

Silver Swan. Horace Gregory & Marya Zaturenska. LC 66-12031. (Illus.). 1968. pap. 1.50 o.s.i. (ISBN 0-02-069550-0, Collier). Macmillan.

Silver Sword. Ian Serraillier. LC 59-6556. (Illus.). (gr. 7-9). 1959. 9.95 (ISBN 0-87599-104-1). S G Phillips.

Silver Thaw. Betty Neels. (Harlequin Romances Ser.). 192p. (Orig.). 1981. pap. 1.25 (ISBN 0-373-02386-3, Pub. by Harlequin). PB.

Silver: The Restless Metal. Roy W. Jastram. 225p. 1981. 23.95 (ISBN 0-471-03912-8, Pub. by Wiley-Interscience). Wiley.

Silver Threads to Love. Ethel Van Pelt. 192p. (YA) 1976. 5.95 (ISBN 0-685-62628-8, Avalon). Bouregy.

Silver Touch & Other Family Christmas Stories. Margaret Rettich. Tr. by Elizabeth D. Crawford. (Illus.). (gr. 4-6). 1978. 7.50 o.p. (ISBN 0-688-22164-5); PLB 7.63 (ISBN 0-688-32164-X). Morrow.

Silver Warriors. Michael J. Moorcock. 1977. pap. 1.75 o.s.i. (ISBN 0-440-17994-7). Dell.

Silver Web. Jean Nash. (Orig.). 1980. pap. 2.25 (ISBN 0-505-51473-7). Tower Bks.

Silverhill. Phyllis Whitney. 1978. pap. 2.25 (ISBN 0-449-24094-0, Crest). Fawcett.

Silversmiths. Leonard E. Fisher. LC 64-17792. (Colonial Americans Ser). (Illus.). (gr. 4-6). 1965. PLB 4.90 o.p. (ISBN 0-531-01036-8). Watts.

Silyated Surfaces, Vol. 7. D. Leyden & W. Collins. (Midland Macromolecular Monographs). 1980. 63.50 (ISBN 0-677-13370-7). Gordon.

Simeon North: First Official Pistol Maker of the United States. North & North. Repr. 9.95 (ISBN 0-88227-001-X). Gun Room.

Similarity Methods in Engineering Dynamics: Theory & Practice of Scale Modeling. Wilfred Baker et al. (Illus.). 1973. 22.95x (ISBN 0-8104-9214-8). Hayden.

Similarity, Self-Similarity & Intermediate Asymptotics. Ed. by Barenblatt. (Illus.). 1979. 35.00 (ISBN 0-306-10956-5, Consultants). Plenum Pub.

Simon & Schuster Book of the Ballet. Ed. by Montadori Editors. (Illus.). 1980. 24.95 (ISBN 0-671-25099-X). S&S.

Simon & Schuster Crossword Book of Quotations. Ed. by Eugene T. Maleska. (Series 12). (Orig.). 1980. pap. write for info. (ISBN 0-671-24090-0, Fireside). S&S.

Simon & Schuster Guide to Shells. Harold Feinberg. (Illus.). 1980. 22.50 (ISBN 0-686-60938-7, 25319); pap. 9.95 (ISBN 0-686-60939-5, 25320). S&S.

Simon Bolivar: The Liberator. Robert N. Webb. LC 66-12146. (Biography Ser). (gr. 7 up). 1966. PLB 5.90 o.p. (ISBN 0-531-00856-8). Watts.

Simon Boom Gives a Wedding. Yuri Suhl. LC 70-161015. (Illus.). 48p. (gr. k-3). 1972. 6.72 (ISBN 0-590-07209-9, Four Winds). Schol Bk Serv.

Simon Cameron: Ante Bellum Years. Lee F. Crippen. LC 76-168674. (American Scene Ser). 1972. Repr. of 1942 ed. lib. bdg. 32.50 (ISBN 0-306-70362-9). Da Capo.

Simon de Montfort: Reformer & Rebel. Luckock. 3.38 (ISBN 0-08-008757-4). Pergamon.

Simon Peter. Martin R. De Haan. 1954. 4.95 (ISBN 0-310-23481-6). Zondervan.

Simon Peter: The Boy Who Became a Fisherman. Gerald N. Battle. LC 75-135353. (Illus.). (gr. 3-7). 1970. 3.95 o.p. (ISBN 0-87680-179-3). Word Bks.

Simon the Coldheart. Georgette Heyer. 1976. Repr. of 1925 ed. lib. bdg. 16.20x (ISBN 0-89966-118-1). Buccaneer Bks.

Simon the Small. Mary Ranger. (Starlight Ser.). (Illus.). (gr. 5-8). 1977. pap. 2.25 (ISBN 0-570-03613-5, 39-1101). Concordia.

Simone de Beauvoir. Konrad Bieber. (World Authors Ser.: No. 532). 1979. lib. bdg. 13.50 (ISBN 0-8057-6374-0). Twayne.

Simone De Beauvoir. Robert D. Cottrell. LC 74-34131. (Modern Literature Ser.). 1975. 10.95 (ISBN 0-8044-2132-3). Ungar.

Simone De Beauvoir: A Life of Freedom. Carol Ascher. LC 80-70361. 256p. 1981. 13.95 (ISBN 0-8070-3240-9). Beacon Pr.

Simone de Beauvoir: Encounters with Death. Elaine Marks. 1973. 14.00 (ISBN 0-8135-0707-3). Rutgers U Pr.

Simone Weil: A Sketch for a Portrait. Richard Rees. LC 66-11154. (Crosscurrents-Modern Critiques Ser.). 215p. 1966. 10.95 (ISBN 0-8093-0191-1). S Ill U Pr.

Simone Weil: A Sketch for a Protrait. Richard Rees. LC 77-24990. (Arcturus Books Paperbacks). 215p. 1978. pap. 6.95 (ISBN 0-8093-0852-5). S Ill U Pr.

Simple Biflagellate Holocarpic Phycomycetes. 2nd ed. J. S. Karling. (Illus.). 1981. lib. bdg. 60.00x. Lubrecht & Cramer.

Simple Celestial Navigation. Maxwell Kelch. (Illus.). 1975. pap. 5.95 o.p. (ISBN 0-87799-051-4). Aztex.

Simple Checkmates. Tony Gillam. 1978. pap. 5.95 (ISBN 0-7134-1482-0, Pub. by Batsford England). David & Charles.

Simple Chess. Michael Stean. 1978. 9.50 o.p. (ISBN 0-571-11215-3, Pub. by Faber & Faber); pap. 4.95 (ISBN 0-571-11257-9). Merrimack Bk Serv.

Simple Chess Tactics. Tony Gillam. 1978. pap. 5.95 (ISBN 0-7134-1480-4, Pub. by Batsford England). David & Charles.

Simple Composition. Charles Wuorinen. (Music Ser.). 1979. pap. text ed. 13.95x (ISBN 0-582-28059-1). Longman.

Simple Cooking for the Epicure. J. H. Campbell & G. Kameron. (Keith Jennison Large Type Bks). 7.95 o.p. (ISBN 0-531-00281-0). Watts.

Simple Craft Jewellery. 3rd ed. Claude Geoffroy-Dechaume. 1963. 6.95 (ISBN 0-571-05733-0, Pub. by Faber & Faber). Merrimack Bk Serv.

Simple Cross Stitch. Ondori Company Staff. (Ondori Young Handicrafts Ser). (Illus.). 104p. 1977. pap. 3.50 o.p. (ISBN 0-87040-399-0). Japan Pubns.

Simple Decoupage: Having Fun with Cutouts. Alice Gilbreath. LC 77-22088. (Illus.). (gr. 3-7). 1978. 6.50 (ISBN 0-688-22134-3); PLB 6.24 (ISBN 0-688-32134-8). Morrow.

Simple Dielectric Liquids: Mobility, Conduction, & Breakdown. T. J. Gallagher. (Oxford Science Research Papers Ser). (Illus.). 180p. 1975. pap. 24.95x (ISBN 0-19-851933-8). Oxford U Pr.

Simple Embroidery. Ondori Publishing Co. Staff. (Ondori Handicrafts Ser.). (Illus.). 72p. 1976. pap. 5.50 (ISBN 0-87040-377-X). Japan Pubns.

Simple Food for the Good Life: An Alternative Cook Book. Helen Nearing. 1980. 12.95 (ISBN 0-440-08479-2). Delacorte.

Simple French Food. Richard Olney. LC 73-80755. (Illus.). pap. 7.95 (ISBN 0-689-70546-8, 229). Atheneum.

Simple Gasoline Engine Repair. Ross R. Olney. LC 72-160876. 1972. pap. 3.50 (ISBN 0-385-03778-3, Dolp). Doubleday.

Simple Geological Structures. John Platt & John Challinor. 1974. pap. text ed. 4.95x (ISBN 0-04-550020-7). Allen Unwin.

Simple Guides to Daily Growth: Problem Solving or Purposeful Relaxation for Comfort or Effectiveness, Set-SG. rev. ed. Russell E. Mason. 1975. pap. 25.00x (ISBN 0-89533-001-6); tape-1a, t-2, t-5a, notes, clinical applications, differential criteria, implications for bioawareness 1979 incl. F I Comm.

Simple Home Repairs. Elizabeth Gundrey. (Orig.). 1980. pap. 6.95x (ISBN 0-8464-1050-8). Beekman Pubs.

Simple IC Test Instruments You Can Build. Rufus P. Turner. LC 79-90832. 1979. pap. 4.95 (ISBN 0-672-21683-3). Sams.

Simple Living. E. K. Ziegler. 1975. pap. 1.25 (ISBN 0-89129-078-8, PV078). Jove Pubns.

Simple Low-Cost Wire Antennas for Radio Amateurs. William I. Orr & S. D. Cowan. LC 76-190590. (Illus.). 192p. 1972. 6.95 (ISBN 0-933616-02-3). Radio Pubns.

Simple Lust: Collected Poems of South African Jail & Exile. Dennis Brutus. 176p. 1973. 7.95 (ISBN 0-8090-8678-6); pap. 3.45 o.p. (ISBN 0-8090-1371-1). Hill & Wang.

Simple Method of Solving Equations of the Fourth Degree. Laughlin. 2.00 o.p. (ISBN 0-686-00168-0). Columbia Graphs.

Simple Methods for Detecting Buying & Selling Points in Securities. James Liveright. Repr. of 1968 ed. flexible cover 3.50 (ISBN 0-87034-028-X). Fraser Pub Co.

Simple Nervous Systems. Ed. by D. R. Newth & P. N. Usherwood. LC 75-7810. 1975. 47.50x (ISBN 0-8448-0713-3). Crane-Russak Co.

Simple Object Lessons for Children. Tom A. Biller & Martie Biller. (Object Lesson Ser.). 160p. 1980. pap. 4.95 (ISBN 0-8010-0793-3). Baker Bk.

Simple Outlines on the Christian Faith. Russell E. Spray. (Dollar Sermon Library). 1977. pap. 1.45 (ISBN 0-8010-8120-3). Baker Bk.

Simple Paper Craft. Gunvor Ask & Harriet Ask. 1971. 16.95 (ISBN 0-7134-2293-9, Pub. by Batsford England). David & Charles.

Simple Pascal. Jim McGregor & Alan Watt. 1981. text ed. price not set (ISBN 0-914894-72-2). Computer Sci. Postponed.

Simple Printing. J. Ben Lieberman. (Root Technologies Ser.: Bk. II). (Illus.). Date not set. write for info. (ISBN 0-918142-09-1); pap. write for info. (ISBN 0-918142-11-3). Myriade. Postponed.

Simple Printing. J. Ben Lieberman. 1980. pap. 6.95 o.p. (ISBN 0-918142-11-3). Caroline Hse.

Simple Propagation: Propagation by Seed, Division, Layering, Cuttings, Budding & Grafting. Noel J. Proktor. (Illus.). 246p. 1981. pap. 8.95 (ISBN 0-571-11707-4, Pub. by Faber & Faber). Merrimack Bk Serv.

Simple Quantum Physics. P. V. Landshoff & A. J. Metherell. LC 78-73244. (Illus.). 1980. 29.95 (ISBN 0-521-22498-5); pap. 9.95 (ISBN 0-521-29538-6). Cambridge U Pr.

Simple Science Experiments. Hans J. Press. 1974. 14.95 (ISBN 0-7134-2894-5, Pub. by Batsford England). David & Charles.

Simple Science Fun: Experiments with Light, Sound, Air & Water. Bob Ridiman. LC 72-664. (Humpty Dumpty Bk). (Illus.). 56p. (gr. k-3). 1972. 5.95 o.s.i. (ISBN 0-8193-0606-1, Four Winds); PLB 5.41 o.s.i. (ISBN 0-8193-0607-X). Schol Bk Serv.

Simple Sermons for Funeral Services. W. Herschel Ford. pap. 3.95 (ISBN 0-310-24461-7). Zondervan.

Simple Sermons for Midweek Services. W. Herschel Ford. pap. 3.95 (ISBN 0-310-24531-1). Zondervan.

Simple Sermons for Modern Man. W. Herschel Ford. pap. 2.95 (ISBN 0-310-24541-9). Zondervan.

Simple Sermons for Special Days & Occasions. W. Herschel Ford. pap. 2.95 (ISBN 0-310-24661-X). Zondervan.

Simple Sermons for Sunday Evening. W. Herschel Ford. 1967. 3.95 (ISBN 0-310-24671-7). Zondervan.

Simple Sermons for Time & Eternity. W. Herschel Ford. pap. 3.95 (ISBN 0-310-24701-2). Zondervan.

Simple Sermons from the Book of Acts. W. Herschel Ford. pap. 6.95 (ISBN 0-310-24401-3). Zondervan.

Simple Sermons on Conversion & Commitment. W. Herschel Ford. pap. 3.95 (ISBN 0-310-24441-2). Zondervan.

Simple Sermons on Evangelistic Themes. W. Herschel Ford. pap. 3.95 (ISBN 0-310-24451-X). Zondervan.

Simple Sermons on Grace & Glory. W. Herschel Ford. 1977. pap. 3.95 (ISBN 0-310-24751-9). Zondervan.

Simple Sermons on Heaven, Hell, & Judgment. W. Herschel Ford. pap. 2.95 (ISBN 0-310-24481-1). Zondervan.

Simple Sermons on Life & Living. W. Herschel Ford. pap. 3.95 (ISBN 0-310-24511-7). Zondervan.

Simple Sermons on Old Testament Texts. W. Herschel Ford. 112p. 1975. pap. 3.95 (ISBN 0-310-24561-3). Zondervan.

Simple Sermons on Prayer. W. Herschel Ford. pap. 3.95 (ISBN 0-310-24581-8). Zondervan.

Simple Sermons on Prophetic Themes. W. Herschel Ford. pap. 3.95 (ISBN 0-310-24591-5). Zondervan.

Simple Sermons on Sevens Churches of the Revelation. W. Herschel Ford. pap. 3.95 (ISBN 0-310-24431-5). Zondervan.

Simple Sermons on Simple Themes. W. Herschel Ford. pap. 2.95 o.p. (ISBN 0-310-24641-5). Zondervan.

Simple Sermons on the Ten Commandments. W. Herschel Ford. pap. 3.95 (ISBN 0-310-24691-1). Zondervan.

Simple Singularities & Simple Algebraic Groups. P. Slodowy. (Lecture Notes in Mathematics: Vol. 815). 175p. 1980. pap. 11.80 (ISBN 0-387-10026-1). Springer-Verlag.

Simple Songs for Young Children. Compiled by Patricia Shely. (Standard Ideas Ser.). (Illus.). 1978. pap. 1.75 (ISBN 0-87239-214-7, 2815). Standard Pub.

Simple Spanish Cookery. PPP Inc. 1977. 2.95 (ISBN 0-442-82575-7). Peter Pauper.

Simple Squeeze in Bridge. Frank P. Schuld. LC 74-6305. (Illus.). 1977. 10.95 (ISBN 0-8069-8662-X); PLB 9.29 (ISBN 0-8069-8663-8); pap. 5.95 (ISBN 0-8069-8664-6). Sterling.

Simple Stuffed Toys. Ondori Company Staff. (Ondori Young Handicrafts Ser). (Illus.). 1977. pap. 3.50 o.p. (ISBN 0-87040-398-2). Japan Pubns.

Simple Subs Book. L. Sellers. 1968. 21.00 (ISBN 0-08-013042-9); pap. 12.75 (ISBN 0-08-013041-0). Pergamon.

Simple Tales for the Very Young. Doris Rust. (Illus.). (ps-5). 1960. 4.95 o.p. (ISBN 0-571-03842-5, Pub. by Faber & Faber). Merrimack Bk Serv.

Simple Welcome Speeches & Other Helps. Amy Bolding. (Pocket Pulpit Library). 1973. pap. 2.25 (ISBN 0-8010-0612-0). Baker Bk.

Simplefied Painless Endodontics for the General Dentist: An Alternative to N 2. David Pyner. (Illus.). 171p. 1980. 48.00 (ISBN 0-931386-12-8). Quint Pub Co.

Simplicity. Elliott Sober. (Clarendon Library of Logic & Philosophy). (Illus.). 160p. 1975. 24.00x (ISBN 0-19-824407-X). Oxford U Pr.

Simplicity of Prayer: A Discussion of the Methods & Results of Christian Prayer. H. A. Williams. LC 77-78649. 80p. 1977. pap. 2.50 (ISBN 0-8006-1315-5, 1-1315). Fortress.

Simplicius Simplicissimus. Johann Grimmelshausen. Tr. by George Schulz-Behrend. LC 63-16934. (Orig.). 1965. pap. 6.95 (ISBN 0-672-60424-8, LLA186). Bobbs.

Simplified Approach to S-370 Assembly Language Programming. Barbara J. Burian. (Illus.). 1977. 17.95 (ISBN 0-13-810119-1); self study guide 7.50 (ISBN 0-13-810101-9). P-H.

Simplified Basic Programming. Gerald A. Silver & J. Silver. (Illus.). 320p. 1974. pap. 15.75 o.p. (ISBN 0-07-057387-5, G). McGraw.

Simplified BASIC Programming: With Companion Problems. Lisa Rosenblatt & Judah Rosenblatt. 1973. pap. text ed. 8.95 (ISBN 0-201-06512-6). A-W.

Simplified Behavior & "Feeling" State Change & Goal Accomplishment, Set-SB. Russell E. Mason. 1975. pap. 50.00x (ISBN 0-89533-002-4); tape-1a, t-2, t-5a, t-3, t-16, t-17 incl., notes, clinical applications, substitution training. F I Comm.

Simplified Boatbuilding: Flat Bottom. Harry V. Sucher. (Illus.). 1973. 24.95 (ISBN 0-393-03173-X). Norton.

Simplified Building Design for Wind & Earthquake Forces. James Ambrose & Dimitry Vergun. LC 79-26660. 1980. 24.00 (ISBN 0-471-05013-X, Pub. by Wiley-Interscience). Wiley.

Simplified Concrete Masonry Planning & Building. 2nd, rev. ed. J. Ralph Dalzell. Rev. by Frederick S. Merritt. LC 81-385. 398p. 1981. Repr. of 1972 ed. lib. bdg. price not set (ISBN 0-89874-278-1). Krieger.

Simplified Design of Building Foundations. James Ambrose. 384p. 1981. 20.00 (ISBN 0-471-06267-7, Pub. by Wiley-Interscience). Wiley.

Simplified Design of Reinforced Concrete. 4th ed. Harry Parker & Harold D. Hauf. LC 75-38840. 1976. 21.95 (ISBN 0-471-66069-8, Pub. by Wiley-Interscience). Wiley.

Simplified Design of Structural Steel. 4th ed. Harry Parker & Harold D. Hauf. LC 73-13562. 326p. 1974. 22.00 (ISBN 0-471-66432-4, Pub. by Wiley-Interscience). Wiley.

Simplified Design of Structural Wood. 2nd ed. Harry Parker & H. D. Hauf. LC 78-9888. 1979. 19.95 (ISBN 0-471-66630-0, Pub. by Wiley-Interscience). Wiley.

Simplified Drugs & Solutions for Nurses, Including Arithmetic. 7th ed. Norma Dison. LC 79-28198. (Illus.). 1980. pap. text ed. 8.50 (ISBN 0-8016-1311-6). Mosby.

Simplified Engineering for Architects & Builders. 5th ed. Harry Parker & Harold D. Hauf. LC 74-18068. 362p. 1975. 24.50 (ISBN 0-471-66201-1, Pub. by Wiley-Interscience). Wiley.

Simplified Extended, Deep, & or Meditative Relaxation, Set-R. Russell E. Mason. 1975. pap. 25.00x (ISBN 0-89533-004-0); tape-1a, t-l, t-6, relaxation training, clinical applications incl. (ISBN 0-89533-026-1). F I Comm.

Simplified Fly Fishing. S. R. Slaymaker, 2nd. LC 69-15262. (Illus.). 1969. 9.95 o.p. (ISBN 0-06-036061-5, HarpT). Har-Row.

Simplified Fortran Programming: With Companion Problems. Lisa Rosenblatt & Judah Rosenblatt. 1973. pap. text ed. 8.95 (ISBN 0-201-06511-8). A-W.

Simplified Golf: There's No Trick to It! Peter Longo. Ed. by Boye De Mente. (Illus.). 144p. (Orig.). 1980. pap. 9.95 (ISBN 0-914778-34-X). Phoenix Bks.

Simplified Guide to Construction Management for Architects & Engineers. James E. Gorman. LC 75-34480. 288p. 1976. 17.95 (ISBN 0-8436-0160-4). CBI Pub.

Simplified Guide to Estate Planning & Administration. Robert Whitman. 192p. 1981. pap. 6.95 (ISBN 0-671-09136-0). Monarch Pr.

Simplified Home Appliance Repairs. Dan Browne. LC 76-4732. (Illus.). 1978. 12.95 o.p. (ISBN 0-03-042636-7); pap. 6.95 o.p. (ISBN 0-03-015621-1). HR&W.

Simplified Indian Cookery. Rebecca Joseph. 1970. pap. 3.00 (ISBN 0-88253-144-1). Ind-US Inc.

Simplified Introduction to the Wisdom of St. Thomas. Peter A. Redpath. LC 80-5230. 180p. 1980. lib. bdg. 17.50 (ISBN 0-8191-1058-2); pap. text ed. 8.50 (ISBN 0-8191-1059-0). U Pr of Amer.

Simplified Mechanics & Strength of Materials. 3rd ed. Harry Parker & Harold D. Hauf. LC 76-56465. 304p. 1977. 22.95 (ISBN 0-471-66562-2, Pub. by Wiley-Interscience). Wiley.

Simplified Medical Dictionary. R. Franks & H. Swartz. 1977. 14.50 (ISBN 0-87489-054-3). Med Economics.

Simplified Medical Dictionary. Richard Franks. 1977. pap. text ed. 12.52 (ISBN 0-8273-1786-7). Delmar.

Simplified Physics for Radiology Students. Barbara Howl. (Illus.). 96p. 1971. 8.75 (ISBN 0-398-02184-8). C C Thomas.

Simplified Quantity Ethnic Recipies. Mabel Caviani et al. (Ahrens Ser.). 272p. 1980. 15.95 (ISBN 0-8104-9474-4). Hayden.

Simplified Quantity Regional Recipes. Mabel Cavaiani et al. 1979. 15.25 (ISBN 0-8104-9453-1). Hayden.

Simplified Radiotelephone License Course, 3 Vols. Leonard C. Lane. (Illus.). 1971. combined ed. 18.50 (ISBN 0-8104-0755-8); Set. pap. 24.05 (ISBN 0-8104-0751-5); Vol. 1. pap. 7.75 (ISBN 0-8104-0752-3); Vol. 2. pap. 8.60 (ISBN 0-8104-0753-1); Vol. 3. pap. 7.70 (ISBN 0-8104-0754-X). Hayden.

Simplified Recipes for Day Care Centers. Patricia D. Asmussen. LC 74-222. 224p. 1976. spiral bdg. 12.95 (ISBN 0-8436-0590-1). CBI Pub.

Simplified Relaxation, Problem Solutions & Substitutions, & Value Considerations, Set-S. Russell E. Mason. 1975. pap. 75.00x (ISBN 0-89533-020-2); tape-1a, t-5a, t-10-11, t-12, t-13, t-14, notes incl., clinical applications, substitution training & goal archievements. F I Comm.

Simplified Stair Layout. 2nd ed. Wilson & Werner. LC 70-188808. 64p. 1973. pap. 3.40 (ISBN 0-8273-0103-0). Delmar.

Simplified Statistical Analysis: Handbook of Methods, Examples & Tables. Harry H. Holscher. LC 78-132672. (Illus.). 1971. 19.95 (ISBN 0-8436-0305-4). CBI Pub.

Simplified Style Manual: For the Preparation of Journal Articles in Psychology, Social Sciences, Education & Literature. Marigold Linton. 200p. 1972. 9.95 (ISBN 0-13-810135-3). P-H.

Simplified Swahili. Peter Wilson. 328p. (Orig.). 1981. pap. text ed. 8.95x (ISBN 0-582-62358-8). Longman.

Simplified TV Trouble Diagnosis. Robert L. Goodman. LC 72-94810. 224p. 1973. 8.95 o.p. (ISBN 0-8306-3633-1); pap. 5.95 o.p. (ISBN 0-8306-2633-6, 633). TAB Bks.

Simplifying Office Work. 2nd ed. Oliver Standingford. (Orig.). 1974. pap. 6.95x o.p. (ISBN 0-8464-0850-3). Beekman Pubs.

Simply Beautiful: Living with the Earth in Mind. Elizabeth Leite. (Illus., Orig.). 1980. lib. bdg. 7.95 (ISBN 0-87961-106-5); pap. 3.95 (ISBN 0-87961-107-3). Naturegraph.

Simply Christmas. Noel Pax. (Illus.). 72p. (Orig.). 1980. pap. 3.95 (ISBN 0-8027-7168-8); 5.95 (ISBN 0-8027-0672-X). Walker & Co.

Simply Elegant: A Guide for Elegant but Simple Entertaining. rev. 8th ed. Pearl S. Gordon. LC 77-13166. (Illus.). 208p. 1981. lib. bdg. 12.95 (ISBN 0-9600492-3-1). Simply Elegant.

Simply Seafood Cookbook of East Coast Fish. R. Marilyn Schmidt. (Illus.). 150p. (Orig.). 1980. pap. 7.95 (ISBN 0-937996-00-9). Barnegat.

Simply Seafood Cookbook of East Coast Shellfish. R. Marilyn Schmidt. (Illus.). 150p. (Orig.). 1980. pap. 7.95 (ISBN 0-937996-01-7). Barnegat.

Simply Stews. Shirley Sarris. 1973. pap. 1.25 (ISBN 0-451-07805-5, Y7805, Sig). NAL.

Sims Reeves, Fifty Years of Music in England. Charles E. Pearce. (Music Reprint Ser.). 1980. Repr. of 1924 ed. lib. bdg. 22.50 (ISBN 0-306-76007-X). Da Capo.

SIMSOC (Simulated Society) 3rd ed. Ed. by William A. Gamson. LC 77-84285. 1978. pap. text ed. 7.95 (ISBN 0-02-911170-6). Free Pr.

Simulated Patients (Programmed Patients) The Development & Use of a New Technique in Medical Education. Howard S. Barrows. (Illus.). 80p. 1971. pap. 9.75 (ISBN 0-398-02227-5). C C Thomas.

Simulating Terrorism. Stephen Sloan. LC 80-5937. (Illus.). 200p. 1981. 12.95 (ISBN 0-8061-1746-X); pap. 5.95 (ISBN 0-8061-1760-5). U of Okla Pr.

Simulating the Housing Allowance Program in Green Bay & South Bend: A Comparison of the Urban Institute Housing Model with the Supply Experiment. Jean Vanski & Larry Ozanne. (Institute Paper). 93p. 1978. pap. 6.50 (ISBN 0-87766-236-3, 23800). Urban Inst.

Simulation & Gaming in Social Science. Michael Inbar & Clarice Stoll. LC 74-143527. 1972. 17.95 (ISBN 0-02-915750-1). Free Pr.

Simulation & the Monte Carlo Method. Reuven Y. Rubenstein. (Probability & Mathematical Statistics Ser.). 300p. 1981. 30.00 (ISBN 0-471-08917-6, Pub. by Wiley-Interscience). Wiley.

Simulation & Training Technology for Nuclear Power Plant Safety. Ed. by Albert E. Hickey. 350p. 1981. pap. 40.00 (ISBN 0-89785-975-8). AIR Systems.

Simulation Games: An Introduction for the Social Studies Teacher. Samuel A. Livingston & Clarice S. Stoll. LC 77-171567. (Orig.). 1973. pap. text ed. 8.95 (ISBN 0-02-919240-4). Free Pr.

Simulation Games: Design & Implementation. Robert Maidment & Russell Bronstein. LC 73-75051. 1973. pap. text ed. 6.95 (ISBN 0-675-08968-9). Merrill.

Simulation Games in Learning. Ed. by Sarane S. Boocock & E. O. Schild. LC 68-21913. 1978. pap. 9.95x (ISBN 0-8039-1002-9). Sage.

Simulation Gaming for Values Education: The Prisoner's Dilemma. Ronald T. Hyman. LC 77-93726. 1978. pap. text ed. 8.50x o.p. (ISBN 0-8191-0428-0). U Pr of Amer.

Simulation Model Building: A Statistical Approach to Modelling in the Social Sciences with the Simulation Methods. Urban Norlen. LC 75-4935. 1976. pap. 21.95 (ISBN 0-470-65090-7). Halsted Pr.

Simulation Modeling & Analysis. Averill M. Law & David Kelton. (Illus.). 416p. 1981. text ed. 25.95 (ISBN 0-07-036696-9). McGraw.

Simulation Models in Corporate Planning. Thomas H. Naylor. LC 78-31258. (Praeger Special Studies). 1979. 24.95 (ISBN 0-03-047061-7). Praeger.

Simulation of Assimilation, Respiration & Transpiration of Crops. C. T. DeWit et al. 1978. pap. 18.95 (ISBN 0-470-26494-2). Halsted Pr.

Simulation of Ecological Processes. 2nd ed. C. T. DeWit & J. Houdriaan. 1978. pap. 20.95 (ISBN 0-470-26357-1). Halsted Pr.

Simulation of Lime Aphid Population Dynamics. 165p. 1980. pap. 28.00 (ISBN 90-220-0706-5, PDC 186, PUDOC). Unipub.

Simulation of the Denver Fire Department for Development Policy Analysis. Donald R. Plane et al. 1975. 2.50 (ISBN 0-686-64196-5). U CO Busn Res Div.

Simulation Studies. Ed. by I. Hodder. LC 78-51670. (Illus.). 1979. 24.95 (ISBN 0-521-22025-4). Cambridge U Pr.

Simulation Using GPSS. T. J. Schriber. LC 73-21896. 608p. 1974. 29.95 (ISBN 0-471-76310-1). Wiley.

Simulation with Gasp PL I: A PL I Based Continuous Discrete Simulation Language. Alan B. Pritzker & Robert E. Young. LC 75-23182. 335p. 1975. 24.00 (ISBN 0-471-70046-0, Pub. by Wiley-Interscience). Wiley.

Simulation with Gpss & Gpssv. P. A. Bobillier et al. LC 75-40316. 1976. 25.95 (ISBN 0-13-810549-9). P-H.

Simulations. Herbert-Sturtridge. (ELT Guide Ser.: No. 2). 1979. pap. text ed. 14.50x (ISBN 0-85633-192-9, NFER). Humanities.

Simulations: A Handbook for Teachers. Ken Jones. 180p. 1980. 25.00x (ISBN 0-89397-090-5). Nichols Pub.

Simulations in Archaeology. Ed. by Jeremy A. Sabloff. (School of American Research Advanced Seminar Ser.). (Illus.). 440p. 1981. 29.95x (ISBN 0-8263-0576-8). U of NM Pr.

Simultaneous Equations. Laurence Halley. LC 77-17637. 1978. 7.95 o.p. (ISBN 0-312-72595-7). St Martin.

Sin & Science: Reinhold Niebuhr As Political Theologian. Holtan P. Odegard. 245p. 1956. 13.00 (ISBN 0-9600524-1-0). Advance Planning.

Sin, Sex & Self-Control. Norman V. Peale. 1978. pap. 2.25 (ISBN 0-449-23921-7, Crest). Fawcett.

Sinai- a Mountain Speaks. Basilea Schlink. 1.25 o.p. (ISBN 0-686-12674-2). Evang Sisterhood Mary.

Sinai Blunder: Withdrawal of the United Nations Emergency Force Leading to the Six-Day War of June 1967. I. J. Rikhye. 240p. 1980. 24.00x (ISBN 0-7146-3136-1, F Cass Co). Biblio Dist.

Sinai Myth. Andrew M. Greeley. LC 72-79390. 200p. 1975. pap. 2.45 (ISBN 0-385-08824-8, Im). Doubleday.

Sinan: The Turkish Michelangelo. Veronica De Osa. 1981. 10.95 (ISBN 0-533-04655-6). Vantage.

Sinatra. Earl Wilson. LC 75-44193. (Illus.). 450p. 1976. 9.95 o.s.i. (ISBN 0-02-630090-7, 63009). Macmillan.

Sinbad, the Sailor. (MacDonald Educational Ser.). (Illus., Arabic.). 3.50 (ISBN 0-686-53088-8). Intl Bk Ctr.

Since Cumorah. Hugh C. Nibley. 7.95 o.p. (ISBN 0-87747-240-8). Deseret Bk.

Since Debussy: A View of Contemporary Music. Andre Hodeir. Tr. by Noel Burch. LC 74-28310. (Illus.). 256p. 1975. Repr. of 1961 ed. lib. bdg. 22.50 (ISBN 0-306-70662-8). Da Capo.

Since Jesus Passed by. Frances Hunter & Charles Hunter. 1973. pap. 1.95 (ISBN 0-917726-38-3). Hunter Bks.

Since Nineteen Forty-Five: Politics & Diplomacy in Recent American History. 2nd ed. Robert A. Divine. LC 79-12157. 1979. pap. text ed. 8.95 (ISBN 0-471-04908-5). Wiley.

Since Nineteen Sixty-Four: New & Selected Poems. Peter Schjeldahl. LC 78-15572. 1978. pap. 4.00 (ISBN 0-915342-26-X). SUN.

Since Silent Spring. Frank Graham, Jr. 1977. pap. 1.75 o.p. (ISBN 0-449-23141-0, Crest). Fawcett.

Since Socrates. Henry Perkinson. 1979. pap. text ed. 8.95x (ISBN 0-582-28098-2). Longman.

Since Socrates: Studies in the History of Western Educational Thought. Henry J. Perkinson. LC 79-9150. 222p. 1980. pap. 8.95 (ISBN 0-582-28098-2). Longman.

Since You Went Away. Donald I. Rogers. LC 72-91642. 320p. 1973. 8.95 o.p. (ISBN 0-87000-195-7). Arlington Hse.

Sincerest Form of Flattery. Paul D. Herbert. LC 80-67699. (Sherlock Holmes Reference Ser.). 128p. 1981. 14.95 (ISBN 0-934468-04-4). Gaslight.

Sinclair Lewis. Sheldon N. Grebstein. (U. S. Authors Ser.: No. 14). lib. bdg. 9.95 (ISBN 0-8057-0448-5). Twayne.

Sinclair Lewis. James Lundquist. LC 72-76774. (Modern Literature Ser.). 10.95 (ISBN 0-8044-2562-0). Ungar.

Sinclair Ross. Lorraine McMullen. (World Authors Ser.: No. 504). 1979. lib. bdg. 14.95 (ISBN 0-8057-6385-6). Twayne.

Sinful Ones. Fritz Lieber. (Science Fiction Ser.). 1980. lib. bdg. 13.95 (ISBN 0-8398-2643-5). Gregg.

Sinful, the Intimate, & the Mysterious Life of Mary Magdalene, 2 vols. Bonaventura Saba. (Illus.). 1978. Set. 79.75 (ISBN 0-89266-133-X). Am Classical Coll Pr.

Sinful Tunes & Spirituals: Black Folk Music to the Civil War. Dena J Epstein. LC 77-6315. (Music in American Life Ser.). (Illus.). 1977. 17.95 (ISBN 0-252-00520-1); pap. 10.95 (ISBN 0-252-00875-8). U of Ill Pr.

Sing a Rainbow: Musical Activities with Mentally Handicapped Children. David Ward. (Illus.). 64p. (Orig.). 1979. pap. text ed. 8.95x (ISBN 0-19-317416-2). Oxford U Pr.

Sing a Sad Song: The Life of Hank Williams. Roger M. Williams. LC 80-15520. (Music in American Life Ser.). 275p. 1981. 18.95 (ISBN 0-252-00844-8); pap. 7.95 (ISBN 0-252-00861-8). U of Ill Pr.

Sing a Song of People. Roberta McLaughlin & Lucille Wood. (ps-3). 1973. songbook 9.00 (ISBN 0-8372-0765-7); 3 lp records 8.49 ea.; sets 1-3, incl. 2 filmstrips lp record & 20 minibks 45.00 ea.; 3 sets incl. 2 filmstrips, 2 cassettes & 20 minibks 45.00 ea.; minibks. sep. sets of 10 6.00 (ISBN 0-685-24085-1); complete kit cassette ed. 171.00 (ISBN 0-8372-0219-1); flannelbd. figures 3.93 (ISBN 0-8372-0220-5); complete kit, record edition 171.00 (ISBN 0-8372-0218-3). Bowmar-Noble.

Sing a Song of Seasons. Sara Brewton & John E. Brewton. (Illus.). (gr. 4-6). 1955. 5.95g o.s.i. (ISBN 0-02-712890-3). Macmillan.

Sing a Song of Solomon. Norman Habel. (Purple Puzzle Tree Bk). (Illus.). (ps-5). 1972. pap. 0.85 (ISBN 0-570-06519-4, 56-1223). Concordia.

Sing a Song to Jenny Next. Lawrence Gardella. 1981. 12.95 (ISBN 0-525-20462-8). Dutton.

Sing Along-Senior Citizens. Ed. by R. E. Grant. 108p. 1973. pap. 7.50 (ISBN 0-398-02722-6). C C Thomas.

Sing & Be Happy: Songs for the Young Child. Clara B. Baker. LC 80-13421. (Illus.). 96p. 1980. pap. 6.95 (ISBN 0-687-38547-4). Abingdon.

Sing Children Sing. Ed. by Carl Miller. (gr. k up). 1972. pap. 3.50 (ISBN 0-935738-05-3, 5027). US Comm UNICEF.

Sing Down the Moon. Scott O'Dell. LC 71-98513. (gr. 5 up). 1970. 9.95 (ISBN 0-395-10919-1). HM.

Sing for Our Execution: Poems. Jensma Wopko. (Illus.). 1973. pap. 10.00 (ISBN 0-86975-021-6, Pub by Ravan Press). Three Continents.

Sing for Your Supper, Snoopy. Charles Schulz. 128p. 1981. pap. 1.75 (ISBN 0-449-24403-2, Crest). Fawcett.

Sing Hey for Christmas Day! Ed. by Lee B. Hopkins. LC 75-6612. (Illus.). 32p. (gr. 1-5). 1975. 4.75 (ISBN 0-15-274960-8, HJ). HarBraceJ.

Sing It! Amy Sit. 1979. pap. 2.95 (ISBN 0-917726-39-1). Hunter Bks.

Sing Me a Love Song. Jacob Benjamin. (Orig.). 1980. pap. 1.75 (ISBN 0-532-23173-2). Manor Bks.

Sing Out Charley. Margaret Hodges. 96p. 1968. 3.50 (ISBN 0-374-36930-5). FS&G.

Sing-Song, Repr. Of 1872 Ed. Christina Rossetti. Bd. with Speaking Likenesses. Repr. of 1874 ed; Goblin Market. Repr. of 1893 ed. LC 75-32176. (Classics of Children's Literature, 1621-1932: Vol. 39). (Illus.). 1977. PLB 38.00 (ISBN 0-8240-2288-2). Garland Pub.

Sing the Faith-Poems of the Spirit. Errol T. Elliott. 1975. 3.00 o.p. (ISBN 0-913408-21-2); pap. 2.00 o.p. (ISBN 0-913408-60-3). Friends United.

Sing the Lord's Song in a Strange Land: The Life of Justin Morgan. Betty Bandel. LC 78-73309. 280p. 1981. 17.50 (ISBN 0-8386-2411-1). Fairleigh Dickinson.

Sing the Lord's Song in a Strange Land: The Life of Justin Morgan. Betty Bandel. LC 78-73309. 264p. 1981. 24.50 (ISBN 0-8386-2411-1). Fairleigh Dickinson.

Sing Through the Seasons: Ninety-Nine Songs for Children. Illus. by Susanna Moneli & Moneli. LC 70-164916. (Illus.). 190p. 9.75 (ISBN 0-87486-006-7); l.p. record 5.25 (ISBN 0-87486-040-7); with record 15.00 (ISBN 0-686-66591-0). Plough.

Sing Together: A Girl Scout Songbook. Girl Scouts of the USA. (Illus.). (gr. 1-12). 1973. 4.50 (ISBN 0-88441-309-8, 20-206). GS.

Sing with Me. (gr. 1-6). 5.00 (ISBN 0-87747-362-5). Deseret Bk.

Sing with Understanding. Harry Eskew & Hugh T. McElrath. LC 79-55293. 1980. 12.95 (ISBN 0-8054-6809-9). Broadman.

Singapore in Southeast Asia: An Economic & Political Appraisal. Iain Buchanan. LC 72-183727. (Illus.). 336p. 1972. 15.00x (ISBN 0-7135-1656-9). Intl Pubns Serv.

Singapore: The Chain of Disaster. S. Woodburn Kirby. (Illus.). 1971. 8.95 o.s.i. (ISBN 0-02-563200-0). Macmillan.

Singer & Accompanist: The Performance of Fifty Songs. Gerald Moore. LC 73-11859. (Illus.). xi, 232p. 1973. Repr. of 1953 ed. lib. bdg. 18.00x (ISBN 0-8371-7090-7, MOSC). Greenwood.

Singer & His Art. Askel Schiotz. LC 69-15259. (Illus.). 1970. 10.95 o.p. (ISBN 0-06-035817-3, HarpT). Har-Row.

Singer & the Voice: Vocal Physiology & Technique for Singers. 2nd ed. Arnold Rose. (Illus.). 267p. 1978. 15.95 (ISBN 0-85967-446-0, Pub. by Scolar Pr England); pap. 7.95 (ISBN 0-85967-447-9). Biblio Dist.

Singer at the Wedding. Bruce Arnold. 285p. 1980. 17.95 (ISBN 0-241-89825-0, Pub. by Hamish Hamilton England). David & Charles.

Singer in the Shadows. I. Litvag. 1972. 7.95 o.s.i. (ISBN 0-02-573350-8). Macmillan.

Singer in the Stone. John Willett. (gr. 5-8). 1981. 6.95 (ISBN 0-395-30374-5). HM.

Singer of the Eclogues: A Study of Virgilian Pastoral. Paul Alpers. 1979. 17.50x (ISBN 0-520-03651-4). U of Cal Pr.

Singer on the Sand. Norma R. Youngberg. LC 64-17655. (Panda Ser). 1974. pap. 4.95 (ISBN 0-8163-0213-8, 19356-5). Pacific Pr Pub Assn.

Singer Sewing Book. Jessie Hutton & Gladys Cunningham. (Illus.). 1976. 14.95 (ISBN 0-307-09870-2, Golden Pr); pap. 9.95 (ISBN 0-307-09871-0). Western Pub.

Singer's & Actor's Throat. 3rd ed. Norman A. Punt. (Illus.). 112p. 1979. pap. text ed. 7.95x (ISBN 0-433-26451-9). Drama Bk.

Singer's & Actor's Throat: The Vocal Mechanism of the Professional Voice User & Its Care in Health & Disease. 4th, rev. ed. Norman A. Punt. (Illus.). 100p. 1979. pap. write for info. o.p. Heinman.

Singers Glossary of Show Business Jargon. Al Berkman. 1961. 3.00 (ISBN 0-934972-06-0). Melrose Pub Co.

Singers' Italian: A Manual of Diction & Phonetics. Evelina Colorni. 1970. pap. text ed. 7.95 (ISBN 0-02-870620-X). Schirmer Bks.

Singer's Manual of English Diction. Madeleine Marshall. 1953. pap. text ed. 7.95 (ISBN 0-02-871100-9). Schirmer Bks.

Singer's Manual of German & French Diction. Richard G. Cox. 1970. pap. text ed. 6.95 (ISBN 0-02-870650-1). Schirmer Bks.

Singer's Pilgrimage. Blanche Marchesi. LC 77-1941. (Music Reprint Ser.: 1978). (Illus.). 1978. Repr. of 1923 ed. lib. bdg. 27.50 (ISBN 0-306-70878-7). Da Capo.

Singer's Repertoire, 4 vols. 2nd ed. Berton Coffin. Incl. Vol. 1. Coloratura, Lyric & Dramatic Soprano (ISBN 0-8108-0188-4); Vol. 2. Mezzo Soprano & Contralto (ISBN 0-8108-0189-2); Vol. 3. Lyric & Dramatic Tenor (ISBN 0-8108-0190-6); Vol. 4. Baritone & Bass (ISBN 0-8108-0191-4). 1960. Set. 36.00 (ISBN 0-8108-0187-6); 11.00 ea. Scarecrow.

Singing. Herbert Witherspoon. (Music Reprint Ser.). (Illus.). 126p. 1980. Repr. of 1925 ed. lib. bdg. 15.00 (ISBN 0-306-76001-0). Da Capo.

Singing--An Extension of Speech. Russell A. Hammar. LC 78-11756. 1978. lib. bdg. 11.00 (ISBN 0-8108-1182-0). Scarecrow.

Singing & Dancing Games for the Very Young. Esther L. Nelson. LC 77-79513. (Illus.). 1977. 8.95 (ISBN 0-8069-4568-0); lib. bdg. 8.29 (ISBN 0-8069-4569-9). Sterling.

Singing Bone. R. Austin Freeman. LC 75-44972. (Crime Fiction Ser). 1976. Repr. of 1912 ed. lib. bdg. 17.50 (ISBN 0-8240-2367-6). Garland Pub.

Singing Bone. R. Austin Freeman. 1976. lib. bdg. 12.95x (ISBN 0-89968-168-9). Lightyear.

Singing Cowboys. David Rothel. LC 77-89646. (Illus.). 272p. (Orig.). 1981. pap. 10.95 (ISBN 0-498-02523-3). A S Barnes.

Singing David. Illus. by Sekiya Miyoshi. LC 74-110722. (Illus.). (gr. k-3). 1971. PLB 4.90 o.p. (ISBN 0-531-01936-5). Watts.

Singing Entertainer. John Davidson & Cort Casady. LC 79-17183. 227p. 1979. pap. 9.95 (ISBN 0-88284-095-9). Alfred Pub.

Singing for Power: The Song Magic of the Papago Indians of Southern Arizona. Ruth M. Underhill. (Library Reprint Ser.). 1977. 15.75x (ISBN 0-520-03310-8); pap. 2.95 (ISBN 0-520-03280-2). U of Cal Pr.

Singing Forest. H. Mortimer Batten. (Illus.). 214p. (gr. 6 up). 1964. 3.95 (ISBN 0-374-26468-6). FS&G.

Singing in the Shrouds. Ngaio Marsh. 1978. pap. 1.50 (ISBN 0-515-04532-2). Jove Pubns.

Singing Men at Cashel. Austin Clarke. 320p. 1980. text ed. 15.75x (ISBN 0-85105-354-8, Dolmen Pr). Humanities.

Singing Mouse Stories. Emerson Hough. 1976. lib. bdg. 12.50x (ISBN 0-89968-047-X). Lightyear.

Singing Penguins & Puffed-up Toads. William L. Coleman. 128p. (ps-4). 1981. pap. 3.95 (ISBN 0-87123-554-4, 210554). Bethany Fell.

Singing Pope: The Story of Pope John Paul II. Rinna Wolfe. (Illus.). 128p. (gr. 6-8). 1980. 8.95 (ISBN 0-8164-0472-0). Seabury.

Singing Soldiers. John J. Niles. LC 68-26595. 1968. Repr. of 1927 ed. 15.00 (ISBN 0-8103-3416-X). Gale.

Singing Swans. Alexandra Manners. 1977. pap. 1.50 o.p. (ISBN 0-425-03290-6). Berkley Pub.

Singing Takes More Than a Voice. Al Berkman. 1961. 3.00 (ISBN 0-934972-00-1). Melrose Pub Co.

Singing Tree & Laughing Waters. Sylvia Hardwick. LC 71-101534. 1970. pap. 4.95 (ISBN 0-8163-0159-X, 19362-3). Pacific Pr Pub Assn.

Singing Voice. Robert Rushmore. (Apollo Eds.). 1971. pap. 2.25 o.s.i. (ISBN 0-8152-0307-1, A307, TYC-T). T Y Crowell.

Singing Word: Youth with a Mission Songbook. enl &rev. 2nd ed. Youth with a Mission. (Illus.). 280p. 1974. plastic spiral bd. 5.95 (ISBN 0-87123-505-6, 280505). Bethany Fell.

Single. Marilyn McGinnis. 1976. pap. 1.50 (ISBN 0-89129-164-4). Jove Pubns.

Single. Peter Stein. 1976. pap. text ed. 2.95x (ISBN 0-13-810564-2, Spec). P-H.

Single Case Experimental Designs: Strategies for Studying Behavior Change. Michel Hersen & David H. Barlow. Ed. by A. P. Goldstein & L. Krasner. 1975. text ed. 40.00 (ISBN 0-08-019512-1); pap. text ed. 14.75 (ISBN 0-08-019511-3). Pergamon.

Single-Field Isodose Charts for High-Energy Radiation: An International Guide. (Technical Reports: No. 8). 1962. pap. 6.50 (ISBN 92-0-115062-8, IAEA). Unipub.

Single Finger Prints: A New & Practical Method of Classifying & Filing Single Finger Prints & Fragmentary Impressions. Harry Battley. (Illus.). 1931. 42.50x (ISBN 0-686-51311-8). Elliots Bks.

Single Girl Goes to Town. Jean Baer. 1968. 5.95 o.s.i. (ISBN 0-02-505190-3). Macmillan.

Single Grandmother. Tracy E. Hyde. LC 73-88510. 250p. 1974. 11.95 (ISBN 0-88229-128-9). Nelson-Hall.

Single-Minded: A Tract on Chastity, Mainly in the Context of Celibacy. Michael Adams. 120p. 1979. pap. 10.00x (ISBN 0-7165-1819-8, Pub. by Irish Academic Pr). Biblio Dist.

Single Nature's Double Name: The Collectedness of the Conflicting in British & American Romanticism. Raymond Benoit. (De Proprietatibus Litterarum Ser.: No. 26). 1973. text ed. 23.50x (ISBN 90-2792-599-2). Mouton.

Single on Sunday: A Manual for Successful Single Adult Ministries. Bobbie Reed. 1979. pap. 5.50 (ISBN 0-570-03781-6, 12-2735). Concordia.

Single Parent. Virginia Watts. 1976. 7.95 (ISBN 0-8007-0823-7). Revell.

Single Parenting: A Practical Resource Guide. Stephen L. Atlas. 256p. 1981. 12.95 (ISBN 0-13-810622-3, Spec); pap. 5.95 (ISBN 0-13-810614-2). P-H.

Single Person's Home-Buying Handbook. Kristelle L. Petersen. 320p. 1980. 14.95 (ISBN 0-8015-6840-4, Hawthorn); pap. 7.95 (ISBN 0-8015-6842-0). Dutton.

Single Photon Emission Computed Tomography & Other Selected Computer Topics. Ed. by Ronald R. Price et al. LC 80-52817. (Illus.). 244p. 1980. pap. 29.50 (ISBN 0-932004-06-7). Soc Nuclear Med.

Single Scattering & Transport Theory. A. Ishimaru. (Wave Propagation & Scattering in Random Media: Vol. 1). 1978. 31.00 (ISBN 0-12-374701-5). Acad Pr.

Single Star: An Anthology of Christmas Poetry. Compiled by David Davis. (Illus.). 1978. 7.95 (ISBN 0-370-01269-0, Pub. by Chatto Bodley Jonathan). Merrimack Bk Serv.

Single-Stranded DNA Phages. Ed. by D. T. Denhardt et al. LC 78-60445. (Monograph: No. 8). (Illus.). 720p. 1978. 65.00 (ISBN 0-87969-122-0). Cold Spring Harbor.

Single Ticket to China. Douglas Hare. pap. 1.55 (ISBN 0-08-017839-1). Pergamon.

Single Vision: The Alienation of American Intellectuals. Ernest Earnest. LC 78-116132. 1970. 10.00x (ISBN 0-8147-0459-X); pap. 5.00x (ISBN 0-8147-0460-3). NYU Pr.

Single-Word Usage, Cognitive Development & the Beginnings of Combinatorial Speech. M. Rodgon. LC 75-7211. (Illus.). 192p. 1976. 27.50 (ISBN 0-521-20884-X). Cambridge U Pr.

Singled Out. Richard Schickel. LC 80-54080. 128p. 1981. 9.95 (ISBN 0-670-64710-1). Viking Pr.

Singles Are Suckers. Lawrence J. Babin. 1981. pap. 6.95 (ISBN 0-912492-16-3). Pyquag.

Single's First Menu Cookbook. Charlotte Adams. LC 72-23480. 192p. 1975. 6.95 (ISBN 0-396-07070-1). Dodd.

Singular Anomaly: Women Novelists of the Nineteenth Century. Vineta Colby. LC 70-92522. (Gotham Library). 1970. 15.00x (ISBN 0-8147-0096-9); pap. 4.95x (ISBN 0-8147-0097-7). NYU Pr.

Singular Perturbations & Syasymptotics. Ed. by Richard Meyer & Seymour Parter. LC 80-24946. 1980. lib ed 22.00 (ISBN 0-12-493260-6). Acad Pr.

Singular Preference: Portraits & Essays. Peter Quennell. LC 70-132091. (Essay & General Literature Index Reprint Ser). 1971. Repr. of 1953 ed. 12.25 (ISBN 0-8046-1419-9). Kennikat.

Singular View. rev. ed. F. Brady. (Illus.). 1979. 16.50 (ISBN 0-87489-224-4). Med Economics.

Singularities: Essays on the Theater 1964-1974. John Simon. LC 75-10260. 256p. 1976. 12.95 (ISBN 0-394-73118-2); pap. 4.95 (ISBN 0-394-73118-2). Random.

Singularity Theory & Introduction to Catastrophe Theory. Y. C. Lu. LC 76-48307. (Illus.). 1976. soft cover 16.80 (ISBN 0-387-90221-X). Springer-Verlag.

Singweisen Bernarts Von Ventadorn Nach Den Handschriften Mitgeteilt. Carl L. Appel. LC 80-2171. 1981. Repr. of 1934 ed. 17.50 (ISBN 0-404-19002-2). AMS Pr.

Sinhalayo. rev. 2nd ed. Senarat Paranavitana. 67p. 1975. text ed. 6.00x o.p. (ISBN 0-8426-0794-3). Verry.

Sinhalese: An Introductory Course. C. Reynolds. 1980. 38.00x (ISBN 0-8364-0661-3, Pub. by London U England). South Asia Bks.

Sinhalese: An Introductory Course. C. H. Reynolds. 1980. 38.00x (ISBN 0-8364-0661-3). South Asia Bks.

Sinister, Strange & Supernatural. Ed. by Helen Hoke. (gr. 6 up). 1981. 9.95 (ISBN 0-525-66703-2). Elsevier-Nelson.

Sinister Tennis-How to Play Against & with Left Handers. Peter Schwed. LC 73-20530. 96p. 1975. 4.95 o.p. (ISBN 0-385-06706-2); pap. 2.50 Softbound (ISBN 0-385-06368-7). Doubleday.

Sink the Haguro! The Last Destroyer of the Second World War. John Winton. (Illus.). x, 182p. 1978. 19.50 (ISBN 0-85422-152-2). Shoe String.

Sinkiang Story. Jack Chen. LC 77-22938. (Illus.). 1977. 17.95 o.s.i. (ISBN 0-02-524640-2). Macmillan.

Sinking of the Odradek Stadium & Other Novels. Harry Mathews. LC 74-15881. 1975. pap. 5.95 o.p. (ISBN 0-06-012841-0, TD-220, HarpT). Har-Row.

Sinking Spell. Edward Gorey. (Illus.). 1965. pap. 7.95 (ISBN 0-8392-1150-3). Astor-Honor.

Sinner's Progress: A Study of Madness in Elizabethan Renaissance Drama. Robert Shenk. (Salzburg Elizabethan & Renaissance Studies: No. 74). 1978. pap. text ed. 25.00x (ISBN 0-391-01520-6). Humanities.

Sino-American Detente & Its Policy Implications. Ed. by Gene T. Hsiao. LC 73-13346. (Special Studies). (Illus.). 352p. 1974. text ed. 23.95 o.p. (ISBN 0-275-28787-4); pap. text ed. 9.95 o.p. (ISBN 0-275-88810-X). Praeger.

Sino-American Juvenile Justice System. Jin-An Liu. LC 80-67051. (Scholarly Monographs). 340p. 1980. pap. 27.50 (ISBN 0-8408-0512-8). Carrollton Pr.

Sino-German Connection: Alexander von Falckenhausen Between China & Germany. Hsi-Huey Liang. (Van Gorcum Historical Library: No. 94). (Illus.). 1978. pap. text ed. 23.75x (ISBN 90-232-1554-0). Humanities.

Sino-Japanese War, 1937-41: From Marco Polo Bridge to Pearl Harbor. Frank Dorn. LC 74-10828. (Illus.). 416p. 1974. 17.50 o.s.i. (ISBN 0-02-532200-1). Macmillan.

Sino-Soviet Intervention in Africa. Ed. by Roger Pearson. 1977. pap. 10.00 (ISBN 0-685-79965-4). Coun Am Affairs.

Sino-Soviet Territorial Dispute: 1949-64. George Ginsburgs & Carl F. Pinkele. LC 78-19458. 1978. 20.95 (ISBN 0-275-99990-3). Praeger.

Sino-Tibetan: A Conspectus. Paul K. Benedict. LC 78-154511. (Princeton-Cambridge Studies in Chinese Linguistics: No. 2). 1972. 75.00 (ISBN 0-521-08175-0). Cambridge U Pr.

Sins of New York As "Exposed" by the Police Gazette. Edward Van Every. LC 70-174130. (Illus.). 299p. 1976. Repr. of 1930 ed. 20.00 (ISBN 0-8103-4038-0). Gale.

Sins of Omission. Charles Q. Yarbro. 1980. pap. 2.25 (ISBN 0-451-09165-5, E9165, Sig). NAL.

Sins of Rachel Ellis. Philip Caveney. 1979. pap. 2.25 o.p. (ISBN 0-425-04144-1). Berkley Pub.

Sins of Rachel Ellis. Philip Caveney. LC 77-16763. 1978. 8.95 o.p. (ISBN 0-312-72603-1). St Martin.

Sins of the Father. Joseph Bellestri. 1981. 7.75 (ISBN 0-8062-1612-3). Carlton.

Sins of the Lion. Annette Motley. 448p. 1981. pap. 2.75 (ISBN 0-445-04647-3). Popular Lib.

Sintering Processes. Ed. by Kuczynski. (Materials Sciences Research Ser.: Vol. 13). 585p. 1980. 55.00 (ISBN 0-306-40336-6, Plenum Pr). Plenum Pub.

Sintesis De las Decisiones Tomadas En las Sesiones y Textos De las Resoluciones Aprobadas. OAS General Secretariat. (Vol. XXXI Enero-Diciembre De 1978). 174p. 1980. pap. text ed. 3.00 (ISBN 0-8270-6300-8). OAS.

Sintesis Del Nuevo Testamento. W. M. Dunnett. Tr. by Jose M. Blanch from Eng. (Curso Para Maestros Cristianos: No. 3). Orig. Title: New Testament Survey. 128p. (Span.). 1972. pap. 2.50 (ISBN 0-89922-012-6); instructor's manual 1.50 (ISBN 0-89922-013-4). Edit Caribe.

Sinusoidal Analysis & Modeling of Weakly Nonlinear Circuits: With Application to Nonlinear Interference Effects. Donald D. Weiner & John F. Spina. (Electrical-Computer Science & Engineering Ser.). 304p. 1980. text ed. 27.50 (ISBN 0-442-26093-8). Van Nos Reinhold.

Sioux: A Critical Bibliography. Herbert T. Hoover. LC 79-2167. (Newberry Library Center for the History of the American Indian Bibliographical Ser.). 96p. (Orig.). 1979. pap. 3.95x (ISBN 0-253-34972-9). Ind U Pr.

Sioux Are Coming. Walter O'Meara. (Illus.). (gr. 3-7). 1971. 6.95 (ISBN 0-395-12759-9). HM.

Sioux Chronicle. George E. Hyde. (Civilization of the American Indian Ser.: Vol. 45). 334p. 1956. 15.95 (ISBN 0-8061-0358-2). U of Okla Pr.

Sioux Indians, Vol. 3. Incl. Ethnohistorical Report on the Yankton Sioux. Alan R. Woolworth; Yankton Chronology. John L. Champe. (American Indian Ethnohistory Ser: Plains Indians). (Illus.). lib. bdg. 42.00 (ISBN 0-8240-0796-4). Garland Pub.

Sioux Indians: Hunters & Warriors of the Plains. Sonia Bleeker. (Illus.). (gr. 3-6). 1962. PLB 6.67 (ISBN 0-688-31457-0). Morrow.

Sioux Indians, Vol. Four: Findings of Fact, & Opinion. Indian Claims Commission. (American Indian Ethnohistory Ser: Plains Indians). (Illus.). lib. bdg. 42.00 (ISBN 0-8240-0797-2). Garland Pub.

Sioux Indians, Vol. One: Mdewakanton Band of Sioux Indians. Harold Hickerson. (American Indian Ethnohistory Ser: Plains Indians). (Illus.). lib. bdg. 42.00 (ISBN 0-8240-0794-8). Garland Pub.

Sioux Indians, Vol. Two: Dakota Sioux Indians. Wesley R. Hurt. (American Indian Ethnohistory Ser: Plains Indians). (Illus.). lib. bdg. 42.00 (ISBN 0-8240-0795-6). Garland Pub.

Sioux of the Rosebud: A History in Pictures. Henry W. Hamilton & Jean T. Hamilton. LC 78-145506. (Civilization of the American Indian Ser.: Vol. 111). (Illus.). 320p. 1981. pap. 12.50 (ISBN 0-8061-1622-6). U of Okla Pr.

Sioux Today. Frank LaPointe. LC 73-189727. 144p. (gr. 7 up). 1972. 5.95g o.s.i. (ISBN 0-02-751600-8, CCPr). Macmillan.

Sioux Uprising. George G. Gilman. (Edge Ser.: No. 11). 1974. pap. 1.75 (ISBN 0-523-41289-4). Pinnacle Bks.

Siphonophores of the Pacific, with a Review of the World Distribution. Angeles Alvarino. (Bulletin of the Scripps Institution of Oceanography: Vol. 16). pap. 8.00x (ISBN 0-520-09321-6). U of Cal Pr.

Sir Andrew. Paula Winter. (Illus.). 32p. (gr. k-2). 1980. PLB 7.95 (ISBN 0-517-53911-X). Crown.

Sir Cecil & the Bad Blue Beast. Glen Dines. LC 70-125868. (Illus.). (gr. k-2). 1970. 8.95 (ISBN 0-87599-175-0). S G Phillips.

Sir Charles V Stanford. J. F. Porte. LC 76-12570. (Music Reprint Ser.). 1976. Repr. of 1921 ed. lib. bdg. 18.50 (ISBN 0-306-70790-X). Da Capo.

Sir Christopher Wren: Renaissance Architect, Philosopher, & Scientist. Heywood Gould. LC 75-101752. (Biography Ser). (Illus.). (gr. 7 up). 1970. PLB 5.90 o.p. (ISBN 0-531-00946-7). Watts.

Sir Donald Bradman: A Biography. Irving Rosenwater. 1978. 35.00 (ISBN 0-7134-0664-X, Pub. by Batsford England). David & Charles.

Sir Edgar. 1810. Francis Hodgson. Ed. by Donald H. Reiman. LC 75-31222. (Romantic Context Ser.: Poetry 1789-1810). 1977. lib. bdg. 47.00 (ISBN 0-8240-2172-X). Garland Pub.

Sir Edward Appleton, C.B.E., K.C.B., F.R.S. Ronald Clark. 256p. 1972. text ed. 27.00 (ISBN 0-08-016093-X). Pergamon.

Sir Edward Coke, 4 vols. Ed. by David S. Berkowitz & Samuel E. Thorne. (English Legal History Ser.). 1468p. 1979. lib. bdg. 55.00 (ISBN 0-8240-3053-2). Garland Pub.

Sir Eglamour. Eglamour. Ed. by Albert S. Cook. 1911. 17.50x (ISBN 0-685-69803-3). Elliots Bks.

Sir Eldon Gorst: The Overshadowed Proconsul. Peter Mellini. LC 76-51878. (Publication Ser: No. 178). (Illus.). 1977. 10.95 (ISBN 0-8179-6781-8). Hoover Inst Pr.

Sir Francis Bacon. A. Wigfall Green. (English Authors Ser.: No. 40). 1966. lib. bdg. 10.95 (ISBN 0-8057-1016-7). Twayne.

Sir Frederic Madden: A Bibliography & Biographical Sketch. Robert W. Ackerman & Gretchen P. Ackerman. LC 78-68237. 150p. 1979. lib. bdg. 18.00 (ISBN 0-8240-9819-6). Garland Pub.

Sir Frederick Banting. Ann M. Mayer. LC 74-2048. (Personal Closeups Ser). 40p. (gr. 4-6). 1974. 5.75 o.p. (ISBN 0-87191-323-2). Creative Ed.

Sir Gawain & the Green Knight. Intro. by B. Raffel. (Orig.). 1970. pap. 1.75 (ISBN 0-451-61848-3, ME1848, Ment). NAL.

Sir Gawain & the Green Knight. 2nd ed. Ed. by J. R. Tolkien & E. V. Gordon. 1967. pap. 8.95x (ISBN 0-19-811486-9). Oxford U Pr.

Sir Gawain & the Green Knight. Ed. by R. A. Waldron. LC 75-129568. (York Medieval Texts Ser). 1970. text ed. 8.95 (ISBN 0-8101-0327-3); pap. text ed. 2.95 o.s.i. (ISBN 0-8101-0328-1). Northwestern U Pr.

Sir Gawain & the Grene Gnome. Ed. by R. T. Jones. 1972. text ed. 3.75x o.p. (ISBN 0-435-14511-8). Heinemann Ed.

Sir Godfrey Kneller. J. Stewart. (Illus.). 10.00 (ISBN 0-685-26748-2). Newbury Bks Inc.

Sir Henry Finch. Edmund Wingate. William Phillips. Ed. by David S. Berkowitz & Samuel E. Thorne. (English Legal History Ser.: Vol. 68). 462p. 1979. lib. bdg. 55.00 (ISBN 0-8240-3055-9). Garland Pub.

Sir Henry Vane the Younger: A Study in Political & Administrative History. Violet A. Rowe. (Univ. of London on Historical Studies: No. 28). 1970. text ed. 15.25x (ISBN 0-485-13128-5, Athlone Pr). Humanities.

Sir Isaac Newton. Edward N. Andrade. LC 79-15162. 140p. 1979. Repr. of 1958 ed. lib. bdg. 14.50x (ISBN 0-313-22022-0). Greenwood.

Sir James Kay-Shuttleworth on Popular Education. Trygve R. Tholfsen. LC 73-15046. 1974. text ed. 8.75 (ISBN 0-8077-2402-5); pap. text ed. 4.00x (ISBN 0-8077-2411-4). Tchrs Coll.

Sir John Betjeman: A Bibliography of Writings by & About Him. Margaret L. Stapleton. (Author Bibliographies Ser.: No. 21). 1974. 10.00 (ISBN 0-8108-0758-0). Scarecrow.

Sir John Brunner, Radical Plutocrat. Stephen Koss. (Conference on British Studies Biographical Ser). (Illus.). 1970. 47.50 (ISBN 0-521-07906-3). Cambridge U Pr.

Sir John Davies. James L. Sanderson. (English Authors Ser.: No. 175). 1975. lib. bdg. 10.95 (ISBN 0-8057-1141-4). Twayne.

Sir John Suckling. Charles L. Squier. (English Authors Ser.: No. 218). 1978. 12.50 (ISBN 0-8057-6721-5). Twayne.

Sir John Vanbrugh. Arthur R. Huseboe. (English Authors Ser: No. 191). 1976. lib. bdg. 12.50 (ISBN 0-8057-6665-0). Twayne.

Sir Joseph Banks. Charles Lyte. (Illus.). 232p. 1980. 32.00 (ISBN 0-7153-7884-8). David & Charles.

Sir Joshua Reynolds: Discourses on Art. Ed. by Robert R. Wark. LC 74-17647. 408p. 1975. 35.00x (ISBN 0-300-01823-1). Yale U Pr.

Sir Josiah Child, Merchant Economist. William Letwin. (Kress Library of Business & Economics: No. 14). (Illus.). 1959. pap. 5.00x (ISBN 0-678-09909-X, Baker Lib). Kelley.

Sir Matthew Hale: The Analysis of the Law: Being a Scheme or Abstract of the Several Titles & Portions of the Law of England, Digested into Method, Repr. Of 1713 Ed. Sir Matthew Hale. Ed. by David Berkowitz & Samuel Thorne. Bd. with Giles Jacob: The Student's Companion: or, the Reason of the Laws of England, Shewing the Principal Reasons & Motives Wherein Our Laws & Statutes Are Criminal Cases; Together with the Law Itself. Giles Jacob. Repr. of 1725 ed. LC 77-86566. (Classics of English Legal History in the Modern Era Ser.: Vol. 70). 1979. lib. bdg. 55.00 (ISBN 0-8240-3057-5). Garland Pub.

Sir Nigel. Arthur Conan Doyle. 15.95 (ISBN 0-7195-3228-0). Transatlantic.

Sir Patches & the Dragon. Tom Tichenor. LC 78-128454. (Illus.). (gr. 1-7). 1971. 5.95 o.s.i. (ISBN 0-87695-108-6). Aurora Pubs.

Sir Pherozeshah Mehta: A Political Biography. Homi Mody. 10.00x (ISBN 0-210-33946-2). Asia.

Sir Philip Sidney. Robert Kimbrough. (English Authors Ser.: No. 114). lib. bdg. 10.95 (ISBN 0-8057-1492-8). Twayne.

Sir Philip Sidney. Kenneth Muir. Ed. by Bonamy Dobree et al. Bd. with Sir Thomas Wyatt. Sergio Baldi; Edmund Spenser. Rosemary Freeman. LC 63-63096. (British Writers & Their Work Ser: Vol. 8). 1965. pap. 1.60x (ISBN 0-8032-5658-2, BB 457, Bison). U of Nebr Pr.

Sir Philip Sidney. John A. Symonds. LC 67-23878. 1968. Repr. of 1886 ed. 15.00 (ISBN 0-8103-3056-3). Gale.

Sir Philip Sidney As a Literary Craftsman. Kenneth Myrick. LC 35-13065. 1966. pap. 3.95x (ISBN 0-8032-5140-8, BB 312, Bison). U of Nebr Pr.

Sir Philip Sidney: Rebellion in Arcadia. Richard C. McCoy. 1979. 16.50 (ISBN 0-8135-0869-X). Rutgers U Pr.

Sir Purshotamdas Thakurdas. Frank Moraes. Repr. 10.00x (ISBN 0-210-33748-6). Asia.

Sir Randal Cremer: His Life & Work. Howard Evans. LC 74-147455. (Garland Library of War & Peace: Peace Leaders: Biographies & Memoirs). xviii, 356p. 1973. Repr. of 1909 ed. lib. bdg. 38.00 (ISBN 0-8240-0250-4). Garland Pub.

Sir Ribbeck of Ribbeck of Havelland. Theodor Fontane. Tr. by Elizabeth Shub. LC 69-12746. (Illus.). (gr. k-3). 1969. 4.95g o.s.i. (ISBN 0-02-735630-2). Macmillan.

Sir Richard Grenville of the Civil War. Amos C. Miller. (Illus.). 215p. 1979. 16.50x (ISBN 0-8476-6160-1). Rowman.

Sir Roland Ashton: A Tale of the Times, 1841. Catherine Long. Ed. by Robert L. Wolff. Bd. with Mary Spencer: A Tale for the Times, 1844. Anne Howard. (Victorian Fiction Ser.). 1975. lib. bdg. 66.00 (ISBN 0-8240-1565-7). Garland Pub.

Sir Samuel Garth. Richard I. Cook. (English Authors Ser.: No. 276). 1980. lib. bdg. 12.50 (ISBN 0-8057-6775-4). Twayne.

Sir Sayyid Ahmad Khan & Muslim Modernization in India & Pakistan. Hafeez Malik. LC 80-13905. (Illus.). 288p. 1980. 25.00x (ISBN 0-231-04970-6). Columbia U Pr.

Sir Thomas Browne. Joan Bennett. 1962. 42.00 (ISBN 0-521-04159-7). Cambridge U Pr.

Sir Thomas Browne's Pseudodoxia Epidemica. Ed. by R. H. Robbins. (Oxford English Texts Ser.). (Illus.). 1000p. 1980. 129.00 (ISBN 0-19-812706-5). Oxford U Pr.

Sir Thomas Elyot & Roger Ascham: A Reference Guide. Jerome S. Dees. (Reference Books Ser.). 1981. 25.00 (ISBN 0-8161-8353-8). G K Hall.

Sir Thomas Elyot's: The Book Named the Governor. Ed. by John M. Major. LC 75-108883. 1970. text ed. 9.75 (ISBN 0-8077-1796-7); pap. 4.25x (ISBN 0-8077-1795-9). Tchrs Coll.

Sir Thomas Malory & the Morte Darthur: A Survey of Scholarship & Annotated Bibliography. Page W. Life. LC 80-16180. 1980. 13.50x (ISBN 0-8139-0868-X). U Pr of Va.

Sir Thomas Malory: King Arthur & His Knights. Ed. by R. T. Davies. 1967. 9.95 o.p. (ISBN 0-571-08030-8, Pub. by Faber & Faber). Merrimack Bk Serv.

Sir Thomas Malory: King Arthur & His Knights. Ed. by R. T. Davies. 1968. pap. 4.95 o.p. (ISBN 0-571-08608-X, Pub. by Faber & Faber). Merrimack Bk Serv.

Sir Thomas Wyatt: The Complete Poems. Ed. by R. A. Rebholz. LC 80-53980. 558p. 1981. text ed. 25.00x (ISBN 0-300-02681-1); pap. 5.95x (ISBN 0-300-02688-9). Yale U Pr.

Sir Walter Raleigh. Henry D. Thoreau. Ed. by Franklin B. Sanborn. LC 80-2523. 1981. Repr. of 1905 ed. 24.50 (ISBN 0-686-28929-3). AMS Pr.

Sir Walter Raleigh As Historian: An Analysis of 'the History of the World' John Racin. (Salzburg Studies in English Literature, Elizabethan & Renaissance Studies: No. 2). 216p. 1976. pap. text ed. 25.00x (ISBN 0-391-01506-0). Humanities.

Sir Walter Raleigh's History of the World. Charles Firth. 49p. 1980. Repr. write for info. (ISBN 0-8492-4707-1). R West.

Sir Walter Scott. John Buchan. LC 67-27580. Repr. of 1932 ed. 12.50 (ISBN 0-8046-0054-6). Kennikat.

Sir Walter Scott. John Lauber. (English Authors Ser.: No. 39). 1966. lib. bdg. 10.95 (ISBN 0-8057-1476-6). Twayne.

Sir Walter Scott: Locality & Landscape. James Reed. 1980. text ed. 40.00x (ISBN 0-485-11197-7, Athlone Pr). Humanities.

Sir Walter Scott: Wizard of the North. Pearle H. Schultz. LC 66-28884. (Illus.). (gr. 7-10). 1967. 5.95 (ISBN 0-8149-0383-5). Vanguard.

Sir William Hamilton: Envoy Extraordinary. Brian Fothergill. (Illus.). 1969. 9.95 o.p. (ISBN 0-571-08958-5, Pub. by Faber & Faber); pap. 3.95 o.p. (ISBN 0-571-10291-3). Merrimack Bk Serv.

Sir William Johnson, Colonial American, 1715-1763. Milton W. Hamilton. (Ser. in American Studies). 1976. 22.50 (ISBN 0-8046-9134-7, Natl U). Kennikat.

Sir William Jones: A Bibliography of Primary & Secondary Sources. Garland Cannon. (Library & Information Sourcesin Linguistics Ser.: No. 7). 1980. text ed. 17.25x (ISBN 90-272-0998-7). Humanities.

Sir William Rowan Hamilton: A Biography. Thomas L. Hankins. LC 80-10627. 512p. 1980. text ed. 32.50 (ISBN 0-8018-2203-3). Johns Hopkins.

Sir William Staunford. William Dickinson. Roger Maynwaring. Robert Sibthorpe. Sir Walter Raleigh. Ed. by David S. Berkowitz & Samuel E. Thorne. (English Legal History Ser.: Vol. 131). 426p. 1979. lib. bdg. 55.00 (ISBN 0-8240-3168-7). Garland Pub.

Sirds Ko Dzili Iemileja, II. 2nd ed. Valdis Mezezers. LC 79-53071. 106p. 1980. Repr. of 1977 ed. 9.00 (ISBN 0-936302-01-1). Pub Vaidava.

Sire Lines. Abram Hewitt. 26.25 (ISBN 0-936032-09-X). Thoroughbred Own and Breed.

Sire Unknown. Marjorie Reynolds. LC 68-20608. (Illus.). (gr. 4-6). 1968. 4.50g o.s.i. (ISBN 0-02-776110-X). Macmillan.

Sirenian Evolution in the North Pacific Ocean. Daryl Domning. (Publications in Geological Science Ser.: Vol. 118). 1978. 11.00x (ISBN 0-520-09581-2). U of Cal Pr.

Sirens. Eric Van Lustbader. Ed. by Herbert M. Katz. 504p. 1981. 12.95 (ISBN 0-87131-346-4). M Evans.

Sirens of Titan. Kurt Vonnegut, Jr. pap. 2.75 (ISBN 0-440-17948-3). Dell.

Sires & Dams of Stakes Winners, 1928-1978. 82.50 (ISBN 0-936032-10-3). Thoroughbred Own and Breed.

Sires of Runners of 1978: Supplement. The Thoroughbread Owners & Breeders Association. 1978. lib. bdg. 15.00 (ISBN 0-936032-17-0); pap. 10.00 (ISBN 0-936032-18-9). Thoroughbred Own and Breed.

Sires of Runners of 1979. Ed. by Blood-Horse. (Annual Supplement). 1980. lib. bdg. 20.00 (ISBN 0-936032-19-7); pap. 10.00 (ISBN 0-936032-20-0). Thoroughbred Own & Breed.

Sires of Runners, 1980. Blood-Horse Editors. 1981. pap. 10.00 (ISBN 0-936032-37-5). Thoroughbred Own & Breed.

Sirian Experiments. Doris Lessing. LC 79-27710. 304p. 1981. 11.95 (ISBN 0-394-51231-6). Knopf.

Sirius Mystery. Robert Temple. LC 74-83583. (Orig.). 1978. pap. 6.95 (ISBN 0-312-72731-3). St Martin.

Sisson's Word & Expression Locater. Sisson. 12.95 (ISBN 0-13-810671-1). P-H.

Sistema de Clasificacion Decimal, con adaptaciones para los paises de habla espanola, basado en la 18a edicion con adiciones de la 19a edicion, 3 vols. Melvil Dewey. Tr. by Jorge Aguayo. LC 80-24527. (Span.). 1980. Set. 75.00x (ISBN 0-910608-26-1); Vol. 1, Introduccion, Tablas Auxiliares. 25.00x (ISBN 0-910608-27-X); Vol. 2, Esquemas. 25.00x (ISBN 0-910608-28-8); Vol. 3, Indice. 25.00x (ISBN 0-910608-29-6). Forest Pr.

Sistema Generalizado De Preferencial De Estados Unidos: Cobertura Y Procedimientos Administrativos Vignetes En 1980. OAS General Secretariat International Trade & Export Development Program. (International Trade Ser.). 58p. pap. text ed. 5.00 (ISBN 0-8270-1125-3). OAS.

Sistema Generalizado De Preferencias De Estados Unidos: Material Informativo. (Programa Sector Externo). (Span. & Eng.). 1977. Span. pap. 6.00 (ISBN 0-8270-3335-4); Eng. pap. 3.00 (ISBN 0-8270-3325-7). OAS.

Sistemas De Ecuaciones. Kenneth Austwick. (Span). 1970. pap. 1.40 (ISBN 0-06-310040-1, IntlDept). Har-Row.

Sister. Eloise Greenfield. LC 73-22182. (gr. 5-12). 1974. 8.95 (ISBN 0-690-00497-4, TYC-J). T Y Crowell.

Sister Act. Max F. Harris. 1981. pap. 1.95 (ISBN 0-8439-0907-2, Leisure Bks). Nordon Pubns.

Sister Carrie. Theodore Dreiser. (Literature Ser). (gr. 10-12). 1970. pap. text ed. 3.75 (ISBN 0-87720-739-9). AMSCO Sch.

Sister Carrie. Theodore Dreiser. LC 78-183140. 472p. 1971. Repr. lib. bdg. 12.50x (ISBN 0-8376-0401-X). Bentley.

Sister Carrie. Theodore Dreiser. LC 69-13798. (Merrill Standard Ser). 6.00 (ISBN 0-675-09527-1); pap. 4.00 (ISBN 0-675-09528-X). Brown Bk.

Sister Carrie. Theodore Dreiser. Ed. by Jack Salzman. LC 69-16530. 1970. 6.95 (ISBN 0-685-91574-3); pap. 4.50 (ISBN 0-672-61014-0). Bobbs.

Sister Carrie. Theodore Dreiser. 557p. 1980. Repr. of 1907 ed. lib. bdg. 17.95x (ISBN 0-89968-207-3). Lightyear.

Sister Carrie: The Pennsylvania Edition. Theodore Dreiser. Ed. by James L. West, III et al. 1981. text ed. 29.95x (ISBN 0-8122-7784-8); pap. text ed. 14.95x (ISBN 0-8122-1110-3). U of Pa Pr.

Sister Fly Goes to Market. Melissa Cannon. LC 80-21120. (Illus., Orig.). 1980. pap. 1.95 (ISBN 0-937212-01-6). Truedog.

Sister for Helen. Grace Hogarth. LC 79-64313. (Illus.). (gr. 4-7). 1980. 8.95 (ISBN 0-233-96817-2). Andre Deutsch.

Sister of the Bride. Beverly Cleary. (Illus.). (gr. 7 up). 1963. PLB 8.48 (ISBN 0-688-31742-1). Morrow.

Sister of the Bride. Beverly Cleary. (gr. 7-12). 1981. pap. 1.75 (ISBN 0-440-97596-4, LE). Dell.

Sister Philomene. Edmond De Goncourt & Jules De Goncourt. Tr. by L. Ensor. 292p. 1975. Repr. of 1890 ed. 16.50 (ISBN 0-86527-304-9). Fertig.

Sistercelebrations: Nine Worship Experiences. Ed. by Arlene Swidler. LC 74-80414. 96p. (Orig.). 1974. pap. 0.50 (ISBN 0-8006-1084-9, 1-1084). Fortress.

Sisters. David Hamilton & Alain Robbe-Grillet. (Illus.). 136p. 1973. 24.95 (ISBN 0-688-00166-1); pap. 9.95 (ISBN 0-688-05166-9). Morrow.

Sisters & Lovers. Nicola Thorne. LC 80-509. 600p. 1981. 14.95 (ISBN 0-385-15857-2). Doubleday.

Sisters of Sacred Song: Selected Listing of Women Hymnodists in Great Britain & America. Samuel J. Rogal. LC 80-8482. 180p. 1981. lib. bdg. 22.00 (ISBN 0-8240-9482-4). Garland Pub.

Sisters of Sorrow. Aola Vandergriff. 1978. pap. 1.95 o.s.i. (ISBN 0-446-89999-2). Warner Bks.

Sisters of the Quill. Alice A. Hufstader. LC 78-2642. (Illus.). 1978. 15.00 (ISBN 0-396-07544-4). Dodd.

Sisters of Valcour. Dorothy Daniels. 416p. (Orig.). 1981. pap. 2.75 (ISBN 0-446-95484-5). Warner Bks.

Sisyphus; or, the Limits of Education. Siegfried Bernfeld. Tr. by Frederic Lilge from Ger. 1973. 14.50x (ISBN 0-520-01407-3). U of Cal Pr.

Sit Down & Shape up: Sit & Exercise? Yes You Can. Fairfax Stephenson. LC 78-6286. 1979. pap. 4.00 (ISBN 0-931490-04-9). Gotuit Ent.

Sit-in Game. Doris Dahlin. Tr. by Joan Tate from Swedish. 96p. (gr. 7 up). 1974. 4.95 o.p. (ISBN 0-670-64730-6). Viking Pr.

Sita. Kate Millett. 1977. 10.00 o.p. (ISBN 0-374-26546-1). FS&G.

Sitanka: The Full Story of Wounded Knee. Forest W. Seymour. 1981. 9.75 (ISBN 0-8158-0399-0). Chris Mass.

Site: Buildings & Spaces. (Illus.). 48p. (Orig.). 1970. pap. 3.50x (ISBN 0-917046-10-2). Va Mus Fine Arts.

Site Carpentry. C. K. Austin. (Illus.). 1979. 19.95x; wire bdg. 14.95x (ISBN 0-7198-2730-2). Intl Ideas.

Site Characterization & Aggregation of Implanted Atoms in Materials. Ed. by A. Perez & R. Coussement. (NATO Advanced Study Institutes, Ser. B, Physics: Vol. 47). 530p. 1980. 55.00 (ISBN 0-306-40299-8, Plenum Pr). Plenum Pub.

Site Characterization & Exploration. Compiled by American Society of Civil Engineers. 408p. 1979. pap. text ed. 15.00 (ISBN 0-87262-186-3). Am Soc Civil Eng.

Site Manual. 4th ed. Eldon Carran. (Illus.). 1975. 17.50x (ISBN 0-7198-2600-4). Intl Ideas.

Site Selection Factors for Repositories of Solid High-Level & Alpha Bearing Wastes in Geological Formations. (Illus.). 1978. pap. 7.50 (ISBN 92-0-125177-7, IDC177, IAEA). Unipub.

Site Value Taxation in Central Business District Redevelopment (Sydney, Aus.) R. W. Archer. LC 72-93820. (Research Report Ser.: No. 19). (Illus.). 44p. 1972. pap. 4.75 (ISBN 0-87420-319-8). Urban Land.

Siting Energy Facilities. Ralph L. Keeney. LC 80-764. 1980. 32.00 (ISBN 0-12-403080-7). Acad Pr.

Siting of Nuclear Facilities: Proceedings. Symposium, Vienna, 1974. (Illus.). 625p. 1975. pap. 55.25 (ISBN 92-0-020175-X, ISP 348, IAEA). Unipub.

Siting of Reactors & Nuclear Research Centres. 1963. 18.75 (ISBN 92-0-020263-2, IAEA). Unipub.

Siting Procedures for Major Energy Facilities: Some National Cases. OECD. (Illus.). 142p. (Orig.). 1980. pap. text ed. 8.00x (ISBN 92-64-11986-8). OECD.

Sitosterol. O. J. Pollak & D. Kritchevsky. (Monographs on Atherosclerosis: Vol. 10). (Illus.). 1980. pap. 75.00 (ISBN 3-8055-0568-X). S Karger.

Sitting Bull, Champion of the Sioux: A Biography. rev.ed ed. Stanley Vestal. (Civilization of the American Indian Ser: No. 46). (Illus.). 1980. Repr. of 1957 ed. 15.95 (ISBN 0-8061-0363-9). U of Okla Pr.

Sitting Bull: War Chief of the Sioux. Julian May. LC 72-89462. 40p. (gr. 2-5). 1972. PLB 5.95 (ISBN 0-87191-221-X). Creative Ed.

Sitting Handbook for Small Wind Energy Conversion Systems. Pacific Northwest Laboratory. 85p. Date not set. 21.95 (ISBN 0-89934-121-7); pap. 10.95 (ISBN 0-89934-122-5). Solar Energy Info.

Sitting Posture. 1976 ed. E. Grandjean. 34.95 (ISBN 0-470-15176-5). Halsted Pr.

Situation Is Hopeless. Ronald Searle. LC 80-15868. (Illus.). 64p. 1981. 12.95 (ISBN 0-670-64731-4, Studio). Viking Pr.

Situation Skiing. Jean-Claude Killy & Mike Halstead. LC 77-16927. 1978. 12.50 o.p. (ISBN 0-385-12189-X). Doubleday.

Situational English Language Picture Series. L. G. Alexander. 14.50x (ISBN 0-582-52114-9). Longman.

Situational Supervision for Banks. John Wells. 1977. text ed. 8.95 (ISBN 0-201-08514-3). A-W.

Situational Supervision for Business. John Wells. 1977. pap. text ed. 8.95 (ISBN 0-201-08515-1). A-W.

Situations. Jean-Paul Sartre. LC 65-14602. 1965. 5.95 o.s.i. (ISBN 0-8076-0292-2). Braziller.

Situations in Human Geography: A Practical Approach. J. P. Cole. pap. 15.00x (ISBN 0-631-16860-5, Pub. by Basil Blackwell). Biblio Dist.

Sitwells. John Pearson. LC 80-14371. 1980. pap. 7.95 (ISBN 0-15-682676-3, Harv). HarBraceJ.

Sitwells: A Family's Biography. John Pearson. 1979. 15.00 o.p. (ISBN 0-15-182703-6). HarBraceJ.

Sivalaya: Explorations of the Eight-Thousand Metre Peaks of the Himalaya. Louis Baume. LC 79-20964. 336p. 1979. 12.95 (ISBN 0-916890-97-X); pap. 9.95 (ISBN 0-916890-71-6). Mountaineers.

Six. David Meltzer. (Illus.). 130p. (Orig.). 1976. ltd. signed o.p. 15.00 (ISBN 0-87685-271-1); pap. 4.00 (ISBN 0-87685-270-3). Black Sparrow.

Six - Million Dollar Cucumber: Riddles & Fun for Children. Richard Churchill. LC 75-23103. (Illus.). 96p. (gr. 3 up). 1976. 2.95 o.p. (ISBN 0-531-02429-6); PLB 4.90 o.p. (ISBN 0-531-01106-2). Watts.

Six Against the Rock. Clark Howard. 1978. pap. 2.25 (ISBN 0-515-04709-0). Jove Pubns.

Six American Families. Paul Wilkes. (Orig.). 1977. pap. 1.95 (ISBN 0-8164-2142-0). Crossroad NY.

Six Anatomists Worth Knowing. Warren Andrew. LC 73-707. 280p. 1981. 13.50 (ISBN 0-87527-174-X). Green.

Six Answers to the Problem of Taste. Ronald Suter. LC 79-84279. 1979. pap. text ed. 6.25 (ISBN 0-8191-0726-3). U Pr of Amer.

Six Approaches to the Person. Ed. & pref. by Ralph Ruddock. 224p. 1972. 18.00x (ISBN 0-7100-7335-6); pap. 8.95 (ISBN 0-7100-7382-8). Routledge & Kegan.

Six Black Masters of American Art. Romare Bearden & Harry Henderson. LC 70-175358. 4.95 o.p. (ISBN 0-385-01211-X). Doubleday.

Six Bloody Summer Days. Nick Carter. (Nick Carter Ser.). 174p. 1981. pap. 1.95 (ISBN 0-441-76839-3). Charter Bks.

Six Blue Horses. Yvonne Escoula. LC 70-103044. (gr. 5-9). 1970. 8.95 (ISBN 0-87599-162-9). S G Phillips.

Six Brandenburg Concertos & the Four Orchestral Suites in Full Score. Johann S. Bach. 273p. 1976. pap. 6.95 (ISBN 0-486-23376-6). Dover.

Six by Lewis. C. S. Lewis. 1978. pap. 12.95 (ISBN 0-02-086770-0). Macmillan.

Six Centuries in East Asia: China, Japan & Korea from the 14th Century to 1912. Peter Lum. LC 72-12582. (Illus.). 288p. 1973. 10.95 (ISBN 0-87599-183-1). S G Phillips.

Six Contemporary British Novelists. Ed. by George Stade. 1976. 20.00x (ISBN 0-231-04054-7). Columbia U Pr.

Six Crises. Richard M. Nixon. 576p. 1981. pap. 2.95 (ISBN 0-446-93101-2). Warner Bks.

Six Days. Elinor Glyn. (Barbara Cartland's Library of Love: Vol. 12). 213p. 1980. 12.95x (ISBN 0-7156-1471-1, Pub. by Duckworth England). Biblio Dist.

Six Days: An Anthology of Canadian Christian Poetry. Ed. by Houtmann. 1973. pap. 2.50 o.p. (ISBN 0-686-11983-5). Wedge Pub.

Six Days & the Seven Gates. Yitzhak Navon. 1980. 6.00 (ISBN 0-930832-57-4); pap. 4.00. Herzl Pr.

Six Days to Sunday. Bernard Brunner. 240p. 1976. pap. 1.75 o.p. (ISBN 0-345-25165-2). Ballantine.

Six Days, 5 Nites. Susana De Lyonne. 1978. pap. 1.75 o.p. (ISBN 0-449-14028-8, GM). Fawcett.

Six Disney Winnie-the-Pooh Hunny Pot Shape Books, 6 bks. (ps). Date not set. pap. 3.50 boxed set (ISBN 0-307-13626-4, Golden Pr). Western Pub.

Six Dramatists in Search of a Language. A. Kennedy. LC 74-76572. 288p. 1975. 45.00 (ISBN 0-521-20492-5); pap. 10.95x (ISBN 0-521-09866-1). Cambridge U Pr.

Six-Eight Hundred Microprocessor: A Self-Study Course with Applications. Lance A. Leventhal. (gr. 10 up). 1978. pap. text ed. 9.55 (ISBN 0-8104-5120-4). Hayden.

Six Eight Zero Nine Assembly Language Programming. Lance Leventhal. (Assembly Language Programming Ser.: No. 6). 530p. 1980. pap. text ed. 16.99 (ISBN 0-931988-35-7). Osborne-McGraw.

Six Extra Years: Health & Longevity Secrets of the Seventh-Day Adventists. Lewis Walton et al. (Illus.). 160p. 1981. pap. 4.95 (ISBN 0-912800-84-4). Woodbridge Pr.

Six-Figure Tables of Trigonometric Functions. L. S. Khrenov. 1965. 33.00 o.p. (ISBN 0-08-010101-1). Pergamon.

Six Golden Look-Look Books, 6 bks. Richard Scarry. (Illus.). Date not set. pap. 5.70 boxed set (ISBN 0-307-15524-2, Golden Pr). Western Pub.

Six Great Englishmen. Aubrey De Selincourt. 221p. 1980. lib. bdg. 20.00 (ISBN 0-8482-3652-1). Norwood Edns.

Six Great Ideas. Mortimer J. Adler. 256p. 1981. 12.95 (ISBN 0-02-500560-X). Macmillan.

Six Great Secular Cantatas in Full Score. Johann S. Bach. 288p. (Orig.). 1980. pap. 7.95 (ISBN 0-486-23934-9). Dover.

Six-Gun Country. Max Brand. LC 79-24209. 180p. 1980. 7.95 (ISBN 0-396-07805-2). Dodd.

Six-Gun Country. May Brand. 1981. pap. 1.95 (ISBN 0-686-69453-8). PB.

Six-Gun Mystique. John Cawelti. 148p. 1970. 7.95 (ISBN 0-87972-007-7); pap. 4.95 (ISBN 0-87972-008-5). Bowling Green Univ.

Six Gun Planet. John Jakes. 1970. pap. 1.75 o.s.i. (ISBN 0-446-84721-6). Warner Bks.

Six-Horse Hitch. Janice H. Giles. 408p. 1980. pap. 2.75 (ISBN 0-380-51532-6, 51532). Avon.

Six Hundred Bible Gems & Outlines. S. R. Briggs & J. H. Elliott. LC 75-42955. 1976. pap. 3.95 (ISBN 0-8254-2255-8). Kregel.

Six Hundred Endings. Lajos Portisch & Balazs Sarkozy. Tr. by Sandor Eszenyi et al. (Pergamon Chess Ser.). (Illus.). 328p. 1981. text ed. 16.75 (ISBN 0-08-024137-9). Pergamon.

Six Hundred More Things to Make for the Farm & Home. G. C. Cook & Lloyd J. Phipps. (Illus.). (gr. 9-12). 1952. 16.65 (ISBN 0-8134-0198-4); text ed. 12.50x (ISBN 0-685-03923-4). Interstate.

Six Hundred Ninety-Nine Ways to Improve the Performance of Your Car. Harry Alexandrowicz. LC 79-93251. (Illus.). 192p. 1980. 14.95 (ISBN 0-8069-5550-3); lib. bdg. 13.29 (ISBN 0-8069-5551-1); pap. 6.95 (ISBN 0-8069-8900-9). Sterling.

Six Hundred Sixty Six Science Tricks & Experiments. Bob Brown. pap. 7.95 (ISBN 0-8306-6881-0, 881). TAB Bks.

Six Impossible Things Before Breakfast. Norma Farber. LC 76-40264. (Illus.). (gr. 5-6). 1977. lib. bdg. 6.95x (ISBN 0-201-01969-8, 1969, A-W Childrens). A-W.

Six in One Complete Milly-Molly-Mandy Stories. Joyce L. Brisley. (gr. k-3). 1980. pap. cancelled o.p. (ISBN 0-679-20955-7). McKay.

Six Inner Hebrides. Noel Banks. 1977. 16.95 (ISBN 0-7153-7368-4). David & Charles.

Six Keyboard Sonatas. Baldassare Galuppi. Ed. by Mary L. Serafine. 62p. (gr. 6-12). pap. 7.95 (ISBN 0-686-64721-1, 05052). Fischer Inc NY.

Six Language Dictionary of Welding Technique. Alfred Dollinger. LC 75-591161. 1974. 45.00x (ISBN 0-8002-0400-X). Intl Pubns Serv.

Six Lectures on Economic Growth. Simon Kuznets. LC 59-13596. 1959. 19.95 (ISBN 0-02-917700-6). Free Pr.

Six Little Ducks. Chris Conover. LC 75-22155. (Illus.). 32p. (gr. k-2). 1976. 7.95 (ISBN 0-690-01036-2, TYC-J); PLB 7.89 (ISBN 0-690-01037-0). T Y Crowell.

Six Little Golden Books by Eloise Wilkin, 6 bks. Illus. by Eloise Wilkin. (Illus.). Date not set. boxed set 4.50 (ISBN 0-307-15517-X, Golden Pr). Western Pub.

Six Looney Tunes Golden Shape Books, 6 bks. 144p. 1980. Set. pap. 3.50 (ISBN 0-307-13625-6). Western Pubs OH.

Six Million Dollar Man: International Incidents, No. 2. Mike Jahn. 1977. pap. 1.25 o.p. (ISBN 0-425-03331-7). Berkley Pub.

Six Million Dollar Man, No. 1: Wine, Women & Wars. Michael Jahn. 1975. pap. 1.25 o.s.i. (ISBN 0-446-76833-2). Warner Bks.

Six Million Dollar Man, No. 3: High Crystal. Martin Caidin. 1975. pap. 1.25 o.s.i. (ISBN 0-446-76408-6). Warner Bks.

Six Million Dollar Man, No. 4: Pilot Error. Jay Barbree. 1975. pap. 1.25 o.s.i. (ISBN 0-446-76835-9). Warner Bks.

Six Million Dollar Man: The Secret of Big Foot Pass. Mike Jahn. 1976. pap. 1.25 o.p. (ISBN 0-425-03307-4). Berkley Pub.

Six Modern American Plays. Ed. by Halline. 1951. 3.95 o.p. (ISBN 0-394-60276-5). Random.

Six Modern British Novelists. Ed. by George Stade. LC 74-6141. 336p. 1974. 17.50x (ISBN 0-231-03846-1). Columbia U Pr.

Six Novelists Look at Society. John Atkins. 1980. 11.95 (ISBN 0-7145-3535-4). Riverrun NY.

Six on Easy Street. Betty Cavanna. pap. 0.95 o.p. (ISBN 0-425-03511-5, Highland). Berkley Pub.

Six Painters: Mondrian, DeKooning, Guston, Kline, Pollock, Rothko. Thomas B. Hess & Morton Feldman. LC 67-30452. (Illus.). 1968. pap. 3.00 (ISBN 0-914412-22-1). Inst for the Arts.

Six Pillars: Introduction to the Major Works of Sri Aurobindo. Robert A. McDermott et al. Ed. by Robert A. McDermott. LC 74-77411. 300p. 1974. pap. 5.95 (ISBN 0-89012-001-3). Anima Pubns.

Six-Place Tables. Edward S. Allen. 256p. 1981. Repr. of 1922 ed. lib. bdg. price not set (ISBN 0-89874-287-0). Krieger.

Six Plays by Lillian Hellman: The Children's Hour, Days to Come, the Little Foxes, Watch on the Rhine, Another Part of the Forest, the Autumn Garden. Lillian Hellman. LC 79-2160. 1979. pap. 3.95 (ISBN 0-394-74112-9, Vin). Random.

Six Plays for Girls. N. L. Clay. pap. text ed. 3.25x o.p. (ISBN 0-435-21004-1). Heinemann Ed.

Six Problems for Don Isidro Parodi. Jorge L. Borges. Ed. by Marian Skedgell. 160p. 1981. 10.95 (ISBN 0-525-20480-6). Dutton.

Six Racy Madams of Colorado. Caroline Bancroft. 1965. pap. 2.50 (ISBN 0-933472-22-6). Johnson Colo.

Six Rags Apiece. Marcia Newfield. LC 76-6776. (Illus.). (ps-3). 1976. 6.95 o.p. (ISBN 0-7232-6132-6). Warne.

Six Reports from the Select Committee on Artizans & Machinery, 23 February - 21 May 1824. Great Britain, Parliament, House of Commons, Select Committee on Artizans & Machinery. LC 68-110405. 1981. Repr. of 1824 ed. lib. bdg. 45.00x (ISBN 0-678-05229-8). Kelley.

Six Rural Problem Areas: Relief-Resources-Rehabilitation. P. G. Beck & M. C. Forster. LC 71-165679. (Franklin D. Roosevelt & the Era of the New Deal Ser). 1971. Repr. of 1935 ed. lib. bdg. 17.50 (ISBN 0-306-70333-5). Da Capo.

Six Russian Men - - Lives in Turmoil. Helen Beier & Eugenia Hanfmann. LC 75-32060. 220p. 1976. pap. 5.95 o.p. (ISBN 0-8158-0333-8). Chris Mass.

Six Scandinavian Novelists: Lie, Jacobsen, Heidenstam, Selma Lagerlof, Hamsun, Sigrid Undset. Alrik Gustafson. LC 69-19835. 1968. Repr. of 1940 ed. 12.00x (ISBN 0-8196-0230-2). Biblo.

Six Score: The 120. W. S. Reese. LC 76-8956. (Illus.). 100p. 1976. 30.00 (ISBN 0-8363-0144-7). Jenkins.

Six Sixty-Six. Jay Anson. 13.95 (ISBN 0-671-25144-9). S&S.

Six Stages in the Process of Learning Mathematics. Z. P. Dienes. Tr. by P. L. Seabourne. (NFER General Ser). 64p. 1973. pap. text ed. 5.75x (ISBN 0-85633-022-1, NFER). Humanities.

Six Stages of Parenthood: Between Generations. Ellen Galinsky. 1981. 12.95 (ISBN 0-686-62160-3). Times Bks.

Six Steps to Sexual Ecstasy. (Illus.). 4.95 (ISBN 0-910550-72-7). Centurion Pr.

Six Stories for Acting. Adapted by Geo. P. McCallum. 1976. pap. 2.95 (ISBN 0-89318-031-9); cassettes 29.50 (ISBN 0-89318-034-3). ELS Intl.

Six Things Everyone Should Know. Charles H. Van Dorn. 201p. 1980. 7.95 (ISBN 0-533-03707-7). Vantage.

Six Thousand Years of Housing, 3 vols. Norbert Schoenauer. Incl. Vol. 31. The Pre-Urban House. lib. bdg. 17.50 (ISBN 0-8240-7172-7); Vol. 2. The Oriental Urban House. lib. bdg. 17.50 (ISBN 0-8240-7173-5); Vol. 3. The Occidental Urban House. lib. bdg. 17.50 (ISBN 0-8240-7174-3). 250p. 1980. Garland Pub.

Six Thousand Years of Housing, 3 vols. Norbert Schoenauer. LC 79-20303. 250p. 1980. lib. bdg. 19.50 ea. Vol. 1, The Pre-urban House (ISBN 0-8240-7172-7). Vol. 2, The Oriental Urban House (ISBN 0-8240-7173-5). Vol. 3, The Occidental Urban House (ISBN 0-8240-7174-3). Garland Pub.

Six to Sixteen. Juliana H. Ewing. LC 75-32179. (Classics of Children's Literature, 1621-1932: Vol. 42). (Illus.). 1977. Repr. of 1875 ed. PLB 38.00 (ISBN 0-8240-2291-2). Garland Pub.

Six-Way Paragraphs. Walter Pauk. (Illus.). 224p. (gr. 9 up). 1974. pap. text ed. 4.00x (ISBN 0-89061-009-6). Jamestown Pubs.

Six Ways of Dying. Lewis B. Patten. 144p. 1976. pap. 1.95 (ISBN 0-441-76843-1). Ace Bks.

Six Weeks in the Sioux Tepees: A Narrative of Indian Captivity, Repr. Of 1863 Ed. Sarah Wakefield. Bd. with Miss Coleson's Narrative of Her Capitivity Among the Sioux Indians. Ann Coleson. Repr. of 1864 ed; Reminiscences of Col. John Ketcham, of Monroe County, Indiana, by His Pastor. Thomas M. Hopkins. Repr. of 1866 ed; Gertrude Moran: Or, Life & Adventures Among the Indians of the Far West. Repr. of 1866 ed. LC 75-7104. (Indian Captivities Ser.: Vol. 79). 1977. lib. bdg. 44.00 (ISBN 0-8240-1703-X). Garland Pub.

Six Weeks to Better Parenting: The Complete Guide for Creative Raising of Children 2-12. Caryl W. Krueger. 348p. 1981. pap. 8.95 (ISBN 0-938632-05-1). Belleridge.

Six Who Protested: Radical Opposition to the First World War. Frederick C. Giffin. (National University Publications Ser. in American Studies). 1977. 12.50 (ISBN 0-8046-9193-2). Kennikat.

Six Wives of Henry Eighth. Gladys Malvern. LC 71-134678. (Illus.). (gr. 7 up). 1969. 7.95 (ISBN 0-8149-0665-6). Vanguard.

Six-Year Experience of Unwed Mothers As Parents: A Continuing Study of These Mothers & Their Children. Mignon Sauber & Eileen M. Corrigan. 1970. pap. 3.50 (ISBN 0-86671-007-8). Comm Coun Great NY.

Six Years in Hell: A Returned POW Views Captivity, Country & the Nation's Future. Jay R. Jensen. 1979. 7.95 o.p. (ISBN 0-88290-043-9). Horizon Utah.

Six Years with God. Jeannie Mills. (Illus.). 1979. 12.95 (ISBN 0-89479-046-3). A & W Pubs.

Six Years with the Texas Rangers, 1875 to 1881. James B. Gillett. Ed. by Milo M. Quaife. LC 76-4495. (Illus.). 1976. 14.95x (ISBN 0-8032-0889-8); pap. 3.95 (ISBN 0-8032-5844-5, BB 624, Bison). U of Nebr Pr.

Sixe Bookes of Politickes or Civil Doctrine. Justus Lipsius. Tr. by W. Jones. LC 79-25633. (English Experience Ser.: No. 287). 1970. Repr. of 1594 ed. 22.00 (ISBN 90-221-0287-4). Walter J Johnson.

Sixes & Sevens. John Yeoman. LC 79-147893. (Illus.). 32p. (ps-1). 1974. pap. 1.25 o.s.i. (ISBN 0-02-045720-0, 04572, Collier). Macmillan.

Sixes & Sevens. John Yeoman & Quentin Blake. (Illus.). (gr. k-3). 1971. 7.95 (ISBN 0-02-793610-4). Macmillan.

Sixguns & Society. Will Wright. 1975. 12.50x o.p. (ISBN 0-520-02753-1); pap. 5.95 (ISBN 0-520-03491-0). U of Cal Pr.

Sixpence in Her Shoe. Phyllis McGinley. 1964. 9.95 (ISBN 0-02-583360-X). Macmillan.

Sixteen-Bit Microprocessors. Rahul Chattergy & Udo Pooch. 256p. 1982. text ed. 19.95 (ISBN 0-8359-7003-5). Reston.

Sixteen Can Be Sweet. Johnson. (gr. 7-12). pap. 1.25 (ISBN 0-590-03860-5, Schol Pap). Schol Bk Serv.

Sixteen Documents of Vatican Two. Daughters Of St. Paul. 6.95 o.s.i. (ISBN 0-8198-0145-3); pap. 3.25 (ISBN 0-8198-0146-1). Dghtrs St Paul.

Sixteen Indices: An Aid in Reviewing State & Local Mental Health & Hospital Programs. 93p. 1976. pap. 5.00, 2-9 copies 4.00 ea., 10 or more copies 3.50 ea. (ISBN 0-685-31184-8, P212-0). Am Psychiatric.

Sixteen MM Film Cutting. Burger. 158p. 1975. 7.95 (ISBN 0-240-50857-2). Focal Pr.

Sixteen PF Codebook. Samuel E. Krug. 1981. pap. price not set (ISBN 0-918296-16-1). Inst Personality & Ability.

Sixteen Quaker Leaders Speak. Leonard S. Kenworthy. LC 79-50101. 1979. pap. 2.95 (ISBN 0-913408-49-2). Friends United.

Sixteen-Thirteen Print of Juan Esquivel Barahona. Robert J. Snow. LC 78-70021. (Detroit Monographs in Musicology: No. 7). 1978. 11.00 (ISBN 0-911772-92-8). Info Coord.

Sixteenth Century Art & Architecture. LC 76-14069. (Garland Library of the History of Art). 1976. lib. bdg. 50.00 (ISBN 0-8240-2417-6). Garland Pub.

Sixteenth-Century Europe. Leonard W. Cowie. (Illus.). 1977. pap. text ed. 10.95x (ISBN 0-05-002828-6). Longman.

Sixteenth-Century North America: The Land & People As Seen by Europeans. Carl O. Sauer. LC 75-138635. 1971. 21.95x (ISBN 0-520-01854-0); pap. 4.95 (ISBN 0-520-02777-9). U of Cal Pr.

Sixteenth Round. Rubin Carter. (Illus.). 1975. pap. 2.50 o.s.i. (ISBN 0-446-91020-1). Warner Bks.

Sixth Amendment to the Constitution of the United States: A Study in Constitutional Development. Francis H. Heller. LC 69-13931. 1969. Repr. of 1951 ed. lib. bdg. 15.00x (ISBN 0-8371-0471-8, HESI). Greenwood.

Sixth Book of Virgil Finlay. Ed. by Gerry De La Ree. (Illus.). 1980. 15.75 (ISBN 0-938192-06-X). De La Ree.

Sixth Commandment. Lawrence Sanders. 1980. pap. 2.75 (ISBN 0-425-04271-5). Berkley Pub.

Sixth Day. Tom Noe. LC 79-55296. (Illus.). 80p. (Orig.). (gr. 3-7). 1979. pap. 2.95 (ISBN 0-87793-190-9). Ave Maria.

Sixth European Conference on Optical Communication. (IEE Conference Publication Ser.: No. 190). (Illus.). 466p. (Orig.). 1980. soft cover 73.00 (ISBN 0-85296-223-1). Inst Elect Eng.

Sixth Form & Its Alternatives. Judy Dean et al. (Orig.). 1979. pap. text ed. 27.50x (ISBN 0-85633-182-1, NFER). Humanities.

Sixth Form Pure Mathematics, Vols. 1-2. C. Plumpton & W. H. Tomkys. 1968. Vol. 1. pap. 9.50 (ISBN 0-686-57456-7); Vol. 2. pap. 11.00 (ISBN 0-08-009383-3). Pergamon.

Sixth LACUS Forum Proceedings, Linguistic Association of Canada & the U.S. Ed. by William G. McCormack & Herbert J. Izzo. pap. 10.95 (ISBN 0-686-64345-3). Hornbeam Pr.

Sixth Meeting of the Italian League Against Parkinson's Disease & Extrapyramidal Disorders, 1981. Ed. by A. Agnoli. (Journal: Pharmacology: Vol. 22, No. 1). (Illus.). 92p. 1981. pap. write for info. (ISBN 3-8055-2322-X). S Karger.

Sixth Report of the United States Geographic Board. United States Geographic Board. LC 67-8571. 1967. Repr. of 1933 ed. 24.00 (ISBN 0-685-11676-X). Gale.

Sixth Sense. Larry Kettelkamp. (Illus.). (gr. 5-9). 1970. PLB 6.96 (ISBN 0-688-31463-5). Morrow.

Sixth Wife. Jean Plaidy. 1975. pap. 1.25 o.p. (ISBN 0-449-22343-4, P2343, Crest). Fawcett.

Sixth Winter. Douglas Orgill & John Gribben. 288p. 1981. pap. 2.75 (ISBN 0-345-29242-1). Ballantine.

Sixty American Poets, Eighteen Ninety-Six - Nineteen Fourty-Four. rev. ed. U. S. Library of Congress, General Reference & Bibliography Division. LC 73-5993. xii, 155p. Repr. of 1954 ed. 15.00 (ISBN 0-8103-3365-1). Gale.

Sixty Challenging Problems with BASIC Solutions. Donald Spencer. LC 79-50793. 1979. pap. 7.70 (ISBN 0-8104-5180-8). Hayden.

Sixty Day Fully Financed Fortune. 2nd ed. Tyler G. Hicks. 150p. 1981. pap. 29.50 (ISBN 0-914306-54-5). Intl Wealth.

Sixty-Eight Hundred Assembly Language Programming. Lance A. Leventhal. (Assembly Language Programming Ser.: No. 2). (Orig.). 1978. pap. text ed. 15.99 (ISBN 0-931988-12-8). Osborne-McGraw.

Sixty-Eight Hundred Family Book. Vito Fiore et al. 1982. text ed. 14.95 (ISBN 0-8359-7005-1). Reston.

Sixty-Eight Thousand Microprocessor Handbook. Adam Osborne. 200p. (Orig.). 1981. pap. 6.99 (ISBN 0-931988-41-1). Osborne-McGraw.

Sixty-Fifth Tape. Frank Ross. 304p. 1980. pap. 2.50 (ISBN 0-553-13747-6). Bantam.

Sixty-Five Plus. Melvin Oss. LC 72-88857. (Better Living Ser.). 64p. 1972. pap. 0.95 (ISBN 0-8127-0063-5). Southern Pub.

Sixty-Five Songs; Sixty-Five Pesen. Bulat Okudzhava. Ed. by V. Frumkin. (Eng. & Rus.). 1980. 18.00 (ISBN 0-88233-637-1); pap. 11.00 (ISBN 0-88233-638-X). Ardis Pubs.

Sixty Million Years of Horses. Lois Darling & Louis Darling. (Illus.). (gr. 3-7). 1960. PLB 6.48 (ISBN 0-688-31000-1). Morrow.

Sixty-Minute Cookbook. Pamela Westland. (Illus.). 224p. 1981. 23.00 (ISBN 0-571-11554-3, Pub. by Faber & Faber); pap. 7.50 (ISBN 0-571-11555-1). Merrimack Bk Serv.

Sixty One Gospel Talks for Children: With Suggested Objects for Illustration. Eldon Weisheit. LC 70-96217. 1969. pap. 3.95 (ISBN 0-570-03713-1, 12-2615). Concordia.

Sixty-One Talks for Orthodox Funerals. A. M. Coniaris. 1969. pap. 4.95 (ISBN 0-937032-02-6). Light & Life Pub Co MN.

Sixty-One Worship Talks for Children. rev. ed. E. Weisheit. LC 68-20728. (gr. 3-6). 1975. pap. 3.95 (ISBN 0-570-03714-X, 12-2616). Concordia.

Sixty Steps to Precis. rev ed. L. G. Alexander. 1975. pap. text ed. 2.50x (ISBN 0-582-52309-5). Longman.

Sixty Things God Said About Sex. Lester Sumrall. 144p. 1981. pap. 3.95 (ISBN 0-8407-5756-5). Nelson.

Sixty-Three: Dream Palace & Other Stories. James Purdy. 176p. 1981. pap. 3.95 (ISBN 0-14-005732-3). Penguin.

Sixty Upanishads, 2 vols. Paul Deussen. Tr. by V. M. Bedekar & G. B. Palsule. 1030p. 1980. text ed. 45.00x (ISBN 0-8426-1645-4). Verry.

Sixty Years in Texas. George Jackson. (Illus.). 200p. 1975. Repr. 12.00 o.p. (ISBN 0-89015-105-9). Nortex Pr.

Sixty Years' Memories of Art & Artists. Benjamin Champney. Ed. by H. Barbara Weinberg. LC 75-28887. (Art Experience in Late 19th Century America Ser.: Vol. 20). (Illus.). 1976. Repr. of 1900 ed. lib. bdg. 37.00 (ISBN 0-8240-2244-0). Garland Pub.

Size. rev. ed. Harlan Wade. LC 78-26785. (Book About Ser.). (Illus.). (gr. k-3). 1979. PLB 7.30 (ISBN 0-8172-1533-6). Raintree Pubs.

Size Exclusion Chromatography (GPC) Ed. by Theodore Provder. LC 80-22015. (ACS Symposium Ser.: No. 138). 1980. 30.75 (ISBN 0-8412-0586-8). Am Chemical.

Size, Growth, & U. S. Cities. Richard P. Appelbaum. LC 78-61885. (Praeger Special Studies). 1978. 20.95 (ISBN 0-03-045336-4). Praeger.

Size Queen & Other Poems. Dennis Kelly. (Illus.). 112p. (Orig.). 1981. ltd. ed. 30.00 (ISBN 0-917342-81-X); pap. 5.95 (ISBN 0-917342-82-8). Gay Sunshine.

Sizes. Jan Pienkowski. LC 74-8308. (Concept Bks). (Illus.). 32p. (ps-2). 1975. PLB 5.29 (ISBN 0-8178-5262-X). Harvey.

Sizes. Gillian Youldon. (Picture Play Ser.). (Illus.). (ps-2). 1979. 3.50 (ISBN 0-531-02390-7); PLB 5.45 s&l (ISBN 0-531-00442-2). Watts.

Sizing of Services, Meters & House Pipes. Goldman. 6.00 o.p. (ISBN 0-686-00163-X). Columbia Graphs.

Sizing up the Soviet Army. Jeffrey Record. (Studies in Defense Policy). 51p. 1975. pap. 3.95 (ISBN 0-8157-7367-6). Brookings.

Sizzle Wheels. Barbara Douglass. LC 80-39750. (Illus.). (gr. 3-6). 1981. 9.95 (ISBN 0-664-32680-3). Westminster.

SJIS State of the Art, Nineteen Eighty. Janowski et al. 500p. 1980. pap. 15.00 (ISBN 0-89656-047-3, F-006). Natl Ctr St Courts.

Skate Patrol. Eve Bunting. Ed. by Kathleen Tucker. LC 80-18640. (First Read Alone Mysteries Ser.). (Illus.). 48p. (gr. 2-5). 1980. 5.50g (ISBN 0-8075-7393-0). A Whitman.

Skateboard Four. Eve Bunting. Ed. by Caroline Rubin. LC 76-16115. (Springboard Sports Ser.). (Illus.). 64p. (gr. 3-6). 1976. 5.75g (ISBN 0-8075-7392-2). A Whitman.

Skateboard Practice: Multiplication & Division. Mary Laycock & Peggy McLean. (Illus.). (gr. 3-6). 1979. pap. text ed. 4.95 (ISBN 0-918932-65-3). Activity Resources.

Skateboarding. Howard Reiser. (First Bks.). (Illus.). (gr. 4 up). 1978. PLB 6.45 s&l (ISBN 0-531-01412-6). Watts.

Skateboards & Skateboarding. Weir La Vada. (gr. 4-6). 1977. pap. 1.75 (ISBN 0-671-41136-5). PB.

Skater's Waltz. Philip Norman. 320p. 1980. 17.95 (ISBN 0-241-10255-3, Pub. by Hamish Hamilton England). David & Charles.

Skates. Ezra J. Keats. LC 73-6707. (Illus.). (ps-2). 1973. PLB 5.95 o.p. (ISBN 0-531-02652-3). Watts.

Skates! Ezra J. Keats. LC 80-70119. (Illus.). 32p. (ps-3). 1981. Repr. of 1974 ed. 10.95 (ISBN 0-590-07812-7, Four Winds). Schol Bk Serv.

Skates of Uncle Richard. Carol Fenner. LC 78-55910. (Illus.). (gr. 2-5). 1978. 4.95 (ISBN 0-394-83553-0, BYR); PLB 5.99 (ISBN 0-394-93553-5). Random.

Skating. Boy Scouts of America. LC 19-600. (Illus.). 32p. (gr. 6-12). 1973. pap. 0.70x (ISBN 0-8395-3250-4, 3250). BSA.

Skating Heidens. Mary V. Fox. LC 80-23066. (Illus.). 128p. (gr. 5-12). 1980. PLB 7.95 (ISBN 0-89490-046-3). Enslow Pubs.

Skating Rink. Mildred Lee. LC 69-13443. (gr. 5 up). 1969. 6.95 (ISBN 0-395-28912-2, Clarion). HM.

Skean. Robert McKay. LC 76-6904. 160p. (YA) 1976. 7.95 o.p. (ISBN 0-525-66486-6). Elsevier-Nelson.

Skein of Legends Around Chopin. Adam Harasowski. LC 77-28829. (Music Reprint Ser., 1978). (Illus.). 1978. Repr. of 1967 ed. lib. bdg. 32.50 (ISBN 0-306-77525-5). Da Capo.

Skeletal Growth of Acquatic Organisms: Biological Records of Environmental Change. Ed. by Donald C. Rhoads & Richard A. Lutz. (Topics in Geobiology Ser.: Vol. I). (Illus.). 720p. 1980. 47.50 (ISBN 0-306-40259-9, Plenum Pr). Plenum Pub.

Skeleto-Muscular Morphogenesis of the Thorax & Wings of the Honey Bee Apis Mellifera (Hymenoptera: Apidea) H. V. Daly. (U. C. Publ. in Entomology: Vol. 39). 1964. pap. 6.75x (ISBN 0-520-09111-6). U of Cal Pr.

Skeleton. Kathleen Elgin. LC 74-152741. (Human Body Ser). (Illus.). (gr. 4 up). 1971. PLB 6.90 (ISBN 0-531-01180-1). Watts.

Skeleton Clocks. 2nd ed. F. B. Royer-Collard. (Illus.). 1977. 24.00x (ISBN 0-7198-0110-9). Intl Ideas.

Skeleton in the Closet. Clarence Darrow. 1936. pap. 2.00 (ISBN 0-8283-1438-1). Branden.

Skeleton Inside You. Philip Balestrino. LC 72-132290. (Let's-Read-and-Find-Out Science Bk). (Illus.). (gr. k-3). 1971. PLB 7.89 (ISBN 0-690-74123-5, TYC-J); filmstrip with cassette 14.95 (ISBN 0-690-74126-X); filmstrip with record 11.95 (ISBN 0-690-74124-3). T Y Crowell.

Skeleton Key to Finnegans Wake. Joseph Campbell & Henry M. Robinson. 1977. pap. 5.95 (ISBN 0-14-004663-1). Penguin.

Skeletons. Glendon Swarthout. 1981. pap. write for info. (ISBN 0-671-83586-6). PB.

Skeletons & Muscles. Donald Reid & Philip Booth. (Biology for the Individual Ser.). pap. text ed. 4.50x o.p. (ISBN 0-435-59768-X). Heinemann Ed.

Skepsis, Dogma, & Belief: Uses & Abuses in Medicine. Edmond A. Murphy. LC 80-8870. 176p. 1981. text ed. 14.95x (ISBN 0-8018-2510-5). Johns Hopkins.

Skeptical Essays. Benson Mates. LC 80-19553. 1981. lib. bdg. 17.00x (ISBN 0-226-50986-9). U of Chicago Pr.

Skeptical Sociology. Dennis H. Wrong. LC 76-18843. 1976. 20.00x (ISBN 0-231-04014-8). Columbia U Pr.

Skepticism & Cognitivism: A Study in the Foundations of Knowledge. Oliver A. Johnson. LC 77-91743. 1979. 16.50x (ISBN 0-520-03620-4). U of Cal Pr.

Sketch & Draw Today. Henry J. Filson. (Draw-Sketch Practice Ser.). (Illus.). 122p. 1976. plastic bdg. 12.00 (ISBN 0-918554-00-4). Old Violin.

Sketch Book. Peter Hurd. LC 70-150951. (Illus.). 121p. 1971. 45.00 (ISBN 0-8040-0531-1, SB). Swallow.

Sketch of a System of the Philosophy of the Human Mind. Thomas Brown. Bd. with Logic of Condillac. (Contributions to the History of Psychology Ser., Pt. A: Orientations). 1978. Repr. of 1820 ed. 30.00 (ISBN 0-89093-150-X). U Pubns Amer.

Sketch of the Laws Relating to Slavery in the Several States of the United States of America. George M. Stroud. LC 68-55917. Repr. of 1956 ed. 11.50x (ISBN 0-8371-0673-7). Negro U Pr.

Sketchbook of Michigan. Reynold H. Weidenaar & Ann Zeller. (Illus.). 128p. 1980. 15.95 (ISBN 0-8010-9620-0). Baker Bk.

Sketchbook of New Zealand Birds. Molly Falla. (Illus.). 1966. 6.75 o.p. (ISBN 0-589-00327-5, Dist. by C E Tuttle). Reed.

Sketches. Ben Burroughs. LC 56-11909. 160p. 1980. pap. 8.50 (ISBN 0-8303-0048-1). Fleet.

Sketches, Historical & Topographical, of the Floridas. James G. Forbes. Ed. by James W. Covington. LC 64-19158. (Floridiana Facsimile & Reprint Ser). 1964. Repr. of 1821 ed. 9.50 (ISBN 0-8130-0078-5). U Presses Fla.

Sketches: Historical, Literary, Biographical, Economic. Thomas E. Watson. (Studies in Populism). 1980. lib. bdg. 75.00 (ISBN 0-686-68884-8). Revisionist Pr.
Sketches of a History of Literature. Robert Alves. LC 67-18714. 1967. Repr. of 1794 ed. 33.00x (ISBN 0-8201-1002-7). Schol Facsimiles.
Sketches of Irish Character, 2 vols. Anna Maria Hall. Ed. by Robert L. Wolff. (Ireland Nineteenth Century Fiction, Ser. Two: Vol. 46). 1979. Set. lib. bdg. 92.00 (ISBN 0-8240-3495-3); lib. bdg. 46.00 ea. Garland Pub.
Sketches of Springfield in 1856. Daily Nonpareil Office. (Annual Monograph Ser.). 96p. 1973. pap. 3.00 facsimile reprint. Clark County Hist Soc.
Sketches of the Judicial History of Massachusetts from 1630 to the Revolution in 1775. Emory Washburn. LC 74-6427. (American Constitutional & Legal History Ser.). 407p. 1974. Repr. of 1840 ed. lib. bdg. 42.50 (ISBN 0-306-70616-4). Da Capo.
Sketches of the Life & Correspondences of Nathanael Green, 2 vols. William Johnson. LC 78-119063. 516p. 1974. Repr. of 1822 ed. lib. bdg. 65.00 (ISBN 0-306-71953-3). Da Capo.
Sketches of the Origin, Process & Effects of Music. R. Eastcott. LC 70-159680. (Music Ser). 1971. Repr. of 1793 ed. lib. bdg. 27.50 (ISBN 0-306-70184-7). Da Capo.
Sketches of the Rise, Progress, & Decline of Secession. 2nd ed. William G. Brownlow. LC 68-23813. (American Scene Ser). 1968. Repr. of 1862 ed. 42.50 (ISBN 0-306-71137-0). Da Capo.
Sketches of the Tennessee Valley in Antebellum Days. H. S. Marks. pap. 5.95 (ISBN 0-915536-02-1). H S Marks.
Sketches of Western Adventure: Containing an Account of the Most Interesting Incidents Connected with the Settlement of the West from 1755 to 1794. John A. McClung. LC 75-7072. (Indian Captivities Ser.: Vol. 50). 1976. Repr. of 1832 ed. lib. bdg. 44.00 (ISBN 0-8240-1674-2). Garland Pub.
Sketchpad: A Man-Machine Graphical Communication System. Ivan E. Sutherland. LC 79-50557. (Outstanding Dissertations in the Computer Sciences Ser.: Vol. 21). 176p. 1980. lib. bdg. 20.00 (ISBN 0-8240-4411-8). Garland Pub.
Skew Field Constructions. P. M. Cohn. LC 76-46854. (London Mathematical Society Lecture Note Series: No. 27). (Illus.). 1977. limp bdg. 26.95x (ISBN 0-521-21497-1). Cambridge U Pr.
Ski California: A Guide to Downhill & Cross-Country Skiing. Luanne Pfeifer. LC 80-13731. (Illus.). 1980. pap. 7.95 (ISBN 0-89141-091-0). Presidio Pr.
Ski Camping. Ron Watters. LC 79-22843. (Illus., Orig.). 1979. pap. 7.95 (ISBN 0-87701-165-6). Chronicle Bks.
Ski Conditioning. Merle L. Foss & James G. Garrick. LC 77-24553. (American College of Sports Medicine Ser.). 1978. text ed. 14.95 (ISBN 0-471-26764-3). Wiley.
Ski-Doo Snowmobile Service-Repair: 1970-1979. David Sales. Ed. by Eric Jorgensen. (Illus.). 1977. pap. 8.95 (ISBN 0-89287-178-4, X953). Clymer Pubns.
Ski Free. Greg Athans. 1978. 12.95 o.p. (ISBN 0-87690-321-9); pap. 7.95 o.p. (ISBN 0-87690-322-7). Dutton.
Ski Magazine's Complete Book of Ski Technique. Morten Lund & Ski Magazine Editors. LC 75-6362. (Illus.). 208p. 1975. 12.95 o.p. (ISBN 0-06-013904-8, HarpT). Har-Row.
Ski Racer. Martin Luray. LC 75-38512. (Target Bks.). (Illus.). 48p. (gr. 3 up). 1976. PLB 6.45 (ISBN 0-531-01186-0). Watts.
Ski Run. Mike Neigoff. LC 70-188433. (Pilot Books Ser.). (Illus.). 128p. (gr. 4-7). 1972. 6.95g (ISBN 0-8075-7396-5). A Whitman.
Ski Touring in California. 2nd ed. David Beck. LC 79-90502. (Illus.). 1979. pap. 7.95 (ISBN 0-686-59506-8). Pika Pr.
Ski Waxing for High Performance. A. Duvillard & J. P. Toussaint. LC 77-21481. 1977. pap. 2.50 (ISBN 0-8120-0865-0). Barron.
Ski with Nitka. Louis Nitka. LC 72-82134. (Illus.). 64p. 1972. pap. 1.25 o.p. (ISBN 0-88208-006-7). Lawrence Hill.
Ski with the Big Boys. Stuart D. Campbell & Malcolm Reiss. 1974. 11.95 (ISBN 0-87691-144-0). Winchester Pr.
Skidarima: An Inquiry into the Written & Printed Texts, References & Commentaries. Ed. by Theo Homan. (Amsterdamer Publikationen Zur Sprache und Literatur: No. 20). 430p. (Orig.). 1975. pap. text ed. 85.50x (ISBN 90-6203-079-3). Humanities.
Skier's Almanac. I. William Berry. LC 78-15441. 1978. 12.95 o.p. (ISBN 0-684-15791-8, ScribT); pap. 5.95 o.p. (ISBN 0-684-15792-6, ScribT). Scribner.
Skier's Handbook. Ski Magazine Editors. (Illus.). 1965. 13.95 (ISBN 0-06-111710-2, HarpT). Har-Row.
Skiffs & Schooners. R. D. Culler. LC 74-17905. (Illus.). 406p. 1975. 20.00 (ISBN 0-87742-047-5). Intl Marine.
Skiing. Boy Scouts Of America. LC 19-600. (Illus.). 64p. (gr. 6-12). 1965. pap. 0.55x o.p. (ISBN 0-8395-3364-0, 3364). BSA.
Skiing. Boy Scouts, of America. (Illus.). 56p. (gr. 6-12). 1980. pap. 0.70x. BSA.
Skiing Fundamentals. Bryan Boswell. (Fundamentals: A Series on Getting It Right the First Time). (Illus.). 80p. (Orig.). 1979. pap. 8.95 (ISBN 0-589-50085-6, Pub. by Reed Books Australia). C E Tuttle.
Skiing Is a Family Sport. John H. Auran. LC 68-31329. 4.95 (ISBN 0-910294-33-X). Brown Bk.
Skiing Mechanics. John G. Howe. 1981. 16.95 (ISBN 0-686-28916-1). Poudre Pub Co.
Skiing Skills. Rudiger Jahn et al. (Illus.). 160p. 1980. 19.95 (ISBN 0-87691-330-3). Winchester Pr.
Skiing the Midwest. Patricia Skalka. 1978. 14.95 o.p. (ISBN 0-8092-7610-0); pap. 7.95 (ISBN 0-8092-7609-7). Contemp Bks.
Skiing the Rockies. Photos by Bruce Barthel. LC 80-65133. (Belding Imprint Ser.). (Illus.). 128p. (Text by Charlie Meyers). 1980. 27.50 (ISBN 0-912856-60-2). Graphic Arts Ctr.
Skill Factor in Politics: Repealing the Mental Commitment Laws in California. Eugene Bardach. LC 79-157820. 300p. 1972. 20.00x (ISBN 0-520-02042-1). U of Cal Pr.
Skillbook in Reading. Jack Norman. (gr. 6-12). 1975. wkbk 5.08 (ISBN 0-87720-322-9). AMSCO Sch.
Skilled Teacher: A System Approach to Teaching Skills. Robert R. Carkhuff. (Illus.). 184p. 1981. pap. 10.95 (ISBN 0-914234-52-8). Human Res Dev Pr.
Skills & Procedures of Emergency & General Medicine. Harvey W. Meislin & Stephen J. Dresnick. 250p. 1982. text ed. 29.95 (ISBN 0-8359-7009-4). Reston.
Skills Development Portfolio for What Every Supervisor Should Know, The Basics of Supervisory Management. 4th ed. Lester R. Bittel. 1979. 5.30 (ISBN 0-07-005562-9). McGraw.
Skills for Effective Communication: A Guide to Building Relationships. Raphael J. Becvar. LC 73-19914. (Self-Teaching Guides Ser). 1974. pap. text ed. 7.95x (ISBN 0-471-06143-3). Wiley.
Skills for Success. Adele M. Scheele. 208p. 1981. pap. 2.95 (ISBN 0-345-29484-X). Ballantine.
Skills in Counterattacks, No. 135. Pu Gill Gwon. 1980. pap. 6.95 (ISBN 0-89750-067-9). Ohara Pubns.
Skills in Life-Career Planning. Karl Bartsch & Louise Sandmeyer. LC 78-24615. (Psychology Ser.). (Illus.). 1979. pap. text ed. 8.95 (ISBN 0-8185-0322-X). Brooks-Cole.
Skills in Neighbourhood Work. Paul Henderson & David N. Thomas. (National Institute Social Services Library: No. 39). (Illus.). 280p. 1981. text ed. 27.50x (ISBN 0-04-361042-0, 2554); pap. text ed. 12.95x (ISBN 0-04-361043-9, 2555). Allen Unwin.
Skills in Spelling: 1973 Ed, Bks. A-H. Bremer. Incl. Bk. A. (gr. 1). pap. text ed. 3.44 (ISBN 0-8009-0551-2); tchr's ed. 5.04 (ISBN 0-8009-0555-5); 1967 ed. of text & tchr's. ed. also avail. Write for further info.; Bk. B. (gr. 2). text ed. 6.88 (ISBN 0-8009-0649-7); pap. text ed. 3.44 (ISBN 0-8009-0564-4); tchr's. ed. for hardcover text 5.04 (ISBN 0-8009-0651-9); tchr's. ed. for pap. text 4.56 (ISBN 0-8009-0568-7); 1967-68 eds. of texts & tchr's ed. also avail. Write for further info.; Bk. C. (gr. 3). text ed. 6.88 (ISBN 0-8009-0653-5); pap. text ed. 3.44 (ISBN 0-8009-0576-8); tchr's. ed. for hardcover text 6.04 (ISBN 0-8009-0655-1); tchr's. ed. for pap. text 4.56 (ISBN 0-8009-0580-6); 1964 & 1967-68 eds. of texts & tchr's. ed. avail. Write for further info.; Bk. D. (gr. 4). text ed. 6.88 (ISBN 0-8009-0657-8); pap. text ed. 3.44 (ISBN 0-8009-0588-1); tchr's. ed. for hardcover text 5.04 (ISBN 0-8009-0659-4); tchr's. ed. for pap. text 4.56 (ISBN 0-8009-0593-8); 1964 & 1967-68 eds. of texts & tchr's. eds. also avail. Write for further info.; Bk. E. (gr. 5). text ed. 6.88 (ISBN 0-8009-0661-6); pap. text ed. 3.44 (ISBN 0-8009-0601-2); tchr's. ed. for hardcover text 5.04 (ISBN 0-8009-0663-2); tchr's. ed. for pap. text 4.56 (ISBN 0-8009-0605-5); 1967-68 eds. of texts & tchr's. eds. also avail. Write for further info.; Bk. F. (gr. 6). text ed. 6.88 (ISBN 0-8009-0665-9); pap. text ed. 3.44 (ISBN 0-8009-0614-4); tchr's. ed. for hardcover text 5.04 (ISBN 0-8009-0667-5); tchr's. ed. for pap. text 4.56 (ISBN 0-8009-0618-7); 1967-68 eds. also avail. Write for further info.; Bk. G. (gr. 7). text ed. 6.88 (ISBN 0-8009-0669-1); pap. text ed. 3.44 (ISBN 0-8009-0626-8); tchr's. ed. for hardcover text 5.04 (ISBN 0-8009-0671-3); tchr's. ed. for pap. text 4.56 (ISBN 0-8009-0630-6); 1964 & 1967-68 eds. also avail. Write for further info.; Bk. H. (gr. 8). text ed. 6.88 (ISBN 0-8009-0674-8); pap. text ed. 3.44 (ISBN 0-8009-0638-1); tchr's. ed. for hardcover text 5.04 (ISBN 0-8009-0676-4); tchr's. ed. for pap. text 4.56 (ISBN 0-8009-0643-8); 1964 & 1967-68 eds. also avail. Write for further info.. (gr. 1-8). McCormick-Mathers.
Skills of Helping: An Introduction to Counseling. Robert Carkhuff et al. LC 78-73987. 262p. 1979. text ed. 13.95x (ISBN 0-914234-09-9); pap. 10.95x (ISBN 0-914234-87-0). Human Res Dev.
Skills of Helping Individuals & Groups. Lawrence Shulman. LC 78-71816. 1979. text ed. 14.95 (ISBN 0-87581-243-0). Peacock Pubs.
Skills of Helping Student Workbook. R. R. Carkhuff et al. 150p. pap. text ed. 5.95 o.p. (ISBN 0-914234-13-7, SHSW). Human Res Dev Pr.
Skills of Management. A. N. Welsh. 247p. 1981. 14.95 (ISBN 0-8144-5670-7). Am Mgmt.
Skills of Managing. Arthur F. Strohmer, Jr. LC 76-136128. (Business Ser). (Prog. Bk.). 1970. pap. 8.95 (ISBN 0-201-07325-0). A-W.
Skills of Selling. Roger W. Seng. (Illus.). 1978. 14.95 (ISBN 0-8144-5458-5). Am Mgmt.
Skills, Outlooks, Passions: A Psychoanalytic Contribution to Lthe Study of Politics. 2nd ed. A. F. Davies. LC 78-54575. (Illus.). 456p. Date not set. 55.00 (ISBN 0-521-22081-5); pap. 14.95 (ISBN 0-521-29349-9). Cambridge U Pr.
Skillseekers, 3 kits. Ed. by R. E. Eicholz. (gr. 3-12). 1977. 185.00 ea. (Sch Div). Kit I (ISBN 0-201-23026-7). tchr's. ed. 5.48 (ISBN 0-201-23027-5); dup. masters 5.48 (ISBN 0-201-23030-5); ans. bk. 8.44 (ISBN 0-201-23028-3). A-W.
Skillseekers 3: Decimal Computation Kit. Ed. by Judith Good. (gr. 5-8). 1978. kit 185.00 (ISBN 0-201-23200-6, Sch Div). A-W.
Skillstuff: Reasoning. Imogene Forte & Joy MacKenzie. LC 80-81737. (Skillstuff Ser.). (Illus.). 232p. (gr. 2-6). 1981. pap. text ed. 10.95 (ISBN 0-913916-81-1). Incentive Pubns.
Skimming & Scanning. Edward Fry. (Illus.). (gr. 9-12). 1978. pap. text ed. 4.00x (ISBN 0-89061-123-8, 781). Jamestown Pubs.
Skin. Kathleen Elgin. LC 72-101746. (Human Body Ser). (Illus.). (gr. 4-6). 1970. PLB 4.90 o.p. (ISBN 0-531-01177-1). Watts.
Skin Book: Looking & Feeling Your Best Through Proper Skin Care. James H. Klein et al. 1980. 10.95 (ISBN 0-02-563920-X). Macmillan.
Skin: Coverings & Linings of Living Things. A. Silverstein & V. Silverstein. 1972. 5.95 (ISBN 0-13-812776-X, 812776). P-H.
Skin Disorders in Clinical Practice. 3rd ed. I. B. Sneddon & R. E. Church. 19.50 (ISBN 0-201-07705-1). A-W.
Skin Diver's Bible. Owen Lee. LC 67-11191. pap. 3.50 (ISBN 0-385-03737-6). Doubleday.
Skin Diving in the Virgins & Other Poems. John M. Brinnin. 1970. 4.50 o.p. (ISBN 0-440-08031-2, Sey Lawr). Delacorte.
Skin Diving Is for Me. Carole S. Briggs. (Sports for Me Bks.). (Illus.). (gr. 2-5). 1981. PLB 5.95 (ISBN 0-8225-1132-0). Lerner Pubns.
Skin Diving Mystery. Mary Adrian. Date not set. 5.95 (ISBN 0-8038-6719-0). Hastings.
Skin Flaps. Ed. by William C. Grabb & M. Bert Myers. LC 74-20219. 440p. 1975. 60.00 (ISBN 0-316-32267-9). Little.
Skin, Heredity, & Malignant Neoplasms. Henry T. Lynch. 1972. spiral bdg. 24.00 o.p. (ISBN 0-87488-744-5). Med Exam.
Skin of Dreams. Raymond Queneau. Tr. by H. J. Kaplan from Fr. LC 77-11668. 1979. Repr. of 1948 ed. 13.50 (ISBN 0-86527-305-7). Fertig.
Skin Problems of the Amputee. William S. Levy. LC 78-50196. (Illus.). 320p. 1981. 55.00 (ISBN 0-87527-181-2). Green.
Skinner. F. M. Parker. LC 80-1863. (Double D Western Ser.). 192p. 1981. 9.95 (ISBN 0-385-17382-2). Doubleday.
Skinner Primer: Behind Freedom & Dignity. Finley Carpenter. LC 73-16603. 1974. 12.95 (ISBN 0-02-905290-4); pap. 2.95 (ISBN 0-02-905310-2). Free Pr.
Skinner's Philosophy. Paul T. Sagal. LC 80-5737. 132p. 1981. lib. bdg. 15.75 (ISBN 0-8191-1432-4); pap. text ed. 7.50 (ISBN 0-8191-1433-2). U Pr of Amer.
Skinnie Minnie Recipe Book. Frances Hunter. 1976. pap. 2.95 (ISBN 0-917726-06-5). Hunter Bks.
Skinny Dynamite & Other Short Stories. Jack Micheline. Ed. by A. D. Winans. LC 79-63969. 96p. (Orig.). 1980. pap. 4.95x (ISBN 0-915016-27-3). Second Coming.
Skinny Willy. W. C. Chalk. 1971. pap. text ed. 2.50x o.p. (ISBN 0-435-11191-4). Heinemann Ed.
Skintelligence: How to Be Smart About Skin. Richard A. Walzer. (Appleton Consumer Health Guides). 256p. 1981. 12.95 (ISBN 0-8385-8569-8); pap. 6.95 (ISBN 0-8385-8568-X). ACC.
Skip Aboard a Space Ship. Jane B. Moncure. LC 77-12958. (Creative Dramatics Ser.). (Illus.). (ps-3). 1978. PLB 5.50 (ISBN 0-89565-009-6); pap. 2.50 (ISBN 0-89565-042-8). Childs World.
Skipper. Paige Dixon. LC 79-10420. (gr. 5-10). 1979. 8.95 (ISBN 0-689-30706-3). Atheneum.
Skipping the Rope. 2nd, rev. ed. Frank Prentup. 36p. 1980. pap. 3.95 (ISBN 0-87108-572-0). Pruett.
Skipping the Rope for Fun & Fitness. Frank B. Prentup. (Illus.). pap. 2.25 o.p. (ISBN 0-87108-021-4). Pruett.
Skippy & Percy Crosby. Jerry Robinson. LC 78-53777. (Illus.). 1978. 16.95 o.p. (ISBN 0-03-018491-6). HR&W.
Skirmish at Fort Phil Kearny. Wayne C. Lee. (YA) 1977. 5.95 (ISBN 0-685-74268-7, Avalon). Bouregy.
Skirmish: The Great Short Fiction of Clifford D. Simak. Clifford D. Simak. LC 77-7176. 1977. 8.95 o.p. (ISBN 0-399-12032-7, Dist. by Putnam). Berkley Pub.
Skirmish Wargaming. Donald F. Featherstone. Ed. by D. Reach. (Illus.). 1979. pap. 11.75 o.p. (ISBN 0-85059-392-1). Aztex.
Skirtmaking Book. Patricia Riley. 1979. 17.95 (ISBN 0-7134-1641-6, Pub. by Batsford England). David & Charles.
Skitch: The Message of the Roses. Vincent G. Perry. 6.95. Green Hill.
Skits & Puppets. Boy Scouts Of America. (Illus.). 68p. 1967. pap. 1.25x (ISBN 0-8395-3842-1). BSA.
Skits, Comedies & Farces for Teen-Agers. Ed. by A. S. Burack. (gr. 7-12). 1970. 10.95 (ISBN 0-8238-0001-6). Plays.
Skitterbrain. Brown. (gr. 3-5). 1980. pap. 1.25 (ISBN 0-590-30906-4, Schol Pap). Schol Bk Serv.
Skitterbrain. Irene B. Brown. LC 78-18349. (gr. 5 up). 1978. 6.95 (ISBN 0-525-66587-0). Elsevier-Nelson.
Skittles Make Believe School. 1976. 2.00 (ISBN 0-686-64104-3). Borden.
Sklansky on Poker Theory. rev. ed. David Sklansky. 176p. 1980. pap. 5.95 (ISBN 0-89650-918-4). Gamblers.
Sklansky's Poker Theory. David Sklansky. 1978. pap. 3.95 o.p. (ISBN 0-89650-917-6). Gamblers.
Skoolplay. Alan Brown. 1980. pap. 3.95 (ISBN 0-7145-3672-5). Riverrun NY.
Skorzeny: Hitler's Commando. Glenn Infield. (Illus.). 304p. 1981. 15.95 (ISBN 0-312-72777-1). St Martin.
Skrebneski Portraits: A Matter of Record. Victor Skrebneski. LC 78-18566. 1978. 19.95 o.p. (ISBN 0-385-14623-X). Doubleday.
Skull in the Snow & Other Folktales. Toni McCarty. LC 80-68730. (Illus.). 96p. (gr. 4-7). 1981. 7.95 (ISBN 0-440-08028-2); PLB 7.45 (ISBN 0-440-08030-4). Delacorte.
Skull of Adam. Stanley Moss. 1980. 7.95 (ISBN 0-8180-1578-0); pap. 3.95 (ISBN 0-686-64570-7). Horizon.

Skunk Baby. Berniece Freschet. LC 72-83781. (Illus.). (gr. 2-5). 1973. PLB 7.89 (ISBN 0-690-74194-4, TYC-J). T Y Crowell.

Skunk in the House. Constance Colby. LC 73-497. (Illus.). 1973. 8.95 (ISBN 0-397-00978-X). Lippincott.

Skunks. Wyatt Blassingame. LC 80-21555. (Skylight Bk.). (Illus.). 64p. (gr. 2-5). 1981. PLB 5.95 (ISBN 0-396-07909-1). Dodd.

Skunny Wundy Seneca Indian Tales. Arthur C. Parker. LC 73-115899. (Folklore Ser). (Illus.). (gr. 3 up). 1970. 5.95g o.p. (ISBN 0-8075-7405-8). A Whitman.

Sky. Michael Benedikt. LC 75-120257. (Wesleyan Poetry Program: Vol. 52). 1970. 10.00x (ISBN 0-8195-2052-7, Pub. by Wesleyan U Pr); pap. 4.95x (ISBN 0-8195-1052-1). Columbia U Pr.

Sky & Sextant. John P. Budlong. 232p. 1981. pap. text ed. 10.95 (ISBN 0-442-20460-4). Van Nos Reinhold.

Sky Clears: Poetry of the American Indians. A. Grove Day. LC 65-38538. 1964. pap. 2.45 (ISBN 0-8032-5047-9, BB 142, Bison). U of Nebr Pr.

Sky Determines: An Interpretation of the Southwest. rev ed. Ross Calvin. LC 48-6466. (Illus.). 1965. pap. 4.95 (ISBN 0-8263-0011-1). U of NM Pr.

Sky Dive. Mary Verdick. Ed. by Thomas J. Mooney. (Pal Paperbacks Kit A Ser.). (Illus., Orig.). (gr. 7-12). 1976. pap. text ed. 1.25 (ISBN 0-8374-3498-X). Xerox Ed Pubns.

Sky Drift. David Dunn. LC 80-80806. (Illus.). 90p. 1979. soft wrap-around cover 15.95. Lingua Pr.

Sky Fighters of France: Aerial Warfare, Nineteen Fourteen to Nineteen Eighteen. Henry Farre. Ed. by James Gilbert. Tr. by Catharine Rush. LC 79-7252. (Flight: Its First Seventy-Five Years Ser.). (Illus.). 1979. Repr. of 1919 ed. lib. bdg. 16.00x (ISBN 0-405-12164-4). Arno.

Sky Heart. Harley Elliott. LC 75-14965. (Illus.). 60p. 1975. pap. 3.00x (ISBN 0-915316-13-7); pap. 7.50 limited signed ed (ISBN 0-915316-14-5). Pentagram.

Sky Is Blue, the Grass Is Green. John E. Johnson. (Cloth Bks.). (Illus.). 8p. (ps). pap. 2.50 (ISBN 0-394-84403-3, BYR). Random.

Sky Is Free. Mavis T. Clark. LC 76-15171. (gr. 5-8). 1976. 8.95 (ISBN 0-02-718910-4, 71891). Macmillan.

Sky on Fire. D. S. Halacy, Jr. (gr. 7 up). 1965. 3.50 o.s.i. (ISBN 0-02-741720-4). Macmillan.

Sky Pilot, a Tale of the Foothills. Ralph Connor. 1976. lib. bdg. 14.25x (ISBN 0-89968-019-4). Lightyear.

Sky Pilot in No Man's Land. Ralph Connor. 1976. lib. bdg. 15.75x (ISBN 0-89968-018-6). Lightyear.

Sky Ride. Steven Otfinoski. Ed. by Thomas J. Mooney. (Beginning Pal Paperbacks Ser.). (Illus., Orig.). (gr. 7-12). 1977. pap. text ed. 1.25 (ISBN 0-8374-3450-5). Xerox Ed Pubns.

Sky Rocket: The Story of a Little Bay Horse. Margaret C. Self. LC 78-111913. (gr. 8 up). 1970. 5.95 (ISBN 0-396-06207-5). Dodd.

Skyblazer. M. Howard. (Illus.). (gr. 7-9). 1966. 2.95 (ISBN 0-394-81642-0, BYR); PLB 5.69 (ISBN 0-394-91642-5). Random.

Skydance. Elizabeth Swados. LC 80-7913. (Illus.). 32p. (ps-3). 1981. 8.95 (ISBN 0-06-026073-4, HarpJ); PLB 8.79g (ISBN 0-06-026074-2). Har-Row.

Skydiving. Eleanor Kay. LC 75-151885. (First Bks). (Illus.). (gr. 7-9). 1971. PLB 4.90 o.p. (ISBN 0-531-00750-2). Watts.

Skye. Derek Cooper. (Illus.). 1970. 22.50 (ISBN 0-7100-6820-4). Routledge & Kegan.

Skye. F. C. Sillar & Ruth Meyler. (Islands Ser). (Illus.). 248p. pap. 10.50 (ISBN 0-7153-5751-4). David & Charles.

Skye O'Malley. Bertrice Small. 1980. 5.95 (ISBN 0-345-29256-1). Ballantine.

Skye Railway. John Thomas. 1977. 8.95 (ISBN 0-7153-7383-8). David & Charles.

Skye Terrier Handbook. 1974. 7.00 (ISBN 0-9600722-1-7). Skye Terrier.

Skyhooks: The Story of Helicopters. Charles Coombs. (Illus.). (gr. 5-9). 1967. 6.25 o.p. (ISBN 0-688-21556-4); PLB 6.00 o.p. (ISBN 0-688-31556-9). Morrow.

Skyjacker: His Flights of Fancy. David G. Hubbard. Ed. by Clement Alexandre. 1971. 5.95 o.p. (ISBN 0-02-555290-2); pap. 1.95 (ISBN 0-02-095920-6). Macmillan.

Skylab. Charles Coombs. LC 79-168471. (Illus.). (gr. 5-9). 1972. PLB 6.96 (ISBN 0-688-31812-6). Morrow.

Skylark DuQuesne. E. E. Smith. 1973. pap. 1.50 o.s.i. (ISBN 0-515-03050-3, N3050). Jove Pubns.

Skylark of Space. Edward E. Smith. 1970. pap. 1.50 o.s.i. (ISBN 0-685-19678-X, V2969). Jove Pubns.

Skylark of Valeron. E. E. Smith. 1973. pap. 1.50 o.s.i. (ISBN 0-515-03022-8, V3022). Jove Pubns.

Skylark Three. E. E. Smith. 1973. pap. 1.50 o.s.i. (ISBN 0-515-03160-7, V3160). Jove Pubns.

Skylight. Carol Muske. LC 80-712. 96p. 1981. pap. 5.95 (ISBN 0-385-17087-4). Doubleday.

Skylights & Windows You Can Install. Peter Jones. Ed. by K. Lawson. (Home Environment "HELP" Ser.). (Illus.). 144p. (Orig.). pap. cancelled (ISBN 0-88421-155-X). Butterick Pub.

Skyriders: History of the 327-401 Glider Infantry. James L. McDonough & Richard S. Gardner. LC 80-67956. (Airborne Ser.: No. 11). (Illus.). 176p. 1980. 20.00 (ISBN 0-89839-034-6). Battery Pr.

Sky's the Limit. Wayne Dyer. 1980. 12.95 (ISBN 0-671-24989-4, 24989). S&S.

Skyscraper Goes Up. Carter Harman. (Illus.). (gr. 5 up). 1973. 4.95 (ISBN 0-394-82147-5). Random.

Skyscraper Nurse. Ann Gilmer. (YA) 1976. 4.95 o.p. (ISBN 0-685-69516-6, Avalon). Bouregy.

Skyscraper Primitives: Dada & the American Avant-Garde, 1910-1925. Dickran L. Tashjian. LC 74-21925. (Illus.). 360p. 1975. 22.50x (ISBN 0-8195-4081-1, Pub. by Wesleyan U Pr). Columbia U Pr.

Skyshooting: Photography for Amateur Astronomers. R. N. Mayall & M. W. Mayall. (Illus.). 7.50 (ISBN 0-8446-2553-1). Peter Smith.

Skywatchers of Ancient Mexico. Anthony F. Aveni. (Texas Pan American Ser.). (Illus.). 360p. 1980. text ed. 20.00x (ISBN 0-686-60148-3); pap. 6.95 (ISBN 0-292-77557-1). U of Tex Pr.

Slab, Coil, & Pinch: A Beginners Pottery Book. Alice Gilbreath. (Illus.). (gr. 3-7). 1977. 6.75 (ISBN 0-688-22105-X); PLB 6.48 (ISBN 0-688-32105-4). Morrow.

Slab Cowboy. Gary Paulsen. LC 79-63130. Date not set. pap. 4.50 cancelled (ISBN 0-931328-04-7). Timely Bks.

Slacks Cut-to-Fit. Doris Ekern. Ed. by Mary Leppert. LC 77-70233. 1977. 3.80 (ISBN 0-933956-00-2); tchrs ed. 3.04. Sew-Fit.

Slade Short Course in Grammar. Slade Schuster. 54p. (Orig.). (gr. 8-11). 1978. pap. text ed. 2.25x (ISBN 0-88334-111-5). Ind Sch Pr.

Slag. David Hare. 1971. pap. 4.95 (ISBN 0-571-09643-3, Pub. by Faber & Faber). Merrimack Bk Serv.

Slam the Big Door. John D. MacDonald. 208p. 1977. pap. 1.95 o.p. (ISBN 0-449-13707-4, GM). Fawcett.

Slamming the Door: The Administration of Immigration Control. Robert Moore & Tina Wallace. 126p. 1975. 23.25x (ISBN 0-85520-107-X, Pub by Martin Robertson England); pap. 8.95x (ISBN 0-85520-106-1). Biblio Dist.

Slang Today & Yesterday: With a Short Historical Sketch & Vocabularies of English, American & Australian Slang. 4th ed. Eric Partridge. 1970. 30.00 (ISBN 0-7100-6922-7). Routledge & Kegan.

Slap Shot. Bill Stokes & Peter Sanders. LC 75-22001. (a Reading Incentive Program). (Illus.). (gr. 7-12). 1975. text ed. 23.25 ea. pack of 5 (RL4, 5-6, 7). Follett.

Slap Shot. Richard Woodley. 1977. pap. 1.50 o.p. (ISBN 0-425-03339-2). Berkley Pub.

Slasher. Michael Collins. LC 81-80081. (Dan Fortune Detective Mysteries Ser.). 208p. 1981. pap. 2.25 (ISBN 0-87216-855-7). Playboy Pbks.

Slate Waste: Engineering & Environmental Aspects. K. L. Watson. (Illus.). xii, 195p. 1980. 37.50x (ISBN 0-85334-880-4, Pub. by Applied Science). Burgess-Intl Ideas.

Slattery Stands Alone. Steven C. Lawrence. (Slattery Ser.). (Orig.). 1976. pap. 0.95 o.p. (ISBN 0-685-64017-5, LB337NK, Leisure Bks). Nordon Pubns.

Slattery's Gun Says No. Steven C. Lawrence. 1975. pap. 0.95 o.p. (ISBN 0-685-52942-8, LB258NK, Leisure Bks). Nordon Pubns.

Slaughter by Auto. W. E. Butterworth. LC 80-66245. 192p. (gr. 7 up). 1980. 8.95 (ISBN 0-590-07589-6, Four Winds). Schol Bk Serv.

Slaughter of the Innocents. John W. Montgomery. (Orig.). 1981. pap. 3.95 (ISBN 0-89107-216-0). Good News.

Slaughter Ranches & Their Makers. Mary W. Clarke. (Illus.). Date not set. 12.95. Jenkins.

Slaughterhouse-Five. Kurt Vonnegut, Jr. pap. 2.50 (ISBN 0-440-18029-5). Dell.

Slave & Citizen: The Life of Frederick Douglas. Nathan I. Huggins. (Library of American Biography). 1980. 9.95 (ISBN 0-316-38001-6); pap. 4.95 (ISBN 0-316-38000-8). Little.

Slave & Freeman: The Autobiography of George L. Knox. George L. Knox. Ed. by Willard B. Gatewood, Jr. LC 78-21058. 256p. 1979. 17.00x (ISBN 0-8131-1384-9). U Pr of Ky.

Slave Community: Plantation Life in the Ante-Bellum South. 2nd rev. enl. ed. John W. Blassingame. (Illus.). 1979. 15.00x (ISBN 0-19-502562-8); pap. text ed. 5.95x (ISBN 0-19-502563-6). Oxford U Pr.

Slave Dancer. Paula Fox. LC 73-80642. (Illus.). 192p. (gr. 6-8). 1973. 9.95 (ISBN 0-87888-062-3). Bradbury Pr.

Slave Girl of Gor. John Norman. (Science Fiction Ser). 1977. pap. 2.25 (ISBN 0-87997-474-5, UE1474). DAW Bks.

Slave Population & the Economy of Jamaica: 1807-1834. B. W. Higman. LC 75-28627. (Illus.). 1977. 47.50 (ISBN 0-521-21053-4); pap. 11.50 (ISBN 0-521-29569-6). Cambridge U Pr.

Slave Religion: The Invisible Institution in the Antebellum South. Albert J. Raboteau. (Illus.). 1980. pap. 6.95 (ISBN 0-19-502705-1, GB 594, GB). Oxford U Pr.

Slave Ships & Slaving. George F. Dow. LC 68-57116. (Illus.). 1927. 10.00 (ISBN 0-87033-112-4). Cornell Maritime.

Slave Society in Cuba During the Nineteenth Century. Franklin W. Knight. LC 76-121770. (Illus.). 1970. 25.00 (ISBN 0-299-05790-9); pap. 7.50x (ISBN 0-299-05793-3). U of Wis Pr.

Slave Soldiers & Islam: The Genesis of a Military System. Daniel Pipes. LC 80-23969. 272p. 1981. text ed. 25.00x (ISBN 0-300-02447-9). Yale U Pr.

Slave to Beauty: The Eccentric Life & Singular Achievements of F. Holland Day Photographer, Publisher, Aesthete. Estelle Jussim. LC 80-66460. (Illus.). 288p. 1981. 30.00 (ISBN 0-87923-346-X). Godine.

Slave Trade. David Killingray. Ed. by Malcolm Yapp & Margaret Killingray. (World History Ser.). (Illus.). (gr. 10). 1980. Repr. of 1977 ed. lib. bdg. 5.95 (ISBN 0-89908-149-5); pap. text ed. 1.95 (ISBN 0-89908-124-X). Greenhaven.

Slave Trade, 95 vols. (British Parliamentary Papers Ser.). 1971. Set. 7515.00x (ISBN 0-7165-1499-0, Pub. by Irish Academic Pr Ireland). Biblio Dist.

Slave Trade & Its Abolition. John Langdon-Davies. (Jackdaw Ser: No. 12). (Illus.). 1970. 5.95 o.s.i. (ISBN 0-670-65082-X, Grossman). Viking Pr.

Slave Trade Today: American Exploitation of Illegal Aliens. Sasha G. Lewis. LC 79-51151. 256p. 1980. pap. 5.95 (ISBN 0-8070-0490-1, BP 610). Beacon Pr.

Slaver's Log Book: Or, 20 Years' Residence in Africa. Theophilus Conneau. 1972. pap. 2.75 (ISBN 0-380-01773-3, 35063, Discus). Avon.

Slavery. Kenneth Hughes. (Greek & Roman Topics Ser.). 1975. pap. text ed. 3.95x (ISBN 0-04-930004-0). Allen Unwin.

Slavery: A Bibliography & Union List of the Microfilm Collection, Part I. Ed. by Henry Barnard. 1980. pap. write for info. (ISBN 0-667-00613-3). Microfilming Corp.

Slavery: A Comparative Perspective: Readings on Slavery from Ancient Times to the Present. Ed. by Robin W. Winks. LC 72-84386. 240p. 1972. 10.00x (ISBN 0-8147-9156-5); pap. 5.00x (ISBN 0-8147-9157-3). NYU Pr.

Slavery, Abolition & Emancipation. M. Craton & J. Walvin. LC 76-18302. 1977. text ed. 21.00x (ISBN 0-582-48092-2); pap. text ed. 11.95x (ISBN 0-582-48093-0). Longman.

Slavery & Plantation Growth in Antebellum Florida, 1821-1860. Julia F. Smith. LC 70-150656. 249p. 1972. 8.50 (ISBN 0-8130-0323-7). U Presses Fla.

Slavery & Segregation: Did the Civil War Change America? Martin W. Sandler et al. (People Make a Nation Ser.). (gr. 7-12). 1971. pap. text ed. 5.20 (ISBN 0-205-03439-X, 783439X). Allyn.

Slavery & Serfdom in the Middle Ages: Selected Papers by Marc Bloch. Mark Bloch. Tr. by William R. Beer. 320p. 1975. 25.75x (ISBN 0-520-01767-6). U of Cal Pr.

Slavery, Colonialism, & Racism. Ed. by Sidney W. Mintz. 213p. 1975. text ed. 10.95x 1975 (ISBN 0-393-01115-1); pap. text ed. 3.95x 1974 (ISBN 0-393-09234-8). Norton.

Slavery in Africa: Historical & Anthropological Perspectives. Ed. by Suzanne Miers & Igor Kopytoff. LC 76-53653. 1977. 25.00 (ISBN 0-299-07330-0); pap. 9.95 (ISBN 0-299-07334-3). U of Wis Pr.

Slavery in the United States. Ingraham. LC 68-27402. (First Bks). (Illus.). (gr. 4-6). 6.45 (ISBN 0-531-02317-6). Watts.

Slavery, Law, & Politics: The Dred Scott Case in Historical Perspective. Don E. Fehrenbacher. (Illus.). 288p. 1981. 16.95 (ISBN 0-19-502882-1). Oxford U Pr.

Slavery, Law & Politics: The Dred Scott Case in Historical Perspective. Don E. Fehrenbacher. (Illus.). 288p. 1981. pap. 6.95 (ISBN 0-19-502883-X, GB639, GB). Oxford U Pr.

Slavery on the Spanish Frontier: The Colombian Choco, 1680-1810. William F. Sharp. LC 76-18767. (Illus.). 253p. 1981. pap. 6.95 (ISBN 0-8061-1759-1). U of Okla Pr.

Slavery, Race & the American Revolution. D. J. MacLeod. LC 74-77382. 269p. 1975. 37.95 (ISBN 0-521-20502-6); pap. 11.50x (ISBN 0-521-09877-7). Cambridge U Pr.

Slavery, the Mere Pretext for the Rebellion. John P. Kennedy. 20p. 1967. Repr. of 1863 ed. pap. 3.65 (ISBN 0-910120-02-1). Americanist.

Slavery Through the Ages. George F. MacMunn. 298p. 1974. Repr. of 1938 ed. 15.00x o.p. (ISBN 0-87471-463-X). Rowman.

Slaves No More: Letters from Liberia, 1833-1869. Ed. by Bell I. Wiley. LC 79-4015. (Illus.). 360p. 1980. 21.50x (ISBN 0-8131-1388-1). U Pr of Ky.

Slaves of the White Myth: The Psychology of Neocolonialism. Thomas Gladwin & Ahmad Saidin. LC 80-14939. 1981. text ed. 12.50 (ISBN 0-391-01936-8). Humanities.

Slaves on Horses. Patricia Crone. LC 79-50234. 1980. 39.50 (ISBN 0-521-22961-8). Cambridge U Pr.

Slaves, Peasants, & Capitalists in Southern Angola: Eighteen Forty to Nineteen Twenty-Six. W. G. Clarence-Smith. LC 78-67805. (African Studies: No. 27). (Illus.). 1979. 21.50 (ISBN 0-521-22406-3). Cambridge U Pr.

Slaves Uprooted & the Mau Mau Massacre. John P. Sykes. 1978. 4.50 o.p. (ISBN 0-682-49035-0). Exposition.

Slaves Without Masters: The Free Negro in the Antebellum South. Ira Berlin. 446p. 1981. pap. 6.95 (ISBN 0-19-502905-4, GB 629, OPB). Oxford U Pr.

Slavic Element in the Old Prussian Elbing Vocabulary. Jules F. Levin. (U. C. Publ. in Linguistics: Vol. 77). pap. 10.50x (ISBN 0-520-09473-5). U of Cal Pr.

Slavic Structuralism. Endre Bojtar. (Linguistic & Literary Studies in Eastern Europe). 130p. 1980. text ed. 28.50x (ISBN 90-272-1507-3). Humanities.

Slavophile Controversy: History of a Conservative Utopia in Nineteenth Century Russian Thought. Andrzei Walicki. Tr. by Hilda Andrews from Polish. 600p. 1975. 59.00x (ISBN 0-19-822507-5). Oxford U Pr.

Slavoteutonica: Lexikalische Untersuchungen Zum Slawisch-deutschen Sprachkontakt Im Ostmitteldeutschen. Guenter Bellman. (Studia Linguistica Germanica Ser.: Vol. 4). (Illus.). 356p. 1971. 51.75x (ISBN 3-11-003344-5). De Gruyter.

Slavs in European History & Civilization. Francis Dvornik. 726p. 1975. pap. 12.50x (ISBN 0-8135-0799-5). Rutgers U Pr.

Slay Ride. Alfred Hitchcock. 1981. pap. 2.95 (ISBN 0-440-13641-5). Dell.

Slaying the Law School Dragon. George J. Roth. LC 80-16974. 284p. 1980. 10.95 (ISBN 0-396-07880-X); pap. 7.95 (ISBN 0-396-07879-6). Dodd.

Slayride. Dick Francis. LC 73-14311. (Harper Novel of Suspense). 256p. (YA) 1974. 8.95 o.p. (ISBN 0-06-011336-7, HarpT). Har-Row.

Sledge Patrol. David A. Howarth. (Illus.). 1957. 5.50 o.s.i. (ISBN 0-02-555040-3). Macmillan.

Sleek & Savage: North America's Weasel Family. Delphine Haley. LC 75-32837. (Illus.). 128p. (YA) 1975. pap. 5.95 (ISBN 0-914718-12-6). Pacific Search.

Sleek for the Long Flight. William Matthews. 1972. pap. 1.95 o.p. (ISBN 0-394-70762-1). Random.

Sleep & Aging. Laughton E. Miles & William C. Dement. (Sleep Ser.: Vol. 3, No. 2). 108p. 1981. text ed. 20.00 (ISBN 0-89004-651-4). Raven.

Sleep & Dreams. Rae Lindsay. LC 78-5519. (First Bks.). (Illus.). (gr. 4-6). 1978. PLB 6.45 s&l (ISBN 0-531-01493-2). Watts.

Sleep & Dreams. Alvin Silverstein & Virginia Silverstein. LC 73-13825. (Illus.). 160p. (gr. 7 up). 1974. 8.95 (ISBN 0-397-31325-X). Lippincott.

Sleep Apnea Syndromes: Proceedings. Ed. by Christian Guilleminault & Christian Guilleminault. LC 78-416. (Kroc Foundation Ser.: Vol. 11). 1978. 39.00 (ISBN 0-8451-0301-6). A R Liss.

Sleep Disorders: Diagnosis & Treatment. R. L. Williams & I. Karacan. LC 78-18896. 1978. 42.95 (ISBN 0-471-94682-6, Pub. by Wiley-Medical). Wiley.

Sleep Disorders: Insomnia & Narcolepsy. Henry Kellerman. 250p. 1981. 17.50 (ISBN 0-87630-264-9). Brunner-Mazel.

Sleep, Dreams & Memory: Advances in Sleep Research. Ed. by William Fishbein. LC 79-23861. (Illus.). 270p. 1981. text ed. 30.00 (ISBN 0-89335-054-0). Spectrum Pub.

Sleep Has His House. Anna Kavan. LC 79-26730. 1980. Repr. 11.95 (ISBN 0-935576-00-2). Unity Pr.

Sleep in the Woods. Dorothy Eden. 1978. pap. 1.95 o.p. (ISBN 0-449-23706-0, Crest). Fawcett.

Sleep Instinct. R. Meddis. 1977. 15.00 (ISBN 0-7100-8545-1). Routledge & Kegan.

Sleep Is for Everyone. Paul Showers. LC 72-83785. (Let's Read-&-Find-Out Science Bk). (Illus.). (ps-3). 1974. 7.89 (ISBN 0-690-01118-0, TYC-J). T Y Crowell.

Sleep My Love. Elizabeth Norman. 1979. pap. 2.50 (ISBN 0-380-48694-6, 48694). Avon.

Sleep Nineteen Eighty. Fifth European Congress on Sleep Research, Amsterdam, September 1980. Ed. by W. P. Koella. (Illus.). 1981. 108.00 (ISBN 3-8055-2045-X). S Karger.

Sleep Nineteen Seventy-Eight. European Congress on Sleep Research, 4th, Tirgu-Mures, September 1978. Ed. by L. Popoviciu et al. 1980. 118.00 (ISBN 3-8055-0778-X). S Karger.

Sleep off the Highway. Patricia J. Sherman. (Orig.). 1979. pap. 1.95 (ISBN 0-686-68910-0). Manor Bks.

Sleep: Our Unknown Life. Richard Deming. 1973. 6.95 o.p. (ISBN 0-525-66230-8). Elsevier-Nelson.

Sleep Out. Carol Carrick. LC 72-88539. (Illus.). 32p. (gr. 1-3). 1973. 7.95 (ISBN 0-395-28780-4, Clarion). HM.

Sleep Research: A Critical Review. Frank R. Freemon. (Illus.). 220p. 1974. 19.75 (ISBN 0-398-02540-1). C C Thomas.

Sleep-Talking: Psychology & Psychophysiology. Arthur M. Arkin. (Illus.). 576p. 1981. text ed. 29.95 (ISBN 0-89859-031-0). L Erlbaum Assocs.

Sleep: The Mysterious Third of Your Life. Jonathan Kastner & Marianna Kastner. LC 67-22392. (Curriculum Related Bks). (Illus.). (gr. 7 up). 1968. 5.75 o.p. (ISBN 0-15-275911-5, HJ). HarBraceJ.

Sleeper. Woody Allen. 1978. 7.95 o.p. (ISBN 0-394-50051-2). Random.

Sleeper. Bruce Crowther. 1977. 6.95 o.s.i. (ISBN 0-8027-5372-8). Walker & Co.

Sleeper Agent. Ib Melchior. LC 74-15882. 312p. (YA) 1975. 8.95 o.p. (ISBN 0-06-012942-5, HarpT). Har-Row.

Sleepers Joining Hands. Robert Bly. LC 72-123916. 96p. 1973. 8.95 (ISBN 0-06-010381-7, HarpT); pap. 3.95 o.p. (ISBN 0-06-010382-5, TD-139, HarpT). Har-Row.

Sleepers of Roraima: A Carib Trilogy. Wilson Harris. (Illus.). 1970. 5.95 (ISBN 0-571-09272-1, Pub. by Faber & Faber). Merrimack Bk Serv.

Sleeping Beauty. Charles Perrault. Tr. & illus. by David Walker. LC 76-22697. (Illus.). (gr. k-5). 1977. 6.95 o.p. (ISBN 0-690-01278-0, TYC-J); PLB 7.89 (ISBN 0-690-01279-9). T Y Crowell.

Sleeping Beauty: Disney Classic. Guy N. Smith. 1976. pap. 1.50 o.s.i. (ISBN 0-515-04165-3). Jove Pubns.

Sleeping Dogs Lie. Julian Gloag. 1981. pap. price not set (ISBN 0-671-42494-7). PB.

Sleeping Fires. George Gissing. (Society & the Victorians: No. 24). 1974. text ed. 17.00x (ISBN 0-85527-032-2). Humanities.

Sleeping Giant & Other Stories. Eleanor Estes. LC 48-9223. (Illus.). (gr. 1-5). 4.50 o.p. (ISBN 0-15-275851-8, HJ). HarBraceJ.

Sleeping Giants. William E. Coffer & Koi Hosh. LC 79-64248. 1979. pap. text ed. 7.50 (ISBN 0-8191-0760-3). U Pr of Amer.

Sleeping Pills, Insomnia, & Medical Practice. Institute of Medicine. 1979. pap. text ed. 6.00 (ISBN 0-309-02881-7). Natl Acad Pr.

Sleepy Heads. Aileen Fisher. (Nature Ser). (gr. k-6). 1973. PLB 6.96 (ISBN 0-8372-0866-1); filmstrip & record 18.00 (ISBN 0-8372-0211-6); filmstrip & cassette 18.00 (ISBN 0-8372-0877-7). Bowmar-Noble.

Slender Human Word: Emerson's Artistry in Prose. William J. Scheick. LC 77-27020. 1978. 10.50x (ISBN 0-87049-222-5). U of Tenn Pr.

Slewfoot, the Despicable Monster. Christine Clements. (Illus.). 100p. (ps-4). Date not set. pap. price not set. C Clements.

Slice of Life - Reflections. Claire Schneider. 48p. (Orig.). pap. 2.95 (ISBN 0-9601982-1-0). Greenwood Hse.

Slice of Snow: A Book of Poems. Joan W. Anglund & Joan Walsh. LC 70-11830. (gr. 1-5). 1970. 3.95 o.p. (ISBN 0-15-183015-0, HJ). HarBraceJ.

Slide Atlas of Coloscopy. Ed. by F. P. Rossini. A. Ferrari. (Illus.). 58p. 1980. Repr. of 1979 ed. text ed. 110.00x (ISBN 88-212-0791-9, Pub. by Piccin Italy). J K Burgess.

Slide Buyers Guide. rev. ed. Ed. by Nancy DeLaurier. LC 80-84877. (Mid-America College Art Association Visual Resources Guides Ser.). 128p. 1980. 8.00 (ISBN 0-938852-07-8). Mid Am Coll.

Slide Guitar. Straw Dog. LC 72-76529. (Green Note Musical Publications Ser.). (Illus.). 1975. 10.95 (ISBN 0-02-871310-9); pap. 6.95 (ISBN 0-02-871000-2). Schirmer Bks.

Slide Guitar: A Book/Record Guide to Electric Lead & Traditional Slide & Bottleneck Styles with Special Chapters on Improvising Blues & Country & Western Lead Guitar Plus a Riff on Open Tunings. Richard Saslow & Straw Dog. LC 72-76529. (Contemporary Guitar Styles Ser.). (Illus.). 82p. (Orig., Prog. Bk.). 1972. pap. 8.95 (ISBN 0-912910-02-X). Green Note Music.

Slide Libraries: A Guide for Academic Institutions, Museums, & Special Collections. 2nd ed. Betty J. Irvine & P. Eileen Fry. LC 79-17354. (Illus.). 1979. lib. bdg. 22.50 (ISBN 0-87287-202-5). Libs Unl.

Slide Rule for the Mariner. H. H. Shufeldt. LC 74-188008. 1972. 8.00 o.s.i. (ISBN 0-87021-655-4). Naval Inst Pr.

Slide Rule: How to Use It. 3rd ed. Calvin C. Bishop. (Orig.). 1955. pap. 1.75 o.p. (ISBN 0-06-463254-7, 254, EH). Har-Row.

Slide Rule Series, 5 bks. Incl. Dividing with the Slide Rule (ISBN 0-8273-0541-9); How the Slide Rule Works (ISBN 0-8273-0539-7); Multiplying with the Slide Rule (ISBN 0-8273-0540-0); Slide-Rule Short Cut to Trigonometry (ISBN 0-8273-0543-5); Squares, Square Roots & Logarithms (ISBN 0-8273-0542-7). 1970. Set. pap. 7.80 o.p. (ISBN 0-8273-0537-0); pap. 1.80 ea. o.p.; ans. key 0.35 o.p. (ISBN 0-8273-0538-9). Delmar.

Slide, Sound, & Film Strip Production. John Sunier. (Illus.). 220p. 1981. 15.95 (ISBN 0-240-51074-7). Focal Pr.

Slides. Roger A. Kueter & Janeen Miller. Ed. by James E. Duane. LC 80-21335. (The Instructional Media Library: Vol. 13). (Illus.). 104p. 1981. 13.95 (ISBN 0-87778-173-7). Educ Tech Pubns.

Sliding Down the Wind. Donald E. Axinn. LC 77-90082. 1977. 5.95 o.p. (ISBN 0-8040-0793-4); pap. 3.50 o.s.i. (ISBN 0-8040-0794-2). Swallow.

Slight Misunderstanding. Prosper Merimee. Tr. by Douglas Parmee. 1980. pap. 2.95 (ISBN 0-7145-0529-3). Riverrun NY.

Sligo: Sinbad's Yellow Shore. T. A. Finnegan. 1979. pap. text ed. 5.25x (ISBN 0-85105-332-7, Dolmen Pr). Humanities.

Slim Chance in a Fat World: Behavioral Control of Obesity. professional ed. Richard B. Stuart & Barbara Davis. (Illus., Orig.). 1972. pap. 10.95 incl. materials (ISBN 0-87822-060-7); (bk. alone) 8.95 (ISBN 0-87822-064-X); (materials alone) 2.95 (ISBN 0-87822-061-5). Res Press.

Slim Down Camp. Stephen Manes. 192p. (gr. 4-8). 1981. 7.95 (ISBN 0-395-30170-X, Clarion). HM.

Slim Goodbody: Your Health & Feelings. A Good Thing Inc. & John Burstein. (gr. 1-3). 1978. pap. text ed. 125.00 (ISBN 0-89290-098-9, CM-43). Soc for Visual.

Slimmanship. Dewey Lipe & Jurgen Wolff. LC 74-17808. (Illus.). 224p. 1974. pap. 13.95 (ISBN 0-88229-161-0). Nelson-Hall.

Sling Braiding of the Andes. Adele Cahlander et al. 96p. (Orig.). 1980. pap. text ed. 11.00 (ISBN 0-937452-03-3). Colo Fiber.

Slipcovers & Bedspreads. Sunset Editors. LC 79-88157. (Illus.). 120p. 1979. pap. 4.95 (ISBN 0-376-01512-8, Sunset Bks). Sunset-Lane.

Slipform Concrete. R. G. Batterham. (Illus.). 96p. 1980. text ed. 19.95 cased (ISBN 0-86095-855-8). Longman.

Slipped Disc: Relieving & Understanding Your Back Troubles. 2nd ed. James Cyriax. LC 74-185562. (Illus.). 180p. 1975. 15.00 (ISBN 0-7161-0142-4). Herman Pub.

Slips of Speech. John H. Bechtel. LC 77-159889. Repr. of 1901 ed. 18.00 (ISBN 0-8103-4041-0). Gale.

Slithery Snakes & Other Aids to Children's Writing. Walter T. Petty & Mary Bowen. (Orig.). 1967. text ed. 7.95 (ISBN 0-13-813097-3). P-H.

Sloan's Almanac & Weather Forecaster. Eric Sloane. 1977. pap. 3.50 (ISBN 0-8015-6877-3, Hawthorn). Dutton.

Sloan's Victorian Buildings: Illustrations & Floor Plans for 60 Residences & Other Structures, 2 vols. in 1. Samuel Sloan. (Illus.). 400p. 1981. pap. 12.95 (ISBN 0-486-24009-6). Dover.

Slocum & the Widow Kate. Jake Logan. LC 75-21634. (John Slocum Ser.: No. 3). 224p. 1975. pap. 1.75 (ISBN 0-87216-744-5, B16287). Playboy Pbks.

Slocums Code. Jake Lagan. LC 80-85107. (Jake Logan Ser.). 224p. (Orig.). 1981. pap. 1.95 (ISBN 0-87216-823-9). Playboy Pbks.

Slocum's Flag. Jake Logan. LC 81-80091. (Slocum Ser.). 224p. (Orig.). 1981. pap. 1.95 (ISBN 0-87216-856-5). Playboy Pbks.

Slocum's Gold. Jake Logan. LC 75-40704. (John Slocum Ser.: No. 6). 1976. pap. 1.75 (ISBN 0-87216-738-0). Playboy Pbks.

Slocum's Woman. Jake Logan. LC 76-9585. (John Slocum Ser.: No. 9). 1977. pap. 1.75 (ISBN 0-87216-745-3). Playboy Pbks.

Slogum House. Mari Sandoz. LC 80-22077. 336p. 1981. 17.95x (ISBN 0-8032-4126-7); pap. 5.95 (ISBN 0-8032-9123-X, BB 756, Bison). U of Nebr Pr.

Sloop of War. Alexander Kent. 1979. pap. 1.95 (ISBN 0-515-05370-8). Jove Pubns.

Sloppy Kisses. Elizabeth Winthrop. LC 80-13673. (Illus.). 32p. (gr. k-3). 1980. PLB 7.95 (ISBN 0-02-793210-9). Macmillan.

Slot Machine Story. Marshall Fey. (Illus.). 1981. 25.00 (ISBN 0-913814-33-4). Nevada Pubns.

Sloth & Heathen Folly. Edward L. Robinson. LC 76-167930. 384p. 1972. 8.95 o.s.i. (ISBN 0-02-604090-5). Macmillan.

Slovak-English, English-Slovak Dictionary. 791p. 1981. 14.95 (ISBN 0-88254-543-4, Pub. by Slovart Czechoslovakia). Hippocrene Bks.

Slovenes of Carinthia. 2nd ed. Thomas M. Barker & Andreas Moritsch. LC 79-15399. (Eastern European Studies of Columbia University). 1981. 22.50x (ISBN 0-231-04862-9). Columbia U Pr.

Slovenian Community in Bridgeport, Conn. John A. Arnez. LC 73-170467. (Studia Slovenica, Special Series). 96p. 1971. 4.00 (ISBN 0-686-28388-0). Studia Slovenica.

Slovenian Village: Zerovnica. Irene Winner. LC 77-127367. (Illus.). 267p. 1971. 14.00x (ISBN 0-87057-128-1, Pub. by Brown U Pr). Univ Pr of New England.

Slovo Pedahoha. Wasyl Luciw. LC 75-541045. (Seriia Shkil'na Biblioteka). (Ukra.). 1971. pap. text ed. 8.00 (ISBN 0-918884-01-2). Slavia Lib.

Slow Coming Dark: Interviews on Death Row. Doug Magee. LC 80-19747. (Illus.). 181p. 1980. 10.95 (ISBN 0-8298-0400-5). Pilgrim NY.

Slow Creatures. Ernest Prescott. (Easy-Read Wildlife Bk.). (Illus.). 31p. (gr. 2-4). 1976. PLB 4.90 o.p. (ISBN 0-531-01219-0). Watts.

Slow Dancing in the Big City. Barra Grant. 1978. pap. 1.95 o.s.i. (ISBN 0-446-89630-6). Warner Bks.

Slow Fade to Black: The Negro in American Film, 1900-1942. Thomas Cripps. LC 76-21818. (Illus.). 1977. 24.95 (ISBN 0-19-501864-8). Oxford U Pr.

Slow Fade to Black: The Negro in American Film, 1900-1942. Thomas Cripps. (Illus.). 1977. pap. 7.95 (ISBN 0-19-502130-4, 484, GB). Oxford U Pr.

Slow Joe. Max Brand. 240p. 1972. pap. 1.95 (ISBN 0-446-90311-6). Warner Bks.

Slow Learner & the Reading Problem. John F. Cawley et al. (Illus.). 328p. 1972. 24.75 (ISBN 0-398-02256-9). C C Thomas.

Slow Learner in the Classroom. 2nd ed. Newell Kephart. LC 77-158613. 1971. text ed. 17.95x (ISBN 0-675-09196-9). Merrill.

Slow Speech Development of a Bright Child. Thelma E. Weeks. LC 73-23019. (Illus.). 1974. 17.95 (ISBN 0-669-91876-8). Lexington Bks.

Slow to Take Offense: Bombers, Cruise Missiles, & Prudent Deterrence. Frank Hoeber. LC 80-80662. (CSIS Monograph). 137p. 1980. pap. text ed. 6.95. CSI Studies.

Slow to Take Offense: Bombers, Cruise Missles & Prudent Deterrence. 136p. 1980. pap. 15.00 (ISBN 0-89206-015-8, CSIS017, CSIS). Unipub.

Slowcrock Cookbook. Michele Evans. 160p. (Orig.). 1975. pap. 1.95 o.s.i. (ISBN 0-446-89033-2). Warner Bks.

Slowing Down the Aging Process. Hans J. Kugler. (Orig.). 1973. pap. 1.95 (ISBN 0-515-05333-3, A3099). Jove Pubns.

Slowly Strangle All Political Rapists: The Story of the Voters' Vendetta. Ed Hertzog. LC 80-83137. 1981. 15.00 (ISBN 0-937894-00-1); pap. 10.00 (ISBN 0-937894-01-X). Life Arts.

Slowth: The Changing Economy & How You Can Successfully Cope. Martin Kupferman. Ed. by Maurice D. Levi. LC 80-18863. 225p. 1980. 13.95 (ISBN 0-471-08090-X). Wiley.

SLR Photography. Derek Watkins. LC 76-54090. 1977. 14.95 (ISBN 0-7153-7301-3). David & Charles.

Sludge & Its Ultimate Disposal. Ed. by Jack Borchardt & William Redman. (Illus.). 1981. 37.50 (ISBN 0-250-40386-2). Ann Arbor Science.

Sludge: Health Risks of Land Application. Ed. by J. M. Davidson & G. T. Edds. (Illus.). 400p. 1980. 37.50 (ISBN 0-250-40374-9). Ann Arbor Science.

Slugger Sal's Slump. Syd Hoff. LC 78-26338. (Illus.). 48p. (ps-2). 1981. pap. 1.95 (ISBN 0-671-42581-1, Pub. by Windmill). S&S.

Slum Silouette. Leela Dharmaraj. 8.00 (ISBN 0-89253-551-2); flexible cloth 4.00 (ISBN 0-89253-552-0). Ind-US Inc.

Slumlord: The True Story of the Man Who Is Beating America's Biggest Problem. Albert Lee. LC 76-4784. 1976. 7.95 o.s.i. (ISBN 0-87000-360-7). Arlington Hse.

Slumps, Grunts, & Snickerdoodles: What Colonial America Ate & Why. Lila Perl. LC 75-4894. (Illus.). 128p. (gr. 6 up). 1975. 7.95 (ISBN 0-395-28923-8, Clarion). HM.

Slums & Community Development. Marshall Clinard. LC 66-10960. 1966. 14.95 (ISBN 0-02-905570-9); pap. text ed. 4.00 (ISBN 0-02-905580-6). Free Pr.

Slums of Hope? Shanty Towns of the Third World. Peter C. Lloyd. LC 78-24770. 1979. 17.95x (ISBN 0-312-72963-4). St Martin.

Slurry Hydrotransport of Minerals & Tailings. V. M. Karasik et al. Ed. by W. C. Cooley. Tr. by A. L. Peabody from Rus. LC 79-67434. (Illus., Eng.). 1979. 60.00x o.p. (ISBN 0-918990-05-X). Terraspace.

Sly Fox & the Little Red Hen. (Illus.). Arabic 2.50x (ISBN 0-685-82872-7). Intl Bk Ctr.

Sly Spy & Other Stories. Marjorie T. Olson. (Educational Ser.). (Illus.). (gr. 2-3). 1979. pap. 5.00 (ISBN 0-89039-242-0). Ann Arbor FL.

Small Airports - Managers Handbook. Earl Seay. (Aviation Maagement Ser.). 1980. write for info. (ISBN 0-89100-140-9). Aviation Maintenance.

Small & Medium Power Reactors - 1960, 2 vols. 1961. Vol 1. 23.75 (ISBN 92-0-050161-3, IAEA); Vol 2. 13.50 (ISBN 92-0-050261-X, ISP 30-2). Unipub.

Small & Medium Power Reactors - 1970. 1971. pap. 32.25 (ISBN 92-0-050171-0, IAEA). Unipub.

Small & Micro Hydroelectric Power Plants: Technology & Feasibility. Ed. by Robert Noyes. LC 80-19099. (Energy Tech. Rev. 60). (Illus.). 457p. 1981. 42.00 (ISBN 0-8155-0819-0). Noyes.

Small Appliance Repair. Phyllis Palmore & Nevin Andre. Ed. by Charles A. Schuler. LC 79-19186. (Basic Skills in Electricity & Electronics Ser.). (Illus.). 192p. (gr. 9-12). 1980. 11.60 (ISBN 0-07-048361-2, G); tchrs. manual 2.00 (ISBN 0-07-048363-9); activities manual 5.96 (ISBN 0-07-048362-0). McGraw.

Small Blessings. Celestine Sibley. LC 76-42394. 1977. 7.95 (ISBN 0-385-12318-3). Doubleday.

Small Boat Against the Sea. Derek King & Peter Bird. 1976. 12.95 (ISBN 0-236-40013-4, Pub. by Paul Elek). Merrimack Bk Serv.

Small Boat Building. Dave Gannaway. 1980. 6.00x (ISBN 0-245-52656-0, Pub. by Nautical England). State Mutual Bk.

Small Boat Building. H. W. Patterson. (Illus.). 144p. pap. 7.50 (ISBN 0-8466-6052-0). Shorey.

Small Boat Design for Beginners. Frank Bailey. (Illus.). 88p. (Orig.). 1980. pap. 8.25 (ISBN 0-589-50203-4, Pub. by Reed Bks Australia). C E Tuttle.

Small-Boat Handbook. David Richey. LC 78-3315. 224p. pap. 3.95 (ISBN 0-06-463535-X, EH 535, EH). Har-Row.

Small Boat Law Nineteen Seventy-Eight Supplement. Herbert L. Markow. LC 79-88475. 1979. pap. 14.95 (ISBN 0-934108-01-3). H L Markow.

Small Boat Law: Nineteen Seventy-Nine to Nineteen Eighty Supplement. Herbert L. Markow. 1981. pap. write for info. (ISBN 0-934108-02-1). H L Markow.

Small Boat Law Supplement 1979-1980. Herbert L. Markow. (Orig.). 1981. pap. write for info. (ISBN 0-934108-02-1). H L Markow.

Small-Boat Sailing. Boy Scouts Of America. LC 19-600. (Illus.). 96p. (gr. 6-12). 1965. pap. 0.70x (ISBN 0-8395-3319-5, 3319). BSA.

Small-Boat Sailor's Bible. rev ed. Hervey Garrett Smith. LC 73-82247. 144p. 1974. pap. 3.50 (ISBN 0-385-05527-7). Doubleday.

Small-Boat Skipper's Safety Book. Denny Desoutter. 224p. 1972. pap. 8.50 (ISBN 0-370-30010-6). Transatlantic.

Small-Bore Heating & Hot Water Supply for Small Dwellings. 2nd ed. J. J. Barton. 1971. 9.75 (ISBN 0-408-00351-0). Transatlantic.

Small-Bore Target Shooting. rev. ed. W. H. Fuller. Ed. by A. J. Palmer. 1978. 11.95 o.p. (ISBN 0-214-20334-4, 8031, Dist. by Arco). Barrie & Jenkins.

Small Boy in the Sixties. George Sturt. 1977. Repr. of 1952 ed. text ed. 13.00x (ISBN 0-85527-244-9). Humanities.

Small Brave City-State: A History of Nembe-Brass in the Niger Delta. Ebiegberi J. Alagoa. (Illus.). 1964. 15.00x (ISBN 0-299-03110-1). U of Wis Pr.

Small Business Computer Evaluation Program. Business Systems Research Group. 1978. ring bdg. 29.95x (ISBN 0-9603584-0-4). Busn Systems Res.

Small Business Development in Brazil: A Study of the UNO Program. Jose G. Schreiber. 64p. (Orig.). 1976. pap. 3.00 (ISBN 0-89192-119-2). Interbk Inc.

Small Business Development in the Inner City Areas of Rochester. Brijan K. Gupta & Arthur D. Lopatin. LC 78-58110. (Illus.). xx, 231p. (Orig.). 1978. pap. 22.50 (ISBN 0-936876-15-8). Learn Res Intl Stud.

Small Business Guide to Borrowing Money. Philip Goldberg & Richard Rubin. (Illus.). 1980. 19.95 (ISBN 0-07-054198-1). McGraw.

Small Business Handbook: Comprehensive Guide to Starting & Running Your Own Business. Irving Burstiner. (Illus.). 1979. text ed. 19.95 (ISBN 0-13-814202-5, Spec); pap. text ed. 10.95 (ISBN 0-13-814194-0). P-H.

Small Business in American Life. Ed. by Stuart Bruchey. LC 80-10994. 450p. 1980. 25.00x (ISBN 0-231-04872-6). Columbia U Pr.

Small Business Index. Wayne D. Kryszak. LC 78-17540. 1978. 12.00 (ISBN 0-8108-1150-2). Scarecrow.

Small Business Investment Company Directory & Handbook. 2nd ed. Tyler G. Hicks. 150p. 1981. pap. 15.00 (ISBN 0-914306-48-0). Intl Wealth.

Small Business: Look Before You Leap; a Catalog of Sources of Information to Help You Start & Manage Your Own Small Business. Louis Mucciolo. 256p. 1981. pap. 7.95 (ISBN 0-668-05173-6, 5173). Arco.

Small Business Management. Hailes & Hubbard. LC 76-3945. 1977. pap. 8.80 (ISBN 0-8273-1400-0); instructor's guide 1.60 (ISBN 0-8273-1401-9). Delmar.

Small Business Management. 2nd ed. H. B. Pickle & R. L. Abrahson. (Wiley Series in Management). 500p. 1981. text ed. 20.95 (ISBN 0-471-06218-9). Wiley.

Small Business Management. Hal B. Pickle & Royce L. Abrahamson. LC 75-29035. 512p. 1976. text ed. 20.95 (ISBN 0-471-68806-1); instr's. guide avail. (ISBN 0-471-68927-0); study guide 7.95 (ISBN 0-471-68811-8). Wiley.

Small Business Management: A Guide to Entrepreneurship. Nicholas C. Siropolis. LC 76-13799. (Illus.). 1977. text ed. 17.95 (ISBN 0-395-24475-7); inst. manual 2.25 (ISBN 0-395-24476-5). HM.

Small Cell Lung Cancer. F. Anthony Greco et al. (Clinical Oncolgy Monograph). 1981. write for info. (ISBN 0-8089-1345-X). Grune.

Small Changes. Marge Piercy. 544p. 1978. pap. 2.75 (ISBN 0-449-23671-4, Crest). Fawcett.

Small Church Library. Charles C. Brown. 1980. 0.75 (ISBN 0-686-28794-0). Forward Movement.

Small Cities Management Training Program. Ed. by Thomas J. Mikulecky. LC 75-27076. 1975. text ed. 40.00 (ISBN 0-87326-011-2). Intl City Mgt.

Small City & Regional Community: Proceeding of the Nineteen Eighty Conference, Vol. 3. Ed. by Robert P. Wolensky & Edward J. Miller. viii, 450p. (Orig.). 1980. pap. text ed. 11.50 (ISBN 0-932310-02-8). UWSP Found Pr.

Small Comforts for Hard Times. Ed. by Michael Mooney & Florian Stuber. LC 77-5851. 1977. 22.50x (ISBN 0-231-04042-3). Columbia U Pr.

Small Computer in Small Business. Brian R. Smith. (Illus.). 160p. 1980. 12.50 (ISBN 0-8289-0407-3). Greene.

Small Computer Systems Handbook. Sol Libes. (gr. 12 up). 1978. pap. 9.95 (ISBN 0-8104-5678-8). Hayden.

Small Computers for Business & Industry. Dermot McKeone. 1979. text ed. 32.50x (ISBN 0-566-02096-3, Pub. by Gower Pub Co Englad). Renouf.

Small Computers for the Small Businessman. Nicolas Rosa & Sharon Rosa. LC 80-68531. 350p. 1980. pap. 12.95 (ISBN 0-918398-31-2). Dilithium Pr.

Small Computers P-058: Markets for Plastics. 1980. cancelled (ISBN 0-89336-259-X). BCC.

Small Craft Warnings. Tennessee Williams. LC 72-80978. 1972. pap. 4.95 (ISBN 0-8112-0460-X). New Directions.

Small Dreams of a Scorpion. Spike Milligan. 1972. 6.95 (ISBN 0-7181-1049-8, Pub. by Michael Joseph). Merrimack Bk Serv.

Small Escapes Under the Sun. John Sinor. 1981. pap. 4.95 (ISBN 0-935572-10-4). Alive Pubns.

Small Farm Development: Understanding & Improving Farming Systems in the Humid Tropics. Richard R. Harwood. LC 79-13169. (IAOS Development-Oriented Literature Ser.). 1979. lib. bdg. 18.50x (ISBN 0-89158-669-5). Westview.

Small Farmer's Guide to Raising Livestock & Poultry. Ed. by Alistair Fraser & Katie Thear. (Illus.). 240p. 1981. 25.00 (ISBN 0-668-04687-2). Arco.

Small Feasts: Soups, Salads, & Sandwiches. Ed. by Marilee Matteson. (Clarkson N. Potter Bks.). 1980. 17.95 (ISBN 0-517-54052-5). Crown.

Small Flowers in Embroidery. Ondori Company Staff. (Ondori Young Handicrafts Ser). (Illus.). 1977. pap. 3.95 (ISBN 0-87040-396-6). Japan Pubns.

Small Folk: A Celebration of Childhood in America. Sandra Brant & Elissa Cullman. (Illus.). 192p. 1981. 29.95 (ISBN 0-525-93131-7). Dutton.

Small Fruit Culture. 5th ed. James S. Shoemaker. (Illus.). 1978. lib. bdg. 20.50 (ISBN 0-87055-248-1). AVI.

Small Game Hunting. rev. ed. Clyde Ormond. LC 67-14557. (Funk & W Bk.). (Illus.). 1977. 8.95 (ISBN 0-308-10328-9, TYC-T); pap. 4.95 o.s.i. (ISBN 0-308-10329-7, TYC-T). T Y Crowell.

Small Garden. John Brookes. (Illus.). 1978. 10.95 o.s.i. (ISBN 0-02-516700-6). Macmillan.

Small Garden Design. M. J. Jefferson-Brown. 1969. 6.25 o.p. (ISBN 0-8231-6032-7). Branford.

Small Gardens for City & Country: A Guide to Designing & Planting Your Own Property. Alice R. Ireys. (Illus.). 1978. 14.95 o.p. (ISBN 0-13-813063-9, Spec); pap. 8.95 (ISBN 0-13-813055-8, Spec). P-H.

Small Gas Engines: Maintenance, Troubleshooting & Repair. George Drake. 500p. 1981. text ed. 16.95 (ISBN 0-8359-7014-0); pap. text ed. 7.95 (ISBN 0-8359-7013-2); soln. manual avail. (ISBN 0-8359-7015-9). Reston.

Small Gasoline Engines. George E. Stephenson. LC 76-51117. 1978. pap. text ed. 6.80 (ISBN 0-8273-1026-9); instructor's guide 1.60 (ISBN 0-8273-1027-7). Delmar.

Small Gasoline Engines Student's Workbook. 2nd ed. K. L. MacDonald. 1973. pap. 2.95 (ISBN 0-672-97632-3). Bobbs.

Small Georgian Houses & Their Details. Stanley C. Ramsey & J. D. Harvey. Date not set. 17.95 o.p. (ISBN 0-8038-0235-8). Hastings.

Small Group. Howard L. Nixon. LC 78-13207. (P-H Ser. in Sociology). (Illus.). 1979. ref. ed. 17.95 (ISBN 0-13-814244-0). P-H.

Small-Group Cultures. Tom McFeat. 1974. text ed. 19.00 (ISBN 0-08-017073-0); pap. text ed. 12.00 (ISBN 0-08-017770-0). Pergamon.

Small Group Decision Making: Communication & the Group Process. B. Aubrey Fisher. (Illus.). 288p. 1974. text ed. 12.95 o.p. (ISBN 0-07-021090-X, C). McGraw.

Small Group in Political Science. Ed. by Robert T. Golembiewski. LC 75-36688. 519p. 1978. 27.50x (ISBN 0-8203-0405-0). U of Ga Pr.

Small Group Ministry in the Contemporary Church. T. Ed Barlow. LC 72-90357. 1972. pap. 4.50 o.p. (ISBN 0-8309-0080-2). Herald Hse.

Small Groups: An Introduction. Charles Palazzolo. 1980. text ed. 15.95 (ISBN 0-442-25868-2). D Van Nostrand.

Small Groups & Political Behavior: A Study of Leadership. Sidney Verba. (Center of International Studies Ser.). 1961. 14.50 (ISBN 0-691-09333-4); pap. 4.45 o.p. (ISBN 0-691-02815-X). Princeton U Pr.

Small Groups & Political Rituals in China. Martin K. Whyte. 1974. 20.00x (ISBN 0-520-02499-0); pap. 5.95x (ISBN 0-520-03053-2). U of Cal Pr.

Small Groups & Self-Renewal. C. Gratton Kemp. 1971. 7.95 (ISBN 0-8164-0191-8). Crossroad NY.

Small Groups: Studies in Social Interaction. rev ed. Ed. by Robert F. Bales et al. 1965. 14.95 o.p. (ISBN 0-394-30227-3). Knopf.

Small Homes for Pleasant Living. 35th ed. W. D. Farmer. (Illus.). 1980. pap. 2.50 (ISBN 0-931518-12-1). W D Farmer.

Small House at Allington. Anthony Trollope. 1963. 12.95x (ISBN 0-460-00361-5, Evman). Dutton.

Small House at Allington. Anthony Trollope. (World's Classics Ser.: No. 472). 15.95 (ISBN 0-19-250472-X). Oxford U Pr.

Small Houses. Jeffrey Weiss & Lila Gault. 1980. pap. 7.95 (ISBN 0-446-97346-7). Warner Bks.

Small Hydroelectric Projects for Rural Development: Planning & Management. Ed. by Louis J. Goodman & Ralph N. Love. (Pergamon Policy Studies). 250p. Date not set. price not set (ISBN 0-08-025966-9). Pergamon.

Small Industries & a Developing Economy. R. V. Rao. 1979. text ed. 11.50x (ISBN 0-391-01829-9). Humanities.

Small Industry Bulletin for Asia & the Pacific, No.16. 189p. 1980. pap. 14.00 (UN80-2F4, UN). Unipub.

Small Investor's Guide to Big Profits in Real Estate. Robert Irwin. (Illus.). 224p. 1980. 12.95 (ISBN 0-07-032062-4, C). McGraw.

Small Investor's Handbook for Long-Term Security or Quick Profit. Ogden D. Scoville. 1971. pap. 3.95 (ISBN 0-06-463324-1, EH 324, EH). Har-Row.

Small Is Beautiful: Economics As If People Mattered. E. F. Schumacher. 1973. pap. 5.95 (ISBN 0-06-090432-1, CN432, CN). Har-Row.

Small Is Possible. George McRobie. LC 79-2634. 256p. 1981. 11.95 (ISBN 0-06-013041-5, CN694, HarpT); pap. 4.95 (ISBN 0-06-090694-4). Har-Row.

Small Mammals. Ed. by F. B. Golley et al. LC 74-25658. (International Biological Programme Ser.: No. 5). (Illus.). 448p. 1975. 65.00 (ISBN 0-521-20601-4). Cambridge U Pr.

Small Motor Cruises. Nigel Warren. 1979. 19.95x (ISBN 0-8464-0064-2). Beekman Pubs.

Small Museums of the West. Gary Hanauer. Ed. by Jane Vandenburgh. LC 80-67476. (Illus.). 288p. (Orig.). 1981. pap. 9.95 (ISBN 0-89395-051-3). Cal Living Bks.

Small Ones. Gary Paulsen. LC 76-12635. (Real Animals Ser.). (Illus.). 64p. (gr. 4 up). 1976. PLB 8.65 (ISBN 0-8172-0600-0). Raintree Pubs.

Small Parrots: Parrakeets. David Seth-Smith. (Illus.). 1979. 9.95 (ISBN 0-87666-978-X, H-1017). TFH Pubns.

Small Patchwork Projects. Barbara Brondolo. (Illus.). 64p. (Orig.). 1981. pap. write for info. (ISBN 0-486-24030-4). Dover.

Small People: How Children Develop & What You Can Do About It. Jean Mercer. LC 78-27345. 1979. 12.95 (ISBN 0-88229-318-4); pap. 6.95 (ISBN 0-88229-664-7). Nelson-Hall.

Small Place in the Country. Toni Mackenzie. 240p. 1980. pap. 6.95 (ISBN 0-00-216408-6, Pub. by W Collins Australia). Intl Schol Bk Serv.

Small Plays for Special Days. Sue Alexander. LC 76-28424. (Illus.). (gr. 2-4). 1977. 7.95 (ISBN 0-395-28761-8, Clarion). HM.

Small Plays for You & a Friend. Sue Alexander. LC 74-4019. (Illus.). 48p. (gr. 1-4). 1974. 6.95 (ISBN 0-395-28762-6, Clarion). HM.

Small Press Record of Books in Print. 9th ed. Ed. by Len Fulton & Ellen Ferber. (Dustbooks Small Press Info. Library). 680p. 1980. 17.95 (ISBN 0-913218-95-2). Dustbooks.

Small-Scale Cane Sugar Processing & Residue Utilization. (FAO Agricultural Services Bulletin: No. 19). 56p. 1981. pap. 6.00 (ISBN 92-5-100935-X, F2069, FAO). Unipub.

Small-Scale Employment & Production in Developing Countries: Evidence from Ghana. William F. Steel. LC 75-44940. (Special Studies). 1977. text ed. 25.95 (ISBN 0-275-56330-8). Praeger.

Small-Scale Fuel Alcohol Prod. U. S. Dept. of Agriculture. 242p. 1980. 24.95 (ISBN 0-89934-047-4, B946-PP); pap. 14.95 (ISBN 0-89934-046-6, B046-PP). Solar Energy Info.

Small-Scale Processing & Storage of Tropical Root Crops. Donald L. Plucknett. (Tropical Agriculture Ser.). 1979. lib. bdg. 30.00x (ISBN 0-89158-471-4). Westview.

Small Scale Retailing in the United Kingdom. David Kirby & John Dawson. 1979. text ed. 28.25 (ISBN 0-566-00164-0, Pub. by Gower Pub Co England). Renouf.

Small Seaports: Revitalization Through Conserving Heritage Resources. John Clark et al. LC 79-67736. (Illus.). 64p. (Orig.). 1979. pap. 6.50 (ISBN 0-89164-059-2). Conservation Foun.

Small State As the Major Troublemaker in History & the Need to Eliminate Its Existence for the Peace of the World. Hugo B. Devereux. (Illus.). 1979. deluxe ed. 49.75 (ISBN 0-930008-34-0). Inst Econ Pol.

Small States & Segmented Societies: National Political Integration Environment. Ed. by Stephanie G. Neuman. LC 75-23986. (Special Studies). 200p. 1976. text ed. 23.95 (ISBN 0-275-55730-8). Praeger.

Small Time Operator: How to Start Your Own Small Business, Keep Your Books, Pay Your Taxes, & Stay Out of Trouble. rev. ed. Bernard Kamoroff. LC 76-29817. (Illus.). 192p. 1980. pap. 7.95 (ISBN 0-917510-00-3). Bell Springs Pub.

Small Town Church. Peter J. Surrey. (Creative Leadership Ser.). 128p. (Orig.). 1981. pap. 4.95 (ISBN 0-687-38720-5). Abingdon.

Small Town in American Literature. 2nd ed. Ed. by David M. Cook & Craig G. Swauger. 1977. pap. text ed. 9.50 scp (ISBN 0-06-041354-9, HarpC). Har-Row.

Small Town Is Best for Waiting & Other Stories. Warren C. Miller. 1979. 2.50 (ISBN 0-686-28279-5). Climate Bks.

Small Town Police & the Supreme Court: Hearing the Word. Stephen L. Wasby. LC 76-5621. 1976. 21.50 (ISBN 0-669-00654-8). Lexington Bks.

Small Town Teacher. Gertrude McPherson. LC 71-188349. (Illus.). 449p. 1972. 12.50 (ISBN 0-674-81100-3); pap. 5.95 (ISBN 0-674-81101-1). Harvard U Pr.

Small Towns & Small Towners: A Framework for Survival & Growth. Bert E. Swanson et al. LC 78-17697. (Sage Library of Social Research: Vol. 79). 1979. 18.00x (ISBN 0-8039-1017-7); pap. 8.95x (ISBN 0-8039-1018-5). Sage.

Small Towns Book. James Robertson & Carolyn Robertson. LC 76-23813. 1978. pap. 5.95 (ISBN 0-385-11012-X, Anch). Doubleday.

Small TV Studio: The Equipment & Facilities. Alan Bermingham et al. (Media Manuals Ser.). Date not set. pap. 7.95 (ISBN 0-8038-6725-5). Hastings.

Small Voices & Great Trumpets: Minorities & the Media. Ed. by Bernard Rubin. 295p. 1980. 24.95 (ISBN 0-03-056973-7); pap. 9.95 (ISBN 0-03-056972-9). Praeger.

Small Wonder: The Story of the Yale Puppeteers & the Turnabout Theatre. Forman Brown. LC 80-17815. 288p. 1980. 12.50 (ISBN 0-8108-1334-3). Scarecrow.

Small World. Tabitha King. 192p. 1981. 10.95 (ISBN 0-02-563190-X). Macmillan.

Small World Cook & Color Book. Beverly Frazier. 40p. (gr. 1-8). 1979. pap. 2.25 (ISBN 0-912300-15-9). Troubador Pr.

Small World of Apes. Ed. by Henry Pluckrose. (Small World Ser.). (Illus.). 1979. (gr. 5-8). 2.95 (ISBN 0-531-03443-7); PLB 5.90 s&l (gr. k-3) (ISBN 0-531-03407-0). Watts.

Small World of Bears. Ed. by Henry Pluckrose. (Small Worlds Ser.). (Illus.). (gr. k-3). 1979. PLB 5.90 s&l (ISBN 0-531-03403-8). Watts.

Small World of Birds. Ed. by Henry Pluckrose. (Small World Ser.). (Illus.). 1979. 9 (gr. 5-8) 5.90 (ISBN 0-531-03444-5); PLB 4.90 s&l (gr. k-3) (ISBN 0-531-03408-9). Watts.

Small World of Elephants. Ed. by Henry Pluckrose. (Small Worlds Ser.). (Illus.). (gr. k-3). 1979. PLB 5.90 s&l (ISBN 0-531-03404-6). Watts.

Small World of Horses. Ed. by Henry Pluckrose. (Small Worlds Ser.). (Illus.). (gr. k-3). 1979. PLB 5.90 s&l (ISBN 0-531-03405-4). Watts.

Small World of Whales. Ed. by Henry Pluckrose. (Small Worlds Ser.). (Illus.). (gr. k-3). 1979. PLB 5.90 s&l (ISBN 0-531-03406-2). Watts.

Small World Vegetable Gardening. John E. Bryan. LC 76-58364. (Illus.). 144p. 1977. 4.95 (ISBN 0-912238-79-8); pap. 4.95 (ISBN 0-912238-78-X). One Hund One Prods.

Smaller Families Through Social & Economic Progress. William Rich. LC 72-97989. (Monographs: No. 7). 74p. 1973. 2.00 (ISBN 0-686-28688-X). Overseas Dev Council.

Smaller Slang Dictionary. Eric Partridge. 1968. 16.95 (ISBN 0-7100-1938-6); pap. 7.95 (ISBN 0-7100-8331-9). Routledge & Kegan.

Smaller Slang Dictionary. Ed. by Eric Partridge. 1961. 6.00 o.p. (ISBN 0-8022-1280-8). Philos Lib.

Smallest Boy in the Class. Jerrold Beim. (Illus.). (gr. k-3). 1949. PLB 7.44 (ISBN 0-688-31442-2). Morrow.

Smallest Freezers. Stella Atterbury. 1977. 11.95 o.p. (ISBN 0-571-10888-1, Pub. by Faber & Faber); pap. 5.95 (ISBN 0-571-11176-9). Merrimack Bk Serv.

Smallest Part. Neal A. Maxwell. LC 73-87240. 104p. 1973. 4.95 o.p. (ISBN 0-87747-505-9). Deseret Bk.

Smallest Pawns in the Game. Peter Townsend. 256p. 1980. 14.95 (ISBN 0-316-85129-9). Little.

Smallest Slavonic Nation. Gerald C. Stone. (Illus.). 214p. 1972. text ed. 12.75x (ISBN 0-485-11129-2, Athlone Pr). Humanities.

Smallholder's Guide. C. J. Munroe. LC 78-74077. 1979. 14.95 (ISBN 0-7153-7652-7). David & Charles.

Smart Aleck. new ed. Howard Teichmann. (Illus.). 352p. 1976. 10.95 o.p. (ISBN 0-688-03034-3). Morrow.

Smart Casino Play. Edwin Silberstang. (Gamblers Book Shelf). 64p. 1976. pap. 2.95 (ISBN 0-89650-560-X). Gamblers.

Smart Keno Play. Keith Hall & Ronald Vikmyhr. (Gamblers Book Shelf). 64p. 1979. pap. 2.95 (ISBN 0-89650-561-8). Gamblers.

Smart Kid Like You. Stella Pevsner. LC 74-19320. 192p. (gr. 4-8). 1974. 7.50 (ISBN 0-395-28876-2, Clarion). HM.

Smart Shopping & Consumerism. Rubie Saunders. LC 72-11707. (Career Concise Guides Ser.). (Illus.). 72p. (gr. 5 up). 1973. PLB 5.90 (ISBN 0-531-02608-6). Watts.

Smart Squash. Austin Francis. 1979. pap. 2.95 (ISBN 0-346-12385-2). Cornerstone.

Smart Squash: Using Your Head to Win. Austin Francis. LC 77-22011. (Illus.). 1977. 10.00 o.s.i. (ISBN 0-397-01238-1). Lippincott.

Smartest Person in the World. Sandy Clifford. LC 79-14138. (Illus.). (gr. k-3). 1979. pap. 4.95 (ISBN 0-395-28411-2). Parnassus.

Smashing: Jimmy Connors. Margaret Ogan & George Ogan. LC 76-10356. (Sports Profiles Ser.). (Illus.). 48p. (gr. 4-11). 1976. PLB 8.50 (ISBN 0-8172-0140-8). Raintree Pubs.

Smell Book: Scent, Sex & Society. Ruth Winter. LC 76-18783. (Illus.). 1976. 7.95 o.p. (ISBN 0-397-01163-6). Lippincott.

Smell of It. Sonallah Ibrahim. Tr. by Denys Johnson-Davies from Arabic. 118p. (Orig.). 1971. pap. 5.00 (ISBN 0-89410-194-3); pap. 5.00 (ISBN 0-89410-195-1). Three Continents.

Smell of Onions. Peggy Appiah. 84p. (Orig.). 1979. pap. 4.00 (ISBN 0-686-27212-9, Dist. by Three Continents Pr). Longman.

Smell of Onions. Peggy Appiah. 84p. (Orig.). 1979. pap. 5.00 (ISBN 0-686-64550-2). Three Continents.

Smile. Harry Bernstein. LC 80-53806. (Illus.). 192p. (Orig.). 1980. pap. 5.00 (ISBN 0-931122-21-X). West End.

Smile! Bil Keane. (Family Circus Ser.). (Illus.). 1979. pap. 1.50 (ISBN 0-449-14172-1, GM). Fawcett.

Smile in a Mad Dog's I. 2nd ed. Richard Stine. 1977. 6.95 (ISBN 0-916860-02-7); pap. 3.95 (ISBN 0-916860-01-9). Bean Pub.

Smile in His Lifetime. Joseph Hansen. LC 80-21420. 312p. 1981. 12.95 (ISBN 0-686-69127-X). HR&W.

Smile on the Void. Stuart Gordon. 264p. 1981. 12.95 (ISBN 0-399-12503-5). Putnam.

Smile or I'll Kick Your Bed. Ted Goen, Jr. (Illus.). 1981. 12.95 (ISBN 0-393-01433-9). Norton.

Smiley Lion Book. Marybob Baker. (Illus.). (ps-1). 1964. PLB 5.38 (ISBN 0-307-68907-7, Golden Pr). Western Pub.

Smiley Snake. Nancy Reese. Ed. by Alton Jordan. (I Can Read Underwater Bks). (Illus.). (gr. k-3). 1974. PLB 3.50 (ISBN 0-89868-010-7, Read Res); pap. text ed. 1.75 (ISBN 0-89868-043-3). ARO Pub.

Smiley Snake's Adventure. Phyllis Barber. Ed. by Alton Jordan. (Buppet Series). (Illus.). (gr. k-3). 1981. PLB 4.50 (ISBN 0-89868-098-0, Read Res); pap. text ed. 1.95 (ISBN 0-89868-109-X). ARO Pub.

Smiley's People. John Le Carre. 1980. pap. 3.50. Bantam.

Smiling Book. Mike Thaler. LC 79-116336. (Illus.). (gr. k-3). 1971. 7.25 o.p. (ISBN 0-688-41441-9); PLB 6.48 o.p. (ISBN 0-688-51435-9). Lothrop.

Smiling Charlie. Max Brand. 224p. 1971. pap. 1.95 (ISBN 0-446-90319-1). Warner Bks.

Smiling Desperado. Max Brand. 1979. pap. 1.50 o.p. (ISBN 0-446-98128-1). Warner Bks.

Smiling Sentences: Sight Word Activities to Cut & Paste. Ellen Sussman. (Spirit Duplicating Masters Ser.). (Illus.). 24p. (gr. 2-3). 1980. 4.95 (ISBN 0-933606-08-7). Monkey Sisters.

Smith Agama Collection: Sanskrit Books & Manuscripts Relating to Pancaratra Studies-a Descrptive Catalog. H. Daniel Smith. LC 78-9149. (Foreign & Comparative Studies-South Asian Special Publications Ser.: No. 2). 1978. pap. text ed. 6.50x (ISBN 0-915984-79-2). Syracuse U Foreign Comp.

Smith College Never Taught Me How to Salute. Ann Combs. LC 80-8227. 216p. 1981. 9.95 (ISBN 0-690-02012-0, HarpT). Har-Row.

Smith-Eight. pap. 3.50 o.p. (ISBN 0-685-78413-4). The Smith.

Smith-Eighteen: The Most General Magazine. pap. 3.00 o.p. (ISBN 0-685-78416-9). The Smith.

Smith-Eleven. pap. 2.50 o.p. (ISBN 0-685-78415-0). The Smith.

Smith-Fifteen. pap. 3.00 o.p. (ISBN 0-685-59103-4). The Smith.

Smith Poets: The Smith-12. LC 70-94633. 224p. 1970. 5.00 o.p. (ISBN 0-685-04836-5); pap. 2.50 o.p. (ISBN 0-685-04837-3). The Smith.

Smith, Ricardo, Marx. Claudio Napoleoni. Tr. by J. M. Gee from It. LC 75-15962. 198p. 1975. lib. bdg. 19.95 (ISBN 0-470-63011-6). Halsted Pr.

Smith Special Issue 20: Poetry. Adrianne Marcus et al. pap. 1.00 o.p. (ISBN 0-685-78412-6). The Smith.

Smith-Ten. pap. 2.50 o.p. (ISBN 0-685-78414-2). The Smith.

Smith's Bible Dictionary. William Smith. Ed. by F. N. Peloubet & M. A. Peloubet. 1979. 8.95 (ISBN 0-8407-5170-2); pap. 5.95 (ISBN 0-8407-5700-X). Nelson.

Smith's Bible Dictionary. William Smith. (Family Library). (YA) (gr. 7-12). 1967. pap. 2.50 (ISBN 0-515-05619-7). Jove Pubns.

Smith's Blood Diseases of Infancy & Childhood. 4th ed. Denis R. Miller & Howard A. Pearson. LC 78-7023. 1978. pap. text ed. 57.50 (ISBN 0-8016-4691-X). Mosby.

Smith's Guide to the Literature of the Life Sciences. 9th ed. Smith et al. 223p. 1980. pap. 12.95 (ISBN 0-8087-3576-4). Burgess.

Smith's Review of Agency & Partnership: For Law School, Bar & College Examinations. 3rd ed. Myron G. Hill et al. LC 79-7186. (Legal Gem Ser.). 264p. 1979. pap. text ed. 8.95 (ISBN 0-8299-2033-1). West Pub.

Smith's Review of Family Law. 2nd ed. Myron G. Hill, Jr. et al. (Smith's Review Ser.). 140p. 1981. pap. text ed. 10.95 (ISBN 0-8299-0515-4). West Pub.

Smith's Review of Federal Income Taxation. Howard M. Rossen et al. LC 79-4396. (Legal Gem Ser.). 364p. 1979. pap. text ed. 8.95 (ISBN 0-8299-2036-6). West Pub.

Smith's Review of Labor Law & Employment Discrimination, for Law School, Bar & College Examinations. 2nd ed. Myron G. Hill et al. LC 79-23934. (Legal Gem Ser.). 235p. 1980. pap. text ed. 8.95 (ISBN 0-8299-2069-2). West Pub.

Smithsonian Collection of Newspaper Comics. Ed. by Bill Blackbeard & Martin Williams. LC 77-608090. (Illus.). 336p. 1978. 29.95; pap. 14.95 (ISBN 0-87474-167-X). Smithsonian.

Smithsonian Experience. Smithsonian Institution. 1977. 21.95. Smithsonian Expo Bks.

Smithsonian Experience. Martin Williams. (Illus.). 1978. 19.95 (ISBN 0-89599-000-8). Norton.

Smocking. Ondori Publishing Co. Staff. (Ondori Handicraft Ser). (Illus.). 64p. 1976. pap. 5.50 (ISBN 0-87040-367-2). Japan Pubns.

Smocks & Smocking. Beverly Marshall. 1981. 14.95 (ISBN 0-442-28268-0). Van Nos Reinhold.

Smoke Across the Prairie. 8.50 o.p. (ISBN 0-685-83391-7). Chatham Pub CA.

Smoke & Products of Combustion, Part 2, Vol. 15. Ed. by Carlos J. Hilado. LC 73-82115. (Fire & Flammability Ser.). (Illus.). 1976. pap. 25.00 (ISBN 0-87762-175-6). Technomic.

Smoke Cooking. Matt Kramer. pap. 3.95 (ISBN 0-8015-6896-X, Hawthorn). Dutton.

Smoke, Dust & Haze: Fundamentals of Aerosol Behavior. S. K. Friedlander. LC 76-26928. 1977. 26.50 (ISBN 0-471-01468-0, Pub. by Wiley Interscience). Wiley.

Smoke Jumpers. Brent Filson. LC 76-56289. (gr. 7 up). 1978. pap. 5.95 (ISBN 0-385-12790-1). Doubleday.

Smokescreen. Dick Francis. LC 72-9095. (Harper Novel of Suspense). 224p. (YA) 1973. 8.95 o.p. (ISBN 0-06-011334-0, HarpT). Har-Row.

Smokestack Lightning. John Eskow. 1980. 10.95 (ISBN 0-440-07688-9); pap. 4.95 (ISBN 0-440-07689-7). Delacorte.

Smokey Bear Saves the Forest. Kennon Graham. (Tell-a-Tale Readers). (Illus.). (gr. k-3). 1971. PLB 4.77 (ISBN 0-307-68463-6, Whitman). Western Pub.

Smokey the Bear. Jane Werner. (Illus.). (ps-3). 1955. PLB 5.00 (ISBN 0-307-60481-0, Golden Pr). Western Pub.

Smokey's, Truckers, CB Radios & You: Complete Guide to Citizen's Band Radio. Thomas Fensch. 1976. pap. 1.75 o.p. (ISBN 0-449-22972-6, Crest). Fawcett.

Smoking. Sherry Sonnett. (First Bks.). (Illus.). (gr. 4-6). 1977. PLB 6.45 (ISBN 0-531-01299-9). Watts.

Smoking & Chemical Abuse. Michael Meftah. 1981. 5.75 (ISBN 0-8062-1616-6). Carlton.

Smoking & Health: A Comprehensive Bibliography. Compiled by Alberta D. Berton. (Biomedical Information Guides Ser.: Vol. 3). 535p. 1980. 95.00 (ISBN 0-306-65184-X, IFI). Plenum Pub.

Smoking & Politics: Policy Making & the Federal Bureaucracy. 2nd ed. A. Lee Fritschler. LC 74-12381. 208p. 1975. pap. text ed. 6.95 (ISBN 0-13-815019-2). P-H.

Smoking for Two: Cigarettes & Pregnancy. Fried & Oxern. 102p. Date not set. 8.95 (ISBN 0-02-910720-2). Macmillan.

Smoking Land: A Novel of Super-Science & Amazing Adventure. Max Brand. (Max Brand Popular Classics Ser.). 112p. 1980. pap. 5.95 (ISBN 0-88496-155-9). Capra Pr.

Smoking, Marijuana & Drugs. Herman Aihara et al. (Illus.). 1973. 1.50 o.p. (ISBN 0-918860-19-9). G Ohsawa.

Smoking Paradox: Public Regulation in the Cigarette Industry. Gideon Doron. LC 79-50400. 1979. text ed. 22.50 (ISBN 0-89011-531-1). Abt Assoc.

Smooth Nonparametric Regression Analysis. Gordon J. Johnston. 88p. 1979. pap. 2.80 (1253). U of NC Pr.

Smoothing Income Numbers: Objectives, Means & Implications. Joshua Ronen & Simcha Sadan. LC 80-21350. (Paperback Series of Accounting). 1981. pap. text ed. 5.95 (ISBN 0-201-06347-6). A-W.

Smouldering Flame. Anne Mather. (Alpha Books). 80p. (Orig.). 1979. pap. text ed. 2.25x (ISBN 0-19-424164-5). Oxford U Pr.

Smudging. Diane Wakoski. 150p. (Orig.). 1974. 10.00 (ISBN 0-87685-131-6); pap. 5.00 (ISBN 0-87685-130-8). Black Sparrow.

Smugglers. Noel Gerson. LC 77-8162. 1977. 8.95 o.s.i. (ISBN 0-690-01468-6, TYC-T). T Y Crowell.

Smugglers. Patrick Pringle. LC 68-1842. (Pegasus Books: No. 6). (Illus.). 1965. 7.50x (ISBN 0-234-77877-6). Intl Pubns Serv.

Smugglers of Buenaventura. S. R. Van Iterson. 192p. (gr. 7 up). 1974. 6.75 o.p. (ISBN 0-688-20116-4); PLB 6.48 (ISBN 0-688-30116-9). Morrow.

Smugglers of Spirits: Prohibition & the Coast Guard Patrol. Harold Waters. 1971. 7.95 (ISBN 0-8038-6705-0). Hastings.

Smugglers' Paradise & Foreign Exchange Law. H. L. Mansukhani. 1977. text ed. 20.00 o.p. (ISBN 0-686-59597-1, Pub. by Vikas India). Advent Bk.

Smuggling Language into the Teaching of Reading. 2nd ed. Arthur W. Heilman & Eliazbeth A. Holmes. (Elementary Education Ser.). 1978. pap. text ed. 8.95x (ISBN 0-675-08360-5). Merrill.

Smuts, 2 vols. William K. Hancock. Incl. Vol. 1. The Sanguine Years, 1870-1919. (ISBN 0-521-05187-8); Vol. 2. The Fields of Force, 1919-1950. (ISBN 0-521-05188-6). 1962. 56.00 ea. Cambridge U Pr.

S.N. Behrman: The Major Plays. William R. Klink. (Costerus: New Ser.: No. 11). 1978. pap. text ed. 25.75x (ISBN 90-6203-512-4). Humanities.

SN Distribution Study Grocery Store Sales - 1980. Book Division Research. 1980. pap. text ed. 27.50 (ISBN 0-87005-313-2). Fairchild.

SN Distribution Study of Grocery Store Sales - 1981. Book Div. Research Staff. 250p. 1981. pap. 30.00 (ISBN 0-87005-370-1). Fairchild.

Snack Food Technology. Samuel A. Matz. (Illus.). 1976. text ed. 36.00 (ISBN 0-87055-193-0). AVI.

Snackers: Kick the Junk Food Habit. Maureen Wallace & Jim Wallace. LC 78-638. 1978. pap. 4.95 (ISBN 0-914842-26-9). Madrona Pubs.

Snacks & Sandwiches. Time-Life Books Editors. (Good Cook Ser.). (Illus.). 1980. 12.95 (ISBN 0-8094-2883-0). Time-Life.

Snaffles. Stephen Cosgrove. (Serendipity Bks.). (Illus.). 32p. 1980. pap. 1.50 (ISBN 0-8431-0576-3). Price Stern.

Snail Transmitted Parasitic Diseases, 2 vols. Emile A. Malek. 1980. Vol. 1, 352p. 79.95 (ISBN 0-8493-5269-X); Vol. 2, 336p. 77.95 (ISBN 0-8493-5270-3). CRC Pr.

Snails. Herbert S. Zim & Lucretia Krantz. LC 74-16262. (Illus.). 64p. (gr. 3-7). 1975. 6.75 (ISBN 0-688-22012-6); PLB 6.48 (ISBN 0-688-32012-0). Morrow.

Snails of Land & Sea. Hilda Simon. LC 75-25140. (Illus.). (gr. k-3). 1977. 7.95 (ISBN 0-8149-0772-5). Vanguard.

Snake. James McClure. 1977. pap. 1.50 (ISBN 0-380-01683-4, 33548). Avon.

Snake & the Olive. Iona MacGregor. 1974. 8.95 (ISBN 0-571-10582-3, Pub. by Faber & Faber). Merrimack Bk Serv.

Snake Book. Roy Pinney. LC 78-68336. (Illus.). 256p. 1981. 12.95 (ISBN 0-385-13547-5). Doubleday.

Snake Eyes. Edwin Silberstang. 1977. 8.95 o.p. (ISBN 0-525-20625-6). Dutton.

Snake In, Snake Out. Linda Banchek. LC 78-51935. (Illus.). (ps-1). 1978. 6.95 (ISBN 0-690-03852-6, TYC-J); PLB 6.89 (ISBN 0-690-03853-4). T Y Crowell.

Snake in the Strawberries. James Hearst. 1979. 5.95 (ISBN 0-8138-0765-4). Iowa St U Pr.

Snake-Lover's Diary. Barbara Brenner. LC 79-98113. (Illus.). (gr. 3-7). 1970. PLB 6.95 (ISBN 0-201-09349-9, A-W Chidrens). A-W.

Snake River Country. Don Moser. (American Wilderness Ser.). (Illus.). 1974. 12.95 (ISBN 0-8094-1241-1). Time-Life.

Snake River Country. Don Moser. LC 74-80283. (American Wilderness). (Illus.). (gr. 6 up). 1974. PLB 11.97 (ISBN 0-8094-1242-X, Pub. by Time-Life). Silver.

Snakedoctor. Christian Garrison. 1980. pap. 1.95 (ISBN 0-686-69263-2, 76232). Avon.

Snakes. Ruth B. Gross. LC 74-13227. (Illus.). 64p. (gr. k-3). 1975. 7.95 (ISBN 0-590-07385-0, Four Winds). Schol Bk Serv.

Snakes. George Shea. LC 80-21294. (Creatures Wild & Free Ser.). (gr. 1-6). 1981. 5.95 (ISBN 0-88436-776-2). EMC.

Snakes. Al Young. 160p. 1981. pap. 5.95 (ISBN 0-916870-34-0). Creative Arts Bk.

Snakes. Herbert S. Zim. (Illus.). (gr. 3-7). 1949. PLB 6.48 (ISBN 0-688-31549-6). Morrow.

Snakes & Lizards. Dean Morris. LC 77-8147. (Read About Animals Ser.). (Illus.). (gr. k-3). 1977. PLB 9.65 (ISBN 0-8393-0007-7). Raintree Child.

Snakes & Snakebite. John Visser & David Chapman. 1980. 30.00x (Pub. by Bailey & Swinton South Africa). State Mutual Bk.

Snakes Around the World. George S. Fichter. LC 78-9774. (Easy Read Fact Bks.). (Illus.). (gr. 2-4). 1980. PLB 6.45 s&l (ISBN 0-531-02275-7). Watts.

Snakes of Texas: A Field Guide. Alan Tennant & John E. Werler. (Illus.). 384p. 1981. text ed. 19.95 (ISBN 0-292-77559-8); pap. 9.95 (ISBN 0-292-77560-1). U of Tex Pr.

Snakes of the World. Raymond L. Ditmars. (Illus.). 1966. 8.50 o.s.i. (ISBN 0-02-531730-X). Macmillan.

Snaketrack. Frank Bonham. (Frank Bonham Ser.). 1978. pap. 1.50 o.p. (ISBN 0-425-03760-6, Medallion). Berkley Pub.

Snap! Photography. Miriam Cooper. (Illus.). (gr. 4-7). 1981. PLB price not set (ISBN 0-671-34021-2). Messner.

Snapping. Flo Conway & Jim Siegelman. LC 78-6627. 1978. 10.00 o.s.i. (ISBN 0-397-01258-6). Lippincott.

Snappy Put-Downs & Funny Insults. Joseph Rosenbloom. LC 80-54348. (Illus.). 128p. (gr. 3-6). 1981. 5.95 (ISBN 0-8069-4646-6); lib. bdg. 6.69 (ISBN 0-8069-4647-4). Sterling.

Snappy Sentences for Church Bulletin Boards. Paul E. Holdcraft. pap. 0.75 o.p. (ISBN 0-687-38803-1). Abingdon.

Snappy Sermon Starters. Paul E. Holdcraft. 1940. pap. 3.95 (ISBN 0-687-38828-7). Abingdon.

Snappy Squibs for the Church Calendar. Paul E. Holdcraft. 1940. pap. 3.95 (ISBN 0-687-38878-3). Abingdon.

Snaps. Victor H. Cruz. LC 69-16456. 1969. 6.95 o.p. (ISBN 0-394-40496-3). Random.

Snapshot, No. One, Vol.19. LC 74-18754. (Illus.). 128p. 1974. 20.00 (ISBN 0-912334-67-3); pap. 12.50 (ISBN 0-912334-68-1). Aperture.

Snare for Catherine. Juliette Benzoni. 1976. pap. 1.95 o.p. (ISBN 0-380-00651-0, 41343). Avon.

Snares & Swindles in Bridge. Terence Reese & Roger Trezel. LC 76-55903. 1977. pap. 3.95 (ISBN 0-8119-0397-4). Fell.

Snares Without Ending. Olympe Bhely-Quenum. Tr. by Dorothy Blair from Fr. (Sun-Lit Ser.). Orig. Title: Un Piege Sans Fin. 220p. (Orig.). 1981. 10.00x (ISBN 0-89410-184-6); pap. 6.00x (ISBN 0-686-64485-9). Three Continents.

Snatching Men Out of the Fire & Other Ser. J. J. Turner. pap. 3.95 (ISBN 0-89315-257-9). Lambert Bk.

Sneakers. Karen Markoe & Louis Phillips. (Funnybones Ser.). (Illus.). 64p. 1981. pap. 1.50 (ISBN 0-671-42117-4). Wanderer Bks.

Snezhnyi Chas: Stikhi, 1931-35. 2nd ed. Boris I. Poplavskii. Ed. by Simon Karlinsky. (Modern Russian Literature & Culture, Studies & Texts: Vol. 8). 110p. (Rus.). 1980. pap. 7.00 (ISBN 0-933884-13-3). Berkeley Slavic.

Sniff, Sniff Al-er-gee. Claude A. Frazier. LC 76-27985. (Illus.). (gr. k-3). 1978. 6.35 (ISBN 0-910812-19-5); pap. 3.00 (ISBN 0-910812-24-1). Johnny Reads.

Snip. Nathaniel Benchley. LC 80-696. (Illus.). 64p. (gr. 4). 1981. 8.95a (ISBN 0-385-15997-8); PLB (ISBN 0-385-15998-6). Doubleday.

Snipp, Snapp, Snurr & the Big Surprise. Maj Lindman. LC 37-35180. (Illus.). (gr. k-2). 1937. 5.75g (ISBN 0-8075-7503-8). A Whitman.

Snipp, Snapp, Snurr & the Buttered Bread. Maj Lindman. LC 34-37832. (Illus.). (gr. k-2). 1934. 5.75g (ISBN 0-8075-7504-6). A Whitman.

Snipp, Snapp, Snurr & the Gingerbread. Maj Lindman. LC 36-32643. (Illus.). (gr. k-2). 1936. 5.75g (ISBN 0-8075-7505-4). A Whitman.

Snipp, Snapp, Snurr & the Seven Dogs. Maj Lindman. LC 59-14391. (Illus.). (gr. k-2). 1959. 5.75g (ISBN 0-8075-7512-7). A Whitman.

Snipp, Snapp, Snurr Learn to Swim. Maj Lindman. LC 54-9945. (Illus.). (gr. k-2). 1954. 5.75g (ISBN 0-8075-7506-2). A Whitman.

Snips & Snails & Walnut Whales. Phyllis Fiarotta. LC 75-9574. (Parents & Children Together). (Illus.). 288p. (ps up). 1975. 9.95 (ISBN 0-911104-75-5); pap. 5.95 (ISBN 0-911104-49-6). Workman Pub.

Snnorra Sagas of Norse Kings. S. Snorra. 1973. 25.00x (ISBN 82-09-00752-1, N-393). Vanous.

Snobol Four Programming Language. 2nd ed. Ralph E. Griswold et al. (Automatic Computation Ser). 1971. pap. 15.95 (ISBN 0-13-815373-6). P-H.

Snooker -How to Become a Champion. Rex Williams. 1976. 4.25 o.p. (ISBN 0-86002-136-X). Transatlantic.

Snoopy Paint with Water Book. (Illus.). 48p. (ps-5). 1979. pap. 1.25 (ISBN 0-448-16768-9). G&D.

Snoopy's Facts & Fun Book About Farms. Charles M. Schulz. LC 79-22307. (Snoopy's Facts & Fun Bks.). (Illus.). 40p. (ps-1). 1980. bds. 2.50 (ISBN 0-394-84300-2); PLB 2.99 (ISBN 0-394-94300-7). Random.

Snoopy's Facts & Fun Book About Nature. Charles M. Schulz. LC 79-22307. (Snoopy's Facts & Fun Bks.). (Illus.). 40p. (ps-1). 1980. bds. 2.50 (ISBN 0-394-84299-5); PLB 2.99 (ISBN 0-394-94299-X). Random.

Snoopy's Facts & Fun Book About Seashores. Charles M. Schulz. LC 79-23362. (Snoopy's Facts & Fun Bks.). (Illus.). 40p. (ps-1). 1980. 2.50 (ISBN 0-394-84298-7); PLB 2.99 (ISBN 0-394-94298-1). Random.

Snoopy's Facts & Fun Book About Trucks. Charles M. Schulz. LC 79-23616. (Snoopy's Facts & Fun Bks.). (Illus.). 40p. (ps-1). 1980. 2.50 (ISBN 0-394-84273-1); PLB 2.99 (ISBN 0-394-94273-6). Random.

Snopp on the Sidewalk & Other Poems. Jack Prelutsky. LC 76-46323. (Illus.). (gr. 3 up). 1977. PLB 6.96 (ISBN 0-688-84084-1). Greenwillow.

Snoqualmie Pass: From Indian Trail to Interstate. Yvonne Prater. Ed. by Rebecca Earnest. (Illus.). 120p. (Orig.). 1981. pap. 6.95 (ISBN 0-89886-015-6). Mountaineers.

Snorri Sturluson. Marlene Ciklamini. (World Authors Ser.: No. 493 (Iceland)). 1978. 13.95 (ISBN 0-8057-6334-1). Twayne.

Snow. John Burningham. LC 75-2492. (Illus.). (ps-1). 1975. 2.50 (ISBN 0-690-00904-6, TYC-J); PLB 4.89 (ISBN 0-690-00905-4). T Y Crowell.

Snow. Ruth Kirk. 1978. 12.50 (ISBN 0-688-03268-0); pap. 5.95 (ISBN 0-688-08268-8). Morrow.

Snow Bunny. Bobbi Katz. Ed. by Caroline Rubin. LC 76-894. (Springboard Sports Ser.). (Illus.). 64p. (gr. 3-7). 1976. 5.75g (ISBN 0-8075-7518-6). A Whitman.

Snow Country. Yasunari Kawabata. Tr. by Edward G. Seidensticker from Jap. (Perigee Japanese Library). 192p. 1981. pap. 4.95 (ISBN 0-399-50525-3, Perigee). Putnam.

Snow Crystals. W. A. Bentley & W. J. Humphreys. (Illus.). 1931. pap. 8.95 (ISBN 0-486-20287-9). Dover.

Snow Falcon. Craig Thomas. 416p. 1981. pap. 2.95 (ISBN 0-553-14625-4). Bantam.

Snow in the River. Carol R. Brink. 1964. 12.95 (ISBN 0-02-515890-2). Macmillan.

Snow Is Falling. Franklyn M. Branley. LC 63-15084. (Let's-Read-&-Find-Out Science Bk). (Illus.). (gr. k-3). 1963. bds. 7.95 (ISBN 0-690-74299-1, TYC-J); PLB 7.89 (ISBN 0-690-74300-9). T Y Crowell.

Snow Job: Canada, the United States & Vietnam (1954-1973) Charles Taylor. LC 74-77028. 209p. 1974. pap. 7.95 (ISBN 0-88784-619-X, Pub. by Hse Anansi Pr Canada). U of Toronto Pr.

Snow Queen. Hans C. Andersen. Ed. by Suria Magito & Rudolf Weil. LC 59-15639. 1960. pap. 2.95x (ISBN 0-87830-538-6). Theatre Arts.

Snow Queen. Marcia Brown & Hans C. Andersen. LC 72-168499. (Encore Ser.). (Illus.). 96p. (gr. 1-5). 1972. 9.95 (ISBN 0-684-16564-3, ScribJ). Scribner.

Snow Queen. Joan Vinge. 1981. pap. 3.25 (ISBN 0-440-17749-9). Dell.

Snow Salmon Reached the Andes Lake. Willis Barnstone. LC 80-65064. 1980. 6.95 (ISBN 0-931604-02-8); pap. 3.95 (ISBN 0-931604-03-6). Curbstone Pub NY TX.

Snow Sculpture & Ice Carving. James S. Haskins. LC 73-20992. (Illus.). 144p. 1974. pap. 4.95 o.s.i. (ISBN 0-02-011500-8, Collier). Macmillan.

Snow, Stars & Wild Honey. George P. Morrill. 1975. 8.95 o.p. (ISBN 0-397-01029-X). Lippincott.

Snow Tiger. Desmond Bagley. 272p. 1977. pap. 1.75 o.p. (ISBN 0-449-23107-0, Crest). Fawcett.

SNOW: Twice Orphaned-Once Rescued. June Gale. LC 80-21941. (Illus.). 168p. 1980. 10.00 (ISBN 0-914016-74-1). Phoenix Pub.

Snow White. Brothers Grimm. Tr. by Paul Heins. LC 73-13585. (Illus.). (gr. k-3). 1979. pap. 3.95 o.p. (ISBN 0-316-35451-1, Pub. by Atlantic-Little Brown); 7.95 o.p. (ISBN 0-316-35450-3). Little.

Snow White & Rose Red. (Illus.). Arabic 2.50x (ISBN 0-685-82873-5). Intl Bk Ctr.

Snow White & the Dwarfs. Patricia Daniels. LC 79-28431. (Raintree Fairy Tales Ser.). (Illus.). 24p. (gr. k-3). 1980. lib. bdg. 8.65 (ISBN 0-8393-0251-7). Raintree Child.

Snow White & the Seven Dwarfs. Caren Caraway. (Stemmer House Story-to-Color Bks). (Illus.). 32p. (ps up). 1980. pap. 2.95 (ISBN 0-916144-57-7). Stemmer Hse.

Snow White & the Seven Dwarfs. Illus. by T. Izawa & S. Hijkata. (Puppet Storybooks). (Illus.). 18p. (gr. k-2). 1981. 3.50 (ISBN 0-448-09757-5). G&D.

Snow White & the Seven Dwarfs. Walt Disney Studios. (Young Reader Ser.). (Illus.). 24p. (gr. k-3). 1976. PLB 5.00 (ISBN 0-307-60066-1, Golden Pr); pap. 1.95 (ISBN 0-307-10451-6). Western Pub.

Snow-White & the Seven Dwarfs: A Tale from the Brothers Grimm. Jacob Grimm & Wilhelm Grimm. Tr. by Randall Jarrell from Ger. LC 72-81489. (Illus.). 32p. (ps-3). 1972. 8.95 (ISBN 0-374-37099-0). FS&G.

Snow White & the Seven Dwarfs: Disney Classic. Guy N. Smith. 1976. pap. 1.50 o.s.i. (ISBN 0-515-04164-5). Jove Pubns.

Snowball Express. Claro. (gr. 3-5). 1980. pap. 1.50 (ISBN 0-590-30359-7, Schol Pap). Schol Bk Serv.

Snowballing. Frank Covino. (Orig.). 1975. pap. 1.50 o.p. (ISBN 0-685-54128-2, LB290DK, Leisure Bks). Nordon Pubns.

Snowbird. Patricia Calvert. LC 80-19139. 192p. (gr. 5 up). 1980. 8.95 (ISBN 0-686-62531-5). Scribner.

Snowbird. Larry Levine. 1977. pap. 1.75 o.p. (ISBN 0-449-13866-6, GM). Fawcett.

Snowbound Mystery. Gertrude C. Warner. LC 68-9124. (Boxcar Children Mysteries-Pilot Bk.). (Illus.). (gr. 3-7). 1968. 6.95g (ISBN 0-8075-7517-8). A Whitman.

Snowbound Six. Richard Martin Stern. LC 77-77551. 1977. 7.95 o.p. (ISBN 0-385-12320-5). Doubleday.

Snowbound with Betsy. Carolyn Haywood. (Illus.). (gr. 3-7). 1962. 7.75 o.p. (ISBN 0-688-21684-6); PLB 7.92 (ISBN 0-688-31684-0). Morrow.

Snowbound with Betsy. Carolyn Haywood. (Illus.). (gr. 3-5). 1980. pap. 1.75 (ISBN 0-671-56048-4). Archway.

Snowdonia & Northern Wales. John B. Hilling. (Illus.). 192p. 1980. 27.00 (ISBN 0-7134-3793-6, Pub. by Batsford England). David & Charles.

Snowfall. Julian May. LC 70-156057. (Investigating the Earth Ser). (Illus.). (gr. 4-8). 1972. PLB 5.95 o.p. (ISBN 0-87191-065-9). Creative Ed.

Snowfire. Phyllis A. Whitney. 1978. pap. 2.25 (ISBN 0-449-24246-3, Crest). Fawcett.

Snowflakes. Ruth Heller. (Creative Coloring Activity Pandabacks). (Illus.). 32p. 1981. pap. 1.25 (ISBN 0-448-49625-9). G&D.

Snowflakes in the Sun. Audrey Brent. 192p. 1981. pap. 1.50 (ISBN 0-671-57063-3). S&S.

Snowing in Paradise. J. R. Williams. (Orig.). 1980. pap. 2.25 (ISBN 0-532-23147-3). Manor Bks.

Snowman. Raymond Briggs. LC 78-55904. (Illus.). (ps-2). 1978. 4.95 (ISBN 0-394-83973-0, BYR); PLB 5.99 (ISBN 0-394-93973-5). Random.

Snowman. Arthur Maling. LC 72-9172. (Harper Novel of Suspense). 1973. 6.95 o.s.i. (ISBN 0-06-012778-3, HarpT). Har-Row.

Snowman's Secret. Robert Barry. LC 75-15801. (Illus.). 32p. (ps-2). 1975. 8.95 (ISBN 0-02-708390-X, 70839). Macmillan.

Snowmelt from Yesteryears: Broadside Poem. 1974. vellum ltd. ed. 3.00 (ISBN 0-918704-03-0). Fels & Firn.

Snowmobile Revolution: Technology & Social Change in the Arctic. Pertti J. Pelto. LC 72-89138. 210p. 1973. 6.95 (ISBN 0-8465-3755-9). Benjamin-Cummings.

Snowmobiler's Companion. Sally Wimer. LC 72-1235. (Illus.). 1972. 9.95 o.p. (ISBN 0-684-13080-7, ScribT). Scribner.

Snowmobiles. Nancy A. Hall. (Illus.). (gr. 6-8). pap. 3.00 o.p. (ISBN 0-513-01315-6). Denison.

Snowmobiling: The Guide. John W. Malo. 1971. pap. 3.95 o.s.i. (ISBN 0-02-029250-3, Collier). Macmillan.

Snows of Craggmoor. Samantha Harte. (YA) 1978. 5.95 (ISBN 0-685-87350-1, Avalon). Bouregy.

Snows of Kilimanjaro & Other Stories. Ernest Hemingway. 1961. 6.95 o.p. (ISBN 0-684-10249-8, ScribT); Hudson River Edition. pap. 2.95 (ISBN 0-684-71807-3, SL32, ScribT); 15.00x (ISBN 0-684-16479-5). Scribner.

Snowy Day. Ezra J. Keats. (Illus.). (ps-1). 1962. PLB 7.95 (ISBN 0-670-65400-0). Viking Pr.

Snowy Hills of Innocence. Ann Boyle. (YA) 1977. 4.95 o.p. (ISBN 0-685-73807-8, Avalon). Bouregy.

Snowy Toes & the Magic Music Box. Patrick Matthews & Mollie Matthews. 1976. 3.95 (ISBN 0-7207-0813-3, Pub. by Michael Joseph). Merrimack Bk Serv.

Snug Little House. Eils M. Lewis. LC 80-24282. (Illus.). 32p. (ps-3). 1981. 8.95 (ISBN 0-689-50177-3, McElderry Bk). Atheneum.

So Called Historical Jesus & the Historic Biblical Christ. Martin Kahler. Tr. by Carl E. Braaten from Ger. LC 64-12994. 168p. 1964. pap. 3.75 (ISBN 0-8006-1960-9, 1-1960). Fortress.

So Desperate the Fight: An Innovative Approach to Chronic Illness. Warren R. Johnson. LC 78-71009. 1981. pap. 6.95 (ISBN 0-917476-16-6). Rational Living.

So Dreadful a Judgement: Puritan Responses to King Philip's War, 1676-1677. Ed. by Richard Slotkin & James K. Folsom. 1978. 25.00x (ISBN 0-8195-6058-8); pap. 10.00x. Wesleyan U Pr.

So Evil My Love. Joseph Shearing. 1961. pap. 0.95 o.s.i. (ISBN 0-02-025190-4, Collier). Macmillan.

So Far Disordered in Mind: Insanity in California, 1870-1930. Richard W. Fox. LC 77-93479. 1979. 11.95x (ISBN 0-520-03620-4). U of Cal Pr.

So Far from Heaven. Richard Bradford. LC 73-7885. 276p. 1973. 6.95 o.s.i. (ISBN 0-397-00853-8). Lippincott.

So Fine Bovine: The Cow Book. Una Edwards et al. 350p. (Orig.). 1980. pap. write for info. Family Pub CA.

So Good, So Far. Grady Nutt. LC 79-90248. 152p. 1981. pap. 4.95 (ISBN 0-914850-68-7). Impact Tenn.

So Good, So Far. Grady Nutt. Frwd. by Ralph Edwards. LC 79-90248. 1979. 5.95 (ISBN 0-914850-53-9). Impact Tenn.

So Great Salvation. W. W. Hammel. 1972. pap. 2.25 (ISBN 0-87148-751-9). Pathway Pr.

So Great the Journey. Bonne B. O'Brien. LC 79-52332. (Illus.). 1980. 5.95 (ISBN 0-8054-5593-0). Broadman.

So Help Me God! Herbert Tarr. 224p. 1980. pap. 2.75 (ISBN 0-553-14135-X). Bantam.

So It Was Just a Simple Wedding. Sara Kasdan. LC 61-13280. 8.95 (ISBN 0-8149-0133-6). Vanguard.

So It Was True: The American Protestant Press & the Nazi Persecution of the Jews. Robert W. Ross. LC 80-196. 1980. 20.00x (ISBN 0-8166-0948-9); pap. 9.95x (ISBN 0-8166-0951-9). U of Minn Pr.

So Long, See You Tomorrow. William Maxwell. 160p. 1981. pap. 2.95 (ISBN 0-345-29194-8). Ballantine.

So Long, See You Tomorrow. William Maxwell. 1980. lib. bdg. 10.95 (ISBN 0-8161-3093-0, Large Print Bks). G K Hall.

So Long Until Tomorrow. Lowell Thomas. 1977. 10.95 o.p. (ISBN 0-688-03236-2). Morrow.

So Many Heroes. 2nd, rev. ed. Alan Levy. LC 80-65002. Orig. Title: Rowboat to Prague. 384p. 1980. 15.95 (ISBN 0-933256-12-4); pap. 7.95 (ISBN 0-933256-16-7). Second Chance.

So Moses Was Born. Joan Grant. 1976. pap. 1.50 (ISBN 0-380-00828-9, 30940). Avon.

So Much Blood. Simon Brett. LC 76-42083. (Encore Editions). 1977. 2.95 (ISBN 0-684-16535-X, ScribT). Scribner.

So Much Blood. Simon Brett. 1981. pap. 2.25 (ISBN 0-425-04935-3). Berkley Pub.

So Much Love. Lucy Walker. 1977. pap. 1.50 o.p. (ISBN 0-345-25858-4). Ballantine.

So Narrow the Bridge & Deep the Water. Lisa Thomas. LC 80-52865. 156p. 1980. pap. 4.95 (ISBN 0-686-28642-1). Seal Pr WA.

So Now You're a Graduate. William J. Krutza. 88p. 1981. 4.95 (ISBN 0-8010-5433-8). Baker Bk.

So This Is Depravity. Russell Baker. 256p. 1980. 10.95 (ISBN 0-312-92782-7). St Martin.

So This Is Depravity & Other Observations. Russell Baker. 1980. 10.95 (ISBN 0-312-92782-7); deluxe signed, limited ed. 40.00 (ISBN 0-312-92783-5). Congdon & Lattes.

So This Is Jazz. Henry O. Osgood. LC 77-17859. (Roots of Jazz Ser.). (Illus.). 1978. Repr. of 1926 ed. lib. bdg. 22.50 (ISBN 0-306-77540-9). Da Capo.

So This Is Where You Work! A Guide to Unconventional Working Environments. Charles A. Fraccia. (Illus.). 1979. pap. 9.95 o.p. (ISBN 0-14-005219-4). Penguin.

So What If I'm a Sore Loser? Barbara Williams. LC 80-24783. (Illus.). 48p. (ps-3). 1981. 8.95 (ISBN 0-15-277260-X, HJ). HarBraceJ.

So What If It's Raining! Miriam Young. LC 75-19340. (Illus.). 40p. (ps-3). 1976. 5.95 o.s.i. (ISBN 0-8193-0803-X, Four Winds); PLB 5.41 o.s.i. (ISBN 0-8193-0804-8). Schol Bk Serv.

So What If You Can't Chew, Eat Hearty! Recipes & a Guide for the Healthy & Happy Eating of Soft & Pureed Foods. Phyllis Z. Goldberg. (Illus.). 152p. 1980. pap. 13.95 (ISBN 0-398-04065-6). C C Thomas.

So White, the Lilies. Mildred L. Reddoch. 1981. 5.95 (ISBN 0-8062-1629-8). Carlton.

So Wild a Dream. C. Florentz. (Pacesetters Ser.). (Illus.). 64p. (gr. 4 up). 1978. PLB 7.95 (ISBN 0-516-02172-9). Childrens.

So You Are Thinking About a Small Business Computer. Richard G. Canning & Nancy C. Leeper. (Computing in Your Business Ser.). (Illus.). 100p. (Orig.). 1980. pap. 12.50 (ISBN 0-938516-01-9). Canning Pubns.

So You Have Asthma! Albert D. Blanc. (Illus.). 280p. 1966. 11.50 (ISBN 0-398-00168-5). C C Thomas.

So You Have Cataracts: What You & Your Family Should Know. Albert E. Sloane. (Illus.). 112p. 1975. 9.50 (ISBN 0-398-01771-9). C C Thomas.

So You Think You Know...? Quiz Book. Dale Crane. (Aviation Training Ser.). (Illus.). 297p. 1980. pap. 6.95 (ISBN 0-89100-071-2, E*A-Q*B). Aviation Maintenance.

So You Think You Want to Be in the Helping Profession As a Community Organizer. Roland Wesley. LC 80-65603. 135p. 1981. perfect bdg. 11.50 (ISBN 0-86548-059-1). Century Twenty One.

So You Think You're Covered? A Consumer's Guide to Home Fire Insurance. Stanley Leinwoll. LC 76-44842. 1978. pap. 2.95 o.p. (ISBN 0-684-15580-X, ScribT). Scribner.

So You Want to Be a Ham. 8th ed. Robert Hertzberg. LC 79-63820. 1979. pap. 6.95 (ISBN 0-672-21600-0). Sams.

So You Want to Be a Leader. R. H. Pierson. LC 66-20341. (Dimension Ser.). pap. 5.95 (ISBN 0-8163-0156-5, 19410-0). Pacific Pr Pub Assn.

So You Want to Be a Nurse. Alan E. Nourse & Eleanore Halliday. LC 61-6189. (So You Want Series). 1961. lib. bdg. 6.79 o.s.i. (ISBN 0-06-005101-9, HarpT). Har-Row.

So You Want to Be a Social Worker. rev. ed. Helen H. Perlman. LC 77-106939. (So You Want to Be Ser). 1970. 8.95 o.p. (ISBN 0-06-013318-X, HarpT); lib. bdg. 6.79 o.p. (ISBN 0-06-013319-8, HarpT). Har-Row.

So You Want to Be an Airline Stewardess. new rev. ed. Keith Saunders. (Illus.). 176p. 1973. pap. 1.50 o.p. (ISBN 0-668-02936-6). Arc Bks.

So You Want to Get into the Race. Chuck Klein. 1980. 2.95 (ISBN 0-8423-6082-4). Tyndale.

So You Want to Learn a Language. F. C. Stork. (Illus., Orig.). 1976. pap. 4.95 (ISBN 0-571-10820-2, Pub. by Faber & Faber). Merrimack Bk Serv.

So You Want to Raise a Boy. W. Cleon Skousen. LC 61-9555. 1962. 9.95 (ISBN 0-385-02408-8). Doubleday.

So You Want to Start a Restaurant? Dewey A. Dyer. LC 71-168741. 1971. 12.95 (ISBN 0-8436-0535-9). CBI Pub.

So You Want to Start a Restaurant? rev. 2nd ed. Dewey A. Dyer. 192p. 1981. 12.95 (ISBN 0-8436-2199-0). CBI Pub.

So You Want to Teach English to Foreigners. C. Leatherdale. 112p. 1980. 16.95x (ISBN 0-85626-191-2, Pub. by Abacus Pr England); pap. 8.95x (ISBN 0-85626-192-0). Intl Schol Bk Serv.

So You'd Like to Know More About Soccer! A Guide for Parents. Paul E. Harris, Jr. 120p. pap. 3.95 (ISBN 0-88839-107-2). Soccer for Am.

So You're Going to Take Tennis Seriously? Jack Roberts. (Illus.). 144p. 1974. pap. 3.50 (ISBN 0-911104-34-8). Workman Pub.

So You're Ready to Drive a Car. David J. Abodaher. (Illus.). 128p. (gr. 7 up). 1981. PLB price not set. Messner.

So You're Ready to Drive a Car. David J. Mbodaher. (Illus.). 128p. (gr. 8 up). 1981. write for info. (ISBN 0-671-32891-3). Messner.

So You're the Pastor's Wife. Ruth Senter. 1979. 6.95 (ISBN 0-310-38820-1). Zondervan.

Soap. rev. ed. Ann Bramson. LC 75-7286. 1975. pap. 3.50 (ISBN 0-911104-57-7). Workman Pub.

Soap Opera Word-Find Puzzles. Ribbon Publications. 1977. pap. 1.50 o.p. (ISBN 0-685-75035-3, 345-25566-6-150). Ballantine.

Soapy Smith. Frank C. Robertson & Beth K. Harris. 1961. 7.95 (ISBN 0-8038-6661-5). Hastings.

Soaramerica. Ed. by John Joss. (Illus.). 216p. 1976. 9.95 o.p. (ISBN 0-930514-04-1, Pub. by Soaring); pap. 6.95 (ISBN 0-930514-06-8). Aviation.

Soaring. William T. Carter. Ed. by Carroll V. Glines. LC 72-92863. (Air Force Academy Ser.). 192p. 1973. 6.95 o.s.i. (ISBN 0-02-522480-8). Macmillan.

Soaring: The Diary & Letters of a Denishawn Dancer in the Far East, 1925-1926. Jane Sherman. LC 75-34445. (Illus.). 1976. 16.95 (ISBN 0-8195-4093-5, Pub. by Wesleyan U Pr). Columbia U Pr.

Sober Living Workbook. Rip O'Keefe. 1980. pap. 5.95. Hazelden.

Soberania De Dios. A. W. Pink. 2.95 (ISBN 0-686-12562-2). Banner of Truth.

Sobranie Sochinenii, Vol. 3. Mikhail Bulgakov. 202p. (Rus.). 1981. 25.00 (ISBN 0-88233-698-3). Ardis Pubs.

Sobranie Sochinenii: Tom. 1, Ranniaia Proza. Mikhail Bulgakov. Tr. by Tom I. Ranniaia. 300p. (Rus.). 1981. 25.00 (ISBN 0-88233-506-5). Ardis Pubs.

Sobriquets & Nicknames. Albert R. Frey. LC 66-22671. 1966. Repr. of 1888 ed. 18.00 (ISBN 0-8103-3003-2). Gale.

Soccer. Howard Liss. (Illus.). pap. 3.50 o.p. (ISBN 0-8015-6910-9). Dutton.

Soccer. 2nd rev. ed. Clive Toye. (First Bks.). (Illus.). (gr. 4-6). 1979. PLB 6.45 s&l (ISBN 0-531-02936-0). Watts.

Soccer. Bob Wilson. (Pelham Pictorial Sports Instructors Ser.). 1977. 8.95 (ISBN 0-7207-0793-5). Transatlantic.

Soccer Book. Don Kowet. LC 76-8131. (gr. 5-9). 1976. pap. 4.95 (ISBN 0-394-93250-1, BYR); pap. 5.95 (ISBN 0-394-83250-7). Random.

Soccer Coaching the Modern Way. 2nd ed. Eric Batty. (Illus., Orig.). 1975. pap. 5.95 o.p. (ISBN 0-571-10648-X, Pub. by Faber & Faber). Merrimack Bk Serv.

Soccer: Coaching to Win. Donald Y. Yonker & Alexander Weide. LC 77-92311. 1978. pap. 5.95 (ISBN 0-8015-6909-5, Hawthorne). Dutton.

Soccer Crazy. Colin McNaughton. LC 80-67834. (Illus.). 32p. (ps-4). 1981. 8.95 (ISBN 0-689-50189-7, McElderry Bk). Atheneum.

Soccer Duel. Thomas J. Dygard. 192p. (gr. 7-9). 1981. 7.95 (ISBN 0-688-00366-4); PLB 7.63 (ISBN 0-688-00367-2). Morrow

Soccer Fever: A Year with the San Jose Earthquakes. Richard B. Lyttle. LC 76-18361. (gr. 4-9). 1977. PLB 7.95 (ISBN 0-385-11297-1). Doubleday.

Soccer for Men. 4th ed. Richard L. Nelson. (Physical Education Activities Ser.). 1981. pap. text ed. 3.25x (ISBN 0-697-07094-8). Wm C Brown.

Soccer for the American Boy. Ted Smits. (Illus.). 1970. 4.95 o.p. (ISBN 0-13-815456-2); pap. 1.50 (ISBN 0-13-815282-9). P-H.

Soccer: Guide to Training & Coaching. Allen Wade. (Funk & W Bk.). (Illus.). 1977. 8.95 (ISBN 0-308-70339-1, TYC-T); pap. 4.95 o.s.i. (ISBN 0-308-10318-1, TYC-T). T Y Crowell.

Soccer Handbook. David Keith. (Physical Education Ser.). (Illus.). 64p. (Orig.). 1980. pap. text ed. 5.95 (ISBN 0-88839-048-3). Hancock Hse.

Soccer Hero. Mike Neigoff. Ed. by Caroline Rubin. LC 76-18750. (Pilot Bks). (Illus.). 128p. (gr. 4-8). 1976. 6.95g (ISBN 0-8075-7529-1). A Whitman.

Soccer! How One Player Made the Pros. Evelyn Kaatz. (Illus.). 128p. (gr. 3 up). 1981. 7.95 (ISBN 0-316-47752-4). Little.

Soccer: How to Become a Champ. Allan Clarke. (Illus.). 1976. pap. 5.95 (ISBN 0-86002-131-9). Transatlantic.

Soccer Illustrated for Coach & Player. 2nd ed. F. F. Di Clemente. 260p. 1968. 14.95 (ISBN 0-471-07138-2). Wiley.

Soccer Illustrated: For Coach & Player. 2nd ed. Frank F. DiClemente. LC 68-8624. (Illus.). 260p. 1968. 14.95 (ISBN 0-8260-2690-7). Ronald Pr.

Soccer Orphans. William MacKellar. LC 78-22435. (gr. 5 up). 1979. 5.95 (ISBN 0-396-07667-X). Dodd.

Soccer Refereeing. Denis Howell. 1978. 10.95 (ISBN 0-7207-1003-0, Pub. by Michael Joseph). Merrimack Bk Serv.

Soccer Statistics Made Easy: A Guide to Rating & Predicting Player & Team Performance. Edward K. Zabrowski. (Illus.). viii, 81p. 1979. 5.95 (ISBN 0-9604994-0-7). Crossbar Ent.

Soccer: World's Most Popular Sport. bilingual ed. Gene Tardy & Al Jackson. (Sports Action Ser.). (Illus.). 64p. (Span. -Eng.). (gr. 3-7). 1975. PLB 6.75 (ISBN 0-914844-11-3). J Alden.

Social Accounting for Development Planning with Special Reference to Sri Lanka. G. Pyatt et al. LC 76-53523. 1978. 34.50 (ISBN 0-521-21578-1). Cambridge U Pr.

Social Accounting: Theory, Issues & Cases. Lee J. Seidler. LC 74-12116. (Management, Accounting & Information Systems Ser.). 547p. 1975. 26.50 (ISBN 0-471-77488-X). Wiley.

Social Action. M. Vasudevamoorthy. 1966. pap. 3.50x (ISBN 0-210-22644-7). Asia.

Social Action - Jesus Style. Larry Christenson. LC 75-44927. Orig. Title: Charismatic Approach to Social Action. 1974. pap. 1.50 (ISBN 0-87123-504-8, 200504). Bethany Fell.

Social & Behavioral Aspects of Female Alcoholism: An Annotated Bibliography. Compiled by H. Paul Chalfant. LC 80-1021. 168p. 1980. lib. bdg. 22.50 (ISBN 0-313-20947-2, CAL/). Greenwood.

Social & Behavioral Sciences Jobs Handbook. R. B. Uleck Associates. (Illus.). 48p. (Orig.). 1979. pap. 9.95 (ISBN 0-937562-02-5). Uleck Assoc.

Social & Biological Predictors of Nutritional Status, Physical Growth & Neurological Development. Ed. by Lawrence S. Green & Francis S. Johnston. 1980. 25.00 (ISBN 0-12-299750-6). Acad Pr.

Social & Business Enterprises. J. S. Boswell. (Economics & Society Ser.). 1976. text ed. 17.95x (ISBN 0-04-338078-6); pap. text ed. 13.50x (ISBN 0-04-338079-4). Allen Unwin.

Social & Cultural Dynamics. Pitirim Sorokin. (Social Science Classics Ser.). 720p. 1982. 19.95 (ISBN 0-87855-363-0); pap. 7.95 (ISBN 0-87855-787-3). Transaction Bks. Postponed.

Social & Cultural Mobility. Pitirim A. Sorokin. LC 59-13122. 1959. 12.95 (ISBN 0-02-930270-6). Free Pr.

Social & Economic Change Among the Northern Ojibwa. R. W. Dunning. LC 60-50269. 1959. 12.50x o.p. (ISBN 0-8020-5073-5); pap. 5.00 (ISBN 0-8020-6131-1). U of Toronto Pr.

Social & Economic Dimensions of Health & Illness Behavior in New Mexico: An Annotated Bibliography. Helen R. Potter. LC 75-99570. 1969. pap. 5.00x o.p. (ISBN 0-8263-0163-0). U of NM Pr.

Social & Economic History of England from Seventeen Hundred to Nineteen Seventy. A. H. Stamp. 334p. 1980. 22.50x (ISBN 0-7050-0070-2, Pub. by Skilton & Shaw England). State Mutual Bk.

Social & Economic History of the Near East in the Middle Ages. E. Ashtor. LC 74-29800. 1976. 25.00x (ISBN 0-520-02962-3). U of Cal Pr.

Social & Economic Impact of Earthquakes on Utility Lifelines: Proceedings. Conference Sponsored by ASCE Construction Division, May 1980, San Francisco, CA. Ed. by J. Isenberg. LC 80-69153. 250p. pap. text ed. 21.00 (ISBN 0-87262-254-1). Am Soc Civil Eng.

Social & Economic Impacts of Coronary Artery Disease. Ed. by Edgar D. Charles & Jennie J. Kronenfeld. LC 79-1554. 160p. 1980. 18.95 (ISBN 0-669-02912-2). Lexington Bks.

Social & Economic Implications of Cancer in the United States. Thomas A. Hodgson. Ed. by Klaudia Cox. (Ser. 3, No. 20). 50p. 1980. pap. text ed. 1.50 (ISBN 0-8406-0203-0). Natl Ctr Health Stats.

Social & Economic Inequality in the Soviet Union: Six Studies. Murray Yanowitch. LC 77-71634. 1977. 15.00 o.p. (ISBN 0-87332-105-7); pap. 6.95 (ISBN 0-87332-148-0). M E Sharpe.

Social & Economic Perspectives on Irrigation. Ed. by Ian Carruthers. 100p. 1980. pap. 22.00 (ISBN 0-08-026780-7). Pergamon.

Social & Environmental Aspects of Desertification. 40p. 1980. pap. 6.75 (ISBN 0-686-68814-7, TUNU085, UNU). Unipub.

Social & Historical Foundations of Modern Medicine. Iago Galdston. 250p. 1981. 25.00 (ISBN 0-87630-259-2). Brunner-Mazel.

Social & Moral Ideas in the Plays of Galsworthy. S. Shukla. (Salzburg Studies in English Literature: 48). 263p. 1979. text ed. 25.00x (ISBN 0-391-01780-2). Humanities.

Social & Moral Theory in Casework. Raymond Plant. (Library of Social Work). 1970. 10.00x (ISBN 0-7100-6808-5); pap. 3.50 (ISBN 0-7100-6809-3). Routledge & Kegan.

Social & Political Change in New York's Chinatown: The Role of Voluntary Associations. Chia-Ling Kuo. LC 77-5328. (Special Studies). 1977. text ed. 24.95 (ISBN 0-03-021951-5). Praeger.

Social & Political Doctrines of Contemporary Europe. Michael Oakeshott. 241p. 1980. Repr. of 1947 ed. lib. bdg. 35.00 (ISBN 0-89987-625-0). Darby Bks.

Social & Political History of the German 1848 Revolution. Rudolph Stadelmann. Tr. by James G. Chastain from Ger. LC 74-27711. Orig. Title: Soziale und Politis Che Geschichet der Revolution Von 1848. xvi, 218p. 1975. 14.00x (ISBN 0-8214-0177-7). Ohio U Pr.

Social & Political Movements. Ed. by Gary B. Rush & R. Serge Denisoff. LC 72-146365. 1971. 34.50x (ISBN 0-89197-411-3). Irvington.

Social & Political Philosophy: Readings from Plato to Gandhi. Ed. by Ronald Santoni & John Somerville. LC 63-18039. 1963. pap. 4.95 (ISBN 0-385-01238-1, A370, Anch). Doubleday.

Social & Political Thought of Herbert Spencer. David Wiltshire. (Oxford Historical Monographs). 1978. 29.95x (ISBN 0-19-821873-7). Oxford U Pr.

Social & Political Thought of Karl Marx. Shlomo Avineri. LC 68-12055. (Studies in the History & Theory of Politics). 1971. 32.50 (ISBN 0-521-04071-X); pap. 8.95x (ISBN 0-521-09619-7). Cambridge U Pr.

Social & Political Thought of Leon Trotsky. Baruch Knei-Paz. 1978. 29.50x o.p. (ISBN 0-19-827233-2). Oxford U Pr.

Social & Religious History of the Jews: Byzantines, Mamelukes, & Maghribians, Vol. 17. Salo W. Baron. 1980. 25.00 (ISBN 0-231-08854-X). Columbia U Pr.

Social & Religious History of the Jews, 16 vols. 2nd, rev. & enl. ed. Salo W. Baron. Incl. Vol. 1. Ancient Times: To the Beginning of the Christian Era. 1952 (ISBN 0-231-08838-8); Vol. 2. Ancient Times: Christian Era: the First Five Centuries. 1952 (ISBN 0-231-08839-6); Vol. 3. High Middle Ages: Heirs of Rome & Persia. 1957 (ISBN 0-231-08840-X); Vol. 4. High Middle Ages: Meeting of the East & West. 1957 (ISBN 0-231-08841-8); Vol. 5. High Middle Ages: Religious Controls & Dissensions. 1957 (ISBN 0-231-08842-6); Vol. 6. High Middle Ages: Laws, Homilies & the Bible. 1958 (ISBN 0-231-08843-4); Vol. 7. High Middle Ages: Hebrew Language & Letters. 1958 (ISBN 0-231-08844-2); Vol. 8. High Middle Ages: Philosophy & Science. 1958 (ISBN 0-231-08845-0); Vol. 9. Late Middle Ages & Era of European Expansion, 1200-1650: Under Church & Empire. 1965 (ISBN 0-231-08846-9); Vol. 10. Late Middle Ages & Era of European Expansion, 1200-1650: On the Empire's Periphery. 1965 (ISBN 0-231-08847-7); Vol. 11. Late Middle Ages & Era of European Expansion, 1200-1650: Citizen or Alien Conjurer. 1967 (ISBN 0-231-08848-5); Vol. 12. Late Middle Ages & Era of European Expansion, 1200-1650: Economic Catalyst. 1967 (ISBN 0-231-08849-3); Vol. 13. Late Middle Ages & Era of European Expansion, 1200-1650: Inquisition, Renaissance & Reformation. 1969 (ISBN 0-231-08850-7); Vol. 14. Late Middle Ages & Era of European Expansion, 1200-1650: Catholic Restoration & Wars of Religion. 1969 (ISBN 0-231-08851-5); Vol. 15. Late Middle Ages & Era of European Expansion, 1200-1650: Resettlement Era. 1973 (ISBN 0-231-08852-3); Index (ISBN 0-231-08877-9). LC 52-404. 27.00x ea. Columbia U Pr.

Social & Religious History of the Jews: Late Middle Ages and Era of European Expansion (1200-1650) Poland-Lithuania 1500-1650, Vol 16. Salo W. Baron. 400p. 1976. 27.00x (ISBN 0-231-08853-1). Columbia U Pr.

Social & Religious Plays of Strindberg. John Ward. 1980. text ed. 32.25x (ISBN 0-485-11183-7, Athlone Pr). Humanities.

Social & Sexual Roles of Hima Women: A Study of Nomadic Cattle Breeders in Nyabushozi County, Ankole. Yizchak Elam. (Illus.). 215p. 1973. text ed. 13.50x (ISBN 0-7190-0534-5). Humanities.

Social & Technological Management in Dry Lands: Past & Present, Indigenous & Imposed. Ed. by Nancie L. Gonzalez. LC 77-93023. (AAAS Selected Symposium Ser.: No. 10). (Illus.). 1978. lib. bdg. 18.75x (ISBN 0-89158-438-2). Westview.

Social Animal. 3rd ed. Elliot Aronson. LC 79-27721. (Psychology Ser.). (Illus.). 1980. text ed. 15.95x (ISBN 0-7167-1229-6); pap. text ed. 7.95x (ISBN 0-7167-1230-X); test & study questions avail. W H Freeman.

Social Anthropology of Radcliffe-Brown. Kuper. 1977. 22.00x (ISBN 0-7100-8556-7); pap. 10.00 (ISBN 0-7100-8557-5). Routledge & Kegan.

Social Appraisal of Projects: A Text in Cost-Benefit Analysis. David Pearce & Christopher Nash. 400p. 1981. 22.95 (ISBN 0-470-27137-X). Halsted Pr.

Social Approaches to Mental Patient Care. Morris S. Schwartz. LC 64-13736. 1964. 20.00x (ISBN 0-231-02698-6). Columbia U Pr.

Social Aspects of Early Christianity. Abraham J. Malherbe. LC 77-3876. 1977. 7.95x (ISBN 0-8071-0261-X). La State U Pr.

Social Aspects of Fertility. R. H. Chowdhury. 200p. 1980. text ed. 22.50x (ISBN 0-7069-1211-X, Pub by Vikas India). Advent Bk.

Social Aspects of Interaction & Transportation. Frederick P. Stutz. Ed. by Salvatore J. Natoli. LC 76-19932. (Resource Papers for College Geography Ser.). 1976. pap. text ed. 4.00 (ISBN 0-89291-117-4). Assn Am Geographers.

Social Aspects of Mental Retardation. Richard A. Kurtz. LC 76-42693. 1977. 18.95 (ISBN 0-669-01054-5). Lexington Bks.

Social Aspects of Sport. Eldon E. Snyder & Elmer Spreitzer. LC 77-26318. (P-H Ser. in Sociology). (Illus.). 1978. pap. 10.95 (ISBN 0-13-815399-X). P-H.

Social Assessment Manual: A Guide to the Preparation of the Social Well-Being Account for Planning Water Resource Projects. S. J. Fitzsimmons et al. LC 76-58332. 1977. lib. bdg. 21.00x (ISBN 0-89158-228-2). Westview.

Social Atlas of London. J. W. Shepherd et al. (Illus.). 100p. 1975. 29.95x (ISBN 0-19-874026-3). Oxford U Pr.

Social Attitudes & Psychophysical Measurement. Ed. by Bernd Wegener. 432p. 1981. professional reference text 24.95 (ISBN 0-89859-083-3). L Erlbaum Assocs.

Social Audit Consumer Handbook: A Guide to the Social Responsibilities of Business to the Consumer. Charles Medawar. (Illus.). 1978. text ed. 23.00x (ISBN 0-333-21665-2); pap. text ed. 10.25x (ISBN 0-333-21666-0). Humanities.

Social Audit Pollution Handbook: How to Assess Environmental & Workplace Pollution. Maurice Frankel. 1978. text ed. 26.00x (ISBN 0-333-21646-6); pap. text ed. 10.00x (ISBN 0-333-21647-4). Humanities.

Social Auditing: Evaluating the Impact of Corporate Programs. David H. Blake et al. LC 76-2901. (Illus.). 1976. text ed. 18.95 o.p. (ISBN 0-275-56700-1); pap. text ed. 9.95 o.p. (ISBN 0-275-85710-7). Praeger.

Social Awareness, Hygiene, & Sex Education for the Mentally Retarded-Developmentally Disabled. Issam B. Amary. (Illus.). 208p. 1980. text ed. 15.50 (ISBN 0-398-04096-6). C C Thomas.

Social Basic for Prewar Japanese Militarism: The Army & the Rural Community. Richard J. Smethurst. (Center for Japanese & Korean Studies). 1974. 24.95x (ISBN 0-520-02552-0). U of Cal Pr.

Social Basis of Religion. Simon Patten. (Neglected American Economists Ser.). 1974. lib. bdg. 50.00 (ISBN 0-8240-1028-0). Garland Pub.

Social Behavior: Fact & Falsehood. Bem P. Allen. LC 77-28709. 1978. 15.95 (ISBN 0-88229-393-1); pap. 7.95 (ISBN 0-88229-611-6). Nelson-Hall.

Social Behavior of Animals. S. J. Dimond. 1970. 32.00 (ISBN 0-7134-0957-6, Pub. by Batsford England). David & Charles.

Social Behavior of Monkeys. Thelma Rowell. (Education Ser.). 1973. pap. 2.95 o.p. (ISBN 0-14-080706-3). Penguin.

Social Behaviorism. Arthur W. Staats. 1975. text ed. 18.95x (ISBN 0-256-01537-6). Dorsey.

Social Behaviour in Vertebrates. Anthony Payne. (Scholarship Series in Biology). 1976. text ed. 12.95x (ISBN 0-435-61670-6). Heinemann Ed.

Social Being: A Theory for Social Psychology. Rom Harre. 438p. 1980. 25.00x (ISBN 0-8476-6284-5). Rowman.

Social Care Research. Jack Barnes. 163p. 1978. pap. text ed. 8.75x (ISBN 0-7199-0947-3, Pub. by Bedford England). Renouf.

Social Casework: A Behavioral Approach. new ed. Arthur Schwartz et al. LC 75-2298. 336p. 1975. 15.00x (ISBN 0-231-03778-3). Columbia U Pr.

Social Casework & Administration. Anthony Forder. 1969. 6.95 (ISBN 0-571-04641-X, Pub. by Faber & Faber). Merrimack Bk Serv.

Social Casework: Theories in Action. Herbert S. Strean. LC 76-160282. 1971. 12.00 (ISBN 0-8108-0408-5). Scarecrow.

Social Change. A. D. Smith. LC 75-42477. (Aspects of Modern Sociology, Social Processes Ser.). 1977. text ed. 9.50x o.p. (ISBN 0-582-48010-8). Longman.

Social Change & History: Aspects of the Western Theory of Development. Robert A. Nisbet. LC 69-17772. 1970. pap. 5.95 (ISBN 0-19-500805-7, 313, GB). Oxford U Pr.

Social Change & Personality in a Puerto Rican Agrarian Reform Community. Eduardo Seda. LC 72-76262. 216p. 1973. text ed. 10.95x o.s.i. (ISBN 0-8101-0394-X). Northwestern U Pr.

Social Change & Political Development in Weimar Germany. Ed. by Richard Bessel & E. J. Feuchtwanger. 297p. 1981. 27.00x (ISBN 0-389-20176-6). B&N.

Social Change & Prejudice. Bruno Bettelheim & M. B. Janowitz. LC 64-11214. 1964. 15.95 (ISBN 0-02-903480-9). Free Pr.

Social Change & Stratification in Postwar Czechoslovakia. Jaroslav Krejci. (Social & Political Processes in Eastern Europe Ser.). 1972. 20.00x (ISBN 0-231-03685-X). Columbia U Pr.

Social Change & the Aged: Recent Trends in the United States. Fred C. Pampel. LC 79-4752. (Illus.). 240p. 1981. 22.95 (ISBN 0-669-02928-9). Lexington Bks.

Social Change at Work: The ICI Weekly Staff Agreement. Joe Roeber. LC 75-11849. 1975. 34.95 (ISBN 0-470-73000-5). Halsted Pr.

Social Change at Work: The Imperial Chemical Industries Weekly Staff Agreement. Joe Roeber. 1975. 22.50x (ISBN 0-7156-0867-3). Intl Ideas.

Social Change: Explorations, Diagnosis, & Conjectures. G. K. Zollschan & W. Hirsch. LC 75-8736. 1976. text ed. 22.50 (ISBN 0-470-98408-2); pap. text ed. 10.50x (ISBN 0-470-98409-0). Halsted Pr.

Social Change in Europe. Ed. by B. W. Frisling. 146p. 1974. pap. text ed. 20.75x (ISBN 90-04-03778-0). Humanities.

Social Change in Indian Society. R. Sinha. 1980. 11.25 (ISBN 0-391-02184-2). Humanities.

Social Change in Modern India. M. N. Srinivas. (Rabindranath Tagore Memorial Lectures). (gr. 9-12). 1966. 17.507 (ISBN 0-520-01203-8); pap. 5.95x (ISBN 0-520-01421-9, CAMPUS21). U of Cal Pr.

Social Change in Rural Society. 2nd ed. Everett M. Rogers & Rabel J. Burdge. (Illus.). 1972. text ed. 17.95 (ISBN 0-13-815464-3). P-H.

Social Change in the Law of Trusts. George W. Keeton. LC 73-9374. 128p. 1974. Repr. of 1958 ed. lib. bdg. 12.50x (ISBN 0-8371-7011-7, KELT). Greenwood.

Social Change: Moderization & Post-Modernization. Eva Etzioni-Halevy. 280p. 1981. price not set (ISBN 0-7100-0767-1); pap. price not set (ISBN 0-7100-0768-X). Routledge & Kegan.

Social Changes During Depression & Recovery. Ed. by William F. Ogburn. LC 72-2381. (FDR & the Era of the New Deal Ser.). 117p. 1974. Repr. of 1935 ed. lib. bdg. 17.50 (ISBN 0-306-70483-8). Da Capo.

Social Class & Mental Illness: A Community Study. A. B. Hollingshead & F. C. Redlich. LC 58-6076. 1958. pap. 16.95 (ISBN 0-471-40685-6). Wiley.

Social Class & Social Change in Puerto Rico. Melvin M. Tumin & Arnold S. Feldman. LC 70-145756. 1971. 28.50x (ISBN 0-672-61375-1); pap. text ed. 14.95x (ISBN 0-89197-939-5). Irvington.

Social Class, Attitudes & Achievement: Two Subsidiary Studies from the Streaming Research Data. Joan C. Lunn. (Research Reports Ser.: No. 1). 35p. (Orig.). 1971. pap. text ed. 3.75x (ISBN 0-901225-92-4, NFER). Humanities.

Social Class Differences in Britain: A Sourcebook. Ivan Reid. (Illus.). 1977. text ed. 15.00x (ISBN 0-7291-0165-7); pap. text ed. 7.75x (ISBN 0-7291-0160-6). Humanities.

Social Class: The Nominal Group & Verbal Strategies. P. Hawkins. (Primary Socialization, Language & Education Ser.). 1977. 22.00x (ISBN 0-7100-8375-0). Routledge & Kegan.

Social Clubs for the Aging. Toni Merrill. (Illus.). 320p. 1973. 13.75 (ISBN 0-398-02644-0). C C Thomas.

Social Cognition: The Ontario Symposium, Vol. 1. Ed. by E. Tory Higgins et al. 512p. 1981. 30.00 (ISBN 0-89859-049-3). L Erlbaum Assocs.

Social Cognitive Development: Frontiers & Possible Futures. Ed. by John Flavell & Lee Ross. (Illus.). 336p. Date not set. price not set (ISBN 0-521-23687-8); pap. price not set (ISBN 0-521-28156-3). Cambridge U Pr.

Social Communication & Movement: Studies of Interaction & Expression in Man & Chimpanzee. Ed. by Mario Von Cranach & Ian Vine. (European Monographs in Social Psychology Ser.). 1974. 66.00 (ISBN 0-12-724750-5). Acad Pr.

Social Comparison Processes: Theoretical & Empirical Perspectives. Jerry Suls & Richard L. Miller. LC 77-8572. (Illus.). 1977. text ed. 23.50 (ISBN 0-470-99174-7). Halsted Pr.

Social Competence: Interventions for Children & Adults. Ed. by Diana P. Rathjen & John P. Foreyt. LC 80-118. (Pergamon General Psychology Ser.: No. 91). (Illus.). 300p. 1980. 26.50 (ISBN 0-08-025965-0). Pergamon.

Social Condition & Education of the People in England & Europe, 2 vols. Joseph Kay. (Development of Industrial Society Ser.). 1156p. 1980. Repr. 50.00x (ISBN 0-7165-1565-2, Pub. by Irish Academic Pr). Biblio Dist.

Social Condition of Humanity: An Introduction to Sociology. Irving M. Zeitlin. 432p. 1981. pap. text ed. 11.95x (ISBN 0-19-502734-5). Oxford U Pr.

Social Conflict & Social Movements. Anthony Oberschall. 1973. text ed. 17.95 (ISBN 0-13-815761-8). P-H.

Social Conflicts in the Roman Republic. P. A. Brunt. (Illus.). 1972. 6.00x (ISBN 0-393-04335-5); pap. 3.95 (ISBN 0-393-00586-0). Norton.

Social Context of Child Abuse & Neglect. Pelton. LC 80-13922. 1980. 24.95 (ISBN 0-87705-504-1). Human Sci Pr.

Social Context of Dentistry. Peter Davis. 189p. 1980. 27.50x (ISBN 0-7099-0152-6, Pub. by Croom Helm Ltd England). Biblio Dist.

Social Context of Health Care. Paul Brearley et al. (Aspects of Social Policy Ser.). 1978. 36.00x (ISBN 0-631-18110-5, Pub. by Basil Blackwell); pap. 14.00x (ISBN 0-631-18120-2). Biblio Dist.

Social Context of Learning & Development. Ed. by John C. Glidewell. LC 76-8867. 239p. 1976. 18.95 (ISBN 0-470-15078-5). Halsted Pr.

Social Context of Premarital Sexual Permissiveness. Ira L. Reiss. LC 67-22609. 1967. 22.50x (ISBN 0-03-064880-7). Irvington.

Social Context of Religiosity. Jerry D. Cardwell. LC 80-67216. 174p. 1980. lib. bdg. 17.50 (ISBN 0-8191-1135-X); pap. text ed. 8.75 (ISBN 0-8191-1136-8). U Pr of Amer.

Social Context of Soviet Science. Ed. by Linda L. Lubrano & Susan G. Solomon. (Special Studies on the Soviet Union & Eastern Europe). 1980. lib. bdg. 25.00x (ISBN 0-89158-450-1). Westview.

Social Context of the School. S. John Eggleston. (Student's Lib. of Ed.). 1967. text ed. 3.75x (ISBN 0-7100-4217-5); pap. text ed. 2.75x (ISBN 0-7100-4210-8). Humanities.

Social Contexts of Health, Illness, & Patient Care. Elliot G. Mishler. LC 80-22604. 256p. Date not set. price not set (ISBN 0-521-23559-6); pap. price not set (ISBN 0-521-28034-6). Cambridge U Pr.

Social Contexts of Research. Ed. by Saad Nagi & Ronald Corwin. LC 78-18770. 422p. 1979. Repr. of 1972 ed. lib. bdg. 19.50 o.p. (ISBN 0-88275-701-6). Krieger.

Social Contract. Jean-Jacques Rousseau. Incl. Discourses. 1976. pap. 3.25 (ISBN 0-460-01660-1, Evman). Dutton.

Social Contract. Jean-Jacques Rousseau. 227p. 1980. Repr. of 1893 ed. lib. bdg. 30.00 (ISBN 0-89987-716-8). Darby Bks.

Social Contract & Discourse on the Origin of Inequality. Jean-Jacques Rousseau. Ed. by Lester G. Crocker. (Orig.). 1971. pap. 2.95 (ISBN 0-671-47864-8). WSP.

Social Contract: Essays by Locke, Hume & Rousseau. Ed. by Ernest Barker. (YA) (gr. 9 up). 1962. pap. 4.95x (ISBN 0-19-500309-8, 68). Oxford U Pr.

Social Contract: Essays by Locke, Hume, & Rousseau. Ed. by Ernest Barker. LC 80-22006. xliv, 307p. 1980. Repr. of 1947 ed. lib. bdg. 27.50x (ISBN 0-313-22409-9, BACT). Greenwood.

Social Control. C. Ken Watkins. (Aspects of Modern Sociology Ser). 176p. 1975. pap. text ed. 8.95x (ISBN 0-582-48714-5). Longman.

Social Control & Deviance in Cuba. Luis Salas. LC 79-19597. (Praeger Special Studies). (Illus.). 416p. 1979. 32.95 (ISBN 0-03-052471-7). Praeger.

Social Control & Socialization: A Study of Class Differences in the Language of Maternal Control. Jenny Cook-Gumperz. (Primary Socialization, Language & Education Ser.). 300p. 1973. 22.50 (ISBN 0-7100-7409-3). Routledge & Kegan.

Social Control in Industrial Organisations. Peter Bowen. (Direct Edition Ser.). (Orig.). 1976. pap. 17.95x (ISBN 0-7100-8312-2). Routledge & Kegan.

Social Control in the Colonial Economy. J. R. Hughes. LC 75-17630. 1976. 13.95x (ISBN 0-8139-0623-7). U Pr of Va.

Social Control of Drugs. Philip Bean. LC 74-1342. 176p. 1974. 15.95 o.p. (ISBN 0-470-06090-5). Halsted Pr.

Social Control of Technology. David Collingridge. 1980. 22.50 (ISBN 0-312-73168-X). St Martin.

Social Cost-Benefit Analysis. Abdul Qayum. 250p. 1979. pap. 9.95 (ISBN 0-913244-16-3). Hapi Pr.

Social Costs & Benefits of Business. Thomas A. Klein. 1977. 12.95 (ISBN 0-13-815837-1); pap. 9.95 (ISBN 0-13-815829-0). P-H.

Social Costs of Solar Energy: A Study of Photovoltaic Energy Systems. Thomas L. Neff. LC 80-23732. (Pergamon Policy Studies on Science & Technology). (Illus.). 110p. Date not set. price not set (ISBN 0-08-026315-1). Pergamon.

Social Criticism of Stephen Leacock: The Unsolved Riddle of Social Justice & Other Essays. Stephen Leacock. LC 73-78960. (Social History of Canada Ser.). 1973. pap. 3.95 (ISBN 0-8020-6201-6). U of Toronto Pr.

Social Darwinism & English Thought: The Interaction Between Biololgical & Social Theory. Greta Jones. (Harvester Studies in Philosophy: No. 20). 1980. text ed. 30.00x (ISBN 0-391-01799-3). Humanities.

Social Darwinism in American Thought. rev. ed. Richard Hofstadter. LC 59-9543. 1959. 7.95 o.p. (ISBN 0-8076-0079-2). Braziller.

Social Democratic Image of Society: A Study of the Achievements & Origins of Scandinavian Social Democracy in Comparative Perspective. Francis G. Castles. 1978. 16.00x (ISBN 0-7100-8870-1). Routledge & Kegan.

Social Development & Personality. Ed. by George G. Thompson. LC 77-146673. (Readings in Educational Research Ser.). 1971. 25.00 (ISBN 0-471-86005-0); text ed. 22.50 ten or more copies (ISBN 0-685-52962-2). McCutchan.

Social Development: The Origins & Plasticity of Interchanges. Robert B. Cairns. LC 78-12199. (Psychology Ser.). (Illus.). 1979. text ed. 19.95x (ISBN 0-7167-0195-2). W H Freeman.

Social Deviance: A Substantive Analysis. rev. ed. Robert R. Bell. 1976. pap. text ed. 10.50 o.p. (ISBN 0-256-01663-1). Dorsey.

Social Deviance in Eastern Europe. Ed. by Ivan Volgyes. LC 78-58836. 1978. lib. bdg. 24.50x (ISBN 0-89158-068-9). Westview.

Social Differentiation of English in Norwich. P. Trudgill. LC 73-77178. (Studies in Linguistics). 208p. 1974. 32.50 (ISBN 0-521-20264-7); pap. text ed. 14.95 (ISBN 0-521-29745-1). Cambridge U Pr.

Social Dimension of Family Treatment. Danuta Mostwin. LC 79-92201. (Illus.). 264p. 1980. pap. 12.50x (ISBN 0-87101-083-6, CBF-083-C). Natl Assn Soc Wkrs.

Social Dimensions of Law & Justice. Julius Stone. LC 73-168258. 1971. Repr. lib. bdg. 50.00x (ISBN 0-912004-08-8). W W Gaunt.

Social Disability: Alcoholism, Drug Addiction, Crime, & Social Disadvantage. Ed. by David Malikin. LC 72-96468. 256p. 1973. 12.00x (ISBN 0-8147-5361-2). NYU Pr.

Social Economics. W. Hagenbuch. (Cambridge Economic Handbook Ser). 1958. 10.95x (ISBN 0-521-08757-0). Cambridge U Pr.

Social Economy of Cities. Ed. by Gary Gappert & Harold M. Rose. LC 73-88911. (Urban Affairs Annual Reviews: Vol. 9). 1975. 25.00x (ISBN 0-8039-0326-X). Sage.

Social Economy: People Transforming Modern Business. S. T. Bruyn. 392p. 1977. 29.95 (ISBN 0-471-01985-2). Wiley.

Social Economy: People Transforming Modern Business. Severyn T. Bruyn. LC 77-14597. 1977. 29.95 (ISBN 0-471-01985-2). Ronald Pr.

Social Effects of Inflation. Ed. by Marvin E. Wolfgang & Richard D. Lambert. (Annals of the American Academy of Political & Social Science: No. 456). 250p. 1981. 7.50 (ISBN 0-87761-264-1); pap. 6.00 (ISBN 0-87761-265-X). Am Acad Pol Soc Sci.

Social Efficiency: A Concise Introduction to Welfare Economics. Peter Bohm. LC 73-9379. 150p. 1975. pap. 11.95 (ISBN 0-470-08636-X). Halsted Pr.

Social Ends & Political Means. Ed. by Ted Honderich. 1976. 20.00x (ISBN 0-7100-8370-X). Routledge & Kegan.

Social England Under the Regency. John Ashton. LC 67-23940. 1968. Repr. of 1899 ed. 15.00 (ISBN 0-8103-3253-1). Gale.

Social Environment & Health. Stewart Wolf. LC 80-50868. (Jessie & John Danz Lecture Ser.). (Illus.). 112p. 1981. 8.95 (ISBN 0-295-95777-8). U of Wash Pr.

Social Environment of the Schools. Maynard C. Reynolds. LC 80-65498. 104p. (Orig.). 1980. pap. 6.75 (ISBN 0-86586-103-X). Coun Exc Child.

Social Ethics Among Southern Baptists, 1917-1969. George D. Kelsey. (Atla Monograph: No. 2). 1973. 10.00 (ISBN 0-8108-0538-3). Scarecrow.

Social Evil, with Special Reference to Conditions Existing in the City of New York. E. R. Segilman. Ed. by Charles Winick. LC 78-60871. (Prostitution Ser.: Vol. 3). 188p. 1979. lib. bdg. 20.00 (ISBN 0-8240-9725-4). Garland Pub.

Social Evolution of Indonesia: The Asiatic Mode of Production & Its Legacy. Fritjov Tichelman. (Studies in Social History: No. 5). 314p. 1980. lib. bdg. 44.75 (ISBN 90-247-2389-2, Pub. by Martinus Nijhoff). Kluwer Boston.

Social Exchange: Advances in Theory & Research. Ed. by Kenneth J. Gergen et al. 320p. 1980. 24.50 (ISBN 0-306-40395-1, Plenum Pr). Plenum Pub.

Social Expectations & Perception: The Case of the Slavic Anthracite Workers. Michael A. Barendse. LC 80-8610. (Penn State Studies: No. 47). (Illus.). 90p. (Orig.). 1981. pap. text ed. 3.50x (ISBN 0-271-00277-8). Pa St U Pr.

Social Experiment in Program Administration: The Housing Allowance Administrative Agency Experiment. William L. Hamilton. LC 79-87501. 1979. text ed. 30.00 (ISBN 0-89011-533-8). Abt Assoc.

Social Fabric: Volume 1. 3rd ed. Cary & Weinberg. (Orig.). 1980. pap. 8.95 (ISBN 0-316-13078-8). Little.

Social Fabric: Volume 2. 3rd ed. Cary & Weinberg. 1980. pap. text ed. 8.95 (ISBN 0-316-13074-5). Little.

Social Forces in Later Life. 3rd ed. Robert C. Atchley. 480p. 1980. text ed. 16.95x (ISBN 0-534-00828-3). Wadsworth Pub.

Social Forces in Later Life: An Introduction to Social Gerontology. 2nd ed. Robert C. Atchley. 1977. 15.95x o.p. (ISBN 0-534-00463-6). Wadsworth Pub.

Social Foundations of Education. Ed. by Dorothy Westby-Gibson. LC 67-15060. 1967. pap. text ed. 3.50 o.s.i. (ISBN 0-02-935200-2). Free Pr.

Social Foundations of Education: A Book of Readings. Cole S. Brembeck. LC 77-76051. text ed. 10.95x o.p. (ISBN 0-471-10191-5). Wiley.

Social Foundations of Education: Environmental Influences in Teaching & Learning. 2nd ed. Cole S. Brembeck. LC 79-135886. 1971. text ed. 19.95x o.p. (ISBN 0-471-10185-0). Wiley.

Social Foundations of Educational Guidance. Carl Weinberg. LC 68-24440. 1969. text ed. 12.95 (ISBN 0-02-934970-2). Free Pr.

Social Foundations of Wage Policy. Barbara Wootton. 1962. pap. text ed. 9.50x o.p. (ISBN 0-04-331034-6). Allen Unwin.

Social Function of Social Science. Duncan MacRae, Jr. LC 75-32282. (Illus.). 376p. 1976. 25.00x (ISBN 0-300-01921-1). Yale U Pr.

Social Function of Social Science. Duncan MacRae, Jr. LC 75-32282. 376p. 1981. pap. 7.95 (ISBN 0-300-02670-6). Yale U Pr.

Social Gamble. Richard J. Tobin. LC 78-19229. 1979. 18.95 (ISBN 0-669-02468-6). Lexington Bks.

Social Geography of Great Britain: An Introduction. Hugh D. Clout & Richard J. Dennis. (Pergamon Oxford Geographies). Date not set. 33.75 (ISBN 0-08-021802-4); pap. 14.50 (ISBN 0-08-021801-6). Pergamon.

Social Geography of the United States. Wreford J. Watson. (Illus.). 1979. 26.00 (ISBN 0-582-48196-1); pap. text ed. 11.95 (ISBN 0-582-48197-X). Longman.

Social Gerontology: An Introduction to the Dynamics of Aging. David L. Decker. 304p. 1980. text ed. 14.95 (ISBN 0-316-17918-3); test bank free (ISBN 0-316-17919-1). Little.

Social Gospel in America: Gladden, Ely, & Rauschenbusch. Ed. by Robert T. Handy. 1966. 14.95 o.p. (ISBN 0-19-501174-0). Oxford U Pr.

Social Grading of Occupations: A New Approach & Scale. John H. Goldthorpe & Keith Hope. (Oxford Studies in Social Mobility). (Illus.). 196p. 1974. pap. 17.95x (ISBN 0-19-827220-0). Oxford U Pr.

Social Groups in Polish Society. David Lane & George Kolankiewicz. (Political Social Processes in Eastern Europe Ser.). 250p. 1973. 22.50x (ISBN 0-231-03729-5). Columbia U Pr.

Social History & Social Policy. Ed. by David Rothman & Stanton Wheeler. LC 80-1772. (Studies in Social Discontinuity). 1981. price not set (ISBN 0-12-598680-7). Acad Pr.

Social History of American Agriculture. Joseph Schafer. LC 70-99471. (American Scene Ser). 1970. Repr. of 1936 ed. lib. bdg. 32.50 (ISBN 0-306-71857-X). Da Capo.

Social History of American Family Sociology, 1865-1940. Ronald L. Howard. Ed. by John H. Mogey & Louis Th. Van Leeuwen. LC 80-1790. (Contributions in Family Studies Ser.: No. 4). 168p. 1981. lib. bdg. 22.50 (ISBN 0-313-22767-5, MOA/). Greenwood.

Social History of American Family Sociology, 1865-1940. Ronald L. Howard et al. Ed. by John H. Mogey & Louis T. Van Leeuwen. LC 80-1790. (Contributions in Family Studies: No. 4). 168p. 1981. lib. bdg. 22.50 (ISBN 0-313-22767-5, MOA/). Greenwood.

Social History of an Indian Caste: The Kayasths of Hyderabad. Karen I. Leonard. LC 76-52031. (Center for South & Southeast Asian Studies). 1978. 19.50x (ISBN 0-520-03431-7). U of Cal Pr.

Social History of Archaeology. K. Hudson. 1980. text ed. 37.50x (ISBN 0-333-25679-4). Humanities.

Social History of Britain in Postcards, 1870 to 1930. Eric J. Evans & Jeffrey Richards. 151p. (Orig.). 1981. 23.00 (ISBN 0-582-50292-6). Longman.

Social History of Housing. John Burnett. LC 77-91461. (Illus.). 1978. 38.00 (ISBN 0-7153-7524-5). David & Charles.

Social History of Medicine. Frederick F. Cartwright. LC 76-41898. (Themes in British Social History Ser.). 1977. pap. text ed. 10.95x (ISBN 0-582-48394-8). Longman.

Social History of the Diocese of Newcastle. W. S. F. Pickering. (Illus.). 1981. 35.00 (ISBN 0-85362-189-6, Oriel). Routledge & Kegan.

Social History of the United States: A Guide to Information Sources. Ed. by Donald F. Tingley. LC 78-13196. (American Government & History Information Guide Ser: Vol. 3). 1979. 30.00 (ISBN 0-8103-1366-9). Gale.

Social Impact of Land Development: An Initial Approach for Estimating Impacts on Neighborhood Usages & Perceptions. Kathleen Christensen. (Land Development Impact Ser.). 144p. 1966. pap. 3.95 (ISBN 0-87766-171-5, 15700). Urban Inst.

Social Impact of Oil in Scotland. Ron Parsler & Dan Shapiro. 192p. 1980. text ed. 27.75x (ISBN 0-566-00375-9, Pub. by Gower Pub Co England). Renouf.

Social Impact of Revenue Sharing: Planning, Participation, & the Purchase of Service. Paul Terrell & Stan Weisner. LC 76-12882. (Illus.). 1976. 22.95 (ISBN 0-275-23470-3). Praeger.

Social Implications of Spina Bifida. Margaret Woodburn. (General Ser.). (Illus.). 285p. 1975. pap. text ed. 23.50x (ISBN 0-85633-061-2, NFER). Humanities.

Social Indicators & Social Theory: Elements of an Operational System. Karl A. Fox. LC 74-16255. (Urban Research Ser). 328p. 1974. 23.95 (ISBN 0-471-27060-1, Pub. by Wiley-Interscience). Wiley.

Social Indicators in Community Research: Proceedings. Committee of Community Social Researchers, 1976. 1976. 2.00 (ISBN 0-86671-034-5). Comm Coun Great NY.

Social Inequality. Louis Kriesberg. (P-H Ser. in Sociology). (Illus.). 1979. ref. ed. 17.95 (ISBN 0-13-815860-6). P-H.

Social Inequality: Classes & Caste in America. Lucile Duberman. LC 75-40327. 314p. 1976. pap. text ed. 9.50 scp (ISBN 0-397-47345-1, HarpC). Har-Row.

Social Inequality: Comparative & Developmental Approaches. Gerald D. Berreman. (Studies in Anthroplogy). 1981. price not set (ISBN 0-12-093160-5). Acad Pr.

Social Inequality, Stratification, & Mobility. Judah Matras. LC 74-18070. (Illus.). 448p. 1975. text ed. 18.95 (ISBN 0-13-815803-7). P-H.

Social Influences on Behavior: Student Booklet. American Psychological Association. (Human Behavior Curriculum Project Ser.). 64p. (Orig.). (gr. 9-12). 1981. pap. text ed. 3.95x (ISBN 0-8077-2619-2). Tchrs Coll.

Social Influences on Behavior: Teachers Handbook. Ameican Psychological Association. (Human Behavior Curriculum Project Ser.). 48p. (Orig.). (gr. 9-12). 1981. pap. 9.95 (ISBN 0-8077-2620-6). Tchrs Coll.

Social Information Processing & Statistical Systems: Change & Reform. Edgar S. Dunn, Jr. LC 74-5289. 246p. 1974. 22.95 (ISBN 0-471-22747-1, Pub. by Wiley-Interscience). Wiley.

Social Inquiry: Instructional Manual to Accompany Mark. Matthew Lipman & Ann M. Sharp. 396p. 1980. tchr's. ed. 30.00 (ISBN 0-916834-15-8). Inst Adv Philo.

Social Insects, Vol. 2. Henry R. Hermann. 1981. write for info. (ISBN 0-12-342202-7). Acad Pr.

Social Integration of the Aged. I. Rosow. LC 67-15059. 1967. 17.95 (ISBN 0-02-927350-1). Free Pr.

Social Interaction. Thomas Kando. LC 76-26614. (Illus.). 1977. pap. text ed. 10.50 (ISBN 0-8016-2614-5). Mosby.

Social Interaction Analysis: Methodological Issues. Ed. by Michael E. Lamb et al. LC 78-53287. 1979. 21.50 (ISBN 0-299-07590-7). U of Wis Pr.

Social Interpretation of the French Revolution. Alfred B. Cobban. LC 64-21535. 1968. 24.95 (ISBN 0-521-04679-3); pap. 7.50xx (ISBN 0-521-09548-4). Cambridge U Pr.

Social Intervention. H. A. Hornstein et al. LC 77-143509. 1971. text ed. 17.95 (ISBN 0-02-914960-6). Free Pr.

Social Issues & Education in the America Urban & Suburban Society: A Textbook for Teacher Education. Kent L. Pillsbury et al. LC 76-6887. 260p. 1977. 16.95 (ISBN 0-88229-154-8). Nelson-Hall.

Social Issues & Problems: The Contradictions of Capitalism. Joan Smith. (Sociology Ser.). 416p. 1981. pap. text ed. 11.95 (ISBN 0-87626-813-0). Winthrop.
Social Issues in Computing. C. C. Gotlieb & A. Borodin. (Computer Science & Applied Mathematics Ser.). 1973. 17.95 (ISBN 0-12-293750-3). Acad Pr.
Social Issues Through Inquiry: Coping in an Age of Crisis. Byron Massialas et al. (Illus.). 288p. 1975. pap. text ed. 10.95 (ISBN 0-13-815852-5). P-H.
Social Judgment: Assimilation & Contrast Effects in Communication & Attitude Change. Muzafer Sherif & Carl I. Hovland. LC 80-21767. (Yale Studies in Attitude & Communication: Vol. 4). xii, 218p. 1981. Repr. of 1961 ed. lib. bdg. 25.00x (ISBN 0-313-22438-2, SHSO). Greenwood.
Social Justice & Preferential Treatment: Women & Racial Minorities in Education & Business. Ed. by William T. Blackstone & Robert D. Heslep. LC 76-28921. 216p. 1977. pap. 5.95x (ISBN 0-8203-0434-4). U of Ga Pr.
Social Justice in the Law of Nations: The ILO Impact After Fifty Years. Wilfred C. Jenks. (Royal Institute of International Affairs Ser.). 1970. pap. 2.50x o.p. (ISBN 0-19-285044-X). Oxford U Pr.
Social Learning & Change: A Cognitive Approach to Human Services. Howard Goldstein. LC 80-23446. 1981. 19.50 (ISBN 0-87249-402-0). U of SC Pr.
Social Learning Approach to Family Intervention: Coercive Family Process, Vol. 3. Gerald R. Patterson. 1981. pap. write for info. Castalia Pub.
Social Learning Approach to Family Intervention, Vol. 1: Families with Aggressive Children. G. R. Patterson et al. LC 75-27000. 179p. 1975. pap. 10.95 (ISBN 0-916154-00-9). Castalia Pub.
Social Learning Theory. A. Bandura. 1977. text ed. 15.95 (ISBN 0-13-816751-6); pap. text ed. 9.95 (ISBN 0-13-816744-3). P-H.
Social Life in Early England: Historical Association Essays. Historical Association, London. Ed. by Geoffrey Barraclough. LC 79-16998. (Illus.). xi, 264p. 1980. Repr. of 1960 ed. lib. bdg. 34.50x (ISBN 0-313-21298-8, HASL). Greenwood.
Social Life in Old New England. Mary C. Crawford. LC 71-102645. (Tower Bks). (Illus.). 1971. Repr. of 1914 ed. 30.00 (ISBN 0-8103-3924-2). Gale.
Social Life in the Reign of Queen Anne: Taken from Original Sources. John Ashton. LC 67-23939. (Illus.). 474p. 1968. Repr. of 1883 ed. 18.00 (ISBN 0-8103-3254-X). Gale.
Social Life of Language. Gillian Sankoff. LC 79-5048. (Conduct & Communication Ser.). 352p. 1980. 35.00x (ISBN 0-8122-7771-6); pap. 12.00x. U of Pa Pr.
Social Life of Monkeys & Apes. 2nd ed. Zuckerman. (Illus.). 496p. 1980. 55.00 (ISBN 0-7100-0691-8). Routledge & Kegan.
Social Life Under the Abbasids. M. M. Ahsan. (Illus.). 1979. text ed. 33.00 (ISBN 0-582-78079-9). Longman.
Social Markers in Speech. Ed. by Klaus R. Scherer & Howard Giles. LC 79-4080. (Illus.). 1980. 49.50 (ISBN 0-521-22321-0); pap. 12.95 (ISBN 0-521-29590-4). Cambridge U Pr.
Social Marketing: Perspectives & Viewpoints. William Lazer & Eugene J. Kelley. 1973. pap. text ed. 12.50x (ISBN 0-256-00284-3). Irwin.
Social Meaning of Human Sexuality. 2nd ed. John Petras. 1978. pap. text ed. 8.35 (ISBN 0-205-06013-7, 8160139). Allyn.
Social Milieu of Alexander Pope: Lives, Examples, & the Poetic Response. Howard Erskine-Hill. LC 74-29719. 352p. 1975. 27.50x (ISBN 0-300-01837-1). Yale U Pr.
Social Mobility in Comparative Perspective. Ed. by Wlodzimierz Wesolowski et al. Tr. by Mach Bogdan W. LC 79-313623. (Illus.). 319p. 1978. 27.50x (ISBN 0-8002-2284-9). Intl Pubns Serv.
Social Models of Teaching: Expanding' Your Teaching Repetoire. Marsha Weil & Bruce Joyce. LC 77-5448. (Illus.). 1978. 14.95 (ISBN 0-13-815944-0); pap. 10.95 (ISBN 0-13-815936-X). P-H.
Social Movements: An Introduction to Political Sociology. Rudolf Heberle. (Century Sociology Ser.). (Illus.). 1951. 24.00x o.p. (ISBN 0-89197-414-8); pap. text ed. 4.95x (ISBN 0-89197-415-6). Irvington.
Social Movements: Between the Balcony & the Barricade. 2nd ed. Ron E. Roberts & Robert M. Kloss. LC 73-12577. (Illus.). 1979. pap. 13.95 (ISBN 0-8016-4135-7). Mosby.
Social Networks in Urban Situations: Analyses of Personal Relationships in Central African Towns. Ed. by J. Clyde Mitchell. (Illus.). 378p. 1969. pap. text ed. 17.50x (ISBN 0-7190-1035-7). Humanities.
Social Novel in England 1830-1850: Dickens, Disraeli, Mrs. Gaskell, Kingsley. Louis Cazamian. Ed. & tr. by Martin Fido. 1973. 22.00 (ISBN 0-7100-7282-1). Routledge & Kegan.
Social Orchestra: A Collection of Popular Melodies Arranged As Duets, Trios, & Quartets. Stephen Foster. Ed. by H. Wiley Hitchcock. LC 79-169645. (Earlier American Music Ser: Vol. 13). (Illus.). 96p. 1973. Repr. of 1854 ed. lib. bdg. 18.50 (ISBN 0-306-77313-9). Da Capo.
Social Organisation of Health Visitor Training. Robert Dingwall. 1977. 30.00x (ISBN 0-85664-487-0, Pub. by Croom Helm Ltd England). Biblio Dist.
Social Organization of Gay Males. Joseph Harry & William B. Devall. LC 78-8381. (Praeger Special Studies). 1978. 25.95 (ISBN 0-03-044696-1). Praeger.
Social Organization of Strikes. Eric Batstone et al. (Warwick Studies in Industrial Relations). 1978. 14.50x (ISBN 0-631-18320-5, Pub. by Basil Blackwell England). Biblio Dist.
Social Organization of the Northern Tungus. S. M. Shirokogoroff. LC 78-66515. (Classics of Anthropology Ser.: Vol. 28). (Illus.). 1979. lib. bdg. 63.00 (ISBN 0-8240-9620-7). Garland Pub.
Social Origins of Christianity. Shirley J. Case. LC 74-84544. 263p. 1975. Repr. of 1923 ed. lib. bdg. 25.00x (ISBN 0-8154-0501-4). Cooper Sq.
Social Origins of Educational Systems. Margaret S. Archer. LC 77-84072. (Illus.). 815p. 1979. 40.00 (ISBN 0-8039-9876-7). Sage.
Social Passion: Religion & Social Reform in Canada, 1914-28. Richard Allen. LC 71-151352. (Illus.). 1971. pap. 8.50 (ISBN 0-8020-6199-0). U of Toronto Pr.
Social Patterns in Australian Literature. T. Inglis Moore. LC 71-133027. 1971. 22.50x (ISBN 0-520-01828-1). U of Cal Pr.
Social Perspectives on Behavior. Ed. by Herman D. Stein & R. A. Cloward. LC 57-12960. 1958. text ed. 12.25 o.s.i. (ISBN 0-02-930830-5). Free Pr.
Social Philosophy. Joel Feinberg. 1973. pap. 7.95 ref. ed. (ISBN 0-13-817254-4). P-H.
Social Planning & Social Change. Robert R. Mayer. LC 75-151511. (Foundations of Social Welfare Ser.). 172p. 1972. 8.95 o.p. (ISBN 0-13-817270-6). P-H.
Social Planning at the Community Level. Armand Lauffer. (P-H Ser. in Social Work Practice). (Illus.). 1978. 15.95 (ISBN 0-13-817189-0). P-H.
Social Planning for Canada. League for Social Reconstruction. LC 72-94917. (Social History of Canada Ser.). 1975. pap. 7.50 (ISBN 0-8020-6178-8). U of Toronto Pr.
Social Poetry of the '30s: An Anthology. Ed. by Jack Salzman & Leo Zanderer. 1978. lib. bdg. 17.85 (ISBN 0-89102-046-2); pap. 5.95 o. p. (ISBN 0-686-68047-2). B Franklin.
Social Policies & Programs on Aging. Louis Lowy. LC 78-55355. 1980. 21.95x (ISBN 0-669-02342-6). Lexington Bks.
Social Policy: A Survey of Recent Developments. Ed. by Michael H. Cooper. (Aspects of Social Policy Series). 1973. 30.50x (ISBN 0-631-15300-4, Pub. by Basil Blackwell); pap. 10.00x (ISBN 0-631-16230-5). Biblio Dist.
Social Policy & It's Administration. J Monie & A. Wise. 1977. 48.00 (ISBN 0-08-021943-8). Pergamon.
Social Policy & Social Services. Alfred J. Kahn. 1973. pap. text ed. 4.50 o.p. (ISBN 0-394-31388-7). Random.
Social Policy & Social Welfare: Structure & Applications. Thomas M. Meenaghan & Robert O. Washington. LC 79-54669. (Illus.). 1980. text ed. 12.95 (ISBN 0-02-920750-9). Free Pr.
Social Policy & Sociology. Ed. by N. J. Demerath et al. (Studies in Quantitative Relations Ser.). 1975. 30.50 (ISBN 0-12-209450-6). Acad Pr.
Social Policy & the Welfare State in New Zealand. Brian Easton. 200p. 1980. text ed. 21.00x (ISBN 0-86861-393-2, 2390); pap. text ed. 11.50x (ISBN 0-86861-002-X, 2391). Allen Unwin.
Social Policy & the Young Delinquent. Peter Boss. (Library of Social Policy & Administration). (Orig.). 1967. text ed. 5.25x (ISBN 0-7100-4030-X); pap. text ed. 2.75x (ISBN 0-7100-4029-6). Humanities.
Social Policy Harmonisation in the European Communities. John Holloway. 1980. text ed. 27.00x (ISBN 0-566-00196-9, Pub. by Gower Pub Co England). Renouf.
Social Policy in Action. Joan L. Eyden. (Library of Social Policy & Administration). 1969. text ed. 5.50x (ISBN 0-7100-6402-0); pap. text ed. 3.25x (ISBN 0-7100-6404-7). Humanities.
Social Policy in Action: Perspectives on the Implementation of Alcoholism Reforms. Marilyn C. Regier. LC 78-20274. 1979. 19.95 (ISBN 0-669-02716-2). Lexington Bks.
Social Policy in Developing Countries. Arthur Livingstone. (Library of Social Policy & Administration). 1969. pap. text ed. 2.50x (ISBN 0-7100-6443-8). Humanities.
Social Policy in the Irish Republic. Ed. by Peter Kaim-Caudle. 1967. text ed. 3.75x (ISBN 0-7100-4023-7). Humanities.
Social Policy of Nazi Germany. C. W. Guillebaud. LC 71-80553. 1971. Repr. 13.00 (ISBN 0-86527-183-6). Fertig.
Social Policy of the European Economic Community. Doreen Collins. LC 75-22282. 286p. 1975. 27.95 (ISBN 0-470-16583-9). Halsted Pr.
Social Policy Research. Martin Bulmer. 373p. 1978. text ed. 31.25x (ISBN 0-333-23142-2); pap. text ed. 13.00x (ISBN 0-333-23143-0). Humanities.
Social Policy: What Is It & How Is It Formed? Cathryn Long & Rudie Tretten. (Crucial Issues in American Government). (gr. 9-12). 1978. pap. text ed. 4.96 (ISBN 0-205-05518-4, 7655185). Allyn.
Social Policy 1830-1914: Individualism, Collectivism & the Origins of the Welfare State. Ed. by Eric J. Evans. (Birth of Modern Britain Ser). 1978. 23.00x (ISBN 0-7100-8613-X); pap. 10.00 (ISBN 0-7100-8626-1). Routledge & Kegan.
Social Portrait in a Rural Society. Andrew Charlesworth. (Historical Geography Research Ser.). 1980. pap. 3.50x (ISBN 0-686-27387-7, Pub. by GEO Abstracts England). State Mutual Bk.
Social Power & Political Freedom. Gene Sharp. LC 80-81479. (Extending Horizons Bks). 456p. 1980. 15.95 (ISBN 0-87558-091-2); pap. 8.95 (ISBN 0-87558-093-9). Porter Sargent.
Social Principles & the Democratic State. S. I. Benn & R. S. Peters. 1959. pap. text ed. 15.95x (ISBN 0-04-300028-2). Allen Unwin.
Social Problems. F. James Davis. LC 76-111934. 1970. text ed. 11.95 (ISBN 0-02-906980-7). Free Pr.
Social Problems. Eitzen. 1980. text ed. 17.95 (ISBN 0-205-06816-2, 8168164); instr's manual o.p. avail. Allyn.
Social Problems. 3rd ed. Joseph Julian. (P-H Ser. in Sociology). (Illus.). 1980. text ed. 17.95 (ISBN 0-13-816777-X); wkbk & study guide 5.95 (ISBN 0-13-816801-6). P-H.
Social Problems. Dennis E. Poplin. 1978. 14.95x (ISBN 0-673-07973-2). Scott F.
Social Problems, 3 pts. Incl. Pt. 1. Drunkenness, 4 vols. Set. 306.00x (ISBN 0-686-01174-0); Pt. 2. Gambling, 2 vols. Set. 117.00x (ISBN 0-686-01175-9); Pt. 3. Sunday Observance, 3 vols. Set. 207.00x (ISBN 0-686-01176-7). (British Parliamentary Papers Ser.). 1971 (Pub. by Irish Academic Pr Ireland). Biblio Dist.
Social Problems & Criminal Justice. Emilio Viano & Alvin W. Cohn. LC 73-92238. (Nelson-Hall Law Enforcement Ser.). 288p. 1975. 18.95 (ISBN 0-88229-115-7). Nelson-Hall.
Social Problems As Human Concerns. John J. Grant & Wayne Pirtle. LC 75-38062. (Illus.). 400p. 1976. text ed. 13.95x (ISBN 0-87835-051-9). Boyd & Fraser.
Social Problems: Human Possibilities. Ron E. Roberts. LC 78-163. (Illus.). 1978. pap. text ed. 12.95 (ISBN 0-8016-4143-8). Mosby.
Social Problems in a Changing Society: Issues & Deviances. Stephen Schafer et al. 272p. 1975. pap. 10.50 o.p. (ISBN 0-87909-771-X). Reston.
Social Problems in America. 2nd ed. Harry C. Bredemeier & Jackson Toby. LC 72-1137. (Illus.). 1972. pap. text ed. 11.50x o.p. (ISBN 0-471-10006-4). Wiley.
Social Problems in American Society. 3rd ed. James M. Henslin & Larry T. Reynolds. 1979. pap. text ed. 12.95 (ISBN 0-205-06575-9, 8165750). Allyn.
Social Problems in Cancer Control. Howard P. Greenwald. LC 79-15385. 304p. 1979. reference 24.50 (ISBN 0-88410-708-6). Ballinger Pub.
Social Problems in Modern Urban Society. 2nd ed. S. Kirson Weinberg. 1970. text ed. 17.95 (ISBN 0-13-817528-4). P-H.
Social Problems: Institutional & Interpersonal Perspectives. Kenneth Henry. 1978. pap. 8.95x (ISBN 0-673-15101-8). Scott F.
Social Problems of Modern Britain. E. Butterworth & D. Weir. 1972. pap. 2.75 o.p. (ISBN 0-531-06036-5, Fontana Pap). Watts.
Social Problems of the Aging: Readings. Mildred M. Seltzer et al. 1978. pap. 10.95x (ISBN 0-534-00484-9). Wadsworth Pub.
Social Problems of the Industrial Revolution. Peter Speed. 160p. 1976. pap. 5.40 (ISBN 0-08-018883-4). Pergamon.
Social Problems of the North: London & Oxford, 1913. C. E. Russell. LC 79-56944. (English Working Class Ser.). 1980. lib. bdg. 20.00 (ISBN 0-8240-0123-0). Garland Pub.
Social Problems of Urban Man. Elmer H. Johnson. 1973. text ed. 17.50x (ISBN 0-256-01124-9). Dorsey.
Social Problems: The Contemporary Debates. 3rd ed. Williamson et al. 1981. pap. text ed. 9.95 (ISBN 0-316-94362-2); test bank avail. (ISBN 0-316-94363-0). Little.
Social Problems Today: Dilemmas & Dissensus. Ed. by Clifton D. Bryant. LC 73-133948. 1971. pap. text ed. 6.95 o.p. (ISBN 0-685-04158-1). Lippincott.
Social Problems: Values & Interests in Conflict. Robert J. Antonio & George Ritzer. 350p. 1975. text ed. 10.95x o.p. (ISBN 0-205-04713-0, 8147132). Allyn.
Social Process of Scientific Investigation. Ed. by Karin D. Knorr et al. (Sociology of the Sciences Ser.: No. IV). 356p. 1980. lib. bdg. 34.50 (ISBN 90-277-1174-7, Pub. by D. Reidel); pap. 15.95 (ISBN 90-277-1175-5). Kluwer Boston.
Social Processes of Scientific Development. Ed. by Richard Whitley. 1974. 22.50x (ISBN 0-7100-7705-X). Routledge & Kegan.
Social Program Administration: The Implementation of Social Policy. Bruce L. Gates. (Illus.). 1980. text ed. 15.95 (ISBN 0-13-817767-8). P-H.
Social Protection Code: A New Model of Criminal Justice. Tadeusz Grygier. (American Series of Foreign Penal Codes: Vol. 22). 1977. text ed. 15.00x (ISBN 0-8377-0605-X). Rothman.
Social Psychiatry. Ed. by F. C. Redlich. LC 68-27002. (ARNMD Research Publications Ser: Vol.47). 1969. 25.00 (ISBN 0-89004-159-8). Raven.
Social Psychiatry in India. Brij Mohan. LC 73-905946. 1973. 10.00x o.p. (ISBN 0-88386-185-2). South Asia Bks.
Social Psychological Theories: A Comparative Handbook. Carl J. Slawski. 1980. pap. text ed. 8.95x (ISBN 0-673-15333-9). Scott F.
Social Psychology. 4th ed. V. V. Akolkar. 1972. pap. 4.75x o.p. (ISBN 0-210-33751-6). Asia.
Social Psychology. Kurt W. Back. LC 76-30835. 1977. text ed. 21.50 (ISBN 0-471-03983-7); instructor's manual avail. (ISBN 0-471-02656-5). Wiley.
Social Psychology. Roger Brown. LC 65-11321. 1965. text ed. 14.95 (ISBN 0-02-904820-6). Free Pr.
Social Psychology. 4th ed. Jonathan Freedman et al. (Illus.). 656p. 1981. text ed. 18.95 (ISBN 0-13-817783-X). P-H.
Social Psychology. Jeffrey H. Goldstein. LC 78-64447. 1980. 17.95 (ISBN 0-12-287050-6); text ed. 11.50 international ed. (ISBN 0-12-287055-7). Acad Pr.
Social Psychology. 2nd ed. William W. Lambert & Wallace E. Lambert. (Foundations of Modern Psychology Ser.). (Illus.). 192p. (Reference eds.). 1973. ref. ed 12.95 (ISBN 0-13-818021-0); pap. 7.95 (ISBN 0-13-818013-X). P-H.
Social Psychology. Ed. by Bernard Seidenberg. Alvin Snadowsky. LC 75-9236. (Illus.). 1976. text ed. 15.95 (ISBN 0-02-928050-8). Free Pr.
Social Psychology. 2nd ed. James W. Vander Zanden. 524p. 1981. text ed. 17.95 (ISBN 0-394-32427-7). Random.
Social Psychology. Robert C. Williamson et al. LC 80-52451. 550p. 1981. text ed. 14.95 (ISBN 0-87581-264-3). Peacock Pubs. Postponed.
Social Psychology: An Attributional Approach. John H. Harvey & William P. Smith. LC 76-17113. (Illus.). 1977. pap. text ed. 13.95 (ISBN 0-8016-2079-1). Mosby.
Social Psychology & Contemporary Society. 2nd ed. Edward E. Sampson. LC 75-30225. 592p. 1976. text ed. 22.95x (ISBN 0-471-75116-2); instructor's manual avail. (ISBN 0-471-01609-8). Wiley.
Social Psychology & Individual Values. 2nd ed. D. W. Harding. 1966. pap. text ed. 2.50x (ISBN 0-09-042632-0, Hutchinson U Lib). Humanities.
Social Psychology & the Study of Deviant Behavior. Andrew J Pavlos. LC 78-65426. 1978. pap. text ed. 12.00 (ISBN 0-8191-0664-X). U Pr of Amer.
Social Psychology for Sociologists. Ed. by D. Field. LC 74-952. 1974. text ed. 16.95 (ISBN 0-470-25813-6). Halsted Pr.
Social Psychology in Athletics. Bryant J. Cratty. (Illus.). 320p. 1981. text ed. 15.95 (ISBN 0-13-817650-7). P-H.
Social Psychology in the Eighties. 3rd ed. Lawrence Wrightsman & Kay Deaux. LC 80-23440. 760p. 1980. 18.95 (ISBN 0-8185-0415-3). Brooks-Cole.
Social Psychology in Transition. Ed. by Lloyd H. Strickland et al. LC 76-22439. 361p. 1976. 29.50 (ISBN 0-306-30918-1, Plenum Pr). Plenum Pub.

Social Psychology, Interdependence, Interaction, & Influence. James T. Tedeschi & Svern Lindskold. LC 75-38883. 1976. 24.50 (ISBN 0-471-85017-9, Pub. by Wiley-Interscience). Wiley.

Social Psychology of Aging. Vern L. Bengtson. LC 73-4918. 1973. pap. 2.95 (ISBN 0-672-61339-5). Bobbs.

Social Psychology of Bargaining. Ian Morley & G. M. Stephenson. 1977. text ed. 35.00x (ISBN 0-04-301081-4). Allen Unwin.

Social Psychology of Education. Alan E. Guskin & Samuel L. Guskin. LC 73-104968. 1970. pap. text ed. 5.95 (ISBN 0-201-02631-7). A-W.

Social Psychology of Organizations. 2nd ed. Daniel Katz & Robert L. Kahn. LC 77-18764. 1978. text ed. 24.95 (ISBN 0-471-02355-8). Wiley.

Social Psychology of Organizing. 2nd ed. Karl E. Weick. LC 79-10015. (Topics in Social Psychology Ser.). 1979. pap. text ed. 7.95 (ISBN 0-201-08591-7). A-W.

Social Psychology of Psychological Research. A. G. Miller. LC 76-143522. 1972. 14.95 (ISBN 0-02-921510-2). Free Pr.

Social Psychology of Reading. Jon Edwards. (Language & Literacy Monograph). 256p. 1981. pap. text ed. 14.95 (ISBN 0-88499-603-4). Inst Mod Lang.

Social Psychology of Religion. Michael Argyle & Benjamin Beit-Hallahmi. 1975. 20.00x (ISBN 0-7100-8043-3); pap. 10.00 (ISBN 0-7100-7997-4). Routledge & Kegan.

Social Psychology of Runaways. Tim Brennan et al. LC 75-42947. 1978. 26.95 (ISBN 0-669-00565-7). Lexington Bks.

Social Psychology of School Learning. Ed. by James H. McMillan. LC 79-6797. (Educational Psychology Ser.). 1980. 21.00 (ISBN 0-12-485750-7). Acad Pr.

Social Psychology of Social Movements. Hans Toch. LC 64-66077. 1965. pap. 5.50 (ISBN 0-672-60847-2). Bobbs.

Social Psychology: People in Groups. Bertran Raven & Jeffrey Rubin. LC 75-32693. 592p. 1976. 21.95 (ISBN 0-471-70970-0); instructor's resource book 2.50 (ISBN 0-471-01498-2). Wiley.

Social Psychology: The Theory & Application of Symbolic Interactionism. Robert H. Lauer & Warren H. Handel. LC 76-10895. 512p. 1977. text ed. 16.95 (ISBN 0-395-24333-5); inst. manual 1.25 (ISBN 0-395-24334-3). HM.

Social Psychology Through Symbolic Interaction. 2nd ed. Gregory P. Stone & Harvey A. Farberman. 450p. 1981. pap. text ed. 13.95 (ISBN 0-471-03029-5). Wiley.

Social Psychology Through Symbolic Interaction. Ed. by Gregory P. Stone & Harvey A. Farberman. LC 79-83731. 1970. text ed. 17.95x o.p. (ISBN 0-471-00575-4). Wiley.

Social Realities & Community Psychiatry. H. Warren Dunham. LC 74-10967. 252p. 1976. 22.95 (ISBN 0-87705-215-8). Human Sci Pr.

Social Reality of Death... Kathleeen C. Charmaz. (Sociology Ser.). 1980. text ed. 9.95 (ISBN 0-201-01033-X). A-W.

Social Reality of Ethics: The Comparative Analysis of Moral Codes. John H. Barnsley. (International Library of Sociology). 464p. 1972. 35.00x (ISBN 0-7100-7286-4). Routledge & Kegan.

Social Rebel in American Literature. Ed. by Robert H. Woodward & James J. Clark. LC 68-21801. (Orig.). 1968. pap. 8.95 (ISBN 0-672-63115-6). Odyssey Pr.

Social Recreation: A Group Dynamics Approach. Richard G. Kraus. LC 79-16634. (Illus.). 1979. pap. text ed. 11.00 (ISBN 0-8016-2742-7). Mosby.

Social Rehabilitation Services for the Blind. Richard E. Hardy & John C. Cull. 420p. 1972. pap. 32.75 photocopy ed. spiral (ISBN 0-398-02309-3). C C Thomas.

Social Relations & Social Roles. Florian Znaniecki. (Reprints in Sociology Ser). lib. bdg. 28.50x (ISBN 0-697-00219-5); pap. 8.95x (ISBN 0-89197-940-9). Irvington.

Social Relations in a Philippine Market: Self-Interest & Subjectivity. William G. Davis. LC 71-145783. 1973. 22.50x (ISBN 0-520-01904-0). U of Cal Pr.

Social Research. Susan G. Philliber et al. LC 79-91097. 189p. 1980. pap. text ed. 6.50 (ISBN 0-87581-252-X). Peacock Pubs.

Social Research & Basic Computer Programming. Elwood W. Guernsey. (Illus.). 336p. 1973. 21.75 (ISBN 0-398-02591-6). C C Thomas.

Social Research & Royal Commissions. Martin Bulmer. 224p. 1980. text ed. 27.50x (ISBN 0-04-351055-8, 2392). Allen Unwin.

Social Research for Policy Decisions. Kurt Finsterbusch & Annabelle B. Motz. 208p. 1980. pap. text ed. 7.95x (ISBN 0-534-00780-5). Wadsworth Pub.

Social Research Methods. D. Forcese & S. Richter. (Illus.). 1973. text ed. 16.95 (ISBN 0-13-818237-X). P-H.

Social Research: Principles & Procedures. Ed. by John Bynner & Keith M. Stribley. (Open University Set Bk.). (Illus.). 1979. pap. text ed. 14.50 (ISBN 0-582-29501-7). Longman.

Social Research Techniques for Planners. Thomas L. Burton & G. E. Cherry. (Illus.). 1970. text ed. 15.95x (ISBN 0-04-711002-3). Allen Unwin.

Social Responsibilities of the Mass Media. Ed. by Allen Casebier & Janet J. Casebier. LC 78-58603. 1978. pap. text ed. 10.25 (ISBN 0-8191-0539-2). U Pr of Amer.

Social Responsibility & the Business Predicament. Ed. by James D. McKie. (Studies in the Regulation of Economic Activity). 361p. 1975. 15.95 (ISBN 0-8157-5608-9); pap. 6.95 (ISBN 0-8157-5607-0). Brookings.

Social Responsibility of Business & the Trusteeship Theory of Mahatma Gandhi. R. B. Upadhyaya. 1976. text ed. 22.50x o.p. (ISBN 0-8426-0927-X). Verry.

Social Responsibility of the Scientist. Ed. by Martin Brown. LC 75-143503. 1971. 9.95 o.s.i. (ISBN 0-02-904790-0); pap. text ed. 5.95 (ISBN 0-02-904730-7). Free Pr.

Social Role of Art. Richard Cork. 128p. 1980. 19.95x (ISBN 0-86092-048-8, Pub. by Douglas & McIntyre Canada). Intl Schol Bk Serv.

Social Science & Philosophical Analysis: Essays in Philosophy of the Social Sciences. Michael Martin. LC 78-51142. 1978. pap. text ed. 12.00 (ISBN 0-8191-0478-7). U Pr of Amer.

Social Science & Political Theory. Walter G. Runciman. 1963. 19.95 (ISBN 0-521-07474-6); pap. 7.50x (ISBN 0-521-09562-X, 562). Cambridge U Pr.

Social Science & Public Policy in the United States. Irving L. Horowitz & James E. Katz. LC 74-33034. (Illus.). 206p. 1975. text ed. 24.95 (ISBN 0-275-05310-5); pap. text ed. 11.95 (ISBN 0-275-89160-7). Praeger.

Social Science & the Ignoble Savage. R. L. Meek. LC 75-22985. (Cambridge Studies in the History & Theory of Politics). 262p. 1976. 32.95 (ISBN 0-521-20969-2). Cambridge U Pr.

Social Science & Utopia: Harvester Studies in Philosophy. Barbara Goodwin. (No. 4). (Illus.). 1978. text ed. 30.00x (ISBN 0-391-00855-2). Humanities.

Social Science Approaches to the Judicial Process. J. B. Grossman et al. LC 74-153371. (Symposia on Law & Society Ser). 1971. Repr. of 1966 ed. lib. bdg. 14.50 (ISBN 0-306-70135-9). Da Capo.

Social Science Education in the Elementary School. 2nd ed. Milton E. Ploghoft & Albert H. Shuster. (Elementary Education Ser.). 400p. 1976. text ed. 17.95 (ISBN 0-675-08692-2). Merrill.

Social Science Laboratories: A Handbook of Design, Management & Organisation. W. F. Archenhold et al. 303p. 1980. 35.00x (ISBN 0-7195-3436-4, Pub. by Murray Pubs England). State Mutual Bk.

Social Science Perspectives of the South, Vol. 1. Merle Black. Ed. by John S. Reed. 1981. price not set (ISBN 0-677-16260-X). Gordon.

Social Science Research in Latin America. Ed. by Charles Wagley. LC 65-11971. 1965. 22.50x (ISBN 0-231-02772-9). Columbia U Pr.

Social Science Research on Business: Product & Potential. Ed. by Robert A. Dahl et al. LC 60-9783. 1959. pap. 10.00 (ISBN 0-231-02407-X). Columbia U Pr.

Social Science Research: Prospects & Purposes. Ed. by Erik Rudeng & Hans-Henrik Holm. 210p. 1981. 36.00x (ISBN 82-00-05521-3). Universitet.

Social Science Researching: Twentieth Century Guide to the Literature. (Specialized Bibliography Ser.: No. 3). 1981. lib. bdg. 8.95 (ISBN 0-915574-11-X). Soc Sci & Soc Res.

Social Science Skills: Activities for the Secondary Classroom, 7 vols. Educational Resources Center. Incl. American Government Issues (ISBN 0-8077-2649-4); American Lifestyle Issues (ISBN 0-8077-2648-6); Consumer Issues (ISBN 0-8077-2647-8); Economic Issues (ISBN 0-8077-2645-1); Energy Issues (ISBN 0-8077-2646-X); Global Issues (ISBN 0-8077-2643-5); Population Issues (ISBN 0-8077-2644-3); Basic Skills (ISBN 0-8077-2650-8). (Orig.). 1981. price not set. Tchrs Coll.

Social Science Theory, Structure & Application. Herbert I. London. LC 74-17461. 361p. 1975. 17.50x (ISBN 0-8147-4958-5). NYU Pr.

Social Sciences & Humanities Index. 1965-74. 30.00 (ISBN 0-685-22255-1). Wilson.

Social Sciences & Planning in India. Ed. by Radhakamal Mukerjee. 1974. 7.95x o.p. (ISBN 0-210-22677-3). Asia.

Social Sciences Index, Vols. 1-6. (Sold on service basis). 1974-80. write for info. Wilson.

Social Sciences View School Administration. D. Tope et al. 1965. 9.95 o.p. (ISBN 0-13-818328-7). P-H.

Social Scientist in American Industry: Self-Perception of Role, Motivation, & Career. Matthew Radom. LC 76-125193. 1970. 15.00 (ISBN 0-8135-0665-4). Rutgers U Pr.

Social Scientist in Industry. Lisl Klein. LC 75-41612. 257p. 1976. 19.95 (ISBN 0-470-15004-1). Halsted Pr.

Social Scientists & Policy Making in the USSR. Ed. by Richard B. Remneck. LC 76-27587. (Praeger Special Studies). 1977. text ed. 22.95 (ISBN 0-275-56890-3). Praeger.

Social Scientists As Advocates: Views from the Applied Disciplines. Ed. by George H. Weber & George J. McCall. LC 77-26798. (Sage Focus Editions: Vol. 4). 1978. 18.95x (ISBN 0-8039-0943-8); pap. 9.95x (ISBN 0-8039-0944-6). Sage.

Social Security: A Reciprocity System Under Pressure. Edward Wynne. (Westview Special Studies in Contemporary Social Issues). 220p. 1980. lib. bdg. 18.50x (ISBN 0-89158-930-9). Westview.

Social Security & Medicine in the USSR: A Marxist Critique. Vincente Navarro. LC 77-227. (Illus.). 1977. 17.95 (ISBN 0-669-01452-4). Lexington Bks.

Social Security Benefits. Consumer Guide Editors. 1980. pap. 2.50 (ISBN 0-449-90029-0, Columbine). Fawcett.

Social Security: Beveridge & After. V. N. George. (International Library of Sociology & Social Reconstruction). 1968. text ed. 13.00x (ISBN 0-7100-6205-2). Humanities.

Social Security Disability Insurance: Problems of Unexpected Growth. Charles W. Meyer. 1979. pap. 4.25 (ISBN 0-8447-3365-2). Am Enterprise.

Social Security Hearings & Appeals: A Study of the Social Security Administration Hearing System. Jerry L. Mashaw et al. LC 78-3129. 1978. 15.95 (ISBN 0-669-02316-7). Lexington Bks.

Social Security in a Changing Society: An Introduction to Programs, Concepts, & Issues. new ed. Yung-Ping Chen. LC 80-81652. (Illus.). 200p. (Orig.). 1980. pap. text ed. 6.00 (ISBN 0-937094-00-5). McCahan Found.

Social Security in International Perspective: Essays in Honor of Eveline M. Burns. Shirley Jenkins. LC 71-94628. (Social Work & Social Issues Ser). 1969. 17.50x (ISBN 0-231-03294-3). Columbia U Pr.

Social Security in the United States: An Analysis & Appraisal of the Federal Social Security Act. 2nd ed. Paul H. Douglas. LC 70-167847. (FDR & the Era of the New Deal). 1971. Repr. of 1939 ed. lib. bdg. 42.50 (ISBN 0-306-70323-8). Da Capo.

Social Security: Perspectives for Reform. Joseph A. M. Pechman et al. LC 68-31836. (Studies in Social Economics). 352p. 1968. 14.95 (ISBN 0-8157-6974-1); pap. 5.95 (ISBN 0-8157-6973-3). Brookings.

Social Security Program in the United States. 2nd ed. Charles I. Schottland. (YA) 1970. text ed. 10.95 (ISBN 0-13-818278-7). P-H.

Social Security Retirement Test: Right or Wrong? Marshall R. Colberg. 1978. pap. 4.25 (ISBN 0-8447-3307-5). Am Enterprise.

Social Security, Savings Plan & Other Retirement Arrangements: Learning Guide CEBS Course III. 1980. spiral 13.00 (ISBN 0-89154-130-6). Intl Found Employ.

Social Security, Savings Plans & Other Retirement Arrangements: Answers to Questions on Subject Matter for Learning Guide CEBS Course III. rev. ed. 101p. (Orig.). 1980. spiral bdg. o.p. 13.00; pap. 10.00 (ISBN 0-89154-131-4). Intl Found Employ.

Social Security: The Fraud in Your Future. Warren Shore. 252p. 1975. 9.95 (ISBN 0-02-610550-0). Macmillan.

Social Security: The Inherent Contradiction. Peter J. Ferrara. LC 80-18949. (Policy Bks.: No. 1). 496p. 1980. 20.00 (ISBN 0-932790-24-0). Cato Inst.

Social Security: Today & Tomorrow. Robert M. Ball. LC 77-13713. 1978. 19.00 (ISBN 0-231-04254-X). Columbia U Pr.

Social Self. R. C. Ziller. 320p. 1973. text ed. 23.00 (ISBN 0-08-017030-7); pap. text ed. 10.75 (ISBN 0-08-017250-4). Pergamon.

Social Service & the Art of Healing. Richard C. Cabot. LC 73-84257. (NASW Classics Ser). 192p. 1973. pap. text ed. 3.50x (ISBN 0-87101-062-3, CBC-062-I). Natl Assn Soc Wkrs.

Social Service Budgets & Social Policy. Howard Glennerster. 1977. pap. text ed. 9.95x (ISBN 0-04-360042-5). Allen Unwin.

Social Service Delivery: A Structural Approach to Social Work Practice. R. Middleman & Gale Goldberg. LC 74-3304. 248p. 1974. 13.00x (ISBN 0-231-03730-9). Columbia U Pr.

Social Service Organizations, 2 vols. Ed. by Peter Romanofsky. LC 77-84754. (Greenwood Encyclopedia of American Institutions: No. 2). 1978. lib. bdg. 65.00 (ISBN 0-8371-9829-1, RSS/). Greenwood.

Social Services by Government Contract. Kenneth Wedel et al. 22.95 (ISBN 0-03-052161-0). Praeger.

Social Services: Federal Legislation vs. State Implemention. Bill Benton et al. (Institute Paper). 157p. 1978. pap. 4.50 (ISBN 0-87766-237-1, 23700). Urban Inst.

Social Significance of Middle Schools. W. A. Blyth & R. Derricott. 1977. 32.00 (ISBN 0-7134-0488-4, Pub. by Batsford England); pap. 16.95 (ISBN 0-686-63737-2). David & Charles.

Social Situations. M. Argyle et al. (Illus.). 450p. Date not set. price not set (ISBN 0-521-23260-0); pap. price not set (ISBN 0-521-29881-4). Cambridge U Pr.

Social Skills for Severely Retarded Adults: An Inventory & Training Program. Sandra E. McClennen et al. LC 80-51546. 265p. 1980. 3-ring binder 34.95 (ISBN 0-87822-220-0, 2200). Res Press.

Social Skills in Interpersonal Communication. Owen Hargie & David Dickson. 208p. 1981. 28.00x (ISBN 0-7099-0279-4, Pub. by Croom Helm LTD England). Biblio Dist.

Social Standing in America: New Dimensions of Class. Richard P. Coleman et al. LC 77-20426. 353p. 1981. pap. 6.95 (ISBN 0-465-07929-6). Basic.

Social Status & Power in Java. L. H. Palmier. (Monographs on Social Anthropology: No. 20). 1969. pap. text ed. 9.00x (ISBN 0-485-19620-4, Athlone Pr). Humanities.

Social Stratification. Carol Owen. (Students Library of Sociology). 1968. text ed. 4.25x (ISBN 0-7100-6086-6). Humanities.

Social Stratification: A Multiple Hierarchy Approach. Jeffries & Ransford. 640p. 1980. text ed. 19.95 (ISBN 0-205-06858-8, 816858X). Allyn.

Social Stratification & Occupations. Alexander Stewart et al. Ed. by Ken Prandy & R. M. Blackburn. LC 80-16282. 320p. 1980. text ed. 36.00x (ISBN 0-8419-0630-0); pap. text ed. 19.95x (ISBN 0-8419-0630-0). Holmes & Meier.

Social Stratification & Trade Unionism. G. S. Bain et al. 184p. 1974. 12.50x o.p. (ISBN 0-8448-0896-2). Crane-Russak Co.

Social Stratification in Africa. Arthur Tuden & Leonard Plotnicov. LC 78-91223. 1970. 17.95 (ISBN 0-02-932780-6). Free Pr.

Social Stratification in Science. Jonathan R. Cole & Stephen Cole. 1973. pap. 9.00 (ISBN 0-226-11339-6). U of Chicago Pr.

Social Stratification: Research & Theory for the 1970's. Ed. by Edward O. Laumann. LC 77-135769. (Illus., Orig.). 1970. 8.50 (ISBN 0-672-51402-8); pap. 6.95 (ISBN 0-672-61195-3). Bobbs.

Social Structure. George P. Murdock. 1965. pap. text ed. 8.95 (ISBN 0-02-922290-7). Free Pr.

Social Structure & Ecology of Elephant-Shrews. G. B. Rathbun. (Advances in Ethology Ser.: Vol. 20). (Illus.). 84p. (Orig.). 1979. pap. text ed. 29.50 (ISBN 3-489-60836-4). Parey Sci Pubs.

Social Structure & Personality. Talcott Parsons. LC 64-11218. 1964. 15.95 (ISBN 0-02-924850-7); pap. 3.45 (ISBN 0-02-924840-X). Free Pr.

Social Structure in Farm Animals. G. J. Syme & L. A. Syme. LC 78-26088. (Developments in Animal & Veterinary Sciences Ser.: Vol. 4). 1979. 39.00 (ISBN 0-444-41769-9). Elsevier.

Social Structure in Italy: Crisis of a System. Sabino Acquaviva & Mario Santuccio. LC 76-13602. 272p. 1976. 35.00x (ISBN 0-89158-615-6). Westview.

Social Structure of Attention. M. R. Chance & R. R. Larsen. 339p. 1976. 46.00 (ISBN 0-471-01573-3). Wiley.

Social Structure of Eastern Europe: Transition & Process in Czechoslovakia, Hungary, Poland, Romania & Yugoslavia. Ed. by Bernard L. Faber. LC 75-23961. (Special Studies). (Illus.). 1976. text ed. 35.95 (ISBN 0-275-55590-9). Praeger.

Social Structure of Modern Britain. 3rd ed. E. A. Johns. 1978. text ed. 30.00 (ISBN 0-08-023343-0); pap. 12.00 (ISBN 0-08-023342-2). Pergamon.

Social Studies. David F. Kellum. 1969. pap. 2.45 o.p. (ISBN 0-8362-0112-4). Andrews & McMeel.

Social Studies. Ed. by Howard Mehlinger & O. L. Davis, Jr. LC 80-83744. (National Society for the Study of Education 80th Yearbooks: Pt. II). 300p. 1981. lib. bdg. 16.00x. U of Chicago Pr.

Social Studies & Social Science Education 1970-1972: An ERIC Bibliography. Educational Resources Information Center. LC 72-82740. 1973. 11.50 o.s.i. (ISBN 0-02-469840-7). Macmillan Info.

Social Studies for Children: A Guide to Basic Instruction. 7th ed. John Michaelis. (Illus.). 1980. text ed. 17.95 (ISBN 0-13-818880-7). P-H.

Social Studies for Children in a Democracy: Recent Trends & Developments. 6th ed. J. U. Michaelis. (Illus.). 1976. 17.95 (ISBN 0-13-818872-6). P-H.

Social Studies for Our Times. Richard E. Gross et al. LC 78-2733. 1978. text ed. 21.95x (ISBN 0-471-02340-X); tchrs. ed. 72.50 (ISBN 0-471-04051-7). Wiley.

Social Studies for the Eighties: In Elementary & Middle Schools. 3rd ed. Leonard S. Kenworthy. LC 80-19096. 480p. 1981. text ed. 12.95 (ISBN 0-471-05983-8). Wiley.

Social Studies for the Preschool-Primary Child. Carol Seefeldt. (Elementary Education Ser.). (Illus.). 1977. pap. text ed. 12.95 (ISBN 0-675-08593-4). Merrill.

Social Studies for the Real World. Maxine Dunfee. 1978. pap. text ed. 15.95 (ISBN 0-675-08366-4); instructor's manual 3.95 (ISBN 0-686-67992-X). Merrill.

Social Studies in a New Era: The Elementary School As a Laboratory for Real-Life Experiences. Byron G. Massialas & Joseph Hurst. LC 77-17716. 1978. pap. 14.95x (ISBN 0-582-28043-5). Longman.

Social Studies in Secondary Schools: Curriculum & Methods. Dorothy M. Fraser & Edith West. 1961. 11.95 o.p. (ISBN 0-8260-3215-X). Wiley.

Social Studies in the Mainstreamed Classroom, K-6. Anna S. Ochoa & Susan K. Shuster. LC 80-12323. 1980. pap. 11.95 (ISBN 0-89994-242-3). Soc Sci Ed.

Social Studies in the Open Classroom: A Practical Guide. Evelyn Berger & Bonnie Winters. LC 72-97667. 108p. 1973. pap. text ed. 5.00x (ISBN 0-8077-2398-3). Tchrs Coll.

Social Studies Sourcebook: Ideas for Teaching in the Elementary & Middle School. new ed. Ryan. 320p. 1980. pap. text ed. 10.45 (ISBN 0-205-06802-2, 2368021). Allyn.

Social Studies Student Investigates Foreign Policy. Arthur Kesselman. (gr. 7-12). 1977. PLB 7.97 o.p. (ISBN 0-8239-0377-X). Rosen Pr.

Social Study: Inquiry in Elementary Classrooms. Millard Clements et al. LC 63-12182. 1966. 28.95x (ISBN 0-672-60644-5). Irvington.

Social System. Talcott Parsons. 1964. pap. text ed. 8.95 (ISBN 0-02-924190-1). Free Pr.

Social System of the Planet Earth. Kenneth E. Boulding et al. LC 79-21022. (Economics Ser.). 1980. text ed. 10.95 o.p. (ISBN 0-201-00207-8). A-W.

Social Systems & Family Patterns: A Propositional Inventory. William J. Goode et al. LC 75-158851. 1971. 38.50x (ISBN 0-672-61151-1). Irvington.

Social Systems & Schizophrenia: Selected Papers. H. Warren Dunham. LC 80-14193. 332p. 1980. 28.95 (ISBN 0-03-056134-5). Praeger.

Social Textures of Western Civilization: The Lower Depths, Vol. 1-2. Ed. by Michael Cherniavsky et al. (Orig.). 1972. pap. 8.95x o.p. (ISBN 0-685-03065-2). Vol. 1 (ISBN 0-471-00673-4). Vol. 2. 8.95x o.p. (ISBN 0-471-00674-2). Wiley.

Social Theories of Jacksonian Democracy, 1825-1850: Representative Writings of the Period, 1825-1850. Ed. by Joseph L. Blau. LC 55-169. (Social Theories of Jacksonian Democracy). 1954. pap. 8.45 o.p. (ISBN 0-672-60001-3, AHS1). Bobbs.

Social Theories of Talcott Parsons: A Critical Examination. Ed. by Max Black. LC 75-40325. (Arcturus Books Paperbacks). 384p. 1976. pap. 8.95 (ISBN 0-8093-0759-6). S Ill U Pr.

Social Theory & Political Practice. Brian Fay. (Controversies in Sociology). 1975. pap. text ed. 8.95x (ISBN 0-04-300048-7). Allen Unwin.

Social Theory & Practice: Philosophical Essays in Honour of Prof. J. A. L. Taljaard. Ed. by B. Van der Walt. 1977. pap. 5.95x (ISBN 0-686-00490-6). Wedge Pub.

Social Theory & Social Policy. Robert Pinker. 240p. 1971. 14.50x (ISBN 0-8448-0185-2). Crane-Russak Co.

Social Theory & Social Practice. Percy Ford. 1968. text ed. 9.50x (ISBN 0-7165-0500-2). Humanities.

Social Theory & Social Practice: An Exploration of Experience. P. Ford. (Bibliography on Parliamentary Papers Ser.). 335p. 1968. 24.00x (ISBN 0-7165-0500-2, Pub. by Irish Academic Pr Ireland). Biblio Dist.

Social Theory & Social Structure. Robert K. Merton. LC 68-28789. 1968. text ed. 17.95 (ISBN 0-02-921130-1). Free Pr.

Social Theory & the Family. D. H. Morgan. (International Library of Sociology). 320p. 1975. 22.50x (ISBN 0-7100-8179-0); pap. 10.00 (ISBN 0-7100-8180-4). Routledge & Kegan.

Social Theory & the Urban Question. Peter Saunders. LC 80-21654. 302p. 1981. text ed. 28.50x (ISBN 0-8419-0622-X); pap. text ed. 11.95x (ISBN 0-8419-0623-8). Holmes & Meier.

Social Theory As Science. Russell Keat & John Urry. 1975. 25.00x (ISBN 0-7100-8125-1); pap. 10.50 (ISBN 0-7100-8126-X). Routledge & Kegan.

Social Thought of Bernard Mandeville: Virtue & Commerce in Early Eighteenth Century England. Thomas A. Horne. LC 77-13573. 1978. 15.00x (ISBN 0-231-04274-4). Columbia U Pr.

Social Usage. 2nd ed. Anne R. Free. (Illus.). 1969. pap. text ed. 9.50 (ISBN 0-13-819607-9). P-H.

Social Usage: A Guide to Good Manners. 2nd ed. Anne R. Free. (Illus.). 1969. 18.95x (ISBN 0-89197-585-3). Irvington.

Social Use of Information: Ownership & Access. Andrew E. Wessel. LC 76-18211. (Information Sciences Ser.). 1976. 25.50 (ISBN 0-471-93377-5, Pub. by Wiley-Interscience). Wiley.

Social Use of Metaphor: Essays on the Anthropology of Rhetoric. Ed. by J. David Sapir & J. Christopher Crocker. LC 76-53200. 1977. 16.00x (ISBN 0-8122-7725-2). U of Pa Pr.

Social Values & Industrial Relations: A Study of Fairness & Inequality. Richard Hyman & Ian Brough. 1975. 20.00x (ISBN 0-631-16640-8, Pub. by Basil Blackwell); pap. 14.00x (ISBN 0-631-16610-6, Pub. by Basil Blackwell). Biblio Dist.

Social Values & Public Policy. Ed. by William Dunn. (Illus., Orig.). 1981. pap. 5.00 (ISBN 0-918592-44-5). Policy Studies.

Social Values, Objectives, & Action. Jimmy Algie. LC 75-12902. 491p. 1975. 34.95 (ISBN 0-470-02250-7). Halsted Pr.

Social Welfare & Family Planning: Concepts, Strategies & Methods Report of a U. N. Project, 1971-1978. 107p. 1979. pap. 8.00 (ISBN 0-686-68972-0, UN79/4/6, UN). Unipub.

Social Welfare: Charity to Justice. John Romanyshyn. 1971. 15.95 (ISBN 0-394-31026-8). Random.

Social Welfare Forum: Official Proceedings. National Conference on Social Welfare. Incl. 94th Annual Forum. 1967 (ISBN 0-231-03136-X); 95th Annual Forum. 1968 (ISBN 0-231-03232-3); 96th Annual Forum. 1969 (ISBN 0-231-03390-7); 97th Annual Forum. 1970 (ISBN 0-231-03473-3); 98th Annual Forum. 1971 (ISBN 0-231-03587-X). LC 8-85377. 20.00x ea. Columbia U Pr.

Social Welfare Forum, 1972: 99th Annual Forum. National Conference on Social Welfare. 376p. 1974. 20.00x (ISBN 0-231-03722-8). Columbia U Pr.

Social Welfare Forum, 1974: 101st Annual Forum 1974. National Conference on Social Welfare. 1975. 20.00x (ISBN 0-231-03948-4). Columbia U Pr.

Social Welfare Forum, 1975: 102nd Annual Forum. National Conference on Social Welfare, May 1975. 256p. 1976. 20.00x (ISBN 0-231-04048-2). Columbia U Pr.

Social Welfare Forum 1977: 104th Annual Forum. National Conference on Social Welfare. 1978. 20.00x (ISBN 0-231-04500-X). Columbia U Pr.

Social Welfare Forum 1979. Ed. by National Conference on Social Welfare. 1980. 25.00x (ISBN 0-231-04990-0). Columbia U Pr.

Social Welfare Forum, 1980. Ed. by National Conference on Social Welfare. 288p. 1981. 27.50 (ISBN 0-231-05290-1). Columbia U Pr.

Social Welfare Manpower in North India. Shankar Pathak. 180p. 1980. text ed. 15.95x (ISBN 0-7069-1075-3, Pub. by Vikas India). Advent Bk.

Social Welfare of the Aging, Proceedings, Vol. 2. International Association Of Gerontology - 5th Congress. Ed. by Jerome Kaplan & G. J. Aldridge. (Aging Around the World Ser.). 1962. 20.00x (ISBN 0-231-08950-3). Columbia U Pr.

Social Welfare, Political Science, Public Administration, Law. Mills & Broughton. (Bliss Bibliographic Classification Ser.). 1977. 19.95 (ISBN 0-408-70833-6). Butterworths.

Social Work: A Profession of Many Faces. 2nd ed. Armando Morales & Bradford Sheafor. 1980. text ed. 16.95 o.p.; instr's manual free o.p. Allyn.

Social Work, Ageing & Society. C. Paul Brearley. (Library of Social Work Ser.). 1975. 12.25x (ISBN 0-7100-8184-7); pap. 6.95 (ISBN 0-7100-8185-5). Routledge & Kegan.

Social Work & Human Problems: Casework, Consultation & Other Topics. Elizabeth E. Irvine. (International Series in Social Work). 1979. 41.00 (ISBN 0-08-023128-4); pap. 19.25 (ISBN 0-08-023127-6). Pergamon.

Social Work & Medical Practice. H. A. Prins & M. B. Whyte. LC 71-184453. 94p. 1972. text ed. 15.00 (ISBN 0-08-016847-7). Pergamon.

Social Work & Mental Retardation. Ed. by Meyer Schreiber. LC 78-101462. (John Day Bk.). 1970. 18.00 o.s.i. (ISBN 0-381-97035-3, A72700, TYC-T). T Y Crowell.

Social Work & Money. Michael Hill & Peter Laing. (Studies in the Personal Social Ser.). (Orig.). 1979. text ed. 17.95x (ISBN 0-04-360051-4); pap. text ed. 7.95x (ISBN 0-04-360052-2). Allen Unwin.

Social Work & Sexual Conduct. John Hart. (Library of Social Work). 1979. 21.50x (ISBN 0-7100-0217-3). Routledge & Kegan.

Social Work & Social Change. Eileen Younghusband. (National Institute Social Services Library). 1964. pap. text ed. 4.95x o.p. (ISBN 0-04-360022-0). Allen Unwin.

Social Work & Social Living. Reynolds. 2.50 (ISBN 0-8065-0332-7). Citadel Pr.

Social Work Careers. Marilyn Granbeck. (Career Concise Guides Ser.). (Illus.). (gr. 7 up). 1977. lib. bdg. 6.45 s&l (ISBN 0-531-01310-3). Watts.

Social Work Ethics. Charles Levy. LC 75-11007. 240p. 1976. text ed. 22.95 (ISBN 0-87705-254-9). Human Sci Pr.

Social Work Ethics. Charles Levy. 266p. 1980. pap. text ed. 9.95 (ISBN 0-87705-493-2). Human Sci Pr.

Social Work Face to Face. Stuart Rees. 1979. 15.50x (ISBN 0-231-04764-9). Columbia U Pr.

Social Work in Conflict: The Practitioner & Bureaucrat. Ed. by Bryan Glastonbury et al. David Cooper & Pearl Hawkins. 178p. 1980. 27.50x (ISBN 0-7099-0314-6, Pub. by Croom Helm Ltd England). Biblio Dist.

Social Work in General Practice. E. Matilda & June E. Neill. (National Institute Social Services Library). 1972. text ed. 18.95x (ISBN 0-04-360025-5); pap. text ed. 8.95x o.p. (ISBN 0-04-360026-3). Allen Unwin.

Social Work in Health Services: An Academic Practice Partnership. Ed. by Phyllis Caroff & Mildred Mailick. 1980. lib. bdg. 15.95 (ISBN 0-88202-131-1); pap. text ed. 9.95 (ISBN 0-88202-130-3). N Watson.

Social Work in Long-Term Care Facilities. Shirley Conger & Kay Moore. 160p. 1981. 15.95 (ISBN 0-8436-0850-1). CBI Pub.

Social Work on Pediatric Settings. Ed. by Harriett Stambaugh. (Social Work in Health Care Ser.: Vol. 1). 350p. 1981. text ed. 22.95 (ISBN 0-917724-29-1). Haworth Pr.

Social Work Perspectives on Poverty. Ed. by R. R. Singh. 1980. text ed. 12.50x (ISBN 0-391-01832-9). Humanities.

Social Work Practice. 2nd ed. Carol H. Meyer. LC 75-20949. (Illus.). 15.95 (ISBN 0-02-921140-9); pap. text ed. 8.95 (ISBN 0-02-921160-3). Free Pr.

Social Work Practice: A Philippine Casebook. abr. ed. Virginia Hebbert et al. 312p. 1980. pap. 5.00x (ISBN 0-686-28649-9). Cellar.

Social Work Practice: A Radical Perspective. Jeffrey Galper. (P-H Ser. Sociology & Social Work). 1980. pap. text ed. 10.95 (ISBN 0-13-819508-0). P-H.

Social Work Practice: Model & Method. Allen Pincus & Anne Minahan. LC 73-82647. 355p. 1973. text ed. 12.95 (ISBN 0-87581-132-9). Peacock Pubs.

Social Work Practice: People & Environments. Ed. by Carel B. Germain. Orig. Title: Ecological Perspective in Social Work Practice. 1979. 22.50x (ISBN 0-231-04332-5); pap. 10.00x (ISBN 0-231-04333-3). Columbia U Pr.

Social Work Practice: Proceedings. National Conference on Social Welfare. Incl. Ninety-Third Annual Meeting. 1966 (ISBN 0-231-03032-0); Ninety-Fourth Annual Meeting. 1967 (ISBN 0-231-03154-8); Ninety-Fifth Annual Meeting. 1968 (ISBN 0-231-03247-1); Ninety-Sixth Annual Meeting. 1969 (ISBN 0-231-03389-3); Ninety-Seventh Annual Meeting. 1970 (ISBN 0-231-03474-1); Ninety-Eighth Annual Meeting. 1971 (ISBN 0-231-03588-8). LC 8-85377. 20.00x ea. Columbia U Pr.

Social Work Practice with Parents of Children in Foster Care: A Handbook. Charles R. Horejsi et al. write for info. (ISBN 0-398-04471-6). C C Thomas.

Social Work Practice with the Mentally Retarded. Martha U. Dickerson. Ed. by Francis J. Turner & Herbert S. Strean. LC 80-2316. (Fields of Practice Ser.). 1981. text ed. 14.95 (ISBN 0-02-907430-4). Free Pr.

Social Work Processes. rev. ed. Beulah Compton & Burt Galaway. 1979. pap. text ed. 14.50x (ISBN 0-256-02194-5). Dorsey.

Social Work: Reform or Revolution? Colin Pritchard & Richard Taylor. (Library of Social Work). 1978. 16.00x (ISBN 0-7100-8882-5); pap. 8.00 (ISBN 0-7100-8884-1). Routledge & Kegan.

Social Work Research & Evaluation. Richard Grinnell. LC 80-52448. 600p. 1981. text ed. 19.50 (ISBN 0-87581-261-9). Peacock Pubs.

Social Work Research & the Analysis of Social Data. J. W. McCulloch et al. LC 74-32369. 252p. 1975. text ed. 25.00 (ISBN 0-08-018213-5); pap. text ed. 12.75 (ISBN 0-08-018212-7). Pergamon.

Social Work Staff Development for Health Care. Society for Hospital Social Work Directors of the American Hospital Association. LC 76-41793. 1976. pap. 7.25 (ISBN 0-87258-322-8, 2550). Am Hospital.

Social Work Supervision in Practice. B. Kent. 1969. pap. 4.95 o.p. (ISBN 0-08-006363-2). Pergamon.

Social Work: The Unloved Profession. Willard C. Richan & Allan R. Mendelsohn. 226p. 1973. 8.95 (ISBN 0-531-05350-4); pap. 4.95 (ISBN 0-531-05550-7). Watts.

Social Work, Welfare & the State. Ed. by Noel Parry et al. LC 79-67578. 202p. 1980. pap. 9.95x (ISBN 0-8039-1415-6). Sage.

Social Work with Adolescents. Ray Jones & Colin Pritchard. (Library of Social Work). 260p. 1981. 16.95 (ISBN 0-7100-0632-2); pap. write for info. (ISBN 0-7100-0633-0). Routledge & Kegan.

Social Work with Children. Juliet Berry. (Library of Social Work). 1972. pap. 7.95 (ISBN 0-7100-7268-6). Routledge & Kegan.

Social Work with Children. Florence Lieberman. LC 78-23287. 1979. text ed. 24.95 (ISBN 0-87705-255-7); pap. text ed. 9.95 (ISBN 0-87705-257-3). Human Sci Pr.

Social Work with Elderly People. Cherry Rowlings. (Studies in the Personal Social Services: No. 3). 144p. (Orig.). 1981. text ed. 19.95x (ISBN 0-04-362036-1, 2603); pap. text ed. 7.95x (ISBN 0-04-362037-X, 2604). Allen Unwin.

Social Work with Families. Eric Sainsbury. (Library of Social Work). 1975. 15.00x (ISBN 0-7100-8039-5); pap. 7.45 (ISBN 0-7100-8040-9). Routledge & Kegan.

Social Work with Groups. Helen Northen. LC 69-19462. 1969. 15.00x (ISBN 0-231-02965-9). Columbia U Pr.

Social Work with Immigrants. Juliet Cheetham. (Library of Social Work). 242p. 1972. 12.95x (ISBN 0-7100-7365-8); pap. 7.95 (ISBN 0-7100-7366-6). Routledge & Kegan.

Social Work with the Aging. Ed. by Carol H. Meyer. LC 75-27193. (NASW Modular Ser.). 140p. 1975. Set. pap. text ed. 8.00x (ISBN 0-87101-002-X, CAB-001-I). Natl Assn Soc Wkrs.

Social Work with the Dying Patient & the Family. Ed. by Elizabeth Prichard & Jean Collard. LC 77-8679. 1977. 22.50x (ISBN 0-231-04021-0). Columbia U Pr.

Social Work with the Dying Patient & the Family. Ed. by Elizabeth Prichard et al. Tr. by Irene Lefkowitz et al. (Foundation of Thanatology Ser.). (Illus.). 1980. pap. 12.50x (ISBN 0-231-08371-8). Columbia U Pr.

Social Worker. Margaret Williamson. 1964. 3.95 o.s.i. (ISBN 0-02-629950-X). Macmillan.

Social Worker As Psychotherapist. Herbert S. Strean. LC 74-5086. 1974. 10.00 (ISBN 0-8108-0721-1). Scarecrow.

Social Workers & Volunteers. Anthea Holme & Joan Maizels. 1978. text ed. 25.00x (ISBN 0-04-361031-5); pap. text ed. 9.95x (ISBN 0-04-361032-3). Allen Unwin.

Social Workers at Work. 2nd ed. Ed. by Tony Tripodi et al. LC 76-41993. 1977. pap. text ed. 8.50 (ISBN 0-87581-216-3). Peacock Pubs.

Social Workers' Perceptions of Clients: A Study of the Caseload of a Social Agency. Edgar F. Borgatta et al. LC 80-27204. 92p. 1981. Repr. of 1960 ed. lib. bdg. 17.50x (ISBN 0-313-22812-4, BOSW). Greenwood.

Social World of Imprisoned Girls. Rose Giallombardo. 314p. 1981. Repr. text ed. price not set (ISBN 0-89874-285-4). Krieger.

Socialism. Ludwig Von Misis. LC 79-21701. Orig. Title: Die Gemeinwirtschaft. 1981. 11.00 (ISBN 0-913966-62-2, Liberty Classics); pap. 5.00 (ISBN 0-913966-63-0). Liberty Fund.

Socialism & American Life, 2 vols. Donald D. Egbert & S. Persons. Incl. Vol. 1. Text (ISBN 0-691-07521-2); Vol. 2. Bibliography (ISBN 0-691-07522-0). (American Civilization). 1952. 35.00x ea.; Set. 59.50x (ISBN 0-685-23098-8). Princeton U Pr.

Socialism & Philosophy. Antonio Labriola. LC 79-90007. 223p. 1980. 12.00 (ISBN 0-914386-21-2); pap. 4.50 (ISBN 0-914386-22-0). Telos Pr.

Socialism & Social Change in the Seventies: A Reader. Winston B. Cox. 1978. pap. text ed. 16.00 (ISBN 0-8191-0375-6). U Pr of Amer.

Socialism & the Cities. Ed. by Bruce M. Stave. (National University Publications Interdisciplinary Urban Ser.). 1975. 15.00 (ISBN 0-8046-9133-9, Natl U); pap. 8.95 (ISBN 0-8046-9189-4). Kennikat.

Socialism & the Great War: The Collapse of the Second International. Georges Haupt. 280p. 1972. 24.95x (ISBN 0-19-827184-0). Oxford U Pr.

Socialism Democracy & Human Rights. Leonid I. Brezhnev. LC 79-42659. 256p. 1981. 50.00 (ISBN 0-08-023605-7). Pergamon.

Socialism for the Dead. J. George. LC 79-67320. 354p. 1980. 12.95 (ISBN 0-533-04454-5). Vantage.

Socialism in Provence Eighteen Seventy-One to Nineteen Fourteen. T. Judt. LC 78-16419. (Illus.). 1979. 42.50 (ISBN 0-521-22172-2); pap. 14.95x (ISBN 0-521-29598-X). Cambridge U Pr.
Socialism in Sub-Saharan Africa: A New Assessment. Ed. by Carl G. Rosberg & Thomas M. Callaghy. LC 79-84635. (Research Ser.: No. 38). (Illus.). 1979. pap. 9.50x (ISBN 0-87725-138-X). U of Cal Intl St.
Socialism in the Third World. Ed. by Helen Desfosses & Jacques Levesque. LC 75-19774. (Special Studies). (Illus.). 340p. 1975. text ed. 23.95 (ISBN 0-275-55560-7); pap. text ed. 10.95 (ISBN 0-275-89460-6). Praeger.
Socialism in Theological Perspective: A Study of Paul Tillich, 1918-1933. John R. Stumme. LC 78-3675. (American Academy of Religion. Dissertation Ser.: No. 21). 1978. pap. 7.50 (ISBN 0-89130-232-8, 010121). Scholars Pr Ca.
Socialism: Its Theoretical Roots & Present-Day Development. James D. Forman. LC 72-6736. (Studies in Contemporary Politics). 128p. (gr. 7-12). 1972. PLB 5.90 o.p. (ISBN 0-531-02581-0). Watts.
Socialism of Fools: Georg Ritter Von Schonerer & Austrian Pan-Germanism. Andrew G. Whiteside. 512p. 1975. 32.50x (ISBN 0-520-02434-6). U of Cal Pr.
Socialism of My Conception. Mohandas K. Gandhi. Ed. by Anand T. Hingorani. 290p. (Orig.). 1981. pap. 4.00 (ISBN 0-934676-29-1). Greenlf Bks.
Socialism of Our Times: A Symposium, Prelude to Depression. Harry W. Laidler & Norman Thomas. LC 76-27725. 1976. Repr. of 1929 ed. lib. bdg. 35.00 (ISBN 0-306-70850-7). Da Capo.
Socialism: Opposing Viewpoints. Ed. by Bruno Leone. (ISMS Ser.). (Illus.). (gr. 9-12). 1978. 8.95 (ISBN 0-912616-55-5); pap. 3.95 (ISBN 0-912616-54-7). Greenhaven.
Socialism, Politics, & Equality. Walter D. Connor. (Illus.). 1979. 27.50x (ISBN 0-231-04318-X). Columbia U Pr.
Socialism, Politics & Equality: Hierarchy & Change in Eastern Europe & the USSR. Walter D. Connor. (Illus.). 1980. pap. 10.00x (ISBN 0-231-04319-8). Columbia U Pr.
Socialism, Social Welfare, & the Soviet Union. Vic George & Nick Manning. (Radical Social Policy Ser.). 224p. (Orig.). 1980. pap. 15.95 (ISBN 0-7100-0608-X). Routledge & Kegan.
Socialism: Utopian & Scientific. Frederick Engels. 1975. pap. 1.50 (ISBN 0-8351-0357-9). China Bks.
Socialist Agriculture in Hungary. Csizmadia. 1971. 12.50 (ISBN 0-9960000-6-2, Pub. by Kaido Hungary). Heyden.
Socialist & Labour Movement in Japan. Arthur M. Young. (Studies in Japanese History & Civilization). 145p. 1979. Repr. of 1921 ed. 18.00 (ISBN 0-89093-268-9). U Pubns Amer.
Socialist Economies of the Soviet Union & Europe. Marie Lavigne. Tr. by T. G. Waywell from Fr. LC 74-83551. 396p. 1974. 25.00 o.p. (ISBN 0-87332-063-8). M E Sharpe.
Socialist Industrial State: Toward a Political Sociology of State Socialism. David Lane. LC 75-33036. 220p. 1976. 24.50x (ISBN 0-89158-523-0). Westview.
Socialist Offensive: The Collectivization of Soviet Agriculture, Nineteen Twenty Nine to Nineteen Thirty. R. W. Davies. (Industrialization of Soviet Russia Ser.: Vol. 1). 576p. 1980. 35.00 (ISBN 0-674-81480-0). Harvard U Pr.
Socialist Origins in the United States: American Forerunners of Marx, 1817-1832. David Harris. (Publications on Social History). 1966. text ed. 10.50x (ISBN 90-232-0269-4). Humanities.
Socialist Ownership & Political Systems Under Socialism. Wlodzimierz Brus. 256p. 1975. 20.00 (ISBN 0-7100-8247-9). Routledge & Kegan.
Socialist Party of Argentina 1890-1930. Richard J. Walter. LC 77-620003. (Latin American Monographs: No. 42). 1977. text ed. 14.95x (ISBN 0-292-77539-3); pap. text ed. 7.95 (ISBN 0-292-77540-7). U of Tex Pr.
Socialist Planning. M. Ellman. LC 78-57757. (Modern Cambridge Economics Ser.). 1979. 44.50 (ISBN 0-521-22229-X); pap. 11.95x (ISBN 0-521-29409-6). Cambridge U Pr.
Socialist Poems of Hugh MacDiarmid. Ed. by T. S. Law & Thurso Berwick. (Orig.). 1978. pap. 8.95 (ISBN 0-7100-8914-7). Routledge & Kegan.
Socialist Register Nineteen Seventy Five. Ed. by Ralph Miliband & John Saville. 372p. 1977. text ed. 15.75x (ISBN 0-85036-224-5). Humanities.
Socialist Register Nineteen Seventy Nine. Miliband & Saville. 346p. 1979. text ed. 15.75x (ISBN 0-85036-252-0). Humanities.
Socialist Register Nineteen Seventy Six. Ed. by Ralph Miliband & John Saville. 1976. text ed. 13.50x (ISBN 0-85036-217-2). Humanities.
Socialist Register Nineteen Seventy Two. Ed. by Ralph Miliband & John Saville. 306p. 1972. text ed. 11.00x (ISBN 0-85036-163-X). Humanities.
Socialist Register 1971: A Survey of Various Movements up to Current Bangladesh. Ralph Miliband & John Saville. 15.00 (ISBN 0-87556-440-2). Saifer.
Socialist Thought: A Documentary History. Ed. by Albert Fried & Ronald Sanders. LC 64-11312. 1964. pap. 3.95 o.p. (ISBN 0-385-01638-7, A384, Anch). Doubleday.
Socialists & European Integration: A Study of the French Socialist Party. Byron Criddle. (Library of Political Studies). 1969. text ed. 7.25x (ISBN 0-7100-6423-3). Humanities.
Socialists & Socialism. Thomas E. Watson. (Studies in Populism). 1980. lib. bdg. 69.95 (ISBN 0-686-68885-6). Revisionist Pr.
Sociality of Christ & Humanity: Dietrich Bonhoeffer's Early Theology, 1927-1933. Clifford J. Green. LC 75-33816. (American Academy of Religion. Dissertation Ser.). 1975. pap. 9.00 (ISBN 0-89130-055-4, 010106). Scholars Pr Ca.
Socialization After Childhood: Two Essays. Q. G. Brim & S. Wheeler. 1966. pap. text ed. 10.95 (ISBN 0-471-10418-3). Wiley.
Socialization & Personality Development. Edward F. Zigler & Irvin L. Child. LC 73-190612. 1973. pap. text ed. 9.95 (ISBN 0-201-08791-X). A-W.
Socialization As Cultural Communication. Ed. by Theodore Schwartz. LC 75-17282. 1976. 15.00x (ISBN 0-520-03061-3); pap. 6.95x (ISBN 0-520-03955-6). U of Cal Pr.
Socialization for Achievement: Essays on the Cultural Psychology of the Japanese. George A. DeVos. LC 78-132420. 613p. 1973. 23.75 o.p. (ISBN 0-520-01827-3); pap. 11.95x (ISBN 0-520-02893-7). U of Cal Pr.
Socialization of Family Size Values: Youth & Family Planning in an Indian Village. Thomas Poffenberger & Kim Sebaly. LC 76-53996. (Michigan Papers on South and Southeast Asia: No. 12). (Illus.). 150p. 1976. pap. 5.00x (ISBN 0-89148-012-9). Ctr S&SE Asian.
Socialization to Politics: A Reader. Ed. by Jack Dennis. LC 72-8329. 527p. 1973. pap. text ed. 16.95 (ISBN 0-471-20926-0). Wiley.
Sociedad Espanola En la Novela de la Postguerra. F. Carenas & Jose Ferrando. 1971. 10.95 (ISBN 0-88303-997-4). E Torres & Sons.
Societa Milanese Nell'eta Precomunale. Cinzio Violante. LC 80-2000. 1981. Repr. of 1953 ed. 35.00 (ISBN 0-404-18602-5). AMS Pr.
Societal Evolution: A Study of the Evolutionary Basis of the Science of Society. Albert G. Keller. 1931. 32.50x (ISBN 0-686-51315-0). Elliots Bks.
Societal Growth: Processes & Implications. Amos H. Hawley. LC 79-7339. (Illus.). 1979. 19.95 (ISBN 0-02-914200-8). Free Pr.
Societal Learning Approach: A New Approach to Social Welfare Policy & Planning in America. Thomas D. Watts. LC 80-69231. 140p. 1981. perfect bdg. 11.95 (ISBN 0-86548-058-3). Century Twenty One.
Societal Marketing Boards. D. Izraeli & J. Zif. LC 77-10606. 1978. 45.95 (ISBN 0-470-99308-1). Halsted Pr.
Societal Structures of the Mind. Uriel G. Foa & Edna B. Foa. (Illus.). 468p. 1974. pap. 37.50 (ISBN 0-398-02932-6). C C Thomas.
Societe Feodale. Joseph L. Calmette. LC 80-1994. 1981. Repr. of 1923 ed. 26.50 (ISBN 0-404-18556-8). AMS Pr.
Societe Feodale Allemande et Ses Institutions Du Xe Au XIIe Siecle. Charles E. Perrin. LC 80-2013. 1981. Repr. of 1956 ed. 34.50 (ISBN 0-404-18583-5). AMS Pr.
Society. R. M. MacIver. 596p. 1980. Repr. of 1937 ed. lib. bdg. 40.00 (ISBN 0-89984-338-7). Century Bookbindery.
Society Against Nature. Serge Moscovici. Tr. by Sacha Rabinowitz from Fr. (European Ideas Ser.). 1976. text ed. 17.00x (ISBN 0-391-00523-5). Humanities.
Society Against the State. Pierre Clastres. Tr. by Robert Hurley. 1977. 12.95 (ISBN 0-916354-38-5); pap. 7.95, 1981 (ISBN 0-916354-39-3). Urizen Bks.
Society & Bureaucracy in Contemporary Ghana. Robert M. Price. LC 74-81439. 275p. 1975. 21.50x (ISBN 0-520-02811-2). U of Cal Pr.
Society & Culture in America: 1830-1860. Russel B. Nye. (New American Nation Ser.). 1974. pap. 7.95x (ISBN 0-06-131826-4, TB1826, Torch). Har-Row.
Society & Development in Contemporary India. Ranjit Tirtha. (Illus.). 368p. 1980. 13.50 (ISBN 0-8187-0040-8). Harlo Pr.
Society & Development in Contemporary India: Geographical Perspectives. Ranjit Tirtha. (Illus.). 368p. 1980. 13.50 (ISBN 0-686-27540-3). R Tirtha.
Society & Drugs, Social & Cultural Observations. Richard H. Blum et al. Incl. Vol. 2. Students & Drugs, College & High School Observations. LC 73-75936. (Social & Behavioral Science Ser.). 1969. 2 vol. set 37.50x (ISBN 0-87589-424-0); Vol. 1. (ISBN 0-87589-033-4); Vol. 2. (ISBN 0-87589-034-2). Jossey-Bass.
Society & Education. 5th ed. Robert J. Havighurst & Daniel U. Levine. LC 78-32024. 1979. text ed. 17.95 (ISBN 0-205-06654-2, 2366541). Allyn.
Society & Education. 4th ed. Robert J. Havighurst & Bernice L. Neugarten. 544p. 1975. text ed. 13.95 o.s.i. (ISBN 0-205-04692-4, 2246929); study guide 4.95 o.s.i. (ISBN 0-205-04915-X). Allyn.
Society & Education in Japan. Herbert Passin. LC 65-19168. (Orig.). 1965. pap. text ed. 7.00x (ISBN 0-8077-1875-0). Tchrs Coll.
Society & Fertility. Malcolm Potts & Peter Selman. (Illus.). 384p. 1979. 27.50x (ISBN 0-7121-1960-4, Pub. by Macdonald & Evans England). Intl Ideas.
Society & Food: The Third World. Manning. (Sicon Bks Ser). 1977. 3.95 (ISBN 0-408-71304-6). Butterworths.
Society & Personality: An Interactionist Approach to Social Psychology. Tamotsu Shibutani. 1961. text ed. 19.95 (ISBN 0-13-820619-X). P-H.
Society & Politics in Ancient Rome: Essays & Sketches. Frank F. Abbott. LC 63-10767. 267p. (gr. 7 up). 1909. 10.50x (ISBN 0-8196-0118-7). Biblo.
Society & Politics in Revolutionary Bordeaux. Alan Forrest. (Oxford Historical Monographs). 320p. 1975. 42.00x (ISBN 0-19-821859-1). Oxford U Pr.
Society & Politics in Wilhelmine Germany. Ed. by Richard J. Evans. LC 77-14746. 1978. text ed. 19.50x (ISBN 0-06-492036-4). B&N.
Society & Politics: Readings in Political Sociology. Richard G. Braungart. (Illus.). 624p. 1976. 21.95 (ISBN 0-13-820555-8). P-H.
Society & Religion During the Age of Industrialization: Christianity in Victorian England. Lee E Grugel. LC 78-65844. (Illus.). 1979. pap. text ed. 7.50 (ISBN 0-8191-0671-2). U Pr of Amer.
Society & Religion in Early Ottoman Egypt. Michael Winter. 230p. 1981. 19.95 (ISBN 0-87855-351-7). Transaction Bks.
Society & Religion in Elizabethan England. Richard L. Greaves. 832p. 1981. 32.50x (ISBN 0-8166-1030-4). U of Minn Pr.
Society & Self: A Reader in Social Psychology. Ed. by Bartlett H. Stoodley. LC 62-11864. 1962. 10.50 o.s.i. (ISBN 0-02-931630-8); pap. text ed. 5.50 o.s.i. (ISBN 0-02-931640-5). Free Pr.
Society & Social Science. Jon H. Huer. LC 79-63563. 1979. pap. text ed. 9.50 o.p. (ISBN 0-8191-0730-1). U Pr of Amer.
Society & the Healthy Homosexual. George Weinberg. 160p. 1973. pap. 1.95 (ISBN 0-385-05083-6, Anch). Doubleday.
Society & the Lyric: A Study of the Song Culture of Eighteenth-Century Scotland. Thomas Crawford. 208p. 1980. text ed. 13.50 (ISBN 0-7073-0227-7, Pub. by Scottish Academic Pr). Columbia U Pr.
Society & the Policeman's Role. Maureen E. Cain. (International Library of Sociology). (Illus.). 326p. 1973. 25.00x (ISBN 0-7100-7490-5). Routledge & Kegan.
Society & the Sex Variant. George W. Henry. (Orig.). 1965. pap. 0.95 o.s.i. (ISBN 0-02-095900-1, Collier). Macmillan.
Society & the Teacher's Role. Frank Musgrove & Philip H. Taylor. 1969. text ed. 4.00x (ISBN 0-7100-6447-0). Humanities.
Society, Crime & Criminal Careers. 3rd ed. Don C. Gibbons. (Illus.). 1977. 18.95 (ISBN 0-13-820100-5). P-H.
Society, Culture & Change in the Middle East. Raphael Patai. LC 70-84742. Orig. Title: Golden River to Golden Road. (Illus.). 1971. pap. 7.95x (ISBN 0-8122-1009-3, Pa Paperbks). U of Pa Pr.
Society, Culture & Drinking Patterns. David J. Pittman & Charles R. Snyder. LC 62-15188. 1962. 28.95 (ISBN 0-471-69102-X, Pub. by Wiley-Interscience). Wiley.
Society, Culture & Drinking Patterns. Ed. by David J. Pittman & Charles R. Snyder. LC 65-15188. (Arcturus Books Paperbacks). 633p. 1968. pap. 12.95 (ISBN 0-8093-0326-4). S Ill U Pr.
Society Finches. Mervin F. Roberts. (Illus.). 1979. 2.95 (ISBN 0-87666-990-9, KW-029). TFH Pubns.
Society Finches, Breeding. Mervin F. Roberts. (Illus.). 1979. 2.95 (ISBN 0-87666-991-7, KW-030). TFH Pubns.
Society in America. Harriet Martineau. Ed. by Seymour M. Lipset. (Socialscience Classics). 357p. 1981. 18.95 (ISBN 0-87855-420-3); pap. 7.95 (ISBN 0-87855-853-5). Transaction Bks.
Society, Law & Morality: Readings in Social Philosophy. Ed. by Fred Olafson. 1961. text ed. 14.95 o.p. (ISBN 0-13-820142-0). P-H.
Society, Literature, Reading: The Reception of Literature Considered in Its Theoretical Context. Ed. by Manfred Naumann et al. (Linguistic & Literary Studies in Eastern Europe). 550p. 1980. text ed. 85.50x (ISBN 90-272-1509-X). Humanities.
Society of Friends. George Gorman. 1978. pap. 2.90 (ISBN 0-08-021412-6). Pergamon.
Society of Nine. Nick Carter. (Nick Carter Ser.). 224p. (Orig.). 1981. pap. 2.25 (ISBN 0-441-77233-1). Charter Bks.
Society of Publication Designers Annual 1977-78. (Illus.). 1978. cancelled o.p. (ISBN 0-8038-6756-5). Hastings.
Society of Women: A Study of a Women's Prison. Rose Giallombardo. LC 66-14132. 1966. pap. text ed. 9.95x (ISBN 0-471-29729-1). Wiley.
Society Scandals. Harriet Bridgeman & Elizabeth Drury. 1977. 8.95 (ISBN 0-7153-7413-3). David & Charles.
Society, Schools & Progress in Australia. P. H. Partridge. LC 68-24067. 1968. 22.00 (ISBN 0-08-012919-6); pap. 11.25 (ISBN 0-08-012918-8). Pergamon.
Society, Schools & Progress in Canada. J. Katz. 1969. 16.50 (ISBN 0-08-006374-8); pap. 8.50 (ISBN 0-08-006373-X). Pergamon.
Society, Schools & Progress in China. Chiu-Sam Tsang LC 68-21109. 1968. 22.00 (ISBN 0-08-012844-0); pap. 11.25 (ISBN 0-08-012843-2). Pergamon.
Society, Schools & Progress in England. G. Baron. 1966. 22.00 (ISBN 0-08-011594-2); pap. text ed. 10.75 (ISBN 0-08-011593-4). Pergamon.
Society, Schools & Progress in India. J. Sargent. LC 68-21106. 1968. 22.00 (ISBN 0-08-012840-8); pap. 11.25 (ISBN 0-08-012839-4). Pergamon.
Society, Schools & Progress in Israel. A. F. Kleinberger. LC 73-92460. 1969. 25.00 (ISBN 0-08-006494-9); pap. 14.50 (ISBN 0-08-006493-0). Pergamon.
Society, Schools & Progress in Japan. Tetzuya Kobayashi. 222p. 1976. text ed. 23.00 (ISBN 0-08-019936-4); pap. text ed. 12.25 (ISBN 0-08-019935-6). Pergamon.
Society, Schools & Progress in Nigeria. L. J. Lewis. 1965. 22.00 (ISBN 0-08-011340-0); pap. 11.25 (ISBN 0-08-011339-7). Pergamon.
Society, Schools & Progress in Peru. Roland G. Paulston. 336p. 1972. text ed. 23.00 (ISBN 0-08-016428-5). Pergamon.
Society, Schools & Progress in Scandinavia. C. W. Dixon. 1965. 25.00 (ISBN 0-08-011405-9); pap. 13.75 (ISBN 0-08-011404-0). Pergamon.
Society, Schools & Progress in Tanzania. J. Cameron & W. A. Dodd. 1970. 22.00 (ISBN 0-08-015564-2); pap. 11.25 (ISBN 0-08-015563-4). Pergamon.
Society, State, & Schools: A Case for Structural & Confessional Pluralism. Gordon Spykman et al. 224p. (Orig.). 1981. pap. 11.95 (ISBN 0-8028-1880-3). Eerdmans.
Society, Stress & Disease, Vol. 1. Ed. by Lennart Levi. 1971. 67.50x (ISBN 0-19-264416-5). Oxford U Pr.
Society, Stress, & Disease: The Productive & Reproductive Age-Male-Female Roles & Relationships, Vol. 3. Lennart Levi. (Illus.). 1978. 67.50x (ISBN 0-19-261306-5). Oxford U Pr.
Society, Stress, & Disease: Working Life, Vol. 4. Ed. by Lennart Levi. 1981. text ed. 75.00x (ISBN 0-19-264421-1). Oxford U Pr.
Society, Systems & Man: Selections for Reading & Composition. Robert G. Wicks & Lawrence Keough. LC 75-161496. 1972. text ed. 10.50 (ISBN 0-471-94290-1). Wiley.
Society, the City & the Space-Economy of Urbanism. D. Harvey. LC 72-77212. (CCG Resource Papers Ser.: No. 18). (Illus.). 1972. pap. text ed. 4.00 (ISBN 0-89291-065-8). Assn Am Geographers.
Society's Victim -- the Policeman: An Analysis of Job Stress in Policing. William H. Kroes. (Illus.). 144p. 1980. 13.75 (ISBN 0-398-03479-6). C C Thomas.
Society's Work. Robert Bridges et al. Ed. by Steele Commager. Incl. Nature of Human Speech; English Handwriting; Notes on Relative Clauses; On Some Disputed Points in English Grammar; English Vowel Sounds; Study of American English; English Handwriting; Shakespeares English; American Pronunciation. (Society for Pure English: Vol. 3). 1979. lib. bdg. 42.00 (ISBN 0-8240-3667-0). Garland Pub.
Socio-Economic Aspects of Urban Hydrology. (Studies & Reports in Hydrology: No. 27). 85p. 1980. pap. 10.00 (ISBN 0-686-60292-7, U965, UNESCO). Unipub.

Socio-Economic Impact of Microelectronics: International Conference on Socio-Economic Problems & Potentialities of Microelectronics, Sept. 1979, Zandvoort, Netherlands. Ed. by Jan Berting et al. LC 80-49810. (Vienna Centre Ser.). (Illus.). 263p. 1980. 50.00 (ISBN 0-08-026776-9). Pergamon.

Socio-Political Aspects of the Palaver in Some African Countries. (Introduction to African Culture Ser.: No. 2). 93p. 1980. pap. 4.75 (ISBN 92-3-101641-5, U937, UNESCO). Unipub.

Socio-Political Complex. A. Khoshkish. 1979. 55.00 (ISBN 0-08-023391-0). Pergamon.

Sociobiology & Human Politics. Elliott White. LC 79-3016. 1981. price not set (ISBN 0-669-03602-1). Lexington Bks.

Sociobiology: Beyond Nature-Nurture. Ed. by George W. Barlow & James Silverberg. (AAAS Selected Symposium: No. 35). 625p. 1980. lib. bdg. 35.00x (ISBN 0-89158-372-6); pap. text ed. 15.00x (ISBN 0-89158-960-0). Westview.

Sociobiology Debate. Ed. by Arthur L. Caplan. LC 77-3742. 1978. 14.95 o.p. (ISBN 0-06-010633-6, HarpT). Har-Row.

Sociocultural Systems. Paul E. Zopf, Jr. LC 78-62250. 1978. 17.75 (ISBN 0-8191-0567-8). U Pr of Amer.

Sociocybernetics, Vols. 1 & 2. Ed. by R. F. Geyer & J. van der Zouwen. 1978. Vol. 1. pap. 17.25 (ISBN 90-207-0854-6, Martinus Nijhoff Pubs); Vol. 2. pap. 17.25 (ISBN 90-207-0855-4). Kluwer Boston.

Socioeconomic History of Argentina: Seventeen Seventy-Six to Eighteen Sixty. J. Brown. LC 78-6800. (Latin American Studies: No. 35). (Illus.). 1979. 35.50 (ISBN 0-521-22219-2). Cambridge U Pr.

Socioeconomic Impact of Resource Development: Methods for Assessment. F. Larry Leistritz & Steven H. Murdock. (Social Impact Assessment Ser.: No. 6). 250p. 1981. lib. bdg. 22.50x (ISBN 0-89158-978-3). Westview.

Socioeconomic Methods in Educational Analysis. William H. Weber, III. LC 74-28195. (Illus.). 125p. 1975. text ed. 13.60x (ISBN 0-8077-2449-1); pap. text ed. 7.50x (ISBN 0-8077-2448-3). Tchrs Coll.

Sociolinguistic Attitudes in India: An Historical Reconstruction. Madhav M. Deshpande. (Linguistica Extranea Ser.: Studia 5). 178p. 1979. lib. bdg. 10.50 (ISBN 0-89720-007-1); pap. 5.50 (ISBN 0-89720-008-X). Karoma.

Sociolinguistic Patterns. William Labov. LC 72-80375. (Conduct & Communication Ser). 360p. 1973. 15.00x (ISBN 0-8122-7657-4); pap. 6.95x (ISBN 0-8122-1052-2, Pa Paperbks). U of Pa Pr.

Sociolinguistics. R. A. Hudson. LC 79-51824. (Cambridge Textbooks in Linguistics Ser.). (Illus.). 1980. 37.50 (ISBN 0-521-22833-6); pap. 10.95x (ISBN 0-521-29668-4). Cambridge U Pr.

Sociological Analysis. Arun Sahay. (International Library of Sociology). 220p. 1972. 17.50x (ISBN 0-7100-7363-1). Routledge & Kegan.

Sociological Aspects of Child Development: A Study of Rural Karnataka. M. A. Khan. 212p. 1980. text ed. 15.75x (ISBN 0-391-02127-3). Humanities.

Sociological Footprints: Introductory Readings in Sociology. Leonard Cargan & Jeanne H. Ballantine. LC 78-69541. (Illus.). 1979. pap. text ed. 8.95 (ISBN 0-395-26718-8); inst. manual 0.45 (ISBN 0-395-26717-X). HM.

Sociological Framework for Patient Care. 2nd ed. J. Folta & E. Deck. LC 78-12073. 1979. pap. 14.95 (ISBN 0-471-04496-2, Pub. by Wiley Medical). Wiley.

Sociological Imagination. C. Wright Mills. 1967. pap. 4.95 (ISBN 0-19-500751-4, GB). Oxford U Pr.

Sociological Methodology Nineteen Eighty-One. Ed. by Samuel Leinhardt. LC 68-54940. (Social & Behavioral Science Series). 1981. text ed. price not set (ISBN 0-87589-490-9). Jossey-Bass.

Sociological Methodology 1979. Ed. by Karl F. Schuessler. LC 78-62564. (Social & Behavioral Science Ser.). (Illus.). 1978. text ed. 17.95x (ISBN 0-87589-387-2). Jossey-Bass.

Sociological Perspective. 2nd rev. & enl. ed. Ely Chinoy. 9.00 (ISBN 0-8446-1855-1). Peter Smith.

Sociological Perspectives on Labor Markets. Ed. by Ivar Berg. (Quantitative Studies in Social Relations). 1981. price not set. Acad Pr.

Sociological Praxis: Current Roles & Settings. Ed. by Elisabeth Crawford & Stein Rokkan. LC 75-31292. (Sage Studies in International Sociology: Vol. 3). 1976. 18.00x (ISBN 0-8039-9956-9); pap. 9.95x (ISBN 0-8039-9973-9). Sage.

Sociological Readings in the Conflict Perspective. Ed. by William J. Chambliss. LC 72-579. 1973. pap. text ed. 9.95 (ISBN 0-201-00959-5). A-W.

Sociological Research: Philosophy & Methods. Henry L. Manheim. 1977. 16.95x (ISBN 0-685-81641-9). Dorsey.

Sociological Self-Images. I. L. Horowitz. 1970. 26.00 (ISBN 0-08-016400-5). Pergamon.

Sociological Study of South Africa. G. C. Kinloch. 1972. text ed. 17.00x (ISBN 0-333-13101-0). Humanities.

Sociological Theories: Race & Colonialism. 499p. 1981. pap. 34.00 (ISBN 92-310-1635-0, U1050, UNESCO). Unipub.

Sociological Theory & Modern Society. Talcott Parsons. LC 67-12517. 1967. 25.00 (ISBN 0-02-924200-2). Free Pr.

Sociological Theory & Research: A Critical Appraisal. Ed. by Hubert M. Blalock, Jr. LC 80-754. (Illus.). 1980. 24.95 (ISBN 0-02-903630-5). Free Pr.

Sociological Theory: Classical Founders & Contemporary Perspectives. Doyle P. Johnson. 600p. 1981. text ed. 16.95 (ISBN 0-471-02915-7); tchrs.' ed. avail. (ISBN 0-471-08958-3). Wiley.

Sociological Theory of C. Wright Mills. Joseph A. Scimecca. (National University Pubns. Series in American Studies). 1976. 11.50 (ISBN 0-8046-9155-X). Kennikat.

Sociological Theory: Pretence & Possibility. Keith Dixon. (Monographs in Social Theory). 142p. 1973. 14.95 (ISBN 0-7100-7601-0); pap. 6.95 (ISBN 0-7100-7698-3). Routledge & Kegan.

Sociological Traditions from Generation to Generation: Glimpses of the American Experience. Ed. by Robert K. Merton & Matilda W. Riley. LC 79-26693. (Modern Sociology: Series of Monographs, Treatises, & Texts). (Illus.). 1980. text ed. 14.95 (ISBN 0-89391-034-1); tchrs' ed. 9.95 (ISBN 0-89391-061-9). Ablex Pub.

Sociology. D. Duane Braun. (Cliffs Course Outlines Ser.). (Orig.). 1971. pap. 4.95 (ISBN 0-8220-1502-1). Cliffs.

Sociology. 2nd ed. Theodore Caplow. LC 74-22417. (Illus.). 448p. 1975. text ed. 17.95 (ISBN 0-13-821363-1); study guide 5.95 (ISBN 0-13-821090-X). P-H.

Sociology. 2nd ed. Ronald C. Federico. LC 78-18637. (Illus.). 1979. text ed. 17.95 (ISBN 0-201-03092-6); instr's man. avail. (ISBN 0-201-03093-4). A-W.

Sociology. Salvador Giner. 296p. 1981. 30.50x (ISBN 0-85520-008-1, Pub. by Martin Robertson England); pap. 12.50x (ISBN 0-85520-007-3). Biblio Dist.

Sociology. 3rd ed. David Popenoe. (Illus.). 1977. text ed. 17.95 (ISBN 0-13-821694-0); wkbk & study guide 4.95x (ISBN 0-13-821660-6). P-H.

Sociology. 4th ed. David Popenoe. 1980. text ed. 17.95 (ISBN 0-13-820944-8); wkbk. 5.95 (ISBN 0-13-820977-4). P-H.

Sociology. Ian Robertson. LC 76-52248. (Illus.). 1977. 15.95x o.p. (ISBN 0-87901-116-5); study guide by Harris & Cole 5.95, o.p. (ISBN 0-87901-071-1). Worth.

Sociology. 2nd ed. Ian Robertson. 1981. text ed. write for info. (ISBN 0-87901-134-3); write for info. study guide (ISBN 0-87901-144-0); write for info. reader (ISBN 0-87901-168-8). Worth.

Sociology. Jack Rudman. (Undergraduate Program Field Test Ser.: UPFT-23). (Cloth bdg. avail. on request). pap. 9.95 (ISBN 0-8373-6023-4). Natl Learning.

Sociology. Jon M. Shepard. (Illus.). 600p. 1980. text ed. 16.95 (ISBN 0-8299-0412-3). West Pub.

Sociology. Neil J. Smelser. (Ser. in Sociology). (Illus.). 640p. 1981. text ed. 18.95 (ISBN 0-13-820829-8). P-H.

Sociology. Walter J. Sprott. (Orig.). 1966. pap. text ed. 2.50x (ISBN 0-09-042622-3, Hutchinson U Lib). Humanities.

Sociology. 4th ed. James W. Vander Zanden. LC 78-14447. 1979. text ed. 17.95 (ISBN 0-471-04341-9); tchrs manual (ISBN 0-471-04846-1); study guide 6.50 (ISBN 0-471-04845-3); tchr's. manual journal entries avail. (ISBN 0-471-05813-0). Wiley.

Sociology: A Multiple Paradigm Science. rev ed. Ritzer. 300p. 1980. pap. text ed. 9.40 (ISBN 0-205-07073-6, 8170738). Allyn.

Sociology: A Multiple Paradigm Science. George Ritzer. 240p. 1975. text ed. 10.95x o.p. (ISBN 0-205-04428-X, 8144281). Allyn.

Sociology: A Student's Introduction. Lester Singer. LC 79-48092. 347p. 1980. pap. text ed. 11.25 (ISBN 0-8191-1011-6). U Pr of Amer.

Sociology: A Text with Adapted Readings. 6th, rev. ed. Leonard Broom & Philip Selznick. (Illus.). 1977. text ed. 19.50 scp (ISBN 0-06-040965-7, HarpC); instructor's manual avail. (ISBN 0-06-360956-8); study guide scp 6.95x (ISBN 0-06-040978-9). Har-Row.

Sociology: Advanced Test for the G. R. E. 2nd ed. Harold J. Reddan. LC 66-16410. (Orig.). 1972. pap. 4.95 o.p. (ISBN 0-668-01444-X). Arco.

Sociology: An Introduction. 2nd ed. Earl R. Babbie. 640p. 1980. text ed. 18.95x (ISBN 0-534-00797-X); 6.95 (ISBN 0-534-00798-8). Wadsworth Pub.

Sociology: An Introduction to the Science of Society. Samuel Koenig. (Orig.). 1957. pap. 3.95 (ISBN 0-06-463268-7, EH 268, EH). Har-Row.

Sociology: An Outline for the Intending Student. Ed. by G. Duncan Mitchell. (Outlines Ser). 1970. 14.00x (ISBN 0-7100-6842-5). Routledge & Kegan.

Sociology & American Social Issues. Leonard Gordon & Patricia Harvey. LC 77-78577. (Illus.). 1978. pap. text ed. 18.95 (ISBN 0-395-25369-1); study guide 6.95 (ISBN 0-395-25371-3); inst. manual 0.70 (ISBN 0-395-25370-5). HM.

Sociology & Everyday Life. Marcello Truzzi. (Orig.). 1968. pap. text ed. 10.95 (ISBN 0-13-821215-5). P-H.

Sociology & History. Peter Burke. (Controversies in Sociology Ser.: No. 10). 128p. (Orig.). 1980. text ed. 14.95x (ISBN 0-04-301114-4, 2409); pap. text ed. 5.95x (ISBN 0-04-301115-2, 2410). Allen Unwin.

Sociology & History of American Music & Dance, 1920-1968. D. Duane Braun. 1969. pap. 3.00 o.p. (ISBN 0-89039-152-1). Ann Arbor FL.

Sociology & Human Destiny: Studies in Sociology, Religion & Society. Ed. by Gregory Baum. 224p. 1980. 12.95 (ISBN 0-8164-0110-1). Crossroad NY.

Sociology & Philosophy. Emile Durkheim. 1953. 12.95 (ISBN 0-02-908570-5). Free Pr.

Sociology & Philosophy. Emile Durkheim. Tr. by D. F. Pocock. LC 54-2835. 1974. pap. text ed. 1.95 (ISBN 0-02-908580-2). Free Pr.

Sociology & Psychology: Essays. Marcel Mauss. Tr. by Ben Brewster from Fr. 1979. 18.50x (ISBN 0-7100-8877-5). Routledge & Kegan.

Sociology & Social Problems: A Conceptual Approach. J. M. Shepard & Stewart. (Illus.). 336p. 1976. pap. text ed. 11.95 (ISBN 0-13-821652-5). P-H.

Sociology & Social Research. Geoff Payne et al. (International Library of Sociology). 272p. 1981. price not set (ISBN 0-7100-0626-8). Routledge & Kegan.

Sociology & Social Work. B. J. Heraud. LC 79-119894. 1971. 18.00 (ISBN 0-08-015855-2); pap. 8.50 (ISBN 0-08-015854-4). Pergamon.

Sociology & Socialism in Contemporary China. Siu-Lun Wong. (International Library of Sociology). 1979. 18.00 (ISBN 0-7100-0089-8). Routledge & Kegan.

Sociology & the Demystification of the Modern World. John Rex. (International Library of Sociology Ser.). 1974. 22.00x (ISBN 0-7100-7858-7). Routledge & Kegan.

Sociology & the Field of Public Health. Edward A. Suchman. LC 63-21228. 1963. pap. 2.00 (ISBN 0-87154-864-X). Russell Sage.

Sociology & the Human Experience. 2nd ed. Donald A. Hobbs & Stuart J. Blank. LC 77-16060. 1978. pap. text ed. 15.95x (ISBN 0-471-03108-9); tchr's manual avail. (ISBN 0-471-04071-1); tests avail. (ISBN 0-471-04078-9). Wiley.

Sociology & the Twilight of Man: Homocentrism & Discourse in Sociological Theory. Charles C. Lemert. LC 78-17146. 274p. 1980. pap. 8.95 (ISBN 0-8093-0975-0). S Ill U Pr.

Sociology & Theology. Ed. by David Martin et al. 170p. 1980. 22.50x (ISBN 0-312-74007-7). St Martin.

Sociology As an Art Form. Robert Nisbet. LC 76-9278. 1976. 12.95 (ISBN 0-19-502102-9). Oxford U Pr.

Sociology: Change & Continuity. Carol A. Warren. 1977. 17.95x (ISBN 0-256-01944-4). Dorsey.

Sociology: Concepts & Characteristics. 4th ed. Judson R. Landis. 416p. 1979. pap. text ed. 13.95x (ISBN 0-534-00784-8). Wadsworth Pub.

Sociology: Concepts & Characteristics. 3rd ed. Judson R. Landis, Jr. 1977. pap. 10.95x o.p. (ISBN 0-534-00492-X). Wadsworth Pub.

Sociology: Focus on Society. Lucile Duberman & Clayton Hartjen. 1979. text ed. 17.95x (ISBN 0-673-15287-1); study guide 4.95x (ISBN 0-673-15294-4). Scott F.

Sociology for a New Day. Thomas F. Hoult. 384p. 1974. pap. text ed. 7.95 o.p. (ISBN 0-394-31736-X). Random.

Sociology for a New Day: Reader. 2nd ed. Thomas F. Hoult. 1979. pap. text ed. 6.95x (ISBN 0-394-32243-6). Random.

Sociology for Pleasure. Marcello Truzzi. (Illus.). 416p. 1974. pap. text ed. 9.95 o.p. (ISBN 0-13-821256-2). P-H.

Sociology for the Modern Mind. Imogen Seger. (Modern Mind Ser.). 336p. 1973. 7.95 o.s.i. (ISBN 0-02-609090-2). Macmillan.

Sociology for the Seventies: A Contemporary Perspective. Ed. by Morris L. Medley & James E. Conyers. LC 70-168640. 1972. pap. text ed. 9.95x o.p. (ISBN 0-471-59015-0). Wiley.

Sociology: Human Society. 2nd brief ed. Melvin L. DeFleur et al. 1977. pap. 12.95x (ISBN 0-673-07928-7). Scott F.

Sociology: Human Society. 3rd ed. Melvin L. DeFleur et al. 1981. text ed. 17.95x (ISBN 0-673-15211-1). Scott F.

Sociology in Action: A Critique of Selected Conceptions of the Role of Sociologist. Christopher G. Bryant. LC 75-9120. 1976. 26.95 (ISBN 0-470-11470-3). Halsted Pr.

Sociology in America: A Bicentennial Review. Ed. by Jack F. Kinton. 1980. pap. 0.95 o.p. (ISBN 0-685-80070-9). Soc Sci & Soc Res.

Sociology in Bondage: An Introduction to Graduate Study. Harold A. Nelson. LC 80-65605. 145p. 1981. perfect bdg. 9.95 (ISBN 0-86548-051-6). Century Twenty One.

Sociology in Medicine. R. K. Jones & P. A. Jones. LC 75-11723. 1976. 15.95 (ISBN 0-470-44936-5). Halsted Pr.

Sociology in Medicine. 2nd ed. Mervyn W. Susser & W. Watson. (Illus.). 1977. pap. text ed. 25.00x (ISBN 0-19-264912-4). Oxford U Pr.

Sociology in the Balance. Johan Goudsblom. LC 77-4368. 1977. 17.50x (ISBN 0-231-04290-6). Columbia U Pr.

Sociology in the USSR: A Collection of Readings from Soviet Sources. Ed. by Stephen P. Dunn. LC 66-23895. 1969. 17.50 o.p. (ISBN 0-87332-029-8). M E Sharpe.

Sociology: Nurses & Their Patients in a Modern Society. 9th ed. Lida F. Thompson et al. LC 74-34417. 1975. text ed. 10.95 (ISBN 0-8016-4942-0). Mosby.

Sociology of Aging. Diana K. Harris & William E. Cole. LC 79-89741. (Illus.). 1980. text ed. 15.95 (ISBN 0-395-28528-3); inst. manual 0.75 (ISBN 0-395-28529-1). HM.

Sociology of America: A Guide to Information Sources. Ed. by Charles Mark & Paula F. Mark. LC 73-17560. (American Studies Information Guide Ser.: Vol. 1). 564p. 1976. 30.00 (ISBN 0-8103-1267-0). Gale.

Sociology of American Corrections. Neal Shover. 1979. pap. text ed. 10.95x (ISBN 0-256-02216-X). Dorsey.

Sociology of Belief. James T. Borhek & Richard F. Curtis. LC 74-26584. 192p. 1975. 11.50 o.p. (ISBN 0-471-08895-1, Pub. by Wiley-Interscience). Wiley.

Sociology of Belief. James T. Borhek & Richard F. Curtis. LC 80-12472. 216p. 1981. Repr. of 1975 ed. lib. bdg. write for info. (ISBN 0-89874-177-7). Krieger.

Sociology of Change & Reaction in Latin America. Dale Johnson. LC 73-7794. (Studies in Sociology Ser). 1973. pap. text ed. 3.50 (ISBN 0-672-61238-0). Bobbs.

Sociology of Childhood. 2nd ed. Marvin R. Koller & Oscar W. Ritchie. LC 77-13314. (P-H Ser. in Sociology). (Illus.). 1978. text ed. 17.95 (ISBN 0-13-821074-8). P-H.

Sociology of Comte: An Appreciation. E. E. Evans-Pritchard. (Orig.). 1970. pap. text ed. 2.00x (ISBN 0-7190-0425-X). Humanities.

Sociology of Corrections: A Book of Readings. Robert G. Leger & John R. Stratton. LC 76-51462. 1977. text ed. 15.95x (ISBN 0-471-01680-2). Wiley.

Sociology of Crime & Delinquency. 2nd ed. Marvin E. Wolfgang et al. LC 73-96041. 1970. pap. text ed. 16.95 (ISBN 0-471-95955-3). Wiley.

Sociology of Developing Societies. Ankie M. M Hoogvelt. LC 77-522. 1977. text ed. 20.00x (ISBN 0-391-00703-3); pap. text ed. 15.75x (ISBN 0-391-00704-1). Humanities.

Sociology of Deviance: An Introduction. Douglas & Waksler. 512p. 1981. text ed. 16.95 (ISBN 0-316-19111-6); tchr's ed free (ISBN 0-316-19112-4). Little.

Sociology of Education. Wilbur Brookover & Edsel L. Ericksen. 1975. 18.50x (ISBN 0-256-01674-7). Dorsey.

Sociology of Education. Ann P. Parelius & Robert J. Parelius. LC 77-10948. (P-H Series in Sociology). (Illus.). 1978. 17.95 (ISBN 0-13-821173-6). P-H.

Sociology of Education: A Guide to Information Sources. Ed. by Francesco Cordasco & David N. Alloway. LC 78-10310. (Education Information Guide Ser.: Vol. 2). 1979. 30.00 (ISBN 0-8103-1436-3). Gale.

Sociology of Education: A Sourcebook. 3rd ed. Holger R. Stub. (Anthropology & Sociology Ser.). 1975. pap. text ed. 11.50x (ISBN 0-256-01630-5). Dorsey.

Sociology of Education: An Introduction. 2nd ed. Sarane S. Boocock. LC 79-88445. (Illus.). 1980. text ed. 17.95 (ISBN 0-395-28524-0). HM.

Sociology of Education: Beyond Equality. Philip Wexler. LC 75-35994. (Studies in Sociology). 64p. 1976. pap. text ed. 3.50 (ISBN 0-672-61338-7). Bobbs.

Sociology of Education: Emerging Patterns of Class Status & Power in the Public Schools. R. Corwin. 1965. 17.95 (ISBN 0-13-821207-4). P-H.

Sociology of Education: Introductory Analytical Perspectives. D. F. Swift. (Students Library of Sociology Ser). 1970. pap. text ed. 2.75x (ISBN 0-7100-6362-8). Humanities.

Sociology of Educational Ideas. Julia Evetts. (Students Library of Education). 176p. 1973. 14.00x (ISBN 0-7100-7609-6); pap. 7.00 (ISBN 0-7100-7619-3). Routledge & Kegan.

Sociology of Emile Durkheim. Robert Nisbet. 320p. 1973. 17.95 (ISBN 0-19-501733-1); pap. 4.95x (ISBN 0-19-501734-X). Oxford U Pr.

Sociology of Everyday Life. Andrew J. Weigert. 272p. 1981. pap. text ed. 10.95 (ISBN 0-582-28199-7). Longman.

Sociology of Georg Simmel. Georg Simmel. Tr. by Kurt H. Wolff. 1964. pap. text ed. 7.95 (ISBN 0-02-928920-3). Free Pr.

Sociology of Health. Andrew C. Twaddle & Richard M. Hessler. LC 76-41215. (Illus.). 1977. pap. text ed. 14.95 (ISBN 0-8016-5153-0). Mosby.

Sociology of Housing: Studies at Berinsfield. R. N. Morris & John Mogey. 1965. text ed. 8.25x o.p. (ISBN 0-7100-3454-7). Humanities.

Sociology of Journalism & the Press. Ed. by Harry Christian. (Sociological Review Monograph: No. 29). 1981. pap. 9.95x (ISBN 0-8476-3257-1). Rowman.

Sociology of Karl Mannheim: Chaos or Planning? With a Bibliographical Guide to the Sociology of Knowledge, Ideological Analysis, & Social Planning. Gunter W. Remmling. (International Library of Sociology). 1974. text ed. 15.75x (ISBN 0-391-00376-3). Humanities.

Sociology of Knowledge: An Essay in Aid of a Deeper Understanding of the History of Ideas. Werner Stark. (International Library of Sociology & Social Reconstruction Ser.). 1958. pap. text ed. 13.00x (ISBN 0-7100-6554-X). Humanities.

Sociology of Language. Joshua A. Fishman. 1972. pap. 9.95 (ISBN 0-912066-16-4). Newbury Hse.

Sociology of Law. Ed. by Pat Carlen. (Sociological Review Monograph: No. 23). 250p. 1976. pap. 23.50x (ISBN 0-8476-2296-7). Rowman.

Sociology of Law. Georges Gurvitch. (International Library of Sociology). 264p. 1973. 18.00x (ISBN 0-7100-7519-7). Routledge & Kegan.

Sociology of Law & Order. Lynn McDonald. LC 76-9753. 330p. 1976. 32.50 o.p. (ISBN 0-89158-614-8); text ed. 15.00 o.p. (ISBN 0-686-67421-9). Westview.

Sociology of Leisure. Ed. by Theodore B. Johannis, Jr. & Neil Bull. LC 73-87853. (Sage Contemporary Social Science Issues: No. 1). 1974. 4.95x (ISBN 0-8039-0318-9). Sage.

Sociology of Literature: Applied Studies. Ed. by Diana Laurenson. (Sociological Review Monograph: No. 26). 284p. 1978. pap. 28.00x (ISBN 0-8476-2299-1). Rowman.

Sociology of Literature: Theoretical Approaches. Ed. by Jane Routh & Janet Wolff. (Sociological Review Monograph: No. 25). 180p. 1977. pap. 18.50x (ISBN 0-8476-2298-3). Rowman.

Sociology of Mental Disorder. William C. Cockerham. (Ser. in Sociology). (Illus.). 300p. 1981. text ed. 17.95 (ISBN 0-13-820886-7). P-H.

Sociology of Mental Disorders. William Eaton. 1979. 19.95 (ISBN 0-03-046466-8). Praeger.

Sociology of Mental Health & Illness. Peter K. Manning & Martine Zucker. LC 76-16067. (Studies in Sociology). 1976. pap. text ed. 5.95 (ISBN 0-672-61265-8). Bobbs.

Sociology of Mental Illness. Bernard J. Gallagher, III. (Ser. in Sociology). (Illus.). 1980. text ed. 14.95 (ISBN 0-13-820928-6). P-H.

Sociology of Organizational Change. E. A. Johns. LC 73-8972. 182p. 1974. text ed. 25.00 (ISBN 0-08-017601-1); pap. text ed. 12.75 (ISBN 0-08-017602-X). Pergamon.

Sociology of Organizations. O. Grusky & G. A. Miller. LC 69-20286. 1970. text ed. 16.95 (ISBN 0-02-913180-4). Free Pr.

Sociology of Organizations: Basic Studies. Ed. by Oscar Grusky & George A. Miller. LC 80-1060. (Illus.). 1981. 18.95 (ISBN 0-02-913060-3); pap. text ed. 12.95 (ISBN 0-02-912930-3). Free Pr.

Sociology of Politics. R. Bhaskaran. 1967. 6.50x o.p. (ISBN 0-210-27169-8). Asia.

Sociology of Power. R. Martin. (International Library of Sociology). 1977. 20.00x (ISBN 0-7100-8563-X). Routledge & Kegan.

Sociology of Race Relations: Reflection & Reform. Thomas F. Pettigrew. LC 79-54666. (Illus.). 1980. pap. text ed. 10.95 (ISBN 0-02-925110-9). Free Pr.

Sociology of Racial Intergration in Guyana. Iris D. Sukedo. 224p. 1981. 9.50 (ISBN 0-682-49686-3). Exposition.

Sociology of Religion: Classical & Contemporary Approaches. Barbara Hargrove. LC 79-50879. 1979. pap. text ed. 11.95x (ISBN 0-88295-211-0). AHM Pub.

Sociology of Science & Research. Ed. by Janos Farkas. (Illus.). 503p. 1979. 47.50x (ISBN 963-05-2204-7). Intl Pubns Serv.

Sociology of Science in Europe. Ed. by Robert K. Merton & Jerry Gaston. LC 77-2996. (Perspectives in Sociology). 397p. 1977. 22.95x (ISBN 0-8093-0633-6). S Ill U Pr.

Sociology of Social Conflicts. Louis Kriesberg. (General Sociology Ser.). (Illus.). 304p. 1973. text ed. 15.95 (ISBN 0-13-821546-4). P-H.

Sociology of Social Problems. 6th ed. Paul B. Horton & Gerald R. Leslie. LC 77-14610. (Illus.). 1978. text ed. 17.95 (ISBN 0-13-821637-1); study guide & wkbk. 4.95 (ISBN 0-13-821611-8). P-H.

Sociology of Social Problems. 7th ed. Paul B. Horton & Gerald R. Leslie. (Illus.). 672p. 1981. text ed. 18.95 (ISBN 0-13-821702-5). P-H.

Sociology of Sociology. Robert W. Friedrichs. LC 77-91882. 1972. pap. text ed. 7.95 (ISBN 0-02-910880-2). Free Pr.

Sociology of Sociology. Halmos. 1970. pap. text ed. 7.75x. Humanities.

Sociology of Southeast Asia: Readings on Social Change & Development. Ed. by Hans-Dieter Evers. (Illus.). 350p. 1980. 32.50 (ISBN 0-19-580408-2). Oxford U Pr.

Sociology of Teaching. W. Waller. 1965. pap. text ed. 14.50 (ISBN 0-471-91890-3). Wiley.

Sociology of the Family: New Directions for Britain. Ed. by Chris Harris et al. (Sociological Review Monograph: No. 28). 240p. 1979. 30.00x (ISBN 0-8476-3265-2); pap. 18.95x (ISBN 0-8476-3258-X). Rowman.

Sociology of the Middle East: A Stocktaking & Interpretation. Ed. by C. Van Nieuwenhuijze. (Social, Economic & Political Studies of the Middle East: Vol. 1). (Illus.). 819p. 1971. text ed. 128.25x (ISBN 90-040-2564-2). Humanities.

Sociology of the Possible. 2nd ed. Richard J. Ofshe. 1977. pap. text ed. 10.95 (ISBN 0-13-821595-2). P-H.

Sociology of the School. Myles W. Rodehaver et al. LC 80-26021. x, 262p. 1981. Repr. of 1957 ed. lib. bdg. 27.50x (ISBN 0-313-22897-3, ROSSC). Greenwood.

Sociology of the School Curriculum. John Eggleston. 1977. 12.00x (ISBN 0-7100-8565-6); pap. 7.95 (ISBN 0-7100-8566-4). Routledge & Kegan.

Sociology of the Third World. J. E. Goldthorpe. LC 74-12979. (Illus.). 336p. 1975. 39.95 (ISBN 0-521-20521-2); pap. 9.95x (ISBN 0-521-09924-2). Cambridge U Pr.

Sociology of the Workplace. Ed. by Malcolm Warner. LC 73-15572. 291p. 1973. 15.95 (ISBN 0-470-92113-7). Halsted Pr.

Sociology of Urban Education: Desegregation & Integration. Charles V. Willie. LC 78-4403. (Illus.). 1978. 18.95 (ISBN 0-669-02348-5). Lexington Bks.

Sociology of Urban Regions. 2nd ed. Alvin Boskoff. (Illus.). 1970. pap. text ed. 17.95 (ISBN 0-13-821751-3). P-H.

Sociology of Urban Women's Image in African Literature. Kenneth Little. 174p. 1980. 27.50x (ISBN 0-8476-6290-X). Rowman.

Sociology of Yiddish: International Journal of the Sociology of Language, No. 24. Ed. by Joshua A. Fishman. 1980. pap. text ed. 21.00x (ISBN 90-279-3058-9). Mouton.

Sociology: Readings on Human Society. John E. Owen. 1981. pap. text ed. 7.95x (ISBN 0-673-15265-0). Scott F.

Sociology: Social Science & Social Concerns. 3rd ed. Ritchie P. Lowry & Robert P. Rankin. 1977. text ed. 16.95x (ISBN 0-669-99648-3); instructor's manual free (ISBN 0-669-03186-0); study guide 5.95x (ISBN 0-669-00339-5). Heath.

Sociology: Traditional & Radical Perspectives. H. J. Sherman. 1981. pap. text ed. 15.70 (ISBN 0-06-318190-8, Pub. by Har-Row Ltd Eng). Har-Row.

Sociology: Understanding Social Behavior. Alan P. Bates & Joseph Julian. 1975. 19.50 (ISBN 0-395-18652-8); instructor's guide & resource manual by patricia a. harvey 1.75 (ISBN 0-395-18794-X). HM.

Sociology, War & Disarmament: Studies in Peace Research. Johan Niezing. (Publications of the Polemological Centre of the Free University of Brussles: Vol. 1). 144p. pap. text ed. 13.50 (ISBN 90-237-6223-1, Pub. by Swets Pub Serv Holland). Swets North Am.

Sociology-with a Human Face: Sociology As If People Mattered. Kloss et al. (Illus.). 352p. 1976. text ed. 13.95 o.p. (ISBN 0-8016-2718-4); pap. 9.50 o.p. (ISBN 0-8016-2712-5). Mosby.

Sociology: Women, Men & Society. Elizabeth Almquist et al. (Illus.). 1978. pap. text ed. 13.95 (ISBN 0-8299-0174-4); instrs.' manual avail. (ISBN 0-8299-0450-6). West Pub.

Sociomedical Health Indicators. Ed. by Jack Elinson & Athilia E. Siegman. 224p. (Orig.). 1979. pap. 9.00x (ISBN 0-89503-013-6). Baywood Pub.

Sociopolitical Effects of Energy Use & Policy. Ed. by Charles T. Unseld et al. LC 79-93181. (Study of Nuclear & Alternative Energy Systems Ser.). xxi, 511p. 1980. pap. text ed. 11.75 (ISBN 0-309-02948-1). Natl Acad Pr.

Sociotechnical Systems: A Sourcebook. Ed. by William A. Pasmore & John J. Sherwood. LC 77-20543. 366p. 1978. pap. 14.95 (ISBN 0-88390-142-0). Univ Assocs.

Sociotechnical Systems: Factors in Analysis, Design & Management. Kenyon De Greene. (Illus.). 416p. 1973. ref. ed. 18.95 (ISBN 0-13-821553-7). P-H.

Socks. Beverly Cleary. LC 72-10298. (Illus.). 192p. (gr. 3-7). 1973. 7.75 (ISBN 0-688-20067-2); PLB 7.44 (ISBN 0-688-30067-7). Morrow.

Socorro: A Historic Study. John P. Conron. LC 79-56821. (Illus.). 144p. 1980. 14.95 (ISBN 0-8263-0528-8). U of NM Pr.

Socrates. William K. Guthrie. 1971. pap. 9.95x (ISBN 0-521-09667-7). Cambridge U Pr.

Socrates & Legal Obligation. R. E. Allen. 176p. 1981. 17.50x (ISBN 0-8166-0962-4); pap. 8.95x (ISBN 0-8166-0965-9). U of Minn Pr.

Socrates, Buddha, Confucius & Jesus: Taken from Vol. 1 of the Great Philosophers. Karl Jaspers. Tr. by Ralph Manheim. Orig. Title: Great Philosophers, Vol. 1 (Pt. 1) 1966. pap. 2.50 (ISBN 0-15-683580-0, HB99, Harv). HarBraceJ.

Socrates: The Original & Its Image. Alan F. Blum. 1978. 20.00x (ISBN 0-7100-8766-7). Routledge & Kegan.

Sod & Stubble: The Story of a Kansas Homestead. John Ise. LC 37-10937. (Illus.). 1967. 13.50x (ISBN 0-8032-0207-5); pap. 3.50 (ISBN 0-8032-5098-3, BB 372, Bison). U of Nebr Pr.

Sod House. Cass G. Barns. LC 73-100812. (Illus.). 1970. 13.95x (ISBN 0-8032-1153-8); pap. 3.95 (ISBN 0-8032-5700-7, BB 511, Bison). U of Nebr Pr.

Sod House. Elizabeth Coatsworth. 1967. 7.95 (ISBN 0-02-721690-X). Macmillan.

Sod-House Frontier: A Social History of the Northern Plains from the Creation of Kansas & Nebraska to the Admission of the Dakotas. Everett Dick. LC 78-24204. (Illus.). 1979. pap. 7.95 (ISBN 0-8032-6551-4, BB 700, Bison). U of Nebr Pr.

Sodeman's Pathologic Physiology: Mechanisms of Disease. 6th ed. William A. Sodeman & Thomas M. Sodeman. LC 78-1790. (Illus.). 1145p. 1979. text ed. 39.50 (ISBN 0-7216-8473-4). Saunders.

Sodium & Water Homeostasis. Ed. by Barry M. Brenner & Jay H. Stein. (Contemporary Issues in Nephrology: Vol. 1). (Illus.). 1978. text ed. 25.00x o.p. (ISBN 0-443-08005-4). Churchill.

Sodium-Cooled Fast Reactor Engineering. (Illus., Orig.). 1970. pap. 52.50 (ISBN 92-0-050270-9, IAEA). Unipub.

Sodom Had No Bible. Leonard Ravenhill. 1979. pap. 2.95 (ISBN 0-87123-496-3, 210496). Bethany Fell.

Soft Contact Lenses: Clinical & Applied Technology. Montague Ruben. LC 77-26918. (Clinical Ophthalmology Ser.). 1978. 44.50 (ISBN 0-471-74430-1, Pub. by Wiley Medical). Wiley.

Soft Hands That Kill. Marcella Powers. LC 77-74001. 1979. 8.00 o.p. (ISBN 0-89430-010-5). Morgan-Pacific.

Soft Machine. William Burroughs. Bd. with Nova Express; Wild Boys. LC 80-8062. 544p. (Orig.). 1981. pap. 5.95 (ISBN 0-394-17749-5, B 446, BC). Grove.

Soft Sculpture. Carolyn V. Hall. LC 80-67546. (Illus.). 112p. 1981. 14.95 (ISBN 0-87192-129-4). Davis Mass.

Soft Skies of France. Samuel Chamberlain. (Illus.). 1953. 12.50 (ISBN 0-8038-6662-3). Hastings.

Soft Skull Sam. Syd Hoff. LC 80-23104. (Let Me Read Bk.). (Illus.). 32p. (ps-3). 1981. pap. 2.95 (ISBN 0-15-277063-1, VoyB). HarBraceJ.

Soft Skull Sam. Syd Hoff. LC 80-24590. (Let Me Read Bk.). (Illus.). 32p. (gr. 4-6). 1981. 6.95 (ISBN 0-15-277062-3, HJ). HarBraceJ.

Soft Stones Cast Upon the Tender Earth. Wilf Redo Castano. 1981. pap. 3.50 (ISBN 0-915016-28-1). Second Coming.

Soft Surface Floor Coverings. Fairchild Market Research Div. (Fact Files Ser.). (Illus.). 75p. 1980. pap. 10.00 (ISBN 0-87005-354-X). Fairchild.

Soft-Tissue Tumors. Association of Bone & Joint Surgeons. Ed. by Anthony F. Depalma. (Clinical Orthopaedics Ser, Vol. 19). (Illus.). 1961. 15.00 (ISBN 0-685-14259-0). Lippincott.

Soft Tissue Tumors. Franz M. Enzinger & Raffaele Lattes. (Anatomic Pathology Seminars). (Illus.). 1975. atlas 78.50 o.p. (ISBN 0-89189-059-9, 15-014-00); pap. text ed. 9.00 o.p. (ISBN 0-89189-060-2, 50-1-039-00); slides 22.50 o.p. (ISBN 0-685-78073-2, 01-1-073-01). Am Soc Clinical.

Soft Touch. John D. MacDonald. 1978. pap. 1.95 (ISBN 0-449-13957-3, GM). Fawcett.

Soft Toys. Delphine Davidson. 1971. 6.50 o.p. (ISBN 0-8231-5028-3). Branford.

Soft Toys. Glen Pownall. 80p. 1980. 7.50 (ISBN 0-85467-008-4, Pub. by Viking Sevenseas New Zealnd). Intl Schol Bk Serv.

Soft Toys & Dolls. Sunset Editors. LC 76-46657. (Illus.). 80p. 1977. pap. 2.95 o.p. (ISBN 0-376-04692-9, Sunset Bks.). Sunset-Lane.

Soft Wheat: Production, Breeding, Milling, & Uses. W. T. Yamazaki. LC 80-65826. (AACC Monograph: Vol. VI). 352p. 1980. 36.00 (ISBN 0-913250-17-1). Am Assn Cereal Chem.

Soft X-Ray Band Spectra & the Electronic Structures of Metals & Materials. Ed. by Derek J. Fabian. 1969. 52.00 (ISBN 0-12-247450-3). Acad Pr.

Software. Ed. by Carl Warren. LC 79-67462. (Best of Interface Age Ser.: Vol. 2). 150p. 1980. pap. 9.95 (ISBN 0-918398-37-1). Dilithium Pr.

Software Debugging for Microcomputers. Robert Bruce. (Illus.). 1980. text ed. 18.95 (ISBN 0-8359-7021-3); pap. text ed. 10.95 (ISBN 0-8359-7020-5). Reston.

Software Design for Microcomputers. Carol A. Ogdin. (Illus.). 1978. ref. ed. 16.95 (ISBN 0-13-821744-0); pap. 12.95 (ISBN 0-13-821801-3). P-H.

Software Design: Methods & Techniques. Lawrence J. Peters. LC 80-50609. (Orig.). 1981. pap. 22.00 (ISBN 0-917072-19-7). Yourdon.

Software Development Tools. W. E. Riddle & R. E. Fairley. (Illus.). 280p. 1980. pap. 19.80 (ISBN 0-387-10326-0). Springer-Verlag.

Software Engineering. Ed. by Herbert Freeman & P. M. Lewis, II. 1980. 21.00 (ISBN 0-12-267160-0). Acad Pr.

Software Engineering, Vols. 1-2. Julius Tou. 1970. Vol. 1. 38.50 (ISBN 0-12-696201-4); Vol. 2. 38.50 (ISBN 0-12-696202-2). Acad Pr.

Software Engineering for Micros: The Electrifying Streamlined Blueprint Speedcode Method. T. G. Lewis. 168p. 1979. pap. 7.70 (ISBN 0-8104-5166-2). Hayden.

Software for Computer Control: Proceedings. IFAC-IFIP Symposium on Software for Computer Control, 2nd, Prague, Czechoslovakia, 11-15, June 1979. Ed. by M. Novak. (IFAC Proceedings). (Illus.). 430p. 1979. 84.00 (ISBN 0-08-024448-3). Pergamon.

Software for Roundoff Analysis of Matrix Algorithms. Webb Miller & Celia Wrathall. LC 80-12662. (Computer Science & Applied Mathematics Ser.). 1980. 18.50 (ISBN 0-12-497250-0). Acad Pr.

Software in BASIC. Ed. by Carl Warren. LC 79-67462. (Best of Interface Age Ser.: Vol. 1). 400p. 1979. pap. 14.95 (ISBN 0-918398-36-3). Dilithium Pr.

Software Maintenance Guidebook. Robert L. Glass & Ronald A. Noiseux. (Illus.). 208p. 1981. text ed. 21.95 (ISBN 0-13-821728-9). P-H.

Software Maintenance Management. Bennet P. Lientz & E. Burton Swanson. LC 80-12154. 160p. 1980. pap. text ed. 8.95 (ISBN 0-201-04205-3). A-W.

Software Manual for the Elementary Functions. William J. Cody, Jr. & William White. (Illus.). 288p. 1980. text ed. 17.95 (ISBN 0-13-822064-6). P-H.

Software Packages, G-032. 1980. 750.00 (ISBN 0-89336-159-3). BCC.

Software Portability. Ed. by P. J. Brown. LC 76-40835. (Illus.). 1977. 32.95 (ISBN 0-521-21485-8); pap. 12.95x (ISBN 0-521-29725-7). Cambridge U Pr.

Software Quality Management. Cooper. 1979. 21.50 (ISBN 0-89433-093-4). Petrocelli.

Software Reliability Guidebook. Robert L. Glass. (Illus.). 1979. text ed. 21.95 (ISBN 0-13-821785-8). P-H.

Software Reliability: Principles & Practices. Glenford J. Myers. LC 76-22202. (Business Data Processing Ser.). 1976. 25.95 (ISBN 0-471-62765-8, Pub. by Wiley-Interscience). Wiley.

Software Soliloquies. Robert L. Glass. 1981. 9.95. Computing Trends.

Software Tools. Brian W. Kernighan & P. J. Plauger. 286p. 1976. pap. text ed. 12.95 (ISBN 0-201-03669-X). A-W.

Sofu Zokei (the Art of Sofu) Sofu Teshigahara. (Illus.). 260p. (Japanese.). 1978. 200.00 (ISBN 0-8048-1344-2, Pub. by Shufunotomo Co Ltd Japan). C E Tuttle.

Sogdian Painting: The Pictorial Epic in Oriental Art. Guitty Azarpay. 300p. 1981. 50.00x (ISBN 0-520-03765-0). U of Cal Pr.

Sogo Shosha: Japanese Multi-National Trading Companies. Alexander Young. LC 78-18935. (Westview Special Studies in International Economics). 1979. lib. bdg. 25.50x (ISBN 0-89158-425-0). Westview.

Sogoshosha: Engines of Export-Based Growth. Y. Tsurumi. 91p. 1980. pap. text ed. 8.95x (ISBN 0-920380-58-1, Pub. by Inst Res Pub Canada). Renouf.

Soho Madonna. Ellen A. Conley. 1980. pap. 2.25 (ISBN 0-380-75614-5, 75614). Avon.

Soho: The Artist in the City. Charles R. Simpson. LC 80-27083. 352p. 1981. 20.00 (ISBN 0-226-75937-7). U of Chicago Pr.

Soil & Civilization. Edward Hyams. 312p. 1980. 15.00x (ISBN 0-7195-3311-2, Pub. by Murray Pubs England). State Mutual Bk.

Soil & Crop Productivity. S. V. Rajan & H. G. Rao. 1973. 10.00x (ISBN 0-210-27100-0). Asia.

Soil & Vegetation Systems. Stephen A. Trudgill. (Contemporary Problems in Geography Ser.). (Illus.). 1977. 29.95x (ISBN 0-19-874058-1); pap. 9.95x (ISBN 0-19-874059-X). Oxford U Pr.

Soil & Water Conservation. Boy Scouts Of America. LC 19-600. (Illus.). 96p. (gr. 6-12). 1968. pap. 0.70x (ISBN 0-8395-3291-1). BSA.

Soil & Water Conservation. Frederick R. Troeh et al. Ed. by Miriam Troeh. (Illus.). 1980. text ed. 25.95 (ISBN 0-13-822155-3). P-H.

Soil & Water Conservation Engineering. 2nd ed. G. O. Schwab et al. LC 66-14131. 1966. 30.00 (ISBN 0-471-76520-1). Wiley.

Soil & Water: Physical Principles & Processes. Daniel Hillel. (Physiological Ecology Ser). 1971. 29.50 (ISBN 0-12-348550-9). Acad Pr.

Soil Animals. Friedrich Schaller. (Ann Arbor Science Library Ser). (Illus.). 1968. pap. 1.95 o.p. (ISBN 0-472-05016-8, 516, AA). U of Mich Pr.

Soil Chemistry. Hinrich Bohn et al. LC 79-14515. 1979. 22.95 (ISBN 0-471-04082-7, Pub. by Wiley-Interscience). Wiley.

Soil Classification for Soil Survey: Monographs on Soil Survey. B. E. Butler. (Illus.). 144p. 1980. 22.50x (ISBN 0-19-854510-X). Oxford U Pr.

Soil Conditions & Plant Growth. 10th ed. E. W. Russell. LC 74-168964. (Illus.). 867p. 1974. text ed. 33.00x (ISBN 0-582-44048-3). Longman.

Soil Conservation. Norman W. Hudson. pap. 21.50 o.p. (ISBN 0-7134-0562-7, Pub. by Batsford England). David & Charles.

Soil Conservation. J. H. Stallings. 1957. 21.95 (ISBN 0-13-821819-6). P-H.

Soil Conservation & Management in the Humid Tropics. Ed. by D. J. Greenland & R. Lal. LC 76-8908. 1977. 58.75 (ISBN 0-471-99473-1, Pub. by Wiley-Interscience). Wiley.

Soil Conservation Districts in Action. W. Robert Parks. (Illus.). 1952. 2.00x o.p. (ISBN 0-685-99406-6). Iowa St U Pr.

Soil Conservation Policies: An Assessment. Pref. by William C. Moldenhauer. LC 80-406. 154p. (Orig.). 1980. pap. 6.50 (ISBN 0-935734-04-X). Soil Conservation.

Soil Dynamics. Shamsher Prakash. (Illus.). 432p. 1981. text ed. 26.95 (ISBN 0-07-050658-2, C); student's manual 4.95 (ISBN 0-07-050659-0). McGraw.

Soil Erosion. R. P. C. Morgan. (Topics in Applied Geography). (Illus.). 1979. pap. text ed. 11.50x (ISBN 0-582-48692-0). Longman.

Soil Erosion & Sedimentation Control. Beckett Jackson Raeder, Inc. (Illus.). 150p. 1980. pap. text ed. 20.00 (ISBN 0-918436-15-X). Environ Design.

Soil Fungi & Soil Fertility. S. D. Garrett. 1963. pap. 15.00 (ISBN 0-08-010475-4). Pergamon.

Soil Fungi & Soil Fertility: An Introduction to Soil Mycology. 2nd ed. S. D. Garrett. (Illus.). 150p. 1981. 19.21 (ISBN 0-08-025507-8); pap. 9.51 (ISBN 0-08-025506-X). Pergamon.

Soil Geography. J. G. Cruickshank. 1972. 14.95 o.p. (ISBN 0-470-18919-3). Halsted Pr.

Soil Improvement: History, Capability & Outlook. Compiled By American Society of Civil Engineers. 192p. 1978. pap. text ed. 8.75 (ISBN 0-87262-126-X). Am Soc Civil Eng.

Soil Management for Conservation & Production. Ray L. Cook. LC 62-8770. (Illus.). 1962. 24.95 (ISBN 0-471-16995-1). Wiley.

Soil Map of the World: Legend, Vol. 1. 59p. 1975. pap. 36.00 with sheet & text (ISBN 92-3-101125-1, M81, UNESCO). Unipub.

Soil Map of the World: Part Four, South America. 1972. with 2 sheets & text 54.75 (ISBN 0-685-27878-6, M91, UNESCO). Unipub.

Soil Map of the World 1: 5 000 000: Mexico & Central America, Vol. 3. (Illus.). 1976. pap. text ed. 13.00 (ISBN 92-3-101127-8, M86, Unesco). Unipub.

Soil Mechanics. T. William Lambe & Robert V. Whitman. LC 68-30915. (Soil Engineering Ser). 1969. 29.95 (ISBN 0-471-51192-7). Wiley.

Soil Mechanics. 2nd ed. Tien Hsing Wu. 464p. 1976. text ed. 25.95x (ISBN 0-205-04863-3, 2748630). Allyn.

Soil Mechanics & Foundations. Parcher. 1968. text ed. 22.95x (ISBN 0-675-09746-0). Merrill.

Soil Mechanics in Engineering Practice. 2nd ed. Karl Terzaghi & R. B. Peck. LC 67-17356. 1967. 34.95 (ISBN 0-471-85273-2, Pub. by Wiley-Interscience). Wiley.

Soil Micro-Organisms. T. R. Gray & S. T. Williams. LC 75-9595. (Illus.). 240p. 1975. pap. text ed. 14.95x (ISBN 0-582-44160-9). Longman.

Soil-Moisture & Irrigation Studies. 1966. pap. 6.50 (ISBN 92-0-011067-3, IAEA). Unipub.

Soil-Moisture & Irrigation Studies - 2. 189p. 1973. pap. 12.00 (ISBN 92-0-011073-8, IAEA). Unipub.

Soil Nitrogen As Fertilizer or Pollutant. (Panel Proceedings Ser.). 398p. 1980. pap. 50.50 (ISBN 92-0-111080-4, ISP535, IAEA). Unipub.

Soil Organic Matter Studies, 2 vols. (Proceedings Ser). (Illus.). 1977. Vol. 1. pap. 36.50 (ISBN 92-0-010077-5, IAEA). Vol. 2. Unipub.

Soil Organic Matter Studies, Vol. 2. 1978. pap. 34.25 (ISBN 92-0-010177-1, ISP 438-2, IAEA). Unipub.

Soil Physics. 4th ed. Leonard D. Baver et al. LC 72-5318. 496p. 1972. 29.95 (ISBN 0-471-05974-9). Wiley.

Soil Physics. T. J. Marshall & J. W. Holmes. LC 78-73809. (Illus.). 1980. 77.50 (ISBN 0-521-22622-8); pap. 21.95x (ISBN 0-521-29579-3). Cambridge U Pr.

Soil-Plant Relationships. 2nd ed. C. A. Black. LC 67-28946. (Orig.). 1968. 41.50 (ISBN 0-471-07723-2). Wiley.

Soil-Plant System in Relation to Inorganic Nutrition. Maurice Fried & Hans Broeshart. (Atomic Energy Commission Monographs). 1967. 22.50 o.s.i. (ISBN 0-12-268050-2). Acad Pr.

Soil Processes. B. J. Knapp. (Process in Physical Geography Ser.: No. 2). (Illus.). 1979. pap. text ed. 5.95x (ISBN 0-04-631011-8). Allen Unwin.

Soil Productivity & Crop Growth. P. C. Raheja. 1967. 15.00x (ISBN 0-210-27008-X). Asia.

Soil Resource: Origin & Behavior. H. Jenny. (Ecological Studies: Vol. 37). (Illus.). 377p. 1981. 29.80 (ISBN 0-387-90543-X). Springer-Verlag.

Soil Sampling & Soil Description. J. M. Hodgson. (Monographs on Soil Survey). (Illus.). 1978. 29.95x (ISBN 0-19-854511-8). Oxford U Pr.

Soil Science Simplified. Milo I. Harpstead & Francis D. Hole. (Illus.). 121p. (gr. 9-12). 1980. pap. text ed. 7.75 (ISBN 0-8138-1515-0). Iowa St U Pr.

Soil Survey of the Horticultural Soils in the Murrumbidgee Irrigation Areas, New South Wales. B. E. Butler. 1980. 20.00x (ISBN 0-686-64952-4, Pub. by CSJRO Australia). State Mutual Bk.

Soil Systems: A Guide for Assisted Learning in Soil Science. C. L. Scrivner & James C. Baker. 1976. pap. text ed. 6.95 o.p. (ISBN 0-8403-1434-5). Kendall-Hunt.

Soil Teaching Aid. Andrew R. Aandahl. LC 79-12843. (Illus.). 1979. pap. text ed. 100.00x with slide carousel (ISBN 0-8032-1012-4); tape cassette 5.00x (ISBN 0-686-65580-X). U of Nebr Pr.

Soil Technological Study on Effectuating & Maintaining Adequate Playing Conditions of Grass Sports Fields. (Agricultural Research Reports Ser.: No. 903). 124p. 1981. pap. 29.50 (ISBN 90-220-0743-X, PDC 220, Pudoc). Unipub.

Soil Testing for Engineers. T. William Lambe. (Soil Engineering Ser.). 1951. pap. text ed. 24.95x (ISBN 0-471-51183-8). Wiley.

Soil, Water & Crop Production. Marlowe D. Thorne & D. Wynne Thorne. 1979. text ed. 18.50 (ISBN 0-87055-281-3). AVI.

Soils. Briggs. (Sources & Methods in Geography). 1977. pap. 6.95 (ISBN 0-408-70911-1). Butterworths.

Soils: An Introduction to Soils & Plant Growth. 4th ed. Roy L. Donahue et al. (Illus.). 1977. 20.95 (ISBN 0-13-821918-4). P-H.

Soils & Other Growth Media. G. W. Flegmann & R. A. George. 1978. text ed. 11.00 (ISBN 0-87055-240-6). AVI.

Soils & Rice. 825p. 1978. pap. 40.00 (R002, IRRI). Unipub.

Soils & Seeds of Sectarianism. James D. Bales. 1977. pap. 4.50 (ISBN 0-89315-264-1). Lambert Bk.

Soils & Soil Management. 2nd ed. Charles Sopher & Jack Baird. 1981. text ed. 16.95 (ISBN 0-8359-7031-0); instr's. manual free (ISBN 0-8359-7032-9). Reston.

Soils & Soil Management. Charles D. Sopher & Jack V. Baird. (Illus.). 1978. text ed. 14.95 (ISBN 0-87909-801-5); instrs'. manual avail. Reston.

Soils in the British Isles. Curtis et al. LC 75-46527. (Illus.). 1976. text ed. 29.00x (ISBN 0-582-48555-X). Longman.

Soils Manual. Earl Kroth et al. (Lucas Text Ser). 1980. text ed. 3.95x unbound (ISBN 0-87543-073-2). Lucas.

Soils of the Humid Tropics. Agricultural Board. LC 78-189475. (Illus.). 224p. 1972. pap. 8.25 (ISBN 0-309-01948-6). Natl Acad Pr.

Soils of the Polar Landscapes. John C. Tedrow. 1977. 65.00 (ISBN 0-8135-0808-8). Rutgers U Pr.

Soils of Wisconsin. Francis D. Hole. LC 75-12209. 264p. 1976. 30.00 (ISBN 0-299-06830-7). U of Wis Pr.

Soils That Support Us. Charles E. Kellogg. 1941. 6.95 o.s.i. (ISBN 0-02-561950-0). Macmillan.

Sojourner Truth: Slave, Abolitionist, Fighter for Women's Rights. Aletha J. Lindstrom. LC 79-25576. (Illus.). 128p. (gr. 4-6). 1980. PLB 7.79 (ISBN 0-671-32988-X). Messner.

Sojourners & Settlers: Chinese Migrants in Hawaii. Clarence E. Glick. LC 80-13799. 480p. 1980. text ed. 20.00x (ISBN 0-8248-0707-3). U Pr of Hawaii.

Sokoto Caliphate. Murray Last. LC 67-16974. (Ibadan History Ser.). (Illus.). 1967. pap. text ed. 8.00x (ISBN 0-582-64504-2). Humanities.

Sol de mi Infancia. Luis Salem. 80p. (Orig., Span.). 1980. pap. 1.95 (ISBN 0-89922-166-1). Edit Caribe.

Sol-Gel Processes for Ceramic Fuels. 1968. pap. 11.25 (ISBN 92-0-141068-9, IAEA). Unipub.

Sola Scriptura: Problems & Principles in Preaching Historical Texts. Sidney Greidanus. 1979. pap. 10.95x (ISBN 0-88906-103-3). Radix Bks.

Solar Access Law: Protecting Access to Sunlight for Solar Energy Systems. Gail B. Hayes. LC 79-9392. (Environmental Law Institute Bk.). (4#320). 1979. reference 18.50 (ISBN 0-88410-091-X). Ballinger Pub.

Solar Active Regions. Ed. by Frank Orrall. LC 79-565371. (Skylab Solar Workshop Ser.). 1981. 17.50x (ISBN 0-87081-085-5). Colo Assoc.

Solar Age Catalog. Solar Vision Inc. Ed. by Solar Age Magazine. LC 79-79117. (Illus.). 232p. 1977. pap. 8.50 (ISBN 0-918984-00-9). Brick Hse Pub.

Solar Age Resource Book: A Complete Guidebook for the Consumer to Harnessing the Power of Solar Energy, in Depth & up-to-Date. Ed. by Solar Age Magazine. LC 78-74580. (Illus.). 1979. pap. 9.95 (ISBN 0-89696-050-1). SolarVision.

Solar & Interplanetary Dynamics. Ed. by Murray Dryer & Einar Tandberg-Hanssen. (International Astronomical Union Symposia: No. 91). 570p. 1980. lib. bdg. 66.00 (ISBN 90-277-1162-3, Pub. by D. Reidel); pap. 28.95 (ISBN 90-277-1163-1). Kluwer Boston.

Solar Boat Book. Pat R. Rose. LC 80-69217. (Illus.). 266p. (Orig.). 1979. pap. 9.95 (ISBN 0-9604874-0-9). Aqua-Sol Ent.

Solar Buyers Guide & Directory. 292p. 1978. 22.00 (ISBN 0-686-62477-7). B Klein Pubns.

Solar Cells. Charles E. Backus. LC 75-46381. (IEEE Press Selected Reprint Ser.). 1976. 29.95 (ISBN 0-471-01981-X); pap. 19.50 o.p. (ISBN 0-471-01980-1, Pub. by Wiley-Interscience). Wiley.

Solar Cells & Photocells. 2nd ed. Rufus P. Turner. LC 80-50048. (Illus.). 1980. pap. 4.95 (ISBN 0-672-21711-2). SAMS.

Solar Census: The Directory for the Eighties. Compiled by Aatec Publications. LC 80-68910. 484p. 1980. perfect-bound 45.00 (ISBN 0-937948-00-4). Aatec Pubns.

Solar Collector Manufacturing Activity. Energy Information Administration. Ed. by J. A. Bereny. 46p. 1980. pap. 9.95 (ISBN 0-930978-12-9). Solar Energy Info.

Solar Compendium, 2 vols. Ken Bossong et al. (Illus.). 1980. 8.00 (ISBN 0-89988-013-4). Citizens Energy.

Solar Cookbook. Stella Andrassy. LC 79-88818. 1981. pap. 4.95 (ISBN 0-87100-142-X, 2142). Morgan.

Solar Cooling & Heating: Architectural, Engineering & Legal Aspects, Proceedings, 3 vols. new ed. Solar Cooling & Heating Forum, Dec. 13-15, 1976, Miami Beach. Ed. by T. N. Veziroglu. LC 77-28813. (Illus.). 1978. Set. text ed. 145.00 (ISBN 0-89116-165-1). Hemisphere Pub.

Solar Critique. Ken Bossong et al. 75p. (Orig.). 1981. 4.00 (ISBN 0-89988-070-3). Citizens Energy.

Solar Decision Book: Your Guide to Making a Sound Investment. R. H. Montgomery. LC 79-762. 1978. pap. text ed. 15.95 (ISBN 0-471-05652-9); tchrs. manual avail. (ISBN 0-471-06319-3). Wiley.

Solar Dwelling Designs. LC 80-52592. (Illus.). 144p. 1980. pap. 5.95 (ISBN 0-8069-8674-3). Sterling.

Solar Electricity: An Economic Approach to Solar Energy. 1978. 52.00 (ISBN 92-3-101427-7, U785, UNESCO). Unipub.

Solar Energy. rev. ed. John Hoke. (Impact Bks.). (Illus.). (gr. 7 up). 1978. PLB 6.90 s&l (ISBN 0-531-01329-4). Watts.

Solar Energy. Ed. by H. Messel & S. T. Butler. LC 75-15144. 350p. 1975. text ed. 25.00 (ISBN 0-08-019817-1); pap. text ed. 13.25 (ISBN 0-08-019781-7). Pergamon.

Solar Energy--International Progress: Proceedings of the International Symposium-Workshop on Solar Energy, 16-22 June 1978, Cairo, Egypt. Ed. by T. Nejat Vezirogly. 330.00 (ISBN 0-08-025077-7); pap. 200.00 (ISBN 0-08-025078-5). Pergamon.

Solar Energy: A Biased Guide. William L. Ewers. LC 76-55551. (International Library of Ecology Ser.). (Illus.). 1977. pap. 4.95 (ISBN 0-89196-013-9, Domus Bks); pap. 4.95 (ISBN 0-89196-013-9). Quality Bks IL.

Solar Energy & Building. 2nd ed. S. V. Szokolay. LC 77-21700. 1977. 21.95x (ISBN 0-470-99235-2). Halsted Pr.

Solar Energy & Conservation: Technology, Commercialization, Utilization: Proceedings. Solar Energy & Conservation Symposium-Workshop, Miami Beach, Florida, 1978. Ed. by T. Nejat Veziroglu. LC 79-19526. (Illus.). 2000p. 1980. 275.00 (ISBN 0-08-025551-5). Pergamon.

Solar Energy & the Consumer Loan: California Ed. (Solarcal Seminar Ser.). 100p. 1981. Repr. of 1979 ed. 25.00 (ISBN 0-89934-082-2). Solar Energy Info.

Solar Energy Applications in the Design of Buildings. Ed. by H. J. Cowan. (Illus.). x, 325p. 1980. 50.00x (ISBN 0-85334-883-9). Burgess-Intl Ideas.

Solar Energy Conversion: An Introductory Course. Solar Energy Conversion Course, 5th, University of Waterloo, Ontario, August 6-19, 1978. Ed. by A. E. Dixon & J. D. Leslie. LC 79-41159. (Illus.). 1979. 69.00 (ISBN 0-08-024744-X). Pergamon.

Solar Energy Employment & Requirements: 1978-1983. Battelle Columbus Labs. 200p. 1981. pap. 24.50 (ISBN 0-89934-102-0). Solar Energy Info.

Solar Energy Experiments. Thomas W. Norton. LC 77-4918. 1977. 8.95 (ISBN 0-87857-179-5). Rodale Pr Inc.

Solar Energy for California's Residential Sector: Progress, Problems, & Prospects. Jennifer K. Hollon. LC 80-29096. (IGS Research Report: No. 80-3). 71p. 1980. pap. text ed. 4.50 (ISBN 0-87772-279-X). Inst Gov Stud Berk.

Solar Energy Handbook. Ed. by Jan F. Kreider & Frank Kreith. (Illus.). 1099p. 1981. 49.50 (ISBN 0-07-035474-X). McGraw.

Solar Energy in America's Future. Stanford Research Institute. 1980. pap. 10.00 (ISBN 0-89934-044-X). Solar Energy Info.

Solar Energy in Buildings. Charles Chauliaguet et al. LC 78-27031. 1979. 30.50 (ISBN 0-471-27570-0, Pub. by Wiley-Interscience). Wiley.

Solar Energy in the Eighties: Conference Proceedings, London, 14-51 Jan 1981. Ed. by C. Stambolis. LC 80-41617. (Illus.). 232p. 1981. 60.00 (ISBN 0-08-026123-X). Pergamon.

Solar Energy in Tomorrow's World. Millard Reed. LC 79-25256. (Illus.). 192p. (gr. 7-12). 1980. PLB 8.79 (ISBN 0-671-33043-8). Messner.

Solar Energy Index. Arizona State University Library. 1980. 150.00 (ISBN 0-08-023888-2). Pergamon.

Solar Energy Information Locator - Nineteen Eighty. Solar Energy Research Institute. 60p. 1981. pap. 3.95 (ISBN 0-89934-089-X). Solar Energy Info.

Solar Energy Program Summary Document Nineteen Eighty One. U.S. Dept. of Energy. 375p. 1981. pap. 34.50 (ISBN 0-89934-093-8). Solar Energy Info.

Solar Energy Reports Available from the National Solar Data Program. Automation Industries. 50p. 1981. pap. 11.95 (ISBN 0-89934-104-7). Solar Energy Info.

Solar Energy Technology Handbook: Part B, Applications. Ed. by W. Dickerson & P. Cheremisinoff. (Energy, Power & Environment Ser.). 1980. 85.00 (ISBN 0-8247-6927-9). Dekker.

Solar Energy Thermal Processes. J. A. Duffie & W. A. Beckman. LC 74-12390. 1974. 27.50 (ISBN 0-471-22371-9, Pub. by Wiley-Interscience). Wiley.

Solar Engineering in Thermal Processes. J. A. Duffie & W. A. Beckman. LC 80-13297. 1980. 25.95 (ISBN 0-471-05066-0, Pub. by Wiley-Interscience). Wiley.

Solar Failure. Kaiman Lee & Linda Donnelly. LC 80-130467. (Illus.). 1980. 30.00 (ISBN 0-915250-36-5). Environ Design.

Solar for Your Present Home. Berkeley Solar Group. 1978. pap. 12.00 (ISBN 0-930978-83-8). Solar Energy Info.

Solar Fun Book. John Barling. 1980. 7.95 (ISBN 0-931790-04-2). Brick Hse Pub.

Solar, Geothermal, Electric & Storage Systems Program Summary Document. U. S. Dept. of Energy. 475p. 1979. pap. 19.95 (ISBN 0-686-63324-5, H031-PP). Solar Energy Info.

Solar Hardware Supplies: A Review Analysis, E-036. Jack T. Miskell. 1980. 875.00 (ISBN 0-89336-192-5). BCC.

Solar Heating & Cooling: Homeowner's Guide. Sunset Editors. LC 78-53673. (Illus.). 96p. 1978. pap. 4.95 (ISBN 0-376-01523-3, Sunset Bks.). Sunset-Lane.

Solar Heating & Cooling of Buildings. Richard S. Greeley et al. 1981. 47.50 (ISBN 0-250-40353-6). Ann Arbor Science.

Solar Heating Design: By the F-Chart Method. William A. Beckman et al. LC 77-22168. 1977. 20.95 (ISBN 0-471-03406-1, Pub. by Wiley-Interscience). Wiley.

Solar Heating Design Process: Active & Passive. Jan F. Kreider. (Illus.). 432p. 1981. 21.50 (ISBN 0-07-035478-2, P&RB). McGraw.

Solar Heating for the Home. Graham M. Hunter. LC 79-52372. (Illus.). 1979. 11.95 (ISBN 0-7153-7726-4). David & Charles.

Solar Heating Systems: Analysis & Design with the Sun-Pulse Method. Gordon F. Tully. (Energy Learning Systems Bks.). (Illus.). 232p. 1981. 23.95 (ISBN 0-07-065441-7). McGraw.

Solar Home Book: Heating, Cooling, & Designing with the Sun. Bruce Anderson & Michael Riordan. LC 76-29494. (Illus.). 1976. o.p. (ISBN 0-917352-02-5); pap. 9.50 (ISBN 0-917352-01-7). Brick Hse Pub.

Solar House. P. Sabady. 1978. 21.95 (ISBN 0-408-00290-5). Butterworths.

Solar Houses for a Cold Climate. Dean Carriere & Fraser Day. (Illus.). 1980. 20.00 (ISBN 0-684-16288-1, ScribT). Scribner.

Solar Houses in Europe: How They Have Worked. Ed. by W Palz & Tc Steemers. LC 80-49715. (Illus.). 320p. 1981. 40.00 (ISBN 0-08-026743-2); pap. 20.00 (ISBN 0-08-026744-0). Pergamon.

Solar-Hydrogen Energy System: An Authoritative Review of Water-Splitting Systems by Solar Beam & Solar Heat; Hydrogen Production, Storage & Utilisation. Ed. by T. Ohta. LC 79-40694. (Illus.). 1979. 48.00 (ISBN 0-08-022713-9). Pergamon.

Solar Installer's Training Program: California Ed. Werner J. Schmidt & Janis Philbin. 1981. Repr. of 1980 ed. 35.00 (ISBN 0-89934-084-9). Solar Energy Info.

Solar Jobs Book. Kay Ericson. LC 80-17886. 220p. 1980. pap. 7.95 (ISBN 0-931790-12-3). Brick Hse Pub.

Solar Materials Science. Ed. by Lawrence E. Murr. LC 80-18959. 1980. 35.00 (ISBN 0-12-511160-6). Acad Pr.

Solar Products Specifications Guide: A Technical Specifications Guide That Continously Monitors the Developments of Solar Products. (Illus.). 1979. binder-1 year of update service. 2 vols bimonthly 165.00 (ISBN 0-686-65545-1). SolarVision.

Solar Projects: Working Solar Devices to Cut Out & Assemble. A. Joseph Garrison. (Illus.). 128p. (Orig.). 1981. lib. bdg. 12.90 (ISBN 0-89471-129-6); pap. 6.95 (ISBN 0-89471-130-X). Running Pr.

Solar Radiation Considerations in Building Planning & Design. Building Research Advisory Board, National Research Council. 1976. pap. 8.75 (ISBN 0-309-02516-8). Natl Acad Pr.

Solar Radiation Control in Buildings. E. L. Harkness & M. L. Mehta. (Illus.). 1978. text ed. 57.00x (ISBN 0-85334-764-6, Pub. by Applied Science). Burgess-Intl Ideas.

Solar Retrofit: Adding Solar to Your Home. Daniel K. Reif. (Illus.). 200p. 1981. 17.95 (ISBN 0-931790-50-6); pap. 8.95 (ISBN 0-931790-15-8). Brick Hse Pub.

Solar Retrofit: How to Evaluate & Install Solar Heating in Existing Homes. Dan Reif. (Illus.). 160p. (Orig.). 1980. 16.95 (ISBN 0-931790-50-6); pap. 8.95 (ISBN 0-931790-15-8). Brick Hse Pub.

Solar Selective Surfaces. O. P. Agnihotri & B. K. Gupta. LC 80-17392. (Alternative Energy Ser.). 250p. 1981. 25.00 (ISBN 0-471-06035-6, Pub. by Wiley Interscience). Wiley.

Solar Still Connection: History, Purpose, & Application. Stella Andrassy. 128p. 1981. pap. 4.95 (ISBN 0-87100-173-X). Morgan.

Solar System. Issac Asimov. LC 73-93548. (Beginning Science Ser.). 32p. (gr. 2-4). 1974. PLB 3.39 o.p. (ISBN 0-695-40473-3). Follett.

Solar System: A Scientific American Book. Scientific American Editors. LC 75-28113. (Illus.). 1975. text ed. 15.95x (ISBN 0-7167-0551-6); pap. text ed. 7.95x (ISBN 0-7167-0550-8). W H Freeman.

Solar System & Back. Isaac Asimov. LC 78-89121. 5.95 o.p. (ISBN 0-385-02345-6). Doubleday.

Solar System & Its Strange Objects. Ed. by Brian J. Skinner. (Earth & Its Inhabitants: Selected Readings from American Scientist Ser.). (Illus.). 200p. (Orig.). 1981. pap. 9.95 (ISBN 0-913232-84-X). W Kaufmann.

Solar System Astronomy. George Payne. 1980. text ed. 7.95 wire coil bdg. (ISBN 0-88252-103-9). Paladin Hse.

Solar-Terrestrial Physics. Syun-Ichi Akasofu & Sidney Chapman. (International Ser. of Monographs on Physics). (Illus.). 1000p. 1972. 112.00x (ISBN 0-19-851262-7). Oxford U Pr.

Solar Thermal Power Systems: Annual Technical Progress Report. Department of Energy. 134p. 1980. pap. 14.95 (ISBN 0-89934-028-8). Solar Energy Info.

Solar Water Heating Reprint Series, 4 pubns. Incl. The Solar Heater - Bulletin No. 469. A. W. Farrall. Repr. of 1929 ed; Domestic Solar Water Heating in Florida - Bulletin No. 18. H. M. Hawkins. Repr. of 1947 ed; Use of Solar Energy for Heating Water. F. A. Brooks. Repr. of 1939 ed; Solar Energy & Its Use for Heating Water in California - Bulletin No. 602. F. A. Brooks. Repr. of 1936 ed. 1978. Set. pap. cancelled (ISBN 0-930978-11-0). Solar Energy Info.

Solaris. Stanislaw Lem. 1976. pap. 1.75 o.p. (ISBN 0-425-03380-5). Berkley Pub.

Soldering. C. J. Thwaites. (Engineering Design Guides Ser). (Illus.). 30p. 1975. pap. 9.95x (ISBN 0-19-859139-X). Oxford U Pr.

Soldering & Welding. B. M. Allen. LC 76-16388. (Drake Home Craftsman Ser.). (Illus.). 160p. 1975. pap. 4.95 o.p. (ISBN 0-8069-8676-X). Sterling.

Soldier & Sailor Words & Phrases. Edward Fraser & John Gibbons. LC 68-30635. 1968. Repr. of 1925 ed. 22.00 (ISBN 0-8103-3281-7). Gale.

Soldier & Social Change: Comparative Studies in the History & Sociology of the Military. Jacques Van Doorn. LC 74-31573. (Sage Ser. on Armed Forces & Society: Vol. 7). (Illus.). 189p. 1975. 20.00 (ISBN 0-8039-9948-8). Sage.

Soldier & the State: The Theory & Politics of Civil Military Relations. Samuel P. Huntington. LC 57-6349. 1957. 25.00x (ISBN 0-674-81735-4, Belknap Pr). Harvard U Pr.

Soldier from Texas. Cecil E. Roberts. Ed. by Carey H. Snyder. LC 78-67480. (Illus.). 1978. 12.50 (ISBN 0-87706-104-1); pap. 6.95. Branch-Smith.

Soldiers. D. Nevin. LC 73-79475. (Old West Ser). (Illus.). (gr. 5 up). 1973. kivar 12.96 (ISBN 0-8094-1463-5, Pub. by Time-Life). Silver.

Soldiers. David Nevin. (Old West Ser.). (Illus.). 1973. 12.95 (ISBN 0-8094-1462-7). Time-Life.

Soldiers: An Anatomy of the British Army. Henry Stanhope. (Illus.). 372p. 1980. 30.00 (ISBN 0-241-10273-1, Pub. by Hamish Hamilton England). David & Charles.

Soldiers & Civilians. Marcus Cunliffe. LC 68-22898. (Illus.). 1973. pap. text ed. 5.95 o.s.i. (ISBN 0-02-906860-6). Free Pr.

Soldiers & Kinsmen in Uganda: The Making of a Military Ethnocracy. Ali Mazrui. LC 75-5017. (Armed Forces & Society Ser.: Vol. 5). 1975. 20.00x o.p. (ISBN 0-8039-0427-4). Sage.

Soldiers & Power: The Development Performance of the Nigerian Military Regime. Victor A. Olorunsola. LC 76-48485. (Publication Ser: No. 168). 1977. pap. 8.95 (ISBN 0-8179-6681-1). Hoover Inst Pr.

Soldiers in Politics: Military Coups & Government. Eric Nordlinger. (Illus.). 1977. pap. text ed. 10.95 (ISBN 0-13-822163-4). P-H.

Soldiers of Fortune. Richard H. Davis. 300p. Repr. lib. bdg. 12.95x (ISBN 0-89966-284-6). Buccaneer Bks.

Soldiers of Light & Love: Northern Teachers & the Georgia Blacks, 1865-1873. Jacqueline Jones. 330p. 1980. 17.50 o.p. (ISBN 0-8078-1435-0). U of NC Pr.

Soldier's Strikes of Nineteen Nineteen. A. Rothstein. 1980. text ed. 27.00x (ISBN 0-333-27693-0). Humanities.

Soldiers When They Go: The Story of Camp Randall, 1861-1865. Carolyn J. Mattern. LC 80-26238. (Illus.). 156p. 1981. 4.95x (ISBN 0-87020-206-5). State Hist Soc Wis.

Soldiers Without Enemies: Preparing the United Nations for Peacekeeping. Larry L. Fabian. 1971. 14.95 (ISBN 0-8157-2726-7); pap. 5.95 (ISBN 0-8157-2725-9). Brookings.

Solfege According to the Kodaly Concept, Vol. I. Erzsebet Hegyi. Tr. by Fred Macnicol from Hungarian. LC 75-21981. (Illus.). 429p. 1975. 24.00 (ISBN 0-913932-09-4). Boosey & Hawkes.

Solid Analytic Geometry. A. Adrian Albert. 1966. pap. 1.95 o.s.i. (ISBN 0-226-01175-5, P530, Phoen). U of Chicago Pr.

Solid Analytic Geometry. John M. Olmsted. (Century Mathematics Ser.). 1947. text ed. 28.50x (ISBN 0-89197-417-2); pap. text ed. 16.50x (ISBN 0-89197-942-5). Irvington.

Solid Contact & Lubrication. Ed. by H. S. Cheng & L. M. Keer. (AMD: Vol. 39). 248p. 1980. 30.00 (G00172). ASME.

Solid-Earth Geophysics: Survey & Outlook. Geophysics Research Board & Division Of Earth Sciences. 1964. pap. 5.00 (ISBN 0-309-01231-7). Natl Acad Pr.

Solid Electrolytes & Their Applications. Ed. by E. C. Subbarao. (Illus.). 310p. 1980. 35.00 (ISBN 0-306-40389-7, Plenum Pr). Plenum Pub.

Solid Electrolytes: Proceedings. International Meeting on Solid Electrolytes, 2nd, University of St. Andrews, Sep. 20-22, 1978. Ed. by R. D. Armstrong. (Illus.). 68p. 1979. pap. 27.50 (ISBN 0-08-025267-2). Pergamon.

Solid Geometry. P. M. Cohn. (Library of Mathematics). 1968. pap. 3.00 (ISBN 0-7100-6343-1). Routledge & Kegan.

Solid Geometry. Qazi Zameeruddin & V. K. Khanna. 1977. 15.00 (ISBN 0-7069-0560-1, Pub. by Vikas India). Advent Bk.

Solid Gold Stethescope. Edgar Berman. 252p. 1976. 7.95 o.s.i. (ISBN 0-02-510050-5). Macmillan.

Solid Ionic & Ionic-Electronic Conductors. Ed. by R. D. Armstrong. LC 77-747. 1977. text ed. 34.00 (ISBN 0-08-021592-0). Pergamon.

Solid-Liquid Equilibrium. T. Haase & H. Schonert. 1969. 44.00 (ISBN 0-08-012663-4). Pergamon.

Solid-Liquid Interface. D. P. Woodruff. LC 72-91362. (Solid State Science Ser.). (Illus.). 150p. 1973. 29.95 (ISBN 0-521-20123-3). Cambridge U Pr.

Solid-Liquid Interface. D. P. Woodruff. LC 72-91362. (Cambridge Solid State Science). (Illus.). 182p. 1980. pap. 11.95 (ISBN 0-521-29971-3). Cambridge U Pr.

Solid Liquid Separation. Svarovsky. (Chemical Engineering Ser). 1977. 64.95 (ISBN 0-408-70795-X). Butterworths.

Solid Liver Tumors. James H. Foster & Martin M. Berman. LC 76-28938. (Major Problems in Clinical Surgery Ser.: Vol. 22). 1977. text ed. 25.00 (ISBN 0-7216-3824-4). Saunders.

Solid Mechanics: Strength of Material & Structural Design. James W. Morrison. LC 77-18555. (Professional Career Exam Ser.). (Illus.). 1978. pap. 10.00 o.p. (ISBN 0-668-04409-8, 4409). Arco.

Solid Particles in the Solar System. Ed. by Ian Halliday & Bruce A. McIntosh. (International Astronomical Union Symposium: No. 90). 432p. 1980. PLB 49.95 (ISBN 90-277-1164-X, Pub. by D. Reidel); pap. 26.50 (ISBN 90-277-1165-8). Kluwer Boston.

Solid Pharmaceutics: Mechanical Properties & Rate Phenomena. Jens T. Carstensen. LC 79-6805. 1980. 35.00 (ISBN 0-12-161150-7). Acad Pr.

Solid Phase Synthesis. Ed. by E. C. Blossey & D. C. Neckers. (Benchmark Papers in Organic Chemistry Ser: Vol. 2). 400p. 1975. 43.50 (ISBN 0-12-786165-3). Acad Pr.

Solid State: An Introduction to the Physics of Crystals. 2nd ed. H. M. Rosenberg. (Physics Ser.). (Illus.). 1979. 15.95x (ISBN 0-19-851844-7); pap. 11.50x (ISBN 0-19-851845-5). Oxford U Pr.

Solid-State & Chemical Radiation Dosimetry in Medicine & Biology. 1967. pap. 22.50 (ISBN 92-0-010167-4, IAEA). Unipub.

Solid State & Molecular Theory: A Scientific Biography. John C. Slater. LC 74-22367. 416p. 1975. text ed. 30.50 (ISBN 0-471-79681-6, Pub. by Wiley-Interscience). Wiley.

Solid State Chemistry. 1980. 5.00 (ISBN 0-910362-14-9). Chem Educ.

Solid State Chemistry: A Contemporary Overview. Ed. by Smith Holt et al. LC 80-17185. (Advances in Chemistry Ser.: No. 186). 1980. 59.50 (ISBN 0-8412-0472-1). Am Chemical.

Solid-State Circuit Design User's Manual. Matthew Mandl. (Illus.). 1977. 18.95 o.p. (ISBN 0-87909-784-1). Reston.

Solid State Circuits. G. J. Pridham. 196p. 1973. text ed. 25.00 (ISBN 0-08-016932-5); pap. text ed. 12.75 (ISBN 0-08-016933-3). Pergamon.

Solid State Devices, 2 vols. I. Tepper. 1974. Vol. 1, Theory. 14.95 (ISBN 0-201-07435-4); Vol. 2. 15.95 (ISBN 0-201-07436-2). A-W.

Solid State Electronic Devices. D. V. Morgan et al. (Wykeham Science Ser.: No. 20). 1972. 6.50x o.p. (ISBN 0-8448-1122-X). Crane Russak Co.

Solid State Electronic Devices. 2nd ed. B. Streetman. 1980. 26.95 (ISBN 0-13-822171-5). P-H.

Solid-State Electronics. George B. Rutkowski. LC 77-131132. 1972. 17.90 o.p. (ISBN 0-672-20801-6). Bobbs.

Solid State Electronics. 2nd ed. George B. Rutkowski. 1980. 19.95 (ISBN 0-672-97315-4); instructors guide 6.67 (ISBN 0-672-97317-0); lab manual 6.95 (ISBN 0-672-97316-2). Bobbs.

Solid State Electronics. F. P. Tedeschi & M. R. Taber. LC 75-27996. 1976. pap. 8.80 (ISBN 0-8273-1171-0); instructor's guide 1.60 (ISBN 0-8273-1172-9). Delmar.

Solid State Maser. D. H. Orton et al. LC 74-101374. 1970. 35.00 (ISBN 0-08-006819-7); pap. 14.50 (ISBN 0-08-006818-9). Pergamon.

Solid-State Microwave Amplifier Design. Tri T. Ha. 350p. 1981. 30.00 (ISBN 0-471-08971-0). Wiley.

Solid-State Motor Controls. John A. Kuecken. (Illus.). 1978. pap. 8.95 (ISBN 0-8306-7929-4, 929). TAB Bks.

Solid State Nuclear Track Detectors: Proceedings. International Conference, 10th, Lyon, July 2-6, 1979. Ed. by H. Francois et al. (Illus.). 1082p. 1980. 235.00 (ISBN 0-08-025029-7). Pergamon.

Solid State Nuclear Track Detectors: Proceedings, 2 vols. Nuclear Track Detection Conference, Neuherberg Munich, Sept. 30 to Oct. 6, 1976. Ed. by F. Granzer et al. 1978. Set. text ed. write for info. (ISBN 0-08-021659-5). Pergamon.

Solid State Physics. H. E. Hall. LC 73-10743. (Manchester Physics Ser.). 372p. 1974. 40.25 (ISBN 0-471-34280-7); pap. 16.75 (ISBN 0-471-34281-5, Pub. by Wiley-Interscience). Wiley.

Solid State Physics: Advances in Research & Applications. Incl. Vol. 1. 1955. 49.25 (ISBN 0-12-607701-0); Vol. 2. 1956. 49.25 (ISBN 0-12-607702-9); Vol. 3. 1956. 49.25 (ISBN 0-12-607703-7); Vol. 4. 1957. 49.25 (ISBN 0-12-607704-5); Vol. 5. 1957. 49.25 (ISBN 0-12-607705-3); Vol. 6. 1958. 49.25 (ISBN 0-12-607706-1); Vol. 7. 1958. 49.25 (ISBN 0-12-607707-X); Vol. 8. 1959. 49.25 (ISBN 0-12-607708-8); Vol. 9. 1959. (ISBN 0-12-607709-6); Vol. 10. 1960. 49.25 (ISBN 0-12-607710-X); Vol. 11. 1960. o.s.i. (ISBN 0-12-607711-8); Vol. 12. 1961. 49.25 (ISBN 0-12-607712-6); Vol. 13. 1962. o.s.i (ISBN 0-12-607713-4); Vol. 14. 1963. (ISBN 0-12-607714-2); Vol. 15. 1963. 49.25 (ISBN 0-12-607715-0); Vol. 16. 1964. 49.25 (ISBN 0-12-607716-9); Vol. 17. 1965. 49.25 (ISBN 0-12-607717-7); Vol 18. 1966. 49.25 (ISBN 0-12-607718-5); Vol. 19. 1967. 49.25 (ISBN 0-12-607719-3); Vol. 20. 1967. o.s.i. (ISBN 0-12-607720-7); Vol. 21. 1968. o.s.i. (ISBN 0-12-607721-5); Vol. 22. 1969. 49.25 (ISBN 0-12-607722-3); Vol. 23. 1970. 49.25 (ISBN 0-12-607723-1); Vol. 24. 1970. 49.25 (ISBN 0-12-607724-X); Vol. 25. 1970. 49.25 (ISBN 0-12-607725-8); Vol. 26. 1971. (ISBN 0-685-59568-4); Vol. 27. 1972. 49.25 (ISBN 0-12-607727-4); Vol. 28. 1973. 49.25 (ISBN 0-12-607728-2); Vol. 29. 1974. 49.25 (ISBN 0-12-607729-0). Acad Pr.

Solid State Physics in Electronics & Telecommunications: Magnetic & Optical Properties. Ed. by M. Desirant. 1960. 76.00 (ISBN 0-12-211503-1); Vol. 4. Part 2. 56.00 (ISBN 0-12-211504-X). Acad Pr.

Solid State Physics in the People's Republic of China: A Trip Report of the American Solid State Physics Delegation. Ed. by Anne Fitzgerald & Charles Slichter. LC 76-49402. (People's Republic of China Ser.: No. 1). 1976. pap. 10.25 (ISBN 0-309-02523-0). Natl Acad Pr.

Solid State Reactions. rev. ed. H. Schmalzried. (Monographs in Modern Chemistry: Vol. 12). Date not set. price not set. Verlag Chemie.

Solid State Semi-Conductors. A. K. Jonscher. (Studies in Solid State Physics). 1965. pap. 16.50 (ISBN 0-7100-4384-8). Routledge & Kegan.

Solid State Theory. Walter A. Harrison. 1980. pap. text ed. 8.95 (ISBN 0-486-63948-7). Dover.

Solid State Theory. Mendel Sachs. LC 74-78777. (Illus.). 384p. 1974. pap. text ed. 4.50 o.p. (ISBN 0-486-61772-6). Dover.

Solid State Theory in Metallurgy. P. Wilkes. LC 72-180020. (Illus.). 480p. (Orig.). 1973. 68.50 (ISBN 0-521-08454-7); pap. 19.95x (ISBN 0-521-09699-5). Cambridge U Pr.

Solid Surface Luminescence Analysis. Hurtubise. 288p. Date not set. 37.50. Dekker.

Solid Waste Research & Development Needs for Emerging Coal Technologies. Compiled by American Society of Civil Engineers. 272p. 1980. pap. text ed. 21.50 (ISBN 0-87262-199-5). Am Soc Civil Eng.

Solid Wastes: Origin, Collection, Processing & Disposal. Charles L. Mantell. LC 74-26930. 1152p. 1975. 74.95 (ISBN 0-471-56777-9, Pub by Wiley-Interscience). Wiley.

Solidarity & Kinship: Essays on American Zionism. Ed. by Nathan M. Kaganoff. (Illus.). 1980. 5.00. Am Jewish Hist Soc.

Solids, Liquids & Gases. Jeanne Bendick. LC 73-13976. (Illus.). 72p. (gr. 4-6). 1974. PLB 4.90 o.p. (ISBN 0-531-01441-X). Watts.

Solipsism & Induction. E. Teensma. 64p. 1974. pap. text ed. 6.50x (ISBN 90-232-1149-9). Humanities.

Solitaire Games. John Belton & Joella Cramblit. LC 75-25956. (Games & Activities Ser.). (Illus.). 48p. (gr. 3 up). 1975. PLB 9.30 (ISBN 0-8172-0027-4). Raintree Pubs.

Solitaries. Ted Walker. LC 67-20026. 3.95 o.p. (ISBN 0-8076-0415-1). Braziller.

Solitary Explorer: Thomas Merton's Transforming Journey. Elena Malits. LC 80-7744. 192p. (Orig.). 1980. pap. 6.95 (ISBN 0-06-065411-2, RD 331, HarpR). Har-Row.

Solitary Heart. Ruth M. Sears. 192p. (YA) 1976. 4.95 o.p. (ISBN 0-685-62629-6, Avalon). Bouregy.

Solitary Nodular Lesions of the Lung: Contribution to Its Diagnosis & Management. Rafael A. Gomez et al. (Illus.). 200p. 1981. 17.50 (ISBN 0-87527-245-2). Green.

Solitary Singer: A Critical Biography of Walt Whitman. Gay Wilson Allen. LC 67-23414. 1967. 20.00x (ISBN 0-8147-0006-3). NYU Pr.

Solitude in the Thought of Thomas Merton. Richard A. Cashen. (Cistercian Studies: No. 40). 208p. 1981. 15.50 (ISBN 0-87907-840-5); pap. 5.50 (ISBN 0-87907-940-1). Cistercian Pubns.

Solitudes of Don Luis De Gongora. Ed. by Edward M. Wilson. 1965. 32.00 (ISBN 0-521-06814-2). Cambridge U Pr.

Solitudes: Premieres Lectures Modernes. Ed. by Edward J. Geary. (Integral French Eds. Ser). (Fr). 1965. pap. text ed. 2.75x o.p. (ISBN 0-685-20247-X). Schoenhof.

Solo. Leo Hamalian & Linda Hamalian. 1977. 10.00 o.s.i. (ISBN 0-440-08068-1). Delacorte.

Solo. Jack Higgins. (Large Print Bks.). 1980. lib. bdg. 13.95 (ISBN 0-8161-3120-1). G K Hall.

Solo Guitar Playing, Book 1. 2nd ed. Frederick M. Noad. LC 76-12833. 1976. pap. 7.95 (ISBN 0-02-871680-9). Schirmer Bks.

Solo Kill. S. Kye Coult. 1977. pap. 1.50 o.p. (ISBN 0-425-03560-3, Medallion). Berkley Pub.

Solo: Nanga Parbat. Reinhold Messner. (Illus.). 1981. 19.95 (ISBN 0-19-520196-5). Oxford U Pr.

Solo Para Muchachos. Frank H. Richardson. 1980. pap. 1.60 (ISBN 0-311-46929-9). Casa Bautista.

Sologub's Literary Children: Keys to a Symbolist's Prose. Stanley J. Rabinowitz. (Illus.). 176p. 1980. pap. 9.95 (ISBN 0-89357-069-9). Slavica.

Solomon & Rehoboam. Gordon Lindsay. (Old Testament Ser.). 1.25 (ISBN 0-89985-145-2). Christ Nations.

Solomon Grundy, Born on Oneday: A Finite Arithmetic Puzzle. Malcolm E. Weiss. LC 76-26560. (Young Math Ser.). (Illus.). (gr. k-3). 1977. PLB 7.89 (ISBN 0-690-01275-6, TYC-J). T Y Crowell.

Solomon Island Society. Douglas L. Oliver. (Illus.). pap. 3.45x o.p. (ISBN 0-8070-4689-2, BP270). Beacon Pr.

Solomon Stoddard. Ralph J. Coffman. (United States Authors Ser.: No. 295). 1978. lib. bdg. 12.50 (ISBN 0-8057-7198-0). Twayne.

Solomon's Daughter. C. E. Poverman. 1981. 12.95 (ISBN 0-670-36144-5). Viking Pr.

Solomon's Folly. Leslie Croxford. LC 75-1458. 1978. 7.95 (ISBN 0-8149-0763-6). Vanguard.

Solomons Seal. Hammond Innes. LC 80-7632. 352p. 1980. 11.95 (ISBN 0-394-51326-6). Knopf.

Solon Robinson, Pioneer & Agriculturalist, 2 Vols. Ed. by H. A. Kellar. LC 68-16242. (American Scene Ser). (Illus.). 1968. Repr. of 1936 ed. lib. bdg. 75.00 (ISBN 0-306-71017-X). Da Capo.

Solos for Unaccompanied Clarinet: An Annotated Bibliography. James E. Gillespie, Jr. LC 73-87277. (Detroit Studies in Music Bibliography Ser.: No. 28). 1973. 7.00 (ISBN 0-685-30213-X); pap. 5.50 (ISBN 0-685-30213-X). Info Coord.

Solovei (Poezy) Igor Severianin. (Rus.). 1981. pap. 5.95 (ISBN 0-89830-011-8). Russica Pubs.

Solstice Cipher. Bruce H. Boyer. 1981. pap. 2.75 (ISBN 0-440-18096-1). Dell.

Solstice III. Paul Payack. (Illus.). 1977. pap. 1.00 o.p. (ISBN 0-686-20639-8). Samisdat.

Solubilities on Inorganic & Organic Compounds, Vol 3. Stephen. 1979. 500.00 (ISBN 0-08-023570-0); pap. 400.00 (ISBN 0-08-023571-9). Pergamon.

Solubility & ph Calculations. James N. Butler. LC 64-15563. (Chemistry Ser). (Orig.). (gr. 9 up). 1964. pap. 5.95 (ISBN 0-201-00733-9). A-W.

Solucion Para los Problemas De la Vida. Paul Y. Cho. Ed. by Esteban Marosi & Angela Whidden. Tr. by C. Julio & O. Orozco. 155p. (Span.). 1980. pap. 1.35 (ISBN 0-8297-0999-1). Vida Pubs.

Solution: Escape. Margaret C. Cooper. LC 80-50496. (Illus.). 94p. (gr. 3-7). 1981. 8.95 (ISBN 0-8027-6404-5); PLB 8.85 (ISBN 0-8027-6405-3). Walker & Co.

Solution of Differential Equation Models for Polynomial Approximation. John Villadsen & Michael Michelson. LC 77-4331. (Illus.). 1977. 29.95 (ISBN 0-13-822205-3). P-H.

Solution of Doctor Resolutus, His Resolutions for Kneeling. David Calderwood. LC 79-84093. (English Experience Ser.: No. 913). 60p. 1979. Repr. of 1619 ed. lib. bdg. 8.00 (ISBN 90-221-0913-5). Walter J Johnson.

Solution of Social Problems: Five Perspectives. 2nd ed. Ed. by Martin S. Weinberg et al. 240p. 1981. pap. text ed. 7.95x (ISBN 0-19-502787-6). Oxford U Pr.

Solution of the Phase Problem, Pt. 1: The Centrosymmetric Crystal. Hauptman & Karle. pap. 3.00 (ISBN 0-686-60369-9). Polycrystal Bk Serv.

Solution Properties of Polysaccharides. Ed. by David A. Brant. (ACS Symposium Ser.: No. 150). 1981. price not set (ISBN 0-8412-0609-0). Am Chemical.

Solution to the Riddle Dyslexia. H. N. Levinson. (Illus.). 398p. 1981. 24.80 (ISBN 0-387-90515-4). Springer-Verlag.

Solutions for Today's Sex Problems & Prostitution. Date not set. 3.70x (ISBN 0-686-68074-X). C C Brown Pub.

Solutions in Statistics & Probability. Edward J. Dudewicz. LC 80-68285. (American Sciences Press Ser. in Mathematical & Management Sciences: Vol. 3). 1980. pap. text ed. 24.95 (ISBN 0-935950-00-1). Am Sciences Pr.

Solutions Manual for Introduction to Probability Models. 2nd ed. Sheldon Ross. (Probability & Mathematical Statistics Ser.). 1980. 2.00 (ISBN 0-12-598462-6). Acad Pr.

Solutions Manual for Modern Genetics. Francisco Ayala & John Kiger. 1980. pap. 2.95 (ISBN 0-8053-0313-8, 800F00). Benjamin Cummings.

Solutions of Problems in Surveying & Field Astronomy. pap. 26.50x (ISBN 0-392-04649-0, SpS). Soccer.

Solutions, Relaxation, or Understanding for Tense, Anxious, Depressive, Hostile (Irritated), & Disgusted States & Problems, Set-ST. Russell E. Mason. 1975. pap. 50.00x (ISBN 0-89533-010-5); tape-1a, t-5a, t-11, t-12, t-13, t-14 incl., notes, clinical applications, substitution training. F I Comm.

Solutions to Advanced Level Physics Questions. 7th ed. M. Nelkon. 1975. pap. text ed. 5.50x o.p. (ISBN 0-435-68336-5). Heinemann Ed.

Solutions to CB Problems. Dave Hicks. (Illus.). 1977. pap. cancelled (ISBN 0-672-21441-5). Sams.

Solutions to Pediatric Problems. Association of Bone & Joint Surgeons. (Clinical Orthopaedics & Related Research Ser No. 79). 15.00 (ISBN 0-685-24743-0). Lippincott.

Solvability of Nonlinear Equations & Boundry Value Problems. Svatopluk Fucik. (Mathematics & Its Applications Ser.: No. 4). 400p. 1980. lib. bdg. 29.95 (ISBN 90-277-1077-5, Pub. by D. Reidel). Kluwer Boston.

Solvent Extraction in Flame Spectroscopic Analysis. Malcolm S. Cresser. 1978. 52.95 (ISBN 0-408-71307-0). Butterworths.

Solventless & High Solids Industrial Finishes: Recent Developments. Ed. by M. T. Gillies. LC 80-21553. (Chemical Technology Review: No. 179). (Illus.). 342p. 1981. 48.00 (ISBN 0-8155-0828-X). Noyes.

Solving Business Problems with Calculators. 5th ed. Richard R. McCready. 1977. 12.95x (ISBN 0-534-00495-4). Wadsworth Pub.

Solving Discipline Problems: Strategies for Classroom Teachers. Charles H. Wolfgang & Carl D. Glickman. 288p. 1980. text ed. 17.95 (ISBN 0-205-06888-X). Allyn.

Solving Educational Problems: Theory & Reality of Innovation in Developing Countries. Ronald G. Havelock & A. M. Huberman. LC 78-52224. (Praeger Special Studies). 1978. 25.95 (ISBN 0-03-044206-0). Praeger.

Solving EEO Problems. 1980. pap. 9.95 (ISBN 0-917386-36-1). Exec Ent.

Solving General Chemistry Problems. 5th ed. R. Nelson Smith & Conway Pierce. LC 79-23677. (Illus.). 1980. 8.95x (ISBN 0-7167-1117-6); answers to b group avail. W H Freeman.

Solving Least Squares Problems. Charles L. Lawson & Richard J. Hanson. (Illus.). 384p. 1974. 22.95 (ISBN 0-13-822585-0). P-H.

Solving Life's Problems. Paul Y. Cho. (Orig.). 1980. pap. 4.95 (ISBN 0-88270-450-8). Logos.

Solving Math Word Problems for Students & Adults. Harold Schneider. 1965. 4.50 (ISBN 0-911642-01-3); pap. 1.95 (ISBN 0-911642-02-1). Word-Fraction.

Solving Problems in Analytical Chemistry. Stephen Brewer. LC 79-17164. 1980. pap. text ed. 13.95x (ISBN 0-471-04098-3). Wiley.

Solving Problems in Meetings. James D. Jorgensen et al. LC 79-21782. 112p. 1981. 8.95 (ISBN 0-88229-521-7). Nelson-Hall.

Solving Problems in Secondary School Administration: A Human Organization Approach. Bill R. Hampton & Robert H. Lauer. 336p. 1980. text ed. 16.95 (ISBN 0-205-06951-7, 2369516). Allyn.

Solving Problems Kids Care About. Randall Souviney. (Illus.). 176p. (Orig.). 1981. pap. 10.95 (ISBN 0-8302-8653-5). Goodyear.

Solving Problems Together. Hogie Wyckoff. LC 80-1003. 272p. 1980. pap. 7.95 (ISBN 0-394-17739-8, E 767, Ever). Grove.

Solving Women's Problems: Through Awareness, Action, & Contact. Hogie Wyckoff. pap. 4.95 (ISBN 0-394-17003-2, E668, Ever). Grove.

Solzhenitsyn at Harvard: The Address, Twelve Early Responses, & Six Later Reflections. Ed. by Ronald Berman. 160p. 1980. 9.50 (ISBN 0-89633-034-6); pap. 5.00 (ISBN 0-89633-023-0). Ethics & Public Policy.

Solzhenitsyn: The Moral Vision. Edward E. Ericson, Jr. 1980. 12.95 (ISBN 0-8028-3527-9). Eerdmans.

Solzhenitsyn, Tvardovsky & Novy Mir. Vladimir Lakshin. 176p. 1980. 10.00 (ISBN 0-262-12086-0). MIT Pr.

Solzhenitsyn's Religion. Niels C. Nielson, Jr. 1976. pap. 1.75 (ISBN 0-89129-141-5). Jove Pubns.

Soma, in Biblical Theology, with Emphasis on Pauline Anthropology. R. Gundry. LC 75-22927. (Society for New Testament Studies: No. 29). 300p. 1976. 42.00 (ISBN 0-521-20788-6). Cambridge U Pr.

Somata. Phillip Foss, Jr. 1981. pap. price not set (ISBN 0-931460-18-2). Bieler.

Somatic Cell Hybridization. Richard L. Davidson & Felix F. De La Cruz. LC 74-75725. 1974. 31.50 (ISBN 0-911216-75-8). Raven.

Somatic Selection & Adaptive Evolution. E. J. Steele. 100p. 1980. 30.00x (Pub. by Croom Helm England). State Mutual Bk.

Somatostatin, Vol. 1. Mary T. McQuillan. Ed. by D. F. Horrobin. (Annual Research Reviews Ser.). 1979. 24.00 (ISBN 0-88831-040-4). Eden Med Res.

Sombra De Galdos: Libra De Lectura, Repaso y Conversacion. Benita Perez Galdos. Ed. by Rudolph Cardona. (Span). 1966. 6.95x (ISBN 0-393-09645-9); pap. 3.25x (ISBN 0-393-09632-7, NortonC); tapes 70.00 (ISBN 0-393-99114-8). Norton.

Sombrero De Tres Picos. 2nd ed. P. A. Alarcon. 1965. 8.95 (ISBN 0-471-00004-3). Wiley.

Some Action of Her Own. Ed. by Helen S. Astin. LC 75-43476. 208p. 1976. 18.95 (ISBN 0-669-00567-3). Lexington Bks.

Some American History. Intro. by Charles Childs. LC 72-153088. (Illus.). 1971. pap. 3.00 o.p. (ISBN 0-913456-86-1). Interbk Inc.

Some Americans: A Personal Record. Charles Tomlinson. (Quantum Bk.). 100p. 1981. 10.00 (ISBN 0-520-04037-6). U of Cal Pr.

Some Applications of Nuclear Physics to Medicine. W. V. Mayneord. 1980. 15.00x (Pub. by Brit Inst Radiology). State Mutual Bk.

Some Architectural Writers of the Nineteenth Century. Nicholas Pevsner. (Illus.). 340p. 1972. 37.50x (ISBN 0-19-817315-6). Oxford U Pr.

Some Aspects of Communicative Competence & Their Implications. A. J. Van Der Geest. 272p. 1975. pap. text ed. 20.75x (ISBN 90-232-1261-4). Humanities.

Some Aspects of Hittite Religion. Oliver R. Gurney. (British Academy - Schweich Lectures). (Illus.). 94p. 1977. text ed. 24.95x (ISBN 0-19-725974-X). Oxford U Pr.

Some Aspects of Hydraulics in Mechanical Handling & Mobile Equipment. (Illus.). 1970. 27.50x (ISBN 0-85461-006-5). Intl Ideas.

Some Aspects of Indian Society. S. C. Bhattacharyya. 1977. 10.00x o.p. (ISBN 0-685-74588-0). South Asia Bks.

Some Aspects of Queueing & Storage Systems. Amitaval Ghosal. LC 78-114016. (Lecture Notes in Operations Research & Mathematical Systems: Vol. 23). 1970. pap. 10.70 o.p. (ISBN 0-387-04947-9). Springer-Verlag.

Some Aspects of the Life & Works of James Augustine Joyce. Peter Allt. 50p. 1980. Repr. of 1942 ed. lib. bdg. 7.50 (ISBN 0-89987-026-0). Darby Bks.

Some Aspects of Vacuum Ultraviolet Radiation Physics. Boris Vodar & J. Romand. LC 73-20163. 1974. text ed. 46.00 (ISBN 0-08-016984-8). Pergamon.

Some Avocado Varieties for Australia. D. M. Alexander. 1980. 10.00x (ISBN 0-643-02276-7, Pub. by CSJRO Australia). State Mutual Bk.

Some Avocado Varieties for Australia. 35p. 1978. pap. 5.00 (ISBN 0-643-02276-7, CO10, CSIRO). Unipub.

Some Basics About Radio-Control Cars. Ed Radlauer. LC 80-22039. (Gemini Bks). 32p. (gr. 4 up). 1981. PLB 8.65g (ISBN 0-516-07691-4, Elk Grove Bks). Childrens.

Some Basics About Rock Climbing. Ed Radlauer. LC 80-22053. (Gemini Bks). 32p. (gr. 4 up). 1981. PLB 8.65g (ISBN 0-516-07692-2, Elk Grove Bks). Childrens.

Some Basics About Women's Gymnastics. Ed Radlauer & Ruth Radlauer. LC 79-21826. (Gemini Bks.). (Illus.). 32p. (gr. 3 up). 1980. PLB 8.65 (ISBN 0-516-07687-6, Elk Grove Bks.); pap. 2.50 (ISBN 0-516-47687-4). Childrens.

Some Beekeepers & Associates, Pt. I. Joseph O. Moffett. (Illus.). 140p. lib. bdg. 19.90; pap. 9.90 (ISBN 0-686-28741-X). Moffett.

Some Birds Have Funny Names. Diana H. Cross. (Illus.). 1980. lib. bdg. 6.95 (ISBN 0-517-54005-3). Crown.

Some Buried Caeser. Rex Stout. 1979. pap. 1.75 (ISBN 0-515-05118-7). Jove Pubns.

Some Cambridge Controversies in the Theory of Capital. G. C. Harcourt. LC 71-161294. (Illus.). 1972. 35.50 (ISBN 0-521-08294-3); pap. 14.95x (ISBN 0-521-09672-3). Cambridge U Pr.

Some Champions: Previously Uncollected Autobiographical Sketches & Fiction. Ring Lardner. Intro. by Matthew J. Bruccoli & Richard Layman. 208p. 1976. encore ed. o.p. 3.50 (ISBN 0-684-15681-4, ScribT); pap. 3.95 (ISBN 0-684-15065-4, SL729, ScribT). Scribner.

Some Chapters on Money. Fred M. Taylor. LC 79-1594. 1981. Repr. of 1906 ed. 23.50 (ISBN 0-88355-899-8). Hyperion Conn.

Some Common BASIC Programs. 3rd ed. Lon Poole & Mary Borchers. 195p. (Orig.). 1979. pap. 14.99 (ISBN 0-931988-06-3). Osborne-McGraw.

Some Common BASIC Programs for Commodore Business Machines. Ed. by Lon Poole. 200p. 1980. pap. 14.99 (ISBN 0-931988-40-3). Osborne-McGraw.

Some Common Crutches. Shirley Schwarzrock & C. Gilbert Wrenn. (Coping with Ser.). (Illus.). 43p. (gr. 7-12). pap. text ed. 1.30 (ISBN 0-913476-15-3). Am Guidance.

Some Common Flowering Plants of Uganda. E. M. Lind & A. C. Tallantire. 1971. pap. 4.50x o.p. (ISBN 0-19-644104-8). Oxford U Pr.

Some Considerations of Early Attempts in Cooperation Between Religion & Psychiatry, Vol. 3. Group for the Advancement of Psychiatry. (Symposium No. 5). 1958. pap. 2.00 (ISBN 0-87318-049-6). Adv Psychiatry.

Some Contemporary Americans. Percy H. Boynton. LC 66-23516. 1924. 9.00x (ISBN 0-8196-0181-0). Biblo.

Some Curios from a Word-Collector's Cabinet. Abram S. Palmer. LC 79-145517. Repr. of 1907 ed. 15.00 (ISBN 0-8103-3670-7). Gale.

Some Day Been Dey: West African Pidgin Folktale. Loreto Todd. (Orig.). 1979. pap. 18.50 (ISBN 0-7100-0024-3). Routledge & Kegan.

Some Details of Water-Works Construction. William R. Billings. LC 72-80387. (History of Technology Ser., Vol. 2). (Illus.). 96p. 1972. Repr. of 1898 ed. 10.00x o.p. (ISBN 0-8155-5006-5, NP). Noyes.

Some Die Eloquent. Catherine Aird. 208p. 1981. pap. 2.25 (ISBN 0-553-14338-7). Bantam.

Some Discourse, Sermons & Remains. Joseph Glanville. Ed. by Rene Wellek. LC 75-11221. (British Philosophers & Theologians of the 17th & 18th Centuries Ser.). lib. bdg. 42.00 (ISBN 0-8240-1775-7). Garland Pub.

Some Distant Shore. Margaret Pemberton. (Orig.). 1981. pap. 2.75 (ISBN 0-671-42772-5). Archway.

Some Early Baha'is of the West. O. Z. Whitehead. (Illus.). 1976. 9.95 (ISBN 0-85398-065-9, 7-32-20, Pub. by George Ronald England); pap. 5.50 (ISBN 0-85398-067-5, 7-32-21, Pub. by George Ronald England). Baha'i.

Some Effects of Technological Change on New England Fishermen. Carl Gersuny et al. (Marine Technical Report Ser.: No. 42). 1975. pap. 1.00 (ISBN 0-938412-14-0). URI MAS.

Some English Books with Coloured Plates. Ronald V. Tooley. LC 75-162521. 1971. Repr. of 1935 ed. 21.00 (ISBN 0-8103-3762-2). Gale.

Some Exercises in Pure Mathematics. J. D. Weston & Herbert J. Godwin. (Orig.). pap. 6.95x (ISBN 0-521-09561-1). Cambridge U Pr.

Some Features of Organization in Nature: A Contribution to Philosophy. Robert E. Bass. 1980. 6.00. Print Mail Serv.

Some Followers of Domenico Ghirlandajo. Everett Fahy. LC 75-23790. (Outstanding Dissertations in the Fine Arts - 15th Century). (Illus.). 1976. lib. bdg. 41.00 (ISBN 0-8240-1986-5). Garland Pub.

Some George Eliot Notebooks: An Edition of the Carl H. Pforzheimer Library's George Eliot Holography Notebooks, Mss. 707, 5 vols. William Baker. (Salzburg Studies in English Literature, Romantic Reassessment: No. 46). 332p. 1977. pap. text ed. 25.00x set (ISBN 0-391-01307-6). Humanities.

Some George Eliot Notebooks: An Edition of the Carl H. Pforzheimer Library's George Eliot Ecolgrph Notebooks Mss 707, 708, 709, 710, Vol.iII-711. William Baker. (Romantic Reassessment Ser.: No.46). 267p. 1980. pap. text ed. 25.00 (ISBN 0-391-01309-2). Humanities.

Some Ghost Stories. A. M. Burrage. 1981. 8.50 (ISBN 0-686-69311-6). Bookfinger.

Some Indian Saints. Gopinath Talwalker. 64p. (Orig.). (gr. 5 up). 1980. pap. 1.50 (ISBN 0-89744-208-3, Pub. by Natl Bk Trust India). Auromere.

Some Issues in Joint Union-Management Quality of Worklife Improvement Efforts. Paul D. Greenberg & Edward M. Glaser. LC 80-14044. 80p. 1980. pap. 4.00 (ISBN 0-911558-70-5). Upjohn Inst.

Some Kannada Poems. Ed. by A. K. Ramanujan & M. G. Krishnamurthi. 1975. 8.00 (ISBN 0-88253-636-2); pap. text ed. 4.00 (ISBN 0-88253-635-4). Ind-US Inc.

Some Kind of Epic Grandeur: The Life of F. Scott Fitzgerald. Matthew J. Bruccoli. LC 80-8740. (Illus.). 384p. 1981. 17.50 (ISBN 0-15-183242-0). HarBraceJ.

Some Lessons in Mathematics. T. J. Fletcher. pap. 12.50x (ISBN 0-521-09248-5, 248). Cambridge U Pr.

Some Lichens of Tropical Africa V: Lecanoraceae to Physiaceae. C. W. Dodge. 1971. pap. 50.00 (ISBN 3-7682-5438-0). Lubrecht & Cramer.

Some Lose Their Way. Frederick J. Lipp. LC 80-13510. 132p. (gr. 5-9). 1980. 7.95 (ISBN 0-689-50178-1, McElderry Bk). Atheneum.

Some Major Tests. Ed. by Bernard Spolsky. LC 78-60576. (Advances in Testing Ser.: No. 1). 1979. pap. text ed. 5.50x (ISBN 0-87281-074-7). Ctr Appl Ling.

Some Mathematical Questions in Biology. Ed. by George F. Oster. (Lectures on Mathematics in the Life Sciences: Vol. 13). 1980. 11.20 (ISBN 0-8218-1163-0). Am Math.

Some Merry Adventures of Robin Hood. Howard Pyle. (Keith Jennison Large Type Bks). (gr. 5 up). 1967. PLB 7.95 o.p. (ISBN 0-531-00283-7). Watts.

Some Merry Adventures of Robin Hood. rev. ed. Howard Pyle. (Illus.). 1954. 4.95 o.p. (ISBN 0-684-13066-1, ScribJ). Scribner.

Some Minor Characters in the New Testament. A. T. Robertson. (A.T. Robertson Library). 194p. 1976. pap. 2.95 o.p. (ISBN 0-8010-7637-4). Baker Bk.

Some Modern Mathematics for Physicists & Other Outsiders, 2 vols. Paul Roman. LC 74-1385. 1975. Vol. 1. text ed. 40.00 (ISBN 0-08-018097-3); Vol. 2. text ed. 34.10 o.p. (ISBN 0-08-018134-1); Vol. 1. pap. text ed. 28.00 (ISBN 0-08-018096-5); Vol. 2. pap. text ed. 28.00 (ISBN 0-08-018133-3). Pergamon.

Some Modern Methods of Organic Synthesis. 2nd ed. W. Carruthers. LC 77-77735. (Cambridge Texts in Chemistry & Biochemistry Ser.). (Illus.). 1978. 85.00 (ISBN 0-521-21715-6); pap. 19.95x (ISBN 0-521-29241-7). Cambridge U Pr.

Some Modern Poets & Other Critical Essays. Edward Davison. 255p. 1980. Repr. of 1928 ed. lib. bdg. 35.00 (ISBN 0-89760-149-1). Telegraph Bks.

Some Modern Poets & Other Critical Essays. Edward Davison. 255p. 1980. Repr. lib. bdg. 35.00 (ISBN 0-89987-157-7). Century Bookbindery.

Some New Directions in Linguistics. Ed. by Roger W. Shuy. LC 73-76752. 149p. 1973. pap. 4.95 o.p. (ISBN 0-87840-202-0). Georgetown U Pr.

Some Nineteenth Century English Woodworking Tools. Kenneth D. Roberts. (Illus.). 496p. 1980. text ed. 40.00x (ISBN 0-913602-40-X). K Roberts.

Some Notes on H. P. Lovecraft. August W. Derleth. 50p. 1980. Repr. of 1959 ed. lib. bdg. 10.00 (ISBN 0-8495-1059-7). Arden Lib.

Some of My Best Friends Are Christians. Zola Levitt. LC 77-90581. 1978. pap. 3.25 o.p. (ISBN 0-8307-0591-0, 54-085-04). Regal.

Some of My Best Friends Are Trees. John S. Wade. (Sparrow Poverty Pamphlets: No. 35). (Orig.). pap. 1.50 o.p. (ISBN 0-686-20776-9). Sparrow Pr.

Some of My Friends Have Tails. Virginia McKenna. LC 76-17730. 1970. 5.50 o.p. (ISBN 0-15-183745-7, HJ). HarBraceJ.

Some of My Years. P. R. Kaikini. (Writers Workshop Redbird Ser.). 1975. 9.00 (ISBN 0-88253-638-9); pap. text ed. 4.80 (ISBN 0-88253-637-0). Ind-US Inc.

Some of the Sonnets. Giuseppe G. Belli. Tr. by Miller Williams from Ital. LC 80-24331. 177p. 1981. 9.95x (ISBN 0-8071-0762-X); pap. 4.95x (ISBN 0-8071-0763-8). La State U Pr.

Some of Your Blood. Theodore Sturgeon. 1977. pap. 1.50 o.p. (ISBN 0-345-25712-X). Ballantine.

Some One Myth: Yeats's Autobiographies. Shirley Neuman. (New Yeats's Papers: No. XIX). (Illus.). 112p. 1980. pap. text ed. 16.50x (ISBN 0-85105-369-6, Dolmen Pr). Humanities.

Some People Are Indians. Ed. by George A. Boyce. LC 75-190224. (Illus.). (gr. 4-6). 1974. 5.95 (ISBN 0-8149-0714-8). Vanguard.

Some People Just Won't Believe a Computer. Donald D. Spencer. 1978. pap. 3.95 (ISBN 0-89218-032-3). Camelot Pub.

Some Physical, Dosimetry & Biomedical Aspects of Californium. (Panel Proceedings Ser.). 1977. pap. 22.50 (ISBN 92-0-111476-1, IAEA). Unipub.

Some Post-Independence Bengali Poems. Tr. by Pradeep Banerjee. (Translated from Bengali). 8.00 (ISBN 0-89253-606-3). Ind-US Inc.

Some Prefer Nettles. Junichiro Tanizaki. Tr. by Edward G. Seidensticker from Jap. (Perigee Japanese Library). 224p. 1981. pap. 4.95 (ISBN 0-399-50521-0, Perigee). Putnam.

Some Presidential Interpretations of the Presidency. Norman J. Small. LC 71-87353. (Politics & Law Ser). 1969. Repr. of 1932 ed. lib. bdg. 27.50 (ISBN 0-306-71663-1). Da Capo.

Some Presidents: Wilson to Nixon. William A. Williams. 1972. pap. 1.95 o.p. (ISBN 0-686-66886-3, 70227). Random.

Some Principles of Fiction. Robert Liddell. LC 73-433. 162p. 1974. Repr. of 1954 ed. lib. bdg. 9.50x o.p. (ISBN 0-8371-6764-7, LIPF). Greenwood.

Some Problems in Chemical Kinetics & Reactivity, Vol. 2. N. N. Semenov. Tr. by M. Boudart. 1959. 19.00x o.p. (ISBN 0-691-08037-2). Princeton U Pr.

Some Problems of Geodynamics. Augustus E. Love. 1967. pap. text ed. 2.50 (ISBN 0-486-61766-1). Dover.

Some Problems of the Constitution. rev. ed. Geoffrey Marshall & G. C. Moodie. (Orig.). 1967. text ed. 6.00x (ISBN 0-09-053243-0, Hutchinson U Lib); pap. text ed. 3.25x (ISBN 0-09-053244-9, Hutchinson U Lib). Humanities.

Some Psychic Experiences & Their Results. Michael Agerskov. LC 79-9596. Orig. Title: Nogle Psykiske Oplevelser. 84p. 1979. pap. 3.25 (ISBN 87-87871-54-8). Toward the Light.

Some Recent Developments in Comparative Medicine. Zoological Society of London - 17th Symposium. 1967. 55.50 (ISBN 0-12-613317-4). Acad Pr.

Some Recent Developments in Operator Theory. Carl M. Pearcy. LC 78-8754. (Conference Board of the Mathematical Sciences Ser.: No. 36). 1980. Repr. of 1978 ed. 8.00 (ISBN 0-8218-1686-1, CBMS 36). Am Math.

Some Recollections of a Western Ranchman, New Mexico 1883-1899, 2 Vols. William French. 1965. Set. 35.00 (ISBN 0-87266-011-7). Argosy.

Some Remarkable Passages in the Life of the Honourable Col. James Gardiner, 1747. Philip Doddridge. Ed. by Michael F. Shugrue. (Flowering of the Novel, 1740-1775 Ser: Vol. 19). 1974. lib. bdg. 50.00 (ISBN 0-8240-1118-X). Garland Pub.

Some Run Crooked. John B. Hilton. LC 77-10182. 1978. 7.95 o.p. (ISBN 0-312-74355-6). St Martin.

Some Sanskrit Poems. Tr. by P. Lal from Sanskrit. 16p. 1973. 8.00 (ISBN 0-88253-266-9); flexible bdg. 4.00 (ISBN 0-89253-520-2). Ind-US Inc.

Some Scale-bearing Polychaetes of Puget Sound & Adjacent Waters. Marian H. Pettibone. LC 53-6933. (Illus.). 136p. 1953. pap. 7.50 (ISBN 0-295-73936-3). U of Wash Pr.

Some Shakespearean Themes & an Approach to Hamlet. L. C. Knights. 1961. 16.50x (ISBN 0-8047-0300-0); pap. 3.95 o.p. (ISBN 0-8047-0301-9). Stanford U Pr.

Some Silent Shore. Sigrid Johannesson. 178p. 1980. 10.95 (ISBN 0-86629-020-6). Sunrise MO.

Some Spanish-American Poets. Tr. by Alice S. Blackwell. LC 68-22694. (Eng. & Span.). 1968. Repr. of 1937 ed. 15.00x (ISBN 0-8196-0217-5). Biblo.

Some Special Problems of Children Aged 2-5. Nina Ridenour & Isabel Johnson. 1976. pap. 1.50 (ISBN 0-686-12268-2). Jewish Bd Family.

Some Statistical Applications in X-Ray Crystallography. B. Srinivasan & S. Parthasarathy. LC 75-9676. 1976. text ed. 42.00 (ISBN 0-08-018046-9). Pergamon.

Some Stories. Walter De La Mare. (Orig.). 1962. pap. 4.95 (ISBN 0-571-04581-2, Pub. by Faber & Faber). Merrimack Bk Serv.

Some Successive Approximation Methods in Control & Oscillation Theory. P. L. Falb & J. L. De Jong. (Mathematics in Science & Engineering Ser.: Vol. 59). 1969. 36.50 (ISBN 0-12-247950-5). Acad Pr.

Some Summer Lands. Jane Gaskell. LC 77-9179. (Atlan Saga: Vol. V). 1979. 8.95 o.p. (ISBN 0-312-74362-9). St Martin.

Some Texas Fusulinidae. M. P. White. (Illus.). 106p. 1932. 0.75 (BULL 3211). Bur Econ Geology.

Some Thermodynamic Aspects of Inorganic Chemistry. D. A. Johnson. LC 68-29118. (Cambridge Chemistry Texts Ser). (Orig.). 1968. pap. 12.50x (ISBN 0-521-09544-1). Cambridge U Pr.

Some Things Dark & Dangerous. Ed. by Joan Kahn. 1970. pap. 1.50 (ISBN 0-380-01556-0, 36038). Avon.

Some Things Strange & Sinister. Ed. by Joan Kahn. 1974. pap. 1.50 (ISBN 0-686-68409-5, 36046). Avon.

Some Things You Just Can't Do by Yourself. (ps-7). 1.50. New Seed.

Some Thoughts Concerning Education. John Locke. Ed. by F. W. Garforth. LC 65-16960. (Orig.). 1964. text ed. 6.00 o.p. (ISBN 0-8120-5057-6); pap. 2.50 o.p. (ISBN 0-8120-0129-X). Barron.

Some Thoughts on Planning in India. H. C. Ganguli. pap. 1.75x o.p. (ISBN 0-210-27181-7). Asia.

Some Thoughts on the Mayor of Casterbridge. W. H. Gardner. 52p. 1980. Repr. of 1930 ed. lib. bdg. 6.00 (ISBN 0-8492-4959-7). R West.

Some Time in the Sun. Tom Dardis. 1981. pap. 4.95 (ISBN 0-14-005831-1). Penguin.

Some Traces of the Pre-Olympian World in Greek Literature & Myth. E. A Butterworth. (Illus.). 1966. 29.50x (ISBN 3-11-005010-2). De Gruyter.

Some Unpublished Letters of Henry D. & Sophia E. Thoreau: A Chapter in the History of a Still-Born Book. Henry D. Thoreau. Ed. by Samuel A. Jones. LC 80-2684. 1981. Repr. of 1899 ed. 15.50 (ISBN 0-404-19078-2). AMS Pr.

Some Vanity of Mine Art: The Masque in English Renaissance Drama, Vols. 1, 2. Catherine Shaw. (SSEL Jacobean Drama Ser.: No. 81). 1980. pap. text ed. 25.00x (ISBN 0-391-01938-4). Humanities.

Some Wine Grape Varieties for Australia. 50p. 1976. pap. 5.00 (ISBN 0-643-00180-8, CO09, CSIRO). Unipub.

Somebody Else's Kids. Torey L. Hayden. 384p. 1981. 11.95 (ISBN 0-399-12602-3). Putnam.

Somebody Killed Her Husband. (Orig.). 1978. 1.95 o.s.i. (ISBN 0-515-04699-X). Jove Pubns.

Somebody Killed Reddy Fox. Susan K. Sibley. Ed. by Ronald H. Bayes. 160p. (Orig.). 1980. pap. 7.00x (ISBN 0-932662-33-1). St Andrews NC.

Somebody Spilled the Sky. Ruth Krauss. LC 78-14306. (Illus.). (gr. k-3). 1979. 7.50 (ISBN 0-688-80186-2); PLB 7.20 (ISBN 0-688-84186-4). Greenwillow.

Somehow Inside of Eternity. Richard C. Halverson. LC 80-21687. (Illus., Orig.). 1981. pap. 8.95 (ISBN 0-930014-51-0). Multnomah.

Someone Cares: The Collected Poems of Helen Steiner Rice. Helen S. Rice. (Illus.). 128p. 1972. 8.95 (ISBN 0-8007-0524-6); keepsake ed. 9.95 (ISBN 0-8007-0528-9). Revell.

Someone Cry for the Children: The Unsolved Girl Scout Murders of Oklahoma & the Case of Gene Leroy Hart. Michael Wilkerson & Dick Wilkerson. 256p. 1981. 10.95 (ISBN 0-8037-8283-7). Dial.

Someone Else's Child: A Book for Foster Parents of Young Children. 2nd ed. Olive Stevenson. 1977. pap. 6.50 (ISBN 0-7100-8706-3). Routledge & Kegan.

Someone Else's Dreams. John Yamrus. LC 80-70611. (Illus.). 60p. (Orig.). 1981. pap. 3.75 (ISBN 0-930090-13-6); pap. 10.00 special ltd. ed. Applezaba.

Someone Had to Hold the Lantern. Florence Burchard & Sharon Boucher. LC 79-17836. (Crown Ser.). 1979. pap. 4.50 (ISBN 0-8127-0238-7). Southern Pub.

Someone in the Dark. August Derleth. 1978. pap. 1.75 o.s.i. (ISBN 0-685-54634-9, 04738-4). Jove Pubns.

Someone in the Dark. August Derleth. 335p. 1980. Repr. of 1941 ed. lib. bdg. 15.50x (ISBN 0-89968-213-8). Lightyear.

Someone Is Killing the Great Chefs of Europe. Nan Lyons & Ivan Lyons. 1978. pap. 1.95 o.s.i. (ISBN 0-515-04834-8). Jove Pubns.

Someone to Love. Iris Weigh. (Aston-Hall Romances Ser.). 192p. (Orig.). Date not set. pap. 1.75 (ISBN 0-523-41131-6). Pinnacle Bks.

Someone Who Cared. Jim Roberts. (Action Bks.). (Illus.). 12p. (ps-3). 1975. pap. 3.50 (ISBN 0-570-07104-6, 56-1281). Concordia.

Someone's in the Kitchen with Dennis. Hank Ketcham. (Dennis the Menace Ser.). (Illus.). 1979. pap. 1.50 o.p. (ISBN 0-449-14253-1, GM). Fawcett.

Somerset & Dorset Locomotive History. D Bradley & David Milton. (Illus.). 1973. 11.50 (ISBN 0-7153-5956-8). David & Charles.

Somerset & Dorset Railway. Robin Atthill. LC 80-69344. (Illus.). 224p. 1981. 12.95 (ISBN 0-7153-4164-2). David & Charles.

Somerset Dreams & Other Fictions. Kate Wilhelm. LC 77-11776. 1978. 9.95 o.s.i. (ISBN 0-06-014649-4, HarpT). Har-Row.

Somerset: From a Draft Translation Prepared by Frank Thorn. Ed. by Caroline Thorn & Frank Thorn. (Domesday Book Ser.). (Illus.). 405p. 1980. 32.50x (ISBN 0-8476-3261-X). Rowman.

Somerset Legends. Berta Lawrence. 11.95 (ISBN 0-7153-6185-6). David & Charles.

Something About a Soldier. Mark Harris. 1976. pap. 1.50 o.p. (ISBN 0-345-24099-5). Ballantine.

Something About Swans: Essays by Madeleine Doran. Madeleine Doran. 100p. 1973. 5.00 (ISBN 0-299-06170-1). U of Wis Pr.

Something About the Author, Vol. 21. Ed. by Anne Commire. LC 72-27107. 300p. 1980. 38.00 (ISBN 0-8103-0093-1). Gale.

Something About the Author, Vol. 22. Ed. by Anne Commire. LC 72-27107. (Illus.). 375p. 1981. 38.00 (ISBN 0-8103-0085-0). Gale.

Something About the Author: Facts & Pictures About Contemporary Authors & Illustrators of Books for Young People. Ed. by Anne Commire. Incl. Vol. 1. 1971 (ISBN 0-8103-0050-8); Vol. 2. 1972 (ISBN 0-8103-0052-4); Vol. 3. 1972 (ISBN 0-8103-0054-0); Vol. 4. 1973 (ISBN 0-8103-0056-7); Vol. 5. 1973 (ISBN 0-8103-0058-3); Vol. 6. 1974 (ISBN 0-8103-0060-5); Vol. 7. 1975 (ISBN 0-8103-0062-1); Vol. 8. 1975. (ISBN 0-8103-0064-8); Vol. 9. 1976. (ISBN 0-8103-0066-4); Vol. 10. 1976. (ISBN 0-8103-0068-0); Vol. 11. 1977. (ISBN 0-8103-0070-2); Vol. 12. 1977. (ISBN 0-8103-0072-9); Vol. 13. 1978. (ISBN 0-685-43929-1); Vol. 14. 1978 (ISBN 0-8103-0095-8); Vol. 15. 1979 (ISBN 0-8103-0096-6); Vol. 16. 1979 (ISBN 0-8103-0097-4); Vol. 17. 1979 (ISBN 0-8103-0098-2); Vol. 18. 1980 (ISBN 0-8103-0099-0). LC 72-27107. (Illus.). (gr. 7-12). 38.00 ea. Gale.

Something Beautiful for God. Malcolm Muggeridge. LC 77-155106. (Illus.). 1971. 10.95 (ISBN 0-06-066041-4, HarpR). Har-Row.

Something Beautiful for God: Mother Teresa of Calcutta. Malcolm Muggeridge. 1977. pap. 2.45 (ISBN 0-385-12639-5, Im). Doubleday.

Something Beautiful from God. Susan S. Macaulay. LC 80-67388. 1980. 11.95 (ISBN 0-89107-189-X, Cornerstone Bks); pap. 6.95 (ISBN 0-89107-186-5). Good News.

Something for Nothing. Sid Roth & Irene Harrell. LC 75-31396. 1976. pap. 1.95 o.p. (ISBN 0-88270-258-0). Logos.

Something Further: Poems. Norma Farber. 1979. 6.95 (ISBN 0-914408-10-0); pap. 3.95. Kylix Pr.

Something Is Stirring in World Orthodoxy. S. Harakas. 1978. pap. 2.95 (ISBN 0-937032-04-2). Light & Life Pub Co MN.

Something Medieval. J. K. Randall. LC 80-80808. 41p. 1981. 14.25. Lingua Pr.

Something Old, Something New. Matilda Nordtvedt & Pearl Steinkuehler. (Orig.). 1981. pap. 1.95 (ISBN 0-8024-0927-X). Moody.

Something Queer at the Ballpark. Elizabeth Levy. LC 74-16332. 48p. (gr. 1-3). 1975. 6.95 o.s.i. (ISBN 0-440-05992-5); PLB 6.46 o.s.i. (ISBN 0-440-05993-3). Delacorte.

Something Queer on Vacation. Elizabeth Levy. LC 78-72858. (gr. 1-3). 1980. 6.95 (ISBN 0-440-08346-X); PLB 6.46 (ISBN 0-440-08347-8). Delacorte.

Something Special. Associated Women's Organization, Mars Hill Bible School. Ed. by Peggy Simpson & Linda Stanley. 1977. pap. 3.75 (ISBN 0-89137-408-6). Quality Pubns.

Something to Count on. Emily Moore. LC 79-23277. 112p. (gr. 5 up). 1980. 7.95 (ISBN 0-525-39595-4). Dutton.

Something to Guard. Cedric Belfrage & James Aronson. 1978. 25.00x (ISBN 0-231-04510-7). Columbia U Pr.

Something to Live By. Dorothea S. Kopplin. 4.95 o.p. (ISBN 0-385-00155-X). Doubleday.

Something to Shout About. Patricia Beatty. LC 76-22185. (gr. 5-9). 1976. PLB 7.92 (ISBN 0-688-32078-3). Morrow.

Something to Tell. Mabel O'Donnell. (Design for Reading Ser). (Illus.). (primer). 1972. text ed. 7.12 (ISBN 0-06-516003-7, SchDept); tchr's ed. 12.20 (ISBN 0-06-516201-3); wkbk. 2.92, (ISBN 0-06-516302-8) tchr's wkbk. 5.76 (ISBN 0-06-516402-4); phonics wkbk. 2.52, (0-06-516311-7) tchr's ed. 5.00 (ISBN 0-06-516411-3); dupl. masters a & b 16.68 ea.; mastery test 14.48 (ISBN 0-06-516611-6); select-a-card for primer & 1st reader 80.92 (ISBN 0-06-516812-7). Har-Row.

Something Weird Is Happening to Matthew, & He's a Little... !! Dina Anastasio. (Write-It-Yourself Bks.). (Illus.). 48p. 1981. pap. 1.75 (ISBN 0-8431-0281-0). Price Stern.

Something Wonderful Happened. Joan C. Bowden. LC 77-6325. (I Can Read a Bible Story Ser.: No. 2). (Illus.). (gr. 2-4). 1977. 4.95 (ISBN 0-570-07324-3, 56-1515); pap. 1.95 (ISBN 0-570-07318-9, 56-1415). Concordia.

Something Wonderful Is Happening. Earnest Larsen. LC 76-24443. (Emmaus Book Ser.). 1977. pap. 1.95 (ISBN 0-8091-1987-0). Paulist Pr.

Something Worse Than Hell & Better Than Heaven. Jerry Barnard. 1979. pap. 1.95 (ISBN 0-917726-31-6). Hunter Bks.

Something's Got to Help - & Yoga Can. Joy F. Herrick & Nancy Schraffenberger. LC 73-80177. (Illus.). 128p. 1974. 5.95 (ISBN 0-87131-126-7). M Evans.

Sometimes I Don't Like School. Paula Z. Hogan. LC 79-24055. (Life & Living from a Child's Point of View Ser.). (Illus.). (gr. k-5). 1980. PLB 9.65 (ISBN 0-8172-1357-0). Raintree Child.

Sometimes I Don't Love My Mother. Hila Colman. (gr. 7 up). 1977. 8.25 (ISBN 0-688-22121-1); PLB 7.92 (ISBN 0-688-32121-6). Morrow.

Sometimes I Feel Like a Blob. Ethel Barrett. LC 79-92649. 1977. pap. 2.75 (ISBN 0-8307-0482-5, 50-003-27). Regal.

Sometimes I Get So Mad. Paula Z. Hogan. LC 79-24057. (Life & Living from a Child's Point of View Ser.). (Illus.). (gr. k-5). 1980. PLB 9.65 (ISBN 0-8172-1359-7). Raintree Child.

Sometimes I Hate Myself. Katie Tonn. (Uplook Ser.). 1978. pap. 0.75 (ISBN 0-8163-0386-X, 19422-5). Pacific Pr Pub Assn.

Sometimes I Hate School. Carol Barkin & Elizabeth James. LC 75-20143. (Moods & Emotions Ser.). (Illus.). 32p. (gr. k-2). 1975. PLB 8.95 (ISBN 0-8172-0034-7). Raintree Pubs.

Sometimes I Like to Cry. Elizabeth Stanton & Henry Stanton. Ed. by Caroline Rubin. LC 77-19131. (Concept Bks.). (Illus.). 32p. (ps-2). 1978. 6.95g (ISBN 0-8075-7537-2). A Whitman.

Sometimes I Weep. Ken Walsh. LC 73-12523. 128p. (Orig.). 1974. tanalin 1.95 o.p. (ISBN 0-8170-0623-0). Judson.

Sometimes I Wonder. Hoagy Carmichael & Stephen Longstreet. LC 76-7577. (Roots of Jazz Ser.). 1976. Repr. of 1965 ed. lib. bdg. 22.50 (ISBN 0-306-70809-4). Da Capo.

Sometimes I'm Afraid. Sylvia R. Tester. LC 78-23262. (Illus.). (ps-3). 1979. PLB 5.95 (ISBN 0-89565-021-5). Childs World.

Sometimes It Happens. Elinor L. Horwitz. LC 79-2687. (Illus.). 40p. (gr. 1-4). 1981. 7.95 (ISBN 0-06-022596-3, HarpJ); PLB 7.89 (ISBN 0-06-022597-1). Har-Row.

Sometimes It Scares Me. Judith Conaway. LC 76-46342. (Moods & Emotions Ser.). (Illus.). (gr. k-3). 1977. PLB 8.95 (ISBN 0-8172-0060-6). Raintree Pubs.

Somewhere Else: A Living-Learning Catalog. Ed. by The Center for Curriculum Design. LC 72-91916. 214p. 1972. pap. 5.95 (ISBN 0-8040-0610-5). Swallow.

Somme. Richard Tames. (Jackdaw Ser: No. 111). 1972. 5.95 o.p. (ISBN 0-670-65714-X, Grossman). Viking Pr.

Somoza. Bernard Diederich. 1981. 16.95 (ISBN 0-525-20670-1). Dutton.

Son. Harlan Wade. Tr. by Claude Potvin & Rose-Ella Potvin. (Book About Ser.). Orig. Title: Sound. (Illus., Fr.). (gr. k-3). 1979. PLB 7.30 (ISBN 0-8172-1450-X). Raintree Pubs.

Son of a Servant: The Story of the Evolution of a Human Being, 1849-1867. August Strindberg. Tr. & intro. by Evert Sprinchorn. 8.50 (ISBN 0-8446-3027-6). Peter Smith.

Son of Apollo: Themes of Plato. F. J. Woodbridge. 272p. (gr. 7 up). 1972. Repr. of 1929 ed. 12.50x (ISBN 0-8196-0278-7). Biblo.

Son of Evil Street. Victor Torres & Don Wilkerson. LC 73-10828. 1977. pap. 1.95 (ISBN 0-87123-516-1, 200516). Bethany Fell.

Son of God to Superstar: Twentieth-Century Interpretation of Jesus. John H. Hayes. 256p. 1976. pap. 5.95 (ISBN 0-687-39091-5); pap. 6.95 o. p. (ISBN 0-687-39092-3). Abingdon.

Son of Man. Robert Silverberg. (Del Rey Bk.). 1977. pap. 2.25 o.p. (ISBN 0-345-28884-X). Ballantine.

Son of Man. A. C. Zenos. (Short Course Ser.). 145p. Repr. of 1914 ed. 2.95 (ISBN 0-567-08312-8). Attic Pr.

Son of Man in the Teaching of Jesus. A. J. Higgins. LC 79-42824. (Society for New Testament Studies Monographs: No. 40). 186p. Date not set. 24.50 (ISBN 0-521-22363-6). Cambridge U Pr.

Son of Minos. David M. Cheney. LC 64-25838. (gr. 7). 8.50x (ISBN 0-8196-0142-X). Biblo.

Son of Old Man Hat: A Navaho Autobiography. Ed. by Walter Dyk. LC 44-2654. 1967. pap. 4.95 (ISBN 0-8032-5054-1, BB 355, Bison). U of Nebr Pr.

Son of Poop. Gerald Locklin. 1980. 2.00 (ISBN 0-917554-14-0). Maelstrom.

Son of Royal Langbrith. W. D. Howells. LC 75-79476. (Selected Edition of W.D. Howells: Center for Editions of American Authors: Vol. 26). (Illus.). 344p. 1970. 17.50x (ISBN 0-253-35393-9). Ind U Pr.

Son of Sam: Based on the Authorized Transcription of the Tapes, Official Documents & Diaries of David Berkowitz. Larry Klausner. (Illus.). 400p. 1980. 12.95 (ISBN 0-07-035027-2). McGraw.

Son of Sato. William Lewis. 1978. 15.00 (ISBN 0-918824-10-9); pap. 3.00 (ISBN 0-918824-09-5). Turkey Pr.

Son of Singapore. Tan Kok Seng. (Writing in Asia Ser.). 1972. pap. text ed. 3.25x (ISBN 0-686-65342-4, 00220). Heinemann Ed.

Son of the Black Stallion. Farley. (gr. 4-6). Date not set. pap. cancelled (ISBN 0-686-68471-0, Schol Pap). Schol Bk Serv.

Son of the Black Stallion. Walter Farley. (Illus.). (gr. 4-6). 1947. 3.95 (ISBN 0-394-80603-4, BYR); PLB 5.99 (ISBN 0-394-90603-9); pap. 1.95 (ISBN 0-394-83612-X). Random.

Son of the Bondwoman. Emilia Pardo Bazan. Tr. by E. H. Hearn. 328p. 1976. Repr. of 1908 ed. 17.50 (ISBN 0-86527-307-3). Fertig.

Son of the Gamblin' Man: The Youth of an Artist. Mari Sandoz. LC 76-17066. 1976. 14.95x (ISBN 0-8032-0895-2); pap. 3.95 (ISBN 0-8032-5833-X, BB 626, Bison). U of Nebr Pr.

Son of the Morning. Joyce C. Oates. LC 78-56428. 1978. 10.95 (ISBN 0-8149-0800-4). Vanguard.

Son of the White Wolf. Robert E. Howard. LC 77-73604. 1977. 12.95 (ISBN 0-913960-09-8). Fax Collect.

Son of the Wolf. Jack London. (Illus.). 250p. 1980. pap. 3.95 (ISBN 0-932458-02-5). Star Rover.

Son-Rise. Barry N. Kaufman. (Illus.). 1977. pap. 2.50 (ISBN 0-446-91828-8). Warner Bks.

Son Songs for Christian Folk, 2 vols. Gary L. Johnson. Incl. Vol. I. pap. 1.25 (ISBN 0-87123-509-9, 280509); Vol. II. pap. 1.50 (ISBN 0-87123-532-3, 280532). 1975. Bethany Fell.

Son Who Said He Wouldn't. Louise Ulmer. (Arch Bks.: No. 18). 1981. pap. 0.79 (ISBN 0-570-06145-8, 59-1262). Concordia.

Sonar & Underwater Sound. Albert W. Cox. LC 74-15547. (Illus.). 1975. 17.95 (ISBN 0-669-95935-9). Lexington Bks.

Sonar Bangla. Asif Currimbhoy. 1972. pap. text ed. 4.80 (ISBN 0-88253-764-4). Ind-US Inc.

Sonata Pathetique. Mykola Kulish. Tr. by George S. Luckyj from Ukrainian. LC 73-91177. (Ukrainian Classics in Translation Ser: No. 3). 120p. 1975. lib. bdg. 11.50x (ISBN 0-87287-092-8). Ukrainian Acad.

Soncino Books of the Bible, 14 Vols. Set. 139.75x (ISBN 0-685-01048-1). Bloch.

Soncino Hebrew-English Talmud. Incl. Tractate Berakoth. 15.75x (ISBN 0-685-23064-3); Tractate Baba Mezia. 23.00x (ISBN 0-685-23065-1); Tractate Gittin. 19.00x (ISBN 0-685-23066-X); Tractate Baba Kamma. 23.00x (ISBN 0-685-23067-8); Tractate Kiddushin. 19.00x (ISBN 0-685-23068-6); Tractate Pesahim. 23.00x (ISBN 0-685-23069-4); Tractate Sanhedrin. 24.75 (ISBN 0-685-23070-8); Tractate Kethuboth. 26.75x (ISBN 0-685-23071-6); Tractate Shabbath, 2 vols. Set. 39.50x (ISBN 0-685-23072-4); Tractate Yoma. 24.50 (ISBN 0-685-23073-2). Bloch.

Soncino Talmud, 18 Vols. (Heb.). Set. 375.00x (ISBN 0-685-01051-1). Bloch.

Sondheim & Company. Craig Zadan. 1976. pap. 4.35 o.s.i. (ISBN 0-380-00607-3, 28639). Avon.

Song & Dance Man: The Films of Gene Kelly. Tony Thomas. LC 73-90949. (Illus.). 256p. 1974. 12.00 (ISBN 0-8065-0400-5). Citadel Pr.

Song Anthology One. rev. 2nd ed. Anne Leyerle & William D. Leyerle. LC 79-90829. 144p. (gr. 9 up). 1980. pap. 8.95 plastic comb. (ISBN 0-9602296-1-2). W D Leyerle.

Song Between Two Stars. Gaston Puel. (Translated from French). 6.75 (ISBN 0-89253-770-1); flexible cloth 4.80 (ISBN 0-89253-771-X). Ind-US Inc.

Song Birds. LC 77-92967. (Wild, Wild World of Animals Ser.). (Illus.). 1978. lib. bdg. 11.97 (ISBN 0-686-51176-X). Silver.

Song Celestial or Bhaggvad-Gita: From the Mahabharata, Being a Discourse Between Arjuna, Prince of India, & the Supreme Being Under the Form of Krishna. Tr. by Edwin Arnold. 1967. pap. 4.00 (ISBN 0-7100-6268-0). Routledge & Kegan.

Song Celestial: Shrimad Bhagavad Gita. 151p. 1980. 6.50x (ISBN 0-89955-328-1, Pub. by Interprint India). Intl Schol Bk Serv.

Song for a Dark Queen. Rosemary Sutcliff. LC 78-19514. (gr. 7 up). 1979. 6.95 (ISBN 0-690-03911-5, TYC-J); PLB 6.89 (ISBN 0-690-03912-3). T Y Crowell.

Song for Joseph. Merv Marquardt. (Arch Bks.: No. 18). (gr. k-4). 1981. pap. 0.79 (ISBN 0-570-06146-6, 59-1263). Concordia.

Song for Sarah. Paula D'Arcy. 128p. 1981. pap. 2.50 (ISBN 0-553-14728-5). Bantam.

Song from the Earth: American Indian Painting. Jamake Highwater. LC 75-37201. (Illus.). 1980. pap. 12.95 (ISBN 0-8212-1091-2, 804061). NYGS.

Song Is a Rainbow: Body Movement, Music, & Rythym Instruments in the Nursery School & Kindergarten. Patty Zeitlin. 336p. (Orig.). pap. 12.95 (ISBN 0-8302-8196-7). Goodyear.

Song-Lines of a Day. Narendra Sethi. 8.00 (ISBN 0-89253-737-X); flexible cloth 4.80 (ISBN 0-89253-738-8). Ind-US Inc.

Song of Enlightenment. Ch'An Master Yung Chia. Ed. by Ch'An Master Hua. Tr. by Bhikshu Heng Yo et al from Chin. (Illus., Orig.). 1981. pap. write for info. (ISBN 0-917512-20-0). Buddhist Text.

Song of Hero. Stephen Du Vall. 1977. 4.00 o.p. (ISBN 0-682-48860-7). Exposition.

Song of Hyemeyohsts: A Novel. Hyemyohsts Storm. LC 80-8359. (Native American Publishing Program). (Illus.). 224p. 1981. 12.95 (ISBN 0-06-452000-5, HarpR). Har-Row.

Song of Love. Barbara Cartland. 208p. 1980. pap. 1.75 (ISBN 0-515-05444-5). Jove Pubns.

Song of Love. Tr. by George Keyt. Orig. Title: Gita Govinda. 123p. 1969. pap. 2.00 (ISBN 0-88253-048-8). Ind-US Inc.

Song of Love. David Miller. Date not set. 5.95 (ISBN 0-533-04741-2). Vantage.

Song of Peace. Frances G. Nachant. 1969. 4.00 o.p. (ISBN 0-8233-0126-5). Golden Quill.

Song of Protest. Pablo Neruda. 1976. 5.95 o.p. (ISBN 0-688-03043-2); pap. 2.95 (ISBN 0-688-08043-X). Morrow.

Song of Roland. Tr. by Frederick Goldin. 1978. 10.00 (ISBN 0-393-04523-4); pap. 3.95x (ISBN 0-393-09008-6). Norton.

Song of Roland. Roland. Tr. by C. Scott Moncrieff. 150p. 1959. pap. 2.95 (ISBN 0-472-06032-5, 32, AA). U of Mich Pr.

Song of Roland. Tr. by Patricia Terry. LC 65-26528. (Orig.). 1965. pap. 5.50 (ISBN 0-672-60476-0, LLA221). Bobbs.

Song of Roland: Formulaic Style & Poetic Craft. Joseph J. Duggan. LC 75-186101. 1973. 16.00x (ISBN 0-520-02201-7). U of Cal Pr.

Song of Saint Francis. Clyde R. Bulla. LC 52-6739. (Illus.). (gr. 2-5). 1952. 8.95 (ISBN 0-690-75222-9, TYC-J). T Y Crowell.

Song of Sedna. Robert Sans Souci & Daniel Sans Souci. LC 80-627. (Illus.). 32p. (gr. 3). 1981. 8.95a (ISBN 0-385-15866-1); PLB (ISBN 0-385-15867-X). Doubleday.

Song of Solomon. George Burrowes. (Geneva Commentaries Ser.). 1977. 11.95 (ISBN 0-85151-157-0). Banner of Truth.

Song of Solomon. H. A. Ironside. Date not set. 4.95 (ISBN 0-87213-389-3). Loizeaux.

Song of Solomon. Toni Morrison. (RL 7). 1978. pap. 2.75 (ISBN 0-451-09443-3, E9443, Sig). NAL.

Song of Songs. Watchman Nee. 1965-1967. 3.00 o.p. (ISBN 0-87508-421-4); pap. 1.75 (ISBN 0-87508-420-6). Chr Lit.

Song of Songs. Illus. by Katie Thamer. Orig. Title: Song of Solomon. (Illus.). 40p. (Orig.). 1981. pap. 9.95 (ISBN 0-914676-46-6). Green Tiger.

Song of the Boat. Lorenz Grahman. LC 74-5183. (Illus.). (gr. 2-5). 1975. 8.95 (ISBN 0-690-75231-8, TYC-J); PLB 7.89 o.p. (ISBN 0-690-75232-6). T Y Crowell.

Song of the Brush: Japanese Paintings from the Sanso Collection. Ed. by John M. Rosenfield. (Illus.). 87p. 1979. text ed. 22.95 (ISBN 0-932216-02-1); pap. text ed. 14.95 (ISBN 0-932216-03-X). Seattle Art.

Song of the Campfire. Robert Service. LC 78-15108. (Illus.). 1978. 6.95 (ISBN 0-396-07623-8). Dodd.

Song of the Cosmos. Devarakunda B. Tilak. (Translated from Telugu). 8.00 (ISBN 0-89253-613-6); flexible cloth 4.80 (ISBN 0-89253-614-4). Ind-US Inc.

Song of the Earth & Other Poems. M. G. Adiga. Tr. by A. K. Ramanujan from Kannada. (Writers Workshop Redbird Ser.). 1975. 8.00 (ISBN 0-88253-640-0); pap. text ed. 4.00 (ISBN 0-88253-639-7). Ind-US Inc.

Song of the Evening. Nandini Satpathi. Tr. by J. B. Mohanty from Oriya. 110p. (Orig.). 1975. pap. 1.50 (ISBN 0-88253-770-9). Ind-US Inc.

Song of the Harp. Linda B. Osborne. LC 76-28047. 1977. 5.95 o.p. (ISBN 0-312-74480-3). St Martin.

Song of the Kingdom. Andy Stone. 256p. 1981. pap. 2.25 (ISBN 0-445-04654-6). Popular Lib.

Song of the Lark. 1915 ed. Willa Cather. LC 77-15596. 1978. pap. 6.95 (ISBN 0-8032-6300-7, BB 670, Bison). U of Nebr Pr.

Song of the Lord, Bhagavadgita. Ed. by Edward J. Thomas. (Wisdom of the East Ser). 3.00 o.p. (ISBN 0-7195-1407-X). Paragon.

Song of the Nightingale. Bruce Arnold. 256p. 1980. 19.95 (ISBN 0-241-10497-1, Pub. by Hamish Hamilton England). David & Charles.

Song of the Pongo. Postgate & Firmin. 1975. 3.95 (ISBN 0-7207-0782-X, Pub. by Michael Joseph). Merrimack Bk Serv.

Song of the Self Supreme. Mukerjee. Date not set. pap. 7.95 (ISBN 0-913922-14-5). Dawn Horse Pr. Postponed.

Song of the Self Supreme: Astavakra Gita. Tr. by Radhakamal Mukerjee. LC 74-24308. 1980. 7.95 (ISBN 0-913922-14-5). Dawn Horse Pr.

Song of the Siren. Philippa Carr. pap. 2.75 (Crest). Fawcett.

Song of the Sirens. Ernest K. Gann. 256p. 1981. pap. 2.50 (ISBN 0-515-05482-8). Jove Pubns.

Song of the Swallows. Leo Politi. (Illus.). (gr. k-3). 1949. reinforced bdg. 8.95 (ISBN 0-684-92309-2, ScribJ); pap. 0.95 o.p. (ISBN 0-684-12780-6, SBF19, ScribJ). Scribner.

Song of the Swallows. Leo Politi. (Illus.). 32p. (gr. k-3). pap. 2.95 (ISBN 0-689-70494-1, A-121, Aladdin). Atheneum.

Song of the Trail. Mabel E. Cason. LC 53-10772. (Destiny Ser.). 1979. pap. 4.95 (ISBN 0-8163-0245-6). Pacific Pr Pub Assn.

Song of the Vineyard: A Guide Through the Old Testament. rev. ed. Davie Napier. LC 78-14672. 360p. 1981. pap. 11.95 (ISBN 0-8006-1352-X, 1-1352). Fortress.

Song of Zion. M. Wohlgemuth. 1977. 5.00 o.p. (ISBN 0-682-48946-8). Exposition.

Song Presentation for Polular Singers: Book II. Al Berkman. 1977. 8.50 (ISBN 0-934972-02-8). Melrose Pub Co.

Song Presentation for Popular Singers: Book I. Al Berkman. 1976. 10.00 (ISBN 0-934972-01-X). Melrose Pub Co.

Song, Speech & Ventriloquism. Larry Kettelkamp. (Illus.). (gr. 5-9). 1967. PLB 6.96 (ISBN 0-688-31799-5). Morrow.

Song to Sing & a Tale to Tell. Jean Brown. 174p. 1980. 14.95 (ISBN 0-906191-43-2, Pub. by Thule Pr England). Intl Schol Bk Serv.

Song Without Music: Chinese Tz'u Poetry. Ed. by Stephen C. Soong. (Renditions Ser). (Illus.). 286p. 1981. 20.00 (ISBN 0-295-95811-1, Pub. by Chinese Univ Hong Kong). U of Wash Pr.

Songbirds. Ed. by Time Life Books Editors. (Wild, Wild World of Animals Ser.). (Illus.). 1978. 10.95 (ISBN 0-913948-18-7). Time-Life.

Songbirds in Your Garden. 3rd st ed. John K. Terres. Ed. by Jeff Conrad. (Illus.). 228p. 1980. pap. 6.95 (ISBN 0-8015-6945-1, Hawthorn). Dutton.

Songbook of Absences. Miguel Hernandez. Tr. by Tom Jones. LC 72-91778. 1980. 7.50 (ISBN 0-685-25407-0). Charioteer.

Songe De Vieil Pelerin of Philippe De Mezieres, 2 Vols. Ed. by G. W. Coopland. LC 69-10194. (Illus.). 1969. Set. 220.00 (ISBN 0-521-07116-X). Cambridge U Pr.

Songes Merveilleux Du Dormeur Eveille: Le Chant Du Dvgne: Contes Parles D'Oscar Wilde. Guillot De Saix. LC 76-25932. (Decadent Consciousness Ser.). lib. bdg. 38.00 (ISBN 0-8240-2785-X). Garland Pub.

Songmaster. Orson S. Card. (Quantum Science Fiction Ser.). 338p. 1980. 10.95 (ISBN 0-8037-7711-6). Dial.

Songs. Henry C. Work. LC 73-5099. (Earlier American Music Ser.: Vol. 19). (Illus.). 180p. 1974. Repr. of 1884 ed. lib. bdg. 25.00 (ISBN 0-306-70586-9). Da Capo.

Songs a Thracian Taught Me. Anne Beresford. 64p. 1981. 8.95 (ISBN 0-7145-2724-6, Pub. by M. Boyars); pap. 4.50 (ISBN 0-7145-2725-4). Merrimack Bk Serv.

Songs Along the Mahantonga: Pennsylvania Dutch Folksongs. Walter E. Boyer et al. 231p. 1964. Repr. of 1951 ed. 15.00 (ISBN 0-8103-5002-5). Gale.

Songs & Ballads of the Maine Lumberjacks. Ed. by Roland P. Gray. LC 73-75944. 1969. Repr. of 1924 ed. 15.00 (ISBN 0-8103-3835-1). Gale.

Songs & Ballads, with Other Short Poems, Chiefly of the Reign of Philip & Mary. Thomas Wright. 214p. 1980. Repr. of 1860 ed. lib. bdg. 45.00 (ISBN 0-8495-5827-1). Arden Lib.

Songs & Motets of Alfonso Ferrabosco, the Younger (1575-1628) John Duffy. Ed. by George Buelow. (Studies in Musicology). 435p. 1981. 39.95 (ISBN 0-8357-1110-2, Pub. by UMI Res Pr). Univ Microfilms.

Songs by Thirty Americans for High Voice. Ed. by Rupert Hughes. LC 77-1948. (Music Reprint Series). 1977. Repr. of 1904 ed. lib. bdg. 25.00 (ISBN 0-306-70824-8). Da Capo.

Songs for Preschool Children. Ed. by Marian Bennett. LC 80-25091. 96p. 1981. pap. 5.95 (ISBN 0-87239-429-8, 5754). Standard Pub.

Songs for Preschoolers. Marie Frost. (Peter Panda Ser.). 1977. pap. 1.25 (ISBN 0-87239-146-9, 42038). Standard Pub.

Songs for the Harvester of Dreams. Duane Niatum. LC 80-50864. 64p. 1980. 7.95 (ISBN 0-295-95758-1). U of Wash Pr.

Songs from the Restoration Theatre. Willard Thorp. LC 76-102003. (Music Ser). 1970. Repr. of 1934 ed. lib. bdg. 17.50 (ISBN 0-306-71867-7). Da Capo.

Songs in the Night. Dorothy Weinberger. 1981. 4.75 (ISBN 0-8062-1699-9). Carlton.

Songs in the Night: A Study of the Book of Job. Horace M. King. (Illus.). 1969. pap. 2.95 (ISBN 0-685-20632-7). Transatlantic.

Songs of a Bridge Builder. D. B. Steinman. 12.00 (ISBN 0-88253-762-8); flexible cloth 4.80 (ISBN 0-88253-761-X). Ind-US Inc.

Songs of a Worker. Arthur O'Shaughnessy. Ed. by Ian Fletcher & John Stokes. LC 76-20159. (Decadent Consciousness Ser.). 1978. lib. bdg. 38.00 (ISBN 0-8240-2782-5). Garland Pub.

Songs of Childhood. Walter De La Mare. LC 75-32200. (Classics of Children's Literature, 1621-1932: Vol. 61). 1976. Repr. of 1902 ed. PLB 38.00 (ISBN 0-8240-2310-2). Garland Pub.

Songs of Cifar & the Sweet Sea. Pablo A. Cuadra. Tr. by Grace Schulman & Ann M. De Zavala. (A Center for Inter-American Relations Book). 1979. 15.00x (ISBN 0-231-04772-X); pap. 7.50x (ISBN 0-231-04773-8). Columbia U Pr.

Songs of Deliverance. Flower A. Newhouse. LC 72-94582. 250p. 1972. 8.00 (ISBN 0-910378-08-8). Christward.

Songs of Duncan MacIntyre. Angus MacLeod. 1978. 25.00x (ISBN 0-7073-0040-1, Pub. by Scottish Academic Pr Scotland). Columbia U Pr.

Songs of God's Grace. M. R. Bawa Muhaiy Addeen. LC 73-91016. (Illus.). 154p. 1974. pap. 3.50 (ISBN 0-914390-02-3). Fellowship Pr PA.

Songs of Highland Emigrants in North America. Margaret Macdonell. 208p. 1981. 18.95x (ISBN 0-8020-5469-2). U of Toronto Pr.

Songs of Homer. Geoffrey S. Kirk. 1962. 55.00 (ISBN 0-521-05890-2). Cambridge U Pr.

Songs of Indonesia. Zainnuddin. 1970. pap. text ed. 3.50x (ISBN 0-686-65419-6, 00508). Heinemann Ed.

Songs of Innocence & Experience. William Blake. Ed. by Margaret Bottrall. LC 70-127566. (Casebook Ser). 1970. pap. text ed. 2.50 o.s.i. (ISBN 0-87695-037-3). Aurora Pubs.

Songs of Irish Rebellion: Political Street Ballads & Rebel Songs, 1780-1900. Georges D. Zimmermann. LC 67-21410. 342p. Repr. of 1967 ed. 15.00 (ISBN 0-8103-5025-4). Gale.

Songs of Jerusalem & Myself. Yehuda Amichai. LC 72-181604. 96p. 1973. 6.95 o.s.i. (ISBN 0-06-010097-4, HarpT); pap. 2.95 o.s.i. (ISBN 0-06-010101-6, TD-124, HarpT). Har-Row.

Songs of Light: The Bruderhof Songbook. Compiled by Society of Brothers & Marlys Swinger. LC 77-1716. (Illus.). 1977. 12.75 o.p. (ISBN 0-87486-017-2). Plough.

Songs of Nova Scotia. Helen Creighton. 1968. pap. 6.00 (ISBN 0-486-21703-5). Dover.

Songs of Peter Rabbit: Music by Dudley Glass. Beatrix Potter. (Illus.). 1952. 3.95 (ISBN 0-7232-1035-7). Warne.

Songs of Richard Rodgers: A Definitive Collection. Richard Rodgers. LC 74-8879. 1974. pap. 8.95 (ISBN 0-394-70966-7). Random.

Songs of Sorrow & Hate. Don Surincik. (Contemporary Poets of Dorrance Ser.). 104p. 1981. 5.00 (ISBN 0-8059-2778-6). Dorrance.

Songs of the Carolina Charter Colonists, 1663-1763. Arthur P. Hudson. 1962. pap. 0.50 o.p. (ISBN 0-86526-104-0). NC Archives.

Songs of the Chassidim. Ed. by Velvel Pasternak. 1968. Vol. 1. 1968. 12.50x (ISBN 0-8197-0170-X); Vol. 2. 1971. 15.00x (ISBN 0-8197-0276-5). Bloch.

Songs of the Good Earth. Margaret Phillips. LC 79-10731. 62p. 1980. pap. 4.95 (ISBN 0-88289-221-5). Pelican.

Songs of the Nativity. William H. Husk. 205p. 1980. Repr. of 1868 ed. lib. bdg. 17.50 (ISBN 0-8414-2094-7). Folcroft.

Songs of the Pacific Northwest. Phil J. Thomas. (Resource Ser). (Illus.). 1979. 14.95 (ISBN 0-87663-551-6). Hancock Hse.

Songs of the People: Lancashire Dialect Poetry of the Industrial Revolution. Ed. by Brian Hollingworth. 1977. text ed. 10.25x (ISBN 0-7190-0612-0). Humanities.

Songs (Opus 40, 47, 56, 58, 60) Edward MacDowell. LC 73-170392. (Earlier American Music Ser.: No. 7). 1972. Repr. lib. bdg. 16.50 (ISBN 0-685-29163-4). Da Capo.

Songs to Krishna. Subramania Bharati. Tr. by David Bunce from Tamil. (Writers Workshop Saffronbird Ser.). 1975. 14.00 (ISBN 0-88253-642-7); pap. text ed. 4.80 (ISBN 0-88253-641-9). Ind-US Inc.

Songs to Poems by Arlo Bates, 1892-1897. George W. Chadwick. LC 73-170928. (Earlier Amer. Music Ser.: Vol. 16). 1976. Repr. of 1897 ed. 18.50 (ISBN 0-306-77316-3). Da Capo.

Songs, 1880 to 1904. Claude Debussy. Ed. by Rita Benson. (Orig.). 1981. pap. price not set (ISBN 0-486-24131-9). Dover.

Songwriter's Handbook. Harvey Rachlin. LC 77-2946. (Funk & W Bk.). (Illus.). 1977. 10.95 (ISBN 0-308-10321-1, TYC-T). T Y Crowell.

Songwriter's Market 1980. 2nd ed. William Brohaugh. (Illus.). 1979. 10.95 o.p. (ISBN 0-89879-003-4). Writers Digest.

Sonia Delaunay: A Retrospective. Ed. by Robert T. Buck et al. LC 79-57450. (Illus.). 236p. 1980. pap. 27.50 (ISBN 0-914782-32-0). Buffalo Acad.

Sonic Design: Practice & Problems. Robert Cogan & Pozzi Escot. (Illus.). 160p. 1981. text ed. 12.95 (ISBN 0-686-68608-X). P-H.

Sonic Design: The Nature of Sound & Music. Robert Cogan & Pozzi Escot. (Illus.). 544p. 1976. 19.95 (ISBN 0-13-822726-8). P-H.

Sonic Scotia. N. R. Baljian-Gara. 53p. 1980. 3.50 (ISBN 0-8059-2751-4). Dorrance.

Sonido. Harlan Wade. Tr. by Mamie M. Contreras from Eng. LC 78-26830. (Book About Ser.). Orig. Title: Sound. (Illus., Sp.). (gr. k-3). 1979. PLB 7.30 (ISBN 0-8172-1475-5). Raintree Pubs.

Sonnenenergie Auf Dem Weg Zur Praktischen Nutzung. (Ger.). 1974. pap. 15.00 o.p. (ISBN 0-89192-173-7). Interbk Inc.

Sonnenenergie: 2 Jahre Praktische Nutzung. 1977. pap. 15.00 o.p. (ISBN 0-89192-185-0). Interbk Inc.

Sonnets. Paul Jacob. 8.00 (ISBN 0-89253-553-9); flexible cloth 4.00 (ISBN 0-89253-554-7). Ind-US Inc.

Sonnets. William Shakespeare. Ed. by Arthur Quiller-Couch et al. (New Shakespeare Ser). 1969. 23.95 (ISBN 0-521-07555-6); pap. 4.50x (ISBN 0-521-09498-4). Cambridge U Pr.

Sonnets. William Shakespeare. 1964. 2.25 o.p. (ISBN 0-212-35868-5). Dufour.

Sonnets, Amatory, Incidental & Descriptive, with Other Poems, Repr. Of 1820. Bd. with Summer; an Invocation to Sleep; Fairy Revels; & Songs & Sonnets. Cornelius Webb. Repr. of 1821 ed; Charles Jeremiah Wells (1800-1879) Joseph & His Brethren: a Scriptural Drama, in Two Acts by H.L. Howard. Jeremiah J. Wells. Repr. of 1824 ed. LC 75-31270. (Romantic Context Ser.: Poetry 1789-1830: Vol. 116). 1978. lib. bdg. 43.00 (ISBN 0-8240-2216-5). Garland Pub.

Sonnets from the Portuguese & Other Love Poems. Elizabeth Barrett Browning. LC 54-10779. 5.95 (ISBN 0-385-01463-5). Doubleday.

Sonnets of Jocelyn Hollis. Jocelyn Hollis. LC 81-90002. 62p. 1981. pap. 3.95 (ISBN 0-933486-21-9). Am Poetry Pr.

Sonnets of the English Renaissance. J. W. Lever. (Athlone Renaissance Library). 192p. 1974. text ed. 18.75x (ISBN 0-485-13604-X, Athlone Pr); pap. text ed. 10.00x (ISBN 0-485-12604-4, Athlone Pr). Humanities.

Sonnets of William Shakespeare. Royal Shakespeare Theatre. 1980. 30.00x (ISBN 0-85683-013-5, Pub. by Shepheard-Walwyn England). State Mutual Bk.

Sonny & Cher. Thomas Braun. (Rock 'n Pop Stars Ser.). (Illus.). (gr. 4-12). 1978. PLB 5.95 (ISBN 0-87191-620-7); pap. 2.95 (ISBN 0-685-81994-9). Creative Ed.

Sonny & the Mountain. Eula K. Darnell. LC 79-63420. (Illus.). 1979. 4.50 (ISBN 0-533-04262-3). Vantage.

Sonoma County Bike Trails. Phyllis L. Neumann. (Illus.). 112p. (Orig.). pap. 3.95 (ISBN 0-686-28739-8). Sonoma County.

Sonoma Mission: San Francisco De Sonoma. R. S. Smilie. LC 74-81641. (Illus.). 1975. 9.95 o.p. (ISBN 0-913548-24-3, Valley Calif). Western Tanager.

Sonoran Desert. Ed. by Christopher L. Helms & Gweneth R. DenDooven. LC 80-82918. (Illus.). 1980. 8.95 (ISBN 0-916122-72-7); pap. 3.75 (ISBN 0-916122-71-9). K C Pubns.

Sons & Lovers. D. H. Lawrence. Ed. by Gamini Salgado. LC 75-127570. (Casebook Ser). 1970. pap. text ed. 2.50 o.s.i. (ISBN 0-87695-041-1). Aurora Pubs.

Sons & Lovers. D. H. Lawrence. 1976. pap. 2.95 (ISBN 0-14-004217-2). Penguin.

Sons & Lovers: A Facsimile of the Manuscript. Ed. by Mark Schorer & D. H. Lawrence. LC 75-46037. 1978. 95.00x (ISBN 0-520-03190-3). U of Cal Pr.

Sons & Mothers: Why Men Behave As They Do. Paul Olsen. Ed. by Fred Graver. 300p. 1981. 11.95 (ISBN 0-87131-338-3). M Evans.

Sons for King Yah. Linda Howard. LC 75-7480. 1975. pap. 2.25 o.p. (ISBN 0-88270-120-7). Logos.

Sons of God Return. Kelly L. Seagraves. 192p. 1975. pap. 1.50 o.p. (ISBN 0-8007-8190-2, Spire Bks). Revell.

Sons of Sam Spade: The Private Eye Novel in the 70s. David Geherin. LC 79-4823. (Recognitions Ser.). 1980. 10.95 (ISBN 0-8044-2231-1). Ungar.

Sons of the Bear God. Norvell W. Page. 1979. pap. 1.75 o.p. (ISBN 0-425-03889-0). Berkley Pub.

Sons of the Pioneers. John Givens. LC 77-73052. 1977. 10.00 o.p. (ISBN 0-15-183775-9); pap. 3.95 o.p. (ISBN 0-15-683815-X, Harv). HarBraceJ.

Sons of the Sheik. E. M. Hull. (Barbara Cartland's Library of Love: Vol. 11). 213p. 1980. 12.95x (ISBN 0-7156-1472-X, Pub. by Duckworth England). Biblio Dist.

Sons or Daughters: A Cross Cultural Survey of Parental Preferences. Nancy E. Williamson. LC 76-26888. (Sage Library of Social Research: Vol. 31). 1976. 18.00x (ISBN 0-8039-0673-0); pap. 8.95x (ISBN 0-8039-0674-9). Sage.

Sonship Training. Harold Vincent. 64p. (Orig.). 1980. pap. 1.50 (ISBN 0-89841-009-6). Zoe Pubns.

Sonya: The Life of Countess Tolstoy. Anne Edwards. 1981. 13.95 (ISBN 0-671-24040-4). S&S.

Soochow Gardens. 1980. 85.00 (ISBN 0-8351-0696-9). China Bks.

Soon-Hee in America. Schi-Zhin Rhie. LC 77-81780. (Illus.). (gr. k-3). 1977. PLB 6.50 (ISBN 0-930878-00-0). Hollym Intl.

Soon to Be a Major Motion Picture. Abbie Hoffman. 1980. 13.95 (ISBN 0-686-68806-6, Perigee); pap. 6.95 (ISBN 0-686-68807-4). Putnam.

Soong Sisters. Roby Eunson. LC 75-5952. 192p. (gr. 7 up). 1975. PLB 6.90 (ISBN 0-531-02835-6). Watts.

Soothsayer's Handbook: A Guide to Bad Signs & Good Vibrations. Elinor Horwitz. LC 76-172143. (Illus.). (gr. 9 up). 1972. 7.95 o.p. (ISBN 0-397-31538-4). Lippincott.

Sophia, 2 vols. in 1. Charlotte Lennox. Ed. by Michael F. Shugrue. (Flowering of the Novel, 1740-1775 Ser: Vol. 61). 1974. Repr. of 1762 ed. lib. bdg. 50.00 (ISBN 0-8240-1160-0). Garland Pub.

Sophie. William Stobbs. 1974. 3.95 (ISBN 0-7207-0769-2, Pub. by Michael Joseph). Merrimack Bk Serv.

Sophie's Choice. William Styron. 640p. 1980. pap. 3.50 (ISBN 0-553-13545-7). Bantam.

Sophists. William K. Guthrie. 1971. pap. 11.50x (ISBN 0-521-09666-9). Cambridge U Pr.

Sophists. Mario Untersteiner. Tr. by Kathleen Freeman. 1954. 24.50x (ISBN 0-631-04600-3, Pub. by Basil Blackwell). Biblio Dist.

Sophocles: Dramatist & Philosopher. LC 80-22360. 64p. 1981. Repr. of 1958 ed. lib. bdg. 22.50x (ISBN 0-313-22625-3, KISD). Greenwood.

Sophocle's Oedipus. Karl Harshbarger. LC 79-66476. 1979. text ed. 15.50 (ISBN 0-8191-0834-0); pap. text ed. 7.50 (ISBN 0-8191-0835-9). U Pr of Amer.

Sophocles the Dramatist. Arthur J. Waldock. pap. 8.50x (ISBN 0-521-09374-0). Cambridge U Pr.

Sophronia; or, Letters to the Ladies. Ed. by Michael F. Shugrue. (Flowering of the Novel Ser.: 1740-1775). Repr. of 1761 ed. lib. bdg. 50.00 (ISBN 0-8240-1158-9). Garland Pub.

Sophus Lie's Eighteen Eighty Transformation Group Paper. M. Ackerman & Robert Hermann. LC 75-17416. (Lie Groups: History, Frontiers on Applications Ser.: No. 1). 1975. 45.00 (ISBN 0-915692-10-4). Math Sci Pr.

Sophus Lie's Eighteen Eighty Transformation Group Paper. Robert Hermann & M. Ackerman. LC 75-43189. (Lie Groups: History Frontiers & Applications Ser.: No. 3). 1976. 26.00 (ISBN 0-915692-13-9). Math Sci Pr.

Sopresa de los Pescadores. Alyce Bergey. Tr. by Fernando Villalobos from Eng. (Libros Arco Ser.). (Illus.). 32p. (Orig., Span.). (gr. 1-3). 1978. pap. 0.95 (ISBN 0-89922-122-X). Edit Caribe.

Sopwith Aircraft Nineteen Twelve to Nineteen Twenty. H. F. King. (Illus.). 320p. 1981. 36.00 (ISBN 0-370-30050-5, Pub. by Chatto-Bodley-Jonathan). Merrimack Bk Serv.

Sorcerer. Eric Ericson. LC 78-19530. 1979. 8.95 o.p. (ISBN 0-312-74506-0). St Martin.

Sorcerer's Apprentice: An Anthropology of Public Policy. Cyril S. Belshaw. 360p. 1976. text ed. 26.00 (ISBN 0-08-018313-1); pap. text ed. 16.75 (ISBN 0-08-018312-3). Pergamon.

Sorceress of the Witchworld. Andre Norton. 224p. 1977. pap. 1.95 (ISBN 0-441-77555-1). Ace Bks.

Sorcery in Its Social Setting. M. G. Marwick. 1970. text ed. 20.25x (ISBN 0-7190-0257-5). Humanities.

Soren Kierkegaard. Robert L. Perkins. Ed. by Dennis E. Nineham & E. H. Robertson. LC 69-14337. (Makers of Contemporary Theology Ser). (Orig.). 1969. pap. 3.45 (ISBN 0-8042-0710-0). John Knox.

Soren Kierkegaard & His Critics: An International Bibliography of Criticism. Compiled by Francois H. Lapointe. LC 80-783. viii, 430p. 1980. lib. bdg. 37.50 (ISBN 0-313-22333-5, LKI/). Greenwood.

Soren Kierkegaard's Journals & Papers, 7 vols. Soren Kierkegaard. Ed. by Howard V. Hong & Edna H. Hong. Incl. Vol. 1. A-E. 572p. 1967. 25.00x (ISBN 0-253-18240-9); Vol. 2. F-K. 640p. 1970. 35.00x (ISBN 0-253-18241-7); Vol. 3. L-R. 944p. 1976. 40.00x (ISBN 0-253-18242-5); Vol. 4. S-Z. 800p. 1976. 40.00x (ISBN 0-253-18243-3); Vol. 5. Autobiographical, Part One, 1829-1848. 576p. 1978. 27.50x (ISBN 0-253-18244-1); Vol. 6. Autobiographical, Part Two, 1848-1855. 648p. 1978. 35.00x (ISBN 0-253-18245-X); Vol. 7. Index & Composite Collation. 160p. 1978. 20.00x (ISBN 0-253-18246-8). LC 67-13025. Set. 175.00x (ISBN 0-253-18239-5). Ind U Pr.

Sorghum: A Bibliography of the World Literature Covering the Years 1930-1963. George Washington University, Biological Sciences Communication Project. LC 67-12060. 1967. 10.00 (ISBN 0-8108-0135-3). Scarecrow.

Sorghum Production & Utilization. J. S. Wall & W. M. Ross. (Illus.). 1970. 39.50 o.p. (ISBN 0-87055-069-1). AVI.

Sorrow of the Snows. Upendranath Askh. Tr. by Jai Ratan. (Translated from Hindi). 9.00 (ISBN 0-89253-639-X); flexible cloth 6.75 (ISBN 0-89253-640-3). Ind-US Inc.

Sorry Dad: An Autobiography. Edward Blishen. 1979. 15.95 (ISBN 0-241-89849-8, Pub. by Hamish Hamilton England). David & Charles.

Sortilego. Abdiasdo Nasciemento. 1980. pap. 2.95 (ISBN 0-88378-086-0). Third World.

Sorting & Sort Systems. Harold Lorin. (Illus.). 480p. 1975. 18.95 (ISBN 0-201-14453-0). A-W.

Sorting Life Out. Purgraski. LC 66-7533. 1978. 24.00x (ISBN 0-930004-00-0). C E M Comp.

Sorting Machine: National Education Policy Since 1945. Joel Spring. LC 75-53801. (Educational Policy, Planning, & Theory Ser.). 1976. pap. 9.95 (ISBN 0-582-28127-X). Longman.

Sorting Out Money Values. I. Purgraski. LC 76-3347. 1979. 6.95x o.p. (ISBN 0-930004-01-9). C E M Comp.

Sorting Out Money Values & Student Packet of Ready-to-Be-Duplicated Worksheets. rev. ed. Carolyn B. Purgraski et al. (Sorting Life Out Ser.). 292p. 1981. tchr's. ed. 25.00 (ISBN 0-930004-02-7); student packet, 68p. free. C E M Comp.

SOS: A Communications Text with a Message. Marlene Ahnne & Sara Burgess. LC 72-81074. 446p. 1973. pap. text ed. 7.95x (ISBN 0-02-470850-X, 47085); tchr's manual free (ISBN 0-02-470860-7). Macmillan.

SOS: The Story of Radio Communication. G. E. Wedlake. LC 73-91529. (Illus.). 240p. 1974. 14.50x (ISBN 0-8448-0270-0). Crane-Russak Co.

Sotheby's Annual Review: 1961-62. 40.00x (ISBN 0-85667-075-8, Pub. by Sotheby Parke Bernet England). Biblio Dist.

Sotheby's: Portrait of an Auction House. Frank Herrmann. (Illus.). 1981. 29.95 (ISBN 0-393-01424-X). Norton.

Soul Afire: Revelations of the Mystics. Ed. by H. A. Reinhold. 440p. 1973. pap. 2.95 (ISBN 0-385-01489-9, Im). Doubleday.

Soul Brothers & Sister Lou. Kristin Hunter. (YA) (gr. 7 up). 1975. pap. 1.50 (ISBN 0-380-00686-3, 42143). Avon.

Soul Building Sermon Outlines. Russell E. Spray. (Dollar Sermon Library). 1977. pap. 1.45 (ISBN 0-8010-8118-1). Baker Bk.

Soul Butter & Hog Wash & Other Essays on the American West. Ed. by Thomas G. Alexander. LC 77-89974. (Charles Redd Monographs in Western History Ser.: No. 8). 1978. pap. 4.95 (ISBN 0-8425-1232-2). Brigham.

Soul Hit. Charlie Haas & Tim Hunter. LC 76-26269. (Harper Novel of Suspense). 1977. 7.95 o.p. (ISBN 0-06-011708-7, HarpT). Har-Row.

Soul in Paraphrase: Prayer & the Religious Affections. Don E. Saliers. 160p. 1980. 8.95 (ISBN 0-8164-0121-7). Seabury.

Soul in the Quad: The Use of Language in Philosophy & Literature. Kathleen Nott. 1969. 25.00 (ISBN 0-7100-6502-7). Routledge & Kegan.

Soul Mates: The Facts & the Fallacies. Robert E. Birdsong. (Aquarian Academy Supplementary Lecture Ser.: No. 9). 22p. (Orig.). 1980. pap. 1.25 (ISBN 0-917108-32-9). Sirius Bks.

Soul Murder Case: A Confession of the Victim. Robert D. Pharr. 1975. pap. 2.95 (ISBN 0-380-00404-6, 26070). Avon.

Soul of Liberty: The Universal Ethic of Freedom & Human Rights. Fred E. Foldvary. LC 79-56782. (Illus.). 330p. 1980. pap. 6.75 (ISBN 0-9603872-1-8). Gutenberg.

Soul of Mbira: Music & Tradition of the Shona People of Zimbabwe. Paul F. Berliner. (Perspectives on Southern Africa Ser.: No. 26). 1978. 20.00x (ISBN 0-520-03315-9); pap. 4.95 (ISBN 0-520-04268-9). U of Cal Pr.

Soul of the Ghost Moth. Philip S. Callahan. (Illus.). 1980. 7.95 (ISBN 0-8159-6840-X). Devin.

Soul of the World. Agnes Mortier. 1977. 5.95 o.p. (ISBN 0-533-02767-5). Vantage.

Soul of the World: An Account of Inwardness of Things. Conrad Bonifazi. LC 78-64826. 1978. pap. text ed. 10.25 (ISBN 0-8191-0638-0). U Pr of Amer.

Soul of Wit: A Study of John Donne. Murray Roston. 250p. 1974. text ed. 29.00x (ISBN 0-19-812053-2). Oxford U Pr.

Soul on Fire. Eldridge Cleaver. LC 77-83335. 1978. 8.95 o.p. (ISBN 0-8499-0046-8, 0046-8). Word Bks.

Soul Sisters: A/Commentary on Enneads IV 3(27), 1-8 of Plotinus. W. Helleman-Elgersma. 485p. 1980. pap. text ed. 51.50x (ISBN 90-6203-931-6, Pub. by Rodopi Holland). Humanities.
Soul So Rebellious. Mary F. Sturlaugson. 88p. 1980. 5.95 (ISBN 0-87747-841-4). Deseret Bk.
Soul Whence & Whither. Hazrat I. Khan. LC 77-15697. (Collected Works of Hazrat Inayat Khan Ser.). 190p. 1977. 6.95 o.p. (ISBN 0-930872-00-2); pap. 4.95 (ISBN 0-930872-01-0). Sufi Order Pubns.
Soul Winner's Secret. Samuel L. Brengle. 1978. pap. 3.25 (ISBN 0-86544-007-7). Salvation Army.
Soul Winning. David Shofner. (Illus.). 96p. (Orig.). 1980. pap. write for info. (ISBN 0-89957-051-8). AMG Pubs.
Soul-Winning Helps for Members of the Healing Profession. Marjorie Gray. LC 75-18268. 1976. pap. 2.95 o.p. (ISBN 0-8163-0219-7, 19467-0). Pacific Pr Pub Assn.
Souldiery Spiritualized: Seven Sermons Preached Before the Artillery Companies of New England, 1674-1774. Ed. by James A. Levernier. LC 79-9727. 1979. 50.00x (ISBN 0-8201-1325-5). Schol Facsimiles.
Souls in Metal: An Anthology of Robot Futures. Mike Ashley. 1978. pap. 1.75 o.s.i. (ISBN 0-515-04546-2). Jove Pubns.
Souls of Black Folk. William E. Du Bois. 1977. pap. 1.75 o.p. (ISBN 0-449-30823-5, Prem). Fawcett.
Soulscript. Ed. by June Meyer Jordan. LC 77-84390. 1970. pap. 2.50 (ISBN 0-385-07325-9, Zenith). Doubleday.
Soulside: Inquiries into Ghetto Culture & Community. Ulf Hannerz. LC 78-96865. 1969. 17.50x (ISBN 0-231-03363-X); pap. 5.00x (ISBN 0-231-08651-2). Columbia U Pr.
Soumchi. Amos Oz. LC 80-8457. (Illus.). 96p. (gr. 4-7). 1981. 8.95 (ISBN 0-06-024621-9, HarpJ); PLB 8.79g (ISBN 0-06-024622-7). Har-Row.
Sound. rev. ed. Harlan Wade. LC 78-20961. (Book About Ser.). (Illus.). (gr. k-3). 1979. PLB 7.30 (ISBN 0-8172-1525-5). Raintree Pubs.
Sound & Hearing. rev. ed. Fred Warshofsky & S. Smith Stevens. LC 65-28353. (Life Science Library). (Illus.). (gr. 5 up). 1969. PLB 8.97 o.p. (ISBN 0-8094-0471-0, Pub. by Time-Life). Silver.
Sound & Poetry. Ed. by Northrop Frye. LC 57-11003. (English Institute Essay). 1957. 12.50x (ISBN 0-231-02209-3). Columbia U Pr.
Sound & Symbol, 2 vols. Victor Zuckerland. Incl. Vol. 1. Music & the External World. Tr. by W. R. Trask. 1956. 20.00 (ISBN 0-691-09828-X); pap. 5.95 (ISBN 0-691-01759-X, 183); Vol. 2. Man the Musician. Tr. by Norbert Guterman. 450p. 1973. 22.00 (ISBN 0-691-09925-1); pap. 5.95 (ISBN 0-691-01812-X). LC 55-11489. (Bollingen Ser.: Vol. 44). Set. 37.50 (ISBN 0-686-64022-5). Princeton U Pr.
Sound & the Fury: A Concordance to the Novel. Noel Polk & Kenneth L. Privratsky. LC 80-12310. (Faulkner Concordances Ser.: No. 5). 412p. 1980. Set. 62.00 (ISBN 0-8357-0513-7, IS-00108, Pub. by Faulkner Concordance). A-L (ISBN 0-8357-0558-7). M-Z (ISBN 0-8357-0559-5). Univ Microfilms.
Sound Doctrine Briefs & Radio Sermons. J. D. Boyd. 3.95 (ISBN 0-89315-258-7). Lambert Bk.
Sound Exploration & Discovery. Palmer. write for info. (ISBN 0-87628-217-6). Ctr Appl Res.
Sound: From Communications to Noise Pollution. Graham Chedd. LC 78-111152. 5.95 o.p. (ISBN 0-385-05992-2). Doubleday.
Sound: In Eight Languages. Ed. by R. W. Stephens. LC 74-16209. (International Dictionaries of Science & Technology Ser). 853p. 1974. 49.95 (ISBN 0-470-82200-7). Halsted Pr.
Sound in the Theatre. rev. ed. Harold Burris-Meyer et al. LC 78-66064. 1979. 12.95 (ISBN 0-87830-157-7). Theatre Arts.
Sound Investment. Soma Sanchez. 1980. pap. 2.95 (ISBN 0-88378-048-8). Third World.
Sound, Man, & Building. L. H. Schaudinischky. (Illus.). 1976. 74.50x (ISBN 0-85334-655-0, Pub. by Applied Science). Burgess-Intl Ideas.
Sound of Dreams. Herman Weiss. 288p. (Orig.). 1981. pap. 2.50 (ISBN 0-380-76976-X, 76976). Avon.
Sound of Edna: Dame Edna's Family Songbook. Edna Everage. (Illus.). 96p. 1980. pap. 11.95 (ISBN 0-903443-34-1, Pub. by Hamish Hamilton England). David & Charles.
Sound of Greek: Studies in the Greek Theory & Practice of Euphony. W. B. Stanford. (Sather Classical Lectures: No. 38). (YA) (gr. 9 up). 1967. 21.50x (ISBN 0-520-01204-6). U of Cal Pr.
Sound of Mad. Nick Meglin & George Woodbridge. (Mad Ser.). (Illus., Orig.). 1980. pap. 1.50 (ISBN 0-446-88844-3). Warner Bks.
Sound of Mountain Water. Wallace Stegner. LC 69-12196. 5.95 o.p. (ISBN 0-385-07138-8). Doubleday.
Sound of Murder. Rex Stout. 1979. pap. 1.75 (ISBN 0-515-05281-7). Jove Pubns.
Sound of One Mind Thinking. Eugene Schwartz. (Illus.). 1981. pap. 6.95 (ISBN 0-89407-040-1). Strawberry Hill.
Sound of Prose. Joseph Collignon. 1971. pap. text ed. 5.95x (ISBN 0-02-474430-1, 47443); tchrs' manual free (ISBN 0-02-474440-9). Macmillan.
Sound of Sunshine, Sound of Rain. Florence P. Heide. LC 77-117555. (Illus.). (gr. k-3). 1970. 5.95 o.s.i. (ISBN 0-8193-0422-0, Four Winds); PLB 5.41 o.s.i. (ISBN 0-8193-0423-9). Schol Bk Serv.
Sound of Surprise. Whitney Balliett. LC 77-17852. (Roots of Jazz Ser.). 1978. Repr. of 1961 ed. lib. bdg. 19.50 (ISBN 0-306-77543-3). Da Capo.
Sound of the Bugle. D. R. Burows. 224p. (gr. 6-9). 1973. pap. 3.50 (ISBN 0-570-03145-1, 12-2529). Concordia.
Sound of the Mountain. Yasunari Kawabata. Tr. by Edward G. Seidensticker from Jap. (Perigee Japanese Library). 288p. 1981. pap. 5.95 (ISBN 0-399-50527-X, Perigee). Putnam.
Sound of the Trumpet. George Reid. (Horizon Ser.). 224p. 1981. price not set (ISBN 0-8127-0328-6); pap. price not set (ISBN 0-8127-0321-9). Southern Pub.
Sound of Thunder. Taylor Caldwell. 576p. 1981. pap. 3.50 (ISBN 0-553-14255-0). Bantam.
Sound Pleasure: A Prelude to Active Listening. Donald Ivey. LC 75-30287. (Illus., Orig.). 1977. pap. text ed. 12.95 (ISBN 0-02-870900-4); record package 12.95 (ISBN 0-02-870870-9). Schirmer Bks.
Sound Production in Fishes. Ed. by William N. Tavolga. LC 76-28352. (Benchmark Papers in Animal Behavior: Vol. 9). 1977. 42.50, by subscription 33.00 (ISBN 0-12-787515-8). Acad Pr.
Sound Recording & Reproduction. Glyn Alkin. LC 80-41481. (Illus.). 208p. 1981. 24.95 (ISBN 0-240-51070-4). Focal Pr.
Sound Recording: From Microphone to Master Tape. David Tombs. (Illus.). 192p. 1980. 24.00 (ISBN 0-7153-7954-2). David & Charles.
Sound Science. Melvin L. Alexenberg. LC 68-15760. (Illus.). (ps-3). 1968. pap. 0.95 o.p. (ISBN 0-13-823047-1). P-H.
Sound Scriptual Sermon Outlines, No. 2. Wade H. Horton. 1974. 5.95 (ISBN 0-87148-769-1); pap. 4.95 (ISBN 0-87148-770-5). Pathway Pr.
Sound Scriptual Sermons. Wade H. Horton. 1973. 5.95 (ISBN 0-87148-775-6); pap. 4.95 (ISBN 0-87148-776-4). Pathway Pr.
Sound Scriptural Outlines: No. 3. Wade H. Horton. 1977. 5.95 (ISBN 0-87148-781-0); pap. 4.95 (ISBN 0-87148-780-2). Pathway Pr.
Sound Shape of Language. Roman Jakobson & Linda R. Waugh. LC 78-19552. (Illus.). 352p. 1979. 17.50x (ISBN 0-253-16417-6). Ind U Pr.
Sound Skill Builder: Use with Sure Steps to Reading & Spelling, 3 bks. Florence W. Blank & Carolyn W. Guertin. Incl. Bk. 1. price not set (ISBN 0-916720-04-7); Bk. 2. price not set (ISBN 0-916720-05-5); Bk. 3. price not set (ISBN 0-916720-06-3). (gr. 1-7). 1981. Weiss Pub.
Sound Sleep. Quentin R. Regestein & James R. Rechs. 1980. 10.95 (ISBN 0-671-24960-6, 24960). S&S.
Sound Structure in Music. Robert Erickson. (Illus.). 1975. 16.50x (ISBN 0-520-02376-5). U of Cal Pr.
Sound Systems Installers Handbook. 3rd ed. Leo G. Sands. LC 73-79074. Orig. Title: Commercial Sound Installers Handbook. (Illus.). 1973. pap. 5.95 o.p. (ISBN 0-672-20980-2, 20980). Sams.
Sound Transmission Through a Fluctuating Ocean. Ed. by S. M. Flatte. LC 77-88676. (Cambridge Monographs on Mechanics & Applied Mathematics). (Illus.). 1979. 44.50 (ISBN 0-521-21940-X). Cambridge U Pr.
Sounder. William H. Armstrong. 1969. pap. 1.95 (ISBN 0-06-080379-7, P379, PL). Har-Row.
Sounding of Storytellers. John Rowe. LC 79-2418. 1980. 13.95 o.p. (ISBN 0-397-31882-0). Lippincott.
Soundings. Rudolph Binion. 275p. 1981. 18.95 (ISBN 0-914434-16-0); pap. 8.95 (ISBN 0-914434-17-9). Psychohistory Pr.
Soundings. Kit Wright. 1975. pap. text ed. 4.95x o.p. (ISBN 0-435-14911-3). Heinemann Ed.
Soundings: Essays Concerning Christian Understanding. A. R. Vidler. 1962. 36.00 (ISBN 0-521-06710-3); pap. 10.95x (ISBN 0-521-09373-2). Cambridge U Pr.
Soundings in Modern South Asian History. Ed. by D. A. Low. LC 68-20442. (Illus.). 1968. 20.00x (ISBN 0-520-00770-0). U of Cal Pr.
Soundless Sound. Edith Smith. 1980. 7.95 o.p. (ISBN 0-8062-1035-4). Carlton.
Soundless Voice: A Discovery in Stillness. David Manners. Date not set. pap. price not set (ISBN 0-916108-10-4). Seed Center. Postponed.
Sounds. Wassily Kandinsky. Tr. by Elizabeth R. Napier from Ger. LC 80-6211. (Illus.). 144p. 30.00 (ISBN 0-300-02510-6); pap. 11.95 (ISBN 0-300-02664-1). Yale U Pr.
Sounds All Around. Joy T. Friedman. LC 80-83935. Orig. Title: Look Around & Listen. (Illus.). 80p. (gr. k-2). 1981. PLB 10.15 (ISBN 0-448-13945-6); pap. 3.95 (ISBN 0-448-14755-6). G&D.
Sounds & Silences: Poems for Performing. Robert W. Boynton & Maynard Mack. (Literature Ser.). 128p. 1975. pap. text ed. 5.95x (ISBN 0-8104-5501-3). Hayden.
Sounds, Feelings, Thoughts: Seventy Poems by Wislawa Szymborska. Wislawa Szymborska. Tr. by Magnus J. Krynski & Robert A. Maguire. LC 80-8579. (Lockert Library of Poetry in Translation). 261p. 1981. 17.50x (ISBN 0-691-06469-5); pap. 7.95x (ISBN 0-691-01380-2). Princeton U Pr.
Sounds for Silents. Charles Hofmann. LC 74-107465. (Illus.). 1969. 10.00 (ISBN 0-910482-14-4); record incl. (ISBN 0-89676-035-9). Drama Bk.
Sounds from the Unknown: A Collection of Japanese-American Tanka. Tr. by Lucille M. Nixon & Tomoe Tana. LC 64-16108. 133p. (Orig.). 1963. 3.75 o.p. (ISBN 0-8040-0278-9); pap. 2.95 (ISBN 0-8040-0279-7, 60). Swallow.
Sounds in the Sea. Francine Jacobs. LC 77-345. (Illus.). (gr. 3-7). 1977. 6.25 (ISBN 0-688-22113-0); PLB 6.00 (ISBN 0-688-32113-5). Morrow.
Sounds of American English. Thomas D. Houchin. (Orig.). 1976. pap. text ed. 3.83 (ISBN 0-87720-974-X). AMSCO Sch.
Sounds of American English: An Introduction to Phonetics. Ralph R. Leutenegger. 1963. pap. 7.95x o.p. (ISBN 0-673-05702-X). Scott F.
Sounds of Controversy: Crucial Arguments in the American Past. Robert Kelley. 640p. 1975. Vol. 1. pap. text ed. 10.95 (ISBN 0-13-823088-9). P-H.
Sounds of Music. Charles Taylor. (Illus.). 1978. 15.95 (ISBN 0-684-15476-5, ScribT). Scribner.
Sounds of People & Places: Readings in the Geography of Music. George O. Carney. 1978. pap. text ed. 11.25x (ISBN 0-8191-0394-2). U Pr of Amer.
Sounds of Railways & Their Recording. Peter Handford. LC 79-56055. (Illus.). 152p. 1980. 14.95 (ISBN 0-7153-7631-4). David & Charles.
Sounds of Silence. Judith Richards. 1981. pap. 2.75 (ISBN 0-671-43117-X). PB.
Soup. Annelike Hoogeweegen. 1977. 6.95 (ISBN 0-8467-0241-X, Pub. by Two Continents). Hippocrene Bks.
Soup & Bread: One Hundred Recipes for Bowl & Board. 2nd ed. Julia Older & Steve Sherman. 128p. 1981. pap. 8.95 (ISBN 0-8289-0338-7). Greene.
Soup on Wheels. Robert N. Peck. LC 80-17661. (Illus.). 128p. (gr. 3 up). 1981. 6.95 (ISBN 0-394-84581-1); PLB 6.99 (ISBN 0-394-94581-6). Knopf.
Soup with Quackers: Funny Cartoon Riddles. Mike Thaler. LC 76-10308. (Illus.). 96p. (gr. 4 up). 1976. PLB 6.45 (ISBN 0-531-00344-2). Watts.
Souper Bowl of Recipes. Dorothy Shula et al. 1980. 15.00 (ISBN 0-89002-164-3); pap. 7.95 (ISBN 0-89002-163-5). Northwoods Pr.
Soups. (Good Cook Ser.). (Illus.). 1979. lib. bdg. 11.97 (ISBN 0-8094-2867-9); kivar bdg. 9.96 (ISBN 0-8094-2868-7). Silver.
Soups. Ed. by Time-Life Books. (Good Cook Ser.). 1980. 12.95 (ISBN 0-8094-2866-0). Time-Life.
Soups, Chowders & Stews. Georgia Orcutt. Ed. by Sandra Taylor. (Flair of New England Ser.). 1981. pap. 8.95 (ISBN 0-911658-17-3, 3078). Yankee Bks.
Soups for All Seasons & a Collation of Sandwiches. Eileen Reece. 1976. 9.50 o.p. (ISBN 0-04-641032-5). Allen Unwin.
Source & Meaning in Spenser's Allegory: A Study of the Faerie Queene. John E. Hankins. 348p. 1972. 29.95x (ISBN 0-19-812013-3). Oxford U Pr.
Source Book. Carol Konek et al. 192p. (Orig.). 1981. pap. text ed. 7.95 (ISBN 0-582-28201-2); tchrs'. manual free (ISBN 0-582-28252-7). Longman.
Source Book for Food Scientists. Herbert W. Ockerman. (Illus.). 1978. lib. bdg. 79.50 (ISBN 0-87055-228-7). AVI.
Source Book for Medieval Economic History. Roy C. Cave & Herbert H. Coulson. LC 64-25840. 1936. 12.00x (ISBN 0-8196-0145-4). Biblo.
Source Book for the Disabled. Ed. by Gloria Hale. 512p. 1981. pap. 3.95 (ISBN 0-553-13753-0). Bantam.
Source Book for the Disabled. Ed. by Gloria Hale. LC 80-50722. (Illus.). 228p. Date not set. 15.95 (ISBN 0-03-057988-0); pap. 10.95 (ISBN 0-03-057654-7). HR&W. Postponed.
Source Book Fro Sociology. Kimball Young. 639p. 1980. Repr. of 1935 ed. lib. bdg. 45.00 (ISBN 0-8495-6105-1). Arden Lib.
Source Book in the History of Psychology. Ed. by Richard J. Herrnstein & Edwin G. Boring. (Source Books in the History of the Sciences Ser). (Illus.). 1965. 20.00x (ISBN 0-674-82410-5); pap. 7.95 (ISBN 0-674-82411-3). Harvard U Pr.
Source Book in Theatrical History. Alois M. Nagler. Orig. Title: Sources of Theatrical History. (Illus.). 1952. pap. 6.95 (ISBN 0-486-20515-0). Dover.
Source Book of a Study of Occupational Values & the Image of the Federal Service. Franklin P. Kilpatrick et al. 1964. 13.95 (ISBN 0-8157-4928-7). Brookings.
Source Book of Advaita Vedanta. Eliot Deutsch & J. A. Van Buitenen. 1971. 15.00x o.p. (ISBN 0-87022-189-2). U Pr of Hawaii.
Source Book of Antiques & Jewelry Designs. Clarence P. Hornung. LC 68-16512. (Illus.). 1968. 12.50 o.s.i. (ISBN 0-8076-0439-9). Braziller.
Source-Book of Biological Names & Terms. 3rd ed. Edmund C. Jaeger. (Illus.). 360p. 1978. 13.75 (ISBN 0-398-00916-3). C C Thomas.
Source Book of Flavors. Henry B. Heath. (Illus.). 1981. lib. bdg. 79.50 (ISBN 0-87055-369-0). AVI.
Source Book of Food Enzymology. Sigmund Schwimmer. (Illus.). 1981. lib. bdg. 79.50 (ISBN 0-87055-369-0). AVI.
Source Book of Gestalt Psychology. Ed. by Willis D. Ellis. 1967. text ed. 28.75x (ISBN 0-7100-6115-3). Humanities.
Source Book of Royal Commissions & Other Major Governmental Inquiries in Canadian Education 1787-1978. Cary F. Goulson. 248p. 1981. 20.00x (ISBN 0-8020-2408-4). U of Toronto Pr.
Source Book of Scottish Economic & Social History. R. H. Campbell & J. B. Dow. 1968. 19.50x (ISBN 0-631-11080-1, Pub. by Basil Blackwell). Biblio Dist.
Source Book on Ductile Iron. (TN 719.5.s68). 1977. 38.00 (ISBN 0-87170-035-2). ASM.
Source Book on Environmental & Safety Considerations for Planning & Design of LNG Marine Terminals. Compiled by American Society of Civil Engineers. 48p. 1976. pap. text ed. 7.00 (ISBN 0-87262-158-8). Am Soc Civil Eng.
Source Book on Forming of Steel Sheet. (TS 360.s68). 1976. 38.00 (ISBN 0-87170-037-9). ASM.
Source-Book on French Law: System, Methods, Outlines of Contract. 2nd ed. Otto Kahn-Freund et al. 1979. pap. 27.00 (ISBN 0-19-825349-4). Oxford U Pr.
Source Book on Maraging Steels. Ed. by Raymond F. Decker. 1979. 38.00 (ISBN 0-87170-079-4). ASM.
Source Book on Materials Selection, 2 vols. (TA 403.s62 (vol. 1) tA 403.s62 (vol. 2)). 1977. 38.00 ea. Vol. 2 (ISBN 0-87170-031-X) (ISBN 0-87170-032-8). ASM.
Source Book on Powder Metallurgy. Ed. by Samuel Bradbury. 1979. 38.00 (ISBN 0-87170-030-1). ASM.
Source Book on Selection & Fabrication of Aluminum Alloys. 1978. 38.00 (ISBN 0-87170-003-4). ASM.
Source Book on Stainless Steels. 1976. 38.00 (ISBN 0-87170-041-7). ASM.
Source Book on Wear Control Technology. Ed. by D. A. Rigney & W. A. Glaeser. 1978. 38.00 (ISBN 0-87170-028-X). ASM.
Source Directory: Assistance to Third World Broadcasters. Ed. by Miriam Williford. LC 79-3610. 1979. loose leaf 5.95 (ISBN 0-916584-14-3). Ford Found.
Source Language Debugging Tools. Edwin H. Satterthwaite, Jr. LC 79-50820. (Outstanding Dissertations in the Computer Sciences). 1980. lib. bdg. 32.00 (ISBN 0-8240-4416-9). Garland Pub.
Source Material for Radiochemistry. rev. ed. Committee On Nuclear Science. LC 59-60042. (Nuclear Sciences Ser). 1971. pap. 3.50 (ISBN 0-309-01867-6). Natl Acad Pr.
Source of Evil. Mary Vigliante. (Orig.). 1979. pap. 1.95 (ISBN 0-532-23104-X). Manor Bks.
Source of Human Good. Henry N. Wieman. LC 63-2226. 318p. 1964. lib. bdg. 10.95x (ISBN 0-8093-0116-4). S Ill U Pr.
Source of Human Good. Henry N. Wieman. LC 63-2226. (Arcturus Books Paperbacks). 318p. 1974. pap. 2.95 (ISBN 0-8093-0117-2). S Ill U Pr.
Source of Light. Reynolds Price. LC 80-69650. 1981. 12.95 (ISBN 0-689-11136-3). Atheneum.

Source Readings in Music History, 5 vols. Ed. by Oliver Strunk. Incl. Vol. 1. Antiquity & the Middle Ages. pap. 4.95x (ISBN 0-393-09680-7); Vol. 2. The Renaissance Era. pap. 4.95x (ISBN 0-393-09681-5); Vol. 3. Baroque Era. pap. 4.95x (ISBN 0-393-09682-3); Vol. 4. Classic Era. pap. 4.95x (ISBN 0-393-09683-1); Vol. 5. Romantic Era. pap. 4.95x (ISBN 0-393-09684-X). 1950. one vol. ed 24.95x (ISBN 0-393-09742-0, NortonC). Norton.

Sourcebook: Activities to Enrich Programs for Infants & Young Children. George Maxim. 208p. 1980. pap. text ed. 11.95x (ISBN 0-534-00854-2). Wadsworth Pub.

Sourcebook for Elementary Science. 2nd ed. Elizabeth B. Hone et al. (Teaching Science Ser.). 475p. 1971. text ed. 14.95 (ISBN 0-15-582855-X, HC). HarBraceJ.

Sourcebook for Programmable Calculators. Texas Instruments Learning Center Staff. LC 78-57030. (Illus.). 1978. pap. text ed. 12.95 o.p. (ISBN 0-89512-025-9, LCB-3521). Tex Instr Inc.

Sourcebook for Substitutes...& Other Teachers. Miriam Freedman & Teri Perl. (gr. k-8). 1974. 10.25 (ISBN 0-201-05786-7). A-W.

Sourcebook in Marriage & the Family. 4th ed. Ed. by Marvin B. Sussman. 432p. 1974. pap. text ed. 11.50 (ISBN 0-395-17538-0). HM.

Sourcebook of Articulation Activities. William J. Worthley. 1981. pap. text ed. price not set. Little.

Sourcebook of Harris National Surveys: Repeated Questions, 1963-1976. Ed. by Elizabeth Martin et al. (IRSS Technical Papers). (Illus.). 515p. 1981. pap. write for info. (ISBN 0-89143-091-1). U NC Inst Res Soc Sci.

Sourcebook of Laboratory Exercises in Plant Pathology. American Phytopathological Society - Sourcebook Committee. Ed. by Arthur Kelman. (Illus.). 1967. 17.95x (ISBN 0-7167-0813-2). W H Freeman.

Sourcebook of Laboratory Techniques for Science Teachers. Rolland Bartholomew & Frank Crawley. (gr. 9-12). 1980. pap. text ed. 12.50 (ISBN 0-201-00354-6, Sch Div). A-W.

Sourcebook of Medical Communications. Robert C. Reeder. (Illus.). 325p. 1981. text ed. 29.00 (ISBN 0-8016-4177-2). Mosby.

Sourcebook of Research & Practice in Behavioral Disorders. Bob Algozzine et al. 375p. 1981. text ed. price not set (ISBN 0-89443-345-8). Aspen Systems.

Sourcebook on Clinical Pharmacy. 2nd ed. American Society of Hospital Pharmacists. LC 79-24069. (Illus.). 404p. 1980. pap. text ed. 20.00 (ISBN 0-88416-303-2). PSG Pub.

Sourcebook on Food & Nutrition. 2nd ed. Ed. by Ioannis S. Scarpa et al. LC 79-91584. 500p. 1980. 39.50 (ISBN 0-8379-4502-X). Marquis.

Sourcebook on Health Sciences Librarianship. Ching-Chih Chen. LC 76-30263. 1977. 15.50 (ISBN 0-8108-1005-0). Scarecrow.

Sourcebook on Mental Health. 2nd ed. 660p. 1981. price not set (ISBN 0-8379-4802-9). Marquis.

Sourcebook on Prison Education: Past, Present, & Future. Albert Roberts. 224p. 1971. pap. 13.50 spiral (ISBN 0-398-02190-2). C C Thomas.

Sourcebook on Probation, Parole & Pardons. 3rd ed. Charles L. Newman. 488p. 1977. 22.75 (ISBN 0-398-01396-9). C C Thomas.

Sourcebook on the Environment: The Scientific Perspective. Charles S. ReVelle & Penelope L. ReVelle. 1974. pap. text ed. 9.95 (ISBN 0-395-17018-4). HM.

Sourcebook, Science Education & the Physically Handicapped. Ed. by Helenmarie Hofman & Kenneth S. Ricker. (Orig.). 1979. pap. 6.00 (ISBN 0-87355-014-5). Natl Sci Tchrs.

Sources & Analogues of Chaucer's Canterbury Tales. Ed. by William F. Bryan & G. C. Dempster. 1958. text ed. 35.00x (ISBN 0-391-00443-3). Humanities.

Sources & Methods in Geography: Sediments. Briggs. 1977. 6.95 (ISBN 0-408-70815-8). Butterworths.

Sources & Shapes of Power. John R. Sherwood & John C. Wagner. LC 80-28125. (Into Our Third Century Ser.). (Orig.). 1981. pap. 3.95 (ISBN 0-687-39142-3). Abingdon.

Sources Cited & Artifacts Illustrated. Ed. by Margaret A. Harrison. (Handbook of Middle American Indians Ser: Vol. 16). 350p. 1976. text ed. 25.00x (ISBN 0-292-73004-7). U of Tex Pr.

Sources et Reflets De l'Histoire De France. Ed. by Madelyn Gutwirth et al. (Illus., Fr). 1972. pap. text ed. 7.95x (ISBN 0-19-501465-0). Oxford U Pr.

Sources for the History of Medieval Europe from the Mid-Eighth to the Mid-Thirteenth Century. Brian Pullan. 228p. 1980. pap. 7.95x (ISBN 0-631-12371-7, Pub. by Basil Blackwell). Biblio Dist.

Sources for the Study of Greek Religion. David G. Rice & John E. Stambaugh. LC 79-18389. (Society of Biblical Literature. Sources for Biblical Study Ser.: No. 14). 1979. 12.00 (ISBN 0-89130-346-4, 060314); pap. 7.50 (ISBN 0-89130-347-2). Scholars Pr Ca.

Sources in Modern East Asian History & Politics. Ed. by Theodore McNelly. LC 67-18502. (Illus., Orig.). 1967. pap. text ed. 7.95x (ISBN 0-89197-419-9). Irvington.

Sources of Art Noveau. Stephan T. Madsen. Tr. by Ragnar Christopherson. LC 74-34464. (Architecture & Decorative Arts Ser). (Illus.). 488p. 1975. Repr. of 1956 ed. lib. bdg. 42.50 (ISBN 0-306-70733-0). Da Capo.

Sources of Art Noveau. Stephan T. Madsen. LC 75-26819. (Architecture & Decorative Arts Ser.). (Illus.). 1976. pap. 8.95 (ISBN 0-306-80024-1). Da Capo.

Sources of Asian-Pacific Economic Information, 2 vols. Ed. by Euan Blauvelt & Jennifer Durlacher. LC 80-28645. 1981. Set. lib. bdg. 125.00 (ISBN 0-313-22963-5). Greenwood.

Sources of Chinese Tradition, 2 Vols. Ed. by William T. De Bary. LC 60-9911. (Records of Civilization, Sources & Studies). 1960. 1 vol. ed. o.p 30.00x (ISBN 0-231-02255-7); Vol. 1. pap. 9.00x (ISBN 0-231-08602-4); Vol. 2. pap. 7.00x (ISBN 0-231-08603-2). Columbia U Pr.

Sources of Compiled Legislative Histories: Bibliography of Government Documents, Periodical Articles & Books, 1st Congress - 94th Congress. Nancy P. Johnson. (AALL Publications Ser.: No. 14). 146p. 1979. loose-leaf in vinyl, 3-ring binder 22.50x (ISBN 0-8377-0112-0). Rothman.

Sources of Construction Information: An Annotated Guide to Reports, Books, Periodicals, Standards, and Codes. Jules B. Godel. LC 77-4671. 1977. 30.00 (ISBN 0-8108-1030-1). Scarecrow.

Sources of Contemporary Radicalism, Vol. 1. Ed. by S. Bialer & S. Sluzar. LC 76-39890. (Studies of the Research Institute of International Change, Columbia University). 1977. lib. bdg. 24.00x (ISBN 0-89158-130-8); lib. bdg. 60.00 3 vol. set. Westview.

Sources of Difference in School Achievement. A. Brimer et al. (General Ser.). (Illus.). 1979. text ed. 33.75x (ISBN 0-85633-168-6, NFER); pap. text ed. 20.00x (ISBN 0-85633-155-4). Humanities.

Sources of European Economic Information. 316p. 1981. 95.00 (ISBN 0-566-02150-1, TEAK 5, CIRS). Unipub.

Sources of Finance for Higher Education in America. James Cunningham. LC 79-6081. 165p. 1980. pap. text ed. 9.00 (ISBN 0-8191-0980-0). U Pr of Amer.

Sources of Gravitational Radiation. Larry Smarr. LC 79-50177. (Illus.). 1979. 24.95 (ISBN 0-521-22778-X). Cambridge U Pr.

Sources of Materials for Minority Languages: A Preliminary List. National Clearinghouse for Bilingual Education. LC 79-103423. 1978. pap. 2.75 o.p. (ISBN 0-89763-003-3). Natl Clearinghse Bilingual Ed.

Sources of Modern Architecture & Design. Nikolaus Pevsner. (World of Art Ser.). (Illus.). 1977. pap. 9.95 (ISBN 0-19-519939-1). Oxford U Pr.

Sources of Physics Teaching: Atomic Energy. Holography. Electrostatics, Vol. 4. Ed. by G. R. Noakes. 1970. pap. text ed. 12.95x (ISBN 0-85066-038-6). Intl Ideas.

Sources of Physics Teaching: Electrolysis, X-Ray Analysis. Electron Diffraction, Vol. 3. Ed. by G. R. Noakes et al. 1969. pap. 11.95x (ISBN 0-85066-031-9). Intl Ideas.

Sources of Physics Teaching: Gravity. Liquids. Gases, Vol. 5. Ed. by G. R. Noakes. 1970. pap. text ed. 12.95x (ISBN 0-85066-040-8). Intl Ideas.

Sources of Progressive Thought in American Education. Philip L. Smith. LC 80-8290. 217p. 1980. lib. bdg. 18.75 (ISBN 0-8191-1300-X); pap. text ed. 9.75 (ISBN 0-8191-1301-8). U Pr of Amer.

Sources of Quantum Mechanics. Ed. by B. L. Van Der Waerden. pap. text ed. 6.00 (ISBN 0-486-61881-1). Dover.

Sources of Self Evaluation: A Formal Theory of Significant Others & Social Influence. Murray Webster, Jr. & Barbara Sobieszek. LC 74-5066. 189p. 1974. 24.50 (ISBN 0-471-92440-7, Pub. by Wiley-Interscience). Wiley.

Sources of Shang History: The Oracle-Bone Inscriptions of Bronze Age China. David N. Keightley. LC 74-29806. 1979. 30.00x (ISBN 0-520-02969-0). U of Cal Pr.

Sources of State Information on Corporations. 1981. pap. 17.50 (ISBN 0-686-26068-6). Wash Res.

Sources of the History of North Africa, Asia, & Oceania in Scandinavia, 2 pts. Incl. Pt. 1. Sources of the History North Africa, Asia, & Oceania in Denmark. lib. bdg. 162.00 (ISBN 3-598-21474-X); Pt. 2. Sources of the History of North Africa, Asia, & Oceania in Finland, Norway, Sweden. lib. bdg. 65.00 (ISBN 3-598-21475-8). (Guides to the Sources for the History of the Nations). 1980 (Dist. by Gale Research Co.). K G Saur.

Sources of the Synoptic Gospels. Carl S. Patton. 263p. 1980. Repr. of 1915 ed. lib. bdg. 50.00 (ISBN 0-89984-385-9). Century Bookbindery.

Sources of Unity in Ben Jonson's Comedy. Mary C. Williams. (Salzburg Studies in English Literature, Jacobean Drama Studies: No. 22). 230p. 1972. pap. text ed. 25.00x (ISBN 0-391-01572-9). Humanities.

Sources of Value. Stephen C. Pepper. 1958. 27.50x (ISBN 0-520-01798-6). U of Cal Pr.

Sources of Vitality in American Church Life. Ed. by Robert L. Moore. LC 78-71065. (Studies in Ministry & Parish Life). 1978. text ed. 12.95x (ISBN 0-913552-14-3); pap. text ed. 5.50x (ISBN 0-913552-15-1). Exploration Pr.

Sources of West Indian History: A Compilation of Writings of Historical Events in the West Indies. Ed. by F. R. Augier & Shirley C. Gordon. (Orig.). (YA) 1962. pap. text ed. 3.75x (ISBN 0-582-76303-7). Humanities.

Sources of Western Literacy: The Middle Eastern Civilizations. Felix Reichmann. LC 79-8292. (Contributions in Librarianship & Information Science: No. 29). 274p. 1980. lib. bdg. 25.00 (ISBN 0-313-20948-0, RWL/). Greenwood.

Sources of World Financial & Banking Information. Ed. by G. R. Dicks. LC 80-28654. 720p. 1981. lib. bdg. 125.00 (ISBN 0-313-22966-X, DSW/). Greenwood.

Sources of Yoruba History. Ed. by S. O. Biobaku. (Oxford Studies in African Affairs). (Illus.). 250p. 1973. 27.00x (ISBN 0-19-821669-6). Oxford U Pr.

Sources, Processes & Methods in Coleridge's Biographia Literaria. Kathleen Wheeler. LC 79-41683. 240p. 1980. 39.50 (ISBN 0-521-22690-2). Cambridge U Pr.

Sousa's Great Marches in Piano Transcription. John P. Sousa. LC 74-93543. (Orig.). 1975. pap. 4.50 (ISBN 0-486-23132-1). Dover.

South. rev. ed. Jerry E. Jennings & Marion H. Smith. LC 78-70052. (United States Ser). (Illus.). 288p. (gr. 5 up). 1979. text ed. 9.93 ea. 1-4 copies (ISBN 0-88296-064-4); 5 or more copies 7.94 ea.; tchrs' annotated ed. 13.68 (ISBN 0-88296-347-3). Fideler.

South Africa. Reuben Musiker. (World Bibliographical Ser.: No. 7). 194p. 1980. 25.25 (ISBN 0-903450-16-X). ABC-Clio.

South Africa: A Short History. 5th ed. Arthur Keppel-Jones. 1975. pap. text ed. 8.75x (ISBN 0-09-042844-7, Hutchinson U Lib, Hutchinson U Lib). Humanities.

South Africa: A Study in Conflict. Pierre Van den Berghe. 1975. pap. 6.95x (ISBN 0-520-01294-1, CAMPUS 159). U of Cal Pr.

South Africa & the United States: The Erosion of an Influence Relationship. Richard E. Bissell. 1981. 19.95 (ISBN 0-03-047026-9); pap. 9.95 (ISBN 0-03-047021-8). Praeger.

South Africa & the World: The Foreign Policy of Apartheid. Amry Vandenbosch. LC 76-111516. (Illus.). 312p. 1970. 13.00x (ISBN 0-8131-1223-0). U Pr of Ky.

South Africa at War: The Crisis in South Africa & U. S. Policy. Richard Leonard. (Orig.). 1981. 12.95 (ISBN 0-88208-108-X); pap. 5.95 (ISBN 0-88208-109-8). Lawrence Hill.

South Africa into the Nineteen Eighties. Ed. by Richard E. Bissel & Chester A. Crocker. (Special Studies on Africa). 1979. lib. bdg. 25.00x (ISBN 0-89158-373-4). Westview.

South Africa: Morality & Action. Henrik Van der Merwe. (Studies in Quakerism). 60p. (Orig.). 1981. pap. 3.00 (ISBN 0-89670-007-0). Progresiv Pub.

South Africa: Sharp Dissection. Christiaan Barnard. LC 77-99151. 1977. 9.95 (ISBN 0-916728-02-1). Bks in Focus.

South Africa: The Vital Link. Ed. by Robert Schuettinger. 1977. pap. 10.00 (ISBN 0-685-79964-6). Coun Am Affairs.

South Africa: White Rule-Black Revolt. Ernest Harsh. 1980. lib. bdg. 25.00 (ISBN 0-913460-78-8); pap. 6.95 (ISBN 0-913460-77-X). Monad Pr.

South Africa Year Book 1978 (State of) Economic, Financial & Statistical Year-Book for the Republic of South Africa. 1978. 35.00 o.p. (ISBN 0-685-81373-8). Heinman.

South African National Bibliography, 1977. Ed. by State Library, Pretoria. 972p. 1977. 35.00x. Intl Pubns Serv.

South African National Bibliography, 1978. Ed. by State Library, Pretoria. 735p. 1978. 35.00x (ISBN 0-8002-2754-9). Intl Pubns Serv.

South African National Bibliography, 1979. Ed. by State Library, Pretoria. 747p. 1979. 66.50x (ISBN 0-8002-2755-7). Intl Pubns Serv.

South Africa's Indians: The Evolution of a Minority. Ed. by Bridglal Pachai. LC 78-65358. 1978. pap. text ed. 17.50 (ISBN 0-8191-0656-9). U Pr of Amer.

South Africa's Transkei: The Politics of Domestic Colonialism. Gwendolen M. Carter et al. (Northwestern African Studies Ser.). 1967. 9.95x o.s.i. (ISBN 0-8101-0062-2). Northwestern U Pr.

South America. Arthur S. Morris. LC 79-13729. (Illus.). 1979. text ed. 17.50x (ISBN 0-06-494981-8); pap. text ed. 14.50x (ISBN 0-06-494982-6). B&N.

South America, Nineteen Eighty-One. Stephen Birnbaum. (Get 'em & Go Travel Guides). 1980. 15.00 (ISBN 0-395-29756-7); pap. 9.95 (ISBN 0-395-29757-5). HM.

South America: Observations & Impressions. James Bryce. (Latin America in the 20th Century Ser.). 1977. Repr. of 1912 ed. lib. bdg. 49.50 (ISBN 0-306-70835-3). Da Capo.

South America on Fifteen & Twenty Dollars a Day, 1981-82. 400p. 1981. pap. 4.95 (ISBN 0-671-43032-7). Frommer-Pasmantier.

South America Overland. Iain Finlay & Trish Sheppard. (Illus.). 1981. 19.95 (ISBN 0-207-14122-3, Pub. by Angus England). Hippocrene Bks.

South America: Problems & Prospects. Ed. by Irwin Isenberg. (Reference Shelf Ser: Vol. 47, No. 2). 1975. 6.25 (ISBN 0-8242-0570-7). Wilson.

South America: River Trips. George Bradt. LC 80-69523. (Illus.). 128p. (Orig.). 1981. pap. 7.95 (ISBN 0-933982-13-5). Bradt Ent.

South American Cookbook: Including Central America, Mexico, & the West Indies. Cora Brown et al. 8.00 (ISBN 0-8446-0041-5). Peter Smith.

South American Handbook, 1979. 19.75 o.p. (ISBN 0-528-84237-4). Rand.

South American Handbook, 1981. 57th ed. Ed. by John Brooks. (Illus.). 1981. 29.95 (ISBN 0-528-84534-9). Rand.

South American Herpetofauna: Its Origin, Evolution, & Dispersal. William E. Duellman et al. (U of KS Museum of Nat. Hist. Monograph: No. 7). (Illus.). 485p. Date not set. 30.00 (ISBN 0-89338-009-1); pap. 25.00 (ISBN 0-89338-008-3). U of KS Mus Nat Hist.

South American Survival: A Handbook for the Independent Traveller. Maurice Taylor. (Illus.). 1977. 19.95x o.p. (ISBN 0-905064-12-7). Intl Learn Syst.

South Asia: A Systematic Geographic Bibliography. Bheru L. Sukhwal. LC 74-10852. 1974. 32.50 (ISBN 0-8108-0761-0). Scarecrow.

South Asian Affairs Two, the Movement for National Freedom in India. Ed. by S. N. Mukherjee. (St. Anthony's Papers Ser). 1966. 5.00x o.p. (ISBN 0-19-827502-1). Oxford U Pr.

South Asian Crisis - India, Pakistan, & Bangladesh: A Political & Historical Analysis of the 1971 War. Robert Jackson. LC 74-8921. (Special Studies). (Illus.). 240p. 1975. text ed. 17.95 o.p. (ISBN 0-275-09560-6). Praeger.

South Asian Culture: An Anthropological Perspective. L. P. Vidyarthi. 1976. 11.00x o.p. (ISBN 0-88386-851-2). South Asia Bks.

South Bay Bargain Guide. Diane Brazil. (Illus.). 96p. (Orig.). 1981. pap. 4.95 (ISBN 0-87701-142-7). Chronicle Bks.

South by West: A Galaxy of Southwestern & Western Scences & Portraits. Everett A. Gillis. 48p. (Orig.). 1981. pap. write for info. Pisces Pr TX.

South Carolina. 28.00 (ISBN 0-89770-116-X). Curriculum Info Ctr.

South Carolina. Louis B. Wright. (States & the Nation). (Illus.). 225p. 1976. pap. 12.95 (ISBN 0-393-05560-4, Co-Pub by AASLH). Norton.

South Carolina: A Guide to the Palmetto State. Federal Writers Project. 514p. 1941. Repr. 45.00 (ISBN 0-403-02189-8). Somerset Pub.

South Carolina Chronology & Factbook, Vol. 40. R. I. Vexler. 1978. 8.50 (ISBN 0-379-16165-6). Oceana.

South Carolina Colony. Marguerite C. Steedman. LC 74-95299. (Forge of Freedom Ser). (Illus.). (gr. 5-8). 1970. 7.95 (ISBN 0-02-786770-6, CCPr). Macmillan.

South Carolina State Directory, 1980. State Industrial Directories Corp. 1980. pap. write for info. (ISBN 0-89910-030-9). State Indus Dir.

South Carolina State Line. Eugene Platt. LC 80-83405. 144p. 1980. 7.95 (ISBN 0-9605064-0-3); pap. 5.00 (ISBN 0-9605064-1-1). Huguley Co.

South Carolina Upcountry, Fifteen Forty to Nineteen Eighty: Historical & Biographical Sketches, Vol. 1. E. Don Herd, Jr. 1981. pap. 11.95 (ISBN 0-87921-062-1). Attic Pr.

South Coast Pleasure Steamers. E. C. Thornton. (Illus.). 1967. pap. 7.95 o.p. (ISBN 0-7153-4203-7). David & Charles.

South Corner of Time. Ed. by Larry Evers. 250p. 1981. 35.00x (ISBN 0-8165-0732-5); pap. 14.95 (ISBN 0-8165-0731-7). U of Ariz Pr.

South Dakota. John R. Milton. (States & the Nation Ser.). (Illus.). 1977. 12.95 (ISBN 0-393-05627-9, Co-Pub by AASLH). Norton.

South Dakota. 23.00 (ISBN 0-89770-117-8). Curriculum Info Ctr.

South Dakota: A Guide to the State. Federal Writers' Project. 421p. 1938. Repr. 45.00 (ISBN 0-403-02190-1). Somerset Pub.

South Dakota Chronology & Factbook, Vol. 41. R. I. Vexler. 1978. 8.50 (ISBN 0-379-16166-4). Oceana.

South Dakota Geographic Names. new ed. Ed. by Virginia D. Sneve. LC 73-80523. 639p. 1973. 19.95 (ISBN 0-88498-008-1); text ed. 17.96 o.p. (ISBN 0-685-46504-7). Brevet Pr.

South Dakota: In Words & Pictures. Dennis Fradin. LC 80-25349. (Young People's Stories of Our States Ser.). (Illus.). 48p. (gr. 2-5). 1981. PLB 8.65g (ISBN 0-516-03941-5, Time Line). Childrens.

South Dakota State Industrial Directory, 1980. State Industrial Directories Corp. 1980. pap. 15.00 (ISBN 0-89910-035-X). State Indus Dir.

South-East Asia: An Introduction. (Illus.). 144p. 1974. pap. 7.95 (ISBN 0-900362-65-0). Transatlantic.

South-East Asia: On a Shoestring. Tony Wheeler. (Illus., Orig.). 1978. pap. 3.95 (ISBN 0-8467-0473-0, Pub. by Two Continents). Hippocrene Bks.

South East Asia 1930-1970: The Legacy of Colonialism & Nationalism. Fred R. Von Der Mehden, pseud. (Library of World Civilization Ser). (Illus.). 144p. 1974. 7.95x (ISBN 0-393-05513-2); pap. 5.95x (ISBN 0-393-09320-4). Norton.

South East England. rev. ed. British Tourist Authority. (Illus.). 114p. 1981. pap. write for info. (ISBN 0-86143-048-4, Pub. by Auto Assn-British Tourist Authority England). Merrimack Bk Serv.

South Fork: The Land & the People of Eastern Long Island. Everett T. Rattray. LC 78-23692. (Illus.). 1979. 10.00 (ISBN 0-394-41860-3). Random.

South from Granada. Gerald Brenan. LC 80-40376. (Illus.). 282p. 1980. pap. 8.95 (ISBN 0-521-28029-X). Cambridge U Pr.

South from Hell-Fer Sartin. Leonard Roberts. 287p. 1964. pap. 2.95. Pikeville Coll.

South German Baroque. T. H. Burrough. (Illus.). 8.50 (ISBN 0-85458-698-9). Transatlantic.

South in Architecture. Lewis Mumford. LC 67-27462. (Architecture & Decorative Art Ser). 1967. Repr. of 1941 ed. lib. bdg. 19.50 (ISBN 0-306-70972-4). Da Capo.

South India: Political Institutions & Political Change 1880-1940. C. J. Baker & D. A. Washbrook. 1975. text ed. 27.50x (ISBN 0-8419-5016-4). Holmes & Meier.

South Indian Cookery. Mary L. Skelton & G. Gopal Rao. 115p. 1975. pap. 2.00 (ISBN 0-89253-030-8). Ind-US Inc.

South Korea. Patricia M. Bartz. (Illus.). 248p. 1972. 24.95x (ISBN 0-19-874008-5). Oxford U Pr.

South of Dusk. Everett E. Eckstein. LC 79-90667. 53p. 1980. 4.95 (ISBN 0-533-04460-X). Vantage.

South of England. rev. ed. British Tourist Authority. (Illus.). 114p. 1981. pap. write for info. (ISBN 0-86143-047-6, Pub. by Auto Assn-British Tourist Authority). Merrimack Bk Serv.

South of No North. Charles Bukowski. 189p. (Orig.). 1979. 14.00 (ISBN 0-87685-190-1); pap. 6.00 (ISBN 0-87685-189-8). Black Sparrow.

South of the Main Offensive. Tr. by Grigory Baklanov from Rus. LC 64-25464. 1963. 6.25 (ISBN 0-8023-1006-0). Dufour.

South Pacific Agriculture: Choices & Constraints. Ed. by R. Gerard Ward & Andrew Proctor. LC 79-56229. (South Pacific Agricultural Survey 1979). 525p. 1980. text ed. 24.95 (ISBN 0-7081-1944-1, 0532). Bks Australia.

South Pacific Coast: A Centennial. rev. ed. Bruce MacGregor. (Illus.). 1981. 34.95 (ISBN 0-87108-545-3). Pruett.

South Pacific Travel Digest. 1981. pap. 8.95 (ISBN 0-528-84336-2). Rand.

South Pass, 1868: James Chisholm's Journal of the Wyoming Gold Rush. James Chisholm. Ed. by Lola M. Homsher. LC 60-12692. (Pioneer Heritage Ser: Vol. 3). (Illus.). vi, 245p. 1960. pap. 2.95 (ISBN 0-8032-5824-0, BB 606, Bison). U of Nebr Pr.

South Pole Station. Melvin Berger. LC 79-132947. (Scientists at Work Ser). (Illus.). (gr. 2-4). 1971. PLB 8.79 (ISBN 0-381-99942-4, A73420, JD-J). John Day.

South Saxons. Ed. by Peter Brandon. (Illus.). 262p. 1978. 29.50x (ISBN 0-8476-6154-7). Rowman.

South Sea Bubble. John Langdon-Davies. (Jackdaw Ser: No. 19). (Illus.). 1968. 5.95 o.p. (ISBN 0-670-65912-6, Grossman). Viking Pr.

South Sea Company. John G. Sperling. (Kress Library of Business & Economics: No. 17). (Illus.). 1962. pap. 5.00x (ISBN 0-678-09911-1, Baker Lib). Kelley.

South Sea Tales. Jack London. 1961. 3.95 o.s.i. (ISBN 0-02-574690-1). Macmillan.

South Seas Odyssey: An Escape. James Y. Kennedy. LC 79-904. (Illus.). 182p. (Orig.). 1979. pap. 5.95 (ISBN 0-9605088-0-5). Kennedy Pub.

South Seas Sailor (John Williams) Cecil Northcott. 1965. 1.95 (ISBN 0-87508-622-5). Chr Lit.

South Shore: America's Last Interurban. William Middleton. LC 70-131244. 18.95 (ISBN 0-87095-003-7). Golden West.

South Since Appomattox: A Century of Regional Change. Thomas D. Clark & Albert D. Kirwan. LC 80-24023. (Illus.). vii, 438p. 1980. Repr. of 1967 ed. lib. bdg. 39.75x (ISBN 0-313-22698-9, CLSS). Greenwood.

South Since Eighteen Sixty-Five. 2nd ed. John S. Ezell. LC 74-15132. 1978. 14.95 (ISBN 0-8061-1480-0). U of Okla Pr.

South Slavic Immigration in America. George J. Prpic. (Immigrant Heritage of America Ser.). 1978. lib. bdg. 13.50 (ISBN 0-8057-8413-6). Twayne.

South Texas Garden Book. Bob Webster. 140p. (Orig.). 1980. pap. 10.95 (ISBN 0-931722-03-9). Corona Pub.

South Texas Uranium Province, Geologic Perspective. W. E. Galloway et al. (Illus.). 81p. 1979. 3.00 (GB 18). Bur Econ Geology.

South Today: 100 Years After Appomattox. Ed. by Willie Morris. 8.00 (ISBN 0-8446-4010-7). Peter Smith.

South Wales. C. Holder & W. H. Manning. 1967. 3.95x o.p. (ISBN 0-435-32963-4). Heinemann Ed.

South Wales. (Regional Guide Ser.). (Illus.). 1979. pap. 2.95 o.p. (ISBN 0-900784-52-0, Pub. by B T a). Merrimack Bk Serv.

South Wales: A Tourist Guide. rev. ed. Wales Tourist Board. (Illus.). 84p. 1981. pap. write for info. (ISBN 0-900784-73-3, Pub. by Auto Assn-British Tourist Authority England). Merrimack Bk Serv.

South-West Africa Case. M. Hidayatullah. 1968. 7.25x (ISBN 0-210-27194-9). Asia.

South West Africa-Namibia Dispute: Documents & Scholarly Writings on the Controversy Between South Africa & the United Nations. Ed. by John Dugard. LC 76-142052. (Perspectives on Southern Africa: No. 9). 1973. 33.75 o.p. (ISBN 0-520-01886-9); pap. 18.50x (ISBN 0-520-02614-4). U of Cal Pr.

South-West Africa Under German Rule, 1894-1914. Helmut Bley. Tr. by Hugh Ridley from Ger. 1971. 13.95k o.s.i. (ISBN 0-8101-0346-X). Northwestern U Pr.

South-West Wales: Pembrokeshire & Camarthenshire: Pembrokeshire & Camarthenshire, a Shell Guide. 2nd ed. Vyvyan Rees. (Shell Guide Ser.). (Illus.). 1976. 13.95 (ISBN 0-571-04810-2, Pub. by Faber & Faber). Merrimack Bk Serv.

Southampton Insurrection. William S. Drewry. (Illus.). 1968. Repr. of 1900 ed. 12.00 (ISBN 0-930230-21-3). Johnson NC.

Southeast: Alaska's Panhandle. Alaska Geographic Staff. LC 72-92087. (Alaska Geographic: Vol. 5, No. 2). (Illus.). 1978. pap. 12.95 album style (ISBN 0-88240-107-6). Alaska Northwest.

Southeast Asia. rev ed. Frederick K. Poole. LC 72-5404. (First Bks.). (Illus.). 96p. (gr. 7-9). 1973. 5.90 (ISBN 0-531-00801-0); text ed. 3.90 (ISBN 0-531-00637-9). Watts.

Southeast Asia. Ed. by W. A. Withington & Margaret Fisher. LC 78-54259. (World Cultures Ser). (Illus.). (gr. 5 up). 1979. text ed. 9.95 1-4 copies o.p. (ISBN 0-88296-134-9); text ed. 7.96 5 or more o.p. (ISBN 0-685-14505-0); tchrs' ed 8.94 o.p. (ISBN 0-88296-369-4). Fideler.

Southeast Asia & China: The End of Containment. Edwin Martin. LC 76-53510. 1977. lib. bdg. 18.00x (ISBN 0-89158-219-3). Westview.

Southeast Asia & the Soviet Union. Philadelphia Suburban School Study Council Group B. LC 66-28972. 1966. pap. text ed. 1.50x o.p. (ISBN 0-8134-0895-4, 895). Interstate.

Southeast Asia: The Politics of National Integration. Ed. by John T. McAlister, Jr. 576p. 1972. text ed. 15.95 (ISBN 0-394-31409-3). Random.

Southeast Asia Under the New Balance of Power. Ed. by Sudershan Chawla et al. LC 73-19441. (Special Studies). 225p. 1974. 19.95 o.p. (ISBN 0-275-28826-9); student ed. 8.95 o.p. (ISBN 0-275-88850-9). Praeger.

Southeast Asian Ceramics: Ninth Through Seventeenth Centuries. Dean F. Frasche. LC 76-20204. (Illus.). 144p. 1976. 25.00 (ISBN 0-87848-047-1). Asia Soc.

Southeast Asia's Chinese Minorities. Mary Somers-Heidhues. (Studies in Contemporary South Asia). 160p. 1974. pap. text ed. 4.50x o.p. (ISBN 0-582-71039-1). Longman.

Southeast Asia's Political Systems. 2nd ed. Lucian W. Pye. (Comparative Asian Government Ser). (Illus.). 128p. 1974. 7.95 (ISBN 0-13-823690-9); pap. text ed. 6.95 (ISBN 0-13-823682-8). P-H.

Southeast Export: Profiles, Typology & the Role of Technology in Selected U. S. Firms. Cedric L. Suzman et al. (Research Monograph: No. 90). 1981. spiral bdg. 15.00 (ISBN 0-88406-146-9). GA St U Busn Pub.

Southeastern Europe Under Ottoman Rule, 1354-1804. Peter F. Sugar. LC 76-7799. (History of East Central Europe Ser.: Vol. 5). 384p. 1977. 18.95 (ISBN 0-295-95443-4). U of Wash Pr.

Southeastern Indians. Charles Hudson. LC 75-30729. (Illus.). 1976. 25.00 (ISBN 0-87049-187-3); pap. 9.50x (ISBN 0-87049-248-9). U of Tenn Pr.

Southeastern Indians Since the Removal Era. Ed. by Walter L. Williams. LC 78-10490. (Illus.). 270p. 1979. 18.50x (ISBN 0-8203-0464-6); pap. 6.00 (ISBN 0-8203-0483-2). U of Ga Pr.

Southern Africa. Ed. by Grant S. McClellan. (Reference Shelf Ser.). 1979. 6.25 (ISBN 0-8242-0633-9). Wilson.

Southern Africa & the United States. Ed. by William A. Hance et al. LC 68-18147. 1969. 15.00x (ISBN 0-231-03117-3). Columbia U Pr.

Southern Africa: Angola, Botswana, Lesotho, Malawi, Mozambique, Namibia, Republic of South Africa, Rhodesia, Swaziland, Zambia. Harry Stein. LC 74-11391. (Illus.). 96p. (gr. 5 up). 1975. PLB 3.90 o.p. (ISBN 0-531-00823-1). Watts.

Southern Africa: Civilizations in Turmoil. Richard W. Hull. (Illus.). 240p. 1981. text ed. 17.50x (ISBN 0-8147-3410-3); pap. text ed. 9.00x (ISBN 0-8147-3411-1). NYU Pr.

Southern Africa in Perspective: Essays in Regional Politics. Ed. by Christian Potholm & Richard Dale. LC 79-143520. 1972. 19.95 (ISBN 0-02-925290-3); pap. text ed. 9.95 (ISBN 0-02-925320-9). Free Pr.

Southern Africa Since 1800. Donald Denoon. 1979. pap. text ed. 9.95x (ISBN 0-582-60321-8). Longman.

Southern Africa, The Critical Land. Clarke Newlon. LC 78-7734. (Illus.). 1978. 6.95 (ISBN 0-396-07589-4). Dodd.

Southern Africa: The Escalation of a Conflict. Stockholm International Peace Research Institute. LC 76-4518. (Special Studies). 400p. 1976. text ed. 32.50 (ISBN 0-275-56840-7). Praeger.

Southern Album. Willie Morris. Ed. by Irwin Glusker. LC 76-49690. 8.95 o.p. (ISBN 0-89104-058-7). A & W Pubs.

Southern Appalachian Resource Catalog, Vol. I. rev. ed. Ed. by Michele L. Boone. (Illus.). 84p. 1980. pap. 4.00 (ISBN 0-937208-00-0). S Appalachian Res.

Southern Appalachians. Jerry Doolittle. (American Wilderness Ser.). (Illus.). 1976. 12.95 (ISBN 0-8094-1346-9). Time-Life.

Southern Appalachians. Jerome Doolittle. LC 75-27179. (American Wilderness). (Illus.). (gr. 6 up). 1976. PLB 11.97 (ISBN 0-8094-1347-7, Pub. by Time-Life). Silver.

Southern Applachian Resource Catalog, Vol. II. Ed. by Michele L. Boone. (Illus.). 76p. 1981. 4.00. S Appalachian Res.

Southern Architecture: An Architectural & Cultural History of the South from the Colonization of America to the 20th Century. Kenneth Severens. 1981. 18.95 (ISBN 0-525-20692-2). Dutton.

Southern Asia: The Politics of Poverty & Peace. Commission on Critical Choices & Donald C. Hellman. LC 75-44731. (Critical Choices for Americans Ser.: Vol. XIII). 1976. 19.95 (ISBN 0-669-00427-8). Lexington Bks.

Southern Blood. Justin Channing. 400p. 1980. pap. 2.50 (ISBN 0-553-13132-X). Bantam.

Southern Calif. Industrial Minerals. 1973. 14.70. Minobras.

Southern California Metropolis: A Study in Development of Government for a Metropolitan Area. Winston W. Crouch & Beatrice Dinerman. (Illus.). 1963. 22.50x (ISBN 0-520-00280-6). U of Cal Pr.

Southern California: Travel Guide. 5th ed. Sunset Editors. LC 78-70269. (Illus.). 128p. 1979. pap. 4.95 (ISBN 0-376-06757-8, Sunset Bks). Sunset-Lane.

Southern Collection. Ed. by Cason J. Callaway, Jr. & Charles M. Flowers. (Illus.). 318p. (Orig.). 1979. pap. 8.50. Jr League Columbus.

Southern Colonial Frontier: Sixteen Hundred Seven to Seventeen Sixty-Three. W. Stitt Robinson. LC 78-21432. (Histories of the American Frontier Ser). 1979. 12.50x o.p. (ISBN 0-8263-0502-4); pap. 6.50x (ISBN 0-8263-0503-2). U of NM Pr.

Southern Commercial Conventions Eighteen Thirty-Seven to Eighteen Fifty-Nine. Herbert Wender. LC 79-1601. 1981. Repr. of 1930 ed. 19.50 (ISBN 0-88355-904-8). Hyperion Conn.

Southern Cordillera Real. R. Pecher & W. Schmiermann. (Illus.). 57p. (Orig.). 1977. pap. 7.95 (ISBN 0-686-69199-7). Bradt Ent.

Southern Country Cookbook. Lena Sturges. LC 72-83975. (Illus.). 1972. 12.95 (ISBN 0-8487-0234-4). Oxmoor Hse.

Southern Directions: Gallimaufry 15. Linney et al. Ed. by Mary MacArthur & Moira Crone. Date not set. pap. cancelled (ISBN 0-916300-19-6). Gallimaufry.

Southern Elections: County & Precinct Data, 1950-1972. Numan V. Bartley & Hugh D. Graham. LC 78-5525. 1977. 24.95x (ISBN 0-8071-0278-4). La State U Pr.

Southern England: An Arcaeological Guide. James Dyer. (Illus., Orig.). 1973. pap. 10.95 (ISBN 0-571-10334-0, Pub. by Faber & Faber). Merrimack Bk Serv.

Southern England (Kent, Sussex, Hampshire, Isle of Wight) Colourmaster. (Travel in England Ser.). (Illus.). 96p. 1975. 7.95 (ISBN 0-85933-007-9). Transatlantic.

Southern Evangelicals & the Social Order Eighteen Hundred to Eighteen Sixty. Anne C. Loveland. LC 80-11200. 368p. 1980. 30.00x (ISBN 0-8071-0690-9); pap. 12.95 (ISBN 0-8071-0783-2). La State U Pr.

Southern Experience in Short Fiction. Allen F. Stein & Thomas N. Walters. 1971. pap. 6.95x (ISBN 0-673-07605-9). Scott F.

Southern Flower Gardening. Williams D. Adams. LC 79-29715. (Illus.). 1980. pap. 3.95 (ISBN 0-88415-291-X). Pacesetter Pr.

Southern Frontier 1670-1732. Verner W. Crane. 1980. pap. 5.95 (ISBN 0-393-00948-3). Norton.

Southern Gardner's Soil Handbook. William Peavy. LC 78-58245. (Illus.). 1979. pap. 3.95 (ISBN 0-88415-817-9). Pacesetter Pr.

Southern Guest House Book. Corinne M. Ross. (Illus.). 192p. 1981. pap. 6.95 (ISBN 0-914788-35-3). East Woods.

Southern Home Landscaping. Ken Smith. (Gardening Ser.). (Orig.). 1981. pap. 7.95 (ISBN 0-89586-063-5). H P Bks.

Southern Home Remedies. Ed. by Bernice K. Harris. (Illus.). 1968. 6.50 (ISBN 0-930230-22-1). Johnson NC.

Southern Indians in the American Revolution. James H. O'Donnell, 3rd. LC 76-146662. 176p. 1973. 10.50x (ISBN 0-87049-131-8). U of Tenn Pr.

Southern Indians: The Story of the Civilized Tribes Before Removal. R. S. Cotterill. LC 54-5931. (Civilization of the American Indian Ser.: Vol. 38). 259p. 1954. 12.50 (ISBN 0-8061-0286-1); pap. 5.95 (ISBN 0-8061-1171-2). U of Okla Pr.

Southern Junior League Cookbook. Ed. by Ann Serrane. 640p. 1981. pap. 7.95 (ISBN 0-345-29518-8). Ballantine.

Southern King Arthur Family. O. S. Nock. LC 76-2885. (Illus.). 96p. 1976. 13.50 (ISBN 0-7153-7156-8). David & Charles.

Southern Lady: From Pedestal to Politics, 1830-1930. Anne F. Scott. LC 73-123750. 1970. 10.00x o.s.i. (ISBN 0-226-74346-2). U of Chicago Pr.

Southern Landscape & Garden Design. J. Carroll Kell. LC 80-473. (Illus.). 1980. pap. 3.95 (ISBN 0-88415-811-X). Pacesetter Pr.

Southern Lawns & Groundcovers. Richard Duble & J. Carroll Kell. LC 77-73533. (Illus.). 1977. pap. 3.95 (ISBN 0-88415-426-2). Pacesetter Pr.

Southern Living Annual Recipes-1980. Southern Living Foods Staff. LC 79-88364. (Illus.). 352p. 1981. 14.95 (ISBN 0-8487-0516-5). Oxmoor Hse.

Southern Living Garden Guide: Your Answer Book to Garden Questions. Southern Living Gardening Staff & John A. Floyd, Jr. LC 80-84409. (Illus.). 224p. 1981. 17.95 (ISBN 0-8487-0518-1). Oxmoor Hse.

Southern Living Travel South - 1981. Rand McNally & Company & Southern Living Travel Editors. (Illus.). 192p. 1981. pap. 9.95 (ISBN 0-686-69039-7). Oxmoor Hse.

Southern Living 1979: Annual Recipes. Ed. by Southern Living Foods Staff. LC 79-88364. 1979. 14.95 (ISBN 0-8487-0513-0). Oxmoor Hse.

Southern Mail. Antoine De Saint-Exupery. Tr. by Curtis Cate. LC 79-182749. 1972. pap. 2.50 (ISBN 0-15-683901-6, HPL55, HPL). HarBraceJ.

Southern Miscellany: Essays in Honor of Glover Moore. Ed. by Frank A. Dennis. LC 80-20373. 202p. 1981. 15.00 (ISBN 0-87805-129-5). U Pr of Miss.

Southern Music American Music. Bill C. Malone. Ed. by Charles P. Ronald. LC 79-4005. (New Perspectives on the South Ser.). (Illus.). 216p. 1979. 11.50 (ISBN 0-8131-0300-2). U Pr of Ky.

Southern Pacific Daylight. 59.95. Chatham Pub CA.

Southern Pacific Motive Power Annual, 1966-67. (Illus.). 10.35 (ISBN 0-89685-001-3). Chatham Pub CA.

Southern Pacific Motive Power Annual, 1967-68. (Illus.). 10.35 (ISBN 0-89685-002-1). Chatham Pub CA.

Southern Pacific Motive Power Annual, 1968-69. (Illus.). 10.35 (ISBN 0-89685-003-X). Chatham Pub CA.

Southern Pacific Motive Power Annual 1977-1980. Donald V. Jewell. LC 80-66138. (Illus.). 88p. 1981. 15.00 (ISBN 0-89685-009-9). Chatham Pub CA.

Southern Pacific Motive Power Annual, 1970. (Illus.). 10.35 (ISBN 0-89685-004-8). Chatham Pub CA.

Southern Pacific Motive Power Annual, 1971. Joseph A. Strapal. (Illus.). 1971. 9.95 (ISBN 0-89685-005-6). Chatham Pub CA.

Southern Pacific Review Nineteen Eighty. Joseph A. Strapac. (Illus.). 1980. pap. 14.00 (ISBN 0-930742-04-4). Shade Tree.

Southern Pacific Review 1978-1979. new ed. Joseph A. Strapac. (Illus.). 1979. pap. 12.00 o.p. (ISBN 0-930742-03-6). Shade Tree.

Southern Pacific Steam Locomotives. Donald Duke. LC 62-6982. (Illus.). 12.95 (ISBN 0-87095-012-6). Golden West.

Southern Plantation: A Study in the Development & the Accuracy of a Tradition. F. P. Gaines. 7.50 (ISBN 0-8446-1193-X). Peter Smith.

Southern Renascence: The Literature of the Modern South. Ed. by Louis D. Rubin, Jr. & Robert D. Jacobs. 456p. 1953. 20.00x (ISBN 0-8018-0568-6); pap. 4.95x (ISBN 0-8018-0569-4). Johns Hopkins.

Southern Reporter & Other Stories. John W. Corrington. LC 80-26204. 168p. 1981. 9.95 (ISBN 0-8071-0869-3). La State U Pr.

Southern Rock: A Climber's Guide to the South. Chris Hall. (Illus.). 192p. 1981. pap. 7.95 (ISBN 0-914788-37-X). East Woods.

Southern Schools: An Evaluation of the Emergency School Assistance Program (EASP) & of School Desegregation. Robert L. Crain. (Report Ser: Nos. 124A-124B). 1973. Set. 10.00 (ISBN 0-932132-21-9). NORC.

Southern Slav Question & the Hapsburg Monarchy. R. W. Seton-Watson. LC 68-9666. 1969. Repr. of 1911 ed. 21.50 (ISBN 0-86527-185-2). Fertig.

Southern South. Albert B. Hart. LC 74-96438. (American Scene Ser). 1969. Repr. of 1969 ed. lib. bdg. 45.00 (ISBN 0-306-71826-X). Da Capo.

Southern Sudan & Eritrea: Aspects of Wider African Problems. Godfrey Morrison. (Minority Rights Group: No. 5). 1973. pap. 2.50 (ISBN 0-89192-094-3). Interbk Inc.

Southern Vegetable Cookbook. Jan Wongrey. Ed. by Del Roberts & Rose Wilkins. LC 80-50790. (Illus.). 152p. 1981. 5.95 (ISBN 0-87844-045-3). Sandlapper Store.

Southerner Discovers the South. Jonathan Daniels. LC 68-16228. (American Scene Ser.). 1970. Repr. of 1938 ed. lib. bdg. 35.00 (ISBN 0-306-71011-0). Da Capo.

Southey. Kenneth Curry. (Author Guides). 1975. 18.00 (ISBN 0-7100-8112-X). Routledge & Kegan.

Southwark & the City. David J. Johnson. 1969. 10.25x o.p. (ISBN 0-19-711630-2). Oxford U Pr.

Southwest, No. XV. new ed. Charles McCarry. LC 78-21450. (Illus.). 1980. 6.95 (ISBN 0-87044-283-X); lib. bdg. 8.50 (ISBN 0-87044-288-0). Natl Geog.

Southwest. Ed. by Alfonso Ortiz. LC 77-17162. (Handbook of North American Indians Ser.: Vol. 9). (Illus.). 700p. 1980. text ed. 17.00x (ISBN 0-87474-189-0). Smithsonian.

Southwest Fiction Anthology. Ed. by Max Apple. 368p. (Orig.). 1981. pap. 2.95 (ISBN 0-553-14256-9). Bantam.

Southwest Indian Painting: A Changing Art. rev. ed. Clara L. Tanner. LC 74-160812. (Illus.). 1980. 50.00 (ISBN 0-8165-0309-5). U of Ariz Pr.

Southwest: Old & New. W. Eugene Hollon. LC 61-9232. (Illus.). 1968. pap. 5.75 (ISBN 0-8032-5091-6, BB 353, Bison). U of Nebr Pr.

Southwest: Three Peoples in Geographical Change, 1600-1970. D. W. Meinig. (Historical Geography of North America Ser). (Orig.). 1971. text ed. 10.95x (ISBN 0-19-501288-7); pap. text ed. 4.95x (ISBN 0-19-501289-5). Oxford U Pr.

Southwestern Arizona Ghost Tours. Stanley W. Paher. (Illus.). 2.95 (ISBN 0-913814-32-6). Nevada Pubns.

Southwestern Indian Arts & Crafts. Tom Bahti. LC 65-499. (Illus.). 1966. 7.95 (ISBN 0-916122-25-5); pap. 2.00 (ISBN 0-916122-00-X). K C Pubns.

Southwestern Indian Ceremonials. Tom Bahti. LC 79-136004. (Illus.). 1970. 7.95 (ISBN 0-916122-27-1); pap. 3.00 (ISBN 0-916122-02-6). K C Pubns.

Southwestern Indian Ritual Drama. Ed. by Charlotte J. Frisbie. LC 79-2308. (School of American Research Advanced Seminar Ser.). (Illus.). 384p. 1980. 30.00 (ISBN 0-8263-0521-0). U of NM Pr.

Southwestern Indian Tribes. Tom Bahti. LC 68-31188. (Illus.). 1968. 7.95 (ISBN 0-916122-26-3); pap. 3.75 (ISBN 0-916122-01-8). K C Pubns.

Southwestern Journals of Adolph F. Bandelier, 3 vols. Ed. by Charles H. Lange et al. Incl. Vol. 1. 1880-1882. 462p. 1966. 15.00x (ISBN 0-8263-0061-8); Vol. 2. 1883-1884. 546p. 1970. 20.00x (ISBN 0-8263-0153-3); Vol. 3. 1885-1888. 702p. 1975. 20.00x o.p. (ISBN 0-8263-0352-8). LC 65-17862. (Illus.). o.p. 30.00x set (ISBN 0-8263-0419-2). U of NM Pr.

Souvenir Buildings: A Collection of Identified Miniatures, 2 vols. Dort F. Brown. (Illus.). 203p. (Orig., Vol. 1, 1977, Vol. 2, 1979). pap. 5.00 set (ISBN 0-9603420-0-1). Indisota Pubs.

Souvenir Programs of Five Great World Series. Ed. by Bert Sugar. (Illus.). 1980. pap. 6.95 (ISBN 0-486-23858-X). Dover.

Souvenirs, Eighteen Seventy-Eight to Eighteen-Ninety-Three. Charles L. Freycinet. LC 73-258. (Europe 1815-1945 Ser.). 524p. 1973. Repr. of 1913 ed. lib. bdg. 49.50 (ISBN 0-306-70560-5). Da Capo.

Sovereign Ghost: Studies in Imagination. Denis Donoghue. 1977. 14.50 (ISBN 0-520-03134-2). U of Cal Pr.

Sovereign Lady: A Life of Elizabeth, Third Lady Holland, with Her Family. Sonia Keppel. (Illus.). 1978. 22.50 (ISBN 0-241-02299-1, Pub. by Hamish Hamilton England). David & Charles.

Sovereignty & Society in Colonial Brazil: The High Court of Bahia & Its Judges, 1609-1751. Stuart B. Schwartz. 1973. 28.50x (ISBN 0-520-02195-9). U of Cal Pr.

Sovereignty for Sale. Rodney P. Carlisle. 336p. 1981. 19.95 (ISBN 0-87021-668-6). Naval Inst Pr.

Sovereignty of God. A. W. Pink. 1976. pap. 3.45 (ISBN 0-85151-133-3). Banner of Truth.

Sovereignty, Security & Arms. Michael Moodie. LC 79-88220. (Washington Papers: No. 67). 1979. pap. 3.50 (ISBN 0-8039-1320-6). Sage.

Soviet Academy of Sciences & the Communist Party, 1927-1932. L. R. Graham. (Studies of the Russian Institute). 1968. 15.00 (ISBN 0-691-08038-0). Princeton U Pr.

Soviet Agrarian Debate: A Controversy in Social Science, 1923-1929. Susan G. Solomon. LC 77-21555. (Special Studies on the Soviet Union & Eastern Europe Ser.). (Illus.). 1978. lib. bdg. 26.50x (ISBN 0-89158-339-4). Westview.

Soviet Agriculture: An Assessment of Its Contributions to Economic Development. Ed. by Harry G. Shaffer. LC 77-7512. (Praeger Special Studies). 1977. text ed. 22.95 (ISBN 0-03-021976-0). Praeger.

Soviet Air & Strategic Rocket Forces, 1939 to 1980: A Guide to Sources in English. Myron J. Smith, Jr. Ed. by Richard D. Burns. (War-Peace Bibliography Ser.: No. 10). 1981. price not set (ISBN 0-87436-306-3). Abc-Clio.

Soviet Air Power in Transition. Robert P. Berman. (Studies in Defense Policy). 1978. pap. 3.95 (ISBN 0-8157-0923-4). Brookings.

Soviet Aircraft of Today. pap. 7.95 (ISBN 0-89747-068-0). Squad Sig Pubns.

Soviet-American Arms Race. Colin S. Gray. LC 75-28542. 208p. 1976. 23.95 (ISBN 0-685-67535-1, 00318-2, Pub. by Saxon Hse). Lexington Bks.

Soviet-American Rivalry. Thomas B. Larson. 320p. 1981. pap. 6.95 (ISBN 0-393-95145-6). Norton.

Soviet-American Trade Negotiations. John W. De Pauw. LC 78-25883. (Praeger Special Studies). 1979. 22.95 (ISBN 0-03-048446-4). Praeger.

Soviet & Chinese Aid to African Nations. Ed. by Warren Weinstein & Thomas H. Henriksen. LC 79-21128. (Praeger Special Studies). 1980. 20.95 (ISBN 0-03-052756-2). Praeger.

Soviet & Chinese Influence in the Third World. Alvin Z. Rubinstein. LC 74-11604. (Special Studies). 246p. 1976. 22.95 o.p. (ISBN 0-275-09640-8); pap. text ed. 9.95 o.p. (ISBN 0-275-64690-4). Praeger.

Soviet and Chinese Personalities. Wilhelm S. Heiliger. LC 80-1383. 221p. 1980. lib. bdg. 17.75 (ISBN 0-8191-1213-5); pap. text ed. 9.50 (ISBN 0-8191-1214-3). U Pr of Amer.

Soviet & East European Agriculture. Ed. by Jerzy F. Karcz. (Russian & East European Studies). 1967. 28.50x (ISBN 0-520-00631-3). U of Cal Pr.

Soviet & East European Foreign Policy: A Bibliography of English- & Russian-Language Publications, 1967-1971. Roger E. Kanet. LC 74-76444. 208p. 1974. text ed. 9.95 (ISBN 0-87436-137-0). ABC-Clio.

Soviet & East European Law & the Scientific-Technical Revolution. Ed. by Gordon B. Smith et al. (Pergamon Policy Studies on International Politics). (Illus.). 330p. 1981. 34.00 (ISBN 0-08-027195-2). Pergamon.

Soviet & Russian Newspapers at the Hoover Institution: A Catalog. Karol Maichel. LC 66-26281. (Bibliographical Ser.: No. 24). 235p. 1966. 8.00 (ISBN 0-8179-2241-5); pap. 6.00 (ISBN 0-8179-2242-3). Hoover Inst Pr.

Soviet & Western Anthrpology. Ed. by Ernest Gellner. LC 80-11676. 300p. 1980. 37.50x (ISBN 0-231-05120-4). Columbia U Pr.

Soviet & Western Perspectives in Social Psychology. Ed. by L. H. Strickland. LC 79-40311. 1979. 41.00 (ISBN 0-08-023389-9). Pergamon.

Soviet Armed Forces Review Annual: Safra, Vol. 4. Ed. by David R. Jones. 1981. 45.00 (ISBN 0-87569-037-8). Academic Intl.

Soviet Army: A Guide to Sources in English. Myron J. Smith, Jr. Ed. by Richard D. Burns. (War-Peace Bibliography Ser.: No. 11). 1982. price not set (ISBN 0-87436-307-1). Abc-Clio. Postponed.

Soviet Asia: Bibliographies. Edward Allworth. LC 73-9061. (Illus.). 756p. 1976. text ed. 54.95 (ISBN 0-275-07540-0). Praeger.

Soviet Asian Ethnic Frontiers. Ed. by William O. McCagg & Brian D. Silver. LC 77-11796. (Pergamon Policy Studies). (Illus.). 1979. 36.00 (ISBN 0-08-024637-0). Pergamon.

Soviet-Asian Relations in the 1970s & Beyond: An Interperceptional Study. Bhabani Sen Gupta. LC 76-24368. 1976. text ed. 32.50 (ISBN 0-275-23740-0). Praeger.

Soviet Attitudes Toward American Writing. Deming O. Brown. 1962. 19.00x o.p. (ISBN 0-691-08712-1). Princeton U Pr.

Soviet Aviation & Air Power: A Historical Review. Ed. by R. Higham & Jacob Kipp. LC 76-30815. (Illus.). 1978. lib. bdg. 35.00x (ISBN 0-89158-116-2). Westview.

Soviet Ballet. Juri Slonimsky. LC 77-107873. (Music Ser). (Illus.). 1970. Repr. of 1947 ed. lib. bdg. 29.50 (ISBN 0-306-71897-9). Da Capo.

Soviet Bargaining Behavior. Christer Jonsson. 1979. 14.50x (ISBN 0-231-04606-5). Columbia U Pr.

Soviet Believers: The Religious Sector of the Population. William Fletcher. LC 80-25495. (Illus.). 276p. 1981. 27.50x (ISBN 0-7006-0211-9). Regents Pr KS.

Soviet Bloc Merchant Ships. Bruno Bock & Klaus Bock. LC 80-81092. (Illus.). 272p. 1981. 29.95 (ISBN 0-87021-669-4). Naval Inst Pr.

Soviet Book Publishing Policy. G. Walker. LC 77-12543. (Soviet & East European Studies). (Illus.). 1978. 23.95 (ISBN 0-521-21843-8). Cambridge U Pr.

Soviet Censorship. Ed. by Martin Dewhirst & Robert Farrell. LC 73-9844. 1973. 10.00 (ISBN 0-8108-0674-6). Scarecrow.

Soviet Chess. Ed. by R. G. Wade. 1976. pap. 3.00 (ISBN 0-87980-311-8). Wilshire.

Soviet City: Ideal & Reality. James H. Bater. LC 80-51193. (Explorations in Urban Analysis: Vol. 2). 196p. 1980. 18.95x (ISBN 0-8039-1466-0); pap. 8.95x (ISBN 0-8039-1467-9). Sage.

Soviet Civil Procedure: History & Analysis. Don W. Chenoweth. LC 77-76427. (Transactions Ser.: Vol. 67, Pt. 7). 1977. pap. 6.00 o.p. (ISBN 0-87169-676-2). Am Philos.

Soviet Codes of Law. William B. Simons. (Law in Eastern Europe Ser.: No. 23). 1288p. 1980. 92.50x (ISBN 90-286-0810-9). Sijthoff & Noordhoff.

Soviet Conquest from Space. Peter N. James. (Illus.). 1974. 8.95 o.p. (ISBN 0-87000-224-4). Arlington Hse.

Soviet Criminologists & Criminal Policy. Peter H. Solomon, Jr. LC 77-3357. (Studies of the Russian Institute Ser.). 1978. 17.50x (ISBN 0-231-04316-3). Columbia U Pr.

Soviet Deserts & Mountains. George St. George. (World's Wild Places Ser.). (Illus.). 184p. 1974. 12.95 (ISBN 0-8094-2012-0). Time-Life.

Soviet Deserts & Mountains. George St. George. (World's Wild Places Ser.). (Illus.). 1978. lib. bdg. 11.97 (ISBN 0-686-51024-0). Silver.

Soviet Design for a World State. Elliot R. Goodman. LC 60-7625. 1960. 25.00x (ISBN 0-231-02339-1). Columbia U Pr.

Soviet Developmental Psychology. Ed. by Michel Cole. Tr. by Michel Vale et al from Rus. LC 77-85709. 1977. 30.00 o.p. (ISBN 0-87332-093-X). M E Sharpe.

Soviet Dissent in Historical Perspective. Marshall S. Shatz. LC 80-13318. 240p. 1981. 19.95 (ISBN 0-521-23172-8). Cambridge U Pr.

Soviet Dissent: Intellectuals, Jews & Detente. Albert Axelbank. LC 74-13635. (Illus.). 112p. (gr. 7 up). 1975. PLB 5.95 o.p. (ISBN 0-531-02800-3). Watts.

Soviet-East European Dialogue: Relations of a New Type? Nish Jamgotch, Jr. LC 68-29991. (Studies: No. 21). 1968. 5.50 (ISBN 0-8179-3211-9); pap. 4.00 (ISBN 0-8179-3212-7). Hoover Inst Pr.

Soviet-East European Dilemmas. Ed. by Karen Dawisha & Philip Hanson. LC 80-28573. 226p. 1981. text ed. 31.00x (ISBN 0-8419-0697-1); pap. text ed. 15.00x (ISBN 0-8419-0698-X). Holmes & Meier.

Soviet Economic Development. Raymond Hutchings. 1971. 36.00x (ISBN 0-631-12830-1, Pub. by Basil Blackwell); pap. 14.00x (ISBN 0-631-13560-X, Pub. by Basil Blackwell). Biblio Dist.

Soviet Economic Development Since 1917. 6th ed. Maurice Dobb. 1966. pap. 16.00 (ISBN 0-7100-4658-8). Routledge & Kegan.

Soviet Economic Structure & Performance. Paul R. Gregory & Robert C. Stuart. (Illus.). 1974. pap. text ed. 16.95 scp o.p. (ISBN 0-06-042509-1, HarpC). Har-Row.

Soviet Economic System. Alec Nove. 1977. text ed. 29.50 (ISBN 0-04-335035-6); pap. text ed. 12.50x (ISBN 0-04-335036-4). Allen Unwin.

Soviet Economic Thought & Political Power in the USSR. Aron Katsenelinboigen. LC 78-17552. (Pergamon Policy Studies). 1980. 28.00 (ISBN 0-08-022467-9). Pergamon.

Soviet Economists of the Twenties: Names to Be Remembered. Naum Jasny. Ed. by M. Kaser. LC 77-168894. (Soviet & East European Studies). 1972. 29.95 (ISBN 0-521-08302-8). Cambridge U Pr.

Soviet Economy. rev. ed. Nicolas Spulber. 1969. 12.95x (ISBN 0-393-09860-5, NortonC). Norton.

Soviet Economy: A Collection of Western & Soviet Views. 2nd ed. Ed. by Harry G. Shaffer. LC 69-16223. (Illus., Orig.). 1969. pap. text ed. 5.95x (ISBN 0-89197-420-2). Irvington.

Soviet Economy: Continuity & Change. Ed. by Morris Bornstein. 532p. (Orig.). 1981. lib. bdg. 26.50x (ISBN 0-89158-958-9); pap. text ed. 12.00x (ISBN 0-89158-959-7). Westview.

Soviet Economy: How It Really Works. Krylov. LC 78-22286. (Illus.). 1979. 18.95 (ISBN 0-669-02743-X). Lexington Bks.

Soviet Empire: Expansion & Detente. Commisiion on Critical Choices. LC 75-44727. (Critical Choices for Americans Ser.: Vol. IX). 1976. 22.95 (ISBN 0-669-00421-9). Lexington Bks.

Soviet Energy Technologies. Robert W. Campbell. LC 80-7562. 288p. 1980. 22.50x (ISBN 0-253-15965-2). Ind U Pr.

Soviet Ethnology & Anthropology Today. Ed. by Yu Bromley. (Studies in Anthropology Ser.: No. 1). 401p. 1974. pap. text ed. 64.70x (ISBN 90-2792-725-1). Mouton.

Soviet Evangelicals Since World War II. Walter Sawatsky. LC 81-94121. (Illus.). 560p. 1981. 19.95 (ISBN 0-8361-1238-5); pap. 14.95 (ISBN 0-8361-1239-3). Herald Pr.

Soviet Far Eastern Policy, 1931-1945. Harriet L. Moore. 16.00 (ISBN 0-86527-187-9). Fertig.

Soviet Foreign Policy. Egbert Jahn. (Allison & Busby's Motive Ser.). 160p. 1981. pap. 7.95 (ISBN 0-8052-8096-0, Pub. by Allison & Busby England). Schocken.

Soviet Foreign Policy Since World War II: Imperial & Global. Alvin Z. Rubinstein. (Political Science Ser.). (Illus.). 354p. 1981. text ed. 15.00 (ISBN 0-87626-810-6); pap. text ed. 9.95 (ISBN 0-87626-809-2). Winthrop.

Soviet Foreign Policy Since World War II. Joseph L. Nogee & Robert H. Donaldson. (Pergamon Policy Studies on International Politics). 300p. Date not set. 35.00 (ISBN 0-08-025997-9); pap. 10.95 (ISBN 0-08-025996-0). Pergamon.

Soviet Foreign Policy Toward Western Europe. George Ginsburgs. Ed. by Alvin Z Rubinstein. LC 78-17925. (Praeger Special Studies). 1978. 24.95 (ISBN 0-03-044331-8). Praeger.

Soviet Foreign Trade. William N. Turpin. LC 76-47337. 1977. 17.95x (ISBN 0-669-01143-6). Lexington Bks.

Soviet Historians in Crisis Nineteen Twenty-Eight to Nineteen Thirty-Two. John Barber. LC 80-13798. 250p. 1981. text ed. 33.00x (ISBN 0-8419-0614-9). Holmes & Meier.

Soviet Images of America. Stephen P. Gibert. LC 76-28569. 1977. pap. 9.95x (ISBN 0-8448-1075-4). Crane-Russak Co.

Soviet Impact on the Western World. E. H. Carr. 1973. 15.00 (ISBN 0-86527-187-9). Fertig.

Soviet Impregnational Propaganda. Baruch Hazan. 1981. 20.00 (ISBN 0-88233-643-6). Ardis Pubs.

Soviet Intelligentsia: An Essay on the Social Structure & Roles of the Soviet Intellectuals During the 1960's. L. G. Churchward. (Illus.). 218p. 1973. 18.00 (ISBN 0-7100-7475-1). Routledge & Kegan.

Soviet Involvement in the Middle East: Policy Formulation, 1966-1973. Ilana Kass. LC 77-8279. (Special Studies on the Soviet Union & Eastern Europe Ser.). 1978. lib. bdg. 26.50x (ISBN 0-89158-063-8). Westview.

Soviet Juggernaut. Time-Life Books Editors & Earl Ziemke. (World War II Ser.). (Illus.). 208p. 1981. 13.95 (ISBN 0-8094-3387-7). Time-Life.

Soviet Land & Housing Law: A Historical & Comparative Study. Stanislaw J. Sawicki. LC 77-3016. (Special Studies). 1977. text ed. 22.95 o.p. (ISBN 0-275-24480-6). Praeger.

Soviet Leadership in Transition. Jerry F. Hough. LC 80-67873. 175p. 1980. 11.95 (ISBN 0-8157-3742-4); pap. 4.95 (ISBN 0-8157-3741-6). Brookings.

Soviet Legal System. 3rd ed. J. N. Hazard. 1977. 20.00. Oceana.

Soviet Legislation on Women's Rights. 1978. 4.80 (ISBN 0-8285-3362-8). Progress Pubs.

Soviet Merchant Marine: Economic Aid & Strategic Challenge to the West. Ed. by David W. Lee et al. 1979. pap. text ed. 6.50x (ISBN 0-686-59447-9). Westview.

Soviet Merchant Ships. 4th ed. Ambrose Greenway. (Illus.). 220p. 1981. text ed. 20.00x (ISBN 0-911378-33-2). Sheridan.

Soviet Military Buildup & U.S. Defense Spending. Barry M. G. Blechman et al. (Studies in Defense Policy). 1977. pap. 3.95 (ISBN 0-8157-0989-7). Brookings.

Soviet Military Policy. Raymond L. Garthoff. 1966. 8.95 o.p. (ISBN 0-571-06788-3, Pub. by Faber & Faber). Merrimack Bk Serv.

Soviet Military Strategy. 3rd ed. V. D. Sokolovskiy. Tr. by Harriet F. Scott from Rus. LC 73-94042. (Illus.). 560p. 1975. pap. 29.50x (ISBN 0-8448-0311-1). Crane-Russak Co.

Soviet Military Strategy in Europe. Joseph D. Douglass, Jr. LC 79-19320. (Pergamon Policy Studies. An Institute for Foreign Policy Analysis Bk.). 270p. 1980. 33.00 (ISBN 0-08-023702-9). Pergamon.

Soviet National Income, 1958-1964: National Accounts of the USSR in the Seven Year Plan Period. Abraham S. Becker. (Illus.). 1969. 35.00x (ISBN 0-520-01437-5). U of Cal Pr.

Soviet Nationality Policies & Practices. Ed. by Jeremy R. Azrael. LC 77-83478. 1978. 35.95 (ISBN 0-03-041476-8). Praeger.

Soviet Natural Gas Development to Nineteen Ninety: The Implications for the CMEA & the West. Jonathan P. Stern. LC 79-2705. 208p. 1980. 21.95x (ISBN 0-669-03233-6). Lexington Bks.

Soviet Naval Developments: Capability & Context. Ed. by Michael McCGwire. LC 73-9058. (Special Studies). (Illus.). 576p. 1973. text ed. 35.00 (ISBN 0-275-07590-7). Praeger.

Soviet Naval Diplomacy. rev. ed. Newton B. Dismukes, Jr. & James M. McConnall. (Pergamon Policy Studies). (Illus.). 450p. 1979. 39.00 (ISBN 0-08-023906-4); pap. 11.25 (ISBN 0-08-023905-6). Pergamon.

Soviet Naval Influence: Domestic & Foreign Dimensions. Ed. by Michael McCgwire & John McDonnell. LC 75-23982. (Special Studies). 1977. text ed. 52.50 (ISBN 0-275-56290-5). Praeger.

Soviet Naval Policy: Objectives & Constraints. Ed. by Michael McCGwire et al. LC 74-11923. (Illus.). 350p. 1975. 45.00 (ISBN 0-275-09720-X). Praeger.

Soviet Navy, Nineteen Fourty-One to Nineteen Seventy Eight: A Guide to Sources in English. Myron J. Smith, Jr. LC 79-26542. (War-Peace Bibliography Ser.: No. 9). 211p. 1980. text ed. 23.75 (ISBN 0-87436-265-2). ABC-Clio.

Soviet Novel: History As Ritual. Katerina Clark. LC 80-18758. 1981. lib. bdg. 20.00x (ISBN 0-226-10766-3). U of Chicago Pr.

Soviet Paradigm. R. D. Laird. LC 75-122278. 1970. text ed. 9.95 o.s.i. (ISBN 0-02-917750-2). Free Pr.

Soviet Partisans in World War Two. Ed. by John A. Armstrong. (Illus.). 1964. 45.00x (ISBN 0-299-03060-1). U of Wis Pr.

Soviet Penal Policy. Ivo Lapenna. (Background Ser.). 1968. 6.25 (ISBN 0-8023-1196-2). Dufour.

Soviet Perceptions of the United States. Morton Schwartz. 1978. 15.95x (ISBN 0-520-03234-9). U of Cal Pr.

Soviet Planning Today, Proposals for an Optimally Functioning Economic System. Michael Ellman. LC 72-145613. (Department of Applied Economics, Occasional Papers: No. 25). (Illus.). 1971. 23.95 (ISBN 0-521-08156-4); pap. 10.95x (ISBN 0-521-09648-0). Cambridge U Pr.

Soviet Policy in Developing Countries. Ed. by W. Raymond Duncan. LC 78-20847. 368p. 1981. Repr. of 1970 ed. lib. bdg. 12.50 (ISBN 0-88275-846-2). Krieger.

Soviet Policy in the Arc of Crisis. Fred Halliday. 90p. 1981. pap. 4.95 (ISBN 0-89758-028-1). Inst Policy Stud.

Soviet Policy in the Third World. W. Raymond Duncan. (Policy Studies). 1980. 35.00 (ISBN 0-08-025125-0). Pergamon.

Soviet Policy Toward the Middle East Since 1970. rev ed. Robert O. Freedman. LC 78-19457. 1978. 28.95 (ISBN 0-03-046601-6); student ed. 10.95 (ISBN 0-03-046606-7). Praeger.

Soviet Policy Towards Pakistan & Bangladesh. J. P. Jain. LC 74-903227. 1974. 15.00x o.p. (ISBN 0-88386-482-7). South Asia Bks.

Soviet Political & Military Conduct in the Middle East. Amnon Sella. 1980. write for info. (ISBN 0-312-74845-0). St Martin.

Soviet Political Indoctrination: Developments in Mass Media & Propaganda Since Stalin. Gayle D. Hollander. LC 70-163927. (Special Studies in International Politics & Government). 1972. 27.00x (ISBN 0-275-28202-3). Irvington.

Soviet Politics & Society in the 1970's. Henry W. Morton & Rudolf L. Tokes. LC 73-10575. (Illus.). 1974. 17.95 (ISBN 0-02-922090-4). Free Pr.

Soviet Politics in the Brezhnev Era. Ed. by Donald R. Kelley. LC 79-24741. (Praeger Special Studies). 282p. 1980. 22.95 (ISBN 0-03-046626-1); pap. 9.95 student edition (ISBN 0-03-046621-0). Praeger.

Soviet Politics: Political Science & Reform. Ronald Hill. LC 79-55751. 256p. 1980. lib. bdg. 27.50 (ISBN 0-87332-156-1). M E Sharpe.

Soviet Population Policy: Conflicts & Constraints. Ed. by Helen Desfosses. (Pergamon Policy Studies). 150p. Date not set. 19.51 (ISBN 0-08-025976-6). Pergamon.

Soviet Prefects: The Local Party Organs in Industrial Decision-Making. Jerry F. Hough. LC 69-18033. (Russian Research Center Studies: No. 58). 1969. 18.50x (ISBN 0-674-82785-6). Harvard U Pr.

Soviet Presence in Latin America. James D. Theberge. LC 74-82929. 1974. pap. 2.95x (ISBN 0-8448-0514-9). Crane-Russak Co.

Soviet Prison Camp Speech: A Survivor's Glossary. Ed. by Meyer Galler & Harlan E. Marquess. LC 75-176411. 216p. 1972. 19.50x (ISBN 0-299-06080-2). U of Wis Pr.

Soviet Procuracy Protests: 1937-1973. Ed. by L. Boim & G. G. Morgan. (Law in Eastern Europe Ser.: No. 21). 324p. 1978. 95.00x (ISBN 90-286-0138-4). Sijthoff & Noordhoff.

Soviet Psychotherapy. Wolf Lauterbach. Date not set. 24.01 (ISBN 0-08-024291-X). Pergamon.

Soviet Quest for Economic Efficiency: Issues, Controversies, & Reforms. George R. Feiwel. LC 72-145952. (Special Studies in International Economics & Development). 1972. 39.50x (ISBN 0-89197-944-1); pap. text ed. 12.95x (ISBN 0-89197-945-X). Irvington.

Soviet Regime in Czechoslovakia. Zdenek Krystufek. (East European Monographs: No. 81). 320p. 1981. text ed. 21.00x (ISBN 0-914710-75-3). East Eur Quarterly.

Soviet Regional Policy: A Quantitative Inquiry into the Social & Political Development of the Soviet Republics. Jan-Ake Dellenbrant. 208p. 1980. text ed. 30.00x (ISBN 0-391-01797-7). Humanities.

Soviet River. Leonid M. Leonov. Tr. by Ivor Montagu & Sergei Nalbandov. LC 72-90298. (Soviet Literature in English Translation Ser.). 383p. 1981. Repr. 21.50 (ISBN 0-88355-009-1). Hyperion Conn.

Soviet Russian Literature Since Stalin. D. Brown. LC 77-73275. 1978. 36.00 (ISBN 0-521-21694-X); pap. 9.95 (ISBN 0-521-29649-8). Cambridge U Pr.

Soviet Russian Literature: Writers & Problems, 1917-1977. 2nd ed. Marc Slonim. 1977. pap. 7.95 (ISBN 0-19-502152-5, GB184, GB). Oxford U Pr.

Soviet Russia's Foreign Policy, 1939-42. David J. Dallin. 1942. 42.50x (ISBN 0-685-88556-9). Elliots Bks.

Soviet Scientific Review: Biology Review, Vol. 2, Section D. Ed. by V. P. Skulachev. 1981. write for info. (ISBN 3-7186-0058-7). Harwood Academic.

Soviet Scientific Review: Chemistry Review, Vol. 3, Section B. Ed. by M. E. Vol'Pin. 1981. write for info. (ISBN 3-7186-0057-9). Harwood Academic.

Soviet Scientific Reviews: Biology Reviews, Vol. 1, Section D. Ed. by V. P. Skulachev. 476p. 1980. lib. bdg. 79.50 (ISBN 0-686-60585-3). Harwood Academic.

Soviet Scientific Reviews: Biology Reviews, Vol. 2, Section D. Ed. by V. P. Skulachev. 1981. write for info. (ISBN 3-7186-0058-7). Harwood Academic.

Soviet Scientific Reviews: Chemistry Reviews, Vol. 3, Section B. Ed. by M. E. Vol'Pin. 1981. price not set (ISBN 3-7186-0057-9). Harwood Academic.

Soviet Scientific Reviews: Physics Reviews, Vol. 1, Section A. Ed. by I. M. Khalatnikov. 322p. 1979. lib. bdg. 67.75 (ISBN 3-7186-0004-8). Harwood Academic.

Soviet Scientific Reviews: Physics Reviews, Vol. 2, Section A. Ed. by I. M. Khalatnikov. 400p. 1980. lib. bdg. 98.00 (ISBN 0-686-65836-1). Harwood Academic.

Soviet Scientific Reviews: Section E, Astrophysics & Space Physics Reviews, Vol. 1, Section E. Ed. by R. Sunyaev. 250p. 1981. 50.00 (ISBN 3-7186-0021-8). Harwood Academic.

Soviet Scientific Reviews 011section B: Chemistry Reviews, Vol.2. Ed. by M. Vol'Pin. (Soviet Scientific Reviews). 480p. 1980. 90.00 (ISBN 3-7186-0018-8). Harwood Academic.

Soviet Secret Services. Otto Heilbrunn. LC 80-27994. 216p. 1981. Repr. of 1956 ed. lib. bdg. 21.75x (ISBN 0-313-22892-2, HESSE). Greenwood.

Soviet Socialized Medicine. Mark G. Field. LC 67-10148. 1967. 9.95 o.s.i. (ISBN 0-02-910130-1). Free Pr.

Soviet Sociology, 1964-75: A Bibliography. Mervyn Matthews. LC 77-83454. (Praeger Special Studies). 1978. 37.95 (ISBN 0-03-022346-6). Praeger.

Soviet Soldier: Soviet Military Management at the Troop Level. Herbert Goldhamer. LC 74-26727. 1975. 22.50x (ISBN 0-8448-0615-3); pap. 8.75x (ISBN 0-8448-0652-8). Crane-Russak Co.

Soviet Sources of Military Doctrine & Strategy. William F. Scott. LC 75-18537. 64p. 1975. 6.50x (ISBN 0-8448-0709-5); pap. 2.75x (ISBN 0-8448-0710-9). Crane-Russak Co.

Soviet South Asian Relations Nineteen Fourty-Seven to Nineteen Seventy-Eight: The Kashmir Question 1952-1964, 2 vols. R. K. Jain. Incl. Vol. 1. The Kutch Conflict Indo-Pak Conflict of 1965 Bangladesh Crisis & Indo-Pak War of 1971 India; Vol. 2. Pakistan, Bangladesh, Nepal. 1979. Set. 55.00x set (ISBN 0-391-00974-5). Humanities.

Soviet State. 2nd ed. Ellsworth Raymond. LC 76-46138. 462p. 1978. 18.00x (ISBN 0-8147-7370-2). NYU Pr.

Soviet Strategic Initiatives: Challenge & Response. C. J. Jacobsen. LC 79-89850. 183p. 1979. 22.95 (ISBN 0-03-053216-7). Praeger.

Soviet Strategy for Nuclear War. Joseph D. Douglass, Jr & Amoretta M. Hoeber. Ed. by Richard F. Staar. LC 79-1787. (Publications 208 Ser.). 1979. pap. 5.95 (ISBN 0-8179-7082-7). Hoover Inst Pr.

Soviet Strategy in Europe. Ed. by Richard Pipes. LC 76-1555. 1976. 19.50x (ISBN 0-8448-0854-7). Crane-Russak Co.

Soviet Succession: Leadership in Transition. Dimitri K. Simes et al. LC 78-62798. (Sage Policy Paper Ser.: Vol. 59). 80p. 1978. pap. 3.50 (ISBN 0-8039-1124-6). Sage.

Soviet Threat: Myths & Realities. Ed. by Grayson Kirk & Nils Wessell. LC 78-56914. 1978. 22.95 (ISBN 0-03-046591-5). Praeger.

Soviet-Type Economic Systems: A Guide to Information Sources. Z. Edward O'Relley. LC 73-17583. (Economics Information Guide Ser.: Vol. 12). 1978. 30.00 (ISBN 0-8103-1306-5). Gale.

Soviet-Type Economies: Performance & Evolution. 3rd ed. Robert W. Campbell. 272p. 1974. pap. text ed. 9.95 (ISBN 0-395-17231-4). HM.

Soviet Union. Ed. by R. W. Davies. (Illus.). 1978. text ed. 16.50x (ISBN 0-04-947022-1); pap. text ed. 8.95x (ISBN 0-04-947023-X). Allen Unwin.

Soviet Union. George Morey. LC 75-44865. (Macdonald Countries). (Illus.). (gr. 6 up). 1976. PLB 7.95 (ISBN 0-382-06103-9, Pub. by Macdonald Ed). Silver.

Soviet Union. Dev Murarka. (Nations & Peoples Library). 1971. 8.50x o.s.i. (ISBN 0-8027-2123-0). Walker & Co.

Soviet Union. 2nd rev. ed. Louis L. Snyder. LC 78-4842. (First Bks.). (Illus.). (gr. 5 up). 1978. PLB 6.45 s&l (ISBN 0-531-02230-7). Watts.

Soviet Union: An Economic Geography. R. S. Mathieson. (Illus.). 342p. 1975. 20.00x (ISBN 0-06-494647-9). B&N.

Soviet Union & Ballistic Missile Defense. Jacquelyn K. Davis et al. LC 79-3298. (Special Reports). 50p. 1980. 6.50 (ISBN 0-89549-021-8). Inst Foreign Policy Anal.

Soviet Union & Ballistic Missile Defense. 71p. 1980. pap. 6.50 (ISBN 0-686-63452-7, IFPA 11, IFPA). Unipub.

Soviet Union & International Oil Politics. Arthur J. Klinghoffer. LC 76-52411. 1977. 22.50x (ISBN 0-231-04104-7). Columbia U Pr.

Soviet Union & Postwar Japan: Escalating Challenge & Response. Rodger Swearingen. LC 78-59866. (Publications Ser.: No. 197). 1978. 14.95 (ISBN 0-8179-6971-3). Hoover Inst Pr.

Soviet Union & SALT. Samuel B. Payne, Jr. 224p. 1980. text ed. 19.95x (ISBN 0-262-16077-3). MIT Pr.

Soviet Union & the Emerging Nations: A Case Study of Soviet Policy Towards India. Harish Kapur. 120p. (Orig.). 1972. pap. text ed. 12.00x (ISBN 0-391-00240-6). Humanities.

Soviet Union & the Palestinian Liberation Organization: Uneasy Alliance. Galia Golan. LC 80-18760. 304p. 1980. 24.95 (ISBN 0-03-057319-X). Praeger.

Soviet Union As a Criminal System. Zaida Stolear. 1981. 7.95 (ISBN 0-533-04601-7). Vantage.

Soviet Union: Figures - Facts - Data. Borys Lewytzki. 614p. 1979. 85.00 (ISBN 0-89664-010-8, Pub. by K G Saur). Gale.

Soviet Union in the Third World: Success & Failures. Ed. by Robert H. Donaldson. (Westview Special Studies in International Relations). 350p. 1980. lib. bdg. 25.00x (ISBN 0-89158-974-0); pap. text ed. 12.00 (ISBN 0-86531-147-1). Westview.

Soviet Union: Looking to the 1980s. Ed. by Robert Wesson. (Special Project Ser.). 298p. 1980. 25.00 (ISBN 0-8179-4251-3). Hoover Inst Pr.

Soviet Union, Nineteen Seventy-Eight to Nineteen Seventy-Nine. Bundesinstitut Fur Ostwissenschaftliche und Internationale Studien. (Soviet Union Ser.: Vol. 5). 220p. 1980. text ed. 29.50x (ISBN 0-8419-0632-7). Holmes & Meier.

Soviet Union Since Stalin. Ed. by Stephen F. Cohen et al. LC 79-3092. 352p. 1980. 22.50x (ISBN 0-253-32272-3); pap. 7.95x (ISBN 0-253-20236-1). Ind U Pr.

Soviet Union Since the Fall of Khrushchev. Ed. by Archie Brown & Michael Kaser. LC 75-39856. 1976. 17.95 (ISBN 0-02-904870-2). Free Pr.

Soviet Union: The Fifty Years. Ed. by Harrison E. Salisbury. LC 67-26001. (New York Times Bk). (Illus.). 1967. 10.00 o.p. (ISBN 0-15-184605-7). HarBraceJ.

Soviet Urban Management: With Comparisons to the United States. Carol Lewis & Stephen Sternheimer. LC 78-19748. (Praeger Special Studies). 1979. 28.95 (ISBN 0-03-046136-7). Praeger.

Soviet View of War, Peace & Neutrality. P. H. Vigor. 1975. 22.00 (ISBN 0-7100-8143-X). Routledge & Kegan.

Soviet Warships of the Second World War. Jurg Meister. LC 76-28690. (Illus.). 1977. 19.95 o.p. (ISBN 0-668-04086-6). Arco.

Soviet Women. William M. Mandel. LC 74-12732. 360p. 1975. pap. 3.50 o.p. (ISBN 0-385-03255-2, Anch). Doubleday.

Soviet Worker: Illusion & Realities. Ed. by Leonard Schapiro & Joseph Godson. Date not set. price not set (ISBN 0-312-74923-6). St Martin.

Sower. Mandeville. (Ladybird Ser.). 1979. 1.49 (ISBN 0-87508-865-1). Chr Lit.

Sower Goes Forth. James D. Bales. 4.50 (ISBN 0-89315-259-5). Lambert Bk.

Soweto I Love. Sipho Sepamla. (Orig.). 1977. pap. 5.00 (ISBN 0-686-64551-0). Three Continents.

Soybean. Charles V. Piper & W. J. Morse. (Illus.). 8.00 (ISBN 0-8446-1350-9). Peter Smith.

Soybean Physiology, Agronomy, & Utilization. Ed. by Geoffrey A. Norman. 1978. 30.50 (ISBN 0-12-521160-0). Acad Pr.

Soybeans: Chemistry & Technology; Vol. 1, Proteins. 2nd ed. Allan K. Smith & Sydney Circle. 1978. text ed. 35.50 (ISBN 0-87055-262-7). AVI.

Space. Anthony Feldman. 336p. 1980. 19.95 (ISBN 0-87196-416-3). Facts on File.

Space. Susan Harris. (Easy-Read Fact Bks.). (Illus.). (gr. 2-4). 1979. PLB 6.45 s&l (ISBN 0-531-02852-6). Watts.

Space. James A. Seevers. LC 77-18976. (Read About Science Ser.). (Illus.). (gr. k-3). 1978. PLB 9.95 (ISBN 0-8393-0076-X). Raintree Child.

Space Adventures Reading Series Sampler. Delia Broad. 1980. pap. 19.95 (ISBN 0-88450-723-8, 4520-B). Communication Skill.

Space & Development: Proceedings of Vikram Sarabhi Symposium of the Twenty-Second Plenary Meeting of the Committee on Space Research, Bangalore, India, 29 May--9 June 1979. Ed. by Yash Pal. LC 79-41358. (Illus.). 100p. 1980. 21.00 (ISBN 0-08-024441-6). Pergamon.

Space & Illusion in the Japanese Garden. Teiji Itoh. (Illus.). 232p. 1980. pap. 9.95 (ISBN 0-8348-1522-2, Pub. by John Weatherhill Inc Japan). C E Tuttle.

Space & Place: The Perspective of Experience. Yi-Fu Tuan. (Illus., LC 77-072910). 1977. 8.95x (ISBN 0-8166-0808-3); pap. 6.95 (ISBN 0-8166-0884-9). U of Minn Pr.

Space & Storage. (Home Repair & Improvement Ser.). (Illus.). 1976. 10.95 (ISBN 0-8094-2350-2). Time-Life.

Space & Storage. Ed. by Time Life Books. LC 75-34852. (Home Repair & Improvement). (Illus.). (gr. 7 up). 1976. PLB 11.97 (ISBN 0-8094-2351-0, Pub. by Time-Life). Silver.

Space & Time in the Modern Universe. P. W. Davies. LC 76-27902. (Illus.). 1977. 28.95 (ISBN 0-521-21445-9); pap. 9.95 (ISBN 0-521-29151-8). Cambridge U Pr.

Space Apprentice. Arkady Strugatsky & Boris Strugatsky. (Best of Soviet Science Fiction Ser.). 141p. 1981. 10.95 (ISBN 0-02-615220-7). Macmillan.

Space Art. R. Miller. 1978. pap. 8.95 (ISBN 0-931064-04-X). Starlog Pr.

Space Art. Ron Miller. Ed. by Jon-Michael Reed. (gr. 3 up). 1978. pap. 13.00 slip case (ISBN 0-931064-06-6); pap. 8.95 (ISBN 0-931064-04-X). Starlog.

Space Art Poster Book. Compiled by Ron Miller. (Illus.). 48p. (Orig.). 1979. pap. 10.95 (ISBN 0-8117-2077-2). Stackpole.

Space Atlas, No. 1447. U. S. Naval Institute. (Illus.). 1979. pap. 2.95 (ISBN 0-8416-1447-4). Am Map.

Space Cats. Steven Kroll. (Illus.). (gr. 1-4). 1981. pap. 1.95 (ISBN 0-380-53371-5, 53371, Camelot). Avon.

Space Colonization: An Annotated Bibliography. Michael Marotta. 1979. pap. 4.00 o.p. (ISBN 0-686-23957-1). Loompanics.

Space Doctor. Lee Corey. 256p. (Orig.). 1981. pap. 2.50 (ISBN 0-345-29263-4, Del Rey). Ballantine.

Space Exploration. Boy Scouts Of America. LC 19-600. (Illus.). 64p. (gr. 6-12). 1966. pap. 0.70x (ISBN 0-8395-3354-3, 3354). BSA.

Space Geology: An Introduction. Elbert A. King. LC 75-45357. 400p. 1976. text ed. 31.95 (ISBN 0-471-47810-5). Wiley.

Space-Gods Revealed. Ronald Story. 160p. 1980. pap. 3.95 (ISBN 0-06-464040-X, BN 4040). Har-Row.

Space Hostages. Nicholas Fisk. LC 69-12743. (gr. 5-8). 1969. 3.95g o.s.i. (ISBN 0-02-735280-3). Macmillan.

Space Lords. Cordwainer Smith. 1979. pap. 1.75 (ISBN 0-515-05122-5). Jove Pubns.

Space Machines. Larry A. Ciupik & James A. Seevers. LC 78-26991. (Machine World Ser.). (Illus.). (gr. 2-4). 1979. PLB 9.95 (ISBN 0-8172-1325-2). Raintree Pubs.

Space Mathematics, 3 vols. American Mathematical Society. Ed. by J. B. Rosser. Incl. Pt.1. (Vol. 5). 1979. 28.40 (ISBN 0-8218-1105-3, LAM-5); Pt. 2. (Vol. 6). 1974. Repr. of 1966 ed. 18.00 (ISBN 0-8218-1106-1, LAM-6); Pt. 3. (Vol. 7). 1966. 18.80 (ISBN 0-8218-1107-X, LAM-7). LC 66-20435. (Lectures in Applied Mathematics Ser). Am Math.

Space Merchants. 2nd ed. Frederik Pohl. 224p. 1981. pap. 1.50 (ISBN 0-345-29697-4). Ballantine.

Space Monster. Dave Ross. (Illus.). 32p. (gr. 2-5). 1981. PLB 6.85 (ISBN 0-8027-6415-0). Walker & Co.

Space Monsters: From Movies, TV & Books. Seymour Simon. LC 77-3566. (gr. 4 up). 1977. 7.95 (ISBN 0-397-31765-4); pap. 2.95 o.p. (ISBN 0-397-31766-2). Lippincott.

Space My Body Fills. Etta Blum. LC 80-26565. 68p. (Orig.). 1980. pap. 4.95 (ISBN 0-913270-93-8). Sunstone Pr.

Space Odysseys. Ed. by Brian Aldiss. 1978. pap. 1.95 o.p. (ISBN 0-425-03681-2, Medallion). Berkley Pub.

Space Operational Analysis. Manuel Marti, Jr. LC 80-81340. (Illus.). 216p. 1981. 19.95 (ISBN 0-914886-11-8). PDA Pubs.

Space Optics: Proceedings. International Commission on Optics International Congress, 9th. Ed. by B. J. Thompson & R. R. Shannon. (Illus.). 849p. 1974. 37.50 (ISBN 0-309-02144-8). Natl Acad Pr.

Space Patrol III. Frances Linke. Ed. by Ray Linke. (Illus.). 205p. 1980. 25.00 (ISBN 0-933276-07-9). Nin-Ra Ent.

Space Patrol III. Frances Linke. (Space Patrol Ser.: No. 3). 205p. 20.00 (ISBN 0-933276-06-0). Nin-Ra Ent.

Space People. Eve Bunting. (Science Fiction Ser.). (Illus.). (gr. 3-9). 1978. PLB 5.95 (ISBN 0-87191-623-1); pap. 2.95 (ISBN 0-89812-053-5). Creative Ed.

Space Physics: The Study of Plasmas in Space. R. L. Boyd. (Oxford Physics Ser). (Illus.). 112p. 1975. text ed. 15.50x (ISBN 0-19-851807-2). Oxford U Pr.

Space Power Systems. Ed. by Nathan W. Snyder. (Progress in Astronautics & Aeronautics Ser.: Vol. 4). (Illus.). 1961. 20.00 o.p. (ISBN 0-12-535104-6). Acad Pr.

Space Puzzles: Curious Questions & Answers About the Solar System. Martin Gardner. (Illus.). (YA) (gr. 7-9). 1972. pap. 1.25 (ISBN 0-671-29838-0). PB.

Space Research, Vols. 13-19. Ed. by Michael J. Rycroft. 1977. Vol. 13, 1977. text ed. 96.00 (ISBN 0-08-021787-7); Vol. 14, 1977. text ed. 115.00 (ISBN 0-08-021788-5); Vol. 15, 1977. text ed. 96.00 (ISBN 0-08-021789-3); Vol. 16, 1977. text ed. 96.00 (ISBN 0-08-021795-8); Vol. 17, 1977. text ed. 96.00 (ISBN 0-08-021636-6); Vol. 18, 1978. text ed. 115.00 (ISBN 0-08-022021-5); Vol. 19, 1979. text ed. 115.00 (ISBN 0-08-023417-8). Pergamon.

Space Research: Directions for the Future. Space Science Board. 1966. pap. 8.75 o.p. (ISBN 0-309-01403-4). Natl Acad Pr.

Space Research, Vol. 20: Proceedings of the Open Meetings of the Working Groups on Physical Sciences of the Twenty-Second Plenary Meeting of the Committee on Space Research, Bangalore, India, 29 May--9 June 1979. M. J. Rycroft. LC 79-41359. (Illus.). 294p. 1980. 58.00 (ISBN 0-08-024437-8). Pergamon.

Space Science Comes of Age: Perspectives in the History of the Space Sciences. Ed. by Paul A. Hanle & Von Del Chamberlain. (Illus.). 220p. 1981. 25.00 (ISBN 0-87474-508-X); pap. 12.50 (ISBN 0-87474-507-1). Smithsonian.

Space Ship in the Park. Louis Slobodkin. LC 70-187799. (Illus.). (gr. 3-7). 1972. 7.95 (ISBN 0-02-784700-4). Macmillan.

Space Ship Under the Apple Tree. Louis Slobodkin. (gr. k-3). 1952. 7.95g (ISBN 0-02-785340-3). Macmillan.

Space Shuttle & Spacelab Utilization: Near-Term & Long-Term Benefits for Mankind, Pt. II. Ed. by G. W. Morgenthaler & M. Hollstein. LC 57-43769. (Advances in the Astronautical Sciences: Vol. 37, Pt. II). 1978. lib. bdg. 45.00 (ISBN 0-87703-097-9). Univelt Inc.

Space Shuttle Coloring Book. Richard Wagner. (Coloring Experience Ser). (Illus., Orig.). (gr. k-6). 1979. pap. 2.95 o.p. (ISBN 0-8431-0651-4). Price Stern.

Space Station Eight. Carlton C. Allen. 1978. 7.95 o.p. (ISBN 0-533-03076-5). Vantage.

Space Technology & Earth Problems. Ed. by C. Quentin Ford. (Science & Technology Ser.: Vol. 23). (Illus.). 1970. lib. bdg. 35.00 (ISBN 0-87703-051-0); microfiche suppl. 20.00 (ISBN 0-87703-134-7). Am Astronaut.

Space Technology Spinoffs. Gene Gurney. (Impact Ser.). (Illus.). (gr. 7 up). 1979. PLB 6.90 s&l (ISBN 0-531-02290-0). Watts.

Space: The Scrapbook of My Divorce. Jan Fuller. 176p. 1975. pap. 1.50 o.p. (ISBN 0-449-22450-3, Q2450-150, Crest). Fawcett.

Space, Time, & Freedom. Major L. Wilson. LC 74-287. 309p. 1974. lib. bdg. 17.50x (ISBN 0-8371-7373-6, WIT/). Greenwood.

Space, Time & Gravitation. Arthur S. Eddington. 26.50 (ISBN 0-521-04865-6). Cambridge U Pr.

Space, Time, & Gravity. Robert M. Wald. LC 77-4038. viii, 132p. 1981. pap. 3.95 (ISBN 0-226-87031-6). U of Chicago Pr.

Space, Time & Gravity: The Theory of the Big Bang & Black Holes. Robert M. Wald. LC 77-4038. (Illus.). 1977. 10.95 (ISBN 0-226-87030-8); pap. 3.95 (ISBN 0-226-87031-6). U of Chicago Pr.

Space-Time & Microphysics: A New Synthesis. Enos E. Witmer. LC 79-66152. 1979. pap. text ed. 9.00 (ISBN 0-8191-0794-8). U Pr of Amer.

Space, Time, & Motion: A Philosophical Introduction. 2nd rev. ed. Wesley C. Salmon. LC 80-18423. (Illus.). 160p. 1981. pap. 8.95x (ISBN 0-8166-1004-5). U of Minn Pr.

Space, Time, & Spacetime. Lawrence Sklar. 1977. pap. 7.75x (ISBN 0-520-03174-1, CAMPUS164). U of Cal Pr.

Space, Time & Structure in the Modern Novel. Sharon Spencer. LC 76-142375. 251p. 1971. pap. 5.95x (ISBN 0-8040-0334-3). Swallow.

Space, Time, Energy, Matter: STEM - Student & Teacher's Editions. Verne N. Rockcastle et al. Incl. Bks. 1-6. Teacher's Guides, 6 bks. 2nd rev. ed. 1975. pap. o.p. Bk. 1. tchr's ed. gr. 1 o.p. (ISBN 0-201-05344-6); Bk. 2. tchr's ed. gr. 2 o.p. (ISBN 0-201-05345-4); Bk. 3. tchr's ed. gr. 3 o.p. (ISBN 0-201-05346-2); Bk. 4. tchr's ed. gr. 4 o.p. (ISBN 0-201-05347-0); Bk. 5. tchr's ed. gr. 5 o.p. (ISBN 0-201-05348-9); Bk. 6. tchr's ed. gr. 6 o.p. (ISBN 0-201-05349-7); Laboratory Record Books. 1976. Bk. 3. pap. text ed. 3.12 gr. 3 o.p. (ISBN 0-201-07591-1); Bk. 3. tchr's ed. 3.56 o.p. (ISBN 0-201-07595-4); Bk. 4. pap. text ed. 3.92 gr. 4 o.p. (ISBN 0-201-07592-X); Bk. 4. tchr's ed. 4.80 o.p. (ISBN 0-201-07596-2); Bk. 5. pap. text ed. 4.72 gr. 5 o.p. (ISBN 0-201-07593-8); Bk. 5. tchr's ed. 5.36 o.p. (ISBN 0-201-07597-0); Bk. 6. pap. text ed. 4.72 gr. 6 o.p. (ISBN 0-201-07594-6); Bk. 6. tchr's ed. 5.36 o.p. (ISBN 0-201-07598-9); Texts. (gr. k-6). 1975. Primer. pap. text ed. 3.60 gr. k o.p. (ISBN 0-201-05280-6); Primer. tchr's ed. 6.92 o.p. (ISBN 0-201-05343-8); text ed. 7.36 gr. 1 o.p. (ISBN 0-201-05281-4); text ed. 7.68 gr. 2 o.p. (ISBN 0-201-05282-2); text ed. 8.20 gr. 3 o.p. (ISBN 0-201-05283-0); text ed. 8.80 gr. 4 o.p. (ISBN 0-201-05284-9); text ed. 10.00 gr. 5 o.p. (ISBN 0-201-05285-7); text ed. 10.00 gr. 6 o.p. (ISBN 0-201-05286-5). (Elementary School Science Ser.). (gr. 1-6, Sch Div). A-W.

Space, Time, Matter. Hermann Weyl. 1922. pap. text ed. 4.50 (ISBN 0-486-60267-2). Dover.

Space-Time Transients & Unusual Events. Michael A. Persinger & Gyslaine F. Lafreniere. LC 76-12634. 224p. 1977. 13.95 (ISBN 0-88229-334-6); pap. 7.95 (ISBN 0-88229-462-8). Nelson-Hall.

Space Travel in Fact & Fiction. Keith Deutsch. (gr. 5 up). 1980. PLB 7.90 (ISBN 0-686-65170-7). Watts.

Space Trip. Carol L. Guest. 48p. 1981. 5.95 (ISBN 0-89962-047-7). Todd & Honeywell.

Space Two: A New Collection of Science Fiction Stories. Richard Davis. 140p. 1975. 8.95 (ISBN 0-200-72275-1). Transatlantic.

Space War Blues. Richard A. Lupoff. 1978. pap. 1.95 o.s.i. (ISBN 0-440-16292-0). Dell.

Space Wars. Joseph Coleman. (Pal Paperbacks, - Pal Skills II Ser.). (Illus.). (gr. 5-12). 1980. pap. text ed. 1.25 (ISBN 0-8374-6809-4). Xerox Ed Pubns.

Space Wars. Rosalynne H. Gillespy. LC 78-730966. 1978. pap. text ed. 175.00 (ISBN 0-89290-111-X, CM-31). Soc for Visual.

Space Witch. Don Freeman. (Illus.). (gr. k-3). 1959. PLB 7.95 (ISBN 0-670-65995-9). Viking Pr.

Spacebread. Steve Senn. LC 80-18326. 224p. (gr. 7 up). 1981. PLB 9.95 (ISBN 0-689-30830-2, Argo). Atheneum.

Spacecraft at Work. Mary Elting. LC 66-10936. (At Work Ser). (Illus.). (gr. 3-6). 1966. PLB 5.39 (ISBN 0-8178-3632-2). Harvey.

Spacecraft Attitude Determination & Control. Ed. by James R. Werz. (Astrophysics & Space Science Library: No. 73). 858p. 1980. PLB 52.00 (ISBN 90-277-0959-9, Pub. by D. Reidel); pap. 28.95 (ISBN 90-277-1204-2). Kluwer Boston.

Spacecraft in Geographic Research. Conference On The Use Of Orbiting Spacecraft In Geographic Research - Houston - Tex 1965. 1966. pap. 4.00 o.p. (ISBN 0-309-01353-4). Natl Acad Pr.

Spacefight Revolution: A Sociological Study. William S. Bainbridge. LC 76-21349. (Science, Culture, & Society Ser.). 1976. 27.50 (ISBN 0-471-04306-0, Pub. by Wiley-Interscience). Wiley.

Spacehounds of IPC. E. E. Smith. 1974. pap. 1.50 o.s.i. (ISBN 0-515-03300-6, N3300). Jove Pubns.

Spaces by a Spaceman. John Schatz. LC 79-91038. (Illus., Orig.). 1979. pap. 4.65 (ISBN 0-9603546-0-3). Spaceman Pr.

Spaces for People: Human Factors in Design. Bennett. LC 76-30847. 1977. pap. 4.95 (ISBN 0-13-823955-X, Spec). P-H.

Spaces with Non-Symmetric Distance. E. M. Zaustinsky. LC 52-42839. (Memoirs: No. 34). 1978. pap. 5.20 (ISBN 0-8218-1234-3, MEMO-34). Am Math.

Spaceship Earth. Barbara Ward. LC 66-18062. (George B Pegram Ser). 1966. 15.00x (ISBN 0-231-02951-9); pap. 5.00x (ISBN 0-231-08586-9). Columbia U Pr.

Spaceships. H. Zimmerman. 1980. pap. 7.95 (ISBN 0-931064-23-6). Starlog Pr.

Spaceships. enl. ed. Howard Zimmerman. 1980. pap. 7.95 (ISBN 0-931064-23-6). O'Quinn Studio.

Spaceships. Ed. by Howard Zimmerman. (Illus.). (gr. 3 up). 1977. pap. 2.95 (ISBN 0-931064-00-7). Starlog.

Spacestone. Theodore L. Harris et al. (Keys to Reading Ser.). (gr. 6). 1974. pap. text ed. 3.60 (ISBN 0-87892-543-0). Economy Co.

Spacetime Physics. Edwin F. Taylor & John A. Wheeler. LC 65-13566. (Physics Ser.). (Illus.). 1966. pap. text ed. 9.95x (ISBN 0-7167-0336-X); answer book avail. W H Freeman.

Spacetrack, Watchdog of the Skies. Charles Coombs. LC 69-14233. (Illus.). (gr. 5-9). 1969. PLB 6.96 (ISBN 0-688-31561-5). Morrow.

Spacewater Blues. Homer Weiner. 1981. 12.95. Sonica Pr.

Spade Coin Types of the Chou Dynasty. Arthur B. Coole. LC 76-86803. (Encyclopedia of Chinese Coins Ser.: Vol. 3). (Illus.). 1973. 35.00x (ISBN 0-88000-011-2). Quarterman.

Spadework in Archaeology. Leonard Woolley. 1953. 4.75 o.p. (ISBN 0-8022-1932-2). Philos Lib.

Spaghetti Westerns: Cowboys & Europeans from Karl May to Sergio Leone. Christopher Frayling. (Cinema & Society Ser.). (Illus.). 352p. 1980. 40.00 (ISBN 0-7100-0503-2); pap. 20.00 (ISBN 0-7100-0504-0). Routledge & Kegan.

Spain. Stephen Clissold. Ed. by Toby Roxburgh. LC 69-11266. (Nations & Peoples Library). 1969. 8.50x o.s.i. (ISBN 0-8027-2116-8). Walker & Co.

Spain. Robert Goldston. (Illus.). (gr. 7 up). 1967. 8.95 (ISBN 0-02-736340-6). Macmillan.

Spain. Robert C. Goldston. LC 72-3717. (First Bks). (Illus.). 72p. (gr. 7-12). 1972. PLB 4.90 o.p. (ISBN 0-531-00781-2). Watts.

Spain. Richard Herr. LC 70-126814. (Modern Nations in Historical Perspective Ser). (Illus.). 1971. pap. 12.95 o.p. (ISBN 0-13-824094-9). P-H.

Spain. Carmen Irizarry. LC 75-44868. (Macdonald Countries). (Illus.). (gr. 6 up). 1976. PLB 7.95 (ISBN 0-382-06100-4, Pub. by Macdonald Ed). Silver.

Spain. Organization for Economic Cooperation & Development. (OECD Economic Surveys, 1980). (Illus.). 62p. (Orig.). 1980. cancelled (ISBN 92-64-12047-5, 1080241). OECD.

Spain: A Brief History. 2nd ed. Pierre Vilar. 1977. text ed. 16.50 (ISBN 0-08-021462-2); pap. text ed. 6.25 (ISBN 0-08-021461-4). Pergamon.

Spain & Morocco on Twenty Dollars a Day, 1981-82. 464p. 1981. pap. 5.95 (ISBN 0-671-41423-2). Frommer-Pasmantier.

Spain & Portugal: Democratic Beginnings. Ed. by Grant S. McClellan. (Reference Shelf Ser.: Vol. 50, No. 5). 1978. 6.25 (ISBN 0-8242-0626-6). Wilson.

Spain in Pictures. Sterling Publishing Company Editors. LC 62-18639. (Visual Geography Ser). (Illus., Orig.). (gr. 6 up). 1962. PLB 4.99 (ISBN 0-8069-1029-1); pap. 2.95 (ISBN 0-8069-1028-3). Sterling.

Spain in the 1970s: Economics, Social Structure, Foreign Policy. Ed. by William T. Salisbury & James D. Theberge. LC 75-19816. (Special Studies). 1976. text ed. 32.95 (ISBN 0-275-55800-2). Praeger.

Spain in Transition: Franco's Regime. Arnold Hottinger. LC 74-21523. (Policy Papers: The Washington Papers, No. 18). 1975. 3.50x (ISBN 0-8039-0204-2). Sage.

Spain in Transition: Prospects & Policies. Arnold Hottinger. LC 74-21523. (Policy Papers: The Washington Papers, No. 19). 1975. 3.50x (ISBN 0-8039-0205-0). Sage.

Spain, the Monarchy & the Atlantic Community. David C. Jordan. LC 79-65887. (Foreign Policy Reports Ser.). 55p. 1979. 5.00 (ISBN 0-89549-010-2). Inst Foreign Policy Anal.

Spain: The Struggle for Democracy Today. Constantine C. Menges. LC 78-62797. (Washington Papers: No. 58). 1978. 3.50x (ISBN 0-8039-1123-8). Sage.

Spain: With Illustrations by the Author. Jan Morris. (Illus.). 1979. 12.95 (ISBN 0-19-520169-8). Oxford U Pr.

Spalding Guide to Fitness for the Weekend Athlete. Gary Rosenthal. 7.95 (ISBN 0-916752-08-9). Green Hill.

Spandau: The Secret Diaries. Albert Speer. 1981. pap. price not set (ISBN 0-671-42447-5). PB.

Spaniards: An Introduction to Their History. Americo Castro. Tr. by Willard F. King & Selma Margaretten. LC 67-14000. 638p. 1980. 32.50x (ISBN 0-520-01617-3); pap. 14.95x (ISBN 0-520-01617-3). U of Cal Pr.

Spaniel Training: For Modern Shooters. Maurice Hopper. (Illus.). 120p. 1974. 14.95 (ISBN 0-7153-6446-4). David & Charles.

Spanish. Holloway Staff. (Harper Phrase Books for the Traveler Ser.). (Orig.). 1977. pap. 1.00 (ISBN 0-8467-0316-5, Pub. by Two Continents). Hippocrene Bks.

Spanish. Alfonso Lowe. 1976. 16.95 o.p. (ISBN 0-86033-006-0). Gordon-Cremonesi.

Spanish. Jack Rudman. (Undergraduate Program Field Test Ser.: UPFT-24). (Cloth bdg. avail. on request). pap. 9.95 (ISBN 0-8373-6024-2). Natl Learning.

Spanish: A Short Course. 2nd ed. Zenia S. Da Silva. (Illus.). 1980. text ed. 16.50 scp (ISBN 0-06-041518-5, HarpC); instr' manual free; scp student wkbk. & tape man. 6.50 (ISBN 0-06-041524-X); scp tapes 250.00 (ISBN 0-06-047492-0). Har-Row.

Spanish-American Frontier, 1783-1795: The Westward Movement & the Spanish Retreat in the Mississippi Valley. Arthur P. Whitaker. LC 27-23368. (Illus.). 1969. pap. 2.95x (ISBN 0-8032-5216-1, BB 398, Bison). U of Nebr Pr.

Spanish American Modernism: A Selected Bibliography. Robert R. Anderson. LC 73-82616. 1970. 2.00 (ISBN 0-8165-0193-9). U of Ariz Pr.

Spanish American Modernista Poets. Ed. by G. Brotherston. LC 68-31793. 1968. 17.00 (ISBN 0-08-012858-0); pap. 8.00 (ISBN 0-08-012857-2). Pergamon.

Spanish American Revolutions, 1808-1862. John Lynch. (Revolutions in the Modern World Ser). (Illus.). 352p. 1973. text ed. 15.00x (ISBN 0-393-05388-1); pap. text ed. 6.95x (ISBN 0-393-09411-1). Norton.

Spanish & English of United States Hispanos: A Critical, Annotated Linguistic Bibliography. Ed. by Richard V. Teschner et al. LC 75-21564. 1975. pap. text ed. 8.95x (ISBN 0-87281-042-9). Ctr Appl Ling.

Spanish Armada. Jay Williams & Lacey B. Smith. LC 66-25994. (Horizon Caravel Bks). (Illus.). 153p. (gr. 5 up). 1966. 9.95 (ISBN 0-8281-0399-2, Dist. by Har-Row); PLB 6.89 o.p. (ISBN 0-06-026541-8). Am Heritage.

Spanish Ballads. Ed. by C. Colin Smith. 1965. 8.75 (ISBN 0-08-010914-4); pap. 6.95 (ISBN 0-08-010913-6). Pergamon.

Spanish Borderlands Frontier, 1513-1821. John F. Bannon. LC 74-110887. (Histories of the American Frontier Series). (Illus.). 308p. 1974. pap. 6.50x (ISBN 0-8263-0309-9). U of NM Pr.

Spanish Caribbean: Trade & Plunder, 1530-1630. K. R. Andrews. LC 77-90944. 1978. 25.00x (ISBN 0-300-02197-6). Yale U Pr.

Spanish Cathedral Music in the Golden Age. Robert Stevenson. LC 76-1013. (Illus.). 523p. 1976. Repr. of 1961 ed. lib. bdg. 39.50x (ISBN 0-8371-8744-3, STSP). Greenwood.

Spanish Central America: A Socioeconomic History, 1520-1720. Murdo J. MacLeod. LC 70-174456. 1973. pap. 8.95x (ISBN 0-520-02632-2). U of Cal Pr.

Spanish Church & the Papacy in the Thirteenth Century. Peter Linehan. LC 75-154505. (Studies in Medieval Life & Thought, Third Ser: No. 4). (Illus.). 1971. 46.95 (ISBN 0-521-08039-8). Cambridge U Pr.

Spanish College at Bologna. Berthe M. Marti. LC 63-15014. 1966. 14.00x o.p. (ISBN 0-8122-7402-4). U of Pa Pr.

Spanish Concise Dictionary. Cassells. 1977. 8.95 (ISBN 0-02-052266-5). Macmillan.

Spanish Dancing. Helen Wingrave & Robert Harrold. (Illus., Orig.). 1978. pap. 2.95 (ISBN 0-8467-0449-8, Pub. by Two Continents). Hippocrene Bks.

Spanish Dictionary. G. H. Calvert. (Routledge Pocket Dictionaries Ser.). 560p. 1980. pap. 7.95 (ISBN 0-7100-0558-X). Routledge & Kegan.

Spanish Drama of the Golden Age. Ed. by Raymond R. MacCurdy. 1979. text ed. 29.50x (ISBN 0-89197-985-9); pap. text ed. 18.95x (ISBN 0-89197-986-7). Irvington.

Spanish-English - English-Spanish Chemical Vocabulary. J. R. Barcelo. vii, 111p. (Orig.). 1980. pap. 7.50 (ISBN 84-205-0696-6). Heinman.

Spanish-English - English-Spanish Medical Guide. Howard H. Hirschhorn. (gr. 11 up). 1968. pap. text ed. 1.95 (ISBN 0-88345-157-3, 17429). Regents Pub.

Spanish-English & English-Spanish Medical Dictionary. 3rd ed. F. Ruiz Torres. 1965. 25.00 o.p. (ISBN 8-4205-0455-6). Heinman.

Spanish-English, English-Spanish Commercial Dictionary. C. R. Orozco. 1969. 21.00 (ISBN 0-08-006381-0); pap. 11.25 (ISBN 0-08-006380-2). Pergamon.

Spanish-English Handbook. G. Howell & J. Perez Y Sabido. 1977. pap. 9.95 (ISBN 0-87489-073-X). Med Economics.

Spanish Explorers in the Southern United States, 1528-1543. Ed. by Frederick W. Hodge & Theodore H. Lewis. (Original Narratives). (Illus.). 1977. Repr. of 1907 ed. 15.00x (ISBN 0-06-480372-4). B&N.

Spanish for Beginners. Charles Duff. (Orig.). 1958. pap. 3.95 (ISBN 0-06-463271-7, EH 271, EH). Har-Row.

Spanish for Careers: Conversational Perspectives. Frank Sedwick. (Orig.). 1980. pap. text ed. 8.95 (ISBN 0-442-20562-7). D Van Nostrand.

Spanish for Conversation. 4th ed. John K. Leslie. LC 75-3774. 1976. text ed. 17.95 (ISBN 0-471-52810-2); instructor's manual avail. (ISBN 0-471-01417-6); wkbk avail (ISBN 0-471-52811-0); tapes avail. (ISBN 0-471-01841-4). Wiley.

Spanish for Hospital Personnel. Josephine Carrenno & Diane Larson. 1974. spiral bdg. 3.50 (ISBN 0-87488-722-4). Med Exam.

Spanish for Teachers: Applied Linguistics. William E. Bull. 1965. 14.95 (ISBN 0-8260-1505-0). Wiley.

Spanish for the Professions. Jorge A. Santana. 256p. 1981. pap. text ed. 7.95 (ISBN 0-394-32652-0). Random.

Spanish for Urban Workers. G. Flynn. LC 72-78445. 1975. pap. 7.95x o.p. (ISBN 0-87108-186-5). Pruett.

Spanish Forger. William Voelkle. LC 78-60193. (Illus.). 77p. 1978. 35.00 (ISBN 0-87598-065-1); pap. 19.50 (ISBN 0-87598-054-6). Pierpont Morgan.

Spanish Glossary of the Petroleum Industry. 316p. 1974. 14.00 (ISBN 0-87814-051-4). Pennwell Pub.

Spanish Golden Age. Joseph L. Laurenti & A. Poqueras-Mayo. (Reference Books). 1979. lib. bdg. 45.00 (ISBN 0-8161-8286-8). G K Hall.

Spanish Grammar. 4th ed. Eric V. Greenfield. (Orig.). 1972. pap. 3.95 (ISBN 0-06-460042-4, CO 42, COS). Har-Row.

Spanish House. Nancy John. 192p. (Orig.). 1980. pap. 1.50 (ISBN 0-671-57034-X). S&S.

Spanish in Context: A Basic Course. C. Dixon Anderson. (Illus.). 1978. text ed. 16.95 (ISBN 0-13-824235-6); pap. 7.95 student wkbk (ISBN 0-13-824243-7). P-H.

Spanish in Review. John B. Dalbor & H. Tracy Sturcken. LC 78-27055. 1979. pap. text ed. 12.95x (ISBN 0-471-03991-8); tchrs. manual (ISBN 0-471-04191-2); wkbk. 3.95 (ISBN 0-471-03992-6); tapes (ISBN 0-471-05673-1). Wiley.

Spanish Inquisition. Cecil Roth. (Orig.). 1964. pap. 4.95 (ISBN 0-393-00255-1, Norton Lib). Norton.

Spanish Kingdoms Twelve Fifty to Fifteen Sixteen, Vol. II: Castilian Hegemony, 1410-1516. J. N. Hillgarth. 1978. 49.50x (ISBN 0-19-822531-8). Oxford U Pr.

Spanish Kingdoms, 1250-1516, Vol. 1: 250-1410 Precarious Balance. J. N. Hillgarth. 1976. 49.50x (ISBN 0-19-822530-X). Oxford U Pr.

Spanish Language. 2nd ed. William J. Entwistle. (Great Language Ser.). 1962. text ed. 13.75 (ISBN 0-571-06404-3). Humanities.

Spanish Language Today. C. H. Stevenson. 1970. text ed. 6.00x (ISBN 0-09-104550-9, Hutchinson U Lib); pap. text ed. 4.75x (ISBN 0-09-104501-0, Hutchinson U Lib). Humanities.

Spanish Leather. John W. Waterer. (Illus.). 1971. 48.00 (ISBN 0-571-09043-5, Pub. by Faber & Faber). Merrimack Bk Serv.

Spanish Level Three: Forty Classroom Tests. Maxim Newmark & Christopher Kendris. LC 58-31609. (Regents Exams & Answers Ser.). (gr. 9-12). 1977. pap. 3.50 (ISBN 0-8120-0120-6). Barron.

Spanish Libertines. Tr. by John Stevens. LC 80-2499. 1981. Repr. of 1707 ed. 83.50 (ISBN 0-404-19135-5). AMS Pr.

Spanish Literature: A Brief Survey. 3rd ed. Nicholson B. Adams et al. (Quality Paperback: No. 38). (Orig.). 1974. pap. 3.50 (ISBN 0-8226-0038-2). Littlefield.

Spanish Made Simple. Eugene Jackson & Antonio Rubio. pap. 3.50 (ISBN 0-385-01212-8, Made). Doubleday.

Spanish Main. Peter Wood. (Seafarers Ser.). (Illus.). 1979. lib. bdg. 11.97 (ISBN 0-8094-2720-6); kivar bdg. 9.96 (ISBN 0-8094-2721-4). Silver.

Spanish Music in the Age of Columbus. Robert Stevenson. LC 78-20496. (Encore Music Editions Ser.). 1981. Repr. of 1960 ed. 29.50 (ISBN 0-88355-872-6). Hyperion Conn.

Spanish Now! A Level One Worktext. 2nd ed. Silverstein et al. Ed. by Nathan Quinones. LC 75-40329. (gr. 7-12). 1977. 14.95 (ISBN 0-8120-5202-1); pap. text ed. 6.95 (ISBN 0-8120-0928-2); tchr's manual 1.25 (ISBN 0-8120-0951-7). Barron.

Spanish Once a Week. rev. ed. Norma Clegg & Patricia Caldwell. 1977. pap. 5.25x (ISBN 0-631-94610-1, Pub. by Basil Blackwell). Biblio Dist.

Spanish One Two-One: From Sound to Letter. Juan Estarellas. (gr. 9-12). 1975. pap. 6.95 (ISBN 0-88345-239-1); cassettes 75.00 (ISBN 0-685-65048-0); tapes 110.00. Regents Pub.

Spanish Oral Drill Book. K. L. Mason & J. C. Sager. 1969. text ed. 8.20 (ISBN 0-08-013363-0); pap. text ed. 7.80 (ISBN 0-08-013362-2). Pergamon.

Spanish Pastoral Romances. Hugo A. Rennert. LC 67-29552. 1968. Repr. of 1912 ed. 11.00x (ISBN 0-8196-0214-0). Biblo.

Spanish Peru, Fifteen Thirty-Two to Fifteen Sixty: A Colonial Society. James Lockhart. LC 68-14032. (Illus.). 1968. 25.00 (ISBN 0-299-04660-5); pap. 7.95x (ISBN 0-299-04664-8). U of Wis Pr.

Spanish Phrase Book. pap. 7.00 (ISBN 0-685-90823-2). Saphrograph.

Spanish Picaresque Novel. Peter N. Dunn. (World Authors Ser.: No. 557). 1979. lib. bdg. 14.50 (ISBN 0-8057-6399-6). Twayne.

Spanish Pocket Dictionary. Donald F. Sola & Frederick B. Agard. 1954. 2.50 (ISBN 0-394-40064-X). Random.

Spanish Poetry of the Golden Age. Ed. by Bruce W. Wardropper. LC 78-132806. (Illus.). 1977. 29.50x (ISBN 0-89197-981-6); pap. text ed. 16.95x (ISBN 0-89197-982-4). Irvington.

Spanish Poetry of the Grupo Poetico De 1927. G. Connell. text ed. 13.75 (ISBN 0-08-016950-3). Pergamon.

Spanish Pole-Cat: The Adventures of Seniora Rufina. Alonso De Castillo Solorzano. Ed. by Roger L'Estrange & John Ozell. LC 80-2472. 1981. Repr. of 1717 ed. 62.50 (ISBN 0-404-19104-5). AMS Pr.

Spanish Political System: Franco's Legacy. E. Ramon Arango. LC 78-8979. (Westview Special Studies in West European Politics & Society). 1978. lib. bdg. 26.50x (ISBN 0-89158-177-4). Westview.

Spanish Politics & Imperial Trade, 1700-1789. Geoffrey J. Walker. LC 78-63107. 320p. 1979. 17.50x (ISBN 0-253-12150-7). Ind U Pr.

Spanish Programmatic Course, Vol. 1. C. Cleland Harris. LC 75-5674. (Spoken Language Ser.). xii, 464p. (Span., Prog. Bk.). (gr. 9-12). 1975. pap. 12.00 (ISBN 0-87950-354-8); cassettes 24 hr dual track 110.00x (ISBN 0-87950-358-0); cassettes with course-bk 115.00x (ISBN 0-87950-359-9). Spoken Lang Serv.

Spanish Programmatic Course, Vol. 2. C. Cleland Harris. LC 75-5674. (Spoken Language Ser.). (Span. Prog. Bk.). 1978. pap. 12.00x (ISBN 0-87950-356-4); 16 dual track cassettes 80.00x (ISBN 0-87950-360-2); cassettes with course book 90.00 (ISBN 0-87950-361-0); vols. 1 & 2 & cassettes 1 & 2 200.00x (ISBN 0-87950-362-9). Spoken Lang Serv.

Spanish Pronunciation in the Americas. D. Lincoln Canfield. LC 80-23664. (Illus.). 1981. lib. bdg. 15.00x (ISBN 0-226-09262-3). U of Chicago Pr.

Spanish Quest. Ray Alan. (Illus.). 1969. 8.95 o.s.i. (ISBN 0-02-500650-9). Macmillan.

Spanish Readings for Conversation. Ed. by Walter A. Dobrian & Coleman R. Jeffers. (Orig., Prog. Bk., Span). 1970. pap. text ed. 8.80 (ISBN 0-395-04367-0). HM.

Spanish Review. pocket ed. 150p. (gr. 7-12). 1981. pap. text ed. 2.50 (ISBN 0-8120-2196-7). Barron. Postponed.

Spanish Review Grammar: Theory & Practice. J. Holton et al. 1977. 14.95 (ISBN 0-13-824409-X). P-H.

Spanish Revolution: The Left & the Struggle for Power During the Civil War. Burnett Bolloten. LC 78-5011. 1979. 29.00x (ISBN 0-8078-1297-8); pap. 14.00x (ISBN 0-8078-4077-7). U of NC Pr.

Spanish Ridge. E. E. Halleran. 160p. 1981. pap. 1.75 (ISBN 0-345-29436-X). Ballantine.

Spanish Romanesque Architecture of the Eleventh Century. Walter M. Whitehill. 1941. 45.00x (ISBN 0-19-817167-6). Oxford U Pr.

Spanish Romantic Theater. John R. Tapia. LC 80-5565. 87p. 1980. lib. bdg. 13.75 (ISBN 0-8191-1276-3); pap. text ed. 6.50 (ISBN 0-8191-1277-1). U Pr of Amer.

Spanish (Ruy Lopez) Marshall. T. D. Harding. 1977. pap. 18.95 (ISBN 0-7134-0252-0, Pub. by Batsford England). David & Charles.

Spanish (Ruy Lopez) Open. K. J. O'Connell. 1978. pap. 15.95 (ISBN 0-7134-0248-2, Pub. by Batsford England). David & Charles.

Spanish Scientists in the New World: The Eighteenth-Century Expeditions. Iris W. Engstrand. LC 80-50863. (Illus.). 304p. 1981. 25.00 (ISBN 0-295-95764-6). U of Wash Pr.

Spanish Texas: Yesterday & Today. Gerald Ashford. LC 72-157044. (Illus.). 1971. 12.50 (ISBN 0-8363-0090-4). Jenkins.

Spanish Textile Tradition of New Mexico & Colorado. Museum of International Folk Art. (Ser. in Southwestern Culture). 1979. 25.95 o.p. (ISBN 0-89013-112-0); pap. 14.95 (ISBN 0-89013-113-9). Museum Nm Pr.

Spanish Traditional Lyric. J. G. Cummins. LC 76-1222. 1977. 18.75 (ISBN 0-08-018117-1); pap. 9.25 (ISBN 0-08-018116-3). Pergamon.

Spanish Treasure in Florida Waters: A Billion Dollar Graveyard. Robert F. Marx. (Illus.). 1979. 12.50case (ISBN 0-913352-06-3). Mariners Boston.

Spanish Twins. Lucy F. Perkins. (Twins Ser). (Illus.). (gr. 4-6). 1969. PLB 4.85 o.s.i. (ISBN 0-8027-6070-8). Walker & Co.

Spanish West. W. W. Johnson. LC 76-1423. (Old West). (Illus.). (gr. 5 up). 1976. kivar 12.96 (ISBN 0-8094-1535-6, Pub. by Time-Life). Silver.

Spanish West. William W. Johnson. (Old West Ser.). (Illus.). 1976. 12.95 (ISBN 0-8094-1533-X). Time-Life.

Spanish Word Machine: Book I. Joyce M. Burkes. LC 79-2122. (Spanish Word Machine Bks.). (Orig.). 1981. pap. 4.95 (ISBN 0-931218-09-8). Joybug.

Spanish Word Machine: Book II. Joyce M. Burkes. LC 79-92122. (Spanish Word Machine Bks.). 26p. (Orig.). 1981. pap. 4.95 (ISBN 0-931218-10-1). Joybug.

Spanish Word Machine: Book III. Joyce M. Burkes. LC 79-2122. (Spanish Word Machine Bks.). 26p. (Orig.). 1981. pap. 4.95 (ISBN 0-931218-11-X). Joybug.

Spanish Workbook: Book 1. Robert J. Nassi & Bernard Bernstein. 1976. pap. text ed. 6.25 (ISBN 0-87720-987-1). AMSCO Sch.

Spanish Workbook 2. Robert Nassi & Bernard Bernstein. 1977. wkbk. 6.25 (ISBN 0-87720-988-X). AMSCO Sch.

Spanish Workbook 3. Robert Nassi et al. 1977. wkbk. 6.25 (ISBN 0-87720-989-8). AMSCO Sch.

Spank Me If You Love Me. Wendel Robley & Grace Robley. LC 76-1067. 128p. 1976. pap. 2.95 o.p. (ISBN 0-89221-019-2). New Leaf.

Spanning the Seven Seas, Level 17. Eldonna Evertts & Byron VanRoekel. (Design for Reading Ser). (Illus.). (gr. 6). 1972. text ed. 11.16 (ISBN 0-06-516009-6, SchDept); tchr's ed. 14.28 (ISBN 0-06-516207-2); wkbk. 3.20 (ISBN 0-06-516308-7); tchr's ed. wkbk. 5.36 (ISBN 0-06-516408-3); dupl. masters 17.68 (ISBN 0-06-516839-9); mastery test pkg. 14.48 (ISBN 0-06-516617-5). Har-Row.

Spare the Rod. George Wesley. LC 78-57982. 1978. pap. text ed. 9.00 (ISBN 0-8191-0660-7). U Pr of Amer.

Spark: A Handbook of Classroom Ideas to Motivate the Teaching of Primary Social Studies. (Spice Ser). 1977. 6.50 (ISBN 0-89273-104-4). Educ Serv.

Sparke of Frendship & Warme Goodwill. Thomas Churchyard. 40p. pap. 10.00 (ISBN 0-913720-18-6). Sandstone.

Sparkle: PR for Library Staff. Virginia Baeckler. LC 80-50566. (Illus.). 80p. (Orig.). 1980. pap. 5.00x (ISBN 0-9603232-1-X). Sources.

Sparkling Words. Ruth K. Carlson. 1979. 8.95 o.p. (ISBN 0-88252-009-1). Paladin Hse.

Sparks at the Grassroots: Municipal Distribution of TVA Electricity in Tennessee. Victor C. Hobday. LC 70-77845. (Illus.). 1969. 14.50x (ISBN 0-87049-099-0). U of Tenn Pr.

Sparks for the Kindling. Harold C. Bonell. 1968. 3.95 o.p. (ISBN 0-8170-0400-9). Judson.

Sparrow on the House Top. Ruth Hunt. 1976. 5.95 o.p. (ISBN 0-8007-0814-8). Revell.

Sparrows Fall. Fred Bosworth. (gr. 7 up). 1975. pap. 1.50 o.p. (ISBN 0-451-08504-3, W8504, Sig). NAL.

Sparrow's Magic. Maria Niklewiczowa. Tr. by Alvin Tresselt. LC 73-99583. Orig. Title: Suzume No Mahou. (Illus., Japanese). (gr. k-3). 1970. 5.95 o.s.i. (ISBN 0-8193-0412-3, Four Winds); PLB 5.41 o.s.i. (ISBN 0-8193-0413-1). Schol Bk Serv.

Sparta & Lakonia: A Regional History Thirteen Hundred to Three Sixty-Two B.C. Paul Cartledge. (States & Cities of Ancient Greece Ser.). 1979. 25.00x (ISBN 0-7100-0377-3). Routledge & Kegan.

Sparta's Bitter Victories: Politics & Diplomacy in the Corinthian War. Charles D. Hamilton. LC 78-58045. 1978. 19.50x (ISBN 0-8014-1158-0). Cornell U Pr.

Spasmic Vistas. Daniel Walter. (Illus.). 1974. pap. 2.50 (ISBN 0-686-22348-9). Oll Korrect.

Spassky's One Hundred Best Games. Bernard Cafferty. 1973. pap. 17.95 (ISBN 0-7134-2409-5, Pub. by Batsford England). David & Charles.

Spastic Dysphonia: A Surgical & Voice Therapy Treatment Program. Herbert H. Dedo & Thomas Shipp. LC 80-65193. (Illus.). 96p. 1980. pap. text ed. 12.95 (ISBN 0-933014-58-9). College-Hill.

Spasticity: Mechanism, Measurement, Management. Ejner Pederson. 144p. 1969. pap. 10.00 spiral (ISBN 0-398-01462-0). C C Thomas.

Spatial Ability: Its Educational & Social Significance. I. MacFarlane Smith. LC 64-22822. 1964. text ed. 8.95 o.p. (ISBN 0-912736-04-6). EDITS Pubs.

Spatial Analysis & Planning Strategies Cityport Industrialization, 15-18 Nov. 1978: Spatial Analysis & Planning Strategies Cityport Industrialization,15-18 Nov. 1978, Univ. Ofsouthampton. Ed. by Brian Hoyle & David Pinder. LC 80-40837. (Urban & Regional Planning Ser.). (Illus.). 350p. 1981. 60.00 (ISBN 0-08-025815-8); prepub. 50.00 (ISBN 0-08-025816-6). Pergamon.

Spatial Analysis for Regional Development. 44p. 1981. pap. 6.75 (ISBN 92-808-0166-X, TUNU 101, UNU). Unipub.

Spatial Analysis in Archaeology. I. Hodder & C. Orton. LC 75-44582. (New Studies in Archaeology Ser.). (Illus.). 1976. 35.00x (ISBN 0-521-21080-1). Cambridge U Pr.

Spatial Analysis in Archaeology. I. Hodder & C. Orton. LC 75-44582. (New Studies in Archaeology). (Illus.). 260p. 1980. pap. 14.50 (ISBN 0-521-29738-9). Cambridge U Pr.

Spatial Analysis, Industry & the Industrial Environment - Progess in Research & Applications: International Industrial Systems, Vol. 2. F. E. Hamilton & G. J. Linge. 1981. price not set (ISBN 0-471-27918-8, Pub. by Wiley-Interscience). Wiley.
Spatial Analysis of the Eletrocardiogram: A Program. Irwin Hoffman et al. (Illus.). 150p. 1975. pap. text ed. 8.25 o.p. (ISBN 0-8016-3124-6). Mosby.
Spatial Analysis of Urban Community Development Policy in India. Derek R. Hall. (Geography & Public Policy Research Studies Ser.). 192p. 1981. 33.75 (ISBN 0-471-27862-9, Pub. by Wiley-Interscience). Wiley.
Spatial & Temporal Uses of English Prepositions: An Essay in Stratificational Semantics. David Bennett. (Longman Linguistics Library). 256p. 1975. text ed. 17.50x (ISBN 0-582-52453-9). Longman.
Spatial Aspects of Aging. Robert Wiseman. Ed. by Salvatore J. Natoli. LC 78-59103. (Resource Papers for College Geography Ser.). (Illus.). 1979. pap. text ed. 4.00 (ISBN 0-89291-133-6). Assn Am Geographers.
Spatial Aspects of Development. Brian S. Hoyle. LC 73-2785. 372p. 1974. 36.50 (ISBN 0-471-41753-X). Wiley.
Spatial Diffusion. P. R. Gould. LC 79-94260. (CCG Resource Papers Ser.: No. 4). (Illus.). 1969. pap. text ed. 4.00 (ISBN 0-89291-051-8). Assn Am Geographers.
Spatial Diffusion: An Historical Geography of Epidemics in an Island Community. A. D. Cliff et al. (Cambridge Geographical Studies: No. 14). (Illus.). 244p. Date not set. price not set (ISBN 0-521-22840-9). Cambridge U Pr.
Spatial Dimensions of Urban Government. I. M. Barlow. (Geographical Research Studies Press Ser.). 900p. 1981. 49.00 (ISBN 0-471-27978-1, Pub by Wiley Interscience). Wiley.
Spatial Econometrics. J. H. Paelinck et al. (Illus.). 1979. 25.95 (ISBN 0-566-00264-7, 02932-7, Pub. by Saxon Hse England). Lexington Bks.
Spatial Economic Theory. R. D. Dean et al. LC 79-90899. 1970. pap. text ed. 10.95 (ISBN 0-02-907110-0). Free Pr.
Spatial Economy of Communist China: A Study on Industrial Location and Transportation. Yuan-li Wu. LC 67-20739. (Publications Ser.: No. 56). 1967. 12.00 (ISBN 0-8179-1561-3). Hoover Inst Pr.
Spatial Interaction: The Geography of Movement. John C. Lowe & S. Moryadas. 1975. text ed. 21.95 (ISBN 0-395-18584-X). HM.
Spatial Organization: The Geographer's View of the World. Ronald Abler et al. LC 71-123081. (Geography Ser). (Illus.). 1971. text ed. 22.95 (ISBN 0-13-824086-8). P-H.
Spatial Perspectives on School Desegregation & Busing. J. Dennis Lord. Ed. by Salvatore J. Natoli. LC 76-57034. (Resource Papers for College Geography Ser.). (Illus.). 1977. pap. text ed. 4.00 (ISBN 0-89291-124-7). Assn Am Geographers.
Spatial Policy Problems of the British Economy. Ed. by M. Chisholm & G. Manners. LC 70-160090. (Illus.). 1971. 38.50 (ISBN 0-521-08235-8). Cambridge U Pr.
Spatial Representation & Behavior: Application & Theory Across the Life Span. Ed. by Lynn S. Liben et al. (Developmental Psychology Ser.). 1980. 27.50 (ISBN 0-12-447980-4). Acad Pr.
Spatial Search: Applications to Planning Problems in the Public Sector. Bryan H. Massam. (Urban & Regional Planning: Vol. 23). (Illus.). 33.00 (ISBN 0-08-024286-3). Pergamon.
Spatial Statistics. Brian D. Ripley. (Probability & Mathematical Statistics Ser.: Applied Probability & Statistics). 352p. 1981. 27.00 (ISBN 0-471-08367-4, Pub. by Wiley-Interscience). Wiley.
Spatial Structure of Administrative Systems. B. H. Massam. LC 75-185557. (CCG Resource Papers Ser.: No. 12). (Illus.). 1972. pap. text ed. 4.00 (ISBN 0-89291-059-3). Assn Am Geographers.
Spatial Synthesis in Computer-Aided Building Design. Ed. by Charles M. Eastman. LC 75-7416. 333p. 1975. 49.95 (ISBN 0-470-22946-2). Halsted Pr.
Spatial Systems: A General Introduction. Leo K. Klaassen et al. 1979. 24.95 (ISBN 0-566-00263-9, 02930-0, Pub. by Saxon Hse England). Lexington Bks.
Spawn. Robert Holles. 1979. pap. cancelled o.s.i. (ISBN 0-515-05182-9). Jove Pubns.
Spawn. Robert Holles. 1980. pap. 2.50 (ISBN 0-425-04570-6). Berkley Pub.
Spawn of the Winds. Brian Lumley & Kirby McCauley. 1978. pap. 1.75 o.s.i. (ISBN 0-515-04571-3). Jove Pubns.
Spawning Problem Fishes. Willy Jocher. Incl. Book 1 (ISBN 0-87666-146-0, PS-302); Book 2 (ISBN 0-87666-147-9, PS-303). (Illus.). 1972. pap. 2.95 ea. (ISBN 0-685-32894-5). TFH Pubns.
Spaziergange Durch Cambridge. Frank A. Reeve. (Illus., Ger.). 1978. pap. 4.00 (ISBN 0-900891-44-0). Oleander Pr.
Speak English, Text 2. Corley & Smallwood. (Speak English Ser.). (Illus.). 96p. (Orig.). 1981. pap. 3.95 (ISBN 0-88499-653-0). Inst Mod Lang.
Speak English, Workbook 2. Corley & Smallwood. (Speak English Ser.). (Illus.). 72p. (Orig.). 1981. pap. 3.95 (ISBN 0-88499-654-9). Inst Mod Lang.
Speak English, Text 3. (Speak English Ser.). (Illus.). 64p. (Orig.). 1981. pap. 3.95 (ISBN 0-88499-655-7). Inst Mod Lang.
Speak English, Workbook 3. (Speak English Ser.). (Illus.). 64p. 1981. pap. write for info. (ISBN 0-88499-656-5). Inst Mod Lang.
Speak English: A Practical Course for Foreign Students. Marie Durel. (Orig.). 1972. pap. 3.95 (ISBN 0-06-463320-9, EH 320, EH). Har-Row.
Speak for Yourself. James H. Byrns. 329p. 1981. pap. text ed. 10.95 (ISBN 0-394-32410-2). Random.
Speak Lord, I'm Listening. Dennis Huse & Geralyn Watson. LC 80-70851. 176p. 1981. pap. 7.95 perfect bnd. (ISBN 0-87793-220-4). Ave Maria.
Speak of the Devil. Alfred Hitchcock. 1980. pap. 2.25 (ISBN 0-440-17654-9). Dell.
Speak Out. W. G. Harkey. LC 76-56659. 7.95 (ISBN 0-87359-022-8); pap. 3.95 (ISBN 0-87359-010-4). Northwood Inst.
Speak Out in Thunder Tones: Letters & Other Writings by Black Northerners, 1787-1865. Ed. by Dorothy Sterling. LC 72-92245. 352p. (gr. 9 up). 1973. 5.95a o.p. (ISBN 0-385-02474-6); PLB (ISBN 0-385-01909-2). Doubleday.
Speak Out with Clout. Charles A. Boyle. LC 77-17265. 196p. 1977. 6.95 (ISBN 0-89709-020-9). Liberty Pub.
Speak Roughly to Your Little Boy: A Collection of Parodies & Burlesques. Ed. by Myra C. Livingston. LC 71-140779. (Illus.). (gr. 3 up). 1971. 8.50 o.p. (ISBN 0-15-277859-4, HJ). HarBraceJ.
Speak to Me. John H. Green. LC 62-14943. (Orig.). 1962. pap. 3.95 (ISBN 0-672-63116-4). Odyssey Pr.
Speak to Me Lord--I'm Listening. Virginia Thompson. LC 78-55479. 1981. pap. 2.25 (ISBN 0-89081-117-2, 1172). Harvest Hse.
Speak Vietnamese. Nguyen-Dinh-Hoa. LC 66-17774. 381p. 1980. pap. 12.50 (ISBN 0-8048-1356-6). C E Tuttle.
Speakers & Lecturers: How to Find Them. 2nd ed. Ed. by Paul Wasserman. 350p. 1981. 68.00 (ISBN 0-8103-0393-0). Gale.
Speakers & Lecturers: How to Find Them. Ed. by Paul Wasserman & Jacqueline R. Bernero. LC 78-26025. 464p. 1979. 62.00 o.p. (ISBN 0-8103-0392-2). Gale.
Speaker's Bible, 18 vols. Ed. by James Hastings & Edward Hastings. 1979. 275.00 (ISBN 0-8010-4036-1). Baker Bk.
Speaker's Bible. Jacob Spatz. 200p. 1981. 12.95 (ISBN 0-8159-6841-8). Devin.
Speaking. Georges Gusdorf. Tr. by Paul T. Brockelman. (Studies in Phenomenology & Existential Philosophy Ser). 1965. 10.95x (ISBN 0-8101-0111-4); pap. 4.25x (ISBN 0-8101-0531-4). Northwestern U Pr.
Speaking Aids Through the Grades. Ruth K. Carlson. LC 74-14719. 1975. pap. text ed. 4.50x (ISBN 0-8077-2421-1). Tchrs Coll.
Speaking & Language: Defense of Poetry. Paul Goodman. 1971. 8.95 o.p. (ISBN 0-394-47089-3). Random.
Speaking & Listening: A Contemporary Approach. 2nd ed. Wayne A. Shrope. 305p. 1979. pap. text ed. 8.95 (ISBN 0-15-583182-8, HC); instructor's manual avail. (ISBN 0-15-583183-6). HarBraceJ.
Speaking Arabic. Abdallah. (Arabic.). pap. 3.50 (ISBN 0-685-82875-1). Intl Bk Ctr.
Speaking As a Farmer: Winning FFA Speeches, Principles of Speech Preparation & Presentation. Dan B. Curtis & Robert S. Brewer. 256p. 1980. pap. text ed. 8.95 (ISBN 0-8403-2248-8). Kendall-Hunt.
Speaking As a Writer. Agnes Smith. Tr. by David Ross-Robertson. LC 78-65831. (Illus.). 76p. (Orig.). 1979. 7.75 (ISBN 0-9602342-0-9); pap. 5.95 (ISBN 0-9602342-1-7). Westwind Pr.
Speaking Clearly: The Basics of Voice & Diction. Noah F. Modisett & James G. Luter. 1979. 9.95 (ISBN 0-8087-3949-2). Burgess.
Speaking for Nature: How Our Literary Naturalists Have Shaped America. Paul Brooks. (Illus.). 288p. 1980. 12.95 (ISBN 0-395-29610-2). HM.
Speaking for Results: Communication by Objectives. John E. Baird, Jr. (Illus.). 301p. 1981. pap. text ed. 10.95 scp (ISBN 0-06-040457-4, HarpC); avail. Har-Row. Postponed.
Speaking for the Master. Batsell B. Baxter. pap. 3.95 (ISBN 0-8010-0588-4). Baker Bk.
Speaking French. Duncan Sidwell & Margaret Sidwell. 1974. pap. text ed. 1.95x o.p. (ISBN 0-435-37800-7); tchr's ed. 3.50x o.p. (ISBN 0-435-37801-5). Heinemann Ed.
Speaking German. Robert L. Politzer. LC 69-10287. 1969. text ed. 10.50 (ISBN 0-13-825794-9). P-H.
Speaking in Public. A. Taylor. 1979. pap. 12.95 (ISBN 0-13-825844-9). P-H.
Speaking in Tongues. Larry Christenson. LC 97-5595. 1968. pap. 2.25 (ISBN 0-87123-518-8, 200518). Bethany Fell.
Speaking in Tongues. Matthew Meyer. pap. 1.95 (ISBN 0-87178-809-8). Brethren.
Speaking Is a Practical Matter. 4th ed. McCabe & Bender. 384p. 1981. pap. text ed. 12.95 (ISBN 0-205-07230-5, 4872304); free tchr's ed. (ISBN 0-205-07231-3). Allyn.
Speaking of Apes: A Critical Anthology of Two-Way Communication with Man. Ed. by Thomas A. Sebeok & D. J. Umiker-Sebeok. (Illus.). 500p. 1980. 37.50 (ISBN 0-306-40279-3, Plenum Pr). Plenum Pub.
Speaking of: Asthma. Dietrich Nolte. Tr. by Francoise Heyden from Ger. LC 80-68766. (Medical Adviser Ser.). Orig. Title: Sprechstunde: Asthma. 128p. (Orig.). 1980. pap. 3.95 (ISBN 0-8326-2250-8, 7460). Delair.
Speaking of: Children's Posture Problems & the Injuries They Cause. Renate Zauner. Tr. by Susan Ray from Ger. LC 80-687464. (Medical Adviser Ser.). (Illus.). 1980. pap. 3.95 (ISBN 0-8326-2244-3, 7459). Delair.
Speaking of: Diabetes. Rudiger Petzoldt. Tr. by Fransois Heyden from Ger. LC 80-68763. (Medical Adviser Ser.). (Illus.). 1980. pap. 3.95 (ISBN 0-8326-2243-5, 7457). Delair.
Speaking of Early Childhood Education. R. D. Hess. (Distinguished Scholars Ser.). 1974. 32.50 o.p. (ISBN 0-07-079432-4, P&RB). McGraw.
Speaking of: Family Planning. Rainer Schrage. Tr. by Fransosis Heyden from Ger. LC 80-68765. (Medical Adviser Ser.). (Illus.). 1980. pap. 3.95 (ISBN 0-8326-2245-1, 7458). Delair.
Speaking of Literature & Society. Lionel Trilling. Ed. by Diana Trilling. LC 80-7944. 448p. 1980. 17.95 (ISBN 0-15-184710-X). HarBraceJ.
Speaking of Mrs. McCluskie. Cecil Maiden & Hilary Knight. LC 62-19862. (Illus.). (gr. 5-9). 1962. 5.95 (ISBN 0-8149-0355-X). Vanguard.
Speaking of My Life: The Art of Living in the Cultural Revolution. Ed. by Jacob Needleman. LC 78-19502. (Illus., Orig.). 1979. pap. 4.95 (ISBN 0-06-250643-9, RD 216, HarpR). Har-Row.
Speaking of Pets. Harry H. Miller. 1962. pap. 0.95 o.s.i. (ISBN 0-02-063410-2, Collier). Macmillan.
Speaking of: Sleeping Problems. Dietrich Langen. Tr. by Martha Humphreys from Ger. LC 78-72874. (Medical Adviser Ser.). (Illus.). 1979. pap. 3.95 (ISBN 0-8326-2234-6, 7452). Delair.
Speaking of Standards. Ed. by Rowen Glie. LC 70-185561. 350p. 1972. 18.00 (ISBN 0-8436-0307-0). CBI Pub.
Speaking of: Vein Problems. Helmut Haid. Tr. by Martha Humphries from Ger. LC 80-68765. (Medical Adviser Ser.). (Illus.). 1980. pap. 3.95 (ISBN 0-8326-2242-7, 7456). Delair.
Speaking Out for America's Children. Milton J. Senn. LC 76-49756. (Fastback Ser.: No. 17). 1977. 15.00x (ISBN 0-300-02107-0); pap. 4.95x (ISBN 0-300-02113-5). Yale U Pr.
Speaking Stones. Sara Cardiff. 1978. pap. 1.75 o.p. (ISBN 0-449-23661-7, Crest). Fawcett.
Speaking to Communicate: An Introduction to Speech. Raymond L. Fischer et al. 1972. pap. text ed. 7.95x (ISBN 0-8221-0076-2). Dickenson.
Speaking Well of God. Edward Vick. LC 79-9336. (Anvil Ser.). 1979. pap. 6.95 (ISBN 0-8127-0245-X). Southern Pub.
Speaking with Confidence. Karen Carlson & Alan Meyers. 1977. pap. 9.95x (ISBN 0-673-15022-4). Scott F.
Speaking with Tongues: Historically & Psychologically Considered. George B. Cutten. 1927. 27.50x (ISBN 0-685-69805-X). Elliots Bks.
Spear & Scepter: Army, Police, & Politics in Tropical Africa. Ernest W. Lefever. 1970. 11.95 (ISBN 0-8157-5200-8). Brookings.
Spearheads for Reform: The Social Settlements & the Progressive Movement, 1890-1914. Allen F. Davis. (Urban Life in America Ser). 15.95 (ISBN 0-19-500527-9); pap. 4.95x (ISBN 0-19-500862-6). Oxford U Pr.
Special Agencies in Metropolitan Calcutta. M. M. Singh et al. 1968. 6.50x o.p. (ISBN 0-210-27119-1). Asia.
Special Atmosphere Themes for Foodservice. Ed. by Jule Wilkinson. LC 78-184740. 1972. 10.95 (ISBN 0-8436-0536-7). CBI Pub.
Special Beverage Study. Ed. by Business Communications Co. 1979. 1000.00 (ISBN 0-89336-237-9, MR-1). BCC.
Special Child Handbook. Joan McNamara & Bernard McNamara. LC 76-41976. 1978. 12.50 o.p. (ISBN 0-8015-6994-X). Dutton.
Special Children: An Integrative Approach. Bernard G. Suran & Joseph V. Rizzo. 1979. text ed. 17.95x (ISBN 0-673-15068-2). Scott F.
Special Class. Brian Kral. (Orig.). 1981. playscript 2.50 (ISBN 0-87602-235-2). Anchorage.
Special Committee for Studies & Recommendations of the Inter-American Commission for the World Conference of International Women's Year (CEER-CIM) Mexico, 1975. (Eng. & Span.). 1976. Eng. Ed. pap. 6.00 (ISBN 0-8270-2870-9); Eng. Ed. pap. 6.00 (ISBN 0-8270-2875-X). OAS.
Special Day Sermons. W. H. Compton. 1972. 2.95 (ISBN 0-87148-752-7); pap. 2.25 (ISBN 0-87148-753-5). Pathway Pr.
Special Education & the Classroom Teacher: Concepts, Perspectives & Strategies. Beverly L. Dexter. (Illus.). 272p. 1977. 22.50 (ISBN 0-398-03607-1). C C Thomas.
Special Education Careers: Training the Handicapped Child. Theodore Huebner. (Career Concise Guides Ser.). (Illus.). (gr. 7up). 1977. lib. bdg. 6.45 (ISBN 0-531-01311-1). Watts.
Special Education for Adolescents: Issues & Perspectives. Douglas Cullinan & Michael Epstein. (Special Education Ser.). 1979. text ed. 17.50 (ISBN 0-675-08407-5). Merrill.
Special Education for the Early Childhood Years. Janet W. Lerner et al. 416p. 1981. text ed. 17.95 (ISBN 0-13-826461-9). P-H.
Special Education for the Eighties. Bill R. Gearheart. LC 79-20647. (Illus.). 1980. text ed. 17.95 (ISBN 0-8016-1759-6). Mosby.
Special Education in the United States: Statistics 1948-1966. Romaine Mackie. LC 69-18776. 1969. pap. 4.25x (ISBN 0-8077-1721-5). Tchrs Coll.
Special Education in Transition: Concepts to Guide the Education of Experienced Teachers with Implications for PL 94-142. Ed. by Dean C. Corrigan & Kenneth R. Howey. LC 80-68281. 208p. 1980. pap. 12.95 (ISBN 0-86586-109-9). Coun Exc Child.
Special Education Index to Assessment Devices. National Information Center for Special Education Materials (NICSEM) LC 79-84457. (Orig.). 1980. pap. 21.00 (ISBN 0-89320-026-3). Univ. SC Natl Info.
Special Education Index to Inservice Training Materials. National Information Center for Special Education Materials (NICSEM) LC 79-84458. (Orig.). 1980. pap. 12.00 (ISBN 0-89320-027-1). Univ. SC Natl Info.
Special Education Index to Learner Materials. National Information Center for Educational Media. LC 79-84454. 462p. 1979. pap. 60.00 (ISBN 0-89320-024-7). Univ SC Natl Info.
Special Education Index to Parent Materials. National Information Center for Special Education Materials (NISCEM) LC 79-84456. (Orig.). 1979. pap. 21.00 (ISBN 0-89320-025-5). Univ SC Natl Info.
Special Education Needs in Bilingual Programs. Victoria Bergin. 64p. (Orig.). 1980. pap. 3.00 (ISBN 0-89763-026-2). Natl Clearinghse Bilingual Ed.
Special Educator: Stress & Survival. Barbara. DeShong. 350p. 1981. text ed. price not set (ISBN 0-89443-358-X). Aspen Systems.
Special Educator's Guide to Vocational Training. Robert A. Weisgerber. (Illus.). 224p. 1980. text ed. 16.50 (ISBN 0-398-03938-0). C C Thomas.
Special Effects, Vol. I. D. Hutchison. 1979. pap. 6.95 (ISBN 0-931064-07-4). Starlog Pr.
Special Effects, Vol. I. David Hutchison. LC 79-63384. 1979. pap. 6.95 (ISBN 0-931064-07-4). Starlog.
Special Effects, Vol. II. David Hutchison. 1980. pap. 7.95 (ISBN 0-931064-22-8). O'Quinn Studio.
Special Effects, Vol. II. 1980. pap. 7.95 (ISBN 0-931064-22-8). Starlog Pr.
Special Forces Combat Firing Techniques. new ed. Frank A. Moyer & Robert J. Scroggie. Ed. by Robert K. Brown. LC 72-180974. (Illus.). 120p. 1971. 15.95 (ISBN 0-87364-010-1). Paladin Ent.
Special Foster Care: A History & Rationale. Bradford A. Bryant. (Orig.). 1980. pap. text ed. 4.50 (ISBN 0-9604068-0-8). People Places.
Special: Fred Freed & the Television Documentary. David Yellin. LC 72-80909. (Illus.). 242p. 1973. 9.95 o.s.i. (ISBN 0-02-632970-0). Macmillan.
Special Functions & Linear Representations of Lie Groups. Jean Dieudonne. (CBMS Regional Conference Ser. in Mathematics: No. 42). 1980. 8.40 (ISBN 0-8218-1692-6). Am Math.
Special Functions & the Theory of Group Representations. N. Ja. Vilenkin. LC 68-19438. (Translations of Mathematical Monographs: Vol. 22). 1978. Repr. of 1968 ed. 26.00 (ISBN 0-8218-1572-5, MMONO-22). Am Math.

Special Functions & Their Approximations, 2 Vols. Yudell L. Luke. LC 68-23498. (Mathematics in Science & Engineering Ser.: Vol. 53). 1969. Vol. 1. 48.00 (ISBN 0-12-459901-X); Vol. 2. 55.00 (ISBN 0-12-459902-8). Acad Pr.

Special Gift for Mother. Gary Bowen. LC 80-68234. (Illus.). (gr. 4 up). 1981. 6.95 (ISBN 0-374-37147-4). FS&G.

Special Index One: Annual Lists & General Index of the Parliamentary Papers Relating to the East Indies 1801-1907. (Bibliography on Parliamentary Papers Ser.). 248p. Repr. of 1909 ed. 61.00x (Pub. by Irish Academic Pr Ireland). Biblio Dist.

Special Issue Dedicated to Dr. Bernard Brodie. Ed. by K. F. Sewing et al. (Pharmacology: Vol. 19, No. 5). (Illus.). 1979. cancelled soft cover o.p. (ISBN 3-8055-0408-X). S Karger.

Special Issue Surveying Electromagnetic Induction in the Earth & Moon. Ed. by B. A. Hobbs. 185p. pap. 23.50 (ISBN 90-277-9041-8, Pub. by D. Reidel). Kluwer Boston.

Special Kind of Love. Kirstin Michaels. Bd. with Enchanted Journey. 1981. pap. 1.95 (ISBN 0-451-09619-3, J9619, Sig). NAL.

Special Kind of Marrying. LC 80-67686. 120p. 1980. pap. 3.50 (ISBN 0-915388-09-X). Buckley Pubns.

Special Lectures. International Congress of Phonetic Sciences, 9th, Copenhagen, 1979. Ed. by Fischer-Jorgensen. (Journal: Phonetica: Vol. 37, No. 1-2). (Illus.). 108p. 1980. pap. 19.75 (ISBN 3-8055-1414-X). S Karger.

Special Librarianship: A New Reader. Ed. by Eugene B. Jackson. LC 80-11530. 773p. 1980. 27.50 (ISBN 0-8108-1295-9). Scarecrow.

Special Libraries: A General Survey with Particular Reference to South Africa. Reuben Musiker. 1970. 10.00 (ISBN 0-8108-0310-0). Scarecrow.

Special Libraries: A Guide for Management. 2nd ed. 1981. write for info. (ISBN 0-87111-258-2). SLA.

Special Library Role in Networks: Proceedings of a Conference. Ed. by Robert W. Gibson. spiral bdg. 10.50 (ISBN 0-87111-279-5). SLA.

Special Look. Karen Koch. 1973. pap. 1.00x (ISBN 0-88323-115-8, 220). Richards Pub.

Special Needs of Long-Term Patients. Carolyn B. Stevens. 250p. 1974. pap. text ed. 5.90 o.p. (ISBN 0-397-54133-3). Lippincott.

Special Offer. Jerry Bumpus. LC 80-20671. 1981. pap. 5.00 (ISBN 0-914140-08-6). Carpenter Pr.

Special Olympics & Paralympics. Lorraine Henroid. (First Bks.). (Illus.). (gr. 4 up). 1979. PLB 6.45 s&l (ISBN 0-531-02263-3). Watts.

Special Optical Effects. Zoran Perisic. LC 80-41005. (Illus.). 1981. 29.95 (ISBN 0-240-51007-0). Focal Pr.

Special People: A Brighter Future for Everyone with Physical, Mental & Emotional Disabilities. Cohen. (Psychology in Action Series). 1977. text ed. 9.95 (ISBN 0-13-826511-9, Spec); pap. text ed. 5.95 (ISBN 0-13-826503-8). P-H.

Special People, Special Times. Irving Wallace. 192p. (Orig.). 1981. pap. 2.25 (ISBN 0-523-41480-3). Pinnacle Bks.

Special People...Getting to Know Them: Resources in Mental Retardation. 1.00. Boston Public Lib.

Special Picture Cookbook. Freida R. Steed. 1974. 5.75 o.p. (ISBN 0-89079-041-8). H & H Ent.

Special Problems. (Life Library of Photography). (Illus.). 1971. 14.95 (ISBN 0-8094-1040-0). Time-Life.

Special Problems in Product Liability Litigation, Vol. 116. (Litigation & Administrative Practice Course Handbook Ser. 1977-78). 1978. softcover 20.00 o.p. (ISBN 0-685-47625-1, H4-3866). PLI.

Special Provision for Reading: When Will They Ever Learn ? David V. Moseley. (General Ser). 240p. 1975. pap. text ed. 20.00x (ISBN 0-85633-063-9, NFER). Humanities.

Special Purpose Rooms. Time-Life Books Editors. (Home Repair & Improvement Ser.). (Illus.). 128p. 1981. 10.95 (ISBN 0-8094-3458-X). Time-Life.

Special Purpose Transistors: A Self-Instructional Programed Manual. Federal Electric Corporation. (Illus.). 1966. pap. 11.95 (ISBN 0-13-826537-2). P-H.

Special Relativity. W. G. Dixon. LC 77-83991. (Illus.). 1978. 49.50 (ISBN 0-521-21871-3). Cambridge U Pr.

Special Relativity. John G. Taylor. (Oxford Physics Ser). (Illus.). 118p. 1975. 10.95x o.p. (ISBN 0-19-851823-4). Oxford U Pr.

Special Report: How to Make Money During Inflation-Recession. Consumer Guide Editors. LC 79-3669. (Illus.). 1980. pap. 4.95 (ISBN 0-06-090782-7, CN 782, CN). Har-Row.

Special Review of Experimental Aging Research: Progress in Biology. Ed. by Merrill F. Elias et al. LC 77-23262. 1976. 24.00 (ISBN 0-933786-00-X); professional individual discount 10.00 (ISBN 0-686-67622-X). Beech Hill.

Special Rooms: Louisville, Kentucky. Ed. by Monica Orr. LC 80-83167. 72p. (Orig.). 1980. pap. 9.95 (ISBN 0-937246-01-8). Hawley Cooke Orr.

Special School. Tom Wakefield. (Orig.). 1977. pap. 7.50 (ISBN 0-7100-8750-0). Routledge & Kegan.

Special Sermons on the Family. George Sweeting. (Special Sermon Ser.). 144p. 1981. pap. 2.95 (ISBN 0-8024-8208-2). Moody.

Special Student: Practical Help for the Classroom Teacher. C. M. Charles & Ida Malian. LC 80-13053. (Illus.). 1980. pap. text ed. 9.95 (ISBN 0-8016-1132-6). Mosby.

Special Techniques in Assertive Training for Women in the Health Profession. Melodie Chenevert. LC 78-11635. (Illus.). 1978. pap. 9.50 (ISBN 0-8016-0971-2). Mosby.

Special Theory of Relativity. C. W. Kilmister. 1970. 35.00 (ISBN 0-08-006996-7); pap. 11.25 (ISBN 0-08-006995-9). Pergamon.

Special Theory of Relativity. S. P. Puri. 1973. text ed. 15.00x (ISBN 0-210-22586-6). Asia.

Special Topics in Endocrinology & Metabolism, Vol. 1. Ed. by Margo P. Cohen & Piero P. Foa. 154p. 1979. 18.00x (ISBN 0-8451-0700-3). A R Liss.

Special Women of the Bible. Kay M. Strom. 1980. pap. 2.95 (ISBN 0-570-03495-7, 56-1712). Concordia.

Special Years: An Autobiography. Val Doonican. (Illus.). 192p. 1981. 17.95 (ISBN 0-241-10499-8, Pub. by Hamish Hamilton England). David & Charles.

Specialist. Chic Sale. 1974. 5.00 (ISBN 0-911416-00-5, 911416). Specialist.

Specialist Techniques in Engineering Mathematics. A. C. Bajpai et al. 416p. 1980. 57.25 (ISBN 0-471-27907-2, Pub. by Wiley-Interscience); pap. 26.00 (ISBN 0-471-27908-0). Wiley.

Specialized Education in Today's Secondary Schools. new ed. David A. Sabatino & August J. Mauser. 1978. text ed. 19.95 (ISBN 0-205-06043-9). Allyn.

Specialty Advertising in Marketing. George Herpel & Richard Collins. LC 78-165355. (Illus.). 1972. 9.95 o.p. (ISBN 0-87094-002-3). Dow Jones-Irwin.

Specialty Agricultural Chemicals, GA-035r. Ed. by Business Communications Co. 1980. 750.00 (ISBN 0-89336-225-5). BCC.

Specialty of the House & Other Stories: The Complete Mystery Tales, 1948-1978. Stanley Ellin. LC 79-67149. 557p. 1979. limited ed. 35.00 (ISBN 0-686-68286-6); 15.00 (ISBN 0-89296-049-3). Mysterious Pr.

Speciation in Wrens of the Genus Campylorhynchus. R. K. Selander. (U. C. Publ. in Zoology: Vol. 74). 1964. pap. 10.00x (ISBN 0-520-09329-1). U of Cal Pr.

Species Identity & Attachment: A Phylogenic Evaluation. M. Aaron Roy. 1979. lib. bdg. 37.50 (ISBN 0-8240-7052-6). Garland Pub.

Species of Eternity. Joseph Kastner. 1978. pap. 8.95 o.p. (ISBN 0-525-47531-1). Dutton.

Species of the Genus Schwagerina & Their Stratigraphic Significance. J. W. Beede & H. T. Kniker. (Illus.). 96p. 1924. 1.00 (BULL 2433). Bur Econ Geology.

Specific Production of Aquatic Invertebrates. V. E. Zaika. Ed. by B. Gollek. Tr. by A. Mercado from Rus. LC 73-12320. 154p. 1973. 39.95 (ISBN 0-470-98111-3). Halsted Pr.

Specific Reading Disability: Advances in Theory & Method. Ed. by Dirk J. Bakker & Paul Satz. (Modern Approaches to the Diagnosis & Instruction of Multi-Handicapped Children: Vol. 3). 166p. 1970. text ed. 21.50 (ISBN 90-237-4103-X, Pub. by Swets Pub Serv Holland). Swets North Am.

Specific Situations in Effective Oral Communication. Don M. Morlan & Goerge E. Tuttle, Jr. (gr. 12). 1977. pap. 9.50 (ISBN 0-672-61410-3); tchr's manual 2.50 (ISBN 0-672-61411-1). Bobbs.

Specific Skill Reading Series: New 1976-1978. Richard A. Boning. Incl. Detecting the Sequence, 14 bks. (gr. 1-12); Drawing Conclusions, 14 bks. (gr. 1-12); Following Directions, 14 bks. (gr. 1-12); Getting the Facts, 14 bks. (gr. 1-12); Getting the Main Idea, 14 bks. (gr. 1-12); Locating the Answer, 14 bks. (gr. 1-12); Using the Context, 14 bks. (gr. 1-12); Working with Sounds, 14 bks. (gr. 1-12). per bk. 1.95 (ISBN 0-685-39281-3); tchr's manuals 3.00ea. (ISBN 0-685-39282-1); Set. spirit masters 6.95 (ISBN 0-685-39283-X); complete elementary set 127.55 (ISBN 0-685-39284-8); complete midway set (4-9) 98.95 (ISBN 0-685-39285-6); complete secondary set (7-12) 98.95 (ISBN 0-685-39286-4). B Loft.

Specific Soil Chemical Characteristics for Rice Production in Asia. (IRRI Research Paper Ser.: No. 2). 18p. 1976. pap. 5.00 (R042, IRRI). Unipub.

Specification & Measurement of Learning Outcomes. Ed. by David A. Payne. (Education & Psychology Ser). (Orig.). 1960. pap. 10.50 (ISBN 0-471-00413-8). Wiley.

Specifications & Criteria for Biochemical Compounds. 3rd ed. Division of Chemistry & Chemical Technology. 224p. 1972. 21.25 (ISBN 0-309-01917-6). Natl Acad Pr.

Specifications & Quantities. 2nd ed. D. Burchess. (Illus.). 136p. 1980. pap. text ed. 12.95x (ISBN 0-7114-5640-2). Intl Ideas.

Specifications for Plant Protection Products Nicotine Sulphate. (FAO Specifications for Plant Protection Products). 1979. pap. 6.00 (ISBN 92-5-100552-4, F1468, FAO). Unipub.

Specifications for Structural Concrete for Buildings. 1976. 19.75 (ISBN 0-685-85100-1, SP-1575) (ISBN 0-685-85101-X). ACI.

Specimen Questions & Answers for Master, Mate, Pilot & Certified Tankerman on the Central Western Rivers. David Metz. LC 63-23041. 1963. pap. 6.50x (ISBN 0-87033-116-7). Cornell Maritime.

Specimens of the British Critics. John Wilson. LC 78-12061. 1979. 34.00x (ISBN 0-8201-1326-3). Schol Facsimiles.

Specimens of the Pre-Shakespearean Drama, 2 Vols. John M. Manly. LC 67-18432. 1897. 20.00x (ISBN 0-8196-0200-0). Biblo.

Specs: The Comprehensive Foodservice Purchasing and Specification Manual. Ray Peddersen. LC 76-56460. 1977. 85.00 (ISBN 0-8436-2084-6). CBI Pub.

Spectacles & Predicaments: Essays in Social Theory. Ernest Gellner. LC 78-67304. 1980. 41.00 (ISBN 0-521-22486-1). Cambridge U Pr.

Spectacles for Aphakia. Curtis D. Benton, Jr. & Robert C. Welsh. (Illus.). 176p. 1977. 17.50 (ISBN 0-398-00135-9). C C Thomas.

Spectaculum: Fuenf Moderne Theaterstuecke und Materialien, Vol. 32. 300p. (Ger.). 1980. text ed. 13.00 (ISBN 0-686-64762-9, 3518-9101, Pub. by Insel Verlag Germany). Suhrkamp.

Spectator, 4 Vols. Joseph Addison et al. 1958. Vol. 1. 6.00x (ISBN 0-460-00164-7, Evman); Vol. 2. 6.00x (ISBN 0-460-00165-5); Vol. 3. 17.95x (ISBN 0-460-00166-3); Vol. 4. 6.00x o.p. (ISBN 0-460-00167-1). Dutton.

Spectators Guide to Sports: Rules, Scoring, Strategy & Competing. Ed. by Consumer Guide Magazine. 1976. pap. 5.95 o.p. (ISBN 0-451-79975-5, G9975, Sig). NAL.

Specter Series. Anita Jackson. Incl. The Actor (ISBN 0-8224-6432-2); Dreams (ISBN 0-8224-6435-7); A Deadly Game (ISBN 0-8224-6434-9); The Ear (ISBN 0-8224-6436-5); Fifty-Seven T-Bird (ISBN 0-8224-6437-3); Homecoming (ISBN 0-8224-6438-1); No Rent to Pay (ISBN 0-8224-6439-X); ZB4 (ISBN 0-8224-6433-0). (gr. 6 up). 1979. pap. 3.56 ea.; Set. pap. 28.00 (ISBN 0-8224-6430-6). Pitman Learning.

Spectra of X Rays Scattered in Low Atomic Number Materials. W. R. Bruce & H. E. Johns. 1980. 10.00x (Pub. by Brit Inst Radiology). State Mutual Bk.

Spectral Analysis & Its Applications. Gwilym M. Jenkins & Donald G. Watts. LC 67-13840. 1968. pap. 36.95x (ISBN 0-8162-4464-2). Holden-Day.

Spectral & Chemical Characterization of Organic Compounds: A Laboratory Handbook. W. J. Criddle & G. P. Ellis. LC 75-23296. 128p. 1976. 19.95 (ISBN 0-471-18767-4, Pub. by Wiley-Interscience); pap. text ed. 8.95 (ISBN 0-471-01499-0, Pub. by Wiley-Interscience). Wiley.

Spectral & Chemical Characterization of Organic Compounds: A Laboratory Handbook. 2nd ed. W. J. Criddle & G. P. Ellis. LC 80-40497. 1980. write for info. (ISBN 0-471-27813-0, Pub. by Wiley-Interscience); pap. write for info. (ISBN 0-471-27812-2). Wiley.

Spectral Atlas of Nitrogen Dioxide: 5530a to 6480a. Donald K. Hsu et al. 1978. 48.50 (ISBN 0-12-357950-3). Acad Pr.

Spectral Boy. Donald Petersen. LC 64-13611. (Wesleyan Poetry Program: Vol. 22). (Orig.). 1964. 10.00x (ISBN 0-8195-2022-5, Pub. by Wesleyan U Pr); pap. 4.95 (ISBN 0-8195-1022-X). Columbia U Pr.

Spectral Emanations: New & Selected Poems. John Hollander. LC 77-20645. 1978. pap. 7.95 (ISBN 0-689-10878-8). Atheneum.

Spectral Properties of Disordered Chains & Lattices. J. Hori. 1968. 34.00 (ISBN 0-08-012359-7). Pergamon.

Spectral Theory of Linear Operators, 2 Vols. A. I. Plesner. Tr. by Merlynd Nestell & Alan G. Gibbs. LC 68-20524. 1969. Vol. 1. 15.00 (ISBN 0-8044-4767-5); Vol. 2. 15.00 (ISBN 0-8044-4768-3); Set. 25.00 (ISBN 0-8044-4766-7). Ungar.

Spectralk Theory of Ordinary Differential Equations. Erich Muller-Pfeiffer. LC 80-42097. (Mathematics & Its Application Ser.). 260p. 1981. 51.95 (ISBN 0-470-27103-5). Halsted Pr.

Spectrometric Indentification of Organic Compounds. 4th ed. Robert M. Silverstein & G. Clayton Bassler. Ed. by Terence C. Morrill. 704p. 1981. text ed. 20.95 (ISBN 0-471-02990-4). Wiley.

Spectrometric Techniques, Vol. II. Ed. by George A. Vanasse. 1981. write for info. (ISBN 0-12-710402-X). Acad Pr.

Spectrophotometric Determination of Elements. Zygmund Marczenko. LC 74-33186. (Ser. in Analytical Chemistry). 643p. 1976. 68.95 (ISBN 0-470-56865-8). Halsted Pr.

Spectroscopic & Chromatographic Analysis of Mineral Oil, 3 vols. S. H. Kagler. LC 72-4105. 559p. 1973. Set. 79.95 (ISBN 0-470-45425-3). Halsted Pr.

Spectroscopic Astrophysics: An Assessment of the Contributions of Otto Struve. Ed. by George H. Herbig. LC 69-15939. 1970. 32.50x (ISBN 0-520-01410-3). U of Cal Pr.

Spectroscopic Data Relative to Diatomic Molecules. S. Bourcier. 1971. 145.00 (ISBN 0-08-016546-X). Pergamon.

Spectroscopic References to Polyatomic Molecules. R. N. Verma. 125p. 1980. 75.00 (ISBN 0-306-65190-4). IFI Plenum.

Spectroscopy, 2 vols. 2nd ed. Ed. by B. P. Straughan & S. Walker. LC 75-45328. 1978. Vol. 1. pap. text ed. 16.50x o.p. (ISBN 0-412-13350-4, Pub. by Chapman & Hall England); Vol. 2. pap. text ed. 22.50x o.p. (ISBN 0-412-13370-9). Halsted Pr.

Spectroscopy, 2 vols. 2nd ed. Ed. by B. P. Straughan & S. Walker. LC 75-45328. 1978. Vol. 1. 15.00 o.p. (ISBN 0-686-00608-9). Vol. 1 (ISBN 0-470-26322-9). Vol. 2. pap. 15.00 o.p. (ISBN 0-470-26323-7). Halsted Pr.

Spectroscopy in Biochemistry, 2 vols. Ed. by J. Ellis Bell. 288p. 1981. 69.95 ea. Vol. 1 (ISBN 0-8493-5551-6). Vol. 2 (ISBN 0-8493-5552-4). CRC Pr.

Spectroscopy in Heterogeneous Catalysis. William Delgass et al. LC 78-27885. 1979. 38.00 (ISBN 0-12-210150-2). Acad Pr.

Spectroscopy in Inorganic Chemistry. C. N. Rao & J. R. Ferraro. 1970-1971. Vol. 1. 48.50 (ISBN 0-12-580201-3); Vol. 2. 48.50 (ISBN 0-12-580202-1). Acad Pr.

Spectroscopy of the Excited State. Ed. by Baldassare De Bartolo. LC 75-38526. (NATO Advanced Study Institutes Ser., Series B: Physics: Vol. 12). 416p. 1976. 37.50 (ISBN 0-306-35712-7, Plenum Pr). Plenum Pub.

Spectrum. David Wise. LC 80-17418. 336p. 1981. 13.95 (ISBN 0-670-66219-4). Viking Pr.

Spectrum of Ritual. Eugene G. D'Aquili et al. 1979. 25.00x (ISBN 0-231-04514-X). Columbia U Pr.

Speculation, Hedging, & Commodity Price Forecasts. Walter Labys & Clive W. Granger. 1971. 19.95 (ISBN 0-669-61051-8). Lexington Bks.

Speculations: Fantasy - Science Fiction. Thomas E. Sanders. LC 72-86794. 608p. 1973. pap. text ed. 8.95x (ISBN 0-02-477630-0). Macmillan.

Speculations on American History. Morton Borden & Otis L. Graham. 1977. pap. text ed. 5.95x (ISBN 0-669-00488-X). Heath.

Speculations on the Fourth Dimension: Selected Writings of C. H. Hinton. Charles H. Hinton. Ed. by Rudolf V. Rucker. (Illus.). 1980. pap. 4.00 (ISBN 0-486-23916-0). Dover.

Speculator: Bernard M. Baruch in Washington, 1917-1965. Jordan A. Schwarz. LC 80-17386. (Illus.). 688p. 1981. 27.50 (ISBN 0-8078-1396-6). U of NC Pr.

Speculum Duorum: Or, a Mirror of Two Men. Giraldus Cambrensis. (University of Wales, History & Law Ser.: No. 27). 1974. 25.00 (ISBN 0-7083-0544-X). Verry.

Speech: A Handbook of Voice Training, Diction & Public Speaking. Dorothy Mulgrave. (Orig.). 1954. pap. 3.95 (ISBN 0-06-460089-0, CO 89, COS). Har-Row.

Speech Acoustics & Perception. Philip Lieberman. LC 70-183114. (Studies in Communicative Disorders Ser). 1972. 2.50 (ISBN 0-672-61293-3). Bobbs.

Speech Acts. John R. Searle. LC 68-24484. 1970. 29.95 (ISBN 0-521-07184-4); pap. 7.95x (ISBN 0-521-09626-X). Cambridge U Pr.

Speech Acts & Happenings. Robert Vas Dias. LC 71-173226. 1972. pap. 2.45 o.p. (ISBN 0-672-51690-X). Bobbs.

Speech After Stroke. S. Stryker. (Illus.). 440p. 1978. pap. 19.00 o.p. (ISBN 0-398-03234-3). C C Thomas.

Speech After Stroke. 2nd ed. S. Stryker. (Illus.). 442p. 1980. pap. 22.75 (ISBN 0-398-04122-9). C C Thomas.

Speech Analysis. Ed. by R. W. Schafer & J. D. Markel. LC 78-65706. (IEEE Press Selected Reprint Ser.). 1979. 33.95 (ISBN 0-471-05830-0); pap. 22.00 (ISBN 0-471-05832-7, Pub. by Wiley-Interscience). Wiley.

Speech & Brain-Mechanisms. Wilder Penfield & Lamar Roberts. 1959. 25.00x (ISBN 0-691-08039-9). Princeton U Pr.

Speech & Brain Mechanisms. Wilder Penfield & Lamar Roberts. LC 59-5602. (Illus.). 304p. 1981. 25.00x; pap. 6.95. Princeton U Pr.

Speech & Cortical Functioning. Ed. by John H. Gilbert. (Based upon a symposium). 1972. 24.50 (ISBN 0-12-282850-X). Acad Pr.

Speech & Hearing Problems: A Guide for Teachers & Parents. Charles E. Palmer. 152p. 1961. pap. 7.25 spiral (ISBN 0-398-01441-8). C C Thomas.

Speech & Hearing Science. 2nd ed. W. R. Zemlin. (Illus.). 704p. 1981. text ed. 23.95 (ISBN 0-13-827378-2). P-H.

Speech & Language: Advances in Basic Research & Practice, Vol. 3. Ed. by Norman J. Lass. (Serial Publication). 1980. 29.50 (ISBN 0-12-608603-6). Acad Pr.

Speech & Language: Advances in Basic Research & Practice, Vol. 4. Ed. by Norman J. Lass. 1980. 35.00 (ISBN 0-12-608604-4). Acad Pr.

Speech & Language Development of the Preschool Child: A Survey. Colleen W. McElroy. (Illus.). 236p. 1978. 16.50 (ISBN 0-398-02368-9). C C Thomas.

Speech & Language Problems: An Overview. Morris V. Jones. (Am. Lec. Special Education Ser.). (Illus.). 420p. 1979. 22.75 (ISBN 0-398-03790-6). C C Thomas.

Speech & Language Rehabilitation: A Workbook for the Neurologically Impaired, Vol. 2. Robert L. Keith. 1977. pap. text ed. 6.95x (ISBN 0-685-84999-6, 1949). Interstate.

Speech & Reason: Language Disorder in Mental Disease & a Translation of Philipp Wegener's The Life of Speech. D. Wilfred Abse. LC 72-163981. 1971. 20.00x (ISBN 0-8139-0344-0). U Pr of Va.

Speech Art Classification. T. Ballmer & W. Brennenstuhl. (Springer Series in Language & Communication: Vol. 8). (Illus.). 304p. 1981. 29.50 (ISBN 0-387-10294-9). Springer-Verlag.

Speech Assessment & Speech Improvement for the Hearing Impaired. Joanne Subtelny. 1980. 19.95 (ISBN 0-88200-138-8). Bell Assn Deaf.

Speech Assessment & Speech Improvement for the Hearing Impaired. Ed. by Joanne D. Subtelny. 420p. 1980. pap. text ed. 19.95 (ISBN 0-88200-138-8, A0138). Alexander Graham.

Speech Bingo, Set 1. Kathleen M. Morrissey. (Illus.). 1980. pap. 7.95x (ISBN 0-8134-2144-6). Interstate.

Speech Chain: The Physics & Biology of Spoken Language. Peter B. Denes & Elliot N. Pinson. LC 74-180069. 192p. 1973. pap. 2.50 (ISBN 0-385-04238-8, Anch). Doubleday.

Speech Clinician & the Hearing-Impaired Child. Ed. by R. L. Cozad. (Illus.). 232p. 1974. 17.50 (ISBN 0-398-02983-0). C C Thomas.

Speech Communication. 4th ed. William D. Brooks. 425p. 1981. pap. text ed. write for info. (ISBN 0-697-04178-6); instr's manual avail. (ISBN 0-697-04190-5); student activities wkbk. avail. (ISBN 0-697-04185-9). Wm C Brown.

Speech Communication: A Career Education Approach. 2nd ed. Ray E. Nadeau & John M. Muchmore. LC 78-18640. (Speech Ser.). 1979. text ed. 12.50 (ISBN 0-201-05007-2). A-W.

Speech Communication: A Career Education Approach. 2nd ed. Raymond E. Nadeau. 1979. text ed. 12.50 (ISBN 0-201-05007-2). A-W.

Speech Communication: A Contemporary Introduction. Gordon I. Zimmerman et al. (Illus.). 1977. pap. text ed. 11.50 (ISBN 0-8299-0055-1); instrs.' manual avail. (ISBN 0-8299-0587-1). West Pub.

Speech Communication & Theatre Arts: A Classified Bibliography of Theses & Dissertations, 1937-1978. Merilyn Merenda & C. W. Polichak. LC 79-9373. 340p. 1979. 75.00 (ISBN 0-306-65182-3). IFI Plenum.

Speech Communication Behavior: Perspectives & Principles. Ed. by Larry L. Barker & Robert J. Kibler. LC 74-143585. 1971. pap. text ed. 14.95 (ISBN 0-13-827337-5). P-H.

Speech Communication: Fundamentals & Practice. 4th ed. Raymond S. Ross. 1977. text ed. 14.95 (ISBN 0-13-827485-1). P-H.

Speech Communication in Society. 2nd ed. Charles R. Gruner et al. 1977. text ed. 13.95 (ISBN 0-205-05732-2, 4857321); instr's manual o.p. free (ISBN 0-205-05733-0). Allyn.

Speech Communication in the Secondary School. 2nd ed. Ron R. Allen et al. 461p. 1976. text ed. 15.95 (ISBN 0-205-05412-9, 4854128). Allyn.

Speech Communication Laboratory Manual. O. David Dye & Gerald D. Baxter. 1977. pap. text ed. 4.95 (ISBN 0-8403-1765-4). Kendall-Hunt.

Speech Corrections: Principles & Methods. 6th ed. Charles Van Riper. (Illus.). 1978. ref. 19.95 (ISBN 0-13-829523-9). P-H.

Speech Criticism. 2nd ed. Lester Thonssen et al. 1970. 18.50 o.p. (ISBN 0-8260-8645-4). Wiley.

Speech Disorder in Nineteenth Century Britain: The History of Stuttering. Denyse Rockey. 280p. 1980. 50.00x (ISBN 0-85664-809-4, Pub. by Croom Helm Ltd England). Biblio Dist.

Speech Disorders in Children. C. E. Renfrew. 78p. 1972. text ed. 8.25 (ISBN 0-08-016828-0). Pergamon.

Speech Disorders: Principles & Practices of Therapy. Mildred F. Berry & Jon Eisenson. (Illus.). 1956. 19.95 (ISBN 0-13-827352-9). P-H.

Speech Education Activities for Children. James N. Blake. (Illus.). 136p. 1970. text ed. 14.50 photocopy ed. spiral (ISBN 0-398-00165-0). C C Thomas.

Speech Education for the Elementary Teacher. 2nd ed. Alan W. Huckleberry & Edward Strother. 1972. text ed. 13.95x o.p. (ISBN 0-205-03320-2, 4833201). Allyn.

Speech Evaluation in Psychiatry. Ed. by John J. Darby & Michael Hecker. 1980. 34.00 (ISBN 0-8089-1315-8). Grune.

Speech Facilitation: Extraoral & Intraoral Stimulation Technique for Improvement of Articulation Skills. Gwenyth R. Vaughn & Ruth M. Clark. (Illus.). 304p. 1979. text ed. 17.75 (ISBN 0-398-03828-7). C C Thomas.

Speech, for Instance. Sidney Goldfarb. LC 69-13743. 1969. pap. 1.95 o.p. (ISBN 0-374-50788-0, N371). FS&G.

Speech for the Actor. rev. ed. Robert Westrom. (Illus.). 87p. (Orig.). 1978. pap. 3.50 (ISBN 0-938230-00-X). Westrom.

Speech for the Stage. new & rev. ed. Evangeline Machlin. LC 80-51639. 1980. 9.95 (ISBN 0-87830-120-8); tchr's manual 2.45 (ISBN 0-87830-573-4). Theatre Arts.

Speech Index. 4th ed. Roberta B. Sutton. LC 66-13749. 1966. 29.50 (ISBN 0-8108-0138-8). Scarecrow.

Speech Index: An Index to Collections of World Famous Orations & Speeches for Various Occasions; Supplement, 1971-1975. 4th ed. Charity Mitchell. LC 66-13749. 1977. 10.00 (ISBN 0-8108-1000-X). Scarecrow.

Speech Index: An Index to Collections of World Famous Orations & Speeches for Various Occasions; Supplement 1966 to 1970. 4th ed. Roberta B. Sutton & Charity Mitchell. LC 66-13749. 1972. 10.00 (ISBN 0-8108-0498-0). Scarecrow.

Speech Is Plurality. Alain Bosquet. Tr. by Melvin B. Yoken & Juliet G. Lapointe. LC 78-61914. 1978. pap. text ed. 7.50 (ISBN 0-8191-0626-7). U Pr of Amer.

Speech, Language & Hearing: Normal Processes & Disorders. Paul H. Skinner & Ralph L. Shelton. LC 77-73956. (Speech Pathology & Audiology Ser.). 1978. text ed. 16.95 (ISBN 0-201-07461-3); instr's man. price not set (ISBN 0-201-07462-1). A-W.

Speech, Language & Learning Disorders: Education & Therapy. James N. Blake. (Illus.). 172p. 1971. 12.75 (ISBN 0-398-00166-9). C C Thomas.

Speech Pathology: An Applied Behavioral Science. 2nd ed. William H. Perkins. LC 76-25839. (Illus.). 1977. text ed. 23.95 (ISBN 0-8016-3785-6). Mosby.

Speech Pathology: An Introduction. Oliver Bloodstein. LC 78-69600. (Illus.). 1979. text ed. 17.75 (ISBN 0-395-27048-0). HM.

Speech Pathology & Audiology. Jack Rudman. (Undergraduate Program Field Test Ser.: UPFT-25). (Cloth bdg. avail. on request). pap. 9.95 (ISBN 0-8373-6025-0). Natl Learning.

Speech Pathology & Dialect Difference. Walt Wolfram. (Dialects & Educational Equity Ser.: No. 3). 1979. pap. 2.50 (ISBN 0-87281-122-0). Ctr Appl Ling.

Speech Pathology & Feedback Theory. Edward D. Mysak. (Illus.). 124p. 1971. 9.75 (ISBN 0-398-01379-9). C C Thomas.

Speech Rehabilitation of the Laryngectomized. 2nd ed. Ed. by John C. Snidecor. (Amer. Lec. in Speech & Hearing Ser). (Illus.). 288p. 1978. 16.75 (ISBN 0-398-01803-0). C C Thomas.

Speech Science: Acoustics in Speech. 2nd ed. Richard A. Hoops. (Illus.). 164p. 1976. 12.75 (ISBN 0-398-00869-8). C C Thomas.

Speech: Science-Art. Elwood Murray et al. LC 79-77823. 1969. text ed. 11.50 (ISBN 0-672-60863-4). Bobbs.

Speech Science Primer: Physiology, Acoustics & Perception of Speech. Gloria J. Borden & Katherine S. Harris. (Illus.). 312p. 1980. pap. 20.95 (ISBN 0-683-00941-9). Williams & Wilkins.

Speech, Silence, Action! The Cycle of Faith. Virginia R. Mollenkott. LC 80-15812. (Journey in Faith Ser.). 144p. 1980. 7.95 (ISBN 0-687-39169-5). Abingdon.

Speech Synthesis. Ed. by J. L. Flanagan & L. R. Rabiner. LC 73-9728. (Benchmark Papers in Acoustics Ser.). 544p. 1973. 43.50 (ISBN 0-12-786476-8). Acad Pr.

Speech Theraphy & ENT Surgery. T. R. Bull & Joyce L. Cook. (Blackwell Scientific Pubns.). (Illus.). 1976. 15.75 (ISBN 0-632-09410-9). Mosby.

Speech Therapy in the Public Schools. Martha E. Black. LC 72-81498. (Studies in Communicative Disorders Ser). 1972. pap. 1.95 (ISBN 0-672-61287-9). Bobbs.

Speech Therapy: Principles & Practice. Betty B. Brown. (Illus.). 288p. 1981. pap. 15.00 (ISBN 0-443-02099-X). Churchill.

Speeches & Writings of Gopal Krishna Gokhale. Ed. by D. G. Karve & D. V. Ambekar. (Educational Series,: Vol. 3). 1968. 9.00x o.p. (ISBN 0-210-31207-6). Asia.

Speeches of the Earl of Shaftesbury. A. A. Cooper. 456p. Repr. of 1868 ed. 32.00x (ISBN 0-686-28328-7, Pub. by Irish Academic Pr). Biblio Dist.

Speeches of the Governors of Massachusetts from 1765 to 1775. Alden Bradford. LC 71-119048. (Era of the American Revolution Ser). 1971. Repr. of 1818 ed. 45.00 (ISBN 0-306-71947-9). Da Capo.

Speed. rev. ed. Harlan Wade. LC 78-21033. (Book About Ser.). (Illus.). (gr. k-3). 1979. PLB 7.30 (ISBN 0-8172-1540-9). Raintree Pubs.

Speed & Power. John Fletcher. (gr. 5 up). 1980. PLB 7.90 (ISBN 0-531-03420-8, G21). Watts.

Speed Culture: Amphetamine Use & Abuse in America. Lester Grinspoon & Peter Hedblom. LC 74-27257. 368p. 1975. 17.50x (ISBN 0-674-83192-6); pap. 5.95 (ISBN 0-674-83194-2). Harvard U Pr.

Speed in the Air. David W. Wragg. LC 74-7456. 1975. 9.95 (ISBN 0-8119-0246-3). Fell.

Speed Kings. Ed. by Thomas J. Mooney. (Pal Paperbacks Kit B Ser.). (Illus., Orig.). (gr. 7-12). 1973. pap. text ed. 1.25 (ISBN 0-8374-3517-X). Xerox Ed Pubns.

Speed Reading. Robert L. Zorn. LC 79-2744. (Everyday Handbook Ser.: EH-502). 128p. (Orig.). 1980. pap. 3.50 (ISBN 0-06-463502-3, EH 502, EH). Har-Row.

Speed Reading Made Easy. Nila B. Smith. 1977. pap. 1.95 (ISBN 0-445-08383-2). Popular Lib.

Speed-Script Secretarial Shorthand, 3 bks. Lenore F. Chalek et al. LC 73-93436. (Speed-Script Secretarial Shorthand Program Ser.). 440p. 1974. Set. text ed. 24.75 set (ISBN 0-913310-23-9). PAR Inc.

Speed Sketching. William T. Lent. LC 77-82957. 1978. 8.95 o.p. (ISBN 0-385-13089-9). Doubleday.

Speedwalking: The Exercise Alternative. Lilian Rowan & D. S. Laiken. 1980. 9.95 (ISBN 0-686-68357-9). Putnam.

Speedway. Joe Scalzo. 192p. 1981. pap. 1.95 (ISBN 0-448-17200-3, Tempo). G&D.

Speedway Challenge. William C. Gault. (gr. 5-8). 1965. pap. 0.95 o.p. (ISBN 0-685-06915-X, Highland). Berkley Pub.

Speedwriting Dictation & Transcription: College Edition. LC 76-41046. 1977. pap. text ed. 12.95 (ISBN 0-672-98051-7); tchr's manual 3.33 (ISBN 0-672-98052-5). Bobbs.

Speedwriting Dictation & Transcription: Secondary Edition. LC 76-41044. (Landmark Ser.). 1976. pap. text ed. 12.95 (ISBN 0-672-98004-5); tchr's manual 3.33 (ISBN 0-672-98005-3). Bobbs.

Speedwriting Dictionary: College Edition. LC 76-41047. (Landmark Ser.). 1977. text ed. 11.95 (ISBN 0-672-98095-9). Bobbs.

Speedwriting Dictionary: Secondary Edition. LC 76-45551. (Landmark Ser.). 1976. text ed. 11.50 (ISBN 0-672-98358-3). Bobbs.

Speedy Extinction of Evil & Misery: Selected Prose of James Thomson (B. V.) Ed. by William D. Schaefer. 1967. 22.75x (ISBN 0-520-01139-2). U of Cal Pr.

Spell in Plains. Phil Grout. LC 78-2230. (Illus.). 1978. 19.95 (ISBN 0-916144-17-8); pap. 9.95 (ISBN 0-916144-18-6). Stemmer Hse.

Spell It Fast. Robert C. Gilboy. 1981. pap. 4.95 (ISBN 0-87491-071-4). Acropolis.

Spell It Right. 2nd ed. Harry Shaw. (Orig.). 1965. pap. 2.95 (ISBN 0-06-463279-2, EH 279, EH). Har-Row.

Spell of Words: Studies in Language Bearing on Custom. Lina Eckenstein. LC 68-23153. 1969. Repr. of 1932 ed. 15.00 (ISBN 0-8103-3892-0). Gale.

Spell Well. Bobbe D'Ambrosio et al. (Makemaster Bk.). 1980. pap. 7.50 (ISBN 0-8224-6455-1). Pitman Learning.

Spell-Write, 8 bks. Educational Development Corporation. (Illus.). (gr. 1-8). 1975. Bks. 2-8. text ed. 4.98 ea.; Bk. 1. text ed. 4.98 ea. (ISBN 0-8107-1350-0); Bks. 2-8. pap. text ed. 3.93 ea.; Bks. 2-8. tchrs'. ed. 4.98 ea.; Bk. 1. tchrs' pap. ed. 3.42 (ISBN 0-685-04625-7); Bks. 2-8. tchrs' pap. eds. 4.80 ea.; Bks. 3-6. activity duplicating masters 9.00 ea. Bowmar-Noble.

Spellbinders. Margaret C. Banning. 1976. lib. bdg. 14.35x (ISBN 0-89968-008-9). Lightyear.

Spellcoats. Diana W. Jones. 1980. pap. write for info. (ISBN 0-671-83599-8). PB.

Spelling. C. D. Buchanan. (gr. 1). 1972. pap. text ed. 2.25 each incl. 8 texts, 4 tchrs' manuals & tests (ISBN 0-8449-2800-3). Learning Line.

Spelling. Mary L. Wallace. Ed. by Alton Raygor. (Communication Skills Ser.). 288p. 1981. pap. text ed. 7.95 (ISBN 0-07-067901-0, C). McGraw.

Spelling Book. Gary Grimm & Don Mitchell. (gr. 3-8). 1976. 7.95 (ISBN 0-916456-05-6, GA60). Good Apple.

Spelling by Principles. Genevie L. Smith. 1966. text ed. 7.95 (ISBN 0-13-834242-3). P-H.

Spelling for the Aviation Technician. David Sanderlin. 75p. (Orig.). 1980. write for info. (ISBN 0-89100-180-8). Aviation Maintenance.

Spelling Made Simple. Stephen V. Ross. LC 61-9566. 1958. pap. 2.50 (ISBN 0-385-01223-3, Made). Doubleday.

Spelling One-Two, 2 bks. (gr. k-3). 1970. pap. text ed. 1.29 ea. (ISBN 0-686-57627-6); Bk. 1. pap. (ISBN 0-440-08214-5); Bk. 2. pap. (ISBN 0-440-08246-3). Dell.

Spelling Plus. Jeffrey Barsch & Betty Creson. 96p. 1980. pap. text ed. 6.00 (ISBN 0-87879-246-5). Acad Therapy.

Spelling Program: Diagnostic & Prescriptive, 30 bks. (gr. 2 up). 1981. Set. 73.95 (ISBN 0-686-69580-1); pap. 2.25 test booklet (ISBN 0-686-69581-X). B Loft.

Spelling Skills. Heidi Hayes. Incl. Bk C. Air Mail (ISBN 0-8372-3500-6). tchr's ed. (ISBN 0-8372-9190-9); Bk D. Space-O-Grams (ISBN 0-8372-3501-4). tchr's ed. (ISBN 0-8372-9191-7); Bk E. Postmarks (ISBN 0-8372-3502-2). tchr's ed. (ISBN 0-8372-9192-5); Bk F. Fan Mail (ISBN 0-8372-3503-0). tchr's ed. (ISBN 0-8372-9193-3). (Illus.). (gr. 3-6). 1977. pap. text ed. 1.35 ea.; tchr's. eds. 1.35 ea. Bowmar-Noble.

Spelling Skills. Peter W. Preksto, Jr. & Patricia S. Schaefer. (Basic Skills Library). (Illus.). (gr. 4 up). 1979. PLB 5.95 (ISBN 0-87191-713-0). Creative Ed.

Spelling: Syllabus. 2nd ed. Delpha Hurlburt. (gr. 7-12). 1980. pap. text ed. 6.95 student syllabus (ISBN 0-89420-053-4, 187898); cassette recordings 133.40 (ISBN 0-89420-185-9, 187900). Natl Book.

Spells, Chants, & Potions. Sue Avent. LC 77-22779. (Myth, Magic & Superstition Ser.). (Illus.). (gr. 4-5). 1977. PLB 9.65 (ISBN 0-8172-1035-0). Raintree Pubs.

Spence & the Holiday Murders. Michael Allen. LC 78-51976. 1978. 7.95 o.s.i. (ISBN 0-8027-5390-6). Walker & Co.

Spence & the Holiday Murders. Michael Allen. 1981. pap. 2.25 (ISBN 0-440-18364-2). Dell.

Spencer's Toothbrush. Diane Tuggle. LC 80-54611. (Illus.). 72p. (Orig.). (gr. k-6). 1981. text ed. 9.95 (ISBN 0-932238-09-2); pap. text ed. 6.95 (ISBN 0-932238-08-4). Word Shop.

Spend Game. Jonathan Gash. LC 80-26266. 204p. 1981. 9.95 (ISBN 0-89919-030-8). Ticknor & Fields.

Spending Advertising Money. 3rd ed. Simon Broadbent. 381p. 1979. pap. 12.25x (ISBN 0-220-67020-X, Pub. by Busn Bks England). Renouf.

Spenser. Richard W. Church. LC 67-23879. 1968. Repr. of 1906 ed. 20.00 (ISBN 0-8103-3057-1). Gale.

Spenser: Fowre Hymnes & Epithalamion: a Study of Edmund Spenser's Doctrine of Love. Enid Welsford. 1967. 16.50x o.p. (ISBN 0-631-10500-X, Pub. by Basil Blackwell). Biblio Dist.

Spenser Handbook. Harry V. Jones. (Illus.). 1930. 28.00x (ISBN 0-89197-423-7); pap. text ed. 14.50 (ISBN 0-89197-632-9). Irvington.

Spenser, Milton, & Renaissance Pastoral. Richard Mallette. LC 78-73154. 224p. 1980. 18.50 (ISBN 0-8387-2412-4). Bucknell U Pr.

Spenser: The Faerie Queene. Ed. by A. C. Hamilton. LC 77-2738. (Longman Annotated English Poets Ser.). 1978. text ed. 60.00x (ISBN 0-582-48106-6). Longman.

Spenser: The Faerie Queene. Ed. by A. C. Hamilton. 768p. (Orig.). 1980. pap. text ed. 19.95 (ISBN 0-582-49705-1). Longman.

Spenser's Image of Life. Clive S. Lewis. Ed. by A. Fowler. 1967. 29.95 (ISBN 0-521-05546-6). Cambridge U Pr.

Spenser's Images of Life. C. S. Lewis. Ed. by A. Fowler. LC 77-82504. (Illus.). 1978. pap. 6.50 (ISBN 0-521-29284-0). Cambridge U Pr.

Spenser's World of Glass: A Reading of The Faerie Queen. Kathleen Williams. (California Library Reprint Series: No. 34). 1973. 18.50x (ISBN 0-520-02369-2). U of Cal Pr.

Sphecid Wasps of the World: A Generic Revision. R. M. Bohart & A. S. Menke. 1976. 62.50x (ISBN 0-520-02318-8). U of Cal Pr.

Sphere Spheroid & Projections for Surveyors: Aspects of Modern Land Surveying. J. E. Jackson. LC 80-82507. 138p. 1980. 37.95 (ISBN 0-470-27044-6). Halsted Pr.

Speech Disorders in Children placeholder removed

Sphereland. Dionys Burger. Tr. by Cornelie J. Rheinboldt. (Apollo Eds.). (Illus.). pap. 3.95 o.s.i. (ISBN 0-8152-0184-2, A184, TYC-T). T Y Crowell.

Spherical & Ellipsoidal Harmonics. Ernest W. Hobson. LC 55-233. 1955. 14.95 (ISBN 0-8284-0104-7). Chelsea Pub.

Spherical Models. Magnus J. Wenninger. LC 78-58806. 1979. 22.50 (ISBN 0-521-22279-6); pap. 9.95 (ISBN 0-521-29432-0). Cambridge U Pr.

Sphinx. Graham Masterton. 1978. pap. 1.95 o.p. (ISBN 0-523-40189-2). Pinnacle Bks.

Sphinx & the Megaliths. John Ivimy. 1976. pap. 3.45 o.p. (ISBN 0-06-090533-6, CN533, CN). Har-Row.

Sphinx: Movie Edition. Robin Cook. 1981. pap. 2.95 (ISBN 0-451-09745-9, E9745, Sig). NAL.

Spice: A Handbook of Classroom Ideas to Motivate the Teaching of Primary Language Arts. (Spice Ser). 1973. 6.50 (ISBN 0-89273-101-X). Educ Serv.

Spice Adventure. Albert Barker. LC 80-18754. (Illus.). 96p. (gr. 4-6). 1980. PLB 7.79 (ISBN 0-671-33097-7). Messner.

Spice & Spirit of Kosher-Jewish Cooking. Ed. by Esther Blau. LC 77-72116. (Illus.). 1977. 13.95 (ISBN 0-8197-0455-5). Bloch.

Spice Box: A Vegetarian Indian Cookbook. Manju S. Singh. (Illus.). 224p. 1981. 12.95 (ISBN 0-89594-052-3); pap. 6.95 (ISBN 0-89594-053-1). Crossing Pr.

Spice Duplicating Masters, 2 vols. (Spice Duplicating Masters Ser). 1973. Vol. 1, Grades K-2. 5.95 (ISBN 0-89273-501-5); Vol. 2, Grades 2-4. 5.25 (ISBN 0-89273-502-3). Educ Serv.

Spice Island Mystery. Betty Cavanna. LC 72-83531. (gr. 7 up). 1969. 8.25 (ISBN 0-688-21706-0). Morrow.

Spice of Life. James M. Hendrickson & Angela LaBarca. 180p. 1979. pap. text ed. 6.95 (ISBN 0-15-583251-4, HC). HarBraceJ.

Spice of Life: Pleasures of the Victorian Age. Patrick Beaver. (Illus.). 1979. 24.00 (ISBN 0-241-89366-6, Pub. by Hamish Hamilton England). David & Charles.

Spices & Civilizations. Duncan Townson. Ed. by Malcolm Yapp et al. (World History Ser.). (Illus.). (gr. 10). 1980. Repr. of 1977 ed. lib. bdg. 5.95 (ISBN 0-89908-029-4); pap. text ed. 1.95 (ISBN 0-89908-004-9). Greenhaven.

Spices & Herbs: Their Lore & Use. Elizabeth S. Hayes. (Illus.). 256p. 1980. pap. 3.50 (ISBN 0-486-24026-6). Dover.

Spices: Their Botanical Origin, Their Chemical Composition, Their Commercial Use Including Seeds, Herbs & Leaves. Joseph K. Jank. 1980. lib. bdg. 49.95 (ISBN 0-8490-3111-7). Gordon Pr.

Spider & Insects. Time-Life Television. (Wild, Wild World of Animals Ser.). (Illus.). 1977. 10.95 (ISBN 0-913948-12-8). Time-Life.

Spider Bomb. W. C. Chalk. pap. text ed. 2.75x o.p. (ISBN 0-435-11226-0). Heinemann Ed.

Spider, Egg, & Microcosm: Three Men & Three Worlds of Science. C. Colebrook. LC 55-9287. 1955. 6.50 (ISBN 0-9600476-1-1). E Kinkead.

Spider Kiss. Harlan Ellison. 1975. pap. 1.50 o.s.i. (ISBN 0-515-03883-0). Jove Pubns.

Spider of Brooklyn Heights. Nancy Veglahn. LC 67-15493. (Encore Edition). (Illus.). (gr. 7-9). 1967. 1.99 o.p. (ISBN 0-684-15858-2, ScribT). Scribner.

Spider Silk. Augusta Goldin. LC 64-18164. (Let's-Read-&-Find-Out Science Bk). (Illus.). (gr. k-3). 1964. bds. 6.95 o.p. (ISBN 0-690-76074-4, TYC-J); PLB 7.89 (ISBN 0-690-76075-2); film with records 11.95 (ISBN 0-690-76076-0); filmstrip with cassette 14.95 (ISBN 0-690-76078-7). T Y Crowell.

Spider Woman Stories. G. M. Mullett. LC 78-11556. 1979. 11.95 o.s.i. (ISBN 0-8165-0669-8); pap. 4.95 (ISBN 0-8165-0621-3). U of Ariz Pr.

Spiderman, No. 3. 1980. pap. write for info. (ISBN 0-671-83495-9). PB.

Spiders. Jane Dallinger. (Lerner Natural Science Bks.). (Illus.). (gr. 4-10). 1981. PLB 7.95 (ISBN 0-8225-1456-7). Lerner Pubns.

Spiders. Dean Morris. LC 77-8115. (Read About Animals Ser.). (gr. k-3). 1977. PLB 9.95 (ISBN 0-8393-0004-2). Raintree Child.

Spiders. Sarah R. Riedman. (Easy-Read Fact Bks.). (Illus.). (gr. 2-4). 1979. PLB 6.45 s&l (ISBN 0-531-02853-4). Watts.

Spiders. Ralph Whitlock. Ed. by Barbara Brenner. LC 76-14935. (Illus.). 80p. (gr. 4 up). 1976. PLB 6.95 o.p. (ISBN 0-8172-0325-7). Raintree Pubs.

Spiders Dance. Joanne Ryder. LC 78-22495. (Illus.). 48p. (gr. 1-4). 1981. 8.95 (ISBN 0-06-025133-6, HarpJ); PLB 8.79 (ISBN 0-06-025134-4). Har-Row.

Spider's Silk of Time. Zella R. Spohrer. (Contemporary Poets of Dorrance Ser.). 64p. 1981. 3.95 (ISBN 0-8059-2771-9). Dorrance.

Spiderweb. Joseph Persico. 224p. 1981. pap. 2.50 (ISBN 0-553-14334-4). Bantam.

Spiegel on the New Testament. Werner Harenberg. Tr. by James H. Burtness. 1970. 6.95 o.p. (ISBN 0-02-548160-6); pap. 1.95 (ISBN 0-02-085410-2). Macmillan.

Spiele Auf Graphen. B. Kummer. (Internationale Schriftenreihe zur numerischen Mathematik: No. 44). 88p. (Ger.). 1979. pap. 18.50 (ISBN 3-7643-1077-4). Birkhauser.

Spielraum Des Verhaltens. Bernhard Waldenfels. (Suhrkamp Taschenbuecher Wissenschaft: 311). 344p. (Ger.). pap. text ed. 9.10 (ISBN 3-518-07911-5, Pub. by Insel Verlag Germany). Suhrkamp.

Spike. Arnaud De Borchgrave & Robert Moss. 1981. pap. 2.95. Avon.

Spiky the Hedgehog. Mirabel Cecil. LC 79-26358. (Illus.). 32p. (gr. k-3). 1980. 3.95 (ISBN 0-07-010322-4). McGraw.

Spin Eigenfunctions: Construction & Use. Ed. by Pauncz. (Illus.). 1979. 35.00 (ISBN 0-306-40141-X, Plenum Pr). Plenum Pub.

Spin Exchange: Principles & Applications in Chemistry & Biology. Y. N. Molin et al. (Springer Series in Chemical Physics: Vol. 8). (Illus.). 242p. 1980. 39.00 (ISBN 0-387-10095-4). Springer-Verlag.

Spin Temperature & Nuclear Spin Relaxation in Matter: Basic Principles & Applications. Dieter Wolf. (International Series of Monographs on Physics). (Illus.). 480p. 1979. text ed. 34.95x (ISBN 0-19-851295-3). Oxford U Pr.

Spin Your Own Wool & Dye It & Weave It. rev. ed. Molly Duncan. (Illus.). 52p. 1978. 7.50 (ISBN 0-589-00334-8, Pub by Reed Books Australia). C E Tuttle.

Spina Bifida & the Total Care of Spinal Myelomeningocele. E. Durham Smith. (Pediatric Surgical Monograph Ser). (Illus.). 168p. 1965. 16.75 (ISBN 0-398-01785-9). C C Thomas.

Spina Bifida: The Treatment & Care of Spina Bifida Children. Nancy Allum. 1975. pap. text ed. 7.95x o.p. (ISBN 0-04-618014-1). Allen Unwin.

Spinal Cord & It's Reaction to Traumatic Injury. Windle. 448p. 1980. 45.00 (ISBN 0-8247-6688-1). Dekker.

Spinal Cord Injuries. Daniel Ruge. 236p. 1969. pap. 16.25 spiral (ISBN 0-398-01630-5). C C Thomas.

Spinal Deformities & Neurological Dysfunction. Ed. by Shelley N. Chou & Edward L. Seljeskog. LC 76-5665. (Seminars in Neurological Surgery). 1978. 33.50 (ISBN 0-89004-183-0). Raven.

Spinal Injury Learning Series. William C. Norris et al. LC 80-26576. (Illus.). 1981. price not set (ISBN 0-87805-131-7). U Pr of Miss.

Spindle Stage: Principles & Practice. Donald F. Bloss. LC 80-21488. (Illus.). 416p. Date not set. price not set (ISBN 0-521-23292-9). Cambridge U Pr.

Spindles & Spires. John R. Earle et al. LC 75-13461. 400p. 1976. 15.95 (ISBN 0-8042-0854-9). John Knox.

Spindletop. Michel Halbouty & James Clark. 336p. 1980. 16.95 (ISBN 0-87201-791-5). Gulf Pub.

Spindrift. rev. ed. Theodore L. Harris et al. (Keys to Reading Ser.). (Illus.). 176p. (gr. 7). 1975. pap. text ed. 3.48 (ISBN 0-87892-459-0); 9.90 (ISBN 0-87892-461-2); thoughtvault student guide 3.96 (ISBN 0-87892-462-0); thoughtvault tchrs' ed. 3.96 (ISBN 0-87892-463-9); duplicating masters 19.53 (ISBN 0-87892-498-1). Economy Co.

Spindrift. Phyllis A. Whitney. 320p. 1978. pap. 2.25 (ISBN 0-449-22746-4, Crest). Fawcett.

Spine, 2 vols. Ed. by Richard H. Rothman & Frederick A. Simeone. LC 74-4584. (Illus.). 922p. 1975. Vol. 1. 32.00 (ISBN 0-7216-7719-3); Vol. 2. 32.00 (ISBN 0-7216-7720-7); Set. 64.00 (ISBN 0-7216-67075-2). Saunders.

Spine Chillers: Unforgettable Tales of Terror. Ed. by Roger Elwood & Howard Goldsmith. LC 77-16887. (gr. 7 up). 1978. PLB 8.95 (ISBN 0-385-09722-0). Doubleday.

Spinner in the Sun. Myrtle Reed. 1976. lib. bdg. 17.25x (ISBN 0-89968-111-5). Lightyear.

Spinning. Ed. by W. A. Blake et al. (Engineering Craftsmen: No. D4). (Illus.). 1968. spiral bdg. 15.95x (ISBN 0-85083-009-5). Intl Ideas.

Spinning & Weaving at Home. Thomas Kilbride. (Illus.). 128p. 1981. pap. 5.95 (ISBN 0-8069-9272-7). Sterling.

Spinning for Trout. Bob Gooch. (Illus.). 192p. 1981. 12.50 (ISBN 0-684-16843-X, ScribT). Scribner.

Spinning Tops. Larry Kettelkamp. (Illus.). (gr. 3-7). 1966. 7.25 (ISBN 0-688-21585-8); PLB 6.96 (ISBN 0-688-31585-2). Morrow.

Spinning Tops & Gyroscopic Motion. Harold Crabtree. LC 66-23755. (Illus.). 1977. text ed. 9.95 (ISBN 0-8284-0204-3). Chelsea Pub.

Spinning Wheel Secret. Lillie V. Albrecht. (Illus.). (gr. 4-6). 1965. PLB 3.99 o.s.i. (ISBN 0-8038-6668-2). Hastings.

Spinning Wheels & Spinning. Patricia Baines. LC 77-78709. (Illus.). 1978. 14.95 o.p. (ISBN 0-684-15307-6, ScribT). Scribner.

Spinning Wheel's Complete Book of Antiques. Albert C. Revi. (Illus.). 9.95 o.p. (ISBN 0-686-51535-8). Wallace-Homestead.

Spinning Wheels, Spinners & Spinning. Patricia Baines. 1980. 14.95 (ISBN 0-686-27277-3). Robin & Russ.

Spinors, Clifford, and Cayley Algebras. Robert Hermann. (Interdisciplinary Mathematics Ser: No. 7). 276p. 1974. 20.00 (ISBN 0-915692-06-6). Math Sci Pr.

Spinoza in Soviet Philosophy: A Series of Essays. George L. Kline. LC 79-2908. 190p. 1981. Repr. of 1952 ed. 18.00 (ISBN 0-8305-0078-2). Hyperion Conn.

Spinoza of Market Street. Isaac B. Singer. Tr. by Elaine Gottleib et al. 1961. 8.95 (ISBN 0-374-26776-6); pap. 4.95 (ISBN 0-374-50256-0). FS&G.

Spinoza's Philosophy of Law. Gail Belaief. LC 78-118275. (Studies in Philosophy: No. 24). (Illus.). 151p. (Orig.). 1971. pap. text ed. 17.65x (ISBN 90-2791-851-1). Mouton.

Spinoza's Philosophy of Man: Proceedings. Jon Wetlesen. 1978. pap. 22.00x (ISBN 82-00-05240-0, Dist. by Columbia U Pr.). Universitet.

Spinsters in Jeopardy. Ngaio Marsh. 1978. pap. 1.75 o.p. (ISBN 0-425-03998-6, Dist. by Putnam). Berkley Pub.

Spinsters in Jeopardy. Ngaio Marsh. (Ngaio Marsh Mystery Ser.). pap. 1.95 (ISBN 0-515-05716-9). Jove Pubns.

Spiral of Conflict: Berkeley, 1964. Max Heirich. LC 73-125073. (Illus.). 502p. 1973. 22.50x (ISBN 0-231-03243-9); pap. 7.50x (ISBN 0-231-08325-4). Columbia U Pr.

Spiral Road. Jan De Hartog. 465p. 1976. Repr. of 1957 ed. lib. bdg. 15.95x (ISBN 0-89244-092-9). Queens Hse.

Spiralings: A Journal into Poems. Karen McKinnon. (Illus.). 48p. (Orig.). 1980. pap. 5.00 (ISBN 0-88235-041-2). San Marcos.

Spirals. Mindel Sitomer & Harry Sitomer. LC 73-9874. (Young Math Ser.). (Illus.). (gr. 1-5). 1974. 7.89 (ISBN 0-690-00180-0, TYC-J). T Y Crowell.

Spirals: A Study in Symbol, Myth & Ritual. Walter L. Brenneman, Jr. LC 77-26365. 1978. pap. text ed. 7.50x (ISBN 0-8191-0463-9). U Pr of Amer.

Spires of Forms: A Study of Emerson's Aesthetic Theory. Vivian C. Hopkins. LC 80-2537. 1981. Repr. of 1951 ed. 33.50 (ISBN 0-404-19263-7). AMS Pr.

Spirit Alive in Prayer: Spirit Masters. Religious Education Staff. (To Live Is Christ Ser.). 1979. 9.95 (ISBN 0-697-01699-4). Wm C Brown.

Spirit Alive in Service: Spirit Masters. Religious Education Staff. (To Live Is Christ Ser.). 1979. 9.95 (ISBN 0-697-01712-5). Wm C Brown.

Spirit Alive in Vocations: Spirit Masters. Religious Education Staff. (To Live Is Christ Ser.). 1980. 9.95 (ISBN 0-697-01755-9). Wm C Brown.

Spirit & Light: Essays in Historical Theology. Ed. by William B. Green & Madeleine L'Engle. 1976. 8.95 (ISBN 0-8164-0310-4). Crossroad NY.

Spirit & Structure of German Fascism. Robert A. Brady. LC 68-9629. 1970. Repr. of 1937 ed. 19.00 (ISBN 0-86527-189-5). Fertig.

Spirit & the Word. Robert E. Coleman. (Spire Bks). 1975. pap. 1.50 (ISBN 0-8007-8192-9). Revell.

Spirit Controlled Family Living. Tim LaHaye & Beverly LaHaye. 1978. 7.95 (ISBN 0-8007-0950-0); pap. 4.95 (ISBN 0-8007-0951-9). Revell.

Spirit Filled Family, No. 11. John F. Stephens. 48p. (Orig.). 1980. pap. 1.50 (ISBN 0-89841-008-8). Zoe Pubns.

Spirit in Galatia: Paul's Interpretation of Pneuma As Divine Power. David J. Lull. LC 79-26094. (Society of Biblical Literature Dissertation: No. 49). 13.50x (ISBN 0-89130-367-7, 06-01-49); pap. 9.00x (ISBN 0-89130-368-5). Scholars Pr CA.

Spirit in the Church. Karl Rahner. 1979. pap. 3.95 (ISBN 0-8164-2189-7). Crossroad NY.

Spirit in the World. Karl Rahner. Tr. by William Lynch. LC 67-29676. 1968. 13.50 (ISBN 0-8164-1122-0). Crossroad NY.

Spirit Is Willing. Betty Baker. LC 73-8576. 128p. (gr. 5-9). 1974. 8.95 (ISBN 0-02-708270-9, 70827). Macmillan.

Spirit-Led Family. Wendell Robley & Grace Robley. 1974. pap. 1.25 o.p. (ISBN 0-88368-033-5). Whitaker Hse.

Spirit Makes a Man. Panzarella, Joseph J., M.D. & Glenn D. Kittler. LC 77-11766. 1978. 6.95 o.p. (ISBN 0-385-12117-2). Doubleday.

Spirit Mountain Speak to Me. Dick Sutphen. 1977. 2.95 o.p. (ISBN 0-911842-15-2). Valley Sun.

Spirit of Bambatse. H. Rider Haggard. LC 79-15278. (Forgotten Fantasy Library: Vol. 22). 1979. Repr. write for info. Newcastle Pub.

Spirit of Bambatse: A Romance. H. Rider Haggard. Ed. by R. Reginald & Douglas Menville. LC 80-19674. (Newcastle Forgotten Fantasy Library Ser.: Vol. 22). 329p. 1980. Repr. of 1979 ed. lib. bdg. 11.95x (ISBN 0-89370-521-7). Borgo Pr.

Spirit of Canoe Camping. Harry Drabik. (Illus.). 126p. 1981. pap. 5.95 (ISBN 0-931714-11-7). Nodin Pr.

Spirit of Christ. 2nd ed. Andrew Murray. LC 79-51335. 1979. pap. 3.50 (ISBN 0-87123-495-5, 200495). Bethany Fell.

Spirit of God. G. Campbell Morgan. (Morgan Library). 240p. 1981. pap. 3.95 (ISBN 0-8010-6119-9). Baker Bk.

Spirit of Islam. A. Tabbarah. 18.00x (ISBN 0-686-63565-5). Intl Bk Ctr.

Spirit of Islam: A History of the Evolution & Ideals of Islam with a Life of the Prophet. rev ed. Syed A. Ali. 515p. 1974. Repr. of 1922 ed. text ed. 17.00x (ISBN 0-391-00341-0). Humanities.

Spirit of Islam: A Summary of the Commentary of Maulana Abul Kalam Azad on A-Fateha, the First Chapter of the Quran. 3rd ed. Ashfaque Huaain. 95p. 1980. text ed. 12.00 (ISBN 0-8426-1664-0). Verry.

Spirit of Laws: A Compendium of the First English Editon with an English Translation of "an Essay on Causes Affecting Mind & Characters", 1737-1743. Montesquieu. Ed. by David W. Carrithers. (No. 192). 1978. 30.00x (ISBN 0-520-02566-0); pap. 6.95x (ISBN 0-520-03455-4, CAMPUS SER., NO. 192). U of Cal Pr.

Spirit of Life. Robert A. Smith. 1978. 5.50 (ISBN 0-912128-13-5); pap. 3.50 (ISBN 0-912128-14-3). Pubns Living.

Spirit of Medieval Philosophy. Etienne Gilson. 1936. lib. rep. ed. 22.50x (ISBN 0-684-14835-8, ScribT). Scribner.

Spirit of Place. Lawrence Durrell. Ed. by Alan G. Thomas. 1971. Repr. of 1969 ed. 10.00 o.p. (ISBN 0-525-20828-3). Dutton.

Spirit of Poland: A Photographic Meditation. Roger J. Radlowski & John Kirvan. (Illus.). 60p. (Orig.). 1980. pap. 6.95 (ISBN 0-03-056666-5). Winston Pr.

Spirit of Prayer & Spirit of Love. William Law. 1969. 13.95 (ISBN 0-227-67720-X). Attic Pr.

Spirit of Protestantism. Robert M. Brown. (YA) (gr. 9 up). 1965. pap. 5.95 (ISBN 0-19-500724-7, GB). Oxford U Pr.

Spirit of St. Louis. hudson river ed. Charles A. Lindbergh. (Illus.). 1953. lib. rep. ed. 20.00x (ISBN 0-684-14421-2, ScribT); slip case ed. 17.50 (ISBN 0-684-10362-1, ScribT). Scribner.

Spirit of Seventy-Six. bicentennial ed. Ed. by Henry S. Commager & Richard B. Morris. LC 75-9349. (Illus.). 1408p. 1975. 25.00 o.p. (ISBN 0-06-010834-7, HarpT). Har-Row.

Spirit of Seventy-Six: The Growth of American Patriotism Before Independence. Carl Bridenbaugh. 192p. 1975. 12.95x (ISBN 0-19-501931-8). Oxford U Pr.

Spirit of Seventy-Six: The Growth of American Patriotism Before Independence, 1607-1776. Carl Bridenbaugh. LC 75-4323. 1977. pap. 3.95 (ISBN 0-19-502179-7, 488, GB). Oxford U Pr.

Spirit of Spring. Penelope Proddow. LC 76-104339. (Illus.). (gr. 5-8). 1970. 4.95 o.p. (ISBN 0-87888-020-8). Bradbury Pr.

Spirit of Sunrise. Bill Bahan et al. 192p. 1980. 16.00x (ISBN 0-7051-0270-X, Pub. by Skilton & Shaw England); pap. 6.00x (ISBN 0-7051-0271-8). State Mutual Bk.

Spirit of Sunrise. Michael Cecil et al. 1979. 7.00 (ISBN 0-686-27655-8); pap. 2.95 (ISBN 0-686-27656-6). Cole-Outreach.

Spirit of Surrealism. Edward B. Henning. LC 79-63387. (Illus.). 228p. 1979. 29.95x (ISBN 0-910386-52-8, Pub. by Cleveland Mus Art). Ind U Pr.

Spirit of the Age: Or, Contemporary Portraits. William Hazlitt. (World's Classics Ser.). 1904. 11.95 (ISBN 0-19-250057-0). Oxford U Pr.

Spirit of the Alberta Indian Treaties. Richard Price. 202p. 1979. pap. text ed. 8.95x (ISBN 0-920380-23-9, Pub. by Inst Res Pub Canada). Renouf.

Spirit of the Border. Zane Grey. 288p. 1980. pap. 1.95 (ISBN 0-448-12393-2, Tempo). G&D.

Spirit of the Circling Stars: Human Problems in a Cosmic Setting. Adam Bittleston. 1975. 8.95 (ISBN 0-900285-25-7, Pub. by Floris Books). St George Bk Serv.

Spirit of the East. Ali Ikbal Shah. 1975. pap. 2.95 o.p. (ISBN 0-525-47395-5). Dutton.

Spirit of the Legal Profession. Robert N. Wilkin. viii, 178p. 1981. Repr. of 1938 ed. lib. bdg. 18.50x (ISBN 0-8377-1308-0). Rothman.

Spirit of the Lord, 12 units. Paulist Press Editorial & Catechetical Team. (Come to the Father Program). (gr. 7-8). 1974. Student Booklets, Units 1-12. pap. text ed. 0.50 ea.; CCD tchr's. manual. gr. 7 6.95 (ISBN 0-8091-9116-4); parochial tchr's. manual gr. 7 7.95 (ISBN 0-8091-9115-6); CCD tchr's. manual gr. 8 6.95 (ISBN 0-8091-9125-3); parochial tchr's. manual gr. 8 7.95 (ISBN 0-8091-9124-5). Paulist Pr.

Spirit of the Old Testament. Sidney B. Sperry. LC 70-119330. (Classics in Mormon Literature Ser.). 246p. 1980. Repr. 5.95 (ISBN 0-87747-832-5). Deseret Bk.

Spirit Seekers: New Religious Movements in Southern Ghana. Robert W. Wyllie. Ed. by Conrad Cherry. LC 79-20486. (Studies in Religion: No. 21). 139p. 13.50 (ISBN 0-89130-355-3); pap. 9.00 (ISBN 0-89130-356-1). Scholars Pr CA.

Spirit Speaks: Are You Listening? Dick Hillis & Don Hillis. LC 80-50260. 96p. 1980. pap. 2.50 (ISBN 0-8307-0752-2, 5016606). Regal.

Spirit Spirit: Shaman Songs. rev. enl. ed. David Cloutier. (Illus.). 100p. 1980. pap. 4.50 (ISBN 0-914278-30-4). Copper Beech.

Spirit Woman: The Spirirtuality of the Feminine in Symbol & Myth. Helen Luke. 144p. 1981. 9.95 (ISBN 0-8245-0018-0). Crossroad NY.

Spirit World of the Bible, the Supernatural, & the Jews. abr. ed. McCandlish Phillips. LC 72-77015. 192p. 1972. pap. 1.75 o.p. (ISBN 0-88207-048-7). Victor Bks.

Spirits in His Parlor. Gail Walker. LC 79-87733. (Destiny Ser.). 1980. pap. 4.95 (ISBN 0-8163-0387-8, 19499-3). Pacific Pr Pub Assn.

Spirits in Rebellion: The Rise & Development of New Thought. Charles S. Braden. LC 63-13245. 584p. 1980. Repr. of 1963 ed. 10.00 (ISBN 0-87074-025-3). SMU Press.

Spirits of Chocamata. S. R. Van Iterson. (gr. 7 up). 1977. 7.25 (ISBN 0-688-22108-4); lib. bdg. 6.96 (ISBN 0-688-32108-9). Morrow.

Spirits of Frederick. Alyce T. Weinberg. LC 79-54039. (Illus.). 73p. (Orig.). 1979. pap. 3.95x (ISBN 0-9604552-0-5). A T Weinberg.

Spirits of Protest. P. Fry. LC 75-20832. (Cambridge Studies in Social Anthropology: No. 14). 134p. 1976. 19.95 (ISBN 0-521-21052-6). Cambridge U Pr.

Spirits, Shamans, & Stars: Perspectives from South America. Ed. by David L. Browman. Ronald A. Schwartz. (World Anthropology Ser.). 1979. text ed. 31.75x (ISBN 90-279-7890-5). Mouton.

Spiritu Santo. Edwin H. Palmer. 3.95 (ISBN 0-686-12551-7). Banner of Truth.

Spiritual Awareness. Ernest Holmes. Ed. by Willis Kinnear. 95p. 1972. pap. 4.50 (ISBN 0-911336-41-9). Sci of Mind.

Spiritual Canticle. John Of The Cross. 1975. pap. 2.95 (ISBN 0-385-08919-8, Im). Doubleday.

Spiritual Cleansing. Draja Mickaharic. 128p. 1981. pap. 6.95 (ISBN 0-87728-531-4). Weiser.

Spiritual Conquest of Mexico. Robert Ricard. Tr. by Lesley B. Simpson. (California Library Reprint Ser: No. 57). 1974. 21.75x (ISBN 0-520-02760-4). U of Cal Pr.

Spiritual Counsel to the Young. J. K. Popham. (Summit Bks). Orig. Title: Letters to the Young. 1977. pap. 1.95 (ISBN 0-8010-7020-1). Baker Bk.

Spiritual Diary, 5 Vols. Emanual Swedenborg. LC 77-93540. Complete Set. 30.00 (ISBN 0-87785-081-X); Vol. 1. 8.50 (ISBN 0-87785-079-8); Vols. 2-5. 25.00 (ISBN 0-87785-080-1). Swedenborg.

Spiritual Diet. Ann Wigmore. (Health Digest Ser.: No. 152). 64p. pap. 1.50. Hippocrates.

Spiritual Direction. Ed. by John Sullivan. LC 80-26654. (Carmelite Studies: No. I). 240p. (Orig.). 1980. pap. 6.95x (ISBN 0-9600876-8-0). ICS Pubns.

Spiritual Dynamics. G. Raymond Carlson. (Radiant Life Ser). 1976. pap. 1.95 (ISBN 0-88243-894-8, 02-0894); teacher's ed 2.50 (ISBN 0-88243-168-4, 32-0168). Gospel Pub.

Spiritual Evolution. Craig C. Downer. Date not set. 10.00 (ISBN 0-533-04704-8). Vantage.

Spiritual Exercises. Robert Kelly. 200p. (Orig.). 1981. signed ed. 20.00 (ISBN 0-87685-508-7); pap. 7.50 (ISBN 0-87685-507-9). Black Sparrow.

Spiritual Fingerprint. Peter Krehel. 1981. 10.95 (ISBN 0-8062-1675-1). Carlton.

Spiritual Folk-Songs of Early America. Ed. by George P. Jackson. 8.50 (ISBN 0-8446-2297-4). Peter Smith.

Spiritual Friend: Reclaiming the Gift of Spiritual Direction. Tilden Edwards. LC 79-91408. 264p. 1980. pap. 7.95 (ISBN 0-8091-2288-X). Paulist Pr.

Spiritual Gifts & the Church. Donald Bridge & David Phypers. LC 73-89303. pap. 1.95 o.p. (ISBN 0-87784-672-3). Inter-Varsity.

Spiritual Healing. Dudley Blades. 128p. (Orig.). 1980. pap. 4.95 o.s.i. (ISBN 0-686-65587-7). Newcastle Pub.

Spiritual Healing. Willis Kinnear. 110p. (Orig.). 1973. pap. 3.95 (ISBN 0-911336-50-8). Sci of Mind.

Spiritual Hunger. Gordon Lindsay. 2.25 (ISBN 0-89985-020-0). Christ Nations.

Spiritual Ideals for Modern Man. Swami Vivididshanando. 198p. 1980. o. p. o.p. (ISBN 0-87481-566-5). Vedanta Pr.

Spiritual Journey of Joel Goldsmith. Lorraine Sinkler. LC 72-13190. 1973. pap. 3.95 o.p. (ISBN 0-06-067388-5, RD 243, HarpR). Har-Row.

Spiritual Journeying: Directions on the Path for Prayer. Mary R. Prose. LC 79-67513. 94p. 1980. 6.95 (ISBN 0-533-04472-3). Vantage.

Spiritual Lessons. J. Oswald Sanders. 440p. 1980. pap. 2.95 (ISBN 0-8024-0106-6). Moody.

Spiritual Letters to Women. Fenelon De Cambrai. LC 80-82324. (Shepherd Classic Ser.). 1980. pap. 5.95 (ISBN 0-87983-233-9). Keats.

Spiritual Liberty. Inayat Khan. (Sufi Message of Hazrat Inayat Khan Ser.: Vol. 5). 1979. 6.95 (ISBN 90-6325-095-9, Pub. by Servire BV Netherlands). Hunter Hse.

Spiritual Life in the Bible. Daughters of St. Paul. 1980. price not set. Dghtrs St Paul.

Spiritual Man in the Modern World. Peter R. De Coppens. 1976. pap. text ed. 5.75x o.p. (ISBN 0-8191-0066-8). U Pr of Amer.

Spiritual Maturity. J. Oswald Sanders. (Orig.). 1969. pap. 1.95 (ISBN 0-8024-0103-1). Moody.

Spiritual Perspective II: The Spiritual Dimension & Implications of Love, Sex, & Marriage. Peter R. De Coppens. LC 80-6302. 175p. (Orig.). 1981. pap. text ed. 8.75 (ISBN 0-8191-1512-6). U Pr of Amer.

Spiritual Perspective: Key Issues & Themes Interpreted from the Standpoint of Spiritual Consciousness. Peter Roche De Coppens. LC 80-487. 163p. 1980. text ed. 17.75 (ISBN 0-8191-1017-5); pap. text ed. 8.00 (ISBN 0-8191-1018-3). U Pr of Amer.

Spiritual Perspectives: Essays in Mysticism & Metaphysics. Ed. by T. M. P. Mahadevan. 303p. 1975. lib. bdg. 15.00 (ISBN 0-89253-021-9). Ind-US Inc.

Spiritual-Physical Survival Through Sprouting. Ann Wigmore. (Health Digest Ser.: No. 153). 63p. pap. 1.50. Hippocrates.

Spiritual Power. rev ed. Don Basham. 92p. 1976. pap. 2.95 (ISBN 0-88368-005-X). Whitaker Hse.

Spiritual Practices of India. pap. 1.25 (ISBN 0-8065-0057-3). Citadel Pr.

Spiritual Psychology: A New Age Course for Body, Mind & Spirit. 2nd ed. Jim Morningstar. (Illus.). 119p. Date not set. pap. 8.00 (ISBN 0-9604856-0-0). Morningstar.

Spiritual Quixote; or, the Summer's Ramble of Mr. Geoffrey Wildgoose, 1773, 3 vols. Richard Graves. Ed. by Michael F. Shugrue. (Flowering of the Novel 1740-1775 Ser: Vol. 102). 1974. Set. lib. bdg. 114.00 (ISBN 0-8240-1201-1); lib. bdg. 50.00 ea. Garland Pub.

Spiritual (Religious) Values in the Black Poet. James D. Tyms. 1977. 10.75 (ISBN 0-8191-0296-2). U Pr of Amer.

Spiritual Renewal of the American Parish. Earnest Larsen. 64p. (Orig.). 1975. pap. 1.50 o.p. (ISBN 0-89243-021-4, 29560). Liguori Pubns.

Spiritual Resources Are Available Today, Vol. 1. Roy A. Cheville. LC 74-21216. 1975. 8.00 o.p. (ISBN 0-8309-0138-8). Herald Hse.

Spiritual Revivals. Ed. by Christian Duquoc & Casiano Floristan. LC 73-6432. (Concilium Ser.: Religion in the Seventies: Vol. 89). 156p. (Orig.). 1973. pap. 4.95 (ISBN 0-8164-2573-6). Crossroad NY.

Spiritual Teaching of Ramana Maharshi. Ramana Maharshi. (Clear Light Ser). 112p. (Orig.). 1972. pap. 5.95 (ISBN 0-394-73015-1). Shambhala Pubns.

Spiritual Unfoldment One. White Eagle. 1942. 5.95 (ISBN 0-85487-012-1). De Vorss.

Spiritual Universe & You. Ernest Holmes. Ed. by Willis H. Kinnear. 1971. pap. 3.50 (ISBN 0-911336-37-0). Sci of Mind.

Spiritual View of Life. Victor Mohr. Tr. by Violet Ozols from Ger. (Victor Mohr Ser.). 364p. Date not set. pap. 15.00 (ISBN 0-934616-15-9). Valkyrie Pr.

Spiritual Well-Being of the Elderly. J. A. Thorson & T. C. Cook, Jr. 1980. 22.50 o.p. (ISBN 0-398-03998-4). C C Thomas.

Spiritualists: The Story of Florence Cook & William Crookes. Trevor H. Hall. 1963. 4.50 o.p. (ISBN 0-912326-06-9). Garrett-Helix.

Spirituality of the Beatitudes: Matthew's Challenge for First World Christians. Michael H. Crosby. 256p. (Orig.). 1981. pap. 7.95 (ISBN 0-88344-465-8). Orbis Bks.

Spirituality of the Future: A Search Apropos of R. C. Zaehner's Study in Sri Auribindo & Teilhard de Chardin. K. D. Sethna. LC 76-14764. 400p. 1981. 22.50 (ISBN 0-8386-2028-0). Fairleigh Dickinson.

Spiritualizing Dietetics. Johnny Lovewisdom. 5.00 (ISBN 0-933278-09-8). OMango.

Spirituals & the Blues. James H. Cone. pap. 3.95 (ISBN 0-8164-2073-4, SP74). Crossroad NY.

Spirochetes in Body Fluids & Tissues: Manual of Investigative Methods. James N. Miller. (Illus.). 86p. 1971. pap. 7.75 (ISBN 0-398-01312-8). C C Thomas.

Spirulina Cookbook: Recipes for Rejuvenating the Body. Sonia Beasley. (Illus.). 160p. (Orig.). 1981. pap. 6.95 (ISBN 0-916438-39-2). Univ of Trees.

Spitfire V Manual. Frwd. by J. M. Bruce. LC 76-393. (RAF Museum Ser.: Vol 1). (Illus.). 336p. 1976. 12.50 o.p. (ISBN 0-88254-376-8). Hippocrene Bks.

Spitsbergen Question: United States Foreign Policy, Nineteen Seven to Nineteen Thirty-Five. Elen C. Singh. 237p. 1981. pap. 18.00x (ISBN 8-20001-971-3). Universitet.

Spitz. pap. 2.00 (ISBN 0-87666-397-8, DS1122). TFH Pubns.

Spleen. A. I. Macpherson et al. (American Lectures in Living Chemistry). (Illus.). 290p. 1973. 22.50 (ISBN 0-398-02806-0). C C Thomas.

Splendid Art: A History of the Opera. Thomas Matthews. LC 78-93717. (Illus.). (gr. 7-12). 1970. 5.95g o.s.i. (ISBN 0-02-765290-4, CCPr). Macmillan.

Splendid Folly. Margaret Pedler. 1976. lib. bdg. 13.75x (ISBN 0-89968-218-9). Lightyear.

Splendid Survivors: San Francisco's Downtown Architectural Heritage. Foundation for San Francisco's Architectural Heritage. Ed. by Charles Hall Page & Assocs. LC 79-53196. (Illus.). 1979. 32.50 (ISBN 0-89395-037-8); pap. 19.95 (ISBN 0-89395-031-9). Cal Living Bks.

Splendid Wayfaring: The Exploits & Adventures of Jedediah Smith & the Ashley-Henry Men, 1822-1831. John G. Neihardt. LC 71-116054. (Illus.). 1970. pap. 5.25 (ISBN 0-8032-5723-6, BB 525, Bison). U of Nebr Pr.

Splendor in Exile: The Ex-Majesties of Europe. Charles Fenyvesi. LC 79-20707. (Illus.). 1979. 12.95 o.p. (ISBN 0-915220-55-5). New Republic.

Splendora. Edward Swift. 264p. 1981. pap. 3.50 (ISBN 0-14-005756-0). Penguin.

Splendors of Dresden: Critical Texts by Licia Collobi Ragghianti. Ed. by Henry A. LaFarge et al. LC 79-3547. (Illus.). 1980. 19.95 (ISBN 0-88225-286-0). Newsweek.

Splendors of Egypt. Davison. pap. 8.98 (ISBN 0-517-28591-6). Bonanza.

Splendors of the Desert World. LC 80-7568. (Illus.). 200p. Date not set. price not set (ISBN 0-87044-331-3). Natl Geog.

Splendors of Tibet. Audrey Topping. 1980. 25.00 (ISBN 0-86519-003-8). Caroline Hse.

Spline Functions: Basic Theory. Larry L. Schumaker. LC 80-14448. (Pure & Applied Mathematics: a Wiley-Interscience Ser. of Texts, Monographs, & Tracts). 500p. 1981. 35.00 (ISBN 0-471-76475-2, Pub. by Wiley Interscience). Wiley.

Splinting of Burn Patients. K. Von Prince & M. H. Yeakel. (Illus.). 136p. 1974. 17.75 (ISBN 0-398-03198-3). C C Thomas.

Splish Splash. Ethel Kessler & Leonard Kessler. LC 72-8137. (Illus.). 48p. (ps-2). 1973. 5.95 o.s.i. (ISBN 0-8193-0654-1, Four Winds); PLB 5.41 o.s.i. (ISBN 0-8193-0655-X). Schol Bk Serv.

Split Decision. Dick Vonier & Peter Sanders. LC 75-20485. (Venture Ser, a Reading Incentive Program). (Illus.). 76p. (gr. 7-12,RL 4.5-6.5). 1975. text ed. 23.25 ea. pack of 5 (ISBN 0-8172-0239-0). Follett.

Split in Two. Michael Daniels. 8.00 (ISBN 0-89253-680-2). Ind-US Inc.

Split Infinity. Anthony Piers. 368p. 1981. pap. 2.50 (ISBN 0-345-28213-2, Del Rey). Ballantine.

Split Rock: Epoch of a Lighthouse. Stephen P. Hall. LC 77-26287. (Minn. Historic Sites Pamphlet Ser.: No. 15). 24p. 1978. pap. 1.50 (ISBN 0-87351-122-0). Minn Hist.

Splitsville. Frank Baginski & Reynolds Dodson. (Illus.). 96p. 1980. pap. 4.95 (ISBN 0-8015-7042-5, Hawthorn). Dutton.

Spoilage: Japanese-American Evacuation & Resettlement During World War Two. Dorothy S. Thomas & Richard Nishimoto. (California Library Reprint Ser.). 1974. Repr. 20.00x (ISBN 0-520-02637-3). U of Cal Pr.

Spoilers. Matt Braun. (Orig.). 1981. pap. 1.95 (ISBN 0-671-82034-6). PB.

Spoils of August. Barbara L. Greenberg. LC 73-15012. (Wesleyan Poetry Program: No. 71). 72p. 1974. 10.00x (ISBN 0-8195-2071-3, Pub. by Wesleyan U Pr); pap. 4.95 (ISBN 0-8195-1071-8). Columbia U Pr.

Spokane Indians: Children of the Sun. Robert H. Ruby & John A. Brown. LC 79-108797. (Civilization of the American Indian Ser.: Vol. 104). (Illus.). 346p. 1981. 19.95 (ISBN 0-8061-0905-X); pap. 9.95 (ISBN 0-8061-1757-5). U of Okla Pr.

Spoken Albanian, Bk. 2. Leonard Newmark et al. LC 79-56549. 348p. 1980. Bk. 2 & Cassettes. pap. 65.00x (ISBN 0-87950-008-5); pap. 10.00x (ISBN 0-87950-005-0); 6 dual track cassettes 60.00x (ISBN 0-87950-007-7). Spoken Lang Serv.

Spoken Amharic, Bk. 1 Units 1-50. S. Obolensky et al. 500p. 1980. pap. text ed. 10.00x (ISBN 0-87950-650-4); cassettes 1, 26 dual track 130.00x (ISBN 0-87950-652-0); Books & cassettes 1, 135.00x (ISBN 0-87950-654-7). Spoken Lang Serv.

Spoken Amharic, Book 2, Units Fifty-One to Sixty-Eight. S. Obolensky et al. (Spoken Language Ser.). 500p. (Amharic.). 1980. pap. text ed. 10.00x (ISBN 0-87950-651-2); 2 cassettes, 5 dual track 30.00x (ISBN 0-87950-653-9); book 2 & cassettes 2 35.00x (ISBN 0-87950-655-5); books 1 & 2 & cassettes 1 & 2 160.00 (ISBN 0-87950-656-3). Spoken Lang Serv.

Spoken Amoy Hokkien: Units 1-30. Nicholas C. Bodman. (Spoken Language Series). 450p. (Amoy Hokkien.). 1981. pap. text ed. 12.00x (ISBN 0-87950-450-1); cassettes, 48 dual track 200.00x (ISBN 0-87950-451-X); bk. & cassettes combined 210.00 (ISBN 0-87950-452-8). Spoken Lang Serv.

Spoken Arabic (Iraqi) Merrill Y. Van Wagoner. LC 75-11338. (Spoken Language Ser.). (Prog. Bk.). 1975. pap. 10.00x (ISBN 0-87950-010-7); records 6 12-inch lP 50.00x (ISBN 0-87950-014-X); records with course-bk. 55.00x (ISBN 0-87950-015-8); cassettes 60.00x (ISBN 0-87950-016-6); cassettes with course-bk. 65.00x (ISBN 0-87950-017-4). Spoken Lang Serv.

Spoken Arabic of the Arabian Gulf. Librarie Du Liban. 1976. pap. 2.95x. Intl Bk Ctr.

Spoken Arabic (Saudi) Merrill Y. Van Wagoner et al. LC 76-17389. (Spoken Language Ser.). (Prog. Bk.). 1979. pap. 8.00x (ISBN 0-87950-410-2); cassettes 5 dual track 60.00 (ISBN 0-87950-411-0); cassettes with course-bk 65.00x (ISBN 0-87950-412-9). Spoken Lang Serv.

Spoken Arts, Inc. Vergilius Ferm. 1952. 3.00 (ISBN 0-8022-0497-X). Philos Lib.

Spoken Baluchi, 2 bks. M. A. Barker. Incl. Bk. I. 526p. cancelled (ISBN 0-87950-425-0); cancelled (ISBN 0-87950-427-7); cancelled (ISBN 0-87950-428-5); Bk. II. 667p. 1980. cancelled (ISBN 0-87950-426-9); cancelled Bks. I & II (ISBN 0-87950-429-3). (Spoken Language Ser.). 1980. Spoken Lang Serv.

Spoken Bengali: Standard, East Bengal. Jack A. Dabbs. LC 66-63243. 1966. 3.00 (ISBN 0-911494-03-0). Dabbs.

Spoken Burmese. William S. Cornyn. Incl. Bk. 1, Units 1-12. pap. 8.00x (ISBN 0-87950-020-4); Bk. 2, Units 13-30. pap. 10.00x (ISBN 0-87950-021-2); Guides Manual (in Burmese) tchrs. guide 5.50x (ISBN 0-87950-022-0). LC 79-1552. (Spoken Language Ser.). (Prog. Bk.). 1979. cancelled cassettes with course book 1 5.50x (ISBN 0-87950-026-3); cancelled (ISBN 0-87950-025-5). Spoken Lang Serv.

Spoken Cambodian, Bk. II. Richard B. Noss & Dale Purtle. 363p. 1980. pap. 10.00x (ISBN 0-87950-667-9); cassettes i 145.00x (ISBN 0-87950-669-5); book iI & cassettes iI 150.00x (ISBN 0-87950-671-7); book i & book iI & cassettes i & iI 240.00x (ISBN 0-87950-672-5). Spoken Lang Serv.

Spoken Cambodian, Bk. I. Richard B. Noss et al. 449p. 1980. pap. 10.00x (ISBN 0-87950-666-0); cassettes i 19 dual track 95.00x (ISBN 0-87950-668-7); book i & cassettes i 100.00x (ISBN 0-87950-670-9); books i & iI & cassettes i & iI 240.00 (ISBN 0-87950-672-5). Spoken Lang Serv.

Spoken Cantonese, Bk I. Elisabeth L. Boyle & Pauline N. Delbridge. 410p. 1980. pap. 10.00x (ISBN 0-87950-675-X); cassettes 1 dual track 75.00x (ISBN 0-87950-677-6); book 1 & cassettes 1 80.00x (ISBN 0-87950-679-2). Spoken Lang Serv.

Spoken Cantonese, Bk. II. Elisabeth L. Boyle & Pauline N. Delbridge. 410p. 1980. pap. 10.00x (ISBN 0-87950-676-8); cassettes iI 75.00x (ISBN 0-87950-678-4); book iI & cassettes iI 80.00x (ISBN 0-686-66052-8); books i & iI & cassettes i & iI 150.00x (ISBN 0-87950-681-4). Spoken Lang Serv.

Spoken Dutch. Leonard Bloomfield. LC 75-15107. (Spoken Language Ser.). (Prog. Bk.). 1975. pap. 9.00x (ISBN 0-87950-054-9); cassettes 5 dual track 50.00x (ISBN 0-87950-060-3); cassettes with course-bk. 55.00x (ISBN 0-87950-061-1). Spoken Lang Serv.

Spoken English in Ireland Sixteen Hundred to Seventeen Forty: Twenty Seven Representative Texts Assembled & Analysed. Ed. by Alan Bliss. (Dolmen Texts: No. 5). 1979. text ed. 36.50x (ISBN 0-391-01119-7, Dolmen Pr). Humanities.

Spoken Finnish. Thomas A. Sebeok. Incl. Book, Units 1-30. xv, 487p. pap. 15.00x (ISBN 0-87950-070-0); Records, Three 12-Inch LP (33.3 rpm) o.p. (ISBN 0-87950-073-5); Record Course-Book & Records. o.p. (ISBN 0-87950-074-3); Cassettes, Three Dual Track. 40.00x (ISBN 0-87950-075-1); Cassette Course-Book & Cassettes. 45.00x (ISBN 0-87950-076-X). LC 74-164345. (Spoken Language Ser.). (Prog. Bk.). 1977. Spoken Lang Serv.

Spoken French. Francois Denoeu & Robert A. Hall, Jr. Incl. Units 1-12. ix, 182p. pap. 8.00x (ISBN 0-87950-080-8); Records, Six 12-Inch LP (33.3 rpm) o.p. (ISBN 0-87950-083-2); Record Course-Bk. & Records. pap. 45.00x (ISBN 0-87950-084-0); Cassettes, Six Dual Track. 60.00x (ISBN 0-87950-085-9); Cassette Course-Bk. & Cassettes. 65.00x (ISBN 0-87950-086-7). LC 74-152740. (Spoken Language Ser.). (Prog. Bk.). 1974. Spoken Lang Serv.

Spoken German. Jenni K. Moulton & William G. Moulton. Incl. Book, Units 1-30. viii, 582p. pap. o.p. (ISBN 0-87950-090-5); Units 1-12. viii, 328p. pap. 8.00x (ISBN 0-87950-091-3); Records, Six 12-Inch Lp (33.3 Rpm) 40.00x (ISBN 0-87950-094-8); Record Course-Bk. & Records. pap. 45.00x (ISBN 0-87950-095-6); Cassettes, Six Dual Track. 60.00x (ISBN 0-87950-096-4); Cassette Course-Bk. & Cassettes. pap. text ed. 65.00x (ISBN 0-87950-097-2). LC 74-176091. (Spoken Language Ser.). (Prog. Bk.). 1976. Spoken Lang Serv.

Spoken Greek. Henry Kahane et al. Incl. Bk. 1, Units 1-12. xi, 279p. pap. 9.00x (ISBN 0-87950-100-6); Bk. 2, Units 13-30. 645p. pap. 12.00x (ISBN 0-87950-101-4); Records, Six 12-Inch LP (33.3 rpm) o.p. (ISBN 0-87950-103-0); Record Course-Bk. 1 & Records. pap. o.p. (ISBN 0-87950-104-9); Cassettes 1, Six Dual Track. 60.00x (ISBN 0-87950-105-7); Cassette Course 1-Bk. 1 & Cassettes 1. 65.00x (ISBN 0-87950-106-5); Cassettes 2, Six Dual Track. 60.00x (ISBN 0-87950-107-3); Cassette Course 2 - Bk. 2 & Cassettes 2. 65.00x (ISBN 0-87950-108-1); Combine Cassette Course-Bks. 1 & 2 & Cassettes 1 & 2. 110.00x (ISBN 0-87950-109-X). LC 74-150404. (Spoken Language Ser.). (Prog. Bk.). 1974. Spoken Lang Serv.

Spoken Hindustani. Henry Hoenigswald. Incl. Bk. 1, Units 1-12. viii, 169p. pap. 9.00x (ISBN 0-87950-110-3); Bk. 2, Units 13-30. pap. 9.00x (ISBN 0-87950-111-1); Cassettes, Six Dual Track. 60.00x (ISBN 0-87950-115-4); Cassette Course-Bk. 1 & Cassettes. 65.00x (ISBN 0-685-73298-3). LC 74-175966. (Spoken Language Ser). (Prog. Bk.). 1976. Spoken Lang Serv.

Spoken Italian. Vincenzo Cioffari. LC 75-15151. (Spoken Language Ser.). 220p. (Prog. Bk.). 1976. pap. 8.00x (ISBN 0-87950-130-8); 12 inch lP records (33.3 rpm) 40.00x (ISBN 0-87950-133-2); records with course-bk. 45.00x (ISBN 0-87950-134-0); cassettes 60.00x (ISBN 0-87950-135-9); cassettes with course-bk. 65.00x (ISBN 0-87950-136-7). Spoken Lang Serv.

Spoken Marathi: Book One. rev. ed. Naresh B. Kavadi & Franklin C. Southworth. LC 64-23368. 1968. text ed. 9.50x (ISBN 0-8122-7457-1). U of Pa Pr.

Spoken Modern Hebrew. Joseph A. Reif & Hanna Levinson. (Spoken Language Ser.). 590p. 1980. pap. 15.00x (ISBN 0-87950-683-0); text & cassette 175.00 (ISBN 0-87950-685-7); cassettes, 34 dual track 165.00x (ISBN 0-87950-684-9) (ISBN 0-87950-685-7). Spoken Lang Serv.

Spoken Norwegian. Einar Haugen. Incl. Book 1, Units 1-12. pap. 10.00x (ISBN 0-87950-170-7); Book 2, Units 13-30. pap. 12.00x (ISBN 0-87950-171-5); Cassettes, Six Dual Track. 60.00x (ISBN 0-87950-175-8); Cassette Course, Bk. 1 & Cassettes. pap. 65.00x (ISBN 0-87950-176-6). LC 75-15152. (Spoken Language Ser.). 1977. Spoken Lang Serv.

Spoken Polish. Alexander M. Schenker. (Spoken Language Ser.). 487p. 1981. pap. 10.00x (ISBN 0-87950-040-9); cassettes, 17 oval track 115.00 (ISBN 0-87950-041-7); cassettes & bk. 120.00x (ISBN 0-87950-042-5). Spoken Lang Serv.

Spoken Russian. I. M. Lesnin & Luba Petrova. Incl. Bk. 1, Units 1-12. vii, 382p. 10.00x (ISBN 0-87950-190-1); Bk. 2, Units 13-30. 397p. 10.00x (ISBN 0-87950-191-X); Records Six 12-Inch lp (33.3 rpm) o.s.i (ISBN 0-87950-194-4); Record Course-Bk. 1 & Records. text ed. o.s.i (ISBN 0-87950-195-2); Cassettes I, Six Dual Track. 60.00x (ISBN 0-87950-196-0); Cassette Course-Bk. 1 & Cassettes I. text ed. 65.00x (ISBN 0-87950-197-9); Cassettes IE for Bk. 1, 28 Dual Track. 135.00 (ISBN 0-87950-200-2); Cassettes IE & Bk. 1. text ed. 140.00 (ISBN 0-87950-202-9); Cassettes II E for Bk. 2, 11 Dual Track. 95.00 (ISBN 0-87950-201-0); Book 2 & Cassettes II. text ed. 100.00 (ISBN 0-87950-203-7); Combined Reel Tape Course, Books 1 & 2 Plus Reel Tapes 1 & 2. text ed. 220.00 (ISBN 0-87950-109-X). LC 74-176010. (Spoken Lang Ser). (Prog. Bk.). 1971. Spoken Lang Serv.

Spoken Serbo-Croatian. Carleton Hodge. Incl. Bk. 1, Units 1-12. viii, 254p. pap. 9.00x (ISBN 0-87950-210-X); Bk. 2, Units 13-30. 432p. 1973. pap. 10.00x (ISBN 0-87950-211-8); Records, Six 12-Inch lp (33.3 rpm) 55.00x (ISBN 0-87950-213-4); Record Course-Bk 1 & Records. pap. 55.00x (ISBN 0-87950-214-2); Cassettes, Six Dual Track. 60.00x (ISBN 0-87950-215-0); Cassette Course-Bk. 1 & Cassettes. pap. text ed. 65.00x (ISBN 0-87950-216-9). LC 74-150403. (Spoken Language Ser). (Prog. Bk.). 1976. Spoken Lang Serv.

Spoken Sinhalese. G. H. Fairbanks et al. (Spoken Languages Ser.). (Prog. Bk.). 1979. Bk. 1, Lessons 1-24. pap. 10.00x (ISBN 0-87950-440-4); Bk. 2, Lessons 25-36. pap. 9.00x (ISBN 0-87950-442-0); cassettes 1 for bk. 1 (21 dual track) 100.00 (ISBN 0-87950-441-2); cassettes 11 for bk. 2 (13 dual track) 65.00x (ISBN 0-87950-443-9). Spoken Lang Serv.

Spoken Spanish. S. N. Trevino. LC 75-15933. (Spoken Language Ser.). (Prog. Bk.). 1975. Book, Units 1-12. pap. 9.00x (ISBN 0-87950-220-7); records 40.00x (ISBN 0-87950-223-1); records 6 12-inch LPs 40.00x (ISBN 0-87950-224-X); cassettes 60.00x (ISBN 0-87950-225-8); cassettes with course-bk. 65.00x (ISBN 0-87950-226-6). Spoken Lang Serv.

Spoken Swedish. Fritz Frauchiger & William R. Van Buskirk. 261p. 1980. pap. text ed. 20.00x (ISBN 0-87950-704-7); cassettes 24 dual track 145.00x (ISBN 0-87950-705-5); bk. & cassettes 160.00 (ISBN 0-87950-706-3). Spoken Lang Serv.

Spoken Taiwanese. N. C. Bodman & Wu Su-Chu. (Spoken Language Ser.). 208p. (Taiwanese.). 1980. pap. 10.00x (ISBN 0-87950-460-9); cassettes 9 dual track 60.00x (ISBN 0-87950-461-7); text & cassettes 65.00x (ISBN 0-87950-462-5). Spoken Lang Serv.

Spoken Telugu. Leigh Lisker. Incl. Bk. Units 1-30. pap. 10.00x (ISBN 0-87950-376-9); Cassettes, Six Dual Track. 60.00x (ISBN 0-87950-377-7); Cassette Course-Bk. & Cassettes. pap. 65.00x (ISBN 0-87950-378-5). LC 63-12992. (Spoken Language Ser). (Prog. Bk.). 1976. cassettes 2 for units 13-30 5 dual trac 50.00x (ISBN 0-87950-379-3). Spoken Lang Serv.

Spoken Urdu, a Course in Urdu. Muhammad Abd-Al-Rahman Barker et al. Incl. Vol. 1. pap. 10.00x (ISBN 0-87950-340-8); Vol. 2. pap. 10.00x (ISBN 0-87950-341-6); Vol. 3. pap. 8.00x (ISBN 0-87950-342-4); Vols 1-3. Set. pap. 25.00x (ISBN 0-87950-343-2); Vol. 1-Cassettes, Six Dual Track. 90.00x (ISBN 0-87950-344-0); Vol. 1-Cassette Course-Bk. & Cassettes. pap. 95.00x (ISBN 0-87950-347-5); Vol. 2-Cassettes Six Dual Track. 75.00x (ISBN 0-87950-345-9); Vol. 2-Cassette Course & Cassettes. pap. 80.00x (ISBN 0-87950-348-3); Combined Cassette Course & Cassettes for Vols. 1 & 2. pap. 165.00x (ISBN 0-87950-349-1). LC 75-15183. (Spoken Language Ser). Orig. Title: Course in Urdu. (Illus.). 520p. (Prog. Bk.). 1976. Set. pap. 25.00 (ISBN 0-87950-343-2). Spoken Lang Serv.

Spoken World Poetry Index, Vol. 1. Herbert H. Hoffman & Rita T. Ludwig. (Reference Aids Ser.). 1981. 45.00x (ISBN 0-89537-012-3) (ISBN 0-89537-012-3). Headway Pubns.

Spoken Yoruba. E. W. Stevick & Odaleye Aremu. (Spoken Language Ser.). 381p. 1980. pap. 10.00x (ISBN 0-87950-708-X); cassettes, 34 oval track 165.00 (ISBN 0-686-64676-2); text & cassettes 170.00x (ISBN 0-87950-712-8). Spoken Lang Serv.

Spoken Yoruba, Units 1-50. Earl Stevick & Odaleye Aremu. 381p. 1980. pap. 10.00x (ISBN 0-87950-708-X); cassettes 34 dual track 165.00 (ISBN 0-87950-710-1); bk. & cassettes 170.00x (ISBN 0-87950-712-8). Spoken Lang Serv.

Spoken (Yucatec) Maya, Bk. 1, Lessons 1-12. Robert W. Blair & Refugio Vermont-Salas. 1979. pap. text ed. 19.00x (ISBN 0-87543-147-X). Lucas.

Spokesman for Freedom: The Life of Archibald Grimke. Janet Stevenson. (Illus.). (gr. 5-8). 1969. 3.95g o.s.i. (ISBN 0-02-788240-3, CCPr). Macmillan.

Sponges. Patricia R. Bergquist. LC 77-93644. 1978. 30.00x (ISBN 0-520-03658-1). U of Cal Pr.

Sponsor: Notes on a Modern Potentate. Erik Barnouw. (Illus.). 1979. pap. 4.95 (ISBN 0-19-502614-4, GB 580, GB). Oxford U Pr.

Sponsored Research of the Carnegie Commission on Higher Education. Carnegie Commission on Higher Education. LC 74-8975. (Illus.). 416p. 1975. 19.50 o.p. (ISBN 0-07-010073-X, P&RB). McGraw.

Sponsor's Guide to Filmmaking. Leo Trachtenberg. 1978. 6.95 o.p. (ISBN 0-911974-26-1); pap. write for info. o.p. (ISBN 0-911974-28-8). Hopkinson.

Sponsorship: The Newest Marketing Skill. Victor Head. 160p. 1980. 39.00x (ISBN 0-85941-151-6, Pub. by Woodhead-Faulkner England). State Mutual Bk.

Spontaneity & Tradition: A Study in the Oral Art of Homer. Michael Nagler. 1975. 18.75x (ISBN 0-520-02244-0). U of Cal Pr.

Spontaneous Images: Relationship Between Psyche & Soma. (Illus.). 123p. (Orig., Eng. Fr. & Ger.). 1980. pap. text ed. 16.00 (ISBN 0-89192-311-X). Interbk Inc.

Spontaneous Intracerebral Haematomas: Advances in Diagnosis & Therapy. Ed. by H. W. Pia et al. (Illus.). 500p. 1981. 116.90 (ISBN 0-387-10146-2). Springer Verlag.

Spontaneous Play in Early Childhood. Mary Sheridan. (Orig.). 1977. pap. text ed. 4.25x (ISBN 0-85633-123-6, NFER). Humanities.

Spontaneous Regression of Cancer. William Boyd. 112p. 1966. pap. 12.75 photocopy ed. spiral (ISBN 0-398-00209-6). C C Thomas.

Spook & the Giant Ant. Donna J. Groskreutz. LC 79-64491. 1980. 4.50 (ISBN 0-533-04298-4). Vantage.

Spook Birds. Eve Bunting. Ed. by Kathleen Tucker. (Illus.). 40p. (gr. 3-7). 1981. 5.50 (ISBN 0-8075-7587-9). A Whitman.

Spook Crooks: Exposing the Secrets of the Propheteers Who Conduct Our Wickedest Industry. Julien J. Proskauer. LC 70-162517. (Illus.). 1971. Repr. of 1932 ed. 18.00 (ISBN 0-8103-3760-6). Gale.

Spooks, Spooks, Spooks. Ed. by Helen Hoke. LC 66-10138. (Terrific Triple Titles Ser). (Illus.). (gr. 7 up). 1956. PLB 7.90 (ISBN 0-531-01797-4). Watts.

Spooky Haunted House Puzzles. Tony Tallarico. Ed. by Meg Schneider. (Puzzlebacks Ser.). 64p. (gr. 3-7). 1981. pap. 1.25 (ISBN 0-671-42655-9, Wanderer). S&S.

Spooky Magic. Larry Kettelkamp. (Illus.). (gr. 4-6). 1955. PLB 6.48 (ISBN 0-688-31581-X). Morrow.

Spoon Bending & Other Feats. Thomas Aylesworth. LC 80-20901. (gr. 4-10). 1980. pap. 1.95 (ISBN 0-88436-767-3). EMC.

Spoon River Anthology with Additional Poems. Edgar L. Masters. 1963. 12.95 (ISBN 0-02-581740-X); pap. text ed. 7.95x 1916 ed. (ISBN 0-02-581730-2). Macmillan.

Spore Seven. Clancy Carlile. 288p. 1979. pap. 2.25 (ISBN 0-380-49031-5, 49031). Avon.

Spores, 4 vols, Vols. 3-6. International Spores Conference, Michigan State University. Ed. by Philipp Gerhardt et al. (Illus.). Vol. 3. 7.00 o.p. (ISBN 0-685-88612-3); Vol. 4. 7.00 (ISBN 0-685-88613-1); Vol. 5. 10.00 o.p. (ISBN 0-685-88614-X); Vol. 6. 1974 15.00 (ISBN 0-685-88615-8). Am Soc Microbio.

Spores VII: Papers Presented at the 7th International Spore Conference, Madison, Wisc., Oct. 1977. Ed. by Glenn Chambliss & James C. Vary. LC 57-14449. (Illus.). 1978. text ed. 20.00 (ISBN 0-914826-17-4). Am Soc Microbio.

Sport. Louise Fitzhugh. (gr. 7-12). 1980. pap. 1.75 (ISBN 0-440-98350-9, LFL). Dell.

Sport: A Philosophic Inquiry. Paul Weiss. LC 69-15326. 286p. 1969. 10.95x (ISBN 0-8093-0358-2). S Ill U Pr.

Sport: A Philosophic Inquiry. Paul Weiss. LC 69-15326. (Arcturus Books Paperbacks). 286p. 1971. pap. 7.95 (ISBN 0-8093-0501-1). S Ill U Pr.

Sport Administration. John J. Jackson. write for info. (ISBN 0-398-04440-6). C C Thomas.

Sport & American Society: Selected Readings. 3rd ed. George H. Sage. LC 79-25573. (Physical Education Ser.). 1980. text ed. 9.50 (ISBN 0-201-06717-X). A-W.

Sport & Leisure. John Skull. pap. text ed. 2.95x o.p. (ISBN 0-435-14488-X); tchr's ed. 1.50x o.p. (ISBN 0-435-14489-8). Heinemann Ed.

Sport & Social Organization. Howard L. Nixon, III. LC 75-31742. (Studies in Sociology). 64p. 1976. pap. text ed. 4.50 (ISBN 0-672-61337-9). Bobbs.

Sport & Social Systems. John W. Loy et al. (Social Significance of Sport Ser.). (Illus.). 1978. text ed. 17.95 (ISBN 0-201-04143-X). A-W.

Sport & Society in Modern France. Richard Holt. 1980. 25.00 (ISBN 0-208-01887-5, Archon). Shoe String.

Sport & the Social Order: Contributions to the Sociology of Sport. Donald W. Ball & John W. Loy. LC 74-30694. 592p. 1975. text ed. 19.95 (ISBN 0-201-00408-9). A-W.

Sport & Work. Bero Rigauer. Ed. by Allen Guttmann. 110p. (Eng.). 1981. 12.50x (ISBN 0-231-05200-6). Columbia U Pr.

Sport Diving: The Instructional Guide to Skin & Scuba. Morton Walker. LC 76-6289. 1977. 14.95 o.p. (ISBN 0-8092-8176-7); pap. 6.95 (ISBN 0-8092-7855-3). Contemp Bks.

Sport Fishing for Sharks. Frank Mundus & Bill Wisner. 392p. 1976. pap. 4.95 o.s.i. (ISBN 0-02-029540-5, Collier). Macmillan.

Sport in Contemporary Society: An Anthology. Ed. by D. Stanley Eitzen. LC 78-65246. Date not set. pap. text ed. 7.95x (ISBN 0-312-75327-6). St Martin.

Sport in Society: Issues & Controversies. Jay J. Coakley. LC 77-23062. (Illus.). 1978. pap. text ed. 11.50 (ISBN 0-8016-0991-7). Mosby.

Sport in Soviet Society. J. Riordan. LC 76-9729. (Soviet & East European Studies Ser.). (Illus.). 1977. 44.50 (ISBN 0-521-21284-7); pap. 14.95 (ISBN 0-521-28023-0). Cambridge U Pr.

Sport in the Socio-Cultural Process. 3rd ed. Marie Hart & Susan Birrell. 544p. 1981. pap. text ed. write for info. (ISBN 0-697-07099-9). Wm C Brown.

Sport of My Mad Mother. Ann Jellicoe. 1964. pap. 3.95 o.p. (ISBN 0-571-05935-X, Pub. by Faber & Faber). Merrimack Bk Serv.

Sport Parachuting. 3rd. ed. Charles Shea-Simonds. (Illus.). 206p. 1975. 18.00 (ISBN 0-7136-1929-5). Transatlantic.

Sport Stars. Ken Lane. Ed. by Thomas Mooney. (Pal Paperbacks Kit A Ser.). (Illus., Orig.). (gr. 7-12). 1974. pap. text ed. 1.25 (ISBN 0-8374-3469-6). Xerox Ed Pubns.

SporTellers, 8 bks. Incl. Catch the Sun. Eve Cowen. LC 80-82983 (ISBN 0-8224-6475-6); Fear on Ice. Earle Rice, Jr. LC 80-82984 (ISBN 0-8224-6476-4); Foul Play. Dick O'Connor. LC 80-82985 (ISBN 0-8224-6477-2); High Escape. Eve Cowen. LC 80-82986 (ISBN 0-8224-6478-0); Race to Win. Eve Cowen. LC 80-82988 (ISBN 0-8224-6479-9); Play-off. Benjamin Swift. LC 80-82987 (ISBN 0-8224-6480-2); Stroke of Luck. Christopher R. Miller. LC 80-82989 (ISBN 0-8224-6482-9); Strike Two. George Shea. LC 80-82990 (ISBN 0-8224-6481-0). 1981. Set. incl. tchrs guide 28.00 (ISBN 0-8224-6484-5); 3.56 ea. Pitman Learning.

Sporting Chance. James E. Amesbury. 242p. 1980. 9.95 (ISBN 0-8037-7865-1). Dial.

Sporting Scene. (Art of Sewing Ser.). (Illus.). 1975. 9.95 (ISBN 0-8094-1745-6). Time-Life.

Sporting Scene. Time-Life Books Editors. LC 75-717. (Art of Sewing). (Illus.). (gr. 6 up). 1975. PLB 11.97 (ISBN 0-8094-1747-2, Pub. by Time-Life). Silver.

Sportman's Eye. James Gregg. (Illus.). 224p. 1974. pap. 2.95 o.s.i. (ISBN 0-02-028850-6, Collier). Macmillan.

Sports. Boy Scouts of America. LC 19-600. (Illus.). 72p. (gr. 6-12). 1972. pap. 0.70x (ISBN 0-8395-3255-5, 3255). BSA.

Sports. Marshall Nunn. LC 75-33869. (Spare Time Guides Ser.: No. 10). 1976. 22.50 (ISBN 0-87287-124-X). Libs Unl.

Sports: A Multimedia Guide for Children and Young Adults. Calvin Blickle & Frances Corcoran. (Selection Guide Ser.: No. 6). 245p. 1980. 16.50 (ISBN 0-87436-283-0). ABC Clio.

Sports Acrobatics. Jill Coulton. (Illus.). 112p. 1981. 12.95 (ISBN 0-8069-9184-4, Pub. by EP Publishing England); pap. 6.95 (ISBN 0-8069-9185-2). Sterling.

Sports Action. Ed. by Robert Vitarelli. (Pal Paperbacks Kit A Ser.). (Illus., Orig.). (gr. 7-12). 1973. pap. text ed. 1.25 (ISBN 0-8374-3484-X). Xerox Ed Pubns.

Sports Afloat. (Library of Boating Ser.). (Illus.). 1976. 14.95 (ISBN 0-8094-2128-3). Time-Life.

Sports Afloat. Time-Life Books Editors. LC 76-17459. (Library of Boating Ser.). (gr. 6 up). 1976. 13.95 (ISBN 0-8094-2129-1, Pub. by Time-Life). Silver.

Sports & Mental Health. Robert Moore. 128p. 1966. pap. 7.50 spiral (ISBN 0-398-01340-3). C C Thomas.

Sports & Pastimes of the People of England: Including Rural & Domestic Recreations. Joseph Strutt. LC 67-23901. (Social History Reference Series). (Illus.). 1968. Repr. of 1903 ed. 18.00 (ISBN 0-8103-3260-4). Gale.

Sports & Psychology. Frank Ryan. 224p. 1981. 9.95 (ISBN 0-13-837856-8). P-H.

Sports & Recreational Activities for Men & Women. 7th ed. David A. Armbruster et al. LC 78-31629. (Illus.). 1979. pap. text ed. 10.95 (ISBN 0-8016-0286-6). Mosby.

Sports & the Courts. Herb Appenzeller & Thomas Appenzeller. 423p. 1980. 15.00 (ISBN 0-87215-243-X). Michie.

Sports Books for Children: An Annotated Bibliography. Barbara K. Harrah. LC 78-18510. 1978. 25.00 (ISBN 0-8108-1154-5). Scarecrow.

Sports Cars, 1907-1927. T. R. Nicholson. 1970. 9.95 (ISBN 0-02-589390-4). Macmillan.

Sports Conditioning & Weight Training: Programs for Athletic Competition. new ed. William J. Stone & William A. Kroll. 1978. pap. 15.95 (ISBN 0-205-06999-1). Allyn.

Sports Conditioning: Getting in Shape, Playing Your Best, & Preventing Injuries. Frank O'Neill & Bill Libby. LC 78-68373. (Illus.). 1979. 10.00 (ISBN 0-385-14108-4). Doubleday.

Sports Doctor's Fitness Book for Women. John L. Marshall & Heather Barbash. 1981. 12.95 (ISBN 0-440-08201-3). Delacorte.

Sports Facilities for Schools in Developing Countries. F. B. Scriven. LC 72-96367. (Educational Studies & Documents). (Illus.). 39p. (Orig.). 1973. pap. 2.50 (ISBN 92-3-101049-2, U629, UNESCO). Unipub.

Sports Fan's Nineteen Seventy-Nine Calender: 365 Great Moments in Sports History. Len Hollreiser. (Illus.). 1978. 3.95 o.p. (ISBN 0-690-01225-X, TYC-T). T Y Crowell.

Sports Firsts. Patrick Clark. 320p. 1981. 14.95 (ISBN 0-87196-302-7). Facts on File.

Sports Fitness & Sports Injuries. Ed. by Thomas Reilly. (Illus.). 304p. 1981. 45.00 (ISBN 0-571-11628-0, Pub. by Faber & Faber); pap. 28.00 (ISBN 0-571-11629-9). Merrimack Bk Serv.

Sports for All. Thomas J. Mooney. Ed. by Mary Verdick. (Beginning Pal Paperbacks Ser.). (Illus., Orig.). (gr. 7-12). 1977. pap. text ed. 1.25 (ISBN 0-8374-3456-4). Xerox Ed Pubns.

Sports Freak. Shannon O'Cork. 1980. 8.95 (ISBN 0-312-75331-4). St Martin.

Sports Hero: Ron Guidry. Marshall Burchard. (Sports Hero Ser.). (Illus.). 96p. (gr. 7-10). 1981. PLB 6.99 (ISBN 0-399-61178-9). Putnam.

Sports Hero: Terry Bradshaw. Marshall Burchard. (Sports Hero Ser.). (Illus.). (gr. 6-8). 1980. PLB 6.29 (ISBN 0-399-61133-9). Putnam.

Sports Illustrated Badminton. rev. ed. J. Frank Devlin et al. LC 72-10556. 1973. 4.95 o.s.i. (ISBN 0-397-00967-4); pap. 2.95 (ISBN 0-397-00968-2, LP80). Lippincott.

Sports Illustrated Basketball. rev. ed. Neil D. Isaacs & Dick Motta. LC 80-7896. (Illus.). 160p. 1981. 8.95 (ISBN 0-690-01990-4, HarpT); pap. 5.95 (ISBN 0-690-01992-0). Har-Row.

Sports Illustrated Basketball. rev. ed. Neil D. Isaacs & Dick Motta. LC 80-7896. (Illus.). 160p. 1981. pap. 5.95 (ISBN 0-690-01992-0, CN 865, CN). Har-Row.

Sports Illustrated Basketball. Sports Illustrated Editors. LC 76-168552. (Illus.). (gr. 7-9). 1971. 5.95 (ISBN 0-397-00881-3); pap. 2.95 (ISBN 0-397-00882-1, LP54). Lippincott.

Sports Illustrated Book of Track & Field: Running Events. rev. ed. Sports Illustrated Editors & James O. Dunaway. LC 76-8268. (Illus.). (gr. 7-9). 1971. 5.95 (ISBN 0-397-01172-5); pap. 2.95 (ISBN 0-397-01171-7). Lippincott.

Sports Illustrated: Bowling. Herm Weiskopf & Chuck Pezzano. LC 80-7887. (Illus.). 160p. 1981. pap. 5.95 (ISBN 0-690-02006-6, CN 866, CN). Har-Row.

Sports Illustrated Canoeing. Dave Harrison. LC 80-8687. (Illus.). 192p. 1981. 8.95 (ISBN 0-06-014853-5, HarpT); pap. 5.95 (ISBN 0-06-090874-2, CN874, HarpT). Har-Row.

Sports Illustrated Dog Training. Sports Illustrated Editors. LC 72-3179. (Illus.). (YA) 1972. 5.95 (ISBN 0-397-00906-2); pap. 2.95 (ISBN 0-397-00907-0, LP-66). Lippincott.

Sports Illustrated Fly Fishing. rev. ed. Vernon S. Hidy & Sports Illustrated Editors. LC 74-38908. (Illus.). (YA) 1972. 5.95 (ISBN 0-397-00859-7); pap. 2.95 (ISBN 0-397-00858-9, LP-63). Lippincott.

Sports Illustrated Football Defense. Bud Wilkinson. 1973. 5.95 (ISBN 0-397-00833-3); pap. 2.95 (ISBN 0-397-00993-3). Lippincott.

Sports Illustrated Football Offense. Bud Wilkinson & Sports Illustrated Editors. LC 72-2924. (Illus.). 1972. 5.95 (ISBN 0-397-00834-1); pap. 2.95 (ISBN 0-397-00910-0, LP-69). Lippincott.

Sports Illustrated Football Quarterback. Bud Wilkinson. LC 75-17678. (Sports Illustrated Ser). (Illus.). 1976. 5.95 (ISBN 0-397-01097-4); pap. 2.95 (ISBN 0-397-01105-9). Lippincott.

Sports Illustrated Golf. Mark Mulvoy. LC 80-8692. (Illus.). 192p. 1981. 8.95 (ISBN 0-06-014871-3, HarpT); pap. 5.95 (ISBN 0-06-090868-8, CN868). Har-Row.

Sports Illustrated Handball. Wayne J. McFarland & Philip Smith. LC 75-28486. (Sports Illustrated Ser). (Illus.). 1976. 5.95 (ISBN 0-397-01095-8); pap. 2.95 (ISBN 0-397-01106-7). Lippincott.

Sports Illustrated Horseback Riding. Sports Illustrated Editors. LC 74-161580. (Illus.). (gr. 7-9). 1971. 5.95 (ISBN 0-397-00736-1); pap. 2.95 (ISBN 0-397-00735-3, LP55). Lippincott.

Sports Illustrated Ice Hockey. Sports Illustrated Editors. LC 78-156366. (Illus.). (gr. 7-9). 1971. 5.95 (ISBN 0-397-00835-X); pap. 2.95 (ISBN 0-397-00836-8). Lippincott.

Sports Illustrated Judo. Paul Stewart. LC 75-15827. (Sports Illustrated Ser). (Illus.). 1976. 5.95 (ISBN 0-397-01096-6); pap. 2.95 (ISBN 0-397-01104-0). Lippincott.

Sports Illustrated Power Boating. Tony Gibbs & Sports Illustrated Editors. LC 72-13277. 1973. 5.95 (ISBN 0-397-00971-2); pap. 2.95 (ISBN 0-397-00972-0, LP81). Lippincott.

Sports Illustrated Racquetball. Victor I. Spear. 1979. 8.95 (ISBN 0-685-93949-9); pap. 5.95 (ISBN 0-685-93950-2). Lippincott.

Sports Illustrated Scuba Diving. Hank Ketels & Jack McDowell. 1979. 8.95 (ISBN 0-397-01304-3); pap. 5.95 (ISBN 0-397-01305-1). Lippincott.

Sports Illustrated Skiing. rev. ed. Sports Illustrated Editors & John Jerome. LC 71-146685. 1971. 5.95 (ISBN 0-397-00840-6); pap. 2.95 (ISBN 0-397-00839-2, LP57). Lippincott.

Sports Illustrated Skin Diving & Snorkeling. Sports Illustrated Editors & Barry Allen. LC 72-14150. 1973. 5.95 (ISBN 0-397-00969-0); pap. 2.95 (ISBN 0-397-00970-4, LP79). Lippincott.

Sports Illustrated Small Boat Sailing. rev. ed. Sports Illustrated Editors. LC 76-37930. (Illus.). (YA) 1972. 4.95 o.s.i. (ISBN 0-397-00861-9); pap. 1.95 o.s.i. (ISBN 0-397-00860-0, LP-62). Lippincott.

Sports Illustrated Soccer. Phil Woosnam & Paul Gardner. LC 72-5629. (Illus.). 96p. 1972. 5.95 (ISBN 0-397-00908-9); pap. 2.95 (ISBN 0-397-00909-7, LP-70). Lippincott.

Sports Illustrated Squash. rev. ed. Sports Illustrated Editors. LC 70-161579. (Illus.). 1971. 4.95 o.s.i. (ISBN 0-397-00837-6); pap. 2.95 (ISBN 0-397-00838-4, LP58). Lippincott.

Sports Illustrated Swimming & Diving. Sports Illustrated Editors. 1973. 5.95 (ISBN 0-397-01002-8); pap. 2.95 (ISBN 0-397-01003-6). Lippincott.

Sports Illustrated Table Tennis. Dick Miles. LC 74-5313. 1974. 5.95 (ISBN 0-397-01024-9); pap. 2.95 (ISBN 0-397-01036-2). Lippincott.

Sports Illustrated Tennis. rev. ed. Bill Talbert & Sports Illustrated Editors. LC 72-37609. (Illus.). (YA) 1972. 5.95 (ISBN 0-397-00863-5); pap. 2.95 (ISBN 0-397-00862-7, LP-61). Lippincott.

Sports Illustrated Track: Field Events. Bill Bowerman & Bobbie Moore. LC 76-8268. (Illus.). 1977. 5.95 (ISBN 0-397-01172-5); pap. 2.95 (ISBN 0-397-01171-7). Lippincott.

Sports Illustrated Track: Running Events. rev. ed. James O. Dunaway & Sports Illustrated Editors. LC 76-8268. (Illus.). 96p. 1972. 5.95 (ISBN 0-397-01172-5); pap. 2.95 (ISBN 0-397-01171-7, LP-64). Lippincott.

Sports Illustrated Volleyball. Bonnie Robison & Sports Illustrated Editors. LC 72-3880. (Sports Illustrated Library Ser). 1970. 5.95 (ISBN 0-397-00842-2); pap. 2.95 (ISBN 0-397-00905-4). Lippincott.

Sports Illustrated Wrestling. Larry Sciacchetano & Jack McCallum. 1979. 5.95 (ISBN 0-397-01275-6); pap. 2.95 (ISBN 0-397-01276-4). Lippincott.

Sports in American Culture, 1980: Proceedings. Sports in American Culture Conference, University of South Florida, May 8-9 1980. Ed. by Don Harkness. (Illus.). 50p. (Orig.). 1980. pap. 2.50 (ISBN 0-934996-09-1). Am Stud Pr.

Sports Injuries. rev. ed. David S. Muckle. 1978. pap. 7.95 (ISBN 0-85362-173-X, Oriel). Routledge & Kegan.

Sports Injuries: The Unthwarted Epidemic. Ed. by Paul F. Vinger & Earl F. Hoerner. LC 79-22195. (Illus.). 450p. 1981. text ed. 49.50 (ISBN 0-88416-260-5). PSG Pub.

Sport's Magazine All-Time All-Stars. Tom Murray. 1977. pap. 2.50 (ISBN 0-451-09169-8, E9169, Sig). NAL.

Sports Medicine Eighty: A Publication by the Members of the American Academy of Podiatric Sports Medicine, Pt. II. American Academy of Podiatric Sports Medicine. Ed. by Robert R. Rinaldi & Michael L. Sabia, Jr. LC 80-66360. (Sports Medicine, Supplement II to the Archives of Podiatric Medicine & Foot Surgery). 250p. 1980. pap. 19.50 monograph (ISBN 0-87993-143-4). Futura Pub.

Sports Medicine Nineteen Eighty: A Review by the Members of the American Academy of Podiatric Sports Medicine, Pt. 1. Members of the American Academy of Podiatric Sports Medicine. Ed. by Robert R. Rinaldi & Michael L. Sabia. LC 80-66360. (Archives of Podiatric Medicine & Foot Surgery: Supplement III). (Illus.). 224p. 1980. pap. 15.00 (ISBN 0-87993-141-8). Futura Pub.

Sports Photography: How to Take Great Action Shots. Arthur Shay. (Illus.). 1981. 14.95 (ISBN 0-8092-5962-1); pap. 7.95 (ISBN 0-8092-5961-3). Contemp Bks.

Sports Skills for Boys & Girls. J. H. Humphrey & J. N. Humphrey. (Illus.). 128p. 1980. pap. 9.75 (ISBN 0-398-04027-3). C C Thomas.

Sports Star: Tommy John. S. H. Burchard. LC 80-8794. (Sports Star Ser.). (Illus.). 64p. (gr. 4-6). 1981. 6.95 (ISBN 0-15-278038-6, HJ). HarBraceJ.

Sports Star: Tommy John. S. H. Burchard. LC 80-8794. (Sports Star Ser.). (Illus.). 64p. (gr. 4-6). pap. 3.95 (ISBN 0-15-278039-4, VoyB). HarBraceJ.

Sports Trader Annual Buyers Guide 1980. (Benn Directories Ser.). 1980. 17.50 (ISBN 0-686-60668-X, Pub. by Benn Pubns). Nichols Pub.

Sports Trip. Lee Mountain. (Attention Span Stories Ser). (Illus., Orig.). (gr. 6-10). 1978. pap. text ed. 3.20x (ISBN 0-89061-147-5, 583). Jamestown Pubs.

Sports Trivia Puzzler, No. 3. 1981. pap. 1.95 (ISBN 0-440-08132-7). Dell.

Sports Trivia Puzzler, No. 4. Robert Kelly. (Orig.). 1981. pap. 1.95 (ISBN 0-440-07807-5). Dell.

Sports Violence: The Interaction Between Private Lawmaking & the Criminal Law. Richard B. Horrow. LC 80-65053. (Scholarly Monographs). 286p. 1980. 27.50 (ISBN 0-8408-0500-4); pap. 17.50 (ISBN 0-686-63392-X). Carrollton Pr.

Sportset: A Math Practice Set. Jerry Funk. 100p. pap. text ed. 5.95 (ISBN 0-686-69610-7); free. Allyn.

Sportsman Head to Toe. John Humphreys. (Illus.). 96p. (Orig.). 1980. pap. 8.50 (ISBN 0-85242-733-6). Intl Pubns Serv.

Sportsmanlike Driving. rev. ed. American Automobile Association. Ed. by Carolyn E. Cranford. (Illus.). (gr. 10-12). 1979. text ed. 10.64 (ISBN 0-07-001330-6); pap. text ed. 6.92 (ISBN 0-07-001331-4); tchr's ed. 12.40 (ISBN 0-07-001332-2). Webster-McGraw.

Sportsmans Book of U.S. Records. Joseph Glogan. (Illus.). 96p. (Orig.). 1980. pap. text ed. 2.50 (ISBN 0-937328-00-6). NY Hunting.

Sportsman's Crafts Book. Paul C. McNair. 1978. 12.95 (ISBN 0-87691-263-3). Winchester Pr.

Sportsman's Dictionary of Fishing & Hunting Lingo. Vin T. Sparano. (Illus.). 1980. 12.95 o.p. (ISBN 0-679-51360-4). McKay.

Sportsman's Digest of Fishing. Hal Sharp. 1953. pap. 3.95 (ISBN 0-06-463247-4, EH 247, EH). Har-Row.

Sportsman's Guide to Game Animals. Leonard L. Rue. LC 68-12140. (Illus.). 1968. 13.95 o.p. (ISBN 0-06-071715-7, HarpT). Har-Row.

Sportsmen & Their Injuries: Fitness, First Aid, Treatment, & Rehabilitations. W. E. Tucker & Molly Castle. (Illus.). 1978. 12.95 o.p. (ISBN 0-7207-0957-1). Transatlantic.

Sportsmen Say. Gene Letourneau. 1977. 8.95 (ISBN 0-930096-01-0). G Gannett.

Spotlight on the Card Sharp. Lawrence Scaife. (Gambler's Book Shelf). (Illus.). 1977. pap. 2.95 (ISBN 0-89650-575-8). Gamblers.

Spotted Cow. Donald Nelsen. LC 73-5738. (Illus.). 48p. (gr. k-3). 1973. 5.95 o.s.i. (ISBN 0-8193-0694-0, Four Winds); PLB 5.41 o.s.i. (ISBN 0-8193-0695-9). Schol Bk Serv.

Spotted Dog: The Strange Tale of a Witch's Revenge. Nancy W. Parker. LC 80-13313. (Illus.). 48p. (gr. 6-9). 1980. PLB 6.95 (ISBN 0-396-07845-1). Dodd.

Spotted Stones: A Story About the Game of Dominoes. Silvio Bedini. LC 78-3283. (Illus.). (gr. 3-6). 1978. 5.95 (ISBN 0-394-83573-5); PLB 5.99 (ISBN 0-394-93573-X). Pantheon.

Spotted Tail's Folk: A History of the Brule Sioux. George E. Hyde. LC 61-6497. (Civilization of the American Indian Ser.: Vol. 57). (Illus.). 361p. 1961. 15.95 (ISBN 0-8061-0484-8); pap. 7.95 (ISBN 0-8061-1380-4). U of Okla Pr.

Spotty & Skunky Kitty Stories. June Sather. 4.00 o.p. (ISBN 0-8062-1193-8). Carlton.

Spousage of a Virgin to Christ. John Alcock. LC 74-80158. (English Experience Ser.: No. 638). (Illus.). 19p. 1974. Repr. of 1496 ed. 3.50 (ISBN 90-221-0638-1). Walter J Johnson.

Sprachen Europas in Systematischer Ubersicht. August Schleicher. (Amsterdam Classics in Linguistics Ser.: No. 4). 325p. (Ger.). 1980. Repr. text ed. 40.00x (ISBN 90-272-0875-1). Humanities.

Sprachliche Rhythmus in Den Buhnenstucken John Millington Synges. Uwe Stork. (Salzburg Studies in Elizabethan Literature: Poetic Drama: No. 55). 1980. pap. text ed. 25.00x (ISBN 0-391-01876-0). Humanities.

Spray: Building & Sailing a Replica of Joshua Slocum's Famous Vessel. R. D. Culler. LC 78-55738. (Illus.). 1978. 10.95 (ISBN 0-87742-099-8). Intl Marine.

Spray Drying Handbook. 3rd ed. K. Masters. 1979. 87.95x (ISBN 0-470-26549-3). Halsted Pr.

Spread Spectrum Systems. R. C. Dixon. LC 75-31707. 1976. text ed. 29.50 (ISBN 0-471-21629-1, Pub. by Wiley-Interscience). Wiley.

Spreading the American Dream. Emily Rosenberg. 1981. 12.95 (ISBN 0-8090-8798-7); pap. 4.95 (ISBN 0-8090-0146-2). FS&G.

Spreading the Word: Daily Homily-Meditation Themes for the Weekdays of the Year. Bernard Mische & Fridolin Mische. pap. 4.75 o.p. (ISBN 0-685-61282-1). Alba.

Sprichwoertersammlungen, 2 vols. Johannes Agricola. Ed. by Sander L. Gilman. (Ausgaben Deutscher Literatur des Xv. Bis Xviii Jahrhunders). 989p. 1971. 182.35x (ISBN 3-11-003710-6). De Gruyter.

Sprig of Holly. new ed. Halford E. Luccock. Ed. & intro. by Charles S. Hartman. LC 78-17096. 64p. 1978. text ed. 3.50 (ISBN 0-8298-0354-8). Pilgrim NY.

Sprig of Sea Lavender. J. R. Anderson. 1980. pap. 2.25 (ISBN 0-440-18321-9). Dell.

Spring. Richard L. Allington & Kathleen Krull. LC 80-25093. (Beginning to Learn About Ser.). (Illus.). 32p. (ps-2). 1981. PLB 9.65 (ISBN 0-8172-1342-2). Raintree Child.

Spring. Alana Willoughby. Ed. by Alton Jordan. (Elephant Ser.). (Illus.). (gr. k-3). 1975. PLB 3.50 (ISBN 0-89868-019-0, Read Res); pap. text ed. 1.75 (ISBN 0-89868-052-2). ARO Pub.

Spring & the Spectacle. Margaret Chatterjee. 4.80 (ISBN 0-89253-555-5); flexible cloth 4.00 (ISBN 0-89253-556-3). Ind-US Inc.

Spring Awakening. Frank Wedekind. Tr. by Tom Osborn from Ger. 1979. pap. 4.95 (ISBN 0-7145-0634-6). Riverrun NY.

Spring Cleaning. Pat Tornborg. (Sesame Street Early Bird Bks). (Illus.). (ps). 1981. 3.50 (ISBN 0-307-11601-8, Golden Pr). Western Pub.

Spring Comes to the Roanoke. Charles S. Manooch, III. (Illus.). 140p. 1979. 7.95 (ISBN 0-9605270-0-1). Era Davidson.

Spring Fires. Leigh Richards. 192p. (Orig.). 1980. pap. 1.50 (ISBN 0-671-57021-8). S&S.

Spring Fires. Leigh Richards. (Silhouette Ser.: No. 21). pap. 1.50 (ISBN 0-686-68329-3). PB.

Spring Flora of Missouri. Julian A. Steyermark. 1964. text ed. 7.95x (ISBN 0-87543-044-9). Lucas.

Spring Flora of Wisconsin. 4th ed. Norman C. Fassett. LC 74-27307. 200p. 1976. 15.00 (ISBN 0-299-06750-5); pap. 5.95 (ISBN 0-299-06754-8). U of Wis Pr.

Spring Gambit. Claudette Williams. 1979. pap. 1.75 o.p. (ISBN 0-449-23891-1, Crest). Fawcett.

Spring Guide to Current American Government 1980. Congressional Quarterly. (Guide to Current American Government Ser.). 1979. pap. 6.95 (ISBN 0-87187-179-3). Congr Quarterly.

Spring House. Ruth Tomalin. 1968. 6.50 (Pub. by Faber & Faber). Merrimack Bk Serv.

Spring in the High Sierras. Kathleen Vyn. LC 79-25450. (Illus.). 64p. (gr. 3-5). 1980. PLB 6.97 (ISBN 0-671-33084-5). Messner.

Spring in This World of Poor Mutts: "the Frank O'Hara Award Series". Joseph Ceravolo. LC 68-56371. (Full Court Rebound Bk.). 1978. 14.95 (ISBN 0-685-60027-0); pap. 6.00 (ISBN 0-685-60028-9). Full Court NY.

Spring Is. Janina Domanska. LC 75-25953. (Illus.). 32p. (gr. k-3). 1976. 8.25 (ISBN 0-688-80026-2); PLB 7.92 (ISBN 0-688-84026-4). Greenwillow.

Spring Is Here! Jane B. Moncure. LC 75-14202. (Illus.). (ps-2). 1975. 5.50 (ISBN 0-913778-11-7). Childs World.

Spring Journal: Poems. Edwin Honig. LC 68-27540. (Wesleyan Poetry Program: Vol. 41). 1968. 10.00x (ISBN 0-8195-2041-1, Pub. by Wesleyan U Pr); pap. 4.95 (ISBN 0-8195-1041-6). Columbia U Pr.

Spring Laughter. Christina Rainsford. 1980. 5.50 (ISBN 0-8233-0316-0). Golden Quill.

Spring, Nineteen Seventy-Seven: An Annual of Archetypal Psychology & Jungian Thought. Ed. by James Hillman. 1977. pap. 12.00 (ISBN 0-88214-012-4). Spring Pubns.

Spring, Nineteen Seventy-Three: An Annual of Archetypal Psychology & Jungian Thought. annual Ed. by James Hillman. 1973. pap. 12.00 o.p. (ISBN 0-88214-008-6). Spring Pubns.

Spring Peepers. Judy Hawes. LC 74-2038. (Let's-Read-&-Find-Out Science Bk). (Illus.). (ps-3). 1975. 7.95 (ISBN 0-690-00522-9, TYC-J); PLB 7.89 (ISBN 0-690-00523-7). T Y Crowell.

Spring Peepers Are Calling. Charlene W. Billings. LC 78-7735. (Illus.). (gr. 3-5). 1979. 5.95 (ISBN 0-396-07584-3). Dodd.

Spring Programs for the Church, No. 1. Ed. by Judy Sparks. (Special-Day Program Bks). 64p. (Orig.). 1979. pap. 2.75 (ISBN 0-87239-253-8, 8731). Standard Pub.

Spring 'seventy-Six: An Annual of Archetypal Psychology & Jungian Thought. Hillman et al. Ed. by James Hillman. 218p. (Orig.). 1976. pap. text ed. 12.00 (ISBN 0-88214-011-6). Spring Pubns.

Spring Wildflowers of N. E. Dwelley. 1980. pap. 6.95 (ISBN 0-89272-008-5). Down East.

Spring Will Come Again. Sylvia Thorpe. 1977. pap. 1.50 o.p. (ISBN 0-449-23346-4, Crest). Fawcett.

Spring 1979: An Annual of Archetypal Psychology & Jungian Thought. James Hillman et al. 1979. pap. 10.00 (ISBN 0-88214-014-0). Spring Pubns.

Spring '80: An Annual of Archetypal Psychology & Jungian Thought. Corbin et al. Ed. by James Hillman. 196p. (Orig.). 1980. pap. text ed. 10.00 (ISBN 0-88214-015-9). Spring Pubns.

Springboard to Discovery. Mary L. Lacy. 1976. 1.25 o.p. (ISBN 0-8042-3595-3). John Knox.

Springboards. Jean Greenlaw & Gretchen Barton. (Design for Reading Ser). (Illus., Personal reading). (gr. 3). 1972. text ed. 10.28 (ISBN 0-06-516031-2, SchDept); tchrs.' ed. 5.12 (ISBN 0-06-516231-5); wkbk. 3.20 (ISBN 0-06-516331-1); tchr's ed. wkbk. 6.36 (ISBN 0-06-516431-8). Har-Row.

Springboards: A College Reader. James Schiavone. 1977. pap. text ed. 7.00 (ISBN 0-87720-955-3). AMSCO Sch.

Springer Tracts in Modern Physics, Vol. 37. Ed. by G. Hoehler. (Illus.). iv, 180p. (Eng. & Ger.). 1965. 34.30 (ISBN 0-387-03404-8). Springer-Verlag.

Springer Tracts in Modern Physics, Vol. 38. Ed. by G. Hoehler. (Illus.). iv, 188p. (Eng. & Ger.). 1965. 34.30 (ISBN 0-387-03405-6). Springer-Verlag.

Springer Tracts in Modern Physics, Vol. 40. Ed. by G. Hoehler. (Illus., Eng. & Ger.). 1966. 34.30 (ISBN 0-387-03669-5). Springer-Verlag.

Springer Tracts in Modern Physics, Vol. 46. Ed. by G. Hoehler. (Illus.). iv, 132p. (Eng. & Ger.). 1968. 34.90 (ISBN 0-387-04340-3). Springer-Verlag.

Springer Tracts in Modern Physics, Vol. 47. Ed. by G. Hoehler. (Illus.). v, 225p. (Eng. & Ger.). 1968. 50.80 (ISBN 0-387-04341-1). Springer-Verlag.

Springer Tracts in Modern Physics, Vol. 49. Ed. by G. Hoehler. (Illus.). iii, 146p. 1969. 34.30 (ISBN 0-387-04712-3). Springer-Verlag.

Springer Tracts in Modern Physics, Vol. 51. Ed. by G. Hoehler. LC 25-9130. (Illus.). 1969. 29.00 (ISBN 0-387-04714-X). Springer-Verlag.

Springer Tracts in Modern Physics, Vol. 53. Ed. by G. Hoehler. (Illus.). 1970. 29.00 (ISBN 0-387-05016-7). Springer-Verlag.

Springer Tracts in Modern Physics, Vol. 54. Ed. by G. Hoehler. LC 25-9130. (Illus.). 1970. 43.70 (ISBN 0-387-05017-5). Springer-Verlag.

Springer Tracts in Modern Physics, Vol. 58. Ed. by G. Hoehler. (Illus.). 1971. 56.70 (ISBN 0-387-05383-2). Springer-Verlag.

Springer Tracts in Modern Physics, Vol. 60. Ed. by G. Hoehler. LC 25-9130. (Illus.). iv, 233p. 1972. 56.70 (ISBN 0-387-05653-X). Springer-Verlag.

Springer Tracts in Modern Physics, Vol. 65. Ed. by G. Hoehler. LC 25-9130. (Illus.). 148p. 1972. 37.80 (ISBN 0-387-05876-1). Springer-Verlag.

Springer's Progress. David Markson. LC 76-43496. 1977. 8.95 o.p. (ISBN 0-03-020341-4). HR&W.

Springs. rev. ed. Harlan Wade. LC 78-21066. (Book About Ser.). (Illus.). (gr. k-3). 1979. PLB 7.30 (ISBN 0-8172-1529-8). Raintree Pubs.

Springs in the Valley. Mrs. Charles E. Cowman. 1938. 5.95 o.p. (ISBN 0-310-22510-8, Pub. by Cowman). Zondervan.

Springs in the Valley. Mrs. Charles E. Cowman. 1977. large-print ed. 6.95 (ISBN 0-310-22517-5). Zondervan.

Springs of... Series, 8 bks. Incl. Springs of Faith (ISBN 0-310-39562-3, 11406); Springs of Grace (ISBN 0-310-39522-4, 11402); Springs of Hope (ISBN 0-310-39552-6, 11405); Springs of Love (ISBN 0-310-39572-0, 11407); Springs of New Life (ISBN 0-310-39542-9, 11404); Springs of Power (ISBN 0-310-39532-1, 11403); Springs of Truth (ISBN 0-310-39512-7, 11401); Springs of Worship (ISBN 0-310-39502-X, 11400). (Illus.). 1980. pap. 0.95 ea. Zondervan.

Springs of Freedom in Czechoslovakia. Victor Weeraratne. (Illus.). 1970. 5.95 o.p. (ISBN 0-8158-0048-7). Chris Mass.

Springs of Living Water. John H. Jowett. (Summit Bks). Orig. Title: My Daily Meditations. 1977. pap. text ed. 2.95 o.p. (ISBN 0-8010-5073-1). Baker Bk.

Springs of Texas, Vol. 1. Gunnar Brune. (Illus.). 534p. 1981. 35.00 (ISBN 0-9604766-0-1). G Brune.

Springs: Troubleshooting & Failure Analysis. Carlson. 216p. 1980. 27.50 (ISBN 0-8247-1003-7). Dekker.

Sprint: Speed Hillclimbs & Speed Trials in Britain, 1889-1925. T. R. Nicholson. 9.95 o.p. (ISBN 0-685-42130-9). David & Charles.

Sprite--MG Midget Service--Repair Handbook: All Models, 1958-1979. Alan Ahlstrand. Ed. by Jeff Robinson. (Illus.). 1977. pap. 10.95 (ISBN 0-89287-164-4, A205). Clymer Pubns.

Sprite MG Midget Handbook & Service Manual: 1958-1968. (Illus.). pap. 5.00 o.p. (ISBN 0-89287-252-7, A188). Clymer Pubns.

Spritual Well-Being of the Elderly. James A. Thorson & Thomas C. Cook, Jr. (Illus.). 260p. 1980. text ed. 22.50 (ISBN 0-398-03998-4). C C Thomas.

Sprout Booklet & Stainless Steel Screen. 3nd ed. Jody Main & Nancy Portugal. (Illus.). 1980. pap. 1.98 (ISBN 0-937148-01-6). Wild Horses Potted Plant.

Sprout for the Love of Everybody: Nutritional Evaluation of Sprouts & Grasses. Viktoras Kulvinskas. pap. 2.45 (ISBN 0-933278-03-9). OMango.

Sprouts on Helicon. Ed. by Judith Earnshaw. (gr. 9 up). 5.95 (ISBN 0-233-95784-7). Transatlantic.

SPSS-Eleven: The SPSS Batch System for the DEC PDP-11. C. Hadlai Hull & Norman H. Nie. 265p. 1980. pap. text ed. 6.95 (ISBN 0-07-046537-1, C). McGraw.

Spud Book: One Hundred One Ways to Cook Potatoes. Houston T. James. LC 80-50166. (Illus.). 134p. 1980. pap. 4.95 (ISBN 0-934726-01-9). Seven Seven Search.

Spudding in: Recollections of Pioneer Days in the California Oil Fields. William Rintoul. 240p. 1978. Repr. of 1976 ed. 12.95 (ISBN 0-910312-37-0). Calif Hist.

Spur of Fame: Dialogues of John Adams & Benjamin Rush 1805 to 1813. Ed. by John A. Schutz & Douglass Adair. LC 66-15694. (Illus.). 301p. 1980. pap. 5.00 (ISBN 0-87328-025-3). Huntington Lib.

Spurgeon's Gems. Charles H. Spurgeon. (Charles H. Spurgeon Ser.). 1980. pap. 3.95 (ISBN 0-8010-8186-6). Baker Bk.

Spurgeon's Lectures to My Students. Charles H. Spurgeon. 1955. 10.95 o.p. (ISBN 0-310-32910-8). Zondervan.

Spurgeon's Morning & Evening. Charles H. Spurgeon. 736p. 1980. Repr. 10.95 (ISBN 0-310-32940-X). Zondervan.

Spurs: Nietzsche's Styles. Jacques Derrida. Tr. by Barbara Harlow from Fr. LC 79-31. vi, 166p. 1981. pap. 4.50 (ISBN 0-226-14333-3). U of Chicago Pr.

Sputum: Fundamentals & Clinical Pathology. Ed. by Mauricio J. Dulfano. (Illus.). 648p. 1973. 48.50 (ISBN 0-398-02737-4). C C Thomas.

SPWAO Showcase. Stephen Gresham et al. Ed. by David Warren. Tr. by Ken Raney. (Illus.). 72p. (Orig.). 1981. pap. 3.00 (ISBN 0-916176-14-2). Sproing.

Spy. James F. Cooper. 1976. lib. bdg. 13.95x (ISBN 0-89968-161-1). Lightyear.

Spy at Tory Hole. Elizabeth Honness. (Bicentennial Historiettes). (Illus.). 64p. (gr. 5-6). 1975. text ed. 4.95x (ISBN 0-915892-03-0); pap. text ed. 1.45 (ISBN 0-915892-17-0). Regional Ctr Educ.

Spy-Counter Spy. Dusko Popov. 4.95 (ISBN 0-686-28850-5). Academy Chi Ltd.

Spy Game. Marc Lovell. LC 80-499. (Crime Club Ser.). 192p. 1980. 8.95 (ISBN 0-385-17073-4). Doubleday.

Spy in the House of Love. Anais Nin. LC 66-6833. 140p. 1959. pap. 5.95 (ISBN 0-8040-0280-0, 82). Swallow.

Spy in the House of Medicine. George A. Silver. LC 76-2184. 1976. 21.75 (ISBN 0-912862-18-1). Aspen Systems.

Spy Lady & the Muffin Man. Sesyle Joslin. LC 74-137757. (Illus.). (gr. 4-6). 1971. 4.75 o.p. (ISBN 0-15-278182-X, HJ). HarBraceJ.

Spy: The Story of Modern Espionage. Clifford Irving & Herbert Burkholz. LC 77-78080. (Illus.). (gr. 7 up). 1969. 8.95g (ISBN 0-02-747330-9). Macmillan.

Spy Vs. Spy Follow-up File. Antonio Prohias. (Mad Ser.). (Illus.). 1975. pap. 1.75 (ISBN 0-446-94424-6). Warner Bks.

Spy Who Loved Me. Christopher Wood. 1977. pap. 1.75 o.s.i. (ISBN 0-446-84544-2). Warner Bks.

Spy Who Never Was & Other True Spy Stories. David C. Knight. LC 77-15162. (Signal Book). (gr. 9 up). 1978. 6.95 (ISBN 0-385-13108-9). Doubleday.

Spyglass. (Illus.). 1978. pap. 4.95 o.p. (ISBN 0-914922-05-X). Spyglass.

Spyglass Nineteen-Eighty. 7th ed. 350p. 5.95 o.p. (ISBN 0-914922-07-6). Western Marine Ent.

Spyglass Seventy-Seven. (Illus.). 1976. pap. 4.95 o.p. (ISBN 0-914922-04-1). Spyglass.

Spyglass Seventy-Six. 1975. pap. 4.95 o.p. (ISBN 0-914922-03-3). Spyglass.

Spy's Wife. Reginald Hill. 1980. 9.95 (ISBN 0-394-51402-5). Pantheon.

Squall Across the Atlantic: American Civil War Prize Cases & Diplomacy. Stuart L. Bernath. LC 76-79042. 1970. 18.50x (ISBN 0-520-01562-2). U of Cal Pr.

Squanto. Matthew G. Grant. LC 73-12813. 1974. PLB 5.95 (ISBN 0-87191-270-8). Creative Ed.

Squanto, Friend of the Pilgrims. Clyde R. Bulla. LC 54-9145. (Illus.). (gr. 2-5). 1954. 8.95 (ISBN 0-690-76642-4, TYC-J). T Y Crowell.

Square Dance. John Wainwright. 1979. pap. text ed. 1.95 o.p. (ISBN 0-425-04160-3). Berkley Pub.

Square Dances of Today & How to Teach & Call Them. R. Kraus. 124p. 1950. 14.95 (ISBN 0-471-07097-1). Wiley.

Square Dances of Today & How to Teach & Call Them. Richard Kraus. (Illus.). (gr. 5-9). 1950. 14.95 (ISBN 0-8260-5120-0). Ronald Pr.

Square Egg. Ronald Searle. (Illus.). 96p. (Orig.). 1981. pap. 2.95 (ISBN 0-14-005467-7). Penguin.

Square Foot Gardening: A New Way to Garden in Less Space with Less Work. Mel Bartholomew. Ed. by Anne Halpin. (Illus.). 288p. 1981. 13.95 (ISBN 0-87857-340-2); pap. 9.95 (ISBN 0-87857-341-0). Rodale Pr Inc.

Square Meal Cookbook. Catherine A. Hunter. 206p. (Orig.). 1980. pap. write for info. Ref Guides.

Square Root of Man. William Tenn. 224p. (Orig.). 1981. pap. 2.25 (ISBN 0-345-29230-8, Del Rey). Ballantine.

Squash. Ted Millman & Paul Millman. (Illus.). 93p. 1980. 10.95 (ISBN 0-7136-1857-4). Transatlantic.

Squash Basics for Men & Women. Betty Constable et al. (Illus.). 1979. pap. 5.95 (ISBN 0-8015-7039-5, Hawthorn). Dutton.

Squash Coaching & Refereeing. R. B. Hawkey. (Illus.). 1975. 10.95 (ISBN 0-571-10539-4, Pub. by Faber & Faber); pap. 9.95 (ISBN 0-571-10810-5). Merrimack Bk Serv.

Squash Cookbook. Yvonne Y. Tarr. 1978. pap. 5.95 (ISBN 0-394-72473-9, Vin). Random.

Squash for Players & Coaches. Cecil J. Zuber. (Illus.). 128p. 1980. 16.95 (ISBN 0-13-839910-7, Spec); pap. 6.95 (ISBN 0-13-839902-6). P-H.

Squash: The Ambitious Player's Guide. Alan Colburn. (Illus.). 112p. 1981. 19.95 (ISBN 0-571-11657-4, Pub. by Faber & Faber); pap. 8.95 (ISBN 0-571-11658-2). Merrimack Bk Serv.

Squaw Man's Son. Evelyn S. Lampman. LC 77-17503. (gr. 5-9). 1978. 7.95 (ISBN 0-689-50102-1, McElderry Bk). Atheneum.

Squawk to the Moon, Little Goose. Edna M. Preston & Barbara Cooney. (Illus.). 32p. (gr. k-3). 1976. pap. 1.50 o.s.i. (ISBN 0-670-05103-9, Puffin). Penguin.

Squeaking by: U.S. Energy Policy Since the Embargo. Richard B. Mancke. 1976. 15.00x (ISBN 0-231-03989-1). Columbia U Pr.

Squirrel & the Harp. David C. De Jong. (Illus.). (gr. k-3). 1966. 3.95g o.s.i. (ISBN 0-02-726530-7). Macmillan.

Squirrel Book. Eugene Kinkead. (Illus.). 160p. 1980. 13.95 (ISBN 0-525-93137-6). Dutton.

Squirrel Book. Jan Pfloog. (Illus.). 24p. (ps-4). 1977. Repr. of 1965 ed. PLB 5.38 (ISBN 0-307-68918-2, Golden Pr). Western Pub.

Squirrel Cage: The Best of Douglass Welch. Ed. by Ruth Welch. LC 76-45418. (Illus.). 1976. pap. 4.95 (ISBN 0-914842-15-3). Madrona Pubs.

Squirrel Hotel. William Pene du Bois. (Children's Literature Ser.). 1980. PLB 5.95 (ISBN 0-8398-2606-0). Gregg.

Squirrels. Brian Wildsmith. LC 74-6193. (Illus.). 32p. (gr. k-3). 1975. PLB 5.95 o.p. (ISBN 0-531-02754-6). Watts.

Squirrels in Britain. Keith Laidler. LC 80-66421. (Illus.). 176p. 1980. 19.95 (ISBN 0-7153-7825-2). David & Charles.

Squirrels of Canada. Shirley E. Woods, Jr. (Illus.). 208p. 1981. lib. bdg. 29.95 (ISBN 0-660-10344-3, 56511-4, Pub. by Natl Mus Canada). U of Chicago Pr.

Squirrels of Canada. Shirley E. Woods, Jr. (Illus.). 208p. 21.95 (ISBN 0-660-10344-3, 56512-2, Pub. by Natl Mus Canada). U of Chicago Pr.

SR Russian. text ed. 4.95 (ISBN 0-88499-116-4); wkbk. 3.95 (ISBN 0-88499-117-2); cassette set 115.00 (ISBN 0-88499-195-4); tape set 225.00 (ISBN 0-88499-194-6); tapebook 3.95 (ISBN 0-88499-118-0). Inst Mod Lang.

Sri Aurobindo. Navajata. (National Biography Ser.). 1979. pap. 2.00 o.p. (ISBN 0-89744-201-6). Auromere.

Sri Aurobindo & the Mother on Education. 6th ed. Sri Aurobindo. 1978. Fifth Ed. 1973. pap. 3.00 (ISBN 0-89744-955-X). Sixth Ed. 1978. Auromere.

Sri Aurobindo: Prophet of Life Divine. Haridas Chaudhuri. 270p. (Orig.). 1973. pap. 3.50 (ISBN 0-89744-994-0, Pub. by Cultural Integration). Auromere.

Sri Lanka. H. A. Goonetileke. (World Bibliographical Ser.: No. 20). 1981. price not set (ISBN 0-903450-33-X). ABC Clio.

Sri Lanka from Dominion to Republic. Lucy M. Jacob. LC 73-906251. 243p. 1973. 11.50x o.p. (ISBN 0-88386-250-6). South Asia Bks.

Sri Ramakrishna: The Great Master, Part I. new, rev. ed. Swami Saradananda. Tr. by Swami Jagadananda. (Illus.). 563p. pap. 8.50x (ISBN 0-87481-495-2). Vedanta Pr.

Sri Ramakrishna: The Great Master, Pt. 2. rev. ed. Swami Saradananda. Tr. by Swami Jagadananda from Bengali. 1980. pap. 8.50x (ISBN 0-87481-496-0). Vedanta Pr.

Sri Sankara Vijayam. Ramachandran. 1977. pap. 2.25 (ISBN 0-89744-123-0, Pub. by Ganesh & Co. India). Auromere.

Srimad Bhagavad Gita. Tr. by Swami Vireswarananda. (Sanskrit & Eng.). 5.25 (ISBN 0-87481-421-9). Vedanta Pr.

Srimad-Bhagavatam: Tenth Canto, Part 3. Swami Prabhupada A. C. Bhaktivedanta. (Illus.). 112p. 1980. 6.95 (ISBN 0-89213-107-1). Bhaktivedanta.

SRS-A & Leukotrienes: Proceedings. Annual Symposium of Basic Medical Sciences, 10th & Priscilla J. Piper. (Prostaglandis Research Studies Press Ser.). 304p. 1981. 63.00 (ISBN 0-471-27959-5, Pub. by Wiley-Interscience). Wiley.

Srygley-Hall Debate on the Church. Ed. by J. W. Shepherd. pap. 3.50 (ISBN 0-89225-169-7). Gospel Advocate.

SS-GB. Len Deighton. 1980. pap. 2.95 (ISBN 0-345-29317-7). Ballantine.

SS Great Britain. Adrian Ball. LC 80-68903. (Illus.). 96p. 1981. 22.50 o.p. (ISBN 0-7153-8096-6); pap. 14.50 o.p. (ISBN 0-7153-8089-3). David & Charles.

SS Great Eastern: The Greatest Iron Ship. George S. Emmerson. LC 80-69345. (Illus.). 216p. 1981. 25.50 (ISBN 0-7153-8054-0). David & Charles.

St.-John Perse: Letters. John Perse. Ed. by Arthur J. Knodel. LC 79-9080. (Bollingen Ser.: LXXXVII: 2). (Illus.). 712p. 1981. 20.00x (ISBN 0-691-09868-9); pap. 8.50 (ISBN 0-691-01836-7). Princeton U Pr.

St Louis Encephalitis. Ed. by Thomas P. Monath. LC 79-53721. (Illus.). 700p. 1980. text ed. 20.00x (ISBN 0-87553-090-7). Am Pub Health.

Stability & Change in an English County Town. A. Armstrong. LC 73-92785. (Illus.). 272p. 1974. 23.95 (ISBN 0-521-20423-2). Cambridge U Pr.

Stability & Constancy in Visual Perception: Mechanisms & Processes. W. Epstein. 1977. 31.50 (ISBN 0-471-24355-8). Wiley.

Stability & Control of Airplanes & Helicopters. Edward Seckel. 1964. text ed. 23.95 (ISBN 0-12-634450-7). Acad Pr.

Stability & Performance of Slopes & Embankments. Compiled by American Society of Civil Engineers. 704p. 1969. text ed. 33.00 (ISBN 0-87262-016-6). Am Soc Civil Eng.

Stability & Trim for the Ship's Officer. 2nd ed. John H. La Dage & Lee Van Gemert. LC 56-6885. 1956. 8.50x (ISBN 0-87033-167-1). Cornell Maritime.

Stability & Trim of Fishing Vessels. J. Anthony Hind. (Illus.). 120p. 9.50 (FN). Unipub.

Stability Constants of Metal Complexes: Critical Survey of Stability Constants of EDTA Complexes. International Union of Pure & Applied Chemistry. Ed. by G. Anderegg. 1977. text ed. 12.00 (ISBN 0-08-022009-6). Pergamon.

Stability Constants of Metal-Ion Complexes, Pt. B: Organic Ligands. Ed. by D. D. Perrin. (Chemical Data Ser.: No. 22). 1280p. 1979. 195.00 (ISBN 0-08-020958-0). Pergamon.

Stability of Elastic Systems. S. J. Britvec. 480p. 1973. text ed. 38.00 (ISBN 0-08-016859-0). Pergamon.

Stability of Heavy Minerals. Ed. by H. Fuechtbauer. LC 74-342080. (Contributions to Sedimentology Ser.: Vol. I). (Illus.). 125p. (Orig.). 1973. pap. 37.50x (ISBN 3-510-57001-4). Intl Pubns Serv.

Stability of Industrial Organisms. 57p. 1981. pap. 12.50 (ISBN 0-85198-470-3, CAB 13, CAB). Unipub.

Stability of Microstructure in Metallic Systems. J. W. Martin & P. D. Doherty. LC 75-38189. (Cambridge Solid State Science Ser.). (Illus.). 180p. 1976. 57.50 (ISBN 0-521-20875-0). Cambridge U Pr.

Stability of Microstructure in Metallic Systems. J. W. Martin & R. D. Doherty. LC 75-38179. (Cambridge Solid State Science Ser.). (Illus.). 298p. 1980. pap. 17.50x (ISBN 0-521-29883-0). Cambridge U Pr.

Stability of Motion. E. J. Routh. Ed. by A. T. Fuller. LC 75-8772. 228p. 1975. Repr. of 1877 ed. 22.95 o.p. (ISBN 0-470-74350-6). Halsted Pr.

Stability of Nonlinear Systems. (Control Theory & Applications Studies Ser.). 208p. 1981. 30.00 (ISBN 0-471-27856-4, Pub. by Wiley-Interscience). Wiley.

Stability of Rock Slopes. Compiled by American Society of Civil Engineers & Edward J. Cording. 1008p. 1972. text ed. 34.50 (ISBN 0-87262-047-6). Am Soc Civil Eng.

Stability of South Africa-or Why South Africa Will Survive. L. H. Gann & Peter Duigan. 320p. 1980. write for info. St Martin.

Stability of Structures Under Static & Dynamic Loads. Compiled by American Society of Civil Engineers. 836p. 1978. pap. text ed. 30.00 (ISBN 0-87262-095-6). Am Soc Civil Eng.

Stability of Unfoldings. G. Wasserman. (Lecture Notes in Mathematics: Vol. 393). xxix, 164p. 1974. pap. 10.40 o.p. (ISBN 0-387-06794-9). Springer-Verlag.

Stability Problems in Engineering Structures & Components. Ed. by T. H. Richards & P. Stanley. (Illus.). 1979. 82.80x (ISBN 0-85334-836-7, Pub. by Applied Science). Burgess-Intl Ideas.

Stability Theory & Its Applications to Structural Mechanics. C. L. Dym. (Mechanics of Elastic Stability Ser.: No. 3). 200p. 1974. 22.50x (ISBN 90-286-0094-9). Sijthoff & Noordhoff.

Stabilization Policy in an African Setting Nineteen Sixty-Three to Seventy-Three. John R. King. LC 79-670197. (Studies in the Economics of Africa). 1979. text ed. 25.95x (ISBN 0-435-97375-4); pap. text ed. 10.95x (ISBN 0-686-65420-X). Heinemann Ed.

Stabilizing America's Economy. Ed. by George A. Nikolaieff. (Reference Shelf Ser: Vol. 44, No. 2). 256p. 1972. 6.25 (ISBN 0-8242-0465-4). Wilson.

Stabilizing World Commodity Markets. Ed. by F. Gerard Adams & Sonia Klein. LC 77-7805. (Wharton Econometric Studies Ser.: No. 1). 1978. 24.95 (ISBN 0-669-01622-5). Lexington Bks.

Stable Homotopy. J. M. Cohen. LC 77-139950. (Lecture Notes in Mathematics: Vol. 165). 1970. pap. 7.80 (ISBN 0-387-05192-9). Springer-Verlag.

Stable Homotopy & Generalized Homology. J. Frank Adams. LC 74-5735. (Chicago Lectures in Mathematics Ser.). x, 374p. 1980. pap. text ed. 10.00x (ISBN 0-226-00524-0). U of Chicago Pr.

Stable Isotope Geochemistry. J. Hoefs. LC 73-75422. (Minerals, Rocks & Inorganic Materials Ser.: Vol. 9). (Illus.). ix, 140p. 1973. 22.70 o.p. (ISBN 0-387-06176-2). Springer-Verlag.

Stable Isotopes in the Life Sciences. 1978. pap. 47.75 (ISBN 92-0-011077-0, ISP 442, IAEA). Unipub.

Stable Mappings & Their Singularities: Second Corrected Printing. M. Golubitsky & V. W. Guillemin. (Graduate Texts in Mathematics: Vol. 14). (Illus.). 209p. 1980. 22.00 o.p. (ISBN 0-387-90072-1). Springer-Verlag.

Stable of Fear. Evelyn Bolton. LC 74-9704. (Evelyn Bolton's Horse Stories Ser). (Illus.). 32p. (gr. 3-7). 1974. PLB 5.95 (ISBN 0-87191-370-4); pap. 2.95 (ISBN 0-89812-129-9). Creative Ed.

Staff & Student Attitudes in Colleges of Education. T. W. Eason & E. J. Croll. (Higher Education Monograph: No. 3). 1971. pap. text ed. 7.00x (ISBN 0-901225-72-X, NFER). Humanities.

Staff & Student Supervision: A Task Centered Approach. Dorothy E. Pettes. (National Institute Social Services Library). 1979. text ed. 16.95x (ISBN 0-04-361033-1); pap. text ed. 7.95x (ISBN 0-04-361034-X). Allen Unwin.

Staff Appraisal-Self Appraisal: A Programmed Guide to Interviews. Nigel Schollick & Peter Bloxsom. (Illus.). 1972. 17.95x (ISBN 0-7114-4919-8). Intl Ideas.

Staff Burnout: Job Stress in the Human Services. Cary Cherniss. LC 80-19408. (Sage Studies in Community Mental Health: Vol. 2). (Illus.). 200p. 1980. 20.00 (ISBN 0-8039-1338-9); pap. 9.95 (ISBN 0-8039-1339-7). Sage.

Staff Development, Vol. 1. Ed. by Journal of Nursing Administration Staff. LC 75-35067. 1975. pap. text ed. 8.95 (ISBN 0-913654-08-6). Nursing Res.

Staff Development in Organizations: A Cost Evaluation for Managers & Trainers. Charles E. Kozoll. 124p. 1974. text ed. 8.95 (ISBN 0-201-03864-1). A-W.

Staff Development in Public Welfare Agencies. Carol H. Meyer. LC 66-10730. 1966. 17.50x (ISBN 0-231-02722-2). Columbia U Pr.

Staff Development: New Demands, New Realities, New Perspectives. Ann Lieberman & Lynn Miller. LC 78-27453. 1979. 10.95 (ISBN 0-8077-2512-9). Tchrs Coll.

Staff Management in University & College Libraries. Peter Durey. Ed. by C. Chandler. 144p. 1976. text ed. 16.00 (ISBN 0-08-019718-3). Pergamon.

Staff Manual for Teaching Patients About Chronic Obstructive Pulmonary Diseases. American Hospital Association. LC 78-27387. (Illus.). 424p. 1979. pap. 39.75 (ISBN 0-87258-249-3, 1317). Am Hospital.

Staff Manual for Teaching Patients About Diabetes Mellitus. Jean E. Espenshade. LC 78-27479. (Illus.). 396p. 1979. pap. 37.75 (ISBN 0-87258-250-7, 1318). Am Hospital.

Staff Manual for Teaching Patients About Hypertension. Betty Chewning. LC 78-27337. (Illus.). 340p. 1979. pap. 37.75 (ISBN 0-87258-251-5, 1319). Am Hospital.

Staff Manual for Teaching Patients About Rheumatoid Arthritis. Roberta Wallace et al. LC 78-20816. (Illus.). 472p. 1979. pap. 39.75 (ISBN 0-87258-252-3, 1320). Am Hospital.

Staff of the Mental Health Center: A Field Study. R. M. Glasscote & Jon E. Gudeman. 207p. 1969. 7.50- (ISBN 0-685-24872-0, P155-0). Am Psychiatric.

Staff Relations in the Civil Service: 50 Years of Whitleyism. Henry Parris. (Royal Institute of Public Administration). 1973. text ed. 35.00x (ISBN 0-04-351046-9). Allen Unwin.

Staffa. new ed. Donald B. MacCulloch. LC 75-26360. (Island Ser.). (Illus.). 224p. 16.95 (ISBN 0-7153-7101-0). David & Charles.

Staffing of Nuclear Power Plants & the Recruitment, Training & Authorization of Operating Personnel. (Safety Ser.: No. 50-Sg-01). pap. 4.50 (ISBN 92-0-123379-5, ISP514, IAEA). Unipub.

Staffing Primary Care in Nineteen Ninety: Physician Replacement & Cost Savings. Jane C. Record. (Health Care & Society Ser.: No. 6). 1981. text ed. 23.50 (ISBN 0-8261-3370-3); pap. text ed. cancelled (ISBN 0-8261-3371-1). Springer Pub.

Staffing Three. Ed. by Journal of Nursing Administration Staff. LC 75-43268. 48p. 1976. pap. text ed. 4.95 (ISBN 0-913654-21-3). Nursing Res.

Staffing Two. Ed. by Journal of Nursing Administration Staff. LC 75-16751. 1975. pap. text ed. 4.95 (ISBN 0-913654-06-X). Nursing Res.

Staffords, Earls of Stafford & Dukes of Buckingham 1394-1521. Carole Rawcliffe. LC 77-71425. (Studies in Medieval Life & Thought: No. 11). (Illus.). 1978. 39.95 (ISBN 0-521-21663-X). Cambridge U Pr.

Staffordshire: a Shell Guide. H. Thorold & T. B. Williams. (Illus.). 1978. 14.95 (ISBN 0-571-10516-5, Pub. by Faber & Faber). Merrimack Bk Serv.

Staffordshire Bull Terrier Owner's Encyclopedia. 2nd ed. John F. Gordon. (Illus.). 1977. 12.95 (ISBN 0-7207-0944-X, Pub. by Michael Joseph). Merrimack Bk Serv.

Staffordshire Bull Terriers. John F. Gordon. (Foyle's Handbks). (Illus.). 1973. 3.95 (ISBN 0-685-55791-X). Palmetto Pub.

Staffordshire Pot Lids & Their Potters. Cyril Williams-Wood. 1972. 26.00 o.p. (ISBN 0-571-09826-6, Pub. by Faber & Faber). Merrimack Bk Serv.

Stag at Large. Roger S. O'Toole. LC 68-19824. 1968. 5.95 o.s.i. (ISBN 0-02-594060-0). Macmillan.

Stag Boy. William Rayner. LC 72-91232. (gr. 7 up). 1973. 4.25 o.p. (ISBN 0-15-278400-4, HJ). HarBraceJ.

Stage: A Handbook of Classroom Ideas to Motivate the Teaching of Elementary Dramatics. (Spice Ser). 1968. 6.50 (ISBN 0-89273-107-9). Educ Serv.

Stage Acquitted: Being a Full Answer to Mr. Collier. LC 77-170448. (English Stage Ser.: Vol. 31). lib. bdg. 50.00 (ISBN 0-8240-0614-3). Garland Pub.

Stage & Image in the Plays of Christopher Marlowe. David H. Zucker. (Salzburg Studies in English Literature, Elizabethan & Renaissance Studies: No. 7). 188p. 1972. pap. text ed. 25.00x (ISBN 0-391-01578-8). Humanities.

Stage & the Page: London's "Whole Show" in the Eighteenth Century Theatre. Ed. by George W. Stone, Jr. 1981. 14.95x (ISBN 0-520-04201-8). U of Cal Pr.

Stage & Theatre, 3 vols. (British Parliamentary Papers Ser.). 1971. Set. 180.00x (ISBN 0-7165-1431-1, Pub. by Irish Academic Pr Ireland). Biblio Dist.

Stage Brat. Susan Terris. LC 80-14065. 192p. (gr. 5-9). 1980. 8.95 (ISBN 0-590-07683-3, Four Winds). Schol Bk Serv.

Stage-Coach & Tavern Days. Alice M. Earle. LC 68-17962. (Illus.). 1968. Repr. of 1900 ed. 20.00 (ISBN 0-8103-3431-3). Gale.

Stage Coach & Tavern Tales of the Old Northwest. Harry E. Cole. Ed. by Louise P. Kellogg. LC 77-137353. 1972. Repr. of 1930 ed. 22.00 (ISBN 0-8103-3073-3). Gale.

Stage Condemn'd. George Ridpath. LC 79-170443. (English Stage Ser.: Vol. 29). lib. bdg. 50.00 (ISBN 0-8240-0612-7). Garland Pub.

Stage Costume Design: Theory, Technique & Style. Douglas A. Russell. 1973. 22.95 (ISBN 0-13-840322-8). P-H.

Stage Costume Techniques. Joy S. Emery. (Ser. in Theatre & Drama). (Illus.). 368p. 1981. 18.95 (ISBN 0-13-840330-9). P-H.

Stage Design. Howard Bay. LC 73-15948. (Illus.). 1978. pap. text ed. 12.95x (ISBN 0-910482-98-5). Drama Bk.

Stage Design Throughout the World Since 1960. 2nd ed. Ed. by Rene Hainaux. Yves Bonnat. LC 72-87117. 1972 39.95 (ISBN 0-87830-129-1). Theatre Arts.

Stage Design Throughout the World: 1970-1975. Ed. by Rene Hainaux. LC 75-7879. 1976. 39.95 (ISBN 0-87830-133-X). Theatre Arts.

Stage Direction in Transition. Hardie Albright. LC 70-163774. (Illus.). 352p. 1972. text ed. 15.95x (ISBN 0-8221-0013-4). Dickenson.

Stage Directions. John Gielgud. 1979. pap. 6.85 (ISBN 0-87830-568-8). Theatre Arts.

Stage in Action. Samuel Selden. LC 67-21040. (Arcturus Books Paperbacks). (Illus.). 367p. 1967. pap. 9.95 (ISBN 0-8093-0275-6). S Ill U Pr.

Stage Is Set. Lee Simonson. LC 62-12338. (Illus.). 1963. pap. 3.95 (ISBN 0-87830-508-4, 8). Theatre Arts.

Stage Lighting Handbook. Francis Reid. LC 76-8319. (Illus.). 1976. 10.45 (ISBN 0-87830-156-9). Theatre Arts.

Stage Makeup. 5th ed. Richard Corson. (Illus.). 384p. 1975. 23.95 (ISBN 0-13-840496-8). P-H.

Stage Makeup. 6th ed. Richard Corson. (Illus.). 464p. 1981. text ed. 23.95 (ISBN 0-13-840512-3). P-H.

Stage Management: A Guidebook of Practical Techniques. Stern. 19.50 (ISBN 0-205-04197-3, 4841972). Allyn.

Stage Management & Theatrecraft. new & rev. ed. Hendrik Baker. LC 68-16449. (Illus.). pap. 14.85 (ISBN 0-87830-559-9). Theatre Arts.

Stage Management Forms & Formats. Barbara Dilker. LC 79-16689. (Illus.). 192p. (Orig.). 1981. pap. text ed 15.00x (ISBN 0-910482-85-3). Drama Bk.

Stage of Aristophanes. C. W. Dearden. (University of London Classical Ser: No. 7). 224p. 1976. text ed. 23.75x (ISBN 0-485-13707-0, Athlone Pr). Humanities.

Stage of Love. Cecily Shelbourne. 1978. pap. 1.95 o.p. (ISBN 0-425-03879-3, Dist. by Putnam). Berkley Pub.

Stage Properties & How to Make Them. Warren Kenton. (Illus.). 119p. pap. 11.50x (ISBN 0-273-43888-3, LTB). Soccer.

Stage Scenery & Lighting. 3rd ed. Samuel Selden & Hunton D. Sellman. (Illus.). 1959. 17.95 o.p. (ISBN 0-13-840470-4). P-H.

Stage Scenery, Machinery, & Lighting: A Guide to Information Sources. Ed. by Richard Stoddard. LC 76-13574. (Performing Arts Information Guide Ser.: Vol. 2). 1977. 30.00 (ISBN 0-8103-1374-X). Gale.

Stage Sound. David Collison. LC 75-6799. (Illus.). 192p. 1976. text ed. 15.00x (ISBN 0-910482-65-9). Drama Bk.

Stage Struck. Simon Gray. 64p. 1981. pap. 4.95 (ISBN 0-394-17882-3). Seaver Bks.

Stage Voices: Twelve Canadian Playwrights Talk About Their Lives & Work. Geraldine Anthony. LC 77-76223. 1978. pap. 7.95 o.p. (ISBN 0-385-13540-8). Doubleday.

Stagecoach Trails in Iowa. Inez E. Kirkpatrick. LC 75-56295. (Illus.). 231p. 1976. 25.00 o.p. (ISBN 0-916170-03-9). J-B Pubs.

Stagecraft & Scene Design. Herbert Philippi. LC 53-6010. 1953. text ed. 18.95 (ISBN 0-395-05053-7). HM.

Stagecraft for Nonprofessionals. 3rd ed. Frederick A. Buerki. (Illus., Orig.). 1972. pap. 5.95 (ISBN 0-299-06234-1). U of Wis Pr.

Stagecraft One: Your Introduction to Backstage Work. William H. Lord. (Illus.). 126p. 1979. pap. 9.45 (ISBN 0-686-27395-8). W H Lord.

Staged Cascades in Chemical Processing. P. L. Brian. (International Ser. in the Physical & Chemical Engineering Sciences). (Illus.). 272p. 1972. ref. ed. 25.95 (ISBN 0-13-840280-9). P-H.

Staged for Death. Patricia Bird. 192p. (YA) 1976. 5.95 (ISBN 0-685-64250-X, Avalon). Bouregy.

Stages & Transition in Conceptual Development: An Experimental Study. J. G. Wallace. (General Ser.). (Illus.). 247p. (Orig.). 1972. pap. text ed. 18.50x (ISBN 0-901225-60-6, NFER). Humanities.

Stages of Economic Growth. 2nd ed. W. W. Rostow. (Illus.). 1971. 32.95 (ISBN 0-521-08100-9); pap. 7.95x (ISBN 0-521-09650-2). Cambridge U Pr.

Stages of Faith: The Psychology of Human Development & the Quest for Meaning. James W. Fowler. LC 80-7757. 224p. 1981. 10.95 (ISBN 0-06-062840-5, HarpR). Har-Row.

Stages of Human Evolution. 2nd ed. C. Brace. 1979. 9.95 (ISBN 0-13-840157-8); pap. 6.95 (ISBN 0-13-840140-3). P-H.

Staging of Plays Before Shakespeare. Richard Southern. LC 73-76707. (Illus.). 1973. 19.95 (ISBN 0-87830-130-5). Theatre Arts.

Stain of Circumstance: Selected Poems. Lloyd Frankenberg. LC 73-85448. 237p. 1974. 10.95 (ISBN 0-8214-0138-6). Ohio U Pr.

Stain Removal Handbook. Max Alth. 1977. 8.95 o.p. (ISBN 0-8015-7072-7); pap. 3.95 o.p. (ISBN 0-8015-7072-7). Dutton.

Stained Glass. William F. Buckley, Jr. 1979. pap. 2.25 o.p. (ISBN 0-446-82323-6). Warner Bks.

Stained Glass: A Guide to Information Sources. Ed. by Darlene Brady & William Serban. LC 79-23712. (Art & Architecture Information Guide Ser.: Vol. 10). 1980. 30.00 (ISBN 0-8103-1445-2). Gale.

Stained Glass Astrology & Tarot Card Designs. Paul Marks. (Illus.). 64p. 1980. pap. 2.95 (ISBN 0-8256-3842-9, Hidden Hse-Flash). Music Sales.

Stained Glass Crafting. rev. ed. Paul W. Wood. LC 67-27750. (Illus.). (gr. 10 up). 1971. 8.95 (ISBN 0-8069-5094-3); PLB 8.29 (ISBN 0-8069-5095-1). Sterling.

Stained Glass Home Studio Guide. Luciano & Gene Mayo. (Illus.). 72p. 1981. pap. 4.95 (ISBN 0-8256-3844-5, Hidden Hse-Flash). Music Sales.

Stained Glass: Music for the Eye. Robert Hill & Jill Hill. LC 79-65725. (Illus.). 108p. (Orig.). 1979. pap. 9.95 (ISBN 0-295-95699-2). U of Wash Pr.

Stained Glass of William Morris & His Circle: A Catalogue, Vol. 2. A. Charles Sewter. LC 72-91307. (Studies in British Art Ser.). 344p. 1975. 95.00x (ISBN 0-300-01836-3). Yale U Pr.

Stained Glass of William Morris & His Circle, Vol. 1. A. Charles Sewter. LC 72-91307. (Studies in British Art Ser.). (Illus.). 384p. 1974. 85.00x (ISBN 0-300-01471-6). Yale U Pr.

Stained Glass Window. Charlotte M. Stein. Date not set. price not set. Double M Pr.

Staining & Finishing Unfinished Furniture & Other Naked Woods. George Grotz. LC 68-25596. 1968. pap. 2.95 (ISBN 0-385-01906-8, Dolp). Doubleday.

Staining & Wood Polishing. Charles H. Hayward. (Illus.). 214p. 1980. pap. 5.95 (ISBN 0-8069-8684-0). Sterling.

Staining Procedures. 3rd ed. George Clark. 16.00 o.p. (ISBN 0-683-01706-3). Williams & Wilkins.

Staining Procedures. 4th ed. George Clark. (Illus.). 444p. 1980. softcover 39.95 (ISBN 0-683-01707-1). Williams & Wilkins.

Stainless Steel Piping, Fittings & Accessories for the Pulp & Paper Industry. 3rd rev. ed. B. L. Merriss et al. (TAPPI PRESS Reports). (Illus.). 1979. pap. 19.85 (ISBN 0-89852-330-3, 01-01-R030). TAPPI.

Staircase Seventeen. Gauri Pant. (Writers Workshop Redbird Ser.). 1975. 8.00 (ISBN 0-88253-644-3); pap. text ed. 4.00 (ISBN 0-88253-643-5). Ind-US Inc.

Staircase to Writing & Reading. 3rd ed. Alan Casty & Donald J. Tighe. (Illus.). 1979. pap. 10.95 (ISBN 0-13-840579-4). P-H.

Stairway to Heaven. Zecharia Sitchin. 384p. 1981. 17.95 (ISBN 0-312-75505-8). St Martin.

Stakes Winners of 1978: Supplement. The Thoroughbread Owners & Breeders Association. 1978. lib. bdg. 15.00 (ISBN 0-936032-21-9); pap. 10.00 (ISBN 0-936032-22-7). Thoroughbred Own and Breed.

Stakes Winners of 1979. Ed. by Blood-Horse. (Annual Supplement, the Blood-Horse). 1980. lib. bdg. 20.00 (ISBN 0-936032-23-5); pap. 10.00 (ISBN 0-936032-24-3). Thoroughbred Own & Breed.

Stakes Winners of 1980. Blood-Horse Editors. (Annual Supplement of the Blood-Horse). 1981. lib. bdg. 20.00 (ISBN 0-936032-39-1); pap. 10.00 (ISBN 0-936032-40-5). Thoroughbred Own & Breed.

Stalag: U.S.A. The Remarkable Story of German POWs in America. Judith M. Gansberg. LC 76-51407. (Illus.). 1977. 10.95 o.s.i. (ISBN 0-690-01223-3, TYC-T). T Y Crowell.

Stale Food vs. Fresh Food: Cause & Cure of Choked Arteries. 6th ed. Robert S. Ford. 48p. 1977. pap. 4.40 (ISBN 0-686-09051-9). Magnolia Lab.

Stalin. David Killingray et al. Ed. by Malcolm Yapp et al. (World History Ser.). (Illus.). 32p. (gr. 10). 1980. Repr. of 1977 ed. lib. bdg. 5.95 (ISBN 0-89908-126-6); pap. text ed. 1.95 (ISBN 0-89908-101-0). Greenhaven.

Stalin: A Political Biography. 2nd ed. Isaac Deutscher. pap. 9.95 (ISBN 0-19-500273-3, GB). Oxford U Pr.

Stalin As Warlord. Albert Seaton. 1976. 27.00 (ISBN 0-7134-3078-8, Pub. by Batsford England). David & Charles.

Stalin File. Martin McCauley. 1979. 14.95 (ISBN 0-7134-1918-0, Pub. by Batsford England). David & Charles.

Stalin Phenomenon. Jean Elleinstein. 1976. text ed. 13.00x (ISBN 0-85315-375-2). Humanities.

Stalin und der Aufstieg Hitlers: Die Deutschlandpolitik der Kommunistischen Internationale, 1929-1934. Thomas Weingartner. (Beitrage zur auswaertigen und international Politik, No. 4). (Ger). 1970. 23.55x (ISBN 3-11-002702-X). De Gruyter.

Stalingrad Elegies. James Schevill. LC 64-16113. 53p. (Orig.). 1964. pap. 2.25 (ISBN 0-8040-0281-9, 59). Swallow.

Stalinism & After. Alec Nove. (Illus.). 1975. text ed. 7.50x (ISBN 0-04-320105-9, 2203). Allen Unwin.

Stalinism: Essays in Historical Interpretation. Ed. by Robert C. Tucker. 1977. 19.95 (ISBN 0-393-05608-2, N892, Norton Lib); pap. 7.95 (ISBN 0-393-00892-4). Norton.

Stalinist Command Economy. Dunmore. LC 79-26712. 224p. 1980. write for info. St Martin.

Stalin's Russia. F. Randall. LC 65-18559. 1965. 12.95 (ISBN 0-02-925810-3). Free Pr.

Stalking Man. William Coughlin. 1979. 8.95 o.s.i. (ISBN 0-440-08334-6). Delacorte.

Stalking the Blue-Eyed Scallop. Euell Gibbons. (Illus.). 1964. 9.95 o.p. (ISBN 0-679-50088-X); pap. 3.95 o.p. (ISBN 0-679-50236-X). McKay.

Stalking the Seattle Bargain: A Complete Bargain Hunter's Catalogue & Consumer Education Guide. Colleen E. Simpson & S. Hirshman. (Illus.). 160p. (Orig.). 1980. pap. 3.95 (ISBN 0-938406-00-0). Simpson-Hirshman.

Stalking the Wild Asparagus. Euell Gibbons. 1970. pap. 3.95 Field Guide ed. (ISBN 0-679-50223-8). McKay.

Stalking the Wild Pendulum: On the Mechanics of Consciousness. Itzhak Bentov. LC 76-46349. 1977. pap. 6.95 (ISBN 0-525-47458-7). Dutton.

Stalking the Wild Taboo. 2nd ed. Garrett Hardin. LC 78-1976. 290p. 1978. 11.95 (ISBN 0-913232-40-8); pap. 6.95 (ISBN 0-913232-41-6). W Kaufmann.

Stallion Register 1979: Annual Supplements to the Blood-Horse. 1979. lib. bdg. 20.00 (ISBN 0-936032-25-1); pap. 10.00 (ISBN 0-936032-26-X). Thoroughbred Own and Breed.

Stallion Register, 1980. Date not set. lib. bdg. 20.00 (ISBN 0-936032-27-8); pap. 10.00 (ISBN 0-936032-28-6). Thoroughbred Own & Breed.

Stallion Register, 1981. Ed. by Blood Horse. (Illus.). 900p. 1980. 20.00 (ISBN 0-936032-33-2); pap. 10.00 (ISBN 0-936032-34-0). Thoroughbred Own & Breed.

Stamme der Insel Hainan, 2 vols. Hans Stubel & Shimizu Mitsuo. (Asian Folklore & Social Life Monographs: Vols. 85-86). (Ger.). 1935. 15.00 (ISBN 0-89986-294-2). E Langstaff.

Stammering & Stuttering: Their Nature & Treatment. James Hunt. 1967. Repr. of 1861 ed. 13.00 o.s.i. (ISBN 0-02-846200-9). Hafner.

Stamp Act: Taxation Without Representation Is Tyranny. Alice Dickinson. LC 75-104187. (Focus Bks). (Illus.). (gr. 7 up). 1970. PLB 4.90 o.p. (ISBN 0-531-01012-0). Watts.

Stamp Collecting. Boy Scouts Of America. LC 19-600. (Illus.). 48p. (gr. 6-12). 1974. pap. 0.70x (ISBN 0-8395-3359-4, 3359). BSA.

Stamp Collecting A-Z. Walter J. Young. LC 80-27181. (Illus.). 150p. 1981. 9.95 (ISBN 0-498-02479-2). A S Barnes.

Stamp Collecting for Fun & Profit. Cetin. pap. 2.00 o.p. (ISBN 0-87980-149-2). Wilshire.

Stamping Ground. Loren D. Estleman. 1981. pap. write for info. (ISBN 0-671-41861-0). PB.

Stamps & Coins. R. H. Rosichan. LC 73-90498. (Spare Time Guides Ser.: No. 5). 225p. 1974. lib. bdg. 13.50 o.p. (ISBN 0-87287-071-5). Libs Unl.

Stamps of the World. Ed. by Stanley Gibbons Ltd. (Illus.). 1979. write for info (ISBN 0-85259-001-6). StanGib Ltd.

Stan. Fred L. Guiles. (Illus.). 1980. cancelled (ISBN 0-7181-1908-8, Pub. by Michael Joseph). Merrimack Bk Serv.

Stan Goes on Safari. Sunny Beach. 1981. 4.95 (ISBN 0-533-04641-6). Vantage.

Stan Jones' Cooking with Bacardi Rum. Stan Jones. LC 80-68071. (Illus.). 192p. 1980. pap. 14.95 (ISBN 0-918338-03-4). Bar Guide.

Stan Place's Guide to Make-Up: How to Look Like Yourself Only Better. Stan Place & Elaine Budd. (Illus.). 192p. 1981. 17.95 (ISBN 0-385-15537-9). Doubleday.

Stan: The Life of Stan Laurel. Fred L. Guiles. LC 80-5806. (Illus.). 272p. 1980. 12.95 (ISBN 0-8128-2762-7). Stein & Day.

Stanbroke Girls. Fiona Hill. 256p. 1981. 10.95 (ISBN 0-312-75570-8). St Martin.

Stand by, Boys! K. Norel. Tr. by Marian Schoolland from Dutch. (Children's Summit Ser.). (Orig.). 1980. pap. 1.65 (ISBN 0-8010-6734-0). Baker Bk.

Stand by-y-y to Start Engines. Daniel V. Gallery. 1967. pap. 1.50 (ISBN 0-446-88921-0). Warner Bks.

Stand Firm: The Teenager's Guide to Self-Defense. James. (gr. 7-12). 1980. pap. 1.25 (ISBN 0-590-30033-4, Schol Pap). Schol Bk Serv.

Stand-in Bride. Carole Halston. 192p. 1981. pap. 1.50 (ISBN 0-671-57062-5). S&S.

Stand on Zanzibar. John Brunner. LC 79-19062. 1979. Repr. of 1968 ed. lib. bdg. 15.00x (ISBN 0-8376-0438-9). Bentley.

Stand Still Like the Hummingbird. Henry Miller. LC 62-10408. 1967. pap. 4.95 (ISBN 0-8112-0322-0, NDP236). New Directions.

Stand up for Your Rights. Roy Cohen. 14.95 (ISBN 0-671-25341-7). S&S.

Stand Watie & the Agony of the Cherokee Nation. Kenny A. Franks. LC 79-124380. 1979. 14.95x (ISBN 0-87870-063-3). Memphis St Univ.

Standard Aircraft Handbook. 3rd ed. Stuart Leavell & Stanley Bungay. LC 80-67736. (Illus.). 1980. pap. 5.95 (ISBN 0-8168-8502-8). Aero.

Standard Alphabet for Reducing Unwritten Languages & Foreign Graphic Systems to a Uniform Orthography in European Letters. Richard Lepsius. (Amsterdam Classics in Linguistics Ser.: No. 5). 375p. 1980. text ed. 45.75x (ISBN 90-272-0876-X). Humanities.

Standard American Bridge Updated. Norma Sands. pap. 4.95 (ISBN 0-686-28759-2). Rocky Mtn Bks.

Standard Bearer: A Story of Army Life in the Time of Caesar. Albert C. Whitehead. (Illus.). (gr. 7-11). 1943. 8.50x (ISBN 0-8196-0116-0). Biblo.

Standard Book of Dog Breeding. Alvin Grossman. LC 76-56010. (Other Dog Bk.). (Illus.). 1981. price not set (ISBN 0-87714-054-5). Denlingers.

Standard Catalog of World Coins. rev. 6th ed. Chester L. Krause & Clifford Mishler. Ed. by Colin R. Bruce. LC 79-65719. (Illus.). 1979. pap. 24.50 o.s.i. (ISBN 0-87341-050-5). Krause Pubns.

Standard COBOL. 2nd ed. Mike Murach. LC 74-34184. (Illus.). 400p. 1975. pap. text ed. 15.95 (ISBN 0-574-18401-5, 13-4010); instr's guide avail. (ISBN 0-574-18402-3, 13-4011). SRA.

Standard COBOL: A Problem-Solving Approach. Marilyn Z. Smith. 308p. 1974. pap. text ed. 14.25 (ISBN 0-395-17091-5). HM.

Standard Data Encryption Algorithm. Harry Katzan, Jr. LC 77-13582. (Illus.). 1977. text ed. 14.00 (ISBN 0-89433-016-0). Petrocelli.

Standard Dictionary of Computers & Information Processing. rev., 2nd ed. Martin H. Weik. 1977. 22.50 (ISBN 0-8104-5099-2). Hayden.

Standard Directory of Advertisers: Classified Edition. National Register Publishing Co. LC 5-21147. 1981. 109.00 (ISBN 0-87217-000-4). Natl Register.

Standard Directory of Advertisers: Geographical Edition. National Register Publishing Co. LC 15-21147. 1981. 109.00 (ISBN 0-87217-001-2). Natl Register.

Standard Directory of Advertising Agencies, 3 vols. National Register Publishing Co. 1981. 52.00 (ISBN 0-87217-003-9); 127.00 set (ISBN 0-686-52432-2). Natl Register.

Standard Education Almanac: 1975-1976. LC 68-3442. 626p. 1975. 29.50 (ISBN 0-8379-2102-3). Marquis.

Standard Education Almanac: 1980-81. 13th ed. LC 68-3442. 600p. 1980. 39.50 (ISBN 0-8379-2107-4, 031097). Marquis.

Standard First Aid & Personal Safety. 2nd ed. American National Red Cross. LC 79-53478. (American Red Cross Bks.). 1979. pap. 2.50 (ISBN 0-385-15736-3). Doubleday.

Standard for Engineering Qualifications: A Comparative Study in Eighteen European Countries. 106p. 1975. pap. 7.00 (ISBN 92-3-101140-5, UNESCO). Unipub.

Standard for Miller: A Community Response to Pornography. Edward J. Shaughnessy & Diana Trebbi. LC 80-5648. (Illus.). 256p. 1980. lib. bdg. 18.75 (ISBN 0-8191-1280-1); pap. text ed. 10.50 (ISBN 0-8191-1281-X). U Pr of Amer.

Standard for the Installation of Centrifugal Fire Pumps. 134p. 5.00 (ISBN 0-686-68287-4). Natl Fire Prot.

Standard Fortran: A Problem-Solving Approach. Laura G. Cooper & Marilyn Z. Smith. LC 72-4395. 288p. (Orig.). 1973. pap. text ed. 13.95 (ISBN 0-395-14028-5). HM.

Standard Fortran Programming. 3rd ed. Donald H. Ford. (Irwin-Dorsey Ser. in Information Processing). 1978. pap. text ed. 11.50 (ISBN 0-256-01998-3). Irwin.

Standard Gauge Great Western Four-Four-Zero's, Vol. 1. O. S. Nock. 1977. 16.95 (ISBN 0-7153-7411-7). David & Charles.

Standard Gauge Great Western Four-Four-Zero's: 1904-1965, Vol. 2. O. S. Nock. LC 78-62486. (Illus.). 1978. 16.95 (ISBN 0-7153-7684-5). David & Charles.

Standard German Vocabulary. C. M. Purin. 1937. text ed. 3.95x o.p. (ISBN 0-669-29678-3). Heath.

Standard Guide to Horse & Pony Breeds. Ed. by Elwyn H. Edwards. LC 79-23921. (Illus.). 352p. 1980. 24.95 (ISBN 0-07-019035-6). McGraw.

Standard Guide to U. S. Coin & Paper Money Valuations. 6th ed. Robert Wilhite & Clifford Mishler. LC 79-67100. (Illus.). 1979. pap. 1.95 o.s.i. (ISBN 0-87341-051-3). Krause Pubns.

Standard Handbook of Salt-Water Fishing. rev. ed. Robert Scharf. (Illus.). 1966. 9.95 o.s.i. (ISBN 0-690-76926-1, TYC-T). T Y Crowell.

Standard Handbook of Stamp Collecting. 2nd ed. Richard M. Cabeen. LC 75-15651. (Illus.). 1965. 14.95 o.s.i. (ISBN 0-690-76997-0, TYC-T). T Y Crowell.

Standard Handbook of Textiles. 8th ed. Archibald J. Hall. 1970. 41.95 (ISBN 0-87245-596-3). Textile Bk.

Standard Lesson Commentary, 1981-1982: Twenty-Ninth Annual Edition. Ed. by James I. Fehl. (Illus.). 456p. 1981. 6.95 (ISBN 0-87239-436-0, 74008); pap. 5.95 (ISBN 0-87239-435-2, 1982). Standard Pub.

Standard Manual of Accounting for Shopping Centers. Touche Ross & Co. LC 73-163156. (Illus.). 40p. 1971. pap. 12.00 (ISBN 0-87420-908-0). Urban Land.

Standard Marine Navigational Vocabulary. 44p. 1977. pap. 8.25 (ISBN 0-686-64013-6, IMCO 38, IMCO). Unipub.

Standard Mechanical & Electrical Details. Jerome F. Mueller. (Illus.). 1980. 24.50 (ISBN 0-07-043960-5). McGraw.

Standard Methods for the Analysis of Oils, Fats & Derivatives. 6th ed. Ed. by C. Paquot. LC 78-40305. 1978. text ed. 25.00 (ISBN 0-08-022379-6). Pergamon.

Standard Methods of Clinical Chemistry. Ed. by Miriam Reiner et al. Incl. Vol. 1. Ed. by Miriam Reiner. 1953. 26.00 (ISBN 0-12-609101-3); Vol. 2. Ed. by David Seligson. 1958. 26.00 (ISBN 0-12-609102-1); Vol. 3. 1961. 26.00 (ISBN 0-12-609103-X); Vol. 4. 1964. 26.00 (ISBN 0-12-609104-8); Vol. 5. Ed. by S. Meites. 1965. 26.00 (ISBN 0-12-609105-6); Vol. 6. Ed. by R. P. MacDonald. 1970. 36.50 (ISBN 0-12-609106-4); Vol. 7. 1972. 42.50 (ISBN 0-12-609107-2). Acad Pr.

Standard on Aircraft Maintenance. 84p. 3.75 (ISBN 0-686-68288-2). Natl Fire Prot.

Standard Operations Manual for the Marine Transportation Sector of the Offshore Mineral & Oil Industry. Ed. by Richard A. Block & Charles B. Collins. 61p. (Orig.). 1979. pap. text ed. 7.50 (ISBN 0-934114-09-9). Marine Educ.

Standard Plant Operators' Manual. 2nd ed. Stephen M. Elonka. (Illus.). 384p. 1975. 22.50 o.p. (ISBN 0-07-019296-0, P&RB). McGraw.

Standard Plumbing Engineering Design. Louis S. Nielsen. (Illus.). 384p. 1981. 21.50 (ISBN 0-07-046541-X). McGraw.

Standard Specifications for Movable Highway Bridges. 1979. pap. 5.00 (ISBN 0-686-27096-7, MHB-70). AASHTO.

Standard Youth Hosteler's Guide to Europe. rev. ed. Youth Hostels Association. (Illus.). 498p. 1981. 6.95 (ISBN 0-02-098950-4, Collier). Macmillan.

Standardization, a New Discipline. Lal C. Verman. 1973. 22.50 o.p. (ISBN 0-208-01285-0, Archon). Shoe String.

Standardization of Analytical Methodology for Feeds. 128p. 1980. pap. 10.00 (ISBN 0-88936-217-3, IDRC 134, IDRC). Unipub.

Standardization of Nomenclature: International Journal of the Sociology of Language, No. 23. Ed. by J. C. Sager. 1980. pap. text ed. 21.95x (ISBN 90-279-3028-7). Mouton.

Standardization of Radiation Dosimetry in the Soviet Union, France, the United Kingdom, the Federal Republic of Germany & Czechoslavakia. (Illus.). 101p. (Orig.). 1973. pap. 6.50 (ISBN 92-0-117073-4, ISTR4, IAEA). Unipub.

Standardization of Radioactive Waste Categories. (Technical Reports: No. 101). (Illus., Orig.). 1970. pap. 2.50 (ISBN 92-0-125070-3, IDC 101, IAEA). Unipub.

Standardization of Radionuclides. 1967. pap. 35.50 (ISBN 92-0-030067-7, IAEA). Unipub.

Standardized Development of Computer Software: Part 1, Methods. Robert C. Tausworthe. 1977. Pt. 2, Standards. 24.95 (ISBN 0-13-842195-1); 24.95 (ISBN 0-13-842203-6); comb. set (pts 1&2) 43.93 (ISBN 0-13-842211-7). P-H.

Standards & Policy Statements of Special Interest to Workers Adopted Under the Auspices of the International Labour Office. International Labour Office, Geneva. 132p. (Orig.). 1980. pap. 7.15 (ISBN 92-2-102441-5). Intl Labour Office.

Standards & Specifications Information Sources. Ed. by Erasmus J. Struglia. LC 65-24659. (Management Information Guide Ser.: No. 6). 1965. 30.00 (ISBN 0-8103-0806-1). Gale.

Standards for Critical Care. Brenda C. Johanson et al. LC 80-15476. (Illus.). 536p. 1980. pap. text ed. 15.95 (ISBN 0-8016-2527-0). Mosby.

Standards for Educational & Psychological Tests. American Psychological Association. LC 74-75734. 1974. pap. 4.00 (ISBN 0-685-56745-1). Am Psychol.

Standards for Evaluations of Educational Programs, Projects & Materials. Joint Committee on Standards for Educational Evaluation. LC 80-12192. 224p. 1980. 8.95 (ISBN 0-07-032725-4). McGraw.

Standards for Juvenile Justice: A Summary & Analysis. Barbara Flicker. (Juvenile Justice Standards Project Ser.). 1977. casebound 16.50 o.p. (ISBN 0-88410-758-2); softcover 7.95 o.p. (ISBN 0-88410-759-0). Ballinger Pub.

Standards for Juvenile Justice: A Summary & Analysis. Barbara Flicker. (Juvenile Justice Standards Project Ser.). 1981. softcover 7.95 (ISBN 0-88410-758-2); casebound 16.50 (ISBN 0-88410-831-7). Ballinger Pub.

Standards for Library Service: An International Survey. E. N. Withers. (Documentation, Libraries & Archives, Studies & Research Ser., No. 6). 421p. (Orig.). 1974. pap. 19.75 (ISBN 92-3-101177-4, U637, UNESCO). Unipub.

Standards for Psychiatric Facilities. 1969. pap. 3.50 (ISBN 0-685-24000-2, P152-0). Am Psychiatric.

Standards for Psychiatric Facilities: Revision-Addendum. 1974. pap. 1.75 (ISBN 0-685-94004-7, P151-2). Am Psychiatric.

Standards for Psychiatric Facilities Serving Children and Adolescents. APA Task Force on Standards for Psychiatric Facilities for Children. 136p. 1971. 5.00 (ISBN 0-685-37536-6, P160-0). Am Psychiatric.

Standards for Pump Makers & Users. 1973. pap. 26.00 (ISBN 0-685-85163-X, Dist. by Air Science Co.). BHRA Fluid.

Standards of Service for the Library of Congress Network of Libraries for the Blind & Physically Handicapped. Association of Specialized & Cooperative Library Agencies. LC 79-22963. 76p. 1980. pap. 4.50 (ISBN 0-8389-0298-7). ALA.

Standards Relating to Abuse & Neglect. Robert A. Burt & Michael Wald. LC 77-3279. (Juvenile Justice Standards Project Ser.). 1977. softcover 7.95 o.p. (ISBN 0-88410-764-7); 16.50, casebound o.p. (ISBN 0-88410-242-4). Ballinger Pub.

Standards Relating to Abuse & Neglect. Robert A. Burt & Michael Wald. (Juvenile Justice Standards Project Ser.). Date not set. softcover 7.95 (ISBN 0-88410-830-9); casebound 16.50 (ISBN 0-88410-242-4). Ballinger Pub.

Standards Relating to Adjudication. Robert O. Dawson. LC 77-1755. (Juvenile Justice Standards Project Ser.). 1977. softcover 5.95 o.p. (ISBN 0-88410-767-1); 12.50, casebound o.p. Ballinger Pub.

Standards Relating to Adjudication. Robert O. Dawson. (Juvenile Justice Standards Project Ser.). 1980. softcover 7.95 (ISBN 0-88410-809-0); casebound 12.50 (ISBN 0-88410-236-X). Ballinger Pub.

Standards Relating to Appeals & Collateral Review. Michael Moran. LC 77-3982. (Juvenile Justice Standards Project Ser.). 1977. softcover 5.95 o.p. (ISBN 0-88410-776-0); 12.50, casebound o.p. (ISBN 0-88410-239-4). Ballinger Pub.

Standards Relating to Appeals & Collateral Review. Michael Moran. (Juvenile Justice Standards Project Ser.). 1980. softcover 5.95 (ISBN 0-88410-815-5); casebound 12.50. Ballinger Pub.

Standards Relating to Architecture of Facilities. Allan M. Greenberg. LC 77-14495. (Juvenile Justice Standards Project Ser.). 1977. soft cover 7.59 o.p. (ISBN 0-88410-778-7); casebound 12.50 o.p. (ISBN 0-88410-249-1). Ballinger Pub.

Standards Relating to Architecture of Facilities. Allan M. Greengerg. (Juvenile Justice Standards Project Ser.). 1980. softcover 6.95 (ISBN 0-88410-813-9); casebound 14.50. Ballinger Pub.

Standards Relating to Corrections Administration. Andrew Rutherford & Fred Cohen. LC 77-3375. (Juvenile Justice Standards Project Ser.). 1977. casebound 16.50 o.p.; softcover 7.95 o.p. (ISBN 0-88410-778-7). Ballinger Pub.

Standards Relating to Corrections Administration. Andrew Rutherford & Fred Cohen. (Juvenile Justice Standards Project Ser.). 1980. softcover 7.95 (ISBN 0-88410-821-X); casebound 16.50 (ISBN 0-88410-750-7). Ballinger Pub.

Standards Relating to Court Organization and Administration. Ted Rubin. LC 76-14413. (Juvenile Justice Standards Project Ser.). 1977. soft cover 5.95 o.p. (ISBN 0-88410-777-9); 12.50, casebound o.p. Ballinger Pub.

Standards Relating to Court Organization & Administration. Ted Rubin. (Juvenile Justice Standards Project Ser.). 1980. softcover 7.95; casebound 16.50 (ISBN 0-88410-231-9). Ballinger Pub.

Standards Relating to Dispositional Procedures. Fred Cohen. LC 76-14414. (Juvenile Justice Standards Project Ser.). 1977. softcover 5.95 o.p. (ISBN 0-88410-766-3); 12.50, casebound o.p. Ballinger Pub.

Standards Relating to Dispositional Procedures. Fred Cohen. (Juvenile Justice Standards Project Ser.). 1980. softcover 5.95 (ISBN 0-88410-808-2); casebound 16.50 (ISBN 0-88410-233-5). Ballinger Pub.

Standards Relating to Dispositions. Linda R. Singer. LC 76-14412. (Juvenile Justice Standards Project Ser.). 1977. soft cover 7.95 o.p. (ISBN 0-88410-779-5); 16.50, casebound o.p. Ballinger Pub.

Standards Relating to Dispositions. Linda R. Singer. (Juvenile Justice Standards Project Ser.). 1980. softcover 7.95 (ISBN 0-88410-816-3); casebound 16.50 (ISBN 0-88410-229-7). Ballinger Pub.

Standards Relating to Interim Status: The Release, Control, & Detention of Accused Juvenile Offenders Between Arrest & Disposition. Daniel J. Freed & Timothy P. Terrell. LC 77-2318. (Juvenile Justice Standards Project Ser.). 1977. softcover 7.95 o.p. (ISBN 0-88410-770-1); 16.50, casebound o.p. Ballinger Pub.

Standards Relating to Interim Status: The Release, Control & Detention of Accused Juvenile Offenders Between Arrest & Disposition. Daniel J. Freed & Timothy P. Terrell. (Juvenile Justice Standards Project Ser.). 1980. softcover 7.95 (ISBN 0-88410-812-0); casebound 16.50 (ISBN 0-88410-244-0). Ballinger Pub.

Standards Relating to Juvenile Delinquency and Sanctions. John M Junker. LC 76-27864. (Juvenile Justice Standards Project Ser.). 1976. soft cover 5.95 o.p. (ISBN 0-88410-774-4); 12.50, casebound o.p. Ballinger Pub.

Standards Relating to Juvenile Delinquency & Sanctions. John M. Junker. (Juvenile Justice Standards Project Ser.). 1980. softcover 5.95 (ISBN 0-88410-829-5); casebound 12.50 (ISBN 0-88410-235-1). Ballinger Pub.

Standards Relating to Juvenile Probation Function: Intake & Predisposition Investigative Services. Josephine Gittler. LC 77-3257. (Juvenile Justice Standards Project Ser.). 1977. 7.95 o.p. (ISBN 0-88410-771-X); casebound 16.50 o.p. Ballinger Pub.

Standards Relating to Juvenile Probation Function: Intake & Predisposition Investigative Services. Josephine Gittler. (Juvenile Justice Standards Project Ser.). 1980. softcover 7.95 (ISBN 0-88410-828-7); casebound 14.50 (ISBN 0-88410-248-3). Ballinger Pub.

Standards Relating to Juvenile Records & Information Systems. Michael L. Altman. LC 77-3228. (Juvenile Justice Standards Project Ser.). 1977. softcover 7.95 o.p. (ISBN 0-88410-760-4); casebound 16.50 o.p. Ballinger Pub.

Standards Relating to Juvenile Records & Information Systems. Michael L. Altman. (Juvenile Justice Standards Project Ser.). 1980. softcover 7.95 (ISBN 0-88410-819-8); casebound 16.50 (ISBN 0-88410-247-5). Ballinger Pub.

Standards Relating to Monitoring. Stephen Bing & Larry Brown. LC 77-3939. (Juvenile Justice Standards Project Ser.). 1977. softcover 5.95 o.p. (ISBN 0-88410-761-2); casebound 12.50 o.p. Ballinger Pub.

Standards Relating to Monitoring. Stephen Bing & Larry Brown. (Juvenile Justice Standards Project Ser.). 1980. softcover 7.95 (ISBN 0-88410-805-8); casebound 16.50 (ISBN 0-88410-753-1). Ballinger Pub.

Standards Relating to Non-Criminal Misbehavior. Aidan Gough. LC 76-14394. (Juvenile Justice Standards Project Ser.). 1977. soft cover 6.95 o.p. (ISBN 0-88410-772-8); 14.00, casebound o.p. (ISBN 0-88410-232-7). Ballinger Pub.

Standards Relating to Non-Criminal Misbehavior. Aidan Gough. (Juvenile Justice Standards Project Ser.). Date not set. softcover 6.95 (ISBN 0-88410-832-5). Ballinger Pub.

Standards Relating to Planning for Juvenile Justice. Leonard Buckle & Suzann Buckle. LC 77-3938. (Juvenile Justice Standards Project Ser.). 1977. final casebound 12.50 o.p.; softcover 5.95 o.p. (ISBN 0-88410-763-9). Ballinger Pub.

Standards Relating to Planning for Juvenile Justice. Leonard Buckle & Suzann Buckle. (Juvenile Justice Standards Project Ser.). 1980. softcover 7.95; final casebound 16.50 (ISBN 0-88410-754-X). Ballinger Pub.

Standards Relating to Police Handling of Juvenile Problems. Egon Bittner & Sheldon Krantz. LC 77-3376. (Juvenile Justice Standards Project Ser.). 1977. final casebound 16.50 o.p.; softcover 7.95 o.p. (ISBN 0-88410-762-0). Ballinger Pub.

Standards Relating to Police Handling of Juvenile Problems. Egon Bittner & Sheldon Krantz. (Juvenile Justice Standards Project Ser.). 1980. softcover 7.95 (ISBN 0-88410-806-6); final casebound 16.50 (ISBN 0-88410-755-8). Ballinger Pub.

Standards Relating to Rights of Minors. Barry Feld & Robert J. Levy. LC 77-1684. (Juvenile Justice Standards Project Ser.). 1977. 6.95 o.p. (ISBN 0-88410-768-X); 14.00, casebound o.p. Ballinger Pub.

Standards Relating to Rights of Minors. Barry Feld & Robert J. Levy. (Juvenile Justice Standards Project Ser.). 1980. softcover 7.95 (ISBN 0-88410-810-4); casebound 16.50 (ISBN 0-88410-243-2). Ballinger Pub.

Standards Relating to Schools and Education. William G Buss & Stephen R. Goldstein. LC 77-1741. (Juvenile Justice Standards Project Ser.). 1977. soft cover 7.95 o.p. (ISBN 0-88410-765-5); 16.50, casebound o.p. (ISBN 0-88410-241-6). Ballinger Pub.

Standards Relating to Schools & Education. William G. Buss & Stephen R. Goldstein. (Juvenile Justice Standards Project Ser.). Date not set. softcover 7.95 (ISBN 0-88410-841-4). Ballinger Pub.

Standards Relating to Transfer Between Courts. Charles Whitebread. LC 76-17798. (Juvenile Justice Standards Project Ser.). 1977. soft cover 5.95 o.p. (ISBN 0-88410-780-9); 12.50, casebound o.p. Ballinger Pub.

Standards Relating to Transfer Between Courts. Charles Whitebread. (Juvenile Justice Standards Project Ser.). 1980. softcover 5.95 (ISBN 0-88410-818-X); casebound 12.50 (ISBN 0-88410-230-0). Ballinger Pub.

Standards Relating to Youth Service Agencies. Judith Areen. LC 77-14496. (Juvenile Justice Standards Project Ser.). 1977. softcover 7.95 o.p. (ISBN 0-88410-782-5); casebound 16.50 o.p. Ballinger Pub.

Standards Relating to Youth Service Agencies. Judith Areen. (Juvenile Justice Standards Project Ser.). 1980. softcover 7.95 (ISBN 0-88410-804-X); casebound 16.50 (ISBN 0-88410-756-6). Ballinger Pub.

Standing Strong. Robrt B. Ruddell et al. (Pathfinder - Allyn & Bacon Reading Program: Level 18). (gr. 5-6). 1978. text ed. 9.12 (ISBN 0-205-05209-6, 5452090); tchr's ed. 14.60 (ISBN 0-205-05211-8, 5452112); 3.88. Allyn.

Standing Tall. Kathryn Kuhlman. LC 74-28755. (Kathryn Kuhlman Ser.). 96p. 1975. pap. 0.95 (ISBN 0-87123-534-X, 200534). Bethany Fell.

Standing Tall in Credit Management. William H. Bryan. (No. 6). 1977. pap. 1.90 (ISBN 0-934914-28-1). NACM.

Standortgemasse Verbesserung und Bewirtschaftung von Alpenweiden-Okologie, Ethologie, Gesundheit. Walter Dietl. Tr. by Regula Grob et al. (Tierhaltung: No. 7). (Illus., Ger.). 1979. pap. 13.00 (ISBN 3-7643-1028-6). Birkhauser.

Stanford, Cambridge Jubilee & Tchaikovsky. Gerald Norris. LC 80-66085. (Illus.). 576p. 1980. 75.00 (ISBN 0-7153-7856-2). David & Charles.

Stanford Mathematics Problem Book: With Hints & Solutions. George Polya & Jeremy Kilpatrick. LC 73-86270. 1974. pap. text ed. 4.50x (ISBN 0-8077-2416-5). Tchrs Coll.

Stanford White. Charles C. Baldwin. LC 78-150512. (Architecture & Decorative Art Ser.: Vol. 39). 1971. Repr. of 1931 ed. lib. bdg. 39.50 (ISBN 0-306-70138-3). Da Capo.

Stanford Wong's Blackjack Newsletters, 1980, Vol. 2. Stanford Wong. (Stanford Wong's Blackjack Newsletters Ser.). (Illus.). 222p. Date not set. pap. 29.95 (ISBN 0-935926-05-4). Pi Yee Pr.

Stanier 4-6-0's of the LMS. Brian Reed & J. W. Rowledge. 1977. 14.95 (ISBN 0-7153-7385-4). David & Charles.

Stanislavski on Opera. Constantin Stanislavski & P. I. Rumyantsev. LC 72-87119. (Illus.). 1975. 18.25 (ISBN 0-87830-132-1); pap. 8.45 (ISBN 0-87830-552-1). Theatre Arts.

Stanislavski's Legacy. rev. ed. Constantin Stanislavski. Tr. by Elizabeth R. Hapgood. LC 68-16450. (Orig.). 1968. pap. 4.25 (ISBN 0-87830-504-1). Theatre Arts.

Stanislavsky Directs. Nikolai M. Gorchakov. Tr. by Miriam Goldina. (Funk & W Bk.). 1968. pap. 4.95 o.s.i. (ISBN 0-308-60064-9, M60, TYC-T). T Y Crowell.

Stanislavsky on the Art of the Stage. Konstantin Stanislavsky. 1967. pap. 9.95 (ISBN 0-571-08172-X, Pub. by Faber & Faber). Merrimack Bk Serv.

Stanislaw Ulam Sets, Numbers, & Universes: Selected Works. Stanislaw M. Ulam. Ed. by William Beyer et al. LC 73-21686. 654p. 1974. 40.00x (ISBN 0-262-02108-0). MIT Pr.

Stanley & Rhoda. Rosemary Wells. LC 78-51874. (Illus.). 40p. (ps-2). 1981. pap. 2.95 (ISBN 0-8037-7995-X, Piper Bk). Dial.

Stanley Elkin's Greatest Hits. Stanley Elkin. 288p. 1980. 10.95 (ISBN 0-525-20940-9). Dutton.

Stanley Gibbons British Commonwealth. Ed. by Stanley Gibbons Ltd. (Illus.). write for info (ISBN 0-85259-086-5). StanGib Ltd.

Stanley Holloway: More Monologues & Songs. Ed. by Michael Marshall. (Illus.). 128p. 1980. pap. 5.95 (ISBN 0-241-10478-5, Pub. by Hamish Hamilton England). David & Charles.

Stanley Meets Do Good & Be Bad. Jacque Mack. (Apple Bks.). (Illus.). 32p. (gr. 5 up). 1978. pap. 3.50 (ISBN 0-570-07900-4, 56-1600). Concordia.

Stanley Morison: Selected Essays, 2 vols. Ed. by D. McKitterick. LC 78-54718. (Illus.). 250p. Date not set. Set. 275.00 (ISBN 0-521-22338-5). Vol. 1 (ISBN 0-521-22456-X). Vol. 2 (ISBN 0-521-22457-8). Cambridge U Pr.

Stanley Plane: A History & Descriptive Inventory. Alvin Sellens. LC 75-9509. (Illus.). 1975. 11.95 (ISBN 0-686-27737-6). Sellens.

Stanley Rule & Level Co. 1879 Price List of Tools & Hardware. Ed. by Kenneth D. Roberts. 1973. 4.50 (ISBN 0-913602-05-1). K Roberts.

Stanley Rule & Level Co. 1888 Price List of Tools. Ed. by Kenneth D. Roberts. 1975. 4.50 (ISBN 0-913602-14-0). K Roberts.

Stanley Rule & Level, Eighteen Ninety-Two Price List Revised to Eighteen Ninety-Seven, Abbrigment. 1980. pap. 3.00 (ISBN 0-913602-36-1). K Roberts.

Stanley Spencer at War. Richard Carline. (Illus.). 1978. 27.00 (ISBN 0-571-11028-2, Pub. by Faber & Faber). Merrimack Bk Serv.

Stanley, the Tale of the Lizard. Peter Meteyard. (Illus.). (gr. k-3). 1979. PLB 7.95 (ISBN 0-233-97071-1). Andre Deutsch.

Stanley's Despatches to the New York Herald, 1871-1872, 1874-1877. Ed. by Norman R. Bennett. LC 72-96999. (Pub. by Boston U Pr). 1970. 24.50x (ISBN 0-8419-8702-5, Africana). Holmes & Meier.

Stanleys Emin Pasha Expedition. Alphonse J. Walters. LC 80-1910. (Illus.). 1981. Repr. of 1890 ed. 43.00 (ISBN 0-404-18988-1). AMS Pr.

Stanton: The Life & Times of Lincoln's Secretary of War. Benjamin P. Thomas & Harold M. Hyman. LC 80-18970. (Illus.). xvii, 642p. 1980. Repr. of 1962 ed. lib. bdg. 49.50x (ISBN 0-313-22581-8, THSL). Greenwood.

Stapedectomy. Harold F. Schuknecht. 119p. 1971. 28.50 o.p. (ISBN 0-316-77511-8). Little.

Star & Planet Spotting: A Field Guide to the Night Sky. Peter L. Brown. (Illus.). 1974. 6.95 (ISBN 0-7137-0655-4, Pub by Blandford Pr England). Sterling.

Star-Apple Kingdom. Derek Walcott. LC 78-11323. 98p. 1979. 10.00 (ISBN 0-374-26974-2); pap. 6.95 (ISBN 0-374-26974-2). FS&G.

Star Beast. Robert A. Heinlein. (Del Rey Bk.). 1977. pap. 1.75 (ISBN 0-345-27580-2). Ballantine.

Star-Chamber Cases, Shewing What Causes Properly Belong to the Cognizance of That Court. Richard Crompton. LC 74-28842. (English Experience Ser.: No. 723). 1975. Repr. of 1630 ed. 6.00 (ISBN 90-221-0723-X). Walter J Johnson.

Star Clusters: Proceedings. Eighty-Fifth Symposium of the International Astronomical Union, Victoria, B. C., Canada, August 27-30, 1979. Ed. by James E. Hesser. (International Astronomical Union Symposium Ser.: No. 85). 540p. 1980. lib. bdg. 63.00 (ISBN 90-277-1087-2); pap. 31.50 (ISBN 90-277-1088-0). Kluwer Boston.

Star Cross. Ira Progoff. LC 70-176111. (Entrance Meditation Ser.). 1971. pap. 2.95 (ISBN 0-87941-001-9). Dialogue Hse.

Star-Crossed. Charlotte Lamb. (Alpha Books). 1978p. (Orig.). 1979. pap. text ed. 2.25x (ISBN 0-19-424160-2). Oxford U Pr.

Star Driver. Lee Correy. 1980. pap. 1.95 (ISBN 0-345-28994-3). Ballantine.

Star Evolution. Ed. by Livio Gratton. (Italian Physical Society: Course 28). (Illus.). 1974. 55.00 (ISBN 0-12-368828-0). Acad Pr.

Star Fall. David Bischoff. (Orig.). 1980. pap. 1.95 o.p. (ISBN 0-686-62032-1). Berkley Pub.

Star for the Latecomer. Paul Zindel & Bonnie Zindel. 160p. (gr. 6 up). 1981. pap. 1.95 (ISBN 0-553-14335-2). Bantam.

Star Force One Take Along Game. Jim Roberts. (gr. 3 up). 1980. pap. 3.95 (ISBN 0-671-95649-3). Wanderer Bks.

Star Gazer. Joachim W. Ekrutt. Tr. by Hugo M. Kellner from Ger. (gr. 9-12). 1981. pap. 2.25 (ISBN 0-8120-2043-X). Barron.

Star Girl. Henry Winterfield. (gr. 2-7). 1976. pap. 1.25 o.s.i. (ISBN 0-380-00659-6, 28506, Camelot). Avon.

Star Guard. Andre Norton. 1978. pap. 1.95 (ISBN 0-449-23646-3, Crest). Fawcett.

Star, Is a Star, Is a Star: The Life & Loves of Susan Hayward. Christopher P. Andersen. LC 80-908. (Illus.). 288p. 1980. 12.95 (ISBN 0-385-15598-0). Doubleday.

Star Ka'at World. Andre Norton & Dorothy Madlee. LC 75-36018. (Illus.). 128p. 1976. 6.95 (ISBN 0-8027-6300-6); PLB 6.85 (ISBN 0-8027-6301-4). Walker & Co.

Star Ka'ats & the Plant People. Andre Norton & Dorothy Madlee. (Illus.). (gr. 3-5). 1980. pap. 1.75 (ISBN 0-671-56045-X). PB.

Star Ka'ats & the Winged Warriors. Andre Norton & Dorothy Madlee. (Star Ka'ats Ser.). (Illus.). 128p. (gr. 2-6). 1981. 8.95 (ISBN 0-8027-6416-9); PLB 9.85 (ISBN 0-8027-6417-7). Walker & Co.

Star Light, Star Bright: The Great Short Fiction of Alfred Bester, Vol. 2. Alfred Bester. LC 76-17377. (YA) 1976. 7.95 o.p. (ISBN 0-399-11816-0). Berkley Pub.

Star Loot. A. Bertram Chancler. (Science Fiction Ser.). 1980. pap. 1.75 (ISBN 0-87997-564-4, UE1564). Daw Bks.

Star Lovers. Robert S. Richardson. 1967. 7.50 o.s.i. (ISBN 0-02-602900-6). Macmillan.

Star-Making Machinery: Inside the Business of Rock & Roll. Geoffrey Stokes. 1977. pap. 3.95 (ISBN 0-394-72432-1, Vin). Random.

Star Masters' Gambit. Gerard Klein. (Daw Science Fiction Ser.). 1979. pap. 1.75 o.p. (ISBN 0-87997-464-8, UE1464). DAW Bks.

Star Mother's Youngest Child. Louise Moeri. (Illus.). (ps-3). 1980. pap. 2.50 (ISBN 0-395-29929-2, Sandpiper). HM.

Star Names: Their Lore & Meaning. Richard H. Allen. Orig. Title: Star-Names & Their Meanings. 11.00 (ISBN 0-8446-1527-7). Peter Smith.

Star of Light. Patricia M. St. John. (gr. 5-8). 1953. pap. 2.50 (ISBN 0-8024-0004-3). Moody.

Star of Redemption. Franz Rosenzweig. Tr. by William W. Hallo. 464p. 1972. pap. 3.95 o.p. (ISBN 0-8070-1129-0, BP441). Beacon Pr.

Star of Song: The Life of Christina Nilsson. Guy Charnace. Tr. by J. C. M. & E. C. LC 80-2264. 1981. Repr. of 1870 ed. 14.50 (ISBN 0-404-18818-4). AMS Pr.

Star of the Sea. Linda Haldeman. 176p. 1981. pap. 2.25 (ISBN 0-380-54114-9, 54114). Avon.

Star Over Adobe. Dorothy L. Pillsbury. LC 63-21376. (Illus.). 1977. pap. 3.95 (ISBN 0-8263-0179-7). U of NM Pr.

Star Pass Receivers of the NFL. John Devaney. (NFL Punt, Pass & Kick Library: No. 17). (Illus.). (gr. 5 up). 1972. 2.50 o.p. (ISBN 0-394-82439-3, BYR); PLB 3.69 (ISBN 0-394-92439-8). Random.

Star People. Brad Steiger & Francie Steiger. (Orig.). 1981. pap. 2.25 (ISBN 0-425-04823-3). Berkley Pub.

Star Power. Leslie Deane. (Orig.). pap. 2.75 (ISBN 0-515-05282-5). Jove Pubns.

Star Power. Leslie Deane. 1980. pap. 2.75 (ISBN 0-515-05282-5, Jove). BJ Pub Group.

Star Prince Charlie. Poul Anderson & Gordon R. Dickson. 1976. pap. 1.75 o.p. (ISBN 0-425-03078-4, Medallion). Berkley Pub.

Star Rangers. Andre Norton. 1979. pap. 1.95 (ISBN 0-449-24076-2, Crest). Fawcett.

Star Riggers Way. Jeffrey Carver. 1978. pap. 1.75 o.s.i. (ISBN 0-440-17619-0). Dell.

Star Rising. Jess Carr. (Orig.). 1980. pap. 3.50 (ISBN 0-505-51575-X). Tower Bks.

Star Rover. Jack London. (gr. 7 up). 1963. 4.95 o.s.i. (ISBN 0-02-759550-1). Macmillan.

Star Running Backs of the NFL. Bill Libby. (NFL Punt, Pass & Kick Library: No. 15). (Illus.). (gr. 5-9). 1971. 2.50 o.p. (ISBN 0-394-82285-4, BYR); PLB 3.69 (ISBN 0-394-92285-9). Random.

Star Sight Reduction Tables for Forty-Two Stars: Assumed Altitude Method of Celestial Navigation. Thomas D. Davies. LC 79-7464. 1980. 28.50x (ISBN 0-87033-250-3). Cornell Maritime.

Star Signs for Lovers. Liz Greene. LC 80-5890. (Illus.). 480p. 1980. 14.95 (ISBN 0-8128-2765-1). Stein & Day.

Star-Spangled Banner. Francis S. Key. LC 66-14940. (Illus.). (gr. 3 up). 1966. 7.95 o.p. (ISBN 0-690-77281-5, TYC-J). T Y Crowell.

Star-Spangled Banner. Oscar G. Sonneck. LC 68-16245. (Music Ser). (Illus.). 1969. Repr. of 1914 ed. lib. bdg. 25.00 (ISBN 0-306-71108-7). Da Capo.

Star Spangled Banner: Words & Music Issued Between 1814-1864. Joseph Muller. LC 79-169653. (Music Ser). (Illus.). 1973. Repr. of 1935 ed. lib. bdg. 25.00 (ISBN 0-306-70263-0). Da Capo.

Star Spangled Books: Books, Sheet Music, Newspapers, Manuscripts, & Persons Associated with the Star-Spangled Banner. P. W. Filby & Edward G. Howard. LC 70-187215. (Illus.). 200p. 1972. 15.00 (ISBN 0-938420-17-8). Md Hist.

Star-Spangled Contract. Jim Garrison. 272p. 1977. pap. 1.95 o.s.i. (ISBN 0-446-89259-9). Warner Bks.

Star-Spangled Fun! Things to Make, Do & See from American History. James Razzi. LC 74-30397. (Illus.). 64p. (ps-4). 1976. 5.95 o.s.i. (ISBN 0-8193-0817-X, Four Winds); PLB 5.41 o.s.i. (ISBN 0-8193-0818-8). Schol Bk Serv.

Star Spangled Retirement Dream: Why It's Going Sour & What You Can Do About It. James Gollin. 224p. 1981. 12.95 (ISBN 0-684-16866-9, ScribT). Scribner.

Star Streak: Stories of Space. Owen. (gr. 7-9). Date not set. pap. cancelled (ISBN 0-590-31264-2, Schol Pap). Schol Bk Serv.

Star Surgeon. James White. 160p. (Orig.). 1981. pap. 1.95 (ISBN 0-345-29169-7, Del Rey). Ballantine.

Star to Steer by: Success Through Positive Experiencing. rev. ed. Patricia Sampson. LC 77-18064. 1979. 9.95 (ISBN 0-8119-0301-X). Fell.

Star Trails, "CH". Valeda Blockcolsky & Joan Frazer. 1980. 20.00 (ISBN 0-88450-726-2, 3150-B). Communication Skill.

Star Trails,"SH". Valeda Blockcolsky & Joan Frazer. 1980. 20.00 (ISBN 0-88450-727-0, 3140-B). Communication Skill.

Star Trails,"TH". Valeda Blockcolsky & Joan Frazer. 1980. 20.00 (ISBN 0-88450-725-4, 3131-B). Communication Skill.

Star Trap. Simon Brett. LC 77-78114. 1978. 7.95 o.p. (ISBN 0-684-15190-1, ScribT). Scribner.

Star Trap. Simon Brett. 1981. pap. 2.25 (ISBN 0-425-04936-1). Berkley Pub.

Star Trek. Jeff Rovin. (Orig.). 1979. pap. text ed. write for info. o.p. (ISBN 0-685-96937-1). Berkley Pub.

Star Trek. (T.V. & Movie Tie-in Ser.). (Illus.). (gr. 4-12). 1979. PLB 5.95 (ISBN 0-87191-718-1); pap. 2.95 (ISBN 0-89812-032-2). Creative Ed.

Star Trek Action Toy Book. James Razzi. (Illus.). (ps-5). 1976. pap. 3.95 (ISBN 0-394-83277-9, BYR). Random.

Star Trek: Good News in Modern Images. Betsy Caprio. 1978. 12.95 o.p. (ISBN 0-8362-3401-4); pap. 5.95 o.p. (ISBN 0-8362-3400-6). Andrews & McMeel.

Star Trek Guide. 1976. pap. 2.25 (ISBN 0-88411-079-6). Amereon Ltd.

Star Trek Maps. New Eye Photography. 1980. pap. 8.95 (ISBN 0-553-01202-9). Bantam.

Star Trip. Lee Mountain. (Attention Span Stories Ser). (Illus., Orig.). (gr. 6-10). 1978. pap. text ed. 3.20x (ISBN 0-89061-149-1, 585). Jamestown Pubs.

Star Visit: A Play for Christmas. Georgianna Summers. 8p. (Orig.). 1980. pap. text ed. 2.30 (ISBN 0-89536-424-7). CSS Pub.

Star Voyage. Joseph DiCerto. Orig. Title: One Hundred Two Questions & Answers About Outer Space. (Illus.). 96p. (gr. 4-7). 1981. PLB price not set (ISBN 0-671-33034-9). Messner.

Star Wars. James A. Lely. (T.V. & Movie Tie-Ins Ser.). (Illus.). (gr. 4-12). 1979. PLB 5.95 (ISBN 0-87191-700-9); pap. 2.95 (ISBN 0-89812-036-5). Creative Ed.

Star Wars. Illus. by Charles Nicholas. (Contemporary Motivators Ser.). (Illus.). (gr. 4-12). 1978. pap. text ed. 1.25 o.p. (ISBN 0-88301-307-X); spirit masters 15.00 o.p. (ISBN 0-685-90747-3). Pendulum Pr.

Star Wars Question & Answer Book About Space. Moche. (Illus.). (gr. 4). Date not set. pap. cancelled (ISBN 0-590-30065-2, Schol Pap). Schol Bk Serv.

Star Wars Question & Answer Book About Space. Dinah L. Moche. LC 78-19684. (Illus.). (gr. 3-6). 1979. PLB 5.99 (ISBN 0-394-84053-4, BYR); 5.99g (ISBN 0-394-94053-9). Random.

Star Wars, Star Trek. Winkie Pratney. 1978. pap. 1.75 (ISBN 0-89728-057-1, 693400). Omega Pubns OR.

Star Wars: The Empire Strikes Back Storybook. Adapted by Shep Steneman. 4.95 (ISBN 0-515-05282-5). Random.

Starart. Ed. by Debby Chesher. (Illus.). 240p. 1979. 32.50 (ISBN 0-9690053-0-X, Pub by Starart Canada). New Glide.

Starch: Chemistry & Technology, 2 vols. Ed. by Roy L. Whistler & Eugene F. Paschall. Incl. Vol. 1. Fundamental Aspects. 1965. 55.25 (ISBN 0-12-746261-9); Vol. 2. Industrial Aspects. 1967. 67.50 (ISBN 0-12-746262-7). Acad Pr.

Starch Industry. J. W. Knight. 1969. 15.00 o.p. (ISBN 0-08-013044-5). Pergamon.

Starch Production Technology. J. A. Radley. (Illus.). 1976. 145.40x (ISBN 0-85334-662-3, Pub. by Applied Science). Burgess-Intl Ideas.

Starchild. Frederik Pohl & Jack Williamson. 1973. pap. 1.25 o.p. (ISBN 0-345-23449-9). Ballantine.

Starcrossed. Ben Bova. 1979. pap. 1.75 (ISBN 0-515-05133-0). Jove Pubns.

Stardrifter. Dale Aycock. 1981. pap. 1.95 (ISBN 0-8439-0855-6, Leisure Bks). Nordon Pubns.

Starets Paisii Velichkovskii: His Life, Teachings & Influence on Orthodox Monasticism. Sergii Chetverikov. Ed. by Carol Janov. Tr. by Vasily Lickwar & Alexander I. Lisenko. LC 75-29632. 340p. (Orig.). 1980. pap. 35.00 (ISBN 0-913124-22-2). Nordland Pub.

Starfinder. Robert F. Yong. 208p. 1980. pap. 2.25 (ISBN 0-671-83282-4). PB.

Starfire. large print ed. Arlene Morgan. 1981. Repr. of 1974 ed. 9.95 (ISBN 0-89621-271-8). Thorndike Pr.

Starfishes. new ed. Ailsa M. Clark. Orig. Title: Starfishes & Their Relations. (Illus.). 1977. pap. 4.95 (ISBN 0-87666-466-4, PS-750). TFH Pubns.

Stark Munro Letters. A. Conan Doyle. LC 80-67705. (Conan Doyle Centennial Ser.). (Illus.). 250p. 1981. price not set (ISBN 0-934468-46-X). Gaslight.

Stark Naked. Rick Masten. 1980. pap. 4.95 (ISBN 0-931104-04-1). Sunflower Ink.

Starkweather. William Allen. 1977. pap. 1.75 o.p. (ISBN 0-380-00973-0, 32508). Avon.

Starleaner Reunion. Cooper Edens. (Illus.). 1979. 16.95 (ISBN 0-914676-31-8, Star & Elephant Bk). Green Tiger.

Starlight on the Rails & Other Songs. U. Utah Phillips. (Illus.). 1973. pap. 3.95 o.s.i. (ISBN 0-8256-9905-3). Wooden Shoe.

Starlight: The Best of Bester. Alfred Bester. 1977. pap. 1.95 o.p. (ISBN 0-425-03451-8, Medallion). Berkley Pub.

Starlore Among the Navaho. Berard Haile. LC 76-53085. 1977. 15.00 (ISBN 0-88307-532-6); pap. 4.95 (ISBN 0-88307-533-4). Gannon.

Starmaker: The Autobiography of Hal Wallis. Hal Wallis & Charles Higham. (Illus.). 256p. 1980. 13.95 (ISBN 0-02-623170-0). Macmillan.

Starr of Wyoming. W. F. Bragg. 1981. pap. 2.25 (ISBN 0-8439-0860-2, Leisure Bks). Nordon Pubns.

Starr-Weiner Report on Sex & Sexuality in the Mature Years. Bernard D. Starr & Marcella B. Weiner. 1981. 12.95 (ISBN 0-8128-2750-3). Stein & Day.

Starring Fred Astaire. Stanley Green & Burt Goldblatt. 436p. 1973. 22.50 o.p. (ISBN 0-396-06877-4). Dodd.

Starring Peter & Leigh. Susan Pfeffer. (gr. 7-12). 1980. pap. 1.75 (ISBN 0-440-98200-6, LFL). Dell.

Starring Rosa. Otto Coontz. (Illus.). 48p. (gr. 1-3). 1980. 7.95g (ISBN 0-316-15535-7). Little.

Starr's Guide to the John Muir Trail & the High Sierra Region. 12th rev. ed. Walter A. Starr, Jr. Ed. by Douglas Robinson. LC 67-25840. (Totebook Ser.). (Illus.). 224p. 1974. pap. 4.95 (ISBN 0-87156-172-7); Starr's Map of the John Muir Trail 1.95 (ISBN 0-87156-173-5). Sierra.

Starry Messenger: The Best of Galileo. Charles C. Ryan. LC 79-16604. 1979. 9.95 (ISBN 0-312-75599-6). St Martin.

Stars. L. Edward Johndro. 1979. pap. 6.95 (ISBN 0-87728-485-7). Weiser.

Stars: A New Way to See Them. 3rd ed. H. A. Rey. (gr. 8 up). 1967. 11.95 (ISBN 0-395-08121-1). HM.

Stars: A New Way to See Them. H. A. Rey. 1976. pap. 6.95 (ISBN 0-395-24830-2). HM.

Stars & Nebulas. William J. Kaufmann, 3rd. LC 78-17544. (Illus.). 1978. text ed. 15.50x o.p. (ISBN 0-7167-0081-6); pap. text ed. 8.95x (ISBN 0-7167-0085-9). W H Freeman.

Stars & Planets. Keith Wicks. (gr. 2-4). 1980. PLB 6.45 (ISBN 0-531-03247-7). Watts.

Stars & Stoves: An Astrological Cookbook. Barbara Morbidoni. (Illus., Orig.). 1979. pap. 5.00 (ISBN 0-933646-07-0). Aries Pr.

Stars Are the Styx. Theodore Sturgeon. 1981. pap. 2.75 (ISBN 0-440-18006-6). Dell.

Stars for Lincoln, Doctors & Dogs. J. Benbow Bullock. LC 80-66936. (Illus.). 100p. (Orig.). 1981. pap. 4.95 (ISBN 0-937024-00-7). Gourmet Guides.

Stars in Flight: Studies in Air Force Leadership. Edgar F. Puryear, Jr. 310p. 1981. 14.95 (ISBN 0-89141-127-5); pap. 8.95 (ISBN 0-89141-128-3). Presidio Pr.

Stars in My Heart. Barbara Cartland. 1978. pap. 1.50 o.p. (ISBN 0-515-04825-9). Jove Pubns.

Stars in My Heart. Barbara Cartland. (Barbara Carrtland Ser.: No. 12). 1981. pap. 1.75 (ISBN 0-515-05570-0). Jove Pubns.

Stars in the Sky. Joseph Jacobs. LC 78-11718. (Illus.). 32p. (ps-3). 1979. 6.95 (ISBN 0-374-37229-2). FS&G.

Stars, Like Dust. Isaac Asimov. 1978. pap. 1.95 (ISBN 0-449-23595-5, Crest). Fawcett.

Stars My Destination. Alfred Bester. 1975. pap. 2.25 (ISBN 0-425-04365-7, Medallion). Berkley Pub.

Stars My Destination. Alfred Bester. (Science Fiction Ser). 244p. 1975. Repr. of 1957 ed. lib. bdg. 12.50 (ISBN 0-8398-2300-2). Gregg.

Stars of God. U. Butler. 5.75 o.p. (ISBN 0-8062-1133-4). Carlton.

Stars of Pro Basketball. Lou Sabin & Dave Sendler. LC 73-117546. (Pro Basketball Library: No. 4). (Illus.). (gr. 5-9). 1970. PLB 3.69 (ISBN 0-394-90621-7); pap. 0.95 (ISBN 0-394-82203-X). Random.

Stars on Ice. Elizabeth Van Steenwyk. LC 80-1012. (Illus.). (gr. 5 up). 1980. 6.95 (ISBN 0-396-07887-7). Dodd.

Stars, Signs, & Salvation in the Age of Aquarius. James Bjornstad & Shildes Johnson. (Orig.). 1971. pap. 1.50 o.p. (ISBN 0-87123-524-2). Bethany Fell.

Stars: Their Birth, Life, & Death. Iosif S. Shklovskii. Tr. by Richard B. Rodman. LC 77-13889. (Illus.). 1978. text ed. 25.95x (ISBN 0-7167-0024-7). W H Freeman.

Stars: Their Structure & Evolution. R. J. Tayler & A. S. Everest. (Wykeham Science Ser.: No. 10). 1970. 11.75x (ISBN 0-8448-1112-2). Crane Russak Co.

Stars To-Night. Sara Teasdale. (Illus.). (gr. 4-6). 1930. 3.95 o.s.i. (ISBN 0-02-789090-2). Macmillan.

Starseekers. Colin Wilson. LC 80-1273. 256p. 1981. 15.95 (ISBN 0-385-17253-2). Doubleday.

Starshine. Theodore Sturgeon. 1977. pap. 1.50 o.s.i. (ISBN 0-515-04459-8). Jove Pubns.

Starship Simulation. Roger Garrett. LC 78-60612. 1978. pap. 7.95 (ISBN 0-918398-10-X). Dilithium Pr.

Starsky & Hutch, No. 7. Max Franklin. 1978. pap. 1.75 o.p. (ISBN 0-345-27340-0). Ballantine.

Starstruck. Linda Palmer. 400p. 1981. 12.95 (ISBN 0-399-12512-4). Putnam.

Starswarm. Brian Aldiss. 160p. (RL 9). Date not set. pap. 1.25 (ISBN 0-451-06883-1, Y6883, Sig). NAL.

Start Golf Young. Doug Ford. LC 77-93324. (gr. 5 up). 1978. 7.95 (ISBN 0-8069-4126-X); PLB 7.49 (ISBN 0-8069-4127-8). Sterling.

Start Point: Six Studies in Violence. Otis Dunbar Richardson. 1973. 8.00 o.p. (ISBN 0-682-47672-2). Exposition.

Start Right with Goldfish. Robert Gannon. (Orig.). pap. 2.00 (ISBN 0-87666-081-2, M504). TFH Pubns.

Start Right with Tropical Fish. (Illus.). pap. 2.50 (ISBN 0-87666-160-6, M510). TFH Pubns.

Start Sailing. L. Messora. (Orig.). 1980. pap. 8.95x (ISBN 0-8464-1051-6). Beekman Pubs.

Start Soaring. Schweizer Aircraft Corporation. 1978. pap. 3.25x (ISBN 0-911721-75-4). Aviation.

Start to Draw. Ann Campbell. LC 68-25727. (Illus.). (gr. k-3). 1968. PLB 4.90 o.p. (ISBN 0-531-01799-0). Watts.

Start-to-Finish Cabinetmaking. Peter Jones. 1980. pap. 7.95 (ISBN 0-8359-7062-0). Reston.

Start to Navigate. Conrad Dixon. (Illus.). 1979. 6.95 (ISBN 0-229-11573-X, ScribT). Scribner.

Start with the Sun: Studies in the Whitman Traditon. James E. Miller, Jr. et al. LC 60-5493. 1963. pap. 1.95x (ISBN 0-8032-5135-1, BB 165, Bison). U of Nebr Pr.

Start Your Own Private School-Legally! Dorie A. Erickson. LC 80-51385. 65p. (Orig.). 1980. pap. 16.00 (ISBN 0-937242-00-4). Scandia Pubs.

Starting a Business in California. Michael D. Jenkins. 185p. 1980. pap. 25.00 (ISBN 0-916378-12-8). Oasis Pr.

Starting a Marine Aquarium. Craig Barker. 1972. pap. 2.95 (ISBN 0-87666-751-5, PS-305). TFH Pubns.

Starting a Small Business: A Simulation Game. Shiv K. Gupta & Ray T. Hamman. (Illus.). 64p. 1974. pap. text ed. 10.95 (ISBN 0-13-842963-4). P-H.

Starting & Succeeding in Small Business: A Guide for the Innercity Businessman. Brijen K. Gupa & Arthur D. Lopatin. LC 78-58105. iv, 100p. (Orig.). 1978. pap. 15.00 (ISBN 0-936876-14-X). Learn Res Intl Stud.

Starting Chess. Tony Gillam. 1978. pap. 5.95 (ISBN 0-7134-1478-2, Pub. by Batsford England). David & Charles.

Starting from Seed. Jack Kramer. 1977. pap. 1.50 o.p. (ISBN 0-685-75040-X, 345-25502-X-150). Ballantine.

Starting, Lighting, Ignition & Generating Systems. 7th ed. S.L.I.G. Buyers Guide. 1981. 7.00 (ISBN 0-685-78814-8). IBMA Pubns.

Starting Millionaire Success Kit. 2nd ed. Tyler G. Hicks. 361p. 1981. pap. 99.50 (ISBN 0-914306-39-1). Intl Wealth.

Starting Mountaineering & Rockclimbing. Donald Law. 1977. 10.50 (ISBN 0-7153-7322-6). David & Charles.

Starting Over. Jacqueline Lapidus. (Illus.). 1977. pap. 3.50 (ISBN 0-918314-03-8). Out & Out.

Starting Over. Damon Stetson. Ed. by Robert Markel. 1971. 5.95 o.s.i. (ISBN 0-02-614390-9). Macmillan.

Starting Over. Dan Wakefield. 304p. 1973. 7.95 o.p. (ISBN 0-440-08256-0, Sey Lawr). Delacorte.

Starting Photography. Michael Langford. (Illus.). (gr. 4 up). 1976. 8.95 o.p. (ISBN 0-8038-6736-0); pap. 6.95 o.p. (ISBN 0-8038-6757-3). Hastings.

Starting Point: A Guide to Basic Writing Skills. R. Swartz. 1980. pap. 9.50 (ISBN 0-13-843029-2). P-H.

Starting Right in Real Estate. Ernest D. Nathan. LC 79-20780. (Illus.). 1980. pap. text ed. 10.95 (ISBN 0-201-05224-5). A-W.

Starting Rock Climbing. Arthur Clarke. (Illus.). 1979. 8.95 o.p. (ISBN 0-214-20488-X, 8050, Dist. by Arco, 8075). Barrie & Jenkins.

Starting Sailing. James Moore & Alan Turvey. 11.95 (ISBN 0-7153-6095-7). David & Charles.

Starting School. Muriel Stanek. Ed. by Ann Fay. (Self-Starter Bks.). (Illus.). 32p. (ps-1). 1981. 6.50 (ISBN 0-8075-7617-4). A Whitman.

Starting to Paint in Oils. John Raynes. LC 79-56681. (Start to Paint Ser.). (Illus.). 104p. 1980. pap. 3.95 (ISBN 0-8008-7386-6, Pentalic). Taplinger.

Starting to Paint with Acrylics. John Raynes. LC 79-56682. (Start to Paint Ser.). (Illus.). 104p. 1980. pap. 3.95 (ISBN 0-8008-7385-8, Pentalic). Taplinger.

Starting with Papier Mache. Chester J. Alkema. (Little Craft Book Ser). (Illus.). 48p. (gr. 2 up). 1974. 4.95 o.p. (ISBN 0-8069-5298-9); PLB 5.89 o.p. (ISBN 0-8069-5299-7). Sterling.

Starting with Stained Glass. Paul W. Wood. (Little Craft Book Ser.). (Illus.). 48p. (gr. 6 up). 1973. 4.95 o.p. (ISBN 0-8069-5244-X); PLB 5.89 o.p. (ISBN 0-8069-5245-8). Sterling.

Starting Your Own Band: Rock, Disco, Folk, Jazz, Country & Western. Lani Van Ryzin. (Illus.). 64p. (gr. 7 up). 1980. 6.95 (ISBN 0-8027-6391-X); PLB 7.85 (ISBN 0-8027-6392-8). Walker & Co.

Startling Revelations. Lucille McNames. 120p. (Orig.). 1979. pap. 3.50 o.p. (ISBN 0-89861-022-2). Esoteric Pubns.

Starving in the Shadow of Plenty. Loretta Schwartz-Nobel. 256p. 1981. 12.95 (ISBN 0-399-12522-1). Putnam.

Starving to Death in a Sea of Objects. John A. Sours. LC 80-68043. 400p. 1980. 25.00 (ISBN 0-87668-426-6). Aronson.

Starworld. Harry Harrison. 208p. (Orig.). 1981. pap. 2.25 (ISBN 0-553-14647-5). Bantam.

State. Ed. by Stephen R. Graubard. 1981. 12.95 (ISBN 0-393-01387-1); pap. text ed. 4.95x (ISBN 0-393-95098-0). Norton.

State. Vladimir I. Lenin. 1965. pap. 0.75 (ISBN 0-8351-0371-4). China Bks.

State Administrative Law, 2 vols. Frank E. Cooper. 1965. slip case 40.00 (ISBN 0-672-81444-7, Bobbs-Merrill Law). Michie.

State & Community Governments in the Federal System. Charles Press & Kenneth VerBerg. LC 78-22064. 1979. text ed. 16.95x (ISBN 0-471-02725-1); tchrs. manual avail. (ISBN 0-471-04909-3). Wiley.

State & Cosmos in the Art of Tenochtitlan. Richard F. Townsend. LC 79-63726. (Sutdies in Pe-Columbian Art & Archaeology: No. 20). (Illus.). 78p. 1979. pap. 5.00 (ISBN 0-88402-083-5, Ctr. Pre-Columbian). Dumbarton Oaks.

State & Economic Development: Peru Since 1968. E. V. Fitzgerald. LC 75-30443. (Department of Applied Economics, Occasional Papers Ser.: No. 49). (Illus.). 140p. 1976. pap. 11.95x (ISBN 0-521-29054-6). Cambridge U Pr.

State & Economics in the Middle East. Alfred Bonne. LC 72-11325. (Illus.). 452p. 1973. Repr. of 1955 ed. lib. bdg. 35.00x (ISBN 0-8371-6661-6, BOSE). Greenwood.

State & Federal Exploratory Wells & Core Holes Drilled off the West Coast of Continental U.S.A. Prior to 1974. 1975. 40.00 (ISBN 0-686-28277-9). Munger Oil.

State & Labour in India. K. N. Vaid. 7.50x (ISBN 0-210-26949-9). Asia.

State & Local Government. Ed. by Alan K. Campbell & Roy W. Bahl. LC 75-43361. 1976. 17.95 (ISBN 0-02-905180-0). Free Pr.

State & Local Government. 4th ed. Maddox & Fuquay. Date not set. pap. text ed. price not set (ISBN 0-442-24454-1). D Van Nostrand.

State & Local Government. Ed. by Herbert L. Marx, Jr. (Reference Shelf Ser: Vol. 34, No. 3). 1962. 6.25 (ISBN 0-8242-0071-3). Wilson.

State & Local Government. 2nd ed. Joseph F. Zimmerman. LC 70-124363. (Illus., Orig.). 1970. pap. 4.95 o.p. (ISBN 0-06-460112-9, 112, COS). Har-Row.

State & Local Government. 3rd ed. Joseph F. Zimmerman. (Illus., Orig.). pap. 4.95 (ISBN 0-06-460181-1, CO 181, COS). Har-Row.

State & Local Government in a Federal System, Cases & Materials. Daniel R. Mandelker & Dawn C. Netsch. (Contemporary Legal Education Ser.). 1977. 25.00 (ISBN 0-672-83047-7, Bobbs-Merrill Law). Michie.

State & Local Government in America. 3rd ed. Daniel R. Grant & H. C. Nixon. 608p. 1975. text ed. 18.95x (ISBN 0-205-04574-X, 7645740); instr's manual o.p. free (ISBN 0-205-05473-0). Allyn.

State & Local Government of Michigan. rev., 8th ed. Ferris E. Lewis & David B. McConnell. LC 78-66807. (Illus.). (gr. 10-12). 1979. pap. text ed. 7.75x (ISBN 0-910726-41-8); questions & answers for tchrs. 3.00x (ISBN 0-910726-42-6). Hillsdale Educ.

State & Local Government: Politics & Public Policies. David C. Saffell. LC 77-76119. (Political Science Ser.). 1978. pap. text ed. 11.95 (ISBN 0-201-06806-0); instr's manual & tests 1.50 (ISBN 0-201-06809-5). A-W.
State & Local Politics. 2nd ed. David R. Berman. 1978. text ed. 16.95 o.p. (ISBN 0-205-05974-0, 765974-1). Allyn.
State & Local Politics. 3rd ed. David R. Berman. 336p. 1980. text ed. 17.95 (ISBN 0-205-07219-4, 767219-5). Allyn.
State & Local Politics: Government by the People. 2nd ed. James M. Burns et al. 1978. pap. text ed. 9.50 (ISBN 0-13-843540-5). P-H.
State & Local Politics: Government by the People. 3rd ed. James M. Burns et al. (Illus.). 1981. 9.95f (ISBN 0-13-843516-2). P-H.
State & Local Tax Performance Nineteen Seventy-Eight. rev. ed. Kenneth E. Quindry & Niles Schoening. 1980. pap. 3.00. S Regional Ed.
State & Local Tax Problems. Ed. by Harry L. Johnson. LC 69-10113. 1969. 12.50x (ISBN 0-87049-089-3). U of Tenn Pr.
State & Revolution. Vladimir I. Lenin. 1965. pap. 1.95 (ISBN 0-8351-0372-2). China Bks.
State & Socialism. Mihaly Vajda. (Allison & Busby Motive Ser.). 160p. 1981. pap. 7.95 (Pub. by Alison & Busby, England). Schocken.
State & Sovereignty in Modern Germany. Rupert Emerson. LC 79-1626. 1981. Repr. of 1928 ed. 22.50 (ISBN 0-88355-931-5). Hyperion Conn.
State & Statecraft in Old Java: A Study of the Later Mataram Period, 16th to 19th Centruy. Soemarsaid Moertono. (Monograph Ser.). 1974. pap. 3.00 o.p. (ISBN 0-685-41682-8). Cornell Mod Indo.
State & the Citizen. Kavalam M. Panikkar. 3.50x o.p. (ISBN 0-210-33763-X). Asia.
State & the Citizen: An Introduction to Political Philosophy. 2nd ed. J. D. Mabbott. 1967. pap. text ed. 6.50x (ISBN 0-391-02081-1, Hutchinson U Lib). Humanities.
State & the Farmer: British Agricultural Policies & Politics. Peter Self & Herbert J. Storing. 1963. 20.00x (ISBN 0-520-01159-7). U of Cal Pr.
State Arts Agencies in Nineteen Seventy-Four: All Present & Accounted for. (Report Ser.: No. 8). 160p. pap. 4.50 (Pub. by Ctr Fot Arts Info). Pub Ctr Cult Res.
State As Defendant: Governmental Accountability & the Redress of Individual Grievances. Leon Hurwitz. LC 80-657. (Contributions in Political Science: No. 51). (Illus.). 224p. 1981. lib. bdg. 27.50 (ISBN 0-313-21257-0, HSD/). Greenwood.
State Assembly Elections. G. G. Mirchandani. 240p. 1980. text ed. 22.50x (ISBN 0-7069-1288-8, Pub. by Vikas India). Advent Bk.
State Birds & Flowers. Olive L. Earle. (Illus.). (gr. 3-7). 1961. Repr. of 1951 ed. PLB 6.48 (ISBN 0-688-31536-4). Morrow.
State Building in Modern China. Robert E. Bedeski. (China Research Monographs: No. 18). 200p. 1981. pap. 8.00 (ISBN 0-912966-28-9). IEAS Ctr Chinese Stud.
State, Bureaucracy & Civil Society: A Critical Discussion of the Political Theory of Karl Marx. Victor M. Perez-Diaz. (New Studies in Sociology Ser.). 1978. text ed. 15.25x (ISBN 0-333-23788-9); pap. text ed. 6.25x (ISBN 0-391-00555-3). Humanities.
State Capital Cities. Delia Goetz. LC 70-155991. (Illus.). (gr. 5-9). 1971. PLB 7.92 (ISBN 0-688-31955-6). Morrow.
State Constitutional Conventions, Revisions & Amendments, 1959-1976: A Bibliography, Supplement One. Compiled by Connie Canning. LC 76-57843. 1977. lib. bdg. 12.50 (ISBN 0-8371-9487-3, CSC/). Greenwood.
State Courts: Options for the Future. National Center for State Courts. 1980. pap. 4.00 (ISBN 0-89656-037-6, R0045). Natl Ctr St Courts.
State Documents on Federal Relations. Ed. by Herman V. Ames. LC 78-77697. (American Constitutional & Legal History Ser). 1970. Repr. of 1900 ed. lib. bdg. 35.00 (ISBN 0-306-71335-7). Da Capo.
State Economic Policies of the Ch'ing Government: 1840-1895. Jerome Chen. LC 78-24797. (Modern Chinese Economy Ser.: Vol. 2). 250p. 1980. lib. bdg. 27.50 (ISBN 0-8240-4251-4). Garland Pub.
State Editions, 51 vols. Set. 650.00 (ISBN 0-89770-127-5). Curriculum Info Ctr.
State Enterprise: Business or Politics? David Coombes. (Political & Economic Planning Ser.). 1971. text ed. 14.95x o.p. (ISBN 0-04-338047-6). Allen Unwin.
State Estimates of Commodity Trade Flows, 1963. John M. Rodgers. LC 73-8811. (Multiregional Input-Output Study: Vol. 5). (Illus.). 272p. 1973. 25.50 (ISBN 0-669-89227-0). Lexington Bks.
State Estimates of Outputs, Employment & Payrolls 1947, 1958, 1963. John M. Rodgers. LC 72-5759. (Multiregional Input-Output Study: Vol. 2). (Illus.). 1972. 25.95 (ISBN 0-669-73494-2). Lexington Bks.
State Estimates of Technology, 1963. Karen R. Polenske. LC 73-1641. (Multiregional Input-Output Study: Vol. 4). (Illus.). 1974. 25.95 (ISBN 0-669-87007-2). Lexington Bks.
State Estimates of the Gross National Product 1947, 1958, 1963. Karen R. Polenske. LC 79-145900. (Output Study: Vol. 1). 320p. 1972. 29.95 (ISBN 0-669-62539-6). Lexington Bks.
State Flowers. Anne O. Dowden. LC 78-51927. (Illus.). (gr. 5 up). 1978. 8.95 (ISBN 0-690-01339-6, TYC-J); PLB 9.89 (ISBN 0-690-03884-4). T Y Crowell.
State Government. Judith Bentley. (American Government Ser.). (Illus.). (gr. 7 up). 1978. PLB 6.90 s&l (ISBN 0-531-01343-X). Watts.
State Government in Georgia. Lawrence R. Hepburn. 200p. (Orig.). (gr. 8-12). 1981. pap. text ed. 10.00 (ISBN 0-89854-067-4). U of GA Inst Govt.
State Government in Transition: Reforms of the Leader Administration, 1955-1959. Reed M. Smith. LC 63-7864. 1963. 9.00x o.p. (ISBN 0-8122-7399-0). U of Pa Pr.
State Government Overviews. Ed. by Justin A. Bereny. (Alcohol Fuels Information Ser.: Vol. 4). 1981. 49.95 (ISBN 0-89934-115-2); pap. 34.95 (ISBN 0-89934-114-4). Solar Energy Info.
State Government Productivity: The Environment for Improvement. Edgar G. Crane et al. LC 76-11716. (Illus.). 1976. text ed. 22.95 o.p. (ISBN 0-275-56850-4). Praeger.
State Government Reference Publications: An Annotated Bibliography. David W. Parish. LC 74-81322. 1974. lib. bdg. 11.50 o.p. (ISBN 0-87287-100-2). Libs Unl.
State Government Reference Publications: An Annotated Bibliography. 2nd ed. David W. Parish. 250p. 1981. lib. bdg. price not set (ISBN 0-87287-253-X). Libs Unl.
State Housing in Britain. Stephen Merrett. (Illus.). 1979. 34.00x (ISBN 0-7100-0264-5). Routledge & Kegan.
State Information Book. 3rd, rev. ed. Ed. by Susan Lukowski & Cary T. Grayson, Jr. LC 73-80718. (Illus.). 310p. 1980. 18.50 (ISBN 0-87107-041-3). Potomac.
State Initiatives on Alcohol Fuels. U.S. National Alcohol Fuels Commission. 102p. 1981. pap. 15.00 (ISBN 0-89934-105-5). Solar Energy Info.
State Land-Use Planning & Regulation: Florida, the Model Code, & Beyond. Thomas G. Pelham. LC 79-2390. (Lincoln Institute of Land Policy Books). 224p. 1979. 23.95 (ISBN 0-669-03062-7). Lexington Bks.
State Level Disclosure Guidelines. Peter F. Rousmaniere. (Municipal Securities Regulation Ser.). 233p. 1980. pap. 40.00 (ISBN 0-916450-20-1). Coun on Municipal.
State Manufacturing Enterprise in a Mixed Economy: The Turkish Case. Bertil Walstedt. LC 78-21398. (World Bank Ser.). 192p. 1980. text ed. 25.00x (ISBN 0-8018-2226-2); pap. text ed. 9.95x (ISBN 0-8018-2227-0). Johns Hopkins.
State Mental Hospitals: Problems & Potentials. John Talbott. LC 79-21928. 1979. 19.95x (ISBN 0-87705-394-4). Human Sci Pr.
State Models of Dynamic Systems. N. H. McClamroch. (Illus.). 248p. 1980. 17.80 (ISBN 0-387-90490-5). Springer-Verlag.
State of Academic Science: Background Papers, Vol. 2. Bruce L. Smith & Joseph J. Karlesky. LC 77-72979. 1977. pap. 5.95 (ISBN 0-915390-13-2). Change Mag.
State of Britain. Colin Buchanan. 1972. 4.95 o.p. (ISBN 0-571-10188-7, Pub. by Faber & Faber). Merrimack Bk Serv.
State of Israel. Israel T. Naamani. LC 79-12757. (Illus.). 1980. pap. 5.95x (ISBN 0-87441-278-1). Behrman.
State of Ming Coin Knives & Minor Knife Coins. Arthur B. Coole. LC 72-86802. (Encyclopedia of Chinese Coins Ser.: Vol. 6). (Illus.). 1977. 35.00x (ISBN 0-88000-013-9). Quarterman.
State of Siege. Janet Frame. LC 66-20188. 1966. 5.00 o.p. (ISBN 0-8076-0373-2). Braziller.
State-of-the-Art of Ecological Modelling: Proceedings of the Conference on Ecological Modelling, Copenhagen, 28 August - 2 September 1978. S. E. Jorgensen. LC 78-41208. (Environmental Sciences & Applications Ser.: Vol. 7). 1979. 125.00 (ISBN 0-08-023443-7). Pergamon.
State of the Arts in North America: Systematic Theology Today. Thor Hall. LC 78-70520. 1978. pap. text ed. 9.00 (ISBN 0-8191-0645-3). U Pr of Amer.
State of the Jews. Marie Syrkin. 1980. 15.95 o.p. (ISBN 0-915220-60-1). New Republic.
State of the Masses. Emil Lederer. 1967. Repr. 14.00 (ISBN 0-86527-190-9). Fertig.
State of the Nation's Air Transportation System. National Academy of Engineering. LC 76-47852. 1976. pap. 5.50 (ISBN 0-309-02534-6). Natl Acad Pr.
State of the Nations: Constraints on Development in Independent Africa. Ed. by Michael F. Lofchie. (African Studies Center, UCLA). 1971. 19.50x (ISBN 0-520-01740-4); pap. 3.25 o.p. (ISBN 0-520-02360-9). U of Cal Pr.
State of the Planet: A Report Prepared by the International Federation of Institutes for Advanced Study, Stockholm. Sam Nilsson. (Illus.). 1980. 27.00 (ISBN 0-08-024717-2); pap. 12.00 (ISBN 0-08-024716-4). Pergamon.
State of the Union III. William Watts & Lloyd A. Free. LC 77-18653. (Illus.). 1978. 15.95x (ISBN 0-669-01507-5). Lexington Bks.
State of the Union Messages of the Presidents Seventeen Eighty-Nine to Nineteen Sixty-Six, 3 vols. Ed. by Fred L. Israel. LC 66-20309. (Illus.). 1981. pap. 42.50 (ISBN 0-87754-131-0). Chelsea Hse.
State of the Union of Europe: Report of the CADMOS Group to the European People. Ed. by Denis De Rougemont. 1979. 14.50 (ISBN 0-08-024483-1); pap. 8.75 (ISBN 0-08-024476-9). Pergamon.
State of the Universe. Ed. by Geoffrey Bath. (Illus.). 200p. 1980. 24.95x (ISBN 0-19-857549-1). Oxford U Pr.
State of the World Atlas. Pluto Press. 1981. 14.95 (ISBN 0-671-42438-6, Touchstone); pap. 9.95 (ISBN 0-671-42439-4). S&S.
State of Welfare. Gilbert Y. Steiner. 1971. 14.95 (ISBN 0-8157-8122-9); pap. 5.95 (ISBN 0-8157-8121-0). Brookings.
State Papers on Nullification. LC 69-16649. (American Constitutional & Legal History Ser). 1970. Repr. of 1834 ed. lib. bdg. 39.50 (ISBN 0-306-71126-5). Da Capo.
State Petroleum Enterprises in Developing Countries. United Nations Centre for Natural Resources, Energy & Transport. LC 79-20681. (Pergamon Policy Studies). 185p. 1980. 28.00 (ISBN 0-08-025126-9). Pergamon.
State Policewoman. Jack Rudman. (Career Examination Ser.: C-1692). (Cloth bdg. avail. on request). pap. write for info. (ISBN 0-8373-1692-8). Natl Learning.
State Policies & Federal Programs: Priorities & Constraints. Peter Passell & Leonard Ross. LC 77-27498. (Praeger Special Studies). 1978. 21.95 (ISBN 0-03-042591-3). Praeger.
State Policy Making for the Public Schools. new ed. Roald F. Campbell & Tim L. Mazzoni, Jr. LC 75-31311. 476p. 1976. 20.00 (ISBN 0-8211-0224-9); pap. text ed. 18.00x (ISBN 0-685-61059-4). McCutchan.
State Politics in China, Nineteen Forty-Nine to Nineteen Eighty. R. K. Jain. 600p. 1980. text ed. 30.75 (ISBN 0-391-02108-7). Humanities.
State Projection of the Gross National Product, 1970, 1980. Raymond C. Scheppach, Jr. LC 72-8038. (Multiregional Input-Output Study: Vol. 3). (Illus.). 320p. 1972. 28.95 (ISBN 0-669-84996-0). Lexington Bks.
State Public Welfare Legislation. Robert C. Lowe. LC 75-165602. (FDR & the Era of the New Deal Ser.). 1971. Repr. of 1939 ed. lib. bdg. 37.50 (ISBN 0-306-70352-1). Da Capo.
State Shareholding: The Role of Local & Regional Authorities. Richard Minns & Jennifer Thornley. 1979. text ed. 35.00x (ISBN 0-333-23739-0). Verry.
State, Society & Self-Destruction. Ed. by Elizabeth Vallance. (Acton Society Studies Ser.). 1975. text ed. 27.50x (ISBN 0-04-350049-8). Allen Unwin.
State, Society & University in Germany, Seventeen Hundred to Nineteen Hundred & Fourteen. Charles McClelland. LC 79-13575. 1980. 34.95 (ISBN 0-521-22742-9). Cambridge U Pr.
State Space Theory of Discrete Linear Control. Vladimir Strejc. 1981. price not set (ISBN 0-471-27594-8, Pub. by Wiley-Interscience). Wiley.
State Succession in Municipal Law & International Law, 2 Vols. Daniel P. O'Connell. (Cambridge Studies in International & Comparative Law). 1967. Vol. 1. 85.00 (ISBN 0-521-05857-0); Vol. 2. 75.00 (ISBN 0-521-05858-9). Cambridge U Pr.
State Systems: International Pluralism, Politics, & Culture. Robert G. Wesson. LC 77-84945. 1978. 17.95 (ISBN 0-02-934940-0). Free Pr.
State Tax Liability & Compliance Manual. Lloyd S. Hale & Ruth Kramer. LC 80-21616. 350p. 1980. 37.50 (ISBN 0-471-08488-3, Pub. by Ronald Pr). Wiley.
State Taxation of Forest & Land Resources: Symposium Proceedings. (Lincoln Institute Monograph: No. 80-6). 149p. 1980. pap. text ed. 12.00. Lincoln Inst Land.
State, the Family, & Education. Miriam E. David. (Radical Social Policy Ser.). 304p. (Orig.). 1980. pap. 17.50 (ISBN 0-7100-0601-2). Routledge & Kegan.
State Trees. rev. ed. Olive L. Earle. LC 73-4932. (Illus.). 64p. (gr. 3-7). 1973. PLB 6.48 (ISBN 0-688-31956-4). Morrow.
State Variables for Engineers. P. M. DeRusso et al. LC 65-21443. 1965. 39.95 (ISBN 0-471-20380-7). Wiley.
State, War & Peace. J. A. Fernandez-Santamaria. LC 76-27903. (Studies in Early Modern History). 1977. 42.50 (ISBN 0-521-21438-6). Cambridge U Pr.
Statecraft: An Introduction to Political Choice & Judgment. Charles W. Anderson. LC 76-22740. 1977. text ed. 16.95 (ISBN 0-471-02896-7); tchrs. manual 2.00 (ISBN 0-471-02429-5). Wiley.
Stateline. John Van Der Zee. LC 75-33627. 216p. 1976. 7.95 o.p. (ISBN 0-15-184905-6). HarBraceJ.
Statement of the Honorable Henry A. Kissinger with Respect to the Treaty on Strategic Arms Limitation Before the Committee on Foreign Relations of the U. S. Senate, July 31, 1979. (Significant Issues Ser.: Vol. I, No. 4). 35p. 1979. pap. 5.00 (ISBN 0-686-68798-1, CSIS005, CSIS). Unipub.
Statement of the Services of Sir Stamford Raffles. Stamford Raffles. (Oxford in Asia Historical Reprints Ser.). 1979. 24.95x (ISBN 0-19-580318-3). Oxford U Pr.
Statements of the Laws of the OAS Member States in Matters Affecting Business. Incl. Brazil. 308p (ISBN 0-8270-5470-X); Colombia. 303p (ISBN 0-8270-5480-7); Dominica; Grenada; St. Lucia; Suriname. 1980. write for info. OAS.
Statements on International Accounting Standards, 13 vols. Set. pap. 29.25 (ISBN 0-685-58522-0). Am Inst CPA.
States & Land-Use Control. R. Robert Linowes & Don T. Allensworth. LC 75-3624. (Special Studies). (Illus.). 262p. 1975. text ed. 27.95 (ISBN 0-275-05210-9). Praeger.
States & Morals: A Study in Political Conflicts. T. D. Weldon. 1973. pap. 4.95 (ISBN 0-685-30027-7). Transatlantic.
States & Social Revolutions. Theda Skocpol. LC 78-14314. 1979. 34.95 (ISBN 0-521-22439-X); pap. 9.95 (ISBN 0-521-29499-1). Cambridge U Pr.
States, Communities, & Control of the Community Colleges. Louis W. Bender. 60p. 1975. pap. 1.50 (ISBN 0-87117-083-3). Am Assn Comm Jr Coll.
States of Consciousness. American Psychological Association et al. (Human Behavior Curriculum Project Ser.). 64p. 1981. pap. text ed. 3.95x (ISBN 0-8077-2615-X); tchrs. manual & dup 9.95, ication masters (ISBN 0-8077-2616-8). Tchrs Coll.
States of Desire. Edmund White. 320p. 1981. pap. 3.95 (ISBN 0-553-14544-4). Bantam.
States Rights Debate: Antifederalism & the Constitution. 2nd ed. Alpheus T. Mason. 224p. 1972. pap. text ed. 3.95x (ISBN 0-19-501553-3). Oxford U Pr.
Statesman. Plato. Ed. by Martin Ostwald. Tr. by B. J. Skemp. LC 57-14633. 1957. pap. 3.95 (ISBN 0-672-60230-X, LLA57). Bobbs.
Statesman's Year-Book World Gazetteer. 2nd ed. Ed. by John Paxton. (Illus.). 800p. 1980. 25.00x (ISBN 0-312-76126-0). St. Martin.
Statesman's Year Book, 1980-81. 117th ed. Ed. by John Paxton. 1700p. 1980. 30.00x (ISBN 0-312-76093-0). St Martin.
Statesmen, Scholars & Merchants: Essays in Eighteenth-Century History. Ed. by Anne Whiteman et al. 396p. 1973. 24.95x (ISBN 0-19-822378-1). Oxford U Pr.
Stat'i. A. Voronsky. (Rus.). 1981. 15.00 (ISBN 0-88233-512-X); pap. 6.00 (ISBN 0-88233-513-8). Ardis Pubs.
Stat'i O Literature. Vladislav Khodasevich. 124p. (Rus.). 1981. 11.50 (ISBN 0-88233-408-5); pap. 3.75 (ISBN 0-88233-409-3). Ardis Pubs.
Static Analysis of Shell Structure. Phillip L. Gould. LC 76-47142. (Illus.). 1977. 45.95 (ISBN 0-669-00966-0). Lexington Bks.
Static & the Dynamic Philosophy of History & the Metaphysics of Reason. Georg W. Hegel. 1977. 37.50 (ISBN 0-89266-052-X). Am Classical Coll Pr.
Static Electrical Equipment Testing. Ed. by D. R. Adams et al. (Engineering Craftsmen: No. G21). (Illus.). 1969. spiral bdg. 23.50x (ISBN 0-685-90174-2). Intl Ideas.
Static Electrical Equipment Winding & Building, 2 vols. Ed. by Engineering Industry Training Board, London. (Engineering Craftsmen: No. G1). (Illus.). 1968. Set spiral bdg. 43.95x (ISBN 0-685-90175-0). Vol. 2 (ISBN 0-85083-128-8). Intl Ideas.
Statically Indeterminate Structures: Their Analysis & Design. Paul Andersen. (Illus.). 1953. 14.95 o.p. (ISBN 0-8260-0395-8). Wiley.
Statics. 2nd ed. J. L. Meriam. Ed. by SI Version. LC 74-11459. 381p. 1975. text ed. 20.95x (ISBN 0-471-59604-3). Wiley.
Statics. 2nd ed. James L. Meriam. LC 71-136719. (Illus.). 1971. text ed. 20.95x (ISBN 0-471-59595-0). Wiley.

Statics: An Individualized Approach. K. C. Muhlbauer. 1972. pap. 13.95 (ISBN 0-201-04888-4). A-W.
Statics & Dynamics Combined Edition. Jerry H. Ginsberg & Joseph Genin. LC 76-30664. 1977. text ed. 28.95 (ISBN 0-471-01795-7). Wiley.
Statics & Strength of Materials. Ladislav Cerny. (Illus.). 382p. 1981. text ed. 21.95 (ISBN 0-07-010339-9, C). McGraw.
Statics & Strength of Materials. Karl K. Stevens. (Illus.). 1979. ref. 24.95 (ISBN 0-13-844688-1). P-H.
Statics & Strength of Materials for Technology. 2nd ed. Don A. Halperin. LC 79-26256. 1981. deluxe ed. 18.95 text (ISBN 0-471-05651-0); tchrs'. manual avail. (ISBN 0-471-06042-9). Wiley.
Statics & Strength of Structures. Mario G. Salvadori. LC 70-138821. 1971. 21.95 (ISBN 0-13-844548-6). P-H.
Statics & Strengths of Materials. Duke L. Golden. LC 76-105328. 1970. text ed. 21.95 (ISBN 0-675-09366-X). Merrill.
Statics of Granular Media. Sokolovskill. 1965. pap. 30.00 (ISBN 0-08-013624-9). Pergamon.
Station Identification: Confessions of a Video Kid. Donald Bowie. 216p. 1980. 9.95 (ISBN 0-87131-300-6); pap. 5.95 (ISBN 0-87131-310-3). M Evans.
Station in the Delta. John Cassidy. 320p. 1981. pap. 2.50 (ISBN 0-345-28846-7). Ballantine.
Stationary Phases in Gas Chromatography. G. E. Baiulescu & A. V. Ilie. 1975. text ed. 55.00 (ISBN 0-08-018075-2). Pergamon.
Stationary Random Processes. Yu A. Rozanov. LC 66-29909. 1967. 19.95x (ISBN 0-8162-7354-5). Holden-Day.
Stationary States. Alan Holden. (Illus.). 1971. pap. text ed. 3.95x (ISBN 0-19-501497-9). Oxford U Pr.
Stationers' Company 1918-1977: A Livery Company in the Modern World. Philip Unwin. 1978. lib. bdg. 16.50 o.p. (ISBN 0-510-00019-3). Westview.
Stations Along the Reading Company's Philadelphia to Williamsport Line (Pa) Edward W. Moul. (RSHS Monograph: No. 5). (Illus.). 1974. softcover 2.50 o.p. (ISBN 0-686-12300-X). Jove Pubns.
Stations of the Mind: New Directions for Reality Therapy. William Glasser & William T. Powers. LC 80-8205. (Illus.). 288p. 1981. 11.95 (ISBN 0-06-011478-9, HarpT). Har-Row.
Statistical Abstract of Colorado, 1978-79. 2nd ed. Compiled by Thomas G. Tyler. (Illus., Orig.). Date not set. pap. cancelled (ISBN 0-918370-04-3). Transrep.
Statistical Abstract of Latin America 1981, Vol. 21. Ed. by James W. Wilkie. LC 56-63569. 1981. lib. bdg. price not set (ISBN 0-87903-239-1). UCLA Lat Am Ctr.
Statistical Abstract of Oklahoma. 1980 ed. 511p. 1980. pap. 15.00 (ISBN 0-931880-01-7). U OK Ctr Econ.
Statistical Account of Assam, 2 vols. new ed. William W. Hunter. LC 75-903409. 1975. Repr. Set. 37.50x o.p. (ISBN 0-88386-078-3). South Asia Bks.
Statistical Aids to Railway Operations. J. Singh. 8.75x o.p. (ISBN 0-210-27042-X). Asia.
Statistical Almanac: New Jersey. LC 79-55809. 1981. 15.95 (ISBN 0-8349-7541-6). W H Wise.
Statistical Analysis. 2nd ed. E. Chou. 1975. 24.95. Dryden Pr.
Statistical Analysis. 2nd ed. Samuel B. Richmond. (Illus.). 1964. 22.50 (ISBN 0-8260-7475-8); manual o.p. (ISBN 0-471-07477-2). Wiley.
Statistical Analysis for Business & Economics. Leonard J. Kazmier. (Illus.). 1978. pap. text ed. 15.95 (ISBN 0-07-033439-0, C); instructors manual 5.95 (ISBN 0-07-033440-4). McGraw.
Statistical Analysis for Business Decisions. new ed. Paul Jedamus et al. (Illus.). 1976. text ed. 18.50 (ISBN 0-07-032302-X, C); inst. manual 5.95 (ISBN 0-07-032306-2). McGraw.
Statistical Analysis for Business Decisions. rev. ed. William A. Spurr & Charles P. Bonini. 1973. text ed. 19.00 (ISBN 0-256-00491-9). Irwin.
Statistical Analysis for Decision Making. Charles A. Nickerson & Ingeborg A. Nickerson. (Illus.). 1979. text ed. 23.00 (ISBN 0-89433-001-2). Petrocelli.
Statistical Analysis for Managerial Decisions. 2nd ed. John C. Boot & Edwin Cox. (Illus.). 672p. 1973. text ed. 18.95 (ISBN 0-07-006518-7, C); instructor's manual 4.95 (ISBN 0-07-006519-5). McGraw.
Statistical Analysis for Sociologists: A Student Manual. Loether & McTavish. 1974. 4.95x o.p. (ISBN 0-205-04434-4, 8144346). Allyn.
Statistical Analysis in Psychology & Education. 4th ed. George Ferguson. 1975. text ed. 22.50x (ISBN 0-07-020480-2, C); instructors' manual 4.95 (ISBN 0-07-020481-0). McGraw.
Statistical Analysis in Psychology & Education. 5th, rev. ed. George A. Ferguson. (Psychology Ser.). (Illus.). 560p. 1981. text ed. 21.00x (ISBN 0-07-020482-9, C); instructor's manual 4.95 (ISBN 0-07-020483-7). McGraw.
Statistical Analysis of Geological Data. George S. Koch, Jr. & Richard F. Link. 850p. 1981. pap. 12.50 (ISBN 0-486-64040-X). Dover.
Statistical Analysis of Spatial Pattern. M. S. Bartlett. LC 75-31673. (Monographs on Applied Probability & Statistics). 1976. 11.95 o.p. (ISBN 0-470-05467-0). Halsted Pr.
Statistical Analysis of Spatial Patterns. M. S. Bartlett. LC 75-31673. 90p. 1978. text ed. 12.95x o.p. (ISBN 0-412-14290-2, Pub. by Chapman & Hall). Methuen Inc.
Statistical Analysis of Time Series. Theodore W. Anderson. LC 70-126222. (Probability & Mathematical Statistics Ser.). 1971. 31.95 (ISBN 0-471-02900-9). Wiley.
Statistical Analysis of Weather Modification Experiments. Wegman & DePrist. 184p. 1980. write for info. (ISBN 0-8247-1177-7). Dekker.
Statistical & Methodological Issues in Psychology & Social Sciences Research. Ed. by Gideon Keren. LC 80-23720. 350p. 1981. text ed. 24.95 (ISBN 0-89859-062-0). L Erlbaum Assocs.
Statistical Concepts in Geography. John Silk. (Illus.). 1979. text ed. 22.50x (ISBN 0-04-910065-3); pap. text ed. 9.95x (ISBN 0-04-910066-1). Allen Unwin.
Statistical Concepts: With Applications to Business & Economics. Richard W. Madsen & Melvin L. Moeschberger. (Illus.). 1980. text ed. 21.00 (ISBN 0-13-844878-7). P-H.
Statistical Considerations in Drug Absorption & Disposition. Ed. by Kenneth S. Albert. 256p. 1980. 18.00 (ISBN 0-917330-28-5). Am Pharm Assn.
Statistical Decision Rules & Optimal Inference. N. N. Cencov. (Mathematical Monographs: Vol. 53). Date not set. cancelled (ISBN 0-8218-4502-0). Am Math.
Statistical Design of Fatigue Experiments. R. E. Little & E. H. Jebe. LC 74-14802. 280p. 1975. 44.95 (ISBN 0-470-54115-6). Halsted Pr.
Statistical Distribution. N. A. Hastings & J. B. Peacock. LC 74-617. 130p. 1974. text ed. 9.95 (ISBN 0-470-35889-0). Halsted Pr.
Statistical Epidemiology in Veterinary Science. Frederick B. Leech & Kenneth C. Sellers. LC 78-75106. 1979. 26.95 (ISBN 0-02-848430-4). Macmillan.
Statistical Exercises in Medical Research. John F. Osborn. LC 79-12451. 1979. 16.95x (ISBN 0-470-26744-5). Halsted Pr.
Statistical Forecasting. Warren Gilchrist. LC 76-13504. 1976. 42.95 (ISBN 0-471-99402-2, Pub. by Wiley-Interscience); pap. 18.50 (ISBN 0-471-99403-0). Wiley.
Statistical Functions & Formulas: A Source of Simplified Derivations Based on Elementary Mathematics. Buddy L. Myers & Norbert L. Enrick. 174p. 1981. Repr. of 1970 ed. text ed. price not set (ISBN 0-89874-286-2). Krieger.
Statistical Inference: Basic Concepts. Richard B. Ellis. (Illus.). 272p. 1975. text ed. 15.95 (ISBN 0-13-844621-0). P-H.
Statistical Inference for Management & Economics. 2nd ed. Huntsberger et al. 640p. 1980. text ed. 18.95 (ISBN 0-205-06803-0, 1068032). Allyn.
Statistical Inference for Management & Economics. David V. Huntsberger et al. 1975. text ed. 15.95x o.p. (ISBN 0-205-04654-1, 1646540); instr's manual free o.p. (ISBN 0-205-04655-X, 1646559); sol. manual 2.95 o.p. (ISBN 0-205-04748-3, 1647482). Allyn.
Statistical Inquiry: Elementary Statistics for the Political, Social & Policy Sciences. George Watson & Dickinson McGaw. LC 79-12109. 1980. text ed. 18.95 (ISBN 0-471-02087-7); tchrs'. manual avail. (ISBN 0-471-05730-4). Wiley.
Statistical Mathematics. Robert Loveday. 1973. text ed. 5.95x (ISBN 0-521-08643-4). Cambridge U Pr.
Statistical Mechanics. rev., 2nd ed. Ralph H. Fowler. 96.00 (ISBN 0-521-05025-1); pap. 29.50 (ISBN 0-521-09377-5). Cambridge U Pr.
Statistical Mechanics. K. M. Khanna. 15.00x (ISBN 0-210-27151-5). Asia.
Statistical Mechanics. T. D. Lee. (Concepts in Contemporary Physics Ser.). 550p. 1981. lib. bdg. 35.00 (ISBN 0-686-65737-3); pap. 14.50 (ISBN 3-7186-0053-6). Harwood Academic. Postponed.
Statistical Mechanics & Field Theory. Ed. by R. N. Sen & C. Weil. LC 72-4108. 1972. 44.95 (ISBN 0-470-77595-5). Halsted Pr.
Statistical Mechanics & Mathematical Problems. Ed. by A. Lenard. (Lecture Notes in Physics: Vol. 20). (Illus.). viii, 246p. 1973. pap. 14.70 o.p. (ISBN 0-387-06194-0). Springer-Verlag.
Statistical Mechanics & Properities of Matter: Theory & Applications. E. S. Gopal. LC 74-3382. 1976. pap. 24.95 (ISBN 0-470-15168-4). Halsted Pr.
Statistical Mechanics & Spectroscopy. G. Allen & H. O. Pritchard. LC 74-7034. 1974. pap. 14.95 (ISBN 0-470-02331-7). Halsted Pr.
Statistical Mechanics, Kinetic, Theory & Stochastic Process. C. V. Heer. 1972. 24.95 (ISBN 0-12-336550-3). Acad Pr.
Statistical Mechanics of the Liquid Surface. Clive A. Croxton. LC 79-40819. 1980. 75.00 (ISBN 0-471-27663-4, Pub. by Wiley-Interscience). Wiley.
Statistical Mechanics, Thermodynamics, & Kinetics. Oscar K. Rice. LC 66-16379. (Chemistry Ser.). (Illus.). 1967. 28.95x (ISBN 0-7167-0133-2). W H Freeman.
Statistical Method for Accounting Students. D. Pitt Francis. 1978. pap. text ed. 15.95x (ISBN 0-434-90580-1). Intl Ideas.
Statistical Methods. 5th ed. Herbert Arkin & Raymond R. Colton. 344p. (Orig.). 1970. pap. 4.95 (ISBN 0-06-460027-0, CO 27, COS). Har-Row.
Statistical Methods. 7th ed. William G. Cochran & George W. Snedecor. 507p. 1980. 21.50 (ISBN 0-8138-1560-6). Iowa St U Pr.
Statistical Methods. 7th ed. William G. Cochran & George W. Snedecor. (Illus.). 608p. 1980. text ed. 21.50 (ISBN 0-8138-1560-6). Iowa St U Pr.
Statistical Methods & the Geographer. 4th ed. S. Gregory. LC 77-7025. (Geographies for Advanced Study Ser). (Illus.). 1978. pap. text ed. 10.95x (ISBN 0-582-48186-4). Longman.
Statistical Methods & the Geographer. S. Gregory. (Geographies for Advanced Study Ser). (Illus.). 1968. pap. text ed. 7.25x (ISBN 0-391-00185-X). Humanities.
Statistical Methods: For Business & Economics. Roger C. Pfaffenberger & James H. Patterson. 1977. 20.95x (ISBN 0-256-01797-2). Irwin.
Statistical Methods for Chemists. W. J. Youden. LC 76-51742. 136p. 1977. Repr. of 1951 ed. 8.50 o.p. (ISBN 0-88275-509-9). Krieger.
Statistical Methods for Comparative Studies: Techniques for Bias Reduction. Sharon Anderson et al. LC 79-27220. (Wiley Series in Probability & Mathematical Statistics: Applied Probability & Statistics). 1980. 24.95 (ISBN 0-471-04838-0, Pub. by Wiley-Interscience). Wiley.
Statistical Methods for Digital Computers. Kurt Enslein et al. LC 60-6509. (Mathematical Methods for Digital Computers Ser.: Vol. 3). 1977. 37.95 (ISBN 0-471-70690-6, Pub. by Wiley-Interscience). Wiley.
Statistical Methods for Rates & Proportion. Joseph L. Fleiss. LC 72-8521. (Probability & Statistics Ser: Applied Section). (Illus.). 223p. 1973. 26.95 (ISBN 0-471-26370-2, Pub. by Wiley-Interscience). Wiley.
Statistical Methods for Rates & Proportions. 2nd ed. Joseph L. Fleiss. (Probability & Statistics Ser.: Applied Probability & Statistics). 300p. 1981. 24.95 (ISBN 0-471-06428-9, Pub. by Wiley-Interscience). Wiley.
Statistical Methods for Survival Data Analysis. Elisa T. Lee. LC 80-24720. 557p. 1980. text ed. 26.95 solutions manual (ISBN 0-534-97987-4). Lifetime Learn.
Statistical Methods for the Behavioral Science: An Introduction. Richard S. Melton. 380p. 1981. pap. text ed. write for info. (ISBN 0-697-06549-9); instr's manual avail. (ISBN 0-697-06550-2). Wm C Brown.
Statistical Methods for the Earth Scientist: An Introduction. Roger Till. LC 73-22704. 1978. pap. 16.95 (ISBN 0-470-26340-7). Halsted Pr.
Statistical Methods in Biology. 2nd ed. Ed. by Norman T. Bailey. LC 80-15774. 1981. pap. 12.95 (ISBN 0-470-27006-3). Halsted Pr.
Statistical Methods in Education & Psychology. Gene V. Glass & Julian C. Stanley. (Educational Measurement, Research & Statistics Ser). 1970. text ed. 19.95x (ISBN 0-13-844928-7). P-H.
Statistical Methods in Hydrology. C. T. Haan. 1977. text ed. 13.50 (ISBN 0-8138-1510-X). Iowa St U Pr.
Statistical Methods in Medical Research. P. Armitage. 509p. 1971. 32.95 (ISBN 0-471-03320-0). Halsted Pr.
Statistical Methods Research. Davies & Goldsmith. 1976. 19.95 (ISBN 0-582-03040-4). Longman.
Statistical Papers of George Udny Yule. Ed. by A. Stuart & M. G. Kendall. 1971. 27.25 (ISBN 0-02-853040-3). Hafner.
Statistical Pattern Classification Using Contextual Information. K. S. Fu & T. S. Yu. (Patterns Recognition & Image Processing Ser.). 208p. 1981. write for info. (ISBN 0-471-27859-9, Pub. by Wiley-Interscience). Wiley.
Statistical Physics. F. Mandl. (Manchester Physics Ser). 1971. 14.25 (ISBN 0-471-56658-6, Pub. by Wiley-Interscience). Wiley.
Statistical Pocketbook of Indonesia 1976. Central Bureau of Statistics, Indonesia. LC 60-18985. 1976. pap. 25.00x o.p. (ISBN 0-686-65036-0). Intl Pubns Serv.
Statistical Portrait of Higher Education. Carnegie Commission on Higher Education. Ed. by E. J. Harris. LC 72-38334. (Illus.). 1024p. 1972. 32.50 o.p. (ISBN 0-07-010039-X, P&RB). McGraw.
Statistical Prediction Analysis. J. Aitchinson & I. R. Dunsmore. LC 74-25649. (Illus.). 276p. 1975. 44.50 (ISBN 0-521-20692-8). Cambridge U Pr.
Statistical Prediction Analysis. J. Aitchison & I. R. Dunsmore. (Illus.). 284p. 1980. pap. 14.95x (ISBN 0-521-29858-X). Cambridge U Pr.
Statistical Problems. Laurence H. Longley-Cook. LC 76-126340. (Illus., Orig.). 1971. pap. 4.50 (ISBN 0-06-460009-2, CO 9, COS). Har-Row.
Statistical Procedures for Agricultural Research. 294p. 1976. pap. 21.50 (R003, IRRI). Unipub.
Statistical Quality Control. 5th ed. Eugene L. Grant & Richard Leavenworth. (Industrial Engineering & Management Science Ser.). (Illus.). 1979. text ed. 25.95x o.p. (ISBN 0-07-024114-7); solutions manual 6.95 o.p. (ISBN 0-685-95714-4). McGraw.
Statistical Reasoning in Psychology & Education. 2nd ed. E. W. Minium. 1978. text ed. 22.95x (ISBN 0-471-60828-9); wkbk (ISBN 0-471-03633-1); instructors' manual avail. (ISBN 0-471-04055-X). Wiley.
Statistical Reasoning in Sociology. 3rd ed. John H. Mueller et al. LC 76-13097. (Illus.). 1977. text ed. 19.95 (ISBN 0-395-24417-X); solutions manual 2.30 (ISBN 0-395-24416-1). HM.
Statistical Report on Catholic Elementary & Secondary Schools for the Years 1967-68 to 1969-70. 104p. 1970. 3.00. Natl Cath Educ.
Statistical Sampling in Auditing. Dan M. Guy. LC 80-17279. (Wiley Series in Accounting & Info. Systems). 224p. 1981. text ed. 17.95 (ISBN 0-471-04232-3). Wiley.
Statistical Study of Wastage at School. (Studies & Surveys in Comparative Education Ser.). (Illus.). 121p. (Orig.). 1973. pap. 7.00 (ISBN 92-3-100942-7, U638, UNESCO). Unipub.
Statistical Survey of Japan's Economy 1979. Economic & Foreign Affairs Research Association. LC 54-43626. (Illus.). 83p. (Orig.). 1980. pap. 15.00x (ISBN 0-8002-2022-6). Intl Pubns Serv.
Statistical System of Communist China. Li, Choh-ming. 1962. 18.50x (ISBN 0-520-00746-8). U of Cal Pr.
Statistical Tables. F. James Rohlf & Robert R. Sokal. LC 68-54121. (Biology Ser.). (Illus.). 1969. text ed. 19.95x (ISBN 0-7167-0673-3); pap. text ed. 9.95x (ISBN 0-7167-0664-4). W H Freeman.
Statistical Tables. 2nd ed. F. James Rohlf & Robert R. Sokal. 1981. text ed. price not set (ISBN 0-7167-1257-1); pap. text ed. price not set (ISBN 0-7167-1258-X). W H Freeman.
Statistical Tables & Formulas. A. Hald. (Wiley Series in Probability & Mathematical Statistics). 1952. 16.50 (ISBN 0-471-34023-5, Pub. by Wiley-Interscience). Wiley.
Statistical Tables of National Income Expenditure & Output of the UK 1855-1965. C. H. Feinstein. LC 76-19627. 1976. limp bdg. 21.50x (ISBN 0-521-21396-7). Cambridge U Pr.
Statistical Techniques in Business & Economics. 4th ed. Robert D. Mason. 1978. text ed. 18.95x (ISBN 0-256-02025-6). Irwin.
Statistical Techniques in Forestry. 2nd ed. Andrew J. Nash. 6.00x (ISBN 0-685-52947-9). Lucas.
Statistical Theories of Mental Test Scores. Frederic M. Lord & Melvin R. Novick. 1968. text ed. 26.95 (ISBN 0-201-04310-6). A-W.
Statistical Theories of Spectra: Fluctuations. Ed. by Charles E. Porter. (Perspectives in Physics Ser.). (Illus., Orig.). 1965. pap. 24.00 (ISBN 0-12-562356-9). Acad Pr.
Statistical Theory & Methodlog of Trace Analysis. C. Liteanu & I. Rica. (Ellis Horwood Ser. in Analytical Chemistry). 1980. 94.95x (ISBN 0-470-26797-6). Halsted Pr.
Statistical Theory & Methodology in Science & Engineering. 2nd ed. Kenneth A. Brownlee. 1965. 37.95 (ISBN 0-471-11355-7). Wiley.
Statistical Theory of Concrete Structures. Milik Tichy & M. Vorlicek. 364p. 1972. 30.00x (ISBN 0-7165-2080-X, Pub. by Irish Academic Pr Ireland). Biblio Dist.
Statistical Theory of Non-Equilibrium Processes in a Plasma. Yu L. Klimontovich. 1967. text ed. 40.00 (ISBN 0-08-011966-2). Pergamon.
Statistical Theory of Signal Detection. 2nd ed. C. W. Helmstrom. 1968. 26.00 (ISBN 0-08-013265-0). Pergamon.
Statistical Thermodynamics. 2nd ed. John F. Lee et al. LC 78-183672. 1973. 20.95 (ISBN 0-201-04214-2). A-W.
Statistical Thermodynamics, 2 vols. A. Munster. Vol. 1, 1969. 72.00 (ISBN 0-12-510901-6); Vol. 2, 1974. 90.00 (ISBN 0-12-510902-4). Acad Pr.

Statistical Thermodynamics. Chang-Lim Tien & John H. Lienhard. (McGraw-Hill Hemisphere Ser. in Thermal & Fluids Engineering). 1979. pap. 25.95 (ISBN 0-07-064570-1, C); solution manual 5.95 (ISBN 0-07-064571-X). McGraw.

Statistical Thinking: A Structural Approach. John L. Phillips, Jr. LC 73-3035. (Psychology Ser). (Illus.). 1973. text ed. 11.95x (ISBN 0-7167-0832-9); pap. text ed. 5.95x (ISBN 0-7167-0831-0). W H Freeman.

Statistical Vocabulary. (Eng., Span., Port. & Fr., Fr). pap. 1.00 o.p. (ISBN 0-8270-6575-2). OAS.

Statistical Yearbook for Asia & the Pacific, 1978: Annuaire Statistique pour l'asie et le Pacifique. 11th ed. United Nations. LC 76-641968. (Illus.). 536p. (Orig.). 1979. pap. 28.00x (ISBN 0-8002-1083-2). Intl Pubns Serv.

Statistical Yearbook for Latin America 1978. 471p. 1980. pap. 32.00 (ISBN 0-686-68973-9, UN79/2G3, UN). Unipub.

Statistical Yearbook for Latin America, 1978. United Nations. 471p. 1979. pap. 32.00x (ISBN 0-8002-1087-5). Intl Pubns Serv.

Statistical Yearbook for Latin America: Nineteen Seventy-Eight. 471p. 1980. pap. 32.00 (UN79-2G3, UN). Unipub.

Statistical Yearbook of Finland, 1978. 75th ed. Central Statistical Office of Finland. Ed. by Elia Laakso. LC 59-42150. (Illus.). 577p. (Eng, Finnish, Swed.). 1980. vinyl bnd. 38.00x (ISBN 0-8002-2731-X). Intl Pubns Serv.

Statistical Yearbook: Poland. (Yearly). text ed. 25.00x (ISBN 0-89918-485-5, P485). Vanous.

Statistics. Ed. by Roland F. Hirsch. LC 78-10508. (Eastern Analytical Symposiam Ser.). 1978. pap. 24.00 (ISBN 0-89168-017-9). Franklin Inst.

Statistics. 2nd ed. Donald J. Koosis & Arthur P. Coladarci. LC 77-10201. (Self-Teaching Guides Ser.). 1977. pap. text ed. 6.95 (ISBN 0-471-03391-X). Wiley.

Statistics. 2nd ed. Robert Loveday. LC 74-96095. Orig. Title: Second Course in Statistics. (Illus.). 1969. text ed. 10.95x (ISBN 0-521-07234-4). Cambridge U Pr.

Statistics. Jane J. Srivastava. LC 72-7559. (Young Math Ser.). (Illus.). (gr. 1-5). 1973. PLB 7.89 (ISBN 0-690-77300-5, TYC-J). T Y Crowell.

Statistics. Witte. LC 78-57922. 315p. 1980. text ed. 16.95 (ISBN 0-03-055231-1, HoltC); wkbk. 6.95 (ISBN 0-03-055236-2). HR&W.

Statistics--Africa: Sources for Social, Economic, & Market Research. 2nd ed. Ed. by Joan M. Harvey. 1978. 98.00 (ISBN 0-900246-26-X, Pub. by CBD Research Ltd.). Gale.

Statistics: A Beginning. Roy R. Kuebler, Jr. & Harry Smith, Jr. LC 75-35719. 1976. text ed. 19.50 (ISBN 0-471-50928-0); instructor's manual avail. (ISBN 0-471-01541-5); wkbk. avail. (ISBN 0-471-02638-7); answers avail. (ISBN 0-471-02757-X). Wiley.

Statistics: A Conceptual Approach. new ed. Sidney J. Armore. LC 74-22892. (Mathematics Ser). 288p. 1975. text ed. 17.95 (ISBN 0-675-08730-9). Merrill.

Statistics: A First Course. 2nd ed. John E. Freund. (Illus.). 1976. pap. 17.95 (ISBN 0-13-846055-8); wkbk. 5.50 (ISBN 0-13-846014-0). P-H.

Statistics: A Guide to Biological & Health Sciences. Ed. by J. M. Tanur et al. 1977. pap. text ed. 5.95x (ISBN 0-8162-8564-0). Holden-Day.

Statistics: A Guide to Business & Economics. Ed. by Judilh M. Tanur et al. LC 76-5708. 120p. 1976. pap. text ed. 5.95x (ISBN 0-8162-8584-5). Holden-Day.

Statistics: A Guide to Political & Social Issues. Ed. by Judith M. Tanur et al. LC 76-50852. 1977. pap. text ed. 5.95x (ISBN 0-8162-8574-8). Holden-Day.

Statistics: A Guide to the Unknown. 2nd ed. Ed. by Judith M. Tanur et al. 1978. pap. text ed. 11.50x (ISBN 0-8162-8605-1). Holden-Day.

Statistics: A New Approach. W. Allen Wallis & Harry V. Roberts. 1956. text ed. 12.95 (ISBN 0-02-933720-8). Free Pr.

Statistics-America: Sources for Market Research (North, Central, & South America) Ed. by Joan M. Harvey. 1973. 40.00 o.p. (ISBN 0-900246-13-8, Pub. by CBD Research Ltd). Gale.

Statistics America: Sources for Social, Economic, & Marketing Research. 2nd ed. Joan M. Harvey. 300p. 1980. write for info. Gale.

Statistics: An Introduction. Harold J. Larson. LC 74-13460. 1975. 20.95 (ISBN 0-471-51770-4); tchrs. manual avail. (ISBN 0-471-51771-2). Wiley.

Statistics: An Introductory Analysis. 3rd ed. Taro Yamane. (Illus.). 1973. text ed. 21.95 scp (ISBN 0-06-047313-4, HarpC); scp problems manual 6.50 (ISBN 0-06-047319-3); solutions manual free (ISBN 0-06-367313-4). Har-Row.

Statistics: An Intuitive Approach. 4th ed. George H. Weinberg et al. 384p. 1980. text ed. 15.95 (ISBN 0-8185-0426-9). Brooks-Cole.

Statistics: An Intuitive Approach. 3rd ed. George M. Weinberg & John A. Schumaker. LC 73-85595. 1974. text ed. 15.95 (ISBN 0-8185-0113-8); solutions manual avail. (ISBN 0-685-42226-7). Brooks-Cole.

Statistics & Behavior: An Introduction. M. Y. Quereshi. LC 79-5514. 1980. pap. text ed. 11.50 (ISBN 0-8191-0901-0). U Pr of Amer.

Statistics & Dynamics. Boothroyd & Poli. 472p. 1980. 23.50 (ISBN 0-8247-6945-7). Dekker.

Statistics & Econometrics: A Guide to Information Sources. Ed. by Joseph Zaremba. (Economics Information Guide Ser.: Vol. 15). 650p. 1980. 30.00 (ISBN 0-8103-1466-5). Gale.

Statistics & Mathematics in the Nuclear Medicine Laboratory. John R. Prince & Lewis D. Schmidt. LC 75-39797. (Illus.). 89p. 1976. pap. text ed. 18.00 perfect bdg. (ISBN 0-89189-020-3, 45-8-007-00). Am Soc Clinical.

Statistics & Probability. J. H. Durran. LC 70-96086. (School Mathematics Project Handbks). 1970. text ed. 24.95 (ISBN 0-521-06933-5). Cambridge U Pr.

Statistics & Probability. 2nd ed. S. E. Hodge & M. L. Seed. (Illus.). 1977. pap. text ed. 12.95x (ISBN 0-216-90450-1). Intl Ideas.

Statistics & Public Policy. William B. Fairley & Frederick Mosteller. LC 76-10415. (Behavioral Science-Quantitative Methods Ser.). 1977. text ed. 20.95 (ISBN 0-201-02185-4). A-W.

Statistics & Urban Planning. Ken Williams. LC 75-23011. 189p. 1975. 21.50 (ISBN 0-686-65294-0, Pub. by Wiley). Krieger.

Statistics As a Tool for Educational Practitioners. new ed. Harriet Talmage. LC 75-31312. (Illus.). 264p. 1976. 16.65x (ISBN 0-8211-1905-2); text ed. 15.00x (ISBN 0-685-61060-8). McCutchan.

Statistics: Concepts & Controversies. David S. Moore. LC 78-12740. (Illus.). 1979. text ed. 18.95x (ISBN 0-7167-1022-6); pap. text ed. 8.95x (ISBN 0-7167-1021-8). W H Freeman.

Statistics: Decisions & Applications in Business & Economics. Moshe Ben-Horim & Haim Levy. Incl. Mastering Business Statistics: A Student Guide to Problem Solving. Ronald L. Coccari. 320p. wkbk. 7.95 (ISBN 0-394-32484-6). 592p. 1981. text ed. 21.95 (ISBN 0-394-32297-5). Random.

Statistics: Difficult Concepts-Understandable Explanations. Dale E. Mattson. (Illus.). 402p. 1981. pap. text ed. 16.95 (ISBN 0-8016-3173-4). Mosby.

Statistics: Discovering Its Power. Thomas J. Wonnacott & Ronald J. Wonnacott. 448p. 1981. text ed. 16.95 (ISBN 0-471-01412-5). Wiley.

Statistics Essential for Police Efficiency. John I. Griffin. (Illus.). 248p. 1972. 12.75 (ISBN 0-398-00734-9). C C Thomas.

Statistics for Biologists. 2nd ed. R. C. Campbell. (Illus.). 300p. 1974. 47.50 (ISBN 0-521-20381-3); pap. 9.95x (ISBN 0-521-09836-X). Cambridge U Pr.

Statistics for Business & Economics. Jerome D. Braverman & William C. Stewart. 500p. 1973. 17.50 (ISBN 0-471-06610-9). Wiley.

Statistics for Business & Economics. Heitzman & Mueller. 1980. text ed. 19.95 (ISBN 0-205-06753-0, 106753-2); solutions manual 7.95 (ISBN 0-205-06754-9, 1067540); study guide 6.95 (ISBN 0-205-06756-5, 1067567). Allyn.

Statistics for Business & Economics. Edwin Mansfield. 1980. text ed. 16.95x (ISBN 0-393-95057-3); May 1980. pap. 8.95x readings & cases (ISBN 0-393-95066-2); pap. 6.95x problems, exercises & case studies (ISBN 0-393-95062-X); solutions manual 1.95x (ISBN 0-393-95070-0). Norton.

Statistics for Business & Economics. 2nd ed. Stephen Shao. 1973. 8.95 (ISBN 0-675-08898-4). Merrill.

Statistics for Business & Economics. Joseph G. Van Matre & Glenn H. Gilbreath. 1980. text ed. 19.50x (ISBN 0-256-02276-3). Business Pubns.

Statistics for Business, Finance, & Accounting. J. P. Dickinson. (Illus.). 328p. 1976. text ed. 21.00x (ISBN 0-7121-1939-6, Pub. by Macdonald & Evans England); pap. text ed. 14.95x (ISBN 0-7121-1948-5). Intl Ideas.

Statistics for Comparative Studies. Michael Hills. LC 74-14542. 194p. 1974. pap. 10.95 o.p. (ISBN 0-470-39960-0). Halsted Pr.

Statistics for Decision Makers. David F. Groebner & Patrick W. Shannon. (General Business Ser.). 800p. 1981. text ed. 20.95 (ISBN 0-675-08083-5); student guide 6.95 (ISBN 0-675-08084-3). Merrill.

Statistics for Decision Making. Gulezian. 1979. 19.95 (ISBN 0-7216-4350-7). Dryden Pr.

Statistics for Experimentalists. B. E. Cooper. 1969. 19.50 (ISBN 0-08-012600-6). Pergamon.

Statistics for Experimenters: An Introduction to Design, Data Analysis & Model Building. George E. Box et al. LC 77-15087. (Wiley Ser. in Probability & Mathematical Statistics). 1978. 26.95 (ISBN 0-471-09315-7, Pub. by Wiley-Inerscience). Wiley.

Statistics for Management. Lincoln L. Chao. LC 79-22706. 1980. text ed. 20.95 (ISBN 0-8185-0367-X); study guide 6.95 (ISBN 0-8185-0409-9). Brooks-Cole.

Statistics for Management: A Simplified Introduction to Statistics. 4th ed. B. J. Mandel. LC 76-39577. 1977. 12.50 (ISBN 0-685-81631-1, 0-910486). Dangary Pub.

Statistics for Management Decisions. Donald R. Plane & Edward B. Oppermann. 1977. 18.50x (ISBN 0-256-01814-6). Business Pubns.

Statistics for Nurses: An Introductory Text. Frederick J. Kviz & Kathleen A. Knafl. 330p. 1980. pap. text ed. 9.95 (ISBN 0-316-50750-4). Little.

Statistics for Public Policy & Management. Matlack. LC 79-11886. 1980. text ed. 19.95 (ISBN 0-87872-226-2). Duxbury Pr.

Statistics for Students in the Behavioral Sciences. William A. Lindner & Rhoda Lindner. 1979. pap. text ed. 17.95 (ISBN 0-8053-6576-1); instr's guide 3.95 (ISBN 0-8053-6577-X); wkbk 5.95 (ISBN 0-8053-6578-8). Benjamin-Cummings.

Statistics for the Allied Health Sciences. Richard J. Larsen. 320p. 1975. text ed. 19.95 (ISBN 0-675-08782-1). Merrill.

Statistics for the Biological Sciences. 2nd ed. William C. Schefler. LC 78-55830. (Illus.). 1979. text ed. 14.95 (ISBN 0-201-07500-8). A-W.

Statistics for the Teacher. A. C. Crocker. 144p. 1974. pap. text ed. 7.75x (ISBN 0-85633-042-6, NFER). Humanities.

Statistics for the Teacher. 2nd ed. D. M. McIntosh. 1967. text ed. 13.75 (ISBN 0-08-012254-X); pap. text ed. 6.25 (ISBN 0-08-012255-8). Pergamon.

Statistics in Geography: A Practical Approach. David Ebdon. 1977. 9.95x (ISBN 0-631-16880-X, Pub. by Basil Blackwell); pap. 12.95x (ISBN 0-631-10131-4). Biblio Dist.

Statistics in Health Administration, 2 vols. Robert Broyles & Colin Lay. Incl. Vol. 1. Basic Concepts & Applications. 1979. 47.50 (ISBN 0-89443-153-6); Vol. II. Advanced Concepts & Applications. 1980. 48.00 (ISBN 0-89443-166-8). LC 79-23280. Aspen Systems.

Statistics in Political & Behavioral Science. 2nd ed. Dennis J. Palumbo. LC 76-15572. 1977. 22.50x (ISBN 0-231-04010-5). Columbia U Pr.

Statistics Made Simple. H. T. Hayslett, Jr. LC 67-10414. pap. 3.50 (ISBN 0-385-02355-3, Made). Doubleday.

Statistics: Methods & Analyses. 2nd ed. L. Chao. 1974. text ed. 18.95 (ISBN 0-07-010525-1, C); solutions manual 5.95 (ISBN 0-07-010526-X). McGraw.

Statistics of Educational Attainment & Illiteracy 1945-1974. (Statistical Reports & Studies: No. 22). 1978. pap. 10.00 (ISBN 92-3-001506-7, U803, UNESCO). Unipub.

Statistics of Extremes. Emil J. Gumbel. LC 57-10160. 1959. 20.50x (ISBN 0-231-02190-9). Columbia U Pr.

Statistics of Students Abroad; 1962-1968. LC 77-187557. (Statistical Reports & Studies, No. 18). 416p. (Orig.). 1972. pap. 10.00 (ISBN 92-3-000941-5, U633, UNESCO). Unipub.

Statistics of World Trade in Steel, 1978. 75p. 1980. 6.00 (ISBN 0-686-65815-9, UN79-2D19, UN). Unipub.

Statistics on Narcotic Drugs for 1978. 99p. 1980. pap. 9.00 (ISBN 0-686-68974-7, UN80/11/4, UN). Unipub.

Statistics Prob. Inf. Dec. 2nd ed. 1975. 24.95 (ISBN 0-03-014011-0). Dryden Pr.

Statistics: Problems & Solutions. J. Murdoch & J. Barnes. LC 72-8592. 352p. 1973. pap. 11.95x (ISBN 0-470-62510-4). Halsted Pr.

Statistics: Step-by-Step. Howard B. Christensen. LC 76-10903. (Illus.). pap. text ed. 18.75 (ISBN 0-395-24527-3); manual with solutions 1.75 (ISBN 0-395-24528-1). HM.

Statistics: The Essentials for Research. 2nd ed. Henry E. Klugh. LC 73-16182. 416p. 1974. text ed. 22.95 (ISBN 0-471-49372-4). Wiley.

Statistics: Tool of the Behavioral Sciences. M. Johnson & Liebert. 1977. 16.95 (ISBN 0-13-844704-7). P-H.

Statistics: With a View Toward Applications. Leo Breiman. LC 72-3131. 480p. 1973. text ed. 22.50 (ISBN 0-395-04232-1, 3-05972). HM.

Statistics Workbook for Social Science Students. M. F. Fuller & D. A. Lury. 256p. 1977. 30.00x (ISBN 0-86003-016-4, Pub. by Allan Pubs England); pap. 15.00x (ISBN 0-86003-117-9). State Mutual Bk.

Statistics 1: A Text for Beginners. F. Dapkus. 1979. pap. text ed. 13.95 (ISBN 0-89669-042-3). Collegium Bk Pubs.

Statius & the Thebaid. D. W. Vessey. LC 72-83578. 300p. 1973. 49.50 (ISBN 0-521-20052-0). Cambridge U Pr.

Statlib: A Statistical Computing Library. William M. Brelsford & Daniel A. Relles. 448p. 1981. text ed. 17.50 (ISBN 0-13-846220-8). P-H.

Statue of Liberty: Heritage of America. Paul Weinbaum. Ed. by Gweneth R. DenDooven. LC 78-78122. (Illus.). 1979. 7.95 (ISBN 0-916122-64-6); pap. 3.00 (ISBN 0-916122-63-8). K C Pubns.

Statue of Pedro Vito. Eli E. Pieters. 1981. 4.95 (ISBN 0-8062-1671-9). Carlton.

Stature of Man. Colin Wilson. Repr. of 1959 ed. lib. bdg. 17.50x (ISBN 0-8371-0273-1, WISM). Greenwood.

Status & Conformity. Richard Murphy. LC 76-11334. (Human Behavior). (Illus.). (gr. 5 up). 1976. PLB 9.99 o.p. (ISBN 0-8094-1955-6, Pub. by Time-Life). Silver.

Status & Conformity. Richard W. Murphy. (Human Behavior Ser.). 9.95 (ISBN 0-8094-1954-8). Time-Life.

Status & Power in Rural Jamaica: A Study of Educational & Political Change. Nancy Foner. LC 72-5943. (Illus.). 1973. text ed. 9.25x (ISBN 0-8077-2366-5); pap. text ed. 5.75x (ISBN 0-8077-2408-4). Tchrs Coll.

Status & Prospects of Thermal Breeders & Their Effect on Fuel Utilization. (Technical Reports Ser.: No. 195). 146p. 1980. pap. 19.75 (ISBN 92-0-155079-0, IDC195, IAEA). Unipub.

Status Book. Gary Blake. LC 77-94863. 1978. pap. 3.95 (ISBN 0-385-13549-1, Dolp). Doubleday.

Status of Aliens in East Africa: Asians & Europeans in Tanzania, Uganda, & Kenya. Daniel D. Don Nanjira. LC 75-19804. (Special Studies). 1976. text ed. 23.95 o.p. (ISBN 0-275-55570-4). Praeger.

Status of Birds in Britain & Ireland. Ed. by D. W. Snow. (Illus.). 354p. 1971. 10.50 o.p. (ISBN 0-397-60204-9, Blackwell). Lippincott.

Status of Hospital Discharge Data, in Denmark, Scotland, West Germany, & the United States. Lola J. Kozak. Ed. by Klaudia Cox. (Ser. Two: No. 88). 55p. 1981. pap. 1.75 (ISBN 0-8406-0211-1). Natl Ctr Health Stats.

Status of Inter-American Treaties & Conventions. rev. ed. Ed. by OAS General Secretariat Bureau of Legal Affairs. (Treaty Ser.: No. 5). 53p. text ed. 5.00 (ISBN 0-8270-1147-4). OAS.

Status of the Arab Woman: A Select Bibliography. Samira R. Meghdessian. LC 80-1028. 176p. 1980. lib. bdg. 32.50 (ISBN 0-313-22548-6, MEA/). Greenwood.

Status of the Curability of Childhood Cancers. Ed. by Jan Van Eys & Margaret P. Sullivan. (M. D. Anderson Clinical Conferences on Cancer: 24th). 350p. 1980. text ed. 34.00 (ISBN 0-89004-478-3). Raven.

Status of the Humanities. John Arthos. LC 80-84732. 1981. 12.50 (ISBN 0-686-68870-8). Philos Lib.

Statutes of Limitation Saving Statutes. William D. Ferguson. 1978. 35.00 (ISBN 0-87215-214-6). Michie.

Stavelot Triptych, Mosan Art, & the Legend of the True Cross. The Pierpont Morgan Library. (Illus.). 48p. 1980. text ed. 24.95x (ISBN 0-19-520225-2). Oxford U Pr.

Stavelot Triptych: Mosan Art & the Legand of the True Cross. William Voelke. LC 80-8970. (Illus.). 80p. 1980. pap. 3.70 (ISBN 0-87598-071-6). Pierpont Morgan.

Stay Healthy with Wine: Natural Cures & Beauty Secrets from the Vineyards. Marjorie Michaels. 256p. 1981. 11.95 (ISBN 0-686-69092-3). Dial.

Stay in the Son-Shine. Hubert S. Beck. (Orig.). 1980. pap. text ed. 3.95 (ISBN 0-89536-460-3). CSS Pub.

Stay of Execution: A Sort of Memoir. Stewart Alsop. LC 73-13691. 1973. 9.95 (ISBN 0-397-00897-X). Lippincott.

Stay Slim for Good: A Proven Seven Week Program for Lifelong Weight Control. E. Ann Sutherland & Zalman Almit. LC 75-36538. (Illus.). 192p. 1976. 8.95 o.s.i. (ISBN 0-8027-0520-0). Walker & Co.

Stay Tuned. Richard Levinson & William Link. 256p. 1981. 10.95 (ISBN 0-312-76136-8). St Martin.

Stay Well Every Year of Your Life: Dr. Molners Guide to Total Health. J. Molner. 1964. 6.95 o.p. (ISBN 0-13-846345-X). P-H.

Stay Where You Were: A Study of Unemployables in Industry. Harland Padfield & Roy Williams. LC 72-11972. 250p. 1973. 7.50 o.p. (ISBN 0-397-47289-7); pap. text ed. 3.25 o.p. (ISBN 0-397-47280-3). Lippincott.

Stay with It Snoopy. Charles Schulz. 128p. 1980. pap. 1.50 (ISBN 0-449-24310-9, Crest). Fawcett.

Stay with Me Lord: A Man's Prayers. Herbert B. West. LC 73-17914. 1974. 4.95 (ISBN 0-8164-0255-8). Crossroad NY.

Stay Young at Heart. John D. Cantwell. LC 75-25958. (Illus.). 212p. 1975. 12.95 (ISBN 0-88229-247-1). Nelson-Hall.

Stay Young Longer. Linda Clark. (Orig.). pap. 1.95 (ISBN 0-515-05076-8). Jove Pubns.

Staying Alive in Alaska's Wild. Andy Nault. Ed. by Tee Loftin. (Illus.). 224p. (Orig.). (gr. 6-12). 1980. pap. 8.00 (ISBN 0-934812-01-2). Loftin Pubs.

Staying Hard. Charles Gaines & George Butler. (Orig.). 1980. pap. 8.95 (ISBN 0-671-41265-5, Kenan Pr). S&S.

Staying Healthy with the Seasons. Elson Haas. LC 80-69469. (Illus.). 192p. (Orig.). 1981. pap. 9.95 (ISBN 0-89087-306-2). Celestial Arts.

Staying in Love: Reinventing Marriage & Other Realationships. Norton F. Kristy. (Orig.). pap. 2.75 (ISBN 0-515-05089-X). Jove Pubns.

Staying Is Nowhere: An Anthology of Kondh & Paraja Poetry. Sitakant Mahapatra. (Saffronbird Bk.). 1976. lib. bdg. 12.00 (ISBN 0-89253-126-6); flexible bdg. 6.75 (ISBN 0-89253-142-8). Ind-US Inc.

Staying on. Paul Scott. 1979. pap. 2.25 (ISBN 0-380-46045-9, 46045). Avon.

Steady Flame. Beth Meyers. (YA) 1972. 5.95 (ISBN 0-685-25149-7, Avalon). Bouregy.

Steady, Freddie. Scott Corbett. LC 78-116881. (Illus.). (gr. 3-6). 1970. 7.95 o.p. (ISBN 0-525-39951-8). Dutton.

Steady-State Economics: The Economics of Biophysical Equilibrium & Moral Growth. Herman E. Daly. LC 77-8264. (Illus.). 1977. text ed. 15.95x (ISBN 0-7167-0186-3); pap. text ed. 7.95x (ISBN 0-7167-0185-5). W H Freeman.

Steal Big. Patrick Mann. 208p. 1981. 9.95 (ISBN 0-312-76139-2). St Martin.

Stealing Home. Philip F. O'Connor. 288p. 1981. pap. 2.75 (ISBN 0-345-28478-X). Ballantine.

Stealing Machine. Eugene Villiod. Tr. by Russell T. Barnhart. LC 76-1271. 225p. 1975. 9.50 (ISBN 0-911996-99-0); pap. 4.50 (ISBN 0-686-67194-5). Gamblers.

Steam & Air Tables, SI Units. new ed. Thomas F. Irvine, Jr. & James P. Hartnett. LC 75-34007. (Illus.). 125p. (Orig.). 1976. pap. text ed. 9.95 (ISBN 0-89116-004-3, Co-Pub. by McGraw Intl); data for other substances incl. Hemisphere Pub.

Steam Cooking Now! Barbara S. Brauer. LC 80-82174. (Illus.). 1980. pap. 2.50 (ISBN 0-915942-15-1). Owlswood Prods.

Steam Engine in Industry-One. George Watkins. 128p. 1980. 25.00x (ISBN 0-686-64742-4, Pub. by Moorland England). State Mutual Bk.

Steam Engine of Thomas Newcomen. L. T. Rolt & J. S. Allen. (Illus.). 1977. 15.00 o.p. (ISBN 0-88202-171-0, Sci Hist). N Watson.

Steam Generation. J. N. Williams. 1969. text ed. 25.00x o.p. (ISBN 0-04-621013-X). Allen Unwin.

Steam House, 2 pts. Jules Verne. Incl. Pt. 1. Demon of Cawnpore. 12.85 ea. (ISBN 0-88411-908-4); Pt. 2. Tigers & Traitors (ISBN 0-88411-909-2). (Illus.). Repr. of 1886 ed. lib. bdg. 12.00 (ISBN 0-686-67026-4). Amereon Ltd.

Steam in the Alleghenies: Western Maryland. Krause & Grenard. (Carstens Hobby Bks.: No. C37). (Illus.). 1980. pap. 10.00 (ISBN 0-911868-37-2). Carstens Pubns.

Steam in the Coalfields. G. T. Heavyside. LC 76-54079. (Illus.). 1977. 11.95 (ISBN 0-7153-7323-4). David & Charles.

Steam in the Village. R. A. Whitehead. 1977. 14.50 o.p. (ISBN 0-7153-7449-4). David & Charles.

Steam Locomotive. W. A. Tuplin. 1980. text ed. 20.75 (ISBN 0-239-00198-2). Humanities.

Steam Locomotive Study Course, 4 vols. Ed. by William C. Fitt. LC 79-65782. (Illus.). 1500p. 1980. Set. 100.00 (ISBN 0-914104-05-5). Wildwood Pubns MI.

Steam Locomotives of the East African Railways. R. Ramaer. 1974. 14.95 (ISBN 0-7153-6437-5). David & Charles.

Steam Nostalgia: Locomotive & Railway Preservation in Great Britain. Gerald Nabarro. (Illus.). 286p. 1972. 22.00 (ISBN 0-7100-7391-7); pap. 7.50 (ISBN 0-7100-8386-6). Routledge & Kegan.

Steam Pig. James McClure. LC 72-410. (Harper Novel of Suspense). 256p. 1972. 7.95 o.p. (ISBN 0-06-012896-8, HarpT). Har-Row.

Steam Power & British Industrialization to 1860. G. N. Von Tunzelman. (Illus.). 1978. 45.00x (ISBN 0-19-828273-7). Oxford U Pr.

Steam-Powered Automobile: An Answer to Air Pollution. Andrew Jamison. LC 78-108211. 1970. 8.50x o.p. (ISBN 0-253-18400-2). Ind U Pr.

Steam Storage Installations. W. Goldstern. 1970. 28.00 (ISBN 0-08-015560-X). Pergamon.

Steam Tables & Mollier Chart M.K.S. System. Ed. by Shyam B. Srivastava. 1966. pap. 1.00x o.p. (ISBN 0-210-22682-X). Asia.

Steam Tables-Thermodynamic Properties of Water Including Vapor, Liquid & Solid Phases. Joseph H. Keenan et al. LC 71-94916. 1969. Eng. units 22.95 (ISBN 0-471-46501-1, Pub by Wiley-Interscience). Wiley.

Steam Tables: Thermodynamic Properties of Water Including Vapor, Liquid, & Solid Phases. Joseph H. Keenan et al. LC 77-28321. 1978. 22.95 (ISBN 0-471-04210-2, Pub. by Wiley-Interscience). Wiley.

Steamboats & Modern Steam Launches. Ed. by Bill Durham. (Illus.). 631p. 1981. Repr. of 1963 ed. 25.00. A S Barnes.

Steamboats & Modern Steam Launches. Ed. by Bill Durham. (Illus.). 631p. 1981. Repr. of 1963 ed. 25.00. Howell-North.

Steamboats & Modern Steam Launches, 3 vols. Ed. by Bill Durham. LC 64-5849. (Illus.). 631p. 1980. Boxed Set. 27.50 (ISBN 0-8310-7126-5); 9.95 ea. Vol. 1, 206 Pp (ISBN 0-8310-7130-3). Vol. 2, 217 Pp (ISBN 0-8310-7131-1). Vol. 3, 208 Pp (ISBN 0-8310-7132-X). Howell-North.

Steamboats on the Mississippi. Ralph K. Andrist. LC 62-10384. (Illus.). 153p. (gr. 6 up). 1962. 9.95 (ISBN 0-8281-0387-9, J009-1); lib. bdg. 12.89 (ISBN 0-06-020136-3, Distr. by Har-Row). Am Heritage.

Steamboats Out of Baltimore. Robert H. Burgess & H. Graham Wood. LC 68-58859. (Illus.). 1968. 10.00 (ISBN 0-87033-120-5, Pub. by Tidewater). Cornell Maritime.

Steamers of British Railways and Associated Companies. W. Paul Clegg & John S. Styring. (Illus.). 140p. 1967. 4.95 o.p. (ISBN 0-7153-4202-9). David & Charles.

Steamers of the Forth. Ian Brodie. LC 76-11099. (Illus.). 168p. 1976. 5.95 (ISBN 0-7153-7155-X). David & Charles.

Steaming into the Eighties: The Standard Gauge Preservation Scene. G. T. Heavyside. 1978. 11.95 (ISBN 0-7153-7513-X). David & Charles.

Steaming Mad. Mad Magazine Editors. (Mad Ser.: No. 39). (Illus.). 1975. pap. 1.75 (ISBN 0-446-94387-8). Warner Bks.

Steamroller: A Fantasy. Margaret W. Brown. LC 74-78107. (Illus.). 32p. (gr. k-3). 1974. 5.95 o.s.i. (ISBN 0-8027-6191-7); PLB 5.85 o.s.i. (ISBN 0-8027-6192-5). Walker & Co.

Steamship Accounting. Phillip C. Cheng. LC 70-80637. 1969. 11.00x (ISBN 0-87033-117-5). Cornell Maritime.

Steel & Its Heat Treatment: Bofors Handbook. K. Thelning. 564p. 1975. 69.95 (ISBN 0-408-70651-1). Butterworths.

Steel Beams & Iron Men. Mike Cherry. LC 80-66246. (Illus.). 96p. (gr. 5 up). 1980. 9.95 (ISBN 0-590-07591-8, Four Winds). Schol Bk Serv.

Steel Boat Construction. K. A. Slade. (Questions & Answers Ser.). (Illus.). 115p. (Orig.). 1979. pap. 7.50 (ISBN 0-686-64487-5). Transatlantic.

Steel Box Girder Bridges. Thomas Telford Ltd, Editorial Staff. 324p. 1980. 60.00x (Pub. by Telford England). State Mutual Bk.

Steel Buildings: Analysis & Design. 2nd ed. Stanley M. Crawley & Robert W. Dillion. LC 76-39934. 1977. text ed. 29.95 (ISBN 0-471-18552-3). Wiley.

Steel Design for Structural Engineers. B. O. Kuzmanovic & N. Williams. (Illus.). 1977. 25.95 (ISBN 0-13-846352-2). P-H.

Steel Designer's Manual. 4th ed. Contruction Steel Research & Development Organization. LC 75-19073. 1089p. 1975. 54.95 (ISBN 0-470-16865-X). Halsted Pr.

Steel-Engraved Book Illustration in England. Basil Hunnisett. LC 79-92108. (Illus.). 288p. 1980. 40.00 (ISBN 0-87923-322-2). Godine.

Steel Hawk & Other Stories. Bhabani Bhattacharya. 143p. 1968. pap. 1.95 (ISBN 0-88253-020-8). Ind-US Inc.

Steel Industry. A. Cockerill & A. Silberton. (Department of Applied Economics, Occasional Papers Ser: No. 42). (Illus.). 128p. 1974. pap. 12.50x (ISBN 0-521-09878-5). Cambridge U Pr.

Steel Industry in Communist China. Yuan-li Wu. LC 64-8250. (Publications Ser.: No. 36). 334p. 1965. 10.00 (ISBN 0-8179-1361-0). Hoover Inst Pr.

Steel Industry of India. William A. Johnson. LC 66-23471. (Rand Corporation Research Studies). 1966. 16.50x (ISBN 0-674-83715-0). Harvard U Pr.

Steel Magic. Andre Norton. (Illus.). (gr. 4-6). 1978. pap. 1.75 (ISBN 0-671-56094-8). PB.

Steel-Making Community: Pittsburg, Pennsylvania. (gr. 2). 1974. pap. text ed. 4.40 (ISBN 0-205-03889-1, 8038899); tchrs'. guide 12.00 (ISBN 0-205-03884-0, 8038848). Allyn.

Steel Mill. Eve Stwertka & Albert Stwertka. LC 78-2319. (Industry at Work Ser.). (Illus.). (gr. 4-6). 1978. PLB 5.90 s&l (ISBN 0-531-02208-0). Watts.

Steel of Raithskar. Randall Garrett & Vicki A. Heydron. 192p. (Orig.). 1981. pap. 2.25 (ISBN 0-553-14607-6). Bantam.

Steel Selection: A Guide for Improving Performance & Profit. Roy F. Kern & Manfred E. Suess. LC 78-13610. 1979. 27.95 (ISBN 0-471-04287-0, Pub. by Wiley-Interscience). Wiley.

Steel Skeleton, 2 vols. J. F. Baker. Incl. Vol. 1. Elastic Behaviour & Design. 1954. 35.50 (ISBN 0-521-04086-8); Vol. 2. Plastic Behaviour & Design. 1956. 57.50 (ISBN 0-521-04088-4). Cambridge U Pr.

Steel String Guitar: Its History & Construction. 2nd rev ed. Donald Brosnac. (Illus.). 112p. 1976. pap. 6.95 (ISBN 0-915572-26-5). Panjandrum.

Steel Structures. William McGuire. 1968. text ed. 38.00 (ISBN 0-13-846493-6). P-H.

Steel: The Metal with Muscle. Walter Harter. (Illus.). 96p. (gr. 4-7). 1981. PLB price not set. Messner.

Steel Titan: The Life of Charles M. Schwab. Robert Hessen. (Illus.). 352p. 1975. 19.95x (ISBN 0-19-501937-7). Oxford U Pr.

Steele Glas & The Complainte of Phylomene: A Critical Edition with Introduction. George Gascoigne. Ed. by William I. Wallace. (Salzburg Studies in English Literature, Elizabethan & Renaissance Studies Ser.: No. 24). 240p. 1975. pap. text ed. 25.00x (ISBN 0-391-01382-3). Humanities.

Steeler Gang. Lou Sahadi. (gr. 7-12). 1977. pap. 1.25 o.p. (ISBN 0-590-10321-0, Schol Pap). Schol Bk Serv.

Steele's Answers. D. Steele. 6.95 (ISBN 0-686-27781-3). Schmul Pub Co.

Steelhead. Mel Marshall. (Illus.). 1980. 10.95 (ISBN 0-87691-093-2). Winchester Pr.

Steer North. Kathrene S. Pinkerton. LC 62-8346. (gr. 7 up). 1962. 4.95 o.p. (ISBN 0-15-280210-X, HJ). HarBraceJ.

Steering & Suspension. John Remling. LC 77-10529. (Automotive Ser.). 1978. 15.95 (ISBN 0-471-71646-4); tchr'. manual avail. (ISBN 0-471-03763-X). Wiley.

Stefan George. Ulrich K. Goldsmith. LC 78-110601. (Columbia Essays on Modern Writers Ser.: No. 50). 48p. 1970. pap. 2.00 (ISBN 0-231-03204-8, MW50). Columbia U Pr.

Steffie Can't Come Out to Play. Fran Arrick. LC 78-4423. (gr. 8 up). 1978. 8.95 (ISBN 0-87888-135-2). Bradbury Pr.

Stehekin: The Enchanted Valley. Fred T. Darvill, Jr. LC 80-16628. (Illus.). 96p. (Orig.). 1980. pap. 5.95 (ISBN 0-913140-42-2). Signpost Bk Pub.

Stein & Day Baseball Date Book, 1981. Rich Marazzi. (Illus.). 128p. 1980. 6.95 (ISBN 0-8128-2770-8). Stein & Day.

Stein on Probate, 2 vols. Ed. by Robert A. Stein. 1976. Set. text ed. 155.00 (ISBN 0-917126-14-9); Vol. I, 477 Pgs. text ed. 45.00 (ISBN 0-917126-15-7); Vol. II, 658 Pgs. text ed. 45.00 (ISBN 0-917126-16-5); Supplement, 523 Pgs. looseleaf text 35.00 (ISBN 0-917126-17-3); Supplement, 43 Pgs. looseleaf pgs. 15.00 (ISBN 0-917126-18-1). Mason Pub.

Steinbeck: A Collection of Critical Essays. Ed. by Robert M. Davis. 1972. 10.95 (ISBN 0-13-846659-9, Spec); pap. 2.95 (ISBN 0-13-846642-4, Spec). P-H.

Steinbeck's Literary Dimension: A Guide to Comparative Studies. Tetsumaro Hayashi. LC 72-7457. 1973. 10.00 (ISBN 0-8108-0550-2). Scarecrow.

Steinberg, No. 205. (Maeght Gallery: Derriere le Miroir Ser.). 1977. pap. 19.95 (ISBN 0-8120-0897-9). Barron.

Steinberg, No. 53-54. (Maeght Gallery: Derriere le Miroir Ser.). (Fr.). 1977. pap. 19.95 (ISBN 0-8120-0912-6). Barron.

Steinberg, No. 157. (Maeght Gallery: Derriere le Miroir Ser.). (Fr.). 1977. pap. 19.95 (ISBN 0-8120-0919-3). Barron.

Steinberg, No. 192. (Maeght Gallery: Derriere le Miroir Ser.). (Fr.). 1977. pap. 19.95 (ISBN 0-8120-0922-3). Barron.

Steinlen Cats. Theophile-Alexandre Steinlen. (Illus.). 48p. 1980. pap. 2.00 (ISBN 0-486-23950-0). Dover.

Steinlen's Lithographs: One Hundred Twenty-One Plates from "Gil Blas Illustre". Theophile-Alexandre Steinlen. (Illus.). 128p. 1980. pap. 6.50 (ISBN 0-486-23943-8). Dover.

Stellar Atmospheres. 2nd ed. Dimitri Mihalas. LC 77-13211. (Astronomy & Astrophysics Ser.). (Illus.). 1978. text ed. 33.95x (ISBN 0-7167-0359-9). W H Freeman.

Stellar Evolution. A. J. Meadows. 1967. 9.90 (ISBN 0-08-012693-6); pap. 4.95 (ISBN 0-08-012224-8). Pergamon.

Stellar Evolution. 2nd ed. A. J. Meadows. 1978. text ed. 23.00 (ISBN 0-08-021668-4); pap. text ed. 7.00 (ISBN 0-08-021669-2). Pergamon.

Stellar Formation. V. C. Reddish. 225p. 1976. text ed. 45.00 (ISBN 0-08-018062-0); pap. text ed. 19.50 (ISBN 0-08-023053-9). Pergamon.

Stellar Science Fiction Stories. Ed. by Judy-Lynn Del Rey. 192p. (Orig.). 1981. pap. 2.25 (ISBN 0-345-28969-2, Del Rey). Ballantine.

Stellar Science Fiction Stories, No. 2. Ed. by Judy-Lynn Del Rey. 1976. pap. 1.50 o.p. (ISBN 0-345-24584-9). Ballantine.

Stellar Short Novels. Ed. by Judy-Lynn Del Rey. 1976. pap. 1.50 o.p. (ISBN 0-345-25501-1). Ballantine.

Stem Cells & Tissue Homeostasis. Ed. by B. I. Lord & C. S. Potten. LC 77-80844. (British Society for Cell Biology Symposium Ser.). (Illus.). 1978. 68.00 (ISBN 0-521-21799-7). Cambridge U Pr.

Stem Dictionary of the English Language. John Kennedy. LC 78-142547. 1971. Repr. of 1870 ed. 26.00 (ISBN 0-8103-3377-5). Gale.

Stencilled Ornament & Illustration. Compiled by Dorothy Abbe. pap. 15.00 (ISBN 0-89073-064-4). Boston Public Lib.

Stendahl: The Life an Egoist. Rudolf Kayber. 278p. 1980. Repr. of 1930 ed. lib. bdg. 30.00 (ISBN 0-89760-427-X). Telegraph Bks.

Stendhal. Wallace Fowlie. Ed. by Louis Kronenberger. (Masters of World Literature Ser.: Vol. 12). 1969. 5.95 o.s.i. (ISBN 0-02-540390-7). Macmillan.

Stendhal. Marcel Gutwirth. (World Authors Ser.: France: No. 174). lib. bdg. 12.50 (ISBN 0-8057-2862-7). Twayne.

Stendhal. Michael Wood. Ed. by Graham Hough. LC 73-164669. (Novelists & Their World Ser). 1971. 14.50x (ISBN 0-8014-0680-3); pap. 4.95 (ISBN 0-8014-9124-X). Cornell U Pr.

Stendhal & the Age of Napoleon: An Interpretive Biography. Gita May. LC 77-8379. 1977. 20.00x (ISBN 0-231-04344-9). Columbia U Pr.

Stendhal: Memoirs of an Egotist. Stendhal. Tr. by David Ellis from Fr. 1975. 6.95 o.p. (ISBN 0-8180-0224-7). Horizon.

Stendhal: The Education of a Novelist. G. Strickland. 276p. 1974. 47.50 (ISBN 0-521-20385-6); pap. 12.50x (ISBN 0-521-09837-8). Cambridge U Pr.

Stenoscript ABC Shorthand - SRA Edition. 1968. text ed. 9.95 (ISBN 0-574-15001-3, 15-1001); tchr's handbook avail. (ISBN 0-574-15003-X, 15-1003); answer key avail. (ISBN 0-574-15002-1, 15-1002); tapes-cassettes 100.00 (ISBN 0-574-15020-X, 15-1020); answer key 0.95 (ISBN 0-574-15030-7, 15-1030). SRA.

Stenospeed Shorthand. Frances A. Greer. 300p. 1974. 8.75 o.p. (ISBN 0-911744-31-2). Intl Educ Systems.

Stenospeed Shorthand 25,000 Word Dictionary. Frances Greer & Frances Greer. (Illus.). 384p. 1971. 8.50 o.p. (ISBN 0-911744-26-6). Intl Educ Systems.

Stenospeed Workbook. Frances A. Greer. 150p. 1974. pap. 3.45 o.p. (ISBN 0-911744-32-0). Intl Educ Systems.

Step-by-Step Guide to Fruits. Harry Baker. (Illus.). 1980. 7.95 (ISBN 0-686-60919-0, 24834). S&S.

Step by Step Guide to Indian Cooking. Khalid Aziz. 1976. 11.95 (ISBN 0-600-38093-9). Transatlantic.

Step by Step Introduction to 8080 Microprocessor Systems. David L. Cohn & James L. Melsa. 1977. pap. 8.95 (ISBN 0-918398-04-5). Dilithium Pr.

Step-by-Step Plumbing. Ann Lambrecht. (Step-by-Step Home Repair Ser.). (Illus.). 96p. 1981. 4.95 (ISBN 0-696-00575-1). Meredith Corp.

Step by Step Through the Parables. John W. Miller. 192p. (Orig.). 1981. pap. 6.95 (ISBN 0-8091-2379-7). Paulist Pr.

Step in the Dark. T. C. Lethbridge. 1967. 12.00 (ISBN 0-7100-1741-3). Routledge & Kegan.

Step into Skiing Discoveries. Jul Kingery. LC 77-91906. (Skiing Your Way Ser.). (Illus.). 1978. pap. 7.97 (ISBN 0-9604574-0-2). Alpine-Tahoe.

Step on It, Andrew. Barbara S. Hazen. LC 80-12522. (Illus.). 32p. (ps-2). 1980. 8.95 (ISBN 0-689-30792-6). Atheneum.

Stepdaughter. Caroline Blackwood. LC 77-3500. 1977. 6.95 o.p. (ISBN 0-684-14934-6, ScribT). Scribner.

Stepfamilies: Myths & Realities. Emily B. Visher & John S. Visher. 1980. pap. 6.95 (ISBN 0-8065-0743-8). Lyle Stuart.

Stephane Mallarme. Stephane Mallarme. 159p. 1980. Repr. of 1927 ed. lib. bdg. 20.00 (ISBN 0-8492-6835-4). R West.

Stephanie. Caroline Arnett. (Regency Romance Ser.). 1979. pap. 1.75 o.p. (ISBN 0-449-24081-9, Crest). Fawcett.

Stephen A. Douglas: A Study in American Politics. Allen Johnson. LC 77-98690. (American Scene Ser). 1970. Repr. of 1908 ed. lib. bdg. 39.50 (ISBN 0-306-71836-7). Da Capo.

Stephen Crane. Edwin H. Cady. (U. S. Authors Ser.: No. 23). 1962. lib. bdg. 9.95 o.p. (ISBN 0-8057-0168-0). Twayne.

Stephen Crane & Literary Impressionism. James Nagel. LC 80-16051. 200p. 1980. 16.50x (ISBN 0-271-00267-0). Pa St U Pr.

Stephen Crane at Brede: An Anglo-American Literary Circle of the Eighteen Nineties. Gordon Milne. LC 80-8126. 69p. 1980. lib. bdg. 12.75 (ISBN 0-8191-1139-2); pap. text ed. 6.25 (ISBN 0-8191-1140-6). U Pr of Amer.

Stephen Crane: The Critical Heritage. Ed. by Richard M. Weatherford. (Critical Heritage Ser.). 362p. 1973. 30.00x (ISBN 0-7100-7636-3). Routledge & Kegan.

Stephen Crane's Artistry. Frank Bergon. 224p. 1975. 17.50x (ISBN 0-231-03905-0). Columbia U Pr.

Stephen Hales: Scientist & Philanthropist. D. G. Allan & R. E. Schofield. (Illus.). 220p. 1980. 50.00x (ISBN 0-85967-482-7, Pub. by Scolar Pr England). Biblio Dist.

Stephen Hero. rev. ed. James Joyce. LC 63-14454. (Illus.). 1969. pap. 4.95 (ISBN 0-8112-0074-4, NDP133). New Directions.

Stephen Long & America Frontier Expedition. Roger Nichols & Patrick L. Halley. LC 78-68878. (Illus.). 280p. 1980. 19.50 (ISBN 0-87413-149-9). U Delaware Pr.

Stephen R. Deane: Early Maine Folk Calligrapher. Marius B. Peladeau. (Illus.). 128p. 1981. 22.50 (ISBN 0-931474-15-9). TBW Bks.

Stephen Remarx: The Story of a Venture into Ethics, 1893. James G. Adderly. Ed. by Robert L. Wolff. Bd. with Christian. Thomas H. Caine. Repr. of 1897 ed. LC 75-485. (Victorian Fiction Ser). 1975. lib. bdg. 66.00 (ISBN 0-8240-1562-2). Garland Pub.

Stephen S. Townsend. Dorothy C. Remick. (Illus.). 160p. 1981. 12.50 (ISBN 0-89962-050-7). Todd & Honeywell.

Stephen Vincent Benet. Parry Stroud. (U. S. Authors Ser.: No. 27). 1962. lib. bdg. 9.95 (ISBN 0-8057-0052-8). Twayne.

Stepparenting. Veryl Rosenbaum & Jean Rosenbaum. LC 77-22070. 160p. 1977. 7.95 (ISBN 0-88316-530-9). Chandler & Sharp.

Steppin' Out: A Guide to Live Music in Manhattan. Susanne Weil & Barry Singer. LC 79-23812. (Illus.). 160p. 1980. lib. bdg. 10.25 o.p. (ISBN 0-914788-24-8). East Woods.

Steppin' Out: New York Nightlife & the Transformation of American Culture, 1890-1930. Lewis A. Erenberg. LC 80-930. (Contributions in American Studies Ser.: No. 50). 296p. 1981. lib. bdg. 23.95 (ISBN 0-313-21342-9, EUN/). Greenwood.

Stepping Stones. Ed. by Robert Gold. (Orig.). (YA) (gr. 7-12). 1981. pap. 1.50 (ISBN 0-440-98269-3, LE). Dell.

Stepping Stones. Jean Greenlaw & Gretchen Barton. (Design for Reading Ser). (Illus., Personal reading). (gr. 2). 1972. text ed. 8.68 (ISBN 0-06-516030-4, SchDept); tchr's ed. 5.12 (ISBN 0-06-516230-7); wkbk. 3.20 (ISBN 0-06-516330-3); tchr's ed. wkbk. 6.36 (ISBN 0-06-516430-X). Har-Row.

Stepping Stones Across the Pacific. Afred M. Bailey & Robert J. Niedrach. (Museum Pictorial: No. 3). 1951. pap. 1.10 o.p. (ISBN 0-916278-32-8). Denver Mus Natl Hist.

Stepping Stones to Go. Shigemi Kishikawa. LC 65-13411. (Illus.). 1965. pap. 5.95 (ISBN 0-8048-0547-4). C E Tuttle.

Steppingstones to Professional Nursing. 5th rev. ed. Kathryn W. Cafferty & Leone K. Sugarman. LC 76-158487. (Illus.). 1971. text ed. 12.95 o.p. (ISBN 0-8016-0929-1). Mosby.

Steps Across Life. Jackie Larsen. LC 80-80720. (Illus.). 1980. soft cover 4.95 (ISBN 0-9602474-3-2). J Larsen.

Steps Heavenward. R. L. Berry. 123p. pap. 1.00. Faith Pub Hse.

Steps in Clothing Skills. Draper & Bailey. (gr. 7-9). 1978. text ed. 13.28 (ISBN 0-87002-265-2); avail. tchr's guide. Bennett IL.

Steps in Composition. 2nd ed. Lynn Q. Troyka & J. Nudelman. 416p. 1976. 9.95 (ISBN 0-13-846501-0). P-H.

Steps in Composition: Alternate. 2nd ed. Lynn Q. Troyka & Jerrold Nudelman. (Illus.). 1979. pap. text ed. 9.95 (ISBN 0-13-846550-9). P-H.

Steps in Darkness. Krishna B. Vaid. 151p. 1972. pap. 2.45 (ISBN 0-88253-120-4). Ind-US Inc.

Steps in Home Living. rev. ed. Florence M. Reiff. (Illus.). (YA) (gr. 7-9). 1971. text ed. 15.96 (ISBN 0-87002-099-4); tchr's guide avail. (ISBN 0-685-06851-X). Bennett IL.

Steps in Mathematics, 5 modules. Leon Ablon et al. 1981. softbound 3.95 ea. Module 1 (ISBN 0-8053-0131-3). Module 2 (ISBN 0-8053-0132-1). Module 3 (ISBN 0-8053-0133-X). Module 4. Module 5 (ISBN 0-8053-0135-6). Benjamin-Cummings.

Steps in Time. Fred Astaire. (Quality Paperbacks Ser.). (Illus.). 327p. 1981. pap. 7.95 (ISBN 0-306-80141-8) Da Capo.

Steps to Christ. Ellen G. White. LC 56-7169. 134p. 1956. 4.95 (ISBN 0-8163-0045-3, 19543-8); pap. 0.95 (ISBN 0-8163-0046-1, 19547-9). Pacific Pr Pub Assn.

Steps to English, Bks. 1-2. D. Kernan. 1974. Bk. 1. text ed. 7.84x (ISBN 0-07-034151-6); Bk. 2. text ed. 7.84x (ISBN 0-07-034156-7). tchrs. eds. 8.76x ea.; ea. wkbks. 3.53 (ISBN 0-686-66128-1); cassettes 161.00 (ISBN 0-07-034153-2). McGraw.

Steps to High-School Education: Students Plus Teachers Plus Parents Equal Success. Stephen J. Drotter. 94p. 1980. 5.95 (ISBN 0-8059-2755-7). Dorrance.

Steps to Independence: A Skills Training Series for Children with Special Needs. Bruce L. Baker et al. Incl. Early Self-Help Skills. pap. text ed. 7.95 spiral bd. (ISBN 0-87822-167-0); Intermediate Self-Help Skills. pap. text ed. 7.95 spiral bdg. (ISBN 0-87822-168-9); Advanced Self-Help Skills. pap. text ed. 7.95 spiral bdg. (ISBN 0-87822-169-7); Behavior Problems. pap. text ed. 7.95 spiral bdg. (ISBN 0-87822-170-0); Training Guide. 1976. pap. 2.95 (ISBN 0-87822-171-9); Toilet Training. LC 77-81303. 1977. pap. text ed. 7.95 spiral bdg. (ISBN 0-87822-144-1); Speech & Language, 2 levels. LC 78-51500. 1978. pap. text ed. 7.95 ea. spiral bdg.; Level 1. (ISBN 0-87822-181-6); Level 2. (ISBN 0-87822-182-4). (Illus., Orig.). Set. 59.95 (ISBN 0-87822-166-2). Res Press.

Steps to Jesus. Ellen G. White. 128p. 1980. 3.95 (ISBN 0-8127-0316-2); pap. 1.95 (ISBN 0-8127-0318-9). Southern Pub.

Steps to Language. I. M. Schlesinger. 448p. 1981. text ed. 24.95 (ISBN 0-89859-045-0). L Erlbaum Assocs.

Steps to Nuclear Power: A Guidebook. (Technical Report Ser.: No. 164). (Illus.). 106p. 1975. pap. 10.75 (ISBN 92-0-155175-4, IAEA). Unipub.

Steps to Prayer Power. Jo Kimmel. 1976. pap. 1.25 (ISBN 0-685-84388-2). Jove Pubns.

Steps to Singing for Voice Classes. 2nd ed. Royal Stanton. 1976. pap. 12.95x (ISBN 0-534-00419-9). Wadsworth Pub.

Steps to Success: A Study Skills Handbook. rev. ed. John W. Crawford. 1978. pap. text ed. 5.50 o.p. (ISBN 0-8403-0975-9). Kendall-Hunt.

Steps to Success in Shorthand, Bk. 1. text ed. 5.00 (ISBN 0-8224-0072-3); pap. 5.40 transcript (ISBN 0-8224-0073-1). Pitman Learning.

Steps to Take to Save a Business Which Is on the Verge of Collaspe. Carl A. Swanson. (International Council for Excellence in Management Library). (Illus.). 105p. 1980. plastic spiral bdg. 24.95 (ISBN 0-89266-243-3). Am Classical Coll Pr.

Steps to the Sermon. Henry C. Brown, Jr. et al. LC 63-19068. 1963. 8.50 (ISBN 0-8054-2103-3). Broadman.

Stereo Infrared Landscapes. Steven Schwartzman. (Illus., Orig.). 1980. pap. 9.00 (ISBN 0-937710-01-6). SunShine.

Stereo Troubleshooting & Repair Manual. Paul Owens. (Illus.). 1979. ref. 16.95 (ISBN 0-8359-7082-5). Reston.

Stereochemistry & Mechanism. David Whittaker. (Oxford Chemistry Ser.). (Illus.). 108p. 1973. pap. text ed. 11.50x (ISBN 0-19-855405-2). Oxford U Pr.

Stereochemistry & the Chemistry of Natural Products. 2nd ed. I. L. Finar. (Organic Chemistry Ser.: Vol. 2). 1959. 13.95 (ISBN 0-471-25888-1). Halsted Pr.

Stereodynamics of Molecular Systems. Ramaswamy H. Sarma. 1979. 66.00 (ISBN 0-08-024629-X). Pergamon.

Stereoscopic Atlas of Ocular Photocoagulation. Francis A. L'Esperance, Jr. LC 75-33111. (Illus.). 338p. 1975. text ed. 77.50 (ISBN 0-8016-2824-5). Mosby.

Stereotactic Brain Operations: Methods, Clinical Aspects, Indications. T. Riechert. (Illus.). 387p. 1980. 120.00 (ISBN 3-456-80457-1, Pub. by Hans Huber). J K Burgess.

Stereotaxic Atlas of the Brain of the Squirrel Monkey. Raimond Emmers & Konrad Akert. (Illus.). 1963. 100.00x (ISBN 0-299-02690-6). U of Wis Pr.

Stereotaxic Atlas of the Chimpanzee Brain. M. R. De Lucchi et al. 1965. 48.50x (ISBN 0-520-00304-7). U of Cal Pr.

Stereotaxic Atlas of the Developing Rat Brain. Nancy Sherwood & Paola Timiras. LC 70-103674. (Illus., Fr. & Ger.). 1970. 45.00x (ISBN 0-520-01656-4). U of Cal Pr.

Stereotaxic Atlas of the Human Brainstem & Cerebellar Nuclei: A Variability Study. F. Afshar et al. LC 76-5676. 1978. 156.00 (ISBN 0-89004-132-6). Raven.

Stereotaxic Brain Atlas for Macaca Nemestrina. W. D. Winters et al. LC 69-16743. (Illus.). 1969. 45.00x (ISBN 0-520-01445-6). U of Cal Pr.

Steric Fit in Quantitative Structure-Activity Relations. Ed. by A. T. Balaban et al. (Lecture Notes in Chemistry: Vol. 15). (Illus.). 178p. 1980. pap. 17.50 (ISBN 0-387-09755-4). Springer-Verlag.

Sterile. Laverne E. Bowers. 1981. 6.95 (ISBN 0-533-04732-3). Vantage.

Sterile-Insect Technique & Its Field Application. (Illus.). 138p. (Orig.). 1974. pap. 9.25 (ISBN 92-0-111374-9, IAEA). Unipub.

Sterile-Male Technique for Control of Fruit Flies. (Illus., Orig.). 1970. pap. 10.75 (ISBN 92-0-111570-9, IAEA). Unipub.

Sterile-Male Technique for Eradication or Control of Harmful Insects. 1969. pap. 8.25 (ISBN 92-0-111369-2, IAEA). Unipub.

Sterility Principle for Insect Control or Eradication. (Illus.). 542p. (Orig.). 1970. pap. 32.25 (ISBN 92-0-010171-2, IAEA). Unipub.

Sterility Principle for Insect Control 1974. (Illus.). 622p. 1975. pap. 55.25 (ISBN 92-0-010275-1, ISP 377, IAEA). Unipub.

Sterilization & Preservation of Biological Tissues by Ionizing Radiation. (Illus., Orig.). 1970. pap. 8.25 (ISBN 92-0-111370-6, IAEA). Unipub.

Stern Drive Service. 192p. 9.00 o.p. (ISBN 0-89287-186-5, B641). Western Marine Ent.

Stern Trawler. Ed. by Peter Hjul. (Illus.). 228p. 22.50 (ISBN 0-85238-025-9, FN). Unipub.

Stern-Wheelers up Columbia: A Century of Steamboating in the Oregon Country. Randall V. Mills. LC 77-7161. (Illus.). 1977. 10.95x (ISBN 0-8032-0937-1); pap. 3.75 (ISBN 0-8032-5874-7, BB 650, Bison). U of Nebr Pr.

Sterne: The Critical Heritage. Ed. by Alan B. Howes. (Critical Heritage Ser). 1974. 40.00x (ISBN 0-7100-7788-2). Routledge & Kegan.

Sterneiana, 22 vols. Incl. Vol. 1. lib. bdg. 47.00 (ISBN 0-8240-1321-2); Vol. 2. lib. bdg. 47.00 (ISBN 0-8240-1322-0); Vol. 3. lib. bdg. 47.00 (ISBN 0-8240-1323-9); Vol. 4. lib. bdg. 47.00 (ISBN 0-8240-1324-7); Vol. 5. lib. bdg. 47.00 (ISBN 0-8240-1325-5); Vols. 6 & 7. Set. lib. bdg. 94.00 (ISBN 0-8240-1326-3); lib. bdg. 47.00 ea.; Vol. 8, 2 vols. in 1. lib. bdg. 47.00 (ISBN 0-8240-1327-1); Vol. 9. lib. bdg. 47.00 (ISBN 0-8240-1328-X); Vols. 10 & 11. Set. lib. bdg. 94.00 (ISBN 0-8240-1329-8); lib. bdg. 47.00 ea.; Vol. 12. lib. bdg. 47.00 (ISBN 0-8240-1330-1); Vols. 13 & 14. Set. lib. bdg. 94.00 (ISBN 0-8240-1331-X); lib. bdg. 47.00 ea.; Vols. 15 & 16. Set. lib. bdg. 94.00 (ISBN 0-8240-1332-8); lib. bdg. 47.00 ea.; Vols. 17 & 18. Set. lib. bdg. 94.00 (ISBN 0-8240-1333-6); lib. bdg. 47.00 ea.; Vol. 19. lib. bdg. 47.00 (ISBN 0-8240-1334-4); Vol. 20. lib. bdg. 47.00 (ISBN 0-8240-1335-2); Vol. 21. lib. bdg. 47.00 (ISBN 0-8240-1336-0); Vol. 22. lib. bdg. 47.00 (ISBN 0-8240-1337-9). (Life & Times of Seven Major British Writers Ser). 1974. Garland Pub.

Sterno Guide to the Outdoors. Ken Anderson. 5.95 (ISBN 0-916752-16-X). Green Hill.

Stern's Handbook of Package Design Research. Walter Stern. 704p. 1981. 42.50 (ISBN 0-471-05901-3, Pub. by Wiley-Interscience). Wiley.

Sternwheel Paddleboats. Gerry Zeck & Pam Zeck. (Illus.). 32p. (gr. k-3). Date not set. PLB 5.95 (ISBN 0-87614-143-2). Carolrhoda Bks.

Steroid Biochemistry: Selected Topics in Biosynthesis & Metabolism, 2 vols. Ronald Hobkirk. 1979. 53.50 ea.; Vol. 1, 176p. (ISBN 0-8493-5193-6); Vol. 2, 208p. (ISBN 0-8493-5194-4). CRC Pr.

Steroid Hormone Action & Cancer. Ed. by K. M. Menon & Jerry R. Reel. LC 76-25873. (Current Topics in Molecular Endocrinology Ser.: Vol. 4). 182p. 1976. 29.50 (ISBN 0-306-34004-6, Plenum Pr). Plenum Pub.

Steroid Hormones. D. B. Gower. 120p. 1980. 35.00x (ISBN 0-85664-838-8, Pub. by Croom Helm England). State Mutual Bk.

Steroid Hormones. D. B. Gower. 1980. pap. 6.95 (ISBN 0-8151-3832-6). Year Bk Med.

Steroid Receptors & Hormone Dependent Neoplasia. James L. Wittliff & Otto Dapunt. (Illus.). 320p. 1979. 46.75 (ISBN 0-89352-043-8). Masson Pub.

Steroid Receptors & the Management of Cancer, 2 vols. E. Brad Thompson & Marc E. Lippman. 1979. Vol. 1, 272p. 64.95 (ISBN 0-8493-5477-3); Vol. 2, 176p. 44.95 (ISBN 0-8493-5478-1). CRC Pr.

Steroids & Non-Steroid Hormones. Kilshaw. 1981. text ed. price not set. Butterworth.

Steroids & Their Mechanisms of Action in Non Mammalian Vertebrates. Ed. by Giovanni Delrio. (Progress in Cancer Research & Theory Ser.). 250p. 1980. text ed. 24.50 (ISBN 0-89004-487-2). Raven.

Steroscopic Atlas of Ophthalmic Surgery of Domestic Animals. Harlan E. Jensen. (Illus.). 1973. text ed. 61.50 o.p. (ISBN 0-8016-2493-2). Mosby.

Steve Biko: Black Consciousness in South Africa. Ed. by Millard Arnold. 1978. 12.95 o.p. (ISBN 0-394-50282-5). Random.

Steve Caney's Toybook. Steven Caney. LC 75-8814. (Parents & Children Together Ser.). (Illus.). 176p. (gr. 3 up). 1972. 8.95 (ISBN 0-911104-15-1); pap. 4.95 (ISBN 0-911104-17-8). Workman Pub.

Steve Martin: A Wild & Crazy Guy. Daly. 1980. pap. 2.25 o.p. (ISBN 0-451-09060-8, Sig). NAL.

Steve: The Life & Times of Steve Donoghue. Michael Seth-Smith. (Illus.). 1974. 8.95 o.p. (ISBN 0-571-10141-0, Pub. by Faber & Faber). Merrimack Bk Serv.

Steve Train's Ordeal. Max Brand. 1980. pap. write for info. (ISBN 0-671-41489-5). PB.

Steven & the Green Turtle. Cromie. (Illus.). (gr. 2). Date not set. pap. cancelled (ISBN 0-590-30904-8, Schol Pap). Schol Bk Serv.

Steven Caney's Playbook. Steven Caney. LC 75-9816. (Parents & Children Together Ser). (Illus.). 240p. (ps-7). 1975. 9.95 (ISBN 0-911104-37-2); pap. 5.95 (ISBN 0-911104-38-0). Workman Pub.

Steve's Ice Cream Book. Stephen Herrel & Michael Schonbach. LC 79-56530. (Illus.). 224p. (Orig.). 1981. pap. 5.95 (ISBN 0-89480-080-9). Workman Pub. Postponed.

Stevie Winwood & His Friends. Stevie Winwood. 1971. pap. 2.95 o.s.i. (ISBN 0-02-061940-5, Collier). Macmillan.

Stevie Wonder. Sam Hasegawa. LC 74-147456. (Rock'n Pop Stars Ser.). (Illus.). 32p. (gr. 3-6). 1974. PLB 5.95 (ISBN 0-87191-395-X); pap. 2.95 (ISBN 0-89812-099-3). Creative Ed.

Stewardess & Pixie Burger. Julia Percival. 1975. pap. 1.75 o.p. (ISBN 0-380-01562-5, 24539). Avon.

Stewardship Myth & Methods: A Program Guide for Ministers & Lay Readers. John H. McNaughton. 128p. 1975. pap. 3.95 (ISBN 0-8164-2112-9). Crossroad NY.

Stick-Carrier. Veronica Maz. 1975. 6.00 o.p. (ISBN 0-682-48423-7). Exposition.

Stickeen: The Story of a Dog. John Muir. LC 73-10825. pap. 2.95 o.p. (ISBN 0-385-08624-5). Doubleday.

Sticklewort & Feverfew. Robert D. Sutherland. LC 79-92898. (Illus.). 360p. 1980. 16.00 (ISBN 0-936044-00-4); pap. 9.00 (ISBN 0-936044-01-2). Pikestaff Pr.

Sticks & Stones. Mary L. Dodge. (Orig.). 1979. pap. 1.75 (ISBN 0-532-23279-8). Manor Bks.

Sticks & Stones & Ice Cream Cones. Phyllis Fiarotta. LC 74-160843. (Parents & Children Together Ser.). (Illus.). 316p. (ps up). 1973. 9.95 (ISBN 0-911104-29-1); pap. 5.95 (ISBN 0-911104-30-5). Workman Pub.

Sticks & Stones Book. Elizabeth Pieper. 1976. 4.00 (ISBN 0-937540-06-4, HPP-8). Human Policy Pr.

Sticky Fingers: A Close Look at Embezzlement---America's Fastest Growing Crime. William W. McCullough. 259p. 1981. 10.95 (ISBN 0-8144-5688-X). Am Mgmt.

Stiff Upper Lip. Peter Israel. 160p. 1979. pap. 1.95 (ISBN 0-380-46086-6, 46086). Avon.

Stigma: A Social Psychological Analysis. Irwin Katz. LC 80-20765. 180p. 1981. ref. 16.50 (ISBN 0-89859-078-7). L Erlbaum Assocs.

Stigma of Poverty: A Critique of Poverty Theories & Policies. Chaim I. Waxman. LC 77-5760. 1977. text ed. 12.75 (ISBN 0-08-021800-8); pap. text ed. 4.95 (ISBN 0-08-021798-2). Pergamon.

Still & I. Melvin Kivley. 1981. 8.95 (ISBN 0-533-04820-6). Vantage.

Still Another Pelican in the Breadbox. Kenneth Patchen. Ed. by Richard Morgan. LC 80-82905. 96p. 1980. pap. 5.95 (ISBN 0-917530-14-4). Pig Iron Pr.

Still Cove Journal. Gladys Taber. Intro. by Constance T. Colby. LC 80-8220. (Illus.). 192p. 1981. 10.95 (ISBN 0-06-014227-8, HarpT). Har-Row.

Still Forms on Foxfield. Joan Slonczewski. 1980. pap. 1.95 (ISBN 0-345-28762-2). Ballantine.

Still Higher for His Highest. Oswald Chambers. 192p. 1970. 5.95. Chr Lit.

Still Hour. Austin Phelps. 1979. pap. 2.45 (ISBN 0-85151-202-X). Banner of Truth.

Still House of Time. Carl S. Criswell. 1980. 5.50 (ISBN 0-8233-0325-X). Golden Quill.

Still I Persist in Wondering. Edward Pangborn. 1978. pap. 1.75 o.s.i. (ISBN 0-440-18277-8). Dell.

Still-Life Painting from Antiquity to the Present. rev. ed. Charles Sterling. LC 78-24827. (Icon Editions Ser.). (Illus.). 320p. 1981. 25.00 (ISBN 0-06-438530-2, HarpT). Har-Row.

Still Life Painting Techniques. Adrian Ryan. 1978. 22.50 (ISBN 0-7134-0635-6). David & Charles.

Still Life with Woodpecker. Tom Robbins. 288p. (Orig.). 1980. 12.95 (ISBN 0-553-05000-1); pap. 6.95 (ISBN 0-553-01260-6). Bantam.

Still Missing. Beth Gutcheon. 252p. 1981. 10.95 (ISBN 0-399-12578-7). Putnam.

Still Missing. Beth Guthean. 336p. 1981. 11.95 (ISBN 0-399-12578-7). Putnam.

Still Moment: Essays on the Art of Eudora Welty. Ed. by John F. Desmond. LC 78-3719. 1978. 10.00 (ISBN 0-8108-1129-4). Scarecrow.

Still More Letters from Camp. Bill Adler. 1973. pap. 0.95 (ISBN 0-451-07106-9, Q7106, Sig). NAL.

Still More of the Best. Ed. by N. Gretchen Greiner. (gr. 3 up). 1979. pap. 1.25 (ISBN 0-307-21519-9, Golden Pr). Western Pub.

Still More Snappy Answers to Stupid Questions. Al Jaffee. (Mad Ser.). (Illus.). 192p. 1976. pap. 1.75 (ISBN 0-446-94411-4). Warner Bks.

Still Pictures. LaMond F. Beatty. Ed. by James E. Duane. LC 80-21448. (Instructional Media Library: Vol. 14). (Illus.). 112p. 1981. 13.95 (ISBN 0-87778-174-5). Educ Tech Pubns.

Still Point: Theme & Variations in the Writings of T. S. Eliot, Coleridge, Yeats, Henry James, Virigina Woolf, & D. H. Lawrence. Ethel F. Cornwell. 1962. 18.00 (ISBN 0-8135-0413-9). Rutgers U Pr.

Still Time to Die. Jack Belden. (China in the 20th Century Ser). xi, 322p. 1975. Repr. of 1944 ed. lib. bdg. 25.00 (ISBN 0-306-70735-7). Da Capo.

Still Water Angling. new ed. Richard Walker. (Illus.). 256p. 1975. 19.95 (ISBN 0-7153-7074-X). David & Charles.

Stillness. Nicholas Delbanco. LC 80-14395. 224p. 1980. 9.95 (ISBN 0-688-03708-9). Morrow.

Stills from a Moving Picture: Paunch No. 39. Lyle Glazier. 1974. pap. 2.00 (ISBN 0-9602478-3-1). Paunch.

Stillwater Trout. John Merwin. LC 80-492. 1980. 15.95 (ISBN 0-385-17140-4, NLB). Doubleday.

Stilt Jack. John Thompson. (House of Anansi Poetry Ser.: No. 36). 48p. (Orig.). 1978. pap. 6.95 (ISBN 0-88784-055-8, Pub. by Hse Anansi Pr Canada). U of Toronto Pr.

Stilts. S. Carl Hirsch. (Illus.). 48p. (gr. 4-6). 1972. PLB 4.75 o.p. (ISBN 0-670-67053-7). Viking Pr.

Stilus Artifex. C. Stace & P. V. Jones. LC 78-164453. 1971. text ed. 5.25x (ISBN 0-521-08143-2). Cambridge U Pr.

Stilwell & the American Experience in China, 1911-45. Barbara W. Tuchman. LC 77-135647. (Illus.). 1971. 19.95 (ISBN 0-02-620290-5). Macmillan.

Stimmt! M. E. Mountjoy. 1975. pap. text ed. 2.95x o.p. (ISBN 0-435-38605-0); tape 20.00x o.p. (ISBN 0-686-67894-X). Heinemann Ed.

Stimulating Environments for Children Who Are Visually Impaired. Carol Halliday & Ina W. Kurzhals. (Illus.). 160p. 1976. 16.25 (ISBN 0-398-03511-3). C C Thomas.

Stimulating Simulations. 2nd ed. Engel Enterprises & C. W. Engel. 112p. 1979. pap. 5.50 (ISBN 0-8104-5170-0); atari version 5.50 (ISBN 0-8104-5197-2). Hayden.

Stimulating Technological Progress. Committee for Economic Development. (CED Statement on National Policy Ser.). lib. bdg. 6.50 (ISBN 0-87186-770-2); pap. 5.00 (ISBN 0-87186-070-8). Comm Econ Dev.

Stimulation of Social Development in School. Ed. by Cornelis F. Lieshout & David J. Ingram. 234p. 1977. pap. text ed. 25.25 (ISBN 90-265-0258-3, Pub. by Swets Pub Serv Holland). Swets North Am.

Sting Man. Robert W. Greene. (Illus.). 256p. 1981. 12.95 (ISBN 0-525-20985-9). Dutton.

Sting of the Honeybee. Frank Parrish. LC 79-10518. 1979. 7.95 (ISBN 0-396-07702-1). Dodd.

Stinger. Nathan Gottlieb. 1978. pap. 1.75 o.s.i. (ISBN 0-685-54635-7, 04749-X). Jove Pubns.

Stir of Echoes. Richard Matheson. 1979. pap. 1.95 o.p. (ISBN 0-425-04107-7). Berkley Pub.

Stitch by Stitch: Needlework for Beginners. Carolyn Meyer. LC 77-117618. (gr. 4-6). 1970. 5.50 o.p. (ISBN 0-15-280350-5, HJ). HarBraceJ.

Stitchery, Step by Step. Ann Sayles. (Step by Step Craft Ser.). 1976. pap. 2.95 (ISBN 0-307-42018-3, Golden Pr). Western Pub.

Stitches & Samplers. Ondori Publishing Company. (Ondori Embroidery Ser: Vol. 2). (Illus.). 104p. 1974. pap. 5.50 (ISBN 0-87040-357-5). Japan Pubns.

Stitches of Bobbin Lace: Structure & Classification. Jules Kliot & Kaethe Kliot. 60p. 1973. spiral bdg. 4.95 o.p. (ISBN 0-916896-02-1). Lacis Pubns.

Stobi: A Guide to the Excavations. James Wiseman. (Illus.). 100p. Date not set. pap. 4.75x (ISBN 0-292-77505-9). U of Tex Pr.

Stochastic Analysis. D. G. Kendall & E. F. Harding. LC 72-8605. (Wiley Series in Probability & Mathematical Statistics: Probability & Mathematical Statistics Section). 1973. 62.95 (ISBN 0-471-46890-8, Pub. by Wiley-Interscience). Wiley.

Stochastic Approximation. M. T. Wasan. LC 69-11150. (Cambridge Tracts in Mathematics & Mathematical Physics). (Illus.). 1969. 35.50 (ISBN 0-521-07368-5). Cambridge U Pr.

Stochastic Control of Economic Models. David Kendrick. (Economic Handbook Ser.). (Illus.). 288p. 1981. text ed. 39.50 (ISBN 0-07-033962-7, C). McGraw.

Stochastic Differential Equations. R. S. Bucy et al. Ed. by H. P. McKean & J. B. Keller. LC 72-13266. (SIAM-AMS Proceedings). 1973. 22.00 (ISBN 0-8218-1325-0). Am Math.

Stochastic Differential Equations & Applications, 2 vols. Avner Friedman. (Probability & Mathematical Statistics Ser.). 1975. 75.00 set (ISBN 0-685-72447-6); Vol. 1, 1975. 40.50 (ISBN 0-12-268201-7); Vol. 2, 1976. 51.50 (ISBN 0-12-268202-5). Acad Pr.

Stochastic Differential Equations: Theory & Applications. Ludwig Arnold. LC 73-22256. 1974. 30.95 (ISBN 0-471-03359-6, Pub. by Wiley-Interscience). Wiley.

Stochastic Differential Systems; Filtering & Control: Proceedings. Ed. by B. Crigelionis. (Lecture Notes in Control & Information Sciences Ser.: Vol. 25). 362p. 1981. pap. 24.20 (ISBN 0-387-10498-4). Springer-Verlag.

Stochastic Dominance. Ed. by G. A. Whitmore & M. C. Findlay. LC 76-55711. (Illus.). 1978. 21.95x (ISBN 0-669-01310-2). Lexington Bks.

Stochastic Dynamic Properties of Linear Econometric Models. J. Wolters. (Lecture Notes in Economics & Mathematical Systems: Vol. 182). (Illus.). 154p. 1981. pap. 15.00 (ISBN 0-387-10240-X). Springer Verlag.

Stochastic Economics: With Applications of Stochastic Processes, Control & Programming. Gerhard Tintner & Jati K. Sengupta. 1972. 35.00 (ISBN 0-12-691650-0). Acad Pr.

Stochastic Geometry. Ed. by E. F. Harding & D. G. Kendall. LC 72-8603. (Ser. in Probability & Mathematical Statistics). 416p. 1974. 55.95 (ISBN 0-471-35141-5). Wiley.

Stochastic Man. Robert Silverberg. 240p. 1977. pap. 1.50 o.p. (ISBN 0-449-13570-5, GM). Fawcett.

Stochastic Processes. Rodney Coleman. (Problem Solves Ser.). (Illus.). 1974. text ed. 12.50x o.p. (ISBN 0-04-519016-X); pap. text ed. 6.50x (ISBN 0-04-519017-8). Allen Unwin.

Stochastic Processes. Joseph L. Doob. LC 52-11857. (Wiley Series in Probability & Mathematical Statistics). 1953. 36.95 (ISBN 0-471-21813-8, Pub. by Wiley-Interscience). Wiley.

Stochastic Processes. S. K. Srinivasan & K. M. Mehata. LC 77-20511. 1978. text ed. 18.95 (ISBN 0-07-096612-5, C); pap. text ed. 8.95 (ISBN 0-07-011548-6). McGraw.

Stochastic Processes & Estimation Theory with Applications. Touraj Assefi. LC 79-17872. 1979. 26.00 (ISBN 0-471-06454-8, Pub. by Wiley-Interscience). Wiley.

Stochastic Processes in Chemical Physics, Vol. 18. Ed. by I. Prigogine. 321p. 1970. 31.50 (ISBN 0-471-69923-3). Krieger.

Stochastic Processes in Control Systems. Ed. by M. T. Hughes. (Iee Control Engineering Ser.). (Illus.). 408p. 1981. write for info. (Pub. by Peregrinus London). Inst Elect Eng.

Stochastic Processes in Mathematical Physics & Engineering: Proceedings, Vol. 16. Symposia in Applied Mathematics-New York-1963. Ed. by R. Bellman. LC 64-18128. 1980. Repr. of 1964 ed. 25.60 (ISBN 0-8218-1316-1, PSAPM-16). Am Math.

Stochastic Processes: Some Problems & Solutions. Chin Long Chiang. 1981. write for info. (ISBN 0-89874-214-5). Krieger.

Stochastic Stability of Differential Equations. 2nd ed. R. Z. Has'Minskii. 360p. 1980. 50.00x (ISBN 90-286-0100-7). Sijthoff & Noordhoff.

Stochastic Storage Processes: Queues, Insurance Risk & Dams. N. U. Prabhu. (Applications of Mathematics Ser.: Vol. 15). 140p. 1981. 19.80 (ISBN 0-387-90522-7). Springer Verlag.

Stochastic Theory of Service Systems. L. Kosten. LC 72-10124. 180p. 1973. text ed. 30.00 (ISBN 0-08-016948-1). Pergamon.

Stochastic Water Resources Technology. N. T. Kottegoda. LC 79-23032. 1980. 53.95x (ISBN 0-470-98975-0). Halsted Pr.

Stock Cars. Sylvia Wilkinson. (World of Racing Ser.). (Illus.). 48p. (gr. 4 up). 1981. PLB 9.25 (ISBN 0-516-04715-9). Childrens.

Stock Control in Manufacturing Industries. 2nd ed. Adin B. Thomas. 240p. 1980. text ed. 29.50 (ISBN 0-566-02140-4, Pub. by Gower Pub Co England). Renouf.

Stock Exchange. E. Victor Morgan & W. A. Thomas. 1970. 39.95 o.p. (ISBN 0-236-30952-8, Pub. by Paul Elek). Merrimack Bk Serv.

Stock Market. 3rd ed. G. L. Leffler & L. C. Farwell. (Illus.). 1963. 18.95 (ISBN 0-8260-5360-2). Ronald Pr.

Stock Market. 3rd ed. G. L. Leffler & L. C. Farwell. 654p. 1963. 18.95 (ISBN 0-471-06571-4). Wiley.

Stock Market & Me: An Independent Approach to Wall Street. Albert A. Spohler. LC 74-78226. 1974. 7.95 (ISBN 0-686-10560-5). A A Spohler.

Stock Market & Wall Street: The Essential Knowledge Which Everybody, but Absolutely Everybody Ought to Have of the Stock Market & Wall Street. C. M. Flumiani. (Essential Knowledge Ser. Books.). (Illus.). 1978. plastic spiral bdg. 28.75 (ISBN 0-89266-115-1). Am Classical Coll Pr.

Stock Market Behavior: The Technical Approach to Understanding Wall Street. Harvey A. Krow. LC 69-18405. Orig. Title: Technical Analysis in the Stock Market. 1969. 15.00 o.p. (ISBN 0-394-44809-X). Random.

Stock Market Charts: The Essential Knowledge of Stock Market Charts, How to Interpret & Apply Them Which Everyone, but Absolutely Everybody Who Is Interested in Speculation Ought to Know. C. M. Flumiani. (Essential Knowldge Ser. Books). (Illus.). 1978. plastic spiral dg. 28.95 (ISBN 0-89266-119-4). Am Classical Coll Pr.

Stock Market Crash, 1929. Ray E. Hiebert & Roslyn Hiebert. LC 73-115411. (Focus Bks). (Illus.). (gr. 7 up). 1970. PLB 4.47 o.p. (ISBN 0-531-01015-5); pap. 1.25 o.p. (ISBN 0-531-02330-3). Watts.

Stock Market Manual for Teenagers. C. M. Flumiani. LC 72-89684. (Illus.). 70p. (YA) 1973. 14.75 (ISBN 0-913314-14-5). Am Classical Coll Pr.

Stock Market Metaphysical Significance of Elliott's Principles & Theories. Augustus Lennox. (Illus.). 1978. deluxe bdg. 79.75 (ISBN 0-918968-07-0). Inst Econ Finan.

Stock Market Strategy for Consistent Profits. Raymond R. Righetti. LC 79-23006. 176p. 1981. 14.95 (ISBN 0-88229-574-8). Nelson-Hall.

Stock Market: Theories & Evidence. James H. Lorie & Mary T. Hamilton. 1973. pap. text ed. 10.95 (ISBN 0-256-01450-7). Irwin.

Stock Photographs: The Fort Worth Fat Stock Show & Rodeo. Garry Winogrand. (Illus.). 128p. Date not set. 19.95 (ISBN 0-292-72433-0). U of Tex Pr.

Stockhausen: Life & Work. Karl H. Worner. Ed. & tr. by Bill Hopkins. LC 76-174460. (Illus.). 1973. 17.95x (ISBN 0-520-02143-6); pap. 3.95 (ISBN 0-520-03272-1). U of Cal Pr.

Stocking up. rev. ed. Carol H. Stoner. LC 77-3942. 1977. 13.95 (ISBN 0-87857-167-1); 13.95 (ISBN 0-87857-221-X); deluxe ed. 15.95 (ISBN 0-686-67634-3). Rodale Pr Inc.

Stockman's Handbook. 5th ed. M. E. Ensminger. LC 76-58206. 1978. 29.95 (ISBN 0-8134-1943-3, 1943); text ed. 22.95x (ISBN 0-686-52293-1). Interstate.

Stocks & Shares Simplified. B. J. Millard. 1980. write for info. (ISBN 0-85501-083-5). Heyden.

Stoic Philosophy. J. M. Rist. LC 79-85736. 1969. 38.00 (ISBN 0-521-07620-X); pap. 9.95 (ISBN 0-521-29201-8). Cambridge U Pr.

Stoic Philosophy of Seneca: Essays & Letters. Seneca. Ed. by Moses Hadas & Moses Hadas. 1968. pap. 4.95 (ISBN 0-393-00459-7, Norton Lib). Norton.

Stoichiometry. Leonard K. Nash. LC 66-21269. (Chemistry Ser). (Orig.). 1966. pap. 6.95 (ISBN 0-201-05234-2). A-W.

Stoicorum Veterum Fragmenta, 4 vols. J. Von Arnim. (Classical Studies Ser.). (Lat. & Gr.). Repr. of 1903 ed. Set. lib. bdg. 96.50x (ISBN 0-89197-950-6); Vol. 1. lib. bdg. 26.00x (ISBN 0-697-00024-9); Vol. 2. lib. bdg. 28.50x (ISBN 0-697-00025-7); Vol. 3. lib. bdg. 28.50x (ISBN 0-697-00026-5); Vol. 4. lib. bdg. 24.00x (ISBN 0-697-00027-3). Irvington.

Stoics. Ed. by John M. Rist. (Major Thinkers Ser.: Vol. 1). 1978. 20.00x o.p. (ISBN 0-520-03135-0); pap. 5.95x (ISBN 0-520-03675-1). U of Cal Pr.

Stolbtsy. N. Zabolotskii. (Rus.). 1974. pap. 3.50 (ISBN 0-88233-191-4). Ardis Pubs.

Stolen Boy: A Story Founded on Facts, Repr. Of 1828 Ed. Barbara H. Hofland. Bd. with Seizure of the Ship Industry, by a Conspiracy, & the Consequent Sufferings of Capt. James Fox & His Companions: Their Captivity Among the Esquimaux Indians in North America; & the Miraculous Escape of the Captain. Repr. of 1830 ed; St. Maur: Or, the Captive Babes Recovered, Pub. by Emory & Waugh for the Tract Society of the Methodist Epescopal Church, New York. Repr. of 1830 ed. LC 75-7066. (Indian Captivities Ser.: Vol. 44). 1976. lib. bdg. 44.00 (ISBN 0-8240-1668-8). Garland Pub.

Stolen Faces. Michael Bishop. LC 76-26262. 1977. 7.95 o.s.i. (ISBN 0-06-010362-0, HarpT). Har-Row.

Stolen Goddess. Richard Purtill. (Science Fiction Ser.). 1980. pap. 1.75 (ISBN 0-87997-584-9, UE1584). DAW Bks.

Stolen House. Jack Remick. LC 79-91912. (Fiction Ser.). 168p. (Orig.). 1980. pap. 4.95 (ISBN 0-917530-13-6). Pig Iron Pr.

Stolen Images. Ulli Beier. 64p. 1976. pap. 2.25x (ISBN 0-521-20901-3). Cambridge U Pr.

Stolen Jew. Jay Neugeboren. 336p. 1981. 14.95 (ISBN 0-03-056223-6). HR&W.

Stolen Telesm. Caroline Baxter. LC 76-17307. (gr. 5-12). 1976. 7.95 o.p. (ISBN 0-397-31686-0). Lippincott.

Stolen Years. Sara Zyskind. (Adult & Young Adult Bks.). 192p. (gr. 4 up). 1981. PLB 9.95 (ISBN 0-8225-0766-8). Lerner Pubns.

Stoma Care. Brigid Breckman. 230p. 1980. 40.00x (Pub. by Beaconsfield England). State Mutual Bk.

Stomach. Ed. by L. Van der Reis. (Frontiers of Gastrointestinal Research: Vol. 6). (Illus.). xii, 188p. 1980. 55.25 (ISBN 3-8055-3071-4). S Karger.

Stomach & Anaemia. L. J. Witts. 1966. text ed. 4.25x (ISBN 0-485-26317-3, Athlone Pr). Humanities.

Stomping Ground. Dennis Hall. 1981. pap. 2.95 (ISBN 0-440-17615-8). Dell.

Stone Age Hunters of the Kafue: The Gwisho A Site. Creighton Gabel. LC 65-22281. (Pub. by Boston U Pr). 1965. 9.50x (ISBN 0-8419-8707-6, Africana). Holmes & Meier.

Stone Age of Mount Carmel, 2 vols. Incl. Vol. 1. Excavations at the Wady el-Mughana. D. A. Garrod & D. M. Bate (ISBN 0-404-16651-2); Vol. 2. Fossil Human Remains from the Levalloiso-Mousterian. T. D. McCown & Arthur Keith (ISBN 0-404-16652-0). LC 77-86432. 1980. Set. 125.00 (ISBN 0-404-16650-4). AMS Pr.

Stone Age Races of Northwest Africa. L. Cabot Briggs. LC 55-1179. (American School of Prehistoric Research Bulletin Ser.: No. 18). (Orig.). 1955. pap. 10.00 (ISBN 0-87365-519-2). Peabody Harvard.

Stone & Elixir. LC 58-5810. 1970. 5.00 (ISBN 0-935490-06-X). Euclid Pub.

Stone Axe Studies: Archaeological, Petrological, Experimental, & Ethnographic. Ed. by T. H. McKClough & W. A. Cummins. 109p. 1980. pap. 35.00x (ISBN 0-900312-63-7, Pub. by Coun Brit Arch England). Intl Schol Bk Serv.

Stone-Campbell Movement. Leroy Garrett. LC 80-65965. 1981. 13.50 (ISBN 0-89900-059-2). College Pr Pub. Postponed.

Stone Doll of Sister Brute. Russell Hoban. LC 68-12089. (ps-3). 1968. 5.95 (ISBN 0-02-744080-X). Macmillan.

Stone Doll of Sister Brute. Russell Hoban. (Snuggle & Read Ser.). (Illus.). 32p. (ps-2). 1980. pap. 1.95 (ISBN 0-380-51169-X, 51169, Camelot). Avon.

Stone Door. Leonora Carrington. LC 77-76629. 1977. 7.95 o.p. (ISBN 0-312-76210-0). St Martin.

Stone Fox. John R. Gardiner. LC 79-7895. (Illus.). 96p. (gr. 2-6). 1980. 7.95 (ISBN 0-690-03983-2, TYC-J); PLB 7.89 (ISBN 0-690-03984-0). T Y Crowell.

Stone God Awakens. Philip J. Farmer. 192p. 1975. pap. 2.25 (ISBN 0-441-78654-5). Ace Bks.

Stone Grinding & Polishing. David F. Olson. LC 73-83453. (Little Craft Book Ser.). (Illus.). 48p. (gr. 7 up). 1973. 5.95 (ISBN 0-8069-5286-5); PLB 6.69 (ISBN 0-8069-5287-3). Sterling.

Stone Harp. John Haines. LC 73-142728. (Wesleyan Poetry Program: Vol. 56). 1971. pap. 4.95 (ISBN 0-8195-1056-4, Pub. by Wesleyan U Pr). Columbia U Pr.

Stone House Murder & Other New England Tales. Clarence E. Hale. LC 77-88189. (Illus.). 1977. casebound 7.95 (ISBN 0-87106-090-6). Globe Pequot.

Stone Idol. Franklin W. Dixon. Ed. by Wendy Barish. (Hardy Boys Ser.). (Illus.). 192p. (gr. 3-5). 1981. price not set (ISBN 0-671-42289-8); pap. price not set (ISBN 0-671-42290-1). Wanderer Bks.

Stone in the Hourglass. Donald Windham. 1981. ltd. ed. 15.00 (ISBN 0-917366-05-0). S Campbell.

Stone Lantern Essays: Services for the Collapse of the Living Room Carpet. Marlene Kamei. LC 79-91969. (Illus.). 75p. (Orig.). 1980. pap. 4.95 (ISBN 0-935684-02-6). Plumbers Ink.

Stone Leopard. Colin Forbes. 288p. 1977. pap. 1.95 o.p. (ISBN 0-449-23129-1, Crest). Fawcett.

Stone Mad: A Sculptor's Life & Craft. Seamus Murphy. (Illus.). 1976. pap. 7.50 (ISBN 0-7100-8542-7). Routledge & Kegan.

Stone Maiden. Velda Johnston. LC 80-16109. 224p. 1980. 8.95 (ISBN 0-396-07882-6). Dodd.

Stone Masonry. Ken Kern et al. (Illus.). 1977. pap. 10.95 (ISBN 0-684-15288-6, SL747, ScribT). Scribner.

Stone of Truth & Other Irish Folk Tales. Ed. & tr. by Douglas Hyde. 126p. 1979. 10.00x (ISBN 0-8476-6232-2). Rowman.

Stone Soup. Marcia Brown. (Illus.). (gr. k-3). 1947. reinforced bdg. 8.95 (ISBN 0-684-92296-7, ScribJ); pap. 2.95 (ISBN 0-684-16217-2, SBF1, ScribJ). Scribner.

Stonecutter: A Japanese Folk Tale. Gerald McDermott. (Illus.). 32p. (gr. k-3). 1975. PLB 9.95 (ISBN 0-670-67074-X). Viking Pr.

Stoned Images. Hans Hoefer. 1979. pap. 7.95 o.p. (ISBN 0-525-47510-9). Dutton.

Stoneflies. Carl Richards et al. (Illus.). 192p. 1980. 19.95 (ISBN 0-87691-327-3). Winchester Pr.

Stonehenge. Theo Bergstrom. (Illus.). 1977. pap. 4.95 (ISBN 0-8467-0323-8, Pub. by Two Continents). Hippocrene Bks.

Stonehenge Decoded. Gerald S. Hawkins & John B. White. LC 65-19933. 1965. 7.95 o.p. (ISBN 0-385-04127-6). Doubleday.

Stonehenge: The Indo-European Heritage. Leon E. Stover & Bruce Kraig. LC 77-25255. 1978. 20.95 (ISBN 0-88229-482-2); pap. 10.95 (ISBN 0-88229-612-4). Nelson-Hall.

Stones. Daisy Aldan. 4.95 (ISBN 0-913152-14-5). Green Hill.

Stones. Marie Clay. (Orig.). (gr. 1-2). 1980. pap. text ed. 2.50x (ISBN 0-686-63229-X, 00556). Heinemann Ed.

Stones. Janet Hickman. LC 76-11037. (gr. 3-6). 1976. 8.95 (ISBN 0-02-743760-4, 74376). Macmillan.

Stones of Fire. Isobel Kuhn. 1951. pap. 2.95 (ISBN 0-85363-049-6). OMF Bks.

Stones of Green Knowe. L. M. Boston. LC 75-44143. (Illus.). (gr. 5-9). 1976. 7.95 (ISBN 0-689-50058-0, McElderry Bk). Atheneum.

Stones of Venice, 3 vols. John Ruskin. Ed. by Sydney J. Freedberg. Incl. Vol. I. Foundation; Vol. II. Sea-Stories; Vol. III. Fall. LC 77-25765. (Connoisseurship, Criticism & Art History Ser.: Vol. 20). 1979. Set. lib. bdg. 100.00 (ISBN 0-8240-3278-0). Garland Pub.

Stones River: Bloody Winter in Tennessee. James L. McDonough. LC 80-11580. 256p. 1980. 14.50 (ISBN 0-87049-301-9). U of Tenn Pr.

Stones: Their Collection, Identification, & Uses. R. V. Dietrich. LC 79-24760. (Geology Ser.). (Illus.). 1980. text ed. 13.95x (ISBN 0-7167-1138-9); pap. text ed. 7.95x (ISBN 0-7167-1139-7). W H Freeman.

Stonewall Jackson. Harrison et al. 35p. (gr. 1-9). 1981. 2.95 (ISBN 0-86575-191-9). Dormac.

Stonewall Jackson: The Good Soldier. Allen Tate. 1957. pap. 2.25 o.p. (ISBN 0-472-06009-0, 9, AA). U of Mich Pr.

Stonewall Ladies. Elizabeth O. Verner. 1963. 6.00 (ISBN 0-937684-07-4). Tradd St Pr.

Stonington Chronology: 1649-1976. Ed. by Willaim Haynes. LC 75-25299. (Illus.). 168p. 1976. casebound 12.50 (ISBN 0-87106-059-0). Globe Pequot.

Stop & Look! Illusions. Robyn Supraner. LC 80-23799. (Illus.). 48p. (gr. 2-5). 1980. PLB 6.92 (ISBN 0-89375-434-X); pap. 1.75 (ISBN 0-89375-435-8). Troll Assocs.

Stop Being Afraid. David Seabury. 1965. pap. 3.95 (ISBN 0-911336-19-2). Sci of Mind.

Stop Crying at Your Own Movies: How to Solve Personal Problems & Open Your Life to Its Full Potential Using the Vector Method. George Burtt. LC 75-4770. 206p. 1975. 12.95 (ISBN 0-911012-83-4). Nelson-Hall.

Stop Dying & Live Forever. Stanley Spears. 1972. pap. 2.95 o.p. (ISBN 0-87516-122-7). De Vorss.

Stop Forgetting. Bruno Furst. Rev. by Lotte Furst & Gerrit Storm. LC 79-7401. (Illus.). 1979. pap. 6.95 (ISBN 0-385-15401-1). Doubleday.

Stop! Go! Word Bird. Jane B. Moncure. LC 80-16273. (Early Bird Reader Ser.). (Illus.). 32p. (ps-2). 1980. PLB 5.50 (ISBN 0-89565-160-2). Childs World.

Stop Procrastinating--Do It! James R. Sherman. LC 80-82893. (Orig.). 1981. pap. 1.75 (ISBN 0-935538-01-1). Pathway Bks.

Stop School Failure. Louise B. Ames et al. LC 79-181603. (Illus.). 256p. 1972. 8.95 o.p. (ISBN 0-06-010114-8, HarpT). Har-Row.

Stop Smoking Book for Teens. Curtis W. Casewit. LC 79-27933. (Illus.). 160p. (gr. 9-12). 1980. PLB 8.29 (ISBN 0-671-33015-2). Messner.

Stop Smoking Diet. Jane Ogle. Ed. by George C. De Kay. 192p. 1981. 8.95 (ISBN 0-87131-337-5). M Evans.

Stop Smoking, Lose Weight. Neil Solomon. 320p. 1981. 11.95 (ISBN 0-399-12600-7). Putnam.

Stop Smoking Soon. The G-Jo Institute. 1980. pap. 4.50 (ISBN 0-916878-09-0). Falkynor Bks.

Stop Talking to Your Plants & Listen. Elvin McDonald. LC 77-9024. (Funk & W Bk.). (Illus.). 1977. 8.95 o.s.i. (ISBN 0-308-10288-6, TYC-T); pap. 4.95 o.s.i. (ISBN 0-308-10333-5, TYC-T). T Y Crowell.

Stop That Rabbit. Sharon Peters. (Illus.). 32p. (gr. k-2). 1980. PLB 2.96 (ISBN 0-89375-388-2); pap. 0.95 (ISBN 0-89375-288-6). Troll Assocs.

Stop the Presses! Alex Barris. LC 74-30718. 300p. 1976. 17.50 o.p. (ISBN 0-498-01603-X). A S Barnes.

Stop Trying to Cheer Me up! Frank Modell. LC 78-17557. 1978. 8.95 (ISBN 0-396-07627-0). Dodd.

Stop Trying to Stop Smoking, & Do It This Time: Secrets of a Mad Smoker. Lee Lamore. LC 80-69207. 112p. pap. 3.95 (ISBN 0-938318-00-4). Britton Pub.

Stop! You're Driving Me Crazy. George R. Bach & Ronald M. Deutsch. 1981. pap. 2.95 (ISBN 0-425-04738-5). Berkley Pub.

Stopford Brooke. Fred L. Standley. (English Authors Ser.: No. 135). lib. bdg. 10.95 (ISBN 0-8057-1060-4). Twayne.

Stopping by Woods on a Snowy Evening. Robert Frost. LC 78-8134. (Illus.). 1978. PLB 8.95 (ISBN 0-525-40115-6). Dutton.

Stopwatch. Victor Mayer. 5.75 o.p. (ISBN 0-8062-1201-2). Carlton.

Storage. 3rd ed. Sunset Editors. LC 74-20021. (Illus.). 96p. 1975. pap. 3.95 (ISBN 0-376-01554-3, Sunset Bks.). Sunset-Lane.

Storage & Handling of Petroleum Liquids. J. R. Hughes. 332p. 1978. 85.00x (ISBN 0-85264-251-2, Pub. by Griffin England). State Mutual Bk.

Storage Batteries. 4th ed. George W. Vinal. LC 54-12826. 1955. 33.00 (ISBN 0-471-90816-9, Pub. by Wiley-Interscience). Wiley.

Storage Battery Manufacturing Manual. 2nd ed. Nels E. Hehner. 1976. 30.00 (ISBN 0-685-65141-X). IBMA Pubns.

Storage, Handling & Movement of Fuel & Related Components at Nuclear Power Plants. (Technical Reports Ser.: No. 189). 1979. pap. 7.50 (ISBN 92-0-125279-X, IDC189, IAEA). Unipub.

Storage Tanks for Liquid Radioactive Wastes: Their Design & Use. (Technical Reports: No. 135). (Illus.). 55p. (Orig.). 1972. pap. 4.50 (ISBN 92-0-125072-X, IAEA). Unipub.

Store. Knight Isaacson. LC 73-93927. 256p. 1974. 6.95 o.s.i. (ISBN 0-8027-0454-9). Walker & Co.

Store. Michael Pearson. 1981. 16.95 (ISBN 0-671-25114-7). S&S.

Store Location Strategy Cases. William Applebaum. (Retailing Ser). 1968. text ed. 19.95 (ISBN 0-201-00290-6); instructor's manual 2.50 (ISBN 0-201-00291-4). A-W.

Store Talk: An Introduction to Retail Merchandising. Edwin C. Greif. LC 78-60034. (gr. 9 up). 1979. pap. 8.60 (ISBN 0-8224-6530-2); pap. 2.40 tchrs'. manual, 1981 (ISBN 0-8224-6531-0). Pitman Learning.

Store up the Anger. Wessel Ebersohn. LC 80-2076. 288p. 1981. 12.95 (ISBN 0-385-17406-3). Doubleday.

Store Windows That Sell, 1980-81. Ed. by Martin Pegler. (Illus.). 178p. 1980. 34.95 (ISBN 0-934590-04-4). Retail Report.

Stored Data Description & Data Translation: A Model & Language. R. W. Taylor. 1977. pap. text ed. 27.50 (ISBN 0-08-021624-2). Pergamon.

Stores. Harry Bornstein. (Signed English Ser.). 56p. 1974. pap. 4.00 (ISBN 0-913580-33-3). Gallaudet Coll.

Stores. Alvin Schwartz. LC 76-47451. (Illus.). (gr. 3 up). 1977. 8.95 (ISBN 0-02-781310-X, 78131). Macmillan.

Stores of the World Directory. 10th, enl. ed. 1978-79. 85.00 o.p. (ISBN 0-7079-6910-7). Heinman.

Stories. Ram Kumar. 1976. lib. bdg. 9.00 (ISBN 0-89253-085-5); flexible bdg. 6.00 (ISBN 0-89253-267-X). Ind-US Inc.

Stories. Leslie De Noronha. 8.00 (ISBN 0-89253-630-6); flexible cloth 4.80 (ISBN 0-89253-631-4). Ind-US Inc.

Stories About Birds & Bird Watchers: From Bird Watcher's Digest. Ed. by Mary B. Bowers. LC 80-7925. (Illus.). 192p. 1981. 12.95 (ISBN 0-689-11093-6). Atheneum.

Stories About Children of the Bible. Hilda L. Rostron. (Ladybird Ser). (Illus.). (gr. k-1). 1962. bds. 1.49 (ISBN 0-87508-860-0). Chr Lit.

Stories About Jesus the Friend. Hilda L. Rostron. (Ladybird Ser). (Illus.). (gr. k-1). 1961. bds. 1.49 (ISBN 0-87508-862-7). Chr Lit.

Stories About Jesus the Helper. Hilda L. Rostron. (Ladybird Ser). (Illus.). (gr. k-1). 1961. bds. 1.49 (ISBN 0-87508-864-3). Chr Lit.

Stories & Fables of Ambrose Bierce. Ambrose Bierce. Ed. by Edward Wagenknecht. LC 77-20146. (Illus.). 1977. 14.95 (ISBN 0-916144-19-4); pap. 7.95 (ISBN 0-916144-20-8). Stemmer Hse.

Stories & Fables: The Reservoir (With Snowman Snowman) Janet Frame. 2 vols. boxed 7.00 o.s.i. (ISBN 0-8076-0233-7). Braziller.

Stories & Lore of the Zodiac. M. A. Jagendorf. LC 76-39724. 1978. 6.95 (ISBN 0-8149-0752-0). Vanguard.

Stories & Sketches. Saros Cowasjee. (Writers Workshop Greenbird Ser.). 85p. 1975. 11.00 (ISBN 0-88253-646-X); pap. text ed. 6.00 (ISBN 0-88253-645-1). Ind-US Inc.

Stories & Texts for Nothing. Samuel Beckett. 1967. pap. 4.95 (ISBN 0-394-17268-X, E466, Ever). Grove.

Stories Behind Everyday Things. Reader's Digest. 19.95 (ISBN 0-89577-068-7). Readers Digest Pr.

Stories Created by Life. Nonna Osipova. (Illus.). 60p. (Rus.). pap. cancelled (ISBN 0-935500-26-X, TX 198-101). Am Samizdat.

Stories for Children. Jacqueline Mehrabi. (Illus.). (gr. 1-5). 1970. pap. 2.00 o.p. (ISBN 0-900125-05-5, 7-52-65). Baha'i.

Stories for Christmas. Alison Uttley. Ed. by Kathleen Lines. (Illus.). 1977. 10.95 (ISBN 0-571-11074-6, Pub. by Faber & Faber). Merrimack Bk Serv.

Stories for Every Holiday. Carolyn S. Bailey. LC 73-20149. 277p. 1974. Repr. of 1918 ed. 26.00 (ISBN 0-8103-3957-9). Gale.

Stories for Five Year-Olds & Other Young Readers. Sara Corrin et al. Ed. by Stephen Corrin. (Illus.). (ps-5). 1973. 8.95 (ISBN 0-571-10162-3, Pub. by Faber & Faber). Merrimack Bk Serv.

Stories for Ramu. Deepak Dubey. 10.00 (ISBN 0-89253-794-9); flexible cloth 5.00 (ISBN 0-89253-795-7). Ind-US Inc.

Stories for Tens & Over. Sara Corrin et al. Ed. by Stephen Corrin. (Illus.). 1976. 9.95 (ISBN 0-571-10873-3, Pub. by Faber & Faber). Merrimack Bk Serv.

Stories for Today, 6 pk. single titles. Carol Bergman. Incl. Paul (ISBN 0-435-11133-7); Donnovan (ISBN 0-435-11134-5); Naomi (ISBN 0-435-11135-3); Junes Work (ISBN 0-435-11136-1); Rescue at Night (ISBN 0-435-11137-X); Big Game (ISBN 0-435-11138-8). (Second Series). 1972. pap. text ed. 9.95 ea. mixed set 1 copy o.p. (ISBN 0-435-11149-3). Heinemann Ed.

Stories for Today: First Series. Peter Abbs. Incl. Ron's Fight (ISBN 0-435-11140-X); Ginger & Sharon (ISBN 0-435-11141-8); Frank's Fire (ISBN 0-435-11142-6); Linda's Journey (ISBN 0-435-11143-4); Joe & Carol (ISBN 0-435-11144-2); Diane's Sister (ISBN 0-435-11145-0). 1972. pap. text ed. 9.75 mixed set-1 copy of ea. o.p. (ISBN 0-435-11150-7); Six-pack Of Single Titles. pap. text ed. 9.95x ea. o.p.; tchrs notes 0.75x o.p. (ISBN 0-435-11139-6). Heinemann Ed.

Stories for Under-Fives. Ed. by Sara Corrin et al. (Illus.). (ps-5). 1974. 9.95 (ISBN 0-571-10371-5, Pub. by Faber & Faber). Merrimack Bk Serv.

Stories from a Snowy Meadow. Carla Stevens. LC 76-3542. 48p. (gr. 2-5). 1976. 6.95 (ISBN 0-395-28883-5, Clarion). HM.

Stories from Around the World. Ed. by Theodore W. Hipple. (Literature Ser.). (gr. 7-12). 1979. pap. text ed. 5.88 (ISBN 0-205-06418-3, 4964187); tchrs'. guide 2.96 (ISBN 0-205-06419-1, 4964195). Allyn.

Stories from El Barrio. Piri Thomas. (YA) (gr. 9 up). 1980. pap. 1.75 (ISBN 0-380-50013-2, 50013). Avon.

Stories from Grandma's Attic. Arleta Richardson. (gr. 6-12). 1980. 5.95 (ISBN 0-89191-310-6). Cook.

Stories from Old-Fashioned Children's Books, Brought Together & Introduced to the Reader. Andrew W. Tuer. LC 68-31438. 1968. Repr. of 1899 ed. 18.00 (ISBN 0-8103-3489-5). Gale.

Stories from The Dawn-Breakers. Zoe Meyer. (Illus.). (gr. 3-5). 1955. 6.00 (ISBN 0-87743-035-7, 7-52-58). Baha'i.

Stories from the Delight of Hearts: The Memoirs of Haji Mirza Haydar-'Ali. A. Q. Faizi. LC 79-91219. (Illus.). 176p. 1980. 8.95 (ISBN 0-933770-11-1). Kalimat.

Stories from the Four Corners. Ralph Cutlip. (gr. 7-12). 1975. pap. text ed. 4.58 (ISBN 0-87720-354-7). AMSCO Sch.

Stories from the Old Ones: As Told to Walter A. Denny. Walter A. Denny. (Illus., Orig.). (gr. 4 up). 1979. pap. 4.95 (ISBN 0-686-27639-6). Rising Wolf.

Stories from the Olympics. Frank Gault & Clare Gault. LC 75-42823. (Illus.). 96p. 1976. 5.95 (ISBN 0-8027-6255-7); PLB 5.85 o.s.i. (ISBN 0-8027-6256-5). Walker & Co.

Stories from Ugidali: Cherokee Story Teller. Piper. 1981. pap. 1.95 (ISBN 0-89992-078-0). MT Coun Indian.

Stories in Verse. rev. ed. Ed. by Max T. Hohn. LC 61-3198. 1961. pap. 5.50 o.p. (ISBN 0-672-73234-3). Odyssey Pr.

Stories Julian Tells. Ann Cameron. LC 80-18023. (Illus.). 96p. (gr. k-5). 1981. 7.95 (ISBN 0-394-84301-0); PLB 7.99 (ISBN 0-394-94301-5). Pantheon.

Stories of a Salesman. Murli D. Melwani. 1976. lib. bdg. 8.00 (ISBN 0-89253-084-7); flexible bdg. 6.75 (ISBN 0-89253-268-8). Ind-US Inc.

Stories of Buddha's Births: A Jataka Reader. C. S. Jossan. LC 76-30762. (Foreign & Comparative Studies-South Asian Special Publications Ser.: No. 1). 1976. pap. text ed. 3.50x (ISBN 0-915984-77-6). Syracuse U Foreign Comp.

Stories of Charlemagne. Jennifer Westwood. LC 74-12435. (gr. 6 up). 1976. 9.95 (ISBN 0-87599-213-7). S G Phillips.

Stories of Elizabeth Spencer. Elizabeth Spencer & Eudora Welty. LC 79-6601. 456p. 1981. 14.95 (ISBN 0-385-15697-9). Doubleday.

Stories of Eric Linklater. Eric Linklater. LC 76-85336. 1969. 6.50 o.p. (ISBN 0-8180-0602-1). Horizon.

Stories of F. Scott Fitzgerald. F. Scott Fitzgerald. 1951. pap. 5.95 o.p. (ISBN 0-684-71737-9, SL135, ScribT); lib. rep. ed. 17.50x o.p. (ISBN 0-684-15366-1). Scribner.

Stories of Faith. John Shea. 1980. 10.95 (ISBN 0-88347-112-4). Thomas More.

Stories of Frank O'Connor. Frank O'Connor. (YA) 1952. 10.00 o.p. (ISBN 0-394-44732-8). Knopf.

Stories of Georgia. Joel C. Harris. LC 73-174943. 1975. Repr. of 1896 ed. 18.00 (ISBN 0-8103-4082-8). Gale.

Stories of Here & Now. Dolores Seidman. (gr. 9 up). 1978. pap. text ed. 4.33 (ISBN 0-87720-309-1). AMSCO Sch.

Stories of Hoaxes. Irving Adler. 1962. pap. 0.95 o.s.i. (ISBN 0-02-016070-4, Collier). Macmillan.

Stories of Home Folks. Mabel Hale. 160p. pap. 1.50. Faith Pub Hse.

Stories of King Arthur. Ed. by Blanche Winder. (Classics Ser). (gr. 4 up). pap. 1.50 (ISBN 0-8049-0167-8, CL-167). Airmont.

Stories of Light & Delight. Manoj Das. (Nehru Library for Children). (Illus.). (gr. 2-8). 1979. pap. 1.50 o.p. (ISBN 0-89744-181-8). Auromere.

Stories of Our American Patriotic Songs. John H. Lyons. LC 42-24375. (Illus.). (gr. 5-12). 7.95 (ISBN 0-8149-0354-1). Vanguard.

Stories of Our Favorite Hymns. Christopher Idle. (Illus.). 80p. 1980. 10.95 (ISBN 0-8028-3535-X). Eerdmans.

Stories of Sicily. Ed. by Alfred Alexander. 1979. 9.95 o.p. (ISBN 0-236-31079-8, Pub. by Paul Elek). Merrimack Bk Serv.

Stories of the Gods & Heroes. Sally Benson. (gr. 4-6). 1979. pap. 1.75 (ISBN 0-440-98291-X, LFL). Dell.

Stories of the Hindus: An Introduction Through Texts & Interpretations. James A. Kirk. LC 72-77651. 224p. 1972. 7.95 o.s.i. (ISBN 0-02-563230-2); pap. 2.95 o.s.i. (ISBN 0-02-086400-0). Macmillan.

Stories of the Irish Peasantry. Anna Maria Hall. Ed. by Robert L. Wolff. (Ireland Nineteenth Century Fiction, Ser. Two: Vol. 49). 1979. lib. bdg. 46.00 (ISBN 0-8240-3498-8). Garland Pub.

Stories of the Months & Days. Reginald C. Couzens. LC 70-124662. (Illus.). 1971. Repr. of 1923 ed. 22.00 (ISBN 0-8103-3013-X). Gale.

Stories of the Old Duck Hunters & Other Drivel. Gordon MacQuarrie. Ed. by Zack Taylor. LC 67-12929. 1967. 6.95 o.p. (ISBN 0-8117-1682-1). Stackpole.

Stories of the Railway. Canon V. Whitechurch. (Illus.). 1977. cased 12.00 (ISBN 0-7100-8635-0). Routledge & Kegan.

Stories of the States: A Reference Guide to the Fifty States & the U. S. Territories. Frank Ross, Jr. LC 68-24585. (Illus.). (gr. 5 up). 1969. 12.95 (ISBN 0-690-77849-X, TYC-J). T Y Crowell.

Stories of the Trees. S. L. Dyson. LC 78-175735. (Illus.). 272p. 1974. Repr. of 1890 ed. 18.00 (ISBN 0-8103-3033-4). Gale.

Stories of the World's Holidays. Grace Humphrey. LC 74-3023. 1974. Repr. of 1923 ed. 22.00 (ISBN 0-8103-3660-X). Gale.

Stories That Live. Ralph Cutlip. (gr. 7-12). 1973. 4.58 (ISBN 0-87720-352-0). AMSCO Sch.

Stories That Must Not Die, Vol. 1. Juan Sauvageau. LC 75-36692. (Illus., Eng. & Span.). 1975. pap. 3.00 (ISBN 0-916378-00-4). PSI Res.

Stories That Must Not Die, Vol. 2. Juan Sauvageau. (Illus., Eng. & Span.). 1976. pap. 3.00 (ISBN 0-916378-01-2). PSI Res.

Stories That Must Not Die, Vol. 3. Juan Sauvageau. (Illus.). 1976. pap. 3.00 (ISBN 0-916378-02-0). PSI Res.

Stories That Must Not Die, Vol. 4. Juan Sauvageau. (Illus.). (gr. k-12). 1978. pap. text ed. 3.00 (ISBN 0-916378-11-X). PSI Res.

Stories to Be Read with the Door Locked. Alfred Hitchcock. 1981. pap. 2.25 (ISBN 0-440-10138-7). Dell.

Stories to See & Share. Maline C. Crockett. 80p. 1980. pap. 2.95 (ISBN 0-87747-828-7). Deseret Bk.

Stories to Teach & Delight. Jack Norman. (gr. 9-10). 1977. pap. text ed. 5.17 (ISBN 0-87720-304-0). AMSCO Sch.

Stories to Tell Children: A Selected List. Ed. by Laura E. Cathon et al. LC 73-13317. (Illus.). 168p. 1974. pap. 3.95 (ISBN 0-8229-5246-7). U of Pittsburgh Pr.

Stories with Holes. Ed. by Mandala Press Staff. 1975. pap. 2.50 (ISBN 0-686-60090-8). Irvington.

Stork. Denison Hatch. 1978. pap. 1.95 o.s.i. (ISBN 0-515-04747-3). Jove Pubns.

Stork Is Dead. Charlie W. Shedd. 1976. pap. 1.50 (ISBN 0-89129-134-2). Jove Pubns.

Storm. Frances S. Moore. 256p. (YA) 1973. 5.95 (ISBN 0-685-27998-7, Avalon). Bouregy.

Storm Alert: Understanding Weather Disasters. Thomas G. Aylesworth. LC 80-19580. (Illus.). 160p. (gr. 7 up). 1980. PLB 8.29 (ISBN 0-671-34052-2). Messner.

Storm & Other Stories. Sharat Kumar. 1976. 9.00 (ISBN 0-89253-815-5); flexible cloth 6.75 (ISBN 0-89253-816-3). Ind-US Inc.

Storm at the Jetty. Leonard E. Fisher. (Illus.). 32p. (gr. k up). 1981. 9.95 (ISBN 0-670-67214-9). Viking Pr.

Storm in the West. rev. ed. Sinclair Lewis & Dore Schary. LC 63-13228. (Illus.). 200p. 1981. pap. 5.95 (ISBN 0-8128-6079-9). Stein & Day.

Storm of Glory. John Beevers. 1977. pap. 2.45 (ISBN 0-385-12617-4, Im). Doubleday.

Storm of Steel. Ernst Junger. Tr. by B. Creighton from Ger. LC 75-22372. xiii, 319p. 1975. Repr. of 1929 ed. 19.00 (ISBN 0-86527-310-3). Fertig.

Storm of Wrath. Alice Dwyer-Joyce. LC 77-6153. 1978. 7.95 o.p. (ISBN 0-312-76248-8). St Martin.

Storm on the Range. Max Brand. 1980. pap. 1.75 (ISBN 0-446-94300-2). Warner Bks.

Storm Over Nashville: A Case Against "Modern" Country Music. Everettt J. Cobin. 202p. (Orig.). 1980. pap. text ed. 9.95 (ISBN 0-932534-01-5). Ashlar Pr.

Storm Over Windhaven. Marie De Jourlet. 1977. pap. 2.75 (ISBN 0-523-41464-1). Pinnacle Bks.

Storm Upon Ulster. Kenneth C. Flint. 320p. (Orig.). 1981. pap. 2.50 (ISBN 0-553-14622-X). Bantam.

Storm Warning: The Story of Hurricanes & Tornadoes. Walter Buehr. LC 71-175815. (Illus.). 64p. (gr. 4-6). 1972 (ISBN 0-688-21921-7). PLB 6.96 (ISBN 0-688-31921-1). Morrow.

Storm Watch. Stephen Longstreet. 1981. pap. 2.50 (ISBN 0-8439-0882-3, Leisure Bks). Nordon Pubns.

Storming of Stony Point on the Hudson, Midnight, July 15, 1779. H. P. Johnston. LC 70-146150. (Era of the American Revolution Ser). 1971. Repr. of 1900 ed. lib. bdg. 22.50 (ISBN 0-306-70141-3). Da Capo.

Storming the Citadel: The Rise of the Woman Doctor. Enid H. Bell. LC 79-2931. 200p. 1981. Repr. of 1953 ed. 17.50 (ISBN 0-8305-0098-7). Hyperion Conn.

Storming the Gates of Hell. Howard F. Sugden. LC 76-50296. 1977. pap. 1.45 o.p. (ISBN 0-916406-63-6). Accent Bks.

Storm's End. Sondrs Stanford. 192p. (Orig.). 1980. pap. 1.50 (ISBN 0-671-57035-8). S&S.

Storms: From the Inside Out. Malcolm E. Weiss. LC 73-5396. (Illus.). 96p. (gr. 4-6). 1973. PLB 5.79 o.p. (ISBN 0-671-32612-0). Messner.

Storms of Fate. Patricia Wright. LC 80-1695. 504p. 1981. 13.95 (ISBN 0-385-17117-X). Doubleday.

Stormy Affair. Margaret Mayo. (Harlequin Romance Ser.). (Orig.). 1980. pap. 1.25 o.p. (ISBN 0-373-02327-8, Pub. by Harlequin). PB.

Stormy Masquerade. Anne Hampson. 192p. (Orig.). 1980. pap. 1.50 (ISBN 0-671-57004-8). S&S.

Stormy: Misty's Foal. Marguerite Henry. LC 63-13334. (Illus.). (gr. 4-9). 1963. 5.95 o.s.i. (ISBN 0-528-82083-4); pap. 2.95 (ISBN 0-528-87690-2). Rand.

Stormy Patriot: The Life of Samuel Chase. James Haw et al. LC 80-83807. (Illus.). 305p. 1980. 14.95 (ISBN 0-938420-00-3). Md Hist.

Story About Ping. Marjorie Flack. (Illus.). (ps-2). 1933. PLB 7.95 (ISBN 0-670-67223-8). Viking Pr.

Story & Discourse: Narrative Structure in Fiction & Film. Seymour Chatman. 1978. pap. 5.95 1980 ed. (ISBN 0-8014-1131-9); pap. 5.95 (ISBN 0-8014-9186-X). Cornell U Pr.

Story & Discourse: Narrative Structure in Fiction & Film. Seymour B. Chatman. LC 78-9329. (Illus.). 1978. 17.50x o.p. (ISBN 0-8014-1131-9). Cornell U Pr.

Story & the Song. Derek Parker & Julia Parker. 1979. 22.50 (ISBN 0-903443-25-2, Pub. by Hamish Hamilton England). David & Charles.

Story As Told. rev. ed. Jalil Mahmoudi. LC 79-65925. (Illus.). 80p. (Orig.). 1980. pap. 5.50 (ISBN 0-933770-10-3). Kalimat.

Story Behind Modern Books. Elizabeth R. Montgomery. LC 49-7920. (gr. 4-6). 1949. 5.95 (ISBN 0-396-03046-7). Dodd.

Story Caravan. new ed. William D. Sheldon et al. (Sheldon Reading Ser). (gr. 3). 1973. text ed. 9.20 (ISBN 0-205-03547-7, 5235472); tchrs'. guide 9.20 (ISBN 0-205-03548-5, 5235480); activity bk. 3.92 (ISBN 0-205-03549-3, 5235499); tchrs'. ed. 3.92 (ISBN 0-205-03550-7, 5235502); independent activ. masters 28.00 (ISBN 0-205-03551-5, 5235510). Allyn.

Story Experience. Jane B. Wilson. LC 79-13888. 177p. 1979. 10.00 (ISBN 0-8108-1224-X). Scarecrow.

Story Hour. K. D. Wiggin & N. A. Smith. 185p. 1980. Repr. PLB 20.00 (ISBN 0-8492-8803-7). R West.

Story Key to Geographic Names. Oscar Dedrich Von Engeln & Jane M. Urquhart. LC 74-13855. 279p. 1976. Repr. of 1924 ed. 20.00 (ISBN 0-8103-4062-3). Gale.

Story-Lives of Great Composers. rev. ed. Katherine L. Bakeless. (Illus.). (gr. 7-9). 1962. 10.00 o.p. (ISBN 0-397-30253-3). Lippincott.

Story of a Bad Boy. Thomas B. Aldrich. LC 75-32173. (Classics of Children's Literature, 1621-1932: Vol. 36). (Illus.). 1976. Repr. of 1870 ed. PLB 38.00 (ISBN 0-8240-2285-8). Garland Pub.

Story of a Musical Life: An Autobiography. George F. Root. LC 70-126072. (Music Ser). 1970. Repr. of 1891 ed. lib. bdg. 29.50 (ISBN 0-306-70031-X). Da Capo.

Story of a Prison: History of Penal Practice, 16th Century to Modern Times. Peter Southerton. (Illus.). 1975. 11.95x o.p. (ISBN 0-8464-0885-6). Beekman Pubs.

Story of a Young Gymnast: Tracee Talavera. Karen Folger. 192p. (Orig.). (gr. 6 up). 1980. pap. 2.25 (ISBN 0-553-14134-1). Bantam.

Story of Adam & Eve. Gordon Lindsay. (Old Testament Ser.). 1.25 (ISBN 0-89985-124-X). Christ Nations.

Story of Adamsville. Riedmann. 128p. 1980. pap. text ed. 3.95x (ISBN 0-534-00823-2). Wadsworth Pub.

Story of Alchemy & the Beginnings of Chemistry. Matthew M. Muir. LC 79-8618. Repr. of 1903 ed. 24.50 (ISBN 0-404-18482-0). AMS Pr.

Story of Algiers. William H. Seymour. (Illus.). 143p. 1981. pap. 6.95 (ISBN 0-911116-33-8). Pelican.

Story of Alice Paul. Inez Irwin. 6.95 (ISBN 0-87714-058-8). Green Hill.

Story of America. Readers Digest Editors. (Illus.). 527p. 1975. 17.95 (ISBN 0-89577-024-5, Pub by Reader's Digest). Norton.

Story of American Methodism. Frederick A. Norwood. LC 74-10621. 448p. 1974. pap. 14.95 (ISBN 0-687-39640-9); pap. 10.95 (ISBN 0-687-39641-7). Abingdon.

Story of American Painting. Abraham A. Davidson. LC 74-5116. (Illus.). 164p. 1975. 15.95 o.p. (ISBN 0-8109-0498-5); pap. 6.95 o.p. (ISBN 0-8109-2069-7). Abrams.

Story of an African Farm. Olive Schreiner. Ed. by Robert L. Wolff. LC 75-1530. (Victorian Fiction Ser). 1975. Repr. of 1883 ed. lib. bdg. 66.00 (ISBN 0-8240-1602-5). Garland Pub.

Story of Ancient History. James T. Shotwell. LC 39-4448. 1961. pap. 6.00x (ISBN 0-231-08518-4, 18). Columbia U Pr.

Story of Arachne. Pamela Espeland. LC 80-66796. (Myths for Modern Children Ser.). (Illus.). 32p. (gr. 1-4). 1980. PLB 5.95g (ISBN 0-87614-130-0). Carolrhoda Bks.

Story of Art. 13th rev. ed. E. H. Gombrich. LC 76-62643. (Illus.). 512p. 1981. 19.95 (ISBN 0-8014-1352-4); pap. 12.95 (ISBN 0-8014-9215-7). Cornell U Pr.

Story of Atomic Energy. Frederick Soddy. 1949. 30.00 (ISBN 0-911268-29-4). Rogers Bk.

Story of Australia. 4th ed. A. G. Shaw. (Story Ser.). (Illus., Orig.). 1973. pap. 6.95 (ISBN 0-571-04775-0, Pub. by Faber & Faber). Merrimack Bk Serv.

Story of Baseball. rev. 3rd ed. John Durant. (Illus.). 302p. (gr. 6 up). 1973. 9.95 (ISBN 0-8038-6715-8). Hastings.

Story of Baucis & Philemon. Pamela Espeland. LC 80-27674. (Myth for Modern Children Ser.). (Illus.). 32p. (gr. 1-4). 1981. PLB 5.95 (ISBN 0-87614-140-8). Carolrhoda Bks.

Story of Bay View. Bernhard C. Korn. LC 80-83069. (Illus.). 136p. (gr. 6-12). 1980. 5.00 (ISBN 0-938076-05-1). Milwaukee County.

Story of Birds of North America. Ruth L. Wheeler. LC 65-14630. (Story of Science Ser.). (Illus.). (gr. 5-10). 1965. PLB 7.29 (ISBN 0-8178-3542-3). Harvey.

Story of Books. Gertrude B. Rawlings. 160p. 1980. Repr. of 1901 ed. lib. bdg. 25.00 (ISBN 0-89984-431-6). Century Bookbindery.

Story of Books & Libraries. Alice D. Rider. LC 76-7596. 183p. 1976. 10.00 (ISBN 0-8108-0930-3). Scarecrow.

Story of Bread. (Ladybird Stories Ser.). (Illus., Arabic.). 2.50x (ISBN 0-686-53071-3). Intl Bk Ctr.

Story of Butterflies & Other Insects. Peter Farb. LC 59-14884. (Story of Science Ser). (Illus.). (gr. 3-6). 1959. PLB 7.29 (ISBN 0-8178-3232-7). Harvey.

Story of Cadmus. Pamela Espeland. LC 80-66795. (Myths for Modern Children Ser.). (Illus.). 32p. (gr. 1-4). 1980. PLB 5.95g (ISBN 0-87614-128-9). Carolrhoda Bks.

Story of Camilla. Vergil. Ed. by Bertha Tilly. text ed. 5.25x (ISBN 0-521-06701-4). Cambridge U Pr.

Story of Canada. Donald Creighton. 1971. pap. 3.95 (ISBN 0-571-09070-2, Pub. by Faber & Faber). Merrimack Bk Serv.

Story of Cancer: On Its Nature, Causes, & Treatment. Armin C. Braun. LC 77-13936. 1978. text ed. 24.50 (ISBN 0-201-00318-X, Adv Bk Prog); pap. text ed. 12.50 (ISBN 0-201-00319-8). A-W.

Story of Captain Jasper Parrish, Captive, Interpreter & United States Sub-Agent to the Six Nations Indians, Repr. Of 1903 Ed. Bd. with Story of My Capture & Escape During the Minnesota Indian Massacre of 1862. with Historical Notes, Description of Pioneer Life, & Sketches & Incidents of the Great Outbreak of the Sioux or Dakota Indians As I Saw Them. Helen M. Tarble. Repr. of 1904 ed; Story of the Rice Boys, Captured by the Indians. Ebenezer Parkman. Repr. of 1906 ed. LC 75-7133. (Indian Captivities Ser.: Vol. 105). 1976. lib. bdg. 44.00 (ISBN 0-8240-1729-3). Garland Pub.

Story of Cars. Howard W. Kanetzke. LC 77-27533. (Read About Science Ser.). (Illus.). (gr. k-3). 1978. PLB 9.95 (ISBN 0-8393-0086-7). Raintree Child.

Story of Cattle Ranching. Oren Arnold. LC 68-22983. (Story of Science Ser.). (Illus.). (gr. 5-8). 1968. PLB 7.29 (ISBN 0-8178-4292-6). Harvey.

Story of Christian Activism: History of the National Baptist Convention U. S. A., Inc. J. H. Jackson. LC 80-17408. (Illus.). 790p. 1980. 19.95 (ISBN 0-935990-01-1). Townsend Pr.

Story of Civil Liberty in the United States. L. Whipple. LC 72-107419. (Civil Liberties in American History Ser). 1970. Repr. of 1927 ed. lib. bdg. 35.00 (ISBN 0-306-71879-0). Da Capo.

Story of Clara Barton of the Red Cross. Jeannette C. Nolan. (Biography Ser.). (gr. 7up). 1941. 4.64 o.p. (ISBN 0-671-32606-6). Messner.

Story of Coins. Sam Rosenfeld. LC 67-16903. (Story of Science Ser). (Illus.). (gr. 5 up). 1968. PLB 7.29 (ISBN 0-8178-3922-4). Harvey.

Story of Colorado, 6 units. Cynthia E. Schmidt. Incl. Unit 1. Colorado - Land & Animals (ISBN 0-913688-50-9); Unit 2. Prehistoric People (ISBN 0-913688-51-7); Unit 3. Tribes & Trailblazers (ISBN 0-913688-52-5); Unit 4. Gold Fever (ISBN 0-913688-53-3); Unit 5. Early Statehood (ISBN 0-913688-54-1); Unit 6. Twentieth Century Colorado (ISBN 0-913688-55-X). (Illus.). Set. 350.00 (ISBN 0-913688-56-8); 65.00 ea.; each set contains a tchr's manual, 2 film strips, 2 cassette tapes, 10 spirit duplications masters, 8 learning center cards, 2 color posters (ISBN 0-685-33322-1). Pawnee Pub.

Story of Computers. Charles T. Meadow. LC 70-89781. (Story of Science Ser). (gr. 5-8). 1970. PLB 7.29 (ISBN 0-8178-4572-0). Harvey.

Story of Computers. Roger Piper. LC 64-20226. (Illus.). (gr. 7 up). 1964. 4.95 o.p. (ISBN 0-15-280847-7, HJ). HarBraceJ.

Story of Computers. Donald D. Spencer. LC 77-7466. 1977. 7.95 o.p. (ISBN 0-89218-000-5); pap. 3.95 (ISBN 0-89218-001-3). Camelot Pub.

Story of Cosmic Rays. Germaine Beiser & Arthur Beiser. (Illus.). (gr. 7 up). 1962. PLB 5.95 o.p. (ISBN 0-525-40121-0). Dutton.

Story of Creation. Holly Zapp & Ivar Zapp. LC 75-2799. 1975. pap. 2.50 o.p. (ISBN 0-88270-119-3). Logos.

Story of Dams: Hydrology for the Young Scientist. Peter Farb. LC 61-15658. (Story of Science Ser). (Illus.). (gr. 5-8). 1961. PLB 7.29 (ISBN 0-8178-3252-1). Harvey.

Story of Daniel. Lucy Diamond. (Ladybird Ser). (Illus.). 1958. bds. 1.49 (ISBN 0-87508-866-X). Chr Lit.

Story of Edward. Philippe Dumas. LC 76-28720. (Illus.). 48p. (gr. k-4). 1977. 5.95 o.s.i. (ISBN 0-8193-0868-4, Four Winds); PLB 5.41 o.s.i. (ISBN 0-8193-0869-2); pap. 1.95 o.s.i. (ISBN 0-8193-0905-2). Schol Bk Serv.

Story of Emmaus. G. A. Pottebaum. (Little People's Paperbacks Ser.). 1979. pap. 0.99 (ISBN 0-8164-2248-6). Crossroad NY.

Story of England. 3rd ed. William McElwee. (Story Ser.). (Illus.). 1972. 6.95 (ISBN 0-571-09951-3, Pub. by Faber & Faber). Merrimack Bk Serv.

Story of England's Architecture. Thomas E. Tallmadge. 363p. 1980. Repr. of 1934 ed. lib. bdg. 40.00 (ISBN 0-8495-5160-9). Arden Lib.

Story of English Literature: A Critical Survey. Anne Tibble. 1970. text ed. 10.50x (ISBN 0-7206-7604-5); pap. text ed. 6.75 (ISBN 0-7206-0244-0). Humanities.

Story of Faith Healing. Sybil Leek. 160p. 1973. 6.95 o.s.i. (ISBN 0-02-570150-9). Macmillan.

Story of Felicity. Anna Aragno. (Illus.). 64p. 1980. 5.00 (ISBN 0-682-49633-2). Exposition.

Story of Fire Fighting. Peter J. Stephens. LC 66-14175. (Story of Science Ser.). (Illus.). (gr. 5-10). 1966. PLB 7.29 (ISBN 0-8178-3722-1). Harvey.

Story of Folk Music. Melvin Berger. LC 76-18159. (Illus.). (gr. 6 up). 1976. PLB 9.95 (ISBN 0-87599-215-3). S G Phillips.

Story of Food. Ira Garard. LC 73-94093. (Illus., Orig.). 1974. pap. 11.00 (ISBN 0-87055-155-8). AVI.

Story of Geology: Our Changing Earth Through the Ages. Jerome Wyckoff. (Illus.). 1976. PLB 13.77 (ISBN 0-307-67750-8, Golden Pr). Western Pub.

Story of Giuseppe Verdi. Gabriele Baldini. Tr. by Roger Parker from Ital. LC 79-41376. 330p. 1980. 34.50 (ISBN 0-521-22911-1); pap. 9.95 (ISBN 0-521-29712-5). Cambridge U Pr.

Story of Gold. Ruth Brindze. LC 55-11840. (Illus.). (gr. 4-8). 1954. 6.95 (ISBN 0-8149-0276-6). Vanguard.

Story of Hans Andersen: Swan of Denmark. Ruth Manning-Sanders. (gr. 7 up). 1966. PLB 5.95 o.p. (ISBN 0-525-40262-4). Dutton.

Story of Helen Keller. L. A. Hickock. 1980. pap. 1.50 (ISBN 0-448-17149-X, Tempo). G&D.

Story of Highway Traffic Control, Eighteen Ninety-Nine-Nineteen Thirty-Nine. William P. Eno. 1939. 34.50x o.p. (ISBN 0-685-89784-2). Elliots Bks.

Story of Hockey. Frank Orr. (Pro Hockey Library: No. 1). (Illus.). (gr. 5-9). 1971. 2.50 o.p. (ISBN 0-394-82303-6, BYR); PLB 3.69 (ISBN 0-394-92303-0). Random.

Story of Horses. Dorothy E. Shuttlesworth. LC 60-6355. (gr. 6-9). PLB 4.95 o.p. (ISBN 0-385-03570-5). Doubleday.

Story of Idaho Teacher's Aid Booklet. rev. ed. Virgil M. Young & Katherine A. Young. LC 80-51706. 1980. 15.00 (ISBN 0-89301-055-3). U Pr of Idaho.

Story of Impacted Wisdom Teeth Kit. Joel M. Berns. 1980. pap. 24.00 (ISBN 0-931386-14-4). Quint Pub Co.

Story of Investment Companies. Hugh Bullock. LC 59-13778. (Illus.). 1959. 22.50x (ISBN 0-231-02378-2). Columbia U Pr.

Story of Inyo. W. A. Chalfant. 1980. 18.95 (ISBN 0-912494-34-4); pap. 12.50 (ISBN 0-912494-35-2). Chalfant Pr.

Story of Japan. Ian Nish. (Story Ser.). (Illus.). 1968. 6.95 (ISBN 0-571-08440-0, Pub. by Faber & Faber). Merrimack Bk Serv.

Story of Jazz. Marshall W. Stearns. (Illus.). 1970. pap. 6.95 (ISBN 0-19-501269-0, GB). Oxford U Pr.

Story of Jesus. rev. ed. Maud Petersham & Miska Petersham. (gr. 2-4). 1967. 6.95g (ISBN 0-02-773850-7). Macmillan.

Story of Jesus: An Interpretation. John Esse. (Illus.). 96p. (Orig.). 1980. pap. 4.95. Pundarika.

Story of Jonah. Illus. by Charles E. Martin. (Look Look Bks). (Illus.). 24p. (ps). 1981. pap. 1.25 (ISBN 0-307-11863-0, Golden Pr). Western Pub.

Story of Joseph. Lucy Diamond. (Ladybird Ser). (Illus.). 1954. bds. 1.49 (ISBN 0-87508-868-6). Chr Lit.

Story of Joseph. 79p. pap. 0.50. Faith Pub Hse.

Story of Judaism. rev. ed. Bernard J. Bamberger. 1970. 6.50 (ISBN 0-8074-0193-5, 959291). UAHC.

Story of King David: Genre & Interpretation. D. M. Gunn. (JSOT Supplement Ser.: No. 6). 164p. 1978. text ed. 29.95x (ISBN 0-905774-11-6, Pub. by JSOT Pr England); pap. text ed. 16.75x (ISBN 0-905774-05-1, Pub. by JSOT Pr England). Eisenbrauns.

Story of King Midas. Pamela Espeland. LC 80-66794. (Myths for Modern Children Ser.). (Illus.). 32p. (gr. 1-4). 1980. PLB 5.95g (ISBN 0-87614-129-7). Carolrhoda Bks.

Story of Kwanza. Safisha Madhubuti. 1980. pap. 2.95 (ISBN 0-88378-001-1). Third World.

Story of Land Warfare. Paul M. Kendall. LC 74-3764. (Illus.). x, 194p. 1981. Repr. of 1957 ed. lib. bdg. 21.75x (ISBN 0-8371-7463-5, KELW). Greenwood.

Story of Life: From the Big Bang to You. Kim Marshall. LC 79-27727. (Illus.). 160p. (gr. 4-7). 1981. 8.95 (ISBN 0-03-054071-2). HR&W.

Story of Life: Plants & Animals Through the Ages. Peter Farb. LC 62-17247. (Story of Science Ser.). (Illus.). (gr. 5 up). 1962. PLB 7.29 (ISBN 0-8178-3292-0). Harvey.

Story of Light. Irving Adler. LC 79-93519. (Story of Science Ser). (Illus.). (gr. 5-8). 1971. PLB 7.29 (ISBN 0-8178-4752-9). Harvey.

Story of Limerick. Robert Wyse Jackson. 1974. pap. 1.75 (ISBN 0-85342-376-8). Irish Bk Ctr.

Story of Little Red Riding Hood. (Children's Library of Picture Bks.). (Illus.). 10p. (ps). 1979. 1.95 o.p. (ISBN 0-89346-128-8, TA21, Pub. by Froebel-Kan Japan). Heian Intl.

Story of Malta. Brian Blouet. (Story Ser.). (Illus., Orig.). 1972. pap. 6.95 (ISBN 0-571-09654-9, Pub. by Faber & Faber). Merrimack Bk Serv.

Story of Mankind. rev. ed. Hendrik W. Van Loon. LC 72-167290. 642p. (gr. 7 up). 1972. 11.95 (ISBN 0-87140-547-4). Liveright.

Story of Maps. Lloyd A. Brown. LC 79-52395. (Illus.). 417p. 1980. Repr. of 1949 ed. 11.95 (ISBN 0-938164-00-7). Vintage Bk Co.

Story of Maryland Politics: An Outline History of the Big Political Battles of the State from 1864 to 1910, with Sketches & Incidents of the Men & Measures That Figured As Factors, & the Names of Most of Those Who Held Office in That Period. Frank R. Kent. LC 68-31444. xiv, 439p. Repr. of 1911 ed. 18.00 (ISBN 0-8103-5035-1). Gale.

Story of Masada. Raphael Rothstein. (Illus.). 296p. 1981. 10.95 (ISBN 0-89961-012-9). SBS Pub.

Story of Medicine in America. Geoffrey Marks & William K. Beatty. LC 73-1369. (Illus.). 416p. 1974. 10.00 o.p. (ISBN 0-684-13537-X, ScribT). Scribner.

Story of Metals. (Illus.). Arabic 2.50x (ISBN 0-685-82877-8). Intl Bk Ctr.

Story of Minstrelsy. Edmondstoune Duncan. LC 69-16802. (Music Story Ser). 1968. Repr. of 1907 ed. 18.00 (ISBN 0-8103-4240-5). Gale.

Story of Miss Moppett. B. Potter. (Peter Possum Paperbacks Ser). 1967. pap. 0.95 o.p. (ISBN 0-531-05118-8). Watts.

Story of Moses. Francine Klagsbrun. LC 68-27403. (Immortals Biography Ser). (gr. 7 up). 1968. PLB 6.90 (ISBN 0-531-00905-X). Watts.

Story of My Boyhood & Youth. John Muir. (Illus.). 1965. 10.00 (ISBN 0-299-03650-2); pap. 5.00 (ISBN 0-299-03654-5). U of Wis Pr.

Story of My Heart: My Autobiography. Richard Jeffries. 144p. 1980. pap. 3.95 (ISBN 0-7043-3257-4, Pub. by Quartet England). Horizon.

Story of My Life. Morarji Desai. LC 78-40613. 1979. text ed. 41.00 (ISBN 0-08-023566-2). Pergamon.

Story of My Life. J. Marion Sims. LC 68-29603. (American Medicine Ser). 1968. Repr. of 1884 ed. lib. bdg. 39.50 (ISBN 0-306-71116-8). Da Capo.

Story of New England. Monroe Stearns. (Landmark Giant Ser). (Illus.). (gr. 5-10). 1967. 4.95 o.p. (ISBN 0-394-81894-6, BYR). Random.

Story of New York State. Schwarz & Goldberg. 1962. pap. 3.00x (ISBN 0-88323-098-4, 282). Richards Pub.

Story of Notation. C. Abdy Williams. LC 69-16797. 1968. Repr. of 1903 ed. 18.00 (ISBN 0-8103-3557-3). Gale.

Story of Nuclear Power. (Illus.). Arabic 2.50x (ISBN 0-685-82878-6). Intl Bk Ctr.

Story of O: Part Two, Return to the Chateau. Pauline Reage. Tr. by Sabine D'Estree from Fr. LC 77-155130. Orig. Title: Retour a Roissy. 158p. 1980. pap. 2.25 (ISBN 0-394-17658-8, B364, BC). Grove.

Story of Oil. Roger Piper. (Junior Reference Ser.). (Illus.). 64p. (gr. 7 up). 7.95 (ISBN 0-7136-1911-2). Dufour.

Story of Oklahoma. Lon Tinkle. (Landmark Ser, No. 100). (Illus.). (gr. 5-8). 1962. PLB 4.39 o.p. (ISBN 0-394-90400-1, BYR). Random.

Story of Opera. Ernest M. Lee. LC 69-16803. (Music Story Ser). 1968. Repr. of 1909 ed. 15.00 (ISBN 0-8103-3359-7). Gale.

Story of Organ Music. C. Abdy Williams. LC 69-16789. 1968. Repr. of 1905 ed. 15.00 (ISBN 0-8103-3558-1). Gale.

Story of Our Names. Elsdon C. Smith. LC 71-109181. 1970. Repr. of 1950 ed. 15.00 (ISBN 0-8103-3858-0). Gale.

Story of Painting. 2nd ed. Agnes Allen. (Illus.). 1966. 5.95 o.p. (ISBN 0-571-06539-2, Pub. by Faber & Faber); pap. 2.95 (ISBN 0-571-09032-X). Merrimack Bk Serv.

Story of Pallas. Vergil. Ed. by Bertha Tilly. 1961. text ed. 5.25x (ISBN 0-521-06703-0). Cambridge U Pr.

Story of Paper. Roy P. Whitney. (TAPPi Press Reports). (Illus.). 28p. 1980. pap. 9.99 (ISBN 0-89852-385-0, 01-01-R085). Tappi.

Story of Paul Bunyan. Barbara Emberley. (Illus.). (ps-3). 1963. PLB 4.95 o.p. (ISBN 0-13-850792-9); pap. 2.50 (ISBN 0-13-850784-8). P-H.

Story of Persephone. Penelope Farmer. LC 73-4923. (Illus.). 48p. 1973. 7.75 (ISBN 0-688-20084-2); PLB 7.44 (ISBN 0-688-30084-7). Morrow.

Story of Peter the Fisherman. D. S. Hare. (Ladybird Ser). 1970. 1.49 (ISBN 0-87508-867-8). Chr Lit.

Story of Photography. Michael Langford. (Illus.). 1980. 14.95 (ISBN 0-240-51044-5). Focal Pr.

Story of Pines. Nicholas T. Mirov & Jean Hasbrouck. LC 74-30899. (Illus.). 160p. 1976. 7.95x (ISBN 0-253-35462-5). Ind U Pr.

Story of Pollination. B. J. Meeuse. (Illus.). 1961. 14.50 o.p. (ISBN 0-8260-5960-0). Ronald Pr.

Story of Pregnancy: In Cartoons. Pax Quigley & Victoria Hodgetts. (Illus.). 1979. pap. 2.50 (ISBN 0-685-46344-3). Budlong.

Story of Printing. Irving B. Simon. LC 65-14386. (Story of Science Ser). (Illus.). (gr. 6-9). 1965. PLB 7.29 (ISBN 0-8178-3552-0). Harvey.

Story of Private Security. John D. Peel. 168p. 1971. 12.75 (ISBN 0-398-01465-5). C C Thomas.

Story of Pueblo Pottery. 4th ed. H. M. Wormington & Arminta Neal. (Museum Pictorial: No. 2). 1974. pap. 1.10 o.p. (ISBN 0-916278-31-X). Denver Mus Natl Hist.

Story of Pygmalion. Pamela Espeland. LC 80-15792. (Myths for Modern Children Ser.). (Illus.). 32p. (gr. 1-4). 1981. PLB 6.95 (ISBN 0-87614-127-0). Carolrhoda Bks.

Story of Quantum Mechanics. Victor Guillemin. LC 68-17354. (Illus.). 1968. pap. 3.95 o.p. (ISBN 0-684-71790-5, SL230, ScribT). Scribner.

Story of Red Rum & Brian Fletcher. Victor Green. 1974. 6.95 o.p. (ISBN 0-7207-0800-1, Pub. by Michael Joseph). Merrimack Bk Serv.

Story of Redemption. large print ed. 1980. pap. 5.95 (ISBN 0-8280-0058-1, 19654-3). Review & Herald.

Story of Roland. J. Baldwin. (Illustrated Classic). (Illus.). (gr. 7 up). 1930. 12.50 o.p. (ISBN 0-684-20731-1, ScribT). Scribner.

Story of St. Paul. D. S. Hare. (Ladybird Ser.). (YA) 1969. pap. 1.49 (ISBN 0-87508-869-4). Chr Lit.

Story of Samuel Chadwick. H. R. Dunning. pap. 1.50 o.p. (ISBN 0-686-12918-0). Schmul Pub Co.

Story of Sandy. rev. ed. Susan S. Wexler. 176p. (RL 10). Date not set. pap. 1.50 (ISBN 0-451-08102-1, W8102, Sig). NAL.

Story of Santa Klaus: Told for Children of All Ages, from Six to Sixty. William S. Walsh. LC 68-58166. (Holiday Ser). (Illus.). 1970. Repr. of 1909 ed. 20.00 (ISBN 0-8103-3370-8). Gale.

Story of Science, Bk. 1. (Illus.). Arabic 2.50x (ISBN 0-685-82879-4). Intl Bk Ctr.

Story of Sculpture. 2nd ed. Agnes Allen. (Illus.). 1967. 7.95 (ISBN 0-571-04601-0, Pub. by Faber & Faber). Merrimack Bk Serv.

Story of Sea Otters. William W. Johnson. (Illus.). (gr. 4-7). 1973. PLB 5.99 (ISBN 0-394-92403-7, BYR). Random.

Story of Search for Meaning: An Autobiography. abr. ed. Swami Kriyananda. 240p. 1980. pap. 3.95 (ISBN 0-916124-19-3). Ananda.

Story of Siddhartha's Release. Richard Bartholomew. (Writers Workshop Redbird Ser.). 1975. 8.00 (ISBN 0-88253-648-6); pap. text ed. 4.00 (ISBN 0-88253-647-8). Ind-US Inc.

Story of Siegfried. J. Baldwin. (Illustrated Classic). (Illus.). (gr. 9 up). 1931. 12.50 o.p. (ISBN 0-684-20732-X, ScribT). Scribner.

Story of Silent Night. John Travers Moore. LC 65-19252. (gr. 2-3). 1965. 5.50 (ISBN 0-570-03430-2, 56-1056). Concordia.

Story of Spiders. Dorothy E. Shuttlesworth. LC 59-5441. (gr. 3-9). 1959. PLB 5.95 o.p. (ISBN 0-385-02286-7). Doubleday.

Story of Submarines. George Weller. (gr. 5-8). 1962. PLB 5.99 (ISBN 0-394-90402-8). Random.

Story of Superman: Four Little Library Books. Ramona Frandon & Dave Hunt. LC 79-67574. (Illus.). (ps). 1980. Set. 4.95 (ISBN 0-394-84416-5, BYR). Random.

Story of Surnames. William D. Bowman. LC 68-8906. 1968. Repr. of 1932 ed. 19.00 (ISBN 0-8103-3110-1). Gale.

Story of Symphony. Ernest M. Lee. LC 69-16804. (Illus.). 1968. Repr. of 1916 ed. 21.00 (ISBN 0-8103-3568-9). Gale.

Story of the Alphabet. Edward Clodd. LC 70-123369. (Illus.). 1970. Repr. of 1938 ed. 15.00 (ISBN 0-8103-3855-6). Gale.

Story of the Arab Legion. John B. Glubb. LC 76-7060. (The Middle East in the 20th Century Ser.). 1976. Repr. of 1948 ed. lib. bdg. 32.50 (ISBN 0-306-70763-2). Da Capo.

Story of the Arabs. M. Hiskett & Sheikh M. Awad. (Illus.). 1963. pap. text ed. 2.50x o.p. (ISBN 0-582-60244-0). Humanities.

Story of the Battersea Dogs' Home. Gloria Cottesloe. 1979. 16.95 (ISBN 0-7153-7704-3). David & Charles.

Story of the Bible. Edgar J. Goodspeed. LC 36-21666. 1936. 5.00 o.s.i. (ISBN 0-226-30375-6). U of Chicago Pr.

Story of the Bicycle. John Woodforde. (Illus.). 1977. pap. 4.95 (ISBN 0-7100-8644-X). Routledge & Kegan.

Story of the Black Beauty. Robert A. Davies. 1981. 10.00 (ISBN 0-8062-1712-X). Carlton.

Story of the Boston Massacre. Mary K. Phelan. LC 75-25961. (Illus.). 160p. (gr. 5-9). 1976. 8.95 (ISBN 0-690-00716-7, TYC-J). T Y Crowell.

Story of the Boston Tea Party. Mary K. Phelan. LC 72-7554. (Illus.). (gr. 5-9). 1973. 8.95 (ISBN 0-690-77653-5, TYC-J). T Y Crowell.

Story of the Cabinet Office. R. K. Mosley. (Library of Political Studies). 1969. text ed. 6.00x (ISBN 0-7100-6600-7). Humanities.

Story of the Carol. Edmondstoune Duncan. LC 69-16805. 1968. Repr. of 1911 ed. 18.00 (ISBN 0-8103-3547-6). Gale.

Story of the Champions of the Round Table. Howard Pyle. (Illus.). (ps-4). 1968. pap. 5.00 (ISBN 0-486-21883-X). Dover.

Story of the Christian Church. rev. ed. Jesse L. Hurlbut. 1970. 8.95 (ISBN 0-310-26510-X). Zondervan.

Story of the Church. George Johnson. LC 80-51329. 521p. (gr. 9). 1980. pap. 10.00 (ISBN 0-89555-156-X). Tan Bks Pubs.

Story of the Church. A. M. Renwick. pap. 3.45 o.p. (ISBN 0-8028-1163-9). Eerdmans.

Story of the Civil War, Vol. 4. John C. Ropes. 749p. 1980. Repr. of 1894 ed. lib. bdg. 375.00 (ISBN 0-8495-4634-6). Arden Lib.

Story of the Crusades: 1097-1291. Alfred Duggan. (Illus., Orig.). 1969. pap. 1.95 o.p. (ISBN 0-571-08990-9, Pub. by Faber & Faber). Merrimack Bk Serv.

Story of the Declaration of Independence. Ira G. Corn, Jr. 1980. 8.95 (ISBN 0-89474-010-5). Green Hill.

Story of the Earth. William H. Matthews, III. LC 67-16904. (Story of Science Ser.). (Illus.). (gr. 5-10). 1968. PLB 7.29 (ISBN 0-8178-3932-1). Harvey.

Story of the Four World Centres: For Girls & Leaders. Girl Scouts of the USA. (Illus.). 51p. (gr. 4-8). 1976. pap. 1.75 (ISBN 0-900827-27-0, 23-123). GS.

Story of the Gems. Herbert P. Whitlock. (Illus.). (gr. 9 up). 13.95 o.s.i. (ISBN 0-87523-053-9). Emerson.

Story of the Glittering Plain, Which Has Been Also Called the Land of Living Men, or the Acre of the Undying. William Morris. Ed. by R. Reginald & Douglas Menville. LC 80-19460. (Newcastle Forgotten Fantasy Library Ser.: Vol. 1). 174p. 1980. Repr. of 1973 ed. lib. bdg. 9.95x (ISBN 0-89370-500-4). Borgo Pr.

Story of the Great American West. (Illus.). 1977. 16.95 (ISBN 0-393-07703-9, Pub. by Reader's Digest). Norton.

Story of the Great Chicago Fire, 1871. Mary K. Phelan. LC 72-109910. (Illus.). (gr. 5-8). 1971. 8.95 (ISBN 0-690-77671-3, TYC-J). T Y Crowell.

Story of the Gypsies. Konrad Bercovici. LC 78-164051. (Illus.). xii, 294p. 1975. Repr. of 1928 ed. 20.00 (ISBN 0-8103-4042-9). Gale.

Story of the House of Witmark: From Ragtime to Swingtime. Isidore Witmark & Isaac Goldberg. LC 76-20707. (Roots of Jazz Ser.). 1975. Repr. of 1939 ed. lib. bdg. 29.50 (ISBN 0-306-70686-5). Da Capo.

Story of the Jesus People. Ronald M. Enroth et al. 1972. pap. 4.95 (ISBN 0-85364-131-5). Attic Pr.

Story of the Kilmarnock Burns. John D. Ross. LC 76-153519. Repr. of 1933 ed. 12.50 (ISBN 0-404-08978-X). AMS Pr.

Story of the Kite. Harry E. Neal. LC 52-11121. (Illus.). (gr. 4-9). 1954. 6.95 (ISBN 0-8149-0373-8). Vanguard.

Story of the Letters & Figures. Hubert M. Skinner. LC 71-175744. (Illus.). 1971. Repr. of 1905 ed. 18.00 (ISBN 0-8103-3035-0). Gale.

Story of the Mine. Charles H. Shinn. LC 79-23102. (Vintage Nevada Ser.). Orig. Title: Story of the Mine. (Illus.). xiv, 277p. 1980. pap. 6.50 (ISBN 0-87417-059-1). U of Nev Pr.

Story of the Naval Academy. Felix Riesenberg. (Landmark Ser, No. 84). (Illus.). (gr. 4-6). 1958. PLB 4.39 o.p. (ISBN 0-394-90384-6). Random.

Story of the Old World. John De Bie. 1954. pap. 6.50 (ISBN 0-8028-1781-5). Eerdmans.

Story of the Olympic Games: 776 B. C. to 1976. John Kieran & Arthur Daley. LC 76-56106. (Illus.). 1977. 12.95 o.s.i. (ISBN 0-397-01168-7). Lippincott.

Story of the Organ. C. F. Williams. LC 78-90250. (Illus.). 328p. 1972. Repr. of 1903 ed. 18.00 (ISBN 0-8103-3067-9). Gale.

Story of the Original Dixieland Jazz Band. H. O. Brunn. LC 77-3791. (Roots of Jazz Ser.). (Illus.). 1977. Repr. of 1960 ed. lib. bdg. 22.50 (ISBN 0-306-70892-2). Da Capo.

Story of the Pennsylvania Germans: Embracing an Account of Their Origin, Their History, Their Dialect. William Beidelman. LC 70-81759. 1969. Repr. of 1898 ed. 20.00 (ISBN 0-8103-3571-9). Gale.

Story of the Pony Express. Glenn D. Bradley. LC 75-141793. 1974. Repr. of 1913 ed. 15.00 (ISBN 0-8103-3632-4). Gale.

Story of the Presidents of the United States of America. rev. ed. Maud Petersham & Miska Petersham. (Illus.). (gr. 4-6). 1966. 6.95g (ISBN 0-02-773890-6). Macmillan.

Story of the Rhinegold: Der Ring Des Nibelungen. Anna Alice Chapin. 138p. 1980. Repr. of 1897 ed. lib. bdg. 25.00 (ISBN 0-89760-119-X). Telegraph Bks.

Story of the Rhodesias & Nyasaland. 2nd ed. A. J. Hanna. (Story Ser.). (Illus.). 1965. 6.95 o.p. (ISBN 0-571-06150-8, Pub. by Faber & Faber). Merrimack Bk Serv.

Story of the Savoy Opera in Gilbert & Sullivan Days. S. J. Fitzgerald. (Music Reprint Ser.). 1979. Repr. of 1925 ed. lib. bdg. 25.00 (ISBN 0-306-79543-4). Da Capo.

Story of the Scottish Rite. Harold V. Voorhis. 1980. Repr. soft cover 5.00 (ISBN 0-686-68271-8). Macoy Pub.

Story of the Seventy Third, the Unofficial History of the Seventy Third Bomb Wing. LC 80-67613. (Aviation Ser.: No. 3). (Illus.). 202p. 1980. Repr. of 1946 ed. 25.00 (ISBN 0-89839-032-X). Battery Pr.

Story of the Stone: The Dream of the Red Chamber, 2 vols. Xueqin Cao. Tr. by David Hawkes from Chinese. Incl. Vol. 1. The Golden Days. 544p. Repr. of 1973 ed (ISBN 0-253-19261-7); Vol. 2. The Crab-Flower Club. 608p. Repr. of 1977 ed (ISBN 0-253-19262-5). LC 78-20279. (Chinese Literature in Translation Ser.). 1979. 25.00x ea. Ind U Pr.

Story of the Terrible Scar. Catherine Storr. (Illus.). (gr. 2-5). 1978. 7.50 (ISBN 0-571-10996-9, Pub. by Faber & Faber). Merrimack Bk Serv.

Story of the Three Bears. Illus. by Lillian Obligado. (Illus.). 24p. (ps). 1980. PLB 6.08 s&l o.p. (ISBN 0-307-61980-X, Golden Pr). Western Pub.

Story of the Ugly Duckling. (Children's Library of Picture Bks.). (Illus.). 10p. 1971. 1.95 (ISBN 0-89346-126-1, TA35, Pub. by Froebel-Kan Japan). Heian Intl.

Story of the Ugly Duckling. (Children's Library of Picture Books). (Illus.). 10p. (ps). 1971. 1.95 (ISBN 0-89346-126-1, TA35, Pub. by Froebel-Kan Japan). Heian Intl.

Story of the Western Railroads: From 1852 Through the Reign of the Giants. Robert E. Riegel. LC 26-9772. 1964. 14.95x (ISBN 0-8032-0903-7); pap. 7.25 (ISBN 0-8032-5159-9, BB 183, Bison). U of Nebr Pr.

Story of Three Little Pigs. (Children's Library of Picture Bks.). (Illus.). 10p. (ps). 1979. 1.95 o.p. (ISBN 0-89346-134-2, TA37, Pub. by Froebel-Kan Japan). Heian Intl.

Story of Toronto. G. P. Glazebrook. LC 78-163815. (Illus.). 1971. 20.00 o.p. (ISBN 0-8020-1791-6); pap. 6.50 o.p. (ISBN 0-8020-6256-3). U of Toronto Pr.

Story of Triumph Motorcycles. 3rd ed. Harry Louis & Bob Curry. (Illus.). 144p. 1981. 37.95 (ISBN 0-85059-480-4). Aztex.

Story of Trojan Aeneas. Vergil. Ed. by E. C. Kennedy & Bertha Tilly. text ed. 4.25x (ISBN 0-521-06704-9). Cambridge U Pr.

Story of Utopias. Lewis Mumford. 8.25 (ISBN 0-8446-1319-3). Peter Smith.

Story of William Penn. Aliki. (gr. k-3). 1964. PLB 5.95 o.p. (ISBN 0-13-850446-6). P-H.

Story of Your Ear. Alvin Silverstein & Virginia Silverstein. (Illus.). 64p. (gr. 5-9). 1981. PLB 6.99 (ISBN 0-698-30704-6). Coward.

Story Programs: A Source Book of Materials. Carolyn S. Peterson & Brenny Hall. LC 80-15112. 300p. 1980. pap. 12.50 (ISBN 0-8108-1317-3). Scarecrow.

Story, Sign, & Self: Phenomenology & Structuralism As Literary-Critical Methods. Robert Detweiler. Ed. by William A. Beardslee. LC 76-9713. (Semeia Studies). 240p. 1978. pap. 5.95 (ISBN 0-8006-1505-0, 1-1505). Fortress.

Story Snail. Anne Rockwell. LC 73-19058. (Ready-to-Read Ser.). (Illus.). 64p. (gr. 1-4). 1974. 7.95g (ISBN 0-02-777560-7). Macmillan.

Story-Teller Retrieves the Past: Historical Fiction & Fictitious History in the Art of Scott, Stevenson, Kipling, & Some Others. Mary Lascelles. 116p. 1980. 29.50x (ISBN 0-19-812802-9). Oxford U Pr.

Story Telling: What to Tell & How to Tell It. 3rd ed. Edna Lyman, pseud. LC 74-167166. 1971. Repr. of 1911 ed. 22.00 (ISBN 0-8103-3403-8). Gale.

Story to Anti-Story. Mary Rohrberger. LC 78-69581. 1978. pap. text ed. 8.50 (ISBN 0-395-26387-5); inst. manual 0.45 (ISBN 0-395-26388-3). HM.

Story Workshop. Wilbur L. Schrammn. 458p. 1980. Repr. of 1938 ed. lib. bdg. 20.00 (ISBN 0-89984-423-5). Century Bookbindery.

Storybook: A Collection of Stories Old & New. Compiled by & illus. by Tomi Ungerer. LC 74-3504. (Illus.). 96p. (gr. k-6). 1974. 4.95 o.p. (ISBN 0-531-02742-2); PLB 5.88 o.p. (ISBN 0-531-02741-4). Watts.

Storybook Cookbook. Carol MacGregor. LC 67-15382. (gr. 3-7). PLB 4.95 o.p. (ISBN 0-385-06329-6). Doubleday.

Storyteller. Leslie M. Silko. 320p. 1981. 16.95 (ISBN 0-394-51589-7); pap. 9.95 (ISBN 0-394-17795-9). Seaver Bks.

Storyteller. Leslie M. Silko. LC 80-20251. (Illus.). 320p. 1981. 16.95 (ISBN 0-394-51589-7); pap. 9.95 (ISBN 0-394-17795-9). Seaver Bks.

Storyteller As Humanist: The Serees of Guillaume Bouchet. Hope H. Glidden. (French Forum Monographs: No. 25). 200p. (Orig.). 1981. pap. 11.50 (ISBN 0-917058-24-0). French Forum.

Storyteller's Pack. Frank R. Stockton. LC 67-23694. 384p. (gr. 6 up). 1968. 7.95 o.p. (ISBN 0-684-12825-X, ScribJ). Scribner.

Storyteller's Sourcebook: An Index to Folklore Collections for Children. Margaret R. McDonald. 500p. 1981. 49.95 (ISBN 0-918212-40-5). Neal-Schuman.

Storytime Tiny Library, 4 bks. Julie Durrell & Ruth Rosner. (Illus.). (ps-2). 1980. slipcased 5.95 (ISBN 0-525-69481-1, Gingerbread). Dutton.

Stouffer Cookbook of Great American Food & Drink. Stouffer. 1974. 10.95 (ISBN 0-394-48810-5). Random.

Stove by a Whale: Owen Chase & the Essex. Thomas F. Heffernan. 256p. 1981. 19.95 (ISBN 0-8195-5052-3). Wesleyan U Pr.

Stover at Yale. Owen Johnson. LC 68-22128. 1968. pap. 1.50 o.s.i. (ISBN 0-02-021780-3, Collier). Macmillan.

Stowell Genealogy: A Record of the Descendants of Samuel Stowell of Hingham, Mass. William H. Stowell. LC 78-87789. (Illus.). 1969. Repr. 27.50 (ISBN 0-8048-0717-5). C E Tuttle.

Strabismus, Heterophoria, Ocular Motor Paralysis (Clinical Ocular Muscle Imbalance) 2nd ed. Rene Hugonnier & Suzanne Clayette-Hugonnier. Tr. by Suzanne Veronneau-Troutman. LC 78-8814. (Illus.). 1969. 49.50 o.p. (ISBN 0-8016-2312-X). Mosby.

Stradivari Memorial. William D. Orcutt. LC 76-58561. (Music Reprint Series). 1977. Repr. of 1978 ed. lib. bdg. 14.95 (ISBN 0-306-70865-5). Da Capo.

Straight. Steve Knickmeyer. 1976. 6.95 o.p. (ISBN 0-394-40190-5). Random.

Straight Down a Crooked Lane. Francena H. Arnold. (gr. 9-12). 1959. pap. 2.25 (ISBN 0-8024-0041-8). Moody.

Straight Hair, Curly Hair. Augusta Goldin. LC 66-12669. (Let's-Read-&-Find-Out Science Bk). (Illus.). (gr. k-3). 1966. PLB 7.89 (ISBN 0-690-77921-6, TYC-J); filmstrip with record 11.95 (ISBN 0-690-77924-0); filmstrip with cassette 14.95 (ISBN 0-690-77926-7). T Y Crowell.

Straight Hearts' Delight: Love Poems & Selected Letters. Allen Ginsberg & Peter Orlovsky. Ed. by Winston Leyland. (Illus.). 240p. 1980. 20.00 (ISBN 0-917342-64-X); pap. 8.95 (ISBN 0-917342-65-8). Gay Sunshine.

Straight Is the Way. Joel French & Jane French. LC 79-169. 1979. pap. 2.95 (ISBN 0-87123-497-1, 210497). Bethany Fell.

Straight Life: The Story of Art Pepper. Art Pepper & Laurie Pepper. LC 79-7363. (Illus.). 1979. 12.95 (ISBN 0-02-871820-8). Schirmer Bks.

Straight Lines, Parallel Lines, Perpendicular Lines. Mannis Charosh. LC 76-106569. (Young Math Ser). (Illus.). (gr. 1-4). 1970. 7.95 (ISBN 0-690-77992-5, TYC-J); PLB 7.89 (ISBN 0-690-77993-3). T Y Crowell.

Straight Shooting. Robert Stack & Mark Evans. 1981. pap. 2.75 (ISBN 0-425-04757-1). Berkley Pub.

Straight Talk About Mental Tests. Arthur R. Jensen. LC 80-83714. (Illus.). 1981. 12.95 (ISBN 0-02-916440-0). Free Pr.

Straight Talk About Sex. Barry Chant. (Illus.). (gr. 10-12). 1977. pap. 1.95 (ISBN 0-88368-078-5). Whitaker Hse.

Straight Talk About Small Business. Kenneth J. Albert. (Illus.). 256p. 1980. 12.95 (ISBN 0-07-000949-X, P&RB). McGraw.

Straight Talk About Your Health Care. Mack Lipkin. LC 75-25046. 1977. 8.95 o.s.i. (ISBN 0-06-012638-8, HarpT). Har-Row.

Straight Talk: How to Improve Your Relationships Through Better Communication. Sherod Miller et al. LC 80-51251. 1980. 12.95 (ISBN 0-89256-143-2). Rawson Wade.

Straight Teeth: Orthodontics & Dental Care for Everyone. Robert Holt. LC 80-10562. (Illus.). 224p. 1980. 13.95 (ISBN 0-688-03625-2); pap. 7.95 (ISBN 0-688-08625-X). Morrow.

Straight Women-Gay Men: A Special Relationship. John Malone. 1980. 8.95 (ISBN 0-8037-8174-1). Dial.

Strain of Violence: Historical Studies of American Violence & Vigilantism. Richard M. Brown. LC 75-7351. 1977. pap. 6.95 (ISBN 0-19-502247-5, GB513, GB). Oxford U Pr.

Strait Is the Gate. Andre Gide. Tr. by Dorothy Bussy from Fr. LC 79-23999. Orig. Title: Porte Etroite. 1980. Repr. of 1924 ed. lib. bdg. 10.00x (ISBN 0-8376-0453-2). Bentley.

Straits Times Dictionary of Singapore. Ed. by Time Periodicals Ltd. 948p. 1980. 58.50x (ISBN 0-8002-2750-6). Intl Pubns Serv.

Strand. Violet V. Englund. LC 77-76176. (Illus.). 1977. pap. 6.95 (ISBN 0-9601258-0-9). Golden Owl Pub.

Strand: A Profile. Mark Strand et al. Tr. by Carol Maier. (Profile Editions Ser.). (Illus.). 1979. pap. 4.00 o.p. (ISBN 0-931238-08-0); pap. 8.00 signed & lettered o. p. o.p. (ISBN 0-931238-09-9). Grilled Flowers Pr.

Strands Entwined. Samuel J. Bernstein. LC 80-12740. 171p. 1980. 17.95x (ISBN 0-930350-07-3). NE U Pr.

Strands of Desire. Antoinette Beaudry. 288p. (Orig.). 1981. pap. 2.50 (ISBN 0-523-40925-7). Pinnacle Bks.

Strands of Organic Chemistry: A Series of Lectures. Claude E. Wintner. LC 78-60358. 1979. pap. text ed. 6.95 (ISBN 0-8162-9661-8). Holden-Day.

Strange Adventures of Roger Ward. George S. Burns. (Illus.). 48p. (gr. 9-12). 1981. 7.95 (ISBN 0-698-20495-6). Putnam.

Strange Allies: The United States & Poland, 1941-1945. Richard C. Lukas. LC 77-8585. 1978. 14.50x (ISBN 0-87049-229-2). U of Tenn Pr.

Strange Animals I Have Known. Raymond Ditmars. (Illus.). 1966. 6.95 o.p. (ISBN 0-15-185631-1). HarBraceJ.

Strange Animals I Have Known. Raymond L. Ditmars. 1966. pap. 0.60 o.p. (ISBN 0-15-685632-8, HPL3, HPL). HarBraceJ.

Strange But True Baseball Stories. Furman Bisher. (Major League Baseball Library). (Illus.). (gr. 5-9). 1966. 2.95 (ISBN 0-394-80184-9, BYR); PLB 4.39 (ISBN 0-394-90184-3); pap. 1.95 (ISBN 0-394-82191-2). Random.

Strange But True Football Stories. Ed. by Zander Hollander. (NFL Punt, Pass & Kick Library: No. 8). (Illus.). (gr. 5-9). 1967. 2.95 (ISBN 0-394-80198-9, BYR); PLB 4.39 (ISBN 0-394-90198-3); pap. 0.95 o.p. (ISBN 0-394-82202-1). Random.

Strange but True: Twenty-Two Amazing Stories. David Duncan. (gr. 4-6). 1974. pap. 1.25 (ISBN 0-590-03528-2, Schol Pap). Schol Bk Serv.

Strange but Wonderful Cosmic Awareness of Duffy Moon. Jean Robinson. LC 73-15526. (Illus.). (gr. 3-6). 1974. 6.50 (ISBN 0-395-28880-0, Clarion). HM.

Strange Career of Jim Crow. 3rd rev. ed. C. Vann Woodward. 256p. 1974. pap. 4.95 (ISBN 0-19-501805-2, GB). Oxford U Pr.

Strange Case of Billy Biswas. Arun Joshi. 1971. 6.00x (ISBN 0-210-22385-5). Asia.

Strange Case of Billy Biswas. Arun Joshi. 1974. pap. 3.50 (ISBN 0-88253-387-8). Ind-US Inc.

Strange Case of Dr. Jekyll & Mr. Hyde. Robert L. Stevenson. (gr. 3 up). 1978. pap. 1.25 (ISBN 0-307-21633-0, Golden Pr). Western Pub.

Strange Case of Dr. M. K. Jessup. 4th ed. Ed. by Gray Barker. (Illus.). 82p. 1975. pap. 7.95 (ISBN 0-685-51759-4). Saucerian.

Strange Case of Edmund Gurney. 2nd ed. Trevor H. Hall. (Illus.). 219p. 1980. 26.50x (ISBN 0-7156-1154-2, Pub. by Duckworth England). Biblio Dist.

Strange Communists I Have Known. Bertram D. Wolfe. LC 65-14401. 232p. 1981. pap. 7.95 (ISBN 0-8128-6120-5). Stein & Day.

Strange Customs of Courtship & Marriage. William J. Fielding. 315p. 1980. Repr. of 1942 ed. lib. bdg. 25.00 (ISBN 0-89987-259-X). Darby Bks.

Strange Death of Franklin Roosevelt: A History of the Roosevelt-Delano Dynasty: America's Royal Family. Emanuel Josephson. (Blacked-Out History Ser.). 284p. 11.00 (Pub. by Chedney); pap. 4.95. Alpine Ent.

Strange Destiny of Rupert Brooke. John Lehmann. LC 80-13822. (Illus.). 228p. 1981. 12.95 (ISBN 0-03-057479-X). HR&W.

Strange Doings. R. A. Lafferty. LC 72-162759. 1972. 5.95 o.p. (ISBN 0-684-12530-7, ScribT). Scribner.

Strange Dreams. Vartan S. Chekijian. 109p. 1980. 5.95 (ISBN 0-533-03227-X). Vantage.

Strange Encounters. Ed. by David Bischoff. LC 76-45662. (Science Fiction Ser.). (Illus.). (gr. 3-6). 1977. 7.75 (ISBN 0-8172-0525-X). Raintree Pubs.

Strange Eons. Robert Bloch. 1979. pap. 1.95 o.p. (ISBN 0-523-40447-6). Pinnacle Bks.

Strange Exile. Laura Saunders. (YA) 1972. 5.95 (ISBN 0-685-28624-X, Avalon). Bouregy.

Strange Experience: How to Become the World's Second Greatest Lover. Strange de Jim. LC 80-69868. (Illus.). 94p. (Orig.). 1980. perfect bdg. 6.95 (ISBN 0-9605308-1-9). Ash-Kar Pr.

Strange Facts About the Bible. Webb Garrison. 1976. pap. 1.95 (ISBN 0-89129-174-1). Jove Pubns.

Strange Fires: The True Story of John Wesley's Love Affair in Georgia. Willie S. Ethridge. LC 77-170902. 7.95 (ISBN 0-8149-0693-1). Vanguard.

Strange Gentleman & Other Plays. Charles Dickens. Ed. by Jeffrey Tillett. 1972. pap. text ed. 2.50x (ISBN 0-435-23225-8). Heinemann Ed.

Strange Happenings. Ed. by Robert Vitarelli. (Pal Paperbacks Kit B Ser.). (Illus., Orig.). (gr. 7-12). 1973. pap. text ed. 1.25 (ISBN 0-8374-3508-0). Xerox Ed Pubns.

Strange Holiness. Robert P. Coffin. LC 78-8151. 1978. lib. bdg. 8.50 o.p. (ISBN 0-89621-003-0); pap. 3.95x (ISBN 0-89621-002-2). Thorndike Pr.

Strange Horizons: The Spectrum of Science Fiction. Sam Moskowitz. LC 76-17088. 1976. 8.95 o.p. (ISBN 0-684-14774-2). Scribner.

Strange Inheritance. Lorena A. Olmsted. (YA) 1978. 5.95 (ISBN 0-685-86415-4, Avalon). Bouregy.

Strange Invasion of Catfish Bend. Ben L. Burman. LC 79-67487. (Catfish Bend Stories). (Illus.). 160p. 1980. 8.95 (ISBN 0-8149-0828-4). Vanguard.

Strange Judgment. Douglas Young. Ed. by Constance Hunting. (Orig.). 1981. pap. 4.95 (ISBN 0-913006-23-8). Puckerbrush.

Strange Legacy. Louise Bergstrom. (YA) 4.95 o.p. (ISBN 0-685-07459-5, Avalon). Bouregy.

Strange Monsters & Great Searches. George Laycock. LC 72-76185. 120p. (gr. 4-7). 1973. 6.95 (ISBN 0-385-03463-6). Doubleday.

Strange Museum. Tom Paulin. 64p. (Orig.). 1980. pap. 9.95 (ISBN 0-571-11511-X, Pub. by Faber & Faber). Merrimack Bk Serv.

Strange Mysteries from Around the World. Seymour Simon. LC 79-6339. (Illus.). 64p. (gr. 3-7). 1980. 6.95 (ISBN 0-590-07639-6, Four Winds). Schol Bk Serv.

Strange Relations. Philip J. Farmer. 1978. pap. 1.75 (ISBN 0-380-00095-4, 41418). Avon.

Strange Schemes of Randolph Mason. Melville D. Post. 280p. 1980. Repr. of 1901 ed. lib. bdg. 14.25x (ISBN 0-89968-200-6). Lightyear.

Strange Stories of Life. Joann A. Lawless. LC 77-10866. (Great Unsolved Mysteries Ser.). (Illus.). (gr. 4-5). 1977. PLB 9.65 (ISBN 0-8172-1062-8). Raintree Pubs.

Strange Story of the Quantum. Banesh Hoffmann. 1959. pap. text ed. 3.00 (ISBN 0-486-20518-5). Dover.

Strange Story of Uri Geller. Jim Collins. LC 77-24501. (Myth, Magic & Superstition Ser.). (Illus.). (gr. 4-5). 1977. PLB 9.65 (ISBN 0-8172-1037-7). Raintree Pubs.

Strange Survivals, Some Chapters in the History of Man. Sabine Baring-Gould. LC 67-23909. (Illus.). 1968. Repr. of 1892 ed. 15.00 (ISBN 0-8103-3422-4). Gale.

Strange Tactics of Extremism. H. A. Overstreet & Bonaro Overstreet. 1964. 5.95 (ISBN 0-393-05268-0); pap. 4.95x (ISBN 0-393-09749-8). Norton.

Strange Things Happen. Chowan College Creative Writing Group & North Carolina Writers Conference. Ed. by Bernice K. Harris. 1971. 7.50 (ISBN 0-930230-24-8). Johnson NC.

Strange Wine. Harlan Ellison. 1979. pap. 2.50 (ISBN 0-446-91946-2). Warner Bks.

Strange Wine: Fifteen New Stories from the Nightside of the World. Harlan Ellison. LC 77-89060. 1978. 9.95 o.s.i. (ISBN 0-06-011113-5, HarpT). Har-Row.

Strange World of Frank Edwards. Ed. by Rory Stuart. 1979. pap. 1.95 o.p. (ISBN 0-425-03877-7). Berkley Pub.

Strange World of Ivan Ivanov. G. Warren Nutter. LC 68-54124. (Principles of Freedom Ser.). 1976. Repr. of 1969 ed. 9.95x o.p. (ISBN 0-916054-25-X, Caroline Hse Inc). Green Hill.

Strange World of Prison. Lou Torok. LC 72-88761. 1973. 6.50 o.p. (ISBN 0-672-51711-6). Bobbs.

Strangely Warmed. Garth Lean. 1979. pap. 3.95 (ISBN 0-8423-6662-8). Tyndale.

Stranger. Max Brand. 208p. 1976. pap. 1.75 (ISBN 0-446-94508-0). Warner Bks.

Stranger. Kjell Ringi. LC 68-23661. (Illus.). (ps-2). 1968. 3.95 (ISBN 0-394-81571-8); PLB 5.39 (ISBN 0-394-91571-2). Random.

Stranger & Friend: The Way of an Anthropologist. Hortense Powdermaker. 1966. 7.50x (ISBN 0-393-07442-0, Norton Lib); pap. 3.95 1967 (ISBN 0-393-00410-4). Norton.

Stranger at the Party: A Memoir. Helen Lawrenson. 1975. 8.95 o.p. (ISBN 0-394-48900-4). Random.

Stranger at the Wedding. Frances Lynch. 1978. pap. 1.75 o.p. (ISBN 0-449-23555-6, Crest). Fawcett.

Stranger Beside Me. Ann Rule. (Illus.). 1981. pap. 3.50 (ISBN 0-451-09888-9, E9888, Sig). NAL.

Stranger City Caper. Ross H. Spencer. 1979. pap. 1.95 (ISBN 0-380-75036-8, 75036). Avon.

Stranger in My Home. C. Raymond Holmes. LC 73-9253. (Crown Ser.). 128p. 1974. pap. 4.50 (ISBN 0-8127-0075-9). Southern Pub.

Stranger in the Mirror. Sidney Sheldon. 1977. pap. 2.95 (ISBN 0-446-93814-9). Warner Bks.

Stranger in the Night. Charlotte Lamb. (Harlequin Presents Ser.). 192p. 1981. pap. 1.50 (ISBN 0-373-10417-0, Pub. by Harlequin). PB.

Stranger in Town. Lois Geumlek. (YA) 4.95 o.p. (ISBN 0-685-07460-9, Avalon). Bouregy.

Stranger in Your Bed: A Guide to Emotional Intimacy. Dean C. Dauw. LC 78-23444. 1979. 10.95 (ISBN 0-88229-472-5). Nelson-Hall.

Stranger Is Watching. Mary H. Clark. 1979. pap. 2.50 o.s.i. (ISBN 0-440-18125-9). Dell.

Stranger Thing. Ruth Tomalin. (Illus.). 1975. 8.95 (ISBN 0-571-10748-6, Pub. by Faber & Faber). Merrimack Bk Serv.

Stranger to the Ground. Richard Bach. LC 63-14370. (Illus.). 192p. (YA) 1972. 10.00 o.p. (ISBN 0-06-010180-6, HarpT). Har-Row.

Stranger Warrior. Ian Fraser. 208p. 1980. 19.50x (ISBN 0-7050-0073-7, Pub. by Skilton & Shaw England). State Mutual Bk.

Stranger Within Me. Clifford Rapp. 176p. 1981. 7.95 (ISBN 0-8059-2780-8). Dorrance.

Stranger Within Thee: Concepts of the Self in Late-Eighteenth-Century Literature. Stephen D. Cox. LC 80-5252. (Illus.). 195p. 1980. 14.95x (ISBN 0-8229-3424-8). U of Pittsburgh Pr.

Strangers. Gardner Dozois. 1978. pap. 1.75 o.p. (ISBN 0-425-03924-2, Dist. by Putnam). Berkley Pub.

Strangers. Gardner Dozois. (YA) 1978. 7.95 o.p. (ISBN 0-399-12095-5, Dist. by Putnam). Berkley Pub.

Strangers, All Strangers. Robert A. Yereance. 1981. 10.95 (ISBN 0-87949-151-5). Ashley Bks.

Strangers & Brothers. C. P. Snow. LC 60-12605. 1960. lib.rep.ed. 17.50x (ISBN 0-684-15367-X, ScribT). Scribner.

Strangers at Home: Essays on "The Holocaust", Zionism, & American Judaism. Jacob Neusner. LC 80-19455. 1981. 15.00 (ISBN 0-226-57628-0). U of Chicago Pr.

Strangers at Home: The Vietnam Veteran Since the War. Charles R. Figley & Seymour Leventman. LC 79-24398. (Praeger Spcial Studies). 1980. student edition 9.95 (ISBN 0-03-049776-0); 24.95 (ISBN 0-03-049771-X). Praeger.

Strangers at the Gate: Social Disorder in South China, 1839-1861. Frederic E. Wakeman, Jr. (Center for Chinese Studies, UC Berkeley). 1966. 18.50x o.p. (ISBN 0-520-01312-3); pap. 3.95x o. p. o.p. (ISBN 0-520-02634-9). U of Cal Pr.

Strangers Become Neighbors. Calvin Redekop. (Studies in Anabaptist & Mennonite History Ser.: No. 22). (Illus.). 312p. 1980. 19.95x (ISBN 0-8361-1228-8). Herald Pr.

Stranger's Eyes. Bettie Wysor. 352p. (Orig.). 1981. pap. 2.75 (ISBN 0-515-05564-6). Jove Pubns.

Strangers' Forest. Pamela Hill. 1979. pap. 1.95 o.p. (ISBN 0-449-23907-1, Crest). Fawcett.

Strangers, Healers. Benjamin Siegal. 352p. (Orig.). 1981. pap. 2.75 (ISBN 0-345-29439-4). Ballantine.

Strangers in African Society. Ed. by William A. Shack & Elliott P. Skinner. LC 77-73501. (Campus Ser.: No. 220). 1979. 22.75x (ISBN 0-520-03458-9); pap. 6.95x (ISBN 0-520-03812-6). U of Cal Pr.

Strangers in the Land: Patterns of American Nativism, 1860 to 1925. John Higham. LC 80-22204. (Illus.). xiv, 431p. 1981. Repr. of 1963 ed. lib. bdg. 35.50x (ISBN 0-313-22459-5, HISL). Greenwood.

Strangers, Lovers, Friends. Urban G. Steinmetz. LC 80-69479. (Illus.). 176p. (Orig.). 1981. pap. 3.95 (ISBN 0-87793-217-4). Ave Maria.

Strangers to These Shores: Race & Ethnic Relations in the United States. Vincent M. Parrillo. LC 79-87856. 1979. text ed. 16.25 (ISBN 0-395-28562-3); inst manual 0.65 (ISBN 0-395-28563-1). HM.

Strangers Within Our Gates. James S. Woodsworth. LC 76-163836. (Social History of Canada Ser.). 1972. pap. 6.50 (ISBN 0-8020-6149-4). U of Toronto Pr.

Strangest Thing Happened... Ethel Barrett. LC 76-84599. (gr. 4-8). 1971. pap. 1.95 (ISBN 0-8307-0005-6, S061104). Regal.

Strangled Cries. Julius Balbin. Ed. by Stanley H. Barkan. Tr. by Charlz Rizzuto. (Cross-Cultural Review Chapbook 8). 24p. (Esperanto & Eng.). 1980. pap. 2.50 (ISBN 0-89304-807-0). Cross Cult.

Strangled Democracy: Czechoslovakia 1948-1969. David Rodnick. LC 70-125284. (Orig.). 1970. pap. 8.00x (ISBN 0-912570-01-6). Caprock Pr.

Strangled Voices: The Story of the Haymarket Affair. Irving Werstein. LC 76-89595. (Illus.). (gr. 5-9). 1970. 4.95g o.s.i. (ISBN 0-02-792560-9). Macmillan.

Strangler's Moon. Family D'Alembert. (E.E. Doc Smith Ser: No. 2). 1976. pap. 1.75 (ISBN 0-515-04731-7). Jove Pubns.

Strasburg Manuscript: A Medieval Painters Handbook. B. Borradaile & R. Borradaile. 10.00 (ISBN 0-685-20636-X). Transatlantic.

Strasburger's Textbook of Botany. 30th ed. Dietrich Von Denffer et al. Tr. by P. Bell from Ger. Tr. by P. Bell & D. E. Coombe. LC 75-11731. (Illus.). 879p. 1976. text ed. 35.00x (ISBN 0-582-44169-2). Longman.

Stratagems & Spoils: A Social Anthropology of Politics. F. G. Bailey. (Pavilion Ser.). 240p. 1980. pap. 12.95x (ISBN 0-631-11760-1, Pub. by Basil Blackwell). Biblio Dist.

Strategic Advertising Decisions: Selected Readings. Ronald D. Michman & Donald W. Jugenheimer. LC 75-28535. (Advertising & Journalism Ser.). 1976. pap. text ed. 9.95 o.p. (ISBN 0-88244-091-8). Grid Pub.

Strategic Alternatives: Selection, Development & Implementation. William E. Rothschild. 1979. 15.95 (ISBN 0-8144-5514-X). Am Mgmt.

Strategic Approach to Urban Research & Development: Social & Behavioral Science Considerations. Committee On Social And Behavioral Urban Research - Division Of Behavioral Sciences. LC 73-601566. 1969. pap. 4.75 (ISBN 0-309-01728-9). Natl Acad Pr.

Strategic Balance, 1972. Edward Luttwak. LC 72-6271. (Washington Papers: No. 3). 1972. 3.50x (ISBN 0-8039-0277-8). Sage.

Strategic Decision Analysis: A Managerial Approach to Policy. Alan Patz. 1981. text ed. 18.95 (ISBN 0-316-69400-2); tchrs'. manual free (ISBN 0-316-69401-0). Little.

Strategic Deterrence in a Changing Environment. Ed. by Christoph Bertram. LC 80-67841. (Adelphi Library: Vol. 6). 200p. 1981. text ed. 29.50 (ISBN 0-916672-75-1). Allanheld.

Strategic Deterrence in the Nineteen Eighty's. Roger D. Speed. LC 78-70887. (Publications Ser.: 214). (Illus.). 1979. pap. 7.95 (ISBN 0-8179-7142-4). Hoover Inst Pr.

Strategic Disarmament: Verification & National Security. SIPRI. LC 77-85318. 1977. 19.50x (ISBN 0-8448-1227-7). Crane-Russak Co.

Strategic Disengagement & World Peace: Toward a Noninterventionist American Foreign Policy. Earl C. Ravenal. (Cato Papers Ser.: No. 7). 64p. 1979. pap. 2.00 (ISBN 0-932790-07-0). Cato Inst.

Strategic Energy Supply & National Security. Carl Vansant. LC 78-139882. (Special Studies in International Politics & Government). 1971. 28.00x (ISBN 0-89197-951-4); pap. text ed. 12.95x (ISBN 0-89197-952-2). Irvington.

Strategic Family Therapy. Cloe Madanes. LC 80-26286. (Social & Behavioral Science Ser.). 1981. text ed. 14.95 (ISBN 0-87589-487-9). Jossey-Bass.

Strategic Financial Planning: A Manager's Guide to Improving Profit Performance. Harold Bierman, Jr. LC 80-1058. (Illus.). 1980. 15.95 (ISBN 0-02-903560-0). Free Pr.

Strategic Financial Planning with Simulation. Dennis E. Grawoig & Charles L. Hubbard. (Illus.). 1980. 35.00 (ISBN 0-89433-115-9). Petrocelli.

Strategic Forces: Issues for the Mid-Seventies. Alton H. Quanbeck & Barry M. D. Blechman. (Studies in Defense Policy). 110p. 1973. pap. 3.95 (ISBN 0-8157-7283-1). Brookings.

Strategic Interaction. Erving Goffman. LC 74-92857. (Conduct & Communication Ser). 1971. 12.00x (ISBN 0-8122-7607-8); pap. 3.95x (ISBN 0-8122-1011-5, Pa Paperbks). U of Pa Pr.

Strategic Interaction. Erving Goffman. 1975. pap. 1.95 o.p. (ISBN 0-345-24842-2). Ballantine.

Strategic Intervention in Schizophrenia: Current Developments in Treatment. Ed. by R. Cancro et al. LC 74-1201. 326p. 1974. text ed. 22.95 (ISBN 0-87705-133-X). Human Sci Pr.

Strategic Issues in Marketing. Gordon Wills. LC 74-14910. 239p. 1974. 20.95 (ISBN 0-470-94958-9). Halsted Pr.

Strategic Land Ridge: Peking's Relations with Thailand, Maylaysia, Singapore, & Indochina. Yuan-li Wu. LC 75-12597. (Publications Ser.: No.147). 1975. 5.95 (ISBN 0-8179-6471-1). Hoover Inst Pr.

Strategic Market Planning: Problems & Analytical Approaches. Derek F. Abell & John Hammond. 1979. text ed. 21.95 (ISBN 0-13-851089-X). P-H.

Strategic Marketing. Kollet et al. 1972. 20.95 (ISBN 0-03-078770-X). Dryden Pr.

Strategic Marketing: A Business Response to Consumerism. Andrew Robertson. LC 78-3. 27.95 (ISBN 0-470-26313-X). Halsted Pr.

Strategic Marketing Problems: Cases & Comments. 2nd ed. Roger A. Kerin & Robert A. Peterson. 1980. pap. text ed. 21.95 (ISBN 0-205-07329-8, 085980X); instr's man. o.p avail. (ISBN 0-205-07330-1). Allyn.

Strategic Materials Geopolitics: How to Avoid Shortages, Cartels, Embargoes, & Supply Disruptions. Bohdan O. Szuprowicz. 336p. 1981. 18.95 (ISBN 0-471-07843-3, Pub. by Wiley-Interscience). Wiley.

Strategic Mineral Dependence: The Stockile Dilemma. Amos A. Jordan & Robert A. Kilmarx. LC 79-66890. (Washington Papers: No. 70). 83p. 1979. pap. 3.50 (ISBN 0-8039-1397-4). Sage.

Strategic Perspectives on Social Policy. Ed. by John E. Tropman et al. LC 74-14737. 1976. text ed. 23.00 (ISBN 0-08-018227-5); pap. text ed. 12.75 (ISBN 0-08-018226-7). Pergamon.

Strategic Persuasion: Arms Limitations Through Dialogue. Jeremy J. Stone. LC 67-25591. 1967. 20.00x (ISBN 0-231-03090-8). Columbia U Pr.

Strategic Planning: An Analytical Approach. K. J. Radford. (Illus.). 1980. text ed. 14.95 (ISBN 0-8359-7068-X). Reston.

Strategic Planning for MIS. Ephraim R. McLean & John V. Soden. LC 77-58483. 1977. 31.50 (ISBN 0-471-58562-9, Pub. by Wiley-Interscience). Wiley.

Strategic Planning in a Rapidly Changing Environment. James B. Whittaker. LC 77-4538. 1978. 19.95 (ISBN 0-669-01484-2). Lexington Bks.

Strategic Planning in London: The Rise & Fall of the Primary Road Network. Douglas Hart. Ed. by Urban & Regional Planning Advisory Committee. 239p. 1976. text ed. 18.75 (ISBN 0-08-019780-9). Pergamon.

Strategic Planning Systems. Peter Lorange & Richard F. Vancil. (Illus.). 1977. ref. ed. 18.95 (ISBN 0-13-851006-7). P-H.

Strategic Planning: What Every Manager Must Know. George A. Steiner. LC 78-20647. (Illus.). 1979. 14.95 (ISBN 0-02-931110-1). Free Pr.

Strategic Questioning. Ronald T. Hyman. LC 79-783. (Illus.). 1979. pap. text ed. 9.95 (ISBN 0-13-851055-5). P-H.

Strategic Styles: Coping in the Inner City. Janet K. Mancini. LC 79-56773. (Illus.). 320p. 1980. 15.95 (ISBN 0-87451-179-8). U Pr of New Eng.

Strategic Survey 1975. International Institute for Strategic Studies. LC 76-24927. 1976. 20.00x (ISBN 0-89158-545-1). Westview.

Strategic Survey 1976. International Institute for Strategic Studies. (Illus.). 1977. pap. text ed. 10.50 o.p. (ISBN 0-86079-006-1). Westview.

Strategic Survey 1977: International Institute for Strategic Studies. (Illus.). 1978. pap. text ed. 10.50x (ISBN 0-86079-021-5). Westview.

Strategic Survey 1978. Ed. by International Institute for Strategic Studies. LC 76-24927. 140p. 1980. pap. text ed. 11.50x (ISBN 0-86079-026-6). Westview.

Strategic Survey 1979. Internation Institute of Strategic Studies. (Illus.). 144p. 1980. lib. bdg. 12.50x (ISBN 0-86079-037-1, International Institute for Strategic Studies). Westview.

Strategies. B. Abbs et al. (Illus.). 1976. pap. text ed. 5.00x (ISBN 0-582-51872-5); tchr's ed. 9.00x (ISBN 0-582-51873-3). Longman.

Strategies: A Rhetoric & Reader. Charlene Tibbetts & A. M. Tibbetts. 1981. pap. text ed. 8.95x (ISBN 0-673-15461-0). Scott F.

Strategies Against Violence: Design for Nonviolent Change. Israel W. Charny. LC 78-3135. 1978. lib. bdg. 26.50x (ISBN 0-89158-151-0). Westview.

Strategies & Impact of Contemporary Radicalism: Radicalism in the Contemporary Age. Ed. by Bialer & Sluzar. LC 76-39890. (Studies of the Research Institute on International Change, Columbia University: Vol. 3). 1977. lib. bdg. 24.00x (ISBN 0-89158-129-4); lib. bdg. 60.00 3 vol. set. Westview.

Strategies & Tactics of Human Behavioral Research. James M. Johnston & H. S. Pennypacker. LC 80-22612. 496p. 1980. text ed. 19.95 (ISBN 0-89859-030-2). L Erlbaum Assocs.

Strategies & Techniques in Family Therapy. James C. Hansen & David Rosenthal. (Illus.). 480p. 1981. 28.50 (ISBN 0-398-04435-X); pap. 19.75 (ISBN 0-398-04154-7). C C Thomas.

Strategies for Change & Reform in Public Management. OECD. (Public Management Ser.: No. 1). 242p. (Orig.). 1980. pap. text ed. 16.00x (ISBN 92-64-12121-8). OECD.

Strategies for Change: How to Make the American Political Dream Work. Dick Simpson & George Beam. LC 75-43482. 258p. 1976. 12.00 (ISBN 0-8040-0696-2). Swallow.

Strategies for Change: Logical Incrementalism. James B. Quinn. LC 80-82098. 230p. 1980. 15.95 (ISBN 0-87094-220-4). Dow Jones-Irwin.

Strategies for Communication Research. Ed. by Paul M. Hirsch et al. LC 77-88630. (Sage Annual Reviews of Communication Research: Vol. 6). 1977. 20.00x (ISBN 0-8039-0891-1); pap. 9.95x (ISBN 0-8039-0892-X). Sage.

Strategies for Conducting Technology Assessments. Joe E. Armstrong & Willis W. Harman. (Westview Special Studies in Science, Technology, & Public Policy). 130p. 1980. lib. bdg. 17.50x (ISBN 0-89158-672-5). Westview.

Strategies for Curriculum Development. Jon Schaffarcick & David Hampson. LC 75-24652. 250p. 1975. 16.60x (ISBN 0-8211-0756-9); text ed. 15.00x (ISBN 0-685-57429-6). McCutchan.

Strategies for Differentiated Staffing. Fenwick W. English & Donald K. Sharpes. LC 75-190058. 1972. 19.00x (ISBN 0-8211-0409-8); text ed. 17.00x (ISBN 0-685-24962-X). McCutchan.

Strategies for Freedom: The Changing Pattern of Black Protest. Bayard Rustin. 100p. 1976. 10.00x (ISBN 0-231-03943-3). Columbia U Pr.

Strategies for Human Settlements: Habitat & Environment. Ed. by Gwen Bell. LC 76-5416. (Illus.). 200p. (Orig.). 1976. 9.95 o.p. (ISBN 0-8248-0414-7, Eastwest Ctr); pap. 3.95 (ISBN 0-8248-0469-4). U Pr of Hawaii.

Strategies for Identifying Words: A Workbook for Teachers & Those Preparing to Teach. 2nd ed. Dolores Durkin. 1980. pap. 9.50 (ISBN 0-205-07229-1, 2372290). Allyn.

Strategies for Implementing Work Experience Programs. Grady Kimbrell & Ben S. Vineyard. 400p. 1975. text ed. 34.67 (ISBN 0-87345-528-2). McKnight.

Strategies for Instructional Management. Lanore A. Netzer et al. 1979. text ed. 18.95 (ISBN 0-205-06448-5). Allyn.

Strategies for Marine Pollution Monitoring. Ed. by Edward D. Goldberg. LC 76-12490. 1976. 35.00 (ISBN 0-471-31070-0, Pub. by Wiley-Interscience). Wiley.

Strategies for Meeting the Information Needs of Society in the Year 2000. Martha Boaz. 250p. 1981. lib. bdg. price not set (ISBN 0-87287-249-1). Libs Unl.

Strategies for Motivation. (Study Units Ser.). 1977. pap. 9.00 (ISBN 0-89401-116-2). Didactic Syst.

Strategies for Planned Change. Gerald Zaltman & Robert Duncan. LC 76-39946. 1977. 25.95 (ISBN 0-471-98131-1, Pub. by Wiley-Interscience). Wiley.

Strategies for Planned Curricular Innovation. Ed. by Marcella R. Lawler. LC 78-106048. 1970. text ed. 9.25x (ISBN 0-8077-1667-7); pap. text ed. 6.00x (ISBN 0-8077-1666-9). Tchrs Coll.

Strategies for Postsecondary Education. Peter Scott. LC 75-8372. 161p. 1975. 21.95 (ISBN 0-470-76860-6). Halsted Pr.

Strategies for Public Health: Promoting Health & Preventing Disease. Ed. by Lorenz K. Ng & Devra Davis. 384p. 1980. text ed. 21.95 (ISBN 0-442-24428-2). Van Nos Reinhold.

Strategies for Reading: Paragraphs. H. Alan Robinson et al. (gr. 7-12). 1978. pap. text ed. 4.96 (ISBN 0-205-05852-3, 5258529); tchr's ed. 4.96 (ISBN 0-205-05853-1, 5258537). Allyn.

Strategies for Reading: Sentences. H. Alan Robinson et al. (gr. 7-12). 1978. pap. text ed. 4.96 (ISBN 0-205-05848-5, 5258480); tchr's ed. 4.96 (ISBN 0-205-05849-3, 5258499). Allyn.

Strategies for Reading: Words in Context. H. Alan Robinson et al. (gr. 7-12). 1978. pap. text ed. 4.96 (ISBN 0-205-05850-7, 5258502); tchr's ed. 4.96 (ISBN 0-205-05128-6, 5258510). Allyn.

Strategies for Research & Development in Higher Education: Proceedings. Educational Research Symposium Organised by the Council of Europe & the Research & Development Unit of the Chancellor of the Swedish Universities, Goteborg, Sweden, September 7-12, 1975. Ed. by Noel Entwistle. 282p. 1976. pap. text ed. 25.50 (ISBN 90-265-0242-7, Pub. by Swets Pub Serv Holland). Swets North Am.

Strategies for Survival: Cultural Behavior in an Ecological Context. Michael Jochim. 1981. price not set (ISBN 0-12-385460-1). Acad Pr.

Strategies for Teachers: Information Processing Models in the Classroom. Paul Eggen et al. (Curriculum & Teaching Ser.). (Illus.). 1979. ref. ed. 17.95 (ISBN 0-13-851162-4). P-H.

Strategies for Teaching. Anthony S. Jones et al. LC 79-20596. 249p. 1979. 13.50 (ISBN 0-8108-1257-6). Scarecrow.

Strategies for Teaching Children Mathematics. Ralph T. Heimer & Cecil R. Trueblood. LC 76-20030. 1977. text ed. 16.95 (ISBN 0-201-02882-4). A-W.

Strategies for Teaching the Mentally Retarded. 2nd ed. James S. Payne et al. (Special Education Ser.). 368p. 1981. text ed. 17.95 (ISBN 0-675-08067-3). Merrill.

Strategies for the Class Struggle in Latin America. Ed. by Marlene Dixon & Susanne Jonas. (Contemporary Marxism Ser.). (Illus.). 104p. (Orig.). 1980. pap. 5.00 (ISBN 0-89935-010-0). Synthesis Pubns.

Strategies for the Control of Cereal Disease: Organized by the British Plant Pathologist, Vol. 2. J. F. Jenkyn & R. T. Plumb. 250p. 1981. 47.50 (ISBN 0-470-27049-7). Halsted Pr.

Strategies for the Options Trader. Claud E. Cleeton. LC 78-11230. 1979. 22.95 (ISBN 0-471-04973-5, Pub. by Wiley-Interscience). Wiley.

Strategies for the Promotion of Health. Gordon DeFriese et al. 1981. price not set (ISBN 0-88410-719-1). Ballinger Pub.

Strategies for the Second Half of Life. Peter Weaver. 1981. pap. 3.50 (ISBN 0-451-09814-5, E9814, Signet Bks). NAL.

Strategies in Business. Shea Smith & John E. Walsh, Jr. LC 77-25091. (Systems & Controls for Financial Management Ser). 1978. 27.95 (ISBN 0-471-80002-3). Ronald Pr.

Strategies in Humanistic Education, 3 vols. Tim Timmermann & Jim Ballard. LC 75-25394. (Mandala Series in Education). 592p. 1976. Vol. 1. pap. 6.95x (ISBN 0-916250-03-2); Vol. 2. pap. 7.95 (ISBN 0-916250-11-3); Vol. 3. pap. 7.95 (ISBN 0-916250-25-3). Irvington.

Strategies of Community Organizations: A Book of Readings. 3rd ed. Ed. by Fred M. Cox et al. LC 77-83396. 1979. pap. text ed. 12.95 (ISBN 0-87581-230-9). Peacock Pubs.

Strategies of Ethics. Bernard Rosen. LC 77-77431. (Illus.). 1978. text ed. 13.50 (ISBN 0-395-25077-3); inst. manual 0.60 (ISBN 0-395-25078-1). HM.

Strategies of Immune Regulation. Ed. by Eli E. Sercarz & Alastair J. Cunningham. LC 79-28392. 1980. 39.50 (ISBN 0-12-637140-7). Acad Pr.

Strategies of International Mass Retailers. Charles Waldman. LC 78-19467. (Praeger Special Studies). 1978. 25.95 (ISBN 0-03-045626-6). Praeger.

Strategies of Political Emancipation. Christian Bay. LC 80-53117. 240p. 1981. text ed. 18.95 (ISBN 0-268-01702-6). U of Notre Dame Pr.

Strategies of Rhetoric. 3rd ed. A. M. Tibbetts & Charlene Tibbetts. 1979. pap. text ed. 10.95x (ISBN 0-673-15179-4). Scott F.

Strategies of Social Research. 2nd ed. H. Smith. 1980. 18.95 (ISBN 0-13-851154-3). P-H.

Strategies of Social Research: The Methodological Imagination. Herman W. Smith. (Methods of Social Science Ser.). (Illus.). 448p. 1975. text ed. 18.95 (ISBN 0-13-851147-0). P-H.

Strategies of Teaching Nursing. Rheba DeTornyay. LC 73-134038. (Paperback Nursing Ser.). 1971. pap. 9.50 (ISBN 0-471-20395-5, Pub. by Wiley Medical). Wiley.

Strategy & Conflict: The Search for Historical Malleability. Christian P Potholm. LC 78-71368. (Illus.). 1979. pap. 7.50 (ISBN 0-8191-0668-2). U Pr of Amer.

Strategy & Organization. rev ed. Hugo E. Uyterhoeven et al. 1977. text ed. 19.50 (ISBN 0-256-01923-1). Irwin.

Strategy & Policy. Arthur A. Thompson, Jr. & A. J. Strickland, III. 1978. text ed. 19.95 (ISBN 0-256-02083-3). Business Pubns.

Strategy & Society. C. Barrett. 161p. 1976. 7.00x (ISBN 0-7190-0627-9, Pub. by Manchester U Pr England). State Mutual Bk.

Strategy & Tactics of War. Ned Willmott & John Pimlott. (Illus.). 240p. 1980. 16.95 (ISBN 0-85685-503-0). Quality Bks IL.

Strategy for Agricultural Development & Other Essays on Economic Policy & Planning. 2nd ed. Samar R. Sen. 1966. 6.50x o.p. (ISBN 0-210-34027-4). Asia.

Strategy for Defeat: Vietnam in Retrospect. U. S. G. Sharp. LC 78-17607. (Illus.). 1978. 12.95 (ISBN 0-89141-053-8). Presidio Pr.

Strategy for Evaluating Health Services. Institute of Medicine. (Contrasts in Health Status Ser. Vol. 2). (Illus.). 256p. 1973. pap. 8.50 (ISBN 0-309-02104-9). Natl Acad Pr.

Strategy for for Rural Development: Saemaeul Undong in Korea. Young-Pyoung Kim. 1980. pap. 5.00 (ISBN 0-89249-032-2). Intl Development.

Strategy for Handling Executive Stress. Ari Kiev. LC 74-7319. 1974. 12.95 (ISBN 0-88229-153-X). Nelson-Hall.

Strategy for Minority Businesses. Luanna C. Blagrove. 67p. (Orig.). 1980. pap. 5.95. Blagrove Pubns.

Strategy for Personal Finance. 2nd ed. Larry Lang. 1981. text ed. 17.95 (ISBN 0-07-036281-5, C); instructor's manual 4.95 (ISBN 0-07-036283-1); wkbk. 5.95 (ISBN 0-07-036282-3). McGraw.

Strategy for Revolution: Essays on Latin America. Regis Debray. Ed. by Robin Blackburn. LC 78-105315. (Illus.). 1970. 6.50 (ISBN 0-85345-127-3, CL-1273); pap. 2.95 o.p. (ISBN 0-85345-180-X, PB-180X). Monthly Rev.

Strategy for Success. Ari Kiev. 1977. 6.95 o.s.i. (ISBN 0-02-563100-4, 56310). Macmillan.

Strategy for Survival. Arthur S. Boughey. LC 75-44541. (Orig.). 1976. pap. text ed. 9.50 (ISBN 0-8053-1095-9). Benjamin-Cummings.

Strategy for Survival. James Thompson. LC 79-67274. (Journey Bks). 144p. 1980. pap. 2.35 (ISBN 0-8344-0113-4). Sweet.

Strategy Formulation & Implementation: Tasks of the General Manager. Arthur A. Thompson, Jr. & A. J. Strickland, 3rd. 1980. pap. 10.50x (ISBN 0-256-02277-1). Business Pubns.

Strategy in Renal Failure. Eli A. Friedman. LC 77-11003. (Nephrology & Hypertension Ser.). 1978. 44.00 (ISBN 0-471-01597-0, Pub. by Wiley Medical). Wiley.

Strategy Management: How to Plan, Execute & Control Strategic Plans for Your Business. Kevin Tourangeau. 1980. 16.95 (ISBN 0-07-065043-8, P&RB). McGraw.
Strategy of Cash: A Liquidity Approach to Maximizing the Company's Profits. S. D. Slater. LC 74-9811. (Systems & Controls for Financial Management Ser). 416p. 1974. 28.50 (ISBN 0-471-79640-9, Pub. by Wiley-Interscience). Wiley.
Strategy of Conflict. Thomas C. Schelling. LC 60-11560. (Illus.). 1960. 15.00x (ISBN 0-674-84030-5); pap. text ed. 6.95 (ISBN 0-674-84031-3). Harvard U Pr.
Strategy of Decision: Policy Evaluation As a Social Process. David Braybrooke & Charles E. Lindblom. LC 63-13537. 1970. 10.95 o.s.i. (ISBN 0-02-904600-9); pap. text ed. 7.95 (ISBN 0-02-904610-6). Free Pr.
Strategy of Joy: An Essay on the Poetry of Samuel Taylor Coleridge. George H. Gilpin. (Salzburg Studies in English Literature, Romantic Reassessment: No.3). 1972. pap. text ed. 25.00x (ISBN 0-391-01384-X). Humanities.
Strategy of Life. 2nd ed. Clifford Grobstein. LC 73-18061. (Biology Ser.). (Illus.). 1974. text ed. 16.95x (ISBN 0-7167-0591-5); pap. text ed. 8.95x (ISBN 0-7167-0590-7). W H Freeman.
Strategy of Marketing Research. Chester R. Wasson. LC 64-15387. (Illus.). 1964. 24.50x (ISBN 0-89197-426-1); pap. text ed. 14.95x (ISBN 0-89197-953-0). Irvington.
Strategy of Peace. John F. Kennedy. Ed. by Allan Nevins. LC 60-7530. 1960. 10.00 o.s.i. (ISBN 0-06-012325-7, HarpT). Har-Row.
Strategy of Puts & Calls. A. Dadeklan. LC 68-57498. 1973. pap. 2.95 o.p. (ISBN 0-684-13310-5, SL430, ScribT). Scribner.
Strategy of Sea Power: Its Development & Application. Stephen W. Roskill. LC 80-27028. (Lees-Knowles Lecture Ser., Cambridge, 1961). 287p. 1981. Repr. of 1962 ed. lib. bdg. 27.50x (ISBN 0-313-22801-9, ROSSP). Greenwood.
Strategy of Social Protest. William A. Gamson. 1975. pap. text ed. 10.50x (ISBN 0-256-01684-4). Dorsey.
Strategy, Politics & Defense Budgets. Warner R. Schilling et al. LC 62-17353. (Institute of War & Peace Studies). 1962. 22.50x (ISBN 0-231-02556-4). Columbia U Pr.
Strathmore. Jessica Stirling. Orig. Title: Call Home the Heart. 1975. 8.95 o.s.i. (ISBN 0-440-05971-2). Delacorte.
Stratification Among the Aged. James J. Dowd. LC 79-25143. (Social Gerontology Ser.). (Orig.). 1980. pap. text ed. 6.95 (ISBN 0-8185-0386-6). Brooks-Cole.
Stratification, Class & Conflict. Irving Krauss. LC 75-12060. (Illus.). 1976. text ed. 15.95 (ISBN 0-02-917690-5). Free Pr.
Stratification of Behavior. David S. Shwayder. 1971. text ed. 14.25x (ISBN 0-391-00145-0). Humanities.
Stratigraphy & Glacial-Marine Sediments of the Amerasian Basin,Central Arctic Ocean. David L. Clark. LC 80-65270. (Special Paper Ser.: No. 181). (Illus., Orig.). 1980. pap. 13.00 (ISBN 0-8137-2181-4). Geol Soc.
Stratigraphy & Life History. Ed. by Marshall Kay & E. H. Colbert. LC 64-20072. 1965. 23.95 (ISBN 0-471-46105-9). Wiley.
Stratigraphy & Sedimentation. 2nd ed. William C. Krumbein & L. L. Sloss. LC 61-11422. 1963. 27.95x (ISBN 0-7167-0219-3). W H Freeman.
Stratigraphy of the British Isles. 2nd ed. D Rayner. LC 79-8523. (Illus.). 400p. Date not set. price not set (ISBN 0-521-23452-2); pap. price not set (ISBN 0-521-29961-6). Cambridge U Pr.
Stratigraphy of the British Isles. D. H. Rayner. (Illus.). 1967. 44.50 (ISBN 0-521-06047-8). Cambridge U Pr.
Stratigraphy of the British Isles. Dorothy H. Rayner. (Illus.). 1980. pap. 15.50 (ISBN 0-521-29820-2). Cambridge U Pr.
Strauss Air Pollution Control, Pt. 4. Gordon M. Bragg & Jennifer Strauss. LC 79-23458. (Environmental Science & Technology Ser.). 416p. 1981. 30.00 (ISBN 0-471-07957-X, Pub. by Wiley-Interscience). Wiley.
Strausser Transfer. Don Smith. (Secret Mission Ser.). 1978. pap. 1.95 (ISBN 0-441-77200-5). Charter Bks.
Stravinsky: Classic Humanist. Heinrich Strobel. LC 73-4338. 186p. 1974. Repr. of 1955 ed. lib. bdg. 18.50 (ISBN 0-306-70580-X). Da Capo.
Stravinsky in the Theatre. Ed. by Minna Lederman. LC 74-34377. (Music Reprint Ser.). (Illus.). 228p. 1975. Repr. of 1949 ed. lib. bdg. 22.50 (ISBN 0-306-70665-2); pap. 4.95 (ISBN 0-306-80022-5). Da Capo.
Straw Decay & Its Effect on Disposal & Utilization. Ed. by E. Grossbard. LC 79-42841. 1979. 50.25 (ISBN 0-471-27694-4, Pub. by Wiley Interscience). Wiley.
Straw Man. Barbara Goldsmith. 1981. pap. 2.75 (ISBN 0-345-29423-8). Ballantine.
Straw Obelisk. Adolph Caso. 296p. 1971. 6.95 (ISBN 0-8283-1293-1). Dante U Am.
Strawberries. Barbara Noda. (Illus.). 1980. pap. 2.95 (ISBN 0-915288-40-0). Shameless Hussy.
Strawberry: A World Bibliography Nineteen Twenty to Nineteen Sixty Six. William Anderson. LC 72-3866. 1969. 20.50 (ISBN 0-8108-0262-7). Scarecrow.
Strawberry Book of Colors. Hefter. 120p. Date not set. 4.50 (ISBN 0-07-027826-1). McGraw.
Strawberry Deficiency Symptoms: A Visual & Plant Analysis Guide to Fertilization. Albert Ulrich et al. LC 79-67379. (Illus.). 58p. pap. text ed. 8.00x (ISBN 0-931876-37-0). Ag Sci Pubns.
Strawberry Look Book. Hefter. 120p. Date not set. 4.95 (ISBN 0-07-027824-5). McGraw.
Strawberry Statement: Notes of a College Revolutionist. James S. Kunen. LC 69-16455. 1969. 6.95 o.p. (ISBN 0-394-44753-0). Random.
Strawcraft. M. Lambeth. 72p. 1974. 9.95 (ISBN 0-212-97010-0). Transatlantic.
Straws in the Wind. R. Rabindranath Menon. (Writers Workshop Redbird Ser.). 1975. 12.00 (ISBN 0-88253-650-8); pap. text ed. 4.80 (ISBN 0-88253-649-4). Ind-US Inc.
Stray. Lynn Hall. (gr. 2-4). 1975. pap. 0.95 (ISBN 0-380-00202-7, 23473, Camelot). Avon.
Stray Cow. Meyer Llewellyn. pap. 2.15 o.p. (ISBN 0-08-015697-5). Pergamon.
Stray Dog. Carol B. York. LC 80-28779. 128p. (gr. 4 up). 1981. 7.95 (ISBN 0-8253-0046-0). Beaufort Bks NY.
Streak of Sunshine. T. L. Nichols. 4.00 o.p. (ISBN 0-8062-1012-5). Carlton.
Stream on the Other Side of the Mind. 300p. 1981. 30.00 (ISBN 0-913028-82-7); pap. 8.95 (ISBN 0-686-69476-7). North Atlantic.
Stream Runner. David Seed. LC 78-21769. 192p. (gr. 5 up). 1979. 7.95 (ISBN 0-590-07568-3, Four Winds). Schol Bk Serv.
Streaming: Two Years Later. Elsa Ferri. (Research Reports Ser.). 1971. text ed. 12.50x (ISBN 0-901225-55-X, NFER). Humanities.
Streamlined. John Kaufmann. LC 74-2357. (Let's-Read-&-Find-Out Science Bk). (gr. k-3). 1974. 6.95 o.p. (ISBN 0-690-00273-4, TYC-J); PLB 7.89 (ISBN 0-690-00565-2). T Y Crowell.
Streams in the Desert, Vol. 2. large print ed. Mrs. Charles E. Cowman. 384p. 1976. kivar bdg. 6.95 (ISBN 0-310-22537-X). Zondervan.
Street. Ann Petry. (gr. 9-12). 1969. pap. 1.25 (ISBN 0-515-01997-6). Jove Pubns.
Street Biking: How to Ride to Save Your Hide. Bob Jackson. 1980. pap. 5.95 (ISBN 0-89586-081-3). H P Bks.
Street Cars of Boston, Vol.6: Birneys, Type 5, Semiconvertibles, Parlor, Private, & Mail Cars. O. R. Cummings. (Illus.). 84p. 1980. pap. 9.00 (ISBN 0-911940-34-0). Cox.
Street Club Work in Tel Aviv & New York. Aryeh Leissner. (Studies in Child Development). (Illus., Orig.). 1969. pap. text ed. 5.75x (ISBN 0-582-32444-0). Humanities.
Street Corner Conservative. William F. Gavin. 1975. 7.95 o.s.i. (ISBN 0-87000-325-9). Arlington Hse.
Street Directory of the Principal Cities of the United States: Embracing Letter-Carrier Offices Established to April 30, 1908. 5th ed. U. S. Post Office Department. LC 76-179692. 904p. Repr. of 1908 ed. 42.00 (ISBN 0-8103-3072-5). Gale.
Street Hustler. Norman Rubington. 1975. pap. 1.50 o.p. (ISBN 0-685-57552-7, LB301DK, Leisure Bks). Nordon Pubns.
Street in Marrakech. Elizabeth Warnock Fernea. LC 74-12686. 1976. pap. 3.50 (ISBN 0-385-12045-1, Anch). Doubleday.
Street Law: A Course in Practical Law. 2nd ed. Lee Arbetman et al. 383p. 1980. pap. text ed. write for info. (ISBN 0-8299-1031-X). West Pub.
Street Life: Afro-American Culture in Urban Trinidad. Michael Lieber. (University Book Ser.). 1981. lib. bdg. 15.95 (ISBN 0-8161-9033-X). G K Hall.
Street Markets Around the World. Winifred Lubell & Cecil Lubell. LC 74-805. (Finding-Out Book). (Illus.). 64p. (gr. 2-4). 1974. PLB 6.95 (ISBN 0-8193-0732-7). Enslow Pubs.
Street of the Five Moons. Elizabeth Peters. LC 74-4278. 1978. 7.95 (ISBN 0-396-07528-2). Dodd.
Street of the Flower Boxes. Peggy Mann. (gr. 3-5). 1971. pap. 0.60 o.s.i. (ISBN 0-671-29322-2). Archway.
Street Smarts. Bruce Reeves. LC 80-28256. 192p. (gr. 6 up). 1981. 8.95 (ISBN 0-8253-0047-9). Beaufort Bks NY.
Streetcar Guide to Uptown New Orleans. Louis Costa et al. Ed. by David Swords. (Illus.). 136p. (Orig.). 1980. pap. 5.00 (ISBN 0-939108-00-3). Transitour.
Streetcar Named Desire. Tennessee Williams. LC 48-5556. 1980. pap. 3.95 (ISBN 0-8112-0765-X, NDP501). New Directions.
Streetcar Named Desire. Tennessee Williams. 1973. pap. 1.75 (ISBN 0-451-07595-1, E9372, Sig). NAL.
Streetfighter in the Courtroom. Charles Garry & Art Goldberg. 1977. 11.95 o.p. (ISBN 0-525-21110-1). Dutton.
Streetful of People. Winston M. Estes. 1978. pap. 1.75 o.p. (ISBN 0-380-01917-5, 37614). Avon.
Streets After Rain. Elizabeth Knies. LC 80-66181. 64p. 1980. pap. 4.95 (ISBN 0-914086-31-6). Alicejamesbooks.
Street's Cruising Guide to the Eastern Caribbean, Vol. 1. Donald M. Street, Jr. 1981. pap. 27.95 spiral bdg. (ISBN 0-393-03250-7). Norton.
Streets for People. Bernard Rudofsky. LC 76-78735. 1969. 14.95 o.p. (ISBN 0-385-04231-0). Doubleday.
Streets of Death. Dell Shannon. LC 80-24140. 315p. 1980. Repr. of 1976 ed. large print ed. 8.95 (ISBN 0-89621-250-5). Thorndike Pr.
Streets of Gold. Karen Branson. 160p. (gr. 10 up). 1981. 7.95 (ISBN 0-399-20791-0). Putnam.
Streets of the Kings. Harry Williams. LC 80-50035. 1980. 8.95 (ISBN 0-533-04584-3). Vantage.
Streets Were Paved with Gold: The Decline of New York--An American Tragedy. Ken Auletta. LC 79-22305. 1980. pap. 4.95 (ISBN 0-394-74355-5, V-355, Vin). Random.
Streetscape Equipment Sourcebook, No. 2. Center for Design Planning. LC 79-56221. (Illus.). 244p. 1979. pap. text ed. 19.50 (ISBN 0-87420-589-1). Urban Land.
Streetwater Saga. Roxanne Dent. 1979. pap. cancelled o.p. (Sig). NAL.
Streetwork: The Exploding School. Colin Ward & Anthony Fyson. 150p. 1974. 14.00 (ISBN 0-7100-7683-5); pap. 7.95 (ISBN 0-7100-7702-5). Routledge & Kegan.
Strega Nona. Tomie De Paola. LC 75-11565. (Illus.). (ps-3). 1975. 8.95 (ISBN 0-13-851600-6); pap. 3.95. P-H.
Streisand. Jonathan Black. 1975. pap. 1.50 o.p. (ISBN 0-685-57553-5, LB298DK, Leisure Bks). Nordon Pubns.
Strength. rev. ed. Harlan Wade. LC 78-26848. (Book About Ser.). (Illus.). (gr. k-3). 1979. PLB 7.30 (ISBN 0-8172-1528-X). Raintree Pubs.
Strength & Failure of Visco-Elastic Materials. G. M. Bartenev & Yu. S. Zuyev. 1968. 60.00 (ISBN 0-08-012183-7). Pergamon.
Strength & Structure of Engineering Materials. N. H. Polakowski & E. Ripling. 1965. text ed. 26.95 (ISBN 0-13-851790-8). P-H.
Strength from Above. E. J. Saleska. 1946. 0.85 (ISBN 0-570-03677-1, 74-1002). Concordia.
Strength of Materials. P. Black. 1966. 22.00 (ISBN 0-08-011555-1). Pergamon.
Strength of Materials. Jacob P. Den Hartog. 1949. pap. 5.00 (ISBN 0-486-60755-0). Dover.
Strength of Materials. R. W. Fitzgerald. 1967. text ed. 20.95 (ISBN 0-201-02050-5); instructor's guide 2.95 (ISBN 0-201-02051-3). A-W.
Strength of Materials. A. A. Ilyushin & V. S. Lenskii. Ed. by L. C. Redshaw. Tr. by J. K. Loshor. 1967. 75.00 (ISBN 0-08-011461-X). Pergamon.
Strength of Materials. Bela I. Sandor. (Illus.). 1978. ref. ed. 24.95 (ISBN 0-13-852418-1). P-H.
Strength of Materials. Surendra Singh. 1980. text ed. 18.95x (ISBN 0-7069-0705-1, Pub. by Vikas India). Advent Bk.
Strength of Materials. Nicholas Willems et al. (Illus.). 576p. 1981. text ed. write for info. (ISBN 0-07-070297-7, C); write for info. solutions manual (ISBN 0-07-070298-5). McGraw.
Strength of Materials - Mechanics of Solids. REA Staff. 896p. 1980. 22.85 (ISBN 0-87891-522-2). Res & Educ.
Strength of Materials & Structures: An Introduction to the Mechanics of Solids & Structures. 2nd ed. John Case & A. H. Chilver. (Illus.). 1971. pap. text ed. 19.95x (ISBN 0-7131-3244-2). Intl Ideas.
Strength of Materials for Technology. Charles D. Bruch. LC 77-27629. 1978. text ed. 19.95 (ISBN 0-471-11372-7); sol. manual (ISBN 0-471-04513-6). Wiley.
Strength of Materials: Fundamentals, Vol. 1. J. M. Alexander. 190p. 1981. 47.95 (ISBN 0-470-27119-1). Halsted Pr.
Strength of Materials: Theory & Examples. R. C. Stephens. (Illus.). 1970. pap. text ed. 16.50x (ISBN 0-7131-3211-6). Intl Ideas.
Strength of Metals & Alloys: International Conference on the Strength of Metals & Alloys, 5th, Aachen, 1979, 3 vols. Ed. by P. Haasen et al. LC 79-40131. (Illus.). 1980. Set. 260.00 (ISBN 0-08-023265-5); Set. pap. 150.00 (ISBN 0-08-024760-1). Pergamon.
Strength of the People: A Study in Social Economics, London Nineteen Three. 2nd ed. Helen Bosanquet. LC 79-56950. (English Working Class Ser.). 1980. lib. bdg. 30.00 (ISBN 0-8240-0104-4). Garland Pub.
Strength Properties of Timber. Building Research Establishment. 208p. 1974. 24.50 (ISBN 0-89047-050-2). Herman Pub.
Strength to Love. Martin L. King, Jr. LC 80-2374. 160p. 1981. pap. 4.25 (ISBN 0-8006-1441-0, 1-1441). Fortress.
Strengthening Bilingual Education. Commissioner of Education. 102p. 1979. pap. 3.50 o.s.i. (ISBN 0-89763-017-3). Natl Clearing Bilingual Ed.
Strengthening Methods in Crystals. Ed. by A. Kelly & R. Nicholson. 627p. 1972. 54.95 (ISBN 0-470-46800-9). Halsted Pr.
Strengths of a Good School Faculty. David Mallery. 1975. pap. 6.50 (ISBN 0-934338-31-0). NAIS.
Streptococcal Diseases & the Immune Response. Ed. by Stanley E. Read & John B. Zabriskie. LC 79-26638. 1980. 45.00 (ISBN 0-12-583880-8). Acad Pr.
Stress. Ogden Tanner. LC 75-33607. (Human Behavior). (Illus.). (gr. 5 up). 1976. PLB 12.40 o.p. (ISBN 0-8094-1929-7, Pub. by Time-Life). Silver.
Stress. Ogden Tanner. (Human Behavior Ser.). 9.95 (ISBN 0-8094-1928-9). Time-Life.
Stress Analysis by the Finite Element Method for Practically Engineers. W. H. Bowes & Leslie T. Russell. 128p. 1975. 22.95 (ISBN 0-669-99903-2). Lexington Bks.
Stress Analysis of Notch Problems. Ed. by G. C. Sih. (Mechanics of Fracture Ser.: No. 5). 312p. 1978. 45.00x (ISBN 90-286-0166-X). Sijthoff & Noordhoff.
Stress Analysis of Polymers. 2nd rev. ed. J. G. Williams. LC 80-40144. (Ellis Horwood Ser. in Engineering Science). 360p. 1980. 77.95x (ISBN 0-470-26964-2). Halsted Pr.
Stress Analysis of Pressure Vessels & Pressure Vessel Components. S. S. Gill. 1970. 90.00 (ISBN 0-08-006729-8). Pergamon.
Stress Analysis Problems in SI Units. D. F. Mallows & W. J. Pickering. LC 71-171465. 1972. 25.00 (ISBN 0-08-016293-2); pap. 11.75 o.p. (ISBN 0-08-016292-4). Pergamon.
Stress & Anxiety, Vol. 7. Ed. by Irwin G. Sarason & Charles D. Spielberger. LC 74-28292. (Clinical & Community Psychology Ser.). (Illus.). 384p. 1980. text ed. 25.50 (ISBN 0-89116-183-X). Hemisphere Pub.
Stress & Anxiety, Vol. 8. Ed. by Charles D. Spielberger et al. LC 74-28292. (Clinical & Community Psychology). (Illus.). 560p. 1981. text ed. 27.50 (ISBN 0-89116-184-8). Hemisphere Pub.
Stress & Campus Response: Current Issues in Higher Education 1968. Ed. by G. Kerry Smith. LC 73-92897. (Higher Education Ser.). 1968. 12.95x o.p. (ISBN 0-87589-025-3). Jossey-Bass.
Stress & Coping: An Anthology. Ed. by Alan Monat & Richard S. Lazarus. LC 77-3264. 1977. 25.00x (ISBN 0-231-08358-0); pap. 10.00x (ISBN 0-685-75645-9). Columbia U Pr.
Stress & Decision Making in the Dental Practice. James M. Dyce. (Illus.). 165p. 1973. 24.00. Quint Pub Co.
Stress & Its Relationship to Health & Illness. Linas A. Bieliauskas. (Behavioral Sciences for Health Care Professionals Ser.). 128p. (Orig.). 1981. lib. bdg. 15.00x (ISBN 0-86531-002-5); pap. text ed. 6.00x (ISBN 0-86531-003-3). Westview.
Stress & Mental Disorder. Ed. by James E. Barrett. LC 79-2202. (American Psychopathological Association Ser.). 1979. text ed. 28.00 (ISBN 0-89004-384-1). Raven.
Stress & Performance Effectiveness. Ed. by Earl A. Alluisi & Edwin A. Fleishman. (Human Performance & Productivity Ser.: Vol.3). 336p. 1981. professional ref. text 19.95 (ISBN 0-89859-091-4). L Erlbaum Assocs.
Stress & Relaxation: Application to Dentistry. Donald R. Morse & Merrick L. Furst. (Illus.). 284p. 1978. 17.75 (ISBN 0-398-03816-3). C C Thomas.
Stress & Survival: The Emotional Realities of Life Threatening Illness. Ed. by Charles A. Garfield. LC 78-31341. (Illus.). 1979. text ed. 16.95 (ISBN 0-8016-1743-X). Mosby.
Stress & Tension Control. Ed. by F. J. McGuigan et al. 330p. 1980. 29.50 (ISBN 0-306-40450-8, Plenum Pr). Plenum Pub.
Stress & the Heart. 2nd ed. Ed. by David Wheatley. 430p. 1981. 39.50 (ISBN 0-89004-520-8). Raven.
Stress & the Heart: Interactions of the Cardiovascular System, Behavioral State, & Psychotropic Drugs. Ed. by David Wheatley. LC 76-55064. 1977. 19.00 (ISBN 0-89004-151-2). Raven.
Stress & the Helping Professions. Sheldon F. Greenberg & Peter J. Valletutti. LC 80-20328. 156p. (Orig.). 1980. pap. text ed. 9.95 (ISBN 0-933716-09-5). P H Brookes.
Stress & the Manager: Making It Work for You. Karl Albrecht. (Illus.). 1978. 14.95 (ISBN 0-13-852681-8, Spec); pap. 5.95 (ISBN 0-13-852673-7). P-H.

Stress & the Organization. Ed. by Richard H. Davis. James E. Birren. LC 78-66074. 1979. pap. 3.00 (ISBN 0-88474-086-2). USC Andrus Geron.

Stress & the Police: A Manual for Prevention. Lynn H Monahan & Richard E. Farmer. LC 80-83671. 1981. pap. 7.95 (ISBN 0-913530-23-9). Palisades Pubs.

Stress & Tiger Juice: How to Manage Your Stress & Improve Your Life & Your Health. Stewart Bedford. LC 79-92277. 128p. 1980. 9.95x (ISBN 0-935930-00-0); pap. 4.95x (ISBN 0-935930-01-9). Scott Pubns CA.

Stress & Work: A Managerial Perspective. John M. Ivancevich & Michael T. Matteson. 1981. pap. text ed. 7.95x (ISBN 0-673-15381-9). Scott F.

Stress at Work. C. L. Cooper & R. Payne. (Studies in Occupational Stress). 293p. 1978. 36.50 (ISBN 0-471-99547-9, Pub. by Wiley-Interscience). Wiley.

Stress Concentration Factors. Rudolph E. Peterson. LC 53-11283. 336p. 1974. 32.50 (ISBN 0-471-68329-9, Pub. by Wiley-Interscience). Wiley.

Stress Control. Vernon Coleman. 214p. 1979. 20.00 (ISBN 0-85117-167-2). Transatlantic.

Stress Corrosion of Metals. Hugh L. Logan. LC 66-2651. (Corrosion Monograph Ser.). 1966. 30.50 o.p. (ISBN 0-471-54340-3, Pub. by Wiley-Interscience). Wiley.

Stress Corrosion Research. H. Arup & R. N. Parkins. (NATO Advanced Study Institute Ser.). 279p. 1979. 30.00x (ISBN 90-286-0647-5). Sijthoff & Noordhoff.

Stress in Hospital. Jenifer Wilson-Barnett. (Illus.). 136p. 1980. pap. text ed. 8.95x (ISBN 0-443-01879-0). Churchill.

Stress: In the Eye of the Beholder the Key to Competent Coping. Blair Justice & Rita Justice. 193p. (Orig.). 1980. pap. cancelled (ISBN 0-915190-29-X). Jalmar Pr.

Stress Management: A Conceptual & Procedural Guide. Ronald G. Nathan & Edward A. Charlesworth. LC 80-70400. (Illus.). 223p. (Orig.). 1980. 19.95 (ISBN 0-938176-01-3). Wendover.

Stress Management: A Conceptual & Procedural Guide. Ronald G. Nathan & Edward A. Charlesworth. (Illus.). 223p. (Orig.). 1980. pap. text ed. 19.95 (ISBN 0-938176-01-3). Biobehavioral Pr.

Stress Management for Health Care Professionals. Steven Appelbaum. 350p. 1980. text ed. 24.95 (ISBN 0-89443-332-6). Aspen Systems.

Stress Mess Solution. George Everly & Daniel Girdano. LC 79-14652. 174p. 1980. text ed. 11.95 (ISBN 0-87619-666-0); pap. 9.95 (ISBN 0-87619-434-X). R J Brady.

Stress of Hot Environments. D. M. Kerslake. LC 74-168896. (Physiological Society Monographs: No. 29). (Illus.). 300p. 1972. 59.50 (ISBN 0-521-08343-5). Cambridge U Pr.

Stress Power: How to Turn Tension into Energy. Robert A. Anderson. LC 78-8308. 225p. 1978. 14.95 (ISBN 0-87705-328-6). Human Sci Pr.

Stress-Strain Behaviour of Soils. Ed. by R. H. Parry. (Illus.). 1973. text ed. 54.00x (ISBN 0-85429-121-0). Intl Ideas.

Stress Survival Foodbook. Margaret C. Dean. 1981. pap. 5.95 (ISBN 0-87491-295-4). Acropolis.

Stress Testing: Principles & Testing. Myrin H. Ellestad. 1980. 35.00 (ISBN 0-8036-3111-1). Davis Co.

Stress, Vibration & Noise Analysis in Vehicles. Ed. by H. G. Gibbs & T. H. Richards. LC 75-14389. 1975. 61.95 (ISBN 0-470-29742-5). Halsted Pr.

Stress Waves in Solids. 2nd ed. H. Kolsky. (Illus.). 1963. pap. text ed. 4.00 (ISBN 0-486-61098-5). Dover.

Stress Without Distress. Hans Selye. LC 74-1314. (Illus.). 1974. 10.95 (ISBN 0-397-01026-5). Lippincott.

Stresses in Plates & Shells. Ansel C. Ugural. (Illus.). 352p. text ed. 29.95x (ISBN 0-07-065730-0, C); solutions manual 6.95 (ISBN 0-07-065731-9). McGraw.

Stresses in Shells. 2nd ed. W. Fluegge. LC 74-183604. (Illus.). 525p. 1973. 28.30 (ISBN 0-387-05322-0). Springer-Verlag.

Stresses in U.S. - Japanese Security Relations. Fred Greene. (Studies in Defense Policy). 120p. 1975. pap. 3.95 (ISBN 0-8157-3271-6). Brookings.

Stretchers: The Story of a Hospital Unit on the Western Front. Frederick A. Pottle. 1929. 34.50x (ISBN 0-685-89785-0). Elliots Bks.

Stretching Fence. Sonya Dorman. LC 75-14550. 61p. 1975. 8.95 (ISBN 0-8214-0188-2); pap. 4.95 (ISBN 0-8214-0209-9). Ohio U Pr.

Stretching for All Sports. John E. Beaulieu. (Illus.). 214p. 7.95 (ISBN 0-87095-079-7). Athletic.

Stretching the Food Dollar Cookbook. Edyth Y. Cottrell. LC 80-36894. (Illus., Orig.). 1981. pap. 3.95 (ISBN 0-912800-80-1). Woodbridge Pr.

Stretching the Food Dollar: Practical Solutions to the Challenges of the 80's. Janet Spiegel. (Urban Life Ser.). (Illus.). 96p. (Orig.). 1981. pap. 4.95 (ISBN 0-87701-172-9). Chronicle Bks.

Stretching Your Meat Dollar. Jon McClure. (Orig.). 1978. pap. 2.50 o.s.i. (ISBN 0-515-04563-2). Jove Pubns.

Strictly for Laughs. Joey Adams. 224p. 1981. 8.95 (ISBN 0-89479-079-X). A & W Pubs.

Strictly for the Chickens. Frances Hamerstrom. 136p. 1980. 11.95 (ISBN 0-8138-0800-6). Iowa St U Pr.

Strictly Personal. John Eisenhower. LC 73-20510. (Illus.). 10.95 o.p. (ISBN 0-385-07071-3). Doubleday.

Strictly Speaking. Edwin Newman. 1975. pap. 2.75 (ISBN 0-446-95945-6). Warner Bks.

Strictly Speaking: Will America Be the Death of English? Edwin Newman. LC 74-6525. 224p. 1974. 9.95 (ISBN 0-672-51990-9). Bobbs.

Strictures on the Modern System of Female Education, 2 vols. Hannah More. Ed. by Gina Luria. (Feminist Controversy in England, 1788-1810 Ser.). 1974. Set. lib. bdg. 100.00 (ISBN 0-8240-0873-1); lib. bdg. 50.00 ea. Garland Pub.

Striding Slippers: Adapted from an Udmurt Tale. Mirra Ginsburg. LC 77-12035. (Illus.). (gr. k-3). 1978. 8.95 (ISBN 0-02-736370-8, 73637). Macmillan.

Strike Force Ten. Heinz G. Konsalik. 320p. 1981. 12.95 (ISBN 0-399-12615-5). Putnam.

Strike in the American Novel. Fay M. Blake. LC 72-623. 1972. 10.00 (ISBN 0-8108-0481-6). Scarecrow.

Strike It Rich! Treasure Hunting with Metal Detectors. Peggy Hardigree. (Illus.). 224p. 1980. 10.95 (ISBN 0-517-54216-1, Harmony); pap. 5.95 (ISBN 0-517-54160-2, Harmony). Crown.

Strike Two. George Shea. (Sportellers Ser.). (Illus.). 64p. (gr. 5 up). 1981. PLB 7.95 (ISBN 0-516-02267-9). Childrens.

Striker Portfolio. Adam Hall. 1970. pap. 1.75 o.s.i. (ISBN 0-685-19679-8). Jove Pubns.

Striker Schneiderman. Jack Gray. LC 72-954459. 1973. pap. 2.50 (ISBN 0-8020-6172-9). U of Toronto Pr.

Strikes. R. Hyman. pap. 1.95 o.p. (ISBN 0-531-06033-0, Fontana Pap). Watts.

Strikes & Industrial Conflict: Britain & Scandinavia. Geoffrey Ingham. (Studies in Sociology). 95p. (Orig.). 1974. pap. 3.25x (ISBN 0-333-13435-4). Humanities.

Strikes, Stoppages & Boycotts 1980, Vol. 160. (Litigation & Administrative Practices Course Handbook Ser. 1979-80). 1980. soft cover 25.00 (ISBN 0-685-47620-0, H4-4826). PLI.

String. Dennis Schmitz. LC 79-9444. (American Poetry Ser.: Vol. 19). 80p. 1981. pap. 4.95 (ISBN 0-912946-69-5). Ecco Pr.

String & List Processing in Snobol 4: Techniques & Applications. Ralph C. Griswold. (Illus.). 304p. 1975. text ed. 14.95 (ISBN 0-13-853010-6). P-H.

String Art Encyclopedia. LC 76-1184. (Illus.). 112p. (YA) 1976. 14.95 o.p. (ISBN 0-8069-5362-4); PLB 13.29 o.p. (ISBN 0-8069-5363-2). Sterling.

String Designs. Glen Saeger. LC 74-31703. (Little Craft Book Ser.). (Illus.). 48p. (gr. 5 up). 1975. 5.95 (ISBN 0-8069-5320-9); PLB 6.69 (ISBN 0-8069-5321-7). Sterling.

String (Double) Bass. David H. Stanton. 8.00 (ISBN 0-686-15896-2). Instrumentalist Co.

String Ensemble Performance, Zone 3, Book A. H. Higa. (University of Hawaii Music Project). (gr. 4-6). 1975. pap. write for info o.p.; tchr's ed. 7.84 o.p. (ISBN 0-201-00816-5). A-W.

String Figures & Other Monographs, 4 vols. in 1. Ed. by W. Rouse Ball et al. Incl. String Figures. W. R. Ball; History of the Slide Rule. F. Cajori; Non Euclidean Geometry. Horatio S. Carslaw; Methods Geometrical Construction. Julius Petersen. LC 59-11780. 12.95 (ISBN 0-8284-0130-6). Chelsea Pub.

String Music in Print. 2nd ed. Ed. by Margaret K. Farish. LC 80-18425. (Music in Print Ser.: Vol. 6). 464p. 1980. Repr. lib. bdg. 60.00 (ISBN 0-88478-011-2). Musicdata.

String of Chinese Peach-Stones. W. Arthur Cornaby. LC 70-175730. (Illus.). xvi, 478p. 1974. Repr. of 1895 ed. 20.00 (ISBN 0-8103-3125-X). Gale.

String Quartet. Arnold Elston. (U. C. Publ. in Contemporary Music: Vol. 1.). (Illus.). 1967. pap. 12.50x (ISBN 0-520-00383-7). U of Cal Pr.

Stringcraft. Roland Cauro & Dominique Cauro. LC 76-1181. (Little Craft Book Ser.). (Illus.). 48p. 1976. 4.95 o.p. (ISBN 0-8069-5364-0); PLB 5.89 o.p. (ISBN 0-8069-5365-9). Sterling.

Stringed Instruments of the Middle Ages. Hortense Panum. LC 73-127279. (Music Ser). (Illus.). 1970. Repr. of 1939 ed. lib. bdg. 39.50 (ISBN 0-306-70039-5). Da Capo.

Strings on Your Fingers: How to Make String Figures. Harry Helfman & Elizabeth Helfman. (Illus.). (gr. 3-7). 1965. PLB 6.48 (ISBN 0-688-31582-8). Morrow.

Strip Method of Design. 2nd ed. Arno Hilleborg. (C & CA Viewpoint Publication Ser.). (Illus.). 1976. pap. text ed. 22.50 (ISBN 0-7210-1012-1). Scholium Intl.

Strip-Mineable Coals Guidebook. LC 80-81269. 1980. 103.00. Minobras.

Strip Spring Making & Forming. Ed. by Spring Research Association, Sheffield. (Engineering Craftsmen: No. H7). (Illus.). 1977. spiral bdg. 18.95x (ISBN 0-85083-331-0). Intl Ideas.

Striped Ice Cream. Joan M. Lexau. LC 68-10774. (gr. 1-6). 1968. 7.95 (ISBN 0-397-31046-3). Lippincott.

Stripping the Trees. Harris Collingwood. (Chapbook Ser.: No. 2). 48p. (Orig.). 1980. pap. 4.95 (ISBN 0-937672-01-7). Rowan Tree.

Stripping Voltammetry in Chemical Analysis. K. Z. Brainina. Tr. by P. Shelnitz from Rus. LC 74-13974. 222p. 1974. 29.50 (ISBN 0-470-09590-3). Halsted Pr.

Stripwell & Claw. Howard Barker. 1980. pap. 4.95 (ISBN 0-7145-3572-9). Riverrun NY.

Stroke. Lowell G. Lubic & Harry P. Palkovitz. (Discussions in Patient Management Ser.). 1979. pap. 9.50 (ISBN 0-87488-893-X). Med Exam.

Stroke. Ed. by Richard A. Thompson & J. R. Green. LC 75-25129. (Advances in Neurology Ser.: Vol. 16). 1977. 25.00 (ISBN 0-89004-098-2). Raven.

Stroke: Cause, Prevention, Treatment & Rehabilitation. Ed. by A. L. Sahs et al. (Illus.). 1978. 36.00x o.p. (ISBN 0-7194-0003-1). Intl Ideas.

Stroke of Death. Josephine Bell. LC 77-79963. 1977. 6.95 o.s.i. (ISBN 0-8027-5378-7). Walker & Co.

Stroke of Luck. Christopher R. Miller. (Sportellers Ser.). (Illus.). 64p. (gr. 5 up). 1981. PLB 7.95 (ISBN 0-516-02268-7). Childrens.

Stroke Rehabilitation: A Guide to the Rehabilitation of an Adult Patient Following a Stroke. Harry T. Zankel. (Illus.). 300p. 1971. text ed. 29.75 photocopy ed. spiral (ISBN 0-398-02446-4). C C Thomas.

Strokes & Their Prevention. Arthur M. Ancowitz. (Orig.). pap. 2.75 (ISBN 0-515-05723-1). Jove Pubns.

Strokes: How to Prevent It- How to Survive. Gloria J. Sessler. 256p. 1980. 14.95 (ISBN 0-13-852913-2, Spec); pap. 6.95 (ISBN 0-686-63391-1). P-H.

Strokes: Natural History, Pathology & Surgical Treatment. E. C. Hutchinson & E. J. Acheson. LC 74-28100. (Major Problems in Neurology: Vol. 4). (Illus.). 283p. 1975. text ed. 28.00 (ISBN 0-7216-4870-3). Saunders.

Stroll Through Historic Salem. Samuel Chamberlain. LC 78-79738. (Illus.). 1969. 8.95 (ISBN 0-8038-6689-5). Hastings.

Strolling Through Istanbul. Hilary Sumner-Boyd & John Freely. (Illus.). 1972. 15.00x (ISBN 0-686-16866-6). Intl Learn Syst.

Strong Americans: The Raging Heart. Arthur Moore. 384p. (Orig.). 1981. pap. 2.75 (ISBN 0-523-41144-8). Pinnacle Bks.

Strong at the Broken Places. Max Cleland. 1980. 6.95 (ISBN 0-912376-55-4). Word Bks.

Strong City. Taylor Caldwell. 544p. 1980. pap. 2.95 (ISBN 0-515-05629-4). Jove Pubns.

Strong Land & a Sturdy: Life in Medieval England. Richard Barber. LC 75-43895. (Illus.). (gr. 6 up). 1976. 8.95 (ISBN 0-395-28888-6, Clarion). HM.

Strong Materials. J. W. Martin & R. A. Hull. LC 72-189452. (Wykeham Science Ser.: No. 21). 1972. 9.95x (ISBN 0-8448-1123-8). Crane Russak Co.

Strong Name. James S. Stewart. (Scholar As Preacher). 268p. Repr. of 1940 ed. text ed. 7.75 (ISBN 0-567-04427-0). Attic Pr.

Strong Opinions. Vladimir Nabokov. 348p. 1981. pap. 6.95 (ISBN 0-07-045725-5). McGraw.

Strong Poison. Dorothy L. Sayers. (Large Print Bks.). 1980. lib. bdg. 15.95 (ISBN 0-8161-3042-6). G K Hall.

Strong Solids. 2nd ed. A. Kelly. (Monographs on the Physics & Chemistry of Materials Ser.). (Illus.). 285p. 1973. 42.00x (ISBN 0-19-851350-X). Oxford U Pr.

Strong Tea. John B. Keane. 1966. pap. 3.95 (ISBN 0-85342-255-9). Irish Bk Ctr.

Strong Weak People. Jay Kesler. 1976. pap. 2.50 o.p. (ISBN 0-88207-739-2). Victor Bks.

Stronger Than Sin. Jackie Collins. Date not set. pap. price not set. Warner Bks.

Strongest One of All. Mirra Ginsburg. LC 76-44326. (Illus.). 1977. 8.25 (ISBN 0-688-80081-5); PLB 7.92 (ISBN 0-688-84081-7). Greenwillow.

Strongholds. Lucy M. Boston. LC 68-24383. 1969. 4.95 o.p. (ISBN 0-15-185988-4, HJ). HarBraceJ.

Strontium Isotope Geology. G. Faure & J. L. Powell. LC 72-75720. (Minerals, Rocks & Inorganic Materials Ser.: Vol. 5). (Illus.). 200p. 1972. 17.80 (ISBN 0-387-05784-6). Springer-Verlag.

Structopathic Children. J. F. Kok. Incl. Pt. 1. Description of Disturbance Type & Strategies. (Modern Approaches to the Diagnosis & Instruction of Milti-Handicapped Children: Vol. 9). 126p (ISBN 90-237-4109-9); Pt. 2. Results of Experimental Research of Structuring Group Therapy. (Modern Approaches to the Diagnosis & Instruction of Multi-Handicapped: Vol. 10). 122p (ISBN 90-237-4110-2). 1972. text ed. 26.00 ea. (Pub. by Swets Pub Serv Holland). Swets North Am.

Structopathic Children, 2 pts. J. F. W. Kok. Incl Pt. 1. Description of Disturbance Type & Strategies. 1126p (ISBN 90-237-4109-9); Pt. 2. Results of Experimental Research of Structuring Group Therapy. 122p (ISBN 90-237-4110-2). (Modern Approaches to the Diagnosis & Instruction of Multi-Handicapped Children Ser.: Vols. 9 & 10). 1972. text ed. 26.00 ea. (Pub. by Swets Pub Serv Holland). Swets North Am.

Structual Stability & Morphogenesis: An Outline of a General Theory of Models. R. Thom. Tr. by D. H. Fowler from Fr. pap. 22.50 (ISBN 0-8053-9279-3). A-W.

Structural Analysis & Design of Nuclear Plant Facilities. Compiled by American Society of Civil Engineers. LC 80-65828. (ASCE Manual & Report on Engineering Practice Ser.: No. 58). 576p. 1980. text ed. 140.00 (ISBN 0-87262-238-X). Am Soc Civil Eng.

Structural Analysis & Design: Some Minicomputer Applications. H. B. Harrison. (Illus.). 1980. text ed. 79.00 (ISBN 0-08-023239-6); pap. text ed. 30.00 (ISBN 0-08-023240-X). Pergamon.

Structural Analysis of Complex Aerial Photographs. Ed. by Makoto Nagao & Takashi Matsuyama. (Advanced Applications in Pattern Recognition Ser.). 200p. 1980. 32.50 (ISBN 0-306-40571-7, Plenum Pr). Plenum Pub.

Structural Analysis of Discrete Data. Ed. by Charles F. Manski & Daniel McFadden. 600p. 1981. text ed. 29.95x (ISBN 0-262-13159-5). MIT Pr.

Structural Analysis of Narrative. Jean Calloud. Ed. by William A. Beardslee. Tr. by Daniel Patte from Fr. LC 75-37158. (Semeia Studies). 128p. 1976. pap. 3.95 (ISBN 0-8006-1503-4, 1-1503). Fortress.

Structural Analysis of Narrative Texts, Conference Papers. Ed. by Andrej Kodjak et al. (New York University Slavic Papers: Vol. II). (Illus.). 203p. (Orig.). 1980. pap. 10.95 (ISBN 0-89357-071-0). Slavica.

Structural Analysis of Shells. 2nd ed. E. H. Baker et al. LC 79-27250. 364p. 1981. Repr. lib. bdg. write for info. (ISBN 0-89874-118-1). Krieger.

Structural & Geotechnical Mechanics: A Volume Honoring Nathan M. Newmark. W. J. Hall. LC 76-28735. (Illus.). 1977. ref. ed. 32.95 (ISBN 0-13-853804-2). P-H.

Structural & Physiological Aspects of Exercise & Sport. Ed. by Warren R. Johnson & E. R. Buskirk. LC 79-91733. (Illus.). 291p. 1980. text ed. 19.50x (ISBN 0-916622-16-9). Princeton Bk Co.

Structural & Thematic Analysis of George Meredith's Novel "Diana of the Crossways". Renate Bruckl. (Salzburg Studies in English Literature: Romantic Reassessment Ser.: No. 73). 1978. pap. text ed. 25.00x (ISBN 0-391-01332-7). Humanities.

Structural Approach in Psychological Testing. M. L. Kaplan et al. LC 70-93755. 1970. 21.00 (ISBN 0-08-006867-7). Pergamon.

Structural Approaches to South India Studies. Ed. by Harry M. Buck & Glenn A. Yocum. LC 74-77412. 1974. pap. 5.95 (ISBN 0-89012-000-5). Anima Pubns.

Structural Aspects of Language Change. James M. Anderson. (Linguistics Library Ser.: No. 13). (Illus.). 1973. 14.95x (ISBN 0-582-55032-7); pap. 10.95x (ISBN 0-582-55033-5). Longman.

Structural Basis of Membrane Function. Ed. by D. Hatefi. 1976. 32.00 (ISBN 0-12-332450-5). Acad Pr.

Structural Change & Economic Growth. L. Pasinetti. (Illus.). 337p. Date not set. price not set (ISBN 0-521-23607-X). Cambridge U Pr.

Structural Changes in Puerto Rico's Economy 1947-1976. Robert J. Tata. LC 80-19080. (Latin America Ser., Ohio University Papers in International Studies). (Illus.). 104p. (Orig.). 1981. pap. 11.95. Ohio U Ctr Intl.

Structural Characteristics of Materials. Ed. by H. M. Finniston. (Illus.). 1971. 48.50x (ISBN 0-444-20045-2, Pub. by Applied Science). Burgess-Intl Ideas.

Structural Chemistry & Molecular Biology: A Volume Dedicated to Linus Pauling by His Students, Colleagues, & Friends. Ed. by Alexander Rich & Norman Davidson. LC 67-21127. (Illus.). 1968. 36.95x (ISBN 0-7167-0135-9). W H Freeman.

Structural Communication. Kieran Egan. LC 74-83215. 1976. pap. text ed. 5.95 (ISBN 0-8224-6550-7). Pitman Learning.

Structural Concepts & Systems for Architects & Engineers. Tung Yen Lin & Sidney D. Stotesbury. 1981. text ed. 23.95 (ISBN 0-471-05186-1). Wiley.

Structural Description of the Macedonian Dialect of Dihovo. B. M. Groen. (PDR Press Publication on Macedonian: No. 2). 1977. pap. text ed. 22.75x (ISBN 9-0316-0143-8). Humanities.

Structural Design of Nuclear Plant Facilities. Compiled by American Society of Civil Engineers. 1975. pap. text ed. 73.00 (ISBN 0-87262-172-3). Am Soc Civil Eng.

Structural Design of Nuclear Plant Facilities. Compiled by American Society of Civil Engineers. 1973. pap. text ed. 52.00 (ISBN 0-87262-155-3). Am Soc Civil Eng.

Structural Design of Tall Steel Buildings. Council on Tall Buildings & Urban Habitats of Fritz Engineering Lab., Lehigh Univ. LC 79-63736. 1080p. 1979. text ed. 60.00 (ISBN 0-87262-228-2). Am Soc Civil Eng.

Structural Drafting Workbook. Rip Weaver. (Illus.). 112p. 1980. pap. text ed. 9.95. Gulf Pub.

Structural Dynamics Heat Conduction. CISM (International Center for Mechanical Sciences) Ed. by B. F. De Veubeke et al. (CISM Pubns. Ser.: No. 126). (Illus.). 256p. 1974. pap. 25.60 (ISBN 0-387-81201-6). Springer-Verlag.

Structural Econometric Model of the Saudi Arabian Economy: 1960-1970. Faisal S. Al-Bashir. LC 77-441. 1977. 29.95 (ISBN 0-471-02177-6). Ronald Pr.

Structural Engineering & Structural Mechanics: A Volume Honoring Egor P. Popov. Ed. by K. Pister. 1980. 29.95 (ISBN 0-13-853671-6). P-H.

Structural Engineering, Combined Edition, 2 vols. in 1. Richard N. White et al. LC 76-202. 570p. 1976. text ed. 27.95 (ISBN 0-471-94067-4). Wiley.

Structural Engineering for Architects. Kenneth R. Lauer. (Illus.). 672p. 1981. text ed. 25.95 (ISBN 0-07-036622-5, C). McGraw.

Structural Engineering for Professional Engineer's Examination. 3rd ed. Max Kurtz. (Illus.). 1978. 19.50 (ISBN 0-07-035657-2, P&RB). McGraw.

Structural Engineering, Vol. 1: Introduction to Design Concepts & Analysis. 2nd ed. Richard N. White et al. LC 75-174772. 288p. 1976. text ed. 21.95 (ISBN 0-471-94066-6). Wiley.

Structural Engineering, Vol. 3: Behavior of Members & Systems. Richard N. White et al. LC 75-174772. 544p. 1974. text ed. 27.50 (ISBN 0-471-94072-0). Wiley.

Structural Fabulation: An Essay on Fiction of the Future. Robert Scholes. LC 74-30167. 104p. 1975. text ed. 2.95 (ISBN 0-268-00570-2). U of Notre Dame Pr.

Structural Fabulation: An Essay on Fiction of the Future. Robert Scholes. LC 74-30167. 111p. 1975. 2.95x o.p. (ISBN 0-268-00571-0). U of Notre Dame Pr.

Structural Failure in Residential Buildings, 3 vols. Erich Schild et al. Incl. Vol. 1. Flat Roofs, Roof Terraces & Balconies. 24.50x (ISBN 0-470-26305-9); Vol. 2. External Walls & Openings. 27.95x (ISBN 0-470-26789-5); Vol. 3. 154p. 29.95x (ISBN 0-470-26846-8). LC 77-28647. 1978-80. Set. 85.85x (ISBN 0-470-26898-0). Halsted Pr.

Structural Failures-Modes, Causes, Responsibilities. Compiled by American Society of Civil Engineers. 112p. 1973. pap. text ed. 5.00 (ISBN 0-87262-051-4). Am Soc Civil Eng.

Structural Features of the Laksevag Gneiss. L. E. Weiss et al. (Geological Survey of Norway Ser: No. 334, Bulletin 43). 1978. pap. 12.00x (ISBN 82-00-31368-9, Dist. by Columbia U Pr). Universitet.

Structural Functions in Music. Wallace Barry. (Illus.). 512p. 1976. 20.95 (ISBN 0-13-853903-0). P-H.

Structural Geology. John G. Dennis. 532p. 1972. 25.50 (ISBN 0-8260-2615-X). Wiley.

Structural Hearing: Tonal Coherence in Music, 2 Vols. Felix Salzer. (Illus.). 1952. text ed. 7.50 ea.; Vol. 1. text ed. (ISBN 0-486-22275-6); Vol. 2. text ed. (ISBN 0-486-22276-4). Dover.

Structural-Induced Response to Explosion-Induced Motions. Compiled by American Society of Civil Engineers & Kenneth G. Medearis. 148p. 1975. pap. text ed. 8.00 (ISBN 0-87262-150-2). Am Soc Civil Eng.

Structural Inorganic Chemistry. 4th ed. A. F. Wells. (Illus.). 1120p. 1975. text ed. 84.00x (ISBN 0-19-855354-4). Oxford U Pr.

Structural Learning & Concrete Operations: An Approach to Piagetian Conservation. Joseph M. Scandura. LC 80-16153. 218p. 1980. 21.95 (ISBN 0-03-056697-5). Praeger.

Structural Linguistics & Human Communication. B. Malmberg. LC 63-12931. (Kommunikation und Kybernetik in Einzeldarstellungen: Band 2). (Illus.). 1976. 33.10 o.p. (ISBN 0-387-03888-4). Springer-Verlag.

Structural Materials in Animals. C. H. Brown. LC 75-1293. 1975. 38.95 o.p. (ISBN 0-470-10641-7). Halsted Pr.

Structural Mechanics. Andrew C. Palmer. (Oxford Engineering Science Texts). (Illus.). 1976. 36.00x (ISBN 0-19-856127-X); pap. 16.95x (ISBN 0-19-856128-8). Oxford U Pr.

Structural Mechanics Software Series, Vol. III. Ed. by Walter D. Pilkey & Nicholas Perrone. (Illus.). 450p. 1980. 25.00x (ISBN 0-8139-0857-4). U Pr of Va.

Structural Mechanics: The Behavior of Plates & Shells. Jack R. Vinson. LC 73-19881. 288p. 1974. 21.95 o.p. (ISBN 0-471-90837-1, Pub. by Wiley-Interscience). Wiley.

Structural Model of the U. S. Government Securities Market. V. Vance Roley. LC 78-75048. (Outstanding Dissertations in Economics Ser.). 1979. lib. bdg. 30.00 (ISBN 0-8240-4127-5). Garland Pub.

Structural Models & African Poetics: Towards a Pragmatic View of Literature. Sunday O. Anozie. 220p. 1981. 37.50 (ISBN 0-7100-0467-2). Routledge & Kegan.

Structural Notes & Details. John C. Maxwell-Cook. (C & CA Viewpoint Publication Ser.). (Illus.). 1976. text ed. 20.00 (ISBN 0-7210-1006-7). Scholium Intl.

Structural Plastics-Properties & Possibilities. Compiled by American Society of Civil Engineers. 248p. 1969. pap. text ed. 6.50 (ISBN 0-87262-015-8). Am Soc Civil Eng.

Structural Polymers: Testing Methods, 2 vols. P. M. Ogibalov et al. Tr. by T. Pelz. LC 73-16434. 612p. 1974. 83.95 (ISBN 0-470-65284-5). Halsted Pr.

Structural Recommendations for Timber Frame Housing. Timber Research & Development Association. (Illus.). 1981. 38.00 (ISBN 0-86095-890-6). Longman.

Structural Responses to the Problems of Volume & Delay in Appellate Courts. National Center for State Courts. Date not set. pap. price not set (ISBN 0-89656-048-1, R-0055). Natl Ctr St Courts.

Structural Safety & Reliability: Proceedings of the International Conference. Ed. by Alfred M. Freudenthal et al. 1972. 115.00 (ISBN 0-08-016566-4). Pergamon.

Structural Steel Design. 3rd ed. Jack C. McCormac. (Illus.). 640p. 1981. text ed. 27.50 scp (ISBN 0-06-044344-8, HarpC); avail. Har-Row.

Structural Studies on Molecules of Biological Interest: A Volume in Honour of Professor Dorothy Hodgkin. Ed. by Guy Dodson et al. (Illus.). 400p. 1981. 115.00 (ISBN 0-19-855362-5). Oxford U Pr.

Structural Surveying. H. E. Desch. 269p. 1970. 33.95 (ISBN 0-85264-167-2, Pub. by Griffin England). State Mutual Bk.

Structural System. Henry J. Cowan. (Illus.). 356p. 1981. price not set (ISBN 0-442-21714-5); pap. price not set (ISBN 0-442-21713-7). Van Nos Reinhold.

Structural Theorems & Their Applications. B. G. Neal. 1964. 19.50 (ISBN 0-08-010872-5); pap. 9.75 (ISBN 0-08-010871-7). Pergamon.

Structural Theory & Analysis. Joseph D. Todd. LC 75-327936. (Illus.). 1975. 28.50x (ISBN 0-333-18021-6); pap. 18.95x (ISBN 0-333-15693-5). Scholium Intl.

Structural Theory of Revolutions: Proceedings, Vol. 5. First International Working Conference on Violence & Non-Violent Action in Industrialized Societies, Brussels, March 13-15th, 1974, Part II & J. Galtung. (Publications of the Polemological Centre of the Free University of Brussels). 78p. 1974. pap. text ed. 9.95 (ISBN 90-237-6252-5, Pub. by Swets Pub Serv Holland). Swets North Am.

Structural Transformation & Economic Development. Birla Institute of Scientific Research. 126p. 1980. text ed. 9.50 (ISBN 0-391-01790-X). Humanities.

Structural Units of Medical & Biological Terms: A Convenient Guide, in English, to the Roots, Stems, Prefixes, Suffixes, & Other Combining Forms Which Are the Building Blocks of Medical & Related Scientific Words. J. E. Schmidt. 180p. 1969. text ed. 11.75 (ISBN 0-398-01676-3). C C Thomas.

Structuralism. Justin Leiber. 1978. lib. bdg. 12.50 (ISBN 0-8057-7721-0). Twayne.

Structuralism: An Introduction-Wolfson College Lectures 1972. Ed. by David Robey. 1973. pap. text ed. 9.95x (ISBN 0-19-874017-4). Oxford U Pr.

Structuralism & Semiotics. Terence Hawkes. 1977. 14.00x (ISBN 0-520-03398-1); pap. 3.95x (ISBN 0-520-03422-8). U of Cal Pr.

Structuralism or Criticism? G. Strickland. 200p. Date not set. 39.50 (ISBN 0-521-23184-1). Cambridge U Pr.

Structuralist Analysis in Contemporary Social Thought: A Comparison of the Theories of Claude Levi-Strauss & Louis Althusser. Miriam Glucksman. (International Library of Sociology). 1974. 26.00 (ISBN 0-7100-7773-4). Routledge & Kegan.

Structuralist Poetics: Structuralism, Linguistics & the Study of Literature. Jonathan Culler. LC 74-11608. 1975. 19.50x (ISBN 0-8014-0928-4); pap. 5.95 (ISBN 0-8014-9155-X). Cornell U Pr.

Structuralists: From Marx to Levi-Strauss. Ed. by Richard T. De George & Fernande De George. LC 76-175409. 3.50 (ISBN 0-385-00930-5, Anchor Pr). Doubleday.

Structure-Activity Relationships & Theory. Ed. by C. J. Cavallito. LC 72-13533. 1973. text ed. 75.00 (ISBN 0-08-016890-6). Pergamon.

Structure-Activity Relationships in Chemoreception: Proceedings. European Chemoreception Research Organisation, 2nd Interdisciplinary Symposium, Switzerland, 1975. 197p. 20.00 (ISBN 0-904147-03-7). Info Retrieval.

Structure-Activity Relationships in Human Chemoreception. Ed. by M. G. Beets. (Illus.). 1978. text ed. 71.30x (ISBN 0-85334-746-8, Pub. by Applied Science). Burgess-Intl Ideas.

Structure Analysis by Electron Diffraction. B. K. Vainshtein. 1964. 33.00 o.p. (ISBN 0-08-010241-7). Pergamon.

Structure & Activity of Natural Peptides: Selected Topics. Ed. by W. Voelter & G. Weitzel. 480p. 1980. 91.00x (ISBN 3-11-008264-0). De Gruyter.

Structure & Application of Galvanomagnetic Devices. H. Weiss. 1969. 60.00 (ISBN 0-08-012597-2). Pergamon.

Structure & Bonding in Solid State Chemistry. M. F. Ladd. LC 78-41289. 1979. 52.95 (ISBN 0-470-26597-3). Halsted Pr.

Structure & Communication: Critical Studies in Mass Media Research. Ed. by Emile McAnany et al. 260p. 1981. 20.95 (ISBN 0-03-057954-6). Praeger.

Structure & Conflict in Nigeria. Kenneth Post & Michael Vickers. 1974. 22.50 (ISBN 0-299-06470-0). U of Wis Pr.

Structure & Conformation of Nucleic Acids & Protein-Nuclein Acid Interactions. Ed. by M. Sundaralingham & S. R. Rao. (Illus.). 1975. 49.50 (ISBN 0-8391-0764-1). Univ Park.

Structure & Control of the Melanocyte: Proceedings. International Pigment Cell Conference - 6th. Ed. by G. Della Porta & O. Muehlbock. (Illus.). 1966. 44.00 (ISBN 0-387-03676-8). Springer-Verlag.

Structure & Creativity in Religion. Douglas Allen. (Religion & Reason Ser.: No. 14). 1978. 28.80x (ISBN 90-279-7594-9). Mouton.

Structure & Crystallization of Glasses. W. Vogel. 1971. 46.00 (ISBN 0-08-006998-3). Pergamon.

Structure & Design of Programming Languages. John E. Nicholls. LC 74-12801. (IBM Systems Programming). (Illus.). 592p. 1975. text ed. 21.95 (ISBN 0-201-14454-9). A-W.

Structure & Development in Child Language: The Preschool Years. Marion Potts et al. LC 78-10968. 1979. 17.50x (ISBN 0-8014-1184-X). Cornell U Pr.

Structure & Development of Vertebrates. Berton J. Leach. (Lucas Text Ser). 1973. text ed. 3.95x (ISBN 0-87543-086-4). Lucas.

Structure & Direction in Thinking. D. E. Berlyne. (Illus.). 378p. 1965. text ed. 14.50 (ISBN 0-471-07035-1, Pub. by Wiley). Krieger.

Structure & Distribution of Coral Reefs. Charles Darwin. (Library Reprint Ser.). 1976. 19.50x (ISBN 0-520-03282-9). U of Cal Pr.

Structure & Dynamics of Organizations & Groups. Eric Berne. 1973. pap. 2.50 o.p. (ISBN 0-345-28473-9). Ballantine.

Structure & Evolution of Vertebrates: A Laboratory Text for Comparative Vertebrate Anatomy. hew ed. Alan Feduccia. 275p. 1974. pap. 7.95x (ISBN 0-393-09291-7). Norton.

Structure & Fabric, 2 pts. Jack S. Foster. (Mitchell's Building Construction Ser.). 1978. Pt. 1. pap. 13.95 (ISBN 0-470-26348-2); Pt. 2. pap. 13.95 (ISBN 0-470-26349-0). Halsted Pr.

Structure & Fuction of Antibodies. L. E. Glynn. Ed. by M. W. Steward. 150p. 1981. pap. 15.00 (ISBN 0-471-27917-X, Pub. by Wiley-Interscience). Wiley.

Structure & Function in Cilia & Flagella. P. Satir. Ed. by M. Alfert et al. Bd. with Trichocystoides. Corps Trichocytoides. Cnidocystes & Colloblastes. R. Horvasse. (Illus.). 57p. 1965. (Protoplasmatologia: Vol. 3, Pt. E). (Illus.). iv, 52p. 1965. pap. 34.90 o.p. (ISBN 0-387-80732-2). Springer-Verlag.

Structure & Function in Primitive Society. Alfred R. Radcliffe-Brown. 1952. 12.95 (ISBN 0-02-925630-5); pap. text ed. 6.95 (ISBN 0-02-925620-8). Free Pr.

Structure & Function in the Nervous Systems of Invertebrates, 2 Vols. Theodore H. Bullock & G. Adrian Horridge. (Biology Ser.). (Illus.). 1965. 160.00x (ISBN 0-7167-0626-1). W H Freeman.

Structure & Function of Inhibitory Neuronal Mechanisms. Ed. by U. S. Von Euler et al. 1968. 79.00 (ISBN 0-08-012414-3). Pergamon.

Structure & Function of Muscle. 2nd ed. Geoffrey H. Bourne. Vol. 1, 1972. 67.00 (ISBN 0-12-119101-X); Vol. 2, 1973. 72.50 (ISBN 0-12-119102-8); Vol. 3, 1973. 67.00 (ISBN 0-12-119103-6); Vol. 4, 1974. 67.00 (ISBN 0-12-119104-4); 223.25 set (ISBN 0-685-36103-9). Acad Pr.

Structure & Function of Oxidation Reduction Enzymes. A. Akeson & A. Ehrenburg. 788p. 1972. 130.00 (ISBN 0-08-016874-4). Pergamon.

Structure & Function of Plant Cells in Saline Habitats. B. P. Strogonov et al. Ed. by B. Gollak. Tr. by A. Mercado from Rus. LC 73-13609. (Illus.). 284p. 1973. 44.95 (ISBN 0-470-83406-4). Halsted Pr.

Structure & Function of the Body. 6th ed. Catherine P. Anthony & Gary A. Thibodeau. LC 75-30936. 1980. text ed. 12.95 (ISBN 0-8016-0273-4); pap. text ed. 9.95 (ISBN 0-8016-0287-4). Mosby.

Structure & Function of the Circulation, Vol. 1. Ed. by Stewart Wolf et al. 825p. 1980. 75.00 (ISBN 0-306-40278-5). Plenum Pub.

Structure & Function of the Gangliosides. Ed. by Lars Svennerholm et al. (Advances in Experimental Medicine & Biology Ser.: Vol. 125). 580p. 1980. 49.50 (ISBN 0-306-40332-3, Plenum Pr). Plenum Pub.

Structure & Function of the Human Body: An Introduction to Anatomy & Physiology. Lee Langley & John B. Christensen. LC 77-75791. 1978. text ed. 16.95 o.p. (ISBN 0-8087-1241-1). Burgess.

Structure & History in Greek Mythology & Ritual. Walter Burkert. (Sather Classical Lectures: Vol. 47). 1980. 16.50x (ISBN 0-520-03771-5). U of Cal Pr.

Structure & Imagery in Ancrene Wisse. Janet Grayson. LC 73-77480. 256p. 1974. text ed. 15.00x (ISBN 0-87451-081-3). U Pr of New Eng.

Structure & Life of Bryopytes. 3rd ed. Eric V. Watson. 1971. pap. text ed. 7.50 (ISBN 0-09-109301-5, Hutchinson U Lib). Humanities.

Structure & Meaning: An Introduction to Literature. Anthony Dube et al. LC 75-31038. (Illus.). 1152p. 1976. text ed. 15.95 (ISBN 0-395-21967-1); inst. manual 1.00 (ISBN 0-395-21968-X). HM.

Structure & Metabolism of the Pancreatic Islets - a Centennial of Paul Langerhan's Discovery. S. Falkmer et al. 1970. 105.00 (ISBN 0-08-015844-7). Pergamon.

Structure & Metabolism of the Pancreatic Islets. Ed. by S. E. Brolin. 1964. 64.00 (ISBN 0-08-010758-3). Pergamon.

Structure & Outcomes of Study Groups: A Method of Determining Several Properties of Group Structure & Some Relationships Observed with Group Outcome. D. Van Kreveld. (Orig.). 1970. pap. text ed. 4.75x (ISBN 90-232-0700-9). Humanities.

Structure & Performance of the Aerospace Industry. H. O. Stekler. 1965. 20.00x (ISBN 0-520-01214-3). U of Cal Pr.

Structure & Process in Modern Societies. Talcott Parsons. 1960. 15.95 (ISBN 0-02-924340-8). Free Pr.

Structure & Process of Organization: A Systems Approach. Arlyn J. Melcher. (Illus.). 480p. 1976. 19.95 (ISBN 0-13-855254-1). P-H.

Structure & Processes of Organization. H. C. Ganguli. 1964. 6.50 o.p. (ISBN 0-210-27005-5). Asia.

Structure & Properties of Inorganic Solids. F. S. Galasso. LC 70-104123. 1970. 42.00 (ISBN 0-08-006873-1). Pergamon.

Structure & Properties of Materials, 4 vols. Ed. by J. Wulff. Incl. Vol. 1. Structures. G. W. Moffatt et al. 236p (ISBN 0-471-61265-0); Vol. 3. Mechanical Behavior. H. W. Hayden et al. 247p (ISBN 0-471-36469-X); Vol. 4. Electronic Properties. R. M. Rose et al. 306p (ISBN 0-471-73548-5). 1964-66. Set. pap. 31.50 (ISBN 0-471-96495-6). Wiley.

Structure & Properties of Oriented Polymers. Ed. by I. M. Ward. LC 74-26599. 500p. 1975. 69.95 (ISBN 0-470-91996-5). Halsted Pr.

Structure & Properties of Water. David Eisenberg & Walter Kauzmann. 1969. 13.95x (ISBN 0-19-500320-9); pap. 6.95x (ISBN 0-19-500321-7). Oxford U Pr.

Structure & Reform of Direct Taxation. James Meade. (Illus.). 1978. text ed. 50.00x (ISBN 0-04-336064-5); pap. text ed. 19.95x (ISBN 0-04-336065-3). Allen Unwin.

Structure & Relationship in Constitutional Law. Charles L. Black, Jr. LC 69-17621. (Edward Douglass White Lectures). 1969. 7.95 (ISBN 0-8071-0305-5). La State U Pr.

Structure & Relationships of Notharctus, an American Eocene Primate. William K. Gregory. LC 78-72719. Repr. of 1920 ed. 47.50 (ISBN 0-404-18294-1). AMS Pr.

Structure & Reproduction of Corn. T. A. Kiesselbach. LC 79-19648. viii, 96p. 1980. 9.50x (ISBN 0-8032-2703-5); pap. 2.95x (ISBN 0-8032-7751-2, BB 724, Bison). U of Nebr Pr.

Structure & Reproduction of the Algae, 2 Vols. Felix E. Fritsch. Vol. 1. 75.00 (ISBN 0-521-05041-3); Vol. 2. 90.00 (ISBN 0-521-05042-1). Cambridge U Pr.

Structure & the Operation of the Japanese Economy. K. Bieda. LC 76-127033. 1970. pap. 14.50 o.p. (ISBN 0-471-07225-7, Pub. by Wiley-Interscience). Wiley.

Structure & Transformation: Development & Historical Aspects. K. F. Riegel & G. C. Rosenwald. (Origins of Behavior Ser.: Vol. 3). 1975. 27.95 (ISBN 0-471-72140-9). Wiley.

Structure Determination by X-Ray Crystallography. Ed. by M. F. Ladd & R. A. Palmer. (Illus.). 393p. 1977. 29.50 (ISBN 0-306-30844-4, Plenum Pr); pap. 14.75 (ISBN 0-306-40032-4). Plenum Pub.

Structure in Architecture: Building of Buildings. 2nd ed. Mario G. Salvadori & Robert Heller. (Illus.). 336p. 1975. 21.95 (ISBN 0-13-854109-4). P-H.

Structure in Early Learning. Alice Yardley. LC 73-94155. 1974. 3.25 o.p. (ISBN 0-590-07395-8, Citation). Schol Bk Serv.

Structure in Teaching. O. Roger Anderson. LC 76-150210. (Illus.). 1969. text ed. 7.50x (ISBN 0-8077-1030-X). Tchrs Coll.

Structure, Law, & Power: Essays in the Sociology of Law. Ed. by Paul J. Brantingham & Jack M. Kress. LC 79-18127. (Sage Research Progress Ser. in Criminology: Vol. 13). (Illus.). 1979. 12.95x (ISBN 0-8039-1318-4); pap. 6.50x (ISBN 0-8039-1319-2). Sage.

Structure Mediation in Divorce Settlements: A Handbook for Marital Mediators. O. J. Coogler. LC 77-15814. 1978. 16.95 (ISBN 0-669-02343-4). Lexington Bks.

Structure of Accounting Theory. S. C. Yu. LC 76-10355. 1976. pap. 9.00 (ISBN 0-8130-0405-5). U Presses Fla.

Structure of Algebras. Abraham A. Albert. LC 41-9. (Colloquium Pbns. Ser.: Vol. 24). 1980. Repr. of 1939 ed. 25.20 (ISBN 0-8218-1024-3, COLL-24). Am Math.

Structure of Ammon's Horn. Santiago Ramon Y Cajal. Tr. by Lisbeth M. Kraft. (Illus.). 100p. 1968. pap. 11.50 photocopy ed. spiral (ISBN 0-398-01543-0). C C Thomas.

Structure of "Anna Karenina". Sidney Schultze. 1981. 15.00 (ISBN 0-88233-587-1). Ardis Pubs.

Structure of Arabic: From Sound to Sentence. Raja Nasr. 1968. 12.00x (ISBN 0-685-77112-1). Intl Bk Ctr.

Structure of Asia. Ed. by J. W. Gregory. LC 75-31680. 240p. 1976. Repr. of 1929 ed. 14.50 o.p. (ISBN 0-88275-361-4). Krieger.

Structure of British Industry. M. Dunn & P. Tranter. (Studies in the British Economy). 1979. pap. text ed. write for info. (ISBN 0-435-84544-6). Heinemann Ed.

Structure of Bushman & Its Traces in Indo-European. Roman Stopa. (Illus.). 216p. 1972. text ed. 11.75x (ISBN 0-7007-0017-X). Humanities.

Structure of Christian Existence. John B. Cobb, Jr. (Library of Contempory Theology). 1979. pap. 6.95 (ISBN 0-8164-2229-X). Crossroad NY.

Structure of Complex Words. 3rd. ed. William Empson. 450p. 1979. Repr. of 1951 ed. 22.50x (ISBN 0-8476-6207-1). Rowman.

Structure of Computers & Computations, Vol. 1. David J. Kuck. LC 78-5412. 1978. text ed. 29.95 (ISBN 0-471-02716-2); tchr's manual avail. (ISBN 0-471-05294-9). Wiley.

Structure of Crystalline Polymers. Hiroyuki Tadokoro. LC 78-5412. 1979. 39.50 (ISBN 0-471-02356-6, Pub. by Wiley-Interscience). Wiley.

Structure of Earnings. Harold Lydall. (Illus.). 1968. 29.95x (ISBN 0-19-828158-7). Oxford U Pr.

Structure of Evil. Ernest Becker. LC 68-12890. (Illus.). 1968. 8.50 o.s.i. (ISBN 0-8076-0446-1). Braziller.

Structure of Field Space: An Axiomatic Formulation of Field Physics. Dominic G. Edelen. 1962. 27.50x (ISBN 0-520-00372-1). U of Cal Pr.

Structure of Human Decisions. David W. Miller & Martin K. Starr. (Orig.). 1967. pap. text ed. 10.95 (ISBN 0-13-854687-8). P-H.

Structure of Human Memory. Ed. by Charles N. Cofer. LC 76-2581. (Psychology Ser.). (Illus.). 1976. pap. text ed. 9.95x (ISBN 0-7167-0715-2). W H Freeman.

Structure of Human Populations. Ed. by G. A. Harrison & A. J. Boyce. (Illus.). 463p. 1972. 24.00x (ISBN 0-19-857117-8); pap. 15.50x (ISBN 0-19-857120-8). Oxford U Pr.

Structure of Human Society. P. Hammond et al. 736p. 1975. text ed. 15.95x (ISBN 0-669-81315-X); instructor's manual free (ISBN 0-669-90266-7). Heath.

Structure of Impartiality. Thomas M. Franck. LC 68-20264. 1968. 8.95 o.s.i. (ISBN 0-02-540580-2). Macmillan.

Structure of Intellect: Its Interpretation & Uses. Mary Meeker. LC 69-17296. 1969. text ed. 17.95 (ISBN 0-675-09516-6). Merrill.

Structure of Intonational Meaning: Evidence from English. D. Robert Ladd, Jr. LC 79-3093. 256p. 1980. 18.50x (ISBN 0-253-15864-8). Ind U Pr.

Structure of Jewish History & Other Essays. Heinrich Graetz. 15.00x (ISBN 0-87068-466-3); pap. 8.95x (ISBN 0-685-56206-9). Ktav.

Structure of Language. Jerry Fodor & J. J. Katz. 1964. 19.95 (ISBN 0-13-854703-3). P-H.

Structure of Language & Its Mathematical Aspects: Proceedings, Vol. 12. Symposia in Applied Mathematics - New York - 1960. Ed. by R. Jakobson. LC 50-1183. 1980. Repr. of 1961 ed. 19.60 (ISBN 0-8218-1312-9, PSAPM-12). Am Math.

Structure of Literary Understanding. Stein H. Olsen. LC 77-77719. 1978. 28.50 (ISBN 0-521-21731-8). Cambridge U Pr.

Structure of Lutheranism: The Theology & Philosophy of Life of Lutheranism, 16th & 17th Centuries, Vol. 1. Werner Elert. Tr. by Walter A. Hansen. LC 62-19955. 1974. pap. 12.95 (ISBN 0-570-03192-3, 12-2588). Concordia.

Structure of Matter: A Survey of Modern Physics. Stephen Gasiorowicz. LC 78-18645. (Physics Ser.). (Illus.). 1979. text ed. 23.95 (ISBN 0-201-02511-6). A-W.

Structure of Metals: Crystallographic Methods, Principles & Data. 3rd rev. ed. C. S. Barrett & T. B. Massalski. LC 80-49878. (International Ser. on Materials Science & Technology: Vol. 14). (Illus.). 675p. 1980. 65.00 (ISBN 0-08-026171-X); pap. 20.00 (ISBN 0-08-026172-8). Pergamon.

Structure of Metaphysics. Morris Lazerowitz. 1963. text ed. 17.75x (ISBN 0-7100-3148-3). Humanities.

Structure of Morality. Hector-Neri Castaneda. (American Lectures in Philosophy Ser.). (Illus.). 256p. 1974. 22.50 (ISBN 0-398-02794-3). C C Thomas.

Structure of Non-Crystalline Materials. Yoshio Waseda. (Illus.). 304p. 1980. text ed. 44.50 (ISBN 0-07-068426-X, C). McGraw.

Structure of Nuclei: Trieste Lectures 1971. (Illus.). 599p. (Orig.). 1973. pap. 33.25 (ISBN 92-0-130072-7, IAEA). Unipub.

Structure of Professionalism. John B. Cullen. (Illus.). 1979. text ed. 17.50 (ISBN 0-89433-084-5). Petrocelli.

Structure of Psychology: An Introductory Text. Ed. by C. I. Howath & W. E. Gillham. (Illus.). 792p. 1981. text ed. 57.50x (ISBN 0-04-150071-7, 2492); pap. text ed. 19.95x (ISBN 0-04-150072-5, 2493). Allen Unwin.

Structure of Russian History. Ed. by Michael Cherniavsky. (Orig.). 1970. pap. text ed. 7.95x (ISBN 0-394-30112-9, RanC). Random.

Structure of Science. Ernest Nagel. LC 60-15504. 1979. lib. bdg. 25.00 (ISBN 0-915144-72-7); pap. text ed. 12.50 (ISBN 0-915144-71-9). Hackett Pub.

Structure of Scientific Inference. Mary Hesse. 1974. 22.50x (ISBN 0-520-02582-2). U of Cal Pr.

Structure of Social Action. Talcott Parsons. LC 49-49353. 1949. 15.95 (ISBN 0-02-924260-6); Vol. 1. pap. text ed. 7.95 (ISBN 0-02-924240-1); Vol. 2. pap. text ed. 6.95 (ISBN 0-02-924250-9). Free Pr.

Structure of Sociological Theory. rev. ed. Jonathan H. Turner. 1978. text ed. 16.95x (ISBN 0-256-02061-2). Dorsey.

Structure of Space. J. Solomon. LC 73-8543. (Illus.). 219p. 1974. 15.95 (ISBN 0-470-81221-4). Halsted Pr.

Structure of Technical English. A. J. Herbert. 1975. pap. text ed. 5.00x (ISBN 0-582-52523-3). Longman.

Structure of the American Economy, 2 vols. in 1. United States National Resources Committee. LC 78-173418. (FDR & the Era of the New Deal Ser). 1972. Repr. of 1939 ed. lib. bdg. 45.00 (ISBN 0-306-70388-2). Da Capo.

Structure of the Book of Job: A Form-Critical Analysis. Claus Westermann. Tr. by Charles A. Muenchow from Ger. LC 80-2379. 160p. 1981. 14.95 (ISBN 0-8006-0651-5, 1-651). Fortress.

Structure of the British Isles. J. G. Anderson & T. R. Owen. 1968. 18.00 (ISBN 0-08-012423-2); pap. 11.25 (ISBN 0-08-012422-4). Pergamon.

Structure of the British Isles. 2nd ed. J. G. Anderson & T. R. Owen. LC 80-41075. (Illus.). 242p. 1980. 28.00 (ISBN 0-08-023998-6); pap. 13.50 (ISBN 0-08-023997-8). Pergamon.

Structure of the Epididymis of Birds & the Seasonal Changes in the Epididymis of the Parrot. Bhrigunath Prasad. 1965. pap. 5.00x (ISBN 0-210-98100-8). Asia.

Structure of the Meat Animals: A Guide to Their Anatomy & Physiology. 2nd ed. Roderick MacGregor. (Illus.). 1965. pap. 14.95 (ISBN 0-291-39536-8). Intl Ideas.

Structure of the Nucleus. M. A. Preston & R. K. Bhaduri. 475p. 1975. 37.50 (ISBN 0-201-05976-2, Adv Bk Prog); pap. text ed. 25.50 (ISBN 0-201-05977-0, Adv Bk Prog). A-W.

Structure of the Quiet Photosphere & the Low Chromosphere: Proceedings. Bilderberg Conference - Arnhem - Holland - 1968. Ed. by C. De Jager. 1968. 9.90 o.p. (ISBN 0-387-91015-8). Springer-Verlag.

Structure of the Retina. Santiago Ramon Y Cajal. Tr. by Sylvia A. Thorpe. (Illus.). 224p. 1972. text ed. 17.75 (ISBN 0-398-02385-9). C C Thomas.

Structure of the Roman De Thebes. Mary Paschal. LC 80-66540. 96p. 1980. pap. 9.95 (ISBN 0-89729-261-8). Ediciones.

Structure of the Terror. Colin R. Lucas. (Oxford Historical Monographs). 1973. 42.00x (ISBN 0-19-821843-5). Oxford U Pr.

Structure of the Transition Zone. Ed. by Shuzo Asano. (Advances in Earth & Planetary Sciences Ser.: No. 8). 184p. 1980. lib. bdg. 26.50 (ISBN 90-277-1149-6, Pub. by D. Reidel). Kluwer Boston.

Structure of the Turkic Languages. Kaare Gronbech. Ed. by Denis Sinor. Tr. by John R. Krueger. (Indiana University Uralic & Altaic Ser.: Vol. 136). 189p. pap. text ed. 8.00 (ISBN 0-933070-04-7). Ind U Res Inst.

Structure of the World Economy & Economic Order: Prospects for a New International. Ed. by Ervin Laszlo & Joel Kurtzman. LC 79-23350. 1980. 16.50 (ISBN 0-686-64334-8). Pergamon.

Structure of the World Economy & Prospects for a New International Economic Order. Ed. by Ervin Laszlo & Joel Kurtzman. LC 79-23350. (Pergamon Policy Studies on the New International Economic Order Ser.). 120p. 1980. 16.50 (ISBN 0-08-025119-6). Pergamon.

Structure of Thucydides' History. Hunter R. Rawlings. LC 80-8572. 312p. 1981. 21.00x (ISBN 0-691-03555-5). Princeton U Pr.

Structure of Turbulent Shear Flow. 2nd ed. A. A. Townsend. LC 74-14441. (Monographs on Mechanics & Applied Mathematics). 300p. 1975. 74.50 (ISBN 0-521-20710-X). Cambridge U Pr.

Structure of Turbulent Shear Flow. 2nd ed. A. A. Townsend. LC 79-8526. (Cambridge Monographs on Mechanics & Applied Mathematics). (Illus.). 441p. 1980. pap. 19.95x (ISBN 0-521-29819-9). Cambridge U Pr.

Structure of Urban Reform. Ronald L. Warren et al. (Illus.). 256p. 1974. 18.95 (ISBN 0-669-92809-7); pap. 9.95 (ISBN 0-669-92817-8). Lexington Bks.

Structure of Western Europe. J. G. Anderson. 1978. text ed. 30.00 (ISBN 0-08-022045-2); pap. text ed. 14.00 (ISBN 0-08-022046-0). Pergamon.

Structure, Properties & Preparation of Perovskite-Type Compounds. F. S. Galasso. 1969. 25.00 (ISBN 0-08-012744-4). Pergamon.

Structure, Size & Costs of Urban Settlements. P. A. Stone. LC 73-80480. (National Institute of Economic & Social Research Economic & Social Studies: No. 28). (Illus.). 300p. 1973. 38.50 (ISBN 0-521-20309-0). Cambridge U Pr.

Structure, System & Economic Policy. Ed. by W. Leontief. LC 77-8581. 1977. 35.50 (ISBN 0-521-21724-5). Cambridge U Pr.

Structured Analysis. Victor Weinberg. LC 78-105808. 1978. pap. 19.00 (ISBN 0-917072-05-7). Yourdon.

Structured Analysis. Victor Weinberg. (Illus.). 1980. text ed. 25.95 (ISBN 0-13-854414-X). P-H.

Structured Approach to BASIC Programming. C. Joseph Sass. 1980. pap. text ed. 15.95 (ISBN 0-205-06726-3, 2067269); solutions manual free (ISBN 0-205-06727-1). Allyn.

Structured Approach to Essential Basic. George Ledin, Jr. 176p. 1979. pap. text ed. 7.95x (ISBN 0-87835-077-2). Boyd & Fraser.

Structured Approach to General BASIC. George Ledin. 1978. pap. 10.95x (ISBN 0-87835-070-5). Boyd & Fraser.

Structured Business Problem Solving with Fortran. Brian C. Honess. 300p. 1981. text ed. 13.95 (ISBN 0-205-07332-8); free (ISBN 0-205-07328-X). Allyn.

Structured COBAL. 2nd ed. Andreas S. Philippakis & Leonard Kazmier. Ed. by Charles E. Stewart. (Illus.). 448p. 1980. pap. text ed. 13.95 (ISBN 0-07-049801-6); instructor's manual 7.95 (ISBN 0-07-049802-4). McGraw.

Structured COBOL. Gary N. Gleason & Lister W. Horn. LC 78-31566. (Illus.). 1979. pap. 10.95x (ISBN 0-87835-079-9). Boyd & Fraser.

Structured COBOL. Mike Murach. 1980. pap. text ed. 13.95 (ISBN 0-574-21260-4, 13-4260); instr's guide avail. (ISBN 0-574-21261-2, 13-4261); oS supplement 4.50 (ISBN 0-574-21263-9, 13-4263); dOS supplement 4.50 (ISBN 0-574-21264-7, 13-4264). SRA.

Structured COBOL. 2nd ed. Andreas S. Philippakis & Leonard J. Kazmier. Ed. by Charles E. Stewart. (Illus.). 448p. 1981. pap. text ed. 13.95 (ISBN 0-07-049801-6); instrs'. manual 5.95 (ISBN 0-07-049802-4). McGraw.

Structured COBOL: A Direct Approach. Gerald Wohl. 1979. pap. text ed. 13.95 (ISBN 0-574-21230-2, 13-4230); instr's guide avail. (ISBN 0-574-21231-0, 13-4231). SRA.

Structured COBOL: A Pragmatic Approach. Robert T. Grauer & Marshal A. Crawford. (Illus.). 544p. 1981. pap. text ed. 19.95 (ISBN 0-13-854455-7). P-H.

Structured Cobol: A Self Teaching Guide. Ruth Ashley. LC 79-27340. (Wiley Self-Teaching Guides). 320p. 1980. pap. text ed. 8.95 (ISBN 0-471-05362-7). Wiley.

Structured COBOL: Fundamentals & Style. Tyler Welburn. (Illus.). 640p. (Orig.). 1981. pap. text ed. price not set (ISBN 0-87484-543-2). Mayfield Pub.

Structured Cobol Programming. 3rd ed. Nancy Stern & Robert A. Stern. 571p. 1980. pap. 16.95 (ISBN 0-471-04913-1). Wiley.

Structured COBOL Report Writer. David Schecter & George Yukoff. 1981. text ed. 17.95 (ISBN 0-8359-7097-3). Reston.

Structured Computer Organization. A. Tanenbaum. 1976. 24.95 (ISBN 0-13-854505-7). P-H.

Structured Computer Vision: Machine Perception Through Hierarchical Computation Structures. Ed. by S. Tanimoto & A. Klinger. LC 80-14878. 1980. 21.00 (ISBN 0-12-683280-3). Acad Pr.

Structured Concurrent Programming with Operating Systems Applications. Richard C. Holt et al. 1978. pap. text ed. 10.95 (ISBN 0-201-02937-5). A-W.

Structured Crowd: Essays in English Social History. Harold Perkin. 224p. 1981. 28.50x (ISBN 0-389-20116-2). B&N.

Structured Design. 2nd ed. Edward Yourdon & Larry L. Constantine. LC 78-24465. 599p. 1978. pap. 21.00 (ISBN 0-917072-11-1). Yourdon.

Structured FORTRAN. 2nd ed. John B. Moore & Leo Maleka. 567p. 1981. text ed. 19.95 (ISBN 0-8359-7104-X); pap. text ed. 13.95 (ISBN 0-8359-7103-1); soln. manual avail. (ISBN 0-8359-7105-8). Reston.

Structured Fortran Seventy-Seven for Business & General Applications. Harice L. Seeds. 496p. 1981. text ed. 15.95 (ISBN 0-471-07836-0). Wiley.

Structured Groups for Facilitating Development: Acquiring Life Skills, Resolving Life Themes, & Making Life Transitions. David J. Drum & J. Eugene Knott. LC 77-1947. (New Vistas in Counseling Ser.: Vol. 1). 1977. 16.95 (ISBN 0-87705-308-1). Human Sci Pr.

Structured Pascal. Jean P. Tremblay & Richard B. Bunt. 448p. 1980. pap. text ed. 10.95 (ISBN 0-07-065159-0, C). McGraw.

Structured PL-One & PL: A Problem Solving Approach. Peter Abel. 1981. text ed. 18.95 (ISBN 0-8359-7120-1); pap. text ed. 12.95 (ISBN 0-8359-7119-8); instr's. manual avail. (ISBN 0-8359-7121-X). Reston.

Structured PL-One (PL-C) Programming. Jean P. Tremblay & Richard B. Bunt. 1979. pap. text ed. 11.95x (ISBN 0-07-065173-6). McGraw.

Structured PL-Zero PL-One. Michael Kennedy & Martin B. Solomon. (Illus.). 1977. pap. 15.95 (ISBN 0-13-854901-X). P-H.

Structured PL-1 Programming with Business Applications. C. J. Rockey. 1981. pap. text ed. 13.95x (ISBN 0-697-08141-9); solutions manual avail. (ISBN 0-697-08145-1). Wm C Brown.

Structured Polymer Properties. Robert J. Samuels. LC 73-21781. 288p. 1974. 29.95 (ISBN 0-471-75155-3, Pub. by Wiley-Interscience). Wiley.

Structured Preoperative Teaching: Using Research to Improve Clinical Practice. Joanne Horsely. 1980. 9.50 (ISBN 0-8089-1311-5). Grune.

Structured Programming & Problem Solving with Algol W. Richard B. Kieburtz. (Illus.). 384p. 1975. 14.95 (ISBN 0-13-854737-8). P-H.

Structured Programming & Problem Solving with Pascal. Richard B. Kieburtz. (Illus.). 1978. Cloth 20.95 (ISBN 0-13-854877-3); pap. 14.95 (ISBN 0-13-854869-2). P-H.

Structured Programming & Problem Solving with PL-One. Richard B. Keiburtz. (Illus.). 1977. 18.95 o.p. (ISBN 0-686-60837-2); pap. 13.95 (ISBN 0-13-854943-5). P-H.

Structured Programming in FORTRAN. Louis A. Hill, Jr. (Illus.). 512p. 1981. text ed. 13.95 (ISBN 0-13-854612-6). P-H.

Structured Programming: Theory & Practice. R. C. Linger et al. LC 78-18641. 1979. text ed. 19.95 (ISBN 0-201-14461-1). A-W.

Structured Programming Using PL-C. J. K. Hughes. 512p. 1981. text ed. 14.95 (ISBN 0-471-04969-7). Wiley.

Structured Questions in "A" Level Chemistry. M. Cane et al. 1976. pap. text ed. 4.95x o.p. (ISBN 0-435-65098-X). Heinemann Ed.

Structured Questions in O Level Chemistry. Robin A. Hillman & Michael C. Cane. 1973. pap. text ed. 3.95x o.p. (ISBN 0-435-64322-3). Heinemann Ed.

Structured Questions in Physics. James M. Wilson & John R. Muckersie. 1975. pap. text ed. 5.25x o.p. (ISBN 0-435-67681-4). Heinemann Ed.

Structured Reading. Lynn Q. Troyka. (Illus.). 1978. pap. text ed. 10.50 (ISBN 0-13-854513-8). P-H.

Structured System Analysis: A New Technique. Barbara F. Medina. 1981. write for info. (ISBN 0-677-05570-6). Gordon.

Structured Walkthroughs. 2nd ed. Ed. by E. Yourdon. 1980. 13.95 (ISBN 0-13-855221-5). P-H.

Structures. Michael Andress. (Model Railway Guide Ser.: No. 3). (Illus.). 1980. pap. 9.95 (ISBN 0-85059-400-6). Aztex.

Structures Analysis & System Specification. Tom DeMarco. (Software Ser.). 1979. text ed. 25.00 o.p. (ISBN 0-13-854380-1). P-H.

Structures & Approximations for Electrons in Molecules. D. B. Cook. LC 77-15665. 1978. 44.95 (ISBN 0-470-99348-0). Halsted Pr.

Structures & Environment Handbook. 10th, rev. ed. Midwest Plan Service Engineers. Ed. by Midwest Plan Service Staff. LC 76-27983. (Illus.). 490p. 1980. pap. 10.00 (ISBN 0-686-68276-9, MWPS-1). Midwest Plan Serv.

Structures & Forces: Stage 3. Albert James. LC 77-82991. (Science 5-13 Ser.). (Illus.). 1977. pap. text ed. 8.25 (ISBN 0-356-04107-7). Raintree Child.

Structures & Forces: Stages 1 & 2. Albert James. LC 77-82991. (Science 5-13 Ser.). (Illus.). 1977. pap. text ed. 8.25 (ISBN 0-356-04007-0). Raintree Child.

Structures for Composition. 2nd ed. Bernard A. Drabeck et al. LC 77-77675. (Illus.). 1978. pap. text ed. 10.50 (ISBN 0-395-25567-8); inst. manual 0.25 (ISBN 0-395-25568-6). HM.

Structures in Context. Nicholas Sikiotis. (Illus.). 1980. pap. text ed. 4.50x (ISBN 0-582-55884-0); key 1.75x (ISBN 0-582-55885-9). Longman.

Structures in the Subjective Lexicon: An Experimental Approach to the Study of Semantic Fields. Samuel Fillenbaum & Amnon Rapoport. 1971. 33.00 (ISBN 0-12-256250-X). Acad Pr.

Structures: Model Railway Guide 3. Michael Andress. 64p. 1980. pap. 9.95 (ISBN 0-85059-400-6). Aztex.

Structures of Broadcasting: A Symposium. E. G. Wedell. 108p. 1970. 27.00x (ISBN 0-686-63741-0, Pub. by Manchester U Pr England). State Mutual Bk.

Structures of the Church. Ed. by Teodoro J. Urresti. (Concilium Ser.: Religion in the Seventies: Vol. 58). 1970. pap. 4.95 (ISBN 0-8164-2514-0). Crossroad NY.

Structures of the Elements. Jerry Donohue. 448p. 1981. Repr. of 1974 ed. lib. bdg. price not set (ISBN 0-89874-230-7). Krieger.

Structuring Child Behavior Through Visual Art: A Therapeutic, Individualized Art Program to Develop Positive Behavior Attitudes in Children. Florence Singer. (Illus.). 144p. 1980. text ed. 15.75. C C Thomas.

Structuring of Organizations. Henry Mintzberg. (Theory of Management Policy Ser.). (Illus.). 1979. ref. ed. 22.95 (ISBN 0-13-855270-3). P-H.

Structuring Speech: A How-to-Do-It-Book About Public Speaking. Gerald M. Phillips & J. Jerome Zolten. (Speech Communication Ser.). 1976. pap. 6.50 (ISBN 0-672-61366-2, SC-22). Bobbs.

Structuring the Journey to Work. Howard S. Lapin. LC 63-15012. 1964. 9.00x o.p. (ISBN 0-8122-7424-5). U of Pa Pr.

Structuring the Therapeutic Process: Compromise with Chaos - a Therapist's Response to the Individual & the Group. Murray Cox. LC 77-4181. 1978. text ed. 37.00 (ISBN 0-08-020403-1); pap. text ed. 12.50 (ISBN 0-08-020402-3). Pergamon.

Structuring Your Novel. Robert C. Meredith & John D. Fitzgerald. 1972. pap. 4.50 (ISBN 0-06-463325-X, EH 325, EH). Har-Row.

Strucured FORTRAN with Watfiv-S. P. Cress et al. 1980. pap. 13.95 (ISBN 0-13-854752-1). P-H.

Struggle Against Terrorism. Ed. by William P. Lineberry. (Reference Shelf Ser.). 1977. 6.25 (ISBN 0-8242-0605-3). Wilson.

Struggle & Contemplation. Schutz, Prior of Taize. 1974. pap. 2.95 (ISBN 0-8164-2106-4). Crossroad NY.

Struggle & Fulfillment: The Inner Dynamics of Religion & Morality. Donald Evans. LC 80-8050. 256p. 1981. pap. 7.95 (ISBN 0-8006-1426-7, 1-1426). Fortress.

Struggle & Lose, Struggle & Win: The United Mine Workers Union. Elizabeth Levy & Tad Richards. LC 76-56703. 144p. (gr. 7-11). 1977. 6.95 (ISBN 0-590-07355-9, Four Winds). Schol Bk Serv.

Struggle & Survival in Colonial America. Ed. by David G. Sweet & Gary B. Nash. 1981. 25.00 (ISBN 0-520-04110-0). U of Cal Pr.

Struggle for a Free Europe. Dean Acheson. 1971. pap. text ed. 3.95x (ISBN 0-393-09983-0). Norton.

Struggle for Asia 1828-1914. David Gillard. 1978. text ed. 31.50x (ISBN 0-8419-7000-9); pap. 13.95 o.p. (ISBN 0-8419-7003-3). Holmes & Meier.

Struggle for Basic Needs in Nepal. M. P. Blaikie et al. (Illus.). 100p. (Orig.). 1980. pap. 6.50 (ISBN 92-64-12101-3). OECD.

Struggle for Black Equality, Nineteen Fifty-Four to Nineteen Eighty. Harvard Sitkoff. Ed. by Eric Forer. 1981. 10.95; pap. 4.95. FS&G.

Struggle for Black Equality, Nineteen Fifty-Four to Nineteen Eighty. Harvard Sitkoff. Ed. by Eric Foner. 1981. 10.95 (ISBN 0-8090-8925-4); pap. 4.95 (ISBN 0-8090-0144-6). Hill & Wang.

Struggle for Democracy: Sung Chiao-Jen & the 1911 Revolution. Kit S. Liew. LC 74-123623. 1971. 20.00x (ISBN 0-520-01760-9). U of Cal Pr.

Struggle for Indochina, 1940-1955. Ellen J. Hammer. 1955. 15.00x (ISBN 0-8047-0458-9). Stanford U Pr.

Struggle for Mastery in Europe: 1848-1918. Alan J. Taylor. 1954. 45.00x (ISBN 0-19-822101-0). Oxford U Pr.

Struggle for Religious Freedom in Virginia: The Baptist. William Thom. pap. 9.00 o.p. (ISBN 0-686-12395-6). Church History.

Struggle for Significance. John H. Brennecke & Robert G. Amick. 1971. pap. text ed. 5.95x (ISBN 0-02-473360-1). Macmillan.

Struggle for Significance. 2nd ed. John H. Brennecke & Robert G. Amick. 1975. pap. text ed. 9.95x (ISBN 0-02-471000-8, 47100); tchrs' manual free (ISBN 0-02-471010-5). Macmillan.

Struggle for Sobriety. Jeanne McCarty. (Southwestern Studies: No. 62). 1980. pap. 3.00 (ISBN 0-87404-121-X). Tex Western.

Struggle for the American Mediterranean: United States-European Rivalry in the Gulf-Caribbean, 1776-1904. Lester D. Langley. LC 74-84527. 240p. 1975. 15.00x (ISBN 0-8203-0364-X). U of Ga Pr.

Struggle for the Constitution, 1603-1689: England in the Seventeenth Century. G. E. Aylmer. (History of England Ser.). 1968. text ed. 6.25x o.p. (ISBN 0-7137-0309-1). Humanities.

Struggle for the Good, 2 pts. Ilija Poplasen. (Illus.). 1981. Repr. of 1978 ed. Pt. I, 61 Pgs. 10.00 (ISBN 0-935352-03-1); Pt. II, 128 Pgs. 20.00 (ISBN 0-935352-04-X). MIR PA.

Struggle for the Gulf Borderlands: The Creek War & the Battle of New Orleans, Eighteen Twelve to Eighteen Fifteen. Frank L. Owsley, Jr. LC 80-11109. 20.00 (ISBN 0-8130-0662-7). U Presses Fla.

Struggle for the Middle East: The Soviet Union & the Middle East 1958-1968. Walter Laqueur. 1969. 12.95 o.s.i. (ISBN 0-02-568320-9). Macmillan.

Struggle for the Ministry of Health. Frank Honigsbaum. 80p. 1970. pap. text ed. 5.00x (ISBN 0-7135-1836-7, Pub. by Bedford England). Renouf.

Struggle in the Andes: Peasant Political Mobilization in Peru. Howard Handleman. (Latin American Monographs: No. 35). 350p. 1974. 14.95x (ISBN 0-292-77513-X). U of Tex Pr.

Struggle of Prayer. Donald G. Bloesch. LC 79-3589. 192p. 1980. 9.95 (ISBN 0-06-060797-1, HarpR). Har-Row.

Struggle That Must Be: An Autobiography. Harry Edwards. 304p. 1980. 13.95 (ISBN 0-02-535040-4). Macmillan.

Struggle to Bring Technology to Cities. Ed. by Urban Institute. 1971. pap. 1.95 o.p. (ISBN 0-87766-013-1, 70001). Urban Inst.

Struktur Des Dramas Bei T. S. Eliot. Gerd Schmidt. (Salzburg Studies in English Literature, Poetic Drama & Poetic Theory Ser.: No. 38). 1978. pap. text ed. 25.00x (ISBN 0-391-01516-8). Humanities.

Struktura Khudozhestvennogo Teksta. Iu. M. Lotman. LC 70-158681. (Slavic Reprint Ser.: No. 9). 381p. (Rus.). 1971. pap. 6.00 (ISBN 0-87057-129-X, Pub. by Brown U Pr). Univ Pr of New England.

Strukturelle und instrumentalphonetische Untersuchungen zur gesprochenen Sprache. Joachim Goeschel. LC 72-76054. (Studia Linguistica Germanica Vol. 9). (Illus.). 1973. 51.00x (ISBN 3-11-003624-X). De Gruyter.

Struve: Liberal on the Left, 1870-1905. Richard Pipes. (Russian Research Center Studies: No. 64). 1970. 20.00x (ISBN 0-674-84595-1). Harvard U Pr.

Stryker Family in America: A History of the Stryker & Striker Families, Vol 2. William N. Stryker. LC 78-75351. (Illus.). 500p. 1981. lib. bdg. 45.00 (ISBN 0-9602936-2-0). W N Stryker.

Stuart Age. Barry Coward. (History of England Ser.). (Illus.). 512p. 1980. text ed. 32.00 (ISBN 0-582-48279-8); pap. 18.95 (ISBN 0-582-48833-8). Longman.

Stuart Age. Peter Lane. 96p. 1980. 16.95 (ISBN 0-7134-0037-4, Pub. by Batsford England). David & Charles.

Stuart & Georgian Moments: Clark Library Seminar Papers on Seventeeth & Eighteenth Century Literature. Ed. by Earl Miner. (Seventeenth & Eighteenth Centuries Studies Group, UCLA: No. 3). 308p. 1972. 18.50x (ISBN 0-520-01641-6). U of Cal Pr.

Stuart Constitution, Sixteen Hundred Three to Sixteen Eighty Eight: Documents & Commentary. John P. Kenyon. (Orig.). 1966. 62.00 (ISBN 0-521-05884-8); pap. 17.95x (ISBN 0-521-09370-8). Cambridge U Pr.

Stuart Davis: Art & Art Theory. John R. Lane. LC 77-17452. (Illus.). 1978. pap. 11.95 o.p. (ISBN 0-87273-067-0). Bklyn Mus.

Stuart England. J. R. Kenyon. 1978. pap. 3.50 (ISBN 0-14-022076-3, Pelican). Penguin.

Stuart People. Madeline Jones. 1978. 16.95 (ISBN 0-7134-0617-8, Pub. by Batsford England). David & Charles.

Stuart Plays. rev. ed. Ed. by A. H. Nethercot et al. LC 72-161203. 1971. 49.50x (ISBN 0-03-083029-X). Irvington.

Stuart Royal Proclamations: Royal Proclamations of King James I 1603-1625, Vol. 1. Ed. by James F. Larkin & Paul L. Hughes. 716p. 1974. 79.00x (ISBN 0-19-822372-2). Oxford U Pr.

Stuart Times. (Picture Panorama of British History Ser.). 1977. pap. 4.95 (ISBN 0-263-06242-2). Transatlantic.

Stubborn Old Woman. Clyde R. Bulla. LC 78-22506. (Illus.). 48p. (gr. 1-4). 1980. 7.95 (ISBN 0-690-03945-X, TYC-J); PLB 7.89 (ISBN 0-690-03946-8). T Y Crowell.

Stubborn Sam. William C. Gault. (gr. 5 up). 1969. PLB 7.95 o.p. (ISBN 0-525-40433-3). Dutton.

Stuck on the Cubs. Rick Schwab. 192p. (Orig.). 1977. pap. 1.95 (ISBN 0-930528-01-8). Sassafras Pr.

Stuck on the Sox. Rick Lindberg. 192p. (Orig.). 1978. pap. 1.95 (ISBN 0-930528-02-6). Sassafras Pr.

Stuck-Up Kitty. Keng Keng. (Illus.). 38p. (gr. 6-10). 1979. 3.95 o.p. (ISBN 0-8351-0693-4); pap. 1.75 o.p. (ISBN 0-8351-0694-2). China Bks.

Stud Farm Diary. Humphrey S. Finney. 5.25 (ISBN 0-85131-194-6, Dist. by Sporting Book Center). J A Allen.

Stud Poker Blue Book. George H. Fisher. (Gamblers Book Shelf). 1968. pap. 2.95 (ISBN 0-89650-508-1). Gamblers.

Student - the College - the Law. William T. O'Hara & John G. Hill, Jr. LC 72-87116. 1972. pap. 6.50x (ISBN 0-8077-2378-9). Tchrs Coll.

Student Activism & Protest: Alternatives for Social Change. Edward E. Samson & Harold A. Korn. LC 77-92898. (Higher Education Ser.). 1970. 14.95x o.p. (ISBN 0-87589-052-0). Jossey-Bass.

Student Activities in Secondary Schools: A Bibliography. Compiled by Jackson et al. Battiste. 92p. 1980. pap. 4.00 (ISBN 0-88210-109-9). Natl Assn Principals.

Student & Singer. Charles Santley. 1981. Repr. of 1892 ed. 39.50 (ISBN 0-404-18866-4). AMS Pr.

Student Assistance Program: How It Works. Roger Svendson & Tom Griffin. 1980. pap. 3.95 (ISBN 0-89486-110-7). Hazelden.

Student Attitudes & Academic Environments: A Study of California Higher Education. Harvey E. Rich & Pamela M. Jolicoeur. LC 78-2953. (Praeger Special Studies). 1978. 19.95 (ISBN 0-03-041431-8). Praeger.

Student Biologist Explores Genetics. Carl Raab & Joan Raab. (gr. 7-12). 1977. PLB 7.97 o.p. (ISBN 0-8239-0378-8). Rosen Pr.

Student-Centered Health Instruction: A Humanistic Approach. Jerrold S. Greenberg. LC 76-55642. (Illus.). 1978. pap. text ed. 7.95 (ISBN 0-201-02627-9). A-W.

Student Centered Language Arts & Reading, K-13: A Handbook for Teachers. 2nd ed. James Moffett & Betty J. Wagner. LC 76-11920. (Illus.). 640p. 1976. 19.50 (ISBN 0-395-20630-8). HM.

Student Characteristics & Teaching. Jere Brophy et al. (Professional Ser.). 224p. 1981. text ed. 22.50 (ISBN 0-582-28152-0). Longman.

Student Competencies Guide: Survival Skills for a Changing World. 1977. 2.75 (ISBN 0-89354-602-X). Northwest Regional.

Student Development Practices. F. B. Newton & K. L. Ender. (Illus.). 348p. 1980. 22.75 (ISBN 0-398-03997-6). C C Thomas.

Student Diagnosis, Placement, & Prescription: A Criterion-Referenced Approach. Roger B. Worner. LC 76-26432. (Illus.). 256p. 1977. 10.95x (ISBN 0-253-35526-5). Ind U Pr.

Student Displacement-Exclusion: Violations of Civil & Human Rights. Conference on Civil & Human Rights in Education, 11th. LC 73-9751. 64p. 1973. pap. 1.50 (ISBN 0-8106-0543-0). NEA.

Student Engineer's Companion: A Handbook for Engineers, Draftsmen & Students. J. Carvill. Orig. Title: Mechanical Engineering Components. (Illus.). 1980. pap. 12.50 (ISBN 0-408-00438-X). Butterworths.

Student Entrepreneur's Guide. Brett M. Kingstone. 192p. (Orig.). 1981. pap. 4.95 (ISBN 0-89815-045-0). Ten Speed Pr.

Student Evaluation of Instruction. Kenneth O. Doyle, Jr. LC 74-7859. (Illus.). 1975. 17.95 (ISBN 0-669-93328-7). Lexington Bks.

Student Guide for Negotiations: Understanding the Bargaining Process. Neal W. Beckmann. 1981. write for info. (ISBN 0-87527-241-X). Green.

Student Guide to Accounting for Life Insurance Companies. Ed. by Life Office Management Association. (FLMI Insurance Education Program Ser.). 97p. (Orig.). 1980. wkbk. 4.00x (ISBN 0-915322-42-0). Loma.

Student Guide to Fellowships & Internships. The Amherst Student. 356p. 1980. 15.95 (ISBN 0-525-93155-4); pap. 7.95 (ISBN 0-525-93147-3). Dutton.

Student Guide to Management Accounting: Concepts & Applications. Ronald Thacker & Loudell Ellis. 336p. 1980. pap. text ed. 8.95 (ISBN 0-8359-4196-5). Reston.

Student Guide to Richards Atlas of New York State. Jeanne Schwarz. 1976. pap. 6.95x ea. (ISBN 0-88323-108-5, 304). Richards Pub.

Student Guide to Sex on Campus. Yale Committee on Human Sexuality. pap. 1.00 (ISBN 0-451-04607-2, N4607, Sig). NAL.

Student Guide to the Dental Aptitude Test. David M. Tarlow & Marc L. Lichtenberg. LC 78-53093. (Illus.). 1978. pap. 6.00 (ISBN 0-931572-01-0). Datar Pub.

Student Guide to the Medical College Admission Test. 3rd ed. David M. Tarlow. LC 78-53092. (Illus.). 1978. pap. 6.00 (ISBN 0-931572-00-2). Datar Pub.

Student Guide to the Optometry College Admission Test. David M. Tarlow. (Illus.). 1978. pap. 7.00 (ISBN 0-931572-04-5). Datar Pub.

Student Guide to the Pharmacy College Admission Test. David M. Tarlow. (Illus.). 1978. pap. 7.00 (ISBN 0-931572-05-3). Datar Pub.

Student Guide to the Plays of Samuel Becket. John Fletcher et al. 1978. 15.00 (ISBN 0-571-10796-6, Pub. by Faber & Faber); pap. 6.95 (ISBN 0-571-10804-0). Merrimack Bk Serv.

Student Guide to the Registered Nurse (R.N.) Examination. Maryanne C. Glynn. Ed. by David M. Tarlow. (Illus.). 1978. pap. 7.00 (ISBN 0-931572-03-7). Datar Pub.

Student Guide to Writing a Journal. 1977. 2.25 (ISBN 0-89354-601-1). Northwest Regional.

Student Handbook: A Review Guide, Activities Manual & Reader for "Understanding Psychology". 2nd ed. Martin Schulman. 1977. wkbk. 6.95 (ISBN 0-394-32022-0). Random.

Student Internationals. Philip G. Altbach & Norman T. Uphoff. LC 72-12980. 1973. 10.00 (ISBN 0-8108-0578-2). Scarecrow.

Student Involvement Manual for Personnel Management. William F. Glueck & Jerry A. Wall. 1979. pap. 6.95x (ISBN 0-256-02253-4). Business Pubns.

Student Journalist & Keys to Successful Reporting. Hazel Presson. LC 65-22256. (Student Journalist Ser). (gr. 7 up). Date not set. PLB 7.97 (ISBN 0-8239-0124-6). Rosen Pr. Postponed.

Student Journalist & Mass Communication. Julian Adams. (Illus.). 190p. 1981. lib. bdg. 8.95 (ISBN 0-8239-0538-1); workbook 1.50 (ISBN 0-8239-0499-7). Rosen Pr.

Student Learning Styles: Diagnosing & Prescribing Programs. National Association of Secondary School Principals. Ed. by Thomas F. Koerner. (Orig.). 1979. pap. text ed. 5.00 (ISBN 0-88210-103-X). Natl Assn Principals.

Student Life in a Class Society. J. Abbott. 1971. 30.00 (ISBN 0-08-015654-1). Pergamon.

Student Map Manual: Historical Geography of the Bible Landa. Richard Cleeve. Ed. by J. Monson et al. 168p. 1980. 34.95 (ISBN 0-310-42980-3). Zondervan.

Student Nurse. Gertrude V. Pyke & Helen G. Pyke. LC 77-70846. (Nova Ser.). 1977. pap. 4.95 (ISBN 0-8127-0134-8). Southern Pub.

Student Personnel Work: A Program of Development Relationships. Edmund G. Williamson & Donald A. Biggs. LC 74-28492. 384p. 1975. text ed. 24.50 (ISBN 0-471-94880-2). Wiley.

Student Personnel Work in General Education: A Humanistic Approach. Ed. by Harold A. Moses. (Illus.). 408p. 1974. 22.75 (ISBN 0-398-03128-2). C C Thomas.

Student Politics in Bombay. Philip G. Altbach. 7.50x (ISBN 0-210-22204-2). Asia.

Student Power in World Missions. 2nd ed. David M. Howard. LC 79-122918. (Orig.). 1979. pap. 2.25 (ISBN 0-87784-493-3). Inter-Varsity.

Student Project Work in Construction. Ed. by Thames Valley Group. 1971. pap. text ed. 11.95x (ISBN 0-7114-4903-1). Intl Ideas.

Student Protest Nineteen Sixty-Nineteen Sixty-Nine: An Analysis of the Issues & Speeches. Donald E. Phillips. LC 79-3716. 1980. text ed. 14.75 (ISBN 0-8191-0911-8); pap. text ed. 9.00 (ISBN 0-8191-0912-6). U Pr of Amer.

Student Record of Community Exploration. 1977. 2.25 (ISBN 0-89354-603-8). Northwest Regional.

Student Resource & Activity Manual to Accompany Koontz & Fulmer's a Practical Introduction to Business. rev. ed. Harold L. Goldman. 1978. pap. text ed. 6.95x (ISBN 0-256-02044-2). Irwin.

Student Rights & Responsibilities. Donald Grault. 1976. pap. text ed. 8.00 (ISBN 0-87545-003-2). Natl Sch Pr.

Student Services: A Handbook for the Profession. Ursula Delworth et al. LC 80-8008. (Higher Education Ser.). 1980. text ed. 25.00x (ISBN 0-87589-476-3). Jossey-Bass.

Student-Structured Learning in Science: A Program for the Teacher. 3rd ed. Charles C. Matthews et al. 1977. pap. text ed. 7.95 o.p. (ISBN 0-8403-1651-8). Kendall-Hunt.

Student, Teacher, & Engineer: Selected Speeches & Articles of Nathan W. Dougherty. Ed. by William K. Stair. LC 76-186707. 1972. 13.50x (ISBN 0-87049-138-5). U. of Tenn Pr.

Student Teacher on the Firing Line. D. Eugene Meyer. LC 80-69236. 135p. 1981. perfect bdg. 11.95 (ISBN 0-86548-048-6). Century Twenty One.

Student Teacher's Handbook: A Step-by-Step Guide Through the Term. Andrew I. Schwebel et al. LC 79-2239. 1979. pap. 3.95 (ISBN 0-06-460186-2, CO 186, COS). Har-Row.

Student Teaching: Attitude & Research Bases for Change in School & University. Carol K. Tittle. LC 73-20477. 1974. 10.00 (ISBN 0-8108-0694-0). Scarecrow.

Student Teaching in Special Classes for the Mentally Retarded. Maxine Mays. (Illus.). 108p. 1974. pap. 7.75 (ISBN 0-398-02861-3). C C Thomas.

Student Teaching: The Entrance to Professional Physical Education. John B. Woods et al. 1973. pap. text ed. 9.50 (ISBN 0-12-763050-3). Acad Pr.

Student Workbook to Accompany Business Law. 3rd ed. John R. Goodwin. 1980. pap. 6.50x (ISBN 0-256-02267-4). Irwin.

Student Workbook to Accompany Lusk's Business Law. 4th ed. Phillip Scaletta et al. 1978. pap. text ed. 6.95 (ISBN 0-256-02022-1). Irwin.

Students Against Tyranny: The Resistance of the White Rose, Munich, 1942-1943. rev. ed. Inge Scholl. Tr. by Arthur R. Schultz from Ger. LC 73-105504. Orig. Title: Weisse Rose. (Illus.). 1970. 12.50x (ISBN 0-8195-4021-8, Pub. by Wesleyan U Pr). Columbia U Pr.

Students & Books. Peter H. Mann. 1974. 16.95x (ISBN 0-7100-7850-1). Routledge & Kegan.

Students & Sex. (Illus.). pap. 5.00 (ISBN 0-910550-71-9). Centurion Pr.

Students & the Law. Peter Sandman. 1971. pap. 1.95 o.s.i. (ISBN 0-02-081470-4, Collier). Macmillan.

Student's Book of College English. 2nd ed. David Skwire & Frances Chitwood. 1978. pap. text ed. 7.95 (ISBN 0-02-478330-7). Macmillan.

Student's Book of English: A Complete Course-Book & Grammar to Advanced Intermediate Level. John L. Cook et al. 448p. 1980. pap. 9.95x (ISBN 0-631-12812-3, Pub. by Basil Blackwell); tapes 35.00 (ISBN 0-631-12893-X); complete pack 40.00x (ISBN 0-631-12903-0). Biblio Dist.

Students, Churches & Higher Education. R. T. Gribbon. 128p. 1981. pap. 6.95 (ISBN 0-8170-0931-0). Judson.

Student's Comprehensive Guide to The Canterbury Tales. Allan H. MacLaine. LC 64-22359. (Orig.). (gr. 10up). 1965. text ed. 5.95 (ISBN 0-8120-5016-9); pap. text ed. 4.50 (ISBN 0-8120-0040-4). Barron.

Student's Dictionary of Anglo-Saxon. Henry Sweet. 1896. 22.00x (ISBN 0-19-863107-3). Oxford U Pr.

Students' Dictionary of Economics. Ed. by Jacqueline M. Lynch. (Students' Dictionary Ser.). 112p. (Orig.). (gr. 7 up). 1980. pap. text ed. 4.95 (ISBN 0-686-28479-8). Mara Pr MA.

Student's Edition of Monograph of the Work of McKim, Mead & White--1879-1915. Ed. by Alan Greenbeg & Michael George. (Illus.). 160p. 1981. 18.95 (ISBN 0-8038-6774-3); pap. 10.95 (ISBN 0-8038-6775-1). Hastings.

Student's English-Sanskrit Dictionary. V. S. Apte. 501p. 1973. text ed. 7.50x (ISBN 0-8426-0507-X). Verry.

Students Guide to Accounting, 2 vols. Edward C. Cavert et al. 512p. 1980. pap. text ed. 15.95 (ISBN 0-8403-2223-2). Kendall-Hunt.

Student's Guide to Basic French. 2nd ed. Julius Arnold. 184p. (gr. 9-11). 1980. pap. text ed. 5.50 (ISBN 0-88334-021-6). Ind Sch Pr.

Student's Guide to Conducting Social Science Research. Barbara Bunker et al. LC 74-11814. 120p. 1975. pap. text ed. 6.95 (ISBN 0-87705-238-7). Human Sci Pr.

Student's Guide to Moliere. Brian Masters. 1970. pap. text ed. 4.95x (ISBN 0-435-37570-9). Heinemann Ed.

Student's Guide to Piaget. D. J. Boyle. LC 77-94056. 1969. 11.25 (ISBN 0-08-006407-8); pap. 5.75 (ISBN 0-08-006406-X). Pergamon.

Student's Hindi-Urdu Reference Manual. Franklin Southworth. LC 71-164367. 256p. 1971. pap. 4.95x o.p. (ISBN 0-8165-0306-0). U of Ariz Pr.

Students Indexed World Atlas, No. 9551. American Map Company. (Illus.). (gr. 7-12). 1979. pap. 1.10 (ISBN 0-8416-9551-2). Am Map.

Students into Teachers: Experiences of Probationers in Schools. Mildred Collins. (Students Library of Education). 1969. text ed. 5.25x (ISBN 0-7100-6338-5); pap. text ed. 2.25x (ISBN 0-7100-6342-3). Humanities.

Student's Introduction to Engineering Design. Harold A. Simon. LC 74-19010. 1975. text ed. 28.00 (ISBN 0-08-017103-6); pap. text ed. 21.00 (ISBN 0-08-018234-8). Pergamon.

Student's Milton. rev. ed. Ed. by Frank A. Patterson. 1930. 44.50x (ISBN 0-89197-430-X). Irvington.

Student's Resource Book & Study Guide to Accompany Psychology & You. Dan G. Perkins et al. 1978. pap. 5.95x (ISBN 0-673-15087-9). Scott F.

Students Resource Manual: Hicks-Gullett Management of Organization. th ed. James D. Powell & C. Aron Kelley. 368p. Date not set. text ed. price not set (ISBN 0-07-028777-5). McGraw.

Students' Survival Guide to San Diego. 3rd ed. Barbara H. Peters & Phil Hopkins. (Illus.). 1980. cancelled (ISBN 0-931854-01-6). Humbird Hopkins.

Students Under Stress: A Study in the Social Psychology of Adaptation. David Mechanic. LC 77-91058. 1978. 20.00 (ISBN 0-299-07470-6); pap. text ed. 6.95 (ISBN 0-299-07474-9). U of Wis Pr.

Students, Values, & Politics: A Cross-Cultural Comparison. Otto Klineberg et al. LC 77-94082. 1979. 19.95 (ISBN 0-02-916770-1). Free Pr.

Student's Workbook for the Buyer's Manual. Murray Krieger. 300p. 1980. pap. text ed. 13.50 (ISBN 0-686-60198-X, M47579). Natl Ret Merch.

Studia Biblica Nineteen Seventy-Eight, I: Papers on Old Testament & Related Themes. Sixth International Congress on Biblical Studies, Oxford, 3-7 April 1978. Ed. by E. A. Livingstone. 272p. 1979. text ed. 36.95x (ISBN 0-905774-16-7, Pub. by JSOT Pr England); pap. text ed. 23.95x (ISBN 0-905774-17-5). Eisenbrauns.

Studia Biblica Nineteen Seventy-Eight II: Papers on the Gospels. International Congress on Biblical Studies. Ed. by E. A. Livingston. (Journal for the Study of the New Testament Supplement Ser.: No. 2). 350p. 1980. text ed. 21.95 (ISBN 0-905774-22-1, Pub. by JSOT Pr England). Eisenbrauns.

Studia Bibliologica. Cornelius Dima-Dragan. 1980. 15.00 (ISBN 0-917944-02-X). Am Inst Writing Res.

Studia Hispanica I in Honor of Rodolfo Cardona. Ed. by Luis A. Ramos-Garcia & Nestor Lugones. 1980. 12.95 (ISBN 0-934840-01-6). U Tex Studia.

Studia Linguistica Alexandro Vasilii Filio Issatschenko a Collegis Amicisque Oblata. Ed. by Henrik Birnbaum et al. 1978. pap. text ed. 70.50x (ISBN 0-685-59424-6). Humanities.

Studia Semitica, 2 vols. Erwin I. Rosenthal. Incl. Vol. 1. Jewish Themes. 57.00 (ISBN 0-521-07958-6); Vol. 2. Islamic Themes. 45.00 (ISBN 0-521-07959-4). (Oriental Publications Ser.: Nos. 16 & 17). Cambridge U Pr.

Studied Madness. Heywood H. Broun. LC 79-84436. 1979. 15.95 (ISBN 0-933256-00-0); pap. 7.95 (ISBN 0-933256-03-5). Second Chance.

Studien Zu Den Klosterprivilegien der Paepste Im Fruehen Mittelalter Unter Besonderer Beruecksichti der Privilegierung Von St. Maurice D'agaune. Hans H. Anton. (Beitraege Zur Geschichte und Quellenkunde Des Mittelalters Ser.: Vol. 4). 1975. pap. 47.00x (ISBN 3-11-004686-5). De Gruyter.

Studien zum Altestamentlichen Hintergrund Des Johannesevangeliums. G. Reim. LC 72-76086. (New Testament Studies Monograph, No. 22). 280p. (Ger.). 1973. 51.00 (ISBN 0-521-08630-2). Cambridge U Pr.

Studien Zum Mahaprajnaparamita (Upadesa) Sastra. Tr. by Mitsuyoshi Saigusa. (Ger.). 1969. 39.50 o.p. (ISBN 0-89346-097-4, Pub. by Hokuseido Pr). Heian Intl.

Studien zum Verstaendnis der Romischen Literatur. Wilhelm Kroll. Ed. by Steele Commager. LC 77-70839. (Latin Poetry Ser.: Vol. 23). 1978. lib. bdg. 41.00 (ISBN 0-8240-2972-0). Garland Pub.

Studies for a Byron Bibliography. Francis L. Randolph. LC 79-13752. 1979. 25.00 (ISBN 0-915010-26-7). Sutter House.

Studies for an Actress & Other Poems. Jean Garrigue. 1973. pap. 1.95 o.s.i. (ISBN 0-02-069370-2, Collier). Macmillan.

Studies in Abstract Phonology. Edmund Gussman. (Linguistic Inquiry Monographs). 160p. (Orig.). 1980. 22.50x (ISBN 0-262-07081-2); pap. text ed. 13.50x (ISBN 0-262-57057-2). MIT Pr.

Studies in Acts. William J. Fallis. pap. 2.25 o.p. (ISBN 0-8054-1346-4). Broadman.

Studies in Alchemy. St. Germain. (Alchemy Ser.). (Illus.). 92p. 1974. pap. 3.95 (ISBN 0-916766-00-4). Summit Univ.

Studies in American Indian Languages. Jesse Sawyer. (California Library Reprint). 1974. 20.00x (ISBN 0-520-02525-3). U of Cal Pr.

Studies in American Minority Life. Eldon L. Seamans. 1976. pap. text ed. 7.50x (ISBN 0-8191-0092-7). U Pr of Amer.

Studies in Ancient Europe: Essays Presented to Stuart Piggott. Ed. by J. M. Coles & D. D. Simpson. (Illus.). 1968. text ed. 14.00x (ISBN 0-7185-1079-8, Leicester). Humanities.

Studies in Ancient Greek Topography, Pt. 2: Battlefields. W. Kendrick Pritchett. (U. C. Publ. in Classical Studies: Vol. 4). 1969. pap. 11.50x (ISBN 0-520-09050-0). U of Cal Pr.

Studies in Animal & Human Behaviour, 2 vols. Konrad Lorenz. LC 75-11087. Vol. 1. 1970. 18.50x (ISBN 0-674-84630-3); Vol. 2. 1971. 18.50x (ISBN 0-674-84631-1). Harvard U Pr.

Studies in Arabic Linguistics. D. Abdo. (Arabic.). 1973. 14.00x (ISBN 0-685-72058-6). Intl Bk Ctr.

Studies in Arabic Philology. A. Bakr. (Arabic.). 1969. 14.00x (ISBN 0-685-72059-4). Intl Bk Ctr.

Studies in Art, Architecture, & Design, 2 vols. Nikolaus Pevsner. 15.00 ea o.s.i. Vol. 1 (ISBN 0-8027-0276-7). Vol. 2 (ISBN 0-8027-0277-5). Walker & Co.

Studies in Asian Genealogy. Ed. by Spencer J. Palmer. LC 70-158453. (Illus.). 281p. 1972. 12.50 o.p. (ISBN 0-8425-0587-3). Brigham.

Studies in Asian History: Proceedings of the Asian History Congress 1961. Indian Council For Cultural Relations. 15.00x o.p. (ISBN 0-210-22748-6). Asia.

Studies in Attribution: Shakespeare & Middleton. MacD. P. Jackson. (SSEL Jacobean Drama Studies: No. 79). (Orig.). 1979. pap. text ed. 25.00x (ISBN 0-391-01699-7). Humanities.

Studies in Bibliography, Vol. 34. Ed. by Fredson Bowers. LC 49-3353. 1981. 20.00x (ISBN 0-8139-0898-1). U Pr of Va.

Studies in Biological Control. Ed. by V. L. Delucchi. LC 75-16867. (International Biological Programme Ser.: No. 9). (Illus.). 380p. 1975. 72.00 (ISBN 0-521-20910-2). Cambridge U Pr.

Studies in British Transport History, 1870-1970. Derek H. Aldcroft. 1974. 17.50 o.p. (ISBN 0-7153-6505-3). David & Charles.

Studies in Byzantine Intellectual History. Milton V. Anastos. 432p. 1980. 78.00x (ISBN 0-86078-031-7, Pub. by Variorum England). State Mutual Bk.

Studies in Caucasian History. V. Minorsky. (Cambridge Oriental Ser). 44.00 (ISBN 0-521-05735-3). Cambridge U Pr.

Studies in Child Language & Multilingualism. Ed. by Virginia Teller & Sheila J. White. LC 80-16810. 187p. 1980. 28.00x (ISBN 0-89766-078-1). NY Acad Sci.

Studies in Childhood. James Sully. (Contributions to the History of Psycholgy Ser.: Psychometrics & Educational Psychology). 1978. Repr. of 1978 ed. 30.00 (ISBN 0-89093-162-3). U Pubns Amer.

Studies in Chinese Buddhism. Anukul C. Banerjee. 1977. 6.00x o.p. (ISBN 0-8364-0047-X). South Asia Bks.

Studies in Chinese Diplomatic History. Ching-Lin Hsia. 226p. 1977. Repr. of 1925 ed. 17.00 (ISBN 0-89093-088-0). U Pubns Amer.

Studies in Chinese Literary Genres. Ed. & intro. by Cyril Birch. LC 77-157825. 1975. 18.50x (ISBN 0-520-02037-5). U of Cal Pr.

Studies in Chinese Price History. Endymion P. Wilkinson. LC 78-24799. (Modern Chinese Economy Ser.). 285p. 1980. lib. bdg. 31.00 (ISBN 0-8240-4257-3). Garland Pub.

Studies in "Christ & Satan". Charles Sleeth. (McMaster Old English Studies & Texts). 160p. 1981. 15.00x (ISBN 0-8020-5484-6). U of Toronto Pr.

Studies in Cistercian Art & Architecture I. Ed. by Meredith Lillich et al. (Cistercian Studies: No. 66). (Illus., Orig.). 1981. pap. price not set (ISBN 0-87907-866-9). Cistercian Pubns.

Studies in Classical & Ottoman Islam (7th-16th Centuries) Bernard Lewis. 414p. 1980. 68.00x (ISBN 0-902089-97-8, Pub. by Variorum England). State Mutual Bk.

Studies in Cognitive Development: Essays in Honor of Jean Piaget. Ed. by David Elkind & John H. Flavell. 1969. 13.95 (ISBN 0-19-500877-4); pap. 8.95x (ISBN 0-19-500878-2). Oxford U Pr.

Studies in Comparative Criminal Law. E. M. Wise & G. O. Mueller. (Criminal Law Education & Research Center Ser.). (Illus.). 338p. 1975. 25.75 (ISBN 0-398-03168-1). C C Thomas.

Studies in Comparative Librarianship: Three Sevensma Prize Essays. 1973. pap. 11.00x (ISBN 0-85365-306-2, Pub. by Lib Assn England). Oryx Pr.

Studies in Constructive Mathematics & Mathematical Logic, Pt. 3. Ed. by A. O. Slisenko. LC 69-12507. (Seminars in Mathematics Ser.: Vol. 16). 1971. 25.00 (ISBN 0-306-18816-3, Consultants). Plenum Pub.

Studies in Creative Partnership: Federal Aid to Public Libraries During the New Deal. Ed. by Daniel F. Ring. LC 80-15762. 154p. 1980. 10.00 (ISBN 0-8108-1319-X). Scarecrow.

Studies in Cryobiology. L. K. Lozina-Lozinskii. Tr. by P. Harry from Rus. LC 74-8277. (Illus.). 259p. 1974. 44.95 (ISBN 0-470-54347-7). Halsted Pr.

Studies in Death of a Salesman. Walter Meserve. LC 79-171570. 1972. pap. text ed. 2.95x (ISBN 0-675-09259-0). Merrill.

Studies in Dependency Syntax. Igor A. Melcuk. Ed. by Paul T. Roberge. Tr. by Lev Stern from Russian. (Linguistica Extranea: Studia 2). 172p. 1979. pap. 7.25 (ISBN 0-89720-001-2). Karoma.

Studies in Dyadic Communication: Proceedings of a Research Conference on the Interview. Aron Wolfe Siegman & Benjamin Pope. 356p. 1972. text ed. 21.00 (ISBN 0-08-015867-6). Pergamon.

Studies in East African Geography & Development. Ed. by S. H. Ominde. (Illus.). 1971. 27.50x (ISBN 0-520-02073-1). U of Cal Pr.

Studies in East African History. Norman R. Bennett. LC 63-11193. (Pub. by Boston U Pr). 1963. 5.50x (ISBN 0-8419-8701-7, Africana). Holmes & Meier.

Studies in Education During the Age of the Renaissance 1400 to 1600. Ed. by William H. Woodward. LC 67-17748. (Orig.). 1967. pap. text ed. 5.25x (ISBN 0-8077-2353-3). Tchrs Coll.

Studies in Eighteenth-Century Culture. Incl. Vol. 1. The Modernity of the Eighteenth Century. Ed. by Louis T. Milic. 1971. 25.00 (ISBN 0-299-07070-0); Vol. 2. Irrationalism in the Eighteenth Century. Ed. by Harold E. Pagliaro. 1972. 25.00 (ISBN 0-299-07080-8); Vol. 3. Racism in the Eighteenth Century. Ed. by Harold E. Pagliaro. 1973. 25.00 (ISBN 0-299-07090-5); Vol. 4. Ed. by Harold E. Pagliaro. 1975. 25.00 (ISBN 0-299-06700-9); Vol. 5. Ed. by Ronald C. Rosbottom. 1976. 25.00 (ISBN 0-299-06930-3); Vol. 6. Ed. by Ronald C. Rosbottom. 1977. 25.00 (ISBN 0-299-07130-8); Vol. 7. Ed. by Roseann Runte. 1978. 25.00 (ISBN 0-299-07400-5). U of Wis Pr.

Studies in Eighteenth-Century Culture, Vol. 8. Ed. by Roseann Runte. 1979. 25.00 (ISBN 0-299-07740-3). U of Wis Pr.

Studies in Eighteenth-Century Culture, Vol. 9. Ed. by Roseann Runte. LC 74-25572. 1980. 25.00 (ISBN 0-299-08020-X). U of Wis Pr.

Studies in Eighteenth Century Culture, Vol. 10. Ed. by Harry C. Payne. 384p. 1981. 25.00 (ISBN 0-299-08170-2). U of Wis Pr.

Studies in Eighteenth Century Music: A Tribute to Karl Geiringer on His 70th Birthday. Robbins H. Landon & Roger Chapman. (Music Reprint Ser.). 1979. Repr. of 1970 ed. lib. bdg. 35.00 (ISBN 0-306-79519-1). Da Capo.

Studies in English Linguistics: For Randolph Quirk. Ed. by S. Greenbaum et al. (Illus.). 320p. 1980. lib. bdg. 45.00 (ISBN 0-582-55079-3). Longman.

Studies in Epistemology. Ed. by Nicholas Rescher. (Monograph Ser.: Vol. 9). 1975. pap. 15.00x (ISBN 0-631-11530-7, Pub. by Basil Blackwell). Biblio Dist.

Studies in Ethics. Ed. by Nicholas Rescher. (Monograph Ser.: No. 7). 1973. pap. 19.00x (ISBN 0-631-11510-2, Pub. by Basil Blackwell). Biblio Dist.

Studies in Ethnomethodology. Harold Garfinkel. 1967. text ed. 16.95 (ISBN 0-13-858381-1). P-H.

Studies in European Politics. Mountstuart E. Grant-Duff. LC 72-110901. 1970. Repr. of 1866 ed. 16.50 (ISBN 0-8046-0884-9). Kennikat.

Studies in Everyday Medical Life. Ed. by Michael Wadsworth & David Robinson. 232p. 1981. 23.50x (ISBN 0-85520-147-9, Pub. by Martin Robertson England). Biblio Dist.

Studies in Extensible Programming Languages. Ben Wegbreit. LC 79-7309. (Outstanding Dissertations in the Computer Sciences Ser.: Vol. 23). 425p. 1980. lib. bdg. 36.00 (ISBN 0-8240-4423-1). Garland Pub.

Studies in Finno-Ugric Linguistics: In Honor of Alo Raun. Ed. by Denis Sinor. (Indiana University Uralic & Altaic Ser.: Vol. 131). 440p. 1977. 70.00 (ISBN 0-933070-00-4). Ind U Res Inst.

Studies in First & Second Samuel. Willard W. Winter. LC 70-1508. (Bible Study Textbook Ser.). 1967. 15.00 (ISBN 0-89900-011-8). College Pr Pub.

Studies in First & Second Thessalonians. Robert R. Taylor, Jr. 1977. pap. 1.95 (ISBN 0-89315-285-4). Lambert Bk.

Studies in French Language Literature & History. Ed. by Fraser Mackenzie et al. 258p. 1980. Repr. of 1949 ed. lib. bdg. 50.00 (ISBN 0-89760-736-8). Telegraph Bks.

Studies in Fundamentals of Arabic Language & Grammar. Fuad Tarazi. (Arabic.). 1969. 14.00x (ISBN 0-685-72060-8). Intl Bk Ctr.

Studies in General & Oriental Linguistics Presented to Shiro Hattori on the Occasion of His Sixtieth Birthday. Ed. by Roman Jakobson & Shigeo Kawamoto. 685p. 1970. 24.95x o.p. (ISBN 0-87774-500-5). Schoenhof.

Studies in Geometry. Leonard M. Blumenthal & Karl Menger. LC 74-75624. (Illus.). 1970. text ed. 25.95x (ISBN 0-7167-0437-4). W H Freeman.

Studies in Greek & Roman History. E. Badian. 1964. 30.50x (ISBN 0-631-08140-2, Pub. by Basil Blackwell). Biblio Dist.

Studies in Greek Elegy & Iambus. Martin West. LC 73-93168. (Untersuchungen zur antiken Literatur & Geschichte, Vol. 14). ix, 198p. 1974. 57.10x (ISBN 3-11-004585-0). De Gruyter.

Studies in Hebrews. James D. Bales. pap. 3.50 (ISBN 0-89315-260-9). Lambert Bk.

Studies in History of Buddhism: Papers Presented at the International Conference on the History of Buddhism at the University of Wisconsin, Madison August 19-21,1976. A. K. Narain. 421p. 1980. text ed. 40.50 (ISBN 0-391-02212-1). Humanities.

Studies in Household Economic Behavior. Thomas F. Dernburg et al. 1958. 32.50x (ISBN 0-686-51317-7). Elliots Bks.

Studies in Human Sexual Behavior: The American Scene. Ed. by Ailon Shiloh. (Illus.). 488p. 1970. text ed. 23.00 (ISBN 0-398-01746-8). C C Thomas.

Studies in Indian Agriculture: The Art of the Possible. Gilbert Etienne. Tr. by Megan Mothersole. (Illus.). 1968. 20.00x (ISBN 0-520-00393-4). U of Cal Pr.

Studies in Indian Music. T. V. Subba Rao. 7.50x (ISBN 0-210-33960-8). Asia.

Studies in Inductive Logic & Probability, Vol. II. Ed. by Richard C. Jeffrey. 312p. 1980. 20.00x (ISBN 0-520-03826-6). U of Cal Pr.

Studies in Inductive Logic & Probability, Vol. 1. Ed. by Rudolf Carnap & Richard C. Jeffrey. LC 77-136025. 1971. 25.00x (ISBN 0-520-01866-4). U of Cal Pr.

Studies in International Environmental Economics. Ed. by Ingo Walter. LC 75-38614. 364p. 1976. 40.95 (ISBN 0-471-91927-6, Pub. by Wiley-Interscience). Wiley.

Studies in International Law. Fritz A. Mann. 500p. 1973. 49.50x (ISBN 0-19-825316-8). Oxford U Pr.

Studies in Islamic Mysticism. R. A. Nicholson. LC 78-73958. 1979. 42.00 (ISBN 0-521-05836-8); pap. 12.50x (ISBN 0-521-29546-7). Cambridge U Pr.

Studies in Israel Law. G. Tedeschi. (Hebrew University Legal Studies: No. 7). 1960. 10.00x (ISBN 0-8377-1200-9). Rothman.

Studies in Italian Renaissance Architecture. Wolfgang Lotz. (Illus.). 256p. 1980. 20.00x (ISBN 0-262-12073-9); pap. 7.95 (ISBN 0-262-62036-7). MIT Pr.

Studies in Jahiliyya & Early Islam. M. J. Kister. 360p. 1980. 75.00x (ISBN 0-86078-068-6, Pub. by Variorum England). State Mutual Bk.

Studies in Jocular Literature. William C. Hazlitt. LC 67-24352. 1969. Repr. of 1890 ed. 15.00 (ISBN 0-8103-3529-8). Gale.

Studies in John Dryden's Dramatic Technique. Richard L. Larson. (Salzburg Studies in English Literature, Poetic Drama & Poetic Theory Ser.: No. 9). 320p. (Orig.). 1975. pap. text ed. 25.00x (ISBN 0-391-01455-2). Humanities.

Studies in Joshua, Judges, Ruth. Willard W. Winter. (Bible Study Textbook Ser.). (Illus.). 1969. 15.00 (ISBN 0-89900-010-X). College Pr Pub.

Studies in Language & Reason. Ilham Dilman. LC 79-55527. 230p. 1981. text ed. 27.50x (ISBN 0-06-491691-X). B&N.

Studies in Language Variation: Semantics, Syntax, Phonology, Pragmatics, Social Situations. Ed. by Ralph W. Fasold & Roger W. Shuy. LC 77-20689. 311p. 1977. pap. text ed. 6.95 (ISBN 0-87840-209-8). Georgetown U Pr.

Studies in Law: An Anthology of Essays on Municipal & International Law. 15.95x o.p. (ISBN 0-210-33961-6). Asia.

Studies in Levitical Terminology, 1: The Encroacher & the Levite, the Term Aboda. Jacob Milgrom. (U. C. Publ. in Near Eastern Studies: Vol. 14). 1970. pap. 9.00x (ISBN 0-520-09308-9). U of Cal Pr.

Studies in Louisiana Tort Law. Malone & Guerry. 1970. with 1975 suppl. 35.00 (ISBN 0-672-82448-5, Bobbs-Merrill Law); 1975 suppl. 12.50 (ISBN 0-672-82024-2). Michie.

Studies in Lucian's De Syria Dea. Robert A. Oden, Jr. LC 76-54988. (Harvard Semitic Monograph). (Illus.). 1977. pap. 7.50 (ISBN 0-89130-123-2, 040015). Scholars Pr Ca.

Studies in Luke-Acts. Ed. by Leander E. Keck & J. Louis Martyn. LC 79-8886. 324p. 1980. pap. 7.95 (ISBN 0-8006-1379-1, 1-1379). Fortress.

Studies in Lutheran Doctrine. Paul F. Keller. LC 60-15574. (YA) (gr. 7-8). 1959. pap. 5.50 (ISBN 0-570-03517-1, 14-1265); correction & profile chart 0.40 (ISBN 0-570-03526-0, 14-1267); tests 0.45 (ISBN 0-570-03525-2, 14-1266). Concordia.

Studies in Malaysian Oral & Musical Traditions: Music in Kelantan - Malaysia & Some of Its Cultural Implications. William P. Malm & Amin Sweeney. LC 74-83599. (Michigan Papers on South & Southeast Asia, No. 8). (Illus.). 100p. 1974. pap. 3.50x o.p. (ISBN 0-89148-008-0). Ctr S&SE Asian.

Studies in Managerial Process & Organizational Behavior. John H. Turner. 493p. 1972. pap. 7.95x o.p. (ISBN 0-673-07624-5). Scott F.

Studies in Maritime Economics. R. O. Goss. LC 68-29328. (Illus.). 1968. 35.50 (ISBN 0-521-07329-4). Cambridge U Pr.

Studies in Mathematics Education. 129p. 1980. pap. 7.00 (ISBN 92-3-101779-9, U 1013, UNESCO). Unipub.

Studies in Medieval & Renaissance Literature. C. S. Lewis. 1980. 23.95 (ISBN 0-521-05545-8); pap. 7.95 (ISBN 0-521-29701-X). Cambridge U Pr.

Studies in Medieval Culture, Vol. 1. Ed. by John R. Sommerfeldt & Thomas H. Seiler. 1977. write for info. Medieval Inst.

Studies in Medieval Culture, Vols. 6 & 7. combined ed. Ed. by John R. Sommerfeldt & E. Rozanne Elder. 1976. write for info. Medieval Inst.

Studies in Medieval Culture, Vols. 8 & 9. combined ed. Ed. by John R. Sommerfeldt & Rozanne E. Elder. 1976. write for info. Medieval Inst.

Studies in Medieval Culture, Vol. 10. Ed. by John R. Sommerfeldt & Thomas H. Seiler. 1977. write for info. Medieval Inst.

Studies in Medieval Culture, Vol. 12. Ed. by John R. Sommerfeldt & Thomas H. Seiler. 1978. write for info. Medieval Inst.

Studies in Medieval Jewish Philosophy. Israel I. Efros. LC 73-12512. 300p. 1974. 20.00x (ISBN 0-231-03194-7). Columbia U Pr.

Studies in Medieval Literature: In Honor of Albert Croll Baugh. Ed. by MacEdward Leach. LC 61-15274. 1961. 9.00x o.p. (ISBN 0-8122-7294-3). U of Pa Pr.

Studies in Medieval Painting. Bernard Berenson. LC 73-153884. (Graphic Art Ser.). (Illus.). 148p. 1971. Repr. of 1930 ed. lib. bdg. 35.00 (ISBN 0-306-70292-4). Da Capo.

Studies in Medieval Philosophy, Science & Logic: Collected Papers, 1933-1969. Ernest Moody. LC 73-91661. 1975. 28.50 (ISBN 0-520-02668-3). U of Cal Pr.

Studies in Medieval Physics & Mathematics. Marshall Clagett. 366p. 1980. 75.00x (ISBN 0-86078-048-1, Pub. by Variorum England). State Mutual Bk.

Studies in Medieval Spanish Frontier History. Charles J. Bishko. 336p. 1980. 75.00x (ISBN 0-86078-069-4, Pub. by Variorum England). State Mutual Bk.

Studies in Modality. Ed. by Nicholas Rescher. Ruth Manor. (Monograph Ser.: No. 8). 1973. pap. 10.00x o.p. (ISBN 0-631-11520-X, Pub. by Basil Blackwell). Biblio Dist.

Studies in Modern Economic Analysis: Proceedings. Association of University Teachers of Economics, Edinburgh, 1976. Ed. by M. J. Artis & A. R. Nobay. 1977. 36.50x (ISBN 0-631-17970-4, Pub. by Basil Blackwell). Biblio Dist.

Studies in Modern Indian Fiction in English, 2 vols. Haydn M. Williams. (Greybird Book). 182p. 1975. Set. text ed. 24.00 (ISBN 0-88253-652-4); Set. pap. text ed. 15.00 (ISBN 0-88253-651-6). Ind-US Inc.

Studies in Moral Philosophy. Nicholas Rescher. (Monograph Ser.: No. 1). 1968. pap. 10.00x o.p. (ISBN 0-631-11450-5, Pub. by Basil Blackwell). Biblio Dist.

Studies in Multilingualism. Ed. by Nels Anderson. (International Studies in Sociology & Social Anthropology: No. 8). 1969. text ed. 10.50x o.p. (ISBN 90-0403-036-0). Humanities.

Studies in Music History: Essays for Oliver Strunk. Ed. by Harold Powers. LC 80-14086. (Illus.). x, 527p. 1980. Repr. of 1968 ed. lib. bdg. 39.75x (ISBN 0-313-22501-X, POSM). Greenwood.

Studies in Musicology, 1935-1975. Charles Seeger. LC 76-19668. 1977. 25.95x (ISBN 0-520-02000-6). U of Cal Pr.

Studies in Neurolinguistics, 2 vols. Ed. by Haiganoosh Whitaker & Harry A. Whitaker. LC 75-13100. (Perspectives in Neurolinguistics & Psycholinguistics). 1976-79. Vol. 1. 32.50, subscription 29.00 (ISBN 0-12-746301-1); Vol. 2. 29.00, subscription 26.50 (ISBN 0-12-746302-X); Vol. 3. 28.00, subscription 21.50 (ISBN 0-12-746303-8); Vol. 4. 28.50, by subscription 24.50 (ISBN 0-12-746304-6). Acad Pr.

Studies in Neurophysiology. Ed. by R. Porter. LC 87-51674. (Illus.). 1978. 110.00 (ISBN 0-521-22019-X). Cambridge U Pr.

Studies in New England Transcendentalism. Harold C. Goddard. 1960. text ed. 12.50x (ISBN 0-391-00599-5). Humanities.

Studies in Nigerian Administration. D. J. Murray. 342p. 1978. pap. text ed. 13.75x (ISBN 0-8419-6602-8). Holmes & Meier.

Studies in Nineteenth Century Literature. Ed. by James Hogg. (SSEL: Salzburg Studies in English Literature: No. 87). 264p. 1980. text ed. 25.00x (ISBN 0-391-01782-9). Humanities.

Studies in Niuean Syntax. William J. Seiter. Ed. by Jorge Hankamer. LC 79-55857. (Outstanding Dissertations in Linguistics Ser.). 367p. 1980. lib. bdg. 41.00 (ISBN 0-8240-4560-2). Garland Pub.

Studies in Numerical Analysis. B. K. Scaife. 1974. 38.50 (ISBN 0-12-621150-7). Acad Pr.

Studies in Old English Phonology. R. Lass & J. M. Anderson. LC 74-80360. (Studies in Linguistics: No. 14). 352p. 1975. 49.50 (ISBN 0-521-20531-X). Cambridge U Pr.

Studies in Ontology. Ed. by Nicholas Rescher. (American Philosophical Quarterly Monograph: No. 12). 1978. pap. 19.00x (ISBN 0-631-11560-9, Pub. by Basil Blackwell England). Biblio Dist.

Studies in Optimization. D. M. Burley. LC 74-8454. 1974. text ed. 17.95 (ISBN 0-470-12410-5). Halsted Pr.

Studies in Paleobotany. Henry N. Andrews, Jr. LC 61-6768. (Illus.). 1961. 24.95 (ISBN 0-471-03168-2). Wiley.

Studies in Perception. Ed. by Gerald M. Murch. LC 74-8398. 1976. pap. text ed. 9.50 (ISBN 0-672-61189-9). Bobbs.

Studies in Personalism: Selected Writings of Edgar Sheffield Brightman. Ed. by Robert N. Beck & Warren E. Steinkraus. LC 75-4133. (Philosophy Ser.: No. 603). 15.00 o.s.i. (ISBN 0-89007-603-0). C Stark.

Studies in Phenomenology & Human Science. Ed. by John Sallis. 1980. text ed. 7.50 (ISBN 0-391-01702-0). Humanities.

Studies in Physical Anthropology, Vols. 1 & 2. A. A. Abbie. (AIAS Research & Regional Ser.: No. 5). (Illus., Orig.). 1975. pap. text ed. 10.00x (ISBN 0-391-01421-8); Vol. 1. pap. text ed. 6.25x (ISBN 0-391-01880-9); Vol. 2. pap. text ed. 7.25x (ISBN 0-391-01881-7). Humanities.

Studies in Physiological Optics. Melvin L. Rubin & Gordon L. Walls. (Illus.). 144p. 1965. 10.50 (ISBN 0-398-01624-0). C C Thomas.

Studies in Plato's Metaphysics. Ed. by Reginald E. Allen. (International Library of Philosophy & Scientific Method). 1968. text ed. 25.50x (ISBN 0-7100-3626-4). Humanities.

Studies in Political Economy of Development. Ignacy Sachs. LC 79-40488. 1980. 45.00 (ISBN 0-685-97187-2) (ISBN 0-685-97188-0). Pergamon.

Studies in Political Science. Ed. by J. S. Bains. 7.50x o.p. (ISBN 0-210-33962-4). Asia.

Studies in Pre-Socratic Philosophy, Vol. 1. Ed. by David J. Furley & R. E. Allen. (International Library of Philogophy & Scientific Method). 1970. text ed. 24.75x (ISBN 0-391-00077-2). Humanities.

Studies in Psalms, Vol. I. Joseph B. Rotherham. Ed. by Don DeWelt. (Bible Study Textbook Ser.). (Illus.). 1970. Repr. 13.50 (ISBN 0-89900-016-9). College Pr Pub.

Studies in Public Employment & Compensation in Canada. Meyer W. Bucovetsky. 177p. 1979. pap. text ed. 14.95x (ISBN 0-409-88601-7, Pub. by Inst Res Pub Canada). Renouf.

Studies in Relevance: Romantic & Victorian Writers in 1972. Ed. by Thomas M. Harwell. (Salzburg Studies in English Literature, Romantic Reassessment: No. 32). 171p. 1973. pap. text ed. 25.00x (ISBN 0-391-01400-5). Humanities.

Studies in Renewable Resource Policy, 10 vols, Vol. 1. Ed. by Michael Barker. 1981. pap. write for info. (ISBN 0-934842-74-4). Coun State Plan.

Studies in Resource Allocation Process. Ed. by K. J. Arrow & L. Hurwicz. LC 76-9171. (Illus.). 1977. 47.50 (ISBN 0-521-21522-6). Cambridge U Pr.

Studies in Revelation. W. Leon Tucker. LC 80-16206. (Kregel Bible Study Classics Ser.). 400p. 1980. Repr. of 1935 ed. 10.95 (ISBN 0-8254-3826-8). Kregel.

Studies in Roman Literature, Culture & Religion. Hendrik Wagenvoort. Ed. by Steele Commager. LC 77-70817. (Latin Poetry Ser.: Vol. 31). 1978. lib. bdg. 33.00 (ISBN 0-8240-2981-X). Garland Pub.

Studies in Roman Property. Ed. by M. I. Finley. (Classical Studies). (Illus.). 192p. 1976. 15.95 (ISBN 0-521-21115-8). Cambridge U Pr.

Studies in Rural Capitalism in West Africa. Polly Hill. LC 77-96093. (Cambridge African Studies: No. 2). (Illus.). 27.95 (ISBN 0-521-07622-6). Cambridge U Pr.

Studies in Scottish Literature, Vol. 13. Ed. by G. Ross Roy. LC 73-138822. 1978. lib. bdg. 14.95x (ISBN 0-87249-368-7). U of SC Pr.

Studies in Seicento Art & Theory. Denis Mahon. LC 73-114544. (Illus.). 1971. Repr. of 1947 ed. lib. bdg. 25.00x (ISBN 0-8371-4743-3, MAST). Greenwood.

Studies in Seventeenth Century Imagery, 2 vols. in 1. Manrio Praz. LC 40-3654. Repr. 40.00 (ISBN 0-403-07208-5). Somerset Pub.

Studies in Six Seventeenth Century Writers. James R. King. LC 65-24645. xv, 236p. 1966. 12.95x (ISBN 0-8214-0013-4). Ohio U Pr.

Studies in Social Anthropology: Essays in Memory of E. E. Evans-Pritchard by His Former Oxford Colleagues. Ed. by J. H. Beattie & R. G. Lienhardt. (Illus.). 408p. 1975. 29.95x (ISBN 0-19-823183-0). Oxford U Pr.

Studies in Social Movements. Ed. by Barry McLaughlin. LC 69-17783. 1969. 16.95 (ISBN 0-02-920560-3). Free Pr.

Studies in Southern Nigerian History. Boniface I. Obichere. 276p. 1981. 28.50x (ISBN 0-7146-3106-X, F Cass Co). Biblio Dist.

Studies in Soviet Input-Output Analysis. Ed. by Vladimir G. Treml. LC 77-2739. (Praeger Special Studies). 1977. text ed. 44.50 (ISBN 0-275-56550-5). Praeger.

Studies in Spinoza: Critical & Interpretative Essays. Ed. by S. Paul Kashap. 360p. 1973. 20.00x (ISBN 0-520-02142-8); pap. 6.50x (ISBN 0-520-02590-3). U of Cal Pr.

Studies in State Development Policy, 9 vols, Vol. 1. Ed. by Michael Barker. 1979. pap. 66.00x (ISBN 0-934842-24-8). Coun State Plan.

Studies in Stock Speculation, 2 vols. J. J. Wolf. Repr. of 1967 ed. Vol. 1. flexible cover 5.00 (ISBN 0-87034-017-4); Vol. 2. flexible cover 5.00 (ISBN 0-87034-018-2). Fraser Pub Co.

Studies in Tape Reading. Richard D. Wyckoff. (New Stock Market Library). (Illus.). 1978. Repr. of 1921 ed. 125.45 (ISBN 0-89266-134-8). Am Classical Coll Pr.

Studies in Tennyson. Ed. by Hallam Tennyson. LC 79-55520. 205p. 1981. text ed. 27.50x (ISBN 0-06-496807-3). B&N.

Studies in Tertullian & Augustine. Benjamin B. Warfield. Repr. of 1930 ed. lib. bdg. 29.00x (ISBN 0-8371-4490-6, WATT). Greenwood.

Studies in the Antiquities of Stobi. Ed. by James Wiseman & Djordje Mano-Zissi. (Illus.). 300p. Date not set. 15.00x (ISBN 0-292-77506-7). U of Tex Pr.

Studies in the Civil Law, & Its Relations to the Law of England & America. William W. Howe. xv, 340p. 1980. Repr. of 1896 ed. lib. bdg. 27.50x (ISBN 0-8377-0631-9). Rothman.

Studies in the Colonial History of Spanish America. M. Gongora. Tr. by R. Southern from Span. LC 74-19524. (Latin American Studies: No. 20). 235p. 1975. 32.95 (ISBN 0-521-20686-3). Cambridge U Pr.

Studies in the Development of Capitalism. rev. ed. Maurice Dobb. LC 64-13744. (Orig.). 1964. 7.50 o.p. (ISBN 0-7178-0198-5); pap. 3.95 (ISBN 0-7178-0197-7). Intl Pub Co.

Studies in the Early English Periodical. Ed. by Richmond Bond. 1957. text ed. 20.00x (ISBN 0-391-01609-1). Humanities.

Studies in the Economic Policy of Frederick the Great. William O. Henderson. LC 64-39262. 1963. 22.50x (ISBN 0-678-05176-3). Kelley.

Studies in the Economics of Overhead Costs. John M. Clark. 1980. pap. write for info. (ISBN 0-226-10851-1). U of Chicago Pr.

Studies in the Economics of Transportation. Martin Beckmann et al. 1956. 42.50x (ISBN 0-685-89787-7). Elliots Bks.

Studies in the Fourth Gospel. Leon Morris. LC 68-12790. 1969. 8.95 (ISBN 0-8028-1818-8). Eerdmans.

Studies in the Grammatical Tradition in Tibet. Roy A. Miller. (Studies in the History of Linguistics: No. 6). 1976. text ed. 23.00x (ISBN 0-391-01651-2). Humanities.

Studies in the History of Educational Opinion from the Renaissance. Simon S. Laurie. LC 72-93272. Repr. of 1903 ed. 22.50x (ISBN 0-678-05086-4). Kelley.

Studies in the History of Indian Philosophy, 3 vols. Ed. by D. P. Chattopadhyaya. 1981. text ed. 37.50x (ISBN 0-391-02084-6). Humanities.

Studies in the History of Musical Pitch. Alexander J. Ellis & Arthur Mendel. (Music Ser.). 238p. 1981. lib. bdg. 22.50 (ISBN 0-306-76020-7). Da Capo.

Studies in the Iconography of Cosmic Kingship in the Ancient World. H. P. L'Orange. (Illus.). 206p. 1981. Repr. of 1953 ed. lib. bdg. 45.00x (ISBN 0-89241-150-3). Caratzas Bros.

Studies in the Language of Homer. 2nd ed. G. P. Shipp. LC 76-149439. (Cambridge Classical Studies). 1972. 42.00 (ISBN 0-521-07706-0). Cambridge U Pr.

Studies in the Lateglacial of North-West Europe: Including Papers Presented at a Symposium of the Quaternary Research Association Held at University College London, January 1979. Ed. by J. J. Lowe et al. (Illus.). 215p. 1980. 44.00 (ISBN 0-08-024001-1). Pergamon.

Studies in the Latin Empire of Constantinople. Robert L. Wolff. 412p. 1980. 60.00x (ISBN 0-902089-99-4, Pub. by Variorum England). State Mutual Bk.

Studies in the Management of Government Enterprise. Ed. by Richard J. Horn. (Social Dimensions of Economics Ser.: Vol. 1). 1981. lib. bdg. price not set (ISBN 0-89838-052-9, Pub. by Martinus Nijhoff). Kluwer Boston.

Studies in the Management of Social R & D: Selected Policy Areas. Ed. by Laurence E. Lynn, Jr. (Study Project on Social Research & Development). vii, 218p. (Orig.). 1979. pap. text ed. 12.50 (ISBN 0-309-02930-9). Natl Acad Pr.

Studies in the New Experimental Aesthetics. Ed. by D. E. Berlyne. LC 74-13600. 1974. 14.95 o.p. (ISBN 0-470-07039-0). Halsted Pr.

Studies in the Philosophy of Biology: Reduction & Related Problems. Ed. by Francisco Ayala & Theodosius Dobzhansky. LC 73-90656. 1975. 30.00x (ISBN 0-520-02649-7). U of Cal Pr.

Studies in the Philosophy of Mind. Ed. by Nicholas Rescher. (Monograph Ser.: No. 6). 1972. pap. 19.00x (ISBN 0-631-11500-5, Pub. by Basil Blackwell). Biblio Dist.

Studies in the Philosophy of Science. Ed. by Nicholas Rescher. (Monograph Ser.: No. 3). 1969. pap. 19.00x (ISBN 0-631-11470-X, Pub. by Basil Blackwell). Biblio Dist.

Studies in the Philosophy of Wittgenstein. Ed. by Peter Winch. (International Library of Philosophy & Scientific Method). 1969. text ed. 18.25x (ISBN 0-7100-6393-8). Humanities.

Studies in the Problem of Sovereignty. Harold J. Laski. 1968. Repr. 17.50 (ISBN 0-86527-191-7). Fertig.

Studies in the Quantity Theory of Money. Ed. by Milton Friedman. LC 56-10999. (Economic Research Ser). 1956. 10.50x o.s.i. (ISBN 0-226-26404-1). U of Chicago Pr.

Studies in the Revolution of English Criticism. Laura J. Wylie. 212p. 1980. Repr. of 1903 ed. text ed. 25.00 (ISBN 0-8492-2997-9). R West.

Studies in the Romano - British Villa. Malcolm Todd. 220p. 1977. pap. text ed. 19.00x (ISBN 0-7185-1149-2, Leicester). Humanities.

Studies in the Romantics. Ed. by James Hogg. (SSEL: Salzburg Studies in English Literature: No. 81). 129p. 1980. text ed. 25.00x (ISBN 0-391-01781-0). Humanities.

Studies in the Russian Historical Song. Carl Stief. LC 79-3073. (Illus.). 274p. 1981. Repr. of 1953 ed. 23.50 (ISBN 0-8305-0092-8). Hyperion Conn.

Studies in the Scientific & Mathematical Philosophy of Charles S. Pierce: Essays by Carolyn Eisele. Ed. by Carolyn Eisele & Richard M. Martin. (Studies in Philosophy). 1979. text ed. 57.00x (ISBN 90-279-7808-5). Mouton.

Studies in the Sermon on the Mount. D. Martyn Lloyd-Jones. 11.95 (ISBN 0-8028-3175-3). Eerdmans.

Studies in the Social Thought of Mahadeo Govind Ranade. P. J. Jagirdar. 5.50x o.p. (ISBN 0-210-27033-0). Asia.

Studies in The Sound & the Fury. James B. Meriwether. LC 70-126048. 1970. pap. text ed. 2.95x (ISBN 0-675-09300-7). Merrill.

Studies in the Theory of Imperialism. Ed. by R. Owen & R. Sutcliffe. (Illus.). 390p. 1972. pap. text ed. 14.95x (ISBN 0-582-48753-6). Longman.

Studies in the Theory of Knowledge. Ed. by Nicholas Rescher. (Monograph Ser.: No. 4). 1970. pap. 19.00x (ISBN 0-631-11480-7, Pub. by Basil Blackwell). Biblio Dist.

Studies in the Theory of Numbers. Leonard E. Dickson. LC 61-13494. 9.95 (ISBN 0-8284-0151-9). Chelsea Pub.

Studies in the Theory of Random Processes. A. V. Skorokhod. cancelled o.s.i. (ISBN 0-201-07021-9, Adv Bk Prog). A-W.

Studies in the Vegetation History of the British Isles. Ed. by D. Walker & R. G. West. 79.00 (ISBN 0-521-07565-3). Cambridge U Pr.

Studies in Theatre & Drama. Ed. & frwd. by Oscar G. Brockett. (De Proprietatibus Litterarum, Ser. Major: No. 23). 217p. 1972. text ed. 43.50 (ISBN 90-2792-112-1). Mouton.

Studies in Tudor & Stuart Politics & Government: Papers & Reviews, 1946-1972, 2 vols. G. R. Elton. LC 73-79305. 700p. 1974. 60.00 set (ISBN 0-521-20388-0); Vol. 1. 41.95 (ISBN 0-521-20282-5); Vol. 2. 29.95 (ISBN 0-521-20288-4). Cambridge U Pr.

Studies in Twentieth-Century Russian Literature. Ed. by Christopher J. Barnes. LC 75-40543. 91p. 1976. text ed. 11.50x (ISBN 0-06-490316-8). B&N.

Studies in Two Literatures. Arthur Symons. LC 76-20002. (Decadent Consciousness Ser.: Vol. 25). 1977. Repr. of 1897 ed. lib. bdg. 38.00 (ISBN 0-8240-2774-4). Garland Pub.

Studies in Verbal Behavior: An Empirical Approach. Kurt Salzinger & Richard S. Feldman. LC 76-179073. 474p. 1974. 26.00 (ISBN 0-08-016926-0). Pergamon.

Studies in Victorian Verse Drama: An Appraisal of the Poetic Plays of Browning, Tennyson & Other Victorians. Virendra Sharma. (SSEL Poetic Drama & Poetic Theory: No. 14). 1979. pap. text ed. 25.00x (ISBN 0-391-01621-0). Humanities.

Studies in Western Australian History II: March 1978. 1978. pap. 7.00x (ISBN 0-686-14374-4, Pub. by U of W Austral Pr). Intl Schol Bk Serv.

Studies in Western Australian History, No. 1. 1978. pap. 7.00x (ISBN 0-686-00545-7, Pub. by U of W Austral Pr). Intl Schol Bk Serv.

Studies in Words. 2nd ed. Clive S. Lewis. 1960. 32.50 (ISBN 0-521-05547-4); pap. 9.95 (ISBN 0-521-09371-6). Cambridge U Pr.

Studies in Yue Dialects 1. Oi-Kan Hashimoto. LC 78-179158. (Cambridge-Princeton Studies in Chinese Linguistics: No. 3). (Illus.). 755p. 1972. 115.00 (ISBN 0-521-08442-3). Cambridge U Pr.

Studies in 18th Century Islamic History. Ed. by Thomas Naff & Roger Owen. LC 77-22012. 462p. 1977. 24.95x (ISBN 0-8093-0819-3). S Ill U Pr.

Studies of Biosynthesis in Escherichiacoli, 2 vols. Richard B. Roberts et al. (Illus.). 521p. 1958. pap. 21.50 ea. (607). Carnegie Inst.

Studies of Early Fossil Primates in North America. LC 78-72713. 1980. Repr. 34.50 (ISBN 0-404-18283-6). AMS Pr.

Studies of Familial Communication & Psychopathology: A Socio-Developmental Approach to Deviant Behavior. Rolv M. Blakar. 192p. 1980. pap. 18.00x (ISBN 8-20001-999-3). Universitet.

Studies of Field Systems in the British Isles. Ed. by A. R. Baker & R. A. Butlin. LC 72-91359. (Illus.). 744p. 1973. 77.50 (ISBN 0-521-20121-7). Cambridge U Pr.

Studies of Field Systems in the British Isles. Ed. by Alan H. Baker & R. A. Butlin. (Illus.). 728p. 1980. pap. 28.95 (ISBN 0-521-29790-7). Cambridge U Pr.

Studies of Fossiliferous Amber Arthropods of Chiapas, Mexico, Pt. II. Alexander Petrunkevitch et al. (U. C. Publ. in Entomology: Vol. 63). 1971. pap. 8.50x (ISBN 0-520-09375-5). U of Cal Pr.

Studies of Neurotransmitters at the Synaptic Level. Ed. by E. Costa et al. LC 73-84113. (Advances in Biochemical Psychopharmacology: Vol. 6). 256p. 1972. 24.50 (ISBN 0-911216-20-0). Raven.

Studies of Normal & Abnormal Devlopment, of the Nervous System. Ed. by W. Lierse & F. Beck. (Bibliotheca Anatomica Ser.: No. 19). (Illus.). viii, 328p. 1980. softcover 112.00 (ISBN 3-8055-1039-X). S Karger.

Studies of the Eighteenth Century in Italy. Vernon Lee & Violet Paget. LC 77-17466. (Music Reprint Ser.: 1978). 1978. Repr. of 1887 ed. lib. bdg. 27.50 (ISBN 0-306-77517-4). Da Capo.

Studies of the Four Gospels, 4 vols. G. Campbell Morgan. Incl. The Gospel According to Matthew. 320p (ISBN 0-8007-0122-4); The Gospel According to Mark. 352p (ISBN 0-8007-0121-6); The Gospel According to Luke. 288p (ISBN 0-8007-0120-8); The Gospel According to John. 336p (ISBN 0-8007-0119-4). Set. 34.95 (ISBN 0-8007-0373-1). Revell.

Studies of the Third Wave: Recent Migration of Soviet Jews to the United States. Ed. by Dan N. Jacobs & Ellen F. Paul. (Replica Edition Ser.). 176p. 1981. lib. bdg. 20.00x (ISBN 0-86531-143-9). Westview.

Studies on Asia. Incl. Volume I - 1960. Ed. by Robert K. Sakai. x, 97p. 1960. pap. 3.25x (ISBN 0-8032-5550-0); Volume II - 1961. Ed. by Robert K. Sakai. viii, 85p. 1961. pap. 3.25x (ISBN 0-8032-5551-9); Volume III - 1962. Ed. by Sidney D. Brown. x, 87p. 1962. pap. 3.25x (ISBN 0-8032-5552-7); Volume IV - 1963. Ed. by Robert K. Sakai. x, 196p. 1963. pap. 4.95x (ISBN 0-8032-5553-5); Volume V - 1964. Ed. by Robert K. Sakai. xii, 186p. 1964. pap. 4.95x (ISBN 0-8032-5554-3); Volume VI - 1965. Ed. by Robert K. Sakai. x, 209p. 1965. pap. 4.95x (ISBN 0-8032-5555-1); Volume VII - 1966. Ed. by Robert K. Sakai. x, 185p. 1967. 10.50x (ISBN 0-8032-0557-0); pap. 4.95x (ISBN 0-8032-5557-8); Volume VIII - 1967. Ed. by Sidney D. Brown. x, 192p. 1968. 9.95x (ISBN 0-8032-0558-9); pap. 3.45x (ISBN 0-8032-5558-6). LC 60-15432. (Studies on Asia Ser). U of Nebr Pr.

Studies on Byzantine History, Literature & Education. Robert Browning. 390p. 1980. 60.00x (ISBN 0-86078-003-1, Pub. by Variorum England). State Mutual Bk.

Studies on Byzantine History of the 9th & 10th Centuries. Romilly J. Jenkins. 386p. 1980. 50.00x (ISBN 0-902089-07-2, Pub. by Variorum England). State Mutual Bk.

Studies on Christiean Huygens: Invited Papers. Symposium on the Life and Work of Christiaan Huygens, Amsterdam, 22-25 August 1979. Ed. by H. J. Bos et al. 1980. text ed. 34.25 (ISBN 90-265-0333-4, Pub. by Swets Pub Serv Holland). Swets North Am.

Studies on Copyright, 2 vols. Copyright Society Of The United States. 1963. 35.00x (ISBN 0-8377-1101-0). Rothman.

Studies on Crisis Management. C. F. Smart & W. T. Stanbury. 195p. 1978. pap. text ed. 9.95x (ISBN 0-920380-03-4, Pub. by Inst Res Pub Canada). Renouf.

Studies on Fronting. Ed. by Frank Jansen. 1978. pap. text ed. 10.25x (ISBN 90-316-0163-2). Humanities.

Studies on Host Selection by Ips confusus (LeConte) (Coleoptera: Scolytidae), with Special Reference to Hopkins' Host Selection Principle. D. L. Wood. (U. C. Publ. in Entomology: Vol. 27.3). 1963. pap. 2.00x o.p. (ISBN 0-520-09092-6). U of Cal Pr.

Studies on Korea: A Scholar's Guide. Ed. by Han-Kyo Kim. LC 79-26491. 576p. 1980. text ed. 25.00x (ISBN 0-8248-0673-5). U Pr of Hawaii.

Studies on Latin Greece A. D. 1205-1715. Peter Topping. 400p. 1980. 60.00x (ISBN 0-86078-012-0, Pub. by Variorum England). State Mutual Bk.

Studies on Mathematical Programming: Proceddings. Conference on Mathematical Programming, 3rd, Matrafured, Hungary, 1975. Ed. by A. Prekopa. (Mathematical Methods of Operations Research). 200p. 1980. 22.50x (ISBN 963-05-1854-6). Intl Pubns Serv.

Studies on Neotropical Water Mites. David Cook. (Memoir Ser.: No. 31). (Illus.). 644p. 1980. 44.00 (ISBN 0-686-27979-4). Am Entom Inst.

Studies on Regulation in Canada. W. T. Stanbury. 249p. 1978. pap. text ed. 9.95x (ISBN 0-920380-04-2, Pub. by Inst Res Pub Canada). Renouf.

Studies on Sri Lanka & India Relations. Urmila Phadnis. 1981. 15.00x (ISBN 0-88386-893-8). South Asia Bks.

Studies on Syntactic Topology & Contrastive Grammar. Laslo Deszoe. (Janua Linguarum, Series Practica). 1979. pap. text ed. 27.75x (ISBN 90-279-3108-9). Mouton.

Studies on the Cavernicole Fauna of Mexico & Adjacent Regions. Ed. by Robert W. Mitchell & James R. Reddell. (Association for Mexican Cave Studies: Bulletin 5). 201p. 1973. 13.00. Speleo Pr.

Studies on the Cavernicole Fauna of Mexico. Ed. by James R. Reddell & Robert W. Mitchell. (Association for Mexican Cave Studies: Bulletin 4). 239p. 1971. 13.00. Speleo Pr.

Studies on the Caves & Cave Fauna of the Yucatan Peninsula. Ed. by James R. Reddell. (Association for Mexican Cave Studies: Bulletin 6). 296p. 1977. 13.00. Speleo Pr.

Studies on the Development of Behavior & the Nervous System, 4 vols. Ed. by Gilbert Gottlieb. Incl. Vol. 1. Behavioral Embryology. 1973. 39.50 o.s.i. (ISBN 0-12-609301-6); Vol. 2. Aspects of Neurogenesis. 1973. 37.57 (ISBN 0-12-609302-4); Vol. 3. Development of Neural & Behavioral Specificity. 1976. 43.00 (ISBN 0-12-609303-2); Vol. 4. Early Influences. 1978. 28.50 (ISBN 0-12-609304-0). Acad Pr.

Studies on the Dream in Greek Literature. A. H. Kessels. 280p. 1980. pap. text ed. 34.25x (ISBN 90-6194-491-0). Humanities.

Studies on the Fifth & Sixth Essays of Proclus: Commentary on the Republic. 1980. pap. 30.00 o.p. (ISBN 0-686-65244-4). Adler.

Studies on the Levantine Trade in the Middle Ages. Eliyahu Ashton. 372p. 1980. 60.00x (ISBN 0-86078-020-1, Pub. by Variorum England). State Mutual Bk.

Studies on the Mamluks of Egypt. David Ayalon. 360p. 1980. 60.00x (ISBN 0-86078-006-6, Pub. by Variorum England). State Mutual Bk.

Studies on the Population of China, 1368-1953. Ping-Ti Ho. LC 59-12970. (East Asian Ser: No. 4). 1959. 17.50x (ISBN 0-674-85245-1). Harvard U Pr.

Studies on the Testament of Abraham. Ed. by George W. Nickelsburg, Jr. LC 76-44205. (Society of Biblical Literature. Septuagint & Cognate Studies). 1976. pap. 9.00 (ISBN 0-89130-117-8, 060406). Scholars Pr Ca.

Studies on the Testament of Joseph. Ed. by George Nicklesburg. LC 75-26923. (Society of Biblical Literature. Septurgint & Cognate Studies). 153p. 1975. pap. 7.50 (ISBN 0-89130-027-9, 060405). Scholars Pr Ca.

Studies on the Testament of Moses. Ed. by George Nickelsburg. LC 73-89039. (Society of Biblical Literature. Septuagint & Cognate Studies). 1973. pap. 7.50 (ISBN 0-89130-167-4, 060404). Scholars Pr Ca.

Studies on the Tolerance to Elevated Temperatures in Pleurotus Ostreatus (Jacq. Ex Fr.) Kummer: A Contribution to Taxonomy & the Genetics of the Fruiting Process. Sui-Fong Li. (Bibliotheca Mycologica: No. 76). (Illus.). 88p. 1981. pap. text ed. 15.00x (ISBN 3-7682-1276-9). Lubrecht & Cramer.

Studies on Vasari's Architecture. Leon Satkowski. LC 78-74377. (Fine Arts Dissertations, Fourth Ser.). 1980. lib. bdg. 38.00 (ISBN 0-8240-3964-5). Garland Pub.

Studio. John G. Dunne. 255p. 1969. 5.95 (ISBN 0-374-27112-7). FS&G.

Studio. (Life Library of Photography). (Illus.). 1971. 14.95 (ISBN 0-8094-1041-9). Time-Life.

Studio Acoustics. M. Rettinger. 1981. 35.00 (ISBN 0-8206-0283-3). Chem Pub.

Studio Porcelain. Peter Lane. LC 80-50884. 244p. Date not set. 30.00 (ISBN 0-8019-7001-6). Chilton.

Studio Potter Book. Gerry Williams et al. 1979. 22.50 (ISBN 0-442-29461-1). Litton Educ Pub.

Studio Sulle Opere Di Giuseppe Verdi. Abramo Basevi. LC 80-2255. 1981. Repr. of 1859 ed. 35.50 (ISBN 0-404-18802-8). AMS Pr.

Studios & Styles of the Italian Renaissance. Andre Chastel. LC 68-20093. (Arts of Mankind Ser). 30.00 o.s.i. (ISBN 0-8076-0504-2). Braziller.

Studs Lonigan. James T. Farrell. 1976. pap. 2.75 (ISBN 0-380-00934-X, 31955, Bard). Avon.

Studs Lonigan. James T. Farrell. LC 78-56426. 1979. 17.50 (ISBN 0-8149-0791-1). Vanguard.

Study Abroad XXIII 1981-82, 1982-83. 1011p. 1981. pap. 12.95 (ISBN 92-3-001840-6, U1061, UNESCO). Unipub.

Study & Analysis of Black Politics: A Bibliography. Hanes Walton, Jr. LC 73-12985. 1973. 10.00 (ISBN 0-8108-0665-7). Scarecrow.

Study & Practice of Astral Projection. Robert Crookall. 1977. pap. 3.95 (ISBN 0-8065-0547-8). Lyle Stuart.

Study & Teaching of Anthropology. 2nd ed. Pertti J. Pelto & Raymond H. Muessig. (Social Science Seminar, Secondary Education Ser.: No. C28). 136p. 1980. pap. text ed. 5.95 (ISBN 0-675-08192-0). Merrill.

Study & Teaching of Geography. 2nd ed. Jan O. Broek et al. (Social Science Seminar, Secondary Education Ser.: No. C28). 120p. 1980. pap. text ed. 5.95 (ISBN 0-675-08163-7). Merrill.

Study & Teaching of History. 2nd ed. Henry S. Commager & Raymond H. Muessig. (Social Science Seminar, Secondary Education Ser.: No. C28). 136p. 1980. pap. text ed. 5.95 (ISBN 0-675-08317-6). Merrill.

Study & Teaching of Political Science. 2nd ed. John A. Straayer & Raymond H. Muessig. (Social Science Seminar, Secondary Education Ser.: No. C28). 112p. 1980. pap. text ed. 5.95 (ISBN 0-675-08191-2). Merrill.

Study & Teaching of Sociology. 2nd ed. James A. Kitchens & Raymond H. Muessig. (Social Science Seminar, Secondary Education Ser.: No. C28). 104p. 1980. pap. text ed. 5.95 (ISBN 0-675-08194-7). Merrill.

Study Course in Homeopathy. Phyllis Speight. 145p. 1979. text ed. 23.95x (ISBN 0-8464-1052-4). Beekman Pubs.

Study English for Science. A. R. Bolitho & P. L. Sandler. 1977. pap. text ed. 3.50x (ISBN 0-582-55248-6); tchr's ed. 2.50x (ISBN 0-582-74821-6). Longman.

Study Game. 4th ed. Laia Hanau. 1979. pap. 3.95 (ISBN 0-06-463489-2, EH 489, EH). Har-Row.

Study Guide & Applied Readings to Introduction to Modern Business: Issues & Environment. 8th ed. Vernon L. Musselman & Eugene H. Hughes. 272p. 1981. pap. text ed. 7.95 (ISBN 0-13-488080-3). P-H.

Study Guide & Solutions Manual for an Introduction to Organic Chemistry. Ronald Starkey. 1978. 11.50x (ISBN 0-8162-8391-5, 8162-8391). Holden-Day.

Study Guide & Test Manual for Correlated Dictation & Transcription. 2nd. ed. Frances A. Brown & Hamden L. Forkner. 1974. pap. 5.64x (ISBN 0-912036-19-2). Forkner.

Study Guide Course 1-B: Capitalization Theory & Techniques. American Institute of Real Estate Appraisers. 1973. pap. 6.00 o.p. (ISBN 0-911780-34-3). Am Inst Real Estate Appraisers.

Study Guide for Basic Statistics: Tales of Distributions. 2nd ed. James O. Johnston & Chris Spatz. 150p. (Orig.). 1981. pap. text ed. 6.95 (ISBN 0-8185-0454-4). Brooks-Cole.

Study Guide for Calculus with Analytic Geometry. 5th ed. Cunsolo & Mokanski. 5.95x o.p. (ISBN 0-205-04220-1, 5642205). Allyn.

Study Guide for College Chemistry: An Introduction to Inorganic, Organic, & Biochemistry. Peter C. Scott. (Orig.). 1980. pap. text ed. 8.95 (ISBN 0-8185-0405-6). Brooks-Cole.

Study Guide for Discipleship Evangelism. Ken Stephens. 1981. pap. 2.50 (ISBN 0-89081-286-1). Harvest Hse.

Study Guide for Educating Exceptional Children. 3rd ed. James J. Gallagher. (Illus.). 208p. 1980. pap. text ed. write for info. (ISBN 0-395-28690-5). HM.

Study Guide for Forkner Shorthand. 4th ed. Hamden L. Forkner et al. 121p. pap. 6.64x (ISBN 0-912036-12-5). Forkner.

Study Guide for Foundations of College Chemistry: Alternate Edition. Peter C. Scott. (Orig.). 1980. pap. text ed. 6.95 (ISBN 0-8185-0404-8). Brooks-Cole.

Study Guide for Human Information Processing. 2nd ed. Ross Bott et al. Ed. by Norman Lindsay. 1977. 6.95 (ISBN 0-12-450962-2). Acad Pr.

Study Guide for Introduction to Statistics. Robert H. Johnstone. 280p. (Orig.). 1980. pap. text ed. 7.95 (ISBN 0-8185-0410-2). Brooks-Cole.

Study Guide for Modern Marketing. Bruce Seaton. 1978. pap. 4.95x (ISBN 0-673-15128-X). Scott F.

Study Guide for Nehemiah & the Dynamics of Effective Leadership. Cyril J. Barber. (Illus.). 96p. 1980. pap. text ed. 3.25 (ISBN 0-87213-022-3). Loizeaux.

Study Guide for Social Psychology in the Eighties. 3rd ed. T. Edward Hannah et al. 192p. (Orig.). 1980. pap. text ed. 6.95 (ISBN 0-8185-0416-1). Brooks-Cole.

Study Guide for Stat. for Management. Lincoln Chao & G. Rodich. 272p. 1980. pap. text ed. 7.95 (ISBN 0-8185-0409-9). Brooks-Cole.

Study Guide for Teaching Reading in the Elementary Schools. rev. ed. Sterl Artley. 1976. pap. text ed. 4.25x (ISBN 0-87543-130-5). Lucas.

Study Guide for the Cult Explosion. Dave Hunt. 128p. (Orig.). 1981. pap. 2.95 (ISBN 0-89081-280-2). Harvest Hse.

Study Guide for the Holy Spirit, Lord & Life-Giver. John Williams. (Illus.). 1980. pap. text ed. 3.25 (ISBN 0-87213-952-2). Loizeaux.

Study Guide for Weinberg, Schumaker & Oltman's Statistics: An Intuitive Approach. 4th ed. Debra Oltman. 250p. (Orig.). 1981. pap. text ed. 7.95 (ISBN 0-8185-0442-0). Brooks-Cole.

Study Guide in Alternating Current Circuits: A Personalized System of Instruction. Irving Kosow. LC 77-22152. (Electronic Technology Ser.). 1977. pap. text ed. 10.95 (ISBN 0-471-02665-4); solutions manual avail. (ISBN 0-471-03218-2). Wiley.

Study Guide in Direct Current Circuits: A Personalized System of Instruction. I. L. Kosow. LC 77-1739. (Ser. in Electronic Technology). 1977. 9.95 (ISBN 0-471-01664-0); solutions manual avail. (ISBN 0-471-03081-3). Wiley.

Study Guide in Physics, 2 vols. Namias. Incl. Vol. 1. Mechanics. 8.95x o.p. (ISBN 0-205-04009-8, 7340095); Vol. 2. Fluid Mechanics, Waves & Thermodynamics. 7.95x o.p. (ISBN 0-205-04210-4, 7342101). Allyn.

Study Guide in Physics: Electricity, Magnetism, Geometrical Optics, & Wave Optics, Vol. 3. Victor Namias. 1976. pap. text ed. 6.95x o.p. (ISBN 0-205-05719-5). Allyn.

Study Guide to Accompany Buffa & Pletcher's Understanding Business Today. Kathy Hegar. 1980. pap. 6.95x (ISBN 0-256-02282-8). Irwin.

Study Guide to Accompany Essential Human Anatomy & Physiology. 2nd ed. Jacob Wiebers & Wallace Rogers. 1980. pap. text ed. 7.95x (ISBN 0-673-15323-1). Scott F.

Study Guide to Accompany in Search of Ourselves. 3rd ed. Randy B. Pollack. 1981. pap. text ed. price not set o.p. (ISBN 0-8087-3326-5). Burgess.

Study Guide to Accompany Intermediate Algebra. 3rd ed. Margaret A. Lial & Charles D. Miller. 1981. pap. text ed. 5.95x (ISBN 0-673-15480-7). Scott F.

Study Guide to Accompany Principles of Economics. 2nd ed. Frank A. Close et al. 1981. pap. text ed. 6.95x (ISBN 0-673-15494-7). Scott F.

Study Guide to Accompany Principles of Macroeconomics. 2nd ed. Frank A. Close et al. 1981. pap. text ed. 4.95x (ISBN 0-673-15496-3). Scott F.

Study Guide to Accompany Principles of Microeconomics. 2nd ed. Frank A. Close et al. 1981. pap. text ed. 4.95x (ISBN 0-673-15495-5). Scott F.

Study Guide to Accompany Psychology: A Brief Introduction. Marianne Bauer & Micheal Wertheimer. 1972. pap. 3.95x o.p. (ISBN 0-673-07786-1). Scott F.

Study Guide to Accompany Pyle & Larson's Financial Accounting. Dan Short. 1980. pap. 5.00x (ISBN 0-256-02331-X). Irwin.

Study Guide to Accompany Sociology: Human Society. 3rd ed. John F. Schnabel. 1981. pap. text ed. 4.95x (ISBN 0-673-15479-3). Scott F.

Study Guide to Accompany Unfinished Democracy. Richard Payne. 1981. pap. 5.95x (ISBN 0-673-15487-4). Scott F.

Study Guide to Accompany Vazsonyi's Introduction to Data Processing. 3rd ed. Herbert F. Spirer & Marilynn Dueker. 1980. pap. 6.50 (ISBN 0-256-02381-6). Irwin.

Study Guide to Activities Therapy. Diana P. Burnell. LC 75-28928. 1976. 7.50 (ISBN 0-89004-081-8). Raven.

Study Guide to "Congregations in Change". James C. Fenhagen & Celia A. Hahn. LC 73-17894. 1974. 1.45 (ISBN 0-8164-2093-9). Crossroad NY.

Study Guide to Physics in the Modern World. 2nd ed. Jerry Marion. 1980. 5.95 (ISBN 0-12-472284-9). Acad Pr.

Study Guide to Principles of Management. Drake et al. 176p. 1980. wkbk. 7.95 (ISBN 0-8359-5597-4). Reston.

Study Guide to Putnam's Geology. E. Lynn Savage & Helen A. Biren. 208p. (Orig.). 1978. pap. text ed. 6.95x (ISBN 0-19-502385-4). Oxford U Pr.

Study Guide to Steinbeck, Pt. II. Tetsumaro Hayashi. LC 74-735. 252p. 1979. 12.00 (ISBN 0-8108-1220-7). Scarecrow.

Study Guide to Steinbeck: A Handbook to His Major Works. Tetsumaro Hayashi. LC 74-735. 1974. 12.00 (ISBN 0-8108-0706-8). Scarecrow.

Study Guide to the Master Plan of Evangelism. R. J. Fish. 64p. 1972. pap. 1.25 (ISBN 0-8007-0479-7). Revell.

Study Guide to the Multiple Choice Examinations for Chief Mate & Master. Richard James & Richard M. Plant. LC 76-48096. (Illus.). 1976. 25.00x (ISBN 0-87033-232-5). Cornell Maritime.

Study Guide to the Multiple Choice Examinations for Third & Second Mates. 3rd ed. Richard James & Richard M. Plant. LC 79-1735. 1979. pap. 20.00x (ISBN 0-87033-252-X). Cornell Maritime.

Study Hour Series. W. Graham Scroggie. Incl. 192p. kivar o.p. 3.95 (ISBN 0-310-32671-0); Gospel of John. 144p. kivar o.p. 3.95 (ISBN 0-310-32681-8); Gospel of Mark. 288p. kivar 6.95 (ISBN 0-310-32691-5). 1976. Zondervan.

Study in Aesthetics. Louis A. Reid. 415p. 1980. Repr. of 1931 ed. lib. bdg. 45.00 (ISBN 0-8495-4635-4). Arden Lib.

Study in Comparative Urban Indicators: Conditions in 18 Large Metropolitan Areas. Michael J. Flax. 1972. pap. 3.50 o.p. (ISBN 0-87766-061-1, 20006). Urban Inst.

Study in Consciousness. 6th ed. Annie Besant. 1972. 6.25 (ISBN 0-8356-7287-5). Theos Pub Hse.

Study in Conservation. Winston Barnett & Cyril Winskell. 1978. 11.95 (ISBN 0-85362-168-3, Oriel); pap. 8.95 (ISBN 0-85362-172-1). Routledge & Kegan.

Study in Neurolinguistics. Simeon Locke et al. (Illus.). 160p. 1973. text ed. 13.75 (ISBN 0-398-02738-2). C C Thomas.

Study in Regional Taste: The May Show 1919-1975. Jay Hoffman et al. LC 77-78145. (Themes in Art Ser.). (Illus.). 72p. 1977. pap. 4.95x (ISBN 0-910386-36-6, Pub. by Cleveland Mus Art). Ind U Pr.

Study in Scarlet. Arthur C. Doyle. 160p. 1975. pap. 1.25 o.p. (ISBN 0-345-24714-0). Ballantine.

Study in Scarlet. Arthur C. Doyle. lib. bdg. 13.95x (ISBN 0-89966-231-5). Buccaneer Bks.

Study in the Dialectics of Sphota. G. Sastri. 106p. 1980. text ed. 10.50 (ISBN 0-8426-1653-5). Verry.

Study Notes for the Biological Sciences. Phillip D. Sparks et al. 1973. pap. text ed. 4.95 o.p. (ISBN 0-8087-6033-5). Burgess.

Study of Acquaintance. Steven Duck. 1977. 24.95 (ISBN 0-566-00160-8, 01085-5, Pub. by Saxon Hse England). Lexington Bks.

Study of Agricultural Systems. Ed. by G. E. Dalton. (Illus.). 1975. 63.30x (ISBN 0-85334-640-2, Pub. by Applied Science). Burgess-Intl Ideas.

Study of Anthropology. Pelto. 1965. pap. text ed. 4.95x (ISBN 0-675-09700-2). Merrill.

Study of Astrology, Vol. II. Henry Weingarten. Date not set. pap. 7.95 (ISBN 0-88231-030-5). ASI Pubs Inc. Postponed.

Study of Ben Jonson. Algernon C. Swinburne. Ed. by Howard B. Norland. LC 69-12400. 1969. pap. 3.65x (ISBN 0-8032-5709-0, BB 326, Bison). U of Nebr Pr.

Study of Bible Leaders. J. J. Turner. pap. 2.50 (ISBN 0-89315-290-0). Lambert Bk.

Study of Biology. 3rd ed. Jeffrey J. Baker & Garland E. Allen. LC 76-15460. (Illus.). 1977. text ed. 21.95 (ISBN 0-201-00349-X); instr's manual 3.00 (ISBN 0-201-00413-5). A-W.

Study of Bird Song. 2nd, enl. ed. Edward A. Armstrong. (Illus.). 1980. 7.50 (ISBN 0-8446-4704-7). Peter Smith.

Study of Boy Life in Our Cities: London, 1904. Ed. by E. J. Urwick. LC 79-56942. (English Working Class Ser.). 1980. lib. bdg. 28.00 (ISBN 0-8240-0125-7). Garland Pub.

Study of Changing Pre-Columbian Commercial Systems: Cozumel, Mexico. Ed. by Jeremy A. Sabloff & William L. Rathje. LC 75-20624. (Peabody Museum Monographs: No. 3). 1975. pap. 12.00 (ISBN 0-87365-902-3). Peabody Harvard.

Study of Combined School-Public Libraries. Shirley L. Aaron. LC 80-19785. 120p. 1980. pap. 7.00 (ISBN 0-8389-3247-9). ALA.

Study of Community Power: A Bibliographic Review. Ed. by Willis D. Hawley & James H. Svara. LC 72-83287. 123p. 1972. text ed. 3.50 (ISBN 0-87436-088-9); pap. text ed. 2.50 (ISBN 0-87436-089-7). ABC-Clio.

Study of Culture at a Distance. Ed. by Margaret Mead & Rhoda Metraux. LC 53-13135. 1953. 20.00x (ISBN 0-226-51508-7). U of Chicago Pr.

Study of Curriculum. Peter Gordon. 192p. 1981. 27.00 (ISBN 0-686-69077-X, Pub. by Batsford England); pap. 13.50 (ISBN 0-7134-2092-8). David & Charles.

Study of Damage to Residential Structures from Blast Vibrations. Compiled by American Society of Civil Engineers. 80p. 1974. pap. text ed. 4.50 (ISBN 0-87262-074-3). Am Soc Civil Eng.

Study of Daniel. John A. Copeland. 1973. pap. 3.45 (ISBN 0-89137-703-4). Quality Pubns.

Study of Data Base Processor Technology. Laura A. Gregory. (Data Base Monograph: No. 8). (Illus.). 77p. (Orig.). pap. 15.00 (ISBN 0-89435-035-8). QED Info Sci.

Study of Deviance: Perspectives & Problems. Don C. Gibbons & John F. Jones. (Illus.). 192p. 1975. pap. text ed. 10.95 (ISBN 0-13-858936-4). P-H.

Study of Dialect: An Introduction to Dialectology. K. M. Petyt. (Andre Deutsch Language Library). 240p. 1980. lib. bdg. 26.50x (ISBN 0-86531-060-2). Westview.

Study of Economic History: Collected Inaugural Lectures, 1893-1970. Ed. by N. B. Harte. 385p. 1971. 29.50x (ISBN 0-7146-2905-7, F Cass Co). Biblio Dist.

Study of Education. Ed. by J. W. Tibble. (Students Library of Education). 1970. text ed. 6.25x (ISBN 0-7100-4205-1). Humanities.

Study of Education: A Collection of Inaugural Lectures, Vol. I--Early & Modern, Vol. II--The Last Decade. Ed. by Peter Gordon. (Woburn Education Ser.). 662p. 1980. Set. 60.00x (ISBN 0-7130-0169-0, Pub. by Woburn Pr England); Set. pap. 30.00x (ISBN 0-7130-4004-1). Biblio Dist.

Study of Elizabethan & Jacobean Tragedy. Thomas B. Tomlinson. 1964. 48.00 (ISBN 0-521-06642-5). Cambridge U Pr.

Study of Engineering in Medicine & Health Care. Committee on Interplay of Engineering with Biology & Medicine. LC 74-7253. 80p. 1974. pap. 3.50 (ISBN 0-309-02148-0). Natl Acad Pr.

Study of Folklore. Alan Dundes. (Illus.). 1965. text ed. 14.95 (ISBN 0-13-858944-5). P-H.

Study of Fossils. J. F. Kirkaldy. 1964. pap. text ed. 3.50x (ISBN 0-09-108391-5, Hutchinson U Lib). Humanities.

Study of Future Worlds. Richard A. Falk. LC 74-10139. (Preferred Worlds for the 1990's Ser.). (Illus.). 1975. pap. text ed. 10.95 (ISBN 0-02-910080-1). Free Pr.

Study of Government: Political Science & Public Administration. F. F. Ridley. 1975. text ed. 25.00x (ISBN 0-04-320106-7); pap. text ed. 8.95x (ISBN 0-04-320107-5). Allen Unwin.

Study of Heart-Rate Variability. R. I. Kitney & O. Rompelman. (Illus.). 220p. 1980. text ed. 65.00x (ISBN 0-19-857533-5). Oxford U Pr.

Study of History. Henry S. Commager. 1966. pap. text ed. 4.95x (ISBN 0-675-09712-6). Merrill.

Study of History. Arnold J. Toynbee. (Royal Institute of International Affairs). 1954. Vols. 1-6. o.p. (ISBN 0-19-500198-2); Vols. 7-10. maroon cloth 60.00 (ISBN 0-19-519689-9); Vols. 11-12 (vol. 11 O.p.) maroon cloth 19.95 (ISBN 0-19-500197-4). Oxford U Pr.

Study of History: A Collection of Inaugural Lectures in Two Volumes. Ed. by Arthur J. Taylor. Incl. Vol. 1. Beginnings to Nineteen Forty-Five; Vol. 2. Nineteen Forty-Five to Present. 1980. 30.00x set (ISBN 0-7146-3125-6, F Cass Co). Biblio Dist.

Study of History: Introduction the Genesis of Civilization, & the Growth of Civilization, 3 vols. 2nd ed. Arnold J. Toynbee. (Royal Institute of International Affairs Ser.). 1935. Vol. 1. 26.50x (ISBN 0-19-215207-6); Vol. 2. 29.95x (ISBN 0-19-215208-4); Vol. 3. 29.00x (ISBN 0-19-215209-2). Oxford U Pr.

Study of History: Reconsideration. Arnold J. Toynbee. 1961. Vol. 12. 26.00x (ISBN 0-19-215225-4). Oxford U Pr.

Study of History: The Disintegrations of Civilization. Arnold J. Toynbee. (Royal Institute of International Affairs Ser.). 1939. Vol. 4. 29.00x (ISBN 0-19-215211-4); Vol. 5. 13.95x (ISBN 0-19-215212-2); Vol. 6. 29.95x (ISBN 0-19-215213-0). Oxford U Pr.

Study of Human Communication. Nan Lin. LC 72-77128. 1973. 7.65 o.p. (ISBN 0-672-61340-9); pap. 6.50 (ISBN 0-672-61206-2). Bobbs.

Study of Human Nature. Ed. by Leslie Stevenson. 352p. 1981. pap. text ed. 7.95x (ISBN 0-19-502827-9). Oxford U Pr.

Study of International Politics: A Guide to the Sources for the Student, Teacher, & Researcher. Dorothy F. LaBarr & J. David Singer. LC 76-12545. 211p. 1976. text ed. 10.00 (ISBN 0-87436-233-4). ABC-Clio.

Study of International Relations: A Guide to Information Sources. Ed. by Robert Pfaltzgraff, Jr. LC 73-17511. (International Relations Information Guide Ser.: Vol. 5). 220p. 1977. 30.00 (ISBN 0-8103-1331-6). Gale.

Study of Intimate Communication. Gerald M. Phillips & Nancy J. Metzger. 464p. 1976. text ed. 12.95x o.p. (ISBN 0-205-04876-5); instr's manual free o.p. (ISBN 0-205-04877-3). Allyn.

Study of Jazz. 4th ed. Paul Tanner & Maurice Gerow. 225p. 1981. pap. text ed. write for info. (ISBN 0-697-03442-9); instr's manual avail. (ISBN 0-697-03443-7). Wm C Brown.

Study of John Webster's Use of Renaissance Natural & Moral Philosophy. William W. Dwyer. (Salzburg Studies in English Literature, Jacobean Drama Studies: No. 18). 206p. 1973. pap. text ed. 25.00x (ISBN 0-391-01368-8). Humanities.

Study of Judaism: Bibliographic Essays. Richard Bavier. 1972. 17.50 (ISBN 0-685-38395-4, 87068-180-4, Pub. by Anti-Defamation League). Ktav.

Study of Juvenal's Tenth Satire. Emin Tengstrom. 1981. pap. text ed. 14.00x (ISBN 91-7346-089-3). Humanities.

Study of Kant. James Ward. Ed. by Lewis W. Beck. Bd. with Immanuel Kant (Seventeen Twenty-Four to Eighteen Hundred Four) The British Academy Annual Philosophical Lecture. LC 75-32045. (Philosophy of Immanuel Kant Ser.: Vol. 9). 1977. Repr. of 1922 ed. lib. bdg. 24.00 (ISBN 0-8240-2333-1). Garland Pub.

Study of Keats's Isabella. Eve Leoff. (Salzburg Studies in English Literature, Romantic Reassessment: No. 17). 217p. 1972. pap. text ed. 25.00x (ISBN 0-391-01457-9). Humanities.

Study of Landforms. 2nd ed. R. J. Small. LC 77-71427. 1978. 57.50 (ISBN 0-521-21634-6); pap. 23.95x (ISBN 0-521-29238-7). Cambridge U Pr.

Study of Language in Seventeenth Century England. Vivian Salmon. (Studies in the History of Linguistics: No. 17). 1978. text ed. 37.25x (ISBN 0-391-01645-8). Humanities.

Study of Liberty & Revolution. Edward Goodman. 1975. 19.95x (ISBN 0-7156-0870-3); pap. 11.95x (ISBN 0-685-88347-7). Intl Ideas.

Study of Life: A Naturalist's View. R. D. Lawrence. (Illus.). 43p. 1980. pap. 1.50 (ISBN 0-913098-37-X). Myrin Institute.

Study of Literature for Readers & Critics. David Daiches. LC 71-152593. 240p. 1972. Repr. of 1948 ed. lib. bdg. 21.00x (ISBN 0-8371-6026-X, DARC). Greenwood.

Study of Liturgy. Ed. by Cheslyn Jones & Geoffrey Wainwright. 1978. 23.95 (ISBN 0-19-520075-6); pap. 9.95 (ISBN 0-19-520076-4). Oxford U Pr.

Study of Maya Art: Its Subject Matter & Historical Development. Herbert J. Spinden. LC 74-20300. (Illus.). 352p. 1975. pap. text ed. 6.95 (ISBN 0-486-21235-1). Dover.

Study of Medieval Records: Essays in Honour of Kathleen Major. Ed. by D. A. Bullough & R. L. Storey. (Illus.). 380p. 1971. 29.95x (ISBN 0-19-822347-1). Oxford U Pr.

Study of Minor Prophets. Brodie Crouch. pap. 2.50 (ISBN 0-89315-291-9). Lambert Bk.

Study of Morton, Bliss & Company. Dolores Greenberg. LC 78-66830. 288p. 1980. 22.50 (ISBN 0-87413-148-0). U Delaware Pr.

Study of Names in Literature: A Bibliography. E. M. Rajec. 261p. 1978. 38.00 (ISBN 0-89664-000-0, Pub. by K G Saur). Gale.

Study of Nietzsche. J. P. Stern. LC 78-54328. (Major European Authors Ser.). 1979. 26.95 (ISBN 0-521-22126-9). Cambridge U Pr.

Study of Nietzsche. J. P. Stern. LC 78-54328. (Major European Authors Ser.). Date not set. pap. price not set (ISBN 0-521-28380-9). Cambridge U Pr.

Study of Nineteenth Century Society. Ed. by E. A. Wrigley. LC 71-174258. (Illus.). 512p. 1972. 46.50 (ISBN 0-521-08412-1). Cambridge U Pr.

Study of Olmec Sculptural Chronology. Susan Milbrath. LC 79-89248. (Studies in Pre-Columbian Art & Archaeology: No. 23). (Illus.). 75p. 1979. pap. 5.00 (ISBN 0-88402-093-2, Ctr Pre-Columbian). Dumbarton Oaks.

Study of Oral Interpretation: Theory & Comment. Richard Haas & David A. Williams. LC 74-13539. 252p. 1975. pap. text ed. 5.95 (ISBN 0-672-61226-7). Bobbs.

Study of Organizational Leadership. Ed. by Office of Military Leadership, United States Military Academy Associates. LC 76-25242. 600p. 1976. pap. 12.95 (ISBN 0-8117-2059-4). Stackpole.

Study of Organizations: Findings from Field & Laboratory. Ed. by Daniel Katz et al. LC 80-15488. (Social & Behavioral Science Ser.). 1980. text ed. 28.95x (ISBN 0-87589-464-X). Jossey-Bass.

Study of Plant Communities: An Introduction to Plant Ecology. 2nd ed. Henry J. Oosting. LC 56-11029. (Illus.). 1956. 21.95x (ISBN 0-7167-0703-9). W H Freeman.

Study of Policy Formation. R. A. Bauer & K. J. Gergen. 1971. pap. text ed. 7.95 (ISBN 0-02-901930-3). Free Pr.

Study of Politics. Charles S. Hyneman. LC 59-10554. 1959. 12.00 (ISBN 0-252-72671-5). U of Ill Pr.

Study of Psychology. George H. Lewes. (Contributions to the History of Psychology Ser.: No. 6, Pt. A Orientations). 1978. Repr. of 1879 ed. 30.00 (ISBN 0-89093-155-0). U Pubns Amer.

Study of Public Policy. Richard I. Hofferbert. LC 73-9826. (Policy Analysis Ser). 1974. 11.95 (ISBN 0-672-51475-3); pap. text ed. 10.50 (ISBN 0-672-61062-0). Bobbs.

Study of Religion & Its Meaning. J. Barnhart. 1977. 27.05x (ISBN 90-279-7762-3). Mouton.

Study of Religion in Two-Year Colleges. C. Freeman Sleeper & Robert A. Spivey. LC 75-28158. (American Academy of Religion, Individual Volumes). 1975. pap. 4.50 (ISBN 0-89130-031-7, 010801). Scholars Pr CA.

Study of Religion on the Campus of Today. Ed. by Karl D. Hartzell & Harrison Sasscer. 1967. 3.00 o.p. (ISBN 0-685-05154-4). ACE.

Study of Religions. Jean Holm. LC 76-15426. 1977. pap. 3.95 (ISBN 0-8164-1227-8). Crossroad NY.

Study of Rhetoric in the Plays of Thomas Dekker. Suzanne K. Blow. (Salzburg Studies in English Literature, Jacobean Drama Studies: No. 3). 1972. pap. text ed. 25.00x (ISBN 0-391-01327-0). Humanities.

Study of Self-Deception. M. R. Haight. 1980. text ed. 20.00x (ISBN 0-391-01803-5). Humanities.

Study of Shelley's "a Defence of Poetry" A Textual & Critical Evaluation, 2 vols. Fanny Delisle. (Salzburg Studies in English Literature,Romantic Reassessment: Nos.27-28). 633p. 1974. Set. pap. text ed. 50.25x (ISBN 0-391-01359-9). Humanities.

Study of Simon Willard's Clocks. R. W. Husher & W. W. Welch. LC 80-65021. (Illus.). 292p. 1980. 35.00x (ISBN 0-9603944-0-0). Husher & Welch.

Study of Social Dialects in American English. Walt Walfman & Ralph W. Fasold. 272p. 1974. ref. ed. 12.95 (ISBN 0-13-858787-6). P-H.

Study of Social Problems: Five Perspectives. 2nd ed. Ed. by Earl Rubington & Martin S. Weinberg. 1977. pap. text ed. 6.95x (ISBN 0-19-502146-0). Oxford U Pr.

Study of Social Problems: Five Perspectives. 3rd ed. Ed. by Earl Rubington & Martin S. Weinberg. 256p. 1981. pap. text ed. 7.95x (ISBN 0-19-502825-2). Oxford U Pr.

Study of Sociology. Rose. 1966. pap. text ed. 4.95x (ISBN 0-675-09717-7). Merrill.

Study of Sociology. Herbert Spencer. 1961. pap. 3.25 o.p. (ISBN 0-472-06060-0, 60, AA). U of Mich Pr.

Study of Speech Patterns in the Former Urban District of Cannock, Staffordshire. Christopher D. Heath. 1980. 22.00x (ISBN 0-631-11611-7, Pub. by Basil Blackwell England). Biblio Dist.

Study of Splashes. Arthur M. Worthington. (gr. 10 up). 1963. 6.25g o.s.i. (ISBN 0-02-793570-1). Macmillan.

Study of Strategy & Policy Formation: A Multifunctional Orientation. Robert C. Shirley et al. LC 75-25814. 232p. 1976. text ed. 10.95x o.p. (ISBN 0-471-78643-8). Wiley.

Study of the Capital Market in Britain from 1919-1936. Alexander T. Grant. LC 67-16365. Repr. of 1937 ed. 26.00x (ISBN 0-678-05052-X). Kelley.

Study of the Child. A. R. Taylor. 215p. 1980. Repr. of 1910 ed. lib. bdg. 35.00. Telegraph Bks.

Study of the Language of Love in the Song of Songs & Ancient Egyptian Poetry. John B. White. LC 77-13399. (Society of Biblical Literature. Dissertation Ser.: Vol. 38). 1978. pap. 7.50 (ISBN 0-89130-192-5, 060138). Scholars Pr Ca.

Study of the Middle East: Research & Scholarship in the Humanities & Social Sciences. Leonard Binder. LC 76-7408. 648p. 1976. 39.95 (ISBN 0-471-07304-0, Pub. by Wiley-Interscience). Wiley.

Study of the Nonprofit Arts & Cultural Industry in New York State. 212p. 1972. pap. 4.00x spiral bound (ISBN 0-89062-013-X, Pub. by National Research Center of the Arts). Pub Ctr Cult Res.

Study of the Quality of Continuing Legal Education in the United States. 29.00; 2 copies 16.24 ea.; 3 or more copies 11.60 ea. ALI-ABA.

Study of the Revelation. John A. Copeland. 1971. pap. 3.45 (ISBN 0-89137-702-6). Quality Pubns.

Study of the Social & Economic Needs Created by the Proposed Craig Power Plant Installation. 119p. 1974. 15.00 (ISBN 0-686-64166-3). U CO Busn Res Div.

Study of Thinking. Jerome S. Bruner et al. LC 56-7999. 1956. pap. 13.95 o.p. (ISBN 0-471-11415-4). Wiley.

Study of Thomas Middleton's Tragicomedies. Carolyn Asp. (Salzburg Studies in English Literature, Jacobean Drama Studies: No. 28). 282p. 1974. pap. text ed. 25.00x (ISBN 0-391-01303-3). Humanities.

Study of Tooth Shapes: A Systematic Procedure. Horst Grundler. (Illus.). 104p. 1976. 24.00 (ISBN 3-87652-561-6). Quint Pub Co.

Study of Trace Fossils: A Synthesis of Principles, Problems, & Procedures in Ichnology. Ed. by R. W. Frey. LC 74-30164. (Illus.). xxiii, 570p. 1975. 66.50 o.p. (ISBN 0-387-06870-8). Springer-Verlag.

Study of Twentieth-Century Harmony: Harmony in France to 1914 & Contemporary Harmony, 2 vols. in 1. Rene Lenormand & Mosco Carner. LC 76-40058. (Music Reprint Ser). 1975. Repr. of 1940 ed. lib. bdg. 22.50 (ISBN 0-306-70717-9). Da Capo.

Study of Urban Geography. 2nd ed. Harold Carter. LC 76-22730. 1976. pap. text ed. 16.95 (ISBN 0-470-98911-4). Halsted Pr.

Study of Vasyl' Stefanyk: The Pain at the Heart of Existence. D. S. Struk. LC 72-89110. 225p. 1973. lib. bdg. 13.50x (ISBN 0-87287-056-1). Ukrainian Acad.

Study on Kresek (Wilt) of the Rice Bacterial Blight Syndrome. (IRRI Research Paper Ser.: No. 39). 8p. 1979. pap. 5.00 (R079, IRRI). Unipub.

Study on the Historiography of the British West Indies to the End of the Nineteenth Century. Elsa V. Goveia. LC 75-20036. 192p. 1981. pap. 8.95 (ISBN 0-88258-048-5). Howard U Pr.

Study on the Origins of Mental Rehabilitation. Matti Iavanainen. (Clinics in Developmental Medicine Ser.: Vol. 51). 173p. 1974. 23.00 (ISBN 0-685-59045-3). Lippincott.

Study on the Origins of Mental Retardation. Matti Iivanainen. 1974. 18.95x (ISBN 0-433-16300-3). Intl Ideas.

Study on the Potentialities of the Use of a Nuclear Reactor for the Industrialization of Southern Tunisia. (Technical Reports: No. 35). 1964. pap. 2.75 (ISBN 92-0-155164-9, IAEA). Unipub.

Study Skills. Carol A. Francis. pap. text ed. 2.95x (ISBN 0-933892-14-4). Child Focus Co.

Study Skills for College. Eleanor Haburton. (Illus.). 176p. 1981. pap. text ed. 6.95 (ISBN 0-87626-860-2). Winthrop.

Study Skills for Information Retrieval, Bk. 1. Donald L. Barnes & Arlene Burgdorf. (gr. 4-8). 1979. pap. text ed. 4.40 (ISBN 0-205-06436-1, 4964365); tchrs'. ed. 4.80 (ISBN 0-205-06440-X, 4964403). Allyn.

Study Skills for Information Retrieval, Bk. 2. Donald L. Barnes & Arlene Burgdorf. (gr. 4-8). 1979. pap. text ed. 4.40 (ISBN 0-205-06437-X, 4964373); tchrs'. ed. 4.80 (ISBN 0-205-06441-8, 4964411). Allyn.

Study Skills for Information Retrieval, Bk. 3. Donald L. Barnes & Arlene Burgdorf. (gr. 4-8). 1979. pap. text ed. 4.40 (ISBN 0-205-06438-8, 496438-1); tchrs'. ed. 4.80 (ISBN 0-205-06442-6, 496442-X). Allyn.

Study Skills for Information Retrieval, Bk. 4. Donald L. Barnes & Arlene Burgdorf. (gr. 4-8). 1974. pap. text ed. 4.40 (ISBN 0-205-03994-4, 4939948); tchrs. ed. 4.80 (ISBN 0-205-03995-2, 4939956). Allyn.

Study Skills Workshop Kit Level I. (gr. 5-9). 1980. pap. 9.95 (ISBN 0-88210-112-9). Natl Assn Principals.

Study Skills Workshop Kit Level II. (gr. 8-10). 1979. pap. 9.95 (ISBN -088210-113-7). Natl Assn Principals.

Study Topics in Physics, 4 vols. W. Bolton. 1980. pap. text ed. 4.50 ea. Vol. 1, 79-41764 (ISBN 0-408-10652-2). Vol. 2, 79-41775 (ISBN 0-408-10653-0). Vol. 3, 80-40009 (ISBN 0-408-10654-9). Vol. 4, 80-40151 (ISBN 0-408-10655-7). Butterworths.

Studying a Study & Testing a Test: How to Read the Medical Literature. 1981. pap. text ed. price not set (ISBN 0-316-74518-9). Little.

Studying Africa in Elementary & Secondary Schools. rev. ed. Leonard S. Kenworthy. LC 70-105869. (Illus.). 1970. pap. text ed. 3.50x (ISBN 0-8077-1606-5). Tchrs Coll.

Studying Birds in the Garden. T. Jennings. 1976. 7.80 (ISBN 0-08-017802-2). Pergamon.

Studying Children: An Introduction to Research Methods. Ross Vasta. LC 78-25941. (Psychology Ser.). (Illus.). 1979. text ed. 15.95x (ISBN 0-7167-1067-6); pap. text ed. 7.95x (ISBN 0-7167-1068-4). W H Freeman.

Studying Children: Observing & Participating. Draper. 1977. pap. text ed. 9.28 (ISBN 0-87002-291-1). Bennett IL.

Studying China. Leonard Kenworthy. LC 74-23808. 1975. pap. text ed. 4.25x (ISBN 0-8077-2456-4). Tchrs Coll.

Studying Civilization. 5th ed. T. Walter Wallbank et al. 1978. pap. 5.95x (ISBN 0-673-15125-5). Scott F.

Studying Civilizations Past & Present, Vol. 1. 8th ed. Richard Wires. 1981. pap. text ed. 5.95x study guide (ISBN 0-673-15502-1). Scott F.

Studying Deductive Logic. F. Berger. 1977. pap. 8.95 (ISBN 0-13-858811-2). P-H.

Studying Effectively. C. Gilbert Wrenn & Robert P. Larsen. 1955. pap. 0.65x (ISBN 0-8047-1071-6). Stanford U Pr.

Studying India. Leonard Kenworthy. LC 74-23809. 1975. pap. text ed. 4.25x (ISBN 0-8077-2457-2). Tchrs Coll.

Studying Japan. Leonard Kenworthy. LC 74-23896. 1975. pap. text ed. 4.25x (ISBN 0-8077-2455-6). Tchrs Coll.

Studying Latin America: Essays in Honor of Preston E. James. David J. Robinson. LC 80-12413. (Dellplain Latin American Studies: No. 4). 290p. (Orig.). 1980. pap. 19.25 (ISBN 0-8357-0515-3, SS-00135, Pub. by Syracuse U Dept Geog). Univ Microfilms.

Studying Life Designs. Marcia Lipetz. 1978. pap. 4.95x (ISBN 0-673-15121-2). Scott F.

Studying Personality: Student Booklet. American Psychological Association. (Human Behavior Curriculum Project Ser.). 64p. (Orig.). (gr. 9-12). 1981. pap. text ed. 3.95x (ISBN 0-8077-2627-3). Tchrs Coll.

Studying Personality: Teachers Manual & Duplication Masters. American Psychological Association. (Human Behavior Curriculum Project Ser.). 48p. (Orig.). (gr. 9-12). 1981. pap. 9.95x (ISBN 0-8077-2628-1). Tchrs Coll.

Studying Politics. Ed. by William A. Welsh. LC 77-189929. 272p. 1973. pap. 5.95 o.p. (ISBN 0-275-84150-2). Praeger.

Studying South America in Elementary & Secondary Schools. rev. ed. Leonard S. Kenworthy. LC 65-19211. (Illus.). 1965. pap. text ed. 3.50x (ISBN 0-8077-1614-6). Tchrs Coll.

Studying Suzuki Piano: More Than Music: A Handbook for Teachers, Parents & Students. Carole L. Bigler & Valery Lloyd-Watts. LC 78-73088. (Illus., Orig.). 1979. pap. 19.95 (ISBN 0-918194-06-7). Accura.

Studying Teaching. 2nd ed. James Raths et al. LC 70-123086. 1971. pap. text ed. 13.95 (ISBN 0-13-858878-3). P-H.

Studying the Middle East in Elementary & Secondary Schools. rev. ed. Leonard S. Kenworthy. LC 65-19213. (Orig.). 1965. pap. text ed. 3.50x (ISBN 0-8077-1611-1). Tchrs Coll.

Studying the U.S.S.R. in Elementary & Secondary Schools. Leonard S. Kenworthy. LC 77-94510. 1970. pap. text ed. 3.50x (ISBN 0-8077-1615-4). Tchrs Coll.

Stuecke. Erwin Sylvanus. 203p. 1980. pap. 11.70 quality paper (ISBN 3-518-04387-0, Pub. by Insel Verlag Stucke). Suhrkamp.

Stuffed Toys. Ondori Publishing Co. Staff. (Ondori Handicraft Ser). (Illus.). 96p. 1976. pap. 5.50 (ISBN 0-87040-368-0). Japan Pubns.

Stumpwork: The Art of Raised Embroidery. Muriel L. Baker. LC 77-13204. (Illus.). 1978. 14.95 o.p. (ISBN 0-684-15360-2, ScribT). Scribner.

Stunts & Tumbling for Girls: A Textbook for Schools & Colleges. Virginia L. Horne. (Illus.). (gr. 9 up). 1943. 13.95 (ISBN 0-8260-4385-2). Ronald Pr.

Stupid Lady. Lope De Vega. 3.00 (ISBN 0-8283-1426-8). Branden.

Stupid Tiger & Other Tales. Upendrakishore Raychaudhuri. Tr. by William Radice. LC 80-2691. (Illus.). 96p. (gr. 1-5). 1981. 8.95 (ISBN 0-233-97256-0). Andre Deutsch.

Stupids Die. Harry Allard. (gr. k-3). 1981. 7.95 (ISBN 0-395-30347-8). HM.

Sturdy Black Bridges: Visions of Black Women in Literature. Roseann P. Bell et al. LC 77-16898. 1979. pap. 6.95 (ISBN 0-385-13347-2, Anch). Doubleday.

Sturdy Statistics: Nonparametrics & Order Statistics. F. R. Mosteller & Robert E. Rourke. LC 70-184162. 1973. text ed. 18.95 (ISBN 0-201-04868-X). A-W.

Sturge Moore & the Life of Art. Frederick L. Gwynn. 159p. 1980. Repr. of 1952 ed. lib. bdg. 30.00 (ISBN 0-89984-249-6). Century Bookbindery.

Sturgeon in Orbit. Theodore Sturgeon. 1978. pap. 1.50 o.s.i. (ISBN 0-515-04477-6). Jove Pubns.

Sturmian Theory for Ordinary Differential Equations. William T. Reid. (Applied Mathematical Sciences: Vol. 31). 559p. 1981. pap. 26.80 (ISBN 0-387-90542-1). Springer-Verlag.

Stutter-Free Speech: A Goal for Therapy. George H. Shames & Cheri L. Florance. (Special Education Ser.). 184p. (Orig.). 1980. pap. text ed. 10.95 (ISBN 0-675-08178-5); recording forms 12.50 (ISBN 0-675-08174-2); media 195.00 (ISBN 0-675-08099-1). Merrill.

Stuttering: Differential Evaluation & Therapy. Hugo H. Gregory. LC 73-4549. (Studies in Communicative Disorders Ser.). 1973. pap. text ed. 2.95 (ISBN 0-672-61291-7). Bobbs.

Stuttering: Learned & Unlearned. Frank J. Falck. (Illus.). 172p. 1969. 16.75 (ISBN 0-398-00541-9). C C Thomas.

Stuttering Manual for the Speech Therapist. Nancy G. Polow. 84p. 1975. pap. 9.75 (ISBN 0-398-03492-3). C C Thomas.

Stuttering Solved. Martin F. Schwartz. LC 75-42456. (Illus.). 1976. 9.95 (ISBN 0-397-01134-2). Lippincott.

Stuttering: The Disorder of Many Theories. Gerald Jonas. 64p. 1977. 5.95 (ISBN 0-374-27118-6); pap. 2.95 (ISBN 0-374-51429-1). FS&G.

Stuttering: Theory & Treatment. 2nd ed. Marcel E. Wingate. (Speech & Hearing Series). 384p. 1981. text ed. 18.50x (ISBN 0-8290-0359-2). Irvington.

Stuttering: Therapy for Children. Harold L. Luper & Robert L. Mulder. 1964. text ed. 13.95 (ISBN 0-13-858985-2). P-H.

Stuttgart Ballet. Leslie Spatt & Horst Koegler. 1978. 14.95 (ISBN 0-903102-42-0). Dance Horiz.

Style a la Pensee: Trois Etudes Sur les Caractires De la Breuyier. LC 80-66328. (French Forum Monographs: No. 20). 90p. (Orig., Fr.). 1980. pap. 9.00 (ISBN 0-917058-19-4). French Forum.

Style & Design, Nineteen Hundred Nine to Nineteen Twenty-Three. Giulia Veronesi. LC 68-20093. (Illus.). 1968. 15.00 o.s.i. (ISBN 0-8076-0448-8). Braziller.

Style & Management of a Pediatric Practice. Lee W. Bass & Jerome H. Wolfson. LC 76-50882. (Contemporary Community Health Ser.). 1977. pap. 7.95 (ISBN 0-8229-3341-1). U of Pittsburgh Pr.

Style & Symbolism in Piers Plowman: A Modern Critical Anthology. Ed. by Robert J. Blanch. LC 69-20115. (Illus., Orig.). 1969. 12.50x (ISBN 0-87049-093-1); pap. text ed. 5.95x (ISBN 0-87049-101-6). U of Tenn Pr.

Style & Vocabulary: Numerical Studies. C. B. Williams. 1970. 8.75 o.s.i. (ISBN 0-02-854850-7). Hafner.

Style for Living: How to Make Where You Live You. Alexandra Stoddard. LC 73-82250. 320p. 1974. 12.50 o.p. (ISBN 0-385-08252-5). Doubleday.

Style in Administration: Readings in British Public Administration. Ed. by Richard A. Chapman & A. Dunsire. (Royal Institute of Public Administration). 1971. text ed. 14.50x o.p. (ISBN 0-04-350027-7). Allen Unwin.

Style in Art History: An Introduction to Theories of Style & Sequence. Margaret Finch. LC 73-14705. 178p. 1974. lib. bdg. 10.00 (ISBN 0-8108-0679-7). Scarecrow.

Style in Fiction. G. N. Leech & M. H. Short. (English Language Ser.). 384p. 1981. text ed. 32.00 (ISBN 0-582-29102-X); pap. text ed. 16.95 (ISBN 0-582-29103-8). Longman.

Style in Piano Playing. Peter Cooper. 1980. 11.95 (ISBN 0-7145-3512-5). Riverrun NY.

Style in Prose Fiction. Ed. by Harold C. Martin. LC 59-11178. (Essays from the English Institute Ser.). 1959. 12.50x (ISBN 0-231-02353-7). Columbia U Pr.

Style in the French Novel. Stephen Ullmann. 1964. 29.50x (ISBN 0-631-07960-2, Pub. by Basil Blackwell). Biblio Dist.

Style Manual for Written Communications. Arno Knapper & Loda Newcomb. (Business English Ser.). 1974. pap. text ed. 8.95 (ISBN 0-88244-053-5). Grid Pub.

Style of J. S. Bach's Chorale Preludes. 2nd ed. Robert L. Tusler. LC 68-13275. (Music Ser). 1968. Repr. of 1956 ed. lib. bdg. 12.50 (ISBN 0-306-70942-2). Da Capo.

Style of Lord Byron's Plays. Paulino Lim, Jr. (Salzburg Studies in English Literature, Poetic Drama & Poetic Theory: No. 3). 177p. 1973. pap. text ed. 25.00x (ISBN 0-391-01461-7). Humanities.

Style: Ten Lessons in Clarity & Grace. Joseph M. Williams. 1981. text ed. 8.95x (ISBN 0-673-15393-2). Scott F.

Style: Writing & Reading As the Discovery of Outlook. 2nd ed. Richard M. Eastman. (Illus.). 1978. pap. 7.95x (ISBN 0-19-502277-7). Oxford U Pr.

Styles & Structures: Alternative Approaches to College Writing. Charles K. Smith. 340p. 1974. pap. text ed. 8.95x (ISBN 0-393-09273-9). Norton.

Styles in Art. Heribert Hutter. LC 73-88460. (Universe History of Art Ser.). (Illus.). 192p. (Orig.). 1981. pap. 6.95 (ISBN 0-87663-558-3). Universe.

Styles in Art: An Historical Survey. Heribert Hutter. LC 73-88460. (Illus.). 189p. 1978. 8.95x (ISBN 0-87663-205-3). Universe.

Styles of Learning & Teaching: An Integrated Outline of Educational Psychology for Students, Teachers, & Lecturers. Noel Entwistle. 1981. price not set (ISBN 0-471-27901-3, Pub. by Wiley-Interscience). Wiley.

Styles of Loving: Why You Love the Way You Do. Marcia Lasswell & Norman Lobsenz. 192p. 1981. pap. 2.50 (ISBN 0-345-29228-6). Ballantine.

Styles of Ornament. Alexander Speltz. (Illus.). 12.50 (ISBN 0-8446-2982-0). Peter Smith.

Stylistic Analysis of Arshile Gorky's Art from 1943-1948. Robert F. Reiff. LC 76-23679. (Outstanding Dissertations in the Fine Arts - American). (Illus.). 1977. Repr. of 1961 ed. lib. bdg. 52.00 (ISBN 0-8240-2719-1). Garland Pub.

Stylistic & Narrative Structures in the Middle English Romances. Susan Wittig. 1977. 15.95x o.p. (ISBN 0-292-77541-5). U of Tex Pr.

Stylistic Variation in Prehistoric Ceramics. Stephen Plog. (New Studies in Archaeology). (Illus.). 130p. 1980. 19.95 (ISBN 0-521-22581-7). Cambridge U Pr.

Stylistics & the Teaching of Literature. Henry G. Widdowson. (Applied Linguistics & Language Study). (Illus.). 144p. 1975. pap. text ed. 8.75x (ISBN 0-582-55076-9). Longman.

Styro-Flyers: How to Build Super Model Airplanes from Hamburger Boxes & Other Fast-Food Containers. Platt Monfort. (Illus.). 32p. (gr. 5 up). 1981. pap. 3.95 (ISBN 0-394-84715-6). Random.

Styx Complex. Russell Rhodes. LC 77-654. 1977. 8.95 (ISBN 0-396-07435-9). Dodd.

Su Man-Shu. Liu Wu-Chi. (World Authors Ser.: China: No. 191). lib. bdg. 10.95 (ISBN 0-8057-2870-8). Twayne.

Su Obstinado Amor. Tr. by Joyce Landorf. (Spanish Bks.). (Span.). 1978. 1.80 (ISBN 0-8297-0600-3). Life Pubs Intl.

Su Tung-P'o: Selections from a Sung Dynasty Poet. Tr. by Burton Watson. LC 65-13619. 1965. 12.50x (ISBN 0-231-02798-2); pap. 6.00x (ISBN 0-231-02799-0). Columbia U Pr.

Suakin & Massawa Under Egyptian Rule, Eighteen Sixty-Five to Eighteen Eighty-Five. Ghada H. Talhami. LC 79-66418. 1979. pap. text ed. 11.50 (ISBN 0-8191-0828-6). U Pr of Amer.

Sub-Regional Planning Studies: An Evaluation. T. M. Cowling & G. C. Steeley. LC 73-4476. 1973. text ed. 16.00 (ISBN 0-08-017019-6). Pergamon.

Sub-Saharan Africa: A Guide to Information Sources. Ed. by W. A. Skurnik. LC 73-17513. (International Relations Information Guide Ser.: Vol. 3). 1977. 30.00 (ISBN 0-8103-1391-X). Gale.

Sub-Saharan Africa: An Introduction. Edmund C. Gannon. 1978. pap. 10.00 (ISBN 0-685-59451-3). Coun Am Affair.

Subacute Bacterial Endocarditis. Andrew Kerr, Jr. (Illus.). 344p. 1956. pap. 32.75 photocopy ed., spiral (ISBN 0-398-01008-0). C C Thomas.

Subantarctic Campbell Island. Alfred M. Bailey & J. H. Sorenson. (Proceedings: No. 10). 1962. 5.50 o.p. (ISBN 0-916278-62-X); pap. 4.00 o.p. (ISBN 0-916278-63-8). Denver Mus Natl Hist.

Subarachnoid Hemorrhage & Cerebrovascular Spasm. R. R. Smith & J. T. Robertson. (Illus.). 284p. 1975. 33.50 (ISBN 0-398-03230-0). C C Thomas.

Subarctic Athabascans: A Selected Bibliography. Arthur E. Hippler & John R. Wood. LC 74-620010. (Joint Institute of Social & Economic Research, Univ. of Alaska Publ. Ser.: No. 39). 360p. 1974. pap. 15.00 (ISBN 0-295-95362-4). U of Wash Pr.

Subaru Service Repair Handbook: All Models, 1972-1979. Ray Hoy. Ed. by Eric Jorgensen. (Illus.). 1977. pap. 10.95 (ISBN 0-89287-146-6, A186). Clymer Pubns.

Subatomic Physics. Hans Frauenfelder & Ernest M. Henley. (Illus.). 544p. 1974. 29.95 (ISBN 0-13-859082-6). P-H.

Subcontinent in World Politics: India, Its Neighbors & the Great Powers. Ed. by Lawrence Ziring. LC 78-19468. (Praeger Special Studies). 1978. 24.95 (ISBN 0-03-042921-8). Praeger.

Subcontract Management Handbook. George Sammet, Jr. & Clifton G. Kelley. 370p. 1981. 24.95 (ISBN 0-8144-5639-1). Am Mgmt.

Subcontracting Policy in the Airframe Industry. J. S. Day. 1970. 28.00 (ISBN 0-08-018745-5). Pergamon.

Subcutaneous Mycoses. Ed. by C. Terrence Dolan. (Atlases of Clinical Mycology: 5). 1976. text & slides 78.00 (ISBN 0-89189-043-2, 15-7-009-00); microfiche ed. 22.00 (ISBN 0-89189-091-2, 17-7-009-00). Am Soc Clinical.

Subdue the Earth. Ralph Walworth. 1977. 9.95 o.s.i. (ISBN 0-440-08434-2). Delacorte.

Subhash Chandra Bose: The Springing Tiger. Hugh Toye. 1970. pap. 2.80 (ISBN 0-88253-190-5). Ind-US Inc.

Subject & Object in Modern English. Barbara H. Partee. Ed. by Jorge Hankamer. LC 78-66576. (Outstanding Dissertations in Linguistics Ser.). 1979. lib. bdg. 15.50 (ISBN 0-8240-9679-7). Garland Pub.

Subject & Psyche: Ricoeur, Jung, & the Search for Foundations. Robert M. Doran. 1977. 10.75 (ISBN 0-8191-0257-1). U Pr of Amer.

Subject & Structure: An Anthology for Writers. 7th ed. John M. Wasson. 1981. pap. text ed. 7.95 (ISBN 0-316-92423-7); tchrs'. manual free (ISBN 0-316-92424-5). Little.

Subject Bibliography of the Second World War: Books in English 1929-1974. Compiled by A. G. S. Enser. LC 76-54230. (Grafton Books on Library Science). 1977. lib. bdg. 36.00x (ISBN 0-89158-722-5). Westview.

Subject Bibliography of the Social Sciences & Humanities. B. M. Hale. LC 78-113358. 1970. 22.00 (ISBN 0-08-015791-2). Pergamon.

Subject Catalog of the Department Library: First Supplement, 4 vols. U. S. Department of Health, Education, & Welfare, Washington, D. C. 1973. Set. 315.00 (ISBN 0-8161-1109-X). G K Hall.

Subject Catalog of the Library of the New York Academy of Medicine, Second Supplement. New York Academy of Medicine. 1979. lib. bdg. 500.00 (ISBN 0-8161-1182-0). G K Hall.

Subject Catalogue-Africa, 3 vols. Ed. by I. D. Wolck. Incl. Vol. 2. Politics; Vol. 3. Literature; Vol. 4. Social & Cultural Anthropology. 1979. Set. 110.00 (ISBN 0-89664-073-6, Pub. by K G Saur); 68.00 ea. Gale.

Subject Compilations of State Laws: Research Guide & Annotated Bibliography. Lynn Foster & Carol Boast. LC 80-1788. 480p. 1981. lib. bdg. 45.00 (ISBN 0-313-21255-4, FOS). Greenwood.

Subject Departmentalized Public Library. M. A. Overton. 1969. 10.00x (ISBN 0-85365-051-9, Pub. by Lib Assn England). Oryx Pr.

Subject Directory of Special Libraries & Information Centers, 5 vol. set. 6th ed. Ed. by Margaret Labash Young & Harold C. Young. 1981. Set. 350.00 (ISBN 0-8103-0305-1). Gale.

Subject Directory of Special Libaries and Information Centers: Education & Information Science Libraries, Including Audiovisual, Picture, Publishing, Rare Book, & Recreational Libaries, Vol. 2. 6th ed. Ed. by Margaret Labash Young & Harold C. Young. 1981. 80.00 (ISBN 0-8103-0307-8). Gale.

Subject Directory of Special Libaries & Information Centers: Social Sciences & Humanities Libraries, Including Area-Ethic, Art, Geography-Map, History, Music, Religion, Theology, Theatre, Urban-Regional Planning Libraries, Vol. 4. 6th ed. Ed. by Margarey Labash Young & Harold C. Young. 1981. 80.00 (ISBN 0-8103-0309-4). Gale.

Subject Directory of Special Libaries & Information Services: Science & Technology Libraries, Including Agriculture, Energy, Environment-Conservation & Food, Vol. 5. 6th ed. Ed. by Margaret Labash Young & Harold C. Young. 1981. 80.00 (ISBN 0-8103-0309-4). Gale.

Subject Directory of Special Libraries & Information Centers, 5 vols. 5th rev. ed. Ed. by Margaret L. Young & Harold C. Young. Incl. Vol. 1. Business & Law Libraries (ISBN 0-8103-0300-0); Vol. 2. Education & Information Science Libraries, Including Audiovisual, Picture, Publishing, Rare Book, & Recreational Libraries (ISBN 0-8103-0301-9); Vol. 3. Health Sciences Libraries, Including All Aspects of Basic & Applied Medical Sciences (ISBN 0-8103-0302-7); Vol. 4. Social Sciences & Humanities Libraries, Including Aera-Ethnic, Art, Geography-Map, History, Music Religion-Theology, Theatre, & Urban-Regional Planning Libraries (ISBN 0-8103-0303-5); Vol. 5. Science & Technology Libraries Including Agriculture, Energy, Environment-Conservation, & Food Sciences Libraries (ISBN 0-8103-0304-3). LC 79-21711. 163p. 1979. Set. 280.00 set (ISBN 0-8103-0299-3); 68.00 ea. Gale.

Subject Directory of Special Libraries & Info. Centers: Business & Law Libaries, Vol. 1. 6th ed. Ed. by Margaret Labash Young & Harold C. Ypung. 1981. 80.00 (ISBN 0-8103-0306-X). Gale.

Subject Directory of Special Libaries & Information Centers: Health Science Libraries, Including All Aspects of Basic & Pplied Medical Sciences, Vol. 3. 6th ed. Ed. by Margaret Labash Young & Harold C. Young. 1981. 80.00 (ISBN 0-8103-0308-6). Gale.

Subject Guide to Books in Print 1980-81, 2 vols. 5700p. 1980. Set. 79.50 (ISBN 0-8352-1308-0). Bowker.

Subject Guide to Children's Books in Print 1980-1981. 540p. 1980. 35.00 (ISBN 0-8352-1312-9). Bowker.

Subject Guide to Government Reference Books. Sally Wynkoop. LC 72-83382. 1972. 18.50 (ISBN 0-87287-025-1). Libs Unl.

Subject Guide to Humor: Anecdotes, Facetiae & Satire from 365 Periodicals, 1968-74. Jean S. Kujoth. LC 76-4865. 206p. 1976. 10.00 (ISBN 0-8108-0924-9). Scarecrow.

Subject Guide to Large Print Book Catalog. LC 76-30595. 110p. 1976. 5.00 (ISBN 0-913578-15-0). Inglewood Ca.

Subjects & Sovereigns: The Grand Controversy Over Legal Sovereignty in Stuart England. Corin Weston & Janelle R. Greenberg. LC 80-40588. 400p. Date not set. 39.50 (ISBN 0-521-23272-4). Cambridge U Pr.

Subjugation & Dishonor: A Brief History of the Travail of the Native Americans. Philip Weeks & James B. Gidney. LC 79-28713. (Orig.). 1980. 12.50 (ISBN 0-89874-076-2); pap. 5.95 (ISBN 0-686-66018-8). Krieger.

Sublanguage: Studies on Language in Restricted Semantic Domains. Ed. by Richard Kittredge & John Lehrberger. (Foundations of Communications Ser.). 240p. 1980. text ed. 52.50x (ISBN 3-11-008244-6). De Gruyter.

Subliminal Politics: Myths & Mythmakers in America. D. Nimmo & J. Combs. 1980. 10.95 (ISBN 0-13-859116-4); pap. 4.95 (ISBN 0-13-859108-3). P-H.

Submarine Commander. Ben Bryant. (Bantam War Books). 272p. 1980. pap. 2.50 (ISBN 0-553-13665-8). Bantam.

Submarine Geology. 3rd ed. Francis P. Shepard. (Harper's Geoscience Ser.). 1973. text ed. 31.50 scp (ISBN 0-06-046091-1, HarpC). Har-Row.

Submarine Permafrost on the Alaskan Continental Shelf. Michael Vigdorchik. (Westview Special Studies in Earth Science). 1979. lib. bdg. 24.50x (ISBN 0-89158-659-8). Westview.

Submarine Telecommunication Systems. (IEE Conference Publication Ser.: No. 183). (Illus.). 43p. 1980. softcover 32.75 (ISBN 0-85296-211-8). Inst Elect Eng.

Submarines of World War Two. Erminio Bagnasco. LC 77-81973. Orig. Title: I Sommergibili. 1978. 24.95 (ISBN 0-87021-962-6). Naval Inst Pr.

Submicroscopic Cytochemistry, 2vols. Ed. by Isidore Gersh. Incl. Vol. 1. Protein & Nucleic Acids. 1974. 49.25 (ISBN 0-12-281401-0); Vol.2. Membranes,Mitochondria, & Connective Tissue. 1974. 36.50 (ISBN 0-12-281402-9). Set. 70.50 (ISBN 0-685-40610-5). Acad Pr.

Submicroscopic Ortho- & Patho-Morphology of the Liver. H. David. 1964. 195.00 (ISBN 0-08-010903-9). Pergamon.

Submillimetre Spectroscopy. G. W. Chantry. 1972. 53.00 (ISBN 0-12-170550-1). Acad Pr.

Submillimetre Waves & Their Applications: Proceedings. International Conference on Submillimetre Waves & Their Applications, 3rd, 1978. LC 79-40065. (Illus.). 1979. 46.00 (ISBN 0-08-023817-3). Pergamon.

Submitting. Churches Alive Inc. (Love One Another Bible Study). 1979. wkbk. 1.50 (ISBN 0-934396-04-3). Churches Alive.

Submolecular Biology & Cancer. Ciba Foundation. LC 79-10949. (Ciba Foundation Ser.: No. 67). 360p. 1979. 42.50 (ISBN 0-444-90078-0, Excerpta Medica). Elsevier.

Subnormal Mind. Cyril Burt. 1977. text ed. 14.95x o.p. (ISBN 0-19-261130-5). Oxford U Pr.

Subnuclear Components: Preparation & Fractionation. G. D. Birnie. 160p. 1976. 31.50 (ISBN 0-408-70729-1). Butterworths.

Subnuclear Resonance Science Unification Key: Old Data-New Concepts. Harold H. Belcher. 1977. 14.50 o.p. (ISBN 0-682-48884-4, University). Exposition.

Subscribe Now! Building Arts Audiences Through Dynamic Subscription Promotion. Danny Newman. LC 77-81452. (Illus.). 1977. text ed. 12.95x (ISBN 0-930452-00-3, Pub. by Theatre Comm); pap. text ed. 7.95x (ISBN 0-930452-01-1). Pub Ctr Cult Res.

Subscribe Now! Building Arts Audiences Through Dynamic Subscription Promotion. Danny Newman. LC 77-81452. (Illus.). 276p. 1977. 12.95x (ISBN 0-930452-00-3, Pub. by Theatre Comm); pap. 7.95x (ISBN 0-930452-01-1). Pub Ctr Cult Res.

Subsidies to Higher Education: The Issues. Ed. by Howard P. Tuckman & Edward L. Whalen. 320p. 1980. 27.95 (ISBN 0-03-055791-7). Praeger.

Subsidized Muse. D. Netzer. LC 77-25441. (Illus.). 1978. 24.95 (ISBN 0-521-21966-3). Cambridge U Pr.

Subsidized Muse. D. Netzer. LC 77-25441. (Illus.). 289p. 1980. pap. 9.95 (ISBN 0-521-29796-6). Cambridge U Pr.

Substance Abuse. Joyce Lowinson & Pedro Ruiz. (Illus.). 900p. 1981. write for info. (5210-1). Williams & Wilkins.

Substance Abuse & Psychiatric Illness: Proceedings of the Second Annual Coatesville--Jefferson Conference on Addiction. Ed. by Edward Gottheil et al. LC 79-25407. 224p. 1980. 28.00 (ISBN 0-08-025547-7). Pergamon.

Substance Abuse: Genetic, Perinatal, & Developmental Aspects. Ed. by Monique Braude. Date not set. text ed. write for info. (ISBN 0-89004-413-9). Raven.

Substance Abuse Problems. Sidney Cohen. 416p. 1981. text ed. 22.95 (ISBN 0-917724-18-6); pap. text ed. 13.95 (ISBN 0-917724-22-4). Haworth Pr.

Substance of Greek & Shakespearean Tragedy. Gerhard W. Kaiser. (Salzburg Studies in English Literature: Elizabethan & Renaissance Studies: No. 67). 1977. pap. text ed. 25.00x (ISBN 0-391-01442-0). Humanities.

Substance of Library Science. Jagdish S. Sharma. 1966. 8.75x o.p. (ISBN 0-210-26952-9). Asia.

Substance of Social Deviance. Victoria L. Swigert & Ronald A. Farrell. LC 78-23970. (Illus.). 1979. pap. text ed. 9.95x (ISBN 0-88284-059-2). Alfred Pub.

Substance P. Ed. by Ulf S. Von Euler & Bengt Pernow. LC 76-52600. (Nobel Symposium Ser: No. 37). 1977. 31.50 (ISBN 0-89004-100-8). Raven.

Substance P, Vol. 1, 1977. P. Skrabanek & D. Powell. 1978. 21.60 (ISBN 0-88831-019-6). Eden Med Res.

Substance P, Vol. 2. Petr Skrabanek & David Powell. Ed. by D. F. Horrobin. LC 80-646426. (Annual Research Reviews Ser.). 175p. 1980. 26.00 (ISBN 0-88831-073-0). Eden Med Res.

Substanz und Qualitaet: Ein Beitrag zur Interpretation der plotinischen Traktate Vi 1, 2, und 3. Klaus Wurm. LC 72-81572. (Quellen und Studien zur Philosophie, Vol. 5). 276p. 1973. 41.75x (ISBN 3-11-001899-3). De Gruyter.

Substitute. Sallie L. Bell. 1976. pap. 2.25 (ISBN 0-310-21042-9). Zondervan.

Substitute. Ann Lawler. LC 77-23303. (Illus.). 40p. (gr. k-4). 1977. 5.95 o.s.i. (ISBN 0-8193-0902-8, Four Winds); PLB 5.41 o.s.i. (ISBN 0-8193-0903-6). Schol Bk Serv.
Substitute Bride. Lynna Cooper. Bd. with My Treasure, My Love. 1981. pap. 2.25 (ISBN 0-451-09739-4, E9739, Sig). NAL.
Substitute Bride. Dorothy Mack. 1977. pap. 1.25 o.s.i. (ISBN 0-440-18375-8). Dell.
Substitute Natural Gas: Manufacture & Properties. W. L. Lom & A. F. Williams. 1976. 44.95 (ISBN 0-470-15018-1). Halsted Pr.
Substitutes for Asbestos, Gb-061: What-Who-How Much. Business Communications Co. 1980. 850.00 (ISBN 0-89336-277-8). BCC.
Substoichiometry in Radiochemical Analysis. J. Ruzicka & J. Stary. 1968. 27.00 (ISBN 0-08-012442-9). Pergamon.
Subsurface Exploration for Underground Excavation & Heavy Construction. Compiled by American Society of Civil Engineers. 414p. 1974. pap. text ed. 13.50 (ISBN 0-87262-105-7). Am Soc Civil Eng.
Subsurface Investigation for Design & Construction for Foundations of Buildings. Compiled by American Society of Civil Engineers. (Manuel & Report on Engineering Practice Ser.: No. 56). 68p. 1976. pap. text ed. 6.00 (ISBN 0-87262-230-4). Am Soc Civil Eng.
Subsurface Space--Environment Protection, Low Cost Storage, Energy Savings: Proceedings of the International Symposium, Stockholm, Sweden, June 23-27, 1980, 3 vols. Ed. by M. Bergman. (Illus.). 1500p. 1980. 250.00 (ISBN 0-08-026136-1). Pergamon.
Subterranean Horses. Yannis Ritsos. Tr. by Minas Savvas from Greek. LC 80-83220. (International Poetry: Vol. 3). (Illus.). xii, 63p. 1980. 10.95 (ISBN 0-8214-0579-9); pap. 6.95 (ISBN 0-8214-0580-2). Ohio U Pr.
Subterranean Hydrology. G. Kovacs et al. 1981. 45.00 (ISBN 0-918334-35-7). WRP.
Subterranean World. Timothy G. Beckley. 1971. pap. 6.95 o.p. (ISBN 0-685-04796-2). Saucerian.
Subtle Art of Choosing Early & Late Leaders in the Operations of the Stock Market. William D. Gann. (Illus.). 123p. 1981. 49.85 (ISBN 0-918968-97-6). Inst Econ Finan.
Subtle Brains & Lissom Fingers. 3rd ed. Andrew Wynter. LC 67-27868. (Social History Reference Ser.). (Illus.). 1968. Repr. of 1863 ed. 15.00 (ISBN 0-8103-3267-1). Gale.
Subtle Revolution: Women at Work. Ed. by Ralph E. Smith. 1979. 15.00 (ISBN 0-87766-259-2, 26800); pap. 7.50 (ISBN 0-87766-260-6, 26700). Urban Inst.
Subtraction 10-0. Kitty Wehrli. (Michigan Arithmetic Program Ser.). (gr. 2-3). 1976. wkbk. 7.00 (ISBN 0-89039-176-9). Ann Arbor Pubs.
Subtraction 20-10, Levels 1 & 2. Kitty Wehrli. (Michigan Arithmetic Program). (gr. 2-3). 1976. Level 1. wkbk 7.00x ea. Level 2. Ann Arbor Pubs.
Suburb: Neighborhood & Community in Forest Park, Ohio, 1935-1976. Zane L. Miller. LC 80-21828. (Twentieth-Century America Ser.). 256p. 1981. 18.50x (ISBN 0-87049-289-6). U of Tenn Pr.
Suburban Economic Network: Economic Activity, Resource Use, & the Great Sprawl. Ed. by John E. Ullmann. LC 76-12883. (Special Studies). 1977. text ed. 28.50 (ISBN 0-275-23560-2). Praeger.
Suburban Environment & Women. Donald N. Rothblatt et al. LC 78-19797. (Praeger Special Studies). 210p. 1979. 25.95 (ISBN 0-03-041031-2). Praeger.
Suburban Growth: Geographical Processes at the Edge of the Western City. J. H. Johnson. LC 73-8195. 272p. 1974. 31.75 (ISBN 0-471-44390-5, Pub. by Wiley-Interscience). Wiley.
Suburban Myth. Scott Donaldson. LC 77-79191. 1969. 17.00x (ISBN 0-231-03192-0); pap. 5.00x (ISBN 0-231-08659-8). Columbia U Pr.
Suburban Press: A Separate Journalism. Hal Lister. 1975. pap. text ed. 5.25x (ISBN 0-87543-124-0). Lucas.
Suburban Tokyo: A Comparative Study in Politics & Social Change. Gary D. Allinson. 1979. 20.00x (ISBN 0-520-03768-5). U of Cal Pr.
Suburban Wilderness. William J. Watkins. (Illus.). 192p. 1981. 9.95 (ISBN 0-399-12552-3). Putnam.
Suburban Woman: Her Changing Role in the Church. Mary G. Durkin. 180p. 1975. 6.95 (ISBN 0-8164-1200-6). Crossroad NY.
Suburbanization & the Ciy. Thomas M. Stanback, Jr. & Richard V. Knight. LC 76-472. (Conservation of Human Resources Ser.: No. 2). 256p. 1976. text ed. 19.50 (ISBN 0-916672-01-8). Allanheld.
Suburbia: A Guide to Information Sources. Ed. by Joseph Zikmund & Deborah E. Dennis. LC 78-10523. (Urban Studies Information Guide Ser: Vol. 9). 1979. 30.00 (ISBN 0-8103-1435-5). Gale.
Suburbia: Civic Denial. Robert Goldston. LC 76-99120. (Portraits in Urban Civilization Ser). (gr. 9 up). 1970. 5.95g o.s.i. (ISBN 0-02-736380-5). Macmillan.
Suburbia: The American Dream & Dilemma. Ed. by Phillip C. Dolce. LC 76-2838. pap. 2.95 o.p. (ISBN 0-385-01336-1). Doubleday.
Subverse: Rhymes for Our Times. Marya Mannes & Robert Osborn. (Illus.). 1959. 4.50 o.s.i. (ISBN 0-8076-0072-5). Braziller.
Subversion & Social Change in Colombia. Orlando Fals-Borda. Tr. by Jacqueline Quayle. LC 69-19458. 1969. 20.00x (ISBN 0-231-03148-3). Columbia U Pr.
Subversive. D. O. Schultz & S. K. Scott. (Illus.). 120p. 1973. 8.75 (ISBN 0-398-02660-2). C C Thomas.
Subversive Science: Essays Toward an Ecology of Man. Ed. by Paul Shepard & Daniel McKinley. LC 69-15029. (Illus., Orig.). 1969. pap. text ed. 11.50 (ISBN 0-395-05399-4). HM.
Subversive Vegetarian. Michael Cox & Dresda Crocket. LC 80-635. (Illus.). 129p. (Orig.). 1980. pap. 3.95 (ISBN 0-912800-83-6). Woodbridge Pr.
Subversive Vegetarian. Michael Cox & Desda Crockett. 128p. (Orig.). 1980. pap. 3.95 o.s.i. (ISBN 0-7225-0559-0). Newcastle Pub.
Subway Stalker. Lou Cameron. (Orig.). 1980. pap. 2.50 (ISBN 0-440-17873-8). Dell.
Subway Survival: The Art of Self Defense on American Public Transit Facility. Bradley J. Steiner. 1980. pap. 7.95. Loompanics.
Subway to Samarkand. J. R. Humphreys. 1979. pap. 2.25 o.p. (ISBN 0-425-03938-2). Berkley Pub.
Succeed as a Job Applicant. Gordon G. Barnewall. LC 75-18877. (Career Guidance Ser.). 160p. (YA) 1976. pap. 3.50 (ISBN 0-668-03861-6). Arco.
Succeed in Spite of Yourself. Everett T. Suters. 1974. pap. 3.95 o.p. (ISBN 0-8015-7314-9). Dutton.
Succeeding in the World of Work. rev. ed. Grady Kimbrell & Ben S. Vineyard. (gr. 10-12). 1975. text ed. 14.64 (ISBN 0-87345-525-8); filmstrip set 330.00 (ISBN 0-685-04243-X). McKnight.
Success & Failure. Eugene Raudsepp. (Best Thoughts Ser.). (Illus.). 80p. (Orig.). 1981. pap. 2.50 (ISBN 0-8431-0390-6). Price Stern.
Success & Failure in Analysis: Proceedings. International Congress for Analytical Psychology, 5th. Ed. by Gerhard Adler. LC 73-76973. (Illus.). 231p. 1974. 15.00 o.p. (ISBN 0-913430-21-8). C G Jung Foun.
Success & Failure in Israeli Elementary Education. Avram Minkowich. 400p. 1981. 29.95 (ISBN 0-87855-370-3). Transaction Bks.
Success & Survival in the Family Owned Business. Pat Alcorn. 256p. 1981. 17.95 (ISBN 0-07-000961-9). McGraw.
Success As a Consultant: The Complete Guide. Sandra L. Dean. 225p. 1981. 14.95 (ISBN 0-913864-61-7). Enterprise Del.
Success Factor. Robert Sharpe & David Lewis. 1979. pap. 2.95 (ISBN 0-446-93980-3). Warner Bks.
Success Fantasy. Anthony Campolo. 1980. pap. 3.50 (ISBN 0-88207-796-1). Victor Bks.
Success Fearing Personality. Donnah Canavan-Gumpert et al. LC 76-42853. 1978. 19.95 (ISBN 0-669-01075-8). Lexington Bks.
Success Guide to Writing for TV & Motion Pictures: Learn the Business Side of Show Business. Arthur C. Simon. LC 78-55986. (Illus.). 1978. softcover 12.95 o.p. (ISBN 0-930490-03-7). Future Shop.
Success in Athletics. Carl Johnson. (Success Sportbooks Ser.). (Illus.). 1977. 9.95 (ISBN 0-7195-3375-9). Transatlantic.
Success in British History Seventeen Sixty to Nineteen Fourteen. Peter Lane. (Success Ser). (Illus.). 1978. pap. 9.95 (ISBN 0-7195-3483-6). Transatlantic.
Success in Football (Soccer) Mike Smith. (Illus.). 96p. 1974. 9.95 (ISBN 0-7195-2822-4). Transatlantic.
Success in Golf. Ken Redford & Nick Tremayne. (Success Sportbooks Ser.). (Illus.). 1977. 9.95 (ISBN 0-7195-2862-3). Transatlantic.
Success in Literature. William M. Colles & Henry Cresswell. 360p. 1980. Repr. of 1911 ed. lib. bdg. 20.00 (ISBN 0-89760-116-5). Telegraph Bks.
Success in Marriage. David R. Mace. (YA) (gr. 9 up). 1965. pap. 1.95 o.p. (ISBN 0-687-40554-8, 405548, Apex). Abingdon.
Success in Swimming. John Hogg. (Success Sportbooks Ser.). (Illus.). 1977. 9.95 (ISBN 0-7195-3376-7). Transatlantic.
Success in Volleyball. Don Anthony. (Illus.). 80p. 1974. 10.95 (ISBN 0-7195-2584-5). Transatlantic.
Success or Failure Begins in the Early School Years. Mary Lu Kost. (Amer. Lec. Special Education Ser.). (Illus.). 500p. 1972. 22.75 (ISBN 0-398-02334-4); pap. 19.50 (ISBN 0-398-02486-3). C C Thomas.
Success Oriented Supervision. rev. ed. Ed. by Albert St. Denis. 1980. 44.15 (ISBN 0-87771-019-8). Grad School.
Success Secrets of Successful Women. Ed. by Dottie Walters. LC 78-68596. (Illus.). 276p. 1978. 11.95 (ISBN 0-8119-0339-7, Pub. by Royal CBC). Fell.
Success Signs. Marlene M. Rathgeb. (Illus.). 224p. 1981. 10.95 (ISBN 0-312-77485-0); pap. 5.95 (ISBN 0-312-77486-9). St Martin.
Success with Mathematics I. Robert E. Eicholz & Phares G. O'Daffer. (Low Track Ser). (gr. 7-9). 1972. pap. text ed. 10.52 o.p. (ISBN 0-201-01580-3, Sch Div). A-W.
Success with Mathematics I: Diagnostic Tests. 2nd ed. Robert E. Eicholz & Phares G. O'Daffer. (Low Track Ser). (gr. 7-9). 1972. 8.72 o.p. (ISBN 0-201-01585-4, Sch Div). A-W.
Success with Mathematics II: Achievement & Diagnostic Tests. 2nd ed. Robert E. Eicholz & Phares G. O'Daffer. (Low Track Ser). (gr. 7-9). 1972. Achievement Tests. 8.72 o.p. (ISBN 0-201-01594-3, Sch Div); Diagnostic Tests. 8.72 o.p. (ISBN 0-201-01595-1). A-W.
Success with People: The Theory Z Approach to Mutual Achievement. Willard I. Zangwill. 1976. pap. text ed. 10.95 (ISBN 0-256-01864-2). Irwin.
Success Without Compromise. Richard H. LeTourneau. 1977. pap. 3.50 (ISBN 0-88207-757-0). Victor Bks.
Success: You Can Make It Happen. Lila Swell. 1978. pap. 1.75 (ISBN 0-515-04711-2). Jove Pubns.
Successful Advertising Management. Henry Obermeyer. LC 69-18719. 1969. 18.50 o.p. (ISBN 0-07-047591-1, P&RB). McGraw.
Successful Alternate Energy Methods. James D. Ritchie. Ed. by Peggy Frohn. LC 80-13103. (Successful Ser.). (Illus.). 1980. 14.95 (ISBN 0-89999-000-2); pap. 8.95 (ISBN 0-89999-001-0). Structures Pub.
Successful & Masonry. Robert Scharff. Ed. by Virginia A. Case. (Successful Ser.). 144p. 1981. 18.95 (ISBN 0-89999-023-1); pap. 8.95 (ISBN 0-89999-024-X). Structures Pub.
Successful Bathrooms. 2nd rev. ed. Joseph Schram. Ed. by Shirley M. Horowitz & Peggy Frohn. LC 80-183. (Successful Series). (Illus.). 1980. 14.95 (ISBN 0-912336-97-8); pap. 6.95 (ISBN 0-912336-98-6). Structures Pub.
Successful Bed Book. John Boeschen. Ed. by Virginia A. Case. (Successful Ser.). (Illus.). 200p. 1981. 18.95 (ISBN 0-89999-030-4); pap. 8.95 (ISBN 0-89999-031-2). Structures Pub.
Successful Bluefishing. Henry Lyman. LC 73-93528. (Illus.). 120p. 1974. 15.00 (ISBN 0-87742-041-6). Intl Marine.
Successful Bonsai Growing. Peter Adams. (Illus.). 102p. 1980. pap. 6.95 (ISBN 0-7063-5376-5, Pub. by Ward Lock England). Hippocrene Bks.
Successful Bridge Partnerships. Pat Sheinwold. 208p. 1981. 4.95 (ISBN 0-686-69323-X). Cornerstone.
Successful Building Primer. Robert Taylor. Ed. by Virginia Case. LC 80-19490. (Successful Ser.). (Illus.). 176p. 1980. pap. 6.95 (ISBN 0-89999-010-X). Structures Pub.
Successful Business Policies. Gerald D. Newbould & George A. Luffman. LC 78-70561. 1979. 25.95 (ISBN 0-03-049386-2). Praeger.
Successful Business Resumes. Ernest Gray. 265p. 1981. 10.95 (ISBN 0-8436-0771-8). CBI Pub.
Successful Businesses for the Abandoned Service Station. A. L. Kerth. (Illus.). 1981. 28.00x (ISBN 0-9601188-2-9). A L Kerth.
Successful Catering. Bernard R. Splaver. LC 75-30645. 1975. 16.95 (ISBN 0-8436-2061-7). CBI Pub.
Successful Celestial Navigation with H.O. 229. G. Dale Dunlap. LC 76-8771. (Illus.). 1977. 19.95 (ISBN 0-87742-075-0). Intl Marine.
Successful Children's Rooms. Joseph Schram. Ed. by Shirley Horowitz. LC 79-11967. (Successful Ser.). (Illus.). 1979. 13.95 (ISBN 0-912336-89-7); pap. 6.95 (ISBN 0-912336-90-0). Structures Pub.
Successful Cold Climate Gardening. Lewis Hill. 288p. (Orig.). 1981. 14.95 (ISBN 0-8289-0421-9). Greene.
Successful Commodity Futures Trading. 2nd ed. T. Watling & J. Morley. 244p. 1974. text ed. 29.50x (ISBN 0-220-66340-8, Pub. by Busn Bks England). Renouf.
Successful Communication & Effective Speaking. Bennett. pap. 3.95 (ISBN 0-13-860437-1, Parker). P-H.
Successful Communication in Business. B. Elizabeth Pryse. 272p. 1981. pap. 10.95x (ISBN 0-631-11601-X, Pub. by Basil Blackwell). Biblio Dist.
Successful Construction Cost Control. H. N. Ahuja. LC 80-10156. (Construction Management & Engineering Ser.). 1980. 33.95 (ISBN 0-471-05378-3, Pub. by Wiley-Interscience). Wiley.
Successful Consultant's Guide to Fee Setting. 167p. 1980. text ed. 34.00 (ISBN 0-930686-11-X). Bermont Bks.
Successful Consultant's Guide to Winning Government Contracts. Consultant's Library Editors. 122p. pap. write for info. leatherette (ISBN 0-930686-12-8). Bermont Bks.
Successful Custom Interiors. Jane Cornell. Ed. by Shirley M. Horowitz. LC 79-15910. (Successful Ser.). (Illus.). 1979. 13.95 (ISBN 0-912336-87-0); pap. 6.95 (ISBN 0-912336-88-9). Structures Pub.
Successful Deaf Americans. Darlene Toole. 88p. 1979. 4.95 (ISBN 0-86575-118-8). Dormac.
Successful Dieter's Sure-Fire Dieting Tips. Consumer-Aid Group. Ed. by Kathe Grooms. (Consumer-Aid Bk.). (Illus.). 130p. 1981. pap. 3.95 (ISBN 0-915658-34-8). Meadowbrook Pr.
Successful Drugstore: How to Build a Million Dollar Business. Thomas E. Coleman. 1973. 32.95 o.p. (ISBN 0-13-860734-6). P-H.
Successful Endurance Riding: The Ultimate Test of Horsemanship. Patricia Ingram & Lewis Hollander. 192p. 1981. 11.95 (ISBN 0-8289-0423-5). Greene.
Successful Family & Recreation Rooms. Jane Cornell. LC 77-719. (Illus.). 136p. 1977. 13.95 (ISBN 0-912336-42-0); pap. 6.95 (ISBN 0-912336-43-9). Structures Pub.
Successful Family Organizations, Record Keeping, & Genealogy in Family Activities. 3rd ed. Arthur Wallace & Shirley Bousfield. (Illus.). 189p. 1978. pap. 3.95 (ISBN 0-937892-02-5). LL Co.
Successful Garage-Yard Sale. M. L. Chaney. 1.00 o.p. (ISBN 0-686-17207-8). Sandollar Pr.
Successful Garages & Carports. Joseph Schram. Ed. by Virginia Case. LC 80-23515. (Successful Ser.). (Illus.). 128p. 1980. 15.95 (ISBN 0-89999-017-7); pap. 6.95 (ISBN 0-89999-018-5). Structures Pub.
Successful Handling of Casualty Claims. Pat Magarick. LC 73-91720. 1974. 37.50 (ISBN 0-87632-168-6). Boardman.
Successful Home Additions. Joseph F. Schram. LC 77-8872. (Successful Book). (Illus.). 1977. 13.95 (ISBN 0-912336-46-3); pap. 6.95 (ISBN 0-912336-47-1). Structures Pub.
Successful Home Appliances: The 1980's Energy & Money Saving Guide. William F. Keefe. Ed. by Virginia Case. (Successful Ser.). (Illus.). 1981. 18.95 (ISBN 0-89999-019-3); pap. 8.95 (ISBN 0-89999-020-7). Structures Pub.
Successful Home Decorating. Brenda McClellan. Ed. by Virginia A. Case. (Successful Ser.). (Illus.). 136p. 1981. 18.95 (ISBN 0-89999-021-5); pap. 7.95 (ISBN 0-89999-022-3). Structures Pub.
Successful Home Electrical Wiring. Larry Mueller. Ed. by Virginia Case. LC 80-18678. (Successful Ser.). (Illus.). 144p. 1980. 15.95 (ISBN 0-89999-008-8); pap. 6.95 (ISBN 0-89999-009-6). Structures Pub.
Successful Home Greenhouses. William Scheller. LC 76-51747. (Illus.). 134p. 1977. 13.95 (ISBN 0-912336-40-4); pap. 6.95 (ISBN 0-912336-41-2). Structures Pub.
Successful Home Plans for the Eighties. Ed. by Peggy Frohn. LC 80-7498. (Successful Ser.). (Illus.). 1980. 15.95 (ISBN 0-89999-002-9); pap. 6.95 (ISBN 0-89999-003-7). Structures Pub.
Successful Home Repair: When Not to Call the Contractor. Gary Paulsen. LC 78-9107. (Illus.). 1978. 13.95 (ISBN 0-912336-69-2); pap. 6.95 (ISBN 0-912336-70-6). Structures Pub.
Successful Homeowner's Tools. James Ritchie. (Successful Ser.). 192p. 1980. 14.95 (ISBN 0-912336-85-4); pap. 7.95 (ISBN 0-912336-86-2). Structures Pub.
Successful How to Build Your Own Home. 2nd ed. Robert C. Reschke. LC 79-91999. (Successful Ser.). (Illus.). 1979. 15.95 (ISBN 0-912336-93-5); pap. 9.95 (ISBN 0-912336-94-3). Structures Pub.
Successful Industrial Real Estate Brokerage. 2nd ed. Grubb & Ellis Company. 327p. (Orig.). 1980. pap. 49.95 (ISBN 0-88462-317-3). Real Estate Ed Co.
Successful Industrial Real Estate Brokerage. 2nd ed. Real Estate Education Company & Grub & Ellis Commercial Brokerage Co. 327p. 1980. 3-ring binder 49.95 o.p. (ISBN 0-695-81501-6). Real Estate Ed Co.
Successful Landlording. Kathleen Abrams & Lawrence Abrams. Ed. by Virginia Case. LC 80-36678. (Successful Ser.). (Illus.). 144p. 1980. 15.95 (ISBN 0-89999-006-1); pap. 6.95 (ISBN 0-89999-007-X). Structures Pub.
Successful Landscaping. Raymond Felice. LC 77-16624. (Illus.). 1978. 13.95 (ISBN 0-912336-55-2); pap. 6.95 (ISBN 0-912336-56-0). Structures Pub.

Successful Leasing & Selling of Office Property. Real Estate Education Co. & Grubb & Ellis Commercial Brokerage Co. 1980. 3-ring binder 49.95 (ISBN 0-88462-312-2). Real Estate Ed Co.

Successful Leasing & Selling of Retail Property. Real Estate Education Company Staff & Grubb & Ellis Company. 250p. 1980. 49.95 (ISBN 0-88462-315-7). Real Estate Ed Co.

Successful Living Rooms. Jay W. Hedden. LC 77-26025. (Illus.). 1978. 13.95 (ISBN 0-912336-60-9); pap. 6.95 (ISBN 0-912336-61-7). Structures Pub.

Successful Log Homes. James D. Ritchie. LC 78-15308. 1978. 13.95 (ISBN 0-912336-71-4); pap. 6.95 (ISBN 0-912336-72-2). Structures Pub.

Successful Management by Objectives: An Action Manual. Karl Albrecht. LC 77-14971. (Illus.). 1978. 14.95 (ISBN 0-13-863266-9, Spec); pap. 4.95 (ISBN 0-13-863258-8, Spec). P-H.

Successful Management Strategies for Small Business. Harvey C. Krentzman. (Illus.). 208p. 1981. text ed. 13.95 o.p. (ISBN 0-13-863126-3, Spec); pap. text ed. 6.95 (ISBN 0-13-863118-2, Spec). P-H.

Successful Marketing for Small Business. William A. Cohen & Marshall E. Reddick. 364p. 1981. 17.95 (ISBN 0-8144-5611-1). Am Mgmt.

Successful Marriage: A Principles Approach. Wesley R. Burr. 1976. text ed. 17.95x (ISBN 0-256-01789-1). Dorsey.

Successful Movement Challenges: Movement Activities for the Developing Child. Jack Capon. Ed. by Frank Alexander & Diane Alexander. (Illus.). 129p. 1981. pap. 7.95 (ISBN 0-915256-07-X). Front Row.

Successful Parole. Franklin H. Evrard. 140p. 1971. 12.75 (ISBN 0-398-00532-X). C C Thomas.

Successful Personnel Recruiting & Selection: Within EEO-Affirmative Action Guidelines. new ed. Erwin S. Stanton. LC 77-21384. 1977. 15.95 (ISBN 0-8144-5450-X). Am Mgmt.

Successful Playhouses. John Boeschen. LC 79-16230. (Successful Ser.). (Illus.). 1979. 13.95 (ISBN 0-912336-91-9); pap. 6.95 (ISBN 0-912336-92-7). Structures Pub.

Successful Plumbing. Robert Scharff. LC 80-24212. (Successful Ser.). (Illus.). 144p. 1980. 15.95 (ISBN 0-89999-014-2); pap. 6.95 (ISBN 0-89999-015-0). Structures Pub.

Successful Policy Implementation. Ed. by Daniel Mazmanian & Paul Sabatier. (Orig.). 1980. pap. 5.00 (ISBN 0-918592-37-2). Policy Studies.

Successful Praying. F. J. Huegel. 1967. pap. 1.95 (ISBN 0-87123-453-X, 200453). Bethany Fell.

Successful Pregnancy. Gary Null. (Orig.). 1976. pap. 1.50 (ISBN 0-515-03622-6). Jove Pubns.

Successful Project Management. W. J. Taylor & T. F. Watling. 269p. 1979. text ed. 29.50x (ISBN 0-220-67004-8, Pub. by Busn Bks England). Renouf.

Successful Project Management: A Step-by-Step Approach with Practical Examples. Milton D. Rosenau, Jr. LC 80-24720. 350p. 1981. text ed. 24.95 (ISBN 0-534-97977-7). Lifetime Learn.

Successful Putting It All Together. Robert Scharff. Ed. by Hope Diefenderfer. LC 79-67828. (Successful Ser.). (Illus.). 1980. 14.95 (ISBN 0-912336-95-1); pap. 7.95 (ISBN 0-912336-96-X). Structures Pub.

Successful Retail Sales. K. Mills & J. Paul. 1979. pap. 12.95 (ISBN 0-13-869602-0). P-H.

Successful Retail Security. Ed. by Mary Margaret Hughes. LC 73-91244. 320p. 1974. 15.95 (ISBN 0-913708-15-1). Butterworths.

Successful Reviving the Older Home. rev. ed. Larry Mueller. Ed. by Virginia Case. (Successful Ser.). (Illus.). 164p. Date not set. price not set (ISBN 0-89999-012-6); pap. price not set (ISBN 0-89999-013-4). Structures Pub.

Successful Roofing & Siding. Robert C. Reschke. LC 76-54145. (Illus.). 160p. 1977. 14.95 (ISBN 0-912336-26-9); pap. 7.95 (ISBN 0-912336-27-7). Structures Pub.

Successful Rules of Artistic Composition. Peter Gianpietri. (Illus.). 1979. deluxe ed. 49.75 (ISBN 0-930582-42-X). Gloucester Art.

Successful Sailing. Lou D'Alpuget. LC 77-180469. (Illus.). 80p. 1973. pap. 2.95 o.s.i. (ISBN 0-02-028200-1, Collier). Macmillan.

Successful Secretary. Eleanor Macdonald & Julia Little. (Illus.). 176p. 1980. pap. 9.95x (ISBN 0-7121-1976-0). Intl Ideas.

Successful Selling. Jay Diamond & Gerald Pintel. (Illus.). 384p. 1980. text ed. 14.95 (ISBN 0-8359-7246-1). Reston.

Successful Selling Skills for Small Business. D. M. Brownstone. 112p. 1978. 4.95 (ISBN 0-471-04029-0). Wiley.

Successful Shelves & Built-Ins. Jay Hedden. LC 78-27234. 1979. 13.95 (ISBN 0-912336-77-3); pap. 6.95 (ISBN 0-912336-78-1). Structures Pub.

Successful Shotgun Shooting. Andrew A. Montague. LC 70-150384. (Illus.). 1971. 8.95 (ISBN 0-87691-034-7). Winchester Pr.

Successful Small Business Management. Forest H. Frantz. LC 77-14385. 1978. text ed. 17.95 (ISBN 0-13-872119-X). P-H.

Successful Small Business Management. rev. ed. Curtis E. Tate, Jr. et al. 1978. 18.50x (ISBN 0-256-02074-4). Business Pubns.

Successful Small Business Management. Leon Wortman. (AMACOM Executive Books). 1978. pap. 5.95 (ISBN 0-8144-7503-5). Am Mgmt.

Successful Small Farms: Building Plans & Methods. Herbert T. Leavy. LC 78-7987. 1978. 14.00 (ISBN 0-912336-67-6); pap. 7.95 (ISBN 0-912336-68-4). Structures Pub.

Successful Space Saving at Home. Patrick J. Galvin. LC 76-27683. (Illus.). 1976. 12.00 (ISBN 0-912336-30-7); pap. 5.95 (ISBN 0-912336-31-5). Structures Pub.

Successful Stock Selecting Methods in Wall Street. William D. Gann. (New Stock Market Reference Library). (Illus.). 118p. 1981. 49.85 (ISBN 0-918968-96-8). Inst Econ Finan.

Successful Striped Bass Fishing. Frank T. Moss. LC 73-93527. (Illus.). 192p. 1974. 15.00 (ISBN 0-87742-040-8). Intl Marine.

Successful Student Teaching: A Handbook for Elementary & Secondary Student Teachers. Fillmer Hevener, Jr. LC 80-69332. 125p. 1981. perfect bdg. 8.95 (ISBN 0-86548-040-0). Century Twenty One.

Successful Student's Handbook: A Step-by-Step Guide to Study Skills. Rita Phipps. LC 80-54427. (Illus.). 160p. (Orig.). 1981. pap. price not set (ISBN 0-295-95813-8). U of Wash Pr.

Successful Studios & Work Centers. Margaret Davidson. LC 76-52980. (Illus.). 144p. 1977. 12.00 (ISBN 0-912336-36-6); pap. 5.95 (ISBN 0-912336-37-4). Structures Pub.

Successful Sunday School & Teachers Guidebook. new ed. Elmer Towns. LC 75-23009. (Illus.). 430p. 1976. pap. 10.95 (ISBN 0-88419-118-4). Creation Hse.

Successful Tax Planning. Edward Mendlowitz. LC 79-25586. 1980. flexible bdg. 50.00 (ISBN 0-932648-07-X). Boardroom.

Successful Teaching Ideas. Marie Chapman. LC 74-82558. (Illus.). 96p. 1975. pap. 5.50 (ISBN 0-87239-032-2, 3195). Standard Pub.

Successful Techniques for Criminal Trials. F. Lee Bailey & Henry B. Rothblatt. LC 72-161700. (Criminal Law Library). 1971. 47.50 (ISBN 0-686-14485-6). Lawyers Co-Op.

Successful Techniques for Higher Profits. Robert Rachlin. 260p. 1981. 16.95 (ISBN 0-938712-02-0). Marr Pubns.

Successful Techniques for Solving Employee Compensation Problems. Don. R. Marshall. LC 77-17964. 1978. 26.95 (ISBN 0-471-57297-7, Pub. by Wiley-Interscience). Wiley.

Successful Track & Field. Ron Clarke & Raelene Boyle. LC 76-51186. (Illus.). (gr. 7 up). 1977. 9.95 (ISBN 0-8069-4116-2); PLB 9.29 (ISBN 0-8069-4117-0). Sterling.

Successful Treatment of Stuttering. Ann Irwin. 1981. 9.95 (ISBN 0-8027-0671-1). Walker & Co.

Successful Vacation Homes. Ronald Derven & Ellen Rand. LC 78-31270. 1979. 13.95 (ISBN 0-912336-79-X); pap. 6.95 (ISBN 0-912336-80-3). Structures Pub.

Successful Wallcoverings & Decoration. 2nd ed. Abel Banov & Marie-Jeanne Lytle. Ed. by Virginia A. Case. (Successful Ser.). (Illus.). 136p. 1981. 17.95 (ISBN 0-89999-021-5); pap. 7.95 (ISBN 0-89999-022-3). Structures Pub.

Successful Waterfowling. Zack Taylor. 288p. (Orig.). 1981. pap. 13.95 (ISBN 0-8117-2147-7). Stackpole.

Successful Wood Book: Selection & Use, Fastening & Finishing. Rachel Bard. LC 78-15547. 1978. 13.95 (ISBN 0-912336-73-0); pap. 6.95 (ISBN 0-912336-74-9). Structures Pub.

Successful Writing: A Short Course for Professionals. G. T. Vardaman & P. B. Vardaman. 1977. 39.95 (ISBN 0-471-02428-7). Wiley.

Succession Aux Fiefs Dans les Coutumes Flamandes. Emile Bellette. LC 80-1997. 1981. Repr. of 1926 ed. 23.50 (ISBN 0-404-18553-3). AMS Pr.

Succession in the Muslim Family. N. J. Coulson. 1971. 44.00 (ISBN 0-521-07852-0). Cambridge U Pr.

Succession to High Office. Jack Goody. LC 79-52487. (Cambridge Papers in Social Anthropology: No. 4). (Illus.). 1979. pap. 7.95x (ISBN 0-521-29732-X). Cambridge U Pr.

Successors of Genghis Khan. Tr. by John A. Boyle from Pers. LC 70-135987. (Illus.). 1971. 20.00x (ISBN 0-231-03351-6). Columbia U Pr.

Succubus. Kenneth R. Johnson. (Orig.). 1980. pap. 2.50 (ISBN 0-440-17716-2). Dell.

Succulents of Southern Africa. B. Barkuizen. 1980. 60.00x (Pub. by Bailey & Swinton South Africa). State Mutual Bk.

Sucessful Problem Management. Michael Sanderson. LC 78-21050. 1978. 19.95 (ISBN 0-471-04871-2, Pub. by Wiley-Interscience). Wiley.

Sucessful Swimming Pools. 2nd ed. Ronald Derven & Carol Nichols. Ed. by Virginia A. Case. (Successful Ser.). (Illus.). 128p. 1981. 18.95 (ISBN 0-89999-025-8); pap. 8.95 (ISBN 0-89999-026-6). Structures Pub.

Such a Pretty Face: Being Fat in America. Marcia Millman. 1981. pap. 2.75 (ISBN 0-425-04849-7). Berkley Pub.

Such Good Friends. Lois Gould. 1970. 6.95 o.p. (ISBN 0-394-43855-8). Random.

Such Holy Song: Music As Idea, Form, & Image in the Poetry of William Blake. B. H. Fairchild, Jr. LC 79-92809. 1980. 11.00x (ISBN 0-87338-238-2). Kent St U Pr.

Such Is the Way of the World. Benjamin Elkin. LC 68-11662. (Illus.). (gr. k-3). 1968. 5.95 o.s.i. (ISBN 0-8193-0347-X, Four Winds); PLB 5.41 o.s.i. (ISBN 0-8193-0348-8). Schol Bk Serv.

Such Sweet Compulsion, the Autobiography of Geraldine Farrar. Geraldine Farrar. LC 70-100656. (Music Ser). 1970. Repr. of 1938 ed. lib. bdg. 25.00 (ISBN 0-306-71863-4). Da Capo.

Suche Nach Gott, Bk I. ARE Study Group No. 1. Tr. by Helge F. Kronberger from Eng. 135p. (Ger.). 1978. pap. 10.00 (ISBN 0-87604-131-4). ARE Pr.

Sucker's Visit to the Mammoth Cave. Ralph S. Thompson. Repr. of 1870 ed. 7.00 (ISBN 0-914264-33-8). Zephyrus Pr.

Sudan. Nick Worrall. (Illus.). 136p. 1980. 30.00 (ISBN 0-7043-2242-0, Pub. by Quqrtet England). Horizon.

Sudan Under Wingate: Administration in the Anglo-Egyptian Sudan, 1899 to 1916. Gabriel Warburg. (Illus.). 245p. 1971. 26.00x (ISBN 0-7146-2612-0, F Cass Co). Biblio Dist.

Sudden Death. Peter Brennan. 1979. pap. 2.25 o.s.i. (ISBN 0-515-04851-8). Jove Pubns.

Sudden Insurrection: Twelve Short Stories. Philip L. Sawyer. LC 75-126427. 1970. pap. 2.75 o.p. (ISBN 0-911308-02-4). P Sawyer.

Sudden Land. Dale Oldham. (Orig.). 1980. pap. 1.75 (ISBN 0-505-51480-X). Tower Bks.

Sudden Shelter. Jesse D. Jennings et al. (University of Utah Anthropological Papers: No. 103). (Illus., Orig.). 1980. pap. 15.00x (ISBN 0-87480-166-4). U of Utah Pr.

Suddenly - a Witch. Irene Bowen. LC 74-117234. (Illus.). (gr. 4-6). 1970. 3.95 o.p. (ISBN 0-397-31164-8). Lippincott.

Suddenly It Was Love. Daisy Thomson. 1977. pap. 1.25 o.s.i. (ISBN 0-515-04447-4). Jove Pubns.

Suddenly While Gardening. Elizabeth Lemarchand. 1978. 7.95 o.s.i. (ISBN 0-8027-5395-7). Walker & Co.

Sudeten-German Tragedy. Austin J. App. (Illus.). 84p. (Orig.). 1979. pap. 3.00x (ISBN 0-911038-66-3, Inst Hist Rev). Noontide.

Sudeten Problem, 1933-38: "Volkstumpolitik" & the Formulation of Nazi Foreign Policy. Ronald M. Smelser. LC 74-5912. 296p. 1975. 20.00x (ISBN 0-8195-4077-3, Pub. by Wesleyan U Pr). Columbia U Pr.

Sudhin N. Ghose. S. A. Narayan. (Indian Writers Ser.). 8.50 (ISBN 0-89253-557-1). Ind-US Inc.

Sue the B-st-rds: The Victim's Handbook. rev. ed. Douglas Matthews. 1981. pap. 7.95 (ISBN 0-87795-288-4). Arbor Hse.

Sue Your Boss. E. Richard Larson. 1981. 14.95 (ISBN 0-374-27161-5); pap. 6.95 (ISBN 0-374-51608-1). FS&G.

Sueno de un Pordiosero. Alyce Bergey. Tr. by Fernando Villalobos from Eng. (Libros Arco Ser.). (Illus.). 32p. (Orig., Span.). (gr. 1-3). 1978. pap. 0.95 (ISBN 0-89922-126-2). Edit Caribe.

Suez Canal. Sean Garrett. Ed. by Malcolm Yapp et al. (World History Ser.). (Illus.). 32p. (gr. 10). 1980. Repr. of 1977 ed. lib. bdg. 5.95 (ISBN 0-686-59707-9); pap. text ed. 1.95 (ISBN 0-89908-205-X). Greenhaven.

Suez Nineteen Fifty-Six. Robert R. Bowie. (International Crisis & the Role of Law Ser). 164p. 1974. 9.95x (ISBN 0-19-519805-0); pap. 4.95x (ISBN 0-19-519804-2). Oxford U Pr.

Suez: The Double War. Geoffrey Powell & Roy Fullick. (Illus.). 240p. 1979. 24.00 (ISBN 0-241-10182-4, Pub. by Hamish Hamilton England). David & Charles.

Suffer a Witch. Rae Foley. 1978. pap. 1.75 o.s.i. (ISBN 0-515-04492-X). Jove Pubns.

Suffer the Children: The Story of Thalidomide. London Sunday Times. 1979. 12.95 o.p. (ISBN 0-670-68114-8). Viking Pr.

Suffering. Louis Evely. 120p. 1974. pap. 1.45 (ISBN 0-385-02996-9, Im). Doubleday.

Suffering to Silence. Bradford K. Felmy & John C. Grady, Jr. (Illus.). 200p. 1975. 9.95 (ISBN 0-89015-098-2). Nortex Pr.

Sufferings & the Glories of the Messiah. John Brown. (Giant Summit Bks.). 352p. 1981. pap. 5.95 (ISBN 0-8010-0792-5). Baker Bk.

Sufferings of Young Werther. Johann W. Von Goethe. Tr. by Harry Steinhauer. 1970. 6.00x (ISBN 0-393-04314-2); pap. 4.45x (ISBN 0-393-09880-X). Norton.

Sufferings of Young Werther. Johann W. Von Goethe. Tr. by J. Q. Morgan. 1980. pap. 4.50 (ISBN 0-7145-0542-0). Riverrun NY.

Suffolk: A Shell Guide. Norman Scharfe. 1976. 14.95 (ISBN 0-571-04901-X, Pub. by Faber & Faber). Merrimack Bk Serv.

Sufi Orders in Islam. J. Spencer Trimingham. 1971. 27.00x (ISBN 0-19-826524-7). Oxford U Pr.

Sufi Orders in Islam. J. Spencer Trimingham. 344p. 1973. pap. 4.95 (ISBN 0-19-501662-9, GB). Oxford U Pr.

Sufi Saint of the Twentieth Century: Shaikh Ahmad al-'Alawi, His Spiritual Heritage & Legacy. Martin Lings. (Illus.). 242p. 1972. 17.50x (ISBN 0-520-02174-6); pap. 4.95 (ISBN 0-520-02486-9). U of Cal Pr.

Sufi Teachings. Inayat Khan. (Sufi Message of Hazrat Inayat Khan Ser.: Vol. 8). 1979. 6.95 (ISBN 90-6077-954-1, Pub. by Servire BV Netherlands). Hunter Hse.

Sufis of Andalusia: The Ruh Al-Quds & Al-Durrat Al-Fakhirah of Ibn 'arabi. R. W. Austin. (Library Reprint Ser.: Vol. 91). 1978. 16.00x (ISBN 0-520-03553-4). U of Cal Pr.

Sufism: Message of Brotherhood, Harmony, & Hope. Nasrollah S. Fatemi et al. LC 75-29692. 256p. 1976. 12.00 o.p. (ISBN 0-498-01869-5). A S Barnes.

Sug, the Trickster Who Fooled the Monk: A Northern Thai Tale with Vocabulary. Viggo Brun. (Scandinavian Institute of Asian Studies Monographs: No. 27). (Orig.). 1976. pap. text ed. 9.25x (ISBN 0-7007-0095-1). Humanities.

Sugar Bee. Rita Micklish. LC 78-176034. (gr. 3-7). 1972. 5.95 o.s.i. (ISBN 0-440-08358-3); PLB 5.47 o.s.i. (ISBN 0-440-08350-8). Delacorte.

Sugar-Beet Nutrition. A. P. Draycott. 1972. 28.95 (ISBN 0-470-22160-7). Halsted Pr.

Sugar Blues. William Dufty. 256p. 1976. pap. 2.95 (ISBN 0-446-93786-X). Warner Bks.

Sugar Chemistry. R. S. Shallenberger & G. G. Birch. 1975. lib. bdg. 24.50 (ISBN 0-87055-166-3). AVI.

Sugar-Coated Teddy. Edyth Y. Cottrell. LC 75-37441. (Illus.). 80p. (Orig.). 1976. pap. 4.95 (ISBN 0-912800-25-9). Woodbridge Pr.

Sugar-Free Cookbook. William I. Kaufman. LC 64-15774. 1964. pap. 1.95 (ISBN 0-385-01549-6, C444, Dolp). Doubleday.

Sugar House. Antonia White. (Virago Modern Classic Ser.). 256p. 1981. pap. 5.95 (ISBN 0-686-69334-5). Dial.

Sugar Industry in Pernambuco, 1840-1910: Modernization Without Change. Peter L. Eisenberg. 1974. 22.50x (ISBN 0-520-01731-5). U of Cal Pr.

Sugar: Science & Technology. Ed. by G. G. Birch & K. J. Parker. (Illus.). 1979. 82.80x (ISBN 0-85334-805-7, Pub. by Applied Science). Burgess-Intl Ideas.

Sugar Year Book 1978. 32nd ed. (Illus.). 1978. 22.50x (ISBN 0-8002-2259-8). Intl Pubns Serv.

Sugarat. A. A. Attanasio. 544p. 1981. 14.95 (ISBN 0-688-00135-1); pap. 7.95 (ISBN 0-688-00508-X). Morrow.

Sugarbush, an Aristocat. C. Hershberger. 4.50 o.p. (ISBN 0-8062-1100-8). Carlton.

Sugarcane Crop Logging & Crop Control: Principles & Practices. Harry F. Clements. (Illus.). 540p. 1980. 30.00 (ISBN 0-8248-0508-9). U Pr of Hawaii.

Sugarcane Island. Packard & Carter. (Make up Your Own Mind Ser.: No. 1). 1976. 4.00 (ISBN 0-915248-12-3). Vermont Crossroads.

Sugarcane Island. Edward Packard. (gr. 3-6). 1978. pap. 1.25 (ISBN 0-671-56104-9). Archway.

Sugarcane Island. Edward Packard. (Illus.). (gr. 3-6). 1978. pap. 1.50 (ISBN 0-686-68480-X). PB.

Sugarless Cooking. Pam Martinez. 5.95 (ISBN 0-934230-05-6). Green Hill.

Sugerencias Para Ayudas Visuales. LeRoy Ford. Tr. by Viola D. Campbell from Eng. Orig. Title: Tool for Teaching & Training. (Illus.). 72p. (Span.). 1980. pap. 1.35 (ISBN 0-311-24302-9). Casa Bautista.

Suggested Pattern Jury Instructions: Civil Cases, Vol. 1. Ed. by Marcus B. Calhoun et al. LC 80-14282. 335p. 1980. ring bind 35.000 (ISBN 0-89854-060-7). U of GA Inst Govt.

Suggestions & Statement in Poetry. Krishna Rayan. 1972. text ed. 19.50x (ISBN 0-485-11134-9, Athlone Pr). Humanities.

Suho & the White Horse. Yuzo Otsuka. Tr. by Ann Herring from Japanese. LC 80-26789. (Illus.). 48p. (gr. k-3). 1981. 10.95 (ISBN 0-670-68149-0). Viking Pr.

Suicidal Behavior. J. W. McCulloch & A. E. Philip. LC 72-188140. 133p. 1972. pap. text ed. 21.00 (ISBN 0-08-016855-8). Pergamon.

Suicidal Patient: Recognition & Management. Ari Kiev. LC 76-47330. 1977. 15.95 (ISBN 0-88229-302-8). Nelson-Hall.

Suicide. Jacques Choron. LC 75-162757. 288p. 1972. pap. 3.95 o.p. (ISBN 0-684-13500-0, SL 457, ScribT). Scribner.

Suicide. Emile Durkheim. 1951. 14.95 (ISBN 0-02-908650-7); pap. text ed. 4.95 (ISBN 0-02-908660-4). Free Pr.

Suicide: A Guide to Information Sources. Ed. by David Lester et al. LC 80-71. (Social Issues & Social Problems Information Guide Ser.: Vol. 3). 30.00 (ISBN 0-8103-1415-0). Gale.

Suicide: A Selective Bibliography of Over 2,200 Items. Ann E. Prentice. LC 74-19231. 1974. 10.00 (ISBN 0-8108-0773-4). Scarecrow.

Suicide & Euthanasia: The Rights of Personhood. Ed. by Samuel E. Wallace & Albin Eser. LC 80-28799. 176p. 1981. 12.50x (ISBN 0-87049-299-3). U of Tenn Pr.

Suicide & Grief. Howard W. Stone. LC 70-171506. 144p. 1972. pap. 3.50 o.p. (ISBN 0-8006-1402-X, 1-402). Fortress.

Suicide & Young People. Arnold Madison. LC 77-13240. (gr. 5 up). 1978. 6.95 (ISBN 0-395-28913-0, Clarion). HM.

Suicide & Young People. Arnold Madison. 144p. (gr. 6 up). 1981. pap. 3.95 (ISBN 0-686-69043-5, Clarion). HM.

Suicide Attempts in Children & Youth. Ed. by Matilda S. McIntire & Carol R. Angle. 96p. 1980. pap. text ed. 7.95 (ISBN 0-686-65758-6, 0-0614160-X). Har-Row.

Suicide Course. Roy Brown. 128p. (gr. 6 up). 1980. 7.95 (ISBN 0-395-29436-3, Clarion). HM.

Suicide Most Foul. J. G. Jeffrys. 192p. 1981. 9.95 (ISBN 0-8027-5430-9). Walker & Co.

Suicide Notes. Brice Marden. (Illus.). 1974. 4.95 o.p. (ISBN 0-685-67985-3). Minneapolis Inst Arts.

Suicide of Christian Theology. John W. Montgomery. LC 70-270170. 1970. 6.95 (ISBN 0-87123-521-8, 210521). Bethany Fell.

Suicide of the Democracies. Claude Julien. 1980. 13.95 (ISBN 0-7145-1061-0). Riverrun NY.

Suicide Prevention: Proceedings. International Congress for Suicide Prevention, 7th, Amsterdam, August 27-30, 1973 et al. 677p. 1974. pap. text ed. 44.50 (ISBN 90-265-0186-2, Pub. by Swets Pub Serv Holland). Swets North Am.

Suicide Syndrome. Ed. by R. D. Farmer & S. R. Hirsch. 272p. 1980. 40.00x (ISBN 0-85664-868-X, Pub. by Croom Helm England). State Mutual Bk.

Suicide Syndrome. Ed. by Richard Farmer & Steven Hirsch. 268p. 1980. 37.50x (ISBN 0-85664-868-X, Pub. by Croom Helm Ltd England). Biblio Dist.

Suing of America. Marlene A. Marks. LC 80-52412. 256p. 1981. 11.95 (ISBN 0-87223-658-7). Seaview Bks.

Suisse. new ed. Ed. by Daniel Moreau. (Collection monde et voyages). (Illus.). 159p. (Fr.). 1973. 21.00 (ISBN 2-03-053103-0). Larousse.

Suit to Fit Your Man. Doris Ekern. LC 80-50504. (Illus.). 56p. 1980. pap. 3.80 (ISBN 0-933956-05-3); 3.04. Sew-Fit.

Suit Yourself...Shopping for a Job. Wider Opportunities for Women, Inc. Ed. by Roberta Kaplan. LC 80-53209. (Illus.). 52p. (Orig.). 1980. pap. text ed. 5.00 (ISBN 0-934966-02-8). WOW Inc.

Suitable for Children? Controversies in Children's Literature. Ed. by Nicholas Tucker. 1976. 17.50x (ISBN 0-520-03236-5). U of Cal Pr.

Suite in E, Serenade in E. Arthur Foote. (Early American Music Ser.: No. 60). 60p. 1980. 18.50. Da Capo.

Suivez la Piste. Emile De Harven. 1972. pap. 3.50 (ISBN 0-912022-30-2). EMC.

Suizer Diesel Locomotives of British Rail. Brian Webb. 1978. 16.95 (ISBN 0-7153-7514-8). David & Charles.

Sukuma Law & Customs. Hans Cory. LC 70-106831. (Illus.). 194p. Repr. of 1953 ed. 15.00x (ISBN 0-8371-3453-6). Negro U Pr.

Suleyman & the Ottoman Empire. John Addison et al. Ed. by Malcolm Yapp & Margaret Killingray. (Illus.). (gr. 10). 1980. lib. bdg. 5.95 (ISBN 0-89908-038-3); pap. text ed. 1.95 (ISBN 0-89908-013-8). Greenhaven.

Sulfur Containing Radio-Protective Agents. Z. M. Bacq. 344p. 1976. text ed. 94.00 (ISBN 0-08-016298-3). Pergamon.

Sulfur in Proteins. Yu. M. Torchinsky. (Illus.). 304p. 1981. 96.00 (ISBN 0-08-023778-9); pap. cancelled. Pergamon.

Sulfur in Texas. S. P. Ellison, Jr. (Illus.). 1971. 2.00 (HB 2). Bur Econ Geology.

Sulfur in the Environment: Atmospheric Cycle, Pt. 1. Jerome O. Nriagu. LC 78-6807. (Environmental Science & Technology Ser.). 464p. 1978. 46.50 (ISBN 0-471-02942-4, Pub. by Wiley-Interscience). Wiley.

Sulfur Nutrition of Wetland Rice. (IRRI Research Paper Ser.: No. 21). 29p. 1979. pap. 5.00 (R061, IRRI). Unipub.

Sulfur Oxides. Board on Toxicology & Environmental Health, National Research Council. pap. text ed. 9.00x (ISBN 0-309-02862-0). Natl Acad Pr.

Sulfur Specialty Chemicals, C-031. Business Communications Co. 1981. 850.00 (ISBN 0-89336-272-7). BCC.

Sulivans & the Slave Trade. Peter Collister. (Illus.). 199p. 1981. 14.95x (ISBN 0-8476-3611-9). Rowman.

Sullen Art: Interviews with Modern American Poets. David Ossman. (Orig.). 1963. pap. 1.45 o.s.i. (ISBN 0-87091-053-1). Corinth Bks.

Sullivan Basal Mathematics Program, 37 bks. Sullivan Assoc. pap. text ed. 3.00 ea. (ISBN 0-8449-0304-3). Learning Line.

Sullivan Fun Readers, 12 vols. Sullivan Assoc. 1972. pap. 3.50 ea. (ISBN 0-8449-4080-1). Learning Line.

Sullivan Reading Plays, 1 bk. Sullivan Assoc. pap. text ed. 4.50 (ISBN 0-8449-4050-X). Learning Line.

Sullivan Reading Program, 25 texts. Sullivan Assoc. 1980. pap. text ed. 2.50 ea. (ISBN 0-8449-1902-0); 6 tchr's manual, 6 tests avail. Learning Line.

Sullivan Topic Readers, 20 vols. Sullivan Assoc. 1972. pap. 2.00 ea. (ISBN 0-8449-4201-4). Learning Line.

Sullivan's Comic Operas: A Critical Appreciation. Thomas F. Dunhill. (Music Ser.). 256p. 1981. Repr. of 1928 ed. lib. bdg. 25.00 (ISBN 0-306-76080-0). Da Capo.

Sulphate Reducing Bacteria. J. R. Postgate. LC 78-73600. (Illus.). 1979. 35.50 (ISBN 0-521-22188-9). Cambridge U Pr.

Sulphide Catalysts, Their Properties & Applications. Otto Weisser & S. Landa. Tr. by Ota Sofr. 506p. 1973. text ed. 75.00 (ISBN 0-08-017556-2). Pergamon.

Sulphur in the Atmosphere: Proceedings. International Symposium, Dubrovnik, Yugoslavia, 7-14 Sept. 1977. Ed. by R. B. Husar et al. 1978. text ed. 75.00 (ISBN 0-08-022932-8). Pergamon.

Sulpiride & Other Benzamides. Ed. by Pier F. Spano et al. 326p. 1979. text ed. 27.00 (ISBN 0-89004-502-X). Raven.

Sultan of Batan. (Sharazad Stories Ser.). (Illus., Arabic.). pap. 3.50 (ISBN 0-686-53109-4). Intl Bk Ctr.

Sultanate of Oman: A Heritage. Ann Hill & Daryl Hill. LC 76-49444. (Illus.). 1977. text ed. 42.00x (ISBN 0-582-78050-0). Longman.

Sultan's Perfect Tree. Jane Yolen. LC 76-18096. (Illus.). (ps-4). 1977. 5.95 o.s.i. (ISBN 0-8193-0864-1, Four Winds); PLB 5.41 o.s.i. (ISBN 0-8193-0865-X). Schol Bk Serv.

Sultan's Snakes. Lorna Turpin. LC 80-10956. (Illus.). 48p. (gr. k-3). 1980. 7.95 (ISBN 0-688-80260-5); PLB 7.63 (ISBN 0-688-84260-7). Greenwillow.

Sultry Month. Alethea Hayter. 1965. 7.95 (ISBN 0-571-06214-8, Pub. by Faber & Faber). Merrimack Bk Serv.

Sum. Alan Stephens. LC 58-13024. (New Poetry Ser.). 1958. 2.50 (ISBN 0-8040-0285-1). Swallow.

Sum of Things. Olivia Manning. LC 80-7924. 1981. 10.95 (ISBN 0-689-11096-0). Atheneum.

Sumatra Alley. Merle Constiner. LC 79-140080. (gr. 6 up). 1971. 6.95 o.p. (ISBN 0-525-66126-3). Elsevier-Nelson.

Sumerian Administrative Documents from the Second Dynasty of Ur. David W. Myhrman. (Publications of the Babylonian Section, Ser.A: Vol. 3). (Illus.). 146p. 1910. soft bound 8.00 o.p. (ISBN 0-686-11912-6). Univ Mus of U PA.

Sumerian Literary Fragments from Nippur. J. Heimerdinger. (Occasional Pubns. of the Babylonian Fund Ser.: Vol. 4). 1980. 20.00 (ISBN 0-934718-31-8). Univ Mus of U PA.

Sumerian Literary Texts in the Ashmolean Museum. Ed. by Oliver R. Gurney & Samuel N. Kramer. (Oxford Editions of Cuneiform Texts). (Illus.). 1976. pap. 45.00x (ISBN 0-19-815450-X). Oxford U Pr.

Sumerian Loanwords in Old-Babylonian Akkadian: Prolegomena & Evidence. Stephen J. Lieberman. LC 76-54167. (Illus.). 1977. 15.00 (ISBN 0-89130-122-4, 040422). Scholars Pr Ca.

Sumerian Mythology. Samuel N. Kramer. (Illus.). 1972. pap. 5.95x (ISBN 0-8122-1047-6, Pa Paperbks). U of Pa Pr.

Sumerian Proverbs: Glimpses of Everyday Life in Ancient Mesopotamia. Edmund I. Gordon. LC 69-10100. 1969. Repr. of 1959 ed. lib. bdg. 39.75x o.p. (ISBN 0-8371-0086-0, GOSP). Greenwood.

Sumi-E in Three Weeks. Sadami Yamada. LC 64-17024. (Illus.). 32p. 1964. pap. 3.50 (ISBN 0-87040-121-1). Japan Pubns.

Summa Theologiae. St. Thomas Aquinas. Ed. by Thomas Gilby. Incl. Vol. 1. Existence of God. LC 70-84399. pap. 3.95 (ISBN 0-385-02768-0, Im). Doubleday.

Summaries of the Leading Cases on the Constitution. 10th ed. Paul C. Bartholomew & Joseph F. Menez. LC 68-7178. (Quality Paperback: No. 50). 1979. pap. 5.95 (ISBN 0-8226-0050-1). Littlefield.

Summarized Bible. Keith L. Brooks. (Direction Bks.). 296p. 1980. pap. cancelled (ISBN 0-8010-0669-4). Baker Bk.

Summary of Christian Doctrine. Edward W. A. Koehler. 1971. 11.95 (ISBN 0-570-03216-4, 15-2117). Concordia.

Summary of International Energy Research & Development Activities 1974-1976. Smithsonian Science Information Exchange Inc. 1978. 61.00 (ISBN 0-08-023248-5). Pergamon.

Summary of Landlord & Tenant Law. A. J. Lomnicki. 1975. 25.00 (ISBN 0-7134-2923-2, Pub. by Batsford England); pap. 14.95 (ISBN 0-7134-2924-0). David & Charles.

Summary of Medicine for Nurses & Medical Auxiliaries. 7th ed. R. Gordon Cooke & Ann Miller. 1978. pap. 4.95 (ISBN 0-571-04942-7, Pub. by Faber & Faber). Merrimack Bk Serv.

Summary of Research in Science Education, 1974. J. Dudley Herron et al. (Supplement Volume of Science Education Ser.). 1976. pap. 8.95 (ISBN 0-471-05189-6, Pub. by Wiley-Interscience). Wiley.

Summary of Research in Science Education, 1975. G. G. Mallinson. (ERIC Bibliography Ser.). 1977. 12.95 (ISBN 0-471-04359-1). Wiley.

Summary of Research in Science Education, 1973. M. B. Rowe & L. DeTure. LC 75-21655. 85p. (Orig.). 1975. pap. 7.95 (ISBN 0-470-74354-9). Halsted Pr.

Summary of the Law of Contracts. C. C. Langdell. xiv, 278p. 1980. Repr. of 1880 ed. lib. bdg. 26.00x (ISBN 0-8377-0809-5). Rothman.

Summary of the Recommendations Made at the Conference on the Communication Responsibilities of the International Agricultural Research Centres. 1980p. 1980. pap. 7.50 (R031, IRRI). Unipub.

Summary of Town & Country Planning Law. A. J. Lomnicki. 1973. pap. 19.95 o.p. (ISBN 0-7134-0531-7, Pub. by Batsford England). David & Charles.

Summary of UNEP Activities: Technical Assistance, 1980. (UNEP Report Ser.: No. 8). 115p. 1980. pap. 11.00 (UNEP 036, UNEP). Unipub.

Summe & Substance of the Conference at Hampton Court, January 14, 1603. William Barlow. LC 74-28829. (English Experience Ser.: No. 711). 1975. Repr. of 1604 ed. 9.50 (ISBN 90-221-0711-6). Walter J Johnson.

Summe & Substance of the Conference. William Barlow. LC 65-10395. 1965. Repr. of 1604 ed. 20.00x (ISBN 0-8201-1004-3). Schol Facsimiles.

Summer. Richard L. Allington & Kathleen Krull. LC 80-25097. (Beginning to Learn About Ser.). (Illus.). 32p. (gr. k-2). 1981. PLB 9.65 (ISBN 0-8172-1341-4). Raintree Child.

Summer. Edith Wharton. 1981. pap. 2.75 (ISBN 0-425-04610-9). Berkley Pub.

Summer & Fall Wildflowers of N. E. Dwelley. 1980. pap. 8.95 (ISBN 0-89272-020-4). Down East.

Summer Anniversaries. Donald Justice. LC 60-7256. (Wesleyan Poetry Program: Vol. 6). (Orig.). 1960. 10.00x (ISBN 0-8195-2006-3, Pub. by Wesleyan U Pr). Columbia U Pr.

Summer at High Kingdom. Louise R. Dickinson. 128p. (gr. 5-9). 1975. 5.90 (ISBN 0-531-02809-7). Watts.

Summer at Sea. Clifford Q. Edwards. LC 73-84576. 1976. pap. 2.25 o.p. (ISBN 0-87680-836-4, 98093). Word Bks.

Summer Brave. William Inge. Orig. Title: Picnic. pap. 2.50 (ISBN 0-686-62807-1). Dramatists Play.

Summer Camp: A Guidebook for Parents. Alice Van Krevelen. LC 80-26726. (Illus.). 168p. 1981. 11.95 (ISBN 0-88229-296-X). Nelson-Hall.

Summer Cat. Howard Knotts. LC 79-9610. (Illus.). 48p. (gr. k-4). 1981. 7.95 (ISBN 0-06-023178-5, HarpJ); PLB 7.89g (ISBN 0-06-023179-3). Har-Row.

Summer Day at Ajaccio. E. G. Bartlett. 168p. 1980. 15.00x (ISBN 0-7050-0075-3, Pub. by Skilton & Shaw England). State Mutual Bk.

Summer Day Is Done. R. T. Stevens. 464p. 1977. pap. 2.50 (ISBN 0-446-91667-6). Warner Bks.

Summer Diary. Ruthven Tremain. (Illus.). (gr. 5 up). 1970. pap. 1.95 o.s.i. (ISBN 0-02-789410-X). Macmillan.

Summer Employment Directory of the U. S. Nineteen Eighty. 29th ed. 1979. lib. bdg. 8.95 o.p. (ISBN 0-89879-006-9); pap. 6.95 o.p. (ISBN 0-89879-005-0). Writers Digest.

Summer Fires. Robert Reiss. 1980. pap. write for info. (ISBN 0-671-83414-2). PB.

Summer Food Service Program for Children in New York City: Part 2, Report on Monitoring the Summer Food Service Program for Children in New York City. 1978. 1.00 o.s.i. (ISBN 0-686-05507-1). Comm Coun Great NY.

Summer Girl. Caroline Crane. 1981. pap. 2.50 (ISBN 0-451-09806-4, E9806, Signet Bks). NAL.

Summer Gold: A Camper's Guide to Amateur Prospecting. John N. Dwyer. LC 73-19267. 1974. 5.95 o.p. (ISBN 0-684-13706-2, ScribT). Scribner.

Summer I Was Lost. Viereck. (gr. 3-5). 1980. pap. 1.25 (ISBN 0-590-30060-1, Schol Pap). Schol Bk Serv.

Summer I Was Lost. Phillip Viereck. LC 65-13735. (Illus.). (gr. 6-9). 1965. 8.95 (ISBN 0-381-99659-X, A75800, JD-J). John Day.

Summer in Sodom with Kitchen Privileges. Florence Holland. 1977. 6.50 o.p. (ISBN 0-682-48968-9). Exposition.

Summer in the Seed. Aelred Squire. LC 79-52126. 1980. pap. 7.95 (ISBN 0-8091-2237-5). Paulist Pr.

Summer in the South. James Marshall. (gr. k-6). 1980. pap. 1.50 (ISBN 0-440-48105-8, YB). Dell.

Summer in the Twenties. Peter Dickinson. 1981. 10.95 (ISBN 0-394-51330-4). Pantheon.

Summer Is from Winter Until Winter. Sigrid Olesen. (Illus.). 80p. 1980. 4.95 (ISBN 0-936748-02-8); pap. 3.50 (ISBN 0-936748-03-6). Fade In.

Summer Is Here! Jane B. Moncure. LC 75-12945. (Illus.). (ps-2). 1975. 5.50 (ISBN 0-913778-12-5). Childs World.

Summer Key to Trees of Tennessee & the Great Smokies. Royal E. Shanks & Aaron J. Sharp. (Illus.). 24p. 1963. pap. 1.50x (ISBN 0-87049-040-0). U of Tenn Pr.

Summer Light. Herbert Mason. 148p. 1980. 9.95 (ISBN 0-374-27176-3). FS&G.

Summer Lightning. Judith Richards. LC 77-16761. 1978. 8.95 o.p. (ISBN 0-312-77544-X). St Martin.

Summer Maker: An Ojibway Indian Myth. Margery Bernstein & Janet Kobrin. LC 76-14875. (Myths You Can Read by Yourself). 48p. (gr. 1-3). 1977. binding 5.95reinforced (ISBN 0-684-14716-5, ScribJ). Scribner.

Summer Masquerade. Blanche Chenier. (Regency Romance Ser.). 1978. pap. 1.75 o.p. (ISBN 0-449-23820-2, Crest). Fawcett.

Summer Meadows. Robert Nathan. 128p. 1973. 5.95 o.p. (ISBN 0-440-08444-X). Delacorte.

Summer of My German Soldier. Bette Green. 208p. 1981. pap. 2.25 (ISBN 0-553-14687-4). Bantam.

Summer of the Dragon. Elizabeth Peters. LC 79-9782. 1979. 8.95 (ISBN 0-396-07689-0). Dodd.

Summer of the Great Grandmother. Madeleine L'Engle. 1980. 5.95 (ISBN 0-8164-2259-1). Seabury.

Summer of the Great Grandmother. Madeline L'Engle. LC 74-13157. 1974. 10.95 (ISBN 0-374-27174-7). FS&G.

Summer of the Green Star. Robert C. Lee. LC 80-27427. (Junior Literary Guild Ser.). (gr. 5-9). 1981. price not set (ISBN 0-664-32681-1). Westminster.

Summer of the Gun. Will Henry. 1978. 9.95 (ISBN 0-397-01309-4). Lippincott.

Summer of the Spanish Woman. Catherine Gaskin. LC 76-56292. 1977. 10.00 o.p. (ISBN 0-385-07414-X). Doubleday.

Summer of the Stallion. June A. Hanson. LC 78-24212. (gr. 5-9). 1979. 8.95 (ISBN 0-02-742620-3, 74262). Macmillan.

Summer of the Wild Pig. Sandy Dengler. (gr. 6-8). 1979. pap. 1.95 (ISBN 0-8024-8429-8). Moody.

Summer Olympics. 4th rev. ed. Frank Litsky. (First Bks.). (Illus.). (gr. 4-6). 1979. PLB 6.45 s&l (ISBN 0-531-02935-2). Watts.

Summer People. John R. Townsend. LC 72-3270. 224p. (gr. 9 up). 1972. 9.95 (ISBN 0-397-31421-3). Lippincott.

Summer Pioneers: Memories of Old Field. Hanford Twitchell. 1977. 4.50 o.p. (ISBN 0-682-48979-4). Exposition.

Summer Pony. Jean S. Doty. 128p. (gr. 3-7). 1973. 8.95 (ISBN 0-02-732750-7). Macmillan.

Summer Rain. Yvonne Kalman. (Orig.). pap. 2.50 (ISBN 0-515-05702-9). Jove Pubns.

Summer Range. L. P. Holmes. 1981. pap. 1.75 (ISBN 0-445-00697-8). Popular Lib.

Summer Rules. Robert Lipsyte. LC 79-2816. (Ursula Nordstrom Bk.). (YA) (gr. 7 up). 1981. 8.95 (ISBN 0-06-023897-6, HarpJ); PLB 8.79g (ISBN 0-06-023898-4). Har-Row.

Summer Saturdays in the West. David S. Thomas & Simon Rocksborough Smith. (Illus.). 1973. 14.95 (ISBN 0-7153-5912-6). David & Charles.

Summer Savory: A Family Resource Book. Mary L. Tietjen. LC 77-78961. 1977. pap. 3.95 (ISBN 0-8091-2034-8). Paulist Pr.

Summer Soldier. Nicholas Guild. 1979. pap. 1.95 o.s.i. (ISBN 0-515-05228-0). Jove Pubns.

Summer Solstice. Michael T. Hinkemeyer. LC 75-33587. (YA) 1976. 7.95 o.p. (ISBN 0-399-11645-1, Dist. by Putnam). Berkley Pub.

Summer Solstice. Michael T. Hinkemeyer. (Orig.). 1980. pap. 2.50 o.p. (ISBN 0-425-04706-7). Berkley Pub.

Summer Stargazer: Astronomy for Beginners. Robert Claiborne. 1981. pap. 3.95 (ISBN 0-14-046487-5). Penguin.

Summer Storm. Letitia Healey. 192p. (Orig.). 1980. pap. 1.50 (ISBN 0-671-57024-2). S&S.

Summer Story. Robert Houston. 1978. pap. 1.75 o.p. (ISBN 0-449-14019-9, GM). Fawcett.

Summer Study Abroad. Gail A. Cohen. LC 73-78423. 1979. pap. 6.00 o.p. (ISBN 0-87206-091-8). Inst Intl Educ.

Summer Theatre Directory: 1980. Ed. by Kevin Hoggard. 1980. pap. 3.50, ATA members 3.00 (ISBN 0-686-18919-1). Am Theatre Assoc.

Summer with Danica. H. G. Gunther. (Gunther Ser.: No. 3). 224p. (Orig.). 1981. pap. 1.95 (ISBN 0-515-05674-X). Jove Pubns.

Summerblood. Anne Rudeen. (Orig.). 1978. pap. 2.25 o.s.i. (ISBN 0-446-82535-2). Warner Bks.

Summerdog. Thom Roberts. 1978. pap. 1.50 (ISBN 0-380-01950-7, 75788, Camelot). Avon.

Summerdog Comes Home. George A. Zabriskie. (Illus.). 1980. pap. 1.75 (ISBN 0-380-75259-X, 75259, Camelot). Avon.

Summerland. Ed. by Alec Shoate & Barbara Y. Main. 242p. 1980. 16.95x (ISBN 0-85564-166-5, Pub. by U of West Australia Pr Australia). Intl Schol Bk Serv.

Summers Fly, Winters Walk, Vol. III. Charles Schulz. 128p. 1980. Repr. cancelled (ISBN 0-449-24310-9, Crest). Fawcett.

Summer's Lease. Marilyn Sachs. (gr. 7-12). Date not set. pap. 1.75 (ISBN 0-440-97787-8, LE). Dell.

Summertime Blues. Ed. by Mary Verdick. (Pal Paperbacks - Pal Skills Ser.). (Illus., Orig.). (gr. 7-12). 1978. pap. text ed. 1.25 (ISBN 0-8374-6702-0). Xerox Ed Pubns.

Summons & Sign. Dagmar Nick. Tr. by Jim Barnes from Ger. LC 80-18367. Orig. Title: Zeugnis & Zeichen. (Illus.). 124p. (Orig.). 1980. pap. 3.00 (ISBN 0-933428-02-2). Chariton Review.

Summons to Life: Mediating Structures & the Prevention of Youth Crime. Robert Woodson. 150p. 1981. 16.50 (ISBN 0-88410-826-0). Ballinger Pub.

Sumner: John Brown, Second Prolog. Mark Dunster. 1980. pap. 4.00 (ISBN 0-89642-065-5). Linden Pubs.

Sumner Street. Rod Townley. 1976. 1.00 o.p. (ISBN 0-685-78417-7). The Smith.

Sumo: The Sport & the Tradition. J. A. Sargeant. LC 59-5993. (Illus.). 1959. pap. 4.25 (ISBN 0-8048-0556-3). C E Tuttle.

Sun. 2nd ed. Giorgio Abetti. (Illus.). 1963. 9.95 (ISBN 0-571-05389-0, Pub. by Faber & Faber). Merrimack Bk Serv.

Sun. Isaac Asimov. LC 70-184458. (Beginning Science Ser.). (Illus.). 32p. (gr. 2-5). 1972. 2.50 o.p. (ISBN 0-695-80320-4); PLB 2.97 o.p. (ISBN 0-695-40320-6). Follett.

Sun. Fields. (gr. 2-4). 1980. PLB 6.45 (ISBN 0-531-03243-4, G23). Watts.

Sun. rev. ed. Herbert S. Zim. LC 74-34461. (Illus.). 64p. (gr. 3-7). 1975. PLB 6.48 (ISBN 0-688-32033-3). Morrow.

Sun a Honeydew, Moon a Cantaloupe. Jack Libert. (Illus., Orig.). 1970. pap. 2.00 (ISBN 0-911732-53-5). Irego.

Sun Also Rises. Ernest Hemingway. (Arabic.). pap. 7.95x (ISBN 0-686-63550-7). Intl Bk Ctr.

Sun & Its Family. rev. ed. Irving Adler. LC 68-57377. (Illus.). (gr. 5-9). 1969. PLB 7.89 (ISBN 0-381-99983-1, A76000, JD-J). John Day.

Sun & Steel. Yukio Mishima. Tr. by John Bester from Japanese. 176p. 1972. pap. 4.95 (ISBN 0-394-17765-7, E583, Ever). Grove.

Sun Chief: The Autobiography of a Hopi Indian. rev. ed. Ed. by Leo W. Simmons. (Illus.). 1942. 30.00x (ISBN 0-300-00949-6); pap. 5.95x 1963 (ISBN 0-300-00227-0, YW8). Yale U Pr.

Sun Comes Up, The Sun Goes Down. Johnny Hart. (B.C. Ser.). (Illus.). 1979. pap. 1.50 (ISBN 0-449-14205-1, GM). Fawcett.

Sun Dance People. Richard Erdoes. (Illus.). 241p. Date not set. pap. 1.95 (ISBN 0-394-70803-2, Vin). Random.

Sun Dances. 2nd ed. Alexander Carmichael. 1977. pap. 3.75 (ISBN 0-903540-07-X, Pub by Floris Books). St George Bk Serv.

Sun Dials & Roses of Yesterday. Alice M. Earle. LC 79-75790. 1969. Repr. of 1902 ed. 20.00 (ISBN 0-8103-3830-0). Gale.

Sun Dogs. Mark J. McGarry. (Orig.). 1981. pap. 1.95 (ISBN 0-451-09620-7, J9620, Sig). NAL.

Sun Dogs & Shooting Stars: A Skywatcher's Calendar. Franklyn M. Branley. (gr. 5 up). 1980. 6.95 (ISBN 0-395-29520-3). HM.

Sun, Earth, & Man. George P. Bischof & Eunice S. Bischof. LC 56-8352. (Illus.). (gr. 5 up). 1957. 4.50 o.p. (ISBN 0-15-282643-2, HJ). HarBraceJ.

Sun Flight. Gerald McDermott. LC 79-5067. (Illus.). 40p. 1980. 10.95 (ISBN 0-590-07632-9, Four Winds). Schol Bk Serv.

Sun Grumble. Claudia Fregosi. LC 73-6046. (Illus.). 32p. (ps-2). 1974. 4.95g o.s.i. (ISBN 0-02-735740-6). Macmillan.

Sun: Mankind's Future Source of Energy, 3 vols. Ed. by F. De Winter. 1979. text ed. 320.00 (ISBN 0-08-022725-2). Pergamon.

Sun Men of the Americas. Grace Cooke. 6.95 (ISBN 0-85487-035-0). De Vorss.

Sun Myung Moon & the Unification Church: An in-Depth Investigation of the Man & the Movement. Frederick Sontag. LC 77-9075. (Illus.). 1977. 8.95 o.p. (ISBN 0-687-40622-6). Abingdon.

Sun of Superlove. L. Tom Letchworth. LC 80-53694. (Illus.). 120p. (Orig.). (gr. 7 up). 1980. pap. 3.95 (ISBN 0-9602334-1-5). Superlove.

Sun on the Wall. Wayne Overholser. 1981. pap. 1.75 (ISBN 0-345-29493-9). Ballantine.

Sun: Our Nearest Star. Franklyn M. Branley. LC 60-13241. (Let's-Read-&-Find-Out Science Bk). (Illus.). (gr. k-3). 1961. PLB 7.89 (ISBN 0-690-79483-5, TYC-J). T Y Crowell.

Sun Placed in the Abyss & Other Texts. Francis Ponge. Tr. by Serge Gavronsky from Fr. LC 77-3631. 1977. pap. 4.00 (ISBN 0-915342-22-7). SUN.

Sun Power: A Bibliography of United States Government Documents on Solar Energy. Compiled by Sandra McAninch. LC 80-29037. 980p. 1981. lib. bdg. 75.00 (ISBN 0-313-20992-8, MSU/). Greenwood.

Sun Records. Colin Escott & Martin Hawkins. (Illus.). 1980. pap. 8.95 (ISBN 0-8256-3161-0). Music Sales.

Sun Reflections: Images for a New Solar Age. John Cole. Ed. by Marcy Posner. (Illus.). 208p. 1981. 14.95 (ISBN 0-87857-318-6); pap. 10.95 (ISBN 0-87857-317-8). Rodale Pr Inc.

Sun Rides High: Pioneering Days in Oklahoma, Kansas & Missouri. Orrin U. Burright. 8.95 (ISBN 0-685-48814-4). Nortex Pr.

Sun Rising on the West: The Saga of Henry Clay & Elizabeth Smith. W. H. Curry. 1979. write for info. Crosby County.

Sun Sight Sailing. S. L. Seaton. 1980. 9.95 (ISBN 0-679-51363-9). McKay.

Sun Signs: The Stars in Your Life. Amy Shapiro. LC 77-21393. (Myth, Magic & Superstition Ser.). (Illus.). (gr. 4-5). 1977. PLB 9.65 (ISBN 0-8172-1028-8). Raintree Pubs.

Sun, Soil, & Survival: An Introduction to Soils. Kermit C. Berger. LC 72-3608. (Illus.). 371p. pap. 8.95 (ISBN 0-8061-1388-X). U of Okla Pr.

Sun-Spaces. Frances Ottesen. (Illus.). 76p. 1981. 7.95 (ISBN 0-9605220-0-X). Otafra.

Sun Valley. Dorice Taylor. (Illus.). 264p. 1980. 20.00 (ISBN 0-9605212-0-8). Ex Libris Sun.

Sun Valley: Ketchum Epicure. Ed. by Elliott Wolf. 1978. pap. 2.50 (ISBN 0-89716-030-4). Peanut Butter.

Sun-Warmed Nudes. Andre De Dienes. (Illus.). 10.00 (ISBN 0-910550-15-8, Dist. by Lyle Stuart). Elysium.

Sun, Weather, & Climate. John R. Herman & Richard A. Goldberg. LC 79-22363. (Illus.). 1980. Repr. of 1978 ed. 30.00 (ISBN 0-8103-1018-X). Gale.

Sun Yat-sen & the Origins of the Chinese Revolution. Harold Z. Schiffrin. (Center for Chinese Studies, UC Berkeley). 1968. 18.50x (ISBN 0-520-01142-2). U of Cal Pr.

Sun Yat-Sen: Frustrated Patriot. C. Martin Wilbur. LC 76-18200. 384p. 1976. 22.50x (ISBN 0-231-04036-9). Columbia U Pr.

Sun Yat Sen, Liberator of China. Henry B. Restarick. LC 79-2837. (Illus.). 167p. 1981. Repr. of 1931 ed. 16.50 (ISBN 0-8305-0014-6). Hyperion Conn.

Sunbeam Frypan Cookbook. 1981. 8.95 (ISBN 0-916752-43-7). Green Hill.

Sunbeam Great Crepe Recipes. Rose-Marie Brooks. 7.95 (ISBN 0-916752-03-8). Green Hill.

Sunbeam Owners Handbook of Maintenance & Repair. Ed. by Clymer Publications. (Illus.). 1965. pap. 8.95 (ISBN 0-89287-253-5, A189). Clymer Pubns.

Sunbelt Retirement: The Complete State-By-State Guide to Retiring in the South & West of the United States. 2nd ed. Peter Dickinson. (Illus.). 1980. 14.95 (ISBN 0-525-93123-6); pap. 8.95 (ISBN 0-525-93107-4). Dutton.

Sunbird. Arthur Dobrin. 64p. signed ed. 15.00 (ISBN 0-89304-046-0); pap. 3.95 (ISBN 0-89304-012-6). Cross Cult.

Sunbonnet: Filly of the Year. Barbara Van Tuyl. (RL 5). 1973. pap. 1.25 (ISBN 0-451-08152-8, Y8152, Sig). NAL.

Sunbound. Cynthia Felice. (Orig.). 1981. pap. 2.50 (ISBN 0-440-18373-1). Dell.

Sunburn. John Lescroart. 224p. (Orig.). 1981. pap. 2.25 (ISBN 0-523-41187-1). Pinnacle Bks.

Sundance: The Marauders. Peter McCurtin. (Orig.). 1980. pap. 1.75 (ISBN 0-8439-0740-1, Leisure Bks). Nordon Pubns.

Sundark. Paige Mitchell. 552p. 1981. 14.95 (ISBN 0-385-14368-0). Doubleday.

Sunday Afternoons. Roy Kingsbury & Patrick O'Shea. 1974. tchrs notes 2.50x (ISBN 0-582-55226-5); record 11.75x (ISBN 0-582-56732-7); cassette 12.50x (ISBN 0-582-56755-6). Longman.

Sunday Morning We Went to the Zoo. Deborah Ray. LC 80-7915. (Illus.). (ps-2). 1981. 8.95 (ISBN 0-06-024841-6, HarpJ); PLB 8.79 (ISBN 0-06-024842-4). Har-Row.

Sunday No Sabbath: A Sermon. John Pocklington. LC 74-28881. (English Experience Ser.: No. 759). 1975. Repr. of 1636 ed. 6.00 (ISBN 90-221-0759-0). Walter J Johnson.

Sunday School Board: Ninety Years of Service. Walter B. Shurden. (Orig.). pap. 5.95 (ISBN 0-8054-6558-8). Broadman.

Sunday School Board: Ninety Years of Service. Walter B. Shurden. (Orig.). 1981. soft cover 5.95 (ISBN 0-8054-6558-8). Broadman.

Sunday School Success. rev. ed. Clarence H. Benson. LC 64-13765. 1964. pap. text ed. 3.75 o.p. (ISBN 0-910566-06-2); instructor's guide by bill bynum 3.75 o.p. (ISBN 0-910566-22-4). Evang Tchr.

Sunday Seducer. Linda DuBreuil. 1975. pap. 1.50 o.p. (ISBN 0-685-52173-7, LB246DK, Leisure Bks). Nordon Pubns.

Sunday Supplement for Kids. Patti Hughes. (Illus.). 63p. (Orig.). (gr. 3-6). 1980. pap. 3.95 (ISBN 0-87747-848-1). Deseret Bk.

Sunday the Rabbi Stayed Home. Harry Kemelman. (Rabbi Ser.). 1979. pap. 2.25 (ISBN 0-449-24116-5, Crest). Fawcett.

Sunday Times Book of Brain Teasers, Bk. 1. Victor Bryant & Ronald Postill. (Unwin Paperbacks Ser.). (Illus.). 176p. (Orig.). 1980. pap. 4.95x (ISBN 0-04-793045-4, AU-452). Allen Unwin.

Sunday Too Far Away! John Dingwall. (Australian Theatre Workshop Ser.). pap. text ed. 6.50x (ISBN 0-686-65422-6, 00532). Heinemann Ed.

Sunday with the Family Circus. Bil Keane. (Illus., Orig.). pap. 1.75 (ISBN 0-8170-0364-9). Judson.

Sunday Zebras. Art Holst. 1980. 10.00 (ISBN 0-9605118-0-6). Forest Pub.

Sundays. Cynthia Applewhite. 1978. pap. 1.95 (ISBN 0-380-42358-8, 42358). Avon.

Sundays. Steve Franks. 1972. 1.00 o.p. (ISBN 0-685-67927-6). Windless Orchard.

Sunday's Child. Claudette Williams. 1979. pap. 1.75 o.p. (ISBN 0-449-23986-1, Crest). Fawcett.

Sunday's Scriptures. rev. ed. Wm Sydnor. 1979. pap. 5.25 o.p. (ISBN 0-8192-1215-6). Morehouse.

Sundials: The Art & Science of Gnomonics. Frank W. Cousins. (Illus.). 248p. 1970. 22.50x o.p. (ISBN 0-87663-704-7, Pica Pr). Universe.

Sundials, Their Theory & Construction. Albert E. Waugh. (Illus.). 8.00 (ISBN 0-8446-4835-3). Peter Smith.

Sundown Jim. Ernest Haycox. 1981. pap. 1.75 (ISBN 0-451-09676-2, E9676, Sig). NAL.

Sundown Man-Sunday in Choctaw Country. Shad Denver & Brett McKinley. 1980. pap. 2.25 (ISBN 0-8439-0732-0, Leisure Bks). Nordon Pubns.

Sundowners. Jon Cleary. 288p. 1981. pap. 2.50 (ISBN 0-445-04642-2). Popular Lib.

Sunfall. C. J. Cherryl. (Science Fiction Ser.). 1981. pap. 2.25 (ISBN 0-87997-618-7, UE1618). DAW Bks.

Sunflakes & Snowshine. Newman & Boulanger. (ps-3). pap. 1.25 (ISBN 0-590-05412-0, Schol Pap). Schol Bk Serv.

Sunflower. Charles B. Heiser, Jr. LC 74-15906. (Illus.). 198p. 1981. pap. 5.95 (ISBN 0-8061-1743-5). U of Okla Pr.

Sunflower. P. S. Vasudev. 15.00 (ISBN 0-89253-776-0); flexible cloth 6.75 (ISBN 0-89253-777-9). Ind-US Inc.

Sunflower! Martha M. Welch. LC 80-1008. (Illus.). 64p. (gr. 2-5). 1980. PLB 6.95 (ISBN 0-396-07885-0). Dodd.

Sunflower Garden. Janice M. Udry. LC 69-17738. (Illus.). (gr. 2-5). 1969. PLB 5.39 o.p. (ISBN 0-8178-4472-4). Harvey.

Sunflowering. Bob Stanish. (gr. 4-12). 1977. 7.95 (ISBN 0-916456-12-9, GA69). Good Apple.

Sunflowers. Cynthia Overbeck. (Lerner Natural Science Bks.). (Illus.). (gr. 4-10). 1981. PLB 7.95 (ISBN 0-8225-1457-5). Lerner Pubns.

Sung Under the Silver Umbrella. Association For Childhood Education International. (Illus.). (gr. k-3). 1972. 4.95g o.s.i. (ISBN 0-02-706180-9). Macmillan.

Sungates: A Testimony Carved in Wood. Victor Hajdu. Tr. by Rose Stein. (Illus., Hungarian.). 1980. 15.00 (ISBN 0-933652-16-X). Domjan Studio.

Sunlight on Your Doorstep. Bradley L. Morison. 3.95 (ISBN 0-87018-044-4); pap. 1.95 (ISBN 0-87018-073-8). Ross.

Sunlight to Electricity: Prospects for Solar Energy Conversion by Photovoltaics. Joseph A. Merrigan. LC 75-6933. 192p. (Orig.). 1975. 15.00x (ISBN 0-262-13116-1); pap. 5.95 (ISBN 0-262-63072-9). MIT Pr.

Sunlit Sea. Augusta Goldin. LC 68-17075. (Let's-Read- & Find-Out Science Bk). (Illus.). (gr. k-3). 1968. bds. 7.95 (ISBN 0-690-79411-8, TYC-J); PLB 7.89 (ISBN 0-690-79412-6). T Y Crowell.

Sunny Sentences: Sight Word Activities to Cut & Paste. Ellen Sussman. (Spirit Duplicating Masters Ser.). (Illus.). 24p. (gr. 1-2). 1980. 4.95 (ISBN 0-933606-07-9). Monkey Sisters.

Sunny Side of Castro Street. Dan Vojir. (Illus., Orig.). 1981. pap. 6.95 (ISBN 0-89407-034-7). Strawberry Hill.

Sunnyside of Chords: An Encyclopedia of Chord & Scale Diagrams for Fingerboard Instruments. Robert R. Whitlock & Linda J. Whitlock. LC 78-71087. (Illus.). 240p. 1979. pap. 22.00 (ISBN 0-9602178-0-0). Pattecky Music.

Sunpower Experiments. Maggie Spooner. LC 79-65077. (Illus.). (gr. 5 up). 1979. 8.95 (ISBN 0-8069-3110-8); PLB 8.29 (ISBN 0-8069-3111-6). Sterling.

Sunrise. White Eagle. 1958. 3.50 (ISBN 0-85487-016-4). De Vorss.

Sunrise, a Whole Grain, Natural Food Breakfast Cook Book. Diane S. Greene. LC 80-20749. 240p. 1980. 12.95 (ISBN 0-89594-041-8); pap. 6.95 (ISBN 0-89594-040-X). Crossing Pr.

Sunrise & Sunset Tables for Key Cities & Weather Stations in the United States. United States. Nautical Almanac Office & Gale Research Company. LC 76-24796. 1977. 40.00 (ISBN 0-8103-0464-3). Gale.

Sunrise Cookbook. Dorothy De Winton. 1976. 3.00 (ISBN 0-686-27657-4). Cole-Outreach.

Sunrise: No. 25. Grace L. Hill. 208p. 1980. pap. 1.95 (ISBN 0-553-14169-4). Bantam.

Sunrise West. William Carlson. LC 79-7043. (Science Fiction Ser.). 192p. 1981. 9.95 (ISBN 0-385-14498-9). Doubleday.

Sun's Eye: West Indian Writing for Young Readers. Ed. by Anne Walmsley. (Illus.). 1977. pap. text ed. 4.00x (ISBN 0-582-76702-4). Longman.

Suns of Independence. Ahmadu Kourouma. Tr. by Adrian Adams from Fr. LC 80-8891. 160p. 1981. text ed. 24.50x (ISBN 0-8419-0626-2, Africana); pap. text ed. 9.75x (ISBN 0-8419-0688-2). Holmes & Meier.

Sun's Wind. Alexei Leonov. (Let There Always Be Sunshine Ser.). (Illus.). (gr. k-3). 1977. 2.75 (ISBN 0-8285-8829-5). Progress Pubs.

Sunset Cloud. Anne Hampson. (Alpha Books). 80p. (Orig.). 1979. pap. text ed. 2.25x (ISBN 0-19-424161-0). Oxford U Pr.

Sunset People. Herbert Kastle. 384p. (Orig.). 1980. pap. 2.75 (ISBN 0-515-05488-7). Jove Pubns.

Sunset Warrior. Eric Van Lustbader. 1978. pap. 1.50 (ISBN 0-515-04714-7). Jove Pubns.

Sunset Warrior. Eric Van Lustbader. 1980. pap. 2.50 (ISBN 0-425-04452-1). Berkley Pub.

Sunsets into Sunrises. Bischof Martin. Tr. by Violet Ozols. 560p. Date not set. 20.00 (ISBN 0-934616-14-0). Valkyrie Pr.

Sunshine. Bob Reese. Ed. by Dan Wasserman. (Ten Word Bks.). (Illus.). (gr. k-1). 1979. PLB 4.50 (ISBN 0-89868-073-5); pap. 1.95 (ISBN 0-89868-084-0). ARO Pub.

Sunshine & Shadow: The Amish & Their Quilts. Phyllis Haders. LC 76-5094. (Illus.). 72p. 1976. 5.95 o.s.i. (ISBN 0-87663-236-3). Universe.

Sunshine & Shadow: The Amish & Their Quilts. Phyllis Haders. LC 76-5094. (Illus.). 72p. 1981. pap. 5.95 (ISBN 0-87663-556-7). Universe.

Sunshine & Shadows. Ed. by Travis D. Anthony. (Illus.). 190p. 1981. price not set (ISBN 0-9604686-1-7). T D Anthony.

Sunshine at Midnight. Genevieve Laporte. 136p. 1975. 6.95 o.s.i. (ISBN 0-02-568300-4). Macmillan.

Sunshine Days. Robert B. Ruddell et al. (Pathfinder - Allyn & Bacon Reading Program: Level 13). (gr. 3). 1978. text ed. 8.40 (ISBN 0-205-05166-9, 5451663); tchr's ed. 12.20 (ISBN 0-205-05167-7, 5451671); 3.60. Allyn.

Sunshine Days & Foggy Nights. James Kavanaugh. (Illus.). 1975. 7.95 (ISBN 0-87690-167-4). Dutton.

Sunshine Family & the Pony. Sharron Loree. LC 71-171859. (Illus.). 48p. (ps-2). 1972. 5.95 (ISBN 0-395-28816-9, Clarion). HM.

Sunshine Makes the Seasons. Franklyn M. Branley. LC 73-19694. (Let's Read & Find Out Science Bk). (Illus.). 40p. (ps-3). 1974. PLB 7.89 (ISBN 0-690-00438-9, TYC-J). T Y Crowell.

Sunshine, Rainbows & Friends. Judith Beyl. LC 80-50828. (Illus.). 1980. pap. 5.95 (ISBN 0-933308-01-9). West Village.

Sunshine Through the Shadows. Hulen Jackson. 4.95 (ISBN 0-89315-283-8). Lambert Bk.

Sunspinners. Theodore L. Harris et al. (Keys to Reading Ser.). (gr. 6). 1974. pap. text ed. 3.60 (ISBN 0-87892-542-2); resource bk 8.85 (ISBN 0-87892-544-9); master key (student guide) 3.96 (ISBN 0-87892-545-7); duplicating masters 19.53 (ISBN 0-87892-547-3). Economy Co.

Sunspots. Steve Baer. LC 75-20779. 1977. pap. 4.00 o.p. (ISBN 0-686-21779-9). Zomeworks Corp.

Sunspots. Steve Baer. write for info. (ISBN 0-88930-062-3); pap. write for info. (ISBN 0-88930-061-5). Zomeworks Corp.

Sunwatch. Frank Dorn. (Orig.). 1980. pap. 1.95 (ISBN 0-532-23239-9). Manor Bks.

Sunworld. Leo P. Kelley. LC 79-51080. (Space Police Bks.). (Illus.). 64p. (gr. 4 up). 1980. PLB 7.95 (ISBN 0-516-02235-0). Childrens.

Suomen Lasi-Finnish Glass. 68p. 1980. pap. 5.95x (ISBN 0-904461-56-4, Pub. by Ceolfrith Pr England). Intl Schol Bk Serv.

Super. John Cornwell. 1972. pap. 2.25 (ISBN 0-8439-0682-0, Leisure Bks). Nordon Pubns.

Super Bowl. Leonard Kessler. LC 80-10171. (Greenwillow Read-Alone Bks.). (Illus.). 56p. (gr. 1-4). 1980. 5.95 (ISBN 0-688-80270-2); PLB 5.71 (ISBN 0-688-84270-4). Greenwillow.

Super-Colossal Book of Puzzles, Tricks & Games. Sheila A. Barry. LC 77-93325. (Illus.). (gr. 4 up). 1978. 17.95 (ISBN 0-8069-4580-X); PLB 15.99 (ISBN 0-8069-4581-8). Sterling.

Super Dan & the Dinosaurs. John Kastner. (Illus.). 32p. (gr. 1 up). 1980. PLB 6.95 (ISBN 0-201-03901-X, 3901, A-W Childrens); pap. 3.95 (ISBN 0-201-03910-9, 3910). A-W.

Super Destroyers. Antony Preston. 72p. 1980. 11.50x (ISBN 0-85177-131-9, Pub. by Cornell England). State Mutual Bk.

Super Duper American History Fun Book. Louis Phillips & Karen Markoe. (Illus.). (gr. 4-6). 1978. PLB 7.90 s&l (ISBN 0-531-01468-1). Watts.

Super Dynamic Kicks, Vol. 3. Chong Lee. LC 80-84496. 1980. pap. 5.50 (ISBN 0-89750-072-5). Ohara Pubns.

Super-Easy Step-by-Step Book of Special Breads. Yvonne Y. Tarr. (Orig.). 1975. pap. 2.95 o.p. (ISBN 0-394-72010-5, Vin). Random.

Super-Easy-Step-by-Step Sausagemaking. Yvonne Y. Tarr. (Orig.). 1975. pap. 3.95 (ISBN 0-394-72011-3, Vin). Random.

Super Easy-Step-by-Step Winemaking. Yvonne Y. Tarr. (Orig.). 1975. pap. 3.95 o.p. (ISBN 0-394-72012-1, Vin). Random.

Super Eight Book. L. Lipton. 1975. 6.95 (ISBN 0-671-22082-9). S&S.

Super Eight Handbook. George D. Glenn & Charles B. Scholz. 1980. pap. 9.95 (ISBN 0-672-21743-0). Bobbs.

Super Eight the Modest Medium. (Monographs on Communication Technology & Utilization: No. 1). (Illus.). 1977. pap. 4.00 (ISBN 92-3-101368-8, U644, UNESCO). Unipub.

Super Food Cookbook for Kids. Sherry G. Loller. Ed. by Bobbie J. Van Dolson. (Illus.). (gr. k-5). 1976. pap. 2.95 (ISBN 0-8280-0060-3). Review & Herald.

Super Games & Projects to Do with Your Home Computer. Fred D'Ignazio. LC 79-6860. (Illus.). 144p. (gr. 6). 1981. 9.95a (ISBN 0-385-15313-9); PLB (ISBN 0-385-15314-7). Doubleday.

Super Hair. Jonathan Zizmor & John Foreman. 1978. pap. 1.95 o.p. (ISBN 0-425-03878-5, Dist. by Putnam). Berkley Pub.

Super Joe: The Life & Legend of Joe Charboneau. Joe Charboneau et al. LC 80-6169. 256p. 1981. 12.95 (ISBN 0-8128-2806-2). Stein & Day.

Super Living Rooms. Emily Malino. 1976. 10.00 o.p. (ISBN 0-394-49901-8); pap. 4.95 o.p. (ISBN 0-394-73103-4). Random.

Super Marriage, Super Sex. H. F. Freedman. 1975. pap. 1.75 o.p. (ISBN 0-345-24949-6). Ballantine.

Super Power Steam Locomotives. Richard J. Cook. LC 66-29787. (Illus.). 1966. 15.95 (ISBN 0-87095-010-X). Golden West.

Super Powers. Roger James. 1978. 14.95 (ISBN 0-7134-0081-1, Pub. by Batsford England). David & Charles.

Super Realism: A Critical Anthology. Ed. & intro. by Gregory Battcock. 352p. 1975. pap. 10.95 (ISBN 0-525-47377-7). Dutton.

Super Self: A Woman's Guide to Self-Management. Dorothy Tennov. LC 76-41721. (Funk & W Bk.). 1977. 8.95 o.s.i. (ISBN 0-308-10273-8, TYC-T). T Y Crowell.

Super Self: A Woman's Guide to Self-Management. Dorothy Tennov. 1978. pap. 1.95 (ISBN 0-515-04510-1). Jove Pubns.

Super Skin. Jonathan Zizmor & John Foreman. LC 75-28443. 224p. 1976. 8.95 (ISBN 0-690-01078-8, TYC-T). T Y Crowell.

Super Spelling Fun. Charlie Daniel & Becky Daniel. (gr. 2-6). 1978. 5.95 (ISBN 0-916456-31-5, GA82). Good Apple.

Super Steelers: The Making of a Dynasty. Lou Sahadi. 256p. 1980. 14.95 (ISBN 0-8129-0950-X). Times Bks.

Super Stickers for Kids: One Hundred & Twenty-Eight Fun Labels. Carolyn Bracken. (Illus.). 16p. (Orig.). 1981. pap. price not set (ISBN 0-486-24092-4). Dover.

Super Strategies: Games & Puzzles for Strategy Training. Saul Levmore. (Illus.). 168p. 1981. 10.95 (ISBN 0-385-17165-X). Doubleday.

Super Sundays -- One to Thirteen. Lou Sahadi. LC 79-50991. (Illus.). 1979. pap. 7.95 o.p. (ISBN 0-8092-7445-0). Contemp Bks.

Super Superintendent: A Layman's Guide to Sunday School Management. Harold J. Westing. LC 80-66721. (Accent Teacher Training Ser.). 160p. (Orig.). 1980. pap. 3.95 (ISBN 0-89636-057-1). Accent Bks.

Super Vee. Sylvia Wilkinson. (World of Racing Ser.). (Illus.). 48p. (gr. 4 up). 1981. PLB 9.25 (ISBN 0-516-04714-0). Childrens.

Super-Vroomer. Northern J. Calloway & Carol Hall. LC 77-26512. (gr. k-3). 1978. PLB 5.95 (ISBN 0-385-14178-5). Doubleday.

Superalloys. Ed. by Chester T. Sims & William C. Hagel. LC 72-5904. (Science & Technology of Materials Ser.). 688p. 1972. 54.50 (ISBN 0-471-79207-1, Pub. by Wiley-Interscience). Wiley.

Superbath - The Blood - Washing Method. Benedict Lust. (Illus.). 1980. pap. 2.95 (ISBN 0-87904-027-0). Lust.

Superbikes. Laurie Caddell & Mike Winfield. (Orig.). 1981. pap. 9.95 (ISBN 0-89586-067-8). H P Bks.

Superbowl. Julian May. LC 75-5855. (Sports Classics Ser.). (Illus.). 48p. (gr. 4-6). 1975. PLB 8.95 o.p. (ISBN 0-87191-446-8). Creative Ed.

Supercars. John Gabriel Navarra. LC 73-10949. (gr. 1-5). 1975. PLB 7.95 (ISBN 0-385-06827-1). Doubleday.

Supercars. Jeremy Sinek. LC 79-10851. (Illus.). 128p. 1979. 14.95 (ISBN 0-89196-041-4, Domus Bks). Quality Bks IL.

Supercharged Mercedes. Halwart Schrader & Carlo Demand. Tr. by D. B. Tubbs. (Illus.). 96p. 1979. 37.50 (ISBN 0-85059-417-0, Pub. by Edita Switzerland). Motorbooks Intl.

Supercold - Superhot: Cryogenics & Controlled Thermonuclear Fusion. Gail K. Haines. (Impact Bks.). (Illus.). 96p. (gr. 7 up). 1976. PLB 4.90 o.p. (ISBN 0-531-01203-4). Watts.

Superconductivity. 2nd ed. David Shoenberg. (Cambridge Monographs on Physics). (Illus.). 1960-1965. pap. 5.00 (ISBN 0-521-09254-X). Cambridge U Pr.

Superconductivity. A. W. Taylor & G. R. Noakes. (Wykeham Science Ser.: No. 11). 1970. 9.95x (ISBN 0-8448-1113-0). Crane Russak Co.

Superconductivity & Quantum Fluids. Z. M. Galasiewicz. 1970. 32.00 (ISBN 0-08-013089-5). Pergamon.

Superconductivity Industry. Ed. by BCC Staff. 1980. 750.00 (ISBN 0-89336-144-5, E-032R). BCC.

Superculture: American Popular Culture & Europe. C. W. Bigsby. LC 74-84638. 1975. 13.95 (ISBN 0-87972-070-0); pap. 7.95 (ISBN 0-87972-163-4). Bowling Green Univ.

Superduper Teddy. Johanna Hurwitz. LC 80-12962. (Illus.). 80p. (gr. k-3). 1980. 6.95 (ISBN 0-688-22234-X); PLB 6.67 (ISBN 0-688-32234-4). Morrow.

Superficial Mycoses. Ed. by C. Terrence Dolan. (Atlases of Clinical Mycology: 4). 1975. text & slides 78.00 (ISBN 0-89189-042-4, 15-7-005-00); microfiche ed. 22.00 (ISBN 0-89189-090-4, 17-7-005-00). Am Soc Clinical.

Superfight No. II: The Story Behind the Fights Between Muhammad Ali & Joe Frazier. Joseph Okpaku. LC 74-74429. 1974. 6.95 (ISBN 0-89388-165-1). Okpaku Communications.

Superfilms: An International Guide to Award Winning Educational Films. Salvatore J. Parlato, Jr. LC 76-10801. 1976. 16.50 (ISBN 0-8108-0953-2). Scarecrow.

Superflirt. Helen Cavanaugh. 176p. (Orig.). (gr. 7 up). 1980. pap. 1.50 (ISBN 0-590-30951-X, Schol Pap). Schol Bk Serv.

Superfluidity & Superconductivity. D. R. Tilley & J. Tilley. LC 73-11584. 1975. 39.95 (ISBN 0-470-86788-4). Halsted Pr.

Superfluidity & Superconductivity. David R. Tilley & John Tilley. LC 74-7081. 262p. 1974. 29.95 (ISBN 0-470-86788-4, Pub. by Wiley). Krieger.

Superfluous Anarchist: Albert Jay Nock. Michael Wreszin. LC 75-154339. (Illus.). 196p. 1971. 8.50 (ISBN 0-87057-130-3). Univ Pr of New England.

Superfluous Man in Russian Letters. Jesse V. Clardy & Betty S. Clardy. LC 80-5080. 189p. 1980. text ed. 17.00 (ISBN 0-8191-1039-6); pap. text ed. 9.00 (ISBN 0-8191-1040-X). U Pr of Amer.

Supergroups. Cynthia Dagnal. (Illus.). 192p. (Orig.). (gr. 6 up). 1981. pap. 1.95 (ISBN 0-448-17228-3, Tempo). G&D.

SuperHair: The Doctor's Book of Beautiful Hair. Jonathan Zizmor & John Foreman. LC 77-22817. (Illus.). (YA) 1978. 7.95 o.p. (ISBN 0-399-12005-X, Pub. by Berkley Pub). Berkley Pub.

Superheavy Elements: Proceedings. International Symposium on Superheavy Elements, March 9-11, 1978, Lubbock, Texas. Ed. by M. A. Lodhi. 604p. 1979. 60.00 (ISBN 0-08-022946-8). Pergamon.

Superinsulated House: A Working Guide for Owner/Builders & Architects. Ed McGrath. (Illus.). 128p. 1981. 13.95 (ISBN 0-918270-11-1); pap. 9.95 (ISBN 0-918270-12-X). That New Pub.

Superinsulated Houses & Double-Envelope Houses. William A. Shurcliff. (Illus.). 228p. 1981. 19.95 (ISBN 0-931790-19-0); pap. 12.00. Brick Hse Pub.

Superintendency Team. Fensch. 1964. text ed. 12.50 (ISBN 0-675-09926-9). Merrill.

Superior Sex. Thomas M. Lister. 237p. 1980. 7.95 (ISBN 0-8059-2732-8). Dorrance.

Superlative Horse. Jean Merrill. (gr. 4-7). 1961. PLB 5.95 o.p. (ISBN 0-685-21701-9, A-W Childrens). A-W.

Superman & Spiderman. Jim Shooter et al. 160p. (Orig.). 1981. pap. 2.50 (ISBN 0-446-91757-5). Warner Bks.

Superman of Letters: R. Reginald & the Borgo Press. John Weeks. LC 80-11112. 64p. 1981. lib. bdg. 8.95x (ISBN 0-89370-811-9); pap. 2.95x (ISBN 0-89370-911-5). Borgo Pr.

Supermarket. Anne Rockwell & Harlow Rockwell. LC 79-11411. (Illus.). (ps-1). 1979. 7.95 (ISBN 0-02-777580-1). Macmillan.

Supermarket Handbook: Access to Whole Foods. Nikki Goldbeck & David Goldbeck. LC 73-4084. (Illus.). 432p. 1973. 9.95 o.p. (ISBN 0-06-011581-5, HarpT). Har-Row.

Supermarket Magic. Jack Kent. LC 78-55908. (Sniffy Bks.). (ps-2). 1978. 3.95 (ISBN 0-394-83921-8, BYR). Random.

Supermarket Merchandising & Management. Hugh S. Peak & Ellen Peak. LC 76-17604. (Illus.). 1977. ref. ed. 15.95 (ISBN 0-13-876037-3). P-H.

Supermarket News Distribution Study of Grocery Store Sales. 257p. 1980. pap. 27.50 o.p. (ISBN 0-87005-313-2). Fairchild.

Supermarket Trap: The Consumer & the Food Industry. rev. ed. Jennifer Cross. LC 75-10806. (Midland Bks.: No. 199). (Illus.). 320p. 1976. 12.50x (ISBN 0-253-35582-6); pap. 3.50x (ISBN 0-253-20199-3). Ind U Pr.

Supermazes: No. 1. Bernard Myers. 1977. pap. 2.95 (ISBN 0-385-11467-2, Dolp). Doubleday.

Superminds. John Taylor. 1977. pap. 1.95 o.s.i. (ISBN 0-446-89032-4). Warner Bks.

Supermonsters. Daniel Cohen. (gr. 4 up). 1978. pap. 1.50 (ISBN 0-671-41190-X). Archway.

Supermonsters. Daniel Cohen. LC 76-48970. (gr. 4-9). 1977. 5.95 (ISBN 0-396-07399-9). Dodd.

Supermonsters. Daniel Cohen. (Illus.). (gr. 4 up). 1978. pap. 1.50 (ISBN 0-671-41190-X, HI-LO). PB.

Supernatural. Douglas Hill & Pat Williams. pap. 6.95 o.p. (ISBN 0-452-25094-3, Z5094, Plume). NAL.

Supernatural. Douglas Hill & Pat Williams. pap. 1.95 (ISBN 0-451-09265-1, J9265, Sig). NAL.

Supernatural: From ESP to UFO's. Melvin Berger. LC 77-2829. (gr. 6 up). 1977. 8.95 (ISBN 0-381-90054-1, JD-J). John Day.

Supernatural in Fiction. Peter Penzoldt. 1952. text ed. 15.00x (ISBN 0-391-00461-1). Humanities.

Supernatural in Romantic Fiction. Edward Yardley. 1979. 28.50 o.p. (ISBN 0-685-94350-X). Porter.

Supernatural Poetry. Michael Hayes. 1980. 10.95 (ISBN 0-7145-3697-0). Riverrun NY.

Supernatural Reader. Ed. by Groff Conklin. 1962. pap. 1.50 o.s.i. (ISBN 0-02-019110-3, Collier). Macmillan.

Supernatural Short Stories of Charles Dickens. Ed. by Michael Hayes. 1979. 9.95 (ISBN 0-7145-3678-4). Riverrun NY.

Supernatural Short Stories of Robert Louis Stevenson. Ed. by Michael Hayes. (Scottish Library). 1976. text ed. 13.00x (ISBN 0-7145-3550-8). Humanities.

Supernatural Short Stories of Sir Walter Scott. Ed. by Michael Hayes. (Scottish Library). 1977. text ed. 13.75x (ISBN 0-7145-3616-4). Humanities.

Supernutrition for Healthy Hearts. Richard Passwater. 1978. pap. 2.95 (ISBN 0-515-05725-8). Jove Pubns.

Superplanes. John Gabriel Navarra. LC 77-16936. (gr. 3-7). 1979. 7.95a (ISBN 0-385-12561-5); PLB (ISBN 0-385-12562-3). Doubleday.

Superplasticizers in Concrete. 1979. 30.95 (SP-62); member 24.50. ACI.

Superposition & Interaction: Coherence in Physics. Richard Schlegel. LC 80-11119. (Illus.). 1980. lib. bdg. 22.50x (ISBN 0-226-73841-8). U of Chicago Pr.

Superpowers & the Balance of Power in the Arab World. Enver M. Koury. LC 79-131974. 208p. 1970. pap. 7.00 (ISBN 0-934484-01-5). Inst Mid East & North Africa.

Superpowers & the Middle East. Tarun C. Bose. 208p. 1972. lib. bdg. 7.50x (ISBN 0-210-22345-6). Asia.

Superpuppy: How to Choose, Raise & Train the Best Possible Dog for You. Jill Pinkwater & D. Manus Pinkwater. LC 76-8825. (Illus.). (gr. 3 up). 1977. 9.95 (ISBN 0-395-28878-9, Clarion). HM.

Superships & Nation-States: The Transnational Politics of the Intergovernmental Maritime Consultative Organization. Harvey Silverstein. LC 77-27662. (Illus.). 1978. lib. bdg. 24.50x (ISBN 0-89158-058-1). Westview.

Superspies: The Secret Side of Government. Jules Archer. LC 77-72640. (gr. 7up). 1977. 7.95 o.p. (ISBN 0-440-08136-X). Delacorte.

Superspill: An Account of the 1978 Grounding at Bird Rocks. Mary K. Becker & Patricia Coburn. LC 74-76954. 1974. pap. 3.95 (ISBN 0-914842-02-1). Madrona Pubs.

Superstars of Golf. Nick Seitz. LC 77-92910. (Illus.). 192p. 1977. 10.95 (ISBN 0-914178-13-X, 22975). Golf Digest.

Superstars of Rock: Their Lives & Their Music. Gene Busnar. LC 80-18912. (Illus.). 224p. (gr. 7 up). 1980. PLB 9.29 (ISBN 0-671-32967-7). Messner.

Superstars, Stars, & Just Plain Heroes. Nathan Salant. LC 79-3877. 288p. 1981. 14.95 (ISBN 0-8128-2716-3). Stein & Day.

Superstition! Willard A. Heaps. LC 72-8114. (gr. 6up). 1972. 7.95 o.p. (ISBN 0-525-66226-X). Elsevier-Nelson.

Superstitions. Daniel Cohen. Ed. by Gene Liberty. LC 74-125916. (Understanding Bks). (Illus.). (gr. 6-9). 1971. PLB 7.95 (ISBN 0-87191-069-1). Creative Ed.

Superstitions from Seven Towns of the United States. Catherine H. Ainsworth. (Folklore Bks.). vi, 58p. 1980. 2.00 (ISBN 0-933190-00-X). Clyde Pr.

Superstitions of Sailors. Angelo S. Rappoport. LC 71-158207. 1971. Repr. of 1928 ed. 20.00 (ISBN 0-8103-3739-8). Gale.

Superstitions of the Highlands & Islands of Scotland. John G. Campbell. 1970. 20.00 (ISBN 0-8103-3589-1). Gale.

SuperStudent! The Student's High School Handbook. rev. ed. Scott C. Mitchell. LC 80-84049. (Illus.). 112p. (gr. 9-12). 1981. pap. text ed. 4.95 (ISBN 0-938494-00-7). Kingsfield.

Supertanker. George Sullivan. LC 77-16870. (gr. 7 up). 1978. 6.95 (ISBN 0-396-07527-4). Dodd.

Superthreats. John Striker. 1981. pap. 2.95 (ISBN 0-440-17828-2). Dell.

Supertraining Your Dog. Jo Loeb & Paul Loeb. LC 80-10623. (Illus.). 1980. 9.95 (ISBN 0-13-876730-0). P-H.

Supertrains. John Gabriel Navarra. LC 74-18820. 80p. (gr. 1-5). 1976. 7.95 (ISBN 0-385-02024-4). Doubleday.

SuperTrust. rev. ed. Frank B. Weisz. LC 78-72975. 1980. 14.95 (ISBN 0-87863-179-8). Farnswth Pub.

Supervising Building Inspector. Jack Rudman. (Career Examination Ser.: C-2840). (Cloth bdg. avail. on request). 1980. Natl Learning.

Supervising Employees Effectively. William F. Cone. (Illus.). 180p. 1974. 8.95 (ISBN 0-201-01154-9). A-W.

Supervising the Reading Program. Nicholas P. Criscuolo. LC 72-98020. 1973. pap. 9.00 o.p. (ISBN 0-87812-049-1). Pendell Pub.

Supervising Today: A Guide for Positive Leadership. Martin M. Broadwell. LC 79-12751. 1979. pap. 8.95 (ISBN 0-8436-0775-0). CBI Pub.

Supervision. rev. ed. George R. Terry. 1978. pap. text ed. 12.50 (ISBN 0-256-02047-7). Irwin.

Supervision: A Guide to Practice. Jon Wiles & Joseph Bondi, Jr. (Educational Administration Ser.: No. C21). 350p. 1980. text ed. 15.95 (ISBN 0-675-08168-8). Merrill.

Supervision: An Introduction to Business Management. Steven L. Shapiro. 1978. 12.50 (ISBN 0-87005-213-6); instructor's guide 2.50 (ISBN 0-87005-306-X). Fairchild.

Supervision & Inspection of Federal Construction. Building Research Advisory Board. (Federal Construction Council Technical Report No. 54). 1968. pap. 4.00 o.p. (ISBN 0-309-01609-6). Natl Acad Pr.

Supervision & Management of Quantity Food Preparation - Principles & Procedures. William J. Morgan, Jr. LC 73-7239. 1974. 24.00x (ISBN 0-8211-1225-2); text ed. 19.50x (ISBN 0-685-72314-3). McCutchan.

Supervision & Management of Quantity Preparation. 2nd, rev ed. William J. Morgan, Jr. LC 80-83876. (Illus.). 1981. price not set (ISBN 0-8211-1254-6); text ed. price not set. McCutchan.

Supervision Decision! Employee Guide. Paul O. Radde. (Illus.). 150p. 1981. price not set vinyl binder (ISBN 0-89384-060-2); price not set wkbk. (ISBN 0-89384-061-0). Learning Concepts.

Supervision in Social Work. Alfred Kadushin. 496p. 1976. 17.50x (ISBN 0-231-03657-4). Columbia U Pr.

Supervision of Construction: A Guide to Site Inspection. John Watts. (Illus.). 208p. 1980. 38.00 (ISBN 0-7134-2173-8, Pub. by Batsford England). David & Charles.

Supervision of Police Personnel. 3rd ed. N. Iannone. 1980. 15.95 (ISBN 0-13-876987-7). P-H.

Supervision of Private Insurance in Europe. Organization for Economic Cooperation & Development. Incl. General Study. 226p; Country Reports. (18 bklets in cardboard box). 1963. 9.00 ea. o.p. OECD.

Supervision: Principles of Management. Robert M. Fulmer. 1976. text ed. 14.95x (ISBN 0-02-473070-X). Macmillan.

Supervision: The Art of Management. J. Halloran. 1981. 17.95 (ISBN 0-13-876276-7); pap. 6.95 study guide (ISBN 0-13-876292-9). P-H.

Supervision: The Management of Organizational Resources. Sterling H. Schoen & Douglas E. Durand. (Illus.). 1979. ref. 15.95 (ISBN 0-13-876235-X). P-H.

Supervisor & on the Job Training. 2nd ed. Martin M. Broadwell. LC 74-30695. (Illus.). 176p. 1975. text ed. 8.95 (ISBN 0-201-00754-1). A-W.

Supervisor As an Instructor: A Guide for Classroom Training. 3rd ed. Martin M. Broadwell. LC 77-81201. (Illus.). 1978. pap. text ed. 8.95 (ISBN 0-201-00329-5). A-W.

Supervisors & Teachers: A Private Cold War. 2nd ed. Arthur Blumberg. LC 79-89771. 1980. 16.60 (ISBN 0-8211-0133-1); text ed. 15.00 in copies of 10 (ISBN 0-686-66218-0). McCutchan.

Supervisor's Manual for Amanecer, 1 bk. Sullivan Assoc. text ed. 15.00 (ISBN 0-8449-4168-9). Learning Line.

Supervisor's Survival Kit: A Mid-Management Primer. 2nd ed. Elwood N. Chapman. LC 75-26903. (Illus.). 192p. 1975. pap. text ed. 7.95 (ISBN 0-574-20000-2, 13-3000); instr's guide avail. (ISBN 0-574-20001-0, 13-3001). SRA.

Supervisory & Middle Managers in Libraries. Martha J. Bailey. LC 80-23049. 218p. 1981. 12.00 (ISBN 0-8108-1400-5). Scarecrow.

Supervisory Behavior in Education. 2nd ed. Ben M. Harris. LC 74-13100. (Illus.). 480p. 1975. ref. ed. 17.95x (ISBN 0-13-877118-9). P-H.

Supervisory Experience. Robert Langs. LC 79-51514. 1979. 30.00 (ISBN 0-87668-342-1). Aronson.

Supervisory Management. Robert W. Eckles & Ronald L. Carmichael. (Management Ser.). 550p. 1981. text ed. 22.95 (ISBN 0-471-05947-1); tchrs.' ed. avail. (ISBN 0-471-08941-9). Wiley.

Supervisory Management for Health Care Institutions. Theo Haimann. LC 72-92380. 1973. 11.00 (ISBN 0-87125-004-7). Cath Health.

Supervisory Management for the Human Services. Michael J. Austin. (P-H Ser. in Social Work Practices). 352p. 1981. text ed. 16.95 (ISBN 0-13-877068-9). P-H.

Supervisory Management: Skill Building Techniques. David M. Hunter. 300p. 1981. text ed. 16.95 (ISBN 0-8359-7155-4); pap. text ed. 12.95 (ISBN 0-8359-7156-2); instr's. manual free (ISBN 0-8359-7157-0). Reston.

Supplement Aux Dictionnaire Arabe (Arabic-French, 2 vols. R. Dozy. 1969. 70.00x (ISBN 0-685-72061-6). Intl Bk Ctr.

Supplement: Depression. 1968. Repr. pap. 1.00 o.p. (ISBN 0-685-84700-4, 194). Am Psychiatric.

Supplement E Chemistry of Ethers Crown Ethers Hydroxyl Group & Their Sulphur Analogs. S. Patai. 1192p. 1980. Set. write for info. (ISBN 0-471-27618-9, Pub. by Wiley-Interscience). Pt. 1 (ISBN 0-471-27771-1). Pt. 2 (ISBN 0-471-27772-X). Wiley.

Supplement Number One to the Nineteen Seventy-Seven Edition of the Code for the Construction & Equipment of Ships Carrying Dangerous Chemicals in Bulk. 24p. 1978. 7.00 (IMCO). Unipub.

Supplement Relating to the Annex to the Convention on Facilitation of International Maritime Traffic, 1965. 62p. 1979. 9.75 (IMCO). Unipub.

Supplement to a California Flora. Philip A. Munz. 1968. 11.50x (ISBN 0-520-00904-5). U of Cal Pr.

Supplement to a Teacher's Notebook: Alternatives for Children with Learning Problems. Sherry R. Migdail & Priscilla L. Vail. 1978. pap. 4.25 (ISBN 0-934338-10-8). NAIS.

Supplement to ACI 318-71 & Commentary, 1975. ACI Committee 318. 1975. 5.00 o.p. (ISBN 0-685-85079-X, 318-71 SUP); members 3.00 o.p. (ISBN 0-685-85080-3). ACI.

Supplement to Allibone's Critical Dictionary of English Literature & British & American Authors, 2 Vols. John F. Kirk. LC 67-296. 1965. Repr. of 1891 ed. 76.00 (ISBN 0-8103-3018-0). Gale.

Supplement to Antiquity Explained. Bernard De Montfaucon. Tr. by David Humphreys. LC 75-27882. (Renaissance & the Gods Ser.: Vol. 37). (Illus.). 1976. Repr. of 1725 ed. lib. bdg. 73.00 (ISBN 0-8240-2086-3). Garland Pub.

Supplement to Bibliography on Deafness: 1977 to 1979. Ed. by George W. Fellendorf. 1980. pap. text ed. 4.95 (ISBN 0-88200-139-6, L9435). Alexander Graham.

Supplement to Checklist of Plant & Soil Nematodes, 1961-1965: A Nomenclatorial Compilation. Armen C. Tarjan. LC 60-10226. 1967. 6.75 (ISBN 0-8130-0224-9). U Presses Fla.

Supplement to Coping with Psychiatric & Psychological Testimony. Jay Ziskin. 1977. 9.50 o.p. (ISBN 0-9603630-1-7). Law & Psych.

Supplement to E. J. Labarre's Dictionary & Encyclopaedia of Paper & Paper-Making. Ed. by E. G. Loeber. 114p. text ed. 23.75 (ISBN 90-265-0038-6, Pub. by Swets Pub Serv). Swets North Am.

Supplement to European Pharmacopoeia, Vols. 1&2. 1973. 10.00 o.p. (ISBN 0-85369-089-8, Pub. by Pharmaceutical). Rittenhouse.

Supplement to European Pharmacopoeia, Vol. 3. 1977. 37.00 o.p. (ISBN 0-685-41509-0, Pub. by Pharmaceutical). Rittenhouse.

Supplement to F. Scott Fitzgerald: A Descriptive Bibliography. Matthew J. Bruccoli. LC 79-21728. (Pittsburgh Ser. in Bibliography). (Illus.). 235p. 1980. 19.95x (ISBN 0-8229-3409-4). U of Pittsburgh Pr.

Supplement to the Blood-Horse: Stallion Register 1980. The Throroughbred Owners & Breeders Association. 1980. lib. bdg. 20.00 o.p. (ISBN 0-936032-28-6); pap. 10.00 o.p. (ISBN 0-686-10833-7). Thoroughbred Own and Breed.

Supplement to the Code of Safe Practice for Ships Carrying Timber Deck Cargoes. 18p. 1979. 7.00 (IMCO). Unipub.

Supplement to the Index Bergeyana. John G. Holt. 387p. 1981. write for info. (4106-1). Williams & Wilkins.

Supplement to the World Trade Annual 1972: Trade of the Industrial Nations with Eastern Europe & the Developing Nations, 5 vols. Incl. Vol. 1. Eastern Europe & U.S.S.R (ISBN 0-8027-5915-7); Vol. 2. South & Central America (Including Caribbean & Bermuda (ISBN 0-8027-5916-5); Vol. 3. Africa (ISBN 0-8027-5917-3); Vol. 4. Near East (ISBN 0-8027-5918-1); Vol. 5. Far East (ISBN 0-8027-5919-X). LC 64-66238. Set. 477.00 o.s.i. (ISBN 0-8027-5920-3). Walker & Co.

Supplemental Security Income: New Federal Program Aged, Blind, & Disabled. Paul L. Grimaldi. 1980. pap. 5.25 (ISBN 0-8447-3356-3). Am Enterprise.

Supplementary English Glossary. Thomas L. Davies. LC 68-23468. 1968. Repr. of 1881 ed. 28.00 (ISBN 0-8103-3245-0). Gale.

Supplementary Field Investigation of Underground Heat Distribution Systems. Federal Construction Council - Building Research Advisory Board. 1966. pap. 3.25 (ISBN 0-309-01481-6). Natl Acad Pr.

Supplementary Studies on the Systematics of the Genus Perdita (Hymenoptera: Andrenidae) P. H. Timberlake. (U. C. Publ. in Entomology: Vol. 66). 1971. pap. 6.00x (ISBN 0-520-09397-6). U of Cal Pr.

Supplementary Studies on the Systematics of the Genus Perdita (Hymenoptera, Andrenidae, Part II. P. H. Timberlake. (U. C. Publications in Entomology Ser.: Vol. 85). 1980. pap. 9.00 (ISBN 0-520-09605-3). U of Cal Pr.

Suppliant Women. Aeschylus. Tr. by Gilbert Murray. 1930. pap. text ed. 3.95x (ISBN 0-04-882017-2). Allen Unwin.

Suppliants. Aeschylus. Ed. by William Arrowsmith. Tr. by Janet Lembke from Greek. (Greek Tragedy in New Translations Ser.). 110p. 1975. 10.95 (ISBN 0-19-501933-4). Oxford U Pr.

Supplicatyon... Unto Henry the Eighth. Robert Barnes. LC 73-6098. (English Experience Ser.: No. 567). 1973. Repr. of 1534 ed. 18.50 (ISBN 90-221-0567-9). Walter J Johnson.

Supplies & Materials Management. 2nd ed. H. K. Compton. (Illus.). 512p. 1979. text ed. 45.00x (ISBN 0-7121-1964-7, Pub. by Macdonald & Evans England). Intl Ideas.

Supply & Demand. Hubert Henderson. (Cambridge Economic Handbook Ser). 1958. pap. 8.95x (ISBN 0-521-08760-0). Cambridge U Pr.

Supply in a Market Economy. Richard Jones. (Studies in Economics Ser.). 1976. text ed. 17.95x (ISBN 0-04-330270-X); pap. text ed. 8.95x (ISBN 0-04-330271-8). Allen Unwin.

Supplying Repression: U. S. Support for Authoritarian Regimes Abroad. rev. ed. Cynthia Arnson & Michael T. Klare. 100p. 1981. pap. 4.95 (ISBN 0-89758-024-9). Inst Policy Stud.

Supplying War. Martin L. Van Creveld. LC 77-5550. 1979. pap. 9.95 (ISBN 0-521-29793-1). Cambridge U Pr.

Supplying War: Logistics from Wallenstein to Patton. Martin L Van Creveld. LC 77-5550. (Illus.). 1977. 27.50 (ISBN 0-521-21730-X). Cambridge U Pr.

Support Costs in the Defense Budget: The Submerged One-Third. Martin Binkin. (Studies in Defense Policy). 49p. 1972. pap. 3.95 (ISBN 0-8157-0957-9). Brookings.

Support of Life. Gene Liberty. (Orig.). (gr. 7-10). 1975. pap. text ed. 6.00 (ISBN 0-87720-011-4). AMSCO Sch.

Support Systems in Social Work. Martin Davies. (Library of Social Work). 1977. 16.00x (ISBN 0-7100-8616-4); pap. 7.95 (ISBN 0-7100-8617-2). Routledge & Kegan.

Supporting Documents: Transborder Data Flows: Concerns in Privacy Protection & Free Flow of Information, Vol. II. Ed. by Rein Turn & Alexander D. Roth. 300p. 1979. pap. 25.00 (ISBN 0-88283-024-4). AFIPS Pr.

Supportive Personnel Training Manuals, 2 vols. (Illus.). 1978. pap. 24.00 set (ISBN 0-917330-22-6); Pharmacist's Manual. pap. 15.00 (ISBN 0-685-29172-3); Trainee's Manual. pap. 15.00 (ISBN 0-685-29173-1). Am Pharm Assn.

Supportive Services for Disadvantaged Workers & Trainees. Deborah Heskes. (Key Issues Ser.: No. 12). 1973. pap. 2.00 (ISBN 0-87546-225-1). NY Sch Indus Rel.

Suppose You Were a Dinka: Teens in Other Societies. Barbara Milbauer. (gr. 7 up). 1981. PLB price not set (ISBN 0-671-32891-3). Messner. Postponed.

Suppressed Inventions & How They Work. Mike Brown. 1974. 5.95 o.p. (ISBN 0-913808-03-2); pap. 1.95 o.p. (ISBN 0-913808-04-0). Madison Pub.

Suppressed Truth About the Assassination of Abraham Lincoln. Burke McCarty. 255p. 1960. Repr. of 1870 ed. 10.00 (Pub. by Chedney). Alpine Ent.

Suppression. Francisco H. Mosti. 64p. 1981. 9.00 (ISBN 0-682-49691-X). Exposition.

Suppression of the African Slave Trade to the United States of America, Sixteen Thirty-Eight to Eighteen Seventy. reprint, orig. pub. 1970 ed. William E. Du Bois. Ed. by Philip S. Foner. LC 70-110748. (Rediscovery Ser). 1970. pap. 2.50 o.p. (ISBN 0-486-22463-5). Dover.

Supremacy of God. Ilon. LC 80-66408. 1980. pap. 3.00 (ISBN 0-9600958-6-1). Birth Day.

Supreme Adventure: Analyses of Psychic Communications. rev. ed. R. Crookall. 288p. 1975. 13.95 (ISBN 0-227-67606-8). Attic Pr.

Supreme Court. David F. Forte. (American Government Ser.). (Illus.). (gr. 7 up). 1979. PLB 6.90 s&l (ISBN 0-531-02267-6). Watts.

Supreme Court & Confessions of Guilt. Otis H. Stephens, Jr. LC 73-8777. 248p. 1973. 13.50x (ISBN 0-87049-147-4). U of Tenn Pr.

Supreme Court & Congress: Conflict & Interaction, 1945-1968. John Schmidhauser & Larry Berg. LC 77-160068. 1972. pap. text ed. 4.50 o.s.i. (ISBN 0-02-927900-3). Free Pr.

Supreme Court & Education. 3rd ed. Ed. by David Fellman. LC 76-14495. 1976. pap. text ed. 7.00x (ISBN 0-8077-2511-0). Tchrs Coll.

Supreme Court & Fundamental Freedoms. 2nd ed. George W. Spicer. (Orig.). 1967. pap. 9.95 (ISBN 0-13-877852-3). P-H.

Supreme Court & Individual Rights. Congressional Quarterly Staff. Ed. by Congressional Quarterly Staff. 310p. (Orig.). 1980. pap. text ed. 6.95 (ISBN 0-87187-195-5). Congr Quarterly.

Supreme Court & Its Publics. Larry C. Berkson. LC 77-14793. (Illus.). 1978. 16.95 (ISBN 0-669-01994-1). Lexington Bks.

Supreme Court & Judicial Review. Robert K. Carr. LC 74-98215. Repr. of 1942 ed. lib. bdg. 19.75x (ISBN 0-8371-3261-4, CAJR). Greenwood.

Supreme Court & Labor-Management Relations Law. Alvin L. Goldman. LC 75-42953. 1976. 19.95 (ISBN 0-669-00496-0). Lexington Bks.

Supreme Court & Libel. Clifton O. Lawhorne. (New Horizons in Journalism Ser.). 1981. 19.95 (ISBN 0-8093-0998-X). S Ill U Pr.

Supreme Court & Political Questions. C. Gordon Post. LC 74-87386. (American History, Politics & Law Ser). 1969. Repr. of 1936 ed. lib. bdg. 19.50 (ISBN 0-306-71610-0). Da Capo.

Supreme Court & Religion. Richard E. Morgan. LC 72-80077. 1972. 12.95 (ISBN 0-02-921970-1). Free Pr.

Supreme Court & Religion. Richard E. Morgan. LC 72-80077. 1974. pap. text ed. 3.95 (ISBN 0-02-922070-X). Free Pr.

Supreme Court & Sovereign States. Charles Warren. LC 75-87626. (American Scene Ser). 160p. 1972. Repr. of 1924 ed. lib. bdg. 19.50 (ISBN 0-306-71807-3). Da Capo.

Supreme Court & the Allocation of Constitutional Power. Otis H. Stephens & Gregory Rathjen. LC 79-26468. (Illus.). 1980. text ed. 21.95x (ISBN 0-7167-1154-0); pap. text ed. 13.95x (ISBN 0-7167-1218-0). W H Freeman.

Supreme Court & the Commander in Chief. Clinton Rossiter. LC 76-98182. 1970. Repr. of 1951 ed. lib. bdg. 17.50 (ISBN 0-306-71832-4). Da Capo.

Supreme Court & the Idea of Progress. Alexander M. Bickel. LC 77-18365. 1978. 17.50x (ISBN 0-300-02238-7); pap. 4.95x (ISBN 0-300-02239-5). Yale U Pr.

Supreme Court & the Presidency. R. Scigliano. LC 76-128475. 1971. pap. text ed. 4.50 o.s.i. (ISBN 0-02-928280-2). Free Pr.

Supreme Court Crisis. Merlo J. Pusey. LC 74-171699. (FDR & the Era of the New Deal Ser). 108p. 1972. Repr. of 1937 ed. lib. bdg. 15.00 (ISBN 0-306-70389-0). Da Capo.

Supreme Court Decision Making. David W. Rohde & Harold J. Spaeth. LC 75-25645. (Illus.). 1976. text ed. 18.95x (ISBN 0-7167-0717-9); pap. text ed. 9.95x (ISBN 0-7167-0716-0). W H Freeman.

Supreme Court: Does It Protect or Limit Our Liberties? Daniel Selakovich. Ed. by Jack R. Fraenkel. (Crucial Issues in American Government Ser.). (gr. 9-12). 1976. pap. text ed. 4.96 (ISBN 0-205-04911-7, 7649118). Allyn.

Supreme Court in Modern Role. rev. ed. Carl B. Swisher. LC 79-26664. (New York University, James Stokes Lectureship on Politics Ser.). ix, 221p. 1980. Repr. of 1965 ed. lib. bdg. 21.00x (ISBN 0-313-22279-7, SWSU). Greenwood.

Supreme Court: Judicial Process & Judicial Politics. Arthur A. North. LC 66-17855. (Orig.). 1966. pap. text ed. 5.95x (ISBN 0-89197-435-0). Irvington.

Supreme Court Justice Is Appointed. David J. Danelski. LC 80-21229. (Studies in Political Science). x, 242p. 1980. Repr. of 1964 ed. lib. bdg. 23.50x (ISBN 0-313-22652-0, DASJ). Greenwood.

Supreme Court of the United States. Charles E. Hughes. LC 66-2855. 1928. pap. 9.50x (ISBN 0-231-08567-2, 67). Columbia U Pr.

Supreme Court on Trial. Charles S. Hyneman. LC 73-20501. 308p. 1974. Repr. of 1963 ed. lib. bdg. 21.75x (ISBN 0-8371-7326-4, HYSC). Greenwood.

Supreme Court Policy Making: Explanation & Prediction. Harold J. Spaeth. LC 78-14493. (Illus.). 1979. text ed. 16.95x (ISBN 0-7167-1013-7); pap. text ed. 8.95x (ISBN 0-7167-1012-9). W H Freeman.

Supreme Court: Politicians in Robes. Ed. by Charles Sheldon et al. (Insight Ser). 1970. pap. text ed. 4.95x (ISBN 0-02-478150-9, 47815). Macmillan.

Supreme Court, the Constitution, & Presidential Power. Michael A. Genovese. LC 80-5695. 345p. 1980. lib. bdg. 20.50 (ISBN 0-8191-1322-0); pap. text ed. 11.75 (ISBN 0-8191-1323-9). U Pr of Amer.

Supreme Doctrine: Discourses on the Kenopanishad. Bhagwan S. Rajneesh. 356p. (Orig.). 1980. pap. 14.95 (ISBN 0-7100-0572-5). Routledge & Kegan.

Supreme Victorie. Tr. by Harold Hill. (French Bks.). (Fr.). 1979. 1.95 (ISBN 0-8297-0942-8). Life Pubs Intl.

Sur le Vif. Madeleine Le Cunff. (Illus., Fr.). 1977. pap. text ed. 5.75 (ISBN 0-88436-454-2). EMC.

Surat in the Seventeenth Century: A Study in Urban Hstory of Pre-Modern India. B. G. Gokhale. (Scandinavian Inst. of Asian Studies: No. 28). 1977. pap. text ed. 12.50x (ISBN 0-7007-0099-4). Humanities.

Sure & There's More. Gahagan O'Sullivan. (Contemporary Poets of Dorrance Ser.). 64p. 1981. 3.95 (ISBN 0-8059-2781-6). Dorrance.

Sure Way to Get Job Interviews. Grandin K. Hammell. Ed. by Karen A. Brown. (Educational Ser.). (Illus.). 78p. (Orig.). (gr. 11-12). 1980. tchrs. ed. 4.50 (ISBN 0-936510-00-5, 101); wkbk. 9.00. Diamond Pubs.

Suretyship. 1981 ed. 75p. 10.00 (ISBN 0-87526-164-7). Gould.

Surf Club. Ed Harsen. 32p. (Orig.). 1981. pap. 3.00 (ISBN 0-935252-27-4). Street Pr.

Surf, Sand & Streetcars. Charles S. McCaleb. Ed. by Jim Walker. LC 77-14900. (Special Ser.: No.67). (Illus.). 1977. 12.50 o.p. (ISBN 0-916374-28-9). Interurban.

Surface. H. B. Griffiths. LC 74-25660. (Illus.). 128p. 1976. 19.95 (ISBN 0-521-20696-0). Cambridge U Pr.

Surface Active Chemicals. H. E. Garrett. 177p. 1973. pap. text ed. 21.00 (ISBN 0-08-016422-6). Pergamon.

Surface Active Ethylene Oxide Adducts. N. Schonfeldt. LC 69-19089. 1970. 115.00 (ISBN 0-08-012819-X). Pergamon.

Surface Anatomy for Coaches & Athletic Trainers. Hubert F. Riegler & Alan P. Peppard. (Illus.). 80p. 1979. pap. 10.75 spiral (ISBN 0-398-03856-2). C C Thomas.

Surface & Radiological Anatomy. 2nd rev. ed. A. Halim & A. C. Das. 1980. text ed. 15.00x (ISBN 0-7069-0640-3, Pub. by Vikas India). Advent Bk.

Surface Effect Vehicles: Principles & Applications. Joseph F. Sladky & Paul C. Klimas. LC 75-27231. (Illus.). 620p. Date not set. cancelled (ISBN 0-271-01211-0). Pa St U Pr. Postponed.

Surface Membrane Receptors: Interface Between Cells & Their Environment. Ed. by Ralph A. Bradshaw et al. LC 76-25821. (NATO Advanced Study Institutes Ser., Series A: Life Sciences: Vol. 11). 482p. 1976. 39.50 (ISBN 0-306-35611-2, Plenum Pr). Plenum Pub.

Surface Mining of Non-Coal Minerals. Board on Mineral & Energy Resources. LC 79-91887. xxiii, 339p. 1979. pap. 11.50 (ISBN 0-309-02942-2). Natl Acad Pr.

Surface Mining of Non-Coal Minerals. Incl. Appendix I: Sand & Gravel Mining, & Quarrying & Blasting for Crushed Stone & Other Construction Minerals. 7.50 (ISBN 0-686-64938-9, -03020-X); Appendix II: Mining & Processing of Oil Shale & Tar Sands. 8.25 (ISBN 0-309-03037-4). 1980. Natl Acad Pr.

Surface Modelling by Computer. 112p. 1980. 28.00x (ISBN 0-7277-0029-4, Pub. by Telford England). State Mutual Bk.

Surface Properties of Oxidized Silicon. E. Kooi. (Illus.). 1967. 5.60 o.p. (ISBN 0-387-91009-3). Springer-Verlag.

Surface Relief Images for Color Reproduction. M. T. Gale. (Illus.). 200p. 1980. pap. 25.00 (ISBN 0-240-51068-2). Focal Pr.

Surface Roughness Effects in Hydrodymanic & Mixed Lubrication. Ed. by S. M. Rohde & H. S. Cheng. 211p. 1980. 30.00 (G00193). ASME.

Surface Science: Proceedings, 2 vols. International Course, Trieste, Jan. 16-April 10, 1974. (Illus.). 503p. 1976. Vol. 1. pap. 37.50 (ISBN 92-0-130375-0, IAEA); Vol. 2. pap. 22.50 (ISBN 0-685-62848-5). Unipub.

Surface Skimmers Nineteen Eighty. McLeavy. 1980. 85.00 (ISBN 0-531-03933-1). Watts.

Surface Structure & Mechanisms of Gasification Catalyst Deactivation. P. J. Reucroft et al. Ed. by R. William De Vore. (Illus.). 86p. (Orig.). 1980. pap. 4.50 (ISBN 0-89779-028-6, IMMR46-PD22-80); 1.50 (ISBN 0-89779-029-4). OES Pubns.

Surface Water Sewerage. R. E. Bartlett. LC 75-46624. 1976. 29.95 (ISBN 0-470-15020-3). Halsted Pr.

Surfaces & Planar Discontinuous Groups: Revised & Expanded Translation. H. Zieschang et al. (Lecture Notes in Mathematics Ser.: Vol. 835). 334p. 1981. pap. 19.50 (ISBN 0-387-10024-5). Springer-Verlag.

Surfacing. Margaret Atwood. 224p. 1981. pap. 2.50 (ISBN 0-445-08465-0). Popular Lib.

Surfactants & Sequestrants-Recent Advances. S. J. Gutcho. LC 77-72960. (Chemical Technology Review Ser.: No. 89). (Illus.). 1977. 39.00 o.p. (ISBN 0-8155-0661-9). Noyes.

Surfboard Builders' Yearbook, Vols. 9 & 10. Stephen M. Shaw. Ed. by Michael Morgan et al. (Illus.). 1973-75. Vol. 9. 4.00 o.p. (ISBN 0-912750-01-4); Vol.10. 5.00 o.p. (ISBN 0-912750-02-2). Transmedia.

Surfboard: How to Build Surfboards & How to Surf. Ed. by Stephen M. Shaw & Aileen Brown. (Illus.). 1980. 8.00 (ISBN 0-912750-03-0). Transmedia.

Surfer & the City Girl. Betty Cavanna. LC 80-25901. (Hiway Bk.). (gr. 7-9). 1981. 8.95 (ISBN 0-664-32679-X). Westminster.

Surficial Geology: Building with the Earth. J. Costa & V. Baker. LC 80-22644. 1981. write for info. (ISBN 0-471-03229-8). Wiley.

Surficial Geology Building with the Earth. John E. Costa & Victor R. Baker. 608p. 1981. text ed. 19.95 (ISBN 0-471-03229-8). Wiley.

Surfiction: Fiction Now & Tomorrow. rev. ed. Ed. by Raymond Federman. 1981. pap. 7.95. Swallow.

Surfing: How to Improve Your Technique. Mark Sufrin. LC 73-2942. (Career Concise Guides Ser.). (gr. 5 up). 1973. PLB 4.90 o.p. (ISBN 0-531-02628-0). Watts.

Surgeon to Washington: Dr. John Cochran (1730-1807) Morris H. Saffron. LC 77-2675. 1977. 20.00x (ISBN 0-231-04186-1). Columbia U Pr.

Surgeon's Family. Carole G. Page. 1980. pap. 4.95 (ISBN 0-8423-6683-0). Tyndale.

Surgeon's Heart: History of Cardiac Surgery. Robert G. Richardson. (Illus.). 1969. 21.00x (ISBN 0-433-27590-1). Intl Ideas.

Surgery. 6th ed. M. D. Ram. (Medical Examination Review Book: Vol. 5). 1977. spiral bdg. 8.50 (ISBN 0-87488-105-6). Med Exam.

Surgery Annual: 1969, Vol. 1. Cooper. (Illus.). 1969. 18.85 o.p. (ISBN 0-8385-8700-3). ACC.

Surgery Annual: 1970, Vol. 2. Cooper. (Illus.). 1970. 17.80 o.p. (ISBN 0-8385-8702-X). ACC.

Surgery Annual: 1971, Vol. 3. Cooper. (Illus.). 1971. 19.50 o.p. (ISBN 0-8385-8703-8). ACC.

Surgery Annual: 1972, Vol. 4. Cooper. (Illus.). 1972. 17.50 o.p. (ISBN 0-8385-8704-6). ACC.

Surgery Annual: 1973, Vol. 5. Nyhus. (Illus.). 1973. 21.00 o.p. (ISBN 0-8385-8705-4). ACC.

Surgery Annual: 1974, Vol. 6. Nyhus. (Illus.). 1974. 25.50 o.p. (ISBN 0-8385-8706-2). ACC.

Surgery Annual: 1975, Vol. 7. Nyhus. (Illus.). 1975. 25.50 o.p. (ISBN 0-8385-8707-0). ACC.

Surgery Annual: 1976, Vol. 8. Nyhus. (Illus.). 1976. 27.50 o.p. (ISBN 0-8385-8708-9). ACC.

Surgery Annual: 1977, Vol. 9. Nyhus. (Illus.). 1977. 28.50 o.p. (ISBN 0-8385-8710-0). ACC.

Surgery Annual 1980. Ed. by Lloyd M. Nyhus. (Surgery Annual Ser.). 512p. 1980. 33.50x (ISBN 0-8385-8713-5). ACC.

Surgery Annual, 1981. Lloyd M. Nyhus. (Surgery Annual Series). 1981. 27.00 (ISBN 0-8385-8715-1). ACC.

Surgery for Cancer of the Larynx. C. E. Silver. 1981. text ed. write for info. (ISBN 0-443-08064-X). Churchill.

Surgery for Phonatory Disorders. Tucker. 1981. text ed. write for info. (ISBN 0-443-08058-5). Churchill.

Surgery in Acute Coronary Problems. Watts R. Webb. (Illus.). 68p. 1974. pap. 9.95 o.p. (ISBN 0-683-08888-2, Pub. by Williams & Wilkins). Krieger.

Surgery in Rheumatoid Arthritis. Ed. by I. Goldie. (Reconstruction Surgery & Traumatology Ser.: Vol. 18). (Illus.). 200p. 1981. 60.00 (ISBN 3-8055-1445-X). S Karger.

Surgery of Conditions Complicating Pregnancy, Vol. 6. David H. Lees & Albert Singer. (Illus.). 1981. write for info. (ISBN 0-8151-5356-2). Year Bk Med.

Surgery of Diseases & Injuries of the Hand, 2 vols. E. V. Usoltseva & K. I. Mashkara. LC 78-26990. (Illus.). 1979. Set. 39.50 (ISBN 0-8016-5198-0). Mosby.

Surgery of Female Incontinence. Ed. by S. L. Stanton & E. A. Tanagho. (Illus.). 203p. 1980. 58.00 (ISBN 0-387-10155-1). Springer-Verlag.

Surgery of Hydatid Disease. F. Saidi. LC 74-4587. (Illus.). 1976. text ed. 50.00 (ISBN 0-7216-7900-5). Saunders.

Surgery of the Adrenal Glands. Frank Glenn et al. (Illus.). 1968. 14.00 o.s.i. (ISBN 0-02-344260-3). Macmillan.

Surgery of the Alimentary Tract, Vol. 2. Richard T. Shackelford & George D. Zuidema. 1981. text ed. price not set (ISBN 0-7216-8084-4). Saunders.

Surgery of the Biliary Tract. Bjorn Thorbjarnarson. LC 74-25482. (Mpcs Ser.: Vol. 16). (Illus.). 166p. 1975. text ed. 18.00 (ISBN 0-7216-8858-6). Saunders.

Surgery of the Ear. 3rd ed. George E. Shambaugh & Michael E. Glasscock. (Illus.). 784p. 1980. text ed. 70.00 (ISBN 0-7216-8142-5). Saunders.

Surgery of the Gall Bladder & Bile Ducts. 2nd ed. Smith & Sherlock. 1981. price not set (ISBN 0-407-00118-2). Butterworths.

Surgery of the Leg & Foot. Rutt. (Hackenbroch Ser.). 1980. text ed. write for info. (ISBN 0-7216-4446-5). Saunders.

Surgery of the Orbit & Adnexa: Proceedings. The New Orleans Academy of Ophthalmology Symposium on Surgery of the Orbit & Adnexa. LC 73-14508. 1974. 38.50 o.p. (ISBN 0-8016-3677-9). Mosby.

Surgery of the Posterior Fossa. Ed. by William Buchheit & Raymond C. Truex. LC 78-73554. (Seminars in Neurological Surgery: Vol. 3). 1979. text ed. 24.00 (ISBN 0-89004-256-X). Raven.

Surgery of the Thyroid & Parathyroid Glands. 2nd ed. Cornelius E. Sedgwick & Blake Cady. (Major Problems in Clinical Surgery Ser.: No. XV). (Illus.). 200p. 1980. text ed. 21.50 (ISBN 0-7216-8054-2). Saunders.

Surgery of the Vulva & Vagina: A Practical Guide. Edward H. Copenhaver. (Illus.). 100p. 1981. text ed. write for info. (ISBN 0-7216-2718-8). Saunders.

Surgery of Traumatized Skin: Management & Reconstruction in the Dog & Cat. Steven F. Swaim. (Illus.). 585p. 1980. text ed. 42.50 (ISBN 0-7216-8688-5). Saunders.

Surgery: PreTest Self-Assessment & Review. Ed. by Wain L. White. LC 77-78445. (Clinical Sciences: PreTest Self-Assessment & Review Ser.). (Illus.). 1978. pap. 9.95 (ISBN 0-07-051605-7). McGraw-Pretest.

Surgery, Renal Disease, & Special Problems, Vol. III, Pt. II. Ed. by Ralph C. Scott. (Clinical Cardiology & Diabetes Monographs). (Illus.). 192p. 1981. 27.00 (ISBN 0-87993-138-8). Futura Pub.

Surgery Review & Assessment: Tumor, Trauma, & Specialties. Richard M. Stillman. 1981. pap. 12.50 (ISBN 0-686-69608-5). ACC.

Surgery Specialty Board Review. 5th ed. Alfred N. Butner. 1973. spiral bdg. 16.50 (ISBN 0-87488-302-4). Med Exam.

Surgery Without Fear. Danise L. Lee. (Illus.). 48p. 1980. pap. 4.95 (ISBN 0-937210-00-5). Time-Lee Pubns.

Surgical Anatomy for Clinical Examination. Andrew M. Munster & George J. Thomas. (Illus.). 144p. 1973. text ed. 14.75 (ISBN 0-398-02715-3). C C Thomas.

Surgical Anatomy of Peripheral Nerves. Anthony M. DeAngelis. LC 72-96490. (Illus.). 152p. 1973. 16.50 (ISBN 0-87993-019-5). Futura Pub.

Surgical Anatomy of the Temporal Bone. 3rd ed. Barry Anson & James A. Donaldson. (Illus.). 500p. 1980. write for info. (ISBN 0-7216-1292-X). Saunders.

Surgical & Medical Equipment Instruments. 1978. 350.00 o.p. (ISBN 0-89336-128-3, GB-044). BCC.

Surgical & Medical Support for Burn Patients. Bruce MacMillan. 1981. write for info. (ISBN 0-88416-301-6). PSG Pub.

Surgical & Nonsurgical Management of Strabismus. E. Howard Bedrossian. (Illus.). 240p. 1969. 24.50 (ISBN 0-398-00123-5). C C Thomas.

Surgical Atlas of Dental Implant Techniques. Charles A. Babbush. LC 78-65373. (Illus.). 280p. 1980. text ed. 49.00 (ISBN 0-7216-1474-4). Saunders.

Surgical Conditions in Pediatrics. Nixon. Ed. by M. J. Apley. (Operative Surgery Ser.). 1978. 68.95 (ISBN 0-407-00090-9). Butterworths.

Surgical Control of Behavior: A Symposium. Ed. by Arthur Winter. (Illus.). 100p. 1971. 11.25 (ISBN 0-398-02091-4). C C Thomas.

Surgical Correction of Dentofacial Deformities. William H. Bell et al. LC 76-27050. 1979. text ed. 150.00 (ISBN 0-7216-1671-2); Vol. 1. 70.00 (ISBN 0-7216-1675-5); Vol. 2. 80.00 (ISBN 0-7216-1707-7). Saunders.

Surgical Diagnosis. 3rd ed. Philip Thorek. LC 77-8532. (Illus.). 1977. 24.75 o.p. (ISBN 0-397-50370-9). Lippincott.

Surgical Gynecological Techniques. Franc Novak. LC 77-92099. 421p. 1978. 100.00 (ISBN 0-471-04276-5, Pub. by Wiley Medical). Wiley.

Surgical Infectious Disease. Richard Simmons. 1981. 65.00 (ISBN 0-8385-8729-1). ACC.

Surgical Nursing. Mary Jo Aspinall & Christine Tanner. 480p. 1981. pap. 14.95 (ISBN 0-8385-2481-8). ACC.

Surgical Nutrition. The American College of Surgeons. Ed. by Walter F. Ballinger. LC 75-19840. (Illus.). 527p. 1975. text ed. 26.00 (ISBN 0-7216-1525-2). Saunders.

Surgical Oncology Case Studies. H. Mason Morift & Erick R. Ratzer. 1977. 18.50 (ISBN 0-87488-063-7). Med Exam.

Surgical Operations in Short-Stay Hospitals, U.S. 1973. Abraham L. Ranofsky. Ed. by Audrey M. Shipp. (Ser. 13: No. 24). 61p. 1976. pap. text ed. 1.25 (ISBN 0-8406-0069-0). Natl Ctr Health Stats.

Surgical Pathology Case Studies, Vol. 1. Majid Ali et al. 1978. spiral bdg. 19.50 (ISBN 0-87488-068-8). Med Exam.

Surgical Pathology Case Studies, Vol. 2. Majid Ali et al. 1978. spiral bdg. 19.50 (ISBN 0-87488-089-0). Med Exam.

Surgical Pathology of the Nervous System & Its Coverings. Peter C. Burger & F. Stephen Vogel. LC 76-6492. 1976. 65.50 (ISBN 0-471-12347-1, Pub. by Wiley Medical). Wiley.

Surgical Pathology of the Uterus. Steven G. Silverberg. LC 77-8569. (Surgical Pathology Ser.). 1977. 25.95 (ISBN 0-471-01476-1, Pub. by Wiley Medical). Wiley.

Surgical Patient: Behavioral Concepts for the Operating Room Nurse. 2nd ed. Barbara J. Gruendemann et al. LC 76-51725. (Illus.). 1977. pap. text ed. 10.50 (ISBN 0-8016-1981-5). Mosby.

Surgical Procedures in Emergency Medicine. Norman McSwain, Jr. & Mary B. Skelton. 300p. 1982. text ed. 29.95 (ISBN 0-8359-7394-8). Reston.

Surgical-Prosthetic Approaches to Speech Rehabilitation. Donald P. Shedd & Bernd Weinberg. (Medical Publications Ser.). 1980. lib. bdg. 32.50 (ISBN 0-8161-2186-9). G K Hall.

Surgical Radiology, 3 vols. J. George Teplick & Marvin E. Haskin. Date not set. text ed. 65.00 ea.; Set. 250.00 (ISBN 0-7216-8783-0). Saunders. Postponed.

Surgical Rehabilitation in Leprosy. Frank McDowell & Carl D. Enna. 450p. 1974. 44.00 o.p. (ISBN 0-683-05853-3). Williams & Wilkins.

Surgical Rehabilitation of the Amputee. Lawrence W. Friedmann. (Illus.). 576p. 1978. 54.50 (ISBN 0-398-03763-9). C C Thomas.

Surgical Repair & Reconstruction in Rheumatoid Disease. Alexander Benjamin & Basil Helal. 256p. 1980. 45.00 (ISBN 0-471-08291-0, Pub. by Wiley Med). Wiley.

Surgical Resident's Manual. Richard M. Stillman & Philip N. Sawyer. 192p. 1980. pap. 12.50x (ISBN 0-8385-8732-1). ACC.

Surgical Skills in Patient Care. Charles W. Van Way & Charles A. Buerk. LC 78-4198. 1978. pap. text ed. 15.95 (ISBN 0-8016-5214-6). Mosby.

Surgical Technology: The 70's. Mark C. Libig. 432p. 1981. text ed. 26.50 (ISBN 0-8403-2336-0). Kendall-Hunt.

Surgical Treatment of Endocrine Disorders. Ed. by W. M. Hamilton. 272p. 1976. 42.95 (ISBN 0-407-00041-0). Butterworths.

Surgical Treatment of Obesity. Edward E. Mason. 512p. 1981. text ed. 32.50 (ISBN 0-7216-6141-6). Saunders.

Surgical Typists Handbook. Norma B. Chernok. 1972. spiral bdg. 6.00 o.p. (ISBN 0-87488-991-X). Med Exam.

Surimono: Prints by Elbow. Edythe Polster & Alfred H. Marks. (Illus.). 494p. 1980. 1500.00 (ISBN 0-8188-0120-4, Lovejoy). Paragon.

Surnames of Ireland. 3rd ed. Edward MacLysaght. 336p. 1978. 15.00x (ISBN 0-7165-2164-4, Pub. by Irish Academic Pr Ireland); pap. 6.00x (ISBN 0-7165-2291-8). Biblio Dist.

Surpassing the Love of Men: Love Between Women from the Renaissance to the Present. Lillian Faderman. Ed. by Maria Guarnaschelli. LC 80-24482. (Illus.). 488p. 1981. 15.95 (ISBN 0-688-03733-X). Morrow.

Surpassing the Love of Men: Love Between Women from the Renaissance to the Present. Lillian Faderman. Ed. by Maria Guarnaschelli. (Illus.). 488p. 1981. pap. 10.95 (ISBN 0-688-00396-6, Quill). Morrow.

Surpassing Wit. James F. Carens. LC 78-12644. 1979. 17.50x (ISBN 0-231-04642-1). Columbia U Pr.

Surprise. Aline Cunningham. (Caterpillar Bk. Ser.). (Illus.). 16p. (ps-k). 0.69 (ISBN 0-570-06906-8, 56Y1271). Concordia.

Surprise Attack in Mathematical Problems. Lloyd A. Graham. (Illus., Orig.). 1968. pap. 3.00 (ISBN 0-486-21846-5). Dover.

Surprise Book: Seventy-Seven Stupendously Silly Practical Jokes You Can Play on Your Friends. Laurence B. White, Jr. & Ray Broekel. (Illus.). 96p. 1981. 7.95a (ISBN 0-385-15832-7); PLB (ISBN 0-385-15833-5). Doubleday.

Surprise for Cashimere. Garfield J. George. Bd. with Cashimere Learns to Skate. Date not set. pap. 4.95 (ISBN 0-533-04770-6). Vantage.

Surprise Island. Gertrude C. Warner. LC 49-49618. (Boxcar Children Mysteries-Pilot Bk.). (Illus.). (gr. 3-7). 6.95g (ISBN 0-8075-7673-5). A Whitman.

Surprise Island. Barbara Willard. (Illus.). 112p. (gr. 3-6). 1981. 7.95 (ISBN 0-525-66734-2). Elsevier-Nelson.

Surprise Kitten. Joseph Palecek. LC 76-4806. (Illus.). 40p. (ps-2). 1976. 5.95 o.s.i. (ISBN 0-8193-0877-3, Four Winds); PLB 5.41 o.s.i. (ISBN 0-8193-0878-1). Schol Bk Serv.

Surprise Party. Pat Hutchins. LC 69-18239. (Illus.). (gr. k-2). 1969. 8.95 (ISBN 0-02-745830-X). Macmillan.

Surprise Party. Pat Hutchins. LC 69-18239. (Illus.). 32p. (gr. k-3). 1972. pap. 0.95 o.s.i. (ISBN 0-02-043760-9, Collier). Macmillan.

Surprise Party: An I Am Reading Book. Annabelle Prager. LC 76-40309. (Illus.). (ps-4). 1977. 4.95 (ISBN 0-394-83235-3); PLB 3.99 (ISBN 0-394-93235-8). Pantheon.

Surprise! Surprise. Ron Shaffer & Kevin Klose. 1979. pap. 2.25 (ISBN 0-380-42853-9, 42853). Avon.

Surprised by Joy: The Shape of My Early Life. Clive S. Lewis. LC 56-5329. 1956. 12.95 (ISBN 0-15-187011-X). HarBraceJ.

Surprised by Light. Ulrich Schaffer. LC 80-7751. (Illus.). 80p. 1980. 22.95 (ISBN 0-06-067086-X, HarpR); pap. 9.95 (ISBN 0-06-067087-8, RD 335). Har-Row.

Surprises. Kenneth G. Mills. 1980. 10.95 (ISBN 0-919842-06-2). Sun-Scape Pubns.

Surprises & Prizes. Robert B. Ruddell et al. 1978. pap. text ed. 3.28 (ISBN 0-205-05113-8) 8.80 (ISBN 0-205-05128-6). Allyn.

Surprising Things Maui Did. Jay Williams. LC 79-5069. (Illus.). 40p. (gr. k-3). 1979. 9.95 (ISBN 0-590-07553-5, Four Winds). Schol Bk Serv.

Surreal Numbers. Donald E. Knuth. LC 74-5998. 1974. pap. text ed. 5.95 (ISBN 0-201-03812-9). A-W.

Surrealism. Jose Pierre. (Masters of Art Ser.). (Illus.). 1979. pap. 3.95 (ISBN 0-8120-2156-8). Barron.

Surrealism. Patrick Waldberg. (World of Art Ser.). (Illus.). 1978. pap. 9.95 (ISBN 0-19-520070-5). Oxford U Pr.

Surrealism & American Feature Films. J. H. Matthews. (Theatrical Arts Ser.). 1979. lib. bdg. 10.95 (ISBN 0-8057-9265-1). Twayne.

Surrealism & Film. J. H. Matthews. LC 75-163624. (Illus.). 1971. 8.50 o.p. (ISBN 0-472-64135-2). U of Mich Pr.

Surrealism & Its Popular Accomplices. Ed. by Franklin Rosemont. (Illus.). 112p. 1980. pap. 5.00 (ISBN 0-87286-121-X). City Lights.

Surrealism & the Novel. J. H. Matthews. LC 66-17021. 1966. 5.95 o.p. (ISBN 0-472-64140-9). U of Mich Pr.

Surrealism in Perspective. Michael Lawrence. LC 79-51630. (Themes in Art Ser.). (Illus., Orig.). Date not set. pap. 7.95 o.p. (ISBN 0-910386-54-4, Pub. by Cleveland Mus Art). Ind U Pr. Postponed.

Surrealism: The Road to the Absolute. rev. ed. Anna Balakian. 1970. 7.95 o.p. (ISBN 0-525-21270-1). Dutton.

Surrealisme: Theories, themes, techniques. new ed. Gerard Du & Bernard Lecherbonnier. (Collection themes et textes). 288p. (Orig., Fr.). 1972. pap. 6.75 (ISBN 2-03-035004-4, 2691). Larousse.

Surrealist Art. Sarane Alexandrian. (World of Art Ser.). (Illus.). 256p. (Orig.). 1978. pap. 9.95 (ISBN 0-19-520009-8). Oxford U Pr.

Surrealists. Simon Wilson. (Tate Gallery: Little Art Books Ser.). (Illus.). 1977. pap. 1.95 (ISBN 0-8120-0861-8). Barron.

Surrender by Moonlight. Bonnie Drake. (Orig.). 1981. pap. 1.50 (ISBN 0-440-18426-6). Dell.

Surrender in Paradise. Sandra Robb. 192p. (Orig.). 1980. pap. 1.50. S&S.

Surrey: A Shell Guide. Bruce Watkin. 1977. 13.95 (ISBN 0-571-09609-3, Pub. by Faber & Faber). Merrimack Bk Serv.

Surrogate. Nick Sharman. (Orig.). 1980. pap. 2.50 (ISBN 0-451-09293-7, E9293, Sig). NAL.

Surrogate's Court Procedure Act (N. Y.) Gould Editorial Staff. (Supplemented annually). looseleaf 8.00 (ISBN 0-87526-129-9). Gould.

Surrounded by Angels. Andre Morea. LC 76-22930. 1976. pap. 1.95 (ISBN 0-87123-503-X, 200503). Bethany Fell.

Surti Touch: Adventures in Indian Cooking. Malvi Doshi. LC 80-21847. (Illus.). 1980. pap. 7.95 (ISBN 0-89407-042-8). Strawberry Hill.

Surtsey: Evolution of Life on a Volcanic Island. S. Fridriksson. LC 74-30850. 198p. 1975. 21.95 (ISBN 0-470-28000-X). Halsted Pr.

Surveillant Sceince: Remote Sensing of the Environment. Ed. by Robert K. Holz. LC 72-7922. (Illus.). 300p. (Orig.). 1973. pap. text ed. 15.25 (ISBN 0-395-14041-2, 3-25711). HM.

Surveiors Dialogue...for All Men to Peruse, That Have to Do with the Revenues of Land, or the Manurance, Use or Occupation. Third Time Imprinted & Enlarged. John Norden. LC 79-84126. (English Experience Ser.: No. 945). 280p. 1979. Repr. of 1618 ed. lib. bdg. 26.00 (ISBN 90-221-0945-3). Walter J Johnson.

Survey & Opinion Research: Procedures for Processing & Analysis. John A. Sonquist & William C. Dunkelberg. (Illus.). 1977. 28.95 (ISBN 0-13-878264-4). P-H.

Survey Design & Analysis. Herbert H. Hyman. 1955. text ed. 10.95 o.s.i. (ISBN 0-02-915770-6). Free Pr.

Survey-Guided Development I: Data-Based Organizational Change. rev. ed. David G. Bowers & Jerome L. Franklin. LC 77-75523. 146p. 1977. pap. 11.50 (ISBN 0-88390-137-4). Univ Assocs.

Survey-Guided Development II: A Manual for Consultants. rev. ed. D. L. Hausser et al. LC 77-75523. 162p. 1977. pap. 11.50 (ISBN 0-88390-138-2). Univ Assocs.

Survey-Guided Development III: A Manual for Concepts Training. rev. ed. Jerome L. Franklin et al. LC 77-75523. 118p. 1977. pap. 11.50 (ISBN 0-88390-139-0). Univ Assocs.

Survey in Combinatorics. Ed. by Bella Bollobas. LC 79-51596. (London Mathematical Society Lecture Note Ser.: No. 38). 1979. pap. 23.95x (ISBN 0-521-22846-8). Cambridge U Pr.

Survey of Academic Resources in Psychiatric Residency Training. Lee Gurel. 117p. 1973. pap. 3.25 o.p. (ISBN 0-685-65570-9, 187). Am Psychiatric.

Survey of Accounting. Gary L. Schugart et al. LC 80-67776. 600p. 1981. text ed. 18.95x (ISBN 0-931920-25-6); study guide 5.95 (ISBN 0-686-68565-2); practice problem 4.95 (ISBN 0-686-68566-0); working papers 6.95 (ISBN 0-686-68567-9). Dame Pubns.

Survey of Allied Health Professions. Alan Weston. (Illus.). 224p. pap. text ed. 12.95 (ISBN 0-933014-63-5). College-Hill.

Survey of American Foreign Relations: 1928, 1929, 1930, 1931. Charles P. Howland. Ea. 47.50x (ISBN 0-686-50174-8). Elliots Bks.

Survey of American Genealogical Periodicals & Periodical Indexes. Ed. by Kip Sperry. LC 78-55033. (Genealogy & Local History Ser.: Vol. 3). 1978. 30.00 (ISBN 0-8103-1401-0). Gale.

Survey of Applied Linguistics. Ed. by Ronald Wardhaugh & H. Douglas Brown. LC 75-31053. 1976. text ed. 14.00 o.p. (ISBN 0-472-08958-7); pap. 7.95x (ISBN 0-472-08959-5). U of Mich Pr.

Survey of Arts Administration Training in the U.S. & Canada. rev. ed. 1977. pap. 5.00 o.p. (ISBN 0-915400-09-X). Interbk Inc.

Survey of Basic Accounting. 3rd ed. R. F. Salmonson et al. 1981. text ed. 19.95x (ISBN 0-256-02471-5). Irwin.

Survey of Bible Doctrine: Leader's Guide. 1978. pap. 3.25 (ISBN 0-8024-8436-0). Moody.

Survey of Chemical Notation Systems. Division Of Chemistry And Chemical Technology. 1964. pap. 8.00 o.p. (ISBN 0-309-01150-7). Natl Acad Pr.

Survey of Chinese-American Manpower & Employment. Betty Lee Sung. LC 76-14435. (Special Studies). (Illus.). 1976. text ed. 28.95 (ISBN 0-275-23090-2). Praeger.

Survey of Climatology. John F. Griffiths & Dennis M. Driscoll. 352p. 1981. text ed. 19.95 (ISBN 0-675-09994-3); instr's. manual 3.95 (ISBN 0-686-69500-3). Merrill.

Survey of Clinical Pediatrics. 7th ed. Edward Wasserman & Donald S. Gromisch. (Illus.). 560p. 1981. text ed. 27.95 (ISBN 0-07-068431-6, HP). McGraw.

Survey of Counseling Methods. Samuel H. Osipow et al. 1980. pap. 10.50x (ISBN 0-256-02189-9). Dorsey.

Survey of Current Structural Research. Compiled by American Society of Civil Engineers. (Manual & Report on Engineering Practice Ser.: No. 51). 336p. 1970. pap. text ed. 29.75 (ISBN 0-87262-225-8). Am Soc Civil Eng.

Survey of Electronics. 2nd ed. Leland Schwartz. (Electronics Technology Ser.). 1977. pap. text ed. 12.50 (ISBN 0-675-08554-3). Merrill.

Survey of Employee Benefits of Engineers - 1977. Date not set. 20.00 (510-77). AAES.

Survey of English Literature: Eighteen Thirty to Eighteen Eighty, 2 vols. Oliver Elton. (Vol. I 434 pp., Vol. II 432 pp.). 1980. Repr. of 1932 ed. Set. lib. bdg. 85.00 (ISBN 0-8492-0786-X). R West.

Survey of European Civilization. 4th ed. Wallace K. Ferguson & Geoffrey Bruun. Incl. Pt. 1. To 1660. text ed. 17.50 (ISBN 0-395-04427-8); Pt. 2. Since 1660. text ed. o.p. (ISBN 0-395-04428-6); Since 1500. text ed. o.p. (ISBN 0-395-04426-X). 1969. 1 vol. ed. 21.95 (ISBN 0-395-04425-1); instr's manual 4.00 (ISBN 0-395-04432-4). HM.

Survey of Functional Neuroanatomy. Bill Garoutte. (Illus.). 240p. 1981. pap. text ed. 9.00x (ISBN 0-930010-04-3). Jones Med.

Survey of Geomedical Problems. Ed. by Jul Lag. 272p. 1980. 24.00x (ISBN 82-00-12654-4). Universitet.

Survey of Geometry. rev. ed. Howard Eaves. 1972. text ed. 25.15x (ISBN 0-205-03226-5, 5632269). Allyn.

Survey of Greek Alchemy. Frank S. Taylor. LC 79-8627. Repr. of 1930 ed. 12.50 (ISBN 0-404-18493-6). AMS Pr.

Survey of Hidden Variables Theories. F. J. Belinfante. 376p. 1973. text ed. 50.00 (ISBN 0-08-017032-3). Pergamon.

Survey of Human Diseases. David T. Purtilo. LC 77-81550. 1978. 21.95 (ISBN 0-201-05782-4, M&N Div). A-W.

Survey of Images of a Phanton Produced by Radioisotope Scanners & Cameras 1976. 1980. 10.00x (Pub. by Brit Inst Radiology). State Mutual Bk.

Survey of Internal Auditing: 1979. Institute of Internal Auditors, Inc. Ed. by Samuel Newman. (Illus.). 250p. 1980. pap. text ed. 20.00 (ISBN 0-89413-085-4). Inst Inter Aud.

Survey of Israel's History. Leon J. Wood. LC 70-120041. (Illus.). 1970. text ed. 12.95 (ISBN 0-310-34760-2). Zondervan.

Survey of London. Greater London Council. Incl. Vol. 31-32. St. James, Westminister, Pt. 2. text ed. 47.50x (ISBN 0-485-41831-2); Vol. 33-34. St. Anne, Soho. text ed. 53.75x (ISBN 0-485-48233-9); Vol. 35. Theatre Royal, Drury Lane, & the Royal Opera House, Covent Garden. text ed. o.p. (ISBN 0-485-48235-5); Vol. 36. St. Paul, Covent Garden. text ed. 75.00x (ISBN 0-485-48236-3); Vol. 37. Northern Kensington. text ed. 46.25x (ISBN 0-485-48237-1). Athlone Pr). Humanities.

Survey of London, Vol. 38: The Museum Area of South Kensington & Westminster. Greater London Council. (Illus.). 480p. 1975. text ed. 80.00x (ISBN 0-485-48238-X, Athlone Pr). Humanities.

Survey of London, Vol. 39: The Grosvenor Estate in Mayfair, Part. 1, General History. Greater London Council. (Survey of London Ser.). 1977. text ed. 75.00x (ISBN 0-485-48239-8, Athlone Pr). Humanities.

Survey of Low Income Aged & Disabled, 1973-1975. Social Security Administration. LC 79-67535. 1979. codebook 20.00 (ISBN 0-89138-965-2). ICPSR.

Survey of Malayalam Literature. K. M. George. 10.00x (ISBN 0-210-22735-4). Asia.

Survey of Materials for the Study of the Uncommonly Taught Languages: Middle East, No. 3. LC 76-44591. 1976. pap. 4.50x (ISBN 0-87281-056-9). Ctr Appl Ling.

Survey of Mathematics: With Applications. Allen R. Angel & Stuart R. Porter. LC 80-19471. (Mathematics Ser.). (Illus.). 576p. 1981. text ed. write for info. (ISBN 0-201-00045-8). A-W.

Survey of Medical Technology. Roger W. Coltey. (Illus.). 1978. pap. text ed. 13.95 (ISBN 0-8016-1020-6). Mosby.

Survey of Numerical Mathematics, Vol. 1. David M. Young & Robert T. Gregory. LC 78-168767. 1972. text ed. 21.95 (ISBN 0-201-08773-1). A-W.

Survey of Numerical Mathematics, Vol. 2. David M. Young & Robert T. Gregory. LC 78-168767. 1973. text ed. 22.95 (ISBN 0-201-08774-X). A-W.

Survey of Numerical Methods for Partial Differential Equations. Ed. by I. Gladwell & R. Wait. (Illus.). 1980. 39.95x (ISBN 0-19-853351-9). Oxford U Pr.

Survey of Organic Syntheses, 2 vols. Calvin A. Buehler & Donald E. Pearson. LC 73-112590. Vol. 1, 1970. 49.50 (ISBN 0-471-11670-X); Vol. 2, 1977. 32.50 (ISBN 0-471-11671-8, Pub. by Wiley-Interscience). Wiley.

Survey of Phenomena in Ionized Gases: Invited Papers. (Eng., Fr., Rus. & Ger.). 1968. pap. 35.50 (ISBN 92-0-030068-5, IAEA). Unipub.

Survey of Printing Processes. 2nd ed. Ernest A. Hutchings. (Illus.). 1978. pap. 13.95x (ISBN 0-434-90801-0). Intl Ideas.

Survey of Progress in Chemistry, 8 vols. Ed. by Arthur F. Scott. Incl. Vol. 1. 1963. 40.50 (ISBN 0-12-610501-4); Vol. 2. 1965. 40.50 (ISBN 0-12-610502-2); Vol. 3. 1966. 40.50 (ISBN 0-686-62064-X); Vol. 4. 1968. 40.50 (ISBN 0-12-610504-9); Vol. 5. 1969. 40.50 (ISBN 0-12-610505-7); Vol. 6. 1974. 51.50 (ISBN 0-12-610506-5); Vol. 7. 1976. 40.00 (ISBN 0-12-610507-3); lib. ed 50.50 (ISBN 0-12-610574-X); microfiche 29.00 (ISBN 0-12-610575-8); Vol. 8. 1978. 43.00 (ISBN 0-12-610508-1); lib. ed. 55.50 (ISBN 0-12-610576-6); microfiche 31.50 (ISBN 0-12-610577-4); Vol. 9. 1980. 35.00 (ISBN 0-12-610509-X); lib. bdg. 45.50 (ISBN 0-12-610578-2); microfiche 24.50 (ISBN 0-12-610579-0). Acad Pr.

Survey of Recent Research in Special Education. Cyril Cave & Pamela Maddison. (General Ser.). 1979. text ed. 27.50x (ISBN 0-85633-148-1, NFER). Humanities.

Survey of Resources & a Production Cycle for the Non-Ferrous Metals. C. Lafkas & J. G. Paterson. 60p. (Orig.). 1978. pap. text ed. 3.00x (ISBN 0-686-63136-6, Pub. by Ctr Resource Stud Canada). Renouf.

Survey of Russian Music. M. D. Calvocoressi. LC 73-6208. (Illus.). 142p. 1974. Repr. of 1944 ed. lib. bdg. 15.00x (ISBN 0-8371-6888-0, CARM). Greenwood.

Survey of Some Japanese Tax Laws. Eric V. De Becker. (Studies in Japanese Law & Government). 182p. 1979. Repr. of 1931 ed. 18.50 (ISBN 0-89093-218-2). U Pubns Amer.

Survey of the Dragonflies (Order Odonata) of Eastern Africa. E. C. Pinhey. (Illus.). vii, 214p. 1961. 18.50x (ISBN 0-565-00216-3, Pub. by Brit Mus Nat Hist England). Sabbot-Natural Hist Bks.

Survey of the Emerging Solar Energy Industry. Justin A. Bereny. Ed. by Francis De Winter. LC 77-71664. (Illus.). 1977. 69.50 (ISBN 0-930978-00-5); pap. cancelled (ISBN 0-930978-01-3). Solar Energy Info.

Survey of the Graphic Arts. F. Matthews. 1974. pap. 7.90x o.p. (ISBN 0-87563-067-7). Stipes.

Survey of the Law of Property. 3rd ed. Ralph E. Boyer. 737p. 1981. text ed. write for info. (ISBN 0-8299-2128-1). West Pub.

Survey of the Pretended Holy Dicipline. Richard Bancroft. LC 78-38148. (English Experience Ser.: No. 428). 472p. 1972. Repr. of 1593 ed. 67.00 (ISBN 90-221-0428-1). Walter J Johnson.

Survey of the Woman Problem. Rosa Mayreder. Tr. by Scheffauer Herman from Ger. LC 79-2944. 275p. 1981. Repr. of 1913 ed. 21.50 (ISBN 0-8305-0108-8). Hyperion Conn.

Survey of Tidal River Systems in the Northern Territory & Their Crocodile Populations: Monographs, Nos. 2-8. H. Messel et al. Incl. No. 2. Victoria & Fitzmaurice River Systems. 52p (ISBN 0-08-023098-9); No. 3. Adelaide, Daly & Moyle Rivers. 58p (ISBN 0-08-023099-7); No. 4. Alligator Region River System: Murgenella & Cooper's Creeks; East, South & West Alligator Rivers & Wildman River. 70p (ISBN 0-08-024789-X); No. 5. Goodmadeer & King River Systems: Majarie, Wurugoij & All Night Creeks. 62p (ISBN 0-08-024790-3); No. 6. Some River & Creek Systems on Melville & Grant Islands: North & South Creeks on Grant Island. 64p (ISBN 0-08-024784-9); No. 7. Liverpool-Tomkinson River Systems & Nungbulgarri Creek. 84p (ISBN 0-08-024785-7); No. 8. Some Rivers & Creeks on the Western Shore of the Gulf of Carpentaria: Rose River, Muntak Creek; Hart, Walker & Koolatong Rivers. 40p (ISBN 0-08-024786-5). (Illus.). 1979. pap. 16.00 ea. Pergamon.

Survey of Urban Indicator Data, 1970-77. Michael J. Flax. (Institute Paper). 52p. 1978. pap. 3.50 (ISBN 0-87766-214-2, 21200). Urban Inst.

Survey of Vegetation in the Curecanti Reservoir Basins. Angus M. Woodbury et al. (University of Utah Anthropological Papers: No. 56). 1962. pap. 8.00x (ISBN 0-87480-173-7). U of Utah Pr.

Survey on the Scientific & Technical Potential of the Countries of Africa. 296p. (Orig.). 1972. pap. 10.00 (ISBN 92-3-000799-4, U647, UNESCO). Unipub.

Survey, or Topographical Description of France. with a New Mappe. John Eliot. LC 79-84104. (English Experience Ser.: No. 923). (Illus.). 116p. 1979. Repr. of 1592 ed. lib. bdg. 11.50 (ISBN 90-221-0923-2). Walter J Johnson.

Survey Report of Starting Salaries & Employment Status of Chemistry & Chemical Engineering Graduates: 1978. 1978. pap. 5.00 (ISBN 0-8412-0548-5). Am Chemical.

Survey Research. 2nd ed. Charles H. Backstrom & Gerald Hursch-Cesar. 400p. 1981. text ed. 8.95 (ISBN 0-471-02543-7). Wiley.

Survey Research & Public Attitudes in Eastern Europe & the Soviet Union. Ed. by William Welsh. LC 79-27902. (Pergamon Policy Studies). 550p. Date not set. 47.51 (ISBN 0-08-025958-8). Pergamon.

Survey Research Methods: A Cookbook & Other Fables. Earl R. Babbie. 320p. 1973. 13.95x (ISBN 0-534-00224-2). Wadsworth Pub.

Survey Sampling. Leslie Kish. LC 65-19479. 1965. 29.95 (ISBN 0-471-48900-X). Wiley.

Surveying. Boy Scouts Of America. LC 19-600. (Illus.). 56p. (gr. 6-12). 1960. pap. 0.70x (ISBN 0-8395-3327-6, 3327). BSA.

Surveying. 3rd ed. C. B. Breed. 495p. 1971. 22.95 (ISBN 0-471-10070-6). Wiley.

Surveying. 3rd ed. R. H. Dugdale. (Illus.). 224p. 1980. pap. text ed. 14.95x (ISBN 0-7114-5641-0). Intl Ideas.

Surveying. Jack S. McCormack. (Illus.). 288p. 1976. 16.95x (ISBN 0-13-879064-7). P-H.

Surveying & Photogrammetry, Computation for Civil Engineers. D. E. Murchison. 1977. 16.00 (ISBN 0-408-00293-X). Transatlantic.

Surveying Crime. Committee on National Statistics, National Research Council. Ed. by Bettye Penick. LC 76-50120. 1976. pap. 11.00 (ISBN 0-309-02524-9). Natl Acad Pr.

Surveying Instruments. Fritz Deumlich. 336p. 1979. text ed. 47.00x (ISBN 3-11-007765-5). De Gruyter.

Surveying Instruments: Their History. Edmond R. Kiely. 1979. Repr. of 1947 ed. 19.50 (ISBN 0-686-25583-6). CARBEN Survey.

Surveying Law for the California Civil Professional Engineering Exam. Michael R. Lindeburg. (Engineering Review Manual Ser.). (Illus.). 154p. 1981. pap. 9.50 (ISBN 0-932276-26-1). Prof Engine.

Surveying Small Craft. Ian Nicolson. LC 73-90687. (Illus.). 224p. 1974. 12.50 o.p. (ISBN 0-87742-039-4). Intl Marine.

Surveyor's Guide. B. F. Dorr. 1978. pap. 8.50 (ISBN 0-686-25542-9, 514). CARBEN Survey.

Surveys in Parapsychology. Rhea A. White. LC 76-119. 496p. 1976. 21.00 (ISBN 0-8108-0906-0). Scarecrow.

Surveys of Australian Economics, Vol. 1. Ed. by F. H. Gruen. LC 78-55055. 1978. text ed. 21.00x (ISBN 0-86861-208-1); pap. text ed. 12.50x (ISBN 0-86861-216-2). Allen Unwin.

Surveys of Consumers 1971-72: Contributions to Behavioral Economics. Lewis Mandell et al. LC 72-619718. 352p. 1973. cloth 11.00 (ISBN 0-87944-140-2); pap. 7.00 (ISBN 0-87944-139-9). U of Mich Soc Res.

Surveys of Tidal River Systems in the Northern Territory & Their Crocodile Populations, 7 vols. Ed. by H. Messel. Incl. Tidal Waterways of Castlereagh Bay & Hutchinson & Cadell Straits: Bennett, Darbitla, Djigaglia Djabura, Ngandadauda Creeks & the Glyde & Woolen Rivers. (Monograph: No. 9). 23.25 (ISBN 0-08-024801-2); Tidal Waterways of Buckingham & Ulundurwi Bays: Buckingham, Kalarwoi, Warawuruwoi & Kurala Rivers & Slippery Creek. (Monograph: No. 10). 18.00 (ISBN 0-08-024802-0); Tidal Waterways of Arnhem Bay: Darwarunga, Habgood, Baralminer, Gobalpa, Coromuro, Cato, Peter John & Burungbirinung Rivers. (Monograph: No. 11). 21.50 (ISBN 0-08-024803-9); Tidal Waterways on the South-Western Coast of the Gulf of Carpentaria: Limmen Bight Towns, Roper, Phelp & Wilson Rivers; Nayarnpi, Wungguliyanga, Painnyilatya, Mangkurdurrungku & Yiwapa Creeks. (Monograph: No. 12). 17.00 (ISBN 0-08-024804-7); Tidal Waterways on the Southern Coast of the Gulf of Carpentaria: Calvert, Robinson, Wearyan & McArthur Rivers & Some Intervening Creeks. (Monograph: No. 13). 19.00 (ISBN 0-08-024805-5); Tidal Waterways of the Van Diemen Gulf: Ilamary; River, Iwalg, Saltwater & Minimini: Creeks & Coastal Arms on Cobourg Peninsula. Resurveys of the Alligator Region Rivers. (Monograph: No. 14). 20.00 (ISBN 0-08-024806-3); Some River & Creek Systems on the West Coast of Cape York Peninsula in the Gulf of Carpentaria: Nassau, Staaten & Gilbert Rivers & Duck Creek. (Monograph: No. 16). write for info. (ISBN 0-08-024807-1). (Illus.). 1980. Pergamon.

Survival. Paul Neimark. (Wilderness World Ser.). (Illus.). 64p. (gr. 3 up). 1981. PLB 9.25 (ISBN 0-516-02454-X). Childrens.

Survival Afloat. Don Biggs. (Illus.). 1976. 9.95 o.p. (ISBN 0-679-50579-2); pap. 4.95 o.p. (ISBN 0-679-50629-2). McKay.

Survival & Peace in the Nuclear Age. Laurence W. Beilenson. LC 80-51729. 169p. 1980. 10.95 (ISBN 0-89526-672-5). Regnery-Gateway.

Survival & Progress: The Afro-American Experience. L. Alex Swan. LC 80-1197. (Contributions in Afro-American & African Studies: No. 58). (Illus.). 280p. 1981. lib. bdg. 25.00 (ISBN 0-313-22480-3, SSU). Greenwood.

Survival at Valley Forge. Carole Charles. LC 75-33159. (Stories of the Revolution Ser.). (Illus.). (gr. 2-6). 1975. PLB 5.50 (ISBN 0-913778-20-6). Childs World.

Survival: Black & White. Florence Halpern. 225p. 1973. text ed. 23.00 (ISBN 0-08-016994-5); pap. text ed. 10.00 (ISBN 0-08-017193-1). Pergamon.

Survival Camp. Eve Bunting. (Young Romance Ser.). (Illus.). (gr. 3-9). 1978. PLB 5.95 (ISBN 0-87191-631-2); pap. 2.95 (ISBN 0-89812-063-2). Creative Ed.

Survival Distributions: Reliability Applications in the Biomedical Sciences. Alan J. Gross & Virginia A. Clark. LC 75-6806. (Probability & Mathematical Statistics Ser). 331p. 1975. 32.95 (ISBN 0-471-32817-0, Pub. by Wiley-Interscience). Wiley.

Survival First Aid. Jacques De Langre. (Illus.). 164p. 1980. 10.00 (ISBN 0-916508-14-5); pap. 8.00 (ISBN 0-916508-13-7). Happiness Pr.

Survival First Aid: Practical Guide to Life's Presercation in Wars & Cataclysms for Self & Others. Skills &Preparedness. LC 80-84992. (Illus.). 1981. 10.00 (ISBN 0-916508-14-5); pap. 8.00 (ISBN 0-686-69456-2). Happiness Pr.

Survival from Infinity: Original Science Fiction Stories for Young Readers. Ed. by Roger Elwood. LC 73-14696. (Illus.). 192p. (gr. 7 up). 1974. PLB 6.90 (ISBN 0-531-02666-3). Watts.

Survival Game. Colin Kapp. 192p. 1976. pap. 1.50 o.p. (ISBN 0-345-25192-X). Ballantine.

Survival Guide for Tough Times. Mike Phillips. LC 79-4261. 1979. pap. 3.50 (ISBN 0-87123-498-X, 210498). Bethany Fell.

Survival Guns & Ammo: Raw Meat. John J. Williams. (Illus.). 1979. pap. 19.00 (ISBN 0-686-24791-4). Consumertronics.

Survival Handbook. W. K. Merrill. (Illus.). 1972. 10.95 (ISBN 0-87691-068-1). Winchester Pr.

Survival Handbook for Salespeople. Paul J. Micali. 160p. 1981. pap. 8.95 (ISBN 0-8436-0853-6). CBI Pub.

Survival Handbook for Small Business. Frieda Carrol. LC 80-70496. 73p. 1980. 16.95 (ISBN 0-9605246-4-9); pap. 12.95. Biblio Pr GA.

Survival in Beirut. Lina M. Tabbara. (Illus.). 186p. 1977. cased 16.00; pap. 7.00. Three Continents.

Survival in Business. Michael Allsopp. 139p. 1977. text ed. 22.00x (ISBN 0-220-66320-3, Pub. by Busn Bks England). Renouf.

Survival in Society. Eugene Heimler. LC 74-12871. 159p. 1975. 11.95 o.p. (ISBN 0-470-36901-9). Halsted Pr.

Survival in the Classroom: Negotiating with Kids, Colleagues & Bosses. Ernest R. House & Stephen D. Lapan. 1978. pap. text ed. 18.95x (ISBN 0-205-06082-X); tchr's ed. 14.95x (ISBN 0-685-89341-3). Allyn.

Survival in the Executive Jungle. Chester Burger. 1966. pap. 1.95 o.s.i. (ISBN 0-02-008100-6, Collier). Macmillan.

Survival in the Face of Crises: Selected Proceedings of the Fifth National Symposium of the Black Economy. Ed. by Gerald F. Whittaker. 1976. pap. 3.50 o.p. (ISBN 0-87712-174-5). U Mich Busn Div Res.

Survival in the Outdoors. Byron Dalrymple. 1972. 6.95 o.p. (ISBN 0-525-21290-6). Dutton.

Survival in Two Worlds: Moshoeshoe of Lesotho, 1786-1870. Leonard Thompson. (Illus.). 366p. 1976. text ed. 36.00x (ISBN 0-19-821693-9). Oxford U Pr.

Survival in Two Worlds: Moshoeshoe of Lesotho 1786-1870. Leonard Thompson. (Illus.). 1975. pap. 12.50x (ISBN 0-19-822702-7). Oxford U Pr.

Survival into the Twenty-First Century. Viktoras Kulvinskas. Ed. by Hermine Hurlbut & Joan Newman. (Illus.). 1975. pap. 12.95 (ISBN 0-933278-04-7). OMango.

Survival Is the Bottom Line. Phil Potts. 58p. (Orig.). 1980. pap. 2.95 (ISBN 0-89260-182-5). Hwong Pub.

Survival Kit for School Publications Advisers. Ed. by Jackie Engel. 274p. (Orig.). 1980. pap. 9.50 (ISBN 0-936352-04-3, B355). U of KS Ind Stud Div.

Survival Management for Industry. Nyles Reinfeld. 1981. text ed. 17.95 (ISBN 0-8359-7410-3); instr's. manual free (ISBN 0-8359-7411-1). Reston.

Survival Manual for the Independent Woman Traveler. Roberta Mendel. (Orig.). 1981. pap. write for info. (ISBN 0-936424-06-0, 007). Pin Prick. Postponed.

Survival Math. Edward Williams & Jacob Cohen. (gr. 9-12). 1981. pap. 4.95 (ISBN 0-8120-2012-X). Barron. Postponed.

Survival Models & Data Analysis. Regina C. Elandt-Johnson & Norman L. Johnson. LC 79-22836. (Wiley Series in Probability & Mathematical Statistics: Applied Probability & Statistics). 1980. 34.95 (ISBN 0-471-03174-7, Pub. by Wiley-Interscience). Wiley.

Survival: My Life in Love & War. Rafael Alberto Rivas. 1977. 8.50 o.p. (ISBN 0-682-48942-5). Exposition.

Survival of Antiquity. Justina Gregory et al. LC 80-53219. (Studies in History Ser.: No. 48). (Illus.). 1980. pap. 10.00 (ISBN 0-87391-019-2). Smith Coll.

Survival of Capitalism. Henri Lefebvre. (Allison & Busby Motive Ser.). 140p. 1981. pap. 7.95 (ISBN 0-8052-8076-6, Pub. by Allison & Busby England). Schocken.

Survival of English Essays in the Criticism of Language. Ian Robinson. 300p. 1973. 34.00 (ISBN 0-521-20191-8); pap. 9.95x (ISBN 0-521-09898-X). Cambridge U Pr.

Survival of Illness: Implications for Nursing. Dorothy W. Smith et al. 1981. pap. text ed. 9.95 (ISBN 0-8261-2871-8). Springer Pub.

Survival of the Bark Canoe. John McPhee. 1977. pap. 4.95 (ISBN 0-446-97326-2). Warner Bks.

Survival of the Habsburg Empire: Radetzky, the Imperial Army & the Class War, 1848. Alan Sked. (Illus.). 289p. 1979. lib. bdg. 35.00 (ISBN 0-582-50711-1). Longman.

Survival of the Unfittest: A Study of Geriatric Patients in Glasgow. Bernard Isaacs et al. 1972. 14.50 o.p. (ISBN 0-7100-7233-3). Routledge & Kegan.

Survival of Vegetative Microbes. Ed. by T. G. Gray & J. R. Postgate. LC 75-31399. (Society for General Microbiology Symposium: NO. 26). (Illus.). 450p. 1976. 57.50 (ISBN 0-521-21094-1). Cambridge U Pr.

Survival Plus. Reuel L. Howe. LC 76-148143. 1974. pap. 2.95 (ISBN 0-8164-2088-2). Crossroad NY.

Survival Prayers for Young Mothers. Deborah A. Holmes. LC 76-12390. 1976. 4.95 (ISBN 0-8042-2195-2). John Knox.

Survival Resource Book. M. A. Henderson. (Illus.). 180p. 1981. pap. 8.95 (ISBN 0-312-77951-8). St Martin.

Survival Sanctuary: A Scouts Guide to Preparedness. Gretchen E. Albright. LC 80-54281. (Illus.). 146p. (Orig.). 1980. pap. 4.95 (ISBN 0-938064-00-2). Secure Futures.

Survival Sense for the Pilot. R. Stoffel & Patrick Lavalla. (Illus.). 160p. (Orig.). 1980. pap. 5.95 (ISBN 0-913724-24-6). Survival Ed Assoc.

Survival Sewing for Men. Ruth Oblander. (Illus.). 56p. 1980. pap. 3.50 cancelled (ISBN 0-933956-06-1). Sew-Fit.

Survival Spanish: Book One. Dorothy H. Mills & Maria D. Mata. LC 80-66641. (Illus.). 180p. (Orig., Eng. & Span.). 1981. pap. text ed. 16.96 (ISBN 0-935356-01-0). Mills Pub Co.

Survival Tactics in the Parish. Lyle E. Schaller. LC 76-54751. (Orig.). 1977. pap. 6.95 (ISBN 0-687-40757-5). Abingdon.

Survival Themes in Fiction for Children & Young People. Binnie T. Wilkin. LC 77-14295. 1978. 12.00 (ISBN 0-8108-1048-4). Scarecrow.

Survival Trip. Lee Mountain. (Attention Span Stories Ser). (Illus., Orig.). (gr. 6-10). 1978. pap. text ed. 3.20x (ISBN 0-89061-146-7, 582). Jamestown Pubs.

Survival: Unity to Live. Jim Bakker. Ed. by John Boneck & Cliff Dudley. LC 80-84504. 150p. 1980. 7.95 (ISBN 0-89221-081-8). New Leaf.

Survivalists. Giles Tippette. 1975. 7.95 o.s.i. (ISBN 0-02-619020-6). Macmillan.

Survivals of Roman Religion. Gordon Laing. LC 63-10280. (Our Debt to Greece & Rome Ser). 1963. Repr. of 1930 ed. 22.50x (ISBN 0-8154-0130-2). Cooper Sq.

Survive! Clay Blair, Jr. pap. 1.95 o.p. (ISBN 0-425-03309-0). Berkley Pub.

Surviving Family Life: The Seven Crises of Living Together. Sonya Thodes & Josleen Wilson. 300p. 1981. 11.95 (ISBN 0-399-12507-8). Putnam.

Surviving in College. David J. Yarington. 1977. pap. text ed. 7.50 (ISBN 0-672-61372-7); tchr's manual 2.50 (ISBN 0-672-61373-5). Bobbs.

Surviving in the Eighties. Michael Boddy & Richard Beckett. (Illus.). 192p. (Orig.). 1980. text ed. 28.50 (ISBN 0-86861-106-9, 2515); pap. text ed. 14.95 (ISBN 0-86861-114-X, 2516). Allen Unwin.

Surviving Popular Psychology: Debriefing the Me Degeneration. Clint Weyand. 148p. (Orig.). 1980. pap. 3.95 (ISBN 0-686-28854-8). Being Bks.

Surviving Sisters. Gail Pass. LC 80-69373. 1981. 10.95 (ISBN 0-689-11134-7). Atheneum.

Surviving Steam Railways. Jeoffry Spence. 1979. pap. 5.95 (ISBN 0-7134-0641-0, Pub. by Batsford England). David & Charles.

Surviving the Long Night: An Autobiographical Account of a Political Kidnapping. Sir Geoffrey Jackson. LC 74-83673. Orig. Title: People's Prison. 222p. 1974. 8.95 (ISBN 0-8149-0756-3). Vanguard.

Surviving the Male Mid-Life Crisis. Henry Still. 1977. 9.95 o.s.i. (ISBN 0-690-01445-7, TYC-T). T Y Crowell.

Surviving Without Governing: The Italian Parties in Parliament. Guiseppe DiPalma. LC 75-46035. 1977. 21.00x (ISBN 0-520-03195-4). U of Cal Pr.

Surviving Your Parent's Divorce. Boekman. (gr. 7 up). 1980. PLB 7.90 (ISBN 0-531-02869-0, B51). Watts.

Survivor. Jack Eisner. LC 80-14184. (Illus.). 288p. 1980. 11.95 (ISBN 0-688-03741-0). Morrow.

Survivor. James Herbert. 1977. pap. 1.95 (ISBN 0-451-08369-5, J8369, Sig). NAL.

Survivors & Other Poems. Carol A. Morizot. LC 77-80488. (Illus., Orig.). 1977. pap. 3.95 o.p. (ISBN 0-930138-00-7). Harold Hse.

Survivor's Manual to Wills, Trusts, Maintaining Emotional Stability. Charlotte Kirsch. LC 80-977. 240p. 1981. 11.95 (ISBN 0-385-15879-3, Anchor Pr). Doubleday.

Survivors of Suicide. Ed. by Albert C. Cain. (Illus.). 324p. 1972. pap. 26.75 photocopy edition, spiral (ISBN 0-398-02252-6). C C Thomas.

Survivors of the Bering Land Bridge. William Laughlin. (Case Studies in Cultural Anthropology). 128p. 1980. pap. text ed. 4.95 (ISBN 0-03-081269-0, HoltC). HR&W.

Survivors of the Stone Age: Nine Tribes Today. Rebecca Marcus. (Illus.). 160p. (gr. 7 up). 1975. PLB 7.95 (ISBN 0-8038-6726-3). Hastings.

Susan & Anna Warner. Edward H. Foster. (United States Authors Ser.: No. 312). 1978. lib. bdg. 12.50 (ISBN 0-8057-7232-4). Twayne.

Susan B. Anthony. Matthew G. Grant. LC 73-15911. 1974. PLB 5.95 (ISBN 0-87191-305-4). Creative Ed.

Susan B. Anthony. Charlotte Koch. LC 78-73539. (Illus.). (gr. 2-5). Date not set. price not set (ISBN 0-89799-162-1); pap. price not set (ISBN 0-89799-080-3). Dandelion Pr. Postponed.

Susan B. Anthony. Iris Noble. LC 74-30230. (Biography Ser). 192p. (gr. 7 up). 1975. PLB 5.29 o.p. (ISBN 0-671-32715-1). Messner.

Susan Ferrier of Edinburgh: A Biography. Aline Grant. 174p. 1957. 4.95 (ISBN 0-8040-0286-X). Swallow.

Susan Hayward & the Movie. Clive Denton. 300p. Date not set. cancelled o.p. (ISBN 0-498-02316-8). A S Barnes. Postponed.

Susan Hayward: Portrait of a Survivor. Beverly Linet. LC 80-66003. 1980. 12.95 (ISBN 0-686-68614-4). Atheneum.

Susan Hoffman's Quilted Tapestries. Patricia Mainardi & Susan Hoffman. LC 79-92444. (Illus.). 80p. Date not set. pap. cancelled (ISBN 0-89659-106-9). Abbeville Pr.

Susan Kahn. Lincoln Rothschild. LC 79-5388. (Illus.). 180p. 1980. 25.00 (ISBN 0-87982-031-4). Art Alliance.

Susan Sometimes. Phyllis Krasilovsky. (Illus.). (gr. k-1). 1962. 1.95 o.s.i. (ISBN 0-02-751160-X). Macmillan.

Susan Witt's Classics for Needlepoint. Susan Witt. LC 80-84410. (Illus.). 160p. 1981. 17.95 (ISBN 0-8487-0525-4). Oxmoor Hse.

Susana y Javier En Espana. Marvin Wasserman & Carol Wasserman. (Orig.). (gr. 7-12). 1975. pap. text ed. 4.58 (ISBN 0-87720-502-7). AMSCO Sch.

Susanna. Joan Dial. 1978. pap. 1.75 o.p. (ISBN 0-449-13961-1, GM). Fawcett.

Susanna Centlivre. F. P. Lock. (English Authors Ser.: No. 254). 1979. lib. bdg. 13.95 (ISBN 0-8057-6744-4). Twayne.

Susanna, Jeanie & the Old Folks at Home: The Songs of Stephen C. Foster from His Time to Ours. William W. Austin. LC 75-17635. 448p. 1975. 17.95 o.s.i. (ISBN 0-02-504500-8, 50450). Macmillan.

Susanna: Mother of the Wesleys. Rebecca L. Harmon. 1968. 8.95 (ISBN 0-687-40765-6). Abingdon.

Susanna Wesley: God's Catalyst for Revival. Donald L. Kline. (Orig.). 1980. pap. text ed. 4.35 (ISBN 0-89536-450-6). CSS Pub.

Susannah & the Blue House Mystery. Patricia Elmore. LC 79-20491. (Illus.). 176p. (gr. 4-7). 1980. PLB 9.95 (ISBN 0-525-40525-9). Dutton.

Susannah, the Pioneer Cow. Miriam E. Mason. (gr. k-3). 1941. 4.95g o.s.i. (ISBN 0-02-765150-9). Macmillan.

Susanna's Candlestick. Lillie V. Albrecht. LC 77-126422. (Illus.). (gr. 4-6). 1970. PLB 4.44 o.s.i. (ISBN 0-8038-6691-7). Hastings.

Susan's Magic. Nan H. Agle. LC 73-7124. (Illus.). 140p. (gr. 3-6). 1973. 6.95 o.p. (ISBN 0-8164-3108-6, Clarion). HM.

Susie Goes Shopping. Rose Greydanus. (Illus.). 32p. (gr. k-2). 1980. PLB 2.96 (ISBN 0-89375-389-0); pap. 0.95 (ISBN 0-89375-289-4). Troll Assocs.

Susie's Girls. Susanna Sheldon. 1975. pap. 1.50 o.p. (ISBN 0-685-61050-0, LB314DK, Leisure Bks). Nordon Pubns.

Suslov: Selected Speeches & Writings. Mikhail A. Suslov. LC 79-41075. 368p. 1980. 46.00 (ISBN 0-08-023602-2). Pergamon.

Suspect. B. M. Gill. 192p. 1981. 9.95 (ISBN 0-684-16885-5, ScribT). Scribner.

Suspected Carcinogens. Ed. by Edward J. Fairchild. 1978. pap. 45.00x o.p. (ISBN 0-7194-0000-7). Intl Ideas.

Suspension of the Power of Alienation, & Postponement of Vesting, Under the Laws of New York, Mich Igan, Minnesota & Wisconsin. Stewart Chaplin. xxxix, 370p. 1981. Repr. of 1891 ed. lib. bdg. 30.00x (ISBN 0-8377-0428-6). Rothman.

Suspensions & Expulsions. Shirley B. Neill. 1976. pap. 8.00 (ISBN 0-87545-004-0). Natl Sch Pr.

Suspicions. Barbara Betcherman. 1981. pap. 2.75 (ISBN 0-425-04839-X). Berkley Pub.

Susquehanna Compact: Guardian of the River's Future. William Voigt, Jr. (Illus.). 352p. 1972. 23.00 (ISBN 0-8135-0722-7). Rutgers U Pr.

Susquehanna: NYS&W. Krause & Crist. (Carstens Hobby Bks.: No. C38). (Illus.). 1980. pap. 12.00 (ISBN 0-911868-38-0). Carstens Pubns.

Sustainable Society: Implications for Limited Growth. Barry Buxton. LC 76-24365. (Special Studies). 1977. text ed. 29.95 (ISBN 0-275-23890-3); pap. 10.95 (ISBN 0-275-64760-9). Praeger.

Sustained Release Medications. Ed. by J. C. Johnson. LC 80-23455. (Chemical Technology Review: No. 177). (Illus.). 412p. 1981. 54.00 (ISBN 0-8155-0826-3). Noyes.

Sutherland: The Wartime Drawings. Roberto Tassi. Ed. & tr. by Julian Andrews. (Illus.). 172p. 1980. 40.00x (ISBN 0-85667-095-2, Pub. by Sotheby Parke Bernet England). Biblio Dist.

Sutra Vimalakirti. Ed. by Kozyun Kawase. Tr. by Jakob Fisher & Takezo Yokota. (Ger.). 1969. 13.95 o.p. (ISBN 0-89346-060-5, Pub. by Hokuseido Pr). Heian Intl.

Sutter Buttes of California: A Study of Plio-Pleistocene Volcanism. Howell Williams & G. H. Curtis. (Library Reprint Ser.: No. 97). 1979. Repr. of 1977 ed. 11.95x (ISBN 0-520-03808-8). U of Cal Pr.

Sutton-Taylor Feud. Robert C. Sutton, Jr. (Illus.). 82p. 1974. 6.95 (ISBN 0-89015-066-4). Nortex Pr.

Suttons Synagogue: Or the English Centurion (A Sermon) Percival Burrell. LC 74-28822. (English Experience Ser.: No. 647). 1974. Repr. of 1629 ed. 3.50 (ISBN 90-221-0647-0). Walter J Johnson.

Suzanne & Nicholas at the Market. Satomi Ichikawa. (Illus.). (gr. k-3). 1978. PLB 6.90 s&l o.p. (ISBN 0-531-01357-X). Watts.
Suzanne & Nicholas in the Garden. Satomi Ichikawa. (Illus.). (gr. k-3). 1978. PLB 6.90 s&l o.p. (ISBN 0-531-01358-8). Watts.
Suzanne & the Pacific. Jean Giraudoux. Tr. by Ben R. Redman from Fr. 286p. 1975. Repr. of 1923 ed. 17.00 (ISBN 0-86527-311-1). Fertig.
Suzanne's Cooking Secrets. Suzanne W. Pierot. (Illus.). 1981. 12.95 (ISBN 0-393-01458-4); pap. 5.95 (ISBN 0-393-00055-9). Norton.
Suzette & Nicholas & the Sunijudi Circus. Michele Lochak & Marie-France Mangin. (Illus.). 32p. (gr. 4-8). 1981. 7.95 (ISBN 0-399-20750-3); lib. bdg. 7.99 (ISBN 0-399-61160-6). Philomel.
Suzuki DS80-185 Singles, 1978-1979: Service, Repair, Maintenance. David Sales. Ed. by Eric Jorgensen. (Illus.). 142p. (Orig.). 1980. pap. text ed. 9.95 (ISBN 0-89287-316-7, M363). Clymer Pubns.
Suzuki GS1000 Fours: 1978-1979 Service-Repair-Performance. David Sales. Ed. by Eric Jorgensen. (Illus.). 216p. (Orig.). 1980. pap. text ed. 9.95 (ISBN 0-89287-315-9, M375). Clymer Pubns.
Suzuki: GS400 Twins 1977-1978--Service, Repair, Performance. David Sales. Ed. by Eric Jorgensen. (Illus.). 1978. pap. 9.95 (ISBN 0-89287-237-3, M372). Clymer Pubns.
Suzuki: GS550 Fours, 1977-1978--Service, Repair, Performance. David Sales. Ed. by Eric Jorgensen. (Illus.). 1978. pap. 9.95 (ISBN 0-89287-273-X, M373). Clymer Pubns.
Suzuki GS750 Fours, 1977-1979: Service, Repair, Performance. Mike Bishop. Ed. by Eric Jorgensen. (Illus.). 1979. pap. 9.95 (ISBN 0-89287-189-X, M370). Clymer Pubns.
Suzuki GS850 Fours, 1979-1980: Service, Repair, Maintenance. David Sales. Ed. by Eric Jorgensen. (Illus.). 295p. (Orig.). 1980. pap. text ed. 9.95 (ISBN 0-89287-305-1, M376). Clymer Pubns.
Suzuki Service-Repair Handbook 125-500cc Twins: 1964-1976. 3rd rev. ed. Ray Hoy. Ed. by Jeff Robinson. (Illus.). 1977. pap. 9.95 (ISBN 0-89287-132-6, M-366). Clymer Pubns.
Suzuki SP-DR Three Hundred Seventy & Four Hundred Singles Nineteen Seventy-Eight to Nineteen Eighty: Service, Repair, Performance. David Sales. Ed. by Eric Jorgensen. (Illus.). 224p. (Orig.). 1980. pap. text ed. 9.95 (ISBN 0-89287-327-2, M374). Clymer Pubns.
Suzuki: 125-400cc Singles, 1964-1979 Service, Repair, Performance. 3rd ed. Ed. by Eric Jorgensen. (Illus.). 1978. pap. 9.95 (ISBN 0-89287-280-2, M369). Clymer Pubns.
Suzuki: 380-750cc Triples, 1972-1977 Service, Repair, Maintenance. Clymer Pubns. (Illus.). 1977. pap. 9.95 (ISBN 0-89287-285-3, M368). Clymer Pubns.
Suzuki: 50-120cc Singles 1964-1979--Service, Repair, Maintenance Handbook. 3rd ed. David Sales. Ed. by Eric Jorgensen. (Illus.). 1978. pap. 9.95 (ISBN 0-89287-292-6, M367). Clymer Pubns.
Suzuki 50-400cc RM Series Singles, 1975-79: Service, Repair, Performance. David Sales. Ed. by Eric Jorgensen. (Illus.). 1977. pap. 9.95 (ISBN 0-89287-196-2, M371). Clymer Pubns.
Suzy & the Rembrandt Kid. Michael T. Brown. LC 78-55986. 1980. softcover 7.95 o.p. (ISBN 0-930490-12-6). Future Shop.
Svayamvara & Other Poems. Jayanta Mahapatra. (Redbird Bk.). 1976. 6.75 (ISBN 0-89253-091-X); flexible bdg. 4.00 (ISBN 0-685-69683-9). Ind-US Inc.
Svensk-Engelsk Modern Ordbok. 4th ed. Rolf Prisma-Lagersson. 1979. 20.00x (ISBN 9-1518-0942-7, SW-204). Vanous.
Svenska Fur Er, Part 1. S. Higelin et al. (Illus.). Set. pap. text ed. 27.50 exercise, wordlist (ISBN 9-1522-1363-3, SW174); 8 tapes 75.00x (ISBN 0-686-05370-2, SW174T); cassettes 75.00x (ISBN 0-686-05371-0, SW174C); lecture outline 6.00 (ISBN 91-522-1395-1); o.p. (ISBN 91-522-1363-3); o.p. (ISBN 91-522-1376-5); o.p. (ISBN 91-522-1381-1). Vanous.
Svenska Fur Er, Part 2. S. Higelin et al. (Illus.). 1971. Set. pap. text ed. 27.50x exercise wordlist (ISBN 0-686-05373-7, SW175); 4 tapes 75.00x (ISBN 0-686-05374-5, SW175T); 3 cassettes 75.00 (ISBN 0-686-05375-3, SW175C); lecture outline 7.50 (ISBN 0-686-05376-1); o.p. (ISBN 91-522-1424-9); o.p. (ISBN 91-522-1425-7); o.p. (ISBN 91-522-1503-2). Vanous.
Svetasvataropanisad. Tr. by Swami Tyagisananda. (Sanskrit & Eng.). pap. 2.00 (ISBN 0-87481-418-9). Vedanta Pr.
Swag. Elmore Leonard. 240p. 1976. 7.95 o.p. (ISBN 0-440-08449-0). Delacorte.
Swahili: A Foundation for Speaking, Reading & Writing. Thomas J Hinnebusch & Sarah M Mirza. LC 78-65430. (Illus., English & Swahili). 1978. pap. 10.50 (ISBN 0-8191-0659-3). U Pr of Amer.
Swahili Dictionary. D. V. Perrot. (Teach Yourself Ser.). 1974. pap. 2.95 o.p. (ISBN 0-679-10015-6). McKay.
Swahili-English Dictionary. F. Johnson. 15.00 (ISBN 0-685-20193-7). Saphrograph.
Swahili Grammar. 2nd ed. E. O. Ashton. 1976. pap. text ed. 6.50x (ISBN 0-582-62701-X). Longman.
SWAK: The Complete Book of Mail Fun for Kides. Randy Harelson. LC 80-54624. (Illus.). 160p. (gr. 3-7). 1981. pap. 3.95 (ISBN 0-89480-150-3). Workman Pub.
Swallow the Lake. Clarence Major. LC 79-120258. (Wesleyan Poetry Program: Vol. 54). (Orig.). 1970. 10.00x (ISBN 0-8195-2054-3, Pub. by Wesleyan U Pr); pap. 4.95 (ISBN 0-8195-1054-8). Columbia U Pr.
Swallows & Amazons. Arthur Ransome. 352p. (gr. 3-7). 1981. 9.95 (ISBN 0-224-60631-X, Pub. by Chatto-Bodley-Jonathan). Merrimack Bk Serv.
Swami. Doug Boyd. 1976. 10.00 o.p. (ISBN 0-394-49603-5). Random.
Swami Adbhutananda: Teachings & Reminiscences. Swami Chetanananda. LC 80-50962. (Illus.). 175p. 1980. pap. 6.95 (ISBN 0-916356-59-0). Vedanta Soc St Louis.
Swami & Friends. R. K. Narayan. LC 80-16119. 192p. 1980. lib. bdg. 13.00x (ISBN 0-226-56829-6); pap. 3.95 (ISBN 0-226-56831-8). U of Chicago Pr.
Swami Vijnanananda: His Life & Sayings. Swami Vishwashrayananda. Tr. by Devavrata Basu Ray from Bongali. 72p. 1981. pap. 1.95 (ISBN 0-87481-502-9). Vedanta Pr.
Swamp. Bill Thomas. (Illus.). 1976. 29.95 (ISBN 0-393-08747-6). Norton.
Swamp Fox, Francis Marion. Noel Gerson. 1980. pap. 2.25 (ISBN 0-89176-001-6, 6001). Mockingbird Bks.
Swamp Spring. Carol Carrick. LC 69-10497. (Illus.). (gr. k-2). 1969. 4.95g o.s.i. (ISBN 0-02-717320-8). Macmillan.
Swamp Water. Vereen Bell. LC 80-24570. (Brown Thrasher Ser.). 272p. 1981. pap. 6.95 (ISBN 0-8203-0546-4). U of Ga Pr.
Swampy Alligator. Jack Gantos. (Illus.). (gr. 3-5). Date not set. 7.95 (ISBN 0-671-96092-X). Dial.
Swan, Cygnets, & Owl: An Anthology of Modernist Poetry in Spanish America. Tr. by Mildred E. Johnson. LC 56-12576. 1956. 15.00x o.p. (ISBN 0-8262-0599-2). U of Mo Pr.
Swan Dive. Keith Korman. 1981. pap. 2.95 (ISBN 0-440-18423-1). Dell.
Swan Song. Violet Ashton. 1979. pap. 2.25 o.p. (ISBN 0-449-14263-9, GM). Fawcett.
Swan Watch. Budd Schulberg. 160p. 1975. 8.95 o.p. (ISBN 0-440-06016-8). Delacorte.
Swans of Brhyadr. Vivienne Couldrey. 224p. 1981. pap. 1.75 (ISBN 0-449-50166-3, Coventry). Fawcett.
Swans of Other Worlds: Kazimir Malevich & the Origins of Abstraction in Russia. Charlotte C. Douglas. (Studies in Fine Arts: The Avant-Garde, No. 2). 1980. 23.95 (ISBN 0-8357-1058-0). Univ Microfilms.
Swastika Poems. William Heyen. LC 76-39729. 1977. 7.95 (ISBN 0-8149-0780-6). Vanguard.
Sweat of the Sun & Tears of the Moon: Gold & Silver in Pre-Columbian Art. Andre Emmerich. LC 77-72685. (Illus.). 1977. Repr. of 1965 ed. 25.00 (ISBN 0-87817-208-4). Hacker.
Sweated Trades: Outwork in the Nineteenth Century. Duncan Bythell. 1978. 50.00 (ISBN 0-7134-1259-3, Pub. by Batsford England). David & Charles.
Sweden. Helen H. Merrick. LC 71-151884. (First Bks). (Illus.). (gr. 4-6). 1971. PLB 4.90 o.p. (ISBN 0-531-00751-0). Watts.
Sweden - a Short Survey of the Kingdom of Sweden. LC 79-84139. (English Experience Ser.: No. 956). 116p. 1979. Repr. of 1632 ed. lib. bdg. 11.50 (ISBN 90-221-0956-9). Walter J Johnson.
Sweden: A Political & Cultural History. Eric Elstob. (Illus.). 209p. 1979. 18.50x (ISBN 0-8476-6220-9). Rowman.
Sweden in Pictures. Sterling Publishing Company Editors. (Visual Geography Ser). (Illus., Orig.). (gr. 6 up). 1966. PLB 4.99 o.p. (ISBN 0-8069-1091-7); pap. 2.95 o.p. (ISBN 0-8069-1090-9). Sterling.
Sweden in World Society: Thoughts About the Future. Secretariat for Futures Studies, Stockholm, Sweden. LC 80-40321. (Illus.). 228p. 1980. 33.00 (ISBN 0-08-025456-X); pap. 16.25 (ISBN 0-08-025455-1). Pergamon.
Sweden Sings. B. Eriksson. pap. 12.50x o.p. (ISBN 0-89918-120-1, SW120). Vanous.
Sweden: The Nation's History. Franklin D. Scott. LC 76-51159. (Illus.). 1979. 30.00x (ISBN 0-8166-0804-0); pap. 10.95x (ISBN 0-8166-0805-9). U of Minn Pr.
Swedenborg: Life & Teaching. George Trobridge. 1976. pap. 1.95 (ISBN 0-89129-058-3). Jove Pubns.
Swedes & Turnips for the Fresh Market. 96p. 1980. pap. 9.95x (ISBN 0-901361-42-9, Pub. by Grower Bks England). Intl Schol Bk Serv.
Swedes in Chicago: A Demographic & Social Study of the 1846-1880 Immigration. Ulf Beijbom. LC 71-182869. (Illus.). 381p. 1971. pap. 20.00 o.p. (ISBN 91-24-68690-5). Chicago Hist.
Swedish. 2nd ed. Gladys Hird. LC 78-74534. 1980. 18.95x (ISBN 0-521-22644-9). Cambridge U Pr.
Swedish Basic Grammar. 3rd ed. Beite Hildeman. 1976. text ed. 18.50x (ISBN 9-1210-1551-1, SW145). Vanous.
Swedish Economic Policy. Assar Lindbeck. 1973. 19.50x (ISBN 0-520-02422-2). U of Cal Pr.
Swedish-English, English-Swedish Dictionary, 2 vols. R. Santesson & Karl K. Kaerre. 1976. Set. cancelled (ISBN 9-1241-9070-5). Heinman.
Swedish-English Fact Ordbok (Technical Terms) 2nd ed. Ingvar E. Gullberg. 1977. 200.00x (ISBN 91-1-775052-0, SW-207). Vanous.
Swedish-English Modern Dictionary. 4th ed. R. Prisma-Lagersson. 1979. 20.00x (ISBN 9-1518-0942-7, SW204). Vanous.
Swedish-English, Swedish Ordbok: Presma Modern Pocket Dictionary. 2nd ed. 1979. 8.50x (ISBN 91-518-1148-0, SW-208). Vanous.
Swedish-English-Swedish Pocket Dictionary. A. Hills. 1978. 7.50x (ISBN 0-89918-134-1, SW134). Vanous.
Swedish Exercises. Paul Jacob. (Writers Workshop Redbird Ser.). 1975. 8.00 (ISBN 0-88253-656-7); pap. text ed. 4.00 (ISBN 0-88253-655-9). Ind-US Inc.
Swedish Exodus. Lars Ljungmark. Tr. by Kermit B. Westerberg from Swedish. LC 79-10498. 192p. 1979. 12.95 (ISBN 0-8093-0905-X). S Ill U Pr.
Swedish Imperial Experience: Fifteen Sixty to Seventeen Eighteen. Michael Roberts. LC 78-58799. (Illus.). 1979. 23.50 (ISBN 0-521-22502-7). Cambridge U Pr.
Swedish Karre Dictionary, Vol. 1: Svensk-Engelsk. K. Karre. 1976. 40.00x (ISBN 91-24-14308-1, SW132). Vanous.
Swedish Karre Dictionary, Vol. 2: Engelsk-Svensk. 3rd ed. K. Karre. 1974. text ed. 60.00x (ISBN 91-24-19070-5, SW133). Vanous.
Swedish, Learn: Reader for Beginners. N. Hildeman et al. (Swedish Language Ser.). 1975. text ed. 18.50x (ISBN 9-1210-3042-1, SW143); 5 45 rpm records 90.00x (ISBN 91-21-90171-6, SW143R); 5 tapes 90.00x (ISBN 91-21-90332-8, SW143T); 2 cassettes 90.00x (ISBN 91-21-90089-2, SW143C). Vanous.
Swedish Modern Pocket Dictionary: Svensk-Engelskt Engelsk-Svensk Grammatik Parlor. E. Gomer. 1978. text ed. 8.50x (ISBN 91-518-1148-0, SW-208). Vanous.
Swedish Practice. N. H. Hildeman et al. 1975. text ed. 8.50x (ISBN 9-1210-2423-5, SW144); key to exercise book 6.00x (SW144K). Vanous.
Sweeney Todd, The Demon Barber of Fleet Street. Hugh Wheeler & Stephen Sondheim. LC 79-18468. 1979. 7.95 (ISBN 0-396-07776-5). Dodd.
Sweep of American History, Vol. 1. Robert Jones & Gustav L. Seligman. 400p. 1981. pap. text ed. 8.95 (ISBN 0-471-07898-0). Wiley.
Sweep of American History, Vol. 2. Robert Jones & Gustav L. Seligman. 400p. 1981. pap. text ed. 8.95 (ISBN 0-471-07897-2). Wiley.
Sweep Westward, 1829-1849. Margaret L. Coit. LC 63-8572. (Life History of the United States). (Illus.). (gr. 5 up). 1974. PLB 9.93 (ISBN 0-8094-0553-9, Pub. by Time-Life). Silver.
Sweeper to Saint: Stories of the Holy India. Baba Hari Dass. Ed. by Ma Denu. (Illus.). 200p. (Orig.). 1980. pap. 6.95 (ISBN 0-918100-03-8). Sri Rama.
Sweepers of Slaughterhouse: A Study of Conflict & Survival in a Karachi Neighbourhood. Pieter Streefland. (Studies of Developing Countries Ser.: No. 23). 1979. pap. text ed. 14.25x (ISBN 90-232-1665-2). Humanities.
Sweepstakes. Judith A. Magarian & Patricia M. Horton. (Illus.). 13p. (gr. 4-6). 1980. pap. 4.95 (ISBN 0-933358-74-1). Enrich.
Sweet Adelaide. Julian Symons. LC 80-7610. 288p. 1980. 11.95 (ISBN 0-06-014207-3, HarpT). Har-Row.
Sweet Adventure, No. 17. Barbara Cartland. 1978. pap. 1.50 (ISBN 0-515-04137-8). Jove Pubns.
Sweet Anarchy. Nathaniel Benchley. (Large Print Bks.). 1980. lib. bdg. 15.50 (ISBN 0-8161-3134-1). G K Hall.
Sweet Anarchy. Nathaniel Benchley. 304p. 1981. pap. 2.50 (ISBN 0-380-53777-X, 53777). Avon.
Sweet & Deadly. Charlaine Harris. 180p. 1981. 8.95 (ISBN 0-395-30532-2). HM.
Sweet & Lowdown: America's Popular Song Writers. Warren Craig. LC 77-20223. 1978. 30.00 (ISBN 0-8108-1089-1). Scarecrow.
Sweet & Sour: Tales from China. Carol Kendall & Li Yao-wen. LC 78-24349. (Illus.). (gr. 3-6). 1979. 7.95 (ISBN 0-395-28958-0, Clarion). HM.
Sweet & Twenty. Joan Smith. 1979. pap. 1.75 o.p. (ISBN 0-449-23818-0, Crest). Fawcett.
Sweet Betsy from Pike: A Song from the Gold Rush Days. Robert A. Parker. (Illus.). (gr. 1-4). 1978. 7.95 o.p. (ISBN 0-670-68632-8). Viking Pr.
Sweet Dreams. Warren Murphy. (Destroyer Ser.: No. 25). 1976. pap. 1.75 (ISBN 0-523-40901-X). Pinnacle Bks.
Sweet Ember. Bonnie Drake. (Candlelight Romance Ser.). (Orig.). Date not set. pap. 1.50 (ISBN 0-440-18459-2). Dell.
Sweet Enchantress. Barbara Cartland. 1979. pap. 1.50 (ISBN 0-515-05100-4). Jove Pubns.
Sweet Evil. Charles Platt. 1977. pap. 1.25 o.p. (ISBN 0-425-03298-1). Berkley Pub.
Sweet Gogarty: A Darkly Comic Novel. Matthew Hochberg. LC 80-28358. 224p. 1981. 10.95 (ISBN 0-8253-0048-7). Beaufort Bks NY.
Sweet Grass Lives on: Fifty Contemporary North American Indian Artists. Jamake Highwater. LC 80-7776. (Illus.). 192p. 1980. 35.00 (ISBN 0-690-01925-4). Lippincott & Crowell.
Sweet Harvest. Kerry Allyne. (Romances Ser.). 192p. (Orig.). 1980. pap. text ed. 1.25 (ISBN 0-373-02341-3, Pub. by Harlequin). PB.
Sweet Home Chicago. Joel Lipmann. 1980. pap. 2.00. Quixote.
Sweet Life of Jimmy Riley. James Reardon. 1981. 13.95 (ISBN 0-686-68760-4, Wyndham Bks). S&S.
Sweet Love, Bitter Honey. Clara Domany. LC 78-66061. 1980. 7.95 (ISBN 0-533-04139-2). Vantage.
Sweet Love, Bitter Love. Anna James. 1978. pap. 2.25 (ISBN 0-515-04697-3, 04697-3). Jove Pubns.
Sweet Music for Gentle Americans. Nicholas Tawa. LC 78-71394. 1980. 21.95 (ISBN 0-87972-130-8); pap. 10.95 (ISBN 0-87972-157-X). Bowling Green Univ.
Sweet Not Always. Karen Van Der Zee. (Harlequin Romance Ser.). (Orig.). 1980. pap. 1.25 o.p. (ISBN 0-373-02334-0, Pub. by Harlequin). PB.
Sweet of Fear. Robert C. Dennis. 176p. 1976. pap. 1.50 o.p. (ISBN 0-345-25148-2). Ballantine.
Sweet Piracy. Patricia Maxwell. 1978. pap. 1.95 o.p. (ISBN 0-449-13990-5, GM). Fawcett.
Sweet Potatoes: Production, Processing, Marketing. Joseph B. Edmond & C. R. Ammerman. LC 73-165213. (Illus.). 1971. 31.00 o.p. (ISBN 0-87055-103-5). AVI.
Sweet Robin: A Biography of Robert Dudley, Earl of Leicester, 1533-1588. Derek Wilson. (Illus.). 304p. 1981. 54.00 (ISBN 0-241-10149-2, Pub. by Hamish Hamilton England). David & Charles.
Sweet Savage Love. Rosemary Rogers. 640p. 1980. pap. 2.95 (ISBN 0-380-00815-7, 76588). Avon.
Sweet Skunks & Sneaky Butter. Wendell Knowles. LC 79-92619. 3.95. Heritage Kansas.
Sweet Spot in Time. John Jerome. LC 80-15793. 348p. 1980. 13.95 (ISBN 0-671-40039-8). Summit Bks.
Sweet Tooth. Yves Navarre. Tr. by Donald Watson. 1980. 8.95 (ISBN 0-7145-3522-2). Riverrun NY.
Sweet Treat Cookery. M&MR Mars, LC 78-61008. (Illus.). 1978. pap. 4.95 (ISBN 0-89586-013-9). H P Bks.
Sweet Wild World: Thoreau on Birds & Small Creatures. William M. White. (Illus.). 146p. (Orig.). 1981. 10.00 (ISBN 0-85699-112-0); pap. 6.95 (ISBN 0-85699-115-5). Chatham Pr.
Sweeteners: Issues & Uncertainties. Academy Forum, National Academy of Sciences. LC 75-29990. vi, 259p. 1975. pap. 8.00 (ISBN 0-309-02407-2). Natl Acad Pr.
Sweetheart Deal. Robert Rosenblum. 1977. pap. 1.95 o.p. (ISBN 0-345-25620-4). Ballantine.
Sweetheart of the Silent Majority. Carol Felsenthal. LC 79-6090. (Illus.). 360p. 1981. 13.95 (ISBN 0-385-14912-3). Doubleday.
Sweetheart, Sweetheart. Bernard Taylor. 1979. pap. 2.25 o.p. (ISBN 0-345-27846-1). Ballantine.
Sweetie Feetie. Harold K. Jones & Connie L. Wakefield. LC 74-19966. (Picture Bk). (Illus.). 32p. (ps-3). 1975. 5.95 o.p. (ISBN 0-695-80546-0); lib. ed. 5.97 o.p. (ISBN 0-695-40546-2). Follett.
Sweetman Curve. Graham Masterton. 1979. pap. 2.50 (ISBN 0-441-79133-6). Ace Bks.
Sweetness & Sweeteners. Ed. by G. G. Birch. (Illus.). 1971. 26.00x (ISBN 0-85334-503-1, Pub. by Applied Science). Burgess-Intl Ideas.
Sweetness of the Fig: The Australian Aboriginal Woman As a Transitional Figure. Virginia Huffer et al. LC 80-21658. (Illus.). 244p. 1981. 15.00 o.p. (ISBN 0-295-95790-5). U of Wash Pr.

Sweetness of the Pig: Aboriginal Women in Transition. Virginia Huffer et al. LC 80-21658. (Illus.). 244p. 1981. 15.00 (ISBN 0-295-95790-5). U of Wash Pr.
Sweetness Readie Penn'd Imagery, Syntax & Metric in the Poetry of George Herbert. Rodney Edgecombe. (Elizabethan Studies). 1980. pap. text ed. 25.00x (ISBN 0-391-02185-0). Humanities.
Sweet's Folly. Fiona Hill. LC 76-22717. (YA) 1977. 8.95 o.p. (ISBN 0-399-11877-2, Dist. by Putnam). Berkley Pub.
Sweets for Saints & Sinners. Janice Feuer. LC 80-21934. (Illus.). 144p. 1980. pap. 5.95 (ISBN 0-89286-180-0). One Hund One Prods.
Sweets 'n' Treats. Ed. by Annette Gohlke & Annette Gohlke. (Illus.). 68p. (Orig.). 1980. pap. 2.95 (ISBN 0-89821-034-8). Reiman Assocs.
Sweets Without Guilt. Minuha Cannon. (Illus.). 128p. (Orig.). 1980. lib. bdg. 9.25 o.p. (ISBN 0-914788-30-2) (ISBN 0-686-27281-1). East Woods.
Sweetsir. Helen Yglesias. 1981. 13.95 (ISBN 0-671-25092-2). S&S.
Swenson's Pediatric Surgery. 4th ed. Ed. by John G. Raffensperger. 960p. 1980. 78.50x (ISBN 0-8385-8756-9). ACC.
Swift Aire Lines: History of an American Commuter Airline. I. E. Quastler. (Illus.). 126p. 1979. pap. 5.50 (ISBN 0-9602554-0-0). Commuter Airlines.
Swift Aire Lines, 1969-79: Commuter Air Lines. I. E. Quastler. (Illus.). 1979. pap. 6.00 (ISBN 0-9602554-0-0, Pub by Commuter). Aviation.
Swift & Enduring: Cheetahs & Wild Dogs of the Serengeti. George Frame & Lory Frame. 1981. 15.95 (ISBN 0-525-93060-4). Dutton.
Swift & Enduring: Cheetahs & Wilddogs of the Serengeti. George Frame & Lory Frame. (Illus.). 256p. 1980. 15.95 (ISBN 0-525-93060-4). Dutton.
Swift Arrow. Josephine C. Edwards. LC 67-17867. 116p. 1967. pap. 4.95 (ISBN 0-8163-0049-6, 19795-4). Pacific Pr Pub Assn.
Swift As a Shadow. Elizabeth Benoist. 256p. 1980. 9.95 (ISBN 0-86629-002-8). Sunrise MO.
Swift to Hear, Slow to Speak. Jerry Butler. 1975. pap. 3.95 (ISBN 0-89137-511-2). Quality Pubns.
Swifter Than Eagles: Bill White and the Battle of Athens-1946. Howard Cook. (Illus.). 354p. 15.00x (ISBN 0-938212-00-1). Friendly City.
Swiftiana, 19 vols. Incl. Vol. 1. On the Tale of a Tub (ISBN 0-8240-1262-3); Vol. 2. Bickerstaffiana, & Other Early Materials on Swift (ISBN 0-8240-1263-1); Vol. 3. On Swift's Remarks on the Barrier Treaty, & His Conduct of the Allies (ISBN 0-8240-1264-X); Vol. 4. On the Drapier's Letters (ISBN 0-8240-1265-8); Vol. 5. Gulliver's Travels, One (ISBN 0-8240-1266-6); Vol. 6. Gulliver's Travels, Two (ISBN 0-8240-1267-4); Vol. 7. Gulliver's Travels, Three (ISBN 0-8240-1268-2); Vol. 8. Smedley on Swift (ISBN 0-8240-1269-0); Vol. 9. Biographical Satire (ISBN 0-8240-1270-4); Vol. 10. In Praise of Swift (ISBN 0-8240-1271-2); Vol. 11. Biography (ISBN 0-8240-1272-0); Vol. 12. Biography (ISBN 0-8240-1273-9); Vol. 13. Biography (ISBN 0-8240-1274-7); Vol. 14. Biography (ISBN 0-8240-1275-5); Vol. 15. Biography (ISBN 0-8240-1276-3); Vol. 16. Biography (ISBN 0-8240-1277-1); Vols. 17-19. Biography (ISBN 0-8240-1278-X). (Life & Times of Seven Major British Writers Ser). 1974. 47.00 ea. Garland Pub.
Swiftly Tilting Planet. Madeleine L'Engle. (YA) 1980. pap. 1.75 (ISBN 0-440-90158-8, LFL). Dell.
Swift's Anatomy of Misunderstanding: A Study of Swift's Epistemological Imagination in "a Tale of a Tub" & "Gulliver's Travels". Frances Louis. 220p. 1980. 18.00x (ISBN 0-389-20074-3). B&N.
Swift's Rhetorical Art: A Study in Structure & Meaning. Martin Price. LC 73-7764. (Arcturus Books Paperbacks). 125p. 1973. pap. 3.95 (ISBN 0-8093-0646-8). S Ill U Pr.
Swim for Fitness. Marianne Brems. LC 78-32033. (Illus.). 1979. pap. 6.95 (ISBN 0-87701-124-9). Chronicle Bks.
Swimmer in the Spreading Dawn. Kathleen Spivack. (Orig.). 1981. pap. 4.95 (ISBN 0-918222-24-9). Apple Wood.
Swimming. Boy Scouts Of America. LC 19-600. (Illus.). 48p. (gr. 6-12). 1960. pap. 0.55x o.p. (ISBN 0-8395-3299-7, 3299). BSA.
Swimming. Boy Scouts of America. (Illus.). 48p. (gr. 6-12). 1980. pap. 0.70x. BSA.
Swimming. Martin Collis & William Kirchoff. 96p. 1974. pap. text ed. 2.95x o.p. (ISBN 0-205-03853-0, 623853X). Allyn.
Swimming. Helen Elkington. LC 76-53514. (Illus.). 1978. pap. 9.95x (ISBN 0-521-29027-9). Cambridge U Pr.
Swimming. David Haller. (Pelham Pictorial Sports Instruction Ser.). (Illus.). 1979. 9.95 (ISBN 0-7207-0954-7). Transatlantic.
Swimming & Flying in Nature. Ed. by Theodore Y. Wu et al. LC 75-33753. 1975. Vol. 1, 420p. 45.00 (ISBN 0-306-37088-3, Plenum Pr); Vol. 2, 583p. 45.00 (ISBN 0-306-37089-1). Plenum Pub.
Swimming for Total Fitness: A Progressive Aerobic Program. Jane Katz & Nancy P. Bruning. LC 80-708. (Illus.). 380p. 1981. pap. 10.95 (ISBN 0-385-15932-3, Dolp). Doubleday.
Swimming Hole. Jerrold Beim. (Illus.). (gr. k-3). 1951. PLB 7.44 (ISBN 0-688-31442-2). Morrow.
Swimming Is for Me. Lowell A. Dickmeyer. LC 80-15366. (Sports for Me Bks.). (Illus.). (gr. 2-5). 1980. PLB 5.95g (ISBN 0-8225-1084-7). Lerner Pubns.
Swimming Mammals. Susan Harris. (Easy-Read Wildlife Bks.). (Illus.). (gr. 2 up). 1977. lib. bdg. 6.45 s&l (ISBN 0-531-00378-7). Watts.
Swimming Pools. 5th ed. Sunset Editors. LC 80-53488. (Illus.). 128p. 1981. pap. 4.95 (ISBN 0-376-01607-8, Sunset Bks.). Sunset-Lane.
Swimming Program for the Handicapped. Ed. by Grace D. Reynolds. 1973. pap. 4.95 o.p. (ISBN 0-8096-0471-X, Assn Pr). Follett.
Swimming Skill Book. (Illus.). 1977. tchrs. guide 0.30x (ISBN 0-8395-6591-7). BSA.
Swimming the Channel. Richard Meade. LC 80-26545. 80p. 1981. 7.95 (ISBN 0-686-69065-6); pap. 3.95 (ISBN 0-931704-06-5). Story Pr.
Swinburne: A Study of Romantic Mythmaking. David G. Riede. LC 78-4940. 1978. 12.95x (ISBN 0-8139-0745-4). U Pr of Va.
Swinburne: Portrait of a Poet. Philip Henderson. LC 74-478. (Illus.). 312p. 1974. 10.95 o.s.i. (ISBN 0-02-550960-8). Macmillan.
Swinburne: The Critical Heritage. Ed. by Clyde K. Hyder. 1970. 24.00x (ISBN 0-7100-6656-2). Routledge & Kegan.
Swinburne: The Poet of His World. Donald Thomas. 1979. 14.95 (ISBN 0-19-520136-1). Oxford U Pr.
Swine. Subcommittee On Standards For Large Domestic Laboratory Animals. LC 75-169293. (Standards & Guidelines for the Breeding, Care, & Management of Laboratory Animals Ser). 1971. pap. text ed. 3.25 o.p. (ISBN 0-309-01923-0). Natl Acad Pr.
Swine Management Packet. 3.25 (ISBN 0-8134-0546-7); text ed. 2.50x (ISBN 0-8134-0547-5, 544-547). Interstate.
Swine Production in Temperate & Tropical Environments. Wilson G. Pond & Jerome H. Maner. LC 73-16068. (Illus.). 1974. text ed. 30.95x (ISBN 0-7167-0840-X). W H Freeman.
Swine Science. 4th ed. M. Eugene Ensminger. LC 68-21886. (Illus.). (gr. 9-12). 1970. 23.35 (ISBN 0-8134-1026-6); text ed. 17.50x (ISBN 0-685-03929-3). Interstate.
Swing. Emily Hanlon. LC 78-26400. (gr. 5-7). 1979. 8.95 (ISBN 0-87888-146-8). Bradbury Pr.
Swing Easy, Hit Hard. Julius Boros. 192p. 1968. pap. 2.95 (ISBN 0-346-12305-4). Cornerstone.
Swing of the Gate. Roy Brown. LC 78-6422. (gr. 6 up). 1978. 6.95 (ISBN 0-395-28895-9, Clarion). HM.
Swing, Swing Together. Peter Lovesey. LC 76-14865. 1976. 6.95 (ISBN 0-396-07327-1). Dodd.
Swinger of Birches: A Portrait of Robert Frost. Sidney Cox. LC 54-6902. 1957. 12.00x (ISBN 0-8147-0105-1). NYU Pr.
Swinging Mad. (Mad Ser.: No.46). (Illus., Orig.). 1977. pap. 1.75 (ISBN 0-446-94388-6). Warner Bks.
Swinging Marriage. (Illus.). pap. 5.00 (ISBN 0-910550-70-0). Centurion Pr.
Swipe File 2. Jean Brodsky. (NonProfit-Ability Ser.). 1976. pap. 9.95 o.s.i. (ISBN 0-914756-11-7). Taft Corp.
Swiss Abduction. Mark Denning. 1981. pap. 1.95 (ISBN 0-8439-0858-0, Leisure Bks). Nordon Pubns.
Swiss Banking Handbook. Robert Roethenmund. LC 79-55800. (Illus.). 1980. 19.95 (ISBN 0-916728-33-1); pap. 8.95 o.s.i. (ISBN 0-916728-34-X). Bks in Focus.
Swiss Conspiracy. Michael Stanley. 1976. pap. 1.95 (ISBN 0-380-00492-5, 34082). Avon.
Swiss Cooking. Anne Mason. 12.00 (ISBN 0-233-96257-3). Transatlantic.
Swiss Family Robinson. (Illustrated Junior Library). (Illus.). 384p. 1981. pap. 4.95 (ISBN 0-448-11022-9). G&D.
Swiss Family Robinson. J. R. Wyss. (Childrens Illustrated Classics Ser). (Illus.). 350p. 1977. Repr. of 1957 ed. 9.00x (ISBN 0-460-05008-7, Pub. by J. M. Dent England). Biblio Dist.
Swiss Men of Letters. Ed. by Alex Natan. 1970. 15.95 (ISBN 0-85496-064-3). Dufour.
Swiss Watchmaking Year-Book, 1980-1981. 83rd ed. Ed. by Chapalay & Mottier. LC 46-34872. Orig. Title: Quid Horloger: Annuaire De L'Horlogerie Suisse. 602p. (Orig.). 1980. pap. write for info. (ISBN 0-8002-2751-4). Intl Pubns Serv.
Switch. Ed. by Mary Verdick. (Pal Paperbacks Kit A Ser.). (Illus., Orig.). (gr. 7-12). 1976. pap. text ed. 1.25 (ISBN 0-8374-3491-2). Xerox Ed Pubns.
Switch, No. 2. Mike Jahn. pap. 1.25 o.p. (ISBN 0-425-03252-3). Berkley Pub.
Switchback. Molly Parkin. 160p. Date not set. cancelled (ISBN 0-686-68789-2). Riverrun NY.
Switchbacks. Andy Holland. Ed. by Cynthia Mallory. LC 80-25407. (Illus.). 144p. (Orig.). 1980. pap. 6.95 (ISBN 0-916890-99-6). Mountaineers.
Switching & Linear Power Supply, Power Converter Design. Abraham I. Pressman. (Illus.). 1977. text ed. 23.95 (ISBN 0-8104-5847-0); net solutions manual 1.95 (ISBN 0-8104-5827-6). Hayden.
Switching Circuits for Engineers. 3rd ed. Mitchell P. Marcus. (Illus.). 336p. 1975. ref. ed. 23.95 (ISBN 0-13-879908-3). P-H.
Switching Circuits: Theory & Logic Design. Torng. 1976. 18.95 (ISBN 0-201-07576-8). A-W.
Switching Power Converters. Peter Wood. 464p. 1981. text ed. 26.50 (ISBN 0-442-24333-2). Van Nos Reinhold.
Switching Regulators & Power Supplies with Practical Inverters & Converters. Irving Gottlieb. LC 75-41722. (Illus.). 252p. 1976. 12.95 o.p. (ISBN 0-8306-6828-4); pap. 6.95 (ISBN 0-8306-5828-9, 828). TAB Bks.
Switzerland. William Martin. 1971. 11.95 (ISBN 0-236-15402-8, Pub. by Paul Elek). Merrimack Bk Serv.
Switzerland Exposed. Jean Ziegler. (Allison & Busby Motive Ser.). 180p. 1981. pap. 7.95 (ISBN 0-8052-8077-4, Pub. by Allison & Busby England). Schocken.
Switzerland in Pictures. Sterling Publishing Company Editors. LC 60-14340. (Visual Geography Ser.). (Orig.). (gr. 6 up). PLB 4.99 (ISBN 0-8069-1017-8); pap. 2.95 (ISBN 0-8069-1016-X). Sterling.
Sword & the Flute - Kali & Krsna: Dark Visions of the Terrible & the Sublime in Hindu Mythology. David R. Kinsley. 175p. 1975. 18.50x (ISBN 0-520-02675-6); pap. 2.95 (ISBN 0-520-03510-0). U of Cal Pr.
Sword & the Grail. Constance Hieatt. LC 78-139097. (Illus.). (gr. 5-8). 1972. 8.95 (ISBN 0-690-79873-3, TYC-J); PLB 6.49 o.p. (ISBN 0-690-79874-1). T Y Crowell.
Sword & the Pen: A Collection of the World's Greatest Military Writings. Hart B. Liddell & Hart A. Liddell. 304p. 1976. 10.95 o.p. (ISBN 0-690-00052-9, TYC-T). T Y Crowell.
Sword Dance & Drama. Violet Alford. 1963. 8.95 o.p. (ISBN 0-85036-035-8). Dufour.
Sword for the Empire. Gene Lancour. LC 77-11750. 1978. 7.95 o.p. (ISBN 0-385-13067-8). Doubleday.
Sword in the Tree. Clyde R. Bulla. LC 56-5699. (Illus.). (gr. 2-5). 1956. 8.95 (ISBN 0-690-79908-X, TYC-J). T Y Crowell.
Sword of Culann. Betty Levin. LC 73-583. 288p. (gr. 5-8). 1973. PLB 8.95 (ISBN 0-02-757340-0). Macmillan.
Sword of His Mouth. Robert C. Tannehill. Ed. by William A. Beardslee. LC 75-18948. (Semeia Studies). 236p. 1976. pap. 4.95 (ISBN 0-8006-1501-8, 1-1501). Fortress.
Sword of Poyana. Gerald E. Bailey. 1979. pap. 1.75 o.p. (ISBN 0-425-04055-0). Berkley Pub.
Sword of Rhiannon. Leigh Brackett. 1975. pap. 1.95 (ISBN 0-441-79142-5). Ace Bks.
Sword of Shahrazar. Robert E. Howard. LC 76-16707. 1976. 12.95 (ISBN 0-913960-08-X). Fax Collect.
Sword of Shannara. Terry Brooks. (Del Rey Bk.). 1978. pap. 3.50 o.p. (ISBN 0-345-29024-0). Ballantine.
Sword of the Nurlingas. Gerald E. Bailey. 1979. pap. 1.75 o.p. (ISBN 0-425-03954-4). Berkley Pub.
Sword of the Prophet. Robert Goldston. 224p. 1981. pap. 2.50 (ISBN 0-449-24393-1, Crest). Fawcett.
Sword of the Republic: The U. S. Army on the Frontier, 1783-1846. Francis P. Prucha. LC 77-74431. (Wars of the United States Ser.). (Illus.). 458p. 1977. pap. 6.95x (ISBN 0-253-28800-2). Ind U Pr.
Sword of the Spirits. John Christopher. LC 74-176419. (Illus.). 192p. (gr. 5-9). 1972. 4.95 o.s.i. (ISBN 0-02-718340-8). Macmillan.
Sword of the Spirits Trilogy, 3 bks. John Christopher. Incl. Beyond the Burning Lands; Prince in Waiting; Sword of the Spirits. (gr. 6 up). 1980. Boxed Set. pap. 7.95 (ISBN 0-02-042770-0, Collier). Macmillan.
Sword of the Wilderness. Elizabeth Coatsworth. (Illus.). (gr. 7 up). 1966. 4.95g o.s.i. (ISBN 0-02-721910-0). Macmillan.
Sword of Vengeance. Sylvia Thorpe. 240p. 1977. pap. 1.50 o.p. (ISBN 0-449-23136-4, Crest). Fawcett.
Sword of Vengence. Alexander Karol. 1977. pap. 1.50 (ISBN 0-505-51150-9). Tower Bks.
Swordplay & the Elizabethan & Jacobean Stage. Robert E. Morsberger. (Salzburg Studies in English Literature, Jacobean Drama Studies: No. 37). (Illus.). 129p. 1974. pap. text ed. 25.00x (ISBN 0-391-01485-4). Humanities.
Swords Against Carthage. Friedrich Donauer. Tr. by F. T. Cooper. LC 61-12878. (Illus.). (gr. 7-11). 1932. 8.50x (ISBN 0-8196-0112-8). Biblo.
Swords Against Wizardry. Fritz Leiber. Ed. by James P. Baen. (Fafhrd & the Grey Mouser Ser.). 1976. pap. 1.95 (ISBN 0-441-79164-6). Ace Bks.
Swords & Ice Magic. Fritz Leiber. 1977. pap. 1.95 (ISBN 0-441-79168-9). Ace Bks.
Swords & Scales: The Development of the Uniform Code of Military Justice. William T. Generous, Jr. LC 72-91173. 1973. 17.50 (ISBN 0-8046-9039-1, Natl U). Kennikat.
Swords in the Mist. Fritz Leiber. Ed. by James P. Baen. (Fafhrd & the Grey Mouser Ser.). 1976. pap. 1.95 (ISBN 0-441-79184-0). Ace Bks.
Swords of December. Robert York. LC 78-24026. 1979. 8.95 o.p. (ISBN 0-684-16142-7, ScribT). Scribner.
Swords of Lankhmar. Fritz Leiber. Ed. by James P. Baen. (Fafhrd & the Grey Mouser Ser.). 1974. pap. 1.95 (ISBN 0-441-79223-5). Ace Bks.
Swords of Mars. Edgar R. Burroughs. 1973. pap. 1.95 (ISBN 0-345-27841-0). Ballantine.
Swords or Ploughshares? the Morgenthau Plan for Defeated Nazi Germany: 1943-1946. Warren F. Kimball. LC 75-33057. (America's Alternatives Ser.). 172p. 1976. pap. text ed. 3.25x o.p. (ISBN 0-397-47350-8). Lippincott.
Swordsmen of the Screen. J. Richards. (Cinema & Society Ser.). (Illus.). 1977. 23.50 (ISBN 0-7100-8478-1). Routledge & Kegan.
Swynden Necklace. Mira Stables. 1977. pap. 1.50 o.p. (ISBN 0-449-23270-0, Crest). Fawcett.
Sybervision: Muscle Memory Programming for Any Sport. Steven DeVore et al. (Illus.). 250p. 1981. 12.95 (ISBN 0-914090-98-4). Chicago Review.
Sybil. Flora R. Schreiber. (Illus.). 464p. 1974. pap. 3.50 (ISBN 0-446-96903-6). Warner Bks.
Sybil Leek's Book of Herbs. Sybil Leek. 1980. pap. 3.95 (ISBN 0-346-12435-2). Cornerstone.
Sybil Leek's Book of the Curious & the Occult. Sybil Leek. 1976. pap. 1.75 o.p. (ISBN 0-345-25385-X). Ballantine.
Sybil's Dreams, Autographed. Mary Helen. 1980. deluxe ed. 14.95 (ISBN 0-912492-15-5). Pyquag.
Sycamore Hill. Francine Rivers. 288p. (Orig.). 1981. pap. 2.50 (ISBN 0-523-41324-6). Pinnacle Bks.
Sycamore Year. Mildred Lee. 160p. (RL 6). Date not set. pap. 1.25 (ISBN 0-451-07073-9, Y7073, Sig). NAL.
Sycamores. Marcia Ford. (YA) 1972. 5.95 (ISBN 0-685-25148-9, Avalon). Bouregy.
Syd Hoff's How to Draw Dinosaurs. Syd Hoff. (Illus.). 64p. (gr. 3 up). 1981. pap. 3.95 (ISBN 0-671-42553-6). Windmill Bks.
Sydney. new ed. Peter Porter. Ed. by Time-Life Books Editors. (Great Cities Ser.). (Illus.). 200p. 1980. 14.95 (ISBN 0-8094-3108-4, Silver Burdett). Time-Life.
Sydney & Frances Lewis Contemporary Art Fund Collection. Rebecca Massie. (Illus.). 112p. (Orig.). 1980. pap. 7.95x (ISBN 0-917046-09-9). VA Mus Fine Arts.
Sydney Omarr's Astrological Guide for You in 1980. Sydney Omarr. (Orig.). 1979. pap. 2.25 o.p. (ISBN 0-451-08835-2, E8835, Sig). NAL.
Sydney Omarr's Astrological Revelation About You. Sydney Omarr. 1973. pap. 1.25 (ISBN 0-451-05674-4, Y5674, Sig). NAL.
Sydney Omarr's Weekly Astrological Guide Series 1980, 12 bks. (Orig.). 1979. pap. 1.25 ea. o.p. (Y8792-Y8805, Sig). Bk. 1 (ISBN 0-451-08792-5). Bk. 2 (ISBN 0-451-08793-3). Bk. 3 (ISBN 0-451-08794-1). Bk. 4 (ISBN 0-451-08796-8). Bk. 5 (ISBN 0-451-08797-6). Bk. 6 (ISBN 0-451-08798-4). Bk. 7 (ISBN 0-451-08799-2). Bk. 8 Isbn 0-451-08801-8 Bk. 9 Isbn 0-451-08802-6 Bk. 10 Isbn 0-451-08803-4 Bbk. 11 Isbn 0-451-08804-2 Bk. 12 Isbn 0-451-08805-0. NAL.
Sydney Smith. Alan Bell. (Illus.). 240p. 1980. 29.95 (ISBN 0-19-812050-8). Oxford U Pr.
Sydney Smith. George W. E. Russell. LC 79-156929. 1971. Repr. of 1905 ed. 15.00 (ISBN 0-8103-3720-7). Gale.
Syllable-Based Generalizations in English Phonology. Daniel Kahn. Ed. by Jorge Hankamer. LC 79-55852. (Outstanding Dissertations in Linguistics Ser.). 218p. 1980. lib. bdg. 26.50 (ISBN 0-8240-4554-8). Garland Pub.
Syllabus der Pflanzenfamilien, 2 vols. 12th ed. A. Engler. Incl. Vol. 1. Allgemeiner Teil: Bakterien Bis Gymnospermen. 1954. 42.20 (ISBN 3-4433-9015-3); Vol. 2. Angiospermen Vebersicht Ueber Die Florengebiete der Erde. 1964. 75.85 (ISBN 3-4433-9016-1). (Illus.). Lubrecht & Cramer.

Syllabus of Chinese Civilization. rev. 2nd ed. J. Mason Gentzler. LC 68-55814. (Companions to Asian Studies). 120p. 1972. pap. text ed. 6.00x (ISBN 0-231-03676-0). Columbia U Pr.
Syllabus of Comparative Literature. 2nd ed. Faculty of Comparative Literature, Livingston College. Ed. by John O. McCormick. LC 72-8502. 1972. 10.00 (ISBN 0-8108-0555-3). Scarecrow.
Syllabus of Complete Dentures. 3rd ed. Charles M. Heartwell, Jr. & Arthur O. Rahn. LC 80-10476. (Illus.). 558p. 1980. text ed. 28.50 (ISBN 0-8121-0711-X). Lea & Febiger.
Syllabus of Indian Civilization. Leonard A. Gordon & Barbara S. Miller. LC 70-168868. (Companions to Asian Studies). 1971. pap. 7.50x (ISBN 0-231-03560-8). Columbia U Pr.
Syllabus of Japanese Civilization. rev. 2nd ed. H. Paul Varley. LC 68-55815. (Companions to Asian Studies). 120p. 1972. pap. 5.00x (ISBN 0-231-03677-9). Columbia U Pr.
Sylloge of Coins of the British Isles-National Museum, Copenhagen, Royal Collection of Coins & Metals: Anglo-Saxon Coins, Aethelred II, Vol. 2. Georg Galster. 1966. 25.75x (ISBN 0-19-725896-4). Oxford U Pr.
Sylloge of Coins of the British Isles, No. 19: Ancient British Coins & Coins of the Bristol & Gloucestershire. L. V. Grinsell et al. (Illus.). 162p. 1973. 22.50x o.p. (ISBN 0-19-725932-4). Oxford U Pr.
Sylloge of Coins of the British Isles, Vol. 28. Ed. by Veronica Smart. 164p. 1981. 74.00 (ISBN 0-19-726002-0). Oxford U Pr.
Sylloge of Coins of the British Isles: Vol. 26, Museums of East Anglia. Ed. by T. H. Clough. 1980. 99.00x (ISBN 0-19-725991-X). Oxford U Pr.
Sylva the Mink. Ewan Clarkson. LC 68-25764. (Illus.). 1968. 4.95 o.p. (ISBN 0-525-21355-4). Dutton.
Sylvanus G. Morley & the World of the Ancient Mayas. Robert L. Brunhouse. LC 78-160489. (Illus.). 1971. pap. 8.95 o.p. (ISBN 0-8061-1294-8). U of Okla Pr.
Sylvester Judd. Francis B. Dedmond. (United States Authors Ser.). 1980. lib. bdg. 11.95 (ISBN 0-8057-7305-3). Twayne.
Sylvia & Bruno. Lewis Carroll. LC 75-32196. (Classics of Children's Literature, 1621-1932: Vol. 58). (Illus.). 1976. Repr. of 1889 ed. PLB 38.00 (ISBN 0-8240-2307-2). Garland Pub.
Sylvia Plath: A Bibliography. Gary Lane & Maria Stevens. LC 78-834. (Author Bibliographies Ser.: No. 36). 1978. 10.00 (ISBN 0-8108-1117-0). Scarecrow.
Sylvia Plath: A Dramatic Portrait. Kyle. 1976. pap. 4.95 (ISBN 0-571-10698-6, Pub. by Faber & Faber). Merrimack Bk Serv.
Sylvia Plath: The Woman & the Work. Ed. by Edward Butscher. LC 77-24700. 1977. 8.95 (ISBN 0-396-07497-9). Dodd.
Sylvia Porter's Money Book. Sylvia Porter. 1976. pap. 6.95 o.s.i. (ISBN 0-380-00638-3, 40089). Avon.
Sylvia's Lovers. Elizabeth Gaskell. 1964. 15.50x (ISBN 0-460-00524-3, Evman). Dutton.
Symbionese Liberation Army: Documents & Communications. Ed. by Robert B. Pearsall. (Melville Studies in American Culture: Vol.4). (Illus.). 158p. (Orig.). 1974. pap. text ed. 9.25x (ISBN 90-6203-128-5). Humanities.
Symbiosis in Cell Evolution: Life & Its Environment on the Early Earth. Lynn Margulis. LC 80-26695. (Illus.). 1981. text ed. 27.95x (ISBN 0-7167-1255-5); pap. text ed. 13.95x (ISBN 0-7167-1256-3). W H Freeman.
Symbiosis Intelligentsia. W. D. Taylor. 224p. 1981. 9.50 (ISBN 0-682-49675-8). Exposition.
Symbiosis: Its Physiological & Biochemical Significance, 2 vols. Ed. by S. Mark Henry. Incl. Vol. 1. Association of Microorganisms, Plants & Marine Organisms. 1966. 49.25 (ISBN 0-12-341101-7); Vol. 2. Association of Invertebrates, Birds, Ruminants & Other Biota. 1967. 49.25 (ISBN 0-12-341102-5). Set. 80.00 (ISBN 0-685-23224-7). Acad Pr.
Symbiote's Crown. Scott Baker. 1978. pap. 1.75 o.p. (ISBN 0-425-03839-4, Medallion). Berkley Pub.
Symbiotic Nitrogen Fixation in Plants. Ed. by P. S. Nutman. LC 75-2732. (International Biological Programme Ser.: No. 7). (Illus.). 652p. 1976. 105.00 (ISBN 0-521-20645-6). Cambridge U Pr.
Symbol & Art in Worship, Concilium 132. Ed. by Luis Maldonado & David Power. (New Concilium 1980). 128p. 1980. pap. 5.95 (ISBN 0-8164-4765-9). Crossroad NY.
Symbol & Theory. J. Skorupski. LC 76-3037. 1976. 32.95 (ISBN 0-521-21200-6). Cambridge U Pr.
Symbol & Truth in Blake's Myth. Leopold Damrosch, Jr. LC 80-7515. (Illus.). 504p. 1980. 25.00x (ISBN 0-691-06433-4); pap. 9.50x (ISBN 0-691-10095-0). Princeton U Pr.
Symbol Communication for the Severely Handicapped. D. Gallender. (Illus.). 272p. 1980. pap. 24.75 spiral (ISBN 0-398-04018-4). C C Thomas.
Symbol Discrimination & Sequencing. W. Edwards & S. Edwards. (Ann Arbor Tracking Program Ser.). 1976. wkbk. 5.00 (ISBN 0-89039-154-8). Ann Arbor Pubs.
Symbol, Myth & Culture: Essays & Lectures of Ernst Cassirer 1935-45. Ernst Cassirer. Ed. by Donald P. Verne. LC 78-9887. 1979. 25.00x (ISBN 0-300-02306-5). Yale U Pr.
Symbol, Myth & Culture: Essays & Lectures of Ernst Cassirer 1935-45. Ernst Cassirer. Ed. by Donald P. Verne. LC 78-9887. 368p. 1981. pap. 9.95x (ISBN 0-300-02666-8). Yale U Pr.
Symbol of the Soul from Holderlin to Yeats: A Study in Metonymy. Suzanne Nalbantian. LC 76-25550. 1976. 17.50x (ISBN 0-231-04148-9). Columbia U Pr.
Symbol Signs. American Institute of Graphic Arts. (Visual Communication Bks). (Illus.). 192p. (Orig.). 1981. pap. 12.95 (ISBN 0-8038-6777-8). Hastings.
Symbol Simons Too. Ed Halperin et al. (Orig.). (gr. 3-7). 1981. pap. 2.50 (ISBN 0-671-42537-4). Wanderer Bks.
Symbolaeographia, Which May Be Termed the Art, Description, or Image of Instruments Covenants, Contracts, 2 vols. William West. Ed. by David S. Berkowitz & Samuel E. Thorne. LC 77-86629. (Classics of English Legal History in the Modern Era Ser.: Vol. 85). 1979. Set. lib. bdg. 110.00 (ISBN 0-8240-3072-9); lib. bdg. 55.00 ea. Garland Pub.
Symbolaeographia Which Termed the Art, Description of Instruments, Covenants, Contracts, Etc. William West. LC 74-28892. (English Experience Ser.: No. 768). 1975. Repr. of 1590 ed. 43.00 (ISBN 90-221-0768-X). Walter J Johnson.
Symbolarum Libri XVII Virgilii, 3 vols. Jacobus Pontanus. LC 75-27860. (Renaissance & the Gods Ser.: Vol. 18). (Illus.). 1976. Repr. of 1599 ed. Set. lib. bdg. 73.00 (ISBN 0-8240-2066-9); lib. bdg. 30.00 (ISBN 0-685-76406-0). Garland Pub.
Symbolic Action in the Plays of the Wakefield Master. Jeffrey Helterman. LC 80-18273. (South Atlantic Modern Language Association Award Study). 216p. 1981. lib. bdg. 17.50x (ISBN 0-8203-0534-0). U of Ga Pr.
Symbolic Anthropology, a Reader in the Study of Symbols & Meanings. Ed. by Janet L. Dolgin et al. LC 77-3176. 1977. text ed. 32.50x (ISBN 0-231-04032-6); pap. 13.50x (ISBN 0-231-04033-4). Columbia U Pr.
Symbolic Aspects of Interaction. Glenn M. Vernon. LC 78-69837. 1978. pap. text ed. 10.25 (ISBN 0-8191-0581-3). U Pr of Amer.
Symbolic Crusade: Status Politics & the American Temperance Movement. Joseph R. Gusfield. LC 80-13342. viii, 198p. 1980. Repr. of 1963 ed. lib. bdg. 18.00x (ISBN 0-313-22423-4, GUSC). Greenwood.
Symbolic Interaction: A Reader in Social Psychology. 3rd ed. Jerome Manis & Bernard Meltzer. 1978. pap. text ed. 12.95 (ISBN 0-205-06062-5, 8160627). Allyn.
Symbolic Interactionism: An Introduction, an Interpretation, an Integration. J. Charon. 1979. pap. 9.95 (ISBN 0-13-870105-9). P-H.
Symbolic Interactionism: Genesis, Varieties & Criticsms. B. N. Meltzer et al. (Monographs in Social Theory). 1977. pap. 6.95 (ISBN 0-7100-8056-5). Routledge & Kegan.
Symbolic Interactionism: Perspective & Method. Herbert Blumer. 1969. text ed. 13.95 (ISBN 0-13-879924-5). P-H.
Symbolic Leaders: Public Dramas & Public Men. Orrin E. Klapp. LC 64-23369. 1964. 24.00x (ISBN 0-202-30024-2); pap. text ed. 2.95. Irvington.
Symbolic Logic. 2nd ed. John Venn. LC 79-119161. 1971. text ed. 15.95 (ISBN 0-8284-0251-5). Chelsea Pub.
Symbolic Stories: Traditional Narratives of the Family Drama in English Literature. Derek Brewer. 190p. 1980. 31.50x (ISBN 0-8476-6900-9). Rowman.
Symbolical Consciousness: A Commentary on Love's Body. William C. Shepherd. LC 76-26582. (American Academy of Religion. Aids for the Study of Religion Ser.). 1976. pap. 6.00 (ISBN 0-89130-083-X, 010304). Scholars Pr Ca.
Symbolicarum Quaestionum de Universo Genere. Achille Bocchi. Ed. by Stephen Orgel. LC 78-68188. (Philosophy of Images Ser: Vol. 5). 1979. lib. bdg. 66.00 (ISBN 0-8240-3679-4). Garland Pub.
Symbolism. John Milner. (Oresko-Jupiter Art Bks). (Illus.). 96p. 1981. 17.95 (ISBN 0-933516-87-8, Pub. by Oresko-Jupiter England). Hippocrene Bks.
Symbolism. Jose Pierre. (Masters of Art Ser.). (Illus.). 1979. pap. 3.95 (ISBN 0-8120-2155-X). Barron.
Symbolism & Art Nouveau. A. Mackintosh. LC 77-76764. (Modern Movements in Art Ser.). 1978. pap. 1.95 (ISBN 0-8120-0882-0). Barron.
Symbolism & Some Implications of the Symbolic Approach: W. B. Yeats During the Eighteen Nineties. Robert O'Driscoll. (New Yeats Papers Ser.: No. 9). 84p. 1975. pap. text ed. 8.00x (ISBN 0-85105-270-3, Dolmen Pr). Humanities.
Symbolism for Artists. Henry T. Bailey & Ethel Pool. LC 68-18018. (Illus.). 239p. 1973. Repr. of 1925 ed. 15.00 (ISBN 0-8103-3870-X). Gale.
Symbolism in Religion & Literature. Ed. by Rollo May. LC 59-8842. 6.95 o.s.i. (ISBN 0-8076-0115-2). Braziller.
Symbolism of the Biblical World Ancient Near Eastern Iconography & the Book of Psalms. Othmar Keel. (Illus.). 1978. 24.50 (ISBN 0-8164-0353-8). Crossroad NY.
Symbolism of the East & West. Harriet G. Murray-Aynsley. LC 77-141748. (Illus.). 1971. Repr. of 1900 ed. 20.00 (ISBN 0-8103-3395-3). Gale.
Symbolist Aesthetic in France, 1885-1895. 2nd ed. A. G. Lehmann. 1968. 30.25x (ISBN 0-631-10380-5, Pub. by Basil Blackwell). Biblio Dist.
Symbolist Art. Edward Lucie-Smith. (World of Art Ser.). (Illus.). 1972. pap. 9.95 (ISBN 0-19-519947-2). Oxford U Pr.
Symbolist Movement: A Critical Appraisal. Anna Balakian. LC 77-76044. 320p. 1977. 15.00x (ISBN 0-8147-0993-1); pap. 6.00x (ISBN 0-8147-0994-X). NYU Pr.
Symbols & Society. Conference On Science - Philosophy And Religion - 14th Symposium. Ed. by L. Bryson et al. 1964. Repr. of 1955 ed. 19.50x (ISBN 0-8154-0039-X). Cooper Sq.
Symbols & Sounds. Bernard Gunther et al. (Essence Books Ser). (YA) 1973. pap. 0.50 o.s.i. (ISBN 0-02-080260-9, Collier). Macmillan.
Symbols & Values. Conference On Science - Philosophy And Religion - 13th Symposium. Ed. by L. Bryson et al. 1964. Repr. of 1954 ed. 35.00x (ISBN 0-8154-0038-1). Cooper Sq.
Symbols for Communication. J. Van Baal. (Studies of Developing Countries). 354p. 1971. pap. text ed. 38.50x (ISBN 9-0232-0896-X). Humanities.
Symbols for Designers. Arnold Whittick. LC 71-175760. (Illus.). xvi, 168p. 1972. Repr. of 1935 ed. 26.00 (ISBN 0-8103-3119-5). Gale.
Symbols of Ancient Egypt in the Late Period (21st Dynasty) Beatrice L. Goff. (Religion & Society Ser.). 1979. text ed. 91.75x (ISBN 90-279-7622-8). Mouton.
Symbols of Church & Kingdom. R. Murray. LC 74-80363. 430p. 1975. 49.95 (ISBN 0-521-20553-0). Cambridge U Pr.
Symbols of Magic: Amulets & Talismans. Clifford L. Alderman. LC 76-51277. (Illus.). (gr. 7 up). 1977. PLB 7.79 o.p. (ISBN 0-671-32837-9). Messner.
Symbols, Standards, Flags & Banners of Ancient & Modern Nations. George H. Preble. 1980. lib. bdg. 12.00 (ISBN 0-8161-8476-3). G K Hall.
Symbols: The Language of Communication. Polly Bolian. LC 74-22464. (First Bks.). (Illus.). 96p. (gr. 5 up). 1975. PLB 4.90 o.p. (ISBN 0-531-00833-9). Watts.
Symeon, the New Theologian: The Discourses. C. J. De Catanzaro. (Classics of Western Spirituality Ser.). 1980. 11.95 (ISBN 0-8091-0292-7); pap. 7.95 (ISBN 0-8091-2230-8). Paulist Pr.
Symmetric Eigenvalue Problem. Beresford N. Parlett. (Illus.). 1980. text ed. 25.95 (ISBN 0-13-880047-2). P-H.
Symmetric Function & Allied Tables. F. N. David et al. 278p. 1966. 27.00x (ISBN 0-85264-702-6, Pub. by Griffin England). State Mutual Bk.
Symmetric Structures in Banach Spaces. W. B. Johnson et al. (Memoirs Ser.: No. 217). 1979. write for info. o.p. (ISBN 0-8218-2217-9). Am Math.
Symmetrical Components. L. J. Myatt. 1968. text ed. 19.50 (ISBN 0-08-012979-X); pap. text ed. 9.75 (ISBN 0-08-012978-1). Pergamon.
Symmetrical Family. Michael Young & Peter Willmott. LC 73-7009. 1974. 10.00 o.p. (ISBN 0-394-48727-3). Pantheon.
Symmetries & Reflections. Eugene P. Wigner. LC 79-89843. 1979. pap. text ed. 9.50 (ISBN 0-918024-16-1). Ox Bow.
Symmetry: A Stereoscopic Guide for Chemists. Ivan Bernal et al. LC 75-178258. (Illus.). 1972. text ed. 25.95x (ISBN 0-7167-0168-5). W H Freeman.
Symmetry Analysis of Upper Gila Area Ceramic Design. Dorothy K. Washburn. LC 76-53125. (Papers of the Peabody Museum Ser.: Vol. 68). (Illus.). 1977. lib. bdg. cancelled (ISBN 0-685-84633-4); pap. 20.00 (ISBN 0-87365-193-6). Peabody Harvard.
Symmetry & Chirality. C. A. Mead. LC 51-5497. (Topics in Current Chemistry: Vol. 49). (Illus.). 90p. 1974. 17.60 (ISBN 0-387-06705-1). Springer-Verlag.
Symmetry & Its Applications in Science. Allan D. Boardman et al. LC 72-13908. 305p. 1973. pap. 24.95 (ISBN 0-470-08412-X). Halsted Pr.
Symmetry & Selectivity in the U. S. Defense Policy: A Grand Design or a Major Mistake? Agatha S. Wong-Fraser. LC 80-5610. 172p. 1980. lib. bdg. 17.50 (ISBN 0-8191-1182-1); pap. text ed. 8.95 (ISBN 0-8191-1183-X). U Pr of Amer.
Symmetry Groups: Theory & Chemical Applications. Robert L. Flurry, Jr. (Illus.). 1980. text ed. 28.95 (ISBN 0-13-880013-8). P-H.
Symmetry in Chemical Theory: The Application of Group Theoretical Techniques to the Solution of Chemical Problems. Ed. by John P. Fackler, Jr. LC 73-12620. (Benchmark Papers in Inorganic Chemistry Ser.). 528p. 1974. text ed. 44.50 (ISBN 0-12-786453-9). Acad Pr.
Symmetry in Coordination Chemistry. John P. Fackler, Jr. 1971. text ed. 9.00 (ISBN 0-12-247540-2); pap. 7.95 (ISBN 0-12-247550-X). Acad Pr.
Symmetry, Orbitals, & Spectra. Milton Orchin & H. H. Jaffe. LC 76-136720. 1971. 36.50 (ISBN 0-471-65550-3, Pub. by Wiley-Interscience). Wiley.
Symmetry Principles in Elementary Particle Physics. W. M. Gibson & B. R. Pollard. LC 74-31796. (Cambridge Monographs on Physics). (Illus.). 395p. 1980. 22.50 (ISBN 0-521-29964-0). Cambridge U Pr.
Symmetry Principles in Solid State & Molecular Physics. Melvin Lax. LC 74-1215. 592p. 1974. 26.95 o.p. (ISBN 0-471-51903-0, Pub. by Wiley-Interscience); pap. 23.95x (ISBN 0-471-51904-9). Wiley.
Symmetry Rules for Chemical Reactions: Orbital Topology & Elementary Processes. Ralph G. Pearson. LC 76-10314. 600p. 1976. 37.50 (ISBN 0-471-01495-8, Pub. by Wiley-Interscience). Wiley.
Sympathetic Magic. Michael Blumenthal. LC 80-50812. (Illus.). 96p. (Orig.). 1980. 25.00 (ISBN 0-931956-04-8); pap. 6.50 (ISBN 0-931956-03-X); handbound 60.00. Water Mark.
Sympathetic Understanding of the Child: Birth to Sixteen. 2nd ed. David Elkind. text ed. 15.95 (ISBN 0-205-06016-1). Allyn.
Sympathy & Ethics: A Study of the Relationship Between Sympathy & Morality with Special Reference to Hume's Treatise. Philip Mercer. 1972. 9.95x o.p. (ISBN 0-19-824363-4). Oxford U Pr.
Symphonic Music: Its Evolution Since the Renaissance. Homer Ulrich. LC 52-12033. 1952. 20.00x (ISBN 0-231-01908-4). Columbia U Pr.
Symphonies De Beethoven. 13th ed. J. G. Prod'Homme. LC 76-52485. (Music Reprint Ser.). (Illus., Fr.). 1978. Repr. of 1906 ed. lib. bdg. 39.50 (ISBN 0-306-70859-0). Da Capo.
Symphonies. Nos. 66, 69, 70, 71 & 75. 2nd ed. Joseph Haydn. LC 65-24150. (Music Ser.). 1967. text ed. 8.00 ea. (ISBN 0-306-77004-0). No. 66 (ISBN 0-306-77005-9). No. 69 (ISBN 0-306-77006-7). No. 70 (ISBN 0-306-77007-5). No. 71 (ISBN 0-306-77008-3). No. 75 (ISBN 0-306-77009-1). Da Capo.
Symphonies of Ralph Vaughan Williams. Elliot S. Schwartz. LC 64-24402. (Illus.). 1965. 12.00x o.p. (ISBN 0-87023-004-2). U of Mass Pr.
Symphony. Preston Stedman. (Illus.). 1979. ref. ed. 16.95 (ISBN 0-13-880062-6). P-H.
Symphony Hall, Boston. H. Earle Johnson. (Music Reprint Ser.). 1979. Repr. of 1950 ed. lib. bdg. 32.50 (ISBN 0-306-79518-3). Da Capo.
Symphony in B Minor: The Passion of Peter Ilitch Tchaikovsky. Larry Holdridge. LC 78-2284. (Illus.). 1978. 10.95 (ISBN 0-916144-26-7); pap. 3.95 (ISBN 0-916144-27-5). Stemmer Hse.
Symphony No. One: Opus 23. John K. Paine. LC 73-171077. (Earlier American Music Ser.: No. 1). 180p. 1972. Repr. of 1908 ed. lib. bdg. 25.00 (ISBN 0-306-77301-5). Da Capo.
Symphony No. Two: In B Flat, Opus 21. facsimile ed. George W. Chadwick. LC 71-170930. (Earlier American Music Ser.: No. 4). 216p. 1972. Repr. of 1888 ed. 22.50 (ISBN 0-306-77304-X). Da Capo.
Symphony Number 35 in D. K. 385: The Haffner Symphony. facsimile ed. Wolfgang A. Mozart. 1968. Set. boxed 22.50 (ISBN 0-19-393180-X); pap. 5.00 (ISBN 0-19-385289-6). Oxford U Pr.
Symplectic Cobordism Ring. Stanley O. Kochman. LC 79-27872. 1980. 9.60 (ISBN 0-8218-2228-4). Am Math.
Symposia, Vols. 5 & 6. Phytochemical Society of North America. Ed. by V. C. Runeckles & T. C. Tso. Incl. Vol. 5. Structural & Functional Aspects of Phytochemistry. 1972. 48.50 (ISBN 0-12-612405-1); Vol. 6. Terpenoids: Structure, Biogenesis, Distribution. 1973. 37.00 (ISBN 0-12-612406-X). Acad Pr.

Symposia Mathematica: Proceedings. Italian National Institute of Higher Mathematics Conventions. Incl. Vol. 1. Group Theory. 1970. 59.50 (ISBN 0-12-612201-6); Vol. 2. Functional Analysis & Geometry. 1970. 56.50 (ISBN 0-12-612202-4); Vol. 3. Problems in the Evolution of the Solar System. 1970. 69.00 (ISBN 0-12-612203-2); Vol. 4. 1971. 60.50 (ISBN 0-12-612204-0); Vol. 5. 1971. 64.00 (ISBN 0-12-612205-9); Vol. 6. 1971. 54.50 (ISBN 0-12-612206-7); Vol. 7. 1972. 68.00 (ISBN 0-12-612207-5); Vol. 8. 1972. 38.50 (ISBN 0-12-612208-3); Vol. 9. 1972. 71.50 (ISBN 0-12-612209-1); Vol. 10. 1973. 56.00 (ISBN 0-12-612210-5); Vol. 18. 1977. 68.00 (ISBN 0-12-612218-0); Vol. 19. 1977. 52.50 (ISBN 0-12-612219-9). Acad Pr.

Symposium. Plato. Tr. by Benjamin Jowett. 1956. pap. 1.95 (ISBN 0-672-60169-9, LLA7). Bobbs.

Symposium, Vol. 13. Millard. LC 76-16519. (Illus.). 432p. 1976. 45.00 (ISBN 0-8016-3413-X). Mosby.

Symposium & Other Dialogues. Plato. Ed. by Michael Joyce et al. 1964. 12.95x (ISBN 0-460-00418-2, Evman). Dutton.

Symposium Held at UCLA in Honor of C. D. O'Malley. Ed. by Allen G. Debus. (Illus.). 1974. 22.50x (ISBN 0-520-02226-2). U of Cal Pr.

Symposium: Major Advances in Cardiovascular Therapy. Paul D. White. 400p. 1973. 37.50 (ISBN 0-685-78090-2, Pub. by Williams & Wilkins). Krieger.

Symposium of Surgery of the Aging Face. Ed. by Dicran Goulian & Eugene H. Courtiss. LC 78-12298. (Symposia of the Educational Foundation of the American Society of Plastic & Reconstructive Surgeons Inc. Ser.). 1978. text ed. 46.50 (ISBN 0-8016-1941-6). Mosby.

Symposium on Advanced Medicine, 9th. Geoffrey Walker. 452p. 1973. 12.00 o.p. (ISBN 0-685-56381-2, Pub. by Williams & Wilkins). Krieger.

Symposium on Aesthetic Surgery of the Breast. John Q. Owsley, Jr. & Rex A. Peterson. LC 78-17489. (Symposia of the Educational Foundation of the American Society of Plastic & Reconstructive Surgeons, Inc. Ser.). 1978. 67.50 (ISBN 0-8016-3793-7). Mosby.

Symposium on Analgesics: 1974. Knoll. 1979. 14.00 (ISBN 0-9960007-4-7, Pub. by Kaido Hungary). Heyden.

Symposium on Anthroscopy & Arthrography of the Knee. American Academy of Orthopaedic Surgeons. LC 78-17015. (Illus.). 1978. text ed. 62.50 (ISBN 0-8016-0056-1). Mosby.

Symposium on Cataracts. 1st ed. New Orleans Academy of Ophthalmology. LC 79-4489. (Illus.). 1979. text ed. 43.50 (ISBN 0-8016-3674-4). Mosby.

Symposium on Comples Analysis. Ed. by J. G. Clunie & W. K. Hayman. LC 73-92787. (London Mathematical Society Lecture Note Ser.: No. 12). 200p. 1974. 21.50 (ISBN 0-521-20452-6). Cambridge U Pr.

Symposium on Diagnosis & Treatment of Craniofacial Anomalies, Vol. 20. John M. Converse et al. LC 79-27063. 1979. text ed. 72.50 (ISBN 0-8016-1030-3). Mosby.

Symposium on Earth Reinforcement. Compiled by American Society of Civil Engineers. 912p. 1979. pap. text ed. 40.00 (ISBN 0-87262-144-8). Am Soc Civil Eng.

Symposium on Geothermal Energy & Its Direct Uses in the Eastern United States, April Fifth to Seventh, Nineteen Seventy-Nine, Roanoke, Virginia. Ed. by Geothermal Resources Council. (Special Report Ser.: No. 5). (Illus., Orig.). 1979. pap. 3.50 (ISBN 0-934412-05-7). Geothermal.

Symposium on Glaucoma. New Orleans Academy of Ophthalmology. (Illus.). 536p. 1981. text ed. 57.95 (ISBN 0-8016-3667-1). Mosby.

Symposium on Glaucoma: Transactions of the New Orleans Academy of Opthalmology. New Orleans Academy of Opthalmology. LC 75-2075. 1975. 39.50 o.p. (ISBN 0-8016-3679-5). Mosby.

Symposium on Medical & Surgical Diseases of the Cornea. New Orleans Academy of Opthalmology. LC 80-13693. (Illus.). 1980. text ed. 72.50 (ISBN 0-8016-3666-3). Mosby.

Symposium on Microsurgery: Practical Use in Orthopaedics. American Academy of Orthopaedic Surgeons. Ed. by James R. Urbaniak. LC 79-14999. 1979. text ed. 52.50 (ISBN 0-8016-0066-9). Mosby.

Symposium on Mineral Resources of the Southeastern United States. Ed. by F. G. Snyder. 1950. 14.50x (ISBN 0-87049-007-9). U of Tenn Pr.

Symposium on Ocular Therapy. Irving H. Leopold & Robert P. Burns. LC 76-645664. (Clinical Opthalmology Ser.: Vol. 11). 1979. 20.95 o.p. (ISBN 0-471-05151-9, Pub. by Wiley Medical). Wiley.

Symposium on Photomorphogenesis. Ed. by Song Pill-Soon. 1978. pap. text ed. 21.00 (ISBN 0-08-022677-9). Pergamon.

Symposium on Rearation Research. Compiled by American Society of Civil Engineers. 376p. 1979. pap. text ed. 26.00 (ISBN 0-87262-142-1). Am Soc Civil Eng.

Symposium on Reconstruction of Jaw Deformity. Ed. by Linton A. Whitaker & Peter Randall. LC 78-4867. (Symposia of the Educational Foundaion of the American Society of Plastic & Reconstructive Surgeons, Inc. Ser.). 1978. text ed. 54.50 (ISBN 0-8016-5610-9). Mosby.

Symposium on Reconstruction of the Auricle, Vol. X. Ed. by Radford C. Tanzer & Milton T. Edgerton. LC 79-7329. 1974. 49.50 (ISBN 0-8016-4852-1). Mosby.

Symposium on Reconstructive Surgery of the Knee. American Academy of Orthopaedic Surgeons. LC 78-6486. (Illus.). 1978. 52.50 (ISBN 0-8016-0132-0). Mosby.

Symposium on Strabismus: Transactions of the New Orleans Academy of Ophthalmology. New Orleans Academy of Ophthalmology. (Illus.). 1978. 49.50 (ISBN 0-8016-3687-6). Mosby.

Symposium on Surface Mining Hydrology, Sedimentology, & Reclamation. Ed. by R. William De Vore & Stanley B. Carpenter. LC 79-91553. (Illus.). 353p. (Orig.). 1979. pap. 33.50 (ISBN 0-89779-024-3, UKY BU119); microfiche 4.50 (ISBN 0-89779-025-1). OEA Pubns.

Symposium on Surface Mining Hydrology, Sedimentology, & Reclamation 1980: Proceedings. Ed. by R. William De Vore & Donald H. Graves. (Illus., Orig.). 1980. pap. 33.50 (ISBN 0-89779-044-8, UKYBU123); microfiche 5.50 (ISBN 0-89779-045-6). OES Pubns.

Symposium on Tendon Surgery in the Hand. American Academy of Orthopaedic Surgeons. LC 75-37577. (Illus.). 314p. 1975. 37.50 o.p. (ISBN 0-8016-0046-4). Mosby.

Symposium on the Athlete's Knee: Surgical Repair & Reconstruction. American Academy of Orthopaedic Surgeons. LC 80-19414. (Illus.). 218p. 1980. text ed. 39.50 (ISBN 0-8016-0077-4). Mosby.

Symposium on the Biology of the California Islands: Proceedings. Ed. by Ralph N. Philbrick. (Illus.). 1967. 12.50 (ISBN 0-916436-01-2). Santa Barb Botanic.

Symposium on the Neurologic Aspects of Plastic Surgery. Ed. by Simon Fredricks & Garry S. Brody. LC 78-7355. (Symposia of the Educational Foundaion of the American Society of Plastic & Reconstructive Surgeons, Inc. Ser.: Vol. 17). 1978. text ed. 51.50 (ISBN 0-8016-1679-4). Mosby.

Symposium: Processing Agricultural & Municipal Wastes. George E. Inglett. (Illus.). 1973. text ed. 23.50 (ISBN 0-87055-139-6). AVI.

Symposium: Progress in Human Nutrition. Ed. by Sheldon Margen. (Illus.). 1971. text ed. 23.50 (ISBN 0-87055-101-9). AVI.

Symposium sur les Tumeurs Cutanees des Enfants. Gent. November 1978. Ed. by J. De Bersaques. (Journal: Dermatologica: Vol. 161, Suppl. 1, 1980). (Illus.). iv, 160p. 1980. pap. 11.00 (ISBN 3-8055-2238-X). S Karger.

Symposium: Sweeteners: Proceedings. Ed. by George E. Inglett. (Illus.). 1974. 24.50 (ISBN 0-87055-153-1). AVI.

Symptom Iceberg: A Study of Community Health. David R. Hannay. 1979. pap. 16.50 (ISBN 0-7100-8982-1). Routledge & Kegan.

Symptoms of Psychopathology: A Handbook. C. G. Costello. LC 78-88310. 1970. 37.95 (ISBN 0-471-17520-X). Wiley.

Synagogue Treasures of Bohemia & Monravia. Hana Volavkova. (Illus.). 10.00x o.p. (ISBN 0-87556-525-5). Saifer.

Synapses & Synaptosomes. D. G. Jones. LC 74-26646. 258p. 1975. text ed. 54.50x o.p. (ISBN 0-412-11270-1, Pub. by Chapman & Hall). Methuen Inc.

Synapses & Synaptosomes: Morphological Aspects. D. G. Jones. LC 74-26646. 1975. 54.50 o.p. (ISBN 0-470-44942-X). Halsted Pr.

Synapsida: A New Look into the Origin of Mammals. John C. McLoughlin. LC 79-56270. (Illus.). 160p. 1980. 14.95 (ISBN 0-670-68922-X). Viking Pr.

Synaptic Constituents in Health & Disease: Proceedings of the Third Meeting of the European Society for Neurochemistry, Bled, August 31st-Sept, 5th, 1980. Ed. by M. Brzin et al. (Illus.). 760p. 1980. 125.00 (ISBN 0-08-025921-9). Pergamon.

Synaptic Transmission & Neuronal Interaction. Ed. by M. V. Bennett. LC 73-83886. (Society of General Physiologists Ser: Vol. 28). 401p. 1974. 34.50 (ISBN 0-911216-56-1). Raven.

Synchro & Resolver Conversion. Ed. by Geoffrey Boyes. (Illus.). 196p. (Orig.). 1980. pap. 11.50 (ISBN 0-916550-06-0). Analog Devices.

Synchrotron Radiation. A. A. Sokolov. 1969. 50.00 (ISBN 0-08-012945-5). Pergamon.

Synchrotron Radiation Research. Ed. by Herman Winick & Seb Doniach. (Illus.). 740p. 1980. 65.00 (ISBN 0-306-40363-3, Plenum Pr). Plenum Pub.

Syncretic Society. Felipe G. Casals. Ed. by Alfred G. Meyer. Tr. by Guy Daniels from Fr. LC 80-5455. 100p. 1980. 15.00 (ISBN 0-87332-176-6). M E Sharpe.

Syndic. C. M. Kornbluth. 1978. pap. 1.50 (ISBN 0-380-00093-8, 39404). Avon.

Syndicalism & Revolution in Spain. Antonio Bar. (History of Anarchism Ser.). 1981. lib. bdg. 69.95 (ISBN 0-8490-3208-3). Gordon Pr.

Syndromes of the Seventies: Population, Sex & Social Change. John Loraine. (Contemporary Issues Ser.: No. 11). 1977. text ed. 15.75x (ISBN 0-7206-0404-4). Humanities.

Synectics: The Development of Creative Capacity. William J. Gordon. 1968. pap. 1.95 o.s.i. (ISBN 0-02-008250-9, Collier). Macmillan.

Synergetics-A Workshop: Proceedings of the International Workshop on Synergetics at Schloss Elmau, Bavaria, Germany, May 2-7,1977. Ed. by H. Haken. (Illus.). 1977. 34.30 (ISBN 0-387-08483-5). Springer-Verlag.

Synergic Power: Beyond Domination, Beyond Permissiveness. 2nd ed. James H. Craig & Marguerite Craig. LC 79-67184. (Illus.). 1979. pap. 4.95x (ISBN 0-914158-28-7). ProActive Pr.

Synergy Session. Lynn M. Buess. LC 80-67932. (Illus.). 113p. (Orig.). 1980. pap. 4.95 (ISBN 0-87516-427-7). De Vorss.

Synfuels: Equipment, Technology, Supplies, Money, People, E-042. Business Communications Co. Staff. 1981. 875.00 (ISBN 0-89336-281-6). BCC.

Synfuels Industry Opportunities. Ed. by Richard F. Hill et al. Elliot B. Boardman & Martin L. Heavner. LC 80-84730. 256p. 1981. 32.50 (ISBN 0-86587-088-8). Gov Insts.

Synodicon Vetus. Ed. by John Duffy. Tr. by John Parker. LC 79-52935. (Dumbarton Oaks Texts: Vol. 5). 209p. 1979. 35.00 (ISBN 0-88402-088-6, Ctr Byzantine). Dumbarton Oaks.

Synonyms Discriminated. Charles J. Smith. Ed. by Percy H. Smith. LC 78-126007. 1970. Repr. of 1903 ed. 26.00 (ISBN 0-8103-3010-5). Gale.

Synopsis of Analysis of Roentgen Signs in General Radiology. Isadore Meschan. LC 75-8181. (Illus.). 655p. 1976. 32.00 (ISBN 0-7216-6301-X). Saunders.

Synopsis of Clinical Pulmonary Diseases. 2nd ed. Roger S. Mitchell. LC 77-11024. (Illus.). 1978. pap. text ed. 15.95 (ISBN 0-8016-3430-X). Mosby.

Synopsis of Contemporary Psychiatry. 6th ed. George A. Ulett & Kathleen Smith. LC 79-14554. (Illus.). 1979. pap. text ed. 18.95 (ISBN 0-8016-5176-X). Mosby.

Synopsis of Endrocrinology & Metabolism. 2nd ed. I. Ramsay. (Illus.). 1980. pap. 18.95 (ISBN 0-8151-7033-5). Year Bk Med.

Synopsis of Gynecologic Oncology. Philip J. DiSaia et al. LC 74-34307. (Clinical Monographs in Obstetrics & Gynecology Ser). 344p. 1975. 32.50 (ISBN 0-471-21590-2, Pub. by Wiley-Med). Wiley.

Synopsis of Gynecologic Oncology. C. Paul Morrow & Duane E. Townsend. 500p. 1981. 29.50 (ISBN 0-471-06504-8, Pub. by Wiley-Med). Wiley.

Synopsis of Gynecology. 9th ed. Daniel W. Beacham & Woodard D. Beacham. LC 77-3544. (Illus.). 1977. pap. 19.95 (ISBN 0-8016-0525-3). Mosby.

Synopsis of North American Desmids Part II: Desmidiaceae: Placodermae Section 3. G. W. Prescott et al. LC 70-183418. (Illus.). x, 720p. Date not set. 58.50x (ISBN 0-8032-3660-3). U of Nebr Pr.

Synopsis of Ophthalmology. 4th ed. William H. Havener. LC 74-14772. 1975. pap. 18.95 o.p. (ISBN 0-8016-2098-8). Mosby.

Synopsis of Opthalmology. 5th ed. William H. Havener. LC 79-12076. (Illus.). 1979. pap. text ed. 28.50 (ISBN 0-8016-2111-9). Mosby.

Synopsis of Oral Pathology. 6th ed. S. N. Bhaskar. (Illus.). 676p. 1981. text ed. 27.50 (ISBN 0-8016-0685-3). Mosby.

Synopsis of Pathology. 10th ed. W. A. Anderson & W. A. Scotti. LC 80-13985. (Illus.). 786p. 1980. pap. text ed. 26.00 (ISBN 0-8016-0231-9). Mosby.

Synopsis of Pathology. 9th ed. W. A. D. Anderson & Thomas M. Scotti. LC 75-31874. (Illus.). 1152p. 1976. 19.95 o.p. (ISBN 0-8016-0230-0). Mosby.

Synopsis of Pediatrics. 5th ed. James G. Hughes. LC 79-14927. 1979. pap. text ed. 26.50 (ISBN 0-8016-2309-X). Mosby.

Synopsis of Surgery. 4th ed. Richard D. Liechty & Robert T. Soper. LC 80-12884. (Illus.). 1980. pap. text ed. 24.50 (ISBN 0-8016-3012-6). Mosby.

Synopsis of the Four Gospels: Greek - English Edition. 3rd ed. Ed. by Kurt Aland. (Eng. & Gr.). 1979. 20.00 (ISBN 3-438-05405-1, 56691). United Bible.

Synopsis Quattuor Evangeliorum. 10th ed. Ed. by Kurt Aland. 1978. 20.00 (ISBN 3-438-05130-3, 56690). United Bible.

Synoptic Approach to the Riddle of Existence. Arthur W. Nunk. LC 77-818. 336p. 1977. 15.00 (ISBN 0-87527-165-0). Fireside Bks.

Synoptic Gospels: An Introduction. Keith F. Nickle. LC 79-92069. (Orig.). 1980. pap. 6.95 (ISBN 0-8042-0422-5). John Knox.

Synopticon. Ed. by William R. Farmer. 1969. 80.00 (ISBN 0-521-07464-9). Cambridge U Pr.

Syntactic Argumentation & the Structure of English. David M. Perlmutter & Scott Soames. 1979. 27.50x (ISBN 0-520-03828-2); pap. 10.50x (ISBN 0-520-03833-9, CAMPUS NO. 231). U of Cal Pr.

Syntactic Pattern Recognition: An Introduction. Rafael C. Gonzalez & Michael G. Thomason. (Applied Mathematics & Computation Ser.: No. 14). 1978. text ed. 33.50 (ISBN 0-201-02930-8, Adv Bk Prog); pap. text ed. 21.50 (ISBN 0-201-02931-6). A-W.

Syntactic Revolution. Abraham L. Gillespie. Ed. by Richard Milazzo. LC 75-22994. (Illus.). 190p. 1981. pap. 12.95 (ISBN 0-915570-05-X). Oolp Pr.

Syntactical Evidence of Semitic Sources in Greek Documents. Raymond Martin. LC 73-89038. (Society of Biblical Literature. Septuagint & Cognate Studies). 1974. pap. 7.50 (ISBN 0-89130-168-2, 060403). Scholars Pr Ca.

Syntactical Study of Epic Formulas. C. W. Aspland. 1970. text ed. 13.25x (ISBN 0-391-00422-0). Humanities.

Syntagma Musicum, 2 vols. Michael Praetorius. Tr. by Harold Blumenfeld from Ger. (Music Reprint Ser.: 1979). Orig. Title: De Organographia, First & Second Parts. (Illus.). 1979. Repr. of 1962 ed. lib. bdg. 19.50 (ISBN 0-306-70563-X). Da Capo.

Syntax: A Linguistic Introduction to Sentence Structure. E. K. Brown & J. E. Miller. 394p. 1981. text ed. 33.75x (ISBN 0-686-69131-8, Hutchinson U Lib); pap. text ed. 15.50x (ISBN 0-686-69132-6). Humanities.

Syntax & Semantics, 13 vols. John P. Kimball et al. Incl. Vol. 1. Studies in Language. 260p. 1973. 30.50 (ISBN 0-12-785421-5); Vol. 2. 1973. 30.50 (ISBN 0-12-785422-3); Vol. 3. 1975. 31.00 (ISBN 0-12-785423-1); Vol. 4. 1975. 35.00 (ISBN 0-12-785424-X); Vol. 5. Japanese Generative Grammar. 1975. 45.50 (ISBN 0-12-785425-8); Vol. 6. 1976. 42.50 (ISBN 0-12-785426-6); Vol. 7. 1976. 30.00 (ISBN 0-12-613507-X); Vol. 8. 1976. 30.00 (ISBN 0-12-613508-8); Vol. 9. Pragmatics. 1978. 27.00 (ISBN 0-12-613509-6); Vol. 10. 1979. 38.00 (ISBN 0-12-613510-X); Vol. 11. Presupposition. 1979. 35.00 (ISBN 0-12-613511-8); Vol. 12. Discourse & Syntax. 1979. 43.00 (ISBN 0-12-613512-6); Vol. 13. Current Approaches to Syntax. 1980. write for info. (ISBN 0-12-613513-4). Acad Pr.

Syntax & Semantics of Questions in Navajo. Ellen Schauber. Ed. by Jorge Hankamer. LC 78-66568. (Outstanding Dissertations in Linguistics Ser.). 1979. lib. bdg. 35.00 (ISBN 0-8240-9676-2). Garland Pub.

Syntax & Semantics, Vol. 14: Tense & Aspect. Ed. by John P. Kimball & Philip Tedesch. 1981. price not set (ISBN 0-12-613514-2). Acad Pr.

Syntax & Speech. William E. Cooper & Jeanne Paccia-Cooper. LC 80-16614. (Cognitive Science Ser.: No. 3). 1980. text ed. 21.00x (ISBN 0-674-86075-6). Harvard U Pr.

Syntax & Style. Clarence E. Schneider. LC 72-97330. 342p. 1974. pap. 7.95x (ISBN 0-88316-019-6). Chandler & Sharp.

Syntax in English Poetry, 1870-1930. William E. Baker. (Perspectives in Criticism: No. 18). 1968. 14.00x (ISBN 0-520-00069-2). U of Cal Pr.

Syntax of Causative Constructions. Judith Aissen. Ed. by Jorge Hankamer. LC 78-66533. (Outstanding Dissertations in Linguistics Ser.). 1979. lib. bdg. 27.50 (ISBN 0-8240-9690-8). Garland Pub.

Syntax of Early Latin, 2 Vols. Charles E. Bennett. Repr. of 1910 ed. Set. 100.60 (ISBN 0-685-05294-X). Adler.

Syntax of Modern Arabic Prose. Vicente Cantarino. Incl. Vol. 1. The Simple Sentence. 184p. 1974. 12.00x (ISBN 0-253-39504-6); Vol. 2. The Expanded Sentence. 544p. 1976. 17.50x (ISBN 0-253-39505-4); Vol. 3. The Compound Sentence. 424p. 1976. 15.00x (ISBN 0-253-39506-2). LC 69-16996. (Oriental Ser.: Vol. 4). Set. 37.50x (ISBN 0-253-39507-0). Ind U Pr.

Syntax of Moods & Tenses of New Testament Greek. 3rd ed. E. Burton. 240p. 1898. text ed. 11.50x (ISBN 0-567-01002-3). Attic Pr.

Syntax of New Testament Greek. James A. Brooks & Carlton L. Winbery. LC 78-51150. 1978. pap. text ed. 7.50x (ISBN 0-8191-0473-6). U Pr of Amer.

Syntax of Urban Hijazi Arabic. M. Sieny. 12.00x (ISBN 0-685-89879-2). Intl Bk Ctr.

Syntax of Welsh. Gwen Awbery. LC 76-11489. (Cambridge Studies in Linguistics: No. 18). 1977. 35.00 (ISBN 0-521-21341-X). Cambridge U Pr.

Syntax Oriented Translator. Peter Z. Ingerman. 1966. text ed. 10.95 (ISBN 0-12-370850-8). Acad Pr.

Synthajoy. D. G. Compton. 1979. pap. 1.95 o.p. (ISBN 0-425-04207-3). Berkley Pub.

Syntheses & Physical Studies of Inorganic Compounds. C. F. Bell. LC 79-178772. 253p. 1972. text ed. 46.00 (ISBN 0-08-016651-2). Pergamon.

Synthesis: An Introduction to the History, Theory, & Practice of Electronic Music. Herbert Deutsch. LC 76-20709. (Illus.). 250p. 1976. pap. text ed. 7.95x (ISBN 0-88284-043-6). Alfred Pub.

Synthesis & Analysis Methods for Safety & Reliability Studies. Ed. by G. Apostolakis et al. 470p. 1980. 49.50 (ISBN 0-306-40316-1, Plenum Pr). Plenum Pub.

Synthesis & Characterization of Inorganic Compounds. W. Jolly. 1970. 23.95 (ISBN 0-13-879932-6). P-H.

Synthesis & Release of Adenohypophyseal Hormones. Ed. by Marian Jutisz & Kenneth W. McKerns. (Biochemical Endocrinology Ser.). (Illus.). 780p. 1980. 69.50 (ISBN 0-306-40247-5, Plenum Pr). Plenum Pub.

Synthesis Fo Economic Performance in Latin America During 1979. OAS General Secretariat Planning & Statistics. (Statistics Ser.). 40p. 1979. pap. 3.00 (ISBN 0-686-68295-5). OAS.

Synthesis of Feedback Systems. Isaac M. Horowitz. 1963. text ed. 24.95 (ISBN 0-12-355950-2). Acad Pr.

Synthesis of Planar Antenna Sources. Donald R. Rhodes. (Oxford Engineering Science Ser.). (Illus.). 230p. 1975. 45.00x (ISBN 0-19-856123-7). Oxford U Pr.

Synthesis of Yoga. Sri Aurobindo. 1976. pap. 8.00 (ISBN 0-89071-268-9). Matagiri.

Synthetic Aperture Radar Systems Theory & Design. R. O. Harger. (Electrical Science Ser). 1969. 30.50 (ISBN 0-12-325050-1). Acad Pr.

Synthetic Aspects of Biologically Active Cyclic Peptides: Gramicidei S & Tyrocidres. Nobuo Izumiya. LC 79-19998. 1979. 32.95x (ISBN 0-470-26863-8). Halsted Pr.

Synthetic Biomedical Polymers: Concepts & Applications. Ed. by Michael Szycher & William J. Robinson. LC 80-52137. (Illus.). 235p. 1980. 39.00 (ISBN 0-87762-290-6). Technomic.

Synthetic Chemistry of Insect Phermones & Juvenile Hormones. K. Mori et al. (Recent Developments in the Chemistry of Natural Carbon Compounds: Vol. 9). (Illus.). 420p. 1979. 40.00x (ISBN 963-05-1632-2). Intl Pubns Serv.

Synthetic Detergents. 6th ed. A. Davidsohn & B. M. Milwidski. LC 77-13133. 1978. 29.95 (ISBN 0-470-99312-X). Halsted Pr.

Synthetic Fibrinolytic Thrombolytic Agents: Chemical, Biochemical, Pharmacological & Clinical Aspects. Ed. by K. N. Von Kaulla & J. F. Davidson. (Illus.). 528p. 1975. text ed. 46.75 (ISBN 0-398-02927-X). C C Thomas.

Synthetic Fuels from Coal: Overview & Assessment. Larry L. Anderson & David A. Tillman. LC 79-17786. 1979. 19.50 (ISBN 0-471-01784-1, Pub. by Wiley-Interscience). Wiley.

Synthetic Fuels Technology Overviews with Health & Environmental Impacts. Edward J. Bentz, Jr. & Eliahi J. Salmon. 136p. 1981. text ed. 19.95 (ISBN 0-250-40423-0). Ann Arbor Science.

Synthetic Oils & Additives for Lubricants: Advances Since 1977. Ed. by M. William Ranney. LC 79-24355. (Chemical Technology Review Ser.: No. 145). (Illus.). 1980. 48.00 (ISBN 0-8155-0781-X). Noyes.

Synthetic Peptides, Vol. 3. George R. Pettit. 1975. 55.25 (ISBN 0-12-552403-X). Acad Pr.

Synthetic Polymers & the Paper Industry. Vladimir M. Wolpert. LC 76-6719. (Pulp & Paper Book). (Illus.). 1977. 42.50 (ISBN 0-87930-056-6). Miller Freeman.

Synthetic Polypeptides: Preparation, Structure, & Properties. C. H. Bamford et al. (Physical Chemistry Ser.: Vol. 5). 1956. 49.00 o.p. (ISBN 0-12-077650-2). Acad Pr.

Synthetic Production & Utilization of Amino Acids. Ed. by Takeo Kaneko et al. LC 74-9924. 312p. 1974. 32.95 (ISBN 0-470-45590-X). Halsted Pr.

Synthetic Reagents, Vols. 1-2. J. S. Pizey. LC 73-14417. 411p. 1974. Vol. 1. 74.95 (ISBN 0-470-69104-2); Vol. 2. 54.95 (ISBN 0-470-69107-7). Halsted Pr.

Synthetic Reagents, Vol. 3. Ed. by J. S. Pizey. LC 73-14417. 1977. 59.95 (ISBN 0-470-99118-6). Halsted Pr.

Synthetic Reagents Vol. 4: Mercuric Acetate Periodic Acid & Periodates Sulfuryl Chloride. J. S. Pizey. 200p. 1981. 110.00 (ISBN 0-470-27133-7). Halsted Pr.

Synthetic Substrates in Clinical Blood Coagulation Assays. Ed. by H. R. Lijnen et al. (Developments in Hematology Ser.: No. 1). 142p. 1981. PLB 23.50 (ISBN 90-247-2409-0, Pub. Bymartinus Nijhoff). Kluwer Boston.

Syntony & Spark - the Origins of Radio Technology. Hugh G. Aitken. LC 75-34247. (Science, Culture & Society Ser.). 1976. 25.50 (ISBN 0-471-01816-3, Pub. by Wiley-Interscience). Wiley.

Syria. Henry Gilfond. (First Bks.). (Illus.). (gr. 4-6). 1978. PLB 6.45 s&l (ISBN 0-531-02238-2). Watts.

Syria & Lebanon. H. Hourani. (Arab Background Ser.). 1968. 14.00x (ISBN 0-685-77096-6). Intl Bk Ctr.

Syria & Lebanon. Nicola Ziadeh. (Arab Background Ser.). 1968. 14.00x (ISBN 0-685-77109-1). Intl Bk Ctr.

Syria & Lebanon Under French Mandate, 1968. Stephen Longrigg. (Arab Background Ser.). 15.00x (ISBN 0-685-72062-4). Intl Bk Ctr.

Syriac Bible, Peshitta Version. Ed. by S. Lee. 9.40 (ISBN 0-564-03212-3, 82566). United Bible.

Syriac Manuscripts in the Harvard College Library: A Catalog. Moshe H. Goshen-Gottstein. LC 77-13132. (Harvard Semitic Studies: No. 23). 1979. 15.00 (ISBN 0-89130-189-5, 040423). Scholars Pr Ca.

Syriac Version of the Ps. Nonnos Mythological Scholia. Sebastian Brock. LC 79-139712. (Oriental Publications: No. 20). 1971. 62.00 (ISBN 0-521-07990-X). Cambridge U Pr.

Syrian-African Rift & Other Poems. Avoth Yeshurun. Ed. by Yehuda Amichai & Allen Mandelbaum. Tr. by Harold Schimmel. 160p. 1980. 11.95 (ISBN 0-8276-0181-6, 464); pap. 7.95 (ISBN 0-8276-0182-4, 463). Jewish Pubn.

Syrian-Lebanese in America. Philip M. Kayal & Joseph M. Kayal. (Immigrant Heritage of America Ser.). 1975. lib. bdg. 13.95 (ISBN 0-8057-8412-8). Twayne.

System Analysis Techniques. Ed. by J. Daniel Couger & Robert W. Knapp. LC 73-14818. 509p. 1974. text ed. 25.50 (ISBN 0-471-17735-0). Wiley.

System & Theory of Geosciences, 2 pts. Ed. by H. Uhlig. 103p. 1975. Vol. 1. pap. text ed. 24.00 (ISBN 0-08-019664-0); Vol. 7, Pt. 1. pap. text ed. 24.00 (ISBN 0-08-019670-5). Pergamon.

System Approach for Developement: Proceedings of the Third IFAC-IFIP-IFORS Conference, Rabat, Morocco, 24-27 November 1980. Ed. by M Najim & Y. M. Abdel-Fettah. LC 80-41530. 600p. 1981. 105.00 (ISBN 0-08-025670-8); pap. 80.00 (ISBN 0-08-027283-5). Pergamon.

System Architecture. John Zarrella. LC 80-82932. (Microprocessor Software Engineering Concepts Ser.). (Illus.). 240p. (Orig.). 1980. pap. 9.95 (ISBN 0-935230-02-5). Microcomputer Appns.

System, Change & Conflict. N. S. Demerath & R. A. Peterson. LC 67-12512. 1967. 15.95 (ISBN 0-02-907180-1). Free Pr.

System Dynamics. Katshuiko Ogata. LC 77-20180. (Illus.). 1978. 29.95 (ISBN 0-13-880385-4). P-H.

System Dynamics: A Unified Approach. Dean C. Karnopp & Ronald C. Rosenberg. LC 74-22466. 496p. 1975. 32.50 (ISBN 0-471-45940-2, Pub. by Wiley-Interscience). Wiley.

System Dynamics: Modeling & Response. E. O. Doebelin. LC 77-187802. 448p. 1972. 26.95x (ISBN 0-675-09120-9). Merrill.

System for Ophthalmic Dispensing. Clifford F. Brooks & Irving Borish. 1979. 48.00 (ISBN 0-87873-025-7). Prof Press.

System Identification: Least Squares Method. Tien C. Hsia. LC 75-3515. (Illus.). 1977. 27.95 (ISBN 0-669-99630-0). Lexington Bks.

System Management: Planning & Control. H. W. Lanford. (National University Publications Ser.). 200p. 1981. 15.00 (ISBN 0-8046-9223-8). Kennikat.

System Methods for Socio-Economic & Environmental Impact Analysis. Glenn R. DeSouza. LC 79-7183. (Arthur D. Little Bk.). 176p. 1979. 19.95 (ISBN 0-669-02953-X). Lexington Bks.

System Modeling & Control. J. Schwarzenbach & K. F. Gill. LC 78-40537. 1978. pap. 19.95 (ISBN 0-470-26457-8). Halsted Pr.

System Modeling & Response: Theoretical & Experimental Approaches. Ernest O. Doebelin. LC 79-27609. 587p. 1980. text ed. 26.95 (ISBN 0-471-03211-5). Wiley.

System of Architectural Ornament. Louis Sullivan. LC 67-17016. 1967. 10.95x o.s.i. (ISBN 0-87130-018-4). Eakins.

System of Ethics. Leonard Nelson. 1956. 42.50x (ISBN 0-685-69846-7). Elliots Bks.

System of Open Star Clusters & Galaxy Atlas of Open Star Clusters. G. Alter & J. Ruprecht. 1963. 36.50 (ISBN 0-12-054250-1). Acad Pr.

System of Ophthalmology Series. Ed. by Stewart Duke-Elder. Incl. Vol. 1. Eye in Evolution. (Illus.). 843p. 1958. 61.50 (ISBN 0-8016-8282-7); Vol. 2. Anatomy of the Visual System. (Illus.). 901p. 1961. 63.50 (ISBN 0-8016-8283-5); Vol. 3, Pt. 1. Normal & Abnormal Development: Embryology. (Illus.). 330p. 1963. 49.00 (ISBN 0-8016-8285-1); Vol. 3, Pt. 2. Normal & Abnormal Development: Congenital Deformities. (Illus.). 1190p. 1964. 69.00 (ISBN 0-8016-8286-X); Vol. 4. Physiology of the Eye & of Vision. (Illus.). xx, 734p. 1968. 75.50 o.p. (ISBN 0-8016-8296-7); Vol. 5. Ophthalmic Optics & Refraction. (Illus.). xix, 879p. 1970. 65.50 o.p. (ISBN 0-8016-8298-3); Vol. 7. Foundations of Ophthalmology: Heredity, Pathology, Diagnosis & Therapeutics. (Illus.). 829p. 1962. 65.50 (ISBN 0-8016-8284-3); Vol. 8. Diseases of the Outer Eye: Conjunctiva, Cornea & Sclera, 2 vols. (Illus.). 1339p. 1965. 100.00 (ISBN 0-8016-8287-8); Vol. 9. Diseases of Uveal Tract. (Illus.). xvi, 978p. 1966. 80.00 (ISBN 0-8016-8290-8); Vol. 10. Diseases of the Retina. (Illus.). xv, 878p. 1967. 80.00 (ISBN 0-8016-8295-9); Vol. 11. Diseases of the Lens & Vitreous: Glaucoma & Hypotony. (Illus.). xx, 779p. 1969. 80.00 (ISBN 0-8016-8297-5); Vol. 12. Neuro-Ophthalmology. (Illus.). xxi, 994p. 1971. 83.50 (ISBN 0-8016-8299-1); Vol. 14. Injuries, 2 vols. 1357p. 1972. Set. 117.00 (ISBN 0-8016-8300-9). Mosby.

System of Quality Control for a CPA Firm. (Statement on Quality Control Standards Ser.: No. 1). 1979. pap. 1.35. Am Inst CPA.

System of Stages for Correlation of Magallanes Basin Sediments. M. L. Natland et al. LC 74-75964. (Memoir: No. 139). (Illus.). 1974. 15.50x (ISBN 0-8137-1139-8). Geol Soc.

System of the Science of Music & Practical Composition: Incidentally Comprising What Is Usally Understood by the Term Through Bass. Johann B. Logier. LC 76-20715. (Music Reprint Ser). 1976. Repr. of 1897 ed. lib. bdg. 32.50 (ISBN 0-306-70793-4). Da Capo.

System of the Vedanta. Paul Deussen. 544p. 1973. pap. 4.00 o.p. (ISBN 0-486-22958-0). Dover.

System of Water Quality from the Biological Point of View. Vladimir Sladecek. Ed. by H. Elster & W. Ohle. LC 74-170857. (Ergebnisse der Limnologie: Vol. 7). (Illus.). 218p. (Orig.). 1973. pap. 57.50x (ISBN 3-510-47005-2). Intl Pubns Serv.

System Simulation. 2nd ed. Geoffrey Gordon. LC 77-24579. (Illus.). 1978. ref. ed. 23.50 (ISBN 0-13-881797-9). P-H.

System Theory: A Unified State-Space Approach to Continuous & Discrete Systems. Louis Padulo & Michael A. Arbib. LC 73-77941. (Illus.). 1974. text ed. 24.95 (ISBN 0-7216-7035-0). Hemisphere Pub.

System-Three-Sixty RPG. Mike Murach. LC 70-178830. (Illus.). 297p. 1972. pap. text ed. 14.95 (ISBN 0-574-16097-3, 13-1415); instr's guide avail. (ISBN 0-574-16128-7, 13-1416); transparency masters 29.95 (ISBN 0-574-16129-5, 13-1417). SRA.

System 360 Assembler Language. Don Stabley. LC 67-30037. 1967. pap. 14.50 (ISBN 0-471-81950-6, Pub. by Wiley-Interscience). Wiley.

System-360 Job-Control Language. Gary D. Brown. 1970. pap. 16.50 (ISBN 0-471-10870-7, Pub. by Wiley-Interscience). Wiley.

System-370 Job Control Language. Gary D. Brown. LC 77-24901. 1977. 14.95 (ISBN 0-471-03155-0, Pub. by Wiley-Interscience). Wiley.

Systematic Analyses of Learning & Motivation. Frank A. Logan & Douglas P. Ferraro. LC 78-6870. 1978. text ed. 21.95x (ISBN 0-471-04130-0). Wiley.

Systematic Approach to Commercial & Clerical Training. K. Oakley & W. Richmond. 1970. pap. 6.25 (ISBN 0-08-015722-X). Pergamon.

Systematic Approach to Digital Logic Design. Frederic J. Mowle. LC 75-18156. (A-W Series in Electrical Engineering). 500p. 1976. text ed. 25.95 (ISBN 0-201-04920-1); solution manual 5.95 (ISBN 0-201-04921-X). A-W.

Systematic Biology. 1969. 16.00 (ISBN 0-309-01692-4). Natl Acad Pr.

Systematic Commercial Refrigeration Service. Raymond K. Schneider. LC 78-14464. (Illus.). 192p. 1979. 15.95x (ISBN 0-912524-18-9). Busn News.

Systematic Counseling. N. Stewart et al. LC 77-24374. (Illus.). 1978. 18.95 (ISBN 0-13-880252-1). P-H.

Systematic Course Design for the Health Fields. Ascher Segall et al. LC 75-20398. 171p. 1975. 20.95 o.p. (ISBN 0-471-77410-3, Pub. by Wiley Med). Wiley.

Systematic Design of Instruction. Walter Dick & Lou Carey. 1978. pap. 8.95x (ISBN 0-673-15122-0). Scott F.

Systematic Empiricism: Critique of a Pseudoscience. David Willer & Judith Willer. (General Sociology Ser.). (Illus.). 176p. 1973. 13.95 (ISBN 0-13-880351-X). P-H.

Systematic Endocrinology. 2nd ed. Calvin Ezrin et al. (Illus.). 1979. text ed. 42.00 (ISBN 0-06-140797-6, Harper Medical). Har-Row.

Systematic Endodontics. Yoshiro Shoji. (Illus.). 126p. 1977. 22.00. Quint Pub Co.

Systematic Glossary of the Terminology of Statistical Methods: English, French, Spanish, Russian. Isaac Paenson. 1971. 120.00 (ISBN 0-08-012285-X). Pergamon.

Systematic Handling Analysis. Richard Muther & Knut Haganas. LC 73-90920. 1969. spiral bdg. 22.95 (ISBN 0-8436-1002-6). CBI Pub.

Systematic Hydrology. J. C. Rodda et al. 1976. 49.95 (ISBN 0-408-00234-4). Butterworths.

Systematic Identification of Organic Compounds. 5th ed. Ralph L. Shriner et al. LC 64-15000. 1964. 17.95 o.p. (ISBN 0-471-78873-2). Wiley.

Systematic Identification of Organic Compounds: A Laboratory Manual. 6th ed. Ralph Shriner et al. 1980. 22.95x (ISBN 0-471-78874-0). Wiley.

Systematic Instruction. W. Popham & Eva Baker. 1970. pap. text ed. 8.95 (ISBN 0-13-880690-X). P-H.

Systematic Instruction for Retarded Children: The Illinois Program. Incl. Part I, Teacher-Parent Guide. James C. Chalfant & Ronald G. Silikovitz. pap. text ed. 1.00x (ISBN 0-8134-1557-8, 1557); Part II, Systematic Language Instruction. James W. Tawney & Lee W. Hipsher. pap. text ed. 4.95x (ISBN 0-8134-1558-6, 1558); Part III, Self-Help Instruction. Maxine D. Linford et al. pap. text ed. 3.25x (ISBN 0-8134-1559-4, 1559); Part IV, Motor Performance & Recreation Instruction. Anthony G. Linford & Claudine Y. Jeanrenaud. pap. text ed. 2.95x (ISBN 0-8134-1560-8, 1560). 1972. Interstate.

Systematic Layout Planning. 2nd ed. Richard Muther. LC 72-91983. 1973. 23.50 (ISBN 0-8436-0814-5); text ed. 16.50 o.p. (ISBN 0-8436-0817-X). CBI Pub.

Systematic Lupus Erythematosus: A Clinical Analysis, Vol. 6. James F. Fries & Halsted R. Holman. LC 74-31837. (Major Problems in Internal Medicine Ser.). (Illus.). 199p. 1975. text ed. 20.00 (ISBN 0-7216-3917-8). Saunders.

Systematic Management of Human Resources. Richard B. Peterson & Lane Tracy. LC 78-55826. 1979. text ed. 17.95 (ISBN 0-201-05814-6); readings book avail. 10.95 (ISBN 0-201-05815-4). A-W.

Systematic Materials Analysis. Ed. by J. H. Richardson & R. V. Peterson. (Materials Science Ser.: Vol. 1). 1974. 48.50, by subscription 42.00 (ISBN 0-12-587801-X). Acad Pr.

Systematic Nursing Care. Rosemary Long. (Illus.). 96p. 1981. 21.00 (ISBN 0-571-11615-9, Pub. by Faber & Faber); pap. 7.95 (ISBN 0-686-28936-6). Merrimack Bk Serv.

Systematic Patient Medication Record Review: A Manual for Nurses. Timothy H. Self et al. LC 80-12481. 1980. pap. text ed. 8.95 (ISBN 0-8016-4479-8). Mosby.

Systematic Planning of Industrial Facilities, Vol. II. Richard Muther & Lee Hales. LC 79-84256. 1980. write for info. (ISBN 0-933684-02-9). Mgmt & Indus Res Pubns.

Systematic Political Geography. 3rd ed. Martin I. Glassner & Harm J. Deblij. LC 79-26750. 1980. text ed. 26.95 (ISBN 0-471-05228-0). Wiley.

Systematic Programming: An Introduction. Niklaus Wirth. (Illus.). 208p. 1973. 22.95 (ISBN 0-13-880369-2). P-H.

Systematic Reading Instruction. 2nd ed. Gerald G. Duffy & George B. Sherman. 1977. pap. text ed. 13.50 scp (ISBN 0-06-041794-3, HarpC). Har-Row.

Systematic Selling: How to Influence the Buying Decision Process. new ed. Terry A. Mort. LC 77-5937. (Illus.). 1977. 14.95 (ISBN 0-8144-5439-9). Am Mgmt.

Systematic Studies of the Genus Pyrrhopappus (Compositae, Cichorieae) David K. Northington. (Special Publications: No. 6). 38p. 1974. pap. 2.00 (ISBN 0-89672-031-4). Tex Tech Pr.

Systematic Theology, 8 vols. Lewis S. Chafer. 2700p. 1981. Repr. 89.95 (ISBN 0-310-22378-4). Zondervan.

Systematic Theology, 3 vols. Ernest S. Williams. Incl. Vol. 1. 6.95 (ISBN 0-88243-665-1, 02-0665); pap. 4.95 (ISBN 0-88243-643-0, 02-0643); Vol. 2. 6.95 (ISBN 0-88243-666-X, 02-0666); pap. 4.95 (ISBN 0-88243-644-9, 02-0644); Vol. 3. 6.95 (ISBN 0-88243-667-8, 02-0667); pap. 4.95 (ISBN 0-88243-645-7, 02-0645). 1953. Set. 18.95 (ISBN 0-88243-668-6, 02-0668); Set. pap. 13.50 (ISBN 0-88243-650-3, 02-0650). Gospel Pub.

Systematic Thinking for Social Action. Alice M. Rivlin. LC 74-161600. 1971. 11.95 (ISBN 0-8157-7478-8); pap. 4.95 (ISBN 0-8157-7477-X). Brookings.

Systematic Training for Effective Parenting (STEP) Parent's Handbook. Don Dinkmeyer & Gary D. McKay. (Illus.). 117p. 1976. pap. text ed. 4.85 (ISBN 0-913476-77-3). Am Guidance.

Systematic Training for Effective Teaching (STET) Teacher's Resource Book: Special Ctivities for Teachers & Students. Don Dinkmeyer et al. (Illus.). 161p. (Orig.). 1980. pap. 7.00 (ISBN 0-913476-76-5). Am Guidance.

Systematic Training for Effective Teaching: Teacher's Handbook. Don Dinkmeyer et al. (Illus.). 291p. (Orig.). 1980. pap. text ed. 12.00 (ISBN 0-913476-75-7). Am Guidance.

Systematic Urban Planning. Darwin G. Stuart. LC 75-19825. (Special Studies). (Illus.). 1976. text ed. 24.50 o.p. (ISBN 0-275-56060-0). Praeger.

Systematics & Biogeography: Cladistics & Vicariance. Gareth Nelson & Norman I. Platnick. LC 80-20828. (Illus.). 592p. 1981. text ed. 35.00x (ISBN 0-231-04574-3). Columbia U Pr.

Systematics & Evolutionary Relationships of Spiny Pocket Mice, Genus Liomys. Hugh H. Genoways. (Special Publications: No. 5). (Illus., Orig.). 1973. pap. 10.00 (ISBN 0-89672-030-6). Tex Tech Pr.

Systematics & Nesting Behavior of Australian Bembix Sand Wasps - Hymenoptera, Sphecidae. Evans & Matthews. (Memoirs Ser: No. 20). (Illus.). 1973. 25.00 (ISBN 0-686-17148-9). Am Entom Inst.

Systematics & Pollination of the "Closed Flowered" Species of Calathea (Marantaceae) Helen Kennedy. (Publications in Botany: No. 71). 1978. pap. 7.75x (ISBN 0-520-09572-3). U of Cal Pr.

Systematics, Distribution & Abundance of the Epiplanktonic Squid. T. Okutani & J. A. McGowan. (U. C. Publ. in Oceanography: Vol. 14). 1969. pap. 7.00x (ISBN 0-520-09319-4). U of Cal Pr.

Systematics of the Genus Coelocnemis (Coleoptera: Tenebrionidae: A Quatitative Study of Variation. John T. Doyen. (U. C. Publ. in Entomology: Vol. 73). 1973. pap. 7.50x (ISBN 0-520-09481-6). U of Cal Pr.

Systematics of the Genus Didelphis (Marsupialia: Didelphidae) in North & Middle America. Alfred L. Gardner. (Special Publications: No. 4). (Illus., Orig.). 1973. pap. 4.00 (ISBN 0-89672-029-2). Tex Tech Pr.

Systematics of the Genus Monochaetum (Melastomataceae) in Mexico & Central America. Frank Almeda, Jr. (Publications in Botany Ser.: Vol. 75). 1978. 11.00x (ISBN 0-520-09587-1). U of Cal Pr.

Systematics of the Neotropical Species of Thlypteris Section Cyclosorus. Alan R. Smith. (U. C. Publ. in Botany: Vol. 59). 1971. pap. 10.50x (ISBN 0-520-09396-8). U of Cal Pr.

Systematics of the Onocleoid Ferns. Robert M. Lloyd. (U. C. Publ. in Botany: Vol. 61). 1972. pap. 7.50x (ISBN 0-520-09411-5). U of Cal Pr.

Systematics of the Tribe Plectoderini in America North of Mexico (Homoptera: Fulgoroidea, Achilidae) Lois B. O'Brien. (U. C. Publ. in Entomology: Vol. 64). 1971. pap. 7.00x (ISBN 0-520-09377-1). U of Cal Pr.

Systematisierung von Infusionsloesungen und Grundlagen der Infusionstherapie. I. W. Hahnefeld. (Beitrage zu Infusionstherapie und klinische Ernaehrung: Band 5). (Illus.). 112p. 1980. pap. 15.00 (ISBN 3-8055-1395-X). S Karger.

Systeme De la Raison, Ou le Prophete Philosophe. J. L. Carra. (Fr.). 1977. Repr. of 1791 ed. lib. bdg. 20.50x o.p. (ISBN 0-8287-0162-8). Clearwater Pub.

Systeme Des Residences D'hiver et D'ete Chez les Nomades et les Chefs Hongrois Au Xe Siecle. G. Gyorffy. (Pdr Press Publications in Early Hungarian History: No. 2). (Illus.). 1976. pap. text ed. 14.00x (ISBN 90-316-0098-9). Humanities.

Systeme D'un Nouveau Gouvernment En France, 2 vols. E. L. De La Jonchere. (Fr.). 1977. Repr. of 1720 ed. lib. bdg. 75.00x o.p. (ISBN 0-8287-0492-9). Clearwater Pub.

Systemes Des Equations Differentielles, 3 Vols. in 1. J. A. Lappo-Danilevskii. LC 53-7110. (Fr). 22.50 (ISBN 0-8284-0094-6). Chelsea Pub.

Systemic Arterial Hypertension. Milton Mendlowitz. (Illus.). 208p. 1974. 16.75 (ISBN 0-398-02884-2). C C Thomas.

Systemic Aspects of Biocompatibility. Ed. by D. F. Williams. 1981. Vol. 1. 69.95 (ISBN 0-8493-5585-0); Vol. 2. 59.95 (ISBN 0-8493-5589-3). CRC Pr.

Systemic Effects of Skin Disease. Sam Shuster & Janet Marks. (Illus.). 1969. 16.50x (ISBN 0-685-83926-5). Intl Ideas.

Systemic Fungicides. 2nd ed. Ed. by R. W. Marsh. LC 76-49542. (Illus.). 1977. text ed. 40.00x (ISBN 0-582-44167-6). Longman.

Systemic Fungicides. Ed. by R. W. Marsh. LC 72-4058. 1972. pap. 21.95 (ISBN 0-470-57250-7). Halsted Pr.

Systemic Manifestations of Inflammatory Bowel Disease. Ed. by William M. Lukash & Raymond B. Johnson. (Illus.). 368p. 1975. 21.75 (ISBN 0-398-03242-4). C C Thomas.

Systemic Mycoses: Deep Seated. Ed. by C. Terrence Dolan. (Atlases of Clinical Mycology: 2). (Illus.). 1975. text & slides 78.00 (ISBN 0-89189-040-8, 15-7-003-00); microfiche ed. 22.00 (ISBN 0-89189-089-0, 17-7-003-00). Am Soc Clinical.

Systemic Mycoses: Opportunistic Pathogens. Ed. by C. Terrence Dolan. (Atlases of Clinical Mycology: 3). 1975. text & slides 78.00 (ISBN 0-89189-041-6, 15-7-004-00); microfiche ed. 22.00 (ISBN 0-89189-089-0, 17-7-004-00). Am Soc Clinical.

Systemic Mycoses: Saprobic Fungi. Ed. by C. Terrence Dolan. (Atlases of Clinical Mycology: 6). (Illus.). 1976. text & slides 78.00 (ISBN 0-89189-044-0, 15-7-010-00); microfiche ed. 22.00 (ISBN 0-89189-092-0, 17-7-010-00). Am Soc Clinical.

Systemic Mycoses: Yeasts. Ed. by C. Terrence Dolan. (Atlases of Clinical Mycology: 1). (Illus.). 1975. text & slides 78.00 (ISBN 0-89189-039-4, 15-7-002-00); microfiche ed. 22.00 (ISBN 0-89189-087-4, 17-7-002-00). Am Soc Clinical.

Systemic Pathology, Vol. 6. 2nd ed. W. St. C. Symmers. LC 75-3574. 1980. 85.00x (ISBN 0-443-01831-6). Churchill.

Systems Analysis. Ed. by Alan Daniels & Donald Yeates. (Illus.). 1971. text ed. 14.95 (ISBN 0-574-17885-6, 13-0885); instr's guide avail. (ISBN 0-574-17886-4, 13-0886). SRA.

Systems Analysis: A Computer Approach to Decision Models. 3rd ed. Claude McMillan & Richard F. Gonzalez. 1973. text ed. 19.00 (ISBN 0-256-01439-6). Irwin.

Systems Analysis & Computing. D. Hatter & J. Eaton. 1974. 14.95 o.p. (ISBN 0-236-30898-X, Pub. by Paul Elek); pap. 7.95x o.p. (ISBN 0-236-31099-2). Merrimack Bk Serv.

Systems Analysis & Design. Elias M. Awad. 1979. 17.95x (ISBN 0-256-02091-4). Irwin.

Systems Analysis & Design. Marjorie Leeson. 464p. 1980. text ed. 14.95 (ISBN 0-574-21279-5, 13-4285); instr's guide avail. (ISBN 0-574-21286-8, 13-4286); write for info. transparency masters (ISBN 0-574-21287-6, 13-4287). SRA.

Systems Analysis & Design in Engineering, Architecture, Construction, & Planning. Rodolfo J. Aguilar. (Civil Engineering & Engineering Mechanics Ser). (Illus.). 448p. 1973. ref. ed. 25.95 (ISBN 0-13-881458-9). P-H.

Systems Analysis & Design of Real-Time Management Information Systems. Robert J. Thierauf. LC 74-28368. (Illus.). 624p. 1975. ref. ed. 21.95 (ISBN 0-13-881219-5). P-H.

Systems Analysis & Operations Management. Richard Hopeman. LC 69-19269. 1969. text ed. 15.95 (ISBN 0-675-09514-X). Merrill.

Systems Analysis & Simulation in Ecology, 3 vols. Ed. by Bernard C. Patten. Vol. 1. 1971. 52.75 ea. (ISBN 0-12-547201-3). Vol. 1, 1971. Vol. 2, 1972 (ISBN 0-12-547202-1). Vol. 3, 1975. Acad Pr.

Systems Analysis & Social Planning. Robert Boguslaw. 1981. text ed. 18.50x (ISBN 0-8290-0111-5). Irvington.

Systems Analysis: Definition Process & Design. Philip C. Semprevivo. LC 75-30539. (Illus.). 352p. 1976. text ed. 16.95 (ISBN 0-574-21045-8, 13-4045); instr's guide avail. (ISBN 0-574-21046-6, 13-4046). SRA.

Systems Analysis for Business Data Processing. 3rd ed. H. D. Clifton. 242p. 1978. text ed. 30.75x (ISBN 0-220-66369-6, Pub. by Busn Bks England). Renouf.

Systems Analysis for Business Management. 3rd ed. Stanford L. Optner. (Illus.). 400p. 1974. ref. ed. 17.95 (ISBN 0-13-881276-4). P-H.

Systems Analysis for Data Transmission. James Martin. (Automatic Computation Ser). 1972. ref. ed. 39.95 (ISBN 0-13-881300-0). P-H.

Systems Analysis for Managerial Decisions: A Computer Approach. P. Ramalingam. LC 76-10534. 1976. 29.95 (ISBN 0-471-70710-4). Wiley.

Systems Analysis for Social Scientists. F. Cortes et al. LC 73-23061. 1974. 29.95 (ISBN 0-471-17509-9, Pub. by Wiley-Interscience). Wiley.

Systems Analysis for the Food Industry. Filmore Bender et al. (Illus.). 1976. pap. text ed. 24.50 (ISBN 0-87055-306-2). AVI.

Systems Analysis in Health Care. Ed. by Vijay Mahajan & C. Carl Pegels. 1979. 34.50 (ISBN 0-03-046656-3). Praeger.

Systems Analysis in Health-Care Delivery. Arnold Reisman. LC 79-3907. 336p. 1979. 24.95 (ISBN 0-669-02855-X). Lexington Bks.

Systems Analysis in Libraries: A Question & Answer Approach. Chester R. Gough & Taverekere Srikantaiah. 1980. pap. cancelled o.p. (ISBN 0-85157-278-2). K G Saur.

Systems Analysis in Public Policy: A Critique. Ida R. Hoos. LC 79-170723. (Institute of Governmental Studies). 300p. 1972. 18.50x (ISBN 0-520-02105-3); pap. 6.95x (ISBN 0-520-02609-8). U of Cal Pr.

Systems Analysis of International Crises. Richard S. Beal. LC 79-66860. 1979. text ed. 19.75 (ISBN 0-8191-0858-8); pap. text ed. 13.75 (ISBN 0-8191-0859-6). U Pr of Amer.

Systems Analysis of the Logic of Research & Information Processes. Werner Kunz & Horst Rittel. 74p. 1977. text ed. 13.00 (ISBN 3-7940-3455-4, Pub. by K G Saur). Shoe String.

Systems Analysis of the New York City Home Attendant Program: With Recommendations for a Home Care Service Delivery System. 1977. 4.00 (ISBN 0-86671-040-X). Comm Coun Great NY.

Systems Analyst: How to Design Computer-Based Systems. Jerry W. Atwood. 1977. text ed. 13.25x (ISBN 0-8104-5102-6). Hayden.

Systems & Procedures: A Handbook for Business & Industry. 2nd ed. Victor Lazzaro. 1968. text ed. 25.95 (ISBN 0-13-881425-2). P-H.

Systems & Procedures Including Office Management Information Sources. Ed. by Chester Morrill, Jr. LC 67-31261. (Management Information Ser.: No. 12). 1967. 30.00 (ISBN 0-8103-0812-6). Gale.

Systems Approach for Development: Proceedings. IFAC Conference, Cairo, A.R.E., November 1977. (International Federation of Automatic Control(IFAC). Proceedings). 1979. text ed. 125.00 (ISBN 0-08-022017-7). Pergamon.

Systems Approach to Learning Environents. Suleiman Zalatimo & Phillip Sleeman. 1975. pap. 12.40 (ISBN 0-913178-68-3). Redgrave Pub Co.

Systems Approach to Library Program Development. Robert L. Goldberg. LC 76-18157. 1976. 10.00 (ISBN 0-8108-0944-3). Scarecrow.

Systems-Based Independent Audits. 2nd ed. Howard F. Stettler. 1974. 21.95 (ISBN 0-13-881375-2). P-H.

Systems: Decomposition, Optimisation & Control. M. G. Singh & A. Titli. 1978. text ed. 90.00 (ISBN 0-08-022150-5); pap. text ed. 28.00 (ISBN 0-08-023238-8). Pergamon.

Systems Development in Adult Language Learning. J. L. Trim et al. LC 79-42775. (Council of Europe Language Learning Series). (Illus.). 150p. 1980. pap. 9.50 (ISBN 0-08-024586-2). Pergamon.

Systems Drafting. Fred A. Stitt. (Illus.). 1980. 19.95 (ISBN 0-07-061550-0). McGraw.

Systems Engineering & Management. David B. Smith & George Rowland. (Advances in Modern Engineering Ser). (Illus.). 150p. 1974. pap. text ed. 8.95 (ISBN 0-201-07079-0). A-W.

Systems Engineering Methods. Harold Chestnut. LC 67-17336. (System Engineering & Analysis Ser.). 1967. 29.50 o.p. (ISBN 0-471-15448-2, Pub. by Wiley-Interscience). Wiley.

Systems Engineering Tools. Harold Chestnut. LC 65-19484. (System Engineering & Analysis Ser.). 1965. 39.50 o.p. (ISBN 0-471-15446-6, Pub. by Wiley-Interscience). Wiley.

Systems Far from Equilibrium: Sitges Conference. Ed. by L. Garrido. (Lecture Notes in Physics Ser.: Vol. 132). 403p. 1981. pap. 27.70 (ISBN 0-387-10251-5). Springer Verlag.

Systems Management of Operations. Martin K. Starr. (Illus.). 1971. ref. ed. 18.95 (ISBN 0-13-881524-0). P-H.

Systems of Cities: Readings on Structure Growth & Policy. Ed. by Larry S. Bourne & James W. Simmons. (Illus.). 1978. pap. text ed. 10.95x (ISBN 0-19-502264-5). Oxford U Pr.

Systems of Demographic Measurement the Dual Record System. Robert J. Myers. LC 77-71086. (Scientific Report Ser.: No. 26). (Illus.). 1976. pap. text ed. 3.50 (ISBN 0-89383-032-1). Intl Program Labs.

Systems of Equality & Inequality in Human Society. Ed. by Morton H. Reied. 240p. 1981. 20.95 (ISBN 0-89789-012-4). J F Bergin.

Systems of Frequency Curves. W. P. Elderton & N. L. Johnson. LC 69-10571. Orig. Title: Frequency Curves & Correlation. (Illus.). 1969. 32.95 (ISBN 0-521-07369-3). Cambridge U Pr.

Systems of Health Care. Douglas R. MacKintosh. LC 78-3134. (Illus.). 1978. lib. bdg. 27.50x (ISBN 0-89158-330-0); pap. text ed. 13.50x (ISBN 0-89158-818-3). Westview.

Systems of Higher Education: Canada. Edward Sheffield et al. 1978. pap. 8.00 o.s.i. (ISBN 0-89192-204-0). Interbk Inc.

Systems of Higher Education: Federal Republic of Germany. Hansgert Peisert. (Design & Management of Systems of Higher Education Ser.). 240p. (Orig.). 1978. pap. text ed. 8.00 (ISBN 0-89192-206-7). Interbk Inc.

Systems of Higher Education: France. Alain Bienayme. 144p. 1978. pap. 7.00 (ISBN 0-89192-205-9). Interbk Inc.

Systems of Higher Education: Iran. M. Reza Vaghefi et al. 43p. 1978. pap. 3.50 (ISBN 0-89192-207-5). Interbk Inc.

Systems of Higher Education: Japan. Katsuya Narita. (Design & Management of Systems of Higher Education Ser.). 154p. (Orig.). 1978. pap. text ed. 5.50 (ISBN 0-89192-202-4). Interbk Inc.

Systems of Higher Education: Poland. Jan Szczepanski. 1978. pap. 5.00 o.p. (ISBN 0-89192-208-3). Interbk Inc.

Systems of Individualized Education. Ed. by Harriet Talmage. LC 74-24478. 200p. 1975. 16.00x (ISBN 0-8211-1904-4); text ed. 14.50x (ISBN 0-685-51465-X). McCutchan.

Systems of Minerology, 3 vols. 7th ed. J. D. Dana et al. Incl. Vol. 1. Elements, Sulfides, Sulfosalts, Oxides. 1944. 46.50 (ISBN 0-471-19239-2); Vol. 2. Halides, Nitrates, Borates, Carbonates, Sulfates, Phosphates, Arsenates, Tungstates, Molybdates. 1951. 42.95 (ISBN 0-471-19272-4); Vol. 3. Silica Minerals. 1962. 23.95 (ISBN 0-471-19287-2). Pub. by Wiley-Interscience). Wiley.

Systems of Order & Inquiry in Later Eighteenth-Century Fiction. Eric Rothstein. LC 74-16716. 284p. 1975. 17.50x (ISBN 0-520-02862-7). U of Cal Pr.

Systems of Ordinary Differential Equations: An Introduction. Jack L. Goldberg & Arthur J. Schwartz. (Herstein-Rota Ser). 1972. text ed. 20.50 o.p. (ISBN 0-06-042384-6, HarpC). Harrow.

Systems of Psychotherapy: A Comparative Study. Donald H. Ford & Hugh B. Urban. LC 63-20630. 1963. 35.95 (ISBN 0-471-26580-2). Wiley.

Systems of Psychotherapy: A Transtheoretical Analysis. James O. Prochaska. 1979. 17.95x (ISBN 0-256-02064-7). Dorsey.

Systems of States. Martin Wight. Intro. by Hedley Bull. 1977. text ed. 18.25x (ISBN 0-7185-1153-0, Leicester). Humanities.

Systems of Therapy in Cerebral Palsy. Harriet E. Gillette. (American Lecture in Cerebral Palsy Ser.). (Illus.). 96p. 1974. text ed. 9.75 (ISBN 0-398-00680-6). C C Thomas.

Systems of Treatment for the Mentally Ill: Filling the Gaps. Richard E. Gordon & Katherine Gordon. 1981. price not set (ISBN 0-8089-1338-7). Grune.

Systems Physiology. Samuel A. Talbot & Urs Gessner. LC 72-10536. (Biomedical Engineering Ser.). 528p. 1973. 43.00 o.p. (ISBN 0-471-84415-2, Pub. by Wiley-Interscience). Wiley.

Systems Selling Strategies: How to Justify Premium Prices for Commodity Products. Mack Hanan et al. 1978. 14.95 (ISBN 0-8144-5460-7). Am Mgmt.

Systems Simulation. Albert M. Colella et al. LC 73-11645. 288p. 1974. 21.50 (ISBN 0-669-90308-6). Lexington Bks.

Systems Simulation in Agriculture. J. B. Dent & M. J. Blackie. (Illus.). 1979. 29.90x (ISBN 0-85334-827-8, Pub. by Applied Science). Burgess-Intl Ideas.

Systems Simulation: The Art & Science. Robert E. Shannon. (Illus.). 368p. 1975. ref. ed. 19.95 (ISBN 0-13-881839-8). P-H.

Systems, States, Diplomacy & Rules. John W. Burton. 256p. 1968. 28.95 (ISBN 0-521-07316-2). Cambridge U Pr.

Systems Theory & Regional Integration: The "Market Model" of International Politics. James P. O'Leary. LC 78-66420. 1978. pap. text ed. 10.25 (ISBN 0-8191-0500-7). U Pr of Amer.

Systems Theory for Organization Development. Ed. by Thomas G. Cummings. LC 79-42906. (Individuals, Groups & Organizations Ser.). 384p. 1980. 49.00 (ISBN 0-471-27691-X, Pub. by Wiley-Interscience). Wiley.

Systems Theory in Immunology. Ed. by C. Bruni. (Lecture Notes in Biomathematics: Vol. 32). 273p. 1980. pap. 16.00 (ISBN 0-387-09728-7). Springer-Verlag.

Systems Thinking, Systems Practice. P. B. Checkland. 320p. 1981. 31.95 (ISBN 0-471-27911-0, Pub. by Wiley-Interscience). Wiley.

Systems View of Man: Collected Essays by Ludwig Von Bertalanffy. Ludwig Von Bertalanffy. Ed. by Paul LaViolette. 190p. 1981. lib. bdg. 16.00 (ISBN 0-86531-084-X); pap. 7.95 (ISBN 0-86531-094-7). Westview.

Systems View of the World. Ervin Laszlo. LC 71-188357. 1972. 7.95 (ISBN 0-8076-0637-5); pap. 3.95 (ISBN 0-8076-0636-7). Braziller.

Systolic Time Intervals. Ed. by W. List et al. (International Boehringer Mannheim Symposia). (Illus.). 300p. 1980. pap. 31.90 (ISBN 0-387-09871-2). Springer-Verlag.

Szczecin-Stettin: Yesterday, Today & Tomorrow. Henryk Maka. Tr. by Susan Brice-Wojciechowska from Polish. LC 79-320867. (Illus.). 1979. 13.50x (ISBN 0-8002-2288-1). Intl Pubns Serv.

Szenische Darstellung der Opern G. F. Haendels Auf der Londoner Buhne Seiner Zeit, 2 vols. in 1. Joachim Eisenschmitt. LC 80-2275. 1981. Repr. of 1940 ed. 29.50 (ISBN 0-404-18843-5). AMS Pr.

Szivarvany, No. 2. 1980. 6.50 (ISBN 0-936398-02-7). Framo Pub.

Szivarvany, No. 3. 1981. 6.50 (ISBN 0-936398-03-5). Framo Pub.

Szivarvany, No. 4. 1981. 6.50 (ISBN 0-936398-04-3). Framo Pub.

Szivarvany (Rainbow, No. 1. Ed. by F. Mozsi. (Illus.). 96p. (Orig.). 1980. pap. 6.50 (ISBN 0-936398-00-0). Framo Pub.

T

T. A. Games: Using Transactional Analysis in Your Life. Adelaide Bry. LC 74-10066. (Illus., Orig.). 1975. pap. 1.50 o.p. (ISBN 0-06-080334-7, P334, PL). Har-Row.

T & B Lymphocytes: Recognition & Function: Symposium, Vol. XVI. ICN-UCLA Symposia on Molecular & Cellular Biology, 1979. Ed. by Fritz H. Bach et al. LC 79-26438. 1979. 39.50 (ISBN 0-12-069850-1). Acad Pr.

T-Boy in Mossland. Timothy Edler. (Tim Edler's Tales from the Atchafalaya). (Illus.). (gr. k-8). 1978. leather 5.00 (ISBN 0-931108-03-9). Little Cajun.

T-Boy the Little Cajun. Timothy Edler. (Tim Edler's Tales from the Atchafalaya). (Illus.). (gr. k-8). 1978. leather 5.00 (ISBN 0-931108-01-2). Little Cajun.

T. E. Brown. Richard Tobias. (English Authors Ser.: No. 213). 1978. 12.50 (ISBN 0-8057-6682-0). Twayne.

T. E. Lawrence. Stephen E. Tabachnick. (English Authors Ser.: No. 233). 1978. lib. bdg. 10.95 (ISBN 0-8057-6704-5). Twayne.

T Factor. Mark L. Stein. 192p. 1981. pap. 2.25 o.p. (ISBN 0-87216-761-5). Playboy Pbks.

T Factor: How to Make Time Work for You. Mark L Stein. LC 76-17275. 1977. pap. 2.25 (ISBN 0-87216-761-5). Playboy Pbks.

T-Group Theory & Laboratory Method: Innovation in Re-Education. Ed. by Leland P. Bradford et al. LC 64-11499. 1964. 26.50 (ISBN 0-471-09510-9). Wiley.

T-Groups & Therapy Groups in a Changing Society. Dee G. Appley & Alvin E. Winder. LC 73-10934. (Social & Behavioral Science Ser.). 224p. 1973. 14.95x o.p. (ISBN 0-87589-201-9). Jossey-Bass.

T. H. Huxley: Man's Place in Nature. James G. Paradis. LC 78-5492. 1978. 16.50x (ISBN 0-8032-0917-7). U of Nebr Pr.

T. H. White. John K. Crane. LC 74-4121. (English Authors Ser.: No. 172). 1974. lib. bdg. 10.95 (ISBN 0-8057-1573-8). Twayne.

T. J. Folger, Thief. Steven Kroll. (gr. k-6). Date not set. pap. price not set (ISBN 0-440-48668-8, YB). Dell.

T. Lucreti Cari De Rerum Natura Libri Sex, 3 vols. 4th ed. H. A. Munro. LC 77-70833. (Latin Poetry Ser.: Vol. 8). 1978. Repr. of 1886 ed. Set. lib. bdg. 97.00 (ISBN 0-8240-2957-7). Garland Pub.

T. S. Eliot. Bernard Bergonzi. (Masters of World Literature). 1972. 6.95 o.s.i. (ISBN 0-02-509960-4). Macmillan.

T. S. Eliot. Bernard Bergonzi. Ed. by Ray Roberts. 1972. pap. 2.95 o.s.i. (ISBN 0-02-048580-8, Collier). Macmillan.

T. S. Eliot. M. C. Bradbrook. Ed. by Bonamy Dobree et al. Bd. with W. H. Auden. Richard Hoggart; Dylan Thomas. G. S. Fraser. LC 64-17226. (British Writers & Their Work Ser: Vol. 5). 1965. pap. 2.95x (ISBN 0-8032-5655-8, BB 454, Bison). U of Nebr Pr.

T. S. Eliot. Philip R. Headings. (U. S. Authors Ser.: No. 57). 1964. lib. bdg. 10.95 (ISBN 0-8057-0236-9). Twayne.

T. S. Eliot. T. S. Pearce. LC 69-16155. (Literary Critiques Ser.). (Illus.). 1969. Repr. lib. bdg. 4.95 o.p. (ISBN 0-668-01883-6). Arco.

T. S. Eliot. Joachim Seyppel. LC 75-143187. (Modern Literature Ser.). 1971. 10.95 (ISBN 0-8044-2818-2). Ungar.

T. S. Eliot: A Bibliography. Donald Gallup. 19.95 (ISBN 0-571-08928-3, Pub. by Faber & Faber). Merrimack Bk Serv.

T. S. Eliot Als Kritiker. Elizabeth Baun. (Salzburg Studies in Elizabethan Literature: Poetic Drama Ser.: No. 58). 1980. pap. text ed. 25.00x (ISBN 0-391-01906-6). Humanities.

T. S. Eliot & the Human Predicament. Audrey F. Cahill. 1967. 7.50x o.p. (ISBN 0-8426-1187-8). Verry.

T. S. Eliot & the Romantic Critical Tradition. Edward Lobb. 208p. 1981. 20.00 (ISBN 0-7100-0636-5). Routledge & Kegan.

T. S. Eliot: Homage from India. P. Lal. 12.00 (ISBN 0-88253-300-2). Ind-US Inc.

T. S. Eliot: The Pattern in the Carpet. Elizabeth W. Schneider. LC 73-90655. 1975. 16.50x (ISBN 0-520-02648-9). U of Cal Pr.

T. S. Eliot: The Wasteland. Ed. by C. B. Cox & Arnold P. Hinchliffe. (Casebook Ser.). 1970. 2.50 o.s.i. (ISBN 0-87695-040-3). Aurora Pubs.

T. S. Eliot's Theory of Poetry. Rajnath. 1980. text ed. 12.50x (ISBN 0-391-01755-1). Humanities.

T. S. Stribling. Wilton Eckley. LC 75-1096. (U. S. Authors Ser.: No. 255). 1975. lib. bdg. 10.95 (ISBN 0-8057-7151-4). Twayne.

T. V. A. & the Grass Roots: A Study in the Sociology of Formal Organization. Philip Selznick. (California Library Reprint Ser.: No. 103). 1980. 18.50x (ISBN 0-520-03979-3). U of Cal Pr.

T. V. A. Lessons for International Application. Herman Finer. LC 77-172008. (FDR & the Era of the New Deal Ser.). (Illus.). 1972. Repr. of 1944 ed. lib. bdg. 29.50 (ISBN 0-306-70378-5). Da Capo.

T V Studio. Judy Lever. LC 78-61232. (Careers Ser.). (Illus.). 1979. lib. bdg. 7.95 (ISBN 0-686-50004-0). Silver.

TA & the Manager. Dudley Bennett. (AMACOM Executive Bks). 1978. pap. 5.95 (ISBN 0-8144-7511-6). Am Mgmt.

TA & the Manager. Dudley Bennett. (Illus.). 1976. 13.95 (ISBN 0-8144-5422-4). Am Mgmt.

TA & Training: The Theory & Use of Transactional Analysis. Dave Barker. 226p. 1980. text ed. 29.50x (ISBN 0-566-02118-8, Pub. by Gower Pub Co England). Renouf.

TA for Tots (and Other Prinzes) Alvyn Freed. LC 76-19650. (Transactional Analysis for Everybody Ser.). (Illus.). 256p. (Orig.). 1973. buckram 11.95 o.p. (ISBN 0-915190-11-7). Jalmar Pr.

TA for Tots (and Other Prinzes) Alvyn M. Freed. LC 76-19650. (Transactional Analysis for Everybody Ser.). (Illus.). (ps-3). 1973. pap. 7.95 (ISBN 0-915190-12-5). Jalmar Pr.

TA for Tots Coloring Book. Alvyn M. Freed. (Transactional Analysis for Everybody Ser.). 1976. pap. 1.95 (ISBN 0-915190-33-8); spirit masters 3.95. Jalmar Pr.

TA on the Job. Charles Albano. 1976. pap. 2.95 (ISBN 0-06-080385-1, P385, PL). Har-Row.

TA Stories for Kids. Ken Ernst. LC 77-79880. (Illus.). (gr. k-8). 1977. pap. 3.95 o.p. (ISBN 0-89087-208-2). Celestial Arts.

TA: The Total Handbook of Transcendental Analysis. Michael Brown & Stan Woolams. (Illus.). 1979. 15.95 (ISBN 0-13-881920-3, Spec); pap. 6.95 (ISBN 0-13-881912-2). P-H.

Tabernacle, God's Dwelling Place. Dean Guest. 64p. (Orig.). Date not set. pap. 1.95 (ISBN 0-89841-012-6). Zoe Pubns.

Tabernacle, Priesthood & the Offerings. Enlarged type ed. Henry W. Soltau. LC 72-88590. 1974. 9.95 (ISBN 0-8254-3703-2). Kregel.

Tabernacle Types & Teaching. Edward Laity. 1980. pap. 1.25 (ISBN 0-86544-011-5). Salvation Army.

Tabernaculo. Tr. by E. F. Blattner. (Spanish Bks.). 1977. 0.75 (ISBN 0-8297-0601-1). Life Pubs Intl.

Taber's Cyclopedic Medical Dictionary. 14th ed. Ed. by Clayton L. Thomas. (Illus.). 1796p. 1981. text ed. write for info. (ISBN 0-8036-8307-3); Thumb-indexed Edition. text ed. write for info. (ISBN 0-8036-8306-5). Davis Co.

Table Games. Ray J. Marran. LC 75-22567. (Illus.). 160p. 1976. 7.95 o.p. (ISBN 0-498-01829-6). A S Barnes.

Table of Integrals. Ralph G. Hudson. 1917. pap. text ed. 8.50 (ISBN 0-471-41877-3, Pub. by Wiley-Interscience). Wiley.

Table of Integrals, Series & Products. I. S. Gradshteyn & I. M. Ryshik. 1966. 21.50 o.p. (ISBN 0-12-294750-9). Acad Pr.

Table of Laser Lines in Gases & Vapors. R. Beck et al. (Springer Series in Optical Sciences: Vol. 2). 1976. 21.70 o.p. (ISBN 3-540-07808-8). Springer-Verlag.

Table of Laser Lines in Gases & Vapors. 3rd rev. & enl. ed. (Springer Ser. in Optical Sciences: Vol. 2). 36.00 (ISBN 0-387-10347-3). Springer Verlag.

Table of Series & Products. Eldon R. Hansen. 544p. 1975. ref. ed. 76.00 (ISBN 0-13-881938-6). P-H.

Table Prayers for Children. new ed. Walter L. Cook. (Illus.). (gr. k-4). 1977. pap. 1.50 (ISBN 0-8272-3621-2). Bethany Pr.

Table Setting Teachers Manual. Sharon Dlugosch. 1980. 7.00 (ISBN 0-918420-02-4). Brighton Pubns.

Table-Talk. large type ed. John Selden. Ed. by Edward Arber. 1972. Repr. of 1869 ed. 7.50x (ISBN 0-87556-314-7). Saifer.

Table Tennis. Harold Myers. (Illus.). 1977. pap. 4.95 (ISBN 0-571-11001-0, Pub. by Faber & Faber). Merrimack Bk Serv.

Table Tennis. Martin Sklorz. (Sports Library). (Illus.). 1979. 12.95 (ISBN 0-8069-9148-8); pap. 6.95 (ISBN 0-8069-9150-X). Sterling.

Tableau de la Population de la France. Louis Brion de Latour. (Principal French Demographic Works of the 18th Century Ser.). (Illus., Fr.). 1977. lib. bdg. 22.50x o.p. (ISBN 0-8287-0140-7); pap. text ed. 12.50x o.p. (ISBN 0-685-75759-5). Clearwater Pub.

Tableau de la Population de la France, 8 Janvier 1780. Abbe Jean-Joseph Expilly. (Principal French Demographic Works of the 18th Century Ser.). (Fr.). 1977. lib. bdg. 32.50x o.p. (ISBN 0-8287-0322-1); pap. text ed. 22.50x o.p. (ISBN 0-685-75757-9). Clearwater Pub.

Tableau De la Population De Toutes les Provinces De France. Chevaliers Des Pommelles. (Principal French Demographic Works of the 18th Century Ser.). (Fr.). 1976. lib. bdg. 32.00x o.p. (ISBN 0-8287-0270-5); pap. text ed. 22.00x o.p. (ISBN 0-685-71499-3). Clearwater Pub.

Tableaux Du Temple Des Muses, Repr. Of 1655 Ed. Michel de Marolles. Bd. with Iconologia or Moral Problems. Cesare Ripa. Repr. of 1709 ed. LC 75-27876. (Renaissance & the Gods Ser.: Vol. 31). (Illus.). 1976. lib. bdg. 73.00 (ISBN 0-8240-2080-4). Garland Pub.

Tables & Chairs: Easy to Make. Sunset Editors. LC 75-26492. (Illus.). 80p. 1976. pap. 3.95 (ISBN 0-376-01653-1, Sunset Bks.). Sunset-Lane.

Tables for Determination of Common Minerals & Rocks. 4th rev. ed. W. A. Tarr. 1951. text ed. 0.95x spiral bdg. (ISBN 0-87543-045-7). Lucas.

Tables for Statisticians. 2nd ed. Herbert Arkin & Raymond R. Colton. (Illus.). 168p. 1963. pap. 2.95 (ISBN 0-06-460075-0, CO 75, COS). Har-Row.

Tables of Co-efficients for the Analysis of Triple Angular Correlations of Gamma-Rays from Aligned Nuclei. G. Kaye et al. 1968. 42.00 (ISBN 0-08-012260-4). Pergamon.

Tables of Experimental Dipole Moments. A. L. McClellan. LC 63-14844. 1963. text ed. 32.95x (ISBN 0-7167-0122-7). W H Freeman.

Tables of Functions with Formulae & Curves. 4th ed. Eugene Jahnke & Fritz Emde. (Ger & Eng). 1945. pap. text ed. 5.00 (ISBN 0-486-60133-1). Dover.

Tables of Indefinite Integrals. G. Petit Bois. 1906. pap. text ed. 5.00 (ISBN 0-486-60225-7). Dover.

Tables of La Place Transforms. William D. Day. 2.50 (ISBN 0-685-20639-4). Transatlantic.

Tables of Nuclear Quadruple Resonance Frequencies. I. P. Biryukov & M. G. Voroknov. LC 70-15351. 1972. 17.50 o.p. (ISBN 0-470-07549-X). Halsted Pr.

Tables of Physical & Chemical Constants. 14th rev. ed. G. W. Kaye & T. H. Laby. Ed. by A. E. Bailey et al. LC 73-85205. (Illus.). 320p. 1973. text ed. 22.00x (ISBN 0-582-46326-2). Longman.

Tables of the Incomplete Beta-Function. K. Pearson. 505p. 1968. 60.00x (ISBN 0-85264-704-2, Pub. by England Griffin). State Mutual Bk.

Tables of the Incomplete Gamma-Function. K. Pearson. 164p. 1965. 30.00x (ISBN 0-85264-703-4, Pub. by Griffin England). State Mutual Bk.

Tables of Thermodynamic Data. (Technical Reports: No. 38). 1964. pap. 4.50 (ISBN 92-0-145264-0, IAEA). Unipub.

Tables of Trigonometric Functions for the Numerical Computation of Electron Density in Crystals. I. M. Kuntsevich & A. V. Sheleg. 1967. 22.95 (ISBN 0-470-51090-0). Halsted Pr.

Tables on the Thermophysical Properties of Liquids & Gases: In Normal & Dissociated States. 2nd ed. N. B. Vargaftik. LC 75-14260. (Advances in Thermal Engineering Ser.). 758p. 1975. 49.50 (ISBN 0-470-90310-4). Halsted Pr.

Tableservice Techniques. Bruce H. Axler. 1974. pap. 3.95 (ISBN 0-672-96116-4). Bobbs.

Tablet Weaving. Ann Sutton & Pat Holtom. LC 74-18323. (Illus.). 104p. 1975. 11.50 (ISBN 0-8231-5045-3). Branford.

Tabletop the Right Way: An Information & Training Guide for the Professional in the Hospitality Industry. rev ed. Edith Gilbert. LC 80-81206. (Illus.). 54p. 1980. 15.00x (ISBN 0-9600786-4-9). Jet'iquette.

Tablets of Baha'u'llah Revealed After the Kitab-i-Aqdas. Baha'u'llah. Tr. by Shoghi Effendi & Habib Taherzadeh. LC 79-670079. 1978. 9.00 (ISBN 0-85398-077-2, 7-03-21, Pub. by Universal Hse. of Justice). Baha'i.

Tablets of the Divine Plan. rev. ed. Abdu'l-Baha. LC 76-10624. 1977. 10.00 (ISBN 0-87743-107-8, 7-06-09). Baha'i.

Tablets of the Divine Plan. rev ed. Abdu'L-Baha. 1980. pap. 4.00 (ISBN 0-87743-154-X, 7-06-11). Baha'i.

Taboos in Criminology. Ed. by Edward Sagarin. LC 80-18175. (Sage Research Progress Ser. in Criminology: Vol. 15). 152p. 1980. 12.95 (ISBN 0-8039-1513-6); pap. 6.50 (ISBN 0-8039-1514-4). Sage.

Tachometric Tables for the Metric User. D. T. Munsey. 1971. 14.95x (ISBN 0-291-39336-5). Intl Ideas.

Tacit Dimension. Michael Polanyi. LC 66-21015. 1967. pap. 2.50 (ISBN 0-385-06988-X, A540, Anch). Doubleday.

Tacitus, 2 vols. Ronald Syme. 874p. 1980. 55.00 (ISBN 0-19-814327-3). Oxford U Pr.

Tack Now, Skipper. Owen Parker. 1979. 18.95x (ISBN 0-8464-0065-0). Beekman Pubs.

Tackle Box Fishing Guide. Philip Barnard. LC 78-69685. (Illus.). 128p. 1981. 7.95 (ISBN 0-498-02254-4). A S Barnes.

Tackling Problems, Pt. 1. Margaret Collis. LC 77-83014. (Using the Environment Ser.). (Illus.). 1977. pap. text ed. 9.30 (ISBN 0-356-04356-8). Raintree Child.

Tackling Problems, Pt. 2. Margaret Collis. LC 77-83014. (Using the Environment Ser.). (Illus.). 1977. pap. text ed. 9.30 (ISBN 0-356-05000-9). Raintree Child.

Tackling, Running, & Kicking--Now & Again. Gary Paulsen. LC 77-7786. (Sports on the Light Side Ser.). (Illus.). (gr. 3-6). 1977. PLB 9.65 (ISBN 0-8172-0966-2). Raintree Pubs.

Tactical Nuclear Weapons: An Examination of the Issues. W. R. Van Cleave & S. T. Cohen. LC 77-83272. 1978. 14.50x (ISBN 0-8448-1260-9). Crane-Russak Co.

Tacticks of Aelign, or Art of Embattailing an Army. Tacitus Aelinanus. Tr. by J. Bingham. LC 68-54606. (English Experience Ser.: No. 14). (Illus.). Repr. of 1616 ed. 42.00 (ISBN 90-221-0014-6). Walter J Johnson.

Tactics in Women's Singles, Doubles & Mixed Doubles. Rex Lardner. LC 74-12731. 125p. 1975. 4.95a o.p. (ISBN 0-385-09044-7); pap. 2.50 o.p. (ISBN 0-385-06733-X). Doubleday.

Tactics of Mistake. Gordon R. Dickson. (Science Fiction Ser.). 256p. 1972. pap. 1.95 (ISBN 0-87997-521-0, U51534). DAW Bks.

Tactics of Resignation: A Study in British Cabinet Government. R. K. Alderman & J. A. Cross. (Library of Political Studies). (Orig.). 1967. text ed. 5.25x (ISBN 0-7100-5130-1); pap. text ed. 2.75x (ISBN 0-7100-5119-0). Humanities.

Tactics of Social Influence. Albert Mehrabian. 1970. pap. text ed. 9.95 (ISBN 0-13-882159-3). P-H.

Tad. Joan Tate. pap. text ed. 1.95x o.p. (ISBN 0-435-11880-3). Heinemann Ed.

Tad Overweight but Violet Eyes to Die for. G. B. Trudeau. 1981. pap. 1.75 (ISBN 0-553-14337-9). Bantam.

Taddeo Alderotti & His Pupils: Two Generations of Italian Medical Learning. Nancy G. Siraisi. LC 80-7554. 488p. 1981. 32.00x (ISBN 0-691-05313-8). Princeton U Pr.

Taffy & Melissa Molasess. Carolyn Haywood. (Illus.). (gr. 1-4). 1969. PLB 7.92 (ISBN 0-688-31690-5). Morrow.

Taft Corporate Foundation Directory. Ed. by Tara McCallum. 1979. pap. 125.00 (ISBN 0-914756-30-3). Taft Corp.

Taft Foundation Reporter: National Edition. Ed. by Tara McCallum. 1980. pap. 150.00 (ISBN 0-914756-44-3). Taft Corp.

Tag. Theodore L. Harris et al. (Keys to Independence in Reading Ser.). (Illus., Orig.). (gr. 1). 1973. text ed. 2.07 (ISBN 0-87892-010-2); tchr's manual 4.38 (ISBN 0-87892-013-7); avail. wkbk. 2.64 (ISBN 0-87892-014-5). Economy Co.

Tagalog-English - English-Tagalog Dictionary. rev. ed. Maria O. Guzman. xxxix, 678p. 1977. pap. 12.50 (ISBN 0-686-68939-9). Heinman.

Tagalog Reference Grammar. Paul Schachter & Fe T. Otanes. LC 73-122946. 1972. pap. 19.50x (ISBN 0-520-01776-5). U of Cal Pr.

Tagalong. M. Ekin. 4.00 o.p. (ISBN 0-8062-1170-9). Carlton.

Tage Frid Teaches Woodworking, Bk. 1-Joinery. Tage Frid. LC 78-65178. (Illus.). 1979. 15.95 (ISBN 0-918804-03-5, Dist. by Van Nostrand Reinhold). Taunton.

Tagemics: Theoretical Discussion Trends in Linguistics, Vol. 2. Ed. by Ruthm M. Brend & Kenneth L. Pike. (Studies & Monographs: No. 2). 1976. pap. 27.05x (ISBN 90-2793-425-8). Mouton.

Tagmemic Comparison of the Structure of English & Vietnamese Sentences. Duong T. Binh. LC 74-123126. (Janua Linguarum, Ser. Practica: No. 110). (Orig.). 1971. pap. text ed. 51.75x (ISBN 90-2791-598-9). Mouton.

Tagore's Last Poems. Rabindranath Tagore. Tr. by P Lal & Shyamashree Devi. (Translated from bengali). 5.00 o.p. (ISBN 0-89253-607-1); flexible cloth 4.00 o.p. (ISBN 0-89253-608-X). InterCulture.

Tahirih the Pure. Martha L. Root. 1980. Repr. of 1938 ed. casebound 6.95 (ISBN 0-933770-14-6). Kalimat.

Tahiti. Hubert Sieben. (Illus.). 1970. bds. 12.00 o.p. (ISBN 0-911268-28-6). Rogers Bk.

Tahltan Indians. G. T. Emmons. (Illus.). 1979. Repr. of 1911 ed. text ed. 17.25x (ISBN 0-391-00957-5). Humanities.

Tahoe. Dorothy Dowdell. LC 77-76126. 1977. pap. 1.95 o.p. (ISBN 0-87216-408-X). Playboy Pbks.

Tahoe Sierra. rev. ed. Jeffrey P. Schaffer. Ed. by Thomas Winnett. LC 78-65937. (Trail Guide Ser). (Illus., Orig.). 1979. pap. 9.95 (ISBN 0-911824-75-8). Wilderness.

Tai-Chi, a Way of Centering. G. Feng & H. Wilkerson. 1969. 6.95 o.s.i. (ISBN 0-02-537290-4). Macmillan.

Tai-Chi: A Way of Centering. G. Feng & H. Wilkerson. 1970. pap. 4.95 o.s.i. (ISBN 0-02-076130-9, Collier). Macmillan.

T'ai Chi Ch'uan & I Ching. Da Liu. 1978. pap. 1.95 o.p. (ISBN 0-06-080452-1, P 452, PL). Har-Row.

Tai-Chi Ch'uan: Its Effects & Practical Applications. Y. K. Chen. LC 80-19810. 184p. 1980. Repr. of 1979 ed. lib. bdg. 10.95x (ISBN 0-89370-643-4). Borgo Pr.

Ta'i Chi Chu'uan & I Ching: A Choreography of Body & Mind. Liu Da. LC 79-183640. (Illus.). 1972. pap. 1.95 o.p. (ISBN 0-06-061667-9, RD-46, HarpR). Har-Row.

Tai Chi for Health. new ed. Edward Maisel. (Illus.). 224p. 1972. 6.95 o.p. (ISBN 0-03-001416-6); tchr's manual 1.00 o.p. (ISBN 0-03-085864-X). HR&W.

Tai Chi Handbook: Exercise, Meditation, Self-Defense. Herman Kauz. LC 73-10552. 192p. 1974. pap. 5.50 (ISBN 0-385-09370-5, Dolp). Doubleday.

Tai Chi: The Supreme Ultimate. Lawrence Galante. 1981. pap. 8.95 (ISBN 0-87728-497-0). Weiser.

Tai-Pan. James Clavell. 1980. pap. 3.25 (ISBN 0-440-18462-2). Dell.

Tail Twisters. Aileen Fisher. (Nature Ser). (gr. k-6). 1973. PLB 6.96 (ISBN 0-8372-0863-7); filmstrip & record 18.00 (ISBN 0-8372-0208-6); filmstrip & cassette 18.00 (ISBN 0-8372-0874-2). Bowmar-Noble.

Taille. Harlan Wade. Tr. by Claude Potvin & Rose-Ella Potvin. (Book About Ser.). Orig. Title: Size. (Illus., Fr.). (gr. k-3). 1979. PLB 7.30 (ISBN 0-8172-1459-3). Raintree Pubs.

Tailor of Gloucester. B. Potter. (Peter Possum Paperbacks Ser). 1967. pap. 0.95 o.p. (ISBN 0-531-05103-X). Watts.

Tailoring Suits the Professional Way. rev. ed. Clarence Poulin. (Illus.). (gr. 9-12). 1973. text ed. 9.20 (ISBN 0-87002-128-1). Bennett IL.

Tailoring the Easy Way. Lucille Milani. (Illus.). 192p. 1976. 11.95x o.p. (ISBN 0-13-882183-6, Spec); pap. 4.95x o.p. (ISBN 0-13-882175-5). P-H.

Tailoring: Traditional & Contemporary Techniques. Linda Thiel & Marie Ledbetter. (Illus.). 384p. 1980. text ed. 18.95 (ISBN 0-8359-7534-7); instrs' manual avail. Reston.

Tails Are Not for Painting. Bernard Wiseman. Tr. by Bernard Wiseman. LC 79-18373. (Bernard Wiseman Bks.). (Illus.). 32p. (gr. k-4). 1980. PLB 5.49 (ISBN 0-8116-6078-8). Garrard.

Tails Up! Ray R. Kepley. LC 80-81060. (Illus.). 466p. 1980. 25.00 (ISBN 0-9604248-0-6). Kepley.

Tails with a Twist: Animal Nonsense Verse. Alfred Douglas. (Illus.). 64p. 1980. 14.95 (ISBN 0-7134-1870-2, Pub. by Batsford England). David & Charles.

Tailypo. Joanna Galdone. LC 77-23289. (ps-4). 1977. 8.95 (ISBN 0-395-28809-6, Clarion). HM.

Tain. Thomas Kinsella. (Illus.). 1970. pap. 8.95x (ISBN 0-19-281090-1, OPB). Oxford U Pr.

Taiping Ideology: Its Sources, Interpretations & Influences. Vincent Y. Shih. LC 66-19571. (Publications on Asia of the School of International Studies: No. 15). 576p. 1967. 16.00 (ISBN 0-295-73957-6, PA115); pap. 4.95 (ISBN 0-295-95243-1). U of Wash Pr.

Taiping Rebel: The Deposition of Li Hsiu-Ch'eng. C. A. Curwen. LC 76-8292. (Cambridge Studies in Chinese History, Literature & Institutions). (Illus.). 1977. 39.95 (ISBN 0-521-21082-8). Cambridge U Pr.

Taiping Rebellion: Documents & Comments. Franz Michael & Chung-Li Chang. Incl. Vol. 2. 756p (ISBN 0-295-73959-2); Vol. 3. 1107p (ISBN 0-295-73958-4). LC 66-13538. (Publications on Asia of the Institute for Foreign & Area Studies: No. 14, Pt. 2). 1971. 30.00 ea. U of Wash Pr.

Taiping Rebellion: History, Vol. 1. Franz Michael & Chung-Li Chang. (Publications on Asia of the Institute for Foreign & Area Studies: No. 14, Pt. 1). 256p. 1966. 10.00 (ISBN 0-295-73958-4); pap. 5.95 (ISBN 0-295-95244-X). U of Wash Pr.

Taittiriya Upanishad. Tr. by Alladi M. Sastry. 93p. 1980. 28.50 (ISBN 0-89744-145-1, Pub. by Samata Bks India). Auromere.

Taiwan Journal: Ten Historic Days. John Tomikel. LC 79-53164. (Illus.). 1979. lib. bdg. 10.00 (ISBN 0-910042-37-3); pap. 4.00 (ISBN 0-910042-36-5). Allegheny.

Taiwan: Mainline Versus Independent Church Growth. Allen J. Swanson. LC 74-126424. 300p. 1973. pap. 5.95 (ISBN 0-87808-404-5). William Carey Lib.

Taiwan Pawn in the China Game. 80p. 1979. pap. 7.50 (ISBN 0-89206-007-7, CSIS002, CSIS). Unipub.

Taiwan Pawn in the China Game: Congress to the Rescue, Vol. I. Robert Downen. LC 79-88334. (Significant Issues Ser.: No. 1). 80p. 1979. 5.95 (ISBN 0-89206-007-7). CSI Studies.

Taiwan Relations Act & the Defense of the Republic of China. Edwin K. Snyder et al. (Policy Papers in International Affairs Ser.: No. 12). 132p. 1980. pap. 3.95x (ISBN 0-87725-512-1). U of Cal Intl St.

Taiwan Statistical Data Book, 1980. Council for Economic Planning & Development (Republic of China) LC 72-219425. (Illus.). 318p. (Orig.). 1980. pap. 12.50x (ISBN 0-8002-2749-2). Intl Pubns Serv.

Taiwan: Studies in Chinese Local History. Ed. by Leonard H. Gordon. LC 78-108096. (East Asian Institute Ser). 1970. 12.50x (ISBN 0-231-03376-1). Columbia U Pr.

Taiwan's Politics: The Provincial Assemblyman's World. Arthur J. Lerman. LC 78-64524. 1978. pap. text ed. 11.25 (ISBN 0-8191-0632-1). U Pr of Amer.

Takamiyama: The World of Sumo. Jesse Kuhaulua & John Wheeler. LC 72-96129. (Illus.). 176p. 1973. 12.95 (ISBN 0-87011-195-7). Kodansha.

Take a Chance with Your Calculator: Probability Problems for Programmable Calculators. Lennart Rade. LC 77-88868. 1977. pap. 9.95 (ISBN 0-918398-07-X). Dilithium Pr.

Take a Long Jump. Marion Renick. LC 71-158885. (Encore Ser.). (Illus.). 160p. (gr. 3-6). 1971. 5.95 (ISBN 0-684-12496-3, ScribJ). Scribner.

Take a Stand: Discussion Topics for Intermediate Adult Students. L. G. Alexander et al. (Illus.). 1978. pap. text ed. 2.50x (ISBN 0-582-79721-7); cassettes 7.95 (ISBN 0-582-79722-5). Longman.

Take AIM, Vol. 1. James H. Clark. 416p. (Orig.). pap. text ed. 16.95 (ISBN 0-686-69549-6). Matrix Pubns.

Take All to Nebraska. Sophus K. Winther. LC 75-11672. vi, 306p. 1976. 12.50x (ISBN 0-8032-0861-8); pap. 4.50 (ISBN 0-8032-5831-3, BB 611, Bison). U of Nebr Pr.

Take Another Look. Tana Hoban. LC 80-21342. (Illus.). 32p. (ps-3). 1981. 7.95 (ISBN 0-688-80298-2); PLB 7.63 (ISBN 0-688-84298-4). Greenwillow.

Take Back the Night: Women on Pornography. Ed. by Laura Lederer. LC 80-23701. 352p. (Orig.). 1980. pap. 7.95 (ISBN 0-688-08728-0, Quill). Morrow.

Take Back the Night: Women on Pornography. Ed. by Laura Lederer. LC 80-17084. 352p. 1980. 14.95 (ISBN 0-688-03728-3). Morrow.

Take Care of Dexter. (ps-3). pap. 1.25 (ISBN 0-686-68469-9, Schol Pap). Schol Bk Serv.

Take Care of Your Elderly Relative. J. A. Gray & Mrs. Heather M. Lovet. (Illus., Orig.). 1980. 23.95 (ISBN 0-04-618015-X); pap. 13.50 (ISBN 0-04-618016-8). Allen Unwin.

Take Care of Your Elderly Relative. Muir Gray & Heather McKenzie. 208p. 1980. 25.00x (Pub. by Beaconsfield England). State Mutual Bk.

Take Command. Vera D. Tait. LC 80-53217. 144p. 1981. 3.95 (ISBN 0-87159-150-2). Unity Bks.

Take Fire. Margaret Honton. LC 80-69778. 64p. (Orig.). 1980. pap. 4.00 (ISBN 0-936014-09-1). Dawn Valley.

Take Five. Fred Waelti. 7.75 (ISBN 0-8062-1627-1). Carlton.

Take It Easy: American Indians & Two Word Verbs for Students of English As a Foreign Language. Pamela McPartland. (ESL Ser.). 176p. 1981. pap. text ed. 6.95 (ISBN 0-13-882902-0). P-H.

Take It Easy Charlie Brown: Selected Cartoons from "You'll Flip, Charlie Brown," Vol. Ii. Charles Schulz. (Peanuts Ser.). (Illus.). 1978. pap. 1.50 (ISBN 0-449-23955-1, Crest). Fawcett.

Take It Off! One Thousand Four Hundred & Fourteen Tax Deductions Most People Overlook: One Thousand Four Hundred & Fourteen Tax Deductions Most Poeple Overlook. 6th, annual ed. Robert S. Holzman. LC 79-18542. 1979. 10.95 o.p. (ISBN 0-690-01843-6, TYC-T); pap. 5.95 o.p. (ISBN 0-690-01844-4, TYC-T). T Y Crowell.

Take It off! One Thousand Six Hundred Ninety-Five Tax Deductions Most People Overlook. rev. ed. Robert S. Holzman. 336p. 1980. 10.95 (ISBN 0-690-01931-9); pap. 5.95 (ISBN 0-690-01933-5). Lippincott & Crowell.

Take It off with Frank. Frank Field. 1979. pap. 1.95 (ISBN 0-345-27921-2). Ballantine.

Take It or Leave It. Molarsky. (gr. 3-5). 1980. pap. 1.25 (ISBN 0-590-30072-5, Schol Pap). Schol Bk Serv.

Take It to the Hoop. Ed. by Daniel Rudman. (Illus.). 300p. (Orig.). 1980. 25.00; pap. 8.95 (ISBN 0-913028-76-2). North Atlantic.

Take Me Back. Richard Bausch. 372p. 1981. 11.95 (ISBN 0-686-69093-1). Dial.

Take Me Like a Photograph. Chocolate Waters. (Illus.). 1977. pap. 4.00 (ISBN 0-935060-02-2). Eggplant Pr.

Take Me Like a Photograph. 2nd ed. Chocolate Waters. 1980. 4.75 (ISBN 0-935060-02-2). Eggplant Pr.

Take Me Out to the Airfield: How the Wright Brothers Invented the Airplane. Robert Quackenbush. LC 76-2558. (Illus.). 40p. (gr. 1-6). 1976. 5.95 o.s.i. (ISBN 0-8193-0879-X, Four Winds); PLB 5.41 o.s.i. (ISBN 0-8193-0880-3). Schol Bk Serv.

Take Me to the Moon! Sal Murdocca. LC 76-6113. (Fun-To-Read Bk.). (Illus.). 64p. (gr. 1-4). 1976. 6.95 (ISBN 0-688-41766-3); PLB 6.67 (ISBN 0-688-51766-8). Lothrop.

Take Me Where the Good Times Are. Robert Cormier. 176p. 1981. pap. 2.25 (ISBN 0-380-52662-X, 52662). Avon.

Take Murder. John Wainwright. 176p. 1981. 9.95 (ISBN 0-312-78357-4). St Martin.

Take My Heart & Other Poems. John G. Caserta. 1981. 4.50 (ISBN 0-8062-1720-0). Carlton.

Take My Wife... Please! My Life & Laughs. Carroll Carroll. pap. 1.50 o.p. (ISBN 0-425-03241-8). Berkley Pub.

Take My Words. Eugene Maleska. 1981. 14.95 (ISBN 0-671-24881-2). S&S.

Take off from Within. Ervin Seale. LC 71-150974. 1971. 5.95 o.p. (ISBN 0-06-067198-X, HarpR). Har-Row.

Take Out Hunger: Two Case Studies of Rural Development in Basutoland. Sandra Wallman. (Monographs in Social Anthropology Ser). 1969. text ed. 16.25x (ISBN 0-485-19539-9, Athlone Pr). Humanities.

Take Shapes, Lines & Letters: New Horizons in Math. Jeanne Bendick & Marcia Levin. (Illus.). (gr. 4-6). 1962. PLB 6.95 o.p. (ISBN 0-07-004487-2, GB). McGraw.

Take the High Road. A. J. Bueltmann. LC 67-24877. (Concordia Sex Education Ser). (gr. 7-9). 1967. pap. 4.50 (ISBN 0-570-06603-4, 14-1503); color filmstrips w. record 10.00 (ISBN 0-685-08641-0, 79-3102). Concordia.

Take the Road to Creatiity & Get off Your Dead End. David P. Campbell. 1977. pap. 2.95 (ISBN 0-913592-95-1). Argus Comm.

Take Them Round, Please: The Art of Judging Dogs. Tom Horner. LC 74-19782. (Illus.). 160p. 1975. 13.50 (ISBN 0-7153-6880-X). David & Charles.

Take Thirty Dictionary. Ernest Beaucamp & Dorothea Hansen. (gr. 12). 1971. pap. 5.25 (ISBN 0-89420-099-2, 219905). Natl Book.

Take Thirty Shorthand: Student Syllabus, 2 vols. Ernest Beaucamp & Dorthea Hansen. (gr. 11-12). 1970. Vol. 1. pap. text ed. 5.95 (ISBN 0-89420-097-6, 218999); cassette recordings 244.75 (ISBN 0-89420-211-1, 219105); Vol. 2. pap. text ed. 5.80 (ISBN 0-89420-098-4, 219105). Natl Book.

Take This House. Evamae B. Crist. (Illus.). 1977. pap. 2.25 (ISBN 0-8361-1817-0). Herald Pr.

Take This Test. Barry J. Pavelec & Stephen M. Kirschner. LC 80-972. 288p. Date not set. pap. 6.95 (ISBN 0-8019-6924-7). Chilton.

Take Two, They're Small. Elizabeth Levy. (Orig.). (gr. k-6). 1981. pap. 1.95 (ISBN 0-440-48517-7, YB). Dell.

Take What You Want. Faith Baldwin. 1980. pap. write for info. (ISBN 0-671-83097-X). PB.

Taken by the Indians: True Tales of Captivity. Alice Dickinson. LC 75-22307. (Illus.). 192p. (gr. 7 up). 1976. PLB 6.90 o.p. (ISBN 0-531-01107-0). Watts.

Takeoff. Randall Garrett. Ed. by Polly Freas & Kelly Freas. LC 79-9140. (Illus.). 1980. pap. 4.95 (ISBN 0-915442-84-1, Starblaze). Donning Co.

Takeoffs & Touchdowns: My Sixty Years of Flying. Fred E. Jacobs. LC 80-28865. (Illus.). 304p. 1981. 12.95 (ISBN 0-498-02540-3). A S Barnes.

Takeovers & the Theory of the Firm: An Empirical Analysis for the United Kingdom 1957-69. Douglas Kuehn. 189p. 1975. 29.75x (ISBN 0-8419-5000-8). Holmes & Meier.

Takeovers: Their Relevance to the Stock Market & the Theory of the Firm. Ajit Singh. (Department of Applied Economics Monographs: No. 19). 1972. 31.50 (ISBN 0-521-08245-5). Cambridge U Pr.

Takers. Robert Ackworth. 1979. pap. 2.50 o.p. (ISBN 0-345-27632-9). Ballantine.

Takers & Returners. Carol B. York. (gr. 5 up). 1979. pap. 1.50 (ISBN 0-448-17100-7, Tempo). G&D.

Taking Action: Writing, Reading, Speaking & Listening Through Simulation Games. Lynn Q. Troyka & Jerrold Nudelman. (Illus.). 176p. 1975. pap. text ed. 7.95 (ISBN 0-13-882571-8). P-H.

Taking Better Pictures with Your Thirty-Five mm Automatic Camera. Jack Manning. Ed. by Ava Swartz. LC 79-3540. (Illus., Orig.). pap. cancelled o.s.i. (ISBN 0-88225-291-7). Newsweek.

Taking Better Pictures with Your Thirty-Five MM SLR. Tom Grill & Mark Scanlon. (Illus.). 1980. 14.95 (ISBN 0-690-01920-3, H&R); pap. 7.95 (ISBN 0-690-01921-1). Lippincott.

Taking Better Pictures with Your 35mm SLR: A Practial Guide--with Special Emphasis on 35mm Automatic Cameras. Tom Grill & Mark Scanlon. LC 80-7855. (Illus.). 128p. 1981. 15.95 (ISBN 0-690-01920-3, HarpT). Har-Row.

Taking Better Pictures with Your 35mm SLR: A Practial Guide--with Special Emphasis on 35mm Automatic Cameras. Tom Grill & Mark Scanlon. LC 80-7855. (Illus.). 128p. 1981. pap. 7.95 (ISBN 0-690-01921-1, CN 864, CN). Har-Row.

Taking Chances: Abortion & the Decision Not to Contracept. Kristin Luker. LC 74-22965. 200p. 1976. 10.95 o.p. (ISBN 0-520-02872-4); pap. 4.95 (ISBN 0-520-03594-1). U of Cal Pr.

Taking Charge of Your Life. Howe W. Leland. LC 77-86340. 1977. pap. 3.95 (ISBN 0-913592-93-5). Argus Comm.

Taking Charge: Personal Effectiveness in Organizations. Claudyne Wilder & William I. Rogers. LC 79-9513. 1980. pap. text ed. 9.95 (ISBN 0-201-08624-7). A-W.

Taking Charge: The Dynamics of Personal Decision-Making & Self-Management. Gordon McMinn & Larry Libby. LC 80-65061. 192p. (Orig.). 1980. pap. 4.95 (ISBN 0-89636-043-1). Accent Bks.

Taking Gamefish: From Dry Flies to Downrigger Freshwater Fishing. Ed. by Todd Swainbank. LC 79-20982. (Illus.). 1979. 15.95 (ISBN 0-89594-026-4); pap. 8.95 (ISBN 0-89594-025-6). Crossing Pr.

Taking Leave. Don Cupitt. 192p. 1981. 9.95 (ISBN 0-8245-0045-8). Crossroad NY.

Taking Liberty. Lawrence Dunning. 496p. (Orig.). 1981. pap. 2.95 (ISBN 0-380-77297-3, 77297). Avon.

Taking Notice. Marilyn Nacker. LC 79-28166. 128p. 1980. 9.95 (ISBN 0-394-51223-5); pap. 5.95 (ISBN 0-394-73917-5). Knopf.

Taking of the Gry. John Masefield. 1967. 4.95 o.s.i. (ISBN 0-02-581500-8). Macmillan.

Taking off. Richard A. Curtiss. Ed. by Peter Schriver. 188p. (Orig.). 1981. pap. 4.95 (ISBN 0-517-53901-2, Harmony). Crown.

Taking on the Local Color. Cynthia Genser. LC 76-41486. (Wesleyan Poetry Program: Vol. 85). 1977. 10.00x (ISBN 0-8195-2085-3, Pub. by Wesleyan U Pr); pap. 4.95 (ISBN 0-8195-1085-8). Columbia U Pr.

Taking Pictures. Nina Leen. (gr. 6-10). 1980. pap. 1.75 (ISBN 0-380-49205-9, 49205, Camelot). Avon.

Taking Root: Israeli Settlement in the West Bank, the Golan & Gaza-Sinai, 1967-1980. William W. Harris. 256p. 1981. 39.25 (ISBN 0-471-27863-7, Pub. by Wiley-Interscience). Wiley.

Taking Sides. Barbara Wilson. (Orig.). 1981. pap. 4.95 (ISBN 0-931188-09-1). Seal Pr WA.

Taking the Christian Life Seriously: Biblical Teaching on Christian Maturity. Sinclair B. Ferguson. Orig. Title: Add to Your Life. 192p. 1981. pap. 5.95 (ISBN 0-310-43891-8). Zondervan.

Taking the Soundings on Third Avenue. David Kherdian. LC 80-14276. 64p. 1980. 10.00 (ISBN 0-87951-116-8); limited & signed deluxe ed. 35.00 (ISBN 0-87951-119-2). Overlook Pr.

Taking Things Apart & Puttings Things Together. John H. Woodburn. LC 76-20448. 1976. 6.00 o.p. (ISBN 0-8412-0314-8); pap. 2.50 (ISBN 0-8412-0314-8). Am Chemical.

Taking Your Faith to Work. Alfred A. Glenn. (Orig.). 1980. pap. 4.95 (ISBN 0-8010-3748-4). Baker Bk.

Taking Your Meetings Out of the Doldrums. Eva Schindler-Rainman & Ronald Lippitt. LC 75-41890. (Illus.). 100p. 1975. 9.50 (ISBN 0-88390-136-6). Univ Assocs.

Takis Papatsonis. Kostas Myrsiades. LC 74-6370. (World Authors Ser.: Greece: No. 313). 168p. 1974. lib. bdg. 12.50 (ISBN 0-8057-2669-1). Twayne.

Talcott Parsons & the Conceptual Dilemma. Hans P. Adriaansens. (International Library of Sociology). (Illus.). 224p. 1980. 27.50x (ISBN 0-7100-0519-9). Routledge & Kegan.

Talcott Parsons & the Social Image of Man. Ken Menzies. (International Library of Sociology). 1976. 17.95x (ISBN 0-7100-8369-6). Routledge & Kegan.

Tale from Tangier. rev. ed. Jean N. Dale. (Reading & Exercise Ser.: No. 6). 1976. pap. 2.50 (ISBN 0-89285-055-8); cassette tapes 29.50 (ISBN 0-89285-073-6). ELS Intl.

Tale from Tangier. Ed. by Jean N. Dale. (Reading & Exercise Ser.). (Illus.). (gr. k-6). 1974. pap. text ed. 2.50x (ISBN 0-19-433624-7). Oxford U Pr.

Tale Goes with the Hide. Rod Paisley. 1980. 4.75 o.p. (ISBN 0-8062-1223-3). Carlton.

Tale of a Tub. Jonathan Swift. LC 71-170512. (Foundations of the Novel Ser: Vol. 8). 322p. 1973. Repr. of 1704 ed. lib. bdg. 50.00 (ISBN 0-8240-0520-1). Garland Pub.

Tale of a Tub, Battle of the Books, & Mechanical Operation of the Spirit. 2nd ed. Jonathan Swift. Ed. by A. C. Guthkelch & D. N. Smith. 1958. 37.50x (ISBN 0-19-811404-4). Oxford U Pr.

Tale of Balain. Tr. by David E. Campbell from Fr. LC 72-77830. (Medieval French Texts). 144p. 1972. text ed. 8.95x o.s.i. (ISBN 0-8101-0385-0). Northwestern U Pr.

Tale of Benjamin Bunny. B. Potter. (Peter Possum Paperbacks Ser). 1967. pap. 0.95 o.p. (ISBN 0-531-05126-9). Watts.

Tale of Csar Saltan: Or the Prince & the Swan Princess. Alexander Pushkin. Tr. by Patricia T. Lowe. LC 75-5655. 1975. 5.95 (ISBN 0-690-00792-2, TYC-J). T Y Crowell.

Tale of Four Dervishes & Other Sufi Tales. Amina Shah. LC 80-8895. 288p. (Orig.). 1981. pap. 5.95 (ISBN 0-06-067256-0). Har-Row.

Tale of Genji-One. Lady Murasaki. LC 50-47132. pap. 2.95 (ISBN 0-385-09275-X, Anch). Doubleday.

Tale of Genji Scroll. Ivan Morris. LC 77-128695. (Illus.). 1971. ltd. ed. 350.00 (ISBN 0-87011-131-0). Kodansha.

Tale of Lumbdoom, the Long-Tailed Langoor. Uma Anand. (Illus.). 1968. 1.00 (ISBN 0-88253-325-8). Ind-US Inc.

Tale of Meshka the Kvetch. Carol Chapman. LC 80-11225. (Illus.). 32p. (gr. k-3). PLB 8.95 (ISBN 0-525-40745-6). Dutton.

Tale of Peter Rabbit. Potter. (ps-3). pap. 1.25 (ISBN 0-590-09141-7, Schol Pap). Schol Bk Serv.

Tale of Peter Rabbit. Beatrix Potter. (Illus.). (gr. k-2). 1970. 1.95 (ISBN 0-307-10486-9, Golden Pr); PLB 7.62 (ISBN 0-307-60486-1). Western Pub.

Tale of Peter Rabbit. Beatrix Potter. pap. 3.50 incl. record (ISBN 0-590-04358-7, Schol Pap). Schol Bk Serv.

Tale of Squirrel Nutkin. B. Potter. (Peter Possum Paperbacks Ser). 1967. pap. 0.95 o.p. (ISBN 0-531-05116-1). Watts.

Tale of the Amazing Tramp. Dan Propper. LC 76-58849. 1977. pap. 2.50x o.p. (ISBN 0-916156-20-6). Cherry Valley.

Tale of the Campaign of Igor. Tr. by Robert C. Howes. 1974. pap. text ed. 2.95x (ISBN 0-393-09310-7). Norton.

Tale of the House of the Wolfings & All the Kindreds of the Mark. William Morris. Ed. by R. Reginald & Douglas Menville. LC 80-19670. (Newcastle Forgotten Fantasy Library Ser.: Vol. 16). 199p. 1980. Repr. of 1978 ed. lib. bdg. 10.95x (ISBN 0-89370-515-2). Borgo Pr.

Tale of the Reed Pipe: Teaching of the Sufis. Massud Farzan. 1974. pap. 1.95 o.p. (ISBN 0-525-47362-9). Dutton.

Tale of the Shining Princess. Sally Fischer. Tr. by Donald Keene. LC 80-1943. (Illus.). 72p. 1981. 10.95 (ISBN 0-670-63971-0). Viking Pr.

Tale of the Tell: Archaeological Studies by Paul W. Lapp. Ed. by Nancy L. Lapp. LC 75-5861. (Pittsburgh Theological Monographs: No. 5). 1975. pap. text ed. 6.50 (ISBN 0-915138-05-0). Pickwick.

Tale of the Times, 3 vols. Jane West. (Feminist Controversy in England, 1788-1810 Ser.). 1974. Set. lib. bdg. 114.00 (ISBN 0-8240-0886-3); lib. bdg. 50.00 ea. Garland Pub.

Tale of the Tribe: Ezra Pound & the Modern Verse Epic. Michael A. Bernstein. LC 80-129. 1980. 22.50 (ISBN 0-691-06434-2); pap. 9.95 (ISBN 0-691-10105-1). Princeton U Pr.

Tale of Thebes. R. L. Green. LC 76-22979. (Illus.). 1977. 14.95 (ISBN 0-521-21410-6); pap. 5.50 (ISBN 0-521-21411-4). Cambridge U Pr.

Tale of Thomas Mead. Pat Hutchins. (Greenwillow Read-Alone Bks.). (Illus.). 32p. (gr. 1-4). 1980. 5.95 (ISBN 0-688-80282-6); PLB 5.71 (ISBN 0-688-84282-8). Greenwillow.

Tale of Two Cities. Charles Dickens. (Literature Ser). (gr. 7-12). 1969. pap. text ed. 4.00 (ISBN 0-87720-716-X). AMSCO Sch.

Tale of Two Cities. Charles Dickens. Ed. by Harry Shefter et al. (YA) pap. 2.50 (ISBN 0-671-48931-3, Re). WSP.

Tale of Two Cities. Charles Dickens. pap. 1.50. Bantam.

Tale of Two Cities. abr. ed. Charles Dickens & Andrea M. Clare. LC 73-80400. (Pacemaker Classics Ser). (Adapted to grade 2 reading level). 1973. pap. 3.80 (ISBN 0-8224-9228-8); tchrs' manual free (ISBN 0-8224-5200-6). Pitman Learning.

Tale of Two Cities: The Mormons-Catholics. Bill Taylor. 1981. pap. 4.00 (ISBN 0-933046-02-2). Little Red Hen.

Tale of Two Cities with Reader's Guide. Charles Dickens. (Amsco Literature Program). (gr. 10-12). 1971. pap. text ed. 4.67 (ISBN 0-87720-813-1); tchrs. ed. s.p. 3.00 (ISBN 0-87720-913-8). AMSCO Sch.

Tale of Two Courts: Judicial Settlement of Controversies Between the States of the Swiss & American Federations. William G. Rice. 1967. 15.00x (ISBN 0-299-04390-8). U of Wis Pr.

Talent Manual for Carpenters, Millwrights & Pile Drivers: Gr. 1st. Year of Apprenticeship Through 4 Years Training. John V. Willis. (Illus.). 100p. 1970. 5.50 (ISBN 0-686-63616-3). J V Willis.

Talent to Deceive: An Appreciation of Agatha Christie. Robert Barnard. LC 79-27435. 208p. 1980. 10.00 (ISBN 0-396-07827-3). Dodd.

Tales & Historic Scenes, in Verse. 1819. Felicia D. Hemans. Ed. by Donald H. Reiman. LC 75-31215. (Romantic Context Ser.: Poetry 1789-1830). 1978. lib. bdg. 47.00 (ISBN 0-8240-2165-7). Garland Pub.

Tales & Other Selected Poems. George Crabbe. Ed. by Howard W. Mills. 1967. 58.00 (ISBN 0-521-04747-1); pap. 14.95x (ISBN 0-521-09420-8, 420). Cambridge U Pr.

Tales & Sketches Illustrating the Character of the Irish Peasantry. (Nineteenth Century Fiction Ser.: Ireland: Vol. 39). 408p. 1979. lib. bdg. 46.00 (ISBN 0-8240-3488-0). Garland Pub.

Tales & Songs of Herrand von Wildonie. Herrandv. Wildonie. Tr. by J. W. Thomas. LC 76-183354. (Studies in Germanic Languages and Literatures: No. 4). 88p. 1972. 7.25x (ISBN 0-8131-1267-2). U Pr of Ky.

Tales & Stories by Hans Christian Andersen. Hans C. Andersen. Tr. by Patricia Conroy & Sven H. Rossel. LC 80-50867. (Illus.). 316p. 1980. 17.50 (ISBN 0-295-95769-7). U of Wash Pr.

Tales by the O'Hara Family, Eighteen Twenty-Five, 3 vols. John Banim & Michael Banim. Ed. by Robert L. Wolff. (Ireland Nineteenth Century Fiction - Ser. Two: Vol. 16). 1278p. 1979. lib. bdg. 96.00 (ISBN 0-8240-3465-1). Garland Pub.

Tales for the New Life Meher Baba. Eruch et al. 191p. 1976. 8.95 (ISBN 0-686-17265-5); pap. 3.95 (ISBN 0-686-17266-3). Meher Baba Info.

Tales from a Taiwan Kitchen. Cora Cheney. LC 75-38364. (Illus.). (gr. 4 up). 1976. 5.95 (ISBN 0-396-07291-7). Dodd.

Tales from a Troubled Land. Alan Paton. 1961. lib.rep. ed. 12.50x (ISBN 0-684-15135-9, ScribT). Scribner.

Tales from Aesop. J. P. Miller. LC 74-2539. (Picturebacks Ser). (Illus.). 32p. (ps-1). 1976. pap. 1.25 (ISBN 0-394-82812-7, BYR). Random.

Tales from Africa. Lila Green. LC 78-54623. (World Folktale Library). (Illus.). 1979. lib. bdg. 7.65 (ISBN 0-686-51162-X). Silver.

Tales from Ancient Greece. Frederick J. Moffitt. LC 78-56059. (World Folktale Library). (Illus.). 1979. lib. bdg. 7.65 (ISBN 0-686-50008-3). Silver.

Tales from Atop a Russian Stove. Tr. by Janet Higonnet-Schnopper. LC 70-188430. (Folklore Ser). (Illus.). 160p. (gr. 3 up). 1973. 5.95g o.p. (ISBN 0-8075-7755-3). A Whitman.

Tales from Austin. Ed. by Luis A. Ramos-Garcia. 1980. 5.95 (ISBN 0-934840-02-4). U Tex Studia.

Tales from Czechoslavakia. Marie Burg. (gr. 3 up). 1967. 7.50 (ISBN 0-340-09142-8). Dufour.

Tales from Hispanic Lands. Lila Green. LC 78-54624. (World Folktale Library). (Illus.). 1979. lib. bdg. 7.65 (ISBN 0-686-50009-1). Silver.

Tales from Indian Mythology. A. S. Raman. (Illus.). 123p. (gr. 7-12). 74. 3.60 (ISBN 0-88253-473-4). Ind-US Inc.

Tales from Old Carolina. F. Roy Johnson. LC 65-8878. (Illus.). 1980. Repr. of 1965 ed. 7.50 (ISBN 0-930230-38-8). Johnson NC.

Tales from Scandinavia. Frederick Laing. LC 78-56060. (World Folktale Library). (Illus.). 1979. lib. bdg. 7.65 (ISBN 0-686-51165-4). Silver.

Tales from Shakespeare. Charles Lamb & Mary Lamb. (New Children's Classics). (Illus.). (gr. 5-8). 1963. 4.95g o.s.i. (ISBN 0-02-751260-6). Macmillan.

Tales from Shakespeare. Charles Lamb & Mary Lamb. Ed. by Shakespeare Library. LC 79-89991. (Illus.). 1979. 35.00 (ISBN 0-918016-04-5); pap. 19.95 (ISBN 0-918016-17-7). Folger Bks.

Tales from Shakespeare. 1981. 28.50 (ISBN 0-686-68310-2). Porter.

Tales from Southern Africa. Retold by A. C. Jordan. (Perspectives on Southern Africa: No. 4). (Illus.). 1973. 18.50x (ISBN 0-520-01911-3); pap. 3.95 (ISBN 0-520-03638-7). U of Cal Pr.

Tales from the Amazon. Elsie S. Eells. LC 20-18503. (Illus.). (gr. 4-6). 1938. 4.95 (ISBN 0-396-01809-2). Dodd.

Tales from the Australian Bush. Doris Rust. (Illus.). (ps-5). 1968. 5.95 (ISBN 0-571-08358-7, Pub. by Faber & Faber). Merrimack Bk Serv.

Tales from the Big Thicket. Ed. by Francis E. Abernethy. (Illus.). 1966. 12.95 (ISBN 0-292-73636-3). U of Tex Pr.

Tales from the British Isles. John Greenway. LC 78-56058. (World Folktale Library). (Illus.). 1979. lib. bdg. 7.65 (ISBN 0-686-51163-8). Silver.

Tales from the First Americans. Moritz A. Jagendorf. LC 78-56057. (World Folktale Library). (Illus.). 1979. lib. bdg. 7.65 (ISBN 0-686-51164-6). Silver.

Tales from the Heptameron. Marguerite De Navarre. Ed. by H. P. Clive. (Athlone Renaissance Library). 1970. text ed. 10.75x (ISBN 0-485-13801-8, Athlone Pr); pap. text ed. 5.50x (ISBN 0-485-12801-2, Athlone Pr). Humanities.

Tales from the Igloo. Ed. & tr. by Maurice Metayer. LC 76-54253. (Illus.). 1977. pap. 4.95 o.p. (ISBN 0-312-78418-X). St Martin.

Tales from the Mabinogion. Owen Bowen. LC 78-155665. (Illus.). 1974. 6.95 (ISBN 0-8149-0706-7). Vanguard.

Tales from the Mohaves. Herman Grey. LC 69-16731. (Civilization of the American Indian Ser.: Vol. 107). 96p. 1980. pap. 5.95 (ISBN 0-8061-1655-2). U of Okla Pr.

Tales from the Nightside. Charles L. Grant. (Illus.). 250p. 1981. 11.95 (ISBN 0-87054-091-2). Arkham.

Tales from the Prairie, 4 vols. Dorothy W. Creigh. Incl. Vol. 1. 1977. pap. 2.95 (ISBN 0-686-19306-7); Vol. 2. 1973. pap. 2.95 (ISBN 0-686-17269-8); Vol. 3. 1976. pap. 5.95 (ISBN 0-686-17321-X); Vol. 4. 1979. pap. 9.95 (ISBN 0-934858-06-3). LC 74-157038. (Illus.). Set. pap. write for info. Adams County.

Tales from the South Pacific Islands. Anne Gittins. LC 76-5411. (Illus.). 96p. (gr. 3 up). 1977. 4.95 (ISBN 0-916144-02-X). Stemmer Hse.

Tales from the Uncertain Country. Jacques Ferron. Tr. by Betty Bednarski from Fr. LC 71-190704. (Anansi Fiction Ser.: No. 19). 102p. 1972. pap. 3.95 (ISBN 0-88784-320-4, Pub. by Hse Anansi Pr Canada); study guide by Mary Ziroff 1.00x (ISBN 0-88784-053-1). U of Toronto Pr.

Tales from the United States. John Greenway. LC 78-54626. (World Folktale Library). (Illus.). 1979. lib. bdg. 7.65 (ISBN 0-686-51166-2). Silver.

Tales from Third Street. Carol Jordan. (Illus.). 100p. 1980. pap. 3.50 (ISBN 0-9605360-0-0). C Jordan.

Tales I Told My Mother. Robert Nye. LC 72-86821. 1969. 4.95 o.p. (ISBN 0-8090-9106-2). Hill & Wang.

Tales of a Chinese Grandmother. Francis Carpenter. 293p. Repr. of 1937 ed. lib. bdg. 12.75x (ISBN 0-89190-481-6). Am Repr-Rivercity Pr.

Tales of a Country Judge. Robert H. Gollmar. LC 79-65286. (Illus.). 192p. 1981. 8.95x (ISBN 0-87319-018-1). C Hallberg.

Tales of an Ashanti Father. Peggy Appiah. LC 80-2697. (Illus.). 160p. (gr. 2-7). 1981. 8.95 (ISBN 0-233-95927-0). Andre Deutsch.

Tales of Ancient Egypt. Roger L. Green. (gr. k-3). 1972. pap. 2.25 (ISBN 0-14-030438-X, Puffin). Penguin.

Tales of Atlantis & the Enchanted Islands. Thomas W. Higginson. LC 80-19670. (Newcastle Mythology Library Ser.: Vol. 3). 259p. 1980. Repr. of 1977 ed. lib. bdg. 10.95x (ISBN 0-89370-642-6). Borgo Pr.

Tales of Canterbury: Complete. Geoffrey Chaucer. Ed. by Robert A. Pratt. LC 72-9380. (Illus.). 587p. 1974. text ed. 17.50 (ISBN 0-395-14052-8). HM.

Tales of Country Folks Down Carolina Way. F. Roy Johnson. (Illus.). 1978. 9.50 (ISBN 0-930230-36-1). Johnson NC.

Tales of Edgar Allan Poe. Edgar A. Poe. LC 80-14064. (Raintree Short Classics). (Illus.). 48p. (gr. 4 up). 1981. PLB 9.95 (ISBN 0-8172-1662-6). Raintree Pubs.

Tales of Espionage & Intrigue. Arthur Liebman. (Masterworks of Mystery Ser). 274p. (gr. 7-12). 1976. PLB 7.97 (ISBN 0-8239-0411-3); tchr's manual 1.50 (ISBN 0-685-66609-3). Rosen Pr.

Tales of Explorers. Edward G. Jerrome. (Pacemaker True Adventures Ser.). (Illus., Orig.). 1973. pap. 2.36 (ISBN 0-8224-9182-6); tchrs'. manual free (ISBN 0-8224-5208-1). Pitman Learning.

Tales of Galloway. Alan Temperley. 319p. 1980. 12.50x (ISBN 0-7050-0076-1, Pub. by Skilton & Shaw England). State Mutual Bk.

Tales of Henry James: Vol. 1, 1864-1869. Henry James. Ed. by Maqbool Aziz. (Illus.). 528p. 1973. 45.00x (ISBN 0-19-812457-0). Oxford U Pr.

Tales of Henry James, Vol. 2: 1870-1874. Henry James. Ed. by Madbool Aziz. 1979. 49.00x (ISBN 0-19-812572-0). Oxford U Pr.

Tales of Horror & the Supernatural, Vol. 1. Arthur Machen. 1976. pap. 1.50 o.p. (ISBN 0-523-23891-6). Pinnacle Bks.

Tales of Invention. Edward G. Jerrome. (Pacemaker True Adventures Ser.). (Illus., Orig.). 1973. pap. 2.36 (ISBN 0-8224-9186-9); tchrs' manual free (ISBN 0-8224-5208-1). Pitman Learning.

Tales of Ireland. William Carleton. Ed. by Robert L. Wolff. (Ireland Nineteenth Century Fiction - Ser. Two: Vol. 36). 384p. 1979. lib. bdg. 32.00 (ISBN 0-8240-3485-6). Garland Pub.

Tales of Moonlight & Rain: Japanese Gothic Tales. Akinari Uyeda. Tr. by Kengi Hamada from Japanese. LC 79-175064. (Illus.). 1972. 15.00x (ISBN 0-231-03631-0). Columbia U Pr.

Tales of My Neighbourhood. Gerald Griffin. (Nineteenth Century Fiction Ser.: Ireland: Vol. 30). 956p. 1979. lib. bdg. 46.00 (ISBN 0-8240-3479-1). Garland Pub.

Tales of Mystery. Moritz A. Jagendorf. LC 78-56056. (World Folktale Library). (Illus.). 1979. lib. bdg. 7.65 (ISBN 0-686-51167-0). Silver.

Tales of Mystery & Suspense. A. Conan Doyle et al. (gr. 9 up). 1980. Boxed Set. pap. text ed. 3.75 (ISBN 0-307-13622-1, Golden Pr). Western Pub.

Tales of Old Cairo. Nagib Mahfouz. pap. 5.50 arabic (ISBN 0-685-82882-4). Intl Bk Ctr.

Tales of Olga Da Polga. Michael Bond. LC 72-89048. (Illus.). 128p. (gr. 3-7). 1973. 4.95g o.s.i. (ISBN 0-02-711730-8). Macmillan.

Tales of Olga De Polga. Michael Bond. (gr. 7 up). 1974. pap. 1.95 (ISBN 0-14-030500-9, Puffin). Penguin.

Tales of One Thousand & One Iranian Days. Henry A. Sarkissian. 1981. 8.95 (ISBN 0-533-04476-6). Vantage.

Tales of Padre Pio: The Friar of San Giovanni. John McCaffrey. 1979. 9.95 o.p. (ISBN 0-8362-3500-2). Andrews & McMeel.

Tales of Persia: A Book for Children. William M. Miller. LC 79-51273. (Illus.). 145p. (gr. 2-8). 1979. 5.00 (ISBN 0-8059-2635-6). Dorrance.

Tales of Peter Parley About America, Repr. Of 1827 Ed. Samuel G. Goodrich. Bd. with Tales of Travels West of the Mississippi, by Solomon Bell. William J. Snelling. Repr. of 1830 ed. LC 75-32158. (Classics of Children's Literature, 1621-1932: Vol. 23). 1976. PLB 38.00 (ISBN 0-8240-2272-6). Garland Pub.

Tales of Pirates. Edward G. Jerrome. (Pacemaker True Adventures Ser.). (Illus., Orig.). 1973. pap. 2.36 (ISBN 0-8224-9189-3); tchrs' manual free (ISBN 0-8224-5208-1). Pitman Learning.

Tales of Polly & the Hungry Wolf. Catherine Storr. (Illus.). 96p. (gr. 2-5). 1980. 10.95 (ISBN 0-571-11585-3, Pub. by Faber & Faber). Merrimack Bk Serv.

Tales of Potosi. Bartolome Arzans de Orsua y Vela. Ed. by R. C. Padden. Tr. by Frances M. Lopez-Morillas from Span. LC 74-6574. 209p. 1975. 12.50 (ISBN 0-87057-144-3, Pub. by Brown U Pr). Univ Pr of New England.

Tales of Poultney. Elton Haynes. 1977. 3.95 o.p. (ISBN 0-682-48935-2). Exposition.

Tales of Pudding Hill: True Animal Stories from New Hampshire. James E. Frazer. 1975. 5.00 o.p. (ISBN 0-682-48096-7). Exposition.

Tales of Railroads. Edward G. Jerrome. (Pacemaker True Adventure Ser.). (Illus., Orig.). 1972. pap. 2.36 (ISBN 0-8224-9188-5); tchrs' manual free (ISBN 0-8224-5208-1). Pitman Learning.

Tales of Rescue. Edward G. Jerrome. (Pacemaker True Adventure Ser). (Illus., Orig.). 1972. pap. 2.36 (ISBN 0-8224-9190-7); tchrs' manual free (ISBN 0-8224-5208-1). Pitman Learning.

Tales of Shipwreck. Edward G. Jerrome. (Pacemaker True Adventure Ser). (Illus., Orig.). 1970. pap. 2.36 (ISBN 0-8224-9187-7); tchrs' manual free (ISBN 0-8224-5208-1). Pitman Learning.

Tales of South Wales. Ken Radford. 192p. 1980. 12.00x (ISBN 0-7050-0080-X, Pub. by Skilton & Shaw England). State Mutual Bk.

Tales of Speed. Edward G. Jerrome. (Pacemaker True Adventures Ser.). (Illus., Orig.). 1973. pap. 2.36 (ISBN 0-8224-9194-X); tchrs' manual free (ISBN 0-685-30383-7). Pitman Learning.

Tales of Spies. Edward G. Jerrome. (Pacemaker True Adventure Ser.). (Illus., Orig.). 1972. pap. 2.36 (ISBN 0-8224-9195-8); tchrs' manual free (ISBN 0-8224-5208-1). Pitman Learning.

Tales of Ten Worlds. Arthur C. Clarke. (RL 7). 1973. pap. 1.50 (ISBN 0-451-08328-8, W8328, Sig). NAL.

Tales of Terror & Mystery. Sir Arthur C. Doyle. (Illus.). 1979. pap. 3.50 (ISBN 0-14-004878-2). Penguin.

Tales of Terror & Tragedy. Edward R. Snow. LC 79-21872. (Illus.). 1979. 8.95 (ISBN 0-396-07775-7). Dodd.

Tales of the Black Cat. Nagib Mahfouz. pap. 5.50 arabic (ISBN 0-685-82881-6). Intl Bk Ctr.

Tales of the Cochiti Indians. Ruth Benedict. 256p. 1981. pap. price not set (ISBN 0-8263-0569-5). U of NM Pr.

Tales of the Fairies in Three Parts, Compleat: As Extracted from the Second Edition in English of Her "Diverting Works". Marie C. D'Aulnoy. Ed. by Alison Lurie & Justin G. Schiller. LC 75-32137. (Classics of Children's Literature Ser.: 1621-1932). PLB 38.00 (ISBN 0-8240-2254-8). Garland Pub.

Tales of the Four Pigs & Brock the Badger. Alison Uttley. (Illus.). (ps-5). 1939. 5.95 (ISBN 0-571-06456-6, Pub. by Faber & Faber). Merrimack Bk Serv.

Tales of the Frontier: From Lewis & Clark to the Last Roundup. Everett Dick. LC 62-14664. (Illus.). 1963. 14.95x (ISBN 0-8032-0038-2); pap. 4.25 (ISBN 0-8032-5744-9, BB 539, Bison). U of Nebr Pr.

Tales of the Great Game Fish. Zane Grey. 304p. Repr. of 1928 ed. lib. bdg. 12.95x (ISBN 0-89190-767-X). Am Repr-Rivercity Pr.

Tales of the Menehune, the Little Pixie Folk of Hawaii. Viola K. Rivenburgh. (Illus.). 48p. 1980. pap. 3.95 (ISBN 0-918146-19-4). Peninsula WA.

Tales of the Munster Festivals. Gerald Griffin. (Nineteenth Century Fiction Ser.: Ireland: Vol. 27). 1044p. 1979. lib. bdg. 46.00 (ISBN 0-8240-3476-7). Garland Pub.

Tales of the Norse Gods & Heroes. Barbara L. Picard. (Illus.). 312p. (gr. 6 up). 1980. Repr. of 1953 ed. 14.95 (ISBN 0-19-274513-1). Oxford U Pr.

Tales of the Northwest: On Sketches of Indian Life & Character. William J. Snelling. LC 75-7067. (Indian Captivities Ser.: Vol. 45). 1976. Repr. of 1830 ed. lib. bdg. 44.00 (ISBN 0-8240-1669-6). Garland Pub.

Tales of the O'Hara Family, 3 vols. John Banim & Michael Banim. Ed. by Robert L. Wolff. (Ireland Nineteenth Century Fiction - Ser. Two: Vol. 18). 1080p. 1979. lib. bdg. 96.00 (ISBN 0-8240-3467-8). Garland Pub.

Tales of the Punjab. Ed. by Flora A. Steel & R. C. Temple. LC 73-175388. (Illus.). 310p. 1980. 10.95 (ISBN 0-370-01271-2, Pub. by Chatto, Bodley Head & Jonathan). Merrimack Bk Serv.

Tales of the Real Gypsy. Paul Kester. LC 77-142004. 1971. Repr. of 1897 ed. 18.00 (ISBN 0-8103-3633-2). Gale.

Tales of the South Pacific. James A. Michener. 192p. 1978. pap. 2.50 (ISBN 0-449-23852-0, Crest). Fawcett.

Tales of the Spooky Natural & Vampire Jokes. Gary Poole. (Illus.). 128p. 1980. lib. bdg. write for info. (ISBN 0-448-13446-2, Tempo); pap. 1.25 (ISBN 0-448-14516-2). G&D.

Tales of the Superstitions: Origins of the Lost Dutchman Legend. Robert Blair. LC 35-35054. 1975. 8.95 (ISBN 0-685-67970-5); pap. 4.95 (ISBN 0-685-67971-3). AZ Hist Foun.

Tales of the West of Ireland. 3rd ed. James Berry. Ed. by Gertrude M. Horgan. (Yeats Cent. Papers Ser.: Vol. 8). 186p. 1975. text ed. 13.25x (ISBN 0-85105-285-1, Dolmen Pr); pap. text ed. 4.50x (ISBN 0-85105-286-X). Humanities.

Tales of Thunder & Lightning. Harry Devlin. LC 74-41057. 48p. (gr. 1-4). 1975. 5.95 o.s.i. (ISBN 0-8193-0805-6, Four Winds); PLB 5.41 o.s.i. (ISBN 0-8193-0806-4). Schol Bk Serv.

Tales of Time & Space. Ed. by Rose R. Olney. (gr. 3 up). 1978. pap. 1.25 (ISBN 0-307-21628-4, Golden Pr). Western Pub.

Tales of Tongue Fu. Paul Krassner. LC 80-16192. (Illus.). 130p. 1981. pap. 4.95 (ISBN 0-915904-55-1). And-or Pr.

Tales Out of Time. Ed. by Barbara Ireson. 224p. (gr. 10 up). 1981. 8.95 (ISBN 0-399-20786-4). Philomel.

Tales Out of Time, Vol. 1: The Mad Compactor & Other Science Fiction Short Stories. Regina Rapier. 1980. 7.50 (ISBN 0-686-69469-4). R C Rapier.

Tales They Tell. Charlotte Huber et al. (Wonder-Story Books Ser). Orig. Title: These Are the Tales They Tell. (gr. 6). text ed. 11.84 (ISBN 0-06-517506-9, SchDept). Har-Row.

Tales Told Again. Walter De La Mare. (Faber Fanfares Ser.). (Illus.). 208p. (Orig.). (gr. 4-7). 1980. pap. 3.25 (ISBN 0-571-18013-2, Pub. by Faber & Faber). Merrimack Bk Serv.

Tales Told at Twilight. Ruskin Bond. 166p. (gr. 4-6). 1970. 1.25 (ISBN 0-88253-394-0). Ind-US Inc.

Tales Told by Hazrat Inayat Khan. Hazrat I. Khan. LC 80-52548. (Collected Works of Hazrat Inayat Khan). (Illus.). 288p. (Orig.). 1980. pap. 7.95 (ISBN 0-930872-15-0). Sufi Order Pubns.

Tales, Treasures, & Pirates of Old Monterey. Randall A. Reinstedt. LC 79-110354. (Illus.). 1976. pap. 4.95 (ISBN 0-933818-03-3). Ghost Town.

TaleSpinners I, 8 bks. Incl. Balloon Spies. Dudley Bromley. LC 80-65914 (ISBN 0-8224-6730-5); Better Than New. Douglas Hiller. LC 80-65915 (ISBN 0-8224-6731-3); Death Angel. Earle Rice, Jr. LC 80-65913 (ISBN 0-8224-6729-1); Dream Pirate. Jack Durish & Nicki Street. LC 80-65918 (ISBN 0-8224-6734-8); Golden God. Jeanne DuPrau. LC 80-65911 (ISBN 0-8224-6727-5); Johnny Tall Dog. Leo P. Kelley. LC 80-65917 (ISBN 0-8224-6733-X); Joker. Nicki Street & A. F. Oreshnik. LC 80-65916 (ISBN 0-8224-6732-1); Man in the Cage. Lisa Eisenberg. LC 80-65912 (ISBN 0-8224-6728-3). (gr. 7 up). 1980. complete set & tchr's guide 31.20 (ISBN 0-8224-6725-9); 3.96 ea. Pitman Learning.

Taliesin. Robert Nye. (Illus.). (gr. 5 up). 1967. 3.95 o.p. (ISBN 0-8090-9110-0). Hill & Wang.

Talis Qualis; or, Tales of the Jury Room. Gerald Griffin. (Nineteenth Century Fiction Ser.: Ireland: Vol. 31). 942p. 1979. lib. bdg. 46.00 (ISBN 0-8240-3480-5). Garland Pub.

Talisman Ring. Georgette Heyer. 1978. pap. 2.25 (ISBN 0-449-23675-7, Crest). Fawcett.

Talk & Contact. Barbara Wilson. LC 77-52008. 76p. (Orig.). 1978. pap. 3.00 (ISBN 0-931188-01-6). Seal Pr WA.

Talk Does Not Cook the Rice: The Teachings of Agni Yoga. Ralph Houston. Ed. by Amelia Phillips. 416p. 1981. pap. 7.95 (ISBN 0-87728-530-6). Weiser.

Talk Down. Brian Lecomber. 1979. pap. 2.25 o.p. (ISBN 0-425-04196-4). Berkley Pub.

Talk It Over: Discussion Topics for Intermediate Students. John Chapman et al. (Illus.). 1978. pap. text ed. 2.50x (ISBN 0-582-79719-5); cassette 7.95 (ISBN 0-582-79720-9). Longman.

Talk of Texas. Jack R. Maguire. LC 73-84554. (Illus.). 160p. 1980. 7.95 (ISBN 0-88319-014-1). Shoal Creek Pub.

Talk of the Town. Joan Smith. (Regency Romance Ser.). 1979. pap. 1.75 o.p. (ISBN 0-449-24137-8, Crest). Fawcett.

Talk to Me! Charlie W. Shedd. (Spire Bk). 1976. pap. 1.50 o.p. (ISBN 0-8007-8244-5). Revell.

Talk to Me. Charlie W. Shedd. 1976. pap. 1.50 (ISBN 0-89129-112-1). Jove Pubns.

Talk to Yourself: Experiencing Intrapersonal Communication. Genelle Austin-Lett & Janet Sprague. LC 75-31037. (Illus.). 160p. 1976. pap. text ed. 7.25 (ISBN 0-395-18576-9). HM.

Talkabout Animals. (Illus.). Arabic 2.50x (ISBN 0-685-82883-2). Intl Bk Ctr.

Talkabout the Beach. (Illus.). Arabic 2.50x (ISBN 0-685-82884-0). Intl Bk Ctr.

Talkabout the Home. (Illus.). Arabic 2.50x (ISBN 0-685-82885-9). Intl Bk Ctr.

Talkative President: The off-the-Record Press Conferences of Calvin Coolidge. Robert H. Ferrell et al. Ed. by Frank Freidel. LC 78-66526. (The History of the United States Ser.: Vol. 6). 287p. 1979. lib. bdg. 23.00 (ISBN 0-8240-9706-8). Garland Pub.

Talking. Richard L. Allington & Kathleen Krull. LC 80-17021. (Beginning to Learn About Ser.). (Illus.). 32p. (ps-2). 1980. PLB 9.65 (ISBN 0-8172-1320-1). Raintree Child.

Talking About Cakes with an Irish & Scottish Accent. Margaret Bates. 1964. text ed. 15.00 (ISBN 0-08-010004-X). Pergamon.

Talking About Particulars. Jack W. Meiland. (International Library of Philosophy & Scientific Method). 1970. text ed. 8.00x (ISBN 0-391-00056-X). Humanities.

Talking About Prayer. Richard Bewes. LC 80-7781. 128p. (Orig.). 1980. pap. 2.95 (ISBN 0-87784-465-8). Inter-Varsity.

Talking About Relationships. 2nd ed. Herbert J. Hess & Charles O. Tucker. 80p. 1980. pap. text ed. 2.95x (ISBN 0-917974-47-6). Waveland Pr.

Talking All Morning. Robert Bly. (Poets on Poetry Ser.). 316p. 1980. pap. 5.95 (ISBN 0-472-15760-4). U of Mich Pr.

Talking Ape. Kieth Laidler. LC 80-5388. (Illus.). 160p. 1980. 11.95 (ISBN 0-8128-2731-7). Stein & Day.

Talking Clowns: From Laurel & Hardy to the Marx Brothers. Frank Manchel. LC 75-37902. (Illus.). 144p. (gr. 7 up). 1976. PLB 6.90 o.p. (ISBN 0-531-01153-4). Watts.

Talking Cure: Essays in Psychoanalysis. Colin MacCabe. 1981. 25.00 (ISBN 0-312-78474-0). St Martin.

Talking Letters. Albert G. Miller. (ABC Serendipity Ser). (Illus.). (gr. 2-6). 1973. 6.57 o.p. (ISBN 0-8372-0824-6); pap. 4.35 o.p. (ISBN 0-685-28631-2). Bowmar-Noble.

Talking Machine. W. C. Chalk. pap. text ed. 2.75x o.p. (ISBN 0-435-11223-6). Heinemann Ed.

Talking Medicine: America's Doctors Tell Their Stories. Ed. by Peter M. Rabinowitz. 1981. 14.95 (ISBN 0-393-01397-9). Norton.

Talking Out of Alcoholism. David Robinson. 160p. 1980. 25.00x (ISBN 0-85664-755-1, Pub. by Croom Helm England). State Mutual Bk.

Talking Purposefully. (Teacher Idea Ser.). 96p. (Orig.). 1981. pap. text ed. 5.95 (ISBN 0-88499-626-3). Inst Mod Lang.

Talking Rock. Ruth Ainsworth. (Illus.). (gr. k-4). 1979. PLB 8.95 (ISBN 0-233-97080-0). Andre Deutsch.

Talking Stone. Dorothy De Wit. LC 79-13798. (gr. 5 up). 1979. 8.95 (ISBN 0-688-80204-4); PLB 8.59 (ISBN 0-688-84204-6). Greenwillow.

Talking Table Mystery. Georgess McHargue. LC 76-23794. (gr. 5 up). 1977. 5.95a o.p. (ISBN 0-385-11353-6); PLB (ISBN 0-385-11354-4). Doubleday.

Talking Time. 2nd ed. Louise B. Scott & Jesse J. Thompson. 1966. text ed. 12.40 o.p. (ISBN 0-07-055818-3, W). McGraw.

Talking to Children. Catherine Snow & C. Ferguson. LC 76-11094. 1977. 35.00 (ISBN 0-521-21318-5); pap. 12.95x (ISBN 0-521-29513-0). Cambridge U Pr.

Talking to Children About Sex. Edna Lehman. pap. 0.95 o.p. (ISBN 0-06-087001-X, HW). Har-Row.

Talking to God. Jackaline Spinelli. (Color Us Wonderful Ser.). (ps). 1972. pap. 0.35 (ISBN 0-8091-6526-0). Paulist Pr.

Talking to My Friend Jesus: Two - Four. Vera Groomer. (Come Unto Me Ser.: Year 2, Bk. 4). 32p. (ps). 1980. pap. 1.50 (ISBN 0-8127-0273-5). Southern Pub.

Talking to the Moon. John J. Mathews. LC 80-50704. (Illus.). 244p. 1980. text ed. 12.95 (ISBN 0-8061-1611-0). U of Okla Pr.

Talking to Yourself: Learning to Communicate with the Most Important Person in Your Life. Pamela E. Butler. LC 80-6161. 192p. 1981. 12.95 (ISBN 0-8128-2779-1). Stein & Day.

Talking with a Child: What to Say After "Hello" What's Your Name, How Old Are You, Where Do You Go to School, When's Your Birthday, Well That's Nice. James D. White. 1976. 8.95 o.s.i. (ISBN 0-02-626570-2). Macmillan.

Talking with Horses. Henry Blake. 1976. 9.95 (ISBN 0-87690-196-8). Dutton.

Talks & Dialogues of J. Krishnamurti. J. Krishnamurti. (Orig.). 1976. pap. 2.25 (ISBN 0-380-01573-0, 38133). Avon.

Talks on Texas Books: A Collection of Book Reviews. Walter P. Webb. Ed. by Llerena B. Friend. LC 76-84083. 1970. 6.00 (ISBN 0-87611-024-3). Tex St Hist Assn.

Tall & Proud. Vian Smith. (gr. 5-7). pap. 1.25 o.p. (ISBN 0-671-29787-2). Archway.

Tall & Proud. Vian Smith. (Illus.). (gr. 5-7). 1968. pap. 1.25 (ISBN 0-671-29787-2). PB.

Tall Are the Hills. Bert G. Boss. 1972. 7.50 o.p. (ISBN 0-682-47448-7). Exposition.

Tall Book of Bible Stories. Katherine Gibson. LC 57-10952. (Tall Bks.). (Illus.). 128p. (gr. k-3). 1980. 5.95 (ISBN 0-06-021935-1, HarpJ); PLB 6.89 (ISBN 0-06-021936-X). Har-Row.

Tall Book of Christmas. Dorothy H. Smith. LC 54-9002. (Tall Bks). (Illus.). 96p. (gr. k-3). 1980. 5.95 (ISBN 0-06-025700-8, HarpJ); PLB 6.89 (ISBN 0-06-025701-6). Har-Row.

Tall Book of Fairy Tales. Eleanor G. Vance. (Tall Bks). (Illus.). 124p. (gr. k-3). 1980. 5.95 (ISBN 0-06-025545-5, HarpJ); PLB 6.89 (ISBN 0-06-025546-3). Har-Row.

Tall Book of Make-Believe. Jane Werner. (Tall Bks.). (Illus.). 92p. (gr. k-3). 1980. 5.95 (ISBN 0-06-026505-1, HarpJ); PLB 6.89 (ISBN 0-06-026506-X). Har-Row.

Tall Buildings: Systems & Concepts. Council on Tall Buildings & Urban Habitat. LC 80-65692. (Monographs on Planning & Design of Tall Buildings: No. 4). 651p. 1980. text ed. 40.00 (ISBN 0-87262-239-8). Am Soc Civil Eng.

Tall Grass & Trouble. Ann Sigford. LC 77-15560. (Story of Environmental Action Ser.). (Illus.). (gr. 7 up). 1978. PLB 8.95 (ISBN 0-87518-153-8). Dillon.

Tall in the West. Vechel Howard. 1978. pap. 1.25 o.p. (ISBN 0-449-13898-4, GM). Fawcett.

Tall Like a Pine. Ferris Weddle. LC 74-17072. (Illus.). 128p. (gr. 4-7). 1974. 5.95g o.p. (ISBN 0-8075-7757-X). A Whitman.

Tall Ships. Hyla M. Clark. LC 76-43112. (Illus.). 1976. pap. 8.95 (ISBN 0-8467-0236-3, Pub. by Two Continents). Hippocrene Bks.

Tall Stranger. Louis L'Amour. (Western Fiction Ser.). 1981. lib. bdg. 10.95 (ISBN 0-8398-2695-8). Gregg.

Tall Tales: American Myths. Tom Lisker. LC 77-11104. (Myth, Magic & Superstition Ser.). (Illus.). (gr. 4-5). 1977. PLB 9.65 (ISBN 0-8172-1039-3). Raintree Pubs.

Talleyrand in America As a Financial Promoter, 1794-96. Ed. by H. Huth & W. Pugh. LC 76-75323. (American Scene Ser). 1971. Repr. of 1942 ed. lib. bdg. 22.50 (ISBN 0-306-71286-5). Da Capo.

Tallgrass Prairie: The Inland Sea. Patricia D. Duncan. LC 78-60177. (Illus.). 1979. 20.00 (ISBN 0-913504-44-0); pap. 12.95 (ISBN 0-913504-56-4). Lowell Pr.

Tallis. 2nd ed. Paul Doe. (Oxford Studies of Composers). (Illus.). 1976. pap. 7.95x (ISBN 0-19-314122-1). Oxford U Pr.

Tally of Types. Stanley Morison. Ed. by B. Crutchley. LC 72-90486. 144p. 1973. 49.50 (ISBN 0-521-20043-1); pap. 14.95 (ISBN 0-521-09786-X). Cambridge U Pr.

Talmadge Girls. Anita Loos. (Illus.). 1978. 12.50 o.p. (ISBN 0-670-69302-2). Viking Pr.

Talmud Today. Ed. by Alexander Feinsilver. 320p. 1980. 14.95 (ISBN 0-312-78479-1). St Martin.

Tamano. Harlan Wade. Tr. by Mamie M. Contreras from Eng. LC 78-26786. (Book About Ser.). Orig. Title: Size. (Illus., Sp.). (gr. k-3). 1979. PLB 7.30 (ISBN 0-8172-1484-4). Raintree Pubs.

Tamara. Sylvia Fusco. 1979. 4.75 o.p. (ISBN 0-8062-1225-X). Carlton.

Tamara. Elinor J. Jones. 1980. pap. 2.75 (ISBN 0-451-09450-6, E9450, Sig). NAL.

Tamara & the Sea Witch. Krystyna Turska. LC 70-164896. (gr. k-3). 1972. PLB 5.95 o.s.i. (ISBN 0-8193-0530-8, Four Winds); PLB 5.41 o.s.i. (ISBN 0-8193-0531-6). Schol Bk Serv.

Tamarind Tree. Romen Basu. (Greenbird Bk.). 1976. lib. bdg. 14.00 (ISBN 0-89253-119-3); flexible bdg. 8.00 (ISBN 0-89253-144-4). Ind-US Inc.

Tamba Pottery: The Timeless Art of a Japanese Village. Daniel Rhodes. LC 74-113180. (Illus.). 1970. 19.95 (ISBN 0-87011-118-3). Kodansha.

Tambo & Bones: A History of the American Minstrel Stage. Carl F. Wittke. LC 69-10174. 1968. Repr. of 1930 ed. lib. bdg. 19.75x (ISBN 0-8371-0276-6, WIAM). Greenwood.

Tamburlaine: Text & Major Criticism, Parts 1 & 2. Christopher Marlowe. Ed. by Irving Ribner. LC 73-7938. 1974. 9.95 (ISBN 0-672-53061-9); pap. 6.95 (ISBN 0-672-63061-3). Odyssey Pr.

Tamburlaine the Great, Parts I & II. Christopher Marlowe. Ed. by John D. Jump. LC 67-10666. (Regents Renaissance Drama Ser). xxvi, 205p. 1967. pap. 2.95x (ISBN 0-8032-5271-4, BB 222, Bison). U of Nebr Pr.

Tame the Restless Wind: The Life & Legends of Sam Bass. Noel Grisham. (Illus.). 6.95 (ISBN 0-685-13279-X). Jenkins.

Tamers of Death: The History of the Alexian Brothers. Christopher J. Kauffman. 1977. 15.00 (ISBN 0-8164-0314-7). Crossroad NY.

Tamil Culture & Civilisation: Readings, the Classical Period. Xavier T. Nayagam. 1971. 8.95x (ISBN 0-210-98163-6). Asia.

Tamil Prose Reader. R. E. Asher & R. Radharkrishnan. LC 73-93705. 1971. text ed. 38.50 (ISBN 0-521-07214-X). Cambridge U Pr.

Tamil Short Stories. Ed. by Ka Naa Subramanyam. 1981. text ed. 10.50x (ISBN 0-7069-1241-1, Pub by Vikas India). Advent Bk.

Tamils of Sri Lenka. (Minority Rights Group: No. 25). 1975. pap. 2.50 (ISBN 0-89192-111-7). Interbk Inc.

Taming of Fidel Castro. Maurice Halperin. 1981. 16.95 (ISBN 0-520-04184-4). U of Cal Pr.

Taming of the Nations: A Study of the Cultural Bases of International Policy. F. S. Northrup. 1971. Repr. of 1952 ed. 16.25 o.s.i. (ISBN 0-02-849740-6). Hafner.

Taming of the Shrew. William Shakespeare. Ed. by Arthur Quiller-Couch et al. (New Shakespeare Ser). 23.95 (ISBN 0-521-07556-4); pap. 4.50x (ISBN 0-521-09499-2). Cambridge U Pr.

Taming of the Troops: Social Control in the United States Army. Lawrence B. Radine. LC 76-5262. (Contributions in Sociology Ser.: No. 22). (Orig.). 1976. lib. bdg. 16.95x (ISBN 0-8371-8911-X, RTT/). Greenwood.

Taming Your Mind. Ken Keyes, Jr. LC 75-4297. Orig. Title: How to Develop Your Thinking Ability. (Illus.). 264p. (Orig.). 1975. 5.95 (ISBN 0-9600688-7-2). Living Love.

Taming Your Turmoil: Managing the Transitions of Adult Life. Peter L. Brill & John P. Hayes. (Illus.). 256p. 1981. 15.95 (ISBN 0-13-884445-3, Spectrum); pap. 6.95 (ISBN 0-13-884437-2). P-H.

Taming Your TV & Other Media. Dave Schwantes. LC 79-16848. (Orion Ser.). 1979. pap. 2.95 (ISBN 0-8127-0246-8). Southern Pub.

Tamirie-Seven Geese. (Sharazad Stories Ser.). (Illus., Arabic.). pap. 3.50 (ISBN 0-686-53111-6). Intl Bk Ctr.

Tampering with the Machinery: Roots of Economic & Political Malaise. Lester O'Shea. 256p. 1980. 11.95 (ISBN 0-07-047749-3, GB). McGraw.

Tamsen Donner: A Woman's Journey. Ruth Whitman. LC 77-90508. 80p. 1977. pap. 4.95 (ISBN 0-914086-20-0). Alicejamesbooks.

Tamsen: The Donner Party. Edna M. Anderson. 1973. pap. 1.50 (ISBN 0-87508-761-2). Chr Lit.

Tamworth Pig Saves the Trees. Gene Kemp. (Fanfares Ser.). (Illus.). (ps-4). 1980. pap. 3.25 (ISBN 0-571-11493-8, Pub. by Faber & Faber). Merrimack Bk Serv.

Tan & Sandy Silence. John D. MacDonald. 1979. 8.95 o.s.i. (ISBN 0-397-01343-4). Lippincott.

Tan-Faced Children. Frank Calkins. LC 78-18556. 1978. 7.95 o.p. (ISBN 0-385-14410-5). Doubleday.

Tanaina Tales from Alaska. Bill Vaudrin. (Civilization of the American Indians Ser.: Vol. 96). 133p. 1980. pap. 3.95 (ISBN 0-8061-1414-2). U of Okla Pr.

Tanamera. Noel Barber. 416p. 1981. 13.95 (ISBN 0-02-506840-7). Macmillan.

Tanaquil. Donald Windham. LC 77-73864. 1977. 8.95 o.p. (ISBN 0-03-022566-3). HR&W.

Tanaquil: The Hardest Thing of All. Donald Windham. (Illus.). 1972. limited ed 75.00x (ISBN 0-917366-05-0). S Campbell.

Tandem. Deborah Camp. (Orig.). 1980. pap. 1.95 (ISBN 0-532-23236-4). Manor Bks.

T'ang Pottery & Porcelain. Margaret Smedley. (Illus.). 168p. 1981. 58.00 (ISBN 0-571-10957-8, Pub. by Faber & Faber). Merrimack Bk Serv.

Tang Soo Do. Hank Murphy. (Illus.). 112p. (Orig.). 1980. pap. 8.00 (ISBN 0-87364-202-3). Paladin Ent.

Tanganyika: Preplanning. Fred G. Burke. (National Planning Ser.: No. 3). (Orig.). 1965. pap. 3.95x (ISBN 0-8156-2089-6). Syracuse U Pr.

Tangent Factor. Lawrence Sanders. 1979. pap. 2.75 (ISBN 0-425-04858-6). Berkley Pub.

Tangier: A Different Way. Lawdom Vaidon. LC 77-8601. (Illus.). 1977. 21.00 (ISBN 0-8108-1072-7). Scarecrow.

Tangier Nights. Clarissa Ross. 288p. (Orig.). 1981. pap. 2.75 (ISBN 0-515-05368-6). Jove Pubns.

Tangle of Roots. Barbara Girion. (gr. 7-12). pap. 1.75 (ISBN 0-440-98889-6, LE). Dell.

Tangle of Roots. Barbara Girion. 192p. (YA) (gr. 7 up). 1979. 7.95 (ISBN 0-684-16074-9). Scribner.

Tangled Chain: The Structure of Disorder in the Anatomy of Melancholy. Ruth Fox. 1976. 16.50x (ISBN 0-520-03085-0). U of Cal Pr.

Tangled Justice: Some Reasons for a Change of Policy in Africa. Charles C. Roberts. LC 72-89011. Repr. of 1937 ed. 11.75x (ISBN 0-8371-1724-0). Negro U Pr.

Tangled Net: Basic Issues in Canadian Communications. Patricia Hindley et al. LC 78-311500. 198p. 1980. pap. 7.95 (ISBN 0-295-95773-5, Pub. by Douglas & McIntyre Canada). U of Wash Pr.

Tangled Vines: A Collection of Mother & Daughter Poems. Ed. by Lyn Lifshin. LC 77-88340. 1978. 9.95 (ISBN 0-8070-6366-5); pap. 4.95 (ISBN 0-8070-6367-3, BP574). Beacon Pr.

Tangled Web. Barbara Hazard. 224p. 1981. pap. 1.95 (ISBN 0-449-50177-9, Coventry). Fawcett.

Tangled Web. Hannelore Valencak. Tr. by Patricia Crampton from Ger. (gr. 7-9). 1978. 7.95 (ISBN 0-688-22169-6); PLB 7.63 (ISBN 0-688-32169-0). Morrow.

Tangles. Marie-Louise Wallin. Tr. by Gerry Bothmer from Swedish. LC 77-72619. (gr. 7up). 1977. 7.95 o.s.i. (ISBN 0-440-08502-0, Sey Lawr). Delacorte.

Tanglewood Murder. Kallen. 1980. 9.95 (ISBN 0-686-62898-5, 61018, Wyndham). S&S.

Tanglewood Murder. Lucille Kallen. LC 80-25148. 325p. 1980. Repr. of 1980 ed. print ed. 10.95large (ISBN 0-89621-257-2). Thorndike Pr.

Tanglewoods' Secret. Patricia M. St. John. (gr. 5-8). 1951. pap. 2.50 (ISBN 0-8024-0007-8). Moody.

Tangram ABC Kit. Susan Johnston. 1979. pap. 1.75 (ISBN 0-486-23853-9). Dover.

Tangram Diary. Clara E. Clark. (Illus.). 64p. (Orig.). (gr. 3-6). 1980. pap. 4.95 (ISBN 0-934734-05-4). Construct Educ.

Tangram: The Ancient Chinese Puzzle. Eiffeis & Schuyt. 12.95 (ISBN 0-8109-2174-X). Abrams.

Tangrams: Three Hundred & Thirty Puzzles. Ronald C. Read. 1978. pap. 2.50 (ISBN 0-486-21483-4). Dover.

Tangu Traditions: A Study of the Way of Life, Mythology & Developing Experience of a New Guinea People. Kenelm Burridge. 1969. 20.50x o.p. (ISBN 0-19-823136-9). Oxford U Pr.

Tangut (Hsi Hsia) Studies: A Bibliography. Luc Kwanten & Susan Hesse. Ed. by Denis Sinor. (Indiana University Uralic & Altaic Ser.: Vol. 137). 125p. 1980. pap. text ed. 9.00 (ISBN 0-933070-05-5). Ind U Res Inst.

Tank Facts & Feats. Kenneth Macksey. (Guinness Superlatives Ser.). (Illus.). 256p. 1980. 17.95 (ISBN 0-8069-9248-4, Pub. by Guinness Superlatives England). Sterling.

Tankas from the Koelz Collection: Museum of Anthropology, University of Michigan. Carolyn Copeland. (Michigan Papers on South & Southeast Asia: No. 18). (Illus.). 100p. (Orig.). 1980. pap. 9.00x (ISBN 0-89148-018-8). Ctr S&SE Asian.

Tanker Cargo Handling. D. L. Rutherford. 128p. 1979. 69.50x (ISBN 0-85264-256-3, Pub. by Griffin England). State Mutual Bk.

Tanker Casuality Report - Analysis of Serious Casualties to Ocean-Going Tankers, 1968-1977. 1979. pap. 8.25 (ISBN 92-801-1086-1, IMCO48, IMCO). Unipub.

Tanker Register Nineteen Eighty. LC 71-565903. (Illus.). 448p. 1980. 180.00x (ISBN 0-8002-2463-9). Intl Pubns Serv.

Tanker Register 1979. LC 71-565903. 1979. 160.00x (ISBN 0-8002-2206-7). Intl Pubns Serv.

Tankerman: All Grades. rev. ed. Ed. by Richard A. Block. (Illus.). 250p. 1981. pap. 21.00 (ISBN 0-934114-30-7). Marine Educ.

Tanks & Other AFVS: 1911-1918. B. T. White. 1917. 8.95 (ISBN 0-02-265400-3). Macmillan.

Tanks & Other Armored Fighting Vehicles 1942-1945. B. T. White. LC 75-28306. (Macmillan Color Ser.). (Illus.). 176p. 1976. 6.95 o.s.i. (ISBN 0-02-626550-8, 62655). Macmillan.

Tanks of World War II. Duncan Crow. (Illus.). 128p. 1979. 16.50x (ISBN 0-85383-006-1). Intl Pubns Serv.

Tanna Debe Eliyyahu. Tr. by William G. Braude & Israel J. Kapstein. 660p. 1980. 27.50 (ISBN 0-8276-0174-3). Jewish Pubn.

Tanners. Leonard E. Fisher. LC 66-10136. (Colonial Americans Ser). (Illus.). (gr. 4-6). 1966. PLB 4.90 o.p. (ISBN 0-531-01038-4). Watts.

Tannisho: A Resource for Modern Living. Alfred Bloom. LC 80-39523. 112p. (Orig.). 1981. pap. 4.95 (ISBN 0-938474-00-6). Buddhist Study.

Tantalizers: A Book of Original Logical Puzzles. Martin Hollis. 1975. 7.95 o.p. (ISBN 0-04-793023-3). Allen Unwin.

Tantalizing Locked Room Mysteries. Ed. by Martin Greenberg & Charles Waugh. LC 80-54817. 224p. 1981. 12.95 (ISBN 0-8027-0680-0). Walker & Co.

Tantalum: Physico-Chemical Properties of Its Compounds & Alloys. (Atomic Energy Review: No. 3). (Illus.). 133p. (Orig.). 1973. pap. 8.75 (ISBN 92-0-149072-0, IAEA). Unipub.

Tantra for the West: A Guide to Personal Freedom. Marcus Allen. LC 80-316. 220p. 1981. pap. 5.95 (ISBN 0-931432-06-5). Whatever Pub.

Tantra: The Indian Cult of Ecstasy. Philip Rawson. (Illus.). 1977. pap. 8.95 (ISBN 0-500-81001-X). Thames Hudson.

Tantra Today. Eleanor M. Montgomery. 200p. 1980. 35.00 (ISBN 0-89975-001-X). World Authors.

Tanzania Under Colonial Rule. Ed. by M. H. Kaniki. (Illus.). 408p. 1980. pap. text ed. 9.95 (ISBN 0-582-64649-9). Longman.

Tao & T'ai Chi Kung. (Illus.). 55p. 1978. pap. 7.95x (ISBN 0-933740-00-X). Inst Self Dev.

Tao of E Wing Chun Do, 2 pts, Vol. 1. 2nd ed. James W. DeMile. (Illus.). 1980. 6.95 ea.; Pt. 1. Pt. 2. Tao of Wing.

Tao of Existence. 2nd ed. Amos I. Chanh. LC 80-8677. (Illus.). 88p. 1981. 14.50x (ISBN 0-691-03963-1); pap. 4.95 (ISBN 0-691-00330-0). Princeton U Pr.

Tao of Medicine. Stephen Fulder. (Illus.). 1981. pap. 8.95. Inner Tradit.

Tao of Psychology: Synchronicity. Jean S. Bolen. LC 79-1778. 1979. 7.95 (ISBN 0-06-250080-5, HarpR). Har-Row.

Tao of Sex. 2nd enl. ed. Akira Ishihara & Howard S. Levy. LC 68-30574. (Sino-Japanese Sexology Classics Ser., Vol. 1). 1969. 15.50x (ISBN 0-685-19350-0). Paragon.

Tao of Wing Chun Do, Vol 1, Part 2. James W. DeMile. (Illus.). 1978. 6.95 (ISBN 0-918642-03-5). Tao of Wing.

Tao-the Subtle Universal Law & the Integral Way of Life. Master Ni Hua-Ching & Hua-Ching. LC 79-91720. 166p. 1980. pap. text ed. 7.50 (ISBN 0-937064-01-7). Wisdom Garden.

Taoism & Chinese Religion. Henri Maspero. Tr. by Frank A. Kierman from Fr. LC 80-13444. Orig. Title: Taoisme et les religions Chinoises. 656p. 1981. lib. bdg. 32.50x (ISBN 0-87023-308-4). U of Mass Pr.

Taoism: The Road to Immortality. John Blofeld. LC 77-90882. 1979. pap. 6.95 (ISBN 0-394-73582-X). Shambhala Pubns.

Taoist Inner View of the Universe & the Immortal Realm. Master Ni Hua-Ching & Hua-Ching. LC 79-91720. 218p. 1980. pap. text ed. 12.50x (ISBN 0-937064-02-5). Wisdom Garden.

Taos Adobes. Bunting et al. 1975. pap. 7.95 (ISBN 0-89013-088-4). Museum NM Pr.

Taos Pueblo. 2nd rev ed. Phillip Reno. LC 72-78538. 1972. pap. 2.50 (ISBN 0-8040-0329-7, SB). Swallow.

Taos Trappers: The Fur Trade in the Far Southwest. David J. Weber. 260p. 1980. pap. 6.95 (ISBN 0-8061-1702-8). U of Okla Pr.

Tapestries of Europe & Colonial Peru in the MFA. Adolph S. Cavallo. 1968. 17.50 (ISBN 0-87846-015-2). Mus Fine Arts Boston.

Tapestry of a Soul. Alzina Mayo. (Illus.). 1980. pap. 4.00 (ISBN 0-933646-13-5). Aries Pr.

Tapestry of Culture. Abraham Rosman & Paula G. Rubel. 1981. pap. text ed. 10.95x (ISBN 0-673-15281-2). Scott F.

Tapestry of Grace. Edward K. Ziegler. 158p. (Orig.). 1980. pap. 5.95 (ISBN 0-87178-834-9). Brethren.

Tappan Creative Cookbook for Microwave Ovens & Ranges. Sylvia Schur. LC 75-24994. 1976. 10.00 o.p. (ISBN 0-03-016806-6). HR&W.

Tappan Creative Cookbook for Microwave Ovens & Ranges. Sylvia Schur. 1981. pap. 2.95 (ISBN 0-451-09742-4, Sig). NAL.

Tapping Solar Markets in Developing Countries, E-041. Business Communications Co. 1981. 800.00 (ISBN 0-89336-274-3). BCC.

Taps at Reveille. F. Scott Fitzgerald. 1935. lib. rep. ed. 15.50x (ISBN 0-684-14742-4, SL274, ScribT); pap. 2.95 (ISBN 0-684-12464-5, SL 274, ScribT). Scribner.

Tar-Aiym Krang. Alan D. Foster. 1979. pap. 2.45 (ISBN 0-345-29232-4, Del Rey Bks). Ballantine.

Tar Baby. Toni Morrison. LC 80-22821. 320p. 1981. 11.95 (ISBN 0-394-42329-1). Knopf.

"Tar Baby" Option: American Policy Toward Southern Rhodesia. Antony Lake. 288p. 1976. 20.00x (ISBN 0-231-04066-0); pap. 6.50x (ISBN 0-231-04067-9). Columbia U Pr.

Tar Heel Ghosts. John Harden. 1954. 7.95 (ISBN 0-8078-0660-9); pap. 4.95 (ISBN 0-8078-4069-6). U of NC Pr.

Tar Heel Stories. Louise Booker. (Illus.). 1968. 4.95 (ISBN 0-930230-34-5). Johnson NC.

Tara: The Dramatic Story of a Brain Injured Child's Courageous Fight to Get Well. Michael Nason & Donna Nason. 1976. pap. 3.50 o.p. (ISBN 0-8015-7455-2). Dutton.

Tarahumara of the Sierra Madre: Beer, Ecology & Social Organization. John G. Kennedy. LC 77-86044. (Worlds of Man Ser.). (Illus.). 1978. text ed. 12.00x (ISBN 0-88295-614-0); pap. text ed. 6.75x (ISBN 0-88295-615-9). AHM Pub.

Tarahumara: Where Night Is the Day of the Moon. Bernard L. Fontana. LC 78-71375. (Illus.). 1979. 37.50 (ISBN 0-87358-183-0). Northland.

Taran Wanderer. Lloyd Alexander. (gr. 4-8). 1969. pap. 1.75 (ISBN 0-440-48483-9, YB). Dell.

Taranath's History of Buddhism in India. Ed. by Debiprasad Chattopadhyaya. Tr. by Alaka Chattopadhyaya Lama Chimpa & Alalca Chattopadhyaya. 500p. 1980. Repr. of 1608 ed. text ed. write for info. (ISBN 0-391-02176-1). Humanities.

Tarantula & the Red Chigger. Mary E. Robertson. 192p. (gr. 5 up). 1980. PLB 7.95 (ISBN 0-316-75115-4). Little.

Tarantulas. Alexander L. Crosby. LC 80-7672. (Illus.). 64p. (gr. 3-7). 1981. 8.50 (ISBN 0-8027-6393-6); PLB 8.85 (ISBN 0-8027-6394-4). Walker & Co.

Taras Bulba & Other Tales. Nikolai V. Gogol. 1977. 7.50x (ISBN 0-460-00740-8, Evman); pap. 2.75 o.p. (ISBN 0-460-01740-3). Dutton.

Tarawa: The Story of a Battle. Robert Sherrod. LC 73-84464. (Illus.). 207p. 1973. 9.00 (ISBN 0-686-05675-2); ltd. presentation vol. 75.00 (ISBN 0-686-05676-0); pap. 1.95 (ISBN 0-686-05677-9). Adm Nimitz Foun.

Tarde Te Ame. Tr. by Joyce Landorf. (Spanish Bks.). (Span.). 1979. 1.95 (ISBN 0-8297-0906-1). Life Pubs Intl.

Tardive Dyskinesia. new ed. Ed. by William Fann et al. LC 79-4468. (Illus.). 1980. text ed. 55.00 (ISBN 0-89335-076-1). Spectrum Pub.

Target America. James L. Tyson. 215p. 1981. 10.95 (ISBN 0-89526-669-5). Regnery-Gateway.

Target Archery. Margaret L. Klann. (Health & Physical Education Ser). 1970. pap. 7.95 (ISBN 0-201-03765-3). A-W.

Target Mayflower. Richard Hirschhorn. 1978. pap. 1.75 o.s.i. (ISBN 0-515-04079-7). Jove Pubns.

Target Rifle Shooting. E. G. Reynolds & Robin Fulton. 1978. 11.95 o.p. (ISBN 0-686-01039-6, 8032, Dist. by Arco). Barrie & Jenkins.

Target Sixteen Hundred. David B. Charnay. 1980. 10.00 (ISBN 0-8184-0290-3). Lyle Stuart.

Target Spelling Skills Program, 2 pts. Bamman et al. (gr. 3-12). 1977. 291.21 ea. (Sch Div); Pt. 1. (ISBN 0-201-21050-9); Pt. 2. (ISBN 0-201-21100-9); tchr's man. incl. A-W.

Targeting the Top: Everything a Woman Needs to Know to Develop a Successful Career in Business Year After Year. Nancy Lee. LC 78-22736. 408p. 1980. 11.95 (ISBN 0-385-13244-1). Doubleday.

Targets of Satire in the Comedies of Etherege, Wycherley & Congreve. Ursula Jantz. (Salzburg Studies in English Literature: Poetic Drama & Poetic Theory Ser.: No. 42). 1978. pap. text ed. 25.00x (ISBN 0-391-01435-8). Humanities.

Targum Onqelos on Genesis 49. Bernard Grossfeld & Moses Aberbach. LC 76-27271. (Society of Biblical Literature. Aramaic Studies). 1976. pap. 6.00 (ISBN 0-89130-078-3, 061301). Scholars Pr Ca.

Targumic Traditions & the New Testament. J. T. Forestell. LC 79-19293. (Society of Biblical Literature Aramaic Studies: No. 4). pap. 12.00 (06 13 04). Scholars Pr CA.

Targums & Rabbinic Literature. John Bowker. LC 71-80817. 1969. 47.50 (ISBN 0-521-07415-0). Cambridge U Pr.

Taride Guide of Paris & Its Suburbs. Cartes Tarides. (Illus.). 368p. 1972. plastic 6.95 o.p. (ISBN 0-88332-014-2, 4896). Larousse.

Tariff Policies for Urban Transport. European Conference of Ministers of Transport, 46th Round Table. 107p. (Fr. & Eng.). 1980. 4.50 (ISBN 9-2821-1060-5). OECD.

Tariff Policy of England & of the United States Contrasted. Erastus B. Bigelow. (Neglected American Economists Ser.). 1974. lib. bdg. 50.00 (ISBN 0-8240-1015-9). Garland Pub.

Tarikh. Incl. Vol. 1, No. 1. Leadership in Nineteenth Century Africa. Ed. by J. B. Webster. 1965. pap. 2.75x (ISBN 0-582-60855-4); Vol. 1, No. 2. African Leadership & European Domination. Ed. by J. B. Webster. 1965. pap. text ed. 2.75x (ISBN 0-686-66972-X); Vol. 1, No. 3. Man in Africa: From the Earliest Beginnings to the Coming of Metal. Ed. by J. B. Webster. 1966. pap. text ed. 2.75x (ISBN 0-582-60857-0); Vol. 1, No. 4. Modernisers in Africa. Ed. by J. B. Webster. 1967. pap. text ed. 2.75x (ISBN 0-582-60858-9); Vol. 2, No. 1. Early African Christianity. Ed. by J. B. Webster & O. Ikime. 1967. pap. text ed. 2.75x (ISBN 0-582-60859-7); Vol. 2, No. 2. African Achievement & Tragedy. Ed. by J. B. Webster & O. Ikime. 1968. pap. text ed. 2.75x (ISBN 0-582-60860-0); Vol. 2, No. 3. Six Aspects of African History. Ed. by Obaro Ikime & Segun Osoba. 1968. pap. text ed. 2.75x (ISBN 0-582-60861-9); Vol. 2, No. 4. France in Africa. Segun Osoba & Obaro Ikime. 1969. pap. text ed. 2.75x (ISBN 0-582-60862-7); Vol. 3, No. 1. Christianity in Modern Africa. Ed. by Segun Osoba & Obaro Ikime. 1969. pap. text ed. 2.75x (ISBN 0-582-60863-5); Vol. 3, No. 2. People of Uganda in the 19th Century. Ed. by Segun Osoba & Obaro Ikime. 1970. pap. text ed. 2.75x (ISBN 0-582-60864-3); Vol. 3, No. 3. Indirect Rule in British Africa. Ed. by Obaro Ikime & Segun Osoba. 1970. pap. text ed. 2.75x (ISBN 0-582-60865-1); Vol. 3, No. 4. Independence Movements in Africa, Pt. 1. Ed. by Obaro Ikime. 1971. pap. text ed. 2.75x (ISBN 0-582-60866-X); Vol. 4, No. 1. Independence Movements in Africa, Pt. 2. Ed. by Obaro Ikime & Segun Osoba. 1971. pap. text ed. 2.75x (ISBN 0-582-60867-8); Vol. 4, No. 2. Government in Pre-Colonial Africa. Ed. by Obaro Ikime & Segun Osoba. 1973. pap. text ed. 2.75x (ISBN 0-582-60868-6); Vol. 4, No. 3-4. European Conquest & African Resistance, Pts. 1-2. Ed. by Obaro Ikime & Segun Osoba. 1973-74. pap. text ed. 2.75x (ISBN 0-582-60316-1). Vol. 4, No. 3 (ISBN 0-582-60869-4). Vol. 4, No. 4. pap. 2.75x (ISBN 0-582-60870-8). Humanities.

Tarikh Al-Ridda: Gleaned from Al-Iktifaq of Al-Balansi. Ed. by Khurshid A. Fariq. 1972. 8.00x o.p. (ISBN 0-210-22334-0). Asia.

Tarikh: Egypt & the Nile Valley, Vol. 5, No. 2. Tarikh. Ed. by Adeniyij Oroge. 65p. 1977. pap. text ed. 2.75x (ISBN 0-582-60874-0). Humanities.

Tarikh: Pan-Africanism, Vol. 6. Ed. by A. I. Asiwaju et al. (Illus.). 69p. 1980. pap. text ed. 3.25x (ISBN 0-582-60374-9). Humanities.

Tarikh: Peoples & Kingdoms of West Africa in the Pre-Colonial Period, Vol. 5, No. 1. 56p. 1974. pap. text ed. 2.75x (ISBN 0-582-60873-2). Humanities.

Tarikh: Protest Against Colonial Rule in West Africa, Vol. 5, No. 3. Tarikh. Ed. by A. I. Asiwaju & M. Crowder. (Illus.). 1977. pap. text ed. 2.75x (ISBN 0-582-60957-7). Humanities.

Tariq Ut-Tahqiq. Bo Utas. (Scandinavian Institute of Asian Studies Monograph: No. 13). 300p. (Orig.). 1975. pap. text ed. 12.50x (ISBN 0-7007-0062-5). Humanities.

Tarjuman Al-Qur'an, 2 Vols. Abul K. Azad. Vol. 1. o.p. (ISBN 0-210-33966-7); Vol. 2. 13.95x (ISBN 0-210-31193-2). Asia.

Tark! Francis Tarkenton. James Hahn & Lynn Hahn. Ed. by Howard Schroeder. (Sports Legends Ser.). (Illus.). 48p. (Orig.). (gr. 3-5). 1981. PLB 5.95 (ISBN 0-89686-121-X); pap. text ed. 2.95 (ISBN 0-89686-136-8). Crestwood Hse.

Tarot: A New Handbook for the Apprentice. Eileen Connolly. LC 79-15303. (Illus.). 1979. pap. 7.95 (ISBN 0-87877-045-3). Newcastle Pub.

Tarot: A New Handbook for the Apprentice. Eileen Connolly. LC 80-22271. 244p. 1980. Repr. of 1979 ed. lib. bdg. 16.95x (ISBN 0-89370-645-0). Borgo Pr.

Tarot Classic Gift Set. Stuart R. Kaplan. (Illus.). 256p. 1972. card deck incl. 14.00 (ISBN 0-913866-55-5). US Games Syst.

Tarot Murders. Mignon Warner. 1981. pap. 2.25 (ISBN 0-440-16162-2). Dell.

Tarot of Cornelius Agrippa. Frederick Morgan. (Illus.). 1978. pap. 4.50 (ISBN 0-915298-11-2). Sagarin Pr.

Tarot Revealed: A Modern Guide to Reading the Tarot Cards. Eden Gray. 239p. Date not set. pap. 1.75 o.p. (ISBN 0-451-09510-3, E9510, Sig). NAL.

Tarot Revelations. Joseph Campbell & Richard Roberts. (Illus., Orig.). 1980. pap. 8.95 (ISBN 0-931290-23-6). Alchemy Bks.

Tarot Shows the Path. Rolla Nordic. 1979. pap. 3.95 (ISBN 0-87728-477-6). Weiser.

Tarot Therapy. Jan Woudhuysen. LC 80-51556. 203p. 1980. 10.00 (ISBN 0-87477-141-2). J P Tarcher.

Tarot's Tower. Jennie Melville. 1979. pap. 1.75 o.p. (ISBN 0-449-24001-0, Crest). Fawcett.

Tarquinia, Villanovans & Early Etruscans. Hugh Hencken. LC 67-24729. (ASPR Bulletin: No. 23). 1968. pap. text ed. 50.00 (ISBN 0-87365-524-9). Peabody Harvard.

Tarry Flynn. Patrick Kavanaugh & P. J. O'Connor. Ed. by John Nemo. (Abbey Theatre Ser.). pap. 2.50 (ISBN 0-912262-40-0). Proscenium.

Tarski Symposium: Proceedings, Vol. 25. Symposia in Pure Mathematics, University of Calif. Berkeley June 1971. Ed. by L. Henkin. LC 74-8666. 1979. Repr. of 1974 ed. with additions 32.00 (ISBN 0-8218-1425-7, PSPUM-25). Am Math.

Tartar Steppe. Dino Buzzati. 1980. pap. 2.75 (ISBN 0-380-50252-6, 50252, Bard). Avon.

Tartarin De Tarascon: Andre Humbert Benedict d'Arlon. Alphonse Daudet. Ed. by E. I. Amateau et al. 1941. 3.95 (ISBN 0-672-73246-7). Odyssey Pr.

Tartarin of Tarascon. Alphonse Daudet. Incl. Tarin on the Alps. 1954. 12.95x (ISBN 0-460-00423-9, Evman). Dutton.

Tartuffe. Jean B. Moliere. Tr. by Robert W. Hartle. LC 60-12946. (Orig.). 1965. pap. 3.95 (ISBN 0-672-60275-X, LLA87). Bobbs.

Tartuffe. Jean B. Moliere. Ed. by Haskell M. Block. LC 58-13149. (Crofts Classics Ser.). 1958. pap. text ed. 2.75x (ISBN 0-88295-059-2). AHM Pub.

Tarumba: The Selected Poems of Jaime Sabines. Jaime Sabines. Tr. by Philip Levine & Ernesto Trejo. 88p. 1979. pap. 6.00 (ISBN 0-918786-21-5). Lost Roads.

Tarzan & Shane Meet the Toad. limited ed. Gerald Locklin et al. 1980. 2.00 (ISBN 0-917554-01-9). Maelstrom.

Tarzan & the Ant Men, No. 10. Edgar R. Burroughs. Date not set. pap. 1.95 (ISBN 0-345-28997-8). Ballantine.

Tarzan & the Castaways. Edgar R. Burroughs. Date not set. pap. 1.95 (ISBN 0-345-24980-1). Ballantine.

Tarzan & the Forbidden City. Edgar R. Burroughs. Date not set. pap. 1.95 (ISBN 0-345-29106-9). Ballantine.

Tarzan & the Foreign Legion. Edgar R. Burroughs. Date not set. pap. 1.95 (ISBN 0-345-24978-X). Ballantine.

Tarzan & the Golden Lion, No. 9. Edgar R. Burroughs. Date not set. pap. 1.95 (ISBN 0-345-28998-6). Ballantine.

Tarzan & the Jewels of Opar, No. 5. Edgar R. Burroughs. 160p. Date not set. pap. 1.95 (ISBN 0-345-28917-X). Ballantine.

Tarzan & the Leopard Man. Edgar R. Burroughs. Date not set. pap. 1.95 (ISBN 0-345-28687-1). Ballantine.

Tarzan & the Lion Men. Edgar R. Burroughs. Date not set. pap. 1.95 (ISBN 0-345-28988-9). Ballantine.

Tarzan & the Lost Empire, No. 12. Edgar R. Burroughs. Date not set. pap. 1.95 (ISBN 0-345-29050-X). Ballantine.

Tarzan & Tradition: Classical Myth in Popular Literature. Erling B. Holtsmark. LC 80-1023. (Contributions to the Study of Popular Culture: No. 1). (Illus.). 216p. 1981. lib. bdg. 22.50 (ISBN 0-313-22530-3, HOT/). Greenwood.

Tarzan at the Earth's Core. Edgar R. Burroughs. Date not set. pap. 1.95 (ISBN 0-345-24483-4). Ballantine.

Tarzan Lord of the Jungle, No. 11. Edgar R. Burroughs. Date not set. pap. 1.95 (ISBN 0-345-28986-2). Ballantine.

Tarzan of the Apes. Edgar R. Burroughs. 1976. Repr. of 1906 ed. lib. bdg. 17.30x (ISBN 0-89966-046-0). Buccaneer Bks.

Tarzan of the Apes, No. 1. Edgar R. Burroughs. 256p. Date not set. pap. 1.95 (ISBN 0-345-28377-5). Ballantine.

Tarzan the Magnificent. Edgar R. Burroughs. Date not set. pap. 1.95 (ISBN 0-345-25961-0). Ballantine.

Tarzan the Terrible, No. 8. Edgar R. Burroughs. Date not set. pap. 1.95 (ISBN 0-345-28745-2). Ballantine.

Tarzan the Triumphant. Edgar R. Burroughs. Date not set. pap. 1.95 (ISBN 0-345-28688-X). Ballantine.

Task & Organization. Ed. by Eric J. Miller. LC 75-12606. (Wiley Series Individuals, Groups & Organizations). 480p. 1976. 41.25 (ISBN 0-471-60605-7, Pub. by Wiley-Interscience). Wiley.

Task Before Us: Audio-Visual Presentation. Ed. by Waldron Scott. (Illus.). 1976. 34.95 (ISBN 0-87808-600-5). William Carey Lib.

Task-Centered Casework. William J. Reid & Laura Epstein. LC 72-4931. 350p. 1972. 13.00x (ISBN 0-231-03466-0). Columbia U Pr.

Task-Centered Practice. William J. Reid & Laura Epstein. LC 76-28177. 1977. 13.00x (ISBN 0-231-04072-5). Columbia U Pr.

Task-Centered System. William J. Reid. 1978. 15.00x (ISBN 0-231-03797-X). Columbia U Pr.

Task Force on Concerns of Physically Disabled Women: Toward Intimacy. 1978. pap. text ed. 2.95 (ISBN 0-87705-337-5). Human Sci Pr.

Task Force Report: The Police. President's Commission on Law Enforcement & Administration of Justice. LC 73-154585. (Police in America Ser). 1971. Repr. of 1967 ed. 17.00 (ISBN 0-405-03383-4). Arno.

Task of Universities in a Changing World. Ed. by Stephen D. Kertesz. LC 71-148191. 1971. 15.00x o.p. (ISBN 0-268-00444-7); pap. 6.95x o.p. (ISBN 0-268-00486-2). U of Notre Dame Pr.

Task Worthy of Travail. Mercer H. Parks. LC 74-11835. 1975. 15.00 (ISBN 0-88415-784-9). Pacesetter Pr.

Tasks of the Youth Leagues. V. I. Lenin. 1975. pap. 0.75 (ISBN 0-8351-0396-X). China Bks.

Tasks to Jobs: Developing a Modular System of Training for Hotel Occupations. International Labour Office. (Hotel & Tourism Management Ser.: No. 3). 302p. 1979. text ed. 17.10 (ISBN 9-22-102148-3). Intl Labour Office.

Tasmanian Tangle. Jane Corrie. (Harlequin Romances Ser.). (Orig.). 1980. pap. text ed. 1.25 o.p. (ISBN 0-373-02335-9, Pub. by Harlequin). PB.

Tassajara Cooking. Edward E. Brown. LC 73-86144. (Illus.). 1980. 11.95 (ISBN 0-394-49523-3). Shambhala Pubns.

Taste & the Antique: The Lure of Classical Sculpture 1500-1900. Francis Haskell & Nicholas Penny. LC 80-24951. (Illus.). 392p. 1981. 45.00x (ISBN 0-300-02641-2). Yale U Pr.

Taste for Life: A High Protein Diet Especially Suited for Hypoglycemia, Diabetes, & Weight Reduction. Marcia Grad. LC 75-22217. (Encore Edition). 160p. 1976. 3.50 o.p. (ISBN 0-684-15678-4, ScribT). Scribner.

Taste in Eighteenth Century France: Critical Reflections on the Origins of Aesthetics, or An Apology for Amateurs. Remy G. Saisselin. LC 65-23460. 1965. 9.00x o.p. (ISBN 0-8156-2083-7). Syracuse U Pr.

Taste of a Rain Forest. Pranab Chatterjee. (Redbird Bk.). 1976. lib. bdg. 10.00 (ISBN 0-89253-121-5); flexible bdg. 4.80 (ISBN 0-89253-137-1). Ind-US Inc.

Taste of Carrot. William Hoest. (Illus.). (gr. 1 up). 1967. pap. 1.95 (ISBN 0-689-20168-0). Atheneum.

Taste of Chaucer: Selections from the Canterbury Tales. Ed. by Anne Malcolmson. LC 64-11493. (Illus.). 184p. (gr. 7 up). 1964. 5.95 o.p. (ISBN 0-15-284270-5, HJ). HarBraceJ.

Taste of Courage: The War 1939-45. Ed. by Desmond Flower & James Reeves. Incl. Vol. 1. The Blitzkrieg. 1971 (ISBN 0-425-03374-0); Vol. 2. The Axis Triumphant. 1971. o.p. (ISBN 0-425-01976-4); Vol. 3. The Tide Turns. 1971. o.p. (ISBN 0-425-01991-8); Vol. 4. The Allies Advance. 1971. o.p. (ISBN 0-425-02008-8); Vol. 5. Victory & Defeat. 1971. o.p. (ISBN 0-425-02018-5). (gr. 9 up). pap. 1.75 o.p. (ISBN 0-685-24476-8, Medallion). Berkley Pub.

Taste of Goodness: Great Aunt Jane's Cook & Garden Book. Jane Birchfield. LC 76-22729. (Illus.). 1976. 8.95 o.p. (ISBN 0-397-01176-8). Lippincott.

Taste of Quality: Favorite Recipes from the Merillat Kitchens of America. Ruth Seighman. 1980. write for info. (ISBN 0-937304-01-8). Impressions.

Taste, Touch & Smell. Irving Adler & Ruth Adler. LC 66-11448. (Reason Why Ser). (Illus.). (gr. 3-6). 1966. PLB 7.89 (ISBN 0-381-99953-X, A76400, JD-J). John Day.

Tasteful Interlude: American Interiors Through the Camera's Eye, 1860 to 1917. William Seale. (Illus.). 288p. 1981. pap. 12.95 (ISBN 0-910050-49-X). AASLH.

Tastemakers: The Development of American Popular Taste. Russell Lynes. (Illus.). 384p. 1980. pap. 6.50 (ISBN 0-486-23993-4). Dover.

Taster's Guide to Beer: Brews & Breweries of the World. Michael A. Weiner. LC 76-30364. 1977. 17.95 (ISBN 0-02-625600-2, 62560). Macmillan.

Tasty Snacks. Aroona Reejhsinghani. 158p. 1975. pap. 2.00 (ISBN 0-88253-773-3). Ind-US Inc.

Tat. Schnurre. (Easy Reader, C). pap. 3.75 (ISBN 0-88436-040-7, GEA201052). EMC.

Tatler. Richard Steele. 1953. 12.95x (ISBN 0-460-00993-1, Evman). Dutton.

Tatler, 4 Vols. Ed. by Richard Steele et al. Repr. of 1898 ed. Set. 163.00 o.p. (ISBN 0-685-05295-8). Adler.

Tatlings. Sydney Tremayne. LC 79-56432. (Illus.). 64p. 1980. 8.95 (ISBN 0-7153-7908-9). David & Charles.

Tatoosh. Martha Hardy. LC 80-8174. (Illus.). 252p. 1980. pap. 6.95 (ISBN 0-89886-005-9). Mountaineers.

Tattercoats. Flora Annie Steel. LC 76-9947. (Illus.). (gr. k-3). 1976. 9.95 (ISBN 0-87888-109-3). Bradbury Pr.

Tattered Tallis. Carol K. Hubner. (Judaica Youth Series: Devorah Doresh Mysteries). (Illus.). 128p. (gr. 3-8). 1979. 5.95 (ISBN 0-910818-19-3); pap. 4.95. Judaica Pr.

Tatting: A New Look at the Old Art of Making Lace. Lael Morgan. LC 76-2808. 1977. pap. text ed. 5.50 o.p. (ISBN 0-385-07707-6). Doubleday.

Tatting: Designs from Victorian Lace Craft. Ed. by Jules Kliot & Kaethe Kliot. (Illus.). 1978. pap. text ed. 5.95 (ISBN 0-916896-13-7). Lacis Pubns.

Tatting Doilies & Edgings. Rita Weiss. (Illus.). 50p. (Orig.). 1980. pap. 2.00 (ISBN 0-486-24051-7). Dover.

Tattoo. Albert Parry. 1971. pap. 1.95 o.s.i. (ISBN 0-02-081080-6, Collier). Macmillan.

Tauben Im Gras. Wolfgang Koeppen. (Suhrkamp Taschenbuecher: No. 37101). (Illus.). 224p. 1980. pap. text ed. 4.55 (ISBN 3-518-37101-0, Pub. by Insel Verlag Germany). Suhrkamp.

Tauberian Theory & Its Applications. A. G. Postnikov. (Trudy Steklov: No. 144). 1980. 26.00 (ISBN 0-8218-3048-1). Am Math.

Taurine. Ed. by Ryan Huxtable & Andre Barbeau. LC 75-14577. 416p. 1976. 41.50 (ISBN 0-89004-064-8). Raven.

Taurine & Neurological Disorders. Ed. by Andre Barbeau & Ryan Huxtable. LC 77-85076. 1978. 45.00 (ISBN 0-89004-202-0). Raven.

Taurus. Julia Parker. (Pocket Guides to Astrology Ser.). (Orig.). 1980. pap. write for info. (ISBN 0-671-25560-6, Fireside). S&S.

Taurus. Kathleen Paul. (Sun Signs Ser.). (Illus.). (gr. 4-12). 1978. PLB 5.95 (ISBN 0-87191-642-8); pap. 2.95 (ISBN 0-89812-072-1). Creative Ed.

Tavern Days in the Hawkeye State. Inez E. Kirkpatrick. (Illus.). 370p. (Orig.). (gr. 7 up). Date not set. pap. price not set (ISBN 0-916170-15-2). J B Pubs. Postponed.

Taverns in Town. Michael Roulstone. (Travel in England Ser.). (Illus.). 96p. 1975. 7.95 (ISBN 0-85944-001-X). Transatlantic.

Tawfiq Al Hakim: Playwright of Egypt. Richard Long. (Illus.). 235p. 1979. 25.00x (ISBN 0-903729-35-0). Three Continents.

Tawny. Chas Carner. LC 77-17411. (gr. 6-9). 1978. 8.95 (ISBN 0-02-716700-3, 71670). Macmillan.

Tawny Gold Man. Amii Loren. 1980. pap. 1.50 (ISBN 0-440-18978-0). Dell.

Tawny McShane. June Wetherell. 1979. pap. 2.25 o.p. (ISBN 0-523-40340-2). Pinnacle Bks.

Tawny, Scrawny Lion. Kathryn Jackson. (Illus.). (ps-3). 1952. PLB 5.00 (ISBN 0-307-60138-2, Golden Pr). Western Pub.

Tawny Scrawny Lion & Clever Monkey. Mary Carey. (ps-3). PLB 5.00 (ISBN 0-307-60128-5, Golden Pr). Western Pub.

Tax Avoidance Strategies. Ed. by Boardroom Reports Editors. LC 80-18256. 178p. 1980. 50.00 (ISBN 0-932648-09-6). Boardroom.

Tax Book of the Cisterian Order. Ed. by Arne O. Johnsen & Peter King. 1980. pap. 14.00x (ISBN 82-00-12653-6, Dist. by Columbia U. Pr.). Universitet.

Tax Breaks for Homeowners: Tax Breaks for Homeowners. Stephen P. Radics, Jr. & Miriam S. Geisman. (Illus.). 96p. 1981. pap. 5.95 (ISBN 0-87863-024-4). Farnswth Pub.

Tax Burdens in American Agriculture: An Intersectoral Comparison. Charles A. Sisson. 1981. write for info. (ISBN 0-8138-1680-7). Iowa St U Pr.

Tax-Exempt Scandal: America's Leftist Foundations. William H. McIlhany, 2nd. 1980. 20.00 (ISBN 0-87000-380-1). Arlington Hse.

Tax Fighter's Guide 1981. Philip Storrer & Brian Williams. 192p. (Orig.). 1981. pap. 6.95 (ISBN 0-936602-08-2). Harbor Pub CA.

Tax-Free Reorganizations (After the Pension Reform Act of 1974) Robert S. Holzman. LC 75-7574. 350p. 1967. 24.95 (ISBN 0-910580-09-X). Farnswth Pub.

Tax Guide for Artists & Arts Organizations. Ed. by Herrick K. Lidstone. LC 76-53905. (Illus.). 1979. 24.95 (ISBN 0-669-01294-7); pap. 14.95 (ISBN 0-669-01295-5). Lexington Bks.

Tax Havens & Measures Against Tax Evasion & Avoidance in the EEC. Ed. by J. F. Avery Jones. 144p. 1974. text ed. 25.00x (ISBN 0-85227-027-5). Rothman.

Tax Havens & Offshore Companies. John R. Seixas. (Illus.). 159p. (Orig.). 1979. pap. 9.95 (ISBN 0-937456-00-4). Dragon Co.

Tax Incentives & Capital Spending. Ed. by Gary Fromm et al. (Studies of Government Finance). 301p. 1971. 14.95 (ISBN 0-8157-2942-1); pap. 5.95 (ISBN 0-8157-2941-3). Brookings.

Tax Incentives for Historic Preservation. LC 79-93052. 232p. 1980. pap. text ed. 12.95 (ISBN 0-89133-041-0). Preservation Pr.

Tax Laws of Korea, 4 vols. Incl. Vol. 1. Income Tax Laws & Enforcemeent Decree; Vol. 2. Value Added Tax Law, Tax Exemption & Reduction Control Law & Asset Revaluation Law & Enforcement Decrees; Vol. 3. Corporation Tax Law & Enforcement Decree. 1979. Set. 30.00 o.p. (ISBN 0-686-17655-3). A M Newman.

Tax on Value Added. Clara K. Sullivan. LC 65-14322. 1965. 20.00x (ISBN 0-231-02807-5). Columbia U Pr.

Tax Philosophers: Two Hundred Years of Thought in Great Britain & the United States. Harold M. Groves. Ed. by Donald J. Curran. LC 74-5901. 256p. 1974. 17.50 (ISBN 0-299-06660-6). U of Wis Pr.

Tax Planning for Investors. rev. ed. Ed. by Sack Prestol & Herman Schneider. LC 79-10505. 1979. pap. 6.95 (ISBN 0-87128-574-6, Pub. by Dow Jones). Dow Jones-Irwin.

Tax Planning for the Closely Held Corporation 1979. (Tax Law & Estate Planning Course Handbook Ser. 1979-80: Vol. 139). 1979. pap. 20.00 (ISBN 0-685-63716-6, J4-3470). PLI.

Tax Planning Techniques for Individuals. (Study in Federal Taxation Ser.: No. 2). 1980. pap. 22.50. Am Inst CPA.

Tax Planning Tips from the Tax Adviser. 1980. pap. 16.50. Am Inst CPA.

Tax Problems in Tax-Exempt Financing. (Tax Law & Estate Planning Course Handbook Ser. 1979-80: Vol. 141). 1980. pap. 20.00 (ISBN 0-685-92234-0, J4-3457). PLI.

Tax Reduction for Small Business & Self Employed. George H. Logan. 1981. pap. 9.95 (ISBN 0-914598-08-2). Padre Prods.

Tax Reform Act of 1976. (Tax Law & Practice Course Handbook Ser., 1976-77: Vol. 104). 1976. pap. 20.00 o.p. (ISBN 0-685-81580-X, J4-3433). PLI.

Tax Revolt Nineteen Eighty. Sheldon D. Engelmayer & Robert J. Wagman. 1980. 12.95 (ISBN 0-87000-469-7). Arlington Hse.

Tax Saving. Julian Block. LC 80-70260. 224p. 1981. 12.95 (ISBN 0-686-69525-9); pap. 7.95 (ISBN 0-686-69526-7). Chilton.

Tax Shelters. 2nd ed. Ed. by Ruth G. Schapiro. LC 80-81333. 425p. 1980. text ed. 40.00 (ISBN 0-686-62638-9, J1-1430). PLI.

Tax Shelters & Tax-Free Income for Everyone, Vol II. 4th ed. William C. Drollinger & William C. Jr. Drollinger. 1981. write for info. (ISBN 0-914244-06-X). Epic Pubns.

Tax Shelters in Plain English: New Strategies for the 1980's. Robert D. Fierro. 180p. 1981. 11.95 (ISBN 0-87863-023-6). Farnswth Pub.

Tax Systems of Latin America: Honduras & Nicaragua. Joint Tax Program OAS IDB. 1967. pap. 1.00 ea. o.p. OAS.

Tax Tactics for Small Business: Pay Less Taxes Legally. Ed. by Dale L. Flesher. 100p. (Orig.). 1980. pap. 5.00 (ISBN 0-938004-06-9). U MS Bus Econ.

Taxation. 8th ed. James Warner. LC 78-65093. 9.00 (ISBN 0-932788-04-1). Bradley CPA.

Taxation & Development. Ed. by N. T. Wang. LC 75-27023. (Special Studies). 1976. text ed. 29.95 (ISBN 0-275-56010-4). Praeger.

Taxation & Economic Development: Twelve Critical Studies. Ed. by J. F. Toye. (Twelve Critical Studies Ser.). 299p. 1978. 26.00x (ISBN 0-7146-3016-0, F Cass Co). Biblio Dist.

Taxation & Governmental Finance in 16th Century Ming China. R. Huang. LC 73-79311. (Studies in Chinese History, Literature & Institutions). (Illus.). 420p. 1975. 55.00 (ISBN 0-521-20283-3). Cambridge U Pr.

Taxation & Multinational Enterprise. 2nd ed. John F. Chown. (International Business Ser.). (Illus.). 1977. text ed. 18.50x o.p. (ISBN 0-686-28509-3). Longman.

Taxation & the Incentive to Work. C. V. Brown. (Illus.). 128p. 1980. 29.95 (ISBN 0-19-877134-7); pap. 12.00 (ISBN 0-19-877135-5). Oxford U Pr.

Taxation for the Computer Industry. Marc J. Lane. 165p. 1980. 24.95 (ISBN 0-471-05710-X). Wiley.

Taxation of American Railroads: A Policy Analysis. Dennis L. Thompson. LC 79-6194. (Contributions in Economics & Economic History: No. 34). (Illus.). 248p. 1981. lib. bdg. 29.95 (ISBN 0-313-22248-7, TTR/). Greenwood.

Taxation of Income from Capital. Ed. by Arnold C. Harberger & Martin J. Bailey. (Studies of Government Finance). 331p. 1969. 12.95 (ISBN 0-8157-3456-5). Brookings.

Taxation of Intercompany Transactions in Selected Countries in Europe & the USA. Ed. by Peat, Marwick, Mitchell & Co. 119p. 1979. pap. 15.80 (ISBN 90-200-0589-8, Pub. by Kluwer Law & Taxation). Kluwer Boston.

Taxation of Mineral Resources. Ed. by Robert Conrad. Bryce Hool. LC 80-8392. (Lincoln Institute of Land Policy Book). 1980. 14.95x (ISBN 0-669-04104-1). Lexington Bks.

Taxation of Multinationals in Communist Countries. Paul Jonas. LC 77-13886. (Praeger Special Studies). 1978. 21.95 (ISBN 0-03-040676-5). Praeger.

Taxation of Municipal Bonds: An Economic Appraisal. Michael L. Mussa & Roger G. Kormendi. 1979. pap. 7.25 (ISBN 0-8447-3331-8). Am Enterprise.

Taxation of Public Utilities in Tennessee. Edward S. Overman. LC 61-13683. 1962. pap. 5.00x o.p. (ISBN 0-87049-038-9). U of Tenn Pr.

Taxation of the Formation & Combination of Business Enterprises. (Statement of Tax Policy Ser.: No. 5). 1980. pap. 6.50. Am Inst CPA.

Taxation of Urban Property in Less Developed Countries. Roy W. Bahl. LC 78-65018. 1979. 19.50 (ISBN 0-299-07860-4). U of Wis Pr.

Taxation, U. S. A. Willard A. Heaps. LC 71-146653. (gr. 7 up). 1971. 6.95 (ISBN 0-395-28906-8, Clarion). HM.

Taxes & Tax Harmonization in Central America. Virginia G. Watkin. LC 67-26564. (Illus.). 534p. (Orig.). 1967. pap. 15.00x (ISBN 0-915506-07-6). Harvard Law Intl Tax.

Taxes, Government & You. Samuel Greenberg. 58p. 1980. 6.95 (ISBN 0-533-04424-3). Vantage.

Taxes 1985: Prospects for Tax Reform in the United States. F. L. Van Voorhees. 1976. 5.00 (ISBN 0-932826-12-1). New Issues MI.

Taxi. Violette Leduc. Tr. by Helen Weaver from Fr. 96p. 1972. 4.95 o.p. (ISBN 0-374-27253-0). FS&G.

Taxi Dog. Svend Otto. LC 77-24127. (Illus.). 40p. (ps-3). 1978. PLB 7.95 (ISBN 0-590-07722-8, Four Winds). Schol Bk Serv.

Taxicab Geometry. E. Krause. (gr. 9-12). 1976. pap. text ed. 4.40 o.p. (ISBN 0-201-03934-6, Sch Div). A-W.

Taxidermy Step by Step. Waddy F. McFall. (Illus.). 256p. 1975. 9.95 (ISBN 0-87691-209-9). Winchester Pr.

Taxila, 3 vols. John Marshall. (Illus.). 1975. Repr. Set. 100.00 (ISBN 0-89684-327-0). Orient Bk Dist.

Taxing & Spending Policy. Ed. by Warren Samuels & Larry Wade. (Orig.). 1980. pap. 5.00 (ISBN 0-918592-41-0). Policy Studies.

Taxing & Spending Policy. Ed. by Warren J. Samuels & Larry L. Wade. LC 79-3689. (A Policy Studies Organization Book). 1980. 19.95 (ISBN 0-669-03469-X). Lexington Bks.

Taxing California Property. 2nd ed. Kenneth Ehrman & Sean Flavin. 1979. 55.00 (ISBN 0-915950-31-6). Bull Pub.

Taxing the Income from U. S. Corporate Investment Abroad. Oswald H. Brownlee. 1979. pap. 3.25 (ISBN 0-8447-3367-9). Am Enterprise.

Taxing Unfair International Trade Practices: A Study of the U. S. Antidumping & Countervailing Duty Law. Greyson Bryan. LC 80-7571. 1980. 34.95x (ISBN 0-669-03752-4). Lexington Bks.

Taxonomia y la Revolucion En las Ciencias Biologicas. rev. ed. (Serie De Biologia: No. 3). (Span.). 1980. pap. 1.25 (ISBN 0-8270-6050-5). OAS.

Taxonomic & Biological Study of the Genus Xyela Dalman in North America. Donald J. Burdick. (U. C. Publ. in Entomology: Vol. 17.3). 1961. pap. 5.00x (ISBN 0-520-09078-0). U of Cal Pr.

Taxonomic Approach to Insecta. V. C. Kapoor. 1980. text ed. 20.00x (ISBN 0-7069-0796-5, Pub. by Vikas India). Advent Bk.

Taxonomic Approach to Insects. V. C. Kapoor. 500p. 1980. 25.00x (Pub. by Croom Helm England). State Mutual Bk.

Taxonomic Keys to the Common Animals of the North Central States. 3rd ed. Samuel Eddy & Alexander C. Hodson. LC 61-11811. 1961. spiral bdg. 8.95 (ISBN 0-8087-0501-6). Burgess.

Taxonomic Review of the Genus Origanum (Labiatae) J. H. Ietswaart. (Leiden Botanical Ser.: No. 4). (Illus.). 1980. pap. 31.60 (ISBN 90-6021-463-3). Kluwer Boston.

Taxonomic Revision of the Genus Dorytomus in North America (Coleoptera: Curculionidae) Charles W. O'Brien. (U. C. Publ. in Entomology: Vol. 60). 1970. pap. 7.00x (ISBN 0-520-09133-7). U of Cal Pr.

Taxonomic Status of Pentachaeta. Gene S. Van Horn. (U. C. Publ. in Botany: Vol. 65). 1973. pap. 7.50x (ISBN 0-520-09468-9). U of Cal Pr.

Taxonomic Study of the Ranunculus hispidus. Thomas Duncan. (U. C. Publications in Botany V Ser.: Vol. 77). 1980. 7.00 (ISBN 0-520-09617-7). U of Cal Pr.

Taxonomic Terminology of the Higher Plants. Henry I. Featherly. 1965. Repr. of 1954 ed. 10.50 o.s.i. (ISBN 0-02-844590-2). Hafner.

Taxonomists' Glossary of Mosquito Anatomy. R. E. Harbach & Kenneth L. Knight. LC 80-83112. (Illus.). 430p. 1980. 17.95 (ISBN 0-517-54149-1). Plexus Pub.

Taxonomy: A Text & Reference Book. Richard E. Blackwelder. LC 67-13520. 1967. 33.50 (ISBN 0-471-07800-X). Wiley.

Taxonomy & Biology of the Lacewing Genus Meleoma (Neuroptera: Chrysopidae) Catherine A. Tauber. (U. C. Publ. in Entomology: Vol. 58). 1969. pap. 8.00x (ISBN 0-520-09131-0). U of Cal Pr.

Taxonomy & Bionomics of the Genus Tetraopes (Cerambycidae Coleoptera). J. A. Chemsak. (U. C. Publ. in Entomology: Vol. 30.1). 1963. pap. 5.00x (ISBN 0-520-09097-7). U of Cal Pr.

Taxonomy of Computer Science & Engineering. AFIPS Taxonomy Committee & Robert L. Ashenhurst. LC 79-57474. ix, 462p. 1980. 35.00 (ISBN 0-88283-008-2). AFIPS Pr.

Taxonomy of Educational Objectives: Handbook 1: Cognitive Domain. Benjamin S. Bloom & David R. Krathwohl. LC 64-12369. 1977. pap. 7.95x (ISBN 0-582-28010-9). Longman.

Taxonomy of Educational Objectives: Handbook 2: Affective Domain. David R. Krathwohl et al. 1969. pap. 7.95x (ISBN 0-582-28239-X). Longman.

Taxonomy of Flowering Plants. 2nd ed. Cedric L. Porter. LC 66-19914. (Illus.). 1967. 24.95x (ISBN 0-7167-0709-8). W H Freeman.

Taxonomy of North American Flies of the Genus Limnia (Diptera: Sciomyzidae) G. C. Steyskal et al. (Publications in Entomology Ser.: No. 83). 1978. pap. 10.00x (ISBN 0-520-09577-4). U of Cal Pr.

Taxonomy of Thelypteris Subgenus Steiropteris (Including Glaphyropteris) Alan R. Smith. (U. C. Publications in Botany Ser.: Vol. 76). 1980. pap. 6.00 (ISBN 0-520-09602-9). U of Cal Pr.

Taxonomy of Viruses. (Illus.). 20p. 1980. pap. 16.75 (ISBN 90-220-0719-7, PDC149, PUDOC). Unipub.

Taxonomy of Visual Processes. William R. Uttal. LC 80-18262. 802p. 1981. text ed. 45.00 (ISBN 0-89859-075-2). L Erlbaum Assocs.

Taxonomy of Water Mite Larvae. Vikram Prasad & David Cook. (Memoirs Ser: No. 18). (Illus.). 326p. 1972. 22.00 (ISBN 0-686-08727-5). Am Entom Inst.

Taxophilus, the Schole of Shootinge, 2 bks. Roger Ascham. LC 75-76431. (English Experience Ser.: No. 79). 184p. 1969. Repr. of 1545 ed. 25.00 (ISBN 90-221-0079-0). Walter J Johnson.

Taxpayer's Audit Survival Manual. Vernon K. Jacobs & Charles W. Schoeneman. 256p. 1980. spiral bdg. 35.00 (ISBN 0-932496-08-3). Alexandria Hse.

Taxpayers' Audit Survival Manual. Vernon K. Jacobs & Charles W. Schoeneman. 1981. 35.00 (ISBN 0-932496-08-3). Green Hill.

Taxpayers Survival Manual. Howard Fishkin. 1979. pap. 2.95 (ISBN 0-933586-06-X). Book Promo Unltd.

Taxpayers, Taxes, & Government Spending: Perspectives on the Taxpayers Revolt. Robert J. Dworak. 272p. 1980. 24.95 (ISBN 0-03-056111-6); pap. 9.95 (ISBN 0-03-056109-4). Praeger.

Tay Bridge Disaster: New Light on the 1879 Tragedy. John Thomas. 1972. 11.95 (ISBN 0-7153-5198-2). David & Charles.

Taylor-Moore Lodge. Suzanne Taylor-Moore. 1981. pap. 2.50 (ISBN 0-686-28090-3). MTM Pub Co.

Tazia's Torment. Sylvie F. Sommerfield. 416p. (Orig.). 1980. pap. 2.50 (ISBN 0-89083-669-8). Zebra.

TCG Survey Nineteen Seventy-Eight. Ed. by Lou Moore. 54p. 1979. 5.00 o.p. (ISBN 0-930452-12-7, Pub. by Theatre Comm). Pub Ctr Cult Res.

TCG Survey 1977. Lindy Zesch. 1978. pap. 4.00 o.p. (ISBN 0-930452-06-2, Pub. by Theatre Comm). Pub Ctr Cult Res.

TCG Survey 1979. Ed. by Lou Moore. (Illus.). 64p. 1980. 5.00x (ISBN 0-930452-10-0, Pub by Theatre Comm). Pub Ctr Cult Es.

Tchaikovsky: A Self-Portrait. Vladimir Volkoff. LC 73-84133. 1975. 15.00 (ISBN 0-8008-7552-4, Crescendo). Taplinger.

Tchaikovsky Ballet Music. John Warrack. LC 79-52144. (BBC Music Guides Ser.: No. 41). (Illus.). 72p. (Orig.). 1980. pap. 2.95 (ISBN 0-295-95697-6). U of Wash Pr.

Tchuck & Gyek. Arkadiy Gaydar. Ed. by Grahame Scott. (Oxford Rapid-Reading Russian Texts Ser). 1969. pap. 1.75x o.p. (ISBN 0-19-832805-2). Oxford U Pr.

Tea. 3rd ed. T. Eden. (Tropical Agriculture Ser.). (Illus.). 1976. text ed. 36.00x (ISBN 0-582-46806-X). Longman.

Tea & Sects. Samuel E. Churchill-Taylor. 64p. (Orig.). 1975. pap. 1.95 (ISBN 0-686-10978-3). MTM Pub Co.

Tea Leaves: A New Look at Resumes. Richard Bolles. 1976. pap. 0.50x (ISBN 0-913668-72-9). Ten Speed Pr.

Tea Leaves: Being a Collection of Letters & Documents Relating to the Shipment of Tea to the American Colonies in the Year 1773, by the East India Tea Company. Francis S. Drake. LC 77-95778. (Illus.). 1970. Repr. of 1884 ed. 18.00 (ISBN 0-8103-3577-8). Gale.

TEA: 8080-8085 Co-Resident Editor-Assembler. Christopher A. Titus. LC 79-65751. 1979. pap. 10.95 (ISBN 0-672-21628-0, 21628). Sams.

Teaacher Behavior & Pupil Self-Concept. Marilynn M. Kash & Gary D. Borich. LC 77-79452. (Education Ser.). (Illus.). 1978. text ed. 13.95 (ISBN 0-201-00843-2). A-W.

Teach 'em Like God Made 'em. June Crabtree. LC 75-28681. (Illus.). 96p. 1976. pap. 5.50 (ISBN 0-87239-034-9, 3230). Standard Pub.

Teach Manual with Task Cards. Rosa A. Hagin et al. LC 76-3338. 186p. 1975. pap. text ed. 47.50 (ISBN 0-8027-9036-4). Walker Educ.

Teach Me in My Way: A Collection for L.D.S. Children. Hope P. Gardner & Sally Gunnell. LC 80-84147. 1980. soft cover 5.95 (ISBN 0-913420-85-9). Olympus Pub Co.

Teach Me to Pray. W. E. Sangster. 1959. pap. 1.25x (ISBN 0-8358-0125-X). Upper Room.

Teach Us, Amelia Bedelia. Parish. (ps-3). 1980. pap. 1.25 (ISBN 0-590-05797-9, Schol Pap). Schol Bk Serv.

Teach Us to Outgrow Our Madness. Kenzaburo Oe. Tr. & intro. by John Nathan. LC 76-54582. 1977. pap. 4.95 (ISBN 0-394-17002-4, E687, Ever). Grove.

Teach Us to Pray. (Aglow Bible Study: Bk. E-2). 64p. 1980. pap. 1.95 (ISBN 0-930756-49-5, 4220-E2). Women's Aglow.

Teach Us to Pray: Learning a Little About God. Andre Louf. 1977. pap. 2.95 (ISBN 0-8091-2001-1). Paulist Pr.

Teach Your Baby to Read. Glenn Doman. 160p. 1980. 9.95 (ISBN 0-224-60064-8, Pub. by Chatto Bodley Jonathan); instruction kit 7.95 (ISBN 0-224-60081-8, Pub. by Chatto Bodley Jonathan). Merrimack Bk Serv.

Teach Your Child Swimming. (Teach Your Child Ser). (Illus.). 1978. pap. 4.95 (ISBN 0-86019-022-6). Transatlantic.

Teach Your Children Woodwork. Christopher Jarman. LC 74-11762. (Illus.). 96p. 1975. 7.95 (ISBN 0-87749-722-2). Sterling.

Teach Your Preschooler to Write. Donna Connell. (Illus.). 132p. (Orig.). 1980. pap. 7.95 (ISBN 0-9604192-0-9). Can Do Bks.

Teach Yourself Bengali. D. F. Hudson. (Teach Yourself Ser). 1965. pap. 2.95 o.p. (ISBN 0-679-10207-8). McKay.

Teach Yourself Biblical Hebrew. Roland K. Harrison. (Teach Yourself Ser). pap. 4.50 (ISBN 0-679-10180-2). McKay.

Teach Yourself Comparative Linguistics. rev. ed. Robert Lord. 1966. pap. 4.95 o.p. (ISBN 0-679-10210-8). McKay.

Teach Yourself Data Processing. K. N. Dodd. 1976. pap. 2.95 o.p. (ISBN 0-679-10379-1). McKay.

Teach Yourself French Revision. Kathleen D. Munro. (Teach Yourself Ser). 1965. pap. 2.95 o.p. (ISBN 0-679-10216-7). McKay.

Teach Yourself German Reader. L. Stringer. (Teach Yourself Ser). 1964. pap. 2.95 o.p. (ISBN 0-679-10218-3). McKay.

Teach Yourself Latvian. Tereza B. Lazdina. (Teach Yourself Ser). 1966. pap. 3.95 o.p. (ISBN 0-679-10219-1). McKay.

Teach Yourself Lip-Reading. Olive M. Wyatt. (Illus.). 172p. 1974. 8.75 (ISBN 0-398-02128-7). C C Thomas.

Teach Yourself Maltese. Joseph Aquilima. (Teach Yourself Ser). pap. 2.95 o.p. (ISBN 0-679-10188-8). McKay.

Teach Yourself Management Accounting. Brian Murphy. (Teach Yourself Ser.). 1978. pap. 2.50 (ISBN 0-679-10477-1). McKay.

Teach Yourself New Mathematics. L. C. Pascoe. (Orig.). 1979. pap. 4.95 (ISBN 0-679-12326-1). McKay.

Teach Yourself Old English. Leslie Blakely. (Teach Yourself Ser). pap. 2.95 o.p. (ISBN 0-679-10192-6). McKay.

Teach Yourself Serbo-Croat Phrase Book. Viola Ellis. (Teach Yourself Ser). pap. 2.95 o.p. (ISBN 0-679-10196-9). McKay.

Teach Yourself Tennis! Stan Smith et al. Ed. by Robert J. LaMarche. LC 80-66688. (Illus.). 224p. Date not set. 12.95 (ISBN 0-914178-39-3). Tennis Mag.

Teach Yourself Tennis! Stan Smith et al. Ed. by Robert J. LaMarche. LC 80-66688. (Tennis Magazine Bks.). (Illus.). 184p. 1980. 12.95 (ISBN 0-914178-39-3, 41418-6). Golf Digest.

Teach Yourself to Swim...Despite Your Fear of Water. Michael Arellano. LC 77-90092. (Illus.). 1978. 7.95 (ISBN 0-8015-7462-5, Hawthorn); pap. 4.95 (ISBN 0-8015-7463-3). Dutton.

Teach Yourself Urdu. T. Grahame Bailey. (Teach Yourself Ser). pap. 3.95 o.p. (ISBN 0-679-10201-9). McKay.

Teach Yourself Welsh. John T. Bowan & P. Jones. (Teach Yourself Ser). pap. 4.50 o.p. (ISBN 0-679-10825-4). McKay.

Teach Yourself Zen, a Way of Life. Christmas Humphreys. (Orig.). 1980. pap. cancelled o.p. (ISBN 0-679-12625-2). McKay.

Teachables from Trashables: Home-Made Toys That Teach. Toys 'n Things Training & Resource Center. LC 79-64910. (Illus., Orig.). 1979. pap. 5.95 (ISBN 0-934140-00-6); spiral bound o.p. 6.95 (ISBN 0-934140-01-4). Toys N Things.

Teacher Absenteeism. Ed. by Richard Kosten. 1977. pap. 9.00 o.p. (ISBN 0-686-00913-4, D-111). Essence Pubns.

Teacher & Child. Haim G. Ginott. Ed. by Robert Markel. LC 70-182448. 228p. 1972. 9.95 (ISBN 0-02-543340-7). Macmillan.

Teacher & Counselling. Douglas H. Hamblin. 1974. 29.00x (ISBN 0-631-15230-X, Pub. by Basil Blackwell); pap. 11.25x (ISBN 0-631-19140-2). Biblio Dist.

Teacher & Pastoral Care. Douglas H. Hamblin. 1978. 29.00x (ISBN 0-631-18670-0, Pub. by Basil Blackwell England); pap. 11.25x (ISBN 0-631-18680-8). Biblio Dist.

Teacher & Research: A Study of Teachers' Priorities & Opinions on Educational Research & Development. Brian Cane & Colin Schroeder. (Research Reports Ser.). (Illus.). 130p. 1970. pap. text ed. 8.25x (ISBN 0-901225-53-3, NFER). Humanities.

Teacher & School Discipline. Ed. by Jean S. Kujoth. LC 75-9770. 1970. 10.00 (ISBN 0-8108-0300-3). Scarecrow.

Teacher & the Needs of Society in Evolution. E. J. King. 1970. text ed. 19.50 (ISBN 0-08-016102-2); pap. text ed. 10.50 (ISBN 0-08-016103-0). Pergamon.

Teacher As Gift. Gertrude A. Sullivan. 64p. 1979. wire coil bdg. 4.95 (ISBN 0-697-01729-X). Wm C Brown.

Teacher As Learning Facilitator: Psychology & the Education Process. Jay M. Smith & Don-David Lusterman. 1979. pap. text ed. 11.95x (ISBN 0-534-00587-X). Wadsworth Pub.

Teacher As Stranger: Educational Psychology for the Modern Age. Maxine Greene. 256p. 1973. 10.95x (ISBN 0-534-00205-6). Wadsworth Pub.

Teacher at Work. Sidney Hilsum. (Exploring Education Ser). 64p. (Orig.). 1972. pap. text ed. 3.75x (ISBN 0-901225-94-0, NFER). Humanities.

Teacher Centers: What Place in Education. Ed. by Sharon Feiman. (Orig.). 1980. pap. 1.50. U Chi Ctr Policy.

Teacher Diagnosis of Educational Difficulties. Robert Smith. LC 69-11433. 1969. text ed. 14.95 (ISBN 0-675-09550-6). Merrill.

Teacher Education & Cultural Change: England, France, West Germany. James Lynch & H. Dudley Plunkett. (Unwin Education Books). 1973. pap. text ed. 8.95x (ISBN 0-04-370046-2). Allen Unwin.

Teacher Education & the New Profession of Teaching. Martin Haberman & T. M. Stinnett. LC 73-7238. 1973. 16.00x (ISBN 0-8211-0751-8); text ed. 15.00x (ISBN 0-685-42633-5). McCutchan.

Teacher Education in America: A Documentary History. Ed. by Merle L. Borrowman. LC 65-17004. 1965. text ed. 9.75 (ISBN 0-8077-1104-7); pap. text ed. 5.25x (ISBN 0-8077-1101-2). Tchrs Coll.

Teacher Education in India: A Study in New Dimensions. K. K. Vasistha. 1979. text ed. 13.50x (ISBN 0-391-01841-8). Humanities.

Teacher Education in the United States: The Responsibility Gap. Study Commission on Undergraduate Education & the Education of Teachers. LC 75-34710. 1976. 10.00x (ISBN 0-8032-0875-8); pap. 2.95x (ISBN 0-8032-5839-9, BB 621, Bison). U of Nebr Pr.

Teacher Education: The Teacher's Point of View. Leeds University Institute of Education. (General Ser.). 85p. (Orig.). 1974. pap. text ed. 5.75x (ISBN 0-85633-050-7, NFER). Humanities.

Teacher in America. Jacques Barzun. LC 80-82370. 496p. 1981. 9.00 (ISBN 0-913966-78-9, Liberty Pr); pap. 4.00 (ISBN 0-913966-79-7). Liberty Fund.
Teacher Moves: An Analysis of Non-Verbal Activity. Barbara M. Grant & Dorothy G. Hennings. LC 71-148592. 1971. pap. text ed. 5.95x (ISBN 0-8077-1456-9). Tchrs Coll.
Teacher My Stomach Hurts! A Guide to Student Health Complaints. Daniel D. Stuhlman & Arnold G. Brody. (Teachers Education Ser.: No. 2). 1980. pap. 1.25 (ISBN 0-934402-04-3). BYLS Pr.
Teacher of Home Economics: Junior High School, High School. David R. Turner. LC 65-23062. (Orig.). 1970. pap. 6.00 o.p. (ISBN 0-668-01316-8). Arco.
Teacher of Social Studies, Junior High School & High School. 6th ed. David R. Turner. LC 63-21436. (Orig.). 1970. pap. 6.00 o.p. (ISBN 0-668-00815-6). Arco.
Teacher of Young Children. Alice Yardley. LC 72-95336. 112p. 1973. 3.25 o.p. (ISBN 0-590-07326-5, Citation). Schol Bk Serv.
Teacher Participation: A Second Look. Robert B. Carson & John W. Friesen. LC 78-64522. 1978. pap. text ed. 7.25 (ISBN 0-8191-0634-8). U Pr of Amer.
Teacher Strategies: Exploration in the Sociology of the School. Ed. by Peter Woods. 282p. 1980. 28.00x (ISBN 0-7099-0115-1, Pub. by Croom Helm Ltd). Biblio Dist.
Teacher Supervision Through Behavioral Objectives: An Operationally Described System. Terrence J. Piper & Denise B. Elgart. LC 79-15648. (Illus., Orig.). 1979. pap. text ed. 6.50 (ISBN 0-933716-03-6). P H Brookes.
Teacher-Teachim: The Toughest Game in Town. Joel Macht. LC 75-2082. 160p. 1975. pap. text ed. 10.95 (ISBN 0-471-56243-2). Wiley.
Teacher Time Savers. Charlie Daniel. (gr. k-3). 1978. 5.95 (ISBN 0-916456-20-X, GA76). Good Apple.
Teacher's Almanack: Practical Ideas for Every Day of the School Year. Dana Newmann. 1973. 12.95x o.p. (ISBN 0-87628-797-6). Ctr Appl Res.
Teachers & Educational Policy. (Educational Studies & Documents, No. 3). 56p. (Orig.). 1972. pap. 2.50 (ISBN 92-3-100885-4, U651, UNESCO). Unipub.
Teachers & Parents: A Guide to Interaction & Cooperation. new ed. Robert B. Rutherford & Eugene Edgar. 1979. text ed. 18.95 (ISBN 0-205-06578-3). Allyn.
Teachers & Parents: A Guide to Interaction & Cooperation. abr. ed. Robert B. Rutherford, Jr. & Eugene Edgar. 1979. pap. text ed. 9.95 (ISBN 0-205-06671-2, 2466716). Allyn.
Teachers & Students: Aspects of American Higher Education. Carnegie Commission on Higher Education. Ed. by Martin Trow. 1975. 21.50 o.p. (ISBN 0-07-010070-5, P&RB). McGraw.
Teachers As Curriculum Evaluators. Ed Davis. (Classroom & Curriculum in Australia Ser.: No. 4). 180p. 1981. text ed. 21.00x (ISBN 0-86861-090-9, 2517); pap. text ed. 9.95x (ISBN 0-86861-098-4, 2518). Allen Unwin.
Teacher's CopeBook: End the Year Better Than You Started. Kay Winters. LC 80-81682. 1980. pap. 8.95 (ISBN 0-8224-6767-4). Pitman Learning.
Teacher's Day. S. Hilsum & B. S. Cane. (Research Report Ser.). 312p. 1971. text ed. 20.75x (ISBN 0-901225-78-9, NFER). Humanities.
Teacher's Dictation Library, 2 pts. Roberta Thomas. (gr. 11-12). 1974. pap. text ed. 19.95 ea. Pt. 1 (ISBN 0-89420-064-X, 139555). Pt. 2 (ISBN 0-89420-065-8, 139666). pt. 1 cassette recordings 229.95 (ISBN 0-89420-212-X, 139000); pt. 2 cassette recordings 289.95 (ISBN 0-89420-213-8, 139300). Natl Book.
Teacher's Enrichment Activities Guide, 1 bk. Sullivan Assoc. pap. text ed. 5.00 (ISBN 0-8449-1980-2). Learning Line.
Teachers for the Disadvantaged. James C. Stone. LC 79-92893. (Higher Education Ser.). 1969. 13.95x o.p. (ISBN 0-87589-043-1). Jossey-Bass.
Teachers Free of Prejudice? H. Larry Winecoff & Eugene W. Kelly, Jr. 1969. 1.25 (ISBN 0-685-59508-0). Integrated Ed Assoc.
Teacher's Guide to Group Vocational Guidance. Bruce Schertzer. LC 79-146112. (Guidance Information Ser). 74p. 1971. pap. 5.55 o.p. (ISBN 0-87442-021-0). Bellman.
Teacher's Guide to Primary Science. Dorothy Diamond. LC 77-82977. (Teaching Primary Science Ser.). (Illus.). 1978. 15.95 (ISBN 0-356-05082-3). Raintree Child.
Teacher's Handbook of Diagnostic Inventories: Spelling, Reading, Handwriting, Arithmetic-a Practical Guide. Philip H. Mann & Patricia A. Suiter. 136p. 1975. text ed. 21.95x o.s.i. (ISBN 0-205-04758-0); duplicating masters incl. o.s.i. (ISBN 0-685-52904-5). Allyn.
Teachers Handbook of Diagnostic Inventories: Spelling, Reading, Handwriting, Arithmetic -- a Practical Guide with Duplicator Masters. 2nd ed. Philip H. Mann et al. 1979. pap. text ed. 29.95 (ISBN 0-205-06625-9). Allyn.
Teacher's Handbook of Diagnostic Screening: Auditory, Visual, Motor, Language-a Practical Guide. Philip H. Mann & Patricia A. Suiter. 117p. 1975. text ed. 21.95x o.p. (ISBN 0-205-04759-9); duplicating masters incl. o.p. (ISBN 0-685-52905-3). Allyn.
Teacher's Handbook of Diagnostic Screening: Auditory, Visual, Motor, Language, Social-Emotional Developmental Skills -- a Practical Guide with Duplicator Masters. 2nd ed. Philip H. Mann et al. 1979. pap. text ed. 29.95 (ISBN 0-205-06626-7). Allyn.
Teacher's Handbook on the School Library Media Center. Betty Martin & Linda Sargent. 399p. 1980. 18.50 (ISBN 0-208-01854-9, Lib Prof Pubns); pap. text ed. 14.50x (ISBN 0-208-01847-6). Shoe String.
Teacher's Handbook to Elementary Social Studies. 2nd ed. Hilda Taba et al. LC 78-147815. (Education Ser). 1971. pap. 9.95 (ISBN 0-201-07426-5). A-W.
Teachers Have Rights, Too: What Educators Should Know About School Law. Leigh Stelzer & Joanna Banthin. (Orig.). 1981. pap. write for info. (ISBN 0-89994-249-0). Soc Sci Ed.
Teachers, Ideology & Control: A Study in Urban Education. Gerald Grace. 1978. 22.50x (ISBN 0-7100-0014-6); pap. 12.00 (ISBN 0-7100-0015-4). Routledge & Kegan.
Teacher's Manual for Beginning Chinese for Intermediate Schools. Juliet Choi. xxii, 331p. 1980. tchrs' ed. 29.00x (ISBN 0-89644-641-7). Chinese Materials.
Teacher's Notebook: Alternatives for Children with Learning Problems. Cynthia A. Clarke et al. 1975. pap. 5.75 (ISBN 0-934338-09-4). NAIS.
Teacher's Notebook: English 5-9, Vol. II. National Association of Independent Schools. 1977. pap. 5.75 (ISBN 0-934338-06-X). NAIS.
Teacher's Notebook: English 5-9, Vol. 1. National Association of Independent Schools. 1975. pap. 4.75 (ISBN 0-934338-05-1). NAIS.
Teacher's Notebook: French. National Association of Independent Schools. 1974. pap. 4.75 (ISBN 0-934338-03-5). NAIS.
Teacher's Notebook: German. National Association of Independent Schools. 1973. pap. 3.25 (ISBN 0-934338-02-7). NAIS.
Teacher's Notebook: Language Arts, K-4. National Association of Independent Schools. 1972. pap. 3.25 (ISBN 0-934338-00-0). NAIS.
Teacher's Notebook: Latin. 1974. pap. 4.75 (ISBN 0-934338-04-3). NAIS.
Teacher's Notebook: Mathematics, K-9. National Association of Independent Schools. (Illus.). 1975. pap. 5.75 (ISBN 0-934338-08-6). NAIS.
Teacher's Notebook: Spanish. NAIS Spanish Committee. 45p. 1973. pap. 3.25 (ISBN 0-934338-01-9). NAIS.
Teachers of Emerson. John S. Harrison. LC 80-2536. 1981. Repr. of 1910 ed. 37.00 (ISBN 0-404-19263-7). AMS Pr.
Teachers of Math. H. Shuard & D. Quadling. 1980. text ed. 18.35 (ISBN 0-06-318174-6, IntlDept); pap. text ed. 9.25 (ISBN 0-06-318175-4). Har-Row.
Teachers of the Deaf: Descriptive Profiles. Edward E. Corbett & Carl J. Jensema. xviii, 158p. 1981. 7.95 (ISBN 0-913580-64-3). Gallaudet Coll.
Teachers of Young Children. 3rd ed. Robert Hess & Doreen J. Croft. LC 80-81928. (Illus.). 528p. 1981. text ed. 17.50 (ISBN 0-395-29172-0); instr's. manual 0.70 (ISBN 0-395-29173-9). HM.
Teachers of Young Children. 2nd ed. Robert D. Hess & Robert J. Croft. 1975. text ed. 16.75 (ISBN 0-395-18711-7); instructor's manual pap. 1.50 (ISBN 0-395-18779-6). HM.
Teacher's Pets, Troublemakers, & Nobodies: Black Children in Elementary School. Helen Gouldner. LC 78-53660. (Contributions in Afro-American & African Studies: No. 41). (Illus.). 1978. lib. bdg. 18.50 (ISBN 0-313-20417-9, GOE/). Greenwood.
Teacher's Practical Guide for Educating Young Children: A Growing Program. Hatoff et al. 344p. 1980. pap. text ed. 16.95 (ISBN 0-205-07126-0, 237126X). Allyn.
Teacher's Reference Manual for Cosmetology. Anthony B. Colletti. 1981. cancelled (ISBN 0-912126-33-7). Keystone Pubns.
Teachers Role in Counseling. Mary G. Ligon & Sarah W. McDaniel. (Foundations of Secondary Education Ser). 1970. pap. 9.95x ref. ed. (ISBN 0-13-891119-3). P-H.
Teacher's Round Table on Sex Education. Mary S. Miller & Patricia Schiller. (Illus.). 1977. pap. 8.00 (ISBN 0-934338-21-3). NAIS.
Teachers Skills. R. H. Rider. 1979. text ed. cancelled (ISBN 0-06-318115-0, Pub. by Har-Row Ltd England). Har-Row.
Teachers, Unions, & Collective Bargaining in Public Education. Anthony M. Cresswell et al. LC 79-91436. 350p. 1980. text ed. 18.50 10 or more copies (ISBN 0-8211-0229-X). McCutchan.
Teacher's Word Book of the Twenty Thousand Words Found Most Frequently & Widely in General Reading for Children & Young People. rev. ed. Edward L. Thorndike. LC 73-5527. 182p. 1975. Repr. of 1932 ed. 22.00 (ISBN 0-8103-4108-5). Gale.
Teachers, Writers, Celebrities: The Intellectuals of Modern France. Regis Debray. 300p. 1981. 17.50 (ISBN 0-8052-7086-8, Pub. by NLB England). Schocken.
Teaching. John Watts. 1973. 11.95 (ISBN 0-7153-6481-2). David & Charles.
Teaching a Child to Read. Roger Farr & Nancy Roser. 514p. 1979. text ed. 16.95 (ISBN 0-15-586650-8, HC). HarBraceJ.
Teaching a Second Language: A Guide for the Student Teacher. (Language in Education Ser.: No. 28). 1980. pap. text ed. 4.95 (ISBN 0-87281-127-1). Ctr Appl Ling.
Teaching About Drugs: A Curriculum Guide, K-12. write for info o.p. (ISBN 0-917160-04-5). Am Sch Health.
Teaching About Television. Len Masterman. (Illus.). 238p. 1980. text ed. 26.00x (ISBN 0-333-26676-5); pap. text ed. 13.00x (ISBN 0-333-26677-3). Humanities.
Teaching About the Other Americans: Minorities in United States History. Ann Curry. LC 80-69120. 110p. 1981. perfect bdg. 8.95 (ISBN 0-86548-028-1). Century Twenty One.
Teaching Abroad. 87p. 1976. 6.00 (IIE). Unipub.
Teaching Adolescent Literature: A Humanistic Approach. Sheila Schwartz. LC 79-2042. 1979. pap. text ed. 9.50x (ISBN 0-8104-6036-X). Hayden.
Teaching Aids Supplement to Teaching Choral Concepts. Duane S. Crowther. 100p. (Orig.). 1981. pap. 5.95 (ISBN 0-88290-162-1, 2022). Horizon Utah.
Teaching an Infant to Swim. Virginia H. Newman. LC 67-11972. (Illus.). 1967. 5.95 o.p. (ISBN 0-15-188110-3). HarBraceJ.
Teaching & Addresses. Edward A. Kimball. 1944. 5.50 (ISBN 0-910964-01-7); deluxe ed. 8.75 o.p. (ISBN 0-686-66491-4). Metaphysical.
Teaching & Coaching Wrestling: A Scientific Approach. 2nd ed. David N. Camaione & Kenneth G. Tillman. LC 79-18686. 1980. text ed. 17.95 (ISBN 0-471-05032-6). Wiley.
Teaching & Counselling. David Galloway. 192p. 1981. pap. 13.50 (ISBN 0-582-48987-3). Longman.
Teaching & Learning About Science & Society. John Ziman. LC 80-40326. (Illus.). 148p. 1980. 22.50 (ISBN 0-521-23221-X). Cambridge U Pr.
Teaching & Learning Adolescent Psychiatry. Ed. by Daniel Offer & James F. Masterson. 180p. 1971. pap. 17.50 photocopy ed. (ISBN 0-398-01414-0). C C Thomas.
Teaching & Learning As a Communication Process. Phillip J. Hills. LC 79-1060. 1979. 15.95x (ISBN 0-470-26700-3). Halsted Pr.
Teaching & Learning Elementary Social Studies. 2nd ed. Arthur K. Ellis. 1981. text ed. 17.50 (ISBN 0-205-07221-6). Allyn.
Teaching & Learning in Higher Education. Alice Heim. (General Ser.). (Orig.). 1976. pap. text ed. 13.25x (ISBN 0-85633-094-9, NFER). Humanities.
Teaching & Learning Mathematics. Peter Dean. (Woburn Educational Ser.). 1981. 18.50x (ISBN 0-7130-0168-2, Pub by Woburn Pr England). Biblio Dist.
Teaching & Media: A Systematic Approach. Vernon S. Gerlach & Donald P. Ely. LC 71-138476. (Illus.). 1971. ref. ed. 17.95x o.p. (ISBN 0-13-891333-1). P-H.
Teaching & Media: A Systematic Approach. 2nd ed. Vernon S. Gerlach & Donald P. Ely. (Illus.). 1980. text ed. 18.95 (ISBN 0-13-891358-7). P-H.
Teaching & Philosophy: A Synthesis. Marie E. Wirsing. LC 79-47998. 238p. 1980. pap. text ed. 9.25 (ISBN 0-8191-0994-0). U Pr of Amer.
Teaching & Social Behavior: Toward an Organizational Theory of Instruction. Phillip C. Schlechty. 348p. 1976. pap. text ed. 7.95x o.p. (ISBN 0-205-05494-3). Allyn.
Teaching & Study Guide to the Principles & Practice of Astrology. Noel Tyl. 1976. 15.00 (ISBN 0-87542-812-6). Llewellyn Pubns.
Teaching & Television: ETV Explained. Ed. by G. Moir. 1967. 22.00 (ISBN 0-08-012355-4); pap. 10.75 (ISBN 0-08-012354-6). Pergamon.
Teaching & Training: A Handbook for Students. 3rd ed. H. R. Mills. 1978. pap. 12.95 (ISBN 0-470-99317-0). Halsted Pr.
Teaching Aphasics & Other Language Deficient Children: Theory & Application of the Association Method. rev. ed. Etoile Dubard. LC 73-93329. (Illus.). 1976. 15.00 (ISBN 0-87805-134-1); pap. 12.50 (ISBN 0-87805-053-1). U Pr of Miss.
Teaching Apprentice Programs in Language & Literature. Ed. by Joseph Gibaldi & James V. Mirollo. (Options for Teaching Ser.: No. 4). 160p. (Orig.). 1981. pap. 7.00x (ISBN 0-87352-303-2). Modern Lang.
Teaching Aquatics. John A. Torney, Jr. & Robert D. Clayton. (Sport Teaching Ser.). 239p. 1980. pap. text ed. 9.95 (ISBN 0-8087-3617-5). Burgess.
Teaching Art. Doreen Roberts. 1978. 19.95 (ISBN 0-7134-0634-8, Pub. by Batsford England); pap. 14.95 (ISBN 0-7134-2314-5). David & Charles.
Teaching Art As a Career. rev. ed. National Art Education Association. 1971. pap. 1.00 (ISBN 0-686-00143-5, 061-25836). Natl Art Ed.
Teaching Art Basics. Roy Sparkes. 1973. 17.95 (ISBN 0-7134-2314-5, Pub. by Batsford England). David & Charles.
Teaching Art in the Elementary School: Enhancing Visual Perception. Phil H. Rueschhoff & M. Evelyn Swartz. (Illus.). 1969. 19.95 (ISBN 0-8260-7655-6). Wiley.
Teaching Authority & Infallibility in the Church, No. 6. Ed. by Paul C. Empie et al. LC 79-54109. (Lutherans & Catholics in Dialogue). 352p. (Orig.). 1979. pap. 4.95 (ISBN 0-8066-1733-0, 10-6222). Augsburg.
Teaching Basic Skills in College: A Guide to Objectives, Skills Assessment, Course Content, Teaching Methods, Support Services, & Administration. Alice S. Trillin et al. LC 79-92469. (Higher Education Ser.). 1980. text ed. 15.95x (ISBN 0-87589-456-9). Jossey-Bass.
Teaching Basketball Fundamentals. Dick Shilts. 1977. 4.95 (ISBN 0-932826-13-X). New Issues MI.
Teaching Bible Stories More Effectively with Puppets. Roland Sylwester. (Illus.). 64p. 1976. pap. 2.95 (ISBN 0-570-03731-X, 12-2633). Concordia.
Teaching Bioethics: Strategies, Problems & Resources. K. Danner Clouser. LC 80-10492. (Teaching of Ethics Ser.). 77p. 1980. pap. 4.00 (ISBN 0-916558-07-X). Hastings Ctr Inst Soc.
Teaching Business Subjects. 3rd ed. Lloyd V. Douglas et al. (Illus.). 1973. ref. ed. 18.95 (ISBN 0-13-891457-5). P-H.
Teaching Child Development. Cynthia Reynolds. 1975. pap. 14.95 (ISBN 0-7134-2990-9, Pub. by Batsford England). David & Charles.
Teaching Children Basic Skills: A Curriculum Handbook for Directive Teaching. Thomas M. Stephens et al. (Special Education Ser.). 1978. pap. text ed. 16.95 (ISBN 0-675-08399-0). Merrill.
Teaching Children Joy. Linda Eyre & Richard Eyre. (Illus.). 194p. 1980. 6.95 (ISBN 0-87747-816-3). Deseret Bk.
Teaching Children of Different Cultures in the Classroom: A Language Approach. Arnold B. Cheyney. (Elementary Education Ser.). 1976. pap. text ed. 8.50 (ISBN 0-675-08622-1). Merrill.
Teaching Children Self-Control: A Fable Mod Manual for Dealing with Behavior Problems of Elementary School-Age Children. Terry L. Stawar. LC 78-71018. (Illus.). Date not set. pap. cancelled (ISBN 0-917476-12-3). Rational Living.
Teaching Children Self-Control: Preventing Emotional & Learning Problems in the Elementary School. new ed. Stanly Fagen et al. (Special Education Ser.). 288p. 1975. pap. text ed. 10.95 (ISBN 0-675-08783-X). Merrill.
Teaching Children Tennis the Vic Braden Way. Vic Braden & Bill Bruns. (Sports Illustrated Bk). (Illus.). 1980. 16.95 (ISBN 0-316-10512-0). Little.
Teaching Children Through Art in the Early Childhood Years. Lendall L. Haskell. 1979. pap. text ed. 10.95 (ISBN 0-675-08307-9). Merrill.
Teaching Children to Read Music. Charles W. Heffernan. LC 68-55077. (Illus., Orig.). 1968. pap. text ed. 4.95x (ISBN 0-89197-439-3). Irvington.
Teaching Children with Developmental Problems, a Family Care Approach. 2nd ed. Kathryn E. Barnard & Marcene L. Erickson. LC 75-31520. (Illus.). 184p. 1976. pap. 10.50 (ISBN 0-8016-0486-9). Mosby.
Teaching Children with Learning & Behavior Problems. 2nd ed. Donald D. Hammil & Nettie R. Bartel. 1978. text ed. 18.95x (ISBN 0-205-06018-8); pap. text ed. 10.95 (ISBN 0-205-06017-X). Allyn.
Teaching Children with Learning Problems. 2nd ed. Gerald M. Wallace & James M. Kauffman. (Special Education Ser.). 1978. text ed. 17.50 (ISBN 0-675-08425-3). Merrill.
Teaching Choral Concepts: Simple Lesson Plans & Teachng Aids for in-Rehearsal Choir Instruction. Duane S. Crowther. LC 79-89356. (Illus.). 1979. 14.95 (ISBN 0-88290-119-2). Horizon Utah.
Teaching Christian Adults. Warren N. Wilbert. 280p. 1980. 9.95 (ISBN 0-8010-9636-7). Baker Bk.

Teaching Clever Children, 7-11. N. R. Tempest. 1974. 10.00 (ISBN 0-7100-7805-6); pap. 4.75 (ISBN 0-7100-7806-4). Routledge & Kegan.
Teaching Composition in Senior High School. Samuel J. Rogal. (Quality Paperback: No. 99). (Orig.). 1969. pap. 2.95 (ISBN 0-8226-0099-4). Littlefield.
Teaching Content Area Reading Skills. 2nd ed. Harry W. Forgan & Charles T. Mangrum. (Illus.). 336p. 1981. pap. text ed. 12.95 (ISBN 0-675-08037-1); instr's. manual 3.75 (ISBN 0-686-69501-1). Merrill.
Teaching Content Area Reading Skills: A Modular Preservice & Inservice Program. new ed. Harry W. Forgan & Charles T. Mangrum. (Elementary Education Ser.). 384p. 1976. pap. text ed. 14.95 (ISBN 0-675-08597-7); instructor's manual 3.95 (ISBN 0-686-67333-6). Merrill.
Teaching: Description & Analysis. John B. Hough & James K. Duncan. (Education Ser). 1970. text ed. 14.95 (ISBN 0-201-02987-1). A-W.
Teaching Disadvantaged Children in the Preschool. Carl Bereiter & S. Englemann. (Illus.). 1966. text ed. 18.95 (ISBN 0-13-892455-4). P-H.
Teaching Discipline: A Positive Approach for Educational Development. 3rd. ed. Madsen & Madsen. 336p. 1980. text ed. 17.95 (ISBN 0-205-07143-0); pap. text ed. 9.95 (0247143-4). Allyn.
Teaching-Discipline: A Positive Approach for Educational Development. 2nd ed. Charles H. Madsen, Jr. & Clifford K. Madsen. 421p. 1975. text ed. 14.95 o.p. (ISBN 0-205-04413-1); pap. text ed. 5.95x o.p. (ISBN 0-205-04407-7). Allyn.
Teaching Eating & Toileting Skills to the Multi-Handicapped in the School Setting. Demos Gallender. (Illus.). 384p. 1980. text ed. 22.75 (ISBN 0-398-03879-1). C C Thomas.
Teaching Educable Mentally Retarded Children: Methods & Materials. James C. Mainord & Harold D. Love. (Illus.). 276p. 1975. 13.75 (ISBN 0-398-02646-7). C C Thomas.
Teaching Elementary Industrial Arts. W. R. Miller & T. Gardner Boyd. LC 70-117395. (Illus.). 1970. text ed. 9.28 (ISBN 0-87006-115-1). Goodheart.
Teaching Elementary Reading. 4th ed. Miles A. Tinker & Constance M. McCullough. (Illus.). 640p. 1975. 18.95x (ISBN 0-13-892083-4). P-H.
Teaching Elementary Reading: Principles & Strategies. Robert Karlin. 488p. 1980. 16.95 (ISBN 0-686-64993-1, HC). HarBraceJ.
Teaching Elementary School Mathematics: An Active Learning Approach. Harold H. Lerch. (Illus.). 416p. 1981. text ed. price not set (ISBN 0-395-29762-1); price not set instr's. manual (ISBN 0-395-29763-X). HM.
Teaching Elementary School Mathematics. 4th ed. Klaas Kramer. 1978. text ed. 18.95 (ISBN 0-205-06054-4, 2360543); instr's man. o.p. avail. (ISBN 0-205-06055-2); performance based study guide 6.95 (ISBN 0-205-06056-0, 2360543). Allyn.
Teaching Elementary School Mathematics. C. Alan Riedesel. (Illus.). 1980. text ed. 18.95 (ISBN 0-13-892549-6). P-H.
Teaching Elementary School Mathematics. 2nd ed. Robert G. Underhill. (Elementary Education Ser.). 1977. text ed. 17.95 (ISBN 0-675-08541-1); instructor's manual 3.95 (ISBN 0-686-67644-0). Merrill.
Teaching Elementary School Mathematics. 3rd ed. Robert G. Underhill. 1981. write for info; instr's. manual 3.95 (ISBN 0-686-69502-X). Merrill.
Teaching Elementary School Science: A Laboratory Approach. Herbert D. Thier. LC 78-113717. (Illus.). 1970. text ed. 10.95x o.p. (ISBN 0-669-51805-0). Heath.
Teaching Elementary School Science Through Motor Learning. James H. Humphrey. 144p. 1975. 11.75 (ISBN 0-398-03252-1). C C Thomas.
Teaching Elementary Science. 2nd ed. William K. Esler. 1976. 17.95x (ISBN 0-534-00489-X). Wadsworth Pub.
Teaching Elementary Science. 2nd ed. William K. Esler & Mary K. Esler. 512p. 1980. text ed. 18.95x (ISBN 0-534-00913-1). Wadsworth Pub.
Teaching English & the Humanities Through Thematic Units. John H. Bushman & Sandra Jones. LC 79-52998. 1979. pap. text ed. 4.50x (ISBN 0-87543-148-8). Lucas.
Teaching English As a Foreign Language. 2nd ed. Ed. by Geoffrey Broughtn et al. (Routledge Education Bks.). 256p. 1980. write for info. (ISBN 0-7100-0642-X); pap. write for info. (ISBN 0-7100-0643-8). Routledge & Kegan.
Teaching English As a Foreign Language. Geoffrey Broughton et al. (Education Bks). 1978. 20.00x (ISBN 0-7100-8950-3); pap. 9.50 (ISBN 0-7100-8951-1). Routledge & Kegan.
Teaching English As a Second Language. John Bright. 1975. text ed. 8.75x (ISBN 0-582-54003-8). Longman.
Teaching English As a Second Language. Robert L. Politzer & Frieda N. Politzer. 264p. 1981. Repr. of 1972 ed. lib. bdg. write for info. (ISBN 0-89874-068-1). Krieger.
Teaching English As an International Language: From Practice to Principle. Peter Strevens. 128p. 1980. pap. 9.95 (ISBN 0-08-025333-4). Pergamon.
Teaching English Grammar. Robert C. Pooley. LC 57-11455. 1957. 24.00x (ISBN 0-89197-440-7); pap. text ed. 12.95x (ISBN 0-89197-441-5). Irvington.
Teaching English in the Secondary School. Robert P. Parker, Jr. & Maxine E. Daly. LC 72-88812. (Orig.). 1973. pap. text ed. 7.95 (ISBN 0-02-923870-6). Free Pr.
Teaching English Today. Dwight L. Burton et al. 1975. text ed. 17.75 (ISBN 0-395-18616-1). HM.
Teaching Ethics in Journalism Education. Clifford G. Christians & Catherine L. Covert. LC 80-10426. (Teaching of Ethics Ser.). 71p. 1980. pap. 4.00 (ISBN 0-916558-08-8). Hastings Ctr Inst Soc.
Teaching Exceptional Adolescents. James E. Smith, Jr. & James S. Payne. (Special Education Ser.). 312p. 1980. pap. text ed. 16.95 (ISBN 0-675-08128-9). Merrill.
Teaching Exceptional Children in All America's Schools: A First Course for Teachers & Principals. Ed. by Jack W. Birch & Maynard C. Reynolds. 1977. text ed. 10.00 (ISBN 0-86586-084-X). Coun Exc Child.
Teaching Experience: An Introduction to Education Through Literature. E. D. Landau et al. (Illus.). 496p. 1976. pap. text ed. 11.95 (ISBN 0-13-892539-9). P-H.
Teaching Faster Reading: A Manual. Edward Fry. 1963. text ed. 7.95x (ISBN 0-521-05047-2). Cambridge U Pr.
Teaching for Changed Attitudes & Values. J. Ruud. LC 71-187577. 1972. pap. 2.50 (ISBN 0-686-14993-9, 265-08378). Home Econ Educ.
Teaching for Employability. P. Murphy. 1973. pap. 1.00 (ISBN 0-686-14994-7, 261-08414). Home Econ Educ.
Teaching for Learning. 2nd ed. Myron Dembo. 1981. pap. text ed. write for info. (ISBN 0-8302-8856-2). Goodyear.
Teaching Foreign Language Skills. 2nd, rev. ed. Wilga M. Rivers. LC 80-24993. 1981. lib. bdg. 22.00x (ISBN 0-226-72098-5); pap. 12.50x (ISBN 0-226-72097-7). U of Chicago Pr.
Teaching Foreign Languages to the Very Young. Ed. by Reinhold Freudenstein. LC 79-42885. (Pergamon Institute of English - Symposium). (Illus.). 112p. 1979. 7.50 (ISBN 0-08-024576-5). Pergamon.
Teaching French: An Introduction to Applied Linguistics. 2nd ed. Robert L. Politzer. LC 65-14561. 1965. text ed. 14.95 (ISBN 0-471-00430-8). Wiley.
Teaching: From Command to Discovery. Muska Mosston. 300p. 1972. pap. 8.95x (ISBN 0-534-00165-3). Wadsworth Pub.
Teaching General Music: Action Learning for Middle & Secondary Schools. Thomas A. Regelski. LC 80-5561. (Illus.). 448p. 1981. text ed. 12.95 (ISBN 0-02-872070-9). Schirmer Bks.
Teaching Geography. Patrick Bailey. (Teaching Ser.). (Illus.). 261p. 1975. 17.95 (ISBN 0-7153-6860-5). David & Charles.
Teaching Handicapped Children Easily: A Manual for the Average Classroom Teacher Without Specialized Training. Herbert Neff & Judith Pilch. (Illus.). 264p. 1976. 16.50 (ISBN 0-398-03439-7). C C Thomas.
Teaching Handicapped Students in the Mainstream: Coming Back...or Never Leaving. 2nd ed. Anne L. Pasanella & Cara B. Volkmor. (Special Education Ser.). (Illus.). 384p. 1981. pap. text ed. 10.95 (ISBN 0-675-08026-6). Merrill.
Teaching Health Education in the Elementary School. Ruth Engs & Molly Wantz. (Illus., LC 77-079371). 1978. text ed. 17.75 (ISBN 0-395-25483-3); inst. manual 0.75 (ISBN 0-395-25484-1). HM.
Teaching Health Science in Middle & Secondary Schools. Linda B. Meeks et al. 400p. write for info (ISBN 0-697-07392-0). Wm C Brown.
Teaching History with Community Resources. Clifford L. Lord. LC 64-15864. (Orig.). 1967. pap. 4.50x (ISBN 0-8077-1710-X). Tchrs Coll.
Teaching Improvised Drama. Peter Chilver. 1978. 17.95 (ISBN 0-7134-1036-1, Pub. by Batsford England). David & Charles.
Teaching in a Multicultural Society: Perspectives & Professional Strategies. Ed. by Dolores E. Cross et al. LC 76-14291. (Illus.). 1977. 15.95 (ISBN 0-02-906710-3). Free Pr.
Teaching in America. Stephen M. Fain et al. 1979. pap. text ed. 10.95x (ISBN 0-673-15056-9). Scott F.
Teaching in an Open Classroom. Nancy Langstaff. (Illus.). 1975. pap. 4.75 o.p. (ISBN 0-934338-24-8). NAIS.
Teaching in Health Professions. Charles W. Ford & Margaret K. Morgan. LC 75-37571. (Illus.). 250p. 1976. text ed. 16.95 (ISBN 0-8016-1622-0). Mosby.
Teaching in Middle Schools. William E. Klingele. 1979. text ed. 16.95 (ISBN 0-205-06526-0, 236526X). Allyn.
Teaching in Schools of Nursing. Stuart M. Shaffer et al. xii, 110p. (Orig.). 1972. 6.95 o.p. (ISBN 0-8016-4531-X). Mosby.
Teaching in the Early Years. 2nd ed. Bernard Spodek. (Early Childhood Ser.). (Illus.). 1978. ref. ed. 17.95 (ISBN 0-13-892562-3). P-H.
Teaching in the Elementary School: A Guide to Placement. Edgar Klugman. LC 77-116889. (Illus., Orig.). 1970. pap. 3.50 o.p. (ISBN 0-8224-6825-5). Pitman Learning.
Teaching in the First School. Mary Goldstein. 1975. pap. 14.95 (ISBN 0-7134-3026-5, Pub. by Batsford England). David & Charles.
Teaching Industrial Education: Princples & Practices. Robert Andrews & E. E. Ericson. 1976. pap. text ed. 7.12 (ISBN 0-87002-079-X). Bennett IL.
Teaching Inefficient Learners. Wineva M. Grzynkowicz. 148p. 1971. 12.75 (ISBN 0-398-00743-8). C C Thomas.
Teaching Job Hunt. Walter Zintz. LC 73-88726. 27p. 1973. pap. 3.00 o.p. (ISBN 0-915254-05-0, 05-0). Nova Venturion.
Teaching Juniors. Ruth Beechick. LC 80-68886. (Teacher Training Ser.). 192p. (Orig.). 1981. pap. 3.95 (ISBN 0-89636-062-8). Accent Bks.
Teaching Language Arts Creatively in the Elementary Grades. A. Barbara Pilon. LC 77-23508. 1978. 13.50 (ISBN 0-471-68980-7). Wiley.
Teaching Language Through Sight & Sound - Set 1. Joan M. Sayre. 1980. 29.75x (ISBN 0-8134-2077-6). Interstate.
Teaching Languages: A Way & Ways. Earl W. Stevick. (Orig.). 1980. pap. text ed. 11.95 (ISBN 0-88377-147-0). Newbury Hse.
Teaching Law with Computers. Russel W. Burris et al. (EDUCOM Series in Computing & Telecommunications in Higher Education). 1979. lib. bdg. 19.50x (ISBN 0-89158-193-6). Westview.
Teaching, Learning, & the Mind. Young Pai. LC 72-3512. 250p. (Orig.). 1973. pap. text ed. 10.95 (ISBN 0-395-12663-0, 3-42835). HM.
Teaching Learning in the Preschool: A Dialogue Approach. Marion Blank. LC 72-97007. 1973. pap. text ed. 11.95 (ISBN 0-675-08971-9). Merrill.
Teaching Library Skills in Schools. James E. Herring. (General Ser.). 1979. pap. text ed. 11.75x (ISBN 0-85633-171-6, NFER). Humanities.
Teaching Low Achieving Children Reading, Spelling & Handwriting: Developing Perceptual Skills with the Graphic Symbols of the Language. Annabelle M. Markoff. (Illus.). 320p. 1976. 22.75 (ISBN 0-398-03483-4). C C Thomas.
Teaching Luther's Catechism, Vol. II. Herbert Girgensohn. Tr. by John W. Doberstein from Ger. LC 59-8463. 1960. 6.00 (ISBN 0-8006-0866-6, 1-866). Fortress.
Teaching Manual for Tutor Librarians. D. Finn et al. 1978. 10.50 (ISBN 0-85365-830-7, Pub. by Lib Assn England). Oryx Pr.
Teaching Materials on Criminal Procedure. Jerry L. Dowling. (Criminal Justice Ser.). 1976. text ed. 17.95 (ISBN 0-685-99576-3); pap. text ed. write for info. (ISBN 0-8299-0616-9); instrs.' manual avail. (ISBN 0-8299-0617-7). West Pub.
Teaching Mathematics: A Source Book for Aids, Activities, & Strategies. Max Sobel & Evan Maletsky. (Illus.). 288p. 1975. pap. text ed. 11.95 (ISBN 0-13-894121-1). P-H.
Teaching Mathematics in the Elementary School. 2nd ed. Lola J. May. LC 73-11694. (Illus.). 1974. 16.95 (ISBN 0-02-920380-5); pap. text ed. 10.95 (ISBN 0-02-920370-8). Free Pr.
Teaching Mathematics in the Secondary School. Alfred Posamentier. 1981. pap. text ed. 15.95 (ISBN 0-675-08033-9). Merrill.
Teaching Mathematics to Children with Special Needs. Fredericka K. Reisman & Samuel H. Kauffman. (Special Education Ser.). 336p. 1980. text ed. 16.95x (ISBN 0-675-08175-0). Merrill.
Teaching Mathematics to the Learning Disabled. Nancy S. Bley & Carol A. Thornton. 350p. 1981. text ed. price not set (ISBN 0-89443-357-1). Aspen Systems.
Teaching Media Skills: An Instructional Program for Elementary & Middle School Students. H. Thomas Walker & Paula K. Montgomery. LC 76-30605. 1977. lib. bdg. 17.50x (ISBN 0-87287-135-5). Libs Unl.
Teaching Mixed Ability Classes: An Individualized Approach. A. V. Kelly. 1975. pap. 4.00 o.p. (ISBN 0-06-318071-5, IntlDept). Har-Row.
Teaching Modern Languages. David Webb. LC 74-82025. (Teaching Ser.). 1975. 17.95 (ISBN 0-7153-6858-3). David & Charles.
Teaching Modern Science. 3rd ed. Arthur A. Carin & Robert B. Sund. (Elementary Education Ser.: No. C22). 352p. 1980. pap. text ed. 12.95 (ISBN 0-675-08193-9). Merrill.
Teaching Moral Reasoning: Theory & Practice. Jack Arbuthnot & David Faust. (Illus.). 304p. 1980. text ed. 18.50 scp (ISBN 0-06-040321-7, HarpC). Har-Row.
Teaching Morality & Religion. Alan Harris. (Classroom Close-Ups Ser.). 1975. text ed. 10.95x o.p. (ISBN 0-04-371029-8); pap. text ed. 6.50x (ISBN 0-04-371030-1). Allen Unwin.
Teaching Morphology Developmentally: Methods & Materials for Teaching Bound Morphology. Kenneth G. Shipley & Carolyn S. Banis. 1981. manual 50.00 (ISBN 0-88450-728-9). Communication Skill.
Teaching Motor Skills. B. Cratty. (Man in Action Ser.). (Illus.). 1973. pap. text ed. 7.95 (ISBN 0-13-893958-6). P-H.
Teaching Music to the Exceptional Child: A Handbook for Mainstreaming. Alice S. Beer & Richard Graham. (Illus.). 1980. text ed. 14.95 (ISBN 0-13-893982-9); pap. text ed. 9.95 (ISBN-0-13-893974-8). P-H.
Teaching Myself About Asthma. 1st ed. Guy S. Parcel et al. LC 79-13166. (Illus.). 1979. pap. 10.00 (ISBN 0-8016-3755-4). Mosby.
Teaching Nutrition. 2nd ed. E. Eppright et al. 1963. 7.95 (ISBN 0-8138-1660-2). Iowa St U Pr.
Teaching Nutrition & Food Science. Margaret Knight. 1976. pap. 13.50 (ISBN 0-7134-3099-0, Pub. by Batsford England). David & Charles.
Teaching Occupational Home Economics. Terrass & Comfort. 1979. 9.24 (ISBN 0-87002-282-2). Bennett IL.
Teaching of Arabic As a Foreign Language. Raja Nasr. 12.00x (ISBN 0-685-89880-6). Intl Bk Ctr.
Teaching of Art. L. Bucher. 1963. 10.00 o.p. (ISBN 0-8022-0193-8). Philos Lib.
Teaching of Charles Fourier. Nicholas V. Riasanovsky. LC 77-84043. 1969. 20.00x (ISBN 0-520-01405-7). U of Cal Pr.
Teaching of Critical Thinking. Edward D'Angelo. (Philosophical Currents Ser: No. 1). 78p. 1971. text ed. 17.25x (ISBN 90-6032-482-X). Humanities.
Teaching of Elementary Science. Bob F. Steere. LC 80-13992. 174p. (Orig.). 1981. pap. text ed. write for info. (ISBN 0-89874-178-5). Krieger.
Teaching of English in Schools 1900-1970. David Shayer. 216p. 1972. 15.00 (ISBN 0-7100-7321-6). Routledge & Kegan.
Teaching of Ethics in Higher Education: A Report by the Hastings Center. Ed. by Daniel Callahan. LC 80-10294. (Teaching of Ethics Ser.). 103p. 1980. pap. 5.00 (ISBN 0-916558-09-6). Hastings Ctr Inst Soc.
Teaching of Ethics in the Social Sciences. Donald P. Warwick. LC 80-10154. (Teaching of Ethics Ser.). 69p. 1980. pap. 4.00 (ISBN 0-916558-11-8). Hastings Ctr Inst Soc.
Teaching of Evolution in Public Schools: A Comparison of Evolution & Special Creation. Lonni R. Erickson. (Illus.). 40p. (Orig.). 1980. pap. 3.95 (ISBN 0-937242-03-9). Scandia Pubs.
Teaching of French As a Foreign Language in Eight Countries. John B. Carroll. LC 75-17945. (International Studies in Evaluation, Vol. 5). 1975. 17.95 (ISBN 0-470-13602-2). Halsted Pr.
Teaching of High School English. 4th ed. J. N. Hook. 593p. 1972. 18.50 (ISBN 0-8260-4325-9, 50645). Wiley.
Teaching of Human Rights. 258p. 1980. pap. 13.25 (ISBN 92-3-101781-0, U1036, UNESCO). Unipub.
Teaching of Instrumental Music. Richard J. Colwell. (Illus.). 1969. 16.95 (ISBN 0-13-893131-3). P-H.
Teaching of Literature. H. L. Moody. 1974. pap. text ed. 5.50x (ISBN 0-582-52602-7). Longman.
Teaching of Philosophy in Universities of the United States. Harold E. Davis & Harold A. Durfee. (Philosophy Ser). 1965. pap. 5.00 (ISBN 0-8270-5845-4). OAS.
Teaching of Pronunciation. B. Haycraft. 1975. pap. text ed. 7.25x (ISBN 0-582-52434-2). Longman.
Teaching of Psychology: Method, Content, & Context. John Radford & David Rose. LC 79-40824. 1980. 40.00 (ISBN 0-471-27665-0, Pub. by Wiley-Interscience). Wiley.
Teaching of Reading: A Developmental Process. Paul A. Witty et al. 1966. text ed. 8.95x o.p. (ISBN 0-669-20305-X). Heath.
Teaching of Social Studies in British Universities. Kathleen Jones. 87p. 1964. pap. text ed. 3.75x (Pub. by Bedford England). Renouf.
Teaching of the Gita. Mohandas K. Ghandhi. Ed. by Anand T. Hingorani. 103p. (Orig.). 1981. pap. 2.00 (ISBN 0-934676-26-7). Greenlf Bks.

Teaching of the Qur'An, with an Account of Its Growth & Subject Index. H. U. Stanton. LC 74-90040. 1969. Repr. 12.50x (ISBN 0-8196-0253-1). Biblo.

Teaching of the Social Sciences in Higher Technical Education: An International Survey. Ed. by Julius Gould & J. H. Smith. (Teaching in the Social Sciences, Vol. 5). 1968. pap. 7.00 (ISBN 92-3-100692-4, U660, UNESCO). Unipub.

Teaching off the Wall. Elaine Prizzi & Jeanne Hoffman. 1980. pap. 6.95 (ISBN 0-8224-6830-1). Pitman Learning.

Teaching Oral English. Donn Byrne. (Longman Handbooks for Language Teachers). (Illus.). 192p. 1976. pap. text ed. 7.25x (ISBN 0-582-55081-5). Longman.

Teaching Physical Education. 2nd ed. Muska Mosston. (Illus.). 256p. 1981. pap. text ed. 12.95 (ISBN 0-675-08036-3). Merrill.

Teaching Physical Education: A Systems Approach. Robert N. Singer & Walter Dick. 400p. 1974. text ed. 17.25 o.p. (ISBN 0-395-17770-7); instructors' manual pap. 2.45 o.p. (ISBN 0-395-17854-1); study guide 6.95 o.p. (ISBN 0-395-17788-X). HM.

Teaching Physical Education: A Systems Approach. 2nd ed. Robert N. Singer & Walter Dick. LC 79-88450. (Illus.). 1980. text ed. 18.25 (ISBN 0-395-28359-0); instrs'. manual 0.75 (ISBN 0-395-28360-4). HM.

Teaching Physically Handicapped Children: Methods & Materials. Harold D. Love. (Illus.). 176p. 1978. 15.75 (ISBN 0-398-03703-5). C C Thomas.

Teaching Piano. Denes Agay. (Illus.). 1981. 29.95 (ISBN 0-8256-8039-5). Music Sales.

Teaching Policy Studies: A Guide to What, How & Where. Ed. by William D. Coplin. LC 77-9186. (Policy Studies Organization Ser.). 1978. 19.95 (ISBN 0-669-01829-5). Lexington Bks.

Teaching Practical Social Work. Hazel Danbury. 85p. 1979. pap. text ed. 7.40x (ISBN 0-7199-0953-8, Pub. by Bedford England). Renouf.

Teaching Preschool Language Arts. Lawrence J. Foster et al. (Illus.). 272p. 1981. pap. text ed. 15.95 (ISBN 0-8425-1933-5). Brigham.

Teaching Preschool Math: Foundations & Activities. Anthony C. Maffei & Patricia Buckley. LC 79-27448. 176p. 1980. text ed. 14.95 (ISBN 0-87705-492-4). Human Sci Pr.

Teaching Preschool Reading. Sandra H. Heater. LC 80-18768. (Illus.). 128p. (Orig.). 1980. pap. text ed. 8.95x (ISBN 0-8425-1837-1). Brigham.

Teaching Preschoolers. Marie Frost. (Peter Panda Ser.). 1977. pap. 1.25 (ISBN 0-87239-147-7, 42039). Standard Pub.

Teaching Primaries. Ruth Beechick. LC 80-66723. (Accent Teacher Training Ser.). 128p. (Orig.). 1980. pap. 3.95 (ISBN 0-89636-054-7). Accent Bks.

Teaching Primary Mathematics: Strategy & Evaluation. J. A. Glenn. 1977. text ed. 9.50 (ISBN 0-06-318071-5, IntlDept); pap. text ed. 6.65 (ISBN 0-06-318072-3, IntlDept). Har-Row.

Teaching Program in Psychiatry, 3 vols. Incl. Vol. 1. Schizophrenia, Paranoid Conditions, Depression. Peter G. Beckett & Thomas H. Bleakley. 7.95 (ISBN 0-8143-1335-3); pap. 5.95 (ISBN 0-8143-1336-1); Vol. 2. Psychoneurosis, Organic Brain Disease, Psychopharmacology. Peter G. Beckett. 270p. text ed. 8.95x (ISBN 0-8143-1392-2); pap. text ed. 5.95x (ISBN 0-8143-1393-0); Vol. 3. Personality Development in Preschool Years, Latency, & Adolescence. Leonard R. Piggott & Joseph Frischoff. LC 67-64750. 185p. text ed. 8.95x (ISBN 0-8143-1532-1); pap. text ed. 5.95x (ISBN 0-8143-1533-X). LC 67-64750. 1975. Wayne St U Pr.

Teaching Psychiatry in Medical School: Proceedings. Conference on Psychiatry & Medical Education, Atlanta, 1967. 589p. 1969. pap. 5.00 o.p. (ISBN 0-685-65581-4, 213). Am Psychiatric.

Teaching Psychosocial Aspects of Patient Care. Ed. by Bernard Schoenberg et al. LC 68-19757. 1968. 22.50x (ISBN 0-231-03162-9). Columbia U Pr.

Teaching Reading & Study Strategies: The Content Areas. 2nd ed. H. Alan Robinson. 1978. text ed. 17.95 (ISBN 0-205-06084-6, 2360845). Allyn.

Teaching Reading & Thinking Skills. Myles I. Friedman & Michael D. Rowls. (Illus.). 1979. pap. 12.95x (ISBN 0-582-29006-6). Longman.

Teaching Reading As a Language Experience. 3rd ed. Mary A. Hall. (Illus.). 160p. 1981. pap. text ed. 6.95 (ISBN 0-686-69503-8). Merrill.

Teaching Reading As a Language Experience. 2nd ed. MaryAnne Hall. (Elementary Education Ser.). 128p. 1976. pap. text ed. 7.95x (ISBN 0-675-08666-3). Merrill.

Teaching Reading: Foundations & Strategies. 2nd ed. Pose Lamb & Richard Arnold. 432p. 1980. text ed. 16.95x (ISBN 0-534-00847-X). Wadsworth Pub.

Teaching Reading in Content Areas. 2nd ed. Harold L. Herber. (Illus.). 1978. ref. ed. 16.95 (ISBN 0-13-894170-X). P-H.

Teaching Reading in High School: Improving Reading in Content Areas. 3rd ed. Robert Karlin. LC 76-48523. 1977. 16.95 (ISBN 0-672-61402-2). Bobbs.

Teaching Reading in the Middle Grades. 2nd ed. Richard J. Smith & Thomas C. Barrett. LC 78-18650. (Education Ser.). (Illus.). 1979. text ed. 9.50 (ISBN 0-201-07057-X). A-W.

Teaching Reading in the Secondary School. Wilma H. Miller. (Illus.). 532p. 1974. 18.75 (ISBN 0-398-03026-X). C C Thomas.

Teaching Reading: Selected Materials. Walter B. Barbe. 1965. pap. 6.95x (ISBN 0-19-500823-5). Oxford U Pr.

Teaching Reading Through Motor Learning. Dorothy D. Sullivan & James H. Humphrey. (Illus.). 160p. 1973. text ed. 11.75 (ISBN 0-398-02732-3). C C Thomas.

Teaching Reading to Children with Special Needs. John F. Savage & Jean F. Mooney. 1978. pap. text ed. 11.95 (ISBN 0-205-06130-3, 2361302). Allyn.

Teaching Reading to Deaf Children. Beatrice O. Hart. 1978. 9.95 (ISBN 0-88200-117-5). Bell Assn Deaf.

Teaching Reading to Individuals with Learning Difficulties. Patrick Ashlock. 216p. 1974. pap. 14.75 (ISBN 0-398-03050-2). C C Thomas.

Teaching Reading to Slow & Disabled Learners. Samuel A. Kirk et al. LC 77-77655. (Illus.). 1978. text ed. 17.75 (ISBN 0-395-25821-9). HM.

Teaching Reading to the Special Needs Child: An Ecological Approach. Patricia Gillespie. (Special Education Ser.). 1979. text ed. 17.95 (ISBN 0-675-08274-9). Merrill.

Teaching Related Subjects in Trade & Industrial & Technical Education. Milton E. Larson. LC 72-80235. 1972. text ed. 19.95 (ISBN 0-675-09073-3). Merrill.

Teaching Religion: The Secularization of Religion Instruction in a West German School System. W. Clinton Terry, III. LC 80-5569. 208p. 1981. lib. bdg. 18.50 (ISBN 0-8191-1366-2); pap. text ed. 9.50 (ISBN 0-8191-1367-0). U Pr of Amer.

Teaching Research Curriculum for Moderately & Severely Handicapped. H. D. Fredericks & Victor Baldwin. (Illus.). 340p. 1978. pap. 23.75 photocopy ed. spiral (ISBN 0-398-03330-7). C C Thomas.

Teaching Research Curriculum for Moderately & Severely Handicapped: Gross & Fine Motor. H. D. Fredericks et al. (Illus.). 264p. 1980. pap. 17.75 (ISBN 0-398-04035-4); developmental chart 3.50. C C Thomas.

Teaching Research Curriculum for Moderately & Severely Handicapped: Gross & Fine Motor. H. D. Fredericks et al. (Illus.). 1980. pap. 17.75 o.p. (ISBN 0-398-04035-4); developmental chart 3.50 o.p. (ISBN 0-686-65145-6). C C Thomas.

Teaching Research Curriculum for Moderately & Severely Handicapped: Self-Help & Cognitive. H. D. Fredericks et al. (Illus.). 288p. 1980. pap. 15.75 o.p. (ISBN 0-398-04034-6). C C Thomas.

Teaching Research Curriculum for Moderately & Severely Handicapped: Self-Help & Cognitive. H. D. Fredericks et al. (Illus.). 280p. 1980. pap. 17.75 (ISBN 0-398-04034-6); developmental chart 3.50 (ISBN 0-686-65146-4). C C Thomas.

Teaching Research Motor-Development Scale: For Moderately & Severely Retarded Children. H. D. Fredericks et al. (Illus.). 80p. 1972. 9.75 (ISBN 0-398-02284-4). C C Thomas.

Teaching School Physics: A UNESCO Source Bk. Ed. by John L. Lewis. (Illus., Orig.). pap. 11.50 (ISBN 92-3-100937-0, U662, UNESCO). Unipub.

Teaching Science at the Secondary Stage. Association For Science Education. text ed. 8.50x (ISBN 0-7195-1707-9). Transatlantic.

Teaching Science by Inquiry in the Secondary School. 2nd ed. Robert B. Sund & Leslie W. Trowbridge. LC 72-86024. 640p. 1973. text ed. 17.95x (ISBN 0-675-09051-2). Merrill.

Teaching Science in the Elementary School. David P. Butts. LC 72-86790. (Orig.). 1973. 8.95 (ISBN 0-02-905010-3); pap. text ed. 6.95 (ISBN 0-02-905060-X). Free Pr.

Teaching Secondary Health Science. Walter D. Sorochan & Stephen J. Bender. LC 78-1760. 1978. text ed. 21.50 (ISBN 0-471-81387-7). Wiley.

Teaching Seminar with Milton H. Erickson, M.D. Milton H. Erickson. Ed. by Jeffrey K. Zeig. LC 80-23804. 340p. 1980. 20.00 (ISBN 0-87630-247-9). Brunner-Mazel.

Teaching Singing. John C. Burgin. LC 72-10594. 1973. 10.00 (ISBN 0-8108-0565-0). Scarecrow.

Teaching Skills to Children with Learning & Behavioral Disorders. Thomas M. Stephens. 1977. text ed. 18.50 (ISBN 0-675-08533-0). Merrill.

Teaching Slow Learners Through Active Games. J. H. Humphrey & Dorothy D. Sullivan. 192p. 1973. 12.75 (ISBN 0-398-00886-8). C C Thomas.

Teaching Social Studies in the Elementary School. John R. Lee. LC 73-14017. (Illus.). 1974. 12.95 (ISBN 0-02-918360-X); pap. text ed. 7.95 (ISBN 0-02-918370-7). Free Pr.

Teaching Social Studies in the Elementary School: The Basics for Citizenship. T. Kaltsournis. 1979. 17.95 (ISBN 0-13-895631-6). P-H.

Teaching Social Studies in the Secondary School. John R. Lee et al. LC 72-91998. (Orig.). 1973. pap. text ed. 7.95 (ISBN 0-02-918380-4). Free Pr.

Teaching Social Studies to Culturally Different Children. Ed. by James A. Banks & William W. Joyce. LC 72-132057. (Education Ser). 1971. pap. 8.95 (ISBN 0-201-00391-0). A-W.

Teaching Spanish in the Secondary School in Trinidad, West Indies: A Curriculum Perspective. Venus E. Deonanan & Carlton R. Deonanan. LC 79-6199. 373p. 1980. pap. text ed. 11.50 (ISBN 0-8191-1005-1). U Pr of Amer.

Teaching Spanish to the Hispanic Bilingual: Issues, Aims, & Methods. Guadalupe Valdes-Fallis et al. 272p. 1981. text ed. 18.95 (ISBN 0-8077-2629-X). Tchrs Coll.

Teaching Speech Communication. Larry E. Sarbaugh. (General Education Ser.). 1979. text ed. 15.95 (ISBN 0-675-08300-1). Merrill.

Teaching Speech Communication in the Secondary School. William D. Brooks & Gustav W. Friedrich. 368p. 1973. text ed. 19.50 (ISBN 0-395-12629-0, 3-06400). HM.

Teaching Strategies: A Guide to Better Instruction. Donald C. Orlich et al. (Orig.). 1979. pap. text ed. 12.95 (ISBN 0-669-02700-6). Heath.

Teaching Strategies for Children in Conflict: Curriculum, Methods & Materials. H. Lee Swanson & Henry R. Reinert. LC 79-40. (Illus.). 1979. pap. text ed. 15.95 (ISBN 0-8016-4106-3). Mosby.

Teaching Strategies for Ethnic Studies. 2nd ed. James A. Banks. 1979. pap. text ed. 10.95 (ISBN 0-205-06585-6, 2365855). Allyn.

Teaching Strategies for the Social Studies: Inquiry, Valuing & Decision-Making. 2nd ed. James A. Banks & Ambrose A. Clegg, Jr. LC 76-5081. (Illus.). 1977. text ed. 16.50 (ISBN 0-201-00412-7). A-W.

Teaching Students Through Their Individual Learning Styles: A Practical Approach. Kenneth Dunn & Rita Dunn. (Illus.). 1978. ref. ed. 15.95 (ISBN 0-87909-808-2). Reston.

Teaching Students with Learning Problems. Cecil Mercer & Ann Mercer. (Orig.). 1981. pap. text ed. 14.95 (ISBN 0-675-08040-1). Merrill.

Teaching Successfully in Industrial Education. rev. ed. G. Harold Silvius & Estell H. Curry. 1967. text ed. 16.09 (ISBN 0-87345-451-0). McKnight.

Teaching Teaching. E. C. Wragg. LC 74-82023. 1975. 17.95 (ISBN 0-7153-6857-5). David & Charles.

Teaching Technique in Primary Maths. J. D. Williams. (Exploring Education Ser). (Illus.). 1971. pap. text ed. 5.75x (ISBN 0-391-02082-X, NFER). Humanities.

Teaching Techniques. rev. ed. Clarence H. Benson. 1974. pap. text ed. 3.75 (ISBN 0-910566-05-4); instr's guide by janet m. loth 3.75 (ISBN 0-686-66315-2). Evang Tchr.

Teaching Techniques: For Retarded & Pre-Reading Students. Mary L. Durbin. (Illus.). 276p. 1973. pap. 14.50 (ISBN 0-398-00487-0). C C Thomas.

Teaching Television: How to Use TV to Your Child's Advantage. Dorothy G. Singer et al. (Illus.). 192p. 1981. 10.95 (ISBN 0-8037-8515-1). Dial.

Teaching the Art of Literature. Bruce E. Miller. (Orig.). 1980. pap. 5.50 (ISBN 0-8141-5192-2, 51922). NCTE.

Teaching the Child Rider. Pamela Roberts. (Illus.). pap. 4.55 (ISBN 0-85131-195-4, Dist. by Sporting Book Center). J A Allen.

Teaching the Child Under Six. 3rd ed. James L. Hymes. (Illus.). 224p. Date not set. pap. text ed. 7.95 (ISBN 0-675-08063-0). Merrill.

Teaching the Child Under Six. 2nd ed. James L. Hymes, Jr. LC 73-84784. (Education - Elementary Ser.). 192p. 1974. pap. text ed. 8.95x (ISBN 0-675-08891-7). Merrill.

Teaching the Disadvantaged Child. Ed. by Sidney W. Tiedt. 1968. 8.95x (ISBN 0-19-501086-8). Oxford U Pr.

Teaching the Educable Mentally Retarded: Practical Methods. 3rd ed. Malinda D. Garton. (Illus.). 356p. 1974. 14.75 (ISBN 0-398-00654-7). C C Thomas.

Teaching the Gifted & Talented in the Regular Classroom. (NAIS Academic Committee Occasional Paper Ser.). 1978. pap. 4.75 (ISBN 0-934338-18-3). NAIS.

Teaching the Hearing Impaired. Sheila Lowenbraun et al. (Special Education Ser.). 224p. 1980. text ed. 14.95 (ISBN 0-675-08199-8). Merrill.

Teaching the Language Arts to Culturally Different Children. Ed. by William W. Joyce & James A. Banks. LC 78-136123. (Education Ser). 1971. pap. 6.95 (ISBN 0-201-03403-4). A-W.

Teaching the Learning-Disabled Adolescent. Lester Mann et al. LC 77-74377. (Illus.). 1977. pap. text ed. 16.75 (ISBN 0-395-25434-5). HM.

Teaching the Learning Disabled Child. Norris Haring & Barbara Bateman. LC 76-15965. (P-H Series in Education). (Illus.). 1977. 17.95 (ISBN 0-13-893503-3). P-H.

Teaching the Linguistically Diverse. Judy J. Schwartz. (New York State English Council Monographs). 1980. text ed. 8.50 (ISBN 0-930348-08-7). NY St Eng Coun.

Teaching the Mentally Handicapped Child. Ed. by Ralph Hyatt & Norma Rolnick. LC 74-2323. 352p. 1974. text ed. 19.95 (ISBN 0-87705-158-5). Human Sci Pr.

Teaching the Mentally Retarded Child. 2nd ed. Natalie Perry. LC 73-20246. 800p. 1974. 20.00x (ISBN 0-231-03652-3). Columbia U Pr.

Teaching the Metric System in the Foreign Language Classroom. B. Stevens. (Language in Education Ser.: No. 32). 1980. pap. 4.95 (ISBN 0-87281-131-X). Ctr Appl Ling.

Teaching the Mildly Handicapped in the Regular Classroom. 2nd ed. James Q. Affleck et al. (Special Education Ser.). 192p. pap. text ed. 7.50 (ISBN 0-675-08132-7). Merrill.

Teaching the Moderately & Severely Handicapped: Curriculum, Objectives, Strategies & Activites, 3 vols. Michael Bender & Peter J. Valletuhi. (Illus.). 1000p. 1976. Set. ed. 3 vol. set 39.50 (ISBN 0-685-64022-1); vol. 1 & 2 28.50 (ISBN 0-685-64023-X); Vol. 1. 14.95 (ISBN 0-8391-0869-9); Vol. 2. 19.95 (ISBN 0-8391-0868-0); Vol. 3. 13.95 (ISBN 0-8391-0963-6). Univ Park.

Teaching the Physically & Multiply Disabled. June L. Bigge & Patrick A. O'Donnell. (Special Education Ser.). 1977. text ed. 18.95 (ISBN 0-675-08527-6). Merrill.

Teaching the Pre-Academic Child: Activities for Children Displaying Difficulties of Processing Information. Mary Mott. 188p. 1974. text ed. 13.75 (ISBN 0-398-03083-9). C C Thomas.

Teaching the Retarded. Kathryn Blake. LC 73-13719. (Special Education Ser.). (Illus.). 384p. 1974. 17.95 (ISBN 0-13-895276-0). P-H.

Teaching the Retarded Child. Barbara A. Abramo et al. 1975. spiral bdg. 9.00 o.p. (ISBN 0-87488-967-7). Med Exam.

Teaching the Retarded Visually Handicapped: Indeed They Are Children. Donna L. Bluhm. LC 68-23679. (Illus.). 1968. 4.50 o.p. (ISBN 0-7216-1760-3). Saunders.

Teaching the Severely Mentally Retarded: Adaptive Skills Training. Allen A. Mori & Lowell F. Masters. LC 79-27489. 407p. 1980. text ed. 26.50 (ISBN 0-89443-173-0). Aspen Systems.

Teaching the Skills of Composition. 1980. pap. 11.95 (ISBN 0-932166-03-2). Instruct Object.

Teaching the Trainable Retarded. William H. Berdine & Patricia T. Cegelka. (Special Education Ser.). 312p. 1980. text ed. 16.95 (ISBN 0-675-08200-5). Merrill.

Teaching the Universe of Discourse. James Moffett. (Orig.). 1968. pap. text ed. 10.95 (ISBN 0-395-04928-8, 3-38140). HM.

Teaching the Vietnam War: A Critical Examination of School Texts. William L. Griffen & John Marciano. LC 78-73553. 203p. 1980. text ed. 14.50 (ISBN 0-916672-23-9); pap. text ed. 6.50 (ISBN 0-916672-27-1). Allanheld.

Teaching the Visually Limited Child. Virginia E. Bishop. (Illus.). 224p. 1978. 16.50 (ISBN 0-398-00158-8). C C Thomas.

Teaching Thinking. Edward De Bono. 1977. 18.00 (ISBN 0-85117-085-4). Transatlantic.

Teaching Through Encouragement: Techniques to Help Students Learn. Robert J. Martin. 208p. 1980. 10.95 (Spec); pap. 4.95. P-H.

Teaching Through Modality Strengths: Concepts & Practices. Walter B. Barbe & Raymond H. Swassing. LC 79-66953. 1979. 10.00 (ISBN 0-88309-100-3). Zaner-Bloser.

Teaching Through Research. A. R. Arasteh. 1966. 22.50 (ISBN 0-685-12048-1). Heinman.

Teaching Tips: A Guidebook for the Beginning College Teacher. 7th ed. Wilbert J. McKeachie. 1978. pap. text ed. 7.95x (ISBN 0-669-01151-7). Heath.

Teaching to Swim, Learning to Swim. Bela Rajki. Tr. by Ferenc Hepp from Hung. Orig. Title: Uszastanitas--Uszastanulas. (Illus.). 83p. 1980. 12.50x (ISBN 963-13-0957-6). Intl Pubns Serv.

Teaching Today & Tomorrow. Charles R. Kniker & Natalie A. Naylor. (Special Education Ser.). (Orig.). 1981. pap. text ed. 15.95 (ISBN 0-675-08034-7); instrs'. manual 3.95. Merrill.

Teaching Toddlers. Ed. by Diane Stortz et al. Kathy Downs & Joy Grewell. (Illus.). 1978. pap. 3.50 (ISBN 0-87239-219-8, 7964). Standard Pub.

Teaching Undergraduate Courses in Adult Development & Aging. Irene M. Hulicka & Susan K. Whitbourne. LC 79-83690. 1979. text ed. 9.95 (ISBN 0-933786-02-6); pap. text ed. 5.95 (ISBN 0-933786-01-8). Beech Hill.

Teaching Values in College: Facilitating Development of Ethical, Moral & Value Awareness in Students. Richard L. Morrill. LC 80-8003. (Higher Education Ser.). 1980. text ed. 13.95x (ISBN 0-87589-475-5). Jossey-Bass.

Teaching Vocational Agriculture-Agribusiness. Harold R. Binkley & Rodney W. Tulloch. (Illus.). 250p. 1981. pap. write for info. (ISBN 0-8134-2153-5). Interstate.

Teaching with a Purpose. James M. McCrimmon. 1.25 (ISBN 0-395-28254-3). HM.

Teaching with Charisma. Duck. 364p. 1980. text ed. 12.95 (ISBN 0-205-07256-9, 2372568). Allyn.

Teaching with Confidence: How to Get off the Classroom Wall. Bill W. Hillman. (Illus.). 284p. 1981. 19.50 (ISBN 0-398-04103-2). C C Thomas.

Teaching with Feeling. H. M. Greenberg. 1969. 11.95 (ISBN 0-02-545460-9). Macmillan.

Teaching with Feeling: Compassion & Self-Awareness in the Classroom Today. Herbert M. Greenberg. LC 69-13393. 1969. pap. 5.50 (ISBN 0-672-63601-8). Pegasus.

Teaching with Flannelgraph. Helen Sizemore. (Illus.). 48p. 1976. pap. 1.75 (ISBN 0-87239-074-8, 3280). Standard Pub.

Teaching with Newspapers: The Living Curriculum. Lynn Rhoades & George Rhoades. LC 80-82682. (Fastback Ser.: No. 149). (Orig.). 1980. pap. 0.75 (ISBN 0-87367-149-X). Phi Delta Kappa.

Teaching with Puppets. Bruce Rodrick. (Illus.). 48p. 1976. pap. 1.75 (ISBN 0-87239-075-6, 3281). Standard Pub.

Teaching Writing Skills. Donn Byrne. (Longman Handbooks for Language Teachers). (Illus.). 1980. pap. text ed. 7.50 (ISBN 0-582-74602-7). Longman.

Teaching Written English. Ronald V. White. (Practical Language Teaching Series). (Illus., Orig.). 1980. pap. text ed. 6.95x (ISBN 0-04-371068-9, 2372). Allen Unwin.

Teaching Written Expression: The Phelps Sentence Guide Program. Diana Phelps-Tersaki & Tricia Phelps. 112p. 1980. pap. text ed. 7.00 (ISBN 0-87879-248-1). Acad Therapy.

Teaching Young Children. Beatrice D. Martin. LC 74-20267. 1975. pap. 7.80 (ISBN 0-8273-0577-X); instructor's guide 1.60 (ISBN 0-8273-0578-8). Delmar.

Teaching Young Children to Read. 3rd ed. Durkin. 544p. 1980. text ed. 17.50 (ISBN 0-205-06903-7, 2369036). Allyn.

Teaching Young Children to Read. 2nd ed. Dolores Durkin. 448p. 1976. text ed. 13.95x o.s.i. (ISBN 0-205-05020-4). Allyn.

Teaching Young Dancers: Muscular Coordination in Classical Ballet. Joan Lawson. LC 75-15369. (Illus.). 1975. 16.95 (ISBN 0-87830-144-5). Theatre Arts.

Teaching Yourself in Libraries. Lillian L. Shapiro. 1978. 5.00 ea. (ISBN 0-8242-0628-2); 25 or more copies 4.00 ea. Wilson.

Teaching Yourself to Teach. Howard E. Walker. 1974. kit 13.95 (ISBN 0-687-41137-8); wkbk. 0.85 (ISBN 0-687-41138-6). Abingdon.

Teaching 1: Classroom Management. Wesley C. Becker et al. LC 74-31012. (Illus.). 1975. pap. text ed. 10.95 (ISBN 0-574-18025-7, 13-6025); instr's guide avail. (ISBN 0-574-18026-5, 13-6026). SRA.

Teaching 2: Cognitive Learning & Instruction. Wesley C. Becker et al. LC 75-5563. (Illus.). 306p. 1975. pap. text ed. 10.95 (ISBN 0-574-18030-3, 13-6030); instr's guide avail. (ISBN 0-574-18026-5, 13-6026). SRA.

Teachings & Miracles of Jesus. Daughters Of St. Paul. LC 76-118182. (Illus.). 136p. (gr. 4-8). 1970. pap. 3.00 o.s.i. (ISBN 0-8198-0154-2). Dghtrs St Paul.

Teachings of Christ Story-N-Puzzle Book. Ruby Maschke. 48p. (Orig.). (gr. 4 up). 1981. pap. 1.25 (ISBN 0-87239-451-4, 2842). Standard Pub.

Teachings of Lord Caitanya. Swami A. C. Bhaktivedanta. LC 75-2060. (Illus.). 1974. 7.95 (ISBN 0-912776-08-0); pap. 2.95 (ISBN 0-912776-07-2). Bhaktivedanta.

Teachings of Osiris. new ed. H. C. Randall-Stevens. 1970. Repr. of 1927 ed. 9.50 (ISBN 0-685-22177-6). Weiser.

Teachings of the Prophet Joseph Smith. Joseph F. Smith. LC 76-111624. 437p. pap. 2.50 (ISBN 0-87747-778-7). Deseret Bk.

Teachings of Yogi Bhajan. Yogi Bhajan. 1977. pap. 5.95 (ISBN 0-8015-7461-7, Hawthorn). Dutton.

TEACHNEG: A Collective Bargaining Simulation in Public Education. Marcus H. Sandver & Harry R. Blaine. 1980. pap. text ed. 3.95 (ISBN 0-88244-209-0). Grid Pub.

Teague Land or a Journey Among the Wilde Irish. John Dunton. 80p. 1981. Repr. 10.00x (ISBN 0-906127-25-4, Pub. by Irish Academic Pr Ireland). Biblio Dist.

Team. K. M. Peyton. LC 75-34092. (Illus.). (gr. 6 up). 1976. 8.95 (ISBN 0-690-01083-4, TYC-J). T Y Crowell.

Team Behind Your Airline Flight. Curt Schleier. LC 80-27174. (gr. 5-8). 1981. 9.95 (ISBN 0-664-32678-1). Westminster.

Team Building: Issues & Alternatives. William G. Dyer. LC 77-76115. 1977. pap. text ed. 6.50 (ISBN 0-201-01191-3). A-W.

Team Development Manual. Mike Woodcock. LC 78-20789. 1979. 24.95x (ISBN 0-470-26636-8). Halsted Pr.

Team Manager. Paul J. Deegan. LC 74-14515. (Dan Murphy Sports Ser.). (Illus.). 40p. (gr. 3-6). 1974. PLB 5.95 (ISBN 0-87191-403-4); pap. 2.95 (ISBN 0-89812-155-8). Creative Ed.

Team Piano Repertoire: A Manual of Music for Multiple Players at One or More Pianos. Frederic Ming Chang & Albert Faurot. LC 76-14927. 201p. 1976. 10.00 (ISBN 0-8108-0937-0). Scarecrow.

Team Practice & the Specialist: An Introduction to Interdisciplinary Teamwork. John J. Horwitz. 172p. 1970. text ed. 12.75 (ISBN 0-398-00873-6). C C Thomas.

Team Sports: A Competency Based Approach. Robert D. Shrader & Sue Everden. 1977. pap. text ed. 10.25 o.p. (ISBN 0-8403-1807-3). Kendall-Hunt.

Team Teaching. David Warwick. 125p. 1971. 9.50x o.p. (ISBN 0-8448-0538-6). Crane-Russak Co.

Team Teaching at the College Level. H. M. La Fauci & P. Richter. LC 73-88573. 1970. 16.50 (ISBN 0-08-006946-0). Pergamon.

Team Teaching Experiments. John J. Close et al. Ed. by Monica Taylor. (Education Ser.). 156p. 1974. pap. text ed. 10.75x (ISBN 0-85633-045-0, NFER). Humanities.

Team That Runs Your Hospital. Mary P. Lee. LC 80-36762. 1980. write for info. (ISBN 0-664-32669-2). Westminster.

Teams in Development Information Systems. Philip C. Semprevivo. LC 80-50608. (Orig.). 1980. pap. 16.75 (ISBN 0-917072-20-0). Yourdon.

Teamwork for Preventive Care, Vol. 1. Nigel Bruce. (Social Policy Research Monographs). 264p. 1980. 55.00 (ISBN 0-471-27883-1, Pub. by Wiley-Interscience). Wiley.

Teamwork in the Dental Practice. Fritz Schon. (Illus.). 88p. 1971. 27.50. Quint Pub Co.

Teapot Dome: Oil & Politics in the 1920's. Burl Noggle. LC 80-15396. (Illus.). ix, 234p. 1980. Repr. of 1962 ed. lib. bdg. 22.50x (ISBN 0-313-22601-6, NOTD). Greenwood.

Teapots. Noritake Kanzaki. LC 78-71255. (Form & Function Ser.: Vol. 5). (Illus.). 80p. (Orig.). 1981. pap. 8.95 (ISBN 0-87011-392-5). Kodansha.

Tear Gas Munitions: An Analysis of Commercial Riot Gas Guns, Tear Gas Projectiles, Grenades, Small Arms Ammunition & Related Tear Gas Devices. Thomas F. Swearengen. (Illus.). 596p. 1966. 59.75 (ISBN 0-398-01888-X). C C Thomas.

Tearing the Veil: Essays on Femininity. Ed. by Susan Lipshitz. (Orig.). 1978. pap. 7.95 (ISBN 0-7100-8721-7). Routledge & Kegan.

Tears & Laughter in My Poetry. Emma S. Mazor. 192p. 1981. 7.50 (ISBN 0-682-49708-8). Exposition.

Tears of Autumn. Charles McCarry. 320p. 1976. pap. 1.95 o.p. (ISBN 0-449-22649-2, C2649, Crest). Fawcett.

Tears of Passion, Tears of Shame. Rochelle Leslie. 384p. (Orig.). 1980. pap. 2.25 (ISBN 0-515-05445-3). Jove Pubns.

Tears of the Prophets. Halper Roe. LC 75-33530. (Illus.). 1975. 15.00 (ISBN 0-916326-01-2). Bloch.

Tears of Venus. Rebecca Stratton. (Harlequin Romances Ser.). (Orig.). 1980. pap. text ed. 1.25 o.p. (ISBN 0-373-02339-1, Pub. by Harlequin). PB.

Teas of the World. Nancy H. Woodward. (Illus.). 128p. 1980. pap. 7.95 (ISBN 0-02-082870-5, Collier). Macmillan.

Teasure Hunters. Elisabeth Beresford. (gr. 3-7). 1980. 7.95 o.p. (ISBN 0-525-66702-4). Elsevier-Nelson.

Teatime. Aubrey A. Franklin. LC 80-70953. (Illus.). 196p. 1981. 9.95 (ISBN 0-8119-0334-6, 1902). Fell.

Teatro De la Vanguardia. Myrna Casas. 288p. 1975. pap. text ed. 7.95x o.p. (ISBN 0-669-75408-0). Heath.

Technical Analysis in Commodities. P. J. Kaufman. LC 79-19513. 1980. 34.95 (ISBN 0-471-05627-8, Pub by Ronald Pr). Wiley.

Technical & Cultural Prerequisites for the Invention of Printing in China & the West. Constance Miller. (Asian Library Ser.: No. 21). 1980. write for info. (ISBN 0-89644-622-0). Chinese Materials.

Technical & Economic Assessment of Solar Hybrid Repowering. Public Servie Co. of New Mexico. 450p. 1981. pap. 39.50 (ISBN 0-89934-083-0). Solar Energy Info.

Technical & Scientific Reader in English. Howard H. Hirschhorn. (gr. 9-12). 1970. pap. text ed. 3.95 (ISBN 0-88345-158-1, 17430). Regents Pub.

Technical & Scientific Writing. Sarah H. Collins & Frederick B. Tuttle, Jr. 127p. 1979. pap. 4.75 (ISBN 0-686-63671-6, 1718-8-06). NEA.

Technical & Vocational Education in Asia & Oceania. (Bulletin of the UNESCO Regional Office for the Education in Asia & Oceania: Vol.21). 316p. 1980. pap. 8.00 (UB 87, UNESCO Regional Office). Unipub.

Technical Aspects of Data Communication. John E. McNamara. LC 77-93590. (Illus.). 1977. 25.00 (ISBN 0-932376-01-0). Digital Pr.

Technical Aspects of Renal Dialysis. T. H. Frost. LC 78-40089. 1978. 32.50 (ISBN 0-471-04524-1, Pub. by Wiley Medical). Wiley.

Technical Bulletins, 23 vols. Incl. Vol. 1. Field Methods of Water Hardness Determination. I. Douglas; Vol. 2. Techniques for Tracing Suberranean Drainage. D. P. Drew & D. I. Smith; Vol. 3. Determination of the Infiltration Capacity of Field Soils Using the Cylinder Infiltrometer. R. C. Hills; Vol. 4. Method for the Direct Measurement of Erosion on Rock Surfaces. C. High & F. C. Hanna; Vol. 5. Techniques of till Fabric Analysis. J. T. Andrews; Vol. 6. Field Method of Hillslope Description. L. B. Leopold & T. Dunne; Vol. 7. Measurement of Soil Frost-Heave in the Field. P. A. James; Vol. 8. System for the Field Measurement of Soil Water Movement. B. J. Knapp; Vol. 9. Instrument System for Shore Process Studies. R. M. Kirk; Vol. 10. Slope Profile Survey. A. Young; Vol. 11. Electrochemical & Fluorometric Tracer Techniques for Streamflow Measurements. M. Church; Vol. 12. Measurement of Soil Moisture. L. F. Curtis & S. Trudgill; Vol. 13. Drainage Method Morphometry. V. Gardiner; Vol. 14. Use of Electrode Instrumentation for Water Analysis. A. M. Edwards et al; Vol. 15. Instruments for Measuring Soil Creep. E. W. Anderson & B. Finlayson; Vol. 16, Pt. 1. Shorter Technical Methods: Survey of Slopes, Multiple Crest Stage Recorder, Erosional Loss of Rock Tablets, Organic Content of Suspended Sediments. B. Finlayson & H. A. Osmaston; Vol. 16, Pt. 2. Shorter Technical Methods: Soil Creep, Slope Profiles, Schmidt Test Hammer, Erosion Pins. B. Finlayson & H. A. Osmaston; Vol. 17. Instrument System for Measuring Soil Movement. B. Finlayson & H. A. Osmaston; Vol. 18. WATSPEC: A Computer Program for Determining the Equilibrium Speciation of Aqueous Solutions. T. M. Wigley; Vol. 19. Automatic Fluid-Scannning Switch Tensionmeter System. T. P. Burt; Vol. 20. Introduction to Pollen Analysis. R. L. Jones & P. R. Cunpill; Vol. 21. HYDRODAT: A System of FORTRAN Computer Programs for the Preparation & Analysis of Hydrological Data from Charts. K. J. Beven & J. L. Callen; Vol. 22. Shorter Technical Methods III. I. C. Grieve; Vol. 23. Soil Aggregate Stability Tests for the Geomorphologist. A. C. Grieve. 1980. Set. pap. text ed. 175.00 (ISBN 0-686-64926-5, Pub. by GEO Abstracts England); pap. text ed. 8.00 ea. State Mutual Bk.

Technical Calculus. Dale Ewen & Michael A. Topper. (Illus.). 1977. 17.95 (ISBN 0-13-898122-1). P-H.

Technical Calculus with Analytical Geometry. 2nd ed. Allyn J. Washington. 1979. 18.95 (ISBN 0-8053-9519-9); instr's guide 3.95 (ISBN 0-8053-9533-4). Benjamin-Cummings.

Technical Choice, Innovation & Economic Growth. P. A. David. (Illus.). 320p. 1975. 39.50 (ISBN 0-521-20518-2); pap. 12.50x (ISBN 0-521-09875-0). Cambridge U Pr.

Technical Commodity Yearbook, 1981. Robert M. Barnes. 128p. 1980. text ed. 37.50 (ISBN 0-686-69348-5). Van Nos Reinhold.

Technical Communication. David E. Fear. 1977. pap. 9.95x (ISBN 0-673-15017-8). Scott F.

Technical Communication. 2nd ed. David E. Fear. 1981. pap. text ed. 9.95x (ISBN 0-673-15401-7). Scott F.

Technical Communication. James Miles et al. 416p. Date not set. text ed. 10.95t (ISBN 0-686-63006-8). SRA. Postponed.

Technical Communication--the Bridge of Understanding: Proceedings. International Technical Communication Conference, 27th, Minneapolis, May 14-17, 1980. Ed. by Society for Technical Communication. 1058p. 1980. pap. text ed. 35.00x (ISBN 0-914548-32-8). Univelt Inc.

Technical Communicator's Handbook of Technology Transfer. Hyman Olken. 144p. 1980. pap. 12.50 (ISBN 0-934818-01-0). Olken Pubns.

Technical Data on Fuel: S. I. Units. 7th rev. ed. Ed. by J. W. Rose & J. Cooper. LC 77-24872. 1978. 88.95 (ISBN 0-470-99239-5). Halsted Pr.

Technical Development in the Small Plant. J. W. Richards. 1970. 16.50x (ISBN 0-249-44024-5). Intl Ideas.

Technical Dictionary: English, Czech, English. Z. Jouklova. 510p. (Czech.). 1970. 12.00x (ISBN 0-89918-301-8). Vanous.

Technical Dictionary of Data Processing, Computers & Office Machines, English, German, French, Russian. E. Burger. 1970. 120.00 (ISBN 0-08-006425-6). Pergamon.

Technical Dictionary of Higher Polymers: English, French, German, Russian. W. Dawydoff. 1969. 120.00 (ISBN 0-08-013112-3). Pergamon.

Technical Dictionary of Hydraulics & Pneumatics. Ed. by Gunter Neubert. 1973. text ed. 37.00 (ISBN 0-08-016958-9). Pergamon.

Technical Dictionary of Production Engineering (English-German) Rudolph Walther. 1973. text ed. 46.00 (ISBN 0-08-016959-7). Pergamon.

Technical Dictionary of Vacuum Physics & Vacuum Technology (English, French, German, Russian) Karl Hurrle et al. 1973. text ed. 37.00 (ISBN 0-08-016957-0). Pergamon.

Technical Drafting, 4 bks. Clifford J. Joens. LC 77-12932. 686p. 1977. Set. pap. text ed. 19.95 (ISBN 0-87618-891-9). R J Brady.

Technical Drafting. Spence & Atkins. (gr. 9-12). 1980. text ed. 18.60 (ISBN 0-87002-305-5). Bennett IL.

Technical Drawing: An Introduction Metric. Edition. Norman Stirling. 370p. 1981. 18.95 (ISBN 0-442-23151-2). Van Nos Reinhold.

Technical Drawing Problems: Series Three. 3rd ed. Henry C. Spencer et al. (Illus.). 1980. pap. text ed. 9.95 (ISBN 0-02-414360-X). Macmillan.

Technical Elites & Soviet Society Under Lenin & Stalin. Kendall E. Bailes. LC 77-85558. (Studies of the Russian Institute, Columbia University). 1978. 33.00x (ISBN 0-691-05260-3); pap. 12.50 (ISBN 0-691-10063-2). Princeton U Pr.

Technical English: Writing, Reading, & Speaking. 3rd ed. Nell A. Pickett & Ann A. Laster. (Illus.). 1980. pap. 14.50 scp (ISBN 0-06-045221-8, HarpC); instr's manual avail. Har-Row.

Technical Glossary of Horticultural & Landscape Terminology. Ed. by Edward B. Ballard et al. LC 78-165521. 1971. 9.95 (ISBN 0-686-26652-8); text ed. 9.95 (ISBN 0-686-26653-6); tchrs' ed. 6.00 (ISBN 0-686-26654-4). Horticult Research.

Technical Guide, Nineteen Eighty: Consumer Prices. Descriptions of Series Published in the Bulletin of Labour Statistics, Vol. 1. International Labour Office, Geneva. (Illus.). 300p. (Orig.). 1980. pap. 17.95 (ISBN 92-2-102285-4). Intl Labour Office.

Technical Guide, 1980: Employment, Unemployment, Hours of Work, Wages, Vol. II. International Labour Office, Geneva. 432p. (Orig.). 1980. pap. 15.70 (ISBN 92-2-102286-2). Intl Labour Office.

Technical Illustrating. George E. Morris. 250p. 1975. 17.95 (ISBN 0-13-898155-8). P-H.

Technical Imagination: Theories & Fictions. Samuel R. Delaney et al. LC 80-18718. (Theories of Contemporary Culture Ser.: Vol. 3). 212p. (Orig.). 1980. 12.95 (ISBN 0-930956-10-9); pap. 5.95 (ISBN 0-930956-11-7). Coda Pr.

Technical Innovation & British Economic Performance. Keith Pavitt. 353p. 1981. text ed. 50.00x (ISBN 0-333-26225-5, Pub. by Macmillan, England). Humanities.

Technical Instruction. Dale Crane. 140p. 1980. pap. text ed. write for info. (ISBN 0-89100-183-2). Aviation Maintenance.

Technical Intelligentsia & the East German Elite: Legitimacy & Social Change in Mature Communism. Thomas A. Baylis. (Illus.). 1974. 21.50x (ISBN 0-520-02395-1). U of Cal Pr.

Technical Manual for ELSA: English Language Skills Assessment in a Reading Context. Cecelia Doherty & Donna Ilyin. (ELSA Tests Ser.). 1981. pap. text ed. 3.95 (ISBN 0-686-69474-0). Newbury Hse.

Technical Marketing to the Government. Robert A. Rexroad. 325p. 1981. 69.50 (ISBN 0-85013-122-7). Dartnell Corp.

Technical Mathematics. Al H. Chew et al. LC 75-25011. (Illus.). 576p. 1976. text ed. 17.50 (ISBN 0-395-24009-3); inst. manual 2.75 (ISBN 0-395-24010-7). HM.

Technical Mathematics. Philip M. Jaffe & Rodolfo Maglio. 1979. 16.95x (ISBN 0-673-15111-5). Scott F.

Technical Metals. Johnson. (gr. 9-12). 1980. text ed. 20.20 (ISBN 0-87002-313-6). Bennett IL.

Technical Metals. rev. ed. Harold V. Johnson. (gr. 10-12). 1973. text ed. 19.96 (ISBN 0-87002-139-7); wrbk. 6.40 (ISBN 0-87002-147-8). Bennett IL.

Technical Papers. National Association of Broadcasters Engineering Conference, 1973. LC 73-86770. 1973. vinyl 10.00 o.p. (ISBN 0-8306-3173-9, 173). TAB Bks.

Technical Physics Laboratory Manual. Olan E. Kruse et al. 1971. Repr. workbook 5.50x (ISBN 0-934786-07-0). G Davis.

Technical Procedure for City Surveys. Compiled by American Society of Civil Engineers. (Manual & Report on Engineering Practice Ser.: No. 10). 128p. 1963. pap. text ed. 4.00 (ISBN 0-87262-205-3). Am Soc Civil Eng.

Technical Reader: Readings in Technical Business & Scientific Communication. W. Steve Anderson & Don R. Cox. LC 79-29677. 378p. (Orig.). 1980. pap. text ed. 7.95 (ISBN 0-03-048771-4, HoltC). HR&W.

Technical Regulations Hydrology & International Codes. 129p. 1981. pap. 20.00 (ISBN 92-63-10555-3, W477, WMO). Unipub.

Technical Report Standards: How to Prepare & Write Effective Technical Reports. Lawrence R. Harvill & Thomas L. Kraft. LC 77-70964. (Illus.). 1979. pap. 4.95 (ISBN 0-930206-01-0). M-A Pr.

Technical Report Writing. 2nd ed. Herman Weisman. (Speech Ser). 192p. 1975. pap. text ed. 9.95 (ISBN 0-675-08791-0). Merrill.

Technical Report Writing Today. 2nd ed. Steven Pauley. LC 78-69557. (Illus.). 1979. text ed. 14.50 (ISBN 0-395-27111-8); inst. manual 0.20 (ISBN 0-395-27110-X). HM.

Technical Secretary: Terminology & Transcription. Dorothy Adams & Margaret Kurtz. (Diamond Jubilee Ser.). 1967. 15.30 (ISBN 0-07-000320-3, G); instructor's manual & key 5.20 (ISBN 0-07-000322-X); wkbk. 5.90 (ISBN 0-07-000321-1); tapes 195.00 (ISBN 0-07-088980-5). McGraw.

Technical Services in Libraries. Maurice F. Tauber. LC 54-10328. (Columbia Library Service Studies, No. 7). 1954. 25.00 (ISBN 0-231-02054-6). Columbia U Pr.

Technical Services Manual for Small Libraries. John B. Corbin. LC 70-156885. 1971. 10.00 (ISBN 0-8108-0388-7). Scarecrow.

Technical Shop Mathematics. John G. Anderson. 510p. 1974. 17.50 (ISBN 0-8311-1085-6); wkd.-out solutions 6.00 (ISBN 0-8311-1106-2). Indus Pr.

Technical Studies in the Field of the Fine Arts, 1932-1942, 10 vols. Harvard University, Fogg Art Museum. Incl. Vol. 1, 1932. (ISBN 0-8240-1066-3); Vol. 2, 1933. (ISBN 0-8240-1067-1); Vol. 3, 1934. (ISBN 0-8240-1068-X); Vol. 4, 1935. (ISBN 0-8240-1069-8); Vol. 5, 1936. (ISBN 0-8240-1070-1); Vol. 6, 1937. (ISBN 0-8240-1071-X); Vol. 7, 1938. (ISBN 0-8240-1072-8); Vol. 8, 1939. (ISBN 0-8240-1073-6). Vol. 9, 1940 (ISBN 0-8240-1074-4); Vol. 10, 1941. (ISBN 0-8240-1075-2). (Illus.). 2665p. 1975. Repr. of 1942 ed. lib. bdg. 42.00 ea.; Set. lib. bdg. 300.00 (ISBN 0-685-51346-7). Garland Pub.

Technical Transformation of Agriculture in Communist China. Leslie T. Kuo. LC 73-181867. (Special Studies in International Economics & Development). 1971. 29.50x (ISBN 0-275-28276-7). Irvington.

Technical Typewriting. M. A. Kurtz & H. L. Phillips. (gr. 9 up). 1968. text ed. 14.95 (ISBN 0-201-03970-2). A-W.

Technical-Vocational Mathematics. L. Mrachek & C. Kromschlies. LC 76-48917. 1978. pap. 14.95 (ISBN 0-13-898569-3). P-H.

Technical Writing for Social Scientists. John S. Harris & Reed H. Blake. LC 75-20129. 128p. 1976. 10.95 (ISBN 0-911012-39-7); pap. 5.95 (ISBN 0-88229-362-1). Nelson-Hall.

Technically Speaking: Oral Communication for Engineers, Scientists & Technical Personnel. Harold Weiss & J. B. McGrath. 1963. 16.75x (ISBN 0-07-069085-5, C). McGraw.

Technically Write! Communicating in a Technological Era. 2nd ed. Ron S. Bricq. (Illus.). 448p. 1981. pap. text ed. 11.95 (ISBN 0-13-898700-9). P-H.

Technically Write: Communication for the Technical Man. Ronald S. Blicq. LC 77-177394. (Illus.). 384p. 1972. pap. text ed. 11.95 (ISBN 0-13-898676-2). P-H.

Technician Writes: A Guide to Basic Technical Writing. Arnold Sklare. LC 72-141220. (Illus.). 1971. pap. text ed. 5.95x o.p. (ISBN 0-87835-013-6). Boyd & Fraser.

Technician's Guide to Solid State Electronics. Morris Grossman. 1976. 14.95 o.p. (ISBN 0-13-898585-5). P-H.

Technician's Handbook of Plastics. Peter A. Grandilli. 272p. 1981. text ed. 19.95 (ISBN 0-442-23870-3). Van Nos Reinhold.

Technicians of the Sacred: A Range of Poetries from Africa, America, Asia & Oceania. Ed. by Jerome Rothenberg. LC 67-15391. 1969. pap. 4.95 (ISBN 0-385-07597-9, A06, Anch). Doubleday.

Technics & Civilization. Lewis Mumford. LC 63-19641. (Illus.). 1963. pap. 6.95 (ISBN 0-15-688254-X, H030, Hbgr). HarBraceJ.

Technics & Human Development: The Myth of the Machine, Vol. 1. Lewis Mumford. LC 67-16088. (Illus.). 342p. 12.00 o.p. (ISBN 0-15-163975-2). HarBraceJ.

Technics for the Crime Investigator. 2nd ed. William Dienstein. 272p. 1974. 16.50 (ISBN 0-398-03112-6). C C Thomas.

Technique & Treatment with Light-Wire Edgewise Appliances, 2 vols. 2nd ed. Joseph R. Jarabak & James A. Fizzell. LC 72-91624. (Illus.). 1300p. 1972. 62.50 (ISBN 0-8016-2429-0); Vol. 1. 62.50 (ISBN 0-8016-2430-4, 2430); Vol. 2. 62.50 (ISBN 0-8016-2431-2, 2431). Mosby.

Technique for the Ballet Artists. Olga Spessivtzeva. (Illus.). 1978. pap. 6.95 (ISBN 0-584-10297-6). Transatlantic.

Technique in the Use of Surgical Tools. Robert M. Anderson & Richard F. Romfh. 208p. 1980. 16.50 (ISBN 0-8385-8843-3). ACC.

Technique of Bernard Shaw's Plays. Augustin F. Hamon. 70p. 1980. Repr. of 1912 ed. lib. bdg. 12.50 (ISBN 0-8492-5274-1). R West.

Technique of Bobbin Lace. Pamela Nottingham. 1976. 27.00 (ISBN 0-7134-3230-6, Pub. by Batsford England). David & Charles.

Techmique of Editing Sixteen Mm. Films. 4th ed. J. Burder. (Illus.). 152p. 1979. 17.95 (ISBN 0-240-51019-4). Focal Pr.

Technique of Electronic Music. 2nd ed. Thomas H. Wells. LC 78-8819. (Illus.). 1981. text ed. 25.00 (ISBN 0-02-872830-0). Schirmer Bks.

Technique of Fashion Design. Brenda Naylor. 1975. 24.00 (ISBN 0-7134-3009-5, Pub. by Batsford England). David & Charles.

Technique of Glass Forming. Keith Cummings. (Illus.). 168p. 1980. 27.00 (ISBN 0-7134-1612-2, Pub. by Batsford England). David & Charles.

Technique of Honiton Lace. Elsie Luxton. 1979. 22.50 o.p. (ISBN 0-7134-1614-9, Pub. by Batsford England). David & Charles.

Technique of Kinetic Art. John Tovey. 1971. 19.95 (ISBN 0-7134-2518-0, Pub. by Batsford England). David & Charles.

Technique of Latin Dancing. rev. ed. Walter Laird. (Illus.). 180p. 1980. pap. text ed. 19.50 (ISBN 0-392-07535-0, LTB). Soccer.

Technique of Macrame. Bonny Schmid-Burleson. LC 73-17335. (Illus.). 1974. 9.50 o.p. (ISBN 0-8231-7034-9). Branford.

Technique of Orchestration. 2nd ed. Kent Kennan. (Music Ser). (Illus.). 1970. 18.95 (ISBN 0-13-900316-9); wkbk. 2 9.50 (ISBN 0-13-900340-1); wkbk. 3.95 (ISBN 0-13-900332-0). P-H.

Technique of Organic Chemistry. A. Weissberger. Incl. Vol. 2. Catalytic, Photochemical & Electrolytic Reactions. 2nd ed. 1956. 42.00 (ISBN 0-470-92862-X); Vol. 3, Pt. 2. Laboratory Engineering. 1957. 36.95 (ISBN 0-470-92928-6). (All other vols. in set o.p., Pub. by Wiley-Interscience). Wiley.

Technique of Political Lying. Robert W. Rasberry. LC 80-5976. 301p. 1981. lib. bdg. 19.75 (ISBN 0-8191-1482-0); pap. text ed. 11.25 (ISBN 0-8191-1483-9). U Pr of Amer.

Technique of Pottery. Dora Billington & John Colbeck. 1979. 27.00 (ISBN 0-7134-2836-8, Pub. by Batsford England). David & Charles.

Technique of Sculpture. John Mills. (Illus.). 160p. 1976. 16.95 o.p. (ISBN 0-8230-5210-9). Watson-Guptill.

Technique of Sea Fishing. 6.50x o.p. (ISBN 0-392-06482-0, SpS). Soccer.

Technique of Special Effects Cinematography. 3rd, rev., enl. ed. Ray Fielding. (Library of Communication Techniques). 24.95 (ISBN 0-8038-7115-5). Hastings.

Technique of the Film Cutting Room. 2nd ed. Ed. by Ernest Walter. (Library of Communication Techniques). Date not set. 15.50 o.p. (ISBN 0-8038-7132-5). Hastings.

Technique of the Novel. Carl H. Grabo. LC 64-8178. 1964. Repr. of 1928 ed. 6.50 (ISBN 0-87752-046-1). Gordian.

Technique of the Sound Studio. 3rd ed. Alec Nisbett. (Library of Communication Techniques). Date not set. 12.50 (ISBN 0-8038-7122-8). Hastings.

Technique of the Spiritual Life. 2nd ed. Clara M. Codd. 1963. 2.95 (ISBN 0-8356-7090-2). Theos Pub Hse.

Technique of Torchon Lace. Pamela Nottingham. 1979. 22.50 o.p. (ISBN 0-7134-0268-7, Pub. by Batsford England). David & Charles.

Technique of Woven Tapestry. Tadek Beutlich. 1979. 22.50 o.p. (ISBN 0-7134-2513-X, Pub. by Batsford England). David & Charles.

Technique Poetique Des Trouveres Dans la Chanson Courtoise: Contribution a l'etude De la Rhetorique Medievale. Roger Dragonetti. LC 80-2163. 1981. Repr. of 1960 ed. 76.00 (ISBN 0-404-19029-4). AMS Pr.

Techniques & Applications of Path Integration. L. S. Schulman. LC 80-19129. 350p. 1981. 25.00 (ISBN 0-471-76450-7, Pub. by Wiley-Interscience). Wiley.

Techniques & Applications of Plasma Chemistry. Ed. by John R. Hollahan & Alexis T. Bell. LC 74-5122. 416p. 1974. 35.00 (ISBN 0-471-40628-7, Pub. by Wiley-Interscience). Wiley.

Techniques & Experiments in Organic Chemistry. 2nd ed. Ed. by Leon B. Gortler & Robert C. Tripp. (Illus.). 1978. lab manual 8.95 (ISBN 0-89529-016-2). Avery Pub.

Techniques & Laws of Japanese Painting. Henry P. Bowie. (Illus.). 129p. 1981. 47.45 (ISBN 0-930582-91-8). Gloucester Art.

Techniques & Materials in Biology. Marjorie P. Behringer. LC 80-12458. 608p. 1981. Repr. of 1973 ed. lib. bdg. write for info. (ISBN 0-89874-175-0). Krieger.

Techniques & Materials of Tonal Music: With an Introduction to Twentieth Century Techniques. 2nd ed. Thomas E. Benjamin et al. LC 78-69578. (Illus.). 1979. text ed. 16.25 (ISBN 0-395-27066-9). HM.

Techniques & Problems of Assessment for Teachers. Ed. by H. G. Macintosh. 1974. pap. 13.95x (ISBN 0-7131-1816-4). Intl Ideas.

Techniques & Problems of Theory Construction in Sociology. Jerald Hage. LC 72-6447. 272p. 1972. 22.95 (ISBN 0-471-33860-5, Pub. by Wiley-Interscience). Wiley.

Techniques & Procedures of Anesthesia. 3rd ed. John Adriani. 668p. 1972. pap. 48.75 photocopy ed. spiral (ISBN 0-398-00015-8). C C Thomas.

Techniques & Psychology of Disarming for Law Enforcement Personnel. Bradley Steiner. (Illus.). 248p. 1980. write for info. o.p. (ISBN 0-398-04039-7). C C Thomas.

Techniques & Public Administration: A Contextual Evaluation. Maurice Spiers. 250p. 1975. 24.50x (ISBN 0-85520-108-8, Pub by Martin Robertson England). Biblio Dist.

Techniques & Topics in Bioinorganic Chemistry. Ed. by C. A. McAuliffe. LC 74-5074. (Aspects of Inorganic Chemistry Ser.). 351p. 1974. 44.95 (ISBN 0-470-58119-0). Halsted Pr.

Techniques: Experiments for Organic Chemistry. 3rd ed. Addison Ault. 1979. text ed. 18.95x (ISBN 0-205-06528-7, 6865283); instr's man. o.p. avail. (ISBN 0-205-06545-7). Allyn.

Techniques for Beginning Conductors. Allan Ross. 1976. pap. text ed. 16.95x (ISBN 0-534-00403-2). Wadsworth Pub.

Techniques for Behavior Change: Applications of Adlerian Theory. Ed. by Arthur G. Nikelly. 224p. 1979. 18.75 (ISBN 0-398-01401-9). C C Thomas.

Techniques for Controlling Air Pollution from the Operation of Nuclear Facilities. (Safety Ser.: No. 17). 1966. pap. 5.50 (ISBN 92-0-123166-0, IAEA). Unipub.

Techniques for Field Experiments with Rice. 46p. 1972. pap. 5.00 (R111, IRRI). Unipub.

Techniques for Police Instructors. John C. Klotter. 180p. 1978. 12.75 (ISBN 0-398-01029-3). C C Thomas.

Techniques for the Solidification of High-Level Waste. (Technical Reports Ser: No. 176). (Illus.). 1978. pap. 14.50 (ISBN 92-0-125077-0, IAEA). Unipub.

Techniques in Bedside Hemodynamic Monitoring. 2nd ed. Elaine K. Daily & John S. Schroeder. LC 80-16594. (Illus.). 198p. 1980. pap. text ed. 11.95 (ISBN 0-8016-4363-5). Mosby.

Techniques in Endocrine Research. Ed. by P. Eckstein & F. Knowles. 1963. 43.50 (ISBN 0-12-230150-1). Acad Pr.

Techniques in Extracorporeal Circulation. 2nd ed. Ionescu. 1981. text ed. price not set (ISBN 0-407-00173-5). Butterworth.

Techniques in Interviewing for Law Enforcement & Corrections Personnel: A Programmed Text. Robert J. Wicks & Ernest H. Josephs, Jr. 152p. 1977. pap. 10.75 (ISBN 0-398-03677-2). C C Thomas.

Techniques in Mineral Exploration: Popular Edition. J. H. Reedman. (Illus.). 1979. 50.00x (ISBN 0-85334-851-0, Pub. by Applied Science). Burgess-Intl Ideas.

Techniques in Nuclear Structure Physics, 2 vols. J. B. England. LC 74-8171. 697p. 1974. 54.95 (ISBN 0-470-24161-6). Halsted Pr.

Techniques in Partial Differential Equations. C. Chester. 1970. 22.50 o.p. (ISBN 0-07-010740-8, C). McGraw.

Techniques in Pedology. Richard T. Smith & Kenneth Atkinson. 1975. 15.95 (ISBN 0-236-30939-0, Pub. by Paul Elek); pap. 8.95 (ISBN 0-236-31020-8). Merrimack Bk Serv.

Techniques in the Clinical Supervision of Teachers. Keith Acheson & Meredith Gall. 1980. pap. 9.95 (ISBN 0-582-28121-0). Longman.

Techniques in Transactional Analysis: For Psychotherapists & Counselors. Muriel James. LC 76-9325. (Psychology Ser.). text ed. 22.95 (ISBN 0-201-03256-2). A-W.

Techniques, Notes, Tips for Teachers. J. O. Proctor. 1968. pap. text ed. 4.40 (ISBN 0-8273-0361-0). Delmar.

Techniques of Astrological Geomancy. Frank Von Hartmann. (Illus.). 137p. 1981. 47.85 (ISBN 0-89920-019-2). Am Inst Psych.

Techniques of Autoradiography. 3rd, rev. & enl. ed. A. W. Rogers. LC 78-16861. 1979. 65.00 (ISBN 0-444-80063-8, North Holland). Elsevier.

Techniques of Biological Preparation. John Simpkins. (Illus.). 1974. 16.50x (ISBN 0-216-89767-X). Intl Ideas.

Techniques of Chemistry. Ed. by A. Weissberger. Incl. Vol. 1. Physical Methods of Chemistry, 5 pts. B. Rossiter. 1971-72; Pt. 1A. Components of Scientific Instruments. 40.50 (ISBN 0-471-92724-4); Pt. 2A. Electrochemical Methods. 68.00 (ISBN 0-471-92727-9); Pt. 3A. o.p. (ISBN 0-471-92729-5); Pt. 1B. Automatic Recording & Control, Computers in Chemical Research. 36.50 (ISBN 0-471-92725-2); Pt. 2B. o.p. (ISBN 0-471-92728-7); Pt. 3B. Spectroscopy & Spectometry in Infrared, Visible & Ultraviolet. 62.50 (ISBN 0-471-92731-7); Pt. 3C. Polarimetry. 47.95 (ISBN 0-471-92732-5); Pt. 3D. X-Ray, Nuclear, Molecular Beam & Radioactivity Methods. 62.95 (ISBN 0-471-92733-3); Pt. 4. Determination of Mass, Transport & Electrical-Magnetic Properties. 54.50; Pt. 5. o.p. (ISBN 0-471-92734-1); Pt. 6. Supplement & Cumulative Index. LC 75-29544. 256p. 1976. 31.50 (ISBN 0-471-92899-2); Vol. 2. Organic Solvents: Physical Properties & Methods of Purification. 3rd ed. John A. Riddick & William B. Bunger. LC 72-114919. 1971. Pt. 1. 60.50 (ISBN 0-471-92726-0); Vol. 3. Photochromism. G. H. Brown. LC 45-8533. 1971. 93.00 (ISBN 0-471-92894-1); Vol. 4. Elucidation of Organic Structures by Physical & Chemical Methods, 3 pts. K. W. Bentley & G. W. Kirby. 1972-73. Pt. 1. 57.00 (ISBN 0-471-92896-8); Pt. 2. 58.00 (ISBN 0-471-92897-6); Pt. 3. o.p. (ISBN 0-471-92898-4); Vol. 5. Techniques of Electroorganic Synthesis, 2 pts. Ed. by N. L. Weingerb. Pt. 1. 84.50; Pt. 2. 75.00 (ISBN 0-471-93272-8); Vol. 6. Investigation of Rates & Mechanisms of Reactions, 2 pts. 3rd ed. Ed. by E. S. Lewis. LC 73-8850. 1974. Pt. 1. 77.00 (ISBN 0-471-93095-4); Pt. 2. 52.50 (ISBN 0-471-93127-6); Vol. 7. Membranes in Separations. S. T. Hwang & K. Kammermeyer. LC 74-2218. 1975. 60.50 (ISBN 0-471-93268-X); Vol. 10. Applications of Biochemical Systems in Organic Chemistry, 2 pts. Ed. by Bryan J. Jone et al. 1976. Pt. 1. 45.00 (ISBN 0-471-93267-1); Pt. 2. 50.00 (ISBN 0-471-93270-1). Pub. by Wiley-Interscience). Wiley.

Techniques of Chemistry Seperation & Purification. 3rd ed. Ed. by Edward S. Perry. A. Weissberger. LC 77-114920. (Techniques of Chemistry Ser.: Vol. 12). 1978. 42.50 (ISBN 0-471-02655-7, Pub. by Wiley-Interscience). Wiley.

Techniques of Chemistry: Thin Layer Chromatography. 2nd ed. Justus G. Kirchner. LC 78-9163. (Techniques of Chemistry Ser.: Vol. 14). 1978. 77.00 (ISBN 0-471-93264-7, Pub. by Wiley-Interscience). Wiley.

Techniques of Chemistry: Vol. 10 Applications of Biochemical Systems in Organic Chemistry, 2 pts. J. B. Jones et al. 522p. 1976. Pt. 1. 50.00 (ISBN 0-471-93267-1); Pt. 2, 575pp. 55.00 (ISBN 0-471-93270-1); Set. 80.95 (ISBN 0-471-02279-9). Wiley.

Techniques of Chemistry: Vol. 13 Laboratory Engineering & Manipulations. 3rd ed. A. Weissberger & E. S. Perry. 531p. 1979. 47.50 (ISBN 0-471-03275-1). Wiley.

Techniques of Chemistry: Vol. 14 Thin Layer Chromatography. 2nd ed. J. G. Kirchner. 1137p. 1978. 77.00 (ISBN 0-471-93264-7). Wiley.

Techniques of Chemistry: Vol. 15 Theory & Application of Electron Spin Resonance. W. Gordy. 625p. 1980. 39.95 (ISBN 0-471-93162-4). Wiley.

Techniques of Chemistry: Vol. 4, 2 Pts. Elucidation of Organic Structures by Physical & Chemical Methods. 2nd ed. K. W. Bentley & G. W. Kirby. 1250p. 1972. Pt. 1. 57.00 (ISBN 0-471-92896-8); Pt. 2. 58.00 (ISBN 0-471-92897-6). Wiley.

Techniques of Chemistry: Vol. 8, Pt. 1, Solutions & Solubilities. M. R. Dack. 475p. 1975. 48.50 (ISBN 0-471-93266-3). Wiley.

Techniques of Chemistry: Vol. 9, Chemical Experimentation Under Extreme Conditions. B. W. Rossiter. 369p. 1980. 28.50 (ISBN 0-471-93269-8). Wiley.

Techniques of China Painting. Gunhild Jorgensen. 112p. 1980. pap. 7.95 (ISBN 0-442-20176-1). Van Nos Reinhold.

Techniques of Circuit Analysis. G. W. Carter & A. Richardson. LC 79-183222. (Illus.). 544p. 1972. 40.75x (ISBN 0-521-08435-0). Cambridge U Pr.
Techniques of Climatology. E. T. Stringer. LC 74-128094. (Illus.). 1972. text ed. 36.95x (ISBN 0-7167-0250-9). W H Freeman.
Techniques of Clinical Chemistry. 3rd ed. Samuel Natelson. (Illus.). 980p. 1971. 49.75 (ISBN 0-398-01384-5). C C Thomas.
Techniques of Critical Reasoning. Annis. LC 73-81554. 1974. pap. text ed. 8.95 (ISBN 0-675-08906-9). Merrill.
Techniques of Effective Communication. R. Wayne Pace et al. LC 78-18634. (Speech Ser.). (Illus.). 1979. pap. text ed. 11.50 (ISBN 0-201-05703-4). A-W.
Techniques of Electrochemistry. Ed. by Ernest Yeager & Alvin J. Salkind. LC 73-37940. 464p. Vol. 1, 1972. 50.00 (ISBN 0-471-97700-4, Pub. by Wiley-Interscience); Vol. 2, 1973. 43.00 (ISBN 0-471-97701-2); Vol. 3, 1978. 34.95 (ISBN 0-471-02919-X). Wiley.
Techniques of Environmental Systems Analysis. R. H. Pantell. LC 76-98. 224p. 1976. 27.00 (ISBN 0-471-65791-3, Pub. by Wiley-Interscience). Wiley.
Techniques of Family Therapy. David S. Freeman. LC 80-69669. 350p. 1981. 25.00 (ISBN 0-87668-431-2). Aronson.
Techniques of Fiction Writing: Measure & Madness. Leon Surmelian. LC 66-24323. 1969. pap. 2.95 (ISBN 0-385-06391-1, A549, Anch). Doubleday.
Techniques of Financial Analysis. 4th ed. Ed. by Erich A. Helfert. 1977. pap. text ed. 10.95 (ISBN 0-256-01916-9). Irwin.
Techniques of Finite Elements. Bruce Irons & Sohrab Ahmad. LC 79-40994. (Engineering Science Ser.: Civil Engineering). 529p. 1979. 87.95x (ISBN 0-470-26855-7). Halsted Pr.
Techniques of Fire Hydraulics. Lawrence Erven. (Fire Science Ser). 1972. text ed. 11.95x (ISBN 0-02-473000-9, 47300). Macmillan.
Techniques of High Magic. Francis King & Stephen Skinner. (Warner Destiny Bk). (Orig.). 1976. pap. 1.95 o.s.i. (ISBN 0-446-89378-1). Warner Bks.
Techniques of Language Teaching. F. L. Billows. 1961. pap. text ed. 9.75x (ISBN 0-582-52505-5). Longman.
Techniques of Legal Investigation. Anthony M. Golec. (Illus.). 280p. 1976. 19.75 (ISBN 0-398-03522-9). C C Thomas.
Techniques of Medication: A Manual of the Administration of Drug Products. Eric W. Martin et al. LC 69-14854. (Illus.). 1969. 20.00 o.p. (ISBN 0-397-50243-5). Lippincott.
Techniques of Multivariate Calculation. R. H. Farrell. (Lecture Notes in Mathematics: Vol. 520). 1976. pap. 15.60 (ISBN 0-387-07695-6). Springer-Verlag.
Techniques of Nursing Management, Vol. 1. Ed. by The Journal of Nursing Administration, Staff. LC 75-1674. 1975. pap. text ed. 4.95 o.s.i. (ISBN 0-913654-07-8). Nursing Res.
Techniques of Nursing Management, Vol. 2. Ed. by The Journal of Nursing Administration Staff. LC 75-1674. 1976. pap. 4.95 o.s.i. (ISBN 0-913654-32-9). Nursing Res.
Techniques of Observation & Learning Retention: A Handbook for the Policeman & the Lawyer. Louis F. Basinger. (Illus.). 88p. 1973. pap. 8.75 (ISBN 0-398-02935-0). C C Thomas.
Techniques of Organizational Change. Stephen R. Michael et al. (Illus.). 363p. 1981. 16.95 (ISBN 0-07-041775-X). McGraw.
Techniques of Persuasion. James A. Brown. (Orig.). 1963. pap. 2.95 o.p. (ISBN 0-14-020604-3, Pelican). Penguin.
Techniques of Photojournalism: Available Light & the 35 mm Camera. Milton Feinberg. LC 73-96959. 1970. 29.95 (ISBN 0-471-25692-7, Pub. by Wiley-Interscience). Wiley.
Techniques of Polymer Synthesis & Characterization. D. Braun et al. 282p. 1972. 24.50 o.p. (ISBN 0-471-09805-1, Pub. by Wiley). Krieger.
Techniques of Population Analysis. G. W. Barclay. LC 58-59899. 1958. 21.95 (ISBN 0-471-04818-6). Wiley.
Techniques of Pressworking Sheet Metal: An Engineering Approach to Die Design. 2nd ed. Donald F. Eary & Edward A. Reed. 1974. ref. ed. 25.95 (ISBN 0-13-900696-6). P-H.
Techniques of Program Structure & Design. Edward Yourdan. (Illus.). 384p. 1976. 23.95 (ISBN 0-13-901702-X). P-H.
Techniques of Radiobiochemistry. S. Aronoff. (Illus.). 1967. Repr. of 1956 ed. 13.75 o.s.i. (ISBN 0-02-840460-2). Hafner.
Techniques of Ship Modelling. Gerald A. Wingrove. (Illus.). 133p. 1974. 12.50x (ISBN 0-85242-366-7). Intl Pubns Serv.
Techniques of Structured Problem Solving. Arthur B. Van Gundy. 320p. 1981. text ed. 18.95 (ISBN 0-442-21223-2). Van Nos Reinhold.
Techniques of the Selling Writer. Dwight V. Swain. LC 73-7419. 330p. 1981. pap. 7.50 (ISBN 0-8061-1191-7). U of Okla Pr.
Techniques Used to Improve Education. Victor S. Mamatey. (Florida State U. Studies: No. 21). 1955. pap. 2.00 o.p. (ISBN 0-8130-0467-5). U Presses Fla.
Techniques with Tangibles: A Manual for Teaching the Blind. Wilber H. Fulker & Mary Fulker. 84p. 1968. 9.50 (ISBN 0-398-00628-8). C C Thomas.
Techno-Economic Analysis of the Port Transport System. Junichi Imakita. 1978. 29.95 (ISBN 0-03-046241-X). Praeger.
Technocracy. J. Meynaud. LC 69-11976. 1969. 10.95 o.s.i. (ISBN 0-02-921210-3). Free Pr.
Technocracy & the American Dream: The Technocrat Movement, 1900-1941. William E. Akin. 1977. 14.50x (ISBN 0-520-03110-5). U of Cal Pr.
Technocracy: Technological Social Design. Ed. by Technocracy Inc. (Illus.). 76p. (Orig.). 1975. pap. 1.00 (ISBN 0-686-28500-X). Technocracy.
Technological Aids to Microbiology. R. E. Trotman. (Illus.). 1978. pap. text ed. 15.95x (ISBN 0-7131-4293-6). Intl Ideas.
Technological & Social Change: A Transdisciplinary Model. Jacob Fried & Paul Molnar. 1979. text ed. 17.50 (ISBN 0-89433-074-8). Petrocelli.
Technological Change: Economics, Management & Environment. Ed. by Bela Gold. LC 74-17112. 1975. 28.00 (ISBN 0-08-018012-4). Pergamon.
Technological Change in Regulated Industries. Ed. by William M. Capron et al. (Studies in the Regulation of Economic Activity). 1971. 11.95 (ISBN 0-8157-1282-0). Brookings.
Technological Changes & the Law: A Reader. Otta G. Gara & Bruce A. Naegeli. LC 92-276. 1979. lib. bdg. 25.00 (ISBN 0-930342-97-6). W S Hein.
Technological Conscience: Survival & Dignity in an Age of Expertise. Manfred Stanley. LC 78-428. 1978. 17.95 (ISBN 0-02-930610-8). Free Pr.
Technological Dependence, Monopoly & Growth. M. Merhav. 1968. 18.00 (ISBN 0-08-012754-1). Pergamon.
Technological Development Strategies for Developing Countries: A Review for Policy Makers. Maximo Halty-Carrere. 155p. 1979. pap. text ed. 12.95x (ISBN 0-920380-24-7, Pub. by Inst Res Pub Canada). Renouf.
Technological Diffusion & the Computer Revolution. P. Stoneman. LC 75-12136. (Department of Applied Economics Monograph: No. 25). (Illus.). 1976. 38.50 (ISBN 0-521-20945-5). Cambridge U Pr.
Technological Eating. Magnus Pyke. (Illus.). 114p. 1972. 10.50 o.p. (ISBN 0-7195-2576-4). Transatlantic.
Technological History of Motion Pictures & Television. Compiled by Raymond Fielding. 1967. 27.50x (ISBN 0-520-00411-6). U of Cal Pr.
Technological Innovation & Forces for Change in the Mineral Industry. Board on Mineral & Energy Resources. 1978. pap. 5.50 (ISBN 0-309-02768-3). Natl Acad Pr.
Technological Innovation & Public Policy. Roy Rothwell & Walter Zegveld. LC 81-493. (Contributions in Economics & Economic History Ser.: No. 42). 400p. 1981. lib. bdg. 35.00 (ISBN 0-313-22989-9, RTE/). Greenwood.
Technological Innovation & Society. Ed. by Dean Morse & Aaron W. Warner. LC 66-18342. (Seminar on Technology & Social Change Ser.) 1966. 20.00x (ISBN 0-231-02927-6). Columbia U Pr.
Technological Innovation in American Local Governments: The Case of Computing. Ed. by James L. Perry & Kenneth L. Kraemer. LC 78-26458. (Pergamon Policy Studies). (Illus.). 22.00 (ISBN 0-08-023707-X). Pergamon.
Technological Level of Soviet Industry. Ed. by R. Amann et al. LC 77-76298. (Illus.). 1977. 45.00x (ISBN 0-300-02076-7). Yale U Pr.
Technological Man. Victor C. Ferkiss. LC 69-13114. 1969. 7.95 o.p. (ISBN 0-8076-0489-5). Braziller.
Technological Progress in Latin America: The Prospects for Overcoming Dependency. Ed. by James H. Street & Dilmus D. James. (Special Studies on Latin America & the Caribbean). 1979. lib. bdg. 24.50x (ISBN 0-89158-255-X). Westview.
Technological Society. Jacques Ellul. 1967. pap. 3.95 (ISBN 0-394-70390-1, V390, Vin). Random.
Technological System. Jacques Ellul. 384p. 1980. 19.50 (ISBN 0-8164-9007-4). Continuum.
Technology: An Introduction. Paul W. DeVore. LC 79-53782. (Technology Ser.). (Illus.). 397p. 1980. text ed. 16.95 (ISBN 0-87192-115-4, 000-5). Davis Pubns.
Technology & Civility: The Skill Revolution in Politics. Heinz Eulau. LC 76-48483. (Publications Ser.: No. 167). 1977. pap. 4.95 (ISBN 0-8179-6672-2). Hoover Inst Pr.
Technology & Communist Culture: The Socio-Cultural Impact of Technology Under Socialism. Ed. by Frederic J. Fleron, Jr. LC 77-7810. (Praeger Special Studies). 1977. text ed. 44.95 (ISBN 0-03-021821-7). Praeger.
Technology & Decisions in Airport Access. Compiled by American Society of Civil Engineers. 168p. 1970. pap. text ed. 19.75 o.p. (ISBN 0-87262-022-0). Am Soc Civil Eng.
Technology & East West Trade. Ed. by Office of Technology Assessment Congress of the United States. LC 80-26121. 312p. 1981. text ed. 25.00 (ISBN 0-86598-041-1). Allanheld.
Technology & East West Trade: Office of Technology Assessment, Congress of the U. S. LC 80-26121. 312p. 1981. text ed. 25.00 (ISBN 0-86598-041-1). Allanheld.
Technology & Economic Development: A Realistic Perspective. Ed. by Samuel M. Rosenblatt. (Special Studies in Social, Political & Economic Development). 1979. lib. bdg. 22.50x (ISBN 0-89158-474-9). Westview.
Technology & Employment in Footwear Manufacturing: A Study Prepared for the Int'l Labour Office Within the Framework of the World Employment Programme. Gerard K. Boon. LC 80-50458. 232p. 1980. 45.00x (ISBN 90-286-0170-8). Sijthoff & Noordhoff.
Technology & Health: Man & World Proceedings. Ed. by G. Wagner et al. (Lecture Notes in Medical Informatics Ser.: Vol. 7). 243p. 1981. pap. 20.70 (ISBN 0-387-10230-2). Springer Verlag.
Technology & Human Affairs. Larry Hickman & Azizah Al-Hibri. 650p. 1980. text ed. 16.95 (ISBN 0-8016-2164-X). Mosby.
Technology & International Relations. John V. Granger. LC 78-15363. (Illus.). 1979. text ed. 19.95x (ISBN 0-7167-1004-8); pap. text ed. 9.95x (ISBN 0-7167-1003-X). W H Freeman.
Technology & Interpretation of Nuclear Medicine Procedures. 2nd ed. D. Bruce Sodee & Paul J. Early. LC 75-15607. (Illus.). 544p. 1975. text ed. 31.95 (ISBN 0-8016-4732-0). Mosby.
Technology & Labour in Japanese Coal Mining. 65p. 1980. pap. 5.00 (ISBN 92-808-0082-5, TUNU090, UNU). Unipub.
Technology & Manufacture of Ammonia. Samuel Strelzoff. 220p. 1981. 22.00 (ISBN 0-471-02722-7, Pub. by Wiley-Interscience). Wiley.
Technology & Productivity in Urban Government: The 1980's. Ed. by Jules J. Duga. (Illus.). 288p. 1981. 24.50 (ISBN 0-935470-06-9). Battelle.
Technology & Science in the People's Republic of China. John Sigurdson. 1980. 30.00 (ISBN 0-08-024288-X); pap. 12.01 (ISBN 0-686-66170-2). Pergamon.
Technology & Social Change. Emmanuel Mesthene. LC 67-23043. (Orig.). 1967. pap. 2.50 (ISBN 0-672-60900-2, CR14). Bobbs.
Technology & Social Progress. R. A. Buchanan. 1965. 10.50 (ISBN 0-08-011141-6); pap. 6.25 (ISBN 0-08-011140-8). Pergamon.
Technology & Society. Ed. by Noel De Nevers. LC 77-172801. 1972. pap. text ed. 7.95 o.p. (ISBN 0-201-01493-9). A-W.
Technology & Survival. Braun & Collingridge. (Sicon Bks.). 1977. 3.95 (ISBN 0-408-71301-1). Butterworths.
Technology & the Curriculum. Ed. by Paul W. Witt. LC 68-9689. 1968. pap. text ed. 5.25x (ISBN 0-8077-2342-8). Tchrs Coll.
Technology & the Future: A Philosophical Challenge. Schuurman & Egbert. 1980. 19.95x (ISBN 0-88906-111-4). Radix Bks.
Technology & the Future of Stockbroking. M. Josephs. 61p. 1980. 57.50 (ISBN 0-85012-228-7). Intl Pubns Serv.
Technology & the Multinationals. Jack Baranson. LC 77-14699. 1978. 18.95 (ISBN 0-669-02021-4). Lexington Bks.
Technology & the Quality of Health Care. Richard H. Egdahl & Paul M. Gertman. LC 78-7307. (Illus.). 1978. text ed. 31.00 (ISBN 0-89443-025-4). Aspen Systems.
Technology & Toil: In 19th Century Britain. Maxine Berg. (Illus.). 1979. text ed. 26.00x (ISBN 0-906336-02-3); pap. text ed. 10.50x (ISBN 0-906336-03-1). Humanities.
Technology & Values in American Civilization: A Guide to Information Sources. Ed. by Stephen H. Cutcliffe et al. (American Information Guide Ser.: Vol. 9). 680p. 1980. 30.00 (ISBN 0-8103-1475-4). Gale.
Technology As a Social & Political Phenomenon. Philip L. Bereano. LC 76-18723. 1976. text ed. 22.95 (ISBN 0-471-06875-6). Wiley.
Technology Assessment & the Oceans. Philip D. Wilmot & Aart Slingerland. LC 77-73026. 1977. lib. bdg. 46.50x (ISBN 0-89158-725-X). Westview.
Technology Assessment for Development. 166p. 1980. pap. 13.00 (ISBN 0-686-68975-5, UN80/2A1, UN). Unipub.
Technology Assessment-State-of-the-Field. 102p. 1976. 20.00 o.p. (ISBN 0-686-27575-6, 118-76). AAES.
Technology, Culture & Language: Selected Essays. Ed. by Randolph Hudson. (Uses of English Ser.). 1966. pap. 2.95x o.p. (ISBN 0-669-21014-5). Heath.
Technology, Development & the Environment: A Re-Appraisal. A. K. Reddy. (Illus.). 60p. 1980. 5.75 (ISBN 0-08-025693-7). Pergamon.
Technology Enrollments, Nineteen Seventy-Nine by School & by Curriculum for All Students Including a Breakdown by Women & Minorities. 45.00 (ISBN 0-686-27584-5, 207-80). AAES.
Technology Evaluation & Acquisition Methods (TEAM) for Hospitals. American Hospital Association. LC 79-21859. (Illus.). 212p. 1979. 200.00 (ISBN 0-87258-293-0, 1288). Am Hospital.
Technology for Developing Nations: New Directions for U. S. Technical Assistance. Rutherford M. Poats. 225p. 1972. 11.95 (ISBN 0-8157-7118-5). Brookings.
Technology for Test-Item Writing. Gale Roid & Tom Haladyna. 1981. price not set. Acad Pr.
Technology for Ujamaa Village Developement in Tanzania. David J. Vail. LC 74-25876. (Foreign & Comparative Studies-Eastern African Ser.: No. 18). 64p. 1975. pap. 3.50x (ISBN 0-915984-15-6). Syracuse U Foreign Comp.
Technology of Artificial Lift Methods, 2 vols. Incl. Vol. 3A. 1088p (ISBN 0-87814-031-X); Vol. 3B. 1152p (ISBN 0-87814-138-3). 1980. Ea. 75.00 (ISBN 0-686-68543-1). Pennwell Pub.
Technology of Artificial Lift Methods, Vols. 2a & 2b. Kermit Brown. 1980. 55.00 ea. Vol. 2a, 736 P (ISBN 0-87814-119-7). Vol. 2b, 607 P (ISBN 0-87814-133-2). Pennwell Pub.
Technology of Cake Making. 5th ed. Edmond Bennion & G. S. Bamford. (Illus.). 1973. 45.00x (ISBN 0-249-44121-7). Intl Ideas.
Technology of Carbon & Graphite Fiber Composites. John Delmonte. 464p. 1981. text ed. 32.00 (ISBN 0-442-22072-3). Van Nos Reinhold.
Technology of Cereals. 2nd ed. N. L. Kent. LC 75-6654. 320p. 1975. text ed. 32.00 (ISBN 0-08-018175-9); pap. text ed. 14.00 (ISBN 0-08-018177-5). Pergamon.
Technology of Efficient Energy Utilization: Report, Nato Science Committee Conference, les Arcs, France, Oct. 1973. Ed. by E. G. Kovach. LC 74-19839. 82p. 1976. pap. text ed. 10.00 (ISBN 0-08-018314-X). Pergamon.
Technology of Food Preservation. 4th ed. Norman W. Desrosier & John N. Desrosier. (Illus.). 1977. text ed. 22.50 o.p. (ISBN 0-87055-232-5); pap. text ed. 17.00 (ISBN 0-87055-286-4). AVI.
Technology of Fortification of Foods. Food & Nutrition Board, Natl Research Council. 114p. 1975. pap. 7.25 (ISBN 0-309-02415-3). Natl Acad Pr.
Technology of Industrial Materials. Kazanas & Klein. 1979. pap. 13.00 (ISBN 0-87002-301-2); lab manual 5.28 (ISBN 0-87002-170-2). Bennett IL.
Technology of Metal Powders: Recent Developments. Ed. by L. H. Yaverbaum. LC 80-31. (Chemical Technology Review: No. 153). (Illus.). 400p. 1980. 45.00 (ISBN 0-8155-0794-1). Noyes.
Technology of Offshore Drilling: Completion & Production 1976. ETA Offshore Seminars, Inc. LC 75-21903. 31.00 (ISBN 0-87814-066-2). Pennwell Pub.
Technology of Plasticizers. J. Kern Sears & Joseph R. Darby. LC 80-10225. (SPE Monographs). 1981. 75.00 (ISBN 0-471-05583-2, Pub. by Wiley-Interscience). Wiley.
Technology of Teaching. B. F. Skinner. (Orig.). 1968. pap. text ed. 9.95 (ISBN 0-13-902163-9). P-H.
Technology of Wine Making. 4th ed. M. A. Amerine et al. (Illus.). 1980. text ed. 39.50 (ISBN 0-87055-333-X). AVI.
Technology of Wine Making. 3rd. ed. Maynard A. Amerine & H. W. Berg. (Illus.). 500p. 1972. text ed. 38.50 o.p. (ISBN 0-87055-116-7). AVI.
Technology, Planning & Self-Reliant Development: A Latin American View. Francisco R. Sagasti. LC 78-26010. (Praeger Special Studies). 1979. 22.95 (ISBN 0-03-047221-0). Praeger.
Technology: Promises & Problems. new ed. Educational Research Council of America. (Challenges of Our Time Ser.). (Orig.). (gr. 7). 1972. pap. text ed. 9.32 (ISBN 0-205-05029-8, 8050295); tchrs'. guide 6.60 (ISBN 0-205-05030-1, 8050309). Allyn.
Technology, Society & Man. R. C. Dorf. LC 74-76445. (Illus.). 1974. text ed. 16.00x (ISBN 0-87835-047-0); pap. 10.95x (ISBN 0-87835-052-7). Boyd & Fraser.

Technology: Strategies for Survival. Vera Lustig-Arecco. Ed. by George Spindler & Louise Spindler. (Basic Anthropological Units Ser.). 96p. pap. text ed. 5.95x (ISBN 0-686-63841-7). Irvington.

Technology, the University, & the Community. Ed. by George Bugliarello & H. A. Simon. 1975. 42.00 (ISBN 0-08-017872-3). Pergamon.

Technology, Trade & the U. S. Economy. Academy of Engineering. 1978. pap. 8.25 (ISBN 0-309-02761-6). Natl Acad Pr.

Technology Transfer & Change in the Arab World: Proceedings of a Seminar, Beirut, Oct. 1977. United Nations Economic Commission for Western Asia, Natural Resources, Science & Technology Division. Ed. by A. B. Zahlan. 1978. text ed. 72.00 (ISBN 0-08-022435-0). Pergamon.

Technology Transfer & International Law. Peter Nanyenya-Takirambudde. LC 79-23571. 190p. 1980. 22.95 (ISBN 0-03-047531-7). Praeger.

Technology Transfer & U.S. Foreign Policy. Henry R. Nau. LC 76-2908. (Illus.). 1976. text ed. 32.50 (ISBN 0-275-56790-7). Praeger.

Technology Transfer in Some Asian Countries. 180p. 1979. pap. 13.25 (ISBN 92-833-1455-7, APO 83, APO). Unipub.

Technology Transfer, Innovation, & International Competitiveness. Sherman Gee. 240p. 1980. 21.00 (ISBN 0-471-08468-9, Pub. by Wiley-Interscience). Wiley.

Technology Transfer to Cities: Process of Choice at the Local Level. W. Henry Lambright et al. (Special Studies in Public Policy & Public Systems Management). 1979. lib. bdg. 21.50x (ISBN 0-89158-366-1). Westview.

Technology Transfer to East Europe: U.S. Corporate Experience. Eric W. Hayden. LC 76-12855. (Illus.). 1976. text ed. 23.95 (ISBN 0-275-23240-9). Praeger.

Technology Transfer to the U. S. S. R., Nineteen Twenty-Eight to Nineteen Thirty-Seven & Nineteen Sixty-Six to Nineteen Seventy-Five: The Role of Western Development in Soviet Economic Development. George D. Holliday. (Westview Replica Edition Ser.). 1979. lib. bdg. 24.50x (ISBN 0-89158-189-8). Westview.

Technology Trap. Leo J. Moser. LC 78-26034. 1979. 14.95 (ISBN 0-88229-419-9); pap. 8.95 (ISBN 0-88229-669-8). Nelson-Hall.

Technology Unbound. S. Rivkin. 1969. 11.50 (ISBN 0-08-006424-8); pap. 6.25 (ISBN 0-08-006391-8). Pergamon.

Technology, World Politics, & American Policy. Victor Basiuk. LC 76-51841. (Institute of War & Peace Studies). 1977. 22.50x (ISBN 0-685-74998-3). Columbia U Pr.

Technology's Future: The Hague Congress Technology Assessment. Thomas J. Knight. 566p. 1981. Repr. of 1976 ed. text ed. price not set (ISBN 0-89874-283-8). Krieger.

Technometry. William Ames. Tr. by Lee W. Gibbs from Lat. LC 78-65117. (Haney Foundation Ser.). (Illus.). 1979. 17.95x (ISBN 0-8122-7756-2). U of Pa Pr.

Technostructures & Inter-Organizational Relations. David F. Gillespie & Dennis S. Mileti. LC 78-19543. (Illus.). 1978. 17.95 (ISBN 0-669-02542-9). Lexington Bks.

Tecnica. J. A. Lopez. (Span.). 7.95 (ISBN 84-241-5628-5). E Torres & Sons.

Tectonic Essays, Mainly Alpine. E. B. Bailey. 1935. 19.50x (ISBN 0-19-854368-9). Oxford U Pr.

Tectonic Processes. Darrell Weyman. (Process in Physical Geography Ser.: No. 4). (Illus.). 128p. (Orig.). 1981. pap. text ed. 8.95x (ISBN 0-04-551044-X, 2653). Allen Unwin.

Tectonics. Jean Goguel. Tr. by H. E. Thalmann. LC 62-7477. (Geology Ser.). (Illus.). 1962. 29.95x (ISBN 0-7167-0217-7). W H Freeman.

Tectonics & Landforms. C. D. Ollier. (Geomorphology Texts Ser.). (Illus.). 304p. 1981. text ed. 50.00 (ISBN 0-582-30032-0). Longman.

Tectonics of Africa: Explanatory Memoir on International Tectonic Map of Africa. 59.50 (ISBN 92-3-000872-9, U666, UNESCO). Unipub.

Tecumseh & the Indian Confederation: The Indian Nations East of the Mississippi Are Defeated. Joseph B. Icenhower. (Focus Bks). (Illus.). 96p. (gr. 8 up). 1975. PLB 4.90 o.p. (ISBN 0-531-02780-5). Watts.

Tecumseh: Destiny's Warrior. David C. Cooke. LC 59-7011. (Biography Ser.). (gr. 6 up). 1959. PLB 4.29 o.p. (ISBN 0-671-32275-3). Messner.

Tecwyn, the Last of the Welsh Dragons. Mary Dawson. LC 67-10354. (Illus.). 72p. (gr. 3-7). 1967. 5.95 o.s.i. (ISBN 0-8193-0189-2, Four Winds); 5.41 o.s.i. (ISBN 0-8193-0190-6). Schol Bk Serv.

Ted Hughes & the Drama: Zur Lyrik Von Ted Hughes, eine Interpretation Nach Leitmotiven. James Hogg & Waltraud Mitgutsch. (Salzburg Studies in English Literature, Poetic Drama & Poetic Theory: No. 22). 282p. 1974. pap. text ed. 25.00x (ISBN 0-391-01418-8). Humanities.

Ted Hughes: The Unaccommodated Universe (with Selected Critical Writings by Ted Hughes & Two Interviews) Ekbert Faas. 250p. 1980. 14.00 (ISBN 0-87685-460-9); pap. 7.50 (ISBN 0-87685-459-5); signed ed. 30.00 (ISBN 0-87685-461-7). Black Sparrow.

Ted Kennedy: The Politician & the Man. Steve Aschburner. LC 79-27299. (Illus.). 48p. (gr. 4-8). 1980. PLB 7.95 (ISBN 0-8172-0430-X). Raintree Pubs.

Ted Nicholas Small Business Course. Ted Nicholas. 500p. (Orig.). 1981. pap. 14.95 (ISBN 0-913864-65-X). Enterprise Del.

Teddy Bare: The Last of the Kennedy Clan. Zad Rust. LC 79-25329. 1971. 7.00 o.p. (ISBN 0-88279-221-0); pap. 4.95 (ISBN 0-88279-109-5). Western Islands.

Teddy Bear Hamsters. Mervin F. Roberts. (Illus.). 96p. (Orig.). 1974. pap. 2.50 (ISBN 0-87666-206-8, PS710). TFH Pubns.

Teddy Bears, One to Ten. Susanna Gretz. LC 68-9563. (Picture Bk). (Illus.). (ps-3). 1968. 5.95 o.p. (ISBN 0-695-88460-3); PLB 5.97 lib. ed. o.p. (ISBN 0-695-48460-5). Follett.

Teddy Bears' Picnic. Jimmy Kennedy. (Dinosaur Ser.). (Illus.). (ps-1). 1978. pap. 1.45 ea. (ISBN 0-85122-067-3, Pub. by Dino Pub); pap. pack of 5 avail. Merrimack Bk Serv.

Teddy Bears' Picnic: A Counting Book. Ruben Tanner. LC 79-1867. (Illus.). (ps-k). 1979. 1.95 (ISBN 0-525-69000-X, Gingerbread Bks); PLB 5.95 (ISBN 0-525-69001-8, Gingerbread Bks.). Dutton.

Teddy Bear's Scrapbook. Deborah Howe & James Howe. LC 79-22794. (Illus.). (gr. 2-5). 1980. 7.95 (ISBN 0-689-30746-2). Atheneum.

Teddy Roosevelt & the Rough Riders. Henry Castor. (Landmark Ser: No. 41). (Illus.). (gr. 4-6). 1963. PLB 4.39 o.p. (ISBN 0-394-90341-2, BYR). Random.

Tee-Bo & the Persnickety Prowler. Mary B. Whitooma. (Tee-Bo Bks.). (gr. 4 up). 1978. pap. 1.25 (ISBN 0-307-21583-0, Golden Pr). Western Pub.

Tee-Bo in the Great Hort Hunt. Mary B. Whitooma. (Tee-Bo Bks.). (gr. 4 up). 1978. pap. 1.25 (ISBN 0-307-21584-9, Golden Pr). Western Pub.

Tee in Japan: A Realistic Vision: the Feasilbility of Theological Education by Extension for Churches in Japan. W. Frederic Sprunger. (Illus., Orig.). Date not set. pap. write for info. (ISBN 0-87808-434-7). William Carey Lib. Postponed.

Teeline. I. C. Hill. 1977. pap. text ed. 9.95x o.p. (ISBN 0-435-45329-7). Heinemann Ed.

Teeline Self-Taught. Harry Butler. 1975. pap. 9.95x manual o.p. (ISBN 0-435-45340-8); pap. 19.95x kit with cassette o.p. (ISBN 0-435-45338-6). Heinemann Ed.

Teen-Age Alcoholism. Jim Haskins. 1976. 7.95 o.p. (ISBN 0-8015-7480-3, Hawthorn); pap. 3.50 (ISBN 0-8015-7481-1, Hawthorn). Dutton.

Teen-Age Guide to Healthy Skin & Hair. rev. ed. Irwin I. Lubowe & Barbara Huss. 1979. 12.50 o.p. (ISBN 0-87690-335-9); pap. 6.95 (ISBN 0-87690-334-0). Dutton.

Teen-Age Party Time Stories. Ed. by Abraham L. Furman. (gr. 6-10). 1966. PLB 6.19 (ISBN 0-8313-0039-6). Lantern.

Teen-Age Pregnancy: Including Management of Emotional & Constitutional Problems. James P. Semmens & William M. Lamers, Jr. 132p. 1968. pap. 9.75 spiral (ISBN 0-398-01722-0). C C Thomas.

Teen Model: Fact Book. Gerry A. Turner. LC 80-18228. (Illus.). 224p. (gr. 7 up). 1980. PLB 9.29 (ISBN 0-671-33022-5). Messner.

Teen Skin. G. C. Sauer. (Illus.). 80p. 1973. pap. 4.75 (ISBN 0-398-02942-3). C C Thomas.

Teenage Behavior in Shopping Centers. Martin B. Millison. 1976. 12.00 (ISBN 0-685-82622-8). Intl Coun Shop.

Teenage Courtship. (Illus.). 4.95 (ISBN 0-910550-69-7). Centurion Pr.

Teenage Marriage. (Illus.). pap. 5.00 (ISBN 0-910550-68-9). Centurion Pr.

Teenage Marriages: A Demographic Analysis. John R. Weeks. LC 76-5330. (Studies in Population & Urban Demography Ser.: No. 2). (Illus.). 192p. (Orig.). 1976. lib. bdg. 16.50 (ISBN 0-8371-8898-9, WTM/). Greenwood.

Teenage Motherhood: Social & Economic Consequences. Kristin A. Moore et al. (Institute Paper). 50p. 1979. pap. 4.00 (ISBN 0-87766-243-6, 24300). Urban Inst.

Teenage Nutrition & Physique. Ruth L. Huenemann et al. (Illus.). 256p. 1974. 13.75 (ISBN 0-398-03135-5). C C Thomas.

Teenage Pregnancy. Daniel J. Baum. 192p. 1980. pap. 6.95 (ISBN 0-8253-0024-X). Beaufort Bks NY.

Teenage Pregnancy in a Family Context: Implications for Policy. Theodora Ooms. (Family Impact Seminar Ser.). 350p. 1981. 19.50x (ISBN 0-87722-204-5). Temple U Pr.

Teenage Pregnant Girl. Ed. by Jack Zackler & Wayne Brandstadt. (Illus.). 336p. 1975. 17.50 (ISBN 0-398-03152-5). C C Thomas.

Teenage Sex. (Illus.). pap. 5.00 (ISBN 0-910550-67-0). Centurion Pr.

Teenage Sexuality, Pregnancy & Childbearing. Ed. by Frank Furstenberg et al. 1980. 22.95x; pap. 10.50x. U of Pa Pr.

Teenagers & Their Hang-Ups. Paul Gelinas. (YA) 1975. PLB 5.97 o.p. (ISBN 0-8239-0328-1). Rosen Pr.

Teenager's Guidebook to Wall Street & the Stock Market. Carlo M. Flumiani. 1979. 27.75 (ISBN 0-89266-162-3). Am Classical Coll Pr.

Teenagers in Other Societies. Barbara Milbauer. 192p. (gr. 7 up). 1981. write for info. (ISBN 0-671-32891-3). Messner.

Teenager's Life Extension Financial Test. C. M. Flumiani. (Seminar for Human Development Books). (Illus.). 1978. plastic spiral bdg. 12.00 (ISBN 0-89266-124-0). Am Classical Coll Pr.

Teenager's Life Extension Test. C. M. Flumiani. (Illus.). 40p. (YA) (gr. 6 up). 1974. 12.00 (ISBN 0-913314-40-4). Am Classical Coll Pr.

Teenagers Pray. William A. Kramer. LC 55-12193. (gr. 8-12). 1956. 3.95 (ISBN 0-570-03018-8, 6-1054). Concordia.

Teenagers: The Continuing Challenge. Shirley G. Gould. 1977. 7.95 (ISBN 0-8015-5800-X, Hawthorn); pap. 3.95 (ISBN 0-8015-5801-8, Hawthorn). Dutton.

Teens Parenting: The Challenge of Babies & Toddlers. Jeanne W. Lindsay. (Illus.). 320p. 1981. 14.95 (ISBN 0-930934-07-5); pap. 9.95 (ISBN 0-930934-06-7); price not set tchr's guide (ISBN 0-930934-09-1); wkbk. 2.50 (ISBN 0-930934-08-3). Morning Glory.

Teetering on the Tightrope. Carol Amen. LC 79-18718. (Orion Ser.). 1979. pap. 1.95 (ISBN 0-8127-0250-6). Southern Pub.

Teeth. (MacDonald Educational Ser.). (Illus., Arabic.). 3.50 (ISBN 0-686-53075-6). Intl Bk Ctr.

Teeth 'n' Smiles. David Hare. 1976. pap. 5.95 (ISBN 0-571-10995-0, Pub. by Faber & Faber). Merrimack Bk Serv.

Teeth of the Tiger. Maurice LeBlanc. 490p. 1980. Repr. of 1914 ed. lib. bdg. 17.95x (ISBN 0-89968-204-9). Lightyear.

Teetoncey. Theodore Taylor. LC 73-13097. 160p. (gr. 5 up). 1974. PLB 4.95 (ISBN 0-385-09587-2). Doubleday.

Teetoncey. Theodore Taylor. (Illus.). (gr. 3-7). 1975. pap. 1.95 (ISBN 0-380-00346-5, 52118, Camelot). Avon.

Teetoncey & Ben O'Neal. Theodore Taylor. LC 74-4875. 160p. (gr. 3-7). 1975. PLB 5.95 (ISBN 0-385-04504-2). Doubleday.

Teetoncey & Ben O'neal. Theodore Taylor. 1976. pap. 1.25 (ISBN 0-380-00764-9, 30536, Camelot). Avon.

TEG's Nineteen Ninety-Four: An Anticipation of the Near Future. Robert Theobald & J. M. Scott. LC 70-150754. 210p. 1972. 7.95x (ISBN 0-8040-0509-5); pap. 3.95 o.s.i. (ISBN 0-8040-0510-9). Swallow.

Tehran-Yalta-Potsdam: The Soviet Protocols. Ed. by Robert Beitzell. 16.00 (ISBN 0-87569-013-0). Academic Intl.

Teilhard. Mary Lukas & Ellen Lukas. 360p. 1981. pap. 6.95 (ISBN 0-07-039047-9). McGraw.

Teilhard De Chardin. Bernard Towers. Ed. by D. E. Nineham & E. H. Robertson. LC 66-15515. (Makers of Contemporary Theology Ser). (Orig.). 1966. pap. 2.25 (ISBN 0-8042-0723-2). John Knox.

Tekhnika Komicheskogo U Gogolia. Aleksandr L. Slonimskii. LC 63-7523. (Slavic Reprint Ser., No. 2). 65p. (Rus.). 1969. pap. 1.50 (ISBN 0-87057-070-6, Pub. by Brown U Pr). Univ Pr of New England.

Tektites. Ed. by Virgil Barnes & Mildred Barnes. LC 72-95942. (Benchmark Papers in Geology Ser). 400p. 1973. 42.50 (ISBN 0-12-786138-6). Acad Pr.

Tel Ngandong Fossil Hominids: A Comparative Study of a Far Eastern Homo Erectus Group. LC 80-50035. (Publications in Anthropology: No. 78). 1980. pap. 13.50. Yale U Anthro.

Telecommunication by Speech: A Transmission Performance-of-Telephone Networks. D. L. Richards. 1973. 52.95 (ISBN 0-470-71949-4). Halsted Pr.

Telecommunication: One World, One Mind. Don Fabun. 1971. pap. text ed. 2.50x (ISBN 0-02-475400-5, 47540). Macmillan.

Telecommunication System Engineering: Analog & Digital Network. Roger Freeman. LC 79-26661. 1980. 32.50 (ISBN 0-471-02955-6, Pub. by Wiley-Interscience). Wiley.

Telecommunication Systems Engineering. William C. Lindsey & Marvin K. Simon. (Illus.). 672p. 1972. ref. ed. 32.95 (ISBN 0-13-902429-8). P-H.

Telecommunication Transmission. (IEE Conference Publication). 1981. pap. price not set. Inst Electrica.

Telecommunications. E. H. Jolley. Ed. by Patrick Moore. (Young Engineer Ser). (Illus.). (gr. 7 up). 1963. 4.25 o.p. (ISBN 0-298-16439-6). Dufour.

Telecommunications--Transportation Tradeoff: Options for Tomorrow. Jack M. Nilles et al. LC 76-18107. 196p. 1976. 34.95 (ISBN 0-471-01507-5, Pub. by Wiley-Interscience). Wiley.

Telecommunications & Productivity. Mitchell L. Moss. 416p. 1980. text ed. 37.50 (ISBN 0-201-04649-0). A-W.

Telecommunications & the Computer. 2nd ed. J. Martin. 1976. 35.00 (ISBN 0-13-902494-8). P-H.

Telecommunications Demand: A Survey & Critique. Lester Taylor. 1980. 29.50 (ISBN 0-88410-496-6). Ballinger Pub.

Telecommunications Energy. (IEE Conference Publication). (Illus., Orig.). 1981. pap. price not set. Inst Electrical.

Telecommunications Function of the British Post Office. Douglas C. Pitt. 1979. text ed. 20.50x (ISBN 0-566-00273-6, Pub. by Gower Pub Co England). Renouf.

Telecommunications Structure & Management in the Executive Branch of Government: 1900-1970. Thomas E. Will. 1978. lib bdg. 25.50x (ISBN 0-89158-286-X). Westview.

Telecommunications Switching Principles. Michael T. Hills. (Illus.). 1979. text ed. 25.00x (ISBN 0-262-08092-3). MIT Pr.

Telecommunications Transmission Handbook. Roger L. Freeman. LC 75-1134. 587p. 1975. 37.50 (ISBN 0-471-27789-4, Pub. by Wiley-Interscience). Wiley.

Telecourse Study Guide for Personal Finance & Money Management. Martin H. Ivener & Robert S. Rosefsky. 1978. pap. text ed. 8.95 (ISBN 0-471-03797-4); Set. 23.90 (ISBN 0-471-03796-6). Wiley.

Telefon. W. Wager. 1975. 7.95 o.s.i. (ISBN 0-02-622430-5). Macmillan.

Telemedicine: Explorations in the Use of Telecommunications in Health Care. Rashid L. Bashshur et al. (Illus.). 376p. 1975. 36.50 (ISBN 0-398-03276-9); pap. 26.75 (ISBN 0-398-03311-0). C C Thomas.

Telempath. Spider Robinson. (YA) 1976. 7.95 o.p. (ISBN 0-399-11796-2, Dist. by Putnam). Berkley Pub.

Teleological Explanations: An Etiological Analysis of Goals & Functions. Larry Wright. LC 75-17284. 1976. 15.95x (ISBN 0-520-02086-3). U of Cal Pr.

Teleology. A. Woodfield. LC 75-44574. (Illus.). 240p. 1976. 32.95 (ISBN 0-521-21102-6). Cambridge U Pr.

Teleology Revisited & Other Essays in the Philosophy & History of Science. Ernest Nagel. 1979. 22.50x (ISBN 0-231-04504-2). Columbia U Pr.

Telepathy. Eileen J. Garrett. 1941. 4.00 o.p. (ISBN 0-912326-00-X). Garrett-Helix.

Telepathy & Clairvoyance: Views on Some Little Investigated Capabilities of Man. W. H. Tenhaeff. (Illus.). 176p. 1973. 16.75 (ISBN 0-398-02455-3). C C Thomas.

Telephone. (Illus.). Arabic 2.50x (ISBN 0-685-82886-7). Intl Bk Ctr.

Telephone Accessories You Can Build. Jules Gilder. (Illus.). 1976. pap. 6.50 (ISBN 0-8104-5748-2). Hayden.

Telephone Book. Joseph Kaufman. (Illus.). (ps-1). 1968. PLB 5.38 (ISBN 0-307-68938-7, Golden Pr). Western Pub.

Telephone Instrument: Access, Business. BCC Staff. 1980. cancelled (ISBN 0-89336-243-3, G-057). BCC.

Telephone Medicine: The Use of the Telephone & the Management of Pediatric Patients. Jeffrey L. Brown. LC 80-16674. (Illus.). 154p. 1980. pap. text ed. 11.95 (ISBN 0-8016-0856-2). Mosby.

Telephone Systems. Ed. by Herbert S. Zim & James R. Skelly. LC 74-151937. (How Things Work Ser). (Illus.). (gr. 3-7). 1974. 5.75 o.p. (ISBN 0-688-21781-8); PLB 6.48 (ISBN 0-688-31781-2); pap. 1.25 (ISBN 0-688-26781-5). Morrow.

Telephone Techniques That Sell. Charles Bury. 1980. pap. 4.95 (ISBN 0-446-97453-6). Warner Bks.

Telephone's First Century & Beyond. Jerome Wiesner et al. 1977. 10.00 o.s.i. (ISBN 0-690-01485-6, TYC-T). T Y Crowell.

Telephones for the Elderly. Peter Gregory. 128p. 1973. pap. text ed. 5.00x (ISBN 0-7135-1889-8, Pub. by Bedford England). Renouf.

Telephoto Photography. Kalton C. Lahue. LC 77-74103. (PhotoGraphic How to Library). (Illus.). (gr. 9-12). 1977. pap. 3.95 o.p. (ISBN 0-8227-4021-4). Petersen Pub.

Teleplay: An Introduction to Television Writing. Coles Trapnell. 256p. 1974. pap. text ed. 5.95 (ISBN 0-8015-7486-2, Hawthorn). Dutton.

Teles: The Cynic Teacher. Ed. by Edward N. O'Neil. LC 76-41800. (Society of Biblical Literature. Texts & Translantion - Graeco-Roman Religion Ser.). 1977. pap. 6.00 (ISBN 0-89130-092-9, 060211). Scholars Pr Ca.

Telescope. Louis Bell. 287p. 1981. pap. price not set (ISBN 0-486-2415[illegible]-3). Dover.

Telescope Handbook & Star Atlas. rev. ed. Neale E. Howard. LC 75-6601. (Illus.). 226p. 1975. 16.95 (ISBN 0-690-00686-1, TYC-T). T Y Crowell.

Teletext: The New Networks of Information & Knowledge in Computer Society. Daniel Bell. LC 78-19820. Date not set. cancelled (ISBN 0-465-08402-8). Basic.

Televised Medicine Advertising & Children. Thomas S. Robertson et al. 21.95 (ISBN 0-03-049161-4). Praeger.

Television. (Illus.). Arabic 2.50x (ISBN 0-685-82887-5). Intl Bk Ctr.

Television: A Guide for Christians. Edward N. McNulty. LC 76-1990. 96p. (Orig.). 1976. pap. 3.50 o.p. (ISBN 0-687-41220-X). Abingdon.

Television Almanac, 1981, Vol. 26. Ed. by Richard Gertner. 650p. 1981. 38.00 (ISBN 0-900610-25-5). Quigley Pub Co.

Television & Delinquency. J. D. Halloran et al. (Television Research Committee Working Papers: No. 3). 1970. pap. text ed. 9.50x (ISBN 0-7185-1088-7, Leicester). Humanities.

Television & Human Behavior. George Comstock et al. 1978. 20.00 (ISBN 0-231-04420-8); pap. 10.00 (ISBN 0-231-04421-6). Columbia U Pr.

Television & Radio. 5th ed. Giraud Chester et al. (Illus.). 1978. ref. ed. 18.95 (ISBN 0-13-902981-8). P-H.

Television & Radio Announcing. 3rd ed. Stuart W. Hyde. LC 78-69615. (Illus.). 1979. text ed. 17.95 (ISBN 0-395-27108-8). HM.

Television & Radio in the United Kingdom. Burton Paulu. 544p. 1981. 39.50x (ISBN 0-8166-0941-1). U of Minn Pr.

Television & Socialization Processes in the Family. International Zentralinstitut Fur das Jugend und Bildung Fernsehen. (Fernschen und Bildung Ser.). 192p. 1976. text ed. 14.80 (ISBN 3-7940-3368-X, Pub. by K G Saur). Shoe String.

Television & the Aging Audience. Richard H. Davis. LC 80-68093. (Illus.). 107p. (Orig.). 1980. 8.50 (ISBN 0-88474-096-X); pap. 6.50 (ISBN 0-686-28656-1). USC Andrus Geron.

Television & the Teaching of English. Neil Postman. LC 61-13519. (Orig.). 1961. pap. text ed. 10.95x (ISBN 0-89197-445-8). Irvington.

Television & Youth: Twenty-Five Years of Research & Controversy. John P. Murray. 278p. (Orig.). 1980. pap. text ed. 10.00 (ISBN 0-938510-00-2, 010-TV). Boys Town Ctr.

Television As a Cultural Force. Ed. by Richard Adler & Douglass Cater. LC 76-10714. (Special Studies). 1976. text ed. 25.95 (ISBN 0-275-23180-1). Praeger.

Television As a Social Force: New Approaches to Tv Criticism. Ed. by Douglass Cater & Richard Adler. LC 75-23951. (Special Studies). 1975. 23.95 (ISBN 0-275-01190-9). Praeger.

Television Audience: Patterns of Viewing. G. J. Goodhardt et al. (Illus.). 174p. 1975. 18.95 (ISBN 0-347-01102-0, 00179-1, Pub. by Saxon Hse). Lexington Bks.

Television Commericals: How to Create Successful TV Advertising. rev. ed. Charles A. Wainwright. (Communication Arts Bks.). (Illus.). 1970. 8.95 o.s.i. (ISBN 0-8038-7101-5); pap. text ed. 5.95x (ISBN 0-8038-7102-3). Hastings.

Television Contacts. rev. ed. Ed. by Michael McMahon. 1980. pap. text ed. 80.00 (ISBN 0-935224-00-9). Larimi Comm.

Television Digests Cable & Station Coverage Atlas. rev. ed. 1980. 96.50 (ISBN 0-686-15419-3). TV Factbk.

Television Drama Series Programming: A Comprehensive Chronicle, 1959-1975. Larry J. Gianakos. LC 78-650. 1978. 32.50 (ISBN 0-8108-1116-2). Scarecrow.

Television Drama Series Programming: A Comprehensive Chronicle, 1947-1959. Larry J. Gianakos. LC 80-17023. 581p. 1980. 29.50 (ISBN 0-8108-1330-0). Scarecrow.

Television Economics. Bruce Owen et al. LC 74-926. (Illus.). 1974. 19.95 (ISBN 0-669-92999-9). Lexington Bks.

Television Engineering. Arvind M. Dhake. (Illus.). 1980. 14.50 (ISBN 0-07-096389-4, P&RB). McGraw.

Television Evening News Covers Inflation: Nineteen Seventy-Eight to Seventy-Nine. Tom Bethell. Ed. by The Media Institute. (Illus.). 52p. (Orig.). 1980. pap. 5.00 (ISBN 0-937790-00-1). Media Inst.

Television for Higher Technical Education of the Employed: A First Report on a Pilot Project in Poland. 1969. pap. 2.50 (ISBN 92-3-100736-X, U667, UNESCO). Unipub.

Television Fraud: The History & Implications of the Quiz Show Scandals. Ed. by Kent Anderson. LC 77-94755. (Contributions in American Studies: No. 39). lib. bdg. 22.50x (ISBN 0-313-20321-0, ATF/). Greenwood.

Television, Imagination & Aggression: A Study of Preschoolers. Jerome L. Singer & Dorothy G. Singer. LC 80-36810. 224p. 1981. text ed. 19.95 (ISBN 0-89859-060-4). L Erlbaum Assocs.

Television in America. George Comstock. LC 80-10891. (Sage Commtext Ser.: No. 1). 155p. 1980. 12.50x (ISBN 0-8039-1244-7); pap. 5.95 (ISBN 0-8039-1245-5). Sage.

Television in Politics: Its Uses & Influences. Jay G. Blumler & Denis McQuail. LC 69-12843. 1969. 15.00x o.s.i. (ISBN 0-226-06175-2). U of Chicago Pr.

Television in the Corporate Interest. Richard Bunce. LC 75-23958. (Praeger Special Studies). 1976. 17.50 o.p. (ISBN 0-275-55950-5). Praeger.

Television in the Public Interest. A. William Bluem et al. (Communication Arts Bks.). (Illus.). 1961. 8.95 o.p. (ISBN 0-8038-7044-2). Hastings.

Television News, Radio News. 3rd, rev. ed. Irving E. Fang. LC 80-50847. Orig. Title: Television News. (Illus.). 414p. 1980. text ed. 16.95x (ISBN 0-9604212-0-3). Rada Pr.

Television News: Writing, Filming, Editing, Broadcasting. 2nd rev. & enl. ed. Irving E. Fang. (Communication Arts Bks.). (Illus.). 384p. 1972. 12.50 o.s.i. (ISBN 0-8038-7117-1); pap. text ed. 7.50x o.s.i. (ISBN 0-8038-7125-2). Hastings.

Television Production. Dan Baker & Bill Weisgerber. Ed. by James E. Duane. LC 80-23479. (Instructional Media Library: Vol. 15). (Illus.). 112p. 1981. 13.95 (ISBN 0-87778-175-3). Educ Tech Pubns.

Television Production Handbook. 3rd ed. Herbert Zettl. 1976. 19.95x (ISBN 0-534-00414-8); 6.95x (ISBN 0-534-00530-6). Wadsworth Pub.

Television Repair & Servicing: A Bibliography & Index for 1960-1976. Russell H. Powell. LC 77-4058. 1977. 16.95x (ISBN 0-918596-00-9). Commonweal Bks.

Television Service Manual. 4th ed. Robert Middleton. LC 76-24074. 1977. 11.95 (ISBN 0-672-23247-2, 23247). Audel.

Television Simplified. 7th ed. Kiver & Kaufman. LC 72-11273. 630p. 1973. pap. 16.40 (ISBN 0-8273-0492-7); instructor's guide 1.60 (ISBN 0-8273-0493-5). Delmar.

Television Studio Operations Manual. rev. ed. William McCavitt. 106p. 1980. pap. 4.50 (ISBN 0-935648-05-4). Halldin Pub.

Television Symptom Diagnosis. Richard W. Tinnell. 1977. instructor's manual 6.67 (ISBN 0-672-97618-8). Bobbs.

Television: The Creative Experience: A Survey of Anglo-American Progress. Ed. by A. William Bluem & Roger Manvell. (Communication Arts Bks.). 1967. 9.95 o.p. (ISBN 0-8038-7039-6). Hastings.

Television: The Critical View. 2nd ed. Ed. by Horace Newcomb. LC 78-13290. 1979. pap. 7.95 (ISBN 0-19-502501-6). Oxford U Pr.

Television: The Director's Viewpoint. John A. Ravage. (Westview Special Studies in Communications). 1978. lib. bdg. 20.00x (ISBN 0-89158-337-8); text ed. 9.50 (ISBN 0-89158-337-8). Westview.

Television Today: A Close-up View, Readings from TV Guide. Ed. by Barry Cole. (Galaxy Book Ser.: No. 618). 448p. 1981. pap. 7.95 (ISBN 0-19-502799-X, GB). Oxford U Pr.

Television Today: A Close-up View. Readings from TV Guide. Ed. by Barry Cole. 448p. 1981. 19.95 (ISBN 0-19-502798-1). Oxford U Pr.

Television Traffic - a One-Way Street? A Survey & Analysis of the International Flow of Television Programme Material. Kaarle Nordenstreng & Tapio Varis. (Reports & Papers on Mass Communication, No. 70). (Illus.). 62p. (Orig.). 1974. pap. 2.50 (ISBN 92-3-101135-9, U669, UNESCO). Unipub.

Television Troubleshooting. Clyde N. Herrick. (Illus.). 240p. 1975. 17.50 o.p. (ISBN 0-87909-830-9). Reston.

Television Violence & the Adolescent Boy. William A. Belson. (Illus.). 1978. 21.00 (ISBN 0-566-00211-6, 02081-8, Pub. by Saxon Hse England). Lexington Bks.

Television's Transformation. Stuart M. De Luca. LC 80-15254. 1980. 9.95 (ISBN 0-498-02474-1). A S Barnes.

Tell & Sell. Martin M. Pegler. 1979. 7.95 (ISBN 0-911380-46-9). Signs of Times.

Tell el Amarna & the Bible. Charles F. Pfeiffer. (Baker Studies in Biblical Archaeology). 1976. pap. 2.95 (ISBN 0-8010-7002-3). Baker Bk.

Tell Him That I Heard. Patricia Hangen. LC 76-40581. (Illus.). 1977. 7.95 o.p. (ISBN 0-06-011788-5, HarpT). Har-Row.

Tell It Goodbye, Kiddo: The Decline of the New England Offshore Fishing Industry. David Boeri & James Gibson. LC 75-37368. (Illus.). 144p. 1976. 9.95 o.p. (ISBN 0-87742-063-7). Intl Marine.

Tell It to the Dead: Memories of a War. Donald Kirk. LC 75-29137. 229p. 1975. 12.95 (ISBN 0-88229-287-0); pap. 6.95 (ISBN 0-88229-354-0). Nelson-Hall.

Tell It to the Mafia. Joseph Donato. 1975. pap. 2.50 o.p. (ISBN 0-88270-322-6). Logos.

Tell It to the World. Mervyn Maxwell. LC 76-6619. 1976. 7.95 (ISBN 0-8163-0217-0, 20077-4). Pacific Pr Pub Assn.

Tell Me About God. rev. ed. Mary A. Jones. LC 67-15727. (ps-3). 1967. pap. 3.95 (ISBN 0-528-87656-2). Rand.

Tell Me About God Kit: 12 Lessons, Vol. 1. Lois J. Haas. (Tiny Steps of Faith Ser.). (ps). 1966. complete kit 9.95 (ISBN 0-86508-011-9); text only 1.95 (ISBN 0-86508-012-7); color & action book 0.60 (ISBN 0-86508-013-5). BCM Inc.

Tell Me About Jesus. Elizabeth E. Watson. 1980. pap. 3.50 (ISBN 0-570-03484-1, 56-1705). Concordia.

Tell Me About Jesus Kit: 16 Lessons, Vol. 2. Lois J. Haas. (Tiny Steps of Faith Ser.). (ps). 1967. complete kit 9.95 (ISBN 0-86508-014-3); text only 1.95 (ISBN 0-86508-015-1); color & action book 0.60 (ISBN 0-86508-016-X). BCM Inc.

Tell Me About Picture Storybooks, 4 bks. Incl. Tell Me About God (ISBN 0-87239-275-9, 2045); Tell Me About God's World. o.p. (ISBN 0-87239-276-7, 2046); Tell Me About Jesus. o.p. (ISBN 0-87239-277-5, 2047); Tell Me About Love. o.p. (ISBN 0-87239-278-3, 2048). (ps). 1976. 0.50 ea. Standard Pub.

Tell Me Again, Lord, I Forget. Ruth H. Calkin. LC 74-76938. 96p. (Orig.). 1974. pap. 2.50 (ISBN 0-912692-37-5). Cook.

Tell Me Everything. Marie Brenner. 1977. pap. 1.95 o.p. (ISBN 0-451-07685-0, J7685, Sig). NAL.

Tell Me How to Please God Kit: 16 Lessons, Vol. 4. Lois J. Haas. (Tiny Steps of Faith Ser.). (ps). 1974. complete kit 9.95 (ISBN 0-86508-020-8); text only 1.95 (ISBN 0-86508-021-6); color & action book 0.60 (ISBN 0-86508-022-4). BCM Inc.

Tell Me How to Trust God Kit: 16 Lessons, Vol. 3. Lois J. Haas. (Tiny Steps of Faith Ser.). (ps). 1970. complete kit 9.95 (ISBN 0-86508-017-8); text only 1.95 (ISBN 0-86508-018-6); color & action book 0.60 (ISBN 0-86508-019-4). BCM Inc.

Tell Me, Mister Owl. Doris V. Foster. LC 56-9155. (Illus.). (ps-3). 1957. PLB 7.92 o.p. (ISBN 0-688-51071-X). Lothrop.

Tell Me No Lies. Itila Colman. (YA) (gr. 7-9). 1979. pap. write for info. (ISBN 0-671-29920-4). PB.

Tell Me Now, & Again. Richard Llewellyn. LC 77-80895. 1978. 8.95 o.p. (ISBN 0-385-12123-7). Doubleday.

Tell Me Papa. Joy Johnson & Marvin Johnson. 1980. pap. 6.95 boards (ISBN 0-930194-02-0). Highly Specialized.

Tell Me That You Love Me, Junie Moon. Marjorie Kellogg. LC 68-24600. 1968. 7.95 (ISBN 0-374-27280-8). FS&G.

Tell Me Who I Am: James Agee's Search for Selfhood. Mark A. Doty. LC 80-22440. 176p. 1981. 15.95x (ISBN 0-8071-0758-1). La State U Pr.

Tell My Horse. Zora N. Hurston. (New World Writing Ser). (Illus.). 296p. 1981. 17.95 (ISBN 0-913666-31-9); pap. 8.95 (ISBN 0-913666-31-9). Turtle Isl Foun.

Tell-Tale Heart. Edgar A. Poe. (Creative's Classics Ser.). (Illus.). 32p. (gr. 4-9). 1980. PLB 6.95 (ISBN 0-87191-772-6). Creative Ed.

Tell-Tale Heart: The Life & Works of Edgar Allan Poe. Julian Symons. 1981. pap. 3.95 (ISBN 0-14-005371-9). Penguin.

Tell the American People: Perspectives on the Iranian Revolution. rev. ed. David H. Albert. LC 80-83577. 1980. 14.95 (ISBN 0-86571-001-5); pap. 4.95 (ISBN 0-86571-003-1). Movement New Soc.

Tell the American People: Perspectives on the Iranian Revolution. Ed. by David H. Albert. LC 80-82242. 1980. pap. text ed. 3.80 (ISBN 0-86571-000-7). Movement New Soc.

Tell the Next Generation: Homilies & Near Homilies. Walter J. Burghardt. LC 79-91895. 256p. 1980. pap. 6.95 (ISBN 0-8091-2252-9). Paulist Pr.

Tell the Time with Benji. bds. 3.99 (ISBN 0-686-64106-X). Borden.

Tell the Truth. Will Metzger. 220p. (Orig.). 1981. pap. 5.95 (ISBN 0-87784-464-X). Inter Varsity.

Tell the World: A Jesus People Manual. Arthur Blessitt. LC 78-177397. (Spire Bk). 64p. (Orig.). 1973. pap. 0.95 o.p. (ISBN 0-8007-8113-9). Revell.

Tell Them from Me. Lesley Gow & Andrew McPherson. 137p. 1980. 30.65 (ISBN 0-08-025738-0); pap. 13.45 (ISBN 0-08-025739-9). Pergamon.

Tell Them My Name Is Amanda. Joanne Wold. Ed. by Caroline Rubin. LC 77-14297. (Concept Books Ser.). (Illus.). 32p. (gr. k-3). 1977. 6.50g (ISBN 0-8075-7768-5). A Whitman.

Tell Time. Stanley Rice. LC 63-15403. (Illus.). (gr. 2-5). 1963. pap. 3.50 o.p. (ISBN 0-15-284380-9, HJ). HarBraceJ.

Tellers & Listeners: The Narrative Imagination. Barbara Hardy. 279p. 1976. text ed. 27.50x (ISBN 0-485-11153-5, Athlone Pr). Humanities.

Telling a Child About Death. Edgar N. Jackson. 1965. 4.95 o.p. (ISBN 0-8015-7488-9); pap. 2.95 (ISBN 0-8015-7494-3, Hawthorn). Dutton.

Telling Fortunes with Cards. Kevin Martin. 1971. pap. 1.50 o.s.i. (ISBN 0-02-077340-4, Collier). Macmillan.

Telling Lives: The Biographer's Art. Leon Edel et al. Ed. by Marc Pachter. LC 79-698. 1979. 9.95 o.p. (ISBN 0-915220-54-7). New Republic.

Telling the Story of the Local Church: The Who, What, When, Where & Why of Communication. Velma Sumrall & Lucille Germany. (Orig.). 1979. pap. 6.95 (ISBN 0-8164-2193-5); wkbk. avail. (ISBN 0-685-59466-1). Crossroad NY.

Telling Tongues: Language Policy in Mexico, Colony to Nation. Shirley B. Heath. LC 72-408. (Illus.). 1972. text ed. 12.95x (ISBN 0-8077-1508-5); pap. text ed. 7.95x (ISBN 0-8077-1507-7). Tchrs Coll.

Telling Writing. 3rd ed. Ken Macrorie. (English Language Ser.). (gr. 10 up). 1980. pap. 8.95x (ISBN 0-8104-6116-1). Hayden.

Telling Yourself the Truth. William Backus & Marie Chapian. LC 80-10136. 192p. (Orig.). 1980. pap. 4.95 (ISBN 0-87123-562-5, 210562); study guide 1.25 (ISBN 0-87123-567-6). Bethany Fell.

Telltale Lilac Bush & Other West Virginia Ghost Tales. Ruth A. Musick. LC 64-14000. (Illus.). 208p. 1976. pap. 5.50 (ISBN 0-8131-0136-0). U Pr of Ky.

Telltale Line: The Secrets of Handwriting Analysis. Peggy Mann. LC 76-8436. (Illus.). 96p. (gr. 5 up). 1976. 8.95 (ISBN 0-02-762240-1, 76224). Macmillan.

Telltale Summer of Tina C. Lila Perl. LC 75-9518. 192p. (gr. 4-8). 1975. 6.95 (ISBN 0-395-28872-X, Clarion). HM.

Telugu Verbal Bases. Bhadriraju Krishnamurti. 1972. 12.50 (ISBN 0-89684-328-9). Orient Bk Dist.

Tempeh Production: The Book of Tempeh, Vol. II. William Shurtleff & Akiko Aoyagi. LC 79-89281. (Soyfood Production Ser.: No. 3). (Illus.). 1980. 22.95 (ISBN 0-933332-04-1); pap. 15.95 (ISBN 0-933332-02-5). Soyfoods-New Age.

Temper of Victorian Belief: Studies in the Religious Novels of Pater, Kingsley, & Newman. David A. Downes. LC 76-147189. 159p. 1972. text ed. 16.50x (ISBN 0-8290-0209-X). Irvington.

Temperament & Behavior Disorders in Children. Alexander Thomas et al. LC 68-13025. 309p. 1968. 15.00x (ISBN 0-8147-0415-8). NYU Pr.

Temperance. Ellen G. White. 1949. pap. 4.50 (ISBN 0-8163-0150-6, 20101-4); pap. 6.50 deluxe ed. (ISBN 0-8163-0151-4, 20100-4). Pacific Pr Pub Assn.

Temperate-Zone Pomology. Melvin N. Westwood. LC 77-26330. (Illus.). 1978. text ed. 29.95x (ISBN 0-7167-0196-0). W H Freeman.

Temperature Regulation. S. A. Richards & P. S. Fielden. LC 73-77794. (Wykeham Science Ser.: No. 27). 1973. pap. 8.75x (ISBN 0-8448-1335-4). Crane-Russak Co.

Temperatures Very Low & Very High. Mark W. Zemansky. 144p. 1981. pap. price not set (ISBN 0-486-24072-X). Dover.

Tempest. William Shakespeare. Ed. by D. J. Palmer. LC 70-127577. (Casebook Ser). 1970. pap. text ed. 2.50 o.s.i. (ISBN 0-87695-053-5). Aurora Pubs.

Tempest. William Shakespeare. Ed. by Arthur Quiller-Couch et al. (New Shakespeare Ser). 1969. 23.95 (ISBN 0-521-07557-2); pap. 4.50x (ISBN 0-521-09500-X). Cambridge U Pr.

Tempest. William Shakespeare. Ed. by Alfred Harbage. LC 47-25589. (Crofts Classics Ser.). 1946. pap. text ed. 1.25x o.p. (ISBN 0-88295-083-5). AHM Pub.

Tempest. Ed. by G. A. Wilkes. (Challis Shakespeare Ser.). 1981. pap. 3.50x (ISBN 0-686-68845-7, Pub. by Sydney U Pr Australia). Intl Schol Bk Serv.

Tempest in a Tea House: American Attitudes Toward Breast-Feeding. Richard Feinberg et al. 50p. (Orig.). 1980. pap. 2.95 (ISBN 0-933522-06-1). Kent Popular.

Tempestuous Affair. Caroline Courtney. (Orig.). 1981. pap. 1.75 (ISBN 0-446-94608-7). Warner Bks.

Tempestuous Heights. Kamala Sanders. 176p. 1981. 8.50 (ISBN 0-682-49741-X). Exposition.

Tempestuous Lovers. Suzanne Simmons. (Orig.). 1981. pap. 1.50 (ISBN 0-440-18551-3). Dell.
Temple-Beau; or, the Town Coquets: A Novel, 1754. Ed. by Michael F. Shugrue. (Flowering of the Novel, 1740-1775 Ser: Vol. 42). 1974. lib. bdg. 50.00 (ISBN 0-8240-1141-4). Garland Pub.
Temple Dogs. Robert L. Duncan. LC 76-51781. 1977. 8.95 o.p. (ISBN 0-688-03181-1). Morrow.
Temple Houston: Lawyer with a Gun. Glenn Shirley. 1980. 14.95 (ISBN 0-8061-1627-7). U of Okla Pr.
Temple of Eternity: Thomas Traherne's Philosophy of Time. Richard D. Jordan. LC 70-189560. (National University Publications). 1972. 11.00 (ISBN 0-8046-9019-7). Kennikat.
Temple of Fear. (Nick Carter Ser.). 1978. pap. 1.75 (ISBN 0-441-80215-X). Charter Bks.
Temple of Solomon: Archaeological Fact & Medieval Tradition in Christian, Islamic & Jewish Art. Ed. by Joseph Gutmann. LC 75-19120. 1976. 9.00 (ISBN 0-89130-013-9, 090103). Scholars Pr Ca.
Temple of the Dawn. Anne Hampson. (Harlequin Romances Ser.). 192p. 1980. pap. 1.25 o.p. (ISBN 0-373-02353-7, Pub. by Harlequin). PB.
Temple of the Mind: Education & Literary Taste in Seventeenth-Century England. John R. Mulder. LC 79-79059. 1969. 23.50x (ISBN 0-672-53602-1). Irvington.
Temple Reflections. Paul F. Schmidt. LC 80-80346. (Illus.). 112p. 1980. 16.50 (ISBN 0-912998-04-0); pap. 6.50 (ISBN 0-912998-05-9). Hummingbird.
Temple Talks: On Willingness to Be Wrong. 56p. 1978. pap. 2.95 (ISBN 0-933740-02-6). Inst Self Dev.
Templeman on Marine Insurance: Its Principles & Practice. 5th ed. R. J. Lambeth. 500p. 1981. 48.00x (ISBN 0-7121-1395-9). Sheridan.
Temples of Bankura District. David McCutchion. 12.00 (ISBN 0-89253-673-X); flexible cloth 6.75 (ISBN 0-89253-674-8). Ind-US Inc.
Temples, Tombs & Hieroglyphs: A Popular History of Ancient Egypt. Barbara Mertz. LC 78-9806. (Illus.). 1978. 12.95 (ISBN 0-396-07576-2); pap. 7.95 (ISBN 0-396-07641-6). Dodd.
Templet Development for the Pipe Trades. R. Jones. LC 63-22021. (Illus.). 175p. 1963. pap. 8.00 (ISBN 0-8273-0077-8); instructor's guide 1.45 (ISBN 0-8273-0078-6). Delmar.
Tempo Daily Crosswords, No. 4. Robert Gillespie. 128p. (gr. 4 up). 1981. pap. 1.50 (ISBN 0-448-05727-1, Tempo). G&D.
Tempo (Golf's Master Key: How to Find It, How to Keep It) Al Geiberger & Larry Dennis. LC 79-52550. (Illus.). 160p. 1980. 9.95 (ISBN 0-914178-34-2). Golf Digest Bks.
Tempo: Life, Work & Leisure. Ed. by Donald W. Cummings & John Herum. (Illus.). 336p. 1974. pap. text ed. 9.95 (ISBN 0-395-17839-8, 3-12925); instructors' guide 1.50 (ISBN 0-395-17867-3, 3-12926). HM.
Tempo Word Finds, No. 4. Linda Doherty. 128p. (gr. 4 up). 1981. pap. 1.25 (ISBN 0-448-05572-4, Tempo). G&D.
Tempo Word Finds: No. 5. Linda Doherty. (No. 5). 128p. (gr. 6 up). 1981. pap. 1.50 (ISBN 0-448-05567-8, Tempo). G&D.
Tempo World Finds, No. 6. Dawn Gerger. 128p. pap. 1.50 (ISBN 0-448-05777-8, Tempo). G&D.
Tempomatic IV: A Management Simulation. 2nd ed. Charles R. Scott, Jr. & Alonzo J. Strickland, III. LC 79-89182. (Illus.). 1980. pap. text ed. 9.50 (ISBN 0-395-28731-6); instrs'. manual 0.80 (ISBN 0-395-28732-4); computer centers manual 1.75 (ISBN 0-395-28733-2); punched card deck avail. (ISBN 0-395-28734-0). HM.
Temporal Lobe Psychomotor Seizures. G. Glaser. 1981. pap. text ed. write for info. (ISBN 0-443-08000-3). Churchill.
Temporal Order in Disturbed Reading: Developmental & Neuropsychological Aspects in Normal & Reading-Retarded Children. Ed. by Dirk J. Bakker. (Modern Approaches to the Diagnosis & Instruction of Multi-Handicapped Children: Vol. 7). 100p. 1972. text ed. 21.50 (ISBN 90-237-4108-0, Pub. by Swets Pub Serv Holland). Swets North Am.
Temporal Organization in Cells. Brian C. Goodwin. 1964. 23.00 (ISBN 0-12-289350-6). Acad Pr.
Temporal Processes in Beethoven's Music. David B. Greene. 1981. price not set (ISBN 0-677-05600-1). Gordon.
Temporary & Semipermanent Splinting: An Atlas of Clinical Procedures. Andrejs Baumhammers. 128p. 1971. pap. 14.75 photovopy ed. spiral (ISBN 0-398-00117-0). C C Thomas.
Temporary Bride. Phyllis Halldorson. 192p. (Orig.). 1980. pap. 1.50 (ISBN 0-671-57031-5). S&S.
Temporary Duty. Wade Everett. 1975. pap. 0.95 o.p. (ISBN 0-345-23911-3). Ballantine.
Temporary Equilibrium & Long-Run Equilibrium. Willem H. Buiter. LC 78-75046. (Outstanding Dissertations in Economics Ser.). 1979. lib. bdg. 30.00 (ISBN 0-8240-4125-9). Garland Pub.
Temporary Work in Modern Society, part 3. International Institute for Temporary Work. 1979. lib. bdg. 25.30 (ISBN 90-312-0088-3). Kluwer Boston.
Temporomandibular Joint Problems: Biological Diagnosis & Treatment. William K. Solberg & Glenn T. Clark. 177p. 1980. 39.00 (ISBN 0-931386-18-7). Quint Pub Co.
Temps. Harlan Wade. Tr. by Claude Potvin & Rose-Ella Potvin. (Book About Ser.). Orig. Title: Time. (Illus., Fr.). (gr. k-3). 1979. PLB 7.30 (ISBN 0-8172-1452-6). Raintree Pubs.
Temptation. Lydia Lancaster. 1979. pap. 2.50 o.s.i. (ISBN 0-446-81771-6). Warner Bks.
Temptation of Saint Anthony. Gustave Flaubert. LC 78-6700. 1978. Repr. of 1904 ed. 17.00 (ISBN 0-86527-312-X). Fertig.
Tempting of Pescara. Conrad F. Meyer. Tr. by C. Bell. LC 75-4902. 184p. 1975. Repr. of 1890 ed. 11.50 (ISBN 0-86527-313-8). Fertig.
Ten Africans. Margery Perham. (Illus.). 1969. 7.95 (ISBN 0-571-05525-7, Pub. by Faber & Faber). Merrimack Bk Serv.
Ten Against Napoleon. Douglas Hilt. LC 75-9724. (Illus.). 224p. 1975. 13.95 (ISBN 0-88229-253-6). Nelson-Hall.
Ten Best Years of Baseball: An Informal History of the Fifties. Harold Rosenthal. 184p. 1981. pap. 5.95 (ISBN 0-442-27063-1). Van Nos Reinhold.
Ten Best Years of Baseball: An Informal History of the 50's. Harold Rosenthal. 1979. 8.95 o.p. (ISBN 0-8092-7362-4). Contemp Bks.
Ten Books on Architecture. Vitruvius. Tr. by Morris H. Morgan. (Illus.). pap. text ed. 4.00 (ISBN 0-486-20645-9). Dover.
Ten Celebrations of the Word: Bible Vigils Ser. pap. 0.50 o.p. (ISBN 0-8198-0314-6). Dghtrs St Paul.
Ten Centuries That Shaped the West: Greek & Roman Art in Texas Collections. Herbert Hofmann. LC 71-131999. (Illus.). 1970. 18.00 (ISBN 0-914412-18-3); pap. 12.00 (ISBN 0-914412-01-9). Inst for the Arts.
Ten Christians: By Their Deeds You Shall Know Them. Boniface Hanley. LC 79-53836. (Illus.). 272p. (Orig.). 1979. pap. 5.95 (ISBN 0-87793-183-6). Ave Maria.
Ten Colloquies. Desiderius Erasmus. Tr. by Craig R. Thompson. 1957. pap. 4.95 (ISBN 0-672-60216-4). Bobbs.
Ten Commandments. Maureen Curley. (Children of the Kingdom Activities Ser.). (gr. 4-7). 1976. 7.95 (ISBN 0-686-13687-X). Pflaum Pr.
Ten Commandments. Thomas Watson. 1976. 9.95 (ISBN 0-85151-146-5). Banner of Truth.
Ten Commandments & Human Rights. Walter Harrelson. Ed. by Walter Brueggemann & John R. Donahue. LC 77-15234. (Overtures to Biblical Theology). 240p. 1980. pap. 9.95 (ISBN 0-8006-1527-1, 1-1527). Fortress.
Ten Commandments for the Long Jaul. Daniel Berrigan. (Journeys in Faith Ser.). 128p. 1981. 7.95 (ISBN 0-687-41240-4). Abingdon.
Ten Commandments for Today. William Barclay. 1977. pap. 1.95 (ISBN 0-89129-228-4). Jove Pubns.
Ten Contemporary Thinkers. Ed. by Victor E. Amend & Leo T. Hendrick. LC 63-13536. (Orig.). 1964. pap. text ed. 6.95 o.s.i. (ISBN 0-02-900600-7). Free Pr.
Ten Days in the Light of 'Akka. rev. ed. Julia M. Grundy. LC 79-12177. 1979. pap. 5.00 (ISBN 0-87743-131-0, 7-32-40). Baha'i.
Ten Days' Wonder. Ellery Queen. Bd. with King Is Dead. 1980. pap. 2.25 (ISBN 0-451-09488-3, E9488, Sig). NAL.
Ten Deadly Men. Ivar Jorgensen. 192p. 1976. pap. 1.25 o.p. (ISBN 0-523-22817-1). Pinnacle Bks.
Ten-Dollar Wildcat. J. P. Allenbright. 1980. 14.95 (ISBN 0-87000-475-1). Arlington Hse.
Ten Easy Pieces: Creative Programming for Fun & Profit. Hans Sagan & Carl D. Meyer, Jr. 192p. 1980. pap. 7.95 (ISBN 0-8104-5160-3). Hayden.
Ten English Poets: An Anthology. Ed. by Michael Schmidt. (Poetry Ser.). 1979. pap. 5.95 o.s.i. (ISBN 0-85635-167-9, Pub. by Carcanet New Pr England). Persea Bks.
Ten Faces of the Universe. Fred Hoyle. LC 76-44336. (Illus.). 1977. text ed. 19.95x (ISBN 0-7167-0384-X); pap. text ed. 9.95x (ISBN 0-7167-0383-1). W H Freeman.
Ten Favorite French Stories. Joseph S. Galland. (Fr.). 1935. 12.50x (ISBN 0-89197-506-3); pap. text ed. 6.95x (ISBN 0-89197-962-X). Irvington.
Ten-Forty Handbook. Prentice-Hall Tax Editorial Staff. 1979. 18.50 (ISBN 0-13-903393-9). P-H.
Ten Golden Shape Books, 10 bks. (ps). Date not set. pap. 5.95 boxed set (ISBN 0-307-13637-X, Golden Pr). Western Pub.
Ten Great Cosmic Powers. S. Shankaranarayanan. 1979. 6.25 o.p. (ISBN 0-89744-956-8). Auromere.
Ten Ideas That Make a Difference. Ernest Holmes. 1966. pap. 3.50 (ISBN 0-911336-32-X). Sci of Mind.
Ten-Key Adding Machine: Student Guide. Marvin W. Hempel. 1970. pap. text ed. 5.55 (ISBN 0-89420-056-9, 126600); cassette recordings 142.40 (ISBN 0-89420-187-5, 156700). Natl Book.
Ten Lessons of the Energy Crisis. Morris Goran. LC 80-130511. 1980. 19.80 (ISBN 0-915250-35-7). Environ Design.
Ten Little Animals. Carl Memling. (Illus.). (ps-1). 1961. PLB 5.00 (ISBN 0-307-60541-8, Golden Pr). Western Pub.
Ten Little Elephants. Robert Leydenfrost. LC 74-19313. 48p. 1975. 5.95 o.p. (ISBN 0-385-08360-2). Doubleday.
Ten Little Fingers. Monica Stuart & Gill Soper. 1975. 8.95 (ISBN 0-571-10828-8, Pub. by Faber & Faber). Merrimack Bk Serv.
Ten Little Fingers & Ten Little Toes. Illus. by Vivienne DeMuth. (Illus.). (ps-k). 1979. 1.95 (ISBN 0-525-69010-7, Gingerbread Bks); PLB 5.95 o.p. (ISBN 0-525-69011-5). Dutton.
Ten Madrigals for Mixed Voices. Luca Marenzio. Ed. by Denis Arnold. 1966. 6.50x (ISBN 0-19-343675-2). Oxford U Pr.
Ten Men & History. Don Cook. LC 80-1062. 528p. 1981. 14.95 (ISBN 0-385-14908-5). Doubleday.
Ten Million Acres of Timber: The Remarkable Story of Forest Protection in the Maine Forestry District 1909-1972. Austin H. Wilkins. (Illus.). xxiv, 312p. 1978. 10.00 (ISBN 0-931474-02-7); pap. 8.95 (ISBN 0-931474-03-5). TBW Bks.
Ten Million Dollar Getaway: The Inside Story of the Lufthansa Heist. Doug Feiden. (Orig.). pap. 2.50 (ISBN 0-515-05452-6). Jove Pubns.
Ten Million Photoplay Plots. W. Aber Hill. Ed. by Bruce S. Kupelnick. LC 76-52108. (Classics of Film Literature Ser.). 1978. lib. bdg. 15.00 (ISBN 0-8240-2879-1). Garland Pub.
Ten Minutes with Me. 3rd ed. Joanne Cohn-Gilletly. (Illus., Orig.). (gr. k-3). 1980. pap. 2.00 (ISBN 0-916634-05-1). Double M Pr.
Ten Notable Women of Latin America. James D. Henderson & Linda R. Henderson. LC 78-15253. (Illus.). 1978. 17.95 (ISBN 0-88229-426-1); pap. 8.95 (ISBN 0-88229-596-9). Nelson-Hall.
Ten Principal Upanishads. Swami S. Patanjali. Tr. by W. B. Yeats. (Orig.). 1970. pap. 4.95 (ISBN 0-571-09363-9, Pub. by Faber & Faber). Merrimack Bk Serv.
Ten Questions to the Zionists or, Zionist Complicity in Nazi War Atrocities. Michael B. Weismandel. 1980. lib. bdg. 59.95 (ISBN 0-686-68886-4). Revisionist Pr.
Ten Red Rods. T. J. Thompson. LC 80-83135. (Illus.). 16p. (Orig.). (ps-1). 1980. pap. text ed. 1.50 (ISBN 0-915676-02-8). Montessori Wkshps.
Ten Religions of the East. Edward Rice. LC 78-6186. (Illus.). 160p. (gr. 7 up). 1978. 8.95 (ISBN 0-590-07473-3, Four Winds). Schol Bk Serv.
Ten Rules for Living. Clovis G. Chappell. (Clovis G. Chappell Library). 1976. pap. 2.95 o.p. (ISBN 0-8010-2385-8). Baker Bk.
Ten Sixty-Six. John Langdon-Davies. (Jackdaw Ser: No. 38). (Illus.). 1969. 5.95 o.p. (ISBN 0-670-69600-5, Grossman). Viking Pr.
Ten Sixty Six: The Year of the Conquest. David Howarth. 1978. 10.95 (ISBN 0-670-69601-3). Viking Pr.
Ten Sixty Six, Year of Destiny. Terence Wise. 1980. text ed. 19.50x (ISBN 0-85045-320-8). Humanities.
Ten Speed Bicycle. Michael J. Kolin & Denise M. De la Rosa. (Illus.). 1979. 12.95 (ISBN 0-87857-268-6); pap. 9.95 (ISBN 0-87857-281-3). Rodale Pr Inc.
Ten-Speed Taylor. Leila B. Gemme. Ed. by Kathy Pacini. LC 78-1263. (Springboard Bks.). (Illus.). (gr. 3-6). 1978. 5.75g (ISBN 0-8075-7771-5). A Whitman.
Ten Statement Fortran Plus Fortran Four. 2nd ed. Michael Kennedy & Martin B. Solomon. (Illus.). 400p. 1975. pap. text ed. 14.95 (ISBN 0-13-903385-8). P-H.
Ten Steps for Church Growth. Donald A. McGavran & Winfield C. Arn. LC 76-62950. 1977. pap. 4.95 (ISBN 0-06-065352-3, RD 215, HarpR). Har-Row.
Ten Steps to the Good Life. Harold J. Brokke. LC 75-44926. 1976. pap. 1.50 (ISBN 0-87123-332-0, 200332). Bethany Fell.
Ten Talents Cookbook: Vegetarian Natural Foods. Frank J. Hurd & Rosalie Hurd. 1968. 9.95 (ISBN 0-9603532-0-8). Ten Talents.
Ten Thousand Answers to Questions. Frederic J. Haskin. LC 79-99074. 1970. Repr. of 1937 ed. 21.00 (ISBN 0-8103-3861-0). Gale.
Ten Thousand Famous Freemasons, 4 vols. William R. Denslow. 1979. Repr. Set. pap. 29.95 slip cover (ISBN 0-686-68268-8). Macoy Pub.
Ten Thousand Garden Questions Answered by Twenty Experts. Ed. by Marjorie J. Dietz. LC 73-17596. (Illus.). 1400p. 1974. 12.95 (ISBN 0-385-08743-8). Doubleday.
Ten Thousand Jokes, Toasts & Stories. Ed. by Lewis Copeland. LC 66-737. 1965. 10.95 (ISBN 0-385-00163-0). Doubleday.
Ten Thousand Leaves: A Translation of Man'yoshu, Japan's Premier Anthology of Classical Poetry, Vol. 1. Tr. by Ian H. Levy from Japanese. LC 80-8561. (Princeton Library of Asian Translations). (Illus.). 280p. 1981. 20.00x (ISBN 0-691-06452-0). Princeton U Pr.
Ten Thousand Miles for a Miracle. Kathryn Kuhlman. LC 74-4851. (Kathryn Kuhlman Ser). 96p. 1974. pap. 0.95 (ISBN 0-87123-536-6, 200536). Bethany Fell.
Ten Thousand-Point Television Trivia Test. Patrick Finnegan & Rose Matthews. 1979. 5.75 o.p. (ISBN 0-8062-1219-5). Carlton.
Ten Thousand Wonderful Things. Ed. by Edmund F. King. LC 75-124587. 1970. Repr. of 1860 ed. 25.00 (ISBN 0-8103-3009-1). Gale.
Ten Top Favorites. Ed. by Robert Vitarelli. (Pal Paperbacks Kit B Ser.). (Illus., Orig.). (gr. 7-12). 1972. pap. text ed. 1.25 (ISBN 0-8374-3511-0). Xerox Ed Pubns.
Ten Trail Trips in Yosemite National Park. William R. Jores. (Illus.). 1980. pap. 3.95 (ISBN 0-89646-064-9). Outbooks.
Ten Trailer Trips in Southwest. Richard L. Hayes. 1.50 o.s.i. (ISBN 0-87593-013-1). Trail-R.
Ten Trailer Trips in the Rockies. Richard L. Hayes. 1.50 o.s.i. (ISBN 0-87593-011-5). Trail-R.
Ten Twentieth Century Indian Poets. Ed. by R. Parthasarathy. (Three Crowns New Poetry from India Ser.). 1977. pap. 3.95x (ISBN 0-19-560665-5). Oxford U Pr.
Ten Types of Table Wine. Philip Delmon. 1973. pap. 2.50 (ISBN 0-263-51788-8). Transatlantic.
Ten Ways of Looking at a Bird. Higgins. pap. write for info. (ISBN 0-914162-55-1). Knowles.
Ten Women & God. Beverly Lauderdale & Margaret Shelgren. LC 78-75316. (Illus.). Date not set. cancelled (ISBN 0-498-02329-X). A S Barnes.
Ten Word Books, 10 bks. Bob Reese et al. Ed. by Dan Wasserman. (Illus.). (gr. k-6). Set. PLB 45.00 (ISBN 0-89868-066-2); Set. pap. 19.50 (ISBN 0-89868-077-8). ARO Pub.
Ten Words That Will Change Your Life. Ervin Seale. 188p. 1972. pap. 5.95 (ISBN 0-911336-38-9). Sci of Mind.
Ten Year Index to Periodical Articles Related to Law (1958-1968) Ed. by Roy M. Mersky & J. Myron Jacobstein. LC 65-29677. 1970. 35.00 (ISBN 0-87802-050-0). Glanville.
Ten Year Index to Vols. 61-70 of Geological Society of America Bulletin. Geological Society Of America. LC 1-23380. (Orig.). 1962. pap. 10.50x o.p. (ISBN 0-8137-9061-1). Geol Soc.
Ten Years After. Gerard Malanga. 160p. 1977. signed o.p. 15.00 (ISBN 0-87685-287-8); pap. 4.00 (ISBN 0-87685-236-X). Black Sparrow.
Ten Years After Ivan Denisovich. Zhores A. Medvedev. LC 74-3433. 1974. pap. 1.95 o.p. (ISBN 0-394-71112-2, Vin). Random.
Ten Years' Captivity in the Mahdi's Camp, 1882-1892. 13th, rev. & abr. ed. Joseph Ohrwalder. LC 80-2199. (Illus.). 1981. Repr. of 1893 ed. 54.00 (ISBN 0-404-18981-4). AMS Pr.
Ten Years of Films on Ballet & Classical Dance, 1955-1965,Catalogue. UNESCO. 1968. pap. 4.25 (ISBN 92-3-100656-8, U674, UNESCO). Unipub.
Ten Years of Training: Developments in France, Federal Republic of Germany & United Kingdom, 1968-1978. International Labour Office, Geneva. 263p. (Orig.). 1980. pap. 10.00 (ISBN 92-2-102254-4). Intl Labour Office.
Ten Years of Upper Canada in Peace & War, 1805-1815, Being the Ridout Letters with Annotations by Matilda Edgar: Also an Appendix of the Narrative of the Captivity Among the Shawanese Indians in 1788 of Thos. Ridout. Matilda R. Edgar. LC 75-7125. (Indian Captivities Ser.: Vol. 98). 1977. Repr. of 1890 ed. lib. bdg. 44.00 (ISBN 0-8240-1722-6). Garland Pub.
Ten Years to Doomsday. Michael Kurland. 1977. pap. 1.50 o.s.i. (ISBN 0-515-04458-X). Jove Pubns.
Tenant for Death. Cyril Hare. 200p. 1981. pap. price not set (ISBN 0-486-24103-3). Dover.
Tenant Management: Findings from a Three-Year Experiment in Public Housing. Manpower Demonstration Research Group. 240p. 1981. write for info. (ISBN 0-88410-694-2). Ballinger Pub.

Tenants. Bernard Malamud. 160p. 1981. pap. 2.25 (ISBN 0-380-53538-6, 53538). Avon.

Tenants of Moonbloom. Edward L. Wallant. LC 63-13501. 245p. 1973. pap. 3.50 (ISBN 0-15-688535-2, HPL59, HPL). HarBraceJ.

Tench Coxe: A Study in American Economic Development. Harold Hutcheson. LC 77-98690. (American Scene Ser.). 1969. Repr. of 1938 ed. lib. bdg. 25.00 (ISBN 0-306-71511-2). Da Capo.

Tendencies in American Economic Thought. S. Sherwood. Repr. of 1897 ed. pap. 7.00 (ISBN 0-384-55110-6). Johnson Repr.

Tendencies of Character Detection in the Domestic Novels of Burney, Edgeworth & Austen: A Consideration of Subjective & Objective World, Vols. 1-3. Patricia Voss-Clesly. (Salzburg Romantic Reassessment Ser.: No. 95). (Orig.). 1979. pap. text ed. 25.00x ea.; Vol. 1. pap. text ed. (ISBN 0-391-01619-9); Vol. 2. pap. text ed. (ISBN 0-391-01622-9); Vol. 3. pap. text ed. (ISBN 0-391-01625-3). Humanities.

Tender Fugitive. Jennifer Roberts. (Orig.). 1980. pap. 2.50 (ISBN 0-505-51504-0). Tower Bks.

Tender Husband. Richard Steele. Ed. by Calhoun Winton. LC 66-25598. (Regents Restoration Drama Ser). 1967. 6.95x (ISBN 0-8032-0370-5); pap. 1.65x (ISBN 0-8032-5370-2, BB 261, Bison). U of Nebr Pr.

Tender Is the Night. F. Scott Fitzgerald. 1960. lib. rep. ed. 17.50x (ISBN 0-684-15151-0, ScribT); pap. 3.95 (ISBN 0-684-71763-8, SL2, ScribT). Scribner.

Tender Offer. Alexandra Marshall. LC 80-23233. 256p. 1981. 10.95 (ISBN 0-394-50757-6). Knopf.

Tender Shoot & Other Stories. Colette. Tr. by Antonia White from Fr. 404p. 1975. 10.00 (ISBN 0-374-27310-3); pap. 6.95 (ISBN 0-374-51258-2). FS&G.

Tender Torment. Alicia Meadowes. (Orig.). 1980. pap. 2.25 (ISBN 0-446-92179-3). Warner Bks.

Tenderfeet & Ladyfingers: A Visceral Approach to Words & Their Origins. Susan K. Sperling. LC 80-51778. (Illus.). 160p. 1981. 9.95 (ISBN 0-670-69633-1). Viking Pr.

Tenderfoot. Max Brand. Orig. Title: Outlaw's Gold. 1976. pap. 1.95 (ISBN 0-446-90653-0). Warner Bks.

Tending the Talking Wire: A Buck Soldier's View of Indian Country, 1863-1866. Ed. by William E. Unrau. LC 73-30154. (University of Utah Publications in the American West: Vol. 12). (Illus.). 1979. 20.00 (ISBN 0-87480-131-1). U of Utah Pr.

Tenement Landlord. George Sternlieb. 1969. 15.00 (ISBN 0-8135-0604-2); pap. 3.25x (ISBN 0-8135-0605-0). Rutgers U Pr.

Teneriffe Lace. Alexandra Stillwell. (Illus.). 144p. 1980. 16.95 (ISBN 0-8231-5056-9). Branford.

Tennessee. 28.00 (ISBN 0-89770-118-6). Curriculum Info Ctr.

Tennessee: A Guide to the State. Federal Writers' Project. 558p. 1939. Repr. 49.00 (ISBN 0-403-02191-X). Somerset Pub.

Tennessee: A Short History. 2nd ed. Robert E. Corlew. LC 80-13553. (Illus.). 568p. 1981. 22.50 (ISBN 0-87049-258-6); pap. text ed. 14.50x (ISBN 0-87049-302-7). U of Tenn Pr.

Tennessee, a Short History. Stanley J. Folmsbee et al. LC 69-20114. (Illus.). 1969. o.p. 15.00 o.p. (ISBN 0-87049-095-8); pap. text ed. 10.00x o.p. (ISBN 0-87049-103-2). U of Tenn Pr.

Tennessee Blue. Patricia B. Griffiths. Ed. by Carol Southern. 192p. 1981. 10.95 (ISBN 0-517-54187-4). Potter.

Tennessee Chronology & Factbook, Vol. 42. R. I. Vexler. 1978. 8.50 (ISBN 0-379-16167-2). Oceana.

Tennessee Code Annotated, 30 vols. write for info (ISBN 0-672-83239-9, Bobbs-Merrill Law); write for info. 1979 suppl (ISBN 0-672-83785-4). Michie.

Tennessee History: A Bibliography. Ed. by Sam B. Smith. LC 74-8504. 512p. 1974. 21.50x (ISBN 0-87049-158-X). U of Tenn Pr.

Tennessee Law of Evidence. Donald F. Paine. 1974. with 1976 suppl. 30.00 (ISBN 0-672-82543-0, Bobb-Merrill Law); 1976 suppl. 9.50 (ISBN 0-672-82452-3). Michie.

Tennessee Life & Health. 1980. 18.00 (ISBN 0-930868-38-2). Merritt Co.

Tennessee Property & Casualty. 1980. 18.00 (ISBN 0-930868-37-4). Merritt Co.

Tennessee Smash. Don Pendleton. (Executioner Ser.: No. 32). 1978. pap. 1.95 (ISBN 0-523-41096-4). Pinnacle Bks.

Tennessee State Industrial Directory, Nineteen Eighty-One. State Industrial Directories Corp. Date not set. pap. price not set (ISBN 0-89910-049-X). State Indus D.

Tennessee Strings: The Story of Country Music in Tennessee. Charles K Wolfe. LC 77-8052. (Tennessee Three Star Bks. Ser.). (Illus.). 1977. lib. bdg. 8.50x (ISBN 0-87049-295-0); pap. 3.50. U of Tenn Pr.

Tennessee Studies in Literature. Incl. Vol. 1. 1956. o.p. (ISBN 0-87049-015-X); Vol. 2. 1957. pap. o.p. (ISBN 0-87049-017-6); Vol. 3. 1958. pap. o.p. (ISBN 0-87049-018-4); Vol. 4. 1959. pap. (ISBN 0-87049-025-7); Vol. 5. 1960. pap. (ISBN 0-87049-027-3); Vol. 6. 1961. pap. (ISBN 0-87049-033-8); Vol. 7. 1962. pap. (ISBN 0-87049-036-2); Vol. 8. 1963. pap. (ISBN 0-87049-043-5); Vol. 9. 1964. pap. o.p. (ISBN 0-87049-048-6); Vol. 10. 1965. pap. o.p. (ISBN 0-87049-055-9); Vol. 11. 1966. pap. (ISBN 0-87049-062-1); Vol. 12. 1967. pap. (ISBN 0-87049-076-1); Vol. 13. 1968. pap. (ISBN 0-87049-084-2); Vol. 14. 1969. pap. (ISBN 0-87049-104-0); Vol. 15. 1970. (ISBN 0-87049-117-2); pap. (ISBN 0-87049-240-3); Vol. 16. 1971. (ISBN 0-87049-132-6); pap. (ISBN 0-87049-241-1); Vol. 17. 1972. (ISBN 0-87049-142-3); pap. o.p. (ISBN 0-87049-242-X); Vol. 18. 1973. (ISBN 0-87049-148-2); pap. (ISBN 0-87049-243-8); Vol. 19. 1974. (ISBN 0-87049-154-7); pap. (ISBN 0-87049-244-6); Vol. 20. 1975. (ISBN 0-87049-172-5); pap. o.p. (ISBN 0-87049-245-4); Vol. 21. 1976. o.p. (ISBN 0-87049-195-4); pap. (ISBN 0-87049-246-2); Vol. 22. 1977. (ISBN 0-87049-212-8); pap. (ISBN 0-87049-236-5); Vol. 23. 1978. (ISBN 0-87049-249-7); pap. (ISBN 0-87049-250-0); Index. pap. 1.00x (ISBN 0-87049-075-3). LC 58-63252. 9.50x ea.; pap. 5.00x ea. U of Tenn Pr.

Tennessee Supplement for Modern Real Estate Practice. William M. Emerson. 130p. (Orig.). 1981. pap. 7.95 (ISBN 0-88462-338-6). Real Estate Ed Co.

Tennessee: The Old River, Frontier to Secession. Donald Davidson. (Rivers of American Ser). (Illus.). 1946. 4.00 o.p. (ISBN 0-03-028870-3). HR&W.

Tennessee Trails. Evan Means & Tennessee Trails Association. LC 79-11566. (Illus.). 192p. (Orig.). 1979. pap. 6.95 (ISBN 0-914788-11-6). East Woods.

Tennessee: Vol. 1: the Old River-Frontier to Secession. Donald Davidson. LC 78-15103. 1979. 12.50 (ISBN 0-87049-265-9). U of Tenn Pr.

Tennessee Williams. 2nd ed. Signi L. Falk. (United States Authors Ser.). 1978. lib. bdg. 10.95 (ISBN 0-8057-7202-2). Twayne.

Tennessee Williams' Letters to Donald Windham. Tennessee Williams. 1976. 110.00x (ISBN 0-917366-01-8). S Campbell.

Tennis. Pancho Gonzales. Ed. by Gladys Heldman. LC 62-8027. (Illus.). 1965. 6.95 (ISBN 0-8303-0011-2). Fleet.

Tennis. Pancho Gonzales. 128p. 1965. pap. 2.95 (ISBN 0-346-12328-3). Cornerstone.

Tennis. 4th ed. Joan D. Johnson & Paul Xanthos. (Pysical Education Activities Ser.). 1981. pap. text ed. 3.25x (ISBN 0-697-07174-X). Wm C Brown.

Tennis. William McCormick. LC 73-3407. (First Bks.). (gr. 3-7). 1973. PLB 4.90 o.p. (ISBN 0-531-00803-7). Watts.

Tennis. R. Elaine Mason. (Illus.). 160p. 1975. pap. text ed. 6.50x (ISBN 0-205-03844-1, 6238440). Allyn.

Tennis. Wayne Pearce & Janice Pearce. (Sport Ser). (Illus.). 1971. pap. 4.25 ref. ed. (ISBN 0-13-903435-8). P-H.

Tennis. Betty Stove & Susan Adams. (Burns Sports Ser.). 156p. Date not set. pap. cancelled (ISBN 0-695-81571-7). Follett.

Tennis Court Book: A Player's Guide to Home Tennis Courts. James L. Bright. LC 79-51373. (Illus.). 1979. 12.50x o.p. (ISBN 0-933122-02-0); pap. 7.50 o.p. (ISBN 0-933122-01-2); customized ed. 7.50x o.p. (ISBN 0-933122-03-9). Brick Hse Pub.

Tennis Courts. USTA Facilities Committee. 1980. pap. text ed. 5.00 (ISBN 0-938822-09-8). USTA.

Tennis Drills: On & off Court Drills & Exercises to Improve Your Game. Robert F. Greene. (Illus.). 1977. pap. 8.95 (ISBN 0-8015-7527-3, Hawthorn). Dutton.

Tennis: Easy on-Easy off. Eleanor Owens et al. 70p. 1975. 3.95 (ISBN 0-938822-10-1). USTA.

Tennis Experience. Eugene L. Scott. LC 79-7519. (Illus.). 1979. 19.95 o.p. (ISBN 0-88332-119-X). Larousse.

Tennis for Life. Peter Burwash & John Tullius. 1981. 14.95 (ISBN 0-8129-0952-6). Times Bks.

Tennis Guide to the USA: Where to Play in the Most Traveled Cities. Dick Zeldin. 1980. pap. 7.95 (ISBN 0-531-09922-9, C25). Watts.

Tennis: How to Become a Champion. C. M. Jones. (gr. 9 up). 1968. 12.00 (ISBN 0-571-04714-9); pap. 6.50 (ISBN 0-571-09415-5). Transatlantic.

Tennis: How to Become a Champion. C. M. Jones. (Illus., Orig.). 1970. pap. 4.95 (ISBN 0-571-09415-5, Pub. by Faber & Faber). Merrimack Bk Serv.

Tennis: How to Play, How to Win. Instruction Advisory Board & Tennis Magazine Editors. LC 77-92906. (Second Instructional Portfolio Ser.). (Illus.). 222p. 1978. 11.95 (ISBN 0-914178-19-9, 24172, Pub. by Tennis Mag). Golf Digest.

Tennis: How to Play, How to Win. Tennis Magazine Eds. & Instruction Advisory Board. LC 77-92906. (Tennis Magazine Bks.). (Illus.). 222p. 1978. 11.95 (ISBN 0-914178-19-9). Golf Digest Bks.

Tennis in Pictures. Tom Okker. 160p. 1976. pap. 2.95 o.s.i. (ISBN 0-346-12308-9). Cornerstone.

Tennis Menace. Alex B. Allen. LC 72-83680. (Springboard Ser). (Illus.). 64p. (gr. 3-7). 1975. 5.75g (ISBN 0-8075-7773-1). A Whitman.

Tennis Notes, Vol. 3 Of 4 Vols. James Wagenvoord. (Illus.). 160p. 1981. 6.95 (ISBN 0-312-79104-6). St Martin.

Tennis Origins & Mysteries. Malcolm D. Whitman. LC 68-58970. 1968. Repr. of 1932 ed. 18.00 (ISBN 0-8103-3542-5). Gale.

Tennis Player's Handbook. Tennis Magazine Editors. LC 79-65033. (Tennis Magazine Bks). (Illus.). 318p. 1980. pap. 8.95 (ISBN 0-914178-32-6). Golf Digest Bks.

Tennis Player's Handbook. LC 79-65033. (Illus.). 318p. (Orig.). 1980. pap. 8.95 (ISBN 0-914178-32-6, 25165-1, Pub. by Tennis Mag). Golf Digest.

Tennis Psychology. Harold Geist & Cecelia Martinez. LC 75-17651. (Illus.). 136p. 1976. 10.95 (ISBN 0-88229-120-3). Nelson-Hall.

Tennis Rebel. Owenita Sanderlin. (Triumph Bks.). (Illus.). (gr. 5 up). 1978. PLB 5.90 s&l o.p. (ISBN 0-531-01466-5). Watts.

Tennis Rebel. Owenita Sanderlin. (gr. 7-12). 1980. pap. 1.25 (ISBN 0-440-98752-0, LFL). Dell.

Tennis Rules Illustrated. George Sullivan. 96p. (Orig.). 1981. pap. 3.95 (ISBN 0-346-12525-1). Cornerstone.

Tennis Strokes & Strategies. Tennis Magazine Editors. LC 75-14065. (Illus.). 217p. 1975. 10.95 (ISBN 0-671-22073-X). Tennis Mag.

Tennis: Styles & Stylists. P. Metzler. 1970. 7.95 o.s.i. (ISBN 0-02-584480-6). Macmillan.

Tennis Umpire's Clinic Kit. Jack Stahr. 1975. 3.00 (ISBN 0-938822-11-X). USTA.

Tennis: Up to Tournament Standard. Rico Ellwanger. (Sports Library). (Illus.). 1979. 12.95 (ISBN 0-8069-9152-6); pap. 6.95 (ISBN 0-8069-9154-2). Sterling.

Tennis Without Lessons. Jim Brown. (Illus.). 1977. 12.95 (ISBN 0-13-903252-5); pap. 6.95 (ISBN 0-13-903245-2). P-H.

Tenno Seiji: Direct Imperial Rule. Shinichi Fujii. (Studies in Japanese History & Civilization). 415p. 1979. Repr. of 1944 ed. 30.00 (ISBN 0-89093-263-8). U Pubns Amer.

Tennyson. Paul Turner. (Routledge Author Guides Ser.). 1980. pap. 6.95 (ISBN 0-7100-0475-3). Routledge & Kegan.

Tennyson Album: A Biography in Original Photographs. Andrew Wheatcroft. (Illus.). 200p. 1980. 25.00 (ISBN 0-7100-0494-X). Routledge & Kegan.

Tennyson & Matthew Arnold. Oliver Elton. 96p. 1980. Repr. of 1924 ed. lib. bdg. 12.50 (ISBN 0-8492-4411-0). R West.

Tennyson & Swinburne As Romantic Naturalists. Kerry McSweeney. 240p. 1981. 25.00x (ISBN 0-8020-2381-9). U of Toronto Pr.

Tennyson Concordance. A. Ernest Baker. 1965. 75.00x (ISBN 0-7100-6557-4). Routledge & Kegan.

Tennyson: Interviews & Recollections. Ed. by Norman Page. 1981. 26.50x (ISBN 0-389-20066-2). B&N.

Tennyson Laureate. Valerie Pitt. LC 63-6002. 1962. 15.00x o.p. (ISBN 0-8020-1228-0); pap. 4.50 o.p. (ISBN 0-8020-6098-6). U of Toronto Pr.

Tennyson: Poet & Prophet. Philip Henderson. (Illus.). 1978. 20.00x (ISBN 0-7100-8776-4). Routledge & Kegan.

Tennyson, Poet, Philosopher, Idealist. J. Cummings Walters. 370p. 1980. Repr. of 1893 ed. lib. bdg. 40.00 (ISBN 0-89984-505-3). Century Bookbindery.

Tennyson: The Critical Heritage. John D. Jump. 1967. 30.00x (ISBN 0-7100-2941-1). Routledge & Kegan.

Tennyson's Maud: The Biographical Genesis. Ralph W. Rader. (Library Reprint Ser.: Vol. 90). 1978. 15.75x (ISBN 0-520-03617-4). U of Cal Pr.

Tense Drills. L. W. Giggins & D. J. Shoebridge. 1975. pap. text ed. 5.00x (ISBN 0-582-52173-4). Longman.

Tense Marking in Black English: A Linguistic and Social Analysis. Ralph Fasold. (Urban Language Ser.). 1972. pap. text ed. 8.00 (ISBN 0-87281-031-3). Ctr Appl Ling.

Tensile Architecture: From the Tent to the Bubble Dome. Philip Drew. (Illus.). 1979. 45.00 (ISBN 0-89158-550-8). Westview.

Tension of the Lyre: Poetry in Shakespeare's Sonnets. Hallett Smith. (Illus.). 180p. 1981. price not set (ISBN 0-87328-114-4). Huntington Lib.

Tensions: A Practical Method for Their Release. Leslie O. Korth. 1980. 4.00x (ISBN 0-8464-1053-2). Beekman Pubs.

Tensions Can Be Reduced to Nuisances. Edmund Bergler. 12.95 (ISBN 0-87140-976-3); pap. 3.95 (ISBN 0-87140-976-3). Liveright.

Tensions in Contemporary Theology. Ed. by Stanley N. Gundry & Alan F. Johnson. 384p. 1979. 12.95 (ISBN 0-8024-8585-5). Moody.

Tensor Analysis: Fundamentals & Applications. Wasley S. Krogdahl. LC 78-62755. 1978. pap. text ed. 18.50 (ISBN 0-8191-0594-5). U Pr of Amer.

Tensor Analysis on Manifolds. Richard Bishop & Samuel Goldberg. (Illus.). 1980. pap. 6.00 (ISBN 0-486-64039-6). Dover.

Tensor Calculus. Synge & Schild. 1978. pap. text ed. 5.00 (ISBN 0-486-63612-7). Dover.

Tensors, Differential Forms, & Variational Principles. David Lovelock & Hanno Rund. LC 75-2261. (Pure & Applied Mathematics Ser). 364p. 1975. 35.00 (ISBN 0-471-54840-5, Pub. by Wiley-Interscience). Wiley.

Tent for the Sun. Mary Ray. 1971. 6.95 (ISBN 0-571-09770-7, Pub. by Faber & Faber). Merrimack Bk Serv.

Tenth Air Force Story. Kenn C. Rust. (Illus.). 1980. pap. 7.50 (Pub. by Hist. Avn. Album). Aviation.

Tenth Air Force Story. Kenn C. Rust. (World War II Forces History). (Illus.). 64p. 1980. pap. 7.50 (ISBN 0-911852-87-5). Hist Aviation.

Tenth Assembling. Ed. by Richard Kostelanetz et al. LC 80-68188. (Assembling Ser.). (Illus.). 200p. 1981. pap. 4.95 (ISBN 0-686-69410-4). Assembling Pr.

Tenth-Century Studies: Essays in Commemoration of the Millennium of the Council of Winchester & Regulars Concordia. Ed. by David Parsons. (Illus.). 270p. 1975. 35.00x (ISBN 0-87471-781-7). Rowman.

Tenth Commandment. Lawrence Sanders. 1980. 12.95 (ISBN 0-686-64422-0). Putnam.

Tenth Good Thing About Barney. Judith Viorst. (Illus.). (gr. k-4). 1975. pap. 2.95 (ISBN 0-689-70416-X, Aladdin). Atheneum.

Tenth Life. Richard Lockridge. LC 77-6673. 1977. 8.95 o.p. (ISBN 0-397-01237-3). Lippincott.

Tenth Man. Wei Wu-Wei. 246p. 1981. pap. 6.00 (ISBN 0-85656-013-8). Great Eastern.

Tenth Measure. Brenda L. Segal. 1981. pap. 3.25 (ISBN 0-425-05095-5). Berkley Pub.

Tenth Muse: Classical Drama in Translation. Ed. by Charles Doria. LC 77-88695. vi, 587p. 1980. 19.95 (ISBN 0-8040-0781-0). Swallow.

Tenth Muse: Women Poets Before Eighteen Hundred. Jean Buyze. 1980. pap. 3.95 (ISBN 0-915288-39-7). Shameless Hussy.

Tents: Architecture of the Nomads. Torvald Faegre. LC 77-25588. 1979. pap. 5.95 (ISBN 0-385-11656-X, Anch). Doubleday.

Tents of Shem. Simha Pearlmutter. LC 79-56104. 1980. 8.95 (ISBN 0-533-04505-3). Vantage.

Tenure Debate. Bardwell L. Smith et al. LC 72-6058. (Higher Education Ser.). 1973. 13.95x o.p. (ISBN 0-87589-148-9). Jossey-Bass.

Tenure: Research Evidence & Practical & Philosophical Considerations. Annette Geier. 47p. 1977. pap. 10.00 o.p. (ISBN 0-686-00914-2, D-106). Essence Pubns.

Teologia Biblica y Sistematica. Tr. by Myer Pearlman. (Spanish Bks.). 1978. 4.25 (ISBN 0-8297-0603-8); pap. 3.25 (ISBN 0-8297-0602-X). Life Pubs Intl.

Teologia Del Nuevo Testamento. Frank Stagg. Tr. by Arnoldo Canclini. 1976. pap. 7.95 (ISBN 0-311-09077-X). Casa Bautista.

Teonanacatl: Hallucinogenic Mushrooms of North America. Ed. by Jonathan Ott & Jeremy Bigwood. LC 78-14794. 1978. 14.50 (ISBN 0-914842-32-3); pap. 8.95 (ISBN 0-914842-29-3). Madrona Pubs.

Tepehuan of Chihuahua: Their Material Culture. Campbell W. Pennington. LC 73-99792. (Illus.). 1969. 10.00x (ISBN 0-87480-013-7); pap. 7.50x (ISBN 0-87480-147-8). U of Utah Pr.

Tera Beyond. Malcolm MacCloud. LC 80-36728. 192p. (gr. 5-9). 1981. PLB 9.95 (ISBN 0-689-30817-5, Argo). Atheneum.

Tercera Parte de la Tragicomedia de Celestina. Gaspar Gomez De Toledo. Ed. by Mac E. Barrick. LC 70-137886. (Haney Foundation Ser.). (Illus.). 570p. 1973. 15.00x (ISBN 0-8122-7602-7). U of Pa Pr.

Terence, the Adelphoe. Ed. by R. H. Martin. LC 75-36173. (Cambridge Greek & Latin Classics Ser.). 250p. 1976. 42.50 (ISBN 0-521-20936-6); pap. 12.95x (ISBN 0-521-29001-5). Cambridge U Pr.

Teresa Carreno "by the Grace of God". Marta Milinowski. LC 76-58931. (Music Reprint Ser.). 1977. Repr. of 1940 ed. lib. bdg. 25.00 (ISBN 0-306-70870-1). Da Capo.

Teresita. William C. Holden. LC 78-2321. (Illus.). 1978. 14.95 (ISBN 0-916144-24-0); pap. 8.95 (ISBN 0-916144-25-9). Stemmer Hse.

Terezin Requiem. Josef Bor. 1978. pap. 1.95 (ISBN 0-380-01673-7, 33449, Bard). Avon.

Term Paper. Ann Rinaldi. LC 80-7686. 202p. (gr. 5 up). 1980. 8.95 (ISBN 0-8027-6395-2). Walker & Co.

Term Paper Step by Step. Mulkerne, Donald, J.D. & Gilbert Kahn. LC 76-40631. 5.95 (ISBN 0-385-12775-8, Anchor Pr); pap. 2.95 (ISBN 0-385-12380-9, Anch). Doubleday.

Terminal Airport Financing & Management. L. L. Bollinger et al. 1970. Repr. of 1946 ed. 31.00 (ISBN 0-08-018746-3). Pergamon.

Terminal Care: Symposium. Derek Doyle. (Illus.). 1979. pap. text ed. 12.50 o.p. (ISBN 0-443-01920-7). Churchill.

Terminal Generation. Hal Lindsey & C. C. Carlson. 1976. pap. 1.95 o.p. (ISBN 0-8007-8305-0, Spire Bks). Revell.

Terminal Patient: Oral Care. Ed. by Bernard Schoenberg et al. LC 72-9892. 1973. 20.00x (ISBN 0-88238-701-4). Columbia U Pr.

Termination: The Closing at Baker Plant. Alfred Slote. LC 69-13100. 360p. 1977. 11.50 (ISBN 0-87944-219-0). U of Mich Soc Res.

Terminators. Donald Hamilton. (Matt Helm Ser.). 224p. 1978. pap. 1.95 (ISBN 0-449-14035-0, GM). Fawcett.

Terminological Data Banks. (Infoterm Ser.). 1980. 45.00 (Dist. by Gale Research Co.). K G Saur.

Terminology & Concepts in Mental Retardation. Joel R. Davitz et al. LC 62-61261. (Orig.). 1964. pap. text ed. 5.00x (ISBN 0-8077-1233-7). Tchrs Coll.

Termites: A Study in Social Behavior. P. E. Howse. 1970. pap. text ed. 5.50x (ISBN 0-09-100841-7, Hutchinson U Lib). Humanities.

Terms in Systemic Linguistics. Alex DeJoia & Adrian Stenton. LC 80-5089. 1980. 17.95 (ISBN 0-312-79180-1). St Martin.

Ternary Chalcopyrite Semiconductors: Growth, Electronic Properties & Applications. J. L. Shay & J. H. Wernick. LC 74-5763. 1975. text ed. 46.00 (ISBN 0-08-017883-9). Pergamon.

Terpenes, Vol. 3 Sesquiterpenes & Diterpenes & Their Derivatives. J. L. Simonsen & D. H. Barton. 65.00 (ISBN 0-521-06476-7). Cambridge U Pr.

Terra in Piazza: An Interpretation of the Palio in Siena. Alan Dundes & Allesandro Falassi. LC 73-91675. (Illus.). 1975. 24.50 (ISBN 0-520-02681-0). U of Cal Pr.

Terra Incognita. Nancy Dorer & Frances Dorer. (Orig.). 1980. pap. 1.95 (ISBN 0-532-23178-3). Manor Bks.

Terra SF. Ed. by Richard D. Nolane. 1981. pap. 2.25 (ISBN 0-87997-595-4, UE1595). Daw Bks.

Terracotta Lamps. Oscar Broneer. LC 76-362971. (Isthmia Ser: Vol. 3). 1977. 25.00x (ISBN 0-87661-933-2). Am Sch Athens.

Terrain Analysis & Remote Sensing. Ed. by J. R. Townshend. (Illus.). 240p. (Orig.). text ed. 45.00x (ISBN 0-04-551036-9, 2597); pap. text ed. 22.50x (ISBN 0-04-551037-7, 2598). Allen Unwin.

Terrain Evaluation. Colin Mitchell. Ed. by J. Houston. LC 74-158517. (Illus.). 224p. 1974. pap. text ed. 10.95x (ISBN 0-582-48426-X). Longman.

Terranova: The Ethos & Luck of Deep-Sea Fishermen. Joseba Zulaika. LC 80-20931. (Illus.). 160p. 1981. text ed. 14.50x (ISBN 0-89727-016-9). Inst Study Human.

Terrarium Book. Charles M. Evans & Roberta L. Pliner. LC 72-11388. (Illus.). 1973. 7.95 (ISBN 0-394-48364-2); pap. 3.95 (ISBN 0-394-70968-3). Random.

Terrarium in Your Home. William White & Sarah L. White. LC 76-19807. (Illus.). (gr. 7 up). 1976. 6.95 o.p. (ISBN 0-8069-3732-7); PLB 6.69 o.p. (ISBN 0-8069-3733-5). Sterling.

Terrariums. John Hoke. LC 70-189761. (First Bks). (Illus.). 96p. (gr. 4-6). 1972. PLB 4.90 o.p. (ISBN 0-531-00777-4). Watts.

Terrariums. Alice Parker. (Easy-Read Fact Bks.). (Illus.). (gr. 2-4). 1977. PLB 6.45 s&l (ISBN 0-531-01315-4). Watts.

Terrestrial Ecology of Aldabra. Royal Society of London. Ed. by D. R. Stoddart & T. S. Westoll. (Illus.). 1979. lib. bdg. 61.00x (ISBN 0-85403-111-1, Pub. by Royal Soc London). Scholium Intl.

Terrestrial Environments. J. D. Cloudesley-Thompson. 262p. 1980. 29.00x (ISBN 0-85664-001-8, Pub. by Croom Helm England). State Mutual Bk.

Terrestrial Environments. J. L. Cloudsley-Thompson. LC 74-16704. 1975. pap. text ed. 14.95x (ISBN 0-470-26743-7). Halsted Pr.

Terrestrial Environments. S. J. Cloudsley-Thompson. LC 74-16704. 350p. 1975. text ed. 16.95x o.p. (ISBN 0-470-16080-2). Halsted Pr.

Terrestrial Propagation of Long Electromagnetic Waves. J. Galejs. 376p. 1972. 82.00 (ISBN 0-08-016710-1). Pergamon.

Terrible, Awful, Deplorable, Loveable Little Troll. Jay A. Meservy & J. Alonzo. (gr. 1-5). Date not set. cancelled (ISBN 0-8197-0464-4). Bloch.

Terrible Beauty: Conversions in Prayers, Politics & Imagination. James Carroll. LC 72-97400. 1973. 4.95 (ISBN 0-8091-0182-3). Paulist Pr.

Terrible Churnadryne. Eleanor Cameron. (Illus.). (gr. 4-6). 1959. 8.95 (ISBN 0-316-12535-0, Pub. by Atlantic Monthly Pr). Little.

Terrible Ordeal of Daniyell Moore. Susie Moore. 1981. 4.50 (ISBN 0-8062-1713-8). Carlton.

Terrible Secret. Walter Laqueur. 276p. 1980. 12.95 (ISBN 0-316-51474-8). Little.

Terrible Shears. D. J. Enright. LC 74-5966. (Wesleyan Poetry Program: Vol. 73). 72p. 1974. 10.00x (ISBN 0-8195-2073-X, Pub. by Wesleyan U Pr); pap. 4.95x (ISBN 0-8195-1073-4). Columbia U Pr.

Terrible Teens: A Guide for Bewildered Parents. Leonard Gross. 256p. 1981. 10.95 (ISBN 0-02-545820-5). Macmillan.

Terrible Thing That Happened at Our House. Marge Blaine. LC 80-15280. (Illus.). 40p. (ps-3). 1980. Repr. of 1975 ed. 8.95 (ISBN 0-590-07780-5, Four Winds). Schol Bk Serv.

Terrible Things. W. C. Chalk. 1971. pap. text ed. 2.50x o.p. (ISBN 0-435-11197-3). Heinemann Ed.

Terrible Tiger. Jack Prelutsky. LC 75-89592. (Illus.). (gr. k-3). 1970. 4.95g o.s.i. (ISBN 0-02-775130-9). Macmillan.

Terrible Troll. Mercer Mayer. LC 68-28730. (Illus.). 32p. (ps-2). 1981. pap. 2.75 (ISBN 0-8037-8636-0, Pied Piper Bk). Dial.

Terrible Tyrannosaurus. Elizabeth Charlton. (Illus.). 32p. (ps-2). 1981. 5.95 (ISBN 0-525-66724-5). Elsevier-Nelson.

Terrier Lovers Cookbook. Ed. by Sandra Goose Allen. 1977. 6.00 (ISBN 0-9600722-2-5). Skye Terrier.

Terriers Vocation. Geoffrey Sparrow. (Illus.). pap. 4.35 (ISBN 0-85131-111-3, Dist. by Sporting Book Center). J A Allen.

Terrific Gifts to Make & Give. Lawson. (gr. 7-12). 1980. pap. 1.25 (ISBN 0-590-30885-8, Schol Pap). Schol Bk Serv.

Terrific Kemble: A Victorian Self-Portrait from the Writings of Fanny Kemble. Eleanor Ransome. 1979. 22.50 (ISBN 0-241-89884-6, Pub. by Hamish Hamilton England). David & Charles.

Terrific Tomatoes: All About How to Grow & Enjoy Them. Organic Gardening & Farming Editors. LC 75-1314. (Illus.). 240p. 1975. 8.95 (ISBN 0-87857-094-2); pap. 3.95 (ISBN 0-87857-111-6). Rodale Pr Inc.

Terrified Heart. Alicia Grace. 1976. pap. 1.25 o.p. (ISBN 0-685-72357-7, LB383ZK, Leisure Bks). Nordon Pubns.

Territorial Asylum. Atle Grahl-Madsen. LC 80-10498. (Monograph in the Uppsala University Swedish Institute of International Law). 231p. 1980. lib. bdg. 28.00 (ISBN 0-379-20706-0). Oceana.

Territorial Politics in Industrial Nations. Sidney Tarrow et al. LC 77-83439. (Praeger Special Studies). 1978. 32.50 (ISBN 0-03-040961-6). Praeger.

Territories & the United States, 1861-1890: Studies in Colonial Administration. Earl S. Pomeroy. LC 70-8872. (Americana Library Ser.: No. 15). 1969. 10.50 (ISBN 0-295-95030-7, AL15); pap. 2.95 (ISBN 0-295-95101-X, ALP15). U of Wash Pr.

Territory & Function. John Friedmann & Clyde Weaver. 1979. 22.50x (ISBN 0-520-03928-9); pap. 6.95x (ISBN 0-520-04105-4). U of Cal Pr.

Terror. Michael D. Albers. (Orig.). 1980. pap. 2.25 (ISBN 0-532-23311-5). Manor Bks.

Terror & Decorum: Poems, 1940-1948. Peter R. Viereck. LC 78-178796. 110p. 1948. Repr. lib. bdg. 13.75x (ISBN 0-8371-6296-3, VTDE). Greenwood.

Terror at Sea. Dean W. Ballenger. (Orig.). 1981. pap. 2.50 (ISBN 0-451-09670-3, E9670, Sig). NAL.

Terror at Tenerife. Norman Williams. 1977. pap. 3.50 (ISBN 0-89728-058-X, 683641). Omega Pubns OR.

Terror by Satellite. Hugh Walters. (Fanfares Ser.). (gr. 4 up). 1980. pap. 3.25 (ISBN 0-571-11492-X, Pub. by Faber & Faber). Merrimack Bk Serv.

Terror in Ireland: The Heritage of Hate. Edgar O'Ballance. (Illus.). 280p. 1981. 14.95 (ISBN 0-89141-100-3). Presidio Pr.

Terror in Room Two-O-One. Tom Mitcheltree. (Orig.). 1980. pap. 1.75 (ISBN 0-505-51475-3). Tower Bks.

Terror in the Starboard Seat. David McIntosh. 208p. 1980. 10.95 (ISBN 0-8253-0025-8). Beaufort Bks NY.

Terror in the Streets. Gordon McLean. LC 77-74159. (Illus.). 1977. pap. 1.95 (ISBN 0-87123-558-7, 200558). Bethany Fell.

Terror in the Tropics: The Army Ants. Tom Lisker. LC 77-10765. (Great Unsolved Mysteries Ser.). (Illus.). (gr. 4-5). 1977. PLB 9.65 (ISBN 0-8172-1060-1). Raintree Pubs.

Terror on the Ice. Mike Neigoff. LC 74-3405. (Pilot Book Ser.). (Illus.). 128p. (gr. 4-7). 1974. 6.95g (ISBN 0-8075-7808-8). A Whitman.

Terrorism & Criminal Justice. Ed. by Ronald D. Crelinsten et al. LC 77-887185. (Illus.). 1978. 16.95 (ISBN 0-669-01983-6). Lexington Bks.

Terrorism & the Liberal State. Paul Wilkinson. LC 78-53992. 1979. pap. 6.00x usa (ISBN 0-8147-9184-0). NYU Pr.

Terrorism & the Liberal State. Paul Wilkinson. LC 77-12115. 1978. 18.95 (ISBN 0-470-99313-8). Halsted Pr.

Terrorism in Latin America. Ernst Halperin. LC 76-4103. (Washington Papers: No. 33). 1976. 3.50x (ISBN 0-8039-0648-X). Sage.

Terrorism in Today's World. Charles Freeman. LC 79-56474. (Illus.). 96p. 1980. 16.95 (ISBN 0-7134-1230-5, Pub. by Batsford England). David & Charles.

Terrorism: Interdisciplinary Perspectives. Ed. by Yonah Alexander & Seymour M. Finger. LC 77-7552. 1977. 15.00 (ISBN 0-89444-004-7). John Jay Pr.

Terrorism: Theory & Practice. Ed. by Yonah Alexander et al. (Westview Special Studies in National & International Terrorism). 200p. 1979. lib. bdg. 25.00x (ISBN 0-89158-089-1); pap. text ed. 12.00x (ISBN 0-86531-041-6). Westview.

Terrorism: Threat, Reality, Response. Robert Kupperman & Darrel Trent. LC 78-70394. (Publications Ser.: No. 204). 1979. 14.95 (ISBN 0-8179-7041-X). Hoover Inst Pr.

Terrorist Attacks. R. P. Siljander. (Illus.). 342p. 1980. 33.50 (ISBN 0-398-04028-1). C C Thomas.

Terrorist Chic. Michael Selzer. 1979. 9.95 (ISBN 0-8015-7534-6, Hawthorn). Dutton.

Terrors & Horrors of a Haunted House. Brian Winston. 1981. 6.95 (ISBN 0-533-04574-6). Vantage.

Terry Bradshaw. Sam Hasegawa. (Sports Superstars Ser.). (Illus.). (gr. 3-9). 1977. PLB 5.95 (ISBN 0-87191-542-1); pap. 2.95 (ISBN 0-89812-212-0). Creative Ed.

Terry Bradshaw: Man of Steel. Terry Bradshaw & Dave L. Diles. (Illus.). 1979. 7.95 o.p. (ISBN 0-310-39460-0). Zondervan.

Terry Bradshaw: Man of Steel. Dave L. Diles & Terry Bradshaw. 224p. 1980. pap. 4.95 (ISBN 0-310-39461-9, 12025P). Zondervan.

Terry Letters: Private Letters of General Alfred Howe Terry to His Sisters During the Eighteen Seventy-Six Indian War. James Willert. (Illus.). 78p. 1980. 20.00x (ISBN 0-930798-03-1). J Willert.

Terry on the Fence. Bernard Ashley. LC 76-39898. (Illus.). (gr. 5-9). 1977. 9.95 (ISBN 0-87599-222-6). S G Phillips.

Terry Street. Douglas Dunn. 1971. pap. 3.95 (ISBN 0-571-09713-8, Pub. by Faber & Faber). Merrimack Bk Serv.

Terry's Guide to Mexico. rev. ed. James Norman. LC 70-171308. 1972. 9.95 o.p. (ISBN 0-385-04181-0). Doubleday.

Terzaghi Lectures. Compiled by American Society of Civil Engineers. 432p. 1974. pap. text ed. 25.00 (ISBN 0-87262-060-3). Am Soc Civil Eng.

Tess of the D'Urbervilles. Thomas Hardy. (Literature Ser). (gr. 7-12). 1969. pap. text ed. 3.75 (ISBN 0-87720-717-8). AMSCO Sch.

Tess of the D'Urbervilles. 2nd ed. Thomas Hardy. Ed. by Scott Elledge. (Critical Editions). 1979. 14.95 (ISBN 0-393-04507-2); pap. text ed. 4.95x (ISBN 0-393-09044-2). Norton.

Tess of the D'urbervilles. Thomas Hardy. pap. 1.75. Bantam.

Tess of the D'Urbervilles. Thomas Hardy. (Movie tie-in ed.). 1981. pap. 2.95 (ISBN 0-451-51522-6, CE1522, Sig Classics). NAL.

Tess of the D'urbervilles with Reader's Guide. Thomas Hardy. (Amsco Literature Program). (gr. 9-12). 1972. pap. text ed. 4.33 (ISBN 0-87720-815-8); with model ans. s.p. 2.80 (ISBN 0-87720-915-4). AMSCO Sch.

Tessa of Destiny. Leigh Ellis. 1979. pap. 2.50 (ISBN 0-380-75028-7, 75028). Avon.

Test. Pierre Boulle. LC 57-12252. 8.95 (ISBN 0-8149-0069-0). Vanguard.

Test & Measurement: A Developmental Approach. A. Bertrand & J. Cebula. 1980. 14.50 (ISBN 0-201-00778-9). A-W.

Test Item Construction in the Cognitive Domain. Home Economics Ducation Association. 1979. pap. 2.00 o.p. (ISBN 0-686-28360-0, A261-8442). Home Econ Educ.

Test Marketing. LC 80-60762. (Marketing Ser.). 1980. pap. 4.95 (ISBN 0-87251-053-0). Crain Bks.

Test Match Career of Freddie Trueman. Chris Clark. LC 80-66089. (Illus.). 208p. 1980. 19.95 (ISBN 0-7153-7944-5). David & Charles.

Test of English As a Foreign Language (TOEFL) rev. ed. Edward C. Gruber. (Exam Preparation Ser.). 528p. (gr. 12). 1981. pap. text ed. 6.95 (ISBN 0-671-18987-5). Monarch Pr.

Test of English As a Foreign Language: TOEFL. 2nd ed. Harriet N. Moreno et al. LC 77-13180. 1978. lib. bdg. 12.00 (ISBN 0-668-04446-2); pap. text ed. 8.95 (ISBN 0-668-04450-0). Arco.

Test of Poetry. Louis Zukofsky. 1981. 12.95 (ISBN 0-393-01446-0); pap. 4.95 (ISBN 0-393-00050-8). Norton.

Test Paper Thief. Mary B. Christian. (Goosehill Gang Ser.). (Illus.). 32p. (gr. 1-4). 1976. pap. 1.10 (ISBN 0-570-03608-9, 39-1033). Concordia.

Test Scores & What They Mean. 3rd ed. Howard B. Lyman. (Illus.). 1978. ref. 10.95 (ISBN 0-13-903823-X); pap. 9.95 ref. ed. (ISBN 0-13-903815-9). P-H.

Test Theory. David Magnusson. 1966. 17.95 (ISBN 0-201-04395-5). A-W.

Test Your Bible Knowledge. Carls Shoup. 1973. pap. 0.95 o.s.i. (ISBN 0-515-02725-1, N2725). Jove Pubns.

Test Your Chemistry. A. H. Johnstone et al. 1968. pap. text ed. 2.95x o.p. (ISBN 0-435-64481-5). Heinemann Ed.

Test Your Chess IQ, 2 bks. A. Lifshitz. Ed. by K. P. Neat. Incl. Bk. 1. 128p. 15.70 (ISBN 0-08-023120-9); pap. 8.90 (ISBN 0-08-024118-2); Bk. 2. 224p. 20.00 (ISBN 0-08-026881-1); pap. 13.40 (ISBN 0-08-026880-3). LC 80-41072. (Pergamon Russian Chess Ser.). (Illus.). 1981. Pergamon.

Test Your Chess: Piece Power. J. N. Walker. 160p. 1980. pap. cancelled o.p. (ISBN 0-19-217597-1). Oxford U Pr.

Test Your Compatibility. Alfred W. Munzert. (Test Yourself Ser.). 1980. pap. 3.95 (ISBN 0-671-34037-9). Monarch Pr.

Test Your E.S.P. Alfred W. Munzert. (Test Yourself Ser.). 1980. pap. 3.95 (ISBN 0-671-34039-5). Monarch Pr.

Test Your I.Q. Alfred W. Munzert. (Test Yourself Ser.). 1980. pap. 3.95 (ISBN 0-671-34035-2). Monarch Pr.

Test Your Own Job Aptitude: Exploring Your Career Potential. James Barrett & Geoffrey Williams. 128p. 1981. pap. 2.95 (ISBN 0-14-005809-5). Penguin.

Test Your Own Mental Health: A Self-Evaluation Workbook. William J Gladstone. LC 77-4678. 1978. lib. bdg. 9.95 o.p. (ISBN 0-668-04192-7, 4192); pap. 4.95 o.p. (ISBN 0-668-04186-2, 4186). Arco.

Test Your Sex Appeal. Karen E. Elskamp & Alfred W. Munzert. LC 80-85277. (Test Yourself Ser.). 64p. 1981. pap. 3.95 (ISBN 0-671-42627-3). Monarch Pr.

Test Your Tennis I.Q. Peter Schwed. LC 80-84954. (Illus.). 224p. 1981. pap. 8.95 (ISBN 0-914178-46-6, 42907-8). Golf Digest Bks.

Test Yourself: Find Your Hidden Talent. Jack Shafer. pap. 3.00 (ISBN 0-87980-259-6). Wilshire.

Testament. David Morrell. 1976. pap. 1.95 o.p. (ISBN 0-449-23033-3, Crest). Fawcett.

Testament. Elie Wiesel. 1981. 12.95 (ISBN 0-671-44833-1). Summit Bks.

Testament of Abraham. Michael E. Stone. LC 72-88770. (Society of Biblical Literature. Texts & Translation-Psuedepigrapha Ser.). 1972. pap. 6.00 (ISBN 0-89130-170-4, 060202). Scholars Pr Ca.

Testament of Adam: An Examination of the Syriac & Greek Traditions. Stephen E. Robinson. LC 80-12209. (Society of Biblical Literature Dissertation Ser.: No. 52). write for info. (ISBN 0-89130-398-7, 06-01-52); pap. write for info. (ISBN 0-89130-399-5). Scholars Pr Ca.

Testament of Adolf Hitler. Adolf Hitler. (Illus.). 1978. pap. 3.00x (ISBN 0-911038-44-2). Noontide.

Testament of Job. Robert A. Kraft. LC 74-15201. (Society of Biblical Literature. Text & Translation-Psuedepigrapha Ser.). 1974. pap. 6.00 (ISBN 0-88414-044-X, 060205). Scholars Pr Ca.

Testament of Nizamulmulk. K. Mahadev. (Writers Workshop Redbird Ser.). 1975. 8.00 (ISBN 0-88253-654-0); pap. text ed. 4.00 (ISBN 0-88253-653-2). Ind-US Inc.

Testament of Paul Keller. Jose Alejandrino. 1981. 7.95 (ISBN 0-533-04819-2). Vantage.

Testament of Youth. Vera Brittain. 1980. 13.95 (ISBN 0-686-68866-X). Seaview Bks.

Testament of Youth. Vera Brittain. 1980. 13.95 (ISBN 0-686-68995-X); pap. 7.45 (ISBN 0-686-68996-8). Wideview Bks.

Testamento "Nueva Vida". Orig. Title: New Life Testament. 600p. (Span.). Date not set. pap. price not set (ISBN 0-311-48712-2). Casa Bautista.

Testaments of Love: A Study of Love in the Bible. Leon Morris. (Orig.). 1981. pap. price not set (ISBN 0-8028-1874-9). Eerdmans.

Testaments of the Twelve Patriarchs: A Critical History of Research. H. Dixon Slingerland. LC 75-34233. (Society of Biblical Literature. Monograph). 1977. 9.00 (ISBN 0-89130-332-4, 060021); pap. 7.50 (ISBN 0-89130-062-7). Scholars Pr Ca.

Testaments of the Twelve Patriarchs: A Study of Their Text, Composition & Origin. M. De Jonge. (Van Gorcum's Theologische Bibliotheek: No. 25). 1975. pap. text ed. 24.50x (ISBN 90-232-1339-4). Humanities.

Tested Studies for Laboratory Teaching: Proceedings. Association for Biology Laboratory Education, 1st Workshop. Ed. by Jon C. Glase. LC 80-82832. 288p. 1980. text ed. 19.95 (ISBN 0-8403-2271-2). Kendall-Hunt.

Testicular Development. Ed. by Anna Steinberger & Emil Steinberger. 1979. text ed. 56.00 (ISBN 0-89004-397-3). Raven.

Testicular Tumors. 2nd ed. Douglas E. Johnson. 1976. 30.00 o.p. (ISBN 0-87488-743-7). Med Exam.

Testicular Tumors: Management & Treatment, Vol. 3. Ed. by Lawrence H. Einhorn. LC 79-89999. (Cancer Management Series). (Illus.). 224p. 1980. 38.00 (ISBN 0-89352-078-0). Masson Pub.

Testifying in Court. J. E. Horsley & J. Carlova. 1972. 8.95 (ISBN 0-87489-039-X). Med Economics.

Testigos De Jehova y Sus Doctrinas. Tr. by Jose Giron. (Spanish Bks.). 1978. 1.50 (ISBN 0-8297-0604-6). Life Pubs Intl.

Testimonie of Antique. Abbot Aelfric. LC 73-36208. (English Experience Ser.: No. 214). Repr. of 1567 ed. 13.00 (ISBN 90-221-0214-9). Walter J Johnson.

Testimonies for the Church, 9 vols. Ellen G. White. 1948. 5.95 ea. (ISBN 0-8163-0152-2); Set. 52.95 (ISBN 0-8163-0153-0, 20140-0). Pacific Pr Pub Assn.

Testimonio De Dios. Ed. by Benjamin Mercado. Tr. by Rhode Flores. 148p. (Span.). 1980. pap. 1.60. Vida Pubs.

Testimonio De Dios. 1980. pap. 1.35 (ISBN 0-686-69355-8). Vida Pubs.

Testimony of Triumph. John M. Drescher. 1980. pap. 4.95 (ISBN 0-310-23920-6). Zondervan.

Testimony of Two Men. Taylor Caldwell. 1978. pap. 2.95 (ISBN 0-449-23935-7, Crest). Fawcett.

Testing & Evaluation: New Views. Ed. by Monroe D. Cohen. LC 74-34211. 64p. 1980. Repr. of 1975 ed. 3.50x (ISBN 0-87173-000-6). ACEI.

Testing & Fair Employment: Fairness & Validity Of Personnel Tests For Different Ethnic Groups. James J. Kirkpatrick et al. LC 68-28006. (Illus.). 1969. 10.00x (ISBN 0-8147-0234-1). NYU Pr.

Testing & Measurement in the Classroom. Dale Scannell & Dick Tracy. 1975. pap. text ed. 9.75 (ISBN 0-395-18608-0). HM.

Testing Hardened Concrete: Nondestructive Methods. V. M. Malhotra. (Monograph: No. 9). 1976. 19.95 (ISBN 0-685-85144-3, M-9) (ISBN 0-685-85145-1). ACI.

Testing in Counseling, Uses & Misuses. Harley D. Christiansen. (Illus.). 96p. (Orig.). 1981. pap. text ed. 8.95 (ISBN 0-915456-03-6). P Juul Pr.

Testing in Foreign Languages, ESL, & Bilingual Education, 1966-1979: A Select, Annotated ERIC Bibliography. Dale L. Lange & Ray T. Clifford. (Language in Education Ser.: No. 24). 337p. 1980. pap. text ed. 7.95 (ISBN 0-87281-112-3, V-24). Ctr Appl Ling.

Testing Language Proficiency. Ed. by Randall L. Jones & Bernard Spolsky. LC 75-13740. 1975. pap. text ed. 8.95x (ISBN 0-87281-040-2). Ctr Appl Ling.

Testing Machine Tools: For the Use of Machine Tool Makers, Users Inspectors & Plant Engineers. 8th ed. G. Schlesinger. 1977. text ed. 18.00 (ISBN 0-08-021685-4). Pergamon.

Testing of Black Students. Ed. by LaMar P. Miller. LC 74-6237. 128p. 1974. 15.95 (ISBN 0-13-911966-3). P-H.

Testing of Organic Coatings. N. I. Gaynes. LC 76-24148. (Illus.). 1977. 24.00 o.p. (ISBN 0-8155-0650-3). Noyes.

Testing of Polymers. Ed. by William E. Brown. LC 65-14733. (Testing of Polymers Ser.: Vol. 4). 1969. 42.50 (ISBN 0-470-11175-5, Pub. by Wiley-Interscience). Wiley.

Testing Oral Communication in the Foreign Language Classroom. Walter H. Bartz. (Language in Education Ser.: No. 17). 1979. pap. 2.95 (ISBN 0-87281-103-4). Ctr Appl Ling.

Testing Program: Up with Math. Ron McCully. Ed. by Helen J. Jacobs. 120p. (Orig.). (gr. 5-12). 1979. pap. 1.95 (ISBN 0-918272-05-X); tchrs. manual 1.50 (ISBN 0-918272-06-8). Jacobs.

Testing Research Hypotheses Using Multiple Linear Regression. Keith McNeil et al. LC 75-6639. 600p. 1975. lib. bdg. 12.50x o.p. (ISBN 0-8093-0732-4); pap. text ed. 7.95x (ISBN 0-8093-0755-3). S Ill U Pr.

Testis. Ed. by Henry Burger & David Dekretser. (Comprehensive Endocrinology Ser.). 450p. 1981. text ed. 40.00 (ISBN 0-89004-247-0). Raven.

Testis. Ed. by A. D. Johnson et al. Vol. 1 1970. 72.50 (ISBN 0-12-386601-4); Vol. 2 1970. 68.50 (ISBN 0-12-386602-2); Vol. 3 1971. 69.00 (ISBN 0-12-386603-0); Vol. 4 1977. 62.50 (ISBN 0-12-386604-9); Set. 222.75 (ISBN 0-685-02412-1). Acad Pr.

Testis in Normal & Infertile Men. Ed. by Philip Troen & Howard Nankin. LC 76-19852. 1977. 48.50 (ISBN 0-89004-129-6). Raven.

Tests & Drills in Spanish Grammar, 2 bks. Juvenal L. Angel & Robert J. Dixson. (Orig., Span. & Eng., Lessons correlated to Conversacion en Espanol). (gr. 9 up). 1973. Bk. 1. pap. text ed. 2.75 (ISBN 0-88345-161-1, 18100); Bk. 2. pap. text ed. 2.75 (ISBN 0-88345-162-X, 18101). Regents Pub.

Tests & Measurements. 3rd ed. W. Bruce Walsh & Leona Tyler. (Foundations of Modern Psychology Ser.). (Illus.). 1979. ref. 12.95 (ISBN 0-13-911859-4); pap. 7.95 ref. (ISBN 0-13-911842-X). P-H.

Tests & Measurements in the Social Sciences. Truman L. Kelley & A. C. Krey. 635p. 1980. Repr. of 1934 ed. lib. bdg. 35.00 (ISBN 0-89987-452-5). Century Bookbindery.

Tests & Teasers. Ed. by Reader's Digest Editors. (Orig.). 1980. pap. 2.50 (ISBN 0-425-04552-8). Berkley Pub.

Tests, Measurement & Evaluation: A Developmental Approach. Arthur Bertrand & Joseph P. Cebula. LC 79-21032. (Education Ser.). (Illus.). 1980. 14.50 (ISBN 0-201-00778-9). A-W.

Tests of Attainment in Mathematics in Schools: Vol. 1, Monitoring Feasability Study. Ray Sumner. (NFER Occasional Reports: Second Ser.). 200p. (Orig.). 1975. pap. text ed. 15.25x (ISBN 0-85633-084-1, NFER). Humanities.

Tests of Attainment Mathematics in Schools: Vol. 2, Continuation of Monitoring Feasibility Study, Vol. 1. I. Kyles & R. Sumner. (Occasional Reports Ser.: No. 2). (Illus.). 1977. pap. text ed. 9.00x (ISBN 0-85633-135-X, NFER). Humanities.

Tests of Faith. J. A. Motyer. LC 76-134726. (Orig.). 1970. pap. 1.50 o.p. (ISBN 0-87784-696-0). Inter-Varsity.

Tests of Functional Adult Literacy. 1977. 7.50 (ISBN 0-89354-825-1). Northwest Regional.

Tests on Transport Packaging for Radioactive Materials. (Illus.). 641p. (Orig.). 1971. pap. 45.00 (ISBN 92-0-020271-3, ISP 285, IAEA). Unipub.

Tete Sur les Epaules. Henri Troyat. (Easy Readers, C). (Illus.). pap. text ed. 3.75 (ISBN 0-88436-285-X). EMC.

Tether, Contracture, & Deformity. John Clark. 1976. 27.50x (ISBN 0-685-83929-X). Intl Ideas.

Tethered Presidency: A Study of New Congressional Restraints on Presidential Power & Their Effect on America's Ability to Conduct an Effective Foreign Policy. Ed. by Thomas M. Franck. 272p. 1981. text ed. 17.50x (ISBN 0-8147-2567-8). NYU Pr.

Teton Sioux Music. Frances Densmore. LC 72-1889. (Music Ser.). (Illus.). 722p. 1972. Repr. of 1918 ed. lib. bdg. 39.50 (ISBN 0-306-70516-8). Da Capo.

Tetradrachmenpragung Von Syrakus, in der Periode der Signierenden Kunstler. L. O. Tudeer. (Illus.). 1979. 40.00 (ISBN 0-916710-53-X). Obol Intl.

Tetraphenylborates. Orest Papovych. (IUPAC Solubility Data Ser.: Vol. 18). 260p. 1981. 100.00 (ISBN 0-08-023928-5). Pergamon.

Tetraplegia & Paraplegia. 2nd ed. Ida Bromley. (Illus.). 264p. 1981. pap. text ed. 15.00 (ISBN 0-443-01992-4). Churchill.

TEVEC Case: An Experiment in Adult Education Using the Multi-Media System. Raymond Lallez. LC 72-93793. (Experiments & Innovations in Education Ser., No. 1). 659p. (Orig.). 1973. pap. 2.50 (ISBN 92-3-101007-7, U676, UNESCO). Unipub.

Texan Came Riding. Frank O'Rourke. Bd. with Desperate Rider. pap. cancelled o.s.i. (ISBN 0-451-09490-5, Sig). NAL.

Texan Women. Corrinne Johnston. 1977. pap. 2.25 o.s.i. (ISBN 0-515-04395-8). Jove Pubns.

Texans. David Nevin. (Old West Ser.). (Illus.). 1976. 12.95 (ISBN 0-8094-1500-3). Time-Life.

Texans. David Nevin. LC 75-15450. (Old West). (Illus.). (gr. 5 up). 1975. kivar 12.96 (ISBN 0-8094-1502-X, Pub. by Time-Life). Silver.

Texans. Amanda Willoughby. 1980. pap. 2.75 (ISBN 0-440-08665-5). Dell.

Texas, 2 vols. Ed. by David C. DeLong. (Historic American Buildings Ser.). 1980. Set. lib. bdg. 180.00 (ISBN 0-686-52663-5); Vol. 1. (ISBN 0-8240-3198-9); Vol. 2. (ISBN 0-8240-3199-7). Garland Pub.

Texas. Joe B. Frantz. (States & the Nation). (Illus.). 1976. 12.95 (ISBN 0-393-05580-9, Co-Pub by AASLH). Norton.

Texas! Dana F. Ross. (Wagons West Ser.). 368p. (Orig.). 1980. pap. 2.75 (ISBN 0-553-13980-0). Bantam.

Texas. 33.00 (ISBN 0-89770-119-4). Curriculum Info Ctr.

Texas. Lon Tinkle. LC 73-5198. 1976. 17.95 (ISBN 0-684-13415-2, ScribT); pap. 12.50 (ISBN 0-684-14643-6, ScribT). Scribner.

Texas, a Brief Account. William H. Wharton. pap. 4.50 wrappers (ISBN 0-8363-0093-9). Jenkins.

Texas: A Guide to the Lone Star State. Federal Writers' Project. LC 40-10658. 717p. 59.00 (ISBN 0-403-02192-8). Somerset Pub.

Texas: A History. Seymour V. Connor. LC 71-136037. (Illus., Orig.). 1971. text ed. 16.50x (ISBN 0-88295-724-4). AHM Pub.

Texas: A Roadside View. Lady Bird Johnson. (Illus.). 51p. 1980. 12.00 (ISBN 0-911536-89-2). Trinity U Pr.

Texas & the American Revolution. (Illus.). 72p. 1975. pap. text ed. 3.50 (ISBN 0-933164-23-8). U of Tex Inst Tex Culture.

Texas Art of Frank Callcott. (Texas Centennial. National History Ser.: Vol. 1). 1978. 39.50 (ISBN 0-89482-032-X). Stevenson Pr.

Texas Business Law. Don Evans. LC 80-17836. 852p. 1980. text ed. 19.95x (ISBN 0-88289-251-7). Pelican.

Texas Chronology & Factbook, Vol. 43. R. I. Vexler. 1978. 8.50 (ISBN 0-379-16168-0). Oceana.

Texas Constitutional Revision Experience in the 70's. Janice C. May. LC 75-26954. (Orig.). 1975. 8.95 o.p. (ISBN 0-88408-027-7). Sterling Swift.

Texas Courthouse Revisited. June R. Welch. (Illus.). Date not set. 14.95g (ISBN 0-685-96874-X). GLA Pr. Postponed.

Texas Dawn. Phillip Finch. LC 80-52414. 512p. 1981. 12.95 (ISBN 0-87223-656-0). Seaview Bks.

Texas Dew: Manual on Conversion of Engines to Propane (Lpg) Ross Smith. (Applied Technology Ser.). (Illus.). 76p. (Orig.). 1979. pap. 8.45 (ISBN 0-938260-00-6). Ashford.

Texas Energy Issues Nineteen Seventy-Nine. LC 79-91227. (Policy Research Project Report Series: No. 36). 1979. 5.95 (ISBN 0-89940-636-X). LBJ Sch Public Affairs.

Texas Epic: An American Story. Martha A. Turner. 11.95 (ISBN 0-685-48782-2). Nortex Pr.

Texas Fact Book 1981. rev. ed. Joseph E. Pluta et al. 200p. (Orig.). 1981. pap. 6.00 (ISBN 0-87755-246-0). U of Tex Busn Res.

Texas Fever. Jordan Allen. 224p. (Orig.). 1980. pap. 1.95 (ISBN 0-89083-664-7). Zebra.

Texas Fever. W. F. Bragg. 1981. pap. 1.75 (ISBN 0-8439-0864-5, Leisure Bks). Nordon Pubns.

Texas Fever. Donald Hamilton. 1979. pap. 1.75 (ISBN 0-449-14122-5, GM). Fawcett.

Texas Fossils: An Amateur Collector's Handbook. W. H. Matthews. (Illus.). 123p. 1960. Repr. 1.00 (GB 2). Bur Econ Geology.

Texas Government Today: Structures, Functions, Political Processes. rev. ed. Beryl E. Pettus & Randall W. Bland. 1979. pap. text ed. 10.95x (ISBN 0-256-02199-6). Dorsey.

Texas Gun. Nelson Nye. 160p. (Orig.). 1976. pap. 1.75 (ISBN 0-441-80402-0). Ace Bks.

Texas Heartland: A Hill Country Year. Jim Bones, Jr. & John Graves. LC 75-16352. (Illus.). 104p. 1975. 21.50 (ISBN 0-89096-002-X). Tex A&M Univ Pr.

Texas Heritage. Archie McDonald & Ben Procter. LC 79-54886. (Orig.). 1980. pap. text ed. 6.95x (ISBN 0-88273-001-0). Forum Pr MO.

Texas in the Confederacy: Military Installations, Economy & People. Bill Winsor. LC 78-68432. (Illus.). 1978. 12.50 (ISBN 0-912172-24-X). Hill Jr Coll.

Texas in the Middle Eighteenth Century: Studies in Spanish Colonial History and Administration. Herbert E. Bolton. (Texas History Paperbacks Ser.: No. 8). 1970. 17.95x (ISBN 0-292-70056-3); pap. 7.95 (ISBN 0-292-70034-2). U of Tex Pr.

Texas Is the Place for Me. Carl Urbantke. Ed. by Robert C. Cotner. (Illus.). 8.50 (ISBN 0-8363-0094-7). Jenkins.

Texas: Lone Star State Government. E. Larry Dickens et al. (Illus.). 152p. (Orig.). 1980. pap. text ed. 6.95 (ISBN 0-88408-135-4). Sterling Swift.

Texas Missions & Landmarks. 2nd ed. Jack Harmon. (Illus.). 57p. 1978. 10.00 (ISBN 0-933164-43-2); pap. 6.95 (ISBN 0-933164-17-3). U of Tex Inst Tex Culture.

Texas Monthly Guidebooks: Houston. 3rd ed. Felicia Coates & Harriet Howle. 288p. 1980. pap. 5.95 (ISBN 0-932012-12-4). Texas Month Pr.

Texas Monthly's Political Reader. 2nd ed. Ed. by Lawrence C. Dodd. 264p. 1980. pap. 8.00 (ISBN 0-932012-09-4). Texas Month Pr.

Texas Notary Law Primer. Editors of The National Notary Magazine of the National Notary Assn. 1981. pap. 5.95 (ISBN 0-933134-06-1). Natl Notary.

Texas Politics. Richard Kraemer & Charldean Newell. (Illus.). 1979. pap. text ed. 11.50 (ISBN 0-8299-0286-4); instrs.' manual avail. (ISBN 0-8299-0499-9). West Pub.

Texas Politics: Economics, Power, & Policy. James W. Lamare. 225p. 1981. pap. text ed. 7.16 (ISBN 0-8299-0390-9). West Pub.

Texas Politics Today. William E. Maxwell & Ernest Crain. (Illus.). 1978. pap. text ed. 10.95 (ISBN 0-8299-0216-3); instrs.' manual avail. (ISBN 0-8299-0556-1). West Pub.

Texas Politics Today. 2nd ed. William E. Maxwell & Ernest Crain. (Illus.). 585p. 1981. pap. text ed. 8.76 (ISBN 0-8299-0395-X). West Pub.

Texas Quilting Primer. Beverly Orbelo. 48p. 1980. pap. 5.00 (ISBN 0-931722-07-1). Corona Pub.

Texas Railroads: A Record of Construction & Abandonment. Charles P. Zlatkovich. (Research Monograph). 100p. (Orig.). 1981. pap. 7.00 (ISBN 0-87755-248-7). U of Tex Busn Res.

Texas Ranger. Herman Toepperwein. pap. 1.50 (ISBN 0-910722-10-2). Highland Pr.

Texas Ranger Indian War Pensions. Robert W. Stephens. 1976. 6.95 (ISBN 0-89015-087-7). Nortex Pr.

Texas Rangers. new ed. Walter P. Webb. 1965. 14.95 (ISBN 0-292-73400-X). U of Tex Pr.

Texas Rangers: Their First 150 Years. John L. Davis. (Illus.). 114p. 1975. 5.95 (ISBN 0-933164-19-X). U of Tex Inst Tex Culture.

Texas Real Estate. Jacobus Harwood. (Illus.). 672p. 1980. ref. ed. 19.95; text ed. 16.95 (ISBN 0-8359-7553-3). Reston.

Texas Real Estate Law. Charles Jacobus. 1979. ref. ed. 19.95; text ed. 15.95 (ISBN 0-8359-7569-X); instr's. manual avail. Reston.

Texas Real Estate Law. 2nd ed. Charles Jacobus. 1981. 19.95 (ISBN 0-8359-7571-1); text ed. 15.95 (ISBN 0-686-68878-3); instr's. manual free (ISBN 0-8359-7572-X). Reston.

Texas Republic: A Social & Economic History. rev. ed. William R. Hogan. LC 68-59357. (Texas History Paperback Ser: No. 3). 1969. pap. 7.95 (ISBN 0-292-78423-6). U of Tex Pr.

Texas Revolution. William C. Binkley. LC 79-63065. 1979. 10.95 (ISBN 0-87611-041-3); pap. 4.50 (ISBN 0-87611-042-1). Tex St Hist Assn.

Texas Rich: The Hunt Dynasty from the Early Oil Days Through the Silver Crash. Harry Hurt, III. 1981. 16.95 (ISBN 0-393-01391-X). Norton.

Texas Rocks & Minerals: An Amateur's Guide. R. M. Girard. (Illus.). 109p. 1964. Repr. 2.00 (GB 6). Bur Econ Geology.

Texas Senator. Illus. by June R. Welch. 1978. 13.95 (ISBN 0-912854-10-3). GLA Pr.

Texas Six Man Football. C. H. Underwood. (Illus.). 107p. 1974. 6.95 (ISBN 0-89015-078-8). Nortex Pr.

Texas State Capitol. Ed. by Robert C. Cotner et al. (Illus.). 7.50 (ISBN 0-8363-0095-5). Jenkins.

Texas Statehouse Blues. Ben Sargent. 144p. 1980. pap. 5.95 (ISBN 0-932012-11-6). Texas Month Pr.

Texas Tales & Tunes: A Suite for Speech, Voices, & Orff Instruments. Millie Burnett & Mary Ann Cummins. 1977. pap. 3.50 (ISBN 0-918812-00-3). Magnamusic.

Texas Tenants' Handbook. Jim Simons et al. 1980. pap. price not set (ISBN 0-201-08302-7). A-W.

Texas: The Lone Star State. 4th ed. Rupert N. Richardson et al. (Illus.). 464p. 1981. text ed. 17.95 (ISBN 0-13-912444-6). P-H.

Texas Trade & Professional Associations (1981 Edition) rev. ed. Ed. by Rita Wright & Mildred Anderson. 75p. (Orig.). 1981. pap. 5.00 (ISBN 0-686-69074-5). U of Tex Busn Res.

Texas Trilogy. Preston Jones. 338p. 1976. pap. 6.95 (ISBN 0-8090-1236-7, Mermaid). Hill & Wang.

Texas Vistas: Selections from the Southwestern Historical Quarterly. Ed. by Ralph A. Wooster & Robert A. Calvert. LC 80-52706. 1980. 11.95 (ISBN 0-87611-047-2); pap. 6.50 (ISBN 0-87611-048-0). Tex St Hist Assn.

Texas vs. Davis: The Only Complete Account of the Cullen Davis Murder Trials. Michael Cochran. LC 80-674. 400p. 1980. 12.95 (ISBN 0-672-52569-0). Bobbs.

Texas Wild Flowers. Eliza G. Johnston. LC 72-77252. (Illus.). 240p. 1972. collectors ed. 100.00 (ISBN 0-88319-006-0). Shoal Creek Pub.

Texas Wind. James M. Reasoner. (Orig.). 1980. pap. 1.95 (ISBN 0-532-23201-1). Manor Bks.

Texastat '74 & '76. Ed. by Douglas S. Harlan. LC 78-52839. 1978. pap. 15.00 (ISBN 0-911536-75-2). Trinity U Pr.

Texians: Pre-Revolutionary Texas. Dan Parkinson & David L. Hicks. LC 79-91599. 272p. 8.95 (ISBN 0-89896-000-2). Larksdale.

Text & Context: Some Explorations in the Semantics & Pragmatics of Discourse. Teun A. Van Dijk. (Longman Linguistics Library). (Illus.). 1977. text ed. 19.95x (ISBN 0-582-55085-8). Longman.

Text & Interpretation. Ed. by E. Best & R. McL. Wilson. LC 78-2962. 1979. 39.00 (ISBN 0-521-22021-1). Cambridge U Pr.

Text-Book of Palaeontology, 2 vols. K. A. Von Zittel. Ed. by C. R. Eastmann & A. Smith Woodward. Incl. Vol. 2. Vertebrates I: Pisces, Amphibia, Reptile, Aves. 25.00 (ISBN 3-7682-7102-1); Vol. 3. Mammalia. 20.00. 1964. Set. 85.00 (ISBN 3-7682-7101-3). Lubrecht & Cramer.

Text-Critical Methodology & the Pre-Caesarean Text. Larry Hurtado. 112p. (Orig.). 1981. pap. 13.00 (ISBN 0-8028-1872-2). Eerdmans.

Text of the Greek Bible. 3rd ed. F. G. Kenyon. (Studies in Theology). 1975. 40.50x o.p. (ISBN 0-7156-0641-7, Pub. by Duckworth England). Biblio Dist.

Text of the New Testament: Its Transmission, Corruption, & Restoration. 2nd ed. Bruce M. Metzger. 1968. 9.95 (ISBN 0-19-500391-8). Oxford U Pr.

Text of the Septuagint: Its Corruption & Their Emendations. Peter Walters. Ed. by D. W. Gooding. LC 74-161292. (Illus.). 440p. 1972. 77.00 (ISBN 0-521-07977-2). Cambridge U Pr.

Text Processing. Ed. by Wolfgang Burghardt & Klaus Hoelker. (Research in Text Theory Ser.). 466p. 1979. text ed. 92.00x (ISBN 3-11-007565-2). De Gruyter.

Textbook for Dental Surgery Assistants. Janet Oakley & S. F. Parkin. (Illus., Orig.). 1963. pap. 8.95 (ISBN 0-571-10253-0, Pub. by Faber & Faber). Merrimack Bk Serv.

Textbook for Laboratory Assistants. 3rd ed. Irwin A. Oppenheim. (Illus.). 190p. 1981. pap. text ed. 12.95 (ISBN 0-8016-3722-8). Mosby.

Textbook for Nursing Assistants. 3rd ed. Gertrude D. Cherescavich. LC 72-12852. (Illus.). 1973. 15.95 (ISBN 0-8016-0957-7). Mosby.

Textbook for Psychiatric Technicians. 2nd rev. ed. Lucille H. McClelland. LC 74-147167. (Illus.). 1971. pap. text ed. 10.95 o.p. (ISBN 0-8016-3216-1). Mosby.

Textbook of Acupuncture Therapy. rev. 2nd ed. Mary Austin. LC 72-78147. (Illus.). 280p. 1975. text ed. 20.00 (ISBN 0-88231-003-8). ASI Pubs Inc.

Textbook of Adolescent Psychopathology & Treatment. Adrian D. Copeland. (Illus.). 152p. 1974. text ed. 14.75 (ISBN 0-398-03114-2); pap. text ed. 9.75 (ISBN 0-398-03115-0). C C Thomas.

Textbook of Anatomy & Physiology. 10th ed. Catherine P. Anthony & Gary A. Thibodeau. LC 79-11405. (Illus.). 1978. text ed. 21.95 (ISBN 0-8016-0255-6). Mosby.

Textbook of Anatomy & Physiology in Radiologic Technology. 2nd ed. Charles A. Jacobi. LC 74-20889. 1975. text ed. 18.95 (ISBN 0-8016-2390-1). Mosby.

Textbook of Basic Emergency Medicine. 2nd ed. Robert H. Miller. LC 79-27337. (Illus.). 1980. pap. text ed. 12.95 (ISBN 0-8016-3449-0). Mosby.

Textbook of Basic Emergency Medicine. Robert H. Miller & James R. Cantrell. LC 75-9765. (Illus.). 272p. 1975. pap. text ed. 13.95 o.p. (ISBN 0-8016-3448-2). Mosby.

Textbook of Basic Nursing. 2nd ed. Ella M. Thompson & Caroline B. Rosdahl. 875p. 1973. text ed. 15.75 o.s.i. (ISBN 0-397-54146-5). Lippincott.

Textbook of Botany, Vol. I: Algae, Fungi, Bacteria, Virus, Lichens, Mycoplasma & Elementary Plant Pathology. S. N. Pandey & P. S. Trivedi. 1976. 18.95 (ISBN 0-7069-0516-4, Pub. by Vikas India). Advent Bk.

Textbook of Botany, Vol. II: Bryophyta, Pteridophyta, Gymnosperms & Paleobotany. S. N. Pandey et al. 1974. 17.50 (ISBN 0-7069-0213-0, Pub. by Vikas India). Advent Bk.

Textbook of Bunion Surgery. Ed. by Joshua Gerbert. LC 80-68895. (Illus.). 300p. 1981. monograph 24.50 (ISBN 0-87993-153-1). Futura Pub.

Textbook of Clinical Cardiology. Emanuel Goldberger. (Illus.). 934p. 1981. text ed. 35.00 (ISBN 0-8016-1864-9). Mosby.

Textbook of Clinical Neuropharmacology. Harold L. Klawans et al. 1981. text ed. write for info. (ISBN 0-89004-430-9). Raven.

Textbook of Contraceptive Practice. J. Peel & D. M. Potts. (Illus.). 1969. 47.50 (ISBN 0-521-07515-7); pap. 14.50x (ISBN 0-521-09598-0). Cambridge U Pr.

Textbook of Coronary Care. E. Meltzer & J. Dunning. LC 72-91695. (Illus.). 820p. 1972. text ed. 24.95 (ISBN 0-913486-11-6). Charles.

Textbook of Cosmetology. Jerry J. Ahern. 330p. 1980. pap. text ed. 7.00 (ISBN 0-8299-0309-7); study guide 4.50 (ISBN 0-8299-0319-4); answers to study guide avail. (ISBN 0-8299-0354-2); state board review questions 0.75 (ISBN 0-8299-0375-5); answers to state board review questions avail. (ISBN 0-8299-0379-8). West Pub.

Textbook of Cytology. 2nd ed. Walter V. Brown & Eldridge M. Bertke. LC 73-14625. 1974. text ed. 21.95 (ISBN 0-8016-0831-7). Mosby.

Textbook of Dental Radiography. rev. ed. Olaf E. Langland & Francis H. Sippy. (Illus.). 400p. 1978. text ed. 24.75 (ISBN 0-398-02746-3). C C Thomas.

Textbook of Dermatology, 2 vols. 3rd ed. A. Rook et al. (Illus.). 1979. Set. 236.00 (ISBN 0-632-00465-7). Mosby.

Textbook of Diagnostic Ultrasonography. Sandra L. Hagen-Ansert. LC 78-4105. 1978. text ed. 47.50 (ISBN 0-8016-2011-2). Mosby.

Textbook of Dynamics. Ed. by Frank Chorlton. LC 77-85395. (Mathematics & Its Applications Ser.). 1978. Repr. of 1963 ed. 28.95 (ISBN 0-470-99325-1). Halsted Pr.

Textbook of Economics. 7th ed. J. L. Hanson. (Illus.). 640p. 1977. pap. text ed. 15.95x (ISBN 0-7121-2020-3, Pub. by Macdonald & Evans England). Intl Ideas.

Textbook of Electroencephalography. Ernest Niedermeyer & F. H. Da Silva. 700p. 1981. 45.00 (ISBN 0-8067-1301-1). Urban & S.

Textbook of Endocrine Pharmacology. John A. Thomas. Date not set. price not set (ISBN 0-8067-1901-X). Urban & S.

Textbook of Endocrine Physiology. Constance R. Martin. (Illus.). 485p. 1976. 19.95x (ISBN 0-19-502295-5). Oxford U Pr.

Textbook of Endocrinology. 5th ed. Ed. by Robert H. Williams. LC 73-76190. (Illus.). 1138p. 1974. text ed. 35.00 (ISBN 0-7216-9397-0). Saunders.

Textbook of Fish Culture: Breeding & Cultivation of Fish. Marcel Huet. (Illus.). 454p. 41.25 (ISBN 0-85238-020-8, FN). Unipub.

Textbook of Fungi, Bacteria & Viruses. H. C. Dube. 1978. 12.50 (ISBN 0-7069-0587-3, Pub. by Vikas India). Advent Bk.

Textbook of Histology. N. N. Majumdar. 450p. 1980. text ed. 35.00 (ISBN 0-7069-1012-5, Vikas India). Advent Bk.

Textbook of Human Anatomy. 2nd ed. Roger C. Crafts. LC 78-11424. 1979. 32.95 (ISBN 0-471-04454-7, Pub. by Wiley Medical). Wiley.

Textbook of Human Biology. 2nd rev. ed. J. K. Inglis. LC 73-21696. 1974. text ed. 14.50 (ISBN 0-08-017846-4); pap. text ed. 6.75 (ISBN 0-08-017847-2). Pergamon.

Textbook of Human Genetics. 2nd ed. Max Levitan & Ashley Montagu. (Illus.). 1977. text ed. 22.95x (ISBN 0-19-502101-0). Oxford U Pr.

Textbook of Immunology. 2nd ed. Baruj Benacerraf & Emil Unanue. 300p. 1981. write for info. softcover (0528-6). Williams & Wilkins.

Textbook of Immunology: An Introduction to Immunochemistry & Immunobiology. 3rd ed. James T. Barrett. LC 77-16208. (Illus.). 1978. text ed. 19.95 (ISBN 0-8016-0500-8). Mosby.

Textbook of Insurance Broking. Roderick Clews. 224p. 1980. 27.00x (ISBN 0-85941-121-4, Pub. by Woodhead-Faulkner England). State Mutual Bk.

Textbook of Limnology. 2nd ed. Gerald A. Cole. LC 78-24532. (Illus.). 1979. text ed. 19.95 (ISBN 0-8016-1016-8). Mosby.

Textbook of Materials Technology. Lawrence H. Van Vlack. LC 70-190614. 1973. text ed. 20.95 (ISBN 0-201-08066-4); instructor's manual 3.95 (ISBN 0-201-08067-2). A-W.

Textbook of Mechanical Engineering. S. B. Srivastava. pap. 5.00x o.p. (ISBN 0-210-22550-5). Asia.

Textbook of Medical-Surgical Nursing. 4th ed. Lillian S. Brunner & Doris S. Suddarth. LC 79-27506. 1500p. 1980. text ed. 33.95 (ISBN 0-397-54238-0). Lippincott.

Textbook of Medicine for Nurses. 3rd ed. Winifred Hector & J. S. Malpas. (Illus.). 1977. pap. text ed. 19.95x (ISBN 0-433-14214-6). Intl Ideas.

Textbook of Microbiology. R. Ananthanarayan & C. K. Paniker. 608p. 1979. 25.00x (ISBN 0-86131-032-2, Pub. by Orient Longman India). State Mutual Bk.

Textbook of Microbiology. 20th ed. William Burrows. LC 72-88845. (Illus.). 1035p. 1973. text ed. 26.00 o.p. (ISBN 0-7216-2195-3). Saunders.

Textbook of Mineralogy. 4th ed. E. S. Dana & W. E. Ford. 1932. 34.95 (ISBN 0-471-19305-4). Wiley.

Textbook of Modern Algebra. B. Balakrishnan & N. Ramabhadran. 1978. 12.95 (ISBN 0-7069-0636-5, Pub. by Vikas India). Advent Bk.

Textbook of Modern Plant Pathology. K. S. Bilgrami & H. C. Dube. 1976. text ed. 16.95 (ISBN 0-7069-0421-4, Pub. by Vikas India). Advent Bk.

Textbook of Nuclear Medicine Technology. 2nd ed. Paul J. Early et al. LC 74-28229. (Illus.). 464p. 1975. pap. text ed. 21.95 o.p. (ISBN 0-8016-1487-2). Mosby.

Textbook of Nuclear Medicine Technology. 3rd ed. Paul J. Early et al. LC 78-31659. (Illus.). 1979. text ed. 32.95 (ISBN 0-8016-1488-0). Mosby.

Textbook of Operative Dentistry. Lloyd Baum et al. (Illus.). 450p. 1981. text ed. price not set (ISBN 0-7216-1601-1). Saunders.

Textbook of Oral & Maxillofacial Surgery. 5th ed. Gustav O. Kruger. (Illus.). 1979. 29.95 o.p. (ISBN 0-8016-2792-3). Mosby.

Textbook of Organic Chemistry. K. S. Tiwari et al. 1978. 35.00 (ISBN 0-7069-0442-7, Pub. by Vikas India). Advent Bk.

Textbook of Otolaryngology. David D. Deweese & William H. Saunders. LC 76-30466. (Illus.). 1977. 29.50 (ISBN 0-8016-1272-1). Mosby.

Textbook of Paediatric Nutrition. D. McLaren & D. Burman. LC 75-46569. (Illus.). 1976. text ed. 47.00x (ISBN 0-443-01413-2). Churchill.

Textbook of Pediatric Dentistry. Raymond L. Braham & Merle E. Morris. (Illus.). 568p. 1980. pap. text ed. 26.95 (ISBN 0-683-01012-3). Williams & Wilkins.

Textbook of Pediatric Nutrition. Ed. by Robert M. Suskind. 680p. 1980. text ed. 55.00 (ISBN 0-89004-253-5). Raven.

Textbook of Pharmaceutical Analysis. 2nd ed. Kenneth A. Connors. LC 74-34134. 611p. 1975. 29.50 (ISBN 0-471-16853-X, Pub. by Wiley-Interscience). Wiley.

Textbook of Physical Chemistry. 2nd ed. Arthur Adamson. 953p. 1979. 26.50 (ISBN 0-12-044260-4); solutions manual 3.00 (ISBN 0-12-044265-5). Acad Pr.

Textbook of Physical Chemistry. 2nd rev. ed. K. K. Sharma & L K. Sharma. 1980. text ed. 15.00x (ISBN 0-7069-0511-3, Pub. by Vikas India). Advent Bk.

Textbook of Physiology. 10th ed. Ed. by George H. Bell et al. (Illus.). 600p. 1980. text ed. 33.00x (ISBN 0-443-02152-X). Churchill.

Textbook of Physiology. 18th ed. Byron A. Schottelius & Dorothy D. Schottelius. LC 77-17844. (Illus.). 1978. text ed. 19.95 (ISBN 0-8016-4356-2). Mosby.

Textbook of Physiology. 2nd ed. Ed. by Sarada Subrahmanyam & K. Madhaven Kutty. 818p. 1979. 30.00x (ISBN 0-86125-415-5, Pub. by Orient Longman India). State Mutual Bk.

Textbook of Pollen Analysis. 3rd ed. Knut Faegri & J. Iversen. LC 74-12235. 1975. 23.50 o.s.i. (ISBN 0-02-844470-1). Hafner.

Textbook of Polymer Science. 2nd ed. Fred W. Billmeyer, Jr. LC 78-142713. 1971. 28.95 (ISBN 0-471-07296-6, Pub. by Wiley-Interscience). Wiley.

Textbook of Psychiatry for Students & Practitioners. 10th ed. David Henderson & R. D. Gillespie. Ed. by Ivor R. Batchelor. 1969. 16.95x o.p. (ISBN 0-19-264412-2); pap. 10.95x (ISBN 0-19-264413-0). Oxford U Pr.

Textbook of Psychology. Johann F. Herbart. Tr. by Margaret K. Smith. Bd. with Study of Psychology; Outlines of Psychology. (Contributions to the History of Psychology Ser., Vol. VI, Pt. A: Orientations). 1978. Repr. of 1891 ed. 30.00 (ISBN 0-89093-155-0). U Pubns Amer.

Textbook of Radiodiagnosis. Ed. by A. E. Van Voorthuisen. (Illus.). 486p. 1980. text ed. 67.50x (ISBN 0-19-261144-5). Oxford U Pr.

Textbook of Radiology & Imaging, 2 vols. 3rd ed. David Sutton. 1981. Vol. 1. text ed. 149.00 (ISBN 0-686-28939-0); Vol. 2. text ed. 175.00 (ISBN 0-686-28940-4). Churchill.

Textbook of Radiology & Imaging. 3rd ed. David Sutton. (Illus.). 1392p. 1980. lib. bdg. 149.00 in 1 vol. (ISBN 0-443-01700-X); lib. bdg. 175.00 in 2 vols. (ISBN 0-686-28870-X). Churchill.

Textbook of Reinsurance. Richard Wassell. 224p. 1980. 27.00x (ISBN 0-85941-166-4, Pub. by Woodhead-Faulkner England). State Mutual Bk.

Textbook of Roman Law. 3rd ed. William W. Buckland. 1964. text ed. 86.50x (ISBN 0-521-04360-3). Cambridge U Pr.

Textbook of Social Welfare Law. David Pearl & Kevin Gray. 240p. 1981. 31.00x (ISBN 0-85664-644-X, Pub. by Croom Helm LTD England). Biblio Dist.

Textbook of Syrian Semitic Inscriptions: Aramaic Inscriptions, Including Inscriptions in the Dialect of Zenjirli, Vol. 2. John C. Gibson. (Illus.). 160p. 1975. 34.50x (ISBN 0-19-813186-0). Oxford U Pr.

Textbook of Syrian Semitic Inscription: Vol. 1, Hebrew & Moabite Inscriptions. John C. L. Gibson. 1971. text ed. 22.50x (ISBN 0-19-813159-3). Oxford U Pr.

Textbook of Theoretical Botany, Vol. 4. R. C. McLean & W. R. Cook. LC 72-6057. 1973. text ed. 52.95 (ISBN 0-470-58558-7). Halsted Pr.

Textbook of Venereal Diseases. V. N. Sehgal. (Illus.). 1979. text ed. 15.00x (ISBN 0-7069-0639-X, Pub. by Vikas India). Advent Bk.

Textbook of Veterinary Histology. Ed. by Horst-Dieter Dellmann & Esther M. Brown. LC 75-16329. (Illus.). 513p. 1976. text ed. 24.50 o.p. (ISBN 0-8121-0528-1). Lea & Febiger.

Textbook of Veterinary Opthalmology. Ed. by Kirk N. Gelatt. LC 80-17291. (Illus.). 788p. 1981. text ed. write for info. (ISBN 0-8121-0686-5). Lea & Febiger.

Textbook on Educational Research. Lokesh Kaul. 432p. 1981. text ed. 22.50x (ISBN 0-7069-1186-5, Pub. by Vikas India). Advent Bk.

Textbook on Geonomy. J. A. Jacobs. LC 74-9662. 328p. 1974. text ed. 28.95 (ISBN 0-470-43445-7). Halsted Pr.

Textbook on Spherical Astronomy. 6th ed. W. M. Smart. LC 76-50643. (Illus.). 1977. 53.50 (ISBN 0-521-21516-1); pap. 16.95x (ISBN 0-521-29180-1). Cambridge U Pr.

Textbook Study Guide of Gynecology. 2nd ed. W. Glenn Hurt. (Medical Examination Review Book: Vol. 4A). 1976. pap. 8.50 (ISBN 0-87488-152-8). Med Exam.

Textbook Study Guide of Internal Medicine. 3rd ed. Ed. by Leslie S. Feinsmith & Jack J. Kleid. (Medical Examination Review Book: Vol. 2B). 1977. pap. 8.50 o.s.i. (ISBN 0-87488-130-7). Med Exam.

Textbook Study Guide of Internal Medicine. 3rd ed. Jack J. Kleid et al. (Medical Examination Review Book: Vol. 2A). 1976. pap. 8.50 spiral bdg. (ISBN 0-87488-123-4). Med Exam.

Textbook Study Guide of Pediatrics. Richard K. Stone et al. (Medical Examination Review Book: Vol. 11A). 1976. spiral bdg. 8.50 o.s.i. (ISBN 0-87488-157-9). Med Exam.

Textbook Study Guide of Psychiatry. 2nd ed. James R. Allen & Barbara A. Allen. (Medical Examination Review Book: Vol. 7A). 1978. 8.50 (ISBN 0-87488-156-0). Med Exam.

Textbook Study Guide of Surgery. 2nd ed. Alfred N. Butner. (Medical Examination Review Book: Vol. 5A). 1975. pap. 8.50 (ISBN 0-87488-150-1). Med Exam.

Texte et l'avant-texte: Les Brouillons d'un poeme de Milosz. new ed. J. Bellimin-Noel. (Collection L). 144p. (Orig., Fr.). 1972. pap. 8.95 (ISBN 2-03-036003-1). Larousse.

Texte und Ubungen: Intermediate Readings & Exercises. H. Knust. 1977. pap. 9.50 (ISBN 0-13-903526-5). P-H.

Textile. Boy Scouts Of America. LC 19-600. 64p. (gr. 6-12). 1972. pap. 0.70x (ISBN 0-8395-3344-6, 3344). BSA.

Textile - Apparrel Industries. Fairchild Market Research Division. (Fairchild Fact File Ser.). 1979. pap. 9.50 (ISBN 0-87005-321-3). Fairchild.

Textile Auxiliaries. J. W. Batty. 1967. pap. 5.75 (ISBN 0-08-012381-3). Pergamon.

Textile Colorist. Faber Birren. 64p. 1980. pap. 12.95 (ISBN 0-442-23854-1). Van Nos Reinhold.

Textile Designs of Japan, Vol. I: Free-Style Designs. Japan Textile Color Design Center. LC 79-89347. (Textile Designs of Japan Ser.). (Illus.). 440p. 1980. 150.00 (ISBN 0-87011-396-8). Kodansha.

Textile Fabrics & Their Selection. 7th ed. Isabel Wingate. 1976. 19.95 (ISBN 0-13-912840-9). P-H.

Textile Flammability & Consumer Safety. 1969. 5.00 o.p. (ISBN 0-913456-61-6). Interbk Inc.

Textile-Garment Screen Printing. Albert Kosloff. (Illus.). 1980. 12.00 (ISBN 0-911380-39-6). Signs of Times.

Textile Industry. Richard P. Olsen. LC 77-9167. (Lexington Casebook Ser. in Industry Analysis). (Illus.). 1978. 21.95 (ISBN 0-669-01807-4). Lexington Bks.

Textile Industry Information Sources. Ed. by Joseph V. Kopycinski. LC 64-25644. (Management Information Guide Ser.: No. 4). 1964. 30.00 (ISBN 0-8103-0804-5). Gale.

Textile Manufacture in the Northern Roman Provinces. J. P. Wild. LC 74-77294. (Cambridge Classical Studies). (Illus.). 1970. 26.50 (ISBN 0-521-07491-6). Cambridge U Pr.

Textile Mathematics, Vol. 3. J. E. Booth. 18.00 (ISBN 0-87245-588-2). Textile Bk.

Textile Mill. Marguerite Raben. LC 78-1614. (Industry at Work Ser.). (Illus.). (gr. 4-6). 1978. PLB 4.90 s&l o.p. (ISBN 0-531-02209-9). Watts.

Textile Processing & Finishing Aids: Recent Advances. J. W. Palmer. LC 77-89629. (Chemical Technology Review Ser.: No. 96). (Illus.). 1978. 39.00 (ISBN 0-8155-0673-2). Noyes.

Textile Processing: High Speed Carding & Continuous Card Feeding. 17.50 (ISBN 0-87245-613-7). Textile Bk.

Textile Products: Selection, Use & Care. Patsy R. Alexander. LC 76-11955. (Illus.). 416p. 1977. text ed. 15.50 (ISBN 0-395-20358-9); inst. manual 1.50 (ISBN 0-395-20357-0). HM.

Textile Technology Monographs. Incl. Decrystallised Cotton. L. Segal (ISBN 0-87245-462-2); Textile Printing. L. W. Miles. o.p. (ISBN 0-87245-463-0); Cotton Modification with Oxiranes (Epoxides) J. B. McKelvey (ISBN 0-87245-464-9); Physiology & Hygiene of Materials & Clothing. E. T. Renbourn. o.p. (ISBN 0-87245-465-7); Permanent Setting of Wool. A. J. Farnworth & J. Delmenico (ISBN 0-87245-466-5); Drycleaning. A. E. Johnson. o.p. (ISBN 0-87245-467-3); Twistless Yarns. H. J. Selling (ISBN 0-87245-468-1); Elastomeric Fibres. R. Meredith (ISBN 0-87245-469-X); Mothproofing of Wool. J. R. McPhee (ISBN 0-87245-470-3); Durable Press Cotton Goods. R. J. Harper, Jr (ISBN 0-87245-471-1); Flame Resistant Cottons. W. A. Reeves & G. L. Drake, Jr. o.p. (ISBN 0-87245-472-X); Tape Yarns. D. C. Hossack (ISBN 0-87245-473-8); Bicomponent Fibres. R. Jeffries (ISBN 0-87245-474-6); Bonded Fabrics. J. R. Holker. 10.00 ea. o.p. Textile Bk.

Textile Tools of Colonial Homes. 6th ed. Marion L. Channing. LC 75-229981. (Illus.). 64p. 1971. pap. 2.75 (ISBN 0-9600496-1-4). Channing Bks.

Textiles. Roz Abisch & Boche Kaplan. LC 74-13430. (Illus.). (gr. 5 up). 1974. PLB 4.47 o.p. (ISBN 0-531-00824-X). Watts.

Textiles Designs of Japan, Vol. III: Okinawan, Ainu, & Foreign Designs. Japan Textile Color Design Center. LC 79-89347. (Illus.). 400p. 1981. 150.00 (ISBN 0-87011-404-2). Kodansha.

Textiles for Teens. 3rd ed. Marcella H. Ellett. LC 67-26196. 1967. pap. text ed. 4.95 o.p. (ISBN 0-8087-0506-7). Burgess.

Textiles Laboratory Manual. Reagan Perenich. 320p. (Orig.). 1980. pap. 10.95 (ISBN 0-933340-03-6). Prince Scientific.

Textiles of the Andes: Catalogue of the Amano Collection. Yokihiro Tsunoyama. Ed. by Karl Ray. Tr. by D. T. Ooka from Japanese. (Illus.). 248p. 1979. Repr. of 1977 ed. 85.00 (ISBN 0-89346-017-6, Pub. by Heian/Dohosha). Heian Intl.

Textos De los Tratados De Montevideo Sobre Derecho Internacional Privado. (Span.). 1973. pap. 1.00 o.p. (ISBN 0-685-65446-X). OAS.

Texts & Testaments: Critical Essays on the Bible & Early Church Fathers. Ed. by W. Eugene March. 321p. 1980. 15.00 (ISBN 0-911536-80-9). Trinity U Pr.

Texts in Transit. Graydon Snyder & Kenneth Shaffer. pap. 2.95 o.p. (ISBN 0-685-61334-8). Brethren.

Textual & Historical Studies in the Book of Jubilees. James Vander Kam. LC 76-45388. (Harvard Semitic Monograph). 1977. text ed. 9.00 (ISBN 0-89130-118-6, 040014). Scholars Pr Ca.

Textual & Literary Criticism. Fredson Bowers. 1959. 28.50 (ISBN 0-521-04290-9); pap. 6.95x (ISBN 0-521-09407-0, 407). Cambridge U Pr.

Textual Commentary on the Greek New Testament. Ed. by Bruce M. Metzger. 1978. 6.45 (ISBN 3-438-06010-8, 08515). United Bible.

Textual Criticism & Editorial Technique. M. L. West. 150p. 1973. 22.00 (ISBN 3-5190-7402-8); pap. 16.75 (ISBN 3-519-07401-X); pap. 16.30 (ISBN 0-686-66955-X). Adler.

Textual Strategies: Perspectives in Post-Structuralist Criticism. Intro. by Josue V. Harari. LC 79-7617. 1979. 22.50x (ISBN 0-8014-1218-8); pap. 7.95 (ISBN 0-8014-9180-0). Cornell U Pr.

Texture of Knowledge: An Essay on Religion & Science. James W. Jones. LC 80-69036. 112p. 1981. lib. bdg. 15.75 (ISBN 0-8191-1360-3); pap. text ed. 6.75 (ISBN 0-8191-1361-1). U Pr of Amer.

Texture of Music: From Purcell to Brahms. Ivor C. Keys. (Illus.). 1961. 6.95 (ISBN 0-234-77414-2). Dufour.

Texturers in Embroidery. Valerie Harding. (Illus.). 1977. 10.95 o.p. (ISBN 0-8230-5341-5). Watson-Guptill.

Textures in Research & Practice: Proceedings. International Symposium Clausthal - Zellerfeld, 1968. Ed. by J. Grewen & G. Wassermann. (Illus.). 1969. 34.30 (ISBN 0-387-04733-6). Springer-Verlag.

Textures of Materials: Proceedings of the 5th Int'l. Conf. on Texture of Materials, March 29-April 1, 1978, Aachen, Germany, 2 vols. Ed. by G. Gottstein & K. Luecke. 1979. pap. 116.90 o.p. (ISBN 0-387-09220-X). Springer-Verlag.

Thackeray. Anthony Trollope. LC 67-23880. 1968. Repr. of 1879 ed. 18.00 (ISBN 0-8103-3060-1). Gale.

Thackeray. Ion M. Williams. LC 78-78852. (Literary Critiques Ser.). (Illus., Orig.). 1969. lib. bdg. 4.95 o.p. (ISBN 0-668-01952-2). Arco.

Thackeray: A Study in Technique. S. K. Sinha. (Salzburg Institute for English Literature: Studies in Romantic Reassessment: No. 86). (Orig.). 1979. pap. text ed. 25.00x (ISBN 0-391-01713-6). Humanities.

Thackeray at Work. John Sutherland. (Illus.). 160p. 1974. text ed. 18.75x (ISBN 0-485-11146-2, Athlone Pr). Humanities.

Thackeray: The Major Novels. Juliet McMaster. LC 76-151380. 1971. pap. 5.95 (ISBN 0-8020-6309-8). U of Toronto Pr.

Thackeray's Novels: A Fiction That Is True. Jack P. Rawlins. 1975. 18.50x (ISBN 0-520-02562-8). U of Cal Pr.

Thai Peasant Personality: The Patterning of Interpersonal Behavior in the Village of Bang Chan. Herbert P. Phillips. 1965. 17.50x (ISBN 0-520-01008-6). U of Cal Pr.

Thailand. Frederick K. Poole. LC 72-10392. (First Bks). (Illus.). 72p. (gr. 5-7). 1973. PLB 4.90 o.p. (ISBN 0-531-00791-X). Watts.

Thailand: A Complete Guide. William R. Duncan. LC 75-28719. (Illus.). 1976. 15.00 (ISBN 0-8048-1158-X); pap. 7.50 (ISBN 0-8048-1158-X). C E Tuttle.

Thailand in Pictures. rev. ed. Sterling Publishing Company Editors. LC 63-11593. (Visual Geography Ser.). (Illus., Orig.). (gr. 6 up). 1978. PLB 4.99 (ISBN 0-8069-1037-2); pap. 2.95 (ISBN 0-8069-1036-4). Sterling.

Thailand: Origins of Military Rule. Elliott. 190p. 1978. 11.95 (ISBN 0-905762-10-X); pap. 5.95 (ISBN 0-905762-11-8). Lawrence Hill.

Thalamus & Basal Telencephalon of the Cat. Alvin Berman & Edward G. Jones. (Illus.). 180p. 1980. write for info. (ISBN 0-299-08440-X). U of Wis Pr.

Thalidomide: My Fight. David Mason. 1976. 10.95 o.p. (ISBN 0-04-920046-1). Allen Unwin.

Thalidomide-the Legal Aftermath. Harvey Teff & Colin Munro. 1976. 21.95 (ISBN 0-566-00120-9, 00317-4, Pub. by Saxon Hse). Lexington Bks.

Thallium--201 Myocardial Imaging. James L. Ritchie et al. LC 78-3004. 1978. 18.50 (ISBN 0-89004-274-8). Raven.

Thallium-201 & Technettium-99m-Pyrophosphate Nyocardial Imaging in the Coronary Care Unit. Ed. by Frans J. Wackers. (Developments in Cardiovascular Medicine Ser.: No. 9). (Illus.). 255p. 1981. PLB 42.00 (ISBN 90-247-2396-5, Pub. by Martinus Nijhoff). Kluwer Boston.

Thalmus & the Midbrain of Man: A Physiological Atlas Using Electrical Stimulatiob. Ronald R. Tasker et al. (American Lecture Neurosurgery Ser.). (Illus.). 464p. write for info. (ISBN 0-398-04475-9). C C Thomas.

Thames. Theo Bergstrom. (Illus.). 1978. 8.95 (ISBN 0-8467-0501-X, Pub. by Two Continents). Hippocrene Bks.

Thames: An Eating, Drinking & Cruising Guide. L. R. Munk. (Illus.). 4.50 o.p. (ISBN 0-8038-7058-2). Hastings.

Thames & Chilterns. rev. ed. British Tourist Authority. (Illus.). 66p. 1981. pap. write for info. (ISBN 0-86143-043-3, Pub. by Auto Assn-British Tourist Authority England). Merrimack Bk Serv.

Thames & Hudson Manual of Silversmithing: The Constructional Processes. Frances Loyen. 1980. pap. 9.95 (ISBN 0-500-68021-3). Thames Hudson.

Thames & Hudson Manual of Typography. Ruari McLean. (Illus.). 192p. 1980. 17.95 (ISBN 0-500-67022-6). Thames Hudson.

Thames Barrier Design. Institute of Civil Engineers, UK. 202p. 1980. 50.00x (ISBN 0-7277-0057-X, Pub. by Telford England). State Mutual Bk.

Thames Groundwater Scheme. Institute of Civil Engineers, UK. 242p. 1980. 60.00x (ISBN 0-7277-0060-X, Pub. by Telford England). State Mutual Bk.

Thanatologic Aspects of Aging. Ed. by Margot Tallmer et al. (Thantology Service Ser.). 190p. 1980. pap. 9.95 (ISBN 0-930194-25-X). Highly Specialized.

Thanatology Library. Roberta Halporn. (Illus.). 50p. 1980. pap. 5.75 (ISBN 0-930194-07-1). Highly Specialized.

Thank God for Circles. Joanne Marxhaussen. LC 75-159012. 32p. 1980. pap. 3.50 (ISBN 0-8066-1805-1, 10-6241). Augsburg.

Thank God for My Breakdown. Walter Reiss. 1980. 4.95 (ISBN 0-8100-0114-4). Northwest Pub.

Thank God for My Heart Attack. Charles Y. Harrison. 1949. 4.50 o.p. (ISBN 0-03-027285-8). HR&W.

Thank God I Have Cancer! Clifford Oden. LC 76-9824. 1976. 7.95 o.p. (ISBN 0-87000-362-3). Arlington Hse.

Thank God, I'M O.K. The Gospel According to T.A. Richard A. Batey. LC 76-14358. 1976. pap. 2.95 o.p. (ISBN 0-687-41389-3). Abingdon.

Thank You, Animal Friends. Jane B. Moncure. LC 75-29241. (Illus.). (ps-3). 1975. 5.95 (ISBN 0-913778-15-X). Childs World.

Thank You, Doctor Lamaze. Marjorie Karmel. pap. 1.95 (ISBN 0-385-03752-X, C458, Dolp). Doubleday.

Thank You Dr. Lamaze. rev. ed. Marjorie Karmel. LC 80-8372. 192p. 1981. 10.95 (ISBN 0-06-014831-4, HarpT). Har-Row.

Thank You for Being My Parents. Ed. by Susan P. Schutz. LC 80-70743. (Illus.). 64p. (Orig.). 1981. pap. 4.95 (ISBN 0-88396-137-7). Blue Mtn Pr CO.

Thank You, God. Lucille E. Hein. (Illus.). 32p. 1981. pap. 3.50 (ISBN 0-8170-0912-4). Judson.

Thank You God, for Quiet Things. Ruth Odor. LC 80-15099. (Illus.). 32p. (ps-2). 1980. PLB 4.95 (ISBN 0-89565-169-6). Childs World.

Thank You God, for the Quiet Things. Ruth Odor. Ed. by Jane Buerger. (Illus.). 1980. 4.95 (ISBN 0-89565-169-6, 4920). Standard Pub.

Thank You God, for Wonderful Things. Ruth Odor. Ed. by Jane Buerger. (Illus.). 1980. write for info. (ISBN 0-89565-170-X, 4921). Standard Pub.

Thank You, God, for Wonderful Things. Ruth Odor. LC 80-16106. (Illus.). 32p. (Orig.). (ps-2). 1980. PLB 4.95 (ISBN 0-89565-170-X). Childs World.

Thank You, Lord, for Little Things. Annice H. Brown. LC 72-11166. (Illus.). 1973. 2.95 (ISBN 0-8042-2580-X). John Knox.

Thank You, Lord, for My Home. Gigi Tchividjian. 1980. Repr. of 1979 ed. 3.95 (ISBN 0-89066-023-9). World Wide Pubs.

Thank You Mr. President. Merriman Smith. LC 75-31769. (FDR & the Era of the New Deal Ser.). 1975. Repr. of 1946 ed. lib. bdg. 32.50 (ISBN 0-306-70740-3). Da Capo.

Thank You, You're Welcome. Louis Slobodkin. LC 57-12259. (Illus.). (gr. k-3). 5.95 (ISBN 0-8149-0404-1). Vanguard.

Thankfulness Unites: The History of the United Thank Offering. Frances M. Young. 1979. 1.75 (ISBN 0-686-28795-9). Forward Movement.

Thanks Lord, I Needed That. Charlene Potterbaum. 1979. Repr. of 1977 ed. pocket size 2.95 (ISBN 0-88270-411-7). Logos.

Thanks Songbook. Gary L. Johnson. 1980. pap. 1.95 (ISBN 0-87123-776-8, 280776). Bethany Fell.

Thanksgiving. Alana Willoughby. Ed. by Alton Jordan. (Holidays Ser.). (Illus.). (gr. k-3). PLB 3.50 (ISBN 0-89868-024-7, Read Res); pap. text ed. 1.75 (ISBN 0-89868-057-3). ARO Pub.

Thanksgiving Book. Frank Jupo. LC 79-12201. (Illus.). 32p. (gr. 1-4). 1980. PLB 6.95 (ISBN 0-396-07703-X). Dodd.

Thanksgiving Day. Robert M. Bartlett. LC 65-16178. (Holiday Ser.). (Illus.). (gr. 1-3). 1965. PLB 7.89 (ISBN 0-690-81045-8, TYC-J). T Y Crowell.

Thanksgiving for a Liberated Prophet: An Interpretation of Isaiah Chapter Fifty-Three. R. N. Whybray. (JSOT Supplement Ser.: No. 4). 184p. 1978. text ed. 29.95x (ISBN 0-905774-09-4, Pub. by JSOT Pr England); pap. text ed. 16.95x (ISBN 0-905774-04-3, Pub. by JSOT Pr England). Eisenbrauns.

Thanksgiving Mystery. Joan L. Nixon. Ed. by Ann Fay. LC 79-27346. (First Read-Alone Mystery Bk.). (Illus.). (gr. 1-3). 1980. PLB 5.50 (ISBN 0-8075-7820-7). A Whitman.

Thanksgiving Story. Alice Dalgliesh. (Illus.). (gr. k-3). 1954. reinforced bdg. 9.95 (ISBN-0-684-12330-4, ScribJ); pap. 2.95 (ISBN 0-684-16005-6, SL823, ScribJ). Scribner.

That Awful Mess on Via Merulana. Carlo Emilio Gadda. Tr. by W. Weaver. LC 65-19320. 1965. 5.95 o.s.i. (ISBN 0-8076-0305-8). Braziller.

That Black Day: The Manuscripts of 'Crazy Jane on the Day of Judgement' David R. Clark. (New Years Papers Ser.: No. XVIII). (Illus.). 56p. 1980. pap. text ed. 11.75x (ISBN 0-85105-355-6, Dolmen Pr). Humanities.

That Book in the Attic. Ellen K. Oswalk. LC 63-22374. 1963. pap. 4.95 (ISBN 0-8163-0146-8, 20240-8). Pacific Pr Pub Assn.

That Boy, That Girl. Beverly Amstutz. LC 80-80372. 24p. (ps-6). 1979. pap. 2.25 (ISBN 0-937836-01-X). Precious Res.

That Championship Season. Jason Miller. LC 72-87905. 1972. pap. 3.95 o.p. (ISBN 0-689-10538-X). Atheneum.

That Crazy April. Lila Perl. LC 73-14812. (gr. 4-8). 1974. 6.95 (ISBN 0-395-28869-X, Clarion). HM.

That Damn Romantic Fool. Michael Daniels. 14.00 (ISBN 0-89253-624-1); flexible cloth 6.75 (ISBN 0-89253-625-X). Ind-US Inc.

That Everyone May Hear. Ed. by Edward R. Dayton. 1979. pap. 3.75 (ISBN 0-912552-29-8). MARC.

That Girl from Boston. Robert H. Rimmer. 224p. 1980. Repr. of 1962 ed. 12.50 (ISBN 0-8290-0226-X). Irvington.

That Good Between Us. Howard Barker. 1981. pap. 9.95 (ISBN 0-7145-3765-9). Riverrun NY.

That Hideous Strength. C. S. Lewis. LC 68-7663. 1968. 11.95 (ISBN 0-02-571250-0). Macmillan.

That Mad Game: War & the Chances for Peace. James D. Forman. LC 80-11600. (gr. 7 up). 1980. 10.95 (ISBN 0-684-16509-0). Scribner.

That Man Gull. Anthony Stuart. 224p. 1981. pap. 1.95 (ISBN 0-445-04637-6). Popular Lib.

That Man Is Talking to His Toes. Jacquie Hann. LC 76-13496. (Illus.). 40p. (gr. k-3). 1976. 5.95 (ISBN 0-590-07456-3, Four Winds). Schol Bk Serv.

That New Baby! Patricia Relf. 24p. (ps). 1980. 1.50 (ISBN 0-307-11989-0); PLB 6.08 (ISBN 0-307-61989-3). Western Pub.

That Noble Cabinet: A History of the British Museum. Edward Miller. LC 73-85452. (Illus.). 400p. 1974. 18.00x (ISBN 0-8214-0139-4). Ohio U Pr.

That Prosser Kid. Lloyd Pye. 1978. pap. 1.95 o.p. (ISBN 0-449-23659-5, Crest). Fawcett.

That Reminds Me. 64p. 1975. 1.50 (ISBN 0-930756-13-4, 4230-AP). Women's Aglow.

That Tent by the Sawdust Pile. Lillian M. Criss. LC 76-41462. (Destiny Ser.). 1976. pap. 4.95 (ISBN 0-8163-0267-7, 20249-9). Pacific Pr Pub Assn.

That Terrible Halloween Night. James Stevenson. LC 79-27775. (Illus.). 32p. (ps). 1980. 7.95 (ISBN 0-688-80281-8); PLB 7.63 (ISBN 0-688-84281-X). Greenwillow.

That Tragic Queen: The Deirdre Legend in Anglo-Irish Literature. Herbert V. Fackler. (Salzburg Studies in English Literature, Poetic Drama & Poetic Theory Ser.: No. 39). 1978. pap. text ed. 25.00x (ISBN 0-391-01374-2). Humanities.

That Vanderbilt Woman. Phillip Van Rensselaer. LC 80-83007. 320p. 1980. pap. 2.75 (ISBN 0-87216-787-9). Playboy Pbks.

That We Might Have Life. Martha Popson. LC 80-2080. 128p. (gr. 6 up). 1981. pap. 2.75 (ISBN 0-385-17438-1, Im). Doubleday.

That Woman Must Be on Drugs. Nicole Hollander. (Illus.). 128p. 1981. pap. 3.95 (ISBN 0-312-79510-6). St Martin.

That Yankee Cat: The Maine Coon. Marilis Hornidge. LC 80-67660. (Illus., Orig.). 1981. 14.95 (ISBN 0-911764-22-4). Durrell.

That Ye May Heal: A Manual for Individual & Group Study of Meditation for Healing, from the Edgar Cayce Records. rev. ed. Compiled by Mary A. Woodward. 53p. 1970. pap. 2.50 (ISBN 0-87604-075-X). ARE Pr.

That You Might Believe. Dr. Henry M. Morris. LC 78-68398. pap. 4.95 (ISBN 0-89107-157-1). Good News.

Thatched Huts & Stucco Places: Peasants & Landlords in Nineteenth Century Nepal. Mahesh C. Regmi. 173p. 1978. 14.00x (ISBN 0-7069-0672-1, Pub. by Croom Helm Ltd. England). Biblio Dist.

That's Hollywood: Beautiful & Special People, No. 7. George Carpozi, Jr. (Orig.). 1980. pap. 1.95 (ISBN 0-532-23281-X). Manor Bks.

That's Hollywood: The Clossal Cowboys, No. 6. George Carpozi, Jr. (Orig.). 1980. pap. 1.95 (ISBN 0-532-23222-4). Manor Bks.

That's Incredible, Vol. 1. Wendy Jeffries. (That's Incredible TV Show Ser.). 192p. (Orig.). 1981. pap. 2.25 (ISBN 0-515-05807-6). Jove Pubns.

That's Incredible, Vol. 2. Wendy Jeffries. (That's Incredible TV Show Ser.). 192p. (Orig.). 1981. pap. 2.25 (ISBN 0-515-05870-X). Jove Pubns.

That's Incredible, Vol. 3. Wendy Jeffries. (That's Incredible TV Show Ser.). 192p. (Orig.). 1981. pap. 2.25 (ISBN 0-515-05986-2). Jove Pubns.

That's Life Snoopy: Selected Cartoons from "Thompson Is in Trouble, Charlie Brown," Vol. II. Charles Schulz. (Peanuts Ser.). (Illus.). 128p. (YA) 1978. pap. 1.50 (ISBN 0-449-23876-8, Crest). Fawcett.

That's My Girl. Klevin. (gr. 7-12). 1980. pap. 1.50 (ISBN 0-590-31274-X, Schol Pap). Schol Bk Serv.

That's Our Cleo. Illus. by Morris Gollub. (Illus.). 1979. pap. 1.25 (ISBN 0-307-21566-0, Golden Pr). Western Pub.

That's Silly. William Sleator. LC 80-21902. (Illus.). (gr. k-3). 1981. 7.95 (ISBN 0-525-40981-5). Dutton.

That's That. Dwight Bolinger. (Janua Linguarum, Ser. Minor: No. 155). 79p. (Orig.). 1972. pap. text ed. 12.95x (ISBN 90-2792-319-1). Mouton.

That's the Way It Is, Amigo. Hila Colman. LC 74-30398. (Illus.). 96p. (gr. 6 up). 1975. 7.95 (ISBN 0-690-00750-7, TYC-J). T Y Crowell.

That's What Friends Are for. Walt Disney Productions. (Look Look Bks.). (Illus.). 24p. (ps-k). 1981. pap. 1.25 (ISBN 0-307-11859-2, Golden Pr). Western Pub.

Thavis Is Here. Harry Homewood. 1978. pap. 1.75 o.p. (ISBN 0-449-13991-3, GM). Fawcett.

Thaw in Bulgarian Literature. Atanas Slavov. (East European Monographs: No. 84). 200p. 1981. 15.00x (ISBN 0-914710-78-8). East Eur Quarterly.

Theaetetus. Plato. Tr. by Benjamin Jowett. 1949. pap. 2.50 (ISBN 0-672-60174-5, LLA13). Bobbs.

Theaetetus (Including Part I of Theory of Knowledge) Plato. Tr. by Francis M. Cornford. pap. 3.95 (ISBN 0-672-60299-7, LLA105). Bobbs.

Theaetetus of Plato. 2nd ed. Lewis Campbell. LC 78-66572. (Ancient Philosophy Ser.). 356p. 1980. lib. bdg. 35.00 (ISBN 0-8240-9606-1). Garland Pub.

Theaetetus of Plato. Plato. Tr. by M. J. Levett. 1981. lib. bdg. 12.50 (ISBN 0-915144-82-4); pap. text ed. 4.95 (ISBN 0-915144-81-6). Hackett Pub. Postponed.

Theasurus of Engineering & Scientific Terms. rev. ed. Engineers Joint Council Editors. LC 68-6569. 1967. flexible cover 50.00 (ISBN 0-685-09289-5). AAES.

Theater. Boy Scouts Of America. LC 19-600. 64p. (gr. 6-12). 1968. pap. 0.70x (ISBN 0-8395-3328-4, 3328). BSA.

Theater & National Awakening. Ed. by Csaszar Malyusz. 350p. 1981. pap. 19.50 (ISBN 0-934214-00-X). Carrollton Pr.

Theater Art of the Medici. Arthur R. Blumenthal. LC 80-22452. (Illus.). 243p. 1981. 15.00 (ISBN 0-87451-191-7). U Pr of New Eng.

Theater East & West: Perspectives Toward a Total Theater. Leonard C. Pronko. 1967. 11.50x o.p. (ISBN 0-520-01041-8); pap. 3.85 (ISBN 0-520-02622-5). U. of Cal Pr.

Theater Event: Modern Theories of Performance. Timothy J. Wiles. Tr. by Fruma Gottschalk. LC 80-12206. 1980. lib. bdg. 17.50x (ISBN 0-226-89801-6). U. of Chicago Pr.

Theater: Five Plays: Silence, It Is Beautiful, Izzum, the Lie, It Is There. Nathalie Sarraute. LC 78-7111. 176p. 1979. 10.00 (ISBN 0-8076-0939-0); pap. 4.95 o.p. (ISBN 0-8076-0940-4). Braziller.

Theater in Britain: A Playgoer's Guide. 2nd ed. Peter Roberts. 192p. 1975. pap. 8.95x o.p. (ISBN 0-8464-0915-1). Beekman Pubs.

Theater in Its Time: An Introduction. Peter Arnott. 1981. text ed. 15.95 (ISBN 0-316-05194-2). Little.

Theater in the Planned Society: Contemporary Drama in the German Democratic Republic in Its Historical, Political & Cultural Context. H. G. Huettich. (Studies in the Germanic Languages & Literatures). 1978. 11.50x (ISBN 0-8078-8088-4). U. of NC Pr.

Theater of Fernando Arrabal: A Garden of Earthly Delights. Thomas J. Donahue. LC 79-2598. (Gotham Library). 1980. 15.00x (ISBN 0-8147-1771-3); pap. 7.00x (ISBN 0-8147-1772-1). NYU Pr.

Theater of Protest & Paradox: Developments in Avant-Garde Drama. rev. ed. George Wellwarth. LC 64-16901. 1971. 15.00x (ISBN 0-8147-0432-8); pap. 3.95x (ISBN 0-8147-0433-6). NYU Pr.

Theater of the Bauhaus. Ed. by Walter Gropius. Tr. by Arthur S. Wensinger from Ger. LC 61-14239. (Illus.). 109p. 1971. pap. 10.95 (ISBN 0-8195-6020-0, Pub. by Wesleyan U Pr). Columbia U Pr.

Theater of the Oppressed. Augusto Boal. Tr. by Charles McBride. 1979. 12.95 (ISBN 0-916354-59-8); pap. 5.95 (ISBN 0-916354-60-1). Urizen Bks.

Theater Wagon Plays of Place & Any Place. Ed. by Margaret Collins & Fletcher Collins, Jr. LC 73-84160. (Illus.). 297p. 1973. pap. 3.95x o.p. (ISBN 0-8139-0535-4). U Pr of Va.

Theatre. Robert Cohen. (Illus.). 500p. (Orig.). 1981. pap. text ed. price not set (ISBN 0-87484-459-2). Mayfield Pub.

Theatre, Vol. 2. Ed. by Barry Hyams. (Orig.). 1965. pap. 1.95 o.p. (ISBN 0-8090-0602-2, Drama). Hill & Wang.

Theatre: A Contemporary Introduction. 3rd ed. Jerry Pickering. (Illus.). 380p. 1981. pap. text ed. 10.36 (ISBN 0-8299-0403-4). West Pub.

Theatre: A Way of Seeing. Milly S. Barranger. 320p. 1980. pap. text ed. 13.95x (ISBN 0-534-00763-5). Wadsworth Pub.

Theatre & Alchemy. Bettina L. Knapp. 320p. 1981. 19.95 (ISBN 0-8143-1656-5). Wayne St U Pr.

Theatre & Cinema Architecture: A Guide to Information Sources. Ed. by Richard Stoddard. LC 78-14820. (Performing Arts Information Guide Ser.: Vol. 5). 1978. 30.00 (ISBN 0-8103-1426-6). Gale.

Theatre & Its Critics in Seventeenth-Century France. Henry Phillips. (Modern Language & Literature Monographs). 272p. 1980. 36.00 (ISBN 0-19-815535-2). Oxford U Pr.

Theatre & National Awakening. Edith C. Malyusz. Tr. by Thomas Szendrey. LC 79-89134. 349p. 1980. write for info. (ISBN 0-914648-10-1). Hungarian Cultural.

Theatre & Performing Arts Collections. Ed. by Louis A. Rachow. (Special Collections Ser.: Vol. 1, No. 1). 128p. 1981. text ed. 19.95 (ISBN 0-917724-47-X). Haworth Pr.

Theatre Arts Publications in the U. S., 1947-52. Ed. by William W. Melnitz. 188p. 1959. 5.00, ATA members 3.00 (ISBN 0-686-05078-9). Am Theatre Assoc.

Theatre Arts Publications in the U. S., 1953-57. Ed. by Roger M. Busfield. 188p. 1964. 5.00, ATA members 3.00 (ISBN 0-686-05077-0). Am Theatre Assoc.

Theatre Check List: A Guide to the Planning & Construction of Proscenium & Open Stage Theatres. The American Theatre Planning Board. LC 69-19619. (Illus.). 1969. pap. 10.00x (ISBN 0-8195-6005-7, Pub. by Wesleyan U Pr). Columbia U Pr.

Theatre, Children & Youth. Jed H. Davis & Mary J. Evans. 1981. text ed. 19.95 (ISBN 0-87602-016-3); pap. 16.25 (ISBN 0-87602-017-1). Anchorage.

Theatre Crafts Book of Costume. Ed. by C. Ray Smith & Theatre Craft Editors. LC 72-80663. (Illus.). 1973. pap. 4.95 (ISBN 0-87857-016-0). Rodale Pr Inc.

Theatre Directory, 1977-1978. 5th ed. Ed. by Arli Epton. LC 77-89021. 1977. pap. 2.00 o.p. (ISBN 0-930452-05-4, Pub by Theatre Comm). Pub Ctr Cult Res.

Theatre Directory: 1980-81. Ed. by Michael Finnegan. 50p. 1980. pap. 3.50x (ISBN 0-930452-13-5, Pub. by Theatre Comm). Pub Ctr Cult Res.

Theatre, Drama, & Audience in Goethe's Germany. Walter H. Bruford. LC 73-10579. 388p. 1974. Repr. of 1950 ed. lib. bdg. 26.25x (ISBN 0-8371-7016-8, BRTD). Greenwood.

Theatre Facts: From Putting the Show Together Through Opening Night. Jan W. Greenberg. LC 80-20295. 1981. 10.95 (ISBN 0-03-051451-7). HR&W.

Theatre Festivals of the Medici, 1539-1637. A. M. Nagler. LC 76-8447. 1976. Repr. of 1964 ed. lib. bdg. 25.00 (ISBN 0-306-70779-9). Da Capo.

Theatre, Film, & TV Biographies Master Index. 1st ed. Ed. by Dennis La Beau. LC 77-2470. (Gale Biographical Index Ser.: No. 5). 1979. 52.00 (ISBN 0-8103-1081-3). Gale.

Theatre Games. Fred Owens. (Illus.). 220p. (Orig.). 1979. pap. 10.00 (ISBN 0-936182-00-8). Diamond Heights.

Theatre in Asia. A. C. Scott. (Illus.). 304p. 1973. 12.95 (ISBN 0-02-608650-6). Macmillan.

Theatre in Early Kentucky, 1790-1820. West T. Hill, Jr. LC 73-132829. (Illus.). 246p. 1971. 12.00x (ISBN 0-8131-1240-0). U Pr of Ky.

Theatre in Search of a Fix. Robert Corrigan. 1973. 10.00 o.p. (ISBN 0-440-08662-0). Delacorte.

Theatre in the Middle Ages. W. Tydeman. LC 77-85683. (Illus.). 1979. 42.00 (ISBN 0-521-21891-8); pap. 10.50x (ISBN 0-521-29304-9). Cambridge U Pr.

Theatre Language, a Dictionary. Walter P. Bowman & Robert H. Ball. LC 60-10495. 1976. pap. 6.95 (ISBN 0-87830-551-3). Theatre Arts.

Theatre Lighting. Louis Hartmann. LC 76-115696. 1970. Repr. of 1930 ed. 5.95x o.p. (ISBN 0-910482-18-7). Drama Bk.

Theatre Lighting Before Electricity. Frederick Penzel. LC 77-14840. 1978. 20.00 (ISBN 0-8195-5021-3, Pub. by Wesleyan U Pr). Columbia U Pr.

Theatre of Aristophanes. Kenneth McLeish. LC 79-3142. (Illus.). 183p. 1980. 11.95 (ISBN 0-8008-7630-X). Taplinger.

Theatre of Friedrich Durrenmatt. Kenneth S. Whitton. (Illus.). 200p. 1978. text ed. 20.75x (ISBN 0-391-01694-6). Humanities.

Theatre of Jean Anoulh. H. G. McIntyre. 1981. 18.00x (ISBN 0-389-20182-0). B&N.

Theatre of Jean-Paul Sartre. Dorothy K. McCall. LC 74-91659. 1969. 20.00x (ISBN 0-231-03180-7); pap. 6.00 (ISBN 0-231-08657-1). Columbia U Pr.

Theatre of Love: A Collection of Novels, 1759. Ed. by Michael F. Shugrue. (Flowering of the Novel, 1740-1775 Ser: Vol. 52). 1974. lib. bdg. 50.00 (ISBN 0-8240-1151-1). Garland Pub.

Theatre of Mixed Means. Richard Kostelanetz. 1978. pap. 15.00 (ISBN 0-932360-06-8). RK Edns.

Theatre of the Absurd. Martin Esslin. LC 61-13814. 1969. pap. 2.95 (ISBN 0-385-08969-4, A279, Anch). Doubleday.

Theatre of the Absurd. rev. ed. Martin Esslin. LC 72-94410. 1973. Repr. of 1961 ed. 12.95 (ISBN 0-87951-005-6). Overlook Pr.

Theatre of the Mind. Ed. by George Soule. (P-H Series in English Literature). 640p. 1974. pap. text ed. 13.95 (ISBN 0-13-913020-9). P-H.

Theatre Perspectives One: Asian Theatre. Ed. by James R. Brandon. 198p. 1980. 10.00. Am Theatre Assoc.

Theatre Profiles Four. (Illus.). 12.95 o.p. (ISBN 0-686-61274-4, Pub. by Theatre Comm). Pub Ctr Cult Res.

Theatre Profiles Four: A Resource Book on Nonprofit Professional Theatres in the United States. rev. ed. Ed. by David J. Skal & Michael Finnegan. (Illus.). 288p. 1979. pap. 12.95 (ISBN 0-930452-01-1, Pub. by Theatre Comm). Pub Ctr Cult Res.

Theatre Profiles-Four: Resource Book of Nonprofit Professional Theatres in the United States. Ed. by David J. Skal & Michael Finnegan. (Illus.). 276p. (Orig.). 1980. pap. 12.95x (ISBN 0-930452-07-0, Pub. by Theatre Comm). Pub Ctr Cult Res.

Theatre Profiles-Three: Resource Book of Nonprofit Professional Theatres in the United States. Ed. by Marsue Cumming & Arli Epton. (Illus., Orig.). 1978. pap. 9.95x (ISBN 0-930452-02-X, Pub. by Theatre Comm). Pub Ctr Cult Res.

Theatre Props. Motley. LC 75-6786. 1976. 12.50x (ISBN 0-910482-66-7). Drama Bk.

Theatre Royal Brighton. Anthony Dale. 180p. 1980. 25.00 (ISBN 0-85362-185-3). Routledge & Kegan.

Theatre Street. Tamara Karsavina. LC 79-7771. (Dance Ser.). (Illus.). 1980. Repr. of 1950 ed. lib. bdg. 21.00x (ISBN 0-8369-9298-9). Arno.

Theatre Student-Diary of Producing a Play. Peter Kline. (Theatre Student Ser.). (Illus.). 140p. 1981. lib. bdg. 12.50 (ISBN 0-8239-0523-3). Rosen Pr.

Theatre Student: Learning Scenes. Gerald L. Ratliff. (Theatre Student Ser.). (Illus.). 140p. 1981. lib. bdg. 12.50 (ISBN 0-8239-0531-4). Rosen Pr.

Theatre: The Rediscovery of Style. Michel Saint-Denis. LC 60-10492. 1968. pap. 4.25 (ISBN 0-87830-523-8, 23). Theatre Arts.

Theatre World: Vol. 36, 1979-80. John Willis. Ed. by Brandt Aymar. (Illus.). 288p. 1981. 18.95 (ISBN 0-517-54264-1). Crown.

Theatres & Auditoriums. R. Aloi. (Illus.). 1972. 50.00 (ISBN 0-685-30575-9). Heinman.

Theatres for Literature. Marion Kleinau & Janet McHughes. LC 79-24492. 1980. pap. 11.50 (ISBN 0-88284-096-7). Alfred Pub.

Theatrical, Composition of the Major English Romantic Poets. Joan M. Baum. (Salzburg Studies in Poetic Drama: No. 57). 1980. pap. text ed. 25.00x (ISBN 0-391-02187-7). Humanities.

Theatrical Costume: A Guide to Information Sources. Ed. by Jackson Kesler. LC 79-22881. (Performing Arts Information Guide Ser.: Vol. 6). 1979. 30.00 (ISBN 0-8103-1455-X). Gale.

Theatrical Direction. David Welker. 1971. text ed. 17.95 (ISBN 0-205-03220-6, 4832205). Allyn.

Theatrical Event: A "Mythos," a Vocabulary, a Perspective. David Cole. LC 74-21922. (Illus.). 1975. 15.00x (ISBN 0-8195-4078-1, Pub. by Wesleyan U Pr); pap. 5.95 (ISBN 0-8195-6047-2). Columbia U Pr.

Theatrical Evolution: 1776-1976. Kenneth Spritz. LC 76-9774. (Illus.). 120p. 1976. 10.00 (ISBN 0-89062-021-0, Pub. by Hudson River Mus); pap. 6.95 (ISBN 0-89062-027-X). Pub Ctr Cult Res.

Theatrical Manager in Britain & America: Players of a Perilous Game. Ed. by Joseph W. Donohue, Jr. LC 72-154992. (Illus.). 1971. 14.50x (ISBN 0-691-06188-2). Princeton U Pr.

Theatrical Performances in the Ancient World: Hellenistic & Early Roman Theatre. Bruno Gentili. (London Studies in Classical Philology: No. 2). 1978. pap. text ed. 17.25x (ISBN 0-391-01164-2). Humanities.

Theatrical Set Design: The Basic Techniques. David Welker. 1969. text ed. 13.95x o.p. (ISBN 0-205-02222-7, 4822226). Allyn.

Theatrical Set Design: The Basic Techniques. 2nd ed. David Welker. 1979. text ed. 19.95 (ISBN 0-205-06451-5). Allyn.

Theban Mysteries. Amanda Cross. 1979. pap. 1.75 (ISBN 0-380-45021-6, 45021). Avon.

Thebes of the Pharaohs. C. F. Nims. 1965. 19.95 o.p. (ISBN 0-236-31027-5, Pub. by Paul Elek). Merrimack Bk Serv.

Thee, Patience. Lois M. Parker. Ed. by Bobbie J. Van Dolson. LC 74-78021. (Illus.). (gr. 4-7). 1974. pap. 4.50 (ISBN 0-8280-0061-1). Review & Herald.

Theft of a Heart, No. 67. Barbara Cartland. 1978. 1.50 o.s.i. (ISBN 0-515-04650-7). Jove Pubns.

Theios Aner in Hellenistic-Judaism: A Critique of the Use of This Category in New Testament Christology. Carl R. Holladay. LC 77-20712. (Society of Biblical Literature. Dissertation Ser.: No. 40). 1977. pap. 7.50 (ISBN 0-89130-205-0, 060140). Scholars Pr Ca.

Their Finest Hour. Charles Ludwig. LC 74-82112. (Illus.). 128p. (Orig.). 1975. pap. 1.95 o.p. (ISBN 0-912692-45-6). Cook.

Their Last Lap at Indy: A Book of Tributes. DeNonie Barber. (Illus.). 1980. 8.95 (ISBN 0-916620-49-2). Portals Pr.

Their Search for God: Ways of Worship in the Orient. Florence M. Fitch. LC 47-11705. (Illus.). (gr. 7-12). 1947. PLB 7.92 o.p. (ISBN 0-688-51599-1). Lothrop.

Their Sister's Keepers: Women's Prison Reform in America, 1830-1930. Estelle B. Freedman. LC 80-24918. (Women & Culture Ser.). 256p. 1981. text ed. 18.50 (ISBN 0-472-10008-4). U of Mich Pr.

Their Universe: A Look into Children's Hearts & Minds. Arlene Uslander et al. LC 72-6164. 1973. 6.95 o.p. (ISBN 0-440-08684-1). Delacorte.

Theism. John S. Mill. Ed. by Richard Taylor. 1957. pap. 2.25 o.p. (ISBN 0-672-60238-5, LLA64). Bobbs.

Theism in Medieval India: London, 1921. Joseph E. Carpenter. LC 78-74266. (Oriental Religions Ser.: Vol. 2). 564p. 1980. lib. bdg. 60.50 (ISBN 0-8240-3901-7). Garland Pub.

Theist & Atheist: A Typology of Non-Belief. Thomas Molnar. 1979. text ed. 33.50x (ISBN 90-279-7788-7). Mouton.

Theistic Evolution. Bert Thompson. pap. 5.50 (ISBN 0-89315-300-1). Lambert Bk.

Theistic Faith for Our Time: An Introduction to the Process Philosophies of Royce & Whitehead. George D Straton. LC 78-65429. 1978. pap. text ed. 11.25 (ISBN 0-8191-0661-5). U Pr of Amer.

Thelwell Goes West. Norman Thelwell. (Illus.). 1975. 4.95 o.p. (ISBN 0-87690-189-5). Dutton.

Thelwell's Horse Box: Angel on Horseback, Leg at Each Corner, Riding Academy, & Thelwell Country. Norman Thelwell. (Illus.). 1971. 8.95 o.p. (ISBN 0-525-21580-8). Dutton.

Thelwell's Riding Academy. Norman Thelwell. (Illus.). 1965. 4.95 o.p. (ISBN 0-525-21593-X). Dutton.

Them. Joyce C. Oates. LC 74-89660. 1969. 10.95 (ISBN 0-8149-0668-0). Vanguard.

Them. 256p. (Orig.). 1981. pap. 2.95 (ISBN 0-553-13650-X). Bantam.

Them & Us: Struggles of a Rank-&-File Union. James J. Matles & James Higgins. LC 73-19656. 324p. 1974. 6.95 o.p. (ISBN 0-13-913079-9). P-H.

Them Children: A Study in Language Learning. Martha C. Ward. Ed. by George Spindler & Louise Spindler. (Case Studies in Education & Culture). 112p. pap. text ed. 6.95x (ISBN 0-8290-0323-1). Irvington.

Them Was the Days: An American Saga of the '70's. Martha F. McKeown. LC 50-7450. (Illus.). 1961. pap. 2.95 (ISBN 0-8032-5131-9, BB 117, Bison). U of Nebr Pr.

Thematic & Topical Stamp Collecting. A. J. Branston. (Illus.). 192p. 1980. 24.00 (ISBN 0-7134-1974-1, Pub. by Batsford England). David & Charles.

Thematic, Bibliographical & Critical Catalogue of the Works of Luigi Boccherini. Ed. by Yves Gerard. Tr. by Andreas Mayor. 1969. 74.00x (ISBN 0-19-711616-7). Oxford U Pr.

Thematic Cartography. P. Muehrcke. LC 72-77214. (CCG Resource Papers Ser.: No. 19). (Illus.). 1972. pap. text ed. 4.00 (ISBN 0-89291-066-6). Assn Am Geographers.

Thematic Catalog of a Manuscript Collection of Eighteenth-Century Italian Instrumental Music in the University of California, Berkeley, Music Library. Vincent Duckles & Minnie Elmer. 1963. 25.00x (ISBN 0-520-00361-6). U of Cal Pr.

Thematic Units in Teaching English & the Humanities. 2nd ed. Ed. by Sylvia Spann & Mary B. Culp. (Orig.). (gr. 6-12). 1980. pap. text ed. 6.00 (ISBN 0-8141-5376-3). NCTE.

Theme & Form: An Introduction to Literature. 4th ed. Ed. by Monroe C. Beardsley et al. 704p. 1975. text ed. 17.95 (ISBN 0-13-912972-3). P-H.

Theme & Paragraph. Phillip Burnham & Richard Lederer. Orig. Title: Basic Composition. (Illus.). 1976. pap. text ed. 3.50x (ISBN 0-88334-078-X). Ind Sch Pr.

Theme & Rhetoric. James B. Hogins & Robert E. Yarber. LC 76-28344. 1977. pap. text ed. 8.95 (ISBN 0-574-22025-9, 13-5025); instr's guide avail. (ISBN 0-574-22026-7, 13-5026). SRA.

Theme & Variations: A Behavior Therapy Casebook. Joseph Wolpe. 200p. 1976. text ed. 21.00 (ISBN 0-08-020422-8); pap. text ed. 12.75 (ISBN 0-08-020421-X). Pergamon.

Theme & Variations: An Autobiography. Bruno Walter. Tr. by James A. Galston from Ger. LC 80-25558. (Illus.). xi, 344p. 1981. Repr. of 1946 ed. lib. bdg. 35.00x (ISBN 0-313-22635-0, WATV). Greenwood.

Theme et Variations. M. P. Hagiwara & F. De Rocher. 592p. 1980. text ed. 16.95 (ISBN 0-471-05609-X); tchrs.' ed. avail. (ISBN 0-471-05612-X); wkbk. avail. (ISBN 0-471-05607-3); transcript avail. (ISBN 0-471-05613-8). Wiley.

Theme et variations: A Practical Introduction to French. Michio P. Hagiwara & Francoise De Rocher. LC 76-43036. 1977. text ed. 17.95x (ISBN 0-471-33880-X); wkbk. 6.50 (ISBN 0-471-33881-8); tchr's manual avail. (ISBN 0-471-02475-9); tapes avail. (ISBN 0-471-02476-7). Wiley.

Theme in English Expository Discourse. rev. 2nd ed. Linda K. Jones. LC 78-100090. (Edward Sapir Monograph Series in Language, Culture, & Cognition: No. 2). xiv, 241p. 1980. pap. 8.00x (ISBN 0-933104-10-3). Jupiter Pr.

Theme of the Pentateuch. David J. Clines. (JSOT Supplement Ser.: No. 10). 152p. 1978. text ed. 29.95x (ISBN 0-905774-14-0, Pub. by JSOT Pr England); pap. text ed. 16.95x (ISBN 0-905774-15-9, Pub. by JSOT Pr England). Eisenbrauns.

Theme on a Pipedream. F. H. Sasse. 7.35 (ISBN 0-85131-027-3, Dist. by Sporting Book Center). J A Allen.

Themes & Conventions of Elizabethan Tragedy. Muriel C. Bradbrook. 1952-1960. 34.50 (ISBN 0-521-04302-6); pap. 10.95 (ISBN 0-521-09108-X, 108). Cambridge U Pr.

Themes & Conventions of Elizabethan Tragedy. 2nd ed. Muriel C. Bradbrook. (History of Elizabethan Drama Ser.). 270p. 1980. 44.50 (ISBN 0-521-22770-4); pap. 12.95 (ISBN 0-521-29695-1). Cambridge U Pr.

Themes & Images in the Medieval English Religious Lyric. Douglas Gray. (Illus.). 1972. 23.00x (ISBN 0-7100-7253-8). Routledge & Kegan..

Themes from the Minor Prophets. David A. Hubbard. LC 74-17861. 1978. pap. 2.25 (ISBN 0-8307-0498-1, S323-1-09). Regal.

Themes in Geographic Thought. Brian P. Holly & Milton E. Harvey. 224p. 1980. write for info. St Martin.

Themes in the Christian History of Central Africa. Ed. by T. O. Ranger & John Weller. 1975. 27.50x (ISBN 0-520-02536-9). U of Cal Pr.

Themes in U.S. History. 2nd ed. J. Wickens. 1973. pap. 7.95x (ISBN 0-02-478960-7, 47896). Macmillan.

Themes of Elizabeth Gaskell. Enid L. Duthie. 217p. 1980. 29.50x (ISBN 0-8476-6224-1). Rowman.

Themes of Indigenous Acculturation in Northwest Mexico. Ed. by Thomas B. Hinton & Phil C. Weigand. (Anthropological Papers: No. 38). 1981. pap. text ed. 7.95x (ISBN 0-8165-0324-9). U of Ariz Pr.

Themes of Islamic Civilization. Ed. by John A. Williams. 1971. 22.75x (ISBN 0-520-01685-8). U of Cal Pr.

Themes of Magic in Nineteenth Century French Fiction. Emile Cailliet. (Studies in Comparative Literature: No. 2). 228p. Repr. of 1932 ed. lib. bdg. 16.00x (ISBN 0-87991-501-3). Porcupine Pr.

Themis. Jane Harrison. (Illus.). 1963. pap. 17.95 (ISBN 0-686-23502-9, Merlin Pr). Carrier Pigeon.

Then Again, Maybe I Won't. Judy Blume. LC 77-156548. (gr. 5-7). 1971. 8.95 (ISBN 0-87888-035-6). Bradbury Pr.

Then Am I Strong. Francena H. Arnold. 1969. pap. 2.50 (ISBN 0-8024-0060-4). Moody.

Then & Now. Ed. by Paul Hodges. 1979. 10.95 (ISBN 0-89002-153-8); pap. 3.50 (ISBN 0-89002-152-X). Northwoods Pr.

Then Comes the Joy. Mary V. Parrish. LC 76-44383. 1977. pap. 3.75 o.p. (ISBN 0-687-41439-3). Abingdon.

Then We Shall Be Gods. Rodolfo Benavides. (Living Path Ser: No. 3). 1975. pap. 6.50 (ISBN 0-914732-03-X). Bro Life Bks.

Thence Round Cape Horn. Robert E. Johnson. LC 79-6111. (Navies & Men Ser.). (Illus.). 1980. Repr. of 1963 ed. lib. bdg. 25.00x (ISBN 0-405-13040-6). Arno.

Theo Van Doesburg, Propagandist & Practitioner of the Avant-Garde: Belletristic Activity in Holland, Germany & France, 1909-1923. Hannah Hedrick. (Studies in Fine Arts: the Avant-Garde: No. 5). 1980. 23.95x (ISBN 0-8357-1060-2). Univ Microfilms.

Theodess Rothke: An Introduction to the Poetry. Karl Malkoff. LC 66-23967. 1971. pap. 6.00x (ISBN 0-231-08650-4). Columbia U Pr.

Theodor Boveri: The Life & Work of a Great Biologist, 1862-1915. Fritz Baltzer. Tr. by Dorothea Rudnick. (Illus.). 1967. 19.00x (ISBN 0-520-00074-9). U of Cal Pr.

Theodor Storm. Arthur T. Alt. (World Authors Ser.: Germany: No. 252). 1971. lib. bdg. 10.95 (ISBN 0-8057-2865-1). Twayne.

Theodora. Caroline Arnett. 1977. pap. 1.50 o.p. (ISBN 0-449-23347-2, Crest). Fawcett.

Theodora De Croix & the Northern Frontier of New Spain 1776-1783. Ed. by Alfred B. Thomas. (American Exploration & Travel Ser.: No. 5). 1968. Repr. of 1941 ed. 13.95 (ISBN 0-8061-0093-1). U of Okla Pr.

Theodore & the Talking Mushroom. Leo Lionni. (Illus.). (gr. k-3). 1971. PLB 6.99 o.s.i. (ISBN 0-394-92312-X). Pantheon.

Theodore Beza's Doctrine of Predestination. John Bray. (Bibliotheca Humanistica & Reformatorica Ser.: No. 12). 1975. text ed. 38.50x o.p. (ISBN 90-6004-334-0). Humanities.

Theodore Dreiser. Philip L. Gerber. (U. S. Authors Ser.: No. 52). 1963. lib. bdg. 9.95 (ISBN 0-8057-0212-1). Twayne.

Theodore Dreiser. James Lundquist. LC 73-84600. (Modern Literature Ser.). 150p. 1974. 10.95 (ISBN 0-8044-2563-9). Ungar.

Theodore Francis Green: The Rhode Island Years, 1906-1936. Erwin L. Levine. LC 63-18096. (Illus.). 222p. 1963. 8.50 (ISBN 0-87057-077-3, Pub. by Brown U Pr). Univ Pr of New England.

Theodore Francis Green: The Washington Years, 1937-1960. Erwin L. Levine. LC 73-127366. (Illus.). 179p. 1971. 8.50 (ISBN 0-87057-126-5, Pub. by Brown U Pr). Univ Pr of New England.

Theodore Parker: American Transcendentalist: A Critical Essay & a Collection of His Writings. Robert E. Collins. LC 73-9593. 1973. 10.00 (ISBN 0-8108-0641-X). Scarecrow.

Theodore Roethke. George Wolff. (United States Authors Ser.: No. 390). 1981. lib. bdg. 9.95 (ISBN 0-8057-7323-1). Twayne.

Theodore Roethke: Poetry of the Earth, Poet of the Spirit. Lynn Ross-Bryant. (National University Publications, Literary Criticism Ser.). 1981. 15.00 (ISBN 0-8046-9270-X). Kennikat.

Theodore Roosevelt. David H. Burton. (World Leaders Ser). 1973. lib. bdg. 9.95 (ISBN 0-8057-3709-X). Twayne.

Theodore Roosevelt. Aloysius A. Norton. (United States Authors Ser.). 1980. lib. bdg. 8.95 (ISBN 0-8057-7309-6). Twayne.

Theodore Roosevelt Among the Humorists: W. D. Howells, Mark Twain, & Mr. Dooley. William M. Gibson. LC 79-17592. (John C. Hodges Lecture Ser.). 1980. 7.50x (ISBN 0-87049-263-2). U of Tenn Pr.

Theodore Roosevelt: An Initial Biography. Genevieve Foster. (Illus.). (gr. 5-7). 1954. write for info. (ISBN 0-684-12690-7, ScribJ). Scribner.

Theodore Roosevelt & the Idea of Race. Thomas G. Dyer. 198p. 1980. 14.95 (ISBN 0-8071-0658-5). La State U Pr.

Theodore Roosevelt & the Rise of America to World Power. Howard K. Beale. 1962. pap. 1.50 o.s.i. (ISBN 0-02-030380-7, Collier). Macmillan.

Theodore Roosevelt: The Story Behind the Scenery. Henry A. Schoch. Ed. by Gweneth R. DenDooven. LC 74-77575. (Illus.). 1974. 7.95 (ISBN 0-916122-38-7); pap. 2.50 (ISBN 0-916122-13-1). K C Pubns.

Theodore Roosevelt, the Strenuous Life. John A. Garraty. LC 67-17820. (American Heritage Junior Library). (Illus.). 153p. (gr. 5 up). 1967. 9.95 (ISBN 0-06-021931-9, Dist. by Har-Row); PLB 12.89 o.p. (ISBN 0-06-021932-7). Am Heritage.

Theodore Spencer: Selected Essays. Ed. by A. C. Purves. 1967. 22.00 (ISBN 0-8135-0539-9). Rutgers U Pr.

Theodore Sturgeon. Lahna Diskin. (Starmont Reader's Guide Ser.: No. 7). 80p. 1981. Repr. lib. bdg. 9.95x (ISBN 0-89370-038-X). Borgo Pr.

Theodore Thomas: A Musical Autobiography. 2nd ed. Ed. by George P. Upton. LC 64-18990. (Music Reprint Ser). 1964. Repr. of 1905 ed. lib. bdg. 35.00 (ISBN 0-306-70904-X). Da Capo.

Theodore Van Doesburg. Joost Baljeu. LC 74-7400. (Illus.). 208p. 1975. 15.95 o.s.i. (ISBN 0-02-506440-1, 50644). Macmillan.

Theodosia. Katherine Talbot. (Orig.). 1980. pap. 1.75 (ISBN 0-446-94142-5). Warner Bks.

Theogony. Hesiod. Tr. by Norman O. Brown. LC 53-4359. 1953. pap. 2.50 (ISBN 0-672-60202-4, LLA36). Bobbs.

Theologial Reflections. Henry Stob. 200p. (Orig.). 1981. pap. 11.95 (ISBN 0-8028-1881-1). Eerdmans.

Theologians & Catechists in Dialogue: The Albany Forum. Ed. by Brennan Hill & Mary R. Newland. 64p. (Orig.). 1977. pap. 2.25 (ISBN 0-697-01671-4). Wm C Brown.

Theologians of Our Time. Ed. by A. W. Hastings & E. Hastings. LC 66-73626. 224p. Repr. of 1966 ed. pap. text ed. 4.95 (ISBN 0-567-22301-9). Attic Pr.

Theological Battleground in Asia & Africa: The Issues Facing the Churches & the Efforts to Overcome Western Divisions. G. C. Oosthuizen. 1116p. 1972. text ed. 28.50x (ISBN 0-391-00230-9). Humanities.

Theological Development of Edwards Amasa Park: Last of the "Consistent Calvinists". Anthony C. Cecil, Jr. LC 74-83338. (American Academy of Religion. Dissertation Ser.). 1974. pap. 9.00 (ISBN 0-88420-118-X, 010101). Scholars Pr Ca.

Theological Dictionary of the Old Testament, 3 vols. Ed. by G. Johannes Botterweck & Helmer Ringgren. Incl. Vol. I. 21.00 (ISBN 0-8028-2325-4); Vol. II. 21.00 (ISBN 0-8028-2326-2); Vol. III. 21.00 (ISBN 0-8028-2327-0). 1978. Eerdmans.

Theological Dictionary of the Old Testament, Vol. 4. Ed. by G. Johannes Botterweck & Helmer Ringgren. 560p. 1981. 21.00 (ISBN 0-8028-2328-9). Eerdmans.

Theological Enterprise. Vernone M. Sparkes. LC 73-89842. 1969. pap. 6.50 o.p. (ISBN 0-8309-0020-9). Herald Hse.

Theological Essays. Frederick D. Maurice. 1980. Repr. of 1891 ed. cancelled (ISBN 0-87921-048-6). Attic Pr.

Theological Ethics, 3 vols. Helmut Thieliche. Incl. Foundations. Vol. I. pap. 10.95 (ISBN 0-8028-1791-2); Politics. Vol. II. pap. 10.95 (ISBN 0-8028-1792-0); Vol. III. Sex. pap. 6.95 (ISBN 0-8028-1794-7). LC 78-31858. Set. 29.50 (ISBN 0-8028-1795-5). Eerdmans.

Theological Investigations, Vols. 1-13. Karl Rahner. Incl. Vol. 1. 12.95 (ISBN 0-8164-1154-9); Vol. 2. 12.95 (ISBN 0-8164-1190-5); Vol. 3. 12.95 (ISBN 0-8164-1155-7); Vol. 4. 12.95 (ISBN 0-8164-1156-5); Vol. 5. 14.95 (ISBN 0-8164-1191-3); Vol. 6. 12.95 (ISBN 0-8164-1157-3); Vol. 7. 13.95 (ISBN 0-8164-1126-3); Vol. 8. 12.95 (ISBN 0-8164-1127-1); Vol. 9. 10.95 (ISBN 0-8164-1128-X); Vol. 10. 14.95 (ISBN 0-8164-1129-8); Vol. 11. 12.95 (ISBN 0-8164-1143-3); Vol. 12. 10.95 (ISBN 0-8164-1179-4); Vol. 13. 12.95 (ISBN 0-8164-1193-X). Crossroad NY.

Theological Investigations, Vol 14. Karl Rahner. 12.95 (ISBN 0-8164-1203-0). Crossroad NY.

Theological Investigations XVI: Experience of the Spirit: Source of Theology. Karl Rahner. 1979. 14.95 (ISBN 0-8164-0417-8). Crossroad NY.

Theological Method & Imagination. Julian N. Hartt. 1977. 12.95 (ISBN 0-8164-0335-X). Crossroad NY.

Theological Method of Karl Rahner. Anne Carr. LC 76-51639. (American Academy of Religion. Dissertation Ser.). 1977. pap. 7.50 (ISBN 0-89130-129-1, 010119). Scholars Pr Ca.

Theological Outlines. Francis J. Hall. 1895. 7.95 o.p. (ISBN 0-8192-1037-4). Morehouse.

Theological Papers of John Henry Newman: On Biblical Inspiration & on Infallibility. John H. Newman. Ed. by J. Derek Holmes. 1979. text ed. 19.95x (ISBN 0-19-920081-5). Oxford U Pr.

Theological Papers of John Henry Newman: On Faith & Certainty, Vol. 1. John H. Newman. Ed. by Derek Holmes. 1976. 19.95x (ISBN 0-19-920071-8). Oxford U Pr.

Theological Self-Understanding of the Catholic Charismatic Movement. James F. Breckenridge. LC 79-6198. 154p. 1980. pap. text ed. 8.00 (ISBN 0-8191-1006-X). U Pr of Amer.

Theological Wordbook of the Old Testament. Ed. by R. Laird Harris et al. 1800p. 1980. text ed. 29.95 (ISBN 0-8024-8631-2). Moody.

Theologico-Political Treatise: Political Treatise. Benedict Spinoza. Tr. by R. H. Elwes. pap. text ed. 4.50 (ISBN 0-486-20249-6). Dover.

Theologies & Evil. John S. Feinberg. LC 79-66474. 1979. text ed. 14.50 (ISBN 0-8191-0838-3); pap. text ed. 9.00 (ISBN 0-8191-0839-1). U Pr of Amer.

Theology - the Quintessence of Science. William B. Turner. LC 80-82649. 1981. 14.95 (ISBN 0-8022-2375-3). Philos Lib.

Theology After Freud: An Interpretive Inquiry. Peter Homans. LC 76-84162. 1970. 18.50x (ISBN 0-672-51245-9); pap. text ed. 5.95x (ISBN 0-672-60802-2). Irvington.

Theology: An Orthodox Standpoint. Apostolos Makrakis. Ed. by Orthodox Christian Educational Society. Tr. by Denver Cummings from Hellenic. (Logos & Holy Spirit in the Unity of Christian Thought Ser.: Vol. 4). 216p. 1977. pap. 3.50x (ISBN 0-938366-03-3). Orthodox Chr.

Theology & Christian Ethics. James M. Gustafson. LC 74-510. 320p. 1974. 9.95 (ISBN 0-8298-0270-3). Pilgrim NY.

Theology & Ethics in Paul. Victor P. Furnish. LC 68-17445. 1978. pap. 8.95 (ISBN 0-687-41499-7). Abingdon.

Theology & Political Society. Charles Davis. LC 80-40014. 180p. 1980. 19.95 (ISBN 0-521-22538-8). Cambridge U Pr.

Theology & Revolution in the Scottish Reformation. Richard L. Greaves. 336p. 1980. pap. 10.95 (ISBN 0-8028-1847-1, Chr Univ Pr). Eerdmans.

Theology & the Church. Dumitru Staniloae. Tr. by Robert Barry from Romanian. LC 80-19313. 240p. 1980. pap. 6.95 (ISBN 0-913836-69-9). St Vladimirs.

Theology & the Church. Dumitru Staniloae. Tr. by Robert Barringer from Romanian. LC 80-19313. 240p. (Orig.). 1980. pap. 6.95 (ISBN 0-913836-69-9, BS695.57 230.19498). St Martin.

Theology As Comedy: Critical & Theoretical Implications. George Aichele, Jr. LC 80-5384. 161p. 1980. lib. bdg. 15.75 (ISBN 0-8191-1082-5); pap. text ed. 8.75 (ISBN 0-8191-1083-3). U Pr of Amer.

Theology Encounters Revolution. J. Andrew Kirk. LC 80-7471. 192p. (Orig.). 1980. pap. 4.95 (ISBN 0-87784-468-2). Inter-Varsity.

Theology, Exegesis, & Proclamation. Ed. by Roland Murphy. LC 74-168652. (Concilium Ser.: Religion in the Seventies: Vol. 70). 1971. pap. 4.95 (ISBN 0-8164-2526-4). Crossroad NY.

Theology for the Nineteen-Eighties. John Carmody. LC 80-19349. 1980. pap. write for info. (ISBN 0-664-24345-2). Westminster.

Theology for the Social Gospel. Walter Rauschenbusch. (Series E). 1978. pap. 6.95 (ISBN 0-687-41580-2). Abingdon.

Theology in America: The Major Protestant Voices from Puritanism to Neo-Orthodoxy. Ed. by Sydney E. Ahlstrom. LC 67-21401. 1967. pap. 13.50 (ISBN 0-672-60118-4, AHS73). Bobbs.

Theology of Christian Education. Lawrence O. Richards. 320p. 1975. 12.95 (ISBN 0-310-31940-4). Zondervan.

Theology of Christian Marriage. Walter Kasper. 112p. 1980. 7.95 (ISBN 0-8164-0209-4). Crossroad NY.

Theology of Christian Mystical Experience. Roy C. LePak. 1977. pap. text ed. 12.00x (ISBN 0-8191-0148-6). U Pr of Amer.

Theology of Church & Ministry. Franklin M. Segler. LC 60-14146. 1960. bds. 7.50 (ISBN 0-8054-2506-3). Broadman.

Theology of Church Growth. George Peters. 368p. 1981. pap. 8.95 (ISBN 0-310-43101-8, 11285P). Zondervan.

Theology of Church Leadership. Lawrence O. Richards & Clyde Hoeldtke. (Illus.). 352p. 1980. 12.95 (ISBN 0-310-31960-9). Zondervan.

Theology of Community. John P. Schanz. 1977. pap. text ed. 11.25x (ISBN 0-8191-0177-X). U Pr of Amer.

Theology of Culture. Paul Tillich. Ed. by Robert C. Kimball. 1964. pap. 5.95 (ISBN 0-19-500711-5, GB). Oxford U Pr.

Theology of Exile: Judgment-Deliverance in Jeremiah & Ezekiel. Thomas M. Raitt. LC 76-62610. 288p. 1977. 15.95 (ISBN 0-8006-0497-0, 1-497). Fortress.

Theology of John. W. Robert Cook. 1979. 10.95 (ISBN 0-8024-8629-0). Moody.

Theology of Jonathan Edwards: A Reappraisal. C. Cherry. 7.50 (ISBN 0-8446-1849-7). Peter Smith.

Theology of Joy. Johannes B. Metz. (Concilium Ser.: Religion in the Seventies: Vol. 95). pap. 4.95 (ISBN 0-8164-2579-5). Crossroad NY.

Theology of Post-Reformation Lutheranism: A Study of Theological Prolegomena. Robert D. Preus. LC 70-121877. 1970. 15.50 (ISBN 0-570-03211-3, 15-2110). Concordia.

Theology of Post-Reformation Lutheranism, Vol. 2. Robert D. Preus. 350p. 1972. 15.50 (ISBN 0-570-03226-1, 15-2123). Concordia.

Theology of Preaching: The Dynamics of the Gospel. Richard Lischer. (Preacher's Library). (Orig.). 1981. pap. 4.95 (ISBN 0-687-41570-5). Abingdon.

Theology of Q: Eschatology, Prophecy & Wisdom. Richard A. Edwards. LC 75-13042. 192p. 1975. 11.95 (ISBN 0-8006-0432-6, 1-432). Fortress.

Theology of Revelation. Gabriel Moran. 1968. pap. 3.95 (ISBN 0-8164-2567-1). Crossroad NY.

Theology of the Christian Word: A Study in History. Frederick E. Crowe. LC 78-51595. 1978. pap. 6.95 (ISBN 0-8091-2106-9). Paulist Pr.

Theology of the Crossroads in Contemporary Latin America: Missiology in Mainline Proestantism 1969-1974. O. E. Costas. (Orig.). 1976. pap. text ed. 27.50x (ISBN 90-6203-259-1). Humanities.

Theology of the Love of God. George Newlands. LC 80-22547. 224p. 1981. 12.50 (ISBN 0-8042-0726-7); pap. 6.95 (ISBN 0-8042-0727-5). John Knox.

Theology of the New Testament. 2nd ed. G. B. Stevens. (International Theological Library). 636p. Repr. of 1918 ed. text ed. 13.95x (ISBN 0-567-07215-0). Attic Pr.

Theology of the New Testament: Jesus & the Gospels, Vol I. Leonard Goppelt. Tr. by John E. Alsup. LC 80-28947. 316p. 1981. 15.95 (ISBN 0-8028-2384-X). Eerdmans.

Theology of the Old Testament. A. B. Davidson. (International Theological Library Ser.). 567p. Repr. of 1904 ed. text ed. 13.95x (ISBN 0-567-27206-0). Attic Pr.

Theology of the Old Testament. Gustave Oehler. 1978. 20.00 (ISBN 0-686-12952-0). Klock & Klock.

Theology of the Older Testament. J. Barton Payne. 1962. kivar 9.95 (ISBN 0-310-30721-X). Zondervan.

Theology of the Program of Restoration of Ezekiel Forty to Forty-Eight. Jon D. Levenson. LC 76-3769. (Harvard Semitic Museum, Monographs). 1976. 7.50 (ISBN 0-89130-105-4, 040010). Scholars Pr Ca.

Theology of the World. Johannes B. Metz. 1969. pap. 3.95 (ISBN 0-8164-2568-X). Crossroad NY.

Theology of Uncreated Energies of God. George S. Maloney. (Pere Marquette Lecture Ser.). 1978. 6.95 (ISBN 0-87462-516-5). Marquette.

Theology on Dover Beach. Nicholas Lash. LC 79-88760. (Orig.). 1979. pap. 9.95 (ISBN 0-8091-2241-3). Paulist Pr.

Theology Primer. John J. Davis. 128p. (Orig.). 1981. pap. 5.95 (ISBN 0-8010-2912-0). Baker Bk.

Theology to Live By. Herman A. Preus. 1977. pap. 7.95 (ISBN 0-570-03739-5, 12-2643). Concordia.

Theomatics: God's Best Kept Secret Revealed. Jerry Lucas & Del Washburn. LC 76-49958. (Illus.). 1977. 8.95 (ISBN 0-8128-2181-5); pap. 6.95 (ISBN 0-8128-6017-9). Stein & Day.

Theophile Gautier. Richard B. Grant. LC 75-4819. (World Authors Ser.: France: No. 362). 1975. lib. bdg. 10.95 (ISBN 0-8057-6213-2). Twayne.

Theophile Gautier. P. E. Tennant. (Athlone French Poets Ser). 150p. 1975. text ed. 20.00x (ISBN 0-485-14604-5, Athlone Pr); pap. text ed. 10.00x (ISBN 0-485-12204-9, Athlone Pr). Humanities.

Theophilus North. Thornton Wilder. 352p. 1981. pap. 3.95 (ISBN 0-380-00160-8, 53108, Bard). Avon.

Theophrastus & the Greek Physiological Psychology Before Aristotle. George Malcolm Stratton. 227p. 1964. Repr. of 1917 ed. text ed. 27.75x (ISBN 90-6031-042-X). Humanities.

Theophrastus Bombastus von Hohenheim Called Paracelsus. John M. Stillman. LC 79-8625. Repr. of 1920 ed. 25.00 (ISBN 0-404-18491-X). AMS Pr.

Theoreme de Picard-Borel. R. Nevanlinna. LC 73-14779. 179p. 1974. Repr. of 1970 ed. text ed. 9.95 (ISBN 0-8284-0272-8). Chelsea Pub.

Theoretical Advances in Behavior Genetics. Ed. by J. R. Royce & L. P. Mos. (NATO Advanced Study Institute Ser.). 722p. 1980. 75.00x (ISBN 90-286-0569-X). Sijthoff & Noordhoff.

Theoretical Analysis of Growth & Cycles. J. J. Paunio. (Illus.). 80p. 1974. 47.50 (ISBN 0-913314-38-2). Am Classical Coll Pr.

Theoretical & Applied Mechanics, Vol. 28. Ed. by Japan National Committee for Theoretical & Applied Mechanics. 579p. 1980. 89.50x (ISBN 0-86008-264-4, Pub. by Univ Tokyo Pr Japan). Intl Schol Bk Serv.

Theoretical & Computational Plasma Physics. 1978. pap. 43.00 (ISBN 92-0-130078-6, ISP474, IAEA). Unipub.

Theoretical & Experimental Bases of the Behavior Therapies. M. P. Feldman & A. Broadhurst. 459p. 1975. 63.50 (ISBN 0-471-25705-2). Wiley.

Theoretical & Practical Aspects of Uranium Geology. Royal Society of London et al. Ed. by S. H. Bowie & W. S. Fyfe. (Illus.). 1979. lib. bdg. 46.00x (ISBN 0-85403-106-5, Pub. by Royal Soc London). Scholium Intl.

Theoretical Approach to Preselection of Carcinogens & Chemical Carcinogenesis. Vello Veljkovic. 150p. 1981. 25.00 (ISBN 0-677-05490-4). Gordon.

Theoretical Approach to the Indian Economy. C. T. Kurien. (Asia Monographs,: No. 18). 1970. 4.00x o.p. (ISBN 0-210-22261-1). Asia.

Theoretical Approaches in Neurobiology. Ed. by Werner E. Reichardt & Tomaso Poggio. (Illus.). 208p. 1980. text ed. 20.00x (ISBN 0-262-18100-2). MIT Pr.

Theoretical Approaches to Non-Numerical Problem Solving: Proceedings. Systems Symposium - 4th - Case Western Reserve University, Institute of Technology. Ed. by R. B. Banerji & M. D. Mesarovic. LC 79-121996. (Lecture Notes in Operations Research & Mathematical Systems: Vol. 28). 1970. pap. 21.90 o.p. (ISBN 0-387-04900-2). Springer-Verlag.

Theoretical Aspects & the New Developments in Megneto-Optics. Ed. by J. T. Devreese. (NATO Advanced Study Institutes Ser.: B Physics: Vol. 60). 635p. 1981. 69.50 (ISBN 0-306-40555-5, Plenum Pr). Plenum Pub.

Theoretical Aspects of Mainly Low Dimensional Magnetic Systems. Hans C. Fogedby. (Lecture Notes in Physics Ser.: Vol. 131). 163p. 1981. pap. 12.00 (ISBN 0-387-10238-8). Springer Verlag.

Theoretical Aspects of Population Genetics. Motoo Kimura & Tomoko Ohta. LC 75-155963. (Monographs in Population Biology: No. 4). 1971. 16.50 o.p. (ISBN 0-691-08096-8); pap. 9.00 (ISBN 0-691-08098-4). Princeton U Pr.

Theoretical Chemistry. Committee for the Survey of Chemistry. 1966. pap. 3.00 (ISBN 0-309-01292-9). Natl Acad Pr.

Theoretical Chemistry: Advances & Perspectives, Vol. 5. Ed. by A. R. Katritzky & A. J. Boulton. LC 75-21963. 1980. 35.00 (ISBN 0-12-681905-X); lib ed. 45.50 (ISBN 0-12-681978-5); microfiche 24.50 (ISBN 0-12-681979-3). Acad Pr.

Theoretical Chemistry: Theory of Scattering-Papers in Honor of Henry Eyring, Vol. 6a. Ed. by Douglas Henderson. (Serial Publication). 1981. write for info. (ISBN 0-12-681906-8). Acad Pr.

Theoretical Chemistry: Theory of Scattering: Papers in Honor of Henry Eyring, Vol. 6B. Ed. by Douglas Henderson. (Serial Publications). 1981. price not set (ISBN 0-12-681907-6). Acad Pr.

Theoretical Criminology. 2nd ed. George B. Vold. 1979. 16.95x (ISBN 0-19-502530-X). Oxford U Pr.

Theoretical Developments in Marketing: Proceedings. Theory Conference, Phoenix, Arizona, February, 1980. Ed. by Charles W. Lamb, Jr. & Patrick M. Dunne. LC 80-12436. (Illus.). 269p. (Orig.). 1980. pap. text ed. 24.00 (ISBN 0-87757-138-4). Am Mktg.

Theoretical Elasticity. 2nd ed. Albert E. Green & Wolfgang Zerna. 1968. 55.00x (ISBN 0-19-853329-2). Oxford U Pr.

Theoretical Issues in Contrastive Linguistics. Ed. by Jacek Fisiak. (Current Issues in Linguistic Theory: Vol. 12). 1979. text ed. 54.25x (ISBN 0-391-01670-9, Pub. by Benjamins Holland). Humanities.

Theoretical Issues in Dakota Phonology & Morphology. Patricia A. Shaw. Ed. by Jorge Hankamer. LC 79-55856. (Outstanding Dissertations in Linguistics Ser.). 404p. 1980. lib. bdg. 44.00 (ISBN 0-8240-4562-9). Garland Pub.

Theoretical Issues in Reading Comprehension: Perspectives from Cognitive Psychology, Linguistics, Artificial Intelligence & Education. Ed. by Rand J. Spiro et al. LC 80-20716. 608p. 1980. text ed. 39.95 (ISBN 0-89859-036-1). L Erlbaum Assocs.

Theoretical Mechanics. Ted C. Bradbury. 656p. 1981. Repr. of 1968 ed. text ed. price not set (ISBN 0-89874-235-8). Krieger.

Theoretical Mechanics in SI Units: In SI Units, Vols. 1-2. 2nd ed. C. Plumpton & W. H. Tomkys. 1972. Vol. 1. pap. 8.55 (ISBN 0-08-016268-1); Vol. 2. pap. 9.25 (ISBN 0-08-016591-5). Pergamon.

Theoretical Methods in Sociology: Seven Essays. Ed. by Lee Freese. LC 79-3998. 1980. 19.95x (ISBN 0-8229-3402-7). U of Pittsburgh Pr.

Theoretical Models & Processes of Reading. rev., 2nd ed. Ed. by Harry Singer & Robert B. Ruddell. 1976. text ed. 25.00 (ISBN 0-87207-436-6); pap. text ed. 18.50 (ISBN 0-87207-432-3). Intl Reading.

Theoretical Numerical Analysis: An Introduction to Advanced Techniques. Peter Linz. LC 78-15178. (Pure & Applied Mathematics: Texts, Monographs & Tracts). 1979. 23.50 (ISBN 0-471-04561-6, Pub. by Wiley-Interscience). Wiley.

Theoretical Orientations in Creole Studies. Ed. by Albert Valdman & Arnold Highfield. LC 80-26273. 1980. lib ed 29.50 (ISBN 0-12-710160-8). Acad Pr.

Theoretical Perspectives on Urban Politics. W. D. Hawley & M. Lipsky. 1976. 18.95 (ISBN 0-13-913202-3). P-H.

Theoretical Physics. Alexander Kompaneyets. Tr. by MIR Publishers. (Illus.). 592p. 1975. text ed. 17.50x o.p. (ISBN 0-8464-0918-6). Beekman Pubs.

Theoretical Physics. 1963. 23.75 (ISBN 92-0-030263-7, IAEA). Unipub.

Theoretical Physics & Astrophysics. V. L. Ginzberg. Tr. by D. Ter Haar. (International Series in Natural Philosophy: Vol. 99). (Illus.). 1979. 75.00 (ISBN 0-08-023067-9); pap. 32.00 (ISBN 0-08-023066-0). Pergamon.

Theoretical Physics: Classical & Modern Views. George H. Duffey. LC 79-23794. 704p. 1980. Repr. of 1973 ed. lib. bdg. 27.50 (ISBN 0-89874-062-2). Krieger.

Theoretical Principles of Psychosomatic Medicine. I. T. Kurtsin. Tr. by N. Kaner from Rus. LC 75-5587. 257p. 1976. 53.95 (ISBN 0-470-51100-1). Halsted Pr.

Theoretical Problems of Typology & the Northern Eurasian Languages. Ed. by L. Dezso & P. Hajdu. 184p. 1970. text ed. 34.25x (ISBN 0-685-75720-X). Humanities.

Theoretical Soil Mechanics. R. B. Peck & Karl Terzaghi. 1943. 35.00 (ISBN 0-471-85305-4, Pub. by Wiley-Interscience). Wiley.

Theoretical Solid State Physics, 2 vols. W. Jones & N. H. March. Incl. Vol. 1. Perfect Lattices in Equilibrium. 107.95 (ISBN 0-471-44900-8); Vol. 2. Non-Equilibrium & Disorder. 92.00 (ISBN 0-471-44901-6). LC 70-165953. 1973 (Pub. by Wiley-Interscience). Wiley.

Theoretical Thinking in Sociology. 2nd ed. William L. Skidmore. LC 78-74540. (Illus.). 1979. 27.50 (ISBN 0-521-22663-5); pap. 9.95x (ISBN 0-521-29606-4). Cambridge U Pr.

Theorie De la Connaissance et Philosophie De la Parole Dans le Brahmanisme Classique. Madeleine Biardeau. (Le Monde D'outre-Mer Passe et Present, Etudes: No. 23). 1963. pap. 51.20x (ISBN 90-2796-178-6). Mouton.

Theorie der Konvexen Koerper. T. Bonnesen & W. Fenchel. LC 49-29452. (Ger). 9.95 (ISBN 0-8284-0054-7). Chelsea Pub.

Theorie Des Fonctions Algebriques De Deux Variables Independantes 2 Vols. in 1. Emile Picard & G. Simart. LC 67-31156. (Fr). 1971. 29.00 (ISBN 0-8284-0248-5): Chelsea Pub.

Theorie Generale Des Surfaces, 4 Vols. 2nd ed. Gaston Darboux. LC 67-16997. (Fr). 1968. Set. 75.00 (ISBN 0-8284-0216-7). Chelsea Pub.

Theories & Approaches to International Politics. 3rd ed. Patrick M Morgan. 302p. 1981. 24.95 (ISBN 0-87855-350-9); text ed. 24.95 (ISBN 0-686-68062-6); pap. 9.95 (ISBN 0-87855-791-1); pap. text ed. 9.95 (ISBN 0-686-68063-4). Transaction Bks.

Theories & Observation in Science. Ed. by Richard E. Gandy. vii, 184p. 1980. lib. bdg. 22.00 (ISBN 0-917930-39-8); pap. 7.50x (ISBN 0-917930-19-3). Ridgeview.

Theories & Observation in Science. Richard E. Grandy. (Central Issues in Philosophy Ser.). (Illus.). 224p. 1973. pap. 8.50 o.p. (ISBN 0-13-913392-5). P-H.

Theories & Systems of Psychology. 2nd ed. Robert W. Lundin. 1979. text ed. 15.95x (ISBN 0-669-01915-1). Heath.

Theories for Social Work with Groups. Robert W. Roberts & Helen Northen. LC 76-4967. 400p. 1976. 17.50x (ISBN 0-231-03885-2). Columbia U Pr.

Theories of Adolescence. 2nd ed. Rolfe Muuss. 9.00 (ISBN 0-8446-2635-X). Peter Smith.

Theories of Attitude Change. Chester A. Insko. (Century Psychology Ser.). (Illus.). 1980. Repr. of 1967 ed. text ed. 24.50x (ISBN 0-8290-0068-2). Irvington.

Theories of Authorship. Ed. by John Caughie. (B. F. I. Readers in Film Studies). (Illus.). 320p. 1981. 28.00 (ISBN 0-7100-0649-7); pap. 14.00 (ISBN 0-7100-0650-0). Routledge & Kegan.

Theories of Career Development. 2nd & rev. ed. Samuel H. Osipow et al. LC 68-15785. (Illus.). 1973. pap. 17.95 (ISBN 0-13-913442-5). P-H.

Theories of Child Development. 2nd ed. Alfred L. Baldwin. LC 80-24517. 675p. 1981. text ed. 22.95 (ISBN 0-471-04583-7). Wiley.

Theories of Comparative Politics: The Search for a Paradigm. Ronald H. Chilcote. 492p. (Orig.). 1981. lib. bdg. 30.00x (ISBN 0-89158-970-8); pap. 15.00x (ISBN 0-89158-971-6). Westview.

Theories of Development: Concepts & Applications. William C. Crain. (Illus.). 1980. text ed. 16.95 (ISBN 0-13-913566-9). P-H.

Theories of Deviance. 2nd ed. Ed. by Stuart H. Traub & Craig B. Little. LC 79-91105. 400p. 1980. pap. text ed. 9.95 (ISBN 0-87581-247-3). Peacock Pubs.

Theories of Differentiation. Max Hamburgh. LC 72-181848. (Contemporary Biology Ser). 181p. 1972. pap. text ed. 19.50 (ISBN 0-7131-2321-4). Univ Park.

Theories of Economic Growth. Ed. by Bert F. Hoselitz et al. LC 60-10898. 1965. pap. text ed. 5.95 (ISBN 0-02-915220-8). Free Pr.

Theories of Elastic Plates. V. Panc. (Mechanics of Surface Structures Ser.: No. 2). 736p. 1975. 80.00x (ISBN 90-286-0104-X). Sijthoff & Noordhoff.

Theories of Error in Indian Philosophy: An Analytical Study. Bijayananda Kar. 1980. text ed. cancelled o.p. (ISBN 0-391-01731-4). Humanities.

Theories of Ethics. Ed. by Philippa Foot. 1967. pap. 5.95x (ISBN 0-19-875005-6). Oxford U Pr.

Theories of History. Ed. by Patrick Gardiner. LC 58-6481. 1959. text ed. 16.95 (ISBN 0-02-911210-9). Free Pr.

Theories of Human Communication. Stephen W. Littlejohn. 1978. text ed. 15.95 (ISBN 0-675-08431-8). Merrill.

Theories of Human Development. Neal Salkind. (Orig.). 1980. pap. text ed. 13.95 (ISBN 0-442-25859-3). D Van Nostrand.

Theories of Illness: A World Survey. George P. Murdock. LC 80-5257. (Illus.). 160p. 1980. 9.95 (ISBN 0-8229-3428-0). U of Pittsburgh Pr.

Theories of Imperialism. Wolfgang J. Mommsen. Tr. by P. S. Falla. LC 80-5279. 156p. 1981. 9.95 (ISBN 0-394-50932-3). Random.

Theories of Knowledge: With a New Preface. Reginald F. O'Neill. 242p. 1980. Repr. of 1959 ed. text ed. 26.50x (ISBN 0-8290-0227-8); pap. text ed. 12.95x (ISBN 0-8290-0386-X). Irvington.

Theories of Landform Development. Ed. by W. N. Melhorn & R. C. Flemal. (Binghamton Symposia in Geomorphology: International Ser.: No. 6). (Illus.). 312p. 1980. text ed. 20.00x (ISBN 0-04-551039-3, 2507). Allen Unwin.

Theories of Learning. 5th ed. Gordon H. Bower & Ernest J. Hilgard. (Illus.). 640p. 1981. text ed. 20.95 (ISBN 0-13-914432-3). P-H.

Theories of Learning. 4th ed. Ernest R. Hilgard & Gordon H. Bower. 1975. text ed. 20.95x (ISBN 0-13-914457-9). P-H.

Theories of Learning: Traditional Perspectives - Contemporary Development. Leland C. Swenson. 1979. text ed. 19.95x (ISBN 0-534-00698-1). Wadsworth Pub.

Theories of Legitimacy in Imperial China: Discussions on "Legitimate Succession" Under the Jurchen-Chin Dynasty, 1115-1234. 1981. price not set o.p. U of Wash Pr.

Theories of Man & Culture. Elvin J. Hatch. Orig. Title: Main Theories of Man & Culture. 396p. 1973. 20.00x (ISBN 0-685-30374-8); pap. 10.00x (ISBN 0-231-03639-6). Columbia U Pr.

Theories of Mass Communication. 3rd ed. Melvin L. De Fleur & Sandra Ball-Rokeach. LC 74-112656. 1975. pap. 9.95x (ISBN 0-582-28017-6). Longman.

Theories of Neurosis. M. Gossop. (Illus.). 261p. 1981. 35.00 (ISBN 0-387-10370-8). Springer-Verlag.

Theories of Personality. 3rd ed. Calvin S. Hall & Gardner Lindzey. LC 77-26692. 1978. text ed. 23.95 (ISBN 0-471-34227-0); wkbk. 6.95 (ISBN 0-471-72926-4); test 1.00 (ISBN 0-471-03755-9). Wiley.

Theories of Personality. 2nd ed. Duane Schultz. 384p. 1981. text ed. 16.95 o.p. (ISBN 0-8185-0439-0). Brooks-Cole.

Theories of Personality. 2nd ed. Duane Schultz. LC 80-26414. 384p. 1981. text ed. 17.95 (ISBN 0-8185-0439-0). Brooks-Cole.

Theories of Personality: Primary Sources & Research. 2nd ed. Ed. by Gardner Lindzey et al. LC 72-6983. 512p. 1973. pap. text ed. 17.95x (ISBN 0-471-53901-5). Wiley.

Theories of Population from Raleigh to Arthur Young. James Bonar. LC 66-5245. Repr. of 1931 ed. 22.50x (ISBN 0-678-05149-6). Kelley.

Theories of Primitive Religion. Edward E. Evans-Pritchard. pap. 6.95x (ISBN 0-19-823131-8). Oxford U Pr.

Theories of Rain & Other Poems. Bill Zavatsky. LC 74-34537. 1975. 10.00 (ISBN 0-915342-08-1); pap. 4.00 (ISBN 0-915342-03-0). SUN.

Theories of Reading, Looking, & Listening. Ed. by Harry R. Garvin. LC 80-20475. (Bucknell Review Ser.). 192p. 1981. 12.00 (ISBN 0-8387-5007-9). Bucknell U Pr.

Theories of Scientific Method: The Renaissance Through the Nineteenth Century. Ralph M. Blake et al. Ed. by Edward H. Madden. LC 60-8577. 350p. 1966. pap. 2.95 (ISBN 0-295-74010-8, WP2). U of Wash Pr.

Theories of Social Casework. Ed. by Robert W. Roberts & Robert H. Nee. LC 70-123358. 1971. text ed. 15.00x (ISBN 0-226-72105-1). U of Chicago Pr.

Theories of Spectral Line Shape. R. G. Breene, Jr. LC 80-20664. 384p. 1981. 35.00 (ISBN 0-471-08361-5, Pub. by Wiley-Interscience). Wiley.

Theories of Talcott Parsons. Stephen P. Savage. LC 80-13828. 1980. write for info. (ISBN 0-312-79699-4). St Martin.

Theories of the Fable in the Eighteenth Century. Thomas Noel. 176p. 1975. 20.00x (ISBN 0-231-03858-5). Columbia U Pr.

Theories of the Mind. Jordan Scher. LC 62-11860. 1962. 14.95 o.s.i. (ISBN 0-02-927870-8). Free Pr.

Theories of the Political System: Classics of Political Thought & Modern Political Analysis. 3rd ed. William T. Bluhm. 1978. ref. ed. 17.95 (ISBN 0-13-913327-5). P-H.

Theories of the Universe: From Babylonian Myth to Modern Science. Ed. by Milton K. Munitz. LC 57-6746. 1965. pap. 6.95 (ISBN 0-02-922270-2). Free Pr.

Theories of Trade Unionism. Michael Poole. 280p. 1981. 35.00 (ISBN 0-7100-0695-0). Routledge & Kegan.

Theories of Urban Location. Brian J. Berry. LC 68-8949. (CCG Resource Papers Ser.: No. 1). (Illus.). 1968. pap. text ed. 4.00 (ISBN 0-89291-048-8). Assn Am Geographers.

Theories of Value & Distribution Since Adam Smith. Maurice Dobb. LC 72-88619. (Illus.). 264p. 1973. 35.50 (ISBN 0-521-20100-4); pap. 13.95 (ISBN 0-521-09936-6). Cambridge U Pr.

Theorike & Practike of Moderne Warres. Robert Barret. LC 74-26523. (English Experience Ser.: No. 155). (Illus.). 247p. 1969. Repr. of 1598 ed. 42.00 (ISBN 90-221-0155-X). Walter J Johnson.

Theory & Analysis of Phased Array Antennas. Noach Amitay et al. LC 70-174768. 1972. 38.00 o.p. (ISBN 0-471-02553-4, Pub. by Wiley-Interscience). Wiley

Theory & Application of Econometric Models. Daniel B. Suits. LC 65-6906. (Center of Economic Research Training Seminar Ser.: No. 3). (Illus.). 147p. 1963. pap. 7.50x (ISBN 0-8002-2421-3). Intl Pubns Serv.

Theory & Application of Field-Effect Transistors. R. S. Cobbold. LC 75-91162. 1970. 35.00 o.p. (ISBN 0-471-16150-0, Pub. by Wiley-Interscience). Wiley.

Theory & Application of Graphs: Fourth International Conference, Western Michigan Univ., May 6-9, 1980. Ed. & Gary Chartrand. 500p. 1981. 30.00 (ISBN 0-471-08473-5, Pub. by Wiley-Interscience). Wiley.

Theory & Applications of Differentiable Functions of Several Variables, VII. Ed. by S. M. Nikol'Skii. (Trudy Steklov: No. 150). Date not set. cancelled (ISBN 0-8218-3047-3). Am Math.

Theory & Applications of Differentiable Functions of Several Variables, Vol. 4. Ed. by S. M. Nikol'ski. LC 68-1677. (Proceedings of the Steklov Institute). 1974. 43.60 (ISBN 0-8218-3017-1, STEKLO-117). Am Math.

Theory & Applications of Distance Geometry. 2nd ed. Leonard M. Blumenthal. LC 79-113117. 1970. text ed. 13.95 (ISBN 0-8284-0242-6). Chelsea Pub.

Theory & Applications of Fourier Analysis. Ed. by C. Rees et al. (Pure & Applied Mathematics Ser.). 1980. 37.50 (ISBN 0-8247-6903-1). Dekker.

Theory & Applications of Molecular Paramagnetism. E. A. Boudreaux & L. N. Mulay. LC 75-28418. 1976. 55.00 (ISBN 0-471-09106-5, Pub. by Wiley-Interscience). Wiley.

Theory & Applications of Some New Classes of Integral Equations. A. Ramm. 344p. 1981. pap. 18.80 (ISBN 0-387-90540-5). Springer-Verlag.

Theory & Applications of Stochastic Differential Equations. Zeev Schuss. LC 80-14767. (Wiley Ser. in Probability & Mathematical Statistics: Applied Probability & Statistics). 375p. 1980. 25.95 (ISBN 0-471-04394-X). Wiley.

Theory & Design of Broadband Matching Networks. Chen Wai-Kai. 360p. 1976. text ed. 64.00 (ISBN 0-08-019702-7); pap. text ed. 26.00 (ISBN 0-08-019918-6). Pergamon.

Theory & Design of Digital Computer Systems. 2nd ed. Douglas Lewin. 472p. 1980. pap. text ed. 24.95x (ISBN 0-470-26959-6). Halsted Pr.

Theory & Design of Surface Structures Slabs & Plates. Gustav Florin. (Structural Engineering Ser.: Vol. 2). (Illus.). 222p. 1980. 38.00x (ISBN 0-87849-034-5); pap. 30.00 (ISBN 0-87849-035-3). Trans Tech.

Theory & Evidence. Clark Glymour. LC 79-3209. 1980. 25.00x o.s.i. (ISBN 0-691-07240-X); pap. 9.95 o.s.i. (ISBN 0-691-10077-2). Princeton U Pr.

Theory & Meaning. David Papineau. 218p. 1979. text ed. 19.95x (ISBN 0-19-824585-8). Oxford U Pr.

Theory & Method in Ethnomusicology. Bruno Nettl. LC 64-16964. (Illus.). 1964. text ed. 15.95 (ISBN 0-02-922860-3). Free Pr.

Theory & Method of Scaling. Warren S. Torgerson. LC 58-10812. (Illus.). 1958. 26.95 (ISBN 0-471-87945-2). Wiley.

Theory & Methodology in Lexicography. Ed. by Ladislav Zgusta. 1980. pap. 5.75 (ISBN 0-686-64344-5). Hornbeam Pr.

Theory & Methods of Police Patrol. Kenneth R. McCreedy. LC 73-11823. 240p. 1974. pap. 9.20 (ISBN 0-8273-1427-2); instructor's guide 1.60 (ISBN 0-8273-1428-0). Delmar.

Theory & Methods of Social Research. Johan Galtung. LC 67-26343. (Illus.). 1967. 17.00x (ISBN 0-231-03088-6). Columbia U Pr.

Theory & Personality: The Significance of T. S. Eliot's Criticism. Brian Lee. 1979. text ed. 26.00x (ISBN 0-485-11185-3, Athlone Pr). Humanities.

Theory & Phenomenology in Particle Physics, 2 pts. Ed. by A. Zichichi. 1969. Pt. A. 49.00 (ISBN 0-12-780571-0); Pt. B. 53.75 (ISBN 0-12-780572-9); Set. 83.50 (ISBN 0-685-05147-1). Acad Pr.

Theory & Power: On the Character of Modern Science. Rolf Gruner. 1977. pap. text ed. 17.25x (ISBN 90-6032-087-5). Humanities.

Theory & Practice: Essays Presented to Gene Weltfish. Ed. by Stanley Diamond. (Studies in Anthropology). 1979. text ed. 49.50 (ISBN 90-279-7958-8). Mouton.

Theory & Practice in Behavior Therapy. Aubrey J. Yates. LC 74-30018. (Personality Processes Ser). 336p. 1975. 23.95 (ISBN 0-471-97230-4, Pub. by Wiley-Interscience). Wiley.

Theory & Practice in Experimental Bacteriology. 2nd ed. G. G. Meynell & Elinor Meynell. LC 72-85729. (Illus.). 1970. 49.50 (ISBN 0-521-07682-X). Cambridge U Pr.

Theory & Practice in Health Education. Helen S. Ross & Paul Mico. LC 80-82564. (Illus.). 338p. 1980. text ed. 14.95 (ISBN 0-87484-406-1). Mayfield Pub.

Theory & Practice in Library Education: The Teaching-Learning Process. Joe Morehead. LC 80-17431. (Research Studies in Library Science: No. 16). 1980. lib. bdg. 25.00x (ISBN 0-87287-215-7). Libs Unl.

Theory & Practice in Medieval Persian Government. A. K. Lambton. 332p. 1980. 75.00x (ISBN 0-86078-067-8, Pub. by Variorum England). State Mutual Bk.

Theory & Practice in the History of American Education: A Book of Readings. Ed. by James W. Hillesheim & George D. Merrill. LC 79-3735. 439p. 1980. Repr. of 1971 ed. 10.50 (ISBN 0-8191-0929-0). U Pr of Amer.

Theory & Practice in the Organic Laboratory. 2nd ed. John A. Landgrebe. 1976. pap. text ed. 15.95x (ISBN 0-669-99937-7). Heath.

Theory & Practice of Alternating Currents. A. T. Dover. 35.00x o.p. (ISBN 0-392-04926-0, SpS). Soccer.

Theory & Practice of American Marxism, Nineteen Fifty-Seven to Nineteen Seventy. Richard Guarasci. LC 80-1376. 170p. 1980. lib. bdg. 19.50 (ISBN 0-8191-1148-1); pap. text ed. 10.50 (ISBN 0-8191-1149-X). U Pr of Amer.

Theory & Practice of Bed-Load Transport. K. Stelczer. 1981. 22.00 (ISBN 0-918334-38-1). WRP.

Theory & Practice of Central Banking 1797-1913. E. Victor Morgan. LC 67-24754. Repr. of 1943 ed. 22.50x (ISBN 0-678-05189-5). Kelley.

Theory & Practice of Ceramo Metal Restorations. Mashiro Kuwata. (Illus.). 150p. 1980. 58.00 (ISBN 0-931386-15-2). Quint Pub Co.

Theory & Practice of Civil Disobedience. Arthur Harvey. 27p. 1961. pap. 1.00 (ISBN 0-934676-04-6). Greenlf Bks.

Theory & Practice of Curriculum Studies. Denis Lawton et al. (Education Bks). 1978. 22.00x (ISBN 0-7100-0028-6); pap. 8.95 (ISBN 0-7100-0029-4). Routledge & Kegan.

Theory & Practice of Econometrics. George G. Judge et al. LC 80-150. (Applied Statistics Ser.). 1980. text ed. 26.95 (ISBN 0-471-05938-2). Wiley.

Theory & Practice of Education. 2nd ed. M. E. Downey & A. V. Kelly. 1979. text ed. 16.95 (ISBN 0-06-318113-4, IntlDept); pap. text ed. 10.45 (ISBN 0-06-318114-2). Har-Row.

Theory & Practice of English Narrative Verse Since Eighteen Thirty-Three. Willem V. Doorn. 253p. 1980. Repr. of 1833 ed. lib. bdg. 25.00 (ISBN 0-8492-4220-7). R West.

Theory & Practice of Environmental Quality Analysis: Water Resources Management, Land Suitability Analysis, Economics & Aesthetics, No. 27. Eric Hyman et al. 103p. 1980. pap. 15.00 (ISBN 0-86602-027-6). CPL Biblios.

Theory & Practice of Group Counseling. Gerald Corey. LC 80-18985. 500p. 1980. text ed. 15.95 (ISBN 0-8185-0400-5). Brooks-Cole.

Theory and Practice of Histological Techniques. Ed. by John D. Bancroft & Alan Stevens. LC 76-20829. 1977. text ed. 37.50 o.s.i. (ISBN 0-443-01534-1). Churchill.

Theory & Practice of History. Leopold Von Ranke. Ed. by Georg G. Iggers & Konrad Von Moltke. Tr. by Wilma Iggers from Ger. LC 79-167691. 1973. pap. text ed. 14.95x (ISBN 0-672-60920-7). Irvington.

Theory & Practice of Histotechnology. 2nd ed. Denza C. Sheehan & Barbara B. Hrapchak. LC 80-11807. 1980. text ed. 29.95 (ISBN 0-8016-4573-5). Mosby.

Theory & Practice of Induced Breeding in Fish. 48p. 1980. pap. 5.00 (ISBN 0-88936-236-X, IDRCTS21, IDRC). Unipub.

Theory & Practice of Lubrication for Engineers. Dudley D. Fuller. LC 56-6483. 1956. 42.50 (ISBN 0-471-28710-5, Pub. by Wiley-Interscience). Wiley.

Theory & Practice of Microelectronics. Sorab K. Ghandhi. LC 68-28501. (Illus.). 1968. 38.00 (ISBN 0-471-29718-6, Pub. by Wiley-Interscience). Wiley.

Theory & Practice of Modern Guerilla Warfare. Baljit Singh & Ko Wang Mei. 1971. 5.75x o.p. (ISBN 0-210-98169-5). Asia.

Theory & Practice of Natural Healing. Carl C. Lindegren. LC 80-50132. 1981. 7.95 (ISBN 0-533-04595-9). Vantage.

Theory & Practice of Nonpar Banking. Paul F. Jessup. 1967. 7.95x- o.s.i. (ISBN 0-8101-0128-9). Northwestern U Pr.

Theory & Practice of Programmed Instruction: A Guide for Teachers. Jerry Pocztar. (Monographs on Education, No. 7). (Illus.). 179p. (Orig.). 1972. pap. 7.00 (ISBN 92-3-100936-2, U679, UNESCO). Unipub.

Theory & Practice of Propellers for Auxiliary Sailboats. J. R. Stanton. LC 75-31778. (Illus.). 1975. pap. 4.00 (ISBN 0-87033-213-9). Cornell Maritime.

Theory & Practice of Psychotherapy with Specific Disorders. Ed. by Max Hammer. 464p. 1972. 23.75 (ISBN 0-398-02539-8). C C Thomas.

Theory & Practice of Seamanship. G. L. Danton. (Illus., Metric ed). 1972. 45.00 (ISBN 0-7100-7487-5). Routledge & Kegan.

Theory & Practice of Seamanship. 8th, rev. ed. Graham Danton. 1980. 45.00 (ISBN 0-7100-0502-4). Routledge & Kegan.

Theory & Practice of Social Case Work. 2nd ed. Gordon Hamilton. LC 51-12493. 1951. 15.00x (ISBN 0-231-01862-2). Columbia U Pr.

Theory & Practice of the Balance of Power 1486-1914. Ed. by Moorehead Wright. (Rowman & Littlefield University Librry). 152p. 1975. 12.50x (ISBN 0-87471-407-9). Rowman.

Theory & Practice of the International Trade of the United States & England, & of the Trade of the United States & Canada. Patrick Barry. (Neglected American Economists Ser.). 1974. lib. bdg. 50.00 (ISBN 0-8240-1014-0). Garland Pub.

Theory & Practice of Translation. Ed. by Eugene A. Nida & C. R. Taber. 1969. 5.50 (ISBN 90-04-03857-4, 08510). United Bible.

Theory & Practice of Vocational Guidance. B. Hopson & J. Hayes. 1969. 34.00 (ISBN 0-08-013284-7); pap. 15.00 (ISBN 0-08-013391-6). Pergamon.

Theory & Processes of History. Frederick J. Teggart. 1977. pap. 6.95x (ISBN 0-520-03176-8, CAMPUS162). U of Cal Pr.

Theory & Reality in International Relations. Ed. by John C. Farrell & Asa P. Smith. LC 68-18993. 1967. pap. 5.00x (ISBN 0-231-08587-7). Columbia U Pr.

Theory & Reality: The Development of Social Systems. W. Bienkowski. (Allison & Busby Motive Ser.). 272p. 1981. 17.95x (ISBN 0-8052-8093-6, Pub. by Allison & Busby England); pap. 8.95 (ISBN 0-8052-8092-8). Schocken.

Theory & Religious Understanding: A Critique of the Hermeneutics of Joachim Wach. Charles M. Wood. LC 75-26839. (American Academy of Religion. Dissertation Ser.). 1975. pap. 7.50 (ISBN 0-89130-026-0, 010112). Scholars Pr Ca.

Theory & Servicing of AM, FM & FM Stereo Receivers. C. Green & R. Bourgue. 1980. 25.95 (ISBN 0-13-913590-1). P-H.

Theory & Techniques of Optimization for Practicing Engineers. Raymond L. Zahradnik. LC 70-146261. 1971. pap. 9.95 (ISBN 0-8436-0311-9). CBI Pub.

Theory Building. rev. ed. Robert Dubin. LC 77-90010. (Illus.). 1978. text ed. 15.95 (ISBN 0-02-907620-X). Free Pr.

Theory Construction: From Verbal to Mathematical Formulations. H. Blalock, Jr. LC 69-17478. 1969. pap. text ed. 10.95 (ISBN 0-13-913343-7). P-H.

Theory Construction in Nursing: An Adaptation Model. Callista Roy & Sharon Roberts. (Illus.). 352p. 1981. text ed. 17.95 (ISBN 0-13-913657-6). P-H.

Theory for Social Work Practice. Ruth E. Smalley. LC 67-14290. 1967. 20.00x (ISBN 0-231-02769-9); pap. 9.00x (ISBN 0-231-08327-0). Columbia U Pr.

Theory Formulations. Ed. by Williard E. Stone. (U of Fla. Accounting Ser.: No. 6). 1970. pap. 2.00 (ISBN 0-8130-0341-5). U Presses Fla.

Theory in Criminology: Contemporary Views. Ed. by Robert F. Meier. LC 77-81151. (Sage Research Progress Series in Criminology: Vol. 1). 1977. 12.95x (ISBN 0-8039-0915-2); pap. 6.50x (ISBN 0-8039-0910-1). Sage.

Theory of Accounting to Investors. George J. Staubus. LC 61-7516. 1971. Repr. of 1961 ed. text ed. 10.00 (ISBN 0-914348-10-8). Scholars Bk.

Theory of Applications of Hopf Bifurcation. D. B. Hassard et al. (London Mathematical Society Lecture Notes Ser.: No. 41). (Illus.). 300p. (Orig.). Date not set. 35.00 (ISBN 0-521-23158-2). Cambridge U Pr.

Theory of Atomic Collisions. 3rd ed. N. F. Mott & H. S. Massey. (International Series of Monographs on Physics). (Illus.). 1965. 65.00x (ISBN 0-19-851242-2). Oxford U Pr.

Theory of Atomic Spectra. Edward U. Condon & George H. Shortley. (Orig.). 1935. pap. 24.95x (ISBN 0-521-09209-4, 209). Cambridge U Pr.

Theory of Auditing. Charles W. Schandl. LC 78-17862. 1978. text ed. 13.00 (ISBN 0-914348-23-X). Scholars Bk.

Theory of Bessel Functions. George N. Watson. pap. text ed. 29.95x (ISBN 0-521-09382-1). Cambridge U Pr.

Theory of Beta-Decay. C. Strachan. LC 72-86202. 1969. 22.00 (ISBN 0-08-006509-0). Pergamon.

Theory of Box Girders. Vladimir Kristek. LC 78-8637. 1980. 40.50 (ISBN 0-471-99678-5, Pub. by Wiley-Interscience). Wiley.

Theory of Business Relativity. Leon Neihouse. 112p. 1981. 6.50 (ISBN 0-682-49707-X). Exposition.

Theory of Cataloguing. Girja Kumar & Krishan Kumar. 1975. 12.50 (ISBN 0-7069-0361-7, Pub. by Vikas India). Advent Bk.

Theory of Catechetics: Language & Experience in Religious Education. Hubert Halbfas. LC 74-114153. 1971. 6.95 (ISBN 0-8164-1130-1). Crossroad NY.

Theory of Catering. Ronald Kinton & Victor Ceserani. (Illus.). 412p. 1978. pap. 15.95x (ISBN 0-7131-0193-8). Intl Ideas.

Theory of Celestial Influence. Rodney Collin. 414p. 1980. 18.00x (ISBN 0-7224-0019-5, Pub. by Watkins England). State Mutual Bk.

Theory of Christian Education Practice: How Theology Affects Christian Education. Randolph C. Miller. LC 80-15886. 312p. (Orig.). 1980. pap. 10.95 (ISBN 0-89135-049-7). Religious Educ.

Theory of Classification. Brian Buchanan. (Outlines of Modern Librarianship Ser.). 141p. 1980. text ed. 12.00 (ISBN 0-89664-410-3, Pub. by K G Saur). Shoe String.

Theory of Classification. Krishnan Kumar. 1980. text ed. 18.95x (ISBN 0-7069-0797-3, Pub. by Vikas India). Advent Bk.

Theory of Collective Bargaining Nineteen Thirty to Nineteen Seventy-Five. W. H. Hutt. LC 80-36792. (Cato Papers Ser.: No. 14). 160p. 1980. pap. 5.00 (ISBN 0-932790-20-8). Cato Inst.

Theory of Collective Bargaining 1930-1975. W. H. Hutt. (Hobart Paperbacks Special Ser.: No. 8). 1976. pap. 7.50 (ISBN 0-255-36072-X). Transatlantic.

Theory of Collective Behavior. Neil J. Smelser. LC 62-15350. (Illus.). 1962. text ed. 12.95 (ISBN 0-02-929390-1); pap. text ed. 5.95 (ISBN 0-02-929400-2). Free Pr.

Theory of Committees & Elections. Duncan Black. 1958. 29.95 (ISBN 0-521-04262-3). Cambridge U Pr.

Theory of Complementation in English Syntax. Joan W. Bresnan. Ed. by Jorge Hankamer. LC 78-66551. (Outstanding Dissertations in Linguistics Ser.). 1979. lib. bdg. 36.00 (ISBN 0-8240-9689-4). Garland Pub.

Theory of Complex Nuclei. V. G. Soloviev. 1976. 67.00 (ISBN 0-08-018053-1). Pergamon.

Theory of Computation. Walter S. Brainerd & Lawrence H. Landweber. LC 73-12950. 336p. 1974. 27.95 (ISBN 0-471-09585-0). Wiley.

Theory of Condensed Matter. 1968. pap. 39.75 (ISBN 92-0-130068-9, IAEA). Unipub.

Theory of Criminal Justice. Jan Gorecki. 1979. 17.50x (ISBN 0-231-04670-7). Columbia U Pr.

Theory of Customs Unions. A. M. El-Agra & A. J. Jones. 1981. 25.00 (ISBN 0-312-79737-0). St Martin.

Theory of Demand: Real & Monetary. Michio Morishima. (Illus.). 326p. 1973. 29.95x (ISBN 0-19-828180-3). Oxford U Pr.

Theory of Discourse. James L. Kinneavy. 496p. 1980. pap. 7.95x (ISBN 0-393-00919-X). Norton.

Theory of Distributions for Locally Compact Spaces. Leon Ehrenpreis. LC 52-42839. (Memoirs: No. 21). 1978. pap. 5.20 (ISBN 0-8218-1221-1, MEMO-21). Am Math.

Theory of Dumping & American Commercial Policy. William A. Wares. LC 76-54611. (Illus.). 1977. 16.95x (ISBN 0-669-01308-0). Lexington Bks.

Theory of Dynamic Economics. Simon N. Patten. LC 79-1587. 1981. 16.00 (ISBN 0-88355-892-0). Hyperion Conn.

Theory of Econometrics: An Introductory Exposition of Econometric Methods. 2d ed. A. Koutsoyiannis. LC 76-53202. 1978. pap. 20.50x (ISBN 0-06-493949-9). B&N.

Theory of Economic Development. Joseph A. Schumpeter. Tr. by Redvers Opie. 1961. pap. 6.95x (ISBN 0-19-500461-2). Oxford U Pr.

Theory of Economic Growth. W. Arhtur Lewis. 1955. pap. text ed. 13.50x (ISBN 0-04-330054-5). Allen Unwin.

Theory of Economic Growth. Michio Morishima. 1969. 29.95x (ISBN 0-19-828164-1). Oxford U Pr.

Theory of Economic Progress. 3rd ed. C. E. Ayres. 1978. pap. 6.95 (ISBN 0-932826-03-2). New Issues MI.

Theory of Economic Statics. 2nd ed. M. Brennan. 1970. 18.95 (ISBN 0-13-913624-X). P-H.

Theory of Education in the Republic of Plato. Richard L. Nettleship. LC 68-54676. 1968. text ed. 8.75 (ISBN 0-8077-1850-5); pap. text ed. 3.50x (ISBN 0-8077-1849-1). Tchrs Coll.

Theory of Electric & Magnetic Susceptibilities. John H. Van Vleck. (International Series of Monographs on Physics). (Illus.). 1932. pap. 29.95x (ISBN 0-19-851243-0). Oxford U Pr.

Theory of Electrical Transport in Semi-Conductors. B. R. Nag. 238p. 1973. text ed. 34.00 (ISBN 0-08-016802-7). Pergamon.

Theory of Electroacoustics. Josef Merhaut. (Illus.). 336p. 1981. 44.95 (ISBN 0-07-041478-5, C). McGraw.

Theory of Elementary Atomic & Molecular Processes in Gases. E. E. Nikitin. Tr. by M. J. Kearsley. (Illus.). 486p. 1974. 55.00x (ISBN 0-19-851928-1). Oxford U Pr.

Theory of English Lexicography, Fifteen Thirty-Seventeen Ninety-One. Tetsuro Hayashi. (Studies in the History of Linguistics: No. 18). 1978. text ed. 25.75x (ISBN 0-391-01669-5). Humanities.

Theory of Environmental Policy: The Externalities, Public Outlays, & the Quality of Life. William J. Baumol & Wallace E. Oates. LC 74-11205. (Illus.). 304p. 1975. ref. ed. 19.95 (ISBN 0-13-913673-8). P-H.

Theory of Equilibrium Growth. Avinash Dixit. (Illus.). 1976. text ed. 14.50x (ISBN 0-19-877080-4); pap. text ed. 9.95x (ISBN 0-19-877081-2). Oxford U Pr.

Theory of Error. 2nd ed. Yardley Beers. LC 53-8616. (Physics Ser). (Orig.). 1957. pap. 4.95 (ISBN 0-201-00470-4). A-W.

Theory of Evolving Tonality. Joseph Yasser. LC 74-34376. (Music Reprint Ser). (Illus.). x, 381p. 1975. Repr. of 1932 ed. lib. bdg. 35.00 (ISBN 0-306-70729-2). Da Capo.

Theory of Excitons. Robert S. Knox. (Solid State Physics: Advances in Research & Applications Suppl. 5). 1964. 31.50 (ISBN 0-12-607765-7). Acad Pr.

Theory of Experiments in Paramagnetic Resonance. J. Talpe. LC 79-137411. 272p. 1971. 32.00 (ISBN 0-08-016157-X). Pergamon.

Theory of Fashion Design. H. L. Brockman. 1965. 22.50 (ISBN 0-87245-041-4). Textile Bk.

Theory of Fashion Design. Helen L. Brockman. LC 65-25852. 1965. 22.50 (ISBN 0-471-10586-4). Wiley.

Theory of Feelings. Agnes Heller. (Dialectic & Society Ser.: No. 6). 1979. pap. text ed. 23.50x (ISBN 90-232-1699-7). Humanities.

Theory of Fiction: Henry James. Henry James. Ed. by James E. Miller, Jr. LC 78-147168. 1972. pap. 6.50x (ISBN 0-8032-5747-3, BB 542, Bison). U of Nebr Pr.

Theory of Film Practice. Noel Burch. Tr. by Helen R. Lane from French. LC 80-8676. (Illus.). 172p. 1981. 18.50x (ISBN 0-691-03962-3); pap. 5.95 (ISBN 0-691-00329-7). Princeton U Pr.

Theory of Film: The Redemption of Physical Reality. Siegfried Kracauer. (Illus.). 1965. pap. 6.95 (ISBN 0-19-500721-2, GB). Oxford U Pr.

Theory of Finance. Jama Miller. 1972. 21.95 (ISBN 0-03-086732-0). Dryden Pr.

Theory of Financial Decisions. 2nd ed. Charles W. Haley & Larry Schall. (Illus.). 1979. text ed. 19.95 (ISBN 0-07-025568-7, C). McGraw.

Theory of Financial Management. Ezra Solomon. LC 63-8405. (Illus.). 1963. 12.50x (ISBN 0-231-02604-8). Columbia U Pr.

Theory of Finitely Generated Commutative Semigroups. L. Redei. (International Series in Pure & Applied Mathematics: Vol. 82). (Illus.). 1966. 42.00 (ISBN 0-08-010520-3). Pergamon.

Theory of Fiscal Economics. Earl R. Rolph. (California Library Reprint Series: No. 21). 1971. 20.00x (ISBN 0-520-01926-1). U of Cal Pr.

Theory of Fish Population Dynamics As the Biological Background for Rational Exploitation & Management of Fishery Resources. G. V. Nikolskii. Ed. by R. Jones. Tr. by J. E. Bradley from Rus. (Illus.). 323p. 1980. Repr. of 1969 ed. lib. bdg. 43.25x (ISBN 3-87429-171-5). Lubrecht & Cramer.

Theory of Functions. 2nd ed. Constantin Caratheodory. LC 60-16838. Vol. 1. 12.95 (ISBN 0-8284-0097-0); Vol. 2. 12.95 (ISBN 0-8284-0106-3). Chelsea Pub.

Theory of Functions, 2 vols. Konrad Knopp. (Illus.). Vol. 1. pap. 2.75 (ISBN 0-486-60156-0); Vol. 2. pap. text ed. 2.75 (ISBN 0-486-60157-9). Dover.

Theory of Functions. 2nd ed. Edward C. Titchmarsh. 1939. 17.95x (ISBN 0-19-853349-7). Oxford U Pr.

Theory of Futures Trading. B. A. Goss. (Students Library of Economics). (Illus.). 128p. 1972. 12.50 (ISBN 0-7100-7217-1). Routledge & Kegan.

Theory of Gambling & Statistical Logic. rev. ed. Richard A. Epstein. 1977. 29.00 (ISBN 0-12-240760-1). Acad Pr.

Theory of Games & Linear Programming. S. Vajda. 1967. pap. 4.95 o.p. (ISBN 0-470-89779-1). Halsted Pr.

Theory of Games & Statistical Decisions. David A. Blackwell & M. A. Girshick. 368p. 1980. pap. 5.00 (ISBN 0-486-63831-6). Dover.

Theory of Games As a Tool for the Moral Philosopher. Richard B. Braithwaite. 1955. 15.50 (ISBN 0-521-04307-7). Cambridge U Pr.

Theory of German Word Order from the Renaissance to the Present. Aldo Scaglione. LC 80-16619. 275p. 1981. 22.50x (ISBN 0-8166-0980-2); pap. 9.95 (ISBN 0-8166-0983-7). U of Minn Pr.

Theory of Good City Form. Kevin Lynch. (Illus.). 526p. 1981. text ed. 25.00x (ISBN 0-262-12085-2). MIT Pr.

Theory of Grammatical Relations. John S. Bowers. LC 80-21018. 304p. 1981. 24.50x (ISBN 0-8014-1079-7). Cornell U Pr.

Theory of Graphs: A Basis for Network Theory. Lee M. Maxwell & Myril B. Reed. LC 77-106387. 181p. 1975. 16.00 (ISBN 0-08-016321-1). Pergamon.

Theory of Groups. 2nd ed. Marshall Hall, Jr. LC 75-42306. xiii, 434p. text ed. 11.95 (ISBN 0-8284-0288-4). Chelsea Pub.

Theory of Groups. Ian D. MacDonald. 1968. pap. 16.95x (ISBN 0-19-853138-9). Oxford U Pr.

Theory of Groups. 2nd ed. Hans J. Zassenhaus. LC 56-13058. 12.95 (ISBN 0-8284-0053-9). Chelsea Pub.

Theory of Groups: An Introduction. 2nd ed. Joseph J. Rotman. 352p. 1973. text ed. 25.15x (ISBN 0-205-03655-4, 5636558). Allyn.

Theory of Groups & Quantum Mechanics. Hermann Weyl. 1950. pap. text ed. 5.50 (ISBN 0-486-60269-9). Dover.

Theory of Growth in a Corporate Economy: Management Preference, Research & Development & Economic Growth. Hiroyuki Odagiri. LC 80-23494. (Illus.). 256p. Date not set. price not set (ISBN 0-521-23132-9). Cambridge U Pr.

Theory of Harmony. Arnold Schoenberg. Tr. by Roy E. Carter. 1978. 49.50x (ISBN 0-520-03464-3). U of Cal Pr.

Theory of Harmony. Matthew Shirlaw. LC 72-87348. (Music Reprint Ser). 1969. Repr. of 1917 ed. lib. bdg. 29.50 (ISBN 0-306-71658-5). Da Capo.

Theory of Human Action. Alvin I. Goldman. 1977. 14.50 (ISBN 0-691-07216-7); pap. 4.95 (ISBN 0-691-01974-6). Princeton U Pr.

Theory of Human Culture. James K. Feibleman. 1968. Repr. of 1946 ed. text ed. 15.00x (ISBN 0-391-00448-4). Humanities.

Theory of Identity, Existence & Publication: A Theory of Identity, Existence & Predication. Panayot Butchvarov. LC 78-13812. 288p. 1979. 15.00x (ISBN 0-253-13700-4). Ind U Pr.

Theory of Imperfect Competition: A Radical Reconstruction. Donald Dewey. LC 73-79190. (Illus.). 1969. 16.00x (ISBN 0-231-03164-5). Columbia U Pr.

Theory of Imperfect Crystalline Solids: Trieste Lectures, 1970. 608p. (Orig.). 1972. pap. 33.25 (ISBN 92-0-130071-9, IAEA). Unipub.

Theory of Income Distribution. Harry G. Johnson. 1973. 18.00x o.p. (ISBN 0-85641-006-3, Pub. by Basil Blackwell England). Biblio Dist.

Theory of Information & Coding: A Mathematical Framework for Communication. R. J. McEliece. (Encyclopedia of Mathematics & Its Applications: Vol. 3). 1977. text ed. 25.50 (ISBN 0-201-13502-7, Adv Bk Prog). A-W.

Theory of Integral Functions. Georges Valiron. LC 51-7375. 9.95 (ISBN 0-8284-0056-3). Chelsea Pub.

Theory of Intelligent Behavior. Dalbir Bindra. LC 75-46519. 1976. 27.50 (ISBN 0-471-07320-2, Pub by Wiley-Interscience). Wiley.

Theory of Interaction of Elementary Particles at High Energies. Ed. by D. V. Skolbel'tsyn. LC 73-83900. (P. N. Lebedev Physics Institute Ser.: Vol. 57). (Illus.). 258p. 1974. 42.50 (ISBN 0-306-10899-2, Consultants). Plenum Pub.

Theory of Interest. Stephen G. Kellison. 1971. Repr. of 1970 ed. text ed. 14.50 (ISBN 0-256-00283-5). Irwin.

Theory of Intermolecular Forces. 2nd ed. H. Margenau & N. Kestner. 1971. 52.00 (ISBN 0-08-016502-8). Pergamon.

Theory of International Trade. A. Dixit & V. D. Norman. (Cambridge Economic Handbooks). 250p. 1980. 34.50 (ISBN 0-521-23481-6); pap. 13.95 (ISBN 0-521-29969-1). Cambridge U Pr.

Theory of Ion Flow Dynamics. Demetrios G. Samaras. LC 78-153896. 1971. pap. text ed. 7.50 (ISBN 0-486-60309-1). Dover.

Theory of Japanese Democracy. Nobutaka Ike. LC 77-8279. (Westview Special Studies on China & East Asia). (Illus.). 178p. 1980. lib. bdg. 16.50x o.p. (ISBN 0-89158-066-2); pap. text ed. 8.50x (ISBN 0-89158-932-5). Westview.

Theory of Knowledge. 2nd ed. Roderick Chisholm. (Foundations of Philosophy Ser.). 1977. text ed. 13.50 (ISBN 0-13-914168-5); pap. text ed. 7.95 (ISBN 0-13-914150-2). P-H.

Theory of Knowledge. D. W. Hamlyn. (Modern Introductions to Philosophy Ser.). 308p. 1980. pap. text ed. cancelled (ISBN 0-333-11548-1). Humanities.

Theory of Knowledge: An Introduction. A. D. Woozley. (Repr. of 1949 ed). 1964. pap. text ed. 8.25x (ISBN 0-09-044571-6, Hutchinson U Lib). Humanities.

Theory of Knowledge Implicit in Goethe's World Conception. 2nd ed. Rudolf Steiner. Tr. by Olin D. Wannamaker from Ger. LC 70-76994. Orig. Title: Grundlinien Einer Erkenntnistheorie der Goetheschen Weltanschauung. 133p. 1978. 6.95 (ISBN 0-910142-94-7); pap. 3.95 (ISBN 0-910142-85-8). Anthroposophic.

Theory of Language, Culture & Human Behavior. Joe E. Pierce. 161p. 1972. pap. 7.95. Hapi Pr.

Theory of Lepton-Hadron Processes at High Energies: Partons, Scale Invariance & Light-Cone Physics. Probir Roy. (Oxford Studies in Physics). (Illus.). 188p. 1975. 33.50x (ISBN 0-19-851452-2). Oxford U Pr.

Theory of Linear Induction Motors. 2nd ed. Sakae Yamamura. LC 78-21550. 1979. 28.95 (ISBN 0-470-26583-3). Halsted Pr.

Theory of Linear Models & Multivariate Analysis. Steven F. Arnold. LC 80-23017. (Wiley Ser. in Probability & Math Statistics). 500p. 1981. 30.00 (ISBN 0-471-05065-2). Wiley.

Theory of Literary Production. Pierre Macherey. Tr. by Geoffrey Wall from Fr. 1978. 27.50x (ISBN 0-7100-8978-3); pap. 12.75 (ISBN 0-7100-0087-1). Routledge & Kegan.

Theory of Logical Types. Irving M. Copi. (Monographs in Modern Logic). 1971. 11.50 (ISBN 0-7100-7026-8). Routledge & Kegan.

Theory of Machines & Mechanisms. Joseph E. Shigley & John J. Uiker. (Mechanical Engineering Ser.). (Illus.). 576p. 1980. text ed. 27.95x (ISBN 0-07-056884-7); solutions manual 13.95 (ISBN 0-07-056885-5). McGraw.

Theory of Macroeconomic Policy. 2nd ed. Nancy S. Barrett. (Illus.). 480p. 1975. 17.95 o.p. (ISBN 0-13-913830-7). P-H.

Theory of Macroeconomic Policy. M. H. Peston. 224p. 1974. pap. 19.50x (ISBN 0-86003-113-6, Pub. by Allan Pubs England). State Mutual Bk.

Theory of Magnetic Resonance. C. P. Poole, Jr. & H. A. Farach. 452p. 1972. 31.95 (ISBN 0-471-69383-9). Wiley.

Theory of Magnetically Confined Plasmas: Proceedings. Ed. by B. Coppi. (Commission of the European Communities Ser.: Eur 5737). (Illus.). 1979. pap. 92.00 (ISBN 0-08-023434-8). Pergamon.

Theory of Man. Francisco Romero. Tr. by William F. Cooper. 1965. 22.75x (ISBN 0-520-01087-6). U of Cal Pr.

Theory of Matrices, 2 Vols. Felix R. Gantmacher. LC 59-11779. Vol. 1. 15.95 (ISBN 0-8284-0131-4); Vol. 2. 12.95 (ISBN 0-8284-0133-0). Chelsea Pub.

Theory of Matrices. 2nd ed. Cyrus C. MacDuffee. LC 49-2197. 8.95 (ISBN 0-8284-0028-8). Chelsea Pub.

Theory of Matrices in Numerical Analysis. Alston S. Householder. LC 74-83763. 288p. 1975. pap. text ed. 4.00 (ISBN 0-486-61781-5). Dover.

Theory of Microeconomics. Trout Rader. 1972. text ed. 22.50 (ISBN 0-12-575050-1). Acad Pr.

Theory of Monetary Policy. rev. ed. Victoria Chick. 1977. pap. 14.50x (ISBN 0-631-18210-1, Pub. by Basil Blackwell England). Biblio Dist.

Theory of Money. 3rd. ed. Walter T. Newlyn. (Illus.). 1978. pap. 24.95x (ISBN 0-19-877099-5); pap. 9.95 (ISBN 0-19-877100-2). Oxford U Pr.

Theory of Money & Credit. Ludwig Von Mises. Tr. by H. E. Batson from Ger. LC 79-25752. (Liberty Classics Ser.). 544p. 1981. 11.00 (ISBN 0-913966-70-3); pap. 5.00 (ISBN 0-913966-71-1). Liberty Fund.

Theory of Moral Sentiments. Adam Smith. (Glasgow Edition of the Works & Correspondence of Adam Smith Ser.). (Illus.). 1976. 54.00x (ISBN 0-19-828189-7). Oxford U Pr.

Theory of Morality. Alan Donagan. LC 76-25634. 1979. pap. 5.95 (ISBN 0-226-15567-6, P838, Phoen). U of Chicago Pr.

Theory of Need in Marx. Agnes Heller. (Allison & Busby Motive Ser.). 136p. 1981. pap. 7.95 (ISBN 0-8052-8075-8, Pub. by Allison & Busby England). Schocken.

Theory of Networks & Lines. James L. Potter & S. Fich. (Illus.). 1963. ref. ed. 24.95 (ISBN 0-13-913228-7). P-H.

Theory of Nuclear Structure: Trieste Lectures, 1969. (Illus., Orig.). 1970. pap. 51.50 (ISBN 92-0-130070-0, ISP 249, IAEA). Unipub.

Theory of Numbers. 2nd ed. George B. Mathews. LC 61-17958. 9.95 (ISBN 0-8284-0156-X). Chelsea Pub.

Theory of Numbers, Mathematical Analysis & Their Applications. LC 79-20552. (Proceedings of the Steklov Institute). 1979. 60.00 (ISBN 0-8218-3042-2, STEKLO 142). Am Math.

Theory of Numbers: Proceedings, Vol. 8. Symposia in Pure Mathematics-Pasadena-1963. Ed. by A. L. Whiteman. LC 65-17382. 1979. Repr. of 1965 ed. with additions 19.20 (ISBN 0-8218-1408-7, PSPUM-8). Am Math.

Theory of Optimum Noise Immunity. Vladimir A. Kotelnikov. Tr. by R. A. Silverman. LC 68-20594. (Illus.). 1960. pap. text ed. 3.50 (ISBN 0-486-61952-4). Dover.

Theory of Ordinary Differential Equations. Randal H. Cole. LC 68-13433. (Illus.). 1968. 32.50x (ISBN 0-8290-0132-8); pap. text ed. 18.50x (ISBN 0-8290-0132-8). Irvington.

Theory of Organizational Structure. Marshall W. Meyer. LC 76-56415. (Studies in Sociology Ser.). 1977. pap. text ed. 3.95 (ISBN 0-672-61193-7). Bobbs.

Theory of Oscillators. Alexander Andronov et al. (Illus.). 1966. text ed. 41.25 o.p. (ISBN 0-08-009981-5). Pergamon.

Theory of Parsing, Translation & Compiling: Vol. 1, Parsing. Alfred V. Aho & Jeffrey D. Ullman. (Illus.). 592p. 1972. ref. ed. 24.95 (ISBN 0-13-914556-7). P-H.

Theory of Pay. A. Wood. LC 78-1038. 1978. 29.95 (ISBN 0-521-22073-4). Cambridge U Pr.

Theory of Photons & Electrons: Second Corrected Printing. 2nd rev. ed. J. M. Jauch & F. Rohrlich. LC 75-8890. (Texts & Monographs in Physics). (Illus.). 533p. 1980. 19.80 (ISBN 0-387-07295-0). Springer-Verlag.

Theory of Poetry. Lascelles Abercrombie. LC 69-17712. 1969. Repr. of 1926 ed. 12.00x (ISBN 0-8196-0223-X). Biblo.

Theory of Power & Organization. Stewart Clegg. 1979. 20.00x (ISBN 0-7100-0143-6). Routledge & Kegan.

Theory of Price Control. John K. Galbraith. (HP Ser.: No. 173). 1980. text ed. 7.95x (ISBN 0-674-88170-2); pap. text ed. 2.95 (ISBN 0-674-88175-3). Harvard U Pr.

Theory of Probability: An Inquiry into the Logical & Mathematical Foundations of the Calculus of Probability. Hans Reichenbach. (California Library Reprint Series: No. 23). 1971. 23.75x (ISBN 0-520-01929-6). U of Cal Pr.

Theory of Probability: With Answers to Exercises. 4th ed. B. V. Gnedenko. LC 67-8772. 14.95 (ISBN 0-8284-0132-2). Chelsea Pub.

Theory of Profits. A. Wood. 192p. 1975. 27.50 (ISBN 0-521-20768-1). Cambridge U Pr.

Theory of Property Rights-with Special Applications to the California Gold Rush. John R. Umbeck. (Illus.). 160p. 1981. text ed. 9.50 (ISBN 0-8138-1675-0). Iowa St U Pr.

Theory of Property Rights: With Special Application to the 1948 California Gold Rush. John R. Umbeck. 1981. write for info. (ISBN 0-8138-1675-0). Iowa St U Pr.

Theory of Prosody in Eighteenth Century England. Paul Fussell, Jr. 1966. Repr. of 1954 ed. 12.50 o.p. (ISBN 0-208-00581-1, Archon). Shoe String.

Theory of Prosperity. Simon Patten. (Neglected American Economists Ser.). 1974. lib. bdg. 50.00 (ISBN 0-8240-1027-2). Garland Pub.

Theory of Protection. W. M. Corden. (Illus.). 1971. 17.95x (ISBN 0-19-828171-4). Oxford U Pr.

Theory of Public Finance: A Study in Public Economy. Richard A. Musgrave. 646p. 1981. Repr. of 1959 ed. lib. bdg. 32.50 (ISBN 0-89874-110-6). Krieger.

Theory of Random Functions. V. S. Pugachev. 1965. text ed. 51.00 (ISBN 0-08-010421-5). Pergamon.

Theory of Rate Processesin Condensed Media. B. Fain. (Lecture Notes in Chemistry Ser.: Vol. 20). (Illus.). 166p. 1981. 17.50 (ISBN 0-387-10249-3). Springer Verlag.

Theory of Relativity. 2nd ed. R. K. Pathria. 1974. text ed. 45.00 (ISBN 0-08-018032-9); pap. text ed. 24.00 (ISBN 0-08-018995-4). Pergamon.

Theory of Relativity & A Priori Knowledge. Hans Reichenbach. 1965. 18.50x (ISBN 0-520-01059-0). U of Cal Pr.

Theory of Relativity Revisited. H. W. Grayson. 272p. 1978. 10.00 (ISBN 0-8059-2529-5). Dorrance.

Theory of Reproduction & Accumulation. Oskar Lange & A. Banasinski. 1969. 27.00 (ISBN 0-08-012256-6). Pergamon.

Theory of Rotating Fluids. H. P. Greenspan. LC 68-12058. (Cambridge Monographs on Mechanics & Applied Mathematics). (Illus.). 1968. text ed. 44.50 (ISBN 0-521-05147-9). Cambridge U Pr.

Theory of Rotating Fluids. H. P. Greenspan. (Cambridge Monographs on Mechanics & Applied Mathematics). (Illus.). 328p. 1980. pap. 17.95 (ISBN 0-521-29956-X). Cambridge U Pr.

Theory of Scheduling. Richard W. Conway et al. 1967. 18.95 (ISBN 0-201-01189-1). A-W.

Theory of Science, (Die Wissenschaftslehre Oder Versuch Einer Neuen Darstellung der Logik) Bernhard Bolzano. Ed. & tr. by Rolf George. LC 71-126765. 1972. 27.50x (ISBN 0-520-01787-0). U of Cal Pr.

Theory of Semiconductor Junction Devices. J. H. Leck. 1967. 7.00 o.p. (ISBN 0-08-012173-X). Pergamon.

Theory of Semiotics. Umberto Eco. LC 74-22833. (Advances in Semiotics Ser.). 368p. 1976. 15.00x (ISBN 0-253-35955-4); pap. 5.95x (ISBN 0-253-20217-5). Ind U Pr.

Theory of Shape. Karol Borsuk. LC 76-359585. 379p. 1975. 37.50x (ISBN 0-8002-2343-8). Intl Pubns Serv.

Theory of Sheaves. Richard G. Swan. LC 64-24979. (Chicago Lectures in Mathematics Ser). (Orig.). 1964. 8.00x (ISBN 0-226-78329-4). U of Chicago Pr.

Theory of Simple Liquids. J. P. Hansen & I. R. McDonald. 1977. 54.50 (ISBN 0-12-323850-1). Acad Pr.

Theory of Social Action: The Correspondence of Alfred Schutz & Talcott Parsons. Ed. by Richard Grathoff. LC 77-15761. (Studies in Phenomenology and Existential Philosophy). 176p. 1978. 12.50x (ISBN 0-253-35957-0). Ind U Pr.

Theory of Social & Economic Organization. Max Weber. Tr. by Talcott Parsons. 1947. 15.95 (ISBN 0-02-934920-6); pap. text ed. 6.95 (ISBN 0-02-934930-3). Free Pr.

Theory of Social Structure. S. F. Nadel. 1969. Repr. of 1957 ed. 16.50x (ISBN 0-7100-1881-9). Routledge & Kegan.

Theory of Sound, 2 vols. 2nd rev. & enl. ed. John W. Strutt & Baron Rayleigh. (Illus.). Set. 22.00 (ISBN 0-8446-3028-4). Peter Smith.

Theory of Space, Time & Gravitation. 2nd ed. V. A. Fock. 1964. 52.00 (ISBN 0-08-010061-9). Pergamon.

Theory of Spectroscopy: Elementary Introduction. O. W. Howarth. LC 73-35. 214p. 1973. pap. text ed. 11.95 (ISBN 0-470-41667-X). Halsted Pr.

Theory of Spinors. Elie Cartan. 160p. 1981. pap. price not set (ISBN 0-486-64070-1). Dover.

Theory of Stochastic Processes, Vol. 1. I. I. Gihman & A. V. Skorohod. (Grundlehren der Mathematischen Wissenschaften: Vol. 210). 570p. 1981. 89.00 (ISBN 0-387-06573-3). Springer-Verlag.

Theory of Strict Liability: Toward a Reformulation of Tort Law. Richard A. Epstein. (Cato Papers Ser.: No. 8). 158p. 1979. pap. 4.00 (ISBN 0-932790-08-9). Cato Inst.

Theory of Structural Semantics. Samuel Abraham & Ferenc Kiefer. (Janua Linguarum, Ser. Minor: No. 49). 1966. 16.50x (ISBN 90-2790-581-9). Mouton.

Theory of Supervision in Teacher Education. Gilles Dussault. LC 76-121817. (Illus.). 1970. pap. text ed. 6.50x (ISBN 0-8077-1261-2). Tchrs Coll.

Theory of Syntax in Modern Linguistics. Olga Akhmanova & Galina Mikael'An. LC 69-13300. (Janua Linguarum, Ser. Minor: No. 68). (Orig.). 1969. pap. text ed. 24.70x (ISBN 90-2790-683-1). Mouton.

Theory of the Electromagnetic Field. David M. Cook. (Illus.). 560p. 1975. ref. ed. 23.95 (ISBN 0-13-913293-7). P-H.

Theory of the Firm: Resource Allocation in a Market Economy. 2nd ed. Kalman J. Cohen & Richard M. Cyert. (Illus.). 640p. 1975. 20.95 (ISBN 0-13-913798-X). P-H.

Theory of the Gene. Thomas H. Morgan. 1964. pap. 18.50 o.s.i. (ISBN 0-02-849280-3). Hafner.

Theory of the Measurement of Enterprise Income. Robert R. Sterling. LC 79-11417. 1979. Repr. of 1970 ed. text ed. 20.00 (ISBN 0-914348-26-4). Scholars Bk.

Theory of the Moral Life. John Dewey. LC 60-9060. 1980. pap. text ed. 6.95x (ISBN 0-8290-0263-4). Irvington.

Theory of the Novel. Ed. by Philip Stevick. LC 67-25335. 1967. pap. text ed. 8.95 (ISBN 0-02-931490-9). Free Pr.

Theory of the Properties of Metals & Alloys. Nevill F. Mott & H. Jones. 1936. pap. 6.00 (ISBN 0-486-60456-X). Dover.

Theory of Thermal Neutron Scattering: The Use of Neutrons for the Investigation of Condensed Matter. W. Marshall & S. W. Lovesey. (International Series of Monographs on Physics). (Illus.). 624p. 1971. 55.00x o.p. (ISBN 0-19-851254-6). Oxford U Pr.

Theory of Thermal Stresses. Bruno A. Boley & Jerome H. Weiner. LC 60-6446. 1960. 39.50 (ISBN 0-685-22215-2, 471-08679-7, Pub. by Wiley-Interscience). Wiley.

Theory of Thin Walled Bars. Atle Gjelsvik. 272p. 1981. 27.95 (ISBN 0-471-08594-4, Pub. by Wiley-Interscience). Wiley.

Theory of Transformations in Metals & Alloys., Part 1: Equilibrium & General Kinetic Theory. 2nd ed. J. W. Christian. LC 74-22470. 564p. 1975. text ed. 57.00 (ISBN 0-08-018031-0). Pergamon.

Theory of Transition-Metal Ions. John S. Griffith. 1961. 83.50 (ISBN 0-521-05150-9). Cambridge U Pr.

Theory of Unemployment Reconsidered. Edmond Malinvaud. LC 77-1117. 1977. 13.95 o.p. (ISBN 0-470-99075-9). Halsted Pr.

Theory of Unemployment Reconsidered. Edmond Malinvaud. LC 77-1117. 128p. 1980. pap. 13.95x (ISBN 0-470-26883-2). Halsted Pr.

Theory of Value, Distribution & Welfare Economics. J. M. Joshi. 1980. text ed. 20.00x (ISBN 0-7069-0689-6, Pub. by Vikas India). Advent Bk.

Theory of Value, Prices & Accumulation: Two Mathematical Integration of Marx, Von Neumann & Straffa. Gilbert Abraham-Frois & E. Berrebi. Tr. by M. P. Kregel-Javaux. LC 78-16277. (Illus., Fr.). 1979. 29.50 (ISBN 0-521-22385-7). Cambridge U Pr.

Theory of Vibration with Applications. William T. Thomson. (Illus.). 480p. 1973. 26.95 (ISBN 0-13-914549-4). P-H.

Theory of Vibrations with Applications. 2nd ed. William Thomson. (Illus.). 608p. 1981. text ed. 26.95 (ISBN 0-13-914523-0). P-H.

Theory of Wages: And Its Application to the Eight Hour Question & Other Labour Problems. Herbert M. Thompson. LC 79-51868. 1981. Repr. of 1892 ed. 16.50 (ISBN 0-88355-960-9). Hyperion Conn.

Theory of Waveguides. Leonard Lewin. LC 72-389. 320p. 1975. 37.95 (ISBN 0-471-53165-0). Halsted Pr.

Theory of Weak Interaction of Particle Physics. R. E. Marshak et al. LC 72-76058. (Interscience Monographs & Texts in Physics & Astronomy). 1969. 62.50 o.p. (ISBN 0-471-57290-X, Pub. by Wiley-Interscience). Wiley.

Theory, Practice & Application of Prevention in Environmental Health & Social Determinants of Human Health. Ed. by Norton Nelson & Lawrence E. Hinkle, Jr. LC 76-15142. 1976. pap. text ed. 4.50 o.p. (ISBN 0-88202-107-9). N Watson.

Theory Practice & Application of Prevention in Personal Health Services: Quality Control & Evaluation of Preventive Health Services. Ed. by Moorehead. LC 76-15083. 1976. pap. text ed. 4.95x o.p. (ISBN 0-88202-105-2). N Watson.

Theosophical Articles: Articles by Wm. Q. Judge Reprinted from Nineteenth-Century Theosophical Periodicals, 2 vols. 1276p. 1980. Set. 25.00. Theosophy.

Theosophical Glossary. Helene P. Blavatsky. LC 74-142546. 1971. Repr. of 1892 ed. 22.00 (ISBN 0-8103-3679-0). Gale.

Theosophical Glossary: A Photographic Reproduction of the Original Edition, As First Issued at London, England, 1892. Helena P. Blavatsky. Ed. & intro. by G. R. Mead. vi, 389p. 1930. Repr. of 1892 ed. 8.50 (ISBN 0-938998-04-8). Theosophy.

Theosophical Movement, 1875-1950. rev. ed. xiii, 351p. 1951. 6.00 (ISBN 0-686-02605-5). Cunningham Pr.

Theosophy: The Path of the Mystic. 3rd rev ed. Katherine Tingley. LC 77-82604. 1977. 6.00 (ISBN 0-911500-33-2); softcover 3.50 (ISBN 0-911500-34-0). Theos U Pr.

Theosophy: What's It All About. Geoffrey Farthing. 1967. 4.95 (ISBN 0-7229-5075-6). Theos Pub Hse.

Therapeutic Activities for the Handicapped Elderly. Charlotte Hamill & Robert C. Oliver. 295p. 1980. text ed. 24.00 (ISBN 0-89443-326-1). Aspen Systems.

Therapeutic Communication with Children: The Mutual Storytelling Technique in Child Psychotherapy. Richard A. Gardner. LC 71-155063. 1238p. 1971. 35.00x (ISBN 0-87668-042-2). Aronson.

Therapeutic Communities. Ed. by R. D. Hinshelwood & Nick Manning. 1979. 26.00x (ISBN 0-7100-0109-6); pap. 14.00 (ISBN 0-7100-0108-8). Routledge & Kegan.

Therapeutic Community: Outside the Hospital. Ed. by Elly Jansen. 392p. 1980. 31.50x (ISBN 0-85664-967-8, Pub. by Croom Helm Ltd England). Biblio Dist.

Therapeutic Effects in Ocular Lesions Obtained by Systemic & Topical Administration of an Activator of the Oxygen Metabolism. Ed. by F. Menna. (Journal: Ophthalmologica: Vol. 180, Suppl. 1). (Illus.). vi, 92p. 1980. 19.75 (ISBN 3-8055-1686-X). S Karger.

Therapeutic Environment. Robert Langs. 1979. 30.00x (ISBN 0-87668-385-5). Aronson.

Therapeutic Medical Devices: Application & Design. Ed. by Albert M. Cook & John G. Webster. (Illus.). 656p. 1981. 39.95 (ISBN 0-13-914796-9). P-H.

Therapeutic Needs of the Family. Ed. by Richard E. Hardy & John G. Cull. (American Lectures in Social & Rehabilitation Psychology Ser.). 256p. 1974. 15.75 (ISBN 0-398-03048-0). C C Thomas.

Therapeutic Program for the Patient with Arthritis. 3rd ed. Kenneth R. Wilske et al. 54p. Date not set. pap. 5.00 (ISBN 0-9601944-3-6). Mason Clinic.

Therapeutic Psychology: Fundamentals of Counseling & Psychotherapy. 3rd ed. L. Brammer & Everett Shostrum. (Clinical & Social Psych. Ser.). (Illus.). 1977. 19.95 (ISBN 0-13-914622-9). P-H.

Therapeutic Radiology Continuing Education Review. John A. Stryker & John A. Clement. 1977. spiral bdg. 12.00 o.p. (ISBN 0-87488-346-6). Med Exam.

Therapeutic Re-Creation: Ideas & Experiences. Ed. by Frank M. Robinson, Jr. (Illus.). 200p. 1974. 15.50 (ISBN 0-398-03160-6); pap. 9.50 (ISBN 0-398-03161-4). C C Thomas.

Therapeutic Recreation: A Helping Profession. 2nd ed. Gerald S. O'Morrow. (Illus.). 336p. 1980. text ed. 14.95 (ISBN 0-8359-7659-9). Reston.

Therapeutic Recreation Service: An Applied Behavioral Science Approach. Elliott M. Avedon. 256p. 1974. ref. ed. 15.95 (ISBN 0-13-914879-5). P-H.

Therapeutic Touch: A Book of Readings. Marianne Borelli & Patricia Heidt. LC 80-14109. 1980. pap. text ed. 14.95 (ISBN 0-8261-3111-5). Springer Pub.

Therapeutic Use of Child's Play. Ed. by Charles E. Schaeffer. LC 75-9556. 684p. 1981. Repr. of 1977 ed. 30.00 (ISBN 0-87668-209-3). Aronson.

Therapies for School Behavior Problems. Howard L. Millman et al. LC 80-8318. (Social & Behavioral Science Ser.). 1980. text ed. 18.95x (ISBN 0-87589-483-6). Jossey-Bass.

Therapist Disclosure: The Use of Self in Psychotherapy. Myron F. Weiner. 1978. 18.95 (ISBN 0-409-95070-X). Butterworths.

Theraputic Community. Ed. by Elly Jansen. 320p. 1980. 35.00x (ISBN 0-85664-967-8, Pub. by Croom Helm England). State Mutual Bk.

Therapy in Child Care: Collected Papers. Barbara Dockar-Drysdale. (Papers on Residential Work Ser.: No. 3). (Orig.). 1974. pap. text ed. 4.00x (ISBN 0-582-42854-8). Humanities.

Therapy in Eucational Environments for Handicapped Children. Ed. by Ruth A. Kalish. 500p. 1981. 17.95 (ISBN 0-8036-5207-0). Davis Co.

Therapy of Poetry. Molly Harrower. (Amer. Lec. Psychology Ser). 128p. 1972. 7.50 (ISBN 0-398-02311-5). C C Thomas.

Therapy with Oxygen & Other Gases: A Programed Unit in Fundamentals. rev. ed. Marie M. Seedor. LC 66-25981. (Orig.). 1971. pap. 8.00x (ISBN 0-8077-2136-0). Tchrs Coll.

Theravada Meditation: The Buddhist Transformation of Yoga. Winston L. King. LC 79-25856. 192p. 1980. 15.00x (ISBN 0-271-00254-9). Pa St U Pr.

There Are Men Too Gentle. James Kavanaugh. 1970. 5.95 (ISBN 0-87690-165-8). Dutton.

There Are Two Kinds of Terrible. Peggy Mann. LC 76-42372. (gr. 3-7). 1977. 6.95a (ISBN 0-385-09588-0); PLB (ISBN 0-385-08185-5). Doubleday.

There I Stood in All My Splendor. Ethel Barrett. pap. 2.25 o.p. (ISBN 0-8307-0016-1, 5000408). Regal.

There Is a Book. Madelyn Galbraith. LC 75-147021. 1971. 8.50 o.p. (ISBN 0-8309-0043-8). Herald Hse.

There Is a Love: A Beautifully Designed Tribute to Christ by a Talented European Illustrator. Brigitta Yavari. 1972. pap. 4.50 o.p. (ISBN 0-88270-006-5). Logos.

There Is a Place Where You Are Not Alone. Hugh Prather. LC 80-912. 224p. 1980. pap. 5.95 (ISBN 0-385-14778-3, Dolp). Doubleday.

There Is a Season. Karen Rose. 1969. pap. 1.25 (ISBN 0-380-39537-1, 39537). Avon.

There Is No Away: Readings & Language Activities in Ecology. Joan G. Roloff & Robert C. Wylder. 1971. pap. text ed. 7.95x (ISBN 0-02-477170-8, 47717). Macmillan.

There Is No Rhyme for Silver. Eve Merriam. (Illus.). (gr. 2-6). 1962. PLB 3.07 o.p. (ISBN 0-689-20272-5). Atheneum.

There Is Only One Me. Julie Gibbons. 20p. (gr. 1-4). 1974. pap. 2.50 (ISBN 0-911336-56-7). Sci of Mind.

There Must Be More to Love Than Death: Three Novellas. Charles Newman. LC 76-17743. 217p. 1976. 11.95 (ISBN 0-8040-0748-9). Swallow.

There Once Was a Book of Limericks. Paul Sawyer. LC 77-27109. (Games & Activities Ser.). (Illus.). (gr. k-3). 1978. PLB 9.30 (ISBN 0-8172-1168-3). Raintree Pubs.

There Shall Be a General Convention of This Church. Robert N. Wallace. 1976. pap. 3.95x (ISBN 0-8164-1212-X). Crossroad NY.

There Shall Be No Poor. Richard G. Hirsch. 1965. pap. 0.50 (ISBN 0-8074-0092-0, 707930). UAHC.

There Should Have Been Castles. Herman Raucher. 1978. 9.95 o.s.i. (ISBN 0-440-09038-5). Delacorte.

There Was a Certain Man: Spoken Art of the Fipa. Ed. by Roy G. Willis. (Library of African Literature). 1979. 24.00x (ISBN 0-19-815146-2). Oxford U Pr.

There Was a Time. Taylor Caldwell. 1979. pap. 2.75 (ISBN 0-515-05244-2). Jove Pubns.

There Was an Old Woman. Steven Kellogg. LC 80-15293. (Illus.). 48p. (ps-3). 1980. Repr. of 1974 ed. 8.95 (ISBN 0-590-07779-1, Four Winds). Schol Bk Serv.

There Was an Old Woman. Ellery Queen. Bd. with Origin of Evil. 1980. pap. 1.95 (ISBN 0-451-09306-2, J9306, Sig). NAL.

There Was an Old Woman Who Swallowed a Fly. Michael Kohn. LC 78-74130. (Illus.). 32p. (gr. k-5). Date not set. price not set (ISBN 0-89799-166-4); pap. price not set (ISBN 0-89799-165-6). Dandelion Pr. Postponed.

There Was This Man Running. N. L. Ray. LC 80-27225. 156p. (gr. 5-9). 1981. PLB 8.95 (ISBN 0-02-775760-9). Macmillan.

There's a Bat in Bunk Five. Paula Danziger. LC 80-64833. 160p. (gr. 5-8). 1980. 7.95 (ISBN 0-440-08605-1); PLB 7.45 (ISBN 0-440-08606-X). Delacorte.

There's a Caterpillar in My Lemonade. Diana Gregory. LC 80-17067. 176p. (gr. 4-8). 1980. PLB 7.95 (ISBN 0-201-03603-7, 3603, A-W Childrens). A-W.

There's a Fly in My Swill. Johnny Hart & Brant Parker. (Wizard of Id Ser.). (Illus.). 1978. pap. 1.50 (ISBN 0-449-13687-6, GM). Fawcett.

There's a Hippopotamus Under My Bed. Mike Thaler. (Easy-Read Story Bks.). (Illus.). (gr. k-3). 1977. PLB 6.45 s&l (ISBN 0-531-01318-9). Watts.

There's a Town in Missouri. Dickson Terry. 136p. (Orig.). 1980. pap. 4.95 (ISBN 0-86629-016-8). Sunrise MO.

There's Always Hope! Advent Christmas Sermons, Ser. A. John Brokhoff & Barbara Brokhoff. 1980. pap. text ed. 3.95 (ISBN 0-89536-452-2). CSS Pub.

There's an Ape Behind the Drape. Bernard Most. LC 80-24280. (Illus.). 32p. (gr. k-3). 1981. 6.95 (ISBN 0-688-00380-X); PLB 6.67 (ISBN 0-688-00381-8). Morrow.

There's One Born Every Minute. Harry Blackstone, Jr. 1978. pap. 1.50 o.s.i. (ISBN 0-515-04465-2). Jove Pubns.

There's Yeast in the Middle East. Willie S. Ethridge. LC 62-19853. 1962. 7.95 (ISBN 0-8149-0091-7). Vanguard.

Thermal Accommodation & Adsorption Coefficients of Gases, Vol. Ii-1. 1st ed. Y. S. Touloukian & C. Y. Ho. (CINDAS Data Ser. on Material Properties). 448p. (Orig.). 1980. 42.50 (ISBN 0-07-065031-4). McGraw.

Thermal Analysis: Comparative Studies in Materials. Ed. by H. Kambe & Paul D. Garn. LC 74-11511. 326p. 1975. 24.95 (ISBN 0-470-45567-5). Halsted Pr.

Thermal Characteristics of Tumors: Applications in Detection & Treatment. Ed. by Rakesh K. Jain & Pietro M. Gullino. LC 80-13379. (N.Y. Academy of Sciences Annals: Vol. 335). 542p. 1980. 95.00x (ISBN 0-89766-046-3). NY Acad Sci.

Thermal Conditions in Freezing Lakes & Rivers. A. A. Pivovarov. Tr. by E. Vilim from Rus. LC 73-12269. 136p. 1973. 32.95 (ISBN 0-470-69103-4). Halsted Pr.

Thermal Conduction in Solids. R. Berman. (Oxford Studies in Physics). 1980. 12.95x (ISBN 0-19-851430-1). Oxford U Pr.

Thermal Conductivity of Uranium Dioxide. (Technical Reports: No. 59). 1966. pap. 3.25 (ISBN 92-0-145166-0, IAEA). Unipub.

Thermal Conversion of Solid Waste & Biomass. Ed. by Jerry L. Jones & Shirley B. Radding. LC 80-14754. (ACS Symposium Ser.: No. 130). 1980. 57.50 (ISBN 0-8412-0565-5). Am Chemical.

Thermal Design of Nuclear Reactors. R. H. Winterton. LC 80-41187. (Illus.). 200p. 30.00 (ISBN 0-08-024215-4); pap. 15.00 (ISBN 0-08-024214-6). Pergamon.

Thermal Discharges at Nuclear Power Stations. (Technical Reports Ser., No. 155). (Illus.). 155p. (Orig.). 1974. pap. 13.00 (ISBN 92-0-125274-9, IAEA). Unipub.

Thermal Effluent Disposal from Power Generation: Proceedings. new ed. International Advanced Course & Workshop on Thermal Effluent Disposal from Power Generation, Aug. 23-28, 1976, Dubrovnik, Yugoslavia. Ed. by Z. Zaric. LC 77-28808. (Thermal & Fluids Engineering Ser.). (Illus.). 1978. text ed. 49.50 (ISBN 0-89116-093-0, Co-Pub. by McGraw Intl). Hemisphere Pub.

Thermal Electrocyclic Reactions. Elliot N. Marvel. (Organic Chemistry Ser.). 1981. 51.00 (ISBN 0-12-476250-6). Acad Pr.

Thermal Energy from the Sea. A. W. Hagen. LC 75-24767. (Energy Technology Review No. 8: Ocean Technology Review No. 5). (Illus.). 150p. 1976. 24.00 (ISBN 0-8155-0597-3). Noyes.

Thermal Energy Recovery. 2nd ed. John L. Boyen. LC 79-19704. 1980. 27.50 (ISBN 0-471-04981-6, Pub. by Wiley-Interscience). Wiley.

Thermal Energy Storage. Ed. by E. G. Kovach. LC 77-71233. 1977. pap. text ed. 9.50 (ISBN 0-08-021724-9). Pergamon.

Thermal Energy Storage & Regeneration. Frank W. Schmidt & A. John Willmott. (Illus.). 352p. 1981. 35.50 (ISBN 0-07-055346-7). McGraw.

Thermal Energy Storage in Aquifiers. Schaetzle. (Design & Applications). 275p. 1980. text ed. 24.50 (ISBN 0-08-025977-4). Pergamon.

Thermal Engineering. Harry L. Solberg et al. LC 60-11730. 1960. text ed. 26.95x (ISBN 0-471-81147-5). Wiley.

Thermal Environmental Engineering. 2nd ed. James L. Threlkeld. 1970. ref. ed. 26.95 (ISBN 0-13-914721-7). P-H.

Thermal Expansion of Crystals. R. S. Krishnan et al. LC 77-30620. (International Ser. in the Science of the Solid State: Vol. 12). 1980. 41.00 (ISBN 0-08-021405-3). Pergamon.

Thermal Geotechnics. Alfred R. Jumikis. 1977. 42.00 (ISBN 0-8135-0824-X). Rutgers U Pr.

Thermal Insulation. Ed. by S. D. Probert & D. R. Hub. (Illus.). 1968. text ed. 26.00x (ISBN 0-444-20025-8, Pub. by Applied Science). Burgess-Intl Ideas.

Thermal Insulation for Buildings: Economic Design for Comfort & Safety in Homes & Buildings. William C. Turner. 1981. write for info. (ISBN 0-88275-985-X). Krieger.

Thermal Insulation Handbook. 2nd ed. John F. Malloy. LC 76-52962. 570p. 1981. lib. bdg. 54.50 (ISBN 0-88275-510-2). Krieger. Postponed.

Thermal Insulation Handbook. William C. Turner & John F. Malloy. 624p. 1981. 62.50 (ISBN 0-07-039805-4). McGraw.

Thermal Machining Processes. E. C. Jameson. LC 79-62917. (Manufacturing Update Ser.). (Illus.). 29.00x (ISBN 0-87263-049-8). SME.

Thermal Mechanical Behavior of VO2 Nuclear Fuel: Multi-Cycle Test Description, Vol. IV. R. Christensen. xiv, 325p. Date not set. 49.50. Entropy Ltd.

Thermal Mechanical Behavior of VO2 Nuclear Fuel: Statistical Analysis of Acoustic Emission Axial Elagation, & Crack Characteristics. R. Christensen. xii, 238p. 1981. 34.50. Entropy Ltd.

Thermal Mechanical Behavior of VO2 Nuclear Fuel: Statistical Analysis of Acoustic Emission, Diametral Expansion,Anrol Elongation & Crash Characteristics. R. Christensen. x, 238p. pap. 34.50. Entropy Ltd.

Thermal Mechanical Behavior of VO2 Nuclear Fuel: Single Cycle Test Discription, Vol. III. R. Christensen. x, 308p. Date not set. 46.50. Entropy Ltd.

Thermal Mechanical Behavior of V02 Nuclear Fuel: Electrothermal Analysis, Vol. II. R. Christensen. x, 122p. Date not set. 19.50. Entropy Ltd.

Thermal Methods in Polymer Analysis. Ed. by S. W. Shalaby. LC 78-8816. (Eastern Analytical Symposium Ser.). 1978. pap. text ed. 21.75 (ISBN 0-89168-016-0). Franklin Inst.

Thermal Neutron Scattering. Ed. by P. A. Egelstaff. 1966. 72.50 (ISBN 0-12-232950-3). Acad Pr.

Thermal Performance of Buildings. J. F. Van Straaten. (Illus.). 1967. text ed. 48.50x (ISBN 0-444-20011-8, Pub. by Applied Science). Burgess-Intl Ideas.

Thermal Physics. 2nd ed. Charles Kittel & Herbert Kroemer. LC 79-16677. (Illus.). 1980. text ed. 22.95x (ISBN 0-7167-1088-9); instrs' guide avail. W H Freeman.

Thermal Radiation Heat Transfer. 2nd ed. Robert Siegel & John R. Howell. LC 79-17242. (Thermal & Fluids Engineering Hemisphere Ser.). (Illus.). 928p. 1980. text ed. 32.00 (ISBN 0-07-057316-6, C); solutions manual 16.95 (ISBN 0-07-057317-4). McGraw.

Thermal Shutters & Shades. William A. Shurcliff. LC 80-11574. 272p. 1980. pap. 12.95 (ISBN 0-931790-14-X). Brick Hse Pub.

Thermal Stress Analysis. D. J. Johns. 1965. 16.00 (ISBN 0-08-011153-X); pap. 7.75 (ISBN 0-08-011152-1). Pergamon.

Thermal Stress & Low-Cycle Fatigue. S. S. Manson. 416p. 1981. lib. bdg. price not set (ISBN 0-89874-279-X). Krieger.

Thermal Vibrations in Crystallography. B. T. Willis & A. W. Pryor. LC 73-94357. (Illus.). 280p. 1975. 49.50 (ISBN 0-521-20447-X). Cambridge U Pr.

Thermionic Energy Conversion, 2 vols. G. N. Hatsopoulos & E. P. Gyftopoulos. Incl. Vol. 1. Processes & Duricy. text ed. 25.00x (ISBN 0-262-08060-5); Vol. 2. Theory, Technology & Application. text ed. 35.00x (ISBN 0-262-08059-1). (Illus.). 1979. MIT Pr.

Thermochemistry of Organic & Organometallic Compounds. J. D. Cox & G. Pilcher. 1970. 90.50 o.s.i. (ISBN 0-12-194350-X). Acad Pr.

Thermodinamica Para Ingenieros. Jose Manrique. 1976. pap. text ed. 9.00 (ISBN 0-06-315512-5, IntlDept). Har-Row.

Thermodynamic Analysis of Combustion Engines. Ashley S. Campbell. LC 78-16181. 1979. text ed. 27.95 (ISBN 0-471-03751-6); tchrs manual (ISBN 0-471-05498-4). Wiley.

Thermodynamic & Transport Properties of Fluids SI Units. 2nd ed. G. F. Rogers & Y. R. Mayhew. 20p. 1976. Repr. of 1964 ed. pap. text ed. 3.25x (ISBN 0-631-96400-2, Pub. by Basil Blackwell). Biblio Dist.

Thermodynamic & Transport Properties of Organic Salts. Ed. by P. Franzosini & P. Sanesi. (IUPAC Chemical Data Ser.: No. 28). 376p. 1980. 105.00 (ISBN 0-08-022378-8). Pergamon.

Thermodynamic & Transport Properties of Uranium Dioxide & Related Phases. (Technical Reports: No. 39). 1965. pap. 5.00 (ISBN 92-0-145065-6, IAEA). Unipub.

Thermodynamic Charts. 2nd ed. F. O. Ellenwood & Charles O. Mackay. 1944. 11.95 o.p. (ISBN 0-471-23793-0, Pub. by Wiley-Interscience). Wiley.

Thermodynamic Diagrams for High Temperature Plasmas of Air-Carbon, Carbon-Hydrogen Mixtures & Argon. H. Kroepelin et al. 1971. 51.00 (ISBN 0-08-017581-3). Pergamon.

Thermodynamic Theory of Structure, Stability & Fluctuations. P. Glansdorff & I. Prigogine. LC 78-147070. 1971. 48.50 (ISBN 0-471-30280-5, Pub. by Wiley-Interscience). Wiley.

Thermodynamics. Enrico Fermi. 1937. pap. 3.00 (ISBN 0-486-60361-X). Dover.

Thermodynamics, 2 Vols. 1966. Vol. 1. 32.00 (ISBN 92-0-040066-3, IAEA); Vol. 2. 39.75 (ISBN 92-0-040166-X). Unipub.

Thermodynamics. Gordon Van Wylen. LC 59-9356. (Illus.). 1959. text ed. 25.95x (ISBN 0-471-90222-5). Wiley.

Thermodynamics: An Introductory Text for Engineering Students. 2nd ed. John E. Lee & Francis W. Sears. 1963. 22.95 (ISBN 0-201-04190-1). A-W.

Thermodynamics & Heat Power. 2nd ed. Irving Granet. (Illus.). 1980. text ed. 21.95 (ISBN 0-8359-7672-6); instrs' manual avail. Reston.

Thermodynamics & Its Applications. Michael Modell & Robert C. Reid. (Physical & Chemical Engr. Sciences Intl Ser.). (Illus.). 528p. 1974. 27.95 (ISBN 0-13-914861-2). P-H.

Thermodynamics & Statistical Physics: A Short Introduction. Robert J. Finkelstein. LC 78-94103. (Illus.). 1970. text ed. 26.95x (ISBN 0-7167-0325-4). W H Freeman.

Thermodynamics & Statistical Physics. Don C. Kelly. 1973. text ed. 22.95 (ISBN 0-12-404050-0). Acad Pr.

Thermodynamics for Chemists & Biologists. Terrell L. Hill. (Chemistry Ser). 1968. text ed. 16.95 (ISBN 0-201-02841-7). A-W.

Thermodynamics of Aqueous Systems: With Industrial Applications. Ed. by Stephen A. Newman. LC 80-16044. (ACS Symposium Ser.: No. 133). 1980. 58.00 (ISBN 0-8412-0569-8). Am Chemical.

Thermodynamics of Certain Refractory Compounds, 2 vols. Ed. by Harold L. Schick. Incl. Vol. 1. Discussion of Theoretical Studies. 56.00 (ISBN 0-12-624501-0); Vol. 2. Thermodynamic Tables, Bibliography & Property File. 56.00 (ISBN 0-12-624502-9). 1966. Set. 83.00 (ISBN 0-12-624566-5). Acad Pr.

Thermodynamics of Fluid Systems. L. C. Woods. (Oxford Engineering Science Ser). (Illus.). 350p. 1975. 58.00x (ISBN 0-19-856125-3). Oxford U Pr.

Thermodynamics of Irreversible Processes. Rolf Haase. (Chemical Engineering Ser). (Illus.). 1969. text ed. 25.95 (ISBN 0-201-02651-1). A-W.

Thermodynamics of Irreversible Processes. B. H. Lavenda. LC 76-22604. 1978. 39.95x (ISBN 0-470-98898-3). Halsted Pr.

Thermodynamics of Nuclear Materials - 1967. (Eng., Fr. & Rus.). 1968. pap. 41.75 (ISBN 92-0-040068-X, IAEA). Unipub.

Thermodynamics of Nuclear Materials - 1962. 1962. 26.75 (ISBN 92-0-040062-0, IAEA). Unipub.

Thermodynamics of Nuclear Materials, Nineteen Seventy-Nine, Vol. 1. 587p. 1980. pap. 68.25 (ISBN 92-0-040080-9, ISP 520-1, IAEA). Unipub.

Thermodynamics of Nuclear Materials 1974, 2 vols. (Illus.). 469p. 1975. Vol. 1. pap. 34.25 (ISBN 92-0-040175-9, IAEA); Vol. 2. pap. 39.75 (ISBN 0-685-54200-9). Unipub.

Thermodynamics of Nuclear Materials: 1979. 427p. 1981. pap. 54.00 (ISBN 92-0-040180-5, ISP 520, IAEA). Unipub.

Thermodynamics of Polymer Solutions. M. Kurata. Tr. by H. Fujita from Jap. (Mmi Press Polymer Monographs). 310p. 1981. 62.00 (ISBN 3-7186-0023-4). Harwood Academic.

Thermodynamics of Salt & Oxide Systems. Ed. by S. F. Pal'guev. LC 61-15178. (Electrochemistry of Molten & Solid Electrolytes Ser.: Vol. 9, Trudy No. 12). (Illus.). 107p. 1972. 30.00 (ISBN 0-306-18009-X, Consultants). Plenum Pub.

Thermodynamics of Solids. 2nd ed. Richard A. Swalin. LC 72-6334. (Science & Technology of Materials Ser.). 448p. 1972. 38.50 (ISBN 0-471-83854-3, Pub. by Wiley-Interscience). Wiley.

Thermodynamics One: An Introduction to Energy. John R. Dixon. (P-H Ser. in Mechanical Engineering). (Illus.). 512p. 1975. 24.95 (ISBN 0-13-914887-6). P-H.

Thermodynamics: Principles & Applications. Frank C. Andrews. LC 77-150607. 1971. 19.50 (ISBN 0-471-03183-6, Pub. by Wiley-Interscience). Wiley.

Thermodynamics: Principles & Applications. Melvin Mark & Arthur R. Foster. 1979. text ed. 23.50 (ISBN 0-205-06631-3, 3266311); solutions man. o.p. avail. (ISBN 0-205-06632-1). Allyn.

Thermodynamics, the Kinetic Theory of Gases & Statistical Mechanics. 3rd ed. Francis W. Sears & Gerhard L. Salinger. 464p. 1975. text ed. 23.95 (ISBN 0-201-06894-X). A-W.

Thermoelasticity. 2nd rev. & enl. ed. H. Parkus. 1976. soft cover 24.80 (ISBN 0-387-81375-6). Springer-Verlag.

Thermoelectricity in Metals & Alloys. R. D. Barnard. LC 72-10919. 259p. 1973. 29.95 (ISBN 0-470-05053-5). Halsted Pr.

Thermographie und Brustkrebs: Diagnose, Prognose, Ueberwachung. M. Gautherie et al. Ed. by E. Pusterla & C. M. Gros. (Gynaekologische Rundschau: Vol. 19, No. 4). (Illus.). 1980. pap. 19.75 (ISBN 3-8055-0716-X). S Karger.

Thermohaline Finestructure of the Ocean. Ed. by K. N. Fedorov. Tr. by D. A. Brown & J. S. Turner. 1978. text ed. 45.00 (ISBN 0-08-021673-0). Pergamon.

Thermoluminescence Dosimetry. A. F. McKinlay. (Medical Physics Handbook: No. 5). 180p. write for info. (ISBN 0-9960020-4-9, Pub. by a Hilger England). Heyden.

Thermomechanics. J. C. Gibbings. 1970. 21.00 (ISBN 0-08-006334-9); pap. 9.75 (ISBN 0-08-006333-0). Pergamon.

Thermomechanics of Magnetic Fluids: Theory & Applications, Proceedings. new ed. International Advanced Course & Workshop on Thermomechanics of Magnetic Fluids, Udine, Italy, Oct. 3-7, 1977. Ed. by Boris Berkovsky. LC 78-15126. 1978. text ed. 45.00 (ISBN 0-89116-143-0, Co-Pub. by McGraw Intl). Hemisphere Pub.

Thermometric Titrations. J. Barthel. (Chemical Analysis Ser: Vol. 45). 209p. 1975. 29.95 (ISBN 0-471-05448-8, Pub. by Wiley-Interscience). Wiley.

Thermometric Titrimetry. L. S. Bark & S. M. Bark. 1969. 22.00 (ISBN 0-08-013047-X). Pergamon.

Thermomicroscopy in the Analysis of Pharmaceuticals. M. Kuhnert-Brandstatter. 424p. 1972. 72.00 (ISBN 0-08-006990-8). Pergamon.

Thermophilic Microorganisms & Life at High Temperatures. Th. D. Brock. LC 78-6110. (Springer Ser. in Microbiology). (Illus.). 1978. 27.10 (ISBN 0-387-90309-7). Springer-Verlag.

Thermophysics & Temperature Control of Spacecraft & Entry Vehicles. Ed. by Gerhardt B. Heller. (Progress in Astronautics & Aeronautics: Vol. 18). 1966. 27.00 (ISBN 0-12-535118-6). Acad Pr.

Thermoplastic Piping for Potable Water Distribution Systems: BRAB Fcc Technical Report No. 61. Building Research Advisory Board. LC 77-180651. 1971. pap. 3.00 (ISBN 0-309-01934-6). Natl Acad Pr.

Thermosense I: Proceedings. Intro. by Thomas M. Lillesand. 244p. 1978. pap. 15.00 (ISBN 0-686-27662-0). ASP.

Thermosense II. 1979. member 15.00; non-member 19.50. ASP.

Thermostatic Control: Principles & Practice. V. C. Miles. (Illus.). 213p. 1974. 22.50x (ISBN 0-408-00131-3). Transatlantic.

Thesaurus-Making: Grow Your Own Word-Stock. Helen M. Townley & Ralph C. Gee. (Grafton Ser.). 208p. 1981. lib. bdg. 25.00x (ISBN 0-86531-107-2). Westview.

Thesaurus of Engineering & Scientific Terms. 690p. 1967. 40.00 o.p. (ISBN 0-686-27586-1, 507-67). AAES.

Thesaurus of Entomology. Ed. by Foote. 1977. 9.00 (ISBN 0-686-22689-5). Entomol Soc.

Thesaurus of Information Science Terminolgy. rev. ed. Claire K. Schultz. LC 78-16878. 1978. 11.50 (ISBN 0-8108-1156-1). Scarecrow.

Thesaurus of Scales & Melodic Patterns. Nicholas Slonimsky. 1947. 27.50 (ISBN 0-684-10551-9, ScribT). Scribner.

Thesaurus of Slang. Howard N. Rose. LC 72-167144. xii, 120p. Repr. of 1934 ed. 18.00 (ISBN 0-8103-3115-2). Gale.

These Are My Rites: A Brief History of the Eastern Rites of Christianity. Edward E. Finn. (Illus.). 1980. pap. 4.95 (ISBN 0-8146-1058-7). Liturgical Pr.

These Are the Endangered. Charles Cadieux. (Illus.). 228p. 1981. 15.00 (ISBN 0-913276-35-9). Stone Wall Pr.

These Are the Sacraments. A. M. Coniaris. 1981. pap. 5.95 (ISBN 0-686-69400-7). Light & Life.

These Came Back. Richard Webb. (Orig.). 1976. pap. 1.75 (ISBN 0-89129-039-7). Jove Pubns.

These Gentle Hills. John Kollock. 14.95 (ISBN 0-932298-14-1). Green Hill.

These Golden Pleasures. Valerie Sherwood. (Orig.). 1977. pap. 2.75 (ISBN 0-446-95744-5). Warner Bks.

These Primal Years. John Bowen. 240p. 1981. 10.00 (ISBN 0-682-49719-3). Exposition.

These Strange Ashes. Elisabeth Elliot. LC 74-25684. 144p. 1975. pap. 3.95 (ISBN 0-06-062233-4, RD 306). Har-Row.

These, Too, Shall Be Loved. Flower A. Newhouse. LC 76-49246. 1976. pap. 4.50 (ISBN 0-910378-11-8). Christward.

These Were the Greeks. H. D. Amos & A. G. Lang. (Illus.). 224p. 1980. 12.95 (ISBN 0-7175-0789-0). Dufour.

These Were the Romans. Tingay & Badcock. (Illus.). pap. 8.95 (ISBN 0-7175-0591-X). Dufour.

These Were the Sioux. Mari Sandoz. 1975. Repr. 6.95 (ISBN 0-8038-7060-4). Hastings.

Theses: Resolutions & Manifestos of the First Four Congresses of the Third International. Ed. by Bertil Hessel. (Rus.). 1980. text ed. 45.50x (ISBN 0-391-01875-2). Humanities.

Theseus & the Road to Athens. Pamela Espeland. LC 80-27713. (Myths for Modern Children Ser.). (Illus.). 32p. (gr. 1-4). 1981. PLB 6.95 (ISBN 0-87614-141-6). Carolrhoda Bks.

Theshold of the McCarthy Era: The Audio Cassette. Ed. by G. D. Days. LC 80-740529. cassette 11.00 (ISBN 0-918628-07-5). Congeros Pubns.

Thesis: Rhetoric of the Essay. 2nd ed. Alan Danzig & Edith Schor. 352p. 1979. pap. text ed. 7.95x (ISBN 0-534-00726-0). Wadsworth Pub.

Thessalonian Epsitles. D. Edmond Hiebert. 1971. 11.95 (ISBN 0-8024-8640-1). Moody.

Thessalonians. J. E. Frame. LC 12-23430. (International Critical Commentary Ser.). 336p. Repr. of 1912 ed. 17.50x (ISBN 0-567-05032-7). Attic Pr.

Thessalonians. D. E. Whiteley. (New Clarendon Bible Ser). (Illus.). 1969. 6.95x (ISBN 0-19-836906-9). Oxford U Pr.

Thessalonians: An Expositional Commentary. Donald G. Barnhouse. 116p. 1980. pap. 3.95 (ISBN 0-310-20501-8). Zondervan.

Theta Functions of Riemann Surfaces. J. D. Fay. (Lecture Notes in Mathematics: Vol. 352). 137p. 1973. pap. 8.70 (ISBN 0-387-06517-2). Springer-Verlag.

Theta Syndrome. Elleston Trevor. LC 76-55904. 1977. 7.95 o.p. (ISBN 0-385-07463-8). Doubleday.

Theurgy. Mouni Sadhu. 1965. 12.75 o.p. (ISBN 0-04-133003-X). Allen Unwin.

They Accepted the Challenge. Charles T. Knutzleman & Lynx Cryderman. (Illus.). 304p. 1981. 11.95 (ISBN 0-312-79971-3). St Martin.

They All Need to Talk: Oral Communication in the Language Arts Program. Wilma M. Possien. (Orig.). 1969. pap. 8.95 (ISBN 0-13-917088-X). P-H.

They Also Ran. rev. ed. Irving Stone. LC 66-21914. 6.95 o.p. (ISBN 0-385-07409-3). Doubleday.

They & We: Racial & Ethnic Relations in the United States. Peter I. Rose. 252p. 1981. pap. text ed. 7.95 (ISBN 0-394-32402-1). Random.

They Call Him the Buffalo Doctor. Jean Cummings. LC 73-147172. 320p. 1980. Repr. of 1971 ed. 7.00 (ISBN 0-8187-0035-1). Harlo Pr.

They Call Me Assassin. Jack Tatum & Bill Kushner. 1980. pap. 2.95 (ISBN 0-380-52480-5, 52480). Avon.

They Called Me Cassandra. Genevieve Tabouis. LC 76-172178. (Europe 1815-1945 Ser.). (Illus.). 448p. 1973. Repr. of 1942 ed. lib. bdg. 39.50 (ISBN 0-306-70298-3). Da Capo.

They Called Me Leni. Zdenka Bezdekova. LC 77-175227. 1973. 4.50 o.p. (ISBN 0-672-51331-5). Bobbs.

They Came from Outer Space. James Wynorski. LC 80-2249. 336p. 1981. 11.95 (ISBN 0-385-18502-2). Doubleday.

They Came from Space. Elwood D. Baumann. LC 76-44435. (Illus.). (gr. 6 up). 1977. PLB 6.90 s&l (ISBN 0-531-00388-4). Watts.

They Came from the North. Merville Luker. 1979. 5.95 o.p. (ISBN 0-8062-1157-1). Carlton.

They Came from the Sea. E. V. Timms. 1977. pap. 1.50 o.s.i. (ISBN 0-515-04400-8). Jove Pubns.

They Came in Chains. rev. ed. J. Saunders Redding. LC 73-401. 1973. 6.25 o.s.i. (ISBN 0-397-00812-0). Lippincott.

They Came This Way: The Humboldt Valley, Highroad to the Gold Rush. Don Chase. (Illus.). 1973. velo-bind 3.50 (ISBN 0-918634-33-4); pap. 3.00 limited ed. (ISBN 0-685-73469-2). D M Chase.

They Came to Pennsylvania Workshop. Lucille Wallower & Ellen J. Wholey. LC 76-14140. (gr. 4-5). 1976. pap. 3.50 (ISBN 0-931992-02-8). Penns Valley.

They Chose Honor: The Problem of Conscience in Custody. Lewis Merklin, Jr. LC 74-5794. 352p. (YA) 1974. 8.95 o.s.i. (ISBN 0-06-012939-5, HarpT). Har-Row.
They Didn't Win the Oscars. Bill Libby. (Illus.). 256p. 1980. 18.95 (ISBN 0-87000-455-7). Arlington Hse.
They Felled the Redwoods. 15.00. Chatham Pub CA.
They Followed the Piper. Lee Hultquist. pap. 2.95 o.p. (ISBN 0-88270-195-9, P195-8). Logos.
They Followed the Rails: History of Childress County. 15.00 o.p. (ISBN 0-685-48794-6). Nortex Pr.
They Know Not What They Do: Baseball. Robert L. Moore. (Illus.). 112p. (Orig.). 1971. pap. 2.00 (ISBN 0-912178-03-5). Mor-Mac.
They Led a Nation. Virginia Sneve. Ed. by N. Jane Hunt. LC 75-254. (Illus.). 1975. 5.95 (ISBN 0-88498-026-X); text ed. 3.95 o.p. (ISBN 0-685-52611-9); pap. 3.95 (ISBN 0-88498-027-8); pap. text ed. 2.66 o.p. (ISBN 0-685-52612-7). Brevet Pr.
They Led the Way: Fourteen American Women. Johnston. (gr. 3-5). pap. 1.50 (ISBN 0-590-11908-7, Schol Pap). Schol Bk Serv.
They Left Footprints. Elmer Kelley. 3.50 o.p. (ISBN 0-685-48818-7). Nortex Pr.
They Lived Like This in Ancient China. Marie Neurath. LC 67-10000. (They Lived Like This Ser). (Illus.). (gr. 4-6). 1967. PLB 3.90 o.p. (ISBN 0-531-01377-4). Watts.
They Lived Like This in Ancient Crete. Marie Neurath. LC 66-14736. (They Lived Like This Ser). (Illus.). (gr. 4-6). 1966. PLB 3.90 o.p. (ISBN 0-531-01378-2). Watts.
They Lived Like This in Ancient Mesopotamia. Marie Neurath. LC 65-10066. (They Lived Like This Ser). (Illus.). (gr. 4-6). 1965. PLB 3.90 o.p. (ISBN 0-531-01383-9). Watts.
They Lived Like This in Ancient Rome. Marie Neurath. LC 68-14093. (They Lived Like This Ser). (Illus.). (gr. 4-6). 1969. PLB 3.90 o.p. (ISBN 0-531-01386-3). Watts.
They Lived Like This in Chaucer's England. Marie Neurath. LC 68-10837. (They Lived Like This Ser). (Illus.). (gr. 4-6). 1967. PLB 5.90 (ISBN 0-531-01388-X). Watts.
They Lived Like This in Old Japan. Marie Neurath. (They Lived Like This Ser). (Illus.). (gr. 4-6). 1967. PLB 3.90 o.p. (ISBN 0-531-01387-1). Watts.
They Lived Like This in the Old Stone Age. Marie Neurath. LC 74-91876. (They Lived Like This Ser). (gr. 4-6). 1971. PLB 3.90 o.p. (ISBN 0-531-01393-6). Watts.
They Lived Like This: The Ancient Maya. Marie Neurath. LC 67-10095. (They Lived Like This Ser). (Illus.). (gr. 4-6). 1967. PLB 3.90 o.p. (ISBN 0-531-01382-0). Watts.
They Lived Their Lives (As Best They Could) Eda Howink. 1981. 5.50 (ISBN 0-8233-0329-2). Golden Quill.
They Looked for a City. LC 58-17705. 1955. pap. 2.50 (ISBN 0-915540-16-9). Friends Israel-Spearhead Pr.
They Loved the Land: History of Foard County. Bailey Phelps. 25.00 (ISBN 0-685-48796-2). Nortex Pr.
They Met Jesus. David A. Hubbard. 1976. pap. 1.25 (ISBN 0-89129-184-9). Jove Pubns.
They of Rome. Lois Parker. 128p. 1980. pap. write for info. (ISBN 0-8127-0308-1). Southern Pub.
They Paved the Way: A History of N. H. Women. Olive Tardiff. vi, 98p. (gr. 9-12). 1980. pap. text ed. 3.95 (ISBN 0-917890-22-1). Heritage Bk.
They Saddled the West. Glen R. Vernam & Lee M. Rice. LC 75-5734. (Illus.). 1975. 10.00 (ISBN 0-87033-199-X). Cornell Maritime.
They Said It Couldn't Be Done. Ross R. Olney. LC 78-12405. (gr. 4-7). 1979. PLB 10.95 (ISBN 0-525-41060-0). Dutton.
They Satisfy: The Cigarette in American Life. Robert Sobel. LC 77-27681. 1978. 8.95 o.p. (ISBN 0-385-12956-4, Anchor Pr). Doubleday.
They Saw It Happen, Vol. 1: An Anthology of Eye-Witnesses Accounts of Events in British History, 55 B. C. to A. D. 1485. W. O. Hassall. 1973. pap. 6.50x o.p. (ISBN 0-631-05280-1, Pub. by Basil Blackwell). Biblio Dist.
They Saw the Second Coming: An Explosive Novel About the End of the World! Doug Clark. LC 78-71427. 1979. 6.95 (ISBN 0-89081-196-2, 1903); pap. 3.95 (ISBN 0-89081-190-3). Harvest Hse.
They Shoot Canoes, Don't They? Patrick McManus. 228p. 1981. 10.95 (ISBN 0-03-058646-1). HR&W.
They Shoot to Kill: A Psycho-Survey of Criminal Sniping. Ronald Tobias. 240p. (Orig.). 1981. 14.95 (ISBN 0-87364-207-4). Paladin Ent.
They Showed the Way: Forty American Negro Leaders. Charlemae H. Rollins. LC 64-20692. (gr. 4 up). 1964. 8.95 (ISBN 0-690-81612-X, TYC-J). T Y Crowell.
They Sought a Country: Mennonite Colonization in Mexico. Harry L. Sawatzky. LC 78-92673. 1971. 24.50x (ISBN 0-520-01704-8). U of Cal Pr.
They Speak with Other Tongues. John L. Sherril. 1976. pap. 1.50 (ISBN 0-685-84387-4). Jove Pubns.
They Tell a Story. Martha Lupton. LC 74-167052. vi, 553p. 1972. Repr. of 1940 ed. 20.00 (ISBN 0-8103-3112-8). Gale.
They Thought They Were Free: The Germans 1933-45. 2nd ed. Milton Mayer. LC 55-5137. 1966. 13.50x o.s.i. (ISBN 0-226-51190-1). U of Chicago Pr.
They Too Made America Great. Adolph Caso. 175p. 1978. 12.50 (ISBN 0-8283-1699-6). Dante U Am.
They Took Their Stand. Emma G. Sterne. (America in the Making Ser.). (Illus.). (gr. 7-12). 1968. 8.95 (ISBN 0-02-788130-X, CCPr). Macmillan.
They Tried to Cut It All; Grays Harbor: Turbulent Years of Greed & Greatness. Edwin Van Syckle. LC 80-16469. (Illus.). 308p. 1980. 17.95 (ISBN 0-9605152-0-8); pap. 9.95 (ISBN 0-9605152-1-6). Friends Aberdeen.
They Turned to Stone. Julian May. (Illus.). 40p. (gr. k-3). 1965. reinforced bdg. 5.95 o.p. (ISBN 0-8234-0118-9). Holiday.
They Went Thataway. James Horwitz. 1978. pap. 1.95 o.p. (ISBN 0-345-27126-2). Ballantine.
They Were There. R. Andersen & R. Barlag. 1977. pap. 4.50 (ISBN 0-570-03769-7, 12-2704). Concordia.
They Wrote on Clay: The Babylonian Tablets Speak Today. Edward Chiera. Ed. by George G. Cameron. LC 38-27631. (Illus.). 1956. pap. 3.50 (ISBN 0-226-10425-7, P2, Phoen). U of Chicago Pr.
They're Never Too Young for Books: Literature for Pre-Schoolers. Edythe M. McGovern. LC 80-80216. 294p. (Orig.). 1980. pap. 10.00 (ISBN 0-9604064-0-9). Mar Vista.
They're Off. Anne Alcock. (Illus.). 1979. 15.75 (ISBN 0-85131-299-3, Dist. by Sporting Book Center). J A Allen.
They've Discovered a Head in the Box for the Bread & Other Laughable Limericks. Ed. by John E. Brewton & Lorraine A. Blackburn. LC 77-26598. (Illus.). (gr. 3-7). 1978. 7.95 (ISBN 0-690-01388-4, TYC-J); PLB 7.89 (ISBN 0-690-03883-6). T Y Crowell.
Thick Film Hybrid Microcircuit Technology. D. W. Hamer & J. V. Biggers. LC 72-3191. 464p. 1972. 38.50 (ISBN 0-471-34700-0, Pub by Wiley-Interscience). Wiley.
Thick Plate Working, Vol. 1. (Engineering Craftsmen: No. D1). (Illus.). 1969. spiral bdg. 14.95x (ISBN 0-85083-025-7). Intl Ideas.
Thick Plate Working, Vol. 2. Ed. by J. M. Rowney et al. (Engineering Craftsmen: No. D21). (Illus.). 1969. spiral bdg. 15.50x (ISBN 0-85083-047-8). Intl Ideas.
Thicket. Patricia Gallagher. 1977. pap. 1.75 (ISBN 0-380-01578-1, 33316). Avon.
Thidwick, the Big-Hearted Moose. Dr. Seuss. LC 48-8129. (Dr. Seuss Paperback Classics Ser.). (Illus.). 48p. (gr. k-3). 1980. pap. 2.95 (ISBN 0-394-84540-4). Random.
Thief & the Dogs. Nagib Mahfouz. (Arabic.). pap. 5.50 (ISBN 0-685-82888-3). Intl Bk Ctr.
Thief in the Night. Jim Grant. 128p. 1974. pap. 2.50 (ISBN 0-8024-8688-6). Moody.
Thief in the Night. William Sears. 1961. 6.50 (ISBN 0-85398-096-9, 7-31-60, Pub. by George Ronald England); pap. 2.50 (ISBN 0-85398-008-X). Baha'i.
Thief of Copper Canyon. Elizabeth Graham. (Harlequin Presents Ser.). 192p. (Orig.). 1981. pap. 1.50 (ISBN 0-373-10403-0, Pub. by Harlequin). PB.
Thief of Hearts. Rachelle Edwards. 1977. pap. 1.50 o.p. (ISBN 0-449-23401-0, Crest). Fawcett.
Thief of State Street: 30 Years of Audacious Advertising with Zareh. Zareh Thomajah. LC 80-82894. (Illus.). 152p. (Orig.). 1980. pap. 15.00 (ISBN 0-686-28877-7). Garabed.
Thief of Time. John Wainwright. LC 77-94461. 1978. 8.95 o.p. (ISBN 0-312-79989-6). St Martin.
Thief Who Hugged a Moonbeam. Harold Berson. LC 70-190382. (Illus.). 40p. (gr. k-3). 1972. 4.50 (ISBN 0-395-28767-7, Clarion). HM.
Thief's Primer: Life of an American Character. Bruce Jackson. 1969. 5.95 o.s.i. (ISBN 0-02-558280-1). Macmillan.
Thieves. T. A. Noton. LC 78-67232. 264p. 1980. pap. 3.95 (ISBN 0-914850-48-2). Impact Tenn.
Thieves' Brand. Giles A. Lutz. LC 80-2905. (Double D Western Ser.). 192p. 1981. 9.95 (ISBN 0-385-17487-X). Doubleday.
Thieves in the Night. Arthur Koestler. 1967. 12.95 (ISBN 0-02-565670-8). Macmillan.
Thin Air. William Marshall. LC 77-20786. 1978. 6.95 o.p. (ISBN 0-03-021071-2). HR&W.
Thin Edge. Anne W. Simon. 1978. pap. 2.50 (ISBN 0-380-42754-0, 42754). Avon.
Thin Edge: Coast & Man in Crisis. Anne W. Simon. LC 76-26253. 1978. 10.00 o.p. (ISBN 0-06-013890-4, HarpT). Har-Row.
Thin Films. K. D. Leaver & B. N. Chapman. LC 75-153871. (Wykeham Science Ser.: No. 17). 1971. 9.95x (ISBN 0-8448-1119-X). Crane Russak Co.
Thin Films: Interdiffusion & Reactions. Ed. by J. M. Poate et al. LC 77-25348. (Electrochemical Society Ser.). 1978. 43.50 (ISBN 0-471-02238-1, Pub. by Wiley-Interscience). Wiley.
Thin Fine Line. Michael C. Giammatteo. (Illus., Orig.). 1975. pap. 5.00 (ISBN 0-918428-05-X). Sylvan Inst.
Thin from Within. Jack Osman & Bobbie J. Van Dolson. 160p. 1981. pap. write for info. (ISBN 0-8280-0027-1). Review & Herald.
Thin Layer Chromatography: Quantitative Environmental & Clinical Applications. Joseph C. Touchstone & Dexter Rogers. LC 80-36871. 384p. 1980. 27.50 (ISBN 0-471-07958-8, Pub. by Wiley-Interscience). Wiley.
Thin Men of Haddam. C. W. Smith. 1975. pap. 1.50 o.s.i. (ISBN 0-380-00422-4, 24943). Avon.
Thin Plate Design for In-Plane Loading. D. G. Williams & B. Aalami. (Constrado Monographs). 210p. 1980. 44.95x (ISBN 0-470-26834-4). Halsted Pr.
Thin Plate Working, Vol. 1. 2nd ed. Ed. by H. Dickson et al. (Illus.). 1977. 15.95x (ISBN 0-686-65561-3). Vol. 1 (ISBN 0-85083-387-6). Vol. 2 (ISBN 0-85083-047-8). Intl Ideas.
Thin Plate Working, Vol. 2. Ed. by H. Dickson et al. (Engineering Craftsmen: No. D22). (Illus.). 1969. spiral bdg. 13.95x (ISBN 0-85083-033-8). Intl Ideas.
Thin Red Line. James Jones. 1962. lib. rep. ed. 20.00x (ISBN 0-684-15555-9, ScribT). Scribner.
Thin Reinforced Concrete Shells: Special Analysis Problems. Victor Gioncu. LC 78-10338. 1980. 57.00 (ISBN 0-471-99735-8, Pub. by Wiley-Interscience). Wiley.
Thin-Shell Concrete Structures. 2nd ed. David P. Billington. (Illus.). 432p. 1981. 24.50. McGraw.
Thin Shell Structures: Theory, Experiment & Design. ref. ed. Ed. by E. E. Sechler & Y. C. Fung. 1974. 34.95 (ISBN 0-13-918193-8). P-H.
Thin Shells: Computing & Theory. J. E. Gibson. (International Series in Structure & Solid Body Mechanics). (Illus.). 1980. 40.00 (ISBN 0-08-023275-2); pap. 18.00 (ISBN 0-08-024204-9). Pergamon.
Thin-Walled Structures. Ed. by J. Rhodes & A. C. Walker. 1980. 54.95x (ISBN 0-470-26906-5). Halsted Pr.
Thine Health. Nicholas C. Eliopoulos. Ed. by Nicholas G. Phistiklakis. (Orig.). 1980. pap. text ed. 12.00 (ISBN 0-9605396-2-X). Phystiklakis & Eliopoulos.
Thine Is the Glory. Augustine Burch. 1981. 4.50 (ISBN 0-8062-1626-3). Carlton.
Things Around the House. Herbert S. Zim. (Illus.). (gr. 1 up). 1954. PLB 6.00 o.p. (ISBN 0-688-31571-2). Morrow.
Things Chinese. Rita Aero. LC 79-6852. (Illus.). 256p. 1980. 24.95 (ISBN 0-385-17258-3). Doubleday.
Things Chinese. Rita Aero. LC 79-6852. (Illus.). 320p. 1980. pap. 10.95 (ISBN 0-385-15673-1, Dolp). Doubleday.
Things Chinese: Or Notes Connected with China. rev. 5th ed. J. Dyer Ball. Ed. by Chalmers Werner. LC 74-164085. (Tower Bks). 1971. Repr. of 1926 ed. 32.00 (ISBN 0-8103-3917-X). Gale.
Things Divine & Supernatural Conceived by Analogy with Things Natural & Human. Peter Browne. Ed. by Rene Wellek. LC 75-11203. (British Philosophers & Theologians of the 17th & 18th Centuries: Vol. 9). 1976. Repr. of 1733 ed. lib. bdg. 42.00 (ISBN 0-8240-1758-7). Garland Pub.
Things Fall Apart. Chinua Achebe. LC 59-7114. 1959. 5.95 (ISBN 0-8392-1113-9); pap. 4.95 (ISBN 0-8392-5006-1). Astor-Honor.
Things I Didn't Know I Loved: Selected Poems of Nazim Hikmet. Nazim Hikmet. Tr. by Randy Blasing & Mutlu Konuk. LC 75-10789. 96p. 7.95 (ISBN 0-89255-000-7); pap. 4.95 (ISBN 0-89255-001-5). Persea Bks.
Things I Learned After It As Too Late: (& Other Minor Truths) Charles M. Schulz. (Illus.). 1981. pap. 4.95 (ISBN 0-686-69128-8). HR&W.
Things I Meant to Say to You When We Were Old. Merrit Malloy. LC 76-26353. 144p. 1977. pap. 3.95 (ISBN 0-385-12326-4, Dolp). Doubleday.
Things in My House. Illus. by Virginia Parsons. (Block Bk.). (ps). 1981. 2.50 (ISBN 0-686-69205-5, Golden Pr). Western Pub.
Things Kids Collect. Shari Lewis. LC 79-3838. (Kids-Only Club Bks.). (Illus.). 96p. (Orig.). (gr. 3-6). 1981. 6.95 (ISBN 0-03-049731-0); pap. 3.95 (ISBN 0-03-049736-1). HR&W.
Things Maps Don't Tell Us: Adventure into Map Interpretation. Armin K. Lobeck. (Illus.). 1956. 10.95 (ISBN 0-02-573790-2). Macmillan.
Things No One Ever Tells You. Jim Aylward. 144p. (Orig.). 1981. pap. 1.95 (ISBN 0-446-90707-3). Warner Bks.
Things Not Generally Known. John Timbs. Ed. by David A. Wells. LC 68-30584. 1968. Repr. of 1857 ed. 24.00 (ISBN 0-8103-3101-2). Gale.
Things Once Secret. Kathy Anselmo. 33p. 1980. 3.95 (ISBN 0-8059-2750-6). Dorrance.
Things That Go! Stella Nathan. (Word Bird Books). (Illus.). 24p. (ps-2). 1977. PLB 5.22 o.p. (ISBN 0-307-66255-1, Golden Pr). Western Pub.
Things That Happen. J. E. Tiles. Ed. by Andrew Brennan & William E. Lyons. (Scots Philosophical Monograph: Vol. 1). (Illus.). 157p. 1980. 13.50 (ISBN 0-08-025724-0). Pergamon.
Things That I Do in the Dark: Selected Poems. June Jordan. 1977. 7.95 o.p. (ISBN 0-394-40937-X); pap. 4.95 (ISBN 0-394-73327-4). Random.
Things That I Do in the Dark: Selected Poems. June Jordan. LC 80-68165. 224p. 1981. pap. 6.95 (ISBN 0-8070-3235-2, BP 615). Beacon Pr.
Things to Come. J. Dwight Pentecost. 1958. 14.95 (ISBN 0-310-30890-9, Pub by Dunhan). Zondervan.
Things to Come. H. G. Wells. (Science Fiction Ser). 184p. 1975. Repr. of 1935 ed. lib. bdg. 12.50 (ISBN 0-8398-2318-5). Gregg.
Things to Come for Planet Earth. Aaron L. Plueger. 1977. pap. 3.50 (ISBN 0-570-03762-X, 12-2691). Concordia.
Things to Do in a Day. Macmillan. LC 76-1991. 1976. pap. 5.95 o.s.i. (ISBN 0-02-011870-8, 01187, Collier). Macmillan.
Things to Make. (Ladybird Stories Ser.). (Illus., Arabic.). 2.50x (ISBN 0-686-53069-1). Intl Bk Ctr.
Things to Make & Do for Christmas. Ellen Weiss. (Things to Make & Do Bks.). (gr. k-3). 1980. PLB 7.90 (ISBN 0-531-02293-5, C02); pap. 3.95 (ISBN 0-531-02145-9). Watts.
Things to Make & Do for Columbus Day. Gail Gibbons. (Things to Make & Do Ser.). (Illus.). (gr. 1-3). 1977. PLB 7.90 s&l (ISBN 0-531-01274-3). Watts.
Things to Make & Do for Easter. Marion Cole & Olivia H. Cole. LC 78-12457. (Things to Make & Do Ser.). (Illus.). (gr. k-3). 1979. PLB 7.90 (ISBN 0-531-01463-0). Watts.
Things to Make & Do for George Washington's Birthday. Michael Cooper. (Things to Make & Do Ser.). (Illus.). (gr. k-3). 1979. PLB 7.90 s&l (ISBN 0-531-02294-3). Watts.
Things to Make & Do for Halloween. Gail Gibbons. LC 75-19396. (Things to Make & Do Ser.). (Illus.). 48p. (gr. k-2). 1976. PLB 7.90 (ISBN 0-531-01103-8). Watts.
Things to Make & Do for Thanksgiving. (Things to Make & Do Ser.). (gr. 1-3). 1977. lib. bdg. 7.90 (ISBN 0-531-01324-3). Watts.
Things to Make & Do for Valentine's Day. Tomie De Paola. (Things to Make & Do Ser.). (Illus.). 48p. (gr. k-3). 1976. PLB 7.90 (ISBN 0-531-01187-9). Watts.
Things to Make & Do for Your Birthday. Gail Gibbons. (Things to Make & Do Ser.). (Illus.). (gr. 1-3). 1978. 3.95 (ISBN 0-531-02380-X); PLB 7.90 s&l (ISBN 0-531-01462-2). Watts.
Things We Cut. Anthony Thomas. (Easy-Read Awareness Book Ser.). (Illus.). 32p. (gr. 1-3). 1976. PLB 4.47 o.p. (ISBN 0-531-01216-6). Watts.
Things We Hear. Anthony Thomas. (Easy-Read Awareness Book Ser.). (Illus.). 32p. (gr. 1-3). 1976. PLB 4.47 o.p. (ISBN 0-531-00363-9). Watts.
Things We See. Anthony Thomas. (Easy-Read Awareness Book Ser.). (Illus.). 32p. (gr. 1-3). 1976. PLB 4.47 o.p. (ISBN 0-531-01217-4). Watts.
Things We Touch. Anthony Thomas. (Easy-Read Awareness Book Ser.). (Illus.). 32p. (gr. 1-3). 1976. PLB 4.47 o.p. (ISBN 0-531-00364-7). Watts.
Think About It-Kindergarten. Imogene Forte. LC 80-84619. (Think About It Ser.). (Illus.). 80p. (ps-k). 1981. pap. text ed. 5.95 (ISBN 0-913916-96-X, IP-96X). Incentive Pubn.
Think About It: Middle Grades. Imogene Forte. LC 80-84619. (Think About It Ser.). (Illus.). 96p. (gr. 4-6). 1981. pap. text ed. 5.95 (ISBN 0-913916-98-6, IP 98-6). Incentive Pubn.
Think About It: Primary. Imogene Forte. LC 80-84619. (Think About It Ser.). (Illus.). 88p. (gr. 1-3). 1981. pap. text ed. 5.95 (ISBN 0-913916-97-8, IP 97-8). Incentive Pubn.
Think & Grow Rich Action Pack. N. Hill. 1966. pap. 4.95 (ISBN 0-8015-7560-5, Hawthorn). Dutton.
Think & Link: An Advanced Course in Reading & Writing Skills. Janelle Cooper. (Illus.). 1979. pap. 9.95x (ISBN 0-7131-0315-9). Intl Ideas.

Think Back on Us. A Contemporary Chronicle of the 1930s. Malcolm Cowley. Ed. by Henry D. Piper. LC 67-10024. 416p. 1967. 19.95x (ISBN 0-8093-0232-2). S Ill U Pr.
Think Back on Us. A Contemporary Chronicle of the 1930s: The Literary Record. Malcolm Cowley. Ed. by Henry D. Piper. LC 72-5606. (Arcturus Books Paperbacks). 210p. (Pt. 2 of the hardbound ed. of Think Back On Us). 1972. pap. 7.95 (ISBN 0-8093-0599-2). S Ill U Pr.
Think Back on Us. A Contemporary Chronicle of the 1930s: The Social Record. Malcolm Cowley. Ed. by Henry D. Piper. LC 72-5606. (Arcturus Books Paperbacks). 213p. (Pt. 1 of the hardbound ed. of Think Back On Us). 1972. pap. 7.95 (ISBN 0-8093-0598-4). S Ill U Pr.
Think Chinese, Speak Chinese. Allan B. Goldenthal. (Illus.). (gr. 10-12). 1978. 16.95 (ISBN 0-88345-367-3); pap. text ed. 12.95 (ISBN 0-88345-358-4); cassettes 40.00 (ISBN 0-686-67814-1). Regents Pub.
Think Good Thoughts About a Pussycat. George Booth. LC 75-12929. (Illus.). 128p. 1975. 6.95 (ISBN 0-396-07224-0). Dodd.
Think Jewish: A Contemporary View of Judaism, a Jewish View of Today's World. Zalman I. Posner. LC 78-71323. 1979. 8.95 (ISBN 0-9602394-0-5); pap. 4.95 (ISBN 0-9602394-1-3). Kesher.
Think Like a Grandmaster. Alexander Kotov. 1976. pap. 12.50 (ISBN 0-7134-3160-1, Pub. by Batsford England). David & Charles.
Think Like a Lawyer: How to Get What You Want by Using Advocacy Skills. Robert J. Dudley. LC 79-26488. 234p. 1980. 15.95 (ISBN 0-88229-571-3); pap. 8.95 (ISBN 0-88229-749-X). Nelson-Hall.
Think Metric! Franklyn M. Branley. LC 72-78279. (Illus.). (gr. 3-6). 1973. 7.95 (ISBN 0-690-81861-0, TYC-J); PLB 7.89 (ISBN 0-690-81862-9). T Y Crowell.
Think of a Number. Anders Bodelsen. 1978. pap. 1.75 o.s.i. (ISBN 0-685-87091-X). Jove Pubns.
Think of Shadows. Lilian Moore. LC 80-13496. (Illus.). 40p. (gr. 2 up). 1980. 8.95 (ISBN 0-689-30782-9). Atheneum.
Think of Something Quiet. Clare Cherry. LC 80-82981. (Early Childhood Library). 1981. pap. 5.95 (ISBN 0-8224-6949-9). Pitman Learning.
Think on Your Feet: The Art of Thinking & Speaking Under Pressure. Kenneth Wydro. 192p. 1981. text ed. 11.95 (ISBN 0-13-917815-5, Spec); pap. text ed. 4.95 (ISBN 0-13-917807-4, Spec). P-H.
Think Rich. H. Stanley Judd et al. 1978. 8.95 o.s.i. (ISBN 0-440-08732-5). Delacorte.
Think Thin. Murray J. Siegel & Dolores Van Keuren. LC 76-151435. (Illus.). 1971. 8.95 o.s.i. (ISBN 0-8397-7992-5); pap. 9.95 (ISBN 0-8397-7993-3). Eriksson.
Think Thin. Murray J. Siegel & Dolores Van Kueren. LC 76-151435. 288p. 1981. pap. 9.95 (ISBN 0-8397-7993-3). Eriksson.
Think Thinner, Snoopy. Charles M. Schulz. 1979. pap. 1.50 (ISBN 0-449-24042-8, Crest). Fawcett.
Think Your Troubles Away. Ernest Holmes. 1963. pap. 3.50 (ISBN 0-911336-29-X). Sci of Mind.
Think Yourself Thin. Frank J. Bruno. 265p. 1973. pap. 3.50 (ISBN 0-06-463348-9, EH 348, EH). Har-Row.
Thinking. Richard L. Allington & Kathleen Krull. LC 80-15390. (Beginning to Learn About Ser.). (Illus.). 32p. (ps-2). 1980. PLB 9.65 (ISBN 0-8172-1319-8). Raintree Child.
Thinking About Art. Edward Lucie-Smith. 1980. pap. 4.95 (ISBN 0-7145-0553-6). Riverrun NY.
Thinking About Change. Ed. by D. Shugarman. LC 74-82285. 1974. pap. 4.95 (ISBN 0-8020-6251-2). U of Toronto Pr.
Thinking About Children. Joan Busfield & M. Paddon. LC 76-22986. (Illus.). 1977. 29.95 (ISBN 0-521-21402-5). Cambridge U Pr.
Thinking About Housing: A Policy Research Agenda. Morton L. Isler. 47p. 1970. pap. 1.25 o.p. (ISBN 0-87766-004-2, 60004). Urban Inst.
Thinking About Photography: Writings from 1816 to the Present. Ed. by Vicki Goldberg. 1981. 14.95 (ISBN 0-671-25034-5, Touchstone); pap. 6.95 (ISBN 0-686-68487-7). S&S.
Thinking About Politics: American Government in Associational Perspective. Paul DeLespinasse. (Orig.). 1980. pap. 14.95 (ISBN 0-442-25409-1). D Van Nostrand.
Thinking About Retirement. John Wallis. LC 72-652. 120p. 1976. text ed. 19.50 (ISBN 0-08-018269-0); pap. text ed. 8.25 (ISBN 0-08-018268-2). Pergamon.
Thinking About the American People. John McClymer. 98p. 4.50 (ISBN 0-686-68744-2). Revisionary.
Thinking About the Curriculum: The Nature & Treatment of Curriculum Problems. William A. Reid. 1978. 16.00 (ISBN 0-7100-8979-1); pap. 7.95 (ISBN 0-7100-8980-5). Routledge & Kegan.
Thinking Animals: Animals & the Development of Human Intelligence. Paul Shepard. 1978. 14.95 o.p. (ISBN 0-670-70061-4). Viking Pr.
Thinking Black: An Introduction to Black Political Power. Frank McQuilkin. 1970. pap. 2.95 (ISBN 0-685-03350-3, 80510). Macmillan.
Thinking Body: A Study of Balancing Forces of Dynamic Man. Mabel E. Todd. LC 68-28048. (Illus.). 1968. pap. 8.25 (ISBN 0-87127-014-5). Dance Horiz.
Thinking Computer: Mind Inside Matter. Bertram Raphael. LC 75-30839. (Psychology Ser.). (Illus.). 1976. pap. text ed. 10.95x (ISBN 0-7167-0723-3). W H Freeman.
Thinking for Writing. Dorothy U. Seyler & M. Noel Sipple. LC 77-22730. 1978. pap. text ed. 9.95 (ISBN 0-574-22035-6, 13-5035); instr's guide avail. (ISBN 0-574-22036-4, 13-5036). SRA.
Thinking, Knowing, Living: An Introduction to Philosophy. Ed. by Richard A. Smith. LC 78-52290. 1978. pap. text ed. 7.75x (ISBN 0-8191-0492-2). U Pr of Amer.
Thinking Machines: A Layman's Introduction to Logic, Boolean Algebra & Computers. rev ed. Irving Adler. LC 73-19704. (Illus.). 1974. 5.95 o.p. (ISBN 0-381-98220-3, A78600, JD-J). John Day.
Thinking Man's Guide to Trout Angling. Leonard Wright, Jr. 1972. 6.95 o.p. (ISBN 0-525-21740-1). Dutton.
Thinking Metric. 2nd ed. Thomas F. Gilbert & Marilyn B. Gilbert. LC 77-20190. (Self-Teaching Guide Ser.). 1978. pap. text ed. 5.95 (ISBN 0-471-03427-4). Wiley.
Thinking of Offerings: Poems Nineteen Seventy - Nineteen Seventy-Three. John Knoepfle. 1979. 9.00 (ISBN 0-686-65851-5); signed ed. 16.00 (ISBN 0-686-61893-9); pap. 4.00 (ISBN 0-686-61894-7). Juniper Pr WI.
Thinking Physics. Lewis C. Epstein & Paul G. Hewitt. (Illus.). 262p. 1979. pap. 5.95x (ISBN 0-935218-00-9). Insight Pr CA.
Thinking Politically. Jean Blondel. LC 75-38746. 1976. 19.50x (ISBN 0-89158-536-2). Westview.
Thinking Processes of the Human Mind. Christopher E. Larrew. (Illus.). 1980. 37.50 (ISBN 0-89266-218-2). Am Classical Coll Pr.
Thinking: Readings in Cognitive Science. Ed. by P. N. Johnson-Laird & P. C. Wason. LC 77-78887. (Illus.). 1978. 49.50 (ISBN 0-521-21756-3); pap. 13.95x (ISBN 0-521-29267-0). Cambridge U Pr.
Thinking Skills Workbook: A Cognitive Skills Remediation Manual for Adults. Lynn T. Carter et al. (Illus.). 220p. 1980. pap. 13.75 (ISBN 0-398-04049-4). C C Thomas.
Thinking Straight & Talking Sense. Mark Gerald & William Eyman. LC 78-71008. 1981. pap. 10.00 (ISBN 0-917476-14-X). Rational Living.
Thinking the Thinkable: Investment in Human Survival. Ed. by Nish Jamgotch, Jr. LC 77-18592. 1978. pap. text ed. 11.50x (ISBN 0-8191-0402-7). U Pr of Amer.
Thinking Through the Bible, 4 vols. in one. John McNicol. LC 76-25079. 1976. text ed. 12.95 (ISBN 0-8254-3214-6). Kregel.
Thinking Visually: A Strategy Manual for Problem-Solving. rev. ed. Robert H. McKim. LC 80-16526. 1980. text ed. 24.95 (ISBN 0-534-97984-X); pap. text ed. 14.95 (ISBN 0-534-97978-5). Lifetime Learn.
Thinking with Concepts. John Wilson. 1970. 26.95 (ISBN 0-521-06825-8); pap. 5.95x (ISBN 0-521-09601-4). Cambridge U Pr.
Thinking with Models: Mathematical Models in the Physical, Biological & Social Sciences. Thomas L. Saaty & Joyce M. Alexander. (I S Modern Applied Mathematics & Computer Science: Vol. 2). (Illus.). 208p. 1981. 35.00 (ISBN 0-08-026475-1); pap. 20.00 (ISBN 0-08-026474-3). Pergamon.
Thinking Without Language. Hans G. Furth. LC 66-10958. 1966. 15.95 (ISBN 0-02-911000-9). Free Pr.
Third Adam: The Mariavite Experiment in Mystical Marriage. Jerzy Peterkiewicz. (Illus.). 256p. 1975. 27.50x (ISBN 0-19-212198-7). Oxford U Pr.
Third Americans: A Selected Bibliography of Asians in America with Annotations. Te-Kong Tong. 1980. 4.50 (ISBN 0-937256-00-5). CHCUS Inc.
Third Anti-Coloring Book. Susan Striker. (Illus.). 96p. (Orig.). 1980. pap. 3.95 (ISBN 0-03-056814-5). HR&W.
Third Arm. Steven Otfinoski. Ed. by Mary Verdick. (Beginning Pal Paperbacks Ser.). (Illus., Orig.). (gr. 7-12). pap. text ed. 1.25 (ISBN 0-8374-3464-5). Xerox Ed Pubns.
Third Avenue. James Fritzhand. (Orig.). 1979. pap. 2.75 (ISBN 0-515-05787-8). Jove Pubns.
Third-Base Rookie. Duane Decker. (gr. 7 up). 1959. 7.25 (ISBN 0-688-21726-5). Morrow.
Third Book About Achim. Uwe Johnson. LC 67-12273. (Helen & Kurt Wolff Bk). 1967. 5.75 (ISBN 0-15-189901-0). HarBraceJ.
Third Book of Virgil Finlay. Ed. by Gerry De La Ree. (Illus.). 1979. 15.50 (ISBN 0-938192-07-8). De La Ree.
Third Century: America As a Post-Industrial Society. Ed. by Seymour M. Lipset. LC 78-70400. (Publications Ser.: No. 203). 468p. 1979. 14.95 (ISBN 0-8179-7031-2). Hoover Inst Pr.
Third Coast: Contemporary Michigan Poetry. Ed. by Conrad Hilberry et al. James Tipton. LC 76-49581. 1977. 8.95 (ISBN 0-8143-1567-4); pap. 3.95 (ISBN 0-8143-1568-2). Wayne St U Pr.
Third Crossword Puzzle Book. Leslie Hill & P. R. Popkin. 64p. 1970. pap. text ed. 2.95x (ISBN 0-19-432553-9). Oxford U Pr.
Third Deadly Sin. Lawrence Sanders. 480p. 1981. 13.95 (ISBN 0-399-12614-7). Putnam.
Third Degree: A Detailed Account of Police Brutality. Emanuel H. Lavine. LC 74-676. (Civil Liberties in American History Ser.). 248p. 1974. Repr. of 1930 ed. lib. bdg. 27.50 (ISBN 0-306-70601-6). Da Capo.
Third Department: The Political Police in the Russia of Nicholas First. P. S. Squire. LC 69-10198. (Illus.). 1968. 33.50 (ISBN 0-521-07148-8). Cambridge U Pr.
Third Digest of Investigations in the Teaching of Science. Francis D. Curtis. LC 74-153694. 1971. Repr. of 1939 ed. text ed. 12.75x (ISBN 0-8077-1226-4). Tchrs Coll.
Third Dimension. Robert E. Spiller. 5.95 o.s.i. (ISBN 0-02-613010-6). Macmillan.
Third European Congress on Information Systems & Networks "Overcoming the Language Barrier" Overcoming the Language Barrier, 2 vols. 888p. 1978. Set. pap. text ed. 72.00 (ISBN 3-7940-5184-X, Pub. by K G Saur). Gale.
Third Eye. T. Rampa. pap. 2.50 (ISBN 0-685-88126-1). Weiser.
Third Face of War. Gene Schulze. LC 76-94463. (Illus.). 1969. 9.50 (ISBN 0-8363-0097-1). Jenkins.
Third French Republic, 1870-1914. Alexander Sedgwick. LC 68-13384. (AHM Europe Since 1500 Ser. 4). (Orig.). 1969. pap. 5.95x (ISBN 0-88295-763-5). AHM Pub.
Third from the Sun. Guy DeMarco. 64p. 1981. 10.00 (ISBN 0-682-49670-7). Exposition.
Third Grave. David Case. (Illus.). 160p. 1981. 9.95 (ISBN 0-87054-089-0). Arkham.
Third Indochina Conflict. Ed. by David W. Elliott. (Westview Replica Edition Ser.). 250p. 1981. lib. bdg. 18.50x (ISBN 0-89158-739-X). Westview.
Third Industrial Age: Strategy for Business Survival. Charles Tavel. LC 79-40199. (Illus.). 356p. 1980. 23.00 (ISBN 0-08-022506-3). Pergamon.
Third Kiss. Austin Clarke. (Dolmen Editions: No. XxIV). 1976. text ed. 19.50x (ISBN 0-85105-292-4, Dolmen Pr). Humanities.
Third LACUS Forum: Proceedings. Linguistic Association of Canada & the U.S. Ed. by Robert J. Di Pietro & Edward L. Blansitt, Jr. pap. text ed. 10.95 (ISBN 0-685-82432-2). Hornbeam Pr.
Third Language: Recurrent Problems of Translation into English. Alan Duff. LC 80-41116. (Language Teaching Methodology Ser.). 160p. 1981. 23.65 (ISBN 0-08-027248-7); pap. 11.95 (ISBN 0-08-025334-2). Pergamon.
Third Life of Grange Copeland. Alice Walker. LC 77-3427. 1977. pap. 3.95 (ISBN 0-15-689960-4, Harv). HarBraceJ.
Third Mad Dossier of Spy vs. Spy. Antonio Prohias. (Mad Ser.). (Illus.). 192p. 1972. pap. 1.75 (ISBN 0-446-94425-4). Warner Bks.
Third Mammoth Book of Word Games. Richard B. Manchester. 512p. 1981. pap. 8.95 (ISBN 0-89104-202-4). A & W Pubs.
Third Man; bd. with The Fallen Idol. Graham Greene. 1981. pap. 3.95 (ISBN 0-14-003278-9). Penguin.
Third Man: Loser Takes All. Graham Greene. Date not set. 14.95 (ISBN 0-670-70084-3). Viking Pr.
Third Meeting of the Eastern African Sub Committee for Soil Correlation & Land Evaluation. (World Soil Resources Report: No. 51). 170p. 1981. pap. 9.25 (ISBN 92-5-100902-3, F2082, FAO). Unipub.
Third Palenque Round Table, Nineteen Seventy-Eight: Part Two, Vol. V. Ed. by Merle G. Robertson. (Illus.). 200p. (Orig.). Date not set. pap. text ed. 35.00x (ISBN 0-292-78037-0). U of Tex Pr.
Third Parties in Presidential Elections. Daniel A. Mazmanian. LC 74-281. (Studies in Presidential Selection). 140p. 1974. 11.95 (ISBN 0-8157-5522-8); pap. 4.95 (ISBN 0-8157-5521-X). Brookings.
Third Peacock. Robert Farrar Capon. LC 73-147357. 120p. 1972. pap. 1.95 (ISBN 0-385-03627-2, Im). Doubleday.
Third Power. Neville Frankel. LC 80-21723. 384p. 1980. 12.95 (ISBN 0-8253-0026-6). Beaufort Bks NY.
Third "R" Mathematics Teaching for Grades K-8. Gerald R. Rising & Joseph B. Harkin. 1978. text ed. 16.95x (ISBN 0-534-00567-5). Wadsworth Pub.
Third R: Towards a Numerate Society. J. A. Glenn. 1978. text ed. 11.95 (ISBN 0-06-318075-8, IntlDept); pap. text ed. 6.60 (ISBN 0-06-318076-6, IntlDept). Har-Row.
Third Reich & the Christian Churches. Peter Matheson. LC 80-26767. 112p. (Orig.). 1981. pap. 5.95 (ISBN 0-8028-1873-0). Eerdmans.
Third Season-Seven Poets: Poetry by Seven Eastern Oregon Poets. Jim Ambrosek et al. Ed. by Sandra S. Gullikson. 28p. (Orig.). 1980. pap. 3.50 (ISBN 0-9605512-0-4). Clearwater OR.
Third Sex? Kent Philpott. LC 75-13177. 1975. 5.95 o.p. (ISBN 0-88270-131-2); pap. 2.50 o.p. (ISBN 0-88270-259-9). Logos.
Third Supplement to the Cumulation of the Library Catalogsupplements of the New York State School of Industrial & Labor Relations. Cornell University. (Library Catalogs-Bib. Guides). 1979. lib. bdg. 180.00 (ISBN 0-8161-0260-0). G K Hall.
Third Thousand Years. W. Cleon Skousen. 1964. 12.50 (ISBN 0-685-48241-3). Bookcraft Inc.
Third Treasury of the Familiar. Ed. by Ralph L. Woods. LC 79-109455. 1970. 10.95 o.s.i. (ISBN 0-02-631420-7). Macmillan.
Third Twin. John Rae. LC 80-16001. 128p. (gr. 5-9). 1981. 8.95 (ISBN 0-7232-6192-X). Warne.
Third United Nations Conference on the Law of the Sea: Official Records, Vol. IX. 191p. 1979. pap. 14.00 (ISBN 0-686-68976-3, UN79/5/3, UN). Unipub.
Third U. N. Conference on the Law of the Sea: Summary Records of Meetings, Documents Resumed Eighth Session, Vol.12. 115p. 1980. pap. 9.00 (UN80-5-12, UN). Uniub.
Third Wave. Alvin Toffler. LC 79-26690. 448p. 1980. 12.95 (ISBN 0-688-03597-3). Morrow.
Third Wave. Alvin Toffler. 576p. (Orig.). 1981. pap. 3.95 (ISBN 0-553-14431-6). Bantam.
Third Way. Paul M. Lederach. LC 80-26280. 152p. 1980. pap. 6.95 (ISBN 0-8361-1934-7). Herald Pr.
Third Woman: Minority Woman Writers of the United States. Dexter Fisher. LC 79-87863. 1979. pap. text ed. 9.95 (ISBN 0-395-27707-8). HM.
Third Word War. Ian Lee. (Illus.). 1978. pap. 4.95 (ISBN 0-89104-115-X). A & W Pubs.
Third World. Christopher Barlow. 1979. 14.95 (ISBN 0-7134-1878-8, Pub. by Batsford England). David & Charles.
Third World & Press Freedom. Ed. by Philip C. Horton. LC 78-17072. (Praeger Special Studies). 1978. 25.95 (ISBN 0-03-045551-0). Praeger.
Third World & the International Economic Order. Mahbub ul Haq. (Development Papers: No. 22). 54p. 1976. pap. 1.50 (ISBN 0-686-28676-6). Overseas Dev Council.
Third World & the Rich Countries: Prospects for the Year 2000. Angelos Angelopoulos. LC 72-75694. (Special Studies in International Economics & Development). 1972. text ed. 28.50x (ISBN 0-275-28608-8); pap. text ed. 9.50x (ISBN 0-89197-963-8). Irvington.
Third World Calamity. Brian May. (Illus.). 272p. 1981. price not set (ISBN 0-7100-0764-7). Routledge & Kegan.
Third World Coalition in International Politics. Robert A. Mortimer. LC 79-23208. 160p. 1980. 19.95 (ISBN 0-03-055286-9). Praeger.
Third World Development: Problems & Prospects. Edward G. Stockwell & Karen A. Laidlaw. LC 79-24088. 362p. 1981. text ed. 21.95 (ISBN 0-88229-532-2); pap. text ed. 10.95 (ISBN 0-88229-751-1). Nelson-Hall.
Third World Reassessed. Elbaki Hermassi. 1980. 16.50x (ISBN 0-520-03764-2). U of Cal Pr.
Third World Surveys: Survey Research in Developing Countries. Ed. by Gerald Hursh-Cesar & Prodipto Roy. 1976. 11.00x o.p. (ISBN 0-333-90099-5). South Asia Bks.
Third World Voices for Children. McDowell & Lavitt. 1981. 7.95. Okpaku Communications.
Third World War. John Hackett et al. 1980. pap. 3.50 (ISBN 0-425-05019-X). Berkley Pub.
Third World Without Superpowers, Vols. 1-4. K. P. Sauvant. 1978. 42.50 ea. Oceana.
Third World Women Speak Out: Interviews in Six Countries on Change, Development, & Basic Needs. Perdita Huston. LC 78-32180. 172p. 1979. pap. 4.95 (ISBN 0-686-28701-0). Overseas Dev Council.
Third World Women Speakout. Perdita Huston. LC 78-32180. (Praeger Special Studies Ser.). 1979. 20.95 (ISBN 0-03-052116-5); student edition 4.95 (ISBN 0-03-052121-1). Praeger.
Third Year Latin. Charles Jenney, Jr. & Robers V. Scudder. (Latin Program Ser.). (gr. 9-12). 1980. text ed. 15.24 (ISBN 0-205-06811-1, 3968111); tchrs.' guide 2.40 (ISBN 0-205-00541-1, 3905411). Allyn.
Thirst. Charles E. Maine. 1978. pap. 1.95 (ISBN 0-441-80676-7). Charter Bks.

Thirst for God. Sherwood Wirt. 176p. 1980. 6.95 (ISBN 0-310-34640-1). Zondervan.
Thirsting for the Lord: Essays in Biblical Spirituality. Carroll Stuhlmueller. LC 76-51736. (Illus.). 1977. 7.95 o.p. (ISBN 0-8189-0341-4). Alba.
Thirsty? Wayne Judd. (Uplook Ser.). 1975. pap. 0.75 (ISBN 0-8163-0177-8, 20728-2). Pacific Pr Pub Assn.
Thirsty Day & Permanent Wave. Kathleen Aguero & Miriam Goodman. LC 76-55615. 88p. 1977. pap. 4.95 (ISBN 0-914086-17-0). Alicejamesbooks.
Thirteen. Remy Charlip & Jerry Joyner. LC 75-8875. (Illus.). 40p. (gr. 1 up). 1975. 7.95 (ISBN 0-590-17712-5, Four Winds); PLB 7.95 (ISBN 0-590-07712-0). Schol Bk Serv.
Thirteen Danish Tales. Mary C. Hatch. LC 49-10046. (Illus.). (gr. 3-6). 1947. 4.50 o.p. (ISBN 0-15-285683-8, HJ). HarBraceJ.
Thirteen Days. Robert Kennedy. (RL 8). pap. 1.95 (ISBN 0-451-09150-7, J9150, Sig). NAL.
Thirteen Days: A Memoir of the Cuban Missile Crisis. Robert F. Kennedy. (Keith Jennison Large Type Bks). 8.95 o.p. (ISBN 0-531-00314-0). Watts.
Thirteen for the Kill. Peter Buck. (Mercenary Ser.: No. 1). (Orig.). 1981. pap. 1.95 (ISBN 0-451-09893-5, J9893, Sig). NAL.
Thirteen Great Stories of Science Fiction. Ed. by Groff Conklin. 1979. pap. 1.50 o.p. (ISBN 0-449-14228-0, GM). Fawcett.
Thirteen Ivenrow. P. Lehman. 4.00 o.p. (ISBN 0-8062-1101-6). Carlton.
Thirteen Lessons on Romans, Vol. II. Sherwood Smith. LC 81-65030. (Bible Student Study Guides Ser.). 180p. 1981. pap. 2.95 (ISBN 0-89900-170-X). College Pr Pub.
Thirteen Lessons on Romans. Sherwood Smith. LC 79-55509. (Bible Student Study Guides). 113p. (Orig.). 1980. pap. 2.95 (ISBN 0-89900-164-5). College Pr Pub.
Thirteen Men Who Changed the World. H. S. Vigeveno. pap. 2.25 o.p. (ISBN 0-8307-0487-6, 5016207). Regal.
Thirteen Perspectives on Regulatory Simplification. Mandelker et al. Ed. by Annette Kolis. LC 79-65686. (ULI Research Report: No. 29). 144p. 1979. pap. text ed. 11.75 (ISBN 0-87420-329-5). Urban Land.
Thirteen Poems. David Hosburgh. (Writers Workshop Redbird Ser.). 1975. 8.00 (ISBN 0-88253-658-3); pap. text ed. 4.00 (ISBN 0-88253-657-5). Ind-US Inc.
Thirteen Weeks to Riches (Which Could Be Glory!) Loren L. Fenton. (Orig.). 1978. pap. 6.00 (ISBN 0-934178-00-3). Christian Success.
Thirteenth Candle. T. Lobsang Rampa. pap. 2.50 (ISBN 0-685-27227-3). Weiser.
Thirteenth Century, 1216-1307. 2nd ed. Frederick M. Powicke. (Illus.). 1962. 33.00x (ISBN 0-19-821708-0). Oxford U Pr.
Thirteenth Child. Antonia Ridge. 1962. 3.95 o.p. (ISBN 0-571-07068-X, Pub. by Faber & Faber). Merrimack Bk Serv.
Thirteenth Hour. John Lee. 1979. pap. 2.50 o.s.i. (ISBN 0-440-18751-6). Dell.
Thirteenth Man. Murray T. Bloom. 1977. 10.95 (ISBN 0-02-511770-X). Macmillan.
Thirteenth of May: The Advent of De Gaulle's Republic. Ed. by Charles S. Maier & Dan S. White. (Problems in European History Ser). (Orig.). 1968. pap. 4.95x (ISBN 0-19-500959-2). Oxford U Pr.
Thirteenth Oil Shale Symposium: Proceedings. Ed. by Joseph H. Gary. (Oil Shale Ser.). (Illus.). 400p. (Orig.). 1980. pap. 16.00x (ISBN 0-918062-39-X). Colo Sch Mines.
Thirteenth Year. Rose Blue. (Illus.). (gr. 5 up). 1977. PLB 5.90 s&l (ISBN 0-531-00382-5). Watts.
Thirties. Alan Jenkins. LC 75-45511. (Illus.). 1976. 35.95x (ISBN 0-8128-1829-6). Stein & Day.
Thirties. Edmund Wilson. Ed. by Leon Edel. 800p. 1980. 17.50 (ISBN 0-374-27572-6). FS&G.
Thirties: A Dream Revolved. Julian Symons. 1975. 11.95 (ISBN 0-571-10715-X, Pub. by Faber & Faber). Merrimack Bk Serv.
Thirties, Nineteen Thirty to Nineteen Forty. Malcolm Muggerbridge. 327p. 1980. Repr. of 1940 ed. lib. bdg. 30.00 (ISBN 0-89987-574-2). Darby Bks.
Thirtieth Year to Heaven: New American Poets. LC 80-22063. 1980. 12.95 (ISBN 0-917492-09-9). Jackpine Pr.
Thirty Arab Refugees in the Middle East. Ed. by A. G. Mezerik. 94p. 1980. 20.00. Intl Review.
Thirty Bike Rides in the Austin Area. Kevin Pratt. 76p. 1973. 3.50 o.p. (ISBN 0-8363-0127-7). Jenkins.
Thirty Birds That Will Build in Bird Houses. Illus. by R. B. Layton. LC 77-81805. 1977. pap. 5.95 (ISBN 0-912542-03-9). Nature Bks Pubs.
Thirty Day Mental Diet. Willis Kinnear. 1965. pap. 4.95 (ISBN 0-911336-20-6). Sci of Mind.
Thirty-Day to a Born-Again Body. Joy Gross. 1981. pap. 2.75 (ISBN 0-425-04733-4). Berkley Pub.
Thirty Days to a Less Stressful You. Don Osgood. LC 80-65434. 96p. (Orig.). 1980. pap. 4.50 (ISBN 0-915684-66-7). Christian Herald.
Thirty Days to a More Powerful Vocabulary. Wilfred Funk & Norman Lewis. LC 72-94340. (Funk & W Bk.). (gr. 9-12). 1970. text ed. 8.95 (ISBN 0-308-40079-8, 430180, TYC-T). T Y Crowell.
Thirty Days to a New You. Bruce Larson. 1977. pap. 2.50 (ISBN 0-310-27242-4). Zondervan.
Thirty Days to Metric Mastery: For People Who Hate Math. Don C. Steinke. (Illus., Orig.). 1981. pap. 9.00x (ISBN 0-9605344-0-7). Hse of Charles.
Thirty Days to More Powerful Writing. Jonathan Price. 192p. (Orig.). 1981. pap. 5.95 (ISBN 0-449-90047-9, Columbine). Fawcett.
Thirty-Eight Basic Speech Experiences. rev. ed. Clark S. Carlile. 1977. lib. bdg. 6.00 (ISBN 0-931054-03-6). Clark Pub.
Thirty-Eight Recipes for Bulletin Boards & Art Projects That Christian Kids Can Make. Jean Staffeld et al. (Illus.). 1978. pap. 4.50 (ISBN 0-570-03774-3, 12-2721). Concordia.
Thirty-Five Millimeter Handbook. Michael Freeman. (Illus.). 320p. 1980. 25.00 (ISBN 0-87165-093-2). Ziff-Davis Pub.
Thirty Instruction Units in Basic Electricity. slow learner ed. Carl E. Matson. (gr. 9-12). 1961. pap. 4.60 o.p. (ISBN 0-87345-254-2). McKnight.
Thirty-One Hymns to the Star Goddess. Frater Achad. 5.00 o.p. (ISBN 0-685-54734-5). Weiser.
Thirty Passages: Comprehension Practice for High Intermediate & Advanced Students. Donn Byrne & Edwin T. Cornelius. (Illus.). 1978. pap. text ed. 2.95x (ISBN 0-582-79704-7). Longman.
Thirty-Second State: A Pictorial History of Minnesota. Bertha L. Heilbron. LC 54-14431. (Illus.). 306p. 1978. pap. 7.50 (ISBN 0-87351-130-1). Minn Hist.
Thirty Seconds. Michael J. Arlen. 224p. 1981. pap. 2.95 (ISBN 0-14-005810-9). Penguin.
Thirty Seconds. Michael J. Arlen. 211p. 1980. 9.95 (ISBN 0-374-27576-9). FS&G.
Thirty Seconds Over Tokyo. Bob Considine & Ted Lawson. (Landmark Ser.: No. 35). (Illus.). (gr. 7-9). 1953. PLB 5.99 (ISBN 0-394-90335-8). Random.
Thirty Seconds Over Tokyo. Ted Lawson. LC 53-6522. (Landmark Bks.). (Illus.). 208p. (gr. 5-9). 1981. pap. 2.95 (ISBN 0-394-84698-2). Random.
Thirty-Six French Poems. Ed. by Albert Sonnenfeld. 1960. pap. text ed. 4.75 o.p. (ISBN 0-395-05420-6). HM.
Thirty-Six German Poems. Ed. by Karl S. Weimar. LC 50-14279. 1950. pap. text ed. 4.75 (ISBN 0-395-05524-5, 3-59405). HM.
Thirty Six Lectures in Biology. Salvador E. Luria. LC 74-19136. (Illus.). 439p. 1975. text ed. 19.95x o.p. (ISBN 0-262-12068-2); pap. text ed. 9.95x (ISBN 0-262-62029-4). MIT Pr.
Thirty-Six Spanish Poems. E. L. Rivers. LC 57-13596. 1957. pap. text ed. 5.00 (ISBN 0-395-05099-5). HM.
Thirty-Three. Marjorie Fletcher. LC 75-32642. 72p. 1976. pap. 4.95 (ISBN 0-914086-12-X). Alicejamesbooks.
Thirty-Three Mail Order Business You Can Operate from Your Home. Bev Shinn & Duane Shinn. 1978. pap. 9.95 o.p. (ISBN 0-912732-38-5). Duane Shinn.
Thirty-Two Basic Programs for the Apple Computer. Tom Rugg & Phil Feldman. 300p. 1981. pap. 17.95 (ISBN 0-918398-34-7). Dilithium Pr.
Thirty-Two BASIC Programs for the Exidy Sorcerer. Tom Rugg et al. 290p. 1981. pap. 16.95 (ISBN 0-918398-35-5). Dilithium Pr.
Thirty-Two Basic Programs for the PET (8k) Computer. Tom Rugg & Phil Feldman. LC 78-24837. 1979. pap. 16.95 (ISBN 0-918398-25-8). Dilithium Pr.
Thirty-Two Basic Programs for the Trs-Eighty (Level 2) Computer. Tom Rugg & Phil Feldman. LC 79-56399. 290p. 1980. pap. 16.95 (ISBN 0-918398-27-4). Dilithium Pr.
Thirty-Two Picture Postcards of Old Philadelphia. Ed. by Robert F. Looney. (Dover Postcard Ser). (Illus., Orig.). 1977. pap. 2.50 (ISBN 0-486-23421-5). Dover.
Thirty-Two Picture Postcards of Old Washington D.C. Ed. by Robert Reed. 1977. pap. 2.75 (ISBN 0-486-23418-5). Dover.
Thirty Typing Tests. 2nd ed. (gr. 9-12). 1959. pap. 6.60 sets of ten only (ISBN 0-8224-0216-5). Pitman Learning.
Thirty Ways to Help You Write. Fran W. Shaw. 192p. (Orig.). 1980. pap. 2.50 (ISBN 0-553-13924-X). Bantam.
Thirty Years a Watchtower Slave. William J. Schnell. (Direction Bks). pap. 1.95 (ISBN 0-8010-7933-0). Baker Bk.
Thirty Years Among the Dead. Carl A. Wickland. LC 80-19669. 390p. 1980. Repr. of 1974 ed. lib. bdg. 12.95x (ISBN 0-89370-625-6). Borgo Pr.
Thirty Years of Foundational Studies: Lectures on the Development of Mathematical Logic & the Study of the Foundations of Mathematics in 1930-1964. Andrej Mostowski. 1966. 10.50x o.p. (ISBN 0-631-09550-0, Pub. by Basil Blackwell). Biblio Dist.
Thirty Years of Musical Life in London. Hermann Klein. LC 78-2565. (Music Reprint Ser., 1978). (Illus.). 1978. Repr. of 1903 ed. lib. bdg. 32.50 (ISBN 0-306-77586-7). Da Capo.
Thirty Years of Rock & Roll Trivia. Fred L. Worth. 288p. (Orig.). 1980. pap. 2.50 (ISBN 0-446-91494-0). Warner Bks.
Thirty Years Peace. Peter O. Chotjewitz. Tr. by Robert Kimber & Rita Kimber. LC 80-24472. 256p. 1981. 11.95 (ISBN 0-394-50182-9). Knopf.
Thirty Years War. Herbert Langer. Orig. Title: Horticus Bellicus. (Illus.). 260p. 1980. 35.00 (ISBN 0-88254-497-7). Hippocrene Bks.
Thirty Years War. J. V. Polisensky. Tr. by Robert Evans. 1971. 22.75x (ISBN 0-520-01868-0). U of Cal Pr.
Thirty Years' War. Sigfrid H. Steinberg. (Foundations of Modern History Series). (Illus.). 1967. pap. 3.95x (ISBN 0-393-09752-8, NortonC). Norton.
Thirty Years' War: Problems of Motive, Extent, & Effect. 2nd ed. Ed. by Theodore K. Rabb. (Problems in European Civilization Ser.). 1972. pap. text ed. 4.95x o.p. (ISBN 0-669-82503-4). Heath.
This Affair of Louisiana. Alexander Deconde. LC 76-12468. 1976. 12.50 o.p. (ISBN 0-684-14687-8, ScribT). Scribner.
This Alien...Native Land. Asif Currimbhoy. 12.00 (ISBN 0-89253-796-5); flexible cloth 6.75 (ISBN 0-89253-527-X). Ind-US Inc.
This Believing World. Lewis Browne. 1944. 9.95 (ISBN 0-02-517600-5); pap. 2.95 (ISBN 0-02-084050-0). Macmillan.
This Book Is for the Birds. Tom Wilson. (Illus.). 1978. pap. 2.50 (ISBN 0-8362-1110-3). Andrews & McMeel.
This Bridge Called My Back: Writings by Radical Women of Color. Ed. by Cherrie M. Lawrence & Gloria Anzaldua. (Orig.). 1981. pap. price not set (ISBN 0-930436-10-5). Persephone.
This Bright Day. Lehman Engel. LC 73-8352. (Illus.). 352p. 1974. 10.95 o.s.i. (ISBN 0-02-536130-9). Macmillan.
This Can Lick a Lollypop: Body Riddles for Kids. Joel Rothman & Argentina Palacios. LC 77-80911. (ps-3). 1979. 6.95a (ISBN 0-385-13071-6); PLB (ISBN 0-385-13072-4). Doubleday.
This Child Is Mine. Celia Strang. LC 80-28457. 160p. (gr. 6 up). 1981. 7.95 (ISBN 0-8253-0049-5). Beaufort Bks NY.
This Church, These Times: The Roman Catholic Church Since Vatican II. Francis X. Murphy. (Illus.). 128p. 1981. cancelled (ISBN 0-695-81446-X, Assn Pr). Follett.
This City Is Ours. Denis Pitts. 1977. pap. 1.95 o.p. (ISBN 0-380-01851-9, 36483). Avon.
This City, This Man: The Cookingham Era in Kansas City. Bill Gilbert. LC 78-13401. (Illus.). 1978. 14.00 (ISBN 0-87326-021-X). Intl City Mgt.
This Cool World. William Sheldon et al. (Breakthrough Ser.). (gr. 7-12). 1979. pap. text ed. 4.96 (ISBN 0-205-05693-8, 5256933); tchrs'. ed. 2.40 (ISBN 0-205-06412-4, 526412X). Allyn.
This Date in Braves History. Marc Onigman. LC 80-6158. (This Date Ser.). 288p. 1981. pap. 9.95 (ISBN 0-8128-6106-X). Stein & Day.
This Date in Detroit Tigers History. John C. Hawkins. LC 80-5435. (This Date Ser.). 288p. 1981. pap. 9.95 (ISBN 0-8128-6067-5). Stein & Day.
This Date in New York Mets History. Dennis D'Agostino. LC 80-6157. (This Date Ser.). 256p. 1981. pap. 9.95 (ISBN 0-8128-6068-3). Stein & Day.
This Day in Oregon. James Cloutier. LC 80-83719. (Illus.). 128p. (gr. 4 up). 1981. pap. 6.95 (ISBN 0-918966-06-X). Image West.
This Day Is Ours. Jacques Leclercq. Tr. by Dinah Livingstone. LC 80-50314. Orig. Title: Le Jour de L'Homme. 160p. 1980. pap. 6.95 (ISBN 0-88344-504-2). Orbis Bks.
This Earth's End: New Testament Prophecy of the End Times. Carmen Benson. 152p. 1972. pap. 1.95 o.p. (ISBN 0-912106-89-1). Logos.
This English Language. E. Denison Ross. LC 73-167147. 266p. 1973. Repr. of 1939 ed. 18.00 (ISBN 0-8103-3184-5). Gale.
This Fabulous Century. Incl. Vol. 1. 1900-1910. 1969 (ISBN 0-8094-0121-5); Vol. 2. 1910-1920. 1969 (ISBN 0-8094-0122-3); Vol. 3. 1920-1930. 1969 (ISBN 0-8094-0123-1); Vol. 4. 1930-1940. 1969 (ISBN 0-8094-0124-X); Vol. 5. 1940-1950. 1969 (ISBN 0-8094-1205-5); Vol. 6. 1950-1960. 1970 (ISBN 0-8094-0125-8); Vol. 7. 1960-1970. 1970 (ISBN 0-8094-0126-6); Vol. 8. Prelude 1870-1900. 1970 (ISBN 0-8094-0127-4). (Illus.). 14.95 ea. Time-Life.
This Fabulous Century, 7 vols. Incl. Vol. I, 1900-1910. 1969; Vol. II, 1910-1920. 1969; Vol. III, 1920-1930. 1969; Vol. IV, 1930-1940. 1969; Vol. V, 1940-1950. 1969; Vol. VI, 1950-1960. 1970; Vol. VII, 1960-1970. 1970. LC 69-16698. (gr. 6 up). lib. bdg. 9.93 o.p. (ISBN 0-686-52172-2). Silver.
This Fabulous Century, 8 vols. Time-Life Books Editors. (gr. 6 up). kivar 9.93 ea. o.p. (Pub. by Time-Life). Silver.
This Fascinating Oil Business. Douglas Ball & Dan S. Turner. LC 64-15660. 1965. 15.95 (ISBN 0-672-50829-X). Bobbs.
This Fascinating Oil Business. Max W. Ball et al. LC 64-15660. (Illus.). 1979. pap. 10.95 (ISBN 0-672-52584-4). Bobbs.
This for Remembrance. Rosemary Clooney & Raymond Strait. 1979. pap. 2.25 (ISBN 0-87216-680-5). Playboy Pbks.
This Fortress World. James Gunn. 1979. pap. 1.75 o.p. (ISBN 0-425-03881-5). Berkley Pub.
This Game Called Hockey. Ross R. Olney. LC 77-16872. (gr. 5 up). 1978. 5.95 (ISBN 0-396-07524-X). Dodd.
This Gift I Present of Poetry from Hawaii. 3rd ed. Janice C. Yee. (Poetry Gift Ser.). (Illus.). 54p. 1980. pap. 5.00. Pi Pr.
This Girl Is Mine. Mary Munro. (Aston Hall Ser.: No. 118). 192p. (Orig.). 1981. pap. 1.75 (ISBN 0-523-41134-0). Pinnacle Bks.
This Golden Rapture. Paula Moore. 1980. pap. 2.50 (ISBN 0-671-41266-3). PB.
This Great Argument: The Rights of Women. Haig Bosmajian & Hamida Bosmajian. LC 73-162463. (Speech Ser). 1972. pap. text ed. 7.50 (ISBN 0-201-00611-1). A-W.
This Great Symbol: Pierre De Courbertin & the Origins of the Modern Olympic Games. John J. MacAloon. LC 80-21898. 1981. lib. bdg. 25.00x (ISBN 0-226-50000-4). U of Chicago Pr.
This Gun Is Still. Frank Gruber. 1979. pap. 1.50 o.p. (ISBN 0-685-93870-0, T8773-8). Bantam.
This Handful of Dust. Feroz Ahmed-Ud-Din. (Redbird Bk.). 31p. 1975. 8.00 (ISBN 0-88253-835-7); pap. 4.80 (ISBN 0-88253-836-5). Ind-US Inc.
This Haunted Land. Bruce Roberts. 5.95 (ISBN 0-87461-956-4). McNally.
This Hebrew Lord. John S. Spong. 1976. pap. 3.95 (ISBN 0-8164-2133-1). Crossroad NY.
This Holyest Erthe. Oliver L. Reiser. (Illus., Orig.). 1981. pap. 5.95 (ISBN 0-89407-022-3). Strawberry Hill.
This House Is Haunted! Elizabeth P. Hoffman. LC 77-10981. (Myth, Magic & Superstition Ser.). (Illus.). (gr. 4-5). 1977. PLB 9.65 (ISBN 0-8172-1033-4). Raintree Pubs.
This House Is Haunted: The True Story of a Poltergeist. Guy L. Playfair. LC 80-5387. (Illus.). 288p. 1980. 11.95 (ISBN 0-8128-2732-5). Stein & Day.
This I Believe-Thank You, Billy Sunday, for the Goodness & Mercy Which I Know. Leslie A. Outterson. 1977. 7.00 o.p. (ISBN 0-682-48685-X). Exposition.
This Immortal. Roger Zelazny. 192p. 1975. pap. 2.25 (ISBN 0-441-80696-1). Ace Bks.
This Is a River: Exploring an Ecosystem. Laurence Pringle. LC 70-160074. (Illus.). (gr. 4 up). 1972. 4.95g o.s.i. (ISBN 0-02-775240-2). Macmillan.
This Is Astronomy. Lloyd Motz. LC 56-12016. (Illus., Orig.). 1958. pap. 5.00 (ISBN 0-231-08549-4). Columbia U Pr.
This Is Australia. Miroslav Sasek. LC 79-117960. (Illus.). (gr. 4-6). 1971. 4.95g o.s.i. (ISBN 0-02-778160-7). Macmillan.
This Is Ballroom Dance. Lois Ellfeldt & Virgil L. Morton. LC 73-84770. (Illus.). 1974. pap. text ed. 4.50 (ISBN 0-87484-244-1). Mayfield Pub.
This Is Earl Nightingale. Earl Nightingale. LC 67-12840. 1969. 8.95 o.p. (ISBN 0-385-08501-X). Doubleday.
This Is Edinburgh. Miroslav Sasek. (Illus.). (gr. 3 up). 1961. 5.95g o.s.i. (ISBN 0-02-778180-1). Macmillan.
This Is Electronics, 2 bks. ITT Educational Services Inc. Incl. Bk. 1. Basic Principles (ISBN 0-672-20740-0); Bk. 2. Circuits & Applications (ISBN 0-672-20741-9). LC 74-105093. 1978. text ed. 21.95 ea. Set. Bobbs.
This Is for Me. Eric P. Hamp & Jean Greenlaw. (Design for Reading Ser). (Illus.). (preprimer 1). 1972. pap. 2.92 (ISBN 0-06-516000-2, SchDept). Har-Row.
This Is for You. Frwd. by Cornelius Greenway. 68p. 1974. Repr. of 1949 ed. text ed. 3.75. Pen-Art.

This Is for You. Dorothy Porter. (Illus.). 57p. 1974. 6.95 o.p. (ISBN 0-89015-064-8). Nortex Pr.
This Is Hong Kong. Miroslav Sasek. (Illus.). (gr. 3 up). 1965. 5.95g o.s.i. (ISBN 0-02-778190-9). Macmillan.
This Is Ireland. Miroslav Sasek. (Illus.). (gr. 3 up). 1965. 6.95g (ISBN 0-02-778350-2). Macmillan.
This Is Israel. Miroslav Sasek. (Illus.). (gr. 3 up). 1962. 4.95g o.s.i. (ISBN 0-02-778340-5). Macmillan.
This Is Jerusalem. rev. ed. Menashe Har-El. Ed. by Rechavam Zeevy. (Illus.). 368p. 1980. pap. 6.95 (ISBN 0-86628-002-2). Ridgefield Pub.
This Is Karate. rev. ed. Masutatsu Oyama. LC 65-17218. (Illus.). 368p. 1973. boxed 28.00 (ISBN 0-87040-254-4). Japan Pubns.
This Is Kendo: The Art of Japanese Fencing. Gordon Warner & Junzo Sasamori. LC 64-22900. 1964. 16.50 (ISBN 0-8048-0574-1). C E Tuttle.
This Is Lebanon. Khairallah. 5.95 (ISBN 0-686-65476-5). Intl Bk Ctr.
This Is London. Philip Prowse. (Illus.). 1977. pap. 1.25x (ISBN 0-435-27045-1). Heinemann Ed.
This Is London. Miroslav Sasek. (Illus.). (gr. 3 up). 1959-62. 4.95g o.s.i. (ISBN 0-02-778510-6); lt. Ed. 3.00 o.s.i. (ISBN 0-685-16098-X). Macmillan.
This Is My Country. rev. ed. Jene Barr. LC 59-14393. (Community Helpers Ser). (Illus.). (gr. k-2). 1966. 4.75g o.p. (ISBN 0-8075-7879-7). A Whitman.
This Is My Father & Me. Dorka Raynor. LC 73-7320. (Concept Bks.). (Illus.). 40p. (ps up). 1973. 6.95g (ISBN 0-8075-7883-5). A Whitman.
This Is My God. Herman Wouk. LC 79-78741. 1959. 10.95 (ISBN 0-385-02158-5). Doubleday.
This Is My God. Herman Wouk. 1980. pap. write for info. (ISBN 0-671-41512-3). PB.
This Is My House. Illus. by John E. Johnson. (Golden Sturdy Shape Bk.). (Illus.). 14p. (ps). 1981. 2.95 (ISBN 0-307-12251-4, Golden Pr). Western Pub.
This Is My Life. Thyra F. Bjorn. (Spire Bk). 1976. pap. 1.50 o.p. (ISBN 0-8007-8234-8). Revell.
This Is My Life. Thyra F. Bjorn. 1976. pap. 1.50 (ISBN 0-89129-137-7). Jove Pubns.
This Is My Life: Personal History Guide. Duane S. Crowther. LC 78-52406. 1979. 4.50 (ISBN 0-88290-089-7). Horizon Utah.
This Is My Opinion About... Linda P. Silbert & Alvin J. Silbert. (Little Twirps, TM Creative Thinking Wkbks.). (Illus.). (gr. 5-12). 1977. 2.25 (ISBN 0-89544-020-2, 020). Silbert Bress.
This Is New York. Miroslav Sasek. (Illus.). (gr. 3 up). 1960. 5.95g o.s.i. (ISBN 0-02-779530-6). Macmillan.
This Is New York City: Facts & Trends for Social Planning. 1980. 2.00. Comm Coun Great NY.
This Is No Place for a Nervous Person. Ann Crawford. (Illus., Orig.). 1981. pap. 5.00x (ISBN 0-915494-12-4). Fibonacci Corp.
This Is Our Land, Vol. 1. Val J. McClellan. LC 77-151749. (Illus.). 1977. 12.50x (ISBN 0-533-02248-7). Western Pubs OH.
This Is Our Land, Vol. 2. Val J. McClellan. LC 77-151749. (Illus.). 1979. 13.95x (ISBN 0-9602218-0-8). Western Pubs OH.
This Is Our St. Rose Church in Proctor Minnesota. Claire W. Schumacher. (Illus.). 100p. 1976. pap. 3.00 (ISBN 0-917378-02-4). Schumacher Pubns.
This Is Our World. Paul B. Sears. (Illus.). 1937. 8.95x (ISBN 0-8061-0932-7); pap. 4.95x (ISBN 0-8061-0933-5). U of Okla Pr.
This Is Poland. LC 78-322440. (Illus.). 220p. 1978. 18.50x (ISBN 0-8002-2297-0). Intl Pubns Serv.
This Is PR: The Realities of Public Relations. Doug Newsom & Alan Scott. 1976. text ed. 19.95x (ISBN 0-534-00421-0). Wadsworth Pub.
This Is Pro Basketball. George Sullivan. LC 77-6497. (Illus.). (gr. 5 up). 1977. 6.50 (ISBN 0-396-07455-3). Dodd.
This Is Pro Hockey. George Sullivan. LC 75-38359. (Illus.). 128p. 1976. 5.95 (ISBN 0-396-07318-2). Dodd.
This Is Pro Soccer. George Sullivan. LC 78-10729. (Illus.). 1979. 6.95 (ISBN 0-396-07643-2). Dodd.
This Is Ragtime. Terry Waldo. 1976. 10.95 (ISBN 0-8015-7618-0, Hawthorn). Dutton.
This Is Rough Weather Cruising. Erroll Bruce. (Illus.). 1980. 17.50 (ISBN 0-393-03245-0). Norton.
This Is San Francisco. Miroslav Sasek. (Illus.). (gr. 3 up). 1962. 7.95 (ISBN 0-02-780830-0). Macmillan.
This Is Texas. Miroslav Sasek. (Illus.). (gr. 3 up). 1967. 5.95g o.s.i. (ISBN 0-02-780740-1). Macmillan.
This Is the Day: Selected Sermons. 2nd ed. Theodore P. Ferris. LC 76-39640. 384p. 1980. pap. 10.00 (ISBN 0-911658-16-5, 3077). Yankee Bks.
This Is the Life. Goodspeed. (gr. 7-12). 1981. text ed. price not set. Bennett Co.
This Is the Old English Sheepdog. Joan McD. Brearley & Marlene Anderson. (Illus.). 320p. 1974. 12.95 (ISBN 0-87666-345-5, PS-702). TFH Pubns.
This Is Truth About the Self. 2nd ed. Ann Davies. 1974. 2.25 (ISBN 0-938002-03-1). Builders of Adytum.
This Is Venice. Miroslav Sasek. (Illus.). (gr. 3 up). 1961. 4.95g o.s.i. (ISBN 0-02-781050-X). Macmillan.
This Is Washington, D. C. Miroslav Sasek. LC 69-13394. (Illus.). (gr. 3 up). 1969. 4.95 o.s.i. (ISBN 0-02-778240-9). Macmillan.
This Is Your Body. Gyles Brandreth. LC 79-65078. (Illus.). (gr. 3-7). 1979. 6.95 (ISBN 0-8069-3112-4); PLB 7.49 (ISBN 0-8069-3113-2). Sterling.
This Is Your Life, Charlie Brown: Selected Cartoons from "It's a Dog's Life, Charlie Brown", Vol. 1. Charles M. Schulz. (Peanuts Series). (Illus.). 1978. pap. 1.50 (ISBN 0-449-23918-7, Crest). Fawcett.
This Is Zion. Allen R. Hagood. (Illus.). 73p. 1977. 1.75 (ISBN 0-915630-06-0). Zion.
This Island, Now. Peter Abrahams. 1971. pap. 1.95 o.s.i. (ISBN 0-02-048040-7, Collier). Macmillan.
This Isn't Quite What I Had in Mind: A Career Planning Program for College Students. John W. Loughary & Theresa M. Ripley. 1978. pap. 3.95 o.p. (ISBN 0-695-80921-0). Follett.
This Land Is Mine. Hess Harley. (Orig.). 1980. pap. 1.75 (ISBN 0-532-23227-5). Manor Bks.
This Land Is Mine: An Anthology of American Verse. Ed. by Al Hine. LC 65-13437. (Illus.). (gr. 7-9). 1965. 8.95 o.p. (ISBN 0-397-30840-X). Lippincott.
This Land Is Your Land. Paul E. Toms. LC 75-23512. 1977. pap. 2.25 (ISBN 0-8307-0365-9, S312-1-07). Regal.
This Land of Liberty. Ernest Bates. LC 73-19817. (Civil Liberties in American History Ser.). 383p. 1974. Repr. of 1930 ed. lib. bdg. 35.00 (ISBN 0-306-70597-4). Da Capo.
This Land: Ours for a Season. pap. 1.95 (ISBN 0-87178-843-8). Brethren.
This Land Was Theirs: A Study of North American Indians. 3rd ed. Wendell H. Oswalt. LC 77-14986. 1978. text ed. 20.95 (ISBN 0-471-02342-6). Wiley.
This Life. Sidney Poitier. 416p. 1981. pap. 2.95 (ISBN 0-345-29407-6). Ballantine.
This Little Light of Mine: A Pre-School Religion Program. Julie Walters. 1974. pap. tchrs. manual 1.95 o.p. (ISBN 0-87793-069-4); pap. parents manual 0.95 o.p. (ISBN 0-87793-070-8). Ave Maria.
This Little Planet. Ed. by Michael Hamilton. 1971. pap. 2.45 o.p. (ISBN 0-684-71791-3, SL250, ScribT). Scribner.
This Loving Darkness: Silent Films & Spanish Writers 1920 - 1936. C. B. Morris. 240p. 1980. 39.50 (ISBN 0-19-713440-8). Oxford U Pr.
This Loving Torment. Valerie Sherwood. (Orig.). 1977. pap. 2.75 (ISBN 0-446-95745-3). Warner Bks.
This Man Jesus: An Essay Toward a New Testament Christology. Vawter, Bruce, C.M. LC 73-78174. 240p. 1975. pap. 2.45 (ISBN 0-385-02797-4, Im). Doubleday.
This Modern World. Derek Wood. 1976. pap. text ed. 8.95x (ISBN 0-435-31951-5). Heinemann Ed.
This New Land. Lester Goran. (Heritage Ser.: Pt. 1). (Orig.). 1980. pap. 2.75 (ISBN 0-451-09480-8, E9480, Sig). NAL.
This Noble Harvest: A Chronicle of Herbs. Anne O. Dowden. LC 79-12021. (Illus.). 1979. 12.95 (ISBN 0-529-05548-1). Philomel.
This Old House: Restoring, Rehabilitating & Renovating. Bob Vila & Jane Davison. (Illus.). 336p. 1980. 22.50 (ISBN 0-316-17704-0); pap. 12.95 (ISBN 0-316-17702-4). Little.
This Old Man Called Moses. Norman Habel. (Purple Puzzle Tree Ser). (Illus., Orig.). (ps-4). 1971. pap. 0.85 (ISBN 0-570-06512-7, 56-1212). Concordia.
This Passover or the Next I Will Never Be in Jerusalem. Hilton Obenzinger. LC 80-20986. 1980. lib. bdg. 12.50 (ISBN 0-917672-13-5); pap. 4.95 (ISBN 0-917672-12-7). Momos.
This Perfect Day. Ira Levin. 1970. 6.95 o.p. (ISBN 0-394-44858-8). Random.
This Powerful Rhyme: A Book of Sonnets. Helen Plotz. LC 79-14037. (gr. 6 up). 1979. 7.95 (ISBN 0-688-80226-5); PLB 7.63 (ISBN 0-688-84226-7). Greenwillow.
This Promise Is for You. David Parry. LC 77-99305. 1978. pap. 2.95 (ISBN 0-8091-2098-4). Paulist Pr.
This Proud Land: The Blue Ridge Mountains. John F. West & Bruce Roberts. LC 74-20051. (Illus., Orig.). 1974. 4.50 (ISBN 0-87461-960-2). McNally.
This Ravished Rose. Carsley. pap. 2.50 (ISBN 0-671-41293-0). PB.
This Room Is Mine: A Story About Sharing. Betty R. Wright. (Tell-a-Tale Readers). (Illus.). (gr. k-3). 1977. PLB 4.77 (ISBN 0-307-68643-4, Whitman). Western Pub.
This Rough Magic. Mary Stewart. 1979. pap. 2.25 (ISBN 0-449-24129-7, Crest). Fawcett.
This Running Life. George Sheehan. 1980. 10.95 (ISBN 0-671-25608-4). S&S.
This Scene of Man: The Role & Structure of the City in the Geography of Western Civilization. James E. Vance, Jr. (Ser. in Geography). 1977. text ed. 22.95 scp o.p. (ISBN 0-06-167407-9, HarpC). Har-Row.
This Sculptured Earth: The Landscape of America. John A. Shimer. LC 59-10628. (Illus.). 1959. 22.50x (ISBN 0-231-02331-6). Columbia U Pr.
This Side of Glory. Gwen Bristow. LC 40-27259. 1968. 9.95 o.s.i. (ISBN 0-690-81896-3, TYC-T). T Y Crowell.
This Side of Love. Paula Christian. LC 78-54181. 1978. pap. 6.50 (ISBN 0-931328-01-2). Timely Bks.
This Side of Paradise. F. Scott Fitzgerald. 1920. lib. rep. ed. 17.50x (ISBN 0-684-15601-6, ScribT); pap. 3.95 (ISBN 0-684-71765-4, SL60, ScribT). Scribner.
This Side of Tomorrow. Ruth L. Hill. 230p. (gr. 7-12). 1973. pap. 2.25 (ISBN 0-310-26062-0). Zondervan.
This Soldier Still at War. John Bryan. LC 74-5528. (Illus.). 352p. 1975. 9.95 o.p. (ISBN 0-15-190060-4). HarBraceJ.
This Song Remembers: Self-Portraits of Native Americans in the Arts. Jane Katz. (gr. 7 up). 1980. 8.95 (ISBN 0-395-29522-X). HM.
This Species of Property: Slave Life & Culture in the Old South. Leslie H. Owens. LC 75-38110. 1977. pap. 4.95 (ISBN 0-19-502245-9, GB517, GB). Oxford U Pr.
This Stubborn Soil. William A. Owens. LC 66-23604. 1966. 6.95 o.p. (ISBN 0-684-10444-X, ScribT). Scribner.
This Time Count Me In. Phyllis A. Wood. LC 80-15068. (Highway Bk.). 1980. 8.95 (ISBN 0-664-32665-X). Westminster.
This Time Forever. Elaine Lowell. 256p. (YA) 1972. 5.95 (ISBN 0-685-27367-9, Avalon). Bouregy.
This Time It's Love. Barbara Cartland. 1979. pap. 1.50 o.s.i. (ISBN 0-515-05101-2). Jove Pubns.
This Time of Darkness. H. M. Hoover. 192p. (gr. 7 up). 1980. 9.95 (ISBN 0-670-50026-7). Viking Pr.
This Time of Morning. Nayantara Sahgal. 221p. 1969. pap. 1.95 (ISBN 0-88253-079-8). Ind-US Inc.
This Treatise Concernynge the Fruytfull Saynges of Davyd..Was Made & Compyled by..John Fyssher..Bysshop of Rochester. John Fisher. LC 79-84106. (English Experience Ser.: No. 925). 296p. 1979. Repr. of 1509 ed. lib. bdg. 28.00 (ISBN 90-221-0925-9). Walter J Johnson.
This Trembling Land. Dag Ryen. 176p. (gr. 5-9). pap. 8.95 (ISBN 0-938578-01-4). How-to Pr.
This Was a Poet: A Critical Biography of Emily Dickinson. George Frisbiewhicher. 337p. 1980. 17.50 (ISBN 0-208-01900-6, Archon); pap. 9.50 tchr.'s ed. (ISBN 0-208-01901-4). Shoe String.
This Was Abe Lincoln. Ernest Lloyd. 30p. 1954. pap. 0.75 (ISBN 0-8163-0077-1, 20365-3). Pacific Pr Pub Assn.
This Was America. Martin W. Sandler. 1980. 19.95 (ISBN 0-316-77022-1). Little.
This Was Early Oil: Contemporary Accounts of the Growing Petroleum Industry, 1848-1885. Ernest C. Miller. 211p. (Orig.). 1968. 7.00 (ISBN 0-911124-15-2); pap. 4.00 (ISBN 0-911124-14-4). Pa Hist & Mus.
This Was John Calvin. Thea B. Van Halsema. (Christian Biography Ser.). 184p. 1981. pap. 3.95 (ISBN 0-8010-9283-3). Baker Bk.
This Was Logging. Ralph W. Andrews. 1954. 19.95 (ISBN 0-87564-901-7). Superior Pub.
This Was Tomorrow. Elswyth Thane. (Williamsburg Ser.: No. 6). 1981. lib. bdg. 14.95 (ISBN 0-8161-3161-9, Large Print Bks). G K Hall.
This Was Toscanini. Samuel Antek & Robert Hupka. LC 63-15196. (Illus.). 1963. 19.50 (ISBN 0-8149-0018-6). Vanguard.
This Way to Better Teaching. Clyne W. Buxton. 1974. 4.50 (ISBN 0-87148-835-3); pap. 3.50 (ISBN 0-87148-836-1). Pathway Pr.
This Way to Happiness. Clyde M. Narramore. (gr. 8 up). pap. 2.95 (ISBN 0-310-29942-X). Zondervan.
This Way to the Apocalypse: The Politics of the 1960's. Sidney Bernard. LC 77-92709. 1969. 5.95 (ISBN 0-912292-09-1). The Smith.
This Way to Wall Street. Patricia B. Egan & Marie Y. Maran. LC 80-82137. (Illus.). 200p. 1980. pap. 9.95 (ISBN 0-937470-00-7); instructor's manual 5.95 (ISBN 0-937470-01-5). Market Ed.
This We Believe. Ed. by James C. Suggs. 1977. pap. 1.95 (ISBN 0-8272-3623-9). Bethany Pr.
This We Believe. (Eng. & Ger.). pap. 0.75 (ISBN 0-8100-0004-0, 04-0622). Northwest Pub.
This We Can Believe. R. C. Miller. 1976. 6.95 (ISBN 0-8164-0376-7). Crossroad NY.
This World. Harvey Shapiro. LC 72-142725. (Wesleyan Poetry Program: Vol. 57). 1971. pap. 10.00x (ISBN 0-8195-2057-8, Pub. by Wesleyan U Pr); pap. 4.95x (ISBN 0-8195-1057-2). Columbia U Pr.
Thistle Hill, the Cattle Baron's Legacy. Roze M. Porter. LC 80-67827. 456p. 1980. 19.95x (ISBN 0-87706-113-0). Branch-Smith.
Thomas Alva Edison. Margaret Cousins. (Landmark Ser.: No. 110). (Illus.). (gr. 4-8). 1965. PLB 5.99 (ISBN 0-394-90410-9, BYR). Random.
Thomas Alva Edison: The Biography of a Myth. Wyn Wachhorst. 288p. 1981. 15.00 (ISBN 0-262-23108-5). MIT Pr.
Thomas & Sarah. Mollie Hardwick. 288p. (Orig.). 1981. pap. 2.50 (ISBN 0-515-06003-8). Jove Pubns.
Thomas Aquinas Dictionary. Ed. by M. Stockhammer. LC 64-21468. 1965. 7.50 o.p. (ISBN 0-8022-1653-6). Philos Lib.
Thomas Arnold on Education. T. W. Bamford. LC 79-108099. (Texts & Studies in the History of Education: No. 8). 1970. 22.95 (ISBN 0-521-07785-0). Cambridge U Pr.
Thomas Babington Macaulay. Margaret L. Cruikshank. (English Author Ser.: No. 217). 1978. lib. bdg. 10.95 (ISBN 0-8057-6686-3). Twayne.
Thomas Becket: A Textual History of His Letters. Anne Duggan. 384p. 1980. 49.50 (ISBN 0-19-822486-9). Oxford U Pr.
Thomas Berryman Number. James Patterson. 1977. pap. 1.75 o.p. (ISBN 0-685-75042-6, 345-255526-175). Ballantine.
Thomas Betterton & the Management of Lincoln's Inn Fields, 1695-1708. Judith Milhous. LC 78-21017. 304p. 1979. 18.95x (ISBN 0-8093-0906-8). S Ill U Pr.
Thomas Bewick & His Pupils. Austin Dobson. LC 69-17340. 1968. Repr. of 1884 ed. 15.00 (ISBN 0-8103-3523-9). Gale.
Thomas Bewick: Vignettes. Thomas Bewick. Ed. by Iain Bain. (Illus.). 1977. 15.95 (ISBN 0-85967-410-X, Pub. by Scolar Pr England). Biblio Dist.
Thomas Birch Seventeen Seventy-Nine to Eighteen Fifty-One: Paintings & Drawings. Philadelphia Maritime Museum. (Illus.). 64p. 1966. pap. 2.00 (ISBN 0-913346-06-3). Phila Maritime Mus.
Thomas Burke Restless Revolutionary. John S. Watterson. LC 79-3875. 302p. 1980. text ed. 18.50 (ISBN 0-8191-0943-6); pap. text ed. 10.75 (ISBN 0-8191-0944-4). U Pr of Amer.
Thomas Campbell. Mary R. Miller. (English Authors Ser.: No. 227). 1978. 12.50 (ISBN 0-8057-6728-2). Twayne.
Thomas Cantimpratensis: Liber De Natura Rerum. Editio Princeps Secundum Codices Manuscriptos, 2pts, Pt. 1. 1973. 85.30x (ISBN 3-11-003789-0). De Gruyter.
Thomas Cardinal Wolsey. Nancy L. Harvey. (Illus.). 256p. 1980. 19.95 o.s.i. (ISBN 0-02-548600-4). Macmillan.
Thomas Carew. Lynn Sadler. (English Authors Ser.: No. 214). 1979. lib. bdg. 10.95 (ISBN 0-8057-6683-9). Twayne.
Thomas Carlyle. Walter Waring. (English Author Ser.: No.238). 1978. 12.50 (ISBN 0-8057-6710-X). Twayne.
Thomas Carlyle - Reminiscences. Thomas Carlyle. Ed. by Charles E. Norton. (Rowman & Littlefield Univerisity Library). 400p. 1972. 7.50x (ISBN 0-87471-656-X); pap. 3.50x (ISBN 0-87471-655-1). Rowman.
Thomas Chatterton. John C. Nevill. 261p. 1980. Repr. of 1948 ed. lib. bdg. 30.00 (ISBN 0-8495-4020-8). Arden Lib.
Thomas Coke: Apostle of Methodism. John A. Vickers. 1969. 14.50 (ISBN 0-687-41856-9). Abingdon.
Thomas Frognall Dibdin: Selections. Ed. by Victor E. Neuburg. LC 77-18012. (Great Bibliographers Ser.: No. 3). 1978. 12.00 (ISBN 0-8108-1077-8). Scarecrow.
Thomas Gage in Spanish America. Norman Newton. (Great Travellers Ser.). (Illus.). 1969. 4.95 o.p. (ISBN 0-571-08799-X, Pub. by Faber & Faber). Merrimack Bk Serv.
Thomas Gage's Travels in the New World. rev. ed. enl. ed. Thomas Gage. Ed. by J. Eric Thompson. LC 58-6856. (American Exploration & Travel Ser.: Vol. 58). (Illus.). 1958. 15.95 (ISBN 0-8061-0881-9). U of Okla Pr.

Thomas Gainsborough: His Life & Art. Jack Lindsay. LC 80-54397. (Illus.). 248p. 1981. 25.00 (ISBN 0-87663-352-1, Pica Pr). Universe.

Thomas George Lawson: African Historian & Administrator in Sierra Leone. David E. Skinner. LC 78-70393. (Publications Ser, No. 222: Hoover Colonial Studies). 1980. pap. 10.95 (ISBN 0-8179-7221-8). Hoover Inst Pr.

Thomas Gray: His Life & Works. A. L. Sells. (Illus.). 320p. 1980. text ed. 29.50x (ISBN 0-04-928043-0, 2411). Allen Unwin.

Thomas Hardy. L. J. Butler. LC 77-23532. (British Authors Ser.). 1978. 23.95 (ISBN 0-521-21743-1); pap. 7.95x (ISBN 0-521-29271-9). Cambridge U Pr.

Thomas Hardy. Richard C. Carpenter. (English Authors Ser.: No. 13). 1964. lib. bdg. 9.95 (ISBN 0-8057-1244-5). Twayne.

Thomas Hardy. Trevor Johnson. LC 78-123553. (Literary Critiques Ser). (Illus.). 1970. lib. bdg. 4.95 o.p. (ISBN 0-668-02362-7). Arco.

Thomas Hardy. Michael Millgate. 1971. 10.00 o.p. (ISBN 0-394-46121-5). Random.

Thomas Hardy. Norman Page. 1977. 18.00 (ISBN 0-7100-8614-8). Routledge & Kegan.

Thomas Hardy. Norman Page. 212p. (Orig.). 1981. pap. price not set (ISBN 0-7100-8615-6). Routledge & Kegan.

Thomas Hardy & Rural England. Merryn Williams. LC 72-318. 1972. 17.50x (ISBN 0-231-03674-4). Columbia U Pr.

Thomas Hardy, Psychologist Novelist. Rosemary Summer. 19.95 (ISBN 0-312-80161-0). St Martin.

Thomas Hardy's Novels: A Study Guide. Maureen Mahon. 1976. pap. text ed. 3.95x (ISBN 0-435-18552-7). Heinemann Ed.

Thomas Hardy's Personal Writings. Ed. by Harold Orel. 295p. 1981. text ed. 10.00x (ISBN 0-333-05493-8, Pub. by Macmillan, England). Humanities.

Thomas Hardy's "The Mayor of Casterbridge: Tragedy or Social History? Laurence Lerner. (Text & Context Ser.). 1975. text ed. 6.25x (ISBN 0-85621-042-0); pap. text ed. 2.75x (ISBN 0-85621-043-9). Humanities.

Thomas Hardy's Women & Men: The Defeat of Nature. Anne Z. Mickelson. LC 76-28366. 1976. 10.00 (ISBN 0-8108-0985-0). Scarecrow.

Thomas Harriott: Renaissance Scientist. John W. Shirley. (Illus.). 1974. 29.50x (ISBN 0-19-858140-8). Oxford U Pr.

Thomas Hart Benton: A Portrait. Polly Burroughs. LC 77-16903. (Illus.). 208p. 1981. 29.95 (ISBN 0-385-12342-6). Doubleday.

Thomas Hill Green & the Social Assumptions of Liberal-Democratic Thought. I. M. Greengarten. 194p. 1981. 25.00x (ISBN 0-8020-5503-6). U of Toronto Pr.

Thomas Hobbes. Charles H. Hinnant. (English Authors Ser.: No. 215). 1977. lib. bdg. 9.95 (ISBN 0-8057-6684-7). Twayne.

Thomas Holley Chivers. Charles M. Lombard. (United States Authors Ser.: No. 325). 1979. lib. bdg. 12.50 (ISBN 0-8057-7258-8). Twayne.

Thomas Hood. Lloyd N. Jeffrey. (English Authors Ser.: No. 137). lib. bdg. 10.95 (ISBN 0-8057-1268-2). Twayne.

Thomas Hooker: Writings in England & Holland, Sixteen Twenty-Six to Sixteen Thirty-Three. George H. Williams et al. LC 75-30570. (Harvard Theological Review & Studies). 1975. pap. 12.00 (ISBN 0-89130-310-3, 020028). Scholars Pr Ca.

Thomas Hope & the Neo-Classical Idea. David Watkins. 1970. 24.00 (ISBN 0-7195-1819-9). Transatlantic.

Thomas J. Rusk: Soldier, Statesman, Jurist. Mary W. Clarke. LC 79-157043. (Illus.). 1971. 9.50 (ISBN 0-685-00320-5). Jenkins.

Thomas Jefferson. William K. Bottorff. (United States Authors Ser.: No. 327). 1979. lib. bdg. 9.95 (ISBN 0-8057-7260-X). Twayne.

Thomas Jefferson. Harrison et al. (Illus.). 35p. (gr. 1-9). 2.95 (ISBN 0-86575-187-0). Dormac.

Thomas Jefferson. John T. Morse, Jr. LC 80-23357. (American Statesmen Ser.). 330p. 1981. pap. 5.95 (ISBN 0-87754-183-3). Chelsea Hse.

Thomas Jefferson: A Biography in His Own Words. Thomas Jefferson. Ed. by Newsweek Books Editors. LC 72-92143. (Founding Fathers Ser.). (Illus.). 416p. (YA) 1974. 15.00 o.s.i. (ISBN 0-06-011148-8, HarpT). Har-Row.

Thomas Jefferson & His Unknown Brother. Ed. by Bernard Mayo. LC 80-25272. 1981. price not set (ISBN 0-8139-0890-6). U Pr of Va.

Thomas Jefferson & His World. Henry Moscow. LC 60-11827. (American Heritage Junior Library). (Illus.). 153p. (gr. 6 up). 1960. 9.95 (ISBN 0-8281-0386-0, J003-0); PLB 12.89 (ISBN 0-06-024346-5, Dist. by Har-Row). Am Heritage.

Thomas Jefferson & the Development of American Public Education. James B. Conant. 1962. 7.50x o.p. (ISBN 0-520-00262-8). U of Cal Pr.

Thomas Jefferson & the New Nation: A Biography. Merrill D. Peterson. LC 70-110394. (Illus.). 1090p. 1975. pap. 9.95 (ISBN 0-19-501909-1, GB436, GB). Oxford U Pr.

Thomas Jefferson & the Stony Mountains: Exploring the West from Monticello. Donald Jackson. LC 80-10546. (Illus.). 290p. 1981. 19.95 (ISBN 0-252-00823-5). U of Ill Pr.

Thomas Jefferson Landscape Architect. Frederick D. Nichols & Ralph E. Griswold. LC 77-10601. (Illus.). 1977. 10.95x (ISBN 0-8139-0603-2). U Pr of Va.

Thomas Jefferson, Landscape Architect. Frederick D. Nichols & Ralph E. Griswold. LC 77-10601. (Illus.). ix, 196p. 1981. pap. 4.95x (ISBN 0-8139-0899-X). U Pr of Va.

Thomas Jefferson: The Apostle of Liberty. Marguerite E. Wilbur. 416p. 1962. 6.95 o.p. (ISBN 0-87140-809-0). Liveright.

Thomas Jefferson: The Complete Man. James Eichner. LC 65-21647. (Biography Ser). (gr. 7 up). 1966. PLB 4.90 o.p. (ISBN 0-531-00886-X). Watts.

Thomas Jefferson's Architectural Drawings. 2nd ed. Ed. by Frederick D. Nichols. LC 76-163982. (Orig.). 1961. pap. 2.95 (ISBN 0-8139-0328-9). U Pr of Va.

Thomas K. Jefferson on Democracy. Ed. by Saul Padover. pap. 1.50 o.p. (ISBN 0-451-61509-3, MW1509, Ment). NAL.

Thomas Ken: Bishop & Non-Juror. Hugh A. L. Rice. 1958. pap. 7.50x (ISBN 0-8401-2008-7). Allenson.

Thomas L. McKenney, Architect of America's Early Indian Policy: 1816-1830. Herman J. Viola. LC 74-18075. (Illus.). xii, 365p. (Orig.). 1981. pap. 8.95x (ISBN 0-8040-0669-5, SB). Swallow.

Thomas Mann. Arnold Bauer. Tr. by Alexander Henderson & Elizabeth Henderson. LC 71-139221. (Modern Literature Ser.). 1971. 10.95 (ISBN 0-8044-2023-8); pap. 3.45 (ISBN 0-8044-6018-3). Ungar.

Thomas Mann. Ignace Feuerlicht. LC 68-24312. (World Authors Ser.: Germany: No. 47). 1969. lib. bdg. 12.50 (ISBN 0-8057-2584-9). Twayne.

Thomas Mann. Joseph P. Stern. LC 67-16891. (Columbia Essays on Modern Writers Ser.: No. 24). 1967. pap. 2.00 (ISBN 0-231-02847-4, MW24). Columbia U Pr.

Thomas Mann: a Critical Study. R. J. Hollingdale. LC 79-161509. 204p. 1971. 12.00 (ISBN 0-8387-1004-2). Bucknell U Pr.

Thomas Mann: A Study. Martin Swales. 117p. 1980. 11.50x (ISBN 0-8476-6270-5). Rowman.

Thomas Mann Studies, Vol. 2. Ed. by Klaus W. Jonas & Ilsedore B. Jonas. LC 66-12543. 1967. 15.00x o.p. (ISBN 0-8122-7527-6). U of Pa Pr.

Thomas Mann: The Uses of Tradition. T. J. Reed. 442p. 1974. 36.00x (ISBN 0-19-815742-8); pap. 8.25x (ISBN 0-19-815747-9). Oxford U Pr.

Thomas Mann, 1875-1955. Stanley Corngold et al. (Illus.). 1975. pap. 3.00 (ISBN 0-87811-021-6). Princeton Lib.

Thomas Medwin (Seventeen Eighty-Eight to Eighteen Sixty-Nine) Thomas Medwin. Ed. by Donald H. Reiman. LC 75-31230. (Romantic Context Ser.: Poetry 1789-1830). 1978. lib. bdg. 47.00 (ISBN 0-8240-2179-7). Garland Pub.

Thomas Merton. Cornelia Sussman & Irving Sussman. LC 80-924. 176p. 1980. pap. 3.95 (ISBN 0-385-17172-2, Im). Doubleday.

Thomas Merton: A Pictorial Biography. James H. Forest. LC 80-82249. (Illus., Orig.). 1980. pap. 5.95 (ISBN 0-8091-2284-7). Paulist Pr.

Thomas Merton: Contemplative Critic. Henri J. Nouwen. LC 80-8898. 176p. 1981. pap. 3.95 (ISBN 0-06-066324-3, HarpR). Har-Row.

Thomas Merton, Monk: A Monastic Tribute. Ed. by Hart, Patrick, Bro. 240p. 1976. pap. 1.95 (ISBN 0-385-11244-0, Im). Doubleday.

Thomas Merton on Mysticism. Raymond Bailey. LC 74-32570. 280p. 1976. pap. 1.95 (ISBN 0-385-12071-0, Im). Doubleday.

Thomas Merton: Prophet in the Belly of a Paradox. Ed. by Gerald Twomey. LC 78-61717. 1978. 9.95 (ISBN 0-8091-0268-4). Paulist Pr.

Thomas Merton Reader. Ed. by Thomas P. McDonnell. LC 74-29. 600p. 1974. pap. 2.95 (ISBN 0-385-03292-7, Im). Doubleday.

Thomas Merton: The Daring Young Man on the Flying Belltower. Irving Sussman & Cornelia Sussman. LC 76-34236. 192p. (gr. 7 up). 1976. 7.95 (ISBN 0-02-788630-1, 78863). Macmillan.

Thomas Middleton. Norman A. Brittin. (English Authors Ser.: No. 139). lib. bdg. 10.95 (ISBN 0-8057-1388-3). Twayne.

Thomas Middleton's No Wit, No Help Like a Woman's & the Counterfeit Bridegroom (1677) & Further Adaptations. Marston S. Balch. (Jacobean Drama Studies: No. 94). 1980. pap. text ed. 25.00x (ISBN 0-391-01921-X). Humanities.

Thomas Moore. Stephen L. Gwynn. 204p. 1980. Repr. of 1905 ed. lib. bdg. 22.50 (ISBN 0-8495-2045-2). Arden Lib.

Thomas Moran: The Grand Canyon Sketches. Timothy J. Priehs. 1978. 2.95 (ISBN 0-938216-07-4). GCNHA.

Thomas More. Raymond W. Chambers. 1958. pap. 4.95x (ISBN 0-472-06018-X, 18, AA). U of Mich Pr.

Thomas More. Judith P. Jones. (English Authors Ser.: No. 247). 1979. lib. bdg. 9.95 (ISBN 0-8057-6711-8). Twayne.

Thomas More. Daniel Sargent. 299p. 1980. Repr. of 1933 ed. lib. bdg. 30.00 (ISBN 0-89984-412-X). Century Bookbindery.

Thomas More & His Utopia. Karl Kautsky. 258p. 1980. pap. text ed. 8.50x (ISBN 0-85315-493-7). Humanities.

Thomas Morley: Editions of Italian Canzonets & Madrigals, 1597-98. Catharine A. Murphy. LC 64-64160. (Florida State U. Studies: No. 42). 1964. 12.00 (ISBN 0-8130-0480-2). U Presses Fla.

Thomas Nast: His Period & His Pictures. Albert B. Paine. LC 80-20105. (American Men & Women of Letters Ser.). (Illus.). 624p. 1981. pap. 8.95 (ISBN 0-87754-169-8). Chelsea Hse.

Thomas Paine. Ellery Sedgwick. 150p. 1980. Repr. of 1899 ed. lib. bdg. 20.00 (ISBN 0-8482-6306-5). Norwood Edns.

Thomas Paine. Jerome D. Wilson & William F. Ricketson. (United States Authors Ser: No. 301). 1978. lib. bdg. 9.95 (ISBN 0-8057-7206-5). Twayne.

Thomas Percy's Life of Dr. Oliver Goldsmith: A Critical Edition. Richard L. Harp. (Salzburg Studies in English Literature, Romantic Reassessment: No. 52). 1976. pap. text ed. 25.00x (ISBN 0-391-01398-X). Humanities.

Thomas Pringle. John R. Doyle, Jr. (World Authors Ser.: South Africa: No. 238). lib. bdg. 10.95 (ISBN 0-8057-2718-3). Twayne.

Thomas Pynchon: The Art of Allusion. David Cowart. LC 79-20157. (Crosscurrents-Modern Critiques-New Ser.). 160p. 1980. 10.95 (ISBN 0-8093-0944-0). S Ill U Pr.

Thomas Reid's Inquiry & Essays. Thomas Reid. Ed. by Keith Lehrer & Ronald E. Beanblossom. LC 75-1197. (LLA Ser: No. 156). 431p. 1975. pap. 8.50 (ISBN 0-672-61173-2). Bobbs.

Thomas Reid's Lectures on Natural Theology (1780) Thomas Reid. Ed. by Elmer H. Duncan. LC 80-5964. 177p. 1981. lib. bdg. 19.00 (ISBN 0-8191-1354-9); pap. text ed. 9.00 (ISBN 0-8191-1355-7). U Pr of Amer.

Thomas Ritchie: A Study in Virginia Politics. Charles H. Ambler. (Law, Politics & History Ser). 1970. Repr. of 1913 ed. lib. bdg. 39.50 (ISBN 0-306-70092-1). Da Capo.

Thomas Sackville. Normand Berlin. (English Authors Ser.: No. 165). 1974. lib. bdg. 10.95 (ISBN 0-8057-1471-5). Twayne.

Thomas Say Foundation Publications. Incl. Vol. 2. Plecoptera or Stoneflies of America North of Mexico. J. G. Needham & P. W. Claassen. (Illus.). 397p. 1925. 12.50 (ISBN 0-686-11692-5); Vol. 3. Plecoptera Nymphs of North America. P. W. Claassen. (Illus.). 199p. 1931. 10.90 (ISBN 0-686-11693-3); Vol. 4. Blow Flies of North America. D. G. Hall. (Illus.). 477p. 1948. 15.00 (ISBN 0-686-11694-1); Vol. 5. Aphids of the Rocky Mountain Region. Miriam A. Palmer. (Illus.). 452p. 1952. 21.70 (ISBN 0-686-11695-X); Vol. 6. Synoptic Catalog of the Mosquitoes of the World. Alan Stone et al. 358p. o.p. (ISBN 0-686-11696-8); suppl. o.p. 1.50 ea.; Vol. 7. Monograph of Cimicidae. Robert L. Usinger. (Illus.). 588p. 1966. 21.70 (ISBN 0-686-11698-4). LC 66-22730. Entomol Soc.

Thomas Say Foundation Publications. Incl. Vol. 1. Sarcophaga & Allies of North America. J. M. Aldrich. (Illus.). 301p. 1916. pap. 11.70 (ISBN 0-686-11699-2). Entomol Soc.

Thomas Stapleton & the Counter Reformation. M. R. O'Connell. 1964. 29.50x (ISBN 0-685-69850-5). Elliots Bks.

Thomas Stearns Eliot: Poet. A. D. Moody. LC 78-54719. (Illus.). 1979. 29.95 (ISBN 0-521-22065-3). Cambridge U Pr.

Thomas Stearns Eliot: Poet. A. D. Moody. LC 78-54719. 376p. 1980. pap. 14.95 (ISBN 0-521-29968-3). Cambridge U Pr.

Thomas Telford. Brian Bracegirdle & Patricia H. Miles. (Great Engineers & Their Works Ser). (Illus.). 112p. 1973. 14.95 (ISBN 0-7153-5933-9). David & Charles.

Thomas Telford: Engineer. Ed. by Alastair Penfold. 192p. 1980. 40.00x (ISBN 0-7277-0084-7, Pub. by Telford England). State Mutual Bk.

Thomas the Contender; The Coptic Text of the Book of Thomas. John D. Turner. LC 75-22446. (Society of Biblical Literature. Dissertation Ser.). 250p. 1975. pap. 7.50 (ISBN 0-89130-017-1, 060123). Scholars Pr Ca.

Thomas Traherne's Centuries of Meditation. Compiled by William J. Wolf. 1980. 1.60 (ISBN 0-686-28796-7). Forward Movement.

Thomas W. Martin: A Biography. William M. Murray, Jr. LC 77-85483. (Illus.). 276p. 1978. 6.50 (ISBN 0-686-27918-2). S Res Inst.

Thomas Weelkes. David Brown. 1979. Repr. of 1969 ed. lib. bdg. 22.50 (ISBN 0-306-79523-X). Da Capo.

Thomas Wentworth Higginson. James W. Tuttleton. (United States Authors Ser.: No. 313). 1978. lib. bdg. 12.50 (ISBN 0-8057-7236-7). Twayne.

Thomas William Robertson: His Plays & Stagecraft. Maynard Savin. (Brown University Studies: No. 13). (Illus.). 146p. 1950. 6.50x (ISBN 0-87057-029-3, Pub. by Brown U Pr). Univ Pr of New England.

Thomas Willis, 1621-1675: Doctor & Scientist. Hansruedi Isler. 1968. 13.75 o.s.i. (ISBN 0-02-846980-1). Hafner.

Thomas Wolfe. Bruce R. McElderry, Jr. (U. S. Authors Ser.: No. 50). 1963. lib. bdg. 9.95 (ISBN 0-8057-0833-2). Twayne.

Thomas Wolfe. Fritz H. Ryssel. Tr. by Helen Sebba. LC 78-190352. (Modern Literature Ser.). 1972. 10.95 (ISBN 0-8044-2749-6). Ungar.

Thomas Wolfe: Beyond the Romantic Ego. Leo Gurko. LC 74-34204. (Twentieth Century American Writers Ser.). 153p. (gr. 6 up). 1975. 8.95 (ISBN 0-690-00751-5, TYC-J). T Y Crowell.

Thomas Wolfe: Three Decades of Criticism. Ed. by Leslie A. Field. LC 68-13024. (Gotham Library). 304p. (Orig.). 1968. 15.00x (ISBN 0-8147-0147-7); pap. 4.95x (ISBN 0-8147-0148-5). NYU Pr.

Thomas Wolfe: Ulysses & Narcissus. William U. Snyder. LC 78-141381. xxiv, 234p. 1971. 12.00x (ISBN 0-8214-0087-8). Ohio U Pr.

Thomasina. Paul Gallico. 256p. 1981. pap. 2.25 (ISBN 0-380-51524-5, 51524). Avon.

Thomism & Aristotelianism: A Study of the Commentary by Thomas Aquinas on the Nicomachean Ethics. Harry V. Jaffa. LC 78-21520. 1979. Repr. of 1952 ed. lib. bdg. 21.75x (ISBN 0-313-21149-3, JATA). Greenwood.

Thomism & Modern Thought. Ed. by Harry R. Klocker. LC 62-9414. 1962. 28.00x (ISBN 0-89197-451-2). Irvington.

Thomistic Bibliography, 1940-1978. Compiled by Terry L. Miethe & Vernon J. Bourke. LC 80-1195. xxii, 318p. 1980. lib. bdg. 39.95 (ISBN 0-313-21991-5, MTH/). Greenwood.

Thompson on Real Property, 24 vols. John S. Grimes. Set. 350.00 (ISBN 0-672-83972-5, Bobbs-Merrill Law); 1980 suppl. 95.00 (ISBN 0-672-84139-8). Michie.

Thompson's Narrative of the Little Big Horn 1876. Daniel O. Magnussen. (Illus.). 1974. 22.50 o.p. (ISBN 0-87062-108-4). A H Clark.

Thonet Bentwood & Other Furniture: The 1904 Illustrated Catalogue & Supplements. Thonet Co. (Illus.). 154p. 1980. pap. 8.95 (ISBN 0-486-24024-X). Dover.

Thonet: One Hundred Fifty Years of Furniture. Christopher Wilk. (Furniture & Design Ser.). 1980. 18.95 (ISBN 0-8120-5384-2). Barron.

Thonger & the Dragon City. Lin Carter. pap. 1.25 o.p. (ISBN 0-425-03572-7). Berkley Pub.

Thongor & the Wizard of Lemuria. Lin Carter. pap. 1.50 o.p. (ISBN 0-425-03435-6). Berkley Pub.

Thongor at the End of Time. Lin Carter. 1968. pap. 1.75 (ISBN 0-446-94332-0). Warner Bks.

Thongor Fights the Pirates of Takakus. Lin Carter. pap. 1.25 o.p. (ISBN 0-425-03147-0). Berkley Pub.

Thongor in the City of Magicians. Lin Carter. 1968. pap. 1.75 (ISBN 0-446-94208-1). Warner Bks.

Thoor Ballylee: Home of William Butler Yeats. 2nd rev. ed. Ed. by Mary Hanley & Liam Miller. 1977. text ed. 3.75x (ISBN 0-85105-300-9, Dolmen Pr). Humanities.

Thor Heyerdahl: Modern Viking Adventurer. Julian May. LC 72-85046. 40p. (gr. 2-5). 1973. PLB 5.75 o.p. (ISBN 0-87191-220-1). Creative Ed.

Thoracic and Cardiovascular Surgery Continuing Education Review. Edwin C. James et al. 1980. pap. 16.00 (ISBN 0-87488-439-X). Med Exam.

Thoracic & Cardiovascular Surgery with Related Pathology. 3rd ed. Glenn. (Illus.). 1975. 65.00 o.p. (ISBN 0-8385-8955-3). ACC.

Thoracic Medicine. Ed. by Peter Emerson. 1981. text ed. price not set (ISBN 0-407-00210-3). Butterworth.

Thoracic Surgery. 2nd ed. H. Bolooki. (Medical Examination Review Book: Vol. 18). 1972. spiral bdg. 16.50 (ISBN 0-87488-118-8). Med Exam.

Thoracic Surgery Case Studies. Gerard A. Kaiser et al. 1979. pap. 15.75 (ISBN 0-87488-056-4). Med Exam.

Thoracic Trauma. Ed. by Dewitt C. Daughtry. 1980. text ed. 35.00 (ISBN 0-316-17380-0). Little.

Thore-Buerger & the Art of the Past. Frances S. Jowell. LC 76-23632. (Outstanding Dissertations in the Fine Arts - 19th Century). (Illus.). 1977. Repr. of 1971 ed. lib. bdg. 63.00 (ISBN 0-8240-2701-9). Garland Pub.

Thoreau. Henry S. Canby. 8.50 (ISBN 0-8446-1100-X). Peter Smith.

Thoreau and Indian Thought: A Study of the Impact of Indian Thought on the Life of Henry David Thoreau. D. G. Deshmukh. LC 80-2505. 1981. Repr. of 1974 ed. price not set (ISBN 0-404-19053-7). AMS Pr.

Thoreau & the Wild Appetite. Kenneth A. Robinson. LC 90-2682. 1981. Repr. of 1957 ed. 12.50 (ISBN 0-404-19079-0). AMS Pr.

Thoreau As World Traveler. John A. Christie. LC 65-24586. (Illus.). 1966. 22.50x (ISBN 0-231-02833-4). Columbia U Pr.

Thoreau Library of Raymond Adams. Raymond Adams. 24.50 (ISBN 0-686-28930-7). AMS Pr.

Thoreau Library of Raymond Adams. Raymond Adams. 80p. 1980. Repr. of 1936 ed. lib. bdg. 12.50 (ISBN 0-8495-0063-X). Arden Lib.

Thoreau on the Lecture Platform. Walter Harding. LC 80-2681. 1981. 12.50 (ISBN 0-404-19077-4). AMS Pr.

Thoreau, Poet-Naturalist. new & enl. ed. William E. Channing. Ed. by F. B. Sanborn. LC 65-27095. (Illus.). 1902. 15.00x (ISBN 0-8196-0173-X). Biblo.

Thoreau Profile. Milton Meltzer & Walter A. Harding. (Illus.). 8.50 (ISBN 0-8446-0797-5). Peter Smith.

Thoreau: Selected Writings. Henry D. Thoreau. Ed. by Lewis Leary. LC 58-5337. (Crofts Classics Ser.). 1958. pap. text ed. 2.95 (ISBN 0-88295-099-1). AHM Pub.

Thoreau the Poet-Naturalist: With Memorial Verses. William E. Channing. LC 80-2679. 1981. Repr. of 1873 ed. 37.50 (ISBN 0-404-19073-1). AMS Pr.

Thoreaus Minnesota Journey: Two Documents. Henry D. Thoreau. Ed. by Walter Harding. LC 80-2524. 1981. Repr. of 1962 ed. 18.50 (ISBN 0-404-19072-3). AMS Pr.

Thoreau's Philosophy of Life, with Special Consideration of the Influence of Hindoo Philosophy. Helene A. Snyder. LC 80-2518. 1981. Repr. of 1900 ed. 18.50 (ISBN 0-404-19066-9). AMS Pr.

Thoreau's Redemptive Imagination. Frederick Garber. LC 77-73031. (Gotham Library). 229p. 1977. pap. 6.00x (ISBN 0-8147-2965-7); pap. 4.95x (ISBN 0-8147-2966-5). NYU Pr.

Thoreau's Travels in Maine. J. Parker Huber. (Illus.). 200p. 1981. pap. 8.95 (ISBN 0-686-69095-8). Appalach Mtn.

Thorians. Finn Hedin. LC 79-66930. 1980. 6.50 (ISBN 0-533-04423-5). Vantage.

Thorn. Fred Saberhagen. 1980. pap. 2.75 (ISBN 0-441-80744-5). Ace Bks.

Thorn in the Rose. Maye Barrett. 192p. (Orig.). 1980. pap. 1.75 (ISBN 0-515-05631-6). Jove Pubns.

Thorn Rose. Charles Perrault. (Illus.). 1978. pap. 2.50 (ISBN 0-14-050222-X, Puffin). Penguin.

Thorne's Better Medical Writing. 2nd ed. S. Lock. 1977. 11.95 (ISBN 0-471-03062-7, Pub. by Wiley-Medical). Wiley.

Thorns & Roses. Ruby A. Newman. LC 79-92510. 1980. pap. 3.50 (ISBN 0-932964-05-2). MN Pubs.

Thorns & Thistles: Juvenile Delinquents in the United States, 1825-1940. Robert M. Mennel. LC 72-95187. 259p. 1973. pap. text ed. 15.00x (ISBN 0-87451-070-8). U Pr of New Eng.

Thornton the Worrier. Marjorie W. Sharmat. LC 78-1286. (Illus.). (ps-3). 1978. PLB 7.95 (ISBN 0-8234-0328-9). Holiday.

Thornton Wilder. 2nd ed. Rex J. Burbank. (United States Authors Ser.: No. 5). 1978. lib. bdg. 10.95 (ISBN 0-8057-7223-5). Twayne.

Thornton Wilder. Hermann Stresau. Tr. by Frieda Schutze. LC 71-149478. (Modern Literature Ser.). 1971. 10.95 (ISBN 0-8044-2844-1); pap. 3.45 (ISBN 0-8044-6884-2). Ungar.

Thorny Paradise: Writers on Writing for Children. Edward Blishen. 1975. 8.50 (ISBN 0-7226-5463-4). Horn Bk.

Thorough Bass Accompaniment According to Johann David Heinichen. George J. Buelow. 1966. 28.50x (ISBN 0-520-00188-5). U of Cal Pr.

Thoroughbred Broodmare Records, Nineteen Seventy-Eight. Date not set. 66.75 (ISBN 0-936032-11-1). Thoroughbred Own & Breed.

Thoroughbred Broodmare Records, 1980. Thoroughbred Owners & Breeders Association. 1981. text ed. 66.75 (ISBN 0-936032-42-1); leather bdg. 77.75 (ISBN 0-936032-43-X). Thoroughbred O.

Thoroughbred Owner & Breeder Directory, 1976. Date not set. 97.50. Thoroughbred Own & Breed.

Thoroughbred Owner & Breeder Directory, 1978. Date not set. 27.50 (ISBN 0-936032-13-8). Thoroughbred Own & Breed.

Thoroughbred Pedigrees Simplified. Miles Napier. 11.37 (ISBN 0-85131-191-1, Dist. by Sporting Book Center). J A Allen.

Thoroughbreds. Michael Geller. 1981. pap. 2.75 (ISBN 0-8439-0901-3, Leisure Bks). Nordon Pubns.

Thoroughbreds of Nineteen Seventy-Nine. 1980. lib. bdg. 36.25 (ISBN 0-936032-16-2). Thoroughbred Own and Breed.

Thoroughbreds of 1976. Bowen. Date not set. 46.25 (ISBN 0-936032-14-6). Thoroughbred Own & Breed.

Thoroughbreds of 1978. Bowen. Date not set. 36.25 (ISBN 0-936032-15-4). Thoroughbred Own & Breed.

Thorpe! Jim Thorpe. James Hahn & Lynn Hahn. Ed. by Howard Schroeder. (Sports Legends Ser.). (Illus.). 48p. (Orig.). (gr. 3-5). 1981. PLB 5.95 (ISBN 0-89686-123-6); pap. text ed. 2.95 (ISBN 0-89686-138-4). Crestwood Hse.

Thor's Goats & Other Crazy Ways to Ride Around. Slim Goatsend. (Odd Books for Odd Moments Ser.). (Illus.). 72p. (Orig.). 1981. pap. 3.95 (ISBN 0-938338-07-2). Winds World Pr.

Thorstein Veblen: The Carleton College Veblen Seminar Essays. Ed. by Carlton C. Qualey. LC 68-28400. 1968. 15.00x (ISBN 0-231-03111-4). Columbia U Pr.

Those Drinking Days: Myself & Other Writers. Donald Newlove. 150p. 1981. 8.95 (ISBN 0-8180-0250-6). Horizon.

Those Earnest Victorians. Esme Wingfield-Stratford. 8.00 (ISBN 0-8446-0966-8). Peter Smith.

Those Extra Chances in Bridge. Terence Reese & Roger Trezel. LC 77-23675. 1978. pap. 3.95 (ISBN 0-8119-0398-2). Fell.

Those Fabulous Film Factories: The History of Motion Picture Studios in California. Bruce Torrence. (Illus.). 240p. Date not set. price not set (ISBN 0-87905-086-1). Peregrine Smith. Postponed.

Those Fascinating Paper Dolls: An Illustrated Handbook for Collectors. Marion Howard. (Illus.). 320p. 1981. pap. 6.95 (ISBN 0-486-24055-X). Dover.

Those Funny Kids! Dick Van Dyke & Ray Parker. 1976. pap. 1.50 o.s.i. (ISBN 0-446-88274-7). Warner Bks.

Those Gasoline Lines & How They Got There. Helmut Merklein & William Murchison. 150p. 1980. lib. bdg. 10.95x (ISBN 0-933028-10-5); pap. 5.95x (ISBN 0-933028-09-1). Fisher Inst.

Those Gentle Voices. George A. Effinger. 1976. pap. 1.75 o.s.i. (ISBN 0-446-94017-8). Warner Bks.

Those Happy Golden Years. Miriam Wood. 1980. 6.95 (ISBN 0-8280-0062-X, 20380-2). Review & Herald.

Those Mysteriuos UFO's: The Story of Unidentitied Flying Objects. David C. Knight. LC 74-31465. (Finding-Out Book). (Illus.). 64p. (gr. 2-4). 1979. Repr. of 1975 ed. PLB 6.95 (ISBN 0-89490-032-3). Enslow Pubs.

Those Oldies but Goodies. S. Propes. 1973. pap. 1.95 o.s.i. (ISBN 0-02-061430-6, Collier). Macmillan.

Those Oldies but Goodies: A Guide to 50's Record Collecting. Stephen Propes. 160p. 1973. 5.95 o.p. (ISBN 0-02-599270-8); pap. 1.95 (ISBN 0-02-061430-6). Macmillan.

Those S. O. B.'s at Tarryall & Other Tales of the Rockies. 1st ed. Fred Huston. (Mesquite Collector Ser.: No. 5). (Illus.). 102p. 1974. 6.95 (ISBN 0-89015-061-3). Nortex Pr.

Those Southern Milners: A Collection of Record Abstracts for the Southern States Between 1606 & 1850 with Biographical & Historical Sketches, Family Records, & Genealogies up to 1900. Virginia S. Hershey. (Illus.). 426p. 1980. 40.00x (ISBN 0-9605320-0-5, TX-578-128). Hershey.

Those Superstitions. Charles Igglesden. LC 73-12798. 1974. Repr. of 1932 ed. 18.00 (ISBN 0-8103-3621-9). Gale.

Those the Sun Has Loved: An American Family Saga. Rose Jourdain. LC 77-82952. 1978. 10.95 o.p. (ISBN 0-385-13028-7). Doubleday.

Those Were the Days. Stan Fischler. LC 75-28233. (Illus.). 1976. 12.50 (ISBN 0-396-07015-9). Dodd.

Those Who Can, Teach. 2nd ed. Kevin Ryan & James M. Cooper. (Illus.). 500p. 1975. text ed. 14.95 o.p. (ISBN 0-395-18622-6); instructor's manual 1.50 o.p. (ISBN 0-395-18790-7). HM.

Those Who Can, Teach. 3rd ed. Kevin Ryan & James M. Cooper. LC 79-89788. (Illus.). 1980. text ed. 16.50 (ISBN 0-395-28495-3); instrs'. manual 0.80 (ISBN 0-395-28496-1); learning guide 6.25 (ISBN 0-395-28497-X). HM.

Those Who Love Him. Basilea Schlink. 96p. 1981. pap. 2.50 (ISBN 0-87123-609-5, 210609). Bethany Fell.

Those Who Remember. G Grimm. 6.50 o.p. (ISBN 0-8062-1059-1). Carlton.

Thou Swell, Thou Witty: The Life & Lyrics of Lorenz Hart. Ed. & memoir by Dorothy Hart. LC 72-23885. (Illus.). 192p. 1976. 25.00 o.p. (ISBN 0-06-011776-1, HarpT). Har-Row.

Though I Walk Through the Valley. Vance Havner. 128p. 1974. 6.95 (ISBN 0-8007-0654-4). Revell.

Though You Die. 2nd ed. Stanley Drake. 1974. pap. 4.50 (ISBN 0-900285-09-5, Pub. by Floris Books). St George Bk Serv.

Thought & Being: Hegel's Criticism of Kant's System of Cosmological Ideas. Frank Peddle. LC 79-9695. 204p. 1980. text ed. 17.75 (ISBN 0-8191-0987-8); pap. text ed. 9.50 (ISBN 0-8191-0988-6). U Pr of Amer.

Thought As Energy: Exploring the Spiritual Nature of Man. Ed. by Willis H. Kinnear. (Illus.). 96p. 1975. pap. 3.50 (ISBN 0-911336-62-1). Sci of Mind.

Thought for Food. Margaret Sumner. (Illus.). 129p. 1981. text ed. 13.95x (ISBN 0-19-217690-0); pap. text ed. 6.95 (ISBN 0-19-286003-8). Oxford U Pr.

Thought for the Day. Robert A. Smith. 1978. pap. 3.50 (ISBN 0-912128-41-0). Pubns Living.

Thought Forms. abr. ed. Annie Besant & Charles W. Leadbeater. (Illus.). 1969. pap. 4.95 (ISBN 0-8356-0008-4, Quest). Theos Pub Hse.

Thought of the Evangelical Leaders: John Newton, Thomas Scott, Charles Simeon, Etc. Ed. by Josiah Pratt. 1978. 15.95 (ISBN 0-85151-270-4). Banner of Truth.

Thought-Patterns for Compositions. H. M. Brown. (Illus.). 400p. 1976. pap. 9.95 (ISBN 0-13-919985-3). P-H.

Thought Probes: Philosophy Through Science Fiction. Ed. by Fred D. Miller & Nicholas D. Smith. (Illus.). 368p. 1981. text ed. 11.95 (ISBN 0-13-920041-X). P-H.

Thought Tracking Level Four: Questions & Answers. Kitty Wehrli. (gr. 2 up). 1976. wkbk. 5.00x (ISBN 0-89039-192-0). Ann Arbor Pubs.

Thought Tracking Level One: Simple Phrases. Kitty Wehrli. (gr. 2). 1976. wkbk. 5.00 (ISBN 0-89039-186-6). Ann Arbor Pubs.

Thought Tracking Level Three: Simple Sentences. Kitty Wehrli. (gr. 2). 1976. wkbk. 5.00 (ISBN 0-89039-190-4). Ann Arbor Pubs.

Thought Tracking Level Two: Sequential Phrases. Kitty Wehrli. (gr. 2). wkbk. 5.00 (ISBN 0-89039-188-2). Ann Arbor Pubs.

Thought Vibrations. A. Victor Segno. LC 80-23853. 208p. 1980. Repr. of 1973 ed. lib. bdg. 10.95x (ISBN 0-89370-625-6). Borgo Pr.

Thought, Words & Creativity: Art & Thought in Lawrence. F. R. Leavis. 1976. 12.95 (ISBN 0-19-519884-0). Oxford U Pr.

Thoughts Are Things. Ernest Holmes & Willis Kinnear. 1967. pap. 3.50 (ISBN 0-911336-33-8). Sci of Mind.

Thoughts for Our Times. Albert Schweitzer. Ed. by Erica Anderson. (Illus.). 64p. 1981. Repr. of 1975 ed. 3.95 (ISBN 0-8298-0448-X). Pilgrim NY.

Thoughts from My Quiet Corner. Noel J. Reyburn. 52p. 1978. 3.50 (ISBN 0-8059-2591-0). Dorrance.

Thoughts from the Mount of Blessing. Ellen G. White. LC 56-7170. 172p. 1956. 4.95 (ISBN 0-8163-0047-X, 20401-6). Pacific Pr Pub Assn.

Thoughts in a Dry Season. G. Brenan. LC 78-4508. 1978. 17.95 (ISBN 0-521-22006-8). Cambridge U Pr.

Thoughts in Springtime. Lewis Walton. 1979. pap. 1.25 (ISBN 0-8163-0247-2). Pacific Pr Pub Assn.

Thoughts of a Shakta. M. P. Sri Pandit. 1979. pap. 1.75 (ISBN 0-89744-130-3, Pub. by Ganesh & Co India). Auromere.

Thoughts of Giants & Other Poems. Shirley Scott. 60p. (Orig.). 1980. pap. 2.50 (ISBN 0-931846-16-1). Wash Writers Pub.

Thoughts of Robert Jacques Turgot As They Apply to the Economic Complexities of Our Present Age. Kenneth R. Rutledge. (Living Thoughts of the Great Economists Ser.). (Illus.). 93p. 1981. 17.55 (ISBN 0-918968-86-0). Inst Econ Finan.

Thoughts of Thomas Robert Malthus As They Apply to the Economic Complexities of Our Present Age. Richard Louis Gamon. (Living Thoughts of the Great Economists Ser.). (Illus.). 97p. 1981. 17.55 (ISBN 0-918968-87-9). Inst Econ Finan.

Thoughts on Death & Immortality. Ludwig Feuerbach. Tr. by James A. Massey from Ger. 263p. 1981. 12.95x (ISBN 0-520-04051-1); pap. 5.95 (ISBN 0-520-04062-7, CAL 486). U of Cal Pr.

Thoughts on Genesis. Horatius Bonar. LC 79-2516. 1979. 8.95 (ISBN 0-8254-2235-3). Kregel.

Thoughts on Preaching. J. W. Alexander. 1975. 8.95 (ISBN 0-85151-210-0). Banner of Truth.

Thoughts on Religious Experience. Archibald Alexander. 1978. 8.95 (ISBN 0-85151-080-9). Banner of Truth.

Thoughts on the Education of Daughters: With Reflections on Female Conduct, in the More Important Duties of Life. Mary Wollstonecraft. Ed. by Gina Luria. (Feminist Controversy in England, 1788-1810 Ser.). 1974. lib. bdg. 50.00 (ISBN 0-8240-0890-1). Garland Pub.

Thoughts on the Future Civil Policy of America. John W. Draper. Incl. Memoir of John William Draper, 1811-1882. George F. Barker. (Neglected American Economists Ser.). 1974. lib. bdg. 50.00 (ISBN 0-8240-1017-5). Garland Pub.

Thoughts on the Proposed Change of Currency. W. Scott & J. W. Croker. 1971. Repr. of 1826 ed. 24.00x (ISBN 0-7165-0306-9, Pub. by Irish Academic Pr Ireland). Biblio Dist.

Thoughts Rule the World. Leonard E. Read. 128p. 1981. 6.00 (ISBN 0-910614-67-9). Foun Econ Ed.

Thoughts, Troubles & Things About Reading from the Cradle Through Grade Three. Carolyn T. Gracenin. LC 80-65611. 180p. 1981. perfect bdg. 14.95 (ISBN 0-86548-038-9). Century Twenty One.

Thousand & One Nights of Opera. Frederick K. Martens. LC 77-25416. (Music Reprint Ser., 1978). 1978. Repr. of 1926 ed. lib. bdg. 32.50 (ISBN 0-306-77565-4). Da Capo.

Thousand Cranes. Yasunari Kawabata. Tr. by Edward G. Seidensticker from Jap. (Perigee Japanese Library). 160p. 1981. pap. 3.95 (ISBN 0-399-50526-1, Perigee). Putnam.

Thousand Errors. Phyllis Nichols. (Orig.). 1980. pap. 1.95 (ISBN 0-532-23121-X). Manor Bks.

Thousand Graduates: Conflict in University Development in Papua New Guinea, 1961-1976. Ian Howie-Willis. Ed. by E. K. Fisk. (Pacific Research Series Monograph: No. 3). 362p. 1980. pap. text ed. 12.95 (ISBN 0-909150-01-X, 0014). Bks Australia.

Thousand Happiness. Berta LaVan Barker. (YA) 1978. 5.95 (ISBN 0-685-87351-X, Avalon). Bouregy.

Thousand Hour Day. W. S. Kuniczak. 628p. 1980. cancelled (ISBN 0-88254-506-X). Hippocrene Bks.

Thousand Images of Loveliness in Percy Bysshe Shelley's Love Poetry. Ingrid R. Kitzberger. (Salzburg Studies in English Literature, Romantic Reassessment: No. 69). 1977. pap. text ed. 25.00x (ISBN 0-391-01447-1). Humanities.

Thousand Lights & Fireflies. Alvin Tresselt. LC 65-11652. (Illus.). (gr. k-3). 1965. 5.95 o.s.i. (ISBN 0-8193-0123-X, Four Winds); PLB 5.41 o.s.i. (ISBN 0-8193-0124-8). Schol Bk Serv.

Thousand Years of London Bridge. C. W. Shepherd. Date not set. 7.95 o.p. (ISBN 0-8038-5368-8). Hastings.

Thousand Years of Travel in Old Hungary. Gyula Antalffy. Tr. by Elisabeth Hoch. Orig. Title: Igy Utaztunk Hajdanaban. (Illus.). 337p. (Orig.). 1980. pap. 8.50x (ISBN 963-13-0909-6). Intl Pubns Serv.

Thousand Years of West African History. 2nd ed. Ed. by J. F. Ajayi & Ian Espie. 1969. text ed. 12.00x (ISBN 0-391-00217-1). Humanities.

Thousands of Creative Kitchen Ideas. Virginia Habeeb. LC 75-23318. (Funk & W Bk.). (Illus.). 256p. 1976. 13.95 o.s.i. (ISBN 0-308-10227-4, TYC-T). T Y Crowell.

Th'overthrow of Stage-Players. John Rainoldes et al. LC 70-170414. (English Stage Ser.: Vol. 11). lib. bdg. 50.00 (ISBN 0-8240-0594-5). Garland Pub.

Thracians. R. F. Hoddinott. (Ancient Peoples & Places Ser.). (Illus.). 192p. 1981. 19.95 (ISBN 0-500-02099-X). Thames Hudson.

Thrales of Streatham Park. Mary Hyde. (Illus.). 1977. 16.50x (ISBN 0-674-88746-8). Harvard U Pr.

Thrall of Love. Riva Carles. 1977. pap. 1.75 o.p. (ISBN 0-425-03405-4, Medallion). Berkley Pub.

Thread. Bob Arnold. 1981. pap. 4.00 (ISBN 0-915316-87-0); pap. 10.00 lmtd. signed ed. (ISBN 0-915316-90-0). Pentagram.

Thread That Runs So True. Jesse Stuart. 1958. lib. rep. ed. 17.50x (ISBN 0-684-15160-X, ScribT); pap. 4.95 (ISBN 0-684-71904-5, SL44, ScribT). Scribner.

Threaded Interpretive Languages. Ronald Loeliger. 272p. 1980. 18.95 (ISBN 0-07-038360-X, BYTE Bks). McGraw.

Threads. Roger Swaybill. 1980. 12.95 (ISBN 0-440-08319-2). Delacorte.

Threads of Destiny. Jean Lyttle. LC 61-9821. 3.00 o.p. (ISBN 0-685-57231-5). Garrett-Helix.

Threads of Public Policy: A Study in Policy Leadership. Robert Eyestone. LC 79-106638. (Urban Governor Ser). 1971. pap. 5.95 (ISBN 0-672-61142-2). Bobbs.

Threads of Public Policy: A Study in Political Leadership. Robert Eyestone. 216p. pap. text ed. 7.95x (ISBN 0-8290-0325-8). Irvington.

Threat. Richard Jessup. LC 80-52001. 288p. 1981. 12.95 (ISBN 0-670-70618-3). Viking Pr.

Threat of Love. Maye Barrett. (Orig.). pap. 1.75 (ISBN 0-515-05727-4). Jove Pubns.

Threat to the Barkers. Joan Phipson. LC 65-10962. (Illus.). (gr. 4-6). 1965. 4.95 o.p. (ISBN 0-15-286310-9, HJ). HarBraceJ.

Threau's Library. Walter R. Harding. LC 80-2507. 1981. Repr. of 1957 ed. 18.50 (ISBN 0-404-19055-3). AMS Pr.

Three Adventures: Galapagos, Titcaca, the Blue Holes. Jacques-Yves Cousteau & Philippe Diole. LC 72-93396. (Undersea Discoveries of Jacques-Yves Cousteau). (Illus.). 1978. pap. 8.95 (ISBN 0-89104-090-0). A & W Pubs.

Three Adventures: Galapagos, Titicaca, the Blue Holes. Jacques-Yves Cousteau & Philippe Diole. LC 72-93396. 304p. 1973. 12.95 o.p. (ISBN 0-385-06921-9). Doubleday.

Three Aesop Fox Fables. Paul Galdone. LC 79-133061. (ps-2). 1971. 6.95 (ISBN 0-395-28810-X, Clarion). HM.

Three-&-a-Half Husbands. Dorothy Fuldheim. 1977. pap. 1.75 o.p. (ISBN 0-451-07793-8, E7793, Sig). NAL.

Three & A Half Powers: The New Balance in Asia. Harold C. Hinton. LC 74-17565. (Midland Bks.: No. 184). 320p. 1975. 15.00x (ISBN 0-253-36013-7); pap. 3.95x (ISBN 0-253-20184-5). Ind U Pr.

Three & Two: The Autobiography of Tom Gorman, the Great National League Umpire. Tom Gorman & Jerome Holtzman. (Encore Edition). (Illus.). 1979. 3.95 (ISBN 0-684-16751-4, ScribT). Scribner.

Three Angels Over Rancho Grande. Viola Payne. LC 75-32711. (Destiny Ser.). 1976. pap. 4.95 (ISBN 0-8163-0218-9, 20407-3). Pacific Pr Pub Assn.

Three Aspects of Crisis in Colonial Kenya. Bismarck Myrick & David L. Easterbrook. LC 75-30552. (Foreign and Comparative Studies Eastern Africa Series XXI). 91p. 1975. pap. text ed. 4.50x (ISBN 0-915984-18-0). Syracuse U Foreign Comp.

Three Autobiographical Fragments. Isaiah Thomas. 1962. pap. 4.50x (ISBN 0-912296-32-1, Dist. by U Pr of Va). Am Antiquarian.

Three Bears. Ed. & illus. by Paul Galdone. LC 78-158833. (Illus.). 32p. (ps-2). 1972. 8.95 (ISBN 0-395-28811-8, Clarion). HM.

Three Bears. Anne McGill-Franzen. LC 79-62977. (Learn-a-Tale). (Illus.). (gr. k-2). 1979. PLB 8.25 (ISBN 0-8393-0182-0). Raintree Child.

Three Bears. Ed. by Bob Ottum. (Illus.). (ps-1). 1973. PLB 5.38 (ISBN 0-307-68971-9, Golden Pr). Western Pub.

Three Bears. Illus. by Gene Sharp. (Illus.). 24p. (gr. k-2). 1976. PLB 7.15 o.p. (ISBN 0-307-69058-X, Golden Pr). Western Pub.

Three Bedtime Stories. Illus. by Garth Williams. (Illus.). (gr. k-3). 1958. 1.95 o.p. (ISBN 0-307-10392-7, Golden Pr); PLB 7.15 o.p. (ISBN 0-307-60392-X). Western Pub.

Three Bells of Civilization. Sydel Silverman. 1978. pap. 7.50x (ISBN 0-231-08365-3). Columbia U Pr.

Three Bells of Civilization: The Life of an Italian Hill Town. Sydel Silverman. LC 75-15916. (Illus.). 304p. 1975. 17.50x (ISBN 0-231-03804-6). Columbia U Pr.

Three Big Hogs. Manus Pinkwater. LC 75-4780. (Illus.). 40p. (ps-3). 1975. 6.95 (ISBN 0-395-28819-3, Clarion). HM.

Three Billy-Goats Gruff. Illus. by Susan Blair. (Illus.). (gr. k-3). 1970. pap. 1.25 (ISBN 0-590-01613-X, Schol Pap); pap. 3.95 three billy goats gruff & gingerbread man (2 bks.) & 1 record (ISBN 0-590-04405-2). Schol Bk Serv.

Three Billy Goats Gruff. Retold by & illus. by Paul Galdone. LC 72-85338. (Illus.). 32p. (ps-2). 1973. 6.95 (ISBN 0-395-28812-6, Clarion). HM.

Three Billy-Goats Gruff. (Illus.). Arabic 2.50x (ISBN 0-685-82889-J). Intl Bk Ctr.

Three Blind Mice. James Wood. LC 73-188691. 1973. 6.95 (ISBN 0-8149-0705-9). Vanguard.

Three Blind Mice & Other Stories. Agatha Christie. 1980. pap. 2.25 (ISBN 0-440-15867-2). Dell.

Three Books of the Potter's Art, 2 vols. Cipriano Piccolpasso. Tr. by Ronald Lightbown & Alan Caiger-Smith. (Illus.). 358p. 1980. Repr. 210.00x set (ISBN 0-85967-452-5, Pub. by Scolar Pr England). Biblio Dist.

Three Boys & H-Two-O. Nan H. Agle & Ellen Wilson. LC 68-12513. (Encore Ser.). (Illus.). (gr. 2-6). 1968. write for info. (ISBN 0-684-13950-2, ScribJ). Scribner.

Three British Revolutions: 1641, 1688, 1776. Ed. by J. G. Pocock. LC 79-27572. (Folger Institute Essays, Published for the Folger Shakespeare Library). 456p. 1980. 32.50 (ISBN 0-691-05293-X); pap. 12.50 (ISBN 0-691-10087-X). Princeton U Pr.

Three by Flannery O'Connor: Wise Blood, the Violent Bear It Away, a Good Man Is Hard to Find. Flannery O'Connor. 1980. pap. 2.50 (ISBN 0-451-09251-1, E9251, Sig). NAL.

Three by Sloane. Eric Sloane. Incl. Diary of an Early American Boy; Museum of Early American Tools; Reverence for Wood. (Funk & W Bk.). 1969. boxed set 29.95 o.p. (ISBN 0-308-70110-0, 711090, TYC-T). T Y Crowell.

Three by the Sea. Edward Marshall. (Easy-to-Read Ser.). (Illus.). 48p. (ps-3). 1981. PLB 5.99 (ISBN 0-8037-8687-5); pap. 2.50 (ISBN 0-8037-8671-9). Dial.

Three by Three. James Kruss. (Illus.). (ps-k). 1965. 4.75 o.s.i. (ISBN 0-02-751210-X). Macmillan.

Three Caravans to Yuma: The Untold Story of Bactrian Camels in Western America. Harlan D. Fowler. LC 80-66268. (Illus.). 173p. 1980. 25.00 (ISBN 0-87062-131-9). A H Clark.

Three Card Monte. John Scarne & Audley V. Walsh. (Gambler's Book Shelf). (Illus.). 1967. pap. 2.95 (ISBN 0-89650-505-7). Gamblers.

Three Case Histories. Sigmund Freud. 1963. pap. 2.95 (ISBN 0-02-076650-5, Collier). Macmillan.

Three Centuries of Architectural Craftsmanship. Ed. by Colin Amery. (Illus.). 1977. pap. 14.50 (ISBN 0-85139-662-3, Pub. by Architectural Pr). Nichols Pub.

Three Centuries of Peace Treaties & Their Teachings, 1582-1913. Walter G. Phillimore. LC 73-147602. (Library of War & Peace; International Law). lib. bdg. 38.00 (ISBN 0-8240-0363-2). Garland Pub.

Three Centuries of Thumb Bibles. Ruth Adomeit. LC 78-68238. (Garland Reference Library of Humanities). (Illus.). 435p. 1980. 60.00 (ISBN 0-8240-9818-8). Garland Pub.

Three Centuries on Winnipesaukee. Paul H. Blaisdell. LC 75-10740. (Illus.). 16p. 1975. 2.95 (ISBN 0-912274-96-4). NH Pub Co.

Three Children of the Universe: Emerson's Views of Shakespeare, Bacon, & Milton. William M. Wynkoop. LC 80-2548. 1981. Repr. of 1966 ed. 25.50 (ISBN 0-404-19272-6). AMS Pr.

Three Christs of Ypsilanti: A Psychological Study. Milton Rokeach. (Morningside Book Ser.). 360p. 1981. pap. 8.00x (ISBN 0-231-05271-5). Columbia U Pr.

Three Classic Don Juan Plays. Ed. by Oscar Mandel. LC 73-149071. 1971. pap. 2.45x (ISBN 0-8032-5739-2, BB 537, Bison). U of Nebr Pr.

Three Clerks. Anthony Trollope. 497p. 1981. pap. price not set (ISBN 0-486-24099-1). Dover.

Three Coffins. John D. Carr. lib. bdg. 11.50x (ISBN 0-89966-048-7). Buccaneer Bks.

Three Comedies: The Birds, the Clouds, the Wasps. Aristophanes. Ed. by William Arrowsmith. (Illus.). 400p. 1969. pap. 5.95 (ISBN 0-472-06153-4, 153, AA). U of Mich Pr.

Three Conceited Kittens: A Collection of Stories for Children. 1979. 2.50 (ISBN 0-8351-0650-0). China Bks.

Three C's of Atmosphere. Jule Wilkinson. 1971. pap. 8.95 (ISBN 0-686-69418-X). CBI Pub.

Three-D. Carol Showalter. LC 77-90947. 144p. 1980. pap. 4.95 (ISBN 0-932260-04-7). Rock Harbor.

Three-D, Two-D, One-D. David A. Adler. LC 74-5156. (Young Math Ser.). (Illus.). 40p. (gr. k-3). 1974. 7.95 (ISBN 0-690-00456-7, TYC-J); 7.89 (ISBN 0-690-00543-1). T Y Crowell.

Three Daughters of Madame Liang. Pearl S. Buck. (John Day Bk.). 1969. 9.95 (ISBN 0-381-98055-3, A79000, TYC-T). T Y Crowell.

Three Day Challenge. Weir. (gr. 3-5). pap. 1.25 o.p. (ISBN 0-590-11929-X, Schol Pap). Schol Bk Serv.

Three Days on a River in a Red Canoe. Vera B. Williams. LC 80-23893. (Illus.). 32p. (gr. k-3). 1981. 8.95 (ISBN 0-688-80307-5); PLB 8.59 (ISBN 0-688-84307-7). Greenwillow.

Three Days Scene at the Temple in Jerusalem. 2nd ed. Jakob Lorber. Tr. by Nordewin Von Koerber from Ger. Date not set. pap. 4.95 (ISBN 0-934616-10-8). Valkyrie Pr.

Three Decades of Collecting: Gifts of Anna Bing Arnold. Los Angeles County Museum of Art Curatorial Staff. Ed. by Jeanne D'Andrea & Stephen West. (Los Angeles County Museum of Art Bulletin 1980: Vol. 26). (Illus.). 96p. (Orig.). 1981. pap. 6.00 (ISBN 0-87587-099-6). La Co Art Mus.

Three Dialogues Between Hylas & Philonous. George Berkeley. Ed. by Colin M. Turbayne. 1954. pap. 3.95 (ISBN 0-672-60206-7, LLA39). Bobbs.

Three Dialogues Between Hylas & Philonous. George Berkeley. Ed. by Thomas J. McCormack. vi, 136p. 1969. 9.95 (ISBN 0-87548-068-3); pap. 3.50 (ISBN 0-87548-069-1). Open Court.

Three-Dimensional Maze Art. Larry Evans. (Illus.). 64p. 1980. pap. 4.95 (ISBN 0-89844-012-2). Troubador Pr.

Three Dimensions of Vocabulary Growth. Lewis M. Paternoster & Ruth L. Frager. (Orig.). (gr. 10-12). 1971. pap. text ed. 5.25 (ISBN 0-87720-345-8). AMSCO Sch.

Three Ducks Went Wandering. Ron Roy. LC 78-12629. (Illus.). (gr. 1-3). 1979. 8.95 (ISBN 0-395-28954-8, Clarion). HM.

Three Eighteenth Century Figures: Sarah Churchill, John Wesley, Giacomo Casanova. Bonamy Dobree. LC 80-19398. xi, 248p. 1981. Repr. of 1962 ed. lib. bdg. 25.00x (ISBN 0-313-22682-2, DOTF). Greenwood.

Three Endeavors or Walter Blount: A Trubute to Dr. Walter P. Blount on His Seventieth Birthday. Association of Bone & Joint Surgeons. Ed. by Marshall R. Urist. (Clinical Orthopaedics Ser., Vol. 77). 1971. 15.00 (ISBN 0-685-22855-X). Lippincott.

Three Essays on Chinese Farm Economy. John L. Buck. LC 78-74308. (Modern Chinese Economy Ser.: Vol. 10). 155p. 1980. lib. bdg. 20.00 (ISBN 0-8240-4259-X). Garland Pub.

Three Faces of Being: Toward an Existential Clinical Psychology. Ernest Keen. LC 78-128900. (Century Psychology Ser.). (Orig.). 1970. 22.50x (ISBN 0-89197-452-0); pap. text ed. 9.50x (ISBN 0-89197-453-9). Irvington.

Three Faces of Eve. Corbett H. Thigpen & Hervey M. Cleckley. 1974. pap. 2.25 (ISBN 0-445-08137-6). Popular Lib.

Three Faces of Love. Emile Zola. Tr. by R. Gant. LC 67-29442. 6.95 (ISBN 0-8149-0247-2). Vanguard.

Three Faces of Pluralism: Political, Ethnic, & Religious. Ed. by Stanislaw Ehrlich & Graham Wooton. 232p. 1980. 18.95x (ISBN 0-566-00313-9, 03274-3, Pub. by Gower Pub Co England). Lexington Bks.

Three Famous Short Novels. William Faulkner. Incl. Spotted Horses; Old Man; Bear. 1958. pap. 1.95 (ISBN 0-394-70149-6, V-149, Vin). Random.

Three Farms: Making Milk, Meat & Money from the American Soil. Mark Kramer. 1980. 12.95 (ISBN 0-316-50315-0). Little.

Three Fates in Taos. Mabel L. Luhan et al. Ed. by Harry T. Moore. (Illus.). 228p. 1981. 20.00x (ISBN 0-933806-10-8). Black Swan CT.

Three Fighters for Freedom. Brian Peachment. pap. 1.55 (ISBN 0-08-017617-8). Pergamon.

Three Fools & a Horse. Betty Baker. LC 75-14272. (Illus.). 64p. (gr. 1-4). 1975. 8.95 (ISBN 0-02-708250-4, 70825). Macmillan.

Three French Treatises. Jean Calvin. Ed. by F. M. Higman. (Athlone Renaissance Library). 1970. text ed. 10.75x (ISBN 0-485-13802-6, Athlone Pr); pap. text ed. 5.50x (ISBN 0-485-12802-0, Athlone Pr). Humanities.

Three French Writers & the Great War. F. Field. LC 35-22982. 1975. 23.50 (ISBN 0-521-20916-1). Cambridge U Pr.

Three Friends: Bedichek, Dobie, Webb - a Personal History. William A. Owens. LC 70-82957. 335p. 1975. pap. 5.95 (ISBN 0-292-78012-5). U of Tex Pr.

Three Further Clinical Faces of Childhood. Ed. by James E. Anthony & Doris C. Gilpin. (Illus.). 340p. 1981. text ed. 25.00 (ISBN 0-89335-110-5). Spectrum Pub.

Three Generals on War. Incl. War Is a Racket. Smedley D. Butler; Men I Killed. Frank P. Crozier; Old Europe's Suicide, or the Building of a Pyramid of Errors. Christopher B. Thomson. LC 73-147661. (Library of War & Peace; Conscip. & Cons. Object.). lib. bdg. 38.00 (ISBN 0-8240-0423-X). Garland Pub.

Three Generations in Twentieth Century America: Family, Community & Nation. John G. Clark. 1977. 12.50x (ISBN 0-256-01932-0); pap. 12.50x (ISBN 0-256-02099-X). Dorsey.

Three German Classics: A Village Romeo & Juliet: Godfried Keller, Immensee: Theodore Storm, Lenz: Georg Buchner. 1980. 9.95 (ISBN 0-7145-0560-9). Riverrun NY.

Three Great Friday Sermons & Other Theological Discourses. Apostolos Makrakis. Ed. by Orthodox Christian Educational Society. Tr. by Denver Cummings from Hellenic. 107p. (Orig.). 1952. pap. 2.00x (ISBN 0-938366-48-3). Orthodox Chr.

Three Great Irishmen: Shaw, Yeats, Joyce. Arland Ussher. LC 68-54235. 1953. 9.00x (ISBN 0-8196-0222-1). Biblo.

Three Great Teachers of Our Own Time. Alexander H. Japp. 255p. 1980. Repr. of 1865 ed. lib. bdg. 30.00 (ISBN 0-8492-1281-2). R West.

Three Hundred & Fifty Ninth Fighter Group. (Aviation Ser.: No. 1). (Illus.). 1978. pap. 15.00 o.p. (ISBN 0-89839-014-1). Battery Pr.

Three Hundred & Sixty-Seventh Fighter Group in World War II. Peter R. Moody. 1980. pap. 13.00 (ISBN 0-89126-080-3). Military Aff Aero.

Three Hundred Best Word Puzzles. Henry E. Dudeney. Ed. by Martin Gardner. LC 68-12499. (Illus.). 1972. pap. 2.25 o.p. (ISBN 0-684-13068-8, SL370, ScribT). Scribner.

Three Hundred Ninety-Seventh White Elephant. Rene Guillot. LC 57-6246. (Illus.). (gr. 4-6). 1957. 8.95 (ISBN 0-87599-043-6). S G Phillips.

Three Hundred Sixty Five Ways to Cook Hamburger. Doyne Nickerson. LC 60-13551. 1960. 4.95 o.p. (ISBN 0-385-00847-3). Doubleday.

Three Hundred Sixty-Six Goodnight Stories. Illus. by Esme Eve & Gwyneth Mamlock. (Illus.). 1969. 5.95 o.p. (ISBN 0-307-15568-4, Golden Pr). Western Pub.

Three Hundred Twenty Ninth Friend. Marjorie W. Sharmat. LC 76-6454. (Illus.). 48p. (gr. k-3). 1979. 8.95 (ISBN 0-590-07558-6, Four Winds). Schol Bk Serv.

Three Hundred Years of American Drama & Theatre. G. Wilson. (Illus.). 1972. ref. ed. 19.95 (ISBN 0-13-920314-1). P-H.

Three in a Hill. M. Minor. 5.95 o.p. (ISBN 0-8062-1114-8). Carlton.

Three in One: Picture of God. Joanne Marxhausen. 48p. (gr. k-4). 1973. 6.95 (ISBN 0-570-03419-1, 56-1148). Concordia.

Three Incredible Weeks with Meher Baba. Malcolm Schloss & Charles Purdom. Ed. by Filis Frederick. (Illus.). 1979. pap. 5.95 (ISBN 0-913078-36-0). Sheriar Pr.

Three Is Company. Friedrich K. Waechter. Tr. by Harry Allard. LC 79-7790. (Illus.). (gr. k-3). 1980. 8.95a (ISBN 0-385-14632-9); PLB (ISBN 0-385-14633-7). Doubleday.

Three Jovial Huntsmen: A Mother Goose Rhyme. Illus. by Susan Jeffers. LC 70-122739. (Illus.). 32p. (gr. k-2). 1973. 9.95 (ISBN 0-87888-023-2). Bradbury Pr.

Three Kings of Israel. Mark E. Petersen. LC 80-36697. 179p. 1980. 6.95 (ISBN 0-87747-829-5). Deseret Bk.

Three Language-Arts Curriculum Models: Pre-Kindergarten Through College. Ed. by Barrett J. Mandel. 1980. pap. 8.50 (ISBN 0-8141-5458-1). NCTE.

Three Levels of Time. Harold Hayes. 1981. 12.95 (ISBN 0-525-21853-X). Dutton.

Three Literary Men. August W. Derleth. 56p. 1980. Repr. of 1963 ed. lib. bdg. 15.00 (ISBN 0-8482-0645-2). Norwood Edns.

Three Little Kittens. Harry Bornstein. (Signed English Ser.). 32p. 1974. pap. 3.00 (ISBN 0-913580-16-3). Gallaudet Coll.

Three Little Kittens. Illus. by Masha. (Illus.). (ps-1). 1942. PLB 7.62 (ISBN 0-307-60410-1, Golden Pr). Western Pub.

Three Little Pigs. Illus. by Nina Barbaresi. (Golden Storytime Bk.). (Illus.). 24p. 1981. 1.95 (ISBN 0-307-11955-6, Golden Pr). Western Pub.

Three Little Pigs. Illus. by Erik Blegvad. LC 80-10410. (Illus.). 32p. (ps-4). 1980. 8.95 (ISBN 0-689-50139-0, McElderry Bk). Atheneum.

Three Little Pigs. Galdone. (ps-3). pap. 1.25 (ISBN 0-590-09272-3, Schol Pap). Schol Bk Serv.

Three Little Pigs. Paul Galdone. LC 75-123456. (Illus.). (ps-1). 1970. 6.95 (ISBN 0-395-28813-4, Clarion). HM.

Three Little Pigs. Anne McGill-Franzen. LC 79-62978. (Learn-a-Tale). (Illus.). (gr. k-2). 1979. PLB 8.25 (ISBN 0-8393-0183-9). Raintree Child.

Three Little Pigs. Elizabeth Ross. (Illus.). (ps-1). 1973. PLB 5.00 (ISBN 0-307-61544-8, Golden Pr). Western Pub.

Three Little Tales. Barbara Hartley-Cox. 1979. 4.50 o.p. (ISBN 0-8062-1210-1). Carlton.

Three Little Witches. Sharon Gordon. (Illus.). 32p. (gr. k-2). 1980. PLB 2.96 (ISBN 0-89375-390-4); pap. 0.95 (ISBN 0-89375-290-8). Troll Assocs.

Three Little Words. Florence Faulkner. 192p. (YA) 1976. 4.95 o.p. (ISBN 0-685-66573-9, Avalon). Bouregy.

Three Lives. T. Lobsang Rampa. pap. 2.50 (ISBN 0-685-91302-3). Weiser.

Three Magic Gifts. Tr. by James Riordan. (Illus.). 28p. (gr. k-4). 1980. 9.95 (ISBN 0-19-520194-9). Oxford U Pr.

Three Magic Words. Uell S. Andersen. pap. 5.00 (ISBN 0-87980-165-4). Wilshire.

Three Major Social, Economic, Political Tragedies in Contemporary United States History, 2 vols. in one. Stanley Edgeworth. (Illus.). 243p. 1976. lib. bdg. 54.75 (ISBN 0-89266-006-6). Am Classical Coll Pr.

Three Maya Relief Panels at Dumbarton Oaks. Michael D. Coe & Elizabeth P. Benson. LC 66-30016. (Studies in Pre-Columbian Art & Archaeology: No. 2). (Illus.). 1966. pap. 2.00 (ISBN 0-88402-079-7, Ctr Pe-Columbian). Dumbarton Oaks.

Three Medieval Rhetorical Arts. Ed. by James J. Murphy. LC 72-132416. 1971. 18.75x (ISBN 0-520-01820-6). U of Cal Pr.

Three Melodramas: Dido Abandoned, Demetrius, the Olimpiad. Pietro Metastasio. Tr. by Joseph G. Fucilla. LC 80-51017. (Studies in Romance Languages: No. 24). 164p. 1981. 11.00x (ISBN 0-8131-1400-4). U Pr of Ky.

Three Men in a Boat. Jerome K. Jerome. Ed. by David A. Jasen. (Continuum Classic of Humor Ser.). 208p. 1980. 11.95 (ISBN 0-8264-0018-3). Continuum.

Three Men in a Boat. K. Jerome. Incl. Three Men on the Bummell. 1957. 5.00x (ISBN 0-460-00118-3, Evman); pap. 8.95 (ISBN 0-460-01118-9, Evman). Dutton.

Three Men of Boston. John R. Galvin. LC 75-20331. 348p. 1976. 10.00 o.s.i. (ISBN 0-690-01018-4, TYC-T). T Y Crowell.

Three Messages for Israel. Derek Prince. 1969. pap. 1.50 jewish ed. (ISBN 0-934920-21-4, BJ-18). Derek Prince.
Three Messages for Israel: Jewish Edition. Derek Prince. 64p. (Orig.). 1977. pap. 1.50 (ISBN 0-934920-21-4). Derek Prince.
Three Mile Island. Mark Stephens. (Illus.). 1981. 11.95 (ISBN 0-394-51092-5). Random. Postponed.
Three Mint Lollipops. Robert Sabatier. Tr. by Patsy Southgate. 1974. 7.95 o.p. (ISBN 0-525-21855-6). Dutton.
Three Modes of Criticism: The Literary Theories of Scherer, Walzel, & Staiger. Peter Salm. 1968. 15.00 (ISBN 0-8295-0128-2). UPBS.
Three Monophysite Christologies: Severus of Antioch, Philoxenus of Mabbug, & Jacob of Sarug. Roberta C. Chesnut. (Oxford Theological Monographs). 1976. 24.95x (ISBN 0-19-826712-6): Oxford U Pr.
Three Months to Earn. Frank A. Philpot. Ed. by Peter M. Sandman. (Career Ser). (Orig.). 1970. pap. 1.25 o.s.i. (ISBN 0-02-081110-1, Collier). Macmillan.
Three Musketeers. Alexander Dumas. (Illus.). (gr. 7 up). 1962. 4.95 o.s.i. (ISBN 0-02-732840-6). Macmillan.
Three Musketeers. abr. ed. Alexandre Dumas. 168p. (RL 7). 1974. pap. 1.50 o.p. (ISBN 0-451-08107-2, W8107, Sig). NAL.
Three Musketeers. Alexandre Dumas. 1974. pap. 1.75 o.s.i. (ISBN 0-515-03492-4, V3492). Jove Pubns.
Three Musketeers. Alexandre Dumas. 1976. lib. bdg. 15.95x (ISBN 0-89968-148-4). Lightyear.
Three Novels. Charles Dickens. Incl. Oliver Twist; Tale of Two Cities; Great Expectations. 1978. 14.00 (ISBN 0-600-32930-5). Transatlantic.
Three Novels by Flaubert: A Study of Techniques. R. J. Sherrington. 1970. 29.99x (ISBN 0-19-815398-8). Oxford U Pr.
Three of a Kind. Louise D. Rich. LC 76-101747. (gr. 4-6). 1970. PLB 4.90 o.p. (ISBN 0-531-01837-7). Watts.
Three of China's Mighty Men. Leslie Lyall. pap. 3.95 (ISBN 0-85363-090-9). OMF Bks.
Three on the Run. Nina Bawden. (Illus.). (gr. 4-6). 1968. pap. 1.25 (ISBN 0-686-68481-8). PB.
Three Out of Four Wives. Alfred A. Lewis & Barrie Berns. 288p. 1975. 7.95 o.s.i. (ISBN 0-02-570500-8). Macmillan.
Three Pamphlets on the Jacobean Antifeminist Controversy. LC 78-5847. 1978. Repr. of 1620 ed. 20.00 (ISBN 0-8201-1307-7). Schol Facsimiles.
Three Papers on Dynamical Systems. (Translations Series Two: Vol. 116). Date not set. cancelled (ISBN 0-8218-3066-X). Am Math.
Three Penny Lane. Fielding Dawson. 150p. (Orig.). 1981. signed ed. 20.00 (ISBN 0-87685-447-1); pap. 5.00 (ISBN 0-87685-446-3). Black Sparrow.
Three Perfections: Chinese Painting, Poetry & Calligraphy. Michael Sullivan. LC 80-18189. (Illus.). 64p. 10.00 (ISBN 0-8076-0996-X); pap. 4.95 (ISBN 0-8076-0997-8). Braziller.
Three Pieces. Ntozake Shange. 160p. 1981. 12.95 (ISBN 0-312-80280-3). St Martin.
Three Places in New Inkland. David Cole et al. 1977. pap. 5.95 (ISBN 0-9605610-1-3). Zartscorp.
Three Plays. Nissim Ezekiel. (Writers Workshop Bluebird Ser.). 95p. 1975. 6.75 (ISBN 0-88253-660-5); pap. text ed. 4.00 (ISBN 0-88253-659-1). Ind-US Inc.
Three Plays. Joyce Carol Oates. LC 80-20210. 160p. 1980. 10.95 (ISBN 0-86538-001-5); pap. 5.95 (ISBN 0-86538-002-3). Ontario Rev NJ.
Three Plays by Thornton Wilder. Thornton Wilder. 1976. pap. 2.25 (ISBN 0-686-68405-2, 48231, Bard). Avon.
Three Plays for Reading. Tom Bowie. LC 79-64092. 1979. 12.50 (ISBN 0-932508-04-9); pap. 3.95 (ISBN 0-932508-05-7). Seven Oaks.
Three Poetic Plays: Jocasta, Flame & Cedar, the Bacchae. Philip Freund. 216p. 1973. 5.75 (ISBN 0-693-01607-8); pap. 4.95 (ISBN 0-693-01608-6). Transatlantic.
Three Psychologies: Perspectives from Freud, Skinner & Rogers. 2nd ed. Robert D. Nye. LC 80-25716. 170p. (Orig.). 1981. pap. text ed. 7.95 (ISBN 0-8185-0438-2). Brooks-Cole.
Three-Quarters of a Century of Drawings. Frank L. Wright. (Illus.). 1981. 27.50 (ISBN 0-8180-0031-7); pap. 17.50 (ISBN 0-8180-0032-5). Horizon.
Three Religions of China: The Interrelationship Between Confucianism, Buddhism & Taoism. new ed. W. E. Soothill. 1973. text ed. 9.50x o.p. (ISBN 0-7007-0031-5). Humanities.
Three-Ring Psychus. John Shirley. 240p. (Orig.). 1980. pap. 1.95 (ISBN 0-89083-674-4). Zebra.
Three Robots. Art Fettig. LC 81-801016. 1981. 5.95 (ISBN 0-9601334-0-2). Growth Unltd.
Three R's of Life Language. Marjorie Francis. (gr. k-6). 1971. 3.25x (ISBN 0-933892-11-X). Child Focus Co.
Three Russian Poets. Margarita Aliger et al. Tr. by Elaine Feinstein from Rus. (Translation Ser.). 1979. pap. 4.95 o.s.i. (ISBN 0-85635-227-6, Pub. by Carcanet New Pr England). Persea Bks.
Three Seventy Three Sixty Assembler Language Programming. Nancy Stern et al. LC 78-10504. 1979. pap. text ed. 21.95 (ISBN 0-471-03429-0); tchrs. manual avail. (ISBN 0-471-05393-7). Wiley.
Three Shall Be One. Francena H. Arnold. (Orig.). (gr. 9-12). 1966. pap. 2.50 (ISBN 0-8024-0085-X). Moody.
Three Short Stories. Robert Musil. Ed. by Hugh Sacker. (Clarendon German Ser). 1970. pap. 5.95x (ISBN 0-19-832467-7). Oxford U Pr.
Three Some Poems. Jeannine Dobbs et al. LC 75-23819. 88p. 1976. pap. 4.95 (ISBN 0-914086-11-1). Alicejamesbooks.
Three Steps Forward, Two Steps Back. Charles R. Swindoll. 176p. 1980. 8.95 (ISBN 0-8407-5187-7); pap. 4.95 (ISBN 0-8407-5723-9). Nelson.
Three Steps to Heaven. Ruth Hall. 1981. 4.95 (ISBN 0-8062-1560-7). Carlton.
Three Stories. Hsun Lu. Ed. by P. Kratochvil. LC 69-19378. (Cambridge Readers in Modern Chinese Ser). 1970. text ed. 9.95x (ISBN 0-521-09589-1). Cambridge U Pr.
Three Stories. Gordon C. Wilson. 1980. 3.00 (ISBN 0-933292-09-0); pap. 1.50 (ISBN 0-933292-06-6). Arts End.
Three Strikes & You're Out. Valjean McLenighan. (Beginning-to-Read Ser.). 32p. 1980. PLB 4.39 (ISBN 0-695-41462-3); pap. 1.50 (ISBN 0-695-31462-9). Follett.
Three Studies on Charles Robert Maturin. Henry W. Hinck. Ed. by Devendra P. Varma. LC 79-8458. (Gothic Studies & Dissertations Ser.). 1980. lib. bdg. 19.00x (ISBN 0-405-12647-6). Arno.
Three Styles in the Study of Kinship. J. A. Barnes. LC 74-142057. 1972. 17.50x (ISBN 0-520-01879-6); pap. 5.85x (ISBN 0-520-02481-8). U of Cal Pr.
Three Tales. Paul Bowles. LC 75-18063. 24p. 1975. pap. 3.50 (ISBN 0-916228-10-X); pap. 3.50 (ISBN 0-685-16636-8). Phoenix Bk Shop.
Three Talking Trees. Francis Timoney. LC 74-18902. (Illus.). 32p. (gr. 4-7). 1974. 3.95 o.p. (ISBN 0-87973-788-3); pap. 1.95 (ISBN 0-87973-388-8). Our Sunday Visitor.
Three Thousand Five Hundred Good Jokes for Speakers. Jerry Lieberman. LC 74-29354. 480p. 1975. pap. 4.50 (ISBN 0-385-00545-8, Dolp). Doubleday.
Three Thousand Futures: The Next Twenty Years for Higher Education. Carnegie Council on Policy Studies in Higher Education. LC 79-9675. (Carnegie Council Ser.). 1980. text ed. 17.95x (ISBN 0-87589-453-4). Jossey-Bass.
Three Thousand Years in Africa: Man & His Environment in the Lake Chad Region of Nigeria. Graham Connah. LC 79-41508. (New Studies in Archaeology). (Illus.). 240p. Date not set. price not set (ISBN 0-521-22848-4). Cambridge U Pr.
Three to Five Semiconductors. Ed. by H. C. Freyhardt. (Crystals. Growth, Properties & Applications Ser.: Vol. 3). (Illus.). 180p. 1980. 39.80 (ISBN 0-387-09957-3). Springer-Verlag.
Three to Win. James E. Adams. (Radiant Life). pap. 1.50 (ISBN 0-88243-906-5, 02-0906); tchr's ed 2.50 (ISBN 0-88243-176-5, 32-0176). Gospel Pub.
Three Tomorrows: American, British & Soviet Science Fiction. John Griffiths. 217p. 1980. 23.50x (ISBN 0-389-20008-5); pap. 8.95x (ISBN 0-389-20009-3). B&N.
Three Towneley Plays. Dennis Hamley. 1963. pap. text ed. 1.95 o.p. (ISBN 0-435-21012-2). Heinemann Ed.
Three Tracts. Elaezer Of Worms. Tr. by Jack Hirschman & Alexander Altmann. pap. 3.00 o.p. (ISBN 0-686-22381-0). Tree Bks.
Three Treatises. rev. ed. Martin Luther. LC 73-114753. 320p. 1970. pap. 3.50 (ISBN 0-8006-1639-1, 1-1639). Fortress.
Three Treatises: On the Brain, the Eye, & the Ear. Alexander Monro. Bd. with Croonian Lectures on Cerebrqal Localization. D. Ferrier. (Contributions to the History of Psychology Ser., Vol. VII, Pt. E: Psysiological Psychology). 1980. Repr. of 1797 ed. 30.00 (ISBN 0-89093-326-X). U Pubns Amer.
Three Tudor Dialogues. LC 78-14887. 1979. 20.00x (ISBN 0-8201-1319-0). Schol Facsimiles.
Three Uses of Christian Discourse in John Henry Newman. Jouett L. Powell. LC 75-29423. (American Academy of Religion. Dissertation Ser.). 1975. pap. 7.50 (ISBN 0-89130-042-2, 010110). Scholars Pr Ca.
Three Versions of the Story of King Lear: Anonymous Ca. 1594-1605; William Shakespeare 1607-1608; Nahum Tate 1681, 2 vols. Dorothy Nameri. (Salzburg Studies in English Literature, Elizabethan & Renaissance Studies: Nos. 50 & 51). (Illus.). 1976. Set. pap. text ed. 50.25x (ISBN 0-391-01489-7). Humanities.
Three Voyagers in Search of Europe. Alan Holder. LC 64-24513. 1966. 9.75x o.p. (ISBN 0-8122-7486-5). U of Pa Pr.
Three Ways of Thought in Ancient China. Arthur Waley. LC 56-5973. 1956. pap. 2.50 (ISBN 0-385-09280-6, A75, Anch). Doubleday.
Three Weeks in Spring. Joan H. Parker & Robert B. Parker. 1979. pap. 2.25 o.p. (ISBN 0-425-04018-6). Berkley Pub.
Three Weeks on - Three Weeks off. Ole Breide. Date not set. 9.95 (ISBN 0-533-04801-X). Vantage.
Three Wise Men. G. A. Pottebaum. (Little People's Paperbacks Ser.). 1979. pap. 0.99 (ISBN 0-8164-2242-7). Crossroad NY.
Three Wishes: A Collection of Puerto Rican Folktales. Ed. by Ricardo E. Alegria. Tr. by Elizabeth Culbert. LC 69-13770. (Illus.). (gr. 4-6). 1969. 6.75 o.p. (ISBN 0-15-286871-2, HJ). HarBraceJ.
Three Wishes for Jamie. Charles O'Neal. LC 79-66116. 248p. 1980. 15.95 (ISBN 0-933256-08-6); pap. text ed. 7.95 (ISBN 0-933256-09-4). Second Chance.
Three Witnesses. Rext Stout. 192p. 1981. pap. 2.25 (ISBN 0-553-14451-0). Bantam.
Three Women. Faith Baldwin. 1980. pap. write for info. (ISBN 0-671-83098-8). PB.
Three Works by the Open Theater. Karen Malpede & Joseph Chaikin. LC 74-13837. (Illus.). 1975. 12.50 (ISBN 0-910482-54-3). Drama Bk.
Three Worlds Cookbook. Gayle Allen & Robert F. Allen. LC 75-19542. (Illus.). 239p. 1975. pap. 7.95 (ISBN 0-87983-096-4). Keats.
Three Worlds of Economics. Lloyd G. Reynolds. (Studies in Comparative Economics: No. 12). (Illus.). 1971. 27.50x (ISBN 0-300-01481-3); pap. 5.45x o.p. (ISBN 0-300-01491-0, Y245). Yale U Pr.
Three Years. Emil Bock. 1980. pap. 12.50 (ISBN 0-903540-41-X, Pub. by Floris Books). St George Bk Serv.
Three Years Among the Camanches, the Narrative of Nelson Lee, the Texan Ranger, Containing a Detailed Account of His Captivity Among the Indians, His Singular Escape Through the Instrumentality of His Watch, & Fully Illustrating Indian Life As It Is on the War Path & in the Camp. LC 75-7100. (Indian CaptivitieS Ser.: Vol. 75). 1977. Repr. of 1859 ed. lib. bdg. 44.00 (ISBN 0-8240-1699-8). Garland Pub.
Three Years in California: Journal of Life at Sonora, 1849-1852. William Perkins. 1964. 16.95 (ISBN 0-520-01000-0). U of Cal Pr.
Three Years of the Agricultural Adjustment Administration. E. Nourse et al. LC 79-173654. (FDR & the Era of the New Deal Ser.). 600p. 1971. Repr. of 1937 ed. lib. bdg. 59.00 (ISBN 0-306-70365-3). Da Capo.
Three Years' Wanderings in the Northern Provinces of China. Robert Fortune & Ramon H. Myers. LC 78-74307. (Modern Chinese Economy Ser.: Vol. 4). 1979. 44.00 (ISBN 0-8240-4253-0). Garland Pub.
Three Years with Grant: As Recalled by War Correspondent Sylvanus Cadwallader. Sylvanus Cadawallader. Ed. by Benjamin P. Thomas. LC 80-21191. (Illus.). xiv, 361p. 1980. Repr. of 1955 ed. lib. bdg. 28.75x (ISBN 0-313-22576-1, CATY). Greenwood.
Threefold Social Order. rev. ed. Rudolf Steiner. Ed. by Frederick C. Heckel. LC 66-29676. Orig. Title: Threefold Commonwealth. (Orig.). 1966. pap. 3.50 o.p. (ISBN 0-910142-40-8). Anthroposophic.
Threes & Fours Go to School. Sylvia Krown. (Early Childhood Ser.). (Illus.). 288p. 1974. ref. ed. 15.95 (ISBN 0-13-920322-2). P-H.
Thresher. Herbert Krause. LC 76-29325. 1976. Repr. of 1946 ed. 9.95 (ISBN 0-88498-046-4); text ed. 9.95 o.p. (ISBN 0-685-71795-X); leatherette 12.95 (ISBN 0-685-71796-8). Brevet Pr.
Threshing Floor. John F. Sheehan. LC 72-81574. 224p. 1972. pap. 5.95 (ISBN 0-8091-1731-2). Paulist Pr.
Threshold: A Doctor Gives Straightfoward Answers to Teenagers' Most Often Asked Questions About Sex. Thomas Mintz & Lorelie Mintz. LC 77-78991. (Illus.). (gr. 5-9). 1978. 7.95 o.s.i. (ISBN 0-8027-6307-3); PLB 7.85 (ISBN 0-8027-6308-1). Walker & Co.
Threshold Level English. J. Van Ek. LC 79-42720. (Council of Europe Language Learning Ser.). 253p. 1980. pap. 7.95 (ISBN 0-08-024588-9). Pergamon.
Threshold Level for Modern Language Learning in Schools. J. A. Van Ek. 1978. pap. text ed. 9.00x (ISBN 0-582-55700-3). Longman.
Threshold of the McCarthy Era & the McCarthy Era - Beginning of the End. Ed. by G. D. Days. 60p. 1980. pap. 19.95 includes cassettes (ISBN 0-918628-54-7, 54/7). Congeros Pubns.
Threshold of the McCarthy Era & the McCarthy Era-Beginning of the End: Print Media Guide to the Audio Cassettes. G. D. Days. Ed. by Marian Haldeman. (Illus.). 56p. 1980. three ring binder 7.00x (ISBN 0-918628-52-0, 52-0). Congeros Pubns.
Threshold: The First Days of Retirement. Alan H. Olmstead. LC 75-6351. 224p. 1975. 8.95 o.p. (ISBN 0-06-013271-X, HarpT). Har-Row.
Threshold to Music, Level 1. 2nd ed. Eleanor Kidd. (gr. 2-4). 1974. pap. 8.80 teacher's resources book (ISBN 0-8224-9062-5); experience charts 48.00 (ISBN 0-8224-9063-3). Pitman Learning.
Threshold to Music, Level 2. 2nd ed. Eleanor Kidd. (gr. 4-7). 1975. pap. 8.80 teacher's resource book (ISBN 0-8224-9064-1); experience charts 48.00 (ISBN 0-8224-9065-X). Pitman Learning.
Threshold to Music: Early Childhood. 2nd ed. Eleanor Kidd. (gr. k-2). 1974. pap. 5.60 teacher's resource book (ISBN 0-8224-9060-9); experience charts 40.00 (ISBN 0-8224-9061-7). Pitman Learning.
Threshold to Music: Higher Grades. 2nd ed. Eleanor Kidd. (gr. 3-5). 1978. pap. 8.80 tchr's. resource book (ISBN 0-8224-9068-4); experience charts 48.00 (ISBN 0-8224-9069-2). Pitman Learning.
Threshold to Nursing. Jillian MacGuire. 271p. 1969. pap. text ed. 5.00x (Pub. by Bedford England). Renouf.
Thresholds in Geomorphology. Ed. by Donald R. Coates & John D. Vitek. (Binghamton Symposia in Geomorphology Ser.: Vol. 9). (Illus.). 512p. (Orig.). 1980. text ed. 35.00x (ISBN 0-04-551033-4, 2393). Allen Unwin.
Thresholds of Initiation. Joseph L. Henderson. LC 67-24110. 1979. pap. 9.00 (ISBN 0-8195-6061-8, Pub. by Wesleyan U Pr). Columbia U Pr.
Thresholds of Peace: German Prisoners & the People of Britain: 1944-1948. Matthew B. Sullivan. (Illus.). 1979. 30.00 (ISBN 0-241-89862-5, Pub. by Hamish Hamilton England). David & Charles.
Thresholds of Reality: George Santayana & Modernist Poetics. Lois Hughson. (Literary Criticism Ser.). 1976. 15.00 (ISBN 0-8046-9154-1, National University Pub). Kennikat.
Thresholds to Adult Living. rev. ed. Hazel T. Craig. (gr. 9-12). 1976. text ed. 18.60 (ISBN 0-87002-175-3); tchr's guide 6.64 (ISBN 0-87002-283-0). Bennett IL.
Thrice Chosen. Edouard Roditi. 135p. (Orig.). 1981. signed edition 17.50 (ISBN 0-87685-351-3); pap. 5.00 (ISBN 0-87685-350-5). Black Sparrow.
Thrice Shy: Cultural Accommodation to Blindness & Other Disasters in a Mexican Community. John L. Gwaltney. LC 71-118635. 1970. 20.00x (ISBN 0-231-03237-4). Columbia U Pr.
Thrie Tailes of the Thrie Priests of Peblis. LC 72-223. (English Experience Ser.: No. 106). 1969. Repr. of 1603 ed. 11.50 (ISBN 90-221-0106-1). Walter J Johnson.
Thriving: Beyond Adjustment. Alan M. Dahms. LC 79-17954. 1980. pap. text ed. 13.95 (ISBN 0-8185-0358-0). Brooks-Cole.
Throat of the Peacock: Japanese Senryo on Filial Devotion. Tr. by Harold J. Isaacson. 4.45 (ISBN 0-87830-158-5); pap. 1.85 (ISBN 0-87830-557-2); ltd. ed 10.00 (ISBN 0-87830-158-5). Theatre Arts.
Thromboembolism: A New Approach to Therapy. Ed. by J. R. Mitchell & J. G. Domenet. 1978. 25.00 (ISBN 0-12-500050-2). Acad Pr.
Throme of the Erril of Sherill. Patricia A. McKillip. LC 73-76324. (Illus.). 80p. (gr. 5 up). 1973. 4.95 o.p. (ISBN 0-689-30115-4). Atheneum.
Throne for Sesame. Helen Young. LC 78-74757. (Illus.). (ps-2). 1979. 7.95 (ISBN 0-233-96871-7). Andre Deutsch.
Throne of Saturn. Allen Drury. 736p. 1977. pap. 1.95 (ISBN 0-380-00792-4, 22996). Avon.
Throne of Wisdom: Wood Sculptures of the Madonna in Romanesque France. Ilene H. Forsyth. LC 72-166372. (Illus.). 336p. 1972. 38.50x o.p. (ISBN 0-691-03837-6). Princeton U Pr.
Through a Glass Darkly. Deb K. Das. (Writers Workshop Redbird Ser.). 53p. 1975. flexible cloth 3.00 (ISBN 0-89253-519-9); pap. 3.00 (ISBN 0-88253-723-7). Ind-US Inc.
Through Black Eyes. Elton C. Fax. LC 73-9270. (Illus.). 250p. 1974. 6.95 o.p. (ISBN 0-396-06842-1). Dodd.
Through Camera Eyes. Nelson B. Wadsworth. LC 75-8657. (Illus.). 180p. 1975. 10.95 o.p. (ISBN 0-8425-0435-4). Brigham.
Through Cloud & Sunshine. William A. Lauterbach. (Illus.). 1979. 4.95 (ISBN 0-570-03056-0, 6-1181). Concordia.

Through Colonial Doorways. Anne H. Wharton. LC 70-141040. 1970. Repr. of 1893 ed. 15.00 (ISBN 0-8103-3588-3). Gale.

Through Europe on the Eve of War: A Record of Personal Expeiences, Including an Account of the First World Conference of the Churches for International Peace. Frederick H. Lynch. LC 78-147456. (Library of War & Peace; Peace Leaders: Biographies & Memoirs). lib. bdg. 38.00 (ISBN 0-8240-0252-0). Garland Pub.

Through Eyes of Evil. Alpha Blair. 1981. pap. 2.50 (ISBN 0-8439-0865-3, Leisure Bks). Nordon Pubns.

Through Golden Meadows. Sallie L. Bell. LC 72-146582. 1971. pap. 1.95 (ISBN 0-310-21052-6). Zondervan.

Through Greek Eyes. Ed. by R. Nichols & K. McLeish. LC 74-80353. (Illus.). 144p. (gr. 7-12). 1975. 17.95 (ISBN 0-521-20632-4); pap. 6.50 (ISBN 0-521-08560-8). Cambridge U Pr.

Through Happy Hours. rev. ed. Theodore L. Harris. (Keys to Independence in Reading Ser.). (Orig.). (gr. 2). 1973. text ed. 2.70 (ISBN 0-87892-025-0); tchrs' manual 3.96 (ISBN 0-87892-027-7); avail. wkbk. 2.64 (ISBN 0-87892-028-5). Economy Co.

Through Lent to Resurrection. Flower A. Newhouse. Ed. by Melodie N. Bengtson. LC 77-77088. (Illus.). 1977. pap. 4.00 (ISBN 0-910378-13-4). Christward.

Through Living Hell...from Alcohol & Back. Herbie A. 1981. 4.95 (ISBN 0-8062-1603-4). Carlton.

Through Masailand with Joseph Thomson. Ed. by Roland Young. (Illus.). 1962. 10.95x o.s.i. (ISBN 0-8101-0248-X). Northwestern U Pr.

Through More History with J. Wesley Smith. Burr Shafer. LC 53-10800. (Illus.). 1953. 6.95 (ISBN 0-8149-0200-6). Vanguard.

Through Peasant Eyes: More Lucan Parables. Kenneth Bailey. LC 80-14297. 208p. 1980. 16.95 (ISBN 0-8028-3528-7). Eerdmans.

Through Roman Eyes. R. Nichols & K. McLeish. LC 75-10043. (Illus.). 128p. 1976. 18.95 (ISBN 0-521-20345-7); pap. 6.95 (ISBN 0-521-20944-7). Cambridge U Pr.

Through Russia. Maxim Gorky. 1959. 5.00x o.p. (ISBN 0-460-00741-6, Evman). Dutton.

Through Some Eventful Years. Susan B. Eppes. Ed. by Joseph D. Cushman, Jr. LC 68-21660. (Floridiana Facsimile & Reprint Ser). 1968. Repr. of 1926 ed. 12.75 (ISBN 0-8130-0074-2). U Presses Fla.

Through Sorrow into Joy. Hugh Salisbury. LC 77-13329. (Illus.). 1977. pap. 2.95 (ISBN 0-87123-559-5, 210559). Bethany Fell.

Through the Belgian Canals. Philip Bristow. 160p. 1980. 9.00x (ISBN 0-245-50975-5, Pub. by Nautical England). State Mutual Bk.

Through the Bible Book by Book, 4 vols. Myer Pearlman. 1935. pap. 1.95 ea.; Vol. 1. (ISBN 0-88243-660-0, 02-0660); Vol. 2. (ISBN 0-88243-661-9, 02-0661); Vol. 3. (ISBN 0-88243-662-7, 02-0662); Vol. 4. (ISBN 0-88243-663-5, 02-0663). Gospel Pub.

Through the Bible in a Year: Pupil Workbook. Dana Eynon. 64p. (gr. 3-7). 1975. wkbk. 1.95 (ISBN 0-87239-011-X, 3239). Standard Pub.

Through the Bible in a Year: Teacher. Dana Eynon. LC 74-27239. 176p. 1975. tchr's manual 6.95 (ISBN 0-87239-028-4, 3237). Standard Pub.

Through the Doors of Truth, Find Thyself. Deborah Morea. 1978. 5.50 (ISBN 0-9603022-0-4). Davida Pubns.

Through the Dutch Canals. Philip Bristow. 250p. 1980. 15.00x (Pub. by Nautical England). State Mutual Bk.

Through the Earth. Clement Fezandie. 2.50 (ISBN 0-913960-00-4). Fax Collect.

Through the Earth. Clement Fezandie. LC 80-23960. 48p. 1980. Repr. lib. bdg. 8.95x (ISBN 0-89370-028-2). Borgo Pr.

Through the Eighties: Thinking Globally, Acting Locally. Ed. by Frank Feather. 1980. 12.50 (ISBN 0-686-64296-1). World Future.

Through the Eye of a Rose Window: A Perspective on the Environment for Worship. Richard S. Vosko. 1981. pap. text ed. 8.95 (ISBN 0-89390-028-1). Resource Pubns.

Through the Eyes of Love. Lionel Whiston. 1981. pap. 4.95 (ISBN 0-8499-2929-6). Word Bks.

Through the Eyes of Social Science. 2nd ed. Frank Zulke. 336p. 1981. pap. text ed. 7.95x (ISBN 0-917974-54-9). Waveland Pr.

Through the First Antarctic Night, Eighteen Ninety-Eight to Eighteen Ninety-Nine. Frederick A. Cook. (Illus.). 478p. 1980. 49.00x (ISBN 0-7735-0514-8). McGill-Queens U Pr.

Through the French Canals. Philip Bristow. 200p. 1980. 18.00 (ISBN 0-245-53403-2, Pub. by Nautical England). State Mutual Bk.

Through the German Waterways. Philip Bristow. 168p. 1980. 15.00x (ISBN 0-245-51000-1, Pub. by Nautical England). State Mutual Bk.

Through the Glass of Soviet Literature. Ernest J. Simmons. LC 53-8757. (Studies of the Russian Institute of Col. Univ.). 1963. pap. 6.00x (ISBN 0-231-08527-3, 27). Columbia U Pr.

Through the Looking Glass: Epistemology & the Conduct of Inquiry, an Anthology. Ed. by Maria J. Falco. LC 79-66471. 1979. pap. text ed. 14.00 (ISBN 0-8191-0841-3). U Pr of Amer.

Through the Magic Mirror. Anthony Browne. LC 76-13024. (Illus.). (gr. k-3). 1977. 9.25 (ISBN 0-688-80064-5); PLB 8.88 (ISBN 0-688-84064-7). Greenwillow.

Through the Night & Such Impossibilities. Trevor Griffiths. 1977. pap. 5.95 (ISBN 0-571-11158-0, Pub. by Faber & Faber). Merrimack Bk Serv.

Through the Night Raptly. Mohinder Monga. 8.00 (ISBN 0-89253-778-7); flexible cloth 4.80 (ISBN 0-89253-779-5). Ind-US Inc.

Through the Porthole. (Illus.). 1965. pap. 2.50 (ISBN 0-914412-25-6). Inst for the Arts.

Through the Porthole: Exhibition Catalog. Intro. by Dominique De Menil. (Illus.). 1965. pap. 2.50 (ISBN 0-913456-89-6). Interbk Inc.

Through the Rain & Rainbow: The Remarkable Life of Richard Kinney. Lyle M. Crist. LC 73-22386. 224p. 1974. 5.95 o.p. (ISBN 0-687-42036-9). Abingdon.

Through the Reality Warp. Donald J. Pfeil. 1976. pap. 1.50 o.p. (ISBN 0-345-25377-9). Ballantine.

Through the Thirties. (Cincinnati Streetcars Ser.: No. 8). 1979. pap. 9.50 (ISBN 0-914196-20-0). Trolley Talk.

Through the Wilderness & Other Stories. Dan Jacobson. 1968. 5.95 o.s.i. (ISBN 0-02-558550-9). Macmillan.

Through the Winds Rain. rev. ed. Daniel B. Comfort, Jr. LC 80-53436. 64p. 1981. 7.95 (ISBN 0-938316-00-1). Bridges Sound.

Through the Wordsworth Country. William A. Knight. 268p. 1980. Repr. of 1887 ed. lib. bdg. 35.00 (ISBN 0-8482-4196-7). Norwood Edns.

Through the Year with Pope John Paul II: Reading for Every Day of the Year. Ed. by Tony Castle. 288p. 1981. 12.95 (ISBN 0-8245-0041-5). Crossroad NY.

Through the Years in Old Winnsboro. Katharine T. Obear. LC 80-23314. xx, 258p. 1980. Repr. of 1940 ed. write for info. (ISBN 0-87152-344-2). Reprint.

Through These Arches. Katherine Milhous. LC 64-13810. (Illus.). (gr. 4-9). 1964. 6.50 o.p. (ISBN 0-397-30785-3). Lippincott.

Throw a Tomato. Jim Erskine. (Illus.). 1979. 5.95 (ISBN 0-517-53865-2); ten copy prepack 59.50 (ISBN 0-517-53971-3). Potter.

Throwing on the Potter's Wheel. Thomas Sellers. 4.95 (ISBN 0-934706-03-4). Prof Pubns Ohio.

Throwing Shadows. E. L. Konigsburg. (gr. 5-9). pap. 2.95 (ISBN 0-689-70491-7, A-118, Aladdin). Atheneum.

Throws: Contemporary Theory, Technique & Training. 2nd ed. Ed. by Jess Jarver. (Illus.). 1980. pap. 7.50 (ISBN 0-911520-98-8). Tafnews.

Thruway. Anne Rockwell & Harlow Rockwell. LC 70-156842. (Illus.). (ps-1). 1972. 7.95 (ISBN 0-02-777510-0). Macmillan.

Thucydides, Bks. 6 & 7. Thucydides. Ed. by K. J. Dover. 1965. Bk.6. 14.95x (ISBN 0-19-831832-4); Bk. 7. 12.50x (ISBN 0-19-831829-4); pap. 12.95x (ISBN 0-19-872098-X). Oxford U Pr.

Thucydides Mythistoricus. Francis M. Cornford. (Illus.). 1971. pap. 4.95x (ISBN 0-8122-1021-2, Pa. Paperbacks). U of Pa Pr.

Thumbeline. Hans C. Andersen. Tr. by Richard Winston & Clara Winston. LC 80-13012. Orig. Title: Tommelise. (Illus.). 40p. (gr. k-3). 1980. 8.95 (ISBN 0-688-22235-8); PLB 8.59 (ISBN 0-688-32235-2). Morrow.

Thumbs up. Tom Christie & Deb Holmes. (gr. 5-12). 1978. 11.95 (ISBN 0-916456-34-X, GA88). Good Apple.

Thump, Blam, Bump Mystery. Louise Armstrong. LC 74-24582. (Illus.). (gr. k-3). 1975. 5.95 o.s.i. (ISBN 0-8027-6208-5); PLB 5.83 o.s.i. (ISBN 0-8027-6207-7). Walker & Co.

Thump Thump Thump! Anne Rockwell. LC 80-22142. (Illus.). (ps-1). 1981. 7.95 (ISBN 0-525-41300-6). Dutton.

Thunder at Dawn. Jack Hoffenberg. 1969. pap. 1.95 (ISBN 0-380-01583-8, 37226). Avon.

Thunder from Heaven: The Story of the 17th Airborne Division in WW II. Don Pay. LC 80-69273. (Airborne Ser.: No. 4). (Illus.). 179p. 1980. Repr. 22.50 (ISBN 0-89839-037-0). Battery Pr.

Thunder from the Mountain: Mau Mau Patriotic Songs. Ed. by Maina W. Kinyatti. 128p. (Orig.). 1980. 10.95 (ISBN 0-905762-83-5, Pub. by Zed Pr); pap. 5.95 (ISBN 0-905762-84-3). Lawrence Hill.

Thunder God's Son. Ariane Dewey. LC 80-16325. (Illus.). 32p. (gr. k-4). 1981. 7.95 (ISBN 0-688-80295-8); PLB 7.63 (ISBN 0-688-84295-X). Greenwillow.

Thunder in the Kerk. Ann Marlowe. LC 79-9803. 1979. 8.95 (ISBN 0-396-07672-6). Dodd.

Thunder in the West. Lewy Olfson. Ed. by Thomas J. Mooney. (Pal Paperbacks Kit A Ser.). (Illus., Orig.). (gr. 7-12). 1976. pap. text ed. 1.25 (ISBN 0-8374-3490-4). Xerox Ed Pubns.

Thunder, Mighty Stallion of the Hills, No. 1. Mike Jahn. 160p. (gr. 4 up). 1981. pap. 1.50 (ISBN 0-448-17275-5, Tempo). G&D.

Thunder of His Power. George Otis. 1978. 5.95 (ISBN 0-89728-012-1). Omega Pubns OR.

Thunder of the Captains: The Short Summer in 1950. David Detzer. LC 76-25472. (Illus.). 1977. 10.00 o.s.i. (ISBN 0-690-01202-0, TYC-T). T Y Crowell.

Thunder on the Right. Mary Stewart. 1978. pap. 2.25 o.p. (ISBN 0-449-23940-3, Crest). Fawcett.

Thunder on the Right. Mary Stewart. 192p. 1981. pap. 2.25 (ISBN 0-449-23940-3, Crest). Fawcett.

Thunder on the Right: The Protestant Fundamentalists. Gary K. Clabaugh. LC 74-9551. 283p. 1974. 13.95 (ISBN 0-88229-108-4). Nelson-Hall.

Thunder Out of China. Theodore H. White & Annalee Jacoby. LC 74-31228. vi, 331p. 1975. Repr. of 1946 ed. lib. bdg. 32.50 (ISBN 0-306-70699-7). Da Capo.

Thunder Out of China. Theodore H. White & Annalee Jacoby. 345p. 1980. pap. 7.95 (ISBN 0-306-80128-0). Da Capo.

Thunderbird Range. W. C. Tuttle. 256p. (YA) 1974. 5.95 (ISBN 0-685-39470-0, Avalon). Bouregy.

Thunderbird Story: Personal Luxury. Richard M. Langworth. LC 80-20358. 1980. 28.95 (ISBN 0-87938-093-4). Motorbooks Intl.

Thunderbolt. William N. Hess. 1975. pap. 1.95 (ISBN 0-345-28307-4). Ballantine.

Thunderbolt: The History of the Eleventh Armored Division. (Divisional Ser.: No. 17). (Illus.). 1980. Repr. of 1948 ed. 22.50 (ISBN 0-89839-041-9). Battery Pr.

Thunderhead. Mary O'Hara. (gr. 7-9). 1943. 10.95 (ISBN 0-397-00007-3). Lippincott.

Thundering Hills. Al Cody. 256p. (YA) 1973. 5.95 (ISBN 0-685-32413-3, Avalon). Bouregy.

Thundering Peacemaker: The B-36 Story. Frederick A. Johnsen. (Illus.). 1978. pap. 3.95 (ISBN 0-911721-31-2, Pub. by Bomber). Aviation.

Thundering Sneakers. Prudence Mackintosh. LC 80-1124. 192p. 1981. 9.95 (ISBN 0-385-12879-7). Doubleday.

Thunderstorm. Tsao Yu. 1978. 4.95 (ISBN 0-8351-0554-7). China Bks.

Thunderstorms, Tornadoes & Building Damage. Joe R. Eagleman et al. LC 74-30674. 320p. 1975. 25.95 (ISBN 0-669-98137-0). Lexington Bks.

Thurber & Company. James Thurber. LC 64-18067. (Illus.). 1966. 10.95 o.p. (ISBN 0-06-014305-3, HarpT). Har-Row.

Thurlow Weed. Glyndon G. Van Deusen. LC 73-87698. (American Scene Ser.). 1969. Repr. of 1947 ed. lib. bdg. 39.50 (ISBN 0-306-71693-3). Da Capo.

Thursday's Child. Faith Baldwin. LC 75-18668. 1976. 7.95 o.p. (ISBN 0-03-014916-9). HR&W.

Thursday's Child. Victoria Poole. 1980. 10.95 (ISBN 0-316-71334-1). Little.

Thursday's Child No. 2. Edward Robbin. LC 80-83893. (Anthology of Short Stories Ser.). (Illus.). 200p. (Orig.). 1980. pap. 5.00 (ISBN 0-9603518-2-5). Glen Pr.

Thus Saith the Lord. Duane S. Crowther. LC 80-83862. 300p. 1981. 7.95 (ISBN 0-88290-168-0, 1061). Horizon Utah.

Thus Spake the Kings. Walter H. Marx. (Illus.). 1978. pap. text ed. 4.95x (ISBN 0-88334-106-9). Ind Sch Pr.

Thy Hidden Ones. Jessie Penn-Lewis. 1962. pap. 3.50 (ISBN 0-87508-998-4). Chr Lit.

Thy Kingdom Come. Huberto C. Medeiros. 1980. write for info. (ISBN 0-8198-7307-1); pap. write for info. (ISBN 0-8198-7308-X). Dghtrs St Paul.

Thy Kingdom Come. Sterling W. Sill. LC 75-37275. 239p. 1975. 6.95 o.p. (ISBN 0-87747-602-0). Deseret Bk.

Thy Kingdom Come: A Blumhardt Reader. Vernard Eller. 160p. (Orig.). 1980. pap. 9.95 (ISBN 0-8028-3544-9). Eerdmans.

Thy Most Precious Gift: Peace in Jewish Tradition. Richard G. Hirsch. (Issues of Conscience Ser.). 128p. (Orig.). 1974. pap. 0.50 (ISBN 0-8074-0093-9, 180203). UAHC.

Thy Neighbor's Wife. Gay Talese. 1981. pap. 3.95 (ISBN 0-440-18689-7). Dell.

Thy Will Be Done. Andrew Murray. (Summit Bks). 200p. 1981. pap. 3.45 (ISBN 0-8010-6109-1). Baker Bk.

Thyestes. Seneca. Tr. by Moses Hadas. LC 57-14639. 1957. pap. 1.95 (ISBN 0-672-60258-X, LLA76). Bobbs.

Thymus Manganese, & Myasthenia Gravis. Emanuel Josephson. (Natural Health Ser.). 124p. 12.00 (Pub. by Chedney); pap. 6.00. Alpine Ent.

Thyristor DC Drives. P. C. Sen. LC 80-21226. 350p. 1981. 30.00 (ISBN 0-471-06070-4, Pub. by Wiley-Interscience). Wiley.

Thyristor Networks for the Transfer of Energy Between Superconducting Coils. R. L. Kustom. LC 79-5410. 1980. 23.00 (ISBN 0-299-08050-1). U of Wis Pr.

Thyristor Phase-Controlled Converters & Cycloconverters: Operation, Control, & Performance. Brian R. Pelly. LC 70-125276. 1971. 44.50 (ISBN 0-471-67790-6, Pub. by Wiley-Interscience). Wiley.

Thyroid & Endocrine System Investigations with Radionuclides & Radioassays. Ed. by F. S. Ashkar. (Illus.). 544p. 1979. 40.50 (ISBN 0-89352-070-5). Masson Pub.

Thyroid Axis, Drugs & Behavior. Arthur J. Prange, Jr. LC 73-90468. 213p. 1974. 24.50 (ISBN 0-911216-34-0). Raven.

Thyroid Cancer. W. Duncan et al. (Recent Results in Cancer Research Ser.: Vol. 73). (Illus.). 190p. 1980. 35.40 (ISBN 0-387-09328-1). Springer-Verlag.

Thyroid Case Studies. Boris Catz. 1975. spiral bdg. 14.00 (ISBN 0-87488-038-6). Med Exam.

Thyroid Diseases. 4th ed. Leslie J. DeGroot & John B. Stanbury. LC 75-17916. 823p. 1975. 51.95 (ISBN 0-471-20530-3, Pub. by Wiley-Medimedia Publications). Wiley.

Thyroid Diseases in Tropics. K. N. Udupa & S. K. Mishra. 320p. Date not set. text ed. 25.00x (ISBN 0-7069-1173-3, Pub. by Vikas India). Advent Bk.

Thyroid Gland. Ed. by Michel De Visscher. (Comprehensive Endocrinology Ser.). 1980. 53.50 (ISBN 0-89004-342-6, 396). Raven.

Thyroid Hormones & Brain Development. Gilman Grave. LC 76-52899. 1977. 36.00 (ISBN 0-89004-146-6). Raven.

Thyroid: Physiology & Treatment of Disease. Ed. by Jerome M. Hershman & G. A. Bray. 1979. text ed. 60.00 (ISBN 0-08-023202-7). Pergamon.

Thyroid: Physiology & Treatment of Disease. Ed. by Jerome M. Hershman & George A. Bray. (International Encyclopedia of Pharmacology & Therapeutics: Vol. 101). (Illus.). 1979. 140.00 (ISBN 0-08-017685-2). Pergamon.

Thyroid Research III: Eighth International Thyroid Congress 3-5 February 1980, Sydney, Australia. Ed. by P. E. Harding et al. 800p. 1980. 130.00 (ISBN 0-08-026361-5). Pergamon.

Thyroiditis. Virginia A. Livolsi & Paul Logerfo. 192p. 1981. 54.95 (ISBN 0-8493-5705-5). CRC Pr.

Thyroiditis & Thyroid Function: Clinical, Morphological, & Physiopathological Studies. Paul A. Bastenie & A. M. Ermans. 360p. 1972. text ed. 82.00 (ISBN 0-08-016628-8). Pergamon.

Thyrza: A Tale. George Gissing. Ed. by Jacob Korg. (Society & Victorians: No. 21). 1974. text ed. 19.50x (ISBN 0-901759-94-5). Humanities.

TI-Fifty-Nine Reservoir Engineering Manual. Reuven Hollo & Haresh Fifadara. 264p. 1980. 50.00 (ISBN 0-87814-134-0). Pennwell Pub.

Ti Jacques: A Story of Haiti. Ruth Eitzen. LC 76-158688. (Stories from Many Lands Ser). (Illus.). (gr. k-4). 1972. 7.95 (ISBN 0-690-82429-7, TYC-J). T Y Crowell.

Tia Tula. Ynamuno. Ed. by E. D'Entremont. 1975. pap. 7.50 (ISBN 0-13-522870-0). P-H.

Tianitolka: Povesti. Vladimir Maramzin. 200p. (Rus.). 1981. 15.00 (ISBN 0-88233-510-3); pap. 7.00 (ISBN 0-88233-511-1). Ardis Pubs.

Tianitolkai: Povesti. Vladimir Maramzin. (Rus.). 1981. 15.00 (ISBN 0-88233-510-3); pap. 7.50 (ISBN 0-88233-511-1). Ardis Pubs.

Tianshan Mountains. 1980. 20.00 (ISBN 0-8351-0738-8). China Bks.

Tiazhelia Lira. Vladislav Khodasevich. 1975. pap. 10.00 (ISBN 0-88233-192-2). Ardis Pubs.

Tib. Mark Dunster. (Holiday Ser.: Pt. 6: Easter). 77p. (Orig.). 1981. pap. 5.00 (ISBN 0-89642-077-9). Linden Pubs.

Tiberius. Robin Seager. LC 74-185511. (Illus.). 1972. 21.50x (ISBN 0-520-02212-2). U of Cal Pr.

Tibet. Pietro P. Mele. (Illus.). 1969. text ed. 30.00 (ISBN 0-685-12304-9, Oxford & IBH Pub Co). Paragon.

Tibet: Being the Recollections & Adventures of the Hermit Yungdrung, Called Small Ears. Gil Ziff. 348p. 1981. pap. 4.95 (ISBN 0-517-54436-9); 18-copy prepack 89.10 (ISBN 0-517-54440-7). Crown.

Tibet: Land of Snows. Giuseppe Tucci. 1973. 21.95 (ISBN 0-236-31094-1, Pub. by Paul Elek). Merrimack Bk Serv.

Tibetan & Himalayan Woodblock Prints. Douglas Weiner. (Illus., Orig.). 1974. pap. 6.00 (ISBN 0-486-22988-2). Dover.

Tibetan Book of the Dead: The Great Liberation Through Hearing in the Bardo. Tr. by Francesca Fremantle & Chogyam Trungpa. LC 74-29615. (Clear Light Ser.). (Illus.). 256p. 1975. pap. 4.50 (ISBN 0-394-73064-X). Shambhala Pubns.

Tibetan Diary: Travels Along the Ancient Silk Route. Charlotte Salisbury. LC 80-54816. 1981. 9.95 (ISBN 0-8027-0683-5). Walker & Co.

Tibetan-English Dictionary of Modern Tibetan. Melvyn C. Goldstein. 1975. 24.95x (ISBN 0-685-89505-X). Himalaya Hse.

Tibetan Foothold. Dervla Murphy. 1967. 8.95 (ISBN 0-7195-0989-0). Transatlantic.

Tibetan Thanka Portfolio. (Sacred Art Ser.: No. 4). (Illus.). 1974. 25.00 o.p. (ISBN 0-913546-46-1). Dharma Pub.

Tibetan Yoga. Bernard Bromage. 192p. (Orig.). 1980. pap. 7.95 o.s.i. (ISBN 0-85030-199-8). Newcastle Pub.

Tibet's Great Yogi, Milarepa. 2nd ed. Ed. by W. Y. Evans-Wentz. (Illus.). 1969. pap. 6.95 (ISBN 0-19-500301-2, 294, GB). Oxford U Pr.

Tibullus: A Hellenistic Poet at Rome. Francis Cairns. LC 79-50231. 1980. 57.00 (ISBN 0-521-22413-6); pap. 17.95 (ISBN 0-521-29683-8). Cambridge U Pr.

Tick, Tock, the Popcorn Clock. Jane B. Monroe. LC 77-13120. (Creative Dramatics Ser.). (Illus.). (ps-3). 1978. PLB 5.50 (ISBN 0-89565-010-X); pap. 2.50 (ISBN 0-89565-043-6). Childs World.

Ticket to Ride Number Three. Ritchie Perry. 192p. 1981. pap. 2.25 (ISBN 0-345-29057-7). Ballantine.

Tickets. Richard P. Brickner. 1981. 12.95 (ISBN 0-671-41209-4). S&S.

Tickle Yourself with Puzzles. Electric Company. LC 78-68684. (Illus.). (gr. 1-5). 1979. pap. 1.50 (ISBN 0-394-84226-X). Random.

Tidal Power & Estuary Management. Ed. by R. T. Severn et al. (Colston Paper Ser.: No. 30). (Illus.). 296p. 1979. 65.00 (ISBN 0-85608-023-3). Transatlantic.

Tidal Swings of the Stock Market. Scribner Browne. (Illus.). 115p. 1980. 59.50 (ISBN 0-918968-75-5). Inst Econ Finan.

Tidal Wave. Martin W. Tyler. (Orig.). 1975. pap. 1.50 o.p. (ISBN 0-685-52938-X, LB271ZK, Leisure Bks). Nordon Pubns.

Tidal Wave Bait. Jackson S. Tamane. LC 79-66394. 1981. 10.95 (ISBN 0-533-04385-9). Vantage.

Tide Flowing. Joan Phipson. LC 80-24375. 168p. (gr. 7 up). 1981. 8.95 (ISBN 0-689-50196-X, McElderry Bk). Atheneum.

Tide of Fish. Clive Gammon. 10.00x (ISBN 0-392-06417-0, SpS). Soccer.

Tide of Terror: An Anthology of Rare Horror Stories. Ed. by Hugh Lamb. LC 73-6181. 1973. 7.95 o.p. (ISBN 0-8008-7695-4). Taplinger.

Tidepool & Nearshore Fishes of California. John E. Fitch & Robert J. Lavenberg. (Illus.). 1976. 12.95x (ISBN 0-520-02844-9); pap. 5.95 (ISBN 0-520-02845-7). U of Cal Pr.

Tides. John Montague. LC 73-135384. 63p. 1971. 6.50 (ISBN 0-8040-0526-5); pap. 3.75 (ISBN 0-8040-0825-6). Swallow.

Tides Among Nations. Karl W. Deutsch. LC 78-57053. 1979. 19.95 (ISBN 0-02-907300-6). Free Pr.

Tides of Power: Conversations on the American Constitution. Bob Eckhardt & Charles Black. LC 75-32630. 250p. 1976. 15.00x (ISBN 0-300-01974-2); pap. 3.95x (ISBN 0-300-02118-6). Yale U Pr.

Tidewater Dynasty: The Lees of Stratford Hall. Carey Roberts & Rebecca Seely. 1981. 12.95 (ISBN 0-15-190294-1). HarBraceJ.

Tidewater Maryland. Paul Wilstach. LC 76-92686. (Illus.). 1969. 10.00 (ISBN 0-87033-137-X, Pub. by Tidewater). Cornell Maritime.

Tidoon. Robert L. Olivier. LC 70-18934. 96p. 1972. 5.95 (ISBN 0-911116-62-1). Pelican.

Tie Dye, Batik & Candlemaking: Step-by-Step. Macmillan. LC 76-8487. (Step-by-Step Craft Ser.). (Illus.). 1976. pap. 5.95 o.s.i. (ISBN 0-02-011790-6, 01179, Collier). Macmillan.

Tie Dyeing & Batik. Astrith Deyrup. LC 73-9020. 64p. (gr. 4-7). 1974. 6.95 o.p. (ISBN 0-385-03626-4). Doubleday.

Tie That Binds: Conversations with Jewish Writers. Harold U. Ribalow. LC 80-19433. 272p. 12.95 (ISBN 0-498-01963-2). A S Barnes.

Tied up in Tinsel. Ngaio Marsh. 1978. pap. 1.75 (ISBN 0-515-04533-0). Jove Pubns.

Tiempo. Harlan Wade. Tr. by Mamie M. Contreras from Eng. LC 78-26772. (Book About Ser.). Orig. Title: Time. (Illus., Sp.). (gr. k-3). 1979. PLB 7.30 (ISBN 0-8172-1477-1). Raintree Pubs.

Tierra Amarilla: Stories of New Mexico, Cuentos De Nuevo Mexico. Sabine R. Ulibarri. LC 75-153942. (Illus.). 167p. (Eng. & Span.). 1978. pap. 4.95 (ISBN 0-8263-0212-2). U of NM Pr.

Tierra Del Fuego: The Fatal Lodestone. Eric Shipton. (Illus.). 175p. 1974. 24.00 (ISBN 0-85314-194-0). Transatlantic.

Tierra Dulce: The Jesse Nusbaum Papers. Rosemary Nusbaum. (Illus.). 128p. 1980. pap. 7.95 (ISBN 0-913270-83-0). Sunstone Pr.

Tierras, Costumbres y Tipos Hispanicos. Ed. by Orlando Gomez-Gil & Irene E. Stanislawczyk. LC 77-114675. (Span). (gr. 9-12). 1970. pap. 7.95 (ISBN 0-672-63126-1). Odyssey Pr.

Tieta. Jorge Amado. 688p. 1980. pap. 4.95 (ISBN 0-380-50815-X, 50815, Bard). Avon.

Tiger. Mark Dunster. (Holiday Ser.: New Years Eve: Pt. 4). 79p. (Orig.). 1980. pap. 4.00 (ISBN 0-89642-068-X). Linden Pubs.

Tiger. Jennifer Justice. (First Look at Nature Bks.). (Illus.). (gr. 2-4). 1979. 2.50 (ISBN 0-531-09143-0); PLB 6.45 s&l (ISBN 0-531-09154-6). Watts.

Tiger & Leopard. Jill Gill. LC 73-134673. (Illus.). 4.95 (ISBN 0-8149-0679-6). Vanguard.

Tiger Beetles, Ground Beetles, & Water Beetles: Families 1-9, Part 1, 10 parts. Richard E. Blackwelder & Ross H. Arnett, Jr. (Checklist of Beetles, Yellow Version). 1977. 20.00 o.p. (ISBN 0-89140-016-8); 200.00 set o.p. (ISBN 0-686-16918-2). World Natural Hist.

Tiger Book. Jan Pfloog. (Illus.). 24p. (gr. k-1). 1976. PLB 5.38 (ISBN 0-307-68983-2, Golden Pr). Western Pub.

Tiger by the Tail. Ruth McCarthy Sears. (YA) 1978. 5.95 (ISBN 0-685-85783-2, Avalon). Bouregy.

Tiger by the Tail: Parenting in a Troubled Society. Kenneth R. Greenberg. LC 73-93103. 1974. 14.95 (ISBN 0-911012-77-X). Nelson-Hall.

Tiger by the Tail: The Keynesian Legacy of Inflation. Friedrich A. Hayek. (Cato Papers Ser.: No. 6). 178p. 1979. pap. 4.00 (ISBN 0-932790-06-2). Cato Inst.

Tiger, Lion, Hawk. Earle Rice, Jr. (Pacesetters Ser.). (Illus.). 64p. (gr. 4 up). 1978. PLB 7.95 (ISBN 0-516-02174-5). Childrens.

Tiger Rose. Lisa Eisenberg. LC 79-52658. (Laura Brewster Mysteries Ser.). (Illus.). 64p. (gr. 4 up). 1980. PLB 7.95 (ISBN 0-516-02210-5). Childrens.

Tiger, Take off Your Hat. Linda P. Silbert & Alvin J. Silbert. (Little Twirps, TM Understanding People Books). (Illus.). (gr. k-4). 1978. pap. 2.25 (ISBN 0-89544-051-2). Silbert Bress.

Tiger Ten. William Blankenship. 1978. pap. 1.95 o.p. (ISBN 0-425-03674-X, Medallion). Berkley Pub.

Tiger with the Bright Blue Eyes & Other Stories. Ed. by Lewis Jones. (Readers Ser.: Stage 2). 1981. pap. text ed. 1.95 (ISBN 0-88377-137-3). Newbury Hse.

Tigerlily. Mama S. Rampa. 1978. pap. 2.50 (ISBN 0-685-90229-3). Weiser.

Tigers. Patricia Hunt. LC 80-2785. (Skylight Bk.). (Illus.). 64p. (gr. 2-5). 1981. PLB 5.95 (ISBN 0-396-07932-6). Dodd.

Tigers Are Better Looking. Jean Rhys. LC 72-9175. 1974. 8.95 o.p. (ISBN 0-06-013561-1, HarpT). Har-Row.

Tigger & Winnie-the-Pooh. Walt Disney Studio. (Illus.). (ps-1). 1968. PLB 5.38 (ISBN 0-307-68948-4, Golden Pr). Western Pub.

Tight End. Matt Christopher. 128p. (gr. 3 up). 1981. 6.95 (ISBN 0-316-32672-0). Little.

Tightrope Men. Desmond Bagley. 256p. 1977. pap. 1.75 o.p. (ISBN 0-449-23159-3, Crest). Fawcett.

Tigran Petrosian - World Champion. A. O. O'Kelly De Galway. 1967. text ed. 9.00 (ISBN 0-08-011013-4); pap. text ed. 5.50 (ISBN 0-08-011012-6). Pergamon.

Tigris Expedition: In Search of Our Beginnings. Thor Heyerdahl. LC 80-1862. 360p. 1981. 17.95 (ISBN 0-385-17357-1). Doubleday.

Tiguas: The Lost Tribe of City Indians. Stan Steiner. LC 77-189728. (Illus.). (gr. 5up). 1972. 4.95g o.s.i. (ISBN 0-02-787900-3, CCPr). Macmillan.

Tijeras Canyon: Analyses of the Past. Ed. by Linda S. Cordell. (Illus.). 232p. 1980. pap. 9.95 (ISBN 0-8263-0565-2). U of NM Pr.

Tijeras Canyon: Analyses of the Past. Ed. by Linda S. Cordell. (Illus.). 232p. 1980. 19.95 (ISBN 0-8263-0553-9, Pub. by Maxwell Mus Anthropology); pap. 9.95 (ISBN 0-8263-0565-2). U of NM Pr.

Tikal Reports, 4 pts. Incl. Pt. 1. Field Director's Report: 1956 & 1957 Seasons. Edwin M. Shook; Pt. 2. Excavations in the Stela 23 Group. William R. Coe & Vivian L. Broman; Pt. 3. The Problem of Abnormal Stela Placements at Tikal & Elsewhere. Linton Satterthwaite; Pt. 4. Five Newly Discovered Carved Monuments at Tikal & New Data on Four Others. Linton Satterthwaite. (Museum Monographs). (Illus.). 150p. 1958. soft bound 5.00 o.p. (ISBN 0-686-11892-8). Univ Mus of U PA.

Tikal Reports, 6 pts. Incl. Pt. 5. Tikal: Numeration, Terminology & Objectives. Edwin M. Shook & William R. Coe; Pt. 6. The Carved Wooden Lintels of Tikal. William R. Coe et al; Pt. 7. Temple I: Post Constructional Activities. Richard E. Adams & Aubrey S. Trik; Pt. 8. Miscellaneous Investigations. Linton Satterhwaite et al; Pt. 9. The Mounds & Monuments of Xutilha, Peten, Guatemala. Linton Satterthwaite; Pt. 10. The Abandonment of Primicias by Itza of San Jose, Guatemala, & Socotz, British Honduras. Ruben E. Reina. (Museum Monographs). (Illus.). 225p. 1961. soft bound 7.00 o.p. (ISBN 0-934718-12-1). Univ Mus of U PA.

Tiki & the Dolphin: The Adventures of a Boy in Tahiti. Christopher Lucas. LC 74-76441. (gr. 4-6). 1974. 6.95 (ISBN 0-8149-0741-5). Vanguard.

Tikta'liktak: An Eskimo Legend. James Houston. LC 65-21696. (Illus.). (gr. 2-4). 1965. 6.25 (ISBN 0-15-287745-2, HJ). HarBraceJ.

Til Night Is Gone. Phyllis Primmer. 1980. pap. 1.95 mass mkt. (ISBN 0-310-26342-5). Zondervan.

Tilak & Gokhale: Revolution & Reform in the Making of Modern India. Stanley A. Wolpert. (California Library Reprint Ser.). 1977. 22.75x (ISBN 0-520-03339-6). U of Cal Pr.

Tile: Indoors & Out. Monte Burch. Ed. by Shirley M. Horowitz & Gail Kummings. (Illus.). 144p. (Orig.). 1980. 14.95 (ISBN 0-932944-27-2); pap. 5.95 (ISBN 0-932944-28-0). Creative Homeowner.

Tile: Remodeling. Sunset Editors. LC 77-90719. (Illus.). 80p. 1978. pap. 3.95 (ISBN 0-376-01672-8, Sunset Bks). Sunset-Lane.

Till Armageddon. Billy Graham. 1981. 8.95 (ISBN 0-8499-0195-2). Word Bks.

Till He Come. C. H. Spurgeon. 3.95 (ISBN 0-686-09089-6). Pilgrim Pubns.

Till Hope Creates. Ray Smith. 1981. price not set. Kirk Pr.

Till No Light Leaps: The Selected Poems. James Magner. 1981. 8.00 (ISBN 0-8233-0327-6). Golden Quill.

Tilly. Catherine Cookson. LC 80-16627. 384p. 1980. 12.95 (ISBN 0-688-03715-1). Morrow.

Tilly. Jennie Tremaine. (Candlelight Romance Ser.). (Orig.). 1981. pap. 1.50 (ISBN 0-440-18637-4). Dell.

Tilly Wed. Catherine Cookson. Orig. Title: Tilly Trotter Wed. 384p. 1980. 12.95 (ISBN 0-688-00188-2). Morrow.

Tilly's Rescue. Faith Jaques. LC 80-14419. (Illus.). 32p. (ps-4). 1981. 9.95 (ISBN 0-689-50175-7, McElderry Bk). Atheneum.

Tilsit Inheritance. Catherine Gaskin. 1976. pap. 1.75 o.p. (ISBN 0-449-22852-5, X2852, Crest). Fawcett.

Tilsit Inheritance. Catherine Gaskin. 384p. 1981. pap. 2.50 (ISBN 0-553-14833-8). Bantam.

Tim. Colleen McCullough. 1977. pap. 2.50 (ISBN 0-445-08545-2). Popular Lib.

Tim & Charlotte. Edward Ardizzone. (Illus.). 48p. (ps-3). 1981. pap. 4.95 (ISBN 0-19-272118-6). Oxford U Pr.

Tim & Ginger. Edward Ardizzone. (Illus.). 48p. (ps-3). 1981. pap. 4.95 (ISBN 0-19-272113-5). Oxford U Pr.

Tim & His Lamb. Fern Stubblefield. 52p. pap. 0.40; pap. 1.00 3 copies. Faith Pub Hse.

Tim Tadpole & the Great Bullfrog. Marjorie Flack. (ps-1). 4.95a o.p. (ISBN 0-385-07530-8); PLB (ISBN 0-385-07658-4). Doubleday.

Tim to the Lighthouse. Edward Ardizzone. (Illus.). (gr. 1-4). 1980. pap. 3.95 (ISBN 0-19-272107-0). Oxford U Pr.

Timaeus. Plato. Tr. by Benjamin Jowett. 1949. pap. 2.95 (ISBN 0-672-60175-3, LLA14). Bobbs.

Timaeus (from Plato's Cosmology) Plato. Ed. by Oskar Piest. Tr. by Francis M. Cornford. pap. 3.95 (ISBN 0-672-60301-2, LLA106). Bobbs.

Timbal Gulch Trail. Max Brand. 1972. pap. 1.95 (ISBN 0-446-90312-4). Warner Bks.

Timber Colony: A Historical Geography of Early Nineteenth Century New Brunswick. Graeme Wynn. 248p. 1980. 20.00x (ISBN 0-8020-5513-3); pap. 7.50 (ISBN 0-8020-6407-8). U of Toronto Pr.

Timber Economy of Puritan New England. Charles F. Carroll. LC 73-7122. (Illus.). 221p. 1973. 12.50 (ISBN 0-87057-142-7, Pub. by Brown U Pr). Univ Pr of New England.

Timber-Frame House in England. Trudy West. (Illus.). Date not set. 8.95 (ISBN 0-8038-0245-5). Hastings.

Timber Frame Raising. Stewart Elliot. LC 79-84581. 129p. (Orig.). 1979. pap. 9.95 (ISBN 0-932302-01-7). Brick Hse Pub.

Timber: Its Structure, Properties, & Utilization. 6th ed. H. E. Desch. 416p. (Orig.). 1980. pap. text ed. 24.95x (ISBN 0-917304-62-4, Pub. by Timber Press). Intl Schol Bk Serv.

Timber Piles & Construction Timbers. Compiled by American Society of Civil Engineers. (Manual & Report on Engineering Practice Ser.: No. 17). 48p. 1953. pap. text ed. 3.00 (ISBN 0-87262-208-8). Am Soc Civil Eng.

Timber Supply, Land Allocation, & Economic Efficiency. William F. Hyde. LC 80-8021. (Illus.). 248p. 1980. text ed. 19.00x (ISBN 0-8018-2489-3). Johns Hopkins.

Timber Trades Journal Special Issue 1980. (Benn Directories Ser.). 1980. 15.00 (ISBN 0-686-60669-8, Pub by Benn Pubns). Nichols Pub.

Timber Trades Journal Telephone Address Book 1980. (Benn Directories Ser.). 1980. write for info (Pub by Benn Pubns). Nichols Pub.

Timberline Tailings: Tales of Colorado's Ghost Town & Mining Camps. Muriel S. Wolle. LC 76-17740. (Illus.). 337p. 1976. 19.95 (ISBN 0-8040-0739-X). Swallow.

Timbers of the World, Vol. 2. T.R.A.D.A. (Illus.). 1980. text ed. 38.00 (ISBN 0-86095-837-X, Construction Pr). Longman.

Timbul Gulch Trail. Max Brand. 224p. (Orig.). 1981. pap. 1.95 (ISBN 0-446-90312-4). Warner Bks.

Time. Robert Claiborne & Samuel Goudsmit. LC 66-28543. (Life Science Library). (Illus.). (gr. 5 up). 1966. PLB 8.97 o.p. (ISBN 0-8094-0478-8, Pub. by Time-Life). Silver.

Time. rev. ed. Harlan Wade. LC 78-26771. (Book About Ser.). (Illus.). (gr. k-3). 1979. PLB 7.30 (ISBN 0-8172-1527-1). Raintree Pubs.

Time. Gillian Youldon. (ps-2). 1980. 3.50 (ISBN 0-531-02128-9, C17); PLB 5.90 (ISBN 0-531-03417-8, C03). Watts.

Time-Ago Lost: More Tales of Jahdu. Virginia Hamilton. LC 72-85187. (Illus.). 96p. (gr. 2-5). 1973. 8.95 (ISBN 0-02-742450-2). Macmillan.

Time-Ago Tales of Jahdu. Virginia Hamilton. LC 70-78089. (Illus.). (gr. 2-5). 1969. 5.95g o.s.i. (ISBN 0-02-742460-X). Macmillan.

Time & Again: A Systematic Analysis of the Foundations of Physics. Stafleu. 1981. 19.95x (ISBN 0-88906-108-4). Radix Bks.

Time & Beyond. Robert B. Ruddell et al. (Pathfinder - Allyn & Bacon Reading Program: Level 20). (gr. 6). 1978. text ed. 9.56 (ISBN 0-205-05230-4, 5452309); tchr's ed. 14.60 (ISBN 0-205-05232-0, 5452325); 3.88. Allyn.

Time & Chance. Marjorie Pegram. 1979. pap. 1.95 (ISBN 0-87508-594-6). Chr Lit.

Time & Clocks. Herta S. Breiter. LC 77-19007. (Read About Science Ser.). (Illus.). (gr. k-3). 1978. PLB 9.95 (ISBN 0-8393-0088-3). Raintree Child.

Time & Clocks: A Description of Ancient & Modern Methods of Measuring Time. Henry H. Cunynghame. LC 77-78127. (Illus.). 1970. Repr. of 1906 ed. 15.00 (ISBN 0-8103-3576-X). Gale.

Time & Free Will. Henri Bergson. (Muirhead Library of Philosophy). 1971. text ed. 20.00x (ISBN 0-04-194002-4). Humanities.

Time & History. Siegfried Herrmann. Tr. by James L. Belvins. LC 80-25323. (Biblical Encounter Ser.). 208p. (Orig.). 1981. pap. 7.95 (ISBN 0-687-42100-4). Abingdon.

Time & Mind in Wordsworth's Poetry. Jeffrey Baker. 216p. 1980. 14.95 (ISBN 0-8143-1655-7). Wayne St U Pr.

Time & Motion Study & Formulas for Wage Incentives. 3rd ed. S. M. Lowry et al. LC 80-12407. 446p. 1981. Repr. of 1940 ed. write for info. (ISBN 0-89874-174-2, Pub. by McGraw). Krieger.

Time & Myth. John S. Dunne. LC 74-32289. 128p. 1975. pap. 3.45 (ISBN 0-268-01828-6). U of Notre Dame Pr.

Time & Social Structure & Other Essays. Meyer Fortes. (Monographs on Social Anthropology Ser: No.40). (Illus.). 1970. text ed. 19.50x (ISBN 0-391-00112-4, Athlone Pr). Humanities.

Time & Space Theatre. Deborah R. Horner. (Illus.). 24p. (gr. 3-7). 1978. pap. 7.95 o.p. (ISBN 0-684-15546-X, ScribJ). Scribner.

Time & Stars. Poul Anderson. 1978. pap. 1.50 o.p. (ISBN 0-425-03621-9, Medallion). Berkley Pub.

Time & the Flowing River. Francois Leydet. 1978. pap. 3.95 (ISBN 0-345-21143-X). Ballantine.

Time & the Highland Maya. Barbara Tedlock. (Illus.). 288p. 1981. 27.50 (ISBN 0-8263-0577-6). U of NM Pr.

Time & the Novel. A. A. Mendilow. 244p. 1972. Repr. of 1952 ed. text ed. 15.00x (ISBN 0-391-00220-1). Humanities.

Time & the Space-Traveller. L. Marder. LC 77-182498. (Illus.). 1974. 9.95x (ISBN 0-8122-7650-7); pap. 4.95x (ISBN 0-8122-1054-9). U of Pa Pr.

Time & Traditions. Bruce G. Trigger. 1978. 15.00x (ISBN 0-231-04548-4). Columbia U Pr.

Time Before Morning: Art & Myth of the Australian Aborigines. Louis A. Allen. LC 75-12812. 1976. 18.95 o.s.i. (ISBN 0-690-00411-7, TYC-T). T Y Crowell.

Time Between the Wars: Armistice to Pearl Harbor. Jonathan Daniels. Ed. by Frank Freidel. LC 78-66523. (The History of the United States Ser.: Vol. 5). 382p. 1979. lib. bdg. 24.00 (ISBN 0-8240-9707-6). Garland Pub.

Time-Binding: The General Theory. Alfred Korzybski. pap. 4.00x (ISBN 0-910780-01-3). Inst Gen Semantics.

Time Cat. Lloyd Alexander. (Illus.). (gr. 2-4). 1975. pap. 1.25 o.s.i. (ISBN 0-380-00195-0, 39560, Camelot). Avon.

Time, Causality & the Quantum Theory, 2 vols. Henry Mehlberg. Tr. by Paul Benecerraf from Fr. Incl. Vol. 1. Essay on the Causal Theory of Time. 299p. lib. bdg. 39.50 (ISBN 90-277-0721-9); pap. 17.00 (ISBN 90-277-1074-0); Vol. 2. Time in a Quantized Universe. 296p. lib. bdg. 34.20 (ISBN 90-277-1075-9); pap. 16.00 (ISBN 90-277-1076-7). (Boston Studies in the Philosophy of Science: No. 19). 1980. Kluwer Boston.

Time Change: An Autobiography. Hope Cooke. 1981. 12.95 (ISBN 0-671-41225-6). S&S.

Time Clock of Death. (Nick Carter Ser.). 1978. pap. 1.75 (ISBN 0-441-81025-X). Charter Bks.

Time-Compressed Speech, 3 vols. Sam Duker. Incl. Vols 1 & 2. An Anthology & Bibliography. 50.00 (ISBN 0-8108-0643-6); Vol. 3. Annotated Bibliography. 10.00 (ISBN 0-8108-0644-4). LC 73-8756. 1974. Set. 50.00 (ISBN 0-685-34676-5). Scarecrow.

Time Dependent Chemical Processes. E. R. Robinson. LC 75-1124. 370p. 1975. 44.95 (ISBN 0-470-72802-7). Halsted Pr.

Time Deposits in Present-Day Commercial Banking. Lawrence L. Crum. LC 64-63739. (U of Fla. Social Sciences Monographs: No. 20). 1963. pap. 3.25 (ISBN 0-8130-0051-3). U Presses Fla.

Time Distortion in Hypnosis. Linn F. Cooper & Milton H. Erickson. (Illus.). 1981. Repr. of 1954 ed. text ed. 18.50x (ISBN 0-89197-967-0). Irvington.

Time Domain Electron Spin Resonance. Larry Kevan. Ed. by Robert N. Schwartz. LC 78-31128. 1979. 37.50 (ISBN 0-471-03814-8, Pub. by Wiley-Interscience). Wiley.

Time Enough. Emily Kimbrough. LC 74-1823. (Illus.). 256p. 1974. 10.00 o.s.i. (ISBN 0-06-012364-8, HarpT). Har-Row.

Time Explorers & the Phoenix & the Carpet. Marie Overton. pap. text ed. 2.50x o.p. (ISBN 0-435-21016-5). Heinemann Ed.

Time for Angels: The Tragicomic History of the League of Nations. Elmer Bendiner. 1975. 12.95 o.p. (ISBN 0-394-48183-6). Knopf.

Time for Clocks. Daphne Trivett & John Trivett. LC 78-4782. (Illus.). (gr. 2-5). 1979. PLB 7.89 (ISBN 0-690-03896-8, TYC-J). T Y Crowell.

Time for Decision, 1776: A Documentary Record. Ed. by Robert L. Scribner & Brent Tarter. LC 72-96023. (Revolutionary Virginia Ser.: The Road to Independence, Vol. VI). 1981. write for info. (ISBN 0-8139-0880-9). U Pr of Va.

Time for Everything. Ray Harrison. 1977. 6.95 o.p. (ISBN 0-533-02907-4). Vantage.

Time for God. Leslie D. Weatherhead. 1981. pap. 1.75 (ISBN 0-687-42113-6). Abingdon.

Time for Learning: A Self-Instructional Handbook for Parents & Teachers of Young Children. Bernice M. Chappel. 144p. 1974. pap. text ed. 5.00x (ISBN 0-89039-059-2). Ann Arbor Pubs.

Time for Love. Kennedy, Eugene C., M.M. LC 75-121952. 1972. pap. 2.45 (ISBN 0-385-09481-7, Im). Doubleday.

Time for Love. Daisy Thomson. 1978. pap. 1.50 o.s.i. (ISBN 0-515-04430-X). Jove Pubns.

Time for Old Magic. May H. Arbuthnot & Mark Taylor. 1970. 11.95x o.p. (ISBN 0-673-05844-1). Scott F.

Time for Pagans. Jack Hoffenberg. 1971. pap. 1.95 (ISBN 0-380-00876-9, 31435). Avon.

Time for Tea. Cecilia H. Hinde. (Illus., Orig.). 1973. pap. 5.95 (ISBN 0-686-24627-6, Pub. by Faber & Faber). Merrimack Bk Serv.

Time for Tenderness. Betty Cavanna. (gr. 7 up). 1962. PLB 7.63 (ISBN 0-688-31625-5). Morrow.

Time for the Stars. Robert A. Heinlein. (Del Rey Bk.). Date not set. pap. 1.95 (ISBN 0-345-29389-4). Ballantine.

Time for Truth. William Simon. 1979. pap. 2.95 (ISBN 0-425-05025-4). Berkley Pub.

Time for Uncle Joe. Nancy Jewell. LC 79-2695. (Illus.). 48p. (gr. k-3). 1981. 8.95 (ISBN 0-06-022843-1, HarpJ); PLB 8.79g (ISBN 0-06-022844-X). Har-Row.

Time for Violence. Anthea Goddard. 1978. 7.95 o.s.i. (ISBN 0-8027-5369-8). Walker & Co.

Time, Form & Style in Boswell's Life of Johnson. David L. Passler. LC 70-151585. 1971. 12.50x o.p. (ISBN 0-300-01427-9). Yale U Pr.

Time Frames: The Meaning of Family Pictures. Michael Lesy. (Illus.). 1980. 20.00 (ISBN 0-394-42456-5); pap. 8.95 (ISBN 0-394-73958-2). Pantheon.

Time Game: Two Views of a Prison. Anthony J. Manocchio & Jimmy Dunn. LC 77-85238. 1977. pap. 8.95x (ISBN 0-8039-0920-9). Sage.

Time In: A Guide to Communication Skills. K. Flachmann. 1973. 8.95 (ISBN 0-201-43031-2); tchrs' guide 4.25 (ISBN 0-201-43032-0, 43032). A-W.

Time in Animal Behaviour. M. Richelle & H. Lejeune. (Illus.). 1980. 51.00 (ISBN 0-08-023754-1); pap. 23.00 (ISBN 0-08-025489-6). Pergamon.

Time in Literature. Hans Meyerhoff. (Library Reprint Ser: No. 6). 1974. 15.75x (ISBN 0-520-00856-1). U of Cal Pr.

Time in Many Places. Nels Olson. 218p. 1980. 9.00 (ISBN 0-87839-036-7). North Star.

Time in New England. Ed. by Nancy Newhall. 1980. 35.00 (ISBN 0-89381-060-6); after dec. 31, 1980 40.00 (ISBN 0-686-65241-X); ltd. ed., 450 copies 175.00 (ISBN 0-89381-061-4). Aperture.

Time Is Money! Tested Tactics That Conserve Time for Top Executives. Ross A. Webber. LC 80-1032. (Illus.). 1980. 10.95 (ISBN 0-02-934030-6). Free Pr.

Time Is Noon. Pearl S. Buck. (John Day Bk.). 1967. 8.95 o.p. (ISBN 0-381-98056-1, A79800, TYC-T). T Y Crowell.

Time Is Now. William Sheldon et al. (gr. 7-12). 1972. pap. text ed. 3.80 (ISBN 0-205-02919-1, 5229197); tchrs'. guide 2.40 (ISBN 0-205-02920-5, 5229200). Allyn.

Time-Lag in Cataloging. S. Elspeth Pope. (Illus.). 1973. 10.00 (ISBN 0-8108-0551-0). Scarecrow.

Time-Life Book of Needlecraft. Time-Life Editors. LC 76-25399. 1976. lib. bdg. 17.70 o.p. (ISBN 0-8094-1938-6). Silver.

Time-Life Gardening Yearbook. Time Life Books Editors. (Encyclopedia of Gardening Ser.). (Illus.). 1978. 11.95 (ISBN 0-685-86572-X). Time-Life.

Time-Life Gardening Yearbook. (Best-Selling Single Titles Ser.). (Illus.). lib. bdg. 11.97 (ISBN 0-686-51033-X). Silver.

Time-Life Holiday Cookbook. Time-Life Books Editors. 1976. 19.95 (ISBN 0-8094-1932-7). Time-Life.

Time Longer Than Rope: A History of the Black Man's Struggle for Freedom in South Africa. 2nd ed. Edward Roux. 1964. pap. 7.95x (ISBN 0-299-03204-3). U of Wis Pr.

Time Machine. George Pal & Jo Mahain. (Orig.). 1981. pap. 2.50 (ISBN 0-440-18632-3). Dell.

Time Machine & the War of the Worlds: A Critical Edition. H. G. Wells. Ed. by Frank D. McConnell. (Illus.). 1977. pap. text ed. 4.95x (ISBN 0-19-502164-9). Oxford U Pr.

Time No Longer. Taylor Caldwell. 1976. pap. 2.75 o.p. (ISBN 0-515-05441-0). Jove Pubns.

Time of Death, Vol. 3. Dobrica Cosic. Tr. by Muriel Heppell. write for info. HarBraceJ.

Time of Hope. C. P. Snow. 1961. lib. rep. ed. 17.50x (ISBN 0-684-15315-7, ScribT). Scribner.

Time of Hope, Time of Despair: Black Texans During Reconstruction. James M. Smallwood. (National University Publications, Ethnic Studies). 1981. 17.50 (ISBN 0-8046-9273-4). Kennikat.

Time of Hunting. Wayne Dodd. LC 75-4779. 128p. (gr. 6 up). 1975. 6.95 (ISBN 0-395-28903-3, Clarion). HM.

Time of Love. Marcel Pagnol. 208p. 1980. 19.95 (ISBN 0-241-10009-7, Pub. by Hamish Hamilton England). David & Charles.

Time of Reckoning. Walter Wager. LC 77-22548. 288p. 1981. pap. 2.75 (ISBN 0-87216-857-3). Playboy Pbks.

Time of Stalin: Portrait of a Tyranny. A. V. O'Seyenko-Antonov. LC 80-8681. (Illus.). 384p. 1981. 15.00 (ISBN 0-06-010148-2, HarpT). Har-Row.

Time of Storm. Marianne Fisher & Gayle Roper. LC 80-69310. 160p. 1981. pap. 5.95 (ISBN 0-915684-82-9). Christian Herald.

Time of the Burning Mask. Deidre Rowan. 1978. pap. 1.50 o.p. (ISBN 0-449-14048-2, GM). Fawcett.

Time of the Doves. Merce Rodoreda. Tr. by David Rosenthall. LC 79-9652. 1980. 8.95 (ISBN 0-8008-7731-4). Taplinger.

Time of the Dragons Shike, Bk. I. Robert Shea. (Orig.). 1981. pap. 2.95 (ISBN 0-515-04874-7). Jove Pubns.

Time of the Emergency. Peter Rand. LC 77-75388. 1977. 6.95 o.p. (ISBN 0-385-07033-0). Doubleday.

Time of the Hedrons. Jack D. Eckstrom. (YA) 5.95 (ISBN 0-685-07461-7, Avalon). Bouregy.

Time of the King & Queen. Susan F. Schaeffer. (Illus.). Date not set. pap. cancelled (ISBN 0-916300-20-X). Gallimaufry.

Time of the Kraken. Jay Williams. LC 77-5696. (YA) 1978. 7.95g o.s.i. (ISBN 0-590-07501-2, Four Winds). Schol Bk Serv.

Time of Transition: The Growth of Families Headed by Women. Heather L. Ross & Isabel V. Sawhill. 1975. 10.00 (ISBN 0-87766-149-9, 12800); pap. 4.95 (ISBN 0-87766-148-0, 12600). Urban Inst.

Time of Trial, Time of Hope: The Negro in America, 1919-1941. Milton Meltzer & August Meier. LC 66-20917. (Illus.). pap. 2.50 o.p. (ISBN 0-385-05978-7, Z8, Zenith). Doubleday.

Time of Triumph & of Sorrow: Spanish Politics During the Reign of Alfonso Xii, Eighteen Seventy-Four to Eighteen Eighty-Five. Earl R. Beck. LC 78-23282. 320p. 1979. 18.95x (ISBN 0-8093-0902-5). S Ill U Pr.

Time of Your Life Is Now. Frank A. Kostyu. 1977. 6.95 (ISBN 0-8164-0375-9). Crossroad NY.

Time Out, Ladies! Dale E. Rogers. (Spire Bk). 1969. 3.95 o.p. (ISBN 0-8007-0317-0). Revell.

Time Out of Mind. Pierre Boulle. LC 66-26792. 1966. 8.95 (ISBN 0-8149-0062-3). Vanguard.

Time Piper. Delia Huddy. LC 78-24339. (gr. 7 up). 1979. 8.50 (ISBN 0-688-80212-5); PLB 8.16 (ISBN 0-688-84212-7). Greenwillow.

Time, Place & Season. Eduard Vala. pap. 4.95 (ISBN 0-933350-15-5). Morse Pr.

Time Research: 1172 Studies. Irving Zelkind & Joseph Sprug. 1974. 10.00 (ISBN 0-8108-0768-8). Scarecrow.

Time-Saving Sermon Outlines. Russell E. Spray. (Sermon Outline Ser.). (Orig.). 1981. pap. 1.45 (ISBN 0-8010-8193-9). Baker Bk.

Time Series Analysis & Forecasting: The Box Jenkins Approach. O. D. Anderson. 168p. 1975. pap. 15.95 (ISBN 0-686-15234-4). Butterworths.

Time Series Analysis, Forecasting & Control. rev. ed. George E. Box & Gwilym Jenkins. LC 76-8713. 500p. 1976. text ed. 38.50x (ISBN 0-8162-1104-3). Holden-Day.

Time Series: Data Analysis & Theory. enl. ed. David R. Brillinger. (Illus.). 552p. 1980. Repr. of 1975 ed. text ed. 25.00 (ISBN 0-8162-1150-7); foreign ed. 29.95 (ISBN 0-686-69028-1). Holden-Day.

Time, Space & Circumstance. rev. ed. Roy E. Davis. LC 73-77614. 1973. 4.95 (ISBN 0-8119-0399-0). Fell.

Time, Space & Designs for Actors. Maxine Klein. 1975. pap. text ed. 12.95 (ISBN 0-395-18612-9). HM.

Time, Space & Structure in King Lear. Mathilda M. Hills. (Salzburg Studies in English Literature, Jacobean Drama Studies: No. 64). (Orig.). 1976. pap. text ed. 25.00x (ISBN 0-391-01410-2). Humanities.

Time: Stages 1 & 2 & Background. Roy Richards. LC 77-82997. (Science 5-13 Ser.). (Illus.). 1977. pap. text ed. 8.25 (ISBN 0-356-04008-9). Raintree Child.

Time Structure in Drama, Goethe's Storm und Drgng Plays. Walter K. Stewart. (Amsterdamer Publikationen Zur Sprache und Literatur: No. 35). 1978. pap. text ed. 34.50x (ISBN 90-6203-682-1). Humanities.

Time Study. Tony A. Jay. (Illus.). 1981. 17.50 (ISBN 0-7137-1085-3, Pub. by Blandford Pr England); pap. 9.95 (ISBN 0-7137-1126-4). Sterling.

Time Study Manual for the Textile Industry. rev. ed. N. L. Enrick. 1981. write for info. (ISBN 0-89874-044-4). Krieger.

Time, Tense, & the Verb: A Study in Theoretical & Applied Linguistics with Particular Attention to Spanish. William E. Bull. (California Library Reprint Series: No. 5). 1971. 15.00x (ISBN 0-520-00189-3). U of Cal Pr.

Time the Boat Came Back. Bonnie Campbell. (Hello World Ser.). 1976. pap. 1.65 (ISBN 0-8163-0268-5, 20475-0). Pacific Pr Pub Assn.

Time, Tide & Tempest: A Study of Shakespeare's Romances. Douglas L. Peterson. LC 72-94155. 1973. 10.00 (ISBN 0-87328-058-X). Huntington Lib.

Time to Be Human. John H. Griffin. LC 76-47468. (Illus.). (gr. 5 up). 1977. 8.95 (ISBN 0-02-737200-6). Macmillan.

Time to Be Myself. Clive Payne. 4.50 o.p. (ISBN 0-8062-1203-9). Carlton.

Time to Care. Nancy Grant. (Royal College of Nursing Research Ser.). 186p. 1980. pap. text ed. 10.00x (ISBN 0-443-02330-1). Churchill.

Time to Change & Other Stories. Mack Jameson & Al Nist. Ed. by Winifred H. Roderman. (Read on - Write on Ser.). (Illus.). (gr. 7-12). 1981. pap. text ed. 2.85 (ISBN 0-915510-56-1). Janus Bks.

Time to Choose: America's Energy Future. Energy Policy Project Staff. LC 74-14787. (Ford's Foundation's Energy Policy Project Ser.). 1974. 17.50 (ISBN 0-88410-023-5); pap. text ed. 9.95 (ISBN 0-88410-024-3). Ballinger Pub.

Time to Destroy - to Discover. Lawrence Fixel. 1972. regular ed 1.50 (ISBN 0-915572-58-3); ltd. signed, numbered ed 3.00 (ISBN 0-915572-58-3). Panjandrum.

Time to Die. Glenn M. Vernon. 1977. 7.50 (ISBN 0-8191-0126-5). U Pr of Amer.

Time to Die. Tom Wicker. (Illus.). 448p. Date not set. pap. 2.50 (ISBN 0-345-28993-5). Ballantine.

Time to Die & a Time to Live: Two Plays. Eric Bentley. 1970. pap. 11.40 (ISBN 0-686-66227-X, ST00047). Grove.

Time to Enjoy: The Pleasures of Aging. Lilliam Dangott & Richard Kalish. (Illus.). 1978. 11.95 (ISBN 0-13-921692-8, Spec); pap. 4.95 (ISBN 0-13-921684-7). P-H.

Time to Fantasize. May Kapela. LC 80-69294. (Illus.). 102p. (Orig.). 1980. pap. 4.50x (ISBN 0-9603118-7-4). Davenport.

Time to Get Out of the Bath, Shirley. John Burningham. LC 76-58503. (Illus.). (gr. k-2). 1978. 8.95 (ISBN 0-690-01378-7, TYC-J); PLB 8.79 (ISBN 0-690-01379-5). T Y Crowell.

Time to Grow. Gladis DePree & Gordon DePree. 112p. (Orig.). 1981. pap. 3.95 (ISBN 0-310-23681-9). Zondervan.

Time to Heal. Ford. pap. 2.95 (ISBN 0-425-04693-1). Berkley Pub.

Time to Keep: The Tasha Tudor Book of Holidays. Tasha Tudor. LC 77-9067. (Illus.). (gr. 4-8). 1977. 6.95 (ISBN 0-528-82019-2); PLB 6.97 o.s.i. Rand.

Time to Mourn: Judaism and the Psychology of Bereavement. Jack D. Spiro. 1968. 4.95 o.p. (ISBN 0-8197-0185-8). Bloch.

Time to Pause & Reflect. Derald E. Brown. 1981. 4.95 (ISBN 0-8062-1632-8). Carlton.

Time to Reap: The Middle Age of Women in Five Israeli Subcultures. Nancy Datan et al. LC 80-26776. 176p. 1981. text ed. 14.00x (ISBN 0-8018-2516-4). Johns Hopkins.

Time to Seek: An Anthology of Contemporary Jewish American Poets. Ed. by Samuel H. Joseloff. 1975. 5.00 (ISBN 0-8074-0199-4, 168000); tchrs'. guide 5.00 (ISBN 0-685-55043-5, 208001). UAHC.

Time to Sing. Frankie Bush. 1978. pap. 2.95 (ISBN 0-89728-007-5). Omega Pubns OR.

Time to Sleep Book. Kathleen Meyer. (Illus.). (gr. k-2). 1978. PLB 5.38 (ISBN 0-307-68889-5, Golden Pr). Western Pub.

Time to Spare in Victorian England. John Lowerson & John Myerscough. 1977. text ed. 13.00x (ISBN 0-391-00744-0). Humanities.

Time to Take Sides. Sharlya Gold. LC 76-8265. (gr. 5 up). 1976. 6.95 (ISBN 0-395-28905-X, Clarion). HM.

Time Toward Home: The American Experience As Revelation. Richard Neuhaus. 250p. 1975. 9.50 (ISBN 0-8164-0272-8). Crossroad NY.

Time Trap. R. Alec Mackenzie. LC 72-82874. 208p. 1972. 11.95 (ISBN 0-8144-5308-2). Am Mgmt.

Time Trilogy: A Wrinkle in Time; A Wind in the Door; A Swiftly Moving Planet, 3 vols. Madeleine L'Engle. (gr. 4 up). 1979. Boxed Set. 23.85 (ISBN 0-374-37592-5). FS&G.

Time Trip. Lee Mountain. (Attention Span Ser). (Illus., Orig.). (gr. 6-10). 1978. pap. text ed. 3.20x (ISBN 0-89061-145-9, 581). Jamestown Pubs.

Time, Uncertainty & Disequilibrium: Exploration of Austrian Themes. Ed. by Mario J. Rizzo. LC 78-13872. 1979. 21.00 (ISBN 0-669-02698-0). Lexington Bks.

Time Was Away: The World of Louis MacNeice. Ed. by Terence Brown & Alec Reid. (Illus.). 151p. 1974. text ed. 12.00x (ISBN 0-85105-237-1, Dolmen Pr). Humanities.

Time, Work, & Culture in the Middle Ages. Jacques Le Goff. Tr. by Arthur Goldhammer. LC 79-25400. 1980. lib. bdg. 22.50x (ISBN 0-226-47080-6). U of Chicago Pr.

Timed Readings. Edward Spargo et al. (Illus., Orig.). (gr. 4-5). 1979. Bk. 1, 120p. pap. text ed. 2.80 (ISBN 0-89061-198-X, 801); Bk. 2, 120p. pap. text ed. 2.80 (ISBN 0-89061-199-8, 802). Jamestown Pubs.

Timeless Moment. D. Bruce Lockerbie. LC 80-65332. 126p. 1980. pap. 3.95 (ISBN 0-89107-181-4, Cornerstone Bks). Good News.

Timeless Moment: Creativity & the Christian Faith. D. Bruce Lockerbie. 1980. pap. 3.95 (ISBN 0-89107-181-4). Good News.

Timeless Spring. Tr. by Thomas Cleary from Japanese. 176p. 1980. pap. 7.95 (ISBN 0-8348-0148-5, Pub. by John Weatherhill Inc Japan). C E Tuttle.

Timeless Truth for Twentieth Century Times. Fred M. Barlow. 123p. 1970. 3.25 (ISBN 0-87398-838-8, Pub. by Bibl Evang Pr). Sword of Lord.

Times & Locations. Michael Smith. 1972. text ed. 5.00x (ISBN 0-85105-219-3, Dolmen Pr). Humanities.

Times Change. Ron Renauld. 288p. (Orig.). 1981. pap. 2.50 (ISBN 0-523-41107-3). Pinnacle Bks.

Time's Fool. Grant Carrington. LC 79-8558. (Science Fiction Ser.). 192p. 1981. 9.95 (ISBN 0-385-15288-4). Doubleday.

Times Four: The Short Story in Depth. Ed. by Donald S. Heines. (Orig.). 1968. pap. text ed. 9.95 (ISBN 0-13-921809-2). P-H.

Times Guide to the European Parliament. Ed. by David Wood & Alan Wood. (Illus.). 360p. 1980. 45.00x (ISBN 0-930466-30-6). Meckler Bks.

Times Guide to the House of Commons. (Illus.). 350p. 1980. 45.00x (ISBN 0-930466-29-2). Meckler Bks.
Times of Christ. L. A. Muirhead. (Handbooks for Bible Classes). 179p. 1907. text ed. 3.50 (ISBN 0-567-08133-8). Attic Pr.
Times of Life. Huub Oosterhuis. Tr. by N. D. Smith from Dutch. LC 79-89653. (Orig.). 1980. pap. 3.95 (ISBN 0-8091-2245-6). Paulist Pr.
Times One Thousand, Nineteen Eighty to Nineteen Eighty One. 360p. 1980. 47.50x (ISBN 0-930466-31-4). Meckler Bks.
Times, Places & Persons: Aspects of the History of Epidemiology. Abraham M. Litlienfeld. LC 80-8090. (Henry F. Sigerist Supplements to the Bulletin of the History of Medicine, New Ser.: No. 4). 160p. 1980. pap. text ed. 9.00x (ISBN 0-8018-2425-7). Johns Hopkins.
Times, Places & Persons: Aspects of the History of Epidemiology. Abraham M. Litlienfeld. LC 80-8090. (Henry E. Sigerist Supplements to the Bulletin of the History of Medicine, New Ser.: No. 4). 160p. pap. text ed. 9.00x (ISBN 0-8018-2425-7). Johns Hopkins.
Times, Spaces & Places: A Chronogeographic Perspective. Don Parkes & Nigel Thrift. 1980. 64.75 (ISBN 0-471-27616-2, Pub. by Wiley-Interscience). Wiley.
Times to Treasure. Alma Barkman. 96p. 1980. text ed. 9.95 (ISBN 0-686-66054-4). Moody.
Timescales in Geomorphology. R. A. Cullingford et al. LC 79-40517. 1980. 77.95 (ISBN 0-471-27600-6, Pub. by Wiley-Interscience). Wiley.
Timescoop. John Brunner. 1981. pap. 2.25 (ISBN 0-440-18916-0). Dell.
Timesharing. Stuart M. Bloch & William B. Ingersoll. LC 77-88799. (Illus.). 136p. 1977. pap. text ed. 19.50 (ISBN 0-87420-575-1). Urban Land.
Timetable. James M. Bryant. (Illus.). 1981. 20.00 (ISBN 0-686-28942-0). J M Bryant.
Timetables of American History. Laurence Urdang. 1981. 24.95 (ISBN 0-686-63196-X). S&S.
Timetables: Structuring the Passage of Time in Hospital Treatment & Other Careers. Julius A. Roth. (Orig.). 1963. pap. 4.95 (ISBN 0-672-60851-0). Bobbs.
Timetabling & Organization in Secondary Schools. Norman Lawrie & Helen Veitch. (General Ser.). 160p. 1975. pap. text ed. 13.75x (ISBN 0-85633-057-4, NFER). Humanities.
Timetabling Models for Secondary Schools: A Practical Handbook. F. B. Salt. (General Ser.). (Illus.). 1978. pap. text ed. 20.75x (ISBN 0-85633-138-4, NFER). Humanities.
Timetouchers. rev. ed. Theodore L. Harris et al. (Keys to Reading Ser.). (Illus.). 176p. (gr. 8). 1975. pap. text ed. 3.99 (ISBN 0-87892-464-7); 9.90 (ISBN 0-87892-467-1); catalog student guide 3.96 (ISBN 0-87892-468-X); catalog tchr's ed. 3.96 (ISBN 0-87892-469-8); 19.53 (ISBN 0-87892-499-X). Economy Co.
Timing for Animation. Harold Whitaker & John Halas. LC 80-41303. (Illus.). 144p. 1981. 25.00 (ISBN 0-240-50871-8). Focal Pr.
Timing Space & Spacing Time, 3 vols. Ed. by Tommy Carlstein et al. Incl. Vol. I. Making Sense of Time. 24.95 (ISBN 0-470-26511-6); Vol. II. Human Activity & Time Geography. 39.95 (ISBN 0-470-26513-2); Vol. III. Time & Regional Dynamics. 24.95 (ISBN 0-470-26512-4). 1979. Halsted Pr.
Timings for Typing. Carl W. Salser. 1969. 3.95 (ISBN 0-89420-013-5, 296955). Natl Book.
Timoleon & the Revival of Greek Cicily, 344-317 BC. R J. Talbert. 248p. 1974. 19.95 (ISBN 0-521-20419-4). Cambridge U Pr.
Timon of Athens. William Shakespeare. Ed. by Arthur Quiller-Couch et al. (New Shakespeare Ser). 23.95 (ISBN 0-521-07558-0); pap. 4.50x (ISBN 0-521-09501-8). Cambridge U Pr.
Timothy & Gramps. Ron Brooks. LC 78-17389. (gr. k-2). 1979. 7.95 (ISBN 0-87888-139-5). Bradbury Pr.
Timothy & the Blanket Fairy. Nita Clarke. (gr. k-6). 1981. 6.95 (ISBN 0-933184-06-9); pap. 4.95 (ISBN 0-933184-16-6). Flame Intl.
Timothy & Titus. Becker. pap. 1.75 (ISBN 0-8024-2646-8). Moody.
Timothy & Titus. Irving Jensen. pap. 2.25 (ISBN 0-8024-1054-5). Moody.
Timothy Goes to School. Rosemary Wells. LC 80-20785. (Illus.). 32p. (ps-2). 1981. 7.50 (ISBN 0-8037-8948-3); PLB 7.28 (ISBN 0-8037-8949-1). Dial.
Timothy Pickering & American Diplomacy 1795-1800. Gerard H. Clarfield. LC 69-13333. 1969. 6.00x o.p. (ISBN 0-8262-8414-0). U of Mo Pr.
Timothy Pickering As the Leader of New England Federalism, 1800-1815. Hervey Putnam Prentiss. LC 71-124882. (American Scene Ser). (Illus.). 118p. 1972. Repr. of 1934 ed. lib. bdg. 17.50 (ISBN 0-306-71052-8). Da Capo.
Timothy, Titus & Philemon. H. A. Ironside. Date not set. 5.95 (ISBN 0-87213-391-5). Loizeaux.
Timothy Todd's Good Things Are Gone. Anne Rockwell. LC 78-6299. (Ready-to-Read Ser.). (Illus.). (gr. 1-4). 1978. 7.95 (ISBN 0-02-777600-X, 77760). Macmillan.
Timothy Turtle. Alice V. Davis. LC 40-32634. (Illus.). (gr. k-3). 1940. 5.95 o.p. (ISBN 0-15-288368-1, HJ). HarBraceJ.
Tim's Friend Towser. Edward Ardizzone. (Illus.). 48p. (ps-3). 1981. pap. 4.95 (ISBN 0-19-272112-7). Oxford U Pr.
Tin Cans. Theodore Roscoe. (War Books). 1979. pap. 2.50 o.p. (ISBN 0-685-92502-1, 13037-4). Bantam.
Tin Cans & Trash Recovery: Saving Energy Through Utilizing Municipal Ferrous Waste. 1980. pap. 2.00. Tech Info Proj.
Tin Drum. Gunter Grass. Tr. by Ralph Manheim. 1971. pap. 3.95 (ISBN 0-394-70300-6, V-300, Vin). Random.
Tin-Glaze Pottery. Alan Craiger-Smith. 1973. 58.00 (ISBN 0-571-09349-3, Pub. by Faber & Faber). Merrimack Bk Serv.
Tin Lizzie: A Model-Making Book. Frank Ross, Jr. LC 80-14482. (Illus.). (gr. 5 up). 1980. 8.95 (ISBN 0-688-41931-3); PLB 8.59 (ISBN 0-688-51931-8). Lothrop.
Tin Pan Alley. Isaac Goldberg. LC 60-63364. (Illus.). 1961. pap. 3.95 (ISBN 0-8044-6196-1). Ungar.
Tin: The Working of a Commodity Agreement. William Fox Mining Journal Books Ltd. 418p. 1980. 21.00x (ISBN 0-900117-05-2, Pub. by Mining Journal England). State Mutual Bk.
Tin Woodman of Oz. L. Frank Baum. 272p. 1981. pap. 2.25 (ISBN 0-345-28234-5, Del Rey). Ballantine.
Tina. Bruce Whiteley. 192p. 1979. 9.95 (ISBN 0-679-51378-7). McKay.
Tina & David. Joan Tate. (gr. 7-12). 1976. pap. 1.25 o.p. (ISBN 0-590-01656-3, Schol Pap). Schol Bk Serv.
Tina Gogo. Judie Angel. (gr. 7-12). 1980. pap. 1.50 (ISBN 0-440-98738-5, LFL). Dell.
Tina Gogo. Judie Angell. LC 77-16439. (gr. 5 up). 1978. 8.95 (ISBN 0-87888-132-8). Bradbury Pr.
Tina's Reluctant Friend. Hilda Stahl. (gr. 4-7). 1981. pap. 2.25 (ISBN 0-8423-7216-4). Tyndale.
Tinfish Run. Ronald Bassett. LC 76-50167. 1977. 8.95 o.s.i. (ISBN 0-06-010233-0, HarpT). Har-Row.
Tinker Tailor Soldier Sailor. Maureen Roffey & Bernard Lodge. (Illus.). 1978. 6.95 (ISBN 0-370-01805-2, Pub. by Chatto Bodley Jonathan). Merrimack Bk Serv.
Tinker Tales. Mary Dawson. LC 73-3496. (Humpty Dumpty Bk.). (Illus.). 72p. (gr. k-3). 1973. 5.95 o.s.i. (ISBN 0-8193-0698-3, Four Winds); PLB 5.41 o.s.i. (ISBN 0-8193-0699-1). Schol Bk Serv.
Tinkerbell Is a Ding-a-Ling. Roy Doty. LC 79-6973. (Illus.). (gr. 4-6). 1980. 4.95a (ISBN 0-385-13490-8); PLB 4.95 (ISBN 0-385-13491-6). Doubleday.
Tinner's Quest. Violet Bibby. (gr. 6-8). 1978. 10.95 (ISBN 0-571-11029-0, Pub. by Faber & Faber). Merrimack Bk Serv.
Tinonc: Son of the Cajun Teche. Robert L. Olivier. (Illus.). 1974. 5.95 (ISBN 0-88289-054-9). Pelican.
Tins & Other Stories. Peter Cowan. (Paperback Prose Ser.). 124p. 1973. 7.25x o.s.i. (ISBN 0-7022-0824-8); pap. 3.50x o.s.i. (ISBN 0-7022-0823-X). U of Queensland Pr.
Tinsel. William Goldman. 1980. pap. 2.75 o.s.i. (ISBN 0-440-18735-4). Dell.
Tinsmiths of Connecticut. Shirleys S. Devoe. (Illus.). 1968. 15.00x (ISBN 0-686-26749-4). Conn Hist Soc.
Tinted Photograph. Howard M. Crilly. 1981. 10.95 (ISBN 0-533-04653-X). Vantage.
Tiny & Tony. Sy Reit. (Golden Book of Picture Postcards Ser.). (Illus.). (ps-4). 1977. pap. 0.95 o.p. (ISBN 0-307-11103-2, Golden Pr). Western Pub.
Tiny Ant Who Scared a Horned Toad. Goldie B. Despain. (Illus.). (ps-3). 1970. 4.25 o.p. (ISBN 0-8313-0029-9); PLB 6.19 o.p. (ISBN 0-685-13787-2). Lantern.
Tiny Giant: Nate Archibald. Jeff Greenfield. LC 75-42035. (Sports Profiles Ser.). (Illus.). 48p. (gr. 4-11). 1976. PLB 8.50 (ISBN 0-8172-0124-6). Raintree Pubs.
Tiny Golden Library: A Dozen Animal Nonsense Tales. Dororthy Kunhardt. (Illus.). 24p. (gr. 4-8). 1980. 6.95 (ISBN 0-307-13618-3, Golden Pr). Western Pub.
Tiny Little Tow Truck. Alvera. (Illus.). 1980. 5.00 (ISBN 0-682-49542-5). Exposition.
Tiny Mouse. Gary L. Wheeler & David M. Strang. 1980. pap. 2.75 (ISBN 0-937172-10-3). JLJ Pubs.
Tiny Mouse. Gary L. Wheeler & David M. Strang. (Orig.). 1980. pap. 2.75 (ISBN 0-937172-10-3). JLJ Pubs.
Tiny Planets: Asteroids of Our Solar System. David Knight. (Illus.). 96p. (gr. 3-7). 1973. PLB 6.96 (ISBN 0-688-30072-3). Morrow.
Tiny, Tawny Kitten. Barbara S. Hazen. (Illus.). (ps-2). 1969. PLB 5.00 (ISBN 0-307-60590-6, Golden Pr). Western Pub.
Tippy. Hazel Krantz. LC 68-14335. (gr. 7-10). 6.95 (ISBN 0-8149-0342-8). Vanguard.
Tips & Notes for the Artist, Bk. 1. Margy L. Elspass. Ed. by Ralph W. Elspass. LC 79-93059. (Illus.). 100p. 1980. pap. 10.00 (ISBN 0-935798-00-5). RaMar.
Tips for You: Thirty-One Ways to Please Customers & Increase Your Earning Power. John F. Bergmann. LC 79-14759. 1979. pap. 4.95 (ISBN 0-8436-2155-9); tips for your poster set 19.95 (ISBN 0-686-66175-3). CBI Pub.
Tips (to Improve Personal Study Skills) New York Personnel & Guidance Assn. LC 68-8175. (Illus.). 60p. 1968. pap. 2.40 (ISBN 0-8273-0370-X). Delmar.
Tiptoes. (Ladybird Stories Ser.). (Illus., Arabic.). 2.50x (ISBN 0-686-53066-7). Intl Bk Ctr.
Tirso De Molina. Margaret Wilson. (World Authors Ser.: No. 445). 1977. lib. bdg. 12.50 (ISBN 0-8057-6281-7). Twayne.
Tirso De Molina & the Drama of the Counter Reformation. Henry W. Sullivan. 1976. pap. text ed. 25.75x (ISBN 90-6203-399-7). Humanities.
Tiruray-English Lexicon. Stuart A. Schlegel. (U. C. Publ. in Linguistics: Vol. 67). 1971. pap. 10.00x (ISBN 0-520-09359-3). U of Cal Pr.
Tiruray Justice: Traditional Tiruray Law & Morality. Stuart A. Schlegel. LC 72-107660. 1970. 17.50x (ISBN 0-520-01686-6). U of Cal Pr.
Tis Pity She's a Whore. John Ford. Ed. by N. W. Bawcutt. LC 65-15339. (Regents Renaissance Drama Ser). 1966. 7.50x o.p. (ISBN 0-8032-0262-8); pap. 3.50x (ISBN 0-8032-5261-7, BB 215, Bison). U of Nebr Pr.
Tissue Adhesives in Surgery. Teruo Matsumoto. 1972. 30.00 o.p. (ISBN 0-87488-756-9). Med Exam.
Tissue Culture in Medical Research (II) Second International Symposium on Tissue Culture in Medical Research, 1-3 April 1980, Cardiff, Wales. Ed. by R. J. Richards & K. T. Rajan. (Illus.). 281p. 1980. 48.00 (ISBN 0-08-025924-3). Pergamon.
Tissue Culture in Neurobiology. Ed. by Ezio Giacobini et al. 536p. 1980. text ed. 52.00 (ISBN 0-89004-461-9). Raven.
Tissue Culture Methods for Plant Pathologists: Organized by the British Plant Pathologists, Vol. 2. D. S. Ingram & J. P. Helgeson. 250p. 1981. 47.50 (ISBN 0-470-27048-9). Halsted Pr.
Tissue Culture Techniques. Luccio Nuzzolo & Augusto Vellucci. LC 67-26015. (Illus.). 284p. 1981. 22.50 (ISBN 0-87527-117-0). Green.
Tissue Fluid Pressure & Composition. Alan R. Hargens. (Illus.). 282p. 1980. lib. bdg. 34.00 (ISBN 0-683-03891-5). Williams & Wilkins.
Tissue Heart Values. M. I. Ionescu. 112p. 1979. text ed. 64.95 (ISBN 0-407-00139-5). Butterworths.
Tissue Interactions & Development. Norman K. Wessells. LC 76-42696. 1977. pap. text ed. 12.95 (ISBN 0-8053-9620-9). Benjamin-Cummings.
Tissue Management in Restorative Dentistry. Ed. by William F. Malone. 230p. 1981. 22.50 (ISBN 0-88416-154-4). PSG Pub.
Tissue Paper Creations. Chester J. Alkema. LC 73-83454. (Little Craft Book Ser.). (Illus.). 48p. (gr. 3-8). 1973. 5.95 (ISBN 0-8069-5288-1); PLB 6.69 (ISBN 0-8069-5289-X). Sterling.
Tissues & Organs: A Text-Atlas of Scanning Electron Microscopy. Richard G. Kessel & Randy H. Kardon. LC 78-23886. (Illus.). 1979. text ed. 34.95x (ISBN 0-7167-0091-3); pap. text ed. 16.95x (ISBN 0-7167-0090-5); slides avail. (ISBN 0-7167-1231-8). W H Freeman.
Tissues of the Body. 6th ed. W. E. Clark. (Illus.). 1977. pap. text ed. 18.95x (ISBN 0-19-857163-1). Oxford U Pr.
Titan. John Varley. 1979. 9.95 o.p. (ISBN 0-425-04468-8). Berkley Pub.
Titan, His Life & Times: With Some Account of His Family, 2 vols. J. A. Crowe & G. B. Cavalcaselle. Ed. by Sydney J. Freedberg. LC 77-19373. (Connoisseurship Criticism & Art History Ser.: Vol. 8). 1032p. 1979. lib. bdg. 80.00 (ISBN 0-8240-3265-9). Garland Pub.
Titanic, the Psychic & the Sea. Rustie Brown. LC 80-70551. (Illus.). 176p. 1981. 12.95 (ISBN 0-9605278-0-X). Blue Harbor.
Titanium & Titanium Alloys: Scientific & Technological Aspects, 3 vols. Ed. by Williams & Belov. 1981. 195.00 (ISBN 0-306-40191-6, Plenum Pr). Plenum Pub.
Titanium, Its Occurrence, Chemistry & Technology. 2nd ed. Jelks Barksdale. 1966. 43.50 (ISBN 0-8260-0725-2, Pub. by Wiley-Interscience). Wiley.
Titanotheres of Ancient Wyoming, Dakota, & Nebraska. Department of the Interior, U. S. Geologicaal Survey, Monograph & Henry F. Osborn. Ed. by Stephen J. Gould. LC 79-83341. (History of Paleontology Ser.: 55 2vols.). (Illus.). 1980. Repr. of 1929 ed. Set. lib. bdg. 195.00x (ISBN 0-405-12729-4); lib. bdg. 97.50 ea. Vol. 1 (ISBN 0-405-12730-8). Vol. 2 (ISBN 0-405-12731-6). Arno.
Titans. John Jakes. (Kent Family Chronicle: No. 3). (Orig.). 1976. pap. 2.95 (ISBN 0-515-05891-2). Jove Pubns.
Titch. Pat Hutchins. LC 77-146622. (Illus.). (gr. k-3). 1971. 8.95g (ISBN 0-02-745880-6). Macmillan.
Tithe Proctor: Being a Tale of the Tithe Rebellion in Ireland. William Carleton. Ed. by Robert L. Wolff. (Ireland Nineteenth Century Proctor Fiction - Ser. Two: Vol. 43). 304p. 1979. lib. bdg. 32.00 (ISBN 0-8240-3492-9). Garland Pub.
Tithe Surveys of England & Wales. Roger Kain & Hugh Prince. (Studies in Historical Geography). (Illus.). Date not set. cancelled (ISBN 0-208-01726-7, Archon). Shoe String. Postponed.
Titian. David Rosand. (Library of Great Painters). (Illus.). 1978. 35.00 (ISBN 0-8109-1654-1). Abrams.
Titian & the Venetian Woodcut. David Rosand & Michelangelo Muraro. LC 75-25621. (Illus.). 1976. pap. 14.95 (ISBN 0-88397-067-8). Intl Exhibit Foun.
Titian's Assistants During the Later Years. M. Roy Fisher. LC 76-23618. (Outstanding Dissertations in the Fine Arts Ser.). 1977. lib. bdg. 56.00x (ISBN 0-8240-2689-6). Garland Pub.
Titius-Bode Law of Planetary Distance. M. Nieto. 173p. 1972. text ed. 25.00 (ISBN 0-08-016784-5). Pergamon.
Title Derivative Indexing Techniques: A Comparative Study. Hilda Feinberg. LC 73-2671. 1973. 20.50 (ISBN 0-8108-0602-9). Scarecrow.
Title Guide to the Talkies, 2 Vols. Richard B. Dimmitt. LC 65-13556. 1965. Set. 60.00 (ISBN 0-8108-0171-X). Scarecrow.
Title Guide to the Talkies, Nineteen Sixty-Four to Nineteen Seventy-Four. Andrew A. Aros. LC 76-40451. 1977. 15.00 (ISBN 0-8108-0976-1). Scarecrow.
Titles in Series: A Handbook for Librarians & Students, 4 vols. 3rd ed. Eleanora A. Baer. LC 78-14452. 1978. Set. 99.50 (ISBN 0-8108-1043-3). Scarecrow.
Titmice of the British Isles. John G. Barnes. LC 74-33156. (Illus.). 224p. 1975. 15.95 (ISBN 0-7153-6955-5). David & Charles.
Tito: A Pictorial Biography. Fitzroy Maclean. LC 80-18683. (Illus.). 128p. 1980. 14.95 (ISBN 0-07-044671-7); pap. 9.95 (ISBN 0-07-044660-1). McGraw.
Tito & His Family. L. Middleton. 4.00 o.p. (ISBN 0-8062-1055-9). Carlton.
Tito: The Story from Inside. Milovan Djilas. 1980. 9.95 (ISBN 0-686-68552-0). HarBraceJ.
Tito's Private Life. Ivo Eterovic. (Illus.). 1978. 19.95 (ISBN 0-8467-0472-2, Pub. by Two Continents). Hippocrene Bks.
Tito's Yugoslavia. Sir Duncan Wilson. LC 79-11009. 1980. 29.95 (ISBN 0-521-22655-4). Cambridge U Pr.
Titters: The First Collection of Humor by Women. Deanne Stillman & Anne Beatts. (Illus.). 1976. 14.95 o.s.i. (ISBN 0-02-614680-0). Macmillan.
Titters: The First Collection of Humor by Women. Deanne Stillman & Anne Beatts. (Illus.). 1976. pap. 7.95 o.s.i. (ISBN 0-02-040700-9, Collier). Macmillan.
Titus Andronicus. William Shakespeare. Ed. by Arthur Quiller-Couch et al. LC 68-133497. (New Shakespeare Ser). 1968. 23.95 (ISBN 0-521-07559-9); pap. 4.50x (ISBN 0-521-09502-6). Cambridge U Pr.
Titus Andronicus. William Shakespeare. Ed. by Gustav Cross. (Shakespeare Ser.). 1966. pap. 2.95 (ISBN 0-14-071433-2, Pelican). Penguin.
Titus of Rome. Alice C. Desmond. LC 75-38353. (Illus.). (gr. 7). 1976. 5.95 (ISBN 0-396-07299-2). Dodd.
Tiv People. 2nd ed. R. C. Abraham. (Illus.). 1968. text ed. 15.00x o.p. (ISBN 0-391-02060-9). Humanities.
Tlingit Indians: Results of a Trip to the Northwest Coast of America & the Bering Straits. Aurel Krause. Tr. by Erna Gunther. LC 56-3408. (American Ethnological Society Monographs: No. 26). (Illus.). 320p. 1970. 9.95 o.p. (ISBN 0-295-73971-1); pap. 6.95 (ISBN 0-295-95075-7, WP58). U of Wash Pr.
TM: An Alphabetical Guide to the Transcendental Meditation Program. Nat Goldhaber & Denise Denniston. (Illus.). 1976. pap. 3.95 (ISBN 0-345-24096-0). Ballantine.
TM & Cult Mania. Michael A. Persinger et al. 208p. 1980. 10.95 (ISBN 0-8158-0392-3). Chris Mass.

TM Book: How to Enjoy the Rest of Your Life. Denise Denniston & Peter McWilliams. 1975. pap. 1.95 o.s.i. (ISBN 0-446-89123-1). Warner Bks.

TM: Discovering Inner Energy & Overcoming Stress. Harold H. Bloomfield et al. 1975. 8.95 o.s.i. (ISBN 0-440-06048-6). Delacorte.

TM or CM? Lynn Sauls. 1978. pap. 0.75 (ISBN 0-8163-0298-7, 20480-0). Pacific Pr Pub Assn.

TM Program & Enlightenment: Dawn of a New Age. Alan Robins & Jane A. Himber. pap. 1.95 o.p. (ISBN 0-425-03250-7). Berkley Pub.

TM Technique: A Skeptic's Guide to the TM Program. Peter Russell. 1977. pap. 6.95 (ISBN 0-7100-8672-5). Routledge & Kegan.

TM Technique & the Art of Learning. Stephen Truch. (Quality Paperback Ser: No. 329). 1977. pap. 4.95 (ISBN 0-8226-0329-2). Littlefield.

To Acquire Wisdom: The Way of Wang Yang-Ming. Julia Ching. LC 75-20038. (Studies in Oriental Culture). 367p. 1976. 22.50x (ISBN 0-231-03938-7). Columbia U Pr.

To Adam with Love. Doug Roberts. pap. 1.95 (ISBN 0-89728-059-8, 533232). Omega Pubns OR.

To Adam with Love. Douglas Roberts. 1975. pap. 1.50 (ISBN 0-89129-009-5). Jove Pubns.

To Adam with Love. Douglas Roberts. Orig. Title: Para Adan Con Amor. 1977. 1.50 (ISBN 0-8297-0745-X). Life Pubs Intl.

To Advance the Gospel: New Testament Essays. J. A. Fitzmyer. 320p. 1981. 19.50 (ISBN 0-8245-0008-3). Crossroad NY.

To Africa with Love. Ernst H. Wendland. 1974. pap. 6.25 (ISBN 0-8100-0033-4, 12N1710). Northwest Pub.

To All Generations, a Study of Church History. Frank Roberts. 276p. (Orig.). 1981. pap. text ed. price not set (ISBN 0-933140-17-7); price not set tchr's manual (ISBN 0-933140-18-5). Bd of Pubns CRC.

To All My Grandchildren: Lessons in Indonesian Cooking. Leonie Samuel-Hool. Ed. by Sherman Hool. LC 80-84766. (Illus.). 120p. 1981. 12.95 (ISBN 0-936016-50-7); pap. 7.95 (ISBN 0-936016-75-2). Liplop.

To America. Eleanor B. Tripp. LC 69-11493. (Curriculum Related Bks). (Illus.). (gr. 8-11). 1969. 5.95 o.p. (ISBN 0-15-289040-8, HJ). HarBraceJ.

To Anchor a Cloud. Dilip Hiro. (Writers Workshop Bluebird Ser.). 96p. 1975. 15.00 (ISBN 0-88253-662-1); pap. text ed. 6.75 (ISBN 0-88253-661-3). Ind-US Inc.

To Antarctica with the Royal Navy. D. G. Sherrard. LC 79-67138. 122p. 1980. 7.95 (ISBN 0-533-04448-0). Vantage.

To Any God Listening. Don Alexander. 46p. 1974. 3.50 o.p. (ISBN 0-89015-069-9). Nortex Pr.

To Augur Well: Early Warning Indicators in World Politics. Ed. by J. David Singer & Michael D. Wallace. LC 79-14277. (Sage Focus Editions: Vol. 11). (Illus.). 1979. 18.95x (ISBN 0-8039-1246-3); pap. 9.95x (ISBN 0-8039-1247-1). Sage.

To Avoid Catastrophe: Towards a Future Nuclear Weapons Policy. Ed. by Michael P. Hamilton. 1978. pap. 4.95 o.p. (ISBN 0-8028-1703-3). Eerdmans.

To Be a Catholic. Joseph V. Gallagher. LC 73-137884. 1970. pap. 1.45 (ISBN 0-8091-5143-X). Paulist Pr.

To Be a Child: A Book of Photographic Essays on the Psychological Rights of the Child. Ed. by P. R. Bursynski. 65p. 1979. 10.00 (ISBN 0-917668-03-0). Intl Schl Psych.

To Be a Doctor. Felix Marti-Ibanez. Bd. with The Young Princes; The Race & the Runner. LC 68-27688. 1968. 4.95 (ISBN 0-910922-18-7), MD Pubns.

To Be a Manager. Ross D. Webber. 1981. 18.95x (ISBN 0-256-02520-7). Irwin.

To Be a Pilgrim (John Bunyan) Joyce Reason. 1961. pap. 1.95 (ISBN 0-87508-625-X). Chr Lit.

To Be a Priest: Perspectives on Vocation & Ordination. Robert E. Terwilliger & Urban T. Holmes. 192p. (Orig.). 1975. pap. 3.95 (ISBN 0-685-54447-8, 8164-2592-2). Crossroad NY.

To Be a Printer. Brooke Crutchley. 200p. 1980. 19.95 (ISBN 0-521-23663-0). Cambridge U Pr.

To Be a Writer: A Course in Creative Writing. Edite Mason. 1971. pap. 4.95 (ISBN 0-7195-2059-2). Transatlantic.

To Be Continued... An Annotated Bibliography of Science Fiction & Fantasy Series & Sequels. R. Reginald. LC 80-11206. (Borgo Reference Library: Vol. 11). 64p. 1981. lib. bdg. 8.95x (ISBN 0-89370-808-9); pap. 2.95x (ISBN 0-89370-908-5). Borgo Pr.

To Be Human: An Introduction to Anthropology. Alexander Alland, Jr. LC 79-19497. 1980. text ed. 19.95 (ISBN 0-471-01747-7); write for info tchr's ed (ISBN 0-471-06054-2). Wiley.

To Be Human: An Introduction to Cultural Anthropology. Alexander Alland. 401p. 1981. text ed. 13.95 (ISBN 0-471-06213-8). Wiley.

To Be in England. Richard D. Altick. LC 68-20813. (Illus.). 1969. 6.95 o.p. (ISBN 0-393-04302-9). Norton.

To Be on an Island. Constance Kiermaier. (Illus., Orig.). 1980. pap. 7.95 (ISBN 0-89272-098-0). Down East.

To Be or Not to Be: A Question of Survival. Duncan Williams. (International Library Ser.). 1976. pap. text ed. 8.25 (ISBN 0-08-019934-8). Pergamon.

To Be or Not to Bop: Memoirs. Dizzy Gillespie & Al Fraser. LC 77-76237. (Illus.). 1979. 15.95 (ISBN 0-385-12052-4). Doubleday.

To Be Self-Evident. Henry H. Williamson, Jr. 280p. 1980. 8.95 (ISBN 0-533-04016-7). Vantage.

To Become a Racehorse Trainer. Joe Hartigan. 7.00 (ISBN 0-85131-234-9, Dist. by Sporting Book Center). J A Allen.

To Believe in God. Joseph Pintauro & Sr. Corita Kent. LC 68-11741. 1968. 4.95 o.p. (ISBN 0-06-066640-4, HarpR). Har-Row.

To Build a Canal: Sault Ste. Marie, 1853 to 1854 & After. (Illus.). 215p. 1981. 21.50 (ISBN 0-8142-0309-4). Ohio St U Pr.

To Build a Fire: Recent Poems & a Prose Piece. Melville Cane. LC 64-14640. 1964. 3.75 (ISBN 0-15-190478-2). HarBraceJ.

To Burn California. Louis Hammer. LC 74-24492. 3.95 (ISBN 0-685-46996-4). Sagarin Pr.

To Carry & to Keep: The Story of Containers. Frank Jupo. LC 75-5543. 1976. 5.95 (ISBN 0-396-07178-3). Dodd.

To Catch a Bird. Jay Williams. 1968. 3.95g o.s.i. (ISBN 0-02-793040-8, CCPr). Macmillan.

To Catch a Golden Ring. William Coleman. (gr. 4-9). 1980. pap. 2.50 (ISBN 0-89191-330-0). Cook.

To Catch a King. Harry Patterson. 1980. pap. 2.95 (ISBN 0-449-24323-0, Crest). Fawcett.

To Catch a Rainbow. Estelle Thompson. LC 80-24246. 278p. 1980. Repr. of 1979 ed. large print ed. 9.95 (ISBN 0-89621-251-3). Thorndike Pr.

To Catch a Rainbow. Estelle Thompson. 192p. 1980. 9.95 o.s.i. (ISBN 0-8027-0652-5). Walker & Co.

To Catch a Rat. Walter Harris. 1978. pap. 1.50 o.p. (ISBN 0-425-03995-1, Dist. by Putnam). Berkley Pub.

To Catch a Tartar. Lynn Hall. LC 72-85582. 96p. (gr. 4-6). 1973. 4.95 o.p. (ISBN 0-695-80370-0, T0370); PLB 5.97 o.p. (ISBN 0-695-40370-2, L0370). Follett.

To Catch an Angel: Adventures in the World I Cannot See. Robert W. Russell. LC 62-11209. (gr. 7 up). 1962. 9.95 (ISBN 0-8149-0194-8). Vanguard.

To Catch the Uncatchable. Bhaskar Bhattacharyya. (Illus.). 1981. 9.95 (ISBN 0-89281-019-X, Destiny Bks). Inner Tradit.

To Catch the Wind. Helen C. Olsen. (YA) 1978. 5.95 (ISBN 0-685-86416-2, Avalon). Bouregy.

To China with Love. Hudson J. Taylor. Orig. Title: Retrospect, China Inland Mission Mid-1900s. 1972. pap. 1.95 (ISBN 0-87123-549-8, 200549). Bethany Fell.

To Choose a Future. Ronald G. Ridker & William D. Watson, Jr. LC 79-3643. (Resources for the Future Ser.). 1980. 33.50x (ISBN 0-8018-2354-4). Johns Hopkins.

To Christ, Dionysus, Odin. Bill Hotchkiss. 1969. 6.00 o.p. (ISBN 0-912950-06-4); pap. 4.00 o.p. (ISBN 0-912950-05-6). Blue Oak.

To Comfort All Who Mourn: A Parish Handbook for Ministry to the Grieving. Carol Luebering. LC 80-82555. 112p. (Orig.). 1980. pap. 4.95 (ISBN 0-934134-07-3, Celebration Bks). Natl Cath Reporter.

To Comfort & to Challenge: The Dilemma of the Contemporary Church. Charles Y. Glock et al. 1967. 17.50x (ISBN 0-520-00486-8). U of Cal Pr.

To Conquer Chaos. John Brunner. 1981. pap. 1.95 (ISBN 0-87997-596-2, JI596). Daw Bks.

To Cross a River. Jimmy Swaggart & Robert P. Lamb. 1977. pap. 2.95 (ISBN 0-88270-293-9). Logos.

To Die & to Live: Christ's Resurrection & Christian Vocation. Paul S. Minear. 1977. 8.95 (ISBN 0-8164-0340-6). Crossroad NY.

To Die Elsewhere. Theodore Wilden. LC 76-21748. 1976. 7.95 o.p. (ISBN 0-15-190480-4). HarBraceJ.

To Die Elsewhere. Theodore Wilden. 1978. pap. 1.95 o.s.i. (ISBN 0-515-04468-7). Jove Pubns.

To Die for a Golden Leaf. Robert P. Hilldrup. (Orig.). 1980. pap. 1.95 (ISBN 0-532-23217-8). Manor Bks.

To Die Game: The Story of the Lowry Band, Indian Guerrillas of Reconstruction. W. McKee Evans. LC 77-142335. 1971. 17.50x (ISBN 0-8071-0816-2); pap. 5.95 (ISBN 0-8071-0379-9). La State U Pr.

To Die Is Gain. L. Neal Carlson. (Contempo Ser.). pap. 0.95 (ISBN 0-8010-2357-2); dozen 9.50 (ISBN 0-686-66984-3). Baker Bk.

To Do Justly: A Junior Casebook for Social Action. rev. ed. Albert Vorspan. (gr. 6 up). 1977. pap. text ed. 3.25 (ISBN 0-8074-0078-5); tchrs'. guide 1.25 (ISBN 0-8074-0079-3, 207272). UAHC.

To Do the Sick No Harm: A Study of the British Voluntary Hospital System to 1875. John Woodward. (International Library of Social Policy Ser.). 1978. pap. 8.95 (ISBN 0-7100-8911-2). Routledge & Kegan.

To Draw, Upset, & Weld: The Work of the Pennsylvania Rural Blacksmith, 1742-1935. Jeannette Lasansky. LC 80-15912. (Illus.). 84p. 1980. pap. 7.95 (ISBN 0-271-00265-4, Keystone Bks). Pa St U Pr.

To Dream Again. Robert D. Dale. 1981. pap. 4.95 (ISBN 0-8054-2541-1). Broadman.

To Drop a Dime. Paul Hoffman & Ira Pecznick. 1977. pap. 1.95 o.s.i. (ISBN 0-515-04424-5). Jove Pubns.

To Eat or Not to Eat: A Young People's Guide to Dietary Goals for the United States. William Franz & Barbara Franz. (Illus.). 160p. (gr. 9-12). 1981. PLB price not set (ISBN 0-671-42563-3). Messner.

To Educate with Love. Herbert M. Greenberg. LC 73-10562. 228p. 1974. 6.95 o.s.i. (ISBN 0-02-545470-6). Macmillan.

To Embrace the Moon: An Illustrated Biography of Mao Zedong. Ed Hammond. 196p. 1980. 14.95 (ISBN 0-89581-455-2); pap. 8.95 (ISBN 0-89581-502-8). Lancaster-Miller.

To Enjoy Is to Live: Psychotherapy Explained. Benjamin Fabriant et al. LC 76-40141. 1977. 14.95 (ISBN 0-88229-148-3). Nelson-Hall.

To Escape the Stars. Robert Hoskins. 1978. pap. 1.75 o.p. (ISBN 0-345-25856-8, Del Rey Bks). Ballantine.

To Feed Their Hopes: A Book of American Women. John Sanford. LC 80-16505. 275p. 1980. 12.95 (ISBN 0-252-00804-9). U of Ill Pr.

To Find a Blessing. Dorothy Johnson. 59p. 1980. 3.95 (ISBN 0-8059-2745-X). Dorrance.

To Flee from Eagles. Anne-Marie Breton. 288p. (Orig.). 1981. pap. 2.75 (ISBN 0-523-40405-0). Pinnacle Bks.

To Fly Like a Bird: The Story of Man-Powered Aircraft. Keith Sherwin. (Illus.). 1977. 8.95 o.p. (ISBN 0-8069-0114-4); lib. bdg. 8.29 o.p. (ISBN 0-8069-0115-2). Sterling.

To Form a More Perfect Union: America's Struggle for a National Identity. James K. Fitzpatrick. 1979. 9.95 o.p. (ISBN 0-87000-446-8). Arlington Hse.

To Free a Generation: The Dialectics of Liberation. Ed. by David Cooper. LC 68-31275. (Orig.). 1969. pap. 1.95 o.s.i. (ISBN 0-02-095300-3, Collier). Macmillan.

To Glory We Steer. Alexander Kent. pap. 2.25 (ISBN 0-515-05732-0). Jove Pubns.

To Grandfather's House We Go: A Roadside Tour of American Homes. Harry Devlin. LC 80-15294. (Illus.). 48p. (gr. 5 up). 1980. Repr. of 1967 ed. 9.95 (ISBN 0-590-07764-3, Four Winds). Schol Bk Serv.

To Handmake a Saddle. J. H. Shields. (Illus.). pap. 7.70 (ISBN 0-85131-222-5, Dist. by Sporting Book Center). J A Allen.

To Have & Have Not. Ernest Hemingway. 1937. 17.50x (ISBN 0-684-15328-9, ScribT); pap. 3.95 (ISBN 0-684-71809-X, SL132, ScribT). Scribner.

To Have & to Hold. Mary Johnston. 1976. lib. bdg. 11.95x (ISBN 0-89968-149-2). Lightyear.

To Have & to Hold. Jill Renich. 145p. 1975. pap. 2.50 (ISBN 0-310-31812-2); study guide 0.95 (ISBN 0-310-31813-0). Zondervan.

To Have or to Be? Erich Fromm. 256p. 1981. pap. 2.95 (ISBN 0-553-10949-9). Bantam.

To Have, To Hold. 2nd ed. Joyce L. Kieffer. (Illus.). 80p. 1981. pap. 4.95 (ISBN 0-933794-02-9). Train Res Assoc.

To Heal & to Reveal: The Prophetic Vocation According to Luke. Paul S. Minear. 1976. 8.95 (ISBN 0-8164-0295-7). Crossroad NY.

To Hear & to Heed. Joseph Pelham et al. 1978. 1.50 (ISBN 0-686-28797-5). Forward Movement.

To Hear the Angels Sing. Dorothy Maclean. 192p. (Orig.). 1980. pap. text ed. 7.00 (ISBN 0-936878-01-0). Lorian Pr.

To Help Children Communicate. Frank B. May. (Elementary Education Ser.: No. C22). 472p. 1980. pap. text ed. 14.95 (ISBN 0-675-08197-1). Merrill.

To Help Children Read. 2nd ed. Frank B. May & Susan B. Eliot. (Elementary Education Ser.). 1978. pap. text ed. 14.95 (ISBN 0-675-08370-2); instructor's manual 3.95 (ISBN 0-685-86843-5). Merrill.

To Him Who Waits. Mary McMaster. (Aston Hall Romances Ser.). 192p. 1981. pap. 1.75 (ISBN 0-523-41129-4). Pinnacle Bks.

To Hold This Soil. Russell Lord. LC 78-171385. (FDR & the Era of the New Deal Ser). (Illus.). 124p. 1972. Repr. of 1938 ed. lib. bdg. 17.50 (ISBN 0-306-70384-X). Da Capo.

To Hunt in the Morning. Janet Siskind. LC 73-82674. (Illus.). 224p. 1975. pap. 5.95 (ISBN 0-19-501891-5, GB430, GB). Oxford U Pr.

To Irrigate a Wasteland: The Struggle to Shape a Public Television System in the United States. John W. Macy, Jr. 1974. 11.95x (ISBN 0-520-02498-2). U of Cal Pr.

To James Bond with Love. Mary W. Bond. LC 80-17134. (Illus.). 224p. 1980. 10.95 (ISBN 0-915010-28-3). Sutter House.

To Keep Our Honor Clean. Ed. by Edwin McDowell. LC 79-56025. 320p. 1980. 10.95 (ISBN 0-8149-0831-4). Vanguard.

To Keep the Peace: The United Nations Condemnatory Resolution. William W. Orbach. LC 75-41989. (Illus.). 168p. 1977. 14.50x (ISBN 0-8131-1341-5). U Pr of Ky.

To Kill a Mockingbird. Harper Lee. LC 60-7847. 1960. 10.95 (ISBN 0-397-00151-7). Lippincott.

To Know a Library: Essays & Annual Reports, 1970-1976. Daniel Gore. LC 77-84769. (New Directions in Librarianship: No. 1). 1978. lib. bdg. 19.95 (ISBN 0-8371-9881-X, GTK/). Greenwood.

To Know Yourself: The Essential Teachings of Swami Satchidananda. Ed. by Philip Mandelkorn. LC 77-80901. 1978. pap. 3.95 (ISBN 0-385-12613-1, Anch). Doubleday.

To Lead & Manage. Jules Bellaschi. LC 80-83869. 70p. (Orig.). 1980. pap. 4.95 (ISBN 0-9605144-0-6). MJ Pubns.

To Leisure: An Introduction. John Neulinger. 276p. 1980. text ed. 16.95 (ISBN 0-205-06936-3, 8469369). Allyn.

To Lhasa & Beyond. Giuseppe Tucci. Tr. by Mario Carelli from Ital. LC 78-56120. (Illus.). 1978. pap. 8.75 o.p. (ISBN 0-87773-703-7, Prajna). Great Eastern.

To Light the Labyrinth. D. Keogh. 7.95 o.p. (ISBN 0-8062-1136-9). Carlton.

To Like & Be Liked. Shirley Schwarzrock & C. Gilbert Wrenn. (Coping with Ser.). (Illus.). 37p. (gr. 7-12). 1970. pap. text ed. 1.30 (ISBN 0-913476-25-0). Am Guidance.

To Linger Is to Die. Lilya Wagner. LC 75-18349. (Crown Ser.). 128p. 1975. pap. 4.50 (ISBN 0-8127-0102-X). Southern Pub.

To Live Again. LC 78-5029. 1978. 8.95 (ISBN 0-396-07570-3). Dodd.

To Live Forever. Jack Vance. 1976. pap. 1.50 o.p. (ISBN 0-345-25198-9). Ballantine.

To Live Happily Ever After: A Guide to a Lasting Relationship. Arthur F. Ide & Charles A. Ide. 60p. (Orig.). 1981. 12.95 (ISBN 0-86663-998-5); pap. 7.50 (ISBN 0-86663-999-3). Ide Hse.

To Live Is to Love. Ernesto Cardenal. 160p. 1974. pap. 1.45 (ISBN 0-385-03055-X, Im). Doubleday.

To Live on Earth. Sterling Brubaker. pap. 1.50 o.p. (ISBN 0-451-61137-3, MW1137, Ment). NAL.

To Live the Good Life: Planning for the Arts. Wolf Von Eckardt. 1981. 9.95 (ISBN 0-915400-24-3). Am Council Arts.

To Look at Any Thing. Ed. by Lee B. Hopkins. LC 77-88962. (Illus.). (gr. 1 up). 1978. 6.95 (ISBN 0-15-289083-1, HJ). HarBraceJ.

To Love a Stranger. Barbara Paul. 1980. lib. bdg. 14.95 (ISBN 0-8161-3169-4, Large Print Bks). G K Hall.

To Make a Difference: Teaching in the Inner City. Larry Cuban. LC 74-102197. 1970. pap. text ed. 3.95 (ISBN 0-02-906890-8). Free Pr.

To Make a Prairie: Essays on Poets, Poetry, & Country Living. Maxine Kumin. LC 79-13289. (Poets on Poetry Ser.). 1979. pap. 5.95 (ISBN 0-472-06306-5). U of Mich Pr.

To Make the Patient Ready for Anesthesia: Medical Care of the Surgical Patient. Leroy Vandam. LC 80-11190. (Clinical Practice Ser.). 1980. 24.95 (ISBN 0-201-07999-2). A-W.

To Marietta from Paris, Nineteen Forty-Five-Nineteen Sixty. Susan Mary Alsop. LC 74-33628. 384p. 1975. 8.95 o.p. (ISBN 0-385-09774-3). Doubleday.

To Market to Market. Corinne Ross. (Illus.). 1980. pap. 4.50 (ISBN 0-89182-022-1). Charles River.

To Michael with Love. Mary S. Sheridan. (YA) 1977. 4.95 o.p. (ISBN 0-685-74271-7, Avalon). Bouregy.

To Music & Children with Love! Reflections for Parents & Teachers. A. Ramon Rivera & Thelma Gruenbaum. 133p. 1979. pap. 6.95 (ISBN 0-936190-03-5). ExPressAll.

To Paris. Samuel Hazo. LC 80-22685. 96p. 1981. 11.95 (ISBN 0-8112-0787-0); pap. 4.95 (ISBN 0-8112-0788-9, NDP512). New Directions.

To Pray As a Jew. Hayim H. Donin. LC 80-50554. 384p. 1980. 15.00 (ISBN 0-465-08628-4). Basic.

To Pray or Not to Pray. John B. Cobb, Jr. (Prayer in My Life Ser.: Ser. I). 1974. pap. 1.00x (ISBN 0-8358-0310-4). Upper Room.

To Preserve These Rights: Remedies for the Victims of Constitutional Deprivations. Robert L. Spurrier, Jr. (National University Pubns. Multi-Disciplinary Studies in the Law). 1977. 12.95 (ISBN 0-8046-9199-1). Kennikat.

To Purge This Land with Blood: A Biography of John Brown. Stephen B. Oates. 1972. pap. 7.95x (ISBN 0-06-131655-5, TB1655, Torch). Har-Row.

To Raise, Destroy, & Create. Henry C. Lacey. LC 80-50078. 1981. 15.00 (ISBN 0-87875-185-8). Whitston Pub.

To Ravensrigg. Hester Burton. LC 76-54292. 1977. 8.95 (ISBN 0-690-01354-X, TYC-J). T Y Crowell.

To Ravish Rani. Nadine McGuyer. (Orig.). 1979. pap. 1.95 (ISBN 0-532-23273-9). Manor Bks.

To Reach the Green Valley. Joseph M. Pugliese. 1977. 4.50 o.p. (ISBN 0-533-02782-9). Vantage.

To Resist or Surrender. Paul Tournier. LC 64-16248. 1977. pap. 1.25 (ISBN 0-8042-3663-1). John Knox.

To Resist or To Surrender? Paul Tournier. Tr. by John S. Gilmour. LC 64-16248. 1964. Repr. 4.25 (ISBN 0-8042-2232-0). John Knox.

To Ride Pegasus. Anne McCaffrey. (Del Rey Bk.). Date not set. pap. 2.25 (ISBN 0-345-28507-7). Ballantine.

To Risks Unknown. Douglas Reeman. pap. 1.95 (ISBN 0-515-05411-9). Jove Pubns.

To Save a Boy: The Story of Boys Home, North Carolina. A. D. Peacock & Edward Uhlan. LC 75-171711. 1971. 6.00 o.p. (ISBN 0-682-47313-8). Exposition.

To See a Fine Lady. Norah Lofts. 272p. 1976. pap. 2.25 (ISBN 0-449-22890-8, Crest). Fawcett.

To See His Face: Homily Themes for Various Occasions. Russel G. Terra. LC 77-24083. 1977. pap. 4.50 o.p. (ISBN 0-8189-0358-9). Alba.

To See Is to Think: Looking at American Art. Joshua C. Taylor. LC 74-26647. (Illus.). 117p. 1975. pap. 7.95 (ISBN 0-87474-177-7). Smithsonian.

To Serve the Public Interest: Educational Broadcasting in the United States. Robert J. Blakely. 1979. 16.00x (ISBN 0-8156-2198-1); pap. 7.95x (ISBN 0-8156-0153-0). Syracuse U Pr.

To Serve Where Sent. Roy Gardner. 1978. 6.95 o.p. (ISBN 0-533-02962-7). Vantage.

To Set at Liberty: Christian Faith & Human Freedom. Delwin Brown. LC 80-21783. 144p. (Orig.). 1981. pap. 6.95 (ISBN 0-88344-501-8). Orbis Bks.

To Set Them Free. Barbara K. Walker et al. 1981. 14.95; pap. 9.95. Tompson & Rutter.

To Set Them Free: The Early Years of Mustafa Kemal Ataturk. Barbara K. Walker et al. LC 80-21127. (Illus.). 96p. 1981. 14.95 (ISBN 0-936988-00-2); pap. 9.95 (ISBN 0-936988-02-9). Tompson & Rutter.

To Sir, with Love. E. R. Braithwaite. (gr. 9-12). 1973. pap. 1.95 (ISBN 0-515-05823-8). Jove Pubns.

To Sir, with Love. Edward Braithwaite. 1960. 7.95 o.p. (ISBN 0-13-923037-8). P-H.

To Speak of God: Theology for Beginners. Urban T. Holmes, 3rd. 1974. 6.95 (ISBN 0-8164-1169-7). Crossroad NY.

To Speak True: A Study of Poetry As a Spoken Art. B. Nulcany. 4.40 o.p. (ISBN 0-08-006444-2). Pergamon.

To Stand at the Pole: The Dr. Cook-Admiral Peary North Pole Controversy. William R. Hunt. LC 80-6156. 272p. 1981. 14.95 (ISBN 0-8128-2773-2). Stein & Day.

To Stretch a Plank: A Survey of Psychokinesis. Diana Robinson. LC 80-12335. 282p. 1981. 15.95 (ISBN 0-88229-404-0). Nelson-Hall.

To Strive to Search, to Find. Marie Shepherd-Moore. 1976. 6.50 o.p. (ISBN 0-682-48568-3). Exposition.

To Struga with Love. Ed. by Stanley H. Barkan. LC 78-67775. (Illus., Orig.). 1978. in-folio 10.00 (ISBN 0-89304-028-2, CCC115); in-folio boxed 15.00 (ISBN 0-89304-050-9). Cross Cult.

To Tame a Land. Louis L'Amour. (Western Fiction Ser.). 1981. lib. bdg. 11.95 (ISBN 0-8398-2697-4). Gregg.

To Tell the World: The Driving Passion of Rex Humbard & the Cathedral of Tomorrow. Rex Humbard. LC 75-19273. (Illus.). 224p. 1975. 7.95 o.p. (ISBN 0-13-923094-7). P-H.

To the Distant Observer: Form & Meaning in Japanese Cinema. Noel Burch. LC 77-20316. 1979. 21.50x (ISBN 0-520-03605-0); pap. 9.75 (ISBN 0-520-03877-0). U of Cal Pr.

To the Ends of the Universe. new ed. Isaac Asimov. LC 75-10524. 144p. 1976. 6.50 (ISBN 0-8027-6236-0); PLB 7.85 (ISBN 0-8027-6235-2). Walker & Co.

To the Far Blue Mountains. Louis L'Amour. 1977. pap. 2.25 (ISBN 0-685-78253-0, T12721-7). Bantam.

To the Farthest Ends of the Earth: One Hundred Fifty Years of World Exploration by the Royal Geographical Society. Ian Cameron. (Illus.). 304p. 1980. 27.00 (ISBN 0-525-22065-8). Dutton.

To the Finland Station: A Study in the Writing & Acting of History. Edmund Wilson. LC 53-3591. 1953. pap. 3.95 (ISBN 0-385-09281-4, A6, Anch). Doubleday.

To the Fountain of Christianity. Vila. pap. 2.95 (ISBN 0-686-12322-0). Christs Mission.

To the Gods the Shades. David Wright. (Poetry Ser.). 1979. 9.95 o.s.i. (ISBN 0-85635-181-4, Pub. by Carcanet New Pr England). Persea Bks.

To the Golden Shore: The Life of Adoniram Judson. Courtney Anderson. 1977. pap. 6.95 (ISBN 0-310-36131-1). Zondervan.

To the Good Long Life: What We Know About Growing Old. Morton Puner. LC 73-80054. 320p. 1974. 10.00x o.p. (ISBN 0-87663-191-X). Universe.

To the Greenland Whaling. Alexander Trotter. 80p. 1980. pap. 9.95 (ISBN 0-906191-24-6, Pub. by Thule Pr England). Intl Schol Bk Serv.

To the King's Taste: Richard the Second's Book of Feasts and Recipes Adapted for Modern Cooking. Lorna J. Sass. LC 75-17859. (Illus.). 136p. 1975. 5.95 o.p. (ISBN 0-87099-133-7). Metro Mus Art.

To the Man Reporter from the Denver Post. rev. ed. Chocolate Waters. 1980. 3.75 (ISBN 0-935060-05-7). Eggplant Pr.

To the Marianas: War in the Central Pacific: 1944. Edwin P. Hoyt. 192p. 1980. deluxe ed. 12.95 (ISBN 0-442-26105-5). Van Nos Reinhold.

To the Opera Ball. Sarah Gainham. 1978. pap. 2.25 o.s.i. (ISBN 0-446-82592-1). Warner Bks.

To the Palace of Wisdom: Studies in Order & Energy from Dryden to Blake. Martin Price. LC 63-10846. 1970. Repr. of 1964 ed. 7.00x o.p. (ISBN 0-8093-0474-0). S Ill U Pr.

To the People: Prepare for War. Donald L. Martin. 64p. 1981. 7.95 (ISBN 0-89962-043-4). Todd & Honeywell.

To the Perplexed. Mohandas K. Gandhi. Ed. by Anand T. Hingorani. 229p. 1981. 6.00 (ISBN 0-934676-27-5). Greenlf Bks.

To the Queen's Taste: Elizabethan Feasts & Recipes Adapted for Modern Cooking. Lorna J. Sass. LC 76-23242. 1976. 6.95 (ISBN 0-87099-151-5). Metro Mus Art.

To the Right High & Mightie Prince James...An Humble Supplication for Toleration & Libertie. Henry Jacob. LC 74-28869. (English Experience Ser.: No. 748). 1975. Repr. of 1609 ed. 5.00 (ISBN 90-221-0748-5). Walter J Johnson.

To the Slaughterhouse. Jean Giono. 11.95 (ISBN 0-7206-3602-7). Dufour.

To the South Pole. Carla Frazier. LC 78-26274. (Raintree Great Adventures). (Illus.). (gr. 3-6). 1979. PLB 8.95 (ISBN 0-8393-0153-7). Raintree Child.

To the South Seas; the Cruise of the Schooner Mary Pinchot to the Galapogos, the Marquesas, & the Tuamotu Islands, & Tahiti. Gifford Pinchot. LC 70-174094. (Illus.). xiv, 500p. 1972. Repr. of 1930 ed. 24.00 (ISBN 0-8103-3933-1). Gale.

To the Sundown Side: The Mountain Man in Idaho. Roland O. Byers. LC 79-65601. (GEM Books-Historical). (Illus.). 214p. (Orig.). 1979. pap. 8.95 (ISBN 0-89301-063-4). U Pr of Idaho.

To the Top of the Mountain: The Life of Father Umberto Olivieri, "Padre of the Otomis". William N. Abeloe. LC 76-7187. 1976. 8.00 o.p. (ISBN 0-682-48558-6). Exposition.

To the Unknown Hero. Hans E. Nossack. Tr. by Ralph Manheim. 1974. 6.95 o.p. (ISBN 0-374-27838-5). FS&G.

To the Walls of Cartagena. Allan Dwight. LC 67-21645. (Young Readers Ser.). (Illus., Orig.). (gr. 4-7). 1967. 3.95 o.p. (ISBN 0-910412-59-6). Williamsburg.

To Touch the Water. Gretel Ehrlich. Ed. by Tom Trusky. LC 80-69276. (Modern & Contemporary Poets of the West Ser.). 60p. (Orig.). 1981. pap. 2.50 (ISBN 0-916272-16-8). Ahsahta Pr.

To Turn the Tide. John F. Kennedy. Ed. by John W. Gardner. LC 61-12221. 1962. 10.00 o.p. (ISBN 0-06-012335-4, HarpT). Har-Row.

To Understand Each Other. Paul Tournier. Tr. by John S. Gilmour. LC 67-15298. (Illus.). 1967. 4.25 (ISBN 0-8042-2235-5). John Knox.

To Understand Each Other. Paul Tournier. 1976. pap. 1.25 o.p. (ISBN 0-8042-3673-9). John Knox.

To Walk & Not Faint. Marva J. Sedore. LC 80-65433. 160p. (Orig.). 1980. pap. 5.95 (ISBN 0-915684-65-9). Christian Herald.

To Walk the Night. Ed. by Jane Land. 192p. (Orig.). Date not set. pap. 2.25 (ISBN 0-345-28603-0). Ballantine.

To Wash an Aethiop White: British Ideas About Black Educability, 1530-1960. Charles H. Lyons. LC 74-23396. 1975. text ed. 9.25x (ISBN 0-8077-2464-5). Tchrs Coll.

To What Should We Be Loyal. William MacDonald. 55p. pap. 0.75 (ISBN 0-937396-47-8). Walterick Pubs.

To Will One Thing: Solar Action at the Local Level. 173p. 1980. pap. 25.00 (ISBN 0-89553-022-8, ISES 12, AS of ISES). Unipub.

To Win a War: Nineteen Eighteen, The Year of Victory. John Terraine. LC 79-7119. (Illus.). 288p. 1981. 14.95 (ISBN 0-385-15316-3). Doubleday.

To Win the Money Game. Venita VanCaspel. 1980. pap. 1.50 (ISBN 0-8359-8692-6). Reston.

To You from Me. Esther Wilkin. (Golden Book of Picture Postcards Ser.). (Illus.). (ps-4). 1977. pap. 0.95 o.p. (ISBN 0-307-11102-4, Golden Pr). Western Pub.

To You Simonides: Versions from Greek Anthology. William J. Philbin. (Dolmen Editions: No. 19). 120p. 1973. bds. 12.00x (ISBN 0-85105-231-2, Dolmen Pr). Humanities.

To Your Good Health! Charlotte A. Resnick & Gloria R. Resnick. (gr. 7-12). 1979. text ed. 14.50 (ISBN 0-87720-164-1); pap. text ed. 8.92 (ISBN 0-87720-163-3). AMSCO Sch.

To Your Scattered Bodies Go. Philip J. Farmer. 1973. pap. 2.25 (ISBN 0-425-04816-0, Medallion). Berkley Pub.

Toastmasters Companion. 256p. 1981. pap. 2.49 (ISBN 0-686-64510-3, Quick Fox). Music Sales.

Toba Indians of the Bolivian Gran Chaco. Rafael Karsten. 1967. text ed. 6.75x (ISBN 90-6234-023-7). Humanities.

Tobacco & Marijuana. Ochsner et al. 1976. perfect bdg. 6.95 (ISBN 0-88252-048-2). Paladin Hse.

Tobacco & Tobacco Smoke. Ed. by Ernest L. Wynder & Dietrich Hoffman. 1967. 64.00 (ISBN 0-12-767450-0). Acad Pr.

Tobacco & Your Life. Loren Lind & Willard Krabill. LC 64-8550. (Family Life Ser.). (Orig.). 1964. pap. 0.35 o.p. (ISBN 0-8361-1498-1). Herald Pr.

Tobacco: Its History & Associations. Frederick W. Fairholt. LC 68-21770. 1968. Repr. of 1859 ed. 15.00 (ISBN 0-8103-3507-7). Gale.

Tobacco Regulations in Colonial Maryland. Vertrees J. Wyckoff. LC 78-64291. (Johns Hopkins University. Studies in the Social Sciences. Extra Volumes.: 22). Repr. of 1936 ed. 21.00 (ISBN 0-404-61391-8). AMS Pr.

Tobacco: The Ants & Elephants. Charles K. Mann. LC 74-29660. 176p. 1976. 8.95 o.p. (ISBN 0-913420-49-2). Olympus Pub Co.

Tobias Smollett: A Reference Guide. Robert D. Spector. (Scholarly Reference Publications). 1980. lib. bdg. 28.00 (ISBN 0-8161-7960-3). G K Hall.

Tobias Smollett: Bicentennial Essays Presented to Lewis M. Knapp. Ed. by G. S. Rousseau & P. G. Bouce. 1971. 14.95 (ISBN 0-19-501370-0). Oxford U Pr.

Tobias Smollett: Travels Through France & Italy. facsimile ed. Tobias Smollett. Ed. by Frank Felsenstein. 45.00x (ISBN 0-19-812611-5). Oxford U Pr.

Toby & Johnny Joe. Robbie Branscum. 80p. 1981. pap. 1.75 (ISBN 0-380-52670-0, 52670). Avon.

Toby, the Rock Hound. Jane Walrath. (Tell-a-Tale Reader Ser.). (Illus.). (gr. k-3). 1979. PLB 4.77 (ISBN 0-307-68408-3, Golden Pr). Western Pub.

Toby Tyler: Or, Ten Weeks with a Circus. James Otis. LC 75-32185. (Classics of Children's Literature, 1621-1932: Vol. 48). 1977. Repr. of 1881 ed. PLB 38.00 (ISBN 0-8240-2297-1). Garland Pub.

Toby's Gift. Melvin Northrup. (Books I Can Read). 32p. (Orig.). (gr. 2). 1980. pap. 1.25 (ISBN 0-8127-0291-3). Southern Pub.

Tocayo: The True Story of a Resistance Leader in Castro's Cuba. Antonio Navarro. 288p. 1981. 14.95 (ISBN 0-87000-508-1). Arlington Hse.

Tod in Venedig. Thomas Mann. Ed. by George Boyd & Henry Rosenwald. (Illus.). 175p. (Ger.). 1973. pap. text ed. 4.95x (ISBN 0-19-501688-2). Oxford U Pr.

Tod on the Tugboat. Leonard Shortall. LC 73-153186. (Illus.). (ps-3). 1971. 7.25 (ISBN 0-688-21804-0); PLB 6.96 (ISBN 0-688-31804-5). Morrow.

Toda la Fotografia En un Solo Libro. W. D. Emanuel. Tr. by Antonio Cuni from Eng. 228p. (Span.). 1975. 7.95 (ISBN 0-240-51098-4, Pub. by Ediciones Spain). Focal Pr.

Toda Lattices, Cosymplectic Manifolds, Baecklund Transformations & Kinks, Pt. B. Robert Hermann. (Interdisciplinary Mathematics Ser.: No. 18). 1979. 15.00 (ISBN 0-915692-24-4). Math Sci Pr.

Toda Songs. Murray Barnson Emeneau. 1052p. 1971. 39.50x (ISBN 0-19-815129-2). Oxford U Pr.

Today. Aline Cunningham. (Caterpillar Bk. Ser.). (Illus.). 12p. (ps-k). 0.69 (ISBN 0-570-06907-6, 56Y1272). Concordia.

Today & Other Days. Ed. by Jo Thebaud. (Illus.). 151p. (Orig.). 1971. pap. 3.25 (ISBN 0-88489-031-7). St Marys.

Today & Yesterday: Tennyson, Burke, Thackeray, Shakespeare. George M. Young. 312p. 1980. lib. bdg. 15.00 (ISBN 0-8482-3125-2). Norwood Edns.

Today I Am a Woman. Linda Lee. 2.95 (ISBN 0-912216-17-4). Green Hill.

Today in Ireland, 3 vols. Eyre E. Crows. Ed. by Robert L. Wolff. (Ireland Nineteenth Century Fiction - Ser. Two: Vol. 14). 1036p. 1979. lib. bdg. 96.00 (ISBN 0-8240-3463-5). Garland Pub.

Today Is Yours, No. 24. Emilie Loring. 224p. 1981. pap. 1.95 (ISBN 0-553-14656-4). Bantam.

Today Nineteen Eighty. World Book-Childcraft International, Inc. Staff. LC 76-27228. (World Book Today Yearly Diaries Ser.). 1979. 8.95 (ISBN 0-7166-2031-6). World Bk-Childcraft.

Today, Tomorrow, Yesterday. Forest S. Prowant. 1981. 5.95 (ISBN 0-533-04777-3). Vantage.

Today 1978. 1977. 8.95 o.p. (ISBN 0-7166-2027-8). World Bk-Chilcraft.

Today 1979. World Book Encyclopedia Inc Staff. (World Book Today Yearly Diaries Ser.). 1978. 8.95 o.p. (ISBN 0-7166-2028-6). World Bk-Chilcraft.

Today, 1981: A Personal Record & Reference Book. World Book-Childcraft International, Inc. LC 76-27228. (World Book Today Yearly Diaries Ser.). (Illus.). 192p. 1980. write for info. (ISBN 0-7166-2032-4). World Bk-Childcraft.

Today's Barbarian. Geno. 1978. 4.50 o.p. (ISBN 0-533-02959-7). Vantage.

Today's Biggest Animals. Kathleen Daly. (Look-Look Ser.). (Illus.). 1977. PLB 5.38 (ISBN 0-307-61836-6, Golden Pr); pap. 0.95 (ISBN 0-307-11836-3). Western Pub.

Today's Business World. W. Kingstather & W. Parish. 1978. 16.95 (ISBN 0-8359-7761-7); study guide 6.95 (ISBN 0-8359-7762-5). instrs'. manual avail. Reston.

Today's Child: A Modern Guide to Baby Care & Child Training. Elizabeth C. Robertson & Margaret I. Wood. LC 71-37204. 288p. 1972. 7.95 o.p. (ISBN 0-684-12727-X, ScribT). Scribner.

Today's Custom Tailoring. Ethel K. Wyllie. 1979. text ed. 15.80 (ISBN 0-87002-245-8); tchr's guide 3.40 (ISBN 0-87002-210-5). Bennett IL.

Today's Family. Elliott D. Landau. LC 74-28592. 246p. 1974. 5.95 o.p. (ISBN 0-87747-543-1); pap. 3.95 o.p. (ISBN 0-87747-552-0). Deseret Bk.

Today's Fleet Maintainance: A Reader for Fleet Executives. Today's Transport International Staff. LC 75-21975. 1975. 12.95 o.p. (ISBN 0-917408-02-0). Intercontinental Pubns.

Today's Gospel. Walter Chantry. 1980. pap. 2.45. Banner of Truth.

Today's Isms. 8th ed. W. Ebenstein & E. Fogelman. 1980. 14.95 (ISBN 0-13-924399-2); pap. 9.95 (ISBN 0-13-924381-X). P-H.

Today's Language: A Vocabulary Workbook. John T. Hiers et al. 272p. 1980. pap. text ed. 7.95 (ISBN 0-669-03078-3); canelled (ISBN 0-669-03080-5). Heath.

Today's Pastor in Tommorrow's World. Carnegie S. Calian. 1977. 6.95 o.p. (ISBN 0-8015-7761-6). Dutton.

Today's Teen. Kelly & Landers. (YA) 1977. 12.40 (ISBN 0-87002-192-3); tchr's guide 6.60 (ISBN 0-87002-264-4); student guide 3.56 (ISBN 0-87002-268-7). Bennett IL.

Today's Teen. rev. ed. Kelly & Landers. (gr. 7-9). 1981. text ed. 14.60 (ISBN 0-87002-323-3). Bennett IL.

Toddler & the New Baby. Sylvia Close. 128p. 1980. 14.50 (ISBN 0-7100-0522-9); pap. 6.95 (ISBN 0-7100-0523-7). Routledge & Kegan.

Todo Es Bello Alrededor. Adolfo Robleto. 80p. Date not set. pap. price not set (ISBN 0-311-08758-2, Edit Mundo). Casa Bautista.

Toff at Butlins. John Creasey. 1976. 6.95 o.s.i. (ISBN 0-8027-5358-2). Walker & Co.

Toffees, Fudges, Chocolates & Sweets. Mary Norwak. 1977. 14.50 (ISBN 0-7207-0956-3). Transatlantic.

Tofu & Soymilk Production: The Book of Tofu, Vol. II. William Shurtleff & Akiko Aoyagi. LC 74-31629. (Soyfood Production Ser.: No. 2). (Illus.). 1979. 22.95 (ISBN 0-933332-03-3); pap. 17.95 (ISBN 0-933332-01-7). Soyfoods-New Age.

Tofu at Center Stage. Gary Landgrebe. LC 80-69560. (Illus.). 112p. (Orig.). 1981. pap. 5.95 (ISBN 0-9601398-3-4). Fresh Pr.

Tofu-Miso High Efficiency Diet. Yoshiaki Omura et al. 208p. 1981. 10.95 (ISBN 0-668-05178-7); pap. 6.95 (ISBN 0-668-05180-9). Arco.

Tofu Primer: A Beginner's Book of Bean Cake Cookery. Jeul Andersen. (Illus.). 50p. (Orig.). 1981. pap. 2.95 (ISBN 0-916870-33-2). Creative Arts Bk.

Toga Party. Victor Miller. 1979. pap. 1.95 o.p. (ISBN 0-449-14261-2, GM). Fawcett.

Togaviruses. Ed. by R. Walter Schlesinger. 1980. 58.00 (ISBN 0-12-625380-3). Acad Pr.

Together-Communicating Interpersonally. 2nd ed. John Stewart & Gary D'Angelo. LC 79-26426. (Speech Communication Ser.). (Illus.). 1980. pap. 11.50 (ISBN 0-201-07506-7). A-W.

Together with Daddy. Mark Moore. (Illus.). 1977. bds. 3.95 (ISBN 0-8054-4153-0, 4241-53). Broadman.

Toil of the Brave. Inglis Fletcher. 560p. 1981. pap. 2.95 (ISBN 0-553-13811-1). Bantam.

Toilet Training in Less Than a Day. 1980. pap. 2.50 (ISBN 0-671-82741-3). PB.

Toiletries, Beauty Aids & Cosmetics. Fairchild Market Research Division. (Fact File Ser). 35p. 1978. pap. 10.00 (ISBN 0-87005-221-7). Fairchild.

Toiletries, Beauty Aids, Cosmetics, Fragrances. Fairchild Market Research Division. (Fact File Ser.). (Illus.). 100p. 1980. pap. 10.00 (ISBN 0-87005-347-7). Fairchild.

Token Economy: A Motivational System for Therapy & Rehabilitation. Teodoro Ayllon & Nathan H. Azrin. (Orig.). 1968. pap. 12.95 (ISBN 0-13-919357-X). P-H.

Token for Children, Being an Exact Account of the Conversion, Holy & Exemplary Lives & Joyful Deaths of Several Young Children, Repr. Of 1676 Ed. James Janeway. Bd. with Holy Bible in Verse. Benjamin Harris. Repr. of 1717 ed; History of the Holy Jesus. Repr. of 1746 ed; School of Good Manners....Rules for Children's Behavior, at the Meeting-House, at Home, at the Table, in Company, in Discourse, at School, Etc. Repr. of 1754 ed; Prodigal Daughter....Who Because Her Parents Would Not Support Her in All of Her Extravagance, Bargained with the Devil to Poison Them, Etc. Pref. by Elizabeth Williams. Repr. of 1771 ed. LC 75-32134. (Classics of Children's Literature, 1621-1932: Vol. 2). 1976. PLB 38.00 (ISBN 0-8240-2251-3). Garland Pub.

Token Mad. Mad Magazine Editors. (Mad Ser.: No. 35). (Illus.). 192p. (Orig.). 1973. pap. 1.75 (ISBN 0-446-94389-4). Warner Bks.

Tokens from the Writings of Baha 'u'llah. Illus. by Jay Conrader & Constance Conrader. LC 73-78441. (Illus.). 1973. 16.00 (ISBN 0-87743-074-8, 7-03-18); pap. 6.50 o.s.i. (ISBN 0-87743-094-2). Baha'i.

Tokens of the Eighteenth Century, Connected with Booksellers & Bookmakers (Authors, Printers, Publishers, Engravers, & Paper Makers) W. Longman. LC 70-78192. (Illus.). 90p. 1970. Repr. of 1916 ed. 15.00 (ISBN 0-8103-3368-6). Gale.

Tokoloshi. Diana Pitcher. 64p. 1980. 14.75x (ISBN 0-7050-0081-8, Pub. by Skilton & Shaw England). State Mutual Bk.

Tokoloshi: African Folk Tales Retold. Diana Pitcher. LC 80-69843. (Illus.). 64p. (gr. 3 up). 1981. Repr. 9.95 (ISBN 0-89742-049-7). Dawne-Leigh.

Tokugawa Religion. Robert N. Bellah. 1959. 8.95 o.s.i. (ISBN 0-02-902400-5). Free Pr.

Tokyo. Fosco Maraini. (The Great Cities Ser.). (Illus.). (gr. 6 up). 1976. lib. bdg. 14.94 (ISBN 0-685-77696-4, Pub by Time-Life). Silver.

Tokyo. Fosco Maraini. (Great Cities Ser). 1976. 14.95 (ISBN 0-8094-2266-2). Time-Life.

Tokyo & Washington: Dilemmas of a Mature Alliance. Frederick L. Shiels. LC 79-3339. 1980. 20.50 (ISBN 0-669-03378-2). Lexington Bks.

Tokyo Puzzles. Kobon Fujimura. Ed. by Martin Gardner. Tr. by Fumie Adachi. (Illus.). 1978. 8.95 o.p. (ISBN 0-684-15536-2, ScribT). Scribner.

Tokyo War Crimes Trial, 22 vols. Ed. by R. John Pritchard & Sonia M. Zaide. Incl. Vol. 1. 1981 (ISBN 0-8240-4750-8); Vol. 2. 1981 (ISBN 0-8240-4751-6); Vol. 3. 1981 (ISBN 0-8240-4752-4); Vol. 4. 1981 (ISBN 0-8240-4753-2); Vol. 5. 1981 (ISBN 0-8240-4754-0); Vol. 6. 1981 (ISBN 0-8240-4755-9); Vol. 7. 1981 (ISBN 0-8240-4756-7); Vol. 8. 1981 (ISBN 0-8240-4757-5); Vol. 9. 1981 (ISBN 0-8240-4758-3); Vol. 10. 1981 (ISBN 0-8240-4759-1); Vol. 11. 1981 (ISBN 0-8240-4760-5); Vol. 12. 1981 (ISBN 0-8240-4761-3); Vol. 13. 1981 (ISBN 0-8240-4762-1); Vol. 14. 1981 (ISBN 0-8240-4763-X); Vol. 15. 1981 (ISBN 0-8240-4764-8); Vol. 16. 1981 (ISBN 0-8240-4765-6); Vol. 17. 1981 (ISBN 0-8240-4766-4); Vol. 18. 1981 (ISBN 0-8240-4767-2); Vol. 19. 1981 (ISBN 0-8240-4768-0); Vol. 20. 1981 (ISBN 0-8240-4769-9); Vol. 21. 1981 (ISBN 0-8240-4770-2); Vol. 22. 1981 (ISBN 0-8240-4771-0). lib. bdg. 77.00 ea. Garland Pub.

Told Under the Blue Umbrella. Association For Childhood Education International. (Illus.). (gr. k-3). 1962. 4.95g o.s.i. (ISBN 0-02-706390-9). Macmillan.

Told Under the Christmas Tree. Association For Childhood Education International. (Illus.). (gr. 4-6). 1962. 6.95g o.s.i. (ISBN 0-02-706500-6). Macmillan.

Told Under the City Umbrella. Ed. by Association for Childhood Education. LC 72-165107. (Illus.). (gr. 4-6). 1972. 8.95 (ISBN 0-02-707600-8). Macmillan.

Told Under the Green Umbrella. Association For Childhood Education International. (gr. 4-6). 1935. 4.95g o.s.i. (ISBN 0-02-706830-7). Macmillan.

Told Under the Magic Umbrella. Association For Childhood Education International. (Illus.). (gr. k-3). 1967. 5.95g o.s.i. (ISBN 0-02-707050-6). Macmillan.

Told Under the Stars & Stripes. Association For Childhood Education International. (Illus.). (gr. 4-6). 1967. 4.25g o.s.i. (ISBN 0-02-707490-0). Macmillan.

Toledo Museum of Art, American Paintings. Toledo Museum Staff. LC 79-66974. (Illus.). 228p. 1980. lib. bdg. 24.50 (ISBN 0-935172-00-9); pap. 14.50 (ISBN 0-935172-01-7). Toledo Mus Art.

Toleration & Parliament, 1660-1719. Raymond C. Mensing. LC 79-63260. 1979. pap. text ed. 9.00 (ISBN 0-8191-0723-9). U Pr of Amer.

Toleration in Religion & Politics. Adam Watson. LC 80-65746. (Second Annual Distinguished Cria Lecture on Morality & Foreign Policy Ser.). 1980. pap. 4.00 (ISBN 0-87641-218-5). Coun Rel & Intl.

Tolkien & the Silmarils. Randel Helms. 128p. 1981. 10.95 (ISBN 0-395-29469-X). HM.

Tolkien Criticism: An Annotated Checklist. rev. ed. Richard C. West. 1981. Repr. of 1970 ed. write for info. Kent St U Pr.

Tolkien: New Critical Perspectives. Ed. & tr. by Neil D. Isaacs. LC 80-51015. 184p. 1981. 10.50 (ISBN 0-8131-1408-X). U Pr of Ky.

Toll for the Brave. Jack Higgins. 1979. pap. 1.75 o.p. (ISBN 0-449-14105-5, GM). Fawcett.

Toll-Free Digest. 1977. pap. 2.50 o.s.i. (ISBN 0-446-91338-3). Warner Bks.

Toll Free Digest 1979-80. 1979. pap. 4.95 o.s.i. (ISBN 0-446-97016-6). Warner Bks.

Toll House Tried & True Recipes. Ruth G. Wakefield. 8.50 (ISBN 0-8446-5684-4). Peter Smith.

Tollbridge. Wilma E. McDaniel. 32p. 1980. 3.00 (ISBN 0-936556-01-3). Contact Two.

Tolstoi in the Seventies. Boris Eikhenbaum. Tr. by A. Kaspin. 1981. 15.00 (ISBN 0-88233-472-7). Ardis Pubs.

Tolstoi in the Sixties. Boris Eikhenbaum. Tr. by White from Rus. 1981. 15.00 (ISBN 0-88233-470-0). Ardis Pubs.

Tolstoy. Romain Rolland. LC 71-147457. (Library of War & Peace; Peace Leaders: Biographies & Memoirs). lib. bdg. 38.00 (ISBN 0-8240-0316-0). Garland Pub.

Tolstoy. Ernest J. Simmons. (Routledge Author Guides). 272p. 1973. 18.00x (ISBN 0-7100-7394-1); pap. 8.95 (ISBN 0-7100-7395-X). Routledge & Kegan.

Tolstoy: A Critical Introduction. Reginald F. Christian. LC 69-19373. 1970. 48.00 (ISBN 0-521-07493-2); pap. 10.95 (ISBN 0-521-09585-9, 585). Cambridge U Pr.

Tolstoy & Chekov. Logan Speirs. 1972. 42.00 (ISBN 0-521-07950-0). Cambridge U Pr.

Tolstoy: The Critical Heritage. Ed. by A. V. Knowles. 1978. 32.00x (ISBN 0-7100-8947-3). Routledge & Kegan.

Tolstoy's Letters, 2 vols. Ed. & tr. by R. F. Christian. LC 77-90494. (Encore Editions). (Illus.). 1978. 9.95 set (ISBN 0-684-15596-6, ScribT). Scribner.

Tom & Sam. Pat Hutchins. LC 68-24104. (Illus.). (gr. k-2). 1968. 5.95g o.s.i. (ISBN 0-02-745840-7). Macmillan.

Tom Ashley, Sam McGee, Bukka White: Tennessee Traditional Singers. Ed. by Thomas G. Burton. LC 79-19655. 1981. 14.50 (ISBN 0-87049-260-8). U of Tenn Pr.

Tom Boyle, Master Privateer. Fred W. Hopkins, Jr. LC 76-6026. (Illus.). 1976. pap. 4.00 (ISBN 0-87033-218-X, Pub. by Tidewater). Cornell Maritime.

Tom Crabtree on Teenagers. Tom Crabtree. 160p. 1980. pap. 14.95 (ISBN 0-241-10398-3, Pub. by Hamish Hamilton England). David & Charles.

Tom Cringle's Log. Michael Scott. 1969. 5.00x (ISBN 0-460-00710-6, Evman); pap. 2.25 o.p. (ISBN 0-460-01710-1). Dutton.

Tom Jones: A Film Script. John Osborne. 1964. 4.95 (ISBN 0-571-05723-3, Pub. by Faber & Faber). Merrimack Bk Serv.

Tom Mix Died for Your Sins. Darryl Ponicsan. 1975. 8.95 o.p. (ISBN 0-440-05969-0). Delacorte.

Tom Moore. De Vere White. 1979. 22.50 (ISBN 0-241-89622-3, Pub. by Hamish Hamilton England). David & Charles.

Tom Paine & the American Revolution. Eric Foner. 250p. 1976. 17.50 (ISBN 0-19-501986-5). Oxford U Pr.

Tom Paine, Revolutionary. Olivia Coolidge. LC 69-17064. (gr. 9 up). 1969. lib. rep. ed. 10.00x o.p. (ISBN 0-684-15152-9, ScribJ). Scribner.

Tom Sawyer. (Illustrated Junior Library). (Illus.). 320p. 1981. pap. 4.95 (ISBN 0-448-11002-4). G&D.

Tom Sawyer. Mark Twain. LC 80-22095. (Raintree Short Classics). (Illus.). 48p. (gr. 4-8). 1981. PLB 9.95 (ISBN 0-8172-1665-0). Raintree Pubs.

Tom Seaver. Paul J. Deegan. LC 73-13650. (Creative Superstars Ser.). 1974. PLB 5.50 o.p. (ISBN 0-87191-280-5). Creative Ed.

Tom Seaver: Portrait of a Pitcher. Malka Drucker & Tom Seaver. LC 77-17519. (Illus.). (gr. 5 up). 1978. 7.95 o.p. (ISBN 0-8234-0322-X). Holiday.

Tom Stoppard. 3rd ed. Ronald Hayman. (Illus.). 160p. 1979. 11.75x (ISBN 0-8476-6225-X). Rowman.

Tom Stoppard: Comedy As Moral Matrix. Joan F. Dean. LC 80-26400. 128p. 1981. text ed. 9.00x (ISBN 0-8262-0332-9). U of Mo Pr.

Tom Sullivan's Adventures in Darkness. Derek Gill. (Illus., Orig.). 1977. pap. 1.50 o.p. (ISBN 0-451-07698-2, W7698, Sig). NAL.

Tom Swift: Terror on the Moons of Jupiter. 192p. (gr. 3-7). 1981. PLB 7.95 (ISBN 0-671-41182-9); pap. 2.50 (ISBN 0-671-41183-7). Wanderer Bks.

Tom Swift: The Alien Probe. Victor Appleton. Ed. by Wendy Barish. (Tom Swift Ser.). 192p. (Orig.). (gr. 3-7). 1981. 7.95 (ISBN 0-671-42538-2); pap. 1.95 (ISBN 0-671-42578-1). Wanderer Bks.

Tom Swift: The City in the Stars. 192p. (gr. 3-7). 1981. PLB 7.95 (ISBN 0-671-41120-9); pap. 2.50 (ISBN 0-671-41115-2). Wanderer Bks.

Tom Swift: The War in Outer Space. Victor Appleton. Ed. by Wendy Barish. (Tom Swift Ser.). 192p. (Orig.). (gr. 3-7). 1981. 7.95 (ISBN 0-671-42539-0); pap. 1.95 (ISBN 0-671-42579-X). Wanderer Bks.

Tom, the Poet & Gadgetmaker. Rose Britt & Doris Ceely. 64p. 1980. 6.00 (ISBN 0-682-49622-7). Exposition.

Tom Thumb. Margaret Hillert. (Just Beginning-to-Read Ser.). (Illus.). 32p. (gr. 1-6). 1981. PLB 4.39 (ISBN 0-695-41542-5); pap. 1.50 (ISBN 0-695-31542-0). Follett.

Tom Thumb. Illus. by Svend S. Otto. (Grimm's Fairy Tales). (Illus.). (gr. 2). 1976. PLB 4.95 (ISBN 0-88332-043-6, 8077). Larousse.

Tom Tit Tot. Edward Clodd. LC 67-23907. 1968. Repr. of 1898 ed. 15.00 (ISBN 0-8103-3459-3). Gale.

Tom Watson: Agrarian Rebel. C. Vann Woodward. 1963. pap. 7.95 (ISBN 0-19-500707-7, GB). Oxford U Pr.

Tom Wesselmann. Slim Stealingworth. (Illus.). 320p. 1980. 75.00 (ISBN 0-89659-072-0); limited ed. 2000.00 (ISBN 0-89659-160-3). Abbeville Pr.

Tomahawk. Lee Deighton. 156p. 1981. pap. 1.75 (ISBN 0-345-29431-9). Ballantine.

Tomahawks & Long Rifles. Jonathan Scofield. 1981. pap. 2.75 (ISBN 0-440-09119-5). Dell.

Tomas de Iriarte. R. Merritt Cox. (World Authors Ser.: Spain: No. 228). lib. bdg. 10.95 (ISBN 0-8057-2456-7). Twayne.

Tomas Onetwo. Ernest Robson. (Illus.). 1971. 6.95. Primary Pr.

Tomaso Campanella in America: A Critical Bibliography & a Profile. Francesco Grillo. 109p. 1954. 5.75x (ISBN 0-913298-43-3). S F Vanni.

Tomato Boy. Mariana B. Prieto. LC 67-10158. (Illus.). (gr. 2-4). 1967. PLB 7.89 (ISBN 0-381-99725-1, A80800, JD-J). John Day.

Tomato Growing Today. Ian G. Walls. 1973. 14.95 (ISBN 0-7153-5435-3). David & Charles.

Tomato Production Processing & Quality Evaluation. Wilbur A. Gould. (Illus.). 1974. text ed. 42.00 (ISBN 0-87055-162-0). AVI.

Tomatoes for Everyone. Frank W. Allerton. (Illus., Orig.). 1971. pap. 3.95 (ISBN 0-571-09749-9, Pub. by Faber & Faber). Merrimack Bk Serv.

Tomatoes in Peat. 76p. 1980. pap. 9.95x (ISBN 0-901361-32-1, Pub. by Grower Bks England). Intl Schol Bk Serv.

Tomatoes in the Tropics. Ruben L. Villareal. (IADS Development-Oriented Ser.). 200p. 1980. lib. bdg. 22.00x (ISBN 0-89158-989-9). Westview.

Tomb of Kheruef: Theban Tomb No. 192. Epigraphic Survey. LC 79-88739. (Oriental Institute Publications Ser.: Vol. 102). 1980. 90.00x (ISBN 0-918986-23-0). Oriental Inst.

Tomb of Nyhetep-Ptah at Giza & the Tomb of 'Ankhm' Ahor at Saqqara. Alexander Badawy. (Occasional Papers Archaeology Ser.: Vol. II). 1978. pap. 18.50x (ISBN 0-520-09575-8). U of Cal Pr.

Tomb of Queen Hetep-heres. Dows Dunham. (Illus.). 1972. pap. 1.00 (ISBN 0-87846-181-7). Mus Fine Arts Boston.

Tomboy. Norma Klein. LC 78-4337. 128p. (gr. 3-7). 1978. 6.95 (ISBN 0-590-07521-7, Four Winds). Schol Bk Serv.

Tomboy. Norma Klein. (gr. 3-5). 1980. pap. 1.75 (ISBN 0-671-56033-6). PB.

Tombs of Iteti, Sekhem'ankh-Ptah, & Kaemnofert at Giza. Alexander Badawy. LC 75-620057. (Publications, Occasional Papers, Archaeology: Vol. 9). 1976. pap. 14.50x (ISBN 0-520-09544-8). U of Cal Pr.

Tombstone. Matt Braun. 1981. pap. 1.95 (ISBN 0-671-82033-8). PB.

Tombstone. William Hattich. LC 80-5947. (Illus.). 64p. 1981. 9.95 (ISBN 0-8061-1753-2). U of Okla Pr.

Tommaso Campanella in America: A Supplement to the Critical Bibliography. Francesco Grillo. 48p. 1957. 5.00x (ISBN 0-913298-49-2). S F Vanni.

Tommaso Traetta di Bitonto (1727-1779) La Vita e le Opere. Franco Casavola. LC 80-22630. 1981. Repr. of 1957 ed. 22.50 (ISBN 0-404-18816-8). AMS Pr.

Tommy Johnson. David Evans. (Paul Oliver Blues Ser.). pap. 2.95 (ISBN 0-913714-46-1). Legacy Bks.

Tommy Learns About Time & Eternity. Peggy J. Buck. (Illus.). 68p. (Orig.). (gr. 1-3). 1980. pap. 2.50 (ISBN 0-89323-006-5). BMA Pr.

Tommy Strangeleaf & Bow. Russell L. Carson. 116p. (gr. 4-6). 1979. 4.95 (ISBN 0-8059-2627-5). Dorrance.

Tommy Visits the Doctor. Jean Seligmann & Milton Levine. (Illus.). (ps-1). 1962. PLB 4.57 o.p. (ISBN 0-307-60480-2, Golden Pr). Western Pub.

Tomol: Chumash Watercraft. Travis Hudson et al. (Ballena Press Anthropological Papers: No. 9). (Illus.). 1978. pap. 8.95 o.p. (ISBN 0-87919-069-8). Ballena Pr.

Tomorrow a New World. Paul Conklin. (FDR & the Era of the New Deal Ser.). 1976. Repr. of 1959 ed. lib. bdg. 32.50 (ISBN 0-306-70805-1). Da Capo.

Tomorrow & Beyond. Ed. by Ian Summers. LC 78-7119. (Illus.). 1978. 19.95 (ISBN 0-89480-062-0, 1996); pap. 10.95 (ISBN 0-89480-055-8, 1988). Workman Pub.

Tomorrow & Tomorrow. Stanwood Cobb. 1951. pap. 1.00 (ISBN 0-87743-059-4, 7-31-35). Baha'i.

Tomorrow File. Lawrence Sanders. 1976. pap. 2.95 (ISBN 0-425-04994-9). Berkley Pub.

Tomorrow Is Theirs. large type ed. Anne Duffield. 1974. pap. 1.25 o.p. (ISBN 0-425-02713-9, Medallion). Berkley Pub.

Tomorrow Morning, Faustus. I. A. Richards. LC 62-14468. 1962. 4.50 o.p. (ISBN 0-15-190490-1). HarBraceJ.

Tomorrow You Can. Dorothy Corey. Ed. by Caroline Rubin. LC 77-12789. (Self-Starter Ser.). (Illus.). (ps-1). 1977. 6.50g (ISBN 0-8075-8015-5). A Whitman.

Tomorrow You Die. Reona Peterson. pap. 2.95 (ISBN 0-89728-060-1, 659262). Omega Pubns OR.

Tomorrow's Alternatives. Ed. by Roger Elwood. 192p. 1973. 5.95 o.s.i. (ISBN 0-686-66803-0). Macmillan.

Tomorrow's Alternatives, Vol. 1. Ed. by Roger Elwood. 192p. 1973. pap. 1.50 o.s.i. (ISBN 0-02-019800-0, Collier). Macmillan.

Tomorrow's Community- the Development of Neighborhood Organisations. Maurice Broady. 86p. 1979. pap. text ed. 7.40x (ISBN 0-7199-0966-X, Pub. by Bedford England). Renouf.

Tomorrow's Decisions Today: The Corporation. Nina Crosby. 51p. (Orig.). 1979. pap. text ed. 4.95 (ISBN 0-914634-72-0, 7910). DOK Pubs.

Tomorrow's Education: The French Experience. J. Capelle. 1967. 23.00 (ISBN 0-08-012517-4); pap. 12.25 (ISBN 0-08-012516-6). Pergamon.

Tomorrow's Parents: A Study of Youth & Their Families. Bernice M. Moore & W. H. Holtzman. (Hogg Foundation Research Series). 1965. 13.50x (ISBN 0-292-73409-3). U of Tex Pr.

Tomorrow's Pulpit. Alec Gilmore. LC 74-18108. 96p. 1975. pap. 3.50 o.p. (ISBN 0-8170-0641-9). Judson.

Tomorrow's Reality. Evieline L. Smith. LC 79-67224. 78p. 1980. 5.95 (ISBN 0-533-04452-9). Vantage.

Tomorrow's Techniques for Today's Salesmen. John J. Tarrant. 1969. 8.95 (ISBN 0-8015-7806-X, Hawthorn). Dutton.

Tomorrow's Tomorrow. Ladner, Joyce A., Ph.D. LC 78-139038. 320p. 1972. pap. 2.95 (ISBN 0-385-00941-0, Anch). Doubleday.

Tom's Weeds. Mea Allan. (Illus.). 1970. 5.95 o.p. (ISBN 0-571-08919-4, Pub. by Faber & Faber). Merrimack Bk Serv.

Tonal Grammar of Etsako. Baruch Elimelech. (Publications in Linguistics Ser.: Vol. 87). 1979. 10.50x (ISBN 0-520-09576-6). U of Cal Pr.

Tone: A Study in Musical Acoustics. 2nd ed. Siegmund Levarie & Ernst Levy. LC 80-29383. (Illus.). xvii, 256p. 1981. Repr. of 1980 ed. lib. bdg. 27.50x (ISBN 0-313-22499-4, LETO). Greenwood.

Tone: A Study in Musical Acoustics. rev. ed. Siegmund Levarie & Ernst Levy. LC 80-16794. (Illus.). 280p. 1980. pap. 6.75x (ISBN 0-87338-250-1). Kent St U Pr.

Tone Languages: A Technique for Determining the Number & Type of Pitch Contrasts in a Language, with Studies in Tonemic Substitution & Fusion. Kenneth L. Pike. 1948. pap. 6.95x (ISBN 0-472-08734-7). U of Mich Pr.

Tonetti Years at Snedens Landing. Isabelle K. Savell. (Illus.). 1977. 11.50 o.p. (ISBN 0-686-00570-8); pap. 7.95 o.p. (ISBN 0-686-00571-6). Rockland County Hist.

Tonga Christianity. Stan Shewmaker. 1971. pap. 3.45. William Carey Lib.

Tongue & Thunder. David Cloutier. (Illus., Orig.). 1980. pap. 4.50 (ISBN 0-914278-32-0). Copper Beech.

Tongue & Thunder. David Cloutier. (Illus.). 64p. (Orig.). 1980. pap. 4.50x (ISBN 0-914278-32-0). Copper Beech.

Tongues & Spirit-Baptism. Anthony A. Hoekema. 264p. 1981. pap. 6.95 (ISBN 0-8010-4243-7). Baker Bk.

Tongues of Men. Stephen N. Dunning. LC 79-10729. (American Academy of Religion, Dissertation Ser.: No. 27). 1979. 12.00 (ISBN 0-89130-283-2, 010127); pap. 7.50 (ISBN 0-89130-302-2). Scholars Pr Ca.

Tongues of the Moon. Philip J. Farmer. 1978. pap. 1.50 (ISBN 0-515-04595-0). Jove Pubns.

Tonight's the Night. Jim Aylesworth. Ed. by Ann Fay. (Self-Starter Bks.). (Illus.). 32p. (ps-1). 1981. 6.50 (ISBN 0-8075-8020-1). A Whitman.

Toning: The Creative Power of the Voice. rev. ed. Laurel E. Keyes. LC 73-88021. 88p. 1973. pap. 3.95 (ISBN 0-87516-176-6). De Vorss.

Tonio Kroger. 2nd ed. Thomas Mann. Ed. by Elizabeth M. Wilkinson. (Blackwell's German Texts Ser.). 1968. pap. 9.95x (ISBN 0-631-01810-7, Pub. by Basil Blackwell). Biblio Dist.

Toni's Crowd. Ellen Rabinowich. LC 78-1549. (Triumph Bks). (Illus.). (gr. 7-10). 1978. PLB 6.90 s&l (ISBN 0-531-02210-2). Watts.

Tonkawa Texts. Harry Hoijer. (U. C. Publ. in Linguistics: Vol. 73). 1973. pap. 8.00x (ISBN 0-520-09451-4). U of Cal Pr.

Tonnage Measurement: Treatment of Shelter-Deck & Other "Open" Spaces. 15p. 1964. 5.50 (IMCO). Unipub.

Tono-Bungay. H. G. Wells. LC 77-28027. 1978. 13.95x (ISBN 0-8032-4702-8); pap. 4.25x (ISBN 0-8032-9701-7, BB669, Bison). U of Nebr Pr.

Tony & Me. Alfred Slote. LC 74-5182. 160p. (gr. 4-6). 1974. 8.95 (ISBN 0-397-31507-4). Lippincott.

Tony & Me. Alfred Slote. (gr. 3-5). 1975. pap. 1.25 (ISBN 0-380-00438-0, 45914, Camelot). Avon.

Tony Dorsett. Marcia Biddle. LC 80-18302. (Illus.). 192p. (gr. 7 up). 1980. PLB 8.79 (ISBN 0-671-34040-9). Messner.

Tony Orlando. Ann Morse. (Rock 'n Pop Stars Ser.). (Illus.). (gr. 4-12). 1978. PLB 5.95 (ISBN 0-87191-616-9); pap. 2.95 (ISBN 0-89812-123-X). Creative Ed.

Tony Valenti Story. Tony Valenti & Grazia P. Yonan. 160p. (Orig.). 1981. write for info. (ISBN 0-88243-752-6, 02-0752). Gospel Pub.

Tony's Tummy. Lucile Jones. Ed. by Bobbie J. Van Dolson. 32p. 1981. pap. price not set (ISBN 0-8280-0039-5). Review & Herald.

Tony's Tunnel. A. McGrath. 1980. 7.95 (ISBN 0-13-925099-9). P-H.

Too Bad About the Haines Girl. Zoa Sherburne. (gr. 9-12). 1967. PLB 7.44 (ISBN 0-688-31646-8); pap. 2.95 (ISBN 0-688-26646-0). Morrow.

Too Big for the Bag. Beverly Amstutz. (Illus.). 1981. pap. 2.50 (ISBN 0-937836-05-2). Precious Res.

Too Big to Spank. Jay Kesler. LC 77-90580. 1978. pap. 4.95 (ISBN 0-8307-0623-2, 54-093-06). Regal.

Too Bright to See. Linda Gregg. 72p. 1981. 9.00. Graywolf.

Too Busy Not to Pray: A Homemaker Talks with God. Jo Carr & Imogene Sorley. 1966. 3.95 o.p. (ISBN 0-687-42379-1). Abingdon.

Too Dear for My Possessing. Pamela H. Johnson. LC 72-2007. 319p. 1973. 7.95 o.p. (ISBN 0-684-13052-1, ScribT). Scribner.

Too Deep for Tears. Lucy Freeman et al. 1980. 12.95 (ISBN 0-8015-7820-5, Hawthorn). Dutton.

Too Early Lilac. E. M. Almedingen. LC 73-155661. 288p. 1974. 7.95 (ISBN 0-8149-0694-X). Vanguard.

Too Far to Go. John Updike. 1979. pap. 2.50 (ISBN 0-449-24002-9, Crest). Fawcett.

Too Little but Not Too Late: Federal Aid to Lagging Areas. Sar A. Levitan & Joyce K. Zickler. LC 76-12363. (Illus.). 1976. 16.95 (ISBN 0-669-00721-8). Lexington Bks.

Too Long a Sacrifice. Mildred D. Broxon. (Orig.). 1981. pap. 2.50 (ISBN 0-440-18603-X). Dell.

Too Long a Sacrifice: Life & Death in Northern Ireland Since Nineteen Sixty-Nine. Jack Holland. LC 80-27267. (Illus.). 240p. 1981. 8.95 (ISBN 0-686-69573-9). Dodd.

Too Long in the West. Bhalchandra Rajan. 1961. pap. 2.00 (ISBN 0-88253-175-1). Ind-US Inc.

Too Many Cooks. Rex Stout. 1976. pap. 1.75 (ISBN 0-515-04866-6). Jove Pubns.

Too Many Cooks. Rex Stout. LC 75-46002. (Crime Fiction Ser). 1976. Repr. of 1938 ed. lib. bdg. 17.50 (ISBN 0-8240-2394-3). Garland Pub.

Too Many Lollipops. Robert Quackenbush. LC 75-12546. (Illus.). 40p. (gr. k-3). 1975. 5.95 o.s.i. (ISBN 0-8193-0825-0, Four Winds); PLB 5.41 o.s.i. (ISBN 0-8193-0826-9). Schol Bk Serv.

Too Many Midnights. Rod McKuen. 1981. pap. price not set (ISBN 0-671-43111-0). PB.

Too Many Mittens. Florence Slobodkin & Louis Slobodkin. LC 58-12198. (Illus.). (gr. 1-4). 1958. 5.95 (ISBN 0-8149-0394-0). Vanguard.

Too Many Monkeys: A Counting Rhyme. (Illus.). (ps). 1980. 1.50 (ISBN 0-307-11984-X, Golden Pr); PLB 6.08 (ISBN 0-307-61984-2). Western Pub.

Too Many Monkeys Paint the Town. Valerie Flournoy. (Golden Storytime Bks.). (Illus.). 24p. 1981. 1.95 (ISBN 0-307-11951-3, Golden Pr); PLB 1.56 (ISBN 0-686-69207-1). Western Pub.

Too Many Rabbits. Peggy Parish. LC 73-11690. (Ready-to-Read Ser). (Illus.). 48p. (gr. 1-4). 1974. 7.95 (ISBN 0-02-769850-5). Macmillan.

Too Many: The Biological Limitations of Our Earth. George Borgstrom. 1969. 7.95 o.s.i. (ISBN 0-02-513660-7). Macmillan.

Too Many Tomatoes...Squash, Beans, & Other Good Things: A Cookbook for When Your Garden Explodes. Lois M. Burrows & Laura G. Myers. LC 75-34581. 1980. pap. 6.95 (ISBN 0-06-090765-7, CN 765, CN). Har-Row.

Too Many Wheels. Ruben Tanner. LC 79-1909. (Illus.). (ps-2). 1979. 1.95 (ISBN 0-525-69014-X, Gingerbread Bks); PLB 5.95 o.p. (ISBN 0-525-69015-8). Dutton.

Too Many Women. Rex Stout. 176p. 1981. pap. 2.25 (ISBN 0-553-14595-9). Bantam.

Too Much in Love. Brisco. (gr. 7-12). 1980. pap. 1.25 (ISBN 0-590-30910-2, Schol Pap). Schol Bk Serv.

Too Much Invested to Quit. Allan I. Teger et al. (Illus.). 1980. 19.25 (ISBN 0-08-022995-6). Pergamon.

Too Old to Cry. Paul Hemphill. LC 80-51776. 288p. 1981. 11.95 (ISBN 0-670-72017-8). Viking Pr.

Too Old, Too Sick, Too Bad: Nursing Homes in America. Frank E. Moss & Val J. Halamandaris. LC 77-72515. 1977. 22.00 (ISBN 0-912862-43-2). Aspen Systems.

Too Rich for Her Pride. Jacqueline Hacsi. (Candlelight Romance Ser.). (Orig.). 1981. pap. 1.50 (ISBN 0-440-18619-6). Dell.

Too Rich to Clothe the Sunne: Essays on George Herbert. Ed. by Claude J. Summers & Ted-Larry Pebworth. LC 80-5255. (Illus.). 0278p. 1980. 16.95x (ISBN 0-8229-3421-3). U of Pittsburgh Pr.

Too Serious a Business: European Armed Forces & the Coming of the Second World War. Donald C. Watt. LC 74-82853. 1975. 16.50x (ISBN 0-520-02829-5). U of Cal Pr.

Too Small for Stove Wood, Too Big for Kindling. John V. Kelleher. 1980. pap. text ed. 10.50x (ISBN 0-85105-312-2, Dolmen Pr). Humanities.

Too Small to Die. Wilner W. Esalen. LC 79-57586. 114p. 1981. 7.95 (ISBN 0-533-04575-4). Vantage.

Too Smart? Francis Puglise. (Illus.). 23p. (Orig.). 1980. 1.00 (ISBN 0-936920-01-7). Ridgeview Jr High Pr.

Too Soon, Mr. Bear. Catherine Runyon. (ps-5). 1979. pap. 1.95 (ISBN 0-8024-8788-2). Moody.

Too Strong for Fantasy. Marcia Davenport. 1979. pap. 3.50 (ISBN 0-380-45195-6, 45195, Discus). Avon.

Too Swift the Morning. Mary Carroll. 192p. (Orig.). 1980. pap. 1.50 (ISBN 0-671-57045-5). S&S.

Too Well Beloved. Laura Conway. 1979. 7.95 o.p. (ISBN 0-525-22086-0). Dutton.

Toobee Players' Handook: The Amazing Flying Can. new ed. Dan Poynter. LC 80-20529. (Illus.). 52p. (Orig.). 1981. pap. 4.95 (ISBN 0-915516-25-X). Para Pub.

Toohey's Medicine for Nurses. 13th ed. Arnold Bloom. (Illus.). 1981. pap. text ed. 17.50 (ISBN 0-443-02201-1). Churchill.

Tool & Die. International Labour Office, Geneva. (Equipment Planning Guide for Vocational & Technical Training & Education Programmes Ser.: No. 2). x, 214p. (Orig.). 1980. pap. 22.80 spiral (ISBN 92-2-101891-1). Intl Labour Office.

Tool Design. Herman Pollack. (Illus.). 528p. 1976. 19.95 (ISBN 0-87909-840-6); students manual avail. Reston.

Tool for Tomorrow: New Knowledge About Genes. Sylvia L. Engdahl & Rick Roberson. LC 78-13777. (Illus.). (gr. 5 up). 1979. 6.95 (ISBN 0-689-30679-2). Atheneum.

Tool of Power: The Political History of Money. William Wiseley. LC 76-57701. 300p. 1977. 28.95 (ISBN 0-471-02235-7, Pub. by Wiley-Interscience). Wiley.

Tool Steel Simplified. rev. ed. Frank R. Palmer et al. LC 78-7181. 1978. 14.50 (ISBN 0-8019-6747-3). Chilton.

Toolbox. Anne Rockwell. LC 72-119836. (Illus.). (gr. k-1). 1971. 7.95 (ISBN 0-02-777540-2). Macmillan.

Toolchest: A Primer of Woodcraft. Jan Adkins. Ed. by Margery Cuyler. LC 72-81374. (Illus.). 48p. 1973. 6.95 (ISBN 0-8027-6153-4); lib. bdg. 6.83 (ISBN 0-8027-6154-2). Walker & Co.

Tooley! Tooley! Frank Modell. LC 76-49645. (Illus.). (gr. k-3). 1979. 7.50 (ISBN 0-688-80092-0); PLB 7.20 (ISBN 0-688-84092-2). Greenwillow.

Tooling up for Curriculum Review. B. Wilcox & P. J. Eustace. 101p. 1981. pap. text ed. 23.50x (ISBN 0-85633-210-0, NFER). Humanities.

Toolmaker. Jill P. Walsh. LC 73-7126. (Illus.). (gr. 3-6). 1974. 4.95 o.p. (ISBN 0-8164-3109-4, Clarion). HM.

Tools & Techniques of Estate Planning. 3rd ed. Stepan R. Leimberg et al. 376p. 1980. pap. 20.00 (ISBN 0-87218-406-4). Natl Underwriter.

Tools & Technologies: America's Wooden Age. Ed. by Paul B. Kebabian & William C. Lipke. (Illus.). 119p. (Orig.). 1979. pap. 10.00 (ISBN 0-87451-987-X). U Pr of New Eng.

Tools for Conviviality. Ivan Illich. LC 72-9125. (World Perspectives Ser). 142p. 1973. 8.95 o.p. (ISBN 0-06-012138-6, HarpT). Har-Row.

Tools for Homesteaders, Gardeners, & Small Scale Farmers. Ed. by Diana Branch. 1978. pap. 12.95 (ISBN 0-87857-235-X). Rodale Pr Inc.

Tools for Teaching & Training. LeRoy Ford. LC 61-5630. (Orig.). 1961. pap. 3.50 (ISBN 0-8054-3411-9). Broadman.

Tools for Theological Research. 6th ed. John L. Sayre & Roberta Hamburger. 100p. (Orig.). 1981. pap. price not set (ISBN 0-912832-20-7). Seminary Pr.

Tools for Woodwork. LC 76-49681. (Drake Home Craftsman Ser.). (Illus.). 1976. pap. 5.95 (ISBN 0-8069-8718-9). Sterling.

Tools of Empire: Technology & European Imperialism in the Nineteenth Century. Daniel R. Headrick. 224p. 1981. text ed. 9.95x (ISBN 0-19-502831-7); pap. text ed. 5.95x (ISBN 0-19-502832-5). Oxford U Pr.

Tools of Managing: Functions, Techniques & Skills. M. Gene Newport. (Illus.). 1972. pap. text ed. 8.95 (ISBN 0-201-05271-7). A-W.

Tools of Modern Biology. Melvin Berger. LC 73-94788. (Illus.). (gr. 5-8). 1970. 7.95 o.p. (ISBN 0-690-83032-7, TYC-J). T Y Crowell.

Tools of the Maritime Trades. John Horsley. LC 78-51829. (Illus.). 1978. 15.00 o.p. (ISBN 0-87742-101-3). Intl Marine.

Tooni, the Elephant Boy. Astrid B. Sucksdorff. LC 73-137762. (Illus.). 48p. (gr. 3 up). 1971. 5.95 o.p. (ISBN 0-15-289426-8, HJ). HarBraceJ.

Toot-Toot-Tootsie, Good-Bye. Ron Powers. 1981. 10.95 (ISBN 0-440-08190-4). Delacorte.

Tooth & Claw: Defensive Strategies in the Animal World. J. L. Cloudsley-Thompson. (Illus.). 252p. 1980. 22.50x (ISBN 0-460-04360-9, Pub. by J M Dent England). Biblio Dist.

Tooth-Gnasher Superflash. Daniel Pinkwater. LC 80-69996. (Illus.). 32p. (gr. k-3). 1981. 9.95 (ISBN 0-590-07624-8, Four Winds). Schol Bk Serv.

Tooth Mutilations & Dentistry in Pre-Columbian Mexico. Samuel Faschlicht. (Illus.). 152p. 1976. 46.00. Quint Pub Co.

Toothed Whales: In Eastern North Pacific & Arctic Waters. 2nd ed. Compiled by Alice Seed. LC 70-173350. (Sea Mammal Ser.). (Illus.). 40p. (Orig.). 1971. pap. 1.75 o.p. (ISBN 0-914718-00-2). Pacific Search.

Toothpick Building Illustrated. Katrina Davis. (Illus.). 48p. (Orig.). 1980. pap. 3.95 (ISBN 0-937242-04-7). Scandia Pubs.

Toothpick Sculpture & Ice-Cream Stick Art. Bruce Bowman. LC 76-19808. (Illus.). (gr. 5 up). 1976. 7.95 (ISBN 0-8069-5372-1); PLB 7.49 (ISBN 0-8069-5373-X). Sterling.

Tootle. Gertrude Crampton. (Illus.). 24p. (gr. k-1). 1976. PLB 5.38 (ISBN 0-307-68949-2, Golden Pr). Western Pub.

Top Down Structured Design Techniques. Gloria H. Swann. LC 77-27092. (PBI Series for Computer & Data Processing Professionals). 1978. text ed. 13.50 (ISBN 0-89433-094-2); pap. 11.50 (ISBN 0-89433-019-5). Petrocelli.

Top Entertainers Are Born Again. Carol Lawrence & Norma Zimmer. LC 77-78464. (Lifeline Ser.). pap. 0.95 o.p. (ISBN 0-88419-142-7). Creation Hse.

Top-Flight Fully-Automated Junior High School Girl Detective. E. W. Hildick & Iris Schweitzer. pap. write for info. (ISBN 0-671-29911-5). PB.

Top Flight Readers Series, 7 bks. Henry A. Bamman & R. J. Whitehead. Incl. Chopper (ISBN 0-201-21501-2); Test Pilot (ISBN 0-201-21502-0); Hang Glider (ISBN 0-201-21503-9); Bush Pilot. o.p.; Barnstormers. o.p. (ISBN 0-201-21505-5); Balloon. o.p. (ISBN 0-201-21506-3). (gr. 5-12). 1977. pap. text ed. 6.92 ea. (Sch Div); tchr's. ed. 4.08 (ISBN 0-201-21500-4). A-W.

Top Flight: Speed Index to Waterfowl of North America. John A. Ruthven & William Zimmerman. 1976. pap. 5.95 o.p. (ISBN 0-684-14752-1, SL675, ScribT). Scribner.

Top Hat & Tails: The Story of Jack Buchanan. Michael Marshall. (Illus.). 1978. 24.00 (ISBN 0-241-89602-9, Pub. by Hamish Hamilton England). David & Charles.

Top Man. Don G. Mitchell. 192p. 1980. 12.95 o.p. (ISBN 0-8144-5205-1). Am Mgmt.

Top Man with a Gun. Lewis B. Patten. 1979. pap. 1.75 (ISBN 0-449-14191-8, GM). Fawcett.

Top Management Strategy. Benjamin B. Tregoe & John W. Zimmerman. 1980. 9.95 (ISBN 0-671-25401-4). S&S.

Top of the Hill. Irwin Shaw. 1980. pap. 2.95 o.s.i. (ISBN 0-440-18976-4). Dell.

Top of the Pizzas. Bill Basso. LC 77-6085. (gr. 2-5). 1977. 6.50 (ISBN 0-396-07463-4). Dodd.

Top of the World. John R. Townsend. LC 76-48219. 1977. 8.95 (ISBN 0-397-31728-X). Lippincott.

Top Pop Records, Nineteen Fifty-Five to Nineteen Seventy-Two. new ed. Joel Whitburn. (Record Research Ser.). (Illus., Orig.). 1973. pap. text ed. 30.00 o.p. (ISBN 0-89820-000-8). Record Research.

Top Pop Records, 1975. Joel Whitburn. 40p. (Orig.). 1976. pap. text ed. 10.00 o.p. (ISBN 0-89820-006-7). Record Research.

Top Pop Records, 1977. Joel Whitburn. 36p. (Orig.). 1978. pap. text ed. 10.00 o.p. (ISBN 0-89820-008-3). Record Research.

Top Pop Records,Nineteen Seventy-Three. new ed. Joel Whitburn. (Record Research Ser.). (Orig.). pap. text ed. 10.00 o.p. (ISBN 0-89820-004-0). Record Research.

Top Secret: National Security & the Right to Know. Morton H. Halperin & Daniel N. Hoffman. LC 77-5349. 1977. 8.95 o.p. (ISBN 0-915220-27-X); pap. 3.95 o.p. (ISBN 0-915220-28-8). New Republic.

Top Secret Ultra. Peter Calvocoressi. (Illus.). 1981. 10.95 (ISBN 0-394-51154-9). Pantheon.

Top Symbols & Trademarks of the World. LC 73-76266. 150.00 (ISBN 0-8379-4201-2). Marquis.

TOPAZ - General Planning Technique & Its Applications at the Regional, Urban, & Facility Planning Levels. J. F. Brotchie et al. (Lecture Notes in Economics & Mathematical Systems: Vol. 180). (Illus.). 356p. 1980. pap. 29.00 (ISBN 0-387-10020-2). Springer-Verlag.

Topeka: A Pictorial History. Roy Bird. Ed. by Donna R. Friedman. (Illus.). 208p. 1981. pap. price not set (ISBN 0-89865-114-X). Donning Co.

Topic in Finite Groups. T. M. Gagen. LC 75-17116. (London Mathematical Society Lecture Note Ser.: No. 16). 80p. 1976. 11.95 (ISBN 0-521-21002-X). Cambridge U Pr.

Topical & Nautical Operas. Ed. by Walter H. Rubsamen. (Ballad Opera Ser.). 1974. lib. bdg. 50.00 (ISBN 0-8240-0913-4). Garland Pub.

Topical Guide to "Folia Primatologica", Volumes 1-30 (1963-1978) Ed. by E. Biegert. 160p. 1980. pap. 23.50 (ISBN 3-8055-0781-X). S Karger.

Topical Index to JOSH: Nineteen Sixty-Three to Nineteen Seventy-Four. non-members 3.00 (ISBN 0-917160-03-7). Am Sch Health.

Topical Stamp Collecting. M. W. Martin. LC 74-19793. (Illus.). 192p. 1975. lib. bdg. 8.95 o. p. o.p. (ISBN 0-668-03754-7); pap. 5.95 o.p. (ISBN 0-668-03662-1). Arco.

Topicals World Stamp Album. Larry Grossman. (Illus.). 1980. 2.00 o.p. (ISBN 0-685-99700-6). Grossman Stamp.

Topics & Terms in Environmental Problems. John R. Holum. LC 77-12805. 1977. 31.00 (ISBN 0-471-01982-8, Pub. by Wiley-Interscience). Wiley.

Topics for the Restless Brown Book. Ed. by Edward Spargo. (College Reading Skills Ser). (Illus.). 176p. (gr. 12 up). 1974. pap. text ed. 4.80x (ISBN 0-89061-007-X). Jamestown Pubs.

Topics for the Restless Olive Book. Ed. by Edward Spargo. (College Reading Skills Ser). (Illus.). 176p. (gr. 12 up). 1974. pap. text ed. 4.80 (ISBN 0-89061-006-1). Jamestown Pubs.

Topics for the Restless Purple Book. Ed. by Edward Spargo. (College Reading Skills Ser). (Illus.). 176p. (gr. 12 up). 1974. pap. text ed. 4.80x (ISBN 0-89061-008-8). Jamestown Pubs.

Topics in Antibiotic Chemistry, Vol. 5. P. G. Sammes. LC 80-41091. 312p. 1980. 87.50 (ISBN 0-470-27050-0). Halsted Pr.

Topics in Antibiotic Chemistry: Mechanisms of Action of Nalidixic Acid & Its Cogeners & New Synthetic B-Lactam Antibiotics, Vol. 3. P. G. Sammes. LC 79-42955. 1980. 59.95x (ISBN 0-470-26882-4). Halsted Pr.

Topics in Antibiotic Chemistry: Vol. 2, Antibiotic from Marine Organisms, Oligosaccharides, Anthnacyclines and Their Biological Receptors. Ed. by P. G. Sammes. LC 78-40228. 1978. 49.95 (ISBN 0-470-26365-2). Halsted Pr.

Topics in Antibiotic Chemistry, Vol. 4: The Chemistry & Antimicrobial Activity of New Synthetic B-Lactam Antibiotics. Ed. by P. G. Sammes. 278p. 1980. 75.00x (ISBN 0-470-26936-7). Halsted Pr.

Topics in Applied Econometrics. Kenneth F. Wallis. 1973. pap. 36.00x (ISBN 0-85641-011-X, Pub. by Basil Blackwell England). Biblio Dist.

Topics in Applied Econometrics. rev. 2nd ed. Kenneth F. Wallis. 176p. 1980. 19.50x (ISBN 0-8166-1014-2); pap. 6.95x (ISBN 0-8166-1017-7). U of Minn Pr.

Topics in Automatic Chemical Analysis, Vol. 1. Ed. by J. K. Foreman & P. B. Stockwell. LC 79-40239. (Series in Analytical Chemistry). 1979. 62.95x (ISBN 0-470-26600-7). Halsted Pr.

Topics in Basic Immunology. Ed. by M. Sela & M. Prywes. 1969. 32.50 (ISBN 0-12-635550-9). Acad Pr.

Topics in Bioelectrochemistry & Bioenergetics, 3 vols. Ed. by G. Milazzo. LC 76-18231. (Topics in Bioelectrochemistry & Bioenergetics Ser.). Vol. 1, 1978. 65.00 (ISBN 0-471-01356-0, Pub. by Wiley-Interscience); Vol. 2, 1978. 45.50 (ISBN 0-471-99533-9); Vol. 3, 1980. 96.95 (ISBN 0-471-99744-7, Pub. by Wiley-Interscience). Wiley.

Topics in Complex Function Theory, 3 vols. C. L. Siegel. Incl. Vol. 1. Elliptical Functions & Uniformization Theory. 1969. 26.95 (ISBN 0-471-79070-2); Vol. 2. Automorphic Functions & Abelian Integrals. 1972. 26.95 (ISBN 0-471-79080-X); Vol. 3. Abelian Functions & Modular Functions of Several Variables. Tr. by M. Tretkoff & E. Gottschling. 244p. 1973. 29.95 (ISBN 0-471-79090-7). LC 69-19931. (Pure & Applied Mathematics Ser., Pub. by Wiley-Interscience). Wiley.

Topics in English Morphology. Dorothy Siegel. Ed. by Jorge Hankamer. LC 78-66592. (Outstanding Dissertations in Linguistics Ser.). 205p. 1980. lib. bdg. 24.00 (ISBN 0-8240-9675-4). Garland Pub.

Topics in Enzyme & Fermentation Biotechnology, Vol. 2. Ed. by Alan Wiseman. LC 76-25441. 1978. 37.95 (ISBN 0-470-99318-9). Vol. 2. Halsted Pr.

Topics in Enzyme & Fermentation Biotechnology, Vol. 4. Ed. by Alan Wiseman. (Topics in Enzyme & Fermentation Biotechnology Ser.). 242p. 1980. 69.95x (ISBN 0-470-26922-7). Halsted Pr.

Topics in Enzyme & Fermentation Biotechnology, Vol. 5. A. Wiseman. 300p. 1980. 95.00 (ISBN 0-470-27089-6). Halsted Pr.

Topics in Enzyme & Fermentation Biotechnology, VI, Vol. 6. Alan Wiseman. LC 76-25441. 1977. 29.95 (ISBN 0-470-98896-7). Halsted Pr.

Topics in Ergodic Theory. W. Parry. LC 79-7815. (Tracts in Mathematics Ser.). Date not set. price not set (ISBN 0-521-22986-3). Cambridge U Pr.

Topics in General Relativity. Robert Hermann. (Interdisciplinary Mathematics Ser: No. 5). 171p. 1973. 12.00 (ISBN 0-915692-04-X). Math Sci Pr.

Topics in Health Care Financing. (A quarterly topical journal). annual subscription 43.50 (ISBN 0-912862-75-0). Aspen Systems.

Topics in Health Care Financing. Incl. Shared Services. 1976. Vol. 2, No. 4. 13.75 (ISBN 0-912862-83-1); Financial Management Under Third Party Reimbursement. 1976. Vol. 3, No. 1. 13.75 (ISBN 0-912862-84-X); Prospective Rate Setting. 1976. Vol. 3, No. 2. 13.75 (ISBN 0-912862-85-8); Pt. 1. Cost Containment. 1977. Vol. 3, No. 3. 13.75 (ISBN 0-912862-86-6); Pt. 2. Cost Containment. 1977. Vol. 3, No. 4. 13.75 (ISBN 0-912862-87-4). Aspen Systems.

Topics in Health Care Financing. Incl. Vol. 2, No. 2, 1975. Capital Projects. 13.75 (ISBN 0-912862-81-5); Vol. 2, No. 3, 1976. Medicare Reimbursement Controversies & Appeals. 13.75 (ISBN 0-912862-82-3); Vol. 1, No. 1, 1974. Financial Overview. 13.75 (ISBN 0-912862-76-9); Vol. 1, No. 3, 1975. Medicare Reimbursement. 13.75 (ISBN 0-912862-78-5); Vol. 2, No. 1, 1975. Private Third Party Reimbursement. 13.75 (ISBN 0-912862-80-7); Vol. 1, No. 2, 1974. Rate Setting. 13.75 (ISBN 0-912862-77-7); Vol. 1, No. 4, 1975. Risk Management. 13.75 (ISBN 0-912862-79-3). 1975-76. Aspen Systems.

Topics in Health Care Financing. Incl. Vol. 6, No. 2. Uniform Reporting (ISBN 0-912862-97-1); Vol. 6, No. 3. Employee Wage & Benefit Administration; Vol. 6, No. 4. Management Contracts (ISBN 0-912862-99-8); Vol. 7, No. 1. Financial Career Opportunities (ISBN 0-89443-175-7). 1979-80. write for info. Aspen Systems.

Topics in Health Care Financing. Incl. Vol. 4, No. 1. Improving Profitability. 1977 (ISBN 0-912862-88-2); Vol. 4, No. 2. Improving Productivity. 1977 (ISBN 0-912862-89-0); Vol. 4, No. 3. Physicians Compensation. 1978 (ISBN 0-912862-90-4); Vol. 4, No. 4. Hospital Information Systems. 1978 (ISBN 0-912862-91-2); Vol. 5, No. 1. Capital Financing. 1978 (ISBN 0-912862-92-0); Vol. 5, No. 2. Theft in the Health Care Industry. 1978 (ISBN 0-912862-93-9); Vol. 5, No. 3. Provider Reimbursement Review Board. 1979 (ISBN 0-912862-94-7); Vol. 5, No. 4. Flexible Budgeting. 1979 (ISBN 0-912862-95-5); Vol. 6, No. 1. Rate Regulation. 1979 (ISBN 0-912862-96-3). 13.75 ea. Aspen Systems.

Topics in Hormone Chemistry, Vol. I. Ed. by Wilfrid R. Butt. LC 77-84147. 1978. 54.95 (ISBN 0-470-99310-3). Halsted Pr.

Topics in Hypertension. Ed. by John H. Laragh. LC 80-52799. (Illus.). 644p. 1980. 49.00 (ISBN 0-914316-20-6). Yorke Med.

Topics in Inorganic & Organometallic Stereochemistry, Vol. 12. Gregory Geoffroy & Ernest L. Elial. (Topics in Stereochemistry Ser.). 344p. 1981. 50.00 (ISBN 0-471-05292-2, Pub. by Wiley-Interscience). Wiley.

Topics in Learning & Performance. Ed. by Richard F. Thompson & James F. Voss. 1972. 27.00 o.p. (ISBN 0-12-689450-7). Acad Pr.

Topics in Light Water Reactor Physics: Final Report of the NORA Project. (Technical Reports: No. 113). (Illus., Orig.). 1970. pap. 6.50 (ISBN 92-0-135170-4, IAEA). Unipub.

Topics in Management Accounting. John Arnold et al. 256p. 1980. 33.00x (ISBN 0-86003-508-5, Pub. by Allan Pubs England); pap. 16.50x (ISBN 0-86003-609-X). State Mutual Bk.

Topics in Management Science. Robert E. Markland. LC 78-17932. (Management & Administration Ser.). 1979. text ed. 26.95 (ISBN 0-471-01745-0); tchrs. manual (ISBN 0-471-01746-9). Wiley.

Topics in Mathematics. Donald R. Burleson. LC 76-27301. (Illus.). 1977. 17.95 (ISBN 0-13-925305-X). P-H.

Topics in Mojave Syntax. Pamela E. Munro. LC 75-25120. (American Indian Linguistics Ser.). 1976. lib. bdg. 42.00 (ISBN 0-8240-1970-9). Garland Pub.

Topics in Non-Ferrous Extractive Metallurgy. A. R. Burkin. (Critical Reports on Applied Chemistry Ser.: Vol. 1). 1980. 25.95 (ISBN 0-470-27016-0, Pub. by Halsted Pr). Wiley.

Topics in Numerical Analysis III. Ed. by J. H. Miller. 1978. 65.50 (ISBN 0-12-496953-4). Acad Pr.

Topics in Phosphorus Chemistry, Vol. 10. Martin Grayson & Edward J. Griffith. 1980. 70.00 (ISBN 0-471-05830-4, Pub. by Wiley-Interscience). Wiley.

Topics in Plant Population Biology. Ed. by Otto T. Solbrig et al. LC 78-27630. (Illus.). 1979. 27.50x (ISBN 0-231-04336-8). Columbia U Pr.

Topics in Precalculus Mathematics. Donald R. Burleson. (Illus.). 544p. 1974. text ed. 17.95 (ISBN 0-13-925451-7); study guide 1.95 (ISBN 0-13-925214-2). P-H.

Topics in Stereochemistry. Ernest L. Eliel & Norman L. Allinger. LC 67-13943. (Topics in Stereochemistry Ser.). 27.50 (ISBN 0-470-23747-3, Pub. by Wiley-Interscience); Vol. 10, 1978. 51.95 (ISBN 0-471-04344-3). Wiley.

Topics in Stereochemistry, Vol. 9. Norman L. Allinger & Ernest L. Eliel. 1976. 37.95 o.p. (ISBN 0-471-02472-4, Pub. by Wiley-Interscience). Wiley.

Topics in the Formal Methodology of Empirical Sciences. Ryszard Wojcicki. Tr. by Ewa Jansen from Polish. (Synthese Library: No. 135). 1980. lib. bdg. 50.00 (ISBN 90-277-1004-X, D. Reidel Pub). Kluwer Boston.

Topics in the Mathematics of Quantum Mechanics. Robert Hermann. (Interdisciplinary Mathematics Ser: No. 6). 250p. 1973. 16.00 (ISBN 0-915692-05-8). Math Sci Pr.

Topics in the Theory of Group Presentations. D. J. Johnson. (London Mathematical Society Lecture Note Ser.: No. 42). (Illus.). 230p. (Orig.). 1980. pap. 29.95x (ISBN 0-521-23108-6). Cambridge U Pr.

Topics in Therapeutics, No. 6. H. F. Woods. 1980. lib. bdg. 25.00 (ISBN 0-8161-2222-9, Hall Medical). G K Hall.

Topics in Trade Coordination in Planned Economics. Alfred Zauberman. 108p. 1980. text ed. 32.50x (ISBN 0-8419-5085-7). Holmes & Meier.

Topics on Contamination in Hydraulic Systems. Society of Automotive Engineers. 1979. 15.00 (ISBN 0-89883-218-7). Soc Auto Engineers.

Topics, Terms, & Research Techniques: Self-Instruction in Using Library Catalogs. Richard R. Strawn. LC 80-12569. 98p. 1980. 10.00 (ISBN 0-8108-1308-4). Scarecrow.

Topografia. R. Brinker & P. Wolf. (Span.). 1980. pap. text ed. 14.00 (ISBN 0-06-310064-9, HarLA Mexico). Har-Row.

Topographical Description of the State of Ohio, Indiana Territory, & Louisiana. Jervis Cutler. Ed. by Wilcomb E. Washburn. LC 75-7056. (Narratives of North American Indian Captivities: Vol. 34). 1975. lib. bdg. 44.00 (ISBN 0-8240-1658-0). Garland Pub.

Topoi: The Categorial Analysis of Logic. R. Goldblatt. (Studies in Logic & the Foundations of Mathematics Ser.: Vol. 98). 1980. 68.50 (ISBN 0-444-85207-7, North Holland). Elsevier.

Topolgical Degree Methods in Non-Linear Boundary Value Problems. Jean Mahwin. LC 78-31906. (CBMS Regional Conference Ser. in Mathematics: No. 40). 1979. 7.60 (ISBN 0-8218-1690-X, CBMS-40). Am Math.

Topologial Vector Spaces. 2nd ed. A. P. Robertson & Wendy Robertson. LC 72-89805. (Cambridge Tracts in Mathematics Ser: No. 53). 1980. 21.50 (ISBN 0-521-20124-1); pap. 10.95 (ISBN 0-521-29882-2). Cambridge U Pr.

Topological Geometry. 2nd ed. I. R. Porteous. LC 79-41611. Date not set. 59.50 (ISBN 0-521-23160-4); pap. 22.50 (ISBN 0-521-29839-3). Cambridge U Pr.

Topological Methods in Walrasian Economics. E. Dierker. (Lecture Notes in Economics & Mathematical Systems: Vol. 92). 130p. 1974. pap. 8.30 o.p. (ISBN 0-387-06622-5). Springer-Verlag.

Topological Riesz Spaces & Measure Theory. D. H. Fremlin. LC 72-95410. 300p. 1974. 42.00 (ISBN 0-521-20170-5). Cambridge U Pr.

Topological Semifields & Their Applications to General Topology. Antonovskii et al. LC 77-11046. (Translation Ser. No 2: Vol. 106). 1979. Repr. of 1977 ed. 16.40 (ISBN 0-8218-3056-2, TRAN 2/106). Am Math.

Topological Uniform Structures. Warren Page. LC 78-930. (Pure & Applied Mathematics. Wiley-Interscience Ser. of Texts, Monographs & Tracts: A Wiley Interscience Series of Texts, Monographs & Tracts). 1978. 41.95 (ISBN 0-471-02231-4, Pub. by Wiley-Interscience). Wiley.

Topological Vector Spaces. H. H. Schaefer. LC 65-24692. (Graduate Texts in Mathematics: Vol. 3). 1971. text ed. 24.00 (ISBN 0-387-90026-8); pap. text ed. 9.50 (ISBN 0-387-05380-8). Springer-Verlag.

Topologie. Paul S. Alexandroff & H. Hopf. LC 65-21833. (Ger.). 18.50 (ISBN 0-8284-0197-7). Chelsea Pub.

Topology. James Dugundji. 1966. text ed. 26.20 (ISBN 0-205-00271-4, 5602718). Allyn.

Topology. John G. Hocking & G. S. Young. 1961. 17.95 o.p. (ISBN 0-201-02855-7). A-W.

Topology. 2nd ed. Solomon Lefschetz. LC 56-11513. 13.95 (ISBN 0-8284-0116-0). Chelsea Pub.

Topology: A First Course. James Munkres. (Illus.). 448p. 1975. ref. ed. 21.95 (ISBN 0-13-925495-1). P-H.

Topology for Analysis. Albert Wilansky. 1970. text ed. 28.50 o.p. (ISBN 0-471-00633-5). Wiley.

Topology for Analysis. Albert Wilansky. 400p. 1981. Repr. of 1970 ed. lib. bdg. price not set (ISBN 0-89874-343-5). Krieger.

Topology of Stiefel Manifolds. I. M. James. LC 76-9646. (London Mathematical Society Lecture Notes Ser.: No. 24). 1977. 14.50x (ISBN 0-521-21334-7). Cambridge U Pr.

Toponyms of Florida: An Alphabetical Listing of Names Approved by the United States Board on Geographic Names Through 1976, with 1977 Addendum. Ed. by Marianne Donnell. LC 78-23662. 1978. pap. 6.50x o.p. (ISBN 0-8130-0622-8). U Presses Fla.

Topophilia: A Study of Environmental Perception, Attitudes & Values. Tuan Yi-Fu. (Illus.). 272p. 1974. pap. text ed. 8.95 (ISBN 0-13-925230-4). P-H.

Topor: Le Courrier Des Lettres Lithograph. 1977. pap. 150.00 (ISBN 0-8120-0950-9). Barron.

Topos Theory. P. T. Johnstone. 1978. 50.50 (ISBN 0-12-387850-0). Acad Pr.

Topper. Thorne Smith. 208p. 1980. pap. 2.25 (ISBN 0-345-28722-3, Del Rey). Ballantine.

Topsoil & Civilization. rev. ed. Vernon G. Carter & Tom Dale. (Illus.). 240p. 1974. pap. 5.95x (ISBN 0-8061-1107-0). U of Okla Pr.

Topsy-Turvy Tale. Pat Jamieson. (Golden Look-Look Bks.). 24p. (ps-3). 1978. PLB 5.38 (ISBN 0-307-61850-1, Golden Pr); pap. 0.95 (ISBN 0-307-11850-9). Western Pub.

Torah: A Modern Commentary: Exodus. W. Gunther Plaut. (Torah Commentary Ser.). 476p. 1981. 17.50 (ISBN 0-8074-0040-8, 381606). UAHC.

Torah Anthology: Mem Lo'ez, 7 vols. Yaakov Culi. Tr. by Aryeh Kaplan. Incl. Vol. 1. Beginnings: From Creation Until Abraham. 540p. 13.95 (ISBN 0-686-28206-X); Vol. 2. Patriarchs: From Abraham Until Jacob. 600p. 14.95 (ISBN 0-686-28207-8); Vol. 3. Twelve Tribes: From Jacob Until Joseph. 708p. 16.95 (ISBN 0-686-28208-6); Vol. 4. Israel in Egypt: Subjugation & Prelude to the Exodus. 280p. 11.95 (ISBN 0-686-28209-4); Vol. 5. Redemption: The Exodus from Egypt. 436p. 14.95 (ISBN 0-686-28210-8); Vol. 6. Ten Commandments: Revelation at Sinai. 534p. 15.95 (ISBN 0-686-28211-6); Vol. 7. Law: The First Codification. 363p. 12.95 (ISBN 0-686-28212-4). (Illus.). 1977-1980. Maznaim.

Torah Nebiim u Ketubim. Ed. by N. Snaith. 1958. 5.30 (ISBN 0-564-00029-9, 60679). United Bible.

Torah Thoughts, Vol. 6. Leo Gartenberg. LC 64-15745. 1971. 5.95 o.p. (ISBN 0-8246-0125-4). Jonathan David.

Torch of Certainty. Jamgon Kontrul. Tr. by Judith Hanson from Tibetan. LC 76-53359. (Illus.). 179p. (Orig.). 1981. pap. 7.95 (ISBN 0-87773-101-2). Great Eastern.

Torch Song. Anne Roiphe. 1978. pap. 1.95 o.p. (ISBN 0-451-07901-9, J7901, Sig). NAL.

Torch Song Trilogy. Harvey Fierstein. 250p. (Orig.). 1981. pap. 5.95 (ISBN 0-9604724-0-1). Gay Pr NY.

Torches. 2nd rev. & enl. ed. James Tate. 1971. 10.00 (ISBN 0-87775-003-3); pap. 5.00 (ISBN 0-87775-093-9). Unicorn Pr.

Torment to Triumph in Southern Africa. Louise Stack & Don Morton. (Orig.). 1976. pap. 2.75 o.p. (ISBN 0-377-00050-7). Friend Pr.

Tormented Genius: The Struggles of Vincent Van Gogh. Alan Honour. (Illus.). (gr. 7 up). 1967. 7.75 (ISBN 0-688-21605-6). Morrow.

Tormented Master: A Life of Rabbi Nahman of Bratslav. Arthur Green. LC 80-14668. 408p. 1981. pap. 11.95 (ISBN 0-8052-0663-9). Schocken.

Tormenting Flame. Nancy John. 192p. (Orig.). 1980. pap. 1.50 (ISBN 0-671-57017-X). S&S.

Tormenting Flame. Nancy John. (Silhouette Ser.: No. 17). pap. 1.50 (ISBN 0-686-68326-9). PB.

Tornado! Poems. Arnold Adoff. LC 76-47241. (Illus.). (gr. 1-3). 1977. 7.95 (ISBN 0-440-08964-6); PLB 7.45 (ISBN 0-440-08965-4). Delacorte.

Tornadoes of the United States. Snowden D. Flora. (Illus.). 1953. pap. 3.95 (ISBN 0-8061-1057-0). U of Okla Pr.

Toroidal Compactification of Siegel Spaces. Y. Namikawa. (Lecture Notes in Mathematics: Vol. 812). 162p. 1980. pap. 11.80 (ISBN 0-387-10021-0). Springer-Verlag.

Torolv the Fatherless. Pauline Clarke. (Illus.). (gr. 6-8). 1978. 6.95 (ISBN 0-571-03620-1, Pub. by Faber & Faber). Merrimack Bk Serv.

Toronto Legal Directory (Metropolitan List) & Tariff Guide. Ed. by Kieran Simpson. 1980. 14.00 (ISBN 0-8020-4581-2). U of Toronto Pr.

Torquato Tasso. Charles P. Brand. 1965. 57.50 (ISBN 0-521-04311-5). Cambridge U Pr.

Torque Wrench. American Institute of Physics. (Physics of Technology Project Ser.). (Illus.). 40p. 1975. pap. text ed. 4.00 o.p. (ISBN 0-07-001725-5, G). McGraw.

Torrens in the United States. Blair C. Shick & Irving H. Plotkin. 18.95 (ISBN 0-669-02666-2). Lexington Bks.

Torrent: A Novel. Joseph Abruquah. 1968. pap. text ed. 2.50x (ISBN 0-582-64009-1). Humanities.

Torrent of Faces. James Blish. 1977. pap. 1.95 (ISBN 0-441-81782-3). Ace Bks.

Torrents. Marie A. Desmarest. Tr. by Lowell Bair. 1977. pap. 1.75 o.p. (ISBN 0-451-07614-1, E7614, Sig). NAL.

Torres Straits Sculpture: A Study in Oceanic Primitive Art. Douglas F. Fraser. LC 77-94696. (Outstanding Dissertations in the Fine Arts Ser.). 1978. lib. bdg. 48.50 (ISBN 0-8240-3228-4). Garland Pub.

Tortoise & the Tree. Janina Domanska. LC 77-14572. (Illus.). (gr. k-3). 1978. 8.95 (ISBN 0-688-80132-3); PLB 8.59 (ISBN 0-688-84132-5). Greenwillow.

Tortoises. Ivor Noel-Hume & Audrey Noel-Hume. Ed. by Christina Foyles. (Foyle's Handbks). (Illus.). 1973. 3.95 (ISBN 0-685-55798-7). Palmetto Pub.

Tortola Valencia & Her Times. Odelot Solrac. 1981. 11.95 (ISBN 0-533-04563-0). Vantage.

Torts. 1981 ed. Theodore Schussler. 171p. Date not set. 7.50 (ISBN 0-87526-166-3). Gould.

Tortula Hedw. Sect. Rurales De Not. Pottiaceae, Musci in der Oestlichen Holarktis. Wolfgang Kramer. (Bryophytorum Bibliotheca: 21). 250p. (Ger.). 1980. lib. bdg. 30.00x (ISBN 3-7682-1266-1). Lubrecht & Cramer.

Torture. Henry C. Lea. (Middle Ages Ser). 192p. 1973. pap. 6.95x (ISBN 0-8122-1062-X, Pa Paperbks). U of Pa Pr.

Torture of Captives by the Indians of Eastern North America: In: Proceedings of the American Philosophical Society, Vol. 8I, No. 2, March 22, 1940, Repr. Of 1940 Ed. Nathaniel Knowles. Bd. with Captivity of Jonathan Alder. Repr. of 1944 ed; Horrors of Captivity: Authentic & Thrilling Sketches of Tragedies That Occurred on the Texas Frontier During Indian Times. John M. Hunter. Repr. of 1954 ed; Indian John: Life of John W. Johnson. Repr. of 1861 ed. LC 75-7139. (Indian Captivities Ser.: Vol. 111). 1977. lib. bdg. 44.00 (ISBN 0-8240-1735-8). Garland Pub.

Torture Trail. Max Brand. 1975. pap. 1.75 (ISBN 0-446-94344-4). Warner Bks.

Tory Crisis in Church & State 1688-1730: The Career of Francis Atterbury, Bishop of Rochester. G. V. Bennett. (Illus.). 260p. 1975. 42.00x (ISBN 0-19-822444-3). Oxford U Pr.

Tory Islanders. R. Fox. LC 77-83992. (Illus.). 1978. 27.95 (ISBN 0-521-21870-5); pap. 7.95x (ISBN 0-521-29298-0). Cambridge U Pr.

Tory's. William Snyder. 384p. (Orig.). 1981. pap. 2.75 (ISBN 0-380-76547-0, 76547). Avon.

Tosa Diary. Kino Tsurayuki. Tr. by William N. Porter from Japanese. LC 80-51194. 160p. 1981. Repr. of 1912 ed. 9.75 (ISBN 0-8048-1371-X). C E Tuttle.

Toscanini. Harvey Sachs. (Da Capo Quality Paperbacks Ser.). (Illus.). 380p. 1981. pap. 8.95 (ISBN 0-306-80137-X). Da Capo.

Toscanini: An Intimate Portrait. Samuel Chotzinoff. LC 76-7576. 1976. Repr. of 1956 ed. lib. bdg. 18.50 (ISBN 0-306-70777-2). Da Capo.

Tosefta, 13 vols. Saul Lieberman. 125.00 ea. (ISBN 0-685-31430-8, Pub. by Jewish Theol Seminary). KTAV.

Total Actor. Raymond Rizzo. LC 74-28493. 264p. 1975. pap. 8.50 (ISBN 0-672-63276-4). Odyssey Pr.

Total Art: Environments, Happenings, & Performances. Andrian Henri. (World of Art Ser.). (Illus.). 1974. pap. 9.95 (ISBN 0-19-519934-0). Oxford U Pr.

Total Auto Body Repair. L. C. Rhone. LC 75-2551. (Illus.). 1975. pap. 19.95 (ISBN 0-685-93194-3). Bobbs.

Total Auto Body Repair. L. C. Rhone. LC 75-2551. 1978. tchr's guide 3.33 (ISBN 0-672-97137-2); student guide 7.95 (ISBN 0-672-97200-X). Bobbs.

Total Breathing. Philip Smith. (McGraw-Hill Paperbacks Ser.). 1980. pap. 6.95 (ISBN 0-07-058989-5). McGraw.

Total Commitment. Robert Shook & Ronald Bingaman. LC 75-12690. (Illus.). 256p. 1975. 9.95 (ISBN 0-8119-0232-3). Fell.

Total Commitment: Blondel's L'Action. James M. Somerville. 1979. 9.50 (ISBN 0-89012-015-3). Anima Pubns.

Total Communication: A Signed Speech Program for Nonverbal Children. Benson Schaeffer et al. LC 80-51545. (Illus.). 260p. 1980. pap. text ed. 9.95 (ISBN 0-87822-218-9, 2189). Res Press.

Total Communication Used in Experience Based Speechreading & Auditory Training Lesson Plans: For Hard of Hearing & Deaf Individuals. Marta E. Baucom & Ralph E. Causby. (Illus.). 96p. 1981. 12.50 (ISBN 0-398-04124-5); pap. 7.75 (ISBN 0-398-04125-3). C C Thomas.

Total Energy. R. M. Diamant. 1970. 37.00 (ISBN 0-08-006918-5). Pergamon.

Total Energy Systems, E-021, E-021. Business Communications Co. Staff. 1981. 875.00 (ISBN 0-89336-282-4). BCC.

Total Experiance of Having Your Baby at Home. Kathy Fielding. 2.95 (ISBN 0-912216-23-9). Green Hill.

Total Golf: A Behavioral Approach to Lowering Your Score & Getting More Out of Your Game. Thomas C. Simek & Richard M. O'Brien. LC 79-6086. (Illus.). 192p. 1981. 14.95 (ISBN 0-385-15404-6). Doubleday.

Total Health. Morton Walker. 276p. Date not set. pap. 3.95 (ISBN 0-346-12444-1). Cornerstone. Postponed.

Total Hip Prosthesis. N. Gschwend & H. U. Debrunner. (Illus.). 31.00 o.p. (ISBN 0-683-03777-3). Williams & Wilkins.

Total Hip Replacement: Clinical Orthopaedics Ser., Vol. 72. Association of Bone & Joint Surgeons. Ed. by Marshall R. Urist. 1970. 12.00 o.p. (ISBN 0-685-22888-6). Lippincott.

Total Investing. Thomas J. Holt. 1976. 8.95 o.p. (ISBN 0-87000-357-7). Arlington Hse.

Total Joy. Marabel Morgan. 1977. pap. 2.25 (ISBN 0-8007-8326-3, Spire). Revell.

Total Knee Replacement. S. Savastano. 256p. 1980. 22.50x (ISBN 0-8385-8690-2). ACC.

Total Learning for the Whole Child. Hendrick. LC 79-20624. 1980. 16.95 (ISBN 0-8016-2150-X). Mosby.

Total-Life Exercise Book: The Official Japanese Physical Fitness Guide. Ken'Ichi Yoshida. (Illus.). 336p. 1980. pap. 8.95 (ISBN 0-02-082880-2, Collier). Macmillan.

Total Loss Farm: A Year in the Life. Raymond Mungo. LC 73-125905. 1977. pap. 4.95 (ISBN 0-914842-16-1). Madrona Pubs.

Total Nonsense Z to A. Gyles Brandreth. LC 80-54349. (Illus.). 96p. (gr. 4 up). 1981. 5.95; lib. bdg. 6.69 (ISBN 0-8069-4645-8). Sterling.

Total Parenteral Nutrition: Premises & Promises. Hossein Ghadimi. LC 74-17152. (Clinical Pediatrics, Maternal & Child Health Ser.). 672p. 1975. 56.95 (ISBN 0-471-29719-4, Pub. by Wiley Medical). Wiley.

Total Patient Care: Foundations & Practice. 5th. ed. Gail H. Hood & Judy Dincher. LC 79-23834. (Illus.). 1980. text ed. 17.95 (ISBN 0-8016-2574-2). Mosby.

Total Patient Care: Foundations & Practice. 4th ed. Dorothy F. Johnston & Gail H. Hood. LC 75-15563. 1976. pap. text ed. 14.95 (ISBN 0-8016-2573-4). Mosby.

Total Preparation for Childbirth. Cher Randall. 1979. pap. 4.95 (ISBN 0-88270-331-5). Logos.

Total Presence: The Language of Jesus & the Language of Today. Thomas J. Altizer. 128p. 1980. 9.95 (ISBN 0-8164-0461-5). Seabury.

Total Quality Control in the Clinical Laboratory. Murali Dharan. LC 76-30688. (Illus.). 1977. pap. 16.95 (ISBN 0-8016-1290-X). Mosby.

Total Rehabilitation. George N. Wright. LC 80-81957. 830p. 1980. text ed. 32.50 (ISBN 0-316-95628-7). Little.

Total Revolution: A Comparative Study of Germany under Hitler, the Soviet union Under Stalin, & China Under Mao. C. W. Cassinelli. Ed. by Peter H. Merkl. LC 76-10302. (Studies in International & Comparative Politics: No. 10). 1976. text ed. 26.50 o.p. (ISBN 0-87436-227-X); pap. 8.75 (ISBN 0-87436-228-8). ABC-Clio.

Total Sailing. Tom Hall. LC 78-75340. (Illus.). 1980. 17.50 (ISBN 0-498-02309-5). A S Barnes.

Total Sex. Dan Abelow. 1977. pap. 2.75 (ISBN 0-441-81792-0). Ace Bks.

Total Synthesis of Natural Products, Vol. 4. John Apsimon. LC 72-4075. (Total Synthesis of Natural Products Ser.). 450p. 1981. 37.00 (ISBN 0-471-05460-7, Pub. by Wiley-Interscience). Wiley.

Total System Development for Information Systems. Francis G. Kirk. LC 73-4359. (Business Data Processing: A Wiley Ser.). 284p. 1973. 32.95 (ISBN 0-471-48260-9, Pub. by Wiley-Interscience). Wiley.

Total Television: A Comprehensive Guide to Programming from 1948 Through 1979. Alex McNeil. (Illus.). 1980. pap. 9.95 (ISBN 0-14-004911-8). Penguin.

Total Thanks. Constance Tharp. 1978. pap. 3.95 o.p. (ISBN 0-88270-267-X). Logos.

Total Trial System. 175p. 1980. 14.95 (ISBN 0-9605222-0-4). Total Trial.

Total Woman. Marabel Morgan. 192p. 1973. 8.95 (ISBN 0-8007-0608-0). Revell.

Totalitarian Rule: Its Nature & Characteristics. Hans Buchheim. Tr. by Ruth Hein from Ger. LC 68-25417. 112p. 1968. 10.00x (ISBN 0-8195-3090-5, Pub. by Wesleyan U Pr); pap. 5.00 (ISBN 0-8195-6021-9). Columbia U Pr.

Totalitarianism Reconsidered. Ed. by Ernest A. Menze. (National University Publications, Political Science Ser.). 1981. 20.00 (ISBN 0-8046-9268-8). Kennikat.

Totem & Taboo. Sigmund Freud. Tr. by Abraham A. Brill. 1960. pap. 2.95 (ISBN 0-394-70124-0, Vin, V124). Random.

Totem Pole Indians. Joseph H. Wherry. (Apollo Eds.). 1974. pap. 3.50 o.s.i. (ISBN 0-8152-0359-4, A-359, TYC-T). T Y Crowell.

Totem Poles & Tribes. Nancy Lyon. LC 77-23748. (Myth, Magic & Superstition Ser.). (Illus.). (gr. 4-5). 1977. PLB 9.65 (ISBN 0-8172-1044-X). Raintree Pubs.

Totem Tales of Seattle. Gordon Newell & Don Sherwood. 1974. pap. 1.50 (ISBN 0-345-24141-X). Ballantine.

Toto the Timid Turtle. Goldsmith. 1980. 8.95 (ISBN 0-87705-525-4). Human Sci Pr.

Tottie: The Tale of the Sixties. Sarah Aldridge. 181p. 1980. 5.95 (ISBN 0-930044-01-0). Naiad Pr.

Toucans Two & Other Poems. Jack Prelutsky. LC 70-102970. (Illus.). (gr. k-3). 1970. 6.95g (ISBN 0-02-775070-1). Macmillan.

Touch & Tell. Mary S. White. LC 62-7103. (Illus.). (ps). 1962. bds. 0.60 (ISBN 0-8054-4126-3). Broadman.

Touch Blue. Ed. by Lillian Morrison. LC 57-10284. (Illus.). (gr. 4 up). 1958. 8.95 (ISBN 0-690-83316-4, TYC-J). T Y Crowell.

Touch of a Poet. Paul C. Holmes & Harry E. Souza. 1976. pap. text ed. 10.50 scp o.p. (ISBN 0-06-042869-4, HarpC). Har-Row.

Touch of Chill. Joan Aiken. LC 79-3331. (YA) (gr. 8-12). 1980. 7.95 (ISBN 0-440-00007-6). Delacorte.

Touch of Evil. Lydia Colby. LC 77-79429. 1977. pap. 1.50 o.p. (ISBN 0-87216-415-2). Playboy Pbks.

Touch of Magic. Elizabeth Hunter. 192p. 1981. pap. 1.50 (ISBN 0-671-57065-X). S&S.

Touch of Nostalgia: A Glimpse of America's Past. John K. Gates. LC 80-84010. (Illus.). 192p. (Orig.). 1980. pap. 14.95 (ISBN 0-9605168-0-8). Photographit.

Touch of Paris: A Selective Guide to Paris in Plain English. Ed. by Andre De Havenon. (Illus.). 255p. (Orig.). 1981. pap. 9.95 (ISBN 0-933982-14-3). Bradt Ent.

Touch of Style: Sewing Simple, Inventive Clothes. Pieke Stuvel. 96p. 1981. pap. 4.95 (ISBN 0-14-046482-4). Penguin.

Touch of the Master's Hand: Christ's Miracles for Today. Charles L. Allen. 1956. pap. 1.25 (ISBN 0-8007-8093-0, Spire Bks). Revell.

Touch of Wonder. Arthur Gordon. (Orig.). pap. 1.75 (ISBN 0-515-04811-9). Jove Pubns.

Touch System for Better Golf. Bob Toski & Dick Aultman. Ed. by Golf Digest Magazine. LC 70-161626. (Illus.). 128p. 1980. pap. 6.95 (ISBN 0-914178-36-9). Golf Digest.

Touch, Tickle & Pain, 2 vols. Y. Zotterman. LC 70-91702. Vol. 1. 1969. 23.00 (ISBN 0-08-015532-4); Vol. 2. 1971. 25.00 (ISBN 0-08-016052-2). Pergamon.

Touch Typewriting. John C. Evans. (Illus., Orig.). 1963. pap. 2.95 (ISBN 0-06-463229-6, EH 229, EH). Har-Row.

Touch Will Tell. Marcia Brown. (Marcia Brown Concept Library Ser.). (Illus.). (gr. 1-4). 1979. 4.95 (ISBN 0-531-02384-2); PLB 7.90 s&l (ISBN 0-531-02931-X). Watts.

Touchdown. Stephen Byers & Peter Sanders. LC 75-1127. (Venture Ser, a Reading Incentive Program). (Illus.). 80p. (gr. 7-12,RL 4.5-6.5). 1975. In Packs Of 5. text ed. 23.25 ea. pack (ISBN 0-8172-0220-X). Follett.

Touchdown for Doc. Marion Renick. (Encore Ser.). (Illus.). (gr. 2-6). 1948. 5.95 (ISBN 0-684-13048-3, ScribJ). Scribner.

Touchdown for Tommy. Matt Christopher. (Illus.). (gr. 4-6). 1959. 6.95 (ISBN 0-316-13938-6). Little.

Touched by the Fire. Ed. by Wayne Warner. 1978. pap. 2.95 o.p. (ISBN 0-88270-270-X). Logos.

Touched with Fire Civil War Letters & Diary of Oliver Wendell Holmes. Mark D. Howe. LC 73-96218. (American Scene Ser). 1967. Repr. of 1947 ed. lib. bdg. 32.50 (ISBN 0-306-71825-1). Da Capo.

Touching. John Neufeld. LC 76-125867. (gr. 8 up). 1970. 9.95 (ISBN 0-87599-174-2). S G Phillips.

Touching Base: Professional Baseball & American Culture in the Progressive Era. Steven A. Riess. LC 79-6570. (Contributions in American Studies: No. 48). (Illus.). xv, 268p. 1980. lib. bdg. 22.95 (ISBN 0-313-20671-6, RTB/). Greenwood.

Touching Closeness. 2nd enl. ed. Carl Thenebe. 1977. 7.00 o.p. (ISBN 0-682-48110-6). Exposition.

Touching Incidents & Remarkable Answers to Prayer. 135p. pap. 1.00. Faith Pub Hse.

Touchlings: Fantasy Creatures That Live on Love, Sunshine & Giving. Michael W. Fox. 1981. 7.95 (ISBN 0-87491-293-8). Acropolis.

Touchstone. Robert L. Stevenson. LC 76-3412. (Illus.). 48p. (gr. 3 up). 1976. 8.25 (ISBN 0-688-80051-3); PLB 7.92 (ISBN 0-688-84051-5). Greenwillow.

Touchstone: Historical Essays on the Reigning Diversions of the Town. James Ralph. LC 78-170491. (English Stage Ser.: Vol. 47). lib. bdg. 50.00 (ISBN 0-8240-0630-5). Garland Pub.

Tough Country. Frank Bonham. 1979. pap. 1.95 o.p. (ISBN 0-425-03873-4). Berkley Pub.

Tough Decision. Dennis St. Sauver. LC 73-8190. (Illus.). 32p. (gr. 3-5). 1973. PLB 4.95 o.p. (ISBN 0-87191-231-7). Creative Ed.

Tough Guy Writers of the Thirties. Ed. by David Madden. LC 68-10115. (Crosscurrents-Modern Critiques Ser.). 287p. 1968. 16.95 (ISBN 0-8093-0287-X). S Ill U Pr.

Tough Guy Writers of the Thirties. Ed. by David Madden. LC 78-24304. (Arcturus Bks Paperbacks). 287p. 1979. pap. 7.95 (ISBN 0-8093-0912-2). S Ill U Pr.

Tough Guys & Gals of the Movies. Edward Edelson. LC 77-17002. (gr. 4-7). 1978. PLB 5.95 (ISBN 0-385-12789-8). Doubleday.

Tough Jim. Miriam Cohen. LC 73-19065. (Illus.). 32p. (ps-1). 1974. 4.95g o.s.i. (ISBN 0-02-722760-X). Macmillan.

Tough-Minded Management. 3rd rev. ed. J. D. Batten. 1978. 14.95 (ISBN 0-8144-5477-1). Am Mgmt.

Tough-Minded Optimist. Norman V. Peale. 1979. pap. 2.25 (ISBN 0-449-24247-1, Crest). Fawcett.

Tough Texan. Will Cook. 160p. 1980. pap. 1.75 o.p. (ISBN 0-553-13759-X). Bantam.

Toujours L'Amour: Poems. Ron Padgett. LC 76-7710. 1976. 10.00 (ISBN 0-915342-11-1); pap. 4.00 (ISBN 0-915342-10-3). SUN.

Toulouse-Lautrec. Douglas Cooper. (Library of Great Painters Ser). (Illus.). 1956. 35.00 (ISBN 0-8109-0512-4). Abrams.

Toulouse-Lautrec. Richard Thompson. LC 77-21483. (Oresko Art Book). (Illus.). 1977. 15.95 (ISBN 0-8467-0372-6, Pub. by Two Continents); pap. text ed. 9.95 (ISBN 0-8467-0382-3). Hippocrene Bks.

Toulouse-Lautrec & the Paris of the Cabarets. Jacques Lassaigne. (Illus.). 1975. Repr. 5.95 o.p. (ISBN 0-88308-005-2). Lamplight Pub.

Tour Guide to Old Forts of New Mexico, Arizona, Nevada, Utah, Colorado, Vol. 2. Herbert M. Hart. (Illus.). 65p. (Orig.). 1981. pap. 3.95 (ISBN 0-87108-581-X). Pruett.

Tour Guide to Old Forts of Oregon, Idaho, Washington, California, Vol. 3. Herbert M. Hart. (Illus.). 65p. (Orig.). 1981. pap. 3.95 (ISBN 0-87108-582-8). Pruett.

Tour Guide to Old Forts of Texas, Kansas, Nebraska, Oklahoma, Vol. 4. Herbert M. Hart. (Illus.). 65p. (Orig.). 1981. pap. 3.95 (ISBN 0-87108-583-6). Pruett.

Tour Guide to the Civil War. Alice H. Cromie. 1975. 12.95 (ISBN 0-87690-153-4). Dutton.

Tour of a German Artist in England, 2 vols. Johann D. Passavant. Ed. by Sydney J. Freedberg. LC 77-25761. (Connoisseurship Criticism & Art History Ser.: Vol. 16). (Illus.). 658p. 1979. Set. lib. bdg. 70.00 (ISBN 0-8240-3274-8). Garland Pub.

Tour of the Summa. Paul J. Glenn. LC 78-66307. 1978. pap. 9.00 (ISBN 0-89555-081-4, 127). TAN Bks Pubs.

Tour of the Universe. Robert Holdstock & Malcolm Edwards. (Illus.). 144p. 17.95 (ISBN 0-8317-8797-X); pap. 11.95 (ISBN 0-8317-8798-8). Mayflower Bks.

Tour Thro' the Whole Island of Great Britain 1724-26, 2 Vols. Daniel Defoe. LC 68-138261. Repr. of 1927 ed. Set. 30.00x (ISBN 0-678-05165-8). Kelley.

Tourguide to Old Forts of Montana, Wyoming North & South Dakota. Herbert M. Hart. (Illus.). 150p. 1980. pap. 3.95 (ISBN 0-87108-570-4). Pruett.

Tourguide to Old Western Forts. Herbert M. Hart. (Illus.). 208p. 1980. 22.50 (ISBN 0-87108-568-2). Pruett.

Touring Cyprus. Philip Ward. (Illus.). 6.50 (ISBN 0-902675-13-3). Oleander Pr.

Touring Guide to Britain. Automobile Association - British Tourist Authority. (Illus.). 1979. pap. 13.95 (ISBN 0-85630-854-4, Pub. by B T a). Merrimack Bk Serv.

Touring Lebanon. Philip Ward. (Illus.). 1971. 9.50 (ISBN 0-571-09433-3). Transatlantic.

Tourism: A Shrinking World. Lloyd E. Hudman. LC 79-22325. 1980. pap. text ed. 16.95 (ISBN 0-88244-208-2). Grid Pub.

Tourism & Development: A Case Study of the Commonwealth Caribbean. J. M. Bryden. (Illus.). 280p. 1973. 42.50 (ISBN 0-521-20263-9). Cambridge U Pr.

Tourism in the Americas: Road to a Better Life. 40p. 1973. pap. 1.00 Eng. ed. (ISBN 0-8270-4960-9); pap. 1.00 Span. ed. (ISBN 0-8270-4855-6). OAS.

Tourism Planning. Clare A. Gunn. LC 79-15931. 1979. 19.50x (ISBN 0-8448-1301-X). Crane-Russak Co.

Tourism Planning & Development. Charles Kaiser, Jr. & Larry E. Helber. LC 77-14474. 1978. 14.95 (ISBN 0-8436-2128-1); student ed. 10.95 (ISBN 0-8436-2169-9). CBI Pub.

Tourism Policy & International Tourism in OECD Member Countries, 1980. OECD. (Illus.). 189p. (Orig.). 1980. pap. text ed. 19.50x (ISBN 92-64-12123-4). OECD.

Tourism: Principles, Practices, Philosophies. 3rd ed. Robert W. McIntosh & Shashikant Gupta. LC 79-18050. 1980. text ed. 19.95 (ISBN 0-88244-198-1). Grid Pub.

Tourism: The Good, the Bad, & the Ugly. John E. Rosenow & Gerreld L. Pulsipher. (Illus.). 1979. 17.95 (ISBN 0-933400-44-6). Century Three.

Tourism's Top Twenty. 86p. 1980. 15.00 (ISBN 0-89478-053-0). U CO Busn Res Div.

Tourist Business. 4th, rev. ed. Donald E. Lundberg. LC 79-27512. 1980. 16.95 o.p. (ISBN 0-8436-2181-8); pap. 14.95x (ISBN 0-8436-2185-0). CBI Pub.

Tourist Guide to Mount McKinley. rev. ed. Bradford Washburn. LC 76-28403. (Illus.). 1976. pap. 4.95 o.p. (ISBN 0-88240-089-4). Alaska Northwest.

Tourist Mecca & the Clock. A. Currimbhoy. 4.75x o.p. (ISBN 0-210-33971-3). Asia.

Tournament of Shadows. Nicholas Carnac. 1979. 9.95 o.p. (ISBN 0-684-16148-6, ScribT). Scribner.

Tournament of Shadows. Nicholas Carnac. 352p. 1981. pap. 2.75 (ISBN 0-345-28772-X). Ballantine.

Tournaments. Paul J. Deegan. LC 74-149436. (Dan Murphy Sports Ser.). 40p. (gr. 3-6). 1975. PLB 5.95 (ISBN 0-87191-404-2); pap. 2.95 (ISBN 0-89812-156-6). Creative Ed.

Toward a Black Feminist Criticism. Barbara Smith. (Out & Out Pamphlet Ser). pap. 1.00 (ISBN 0-918314-14-3). Out & Out.

Toward a Comprehensive Quality Assurance Program. (QRB Special Exition Ser.). 1979. 35.00 (ISBN 0-686-28423-2, QRB-203). Joint Comm Hosp.

Toward a Critical Sociology. Norman Birnbaum. 468p. 1973. pap. 5.95 (ISBN 0-19-501664-5, GB). Oxford U Pr.

Toward a Definition of Clinical Social Work. Ed. by Patricia L. Ewalt. LC 80-81821. (NASW Conference Proceedings Ser.). 108p. 1980. pap. 5.00x (ISBN 0-87101-086-0, CBP-086-C). Natl Assn Soc Wkrs.

Toward a Democratic Left. Michael Harrington. 1968. 12.95 o.s.i. (ISBN 0-02-548450-8). Macmillan.

Toward a Further Definition. Ed. & intro. by Michael Tarachow. LC 76-21409. (Illus.). 1980. 18.50x (ISBN 0-915316-42-0); pap. 8.50 (ISBN 0-915316-41-2). Pentagram.

Toward a Future for Religious Education. Ed. by James M. Lee & Patrick Rooney. 1969. 2.95 o.p. (ISBN 0-8278-9043-5); pap. 2.95 o.p. (ISBN 0-685-19394-2, 90043). Pflaum Pr.

Toward a General Theory of the Paranormal. 3rd ed. Lawrence LeShan. LC 73-80027. (Parapsychological Monograph No. 9). 1969. pap. 4.00 (ISBN 0-912328-13-4). Parapsych Foun.

Toward a Geography of Price. William Warntz. LC 57-7220. 1959. 5.00x o.p. (ISBN 0-8122-7124-6). U of Pa Pr.

Toward a Healthy Lifestyle: Through Elementary Education. John J. Burt et al. 608p. 1980. text ed. 17.95x (ISBN 0-534-00776-7). Wadsworth Pub.

Toward a History of Needs. Ivan Illich. (Bantam New Age Bk.). 192p. 1980. pap. 2.95 (ISBN 0-553-12276-2). Bantam.

Toward a History of Twentieth Century American Linguistics: Papers from the First Conference on Oral Linguistics. Ed. by Boyd H. Davis & Raymond K. O'Cain. (Studies in the History of Linguistics Ser.: No. 21). 300p. 1980. text ed. 34.25x (ISBN 90-272-4502-9). Humanities.

Toward a Human World Order: Beyond the National Security Straitjacket. Gerald Mische & Patricia Mische. LC 76-41440. 1977. 9.95 (ISBN 0-8091-0216-1); pap. 2.95 (ISBN 0-8091-1977-3). Paulist Pr.

Toward a Humanitarian Diplomacy: A Primer for Policy. Tom J. Farer. LC 79-3514. 1981. 15.00x (ISBN 0-8147-2565-1). NYU Pr.

Toward a Just & Effective Sentencing System: Agenda for Legislative Reform. Pierce O'Donnell et al. LC 76-24362. (Special Studies). 1977. text ed. 21.95 (ISBN 0-275-23990-X). Praeger.

Toward a Marxist Theory of Nationalism. Horace B. Davis. 1978. 17.50 o.p. (ISBN 0-85345-441-8, CL 441-8). Monthly Rev.

Toward a National Health Policy: Public Policy & the Control of Health Care Costs. Kenneth M. Friedman & Stuart H. Rakoff. 1977. 20.50 (ISBN 0-669-00563-0). Lexington Bks.

Toward a National Policy for Children & Families. Assembly of Behavioral and Social Sciences, National Research Council. LC 76-56640. 1976. pap. 6.25 (ISBN 0-309-02533-8). Natl Acad Pr.

Toward a New Catholic Morality. John Giles Milhaven. LC 77-116235. 1972. pap. 1.95 (ISBN 0-385-03000-2, Im). Doubleday.

Toward a New Definition of Health: Psychosocial Dimensions. Ed. by Ahmed & Coelho. LC 79-9066. (Current Topics in Mental Health Ser.). (Illus.). 504p. 1979. 25.00 (ISBN 0-306-40248-3, Plenum Pr). Plenum Pub.

Toward a New International Economic Order. Fred C. Bergsten. LC 74-16635. 1975. 23.95 (ISBN 0-669-96677-0). Lexington Bks.

Toward a New Music: Music & Electricity. Carlos Chavez. Tr. by Herbert Weinstock from Span. LC 74-28308. (Illus.). 180p. 1975. Repr. of 1937 ed. lib. bdg. 19.50 (ISBN 0-306-70719-5). Da Capo.

Toward a New Philosophical Basis for Parapsychological Phenomena. Hornell Hart. LC 65-15951. (Parapsychological Monograph No. 6). 1965. pap. 2.00 (ISBN 0-912328-09-6). Parapsych Foun.

Toward a New Politics in the South. Jasper B. Shannon. 1949. 8.50x (ISBN 0-87049-006-0). U of Tenn Pr.

Toward a New Sociology. 3rd ed. Charles H. Anderson & Jeffry R. Gibson. 1978. pap. text ed. 10.95x (ISBN 0-256-02062-0). Dorsey.

Toward a New Strategy for Development. Compiled by Husseiny. LC 79-9861. 1979. 25.00 (ISBN 0-08-023913-7); pap. 8.95 (ISBN 0-08-023912-9). Pergamon.

Toward a New World: Trade Policy. Ed. by C. Fred Bergsten. LC 74-22304. 1975. 24.95 (ISBN 0-669-96743-2). Lexington Bks.

Toward a People's Art. Eva Cockcroft et al. 1977. 12.95 o.p. (ISBN 0-525-22165-4); pap. 7.95 (ISBN 0-525-47426-9). Dutton.

Toward a Philosophy of Praxis. Pope John Paul. Ed. by Alfred Bloch & George T. Czuczka. 160p. Date not set. 10.95 (ISBN 0-8245-0463-1). Crossroad NY.

Toward a Philosophy of Sport. Harold J. Vanderzwaagg. LC 71-174337. 1972. text ed. 15.95 (ISBN 0-201-08158-X). A-W.

Toward a Philosophy of Zen Buddhism. Toshihiko Izutsu. 1978. 12.50 o.p. (ISBN 0-87773-732-0). Great Eastern.

Toward a Planned Society: From Roosevelt to Nixon. Otis L. Graham, Jr. LC 75-10189. 1977. pap. 4.95 (ISBN 0-19-502181-9, 486, GB). Oxford U Pr.

Toward a Political Sociology of Science. Stuart S. Blume. LC 73-5291. 1974. text ed. 16.95 (ISBN 0-02-904350-6). Free Pr.

Toward a Post-Industrial Psychology: Emerging Perspectives on Technology, Work, Education & Leisure. Don Mankin. LC 78-5302. 1978. pap. text ed. 12.95x (ISBN 0-471-02086-9). Wiley.

Toward a Psychology of Art. Rudolf Arnheim. 1966. 18.50x (ISBN 0-520-00038-2); pap. 5.95 (ISBN 0-520-02161-4, CAL242). U of Cal Pr.

Toward a Psychology of Language & Reading: Selected Papers of Wendell W. Weaver. Ed. by Albert J. Kingston. LC 75-3816. 280p. 1976. 17.50x (ISBN 0-8203-0386-0). U of Ga Pr.

Toward a Psychology of Situations. David Magnusson. 488p. 1981. ref. ed. 24.95 (ISBN 0-89859-061-2). L Erlbaum Assocs.

Toward a Public Policy on Mental Health Care of the Elderly, Vol. 7. GAP Committee on Aging. LC 62-2872. (Report No. 79). 1970. pap. 2.00 (ISBN 0-87318-110-7). Adv Psychiatry.

Toward a Rational Society: Student Protest, Science, & Politics. Jurgen Habermas. Tr. by Jeremy Shapiro from Ger. LC 73-121827. 1971. pap. 3.95 (ISBN 0-8070-4177-7, BP404). Beacon Pr.

Toward a Science of Accounting. Robert R. Sterling. LC 80-14502. 247p. 1980. text ed. 13.00 (ISBN 0-914348-31-0). Scholars Bk.

Toward a Scientific Architecture. Yona Friedman. Tr. by Cynthia Lang. LC 75-8769. 208p. 1975. 14.50x o.p. (ISBN 0-262-06058-2). MIT Pr.

Toward a Scientific Architecture. Yona Friedman. Tr. by Cynthia Lang from Fr. 208p. 1980. pap. 4.95 (ISBN 0-262-56019-4). MIT Pr.

Toward a Sociology of Death & Dying. Ed. by Lyn H. Lofland. LC 75-32378. (Sage Contemporary Social Science Issues Ser.: Vol. 28). 1976. 4.95x (ISBN 0-8039-0586-6). Sage.

Toward a Sociology of Women. Ed. by Constantina Safilios-Rothschild. LC 70-168398. (Illus., Orig.). 1972. pap. text ed. 12.95 (ISBN 0-471-00685-8). Wiley.

Toward a Solar Civilization. Ed. by Robert H. Williams. (Illus.). 264p. 1980. 15.00x (ISBN 0-262-23089-5); pap. 6.95 (ISBN 0-262-73054-5). MIT Pr.

Toward a Strategic Arms Limitation Agreemet. Herbert Scoville, Jr. 1970. pap. 1.50 (ISBN 0-87003-025-6). Carnegie Endow.

Toward a Theology of Aging: A Special Issue of Pastoral Psychology. Ed. by Seward Hiltner. LC 74-19593. 1975. 12.95 (ISBN 0-87705-278-6); pap. 6.95 (ISBN 0-87705-287-5). Human Sci Pr.

Toward a Theory for Nursing: General Concepts of Human Behavior. Imogene M. King. LC 70-136716. (Nursing Ser). 1971. pap. 9.50 (ISBN 0-471-47800-8, Pub. by Wiley-Medical). Wiley.

Toward a Theory of Popular Culture: The Sociology & History of American Music & Dance 1920-1968. D. Duane Braun. (gr. 10-12). 1969. pap. text ed. 3.00x o.p. (ISBN 0-89039-152-1). Ann Arbor Pubs.

Toward a Theory of Psychological Development. Ed. by Celia Modgil & Sahan Modgil. 814p. 1980. text ed. 47.50x (ISBN 0-85633-185-6, NFER). Humanities.

Toward a Theory of Rationally Based Grammar. David E. Johnson. Ed. by Jorge Hankamer. LC 78-66553. (Outstanding Dissertations in Linguistics Ser.). 1979. lib. bdg. 21.00 (ISBN 0-8240-9682-7). Garland Pub.

Toward Actualizing Human Potential. Robert R. Carkhuff. (Illus.). 184p. 1981. 10.95x (ISBN 0-914234-15-3). Human Res Dev Pr.

Toward an Ecology of the Brain. R. Walsh. (Illus.). 285p. 1981. text ed. 35.00 (ISBN 0-89335-087-7). Spectrum Pub.

Toward an Evaluation of the Property Tax System in New York State. League of Women Voters of New York State. Ed. by Susan Amlung. (Illus.). 125p. (Orig.). 1979. pap. 4.00 (ISBN 0-938588-02-8). LWV NYS.

Toward an Exegetical Theology. Walter C. Kaiser, Jr. 224p. 1981. 9.95 (ISBN 0-8010-5425-7). Baker Bk.

Toward an Interpretive Sociology. Anthony J. Blasi et al. 1978. pap. text ed. 13.75x (ISBN 0-8191-0382-9). U Pr of Amer.

Toward an Urban Vision: Ideas & Institutions in 19th-Century America. Thomas Bender. LC 74-18930. (Illus.). 296p. 1975. 17.00x (ISBN 0-8131-1326-1). U Pr of Ky.

Toward Better Kindergartens. Ed. by Sylvia Sunderlin. (Illus.). 1968. pap. 1.25x- o.p. (ISBN 0-87173-044-8). ACEI.

Toward Conceptual Codification: In Race & Ethnic Relations. Jonathan Udell. LC 79-84196. 1980. 7.95 (ISBN 0-87212-119-4). Libra.

Toward Creative Systems Design. Henry C. Lucas. LC 74-4129. 1974. text ed. 15.00x (ISBN 0-231-03791-0). Columbia U Pr.

Toward Distant Suns. T. A. Heppenheimer. (Illus.). 256p. 1979. 19.95 (ISBN 0-8117-1578-7). Stackpole.

Toward Economic Cooperation in Asia. David Wightman. 1963. 42.50x (ISBN 0-685-69884-X). Elliots Bks.

Toward Economic Understanding. Paul T. Heyne & Thomas Johnson. LC 75-31554. (Illus.). 720p. 1976. text ed. 17.95 (ISBN 0-574-19255-7, 13-2255); instr's guide avail. (ISBN 0-574-19256-5, 13-2256); study guide 6.95 (ISBN 0-574-19257-3, 13-2257). SRA.

Toward Education for Health Professions. Jeannette Regensburg. 1978. text ed. 14.95 scp (ISBN 0-06-045357-5, HarpC). Har-Row.

Toward Effective Instruction in Secondary Social Studies. Ed. by Lee Ehman et al. 448p. 1974. text ed. 19.50 (ISBN 0-395-17625-5); instructors' manual 1.85 (ISBN 0-395-17857-6). HM.

Toward Equal Opportunity in Employment, the Role of State & Local Government: Proceedings. J. D. Hyman et al. LC 74-15228. (Symposia on Law and Society Ser). 1971. Repr. of 1964 ed. lib. bdg. 17.50 (ISBN 0-306-70120-0). Da Capo.

Toward Explaining Human Culture. David Levinson & Martin Malone. LC 80-83324. (Comparative Studies Ser.). 400p. 1980. 25.00 (ISBN 0-87536-339-3); pap. 15.00 (ISBN 0-87536-340-7). HRAFP.

Toward Fair Employment. Paul H. Norgren & Samuel E. Hill. LC 64-17756. 1964. 20.00x (ISBN 0-231-02716-8). Columbia U Pr.

Toward Fitness: Guided Exercise for Those with Health Problems. Robert Cantu. LC 79-27686. 256p. 1980. 12.95 (ISBN 0-87705-496-7). Human Sci Pr.

Toward Fulfillment of a National Ocean Commitment. Marine Board. LC 70-183067. (Illus.). 572p. 1972. 5.25 (ISBN 0-309-01936-2). Natl Acad Pr.

Toward Healthy Aging: Human Needs & Nursing Response. Priscilla Ebersole & Patricia Hess. LC 80-26668. (Illus.). 600p. 1981. text ed. 18.95 (ISBN 0-8016-1491-0). Mosby.

Toward Humanistic Teaching in High School. Weems A. Saucier & Robert L. Wendel. 384p. 1974. pap. text ed. 6.95x o.p. (ISBN 0-669-90381-7). Heath.

Toward Independent Living: A Skills Training Series for Children with Special Needs. Bruce L. Baker et al. LC 80-51922. (Steps to Independence Ser.). (Illus.). 118p. 1980. pap. text ed. 7.95 spiral bdg. (ISBN 0-87822-221-9, 2219). Res Press.

Toward Individualized Learning: A Developer's Guide to Self-Instruction. Rita B. Johnson & Stuart R. Johnson. LC 74-19692. 1975. text ed. 12.95 (ISBN 0-201-03420-4). A-W.

Toward Jazz. Andre Hodeir. LC 76-7568. (The Roots of Jazz Ser.). 1976. Repr. of 1962 ed. lib. bdg. 22.50 (ISBN 0-306-70810-8). Da Capo.

Toward Liberty: Essays in Honor of Ludwig Von Mises on the Occasion of His 90th Birthday, 2 vols. F. A. Harper. LC 77-181817. 1976. Repr. of 1971 ed. Set. 20.00x o.p. (ISBN 0-916054-26-8, Caroline Hse Inc). Green Hill.

Toward Nineteen Eighty-Four: The Future of Appalachia? Southern Appalachian Regional Conference. LC 75-521. 1975. pap. 2.95 (ISBN 0-686-27853-4). Appalach Consortium.

Toward Perfection in Learning. Clyde Campbell. LC 68-59444. 142p. 1969. 5.50. Pendell Pub.

Toward Positive Classroom Discipline. 3rd ed. Harvey F. Clarizio. LC 75-25583. 183p. 1976. text ed. 10.50 o.p. (ISBN 0-471-15850-X). Wiley.

Toward Rational Technology in Medicine: Considerations for Health Policy. David Banta. (Health Care & Society Ser.: No. 5). 1981. text ed. 28.50 (ISBN 0-8261-3200-6); pap. text ed. cacelled (ISBN 0-8261-3201-4). Springer Pub.

Toward Reading Comprehension. 2nd ed. Julia F. Sherbourne. 1977. pap. text ed. 9.95x (ISBN 0-669-91371-5). Heath.

Toward Recovery of the Primordial Tradition: Ancient Insights & Modern Discoveries, 2 bks, Vol. 1. John Rossner. Incl. Bk. 1. From Ancient Magic to Future Technology. LC 79-66892 (ISBN 0-8191-0861-8); Bk. 2. Toward a Parapsychology of Religion: from Ancient Religion to Future Science. LC 79-66893 (ISBN 0-8191-0862-6). 1979. pap. text ed. 11.25 ea. U Pr of Amer.

Toward Reform of Program Evaluation: Aims, Methods, & Institutonal Arrangements. Lee J. Cronbach et al. LC 80-8013. (Social & Behavioral Science & Higher Education Ser.). 1980. text ed. 16.95x (ISBN 0-87589-471-2). Jossey-Bass.

Toward Responsible Discipleship. William B. Ward. LC 61-7078. (Orig.). 1961. pap. 2.95 (ISBN 0-8042-4049-3); leader's guide o.p. 1.00 (ISBN 0-8042-4050-7). John Knox.

Toward Restoration: The Growth of Political Consciousness in Tokugawa Japan. H. D. Harootunian. LC 79-94993. (Center for Japanese & Korean Studies, UC Berkeley). 1970. 24.50x (ISBN 0-520-01566-5). U of Cal Pr.

Toward Reunion: The Orthodox & Roman Catholic Churches. Edward Kilmartin. LC 79-88570. 1979. pap. 4.95 (ISBN 0-8091-2236-7). Paulist Pr.

Toward Self-Discipline: Guide for Parents & Teachers. Association for Childhood Education International. 1980. write for info. (ISBN 0-87173-089-8). ACEI.

Toward Self-Understanding: Group Techniques in Self-Confrontation. Daniel I. Malamud & Solomon Machover. (American Lecture Psychology Ser.). 288p. 1975. 15.50 (ISBN 0-398-01204-0). C C Thomas.

Toward Social Economy. Howard Bowen. LC 76-43973. (Political & Social Economy Ser.). 367p. 1977. Repr. of 1948 ed. 19.95x (ISBN 0-8093-0813-4). S Ill U Pr.

Toward Social Welfare: An Analysis of Programs & Proposals Attacking Poverty, Insecurity, & Inequality of Opportunity. Clair Wilcox. 1969. text ed. 16.00 (ISBN 0-256-00589-3). Irwin.

Toward Standards. Norman Foerster. LC 66-13476. 1928. 9.00x (ISBN 0-8196-0166-7). Biblo.

Toward Stewardship: An Interim Ethic of Poverty, Power & Pollution. William J. Byron. LC 74-30806. (Topics in Moral Argument Ser.). 1975. pap. 1.95 (ISBN 0-8091-1865-3). Paulist Pr.

Toward the Future. Pierre Teilhard De Chardin. Tr. by Rene Hague from Fr. LC 74-23802. 224p. 1975. pap. 3.95 o.p. (ISBN 0-15-690780-1, HB310, Harv). HarBraceJ.

Toward the Great Change: Crystal & Max Eastman on Feminism, Anti-Militarism, & Revolution. Blanche Cook. (Library of War & Peace: Documentary Anthologies). 1974. lib. bdg. 38.00 (ISBN 0-8240-0502-3). Garland Pub.

Toward the Integration of World Agriculture. Tripartite report by fourteen experts from North America, the European Community, & Japan. 29p. 1973. pap. 2.00 (ISBN 0-8157-8511-9). Brookings.

Toward the Light: A Message to Mankind from the Transcendental World. Ed. by Michael Agerskov. LC 79-9599. Orig. Title: Vandrer Mod Lyset. 348p. 1979. 11.95 (ISBN 87-87871-50-5); pap. 7.95 (ISBN 0-686-27618-3). Toward the Light.

Toward the Measurement of Competence in Medicine. 1977. pap. text ed. 4.95 o.p. (ISBN 0-685-75086-8). Rittenhouse.

Toward the Morning: The City in the Dawn, Pt. 3. Hervey Allen. 1978. pap. 2.50 o.s.i. (ISBN 0-446-81438-5). Warner Bks.

Toward the Next Economics & Other Essays. Peter F. Drucker. LC 80-8370. 256p. 1981. 11.95 (ISBN 0-06-014828-4, HarpT). Har-Row.

Toward the One. Pir V. Khan. (Orig.). 1974. pap. 10.00 o.p. (ISBN 0-06-090352-X, CN352, CN). Har-Row.

Toward the Poems of Mallarme. Robert G. Cohn. 1965. 12.50x (ISBN 0-520-00250-4, CAMPUS 221); pap. 5.95x (ISBN 0-520-03846-0). U of Cal Pr.

Toward the Responsive Organization: The Theory & Practice of Survey Feed. Robert T. Golembiewski & Richard J. Hilles. 1979. pap. text ed. 12.95 (ISBN 0-89832-001-1). Brighton Pub.

Toward the Soul: A Inquiry into the Meaning of XUXN Before Plate. David B. Claus. LC 80-13559. (Classical Monographs). 232p. 1981. text ed. 17.50x (ISBN 0-300-02096-1). Yale U Pr.

Toward Understanding Macroeconomics. Paul Heyne & Thomas Johnson. LC 76-22501. 1976. pap. text ed. 10.95 (ISBN 0-574-19275-1, 13-2275); instr's guide avail. (ISBN 0-574-19256-5, 13-2256). SRA.

Toward Understanding Microeconomics. Paul Heyne & Thomas Johnson. LC 76-22434. 1976. pap. text ed. 10.95 (ISBN 0-574-19270-0, 13-2270); instr's guide avail. (ISBN 0-574-19256-5, 13-2256). SRA.

Toward World Order & Human Dignity: Essays in Honor of Myres S. McDougal. Ed. by W. Michael Reisman & Burns H. Weston. LC 75-36109. (Illus.). 1976. 25.00 (ISBN 0-02-926290-9). Free Pr.

Towards a Better Life: Being a Series of Epistles, or Declamations. Kenneth Burke. 1966. 15.95x (ISBN 0-520-00193-1). U of Cal Pr.

Towards a Church of the Poor. Julio De Santa Ana. LC 80-25667. (Orig.). 1981. pap. 8.95 (ISBN 0-88344-502-6). Orbis Bks.

Towards a Global Congress of the World's Religions. Ed. by Warren Lewis. LC 80-53764. (Conference Ser.: No. 7). (Illus.). xiv, 78p. (Orig.). 1980. pap. text ed. 3.25x (ISBN 0-932894-07-0). Unif Theol Seminary.

Towards a History of Archaeology. Ed. by Glyn Daniel. 192p. 1981. 27.50 (ISBN 0-500-05039-2). Thames Hudson.

Towards a History of Phonetics. E. J. Henderson & R. Asher. 256p. 1980. 32.50x (ISBN 0-85224-374-X, Pub. by Edinburgh U Pr Scotland). Columbia U Pr.

Towards a Lasting Settlement. Ed. by Charles R. Buxton. LC 78-147578. (Library of War & Peace; Int'l. Organization, Arbitration & Law). lib. bdg. 38.00 (ISBN 0-8240-0343-8). Garland Pub.

Towards a Modern Iran: Studies in Thought, Politics & Society. Ed. by Elie Kedourie & Sylvia G. Haim. 1980. 29.50x (ISBN 0-7146-3145-0, F Cass Co). Biblio Dist.

Towards a National Spirit. Whitfield J. Bell, Jr. 1979. pap. 3.00 (ISBN 0-89073-057-1). Boston Public Lib.

Towards a New American Poetics: Essays & Interviews: Olson, Duncan, Snyder, Creeley, Bly, Ginsberg. Ekbert Faas. 300p. 1979. 14.00 (ISBN 0-87685-389-0); pap. 6.00 (ISBN 0-87685-388-2). Black Sparrow.

Towards a New Marxism: Proceedings. International Telos Conference, 1st, Waterloo, Ont., Oct. 8-11, 1970. Ed. by Paul Piccone & Bart Grahl. LC 73-87129. 240p. 1973. 12.00 (ISBN 0-914386-03-4); pap. 3.95 (ISBN 0-914386-04-2). Telos Pr.

Towards a New Mysticism: Teilhard de Chardin & Eastern Religions. Ursula King. 320p. 1980. 14.95 (ISBN 0-8164-0475-5). Seabury.

Towards a New Poetry. Diane Wakoski. (Poets on Poetry Ser.). 1979. pap. 5.95 (ISBN 0-472-06307-3). U of Mich Pr.

Towards a New Social Work. Ed. by Howard Jones. (Library of Social Work). 1975. 15.00 (ISBN 0-7100-8045-X); pap. 7.95 (ISBN 0-685-52096-X). Routledge & Kegan.

Towards a Philosophy of the Modern Corporation. Dwijendra L. Mazumdar. 1967. 8.50x (ISBN 0-210-26968-5). Asia.

Towards a Plan of Actions for Mankind, 5 vols. Ed. by Maurice Marois. Incl. Vol. 1. Long Range Mineral Resources & Growth. text ed. 60.00 (ISBN 0-08-021445-2); Vol. 2. Long Range Energetic Resources & Growth. text ed. 40.00 (ISBN 0-08-021446-0); Vol. 3. Biological Balance & Thermal Modification. text ed. 60.00 (ISBN 0-08-021447-9); Vol. 4. Design of Global System Models & Their Limitations. text ed. 55.00 (ISBN 0-08-021448-7); Vol. 5. Conclusions & Perspectives. text ed. 100.00 (ISBN 0-08-021449-5). 1977. Set. 445.00 (ISBN 0-08-021850-4). Pergamon.

Towards a Science of Teaching. Ed. by Gabriel Chanan. (General Ser.). 144p. 1973. pap. text ed. 17.00x (ISBN 0-85633-001-9, NFER). Humanities.

Towards a System of Lifelong Education: Some Practical Considerations. A. J. Cropley. LC 80-40417. (Advances in Lifelong Education: Vol. 7). (Illus.). 234p. 1980. 23.00 (ISBN 0-08-026068-3); pap. 11.50 (ISBN 0-08-026067-5). Pergamon.

Towards a Transformation of Philosophy. Karl-Otto Apel. (International Library of Phenomenology & Moral Sciences). 1980. 30.00x (ISBN 0-7100-0403-6). Routledge & Kegan.

Towards a Visual Culture. Caleb Gattegno. 1971. pap. 1.65 o.s.i. (ISBN 0-380-01455-6, 11940, Discus). Avon.

Towards a World Theology: Faith & the Comparative History of Religion. Wilfred C. Smith. 1980. write for info. (ISBN 0-664-21380-4). Westminster.

Towards African Literary Independence: A Dialogue with Contemporary African Writers. Phanuel A. Egejuru. LC 79-6188. (Contributions in Afro-American & African Studies: No. 53). vii, 173p. 1980. lib. bdg. 23.95 (ISBN 0-313-22310-6, EAL/). Greenwood.

Towards Alternative Settlement Strategies: The Role of Small & Intermediate Centers in Development Process. Ed. by B. S. Bhooshan. x, 404p. 1980. text ed. 25.00x (ISBN 0-86590-005-1). Apt Bks.

Towards an African Literature: The Emergence of Literary Form in Xhosa. A. C. Jordan. (Perspectives on Southern Africa: No. 6). 1973. 15.75x (ISBN 0-520-02079-0). U of Cal Pr.

Towards an Enduring Peace. Randolph S. Bourne. LC 73-147574. (Library of War & Peace; Int'l. Organization, Arbitration & Law). lib. bdg. 38.00 (ISBN 0-8240-0340-3). Garland Pub.

Towards an Integrated Social Paradigm: The Search for an Exemplar & an Image of the Subject Matter. George Ritzer. 300p. 1981. pap. text ed. 13.95 (ISBN 0-205-06721-2). Allyn.

Towards an Open Society in South Africa: The Role of Voluntary Organisations. Ed. by Hendrik W. Van Der Merwe et al. 140p. 1980. pap. 10.00x (ISBN 0-8476-3283-0). Rowman.

Towards Analysis of Marmoset Motor Cortex. Thomas J. Tobias. (Illus.). 50p. 1980. pap. text ed. 16.00 (ISBN 0-9604634-0-2). Learn Mich.

Towards Community Education: An Evaluation of Community Schools. John Nisbet et al. 144p. 1980. 20.25 (ISBN 0-08-025735-6). Pergamon.

Towards Dance & Art. Elizabeth Watts. (Illus.). 1978. 14.95 (ISBN 0-86019-027-7). Transatlantic.

Towards Distant Suns. T. A. Heppenheimer. (Illus.). 1980. pap. 8.95 (ISBN 0-449-90035-5, Columbine). Fawcett.

Towards Efficient Regulation of Air Pollution from Coal-Fired Power Plants. Robert O. Mendelsohn. LC 78-75020. (Outstanding Dissertations in Economics Ser.). 1979. lib. bdg. 24.00 (ISBN 0-8240-4055-4). Garland Pub.

Towards Financial Independence in a Developing Economy: An Analysis of the Monetary Experience of the Federation of Rhodesia & Nyasaland. R. A. Sowelem. (Charts). 1967. text ed. 11.00x (ISBN 0-04-332028-7). Humanities.

Towards Global Action for Appropriate Technology: Expert Meeting on International Action for Appropriate Technology, December 5-9 1977, Geneva. Ed. by A. S. Bhalla. LC 78-41191. (Illus.). 240p. 1979. 30.00 (ISBN 0-686-60416-4); pap. 13.00 (ISBN 0-686-60417-2). Pergamon.

Towards Greater Freedom & Happiness. new ed. Alfred A. Barrios. LC 78-63152. 1978. 12.95 (ISBN 0-9601926-1-1); pap. 8.95 (ISBN 0-9601926-0-3). Self-Prog Control.

Towards India's Freedom & Partition. S. R. Mehrotra. LC 79-108398. 322p. 1979. 13.50x (ISBN 0-7069-0712-4). Intl Pubns Serv.

Towards Integration: A Study of Blind & Partially Sighted Children in Ordinary Schools. Monika Jamieson et al. (Orig.). 1977. pap. text ed. 22.00x (ISBN 0-85633-119-8, NFER). Humanities.

Towards International Government. John A. Hobson. LC 70-147581. (Library of War & Peace; Int'l. Organization, Arbitration & Law). lib. bdg. 38.00 (ISBN 0-8240-0345-4). Garland Pub.

Towards Liberty. F. A. Harper. (Humane Studies). 914p. 1980. text ed. 20.00x (ISBN 0-391-02090-0). Humanities.

Towards Lifelong Education: A New Role for Higher Education Institutions. 1978. pap. 15.75 (ISBN 92-3-101449-8, U834, UNESCO). Unipub.

Towards Presidential Governance. Ed. by Arnold J. Meltsner. 300p. (Orig.). 1981. pap. write for info. (ISBN 0-917616-40-5). Inst Contemporary.

Towards Quiescence & Immortality. Barenya K. Banerji. LC 80-81693. 1981. 10.00 (ISBN 0-8022-2366-4). Philos Lib.

Towards Reconstruction of an un-Paired Random Sample. Donna Lucas. 115p. 1979. pap. 3.60 (1252). U of NC Pr.

Towards Socialism. Ed. by Perry Anderson & Robin Blackburn. 397p. 1966. 25.00x o.p. (ISBN 0-8014-0012-0). Cornell U Pr.

Towards Socialism in Tanzania. Ed. by Bismarck Mwansasu & Cranford Pratt. LC 78-10350. 1979. 20.00x (ISBN 0-8020-2330-4); pap. 7.50 (ISBN 0-8020-6433-7). U of Toronto Pr.

Towards Socialist Welfare Work: Working in the State. Ed. by Steve Bolger et al. (Critical Texts in Social Work & the Welfare State). 176p. 1980. text ed. 32.50x (ISBN 0-333-28905-6); pap. text ed. 10.50x (ISBN 0-333-28906-4). Humanities.

Towards Standards of Criticism. F. R. Leavis. 200p. 1981. pap. 7.25x (ISBN 0-85315-388-4, Pub. by Lawrence & Wishart Ltd England). Humanities.

Towards Team Care. Ed. by J. H. Barber & Charlotte R. Kratz. (Illus.). 176p. 1980. pap. text ed. 10.00x (ISBN 0-443-02031-0). Churchill.

Towards the Creative Teaching of English. Ed. by Lou Spaventa. (Illus., Orig.). 1980. pap. text ed. 8.95x (ISBN 0-04-371074-3, 2558). Allen Unwin.

Towards the Elimination of Racism. Ed. by Phyllis A. Katz. 1976. 32.00 (ISBN 0-08-018316-6); pap. 12.75 (ISBN 0-08-018317-4). Pergamon.

Towards the Integration of Indian States, 1919-1947. U. Phadnis. 8.50x (ISBN 0-210-31180-0). Asia.

Towards the New Pattern of Education in India. P. D. Shukla. 1976. text ed. 12.00x o.p. (ISBN 0-8426-0918-0). Verry.

Towards the Sociology of Knowledge: Origin & Development of a Sociological Thought Style. Ed. by Gunter W. Remmling. (International Library of Sociology). (Illus.). 463p. 1974. text ed. 32.50x (ISBN 0-391-00291-0). Humanities.

Towards the Sun. Margaret Chatterjee. (Writers Workshop Redbird Ser.). 1975. 8.00 (ISBN 0-88253-664-8); pap. text ed. 3.00 (ISBN 0-88253-663-X). Ind-US Inc.

Towards the Unknown. Dada. LC 81-65123. (Illus.). 128p. (Orig.). 1981. pap. 4.95 (ISBN 0-930608-02-X). Dada Ctr.

Towards Understanding India. 3rd ed. 1967. pap. 2.00 (ISBN 0-88253-398-3). Ind-US Inc.

Towards Universal Man. Rabindranath Tagore. 1969. Repr. 10.00x (ISBN 0-210-33972-1). Asia.

Towards Utopia: A Study of Brecht. Keith A. Dickson. 1978. 36.00x (ISBN 0-19-815750-9). Oxford U Pr.

Towards Vatican III: The Work That Has to Be Done. Ed. by David Tracy et al. 1978. 14.95 (ISBN 0-8164-0379-1); pap. 5.95 (ISBN 0-8164-2173-0). Crossroad NY.

Tower & the Dome: A Free University Vs Political Control. Homer P. Rainey. LC 76-161831. 1971. 5.95 o.p. (ISBN 0-87108-047-8). Pruett.

Tower of Babel. Illus. by Marilyn Hirsh. LC 80-21196. (Illus.). 32p. (ps-2). 1981. PLB 6.95 (ISBN 0-8234-0380-7). Holiday.

Tower of Polished Black Stones. William B. Yeats. Ed. by David R. Clarke & George P. Mayhew. (Dolmen Editions Ser.: No. II). 1971. text ed. 18.00x (ISBN 0-85105-192-8, Dolmen Pr). Humanities.

Tower Room. Dorothy Spicer. 1973. pap. 0.75 o.s.i. (ISBN 0-380-01589-7, 14506). Avon.

Towers. Archie Gordon. LC 79-52374. (Illus.). 1979. 17.95 (ISBN 0-7153-7787-6). David & Charles.

Town & Country. Rhodri Jones. pap. text ed. 2.95x o.p. (ISBN 0-435-14492-8); tchr's ed. 1.50x o.p. (ISBN 0-435-14493-6). Heinemann Ed.

Town & Country. new ed. William D. Sheldon et al. (gr. 2). 1973. text ed. 8.60 (ISBN 0-205-03537-X, 5235375); tchrs'. guide 8.60 (ISBN 0-205-03538-8, 5235383); activity bk. 3.92 (ISBN 0-205-03539-6, 5235391); tchrs.' ed. 3.92 (ISBN 0-205-03540-X, 5235405); independent activities masters 28.00 (ISBN 0-205-03541-8, 5235413). Allyn.

Town & Country Homes. Hiawatha T. Estes. (Illus.). 1981. 2.00 (ISBN 0-911008-23-3). H Estes.

Town & Country in Central & Eastern Africa: International African Seminar, 12th, Lusaka, Sept. 1972. Ed. by David Parkin. (Illus.). 1976. 36.00x (ISBN 0-19-724199-9). Oxford U Pr.

Town Burning. Thomas Williams. 1970. 6.95 o.p. (ISBN 0-394-44918-5). Random.

Town Cats & Other Tales. Lloyd Alexander. (gr. k-6). 1981. pap. 1.50 (ISBN 0-440-48989-X, YB). Dell.

Town House. Norah Lofts. 384p. 1976. pap. 1.75 o.p. (ISBN 0-449-22793-6, X2793, Crest). Fawcett.

Town in the Empire: Government, Politics, & Society in Seventeenth-Century Popayan. Peter Marzahl. LC 77-620062. (Latin American Monographs: No. 45). 1979. text ed. 14.95x (ISBN 0-292-78028-1); pap. text ed. 6.95x (ISBN 0-292-78029-X). U of Tex Pr.

Town into City: Springfield, Massachusetts & the Meaning of Community, 1840-1880. Michael H. Frisch. LC 72-178075. (Studies in Urban History). (Illus.). 464p. 1972. 15.00x (ISBN 0-674-89820-6); pap. 6.95x (ISBN 0-674-89826-5). Harvard U Pr.

Town Labourer. new ed. J. L. Hammond & B. Hammond. Ed. by John Lovell. LC 77-14533. (Illus.). 1978. text ed. 21.00x (ISBN 0-582-48519-3); pap. text ed. 11.50x (ISBN 0-582-48081-7). Longman.

Town Labourer, 1760-1832: The New Civilization. J. L. Hammond & Barbara Hammond. 342p. 1980. Repr. of 1932 ed. lib. bdg. 25.00 (ISBN 0-89984-293-3). Century Bookbindery.

Town Meeting Time: A Handbook of Parliamentary Law. Richard B. Johnson et al. 1962. 8.95 (ISBN 0-316-46736-7). Little.

Town Mouse & the Country Mouse. new ed. Aesop. LC 78-18062. (Illus.). (gr. 1-4). 1979. PLB 5.21 (ISBN 0-89375-131-6); pap. 1.50 (ISBN 0-89375-109-X). Troll Assocs.

Town Organizations in Prewar Tokyo. 51p. 1980. pap. 5.00 (ISBN 92-808-0086-8, TUNU-060, UNU). Unipub.

Town Planning in Frontier America. John W. Reps. 320p. 1980. pap. 9.95 (ISBN 0-8262-0316-7). U of Mo Pr.

Town Swamps & Social Bridges. George Godwin. (Victorian Library). 110p. 1972. Repr. of 1859 ed. text ed. 8.25x (ISBN 0-391-00158-2, Leicester). Humanities.

Town Traveller. George Gissing. 247p. 1980. Repr. of 1927 ed. lib. bdg. 25.00 (ISBN 0-89984-231-3). Century Bookbindery.

Towneley Cycle. Intro. by A. C. Cawley. Martin Stevens. LC 75-42854. 250p. 1976. softcover 12.00 (ISBN 0-87328-113-6). Huntington Lib.

Townhouses & Condominiums: Residents' Likes & Dislikes. Carl Norcross. LC 73-82886. (Special Report Ser.). (Illus.). 1973. pap. 14.50 (ISBN 0-87420-558-1). Urban Land.

Towns: A Structural Analysis. Krishna Prabha. 1979. text ed. 13.50x (ISBN 0-391-01860-4). Humanities.

Towns & Cities. rev. ed. Bacon & Boyce. (People: Cultures, Times, Places). (gr. 2-4). 1976. text ed. 11.00 (ISBN 0-201-42474-6, Sch Div); tchr's. ed. 15.48 (ISBN 0-201-42475-4). A-W.

Towns & Cities. Emrys Jones. LC 80-24687. (Illus.). viii, 152p. 1981. Repr. of 1966 ed. lib. bdg. 19.50x (ISBN 0-313-22724-1, JOTC). Greenwood.

Towns in Societies. Ed. by P. Abrams & E. A. Wrigley. LC 77-82481. (Past & Present Publications). 1978. 32.95 (ISBN 0-521-21826-8); pap. 10.50 (ISBN 0-521-29594-7). Cambridge U Pr.

Towns of Roman Britain. John Wacher. LC 73-91663. (Illus.). 1975. 34.50x (ISBN 0-520-02669-1). U of Cal Pr.

Townsmen. Keith Wheeler. (Old West Ser). (Illus.). 240p. 1975. 12.95 (ISBN 0-8094-1488-0). Time-Life.

Townsmen. Keith Wheeler. LC 74-2180. (Old West Ser.). (Illus.). 240p. (gr. 5 up). 1975. lib. bdg. 12.96 kivar (ISBN 0-8094-1490-2). Silver.

Towpath Guides to the C & O Canal, 4 sections. T. F. Hahn. Incl. Section 1. Georgetown to Seneca (ISBN 0-933788-50-9); Section 2. Seneca to Harper's Ferry (ISBN 0-933788-51-7); Section 3. Harper's Ferry to Ft. Frederick (ISBN 0-933788-52-5); Section 4. Ft. Frederick to Cumberland (ISBN 0-933788-53-3). 1977-78. 3.00 ea. Am Canal & Transport.

Toxic Constitutuents of Plant Foodstuffs. 2nd ed. Irvin E. Liener. LC 79-51681. (Food Science & Technology Ser.). 1980. 39.50 (ISBN 0-12-449960-0). Acad Pr.

Toxic Plants. Ed. by A. Douglas Kinghorn. LC 79-16180. 1979. 21.50x (ISBN 0-231-04686-3). Columbia U Pr.

Toxic Properties of Inorganic Flourine Compounds. R. Y. Eagers. 1969. 26.00x (ISBN 0-444-20044-4, Pub. by Applied Science). Burgess-Intl Ideas.

Toxic Substances & Trade Secrecy. 1977. 8.00 o.p. (ISBN 0-686-27469-5). Tech Info Proj.

Toxic Substances: Decisions & Values. Incl. Vol. 1. Decision Making. 4.00 (ISBN 0-686-27531-4); Vol. 2. Information Flow. 5.00 (ISBN 0-686-27532-2); Vol. 3. Compensation. 6.00 (ISBN 0-686-27533-0); Vol. 4. Worldwide Problems. 8.00 (ISBN 0-686-27534-9). (Toxnet Ser.). 1979. Set. 21.00. Tech Info Proj.

Toxicants & Drugs: Kinetics & Synamics. Ellen O'Flaherty. 320p. 1981. 27.50 (ISBN 0-471-06047-X, Pub. by Wiley-Interscience). Wiley.

Toxicants Occurring Naturally in Foods. rev. 2nd ed. Food & Nutrition Board. (Illus.). 704p. 1973. 17.25 (ISBN 0-309-02117-0). Natl Acad Pr.

Toxicity of Chemicals & Pulping Wastes to Fish. Louise Louden. LC 79-64742. (Bibliographic Ser.: No. 265, Suppl. I). 1979. pap. 60.00 (ISBN 0-87010-058-0). Inst Paper Chem.

Toxicological Evaluation of Parathion & Azinphosmethyl in Freshwater Model Ecosystems. (Agricultural Research Reports: No. 898). 112p. 1980. pap. 20.75 (ISBN 90-220-0732-4, PDC210, Pudoc). Unipub.

Toxicology & Toxicological Health Assessment for Polycyclic Agents. Ed. by Si D. Lee & Lester Grant. 1980. pap. text ed. 13.50 (ISBN 0-930376-20-X). Pathotox Pubs.

Toxicology, Biochemistry & Pathology of Mycotoxins. Ed. by Kenji Uraguchi & Mikio Yamazaki. LC 78-8992. 1978. 34.95 (ISBN 0-470-26423-3). Halsted Pr.
Toxicology, Biodegradation & Efficacy of Livestock Pesticides: Proceedings. Advanced Study Institute on Toxicity of Pesticides Used on Livestock, Lethbridge, 13-21 July, 1970 & M. A. Khan. 444p. 1972. text ed. 42.25 (ISBN 90-265-0158-7, Pub. by Swets Pub Serv Holland). Swets North Am.
Toxicology in the Tropics. E. A. Bababunmi & R. L. Smith. 280p. 1980. 37.50 (ISBN 0-85066-194-3, Pub. by Taylor & Francis England). J K Burgess.
Toxicology: Mechanisms & Analytical Methods, 2 vols. Ed. by C. P. Stewart & A. Stolman. 1960-61. Vol. 2. 67.25 o.s.i. (ISBN 0-12-669702-7). Acad Pr.
Toxicology of the Eye: Drugs, Chemicals, Plants, Venoms, 2 vols. 2nd ed. W. Morton Grant. (Illus.). 1216p. 1974. pap. 60.25 photocopy (ISBN 0-398-02299-2). C C Thomas.
Toxicology of the Kidney. Ed. by Jerry B. Hook. (Target Organ Toxicity Ser.). 275p. 1981. 27.50 (ISBN 0-89004-475-9). Raven.
Toxicology: Principles & Practice, Vol. 1. Andrew L. Reeves. LC 80-19259. 240p. 1981. 24.50 (ISBN 0-471-71340-6, Pub. by Wiley-Interscience). Wiley.
Toxigenic Fusaria, Their Distribution & Significance As Causes of Disease in Animal & Man. Josef Palti. (Acta Phytomedica Ser.: Vol. 6). (Illus.). 112p. (Orig.). 1978. pap. text ed. 24.00 (ISBN 3-489-60326-5). Parey Sci Pubs.
Toxins: Animal, Plant & Microbial. Ed. by Philip Rosenberg. 1978. text ed. 145.00 (ISBN 0-08-022640-X). Pergamon.
Toy Bear. Ron Reese. Ed. by Alton Jordan. (Elephant Ser.). (Illus.). (gr. k-3). 1975. PLB 3.50 (ISBN 0-89868-016-6, Read Res); pap. text ed. 1.75 (ISBN 0-89868-049-2). ARO Pub.
Toy Book. Joe Kaufman. (Illus.). (ps-1). 1965. PLB 5.38 (ISBN 0-307-68915-8, Golden Pr). Western Pub.
Toy Book. James Razzi. (Illus.). (ps-4). 1976. pap. 3.95 (ISBN 0-394-83146-2, BYR). Random.
Toy Making in Wood. Gordon Stokes. (Pelham Craft Ser.). (Illus.). 1978. 16.50 (ISBN 0-7207-0999-7). Transatlantic.
Toyko-Montana Express. Richard Brautigan. 1980. 10.95 (ISBN 0-440-08770-8, Sey Lawr); pap. 2.50 (ISBN 0-440-03725-5). Delacorte.
Toyota Celica & Supra 1971-81. LC 80-70267. (Illus.). 224p. pap. 8.95. Chilton.
Toyota Corolla-Carina-Tercel 1970-81. LC 80-70345. (Illus.). 224p. 1980. pap. 8.95. Chilton.
Toyota Corolla Tercel Service Manual 1980-1981. Robert Bentley, Inc. pap. 18.50 (ISBN 0-8376-0250-5). Bentley.
Toyota Corolla 1.8 Service Manual 1980-1981. Robert Bentley, Inc. pap. 18.50 (ISBN 0-8376-0245-9). Bentley.
Toyota Pick-Ups Nineteen Seventy to Eighty-One. LC 80-70344. (Illus.). 224p. 1980. pap. 8.95. Chilton.
Toyota Service Repair Handbook: Corolla & Carina, 1968-78. 4th ed. Clymer Publications. 1978. pap. 9.95 o.p. (ISBN 0-89287-232-2, A198). Clymer Pubns.
Toyota Service-Repair Handbook: Corona, Mark II & Celica, 1970-1978. Alan Ahlstrand. Ed. by Eric Jorgensen. (Illus.). 1978. pap. 10.95 (ISBN 0-89287-217-9, A192). Clymer Pubns.
Toyota Service Repair Handbook: Pickups, 1968-1979. Alan Ahlstrand. Ed. by Eric Jorgensen. (Illus.). 1978. pap. 10.95 (ISBN 0-89287-205-5, A193). Clymer Pubns.
Toyota Tune-up & Repair. Ed. by Al Hall. LC 79-64836. (Tune-up & Repair Ser.). (Illus.). 198p. (Orig.). 1979. pap. 4.95 (ISBN 0-8227-5048-1). Petersen Pub.
Toyota, 1970-1979. Chilton's Automotive Editorial Dept. LC 78-20250. (Chilton's Repair & Tune-up Guides). (Illus., Orig.). 1979. pap. 8.95 (ISBN 0-8019-6838-0, 6838). Chilton.
Toys. Robert Broomfield. (Illus.). (ps). 1979. 1.25 (ISBN 0-370-02009-X, Pub. by Chatto Bodley Jonathan). Merrimack Bk Serv.
Toys. DiFiore. 121p. Date not set. 2.95 (ISBN 0-07-016921-7). McGraw.
Toys & Games. Stella Nathan. (Word Bird Books). (Illus.). 24p. (ps-2). 1977. PLB 5.22 o.p. (ISBN 0-307-66253-5, Golden Pr). Western Pub.
Toys & Games. S. Sansweet. 1980. pap. 3.95 (ISBN 0-931064-27-9). Starlog Pr.
Toys & Games. (Ladybird Stories Ser.). (Illus., Arabic.). 2.50x (ISBN 0-686-53070-5). Intl Bk Ctr.
Toys & Gifts for You to Make. Hermyone Fremlin-Key. LC 70-108784. (Illus.). 1970. 8.75 (ISBN 0-8231-5022-4). Branford.
Toys for Your Delight. Winsome Douglass. (Illus.). 208p. 1973. 9.95 o.p. (ISBN 0-263-70035-6). Transatlantic.
Toys, Play & Discipline in Childhood. Beatrice Tudor-Hart. 1972. pap. 8.00 (ISBN 0-7100-6872-7). Routledge & Kegan.
Toys Through the Ages. 32p. 1980. pap. 3.50 (ISBN 0-89844-016-5). Troubador Pr.
Toys You Can Build. C. J. Maginley. 1975. pap. 3.95 (ISBN 0-8015-7860-4, Hawthorn). Dutton.
Toys You Can Build. C. J. Maginley. 8.95 o.p. (ISBN 0-498-01179-8). A S Barnes.
Trabajando Con los Padres De Ninos Con Impedimentos. Joyce Evans. LC 76-11644. 1976. pap. text ed. 3.50 o.p. (ISBN 0-86586-087-4). Coun Exc Child.
Trabajo y Justicia. Joseph McLelland. 1978. 1.95 (ISBN 0-311-46060-7). Casa Bautista.
Trabajos Realizados Por el Comite Juridico Interamericano Durante el Periodo Ordinario De Sesiones. OAS General Secretariat. (International Law Ser.). 147p. 1980. text ed. 10.00 (ISBN 0-8270-1156-3). OAS.
Trabajos Realizados Por el Comite Juridico Interamericano Durante el Periodo Ordinario De Sesiones: Celebrado Del 4 Al 29 De Agosto De 1980. OAS General Secretariat. (Comite Juridico Interamericano). 155p. (Span.). 1980. pap. text ed. 10.00 (ISBN 0-8270-1267-5). OAS.
Trabajos Realizados por el Comite Juridico Interamericano Durante el Periodo Ordinario De Sessiones Celebrado del 12 de Julio al 13 de agosto de 1976. (Eng. & Span.). 1976. 8.00 o.p. (ISBN 0-685-80061-X). OAS.
Trabalhos Realizados Pela Comissao Juridica Interamericana Durante Seu Periodo Ordinario De Sessoes: 30 de Julho a 16 de Agosto de 1979. OAS General Secretariat. 165p. (Port.). 1980. pap. text ed. 7.00 (ISBN 0-8270-1146-6). OAS.
Trabjos Realizados Por el Comite Juridico Interamericano Durante Superiodo Extraordinario De Sesiones 31 De Agosto a 6 De Octobre De 1970. (Span. & Port.). 1971. pap. 1.00 o.p. (ISBN 0-685-65452-4). OAS.
Trace Analysis of Atmospheric Samples. Kikuo Oikawa. LC 77-3458. 1977. 29.95 (ISBN 0-470-99013-9). Halsted Pr.
Trace Analysis of Semiconductor Materials. Ed. by J. P. Cali. 1963. 34.00 (ISBN 0-08-010031-7). Pergamon.
Trace Analysis: Spectroscopic Methods for Elements. Ed. by J. D. Winefordner. LC 75-41460. (Chemical Analysis Ser.: Vol. 46). 1976. 40.00 (ISBN 0-471-95401-2, Pub. by Wiley-Interscience). Wiley.
Trace Components of Plasma: Isolation & Clinical Significance, Proceedings. American Red Cross Seventh Annual Scientific Symposium, Washington, D.C., May 1975. Ed. by G. A. Jamieson & Tibor J. Greenwalt. LC 75-38563. (Progress in Clinical & Biological Research: Vol. 5). 440p. 1976. 43.00 (ISBN 0-8451-0005-X). A R Liss.
Trace Contaminants of Agriculture, Fisheries & Food in Developing Countries. LC 76-8895. (Panel Proceedings). (Illus.). 1977. pap. 10.25 (ISBN 92-0-111576-8, IAEA). Unipub.
Trace Element Analysis of Geological Materials. R. D. Reeves & R. R. Brooks. LC 78-8064. (Chemical Analysis: Monographs on Analytical Chemistry & Its Applications). 1978. 35.00 (ISBN 0-471-71338-4, Pub. by Wiley-Interscience). Wiley.
Trace Element Geochemistry of Coal Resource Development Related to Environmental Quality & Health. 1980. 11.00 (ISBN 0-309-03048-X). Natl Acad Pr.
Trace Elements: Analytical Chemistry in Medicine & Biology. Ed. by P. Schramel. 1000p. 1980. text ed. 113.00x (ISBN 3-11-008357-4). De Gruyter.
Trace Elements & Dental Disease. Martin E. Curzon. 1981. write for info. (ISBN 0-88416-172-2). PSG Pub.
Trace Fossils Two: Geological Journal Special Issue, No. 9. T. P. Crimes & J. C. Harper. (Liverpool Geological Society & the Manchester Geological Association). 360p. 1980. 64.95 (ISBN 0-471-27756-8, Pub. by Wiley-Interscience). Wiley.
Trace Ideals & Their Applications. Barry Simon. LC 78-20867. (London Mathematical Society Lecture Notes Ser.: No. 35). 1979. pap. 16.95x (ISBN 0-521-22286-9). Cambridge U Pr.
Trace Metals: Exposure & Health Effects. R. K. Di Ferrante. 1979. text ed. 41.00 (ISBN 0-08-022446-6). Pergamon.
Trace Metals in Health & Disease: Conference Proceedings, Santa Monica, California, Nov-Dec., 1978. Ed. by Norman Kharasch. 1979. 32.00 (ISBN 0-89004-389-2). Raven.
Trace Mineral Studies with Isotopes in Domestic Animals. 1969. pap. 9.75 (ISBN 92-0-011069-X, IAEA). Unipub.
Trace-Organic Sample Handling. E. Reid. (Methodological Surveys Analysis). 400p. 1981. 110.00 (ISBN 0-470-27071-3). Halsted Pr.
Traceability & Quality Control in the Measurement of Environmental Radioactivity: Seminar Sponsored by the International Committee for Radionuclide Metrology in Braunschweig, June 18-19, 1979. 80p. 1980. pap. 15.00 (ISBN 0-08-026253-8). Pergamon.
Tracer Kinetic Methods in Medical Physiology. Niels A. Lassen & William Perl. LC 75-43198. 1979. text ed. 26.00 (ISBN 0-89004-114-8). Raven.
Tracer Manual on Crops & Soils. (Technical Reports Ser.: No. 171). (Illus.). 1976. pap. 27.50 (ISBN 92-0-115076-8, IAEA). Unipub.
Tracer Studies on Non-Protein Nitrogen for Ruminants. 1972. pap. 14.50 (ISBN 92-0-111072-3, ISP 302-1, IAEA). Unipub.
Tracer Studies on Non-Protein Nitrogen for Ruminants II: Proceedings. Research Co-Ordination Meeting & Panel. (Illus.). 208p. 1975. pap. 15.50 (ISBN 92-0-111175-4, IAEA). Unipub.
Tracer Studies on Non-Protein Nitrogen for Ruminants III: Proceedings (Egypt) pap. 14.50 (ISBN 92-0-111376-5, IAEA). Unipub.
Tracer Techniques for Plant Breeding: Proceedings. Joint FAO-IAEA Division of Atomic Energy in Food & Agriculture, Vienna, December 2-6, 1974. (Illus.). 1976. pap. 9.75 (ISBN 92-0-111675-6, IAEA). Unipub.
Tracer Techniques in Sediment Transport. (Technical Reports: No. 145). (Illus.). 234p. (Orig.). 1973. pap. 17.75 (ISBN 92-0-145073-7, IAEA). Unipub.
Tracer Techniques in Tropical Animal Production. (Illus.). 209p. (Orig.). 1974. pap. 14.50 (ISBN 92-0-111074-X, IAEA). Unipub.
Traces. Robie Liscomb. 1981. pap. 3.00 (ISBN 0-915316-88-9). Pentagram.
Traces: A Field Guide to the History on Your Doorstep. David Weitzman. (Illus.). 1980. 17.95 (ISBN 0-684-16107-9, ScribT). Scribner.
Traces: An Investigation in Reason. John A. Chakeres. LC 76-47816. (Illus., Orig.). 1977. pap. 7.95 (ISBN 0-917924-00-2). Nuance Pr.
Traces of God. Diogenes Allen. LC 80-51570. 170p. (Orig.). 1981. pap. 5.00 (ISBN 0-936384-03-4). Cowley Pubns.
Traces of Mercury. Clark Howard. (Orig.). 1979. pap. 1.95 o.s.i. (ISBN 0-515-04339-7). Jove Pubns.
Traces of the Brush: Studies in Chinese Calligraphy. Shen C. Y. Fu et al. LC 79-24080. 1980. text ed. 45.00 (ISBN 0-300-02487-8); pap. 17.50x (ISBN 0-300-02490-8). Yale U Pr.
Traces of Thomas Hariot. Muriel Rukeyser. 1971. 12.50 o.p. (ISBN 0-394-44923-1). Random.
Tracheal Intubation. Edward L. Applebaum & David L. Bruce. LC 75-19837. (Illus.). 130p. 1976. text ed. 13.95 (ISBN 0-7216-1311-X). Saunders.
Tracing Your Ancestry: A Step-by-Step Guide to Researching Your Family History. F. Wilbur Helmbold. LC 76-14109. (Illus.). 1976. 9.95 (ISBN 0-8487-0415-0); logbook o.p. 3.95 (ISBN 0-8487-0414-2). Oxmoor Hse.
Tracing Your Ancestry Logbook. F. Wilbur Helmbold. LC 76-14113. (Illus.). 256p. 1978. pap. 4.95 (ISBN 0-8487-0414-2). Oxmoor Hse.
Tracings. Marilyn Gillies. LC 80-67934. 84p. 1981. pap. 4.95 (ISBN 0-9605170-0-6). Earth-Song.
Track. William Surface. LC 75-43560. 325p. 1976. 9.95 o.s.i. (ISBN 0-02-615410-2, 61541). Macmillan.
Track & Field. Ken Foreman & Virginia Husted. (Physical Education Ser.). 1966. pap. text ed. 3.25x (ISBN 0-697-07033-6); teacher's manual available. Wm C Brown.
Track & Field. Walt Marusyn et al. LC 77-74306. (Sports Playbook). (Illus.). 1978. pap. 3.50 o.p. (ISBN 0-385-06109-9). Doubleday.
Track & Field. Earl Myers & Rich Hacker. (Creative Sports Ser). (Illus.). (gr. 4 up). 1962. PLB 7.95 o.p. (ISBN 0-87191-022-5). Creative Ed.
Track & Field. 4th ed. Frances Wakefield & Dorothy Harkins. LC 77-170. (Fundamentals for Girls & Women). 1977. 9.95 (ISBN 0-8016-5328-2). Mosby.
Track & Field: An Administrative Approach to the Science of Coaching. Ralph E. Steben & Sam Bell. LC 77-2001. 1978. text ed. 19.95 (ISBN 0-471-02546-1). Wiley.
Track & Field: An Almanac of Facts & Records. David Paige. (Sports Records Ser.). (Illus.). (gr. 3-12). 1977. PLB 6.75 (ISBN 0-87191-606-1). Creative Ed.
Track & Field Athletics. 8th ed. Francis X. Cretzmeyer et al. LC 74-2486. (Illus.). 1974. 15.00 (ISBN 0-8016-1075-3). Mosby.
Track & Field Events. Richard Bowers. LC 73-83432. 1974. pap. 5.95 (ISBN 0-675-08893-3). Merrill.
Track & Field Omnibook. 3rd ed. J. K. Doherty. (Illus.). 1980. 16.95x (ISBN 0-911520-99-6). Tafnews.
Track & Field Series. Don Canham & T. Micoleau. Incl. Vol. 1. Cross-Country Techniques Illustrated. 1953. 11.50 o.p. (ISBN 0-8260-1745-2); Vol. 2. Field Techniques Illustrated. 1952. o.p. (ISBN 0-8260-1760-6); Vol. 3. Track Techniques Illustrated. 1952. o.p. (ISBN 0-8260-1775-4). (Illus.). Ronald Pr.
Track Athletics. N. J. Whitehead. (Sports Library). (Illus.). 1979. 12.95 (ISBN 0-8069-9156-9); pap. 6.95 (ISBN 0-8069-9158-5). Sterling.
Track, Enduro, & Motocross--Unless You Fall Over. Gary Paulsen. LC 78-21022. (Sports on the Light Side Ser.). (Illus.). (gr. 4-6). 1979. PLB 9.65 (ISBN 0-8172-0181-5). Raintree Pubs.
Track of the Cat. Walter V. Clark. LC 80-22458. 344p. 1981. 18.50x (ISBN 0-8032-1412-X); pap. 5.95 (ISBN 0-8032-6307-4, BB 734, Bison). U of Nebr Pr.
Track Planning Ideas from Model Railroader. Ed. by Bob Hayden. LC 80-84022. (Illus.). 96p. (Orig.). 1981. pap. 5.95 (ISBN 0-89024-555-X). Kalmbach.
Track Watching. David Webster. LC 75-180167. (Illus.). 96p. (gr. 4 up). 1972. PLB 5.88 o.p. (ISBN 0-531-02030-4). Watts.
Trackdown. Arthur Moore. (Orig.). 1980. pap. 1.75 (ISBN 0-505-51501-6). Tower Bks.
Trackdown. Dean Owen. (Latigo Ser.: Vol. I). 224p. 1981. pap. 1.95 (ISBN 0-445-04644-9). Popular Lib.
Tracker. Tom Brown & William J. Watkins. 1979. pap. 2.50 (ISBN 0-425-04222-7). Berkley Pub.
Tracking Down Hidden Food Allergy. 2nd ed. William G. Crook. (Illus.). 104p. (Orig.). 1980. pap. 5.95 (ISBN 0-933478-05-4). Prof Bks.
Tracking Down the Sickle Cell. Edgar Jackson et al. (gr. 9-12). 1976. kit 212.00 (ISBN 0-205-05006-9, 7150067). Allyn.
Tracking Ghost RR's in Colorado. 12.50 (ISBN 0-685-83409-3). Chatham Pub CA.
Tracking the Snow-Shoe Itinerant. Photos by Kent Gunnufson. LC 80-54041. (Illus.). 128p. 1981. text ed. 18.95 (ISBN 0-9605366-0-4); pap. text ed. 11.95 (ISBN 0-9605366-1-2). Snowstorm.
Tracking the Wolfpack. J. Farragut Jones. (Silent Service Ser.: No. 5). (Orig.). 1981. pap. 2.75 (ISBN 0-440-18589-0). Dell.
Tracks. Robyn Davidson. (Illus.). 1981. 11.95 (ISBN 0-394-51473-4). Pantheon.
Tracks & Trailcraft. Ellsworth Jaeger. (Illus.). 1948. 9.95 (ISBN 0-02-558830-3). Macmillan.
Track's Magnificent Milers. Nathan Aaseng. LC 80-27404. (Sports Heroes Library). (Illus.). (gr. 4 up). 1981. PLB 5.95 (ISBN 0-8225-1066-9). Lerner Pubns.
Tracks of a Fellow Struggler. John Claypool. 1976. pap. 1.25 (ISBN 0-89129-208-X). Jove Pubns.
Tractatus Logico-Philosophicus. Ludwig Wittgenstein. Tr. by D. F. Pears & B. F. McGuinness. 114p. 1972. text ed. 15.00x (ISBN 0-391-00359-3); pap. text ed. 3.50x. Humanities.
Tracte Containing the Artes of Curious Paintinge. Giovanni P. Lomazzo. Tr. by R. Haydocke. LC 75-25632. (English Experience Ser.: No. 171). 1969. Repr. of 1598 ed. 42.00 (ISBN 90-221-0171-1). Walter J Johnson.
Traction Engines Past & Present. Anthony Beaumont. 1974. 11.95 o.p. (ISBN 0-7153-6379-4). David & Charles.
Tractor & Farm Implement Lubrication Guide, 1980. (Illus.). 1979. pap. 25.35 (ISBN 0-913040-57-6). H M Gousha.
Tractor & Small Engine Maintenance. 4th ed. Arlen D. Brown. LC 72-95181. 1973. 12.00 (ISBN 0-8134-1546-2); text ed. 9.00x (ISBN 0-685-34828-8). Interstate.
Tractor Operator. David R. Turner. LC 80-11822. 224p. 1980. pap. 5.00 (ISBN 0-668-04971-5, 4971-5). Arco.
Tractor Pioneer: The Life of Harry Ferguson. Colin Fraser. LC 73-85451. (Illus.). vi, 294p. 1973. 12.95x (ISBN 0-8214-0134-3). Ohio U Pr.
Tractorization in the United States & Its Relevance for the Developing Countries. Nicholas P. Sargen. LC 78-75050. (Outstanding Dissertations in Economics Ser.). 1979. lib. bdg. 30.00 (ISBN 0-8240-4128-3). Garland Pub.
Tractors. Herbert S. Zim & James R. Skelly. LC 78-189893. (Illus.). 64p. (gr. 3-7). 1974. PLB 6.48 (ISBN 0-688-31782-0); pap. 1.25. Morrow.
Tractors & Their Power Units. 3rd ed. J. B. Liljedahl et al. LC 79-10180. 1979. text ed. 25.95 (ISBN 0-471-01905-4). Wiley.
Tractors, Plows & Harvesters: A Book About Farm Machines. Norman Richards. LC 77-83821. (gr. 1-3). 1978. 7.95 (ISBN 0-385-12347-7); PLB (ISBN 0-385-12348-5). Doubleday.

Tracts Chiefly Relating to the Antiquities & Laws of England. 3rd ed. Sir William Blackstone. 1979. Repr. of 1771 ed. lib. bdg. 30.00x (ISBN 0-87991-750-4). Porcupine Pr.
Tracts of the American Revolution, 1763-1776. Ed. by Merrill Jensen. LC 66-26805. (Orig.). 1967. 10.95 (ISBN 0-672-60046-3, AHS35). Bobbs.
Tracy. Nancy Mack. LC 76-12557. (Moods & Emotions Ser.). (Illus.). 32p. (gr. k-4). 1976. PLB 8.95 (ISBN 0-8172-0013-4). Raintree Pubs.
Tracy Austin: Teen Tennis Champ. rev. ed. Nancy L. Robison. LC 79-56009. (Star People Ser.). (Illus.). 80p. (gr. 4 up). 1980. PLB 5.79 (ISBN 0-8178-5920-9). Harvey.
Tradd Street Follies. Julian Wiles. LC 76-45729. 1978. 6.50 (ISBN 0-937684-08-2). Tradd St Pr.
Trade. William Hallahan. LC 80-22248. 384p. 1981. 11.95 (ISBN 0-688-00103-3). Morrow.
Trade Amongst Growing Economies. Ian Steedman. LC 78-73818. 1980. 24.95 (ISBN 0-521-22671-6). Cambridge U Pr.
Trade & Culture Change in Asia. Gregory L. Possehl. (Illus.). 165p. 1980. lib. bdg. write for info. (ISBN 0-89089-173-7). Carolina Acad Pr.
Trade & Developing Countries. K. Morton & P. Tulloch. LC 76-30567. 1977. 24.95 (ISBN 0-470-99054-6). Halsted Pr.
Trade & Employment in Developing Countries, Vol. 1: Individual Studies. Anne O. Krueger et al. LC 80-15826. (National Bureau of Economic Research Ser.). (Illus.). 1981. lib. bdg. 39.00x (ISBN 0-226-45492-4). U of Chicago Pr.
Trade & Expansion in Han China. Ying-shih Yu. 1967. 20.00x (ISBN 0-520-01374-3). U of Cal Pr.
Trade & Industry, 6 pts. Incl. Pt. 1. Navigation Laws, 2 vols. Set. 171.00x (ISBN 0-686-01135-X); Pt. 2. Trade Depression, 3 vols. Set. 216.00x (ISBN 0-686-01136-8); Pt. 3. Insurance (Friendly Soc, 10 vols. Set. 783.00x (ISBN 0-686-01137-6); Pt. 4. Explosives, 2 vols. Set. 153.00x (ISBN 0-686-01138-4); Pt. 5. Silver & Gold Wares, 2 vols. Set. 117.00x (ISBN 0-686-01139-2); Pt. 6. Tobacco, 2 vols. Set. 171.00x (ISBN 0-686-01140-6). (British Parliamentary Papers Ser.). 1971 (Pub. by Irish Academic Pr Ireland). Biblio Dist.
Trade & Politics in Ancient Greece. Johannes Hasebroek. LC 65-15245. 1933. 10.00x (ISBN 0-8196-0150-0). Biblo.
Trade & Poor Economies. Ed. by Sheila Smith & John Toye. 166p. 1979. 26.00x (ISBN 0-7146-3137-X, F Cass Co). Biblio Dist.
Trade & Statecraft in the Age of the Cholas. Kenneth Hall. 1980. 16.00x (ISBN 0-8364-0597-8). South Asia Bks.
Trade & Technology in Soviet-Western Relations. Philip Hanson. 300p. 1981. 30.00x (ISBN 0-231-05276-6). Columbia U Pr.
Trade & Travel in Early Barotseland: The Diaries of George Westbeech, 1885-1888, & Captain Norman Macleod 1875-1876. Ed. by Edward C. Tabler. (Illus.). 1963. 25.00x (ISBN 0-520-01248-8). U of Cal Pr.
Trade Directories of the World, 1971. LC 52-6569. 55.00 (ISBN 0-87514-003-3). Croner.
Trade, Distortions & Employment Growth in Korea. Wontack Hong. 410p. 1979. 25.00x (ISBN 0-8248-0678-6, Korea Devel Inst). U Pr of Hawaii.
Trade for Development. Harald B. Malmgren. LC 76-152712. (Monographs: No. 4). 88p. 1971. 1.00 (ISBN 0-686-28691-X). Overseas Dev Council.
Trade for Freedom. Morris Brafman & David Schimel. LC 75-26371. 96p. 1975. 5.95 (ISBN 0-88400-044-3). Shengold.
Trade, Inflation & Ethics. LC 75-44723. (Critical Choices for Americans Ser.: Vol. 5). 1976. 18.95 (ISBN 0-669-00419-7). Lexington Bks.
Trade Liberalization & the National Interest. (Significant Issues Ser.: Vol. II, No. 2). 52p. 1980. pap. 7.50 (ISBN 0-89206-016-6, CSIS010, CSIS). Unipub.
Trade Liberalization & the National Interest, Vol. II. Leonard Weiss. LC 80-80932. (Significant Issues Ser.: No. 2). 60p. 1980. 5.95 (ISBN 0-89206-016-6). CSI Studies.
Trade Marks of the Jewelry & Kindred Trades 1915. (Illus.). 1980. Repr. 9.95 (ISBN 0-915706-20-2). Am Reprints.
Trade Names Dictionary, 2 vols. 2nd ed. Ed. by Ellen T. Crowley. LC 79-12685. 907p. 1979. 120.00 (ISBN 0-8103-0694-8). Gale.
Trade Names Dictionary: Company Index. 2nd ed. Ed. by Ellen T. Crowley. LC 79-19239. 1979. 135.00 (ISBN 0-8103-0695-6). Gale.
Trade Negotiations in the Tokyo Round: A Quantitative Assessment. William R. Cline et al. 1978. 12.95 (ISBN 0-8157-1472-6). Brookings.
Trade-Offs: For the Person Who Can't Have Everything. David C. Hon. (Illus.). 150p. 1981. text ed. 14.95 (ISBN 0-89384-048-3). Learning Concepts.
Trade Policy & Economic Welfare. W. M. Corden. (Illus.). 400p. 1974. text ed. 39.00x (ISBN 0-19-828199-4); pap. text ed. 17.95x (ISBN 0-19-828401-2). Oxford U Pr.
Trade Policy & the U. S. Automobile Industry. Eric J. Toder et al. LC 77-16273. (Praeger Special Studies). 1978. 25.95 (ISBN 0-03-040956-X). Praeger.
Trade Policy in the Seventies. G. L. Weil. LC 73-4787. 1969. pap. 1.00 (ISBN 0-527-02847-9). Kraus Repr.
Trade Preferences for Developing Countries. R. Murray. LC 76-58546. (Problems of Economic Integration Ser.). 1977. 22.95 (ISBN 0-470-99080-5). Halsted Pr.
Trade Problems Between Japan & Western Europe. Masamichi Hanabusa. LC 79-88567. (Illus.). 138p. 1979. 24.95 (ISBN 0-03-053361-9). Praeger.
Trade Relations Under Flexible Exchange Rates. (Studies in International Trade: No. 8). 80p. 1981. pap. 8.00 (G143, GATT). Unipub.
Trade Secrets & Know-How Throughout the World, 5 vols. rev. ed. Aaron N. Wise. 1977. looseleaf 265.00 (ISBN 0-87632-128-7). Boardman.
Trade Shows in the Marketing Mix: Where They Fit & How to Make Them Pay off. Al Hanlon. 1980. 22.50 (ISBN 0-8015-1814-8). Herman Pub.
Trade, Taxes, & Transnational. Kent H. Hughes. LC 79-13795. (Praeger Special Studies Ser.). 271p. 1979. 24.95 (ISBN 0-03-051111-9). Praeger.
Trade Union Mergers & Labor Conglomerates. Gideon Chitayat. LC 79-2966. (Praeger Special Studies Ser.). 240p. 1979. 23.95 (ISBN 0-03-051326-X). Praeger.
Trade Union Recognition. Institute of Personnel Management's National Committee on Employee Relations. LC 77-372028. (Orig.). 1977. pap. 22.50x (ISBN 0-85292-148-9). Intl Pubns Serv.
Trade Union Women: A Study of Their Participation in New York City Locals. Barbara M. Wertheimer & Ann H. Nelson. LC 74-32398. (Special Studies). (Illus.). 206p. 1975. text ed. 24.95 (ISBN 0-275-05850-6). Praeger.
Trade Unionism in North Carolina: The Strike in Reynolds Tobacco, 1947. Akosua Barthwell. 1977. 1.25 (ISBN 0-89977-029-0). Am Inst Marxist.
Trade Unionism in Television. Peter Seglow. 1978. text ed. 23.00x (ISBN 0-566-00203-5, Pub. by Gower Pub Co England). Renouf.
Trade Unionism Under Collective Bargaining: A Theory Based on Comparisons of Six Countries. H. A. Clegg. 1976. 13.75x o.p. (ISBN 0-631-17210-6, Pub. by Basil Blackwell); pap. 12.50x (ISBN 0-631-17220-3, Pub. by Basil Blackwell). Biblio Dist.
Trade Unions. 7th ed. Allan Flanders. 1968. text ed. 5.50x (ISBN 0-09-045561-4, Hutchinson U Lib); pap. text ed. 3.00x (ISBN 0-09-045562-2, Hutchinson U Lib). Humanities.
Trade Unions & Labor Relations in the USSR. Dan C. Heldman. 1977. pap. 10.00 (ISBN 0-685-85742-5). Coun Am Affairs.
Trade Unions & Politics in Ceylon. Robert N. Kearney. LC 76-115495. (Center for South & Southeast Asia Studies, UC Berkeley). 1971. 21.50x (ISBN 0-520-01713-7). U of Cal Pr.
Trade Unions & Politics in Western Europe. Ed. by Jack Hayward. 138p. 1980. 25.00x (ISBN 0-7146-3155-8, F Cass Co). Biblio Dist.
Trade Unions & the Economy. B. Burkitt & D. Bowers. 1979. text ed. 23.75 (ISBN 0-8419-5064-4). Holmes & Meier.
Trade Unions & the Media. Ed. by Peter Beharrel. Philo Greg. (Critical Social Studies). 1977. pap. text ed. 6.50x (ISBN 0-333-22055-2). Humanities.
Trade Unions & the Professional Engineer. Will Howie. 80p. 1980. 15.00x (ISBN 0-7277-0044-8, Pub. by Telford England). State Mutual Bk.
Trade Unions in Europe. (Illus.). 220p. (Orig.). 1975. 22.50 o.p. (ISBN 0-7161-0216-1, Gower). Unipub.
Trade Unions Under Capitalism. Ed. by Tom Clarke & Laurie Clements. 1978. text ed. 24.75x (ISBN 0-391-00728-9). Humanities.
Trade Unions, What Are They? T. Van Den Bergh. LC 79-97952. 1970. 19.50 (ISBN 0-08-006517-1); pap. 9.75 (ISBN 0-08-006516-3). Pergamon.
Trade with China: Assessments by Leading Businessmen & Scholars. Patrick M. Boarman & Jayson Mugar. LC 74-1727. 208p. 1974. text ed. 23.95 (ISBN 0-275-08830-8). Praeger.
Trade Without Rulers: Pre-Colonial Economic Development in South-Eastern Nigeria. David Northrup. (Studies in African Affairs). (Illus.). 1978. 36.00x (ISBN 0-19-822712-4). Oxford U Pr.
Trademark Problems & How to Avoid Them. 2nd ed. Sidney A. Diamond. 1981. 19.95 (ISBN 0-87251-059-X). Crain Bks.
Trademark Problems in Acquisitions & Mergers. 1968. pap. 1.00 (ISBN 0-686-20593-6). US Trademark.
Trademark Register of the United States: 1881-1981. rev. ed. Cyril W. Sernak. LC 73-86256. 1981. pap. 97.00 (ISBN 0-685-76665-9, 0082-5786). Trademark Reg.
Trademark Scandinavia. Barbara Bader. LC 76-8502. (Illus.). (gr. 4-7). 1976. 8.25 (ISBN 0-688-80015-7); PLB 7.92 (ISBN 0-688-84015-9). Greenwillow.
Trademarks, No. 7. The Annual of Trade Mark Design. Ed. by David E. Carter. LC 72-76493. (Book of American Trade Marks). (Illus.). Date not set. price not set (ISBN 0-910158-61-4). Art Dir
Trademarks & Brand Management: Selected Annotations. 1976. 7.50 (ISBN 0-686-20595-2). US Trademark.
Trademarks & Unfair Competition, 2 vols. J. Thomas McCarthy. LC 72-91430. 1973. 100.00 (ISBN 0-686-14481-3). Lawyers Co-Op.
Trademarks in Advertising & Selling. (Illus.). 1966. pap. 1.00 (ISBN 0-686-20592-8). US Trademark.
Trademarks in the Marketplace. John D. Oathout. (Illus.). 192p. 1981. 12.95 (ISBN 0-684-16844-8, ScribT). Scribner.
Trademarks in the Marketplace. (Illus.). 1964. pap. 1.00 (ISBN 0-686-20589-8). US Trademark.
Trademarks Throughout the World. 3rd ed. 1979. looseleaf with current service 85.00 (ISBN 0-87632-126-0). Boardman.
Tradeoffs: Executive, Family, & Organizational Life. Barrie S. Greiff & Preston K. Munter. 1981. pap. 3.50 (ISBN 0-451-61960-9, ME1960, Ment). NAL.
Traders & Diplomats: An Analysis of the Kennedy Round of Negotiations Under the General Agreement on Tariffs & Trade. Ernest H. Preeg. LC 69-19693. 1970. 12.95 (ISBN 0-8157-7176-2). Brookings.
Traders, Artists, Burghers: A Cultural History of Amsterdam in the 17th Century. Deric Regin. (Illus.). 1976. pap. text ed. 18.00x (ISBN 9-0232-1427-7). Humanities.
Trader's Cat. Rebecca Stratton. (Harlequin Romances Ser.). 192p. 1980. pap. 1.25 (ISBN 0-373-02376-6, Pub. by Harlequin). PB.
Trading Blocs, U.S. Exports, & World Trade. Penelope Hartland-Thunberg. (Westview Special Studies in International Economics & Business). 197p. 1980. lib. bdg. 22.00x (ISBN 0-89158-967-8). Westview.
Trading in Financial Futures. Paul Sarnoff. 144p. 1980. 30.00x (ISBN 0-85941-133-8, Pub. by Woodhead-Faulkner England). State Mutual Bk.
Trading in Gold. Paul Sarnoff. 144p. 1981. limeted professional ed. 22.50 (ISBN 0-89047-039-1). Herman Pub.
Trading in Options. G. H. Chamberlain. 144p. 1980. 30.00x (ISBN 0-85941-168-0, Pub. by Woodhead-Faulkner England). State Mutual Bk.
Trading-off Environment, Economics, & Energy. Peter W. House. LC 76-50435. (Illus.). 1977. 17.95 (ISBN 0-669-01284-X). Lexington Bks.
Trading with Saudi Arabia: A Guide to the Shipping, Trade, Investment & Tax Laws of Saudi Arabia. Leslie A. Glick. LC 79-55002. 620p. 1980. text ed. 55.00 (ISBN 0-916672-43-3). Allanheld.
Tradition. Edward Shils. LC 80-21643. 320p. 1981. lib. bdg. price not set (ISBN 0-226-75325-5). U of Chicago Pr.
Tradition & Change in Education: A Comparative Study. Andreas M. Kazamias & Byron G. Massialas. 1965. 9.95 (ISBN 0-13-925982-1). P-H.
Tradition & Change in Three Generations of Japanese Americans. John N. Connor. LC 76-28999. 1977. 19.95 (ISBN 0-88229-288-9). Nelson-Hall.
Tradition & Composition in the Parables of Enoch. David W. Suter. LC 79-17441. (Society of Biblical Literature. Dissertation Ser.: No. 47). 1979. 12.00 (ISBN 0-89130-335-9, 060147); pap. 7.50 (ISBN 0-89130-336-7). Scholars Pr Ca.
Tradition & Convention: A Study of Periphrasis in English Pastoral Poetry from 1557-1715. Dorothy S. McCoy. (Studies in English Literature: No. 5). 1979. pap. text ed. 23.00x (ISBN 0-391-01604-0). Humanities.
Tradition & Creativity in Tribal Art. Daniel Biebuyck. LC 69-12457. 1969. 30.00x (ISBN 0-520-01509-6); pap. 4.95 (ISBN 0-520-02487-7). U of Cal Pr.
Tradition & Dissent: A Rhetoric Reader. 2nd ed. Florence Greenberg & Anne P. Heffley. LC 76-145858. 1971. pap. 8.50 (ISBN 0-672-61179-1). Bobbs.
Tradition & Experiment in English Poetry. Philip Hobsbaum. 343p. 1979. 22.50x (ISBN 0-8476-6128-8). Rowman.
Tradition & Folk Life. Iorwerth C. Peate. (Illus.). 1972. 12.95 (ISBN 0-571-09804-5, Pub. by Faber & Faber). Merrimack Bk Serv.
Tradition & Revolt in Latin America: & Other Essays. Robert A. Humphreys. LC 69-12966. 1969. 17.50x (ISBN 0-231-03238-2). Columbia U Pr.
Tradition & Transition in East Africa: Studies of the Tribal Factor in the Modern Era. Ed. by P. H. Gulliver. LC 78-84787. 1969. 21.50x (ISBN 0-520-01402-2). U of Cal Pr.
Tradition, Change, & Modernity. S. N. Eisenstadt. LC 73-7560. 367p. 1973. 25.95 (ISBN 0-471-23471-0, Pub. by Wiley-Interscience). Wiley.
Tradition for Crisis: A Study in Hosea. Walter Brueggemann. LC 68-21008. 1981. pap. 6.95 (ISBN 0-8042-0181-1). John Knox.
Tradition for Crisis: A Study in Hosea. LC 68-21008. 164p. 1981. pap. 6.95 (ISBN 0-8042-0181-1). John Knox.
Tradition of Fine Bookbinding in the Twentieth Century. Compiled by Bernadette G. Callery & E. A. Mosimann. (Illus.). 120p. 1979. 25.00 (ISBN 0-913196-28-2); unbd. 22.00 (ISBN 0-686-65642-3). Hunt Inst Botanical.
Tradition of Pride. Janet Dailey. (Harlequin Presents Ser.). 192p. 1981. pap. 1.50 (ISBN 0-373-10421-9, Pub. by Harlequin). PB.
Tradition of Resistance in Mozambique: The Zambesi Valley. Allen Isaacman. 1977. 20.00x (ISBN 0-520-03065-6). U of Cal Pr.
Tradition of Western Music. Gerald Abraham. (Ernest Bloch Lectures Ser). 1974. 14.50x (ISBN 0-520-02414-1); pap. 5.50x (ISBN 0-520-02615-2). U of Cal Pr.
Tradition, Phase & Style of Shang & Chow Bronze Vessels. Katheryn M. Linduff. LC 77-94705. (Outstanding Dissertations in the Fine Arts Ser.). (Illus.). 254p. 1980. lib. bdg. 27.50 (ISBN 0-8240-3237-3). Garland Pub.
Tradition, Values & Development. Ed. by Denis Goulet & Valeriana Kallab. 322p. 1981. write for info. Overseas Dev Council.
Traditional Africa. John Addison et al. Ed. by Malcolm Yapp et al. (World History Ser.). (Illus.). 32p. (gr. 10). 1980. lib. bdg. 5.95 (ISBN 0-89908-034-0); pap. text ed. 1.95 (ISBN 0-89908-009-X). Greenhaven.
Traditional & National Music of Scotland. Francis Collinson. (Illus.). 1970. Repr. of 1966 ed. 25.00 (ISBN 0-7100-1213-6). Routledge & Kegan.
Traditional Architecture of the Kathmandu Valley. Wolfgang Korn. (Ratna Pustak Bhandar Bibliotheca Himalayica Ser.). (Illus.). 1977. 17.50x (ISBN 0-685-89504-1). Himalaya Hse.
Traditional Artist in African Societies. Ed. by Warren L. D'Azevedo. LC 79-160126. (Illus.). 480p. 1973. pap. 5.95x (ISBN 0-253-39902-5). Ind U Pr.
Traditional Aspects of Hell. James Mew. LC 73-140321. 1971. Repr. of 1903 ed. 24.00 (ISBN 0-8103-3693-6). Gale.
Traditional Authority, Islam, & Rebellion: A Study of Indonesian Political Behavior. Karl D. Jackson. 1980. 22.50x (ISBN 0-520-03769-3). U of Cal Pr.
Traditional British Cookery. Maggie M. Pearse. (International Wine & Food Society Ser.). (Illus.). 15.00 o.p. (ISBN 0-7153-5183-4). David & Charles.
Traditional China. Islay Doncaster. Ed. by Margaret Killingray & Edmund O'Connor. (World History Ser.). (Illus.). (gr. 10). 1980. Repr. of 1977 ed. lib. bdg. 5.95 (ISBN 0-89908-032-4); pap. text ed. 1.95 (ISBN 0-89908-007-3). Greenhaven.
Traditional Chinese Bookbinding. Edward Martinique. (Asian Library: No. 19). (Illus.). xiii, 87p. 1980. write for info. (ISBN 0-89644-596-8). Chinese Materials.
Traditional Chinese Plays, 3 vols. Ed. by A. C. Scott. Incl. Vol. 1. Ssu Lang Visits His Mother; the Butterfly Dream. (Illus.). 1967. pap. 5.95x (ISBN 0-299-04134-4); Vol. 2. Longing for Worldly Pleasures; Fifteen Strings of Cash. (Illus.). 1969. 15.00x (ISBN 0-299-05370-9); pap. 5.95x (ISBN 0-299-05374-1); Vol. 3. Picking up the Jade Bracelet; a Girl Setting Out for Trial. LC 66-22854. 1975. 10.00x (ISBN 0-299-06630-4). U of Wis Pr.
Traditional Chinese Stories. Ed. by Y. W. Ma & Joseph S. Lau. LC 77-21133. 1978. 32.50x (ISBN 0-231-04058-X); pap. 12.00 (ISBN 0-231-04059-8). Columbia U Pr.
Traditional Country Craftsmen. J. Geraint Jenkins. (Illus.). 1968. Repr. of 1965 ed. 20.00 (ISBN 0-7100-1610-7). Routledge & Kegan.
Traditional Crafts. Linda Hetzer. LC 77-28740. (Illustrated Crafts for Beginners). (Illus.). (gr. 3-7). 1978. PLB 9.95 (ISBN 0-8172-1190-X). Raintree Pubs.
Traditional Designs from India for Artists & Craftsmen. Pradumna Tana Tana & Roselba Tana. (Illus.). 112p. (Orig.). 1981. pap. price not set (ISBN 0-486-24129-7). Dover.

Traditional Designs of Armenia & the Near East to Color. Ramona Jablonski. LC 79-15212. (International Design Library). (Illus., Orig.). 1979. pap. 2.95 (ISBN 0-916144-41-0). Stemmer Hse.

Traditional Ethiopian Church Education. Alaka I. Kalewold. LC 70-93506. pap. text ed. 4.00x (ISBN 0-8077-1597-2). Tchrs Coll.

Traditional Favorites. Editors of Time-Life Books. LC 73-94381. (Art of Sewing). (Illus.). (gr. 6 up). 1974. PLB 11.97 (ISBN 0-8094-1715-4, Pub. by Time-Life). Silver.

Traditional Favorites. (Art of Sewing Ser.). (Illus.). 1974. 9.95 (ISBN 0-8094-1713-8). Time-Life.

Traditional Guide to Home Lighting. (Bantam Hudson Plan Bk.). 1980. pap. 6.95 (ISBN 0-553-01234-7). Bantam.

Traditional Health Care Delivery in Contemporary Africe. Ed. by Marshall Segall & Priscilla Ulin. (Foreign & Comparative Studies - African Ser.: No. 35). 100p. 1980. pap. 8.00x (ISBN 0-915984-57-1). Syracuse U Foreign Comp.

Traditional Health Care Delivery in Contemporary Africa. Ed. by Priscilla Ulin & Marshall Segall. LC 80-27442. (African Foreign & Comparative Studies Program: Vol. 35). vii, 98p. (Orig.). 1980. 8.00x (ISBN 0-915984-57-1). Syracuse U Foreign Comp.

Traditional History of the Jie of Uganda. John Lamphear. (Oxford Studies in African Affairs). (Illus.). 1976. 37.50x (ISBN 0-19-821692-0). Oxford U Pr.

Traditional Hungarian Songs. Tr. by W. D. Snodgrass from Hungarian. (Fine Press Poetry Ser.). (Illus.). 1978. ltd. signed ed. 60.00 (ISBN 0-931356-01-6). Seluzicki Poetry.

Traditional Islamic Craft in Moroccan Architecture, 2 vols. Andre Paccard. 1980. 495.00x (Pub. by Editions Atelier England). State Mutual Bk.

Traditional Knitting Patterns from Scandinavia, the British Isles, France, Italy & Other European Countries. James Norbury. LC 73-79490. (Illus.). 240p. 1973. pap. 4.50 (ISBN 0-486-21013-8). Dover.

Traditional Korean Legan Attitudes. Bong D. Chun et al. (Korean Research Monographs: No. 2). 101p. 1980. pap. 8.00 (ISBN 0-912966-30-0). IEAS Ctr Chinese Stud.

Traditional Literatures of the American Indian: Texts & Interpretations. Ed. by Karl Kroeber. LC 80-18338. x, 162p. 1981. 16.50x (ISBN 0-8032-2704-3, Bison); pap. 5.95 (ISBN 0-8032-7753-9, BB 765). U of Nebr Pr.

Traditional Modes of Contemplation & Action. Ed. by Yusuf Ibish & Peter L. Wilson. 1978. 25.00 (ISBN 0-87773-729-0). Great Eastern.

Traditional Music in Ireland. Tomas O Canainn. (Illus.). 1978. pap. 10.00 (ISBN 0-7100-0021-9). Routledge & Kegan.

Traditional Music in Modern Java. Judith Becker. LC 80-19180. (Illus.). 1980. text ed. 30.00x (ISBN 0-8248-0563-1). U Pr of Hawaii.

Traditional Music of America. Ira W. Ford. (Music Reprint Ser., 1978). 1978. Repr. of 1940 ed. lib. bdg. 35.00 (ISBN 0-306-77588-3). Da Capo.

Traditional Music of Thailand. David Morton. LC 70-142048. 1976. 28.50x (ISBN 0-520-01876-1). U of Cal Pr.

Traditional Patchwork Patterns: Full-Size Cut-Outs & Instructions for 12 Quilts. Carol B. Grafton. (Illus.). 64p. (Orig.). 1974. pap. 3.00 (ISBN 0-486-23015-5). Dover.

Traditional Quilt Block Patterns for Crocheting. Antoinette Lep. 48p. (Orig.). 1981. pap. write for info. (ISBN 0-486-23967-5). Dover.

Traditional Quilts & Bed Coverings. Ruth McKendry. 240p. 1980. 37.50 (ISBN 0-442-29790-4). Van Nos Reinhold.

Traditional Romanian Village Communities. Henri Stahl. Tr. by D. Chirot & H. C. Chirot. LC 79-52855. (Studies in Modern Capitalism). (Illus.). 1980. 39.95 (ISBN 0-521-22957-X). Cambridge U Pr.

Traditional Sculpture from Upper Volta. (Illus.). 48p. (Orig.). 1978. pap. text ed. 5.00 (ISBN 0-89192-279-2). Interbk Inc.

Traditional Singers & Songs from Ontario. Edith F. Fowke. LC 65-26777. (Illus.). x, 210p. Repr. of 1965 ed. 18.00 (ISBN 0-8103-5011-4). Gale.

Traditional Smocks & Smocking. Oenone Cave. (Illus.). 101p. (Orig.). 1979. pap. 14.00 (ISBN 0-263-06408-5). Transatlantic.

Traditional Tole Painting: With Authentic Antique Designs & Working Diagrams for Stenciling & Brush-Stroke Painting. Roberta R. Blanchard. LC 77-78208. (Illus.). 1977. pap. 3.50 (ISBN 0-486-23531-9). Dover.

Traditional Use of Malay Plants & Herbs. J. Kloppenburg-Versteegh. Tr. by Aileen Kaufman from Dutch. LC 79-89939. Orig. Title: Het Gebruik Van Indische Planten. (Illus.). Date not set. price not set (ISBN 0-89793-014-2). Hunter Hse.

Traditions & Memories of American Yachting: Complete Edition. W. P. Stephens. LC 80-83038. (Illus.). 384p. write for info. (ISBN 0-87742-132-3). Intl Marine.

Traditions & Revisions: Themes from the History of Sculpture. Gabriel P. Weisberg. LC 75-26708. (Illus.). 162p. 1975. pap. 10.00x (ISBN 0-910386-23-4, Pub. by Cleveland Mus Art). Ind U Pr.

Traditions in Transformation: Turning Points in Biblical Faith. Ed. by Baruch Halpern & Jon D. Levenson. 1981. text ed. write for info. (ISBN 0-931464-06-4). Eisenbrauns.

Traditions of African Education. David G. Scanlon. LC 60-14305. (Orig.). 1964. text ed. 8.75 (ISBN 0-8077-2107-7); pap. text ed. 4.00x (ISBN 0-8077-2104-2). Tchrs Coll.

Traditions of Eleazar Ben Azariah. Tzvee Zahavy. LC 76-46373. (Brown University. Brown Judaic Studies: No. 2). 1977. pap. 9.00 (ISBN 0-89130-095-3, 140002). Scholars Pr Ca.

Traditions of Independence: British Cinema in the 30's. Donald McPherson. (BFI Ser.). (Orig.). 1980. pap. 11.50 (ISBN 0-85170-093-4). NY Zoetrope.

Traditions of Indian Classical Dance. Mohan Khokar. (Illus.). 1980. text ed. 23.25x (ISBN 0-7206-0574-1). Humanities.

Traditions of Social Policy: Essays in Honour of Violet Butler. Ed. by A. H. Halsey. 1976. 29.00x (ISBN 0-631-17130-4, Pub by Basil Blackwell). Biblio Dist.

Traditions of the Classical Guitar. Graham Wade. 1981. 25.00 (ISBN 0-7145-3794-2). Riverrun NY.

Trado Asian-African Directory of Exporters-Importers & Manufacturers, 1980. 25th ed. LC 60-41792. 1640p. 1980. 50.00x (ISBN 0-8002-2736-0). Intl Pubns Serv.

Traffic Accident Investigation & Physical Evidence. D. R. McGrew. (Illus.). 132p. 1976. pap. 16.75 (ISBN 0-398-03503-2). C C Thomas.

Traffic Congestion Goes Through the Issue-Machine: A Case-Study in Issue Processing, Illustrating a New Approach. David Braybrooke. 74p. 1974. 16.50x (ISBN 0-7100-7749-1). Routledge & Kegan.

Traffic Courts. George Warren. Repr. of 1942 ed. lib. bdg. 15.75x (ISBN 0-8371-2568-5, WATC). Greenwood.

Traffic Data Collection. Institute of Civil Engineers, UK. 178p. 1980. 40.00x (ISBN 0-7277-0061-8, Pub. by Telford England). State Mutual Bk.

Traffic Engineering. T. M. Matson et al. 1955. text ed. 25.50 o.p. (ISBN 0-07-040910-2, C). McGraw.

Traffic Engineering: An Introduction. G. R. Wells. 190p. 1979. 34.50x (ISBN 0-85264-254-7, Pub. by Griffin England). State Mutual Bk.

Traffic Engineering: Theory & Practice. Louis J. Pignataro. (Illus.). 512p. 1973. 28.95 (ISBN 0-13-926220-2). P-H.

Traffic Environment & the Driver: Driver Behavior & Training in International Perspective. Julius Marek & Terje Sten. (Illus.). 284p. 1977. 24.75 (ISBN 0-398-03508-3); pap. 17.75 (ISBN 0-398-03509-1). C C Thomas.

Traffic Flow on Transportation Networks. G. F. Newell. (MIT Press Series Intransportation Studies: No. 5). (Illus.). 288p. 1980. 30.00x (ISBN 0-262-14032-2). MIT Pr.

Traffic Investigation & Control. 2nd ed. Bruce A. Hand et al. (Public Service Technology Ser.). 272p. 1980. text ed. 15.95 (ISBN 0-675-08112-2). Merrill.

Traffic Jam! abr. ed. Sylvia R. Tester. LC 80-16303. (Picture Word Bks.). (Illus.). 32p. (ps-1). 1980. PLB 5.50 (ISBN 0-89565-158-0). Childs World.

Traffic Law Enforcement: A Guide for Patrolmen. Southwestern Law Enforcement Institute. (Illus.). 116p. 1971. 9.75 (ISBN 0-398-01816-2). C C Thomas.

Traffic Planning & Engineering. 2nd, rev. ed. F. D. Hobbs. 1975. text ed. 29.70 o.p. (ISBN 0-08-017926-6); pap. text ed. 17.00 o.p. (ISBN 0-08-017927-4). Pergamon.

Traffic Planning & Engineering. 3rd ed. F. D. Hobbs. (Pergamon International Library, Civil Engineering Series). (Illus.). 1979. 82.00 (ISBN 0-08-022696-5); pap. 28.00 (ISBN 0-08-022697-3). Pergamon.

Traffic Safety. Boy Scouts of America. LC 19-600. (Illus.). 64p. (gr. 6-12). 1975. pap. 0.70x (ISBN 0-8395-3391-8, 3391). BSA.

Traffic Science. Denos C. Gazis. LC 73-21947. 304p. 1974. 37.95 (ISBN 0-471-29480-2, Pub. by Wiley-Interscience). Wiley.

Traffic World's Question & Answer Book, Vol. 27. Editors of Traffic World. 1979. text ed. 16.00 (ISBN 0-87408-015-0). Traffic Serv.

Tragaluz: Experimento En Dos Partes. A. Buero Vallejo. Ed. by Anthony Pasquariello & Patricia W. O'Connor. 1977. pap. text ed. 6.95x (ISBN 0-684-14875-7, ScribC). Scribner.

Tragedie au seizieme siecle. (Classiques Larousse). (Illus., Fr.). pap. 1.95 o.p. (ISBN 0-685-14085-7, 327). Larousse.

Tragedie of Darius. William Alexander. LC 72-6936. (English Experience Ser.: No. 293). 80p. Repr. of 1603 ed. 11.50 (ISBN 90-221-0293-9). Walter J Johnson.

Tragedies of the Last Age Consider'd & Examin'd. Thomas Rymer. Bd. with Short View of Tragedy. (English Stage Ser.: Vol. 18). lib. bdg. 50.00 (ISBN 0-8240-0601-1). Garland Pub.

Tragedy & Civilization: An Interpretation of Sophocles. Charles Segal. LC 80-19765. (Modern Classical Lectures: No. 26). 544p. 1981. text ed. 30.00 (ISBN 0-674-90206-8). Harvard U Pr.

Tragedy & Myth in Ancient Greece. Jean-Pierre Vernant & Pierre Vidal-Naquet. Tr. by Janet Lloyd from Fr. (European Philosophy & the Human Sciences: No. 7). 1981. text ed. 50.00x (ISBN 0-391-01978-3). Humanities.

Tragedy & Social Evolution. Eva Figes. 1976. 10.95 (ISBN 0-7145-3516-8). Riverrun NY.

Tragedy & the Jacobean Temper: The Major Plays of John Webster. Richard Bodtke. (Salzburg Studies in English Literature, Jacobean Drama Studies: No. 2). 1972. pap. text ed. 25.00x (ISBN 0-391-01328-9). Humanities.

Tragedy & Tragicomedy in the Plays of John Webster. Jacqueline Pearson. 151p. 1980. 20.50x (ISBN 0-389-20030-1). B&N.

Tragedy & Truth: Studies in the Development of a Neoclassical Discourse. Timothy J. Reiss. LC 80-10413. 320p. 1980. 24.50x (ISBN 0-300-02461-4). Yale U Pr.

Tragedy Is My Parish: Working for God in the Streets of New Orleans. Peter V. Rogers. 1979. 9.95 (ISBN 0-02-604390-4). Macmillan.

Tragedy of Enlightenment. P. Connerton. LC 79-16102. (Cambridge Studies in the History & Theory of Politics). 1980. 29.95 (ISBN 0-521-22842-5); pap. 7.95 (ISBN 0-521-29675-7). Cambridge U Pr.

Tragedy of Jane Shore. Nicholas Rowe. Ed. by Harry W. Pedicord. LC 73-85439. (Regents Restoration Drama Ser.). 1974. 8.95x (ISBN 0-8032-0381-0); pap. 1.85x (ISBN 0-8032-5381-8, BB 277, Bison). U of Nebr Pr.

Tragedy of Labour. Stephen Haseler. (Mainstream Ser.). 249p. 1980. 19.50x (ISBN 0-631-11341-X, Pub. by Basil Blackwell). Biblio Dist.

Tragedy of Lady Jane Gray. Nicholas Rowe. Tr. by Richard J. Sherry. (SSEL Poetic Drama Ser.: No. 59). (Orig.). 1980. pap. text ed. 25.00x (ISBN 0-391-01955-4). Humanities.

Tragedy of Macbeth. Ron Chaddock. LC 80-82092. (Understand Ye Shaskespeare Ser.). 1980. pap. 8.95 deluxe ed. (ISBN 0-933350-33-3). Morse Pr.

Tragedy of MacBeth: Armchair Exposition. Ron Chaddock. 1979. pap. 3.85 (ISBN 0-933350-20-1). Morse Pr.

Tragedy of Nero. Thomas Jones. Ed. by Elliott M. Hill & Stephen Orgel. LC 78-66763. (Renaissance Drama Ser.). 1979. lib. bdg. 33.00 (ISBN 0-8240-9745-9). Garland Pub.

Tragedy of Quebec: The Expulsion of Its Protestant Farmers, 1916. Robert Sellar. LC 73-90925. (Social History of Canada Ser.). 1974. pap. 6.50 (ISBN 0-8020-6195-8). U of Toronto Pr.

Tragedy of Sin. Stanley E. Sayers. 1974. 4.50 o.p. (ISBN 0-89137-510-4); pap. 2.50 o.p. (ISBN 0-89137-509-0). Quality Pubns.

Tragedy of the Baltic States: A Report from Official Documents & Eyewitnesses' Stories. John A. Swettenham. LC 79-2924. (Illus.). 216p. 1981. Repr. of 1952 ed. 19.75 (ISBN 0-8305-0093-6). Hyperion Conn.

Tragedy of the Korosko. A. Conan Doyle. LC 80-67706. (Conan Doyle Centennial Ser.). (Illus.). 250p. 1981. price not set (ISBN 0-934468-47-8). Gaslight.

Tragedy of the Victorian Novel. Jeannette M. King. LC 77-77762. 1978. 36.00 (ISBN 0-521-21670-2). Cambridge U Pr.

Tragedy: Serious Drama in Relation to Aristotle's "Poetics". rev. & enl. ed. F. L. Lucas. 1981. pap. 5.95x (ISBN 0-389-20141-3). B&N.

Tragedy: Vision & Form. 2nd ed. Robert W. Corrigan. 384p. 1980. pap. text ed. 10.95 scp (ISBN 0-06-041371-9, HarpC). Har-Row.

Tragi-Comedy of Pen Browning. Maisie Ward. LC 72-1865. (Illus.). 1972. 10.00x (ISBN 0-8362-0494-8, Pub by Browning Inst). Pub Ctr Cult Res.

Tragi-Comoedia. John Rowe. LC 70-170430. (English Stage Ser.: Vol. 16). lib. bdg. 50.00 (ISBN 0-8240-0599-6). Garland Pub.

Tragic Deception: Marx Ontra Engels. new ed. Norman Levine. LC 74-14193. (Twentieth Century Ser.: No. 8). 259p. 1975. text ed. 5.75 (ISBN 0-87436-192-3); pap. text ed. 2.50 (ISBN 0-87436-193-1). ABC-Clio.

Tragic Drama & Modern Society: Studies in the Social & Literary Theroy of Drama from 1870 to the Present. John Orr. LC 80-18156. Date not set. price not set (ISBN 0-312-81354-6). St Martin.

Tragic Drama of William Butler Yeats: Figures in a Dance. Leonard E. Nathan. LC 65-16513. 1965. 17.50x (ISBN 0-231-02765-6). Columbia U Pr.

Tragic Effect. Andre Green. Tr. by Alan Sheridan. LC 76-12629. 1979. 28.50 (ISBN 0-521-21377-0). Cambridge U Pr.

Tragic Knowledge: Yeat's Autobiography & Hermeneutics. Daniel T. O'Hara. LC 80-26825. 224p. 1981. 20.00x (ISBN 0-231-05204-9). Columbia U Pr.

Tragic Magic. Wesley Brown. 1978. 7.95 (ISBN 0-394-50224-8). Random.

Tragic Occasions: Essays on Several Forms. B. L. Reid. LC 72-154032. 1971. 12.95 (ISBN 0-8046-9016-2, Natl U). Kennikat.

Tragic Sense of Life. Miguel De Unamuno. 8.50 (ISBN 0-8446-3100-0). Peter Smith.

Tragic Vision of John Ford. Tucker Orbison. (Salzburg Studies in English Literature, Jacobean Drama Studies: No. 21). 1974. pap. text ed. 25.00x (ISBN 0-391-01492-7). Humanities.

Tragical Comedy or Comical Tragedy of Punch & Judy. George Cruikshank. (Illus.). 1976. pap. 2.25 (ISBN 0-7100-8199-5). Routledge & Kegan.

Tragicomic Construction of Cymberline & the Winter's Tale. Caesarea Abartis. (Salzburg Studies in English Literature: Jacobean Drama Studies: Vol. 73). (Orig.). 1977. pap. text ed. 25.00x (ISBN 0-391-01289-4). Humanities.

Tragiques, a Selection. Agrippa D'Aubigne. Ed. by I. D. McFarlane. 1970. text ed. 10.75x (ISBN 0-485-13803-4, Athlone Pr); pap. text ed. 5.50x (ISBN 0-485-12803-9, Athlone Pr). Humanities.

Tragoedy of Cleopatra Queene of Aegypt. Thomas May. Ed. by Denzell S. Smith & Stephen Orgel. LC 78-66784. (Renaissance Drama Ser.). 1979. lib. bdg. 35.00 (ISBN 0-8240-9732-7). Garland Pub.

Trail Blazers. J. Portr Wilhite. 4.95 (ISBN 0-89315-302-8). Lambert Bk.

Trail Boss. Peter Dawson. 192p. (Orig.). 1981. pap. 1.95 (ISBN 0-553-12968-6). Bantam.

Trail Drive. Peter McCurtin. (Sundance Ser.: No. 36). 1981. pap. 1.95 (ISBN 0-8439-0878-5, Leisure Bks). Nordon Pubns.

Trail Dust. Douglas Meador. 7.95 (ISBN 0-685-48784-9). Nortex Pr.

Trail Maker (David Livingstone) Robert O. Latham. 1973. pap. 1.95 (ISBN 0-87508-626-8). Chr Lit.

Trail North. Hawk Greenway. (Illus.). 180p. (Orig.). 1981. pap. 6.00 (ISBN 0-933280-04-1). Island CA.

Trail of Blood. Michael Angelella. 1981. pap. 1.95 (ISBN 0-451-09673-8, J9673, Sig). NAL.

Trail of Conflict. Emilie Loring. 208p. 1981. pap. 1.95 (ISBN 0-553-14521-5). Bantam.

Trail of Cthuthu. August Derleth. 1976. pap. 1.50 o.p. (ISBN 0-345-25017-6). Ballantine.

Trail of the Apache Kid. Lewis B. Patten. (Large Print Bks.). 1980. lib. bdg. 10.95 (ISBN 0-8161-3130-9). G K Hall.

Trail of the Fox. David Irving. 1978. pap. 2.50 (ISBN 0-380-40022-7, 40022). Avon.

Trail of the Fox: The True Story of a Perfect Crime. Lawrence Taylor. 1980. 13.95 (ISBN 0-671-25227-5). S&S.

Trail of the Invisible Light: From X-Strahlen to Radiobiology. E. R. Grigg. (American Lectures in Roentgen Diagnosis Ser.). (Illus.). 1106p. 1965. 49.75 (ISBN 0-398-00739-X). C C Thomas.

Trail of the Lonesome Pine. John Fox. 1976. lib. bdg. 18.25x (ISBN 0-89968-040-2). Lightyear.

Trail Partners. Max Brand. 1974. pap. 1.50 (ISBN 0-446-98138-9). Warner Bks.

Trail to Bear Pawn Mountain. William Rayner. 1976. pap. 1.50 o.p. (ISBN 0-345-25391-4). Ballantine.

Trail to Dismal River. Archie Joscelyn. 192p. (YA) 1975. 5.95 (ISBN 0-685-53494-4, Avalon). Bouregy.

Trail to Lometa. Leroy Donald. 192p. (YA) 1976. 5.95 (ISBN 0-685-62630-X, Avalon). Bouregy.

Trail to Lost Horse Ranch. Archie Joscelyn. (YA) 1977. 4.95 o.p. (ISBN 0-685-73810-8, Avalon). Bouregy.

Trailblazers. B. Gilbert. LC 73-76268. (Old West Ser). (Illus.). 1973. kivar 12.96 (ISBN 0-8094-1459-7, Pub. by Time-Life). Silver.

Trailblazers. Bil Gilbert. (Old West Ser.). (Illus.). 1973. 12.95 (ISBN 0-8094-1458-9). Time-Life.

Trailer Life 1980 R. V. Campground & Service Directory. 1980. pap. 8.95 o.p. (ISBN 0-451-82059-2, XE2059, Sig). NAL.

Trailer Life's Nineteen Eighty-One R. V. Campground & Service Directory. 1981. pap. 9.95 (ISBN 0-451-82063-0, XE2063, Sig). NAL.

Trailer Life's RV Travel Guide & Atlas: Everything You Need to Know to RV America: Where to Go, What to See, How to Get There. Bob Longsdorf & Trailer Life Editors. LC 79-66971. (Illus.). 1980. 14.98 (ISBN 0-934798-01-X); pap. 12.98 (ISBN 0-686-25974-2). Trailer Life.

Trailer Tramp-Gone Fishing. Al Redenbaugh. Ed. by Paul Martin & Al Whattam. (Illus.). 101p. 1979. pap. 3.95 (ISBN 0-918146-15-1). Peninsula WA.

Trailerboater's Guide to the Sea of Cortez. Dix Brow. (Illus.). 1980. pap. 12.95 o.p. (ISBN 0-89404-027-8). Aztex.

Trailering America's Highways & Byways. Richard L. Hayes. (Illus.). 1965. Vol. 1: The West. 3.95 o.s.i. (ISBN 0-87593-008-5). Trail-R.

Trails of the Cordillaras Blanca & Huayhuash of Peru. Jim Bartle. (Illus.). 160p. (Orig.). 1980. pap. 7.95 (ISBN 0-933982-10-0). Bradt Ent.

Trails of the Smoky Hill. Wayne C. Lee. LC 79-67199. (Illus., Orig.). 1980. cancelled (ISBN 0-87004-288-2); pap. 12.95 (ISBN 0-87004-276-9). Caxton.

Trails of Thinking, Feeling & Willing. Carl Unger. 1980. pap. 3.00 (ISBN 0-916786-47-1). St George Bk Serv.

Trails Plowed Under. Charles M. Russell. 1953. 12.95 (ISBN 0-385-04494-1). Doubleday.

Trails to Hoosier Heritage. Harry G. Black. LC 80-81608. (Illus.). 114p. (Orig.). 1981. pap. 3.95 (ISBN 0-937086-00-2). HMB Pubns.

Trails to Nature's Mysteries. Ross E. Hutchins. LC 76-50554. (gr. 7 up). 1977. 6.95 (ISBN 0-396-07401-4). Dodd.

Trails to Texas: Southern Roots of Western Cattle Ranching. Terry G. Jordan. LC 80-14169. (Illus.). xviii, 225p. 1981. 15.95 (ISBN 0-8032-2554-7). U of Nebr Pr.

Trailsman No. Three: Mountain Man Kiel. Jon Sharpe. (Orig.). 1980. pap. 1.75 (ISBN 0-451-09353-4, J9353, Sig). NAL.

Trailsman No. 4: The Sundown Searchers. Jon Sharpe. (Orig.). 1980. pap. 1.75 (ISBN 0-451-09533-2, E9533, Sig). NAL.

Trailsman No. 5. Jon Sharpe. (Orig.). 1981. pap. 1.95 (ISBN 0-451-09615-0, J9605, Sig). NAL.

Train Book. (Golden Play & Learn Ser.). 14p. (ps). Date not set. pap. 2.95 (ISBN 0-307-10740-X, Golden Pr). Western Pub.

Train Like a Grandmaster. Alexander Kotov. (Clubplayer's Library Ser.). (Illus.). 112p. 1981. pap. 11.95 (ISBN 0-7134-3609-3, Pub. by Batsford England). David & Charles.

Train Robbers. Piers Paul Read. LC 78-4890. (Illus.). 1978. 10.95 o.s.i. (ISBN 0-397-01283-7). Lippincott.

Train to Pakistan (Mano Majra) Khushwant Singh. LC 80-8920. (YA) (gr. 9 up). 1981. pap. 3.25 (ISBN 0-394-17887-4, B456, BC). Grove.

Train to Timbuctoo. Margaret W. Brown. (Young Reader Ser.). (Illus.). (gr. k-3). 1979. PLB 5.00 (ISBN 0-307-60118-8, Golden Pr). Western Pub.

Train Trips: Exploring America by Rail. William G. Scheller. (Illus.). 270p. (Orig.). 1981. pap. 6.95 (ISBN 0-914788-34-5). East Woods.

Train Whistle Blues. Mike Cherry. LC 77-11229. 1978. 7.95 o.p. (ISBN 0-385-11374-9). Doubleday.

Train Whistle's Echo: Story of Western Railroading. Phyllis Zauner. (Western Mini-Histories Ser.). (Illus.). 64p. (Orig.). 1980. pap. 3.00 (ISBN 0-936914-05-X). Zanel Pubns.

Train Windows. David A. Evans. LC 75-36977. 56p. 1976. 6.95 (ISBN 0-8214-0204-8); pap. 2.50 o.s.i. (ISBN 0-8214-0213-7). Ohio U Pr.

Train Your Human: A Manual for Caring Dogs. Bonzo Jones. LC 79-52365. (Illus.). 1979. 10.50 (ISBN 0-7153-7678-0). David & Charles.

Trainable Children. rev. ed. Julia S. Molloy. LC 70-155017. (John Day Bk.). 256p. 1972. text ed. 18.00 (ISBN 0-381-97028-0, A82402, TYC-T); pap. 13.95 o.s.i. (ISBN 0-381-97027-2, A82401, JD-T). T Y Crowell.

Trainable Retarded: A Foundations Approach. 2nd ed. Bill R. Gearheart & Freddie W. Litton. LC 78-13959. (Illus.). 1979. 16.95 (ISBN 0-8016-1761-8). Mosby.

Trained Manpower for Agricultural & Rural Development. (FAO Economic & Social Development Paper Ser.: No. 10). 132p. 1980. pap. 7.50 (ISBN 92-5-100861-2, F1963, FAO). Unipub.

Trainer's Guide to Time Management. J. Hyland. 1981. write for info. (ISBN 0-201-03109-4). A-W.

Training a Dog to Live in Your Home. John D. Weiss. LC 80-67749. (Housebreaking Chewing Ser.: Bk. One). (Illus.). 84p. (Orig., Prog. Bk.). 1980. pap. 6.95 (ISBN 0-686-64627-4). Animal Owners.

Training & Development Handbook. American Society for Training & Development. 1967. 25.00 o.p. (ISBN 0-07-001520-1, G). McGraw.

Training & Development Organizations Directory. 2nd ed. Ed. by Paul Wasserman. 1980. 125.00 (ISBN 0-8103-0314-0). Gale.

Training & Fighting Skills. Benny Urquidez. Ed. by Stuart Sobel & Emil Farkas. (Illus.). 200p. (Orig.). 1981. pap. 10.95 (ISBN 0-86568-015-9). Unique Pubns.

Training: Challenge of the 1980s. Offprint of Part 1 of the Report of the Director-General to the International Labour Conference, Geneva, 1980. 50p. (Orig.). 1980. pap. 7.15 (ISBN 92-2-102554-3). Intl Labour Office.

Training Effective Teachers: A Competency-Based Practicum Model for Teachers of Emotionally Disturbed Children. Betty R. Damren et al. 53p. 1975. pap. text ed. 4.00x (ISBN 0-89039-134-3). Ann Arbor Pubs.

Training Fishermen at Sea. 1979. pap. 8.75 (ISBN 0-85238-094-1, FN77, FN). Unipub.

Training for Capstan, Turret, & Sequence Controlled Lathe Setters & Operators, 21 vols. Ed. by Engineering Industry Training Board. (Illus.). 1973. Set. 39.95x (ISBN 0-685-90180-7). Intl Ideas.

Training for Change Agents: A Guide to the Design of Training Programs in Education & Other Fields. Ronald G. Havelock & Mary C. Havelock. LC 72-86337. 262p. 1973. cloth 10.00 (ISBN 0-87944-126-7). U of Mich Soc Res.

Training for Drilling Machine Operators, 17 vols. Ed. by Engineering Industry Training Board. (Illus.). 1978. Set. 36.50x (ISBN 0-685-90182-3). Intl Ideas.

Training for Industrial Site Radiography, 14 vols. Ed. by Engineering Industry Training Board. Incl. Vol. 1. Introduction to Radiography; Vol. 2. Ionizing Radiations; Vol. 4. Image Formation; Vol. 5. Safety; Vol. 6. X-Ray Equipment; Vol. 7. Gamma-Ray Equipment; Vol. 8. Exposure; Vol. 9. Operations; Vol. 10. Pipe-Crawler Equipment. (Illus.). 1977. Set. 28.95x (ISBN 0-685-91100-4). Intl Ideas.

Training for Manual Metal-Arc Welders, 14 vols. Ed. by Engineering Industry Training Board. Incl. Vol. 1. Metal-Arc Welding; Vol. 2. Welding Electrodes; Vol. 3. Joints & Weld Symbols; Vol. 4. Limiting Distortion; Vol. 5. Basic Welding; Vol. 6. Plate Surfaces; Vol. 7. Fillet Joints; Vol. 8. Single Vee Butt Joints; Vol. 9. Pipe Welding; Vol. 10. Fault Diagnosis; Vol. 11. Branch Connections. (Illus.). 1974. Set. 28.95x (ISBN 0-685-91101-2). Intl Ideas.

Training for Mass Communication. (Reports & Papers on Mass Communication: No. 73). 44p. 1975. pap. 2.50 (ISBN 92-3-101234-7, U684, UNESCO). Unipub.

Training for Milling Machine Operators & Setters, 22 vols. Ed. by Engineering Industry Training Board. (Illus.). 1977. Set. 38.95x (ISBN 0-685-90183-1). Intl Ideas.

Training for Negotiating. Bromley Kniveton & Brian Towers. 213p. 1978. text ed. 21.00x (ISBN 0-220-66347-5, Pub. by Busn Bks England). Renouf.

Training for Operators of Numerically Controlled Machines, 17 vols. Ed. by Engineering Industry Training Board. Incl. Vol. 1. Introduction to NC Machine Tool; Vol. 2. Rotating Tool; Vol. 3. Rotating Work; Vol. 4. Milling Cutters; Vol. 5. Tape NC Machines; Vol. 6. Automatic Tool & Work Exchanging; Vol. 7. X, Y, & Z Axes; Vol. 8. Positioning of the Tool & Workpiece; Vol. 9. Emergency Stop & Switching Operations; Vol. 10. Operation. 1973. Set. 37.50x (ISBN 0-685-91102-0). Intl Ideas.

Training for Pipe Fitters, 23 vols. Engineering Industry Training Board. 1976. 41.95x. Intl Ideas.

Training for Results: A Systems Approach to the Development of Human Resources in Industry. 2nd ed. Malcom W. Warren. 1979. pap. text ed. 8.95 (ISBN 0-201-08504-6). A-W.

Training for Riggers-Erectors, 15 vols. Ed. by Engineering Industry Training Board. (Illus.). 1976. Set. 31.50x (ISBN 0-685-90181-5). Intl Ideas.

Training for Series (Trilogy) J. Adair & Blitt. 1978. text ed. 17.50x ea. (ISBN 0-685-96474-4, Pub. by Gower Pub Co England); No. 1. (ISBN 0-566-02110-2); No. 2. (ISBN 0-566-02111-0); No. 3. (ISBN 0-566-02112-9). Renouf.

Training for Service: a Survey of the Bible: Instructor's Edition. Orrin Root. (Illus., Orig.). 1964. pap. 2.50 (ISBN 0-87239-325-9, 3219). Standard Pub.

Training for Service: a Survey of the Bible: Pupil's Edition. Orrin Root. (Illus., Orig.). 1964. pap. 1.95 (ISBN 0-87239-326-7, 3220). Standard Pub.

Training in Libraries: Report of the Library Association Working Party on Training. Ed. by N. Simpson. 1977. pap. 2.75x (ISBN 0-85365-339-9, Pub. by Lib Assn England). Oryx Pr.

Training in Radiological Protection: Curricula & Programming. M. Suzuki et al. (Technical Reports: No. 31). 1964. pap. 5.00 (ISBN 92-0-125164-5, IAEA). Unipub.

Training in Radiological Protection for Nuclear Programmes. (Technical Reports: No. 166). 116p. 1975. pap. 12.00 (ISBN 92-0-125075-4, IAEA). Unipub.

Training in Safe Working Practice for Power Press Tool Setters & Operators, 9 vols. Ed. by Engineering Industry Training Board. Incl. Vol. 1. Introduction to Power Press; Vol. 3. Press Brakes; Vol. 4. Safety Tool Setting; Vol. 5. Guards; Vol. 6. Testing Press Guards; Vol. 7. Accident Prevention. 1973. Set. 21.00x (ISBN 0-685-91103-9). Intl Ideas.

Training in Small Groups: A Study of Five Methods. rev. ed. Ed. by B. Babington Smith. B. A. Farrell. 114p. 1979. 23.00 (ISBN 0-08-023689-8). Pergamon.

Training in the Small Department. James H. Auten. 144p. 1973. 12.75 (ISBN 0-398-02719-6). C C Thomas.

Training Interventions in Job Skill Development. James E. Gardner. LC 80-23810. (Illus.). 224p. 1981. text ed. 12.95 (ISBN 0-201-03097-7). A-W.

Training, Licensing & Guidance of Private Security Officers. John D. Peel. 288p. 1973. 14.75 (ISBN 0-398-02813-3). C C Thomas.

Training Manual for Meat Cutting & Merchandising. Thomas Fabbricante. (Illus.). 1977. pap. text ed. 10.50 (ISBN 0-87055-243-0). AVI.

Training Manual for Rice Production. 140p. 1976. pap. 12.00 (R035, IRRI). Unipub.

Training Manual on Food Irradiation Technology & Techniques. (Technical Reports: No. 114). (Illus., Orig.). 1970. pap. 8.25 (ISBN 92-0-115570-0, IAEA). Unipub.

Training of Adult Middle-Level Personnel. Armin Gretler. LC 72-89860. (Illus.). 164p. (Orig.). 1973. pap. 7.00 (ISBN 92-3-100935-4, U685, UNESCO). Unipub.

Training of Functional Literacy Personnel: A Practical Guide. 104p. (Orig.). 1974. pap. 4.75 (ISBN 92-3-101043-3, U686, UNESCO). Unipub.

Training of the Developmentally Handicapped Adult. R. I. Brown & E. A. Hughson. (Illus.). 214p. 1980. 14.75 (ISBN 0-398-03993-3). C C Thomas.

Training of the Twelve: How to Teach Yourself & Others to Pray. Donald W. Barton. 165p. (Orig.). 1981. pap. 3.95 (ISBN 0-938736-01-9). Life Enrich.

Training Officer's Handbook. Thomas F. Adams. 176p. 1964. pap. 14.50 photocopy ed. spiral (ISBN 0-398-00007-7). C C Thomas.

Training Programs for Health Care Workers: Ward Clerks. Incl. Being a Ward Clerk. 247p. student manual 9.95 (ISBN 0-87914-013-5, 9780); Training the Ward Clerk. 216p. instructor's guide 9.95 (ISBN 0-87914-014-3); span. ed. (1972) o.p.. 1967. Hosp Res & Educ.

Training Recommendations for Training Officers, 14 vols. Ed. by Engineering Industry Training Board. Incl. Vol. 1. The Training of Supervisors; Vol. 2. Adult Operators; Vol. 3. Juvenile Operators; Vol. 4. Professional Engineers; Vol. 5. Managers; Vol. 6. Systems Analysts; Vol. 7. Clerks; Vol. 8. Technicians; Vol. 9. Supervisors; Vol. 10. Computer Operators; Vol. 11. Computer Programmers; Vol. 12. Secretaries; Vol. 13. Typists; Vol. 14. Machine Operators. (Illus.). 1973. Set. pap. text ed. 72.50x (ISBN 0-685-91104-7). Intl Ideas.

Training Retarded Babies & Preschoolers. T. F. Linde & T. Kopp. (Illus.). 200p. 1974. 17.50 (ISBN 0-398-02825-7). C C Thomas.

Training Showjumpers. Anthony Paalman. Tr. by G. Holstein from Ger. (Illus.). 1978. 38.35 (ISBN 0-85131-260-8, Dist. by Sporting Book Center). J A Allen.

Training Spaniels. Joe Irving. (Illus.). 230p. 1980. 19.95 (ISBN 0-7153-8008-7). David & Charles.

Training the Boy's Changing Voice. Duncan McKenzie. 1956. 10.00x (ISBN 0-8135-0249-7). Rutgers U Pr.

Training the Food Service Worker. Hospital Research & Educational Trust of the AHA. (Illus.). 1967. pap. 9.95 (ISBN 0-87618-047-0). R J Brady.

Training the Gunfighter. Timothy J. Mullin. (Illus.). 1981. 24.95 (ISBN 0-87364-185-X). Paladin Ent.

Training the Handicapped for Productive Employment. Robert A. Weisgerber et al. 450p. 1980. text ed. 29.50 (ISBN 0-89443-331-8). Aspen Systems.

Training the Housekeeping Aide. Hospital Research & Educational Trust of the AHA. (Illus.). 1968. pap. 9.95 (ISBN 0-87618-049-7). R J Brady.

Training the Mind of Your Gun Dog. J. A. Kersley & F. Haworth. (Illus.). 1977. 15.95 (ISBN 0-7207-0948-2). Transatlantic.

Training the Psychiatrist to Meet Changing Needs. Conference on Graduate Psychiatric Education, 1962. 1963. 3.00 o.p. (ISBN 0-685-24853-4, 150). Am Psychiatric.

Training the Singing Voice: An Analysis of the Working Concepts Contained Contained in Recent Contributions to Vocal Pedagogy. Victor A. Fields. (Music Reprint Ser.). 1979. Repr. of 1966 ed. lib. bdg. 27.50 (ISBN 0-306-79510-8). Da Capo.

Training the Speaking Voice. 3rd ed. Virgil A. Anderson. (Illus.). 1977. text ed. 14.95x (ISBN 0-19-502150-9). Oxford U Pr.

Training the Ward Clerk. Hospital Research & Educational Trust of the AHA. (Illus.). 1967. pap. 9.95 (ISBN 0-87618-053-5). R J Brady.

Training the Young Actor. Michael R. Malkin. 166p. 1981. Repr. of 1979 ed. 9.95 (ISBN 0-498-01957-8). A S Barnes.

Training Thoroughbred Horses. 2nd rev. ed. Burch. 1973. lib. bdg. 10.75 (ISBN 0-936032-29-4). Thoroughbred Own & Breed.

Training to Run the Perfect Marathon. Michael Schreiber. LC 80-82638. (Illus.). 181p. (Orig.). 1980. pap. 7.50 (ISBN 0-912528-19-2). John Muir.

Training with Cerutty. Larry Myers. LC 77-85323. (Illus.). 174p. 1977. pap. 4.95 (ISBN 0-89037-081-8); handbk. 6.95 (ISBN 0-89037-080-X). Anderson World.

Training You to Train Your Cat. Whitney, Leon F., D.V.M. LC 68-14215. 1968. 5.95 o.p. (ISBN 0-385-08381-5). Doubleday.

Training Your Dog. David Kerr. 1978. 8.95 (ISBN 0-7153-7541-5). David & Charles.

Training Your Memory & Your Mind. Harry Caldwell. (Illus.). 1980. pap. 12.95 o.p. (ISBN 0-930490-20-7). Future Shop.

Trains & Railroads. Howard W. Kanetzke. LC 77-27599. (Read About Science Ser.). (Illus.). (gr. k-3). 1978. PLB 9.95 (ISBN 0-8393-0087-5). Raintree Child.

Trains at Work. Mary Elting. LC 62-17252. (Illus.). (gr. 3-6). 1962. 5.35 o.p. (ISBN 0-8178-3391-9); PLB 5.39 (ISBN 0-8178-3392-7). Harvey.

Trains, Tressels, & Tunnels. Lou Harshaw. 1981. 8.95 (ISBN 0-932298-10-9). Green Hill.

Trains, Trestles & Tunnels: Railroad of the Southern Appalachians. Lou Harshaw. (Illus.). pap. 5.95 (ISBN 0-686-27854-2). Appalach Consortium.

Traite De Science Administrative: Anatomie et Physiologie De L'administration Publique. J. M. Auby et al. 1966. 61.75x (ISBN 90-2796-376-2). Mouton.

Traite De Tournois, Joustes, Carrousels et Autres Spectacles Publics. Claude Menestrier. Ed. by Stephen Orgel. LC 78-68198. (Philosophy of Images Ser.: Vol. 16). (Illus.). 1980. Repr. of 1669 ed. lib. bdg. 66.00 (ISBN 0-8240-3690-5). Garland Pub.

Traite d'Iconographie Chretienne. X. Barbier De Montault. (Illus.). 972p. (Fr.). 1981. Repr. of 1890 ed. lib. bdg. 200.00x (ISBN 0-89241-137-6). Caratzas Bros.

Traitor. George Markstein. 192p. 1981. pap. 2.75 (ISBN 0-345-28609-X). Ballantine.

Traitor. James Shirley. Ed. by John S. Carter. LC 65-11520. (Regents Renaissance Drama Ser). 1965. 7.95x (ISBN 0-8032-0282-2); pap. 1.65x (ISBN 0-8032-5283-8, BB 212, Bison). U of Nebr Pr.

Traitors. William S. Long. (Orig.). 1981. pap. 3.50 (ISBN 0-440-18131-3). Dell.

Traitor's Bride. Jessica Howard. (Orig.). 1979. pap. 2.25 (ISBN 0-515-04728-7). Jove Pubns.

Traits & Confidences. Emily Lawless. Ed. by Robert L. Wolff. (Ireland Nineteenth Century Fiction - Ser. Two: Vol. 75). 280p. 1979. lib. bdg. 32.00 (ISBN 0-8240-3524-0). Garland Pub.

Traits & Stories of the Irish Peasantry, 2 vols. William Carleton. (Nineteenth Century Fiction Ser.: Ireland: Vol. 34). 596p. 1979. Set. lib. bdg. 46.00 (ISBN 0-8240-3483-X). Garland Pub.

Traits & Stories of the Irish Peasantry: Second Series, 3 vols. William Carleton. Ed. by Robert L. Wolff. (Ireland Nineteenth Century Fiction - Ser. Two: Vol. 35). 1412p 1979. lib. bdg. 96.00 (ISBN 0-8240-3484-8). Garland Pub.

Trajectories. rev. ed. Theodore L. Harris et al. (Keys to Reading Ser.). (Illus.). 192p. (gr. 7). 1975. pap. text ed. 3.48 (ISBN 0-87892-460-4); resource bk. 9.90 (ISBN 0-87892-461-2); thoughtvault student guide 3.96 (ISBN 0-87892-462-0); thoughtvault tchrs' ed. 3.96 (ISBN 0-87892-463-9); duplicating masters 19.53 (ISBN 0-87892-498-1). Economy Co.

Trajectories of Artificial Celestial Bodies As Determined from Observations: Proceedings. COSPAR-IAU-IUTAM Symposium, Paris, 1965. Ed. by J. Kovalevsky. (Illus.). 1966. 52.00 (ISBN 0-387-03681-4). Springer-Verlag.

Trajectories through Early Christianity. James M. Robinson & Helmut Koester. LC 79-141254. 312p. 1971. pap. 7.95 (ISBN 0-8006-1362-7, 1-1362). Fortress.

Tramp Art. Helaine Fendelman. 96p. 1975. pap. 6.95 o.p. (ISBN 0-525-47407-2). Dutton.

Tramp for the Lord. Corrie T. Boom. 1976. pap. 1.50 (ISBN 0-89129-027-3). Jove Pubns.

Tramp for the Lord. Corrie T. Boom. (Orig.). pap. 2.25 (ISBN 0-515-05828-9). Jove Pubns.
Trampolining: A Complete Handbook. rev. 2nd ed. Dennis Horne. (Illus.). 1978. 11.95 o.p. (ISBN 0-571-04868-4, Pub. by Faber & Faber); pap. 6.95 (ISBN 0-571-04945-1). Merrimack Bk Serv.
Trampolining for Women & Men. Coons. 1980. pap. 6.95 (ISBN 0-8015-7886-8, Hawthorn). Dutton.
Tramps & Ladies. James Bisset & P. R. Stephensen. LC 59-12193. (Illus.). 1959. 14.95 (ISBN 0-87599-014-2). S G Phillips.
Trancas. Adriana Rowan. 288p. Date not set. pap. 2.75 (ISBN 0-445-04641-4). Popular Lib. Postponed.
Trance. Joy Fielding. 1978. pap. 1.95 o.s.i. (ISBN 0-515-04702-3). Jove Pubns.
Tranportez-Vous Montagnes. Tr. by Jim Baker. (French Bks.). (Fr.). 1979. 1.80 (ISBN 0-8297-0817-0). Life Pubs Intl.
Tranquilization with Harmless Herbs. Eric F. Powell. 1980. 3.00x (ISBN 0-8464-1054-0). Beekman Pubs.
Tranquilizing of America. Richard Hughes & Robert Brewin. 1980. pap. 2.95 (ISBN 0-446-93638-3). Warner Bks.
Tranquillitie of the Minde. John Bernard. LC 73-6099. (English Experience Ser.: No. 568). 1973. Repr. of 1570 ed. 15.00 (ISBN 90-221-0568-7). Walter J Johnson.
Trans-Appalachian Frontier. Malcolm J. Rohrbough. (Illus.). 1978. 22.50x (ISBN 0-19-502209-2). Oxford U Pr.
Trans-Asia Motoring. Colin McElduff. (Illus.). 1976. 26.00 (ISBN 0-905064-01-1). Intl Learn Syst.
Trans-Atlantica: Memoirs of a Norwegian Americanist. Sigmund Skard. 1978. 20.50x (ISBN 82-00-05224-9, Dist. by Columbia U Pr.). Universitet.
Trans-Parent: Sexual Politics in the Lanuage of Emerson. Eric Cheyfitz. LC 80-25750. 224p. 1981. text ed. 13.50 (ISBN 0-8018-2450-8). Johns Hopkins.
Trans-Pennine Heritage: People & Transport. Keith Parry. LC 80-68691. (Illus.). 1981. 19.95 (ISBN 0-7153-8019-2). David & Charles.
Trans-per: Understanding Human Communication. Kenneth Sereno & Edward Bodaken. 1975. 14.95 (ISBN 0-395-18701-X); teaching strategies guide 1.50 (ISBN 0-395-18783-4). HM.
Trans-Siberian Railway. Cornelia Veenendaal. LC 73-86246. 64p. 1973. pap. 4.95 (ISBN 0-914086-01-4). Alicejamesbooks.
Transactional Analysis for Police Personnel. Anne T. Romano. write for info. (ISBN 0-398-04175-X). C C Thomas.
Transactional Analysis in Health Care. Jean Elder. LC 78-57376. 1978. 9.95 (ISBN 0-201-01512-9, M&N Div). A-W.
Transactional Analysis: Principles & Applications. Gerald M. Goldhaber & Marylynn B. Goldhaber. 368p. 1976. pap. text ed. 6.95x o.p. (ISBN 0-205-05424-2). Allyn.
Transactional Manager: How to Solve People Problems with Transactional Analysis. Abe Wagner. (Illus.). 208p. 1981. 11.95 (ISBN 0-13-928192-4, Spec); pap. 5.95 (ISBN 0-13-928184-3). P-H.
Transactions, Vol. 88. (Illus.). 400p. 1981. 35.00 (ISBN 0-9603048-2-7). Soc Naval Arch.
Transactions: International Vacuum Congress - 3rd - Stuttgart - 1965, Vol. 2, 3 Pts. Ed. by H. Adam. text ed. 46.00 (ISBN 0-08-012127-6). Pergamon.
Transactions of the American Association of G-U Surgeons: Symposium, Vol. 69. American Association of Genito-Urinary Surgeons. 1978. pap. 19.00 o.p. (ISBN 0-683-00107-8). Williams & Wilkins.
Transactions of the ANA, Vol. 105, 1980. American Neurological Association. 1981. text ed. price not set. Springer Pub.
Transactions of the Blavatsky Lodge of the Theosophical Society. Helena P. Blavatsky. xxiv, 149p. 1923. Repr. of 1890 ed. 5.00 (ISBN 0-938998-05-6). Theosophy.
Transactions of the International Astronomical Union, Vol. XVIIB. Ed. by Patrick A. Wayman. 536p. 1980. PLB 68.50 (ISBN 90-277-1159-3). Kluwer Boston.
Transactions of the International Ophthalmic Optical Congress, 1961. International Ophthalmic Congress. 1962. 19.25 o.s.i. (ISBN 0-02-846270-X). Hafner.
Transactions of the Moscow Mathematical Society. Incl. Vol. 12. 1963. 31.60 (ISBN 0-8218-1612-8, MOSCOW-12); Vol. 13. 1967. 26.00 (ISBN 0-8218-1613-6, MOSCOW-13); Vol. 14. 1967. 26.00 (ISBN 0-8218-1614-4, MOSCOW-14); Vol. 15. 1967. 31.60 (ISBN 0-8218-1615-2, MOSCOW-15); Vol. 16. 1968. 26.80 (ISBN 0-8218-1616-0, MOSCOW-16); Vol. 17. 1969. 27.60 (ISBN 0-8218-1617-9, MOSCOW-17); Vol. 18. 1969. 25.60 (ISBN 0-8218-1618-7, MOSCOW-18); Vol. 19. 1969. 22.40 (ISBN 0-8218-1619-5, MOSCOW-19); Vol. 20. 1971. 33.60 (ISBN 0-8218-1620-9, MOSCOW-20); Vol. 21. 1971. 29.20 (ISBN 0-8218-1621-7, MOSCOW-21); Vol. 22. 1972. 26.00 (ISBN 0-8218-1622-5). LC 65-7413. Am Math.
Transactions of the Moscow Mathematical Society, 1975. N. Ali et al. LC 65-4713. 1977. 37.20 (ISBN 0-8218-1632-2, MOSCOW-32). Am Math.
Transactions of the National Association for the Advancement of Art, & Its Application to Industry, 1889-91, 3 vols. Ed. by Peter Stansky & Rodney Shewan. (Aesthetic Movement & the Arts & Crafts Movement Ser.: Periodicals: Vol. 1). 1979. lib. bdg. 53.00 ea. (ISBN 0-8240-3617-4). Garland Pub.
Transactions of the Philological Society 1980. 224p. 1981. 35.00x (ISBN 0-631-12574-4, Pub. by Basil Blackwell). Biblio Dist.
Transatlantic Mail. Frank Staff. LC 79-67394. 192p. 1980. Repr. of 1956 ed. lib. bdg. 35.00x (ISBN 0-88000-113-5). Quarterman.
Transatlantic Sketches. Henry James. 448p. 1981. cancelled (ISBN 0-8180-1177-7). Horizon.
Transcend: A Guide to the Spiritual Quest. Morton T. Kelsey. 240p. (Orig.). 1981. pap. 5.95 (ISBN 0-8245-0015-6). Crossroad NY.
Transcendence & Immanence: A Study in Catholic Modernism & Integralism. Gabriel Daly. 266p. 1980. 34.95x (ISBN 0-19-826652-9). Oxford U Pr.
Transcendence of the Cave: Sequel to the Discipline of the Cave. John N. Findlay. LC 67-16869. (Muirhead Library of Philosophy Ser.). 1978. text ed. 15.00x (ISBN 0-04-111002-1). Humanities.
Transcendent Selfhood: The Loss & Rediscovery of the Inner Life. Louis Dupre. 1976. 8.95 (ISBN 0-8164-0306-6). Crossroad NY.
Transcendental Meditation: Relation or Religion. Ronald L. Carlson. 1978. pap. 2.50 (ISBN 0-8024-8800-5). Moody.
Transcendental Mirage. James Bjornstad. LC 76-6614. 1976. pap. 1.50 (ISBN 0-87123-556-0, 200556). Bethany Fell.
Transcendental Style in Film: Ozu-Bresson-Dreyer. Paul Schrader. 1972. 14.95 (ISBN 0-520-02038-3). U of Cal Pr.
Transcendentalism in America. Donald N. Koster. (World Leaders Ser.). 1975. lib. bdg. 10.95 (ISBN 0-8057-3727-8). Twayne.
Transcendentalism in New England: A History. Octavius B. Frothingham. LC 59-10346. 1972. pap. 6.50x (ISBN 0-8122-1038-7, Pa. Paperbacks). U of Pa Pr.
Transcendentalist Constant in American Literature. Roger Asselineau. (Gotham Library). 1981. 17.50x (ISBN 0-686-64289-9); pap. 7.00 (ISBN 0-8147-0573-1). NYU Pr.
Transcending Dimensions to Another World. R. Kinney. 6.95 o.p. (ISBN 0-8062-1069-9). Carlton.
Transcending the Power Game: The Way to Executive Serenity. Ralph G. Siu. LC 79-25299. 1980. 14.95 (ISBN 0-471-06001-1, Pub. by Wiley-Interscience). Wiley.
Transcontinental Railroad, 1862-69: A Great Engineering Feat Links America Coast to Coast. Frank B. Latham. LC 73-1222. (Focus Bks). (Illus.). (gr. 7-12). 1973. text ed. 4.47 o.p. (ISBN 0-531-01025-2). Watts.
Transcontinental Rails. Thomas K. Hinckley. LC 71-43562. (Wild & Woolly West Ser., No. 12). (Illus., Orig.). 1969. 7.00 (ISBN 0-910584-92-3); pap. 2.00 (ISBN 0-910584-13-3). Filter.
Transcontinental Railway Strategy, 1869-1893: A Study of Businessmen. Julius Grodinsky. LC 61-6624. 1962. 15.00x o.p. (ISBN 0-8122-7268-4). U of Pa Pr.
Transcreation: Two Essays. P. Lal. 29p. 1973. 8.00 (ISBN 0-88253-269-3). Ind-US Inc.
Transcriber's Guide to Medical Terminology. Peggy F. Bradbury. 1973. spiral bdg. 7.00 (ISBN 0-87488-972-3). Med Exam.
Transcription Office Practice Set. 3rd ed. Esther Sandry. (gr. 9-12). 1973. pap. 6.20 (ISBN 0-8224-2076-7); key 3.16 (ISBN 0-8224-2077-5). Pitman Learning.
Transcription Skills for Information Processing, Module 1. Anne E. Schatz & Beverley M. Funk. 96p. 1981. pap. text ed. 2.92 (ISBN 0-07-055200-2). McGraw.
Transcription Skills for Information Processing, Module 2. Anne E. Schatz & Berverley M. Funk. 112p. 1981. pap. text ed. 2.92 (ISBN 0-07-055201-0). McGraw.
Transcualisticas. bilingual ed. Ernest Robson. Tr. by Lucy Lopez de Thorogood. (Eng. & Span.). 1978. signed limited ed. 25.00; pap. 8.95. Primary Pr.
Transcultural Counseling: Needs, Programs & Techniques. Garry R. Walz & Libby Benjamin. LC 77-26253. (New Vistas in Counseling Ser.: Vol. 7). 1978. text ed. 16.95 (ISBN 0-87705-320-0). Human Sci Pr.
Transcultural Nursing: A Book of Readings. P. J. Brink. (Illus.). 320p. 1976. pap. 11.95 (ISBN 0-13-928101-0). P-H.
Transcultural Nursing: Concepts, Theories & Practices. Madeleine Leininger. LC 77-28250. 1977. text ed. 22.50 (ISBN 0-471-52608-8, Pub by Wiley Medical). Wiley.
Transcultural Nursing, 1979. Ed. by Madeline Leininger. (Illus.). 742p. 1979. text ed. 32.50 (ISBN 0-89352-079-9). Masson Pub.
Transcultural Psychiatry. Ari Kiev. LC 73-163235. 1973. 12.95 (ISBN 0-02-917180-6); pap. 3.50 (ISBN 0-02-917170-9). Free Pr.
Transculture; Universal Heritage: Sixty-Five Timeless Allegories. Mel Yosso. 160p. 1980. pap. 6.50 (ISBN 0-935862-00-5). Transculture Inc.
Transcutaneous Neuro Stimulation: Principles & Practice. Robert A. Ersek. LC 78-50175. 1981. 23.95 (ISBN 0-87527-168-5). Green.
Transducers for Biomedical Measurements: Principles & Applications. Richard S. Cobbold. LC 74-2480. (Biomedical Engineering & Health Systems Ser). 486p. 1974. 36.50 (ISBN 0-471-16145-4, Pub. by Wiley-Interscience). Wiley.
Transducers in Measurement & Control. rev ed. Peter H. Sydenham. 1980. pap. text ed. 17.50 (ISBN 0-87664-460-4). Instru Soc.
Transfer. Silvano Ceccherini. Tr. by Isabel Quigley. LC 66-20533. 1966. 6.00 o.s.i. (ISBN 0-8076-0399-6). Braziller.
Transfer at Eleven. C. J. Hill. 1972. pap. text ed. 3.75x (ISBN 0-901225-99-1, NFER). Humanities.
Transfer Cost of a Housing Allowance: Conceptual Issues & Benefit Patterns. John D. Heinberg. 80p. 1971. pap. 2.50 o.p. (ISBN 0-87766-068-9, 30004). Urban Inst.
Transfer of Cell Constituents into Eukaryotic Cells. Ed. by J. E. Celis et al. (NATO Advanced Study Institutes Ser., A: Life Sciences: Vol. 31). 450p. 1980. 45.00 (ISBN 0-306-40425-7, Plenum Pr). Plenum Pub.
Transfer of Manufacturing Technology Within Multinational Enterprises. Jack H. Behrman & Harvey W. Wallender. LC 76-5866. 272p. 1976. text ed. 20.00 o.p. (ISBN 0-88410-048-0). Ballinger Pub.
Transfer of Power in India: Nineteen Forty-Five to Nineteen Forty-Seven. Edmond W. Lumby. LC 79-1634. 1981. Repr. of 1954 ed. 22.50 (ISBN 0-88355-938-2). Hyperion Conn.
Transfer of Stock, 2 vols. 5th ed. Francis M. Christy. LC 72-84858. 1972. 90.00 (ISBN 0-686-14484-8). Lawyers Co-Op.
Transfer of Technology Among the Developing Countries. B. N. Bhattasali. LC 70-186286. 94p. 1972. 10.50 o.p. (ISBN 92-833-1013-6, APO5, APO). Unipub.
Transfer Pricing & Multinational Corporation: An Overview of Concepts, Mechanisms & Regulations. Sylvain R. Plasschaert. LC 79-84708. (Praeger Special Studies Ser.). 126p. 1979. 21.95 (ISBN 0-03-052396-6). Praeger.
Transfer Pricing in Multinational Firms: A Heuristic Programming Approach & Case Studies. Lars Nieckels. LC 76-6174. 1976. 21.95 (ISBN 0-470-15084-X). Halsted Pr.
Transfer Pricing Practices in the United States & Japan. Roger Y. Tang. LC 78-19780. (Praeger Special Studies). 1979. 20.95 (ISBN 0-03-046551-6). Praeger.
Transfer Station Techniques Manual. Brown. 1981. text ed. 39.95 (ISBN 0-250-40426-5). Ann Arbor Science.
Transfer to Yesterday. Isidore Haiblum. LC 80-2248. (Science Fiction Ser.). 192p. 1981. 9.95 (ISBN 0-385-17136-6). Doubleday.
Transference Neurosis & Transference Psychosis. Margaret Little. LC 80-66925. 350p. 1980. 25.00 (ISBN 0-87668-421-5). Aronson.
Transferencia De Calor. Jose Manrique. 1977. pap. text ed. 8.00 (ISBN 0-06-315511-7, IntlDept). Har-Row.
Transfers Through the Transport Sector: Evaluation of Re-Distribution Effects. (ECMT Roundtable Ser.: No. 48). (Illus.). 93p. (Orig.). 1980. pap. text ed. 6.00x (ISBN 92-821-1064-8). OECD.
Transfiguration of the Commonplace: A Philosophy of Art. Arthur C. Danto. 1981. text ed. 17.50x (ISBN 0-674-90345-5). Harvard U Pr.
Transfigured Hart. Jane Yolen. LC 75-2377. (Illus.). (gr. 4 up). 1975. 7.95 (ISBN 0-690-00736-1, TYC-J). T Y Crowell.
Transform Methods with Applications to Engineering & Operations Research. Eginhard J. Muth. (Illus.). 1977. ref. ed. 25.95 (ISBN 0-13-928861-9). P-H.
Transformation. George B. Leonard. 288p. 1972. 7.95 o.s.i. (ISBN 0-440-09031-8). Delacorte.
Transformation. George B. Leonard. 288p. 1981. pap. 5.95 (ISBN 0-87477-169-2). J P Tarcher.
Transformation & Development of Technology in the Japanese Cotton Industry. 86p. 1980. pap. 5.00 (ISBN 92-808-0091-4, TUNU093, UNU). Unipub.
Transformation Geometry. Max Jeger. (Mathematical Studies Ser.). 1971. text ed. 6.50x o.p. (ISBN 0-04-513002-7). Allen Unwin.
Transformation Groups. Ed. by C. Kosniowski. LC 76-40837. (London Mathematical Society Lecture Notes Ser.: No. 26). 1977. limp bdg. 17.95x (ISBN 0-521-21509-9). Cambridge U Pr.
Transformation of American Foreign Policy. Charles E. Bohlen. 1969. 3.95x (ISBN 0-393-05385-7, NortonC); pap. text ed. 2.95x (ISBN 0-393-09878-8). Norton.
Transformation of American Law, 1790-1860. Morton J. Horwitz. (Studies in Legal History). 1977. 18.50x (ISBN 0-674-90370-6). Harvard U Pr.
Transformation of Europe, 1558-1648. Charles Wilson. LC 75-17283. 1976. 30.00x (ISBN 0-520-03075-3). U of Cal Pr.
Transformation of Man. Rosemary Haughton. 1967. 6.95 o.p. (ISBN 0-87243-010-3). Templegate.
Transformation of Man. rev. ed. Rosemary Haughton. 1980. pap. 6.95 (ISBN 0-87243-127-4). Templegate.
Transformation of Palestine: Essays on the Origin & Development of the Arab-Israeli Conflict. Ed. by Ibrahim Abu-Lughod. 1971. 15.75x o.s.i. (ISBN 0-8101-0345-1). Northwestern U Pr.
Transformation of Political Culture in Cuba. Richard R. Fagen. LC 77-83117. (Illus.). xii, 270p. 1969. 10.00x (ISBN 0-8047-0702-2); pap. 5.95 (ISBN 0-8047-0814-2). Stanford U Pr.
Transformation of Positivism: Alexius Meinong & European Thought, 1880-1920. David Lindenfield. 304p. 1981. 25.00x (ISBN 0-520-03994-7). U of Cal Pr.
Transformation of Sikh Society. Ethne K. Marenco. 342p. pap. 10.95 (ISBN 0-913244-08-2). Hapi Pr.
Transformation of the Roman World: Gibbon's Problem After Two Centuries. Lynn White, Jr. (UCLA Center for Medieval & Renaissance Studies). 1966. 11.00 o.p. (ISBN 0-520-01334-4); pap. 4.95x (ISBN 0-520-02491-5). U of Cal Pr.
Transformational Grammar & the Rumanian Language. Ed. by Sorin Alexanderescu. (PDR Press Publications on Rumanian Ser.: No. 1). 1977. pap. text ed. 9.25x (ISBN 90-316-0144-6). Humanities.
Transformational Grammar of Russian Adjectives. Leonard H. Babby. LC 73-83929. (Janua Linguarum, Ser. Practica: No. 235). 242p. 1975. pap. text ed. 52.65x (ISBN 90-2793-022-8). Mouton.
Transformationi. Ludovico Dolce. Ed. by Stephen Orgel. LC 78-68191. (Philosophy of Images Ser.: Vol. 4). (Illus.). 1980. lib. bdg. 66.00 (ISBN 0-8240-3678-6). Garland Pub.
Transformations of Allegory. Gay Clifford. 1974. 12.50 (ISBN 0-7100-7976-1). Routledge & Kegan.
Transformations of Godot. Frederick Busi. LC 79-4002. 160p. 1980. 12.00x (ISBN 0-8131-1392-X). U Pr of Ky.
Transformations of the American Party System: Political Coalitions from the New Deal to the 1970's. 2nd ed. Everett C. Ladd, Jr. & Charles D. Hadley. 1978. 16.95 (ISBN 0-393-05660-0); pap. 6.95x (ISBN 0-393-09065-5). Norton.
Transformations of the War Oracle in Old Testament Prophecy. Duane L. Christensen. LC 75-34264. (Harvard Dissertations in Religion Ser.). 1975. pap. 9.00 (ISBN 0-89130-064-3, 020103). Scholars Pr Ca.
Transformations on the Highveld: The Tswana & Southern Sotho. William F. Lye & Colin Murray. (People of Southern Africa Ser.). (Illus.). 160p. 1980. bds. 21.50x (ISBN 0-389-20112-X). B&N.
Transformationsgruppen, 3 Vols. 2nd ed. Sophus Lie. LC 76-113135. (Ger). 1970. 79.50 set (ISBN 0-8284-0232-9). Chelsea Pub.
Transformed Cell. Ed. by Ivan L. Cameron & Thomas B. Pool. (Cell Biology Ser.). 1981. price not set (ISBN 0-12-157160-2). Acad Pr.
Transformer Principles & Practice. 2nd ed. Jesse B. Gibbs. (Engineering Books for Industry Ser). (Illus.). 1950. 24.50 o.p. (ISBN 0-07-023179-6, P&RB). McGraw.
Transforming Bible Study: A Leader's Guide. Walter Wink. LC 80-16019. 176p. 1980. pap. 6.50 (ISBN 0-687-42499-2). Abingdon.
Transforming Moment: Understanding Convictional Experiences. James E. Loder. LC 80-8354. 256p. 1981. 12.95 (ISBN 0-06-065276-4, HarpR). Har-Row.

Transfusion Therapy in Infancy & Childhood: The Fetus, Infant, & Child. Ed. by William Sherwood & Alan Cohen. LC 80-80304. (Masson Monographs in Pediatrics). (Illus.). 232p. 1980. text ed. 34.50 (ISBN 0-89352-074-8). Masson Pub.

Transgenerational Family Therapy. Stuart Lieberman. 240p. 1980. 39.00x (ISBN 0-85664-776-4, Pub. by Croom Helm England). State Mutual Bk.

Transgenerational Family Therapy. Stuart Lieberman. (Illus.). 234p. 1979. 35.00x (ISBN 0-85664-776-4, Pub. by Croom Helm Ltd England). Biblio Dist.

Transgrammar: English Structure, Style, & Dialects. Jean Malmstrom & Constance Weaver. 1973. pap. 9.95x (ISBN 0-673-07802-7). Scott F.

Transguide: A Guide to Sources of Freight Transportation Information. Reebie Associates et al. LC 80-53144. 392p. 1980. 40.00 (ISBN 0-9604776-0-8). Reebie Assoc.

Transient Unemployed. John N. Webb. LC 71-166337. (FDR & the Era of the New Deal Ser.). 1971. Repr. of 1935 ed. lib. bdg. 15.00 (ISBN 0-306-70335-1). Da Capo.

Transistor Basics: A Short Course. rev. 2nd ed. George C. Stanley, Jr. (Illus.). 128p. 1975. pap. 7.25 (ISBN 0-8104-5866-7). Hayden.

Transistor Circuit Analysis & Application. Ben Zeines. (Illus.). 448p. 1976. 18.95x o.p. (ISBN 0-87909-837-6); instrs' manual avail. o.p. Reston.

Transistor Fundamentals, 3 vols. Training & Retraining Inc. Incl. Vol. 1. Basic Semiconductor & Circuit Principles (ISBN 0-672-20641-2, 20641); Vol. 2. Basic Transistor Circuits (ISBN 0-672-20642-0, 20642); Vol. 3. Digital & Special Circuits (ISBN 0-672-20644-7, 20644). LC 68-21313. (Illus., Prog. Bk.). 1968. pap. 5.75 ea.; pap. 15.75 set (ISBN 0-672-21796-1). Sams.

Transistor Fundamentals. Training & Retraining, Inc. LC 68-21313. 1968. 10.35 o.p. (ISBN 0-672-20744-3); Bk 2. 10.35 o.p. (ISBN 0-672-20745-1); instructor's guide 5.00 o.p. (ISBN 0-672-20647-1). Bobbs.

Transistor Fundamentals & Servicing. Boyd Larson. (Illus.). 480p. 1974. 20.95 (ISBN 0-13-929992-0). P-H.

Transistor Ignition Systems. Carroll Brant. LC 76-43635. (Illus.). 1976. 8.95 o.p. (ISBN 0-8306-6882-9); pap. 5.95 (ISBN 0-8306-5882-3, 882). TAB Bks.

Transistor Switching & Sequential Circuits. J. J. Sparkes. 1969. 22.00 (ISBN 0-08-012982-X); pap. 10.75 (ISBN 0-08-012981-1). Pergamon.

Transistors. Ed. by E. J. Kendall. LC 70-88307. 1969. 25.00 (ISBN 0-08-006511-2); pap. 12.75 (ISBN 0-08-006510-4). Pergamon.

Transit Improvements in Atlanta-the Effects of Fare & Service Changes. Michael A. Kemp. 46p. 1974. pap. 2.50 o.p. (ISBN 0-87766-117-0, 71000). Urban Inst.

Transit of Cassidy. George Turner. 1979. 14.95 (ISBN 0-241-10093-3, Pub. by Hamish Hamilton England). David & Charles.

Transit Systems Theory. J. Edward Anderson. LC 77-11856. (Illus.). 1978. 24.95 (ISBN 0-669-01902-X). Lexington Bks.

Transition: An Author Index. Charles L. P. Silet. LC 79-67477. 186p. 1979. 15.00x (ISBN 0-87875-168-8). Whitston Pub.

Transition from Capitalism to Socialism. John D. Stephens. (New Studies in Sociology). 1980. text ed. 25.00x (ISBN 0-391-01623-7); pap. text ed. 13.00x (ISBN 0-333-23407-3). Humanities.

Transition in India & Other Essays. K. Santhanam. 1964. 7.00x o.p. (ISBN 0-210-27002-0). Asia.

Transition Metal Clusters. Ed. by Brian F. Johnson. 1980. 96.50 (ISBN 0-471-27817-3, Pub. by Wiley-Interscience). Wiley.

Transition Metal Mediated Organic Syntheses. Ed. by D. W. Slocum & O. R. Hughes. LC 79-24735. (N.Y. Academy of Sciences Annals: Vol. 333). 301p. 1980. 55.00x (ISBN 0-89766-039-0). NY Acad Sci.

Transition of Youth to Adulthood: A Bridge Too Long. Frank B. Brown. 1980. lib. bdg. 24.50x (ISBN 0-89158-675-X); pap. text ed. 11.00 (ISBN 0-89158-756-X). Westview.

Transition to Socialist Economy. Charles Bettelheim. Ed. by John Mepham. Tr. by Brian Pearce from Fr. (Marxist Theory & Contemporary Capitalism Ser). 248p. 1975. text ed. 18.50x (ISBN 0-391-00396-8); pap. text ed. 10.00x (ISBN 0-391-00884-6). Humanities.

Transition: Understanding & Managing Personal Change. John Adams et al. LC 77-5833. 1977. text ed. 18.50x o.s.i. (ISBN 0-916672-98-0). Allanheld.

Transitional Energy Policy 1980-2030: Alternative Nuclear Technologies. Hugh B. Stewart. (Pergamon Policy Studies on Science & Technology). 266p. 1981. 30.00 (ISBN 0-08-027183-9); pap. 12.50 (ISBN 0-08-027182-0). Pergamon.

Transitional Phenomena, Vicissitudes of Symbolization, & Creativity. Susan Deri. 1981. write for info. (ISBN 0-8236-6641-7). Intl Univs Pr.

Transitional Trade & Rural Development: The Nature & Role of Agricultural Trade in a South Indian District. Barbara Harriss. 400p. text ed. 35.00 (ISBN 0-7069-1036-2, Pub. by Vikas India). Advent Bk.

Transitions: Making Sense of Life's Changes. William Bridges. 160p. 1980. 10.95 (ISBN 0-201-00081-4); pap. 6.95 (ISBN 0-201-00082-2). A-W.

Transitions: The Family & the Life Course in Historical Perspectives. Ed. by Tamara K. Hareven. (Studies in Social Discontinuity Ser.). 1978. 24.50 (ISBN 0-12-325150-8). Acad Pr.

Transits: The Time of Your Life. Betty Lunsted. 1980. pap. 7.95 (ISBN 0-87728-503-9). Weiser.

Translantic Summer. John E. McKelvy, Jr. 1981. 10.00 (ISBN 0-533-04786-2). Vantage.

Translating Evaluation into Policy. Ed. by Robert F. Rich. LC 79-21453. (Sage Research Progress Ser. in Evaluation: Vol. 3). (Illus.). 1979. 12.95x (ISBN 0-8039-1283-8); pap. 6.50x (ISBN 0-8039-1284-6). Sage.

Translating Neruda: The Way to Macchu Picchu. John Felstiner. LC 79-67773. (Illus.). 240p. 1980. 18.50x (ISBN 0-8047-1079-1). Stanford U Pr.

Translating Translating Apollinaire. B. P. Nichol. 1979. pap. 4.00 (ISBN 0-87924-031-8). Membrane Pr.

Translation Debate. Eugene H. Glassman. 128p. (Orig.). 1981. pap. 4.25 (ISBN 0-87784-467-4). Inter Varsity.

Translation of Art: Essays on Chinese Painting & Poetry. Ed. by James C. Watt. LC 76-28572. (Renditions Ser.). (Illus.). 218p. 1977. 15.00 (ISBN 0-295-95535-X). U of Wash Pr.

Translation of French Foot-notes of The Dawn-Breakers. Emily M. Perigord. 1939. pap. 3.60 o.p. (ISBN 0-87743-075-6, 7-31-55). Baha'i.

Translation of Glanville: (A Treatise on the Laws & Customs of the Kingdom of England) Ranulph de Glanville. Tr. by John Beames from Latin. xl, 362p. 1980. Repr. of 1812 ed. lib. bdg. 30.00x (ISBN 0-8377-0313-1). Rothman.

Translation Planes. Ed. by H. Lueneburg. 256p. 1980. 29.80 (ISBN 0-387-09614-0). Springer-Verlag.

Translations. Brian Friel. 72p. 1981. pap. 8.50 (ISBN 0-571-11742-2). Merrimack Bk Serv.

Translations by American Poets. Ed. by Jean Garrigue. LC 76-86309. 371p. 1970. 15.00x (ISBN 0-8214-0062-2). Ohio U Pr.

Translations from the Philosophical Writings of Gottlob Frege. Gottlob Frege. Ed. by Peter Geach & Max Black. 1977. Repr. of 1952 ed. 19.00x o.p. (ISBN 0-87471-325-0). Rowman.

Translations from the Philosophical Writings of Gottlob Frege. 3rd ed. Gottlob Frege. Ed. by Peter Geach & Max Black. 228p. 1980. 25.00x (ISBN 0-8476-6286-1); pap. 10.95x (ISBN 0-8476-6287-X). Rowman.

Translations of Ancient Arabian Poetry. Charles J. Lyall. LC 79-2872. 142p. 1981. Repr. of 1885 ed. 18.00 (ISBN 0-8305-0042-1). Hyperion Conn.

Translations of Beowulf: A Critical Biography. Chauncey B. Tinker. LC 67-21717. 1967. Repr. of 1903 ed. 6.00 (ISBN 0-87752-114-X). Gordian.

Translations of German Poetry in American Magazines, 1741-1810. Edward Z. Davis. LC 66-27663. 1966. Repr. of 1905 ed. 15.00 (ISBN 0-8103-3209-4). Gale.

Translators Handbook on Mark. R. G. Bratcher & E. A. Nida. (Helps for Translators Ser.). 1976. Repr. of 1961 ed. soft cover 4.60 (ISBN 0-8267-0135-3, 08501). United Bible.

Translators Handbook on Paul's Letters to the Colossians & to Philemon. Robert G. Bratcher & Eugene A. Nida. (Helps for Translators Ser.). 1977. softcover 2.40 (ISBN 0-8267-0145-0, 08529). United Bible.

Translators Handbook on Paul's Letter to the Galatians. D. C. Arichea, Jr. & E. A. Nida. (Helps for Translators Ser.). 1979. Repr. of 1976 ed. soft cover 2.95 (ISBN 0-8267-0142-6, 08527). United Bible.

Translators Handbook on Paul's Letter to the Philippians. I. Loh & E. A. Nida. (Helps for Translators Ser.). 1979. Repr. of 1977 ed. soft cover 1.70 (ISBN 0-8267-0144-2, 08528). United Bible.

Translators Handbook on Paul's Letter to the Romans. B. M. Newman, Jr. & E. A. Nida. (Helps for Translators Ser.). 1979. Repr. of 1973 ed. soft cover 2.95 (ISBN 0-8267-0139-6, 08517). United Bible.

Translators Handbook on Paul's Letter to the Thessalonians. P. Ellingworth & E. A. Nida. (Helps for Translators Ser.). 1975. soft cover 2.10 (ISBN 0-8267-0146-9, 08526). United Bible.

Translators Handbook on the Acts of the Apostles. B. M. Newman, Jr. & E. A. Nida. (Helps for Translators Ser.). 1979. Repr. of 1972 ed. 3.85 (ISBN 0-8267-0138-8, 08514). United Bible.

Translators Handbook on the Book of Amos. J. De Waard & W. A. Smalley. (Helps for Translators Ser.). 1979. softcover 2.50 (ISBN 0-8267-0128-0, 08577). United Bible.

Translators Handbook on the Book of Jonah. Brynmor F. Price & Eugene A. Nida. (Helps for Translators Ser.). 1978. soft cover 2.80 (ISBN 0-8267-0199-X, 08552). United Bible.

Translators Handbook on the Book of Ruth. J. De Waard & E. A. Nida. (Helps for Translators Ser.). 1976. Repr. of 1973 ed. softcover 2.00 (ISBN 0-8267-0107-8, 08518). United Bible.

Translators Handbook on the First Letter from Peter. D. C. Arichea & E. A. Nida. (Helps for Translators Ser.). 1980. softcover 2.35 (ISBN 0-8267-0152-3, 08624). United Bible.

Translators Handbook on the Gospel of John. B. M. Newman & E. A. Nida. (Helps for Translators Ser.). 1980. softcover 4.85 (ISBN 0-8267-0137-X, 08620). United Bible.

Translators Handbook on the Gospel of Luke. J. Reiling & J. L. Swellengrebel. (Helps for Translators Ser.). 1971. 11.75 (ISBN 0-8267-0136-1, 08512). United Bible.

Translators Handbook on the Letters of John. C. Haas et al. (Helps for Translators Ser.). 1979. Repr. of 1972 ed. softcover 1.90 (ISBN 0-686-14401-5, 08516). United Bible.

Translator's Son. Joseph Bruchac. Ed. by Stanley H. Barkan. (Cross-Cultural Review Chapbook 10). 40p. 1980. pap. 3.50 (ISBN 0-89304-809-7). Cross Cult.

Transmembrane Signaling: Proceedings. ICN-UCLA Symposium on Transmembrane Signaling, Keystone, Colorado, February, 1978. Ed. by M. Bitensky et al. LC 79-5061. (Progress in Clinical & Biological Research Ser.: Vol. 31). 1979. 78.00x (ISBN 0-8451-0031-9). A R Liss.

Transmission & Propagation of Electromagnetic Waves. K. F. Sander & G. A. Reed. LC 77-87390. (Illus.). 1978. 80.50 (ISBN 0-521-21924-8); pap. 17.50x (ISBN 0-521-29312-X). Cambridge U Pr.

Transmission: Communication Skills for Technicians. Long. (Illus.). 1980. pap. text ed. 12.95 (ISBN 0-8359-7816-8); instrs' manual avail. Reston.

Transmission Electron Microscopy of Materials. Gareth Thomas & Michael J. Goringe. LC 79-449. 1979. 27.95 (ISBN 0-471-12244-0, Pub. by Wiley-Interscience). Wiley.

Transmission Error. Michael Kurland. 1978. pap. 1.50 o.s.i. (ISBN 0-515-04514-4). Jove Pubns.

Transmission Lines & Waveguides. Lamont V. Blake. LC 69-16039. (Electronic Engineering & Technology Ser). 1969. text ed. 17.95x (ISBN 0-471-07929-4). Wiley.

Transmission Lines for Communications. C. W. Davidson. 1978. 29.95 (ISBN 0-470-99160-7). Halsted Pr.

Transmission of External Price Disturbances in Small, Open Economies. Louka T. Papaefstratiou. LC 78-75064. (Outstanding Dissertations in Economics Ser.). 1979. lib. bdg. 20.00 (ISBN 0-8240-4141-0). Garland Pub.

Transmission of Information in the Optical Waveband. L. G. Kazovsky. LC 77-28102. 1978. 24.95 (ISBN 0-470-26294-X). Halsted Pr.

Transmission of Rice Tungro Virus at Various Temperatures: A Transitory Virus-Vector Interaction. (IRRI Research Paper Ser.: No. 4). 26p. 1977. pap. 5.00 (R044, IRRI). Unipub.

Transmission Planning of Telephone Networks. R. W. Whorwood & P. K. Webb. (IEE Telecommunications Ser.). 256p. 1981. price not set. Inst Elect Eng. Postponed.

Transmission Systems for Technicians, No. 2. Danielson. 1981. text ed. price not set (ISBN 0-408-00562-9). Butterworth.

Transmutation of Attitudes. Deborah Morea. 1979. pap. 6.50 (ISBN 0-9603022-1-2). Davida Pubns.

Transnational Control of Multinational Corporations. Rainer Hellman. LC 77-7342. (Praeger Special Studies). 1977. text ed. 21.95 (ISBN 0-03-021941-8). Praeger.

Transnational Corporations & World Order: Readings in International Political Economy. Ed. by George Modelski. LC 78-12964. (Illus.). 1979. text ed. 21.95x (ISBN 0-7167-1026-9); pap. text ed. 10.95x (ISBN 0-7167-1025-0). W H Freeman.

Transnational Corporations, Technology Transfer & Development: A Bibliographic Sourcebook. Tagi Sagafi-nejad & Robert Belfield. LC 80-36887. (Pergamon Policy Studies on International Development). 150p. Date not set. 25.00 (ISBN 0-08-026299-6). Pergamon.

Transnational Law. Philip C. Jessup. 1956. 24.50x (ISBN 0-685-89792-3). Elliots Bks.

Transnational Law in a Changing Society: Essays in Honor of Philip C. Jessup. Ed. by Wolfgang G. Friedmann et al. LC 71-187029. 290p. 1972. 20.00x (ISBN 0-231-03619-1). Columbia U Pr.

Transnational Mergers & Acquisitions in the United States. Sarkis J. Khoury. 1980. 27.95 (ISBN 0-669-03960-8). Lexington Bks.

Transnational Party Co-Operation & European Integration. Geoffrey Pridham & Pippa Pridham. 304p. 1981. text ed. 34.00x (ISBN 0-04-329032-9, 2591). Allen Unwin.

Transnational Terrorism: A Chronology of Events, 1968-1979. Edward F. Mickolus. LC 79-6829. xxxviii, 967p. 1980. lib. bdg. 75.00 (ISBN 0-313-22206-1, MTT/). Greenwood.

Transnationalism in World Politics & Business. Ed. by Forest L. Grieves. LC 79-1397. (Pergamon Policy Studies). 240p. 1979. 33.00 (ISBN 0-08-023892-0). Pergamon.

Transonic Flow Problems in Turbomachinery: Proceedings. new ed. Project SQUID Workshop on Transonic Flow Problems in Turbomachinery, Feb. 1976. Ed. by T. C. Adamson & M. F. Platzer. LC 77-22185. (Illus.). 1977. text ed. 57.50 (ISBN 0-89116-069-8). Hemisphere Pub.

Transparent God. Claude Esteban. Tr. by David Cloutier from Fr. LC 80-84603. (Modern Poets in Translation Ser.). 200p. 1981. price not set (ISBN 0-916426-07-6). Kosmos.

Transparent Plastics: Developments Trends, P-053. BCC Staff. 1981. 950.00 (ISBN 0-89336-201-8). BCC.

Transparenz der Wirklichkeit: Edzard Schaper und die innere Spannung in der christlichen Literatur des zwanzigstes Jahrhunderts. Irene Sonderegger-Kummer. (Quellen und Forschungen zur Sprach- und Kulturgeschichte der germanischen Voelker, No. 37). (Ger). 1971. 60.60x (ISBN 3-11-001845-4). De Gruyter.

Transpersonal Education: A Curriculum for Feeling & Being. C. Gaylord Hendricks & James Fadiman. 1976. pap. text ed. 4.95x (ISBN 0-13-930461-4, Spec). P-H.

Transplanted & Artificial Body Organs. Arnold Madison. (Illus.). 192p. (gr. 7 up). 1981. 8.95 (ISBN 0-8253-0050-9). Beaufort Bks NY.

Transporation Economic Analysis. James T. Kneafsey. LC 74-2203. (Illus.). 1975. 21.95x (ISBN 0-669-93211-6). Lexington Bks.

Transport & Communications, 3 pts. Incl. Pt. 1. General, 22 vols. Set. 1845.00x (ISBN 0-686-01146-5); Pt. 2. Shipping (Safety, 9 vols. Set. 792.00x (ISBN 0-686-01147-3); Pt. 3. Posts & Telegraphs, 8 vols. Set. 684.00x (ISBN 0-686-01148-1). (British Parliamentary Papers Ser.). 1971 (Pub. by Irish Academic Pr Ireland). Biblio Dist.

Transport & Distribution. 2nd ed. G. J. Murphy. 300p. 1978. text ed. 24.50x (ISBN 0-220-66321-1, Pub. by Busn Bks England). Renouf.

Transport & Regional Development. W. A. Blonk. 1979. text ed. 43.25x (ISBN 0-566-00285-X, Pub. by Gower Pub Co England). Renouf.

Transport & the Challenge of Structural Change: Proceedings. International Symposium on Theory & Practice in Transport Economics, 8th, Istanbul, 24-28 Sept. 1979. (Illus.). 539p. (Orig.). 1980. pap. 20.00x (ISBN 92-821-1061-3). OECD.

Transport & the Environment. Clifford Sharp & Tony Jennings. 1976. pap. text ed. 9.25x (ISBN 0-7185-1133-6, Leicester). Humanities.

Transport & the Urban Environment: Proceedings of a Conference Held by the International Economic Assoc. at Lyngby. J. Rothenberg & I. G. Heggie. LC 73-15142. (International Economic Association Ser.). 273p. 1974. 20.95 (ISBN 0-470-73969-X). Halsted Pr.

Transport Economics. P. C. Stubbs et al. (Studies in Economics). (Illus.). 1980. text ed. 24.95x (ISBN 0-04-338088-3); pap. text ed. 12.50x (ISBN 0-04-338089-1). Allen Unwin.

Transport for Society. Institute of Civil Engineers, UK. 180p. 1980. 75.00x (ISBN 0-7277-0015-4, Pub. by Telford England). State Mutual Bk.

Transport in High Resistance Epithelia, Vol. 1, 1977. Thomas W. Ziegler. Ed. by D. Horrobin. 1978. 21.60 (ISBN 0-88831-012-9). Eden Med Res.

Transport Manager's Handbook: United Kingdom 1980. D. Lowe. 1979. 20.00 (ISBN 0-686-60661-2, Pub. by Kogan Pg). Nichols Pub.

Transport Mechanisms in Epithelia. Alfred Benzon Symposium 5th. Ed. by H. H. Ussing et al. 1973. 51.00 (ISBN 0-12-709550-0). Acad Pr.

Transport of Charged Aerosols. Richard S. Withers. LC 78-74993. (Outstanding Dissertations on Energy Ser.). 1979. lib. bdg. 38.00 (ISBN 0-8240-3993-9). Garland Pub.

Transport of Hazardous Materials. Institute of Civil Engineers, UK. 160p. 1980. 39.00x (ISBN 0-7277-0058-8, Pub. by Telford England). State Mutual Bk.

Transport of Love: The Meghaduta of Kalidasa. Tr. by Leonard Nathan. 1976. 11.95x (ISBN 0-520-03031-1); pap. 2.95 (ISBN 0-520-03271-3, CAL348). U of Cal Pr.

Transport of Neurotransmitters. Ed. by D. M. Paton. (Journal: Pharmacology: Vol. 21, No. 2). (Illus.). 74p. 1980. pap. 14.50 (ISBN 3-8055-1316-X). S Karger.

Transport of Nutrients in Plants. A. J. Peel. LC 73-17354. 1974. 19.95 (ISBN 0-470-67717-1). Halsted Pr.

Transport Operators Guide to Professional Competence. G. J. Murphy. 314p. 1980. pap. 21.00x (ISBN 0-09-141591-8, Pub. by Busn Bks England). Renouf.

Transport Organization in a Great City: The Case of London. Michael F. Collins & Timothy M. Pharoah. LC 74-77339. 1974. 40.00x (ISBN 0-8039-0434-7). Sage.

Transport Packaging for Radioactive Materials: Proceedings. International Atomic Energy Agency Seminar, Vienna Austria. (Illus.). 1977. pap. 54.25 (ISBN 92-0-020576-3, ISP 437, IAEA). Unipub.

Transport Phenomena & Living Systems: Biomedical Applications of Momentum & Mass Transfer. E. N. Lightfoot. LC 73-9541. 495p. 1974. 36.50 (ISBN 0-471-53515-X, Pub. by Wiley-Interscience). Wiley.

Transport Phenomena in Aqueous Solutions. Tibor Erdey-Gruz. LC 74-13613. 512p. 1974. 54.95 (ISBN 0-470-24371-6). Halsted Pr.

Transport Phenomena in Metallurgy. G. H. Geiger & D. R. Poirier. LC 75-164648. 1973. text ed. 27.95 (ISBN 0-201-02352-0). A-W.

Transport Phenomena in the Nervous System: Physiological & Pathological Aspects. Ed. by Giulio Levi. LC 76-4839. (Advances in Experimental Medicine & Biology Ser.: Vol. 69). 541p. 1976. 45.00 (ISBN 0-306-39069-8, Plenum Pr). Plenum Pub.

Transport Planning for Greater London. Malcolm Buchanan et al. 315p. 1980. text ed. 42.75x (ISBN 0-566-00314-7, Pub. by Gower Pub Co England). Renouf.

Transport Policy: Geographic, Economic & Planning Aspects. Patrick O'Sullivan. 1981. 22.50x (ISBN 0-389-20143-X). B&N.

Transport Processes & Unit Operations. Geankoplis. 1978. text ed. 29.95 (ISBN 0-205-05939-2, 3259390). Allyn.

Transport Revolution, from Seventeen Seventy. Philip S. Bagwell. 1974. 16.95 (ISBN 0-7134-1386-7, Pub. by Batsford England). David & Charles.

Transport Without Wheels. Ed. by E. R. Laithwaite. LC 76-53107. (Illus.). 1977. lib. bdg. 50.00x (ISBN 0-89158-724-1). Westview.

Transportation. H. K. Idleman & M. O. McKitrick. (Contemporary Consumer Ser.). 1974. text ed. 4.24 (ISBN 0-07-031691-0, G); tchr's. manual & key 4.95 (ISBN 0-07-031692-9). McGraw.

Transportation. Etta S. Ress. LC 64-8099. (Illus.). (gr. 4-8). 1967. PLB 7.95 (ISBN 0-87191-003-9). Creative Ed.

Transportation & Energy. Compiled by American Society of Civil Engineers. 456p. 1978. pap. text ed. 15.00 (ISBN 0-87262-135-9). Am Soc Civil Eng.

Transportation & the Environment. John G. B. Hutchins. Ed. by J. Rose & Edward W. Weidner. LC 77-2350. (Environmental Studies: Vol. 5). 1977. lib. bdg. 18.00x (ISBN 0-89158-738-1). Westview.

Transportation & the Prospects for Improved Efficiency. National Academy of Engineering. (Illus.). 1973. pap. 9.75 (ISBN 0-309-02120-0). Natl Acad Pr.

Transportation & Traffic Engineering Handbook. Institute of Traffic Engineers. 1976. 35.95 (ISBN 0-13-930578-5). P-H.

Transportation Economics: A Guide to Information Sources. Ed. by James P. Rakowski. LC 73-17584. (Economics Information Guide Series: Vol. 5). 200p. 1976. 30.00 (ISBN 0-8103-1307-3). Gale.

Transportation Economics & Public Policy: With Urban Extensions. Alan Abouchar. LC 76-51828. 1977. 29.95 (ISBN 0-471-02101-6, Pub. by Wiley-Interscience). Ronald Pr.

Transportation Energy Use Forcasting Model: An Integrated Modal Approach. Jeffrey L. Staley. LC 78-75009. (Outstanding Dissertations on Energy Ser.). 1979. lib. bdg. 16.50 (ISBN 0-8240-3982-3). Garland Pub.

Transportation Engineering. Institute of Civil Engineers, UK. 174p. 1980. 50.00x (Pub. by Telford England). State Mutual Bk.

Transportation Engineering: Planning & Design. Radnor J. Paquette et al. 760p. 1972. 25.95 (ISBN 0-471-06670-2). Wiley.

Transportation Facilities Workshop. Compiled by American Society of Civil Engineers. 576p. 1975. pap. text ed. 24.75 (ISBN 0-87262-107-3). Am Soc Civil Eng.

Transportation for Cities: The Role of Federal Policy. Wilfred Owen. 1976. pap. 3.95 (ISBN 0-8157-6773-0). Brookings.

Transportation for the Elderly: Changing Lifestyles, Changing Needs. Martin Wachs. 1979. 19.50x (ISBN 0-520-03691-3). U of Cal Pr.

Transportation Frontier: Trans-Mississippi West, 1865-1890. Oscar O. Winther. LC 64-10639. (Histories of the American Frontier Ser.). (Illus.). 238p. 1974. pap. 6.50x (ISBN 0-8263-0317-X). U of NM Pr.

Transportation Impact of the Canadian Mining Industry. Iain Wallace. 155p. (Orig.). 1977. pap. text ed. 8.00x (ISBN 0-88757-002-X, Pub. by Ctr Resource Stud Canada). Renouf.

Transportation Improvements in Madison, Wisconsin: Preliminary Analysis of Pricing Programs for Roads & Parking in Conjunction with Transit Changes. Franklin Spielberg. (Institute Paper). 65p. 1978. pap. 5.00 (ISBN 0-87766-234-7, 22400). Urban Inst.

Transportation in Cities. E. O. Pederson. 1980. 12.50 (ISBN 0-08-024666-4). Pergamon.

Transportation in Eastern Europe. Bogdan Mieczkowski. (Eastern European Monographs: No. 38). 1978. 14.50x (ISBN 0-914710-31-1, Dist. by Columbia U Pr). East Eur Quarterly.

Transportation Information Sources. Ed. by Kenneth N. Metcalf. LC 65-24657. (Management Information Guide Ser.: No. 8). 1965. 30.00 (ISBN 0-8103-0808-8). Gale.

Transportation: Management, Economics, Policy. John L. Hazard. LC 77-22414. (Illus.). 1977. 18.00x (ISBN 0-87033-229-5). Cornell Maritime.

Transportation Planning & Policy Decision Making: Behavioral Science Contributions. Richard M. Michaels. 264p. 1980. 24.95 (ISBN 0-03-055786-0). Praeger.

Transportation Planning for a Better Environment. Ed. by Peter Stringer & K. Wenzel. LC 76-46276. (NATO Conference Ser., Series II: Systems Science: Vol. 1). 439p. 1976. 37.50 (ISBN 0-306-32841-0, Plenum Pr). Plenum Pub.

Transportation Policy in Comparative Perspective. James A. Dunn, Jr. (Transportation Ser.). 288p. 1981. text ed. 25.00x (ISBN 0-262-04062-X). MIT Pr.

Transportation: Problems & Prospects. Bill Gunston. Ed. by Robin Clarke. (World of Science Lib.). 1973. 7.95 o.p. (ISBN 0-525-22228-6). Dutton.

Transportation Supply Models. Ed. by Michael Florian & Marc Gaudry. 225p. 1981. 30.00 (ISBN 0-08-026075-6). Pergamon.

Transportation-System Safety. Michael Horodniceanu & Edmund J. Cantilli. LC 78-7126. (Illus.). 1979. 21.00 (ISBN 0-669-02467-8). Lexington Bks.

Transportation Systems Evaluation. Peter R. Stopher & Arnim Meyberg. 1976. 18.95 (ISBN 0-669-96958-3). Lexington Bks.

Transportation, Temporal & Spatial Components of Accessibility. Lawrence D. Burns. LC 79-1725. (Illus.). 176p. 1979. 19.95 (ISBN 0-669-02916-5). Lexington Bks.

Transportation: The Domestic System. 2nd ed. Robert Lieb. 1980. text ed. 18.95 (ISBN 0-8359-7826-5). Reston.

Transportation: The Domestic System. Robert C Lieb. LC 77-5432. 1978. 16.95 (ISBN 0-87909-843-0); instrs'. manual avail. Reston.

Transported to Van Diemen's Land. Judith O'Neill. (Introduction to the History of Mankind Ser.). (Illus.). 1977. 3.95 (ISBN 0-521-21231-6). Cambridge U Pr.

Transports & Disgraces. Robert Henson. LC 80-19131. (Illinois Short Fiction Ser.). 140p. 1980. 10.00 (ISBN 0-252-00840-5); pap. 3.95 (ISBN 0-252-00841-3). U of Ill Pr.

Transracial Adoption. Rita J. Simon & Howard Altstein. LC 76-44817. 1977. 19.95 (ISBN 0-471-79208-X, Pub. by Wiley-Interscience). Wiley.

Transsexual Phenomenon. Harry Benjamin. (Illus.). 1977. pap. 2.25 o.s.i. (ISBN 0-446-82426-7). Warner Bks.

Transsexualism & Sex Reassignment. Ed. by Richard Green & John Money. LC 69-15761. (Illus.). 534p. 1969. 32.50x o.p. (ISBN 0-8018-1038-8). Johns Hopkins.

Transsexuality in the Male: The Spectrum of Gender Dysphoria. Erwin K. Koranyi. (Behavioral Science & Law Ser.). (Illus.). 192p. 1980. text ed. 18.75 (ISBN 0-398-03924-0). C C Thomas.

Transuranium Elements. Glenn T. Seaborg. 1958. 42.50x o.p. (ISBN 0-685-69863-7). Elliots Bks.

Transuranium Nuclides in the Enviroment: Proceedings. (Illus.). 1976. pap. 69.75 (ISBN 92-0-020076-1, ISP 410, IAEA). Unipub.

Transvestism: A Handbook for Psychologists, Psychiatrists & Counsellors. Harry Brierley. (Illus.). 160p. 1979. 36.00 (ISBN 0-08-022268-4); pap. 15.50 (ISBN 0-08-024686-9). Pergamon.

Transvestites & Transsexuals: Mixed Views. Deborah H. Feinbloom. 1976. 12.50 o.s.i. (ISBN 0-440-08513-6, Sey Lawr). Delacorte.

Transwhichics. Ernest Robson. 1970. 15.00; pap. 7.95. Primary Pr.

Transzendentalienlehre der alten Ontologie, Pt. 1: Transzendentalienlehre im Corpus Aristotelicum. Karl Baerthlein. 415p. 1972. 52.00x (ISBN 3-11-004021-2). De Gruyter.

Trap for Cinderella. Sebastien Japrisot. (Crime Monthly Ser). 1979. pap. 2.50 (ISBN 0-14-005364-6). Penguin.

Trapdoor Springfield. M. O. Waite & Bernard D. Ernst. (Illus.). 300p. 1980. 29.95 (ISBN 0-917714-20-2). Beinfeld Pub.

Trapped Charges. Ed. by F. Kieffer. 236p. 1976. pap. text ed. 42.00 (ISBN 0-08-019961-5). Pergamon.

Trapped in Death Valley. Vinnie Ruffo. LC 72-76832. 121p. 1972. pap. 4.95 (ISBN 0-8163-0050-X, 20608-6). Pacific Pr Pub Assn.

Trapping: A Practical Guide. J. E. Bateman. (Illus.). 190p. 1979. 14.95 (ISBN 0-8117-1743-7). Stackpole.

Trapping & Tracking. George Clawson. (Illus.). 1977. 10.95 (ISBN 0-87691-198-X). Winchester Pr.

Trappings of Gold. Manoje Basu. Tr. by S. L. Ghosh. 176p. 1969. pap. 2.00 (ISBN 0-88253-013-5). Ind-US Inc.

Trash Dragon of Shensi. Andrew Glaze. (Illus., Orig.). 1978. pap. 4.50 (ISBN 0-914278-15-0). Copper Beech.

Tratado De Instrumentos Negociables. 2nd, enl.,rev. ed. Basilio Santiago Romero. LC 79-22321. (Illus.). 1980. write for info. (ISBN 0-8477-2636-3). U of PR Pr.

Tratados Sobre el Canal De Panama Suscritos Entre la Republica De Panama y los Estados Unidos De America. OAS General Secretariat Bureau of Legal Affairs. (Serie Sobre Tratados: No. 57 & 57a). 157p. 1979. text ed. 9.00 (ISBN 0-8270-0715-9). OAS.

Tratados y Convenciones Interamerianos. OAS General Secretariat. (Serie Sobre Tratados: No. 9). 303p. 1980. pap. text ed. 15.00 (ISBN 0-8270-1159-8). OAS.

Trattato della natura, Vol. 129. Pietro Aaron. 1980. 30.00x (ISBN 0-8450-2329-2). Broude.

Trattato dell'arte della pittura, scoltura, et architettura. Giovanni P. Lomazzo. (Documents of Art & Architectural History Series 2: Vol. 4). 754p. (Italian.). 1981. Repr. of 1585 ed. 65.00x (ISBN 0-89371-204-3). Broude Intl Edns.

Traum Ein Leben. F. Grillparzer. Ed. by W. E. Yates. 1968. text ed. 7.50x (ISBN 0-521-05154-1). Cambridge U Pr.

Traum Vom Rueckenwind. Walter Schmoegner. (Illus.). 64p. (Ger.). 1980. text ed. 26.00 (ISBN 3-458-04939-8, Pub. by Insel Verlag Germany). Suhrkamp.

Trauma. P. J. O'Shaughnessy. 1978. pap. 1.95 o.p. (ISBN 0-523-40359-3, Dist. by Independent News Co.). Pinnacle Bks.

Trauma, Vol. 1. Mills. 1981. pap. text ed. 25.00 (ISBN 0-443-02018-3). Churchill.

Trauma & Cancer: Pathology for the Lawyer. R. H. Rigdon. 232p. 1975. 21.75 (ISBN 0-398-03441-9). C C Thomas.

Trauma & No-Trauma of the Cervical Spine. Kenneth R. Kattan. (Illus.). 328p. 1975. 32.75 (ISBN 0-398-03371-4). C C Thomas.

Trauma Surgery. Kimball I. Maull & Ward O. Griffen, Jr. (Medical Examination Review Book: Vol. 36). 1977. spiral bdg. 15.00 o.s.i. (ISBN 0-87488-179-X). Med Exam.

Traumatic Injuries of the Genitourinary System. W. Scott McDougal. (Illus.). 139p. 1980. 26.95. Williams & Wilkins.

Traumatic Injuries of the Heart & Great Vessels. Panagiotis N. Symbas. (Illus.). 204p. 1972. text ed. 19.75 (ISBN 0-398-02425-1). C C Thomas.

Traumatic Surgery. Norman E. McSwain, Jr. (Medical Outline Ser.). 1976. spiral bdg. 12.00 o.p. (ISBN 0-87488-619-8). Med Exam.

Travail & Triumph: Black Life & Culture in the South Since the Civil War. Arnold H. Taylor. LC 76-5264. (Contributions in Afro-American & African Studies: No. 26). (Orig.). 1976. lib. bdg. 17.95x (ISBN 0-8371-8912-8, TTT/). Greenwood.

Travail et Travailleurs En Algerie. Pierre Bourdieu et al. (Recherches Mediterraneennes Documents). 1963. pap. text ed. 40.50x (ISBN 90-279-6224-3). Mouton.

Travailleurs Estrangers En Europe Occidentale: Actes Du Colloque Organise Par la Commission Nationale Pour les Etudes et les Recherches Inter-Ethniques, Paris-Sorbonne, Du 5 Au 7 Juin 1974. Philippe J. Bernard. (Publications De l'Institut d'Etudes et De Recherches Interethniques et Inter Culturelles: No. 6). (Fr.). 1976. pap. text ed. 39.40x (ISBN 0-686-22611-9). Mouton.

Travaux Pratiques. 2nd ed. Leon-Francois Hoffman. LC 73-8687. 1973. pap. text ed. 7.95 (ISBN 0-684-13577-9). Scribner.

Travel Agency: A How-to-Do-It Manual for Starting One of Your Own. Anne Stenholm. LC 78-67643. 1979. 8.95 o.p. (ISBN 0-9602050-0-4). Freelance Pubns.

Travel Agency: A How-to-Do-It Manual for Starting One of Your Own. Anne Stenholm. 1981. price not set (ISBN 0-9602050-3-9). Freelance Pubns.

Travel & Lodging Law. John R. Goodwin & James M. Rovelstad. LC 79-12189. (Grid Series in Law). 1980. text ed. 24.50 (ISBN 0-88244-188-4). Grid Pub.

Travel & Tourism: An Introduction to Travel Agency Operations. Armin D. Lehmann. LC 77-12589. 1978. pap. 18.95 (ISBN 0-672-97090-2). Bobbs.

Travel & Tourism Audiovisual Guide. Ed. by Jeanne Gay & Bernard Mead. 530p. (Orig.). 1980. pap. 15.00x (ISBN 0-935638-01-6). Travel & Tourism.

Travel & Tourism Bibliography & Resource Handbook. Ed. by Jeanne Gay. 1342p. 1980. pap. 35.00 (ISBN 0-935638-00-8). Travel & Tourism.

Travel & Tourism Education Guide. Ed. by Jeanne Gay & Bernard Mead. (Orig.). 1980. pap. cancelled (ISBN 0-935638-02-4). Travel & Tourism.

Travel & Tourism Marketing Techniques. Robert T. Reilly. LC 79-92385. 1980. 14.95 (ISBN 0-916032-08-6). Merton Hse.

Travel & Tourism Personnel Directory. Ed. by Jeanne Gay. (Orig.). 1981. pap. 10.00x (ISBN 0-935638-03-2). Travel & Tourism.

Travel Books: Guide to the Travel Guides. Ed. by Jon O. Heise. (Popular Bks.). 304p. 1981. pap. 24.95 (ISBN 0-8352-1337-4). Bowker.

Travel Careers. Ralph H. Peck. (Career Concise Guides Ser.). (Illus.). 96p. (gr. 7 up). 1976. PLB 6.45 (ISBN 0-531-01154-2). Watts.

Travel Catalogue. Karen Cure. 1978. 9.95 o.p. (ISBN 0-03-020711-8); pap. 6.95 o.p. (ISBN 0-03-020706-1). HR&W.

Travel Games. Maurice Pipard. (Panda Paperbacks). (Illus.). 96p. (gr. 3-7). 1975. pap. 1.95 (ISBN 0-531-02734-1). Watts.

Travel Guide to the People's Republic of China. Ruth L. Malloy. LC 75-8510. (Illus.). 224p. 1975. 7.95 o.p. (ISBN 0-688-02933-7). Morrow.

Travel Guide to the People's Republic of China. Ruth L. Malloy. LC 80-16428. (Illus.). 416p. 1980. 17.50 (ISBN 0-688-03690-2); pap. 10.95 (ISBN 0-688-08690-X). Morrow.

Travel in Oceania, Australia & New Zealand: A Guide to Information Sources. Ed. by Robert E. Burton. LC 80-15333. (Geography & Travel Information Guide Ser.: Vol. 2). 150p. 1980. 30.00 (ISBN 0-8103-1421-5). Gale.

Travel in the Nick of Time. Jack C. Street. 1981. 4.50 (ISBN 0-8062-1707-3). Carlton.

Travel in the United States: A Guide to Information Sources. Ed. by Joyce Post & Jeremiah Post. (Geography & Travel Information Guide Ser.: Vol. 3). 600p. 1981. 30.00 (ISBN 0-8103-1423-1). Gale.

Travel Instruction for the Handicapped. Michael D. Laus. 164p. 1977. 14.75 (ISBN 0-398-03637-3). C C Thomas.

Travel Ontario. John Pekkanen. 1971. 3.95 o.p. (ISBN 0-695-80233-X). Follett.

Travel Photography. (Life Library of Photography). (Illus.). 1972. 14.95 (ISBN 0-8094-1065-6). Time-Life.

Travel Trends, Nineteen Eighty-One. 1981. 25.00 (ISBN 0-686-69389-2). U CO Busn Res Div.

Travel with Health. Herbert Dupont & Margaret Dupont. (Appleton Consumer Health Guides). 195p. 1981. 13.95 (ISBN 0-8385-9009-8); pap. 7.95 (ISBN 0-8385-9008-X). ACC.

Travel Your Taste with Kraft Foodservice: International Recipes from the World of Foodservice. Kraft Kitchens. LC 78-5909. (Illus.). 1978. 25.95 (ISBN 0-8436-2171-0). CBI Pub.

TravelAbility: A Guide for Physically Disabled Travelers in the United States. Lois Reamy. 1978. 11.95 (ISBN 0-02-601170-0). Macmillan.

Travelaid Guide to Egypt. 192p. 1980. pap. 9.95 (ISBN 0-902743-14-7, Pub. by Travelaid England). Hippocrene Bks.

Travelaid Guide to Greece. Travelaid Staff. (Travelaid Guides Ser.). (Illus., Orig.). 1978. pap. 5.95 (ISBN 0-8467-0435-8, Pub. by Two Continents). Hippocrene Bks.

TraveLeer Guide to Mexico City. 2nd ed. Loraine Carlson. LC 80-26850. (Illus.). 220p. 1981. pap. 4.50 (ISBN 0-932554-02-4). Upland Pr.

TraveLeer Guide to Yucatan & Guatemala. Loraine Carlson. LC 79-53283. (Illus.). 365p. (Orig.). 1980. pap. 6.95 (ISBN 0-932554-01-6). Upland Pr.

Travelers. Ruth P. Jhabvala. LC 72-9765. 256p. (YA) 1973. 8.95 o.p. (ISBN 0-06-012193-9, HarpT). Har-Row.

Traveler's Africa. Philip M. Allen & Aaron Segal. 1975. 14.95 o.p. (ISBN 0-911974-07-5, ScribT). Scribner.

Travelers & Travel Liars, Sixteen Sixty-Eighteen Hundred. Percy G. Adams. (Illus.). 1980. pap. 4.50 (ISBN 0-486-23942-X). Dover.

Traveler's Choice: A Treasury of America's Regional Restaurants & Their Favorite Recipes. Discovery Magazine Editors. LC 80-53813. (Illus.). 256p. (Orig.). 1981. pap. 4.95 (ISBN 0-528-88042-X). Rand.

Traveler's Guide to Cuba. Lionel Martin. LC 77-11536. (Illus.). Date not set. pap. cancelled (ISBN 0-06-090644-8, CN-644, CN). Har-Row. Postponed.

Traveler's Guide to Running in Major American Cities. Mary-Jo Carroll & Randy Sloane. LC 79-949. 224p. (Orig.). 1979. pap. 6.95 (ISBN 0-8117-2091-8). Stackpole.

Traveler's Health Guide: A Nutritional, Medical & Fitness Handbook for Travelers & People Away from Home. Lanny J. Nalder. LC 80-82454. 120p. (Orig.). 1981. pap. 4.95 (ISBN 0-88290-094-3, 4025). Horizon Utah.

Traveler's Narrative: Written to Illustrate the Episode of the Bab. rev. ed. Abdu'l-Baha. Tr. by Edward G. Browne from Persian. LC 79-19025. 1980. 9.00 (ISBN 0-87743-134-5, 7-06-27); pap. 4.00 (ISBN 0-87743-134-5, 7-06-28). Baha'i.

Traveler's Reading Guides: Background Books, Novels, Travel Literature & Articles, Vol. 1. Europe. new ed. Ed. by M. Simony et al. LC 80-65324. 1981. pap. 11.95 (ISBN 0-9602050-1-2). Freelance Pubns.

Travelers: Stories of Americans Abroad. Ed. by L. M. Schulman. (gr. 9 up). 1972. 5.95 o.s.i. (ISBN 0-02-781410-6). Macmillan.

Traveler's Survival Kit to the East. Vacation Work. (Illus.). 130p. pap. 7.95 (ISBN 0-901205-65-6). Bradt Ent.

Traveler's Tale: Memories of India. Enid Saunders Candlin. LC 73-16902. 360p. 1974. 12.95 o.s.i. (ISBN 0-02-521110-2). Macmillan.

Traveler's Tree: New & Selected Poems. William J. Smith. (Illus.). 200p. 1980. text ed. 13.95 (ISBN 0-686-64515-4); text ed. 13.95 (ISBN 0-89255-049-X). Persea Bks.

Travelin' Woman. Katherine Gibbs. (Orig.). 1980. pap. 1.95 (ISBN 0-8439-0728-2, Leisure Bks). Nordon Pubns.

Traveling America with Today's Poets. Ed. by David Kherdian. LC 76-47535. (gr. 7 up). 1977. 9.95 (ISBN 0-02-750260-0, 75026). Macmillan.

Traveling Games for Babies: A Handbook of Games for Infants to Five-Year-Olds. Julie Hagstrom. (Illus.). 96p. 1981. pap. 4.95 (ISBN 0-89104-203-2). A & W Pubs.

Traveling Light. Daniel F. Manning. (Illus., Orig.). 1979. pap. 5.00x (ISBN 0-933192-00-2). Dancin Bee.

Traveling Runner's Guide: Where to Run in 21 Cities Around the U. S. Penelope Scheerer & John Schwanbeck. 1978. pap. 5.95 o.p. (ISBN 0-525-47530-3). Dutton.

Traveling Salesman: How to Find Answers for Lots of Things for Lots of People Especially Salesman. Larry Moriarty. LC 81-50012. (Illus.). 200p. 1981. 14.95 (ISBN 0-939102-13-7). MLM Pubs.

Traveling the Trade Winds. 2nd ed. Eldonna Evertts & Byron VanRoekel. (Design for Reading Ser). (Illus.). (gr. 4). 1972. text ed. 10.68 (ISBN 0-06-516007-X, SchDept); tchr's ed. 14.28 (ISBN 0-06-516205-6); wkbk. 3.20 (ISBN 0-06-516306-0); tchr's wkbk. 6.36 (ISBN 0-06-516406-7); masterly tests pkg. 14.48 (ISBN 0-06-516615-9); dupl.masters with ans. key 17.68 (ISBN 0-06-516837-2). Har-Row.

Traveling Wave Antennas. Carlton H. Walter. 1970. pap. text ed. 5.00 o.p. (ISBN 0-486-62669-5). Dover.

Traveling Woman. Dena Kaye. 384p. 1981. pap. 2.95 (ISBN 0-553-14714-5). Bantam.

Traveller & His Road. Gostan Zarian. Tr. by Ara Baliozian from Armenian. LC 80-22809. 160p. (Orig.). 1981. pap. 5.95 (ISBN 0-935102-04-3). Ashod Pr.

Traveller Discovering Norway. F. Dreyers. 1968. 25.00x (N499). Vanous.

Traveller in Time. Alison Uttley. (Illus.). 331p. (gr. 3-7). 1981. 8.95 (ISBN 0-571-06182-6, Pub. by Faber & Faber). Merrimack Bk Serv.

Traveller,Or,a Prospect of Society. Oliver Goldsmith. Incl. Deserted Village; Prospect of Society: Preliminary Version of the "Traveller", Dating from 1964. 1975. text ed. 8.50x o.p. (ISBN 0-8277-3845-5); pap. text ed. 5.95x o.p. (ISBN 0-8277-2197-8). British Bk Ctr.

Travellers. Horace Sutton. LC 80-14931. (Illus.). 320p. 1980. 12.50 (ISBN 0-688-03694-5). Morrow.

Travellers' Foreign Phrase Book. J. O. Kettridge. 1967. Repr. of 1960 ed. limp 5.00 (ISBN 0-7100-1674-3). Routledge & Kegan.

Travellers' Guide to Corfu & the Other Ionian Islands. Martin Young. LC 77-363313. (Travellers' Guide Ser.). (Illus.). 1979. 9.95 (ISBN 0-224-01307-6, Pub. by Chatto Bodley Jonathan). Merrimack Bk Serv.

Travellers' Guide to Elba & the Tuscan Archipelago. Christopher Serpell & Jean Serpell. (Travellers' Guide Ser.). (Illus.). 1979. 9.95 (ISBN 0-224-01352-1, Pub. by Chatto Bodley Jonathan). Merrimack Bk Serv.

Travellers' Guide to Morocco. rev. ed. Christopher Kininmonth. (Illus.). 356p. 1981. pap. 10.95 (ISBN 0-224-01897-3, Pub. by Chatto-Bodley-Jonathan). Merrimack Bk Serv.

Travellers' Guide to Rhodes & the Dodecanese. Jean Currie. LC 76-351618. (Travellers' Guide Ser.). (Illus.). 1979. 9.95 (ISBN 0-224-61836-9, Pub. by Chatto Bodley Jonathan). Merrimack Bk Serv.

Travellers' Guide to Sardinia. rev. ed. T. Holme et al. (Travellers' Guide Ser.). (Illus.). 1979. 9.95 (ISBN 0-224-01283-5, Pub. by Chatto Bodley Jonathan). Merrimack Bk Serv.

Travellers' Guide to Sicily. rev. ed. Christopher Kininmonth. LC 74-158691. (Travellers' Guide Ser.). (Illus.). 1979. 9.95 (ISBN 0-224-00612-6, R75, Pub. by Chatto Bodley Jonathan). Merrimack Bk Serv.

Travellers' Guide to Sicily. rev. ed. Christopher Kininmonth. (Illus.). 306p. 1981. pap. 7.95 (ISBN 0-224-01854-X, Pub. by Chatto-Bodley-Jonathan). Merrimack Bk Serv.

Traveller's Guide to Spurgeon Country. Eric W. Hayden. 1975. pap. 1.95 (ISBN 0-686-10527-3). Pilgrim Pubns.

Traveller's Guide to the Art Museums of Europe. David L. Morton. LC 80-67766. 175p. Date not set. pap. price not set (ISBN 0-912944-62-5). Berkshire Traveller. Postponed.

Travellers' Guide to Tunisia. Hazel Thurston. LC 73-174608. (Travellers' Guide Ser.). (Illus.). 1979. 9.95 (ISBN 0-224-00803-X, Pub. by Chatto Bodley Jonathan). Merrimack Bk Serv.

Travellers' Guide to Yugoslavia. Sylvia Nickels. LC 79-427483. (Travellers' Guide Ser.). (Illus.). 1979. 9.95 (ISBN 0-224-61593-9, Pub. by Chatto Bodley Jonathan). Merrimack Bk Serv.

Travellers' India: An Anthology. H. K. Kaul. 535p. 1980. 24.00x (ISBN 0-19-560654-X). Oxford U Pr.

Travellers' Songs from England & Scotland. Ewan MacColl & Peggy Seeger. LC 76-2854. 1977. 23.50x (ISBN 0-87049-191-1). U of Tenn Pr.

Travellers Survival Kit Europe. 2nd ed. Roger Brown. 1980. pap. 6.95 o.p. (ISBN 0-901205-72-9). Writers Digest.

Travelling by Sea in the Nineteenth Century. Basil Greenhill & Ann Giffard. (Illus.). 1974. 12.50 o.s.i. (ISBN 0-8038-7151-1). Hastings.

Travelling Kind. Janet Dailey. (Harlequin Presents Ser.). 192p. 1981. pap. 1.50 (ISBN 0-373-10427-8, Pub. by Harlequin). PB.

Travelling Light. William B. McClain. (Orig.). 1981. pap. 3.75 (ISBN 0-377-00109-0). Friend Pr.

Travelling Soul. Hugh C. Rae. 1977. pap. 1.50 o.p. (ISBN 0-380-01854-3, 36517). Avon.

Travels. William Bartram. Ed. by Mark Van Doren. (Illus.). 9.00 (ISBN 0-8446-1600-1). Peter Smith.

Travels. Jan Morris. LC 76-2531. (Helen & Kurt Wolff Book). (Illus.). 160p. 1976. 7.95 o.p. (ISBN 0-15-191075-8). HarBraceJ.

Travels & Adventures in Canada & the Indian Territories Between the Years 1760 & 1776. Alexander Henry. LC 75-7053. (Indian Captivities Ser.: Vol. 31). 1976. Repr. of 1809 ed. lib. bdg. 44.00 (ISBN 0-8240-1655-6). Garland Pub.

Travels & Adventures of Edward Brown, Esq. John Campbell. LC 75-170599. (Foundations of the Novel Ser.: Vol. 70). lib. bdg. 50.00 (ISBN 0-8240-0582-1). Garland Pub.

Travels & Discoveries in North & Central Africa, 3 vols. Ed. by Heinrich Barth. 1965. 150.00x set (ISBN 0-7146-1790-3, F Cass Co). Biblio Dist.

Travels Between the Hudson & the Mississippi, 1851-1952. Moritz Busch. Tr. by Norman H. Binger. LC 74-147857. 1971. 15.00x (ISBN 0-8131-1251-6). U Pr of Ky.

Travels in Arabia. John L. Burckhardt. (Arab Background Ser.). 25.00x (ISBN 0-685-77092-3). Intl Bk Ctr.

Travels in North America, Including a Summer with the Pawnees. 2nd ed. Charles A. Murray. LC 68-54845. (American Scene Ser.). 878p. 1974. Repr. of 1839 ed. lib. bdg. 69.50 (ISBN 0-306-71021-8). Da Capo.

Travels in North America, 1822-1824. Paul Wilhelm. Ed. by Savoie Lottinville. Tr. by W. Robert Nitske. (Illus.). 1974. pap. text ed. 9.95 (ISBN 0-8061-1501-7). U of Okla Pr.

Travels in South Kensington. Moncure D. Conway. LC 76-17754. (Aesthetic Movement & the Arts & Crafts Movement Ser.: Vol. 8). 1977. Repr. of 1882 ed. lib. bdg. 44.00 (ISBN 0-8240-2457-5). Garland Pub.

Travels in the Great Western Prairies, 2 vols. in 1. Thomas J. Farnham. LC 68-16231. (American Scene Ser.). 612p. 1973. Repr. of 1843 ed. lib. bdg. 35.00 (ISBN 0-306-71012-9). Da Capo.

Travels in the Island of Cyprus. Giovanni Mariti. Tr. by Claude D. Cobham et al from Gr. (Bibliotheca Historica Cypria). 1971. text ed. 11.75x (ISBN 0-900834-20-X). Humanities.

Travels in the New South, 2 vols. Ed. by Thomas D. Clark et al. Incl. Vol. 1. The Postwar South, 1867-1900. (Illus.). xvi, 267p; Vol. 2. The Twentieth-Century South, 1900-1955. (Illus.). xiv, 301p. (American Exploration & Travel Ser: No. 36). 1962. Set. 37.50 (ISBN 0-8061-0524-0). U of Okla Pr.

Travels in the Old South: A Bibliography, 3 vols. Thomas D. Clark. Incl. Vol. 1. The Formative Years, 1527-1783: from the Spanish Explorations Through the American Revolution. (Illus.). 330p. 1956; Vol. 2. The Expanding South, 1750-1825: the Ohio Valley & the Cotton Frontier. (Illus.). 292p. 1959; Vol. 3. The Ante Bellum South, 1825-1860: Cotton, Slavery, & Conflict. (Illus.). 406p. 1969. (American Exploration & Travel Ser: No. 19). boxed set 52.50 (ISBN 0-8061-0878-9). U of Okla Pr.

Travels in the Old South, 1783-1860, Selected from Periodicals of the Times, 2 vols. Ed. by Eugene L. Schwaab. LC 70-119814. (Illus.). 600p. 1973. Set. 35.00 (ISBN 0-8131-1229-X). U Pr of Ky.

Travels of Alexine. Penelope Gladstone. (Illus.). 1971. 12.50 (ISBN 0-7195-2044-4). Transatlantic.

Travels of Lao Ts'an. Harold Shadick & Liv Tieh-Yua. 1966. 15.00x o.p. (ISBN 0-8014-0376-6). Cornell U Pr.

Travels of William Bartram. William Bartram. Ed. & intro. by Robert M. Peck. (Literature of the American Wilderness). 388p. 1980. pap. 3.95 (ISBN 0-87905-079-9). Peregrine Smith.

Travels Through North & South Carolina, Georgia, East & West Florida. William Bartram. LC 73-84685. (Illus.). 520p. 1980. Repr. of 1973 ed. 14.95 (ISBN 0-8139-0871-X). U Pr of Va.

Travels Thru Arabia & Other Countries in the East, 2 vol. C. Niebuhr. (Arab Background Ser.). 30.00x (ISBN 0-685-77101-6). Intl Bk Ctr.

Travels Thru Interior Parts of North America. Jonathan Carver. Repr. 15.00 o.p. (ISBN 0-87018-007-X). Ross.

Travels with a Donkey in the Cevennes. Robert L. Stevenson. 1980. 12.95 (ISBN 0-906223-17-2). Dufour.

Travels with Farley. Phil Frank. (Illus.). 96p. 1980. pap. 6.95 (ISBN 0-89844-023-8). Troubador Pr.

Travels with Henry. Richard Valeriani. 1980. pap. 2.95 (ISBN 0-425-04649-4). Berkley Pub.

Travels with My Aunt. Graham Greene. LC 72-94848. 324p. 1981. 14.95 (ISBN 0-670-72524-2). Viking Pr.

Travels with Myself & Another. Martha Gellhorn. LC 79-15274. 1979. 8.95 (ISBN 0-396-07736-6). Dodd.

Travis. Archie McDonald. LC 76-55914. (Illus.). 1976. 15.00 (ISBN 0-8363-0147-1). Jenkins.

Travolta: A Photo Bio. Michael Reeves. (Illus.). 1978. pap. 1.95 (ISBN 0-515-04850-X). Jove Pubns.

Trawthe & Treason: The Sin of Gawain Reconsidered; A Thematic Study of "Sir Gawain & the Green Knight". W. R. Barron. 150p. 1980. 23.00x (ISBN 0-389-20028-X). B&N.

Treacherous Heart. Helen Nuelle. (Orig.). 1981. pap. 1.50 (ISBN 0-440-18561-0). Dell.

Treachery in Type. Josephine Bell. (Walker Mystery Ser.). 1980. 8.95 o.s.i. (ISBN 0-8027-5402-3). Walker & Co.

Treason at Michilimackinac. Ed. by David Armour. LC 67-81179. (Illus.). 103p. 1967. pap. 2.50 (ISBN 0-911872-32-9). Mackinac Island.

Treason of Benedict Arnold, 1780: An American General Becomes His Country's First Traitor. Robert Kraske. LC 72-115774. (Focus Bks). (Illus.). (gr. 7 up). 1970. PLB 4.47 o.p. (ISBN 0-531-01016-3). Watts.

Treasure & the Song. Mildred Lawrence. LC 66-10203. (gr. 7 up). 1966. 4.95 o.p. (ISBN 0-15-289950-2, HJ). HarBraceJ.

Treasure Chest. Compiled by Charles L. Wallis. LC 65-15395. (Illus.). 1965. 17.95 (ISBN 0-06-069010-0, HarpR); deluxe ed. 16.95 (ISBN 0-06-069011-9); deluxe ed. 17.95 (white) (ISBN 0-06-069051-8). Har-Row.

Treasure Chest of Tales. Paul Stroyer. (Illus.). (gr. 3 up). 1959. 8.95 (ISBN 0-8392-3039-7). Astor-Honor.

Treasure for My Daughter. Ed. by Bessie Batist. pap. 3.95 (ISBN 0-8015-7939-2, Hawthorn). Dutton.

Treasure from Hell. John Tominsky. 1981. 5.75 (ISBN 0-8062-1695-6). Carlton.

Treasure House: Museums of the Empire State. Ed. by Terry M. Kuehnemund. LC 79-53226. (Illus.). 1979. pap. 10.00 (ISBN 0-89062-042-3). Pub Ctr Cult Res.

Treasure Hunters. Elisabeth Beresfod. (Illus.). (gr. 3-7). 1980. 7.95 (ISBN 0-525-66702-4). Elsevier-Nelson.

Treasure Hunter's Manual. Karl Von Mueller. 1976. pap. 6.50 o.p. (ISBN 0-915920-09-3, SL625, ScribT). Scribner.

Treasure in Clay: The Autobiography of Fulton J. Sheen. Fulton J. Sheen. (Illus.). 384p. 1980. 15.95 (ISBN 0-385-15985-4). Doubleday.

Treasure in Earthen Vessels: Protestant Christianity in New South Wales Society 1900-1914. Richard Broome. 216p. 1981. text ed. 36.25x (ISBN 0-7022-1525-2). U of Queensland Pr.

Treasure Island. Malcolm Morgan. pap. text ed. 2.50x o.p. (ISBN 0-435-21001-7). Heinemann Ed.

Treasure Island. abr. ed. Robert L. Stevenson. Ed. by Jenny Gray. LC 70-133537. (Pacemaker Classics Ser.). (Illus., Orig., Adapted to grade 2 reading level). (RL 2.5). 1970. pap. 3.80 (ISBN 0-8224-9230-X); tchrs' manual free (ISBN 0-8224-5200-6). Pitman Learning.

Treasure Island. Robert L. Stevenson. (Literature Ser). (gr. 7-12). 1969. pap. text ed. 3.50 (ISBN 0-87720-718-6). AMSCO Sch.

Treasure Island. Robert L. Stevenson. (Keith Jennison Large Type Bks). (Illus.). (gr. 9 up). 1964. PLB 7.95 o.p. (ISBN 0-531-00296-9). Watts.

Treasure Island. Robert L. Stevenson. LC 78-3553. (Raintree's Illustrated Classics). (Illus.). (gr. 5-8). 1978. PLB 9.65 (ISBN 0-8393-6211-0). Raintree Child.

Treasure Island. Robert L. Stevenson. (Tempo Classic Ser.). 1979. pap. 1.50 (ISBN 0-448-17121-X, Tempo). G&D.

Treasure Island. (Illustrated Junior Library). (Illus.). 352p. 1981. pap. 4.95 (ISBN 0-448-11025-3). G&D.

Treasure Island: Church Growth Among Taiwan's Urban Minnan Chinese. Robert J. Bolton. LC 76-20828. (Illus.). 1976. pap. 8.95 (ISBN 0-87808-315-4). William Carey Lib.

Treasure Island with Reader's Guide. Robert Louis Stevenson. (Amsco Literature Program). (gr. 10-12). 1972. pap. text ed. 4.17 (ISBN 0-87720-817-4); model ans. bk. 2.70 (ISBN 0-87720-917-0). AMSCO Sch.

Treasure Nobody Saw. (Meg Bks.). (gr. 3 up). 1978. pap. 1.25 (ISBN 0-307-21529-6). Western Pub.

Treasure of Alpheus Winterborn. John Bellairs. 192p. (gr. 3-8). 1980. pap. 1.95 (ISBN 0-553-15095-2). Bantam.

Treasure of Diogenes Sampuez. James Munves. LC 78-21768. 192p. (gr. 5-9). 1979. 7.95 (ISBN 0-590-07384-2, Four Winds). Schol Bk Serv.

Treasure of Li-Po. Alice Ritchie. LC 49-10204. (Illus.). (gr. 4-6). 1949. 4.50 o.p. (ISBN 0-15-290158-2, HJ). HarBraceJ.

Treasure of Sierra Madre. Ed. by Tino Balio. LC 78-53298. (Screenplay Ser.). (Illus.). 1979. 15.00 (ISBN 0-299-07680-6); pap. 5.95 (ISBN 0-299-07684-9). U of Wis Pr.

Treasure of the Caves: The Story of the Dead Sea Scrolls. Iris Noble. LC 69-11303. (Illus.). (gr. 7 up). 1971. 5.95 o.s.i. (ISBN 0-02-768130-0). Macmillan.

Treasure of the Lost City. Aaron Fletcher. 1976. pap. 1.25 o.p. (ISBN 0-685-73461-7, LB391, Leisure Bks). Nordon Pubns.

Treasure of the Sangre De Cristos: Tales & Traditions of the Spanish Southwest. Arthur L. Campa. (Illus.). 1963. 7.95 (ISBN 0-8061-0574-7); pap. 4.95 (ISBN 0-8061-1176-3). U of Okla Pr.

Treasure of the Stars. Jeffrey Lord. (Blade Ser.: No. 29). 1978. pap. 1.50 (ISBN 0-523-40207-4, Dist. by Independent News Co.). Pinnacle Bks.

Treasure of Wonderwhat. Bill Starr. pap. 1.95 (ISBN 0-345-28286-8). Ballantine.

Treasure of Wycliffe House. Jeanne Judson. (YA) 5.95 (ISBN 0-685-07462-5, Avalon). Bouregy.

Treasure, People, Ships & Dreams. John L. Davis. (Illus.). 75p. 1977. pap. 5.95 (ISBN 0-933164-20-3). U of Tex Inst Tex Culture.

Treasure Tales of the Rockies. 3rd ed. Perry Eberhart. (Illus.). 315p. 1969. 12.95 (ISBN 0-8040-0295-9, SB). Swallow.

Treasure Trails. R. J. Santschi. (Doodlebug Edition Ser.). 1974. plastic bag 6.00 (ISBN 0-89316-612-X); pap. 4.00 (ISBN 0-89316-601-4). Exanimo Pr.

Treasured Recipes of Country Inns. new ed. Berkshire Traveller. LC 73-91008. (Illus.). 128p. 1973. pap. 3.95x (ISBN 0-912944-08-0). Berkshire Traveller.

Treasures from Earth's Storehouse. Juliet B. Ballard. 311p. (Orig.). 1980. pap. 7.95 (ISBN 0-87604-128-4). ARE Pr.

Treasures from Paul's Letters, Vol. I. A. M. Coniaris. 1978. pap. 5.95 (ISBN 0-937032-05-0). Light & Life Pub Co MN.

Treasures from Paul's Letters, Vol. II. A. M. Coniaris. 1979. pap. 5.95 (ISBN 0-937032-06-9). Light & Life Pub Co MN.

Treasures from the Bodleian Library. W. O. Hassall. 1976. 80.00x (ISBN 0-231-04060-1). Columbia U Pr.

Treasures from the Bronze Age of China: An Exhibition from the People's Republic of China. The Metropolitan Museum of Art. (Illus.). 192p. 12.95 (ISBN 0-345-29051-8). Ballantine.

Treasures from the Great Bronze Age of China: An Exhibition from the People's Republic of China. Compiled by Kitty S. Gilbert. (Illus.). 192p. 1980. pap. 9.95 (ISBN 0-87099-230-9). Metro Mus Art.

Treasures from the Rietberg Museum. Helmut Brinker & Eberhard Fischer. LC 80-12528. (Illus.). 176p. 1980. 19.95 (ISBN 0-87848-055-2). Asia Soc.

Treasures of American Folk Art. Robert Bishop. 12.50 (ISBN 0-8109-2218-5). Abrams.

Treasures of Britain. 3rd ed. Ed. by Automobile Association of England. (Illus.). 1976. 24.95 (ISBN 0-393-08743-3). Norton.

Treasures of Darkness: A History of Mesoptamian Religon. Thorkild Jacobsen. LC 75-27576. (Illus.). 1976. 18.50x (ISBN 0-300-01844-4); pap. 4.95x (ISBN 0-300-02291-3). Yale U Pr.

Treasures of Galveston Bay. Carroll Lewis. (Illus.). 1967. 8.95 (ISBN 0-87244-052-4). Texian.

Treasures of Hope. Alfred Doerffler. 1945. pap. 6.95 (ISBN 0-570-03763-8, 12-2697). Concordia.

Treasures of Independence. John Milley. (Illus.). 224p. 1980. 25.00 (ISBN 0-8317-8593-4). Mayflower Bks.

Treasures of Mechanical Music. Arthur A. Reblitz & Q. David Bowers. (Illus.). 634p. 1981. 25.00 (ISBN 0-911572-20-1). Vestal.

Treasures of Morrow. H. M. Hoover. LC 75-28098. 176p. (gr. 5-9). 1976. 6.95 (ISBN 0-590-07420-2, Four Winds). Schol Bk Serv.

Treasures of the Churches of France. Jean Taralon. LC 66-23097. (Illus.). 1966. 25.00 o.s.i. (ISBN 0-8076-0383-X). Braziller.

Treasures of the Hermitage. Vitaly Suslov. LC 80-81382. (Illus.). 1980. 19.95 (ISBN 0-88225-301-8). Newsweek.

Treasures of the Library of Congress. Charles A. Goodrum. (Illus.). 456p. 1980. 50.00 (ISBN 0-8109-1661-4, 1661-4); pre-Jan 45.00 (ISBN 0-686-62680-X). Abrams.

Treasures of the National Trust. Ed. by Robin Fedden. (Illus.). 1976. 24.00 (ISBN 0-224-01241-X). Transatlantic.

Treasures of the Night: Collected Poems of Jean Genet. Jean Genet. Tr. by Steven Finch from Fr. (Illus.). 120p. (Orig.). 1981. 25.00 (ISBN 0-917342-75-5, Pub. by Gay Sunshine); pap. 5.95 (ISBN 0-917342-76-3). Bookpeople.

Treasures of the Nile. Kamal El Mallakh & Robert S. Bianchi. Ed. by Henry A. LaFarge. LC 80-80044. (Illus.). 176p. 1980. 19.95 (ISBN 0-88225-293-3). Newsweek.

Treasures of the Snow. Patricia St. John. (gr. 5-8). 1950. pap. 2.50 (ISBN 0-8024-0008-6). Moody.

Treasures on the Tibetan Middle Way. Herbert V. Guenther. LC 75-40260. 166p. 1981. pap. 5.95 (ISBN 0-87773-002-4). Great Eastern.

Treasures Underground. Brian Mason. (Illus.). (gr. 4-6). 1960. PLB 6.95 (ISBN 0-87396-015-7). Stravon.

Treasury Alarm. Jocelyn Davey. 229p. 1981. 9.95 (ISBN 0-8027-5431-7). Walker & Co.

Treasury Control & Social Administration. Roy M. MacLeod. 62p. 1968. pap. text ed. 5.00x (Pub. by Bedford England). Renouf.

Treasury for Young Readers. Readers Digest. 1979. 14.95 (ISBN 0-89577-064-4, Pub. by Readers Digest Assoc). Norton.

Treasury Holiday. William Harmon. LC 78-120263. (Wesleyan Poetry Program: Vol. 53). (Orig.). 1970. 10.00x (ISBN 0-8195-2053-5, Pub. by Wesleyan U Pr); pap. 4.95 (ISBN 0-8195-1053-X). Columbia U Pr.

Treasury of Albert Schweitzer. Albert Schweitzer. LC 65-20328. 352p. 1965. 6.00 (ISBN 0-8022-1518-1). Philos Lib.

Treasury of American Antiques. concise ed. Clarence P. Hornung. LC 76-49914. (Illus.). 1977. 17.50 (ISBN 0-8109-1670-3); pap. 8.95 o.p. (ISBN 0-8109-2060-3). Abrams.

Treasury of American Clocks. 2nd ed. Brooks Palmer. 1967. 19.95 (ISBN 0-02-594580-7). Macmillan.

Treasury of American Folklore. B. A. Botkin. 640p. 1981. pap. 3.95 (ISBN 0-553-14149-X). Bantam.

Treasury of American Wildlife, 4 vols. Set. 29.50 (ISBN 0-686-60364-8). Ency Brit Ed.

Treasury of Art Nouveau Design & Ornament. Carol B. Grafton. (Pictorial Archive Ser.). (Illus.). 144p. (Orig.). 1980. pap. 4.50 (ISBN 0-486-24001-0). Dover.

Treasury of Best-Loved Rhymes. (Peter Possum Paperbacks Ser). 1967. pap. 0.95 o.p. (ISBN 0-531-05111-0). Watts.

Treasury of Business Opportunities...Featuring Over 400 Ways to Make a Fortune Without Leaving Your House. David D. Seltz. LC 76-47103. 1976. 15.00 (ISBN 0-87863-097-X). Farnswth Pub.

Treasury of Charted Designs for Needleworkers. Georgia Gorham & Jeanne Warth. (Dover Needlework Ser.). (Illus.). 1978. pap. 1.75 (ISBN 0-486-23558-0). Dover.

Treasury of Chassidic Tales: On the Torah, Vol. 2. Schlomo Y. Zevin. Tr. by Uri Kaploun. (Art Scroll Judaica Classics). 352p. 1980. 11.95 (ISBN 0-89906-902-9); pap. 8.95 (ISBN 0-89906-903-7); gift box ed. 25.95 (ISBN 0-89906-904-5). Mesorah Pubns.

Treasury of Clean Jokes. Tal D. Bonham. LC 80-67639. (Orig.). 1981. pap. 2.95 (ISBN 0-8054-5703-8). Broadman.

Treasury of Design for Artists & Craftsmen. Gregory Mirow. LC 69-18877. (Pictoral Archive Ser). 1969. pap. 4.00 (ISBN 0-486-22002-8). Dover.

Treasury of Embroidery Samples. Ondori Staff. LC 80-84416. (Illus.). 96p. 1981. pap. 5.95 (ISBN 0-87040-496-2). Japan Pubns.

Treasury of Flower Designs for Artists, Embroiderers & Craftsmen: 100 Garden Favorites. Susan Gaber. (Illus.). 80p. (Orig.). 1981. pap. price not set (ISBN 0-486-24096-7). Dover.

Treasury of Frontier Relics. 2nd,rev. ed. Les Beitz. 12.00 o.p. (ISBN 0-498-01688-9). A S Barnes.

Treasury of Houseplants. Rob Herwig & Margot Schubert. LC 75-34283. (Illus.). 368p. 1976. 12.95 o.s.i. (ISBN 0-02-551171-8). Macmillan.

Treasury of Jewish Folklore. Ed. by Nathan Ausubel. 544p. 1980. pap. 3.95 (ISBN 0-553-13807-3). Bantam.

Treasury of Little Golden Books. 1972. 5.95 (ISBN 0-307-16540-X, Golden Pr); PLB 12.23 o.p. (ISBN 0-307-66540-2). Western Pub.

Treasury of Mandaya & Mansaka Folk Literature. Tr. by Milma M. Fuentes & Edito T. De La Cruz. (Illus.). 130p. (Mandaya, Mansaka.). 1980. pap. 8.25x (ISBN 0-686-28808-4). Cellar.

Treasury of Needlework Projects from Godey's Lady's Book. Ed. by Arlene Z. Wiczyk. LC 72-3698. (Illus.). 320p. 1972. pap. 3.95 o.p. (ISBN 0-668-02692-8). Arco.

Treasury of Negro Spirituals. Ed. by Henry A. Chambers. (gr. 7 up). 1963. 10.95 o.s.i. (ISBN 0-87523-145-4). Emerson.

Treasury of Old & Historical American & British Furniture. Charles E. Dunsworth. (Illus.). 1979. deluxe ed. 37.85 (ISBN 0-930582-33-0). Gloucester Art.

Treasury of Poetry. Melanie Janae. 1981. 4.50 (ISBN 0-8062-1687-5). Carlton.

Treasury of Quotations on Christian Themes. C. Simcox. 1975. 12.95 (ISBN 0-8164-0274-4). Crossroad NY.

Treasury of Russian Literature. Ed. by Bernard G. Guerney. LC 43-17369. (Illus.). 15.00 (ISBN 0-8149-0113-1). Vanguard.

Treasury of the Familiar. Ed. by Ralph L. Woods. 1942. 16.95 (ISBN 0-02-631490-8). Macmillan.

Treasury of the Saturday Evening Post. LC 75-16576. (Illus.). write for info. (ISBN 0-89387-029-3). Sat Eve Post.

Treasury of Traditional Stained Glass Designs. Ann V. Winterbotham. (Illus.). 80p. (Orig.). 1981. pap. price not set (ISBN 0-486-24084-3). Dover.

Treasury of Witchcraft & Devilry. Marie Gupta & Frances Brandon. LC 74-6571. 1974. 8.95 o.p. (ISBN 0-685-50510-3). Jonathan David.

Treasury: The Evolution of a British Institution. Henry Roseveare. 1970. 17.50x (ISBN 0-231-03405-9). Columbia U Pr.

Treat It Gentle: An Autobiography. Sidney Bechet. LC 74-23412. (Roots of Jazz Ser). (Illus.). vi, 245p. 1975. lib. bdg. 22.50 (ISBN 0-306-70657-1); pap. 5.95 (ISBN 0-306-80086-1). Da Capo.

Treat Rebellion. Ramon Ruiz. 1980. write for info. Norton.

Treat Yourself to a Better Sex Life. Harvey L. Gochros & Joel Fischer. (Illus.). 1980. 16.95 (ISBN 0-13-930685-4, Spec); pap. 7.95 (ISBN 0-13-930677-3). P-H.

Treaties & Agreements with & Concerning China, 1894-1919, 2 vols. Ed. by John V. MacMurray. LC 77-114588. 1729p. 1974. Repr. of 1921 ed. Set. 80.00 (ISBN 0-86527-195-X). Fertig.

Treating Families in the Home: An Alternative to Placement. Marvin Bryce & June C. Lloyd. (Illus.). 352p. 1980. text ed. 24.75 (ISBN 0-398-04085-0). C C Thomas.

Treating the Offender: Problems & Issues. Ed. by Marc Riedel & Pedro A. Vales. LC 76-12870. 1977. text ed. 24.50 (ISBN 0-275-56350-2). Praeger.

Treatise Concerning Enthusiasme. Meric Casaubon. LC 77-119864. 1970. Repr. of 1656 ed. 32.00x (ISBN 0-8201-1077-9). Schol Facsimiles.

Treatise Concerning Eternal & Immutable Morality. Ralph Cudworth. Ed. by Rene Wellek. LC 75-11214. (British Philosophers & Theologians of the 17th & 18th Centuries: Vol. 17). 1976. Repr. of 1731 ed. lib. bdg. 42.00 (ISBN 0-8240-1768-4). Garland Pub.

Treatise Concerning Political Enquiry & the Liberty of the Press. Tunis Wortman. LC 78-122162. (Civil Liberties in American History Ser). 1970. Repr. of 1800 ed. lib. bdg. 35.00 (ISBN 0-306-71967-3). Da Capo.

Treatise, Concerning the Causes of the Magnificence & Greatness of Cities. Giovanni Botero. LC 79-84090. (English Experience Ser.: No. 910). 128p. (Eng.). 1979. Repr. of 1606 ed. lib. bdg. 13.00 (ISBN 90-221-0910-0). Walter J Johnson.

Treatise Concerning the Principles of Human Knowledge. George Berkeley. Ed. by Colin M. Turbayne. LC 57-1290. 1957. pap. 3.95 (ISBN 0-672-60225-3, LLA53). Bobbs.

Treatise Concerning the Principles of Human Knowledge: Text & Critical Essays. George Berkeley. Ed. by Colin M. Turbayne. LC 69-16531. (Text & Critical Essays Ser). 1970. pap. 6.55 (ISBN 0-672-61115-5, TC2). Bobbs.

Treatise of Civil Government & a Letter Concerning Toleration. John Locke. Ed. by Charles L. Sherman. 1965. pap. text ed. 5.95x (ISBN 0-89197-519-5). Irvington.

Treatise of Daunces. Bd. with Godly Exhortation by Occasion of the Late Judgement of God at Parris Garden. John Fields. (English Stage Ser.: Vol. 5). lib. bdg. 50.00 (ISBN 0-8240-0588-0). Garland Pub.

Treatise of Ecclesiasticall Dicipline. Matthew Sutcliffe. LC 73-7082. (English Experience Ser.: No. 626). 1973. Repr. of 1590 ed. 21.00 (ISBN 90-221-0626-8). Walter J Johnson.

Treatise of Equity. John Fonblanque. Rev. by Henry Ballow et al. LC 77-86649. (Classics of English Legal History in the Modern Era Ser.: Vol. 34). 775p. 1979. lib. bdg. 40.00 (ISBN 0-8240-3083-4). Garland Pub.

Treatise of Feme Converts; or, Lady's Law. Containing All the Laws & Statutes Relating to Women. Ed. by David Berkowitz & Samuel Thorne. LC 77-86663. (Classics of English Legal History in the Modern Era Ser.: Vol. 44). 1979. Repr. of 1732 ed. lib. bdg. 60.50 (ISBN 0-8240-3093-1). Garland Pub.

Treatise of Ghosts. Noel Taillepied. LC 71-162520. 1971. Repr. of 1933 ed. 18.00 (ISBN 0-8103-3741-X). Gale.

Treatise of Human Nature. David Hume. Ed. by L. A. Selby-Bigge & P. H. Nidditch. 1978. text ed. 19.95x (ISBN 0-19-824587-4); pap. text ed. 5.50x (ISBN 0-19-824588-2). Oxford U Pr.

Treatise of Morall Philosophie. rev. ed. William Baldwin. LC 67-10126. 1967. Repr. of 1620 ed. 41.00 (ISBN 0-8201-1003-5). Schol Facsimiles.

Treatise of Musick, Speculative, Practical & Historical. A. Malcolm. LC 69-16676. (Music Ser). 1970. Repr. of 1721 ed. lib. bdg. 49.50 (ISBN 0-306-71099-4). Da Capo.

Treatise of One Hundred & Thirteene Diseases of the Eyes. Richard Banister. LC 79-37135. (English Experience Ser.: No. 297). 480p. Repr. of 1622 ed. 35.00 (ISBN 90-221-0297-1). Walter J Johnson.

Treatise of the Donation of Gyfts & Endowment of Possessyons Gyven & Graunted Unto Sylvester Pope of Rome by Constantyne Emperour of Rome. Constantine I. Tr. by William Marshall. LC 79-84096. (English Experience Ser.: No. 916). 152p. (Eng.). 1979. Repr. of 1534 ed. lib. bdg. 24.00 (ISBN 90-221-0916-X). Walter J Johnson.

Treatise of the Lawes of the Forest. John Manwood. LC 76-57398. (English Experience Ser.: No. 814). 1977. Repr. of 1615 ed. lib. bdg. 51.00 (ISBN 90-221-0814-7). Walter J Johnson.

Treatise of the Laws for the Relief & Settlement of the Poor, 2 vols. Michael Nolan. Ed. by David Berkowitz & Samuel Thorne. LC 77-89221. (Classics of English Legal History in the Modern Era Ser.: Vol. 130). 1979. Repr. of 1805 ed. Set. lib. bdg. 55.00 ea. (ISBN 0-8240-3167-9). Garland Pub.

Treatise of the Laws of Nature, Made English from the Latin by John Maxwell. Richard Cumberland. Ed. by Rene Wellek. LC 75-11216. (British Philosophers & Theologians of the 17th & 18th Centuries: Vol. 19). 1977. Repr. of 1727 ed. lib. bdg. 42.00 (ISBN 0-8240-1770-6). Garland Pub.

Treatise of the Plague: Containing the Nature, Signes, & Accidents of the Same. Thomas Lodge. LC 79-84119. (English Experience Ser.: No. 938). 92p. 1979. Repr. of 1603 ed. lib. bdg. 10.50 (ISBN 90-221-0938-0). Walter J Johnson.

Treatise on American Citizenship. John S. Wise. (Studies in Constitutional Law). viii, 340p. 1981. Repr. of 1906 ed. lib. bdg. 30.00x (ISBN 0-8377-1306-4). Rothman.

Treatise on Analysis, 6 vols. J. A. Dieudonne. Incl. Vol. 1. 1960. 22.95 (ISBN 0-12-215550-5); Vol. 2. rev. ed. 1970. 44.50 (ISBN 0-12-215502-5); Vol. 3. 1972. 48.50 (ISBN 0-12-215503-3); Vol. 4. 1974. 49.00 (ISBN 0-12-215504-1); Vol. 5. 1977. 34.50 (ISBN 0-12-215505-X); Vol. 6. 1978. 32.00 (ISBN 0-12-215506-8). (Pure & Applied Mathematics Ser.). Acad Pr.

Treatise on Analytical Chemistry, 3 pts. I. M. Kolthoff & P. J. Elving. Incl. Pt. 1, Vols. 10-12. Theory & Practice of Analytical Chemistry. Vol. 10, 1972, 595p. 46.50 (ISBN 0-470-49966-4); Vol. 11, 1975. 60.00 (ISBN 0-471-49967-6); Vol. 12, 1976. 32.50 (ISBN 0-471-49968-4); Pt. 2, Vols. 4, 10, 12 & 14-15. Analytical Chemistry of the Elements & of Inorganic & Organic Compounds. Vol. 4, 1966, 452p. 39.50 (ISBN 0-470-49986-9); Vol. 10, 1978. 50.00 (ISBN 0-471-49998-6); Vol. 12, 1976. 27.25 (ISBN 0-470-50002-6); Vol. 14, 1971. 44.95 (ISBN 0-471-50005-4); Vol. 15, 1976. 50.00 (ISBN 0-471-50009-7); Pt. 3, Vols. 3-4. Analytical Chemistry in Industry. 60.00 (ISBN 0-471-50012-7); 60.00 (ISBN 0-471-02765-0). LC 59-12439 (Pub. by Wiley-Interscience). Wiley.

Treatise on Analytical Chemistry, 3 pts. I. M. Kolthoff & P. J. Elving. Incl. Pt. 1, Vols. 1-9. Theory & Practice of Analytical Chemistry. Vol. 1, 1959, 835p (ISBN 0-470-49950-8). Vol. 2, 1961, 520p (ISBN 0-470-49952-4). Vol. 3, 1961, 458p (ISBN 0-470-49954-0). Vol. 4, 1963, 955p (ISBN 0-470-49956-7). Vol. 5, 1964, 640p (ISBN 0-470-49958-3). Vol. 6, 1965, 899p (ISBN 0-470-49960-5). Vol. 7, 1967. 622p (ISBN 0-470-49962-1). Vol. 8, 1968, 515p (ISBN 0-470-49964-8). Vol. 9, 1971, 552p (ISBN 0-471-49965-X); Pt. 2, Vols. 1-3, 5-9, 11 & 13. Analytical Chemistry of the Elements & of Inorganic & Organic Compounds. 1966. Vol. 1, 1961, 471p (ISBN 0-470-49980-X). Vol. 2, 1962, 471p (ISBN 0-470-49982-6). Vol. 3, 1961, 398p (ISBN 0-470-49984-2). Vol. 5, 1961, 409p (ISBN 0-470-49988-5). Vol. 6, 1964, 627p (ISBN 0-470-49990-7); Vol. 7, 1962, 568p (ISBN 0-470-49992-3). Vol. 8, 1963, 556p (ISBN 0-470-49994-X). Vol. 9, 1962, 491p (ISBN 0-470-49996-6). Vol. 11 (ISBN 0-470-50000-X). Vol. 13, 1966, 528p (ISBN 0-470-50004-2); Pt. 3, Vols. 1-2. Analytical Chemistry in Industry. Vol. 1, 1967, 457p (ISBN 0-470-50010-7). Vol. 2, 1971, 597p (ISBN 0-471-50011-9). LC 59-12439. (Pub. by Wiley-Interscience). Wiley.

Treatise on Constitutional Conventions Their History, Powers, & Modes of Proceeding. John A. Jameson. LC 73-166332. (American Constitutional & Legal History Ser). 1972. Repr. of 1887 ed. lib. bdg. 59.50 (ISBN 0-306-70243-6). Da Capo.

Treatise on Contempt Including Civil & Criminal Contempts of Judicial Tribunals, Justices of the Peace, Legislative Bodies, Municipal Boards, Committees, Notaries, Commissioners, Referees & Other Officers Exercising Judicial & Quasi-judicial Functions: With Practice & Forms. Stewart Rapalje. xliv, 273p. 1981. Repr. of 1890 ed. lib. bdg. 32.50x (ISBN 0-8377-1030-8). Rothman.

Treatise on Crimes & Misdemeanors, 6 vols. Sir William O. Russell. Ed. by David S. Berkowitz & Samuel E. Thorne. LC 77-86641. (Classics of English Legal History in the Modern Era Ser.: Vol. 94). 1979. Set. lib. bdg. 55.00 ea. (ISBN 0-8240-3081-8). Garland Pub.

Treatise on Fishing with a Hook. Juliana Berners. LC 79-20603. (Angling Classics Ser.). 1979. Repr. 9.95 (ISBN 0-88427-038-6, Dist. by Caroline Hse). North River.

Treatise on Fishing with a Hook. Juliana Berners. 9.95. Green Hill.

Treatise on Fracture, 7 vols. Harold A. Liebowitz. Incl. Vol. 1. Microscopic & Macroscopic Fundamentals of Fracture. 1969. 62.50 (ISBN 0-12-449701-2); Vol. 2. Mathematical Fundamentals of Fracture. 1969. 75.50 (ISBN 0-12-449702-0); Vol. 3. Engineering Fundamentals & Environmental Effects. 1971. 75.50 (ISBN 0-12-449703-9); Vol. 4. 1969. 51.25 (ISBN 0-12-449704-7); Vol. 5. 1969. 58.50 (ISBN 0-12-449705-5); Vol. 6. 1969. 58.50 (ISBN 0-12-449706-3); Vol. 7. 1972. 97.50 (ISBN 0-12-449707-1). Set. 387.75 (ISBN 0-685-23225-5). Acad Pr.

Treatise on Insanity. Philippe Pinel. Tr. by D. D. Davis from Fr. Bd. with Responsibility in Mental Disease. (Contributions to the History of Psychology Ser., Vol. III, Pt. C: Medical Psychology). 1978. Repr. of 1806 ed. 30.00 (ISBN 0-89093-167-4). U Pubns Amer.

Treatise on International Criminal Law, Vol.2: Jurisdiction & Cooperation. M. Cherif Bassiouni & Ved P. Nanda. 448p. 1973. 59.50 (ISBN 0-398-02573-8); pap. 49.50 (ISBN 0-398-02628-9). C C Thomas.

Treatise on International Criminal Law, Vol. 1: Crimes & Punishment. Ed. by M. Cherif Bassiouni & Ved P. Nanda. 778p. 1973. pap. text ed. 54.75 (ISBN 0-398-02557-6). C C Thomas.

Treatise on Invertebrate Paleontology: Introduction (Fossilization, Biogeography & Biostratigraphy, Pt. A. Ed. by Richard A. Robison & Curt Tiechert. LC 53-12913. 1979. 25.00x (ISBN 0-8137-3001-5). Geol Soc.

Treatise on Invertebrate Paleontology: Part T: Echinodermata 2 (Crinoidea, 3 vols. Ed. by Raymond C. Moore & Curt Teichert. LC 53-12913. (Treatise on Invertebrate Paleontology). (Illus.). 1978. Set. 55.00x (ISBN 0-8137-3021-X); Vol. 1. 27.00x (ISBN 0-686-52382-2); Vol. 2. 26.00x (ISBN 0-686-52383-0); Vol. 3. 13.00x (ISBN 0-686-52384-9). Geol Soc.

Treatise on Invertebrate Paleontology, Pt. W. Suppl.1 Miscellanea, Trace Fossils & Problematica. 2nd. rev. & enl. ed. Walter Hartzschel. LC 53-12913. (Illus.). 1975. 20.00x (ISBN 0-8137-3027-9). Geol Soc.

Treatise on Judicial Evidence, Extracted from the Manuscripts of Jeremy Bentham. Jeremy Bentham. Ed. by M. Dumont. xvi, 366p. 1981. Repr. of 1825 ed. lib. bdg. 35.00x (ISBN 0-8377-0318-2). Rothman.

Treatise on Language. Alexander B. Johnson. Ed. by David Rynin. LC 68-25841. 1969. pap. text ed. 4.00 (ISBN 0-486-22019-2). Dover.

Treatise on Liminology, 3 vols. G. Evelyn Hutchinson. Incl. Vol. 1, 2 pts. 1975. Set. 29.95 (ISBN 0-471-42567-2); Pt. 1. Geography & Physics of Lakes. 672p. 17.95 (ISBN 0-471-42567-2); Pt. 2. Chemistry of Lakes. 474p. 16.50 (ISBN 0-471-42569-9); Vol. 2. Introduction to Lake Biology & the Limnoplankton. 1957. 79.50 (ISBN 0-471-42572-9); Vol. 3. Limnological Biology. 704p. 1975. 43.50 (ISBN 0-471-42574-5). LC 57-8888 (Pub. by Wiley-Interscience). Wiley.

Treatise on Man & the Development of His Faculties, 1842. Lambert A. Quetelet. LC 77-81364. (Hist. of Psych. Ser.). (Illus., Fr.). 1969. 22.00x (ISBN 0-8201-1061-2). Schol Facsimiles.

Treatise on Markets: Spot, Futures, & Options. Joseph M. Burns. 1979. pap. 5.25 (ISBN 0-8447-3340-7). Am Enterprise.

Treatise on Naval Architecture. William Hutchinson. 303p. 1980. 49.95x (ISBN 0-85177-002-9, Pub. by Conway Maritime England). State Mutual Bk.

Treatise on Practical Seamanship. William Hutchinson. (Scolar Maritime Library). (Illus.). 240p. 1979. Repr. of 1777 ed. 60.00x (ISBN 0-85967-566-1, Pub. by Scolar Pr England). Biblio Dist.

Treatise on Solid State Chemistry. Ed. by N. Bruce Hannay. Incl. Vol. 1. The Chemical Structure of Solids. 540p. 1973 (ISBN 0-306-35051-3); Vol. 2, Defects in Solids. 527p. 1975 (ISBN 0-306-35052-1); Crystalline & Non Crystalline Solids. 774p. 1976 (ISBN 0-306-35053-X); Vol. 4, Reactivity of Solids. 721p. 1976 (ISBN 0-306-35054-8); Vol. 5, Changes of State. 600p. 1975 (ISBN 0-306-35055-6); Vol. 6A, Surfaces, I. 491p. 1976 (ISBN 0-306-35056-4); Vol. 6B, Surfaces, II. 418p. 1976 (ISBN 0-306-35057-2). LC 73-79421. (Illus.). 45.00 ea. (Plenum Pr). Plenum Pub.

Treatise on Sunday Laws: The Sabbath-the Lord's Day, Its History & Observance, Civil & Criminal. George E. Harris. xxiii, 338p. 1980. Repr. of 1892 ed. lib. bdg. 32.50x (ISBN 0-8377-2232-2). Rothman.

Treatise on the Calculus of Finite Differences. 5th ed. George Boole. LC 76-119364. text ed. 10.95 (ISBN 0-8284-1121-2). Chelsea Pub.

Treatise on the Circle & the Sphere. Julian L. Coolidge. LC 78-128872. 1971. text ed. 19.50 o.p. (ISBN 0-8284-0236-1). Chelsea Pub.

Treatise on the Constitutional Limitations. Thomas M. Cooley. LC 78-87510. (American Constitutional & Legal History Ser). 720p. 1972. Repr. of 1868 ed. lib. bdg. 59.50 (ISBN 0-306-71403-5). Da Capo.

Treatise on the Fundamental Principles of Violin Playing. 2nd ed. Leopold Mozart. Tr. by Editha Knocher. (Illus.). 1951. 27.00x (ISBN 0-19-318502-4). Oxford U Pr.

Treatise on the Game Laws & on Fisheries, 2 vols. Joseph Chitty. Ed. by David S. Berkowitz & Samuel E. Thorne. LC 77-86657. (Classics of English Legal History in the Modern Era Ser.: Vol. 41). 1662p. 1979. lib. bdg. 80.00 (ISBN 0-8240-3090-7). Garland Pub.

Treatise on the Horse. Earl S. Sloan. (Illus.). 1980. Repr. of 1897 ed. softcover 5.00 (ISBN 0-686-64453-0). S J Durst.

Treatise on the Law of Citizenship in the United States. Prentice Webster. xxiii, 338p. 1980. Repr. of 1891 ed. lib. bdg. 30.00 (ISBN 0-8377-1307-2). Rothman.

Treatise on the Law of Corporations, 2 vols. Stewart Kyd. Ed. by David Berkowitz & Samuel Thorne. LC 77-86637. (Classics of English Legal History in the Modern Era Ser.: Vol. 89). 1979. Repr. of 1794 ed. Set. lib. bdg. 55.00 ea. (ISBN 0-8240-3076-1). Garland Pub.

Treatise on the Law of Libel & the Liberty of the Press. Thomas Cooper. LC 71-107408. (Civil Liberties in American History Ser). 1970. Repr. of 1833 ed. lib. bdg. 19.50 (ISBN 0-306-71892-8). Da Capo.

Treatise on the Law of Property in Intellectual Productions in Great Britain & the United States. Eaton S. Drone. LC 70-189788. liv, 774p. 1972. Repr. of 1879 ed. lib. bdg. 45.00x (ISBN 0-8377-2027-3). Rothman.

Treatise on the Law of the Prerogative of the Crown. Joseph Chitty, Jr. Ed. by David S. Berkowitz & Samuel E. Thorne. LC 77-89235. (Classics of the English Legal History in the Modern Era Ser.: Vol. 72). 515p. 1979. lib. bdg. 40.00 (ISBN 0-8240-3171-7). Garland Pub.

Treatise on the Law of Warranties in the Sale of Chattels. Arthur Biddle. xx, 308p. 1981. Repr. of 1884 ed. lib. bdg. 30.00x (ISBN 0-8377-0316-6). Rothman.

Treatise on the Limitations of Police Power in the United States. C. G. Tiedeman. LC 73-150421. (American Constitutional & Legal History Ser). 1971. Repr. of 1886 ed. lib. bdg. 59.00 (ISBN 0-306-70104-9). Da Capo.

Treatise on the Mathematical Theory of Elasticity. 4th ed. Augustus E. Love. (Illus.). 1927. pap. text ed. 8.00 (ISBN 0-486-60174-9). Dover.

Treatise on the Method of Government Surveying. Shobal V. Clevenger. 1978. pap. 8.50 (ISBN 0-686-25541-0). CARBEN Survey.

Treatise on the Pleas of the Crown, 2 vols. William Hawkins. Ed. by David S. Berkowitz & Samuel E. Thorne. LC 77-86643. (Classics of English Legal History in the Modern Era Ser.: Vol. 30). 874p. 1979. lib. bdg. 80.00 (ISBN 0-8240-3079-6). Garland Pub.

Treatise on the Principal Trades & Manufactures of the United States: Showing the Progress, State & Prospects of Business, & Illustrated by Sketches of Distinguished Mercantile & Manufacturing Firms. Edwin T. Freedley. (Neglected American Economists Ser.). 1974. lib. bdg. 50.00 (ISBN 0-8240-1012-4). Garland Pub.

Treatise on the Principles of Evidence & Practice As to Proofs in the Court of Common Law. William M. Best & James F. Stephen. Ed. by David S. Berkowitz & Samuel E. Thorne. LC 77-86653. (Classics of English Legal History in the Modern Era Ser.: Vol.37). 594p. 1979. lib. bdg. 40.00 (ISBN 0-8240-3086-9). Garland Pub.

Treatise on the Right of Personal Liberty & on Writ of Habeas Corpus. Rollin Carlos Hurd. LC 77-37767. (American Constitutional & Legal History Ser). 670p. 1972. Repr. of 1876 ed. lib. bdg. 59.50 (ISBN 0-306-70431-5). Da Capo.

Treatise on the Rules Which Govern the Interpretation & Construction of Statutory & Constitutional Law. 2nd ed. Theodore Sedgwick. Ed. by John N. Pomeroy. xlviii, 692p. 1981. Repr. of 1874 ed. lib. bdg. 49.50x (ISBN 0-8377-1115-0). Rothman.

Treatise on the Seven Rays, 5 vols. Alice A. Bailey. Incl. Vol. 1. Esoteric Psychology. 1979. 17.00 (ISBN 0-85330-018-6); pap. 5.75 (ISBN 0-85330-118-2); Vol. 2. Esoteric Psychology. 1970. 12.00 (ISBN 0-85330-019-4); pap. 7.25 (ISBN 0-85330-119-0); Vol. 3. Esoteric Astrology. 1975. 15.00 (ISBN 0-85330-020-8); pap. 7.75 (ISBN 0-85330-120-4); Vol. 4. Esoteric Healing. 1978. 22.00 (ISBN 0-85330-021-6); pap. 8.00 (ISBN 0-85330-121-2); Vol. 5. The Rays & the Initiations. 1970. 11.50 (ISBN 0-85330-022-4); pap. 7.25 (ISBN 0-85330-122-0). Lucis.

Treatise on the Theory & Practice of Midwifery. W. Smellie. 480p. 1974. Repr. of 1752 ed. 29.50 o.p. (ISBN 0-88275-159-X). Krieger.

Treatise on Thoroughbred Selection. new ed. Donald Lesh. 12.25 (ISBN 0-85131-296-9, Dist. by Sporting Book Center). J A Allen.

Treatise on Trusts & Monopolies, Containing an Exposition of the Rule of Public Policy Against Contracts & Combinations in Restraint of Trade, & a Review of Cases, Ancient & Modern. Thomas C. Spelling. xxvii, 274p. 1981. Repr. of 1893 ed. lib. bdg. 27.50x (ISBN 0-8377-1116-9). Rothman.

Treatise on Wood Engraving, Historical & Practical. William A. Chatto. LC 69-16477. (Illus.). 1969. Repr. of 1861 ed. 32.00 (ISBN 0-8103-3531-X). Gale.

Treatise Wherein Dicing, Dauncing, Vaine Playes or Enterluds Are Reproved. John Northbrooke. LC 72-170401. (English Stage Ser.: Vol. 1). lib. bdg. 50.00 (ISBN 0-8240-0584-8). Garland Pub.

Treatises of Benvenuto Cellini on Goldsmithing & Sculpture. Benvenuto Cellini. Tr. by C. R. Ashbee. (Illus.). 10.00 (ISBN 0-8446-1828-4). Peter Smith.

Treatises Upon Several Subjects. John Norris. Ed. by Rene Wellek. LC 75-11244. (British Philosophers & Theologians of the 17th & 18th Centuries Ser.). 1978. Repr. of 1698 ed. lib. bdg. 42.00 (ISBN 0-8240-1796-X). Garland Pub.

Treatment & Control of Infectious Diseases in Man. P. J. Imperato. (Illus.). 760p. 1974. 46.75 (ISBN 0-398-02979-2). C C Thomas.

Treatment & Disposal of Liquid & Solid Industrial Wastes: Proceedings of the Third Turkish-German Environmental Engineering Symposium, Istanbul, July 1979. K. Curi. LC 80-40993. (Illus.). 515p. 1980. 75.00 (ISBN 0-08-023999-4). Pergamon.

Treatment & Prevention of Reading Problems: The Neuro-Psychological Approach. Carl H. Delacato. 136p. 1971. pap. 14.50 photocopy ed. spiral (ISBN 0-398-00421-8). C C Thomas.

Treatment in Crisis Situations. Naomi Golan. LC 77-85350. (Treatment Approaches in the Human Services Ser., Gen. Ed. Francis J. Turner). 1978. text ed. 15.95 (ISBN 0-02-912060-8). Free Pr.

Treatment of Airborne Radioactive Wastes. 1968. pap. 39.75 (ISBN 92-0-020068-0, IAEA). Unipub.

Treatment of Bleeding Disorders with Blood Compounds. Ed. by Mammen et al. LC 80-80246. (Reviews of Hematology: Vol. I). 384p. 1980. 39.95. PJD Pubns.

Treatment of Cancer with Herbs. John Heinerman. 1980. 12.95 (ISBN 0-89557-047-5). Bi World Indus.

Treatment of Cats by Homoeopathy. K. Sheppard. 62p. 1960. 3.50x (ISBN 0-8464-1055-9). Beekman Pubs.

Treatment of Delirium Tremens & Related States. Ronald W. McNichol. (Illus.). 160p. 1970. 11.75 (ISBN 0-398-01270-9). C C Thomas.

Treatment of Different Languages in the United States: A Brief Historical Survey. Fred Rodriguez. 1979. text ed. 2.50x saddle stitched o.p. (ISBN 0-87543-153-4). Lucas.

Treatment of Disease by Acupuncture. 3rd ed. Felix Mann. 1974. 24.00x (ISBN 0-433-20308-0). Intl Ideas.

Treatment of Dogs by Homoeopathy. K. Sheppard. 1980. 4.00 (ISBN 0-8464-1056-7). Beekman Pubs.

Treatment of Domestic & Industrial Wastewaters in Large Plants: Proceedings of a Workshop Held in Vienna, Austria, Sept. 1979. S. H. Jenkins. (Progress in Water Technology: Vol. 12, Nos. 3 & 5). 550p. 1980. 90.00 (ISBN 0-08-026033-0). Pergamon.

Treatment of Drug Abuse: Programs, Problems, Prospects, 1972. R. M. Glasscote et al. 250p. 1972. pap. 8.00 (ISBN 0-686-57639-X, P197-0). Am Psychiatric.

Treatment of Epilepsy Today. Ed. by G. Ferriss. 1978. 15.95 o.p. (ISBN 0-87489-201-5); pap. 12.95 o.p. (ISBN 0-87489-202-3). Med Economics.

Treatment of Families in Conflict: The Clinical Study of Family Process. Group For The Advancement Of Psychiatry. LC 78-130635. 1970. 30.00x (ISBN 0-87668-036-8). Aronson.

Treatment of Fractures, 3 Vols. Lorenz Bohler & Jorg Bohler. Tr. by Tretter. LC 55-5445. (Illus.). 1956-58. Set. 177.00 (ISBN 0-685-11775-8); Vol. 1. 70.00 o.p. (ISBN 0-8089-0064-1); Vol. 2. 48.00 (ISBN 0-8089-0065-X); Vol. 3. 59.00 (ISBN 0-8089-0066-8). Grune.

Treatment of Hyperactivity & Learning Disorders. R. Knights. 1979. 24.50 (ISBN 0-8391-1515-6). Univ Park.

Treatment of Incorporated Transuranium Elements. (Technical Reports Ser.: No. 184). 1978. pap. 15.00 (ISBN 92-0-125278-1, IDC184, IAEA). Unipub.

Treatment of Industrial Effluents. A. Calleley & C. Forster. LC 76-54909. 1977. 27.95 (ISBN 0-470-98934-3). Halsted Pr.

Treatment of Low- & Intermediate-Level Radioactive Waste Concentrates. 1968. pap. 6.50 (ISBN 92-0-125068-1, IAEA). Unipub.

Treatment of Market Power: Antitrust Regulation & Public Enterprise. William G. Shepherd. 272p. 1975. 20.00x (ISBN 0-231-03773-2). Columbia U Pr.

Treatment of Neuromuscular Diseases. Ed. by Robert C. Griggs & R. T. Moxley. LC 75-43197. (Advances in Neurology Ser: Vol. 17). 1977. 32.00 (ISBN 0-89004-113-X). Raven.

Treatment of Pain. Harold C. Voris & Walter W. Whisler. (Illus.). 176p. 1975. 19.50 (ISBN 0-398-03353-6). C C Thomas.

Treatment of Phobic & Obsessive Compulsive Disorders. Ed. by John C. Boulougouris & Andreas D. Rabavilas. 1977. text ed. 23.00 (ISBN 0-08-021472-X); pap. text ed. 11.25 o.p. (ISBN 0-08-021471-1). Pergamon.

Treatment of Radioresistant Cancers. Ed. by M. Abe et al. 230p. 1979. 46.50 (ISBN 0-444-80179-0, North Holland). Elsevier.

Treatment of Renal Failure. G. M. Yuill. 214p. 1975. 12.00x (ISBN 0-7190-0628-7, Pub. by Manchester U Pr England). State Mutual Bk.

Treatment of the Aging Skin & Dermal Defects. Perry A. Sperber. (Illus.). 116p. 1965. 11.75 (ISBN 0-398-01826-X). C C Thomas.

Treatment of the Borderline Adolescent: A Developmental Approach. James F. Masterson. LC 78-39721. (Personality Processes Ser). 1972. 28.95 (ISBN 0-471-57615-8, Pub. by Wiley-Interscience). Wiley.

Treatment of the Severly Disturbed Adolescent. Donald Rinsley. 1979. 30.00 (ISBN 0-87668-320-0). Aronson.

Treatment of the Violent Incorrigible Adolescent. Vicki L. Agee. LC 78-24653. (Illus.). 1979. 17.95 (ISBN 0-669-02811-8). Lexington Bks.

Treatment Planning: A Pragmatic Approach. Ed. by Norman K. Wood. LC 78-18375. (Illus.). 1978. 21.95 (ISBN 0-8016-5615-X). Mosby.

Treatment Simulators: Applications of Modern Technology in Radiotherapy-1976. 1980. 10.00x (Pub. by Brit Inst Radiology). State Mutual Bk.

Treaty of Medicine Lodge. Douglas C. Jones. LC 66-22709. (Illus.). 237p. 1966. 12.95 o.p. (ISBN 0-8061-0712-X); pap. 5.95 (ISBN 0-8061-1165-8). U of Okla Pr.

Treaty of Portsmouth: An Adventure in American Diplomacy. Eugene P. Trani. LC 69-19767. (Illus.). 208p. 1969. 10.00x (ISBN 0-8131-1174-9). U Pr of Ky.

Treaty Ports in China: A Study in Diplomacy. En-Sai Tai. (Studies in Chinese History & Civilization). 202p. 1977. 17.50 (ISBN 0-89093-083-X). U Pubns Amer.

Treaty Profiles. new ed. Peter H. Rohn. LC 73-83352. 300p. 1974. text ed. 35.00 (ISBN 0-87436-131-1). ABC-Clio.

Treaty Veto of the American Senate. Denna F. Fleming. LC 72-147598. (Library of War & Peace; International Law). lib. bdg. 38.00 (ISBN 0-8240-0359-4). Garland Pub.

Trecento Commentaries on the Divina Commedia & the Epistle to Cangrande. L. Jenaro-Maclennan. (Oxford Modern Languages & Literature Monographs). 164p. 1974. 29.95x (ISBN 0-19-815519-0). Oxford U Pr.

Tree. Donald Carrick. LC 70-133556. (Illus.). (gr. k-3). 1971. 4.95g o.s.i. (ISBN 0-02-717290-2). Macmillan.

Tree. Joan Tate. pap. text ed. 1.95x o.p. (ISBN 0-435-11879-X). Heinemann Ed.

Tree & Field Crops of the Wetter Regions of the Tropics. C. N. Williams & W. Y. Chew. (Intermediate Tropical Agriculture Series). (Illus.). 262p. 1981. pap. text ed. 5.95x (ISBN 0-582-60319-6). Longman.

Tree & Four Friends. Aline Cunningham. (Caterpillar Bk. Ser.). (Illus.). 12p. (ps-k). 0.69 (ISBN 0-570-06908-4, 56Y1273). Concordia.

Tree Army: A Pictorial History of the Civilian Conservation Corps 1933-1943. Stan Cohen. LC 80-81071. 172p. 1980. 11.95 (ISBN 0-933126-11-5); pap. 7.95 (ISBN 0-933126-10-7). Pictorial Hist.

Tree-Bird. Lalitha Venkateswaran. 8.00 (ISBN 0-89253-749-3); flexible cloth 4.80 (ISBN 0-89253-750-7). Ind-US Inc.

Tree Boy. Shirley Nagel. (Sierra Club-Scribner's Juvenile Ser.). (Illus.). 96p. (gr. 5 up). 1978. 6.95 (ISBN 0-684-15722-5). Sierra.

Tree Climber: A Play in Two Acts. Hakim Tewfik Al. Tr. by D. Johnson-Davies. (Three Crown Bks.). 1966. pap. 1.95x o.p. (ISBN 0-19-911058-1). Oxford U Pr.

Tree Fruit Production. 3rd ed. Benjamin J. Teskey & James S. Shoemaker. (Illus.). 1978. text ed. 22.50 (ISBN 0-87055-265-1). AVI.

Tree Growth. Ed. by Theodore T. Kozlowski. (Illus.). 1962. 21.50 (ISBN 0-8260-5090-5, Pub. by Wiley-Interscience). Wiley.

Tree House Fun. Rose Greydanus. (Illus.). 32p. (gr. k-2). 1980. PLB 2.96 (ISBN 0-89375-391-2); pap. 0.95 (ISBN 0-89375-291-6). Troll Assocs.

Tree House Mystery. Gertrude C. Warner. LC 77-91744. (Boxcar Children Mysteries-Pilot Bk.). (Illus.). 128p. (gr. 3-7). 1969. 6.95g (ISBN 0-8075-8086-4). A Whitman.

Tree Hurts, Too. U. S. Department of Agriculture Forest Service. (Encore Edition). 32p. 1975. 1.79 o.p. (ISBN 0-684-15857-4, ScribT). Scribner.

Tree Is a Plant. Clyde R. Bulla. LC 60-11540. (Let's-Read-&-Find-Out Science Bk). (Illus.). (gr. k-3). 1960. PLB 7.89 (ISBN 0-690-83529-9, TYC-J). T Y Crowell.

Tree Maintenance. 5th ed. P. P. Pirone. (Illus.). 1978. 29.95 (ISBN 0-19-502321-8). Oxford U Pr.

Tree May Fall. Jonah Jones. 213p. 1981. 10.95 (ISBN 0-370-30320-2, Pub. by Chatto-Bodley-Jonathan). Merrimack Bk Serv.

Tree Meditation & Others. Alan Stephens. LC 70-132580. 53p. 1971. 6.00 (ISBN 0-8040-0296-7); pap. 3.75 (ISBN 0-8040-0622-9). Swallow.

Tree Nuts. 2nd ed. J. G. Woodroof. (Illus.). 1979. lib. bdg. 54.00 (ISBN 0-87055-254-6). AVI.

Tree of Animal Life: A Tale of Changing Forms & Fortunes. John C. McLoughlin. (Illus.). 128p. (gr. 5 up). 1981. PLB 8.95 (ISBN 0-396-07939-3). Dodd.

Tree of Liberty. Iona MacGregor. 1972. 6.50 (ISBN 0-571-10121-6, Pub. by Faber & Faber). Merrimack Bk Serv.

Tree of Life. Jo A. Merrell. (Orig.). 1980. 3.50 (ISBN 0-87123-564-1, 210564). Bethany Fell.

Tree of Life: An Anthology of Articles Appearing in the Jewish Vegetarian, 1966-1974. Ed. by Philip L. Pick. LC 76-18476. 1977. 6.95 o.p. (ISBN 0-498-01945-4). A S Barnes.

Tree Surgery: The Complete Guide. Peter Bridgman. LC 75-31320. (Illus.). 160p. 1976. 19.95 (ISBN 0-7153-7050-2). David & Charles.

Tree, Turf & Ornamental Pesticide Guide, 1976. rev. ed. W. T. Thomson. 1979. pap. 10.00 (ISBN 0-913702-02-1). Thomson Pub CA.

Treeful of Pigs. Arnold Lobel. LC 78-1810. (Illus.). (gr. k-3). 1979. 8.50 (ISBN 0-688-80177-3); PLB 8.16 (ISBN 0-688-84177-5). Greenwillow.

Treehouse Gang to the Rescue. Tim Mewees. (Better Living Ser.). 32p. (ps). 1981. write for info. (ISBN 0-8127-0311-1). Southern Pub.

Treen & Other Wooden Bygones. Edward H. Pinto. (Illus.). 1978. 50.00 o.p. (ISBN 0-684-15906-6, ScribT). Scribner.

Trees. H. Angel. 1975. pap. 5.00 o.p. (ISBN 0-85242-401-9, Pub. by Fountain). Morgan.

Trees. James U. Crockett. (Encyclopedia of Gardening Ser.). (Illus.). 160p. 1972. 11.95 (ISBN 0-8094-1117-2); lib. bdg. avail. (ISBN 0-685-27223-0). Time-Life.

Trees. James U. Crockett. LC 78-140420. (Time-Life Encyclopedia of Gardening Ser.). (Illus.). 1972. lib. bdg. 11.97 (ISBN 0-686-51063-1). Silver.

Trees. Francis Donaldson. (Easy-Read Fact Bks.). (Illus.). 48p. (gr. 2-4). 1976. PLB 3.90 o.p. (ISBN 0-531-00360-4). Watts.

Trees. Conrad Richter. (Keith Jennison Large Type Bks). (gr. 7 up). PLB 8.95 o.p. (ISBN 0-531-00297-7). Watts.

Trees. J. P. Serre. 140p. 1980. 29.80 (ISBN 0-387-10103-9). Springer-Verlag.

Trees and Buildings. Ed. by Tony Aldous. 95p. 1980. pap. 9.50 (ISBN 0-900630-73-6, Pub. by RIBA). Intl Schol Bk Serv.

Trees & Man. Herbert L. Edlin. 1976. 27.50x (ISBN 0-231-04158-6). Columbia U Pr.

Trees & Other Woody Plants of Maine. Fay Hyland & Ferdinand H. Steinmetz. LC 78-18706. 1978. lib. bdg. 7.50x o.p. (ISBN 0-89621-019-7); pap. 3.50x o.p. (ISBN 0-89621-018-9). Thorndike Pr.

Trees & Shrubs. Kurt Harz. (Illus.). 144p. 1981. pap. 5.95 (ISBN 0-7011-2542-X, Pub. by Chatto-Bodley-Jonathan). Merrimack Bk Serv.

Trees & Shrubs. Southern Living Garden & Landscape Staff. 1980. cancelled o.p. (ISBN 0-8487-0512-2). Oxmoor Hse.

Trees & Shrubs: A Complete Guide. Richard Gorer. (Illus.). 240p. 1976. 25.00 (ISBN 0-7153-6850-8). David & Charles.

Trees & Shrubs: Ground Covers Vines. John A. Floyd, Jr. LC 79-92605. (Illus.). 256p. 1980. 17.95 (ISBN 0-8487-0512-2). Oxmoor Hse.

Trees & Shrubs: Hardy in the British Isles, 4 vols. 8th ed. Compiled by W. J. Bean. Ed. by D. L. Clarke & George Taylor. (Illus.). 850p. 1981. 280.00x set (ISBN 0-312-81742-8). St Martin.

Trees & Shrubs in the Modern Garden. Cyril Harris. 1975. 12.95 (ISBN 0-7207-0855-9, Pub. by Michael Joseph). Merrimack Bk Serv.

Trees & Shrubs of New England. Dwelley. 425p. 1980. 12.95 (ISBN 0-89272-064-6). Down East.

Trees & Shrubs of the British Isles. Dartnell. 8.50x (ISBN 0-392-06756-0, LTB). Soccer.

Trees & Shrubs of the Southwestern Deserts. rev. ed. Lyman Benson & Robert A. Darrow. 1981. text ed. 49.50x (ISBN 0-8165-0591-8). U of Ariz Pr.

Trees Are Forever: How They Grow from Seeds to Forests. Eleanor B. Heady. LC 76-46541. (Finding-Out Books for Science & Social Studies, Grades 1-4). (Illus.). (gr. 2-4). 1978. PLB 6.95 (ISBN 0-8193-0897-8, Pub. by Parents). Enslow Pubs.

Trees: East Coast Edition. Ed. by Little, Brown Editors. (Explorer's Notebooks). (Illus.). 32p. (Orig.). (gr. 5 up). 1981. pap. 1.95 (ISBN 0-316-52769-6). Little.

Trees Every Boy & Girl Should Know. American Forestry Association. Date not set. 3.50 (ISBN 0-686-26729-X, 31). Am Forestry.

Trees for American Gardens. rev. & enl. ed. Donald Wyman. 1965. 16.95 (ISBN 0-02-632200-5). Macmillan.

Trees for Southern Landscapes. Bill Adams. LC 76-15457. (Illus.). 1976. pap. 3.95 (ISBN 0-88415-881-0). Pacesetter Pr.

Trees in the City. Ira B. Nadel & Cornelia H. Oberlander. LC 77-1713. 1978. text ed. 15.00 (ISBN 0-08-021489-4); pap. text ed. 7.75 (ISBN 0-08-021488-6). Pergamon.

Trees Jobs Grow on: And How to Find the One for You. James J. Gallagher & Kurt C. Nathan. LC 80-70399. (Illus.). 80p. (Orig.). 1980. 9.95 (ISBN 0-938176-00-5). Wendover.

Trees of Central Florida. Olga Lakela & Richard P. Wonderlin. (Illus.). 1980. 14.95 (ISBN 0-916224-51-1). Banyan Bks.

Trees of Christmas. Ed. by Edna Metcalfe. (Illus.). (gr. 3 up). 1969. 8.95 o.p. (ISBN 0-687-42590-5). Abingdon.

Trees of East Texas. Robert A. Vines. (Illus.). 640p. 1977. text ed. 24.95x (ISBN 0-292-78016-8); pap. 9.95 (ISBN 0-292-78017-6). U of Tex Pr.

Trees of Eastern & Central United States & Canada. William M. Harlow. (Illus.). 7.50 (ISBN 0-8446-0679-0). Peter Smith.

Trees of Heaven. Jesse Stuart. LC 80-51020. 344p. 1980. 17.50 (ISBN 0-8131-1446-2); pap. 6.50 (ISBN 0-8131-0150-6). U Pr of Ky.

Trees of Pennsylvania, the Atlantic States, & the Lake States. Li Hui-Lin. LC 72-80377. (Illus.). 1972. 17.50 (ISBN 0-8122-7665-5); pap. 9.95 (ISBN 0-8122-1064-6, Pa Paperbks). U of Pa Pr.

Trees of Santa Barbara. Katherine K. Muller et al. (Illus.). 1974. 10.00 (ISBN 0-916436-00-4). Santa Barb Botanic.

Trees of the Adirondack High Peak Region. 2nd ed. E. H. Ketchledge. LC 67-28444. (Illus.). pap. 2.50 (ISBN 0-935272-07-0). ADK Mtn Club.

Trees of the Sydney Region. John Child. pap. 6.50x (ISBN 0-392-06871-0, ABC). Soccer.

Trees of the World. Scott Leathart. LC 76-52282. (Illus.). 1977. 19.95 o.p. (ISBN 0-89479-000-5). A & W Pubs.

Trees: Stages 1 & 2. Sheila Parker. LC 77-83008. (Science 5-13 Ser.). (Illus.). 1977. pap. text ed. 9.30 (ISBN 0-356-04347-9). Raintree Child.

Trees: West Coast Ed. Ed. by Little, Brown Editorial Staff. (Explorer's Notebooks Ser.). (Illus.). 32p. (Orig.). (gr. 5 up). 1981. pap. 1.95 (ISBN 0-316-52769-6). Little.

Tregaron's Daughter. Madeleine Brent. LC 78-150878. 1971. 6.95 o.p. (ISBN 0-385-00323-4). Doubleday.

Tregaron's Daughter. Madeleine Brent. 320p. 1981. pap. 2.50 (ISBN 0-449-24391-5, Crest). Fawcett.

Trelawny: The Incurable Romancer. William St. Clair. LC 77-84020. (Illus.). 1978. 12.95 (ISBN 0-8149-0792-X). Vanguard.

Trellis Garden Book: How to Build It, How to Grow It, How to Show It. Jack Kramer. LC 75-43989. (Illus.). 96p. 1976. 7.95 o.s.i. (ISBN 0-8027-0532-4). Walker & Co.

Trematoda. Benjamin Dawes. 1946. 79.00 (ISBN 0-521-07219-0). Cambridge U Pr.

Trembling of a Leaf. John Colleton. 1981. pap. 2.50 (ISBN 0-671-41612-X). PB.

Trembling Years. Elsie M. Barber. (gr. 7 up). 1949. 5.95 o.s.i. (ISBN 0-02-506850-4). Macmillan.

Tremendum: A Theological Interpretation of the Holocaust. Arthur A. Cohen. 144p. 1981. 9.95 (ISBN 0-8245-0006-7). Crossroad NY.

Tremor in the Blood: Uses & Abuses of the Lie Detector. David T. Lykken. LC 80-10697. 320p. 1980. 14.95 (ISBN 0-07-039210-2). McGraw.

Tremor Violet. David Lippincott. 1976. pap. 1.75 (ISBN 0-451-06947-1, E6947, Sig). NAL.

Trench Warfare. Tony Ashworth. LC 80-13696. 258p. 1980. text ed. 43.50x (ISBN 0-8419-0615-7). Holmes & Meier.

Trend of Reading Standards. K. B. Start & B. K. Wells. (General Ser.). 80p. (Orig.). 1972. pap. text ed. 5.00x (ISBN 0-901225-96-7, NFER). Humanities.

Trends Affecting the U. S. Banking System. Cambridge Research Institute & Paul V. Teplitz. LC 75-37754. 1976. 17.50 o.p. (ISBN 0-88410-291-2). Ballinger Pub.

Trends & Characteristics of International Migrations Since 1950. (Demographic Studies: No. 64). 172p. 1979. pap. 12.00 (ISBN 0-686-68977-1, UN78/13/5, UN). Unipub.

Trends & Issues Affecting Curriculum: Programs and Practices. Ed. by Lutian R. Wootton et al. LC 80-5784. 281p. 1980. lib. bdg. 18.75 (ISBN 0-8191-1224-0); pap. text ed. 10.75 (ISBN 0-8191-1225-9). U Pr of Amer.

Trends & Issues in OD: Current Theory & Practice. Ed. by W. Warner Burke & Leonard D. Goodstein. LC 80-52929. 351p. (Orig.). 1980. pap. 18.50 (ISBN 0-88390-162-5). Univ Assocs.

Trends in African Contemporary Art. Kojo Fosu. LC 79-51527. (Illus.). 1980. 45.00 (ISBN 0-933184-02-6); pap. 35.00 (ISBN 0-933184-03-4). Flame Intl.

Trends in Allocation Procedures: An NFER Report. 1969. pap. text ed. 2.25x (ISBN 0-901225-05-3, NFER). Humanities.

Trends in Canada's Mineral Trade. Bruce W. Wilkinson. 64p. (Orig.). 1978. pap. text ed. 3.50x (ISBN 0-686-63145-5, Pub. by Ctr Resource Stud Canada). Renouf.

Trends in Energy Use in Industrial Countries. Joy Dunkerley. LC 80-8022. (Resources for the Future Research Ser.: Paper R-19). (Illus., Orig.). 1980. pap. text ed. 8.00x (ISBN 0-8018-2487-7). Johns Hopkins.

Trends in Environmental Policy & Law. (IUCN Environmental Policy & Law Paper Ser.: No. 15). 404p. 1981. pap. 30.75 (ISBN 2-88032-085-2, IUCN94, IUCN). Unipub.

Trends in Enzymology: Proceedings, 2 vols. Incl. Enzyme Regulation & Mechanism of Action. Ed. by P. Mildner & B. Bries. 100.00 (ISBN 0-08-024417-3); Industrial & Clinical Enzymology. Ed. by L. J. Vitale & V. Simeon. 60.00 (ISBN 0-08-024418-1). (FEBS Ser.: Vols. 60 & 61). (Illus.). 730p. 1980. Pergamon.

Trends in Epidemiology: Application to Health Service Research & Training. Ed. by Gordon T. Stewart. (Amer. Lec. Epidemiology Ser). (Illus.). 624p. 1972. 40.75 (ISBN 0-398-02422-7). C C Thomas.

Trends in Ethnic Group Relations in Asia & Oceania: Race & Society. 292p. 1980. pap. 14.50 (ISBN 92-3-101603-2, U 1008, UNESCO). Unipub.

Trends in Genetic Analysis. G. Pontecorvo. LC 58-8805. (Columbia Biological Ser.: No. 18). 1958. 19.00x (ISBN 0-231-02268-9). Columbia U Pr.

Trends in Geography: An Introductory Survey. R. V. Cooke & J. H. Johnson. 1969. 13.75 (ISBN 0-08-006675-5); pap. 6.25 (ISBN 0-08-006674-7). Pergamon.

Trends in Managemment Development Educations: An Economic Study. Gilbert J. Black. LC 79-4435. (Communications Library). 1979. 24.95x (ISBN 0-914236-24-5). Knowledge Indus.

Trends in Relief Expenditures, 1910-1935. Ann E. Geddes. LC 74-166327. (FDR & the Era of the New Deal Ser). 1971. Repr. of 1937 ed. lib. bdg. 15.00 (ISBN 0-306-70342-4). Da Capo.

Trends in Research & in the Application of Science & Technology for Arid Zone Development. (MAB Technical Note Ser.: No. 10). 1979. pap. 7.00 (ISBN 92-3-101597-4, U907, UNESCO). Unipub.

Trends in School Segregation: Nineteen Sixty-Eight to Seventy-Three. James S. Coleman et al. (Institute Paper). 133p. 1975. pap. 3.50 o.p. (ISBN 0-685-99499-6, 12300). Urban Inst.

Trends in Social Work, Eighteen Seventy-Four to Nineteen Fifty-Six: A History Based on the Proceedings of the National Conference of Social Work. 2nd ed. Frank J. Bruno. LC 80-19210. xviii, 462p. 1980. Repr. of 1957 ed. lib. bdg. 39.75x (ISBN 0-313-22665-2, BRTI). Greenwood.

Trends in Speech Recognition. W. Lea. 1980. text ed. 30.00 (ISBN 0-13-930768-0). P-H.

Trends in the Services for Youth. Ed. by J. H. Leicester & W. A. Farndale. 1967. 46.00 (ISBN 0-08-011604-3). Pergamon.

Trends in World Anthropology. L. P. Vidyarthi. 112p. 1979. text ed. 8.00x (ISBN 0-391-01783-7). Humanities.

Trends Toward Corporatist Intermediation. Ed. by Philippe C. Schmitter & Gerhard Lehmbruch. LC 79-63824. (Contemporary Political Sociology: Vol. 1). 328p. 1979. 20.00x (ISBN 0-8039-9836-8); pap. 9.95x (ISBN 0-8039-9837-6). Sage.

Trent Affair, November, 1861: U.S. Detainment of a British Ship Nearly Brings War with England. Theodore Roscoe. LC 76-186758. (Focus Books). (Illus.). 72p. (gr. 7 up). 1972. PLB 6.45 (ISBN 0-531-02455-5). Watts.

Trent & Mersey Canal. Jean Lindsay. LC 78-51089. (Illus.). 1979. 17.95 (ISBN 0-7153-7781-7). David & Charles.

Trent Intervenes. E. C. Bentley. 259p. 1981. pap. price not set (ISBN 0-486-24098-3). Dover.

Trenton Pickle Ordinance & Other Bonehead Legislation. Dick Hyman. LC 75-41874. (Illus.). 132p. 1976. 6.95 (ISBN 0-8289-0278-X). Greene.

Trent's Last Case. E. C. Bentley. LC 75-44955. (Crime Fiction Ser). 1976. Repr. of 1912 ed. lib. bdg. 17.50 (ISBN 0-8240-2353-6). Garland Pub.

Trent's Last Case. E. C. Bentley. 1976. lib. bdg. 13.95x (ISBN 0-89968-165-4). Lightyear.

Trent's Own Case. E. C. Bentley. LC 80-7836. 1980. pap. 1.95 (ISBN 0-06-080516-1, P 516, PL). Har-Row.

Tres Cuentos. 2nd ed. Carlos Garcia-Prada & William E. Wilson. LC 59-4973. (Span). 1959. pap. text ed. 7.20 (ISBN 0-395-04482-0). HM.

Tres de la Madrugada. Bunuel. (Easy Reader, A). pap. 2.90 (ISBN 0-88436-061-X, SPA112051). EMC.

Tres Factores Para Mover Montanas. Tr. by Jim Bakker. (Spanish Bks.). (Span.). 1978. 1.60 (ISBN 0-8297-0488-4). Life Pubs Intl.

Tres Farsas Contemporaneas y un Secuestro. Antonio M. Ballesteros. Ed. by Angel R. Maroto & Charles E. Whitehead. (Orig.). (gr. 10-12). 1980. pap. text ed. 3.25x (ISBN 0-88334-125-5). Ind Sch Pr.

Tres Magnificos, Os. Tr. by Dean Merrill. (Portugese Bks.). (Port.). 1979. 2.20 (ISBN 0-8297-0892-8). Life Pubs Intl.

Tresors Du Temps. Yvone Lenard. (Verbal-Active French Ser.). text ed. 15.68 (ISBN 0-06-582102-5, SchDept); tchr's. ed. 12.36 (ISBN 0-06-582206-4). Har-Row.

Trespasser. Gilbert Parker. 1976. lib. bdg. 13.85x (ISBN 0-89968-083-6). Lightyear.

Trespassing Stoplights & Attitudes. Mary McGrath. (Illus.). 44p. (Orig.). 1980. pap. 5.00 (ISBN 0-930012-43-7). Mudborn.

Trewe Mirrour of Glase Wherin We Maye Beholde the Wofull State of Thys Our Realme of Englande. Laurence Saunders. LC 74-28884. (English Experience Ser.: No. 761). 1975. Repr. of 1556 ed. 3.50 (ISBN 90-221-0761-2). Walter J Johnson.

Triad Imperative. Dwight Martin. 288p. 1980. 10.95 (ISBN 0-312-92829-7). Congdon & Lattes.

Triad Optical Illusions & How to Design Them. Harry Turner. LC 77-81212. (Illus.). 1977. pap. 1.95 (ISBN 0-486-23549-1). Dover.

Triage. Douglas A. Rund & Tondra S. Rausch. (Illus.). 256p. 1981. pap. text ed. 13.95 (ISBN 0-8016-4221-3). Mosby.

Triage: Problem Oriented Sorting of Patients. D. M. Vickery. (Illus.). 1976. pap. 13.95 (ISBN 0-87618-133-7). R J Brady.

Trial. Linda DuBreuil. 1975. pap. 1.50 o.p. (ISBN 0-685-52172-9, LB245DK, Leisure Bks). Nordon Pubns.

Trial & Achievement: Currents in Jewish History. H. H. Ben-Sasson. (Illus.). 327p. 1975. 10.95 (ISBN 0-7065-1420-3). Bloch.

Trial & Error. Anthony Berkeley. 1981. pap. 2.25 (ISBN 0-440-18766-4). Dell.

Trial & Error. D. Michael Tomkins. LC 80-39757. 1981. 9.95 (ISBN 0-396-07944-X). Dodd.

Trial & Error: The Detroit School Segregation Case. Eleanor P. Wolf. 400p. 1981. 19.95 (ISBN 0-8143-1673-5). Wayne St U Pr.

Trial & Triumph. Gayle Turk. (Illus.). 60p. (Orig.). 1978. pap. 2.50 (ISBN 0-936564-11-3). Little London.

Trial by Death & Fire. D. Carl Anderson. LC 80-14446. (Orion Ser.). 160p. 1980. pap. 2.95 (ISBN 0-8127-0292-1). Southern Pub.

Trial by Medicine: The Insanity Defense in Victorian England. Roger Smith. 280p. 1981. 33.00x (ISBN 0-85224-407-X, Pub.by Edinburgh U Pr Scotland). Columbia U Pr.

Trial by Prejudice. Arthur G. Hays. LC 79-109550. (Civil Liberties in American History Ser). 1970. Repr. of 1933 ed. lib. bdg. 35.00 (ISBN 0-306-71904-5). Da Capo.

Trial in the Upper Room. Paul Sann. Ed. by Herbert Michaelman. 1981. price not set (ISBN 0-517-54284-6, Michaelman Books). Crown.

Trial Judge: The Candid, Behind the Bench Story of Justice Bernard Botein. Bernard Botein. (American Constitutional & Legal History Ser.). 337p. 1974. Repr. of 1952 ed. lib. bdg. 32.50 (ISBN 0-306-70630-X). Da Capo.

Trial of Andrew Johnson. Andrew Johnson. LC 69-11326. (Law, Politics, & History Ser). 1970. Repr. of 1868 ed. lib. bdg. 95.00 (ISBN 0-306-71184-2). Da Capo.

Trial of D. M. Bennett: Upon the Charge of Depositing Prohibited Matter in the Mail. Bennet De Robigne. LC 72-8110. (Civil Liberties in American History Ser). 202p. 1973. Repr. of 1879 ed. lib. bdg. 22.50 (ISBN 0-306-70525-7). Da Capo.

Trial of Faith. R. J. Owen. 1.55 (ISBN 0-08-017609-7). Pergamon.

Trial of Generals: Homma, Yamashita, MacArthur. Lawrence Taylor. (Illus.). 260p. 1981. 13.95 (ISBN 0-89651-775-6). Icarus.

Trial of Jesus Christ. Aristarchus Vassilakos. Ed. by Orthodox Christian Educational Society. 64p. (Orig.). 1950. pap. 2.00x (ISBN 0-938366-47-5). Orthodox Chr.

Trial of John Peter Zenger, August 1735: An Early Fight for America's Freedom of the Press. Frank B. Latham. LC 71-101751. (Focus Books). (Illus.). (gr. 7 up). 1970. PLB 1.25 o.p. (ISBN 0-531-02333-8). Watts.

Trial of Luther. Daniel Olivier. 1979. pap. 8.50 (ISBN 0-570-03785-9, 12-2743). Concordia.

Trial of Martin Luther King. Alan P. Westin & Barry Mahoney. LC 74-9945. (Apollo Eds.). (Illus.). 1976. pap. 4.95 o.s.i. (ISBN 0-8152-0421-3, TYC-T). T Y Crowell.

Trial of Samuel Chase, an Associate Justice of the Supreme Court Impeached by the House of Representatives, 2 Vols. Samuel Chase. LC 69-11324. (Law, Politics, & History Ser). Repr. of 1805 ed. 59.50 (ISBN 0-306-71181-8). Da Capo.
Trial of Scott Nearing & the the American Socialist Party. Rand School of Social Science. LC 73-147523. (Library of War & Peace; Labor, Socialism & War). lib. bdg. 38.00 (ISBN 0-8240-0311-X). Garland Pub.
Trial of the Constitution. Sidney G. Fisher. LC 70-164511. (American Constitutional & Legal History Ser.). Repr. of 1864 ed. lib. bdg. 39.50 (ISBN 0-306-70281-9). Da Capo.
Trial of the Germans: An Account of the Twenty-Two Defendants Before the International Tribunal at Nuremburg. Eugene Davidson. 1972. pap. 3.95 o.s.i. (ISBN 0-02-031270-9, Collier). Macmillan.
Trial of the Kaohsiung Defendants. John Kaplan. (Research Papers & Policy Studies: No. 2). 100p. 1981. pap. price not set (ISBN 0-912966-35-1). IEAS Ctr Chinese Stud.
Trial of the Poet: An Interpretation of the First Edition of Leaves of Grass. Ivan Marki. LC 76-18792. 1976. 20.00x (ISBN 0-231-03984-0). Columbia U Pr.
Trial of the Templars. M. C. Barber. LC 77-85716. 320p. 1978. 41.50 (ISBN 0-521-21896-9); pap. 11.95x (ISBN 0-521-21896-9). Cambridge U Pr.
Trial Process. Ed. by Bruce D. Sales. (Perspectives in Law & Psycology Ser.: Vol. 2). 530p. 1981. 39.50 (ISBN 0-306-40491-5, Plenum Pr). Plenum Pub.
Trial Tactics. West Virginia Trial Lawyers Association. 466p. 1966. 12.00 (ISBN 0-913338-21-4). Trans-Media Pub.
Trials & Triumphs of Eva Grant. Effie M. Williams. 94p. pap. 1.00. Faith Pub Hse.
Trials Bike Riding. Don Smith. (EP Sports Ser.). (Illus.). 112p. 1981. 12.95 (ISBN 0-8069-9050-3, Pub. by EP Publishing England). Sterling.
Trials of Oscar Wilde. H. Montgomery Hyde. (Illus.). 8.50 (ISBN 0-8446-5049-8). Peter Smith.
Trials of Rumpole. John Mortimer. 206p. 1981. pap. 2.95 (ISBN 0-14-005162-7). Penguin.
Trials on Trial: The Pure Theory of Legal Procedure. Gordon Tullock. LC 80-13113. 264p. 1980. 20.00x (ISBN 0-231-04952-8). Columbia U Pr.
Trials, Tears & Triumph. Dale E. Rogers. 1977. 4.95 o.p. (ISBN 0-8007-0847-4). Revell.
Triangle of Death. Jon Hart. LC 80-71034. (Mercenaries Ser.). 128p. 1981. pap. 2.95 (ISBN 0-87754-228-7). Chelsea Hse.
Triangle of Death: The Inside Story of the Triads--the Chinese Mafia. Frank Robertson. (Illus.). 1978. 14.95 (ISBN 0-7100-8732-2). Routledge & Kegan.
Triangle Shirtwaist Fire, March 25, 1911: The Blaze That Changed an Industry. Corinne Naden. LC 70-137153. (Focus Bks). (Illus.). (gr. 7 up). 1971. PLB 4.47 o.p. (ISBN 0-531-01023-6); pap. 1.25 o.p. (ISBN 0-531-02334-6). Watts.
Triangle: The Betrayed Wife. Evelyn M. Berger. LC 70-170883. 1971. 13.95 (ISBN 0-911012-13-3). Nelson-Hall.
Trianglepoint. Sherlee Lantz. LC 76-3550. 1976. 12.95 o.p. (ISBN 0-670-73030-0, Studio). Viking Pr.
Triazoles. K. T. Finley. (Chemistry of Heterocyclic Compounds, Series of Monographs: Vol. 39). 368p. 1980. write for info (ISBN 0-471-07827-1). Wiley.
Triazoles, One, Two, Four. Carroll Temple. (Monographs). 752p. 1980. 175.00 (ISBN 0-471-04656-6, Pub. by Wiley-Interscience). Wiley.
Tribal Cohesion in a Money Economy: A Study of the Mambwe People of Zambia. W. Watson. (Institute for African Studies). (Illus.). 286p. 1971. pap. text ed. 13.00x (ISBN 0-7190-1037-3). Humanities.
Tribal Culture of India. Vidyarthi. 1980. text ed. write for info. (ISBN 0-391-01167-7). Humanities.
Tribal Innovators: Tswana Chiefs & Social Change 1795-1940. I. Schapera. (Monographs on Social Anthropology Ser: No. 43). (Illus.). 1970. text ed. 25.00x (ISBN 0-391-00115-9, Athlone). Humanities.
Tribe. Bari Wood. 1981. 12.95 (ISBN 0-453-00393-1, H393). NAL.
Tribe & State in Bahrain: The Transformation of Social & Political Authority in an Arab State. Fuad I. Khuri. LC 80-13528. (Publications of the Center for Middle Eastern Studies: No. 14). (Illus.). 1981. lib. bdg. 16.00x (ISBN 0-226-43473-7). U of Chicago Pr.
Tribe, Caste & Nation. Frederick G. Bailey. 1971. Repr. of 1960 ed. text ed. 19.50x (ISBN 0-7190-0250-8). Humanities.
Tribes of California. Stephen Powers. LC 75-13150. 1977. 27.50x (ISBN 0-520-03023-0); pap. 5.95 (ISBN 0-520-03172-5, CAL 327). U of Cal Pr.
Tribes of the Amazon Basin in Brazil, 1972: Report for the Aborigines Protection Society. Edwin Brooks et al. 201p. 1974. 12.50x o.p. (ISBN 0-85314-210-6). Transatlantic.
Tribes That Slumber: Indians of the Tennessee Region. Thomas M. Lewis & Madeline Kneberg. LC 58-12085. (Illus.). 1958. pap. 7.95 (ISBN 0-87049-021-4). U of Tenn Pr.
Tribes Without Rulers: Studies in African Segmentary Systems. Ed. by John Middleton & David Tait. 1970. pap. text ed. 7.75x (ISBN 0-391-00090-X). Humanities.
Tribesmen. Marshall D. Sahlins. (Illus., Orig.). 1968. pap. 6.95 ref. ed. (ISBN 0-13-930925-X). P-H.
Tribesmen & Patriots: Political Culture in a Poly-Ethnic African State. Ndiva Kofele-Kale. LC 80-5734. 375p. 1981. lib. bdg. 22.00 (ISBN 0-8191-1395-6); pap. text ed. 12.75 (ISBN 0-8191-1396-4). U Pr of Amer.
Trible Candle. Louise Louis. 74p. 1977. pap. 4.95. Pen-Art.
Tribunals in the Social Services, an Introductory Study. Kathleen Bell. (Library of Social Policy & Administration). 1969. text ed. 6.00x (ISBN 0-7100-6339-3); pap. text ed. 3.00x (ISBN 0-7100-6345-8). Humanities.
Tribute to Don Bernardo De Galvez. Ed. by Ralph L. Woodward, Jr. LC 80-116160. (Illus.). xxviii, 148p. 1979. 14.95x (ISBN 0-917860-04-7). Historic New Orleans.
Tribute to Papa & Other Poems. Mamta Kalia. 8.00 (ISBN 0-89253-691-8); flexible cloth 4.80 (ISBN 0-89253-692-6). Ind-US Inc.
Tribute to Thomas Davis. William B. Yeats. 55p. 1980. Repr. of 1947 ed. lib. bdg. 8.50 (ISBN 0-8492-3121-3). R West.
Tribute to Wolfgang Stechow. Ed. by Walter L. Strauss. LC 75-44736. (Illus.). 29.50 (ISBN 0-87920-002-2). Abaris Bks.
Tribute to Yesterday. Sharron L. Hale. LC 80-50118. (Illus.). 224p. 1980. 25.00 (ISBN 0-913548-73-1, Valley Calif). Western Tanager.
Trichology: The Keystone Guide to Hair Analysis As Related to the Practice of Cosmetology & Barbering. Anthony B. Colletti. (Illus.). 1981. text ed. 11.36 (ISBN 0-912126-57-4). Keystone Pubns.
Trick Book. Charles F. Herrmann, III. Ed. by Pat McCarthy. (Pal Paperbacks Kit B Ser.). (Illus., Orig.). (gr. 7-12). 1974. pap. text ed. 1.25 (ISBN 0-8374-3514-5). Xerox Ed Pubns.
Trick or Treat! Ray Connolly. 1977. pap. 1.75 o.p. (ISBN 0-345-26050-3). Ballantine.
Trick or Treat. Louis Slobodkin. (gr. k-3). 1967. 4.95g o.s.i. (ISBN 0-02-785690-9). Macmillan.
Trick or Treat Halloween. Sharon Peters. (Illus.). 32p. (gr. k-2). 1980. PLB 2.96 (ISBN 0-89375-392-0); pap. 0.95 (ISBN 0-89375-292-4). Troll Assocs.
Trick Photography: Crazy Things You Can Do with Cameras. Robert Fischer. (Illus.). 160p. (gr. 8 up). 1980. 8.95 (ISBN 0-87131-335-9); pap. 4.95 (ISBN 0-87131-335-9). M Evans.
Tricks & Games on the Pool Table. Fred Herrmann. Orig. Title: Fun on the Pool Table, Illustrated. pap. 1.75 (ISBN 0-486-21814-7). Dover.
Tricks of Eye & Mind, the Story of Optical Illusion: The Story of Optical Illusion. Larry Kettelkamp. LC 74-5935. (Illus.). 128p. (gr. 5-9). 1974. PLB 6.96 (ISBN 0-688-31829-0). Morrow.
Tricks: Twenty-Five Encounters. Renaud Camus. 252p. 1981. pap. 10.95 (ISBN 0-312-81823-8). St Martin.
Tricks with Your Fingers. Harry Helfman. (Illus.). (gr. 3-7). 1967. PLB 6.48 (ISBN 0-688-31583-6). Morrow.
Trickster in West Africa: A Study of Mythic Irony & Sacred Delight. Robert D. Pelton. (Hermeneutics: Studies in the History of Religions). 1980. 27.50x (ISBN 0-520-03477-5). U of Cal Pr.
Tricky Ground. Indira Parthasarathy. (Indian Novels Ser.). 191p. 1975. 9.50 (ISBN 0-89253-014-6). Ind-US Inc.
Tricky Troggle. Jim Slater. LC 80-53064. (A. Mazing Monsters Ser.). (Illus.). 1981. pap. 1.25 (ISBN 0-394-84738-5). Random.
Trig Goes Ape. Robert N. Peck. (Illus.). 96p. (gr. 3-6). 1980. 7.95g (ISBN 0-316-69657-9). Little.
Triggerman. Bruno Rossi. (Sharpshooter Ser: No. 11). 1975. pap. 0.95 o.p. (ISBN 0-685-51411-0, LB229NK, Leisure Bks). Nordon Pubns.
Trigonometric Series. A. Zygmund. LC 77-82528. 1977. 79.50 (ISBN 0-521-07477-0). Cambridge U Pr.
Trigonometry. Isidore Dressler & Barnett Rich. (gr. 10-12). 1975. pap. text ed. 5.83 (ISBN 0-87720-219-2). AMSCO Sch.
Trigonometry. Harley Flanders & Justin Price. 235p. 1975. text ed. 15.95 (ISBN 0-12-259667-6); instrs'. manual 3.00 (ISBN 0-12-259670-6). Acad Pr.
Trigonometry. 2nd ed. Margaret L. Lial & Charles D. Miller. 1981. text ed. 16.95x (ISBN 0-673-15432-7). Scott F.
Trigonometry. 2nd ed. Elbridge P. Vance. 1969. 9.95 (ISBN 0-201-08053-2); pap. 7.95 (ISBN 0-686-68494-X). A-W.
Trigonometry: A Complete & Concrete Approach. Harold S. Engelsohn. (Illus.). 1980. text ed. 14.95 (ISBN 0-07-019419-X); instructor's manual avail. (ISBN 0-07-019420-3). McGraw.
Trigonometry: A Modern Approach. Jack Ceder. LC 77-21688. 224p. 1978. text ed. 11.95 (ISBN 0-03-020901-3, HoltC). HR&W.
Trigonometry: A Skills Approach. J. Louis Nanney & John L. Cable. 1979. pap. text ed. 15.25 (ISBN 0-205-06603-8, 5666031); instr's man. o.p. avail. (ISBN 0-205-06608-9). Allyn.
Trigonometry: A Skills Approach, Lecture Version. Nanney & Calbe. 301p. 1980. text ed. 14.65 (ISBN 0-205-06920-7, 5669200); study goide 5.95 (ISBN 0-205-06922-3, 5669200). Allyn.
Trigonometry: A Unitized Approach. Reuben W. Farley et al. (Illus.). 1975. pap. text ed. 15.95 (ISBN 0-13-930909-8). P-H.
Trigonometry at Ordinary Level. L. Harwood Clarke. 1970. pap. text ed. 4.95x o.p. (ISBN 0-435-50207-7). Heinemann Ed.
Trigonometry for College Students. 2nd ed. Karl J. Smith. LC 79-9122. 1980. text ed. 16.95 (ISBN 0-8185-0340-8). Brooks-Cole.
Trigonometry for College Students. Karl J. Smith. LC 76-19454. (Contemporary Undergraduate Mathematics Ser.). (Illus.). 1977. text ed. 14.95 o.p. (ISBN 0-8185-0198-7). Brooks-Cole.
Trigonometry for Today. Robert E. Mosher. 336p. 1976. text ed. 16.95 scp o.p. (ISBN 0-06-044630-7, HarpC); scp study guide 7.50 o.p. (ISBN 0-06-044631-5); instructor's manual free o.p. (ISBN 0-06-364583-1). Har-Row.
Trigonometry: Triangles & Functions. 2nd ed. Mervin L. Keedy & Marvin L. Bittinger. 1978. pap. text ed. 13.95 (ISBN 0-201-03868-4). A-W.
Triiodothyronines in Health & Disease. I. J. Chopra. (Monographs in Endocrinology: Vol. 18). (Illus.). 160p. 1981. 46.00 (ISBN 0-387-10400-3). Springer-Verlag.
Trilateral Commission Task Force Reports: 9-14. LC 78-55063. 1978. 15.00x (ISBN 0-8147-8163-2). NYU Pr.
Trilaterals Over Washington. Antony C. Sutton & Patrick M. Wood. 206p. 1979. pap. 5.95 (ISBN 0-933482-01-9). August Corp.
Trilby. George Du Maurier. 1956. 7.50x (ISBN 0-460-00863-3, Evman); pap. 5.95 (ISBN 0-460-01863-9). Dutton.
Trilingual Dictionary of Fisheries Technological Terms-Curing. (FAO Fisheries Ser.: No. 12). 91p. 1980. pap. 10.25 (ISBN 0-686-68188-6, F483, FAO). Unipub.
Trilogy. H. D., pseud. Incl. The Walls Do Not Fall; Tribute to the Angels; The Flowering of the Rod. LC 73-78848. 128p. 1973. 4.95 (ISBN 0-8112-0490-1); pap. 3.95 (ISBN 0-8112-0491-X, NDP362). New Directions.
Trilogy, 3 vols. Klass Schilder. 1978. 48.00 (ISBN 0-686-12940-7). Klock & Klock.
Trilogy: An Experiment in Multi-Media. Truman Capote et al. (Illus.). 1969. 9.95 (ISBN 0-02-488810-9). Macmillan.
Trilogy: An Experiment in Multimedia. Truman Capote et al. (Illus.). 1971. pap. 2.95 o.s.i. (ISBN 0-02-079340-5, Collier). Macmillan.
Trilogy of Personalities: Chaucer, Milton, Shakespeare, 3 vols. Edward Wagenknecht. 22.50x o.p. (ISBN 0-8061-1268-9). U of Okla Pr.
Trinidad-Tobago. Anthony D. Marshall. LC 75-5527. (First Bks.). (Illus.). (gr. 5-7). 1975. PLB 4.47 o.p. (ISBN 0-531-00835-5). Watts.
Trinitarian Concept of God. Wade H. Horton. 1964. pap. 1.50 (ISBN 0-87148-833-7). Pathway Pr.
Trinity. Karl Rahner. LC 72-87766. 128p. 1970. 5.95 (ISBN 0-8164-1133-6). Crossroad NY.
Trinity. Leon Uris. LC 75-14844. 384p. 1976. 13.95 (ISBN 0-385-03458-X). Doubleday.
Trinity & Duke, 1892-1924: Foundations of Duke University. Earl W. Porter. LC 64-15199. (Illus.). 1964. 9.75 o.p. (ISBN 0-8223-0137-7); pap. 5.75 (ISBN 0-8223-0350-7). Duke.
Trinity & the Kingdom. Jurgen Moltmann. LC 80-8352. 320p. 1981. 15.00 (ISBN 0-06-065906-8, HarpR). Har-Row.
Trinity College Library. P. Gaskell. LC 79-41415. (Illus.). 256p. Date not set. 67.50 (ISBN 0-521-23100-0). Cambridge U Pr.
Trinity Factor. Sean Flannery. 418p. (Orig.). 1981. pap. 2.95 (ISBN 0-441-03298-2). Charter Bks.
Trinity in the Universe. Nathan R. Wood. LC 78-5483. Orig. Title: Secret of the Universe. 1978. Repr. 6.95 (ISBN 0-8254-4013-0). Kregel.
Trinity, or the Tri-Personal Being of God. J. A. Synan. pap. 2.95 (ISBN 0-911866-00-0). Advocate.
Trio for Piano, Violin & Cello. Rebecca Clarke. (Women Composer Ser.). (Illus.). 64p. 1980. 16.95 (ISBN 0-306-76053-3). Da Capo.
Trio in E Minor: Opus Forty Five for Piano, Flute, (Violin) & Cello. Louise Farrenc. (Women Composers Ser.). 1979. Repr. of 1862 ed. 16.95 (ISBN 0-306-79553-1). Da Capo.
Trio of Tales. Elbert Rijnberg. 64p. 1981. 5.00 (ISBN 0-682-49735-5). Exposition.
Trip. Ezra Keats. LC 77-24907. (Illus.). (gr. k-3). 1978. 8.95 (ISBN 0-688-80123-4); PLB 8.59 (ISBN 0-688-84123-6). Greenwillow.
Trip to Italy & France. Lawrence Ferlinghetti. LC 80-36778. 64p. 1981. signed limited ed. 50.00 (ISBN 0-8112-0782-X). New Directions.
Trip to Panama. Janosch. (Illus.). 48p. (ps-3). 1981. 8.95 (ISBN 0-316-45766-3, Atlantic). Little.
Trip to the Moon: Containing an Account of the Island of Noibla, 2 vols. in 1. Francis Gentleman. Ed. by Michael F. Shugrue. (Flowering of the Novel, 1740-1775 Ser.: Vol. 68). 1974. lib. bdg. 50.00 (ISBN 0-8240-1167-8). Garland Pub.
Trip to the Yellowstone National Park in July, August, & September, 1875. W. E. Strong. LC 68-15670. (Western Frontier Library: No. 39). (Illus.). 1968. 4.95 o.p. (ISBN 0-8061-0791-X). U of Okla Pr.
Tripartite Structure of Christopher Marlowe's Tamburlaine Plays & Edward II. Lawrence M. Benaquist. (Salzburg Studies in English Literature; Elizabethan & Renaissance Studies: No. 43). 223p. (Orig.). 1975. pap. text ed. 25.00x (ISBN 0-391-01324-6). Humanities.
Triplanetary. Edward E. Smith. (Lensman Ser.). 1970. pap. 1.75 (ISBN 0-515-05331-7). Jove Pubns.
Triple Exposure. Peter Townend. (Quest Ser.: No. 1). 1979. pap. 1.75 o.p. (ISBN 0-523-40163-9). Pinnacle Bks.
Triple Jump Encyclopedia. Ernie Bullard & Larry Knuth. LC 77-4265. 1977. pap. 8.95 (ISBN 0-87095-057-6). Athletic.
Triple Knowledge: Heidelberg Catechism, 3 Vols. Herman Hoeksema. LC 71-129740. 1972. Set. 29.95 (ISBN 0-8254-2813-0). Kregel.
Triple Secreto Del Espiritu Santo. James H. McConkey. Tr. by Beatrice Agostini from Eng. Orig. Title: Three Fold Secret of the Holy Spirit. 106p. (Span.). Date not set. pap. price not set (ISBN 0-311-09090-7). Casa Bautista.
Tripods Trilogy, 3 bks. John Christopher. Incl. White Mountains; the City of Gold & Lead; Pool of Fire; White Mountains. (gr. 6 up). 1980. Boxed Set. pap. 7.95 (ISBN 0-02-042570-8, Collier). Macmillan.
Tripper, the Sound Hound Book One: The Round Sounds. John H. Butterworth, 3rd. (Illus.). 1981. 4.50 (ISBN 0-533-04390-5). Vantage.
Trips & Trails, 2. 2nd ed. E. M. Sterling. LC 67-26501. (Illus.). 228p. 1978. pap. 6.95 (ISBN 0-916890-13-9). Mountaineers.
Triptych & the Cross: A Key to George Eliot's Poetic Imagination. Felicia Bonaparte. LC 78-20542. 1979. 15.00x (ISBN 0-8147-1012-3); pap. 6.00x (ISBN 0-8147-1013-1). NYU Pr.
Triptych: Three Scenic Panels. Max Frisch. Tr. by Geoffrey Skelton. (Helen & Kurt Wolff Bk.). 1981. 8.95 (ISBN 0-15-191157-6). HarBraceJ.
Trish. Margaret M. Craig. (gr. 7-10). pap. 0.95 o.p. (ISBN 0-425-03180-2, Highland). Berkley Pub.
Tristan. Gottfried Von Strassburg. (Classics Ser). 1960. pap. 3.95 (ISBN 0-14-044098-4). Penguin.
Tristan Corbiere. Robert L. Mitchell. (World Authors Ser.: No. 511). 1979. lib. bdg. 13.50 (ISBN 0-8057-6352-X). Twayne.
Tristan De Luna, Conquistador of the Old South: A Study of Spanish Imperial Strategy. Herbert I. Priestley. (Perspectives in American History Ser.: No. 49). (Illus.). Repr. lib. bdg. 16.00x (ISBN 0-87991-375-4). Porcupine Pr.
Tristan Tzara: Dada & Surrational Theorist. Elmer Peterson. 1971. 17.50 (ISBN 0-8135-0673-5). Rutgers U Pr.
Tristan und Isolt. Gottfried Von Strassburg. Ed. by A. Closs. (Blackwell's German Text Ser.). 1974. pap. 9.95x (ISBN 0-631-01750-X, Pub. by Basil Blackwell). Biblio Dist.
Tristia. Ovid. Tr. by L. R. Lind. LC 73-88363. 177p. 1975. 10.00x (ISBN 0-8203-0330-5). U of Ga Pr.
Tristnam Shandy. Laurence Sterne. pap. 1.95 (ISBN 0-451-51051-8, CJ1051, Sig Classics). NAL.
Tristram Shandy. Laurence Sterne. 1979. 7.00x (ISBN 0-460-00617-7, Evman); pap. 4.95 (ISBN 0-460-01617-2, Evman). Dutton.
Tristram Shandy Notes. Charles Parish. (Orig.). 1968. pap. 2.25 (ISBN 0-8220-1311-8). Cliffs.
Tristram Shandy: The Life & Opinions of Tristram Shandy, Gentleman. Laurence J. Sterne. Ed. by James A. Work. 1940. pap. 7.95 (ISBN 0-672-63128-8). Odyssey Pr.
Triticale: Results & Problems. Arne Muentzig. (Advances in Plant Breeding Ser.: Vol. 10). (Illus.). 103p. (Orig.). 1979. pap. text ed. 35.00 (ISBN 3-489-76210-X). Parey Sci Pubs.

Tritium & Other Environmental Isotopes in the Hydrological Cycle. (Technical Reports: No. 73). 1967. pap. 4.50 (ISBN 92-0-145067-2, IAEA). Unipub.

Tritonian King. L. Sprague De Camp. (Del Rey Bk.). 1977. pap. 1.50 (ISBN 0-345-25803-7, 345-25803-7-150). Ballantine.

Tritton's Guide to Better Wine & Beer Making for Beginners. S. M. Tritton. (Illus., Orig.). 1969. pap. 4.50 (ISBN 0-571-09171-7, Pub. by Faber & Faber). Merrimack Bk Serv.

Triumph of Art for the Public: The Emerging Role of Exhibitions & Critics. Ed. by Elizabeth Gilmore Holt. LC 77-27708. 1979. pap. 5.95 (ISBN 0-385-13511-4, Anch). Doubleday.

Triumph of Bolshevism: Revolution or Reaction? Stuart R. Tompkins. LC 66-22714. (Illus.). 331p. (Orig.). 1967. pap. 7.95x (ISBN 0-8061-1158-5). U of Okla Pr.

Triumph of Conservatism: A Reinterpretation of American History, 1900-1916. Gabriel Kolko. LC 63-16588. 1977. pap. text ed. 7.95 (ISBN 0-02-916650-0). Free Pr.

Triumph of Death. Gabriele D'Annunzio. Tr. by G. Harding. 315p. 1975. Repr. of 1898 ed. 18.00 (ISBN 0-86527-318-9). Fertig.

Triumph of Death & Other Unpublished & Uncollected Poems by Mary Sidney, Countess of Pembroke (1561-1621) G. F. Waller. (Salzburg Studies in English Literature: Elizabethan & Renaissance Studies Ser.: No. 65). 1977. pap. text ed. 25.00x (ISBN 0-391-01554-0). Humanities.

Triumph of Evolution: American Scientists & the Heredity-Environment Controversy, 1900-1941. Hamilton Cravens. LC 77-20570. (Illus.). 1978. 19.95x (ISBN 0-8122-7744-9). U of Pa Pr.

Triumph of Failure, Repr. Of 1899 Ed. Patrick A. Sheehan. Bd. with Flower of Asia. Henry E. Dennehy. Repr. of 1901 ed. LC 75-467. (Victorian Fiction Ser.). 1975. lib. bdg. 66.00 (ISBN 0-8240-1545-2). Garland Pub.

Triumph of Form. Wallace C. Brown. LC 73-13452. 212p. 1973. Repr. of 1948 ed. lib. bdg. 16.50x (ISBN 0-8371-7135-0, BRTF). Greenwood.

Triumph of Horus: An Ancient Egyptian Sacred Drama. Ed. & tr. by H. W. Fairman. 1974. 16.50x (ISBN 0-520-02550-4). U of Cal Pr.

Triumph of Tchaikovsky. John Gee & Elliot Selby. LC 60-15068. (Illus.). 1960. 8.95 (ISBN 0-8149-0103-4). Vanguard.

Triumph of the Body. Ray Stedman. (Orig.). 1981. pap. 3.95 (ISBN 0-88449-041-6). Vision Hse.

Triumph of the Classical. D. Watkin. LC 77-12164. (Illus.). 1977. 16.00 (ISBN 0-521-21854-3); pap. 8.95 (ISBN 0-521-29292-1). Cambridge U Pr.

Triumph or Triage? The World Food Problem in Geographical Persective. C. Gregory Knight & R. Paul Wilcox. Ed. by Salvatore J. Natoli. LC 76-29265. (Resource Papers for College Geography Ser.). 1977. pap. text ed. 4.00 (ISBN 0-89291-115-8). Assn Am Geographers.

Triumph Over Disease: By Fasting & Natural Diet. Jack Goldstein. LC 76-44863. 1978. pap. 2.50 o.p. (ISBN 0-668-04140-4, 4140). Arco.

Triumph Over Tension. Ruth Winter. 1978. pap. 1.50 (ISBN 0-441-82411-0). Charter Bks.

Triumph Over Tragedy. Iona H. McLaughlin. (Festival Ser.). 128p. 1981. pap. 1.50 (ISBN 0-687-42640-5). Abingdon.

Triumph Service-Repair Handbook: TR 7 Series, 1975-1978. Alan Ahlstrand. Ed. by Eric Jorgensen. (Illus.). 1978. pap. 10.95 (ISBN 0-89287-206-3, A211). Clymer Pubns.

Triumph Service-Repair Handbook: TR2-TR6 & GT6, 1954-1976. Brick Price. Ed. by Jeff Robinson. (Illus.). 1976. pap. text ed. 10.95 (ISBN 0-89287-103-2, A210). Clymer Pubns.

Triumph Service Repair Handbook: 500-750cc Twins, 1963-1979. Jim Combs. Ed. by Jeff Robinson. (Illus.). 1979. pap. 9.95 (ISBN 0-89287-195-4, M382). Clymer Pubns.

Triumph Spitfire Owner's Handbook: 1962-1970. Ed. by Clymer Publications. (Illus.). 1971. pap. 8.95 (ISBN 0-89287-254-3, A215). Clymer Pubns.

Triumph Through Tragedy. Robert Lightner. 70p. (Orig.). (gr. 7 up). 1980. pap. 2.00 (ISBN 0-89323-008-1). BMA Pr.

Triumphal Forms, Structural Patterns in Elizabethan Poetry. Alastair Fowler. LC 75-105498. (Illus.). 1970. 42.00 (ISBN 0-521-07747-8). Cambridge U Pr.

Triumphal Sun: A Study of the Works of Jalaloddin Rumi. Annemarie Schimmel. (Illus.). 1978. 27.50 (ISBN 0-87773-750-9). Great Eastern.

Triumphant Journey. Dick Miller. LC 80-10834. (Illus.). 272p. 1980. 13.95 (ISBN 0-03-045331-3). HR&W.

Triumphs of Medicine. Harry Keen & John Jarrett. (Illus.). 1976. 19.95 o.p. (ISBN 0-236-30925-0, Pub. by Paul Elek). Merrimack Bk Serv.

Triumphs of Providence. Jane Garrett. (Illus.). 250p. 1981. 19.50 (ISBN 0-521-23346-1). Cambridge U Pr.

Triunfa En la Vida. A. Pereira Alves. (Illus.). 1977. pap. 1.90 (ISBN 0-311-46033-X). Casa Bautista.

Triuwe & Vriunt in the Nibelungenlied. Francis G. Gentry. Ed. by Cola Minis. (Amsterdamer Publikationen Zur Sprache und Literatur: Vol. 19). 94p. 1975. pap. text ed. 17.25x (ISBN 90-6203-368-7). Humanities.

Trixie Belden & the Mystery of the Velvet Gown. Campbell. lib. bdg. 5.52 (ISBN 0-307-61550-2, Golden Pr); pap. 1.25 (ISBN 0-307-21550-4). Western Pub.

Trixie Belden Gift Set, 3 bks. Kathryn Kenny. (gr. 9 up). Date not set. pap. 3.75 boxed set (ISBN 0-307-13623-X, Golden Pr). Western Pub.

Trobador Pistolta. Pistoleta. Bd. with Trobador Guillem Margret. Guillem Magret. LC 80-2184. 1981. 27.00 (ISBN 0-404-19013-8). AMS Pr.

Trobador Uc Brunec Oder Brunenc: Abhandlungen Herrn Prof. Adolf Tobler. Carl L. Appel. LC 80-2177. 1981. Repr. of 1895 ed. 15.00 (ISBN 0-404-19003-0). AMS Pr.

Troika. David Gurr. 1980. pap. 2.75 (ISBN 0-425-04662-1). Berkley Pub.

Troika: Introduction to Russian Letters & Sounds. Reason A. Goodwin. LC 80-817888. (Orig.). (gr. 11-12). 1980. text ed. 14.50 (ISBN 0-936368-00-4); pap. text ed. 6.95 (ISBN 0-936368-01-2). Lexik Hse.

Troilus & Cressida. William Shakespeare. Ed. by Arthur Quiller-Couch et al. (New Shakespeare Ser). 1969. 23.95 (ISBN 0-521-07560-2); pap. 4.50x (ISBN 0-521-09503-4). Cambridge U Pr.

Troilus & Cressida. William Shakespeare. 1967. pap. text ed. 3.50x o.p. (ISBN 0-471-00542-8). Wiley.

Troilus & Criseyde. Geoffrey Chaucer. Tr. by Nevill Coghill. (Classics Ser). 1971. pap. 2.95 (ISBN 0-14-044239-1). Penguin.

Troilus & Criseyde (Abridged) Geoffrey Chaucer. Ed. by D. S. Brewer & L. E. Brewer. 1977. pap. 7.25 (ISBN 0-7100-8719-5). Routledge & Kegan.

Trois Aspects du francais contemporain. A. Dappagne. (Langue vivante). (Fr). pap. 8.25 (ISBN 0-685-14087-3, 3629). Larousse.

Trois Chansonniers Francais Du XV Siecle. Ed. by Eugenie Droz et al. (Music Reprint Ser., 1978). 1978. lib. bdg. 27.50 (ISBN 0-306-77561-1). Da Capo.

Trois Nouvelles de Georges Simenon. Georges Simenon. Ed. by Frank W. Lindsay & Anthony M. Nazzaro. (gr. 10-12). 1966. pap. text ed. 7.95 o.p. (ISBN 0-13-930917-9). P-H.

Troisieme Defaite Du Proletariat Francais. Benoit Malon. (Commune De Paris En 1871 Ser). 539p. (Fr.). 1977. lib. bdg. 28.75x o.p. (ISBN 0-8287-0565-8); pap. text ed. 18.75x o.p. (ISBN 0-685-75629-7). Clearwater Pub.

Troisieme Proces de l'Association Internationale des Travailleurs a Paris. (Fr.). 1977. lib. bdg. 18.75x o.p. (ISBN 0-8287-0833-9); pap. text ed. 8.75x o.p. (ISBN 0-685-75761-7). Clearwater Pub.

Trojan Heritage: A Pictorial History of USC Football. Mal Florence. LC 80-84556. (Illus.). 184p. 1980. 16.95 (ISBN 0-938694-01-4). JCP Corp VA.

Trojan Horse. Paul Nizan. 1975. Repr. 15.50 (ISBN 0-86527-317-0). Fertig.

Trojan Women. Euripides. Tr. by Gilbert Murray. 1905. pap. text ed. 3.95x (ISBN 0-04-882042-3). Allen Unwin.

Troll Country. Edward Marshall. LC 79-19324. (Easy-to-Read Bk.). (Illus.). (ps-3). 1980. PLB 5.89 (ISBN 0-8037-6211-9); pap. 1.95 (ISBN 0-8037-6210-0). Dial.

Troll Tales. new ed. Corinne Denan. LC 79-66327. (Illus.). 48p. (gr. 2-6). 1980. lib. bdg. 4.89 (ISBN 0-89375-322-X); pap. 1.50 (ISBN 0-89375-321-1). Troll Assocs.

Trolley Trails Through the West: Southern California, Vol. 8. Robert S. Wilson. (Illus., Orig.). 1980. pap. 4.00 (ISBN 0-934944-08-3). Wilson Bros.

Trolleys from the Mines: Street Railways of Centre, Clearfield, Indiana & Jefferson Counties, Pennsylvania. Richard C. Albert. (Illus.). 100p. (Orig.). 1980. pap. 9.00 (ISBN 0-911940-32-4). Cox.

Trolleys to the Surf. William Myers & Ira Swett. LC 76-9685. (Special Ser.: No. 63). (Illus.). 1976. 13.75 (ISBN 0-916374-22-X). Interurban.

Trollope Critics. Ed. by N. John Hall. 1981. 28.50x (ISBN 0-389-20044-1). B&N.

Trollope in the Post Office. Robert H. Super. 1981. text ed. 10.00 (ISBN 0-472-10013-0). U of Mich Pr.

Trollope's Later Novels. Robert Tracy. LC 76-55572. 1978. 17.50x (ISBN 0-520-03407-4). U of Cal Pr.

Trombone Technique. Denis Wick. 160p. 1971. pap. 7.75 (ISBN 0-19-318704-3). Oxford U Pr.

Tropes and Figures: A Psychological Study of Henry David Thoreau. Raymond Gozzi. LC 80-2506. 1981. 62.50 (ISBN 0-404-19054-5). AMS Pr.

Trophees. Heredia. Ed. by W. N. Ince. (French Poets Ser.). 1979. text ed. 25.00x (ISBN 0-485-14709-2, Athlone Pr); pap. text ed. 11.25x (ISBN 0-485-12709-1). Humanities.

Tropic Death. Eric Walrond. 192p. 1972. pap. 1.95 o.s.i. (ISBN 0-02-055250-5, Collier). Macmillan.

Tropic Sun: Kipling & the Raj. 5th ed. K. Jamiluddin. 1975. 10.00x o.p. (ISBN 0-88386-950-0). South Asia Bks.

Tropica: Color Cyclopedia of Exotic Plants. Alfred B. Graf. (Illus.). 1978. 115.00x (ISBN 0-684-15568-0, ScribT). Scribner.

Tropica: Color Encyclopedia of Exotic Plants. 2nd ed. Alfred B. Graf. LC 77-82461. (Illus.). 1981. 115.00x (ISBN 0-911266-16-X). Roehrs.

Tropical American Plant Disease. Frederick L. Wellman. LC 71-175527. (Neotropical Phytopathology Problems). (Illus.). 1972. 32.50 (ISBN 0-8108-0459-X). Scarecrow.

Tropical & Subtropical Fruits. Ed. by Steven Nagy & Philip E. Shaw. (Illus.). 1980. lib. bdg. 45.00 (ISBN 0-87055-350-X). AVI.

Tropical Architecture in the Dry & Humid Zones. 2nd ed. Maxwell Fry & Jane Drew. 1980. lib. bdg. 22.50 (ISBN 0-89874-126-2). Krieger.

Tropical Butterflies: The Ecology & Behaviour of Butterflies in the Tropics with Special Reference to African Species. D. F. Owen. (Illus.). 1971. 34.95x (ISBN 0-19-857351-0). Oxford U Pr.

Tropical Climate & Its Influence on Rice. (IRRI Research Paper Ser.: No. 20). 25p. 1979. pap. 5.00 (R060, IRRI). Unipub.

Tropical Crops: Monocotyledons, Vol. 3. J. W. Purseglove. 1972-73. Pt. 2. 18.95 (ISBN 0-471-70242-0). Halsted Pr.

Tropical Crops: Monocotyledons, Vol 3, Pts. 1 & 2. J. W. Purseglove. LC 68-16628. 607p. 1972. pap. 38.95 (ISBN 0-470-70228-1). Halsted Pr.

Tropical Deco: The Architecture & Design of Old Miami Beach. Laura Cerwinske. LC 80-51596. (Illus.). 96p. (Orig.). 1981. pap. 14.95 (ISBN 0-8478-0345-7). Rizzoli Intl.

Tropical Diseases: Responses of Pharmaceutical Companies. Jack N. Behrman. 1980. pap. 4.25 (ISBN 0-8447-3393-8). Am Enterprise.

Tropical Enterprise: Standard Fruit & Steamship Company in Latin America. Thomas Karnes. LC 78-9641. 1979. 20.00x (ISBN 0-8071-0395-0). La State U Pr.

Tropical Exports & Economic Development. Barbara Ingham. Date not set. 22.50 (ISBN 0-312-81918-8). St Martin.

Tropical Fish. Derek McInerny. LC 76-10815. (Illus.). 1976. bds. 2.25 o.p. (ISBN 0-668-03991-4). Arco.

Tropical Fish. Loren P. Woods. LC 74-118956. (Beginning-to-Read Bks). (Illus.). (gr. 2-4). 1971. PLB 2.97 o.p. (ISBN 0-695-40175-0); pap. 1.50 o.p. (ISBN 0-695-30175-6). Follett.

Tropical Fish for Beginners. Herbert R. Axelrod. (Illus.). 1972. 4.95 (ISBN 0-87666-752-3, PS-304). TFH Pubns.

Tropical Fish Identifier. Braz Walker. LC 76-126851. (Illus.). 256p. 1981. pap. 6.95 (ISBN 0-8069-8968-8). Sterling.

Tropical Fish in Your Home. Herbert Axelrod & W. Vorderwinkler. LC 56-7698. (gr. 10 up). 8.95 (ISBN 0-8069-3710-6); PLB 8.29 (ISBN 0-8069-3711-4). Sterling.

Tropical Fish in Your Home. Herbert R. Axelrod & William Vorderwinkler. (Illus.). 144p. 1973. pap. 2.25 (ISBN 0-06-463356-X, E*H 356, EH). Har-Row.

Tropical Fish: Their Care & Breeding. May. (Illus.). 96p. 1981. 3.95 (ISBN 0-903264-23-4, 5216-3, Pub. by K & R Bks England). Arco.

Tropical Forest Trees: Variation Breeding & Conservation. Ed. by J. Burley & B. T. Styles. 1976. 34.00 o.s.i. (ISBN 0-12-145150-X). Acad Pr.

Tropical Fruits. J. A. Samson. LC 74-40498. (Tropical Agriculture Ser.). (Illus.). 288p. 1980. lib. bdg. 38.00 (ISBN 0-582-46032-8). Longman.

Tropical Gardening Along the Gulf Coast. Gerald Arp. LC 78-53815. (Illus.). 1978. pap. 3.95 (ISBN 0-88415-883-7). Pacesetter Pr.

Tropical Geomorphology: A Study of Weathering & Land Form Development in Warm Climates. Michael F. Thomas. LC 73-13428. 1976. pap. 12.95 (ISBN 0-470-98939-4). Halsted Pr.

Tropical Grazing Land Ecosystems. (Natural Resources Research Ser.: No. 16). 655p. 1980. pap. 64.75 (ISBN 92-3-101611-3, U-999, UNESCO). Unipub.

Tropical Health Science. 2nd ed. D. T. Hughes & P. T. Marshall. LC 73-84315. (Illus.). 160p. 1974. pap. text ed. 8.50x (ISBN 0-521-20304-X). Cambridge U Pr.

Tropical Marine Invertebrates of Southern Florida & the Bahama Islands. Warren Zeiller. LC 74-2467. (Illus.). 144p. 1974. 32.95x (ISBN 0-471-98153-2, Pub. by Wiley-Interscience). Wiley.

Tropical Mycorrhiza Research. Ed. by Peitsa Mikola. 288p. 1980. 45.00x (ISBN 0-19-854553-3). Oxford U Pr.

Tropical Nature Study. R. H. Stone. 9.95 (ISBN 0-521-06559-3). Cambridge U Pr.

Tropical Pasture & Fodder Plants. A. V. Bogdan. LC 76-14977. (Tropical Agriculture Ser.). (Illus.). 1977. text ed. 48.00x (ISBN 0-582-46676-8). Longman.

Tropical Plant Types. B. G. Jamieson & J. F. Reynolds. 1967. 29.00 (ISBN 0-08-012119-5); pap. 17.00 (ISBN 0-08-012120-9). Pergamon.

Tropical Pulses. J. Smartt. (Tropical Agriculture Ser.). (Illus.). 1976. text ed. 36.00x (ISBN 0-582-46679-2). Longman.

Tropical Rain Forest. Paul W. Richards. LC 79-50507. (Illus.). 1952. 65.50 (ISBN 0-521-06079-6); pap. 22.50 (ISBN 0-521-29658-7). Cambridge U Pr.

Tropical Soils & Soil Survey. A. Young. LC 75-19573. (Geographical Studies: No. 9). 1976. 65.50 (ISBN 0-521-21054-2). Cambridge U Pr.

Tropical Soils & Soil Survey. A. Young. LC 75-19573. (Cambridge Geographical Studies: No. 9). 468p. Date not set. pap. 15.95 (ISBN 0-521-29768-0). Cambridge U Pr.

Tropical Trees As Living Systems. Ed. by P. B. Tomlinson & M. H. Zimmermann. LC 77-8579. (Illus.). 1978. 75.00 (ISBN 0-521-21686-9). Cambridge U Pr.

Tropical World: Its Social & Economic Conditions & Its Future Status. 4th ed. Pierre Gourou. Tr. by S. H. Beaver & E. D. Laborde. (Geography for Advanced Study Ser.). (Illus.). 200p. 1974. pap. 11.95 o.p. (ISBN 0-470-31919-4). Halsted Pr.

Tropospheric Transport of Pollutants & Natural Substances to the Ocean. Ocean Science Board. 1978. pap. 11.75 (ISBN 0-309-02735-7). Natl Acad Pr.

Tropospheric Waves, Jet Streams & United States Weather Patterns. J. F. Harman. LC 77-182881. (CCG Resource Papers Ser.: No. 11). (Illus.). 1971. pap. text ed. 4.00 (ISBN 0-89291-058-5). Assn Am Geographers.

Trotsky. Ed. by Irving H. Smith. (Great Lives Observed Ser). 192p. 1973. pap. 2.45 o.p. (ISBN 0-13-930966-7, Spec). P-H.

Trotsky: Fate of a Revolutionary. Robert Wistrich. LC 80-6163. 235p. 1981. 14.95 (ISBN 0-8128-2774-0). Stein & Day.

Trotsky: Fate of a Revolutionary. Robert Wistrich. 235p. 1980. 19.00x (ISBN 0-8476-3105-2). Rowman.

Troubador: An American Autobiography. Alfred Kreyemborg. 1957. pap. 1.75 o.p. (ISBN 0-8090-0022-9, AmCen). Hill & Wang.

Troubador Revival: A Study of Social Change & Traditionalism in Late Medieval Spain. Roger Boase. (Illus.). 1978. 28.00 (ISBN 0-7100-8956-2). Routledge & Kegan.

Troubadour Raimon Jordan Vicomte De Saint-Antonin. Raimon Jordan. LC 80-2189. Repr. of 1922 ed. 25.00 (ISBN 0-404-19017-0). AMS Pr.

Troubadours & Courts of Love. John R. Rowbotham. LC 68-22048. 1969. Repr. of 1895 ed. 15.00 (ISBN 0-8103-3840-8). Gale.

Troubadours & Eloquence. Linda M. Paterson. 244p. 1975. 36.00x (ISBN 0-19-815711-8). Oxford U Pr.

Troubadours & Love. L. T. Topsfield. LC 74-14440. (Illus.). 304p. 1975. 42.00 (ISBN 0-521-20596-4); pap. 11.95x (ISBN 0-521-09897-1). Cambridge U Pr.

Trouble at Choctaw Bend. Dan James. (YA) 1972. 5.95 (ISBN 0-685-28626-6, Avalon). Bouregy.

Trouble at Goodewoode Manor. Linda Heller. LC 80-27417. (Illus.). 32p. (gr. k-3). 1981. PLB 8.95 (ISBN 0-02-743570-9). Macmillan.

Trouble at Home. Sara Gilbert. 192p. (gr. 7 up). 1981. 7.95 (ISBN 0-688-41995-X); PLB 7.63 (ISBN 0-688-51995-4). Morrow.

Trouble Book. E. Kennedy. 1977. pap. 3.50 (ISBN 0-346-12287-2). Cornerstone.

Trouble Book. Eugene Kennedy. 1976. 10.95 (ISBN 0-88347-064-0). Thomas More.

Trouble for Tallon. John Ball. LC 80-1983. (Crime Club Ser.). 192p. 1981. 9.95 (ISBN 0-385-17329-6). Doubleday.

Trouble in Form Six. Cyprian O. Ekwensi. 1966. text ed. 2.95x (ISBN 0-521-04884-2). Cambridge U Pr.

Trouble in Paradise. Zuleyka Benitez. Intro. by C. D. Wright. (Lost Roads Ser.: No. 19). (Illus.). 56p. (Orig.). 1980. pap. 9.00 (ISBN 0-918786-20-7). Lost Roads.

Trouble in Thor. Charlotte Armstrong. 1977. pap. 1.50 o.p. (ISBN 0-425-03631-6, Medallion). Berkley Pub.

Trouble Is My Business. Raymond Chandler. pap. 2.25 (ISBN 0-345-27671-X). Ballantine.

Trouble Is My Business. Jay Flynn. 1976. pap. 1.25 o.p. (ISBN 0-685-72358-5, LB384ZK, Leisure Bks). Nordon Pubns.
Trouble River. Betsy Byars. (gr. 5-9). 1975. pap. 1.50 (ISBN 0-380-00345-7, 47001, Camelot). Avon.
Trouble Trail. Max Brand. 1972. pap. 1.95 (ISBN 0-446-90314-0). Warner Bks.
Trouble Twisters. Poul Anderson. pap. 1.25 o.p. (ISBN 0-425-03245-0). Berkley Pub.
Trouble with Jenny's Ear. Oliver Butterworth. (Illus.). (gr. 4-6). 1960. 8.95 (ISBN 0-316-11907-5, Pub. by Atlantic Monthly Pr). Little.
Trouble with Lichen. John Wyndham. 1977. pap. 1.50 o.p. (ISBN 0-345-25847-9). Ballantine.
Trouble with Magic. Chew. (ps-3). pap. 1.50 (ISBN 0-590-10343-1, Schol Pap). Schol Bk Serv.
Trouble with Nowadays: A Curmudgeon Strikes Back. Cleveland Amory. 272p. 1981. pap. 6.95 (ISBN 0-345-29720-2). Ballantine.
Trouble with Rape: A Psychologist's Report on the Legal, Medical, Social, & Psychological Problems. Carolyn J. Hursch. LC 76-28757. (Illus.). 1977. 12.95 (ISBN 0-88229-323-0); pap. 6.95 (ISBN 0-88229-470-9). Nelson-Hall.
Trouble with Thirteen. Betty Miles. (gr. 3-7). 1980. pap. 1.95 (ISBN 0-380-51136-3, 51136, Camelot). Avon.
Trouble with Tickle the Tiger. Norman Habel. LC 56-1218. (Purple Puzzle Tree Bk). (Illus.). (ps-5). 1972. pap. 0.85 (ISBN 0-570-06514-3). Concordia.
Trouble with Tribbles. David Gerrold. pap. 2.25 (ISBN 0-345-27671-X). Ballantine.
Trouble with You Earth People. Katherine MacClean. Ed. by Polly Freas & Kelly Freas. LC 79-15246. (Illus.). 1980. pap. 4.95 (ISBN 0-915442-95-7, Starblaze). Donning Co.
Troubled Campus: Current Issues in Higher Education 1970. Ed. by G. Kerry Smith. LC 71-128700. (Higher Education Ser.). 1970. 12.95x o.p. (ISBN 0-87589-078-4). Jossey-Bass.
Troubled Detente. Albert Weeks. LC 75-27166. 1976. 12.00 (ISBN 0-8147-9166-2). NYU Pr.
Troubled Philosopher: John Dewey & the Struggle for World Peace. Charles F. Howlett. 1977. 15.00 (ISBN 0-8046-9153-3). Kennikat.
Troubled Vision: An Anthology of Contemporary Short Novels & Passages. Ed. by Jerome Charyn. 1970. pap. 2.95 o.s.i. (ISBN 0-02-049370-3, Collier). Macmillan.
Troubled Waters. Peter H. Fine. 192p. (Orig.). 1981. pap. 1.95 (ISBN 0-523-41213-4). Pinnacle Bks.
Troubled Waters. Alice S. Watson. 6.95 (ISBN 0-8062-1587-9). Carlton.
Troubled Waters. Maurice Wiggin. 10.95x (ISBN 0-392-06465-0, SpS). Soccer.
Troublemaker. Lynn Hall. LC 74-78455. (Illus.). 96p. (gr. 3-6). 1974. 4.95 o.p. (ISBN 0-695-80479-0); lib. bdg. 4.98 o.p. (ISBN 0-695-40479-2). Follett.
Troublemaker. Lynn Hall. (Illus.). (gr. 3-5). 1975. pap. 1.25 o.s.i. (ISBN 0-380-00434-8, 26203, Camelot). Avon.
Troubles. Naomi May. 1979. 11.95 (ISBN 0-7145-3555-9); pap. 5.95 (ISBN 0-7145-3606-7). Riverrun NY.
Troubles with Bird Dogs & What to Do About Them: Training Experiences with Actual Dogs Under the Gun. George Bird Evans. (Illus.). 1975. 12.95 (ISBN 0-87691-204-8). Winchester Pr.
Troubleshooting Solid State Circuits. George C. Loveday & Arthur H. Seidman. LC 80-21954. 112p. 1981. pap. text ed. 7.95 (ISBN 0-471-08371-2). Wiley.
Troubleshooting with the Oscilloscope. 3rd ed. Robert G. Middleton. LC 74-15456. (Illus.). 1975. 5.95 o.p. (ISBN 0-672-21103-3). Sams.
Troubleshooting with the Oscilloscope. 4th ed. Robert G. Middleton. LC 80-51719. 1980. 9.95 (ISBN 0-672-21738-4). Sams.
Troublesome Children in Class. Irene E. Caspari. (Students Library of Education). 130p. 1975. 14.00x (ISBN 0-7100-8261-4); pap. 7.50 (ISBN 0-7100-8262-2). Routledge & Kegan.
Troublesome Raigne of John King of England. Ed. by J. W. Sider & Stephen Orgel. LC 78-66778. (Renaissance Drama Ser.). 1979. lib. bdg. 31.00 (ISBN 0-8240-9733-5). Garland Pub.
Trousered Apes: The Influence of Literature on Contemporary Society. Duncan Williams. 160p. 1972. 6.95 o.p. (ISBN 0-87000-182-5). Arlington Hse.
Trout. Ray Bergman & Edward C. Janes. 1976. 15.00 (ISBN 0-394-49957-3); pap. 9.95 (ISBN 0-394-73144-1). Knopf.
Trout & How to Catch Them. Kenneth Mansfield. 1978. 4.95 o.p. (ISBN 0-214-20234-8, 8005, Dist. by Arco). Barrie & Jenkins.
Trout & Salmon Culture (Hatchery Methods) Earl Leitritz & Robert C. Lewis. (Illus.). 1980. pap. 5.00x (ISBN 0-931876-36-2, 4100). Ag Sci Pubns.
Trout & Salmon Fishing. Roy Eaton. LC 80-68897. (Illus.). 192p. 1981. 22.50 (ISBN 0-7153-8117-2). David & Charles.
Trout & Salmon Fly Index. Dick Surette. LC 78-24196. (Illus.). 128p. 1979. pap. 9.95 (ISBN 0-8117-2093-4). Stackpole.
Trout & the Fly. Brian Clarke & John Goddard. LC 80-493. 1980. 20.00 (ISBN 0-385-17141-2, NLB). Doubleday.
Trout & the Fly. Ray Ovington. 1977. 9.95 o.p. (ISBN 0-8015-7982-1, Hawthorn); pap. 5.95 (ISBN 0-8015-7983-X, Hawthorn). Dutton.
Trout Farming Manual. John P. Stevenson. 1980. 60.75x (ISBN 0-686-64739-4, Pub. by Fishing News England). State Mutual Bk.
Trout Farming Manual. John P. Stevenson. (Illus.). 1980. text ed. 26.50x (ISBN 0-85238-102-6). Scholium Intl.
Trout Fishing the Southern Appalachians. J. Wayne Fears. LC 79-1277. (Illus.). 192p. 1979. lib. bdg. 10.25 o.p. (ISBN 0-914788-10-8). East Woods.
Trout Flies: Naturals & Imitations. Charles M. Wetzel. (Illus.). 154p. 1979. 15.00 (ISBN 0-8117-1739-9). Stackpole.
Trout from the Hills. Ian Neill. 10.00x (ISBN 0-392-06403-0, SpS). Soccer.
Trout Hunting. Frank Woolner. 1977. 12.95 (ISBN 0-87691-196-3). Winchester Pr.
Trout, the Whole Trout, & Nothing but the Trout: Solemnly Sworn Testimony on America's No. 1 Gamefish & How to Hook Him. John D. Shingleton. (Illus.). 144p. 1974. 7.95 (ISBN 0-87691-138-6). Winchester Pr.
Trouveres et Protecteurs De Trouveres Dans les Cours Seigneuriales De France. Holgern. Petersen-Dyggve. LC 80-2168. 1981. Repr. of 1942 ed. 41.50 (ISBN 0-404-19032-4). AMS Pr.
Trova. Udo Kultermann. LC 77-1915. (Contemporary Artist Ser.). (Illus.). 1978. 65.00 o.p. (ISBN 0-8109-0502-7); ltd. ed. signed 600.00 o.p. (ISBN 0-686-68042-1). Abrams.
Troy. M. Millard. 4.50 o.p. (ISBN 0-8062-1074-5). Carlton.
Troy State University: Nineteen Thirty-Seven to Nineteen Seventy, Troy Alabama. Charles B. Smith. (Illus.). 1972. pap. 3.50 (ISBN 0-916624-34-X). TSU Pr.
TRS-Eighty Disk! And Other Mysteries. Harvard C. Pennington. (TRS-80 Information Ser.: Vol. 1). (Illus.). 133p. (Orig.). 1979. pap. 22.50 (ISBN 0-936200-00-6). IJG Inc.
TRS-80 Assembly Language. Hubert S. Howe, Jr. (Illus.). 192p. 1981. text ed. 15.95 (ISBN 0-13-931139-4, Spec); pap. text ed. 6.95 (ISBN 0-13-931121-1, Spec). P-H.
Truants from Life: The Rehabilitation of Emotionally Disturbed Children. Bruno Bettelheim. LC 55-7331. 1955. 15.95 (ISBN 0-02-903440-X); pap. 4.95 (ISBN 0-02-903450-7). Free Pr.
Trubner's Bibliographical Guide to American Literature. Nikolaus Trubner. 1966. Repr. of 1859 ed. 32.00 (ISBN 0-8103-3315-5). Gale.
Trucial States. Donald Hawley. (Illus.). 379p. 1970. text ed. 24.50x (ISBN 0-686-66022-6); pap. text ed. 12.95x (ISBN 0-8290-0454-8). Irvington.
Truck Book. (Golden Play & Learn Bk.). (ps). Date not set. pap. 2.95 (ISBN 0-307-10738-8, Golden Pr). Western Pub.
Truck Book. (Sturdy Shape Bks.). (Illus.). 14p. (ps). 1980. 2.95 (ISBN 0-307-12255-7, Golden Pr). Western Pub.
Truck Book. Robert L. Wolfe. LC 80-15683. (Illus.). 32p. (ps-3). 1981. PLB 5.95 (ISBN 0-87614-125-4). Carolrhoda Bks.
Truck Drivers in America. D. Daryl Wyckoff. LC 78-24793. (Illus.). 1979. 16.95 (ISBN 0-669-02818-5). Lexington Bks.
Truck Facts Buyer's Guide, 1981. rev. ed. Ed. by Michael Green. 96p. (Orig.). write for info. DMR Pubns.
Truck Transport (Wayside Amenities) 88p. 1980. pap. 12.00 (ISBN 92-833-1457-3, APO 84, APO). Unipub.
Truck Transportation. Boy Scouts of America. LC 19-600. (Illus.). 32p. (gr. 6-12). 1973. pap. 0.70x (ISBN 0-8395-3371-3, 3371). BSA.
Trucking: A Truck Driver's Training Handbook. Ken Gilliland & J. Millard. Ed. by S. Michele McFadden. LC 79-90760. 1981. pap. 19.50x (ISBN 0-89262-025-0). Career Pub.
Trucking: A Truck Driver's Workbook. Ken Gilliland & J. Millard. Ed. by S. Michele McFadden. 1981. pap. text ed. 16.50 (ISBN 0-89262-029-3). Career Pub. Postponed.
Trucking: Instructor's Guide. Ken Gilliland & J. Millard. Ed. by S. Michele McFadden. 1981. pap. text ed. 12.50 (ISBN 0-89262-030-7). Career Pub. Postponed.
Trucks. Herbert S. Zim & James R. Skelly. LC 75-107973. (Illus.). (gr. 3-7). 1974. PLB 6.48 (ISBN 0-688-31565-8); pap. 1.25 (ISBN 0-688-26565-0). Morrow.
Trucks: An Illustrated History 1892-1921. G. N. Georgano & Carlo Demand. (Illus.). 1978. 24.95 (ISBN 0-8467-0500-1, Pub. by Two Continents). Hippocrene Bks.
Trucks & Vans Before 1927. Prince Marshall. (Illus.). 150p. 1972. 8.95 (ISBN 0-02-580190-2). Macmillan.
Trucks at the Track. Aille X. West. (Pal Paperbacks, - Pal Skills II Ser.). (Illus.). (gr. 5-12). 1980. pap. text ed. 1.25 (ISBN 0-8374-6806-X). Xerox Ed Pubns.
Trucks of the Sixties & Seventies. Nick Baldwin. (Warne's Transport Library). (Illus.). 1980. 10.95 (ISBN 0-7232-2364-5). Warne.
Trucks of the World Highways. Ed. by Arthur Ingram. (Illus.). 1979. 17.50 (ISBN 0-7137-0994-4, Pub by Blandford Pr England). Sterling.
Trucks That Haul by Night. Leonard A. Stevens. LC 66-10066. (Illus.). (gr. k-3). 1966. 7.89 (ISBN 0-690-83743-7, TYC-J). T Y Crowell.
Trucks, Trucking, & You. Hope I. Marston. LC 78-7725. (Illus.). (gr. 5 up). 1978. 6.95 (ISBN 0-396-07602-5). Dodd.
Trudeau Decade. Rick Butler & Jean-Guy Carrier. LC 78-22730. 1979. 16.95 o.p. (ISBN 0-385-14806-2); pap. 9.95 (ISBN 0-385-15543-3). Doubleday.
True & False Universality of Christianity, Concilium 135. Ed. by Claude Geffre & Jean-Pierre Jossua. (New Concilium 1980). 128p. 1980. pap. 5.95 (ISBN 0-8245-4768-3). Crossroad NY.
True & Scandalous History of Howe & Hummel. Richard H. Rovere. (Illus.). 190p. 1979. pap. 5.95 (ISBN 0-89062-093-8, Pub. by Hughes Press). Pub Ctr Cult Res.
True Authorship of the New Testament. Abelard Reuchlin. 1979. pap. 2.00. Vector Assocs.
True Book of the Moon Ride Rock Hunt. Margaret Friskey. LC 72-1457. (True Bks). (Illus.). 48p. (gr. 3-5). 1972. PLB 8.65 o.p. (ISBN 0-516-01144-8). Childrens.
True Bounds of Christian Freedom. 1978. pap. 3.95 (ISBN 0-85151-083-3). Banner of Truth.
True Britt. Britt Ekland. (Illus.). 242p. 1981. 9.95 (ISBN 0-13-931089-4). P-H.
True Confession of the Faith, Which Wee Falsley Called Brownists, Doo Hold. Henry Ainsworth. LC 78-26338. (English Experience Ser.: No. 158). 24p. 1969. Repr. of 1956 ed. 7.00 (ISBN 90-221-0158-4). Walter J Johnson.
True Copie of a Discourse Written by a Gentleman, Employed in the Late Voyage of Spaine & Portingale. Robert Devereux & Anthony Wingfield. LC 78-38172. (English Experience Ser.: No. 449). 1972. Repr. of 1589 ed. 9.50 (ISBN 90-221-0449-4). Walter J Johnson.
True Discipleship. enl. ed. William MacDonald. 58p. pap. 1.95 (ISBN 0-937396-50-8). Walterick Pubs.
True Doctrine of Ultra Vires in the Law of Corporations, Being a Concise Presentation of the Doctrine in Its Application to the Powers & Liabilities of Private & Municipal Corporations. Reuben A. Reese. lxxi, 338p. 1981. Repr. of 1897 ed. lib. bdg. 30.00x (ISBN 0-8377-1031-6). Rothman.
True Escape & Survival Stories. Gurney Williams. LC 77-1421. (Illus.). (gr. 4-6). 1977. PLB 6.90 (ISBN 0-531-00119-9). Watts.
True Founder of Christianity & the Hellenistic Philosophy. Max Rieser. 1980. text ed. 14.25x (ISBN 90-6296-081-2). Humanities.
True Francine. Marc Brown. (Illus.). 32p. (gr. 1-3). 1981. 8.95 (ISBN 0-316-11212-7, Atlantic). Little.
True Ghost Stories. Ed. by Pat McCarthy. (Pal Paperbacks Kit A Ser.). (Illus., Orig.). (gr. 7-12). 1974. pap. text ed. 1.25 (ISBN 0-8374-3478-5). Xerox Ed Pubns.
True Ghost Stories. Isabella Taves. (Illus.). (gr. 5 up). 1978. PLB 6.90 s&l (ISBN 0-531-02225-0). Watts.
True Grit. Charles Portis. (RL 8). pap. 1.25 (ISBN 0-451-05419-9, Y5419, Sig). NAL.
True History of Joshua Davidson, 1872. Eliza L. Linton. Ed. by Robert L. Wolff. LC 75-1524. (Victorian Fiction Ser). 1975. lib. bdg. 66.00 (ISBN 0-8240-1596-7). Garland Pub.
True History of the Captivity & Restoration of Mrs. Mary Rowlandson, Repr. Of 1682 Ed. Bd. with Humiliations Follow'd with Deliverances...with a Narrative, of a Notable Delivarance Lately Recieved by Some English Captives, from the Hands of Cruel Indians. Cotton Mather. Repr. of 1697 ed. LC 75-7020. (Indian Captivities Ser.: Vol. 1). 1977. lib. bdg. 44.00 (ISBN 0-8240-1625-4). Garland Pub.
True History of the Elephant Man. Michael Howell & Peter Ford. 1980. pap. 2.95 (ISBN 0-14-005622-X). Penguin.
True Intellectual System of the Universe, 2 vols. Ralph Cudworth. Ed. by Rene Wellek. LC 75-11213. (British Philosophers & Theologians of the 17th & 18th Centuries Ser.: Vol. 16). 1978. Repr. of 1678 ed. Set. lib. bdg. 76.00 (ISBN 0-8240-1767-6); lib. bdg. 42.00 ea. Garland Pub.
True Life of Billy the Kid. Edmund Fable. LC 80-18408. 75p. (Orig.). 1980. Repr. 19.95 (ISBN 0-932702-11-2); collector's edition 75.00. Creative Texas.
True Likeness: An Anthology of Lesbian and Gay Writing Today. Ed. by Felice Picano. 320p. 1980. pap. 9.95 (ISBN 0-933322-04-6). Sea Horse.
True Love & Perfect Union: The Feminist Reform of Sex & Society. William Leach. LC 80-50557. 320p. 1980. 17.50 (ISBN 0-465-08752-3). Basic.
True Men. Mary Q. Steele. LC 76-5482. (gr. 5-9). 1976. 8.25 (ISBN 0-688-80052-1); PLB 7.92 (ISBN 0-688-84052-3). Greenwillow.
True Mother Goose. Illus. by Eulalie. LC 79-1948. (Illus.). (ps-2). 1979. 1.95 (ISBN 0-525-69004-2, Gingerbread Bks); PLB 5.95 (ISBN 0-525-69005-0, Gingerbread Bks.). Dutton.
True Ocean Found: Paludanus's Letters on Dutch Voyages to the Kara Sea, 1595-1596. Ed. by James D. Tracy. LC 80-13962. (Publication from the James Ford Bell Library at the University of Minnesota). (Illus.). 1980. 10.00x (ISBN 0-8166-0961-6). U of Minn Pr.
True Order & Method of Wryting & Reading Hystories. Thomas Blundeville. LC 79-84088. (English Experience Ser.: No. 908). 68p. (Eng.). 1979. Repr. of 1574 ed. lib. bdg. 7.00 (ISBN 90-221-0908-9). Walter J Johnson.
True Prayer: An Invitation to Christian Spirituality. Kenneth Leech. 208p. 1981. 9.95 (ISBN 0-06-065227-6, HarpR). Har-Row.
True Relation of the Lives & Deaths of the Two English Pyrats, Purser & Clinton. LC 77-171784. (English Experience Ser.: No. 408). 1971. Repr. of 1639 ed. 7.00 (ISBN 90-221-0408-7). Walter J Johnson.
True Relation of the Unjust Proceedings Against the English of Amboyna. LC 72-228. (English Experience Ser.: No. 306). 38p. Repr. of 1624 ed. 14.00 (ISBN 90-221-0306-4). Walter J Johnson.
True Reporte of the Late Discoueries of the Newfound Landes. Sir George Peckham. LC 78-25630. (English Experience Ser.: No. 341). 1971. Repr. of 1583 ed. 11.50 (ISBN 90-221-0341-2). Walter J Johnson.
True Reporte of the Successe Which God Gave Unto Our Elnglish Souldiours in Ireland, 1580. LC 72-6016. (English Experience Ser.: No. 541). 1973. Repr. of 1581 ed. 5.00 (ISBN 90-221-0541-5). Walter J Johnson.
True Service. Harold Cooper. (Illus.). 110p. 1978. pap. text ed. 1.50 (ISBN 0-89114-081-6); tchrs. ed. 1.25 (ISBN 0-89114-082-4). Baptist Pub Hse.
True Stories from the Moscow Zoo. Vera Chaplina. Tr. by Estelle Titiev & Lila Pargment. (Illus.). (gr. 5 up). 1970. PLB 4.50 o.p. (ISBN 0-13-930990-X). P-H.
True Stories of New England Captives Carried to Canada During the Old French & Indian Wars. Charlotte A. Baker. LC 75-7128. (Indian Captivities Ser.: Vol. 101). 1976. Repr. of 1897 ed. lib. bdg. 44.00 (ISBN 0-8240-1725-0). Garland Pub.
True Story of Ah Q. 1969. pap. 1.95 (ISBN 0-8351-0408-7). China Bks.
True Tragedy of Herod & Antipater. Gervase Markham & Willliam Sampson. Ed. by Gordon N. Ross & Stephen Orgel. LC 78-66833. (Renaissance Drama Ser.). 1979. lib. bdg. 28.00 (ISBN 0-8240-9734-3). Garland Pub.
True Transcript of His Majesties Letters Patent for the Publicke Register for General Commerce. LC 74-80219. (English Experience Ser.: No. 655). 1974. Repr. of 1611 ed. 5.00 (ISBN 90-221-0655-1). Walter J Johnson.
True Vine. Andrew Murray. pap. 1.50 (ISBN 0-8024-8798-X). Moody.
True Visual Magnitude Photographic Star Atlas, 2 vols. C. Papadopoulos. LC 78-41254. 1979. Set. 550.00 (ISBN 0-08-021622-6); Vol. 1. 225.00 (ISBN 0-08-023435-6); Vol. 2. 325.00 (ISBN 0-08-021623-4). Pergamon.
True Worlds: A Transnational Experience. Johan Galtung. LC 79-7351. (Preferred World for the 1990's Ser.). (Illus.). 469p. 1981. pap. text ed. 9.95 (ISBN 0-02-911070-X). Free Pr.
Truffles for Lunch. Harold Berson. LC 80-13367. (Illus.). (gr. k-3). 1980. PLB 8.95 (ISBN 0-02-709800-1). Macmillan.
Truganinni. Bill Reed. (Austalian Theatre Workshop Ser.). 1977. pap. text ed. 4.50x (ISBN 0-686-65425-0, 00529). Heinemann Ed.
Trukese-English Dictionary. Ward H. Goodenough & Hiroshi Sugita. LC 79-54277. (Memoir Ser.: Vol. 141). 1980. 10.00 (ISBN 0-87169-141-8). Am Philos.
Trullion: Alastor Two Thousand, Two Hundred & Sixty-Two. Jack Vance. 1981. pap. 2.25 (ISBN 0-87997-590-3, UE1590). Daw Bks.
Truly Bizarre. Harold E. Priestley. LC 78-68689. (Illus.). 1979. 9.95 (ISBN 0-8069-0134-9); lib. bdg. 9.29 (ISBN 0-8069-0135-7). Sterling.
Truman & the Eightieth Congress. Susan Hartmann. LC 78-149008. 1971. 15.00x (ISBN 0-8262-0105-9). U of Mo Pr.

Truman & the Steel Seizure Case. Maeva Marcus. LC 77-4095. (Contemporary American History Ser.). 1977. text ed. 17.50x (ISBN 0-231-04126-8). Columbia U Pr.

Truman & the Steel Seizure Case: The Limits of Presidential Power. Maeva Marcus. 1979. pap. 8.00x (ISBN 0-231-04553-0). Columbia U Pr.

Truman Capote. Helen S. Garson. LC 80-5336. (Modern Literature Ser.). (Illus.). 160p. 1980. 10.95 (ISBN 0-8044-2229-X); pap. 4.95 (ISBN 0-8044-6172-4). Ungar.

Truman Capote. Kenneth Reed. (United States Authors Ser.: No. 388). 1981. lib. bdg. 9.95 (ISBN 0-8057-7321-5). Twayne.

Truman of St. Helens: The Man & His Mountain. Shirley Rosen. (Illus.). 200p. 1981. 9.95 (ISBN 0-914842-57-9). Madrona Pubs.

Truman Period As a Research Field. Ed. by Richard S. Kirkendall. 1967. 12.00 o.p. (ISBN 0-8262-0598-4). U of Mo Pr.

Truman Period As a Research Field: A Reappraisal, 1972. Richard S. Kirkendall. LC 73-80585. 1973. 12.50x (ISBN 0-8262-0152-0). U of Mo Pr.

Truman Persuasions. William R. Underhill. 1981. 19.95 (ISBN 0-8138-1640-8). Iowa St U Pr.

Truman Speaks: On the Presidency, the Constitution, and Statecraft. Harry S. Truman. LC 60-8389. 160p. 1975. 12.50x (ISBN 0-231-02384-7); pap. 5.00 (ISBN 0-231-08339-4). Columbia U Pr.

Trumpet for a Walled City. Dolores Pala. 1979. pap. 1.75 o.p. (ISBN 0-449-23913-6, Crest). Fawcett.

Trumpet in the Morning. Stuart Blanch. 1979. 12.95 (ISBN 0-19-520167-1). Oxford U Pr.

Trumpet in the Twilight of Time. Raymond McCarty. LC 80-53734. (Illus.). 144p. (Orig.). 1981. 10.95 (ISBN 0-938310-00-3); pap. 6.95 (ISBN 0-938310-01-1). Volunteer Pubns.

Trumpet of Conscience. Martin L. King, Jr. LC 68-31061. 1968. 11.95 o.p. (ISBN 0-06-012396-6, HarpT). Har-Row.

Trumpet of Prophecy: A Sociological Study of Jehovah's Witnesses. James A. Beckford. LC 75-14432. 246p. 1975. 24.95 (ISBN 0-470-06138-3). Halsted Pr.

Trumpet Soundeth: William Jennings Bryan & His Democracy, 1896-1912. Paul W. Glad. LC 60-12259. (Illus.). 1966. pap. 3.75x (ISBN 0-8032-5073-8, BB 344, Bison). U of Nebr Pr.

Trumpet Technique. Delbert A. Dale. (YA) (gr. 9 up). 1965. 7.75 (ISBN 0-19-318702-7). Oxford U Pr.

Trumpet to Arms: Alternative Media in America. David Armstrong. 384p. 1981. 12.95 (ISBN 0-87477-158-7). J P Tarcher.

Trumpeter of Krakow. new ed. Eric P. Kelly. (gr. 7 up). 1966. 8.95 (ISBN 0-02-750140-X). Macmillan.

Trumpeter Swan: Its History, Habits, & Population in the United States. Winston E. Banko. LC 80-12533. (Illus.). x, 214p. 1980. pap. 5.95 (ISBN 0-8032-6057-1, BB 731, Bison). U of Nebr Pr.

Trumpets Sound No More. F. Van Wyck Mason. pap. 1.95 o.p. (ISBN 0-425-03171-3). Berkley Pub.

Trundlewheel. Katrina Van Tassel. (Lamont Hall Chapbook Ser. for Poetry). 16p. (Orig.). 1981. 1.25 (ISBN 0-9603840-1-4). Andrew Mtn Pr.

Trust: A New View of Personal & Organizational Development. Jack R. Gibb. LC 77-93139. 1978. 15.00 (ISBN 0-89615-002-X); pap. 8.95 (ISBN 0-89615-006-2). Guild of Tutors.

Trust of Self & Others. Kim Giffin & Richard Barnes. (Interpersonal Communication Ser.). (Illus.). 96p. 1976. pap. text ed. 5.95 (ISBN 0-675-08647-7). Merrill.

Trusting Yourself: Psychotherapy As a Beginning. Stephen Shapiro & Hilary Tyrka. 128p. 1975. pap. 2.45 (ISBN 0-13-931022-3, Spec). P-H.

Trusts & Estate Taxation. Gerald R. Jantscher. (Studies of Government Finance). 11.95 (ISBN 0-8157-4576-1); pap. 4.95 (ISBN 0-8157-4575-3). Brookings.

Trustworthiness of Religious Experience. D. E. Trueblood. LC 78-24656. 1979. pap. 2.45 (ISBN 0-913408-45-X). Friends United.

Truth. Robert Firestone & Joyce Catlett. 320p. 1981. 12.95 (ISBN 0-02-538380-9). Macmillan.

Truth About CB Antennas. William I. Orr & Stuart D. Cowan. LC 70-164932. (Illus.). 240p. 1971. 6.95 (ISBN 0-933616-08-2). Radio Pubns.

Truth About Corporate Accounting. Abraham J. Briloff. LC 80-7584. (Illus.). 416p. 1981. 17.95 (ISBN 0-06-010479-1, HarpT). Har-Row.

Truth About Cottages. John Woodforde. (Illus.). 1979. pap. 6.95 (ISBN 0-7100-0165-7). Routledge & Kegan.

Truth About Dragons. Rhoda Blumberg. LC 79-19589. (Illus.). 64p. (gr. 5 up). 1980. 8.95 (ISBN 0-590-07570-5, Four Winds). Schol Bk Serv.

Truth About Elvis. Jess Stearn & Larry Geller. 288p. (Orig.). 1980. pap. 2.50 (ISBN 0-515-05154-3). Jove Pubns.

Truth About Geronimo. Britton Davis. Ed. by M. M. Quaife. LC 75-37958. (Illus.). xxx, 253p. 1976. 15.50x (ISBN 0-8032-0877-4); pap. 5.25 (ISBN 0-8032-5840-2, BB 622, Bison). U of Nebr Pr.

Truth About Gorillas. Susan Meyers. LC 79-19393. 40p. (gr. 1-4). 1980. PLB 7.95 (ISBN 0-525-41564-5, Smart Cat). Dutton.

Truth About Mary Rose. Marilyn Sachs. LC 72-89128. 160p. (gr. 4-7). 1973. PLB 5.95 (ISBN 0-385-09449-3). Doubleday.

Truth About Mesopotamia, Palestine & Syria. John D. Wakehurst. LC 79-2887. 221p. 1981. Repr. of 1923 ed. 19.50 (ISBN 0-8305-0054-5). Hyperion Conn.

Truth About Reparations & War Debts. David Lloyd George. LC 68-9609. 1970. Repr. 12.50 (ISBN 0-86527-197-6). Fertig.

Truth About Shylock: The Jew of Venice Revisited. Bernard Grebanier. 1962. 8.95 o.p. (ISBN 0-394-44978-9). Random.

Truth About the Panama Canal. Denison Kitchel. (Illus.). 1978. 8.95 o.p. (ISBN 0-87000-409-3). Arlington Hse.

Truth & Actuality: Conversations on Science & Consciousness. J. Krishnamurti. LC 77-20450. 176p. 1980. pap. 5.95 (ISBN 0-06-064875-9, RD 334, HarpR). Har-Row.

Truth & Art. Albert Hofstadter. LC 65-12521. (Illus.). 1965. 15.00x (ISBN 0-231-02794-X). Columbia U Pr.

Truth & Certainty. Ed. by E. Schillebeeckx & B. Van Iersel. (Concilium Ser.: Religion in the Seventies: Vol. 83). 144p. 1973. pap. 4.95 (ISBN 0-8164-2539-6, 73613). Crossroad NY.

Truth & Ideology. Hans Barth. LC 74-81430. Orig. Title: Wahrheit und Ideologie. 1977. 19.50x (ISBN 0-520-02820-1). U of Cal Pr.

Truth & Life of Myth. Robert Duncan. 1968. pap. 2.45 o.s.i. (ISBN 0-912090-18-9). Sumac Mich.

Truth & Light: Brief Explanations. M. R. Bawa Muhaiyaddeen. LC 74-76219. (Illus.). 144p. 1974. pap. 2.95 (ISBN 0-914390-04-X). Fellowship Pr PA.

Truth & Meaning in Political Science: An Introduction to Political Inquiry. Maria J. Falco. LC 73-75328. 1973. pap. text ed. 7.50 (ISBN 0-675-08934-4). Merrill.

Truth & the War. Edmund D. Morel. LC 70-147478. (Library of War & Peace; the Character & Causes of War). lib. bdg. 38.00 (ISBN 0-8240-0270-9). Garland Pub.

Truth & Unity of Man: Letters in Response to a Crisis. M. R. Bawa Muhaivaddeen. LC 80-18050. 144p. 1980. 10.00 (ISBN 0-914390-15-5); pap. 3.95 (ISBN 0-914390-14-7). Fellowship Pr PA.

Truth-Antidote for Error. Anthony D. Palma. LC 76-52177. (Radiant Life). 1977. pap. 1.95 (ISBN 0-88243-904-9, 02-0904); teacher's ed 2.50 (ISBN 0-88243-174-9, 32-017X). Gospel Pub.

Truth Barriers: Poems by Tomas Transtromer. Tomas Transtromer. Tr. by Robert Bly from Swedish. LC 80-13310. (Illus.). 64p. 1980. 9.95 (ISBN 0-87156-235-9); pap. 5.95 (ISBN 0-87156-239-1). Sierra.

Truth: Cossacks, the Glory of Russia. Nicholas V. Feodoroff. 1981. 6.75 (ISBN 0-8062-1704-9). Carlton.

Truth: God or Evolution. Marshall Hall & Sandra Hall. 192p. 1975. pap. 3.45 (ISBN 0-8010-4139-2). Baker Bk.

Truth in Accounting. Kenneth MacNeal. LC 74-75709. 1970. Repr. of 1939 ed. text ed. 15.00 (ISBN 0-914348-04-3). Scholars Bk.

Truth in Advertising. Arthur Gibson et al. 1981. Repr. of 1972 ed. soft cover 4.95x (ISBN 0-88946-912-1). E Mellen.

Truth, Invention & the Meaning of Life. David Wiggins. 1976. pap. 2.50x o.p. (ISBN 0-8476-6067-2). Rowman.

Truth Is One. Henry J. Forman & Roland Gammon. (Illus.). 1954. 10.00 o.s.i. (ISBN 0-06-001680-9, HarpT). Har-Row.

Truth, Love, & Immortality: An Introduction to McTaggart's Philosophy. P. T. Geach. 1979. 15.95x (ISBN 0-520-03755-3). U of Cal Pr.

Truth Machine. Jane Clarke. LC 77-70857. (Star Trek Bks.). (Illus.). (gr. 2-5). 1977. 2.95 (ISBN 0-394-83575-1); PLB 3.99 (ISBN 0-394-93575-6). Random.

Truth of Human Nature. Paul D. Harrison. (Illus.). 300p. (Orig.). Date not set. 14.95 (ISBN 0-938058-25-8); pap. 11.95 (ISBN 0-938058-26-6). Wrightwill Pub.

Truth, Probability, & Paradox: Studies in Philosophical Logic. J. L. Mackie. (Clarendon Library of Logic & Philosophy Ser). (Illus.). 320p. 1973. 32.00x (ISBN 0-19-824402-9). Oxford U Pr.

Truth Restored. Gordon B. Hinckley. 168p. 1979. pap. 1.50 (ISBN 0-87747-765-5). Deseret Bk.

Truth, the Whole Truth, Nothing but the Truth. Charles C. Ryrie. 96p. 1981. pap. 2.95 (ISBN 0-8024-8785-8). Moody.

Try Another Way Training Manual. Marc Gold. LC 80-52142. 105p. (Orig.). 1980. pap. 5.95 (ISBN 0-87822-222-7, 2227). Res Press.

Try Being Healthy. Alec Forbes. 184p. 1976. pap. 5.50x (ISBN 0-8464-1057-5). Beekman Pubs.

Try: Experiences for Young Children, Tasks 1-3. George Manolakes et al. (gr. k-1,RL 1-3). 1967. Tasks 1-3. activity bks 2.52 ea.; tchrs'. guides 2.70 ea.; spanish teacher's guide 4.50 (ISBN 0-8372-9800-8). Bowmar-Noble.

Try God. Laura Hobe. 1978. pap. 1.95 o.s.i. (ISBN 0-446-89708-6). Warner Bks.

Try God, You'll Like Him. Katie Tonn. (Uplook Ser.). 1975. pap. 0.75 (ISBN 0-8163-0178-6, 20340-6). Pacific Pr Pub Assn.

Try on a Shoe. Jane B. Moncure. LC 73-4738. (Illus.). (ps-2). 1973. 5.95 (ISBN 0-913778-00-1). Childs World.

Try to Live to See This! Kabir. Tr. by Robert Bly. 1976. pap. 2.00 (ISBN 0-915408-12-0). Ally Pr.

Tryal of the Witnesses of the Resurrection of Jesus, 1973 & the Use & Extent of Prophecy, 1728. Thomas Sherlock. Ed. by Rene Wellek. LC 75-25131. (British Philosophers & Theologians of the 17th & 18th Centuries Ser.). 1978. lib. bdg. 42.00 (ISBN 0-8240-1761-7). Garland Pub.

Trying Hard to Hear You. Sandra Scoppetone. 324p. (gr. 7-9). 1981. pap. 1.95 (ISBN 0-553-13852-9). Bantam.

Trying-Out of Moby Dick. Howard P. Vincent. LC 80-16962. (Illus.). 417p. 1980. pap. 8.50x (ISBN 0-87338-247-1). Kent St U Pr.

Trying Sociology. Kurt H. Wolff. 448p. 1974. 26.50 (ISBN 0-471-95940-5, Pub. by Wiley-Interscience). Wiley.

Trying to Explain. Donald Davie. (Poets on Poetry Ser.). 1979. pap. 5.95 (ISBN 0-472-06310-3). U of Mich Pr.

Trying to Surprise God. Peter Meinke. LC 80-54062. (Pitt Poetry Ser). x, 78p. 1981. 9.95 (ISBN 0-8229-3434-5); pap. 4.50 (ISBN 0-8229-5326-9). U of Pittsburgh Pr.

Tryouts. Elizabeth Levy. LC 78-22125. (Illus.). 112p. (gr. 3-7). 1979. 7.95 (ISBN 0-590-07487-3, Four Winds). Schol Bk Serv.

Ts'Ao Yu. John Y. Hu. (World Authors Ser.: China: No. 201). lib. bdg. 10.95 (ISBN 0-8057-2894-5). Twayne.

Tsar Alexander First: Paternalistic Reformer. Allen McConnell. LC 70-101949. (AHM Europe Since 1500 Ser.). 1970. pap. 5.95x (ISBN 0-88295-745-7). AHM Pub.

Tsar Alexis, His Reign & His Russia. (Russian Ser.: No. 34). 1981. 15.00 (ISBN 0-87569-040-8). Academic Intl.

T.S.K.H. Tickle, Snug, Kiss, Hug. Elizabeth May. LC 77-70643. 1977. 10.00 (ISBN 0-8091-0226-9); pap. 6.95 (ISBN 0-8091-2022-4). Paulist Pr.

Tsubo: Vital Points for Oriental Therapy. Katsusuke Serizawa. (Illus.). 256p. 1976. 22.00 (ISBN 0-87040-350-8). Japan Pubns.

Tsujigahana: The Flower of Japanese Textile Art. Toshiko Ito. Tr. by Monica Bethe. LC 80-82525. (Illus.). 144p. 1981. 200.00 (ISBN 0-87011-397-6). Kodansha.

Tsvetaeva: A Pictorial Biography. Ed. by Ellendea Proffer. 1980. 20.00 (ISBN 0-88233-358-5); pap. 11.00 (ISBN 0-88233-359-3). Ardis Pubs.

Tu Tze-Chun. Ryunosuke Akutagawa. Tr. by Dorothy Britton. LC 65-12283. (Illus.). 64p. 1965. 10.00x (ISBN 0-87011-013-6). Kodansha.

Tu Wan's Stone Catalogue of Cloudy Forest: A Commentary & Synopsis. Edward H. Schafer. (Illus.). 1961. 14.50x (ISBN 0-520-01143-0). U of Cal Pr.

Tuala Speaks. Tuala. Ed. by Jeanne Tamalelagi. LC 80-67870. 220p. (Orig.). 1980. pap. 8.95 (ISBN 0-87516-425-0). De Vorss.

Tuba Music Guide. Ed. by R. Winston Morris. pap. 7.00 (ISBN 0-686-15895-4). Instrumentalist Co.

Tubby Book Featuring Snoopy. Illus. by Charles M. Schulz. (Tubby Bks.). (Illus.). 10p. (ps). 1980. vinyl book 2.95 (ISBN 0-671-41335-X, Pub. by Windmill). S&S.

Tube Substitution Handbook. 20th ed. Howard W. Sams Engineering Staff. LC 76-42880. 1977. pap. 2.95 o.p. (ISBN 0-672-21405-9, 21405). Sams.

Tube Substitution Handbook. 21st ed. Howard W. Sams Engineering Staff. LC 80-13842. 1980. pap. 3.95 (ISBN 0-672-21746-5). Sams.

Tuberculin Test in Clinical Practice. Maxwell Caplin. (Illus.). 1980. pap. text ed. 18.50 (ISBN 0-02-857390-0). Macmillan.

Tuberculosis. Douglas R. Gracey. Ed. by Whitney W. Addington. LC 79-88043. (Discussions in Patient Management Ser.). 1979. pap. 9.50 (ISBN 0-87488-875-1). Med Exam.

Tuberculosis & Its Prevention. Stefan Grzybowski. (Illus.). 224p. 1981. 19.75 (ISBN 0-87527-210-X). Green.

Tuberous Sclerosis. Ed. by Manuel R. Gomez. LC 78-94312. 1979. text ed. 26.00 (ISBN 0-89004-313-2). Raven.

Tuc: The Growth of a Pressure Group Eighteen Sixty Eight to Nineteen Seventy Six. Ross M. Martin. 408p. 1980. text ed. 42.00x (ISBN 0-19-822475-3). Oxford U Pr.

Tuck. Mark Dunster. (Holiday Series, Thanksgiving: Pt. 2). 55p. (Orig.). 1981. pap. 4.00 (ISBN 0-89642-073-6). Linden Pubs.

Tucker's Countryside. George Selden. (gr. 3-7). 1972. pap. 1.50 (ISBN 0-380-01584-6, 55046, Camelot). Avon.

Tudo Sobre Anjos. (Portuguese Bks.). 1979. 1.20 (ISBN 0-8297-0748-4). Life Pubs Intl.

Tudor Age. James A. Williamson. (A History of England). (Illus.). 496p. 1979. pap. text ed. 13.95 (ISBN 0-582-49074-X). Longman.

Tudor & Jacobean Portraits, 2 vol. Roy Strong. (Illus.). 700p. 1980. Set. 160.00x (ISBN 0-312-82220-0). St Martin.

Tudor Church Music. Dennis Stevens. LC 73-4335. 144p. 1973. Repr. of 1955 ed. lib. bdg. 19.50 (ISBN 0-306-70579-6). Da Capo.

Tudor Constitution: Documents & Commentary. Geoffrey R. Elton. (Orig.). 1960. 47.00 (ISBN 0-521-04891-5); pap. 15.95x (ISBN 0-521-09120-9, 120). Cambridge U Pr.

Tudor Dynastic Problems, 1462-1571. Mortimer Levine. (Historical Problems: Studies & Documents). 1973. pap. text ed. 8.95x o.p. (ISBN 0-04-942111-5). Allen Unwin.

Tudor England. S. T. Bindoff. lib. bdg. 10.50x (ISBN 0-88307-022-7). Gannon.

Tudor England. Peter Lane. (Visual Source Ser.). 96p. 1980. 14.95 (ISBN 0-7134-0035-8, Pub. by Batsford England). David & Charles.

Tudor Interlude. T. W. Craik. 1958. text ed. 9.75x (ISBN 0-7185-1014-3, Leicester). Humanities.

Tudor People. John Fines. 1977. 16.95 (ISBN 0-7134-0283-0, Pub. by Batsford England). David & Charles.

Tudor Play of Mind: Rhetorical Inquiry & the Development of Elizabethan Drama. Joel B. Altman. LC 76-52022. 1978. 22.00x (ISBN 0-520-03427-9). U of Cal Pr.

Tudor Regime. Penry Williams. 1979. 45.00x (ISBN 0-19-822491-5). Oxford U Pr.

Tudor Revolution in Government. Geoffrey R. Elton. 1959. 54.00 (ISBN 0-521-04892-3); pap. 15.95x (ISBN 0-521-09235-3, 235). Cambridge U Pr.

Tudor Story. W. S. Pakenham-Walsh. 1963. 8.95 (ISBN 0-227-67678-5). Attic Pr.

Tudor Times. (Picture Panorama of British History Ser.). 1977. pap. 3.95 (ISBN 0-263-06241-4). Transatlantic.

Tudors: Personalities & Practical Politics in Sixteenth-Century England. Conyers Read. (Illus.). 1969. pap. 6.95 (ISBN 0-393-00129-6, Norton Lib). Norton.

Tuesday Blade. Bob Ottum. 368p. 1978. pap. 2.75 (ISBN 0-446-95643-0). Warner Bks.

Tuesdays & Thursdays. Abby Mann. LC 76-2809. 1978. 8.95 o.p. (ISBN 0-385-08764-0). Doubleday.

Tuesday's Song. Vicki J. Hartley. 64p. 1979. 3.50 (ISBN 0-8059-2648-8). Dorrance.

Tuffy's Bike Race. Linda P. Silbert & Alvin J. Silbert. (Little Twirps, TM Understanding People Books). (Illus.). (gr. k-4). 1978. pap. 2.25 (ISBN 0-89544-058-X). Silbert Bress.

Tufted Puffin. David A. Johnson & Michael Graybill. (Life Forms of the Oregon Coast: Vol. I). (Illus.). 22p. (Orig.). (gr. 6 up). 1979. pap. 2.75 (ISBN 0-932368-07-7). Bandon Hist.

Tug of Loyalties: Anglo-American Relations 1765-85. Ed. by Esmond Wright. (Institute of U. S. Studies Monographs Ser: No. 2). 92p. 1975. pap. text ed. 7.50x (ISBN 0-485-12902-7, Athlone Pr). Humanities.

Tugboat. David Plowden. LC 76-13464. (Illus.). (gr. 3 up). 1976. 8.95 (ISBN 0-02-774550-3, 774550). Macmillan.

Tugboat Annie: Great Stories from the Saturday Evening Post. LC 77-78985. 1977. 5.95 (ISBN 0-89387-010-2). Sat Eve Post.

Tuhurahura & the Whale. Anne Rockwell. LC 71-153791. (Illus.). (gr. k-3). 1971. 5.95 o.s.i. (ISBN 0-8193-0509-X, Four Winds); PLB 5.41 o.s.i. (ISBN 0-8193-0510-3). Schol Bk Serv.

Tujunga Canyon Contacts: A Continuing "Chain Reaction" of UFO Encounters & Abductions. Ann Druffel & D. Scott Rogo. (Illus.). 264p. 1980. 9.95 (ISBN 0-13-932541-7). P-H.

Tulapai to Tokay: A Bibliography of Alcohol Use & Abuse Among Native Americans of North America. David R. McDonald & Patricia D. Mail. LC 80-81243. (Bibliography Ser.). 1981. 18.00 (ISBN 0-87536-253-2). HRAFP.

Tularosa. Jessica Richards. 336p. (Orig.). pap. 2.25 (ISBN 0-515-04761-9). Jove Pubns.

Tularosa--Last of the Frontier West. C. L. Sonnichsen. 356p. 1980. 14.95x (ISBN 0-8263-0563-6); pap. 7.95 (ISBN 0-8263-0561-X). U of NM Pr.

Tularosa: Last of the Frontier West. rev. ed. C. L. Sonnichsen. (Illus.). 1971. 10.00 o.s.i. (ISBN 0-685-40705-5). Devin.

Tulasi Das. Madan Gopal. 120p. 1980. 6.95x (ISBN 0-89955-320-6, Pub. by Interprint India). Intl Schol Bk Serv.

Tule Elk: Its History, Behavior & Ecology. D. R. McCullough. (California Library Reprint Series: No. 16). 1971. 20.00x (ISBN 0-520-01921-0); pap. 10.50x (ISBN 0-520-09345-3). U of Cal Pr.
Tullus & the Kidnapped Prince. LC 74-24845. (Tullus Bks.). (Illus.). 128p. (gr. 4-6). 1975. pap. 1.25 o.p. (ISBN 0-912692-52-9). Cook.
Tullus & the Ransom Gold. LC 74-75544. (Illus.). 96p. (Orig.). (gr. 4-5). 1974. pap. 1.25 o.p. (ISBN 0-912692-33-2). Cook.
Tullus & the Vandals of the North. LC 74-81664. (Illus.). 112p. (Orig.). (gr. 5-8). 1974. pap. 1.25 o.p. (ISBN 0-912692-44-8). Cook.
Tullus in the Deadly Whirlpool. LC 74-75546. (Illus.). 96p. (Orig.). (gr. 4-5). 1974. pap. 1.25 o.p. (ISBN 0-912692-34-0). Cook.
Tulsa Art Deco: An Architectural Era Nineteen Twenty-Five to Nineteen Forty-Two. The Junior League of Tulsa, Inc. 204p. 1980. 40.00 (ISBN 0-9604368-1-2); pap. 15.95 (ISBN 0-9604368-2-0). Jr League Tulsa.
Tulsidas. Devendra Singh. (National Biography Ser.). (Orig.). 1979. pap. 2.25 (ISBN 0-89744-207-5, Pub. by Natl Bk Trust India). Auromere.
Tuluak & Amaulik. Stacey Day. LC 73-93517. (Illus.). 176p. 1973. 6.50 (ISBN 0-912922-07-9); pap. 3.75 (ISBN 0-912922-07-9). U of Minn Bell Mus.
Tumbled Wall. Dixie Browning. 192p. (Orig.). 1980. pap. 1.50 (ISBN 0-671-57038-2). S&S.
Tumbleweed Express. Tom K. Ryan. 128p. (Orig.). 1981. pap. 1.75 (ISBN 0-449-14407-0, GM). Fawcett.
Tumbleweeds, No. 3. Tom K. Ryan. (Tumbleweed Ser.). (Illus.). 1979. pap. 1.50 (ISBN 0-449-13672-8, GM). Fawcett.
Tumbleweeds & Company. Tom K. Ryan. (Tumbleweed Ser.). (Illus.). 1979. pap. 1.50 (ISBN 0-449-14198-5, GM). Fawcett.
Tumbleweeds, No. 5. Tom K. Ryan. (Tumbleweed Ser.). (Illus.). 1977. pap. 1.50 (ISBN 0-449-13789-9, GM). Fawcett.
Tumbling & Trampolining. Newton C. Loken. LC 78-90802. (Athletic Institute Ser). (Illus.). (gr. 5 up). 1969. 6.95 (ISBN 0-8069-4336-X); PLB 7.49 (ISBN 0-8069-4337-8). Sterling.
Tumor Associated Markers: The Importance of Identification in Clinical Medicine. Ed. by P. Wolf. LC 79-87540. (Illus.). 208p. 1979. 25.50 (ISBN 0-89352-065-9). Masson Pub.
Tumor Cell Surfaces & Malignancy: Proceedings. Ed. by R. Hynes & C. Fred Fox. LC 80-7798. (Progress in Clinical & Biological Research Ser.: Vol. 41). 214p. 1980. 130.00 (ISBN 0-8451-0041-6). A R Liss.
Tumors & Tumor Like Lesions of Bone & Joints. F. Schajowicz. (Illus.). 650p. 65.00 (ISBN 0-387-90492-1). Springer-Verlag.
Tumors in Domestic Animals. 2nd ed. Ed. by Jack Moulton. 1978. 36.75 (ISBN 0-520-02386-2). U of Cal Pr.
Tumors of the Central Nervous System. Chang. 1981. write for info. Masson Pub.
Tumors of the Large Bowel. Raymond J. Jackman & Oliver H. Beahrs. LC 28-23685. (Major Problems in Clinical Surgery Ser.: Vol. 8). (Illus.). 1968. 16.00 (ISBN 0-7216-5060-0). Saunders.
Tumors of the Nervous Acustious & the Syndrome of the Cerebellopontile Angle. Harvey W. Cushing. (Illus.). 1963. Repr. of 1917 ed. 23.00 o.s.i. (ISBN 0-02-843340-8). Hafner.
Tumors of the Ocular Adnexa & Orbit. Albert Hornblass. LC 79-11089. (Illus.). 1979. text ed. 49.50 (ISBN 0-8016-2246-8). Mosby.
Tumors of the Pancreas. A. R. Moossa. (Illus.). 576p. 1980. lib. bdg. 62.00 (ISBN 0-683-06147-X). Williams & Wilkins.
Tumors That Secrete Catecholamines: A Study Their Natural History & Their Diagnosis. Ronald Robinson. LC 79-41731. 132p. 1980. 40.00 (ISBN 0-471-27748-7). Wiley.
Tumour Localization with Radioactive Agents. LC 76-7616. (Panel Proceedings Ser.). (Illus.). 1977. pap. 13.00 (ISBN 92-0-111276-9, IAEA). Unipub.
Tumours in Children. H. B. Marsden & J. K. Steward. (Recent Results in Cancer Research: Vol. 13). (Illus.). 1968. 39.40 o.p. (ISBN 0-387-04304-7). Springer-Verlag.
Tumult in the Clouds. John Hoare. 1976. 10.95 o.p. (ISBN 0-7181-1410-8, Pub. by Michael Joseph). Merrimack Bk Serv.
Tuna & Billfish: Fish Without a Country. 2nd ed. James Joseph et al. LC 80-81889. (Illus.). 53p. (Orig.). (gr. 7-12). 1980. pap. 7.95 (ISBN 0-686-65904-X). Inter-Am Tropical.
Tuna: Distribution & Migration. Hiroshi Nakamura. (Illus.). 84p. 8.25 (ISBN 0-85238-002-X, FN). Unipub.
Tuna Fishing with Pole & Line. M. Ben-Yami. 1980. 21.50x (ISBN 0-686-64740-8, Pub. by Fishing News England); pap. 19.50x. State Mutual Bk.
Tunde et Ses Amis, 2 bks. David Weckselmann & Elizabeth Bevan. 1962-65. text ed. 2.25x ea. Vol. 1 (ISBN 0-521-06757-X). Vol. 2 (ISBN 0-521-06758-8). Cambridge U Pr.
Tune in Yesterday. T. Ernesto Bethancourt. LC 77-15640. (YA) 1978. 8.95 (ISBN 0-8234-0316-5). Holiday.
Tune in Yesterday. T. Ernesto Bethancourt. 144p. 1981. pap. 1.75 (ISBN 0-553-13324-1). Bantam.
Tuneup for Partners in Love. Clark Swain. LC 80-84568. 250p. 1981. 7.95 (ISBN 0-88290-171-0, 2015). Horizon Utah.
Tung Yueh. Frederick P. Brandauer. (World Authors Ser.: No. 498 (China)). 1978. 13.95 (ISBN 0-8057-6339-2). Twayne.
Tungsten. Mining Journal Books Ltd. 190p. 1980. 28.00x (ISBN 0-900117-21-4, Pub. by Mining Journal England). State Mutual Bk.
Tungsten-Arc Gas Shielded Welding. Ed. by N. C. Balchin et al. (Engineering Craftsmen: No. F22). (Illus.). 1977. spiral bdg. 15.95x (ISBN 0-85083-394-9). Intl Ideas.
Tunhuang Painted Sculptures. 1978. 125.00 (ISBN 0-8351-0654-3). China Bks.
Tunica Treasure. Jeffrey P. Brain. (Peabody Museum Papers: Vol. 71). (Orig.). 1979. pap. 35.00 (ISBN 0-87365-196-0). Peabody Harvard.
Tuning & Temperament: A Historical Survey. James Murray Barbour. LC 74-37288. (Illus.). 228p. 1972. Repr. of 1951 ed. lib. bdg. 21.50 (ISBN 0-306-70422-6). Da Capo.
Tuning in to Nature. Philip Allahan. (Illus.). 1980. 10.00 (ISBN 0-8159-6309-2). Devin.
Tuning of the World: Toward a Theory of Soundscape Design. R. Murray Schafer. 1980. write for info.; pap. text ed. 11.50x (ISBN 0-8122-1109-X). U of Pa Pr.
Tuning the Historical Temperments by Ear. Jorgensen. LC 77-70993. 1977. 30.00 o.p. (ISBN 0-918616-00-X). Northern Mich.
Tuning the School Band & Orchestra. 3rd ed. Ralph R. Pottle. Orig. Title: Tuning the School Band. (Illus.). (gr. 7-12). 1980. lib. bdg. 9.00 (ISBN 0-911162-01-1). Pottle.
Tunisia in Pictures. Sterling Publishing Company Editors. LC 72-81053. (Visual Geography Ser.). (Illus.). 64p. (gr. 6 up). 1972. pap. 2.95 (ISBN 0-8069-1158-1). Sterling.
Tunnel at Loibl Pass. Andre Lacaze. Tr. by W. Barrett Dower. LC 79-7112. 1981. 14.95 (ISBN 0-385-15015-6). Doubleday.
Tunnel in the Sky. Robert A. Heinlein. (Del Rey Bk.). Date not set. pap. 1.75 (ISBN 0-345-28195-0). Ballantine.
Tunnel Vision. Fran Arrick. LC 79-25939. (YA) (gr. 8 up). 1980. 9.95 (ISBN 0-87888-163-8). Bradbury Pr.
Turbo. Douglas Rutherford. 224p. 1980. 9.95 (ISBN 0-312-82332-0). St Martin.
Turbochargers & Turbocharged Engines. Society of Automotive Engineers. 1979. 24.95 (ISBN 0-89883-214-4). Soc Auto Engineers.
Turbomechanics: A Guide to Design, Selection & Theory. O. E. Balje. LC 80-21524. 525p. 1981. 35.00 (ISBN 0-471-06036-4, Pub. by Wiley-Interscience). Wiley.
Turbulence. Ed. by P. Bradshaw. (Topics in Applied Physics: Vol. 12). 1976. 43.80 o.p. (ISBN 0-387-07705-7). Springer-Verlag.
Turbulence in Internal Flows: Turbomachinery & Other Engineering Applications, Proceedings. new ed. Project Squid Workshop on Turbulence in Internal Flows: Turbomachinery & Other Applications, Airlie House, Warrenton, Va., June 14-15, 1976. Ed. by S. N. Murthy. LC 77-15615. (Illus.). 1977. text ed. 57.50 (ISBN 0-89116-073-6). Hemisphere Pub.
Turbulent Covenent. Jessica Steele. (Harlequin Romances Ser.). 192p. 1980. pap. 1.25 o.p. (ISBN 0-373-02355-3, Pub. by Harlequin). PB.
Turbulent Forced Convection in Channels & Bundles: Theory & Applications to Heat Exchangers & Nuclear Reactors, 2 vols. Ed. by Sadik Kakac & D. Brian Spalding. LC 79-12842. 1132p. 1979. Set. 92.50 (ISBN 0-89116-148-1). Hemisphere Pub.
Turbulent Reacting Flows. Ed. by P. A. Libby & F. Williams. (Topics in Applied Physics Ser.: Vol. 44). (Illus.). 260p. 1981. 49.50 (ISBN 0-387-10192-6). Springer Verlag.
Turbulent Shear Flows, Two. Ed. by J. S. Bradbury et al. (Illus.). 480p. 1980. 68.00 (ISBN 0-387-10067-9). Springer-Verlag.
Turbulent Thirties. Edmund Lindop. LC 78-114923. (Illus.). (gr. 7 up). 1970. PLB 3.90 o.p. (ISBN 0-531-01945-4). Watts.
Turf Culture. Frank Hope. (Illus.). 1978. 22.50 (ISBN 0-7137-0873-5, Pub. by Blandford Pr England). Sterling.
Turf Management Handbook. 2nd ed. Howard B. Sprague. LC 74-19656. 1976. 14.65 (ISBN 0-8134-1692-2); text ed. 11.00x (ISBN 0-685-71186-2). Interstate.
Turfgrass Management. A. J. Turgeon & Floyd Giles. (Illus.). 1980. text ed. 16.95 (ISBN 0-8359-7885-0); instrs' manual avail. Reston.
Turfgrass Management: The Golf Course. James B. Beard. (Orig.). 1981. write for info. (ISBN 0-8087-2872-5). Burgess.
Turfgrass: Science & Culture. J. Beard. (Illus.). 1972. ref. ed. 23.95 (ISBN 0-13-933002-X). P-H.
Turgenev. Lev Shestov. 110p. (Rus.). 1981. 12.50 (ISBN 0-88233-504-9); pap. 4.00 (ISBN 0-88233-505-7). Ardis Pubs.
Turgenev & George Sand: An Improbable Entente. Patrick Waddington. (Illus.). 146p. 1981. text ed. 28.50x (ISBN 0-389-20152-9). B&N.
Turi's Book of Lappland. Johan O. Turi. (Illus.). 1966. pap. text ed. 8.75x (ISBN 0-391-02064-1). Humanities.
Turk. John Mason. (Salzburg Studies in English Literature: Jacobean Drama Studies: No. 30). 1979. pap. text ed. 25.00x (ISBN 0-391-01580-X). Humanities.
Turkey. David Hotham. LC 77-70192. (Countries Ser.). (Illus.). 1977. lib. bdg. 7.95 (ISBN 0-686-51153-0). Silver.
Turkey. Andrew Mango. (Nations & Peoples Library). (Illus.). (YA) 1968. 8.50x o.s.i. (ISBN 0-8027-2119-2). Walker & Co.
Turkey. Organization for Economic Cooperation & Development. (OECD Economic Surveys, 1980). (Illus.). 61p. (Orig.). 1980. cancelled (ISBN 92-64-12066-1, 1080271). OECD.
Turkey: A Delicately Poised Ally. Andrew Mango. LC 75-31332. (Policy Papers Ser.: The Washington Papers, No. 28). 1975. 3.50x (ISBN 0-8039-0578-5). Sage.
Turkey Brother & Other Tales: Iroquois Folk Stories. Joseph Bruchac. LC 75-35580. (Illus.). 64p. (gr. 3-6). 1975. 6.95 o.p. (ISBN 0-912278-68-4); pap. 3.95 o.p. (ISBN 0-912278-85-4). Crossing Pr.
Turkey Red. Esther L. Vogt. LC 75-4455. (Illus.). 128p. (Orig.). (gr. 6-7). 1975. pap. 1.95 (ISBN 0-912692-68-5). Cook.
Turkeys, Pilgrims, & Indian Corn: The Story of the Thanksgiving Symbols. Edna Barth. LC 75-4703. (Illus.). 96p. (gr. 2-6). 1975. 8.95 (ISBN 0-395-28846-0, Clarion). HM.
Turkish & English Lexicon. James Redhouse. 80.00x (ISBN 0-685-72063-2). Intl Bk Ctr.
Turkish Art. Ed. by Esin Atil. LC 79-22171. (Illus.). 386p. 1981. 65.00 (ISBN 0-87474-218-8). Smithsonian.
Turkish Art. Ed. by Esin Atil. (Illus.). 400p. 1980. 65.00 (ISBN 0-686-62717-2, 1659-2). Abrams.
Turkish Art & Architecture. Oktay Aslanapa. 1971. 68.00 (ISBN 0-571-08781-7, Pub. by Faber & Faber). Merrimack Bk Serv.
Turkish Bloodbath. Nick Carter. (Nick Carter Ser.). 224p. (Orig.). 1981. pap. 2.25 (ISBN 0-441-82726-8). Charter Bks.
Turkish Case: The Turkishcase. Bertil Walstedt. LC 78-21398. 1979. 14.00x o.p. (ISBN 0-8018-2226-2); pap. 5.95 o.p. (ISBN 0-8018-2227-0). Johns Hopkins.
Turkish Code of Criminal Procedure. (American Series of Foreign Penal Codes: Vol. 5). 1962. 15.00x (ISBN 0-8377-0025-6). Rothman.
Turkish Criminal Code. (American Series of Foreign Penal Codes: Vol. 9). 1965. 15.00x (ISBN 0-8377-0029-9). Rothman.
Turkish Empire. George J. Eversley & Valentine Chirol. LC 68-9623. (Illus.). 1969. Repr. of 1892 ed. 22.50 (ISBN 0-86527-198-4). Fertig.
Turkish-English Dictionary. 2nd ed. H. C. Hony. 1957. 24.00x (ISBN 0-19-864108-7). Oxford U Pr.
Turkish Experiment in Democracy: 1950 to 1975. Feroz Ahmad. LC 76-25499. 1977. lib. bdg. 35.00x (ISBN 0-89158-629-6). Westview.
Turkish Fairy Tales & Folk Tales. R. Nisbet Bain. (Illus.). (gr. k-8). 1969. pap. 2.50 o.p. (ISBN 0-486-22344-2). Dover.
Turkish Grammar. Geoffrey L. Lewis. 1967. 24.95x (ISBN 0-19-815375-9). Oxford U Pr.
Turkish Letters of Ogier Ghiselin De Busbecq. Ogier G. De Busbecq. Tr. by Edward S. Forster. 1927. 22.50x o.p. (ISBN 0-19-821473-1). Oxford U Pr.
Turkish Ordeal. Halide E. Adivar. LC 79-3081. (Illus.). 407p. 1981. Repr. of 1928 ed. 32.50 (ISBN 0-8305-0057-X). Hyperion Conn.
Turkish Straits & NATO. Ferenc Vali. LC 70-170205. (Studies Ser.: No. 32). (Illus.). 200p. 1972. pap. 6.95 (ISBN 0-8179-3322-0). Hoover Inst Pr.
Turkish White. Mel Arrighi. LC 76-54620. 1977. 7.95 o.p. (ISBN 0-15-191390-0). HarBraceJ.
Turkish White. Mel Arrighi. 1978. pap. 1.95 o.s.i. (ISBN 0-515-04549-7). Jove Pubns.
Turks, Iran & the Caucasus in the Middle Ages. Vladimir Minorsky. 368p. 1980. 69.00x (ISBN 0-86078-028-7, Pub. by Variorum England). State Mutual Bk.
Turmoil & Consensus: A Reader in Basic Political Issues. Ed. by Barbara Calloway & Alan Stone. 300p. 1981. 14.50 (ISBN 0-87073-868-2); pap. 7.95 (ISBN 0-87073-867-4). Schenkman.
Turmoil on the Campus. Ed. by Edward J. Bander. (Reference Shelf Ser: Vol. 42, No. 3). 1970. 6.25 (ISBN 0-8242-0411-5). Wilson.
Turn Around. Giles A. Lutz. LC 78-3258. 1978. 7.95 o.p. (ISBN 0-385-14344-3). Doubleday.
Turn of the Balance. Brand Whitlock. LC 76-104765. (Novel As American Social History). 650p. 1970. 10.00x (ISBN 0-8131-1213-3). U Pr of Ky.
Turn-of-the-Century Party. Vida A. Hardesty. LC 77-82129. (National History Ser.). (Illus.). (gr. 4 up). 1980. 10.95 (ISBN 0-89482-001-X); write for info. ltd. ed. (ISBN 0-89482-023-0); pap. 6.95 (ISBN 0-89482-008-7). Stevenson Pr.
Turn of the Screw. Henry James. Incl. Aspern Papers. 1957. 10.50x (ISBN 0-460-00912-5, Evman); pap. 2.95 (ISBN 0-460-01912-0). Dutton.
Turn of Zero. Won Ko. (Poetry Ser.). (Illus.). 1974. o.p. 10.00x (ISBN 0-89304-021-5, CCC103); signed ltd. ed. 15.00x (ISBN 0-89304-048-7); pap. 4.50x (ISBN 0-89304-003-7); pap. 4.00x signed ltd. ed. o.p. (ISBN 0-89304-049-5). Cross Cult.
Turn off Your Age. Elsye Birkinshaw. LC 79-27693. 1980. pap. 4.95 (ISBN 0-912800-77-1). Woodbridge Pr.
Turn Right at the Fountain. 3rd ed. George Oakes & Alexandra Chapman. 1971. 5.95 o.p. (ISBN 0-03-086006-7). HR&W.
Turn Right at the Fountain. 4th, rev. ed. George W. Oakes & Alexandra Chapman. LC 80-17568. (Illus.). 352p. 1981. 14.95 (ISBN 0-03-047171-0); pap. 7.95 (ISBN 0-686-69129-6). HR&W.
Turn South at the Second Bridge. Leon Hale. LC 80-5517. 224p. 1980. Repr. of 1965 ed. 12.95 (ISBN 0-89096-100-X). Tex A&M Univ Pr.
Turn to the Right: The Ideological Origins & the Development of Ukrainina Nationalism, 1919-1929. Alexander J. Motyl. (East European Monographs: No. 65). 1980. 15.00x (ISBN 0-914710-58-3). East Eur Quarterly.
Turn West, Turn East: Mark Twain & Henry James. Henry S. Canby. LC 65-23485. 1951. 12.00x (ISBN 0-8196-0154-3). Biblo.
Turn Your Ideas into Money. Donald W. Cantin. 1977. 6.95 o.p. (ISBN 0-8015-7996-1, Hawthorn); pap. 4.95 (ISBN 0-8015-7996-1, Hawthorn). Dutton.
Turn Your Life Around: Self-Knowledge for Self Improvement. Stanley Nass & Manfred Weidhorn. LC 78-15360. 1978. 11.95 (ISBN 0-13-933069-0, Spec); pap. 4.95 (ISBN 0-13-933051-8). P-H.
Turnabout. Elaine Raphael & Don Bolognese. LC 80-11866. (Illus.). 32p. (gr. 1-3). 1980. 8.95 (ISBN 0-670-73281-8). Viking Pr.
Turnabout. William Wiesner. LC 72-190380. (Illus.). 40p. (ps-3). 1972. 5.95 (ISBN 0-395-28832-0, Clarion). HM.
Turnaround. Don Carpenter. 13.95 (ISBN 0-671-25353-0). S&S.
Turnbulls. Taylor Caldwell. (Orig.). pap. 2.75 (ISBN 0-515-05291-4). Jove Pubns.
Turncoat. Jack Lynn. 1976. 8.95 o.p. (ISBN 0-440-09133-0). Delacorte.
Turner. William Gaunt. (Illus.). 96p. 1976. pap. text ed. 5.95 (ISBN 0-8120-0704-2). Barron.
Turner. Graham Reynolds. (World of Art Ser.). (Illus.). 1969. pap. 9.95 (ISBN 0-19-519932-4). Oxford U Pr.
Turner. John Rothenstein & Martin Butlin. LC 64-23604. (Illus.). 1964. 22.50 o.s.i. (ISBN 0-8076-0280-9). Braziller.
Turner. John Walker. LC 76-4090. (Library of Great Painters). (Illus.). 1976. 35.00 (ISBN 0-8109-0513-2). Abrams.
Turner & Beard, American Historical Writing Reconsidered. Lee Benson. 1965. pap. 1.95 o.s.i. (ISBN 0-02-902710-1). Free Pr.
Turner & the Sublime. Andrew Wilton. (Illus.). 192p. 1981. 40.00 (ISBN 0-930606-24-8, 06188-4, Pub. by British Museum). U of Chicago Pr.
Turner, Bolton, & Webb: Three Historians of the American Frontier. Wilbur R. Jacobs et al. (Illus.). 127p. (Orig.). 1979. pap. 4.95 (ISBN 0-295-95677-1). U of Wash Pr.
Turner Diaries. 2nd ed. Andrew Macdonald. LC 80-82692. 216p. (Orig.). 1980. pap. 4.95 (ISBN 0-937944-02-5). Natl Alliance.
Turner: Early Works. Mary Chamot. (Tate Gallery: Little Art Book Ser.). (Illus.). 1977. pap. 1.95 (ISBN 0-8120-0857-X). Barron.
Turner in the British Museum: Drawings & Watercolours. Wilton. Date not set. pap. 7.95 (ISBN 0-8120-0905-3). Barron. Postponed.
Turner: Later Works. Martin Butlin. (Tate Gallery: Little Art Book Ser.). (Illus.). 1977. pap. 1.95 (ISBN 0-8120-0858-8). Barron.
Turner Watercolors. Andrew Wilton. LC 77-79293. (Illus.). 195p. (Orig.). 1977. pap. 12.00 (ISBN 0-88397-002-3). Intl Exhibit Foun.
Turner's Personal & Community Health. 15th ed. Natalie Brooks & Stewart M. Brooks. LC 78-31647. (Illus.). 1979. text ed. 15.95 (ISBN 0-8016-5536-6). Mosby.

Turning, Vol. 1. 2nd ed. Ed. by L. Annis et al. (Engineering Craftsmen: No. H2). (Illus.). 1977. spiral bdg. 14.95x (ISBN 0-85083-403-1). Intl Ideas.

Turning, Vol. 2. Ed. by S. G. Fletcher et al. (Engineering Craftsmen: No. H23). 1969. spiral bdg. 13.95x (ISBN 0-85083-038-9). Intl Ideas.

Turning Behavior Inside Out. Donald E. Tarter. LC 79-63749. 1979. pap. text ed. 11.00 (ISBN 0-8191-0736-0). U Pr of Amer.

Turning Complaints into Money. G. N. Brown. 1979. 12.50 o.p. (ISBN 0-685-67819-9). Porter.

Turning Kids on to Print Using Nonprint. James L. Thomas. LC 78-9075. (Illus.). 1978. lib. bdg. 17.50x (ISBN 0-87287-184-3). Libs Unl.

Turning People on: How to Be an Encouraging Person. Losoncy. LC 77-4686. 1977. 11.95 (ISBN 0-13-933242-1, Spec); pap. 5.95 (ISBN 0-13-933234-0). P-H.

Turning Point for Literacy-Adult Education for Development-Spirit & Declaration of Persepolis: Proceedings of the International Symposium for Literacy, Iran, 1975. Ed. by Leon Bataille. LC 76-46206. 1976. text ed. 29.00 (ISBN 0-08-021385-5); pap. text ed. 16.00 (ISBN 0-08-021386-3). Pergamon.

Turning Points: Essays on the Art of Science Fiction. Ed. by Damon Knight. LC 76-5135. (YA) 1977. 12.50 o.s.i. (ISBN 0-06-012432-6, HarpT). Har-Row.

Turning Points in American Educational History. David B. Tyack. 1967. pap. 16.50 (ISBN 0-471-00596-7). Wiley.

Turning Points in Economic Development. Rudolf Bicanic. 1972. text ed. 48.25x (ISBN 90-2792-101-6). Mouton.

Turning Points in Twentieth Century Art: 1890-1917. Hofmann Werner. (Illus.). 1966. 15.00 o.s.i. (ISBN 0-8076-0456-9). Braziller.

Turning Points of the Civil War. James A. Rawley. LC 66-19266. (Illus.). 1974. pap. 5.50x (ISBN 0-8032-5155-6, BB 382, Bison). U of Nebr Pr.

Turning Road. Ralph Kibildis. 112p. 1981. 1.95 (ISBN 0-914544-34-9). Living Flame Pr.

Turning Technology: Engine & Turret Lathes. S. F. Krar & J. W. Oswald. LC 78-153723. 1971. pap. text ed. 11.60 (ISBN 0-8273-0206-1); instructor's guide 1.60 (ISBN 0-8273-0207-X). Delmar.

Turning Things Upside Down: A Theological Workbook. Thomas Woodward. 128p. 1975. 4.50 (ISBN 0-8164-0279-5). Crossroad NY.

Turning to God: A Study of Conversion in the Book of Acts & Today. William Barclay. pap. 2.95 (ISBN 0-8010-0564-7). Baker Bk.

Turning Your Stress into Strength. Robert Schuller. 1979. pap. 1.95 o.p. (ISBN 0-449-14262-0, GM). Fawcett.

Turnip. Janina Domanska. LC 69-18235. (Illus.). (gr. k-3). 1969. 5.95g o.s.i. (ISBN 0-02-732810-4). Macmillan.

Turnkey CAD-CAM Computer Graphics: A Survey & Buyers' Guide for Manufacturers, 3 pts, Pts. 1,2, & 3. Charles M. Foundyller. (Illus.). 476p. 1980. Set. spiral with laminated covers 199.00x (ISBN 0-938484-04-4). Daratech.

Turnkey CAD-CAM Computer Graphics: A Survey & Buyers' Guide for Manufacturers, Pts. 1 & 2. Charles M. Foundyller. Incl. Pt. 1. 254p. 84.00x (ISBN 0-938484-01-X); Pt. 2. 120p. 69.00x (ISBN 0-938484-02-8). (Illus.). 374p. 1980. Set. spiral with laminated covers 153.00x (ISBN 0-938484-00-1). Daratech.

Turnkey CAD-CAM Computer Graphics: A Survey & Buyers' Guide for Manufacturers, Pt. 3. Charles M. Foundyller. (Illus.). 102p. 1980. spiral with laminated covers 46.00x (ISBN 0-938484-03-6). Daratech.

Turnpike Road System, 1663-1840. William Albert. LC 78-163062. (Illus.). 1972. 35.50 (ISBN 0-521-08221-8). Cambridge U Pr.

Turns. John Matthias. LC 75-535. 111p. 1975. 7.95 (ISBN 0-8040-0689-X). Swallow.

Turpin. Stephen Jones. 1968. 5.95 o.s.i. (ISBN 0-02-559820-1). Macmillan.

Turquie. new ed. Ed. by Daniel Moreau. (Collection monde et voyages). (Illus.). 159p. (Fr.). 1973. 21.00 (ISBN 2-03-053110-3). Larousse.

Turquois & Spanish Mines in New Mexico. Stuart A. Northrop. LC 75-7474. (Illus.). 96p. 1975. pap. 3.45 o.p. (ISBN 0-8263-0371-4). U of NM Pr.

Turquoise. Anya Seton. 1977. pap. 1.95 o.p. (ISBN 0-449-23088-0, Crest). Fawcett.

Turquoise Land: Anthology of New Mexico Poetry. Ed. by New Mexico State Poetry Society. 115p. 1974. 4.95 o.p. (ISBN 0-89015-067-2). Nortex Pr.

Turquoise Mask. Phyllis Whitney. 1980. pap. 2.50 (ISBN 0-449-23470-3, Crest). Fawcett.

Turquoise Treasures. Photos by Jerry Jacka. LC 75-7141. (Illus.). 96p. (Text by Spencer Gill). 1975. 19.50 (ISBN 0-912856-21-1); pap. 9.95 o.p. (ISBN 0-912856-25-4). Graphic Arts Ctr.

Turret. Margery Sharp. (Illus.). (gr. 7 up). 1963. 6.95 o.p. (ISBN 0-316-78318-8). Little.

Turtle. Betty S. Cummings. LC 80-24062. (Illus.). (gr. 2-5). 1981. PLB 9.95 (ISBN 0-689-30805-1). Atheneum.

Turtle & Snail. Zibby Oneal. LC 78-14826. (Lippincott I-Like-to-Read Book). (Illus.). (gr. k-2). 1979. 6.95 (ISBN 0-397-31829-4). Lippincott.

Turtle Book. Mel Crawford. (Illus.). (ps-4). 1965. PLB 5.38 (ISBN 0-307-68922-0, Golden Pr). Western Pub.

Turtle Geometry: The Computer As a Medium for Exploring Mathematics. Harold Abelson & Andrea DiSessa. (Illus.). 576p. 1981. text ed. 35.00 (ISBN 0-262-01063-1). MIT Pr.

Turtle Is Born. William White, Jr. (Illus.). 96p. (gr. 5 up). 1973. 6.95 o.p. (ISBN 0-8069-3528-6); PLB 6.69 o.p. (ISBN 0-8069-3529-4). Sterling.

Turtle Tale. Asch. (Illus.). (gr. 3). Date not set. pap. cancelled (ISBN 0-590-30386-4, Schol Pap). Schol Bk Serv.

Turtles. Robert Church. (Illus., Orig.). pap. 2.00 (ISBN 0-87666-226-2, M515). TFH Pubns.

Turtles. Lois Darling & Louis Darling. (Illus.). (gr. 3-7). 1962. PLB 6.48 (ISBN 0-688-31547-X). Morrow.

Turtles. Mervin F. Roberts. (Illus.). 96p. 1980. 2.95 (ISBN 0-87666-928-3, KW051). TFH Pubns.

Turtles & Tortoises. Fred Johnson. Ed. by Russell Bourne & Natalie Rifkin. LC 73-91357. (Ranger Rick's Best Friends Ser.: No. 2). (Illus.). 32p. (gr. 1-6). 1974. 2.50 o.p. (ISBN 0-912186-10-0). Natl Wildlife.

Turtles of the World. Peter Pritchard. 1966. 20.00 o.p. (ISBN 0-87666-228-9, H922). TFH Pubns.

Tuscarora Language. Elton Green. 1969. 4.95 (ISBN 0-930230-27-2). Johnson NC.

Tuscaroras. Shirley H. Witt. LC 75-189730. (Illus.). (gr. 5up). 1972. 6.95 (ISBN 0-02-793270-2, CCPr). Macmillan.

Tuscon Temptress. Chet Cunningham. (Agent Brad Spear Ser.: No. 3). (Orig.). 1981. pap. 2.25 (ISBN 0-440-09140-3, Banbury). Dell.

Tutankhamen. Christiane Desroches-Noblecourt. LC 63-15145. (Illus.). 1963. 19.95 (ISBN 0-8212-0151-4, 857009). NYGS.

Tutankhamun & the Mysteries of Ancient Egypt. Ron Knapp. LC 79-15504. (Illus.). 96p. (gr. 4-6). 1979. PLB 7.79 (ISBN 0-671-33036-5). Messner.

Tutelle: Etudes De Droit Prive Normand, Vol. 3. Robert Genestal. LC 80-2027. 1981. Repr. of 1930 ed. 26.00 (ISBN 0-404-18564-9). AMS Pr.

Tuti-Nama & the Tuti-Nama of the Cleveland Museum of Art & the Origins of Mughal Painting, 2 vols. Incl. Tuti-Nama (Facsimile) Ziya'U'D-Din Nakhshabi. (Illus.). 698p. 1974; Tuti-Nama of the Cleveland Museum of Art & the Origins of Mughal Painting. Pramod Chandra. (Illus.). 236p. 1976. (Illus.). 934p. Set. 460.00 o.p. (ISBN 0-686-64200-7, Pub. by Cleveland Mus Art). Ind U Pr.

Tutor-Notetaker. Russel T. Osguthorpe. 98p. (Orig.). 1980. pap. text ed. 6.00 (ISBN 0-88200-131-0, N6680). Alexander Graham.

Tutorial Essays in Psychology: A Guide to Recent Advances, 2 vols. Ed. by N. S. Sutherland. LC 78-31703. (Tutorial Essays in Psychology Ser.). Vol. 1, 1977. 10.95 (ISBN 0-470-99138-0); Vol. 2, 1979. 14.95 (ISBN 0-470-26652-X). Halsted Pr.

Tutorial System & Its Future. W. G. Moore. 1968. text ed. 11.25 (ISBN 0-08-012659-6); pap. text ed. 6.25 (ISBN 0-08-012658-8). Pergamon.

Tutoring Is Caring -- You Can Help Someone to Read. Aline D. Wolf. LC 76-15777. (Illus.). 1976. spiral bdg. 12.50 (ISBN 0-9601016-1-6). Parent-Child Pr.

Tutor's Guidebook for Remedial Reading. Nicholas Criscuolo. LC 72-80433. 1972. pap. 3.00 o.p. (ISBN 0-87812-042-4). Pendell Pub.

Tutti-Frutti Case. Harry Allard. (Illus.). (ps-2). 1975. 5.95 (ISBN 0-13-933200-6, 933218); pap. 1.50 (ISBN 0-13-933218-9). P-H.

Tuttle's Shell. Sal Murdocca. (Illus.). 64p. (gr. 1-4). 1976. PLB 6.67 (ISBN 0-688-51724-2). Lothrop.

Tutu: The True Story of a Budgie. Alix Weill. LC 79-21793. (Illus., Orig.). 1979. pap. 3.95 (ISBN 0-89127-056-6). Omni Pubs.

TV Ad Trivia Quiz Book. John Di Prete. LC 80-15375. (Illus.). 96p. 1980. pap. 3.95 (ISBN 0-498-02464-4). A S Barnes.

TV & Movie Animals. Gary Paulsen & Art Browne, Jr. LC 79-25861. (Illus.). 96p. (gr. 4-6). 1980. PLB 7.29 (ISBN 0-671-32989-8). Messner.

TV & Radio Careers. D. X. Fenten. (Career Concise Guides Ser.). (Illus.). 72p. (gr. 7 up). 1976. PLB 6.45 (ISBN 0-531-01131-3). Watts.

TV Facts. Cobbett Steinberg. 1980. 17.95 (ISBN 0-87196-312-4). Facts on File.

TV Guide Book of Crossword Puzzles. TV Guide. (Puzzle Ser: No. 5). pap. 1.50 (ISBN 0-445-08342-5). Popular Lib.

TV Guide Book of Crossword Puzzles. T.V. Guide. (Puzzle Ser.: No. 8). (Orig.). 1979. pap. 1.50 (ISBN 0-445-04479-9). Popular Lib.

TV Guide Twenty-Five Year Index: Nineteen Fifty-Three to Nineteen Seventy-Seven. Catherine E. Johnson. LC 79-67725. 506p. 1980. text ed. 77.50 (ISBN 0-9603684-0-X). Triangle Pubns.

TV Jokes. Dachs. (gr. 7-12). pap. 1.25 (ISBN 0-590-05402-3, Schol Pap). Schol Bk Serv.

TV Movies (Revised 1979 Edition) Leonard Maltin. (RL 6). 1978. pap. 2.95 o.p. (ISBN 0-451-08293-1, E8293, Sig). NAL.

TV Nineteen Seventy-Seven to Nineteen Seventy-Eight. 1979. 15.95x (ISBN 0-912700-23-8). Oryx Pr.

TV Olympics Program Guide. Weber. (gr. 7-12). Date not set. pap. cancelled o.p. (ISBN 0-590-30362-7, Schol Pap). Schol Bk Serv.

TV on-off: Better Family Use of Television. Ellen B. DeFranco. 1980. pap. text ed. 7.95 (ISBN 0-8302-9128-8). Goodyear.

TV or Not TV: An Irreverent Look at Television. Bart Andrews & Judy Ervin. (Orig.). 1977. pap. 1.25 o.p. (ISBN 0-451-07660-5, Y7660, Sig). NAL.

TV Ritual: Worship at the Video Altar. Gregor Goethals. LC 80-66072. (Illus.). 192p. 1981. 11.95 (ISBN 0-8070-3222-0). Beacon Pr.

TV Scriptwriter's Handbook. Alfred Brenner. LC 80-23700. 288p. 1980. 10.95 (ISBN 0-89879-024-7). Writers Digest.

TV Sound Operation. Glyn Alkin. (Media Manuals Ser.). pap. 7.95 (ISBN 0-8038-7148-1). Hastings.

TV the Most Popular Art. Horace Newcomb. LC 74-3559. 280p. 1974. pap. 2.50 (ISBN 0-385-03602-7, Anch). Doubleday.

TV: The Television Annual, 1979-80. Steven H. Scheuer. (Illus.). 352p. Date not set. 19.95 (ISBN 0-02-607080-4). Macmillan. Postponed.

TV Time Seventy-Nine. Peggy Herz. (gr. 4-6). 1979. pap. 1.25 o.p. (ISBN 0-590-12105-7, Schol Pap). Schol Bk Serv.

TV '80. Freeman. (gr. 7-12). 1980. pap. 1.25 (ISBN 0-590-30877-7, Schol Pap). Schol Bk Serv.

TVA & the Power Fight: 1933-1939. Thomas K. McCraw. LC 75-129670. (Critical Periods of History Ser). 1971. 5.95 o.p. (ISBN 0-397-47257-9); pap. text ed. 2.95 o.p. (ISBN 0-397-47256-0). Lippincott.

Tvorcheskie Raboty Uchenikov Tolstogo V Yasnoi Polyane. Ed. by Thomas G. Winner. LC 72-2453. (Slavic Reprint Ser: No. 10). 136p. (Rus.). 1974. pap. 4.00 (ISBN 0-87057-135-4, Pub. by Brown U Pr). Univ Pr of New England.

Tvortsi Netlinnoi Krasy. Wasyl Luciw. (Ukra.). 1972. pap. text ed. 6.00 (ISBN 0-918884-05-5). Slavia Lib.

TV's Fabulous Faces. Peggy Herz. (gr. 4-6). 1977. pap. 1.25 o.p. (ISBN 0-590-10428-4, Schol Pap). Schol Bk Serv.

Twain Unabridged. Mark Twain. Ed. by Lawrence Teacher. LC 76-43094. (Illus.). 1250p. (Orig.). 1976. lib. bdg. 19.80 (ISBN 0-914294-53-9); pap. 9.95 (ISBN 0-914294-54-7). Running Pr.

Twain Unabridged Two. Mark Twain. Ed. by Lawrence Teacher. LC 79-9576. 1979. 21.50 (ISBN 0-89471-071-0); lib. bdg. 19.80 (ISBN 0-89471-087-7); pap. 9.95 (ISBN 0-89471-086-9). Running Pr.

Tweed's New York-Another Look. Leo Hershkowitz. LC 76-5338. (Illus.). 1977. 12.50 o.p. (ISBN 0-385-07656-8). Doubleday.

Tweety & Sylvester at the Farm. Cecily Hogan. (Tell-a-Tale Readers). (gr. k-3). 1978. PLB 4.77 (ISBN 0-307-68642-6, Whitman). Western Pub.

Tweety & Sylvester: Birds of a Feather. Seymour Reit. (Look-Look Ser.). (Illus.). 1977. PLB 5.38 (ISBN 0-307-61833-1, Golden Pr); pap. 0.95 (ISBN 0-307-11833-9). Western Pub.

Twelfth-Century Europe & the Foundations of Modern Society. Ed. by Marshall Clagett et al. (Illus.). 1961. pap. 7.50x (ISBN 0-299-02304-4). U of Wis Pr.

Twelfth-Century Europe & the Foundations of Modern Society. University of Wisconsin, Division of Humanities. Ed. by Marshall Clagett et al. LC 80-21872. (Illus.). xvi, 219p. 1980. Repr. of 1966 ed. lib. bdg. 29.75x (ISBN 0-313-22798-5, WITC). Greenwood.

Twelfth Night. William Shakespeare. Ed. by Arthur Quiller-Couch et al. (New Shakespeare Ser). 1968. 23.95 (ISBN 0-521-07561-0); pap. 4.50x (ISBN 0-521-09504-2). Cambridge U Pr.

Twelve Adventures of the Celebrated Baron Munchausen. Brian Robb. (Illus.). (gr. 2 up). 1979. PLB 7.95 (ISBN 0-233-97019-3). Andre Deutsch.

Twelve African Writers. Gerald Moore. LC 80-7988. (Illus.). 320p. 1980. 22.50x (ISBN 0-253-19619-1). Ind U Pr.

Twelve American Women. Elizabeth Anticaglia. LC 74-23229. (Illus.). 272p. 1975. 17.95 (ISBN 0-88229-102-5). Nelson-Hall.

Twelve Angels from Hell. David Wilkerson. (gr. 9 up). 1967. pap. 1.25 o.s.i. (ISBN 0-89129-082-6). Jove Pubns.

Twelve Angry Men: A Screen Adaptation, Directed by Sidney Lumet. Reginald Rose. Ed. by George P. Garrett et al. LC 71-135273. (Film Scripts Ser.). 1971. pap. text ed. 6.95x (ISBN 0-89197-970-0). Irvington.

Twelve Apostles. Ronald Brownrigg. (Illus.). 248p. 1974. 12.95 o.s.i. (ISBN 0-02-517400-2). Macmillan.

Twelve Best RV Trips in America. pap. 2.95 (ISBN 0-685-88022-2). Woodall.

Twelve Caesars: An Illustrated Edition. Gaius S. Tranquillus. Tr. by Robert Graves. 1979. pap. 14.95 (ISBN 0-14-005416-2). Penguin.

Twelve Centuries of Bookbindings: Four Hundred to Sixteen Hundred. Paul Needham. LC 79-52345. (Illus.). 368p. 1979. 75.00 (ISBN 0-19-211580-4); pap. 39.95 (ISBN 0-686-68488-5). Pierpont Morgan.

Twelve Centuries of Bookbindings: Four Hundred to Sixteen Hundred. Paul Needham. (Illus.). 1979. 75.00x (ISBN 0-19-211580-4). Oxford U Pr.

Twelve Dancing Princesses & Other Fairy Tales. Alfred David & Mary E. Meek. LC 73-16517. (Midland Bks.: No. 173). (Illus.). 320p. (gr. 1-6). 1974. 10.00x (ISBN 0-253-36100-1); pap. 3.95x (ISBN 0-253-20173-X). Ind U Pr.

Twelve Days of Christmas Cookbook. Ruth Moorman & Lalla Williams. (Illus.). 80p. 1978. pap. 4.95 (ISBN 0-937552-00-3). Quail Ridge.

Twelve Deaths of Christmas. Marian Babson. 180p. 1980. 9.95 (ISBN 0-8027-5426-0). Walker & Co.

Twelve Facets of Reality: The Jain Path to Freedom. Gurudev S. Chitrabkanu. Ed. by Clare Rosenfeld. LC 80-16773. 200p. 1980. 8.95 (ISBN 0-396-07902-4). Dodd.

Twelve Fair Kingdoms: Book One of the Ozark Fantasy Trilogy. Suzette E. Elgin. LC 80-2837. 192p. 1981. 9.95 (ISBN 0-385-15876-9). Doubleday.

Twelve German Novellas. Tr. by Harry Steinhauer. (Campus Ser.). 1977. 22.75x (ISBN 0-520-03002-8); pap. 8.95x (ISBN 0-520-03504-6). U of Cal Pr.

Twelve Hundred & Four - the Unholy Crusade. John Godfrey. (Illus.). 256p. 1980. 28.50 (ISBN 0-19-215834-1). Oxford U Pr.

Twelve Hundred MCQs in Medicine. Ed. by P. R. Fleming. 168p. 1980. pap. text ed. 11.50 (ISBN 0-443-01571-6). Churchill.

Twelve Hundred Multiple Choice Questions in Pharmacology. R. W. Foster. LC 79-42816. (Illus.). 188p. 1980. pap. write for info. Butterworths.

Twelve Hundred Scripture Outlines. A. Naismith. (Source Book for Ministers). 1978. pap. 3.95 (ISBN 0-8010-6692-1). Baker Bk.

Twelve Labors of Hercules. Robert Newman. LC 75-132300. (Hero Tales Ser.). (Illus.). 150p. (gr. 3-5). 1972. 8.95 (ISBN 0-690-83920-0, TYC-J). T Y Crowell.

Twelve Lectures on the Technique of Fiction Writing. Kenneth Macnichol. 385p. 1980. lib. bdg. 40.00 (ISBN 0-89760-545-4). Telegraph Bks.

Twelve Little Housemates. Karl Von Frisch. Tr. by A. T. Sugar. LC 78-40341. 1978. text ed. 15.75 (ISBN 0-08-021959-4); pap. text ed. 7.75 (ISBN 0-08-021958-6). Pergamon.

Twelve Minor Prophets. Hans C. von Orelli. 1977. 13.50 (ISBN 0-686-12973-3). Klock & Klock.

Twelve Missionary Sermons. Charles H. Spurgeon. (Charles H. Sprugeon Library). 1978. pap. 2.95 (ISBN 0-8010-8135-1). Baker Bk.

Twelve Months. Aliki. LC 78-3554. (Illus.). (gr. k-3). 1978. 7.95 (ISBN 0-688-80164-1); PLB 7.63 (ISBN 0-688-84164-3). Greenwillow.

Twelve Months Harvest. (Illus.). 1977. pap. 4.95 (ISBN 0-917102-12-6). Ortho.

Twelve Months of the Year (Almanac) LC 80-66109. (Illus.). 120p. 1980. 17.95 (ISBN 0-7153-7918-6); pap. 11.95 (ISBN 0-7153-7919-4). David & Charles.

Twelve Mormon Homes. Elizabeth W. Kane. (Utah, the Mormons, & the West: No. 4). 1974. 12.00 (ISBN 0-87480-162-1, Tanner). U of Utah Pr.

Twelve O'Clock High. Beirne Lay, Jr. & Sy Bartlett. LC 80-16525. (Great Classic Stories of World War II Ser.). 1980. pap. 5.95 (ISBN 0-396-07867-2). Dodd.

Twelve One Act Plays. Sam Shepard. Date not set. cancelled (ISBN 0-89396-018-7); pap. cancelled (ISBN 0-89396-019-5). Urizen Bks.

Twelve Original Essays on Great English Novels. Ed. by Charles Shapiro. (Waynebooks Ser: No. 14). 1960. text ed. 7.95x o.p. (ISBN 0-8143-1126-1). Wayne St U Pr.

Twelve Papers in Logic & Algebra. (Translation Ser.: Vol. 113). 1979. write for info. o.p. (ISBN 0-8218-3063-5). Am Math.

Twelve Papers on Analysis. (Translations Series Two: Vol. 115). 1980. 31.60 (ISBN 0-8218-3065-1). Am Math.

Twelve Ravens. Howard Rose. Ed. by R. Marek. 1970. 6.95 o.s.i. (ISBN 0-02-604880-9). Macmillan.

Twelve Sermons on Backsliding. Charles H. Spurgeon. (Charles H. Spurgeon Library). 1979. pap. 2.95 (ISBN 0-8010-8162-9). Baker Bk.

Twelve Sermons on Hope. Charles H. Spurgeon. (Charles H. Spurgeon Library Ser.). 1979. pap. 2.95 (ISBN 0-8010-8145-9). Baker Bk.

Twelve Sermons on the Prodigal Son & Other Texts in Luke 15. Charles H. Spurgeon. (Charles H. Spurgeon Library). 1976. pap. 2.95 (ISBN 0-8010-8084-3). Baker Bk.

Twelve Steps & Twelve Traditions. LC 53-5454. 192p. 1953. 4.00 (ISBN 0-916856-01-1). AAWS.

Twelve String Quartets: Opus 55, 64 & 71 Complete. Joseph Haydn. 288p. 1980. pap. 6.95 (ISBN 0-486-23933-0). Dover.

Twelve Systems of Higher Education: Six Decisive Issues. Clark Kerr et al. 214p. (Orig.). 1978. pap. text ed. 8.00 (ISBN 0-89192-211-3). Interbk Inc.

Twelve Tales of Suspense & the Supernatural. Davis Grubb. 144p. 1977. pap. 1.25 o.p. (ISBN 0-449-13727-9, GM). Fawcett.

Twelve Ten from San Antone: Only the Swift. Kirk Hamilton. (Orig.). 1980. pap. 2.25 (ISBN 0-8439-0741-X, Leisure Bks). Nordon Pubns.

Twelve-Tone Tonality. George Perle. 1978. 18.50x (ISBN 0-520-03387-6). U of Cal Pr.

Twelve Towers. Li Yu. Tr. by Nathan K. Mao from Chinese. LC 73-92416. 154p. 1979. pap. 5.95 (ISBN 0-295-95640-2). U of Wash Pr.

Twelve Ways to Build a Vocabulary. Archibald Hart. (Orig.). 1964. pap. 2.95 (ISBN 0-06-463293-8, EH 293, EH). Har-Row.

Twelve-Year Reich: A Social History of Nazi Germany, 1933-1945. Richard Grunberger. (Illus.). 1971. 10.00 o.p. (ISBN 0-03-076435-1). HR&W.

Twelve Years a Slave. Solomon Northup. Ed. by Sue Eakin & Joseph Logsdon. LC 68-13454. (Library of Southern Civilization: No. 1). (Illus.). 1968. 14.95x (ISBN 0-8071-0633-X); pap. text ed. 5.95 (ISBN 0-8071-0150-8). La State U Pr.

Twelve Years: An American Boyhood in East Germany. Joel Agee. 1981. 10.95 (ISBN 0-374-27958-6). FS&G.

Twenties: American Writing in the Postwar Decade. Frederick J. Hoffman. 1965. pap. text ed. 6.95 (ISBN 0-02-914780-8). Free Pr.

Twenties: Fiction, Poetry, Drama. rev. ed. Ed. by Warren French. LC 74-24534. 1976. lib. bdg. 16.00 o.p. (ISBN 0-912112-05-0). Everett-Edwards.

Twentieth Anniversary of Fluidics Symposium. Ed. by T. M. Drzewiecki & M. E. Franke. 232p. 1980. 30.00 (G00177). ASME.

Twentieth Century. Joel Colton. LC 68-54204. (Great Ages of Man). (Illus.). (gr. 6 up). 1968. PLB 11.97 (ISBN 0-8094-0383-8, Pub. by Time-Life). Silver.

Twentieth Century. Rosemary Lambert. LC 80-40456. (Cambridge Introduction to the History of Art: No. 7). (Illus.). 90p. Date not set. 19.95 (ISBN 0-521-22715-1); pap. 6.95 (ISBN 0-521-29622-6). Cambridge U Pr.

Twentieth Century. Peter Lane. (Visual Sources Ser.). 1972. 16.95 (ISBN 0-7134-1722-6, Pub. by Batsford England). David & Charles.

Twentieth-Century Africa. Ed. by P. J. McEwan. (Readings in African History Ser). 1968. 28.50x (ISBN 0-19-215663-2). Oxford U Pr.

Twentieth-Century American Dramatists, 2 vols. Ed. by John MacNicholas. (Dictionary of Literary Biography Ser.: Vol. 7). (Illus.). 300p. 1980. 108.00 set (ISBN 0-8103-0928-9). Gale.

Twentieth Century American Foreign Policy, Security, & Self Interest. R. Caridi. 1974. 15.95 (ISBN 0-13-934935-9); pap. 12.95 (ISBN 0-13-934927-8). P-H.

Twentieth Century American Literature. Warren French. 672p. 1981. pap. 12.95 (ISBN 0-312-82401-7). St Martin.

Twentieth-Century American Nicknames. Ed. by Laurence Urdang. 1979. 18.00 (ISBN 0-8242-0642-8). Wilson.

Twentieth-Century American Science Fiction Writers. Ed. by David Cowart. (Dictionary of Literary Biography Ser.). 1981. 54.00 (ISBN 0-8103-0918-1, Bruccoli Clark). Gale.

Twentieth Century Authors. Ed. by Stanley J. Kunitz & Howard Haycraft. (Illus.). 1942. 35.00 (ISBN 0-8242-0049-7); 1st suppl. 1955. 27.00 (ISBN 0-8242-0050-0). Wilson.

Twentieth Century Biographical Dictionary of Notable Americans, 10 V0ls. LC 68-19657. 1968. Repr. of 1904 ed. Set. 180.00 (ISBN 0-8103-3162-4). Gale.

Twentieth Century China. 3rd ed. O. Edmund Clubb. 1978. 24.00x (ISBN 0-231-04518-2); pap. 9.00x (ISBN 0-231-04519-0). Columbia U Pr.

Twentieth Century Chinese Stories. Ed. by Chih-Tsing Hsia & Joseph S. Lau. LC 72-173986. 250p. 1972. 17.50x (ISBN 0-231-03589-6); pap. 5.00x (ISBN 0-231-03590-X). Columbia U Pr.

Twentieth Century Church Music. Erik Routley. 1964. 5.75x o.p. (ISBN 0-19-519067-X). Oxford U Pr.

Twentieth Century Civilization. Kerry Davidson. 1976. pap. 3.95 o.p. (ISBN 0-06-460146-3, Cos). Har-Row.

Twentieth Century Crime & Mystery Writers. Ed. by John M. Reilly. (Twentieth Century Writers Ser.). 1600p. 1980. 50.00x (ISBN 0-312-82417-3). St Martin.

Twentieth Century Criticism: The Major Statements. William J. Handy & Max Westbrook. LC 73-3898. (Illus.). 1974. text ed. 14.95 (ISBN 0-02-913710-1). Free Pr.

Twentieth Century Czechoslovakia: The Meanings of Its History. Josef Korbel. LC 76-54250. 1977. 20.00x (ISBN 0-231-03724-4). Columbia U Pr.

Twentieth Century Decorating Architecture & Gardens. Ed. by House & Garden. LC 80-12593. (Illus.). 320p. 1980. 34.95 (ISBN 0-03-047581-3); pre-Jan. 29.95. HR&W.

Twentieth Century Discovery. Isaac Asimov. 1976. pap. 1.95 (ISBN 0-441-83227-X). Ace Bks.

Twentieth Century Drama: England, Ireland, the United States. Ed. by Ruby Cohn & Bernard Dukore. 1966. pap. text ed. 9.95x (ISBN 0-394-30141-2, RanC). Random.

Twentieth Century Ethics. Roger N. Hancock. LC 74-12023. 256p. 1974. 20.00x (ISBN 0-231-03877-1). Columbia U Pr.

Twentieth Century Europe: A History. 4th ed. C. E. Black & E. C. Helmreich. (Illus.). 1972. 18.95 o.p. (ISBN 0-394-47274-8); text ed. 18.95 (ISBN 0-394-31638-X). Knopf.

Twentieth-Century European Painting: A Guide to Information Sources. Ed. by Ann-Marie Cutul. LC 79-24249. (Art & Architecture Information Guide Ser.: Vol. 9). 1980. 30.00 (ISBN 0-8103-1438-X). Gale.

Twentieth Century European Paintings. Art Institute of Chicago & A. James Speyer. (Illus.). 112p. 1981 incl fiche 60.00x (ISBN 0-226-68804-6). U of Chicago Pr.

Twentieth Century French Drama. David I. Grossvogel. LC 65-7487. Orig. Title: Self-Conscious Stage in Modern French Drama. 1958. pap. 6.00x (ISBN 0-231-08522-2). Columbia U Pr.

Twentieth-Century French Fiction: Essays for Germaine Bree. Ed. by George Stambolian. 1975. 20.00 (ISBN 0-8135-0786-3). Rutgers U Pr.

Twentieth Century French Reader. C. D. James. 1966. 8.00 (ISBN 0-08-011232-3); pap. 6.70 (ISBN 0-08-011231-5). Pergamon.

Twentieth Century Furniture. Philippe Garner. 224p. 1980. 24.95 (ISBN 0-442-25421-0). Van Nos Reinhold.

Twentieth-Century Germany. A. J. Ryder. 300p. 1972. 22.50x (ISBN 0-231-03692-2); pap. 10.00x (ISBN 0-231-08350-5). Columbia U Pr.

Twentieth-Century History Nineteen Hundred to Nineteen Forty-Five. C. A. Leeds. (Illus.). 224p. 1979. pap. text ed. 9.95x (ISBN 0-7121-2025-4, Pub by Macdonald & Evans England). Intl Ideas.

Twentieth-Century Indonesia. Wilfred T. Neill. (Illus.). 413p. 1973. 25.00 (ISBN 0-231-03547-0); pap. 10.00x (ISBN 0-231-08316-5). Columbia U Pr.

Twentieth Century Interpretations of Coriolanus. Ed. by James E. Phillips. (Twentieth Century Interpretations Ser). 1970. 8.95 (ISBN 0-13-172676-5, Spec); pap. 1.25 (ISBN 0-13-172668-4, Spec). P-H.

Twentieth Century Interpretations of Hamlet. Ed. by S. Bevington. (Orig.). (YA) (gr. 9-12). 1968. 8.95 (ISBN 0-13-372375-5, Spec); pap. 2.95 (ISBN 0-13-372367-4, Spec). P-H.

Twentieth Century Interpretations of Macbeth. Howkes. 1977. 7.95 (ISBN 0-13-541458-X, Spec); pap. 2.45 (ISBN 0-13-541441-5, Spec). P-H.

Twentieth Century Interpretations of Moby Dick. Ed. by M. Gilmore. 1977. 8.95 (ISBN 0-13-586057-1, Spec); pap. 2.45 (ISBN 0-13-586032-6, Spec). P-H.

Twentieth Century Interpretations of Oedipus Rex. Ed. by M. O'Brien. 1968. 8.95 (ISBN 0-13-630467-2, Spec) P-H.

Twentieth Century Interpretations of Poe's Tales. Ed. by William L. Howarth. LC 69-15337. (Twentieth Century Interpretations Ser). 1971. 8.95 (ISBN 0-13-684654-8, Spec). P-H.

Twentieth Century Interpretations of Vanity Fair. Ed. by Michael G. Sundell. LC 73-79446. 1969 7.95 o.p. (ISBN 0-13-940395-7, Spec); pap. 1.25 o.p. (ISBN 0-13-940387-6, Spec). P-H.

Twentieth Century Interpretations of Walden. Ed. by Richard Ruland. 1968. pap. 8.95 (ISBN 0-13-944306-1, Spec). P-H.

Twentieth Century Interpretations of Anthony & Cleopatra. Ed. by Mark Rose. 1977. 8.95 (ISBN 0-13-038612-X, Spec); pap. 2.45 (ISBN 0-13-038604-9). P-H.

Twentieth Century Interpretations of A Farewell to Arms. Ed. by Jay Gellens. (Twentieth Century Interpretations Ser). 1970. 8.95 (ISBN 0-13-303180-2, Spec). P-H.

Twentieth Century Interpretations of All the Kings Men. Ed. by R. Chambers. 1977. 8.95 (ISBN 0-13-022434-0, Spec); pap. 3.45 (ISBN 0-13-022426-X, Spec). P-H.

Twentieth Century Interpretations of Crime & Punishment. Ed. by Robert L. Jackson. (Twentieth Century Interpretations Ser.). (Illus.). 128p. 1973. 8.95 (ISBN 0-13-193086-9, Spec). P-H.

Twentieth Century Interpretations of Gulliver's Travels. Ed. by Frank Brady. LC 68-23699. 8.95 (ISBN 0-13-371575-2, Spec); pap. 1.25 (ISBN 0-13-371567-1, Spec). P-H.

Twentieth Century Interpretations of Henry Fourth, Pt. 2. Ed. by David P. Young. LC 68-23698. (Twentieth Century Interpretations Ser). (YA) 1968. pap. 1.25 o.p. (ISBN 0-13-386987-3, Spec). P-H.

Twentieth Century Interpretations of Julius Caesar. Ed. by Leonard F. Dean. LC 69-11355. 1968. 8.95 (ISBN 0-13-512285-6, Spec). P-H.

Twentieth Century Interpretations of Moll Flanders. Ed. by Robert C. Elliott. (Twentieth Century Interpretations Ser). 1970. pap. 1.25 (ISBN 0-13-322230-6, Spec). P-H.

Twentieth Century Interpretations of Measure for Measure. Ed. by George L. Geckle. 7.95 o.p. (ISBN 0-13-567727-0, Spec); pap. 1.25 o.p. (ISBN 0-13-567719-X, Spec). P-H.

Twentieth Century Interpretations of Murder in the Cathedral. Ed. by D. Clark. 1971. 7.95 o.p. (ISBN 0-13-606400-0, Spec). P-H.

Twentieth Century Interpretations of Robinson Crusoe. Ed. by Frank H. Ellis. (Interpretations Ser). 1969. 8.95 (ISBN 0-13-781997-8, Spec); pap. 1.25 (ISBN 0-13-781989-7). P-H.

Twentieth Century Interpretations of Sons & Lovers. Ed. by Judith Farr. 1970. 7.95 o.p. (ISBN 0-13-822700-4, Spec); pap. 1.95 o.p. (ISBN 0-13-822692-X, Spec). P-H.

Twentieth Century Interpretations of The Great Gatsby. Ed. by Ernest Lockridge. (Orig.). (YA) (gr. 9-12). 1968. 8.95 (ISBN 0-13-363820-0, Spec); pap. 2.95 (ISBN 0-13-363812-X, Spec). P-H.

Twentieth Century Interpretations of The Pardoner's Tale. Ed. by Dewey R. Faulkner. LC 73-9998. (Twentieth Century Interpretations Ser.). 128p. 1973. pap. 1.45 (ISBN 0-13-648741-6, Spec). P-H.

Twentieth Century Interpretations of The Scarlet Letter. Ed. by John C. Gerber. LC 68-23438. (Twentieth Century Interpretations Series). (Orig.). 1968. 8.95 (ISBN 0-13-791582-9, Spec). P-H.

Twentieth Century Italian Poetry: A Bilingual Anthology. Ed. by L. R. Lind. LC 73-11343. (LLA Ser). 432p. 1974. 10.50 (ISBN 0-672-51409-5); pap. 9.70 (ISBN 0-672-61220-8). Bobbs.

Twentieth-Century Literary Criticism. Ed. by Sharon Hall. (Twentieth-Century Literary Criticism Ser.: Vol. 4). 650p. 1981. 58.00 (ISBN 0-8103-0178-4). Gale.

Twentieth-Century Literary Criticism. Ed. by Sharon K. Hall. LC 76-46132. (Vol. 3). 600p. 1980. 58.00 (ISBN 0-8103-0177-6). Gale.

Twentieth-Century Literary Criticism, Vol. 1. Ed. by Sharon Hall & Phyllis C. Mendelson. LC 76-46132. 1978. 54.00 (ISBN 0-8103-0175-X). Gale.

Twentieth-Century Literary Criticism, Vol. 2. LC 76-46132. 1979. 58.00 (ISBN 0-8103-0176-8). Gale.

Twentieth Century Literary Criticism: A Reader. Ed. by David Lodge. 1977. pap. text ed. 14.95x (ISBN 0-582-48422-7). Longman.

Twentieth Century Man. Gloria North. 16p. 1979. pap. 1.00 (ISBN 0-686-27736-8). Samisdat.

Twentieth-Century Mind: History, Ideas, & Literature in Britain, Vol. I: Nineteen Hundred to Nineteen Eighteen. Ed. by C. B. Cox & A. E. Dyson. 540p. 1972. pap. text ed. 6.95x (ISBN 0-19-281118-5). Oxford U Pr.

Twentieth-Century Mind: History, Ideas, & Literature in Britain, Vol. II: Nineteen Eighteen to Nineteen Forty-Five. Ed. by C. B. Cox & A. E. Dyson. 526p. 1972. pap. text ed. 16.75x (ISBN 0-19-212192-8). Oxford U Pr.

Twentieth Century Mind: History, Ideas, & Literature in Britain, Vol. III: Nineteen Forty-Five to Nineteen Sixty-Five. Ed. by C. B. Cox & A. E. Dyson. 522p. 1972. pap. text ed. 16.75x (ISBN 0-19-212193-6). Oxford U Pr.

Twentieth Century Miracle. Jerry Parrick. (Orig.). 1981. pap. 4.95 (ISBN 0-88270-488-5). Logos.

Twentieth-Century Montana: A State of Extremes. K. Ross Toole. LC 75-177348. 300p. 1979. Repr. of 1972 ed. 10.95 (ISBN 0-8061-0992-0). U of Okla Pr.

Twentieth Century Music: An Introduction. 2nd ed. E. Solzman. 1974. pap. 10.95 (ISBN 0-13-935007-1). P-H.

Twentieth Century Music: How It Developed, How to Listen to It. Marion Bauer. (Music Ser.). 1978. Repr. of 1933 ed. lib. bdg. 24.50 (ISBN 0-306-79503-5). Da Capo.

Twentieth-Century Music in Western Europe: The Compositions & Recordings. Arthur Cohn. LC 70-39297. 510p. 1972. Repr. of 1965 ed. lib. bdg. 37.50 (ISBN 0-306-70460-9). Da Capo.

Twentieth Century Music: Its Evolution from the End of the Harmonic Era into the Present Era of Sound. Peter Yates. LC 80-23310. xv, 367p. 1981. Repr. of 1967 ed. lib. bdg. 28.75x (ISBN 0-313-22516-8, YATC). Greenwood.

Twentieth-Century Music: The Sense Behind the Sound. Joan Peyser. LC 79-57286. (Illus.). 1980. pap. 5.95 (ISBN 0-02-871880-1). Schirmer Bks.

Twentieth Century Painting. Sam Hunter. (Abbeville Library of Art: No. 8). (Illus.). 112p. 1980. pap. 4.95 (ISBN 0-89659-123-9). Abbeville Pr.

Twentieth-Century Philosophy: The Analytic Tradition. M. Weitz. LC 66-10366. 1966. pap. text ed. 6.95 (ISBN 0-02-934990-7). Free Pr.

Twentieth Century Physics. J. Norwood. 1976. 22.95 (ISBN 0-13-935155-8). P-H.

Twentieth-Century Polish Avant-Garde Drama: Plays, Scenarios, Documents. Ed. by Daniel C. Gerould. LC 76-13659. (Illus.). 1977. 18.50x (ISBN 0-8014-0952-7). Cornell U Pr.

Twentieth Century Polish Theatre. Ed. by Bohdan Drosdowski. Tr. by Cathy Itzin. 1980. 16.95 (ISBN 0-7145-3738-1). Riverrun NY.

Twentieth Century Prophecy. James Bjornstad. 1976. pap. 1.25 (ISBN 0-89129-150-4). Jove Pubns.

Twentieth Century Prophecy: Jean Dixon-Edgar Cayce. James Bjornstad. 1969. pap. 1.95 (ISBN 0-87123-546-3, 200546). Bethany Fell.

Twentieth Century Pulpit, Vol. II. Ed. by James W. Cox & Patricia P. Cox. 1981. pap. 8.95 (ISBN 0-687-42716-9). Abingdon.

Twentieth-Century Russian Drama from Gorky to the Present. Harold B. Segel. LC 79-11673. (Illus.). 1979. 30.00x (ISBN 0-231-04576-X); pap. 15.00x (ISBN 0-231-04577-8). Columbia U Pr.

Twentieth Century Science Fiction Writers. Curtis S. Smith. (Twentieth Century Writers Ser.). 1600p. 1981. 65.00x (ISBN 0-312-82420-3). St Martin.

Twentieth-Century Short Story Explication: Supplement 1 to Third Edition. Warren S. Walker. (Short Story Explication Ser.). v, 257p. 1980. 27.50 (ISBN 0-208-01813-1, SSP). Shoe String.

Twentieth Century Spanish-American Novel: A Bibliographic Guide. David W. Foster. LC 75-25787. 1975. 10.00 (ISBN 0-8108-0871-4). Scarecrow.

Twentieth Century Table of Houses. A. LeRoi Simmons. 202p. 1972. text ed. 6.00 (ISBN 0-9605126-2-4). Aquarian Bk Pubs.

Twentieth-Century Theatre. Frank Vernon. 159p. 1980. Repr. of 1924 ed. lib. bdg. 30.00 (ISBN 0-89760-927-1). Telegraph Bks.

Twentieth Century Views of Musical History. William Hays. 1972. lib. rep. ed. 22.50x (ISBN 0-684-15149-9, ScribT). Scribner.

Twentieth Century World. 3rd ed. John Martell. (Illus.). 1981. pap. 13.95x. Intl Ideas.

Twentieth Century Writing: A Reader's Guide to Contemporary Literature. Ed. by Kenneth Richardson. 1970. 20.00 (ISBN 0-693-01700-7). Transatlantic.

Twentieth Century Yugoslavia. Fred Singleton. 340p. 1976. 22.50x (ISBN 0-231-04016-4); pap. 10.00x (ISBN 0-231-08341-6). Columbia U Pr.

Twentieth Century: 1914 to the Present. Ed. by Norman F. Cantor & Michael S. Werthman. LC 67-16644. (AHM Structure of European History Ser.: Vol. 6). 251p. 1967. pap. text ed. 5.95x (ISBN 0-88295-715-5). AHM Pub.

Twentieth Maine. John Pullen. 1980. 17.50 (ISBN 0-686-68805-8). Pr of Morningside.

Twentieth Son of Ornon. Mike Sirota. (Orig.). 1980. pap. 1.95 (ISBN 0-89083-685-X). Zebra.

Twenty American Peaks & Crags. Thomas Morrisey. 1978. 11.95 o.p. (ISBN 0-8092-7569-4); pap. 6.95 o.p. (ISBN 0-8092-7568-6). Contemp Bks.

Twenty & Ten. Claire H. Bishop. (Illus.). (gr. 4-6). 1952. 6.50 o.p. (ISBN 0-670-73407-1); pap. 1.95 o. p. o.p. (ISBN 0-685-59582-X). Viking Pr.

Twenty Artists: Yale School of Art, 1950-1970. Irving Sandler. LC 80-54616. (Illus.). 64p. 1981. pap. write for info. (ISBN 0-89467-016-6). Yale Art Gallery.

Twenty Best Sights of Sydney. John Yeomans. 128p. 1980. pap. 4.95x (ISBN 0-686-68862-7, Pub. by W Collins Australia). Intl Schol Bk Serv.

Twenty Cases Suggestive of Reincarnation. 2nd rev. ed. Ian Stevenson. LC 73-93627. Orig. Title: Proceedings of the American Society for Psychical Research, Vol. 26. xvi, 368p. 1974. 15.00x o.p. (ISBN 0-8139-0546-X). U Pr of Va.

Twenty Centuries of Christianity. Maureen Curley. (Children of the Kingdom Acitivites Ser.). (gr. 7-12). 1977. 7.95 (ISBN 0-686-13698-5). Pflaum Pr.

Twenty Cuentistas Cubanos. Leonardo Fernandez-Marcane. LC 77-89099. 1978. pap. 4.95 (ISBN 0-89729-164-6). Ediciones.

Twenty Drawings. Kahlil Gibran. LC 74-9154. 1974. pap. 4.95 o.p. (ISBN 0-394-71123-8, V-123, Vin). Random.

Twenty-Eight Days to a Better Job. Tom Jackson. 1977. pap. 6.95 (ISBN 0-8015-8013-7, Hawthorn). Dutton.

Twenty-Elephant Restaurant. Russell Hoban & Emily Arnold McCully. LC 77-1056. (gr. k-5). 1978. 9.95 (ISBN 0-689-30593-1). Atheneum.

Twenty Episodes in the Life of Pancho Villa. Elias L. Torres. Tr. by Sheila Ohlendorf from Spanish. 1973. 7.50 o.p. (ISBN 0-88426-017-8). Encino Pr.

Twenty Ethnic Songs from Western Canada. Kenneth Peacock. (Illus.). 1966. pap. 5.00 (ISBN 0-660-02053-X, 56524-6, Pub. by Natl Mus Canada). U of Chicago Pr.

Twenty-Fifth Congress of the CPSU: Assessment & Context. Ed. by Alexander Dallin. LC 77-2445. (Publication Ser: No. 184). (Illus.). 1977. pap. 5.95 (ISBN 0-8179-6842-3). Hoover Inst Pr.

Twenty-Five Hundred Dollars a Year. Mordecai Ezekiel. LC 72-2369. (FDR & the Era of the New Deal Ser). 348p. 1973. Repr. of 1936 ed. lib. bdg. 32.50 (ISBN 0-306-70468-4). Da Capo.

Twenty-Five Hundred Historical Woodwind Instruments: An Inventory of the Major Collections. Phillip T. Young. (Illus.). 1981. lib. bdg. price not set (ISBN 0-918728-17-7). Pendragon NY.

Twenty-Five Oregon Weekend Adventures, Vol. II. Ione Reed. LC 75-27462. (Illus.). 1979. pap. 4.95 (ISBN 0-89802-064-6). Beautiful Am.

Twenty-Five Planets Speak to Planet Earth. Ruth E. Norman. (Tesla Speaks Ser.: Vol. V). (Illus.). 1975. 7.95 (ISBN 0-932642-26-8); pap. 5.95 (ISBN 0-932642-27-6). Unarius.

Twenty-Five Ski Tours in & Around Greater Boston. Irwin Grossman & Ron Wolanin. (Illus.). Date not set. pap. 5.95 (ISBN 0-89725-007-9). NH Pub Co. Postponed.

Twenty-Five Ski Tours in Central New York. Bill Ehling. (Illus.). 128p. 1980. pap. 5.95 (ISBN 0-89725-019-2). NH Pub Co.

Twenty-Five Verses. Mirza Ghalib. (Translated from Urdu). 6.75 (ISBN 0-89253-754-X); flexible cloth 4.80 (ISBN 0-89253-755-8). Ind-US Inc.

Twenty-Five Years of Accounting Responsibility 1911-1936, Vols. I & II. George O. May. Ed. by Carleton Hunt. 1971. Repr. of 1936 ed. text ed. 26.00 (ISBN 0-914348-03-5). Scholars Bk.

Twenty-Five Years of the American Astronautical Society, Historical Reflections & Projections. Ed. by Eugene M. Emme. (AAS History Ser.: Vol. 2). (Illus.). 248p. 1980. lib. bdg. 25.00x (ISBN 0-87703-117-7); pap. 15.00x (ISBN 0-87703-118-5). Univelt Inc.

Twenty-Five Years: 1945 to 1970. Ed. by G. Kerry Smith. LC 73-110640. (Higher Education Ser.). 1970. 14.95x o.p. (ISBN 0-87589-058-X). Jossey-Bass.

Twenty-Four Architectural Plans of Chan Chan, Peru. Michael E. Moseley & Carol Mackey. LC 73-92493. 1974. maps 30.00 (ISBN 0-87365-778-0). Peabody Harvard.

Twenty-Four Caprices in Form Etudes for Violin. Pierre Rode. Ed. by Gustave Saenger. (Carl Fischer Music Library: No.583). 52p. (gr. 6-12). 1910. pap. 4.00 (ISBN 0-686-64060-8, L583). Fischer Inc NY.

Twenty-Four Favorite One-Act Plays. Ed. by Van H. Cartmell & Bennett Cerf. LC 58-13274. pap. 3.95 (ISBN 0-385-06617-1, C423, Dolp). Doubleday.

Twenty-Four Hours a Day. large print ed. Alan L. Roeck. 1980. pap. 4.95 (ISBN 0-89486-108-5). Hazelden.

Twenty-Four Practice Hairstyles. rev. ed. Anthony B. Colletti. 1981. pap. text ed. 5.00 (ISBN 0-912126-47-7, 1265-00). Keystone Pubns.

Twenty-Four Questions in Group Leadership. 2nd ed. Ernest D. Nathan. 1979. pap. 8.95 (ISBN 0-201-05263-6). A-W.

Twenty-Four Stories by Premchand. Ed. by Nandini Nopany & P. Lal. 208p. 1981. text ed. 17.95 (ISBN 0-7069-1199-7, Pub by Vikas India). Advent Bk.

Twenty-Four Ways of Becoming a Millionaire in Less Than One Year. Merton Lansdale. (Essential Knowledge Library). (Illus.). 1979. spiral bdg. 6.00 (ISBN 0-89266-174-7). Am Classical Coll Pr.

Twenty-Four Worked Engineering Drawing Examples. A. J. Jones & N. Barlow. 1966. pap. text ed. 4.20 (ISBN 0-08-012080-6). Pergamon.

Twenty Gallant Horses. Clarence W. Anderson. (gr. 5 up). 1965. 8.95 (ISBN 0-02-705530-2). Macmillan.

Twenty Great Trophy Hunts. Ed. by John O. Cartier. 1980. 17.95 (ISBN 0-679-51379-5). McKay.

Twenty Havoc at War. William Hess. (Illus.). 1980. 17.50 (ISBN 0-684-16453-1, ScribT). Scribner.

Twenty Jataka Tales. Noor I. Khan. (Illus.). 1978. 8.95; pap. 5.95 (ISBN 0-87773-747-9). Great Eastern.

Twenty Lectures on Chinese Culture: An Intermediary Chinese Textbook. Parker P. Huang et al. 1967. 0.p. 13.00 (ISBN 0-300-00579-2); pap. text ed. 8.50x (ISBN 0-300-00127-4). Yale U Pr.

Twenty Lectures on Chinese Culture: Exercise Book. Parker Po-fei Huang. LC 66-21520. 1967. pap. text ed. 8.50x (ISBN 0-300-00128-2). Yale U Pr.

Twenty Lectures on Thermodynamics. H. A. Buchdahl. 1975. text ed. 21.00 (ISBN 0-08-018299-2); pap. text ed. 12.75 (ISBN 0-08-018951-2). Pergamon.

Twenty Longest Days. Lindy Washburn & Lloyd Van Vactor. 197p. (Orig.). 1981. pap. 7.95 (ISBN 0-8298-0450-1). Pilgrim NY.

Twenty Love Poems. Steven Osterlund. 1977. pap. 2.95 (ISBN 0-931534-05-4). Windflower Pr.

Twenty Love Poems & a Song of Despair. Pablo Neruda. LC 70-481699. (Cape Editions Ser). 1976. pap. 2.95 (ISBN 0-14-042205-6, Grossman). Penguin.

Twenty Minutes to Live. Richard Uhlich. Ed. by Richard Uhlich. (Bluejeans Paperback Ser.). (Illus., Orig.). (gr. 7-12). 1978. pap. text ed. 1.25 (ISBN 0-8374-5004-7). Xerox Ed Pubns.

Twenty Modern Americans. Ed. by Alice C. Cooper & Charles A. Palmer. LC 42-1234. (gr. 7 up). 1942. 6.50 o.p. (ISBN 0-15-291590-7, HJ). HarBraceJ.

Twenty One. Koko Ita. (Gambler's Book Shelf). 64p. 1976. pap. 2.95 (ISBN 0-89650-563-4). Gamblers.

Twenty-One Afternoons of Biology: A Laboratory Manual. S. O. Schiff & D. A. Griffith. Ed. by Houston. 155p. 1975. lab manual 6.95x o.p. (ISBN 0-205-04572-3); instr's manual free o.p. (ISBN 0-685-52902-9). Allyn.

Twenty-One Afternoons of Biology: A Laboratory Manual. 2nd ed. S. O. Schiff et al. 1979. pap. text ed. 10.95x o.p. (ISBN 0-205-06132-X, 6761321); instr's man. o.p. avail. o.p. (ISBN 0-205-06193-1). Allyn.

Twenty One Custom Speaker Enclosure Projects You Can Build. David B. Weems. (Illus.). 240p. (Orig.). 1980. 12.95 (ISBN 0-8306-9962-7); pap. 7.95 (ISBN 0-8306-1234-3, 1234). TAB Bks.

Twenty-One Days to a Trained Dog. Dick Maller & Jeffrey Feinman. 1979. pap. 2.95 (ISBN 0-671-25193-7, Fireside). S&S.

Twenty-One Fifty A.D. The Macro Love Story. Thea Alexander. 281p. (Orig.). 1971. pap. 4.00 (ISBN 0-913080-03-9). Macro Bks.

Twenty-One Great Stories. Ed. by Abraham Lass & Norma Tasman. (Orig.). 1969. pap. 1.95 (ISBN 0-451-61843-2, MJ1843, Ment). NAL.

Twenty-One Language Dictionary: International Dictionary. H. L. Ouseg. write for info. Philos Lib.

Twenty-One Mile Swim. Matt Christopher. LC 79-15197. (gr. 3-7). 1979. 8.95g (ISBN 0-316-13979-3). Little.

Twenty-One Stereo Hi-Fi Stereo Speaker Cabinets You Can Build. Christopher Robin. (Illus.). 80p. 1980. pap. 4.95 (ISBN 0-8359-7896-6). Reston.

Twenty-One Stories. Graham Greene. 200p. 1981. pap. 2.95 (ISBN 0-14-003093-X). Penguin.

Twenty Plays of the No Theatre. Ed. by Donald Keene. Tr. by Tyler et al from Jap. LC 74-121556. 1970. 22.50x (ISBN 0-231-03454-7); pap. 12.00x (ISBN 0-231-03455-5). Columbia U Pr.

Twenty Poems of Rolf Jacobsen. Rolf Jacosen. Ed. by Robert Bly. 1977. pap. 3.50 (ISBN 0-685-88845-2). Eighties Pr.

Twenty Problems--Twenty Solutions: The Basic Design Workbook. Raymond Dorn. (Illus.). 88p. 1980. pap. 9.95 (ISBN 0-931368-03-0). Ragan Comm.

Twenty-Seven Lines Upon the Cubic Surface. A. Henderson. (Cambridge Tracts in Mathematics & Mathematical Physics Ser.: No. 13). (Illus.). 1969. Repr. of 1911 ed. 7.50 o.s.i. (ISBN 0-02-845930-X). Hafner.

Twenty Seven Poems. Roger Hecht. LC 66-20099. 64p. 1966. 5.95 (ISBN 0-8040-0300-9). Swallow.

Twenty Seven Wagons Full of Cotton. 3rd ed. Tennessee Williams. LC 53-12488. 1966. pap. 4.95 (ISBN 0-8112-0225-9, NDP217). New Directions.

Twenty-Seven Wagons Full of Cotton & Other Short Stories. Tennessee Williams. LC 78-159743. (Theatre of Tennessee Williams: Vol. VI). 288p. 1981. 17.95 (ISBN 0-8112-0794-3). New Directions.

Twenty Silver Ghosts: The Incomparable Pre-World War 1 Rolls-Royce. Melbourne Brindle & Phil May. LC 78-8806. 1978. 17.95 o.p. (ISBN 0-385-14668-X). Doubleday.

Twenty-Six Afternoons of Biology: An Introductory Laboratory Manual. 2nd ed. G. Wald et al. (gr. 9-12). 1966. pap. text ed. 11.95 (ISBN 0-201-08461-9); individual experiments 1.00 ea. A-W.

Twenty-Six Centuries of Agrarian Reform: A Comparative Analysis. Elias H. Tuma. (Near Eastern Center, UCLA). 1965. 20.00x (ISBN 0-520-01286-0). U of Cal Pr.

Twenty-Six Lessons on Luke, Vol. 1. Paul Butler. LC 79-57089. (Bible Student Study Guides Ser.). 220p. (Orig.). 1981. pap. 3.95 (ISBN 0-89900-166-1). College Pr Pub. Postponed.

Twenty-Six Lessons on Matthew, Vol. II. John Raymond. (Bible Student Study Guide Ser.). 180p. 1981. pap. 2.95 (ISBN 0-89900-171-8). College Pr Pub.

Twenty-Six Lessons on Matthew, Vol. 1. John Raymond. LC 80-67734. (Bible Student Study Guides). 150p. (Orig.). 1980. pap. 2.95 (ISBN 0-89900-167-X). College Pr Pub.

Twenty-Six Lessons on the First Corinthians. Wallace Wartick. (Bible Study Guide Ser.). 210p. (Orig.). 1980. pap. 3.95 (ISBN 0-89900-168-8). College Pr Pub.

Twenty Six Mountains for Viewing the Sunset from. Higgins. pap. write for info. (ISBN 0-914162-54-3). Knowles.

Twenty-Six Riddles from A to Z. Albert G. Miller. (ABC Serendipity Ser). (gr. 2-6). 1973. 6.57 o.p. (ISBN 0-8372-0821-1); pap. 4.35 o.p. (ISBN 0-686-66687-9). Bowmar-Noble.

Twenty-Six Starlings Will Fly Through Your Mind. Barbara Wersba. LC 77-3811. (Illus.). 40p. 1980. 8.95 (ISBN 0-06-026376-8, HarpJ); PLB 8.79 (ISBN 0-06-026377-6). Har-Row.

Twenty Tasks. Frei Otto et al. (Illus.). 334p. (Orig., Eng. & Ger.). 1979. lib. bdg. write for info. (ISBN 0-8150-0905-4). Wittenborn.

Twenty-Third Stamp Car Crash Conference. Society of Automotive Engineers. 1979. 35.00 (ISBN 0-89883-052-4). Soc Auto Engineers.

Twenty Thousand Alarms. Richard Hamilton & Charles N. Barnard. LC 74-33553. 256p. 1981. pap. 2.50 (ISBN 0-87216-810-7). Playboy Pbks.

Twenty Thousand Leagues Under the Sea. Retold by John Kennett. 1977. pap. text ed. 2.95 o.p. (ISBN 0-8277-5383-7). British Bk Ctr.

Twenty Thousand Leagues Under the Sea. Jules Verne. (Literature Ser). (gr. 7-12). 1970. pap. text ed. 3.67 (ISBN 0-87720-740-2). AMSCO Sch.

Twenty Thousand Leagues Under the Sea. Jules Verne. (Illus.). (gr. 7 up). 1962. 5.95 (ISBN 0-02-791640-5). Macmillan.

Twenty Thousand Quips & Quotes. Evan Esar. LC 68-18096. 1968. 12.95 (ISBN 0-385-00047-2). Doubleday.

Twenty-Three Hundred Holley Carburetor Handbook. Mike Urich. (Orig.). 1981. pap. 3.95 (ISBN 0-89586-048-1). H P Bks.

Twenty Three Hundred Steps to Word Power. Edward C. Gruber. LC 62-20285. (Orig.). 1963. pap. 2.95 (ISBN 0-668-01032-0). Arc Bks.

Twenty-Three Modern British Poets. Ed. by John Matthias. LC 71-150757. 338p. 1971. 15.00x (ISBN 0-8040-0507-9); pap. 8.95x (ISBN 0-8214-0508-X). Swallow.

Twenty-Three Steps to Success & Achievement. Robert J. Lumsden. 1978. pap. 3.95 (ISBN 0-85454-024-5). Newcastle Pub.

Twenty Twentieth Century Jews. S. J. Goldsmith. LC 62-21948. (Illus.). 142p. 1962. 6.95 (ISBN 0-88400-021-4). Shengold.

Twenty-Two Caliber Rifle. David Petzal. (Illus.). 1973. 9.95 (ISBN 0-87691-077-0). Winchester Pr.

Twenty-Two Keys of the Tarot. Arland Ussher. Tr. by L. Mac Weeney. (Illus.). 1976. pap. text ed. 2.75x (ISBN 0-85105-297-5, Dolmen Pr). Humanities.

Twenty Years at Hull-House. Jane Addams. (Illus.). 1966. 6.95 o.s.i. (ISBN 0-02-500480-8). Macmillan.

Twenty Years Indonesian Foreign Policy 1945-1965. Gde Agung Anak. LC 72-93180. 1973. text ed. 67.65x (ISBN 0-686-22635-6). Mouton.

Twenty Years of Award Winners from the Society of Illustrators. Ed. by Art Weithas. (Illus.). 352p. 1981. 45.00 (ISBN 0-8038-7224-0, Visual Communication). Hastings.

Twenty Years of Silents, Nineteen Hundred & Eight to Nineteen Twenty-Eight. John T. Weaver. LC 73-157729. 514p. 1971. lib. bdg. 20.50 (ISBN 0-8108-0299-6). Scarecrow.

Twenty Years of the Literary Review: Essays, Stories, Poems, Plays, Epigrams. Ed. & frwd. by Charles Angoff. LC 77-92563. 500p. 1981. 18.00 (ISBN 0-8386-2221-6). Fairleigh Dickinson.

Twice a Minority: Mexican-American Woman. Margarita B. Melville. LC 80-11177. (Illus.). 1980. pap. text ed. 11.95 (ISBN 0-8016-3386-9). Mosby.

Twice Freed. Patricia St. John. pap. 1.95 (ISBN 0-8024-8979-6). Moody.

Twice the Heartache. Judy Campbell & Susan Lowe. 200p. (Orig.). 1981. 1.95 (ISBN 0-89896-050-9). Larksdale.

Twice-Told Tales: An Anthology of Short Fiction. Gerard A. Barker. LC 78-69561. 1978. pap. text ed. 8.75 (ISBN 0-395-26635-1); inst. manual 0.65 (ISBN 0-395-26636-X). HM.

Twice Turned Tales. Donald B. Miller. LC 77-88730. (Illus.). 1977. pap. 3.50 o.p. (ISBN 0-930918-00-2). Vitality Assocs.

Twickenham: The Story of a Rugby Ground. Wallace Reyburn. 1976. 14.95 o.p. (ISBN 0-04-796044-2). Allen Unwin.

Twiggy & Justin. Thomas Whiteside. (Photos). 1968. 4.50 o.p. (ISBN 0-374-27980-2). FS&G.

Twilight. Moni Moulik. 1976. 9.00 (ISBN 0-89253-829-5); flexible cloth 6.75 (ISBN 0-89253-830-9). Ind-US Inc.

Twilight in Dehli. 2nd ed. Ahmed Ali. 290p. 1974. pap. 3.00 (ISBN 0-88253-281-2). Ind-US Inc.

Twilight in Djakarta. Mochtar Lubis. Tr. by Claire Holt. LC 64-16196. 1964. 7.95 (ISBN 0-8149-0148-4). Vanguard.

Twilight of Authority. Robert Nisbet. 272p. 1975. 14.95x (ISBN 0-19-501942-3). Oxford U Pr.

Twilight of Authority. Robert Nisbet. LC 75-7357. 1977. pap. 5.95 (ISBN 0-19-502177-0, 485, GB). Oxford U Pr.

Twilight of Evolution. Henry M. Morris. 1963. pap. 2.95 (ISBN 0-8010-5862-7). Baker Bk.

Twilight of France, 1933-1940. Alexander Werth. 21.00 (ISBN 0-86527-199-2). Fertig.

Twilight of Progressivism: The Western Republican Senators & the New Deal. Ronald L. Feinman. LC 80-20124. (Johns Hopkins Studies in Historical & Political Science). (Illus.). 288p. 1981. text ed. 18.50x (ISBN 0-8018-2373-0). Johns Hopkins.

Twilight of Subjectivity: Contributions to a Post-Individualist Theory of Politics. Fred R. Dallmayr. LC 80-23433. 416p. 1981. lib. bdg. 20.00x (ISBN 0-87023-314-9); pap. text ed. 10.00x (ISBN 0-87023-315-7). U of Mass Pr.

Twilight of the City. Charles Platt. LC 76-40913. 1977. 8.95 o.s.i. (ISBN 0-02-597620-6, 59762). Macmillan.

Twilight of the Gods: The Music of the Beatles. Wilfrid Mellers. LC 73-3508. (Illus.). 1975. pap. 5.95 (ISBN 0-02-871390-7). Schirmer Bks.

Twilight of the Primitive. Lewis Cotlow. (Walden Editions). 1973. pap. 1.65 o.p. (ISBN 0-685-32483-4, 345-23568-1-165). Ballantine.

Twilight of the Sioux. John G. Neihardt. LC 74-134771. Orig. Title: A Cycle of the West. 1971. pap. 4.50 (ISBN 0-8032-5734-1, BB 532, Bison). U of Nebr Pr.

Twilight Over England. William Joyce. 1978. pap. 4.50x (ISBN 0-911038-37-X). Noontide.

Twilight Tapestry. Frieda Bair. 1977. 3.95 (ISBN 0-8059-2470-1). Dorrance.

Twilight, 1977. T. Lobsang Rampa. pap. 2.50 (ISBN 0-685-91303-1). Weiser.

Twin Playlets for Children: Mr. Wishing Match & Community Sing, 2 bks. Louise Louis. (gr. 4-11). 1979. pap. 3.99 (ISBN 0-345-54321-1). Pen-Art.

Twin Research: Proceedings, 3 vols. International Congress on Twin Studies, 2nd. Ed. by Walter E. Nance et al. Incl. Pt. A. Psychology & Methodology. 32.00 (ISBN 0-8451-0150-1); Pt. B. Biology & Epidemiology. 26.00 (ISBN 0-8451-0151-X); Pt. C. Clinical Studies. 35.00 (ISBN 0-8451-0152-8). LC 78-8480. (Progress in Clinical & Biological Research: Vols. 24A, 24B, 24C). 1978. Set. 93.00 (ISBN 0-8451-0024-6). A R Liss.

Twinkie Flickertail. Prudence R. McGowan. (Illus.). 1977. 3.95 (ISBN 0-8059-2379-9). Dorrance.

Twinkle. James Eldridge, pseud. (Illus.). 64p. (Orig.). 1980. pap. 3.25 (ISBN 0-938900-00-5). Creations Unltd.

Twins. Gurney Williams. (First Bks.). (Illus.). (gr. 4 up). 1979. PLB 6.45 s&l (ISBN 0-531-02265-X). Watts.

Twins. Carola Zentner. LC 75-2914. (Illus.). 128p. 1975. 11.95 (ISBN 0-7153-6997-0). David & Charles.

Twins of Ceylon. Harry Williams. (Twins Ser). (Illus.). (gr. 6-9). 1965. 6.00 (ISBN 0-8023-1108-3). Dufour.

Twins of the Rain Forest. Neville M. Ukoli. (Orig.). 1968. pap. text ed. 2.25x (ISBN 0-582-64005-9). Humanities.

Twins on Twins. Frances M. Gill & Kathryn M. Abbe. 1980. 17.95 (ISBN 0-517-54149-1, 541491). Potter.

Twins, the Story of Multiple Births. Joanna Cole & Madeleine Edmondson. LC 75-168470. (Illus.). 64p. (gr. 3-7). 1972. PLB 6.00 (ISBN 0-688-31981-5). Morrow.

Twist of Lennon. Cynthia Lennon. 1979. pap. 2.50 (ISBN 0-380-45450-5, 45450). Avon.

Twist of Sand. Jeffrey Jenkins. (Keith Jennison Large Type Bks). 8.95 (ISBN 0-531-00299-3). Watts.

Twist, Wiggle, & Squirm: A Book About Earthworms. Laurence Pringle. LC 74-184983. (Let's-Read-&-Find-Out Science Bk). (Illus.). 33p. (gr. k-3). 1973. 7.95 (ISBN 0-690-84154-X, TYC-J); PLB 7.89 (ISBN 0-690-84155-8). T Y Crowell.

Twisted Cubic, with Some Account of the Metrical Properties of the Cubic Hyperbla. P. W. Wood. (Cambridge Tracts in Mathematics & Mathematical Physics Ser: No. 14). (Illus.). 1960. Repr. of 1913 ed. 7.50 o.s.i. (ISBN 0-02-854980-5). Hafner.

Twisted Kicks. Tom Carson. 264p. 1981. 11.95 (ISBN 0-934558-03-5); pap. 69.95 (ISBN 0-934558-05-1). Entwhistle Bks.

Twister of Twists, a Tangler of Tongues. Alvin Schwartz. LC 72-1434. (Illus.). 126p. (gr. 6 up). 1972. 8.95 (ISBN 0-397-31387-X); pap. 1.95 (ISBN 0-397-31412-4, LSC-22). Lippincott.

Twists & Turns of Love. Barbara Cartland. LC 78-486. 1978. 6.95 (ISBN 0-87272-036-5, Duron Bks). Brodart.

Twitchwell the Wishful. Marjorie W. Sharmat. LC 80-16845. (Illus.). 40p. (ps-3). 1981. PLB 7.95 (ISBN 0-8234-0379-3). Holiday.

Twits. Mary Tannen. LC 80-18410. (Illus.). 96p. (ps-5). 1981. 7.95 (ISBN 0-394-84599-4); PLB 7.99 (ISBN 0-394-94599-9). Knopf.

Twixt Twelve & Twenty. Pat Boone. 1973. pap. 1.25 o.s.i. (ISBN 0-89129-147-4, FV2933). Jove Pubns.

Two Addresses Delivered to Members of The Grolier Club. William Thorp & Henry S. Drinker. (Incl. I. Trollope's (Willard Thorp) & II, The Lawyers of Anthony Trollope (Henry S. Drinker)). 1950. 6.00x o.p. (ISBN 0-8139-0463-3, Grolier Club). U Pr of Va.

Two Addresses Delivered to Members of the Grolier Club: Trollope's America; the Lawyers of Anthony Trollope. Willard Thorp & Henry S. Drinker. 1950. 6.00x o.p. (ISBN 0-686-28528-X, Dist. by U Pr of Va). Grolier Club.

Two African Tales. Abioseh Nicol. 1965. text ed. 3.95x (ISBN 0-521-05826-0). Cambridge U Pr.

Two Angry Women of Abington: A Critical Edition. Henry Porter. Ed. by Marianne B. Evett. LC 79-54336. (Renaissance Drama Ser.). 304p. 1980. lib. bdg. 33.00 (ISBN 0-8240-4454-1). Garland Pub.

Two Are Better Than One. Carol R. Brink. LC 68-20615. (Illus.). (gr. 4-6). 1968. 6.95g o.s.i. (ISBN 0-02-714320-1). Macmillan.

Two Articles: Collinearity-Preserving Functions Between Affine Desarguesian Planes. David S. Carter & Andrew Vogt. LC 80-20427. (Memoirs: No. 235). 1980. 5.20 (ISBN 0-8218-2235-7). Am Math.

Two Babylons. Alexander Hislop. 1932. 6.95 (ISBN 0-87213-330-3). Loizeaux.

Two Basic Psychological Forces Prompting Men to Action & How to Utilize Them Effectively. Roy T. Lawrence. (Essential Knowledge Library Bk.). (Illus.). 1979. 6.00 (ISBN 0-89266-158-5). Am Classical Coll Pr.

Two Bishops. Agnes S. Turnbull. 1980. lib. bdg. 14.95 (ISBN 0-8161-3173-2, Large Print Bks). G K Hall.

Two Blades of Grass: Rural Cooperatives in Agricultural Modernization. Peter Worsley. 1971. text ed. 21.00x (ISBN 0-7190-0444-6). Humanities.

Two Blocks Down. Jina Delton. LC 80-8458. (YA) (gr. 7 up). 1981. 8.95 (ISBN 0-06-021590-9, HarpJ); PLB 8.79g (ISBN 0-06-021591-7). Har-Row.

Two Books...of the Proficience & Advancement of Learning. Francis Bacon. LC 70-25525. (English Experience Ser.: No. 218). 236p. Repr. of 1605 ed. 39.00 (ISBN 90-221-0218-1). Walter J Johnson.

Two-Boss Business. Elyse Sommer & Mike Sommer. Ed. by K. Lawson. (Illus.). 160p. 1980. 12.95 (ISBN 0-88421-071-5). Butterick Pub.

Two Brahman Sources of Emerson & Thoreau, 1822-1832. Ed. by William B. Stein. LC 67-10340. 1967. 33.00x (ISBN 0-8201-1043-4). Schol Facsimiles.

Two by Norah Lofts. Norah Lofts. Bd. with Requiem for Idols; You're Best Alone. 240p. 1981. 12.95 (ISBN 0-385-01768-5). Doubleday.

Two by Two. Tony Talbot. (gr. 1-3). 1974. 4.95 o.p. (ISBN 0-695-80484-7); lib ed. 4.98 o.p. (ISBN 0-695-40484-9). Follett.

Two Came Calling. Nancy Dorer & Frances Dorer. (Orig.). 1980. pap. 1.95 (ISBN 0-532-23226-7). Manor Bks.

Two-Career Couple. Francine S. Hall & Douglas T. Hall. (Illus.). 1979. 10.95 (ISBN 0-201-02733-X); pap. 5.95 (ISBN 0-201-02734-8). A-W.

Two-Career Family: Issues & Alternatives. Samiha S. Peterson et al. LC 78-66418. 1978. pap. text ed. 10.25 (ISBN 0-8191-0020-X). U Pr of Amer.

Two Carolines. Gloria Martinis. (Orig.). 1976. pap. 1.50 o.p. (ISBN 0-685-64018-3, LB339DK, Leisure Bks). Nordon Pubns.

Two Centuries of Bach. Friedrich Blume. Tr. by Stanley Godman. (Music Reprint Ser., 1978). 1978. Repr. of 1950 ed. lib. bdg. 14.50 (ISBN 0-306-77567-0). Da Capo.

Two Centuries of Black American Art. David C. Driskell. LC 76-13691. 1976. pap. text ed. 7.95 o.p. (ISBN 0-87587-070-8). LA Co Art Mus.

Two Centuries of Black American Art. Compiled by David Driskell. 1976. 15.00 o.p. (ISBN 0-394-40887-X). Knopf.

Two Centuries of Philosophy: American Philosophy Since the Revolution -- Papers from the Bicentennial Symposium. Ed. by Peter Caws. (American Philosophical Quarterly Library of Philosophy). 381p. 1980. 30.00x (ISBN 0-8476-6249-7). Rowman.

Two Centuries of Royal Weddings. Christopher Warwick. LC 79-49276. (Illus.). 145p. 1980. 14.95 (ISBN 0-396-07838-9). Dodd.

Two Choice & Useful Treatises. Joseph Glanville. Ed. by Rene Wellek. LC 75-11223. (British Philosophers & Theologians of the 17th & 18th Centuries Ser.). 1978. lib. bdg. 42.00 (ISBN 0-8240-1777-3). Garland Pub.

Two Christmases. Aleda Renken. LC 74-37. (Haley Adventure Bks.). (Illus.). 96p. (gr. 3-7). 1974. pap. 2.50 (ISBN 0-570-03604-6, 39-1026). Concordia.

Two-Color New Phonics Workbook, Level D. Jane Ervin. (gr. 4). 1977. 3.76 (ISBN 0-87895-442-2). Modern Curr.

Two-Color New Phonics Workbooks. Elwell. Incl. Bk. A. (gr. 1). pap. text ed. 3.96 (ISBN 0-87895-136-9); tchr's ed. 2.00 (ISBN 0-87895-135-0); Bk. B. (gr. 2). pap. text ed. 3.88 (ISBN 0-87895-223-3); teacher's ed 2.00 (ISBN 0-87895-228-4); Bk. C. (gr. 3). pap. text ed. 3.80 (ISBN 0-87895-320-5); teacher's ed 2.00 (ISBN 0-87895-322-1). (MCP Basic Program Ser.). 1976. Modern Curr.

Two Continents Book of Childrens Verse. Ed. by Howard Sergeant. 1977. Repr. of 1972 ed. 7.95 (ISBN 0-8467-0238-X, Pub. by Two Continents). Hippocrene Bks.

Two Contrariant Schools, Concerning the Establishment of a Christian University. Apostolos Makrakis. Ed. by Orthodox Christian Educational Society. Tr. by Denver Cummings from Hellenic. 87p. (Orig.). 1949. pap. 2.00x (ISBN 0-938366-27-0). Orthodox Chr.

Two Crows Came. Jonni Dolan. LC 80-18252. 156p. 1980. pap. 5.95 (ISBN 0-914718-53-3). Pacific Search.

Two Cultures: And a Second Look. Charles P. Snow. LC 64-1425. 1969. 15.50 (ISBN 0-521-06520-8); pap. 3.95 (ISBN 0-521-09576-X). Cambridge U Pr.

Two Dantes & Other Studies. Kenelm Foster. 1978. 20.00x (ISBN 0-520-03326-4). U of Cal Pr.

Two Death Tales: from the Ulster Cycle: The Death of Cu Roi & the Death of Cu Chulainn. Tr. by Maria Tymoczko. (Dolmen Texts: No. 2). 1980. text ed. 31.25x (ISBN 0-85105-342-4, Dolmen Pr). Humanities.

Two Dialogues: Containing a Comparative View of the Lives, Characters, & Writings of Philip, the Late Earl of Chesterfield, & Dr. Samuel Johnson. William Hayley. LC 71-122486. 1970. Repr. of 1787 ed. 28.00x (ISBN 0-8201-1080-9). Schol Facsimiles.

Two Different Girls. Eve Bunting. (Young Romance Ser.). (Illus.). (gr. 3-9). 1978. PLB 5.95 (ISBN 0-87191-637-1); pap. 2.95 (ISBN 0-89812-067-5). Creative Ed.

Two-Dimensional Digital Signal Processing I: Linear Filters. Ed. by T. S. Huang. (Topids in Applied Physics Ser.: Vol. 42). (Illus.). 1981. 46.60 (ISBN 0-686-69432-5). Springer-Verlag.

Two-Dimensional Digital Signal Processing II: Transforms & Median Filters. Ed. by T. S. Huang. (Topics in Applied Physics Ser.: Vol. 43). (Illus.). 260p. 1981. 46.60 (ISBN 0-686-69433-3). Springer-Verlag.

Two-Dimensional Echocardiography. Joseph Kisslo. (Clinics in Diagnostic Ultrasound: Vol. 4). 1980. text ed. 20.50 (ISBN 0-443-08076-3). Churchill.

Two Dimensional Echocardiography. Navin Nanda. 1981. write for info. (ISBN 0-87993-134-5). Futura Pub.

Two-Dimensional Man. Abner Cohen. 1974. pap. 4.95x (ISBN 0-520-03241-1). U of Cal Pr.

Two Dissertations Concerning Sense, & the Immagination, with an Essay on Consciousness. Zachary Mayne. Ed. by Rene Wellek. LC 75-11234. (British Philosophers & Theologians of the 17th & 18th Centuries: Vol. 35). 1976. Repr. of 1728 ed. lib. bdg. 42.00 (ISBN 0-8240-1787-0). Garland Pub.

Two Dog Biscuits. Beverly Cleary. (Illus.). (ps-1). 1961. PLB 7.92 (ISBN 0-688-31656-5). Morrow.

Two-Edged Sword: An Interpretation of the Old Testament. John L. McKenzie. pap. 2.45 (ISBN 0-385-06969-3, D215, Im). Doubleday.

Two Energy Futures: A National Choice for the 80's. American Petroleum Institute. LC 80-24004. (Illus.). 166p. (Orig.). 1980. pap. text ed. write for info. (ISBN 0-89364-037-9). Am Petroleum.

Two Essays on Entropy. Rudolf Carnap. Ed. by Abner Shimony. 1978. 18.00x (ISBN 0-520-02715-9). U of Cal Pr.

Two Essays on the Mind. Benjamin Rush. 1972. 7.50 (ISBN 0-87630-061-1). Brunner-Mazel.

Two Faces of Indira Gandhi. Uma Vasudev. 208p. 1977. 8.50x (ISBN 0-686-63736-4). Intl Pubns Serv.

Two Faces of Life. Leon Reed. 60p. (Orig.). 1980. pap. 3.95 (ISBN 0-89260-197-3). Hwong Pub.

Two Feet Between the Rails: The Early Years, Vol. 1. Robert C. Jones. Ed. by Russ Collman. (Illus.). 1979. 40.00 (ISBN 0-913582-17-4). Sundance.

Two Feet Between the Rails: The Mature Years, Vol. II. Robert C. Jones. (Illus.). 1980. 40.00 (ISBN 0-913582-18-2). Sundance.

Two for Joy: Reflections for a Husband & Wife on Their Spirit Led Journey Through Jesus to the Father. Tom Scheuring & Lynn Scheuring. LC 76-28274. 1976. pap. 4.95 (ISBN 0-8091-1985-4). Paulist Pr.

Two for the Price of One. Tony Kenrick. 1981. pap. 2.50 (ISBN 0-451-09809-9, E9809, Signet Bks). NAL.

Two for the Seesaw, One for the Road. Gerald Locklin. LC 80-80783. 1980. 10.95 (ISBN 0-89002-155-4); pap. 3.50 (ISBN 0-89002-154-6). Northwoods Pr.

Two Forms of Subject Inversion in Modern French. James C. Atkinson. (Janua Linguarum Ser. Practica: No. 168). 1973. pap. text ed. 18.25x (ISBN 90-2792-481-3). Mouton.

Two, Four, Six, Eight: A Book About Legs. Ethel Kessler & Leonard Kessler. LC 80-12574. (Illus.). 48p. (ps-3). 1980. PLB 7.95 (ISBN 0-396-07842-7). Dodd.

Two French Moralists. Odette De Mourgues. LC 77-82506. (Major European Authors Ser.). 1978. 32.50 (ISBN 0-521-21823-3). Cambridge U Pr.

Two Geese. Theodore Enslin. 1980. pap. 3.00 (ISBN 0-915316-86-2). Pentagram.

Two Generations of Zionism. Bernard A. Rosenblatt. LC 67-18134. 1967. 6.95 (ISBN 0-88400-017-6). Shengold.

Two Gentle Men: The Lives of George Herbert & Robert Herrick. Marchette Chute. 1959. 6.95 o.p. (ISBN 0-525-22528-5). Dutton.

Two Gentlemen of Verona. William Shakespeare. Ed. by Arthur Quiller-Couch et al. (New Shakespeare Ser). 1969. 23.95 (ISBN 0-521-07562-9); pap. 4.50x (ISBN 0-521-09505-0). Cambridge U Pr.

Two Gentlemen of Verona. William Shakespeare. Ed. by Berners Jackson. (Shakespeare Ser.). 1965. pap. 2.50 (ISBN 0-14-071431-6, Pelican). Penguin.

Two Germanies: A Modern Geography. Roy E. Mellor. 1978. text ed. 15.70 (ISBN 0-06-318066-9, IntlDept, IntlDept). Har-Row.

Two Germanies: A Modern Geography. Roy E. H. Mellor. (Illus.). 1978. text ed. 19.50x (ISBN 0-06-494778-5); pap. 9.95x (ISBN 0-06-494779-3). B&N.

Two Great Scouts & Their Pawnee Battalion. George B. Grinnell. LC 29-2718. (Illus.). vi, 299p. 1973. pap. 3.45 (ISBN 0-8032-5775-9, BB 564, Bison). U of Nebr Pr.

Two Greedy Bears: Adapted from a Hungarian Folk Tale. Mirra Ginsburg. LC 76-8819. (Illus.). 32p. (ps-2). 1976. 8.95 (ISBN 0-02-736450-X, 73645). Macmillan.

Two Gringos Visit South America. Forrest J. Wright. Bd. with Journey to Bhutan. LC 79-67523. (Illus.). 1980. 6.95 (ISBN 0-533-04475-8). Vantage.

Two Group R. A. F: A Complete History, 1936-1945. Michael J. Bowyer. (Illus.). 1974. 21.95 o.p. (ISBN 0-571-09491-0, Pub. by Faber & Faber). Merrimack Bk Serv.

Two Groups of Thessalian Gold. Stella Miller. LC 77-80473. (UC Publications in Classical Studies: Vol. 18). 1979. pap. 13.00x (ISBN 0-520-09580-4). U of Cal Pr.

Two Guests for Swedenborg. March Cost. LC 74-155664. 7.95 (ISBN 0-8149-0695-8). Vanguard.

Two Guitars: A Galaxy of Duets for Guitar. Vladimir Bobri & Carl Miller. LC 78-181572. 176p. 1972. 7.95 o.s.i. (ISBN 0-02-511980-X). Macmillan.

Two Hague Conferences & Their Contributions to International Law. William I. Hull. LC 73-147582. (Library of War & Peace; Int'l. Organization, Arbitration & Law). lib. bdg. 38.00 (ISBN 0-8240-0346-2). Garland Pub.

Two Hands of God. Alan W. Watts. 1969. pap. 3.95 (ISBN 0-02-068110-0, Collier). Macmillan.

Two-Headed Poems. Margaret Atwood. 1981. 9.95 (ISBN 0-686-68755-8, Touchstone Bks); pap. 5.95 (ISBN 0-686-68756-6). S&S.

Two-Headed Woman. Lucille Clifton. LC 80-5379. 72p. 1980. lib. bdg. 8.00x (ISBN 0-87023-309-2); pap. 3.95 (ISBN 0-87023-310-6). U of Mass Pr.

Two Hearts Adrift. Wendy Martin. 192p. (YA) 1976. 5.95 (ISBN 0-685-62026-3, Avalon). Bouregy.

Two Humorous Novels: A Diverting Dialogue Between Scipio & Bergansa & the Comical History of Rinconete & Cortadillo. Miguel De Cervantes Saavedra. Tr. by Robert Goadby. LC 80-2474. 1981. Repr. of 1741 ed. 39.50 (ISBN 0-404-19106-1). AMS Pr.

Two Hundred & One Turkish Verbs Fully Conjugated in All the Tenses. T. S. Halman. 1980. pap. text ed. 7.95 (ISBN 0-8120-2034-0). Barron.

Two Hundred & Thirty-Nine Days: Abdu'l-Baha's Journey in America. Allan L. Ward. LC 79-14713. (Illus.). 1979. 10.00 (ISBN 0-87743-129-9, 7-32-05). Baha'i.

Two Hundred & Twenty-Two Ways to Save Gas: And Get the Best Possible Mileage. Chet Cunningham. LC 80-26423. (Illus.). 96p. 1981. pap. 3.95 (ISBN 0-13-935213-9). P-H.

Two Hundred Brilliancies. Kevin Wicker. LC 80-54188. (Illus.). 144p. 1981. 15.00 (ISBN 0-668-05214-7, 5214). Arco.

Two Hundred Carp Tips. de Boer Langhenkel. (Illus.). 96p. (Orig.). 1979. pap. 5.00x (ISBN 0-85242-614-3). Intl Pubns Serv.

Two Hundred Darkroom Tips: Black & White. E. Voogel & P. Keyzer. 1978. pap. 5.00 o.p. (ISBN 0-85242-573-2, Pub. by Fountain). Morgan.

Two Hundred Darkroom Tips: Color. J. Van Welzen. 1978. pap. 5.00 o.p. (ISBN 0-85242-574-0, Pub. by Fountain). Morgan.

Two Hundred Decorative Title Pages. Alexander Nesbitt. (Illus., Orig.). 1964. pap. 6.00 (ISBN 0-486-21264-5). Dover.

Two-Hundred Fifty Home Plans for Today's Living. William G. Chirgotis. LC 78-65787. (Illus.). 1979. 11.95 o.p. (ISBN 0-8069-7150-9); pap. 6.95 o.p. (ISBN 0-685-91095-4). Sterling.

Two Hundred Filter & Lens Tips. 1978. pap. 5.00 o.p. (ISBN 0-85242-612-7, Pub. by Fountain). Morgan.

Two Hundred Fishing Tips: Zander. Kees Ketting & Henk Peeters. (Illus.). 88p. (Orig.). 1980. pap. 5.00 (ISBN 0-85242-615-1). Intl Pubns Serv.

Two Hundred Good Restaurants: A Guide to Eating in San Francisco & the Bay Area. 2nd ed. Russell S. Riera & Chris Smith. LC 80-81377. 1980. pap. 3.25 (ISBN 0-930870-02-6). Moss Pubns.

Two-Hundred Ninety-Five Golf Lessons. Billy Casper. 1973. pap. 2.95 o.p. (ISBN 0-695-80403-0). Follett.

Two Hundred One Danish Verbs Fully Conjugated in All the Tenses. Date not set. 7.95 (ISBN 0-8120-2120-7). Barron. Postponed.

Two Hundred One Englische Verben. Strutz. Date not set. pap. 3.95 (ISBN 0-8120-0605-4). Barron. Postponed.

Two Hundred One Franzoische Verben. Strutz. Date not set. pap. 3.95 (ISBN 0-8120-0689-5). Barron. Postponed.

Two Hundred One Modern Greek Verbs. Constantine Tsirpanlis. LC 80-13900. 1980. pap. 8.95 (ISBN 0-8120-0475-2). Barron.

Two Hundred One Verbos Alemanes. Date not set. 6.95 (ISBN 0-8120-2119-3). Barron. Postponed.

Two Hundred Open Games. David Bronstein. (Illus.). 256p. 1975. 11.95 (ISBN 0-02-516500-3). Macmillan.

Two Hundred Patterns for Multiple Harness Looms. Russell E. Groff. (Illus.). 1980. 14.95 (ISBN 0-686-27272-2); pap. 9.95 (ISBN 0-686-28458-5). Robin & Russ.

Two Hundred Photo Tips. G. Spitzing. 1978. pap. 5.00 o.p. (ISBN 0-85242-507-4, Pub. by Fountain). Morgan.

Two Hundred Slide Tips. G. Spitzing. 1978. pap. 5.00 o.p. (ISBN 0-85242-502-3, Pub. by Fountain). Morgan.

Two Hundred Ways to Help Children Learn While You're at It. Board of Cooperative Education Services, Nassau County. 1976. 12.95 (ISBN 0-87909-845-7). Reston.

Two Hundred Years of American Educational Thought. Ed. by Henry J. Perkinson. LC 75-43907. (Educational Policy, Planning, & Theory Ser.). 1976. pap. 8.95x o.p. (ISBN 0-679-30305-7, Pub. by MacKay). Longman.

Two Hundred Years of American Educational Thought. Ed. by Henry J. Perkinson. LC 75-43907. (Educational Policy, Planning, & Theory Ser.). 1980. pap. 9.95x (ISBN 0-582-28198-9). Longman.

Two Hundred Years of Flight in America. Ed. by Eugene M. Emme. (AAS History Ser.: Vol. 1). (Illus.). 1979. softcover 20.00 (ISBN 0-87703-101-0); lib. bdg. 30.00 (ISBN 0-87703-091-X). Am Astronaut.

Two Hundred Years of Flight in America. 2nd ed. Ed. by Eugene M. Emme. (AAS History Ser.: Vol. 1). (Illus.). 1977. lib. bdg. 30.00x (ISBN 0-87703-091-X); soft cover 20.00 (ISBN 0-87703-101-0). Univelt Inc.

Two Hundred Years of Geology in America: Proceedings of the New Hampshire Bicentennial Conference. Ed. by Cecil J. Schneer. LC 78-63149. (Illus.). 401p. 1979. text ed. 22.50x (ISBN 0-87451-160-7). U Pr of New Eng.

Two Hundred Years of Mental Health Care in America. 1977. 2.00 o.p. (ISBN 0-685-83140-X, 123). Am Psychiatric.

Two Irelands. Harold Jackson. (Minority Rights Group: No. 2). 1972. pap. 2.50 (ISBN 0-89192-092-7). Interbk Inc.

Two Is Company, Three's a Crowd. Berta Hader & Elmer Hader. (Illus.). (gr. k-3). 1965. 7.95 (ISBN 0-02-741030-7). Macmillan.

Two Italies. D. Abulafia. LC 76-11069. (Cambridge Studies in Medieval Life & Thought Ser.: No. 9). (Illus.). 1977. 49.50 (ISBN 0-521-21211-1). Cambridge U Pr.

Two Jamaicas: The Role of Ideas in a Tropical Colony, 1830-1865. Philip D. Curtin. LC 69-10082. (Illus.). 1968. Repr. of 1955 ed. lib. bdg. 22.75 (ISBN 0-8371-0055-0, CUTJ). Greenwood.

Two Kinds of Power: An Essay on Bibliographic Control. Patrick Wilson. (California Library Reprint Ser.). 1978. 17.50x (ISBN 0-520-03515-1). U of Cal Pr.

Two Kinds of Values. L. M. Loring. 1966. text ed. 11.50x (ISBN 0-7100-1760-X). Humanities.

Two Layers of Carious Dentin & New Conservative Restoration. Takao Fusayama. 190p. 1981. 42.00. Quint Pub Co.

Two Lectures on Machinery. T. Twiss. 76p. 1971. Repr. of 1844 ed. 17.00x (ISBN 0-7165-0619-X, Pub. by Irish Academic Pr Ireland). Biblio Dist.

Two Little Confederates, Repr. Of 1888 Ed. Thomas N. Page. Bd. with Little Colonel. Annie F. Johnston. Repr. of 1896 ed. LC 75-32194. (Classics of Children's Literature, 1621-1932: Vol. 56). 1976. PLB 38.00 (ISBN 0-8240-2305-6). Garland Pub.

Two Lives of Charlemagne. Einhard & Nofker The Stammerer. Tr. & intro. by Lewis Thorpe. (Classics Ser.). 240p. 1969. pap. 2.95 (ISBN 0-14-044213-8). Penguin.

Two Lives of Joseph Conrad. Leo Gurko. LC 65-16180. (gr. 7 up). 1965. 8.95 (ISBN 0-690-84310-0, TYC-J). T Y Crowell.

Two Lives to Live. Donald Deffner. LC 80-81840. 1981. pap. 4.50 (ISBN 0-933350-40-6). Morse Pr.

Two Lives, Two Lands. Ruth F. Solomon. 384p. 1980. pap. 2.75 (ISBN 0-515-05250-7). Jove Pubns.

Two Logs Crossing. Walter D. Edmonds. LC 43-17980. (Illus.). (gr. 7-9). 1943. 4.50 (ISBN 0-396-02505-6). Dodd.

Two Lucky People. Tony Kenrick. 1981. pap. 2.50 (ISBN 0-451-09725-4, E9725, Sig). NAL.

Two Memoirs of Renaissance Florence: The Diaries of Buonaccorso Pitti & Gregorio Dati. Buonaccorso Pitti & Gregorio Dati. pap. 2.95x (ISBN 0-06-131333-5, TB1333, Torch). Har-Row.

Two Merry Milkmaids. J. C. Metz. Ed. by Stephen Orgel. LC 78-66811. (Renaissance Drama Ser.). 1979. lib. bdg. 33.00 (ISBN 0-8240-9740-8). Garland Pub.

Two Millenia of International Relations in Higher Education. William W. Brickman. 263p. 1980. Repr. of 1976 ed. lib. bdg. 25.00 (ISBN 0-8414-1660-5). Folcroft.

Two Minute Warning. George La Fountaine. 240p. 1977. pap. 1.75 o.p. (ISBN 0-449-23080-5, Crest). Fawcett.

Two Monsoons. Theon Wilkinson. (Illus.). 240p. 1976. 13.50x (ISBN 0-7156-1015-5, Pub. by Duckworth England). Biblio Dist.

Two Monsters. Lucretia Fisher. LC 76-21684. (Illus.). 48p. (ps up). 1976. pap. 2.95 (ISBN 0-916144-08-9). Stemmer Hse.

Two Months in the Camp of Big Bear: The Life & Adventures of Theresa Gowanlock & Theresa Delaney, Repr. Of 1885 Ed. Theresa Gowanlock. Bd. with Cynthia Ann Parker, the Story of Her Capture at the Massacre of the Inmates of Parker's Fort: Of Her Quarter of a Century Spent Among the Comanches As the Wife of the War Chief Peta Nocona: and of Her Recapture at the Battle of Pease River by Captain L. S. Ross of the Texian Rangers. Repr. of 1886 ed. LC 75-7121. (Indian Captivities Ser.: Vol. 95). 1976. lib. bdg. 44.00 (ISBN 0-8240-1719-6). Garland Pub.

Two Most Miraculous Words in the English Language & How to Use Them Successfully. Vincent H. Navarette. (Essential Knowledge Library Bk.). (Illus.). 1979. 6.00 (ISBN 0-89266-159-3). Am Classical Coll Pr.

Two New Houses. Mandeville. (Ladybird Ser.). 1977. 1.49 (ISBN 0-87508-871-6). Chr Lit.

Two Noble Kinsmen. John Fletcher & William Shakespeare. Ed. by G. R. Proudfoot. LC 74-80902. (Regents Renaissance Drama Ser). xxvi, 141p. 1970. 9.25x (ISBN 0-8032-0286-5); pap. 2.65x (ISBN 0-8032-5287-0, BB 234, Bison). U of Nebr Pr.

Two Novellas. Julia Markus & Barbara Reid. 1977. lib. bdg. 17.50 o.s.i. (ISBN 0-918222-03-6); pap. 2.95 (ISBN 0-918222-04-4). Apple Wood.

Two Novellas: A Patron of the Arts & the Tears of San Lorenzo. 2nd ed. Julia Markus & Barbara Reid. 96p. 1981. pap. 4.95 (ISBN 0-918222-23-0). Apple Wood.

Two Novels by Peter Handke. Peter Handke. 1979. pap. 2.75 (ISBN 0-380-48033-6, 48033, Bard). Avon.

Two-Ocean War. 1974. pap. 2.25 o.p. (ISBN 0-345-24046-4). Ballantine.

Two of Them. Aliki. LC 79-10161. (Illus.). (gr. k-3). 1979. 7.95 (ISBN 0-688-80225-7); PLB 7.63 (ISBN 0-688-84225-9). Greenwillow.

Two of Them. Joanna Russ. LC 77-26137. (YA) 1978. 8.95 o.p. (ISBN 0-399-12149-8, Dist. by Putnam). Berkley Pub.

Two on First. Mike Neigoff. LC 67-17419. (Pilot Book Ser). (Illus.). (gr. 3-5). 1967. 6.95g (ISBN 0-8075-8161-5). A Whitman.

Two Passengers for Chelsea & Other Plays. Oscar W. Firkins. LC 77-94340. (One-Act Plays in Reprint Ser.). 1978. Repr. of 1928 ed. 23.75x (ISBN 0-8486-2038-0). Core Collection.

Two-Person Game Theory: The Essential Ideas. Anatol Rapoport. LC 66-11082. (Ann Arbor Science Library Ser). 1966. 5.95 o.p. (ISBN 0-472-00115-9). U of Mich Pr.

Two-Person Game Theory: The Essential Ideas. Anatol Rapoport. (Ann Arbor Science Library Ser). (Orig.). 1966. pap. 4.95 (ISBN 0-472-05015-X, 515, AA). U of Mich Pr.

Two-Phase Flow & Heat Transfer. D. Butterworth & G. F. Hewitt. (Harwell Ser.). (Illus.). 1977. 49.50x (ISBN 0-19-851715-7); pap. 29.00x (ISBN 0-19-851718-1). Oxford U Pr.

Two-Phase Flow & Heat Transfer in the Power & Process Industries. Ed. by Arthur E. Bergles et al. LC 80-22025. (Illus.). 450p. 1980. text ed. 55.00 (ISBN 0-89116-197-X). Hemisphere Pub.

Two-Phase Flow Dynamics & Reactur Safety: The Japan-U. S. Seminar 1979. Ed. by Arthur E. Bergles & Seiken Ishigai. (Illus.). 1981. text ed. 75.00 (ISBN 0-89116-198-8). Hemisphere Pub.

Two-Phase Flows & Heat Transfer: Proceedings, 3 vols. new ed. NATO Advanced Study Institute on Two-Phase Flows & Heat Transfer, Istanbul, Aug. 1976. Ed. by S. Kakac et al. LC 77-8801. 1977. Set. text ed. 155.00 (ISBN 0-89116-167-8). Hemisphere Pub.

Two Phase Flows & Heat Transfer with Application to Nuclear Reactor Design Problems. Jean J. Ginoux. LC 77-2090. (McGraw-Hill - Hemisphere Thermal & Fluids Engineering Ser). (Illus.). 1978. text ed. 39.50x (ISBN 0-07-023305-5, C). McGraw.

Two Phase Flows in Chemical Engineering. David Azbel. LC 80-20936. (Illus.). 400p. Date not set. price not set (ISBN 0-521-23772-6). Cambridge U Pr.

Two-Phase Momentum, Heat & Mass Transfer in Chemical, Process, & Energy Engineering Systems, 2 vols. Ed. by Franz Durst et al. LC 79-12405. (Thermal & Fluid Engineering & Proceedings of the International Centre for Heat & Mass Transfer Ser.). (Illus.). 1079p. 1979. text ed. 105.00 set (ISBN 0-89116-154-6, Co-Pub by McGraw International). Hemisphere Pub.

Two-Phase Steam Flow in Turbines & Separators: Theory, Instrumentation, Engineering. M. J. Moore & C. H. Sieverding. LC 76-9125. 1976. text ed. 34.50 (ISBN 0-07-042992-8, C). McGraw.

Two-Phase Transport & Reactor Safety: Proceedings, 4 vols. Two-Phase Flow & Heat Transfer Workshop, Ft. Lauderdale, Oct. 1976. Ed. by T. N. Veziroglu & S. Kakac. LC 77-14094. 1978. Set. text ed. 225.00 (ISBN 0-89116-168-6). Hemisphere Pub.

Two Plays. Brian Friel. Incl. Crystal & Fox; The Mundy Scheme. 317p. 1970. 6.50 o.p. (ISBN 0-374-13248-8); pap. 2.45 o.p. (ISBN 0-374-50796-1). FS&G.

Two Plays by Wilberto Canton. Tr. by Carl R. Shirley. 99p. 1980. 5.95 (ISBN 0-8059-2706-9). Dorrance.

Two Plays of Ancient India. Tr. by J. A. Van Buitenen. Incl. The Little Clay Cart; The Minister's Seal. LC 67-25441. viii, 278p. 1968. 17.00x (ISBN 0-231-03046-0). Columbia U Pr.

Two Plus Two. Alan Cochran. LC 79-8964. (Illus.). 288p. 1980. 10.95 (ISBN 0-385-15603-0). Doubleday.

Two Plus Two Equals Minus Seven. John F. Adams. LC 73-75392. (Cock Robin Mystery Ser). 1969. 4.50 o.s.i. (ISBN 0-02-500190-6). Macmillan.

Two Poems. Emily Dickinson. (Illus.). 1968. 4.95 o.p. (ISBN 0-8027-0291-0); boxed ed. 10.00 o.p. (ISBN 0-8027-0292-9). Walker & Co.

Two Process Philosophers: Hartshorne's Encounter with Whitehead. Ed. by Lewis S. Ford. LC 73-85592. (American Academy of Religion. Studies in Religion). 1973. pap. 7.50 (ISBN 0-88420-104-X, 010005). Scholars Pr Ca.

Two P's in a Pod. Susan Terris. LC 77-8488. (gr. 5-9). 1977. 8.25 (ISBN 0-688-80107-2); PLB 7.92 (ISBN 0-688-84107-4). Greenwillow.

Two Queens of Heaven: Aphrodite & Demeter. Doris Gates. (Greek Myths Ser). (Illus.). 96p. (gr. 4-6). 1974. PLB 7.95 (ISBN 0-670-73680-5). Viking Pr.

Two Rebels. Meta M. Reid. 1969. 6.50 (ISBN 0-571-08967-4, Pub. by Faber & Faber). Merrimack Bk Serv.

Two Renaissance Book Hunters: The Letters of Poggius Bracciolini to Nicolaus De Niccolis. Ed. by Phyllis G. Gordan. (Records of Civilization, Sources & Studies: No. 91). 384p. 1974. 25.00x (ISBN 0-231-03777-5). Columbia U Pr.

Two Riders of the Storm: A Novel. Jean Giono. Tr. by Alan Brown. 1967. 11.95 (ISBN 0-7206-9198-2). Dufour.

Two Roads & Two Destinies. Caleb Baker. 59p. pap. 0.25; chart 0.50. Walterick Pubs.

Two Roads to Ignorance: A QuasiBiography. Eliseo Vivas. LC 79-757. 318p. 1979. 18.95 (ISBN 0-8093-0916-5). S Ill U Pr.

Two R's: Paragraph to Essay. Shirley Fencl & Susan G. Jager. LC 78-16026. 1979. pap. text ed. 10.95 (ISBN 0-471-01947-X). Wiley.

Two Short Paris Summertime Plays of Nineteen Seventy-Four. William Saroyan. (Santa Susana Press Ser.). 1979. numbered 50.00 (ISBN 0-937048-17-8); lettered 75.00 (ISBN 0-937048-26-7); with laid-in block print 100.00 (ISBN 0-937048-17-8). CSUN.

Two Sides of a Coin. Charles Hunter & Frances Hunter. 1973. pap. 1.95 (ISBN 0-917726-36-7). Hunter Bks.

Two-Six Compounds. B. Ray. LC 72-93126. 1970. 37.00 (ISBN 0-08-006624-0). Pergamon.

Two Spanish Chap-Books. facsimile ed. F. J. Norton & E. M. Wilson. 1969. 58.00 (ISBN 0-521-05843-0). Cambridge U Pr.

Two Spruce Lane. Gretchen Travis. 224p. 1976. pap. 1.50 o.p. (ISBN 0-345-25164-4). Ballantine.

Two Standards. William F. Barry. Ed. by Robert L. Wolff. LC 75-466. (Victorian Fiction Ser). 1975. Repr. of 1898 ed. lib. bdg. 66.00 (ISBN 0-8240-1544-4). Garland Pub.

Two Stochastic Processes. John A. Beekman. LC 73-21380. 176p. 1974. text ed. 25.95 o.p. (ISBN 0-470-06175-8). Halsted Pr.

Two Stories. Thomas Mann. Ed. by W. Witte. Incl. Unordnung und Fruhes Leid; Mario und der Zauberer. (Blackwell's German Text Ser.). 1971. pap. 4.50x o.p. (ISBN 0-631-01870-0, Pub. by Basil Blackwell). Biblio Dist.

Two Stories. Brian Moore. (Santa Susana Press Ser.). 1979. numbered 35.00 (ISBN 0-937048-22-4); lettered 60.00 (ISBN 0-937048-29-1). CSUN.

Two Stories Jesus Told. Lucy Diamond. (Ladybird Ser). (Illus.). 1959. bds. 1.49 (ISBN 0-87508-870-8). Chr Lit.

Two Studies in Roman Nomenclature. D. R. Bailey. (American Philological Association, American Classical Studies). 1976. pap. 6.00 (ISBN 0-89130-243-3, 400403). Scholars Pr Ca.

Two Studies in Romantic Reviewing: Edinburgh Reviewers & the English Tradition, Vol. 1. J. H. Alexander. (Salzburg Studies in English Literature: No. 49). (Orig.). 1976. pap. text ed. 25.00x (ISBN 0-391-01293-2). Humanities.

Two Studies in Romantic Reviewing: The Reviewing of Walter Scott's Poetry, 1805-1817, Vol. 2. J. H. Alexander. (Salzburg Studies in English Literature Romantic Reassessment: No. 49). 1976. pap. text ed. 25.00x (ISBN 0-391-01294-0). Humanities.

Two Studies on Ethnic Group Relations in Africa: Senegal, United Republic of Tanzania. 156p. 1980. pap. 7.00 (ISBN 92-3-101101-4, U-688, UNESCO). Unipub.

Two Studies on Unemployment Among Educated Young People. 133p. 1980. pap. 6.00 (ISBN 92-3-101618-0, U-996, UNESCO). Unipub.

Two Summer Sequences. Gerald Locklin. 1980. 2.50 (ISBN 0-917554-10-8). Maelstrom.

Two Sung Texts on Chinese Painting & the Landscape Styles of the 11th & 12th Centuries. Robert J. Maeda. LC 77-94706. (Outstanding Dissertations in the Fine Arts Ser.). 1978. lib. bdg. 27.50 (ISBN 0-8240-3238-1). Garland Pub.

Two Tactics of Social Democracy in the Democratic Revolution. Vladimir I. Lenin. 1965. pap. 1.95 (ISBN 0-8351-0413-3). China Bks.

Two Tales for Autumn. Berry Fleming. LC 79-88065. 1979. 9.95 (ISBN 0-9604810-0-1); pap. 4.95 (ISBN 0-9604810-1-X). Cotton Lane.

Two That Count. Dennis St. Sauver. LC 73-8192. (Illus.). 32p. (gr. 3-5). 1973. PLB 4.95 o.p. (ISBN 0-87191-232-5). Creative Ed.

Two That Were Tough. Robert Burch. (Illus.). (gr. 6-8). 1976. 7.95 (ISBN 0-670-73684-8). Viking Pr.

Two Thousand & One Churches. W. M. Ramsay & Gertrude L. Bell. (Illus.). xiv, 580p. Repr. of 1905 ed. lib. bdg. 80.00x (ISBN 0-89241-121-X). Caratzas Bros.

Two Thousand & One French & English Idioms: Idiotismes Francais et Anglais 2001. Francois Denoeu & David Sices. Date not set. pap. text ed. 7.50 (ISBN 0-8120-0435-3). Barron. Postponed.

Two Thousand & One German & English Idioms: 2001 Deutsche und Englische Idiome. Bernard Rechtschaffen & Louis Marck. Date not set. pap. 9.95 (ISBN 0-8120-0474-4). Barron. Postponed.

Two Thousand & One Italian & English Idioms: 2001 Locuzione Italiane e Inglese. Robert R. Hall, Jr. & Frances A. Hall. 1980. pap. text ed. 9.95 (ISBN 0-8120-0467-1). Barron.

Two Thousand & One Martial Arts Questions, Kung Fu, Karate, Tae Kwon Do, Kenpo Students Should Know. Sid Campbell et al. LC 80-67769. (Illus.). 150p. 1980. pap. text ed. 8.95 (ISBN 0-686-28062-8). Dimond Pubs.

Two Thousand & One Modismos Espanoles e Ingleses. Eugene Savaiano & Lynn W. Winget. (Barron's Educational Ser.). 336p. 1981. pap. 3.95 (ISBN 0-8120-2314-5). Barron.

Two Thousand & One Spanish & English Idioms: 2001 Modismos Espanoles E Ingleses. Eugene Saviano & Lynn W. Winget. LC 75-11955. 1977. pap. text ed. 6.50 (ISBN 0-8120-0438-8). Barron.

Two Thousand & Ten: Living in the Future. Geoffrey Hoyle. LC 73-12832. (Finding-Out Books for Science & Social Studies, Grades 1-4). (Illus.). 64p. (gr. 2-4). 1974. PLB 6.95 (ISBN 0-8193-0708-4, Pub. by Parents). Enslow Pubs.

Two Thousand Down Home Skills & Secret Formulas for Practically Everything. new ed. LC 76-180143. (Illus.). 384p. 1971. pap. 4.00 o.p. (ISBN 0-912448-04-0). Gala Bks.

Two Thousand Five Hundred One Line Quotations for Speakers, Writers & Raconteurs. Edward Murphy. Ed. by Herbert Michaelman. 1981. 12.95 (ISBN 0-517-54281-1, Michaelman Books). Crown.

Two Thousand Five Hundred Years of European Helmets. Howard M. Curtis. LC 76-20423. 346p. 1978. 19.75 (ISBN 0-917714-06-7). Beinfeld Pub.

Two Thousand Miles on the Appalachian Trail. Donald J. Fortunato. 1981. 5.50 (ISBN 0-686-26176-3). D J Fortunato.

Two Thousand One Hundred & Fifty A. D. Thea Alexander. 288p. (Orig.). 1976. pap. 2.50 (ISBN 0-446-91530-0). Warner Bks.

Two Thousand Plus Index & Glossary. Margaret Reuter. (gr. k-3). 1977. PLB 7.30 (ISBN 0-8172-1025-3). Raintree Pubs.

Two Thousand Seasons. Ayi Armah. 1980. 10.00 (ISBN 0-88378-084-4); pap. 6.95 (ISBN 0-88378-046-1). Third World.

Two to Get Ready. Anthony Florio. 1978. pap. 3.95 (ISBN 0-88207-635-3). Victor Bks.

Two-Ton Secret. Mary B. Christian. Ed. by Ann Fay. (First Read-Alone Mysteries Ser.). (Illus.). 32p. (gr. 1-3). 1981. 5.50 (ISBN 0-8075-8165-8). A Whitman.

Two Tracts on Civil Liberties. Richard Price. LC 74-169641. (Era of the American Revolution Ser.). 1972. Repr. lib. bdg. 35.00 (ISBN 0-306-70233-9). Da Capo.

Two Tracts on Government. John Locke. Ed. by Philip Abrams. 1967. 32.50 (ISBN 0-521-05583-0). Cambridge U Pr.

Two Tragedies: Hector & la Reine D'Escosse. Antoine De Montchrestien. Ed. by C. N. Smith. 1972. text ed. 13.00x (ISBN 0-485-13805-0, Athlone Pr); pap. text ed. 6.50x (ISBN 0-485-12805-5). Humanities.

Two Tragedies: Hippolyte and Marc Antoine. Robert Garnier. Ed. by Christine M. Hill & Mary G. Morrison. (Renaissance Ser). 181p. 1975. text ed. 14.25x (ISBN 0-485-13809-3, Athlone Pr); pap. text ed. 6.75x (ISBN 0-485-12809-8). Humanities.

Two Treatises Concerning the Perservation of Eye-Sight. Walter Bailey. LC 74-28827. (English Experience Ser.: No. 709). 1975. Repr. of 1616 ed. 5.00 (ISBN 90-221-0709-4). Walter J Johnson.

Two Treatises of Government. John Locke. Ed. by Peter Laslett. 1960. 39.95 (ISBN 0-521-06903-3). Cambridge U Pr.

Two Treatises: The Nature of Bodies; the Nature of Man's Soule, 1644. Sir Kenelm Digby. Ed. by Rene Wellek. LC 75-11217. (British Philosophers & Theologians of the 17th & 18th Centuries Ser.). 1978. lib. bdg. 42.00 (ISBN 0-8240-1771-4). Garland Pub.

Two Tudor Conspiracies. D. M. Loades. 1965. 41.95 (ISBN 0-521-05580-6). Cambridge U Pr.

Two University Latin Plays: Philip Parsons' "Atlanta" & Thomas Atkinson's "Homo". William E. Mahaney & Walter K. Sherwin. Tr. by W. K. Sherwin et al. (Salzburg Studies in English Literature, Elizabethan & Renaissance Studies: No. 16). 191p. 1973. pap. text ed. 25.00x (ISBN 0-391-01470-6). Humanities.

Two Variants in Caribbean Race Relations: A Contribution to the Sociology of Segmented Societies. Harry Hoetink. Tr. by Eva M. Hooykaa. 1967. 7.00x o.p. (ISBN 0-19-218164-5). Oxford U Pr.

Two Views of Freedom in Process & Thought. George R. Lucas. LC 79-12287. (American Academy of Religion, Dissertation Ser.: No. 28). 1979. 12.00 (ISBN 0-89130-285-9, 010128); pap. 7.50 (ISBN 0-89130-304-9). Scholars Pr Ca.

Two Voices: Writing About Literature. Kenneth M. Symes. LC 75-31015. (Illus.). 320p. 1976. pap. text ed. 7.95 (ISBN 0-395-20607-3). HM.

Two-Way Street: Home-School Cooperation in Curriculum Decisionmaking. Ed. by Robert L. Sinclair. 92p. (Orig.). 1980. pap. 6.00 (ISBN 0-917754-16-6). Inst Responsive.

Two-Way Talking with Parents of Special Children. Philip C. Chinn et al. LC 77-26980. (Illus.). 1978. pap. text ed. 12.95 (ISBN 0-8016-0973-9). Mosby.

Two-Way Words. C. Imbior Kudrna. LC 80-10468. (Illus.). 32p. (gr. 1-3). 1980. 5.95g (ISBN 0-687-42785-1). Abingdon.

Two Ways to Look South: A Guide to Latin America. R. Dwight Wilhelm. (Orig.). 1980. pap. 2.25 (ISBN 0-377-00098-1). Friend Pr.

Two Wheels of Dhamma: Essays on the Theravada Tradition in India & Ceylon. Ed. by Bardwell L. Smith. LC 70-188906. (American Academy of Religion. Studies in Religion). 1972. pap. text ed. 7.50 (ISBN 0-89130-155-0, 010003). Scholars Pr Ca.

Two Winchester Bibles. Walter Oakshott. (Illus.). 260p. 1981. 395.00 (ISBN 0-19-818235-X). Oxford U Pr.

Two Women. Harry Mulisch. Tr. by Els Early. 1981. 11.95 (ISBN 0-7145-3810-8); pap. 5.95 (ISBN 0-7145-3839-6). Riverrun NY.

Two Wonder of Women, or the Tragedy of Sophonisba. William Kemp. Ed. by Stephen Orgel. LC 78-66805. (Renaissance Drama Ser.). 1979. lib. bdg. 24.00 (ISBN 0-8240-9744-0). Garland Pub.

Two Works of Grace. H. M. Riggle. 56p. pap. 0.40; pap. 1.00 3 copies. Faith Pub Hse.

Two World Wars. David Killingray. Ed. by Malcolm Yapp & Margaret Killlingray. (World History Ser.). (Illus.). 32p. (gr. 10). 1980. Repr. of 1977 ed. lib. bdg. 5.95 (ISBN 0-89908-234-3); pap. text ed. 1.95 (ISBN 0-89908-209-2). Greenhaven.

Two Worlds. David Daiches. 1971. 12.50x (ISBN 0-85621-001-3, Pub. by Scottish Academic Pr Scotland). Columbia U Pr.

Two Worlds. Ivan Molek. Tr. by Mary Molek from Slovene. LC 77-88259. Orig. Title: Dva svetova. 166p. softcover 3.45 (ISBN 0-9603142-2-9). M Molek Inc.

Two Worlds Are Ours (Islamic Studies) Trimingham. 6.00 o.p. (ISBN 0-685-85424-8). Intl Bk Ctr.

Two Worlds of Tracy Corbett. Carole G. Page. LC 79-54117. 128p. 1980. pap. 2.75 (ISBN 0-8066-1767-5, 10-6727). Augsburg.

Two Writers & the Cultural Revolution: Lao She & Chen Jo-hsi. Ed. by George Kao. (Renditions Ser.). 170p. 1980. 19.50 (ISBN 0-295-95747-6, Pub by Chinese Univ Hong Kong). U of Wash Pr.

Two-Year College Instructor Today. Arthur M. Cohen & Florence B. Brawer. LC 77-83482. (Praeger Special Studies). 1977. 23.95 (ISBN 0-03-039706-5). Praeger.

Two Years Before the Mast. Richard H. Dana. 1969. 11.50x (ISBN 0-460-00588-X, Evman); pap. 4.95 (ISBN 0-460-01588-5). Dutton.

Two Years for Freedom. 3rd,rev. ed. 307p. 1980. 16.00 o.p. (ISBN 0-934668-02-7). B Greene.

Twyla. Pamela Walker. pap. 0.95 o.p. (ISBN 0-425-03076-8). Berkley Pub.

Tyco Model Railroad Manual. Robert Schleicher. LC 78-14628. (Chilton's Creative Crafts Ser.). Date not set. pap. 7.95 (ISBN 0-8019-6785-6). Chilton.

Tycoons. Arthur Louis. 1981. 11.95 (ISBN 0-671-24974-6). S&S.

Tye May & the Magic Brush. Molly G. Bang. LC 80-16488. (Read-Along Books). (Illus.). 56p. (gr. 1-3). 1981. 5.95 (ISBN 0-688-80290-7); PLB 5.71 (ISBN 0-688-84290-9). Greenwillow.

Tygers of Wrath: Poems of Hate, Anger, & Invective. Ed. by X. J. Kennedy. LC 80-23212. 272p. 1981. 15.00 (ISBN 0-8203-0535-9). U of Ga Pr.

Tying & Fishing the Fuzzy Nymphs. E. H. Rosborough. LC 78-13949. (Illus.). 192p. 1979. 14.95 (ISBN 0-8117-1811-5). Stackpole.

Tyler-Browns of Brattleboro. Dorothy Sutherland Melville. 1973. 10.00 o.p. (ISBN 0-682-47687-0). Exposition.

Tyler Lane & the Gold Nugget Mystery. Lucille Meyst. 128p. (Orig.). (gr. 4-6). 1976. pap. 1.50 (ISBN 0-8024-3849-0). Moody.

Tyler Toad & the Thunder. Robert L. Crowe. LC 80-347. (Illus.). 32p. (ps-1). 1980. 9.95 (ISBN 0-525-41795-8). Dutton.

Tylman's Theory & Practice of Crown & Fixed Partial Prosthodontics (Bridge) 7th ed. Stanley D. Tylman & William F. Malone. LC 78-17821. 1978. text ed. 37.50 (ISBN 0-8016-5166-2). Mosby.

Tynedale Daughters. Norma L. Clark. LC 80-54482. 192p. 1981. 9.95 (ISBN 0-8027-0676-2). Walker & Co.

Type & Motif-Index of the Folktales of England & North America. Ernest W. Baughman. 1966. pap. text ed. 65.90x (ISBN 90-2790-046-9). Mouton.

Type Foundries of America & Their Catalogs. Maurice Annenberg. LC 73-94198. 1978. Repr. of 1975 ed. 30.00 o.p. (ISBN 0-916526-03-8). Maran Pub.

Type Sign Symbol. Adrian Frutiger. 156p. 1980. 67.50 (ISBN 0-8038-7221-6, Visual Communications). Hastings.

Type Two Superconductivity. D. Saint-James et al. LC 67-27491. 1970. 42.00 (ISBN 0-08-012392-9). Pergamon.

Typefoundry. Dennis Saleh. 1978. 4.00 o.p. (ISBN 0-686-63955-3). Bieler.

Types of Drama. 3rd ed. Barnet et al. Date not set. pap. text ed. 11.95 (ISBN 0-316-08208-2). Little.

Types of Drug Abusers & Their Abuses. Ed. by John G. Cull & Richard E. Hardy. (American Lectures in Social & Rehabilitation Psychology Ser.). (Illus.). 228p. 1974. 16.75 (ISBN 0-398-02928-8). C C Thomas.

Types of English Poetry. Ed. by Rudolf Kirk & Clara M. Kirk. LC 79-51972. (Granger Poetry Library). 1981. Repr. of 1940 ed. 42.50x (ISBN 0-89609-184-8). Granger Bk.

Types of International Society. Evan Luard. LC 75-43173. 1976. 19.95 (ISBN 0-02-919450-4). Free Pr.

Types of Society in Medieval Literature. Frederick Tupper. LC 67-29555. 1968. Repr. of 1926 ed. 7.00x (ISBN 0-8196-0212-4). Biblo.

Types of the Scandinavian Medieval Ballad. Bengt R. Jonsson & Eva Danielson. 1978. 23.00x (ISBN 82-00-01654-4, Dist. by Columbia U Pr). Universitet.

Typewell Typewriting Course. S. T. Stanwell et al. Incl. Vol. 1. Keyboard Mastery. 1974. wire bound 11.00x (ISBN 0-685-85702-6); Vol. 2. Speed Development. 1975. wire bound 12.00x (ISBN 0-685-85703-4); Vol. 3. Intermediate Display. 1975. wire bound 12.00x (ISBN 0-685-85704-2). 1975. Intl Ideas.

Typewell Typewriting Course: Advanced Display, Vol. 4. S. T. Stanwell et al. 1977. wire bound 13.00x (ISBN 0-7131-1842-3). Intl Ideas.

Typewriter Guerillas: Closeups of Twenty Top Investigative Reporters. John C. Behrens. LC 77-3439. 1977. 13.95 (ISBN 0-88229-266-8); pap. 7.95 (ISBN 0-88229-506-3). Nelson-Hall.

Typewriting for Business. rev. ed. Leger R. Morrison. LC 74-23629. (Illus.). 1981. pap. text ed. 9.00 (ISBN 0-913310-05-0). PAR Inc.

Typewriting for the Modern Office: A Self-Paced Learning Activity Program. Ellen Pate & Barbara Spengler. 288p. 1980. 10.95 (ISBN 0-8403-2196-1). Kendall-Hunt.

Typewriting Office Practice Set. 2nd ed. Esther Sandry. (gr. 9-12). pap. 3.32 (ISBN 0-8224-2083-X); supplies 6.20 (ISBN 0-8224-2084-8); tchr's. man. & key 1.72 (ISBN 0-8224-2085-6). Pitman Learning.

Typewriting Techniques for the Technical Secretary. Grace R. Lojko. LC 70-148198. 1972. pap. 10.95 ref. ed. (ISBN 0-13-935288-0). P-H.

Typing. college ed. Verleigh Ernest. LC 72-142516. 1971. 12.95 (ISBN 0-672-96001-X); pap. 10.50 (ISBN 0-672-96002-8); tchrs' manual 5.00 (ISBN 0-672-96003-6); wkbk. 9.50 (ISBN 0-672-96004-4). Bobbs.

Typing for Individual Achievement. Jack Heller. Ed. by Audrey Rubin. LC 80-26244. (Illus.). 192p. 1981. text ed. 13.80 (ISBN 0-686-69551-8). McGraw.

Typing Made Simple. Nathan Levine. 1958. pap. 3.50 (ISBN 0-385-01224-1, Made). Doubleday.

Typing One: General Course. Alan C. Lloyd et al. (Illus.). (gr. 9-12). 1976. text ed. 11.28x (ISBN 0-07-038241-7, G); wkbks. 3.96x ea.; course management manual 12.75x (ISBN 0-07-038247-6). McGraw.

Typing Power -- Spelling Power, Vol. I. Norman W. Elliott et al. LC 75-8458. pap. 6.50 (ISBN 0-672-96415-5); tchr's manual 2.50 (ISBN 0-672-96791-X). Bobbs.

Typing Skill Drills. E. C. Archer & LeRoy A. Pemberton. 1973. pap. text ed. 3.85 (ISBN 0-89420-103-4, 143000). Natl Book.

Typing Sourcebook. 2nd ed. Jordan Hale. LC 77-25064. 1978. pap. 6.95 (ISBN 0-672-97324-3); pap. 6.67 (ISBN 0-672-97184-4). Bobbs.

Typing Two, Advanced Course. Alan C. Lloyd et al. (Illus.). (gr. 9-12). 1977. text ed. 10.72 (ISBN 0-07-038257-3, G); wkbks. 3.76 ea.; tchrs manual & key 11.65 (ISBN 0-07-038247-6). McGraw.

Typographia Scoto-Gadelica. D. Maclean. 384p. 1972. Repr. of 1915 ed. 31.00x (ISBN 0-7165-2058-3, Pub. by Irish Academic Pr Ireland). Biblio Dist.

Typographical Gazetteer. Henry Cotton. LC 76-159922. 1975. Repr. of 1825 ed. 18.00 (ISBN 0-8103-4121-2). Gale.

Typographical Journey Through the Inland Printer. Compiled by Maurice Annenberg. LC 77-89269. 1977. write for info. Maran Pub.

Typographical Journey Through the Inland Printer 1880-1900. Intro. by Maurice Annenberg. LC 77-89269. casebound 45.00 (ISBN 0-916526-04-6). Maran Pub.

Typographical Printing-Surfaces: The Technology & Mechanism of Their Production. Lucien Legros & John C. Grant. Ed. by John Bidwell. LC 78-74403. (Nineteenth-Century Book Arts & Printing History Ser.: Vol. 16). (Illus.). 1980. lib. bdg. 87.00 (ISBN 0-8240-3890-8). Garland Pub.

Typography: A Manual of Design. Emil Ruder. (Visual Communication Bks.). (Illus.). 1967. 42.50 o.p. (ISBN 0-8038-7086-8). Hastings.

Typography: A Manual of Design. 2nd ed. Emil Ruder. (Illus.). 128p. 1981. pap. text ed. 12.95 (ISBN 0-8038-7223-2, Visual Communication). Hastings.

Typologia: Studies in Type Design & Type Making with Comments on the Invention of Typography, the First Types, Legibility & Fine Printing. Frederic W. Goudy. 1978. 17.50x (ISBN 0-520-03308-6); pap. 3.95 (ISBN 0-520-03278-0, CAL 334). U of Cal Pr.

Typology of the Racehorse. Franco Varola. (Illus.). 29.75 (ISBN 0-85131-196-2, Dist. by Sporting Book Center). J A Allen.

Tyranny & Fall of Edward II: 1321-1326. Natalie Fryde. LC 78-56179. 1979. 32.95 (ISBN 0-521-22201-X). Cambridge U Pr.

Tyranny of Change: America in the Progressive Era, 1900-1917. John W. Chambers. (St. Martin's Series in Twentieth Century United States History). 280p. Date not set. text ed. 12.95x (ISBN 0-312-82757-1); pap. text ed. 5.95x (ISBN 0-312-82758-X). St Martin.

Tyranny of Testing. Banesh Hoffman. LC 77-26028. 1978. Repr. of 1962 ed. lib. bdg. 18.75x (ISBN 0-313-20097-1, HOTT). Greenwood.

Tyrants & Conquerors. Fon Boardman, Jr. (Illus.). (gr. 7 up). 1977. 8.95 o.p. (ISBN 0-8098-0010-1). Walck.

Tyrants Destroyed & Other Stories. Vladimir Nabokov. 252p. 1981. pap. 5.95 (ISBN 0-07-045718-2). McGraw.

Tyro: A Review of the Arts of Painting, Sculpture & Design, Nos. 1 & 2, 1921-22. new ed. Ed. by Wyndham Lewis. (Illus.). 120p. 1970. 55.00x (ISBN 0-7146-2116-1, F Cass Co). Biblio Dist.

Tyrone Goes Camping. Linda P. Silbert & Alvin J. Silbert. (Little Twirps, TM Understanding People Books). (Illus.). (gr. k-4). 1978. pap. 2.25 (ISBN 0-89544-055-5). Silbert Bress.

Tyrone Guthrie: The Authorized Biography. James Forsyth. (Illus.). 1978. 22.50 (ISBN 0-241-89471-9, Pub. by Hamish Hamilton England). David & Charles.

Ty's One-Man Band. Mildred P. Walter. LC 80-11224. (Illus.). 40p. (gr. k-3). 1980. 9.95 (ISBN 0-590-07580-2, Four Winds). Schol Bk Serv.

Tzeena U-Reenah of Jacob ben Isaac Ashkenazy. Norman C. Gore. 1965. 10.00 (ISBN 0-685-22508-9). Ktav.

Tzeltal Numerical Classifiers: A Study in Ethnographic Semantics. Brent Berlin. (Janua Linguarum, Ser. Practica: No. 70). (Orig.). 1968. pap. text ed. 52.50x (ISBN 0-686-22422-1). Mouton.

Tzintzuntzan. G. M. Foster. 416p. 1979. pap. 7.95 (ISBN 0-444-99070-4). Elsevier.

U

U-Boat Hunters. Anthony Watts. (Nagel Encyclopedia Guides). 1980. 12.95 (ISBN 0-356-08244-X, Pub. by MacDonald & Jane's England). Hippocrene Bks.

U-Boat Nine Hundred Seventy-Seven. Heinz Schaeffer. (War Book). 208p. 1981. pap. 2.50 (ISBN 0-553-14591-6). Bantam.

U-Boats in the Atlantic. Paul Beaver. (WW 2 Photo Album Ser.: No. 11). 1980. 17.95 o.p. (ISBN 0-85059-386-7); pap. 11.50 o.p. (ISBN 0-85059-388-3). Aztex.

U-Boats in the Atlantic: World War Two Photo Album. Paul Beaver. (Illus.). 96p. 1981. pap. 5.95 (ISBN 0-89404-057-X). Aztex.

U F O Encyclopedia. Sachs. 1980. 14.95 (ISBN 0-399-12365-2). Putnam.

U. F. O. Unidentified Flying Object. Stubbs. 7.95 (ISBN 0-233-97197-1). Andre Deutsch.

U. K. in 1980: The Hudson Report. Hudson Institute. LC 74-25234. 127p. 1974. 17.95 (ISBN 0-470-41855-9). Halsted Pr.

U N & the Middle East Crisis. Arthur Lall. LC 68-8879. (Paperback Ser.: No. 103). 1970. 20.00x (ISBN 0-231-03173-4); pap. 5.00x (ISBN 0-231-08635-0). Columbia U Pr.

U R T A-A T A Humanities & the Theatre, 2 vols. Set. 5.00; ATA members 3.00. Am Theatre Assoc.

U. S. A., the Permanent Revolution. Fortune Magazine & Russell W. Davenport. LC 80-15776. 267p. 1980. Repr. of 1951 ed. lib. bdg. 22.50x (ISBN 0-313-22500-1, FMUS). Greenwood.

U. S. A. West: A Travel Guide to Hawaii, the Pacific States & the Southwest. Joan Storey & Daphne E. Reece. (Illus.). 1981. pap. 6.95 (ISBN 0-908086-09-1). Hippocrene Bks.

U. S. A. y Yo. Miguel Delibes. Ed. by F. L. Gordon. LC 77-117216. 1970. pap. 4.50 (ISBN 0-672-63133-4). Odyssey Pr.

U. S., Cuba & the Cold War: American Failure or Communist Conspiracy. Lester D. Langley. (Problems in American Civilization Ser). 1970. pap. text ed. 4.95x o.p. (ISBN 0-669-51839-5). Heath.

U. S.-European Monetary Relations. Ed. by Samuel I. Katz. 1979. 13.25 (ISBN 0-8447-2150-6); pap. 7.25 (ISBN 0-8447-2149-2). Am Enterprise.

U S Foreign Trade Zones. Ed. by Raymond J. Waldmann. (Orig.). 1981. pap. 45.00 (ISBN 0-933678-02-9). Transnatl Invest.

U. S., Interdependence & World Order. Lincoln P. Bloomfield & Irirangi C. Bloomfield. LC 75-36296. (Headline Ser.: 228). (Orig.). 1975. pap. 2.00 (ISBN 0-87124-033-5). Foreign Policy.

U. S.-Mexico Economic Relations. Ed. by Barry W. Poulson et al. (Special Studies in International Economics & Business). 1979. lib. bdg. 35.00x (ISBN 0-89158-469-2). Westview.

U S Navy in Pensacola: From Sailing Ships to Naval Aviation, Eighteen Twenty-Five to Nineteen Thirty. George F. Pearce. LC 80-12167. (Illus.). vii, 207p. 1980. 17.00 (ISBN 0-8130-0665-1). U Presses Fla.

U. S Programs That Impede U. S. Export Competitiveness: The Regulatory Environment, Vol. II. Robert Flammang. LC 80-80933. (Significant Issues Ser.: No. 3). 45p. 1980. 5.95 (ISBN 0-89206-017-4). CSI Studies.

U S S R Facts & Figures Annual (UFFA, Vol. 4 1980. Ed. by John L. Scherer. 42.50 (ISBN 0-87569-035-1). Academic Intl.

U S S R in World War II: An Annotated Bibliography of Books Published in the Soviet Union, 1945 to 1975. Michael Parrish. LC 80-8502. 925p. 1981. lib. bdg. 110.00 (ISBN 0-8240-9485-9). Garland Pub.

U. T. Austin Traditions & Nostalgia. new ed. Margaret C. Berry. LC 75-8061. 126p. 1980. 6.75 (ISBN 0-88319-021-4); pap. 3.95. Shoal Creek Pub.

U-2 Incident, May, 1960: An American Spy-Plane Downed Over Russia Intensifies the Cold War. Fred J. Cook. LC 73-6796. (World Focus Bks). (gr. 7 up). 1973. PLB 4.47 o.p. (ISBN 0-531-02170-X). Watts.

UAW & Walter Reuther. I. Howe & B. J. Widick. LC 72-2375. (FDR & the Era of the New Deal Ser.). 324p. 1973. Repr. of 1949 ed. lib. bdg. 29.50 (ISBN 0-306-70485-4). Da Capo.

Uber den Umlaut: Zwei Abhandlungen & Uber den Ablaut. Adolf Holtzmann. (Amsterdam Classics in Linguistics 1800-1925: No. 12). 1979. text ed. 27.50x (ISBN 90-272-0871-9). Humanities.

Ubu Plays. Alfred Jarry. Tr. by Cyril Connolly & Simon W. Taylor. Incl. Ubu Rex; Ubu Cuckolded; Ubu Enchained. 1969. pap. 4.95 (ISBN 0-394-17485-2, E496, Ever). Grove.

UCLA Business Forecast for the Nation & California. 1981. 40.00 (ISBN 0-686-69435-X). UCLA Busn Forecasting.

Ucla Business Forecast for the Nation & California in 1980. Ed. by Robert M. Williams. 1980. 35.00 (ISBN 0-686-52633-3). UCLA Busn Forecasting.

UDAG Partnerships: Nine Case Studies. J. Thomas Black et al. (Illus.). 108p. 1980. pap. 10.00 (ISBN 0-87420-594-8, U12). Urban Land.

Udo Fahrt Nach Koln. Peter Lunt. LC 73-20464. (Ger). 1971. pap. text ed. 7.84 (ISBN 0-395-11058-0, 2-34500). HM.

Ueber Kie Beeinflussbarkeit Psychiatrischer Krankheitsverlaeufe, 1980, Vol. 13, No. 3-4. Ed. by E. Gabriel. (Illus.). iv, 136p. 1981. pap. write for info. (ISBN 3-8055-2336-X). S Karger.

Ueber Reinhold Schneider. Carsten Thiede & Peter Thiede. (Suhrkamp Taschenbuecher: No. 504). 368p. (Orig.). 1980. pap. text ed. 6.50 (ISBN 3-518-37004-9, Pub. by Insel Verlag Germany). Suhrkamp.

Uffizi. Luciano Berti. (Illus.). 1978. pap. 9.95 (ISBN 0-8467-0453-6, Pub. by Two Continents). Hippocrene Bks.

Uffizi of Florence. Ed. by Sergio Negrini. LC 72-94912. (Great Galleries of the World Ser.). (Illus.). 104p. 1974. 6.95 o.p. (ISBN 0-668-02923-4). Arco.

UFO. Rhoda Blumberg. (First Books). (Illus.). (gr. 4-6). 1977. PLB 6.45 (ISBN 0-531-00397-3). Watts.

UFO. Milt Machlin & Tim Beckley. (Illus.). 192p. 1981. pap. 8.95 (ISBN 0-8256-3182-3, Quick Fox). Music Sales.

UFO Abductions: True Cases of Alien Kidnappings. (Orig.). 1980. pap. 2.25 (ISBN 0-451-09472-7, E9472, Sig). NAL.

UFO Guidebook. Norman J. Briazack & Simon Mennick. 1978. 10.00 (ISBN 0-8065-0636-9). Citadel Pr.

UFO Invaders Deceive Every Nation. Dennis M. Battle. LC 80-65199. 52p. 1980. pap. 2.50 (ISBN 0-933464-06-1). D M Battle Pubns.

UFO Phenomena & the Behavioral Scientist. Ed. by Richard F. Haines. LC 79-14878. 464p. 1979. 20.00 (ISBN 0-8108-1228-2). Scarecrow.

UFO Prophecy. Arthur Shuttlewood. 266p. (Orig.). 1978. pap. 7.95 (ISBN 0-910122-42-3, Pub. by Global Commun). Amherst Pr.

UFO Verdict: Examining the Evidence. Robert Sheaffer. LC 80-84406. (Critiques of the Paranormal Ser.). 275p. 1981. 15.95 (ISBN 0-87975-146-0). Prometheus Bks.

UFO Warning. John Stuart. 1976. pap. 7.95 (ISBN 0-685-81681-8). Saucerian.

Ufonauts. Hans Holzer. 304p. (Orig.). 1978. pap. 1.75 o.p. (ISBN 0-449-13569-1, GM). Fawcett.

UFO's & Bible Prophecy. R. L. Hymers. pap. 1.95 (ISBN 0-89728-061-X, 665117). Omega Pubns OR.

UFOs & Related Subjects: An Annotated Bibliography. Ed. by Lynn E. Catoe. LC 78-26124. 1979. Repr. of 1969 ed. 38.00 (ISBN 0-8103-2021-5). Gale.

UFO's & the Limits of Science. Ronald D. Story. LC 80-25543. (Illus.). 224p. 1981. 10.95 (ISBN 0-688-00144-0). Morrow.

UFO's Past, Present & Future. Robert Emenegger. Date not set. pap. 2.50 (ISBN 0-345-29047-X). Ballantine.

Uganda. Robert L. Collison. (World Bibliographical Ser.: No. 11). 1981. write for info. (ISBN 0-903450-17-8). ABC Clio.

Uganda: Fire & Blood. Elaine M. Stone. 1977. pap. 1.95 o.p. (ISBN 0-88270-237-8). Logos.

Uganda: The Asian Exiles. Thomas Melady & Margaret Melady. LC 76-10321. 1976. 6.95x o.p. (ISBN 0-88344-506-9). Orbis Bks.

Ugandan: Defiant & Triumphant. Benjamin N. H. Kagwa. (Illus.). 1978. 10.00 o.p. (ISBN 0-682-49032-6). Exposition.

Ugandi Safaris. Brian Herne. 1980. 12.95 (ISBN 0-87691-316-8). Winchester Pr.

Ugarit in Retrospect. Ed. by Gordon D. Young. 1981. text ed. price not set (ISBN 0-931464-07-2). Eisenbrauns.

Ugaritic Textbook. Cyrus H. Gordon. 1965. pap. 56.00 (ISBN 0-911566-08-2). Ventnor.

Ugly American. E. Burdick & W. Lederer. 1977. pap. 2.25 (ISBN 0-449-24201-3, Crest). Fawcett.

Ugly Bird. Russell Hoban. LC 69-11301. (Illus.). (gr. k-2). 1969. 3.95 o.s.i. (ISBN 0-02-744100-8). Macmillan.

Ugly Palaces: Housing in America. Robert A. Liston. LC 74-1044. 160p. (gr. 7 up). 1974. PLB 6.88 o.p. (ISBN 0-531-02673-6). Watts.

Ugly Swans. Arkady Strugatsky & Boris Strugatsky. Tr. by Alexander Nakhimovsky. 1979. 10.95 (ISBN 0-02-615190-1). Macmillan.

Ugly Truth About Milton Friedman. Lyndon H. LaRouche, Jr. & David Goldman. LC 80-20623. (Illus.). 350p. (Orig.). 1980. pap. 3.95 (ISBN 0-933488-09-2). New Benjamin.

Ugly Unicorn. Russell Rinehart. LC 79-84875. 1979. pap. 2.00 (ISBN 0-934020-01-9). Illusive Unicorn.

Ugo Foscolo: Poet of Exile. Glauco Cambon. LC 79-3193. 360p. 1980. 21.50x (ISBN 0-691-06424-5). Princeton U Pr.

Uhuru. Robert Ruark. 1977. pap. 2.25 o.p. (ISBN 0-449-23241-7, Crest). Fawcett.

Uhuru's Fires: African Literature East to South. A. A. Roscoe. LC 76-3038. 280p. 1977. 42.50 (ISBN 0-521-21295-2); pap. 11.95x (ISBN 0-521-29089-9). Cambridge U Pr.

Uists & Barra. Francis Thompson. LC 74-81056. (Islands Ser). (Illus.). 192p. 1974. 16.95 (ISBN 0-7153-6676-9). David & Charles.

UJ Magyar Lexikon, 7 vols. (Hung.). 1960-1972. Set. 240.00 (ISBN 0-8277-3103-5). Maxwell Sci Intl.

Ujamaa - Socialism from Above. Jannik Boese et al. (Scandinavian Institute of African Studies, Uppsala). (Illus.). 1978. text ed. 25.25x (ISBN 0-8419-9730-6). Holmes & Meier.

Ujamaa: Essays on Socialism. Julius K. Nyerere. 1971. pap. 3.95 (ISBN 0-19-501474-X, GB359, GB). Oxford U Pr.

UK Publishing Industry. Peter J. Curwen. (Illus.). 176p. 1981. 24.00 (ISBN 0-08-024081-X). Pergamon.

Ukiyo: Stories of "The Floating World" of Postwar Japan. Ed. by Jay Gluck. LC 63-21851. 1964. 6.95 (ISBN 0-8149-0108-5). Vanguard.

Ukraine Within the USSR: An Economic Balance Sheet. Ed. by I. S. Koropeckyj. LC 77-7817. (Praeger Special Studies). 1977. text ed. 32.50 (ISBN 0-03-022356-3). Praeger.

Ukrainian American Index: The Ukrainian Weekly, Nineteen Seventy-Nine. Christine G. Wynar. 119p. (Orig.). 1980. pap. 9.50 (ISBN 0-934760-02-0). Ukrainian Res.

Ukrainian Nationalism in the Post-Stalin Era: Myth, Symbols & Ideology in Soviet Nationalities Policy. Kenneth C. Farmer. (Studies in Contemporary History: Vol. 4). 253p. 1980. lib. bdg. 36.50 (ISBN 90-247-2401-5, Pub. by Martinus Nijhoff). Kluwer Boston.

Ukrainian Poets, Eleven Hundred & Eight-Nine to Nineteen Sixty-Two. Tr. by C. H. Andrusyshen & Watson Kirkconnell. (Scholarly Reprint Ser.). 1980. Repr. of 1963 ed. 15.00 (ISBN 0-8020-3100-5). U of Toronto Pr.

Ukrainians & the Polish Revolt of 1863: A Contribution to the History of Ukrainian-Polish Relations. Wasyl Luciw. LC 62-67800. 1961. pap. text ed. 2.00 o.p. (ISBN 0-918884-08-X). Slavia Lib.

Ukrainians in Canda & the United States: A Guide to Information Sources. Ed. by Aleksander Sokolyszyn & Vladimir Wertsman. (Ethnic Studies Information Guide Ser.: Vol. 7). 375p. 1981. 32.00 (ISBN 0-8103-1494-0). Gale.

Ukrains'ka Radians'ka Entsyklopediia, 17 vols. (Ukrainian.). 1960-1966. 285.00 (ISBN 0-8277-3062-4). Maxwell Sci Intl.

Ukranian Nationalism. 2nd ed. John A. Armstrong. LC 79-25529. 361p. 1980. Repr. of 1963 ed. 30.00x (ISBN 0-87287-193-2). Libs Unl.

UKSC Eighty-One. 1981. text ed. price not set (ISBN 0-86103-041-9, Westbury Hse). Butterworth.

Ukubamba Amadolo. Bettie Du Toit. 155p. 1980. text ed. 15.75x (ISBN 0-906383-00-5). Humanities.

Ulcerated Milkman. William Sansom. 1979. 7.95 (ISBN 0-7012-0220-3, Pub. by Chatto Bodley Jonathan). Merrimack Bk Serv.

Ulcerative Colitis. Michael J. Goodman & Marshall Sparberg. LC 78-8686. (Clinical Gastroenterology Monographs). 1978. 26.95 (ISBN 0-471-48895-X, Pub. by Wiley Medical). Wiley.

Ulitimate Foundation of Economic Science: An Essay on Method. Ludwig Von Mises. 1978. wrtie for info. NYU Pr.

Ullmanns Encyklopadie der technichen Chemie, Vols. 6 & 20-25. 4th ed. 1980. 328.20. Verlag Chemie.

Ullmanns Encyklopaedie der Technichen Chemie, 18 vols. 4th ed. Vols. 1-3. 203.00 ea.; Vols. 4 & 7-11. 244.20 ea.; Vols. 12-14. 261.80 ea.; Vols. 15-17. 279.50 ea. (ISBN 3-527-20000-2); Vol. 18. 296.90. Verlag Chemie.

Ulrich's International Periodicals. 19th ed. 1980. 69.50 (ISBN 0-8352-1297-1). Bowker.

Ulrich's International Periodicals Directory 1980. 2200p. 1980. 69.50 (ISBN 0-8352-1297-1). Bowker.

Ulrich's International Periodicals Directory 1979-1980. 18th ed. LC 32-16320. 1979. 64.50 o.p. (ISBN 0-8352-1182-7). Bowker.

Ulster: A Case Study in Conflict Theory. R. S. Elliot & John Ickie. LC 78-182186. 180p. 1971. text ed. 14.95x (ISBN 0-8290-0213-8). Irvington.

Ulster Crisis. A. T. Stewart. (Illus., Orig.). 1969. pap. 6.50 (ISBN 0-571-08066-9, Pub. by Faber & Faber). Merrimack Bk Serv.

Ulster: Regional Archaeology. Laurence Flanagan. 1970. 3.95x o.p. (ISBN 0-435-32970-7). Heinemann Ed.

Ultimate. James Lund. 1979. 9.95 (ISBN 0-7145-3595-8). Riverrun NY.

Ultimate Baseball Quiz Book. Dom Forker. (Orig.). 1981. pap. 1.95 (ISBN 0-451-09679-7, J9679, Sig). NAL.

Ultimate Bay Book: A Guide to the Pleasures of the San Francisco Bay. Terry Milne. Ed. by Elaine Ratner & Jay Stewart. LC 78-52509. (Illus.). 1979. pap. 9.95 (ISBN 0-89395-010-6). Cal Living Bks.

Ultimate Code. Nick Carter. (Nick Carter Ser.). 172p. 1981. pap. 2.25 (ISBN 0-441-84309-3). Charter Bks.

Ultimate Dessert Book. Linda Lewis. (Illus.). 1979. cancelled o.p. (ISBN 0-394-41276-1). Random.

Ultimate Foundation of Economic Science: An Essay on Method. Ludwig von Mises. LC 77-20127. (Studies in Economic Theory Ser.). 148p. 1978. Repr. of 1962 ed. 15.00x; pap. 4.95x. NYU Pr.

Ultimate Game. Ralph Glendinning. 1981. 13.95 (ISBN 0-671-42016-X, Wyndham Bks). S&S.

Ultimate Good Luck. Richard Ford. 216p. 1981. 9.95 (ISBN 0-686-69063-X). HM.

Ultimate Load Design of Concrete Structures. Thomas Telford Ltd. Editorial Staff. 104p. 1980. 25.00 (Pub. by Telford England). State Mutual Bk.

Ultimate North: Canoeing Mackenzie's Arctic Great River. Robert Douglas Mead. LC 75-35418. 356p. 1976. 10.00 o.p. (ISBN 0-385-07252-X). Doubleday.

Ultimate Porno. PierNico Solinas. LC 80-69871. 1981. 14.95 (ISBN 0-938112-00-7). Eyecontact.

Ultimate Resource. Julian L. Simon. LC 80-8575. 336p. 1981. 14.50x (ISBN 0-691-09389-X). Princeton U Pr.

Ultimate Revolution. Walter Starcke. LC 73-85058. 1973. pap. 3.95 o.p. (ISBN 0-06-067524-1, RD65, HarpR). Har-Row.

Ultimate Sex. Linda Du Breuil. 1976. pap. 1.50 o.p. (ISBN 0-8439-0347-3, Leisure Bks). Nordon Pubns.

Ultimate Soup Book. Mary Spencer & Mike Spencer. LC 75-9085. (Illus.). 128p. 1975. pap. 4.95 o.p. (ISBN 0-89087-057-8). Celestial Arts.

Ultimate Stranger: The Autistic Child. Delacato, Carl H., Dr. LC 73-9019. 240p. 1974. 6.95 o.p. (ISBN 0-385-01074-5). Doubleday.

Ultimate Values of the American Population. William C. McCready & Andrew M. Greeley. LC 75-40337. (Sage Library of Social Research: Vol. 23). 1976. 18.00x (ISBN 0-8039-0502-5); pap. 8.95x (ISBN 0-8039-0503-3). Sage.

Ultimatum. Paul Bonnecarrere. 1976. pap. 1.75 o.p. (ISBN 0-345-25101-6). Ballantine.

Ultimatum. Antony Trew. LC 76-5379. 1976. 8.95 o.p. (ISBN 0-312-82845-4). St Martin.

Ultra in the West. Ralph Bennett. (Illus.). 306p. 1980. 17.50 (ISBN 0-684-16704-2, ScribT). Scribner.

Ultra-Violet Catastrophe. Margaret Mahy. LC 74-12445. (Illus.). (gr. k-3). 1975. 5.95 o.s.i. (ISBN 0-8193-0748-3, Four Winds); PLB 5.41 o.s.i. (ISBN 0-8193-0749-1); pap. 1.95 o.s.i. (ISBN 0-8193-0908-7). Schol Bk Serv.

Ultrafiltration Membranes & Applications. Ed. by Anthony R. Cooper. (Polymer Science & Technology Ser.: Vol. 13). 700p. 1981. 75.00 (ISBN 0-306-40548-2, Plenum Pr). Plenum Pub.

Ultramafic & Related Rocks. Ed. by Peter J. Wyllie. LC 78-12080. 484p. (Orig.). 1979. Repr. of 1967 ed. 35.00 (ISBN 0-88275-755-5). Krieger.

Ultrasoft X-Ray Microscopy: Its Application to Biological & Physical Sciences. Ed. by Donald F. Parsons. (N.Y. Academy of Sciences: Vol. 342). 402p. 1980. 70.00 (ISBN 0-89766-066-8); pap. write for info. (ISBN 0-89766-067-6). NY Acad Sci.

Ultrasonic Biophysics. Ed. by F. Dunn & W. D. O'Brien, Jr. LC 75-30715. (Benchmark Papers in Acoustics: Vol. 7). 400p. 1976. 44.50 (ISBN 0-12-786395-8). Acad Pr.

Ultrasonic Diagnosis of Ectopic Pregnancy. Nabil F. Maklad. 260p. (Orig.). 1981. 27.50 (ISBN 0-87527-222-3). Green. Postponed.

Ultrasonic Fragmentation for Intraocular Surgery. Louis J. Girard. LC 78-20733. (Illus.). 1979. text ed. 79.50 (ISBN 0-8016-1837-1). Mosby.

Ultrasonic Testing of Materials. J. Krautkramer & H. Krautkramer. LC 76-12561. 1977. 71.70 (ISBN 0-387-07716-2). Springer-Verlag.

Ultrasonic Therapy in Periodontics. Sol J. Ewen & Cyrus Glickstein. (Illus.). 144p. 1968. pap. 19.75 photocopy ed. spiral (ISBN 0-398-00535-4). C C Thomas.

Ultrasonics in Packaging & Plastics Fabrication. Ralph H. Thomas. LC 73-76443. 1974. 21.50 (ISBN 0-8436-1102-2). CBI Pub.

Ultrasonography of Digestive Diseases. Francis W. Weill. LC 77-13046. (Illus.). 1978. 57.50 (ISBN 0-8016-5374-6). Mosby.

Ultrasound in Cancer. Barry B. Goldberg. (Clinics in Diagnostic Ultrasound Ser.: Vol. 6). (Illus.). 224p. 1980. 20.50 (ISBN 0-443-08144-1). Churchill.

Ultrasound in Clinical Obstetrics. William J. Garrett & David E. Robinson. (Illus.). 128p. 1970. 16.50 (ISBN 0-398-00652-0). C C Thomas.

Ultrasound in Emergency Medicine. Kenneth J. Taylor & Gregory N. Viscomi. (Clinics in Diagnostic Ultrasound). (Illus.). 225p. 1981. lib. bdg. 20.50 (ISBN 0-443-08156-5). Churchill.

Ultrasound in Obstetrics & Gynecology. Patricia A. Athey & Frank P. Hadlock. (Illus.). 400p. 1981. text ed. 45.00 (ISBN 0-8016-0374-9). Mosby.

Ultrasound in the Production & Inspection of Concrete: Pt. 1, Production Applications. Yu. E. Kornilovich & V. I. Belokhovstikova. 1965. 29.50 (ISBN 0-306-17035-3, Consultants). Plenum Pub.

Ultrasound in the Production & Inspection of Concrete: Pt. 2, Inspection of Hydraulic Construction. A. K. Tret'yakov & A. M. Filonidov. 1965. 29.50 (ISBN 0-306-17036-1, Consultants). Plenum Pub.

Ultrastructural Aspects of the Liver & Its Disorders. 2nd ed. Kyuichi Tanikawa. LC 79-84646. (Illus.). 1979. 62.50 (ISBN 0-89640-034-4). Igaku-Shoin.

Ultrastructural Pathology of Human Tumors, Vol. 1. Ivan Damjanov. Ed. by D. F. Horrobin. LC 79-319782. (Annual Research Reviews Ser.). 1979. 24.00 (ISBN 0-88831-045-5). Eden Med Res.

Ultrastructural Pathology of Human Tumors, Vol. 2. Ivan Damjanov. Ed. by D. F. Horrobin. (Annual Research Reviews). 144p. 1980. 24.00 (ISBN 0-88831-082-X). Eden Med Res.

Ultrastructural Pathology of the Cell. new ed. Feroze N. Ghadially. 530p. 1975. 149.00 (ISBN 0-407-00011-9). Butterworths.

Ultrastructural Study of the Human Diseased Peripheral Nerve. Claude Vital & Jean M. Vallat. (Illus.). 200p. 1980. 35.00 (ISBN 0-89352-096-9). Masson Pub.

Ultrastructure of Collagen: Its Relation to the Healing of Wounds & to the Management of Hypertrophic Scars. J. J. Longacre. (American Lectures in Plastic & Reconstructive Surgery Ser.). (Illus.). 538p. 1976. 54.75 (ISBN 0-398-03254-8). C C Thomas.

Ultrastructure of the Animal Cell. 2nd ed. L. T. Threadgold. Ed. by G. A. Kerkut. 472p. 1976. text ed. 55.00 (ISBN 0-08-018958-X); pap. text ed. 25.00 (ISBN 0-08-018957-1). Pergamon.

Ultrastructure of the Dormant & Active Cambial Zones & the Dormant Phloem Associated with Formation of Normal & Compression Woods in Picea Abies, No. 96. write for info. o.p. (ISBN 0-686-20706-8). SUNY Environ.

Ultrastructure,Macromolecules, & Evolution. Lawrence S. Dillon. 750p. 1981. 69.50 (ISBN 0-306-40528-8, Plenum Pr). Plenum Pub.

Ulysses: "Aeolus" "Lestrygonians," & "Scylla & Charybdis" a Facsimile of Page Proofs for Episodes 7-9. James Joyce. Ed. by Michael Groden. LC 77-14621. (James Joyce Archive Ser.). 1978. lib. bdg. 104.00 (ISBN 0-8240-2817-1). Garland Pub.

Ulysses: "Aeolus," "Lestrygonians," "Scylla & Charybdis," & "Wandering Rocks": A Facsimile of Placards for Pisodes 7-10. James Joyce. Ed. by Michael Groden. LC 78-16031. (James Joyce Archive Ser.: Vol. 13). 1978. lib. bdg. 104.00 (ISBN 0-8240-2812-0). Garland Pub.

Ulysses & the Sirens. J. Elster. LC 78-15444. 1979. 26.95 (ISBN 0-521-22388-1). Cambridge U Pr.

Ulysses: "Circe": A Facsimile of Page Proofs for Episode 15. James Joyce. Ed. by Michael Groden. LC 77-14656. (James Joyce Archive Ser.). 1978. lib. bdg. 104.00 (ISBN 0-8240-2820-1). Garland Pub.

Ulysses: "Circe" & "Eumaeus": A Facsimile of Manuscripts & Typescripts for Episodes 15 (Part II) & 16. James Joyce. Ed. by Michael Groden. LC 77-11971. (James Joyce Archive Ser.). 1978. lib. bdg. 104.00 (ISBN 0-8240-2825-2). Garland Pub.

Ulysses: "Cyclops" & "Nausicaa", & "Oxen of the Sun": a Facsimile of Page Proofs of Episode 12-14. James Joyce. Ed. by Michael Groden. LC 77-14655. (James Joyce Archive Ser.). 1978. lib. bdg. 104.00 (ISBN 0-8240-2819-8). Garland Pub.

Ulysses: "Eumaeus," "Ithaca," & "Penelope": A Facsimile of Page Proofs for Chapters 16-18. James Joyce. Ed. by Michael Groden. LC 77-14657. (James Joyce Archive Ser.). 1978. lib. bdg. 104.00 (ISBN 0-8240-2821-X). Garland Pub.

Ulysses: "Ithaca" & "Penelope." A Facsimile of Manuscripts & Typescripts for Episodes 17 & 18. Ed. by Michael Groden. LC 77-10882. (James Joyce Archive Ser.: Vol. 16). 1979. lib. bdg. 104.00 (ISBN 0-8240-2826-0). Garland Pub.

Ulysses: Notes & "Telemachus" - "Scylla" & "Charybdis": A Facsimile of Notes for the Book & Mauscripts for Episodes 1-9. James Joyce. Ed. by Michael Groden. LC 78-16032. (James Joyce Archive Ser.). 1978. lib. bdg. 104.00 (ISBN 0-8240-2822-8). Garland Pub.

Ulysses: "Oxen of the Sun," & "Circe": A Facsimile of Drafts, Manuscripts, & Typescripts 14 & 15 (Part 1) James Joyce. Ed. by Michael Groden. LC 77-22764. (James Joyce Archive Ser.). 1978. lib. bdg. 104.00 (ISBN 0-8240-2824-4). Garland Pub.

Ulysses: "Sirens," "Cyclops," "Nausicaa," & "Oxen of the Sun." A Facsimile of Placards for Episodes 11-14. Ed. by Michael Groden. LC 78-11931. (James Joyce Archive Ser.: Vol. 19). 1979. lib. bdg. 104.00 (ISBN 0-8240-2813-9). Garland Pub.

Ulysses: "Telemachus," "Nestor," "Proteus" Calypso" "Lotus Eaters," & "Hades": a Facsimile of Placards for Episodes 1-6. James Joyce. Ed. by Michael Groden. LC 78-16032. (James Joyce Archive Ser.: Vol. 17). 1978. lib. bdg. 104.00 (ISBN 0-8240-2811-2). Garland Pub.

Ulysses, The Waste Land, & Modernism. Stanley Sultan. (Literary Criticism Ser). 1977. 8.95 (ISBN 0-8046-9144-4, Natl U). Kennikat.

Ulysses: "Wandering Rocks" & "Sirens" A Facsimile of Page Proofs for Episodes 10-11. James Joyce. Ed. by Michael Groden. LC 77-14654. (James Joyce Archive Ser.). 1978. lib. bdg. 104.00 (ISBN 0-8240-2818-X). Garland Pub.

Ulysses: "Wandering Rocks," "Sirens," "Cyclops," "Nausicaa": Facsimile of Drafts & Typescripts for Episodes 10-13. Ed. by Michael Groden. LC 77-10196. (James Joyce Archive Ser.). 1978. lib. bdg. 104.00 (ISBN 0-8240-2823-6). Garland Pub.

Um Guia Para Fundacao De Igrejas. Tr. by Melvin Hodges. (Portuguese Bks.). 1979. 1.10 (ISBN 0-686-28807-6). Vida Pub.

Umayyads & Abbasids. Jirji Zaydan. Tr. by D. S. Margoliuth from Arabic. LC 79-2889. 325p. 1981. Repr. of 1907 ed. 26.50 (ISBN 0-8305-0056-1). Hyperion Conn.

Umericks for Children. Veronica Potz. (See-Hear-Color Me Bk). 1981. 8.95 (ISBN 0-912492-15-5). Pyquag.

U.N. in the Congo: The Political & Civilian Efforts. Arthur H. House. LC 78-56052. 1978. pap. text ed. 14.25 (ISBN 0-8191-0516-3). U Pr of Amer.

Una Carrera De Amor. Tr. by Keith Leenhouts. (Spanish Bks.). (Span.). 1978. 1.75 (ISBN 0-8297-0849-9). Vida Pub.

Una Interpretacion Del Apocalipsis. Domingo S. Fernandez. 234p. (Span.). 1980. pap. 2.85 (ISBN 0-311-04312-7). Casa Bautista.

Unabashed Career Guide. Peter Sandman & Dan Goldenson. 1969. pap. 1.95 o.s.i. (ISBN 0-02-081490-9, Collier). Macmillan.

Unabridged Crossword Puzzle Dictionary. A. F. Sisson. 1963. 6.95 (ISBN 0-385-02843-1); thumb-indexed edition 8.95 (ISBN 0-385-01350-7). Doubleday.

Unabridged Jack London. Jack London. Ed. by Lawrence Teacher. 1250p. (Orig.). 1981. lib. bdg. 19.80 (ISBN 0-89471-123-7); pap. 9.95 (ISBN 0-89471-124-5). Running Pr.

Unaccompanied Sonata & Other Stories. Orson S. Card. 288p. 1981. 10.95 (ISBN 0-8037-9175-5). Dial.

Unacknowledged Legislator: Shelley & Politics. P. M. Dawson. 320p. 1980. 48.00x (ISBN 0-19-812095-8). Oxford U Pr.

Unadjusted Man: A New Hero for Americans. Peter R. Viereck. LC 74-178795. 339p. 1973. Repr. of 1956 ed. lib. bdg. 25.00x (ISBN 0-8371-6285-8, VUMA). Greenwood.

Unarmed Victory. Betrand Russell. 1963. text ed. 12.50x (ISBN 0-04-327024-7). Allen Unwin.

Unbind Your Sons: The Captivity of America in Asia. Alex Campbell. LC 79-114382. (Illus.). 1970. 7.95 o.p. (ISBN 0-87140-500-8); pap. 2.45 o.p. (ISBN 0-87140-027-8). Liveright.

Unblessed. Berneice Lunday. LC 78-15244. (Orion Ser). 1979. pap. 1.95 (ISBN 0-8127-0200-X). Southern Pub.

Unblinding. Laurence Lieberman. 1968. 9.95 (ISBN 0-02-571830-4). Macmillan.

Unblocking Your Organization. Mike Woodcock & Dave Francis. LC 78-62929. Orig. Title: People at Work. 254p. 1979. pap. 15.50 (ISBN 0-88390-148-X). Univ Assocs.

Unborn. David Shobin. 1981. 11.95 (ISBN 0-671-25626-2, Linden). S&S.

Unbottled Poison. Ruth J. Buntain. 32p. 1973. pap. 0.75 (ISBN 0-8163-0078-X, 21040-1). Pacific Pr Pub Assn.

Unbound Prometheus: Technological Change & Industrial Development in Western Europe from 1750 to the Present. David S. Landes. 41.50 (ISBN 0-521-07200-X); pap. 9.95x (ISBN 0-521-09418-6). Cambridge U Pr.

Unbounded Love: God & Man in Process. Norman Pittenger. (Orig.). 1976. pap. 3.95 (ISBN 0-8164-2119-6). Crossroad NY.

Unbroken Chain. Neil Rosenstein. LC 75-2648. 1976. 18.95 (ISBN 0-88400-043-5). Shengold.

Uncensored Mad. Mad Magazine Editors. (Mad Ser.: No. 55). 192p. (Orig.). 1980. pap. 1.75 (ISBN 0-446-94462-9). Warner Bks.

Uncertain Glory: Letters of Cautious but Sound Advice. Frederic W. Ness. LC 74-152812. (Higher Education Ser.). 1971. 10.95x o.p. (ISBN 0-87589-098-9). Jossey-Bass.

Uncertain Passage: China's Transition to the Post-Mao Era. A. Doak Barnett. LC 73-22482. 378p. 1974. 14.95 (ISBN 0-8157-0820-3); pap. 5.95 (ISBN 0-8157-0819-X). Brookings.

Uncertain Phoenix: Adventures Toward a Post-Cultural Sensibility. David L. Hall. LC 80-67033. 160p. 1981. 17.50x (ISBN 0-8232-1053-7); pap. 7.50 (ISBN 0-8232-1054-5). Fordham.

Uncertain Promise: Value Conflicts in Technology Transfer. Denis Goulet. LC 77-80314. 324p. 1977. 12.95 (ISBN 0-89021-045-4); pap. 5.95 (ISBN 0-686-28704-5). Overseas Dev Council.

Uncertain Verdict: A Study of the 1969 Elections in Four Indian States. Ramashray Roy. (Illus.). 1975. 18.50x (ISBN 0-520-02475-3). U of Cal Pr.

Uncertainties in French Grammar. Lewis Harmer. Ed. by P. Rickard & G. S. Combe. LC 78-58793. 1980. 80.00 (ISBN 0-521-22233-8). Cambridge U Pr.

Uncertainties in Peasant Farming. Sutti R. De Ortiz. (London School of Economics Monographs on Social Anthropology Ser). (Illus.). 312p. 1973. text ed. 27.50x (ISBN 0-391-00268-6, Athlone Pr). Humanities.

Uncertainties: The Smith - 9. H. L. Van Brunt. 4.50 (ISBN 0-685-78418-5); pap. 2.25 (ISBN 0-912292-01-6). The Smith.

Uncertainty: Behavioral & Social Dimensions. Ed. by Seymour Fiddle. LC 80-82073. 410p. 1980. 26.95 (ISBN 0-03-057022-0). Praeger.

Uncertainty Modeling: With Applications to Multidimensional Civil Engineering. Ove Ditlevsen. (Illus.). 448p. 1980. text ed. 69.50 (C). McGraw.

Unchallenged Violence: An American Ordeal. Robert B. Toplin. LC 75-72. 1975. lib. bdg. 17.95 (ISBN 0-8371-7748-0, TLV/). Greenwood.

Unchaste. Thakazhi S. Pillai. Tr. by M. K. Bhaskaran. 112p. 1971. pap. 2.10 (ISBN 0-88253-067-4). Ind-US Inc.

Unchosen Presidents: The Vice-President & Other Frustrations of Presidential Succession. Allan P. Sindler. (Quantum Book). 1976. 11.95 (ISBN 0-520-03185-7); pap. 2.95 (ISBN 0-520-03493-7). U of Cal Pr.

Uncle Bill's Ice Cream Shop. Gerald H. Krockover & Sharon D. Krockover. 1978. 4.50 o.p. (ISBN 0-533-03191-5). Vantage.

Uncle Bolpenny Tries Things Out. John Bowker. (Illus.). (ps-5). 1973. 5.95 (ISBN 0-571-09973-4, Pub. by Faber & Faber). Merrimack Bk Serv.

Uncle Charlie. Richard Utt. LC 77-85499. 1977. 6.95 (ISBN 0-8163-0288-X, 21070-8); pap. 4.95 (ISBN 0-8163-0289-8, 21069-0). Pacific Pr Pub Assn.

Uncle Dick Wootton: The Pioneer Frontiersman of the Rocky Mountain Region. Howard L. Conard. Ed. by Milo M. Quaife. LC 79-19038. (Illus.). xxiv, 462p. 1980. 22.50x (ISBN 0-8032-1408-1); pap. 7.50 (ISBN 0-8032-6306-6, BB 730, Bison). U of Nebr Pr.

Uncle Ike. Linda S. Chhandler. (gr. 1-6). 1981. 4.95 (ISBN 0-8054-4264-2). Broadman.

Uncle Joe Shannon. Burt Young. 1979. pap. 2.25 o.p. (ISBN 0-523-40572-3). Pinnacle Bks.

Uncle John's Original Bread Book. John R. Brave. 1976. pap. 2.25 (ISBN 0-515-05830-0). Jove Pubns.

Uncle Juan. James Washington. 1981. 4.50 (ISBN 0-8062-1661-1). Carlton.

Uncle Lemon's Spring. Jane Yolen. LC 80-22145. (Illus.). (gr. 2-6). 1981. PLB 8.95 (ISBN 0-525-41830-X). Dutton.

Uncle Misha's Partisans. Yuri Suhl. LC 73-76459. 224p. (gr. 5-10). 1973. 6.95 (ISBN 0-590-07295-1, Four Winds). Schol Bk Serv.

Uncle Robert's Secret. Wylly F. St. John. 1978. pap. 1.50 (ISBN 0-380-00909-9, 46326, Camelot). Avon.

Uncle Sam's Stepchildren: The Reformation of United States Indian Policy, 1865-1887. Loring B. Priest. LC 75-5983. x, 310p. 1975. pap. 3.95 (ISBN 0-8032-5818-6, BB 601, Bison). U of Nebr Pr.

Uncle Sam's Two Hundredth Birthday Parade. Irwin Shapiro. 1974. PLB 9.15 o.p. (ISBN 0-307-63745-X, Golden Pr). Western Pub.

Uncle Scrooge & the Secret of Old Castle. Illus. by Carl Barks. (Illus.). 36p. 1981. 3.95 (ISBN 0-89659-180-8). Abbeville Pr.

Uncle Silas. J. Sheridan Le Fanu. 1966. pap. 6.00 (ISBN 0-486-21715-9). Dover.

Uncle Tom's Cabin. Howard Jones. LC 74-92333. (gr. 6-8). 1969. pap. text ed. 3.50x (ISBN 0-675-09414-3). Merrill.

Uncle Tom's Cabin. Harriet B. Stowe. LC 66-20534. (Illus.). (gr. 5 up). 1966. 7.95 o.s.i. (ISBN 0-8076-0377-5). Braziller.

Uncle Tom's Cabin. (Arabic.). pap. 7.95x (ISBN 0-686-63555-8). Intl Bk Ctr.

Uncle Whiskers. Philip Brown. 1976. pap. 1.95 (ISBN 0-685-96256-3). Warner Bks.

Unclean Sky: A Meteorologist Looks at Air Pollution. Louis J. Battan. LC 80-23434. (Selected Topics in the Atmospheric Sciences, Science Study Ser.). (Illus.). xii, 141p. 1980. Repr. of 1966 ed. lib. bdg. 19.50x (ISBN 0-313-22710-1, BAUS). Greenwood.

Uncollected Letters of James Gates Percival, Poet & Geologist, 1795-1856. James G. Percival. Ed. by Harry R. Warfel. LC 59-62964. (U of Fla. Humanities Monographs: No. 1). 1959. pap. 3.00 (ISBN 0-8130-0186-2). U Presses Fla.

Uncollected Poems, 1604-1617. Samuel Rowlands. Incl. Humors Ordinairie; Theater of Delightful Recreation; Humors Antique Faces; Bride. LC 78-119867. 210p. 1970. 21.00x (ISBN 0-8201-1074-4). Schol Facsimiles.

Uncollected Prose: Early Reviews & Articles 1897-1939, Vol. 1. W. B. Yeats. LC 74-101295. 1975. 30.00x (ISBN 0-231-02845-8). Columbia U Pr.

Uncollected Prose: Later Reviews, Articles & Other Miscellaneous Prose, 1897-1939, Vol. 2. W. B. Yeats. Ed. by John P. Frayne & Colton Johnson. LC 74-101295. 543p. 1976. 30.00x (ISBN 0-231-03660-4). Columbia U Pr.

Uncollected Writings 1785-1822. William Godwin. LC 68-24208. (Illus.). 1968. 52.00x (ISBN 0-8201-1023-X). Schol Facsimiles.

Uncommon Birds in New Zealand. Janet Marshall et al. (Mobil New Zealand Nature Ser.). (Illus.). 96p. 1975. pap. 7.50 (ISBN 0-589-00941-9, Pub. by Reed Bks Australia). C E Tuttle.

Uncommon Child. Ed. by Michael Lewis & Leonard Rosenblum. (Genesis of Behavior Ser.: Vol. 3). 335p. 1981. 25.00 (ISBN 0-306-40499-0, Plenum Pr). Plenum Pub.

Uncommon Controversy: Fishing Rights of the Muckleshoot, Puyallup, & Nisqually Indians. American Friends Service Committee. LC 73-103297. (Illus.). 264p. 1970. 7.50 o.s.i. (ISBN 0-295-95077-3). U of Wash Pr.

Uncommon Guide to Europe. John Whitman. LC 77-10376. (Illus.). 1978. 13.95 o.p. (ISBN 0-312-82862-4); pap. 5.95 o.p. (ISBN 0-312-82863-2). St Martin.

Uncommon Guide to San Luis Obispo County, California. Georgia Lee et al. LC 75-2794. (Padre Productions Uncommon Guide Ser.). (Illus.). 1977. pap. 4.95 o.p. (ISBN 0-914598-18-X). Padre Prods.

Uncommon Guide to San Luis Obispo County California. rev. 2nd ed. Lachlan P. Macdonald. LC 75-2794. (Illus.). 1981. pap. 5.95 (ISBN 0-686-69421-X). Padre Prods.

Uncommon Prayer: A Book of Psalms. Daniel Berrigan. (Illus.). 1978. 7.95 (ISBN 0-8164-0382-1). Crossroad NY.

Uncommon Problems in Emergency Medicine. Michael I. Greenberg & James R. Roberts. 1981. 15.00 (ISBN 0-8036-4331-4). Davis Co.

Uncommon Sense: Manuscript 2 of the Humanist Papers. pap. 5.00 (ISBN 0-938722-02-6). Word Ent.

Uncommon Therapy: The Psychiatric Techniques of Milton H. Erickson, M. D. Jay Haley. 1977. Repr. of 1973 ed. 10.00x (ISBN 0-393-01100-3, Norton Lib); pap. 3.95 (ISBN 0-393-00846-0). Norton.

Uncomplicated Christian. LeRoy Dugan. LC 78-66886. 1978. pap. 1.95 (ISBN 0-87123-572-2, 200572). Bethany Fell.

Unconditional in Human Knowledge: Four Early Essays (1794-1796) by F. W. J. Schelling. Fritz Marti. Tr. by F. W. Schelling. LC 77-74407. 1980. 18.50 (ISBN 0-8387-2020-X). Bucknell U Pr.

Unconquered: Journal of a Year's Adventure Among the Fighting Peasants of North China. James M. Bertram. (China in the 20th Century Ser). (Illus.). ix, 340p. 1975. Repr. of 1939 ed. lib. bdg. 29.50 (ISBN 0-306-70688-1). Da Capo.

Unconscious As Infinite Sets: An Essay in Bi-Logic. Ignacio M. Blanco. 1976. text ed. 35.00x o.p. (ISBN 0-7156-0718-9). Humanities.

Unconscious Conspiracy: Why Leaders Can't Lead. Warren Bennis. (AMACOM Executive Bks). 1978. pap. 5.95 (ISBN 0-8144-7507-8). Am Mgmt.

Unconscious in Culture: The Structuralism of Claude Levi-Strauss in Perspective. Ed. by Ino Rossi. 1974. pap. 6.95 o.p. (ISBN 0-525-47358-0). Dutton.

Unconscious Motives of War. Alix Strachey. 1957. text ed. 5.75x (ISBN 0-391-02065-X). Humanities.

Uncontrollable Spending for Social Services Grants. Martha Derthick. 80p. 1975. pap. 4.95 (ISBN 0-8157-1813-6). Brookings.

Uncook Book: Raw Food Adventures to a New Health High. Elizabeth Baker & Elton Baker. 210p. 1981. pap. 5.95 (ISBN 0-937766-05-4). Comm Creat.

Uncook Book: Raw Food Adventures to a New Health High. Elizabeth Baker & Elton Baker. (Illus.). 198p. 1981. pap. 5.95 (ISBN 0-937766-05-4). Drelwood Pubns.

Uncorrected World. Kenneth Hanson. LC 73-6012. (Wesleyan Poetry Program: Vol. 67). 1973. pap. 4.95x (ISBN 0-8195-1067-X, Pub. by Wesleyan U Pr). Columbia U Pr.

Und Wenn Sie Nicht Gestorben Sind... Maerchenim Spiegel Heutigen Bewusstseins. Ed. by Helmut Brackert. (Edition Suhrkamp: No. 973). (Orig.). 1980. pap. text ed. 6.50 (ISBN 3-518-10973-1, Pub. by Insel Verlag Germany). Suhrkamp.

Undefended City. Sophie Weston. (Harlequin Romances Ser.). 192p. 1980. pap. 1.25 o.p. (ISBN 0-373-02362-6, Pub. by Harlequin). PB.

Under a Changing Moon. Margot Benary-Isbert. LC 64-17084. (gr. 10 up). 1964. 5.95 o.p. (ISBN 0-15-292800-6, HJ). HarBraceJ.

Under a Dancing Star. Ethel M. Comins. (YA) 1977. 4.95 o.p. (ISBN 0-685-75643-2, Avalon). Bouregy.

Under a Glass Bell. Anais Nin. LC 61-65444. 101p. 1948. pap. 3.95 (ISBN 0-8040-0302-5, 30). Swallow.

Under a Raging Sky. Daniel Carney. 322p. 1981. 10.95 (ISBN 0-312-83013-0). St Martin.

Under Christophers Hat. Dorothy Callahan. LC 79-37186. (Encore Ser.). (Illus.). (gr. k-1). 1972. write for info. (ISBN 0-684-12685-0, ScribJ). Scribner.

Under Cover of Darkness. Donald Smith. 1981. pap. 2.50 (ISBN 0-8439-0903-X, Leisure Bks). Nordon Pubns.

Under-Development in Spanish America. Keith Griffin. 1969. text ed. 16.95x (ISBN 0-04-330150-9). Allen Unwin.

Under Gemini. Rosamunde Pilcher. LC 75-26192. 1976. 8.95 o.p. (ISBN 0-312-82915-9). St Martin.

Under God. William C. Hendricks. 1966. 5.50 o.p. (ISBN 0-8028-3108-7). Eerdmans.

Under One Cover: Gifted & Talented Education in Perspective. Ed. by Joseph S. Renzulli & Elizabeth P. Stoddard. LC 80-68284. 248p. 1980. pap. 11.25 (ISBN 0-86586-108-0). Coun Exc Child.

Under One Cover: Implementing the Least Restrictive Environment Concept. Susan E. Hasazi. LC 80-68096. 208p. 1980. pap. 11.25 (ISBN 0-86586-106-4). Coun Exc Child.

Under Orion. K. N. Daruwalla. (Writers Workshop Redbird Ser.). 93p. 1975. 8.00 (ISBN 0-88253-728-8); flexible bdg. 4.80 (ISBN 0-89253-597-0). Ind-US Inc.

Under Stars. Tess Gallagher. LC 77-95331. 1978. 9.00 (ISBN 0-915308-19-3); pap. 5.00 (ISBN 0-915308-20-7). Graywolf.

Under the Axe of Fascism. Gaetano Salvemini. LC 68-9589. 1970. Repr. of 1936 ed. 18.00 (ISBN 0-86527-201-8). Fertig.

Under the Black Flag. Don C. Seitz. LC 78-167167. 1971. Repr. of 1925 ed. 20.00 (ISBN 0-8103-3805-X). Gale.

Under the Blood Banner. Eric Kreye & Norma R. Youngberg. LC 68-21461. 1968. pap. 4.95 (ISBN 0-8163-0148-4, 21190-4). Pacific Pr Pub Assn.

Under the Bo Tree: Studies in Caste, Kinship & Marriage in the Interior of Ceylon. Nur Yalman. 1967. 20.00x (ISBN 0-520-01368-9); pap. 5.95x (ISBN 0-520-02054-5, CAMPUS62). U of Cal Pr.

Under the City of Angels. Jerry E. Brown. 304p. (Orig.). 1981. pap. 1.95 (ISBN 0-553-14605-X). Bantam.

Under the City Streets. Pamela Jones. (Illus.). 1979. 12.95 o.p. (ISBN 0-03-021596-X). HR&W.

Under the Colors. Milovan Djilas. LC 76-134576. 1971. 9.75 o.p. (ISBN 0-15-153470-5). HarBraceJ.

Under the Fifth Sun. 1980. 14.95 (ISBN 0-440-09388-0). Delacorte.

Under the Green Willow. Elizabeth Coatsworth. LC 73-123131. (Illus.). (gr. k-2). 1971. 4.50 o.s.i. (ISBN 0-02-722600-X). Macmillan.

Under the Ground. Eugene Booth. LC 77-8037. (Raintree Spotlight Book). (Illus.). (gr. k-3). 1977. PLB 8.25 (ISBN 0-8393-0110-3). Raintree Child.

Under the Influence. W. E. Butterworth. LC 78-22127. 256p. (gr. 7 up). 1979. 8.95 (ISBN 0-590-07465-2, Four Winds). Schol Bk Serv.

Under the Infulence: Congress, Lobbies, & the American Park Barreling System. William Ashworth. 1981. pap. 7.95 (ISBN 0-8015-5929-4, Hawthorn). Dutton.

Under the Ivi Tree: Society & Economic Growth in Rural Fiji. Cyril S. Belshaw. 1964. 18.50x (ISBN 0-520-00106-0). U of Cal Pr.

Under the Mask: An Anthology About Prejudice in America. Ed. by Karl Weiss. LC 71-176035. (gr. 7 up). 1972. 7.95 o.s.i. (ISBN 0-440-09171-3). Delacorte.

Under the Moorish Wall: Adventures in Andalusia. Peter Luke. 176p. 1980. text ed. 18.75x (ISBN 0-85105-371-8, Dolmen Pr). Humanities.

Under the North Star. Ted Hughes. LC 80-17894. (Illus.). 48p. 1981. 14.95 (ISBN 0-670-73942-1, Studio). Viking Pr.

Under the Ocean. Eugene Booth. LC 77-7983. (Raintree Spotlight Book). (Illus.). (gr. k-3). 1977. PLB 8.25 (ISBN 0-8393-0108-1). Raintree Child.

Under the Rainbow. Lawrence R. Roszkowiak. LC 80-68893. 94p. (Orig.). 1980. pap. 3.95 (ISBN 0-9604986-0-5). Brandywine Bks.

Under the Sign of Saturn. Susan Sontag. 300p. 1980. 10.95 (ISBN 0-374-28076-2). FS&G.

Under the Sunset. Bram Stoker. Ed. by R. Reginald & Douglas Menville. LC 80-19564. (Newcastle Forgotten Library Ser.: Vol. 17). 190p. 1980. Repr. of 1978 ed. lib. bdg. 10.95x (ISBN 0-89370-516-0). Borgo Pr.

Under the Tent of the Sky. Ed. by John E. Brewton. (Illus.). (gr. 4-6). 1937. 8.95 (ISBN 0-02-712470-3). Macmillan.

Under the Wall. (Nick Carter Ser.). 1978. pap. 1.75 (ISBN 0-441-84499-5). Charter Bks.

Under the Wire. William Sheldon et al. (Breakthrough Ser.). (gr. 7-12). 1979. pap. text ed. 4.96 (ISBN 0-205-06072-2, 5260728); tchrs'. ed. 2.40 (ISBN 0-205-06075-7, 5260752). Allyn.

Under This Roof: Family Homes of Southern Ontario. Terry Boyle. LC 79-8925. (Illus.). 160p. 1980. 19.95 (ISBN 0-385-15636-7). Doubleday.

Under Which Lord? A Novel, 1879. Eliza L. Linton. LC 75-482. (Victorian Fiction Ser). 1975. lib. bdg. 66.00 (ISBN 0-8240-1559-2). Garland Pub.

Under World. Subhas C. Saha. (Redbird Ser.). 1975. 8.00 (ISBN 0-88253-666-4); pap. text ed. 4.00 (ISBN 0-88253-665-6). Ind-US Inc.

Underbelly Poems. James A. Costello. 1981. pap. 2.95 (ISBN 0-9605098-0-1). En Passant Poet.

Undercover Operations & Persuasion. R. D. Hicks. (Illus.). 104p. 1973. 8.75 (ISBN 0-398-02807-9). C C Thomas.

Undercover: The Men & Women of the Special Operations Executive. Patrick Howarth. 224p. 1980. 18.95 (ISBN 0-7100-0573-3). Routledge & Kegan.

Undercurrents in American Foreign Relations. M. S. Ventakataramani. 7.50x (ISBN 0-210-22635-8). Asia.

Underdeveloped Europe: Studies in Core-Periphery Relations. Ed. by Dudley Seers et al. (Harvester Studies in Development: No. 1). 1979. text ed. 30.00x (ISBN 0-391-00962-1). Humanities.

Underdevelopment & Agrarian Structure in Pakistan. Mahmood H. Khan. (Replica Edition Ser.). 275p. 1981. lib. bdg. 20.00x (ISBN 0-86531-134-X). Westview.

Underdevelopment & Modernization of the Third World. A. R. DeSouza & P. W. Porter. LC 74-20053. (CCG Resource Papers Ser.: No. 28). (Illus.). 1974. pap. text ed. 4.00 (ISBN 0-89291-075-5). Assn Am Geographers.

Underdevelopment & the Transition to Socialism: Mozambique & Tanzania. James H. Mittelman. (Studies in Social Discontinuity Ser.). 1981. price not set (ISBN 0-12-500660-8). Acad Pr.

Underdevelopment in Kenya: The Political Economy of Neo-Colonialism, 1964-71. Colin Leys. LC 74-76387. 1975. 17.50x (ISBN 0-520-02731-0); pap. 6.95x (ISBN 0-520-02770-1). U of Cal Pr.

Underfoot: A Guide to Exploring and Preserving America's Past. David Weitzman. LC 76-11475. (Illus.). 192p. 1976. pap. 4.95 encore ed. (ISBN 0-684-16205-9, ScribT). Scribner.

Underfoot in Show Business. Helene Hanff. 192p. 1980. 10.95 (ISBN 0-316-34319-6). Little.

Underglaze Decoration. Marc Bellaire. 3.95 (ISBN 0-934706-01-8). Prof Pubns Ohio.

Undergraduate Admissions: The Realities of Institutional Policies, Practices, & Procedures. LC 80-70480. (Illus.). 72p. (Orig.). 1980. pap. 8.50 (ISBN 0-87447-136-2). College Bd.

Undergraduate Curriculum: A Guide to Innovation & Reform. Clifton Conrad. (Westview Special Studies in Higher Education). 1979. lib. bdg. 19.75x (ISBN 0-89158-196-0). Westview.

Undergraduate Education in the Biological Sciences for Students in Agriculture & Natural Resources. Commission On Education In Agriculture And Natural Resources. 1967. pap. 4.25 (ISBN 0-309-01495-6). Natl Acad Pr.

Undergraduate Education in the Plant & Soil Sciences. Commission On Education In Agriculture And Natural Resources. LC 71-600161. (Orig.). 1969. pap. 3.25 (ISBN 0-309-01704-1). Natl Acad Pr.

Undergraduate Education in the Sciences for Students in Agriculture & Natural Resources. Commission On Education In Agriculture And Natural Resources. 1971. pap. text ed. 7.50 (ISBN 0-309-01921-4). Natl Acad Pr.

Undergraduate Personality by Factored Scales: A Large Scale Study on Cattell's 16PF & the Eysenck Personality Inventory. P. Saville & S. Blinkhorn. (NFER General Ser.). 1976. pap. text ed. 21.25x (ISBN 0-85633-104-X, NFER). Humanities.

Undergraduate Program Field Test Series. Jack Rudman. (Cloth bdg. avail. on request). pap. 9.95 ea. (ISBN 0-8373-6000-5). Natl Learning.

Undergraduate Teaching in the Animal Sciences. Commission On Education In Agriculture And Natural Resources. 1967. pap. 4.25 (ISBN 0-309-01486-7). Natl Acad Pr.

Underground Corrosion, Cathodic Protection & Required Field Measurements. Building Research Advisory Board. 1962. pap. 3.00 o.p. (ISBN 0-309-00991-X). Natl Acad Pr.

Underground Design. 100p. 1981. pap. 7.95 (ISBN 0-931790-20-4). Brick Hse Pub.

Underground Disposal of Coal Mine Wastes. Environmental Studies Board. 1975. pap. 8.50 (ISBN 0-309-02324-6). Natl Acad Pr.

Underground Disposal of Radioactive Wastes, Vol. II. 613p. 1980. pap. 76.75 (ISBN 92-0-020280-2, ISP528-2, IAEA). Unipub.

Underground Disposal of Radioactive Wastes, Vol. 1. 517p. 1980. pap. 60.75 (ISP 528-1, IAEA). Unipub.

Underground Furnaces, the Story of Geothermal Energy. Irene Kiefer. LC 76-3606. (Illus.). (gr. 3-7). 1976. PLB 6.00 (ISBN 0-688-32075-9). Morrow.

Underground Homes. rev ed. Louis Wampler. LC 80-18701. (Illus.). 120p. 1980. pap. 5.95 (ISBN 0-88289-273-8). Pelican.

Underground Houses: How to Build a Low-Cost Home. Robert L. Roy. LC 79-64505. (Illus.). 1979. pap. 5.95 o.p. (ISBN 0-8069-8856-8). Sterling.

Underground Marketplace. Jonathan Webster & Harriet Webster. LC 80-54401. (Illus.). 208p. 1981. text ed. 12.50x (ISBN 0-87663-348-3); pap. 6.95 (ISBN 0-87663-555-9). Universe.

Underground Power Transmission: The Science, Technology, & Economics of High Voltage Cables. Peter Graneau. LC 79-15746. 1979. 34.50 (ISBN 0-471-05757-6, Pub. by Wiley-Interscience). Wiley.

Underground Railroad in Connecticut. Horatio T. Strother. LC 62-15122. 1962. 15.00x (ISBN 0-8195-3025-5, Pub. by Wesleyan U Pr); pap. 6.95 (ISBN 0-8195-6012-X). Columbia U Pr.

Underground Railroad in Pennsylvania. Charles L. Blockson. LC 80-69847. (Illus.). 1981. 12.95 (ISBN 0-933184-21-2); pap. 6.95 (ISBN 0-933184-22-0). Flame Intl.

Underground Rock Chambers. Compiled by American Society of Civil Engineers. 608p. 1972. text ed. 29.50 (ISBN 0-87262-033-6). Am Soc Civil Eng.

Underground Shadows. Valery Oistenau. 1977. pap. 1.50 (ISBN 0-9601870-0-6). Pass.

Underground Waters & Subsurface Temperatures of the Woodbine Sand in Northeast Texas. F. B. Plummer & E. C. Sargent. (Illus.). 178p. 1931. 1.00 (BULL 3138). Bur Econ Geology.

Undergrounding Electric Lines. Anthony J. Pansini. (gr. 10 up). 1978. pap. 7.15 (ISBN 0-8104-0827-9); final exam 0.30 (ISBN 0-686-67928-8). Hayden.

Underhanded Backgammon. Arthur Prager. 1977. pap. 4.95 (ISBN 0-8015-8125-7, Hawthorn). Dutton.

Underhanded Bridge. Jerry Sohl. 128p. 1975. pap. 3.95 (ISBN 0-8015-8128-1, Hawthorn). Dutton.

Underhanded Chess. Jerry Sohl. 1973. pap. 3.50 (ISBN 0-8015-8130-3, Hawthorn). Dutton.

Underhanded Serve, or How to Play Dirty Tennis. Rex Lardner. (Illus.). 1968. pap. 2.95 (ISBN 0-8015-8142-7, Hawthorn). Dutton.

Underhill Edge Tool Co., Eighteen Fifty-Nine Price List Axes & Mechanics' Tools. 1980. pap. 3.00 (ISBN 0-913602-37-X). K Roberts.

Underhill's Criminal Evidence, 3 vols. Set. with 1979 suppl. 95.00 (ISBN 0-672-82967-3, Bobbs-Merrill Law); 1979 suppl. 50.00 (ISBN 0-672-83935-0). Michie.

Undersea Base. Mae Freeman. LC 73-9996. (Illus.). 64p. (gr. 3-4). 1974. PLB 4.90 o.p. (ISBN 0-531-02664-7). Watts.

Undersea Fleet. Frederick Pohl & Jack Williamson. 1977. pap. 1.50 o.p. (ISBN 0-345-25618-2). Ballantine.

Undersea Machines. Christopher C. Pick. LC 78-27420. (Machine World Ser.). (Illus.). (gr. 2-4). 1979. PLB 9.95 (ISBN 0-8172-1326-0). Raintree Pubs.

Undersea People. Eve Bunting. (Science Fiction Ser.). (Illus.). (gr. 3-9). 1978. PLB 5.95 (ISBN 0-87191-624-X); pap. 2.95 (ISBN 0-89812-052-7). Creative Ed.

Undersea Vechicles & Habitats: The Peaceful Uses of the Ocean. Frank Ross, Jr. LC 76-106577. (Illus.). (gr. 5-8). 1970. 10.95 (ISBN 0-690-84416-6, TYC-J). T Y Crowell.

Undersea Work Systems. Talkington. 240p. 1981. write for info. (ISBN 0-8247-1226-9). Dekker.

Underseas Victory I. W. J. Holmes. (Zebra World at War Ser.: No. 10). 352p. 1980. pap. 2.50 (ISBN 0-89083-613-2). Zebra.

Underside of History: A View of Women Through Time. Elise Boulding. LC 75-30558. 750p. 1976. lib. bdg. 32.50x (ISBN 0-89158-009-3); text ed. 15.00 (ISBN 0-89158-056-5). Westview.

Understand the Weapon Understand the Wound: Selected Writings of John Cornford. Ed. by Jonathan Galassi. (Essays, Prose, & Scottish Literature). 1979. 12.50 o.s.i. (ISBN 0-85635-152-0, Pub. by Carcanet New Pr England). Persea Bks.

Understanding. Churches Alive Inc. (Love One Another Bible Study). 1979. wkbk. 1.50 (ISBN 0-934396-02-7). Churches Alive.

Understanding. Ann Dally. LC 78-66254. 192p. 1981. pap. 6.95 (ISBN 0-8128-6104-3). Stein & Day.

Understanding Adolescence: Current Developments in Adolescent Psychology. 4th ed. Adams. 512p. 1980. text ed. 17.50 (ISBN 0-205-06931-2, 2469316). Allyn.

Understanding Adolescence: Current Developments in Adolescent Psychology. 3rd ed. James F. Adams. 576p. 1976. text ed. 15.95x o.s.i. (ISBN 0-205-05410-2); tests free o.s.i. (ISBN 0-685-61042-X). Allyn.

Understanding Africa. rev. ed. E. Jefferson Murphy. LC 77-11560. (Illus.). (gr. 7 up). 1978. 8.95 (ISBN 0-690-03834-8, TYC-J); PLB 9.79 (ISBN 0-690-03846-1). T Y Crowell.

Understanding Aging Parents. Andrew D. Lester & Judith L. Lester. LC 80-17832. (Christian Care Bk.). 1980. pap. 5.95 (ISBN 0-664-24329-0). Westminster.

Understanding Alcoholism for the Patient, the Family, & the Employer. C. D. Foundation Smithers. pap. 5.95 (ISBN 0-684-71891-X, SL200, ScribT). Scribner.

Understanding Algebra & Trigonometry. Gene Sellers. 1979. text ed. 17.95 (ISBN 0-675-08306-0); instructor's manual 3.95 (ISBN 0-685-96157-5); test 3.95 (ISBN 0-686-67369-7). Merrill.

Understanding Allergies. John W. Gerrard. 88p. 1977. pap. 6.95 (ISBN 0-398-02768-4). C C Thomas.

Understanding America's Industries. Carl Gerbracht & Frank E. Robinson. (gr. 7-9). 1971. text ed. 14.64 (ISBN 0-87345-499-5). McKnight.

Understanding & Changing Criminal Behavior. Michael J. Lillyquist. (Ser. in Criminal Justice). 1980. text ed. 17.95 (ISBN 0-13-935528-6). P-H.

Understanding & Counseling the Alcoholic. rev. ed. Howard J. Clinebell, Jr. 1968. 8.95 (ISBN 0-687-42801-7). Abingdon.

Understanding & Evaluating Educational Research. Jean R. Dyer. LC 78-67952. (Education Ser.). (Illus.). 1979. text ed. 17.95 (ISBN 0-201-01184-0). A-W.

Understanding & Guiding Young Children. 3rd ed. K. Baker & X. Fane. 1975. 13.32 (ISBN 0-13-935825-0). P-H.

Understanding & Helping the Schizophrenic: A Guide for Family & Friends. Silvano Arieti. 1981. pap. 4.95 (ISBN 0-671-41252-3, Touchstone Bks). S&S.

Understanding & Influencing Human Behavior. Hugh Russell & Kenneth Black. (Illus.). 240p. 1981. text ed. 12.95 (ISBN 0-13-936674-1, Spec). P-H.

Understanding & Living with Brain Damage. Patrick E. Logue. 116p. 1975. 11.75 (ISBN 0-398-03419-2); pap. 7.75 (ISBN 0-398-03420-6). C C Thomas.

Understanding & Managing Stress: A Book of Readings. Ed. by John D. Adams. LC 80-50474. 217p. 1980. pap. 14.50; Set Of 5. pap. 62.50 (ISBN 0-88390-158-7). Univ Assocs.

Understanding & Managing Stress: A Facilitator's Guide. John D. Adams. LC 80-50474. 137p. 1980. pap. 39.50 with readings and workbook (ISBN 0-88390-157-9). Univ Assocs.

Understanding & Managing Stress: A Workbook in Changing Life Styles, 5 vols. John D. Adams. LC 80-50474. 101p. 1980. Set Of 5. pap. 44.50 (ISBN 0-88390-157-9). Set. Univ Assocs.

Understanding & Measuring Vibrations. R. H. Wallace. LC 78-135386. (Wykeham Technology Ser.: No. 4). 1970. 9.95x (ISBN 0-8448-1125-4). Crane Russak Co.

Understanding & Prediction. Stefan Nowak. (Synthese Library: No. 94). 482p. 1980. pap. 15.95 (ISBN 90-277-1199-2, Pub. by D. Reidel). Kluwer Boston.

Understanding & Servicing Alarms. Trimmer. 1981. text ed. price not set. Butterworth.

Understanding & Teaching Emotionally Disturbed Children. new ed. Newcomer. 456p. 1979. text ed. 17.95 (ISBN 0-205-06843-X, 2468433). Allyn.

Understanding & Teaching the Bible. Richard L. Jeske. Ed. by Harold W. Rast. LC 80-69756. (Lead Book). 128p. (Orig.). 1981. pap. 3.25 (ISBN 0-8006-1601-4, 1-1601). Fortress.

Understanding & Training Horses. A. James Ricci. LC 64-14466. (Illus.). (gr. 10 up). 1964. 10.95 (ISBN 0-397-00356-0). Lippincott.

Understanding & Troubleshooting Microprocessors. J. Coffron. 1980. 19.95 (ISBN 0-13-936625-3). P-H.

Understanding & Using Electricity. Bruce A McKenzie & Gerald Zachariah. LC 75-18492. 1975. text ed. 1.95x o.p. (ISBN 0-8134-1754-6, 1754). Interstate.

Understanding & Using Electricity. 2nd ed. Bruce A. McKenzie & Gerald Zachariah. 1981. text ed. 1.95x. Interstate.

Understanding & Using English. 5th ed. Newman P. Birk & Genevieve B. Birk. LC 71-179751. 1972. 12.50 (ISBN 0-672-63214-4). Odyssey Pr.

Understanding & Using English Grammar. Betty S. Azur. (Illus.). 416p. 1981. pap. text ed. 10.95 (ISBN 0-13-936492-7, Spec). P-H.

Understanding & Using Modern Electronic Servicing Test Equipment. Charles M. Gilmore. LC 76-45062. (Illus.). 1976. 8.95 o.p. (ISBN 0-8306-6777-6); pap. 5.95 (ISBN 0-8306-5777-0, 777). TAB Bks.

Understanding & Using Modern Signal Generators. Charles Gilmore. LC 76-45060. (Illus.). 1976. 9.95 o.p. (ISBN 0-8306-6877-2); pap. 6.95 (ISBN 0-8306-5877-7, 877). TAB Bks.

Understanding & Using the Oscilloscope. Clayton Hallmark. LC 73-84546. 1973. pap. 7.95 (ISBN 0-8306-2664-6, 664). TAB Bks.

Understanding Attitudes & Predicting Social Behavior. Martin Fishbein & Icek Ajzen. (Illus.). 1980. text ed. 14.95 (ISBN 0-13-936443-9); pap. text ed. 8.95 (ISBN 0-13-936435-8). P-H.

Understanding Audio. Kenneth W. Johnson & Willard C. Walker. (Illus.). 256p. 1980. pap. text ed. 5.75 (ISBN 0-8403-2216-X). Kendall-Hunt.

Understanding Baking. Donald E. Lundberg & Joseph Amendola. 1970. pap. 9.95 (ISBN 0-8436-0521-9). CBI Pub.

Understanding Basic Calculus: With Application from the Managerial, Social & Life Sciences. Monte B. Boisen, Jr. & Max D. Larsen. (Mathematics Ser.). 1978. text ed. 18.95 (ISBN 0-675-08430-X); manual 3.95 (ISBN 0-686-67993-8). Merrill.

Understanding Basic Energy Terms. Robert V. Nelson. Ed. by Arthur F. Ide. LC 79-9940. (E Equals MC Squared Ser.). (Illus.). 60p. 1980. 9.00 (ISBN 0-86663-806-7); pap. 6.25 (ISBN 0-86663-807-5). Ide Hse.

Understanding Basic Statistics. Harvey W. Kushner & Gerald De Maio. LC 78-54195. 1980. text ed. 17.95 (ISBN 0-8162-4874-5); sol. manual 5.00 (0-8162-8475). Holden-Day.

Understanding Behavioral Research. Nancy S. Harrison. 1979. text ed. 16.95x (ISBN 0-534-00597-7). Wadsworth Pub.

Understanding Biblical Symbols. Charles L. Edwards. 96p. 1981. 6.00 (ISBN 0-682-49704-5). Exposition.

Understanding Bisexuals. (Illus.). pap. 5.00 (ISBN 0-910550-66-2). Centurion Pr.

Understanding Boat Design. 3rd ed. Edward S. Brewer & Jim Betts. LC 70-147872. (Illus.). 1980. pap. 7.95 (ISBN 0-87742-015-7). Intl Marine.

Understanding Body Talk. Thomas G. Aylesworth. LC 78-12446. (Impact Bks.). (Illus.). (gr. 7 up). 1979. PLB 6.90 s&l (ISBN 0-531-02200-5). Watts.

Understanding Britain: A History of the British People & Their Culture. John Randle. (Illus.). 288p. 1981. 25.00x (ISBN 0-631-12471-3, Pub. by Basil Blackwell England); pap. 8.95x (ISBN 0-631-12883-2). Biblio Dist.

Understanding Broadcasting. Eugene S. Foster. LC 77-74323. (Mass Communication Ser.). (Illus.). 1978. text ed. 16.95 (ISBN 0-201-02468-3). A-W.

Understanding Business Today. Elwood S. Buffa & Barbara A. Pletcher. 1980. 16.95x (ISBN 0-256-02257-7). Irwin.

Understanding Cancer. Bryan N. Brooke. LC 72-89655. 128p. 1973. 4.95 o.p. (ISBN 0-03-006181-4). HR&W.

Understanding Cancer. Ron Hicks. 141p. (Orig.). 1980. pap. 4.75 (ISBN 0-7022-1425-6). U of Queensland Pr.

Understanding Capital Markets, 2 vols. Patric H. Hendershott et al. Incl. Vol. 1. Flow of Funds Financial Model. LC 76-55112 (ISBN 0-669-01006-5). 29.50 (ISBN 0-686-67901-6); Vol. 2. Financial Environment & the Flow of Funds in the Next Decade. LC 76-55113. 22.00 (ISBN 0-669-01007-3). 1977. Lexington Bks.

Understanding Cell Structure. M. W. Steer. (Illus.). 120p. Date not set. price not set (ISBN 0-521-23745-9); pap. text ed. price not set (ISBN 0-521-28198-9). Cambridge U Pr.

Understanding Characters: Advanced Level. James A. Giroux & Glenn R. Williston. (Comprehension Skills Ser.). (Illus.). (gr. 12 up). 1974. pap. text ed. 2.40x (ISBN 0-89061-014-2). Jamestown Pubs.

Understanding Characters: Middle Level. Glenn R. Williston. (Comprehension Skills Ser.). (Illus.). 64p. (gr. 6-8). 1976. pap. text ed. 2.40x (ISBN 0-89061-066-5, CB3M). Jamestown Pubs.

Understanding Chemistry. Dudley Herron. Incl. Elizabeth Kean. wkbk. 6.95 (ISBN 0-394-32423-4); Jane Copes. lab manual 6.95 (ISBN 0-394-32437-4). 515p. 1981. text ed. 16.95 (ISBN 0-394-32087-5). Random.

Understanding Chemistry. George C. Pimentel & Richard D. Spratley. LC 70-142944. 1971. 26.50x (ISBN 0-8162-6761-8); solution manual o.p. 6.95 (ISBN 0-8162-6741-3). Holden-Day.

Understanding Children. Kay Kuzma. LC 78-50449. (Harvest Ser.). 1978. pap. 3.95 (ISBN 0-8163-0212-X, 21198-7). Pacific Pr Pub Assn.

Understanding Children's Art for Better Teaching. 2nd ed. Betty Lark-Horovitz et al. LC 73-81970. 1973. text ed. 17.95 (ISBN 0-675-08927-1). Merrill.

Understanding Christian Missions. J. Herbert Kane. 10.95 (ISBN 0-8010-5344-7). Baker Bk.

Understanding Christian Morality. Ronald J. Wilkins. (To Live Is Christ Ser). 256p. 1977. pap. 4.25 (ISBN 0-697-01660-9). Wm C Brown.

Understanding Christian Morality: Short Edition. Ronald J. Wilkins. (To Live Is Christ Ser.). 112p. 1977. pap. 3.25 (ISBN 0-697-01661-7). Wm C Brown.

Understanding Christian Worship: Extended Edition. Ronald J. Wilkins. (To Live Is Christ Ser.). 216p. 1977. pap. 4.10 (ISBN 0-697-01662-5). Wm C Brown.

Understanding Christian Worship: Short Edition. Ronald J. Wilkins. (To Live Is Christ Ser.). 80p. 1977. pap. 3.00 (ISBN 0-697-01663-3); tchr's ed. 3.50 (ISBN 0-697-01669-2). Wm C Brown.

Understanding Church Growth & Decline, 1950-78. Ed. by Dean R. Hoge & David A. Roozen. LC 79-4166. (Illus.). 1979. pap. 9.95 (ISBN 0-8298-0358-0). Pilgrim NY.

Understanding Classroom Life. Ed. by Ray McAleese & David Hamilton. (General Ser.). 1978. pap. text ed. 15.00x (ISBN 0-85633-158-9, NFER). Humanities.

Understanding Climatic Change: A Program for Action. LC 79-22423. (Illus.). 1980. Repr. of 1975 ed. 28.00 (ISBN 0-8103-1019-8). Gale.

Understanding Climatic Change: A Program for Action. U. S. Committee for the Global Atmospheric Research Program. 1975. pap. 9.00 (ISBN 0-309-02323-8). Natl Acad Pr.

Understanding Collective Bargaining in Education: Negotiations, Contracts & Disputes Between Teachers & Boards. Robert C. O'Reilly. LC 78-64495. 1978. 11.00 (ISBN 0-8108-1167-7). Scarecrow.

Understanding College Algebra. Gene R. Sellers. 1979. text ed. 14.95 (ISBN 0-675-08294-3); instructor's manual 3.95 (ISBN 0-686-67292-5); tests 3.95 (ISBN 0-686-67293-3). Merrill.

Understanding Communities. James A. Conway et al. LC 73-22370. (Illus.). 288p. 1974. 14.95 (ISBN 0-13-936393-9). P-H.

Understanding Computers. Paul M. Chirlian. LC 78-60611. 1978. pap. 9.95 (ISBN 0-918398-15-0). Dilithium Pr.

Understanding Computers: All the Basics for Managers & Users. Myles E. Walsh. LC 80-20547. 296p. 1981. 20.95 (ISBN 0-471-08191-4, Pub. by Wiley-Interscience). Wiley.

Understanding Conflict & War, 2 vols. Rudolph J. Rummel. Incl. Vol. 1. 342p. 18.95 (ISBN 0-470-74501-0); Vol. 2. Conflict Helix. 17.50 (ISBN 0-470-15123-4). LC 74-78565. 1975-76. Halsted Pr.

Understanding Contact Lenses. Montague Ruben. 1976. pap. 10.00x (ISBN 0-685-83938-9). Intl Ideas.

Understanding Cooking. Donald Lunberg & Lendal H. Kotschevar. 382p. 1970. pap. 10.95 (ISBN 0-685-04750-4). Radio City.

Understanding Crime. Committee on Research on Law Enforcement & Criminal Justice. 1977. pap. 12.00 (ISBN 0-309-02635-0). Natl Acad Pr.

Understanding Crime: Current Theory & Research. Ed. by Travis Hirshi & Michael Gottfredson. LC 80-19376. (Sage Research Progress Ser. in Criminology: Vol. 18). (Illus.). 144p. 1980. 12.95 (ISBN 0-8039-1517-9); pap. 6.50 (ISBN 0-8039-1518-7). Sage.

Understanding Criminal Law. Jay A. Sigler. 1981. text ed. 16.95 (ISBN 0-316-79054-0); training manual free (ISBN 0-316-79055-9). Little.

Understanding Crop Production. Neal C. Stoskopf. 420p. 1981. text ed. 16.95 (ISBN 0-8359-8027-8). Reston.

Understanding Cystitis. Angela Kilmartin. 1973. pap. 10.00x (ISBN 0-685-83939-7). Intl Ideas.

Understanding Death & Dying. 2nd ed. Wilcox & Sutton. 1981. 10.95 (ISBN 0-88284-122-X). Alfred Pub.

Understanding Death & Dying. 2nd ed. Sandra Wilcox & Marilyn Sutton. LC 76-30406. (Illus.). 1977. 10.95 (ISBN 0-88284-051-7); pap. 9.95x (ISBN 0-88284-052-5). Alfred Pub.

Understanding Disability for Social & Rehabilitation Services. Ed. by John G. Cull & Richard E. Hardy. (American Lectures in Social & Rehabilitation Psychology Ser.). (Illus.). 220p. 1973. 18.75 (ISBN 0-398-02889-3). C C Thomas.

Understanding Ecology. James L. Mariner. 207p. (gr. 9-12). 1975. pap. text ed. 4.50x (ISBN 0-88334-070-4). Ind Sch Pr.

Understanding Econometrics. Jon Stewart. 1980. text ed. 18.25x (ISBN 0-09-126230-5, Hutchinson U Pr); pap. text ed. 10.25x (ISBN 0-09-126231-3). Humanities.

Understanding Educational Organizations: A Field Study Approach. Frank W. Lutz & Laurence Iannacconne. 1969. text ed. 12.95 (ISBN 0-675-09540-9). Merrill.

Understanding Educational Research: An Inquiry Approach. 2nd ed. Charles D. Hopkins. (Illus.). 544p. 1980. text ed. 17.95 (ISBN 0-675-08162-9); instr's manual avail. (ISBN 0-686-63195-1). Merrill.

Understanding Electrocardiography: Physiological & Interpretive Concepts. 3rd ed. Mary B. Conover. LC 80-14104. (Illus.). 254p. 1980. pap. text ed. 12.50 (ISBN 0-8016-5676-1). Mosby.

Understanding Elementary Algebra. Richard G. Moon. (Mathematics Ser.). 1978. text ed. 15.95 (ISBN 0-675-08406-7); instructor's manual 3.95 (ISBN 0-686-67994-6). Merrill.

Understanding English Place-Names. William Addison. 1978. 17.95 (ISBN 0-7134-0295-4, Pub. by Batsford England). David & Charles.

Understanding English Surnames. William Addison. 1978. 19.95 (ISBN 0-7134-0295-4). David & Charles.

Understanding Ernest Hemingway: A Study & Research Guide. Robert B. Harmon. LC 77-14893. 1977. 8.00 o.p. (ISBN 0-8108-1074-3). Scarecrow.

Understanding Events. David R. Heise. LC 78-24177. (ASA Rose Monograph). (Illus.). 1979. 19.95 (ISBN 0-521-22539-6); pap. 6.95x (ISBN 0-521-29544-0). Cambridge U Pr.

Understanding Evolution. Earl D. Hanson. (Illus.). 560p. 1981. text ed. 19.95x (ISBN 0-19-502784-1). Oxford U Pr.

Understanding Evolution. Herbert H. Ross. (Orig.). 1967. pap. 2.45 o.p. (ISBN 0-13-935890-0, Spec). P-H.

Understanding Evolution. 4th ed. Peter E. Volpe. 240p. 1981. pap. text ed. write for info. (ISBN 0-697-04646-X). Wm C Brown.

Understanding Exceptional Children. Colleen J. Mandell & Edward D. Fiscus. (Illus.). 550p. 1981. text ed. 12.76 (ISBN 0-8299-0394-1). West Pub.

Understanding Executive Stress. Cary L. Cooper & Judi Marshall. LC 77-16077. 1978. text ed. 14.00 (ISBN 0-89433-059-4). Petrocelli.

Understanding Exodus. Moshe Greenberg. 1969. pap. 5.95x o.p. (ISBN 0-87441-029-0). Behrman.

Understanding Faculty Unions & Collective Bargaining. Frank R. Kemerer. 1976. pap. 6.50 (ISBN 0-934338-32-9). NAIS.

Understanding Fiction. 3rd ed. Robert P. Warren & Cleanth Brooks. 1979. pap. text ed. 9.50 (ISBN 0-13-936690-3). P-H.

Understanding Figurative Language: What Effect Did the Author Intend? Walter Pauk. (Skill at a Time Ser). 64p. (gr. 9 up). 1975. pap. text ed. 2.40x (ISBN 0-89061-023-1). Jamestown Pubs.

Understanding Foreign Policy Decisions: The Chinese Case. David B. Bobrow et al. LC 78-24667. (Illus.). 1979. 19.95 (ISBN 0-02-904410-3). Free Pr.

Understanding FORTRAN. 2nd ed. Michel Boillot. (Illus.). 500p. 1981. pap. text ed. 11.16 (ISBN 0-8299-0355-0). West Pub.

Understanding Gambling Systems. Dean Wiley. (Gambler's Book Shelf). 64p. 1975. pap. 2.95 (ISBN 0-89650-554-5). Gamblers.

Understanding Gay Relatives & Friends. Clinton R. Jones. 1978. pap. 3.95 (ISBN 0-8164-2179-X). Crossroad NY.

Understanding God. 2nd ed. Patricia B. Gruits. 415p. 1972. pap. 7.95 (ISBN 0-88368-011-4). Whitaker Hse.

Understanding Government. David Potter. 1975. 17.95 (ISBN 0-7134-2910-0, Pub. by Batsford England). David & Charles.

Understanding Grammar. Paul M. Roberts. 1954. text ed. 15.95x scp (ISBN 0-06-045480-6, HarpC). Har-Row.

Understanding Hamlet. P. Winders. pap. 4.30 o.p (ISBN 0-08-018304-2). Pergamon.

Understanding Hematology. Murray Nussbaum. 1973. 12.00 (ISBN 0-87488-977-4). Med Exam.

Understanding Hospital Financial Management. Allen G. Herkimer. LC 78-12182. 1978. text ed. 25.95 (ISBN 0-89443-047-5). Aspen Systems.

Understanding Hospital Labor Relations: An Orientation for Supervisors. Joseph J. Bean, Jr. & Rene Laliberty. LC 76-20014. 110p. 1977. pap. text ed. 8.95 (ISBN 0-201-00496-8). A-W.

Understanding: How It Grows on You & How You Grow on It. Hubert R. Finke. 1977. 4.50 o.p. (ISBN 0-682-48914-X). Exposition.

Understanding Human: A New Synthesis. Farhang Zabeeh. LC 78-65843. 1979. pap. 10.25 (ISBN 0-8191-0670-4). U Pr of Amer.

Understanding Human Behavior. Mary E. Milliken. 224p. pap. 6.00 o.p. (ISBN 0-8273-0338-6). Delmar.

Understanding Human Behavior. Mary E. Milliken. LC 80-51266. (Practical Nursing Ser.). 256p. 1981. 9.20 (ISBN 0-8273-1968-1); pap. 6.80 (ISBN 0-8273-1439-6); instr's. guide 1.70 (ISBN 0-8273-1445-0). Delmar.

Understanding Human Behavior in Health & Illness. 2nd ed. Richard C. Simons & Herbert Pardes. (Illus.). 760p. 1981. write for info. (7740-6). Williams & Wilkins.

Understanding Human Engineering: An Introduction to Ergonomics. John Hammond. 1979. 14.95 (ISBN 0-7153-7670-5). David & Charles.

Understanding Human Nature. Alfred Adler. Tr. by Walter B. Wolfe. 1928. text ed. 19.50x (ISBN 0-04-150002-4). Allen Unwin.

Understanding Human Nature. Alfred Adler. 1978. pap. 1.95 o.p. (ISBN 0-449-30833-2, Prem). Fawcett.

Understanding Human Sexuality. Frederick Cohn & C. Moritz. (Illus.). 304p. 1974. 13.95 (ISBN 0-13-937425-6); pap. 11.95 (ISBN 0-13-937417-5). P-H.

Understanding Human Sexuality. Joann S. Delora et al. LC 79-89744. (Illus.). 1980. pap. text ed. 12.50 (ISBN 0-395-28255-1); inst manual 0.75 (ISBN 0-395-28256-X); study guide 4.95 (ISBN 0-395-28981-5). HM.

Understanding Infancy. Eleanor W. Willemsen. LC 78-21181. (Psychology Ser.). (Illus.). 1979. text ed. 16.95x (ISBN 0-7167-1002-1); pap. text ed. 8.95x (ISBN 0-7167-1001-3). W H Freeman.

Understanding Inflation. John Case. (Illus.). 224p. 1981. 9.95 (ISBN 0-688-00399-0). Morrow.

Understanding Inflation & Unemployment. Allen W. Smith. LC 75-29492. 176p. 1976. 11.95 (ISBN 0-88229-276-5); pap. 6.95 (ISBN 0-88229-492-X). Nelson-Hall.

Understanding Integrated Circuits. Murray P. Rosenthal. (Illus.). 128p. 1975. pap. text ed. 5.95 (ISBN 0-8104-5526-9). Hayden.

Understanding Intercultural Communication. Larry A. Samovar et al. 240p. 1980. pap. text ed. 8.95x (ISBN 0-534-00862-3). Wadsworth Pub.

Understanding Interpersonal Communication. Richard L. Weaver, II. 1978. pap. 9.95x (ISBN 0-673-15089-5). Scott F.

Understanding Interpersonal Communication. 2nd ed. Richard L. Weaver, II. 1981. pap. text ed. 10.95x (ISBN 0-673-15436-X). Scott F.

Understanding Islam. Frithjot Schuon. Tr. by D. M. Matheson. (Mandala Bks.). 1976. pap. 5.25 (ISBN 0-04-297035-0). Allen Unwin.

Understanding Job Satisfaction. Michael M. Gruneberg. LC 78-20782. 1979. 27.95x (ISBN 0-470-26610-4). Halsted Pr.

Understanding Language: An Introduction to Linguistics. Roger Fowler. 1974. 12.50x (ISBN 0-7100-7755-6); pap. 7.95 (ISBN 0-7100-7756-4). Routledge & Kegan.

Understanding Laughter: The Workings of Wit & Humor. Charles R. Gruner. LC 78-16759. 1978. 17.95 (ISBN 0-88229-186-6). Nelson-Hall.

Understanding Learning Disabilities. 2nd ed. Tanis Bryan & James Bryan. LC 77-25987. 1978. text ed. 15.95x (ISBN 0-88284-056-8). Alfred Pub.

Understanding Literature. Robin Mayhead. (Orig.). 1965. 32.50 (ISBN 0-521-05705-1); pap. 7.95x (ISBN 0-521-09282-5). Cambridge U Pr.

Understanding Local Government. Jeffrey Stanyer. 320p. 1976. 30.50x (ISBN 0-85520-140-1, Pub. by Martin Robertson England). Biblio Dist.

Understanding Local Government. Jeffrey Stanyer. 320p. 1981. pap. 9.95x (ISBN 0-85520-373-0, Pub. by Martin Robertson England). Biblio Dist.

Understanding Macroeconomics. 6th ed. Robert L. Heilbroner & Lester C. Thurow. LC 77-28332. Orig. Title: Economic Problem. 1978. pap. 10.95 ref. ed. (ISBN 0-13-936575-3). P-H.

Understanding Management. David R. Wilings. 320p. 1979. text ed. 14.35 (ISBN 0-7715-5728-0); instr's. manual 7.41 (ISBN 0-7715-5730-2). Forkner.

Understanding Management Policy & Making It Work. new ed. Victor Z. Brink. (Illus.). 1978. 19.95 (ISBN 0-8144-5455-0). Am Mgmt.

Understanding Management: Study Guide to Management: A Problem-Solving Process. Robert Kreitner & Margaret Sova. LC 79-88719. (Illus.). pap. 6.95 (ISBN 0-395-28492-9). HM.

Understanding Mass Communication. Melvin L. DeFleur & Everette E. Dennis. LC 80-82762. (Illus.). 528p. 1981. pap. text ed. 11.95 (ISBN 0-395-29722-2); price not set instr's. manual (ISBN 0-395-29723-0). HM.

Understanding Mathematics. Raymond W. Hodges et al. Ed. by Barry M. Smith. LC 73-80234. (Basic Studies Program). (Illus.). 166p. 1973. pap. text ed. 7.65 (ISBN 0-913310-30-1). PAR Inc.

Understanding Media: The Extensions of Man. Marshall McLuhan. 1964. pap. 3.95 (ISBN 0-07-045436-1, GB). McGraw.

Understanding Medical Terms: A Self-Instructional Course. Ralph Rickards. (Illus.). 112p. 1980. pap. text ed. 7.95 (ISBN 0-443-02029-9). Churchill.

Understanding Medicare. T. J. Steskal. 93p. (Orig.). 1980. pap. 9.95 (ISBN 0-937978-00-0, MC-1). Info Prods.

Understanding Microcomputers & Small Computer Systems. Nat Wordsworth. (Da Capo Quality Paperbacks Ser.). (Illus.). 312p. 1981. pap. 8.95 (ISBN 0-306-80143-4). Da Capo.

Understanding Microeconomics. 5th ed. R. Heilbroner & L. Thorou. 1981. pap. 10.95 (ISBN 0-13-936567-2); pap. 7.95 study guide (ISBN 0-13-233296-5). P-H.

Understanding Microeconomics. 4th ed. Robert L. Heilbroner & Lester C. Thurow. LC 77-26296. 1978. pap. 10.95 ref. ed. (ISBN 0-13-936583-4). P-H.

Understanding Microprocessors. Lloyd Rich. (Illus.). 336p. 1980. text ed. 17.95 (ISBN 0-8359-8057-X). Reston.

Understanding Minority Dominant Relations: Sociological Contributions. F. James Davis. LC 77-90671. 1979. 12.95x (ISBN 0-88295-210-2). AHM Pub.

Understanding Modern Government: The Rise & Decline of the American Political Economy. Edward S. Greenberg. LC 78-10104. 1979. pap. text ed. 8.95x (ISBN 0-470-26879-4). Wiley.

Understanding Money. Elizabeth James & Carol Barkin. LC 76-47030. (Money Ser.). (Illus.). (gr. 2-3). 1977. PLB 8.65 (ISBN 0-8172-0277-3). Raintree Pubs.

Understanding Money. David Potter. 1972. 17.95 (ISBN 0-7134-2163-0, Pub. by Batsford England). David & Charles.

Understanding Moral Philosophy. James Rachels. 1976. text ed. 17.95x (ISBN 0-8221-0172-6). Dickenson.

Understanding Movies. 2nd ed. Louis D. Giannetti. (Illus.). 512p. 1976. ref. ed. 16.95 (ISBN 0-13-936302-5); pap. 11.95x (ISBN 0-13-936294-0). P-H.

Understanding Neurological Disease: A Textbook for Therapists. John H. Warfel & Reinhold E. Schlagenhauff. LC 79-28455. (Illus.). 147p. 1980. 9.75 (ISBN 0-8067-2131-6). Urban & S.

Understanding Nutrition. Eleanor N. Whitney & Eva M. Hamilton. (Illus.). 1977. text ed. 18.50 (ISBN 0-8299-0052-7); instrs.' manual avail. (ISBN 0-8299-0583-9). West Pub.

Understanding Nutrition. 2nd ed. Eleanor N. Whitney & Eva M. Hamilton. (Illus.). 650p. 1981. text ed. 18.95 (ISBN 0-8299-0419-0). West Pub.
Understanding of Faith: Interpretation & Criticism. Edward Schillebeeckx. 1974. 8.95 (ISBN 0-8164-1185-9). Crossroad NY.
Understanding of Music. 3rd ed. Charles R. Hoffer. 1976. 15.95x (ISBN 0-534-00443-1); study guide 5.95x (ISBN 0-534-00458-X); enrichment record album 16.95x (ISBN 0-534-00457-1). Wadsworth Pub.
Understanding Organizational Behavior. Stuart M. Klein & Richard R. Ritti. 592p. 1980. text ed. 19.95x (ISBN 0-534-00755-4, Kent Pub.). Kent Pub Co.
Understanding Our Atmospheric Environment. Morris Neiburger et al. LC 72-4753. (Illus.). 1973. text ed. 20.95x (ISBN 0-7167-0257-6). W H Freeman.
Understanding People: Models & Concepts. Walton C. Boshear & Karl G. Albrecht. LC 75-41686. (Illus.). 276p. 1977. pap. 15.50 (ISBN 0-88390-115-3). Univ Assocs.
Understanding People or, How to Be Your Very Own Shrink. Julia Rogers. LC 78-31175. 1979. 12.95 (ISBN 0-88229-273-0); pap. 7.95 (ISBN 0-88229-678-7). Nelson-Hall.
Understanding Persons: Personal & Impersonal Relations. F. M. Berenson. 19.95 (ISBN 0-312-83154-4). St Martin.
Understanding Persuasion. Raymond S. Ross & Mark Ross. (P-H Speech Communication Ser.). (Illus.). 224p. 1981. pap. text ed. 10.95 (ISBN 0-13-936484-6). P-H.
Understanding Physics, 3 Vols. Isaac Asimov. LC 66-17227. 8.95 ea. Vol.1 O.s.i (ISBN 0-8027-0294-5). Vol. 2 (ISBN 0-8027-0295-3). Vol.3 (ISBN 0-8027-0296-1). Walker & Co.
Understanding Physics. Ludwik Kowalski & Hal Hellman. 1978. text ed. 17.95x (ISBN 0-534-00596-9). Wadsworth Pub.
Understanding Physics Today. William H. Watson. 1963. 27.50 (ISBN 0-521-06745-6). Cambridge U Pr.
Understanding Piaget. rev. ed. Mary Ann Pulaski. LC 80-7595. 256p. 1980. 11.95 (ISBN 0-06-013454-2, HarpT). Har-Row.
Understanding Poetry. James Reeves. 1965. text ed. 9.95x (ISBN 0-435-18768-6). Heinemann Ed.
Understanding Political Variables. 2nd ed. William Buchanan. LC 73-1347. (Orig., Tables, Graphs). 1974. pap. text ed. 9.95x o.p. (ISBN 0-684-13654-6, ScribC). Scribner.
Understanding Political Variables. 3rd ed. William Buchanan. LC 80-23707. (Illus.). 1980. pap. text ed. 12.95x (ISBN 0-684-16673-9, ScribC). Scribner.
Understanding Politics in Modern Britain. John Sutton. 1977. pap. text ed. 11.00x (ISBN 0-245-52880-6). Intl Ideas.
Understanding Pottery Glazes. David Green. 1963. 11.95 (ISBN 0-571-06987-8, Pub. by Faber & Faber). Merrimack Bk Serv.
Understanding Psychological Research: The Student Researcher's Handbook. Miriam Lewin. LC 78-27842. 1979. text ed. 21.95 (ISBN 0-471-65837-5); tchrs. manual avail. (ISBN 0-471-05037-7). Wiley.
Understanding Public Policy. 3rd ed. Thomas R. Dye. (Illus.). 1978. text ed. 16.95 (ISBN 0-13-936195-2). P-H.
Understanding Public Policy. 4th ed. Thomas R. Dye. (Illus.). 464p. 1981. text ed. 16.95 (ISBN 0-13-936260-6). P-H.
Understanding Rabbinic Judaism: From Talmudic to Modern Times. Jacob Neusner. 1974. pap. 8.95x (ISBN 0-685-56200-X). Ktav.
Understanding Radiography. Stephen S. Hiss. (Illus.). 392p. 1980. 29.50 (ISBN 0-398-03685-3). C C Thomas.
Understanding Religion & Culture: Anthropological & Theological Perspectives. Ed. by John H. Morgan. LC 79-66684. 1979. pap. text ed. 9.50 (ISBN 0-8191-0848-0). U Pr of Amer.
Understanding-Responding. Long & Prophit. (Illus.). 225p. 1980. pap. text ed. 9.95 (ISBN 0-87872-284-X). Duxbury Pr.
Understanding Risk Management: A Guide for Governments. Charles Coe. 70p. (Orig.). 1980. pap. 7.50x. U of GA Inst Govt.
Understanding Science & Technology in India & Pakistan. Ward Morehouse. (Occasional Publication). 78p. 1967. pap. 2.00 (ISBN 0-89192-136-2). Interbk Inc.
Understanding Self & Society. Dorothy B. Fardan. LC 80-81696. 1980. 13.95 (ISBN 0-8022-2370-2). Philos Lib.
Understanding Sexual Interaction. Joann S. DeLora & Carol A. Warren. LC 76-10902. (Illus.). 1976. pap. text ed. 16.50 (ISBN 0-395-24314-9); inst. manual 1.50 (ISBN 0-395-24316-5). HM.
Understanding Sexual Interaction. 2nd ed. Joann S. Delora et al. (Illus.). 672p. 1981. text ed. 16.95 (ISBN 0-395-29724-9); write for info. instr's manual (ISBN 0-395-29725-7). HM.
Understanding Shakespeare. Evelyn F. Ludowyk. 1962. 32.50 (ISBN 0-521-05611-X); pap. 9.95x (ISBN 0-521-09242-6). Cambridge U Pr.
Understanding Siddha Yoga, Vol. 1. Swami Muktananda. (Orig.). 1979. pap. text ed. 7.95 (ISBN 0-686-53153-1). SYDA Found.
Understanding Social Anthropology. David Pocock. (Teach Yourself Ser). (gr. 7 up). 1976. pap. 4.95 o.p. (ISBN 0-679-10496-8). McKay.
Understanding Social Impacts: Assessing the Effects of Public Projects. Kurt Finsterbusch. LC 80-17586. (Sage Library of Social Research: Vol. 110). (Illus.). 311p. 1980. 18.00 (ISBN 0-8039-1015-0); pap. 8.95 (ISBN 0-8039-1016-9). Sage.
Understanding Social Policy. Michael Hill. (Aspects of Social Policy Ser.). 272p. 1981. pap. 10.00x (ISBN 0-631-18180-6, Pub. by Basil Blackwell England). Biblio Dist.
Understanding Social Policy. Michael Hill. (Aspects of Social Policy Ser.). 1980. 27.50x (ISBN 0-631-08190-9, Pub. by Basil Blackwell). Biblio Dist.
Understanding Social Psychology. rev. ed. Stephen Worchel & Joel Cooper. 1979. text ed. 18.50x (ISBN 0-256-02200-3); study guide 3.95 (ISBN 0-256-02223-2). Dorsey.
Understanding Social Research: An Introduction. Alan Orenstein & William R. Phillips. 1978. text ed. 16.95 (ISBN 0-205-05947-3, 8159475); instr's manual o.p. avail. (ISBN 0-205-05948-1). Allyn.
Understanding Sociology Through Research. Ed. by Donald R. MacQueen. LC 72-581. 1973. pap. text ed. 12.50 (ISBN 0-201-04381-5). A-W.
Understanding Statistical Reasoning: How to Evaluate Research Literature in the Behavioral Sciences. Eleanor W. Willemsen. LC 73-13647. (Psychology Ser.). (Illus.). 1974. text ed. 19.95x (ISBN 0-7167-0838-8); pap. text ed. 9.95x (ISBN 0-7167-0837-X). W H Freeman.
Understanding Statistics. 3rd ed. Mendenhall & Ott. LC 79-20914. (Illus.). 1980. text ed. 15.95 (ISBN 0-87872-241-6); study guide 7.95 (ISBN 0-686-65952-X). Duxbury Pr.
Understanding Statistics in the Behavioral Sciences. Robert R. Pagano. (Illus.). 520p. 1981. text ed. write for info. (ISBN 0-8299-0316-X). West Pub.
Understanding T-Boat Regulations. Ed. by Richard A. Block. (Illus.). 143p. 1979. pap. text ed. 12.00 (ISBN 0-934114-22-6). Marine Educ.
Understanding Technical English, 3 bks. K. Methold & D. D. Waters. (Illus.). 1975. pap. text ed. 3.75x ea. (ISBN 0-582-69032-3); Bk. 1. pap. text ed. 3.75x student's bk. 2 (ISBN 0-582-69032-3); Bk. 2. pap. text ed. 3.75 student's bk 3 (ISBN 0-582-69035-8). Bk. 3 (ISBN 0-582-69036-6). Longman.
Understanding the Aging Patient. Patricia Hess & Candra Day. LC 77-2596. 1977. 13.95 (ISBN 0-87618-733-5). R J Brady.
Understanding the Antitrust Laws. 7th ed. Jerrold G. Van Cise. 1976. text ed. 30.00 o.p. (ISBN 0-685-85358-6, B1-1237). PLI.
Understanding the Antitrust Laws. 8th ed. Jerrold G. Van Cise & William T. Lifland. LC 80-83813. 400p. 1980. text ed. 45.00 (ISBN 0-686-69172-5, B1-1276). PLI.
Understanding the Balance Sheet & Profit & Loss Statement. rev. ed. Dr. Israel Unterman. LC 73-77431. 1976. 7.95 (ISBN 0-910580-14-6). Farnswth Pub.
Understanding the Bible: A Reader's Guide & Reference. Stephen L. Harris. LC 79-91833. (Illus.). 391p. 1980. pap. text ed. 9.95 (ISBN 0-87484-472-X). Mayfield Pub.
Understanding the Bible: Extended Edition. Ronald J. Wilkins. (To Live Is Christ Ser). 212p. 1977. pap. 4.10 (ISBN 0-697-01658-7). Wm C Brown.
Understanding the Books of the New Testament. rev. ed. Ed. by Patrick H. Carmichael. LC 61-9583. 1961. pap. 4.50 (ISBN 0-8042-3304-7). John Knox.
Understanding the Books of the Old Testament. rev. ed. Ed. by Patrick H. Carmichael. LC 61-9225. 1961. pap. 4.50 (ISBN 0-8042-3316-0). John Knox.
Understanding the Christian Faith. Charles D. Barrett. (Illus.). 1980. text ed. 15.00 (ISBN 0-13-935882-X). P-H.
Understanding the Christian Faith. Georgia Harkness. (Series B). 1957. pap. 2.50 o.p. (ISBN 0-687-42954-4, Apex). Abingdon.
Understanding the Christian Faith. Georgia Harkness. (Festival Ser.). 192p. 1981. pap. 1.95 (ISBN 0-687-42955-2). Abingdon.
Understanding the Economy: For Those Who Can't Stand Economics. Alfred L. Malabre, Jr. LC 76-2465. 1976. 8.95 (ISBN 0-396-07309-3). Dodd.
Understanding the Essay. Edward O. Shakespeare et al. 1978. pap. text ed. 4.50x (ISBN 0-88334-109-3). Ind Sch Pr.
Understanding the Family. Kathleen Getty & Winifred Humphries. 608p. 1981. pap. 12.95 (ISBN 0-8385-9265-1). ACC.
Understanding the Federal Air Regulations. James Rardon. (Aviation Technician Training Course Ser.). 96p. (Orig.). 1980. pap. text ed. 4.95 (ISBN 0-89100-123-9). Aviation Maintenance.
Understanding the Heart. rev. ed. Francis Larkin. LC 80-81066. 127p. 1980. pap. write for info. (ISBN 0-89870-007-8). Ignatius Pr.
Understanding the Human Form: A Practical Study & Workbook for Surface Anatomy. Frank D. Shapiro & A. Burchess. (Illus.). 1980. 7.95 (ISBN 0-89529-024-3). Avery Pub.
Understanding the IBM Three-Sixty & Three-Seventy Computer with Machine Language Programming. William T. Batten. (Illus.). 480p. 1974. 17.95 (ISBN 0-13-936096-4). P-H.
Understanding the Language of Medicine: A Programmed Learning Text. Patricia J. Bernthal & James D. Spiller. (Illus.). 300p. 1981. pap. text ed. 11.95x (ISBN 0-19-502879-1). Oxford U Pr.
Understanding the Law: An Advocates Guide to the Law & Developmental Disabilities. Steven J. Taylor & Douglas Biklen. 67p. 1980. pap. 3.25 (ISBN 0-937540-10-2, HPP-13). Human Policy Pr.
Understanding the Law of Our Land. Shirley Schwarzrock & C. Gilbert Wrenn. (Coping with Ser.). (Illus.). 51p. (gr. 7-12). 1973. pap. text ed. 1.30 (ISBN 0-913476-21-8). Am Guidance.
Understanding the Main Idea: Advanced Level. James A. Giroux & Glenn R. Williston. (Comprehension Skills Ser). (Illus.). (gr. 9-12). 1974. pap. text ed. 2.40x (ISBN 0-89061-012-6). Jamestown Pubs.
Understanding the Main Idea: Middle Level. Glenn R. Williston. (Comprehension Skills Ser.). (Illus.). 64p. (gr. 6-8). 1976. pap. text ed. 2.40x (ISBN 0-89061-064-9, CB1M). Jamestown Pubs.
Understanding the Male Temperament: What Every Man Would Like to Tell His Wife About Himself...but Won't. Tim La Haye. 1977. 6.95 o.p. (ISBN 0-8007-0863-6); pap. 3.95 (ISBN 0-8007-0864-4); power ed. o.p. 3.95 (ISBN 0-8007-5009-8). Revell.
Understanding the Metric System. Mary J. Carrell. 1978. pap. text ed. 2.25x (ISBN 0-88323-140-9, 229). Richards Pub.
Understanding the Metric System: A Programed Text. new ed. David M. Miller. (gr. 9-12). 1979. pap. text ed. 4.80 (ISBN 0-205-06581-3, 566581-7); tchrs'. guide 2.40 (ISBN 0-205-06582-1, 566582-5). Allyn.
Understanding the New Religions. Ed. by Jacob Needleman & George Baker. 1978. 17.50 (ISBN 0-8164-0403-8); pap. 6.95 (ISBN 0-8164-2188-9). Crossroad NY.
Understanding the New Testament. 3rd ed. Howard C. Kee et al. (Illus.). 496p. 1973. 17.95 (ISBN 0-13-936104-9). P-H.
Understanding the New Testament. Francis B. Rhein. LC 65-23532. Orig. Title: Analytical Approach to the New Testament. 1974. pap. text ed. 5.25 (ISBN 0-8120-0027-7). Barron.
Understanding the Old Testament. 3rd ed. Bernhard W. Anderson. 608p. 1975. 18.95 (ISBN 0-13-936153-7). P-H.
Understanding the Old Testament. Jay G. Williams. LC 74-162825. (gr. 10 up). 1972. pap. 5.75 (ISBN 0-8120-0424-8). Barron.
Understanding the Preschool Retarded Child. John Fotheringham & Joan Morris. 1976. pap. text ed. 4.25x (ISBN 0-8077-8006-5). Tchrs Coll.
Understanding the Pupil, 3 pts. Marjorie E. Soderholm. Incl. Pt. 1. Pre-School Child. pap. 2.50 (ISBN 0-8010-7906-3); Pt. 2. Primary & Junior Child. pap. 2.50 (ISBN 0-8010-7953-5); Pt. 3. Adolescent. pap. 2.50 (ISBN 0-8010-7922-5). Baker Bk.
Understanding the Rape Victim: A Synthesis of Research Findings. Sedelle Katz & Mary Ann Mazur. LC 78-25704. (Personality Processes Ser.). 1979. 25.95 (ISBN 0-471-03573-4, Pub. by Wiley-Interscience). Wiley.
Understanding the Recovering Alcoholic. Kenneth Anonym. 1980. pap. 3.95 (ISBN 0-89486-103-4). Hazelden.
Understanding the Short Story. Annelle S. Houk & Carlotta L. Bogart. LC 68-55259. (Orig.). (gr. 9-12). 1969. pap. 6.50 (ISBN 0-672-63132-6). Odyssey Pr.
Understanding the Sunday Readings: July, August, September 1980. Ed. by Georgia Bain. (Understanding the Sunday Readings Ser.). 173p. 1980. 8.95 (ISBN 0-8434-0741-7, Consortium). McGrath.
Understanding the Sunday Readings: October, November, December 1980. (Understanding the Sunday Readings Ser.). Date not set. 8.95 (ISBN 0-8434-0758-1, Consortium). McGrath.
Understanding the Twentieth Century: A Course Guide. Open University Staff. (New Viewpoints-Vision Bks.). 1980. pap. 8.95 (ISBN 0-531-06505-7, EE59). Watts.
Understanding the United Methodist Church, 1977 Edition. Nolan B. Harmon. 1974. pap. 4.95 (ISBN 0-687-43005-4). Abingdon.
Understanding Through Communication: Structural Experiments in Self-Exploration. Lois Timmins. 336p. 1972. 17.75 (ISBN 0-398-02430-8). C C Thomas.
Understanding Today's Economics. Robert Crane. (Impact Ser.). (Illus.). (gr. 7 up). 1979. PLB 6.90 s&l (ISBN 0-531-02285-4). Watts.
Understanding Us: Family Development 1. 8.95 (ISBN 0-917340-10-8). Interpersonal Comm.
Understanding Wall Street. Jeffrey B. Little & Lucien Rhodes. LC 78-54787. (Illus.). 220p. 1980. pap. 7.95 (ISBN 0-89709-010-1). Liberty Pub.
Understanding Watchman Nee. Dana Roberts. (Orig.). 1981. pap. 4.95 (ISBN 0-88270-489-3). Logos.
Understanding Weather. Harry Milgrom. (Illus.). (gr. 4-8). 1970. 4.95g o.s.i. (ISBN 0-02-766940-8, CCPr). Macmillan.
Understanding Wood. R. Bruce Hoadley. (Illus.). 1979. 14.95 o.p. (ISBN 0-918804-05-1, ScribT); pap. 9.95 o.p. (ISBN 0-918804-06-X). Scribner.
Understanding Wood: A Craftsman's Guide to Wood Technology. R. Bruce Hoadley. LC 78-65177. (Illus.). 1980. 17.95 (ISBN 0-918804-05-1. Dist. by Van Nostrand Reinhold). Taunton.
Understanding Words: Systematic Spelling & Vocabulary Building. Fred Brengelman. 112p. 1980. pap. 6.95 (ISBN 0-8403-2252-6). Kendall-Hunt.
Understanding Your Body. Lawrence G. Blochman. LC 68-20263. (Illus.). (gr. 4-8). 1968. 3.95g o.s.i. (ISBN 0-02-710930-5, CCPr). Macmillan.
Understanding Your Child from Birth to Three: A Guide to Your Child's Psychological Development. Joseph Church. 1973. 6.95 o.p. (ISBN 0-394-47314-0). Random.
Understanding Your Churches Curriculum. Howard Colson & Raymond Rigdon. LC 77-93915. 1970. pap. 3.00 o.p. (ISBN 0-8054-3201-9). Broadman.
Understanding Your Church's Curriculum. rev. ed. Howard P. Colson & Raymond M. Rigdon. LC 80-67351. 1981. pap. 4.95. Broadman.
Understanding Your Dog. Peter Griffiths. 1977. 11.50 o.p. (ISBN 0-7153-7353-6). David & Charles.
Understanding Your Dog. Eberhard Trumbler. (Illus.). 1973. 9.95 (ISBN 0-571-10373-1, Pub. by Faber & Faber). Merrimack Bk Serv.
Understanding Your Dog: The Intelligent Person's Guide to a Lifelong Relationship with Another Species. Peter Messent. LC 80-51643. (Illus.). 160p. 1980. 12.95 (ISBN 0-8128-2746-5). Stein & Day.
Understanding Your Faith: An Introduction to Catholic Christianity for Freshmen. Thomas Zanzig. LC 80-50258. (Illus.). 192p. (gr. 9). 1980. pap. text ed. 5.20x (ISBN 0-88489-115-1); tchr's guide 5.00x (ISBN 0-88489-122-4); spiritmasters 9.95 (ISBN 0-88489-131-3). St Mary's.
Understanding Your Feelings & Emotions. Paul T. Young. (Illus.). 192p. 1976. pap. 4.95 o.p. (ISBN 0-13-936500-1, Spec). P-H.
Understanding Your New Life with Dialysis: Patient Guide for Physical & Psychological Adjustment to Maintenance Dialysis. 2nd ed. Edith T. Oberley & Terry D. Oberley. (Illus.). 168p. 1979. 16.75 (ISBN 0-398-03797-3); pap. 11.75 (ISBN 0-398-03798-1). C C Thomas.
Understanding Your Sexuality. Jane M. Kahan et al. (Illus.). 1980. pap. text ed. 104.00 (ISBN 0-89290-100-4, A793-SATC). Soc for Visual.
Understanding Your Social Agency. Armand Lauffer et al. LC 77-10012. (Sage Human Services Guides: Vol. 3). 1977. pap. 6.00x (ISBN 0-8039-0882-2). Sage.
Understanding Yourself. Intro. by Christopher Evans. 1980. pap. 2.95 (ISBN 0-451-09303-8, E9303, Sig). NAL.
Understanding Yourself. Kathleen F. Leicht. LC 73-3156. (Concise Guides Ser.). (gr. 7-12). 1973. PLB 4.47 o.p. (ISBN 0-531-02629-9). Watts.
Understanding Yourself & Others. Bill Kvols-Riedler & Kathy Kvols-Riedler. (Illus.). 222p. (Orig.). 1981. pap. 6.95 (ISBN 0-933450-01-X). RDIC Pubns.
Underwater Adventure Book Featuring "20,000 Leagues Under the Sea". Walt Disney Productions. LC 77-90198. (Disney's World of Adventure Ser). (gr. 3-7). 1978. 3.95 (ISBN 0-394-83602-2, BYR); PLB 4.99 (ISBN 0-394-93602-7). Random.
Underwater Attack: The First Submarines. Kelsey McManners. LC 78-15101. (Famous Firsts Ser.). (Illus.). 1978. lib. bdg. 7.35 (ISBN 0-686-51117-4). Silver.
Underwater Engineering. Ron Goodfellow. 1977. 23.00 (ISBN 0-87814-065-4). Pennwell Pub.
Underwater Gardens. Jack Kramer. LC 73-8031. (Illus.). 128p. 1974. 6.95 o.p. (ISBN 0-684-13601-5, ScribT). Scribner.

Underwater Life: The Oceans. Dean Morris. LC 77-23051. (Read About Animals Ser.). (Illus.). (gr. k-3). 1977. PLB 9.95 (ISBN 0-8393-0009-3). Raintree Child.

Underwater Logging. John E. Cayford & Ronald E. Scott. LC 64-18585. (Illus.). 1964. pap. 3.00 (ISBN 0-87033-128-0). Cornell Maritime.

Underwater Man. Joe Macinnis. LC 75-680. (Illus.). 144p. 1975. 6.95 (ISBN 0-396-07142-2). Dodd.

Underwater Photography for Everyone. Flip Schulke. 1978. 17.95 (ISBN 0-13-936450-1). P-H.

Underwater Swimming. John Emmett & Gordon Ridley. 120p. 1980. 12.95 (ISBN 0-8069-9158-5, Pub. by EP Publishing England). Sterling.

Underwater Technology-Offshore Petroleum: Proceedings of the International Conference, Bergen, Norway, April 14-16 1980. Ed. by L. Atteraas et al. LC 80-40414. 450p. 1980. 66.00 (ISBN 0-08-026141-8). Pergamon.

Underwater Tools. Donald J. Hackman & Don W. Caudy. (Illus.). 176p. 1981. 32.95 (ISBN 0-935470-08-5). Battelle.

Underwater Work: A Manual of Scuba Commercial Salvage & Construction Operations. 2nd ed. John E. Cayford. LC 66-28081. (Illus.). 1966. 10.00 (ISBN 0-87033-129-9). Cornell Maritime.

Underwater World of the Coral Reef. Ann McGovern. LC 75-44305. (Illus.). 40p. (gr. k-3). 1977. 6.95 (ISBN 0-590-07467-9, Four Winds). Schol Bk Serv.

Underwear: A History. Elizabeth Ewing. (Illus.). 1972. 6.75 (ISBN 0-87830-145-3). Theatre Arts.

Undiminished Man: A Political Biography of Robert Walker Kenny. Janet Stevenson. LC 80-10889. (Illus.). 218p. 1980. 10.95 (ISBN 0-88316-538-4). Chandler & Sharp.

Undiscovered Country. Arthur Schnitzler. Tr. by Tom Stoppard. 94p. 1981. pap. 8.50 (ISBN 0-571-11575-6, Pub. by Faber & Faber). Merrimack Bk Serv.

Undisputed Andy Capp. Smythe. 128p. 1976. pap. 1.50 (ISBN 0-449-13668-X, GM). Fawcett.

Undivided Hindu Family: A Study of Its Tax Privileges. I. S. Gulati & K. S. Gulati. 4.50x o.p. (ISBN 0-210-34070-3). Asia.

Uneasy Breather. Wayne Judd. (Uplook Ser.). 1975. pap. 0.75 (ISBN 0-8163-0179-4, 20728-2). Pacific Pr Pub Assn.

Uneasy Case for Progressive Taxation. Walter J. Blum & Harry Kalven, Jr. LC 53-3592. (Midway Reprint Ser.). 90p. 1963. pap. 6.00x (ISBN 0-226-06152-3). U of Chicago Pr.

Uneasy Survivors: Five Women Writers. Jeri Parker. LC 75-37705. 224p. 1975. pap. 5.95 o.s.i. (ISBN 0-87905-061-6). Peregrine Smith.

Uneasy Victorian: Thackery the Man 1811-1863. Ann Monsarrat. LC 80-20640. (Illus.). 480p. 1980. 15.00 (ISBN 0-396-07866-4). Dodd.

Unedited Part of Roger Bacon's Opus maius: De signis. K. M. Fredborg et al. (Illus.). 62p. (Orig.). 1978. pap. 6.00 (ISBN 0-8232-0095-7). Fordham.

Unemployment: A Problem of Industry, London 1912. W. H. Beveridge. LC 79-59646. (English Workinh Class Ser.). 1980. lib. bdg. 35.00 (ISBN 0-8240-0101-X). Garland Pub.

Unemployment: A Social Study, London, 1911. B. Seebohm Rountree & Bruno Lasker. LC 79-56970. (English Workinh Class Ser.). 1980. lib. bdg. 28.00 (ISBN 0-8240-0121-4). Garland Pub.

Unemployment & Inflation: Institutional & Structuralist Views. Ed. by Michael J. Piore. LC 79-55274. 1980. 20.00 (ISBN 0-87332-143-X); pap. 7.95 (ISBN 0-87332-165-0). M E Sharpe.

Unemployment & the Multinationals: A Strategy for Technological Change in Latin America. Stephen H. Hellinger & Douglas A. Hellinger. 1976. 13.95 (ISBN 0-8046-9126-6, National University Pub). Kennikat.

Unemployment Benefits: Should There Be a Compulsory Federal Standard? Joseph M. Becker. 1980. pap. 4.25 (ISBN 0-8447-3389-X). Am Enterprise.

Unemployment in Western Countries. Ed. by Edmond Malinvaud & Jean-Paul Fitouss. LC 79-29710. 560p. 1980. 40.00 (ISBN 0-312-83268-0). St Martin.

Unemployment-Inflation Dilemma: A Manpower Solution. Charles C. Holt et al. 1970. pap. 2.95 o.p. (ISBN 0-87766-009-3, 60003). Urban Inst.

Unemployment: Insurance & the Older American. Daniel S. Hamermesh. LC 80-18946. 117p. 1980. 4.00 (ISBN 0-911558-72-1). Upjohn Inst.

Unemployment Insurance Hearing Representative. Jack Rudman. (Career Examination Ser.: C-2728). (Cloth bdg. avail. on request). 1980. pap. 10.00 (ISBN 0-8373-2728-8). Natl Learning.

Unemployment Insurance in the American Economy. William Haber & Merrill G. Murray. 1966. text ed. 12.50x o.p. (ISBN 0-256-00201-0). Irwin.

Unemployment Insurance: The American Experience, 1915-1935. Daniel Nelson. (Illus.). 1969. 25.00x (ISBN 0-299-05200-1). U of Wis Pr.

Unemployment, Vacancies & the Rate of Change of Earnings: Regional Rates of Growth of Employment. A. E. Webb & R. Weeden. (National Inst. of Economic & Social Research, Regional Papers: No. 3). 1974. pap. 13.95 (ISBN 0-521-09895-5). Cambridge U Pr.

Unequal Alliance: The Inter-American Military System, Nineteen Thirty-Eight to Nineteen Seventy-Nine. John Child. (Westview Replica Edition Ser.). 254p. 1980. 24.00x (ISBN 0-89158-677-6). Westview.

Unequal Care: A Case Study of Interorganizational Relations. Murray Milner, Jr. (Illus.). 224p. 1980. 22.50x (ISBN 0-231-05006-2). Columbia U Pr.

Unequal Exchange: A Study of the Imperialism of Trade. Arghiri Emmanuel. Tr. by Brian Pearce from Fr. LC 78-158920. (Illus.). 1972. 16.50 o.p. (ISBN 0-85345-152-4, CL-1524); pap. 6.95 (ISBN 0-85345-188-5, PB-1885). Monthly Rev.

Unequal Justice. Jerold S. Auerbach. 1976. 19.95 (ISBN 0-19-501939-3). Oxford U Pr.

Unequal Treaties: China & the Foreigner. Rodney V. Gilbert. (Studies in Chinese History & Civilzation). 248p. 1977. Repr. of 1929 ed. 19.50 (ISBN 0-89093-075-9). U Pubns Amer.

Unequal Treaty Eighteen Ninety-Seven to Nineteen Ninety-Seven. P. Wesley-Smith. (East Asian Historical Monographs). (Illus.). 296p. 26.00 (ISBN 0-19-580436-8). Oxford U Pr.

Unequivocal Americanism: Right-Wing Novels in the Cold War Era. Macel D Ezell. LC 77-3725. 1977. 10.00 (ISBN 0-8108-1033-6). Scarecrow.

UNESCO Dictionary of the Social Sciences. Julius Gould & W. J. Kolb. LC 64-20307. 1964. 35.00 (ISBN 0-02-917490-2). Free Pr.

UNESCO Educational Simulation Model (ESM) (Reports & Papers in the Social Sciences, No. 29). 29p. (Orig.). 1974. pap. 2.50 (ISBN 92-3-101149-9, U755, UNESCO). Unipub.

UNESCO General History of Africa, 8 vols. Incl. Vol. I. Methodology & African Prehistory. Ed. by J. KiZerbo (ISBN 0-520-03912-2); Vol. II. Ancient Africa. Ed. by G. Mokhtar (ISBN 0-520-03913-0). 1980. 25.00x ea. U of Cal Pr.

UNESCO Handbook for Science Teachers. 199p. 1980. pap. 14.95 (ISBN 0-89059-006-0, U1029, UNESCO). Unipub.

UNESCO Report of the Director General on the Activities of the Organizations in 1977-1978. 256p. 1980. pap. 18.75 (ISBN 92-3-101738-1, U967, UNESCO). Unipub.

UNESCO Statistical Yearbook 1978-1979. 1226p. 1980. pap. 88.75 (ISBN 92-3-001800-7, U1020, UNESCO). Unipub.

UNESCO Statistical Yearbook 1980. 1280p. 1981. pap. 104.00 (ISBN 92-3-001835-X, U1062, UNESCO). Unipub.

UNESCO's Activities in Science & Technology in the European & North American Region. (Science Policy Studies & Documents: No. 45). 1979. pap. 3.25 (ISBN 92-3-101727-6, U930, UNESCO). Unipub.

Unexpected Community: Portrait of an Old Age Subculture. Arlie R. Hochschild. 1978. 18.50x (ISBN 0-520-03663-8); pap. 3.95 (ISBN 0-520-03624-7). U of Cal Pr.

Unexpected Mrs Pollifax. Dorothy Gilman. 1978. pap. 1.95 (ISBN 0-449-23923-3, Crest). Fawcett.

Unexpected Rebellion: Ethnic Activism in Contemporary France. William R. Beer. LC 79-3515. 1980. 18.50x (ISBN 0-8147-1029-8). NYU Pr.

Unexplored Model Systems in Modern Biology. Robert M. Friedenberg. (Pioneering Concepts in Modern Science Ser.: No. 1). 1968. 9.75 o.s.i. (ISBN 0-02-844870-7). Hafner.

Unexpurgated Code: A Complete Manual of Survival & Manners. J. P. Donleavy. (Illus.). 304p. 1975. 10.00 o.s.i. (ISBN 0-440-07794-X, Sey Lawr). Delacorte.

Unfair at Any Gridiron. C. W. Staley. LC 80-66404. 250p. 1981. 14.95 (ISBN 0-9604324-0-X, 8012 800326). CWS Group Pr.

Unfair Contracts: The Doctrine of Unconscionability. Sinai Deutch. LC 76-20048. 1977. 24.95 (ISBN 0-669-00875-3). Lexington Bks.

Unfair Dismissal. D. Jackson. (Department of Applied Economics, Occasional Papers Ser.: No. 1). (Illus.). 200p. 1975. 18.95 (ISBN 0-521-20751-7); pap. 11.95x (ISBN 0-521-09942-0). Cambridge U Pr.

Unfashionable Human Body. Bernard Rudofsky. LC 74-160871. 288p. 1974. pap. 5.95 (ISBN 0-385-07818-8, Anch). Doubleday.

Unfinished Agenda. Ed. by Gerald O. Barney. LC 76-30486. 1977. 8.95 o.s.i. (ISBN 0-690-01481-3, TYC-T). T Y Crowell.

Unfinished Animal. Theodore Roszak. LC 75-9333. (Illus.). 288p. 1975. 4.95 (ISBN 0-06-067016-9, CN 537, HarpR). Har-Row.

Unfinished Democracy: The American Political Systems. Harrell R. Rodgers & Michael Harrington. 1981. text ed. 17.95x (ISBN 0-673-15458-0); pap. text ed. 14.95x (ISBN 0-673-15415-7). Scott F.

Unfinished Man. Nissim Ezekiel. 6.75 (ISBN 0-89253-686-1); flexible cloth 4.00 (ISBN 0-89253-687-X). Ind-US Inc.

Unfinished Mystery. John Walchars. (Orig.). 1978. pap. 4.95 (ISBN 0-8164-2184-6). Crossroad NY.

Unfinished Rebellions. De Vere Pentony et al. LC 72-148658. (Higher Education Ser.). 1971. 14.95x o.p. (ISBN 0-87589-095-4). Jossey-Bass.

Unfinished Revolution. Adam B. Ulam. 1979. lib. bdg. 24.50x (ISBN 0-89158-485-4); pap. 9.50 (ISBN 0-89158-496-X). Westview.

Unfinished Revolution: Russia,1917-1967. Isaac Deutscher. LC 67-23012. 1969. pap. 3.95 (ISBN 0-19-500786-7, GB). Oxford U Pr.

Unfinished Sequence. Edward Butscher. Ed. by Stanley H. Barkan. (Cross-Cultural Review Chapbook 6). 16p. 1980. pap. 2.00 (ISBN 0-89304-805-4). Cross Cult.

Unfinished Sequence & Other Poems. Sean Lucy. 63p. 1980. pap. text ed. 5.25x (ISBN 0-905473-38-8). Humanities.

Unfinished Symphony Conductor. Don Gillis. LC 68-1408. (Illus.). 1967. 6.95 o.p. (ISBN 0-8363-0098-X). Jenkins.

Unfinished Tales. J. R. Tolkien. Ed. by Christopher Tolkien. (Illus.). 368p. 1980. 15.95 (ISBN 0-395-29917-9). HM.

Unfolding of Artistic Activity: Its Basis, Processes, & Implications. Henry Schaefer-Simmern. (Illus.). 1948. 18.50x (ISBN 0-520-01141-4). U of Cal Pr.

Unfolding of Neo-Confucianism. Ed. by W. Theodore De Bary. LC 74-10929. (Studies in Oriental Culture Ser.: No. 10). 672p. 1975. 25.00x (ISBN 0-231-03828-3); pap. 12.50x (ISBN 0-231-03829-1). Columbia U Pr.

Unfolding the Prophecies of Daniel. R. E. Anderson. LC 75-16526. (Dimension Ser.). 1975. pap. 4.50 o.p. (ISBN 0-8163-0180-8, 21390-0). Pacific Pr Pub Assn.

Unfolding the Revelation. Roy A. Anderson. LC 61-10884. (Dimension Ser.). 223p. 1961. pap. 5.95 (ISBN 0-8163-0027-5, 21400-7). Pacific Pr Pub Assn.

Unforgetable Season. G. H. Fleming. LC 80-18299. (Illus.). 336p. 1981. 16.95 (ISBN 0-03-056221-X). HR&W.

Unforgetable Sounds. Elbert D. Godfrey. (Mental Therapy Ser.). 128p. Date not set. 6.50 (ISBN 0-89962-030-2). Todd & Honeywell.

Unforgettable. rev. ed. Gene F. Larson. 1978. 10.00 (ISBN 0-686-68574-1, 1491). Hospital Finan.

Unforgettable Characters. 1980. pap. 2.50 (ISBN 0-425-04722-9). Berkley Pub.

Unforgettable Fire: Pictures Drawn by Atomic Bomb Survivors. Ed. by Japan Broadcasting Corporation. (Illus.). 1981. 15.95 (ISBN 0-394-51585-4); pap. 7.95 (ISBN 0-394-74823-9). Pantheon.

Unfortunate Traveler: Or the Life of Jack Wilton. Thomas Nashe. 194p. 1980. Repr. of 1926 ed. 30.00 (ISBN 0-89760-605-1). Telegraph Bks.

Unfriendly Governor. Anthony A. Lee. (Stories About Abdul'l-Baha Ser.). (Illus.). 24p. (gr. k-5). 1980. pap. 2.50 (ISBN 0-933770-02-2). Kalimat.

Ungentlemanly Art. S. Hess & M. Kaplan. 1968. 14.95 o.s.i. (ISBN 0-02-551280-3). Macmillan.

Ungentlemanly Art: A History of American Political Cartoons. Stephen Hess & Milton Kaplan. (Illus.). 252p. 1975. 12.95 o.s.i. (ISBN 0-02-551320-6). Macmillan.

Unger's Bible Commentary: Genesis-Song of Solomon. Merrill F. Unger. (Commentary Series on the Entire Bible). 360p. 1981. text ed. 17.95 (ISBN 0-8024-9028-X). Moody.

Unger's Bible Dictionary (Thumb Indexed Edition) Merrill Unger. 1961. 22.95 (ISBN 0-8024-9036-0). Moody.

Unhappy Returns. Elizabeth Lemarchand. LC 77-80205. 1978. 7.95 o.s.i. (ISBN 0-8027-5375-2). Walker & Co.

Unhappy Secrets of the Christian Life: Study Guide. Ruth Senter. 80p. 1980. pap. 1.50 (ISBN 0-310-35463-3). Zondervan.

Unheated Greenhouse: How to Maximize Its Potential. Ronald H. Menage. LC 80-52346. (Illus.). 128p. 1980. pap. 5.95 (ISBN 0-8069-8954-8). Sterling.

Unholy Alliance. C. Gregg Singer. 1975. 11.95 o.p. (ISBN 0-87000-327-5). Arlington Hse.

Unholy Child. Catherine Breslin. 1980. pap. 3.50 (ISBN 0-451-09477-8, E9477, Sig). NAL.

Unholy Desires. Stephanie Blake. LC 80-82849. 368p. (Orig.). 1981. pap. 2.95 (ISBN 0-87216-785-2). Playboy Pbks.

Unholy Loves. Joyce C. Oates. LC 79-64396. 1979. 11.95 (ISBN 0-8149-0813-6). Vanguard.

Unholy Pilgrimage: A Visit to Russia to Find What Twenty Years of Official Atheism Had Done for the Russian People. T. L. Harris. 195p. Repr. of 1937 ed. text ed. 2.95. Attic Pr.

Unhurry Harry. Eve Merriam. LC 78-1302. (Illus.). 32p. (gr. k-3). 1978. 5.95 (ISBN 0-590-07480-6, Four Winds). Schol Bk Serv.

UNIA & Black Los Angeles: Ideology & Community in the American Garvey Movement. Emory J. Tolbert. Ed. by Robert A. Hill. LC 80-18054. (Afro-American Culture & Society Monograph: No. 3). (Illus.). 138p. 1980. 13.95 (ISBN 0-934934-04-5); pap. 8.95 (ISBN 0-934934-05-3). Ctr Afro-Am Stud.

Unicorn Affair. James Fritzhand & Frank Glickman. (Orig.). 1981. pap. 2.50 (ISBN 0-451-09605-3, E9605, Sig). NAL.

Unicorn Poem. E. A. Mares. 30p. (Orig.). 1980. pap. 3.00 (ISBN 0-88235-045-5). San Marcos.

Unicorns for Everyone: Large Type. Marilyn R. Riddle. (Illus.). 24p. (Orig.). (gr. k-12). 1980. pap. 3.00 (ISBN 0-9603748-1-7, 200). Sandpiper OR.

Unidentified Flying Objects. Jim Collins. LC 77-13040. (Great Unsolved Mysteries Ser.). (Illus.). (gr. 4-5). 1977. PLB 9.65 (ISBN 0-8172-1065-2). Raintree Pubs.

Unidentified Flying Oddball. Crume. (gr. 3-5). 1980. pap. 1.50 (ISBN 0-590-30061-X, Schol Pap). Schol Bk Serv.

Unidimensional Scaling of Social Variables: Concepts and Procedures. Raymond L. Gorden. LC 76-26443. 1977. 15.95 (ISBN 0-02-912580-4). Free Pr.

Unification of Central Arabia Under Ibn Saud 1909-1925. Ed. by Ibrahim Al-Rashid. (Documents on the History of Saudi Arabia: Vol. 1). 1976. 60.00 (ISBN 0-89712-053-1). Documentary Pubns.

Unified Concepts in Applied Physics. E. Dierauf, Jr. & J. Court. 1979. 20.95 (ISBN 0-13-938753-6). P-H.

Unified Mathematics: Content, Methods, Materials for Elementary School Teachers. Arnold L. Fass & Claire M. Newman. 448p. 1975. text ed. 14.95x o.p. (ISBN 0-669-89359-5). Heath.

Unified Model of the Universe: The Geometrically Unified Field Solution. Sean Sheeter. (Unified Theory of Process: Vol. 1). (Illus.). 150p. 1981. 18.98 (ISBN 0-9605378-0-5); pap. 9.50 (ISBN 0-9605378-1-3). Process Pr.

Unified Operations Management: A Practical Approach to a Management Information System. rev. ed. Arnold O. Putnam et al. LC 63-1546. (Illus.). 1969. 10.95 (ISBN 0-89047-024-3). Herman Pub.

Unified Social Science: A System-Based Introduction. Alfred Kuhn. 1975. text ed. 17.95x (ISBN 0-256-01444-2). Dorsey.

Unified Vocational Preparation: An Evaluation of the Pilot Programme. Monika J. Wray et al. (Report of the National Foundation for Educational Research in England & Wales). 289p. 1980. pap. text ed. 19.25x (ISBN 0-85633-199-6). Humanities.

Uniform Algebras & Jensen Measures. T. W. Gamelin. LC 78-16213. (London Mathematical Society Lecture Note Ser.: No. 32). 1979. pap. 17.95x (ISBN 0-521-22280-X). Cambridge U Pr.

Uniform Commercial Code, 5 vols. 2nd ed. Ronald A. Anderson. LC 77-138263. 1970. 200.00 (ISBN 0-686-14491-0); legal forms vol. 65.00 (ISBN 0-686-14492-9); pleading & practice forms 2 vols. 65.00 (ISBN 0-686-14493-7). Lawyers Co-Op.

Uniform Commercial Code: An Operational Translation. Robert LeVine. LC 80-68569. 1980. 16.50 (ISBN 0-933718-00-4). Browning Pubns.

Uniform Distribution of Sequences. L. Kuipers & H. Niederreiter. LC 73-20497. (Pure & Applied Mathematics Ser.). 416p. 1974. 37.50 (ISBN 0-471-51045-9, Pub. by Wiley-Interscience). Wiley.

Uniform Insignia of the United States Military Forces. Jack L. Britton. (Illus.). 1980. pap. 6.50 (ISBN 0-912958-06-5). Military Coll.

Uniform National Examination in Landscape Architecture: Candidate Review Manual. Reimann et al. LC 78-55457. 1978. pap. 25.00 (ISBN 0-918436-04-4). Environ Des VA.

Uniform System of Accounts for Restaurants. 12.95x (ISBN 0-686-52777-1). Radio City.

Uniforms & Weapons of the Crimean War. Wilkinson. pap. 14.95 (ISBN 0-7134-0666-6). David & Charles.

Uniforms of the American Revolution. John Mollo. LC 74-23543. (Illus.). 208p. 1975. 8.95 (ISBN 0-02-585580-8, 58558). Macmillan.

Uniforms of the Civil War 1861-1865. Philip Haythornthwaite. LC 75-28111. (Macmillan Color Ser). (Illus.). 208p. 1976. 9.95 (ISBN 0-02-549200-4, 54920). Macmillan.

Uniforms of the French Foreign Legion 1831-1981. Martin Windrow. (Illus.). 160p. 1981. 19.95 (ISBN 0-7137-1010-1, Pub. by Blandford Pr England). Sterling.

Uniforms of the French Revolutionary Wars 1789-1802. Philip J. Haythornthwaite. (Illus.). 160p. 1981. 19.95 (ISBN 0-7137-0936-7, Pub. by Blandford Pr England). Sterling.

Uniforms of the Imperial Russian Army. Boris Mollo. (Illus.). 1979. 13.95 (ISBN 0-7137-0893-X, Pub by Blandford Pr England). Sterling.

Uniforms of the Retreat from Moscow, 1812. Philip Haythornthwaite. LC 76-17456. (Color Guides Ser.). (Illus.). 1976. 7.95 o.p. (ISBN 0-88254-421-7). Hippocrene Bks.

Uniforms of Waterloo in Color. Philip Haythornthwaite. (Illus.). 190p. 1980. 9.95 (ISBN 0-7137-0714-3, Pub. by Blandford Pr England). Sterling.

Uniforms, Organization & History of the Panzertruppe. Roger J. Bender & Warren W. Odegard. (Illus.). 336p. 1980. 24.95 (ISBN 0-912138-18-1). Bender Pub CA.

Unifying Concepts & Processes in Elementary Mathematics. University of Maryland Mathematics Project. 1978. pap. text ed. 20.95 (ISBN 0-205-05844-2, 5658446); instr's manual avail. (ISBN 0-205-05845-0). Allyn.

Unifying Influence: Essays of Raynard Coe Swank. Ed. by David W. Heron. LC 80-28595. 237p. 1981. 13.50 (ISBN 0-8108-1407-2). Scarecrow.

Unifying Role of the Bishop. Edward Schillebeeckx. LC 70-168651. (Concilium Ser.: Religion in the Seventies: Vol. 71). 1972. pap. 4.95 (ISBN 0-8164-2527-2). Crossroad NY.

Unilateral Force in International Relations. Incl. Some Neglected Aspects of War. Alfred T. Mahan; Power That Makes for Peace. Henry S. Pritchett; Capture of Private Property at Sea. Julian S. Corbett; Ewige Friede. Karl Von Stengel. (Library of War & Peace; Int'l. Organization, Arbitration & Law). lib. bdg. 38.00 (ISBN 0-8240-0348-9). Garland Pub.

Unilever Overseas: The Anatomy of a Multinational. David K. Fieldhouse. LC 78-20358. (Publications Ser.: No. 205). 1979. pap. 22.00 (ISBN 0-8179-7051-7). Hoover Inst Pr.

Uninvited. Dorothy Macardle. 342p. 1976. Repr. of 1942 ed. lib. bdg. 15.95x (ISBN 0-89244-068-6). Queens Hse.

Uninvited Visitors: A Biologist Looks at UFO's. Ivan T. Sanderson. (Illus.). 1967. 6.95 o.p. (ISBN 0-8092-9225-4). Contemp Bks.

Unioes Legais e Consensuais: Incidencia e Fecundidade na America Latina. Maria H. Henriques. (Port.). 1980. pap. text ed. 2.00 (ISBN 0-89383-069-0). Intl Program Labs.

Union & Communion. Hudson Taylor. 1971. pap. 1.95 (ISBN 0-87123-571-4, 200571). Bethany Fell.

Union & Its Retired Workers: A Case Study of the UMW. Richard Korn. (Key Issues Ser.: No. 21). 1976. pap. 3.00 (ISBN 0-87546-230-8). NY Sch Indus Rel.

Union Democracy: The Internal Politics of the International Typographical Union. Seymour M. Lipset et al. LC 56-6202. (Illus.). 1977. pap. text ed. 8.95 (ISBN 0-02-919210-2). Free Pr.

Union Epidemic: A Prescription for Supervisors. Warren H. Chaney & Thomas R. Beech. LC 76-24132. 1976. 24.00 (ISBN 0-912862-28-9). Aspen Systems.

Union Growth & the Business Cycle: An Econometric Analysis. G. S. Bain & Farouk Elsheikh. 1976. 35.50x (ISBN 0-631-16650-5, Pub. by Basil Blackwell). Biblio Dist.

Union in Crisis, Eighteen Fifty-Eighteen Seventy-Seven. Ed. by Robert W. Johannsen. LC 65-11899. (Orig.). 1965. pap. text ed. 3.50 o.s.i. (ISBN 0-02-916500-8). Free Pr.

Union List of Conference Proceedings in Libraries of the Federal Republic of Germany Including Berlin (West, 2 vols. 907p. 1978. Set. 375.00 (ISBN 3-7940-3004-4, Dist by Gale Research Co). K G Saur.

Union of Individuals: The Formation of the American Newspaper Guild, 1933-36. Daniel J. Leab. LC 75-110603. 1970. 20.00x (ISBN 0-231-03367-2). Columbia U Pr.

Union of Tanganyika & Zanzibar-a Study in Political Intergration. Martin Baily. (Foreign & Comparative Studies-Eastern African Ser.: No.9). 114p. 1973. pap. 4.50x (ISBN 0-915984-05-9). Syracuse U Foreign Comp.

Union Ouvrieve, Troisieme Edition. Flora Tristan. (Fr.). 1977. lib. bdg. 23.75x o.p. (ISBN 0-8287-0832-0); pap. 13.75x o.p. (ISBN 0-685-76998-4). Clearwater Pub.

Union Pacific Eight Thousand, Four Hundred Forty-Four. Ronald C. Hill. (Illus.). 1978. pap. 9.00 (ISBN 0-918654-28-9). CO RR Mus.

Union Pacific FEF-3 Class 4-8-4 Locomotive Drawings. Ed. by William C. Fitt. LC 75-27822. (Illus.). 54p. 1975. pap. 15.50 (ISBN 0-914104-02-0). Wildwood Pubns MI.

Union Power & the Public Interest. Emerson P. Schmidt. LC 72-95239. (Principles of Freedom Ser.). 1976. pap. 6.95x (ISBN 0-916054-88-8, Caroline Hse Inc). Green Hill.

Union Power & the Public Interest. Emerson P. Schmidt. LC 72-95239. (Illus.). 204p. 1973. 10.00x o.p. (ISBN 0-8402-5004-5). Nash Pub.

Union Prayerbook, 2 vols. 1977. Vol. 1. 5.50 (ISBN 0-916694-09-7); Vol. 2. 5.50 (ISBN 0-916694-10-0); lea. bd. 12.50 (ISBN 0-686-67881-8); pulpit ed. o.p. 15.00 (ISBN 0-686-67882-6); Vol. 1. Central Conf.

Union Restored, 1861-1876. T. Harry Williams. LC 63-8572. (Life History of the United States). (Illus.). (gr. 5 up). 1974. PLB 9.96 (ISBN 0-8094-0555-5, Pub. by Time-Life). Silver.

Union Rule in the Schools: Big-City Politics in Transformation. Grimshaw. LC 78-24631. (Politics of Education Ser.). (Illus.). 1979. 18.95 (ISBN 0-669-02769-3). Lexington Bks.

Union Songster: Songs & Prayers for Jewish Youth. 1960. 3.50 o.p. (ISBN 0-916694-16-X). Central Conf.

Union State Relations in India. K. Santhanam. 3.25x o.p. (ISBN 0-210-33973-X). Asia.

Union Steward: Duties, Rights, & Status. Al Nash. (Key Issues Ser.: No. 22). 1977. pap. 3.00 (ISBN 0-87546-235-9). NY Sch Indus Rel.

Union Sundered, 1849-1865. T. Harry Williams. LC 63-8572. (Life History of the United States). (Illus.). (gr. 5 up). 1974. PLB 9.96 (ISBN 0-8094-0554-7, Pub. by Time-Life). Silver.

Union, the Civil War & John W. Tuttle: A Kentucky Captains Account. Ed. by Hambleton Tapp & James C. Klotter. LC 79-89244. 1980. 20.00 (ISBN 0-916968-08-1). Kentucky Hist.

Unionism in Catholic Schools. 70p. 1976. 4.00. Natl Cath Educ.

Unions & Leaders in Ghana: A Model of Labor & Development. Paul S. Gray. LC 80-18482. 1981. 35.00 (ISBN 0-914970-57-7); pap. text ed. 17.50 (ISBN 0-914970-58-5). Conch Mag.

Unions & the Cities. Harry H. Wellington & Ralph K. Winter. LC 79-179327. (Studies of Unionism in Government). 1972. 14.95 (ISBN 0-8157-9294-8); pap. 5.95 (ISBN 0-8157-9293-X). Brookings.

Unions & Universities: The Rise of the New Labor Leader. Joel S. Denker. LC 80-67093. 192p. 1981. text ed. 20.00 (ISBN 0-916672-58-1). Allanheld.

Unions' Rights to Company Information. James T. O'Reilly. 1980. pap. 18.00 (ISBN 0-89546-023-8). Indus Res Unit-Wharton.

Unions, Wages & Inflation. Daniel J. B. Mitchell. 1980. 16.95 (ISBN 0-8157-5752-2); pap. 6.50 (ISBN 0-8157-5751-4). Brookings.

Unique Advantages of Being a Mormon. W. Lynn Fluckiger. pap. 3.95 (ISBN 0-89036-138-X). Hawkes Pub Inc.

Unique & the Universal. J. L. Talmon. LC 65-19565. 1965. 6.50 o.s.i. (ISBN 0-8076-0319-8). Braziller.

Uniqueness of the Individual. Peter B. Medawar. 192p. 1981. pap. write for info. (ISBN 0-486-24042-8). Dover.

Uniqueness: The Human Pursuit of Difference. C. R. Snyder & Howard L. Fromkin. (Perspectives in Social Psychology Ser.). (Illus.). 250p. 1980. 16.95 (ISBN 0-306-40376-5, Plenum Pr). Plenum Pub.

Unit Load Handling. Malcolm Hulett. 351p. 1970. 39.95 (ISBN 0-7161-0035-5). CBI Pub.

Unit Operations for Treatment of Hazardous Industrial Wastes. Ed. by Joan B. Berkowitz et al. LC 78-62520. (Pollution Technology Review: No. 47). (Illus.). 1979. 42.00 (ISBN 0-8155-0717-8). Noyes.

Unit Operations in Mineral Processing. John M. Currie & British Columbia Institute of Technology. 1978. Repr. of 1973 ed. 15.00 (ISBN 0-918062-13-6). Colo Sch Mines.

Unit Operations in Resource Recovery Engineering. P. Vesiland et al. (Illus.). 1980. text ed. 28.95 (ISBN 0-13-937953-3). P-H.

Unit Plan: A Plan for Curriculum Organizing & Teaching. Earl J. Ogletree et al. LC 79-48018. 499p. 1980. pap. text ed. 13.75 (ISBN 0-8191-0996-7). U Pr of Amer.

Unit Pride. John McAleer & Billy Dickson. LC 80-1066. 528p. 1981. 13.95 (ISBN 0-385-15925-0). Doubleday.

United Arab Emirates. 2nd ed. K. G. Fenelon. LC 75-42139. (Illus.). 1977. text ed. 15.00x (ISBN 0-582-78066-7). Longman.

United Arab Emirates: Its Political System & Politics. Enver M. Koury. LC 79-90997. 147p. (Orig.). 1980. pap. 8.00 (ISBN 0-934484-15-5). Inst Mid East & North Africa.

United Arab Emirates: Unity in Fragmentation. Ali M. Khalifa. (Special Studies on the Middle East). 1979. lib. bdg. 26.00x (ISBN 0-89158-394-7). Westview.

United Artists: The Company Built by the Stars. Tino Balio. LC 75-12208. (Illus.). 304p. 1976. 22.50x (ISBN 0-299-06940-0); pap. 7.95 (ISBN 0-299-06944-3). U of Wis Pr.

United Arts Fundraising Manual. Ed. by Robert Porter. 77p. (Orig.). 1980. pap. text ed. 7.95 (ISBN 0-915400-19-7). Am Council Arts.

United Arts Fundraising: Nineteen Eighty Campaign Analysis. Ed. by Robert Porter. (Illus., Orig.). 1980. pap. 9.95 (ISBN 0-915400-29-4). Am Council Arts.

United Front: The TUC & the Russians 1923-1928. D. F. Calhoun. (Soviet & East European Studies). 432p. 1976. 44.50 (ISBN 0-521-21056-9). Cambridge U Pr.

United Kingdom Facts. Richard Rose & Ian McAllister. 240p. 1981. text ed. 48.50x (ISBN 0-8419-5578-6). Holmes & Meier.

United Nations. rev ed. Edna Epstein. LC 73-5965. (First Bks). (Illus.). (gr. 3-7). 1973. PLB 4.90 o.p. (ISBN 0-531-00657-3). Watts.

United Nations & Domestic Jurisdiction. M. S. Rajan. 1958. 25.00x (ISBN 0-210-33974-8). Asia.

United Nations & Rhodesia: A Study in International Law. Ralph Zacklin. LC 74-1751. (Special Studies). (Illus.). 202p. 1974. text ed. 21.50 o.p. (ISBN 0-275-09260-7). Praeger.

United Nations & World Realities. M. J. Lee. 1966. 22.00 (ISBN 0-08-011350-8); pap. 10.75 (ISBN 0-08-011349-4). Pergamon.

United Nations As a Political Institution. 5th ed. H. G. Nicholas. 270p. 1975. pap. 5.95 (ISBN 0-19-519826-3, 105, GB). Oxford U Pr.

United Nations Capital Development Fund: Poor & Rich Worlds in Collision. Marjon V. Kamara & Jack C. Plano. 1974. 5.00 (ISBN 0-932826-14-8). New Issues MI.

U. N. Convention on the Elimination of Al Forms of Racial Discrimination. Natan Lerner. LC 80-51738. 278p. 1980. 37.50x (ISBN 90-286-0160-0). Sijthoff & Noordhoff.

United Nations Demographic Yearbook 1978. 463p. 1980. pap. 36.00 (ISBN 0-686-68978-X, UN79/13/1, UN). Unipub.

United Nations Disarmament Yearbook: 1978, Vol. 3. 535p. 1979. 30.00 (ISBN 0-686-68979-8, UN79/9/2, UN). Unipub.

United Nations Disaster Relief Office: The Politics & Administration of International Relief Assistance. Thomas W. Stephens. LC 78-60792. 1978. pap. text ed. 13.25 o.p. (ISBN 0-8191-0414-0). U Pr of Amer.

United Nations Economic & Social Council. Walter R. Sharp. LC 72-87888. (Columbia Univ. Studies in International Organization: No. 5). 1969. 20.00x (ISBN 0-231-03239-0). Columbia U Pr.

United Nations Environment Programme Annual Review, 1978. 86p. 1981. pap. 10.00 (ISBN 92-807-1013-3, UNEP45, UNEP). Unipub.

United Nations in a Changing World. Leland M. Goodrich. (Columbia University Studies in International Organization). 280p. 1976. 20.00x (ISBN 0-231-03824-0); pap. 7.50x (ISBN 0-231-08343-2). Columbia U Pr.

United Nations in International Politics. Ed. by Leon Gordenker. LC 71-132239. (Center of International Studies Ser.). 224p. 1971. 14.50x (ISBN 0-691-05615-3). Princeton U Pr.

UN Law Reports, Vol. 15: Sept. 1980 to Aug. 1981. 1981. 50.00. Walker & Co.

United Nations List of National Parks & Equivalent Reserves: 1980 Edition. 121p. 1980. pap. 7.50 (ISBN 2-88032-406-8, IUCN 80, IUCN). Unipub.

United Nations Operation in the Congo, 1960-1964. Georges Abi-Saab. (International Crises & the Role of Law Ser.). 1979. pap. 7.95x (ISBN 0-19-825323-0). Oxford U Pr.

United Nations Peacekeeping, 1946-1967: Documents & Commentary, Africa, Vol. 3 Africa. Rosalyn Higgins. 486p. 1980. 87.00x (ISBN 0-19-218321-4). Oxford U Pr.

United Nations Peacekeeping, 1946-1967: Documents & Commentary Vol. 1: The Middle East. Rosalyn Higgins. 1969. 34.95x o.p. (ISBN 0-19-214975-X). Oxford U Pr.

United Nations Philately. Ed. by Arleigh Gaines. LC 80-53294. (Illus.). 704p. 1980. write for info. looseleaf (ISBN 0-938152-00-9). R & D Pubns.

United Nations Secretariat. Syracuse University. Maxwell Graduate School of Citizenship & Public Affairs. Ed. by W. S. Sayre. LC 78-2884. (Carnegie Endowment for International Peace, United Nations Studies: No. 4). 1978. Repr. of 1950 ed. lib. bdg. 14.50x (ISBN 0-313-20331-8, UNNS). Greenwood.

United Nations System; Internaional Bibliography: Vol. 2B, Learned Journals Nineteen Seventy-One to Nineteen Seventy-Five. Ed. by Klaus Hufner & Jens Naumann. 436p. 1977. 68.00 (ISBN 3-7940-2252-1, Dist. by Gale Research Co). K G Saur.

United Nations System: International Bibliography. Ed. by Klaus Hufner. Jens Naumann. 286p. 1977. 58.00 (ISBN 3-7940-2251-3, Dist. by Gale Research Co). K G Saur.

United Nations System International Bibliography, Vol. 3B. new ed. Klaus Hufner & Jens Naumann. (Monographs & Articles in Collective Vols. 1971-75). 692p. 1979. 78.00 (ISBN 0-686-52995-2, Pub. by K G Saur). Gale.

United Nations System; International Bibliography: Vol. 1, Learned Journals & Monographs Nineteen Forty-Five to Nineteen Sixty-Five. Ed. by Klaus Hufner. Jens Naumann. 520p. 1976. 65.00 (ISBN 3-7940-2250-5, Dist. by Gale Research Co). K G Saur.

United Nations System; International Bibliography: Vol. 3A, Monographs & Articles in Collective Volumes Nineteen Sixty-Five to Nineteen Seventy. Ed. by Klaus Hufner & Jens Naumann. 492p. 1978. 68.00 (ISBN 3-7940-2253-X, Dist. by Gale Research Co). K G Saur.

United Nations Water Conference: Summary & Main Documents. new ed. Ed. by Asit K. Biswas. LC 77-30461. 1978. text ed. 42.00 (ISBN 0-08-022392-3). Pergamon.

United Reformed Church. Kenneth Slack. 1978. pap. 2.90 (ISBN 0-08-021414-2). Pergamon.

United States. 4th ed. Hofstader & Miller. 464p. 1976. Pt. 1. pap. 13.95 (ISBN 0-13-938639-4); Pt. 2. pap. 13.95 (ISBN 0-13-938647-5); combined ed. 17.95 (ISBN 0-13-938654-8). P-H.

United States. Ed. by Jerry E. Jennings. LC 78-62083. (Illus.). (gr. 4 up). 1979. text ed. 13.68 1-4 copies, 5 or more 10.94 o.p. (ISBN 0-88296-477-1); tchr's annotated ed. 13.68 o.p. (ISBN 0-686-66762-X). Fideler.

U. S. - Canadian Tables of Feed Composition. Division Of Biology And Agriculture Of The Agricultural Board. 1969. pap. 4.50 (ISBN 0-309-01684-3). Natl Acad Pr.

U. S. - South Asian Relations, Nineteen Forty-Seven to Nineteen Eighty, 2 vols. R. K. Jain. 1400p. 1981. text ed. 61.50x (ISBN 0-391-02119-2). Humanities.

U. S. Air Force Academy Fitness Program for Women. Jack Galub. LC 78-21218. (Illus.). 1979. 14.95 o.p. (ISBN 0-13-938142-2); pap. 7.95 o.p. (ISBN 0-13-938134-1). P-H.

U. S. Airfreight Industry. Nawal K. Taneja. LC 78-24840. 272p. 1979. 21.00 (ISBN 0-669-02853-3). Lexington Bks.

United States Airlines: Trunk & Regional Carriers, Their Operations & Management. Leo G. Fradenburg. (Orig.). 1980. pap. text ed. 18.95 (ISBN 0-8403-2128-7). Kendall-Hunt.

United States & Canada: A Regional Geography. W. R. Mead & E. H. Brown. 1964. text ed. 7.25x (ISBN 0-09-103750-6, Hutchinson U Pr). Humanities.

United States & Canada: Present & Future. Richard S. Thoman. (Geography Ser.). 1978. text ed. 19.95 (ISBN 0-675-08410-5); instructor's manual 3.95 (ISBN 0-686-66348-9). Merrill.

United States & China in the Twentieth Century. Michael Schaller. (Illus.). 1980. pap. text ed. 3.95x (ISBN 0-19-502599-7). Oxford U Pr.

United States & East Asia. Richard W. Van Alstyne. (Library of World Civilization Ser). 1973. pap. 5.95x (ISBN 0-393-09368-9). Norton.

United States & France: Civil War Diplomacy. Lynn M. Case & Warren F. Spencer. LC 75-105108. 680p. 1974. 25.00x (ISBN 0-8122-7604-3). U of Pa Pr.

United States & Iran: A Documentary History. Ed. by Yonah Alexander & Allan Nanes. 450p. 1980. 24.00 (ISBN 0-89093-183-6); pap. 8.00 (ISBN 0-89093-184-4). U Pubns Amer.

United States & Japan in the Western Pacific. Ed. by Grant K. Goodman & Felix Moos. (Westview Replica Edition Ser.). (Illus.). 225p. 1980. lib. bdg. 20.00x (ISBN 0-89158-840-X). Westview.

United States & Korea: Looking Ahead. Robert A. Scalapino. LC 79-54241. (Washington Papers: No. 69). 88p. 1979. pap. 3.50 (ISBN 0-8039-1374-5). Sage.

United States & Latin America. Ed. by Earl T. Glauert & Lester D. Langley. LC 79-133376. (History Ser). 1971. pap. 5.95 (ISBN 0-201-02404-7). A-W.

United States & Latin America. Richard J. Walton. LC 76-171860. 192p. (gr. 7 up). 1972. 5.95 (ISBN 0-395-28930-0, Clarion). HM.

United States & Latin America Wars, 1932-1942. Bryce Wood. LC 65-25493. 1966. 25.00x (ISBN 0-231-02868-7). Columbia U Pr.

United States & Morocco, 1776-1956. Luella J. Hall. LC 71-142233. 1971. 35.00- (ISBN 0-8108-0338-0). Scarecrow.

United States & Peace. William H. Taft. LC 78-147594. (Library of War & Peace; Int'l. Organization, Arbitration & Law). lib. bdg. 38.00 (ISBN 0-8240-0355-1). Garland Pub.

United States & Puerto Rico. Leo S. Rowe. LC 74-14249. (Puerto Rican Experience Ser). 290p. 1975. Repr. 16.00x (ISBN 0-405-06235-4). Arno.

United States & the Contemporary World, 1945-1962. Ed. by Richard L. Watson, Jr. LC 65-11901. (Orig.). 1965. pap. text ed. 3.25 o.s.i. (ISBN 0-02-934000-4). Free Pr.

United States & the Developing Countries. Atlantic Council Working Group on the U.S. & the Developing Countries & Edwin M. Martin. LC 77-9102. (Atlantic Council Policy Ser.). (Illus.). 1977. text ed. 19.50x (ISBN 0-89158-400-5); pap. 9.25x (ISBN 0-89158-401-3). Westview.

United States & the Developing Economies. rev. ed. Gustav Ranis. 1973. 8.95x (ISBN 0-393-05461-6, NortonC); pap. 5.95x (ISBN 0-393-09999-7). Norton.

U. S. & the Developing World: Agenda for Action, 1974. James W. Howe & Overseas Development Council Staff. LC 74-4234. (Agenda Ser.). 228p. 1974. pap. 3.95 (ISBN 0-686-28670-7). Overseas Dev Council.

United States & the Developing World: Agenda for Action, 1973. Robert E. Hunter & Overseas Development Council Staff. LC 73-76292. (Agenda Ser.). 172p. 1973. pap. 2.50 (ISBN 0-686-28671-5). Overseas Dev Council.

United States & the Far East. Richard J. Walton. LC 73-14859. 192p. (gr. 6 up). 1974. 6.95 (ISBN 0-395-28931-9, Clarion). HM.

United States & the First Hague Peace Conference. Calvin D. Davis. (Beveridge Award Books Ser.). 248p. 1962. 19.50x (ISBN 0-8014-0099-6). Cornell U Pr.

United States & the Global Struggle for Minerals. Alfred E. Eckes. LC 78-11082. 1979. text ed. 19.95 (ISBN 0-292-78506-2). U of Tex Pr.

United States & the Hawaiian Kingdom: A Political History. Merze Tate. LC 80-14045. (Illus.). ix, 374p. 1980. Repr. of 1965 ed. lib. bdg. 29.25x (ISBN 0-313-22441-2, TAUS). Greenwood.

U. S. & the Independence of Latin America, 1800-1830. Arthur P. Whitaker. 1964. pap. 3.95 o.p. (ISBN 0-393-00271-3, Norton Lib). Norton.

United States & the Jewish State Movement: The Crucial Decade 1939-1949. Joseph B. Schechtman. (Return to Zion Ser.). (Illus.). 474p. 1980. Repr. of 1963 ed. lib. bdg. 27.50x (ISBN 0-8799-123-9). Porcupine Pr.

United States & the Origins of the Cold War, 1941-1947. John L. Gaddis. LC 75-186388. (Contemporary American History Ser). 448p. 1972. text ed. 22.50x (ISBN 0-231-03289-7); pap. 7.50x (ISBN 0-231-08302-5, 133). Columbia U Pr.

United States & the Pacific Economy in the 1980's. Ed. by Kermit Hanson & Thomas Roehl. LC 80-16599. (ITT Key Issue Lecture Ser.). 160p. 1980. pap. text ed. 6.95. Bobbs.

United States & the Philippines: A Study of Neocolonialism. Stephen R. Shalom. (Illus.). 302p. 1981. 17.50 (ISBN 0-89727-014-2). Inst Study Human.

United States & the Soviet Union: The Decision to Recognize. John Richman. LC 79-92564. 287p. 1980. 11.95 (ISBN 0-935880-00-3). Camberleigh & Hall.

United States & the World Court. Philip C. Jessup. Incl. What's Wrong with International Law? Wolfgang Friedman; Foreign Policy of a Free Democracy. Philip C. Jessup; Fallacy of a "Preventive" War. Philip C. Jessup; Legal Process & International Order. Hans Kelsen. LC 70-147750. (Library of War & Peace; International Law). lib. bdg. 38.00 (ISBN 0-8240-0490-6). Garland Pub.

U. S. & U. K. Education Policy: A Decade of Reform. Edgar Litt & Michael Parkinson. LC 78-19759. (Praeger Special Studies). 1979. 22.95 (ISBN 0-03-046706-3). Praeger.

U. S. & World Development: Agenda for Action, 1976. Roger D. Hansen & Overseas Development Council Staff. LC 76-4936. (Agenda Ser.). 240p. 1976. pap. 4.95 (ISBN 0-275-85670-4). Overseas Dev Council.

U. S. & World Development: Agenda for Action, 1975. James W. Howe & Overseas Development Council Staff. LC 75-11641. (Agenda Ser.). 288p. 1975. pap. 4.95 (ISBN 0-275-89310-3). Overseas Dev Council.

United States & World Development: Agenda 1979. Martin M. McLaughlin & Overseas Development Council. 1979. 23.95 (ISBN 0-03-049146-0); pap. 4.95 student ed (ISBN 0-03-049151-7). Praeger.

United States & World Development: Agenda 1979. Martin M. McLaughlin & Overseas Development Council Staff. LC 78-71589. (Agenda Ser.). 280p. 1979. pap. 5.95 (ISBN 0-686-28666-9). Overseas Dev Council.

United States & World Development: Agenda 1977. John Sewell & Overseas Development Council Staff. LC 76-30725. (Agenda Ser.). 272p. 1977. pap. 4.95. Overseas Dev Council.

United States & World Development: Agenda 1977. John W. Sewell. LC 76-30725. (Special Studies). 1977. text ed. 24.95 (ISBN 0-275-24440-7); pap. 4.95 (ISBN 0-275-65000-6). Praeger.

United States & World Development: Agenda 1980. John W. Sewell. 256p. 1980. 24.95 (ISBN 0-03-058993-2); pap. 6.95 (ISBN 0-03-058992-4). Praeger.

United States & World Development: Agenda 1980. John W. Sewell & Overseas Development Council Staff. LC 80-82415. 242p. 1980. pap. 6.95. Overseas Dev Council.

United States & World Trade: Changing Patterns & Dimensions. Robert T. Green & James Lutz. LC 78-19762. 336p. 1979. 29.95 (ISBN 0-03-045351-8). Praeger.

U. S. Apparel Industry: International Challenge - Domestic Response. Jeffrey S. Arpan et al. (Research Monograph: No. 88). 1981. pap. 14.95 (ISBN 0-88406-141-8). Ga St U Busn Pub.

U. S. Army Airborne Forces, Europe 1942-45. Brian L. Davis. LC 73-83746. (Key Uniform Guides). 1974. pap. 1.95 o.p. (ISBN 0-668-03366-5). Arco.

United States Army & Reconstruction, 1865-1877. James E. Sefton. LC 80-15136. (Illus.). xx, 284p. 1980. Repr. of 1967 ed. lib. bdg. 26.50x (ISBN 0-313-22602-4, SEUS). Greenwood.

U. S. Army Order of Battle in Vietnam. Shelby L. Stanton. (Illus.). 400p. 1980. cancelled (ISBN 0-88254-519-1). Hippocrene Bks.

U. S. Army Standard Military Motor Vehicles Nineteen Forty-Three. (Illus.). 556p. 1979. 25.00x (ISBN 0-905418-46-8). Intl Pubns Serv.

United States Art Directory & Year-Book. S. R. Koehler. Ed. by H. Barbara Weinberg. Incl. Vol. 1. Guide for Artists, Art Students, Travellers, Etc; Vol. 2. Chronicle of Events in the Art World, & a Guide for All Interested in the Progress of Art in America. LC 75-28874. (Art Experience in Late 19th Century America Ser.: Vol. 10). (Illus.). 1976. Repr. of 1884 ed. lib. bdg. 72.50 (ISBN 0-8240-2234-3). Garland Pub.

United States at War. United States, Bureau of the Budget, Committee on Records of War Administration. LC 79-169909. (FDR & the Era of the New Deal Ser.). 553p. 1972. Repr. of 1946 ed. lib. bdg. 55.00 (ISBN 0-306-70330-0). Da Capo.

U. S. Balance of Payments & the Sinking Dollar. Wilson Schmidt. LC 78-65582. 1979. 10.00x (ISBN 0-8147-7797-X); pap. 5.00x (ISBN 0-8147-7798-8). NYU Pr.

U. S. Battleships in Action. 1980. pap. 4.95 (ISBN 0-89747-107-5). Squad Sig Pubns.

U. S. Bombers. 3rd ed. Lloyd Jones. LC 80-66808. 272p. 1980. 14.95 (ISBN 0-8168-9128-1). Aero.

U. S. Book Publishing Yearbook & Directory: 1980-1981. 2nd ed. Ed. by Terry Mollo. LC 79-649219. (Communications Library). 225p. 1980. pap. 35.00 (ISBN 0-914236-63-6). Knowledge Indus.

United States: Brief Edition. Richard Hofdstadter et al. (Illus.). 1979. pap. text ed. 13.95 (ISBN 0-13-938860-5). P-H.

United States, Canada & the New International Economic Order. Ed. by Ervin Laszlo & Joel Kurtzman. (Policy Studies). 1979. 20.00 (ISBN 0-08-025113-7). Pergamon.

United States Capitol: An Annotated Bibliography. Ed. by John R. Kerwood. LC 72-870. 534p. 1973. 27.50x (ISBN 0-8061-1030-9); pap. 9.95x (ISBN 0-8061-1253-0). U of Okla Pr.

U. S. Cartridges & Their Handguns. Charles R. Suydam. (Illus.). 333p. 1976. 15.95 (ISBN 0-917714-04-0); pap. 9.95 (ISBN 0-917714-07-5). Beinfeld Pub.

United States, Chile & Peru in the Tacna & Arica Plebiscite. Joe F. Wilson. LC 78-66124. (Orig.). 1979. pap. text ed. 11.50 (ISBN 0-8191-0685-2). U Pr of Amer.

United States, China & Arms Control. Ralph N. Clough et al. 153p. 1975. 11.95 (ISBN 0-8157-1478-5); pap. 4.95 (ISBN 0-8157-1477-7). Brookings.

U. S. Civil Aircraft, Vol. 8. Joseph Juptner. 351p. 1980. 13.95 (ISBN 0-8168-9178-8). Aero.

U. S. Coal Industry: The Economics of Policy Change. Martin B. Zimmerman. 256p. 1982. text ed. 27.50. MIT Pr.

U. S. Coast Guard in World War II. Malcolm F. Willoughby. LC 79-6163. (Navies & Men Ser.). (Illus.). 1980. Repr. of 1957 ed. lib. bdg. 35.00x (ISBN 0-405-13081-3). Arno.

United States Coin Prices, 1980 to 1981. Ed. by Robert A. Bowse. (Illus.). 304p. (Orig.). 1980. pap. 3.95 (ISBN 0-937458-04-X). Harris & Co.

U. S. Coins of Value. Norman Stack. (Orig.). pap. 2.25 o.s.i. (ISBN 0-440-19102-5). Dell.

U. S. Coins of Value. Norman Stack. (Orig.). 1981. pap. 2.50 (ISBN 0-440-18759-1). Dell.

United States, Communism & the Emergent World. Bernard P. Kiernan. LC 72-75636. 256p. 1972. 10.00x (ISBN 0-253-19009-6). Ind U Pr.

U. S. Congress House: Report...Washington, 1813. U. S. Congress. Ed. by Wilcomb E. Washburn. LC 75-7057. (Narratives of North American Captivities Ser.). 1977. lib. bdg. 44.00 (ISBN 0-8240-1659-9). Garland Pub.

United States Congressional Directories, 1789-1840. Ed. by James S. Young et al. 400p. 1973. 25.00x (ISBN 0-231-03365-6). Columbia U Pr.

United States Congressional Districts, 1788-1841. Stanley Parsons et al. LC 77-83897. (Illus.). 1978. lib. bdg. 37.50x (ISBN 0-8371-9828-3, PUS/). Greenwood.

United States Constitution. Paul N. McCloskey. (gr. 10-12). 1972. pap. text ed. 9.00 incl. tchrs' manual & test (ISBN 0-8449-0901-7). Learning Line.

United States Constitution: A Guide to Information Sources. Ed. by Earlean M. McCarrick. LC 74-15403. (American Government & History Information Guide Ser.: Vol. 4). 1980. 28.00 (ISBN 0-8103-1203-4). Gale.

United States Constitution in Perspective. rev. ed. Claude L. Heathcock. (Studies in Political Science Ser.). 1972. pap. 7.20 (ISBN 0-205-03479-9, 763479X). Allyn.

United States Constitutions Subject Index, Release 1. B. F. Sachs. 1980. 35.00 (ISBN 0-379-20413-4). Oceana.

U. S. Copyright Documents: An Annotated Collection for Use by Educators & Librarians. Jerome K. Miller. LC 80-24768. 360p. 1980. lib. bdg. 25.00x (ISBN 0-87287-239-4). Libs Unl.

U. S. Corporate Profitability & Capital Formation: Are Rates of Return Sufficient? Herman I. Liebling. (Pergamon Policy Studies). 1980. 22.00 (ISBN 0-08-024622-2). Pergamon.

U. S. Crusade in China, Nineteen Thirty-Eight to Nineteen Forty-Five: The United States & China, 1938-1945. Michael Schaller. 1979. 17.50 (ISBN 0-231-04454-2). Columbia U Pr.

United States Cultural History: A Guide to Information Sources. Ed. by Philip I. Mitterling. LC 79-24061. (American Government & History Information Guide Ser.: Vol. 5). 1980. 30.00 (ISBN 0-8103-1369-3). Gale.

U. S. Dept. of the Interior. Paul Metcalf. LC 80-66485. (Illus.). 88p. (Orig.). 1980. pap. 5.00 (ISBN 0-917788-23-0). Gnomon Pr.

United States Diplomatic History, Vol. 1. Gerard H. Clarfield. LC 72-5519. 256p. 1973. pap. text ed. 8.25 (ISBN 0-395-14026-9). HM.

United States Diplomatic History: Readings for the Twentieth Century, Vol. 2. Ed. by Walter V. Scholes. LC 72-6699. 1973. pap. text ed. 8.25 (ISBN 0-395-14057-9, 3-50121). HM.

U. S. Directory of Marine Scientists 1975. Ocean Affairs Board, National Research Council. vii, 325p. 1975. pap. 6.50 (ISBN 0-309-02408-0). Natl Acad Pr.

United States Doctoral Dissertations in Third World Studies, 1869-1978. Michael Sims. 436p. 1980. 60.00. African Studies Assn.

United States Energy Atlas. David J. Cuff & William J. Young. (Illus.). 1980. 75.00 (ISBN 0-02-691250-3). Free Pr.

U. S. Energy Policy: A Primer. Edward J. Mitchell. 103p. 1974. pap. 5.25 (ISBN 0-8447-3131-5). Am Enterprise.

U. S. Energy Prospects: An Engineering Viewpoint. National Academy of Engineering. 1974. 8.00 o.p. (ISBN 0-309-02237-1). Natl Acad Pr.

U. S. Energy Supply Prospects to 2010. Committee on Nuclear & Alternative Energy Systems. 1979. pap. 8.75 (ISBN 0-309-02936-8). Natl Acad Pr.

U. S. Expansionism: The Imperialist Urge in the 1890's. David Healy. LC 71-121769. (Illus.). 1970. 25.00 (ISBN 0-299-05851-4). U of Wis Pr.

U. S. Export Competitiveness in Manufactures in Third World Countries, Vol. II. Raymond F. Mikesell & Mark G. Farah. LC 80-67711. (Significant Issues Ser.: No. 9). 144p. 1980. 5.95 (ISBN 0-89206-026-3). CSI Studies.

U. S. Federal Official Publications: The International Dimension. J. A. Downey. 1978. text ed. 60.00 (ISBN 0-08-021839-3). Pergamon.

U. S. Financial Systems: The Money Markets & Institutions. G. Kaufman. 1980. 19.95 (ISBN 0-13-938084-1). P-H.

U. S. Financing of East-West Trade: Studies in East European & Soviet Planning, Development, & Trade. Paul Marer. (No. 22). 1975. pap. text ed. 8.00 (ISBN 0-89249-030-6). Intl Development.

U. S. Force Structure in NATO: An Alternative. Richard D. Lawrence & K. Jeffrey Record. (Studies in Defense Policy). 136p. 1974. pap. 3.95 (ISBN 0-8157-5171-0). Brookings.

U. S. Foreign Policy & the New International Economic Order. Robert K. Olson. (Special Studies in International Relations). 184p. 1981. lib. bdg. 20.00x (ISBN 0-86531-125-0). Westview.

U. S. Foreign Policy & World Order. 2nd ed. Nathan & Oliver. 475p. (Orig.). 1981. pap. text ed. 10.95 (ISBN 0-316-59851-8). Little.

United States Foreign Policy Toward Yugoslavia, 1943-1963. David L Larson. LC 78-71369. 1979. pap. 12.25 (ISBN 0-8191-0669-0). U Pr of Amer.

U. S. Foreign Policy 1972-1973. Foreign Policy Association. 1972. pap. 1.25 o.s.i. (ISBN 0-02-073510-3, Collier). Macmillan.

U. S. Foreign Relations Law, Vol. 1. Franck. 1980. 40.00 (ISBN 0-379-20355-3). Oceana.

United States Foreign Relations Law, Documents & Sources, 3 vols. Michael J Glennon & Thomas M. Franck. Ed. by Ronald C. Bowman. Incl. Vol. 1. Executive Agreements. 1200p. (ISBN 0-379-20355-3); Vol. 2. Treaties. 1200p. (ISBN 0-379-20356-1); Vol. 3. The War Power. 1200p. (ISBN 0-379-20357-X). LC 80-18165. 40.00 set (ISBN 0-686-68787-6). Oceana.

United States Generalized System of Preferences: Coverage & Administrative Procedures in Force in 1980. OAS General Secretariat International Trade & Export Development Program. (International Trade Ser.). 58p. 1980. text ed. 5.00 (ISBN 0-8270-1101-6). OAS.

United States Government. J. R. Reich & Michael S. Reich. (Illus.). 207p. (Orig.). (gr. 7-12). 1979. pap. text ed. 4.50 (ISBN 0-8372-3552-9); tchrs' guide 1.26 (ISBN 0-8372-3553-7). Bowmar-Noble.

United States Government Documents & Reports Pertaining to Conscription & Conscientious Objection, 1917-1968. John Chambers. LC 76-147694. (Library of War & Peace: Documentary Anthologies). 1974. lib. bdg. 38.00 (ISBN 0-8240-0450-7). Garland Pub.

U. S. Government Publications for the School Media Center. J. Alice Wittig. LC 79-24798. 1979. lib. bdg. 11.50 (ISBN 0-87287-214-9). Libs Unl.

U. S. Government Scientific & Technical Periodicals. Philip A. Yannarella & Rao Aluri. LC 75-38740. 1976. 12.00 (ISBN 0-8108-0888-9). Scarecrow.

U. S. Government Surplus: A Complete Buyer's Manual. James J. Senay. LC 80-18466. 120p. (Orig.). 1981. 12.95 (ISBN 0-936218-00-2); pap. 7.95 (ISBN 0-936218-01-0). Rainbow Pub Co.

United States, Great Britain, & the Cold War: 1944-1947. Terry H. Anderson. LC 80-25838. 256p. 1981. text ed. 23.00x (ISBN 0-8262-0328-0). U of Mo Pr.

United States Half Dimes. Daniel W. Valentine. LC 74-80917. (Illus.). 384p. 1975. Repr. 35.00x (ISBN 0-88000-049-X). Quarterman.

U. S. Health System: Origins & Functions. Marshall Raffel. LC 80-86. 1980. 17.95 (ISBN 0-471-04512-8, Pub. by Wiley Med). Wiley.

U. S. Higher Education: A Guide to Information Sources. Ed. by Franklin Parker & Betty J. Parker. (Education Information Guide Ser.: Vol. 9). 400p. 1980. 30.00 (ISBN 0-8103-1476-2). Gale.

U. S. History, 2 vols. rev. ed. Nelson Klose. 480p. (gr. 7-12). Date not set. Vol. 1. pap. text ed. 5.50 (ISBN 0-8120-2250-5); Vol. 2. pap. text ed. 5.50 (ISBN 0-8120-2251-3). Barron. Postponed.

United States History & Historiography in Post-War Soviet Writings, 1945-1970: A Bibliography. new ed. Leo Okinshevich. LC 76-3756. 431p. 1976. text ed. 10.25 (ISBN 0-87436-208-3). ABC-Clio.

U. S. Identification Manual. rev. ed. Drivers License Guide Co. (Illus.). 700p. 1981. text ed. 90.00. Drivers License.

United States in Cuba, 1898-1902: Generals, Politicians, & the Search for Policy. David F. Healy. (Illus.). 1963. 17.50x (ISBN 0-299-02930-1). U of Wis Pr.

United States in Prague, 1945-1948. Walter Ullmann. (East European Monographs: No. 36). 1978. text ed. 13.00x (ISBN 0-914710-29-X, Dist. by Columbia U Pr). East Eur Quarterly.

United States in the Twentieth Century. Melvyn Dubofsky et al. LC 77-13246. (Illus.). 1978. pap. 16.95 ref. ed. (ISBN 0-13-938712-9). P-H.

United States in the 1980's. Ed. by Peter Duignan & Alvin Rabushka. LC 79-5475. (Publication Ser.: No. 228). 1980. 20.00 (ISBN 0-8179-7281-1). Hoover Inst Pr.

United States in the 20th Century: A Programed Approach. 2nd ed. Melvin P. Lesser. 1975. spiral bdg. 8.50x (ISBN 0-87543-158-5). Lucas.

United States in World Affairs: What Is Its Role? Francis Pratt. Ed. by Jack R. Fraenkel. (Crucial Issues in American Government Ser.). (gr. 9-12). 1976. pap. text ed. 4.96 (ISBN 0-205-04906-0, 7649061). Allyn.
U. S. Income Tax Guide, 1981. rev. ed. Ed. by Michael L. Green. (Buyer's Guide Ser.). 80p. (Orig.). Date not set. pap. 2.50 (ISBN 0-89552-074-5). DMR Pubns.
U. S. International Aviation Policy. Nawal K. Taneja. LC 79-3039. 176p. 1980. 21.95x (ISBN 0-669-03320-0). Lexington Bks.
United States-Japanese Economic Relations: Cooperation, Competition & Confrontation. Ed. by Diane Tasca et al. (Policy Studies). 1980. 18.25 (ISBN 0-08-025129-3). Pergamon.
United States-Latin America: A Special Relationship? Edmund Gaspar. 1978. pap. 4.25 (ISBN 0-8447-3287-7). Am Enterprise.
U. S. Maritime Industry in the National Interest: A Comprehensive History & Statistical Reference. Irwin M. Heine. 1981. pap. 11.95 (ISBN 0-87491-518-X). Acropolis.
United States Metallurgical Coal Industry. James E. Spearman. 209p. 1980. 12.50 (ISBN 0-937058-00-9). West Va U Lib.
United States-Mexico Energy Relationships: Realities & Prospects. Ed. by Jerry R. Ladman et al. 350p. 1980. lib. bdg. cancelled (ISBN 0-86531-066-1). Westview.
United States-Middle East Diplomatic Relations 1784-1978: An Annotated Bibliography. Thomas A. Bryson. LC 78-26754. 1979. lib. bdg. 11.00 (ISBN 0-8108-1197-9). Scarecrow.
U. S. Military Dilemma. Ed. by Lester A. Sobel. 200p. 1981. 17.50x (ISBN 0-87196-202-0, Checkmark). Facts on File.
U. S. Military Shoulder Patches of the U.S. Armed Forces. rev ed. Jack Britton & George Washington. LC 79-112480. (Illus.). 1978. pap. 6.50 o.p. (ISBN 0-912958-04-9). Military Coll.
U. S. Monetary System: Money, Banking, & Financial Markets. Daniel Hamberg. 1981. text ed. 16.95 (ISBN 0-316-34096-0). Little.
U. S. Motor-Carrier Industry. D. Daryl Wyckoff & David H. Maister. (Lexington Casebook Series in Industry Analysis). (Illus.). 1977. 18.95x (ISBN 0-669-01113-4); instructors manual free (ISBN 0-669-01454-0). Lexington Bks.
U. S. Multinationals & Worker Participation in Management: The American Experience in the European Community. Ton DeVos. LC 80-23597. 1981. lib. bdg. 29.95 (ISBN 0-89930-004-9, DUM/, Quorum Bks). Greenwood.
United States Multiregional Input-Output Accounts & Model. Karen R. Polenske. LC 78-332. (Illus.). 1980. 36.00x (ISBN 0-669-02173-3). Lexington Bks.
United States National Interests in a Changing World. Donald E. Nuechterlein. LC 73-77255. (Illus.). 216p. 1973. 10.00x (ISBN 0-8131-1287-7). U Pr of Ky.
U. S. Navy: An Illustrated History. Nathan Miller. LC 77-24139. (Illus.). 416p. 1977. 12.95 (ISBN 0-8281-0204-X, Dist. by Scribner); deluxe ed. 39.95 slipcased (ISBN 0-8281-0205-8, Dist. by Scribner). Am Heritage.
U. S. Navy & Marine Corps Fighters. William Green & Gordon Swanborough. (World War II Aircraft Fact Files Ser.). (Illus.). 1977. 6.95 o.p. (ISBN 0-668-04174-9); pap. 4.95 o.p. (ISBN 0-668-04121-8). Arco.
U. S. Navy in Pensacola: From Sailing Ships to Naval Aviation, Eighteen Twenty-Five to Nineteen Thirty. George F. Pearce. LC 80-12167. 1980. write for info. (ISBN 0-8130-0665-1). U Presses Fla.
United States Navy in the Pacific, 1909-1922. William R. Braisted. 1971. 25.00 (ISBN 0-292-70037-7). U of Tex Pr.
United States Navy of Tomorrow. Malcolm W. Cagle. LC 75-11444. (Illus.). 160p. (gr. 7 up). 1975. PLB 5.95 (ISBN 0-396-07228-3). Dodd.
U. S. Nuclear Weapons in Europe: Issues & Alternatives. Jeffrey Record. (Studies in Defense Policy). 70p. 1974. pap. 3.95 (ISBN 0-8157-7365-X). Brookings.
U. S. Numbered Highways. 1979. 10.00 (ISBN 0-686-27097-5, US-4). AASHTO.
U. S. Nutrition Policies in the Seventies. Ed. by Jean Mayer. LC 72-6548. 1973. text ed. 17.95x (ISBN 0-7167-0599-0); pap. text ed. 9.95x (ISBN 0-7167-0596-6). W H Freeman.
U. S. Occupation in Europe After World War II. Ed. by Hans A. Schmitt. LC 78-51611. 1978. 11.00x (ISBN 0-7006-0178-3); pap. text ed. 6.95x (ISBN 0-7006-0179-1). Regents Pr KS.
United States Occupation of Haiti, 1915-1934. Hans R. Schmidt, Jr. 1971. 22.00 (ISBN 0-8135-0690-5). Rutgers U Pr.
United States of America. John Bear. LC 75-44862. (Macdonald Countries). (Illus.). (gr. 6 up). 1976. PLB 7.95 (ISBN 0-382-06109-8, Pub. by Macdonald Ed). Silver.
United States of America. Sheila Herstein & Naomi Robbins. (World Bibliographical Ser.: No. 16). 1981. write for info. (ISBN 0-903450-29-1). Abc-Clio.
United States of Europe on the Eve of the Parliament of Peace. William T. Stead. LC 70-147592. (Library of War & Peace; Int'l. Organization, Arbitration & Law). lib. bdg. 38.00 (ISBN 0-8240-0353-5). Garland Pub.
U. S. on the Moon. U. S. News And World Report. 1970. 9.95 (ISBN 0-02-620990-X). Macmillan.
U. S. on the Moon. U. S. News & World Report. (gr. 7 up). 1969. pap. 2.95 o.s.i. (ISBN 0-02-074860-4, Collier). Macmillan.
United States One Cent Stamp of 1851-1857. Stanley Ashbrook. Date not set. 100.00x (ISBN 0-88000-082-1). Quarterman. Postponed.
United States, OPEC & Multinational Oil. Frank R. Wyant. LC 77-217. 1977. 21.95x (ISBN 0-669-01433-8). Lexington Bks.
United States Penetration of Brazil. Jan K. Black. LC 76-53192. 1977. 17.00x (ISBN 0-8122-7720-1). U of Pa Pr.
U. S. Petrochemicals: Technologies, Markets & Economics. A. M. Brownstein. LC 77-184571. 1972. 25.50 o.p. (ISBN 0-87814-008-5). Pennwell Pub.
United States Pharmacopeia: National Formulary XV. 20th ed. 1980. 65.00x (ISBN 0-912734-30-2). Mack Pub.
U. S. Policies Toward Mexico: Perceptions & Perspectives. Ed. by Richard D. Erb & Stanley R. Ross. 1979. pap. 4.25 (ISBN 0-8447-2166-2). Am Enterprise.
U. S. Policy & Low-Intensity Conflict: Potentials for Military Struggles in the 1980s. Ed. by Sam C. Sarkesian. 224p. (Orig.). 1981. pap. 9.95 (ISBN 0-87855-851-9). Transaction Bks.
United States Policy in Foreign Affairs. Pat M. Holt. (Studies in Political Science). (Orig.). (gr. 10-12). 1971. pap. text ed. 3.60 o.p. (ISBN 0-205-02871-3, 7628714). Allyn.
U. S. Policy in International Institutions: Defining Reasonable Options in an Unreasonable World. rev. & updated ed. Ed. by Seymour M. Finger & Joseph R. Harbert. (Special Studies in International Relations). 200p. (Orig.). 1981. lib. bdg. 20.00x (ISBN 0-86531-105-6); pap. 8.50x (ISBN 0-86531-106-4). Westview.
U. S. Policy in Latin America. Ed. by Grant S. McClellan. (Reference Shelf Ser: Vol. 35, No. 1). 1963. 6.25 (ISBN 0-8242-0074-8). Wilson.
U. S. Policy Toward Africa. Ed. by Frederick S. Arkhurst. LC 74-33028. (Illus.). 272p. 1975. text ed. 27.95 (ISBN 0-275-05330-X); pap. 9.95 o.p. (ISBN 0-275-64250-X). Praeger.
United States Politics & Elections: A Guide to Information Sources. Ed. by David J. Maurer. LC 78-13669. (American Government & History Information Guide Ser.: Vol. 3). 1978. 30.00 (ISBN 0-8103-1367-7). Gale.
U. S. Power in a World Conflict. (Significant Issues Ser.: Vol. II, No. 7). (Illus.). 45p. 1980. pap. 5.00 (ISBN 0-89206-021-2, CSIS015, CSIS). Unipub.
U. S. Power in a World of Conflict, Vol. II. Ray S. Cline. (Significant Issues Ser.: No. 7). 45p. 1980. 5.95 (ISBN 0-89206-021-2). CSI Studies.
U. S. Productivity & Competitiveness in International Trade, Vol. II. Thibaut De Saint Phalle. LC 80-68434. (Significant Issues Ser.: No. 12). 115p. 1980. 5.95 (ISBN 0-89206-028-X). CSI Studies.
U. S. Program for the Geodynamics Project: Scope & Objectives. 1973. pap. 4.50 (ISBN 0-309-02211-8). Natl Acad Pr.
U. S. Programs That Impede U. S. Export Competitiveness: The Regulatory Environment. (Significant Issues Ser.: Vol. II, No. 3). 45p. 1980. pap. 7.50 (ISBN 0-89206-017-4, CSIS011, CSIS). Unipub.
U. S. Publicity Directory, 5 vols. Craig T. Norback. Incl. Vol. 1. Radio-TV (ISBN 0-471-06372-X); Vol. 2. Newspapers (ISBN 0-471-06375-4); Vol. 3. Magazines (ISBN 0-471-06373-8); Vol. 4. Business & Finance (ISBN 0-471-06371-1); Vol. 5. Communication Services (ISBN 0-471-06374-6). 1980. 65.00 ea. (Pub. by Wiley-Interscience); Set. write for info. (ISBN 0-471-06369-X). Wiley.
U. S. Ratification of the Human Rights Treaties: With or Without Reservations? Ed. by Richard B. Lillich. (Procedural Aspects of International Law Ser.). 1980. write for info. (ISBN 0-8139-0881-7). U Pr of Va.
U. S. Refinery Policy in the Nineteen Eighties: Security, Economics & Equity. Ed. by Bettina Silber & Clarice R. Feldman. LC 80-68123. (Energy Policy Ser.). (Orig.). 1980. 7.00 (ISBN 0-934458-02-2). Americans Energy Ind.
U. S. Reserve Forces: The Problem of the Weekend Warrior. Martin Binkin. (Studies in Defense Policy). 63p. 1974. pap. 3.95 (ISBN 0-8157-0959-5). Brookings.
U. S. Senators & Their World. Donald R. Matthews. LC 80-17163. (Illus.). xvi, 303p. 1980. Repr. of 1960 ed. lib. bdg. 25.00x (ISBN 0-313-22664-4, MASE). Greenwood.
U. S. Soviet Relations in the Era of Detente: A Tragedy of Errors. Richard Pipes. 230p. (Orig.). 1981. lib. bdg. 22.00x (ISBN 0-86531-154-4); pap. text ed. 10.00x (ISBN 0-86531-155-2). Westview.
U. S. Strategic Bomber. Roger Foreman. 1979. 8.95 (ISBN 0-88254-562-0, Pub by Macdonald & Jane's England). Hippocrene Bks.
United States Strategic Bombing Survey, 10 vols. Ed. by David MacIsaac. Incl. Vol. 1 (ISBN 0-8240-2026-X); Vol. 2 (ISBN 0-8240-2027-8); Vol. 3 (ISBN 0-8240-2028-6); Vol. 4 (ISBN 0-8240-2029-4); Vol. 5 (ISBN 0-8240-2030-8); Vol. 6 (ISBN 0-8240-2031-6); Vol. 7 (ISBN 0-8240-2032-4); Vol. 8 (ISBN 0-8240-2033-2); Vol. 9 (ISBN 0-8240-2034-0); Vol. 10 (ISBN 0-8240-2035-9). LC 75-26396. 1976. 44.00 ea. Garland Pub.
U. S. Strategic-Nuclear Policy & Ballistic Missile Defense: The 1980s & Beyond. William S. Schneider, Jr. et al. LC 79-3296. (Special Reports). 61p. 1980. 6.50 (ISBN 0-89549-018-8). Inst Foreign Policy Anal.
U. S. Strategic Nuclear Policy & Ballistic Missile Defense: The 1980's & Beyond. 61p. 1980. pap. 6.50 (ISBN 0-89549-018-8, IFPA 12, IFPA). Unipub.
U. S. Strategy in the Indian Ocean: The International Response. Monoranjan Bezboruah. LC 77-2786. (Praeger Special Studies). 1977. 29.95 (ISBN 0-03-021811-X). Praeger.
United States Supreme Court Decisions: An Index to Their Locations. Nancy Anderman. LC 76-8479. 323p. 1976. 14.50 (ISBN 0-8108-0932-X). Scarecrow.
U. S. Tactical Air Power: Missions, Forces, & Costs. William D. White. (Studies in Defense Policy). 121p. 1974. pap. 3.95 (ISBN 0-8157-9371-5). Brookings.
United States Tax Court Practice & Procedure. L. Ponder. 1976. 29.95 o.p. (ISBN 0-13-938688-2). P-H.
United States: The Destiny of a Democracy, 2 vols. Henry L. Ingham, Jr. 1978. Vol. 1. pap. text ed. 14.00 (ISBN 0-8191-0384-5); Vol. 2. pap. text ed. 15.00 (ISBN 0-8191-0385-3). U Pr of Amer.
United States to Eighteen Seventy-Seven. 7th rev. ed. John A. Krout. (Orig.). 1971. pap. 3.95 (ISBN 0-06-460029-7, CO 29, COS). Har-Row.
U. S. Treasury Bills Table No. 66. Financial Publishing Co. 30.00 (ISBN 0-685-02560-8). Finan Pub.
U. S. Troops in Europe: Issues, Costs & Choices. John Newhouse et al. LC 71-179325. 1971. 11.95 (ISBN 0-8157-6046-9); pap. 4.95 (ISBN 0-8157-6045-0). Brookings.
U. S. Voluntary Aid to the Third World: What Is Its Future? John G. Sommer. LC 75-43481. (Development Papers: No. 20). 68p. 1975. pap. 1.50 (ISBN 0-686-28677-4). Overseas Dev Council.
United States Vs. Nixon: The President Before the Supreme Court. Ed. by Leon Friedman. LC 74-16403. 644p. 1980. pap. 11.95 (ISBN 0-87754-144-2). Chelsea Hse.
United States Waterway Packet-Marks. Eugene Klein. 1981. 35.00x (ISBN 0-88000-076-7). Quarterman.
United States, Western Europe, & the Third World: Allies & Adversaries, Vol. II. Simon Serfaty. LC 80-50588. (Significant Issues Ser.: No. 4). 53p. 1980. 5.95 (ISBN 0-89206-018-2). CSI Studies.
United States, Western Europe, & the Third World: Allied & Adversaries. (Significant Issues Ser.: Vol. II, No. 4). 53p. 1980. pap. 7.50 (ISBN 0-89206-018-2, CSIS012, CSIS). Unipub.
United Synagogue, 1870-1970. Aubrey Newman. 1976. 21.00 (ISBN 0-7100-8456-0). Routledge & Kegan.
United We Fall. Ed. by Pat Works & Jan Works. LC 77-84030. 17.95 (ISBN 0-930438-03-5); pap. 11.95 (ISBN 0-930438-02-7). RWU Parachuting.
Units & Bulk Materials Handling. Ed. by F. J. Loeffler & C. R. Proctor. 289p. 1980. 60.00 (H00163). ASME.
Units & Standards of Electromagnetism. P. Vigoureux & R. A. Tricker. LC 77-153869. (Wykeham Science Ser.: No. 15). 1971. 9.95x (ISBN 0-8448-1117-3). Crane Russak Co.
Units in Woodworking. J. Douglas et al. (Construction-Industrial Arts Ser.). 208p. pap. text ed. 7.80 o.p. (ISBN 0-8273-0112-X); instr's guide 0.50 o.p. (ISBN 0-8273-0115-4); extra test bks free o.p. (ISBN 0-8273-0114-6). Delmar.
Units in Woodworking. Douglass et al. 208p. 1973. 7.80 o.p. (ISBN 0-8273-0112-X); pap. 6.20 o.p. (ISBN 0-8273-0113-8); tests & ans. avail. o.p. Delmar.
Units in Woodworking. J. H. Douglass et al. LC 79-8737. (Industrial Arts Ser.). 320p. 1981. text ed. 12.00 (ISBN 0-8273-1332-2); pap. text ed. 9.00 (ISBN 0-8273-1333-0); comprehensive tests 0.60 (ISBN 0-8273-1334-9); instr's guide 1.30. Delmar.
Units of Life. Richard Gliddon. (Investigations in Biology Ser.). 1970. text ed. 3.95x o.p. (ISBN 0-435-60282-9). Heinemann Ed.
Unity & Diversity in the New Testament. Robert A. Guelich. 1978. 9.95 o.p. (ISBN 0-8028-3504-X). Eerdmans.
Unity & Fellowship & Ecumenicity. H. Hamann. (Contemporary Theology Ser. II). 1973. 3.25 (ISBN 0-570-06725-1, 12RT2564). Concordia.
Unity from Diversity: Extracts from Selected Pennsylvania Colonial Documents, 1681 to 1780, in Commeration of the Tercentenary of the Commonwealth. Louis M. Waddell. (Illus.). 89p. 1980. pap. 4.00 (ISBN 0-89271-009-8). Pa Hist & Mus.
Unity in Hardy's Novels: "Repetitive Symmetries". Peter J. Casagrande. 272p. Date not set. 20.00x (ISBN 0-7006-0209-7). Regents Pr KS. Postponed.
Unity in Marriage. Wilbert J. Fields. LC 61-18222. 1962. 4.95 (ISBN 0-570-03191-5, 12-2593). Concordia.
Unity in the Ghazals of Hafez. Michael C. Hillmann. LC 74-27614. (Studies in Middle Eastern Literatures: No. 6). 1976. 20.00x (ISBN 0-88297-010-0). Bibliotheca.
Unity in Theology: Lonergan's Framework for Theology in Its New Context. Michael C. O'Callaghan. LC 80-8177. 596p. 1980. lib. bdg. 24.50 (ISBN 0-8191-1151-1); pap. text ed. 16.75 (ISBN 0-8191-1152-X). U Pr of Amer.
Unity in Variety. Christopher Dresser. Ed. by Peter Stansky & Rodney Shewan. LC 76-17748. (Aesthetic Movement & the Arts & Crafts Movement Ser.). 1978. Repr. of 1859 ed. lib. bdg. 44.00x (ISBN 0-8240-2451-6). Garland Pub.
Unity of European History: A Political & Cultural Survey. rev. ed. John Bowle. 1970. pap. 6.95 (ISBN 0-19-501249-6, GB329, GB). Oxford U Pr.
Unity of Homer. John A. Scott. LC 65-15246. 1921. 10.50x (ISBN 0-8196-0152-7). Biblo.
Unity of Mankind in Greek Thought. H. C. Baldry. 1965. 36.00 (ISBN 0-521-04091-4). Cambridge U Pr.
Unity of Religious Ideals. Hazrat I. Khan. (Collected Works of Hazrat Inayat Khan Ser.). 264p. 1979. 8.95 (ISBN 0-930872-09-6); pap. 5.95 (ISBN 0-930872-10-X). Sufi Order Pubns.
Unity of Religious Ideals. Inayat Khan. (Sufi Message of Hazrat Inayat Khan Ser.: Vol. 9). 1979. 6.95 (ISBN 90-6325-097-5, Pub. by Servire BV Netherlands). Hunter Hse.
Unity of "The Faerie Queene". Ronald A. Horton. LC 77-15793. 240p. 1978. 15.00x (ISBN 0-8203-0440-9). U of Ga Pr.
Unity of the Platonic Dialogue: The Cratylus, the Protagras, the Parmenides. Ed. by Rudolf H. Weingartner. 1973. pap. 4.50 (ISBN 0-672-61310-7, LLA224). Bobbs.
Unity of the Platonic Dialogue: The Cratylus, the Protagoras, the Parmenides. Rudolph H. Weingartner. LC 73-186244. 1973. text ed. 24.00x (ISBN 0-672-51658-6). Irvington.
Universal Conversion Factors. Steven Gerolde. LC 71-164900. 1971. 14.00 (ISBN 0-87814-005-0). Pennwell Pub.
Universal English Dictionary. Henry C. Wyld. 1960. 45.00 (ISBN 0-7100-2333-2). Routledge & Kegan.
Universal Flame. Ed. by L. H. Lester-Smith. 263p. 1975. 6.50 (ISBN 0-8356-7506-8). Theos Pub Hse.
Universal Joint & Driveshaft Design Manual. Society of Automotive Engineers. 1979. 37.95 (ISBN 0-89883-007-9). Soc Auto Engineers.
Universal Mathematics in Aristotelian-Thomistic Philosophy: The Hermeneutics of Aristotelian Texts Relative to Universal Mathematics. Charles B. Crowley. LC 79-48093. 239p. 1980. text ed. 18.50 (ISBN 0-8191-1009-4); pap. text ed. 9.50 (ISBN 0-8191-1010-8). U Pr of Amer.
Universal Multiplication of Intelligence. Glenn Doman & J. Michael Armentrout. (Gentle Revolution Ser.). 223p. 1980. 12.50 (ISBN 0-936676-02-7). Better Baby.
Universal Pronouncing Dictionary of Biography & Mythology, 2 vols. Joseph Thomas. LC 79-167222. 1976. Repr. of 1870 ed. Set. 135.00 (ISBN 0-8103-4221-9). Gale.
Universal Reference System - Nineteen Seventy-Nine Annual Supplement, 3 vols. Ed. by Samual Long. 2412p. 1980. Set. 350.00 (ISBN 0-306-69029-2, IFI). Plenum Pub.
Universal Reference System: 1979 Annual Supplement, 3 vols. 2412p. 1980. Set. 350.00 (ISBN 0-306-69029-2). IFI Plenum.
Universal Rome. Ed. by Anthony Birley. LC 68-78675. (Selections from History Today Ser.: No. 4). (Illus.). 1969. pap. 3.95 (ISBN 0-05-000020-9). Dufour.

Universal Secrets of Telecosmic Power. Norvell. 1975. pap. 1.50 o.p. (ISBN 0-451-06810-6, W6810, Sig). NAL.
Universal Sikhism. A. S. Sethi. 1972. 5.95 (ISBN 0-88253-767-9). Ind-US Inc.
Universal Soldier: Fourteen Studies in Campaign Life, A.D. 43-1944. Ed. by Martin Windrow & Frederick Wilkinson. (Illus.). 1977. 12.45 o.p. (ISBN 0-85112-176-4). Presidio Pr.
Universal Supplementary Exercisebook. Kathleen Ruhl. 1981. pap. text ed. 6.95x (ISBN 0-673-15453-X). Scott F.
Universal Theory of Automata. H. Ehrig. (Illus.). 1976. pap. 18.75 (ISBN 3-5190-2054-8). Adler.
Universalism in America: A Documentary History. Ernest Cassara. LC 77-136226. 1971. 10.00 o.p. (ISBN 0-8070-1664-0). Beacon Pr.
Universals & Scientific Realism: A Theory of Universals, Vol. 2. D. M. Armstrong. LC 77-80824. 1978. 26.95 (ISBN 0-521-21950-7). Cambridge U Pr.
Universals & Scientific Realism: Nominalism & Realism, Vol. 1. D. M. Armstrong. LC 77-80824. 1978. 23.95 (ISBN 0-521-21741-5). Cambridge U Pr.
Universals & Scientific Realism: Vol. 1, Nominalism. D. M. Armstrong. LC 77-80824. 165p. 1980. pap. 8.95 (ISBN 0-521-28033-8). Cambridge U Pr.
Universals & Scientific Realism: Vol. 2, A Theory of Universals. D. M. Armstrong. LC 77-80824. 200p. 1980. pap. 8.95 (ISBN 0-521-28032-X). Cambridge U Pr.
Universals of Human Thought. Ed. by Barbara Lloyd & J. Gay. LC 79-41471. (Illus.). 300p. Date not set. 47.50 (ISBN 0-521-22953-7); pap. 14.95 (ISBN 0-521-29818-0). Cambridge U Pr.
Universe. David Bergamini. LC 62-18337. (Life Nature Library). (Illus.). (gr. 5 up). 1969. PLB 8.97 o.p. (ISBN 0-8094-0619-5, Pub. by Time-Life). Silver.
Universe. David Bergamini. (Young Readers Library). (Illus.). 1977. lib. bdg. 7.95 (ISBN 0-686-51095-X). Silver.
Universe. Larry A. Ciupik. LC 77-27567. (Read About Science Ser.). (Illus.). (gr. k-3). 1978. PLB 9.95 (ISBN 0-8393-0089-1). Raintree Child.
Universe. Donald Goldsmith. LC 75-28643. 1976. 18.95 o.p. (ISBN 0-8053-3324-X). Benjamin-Cummings.
Universe. rev. ed. Herbert S. Zim. (Illus.). 64p. (gr. 3-7). 1973. PLB 6.48 (ISBN 0-688-31976-9); pap. 1.25 (ISBN 0-688-25096-3). Morrow.
Universe - Its Beginning & End. Lloyd Motz. LC 75-6635. (Illus.). 416p. 1976. 14.95 o.p. (ISBN 0-684-14239-2); pap. 4.95 (ISBN 0-684-15062-X, SL726, ScribT). Scribner.
Universe Against Her. James H. Schmitz. (Science Fiction Ser.). 1981. PLB 13.50 (ISBN 0-8398-2597-8). Gregg.
Universe Between. Alan E. Nourse. (gr. 7 up). 1965. 4.95 o.p. (ISBN 0-679-20226-9); PLB 4.19 o.p. (ISBN 0-685-14519-0). McKay.
Universe, Earth & Atom: The Story of Physics. Alan E. Nourse. LC 69-13493. (Illus.). 1969. 15.00 o.s.i. (ISBN 0-06-004972-3, HarpT). Har-Row.
Universe: From Flat Earth to Quasar. Isaac Asimov. 1976. pap. 2.95 (ISBN 0-380-01596-X, 42192, Discus). Avon.
Universe of Experience: A World View Beyond Science & Religion. Lancelot L. Whyte. 1974. pap. 3.45x o.p. (ISBN 0-06-131821-3, TB1821, Torch). Har-Row.
Universe Ten. Terry Carr. LC 79-6534. (Double Science Fiction Ser.). 1980. 8.95 (ISBN 0-385-15477-1). Doubleday.
Universe Two. Terry Carr. LC 80-2790. (Science Fiction Ser.). 192p. 1981. 9.95 (ISBN 0-385-17226-5). Doubleday.
Universe Unfolding. Ivan King. LC 75-33369. (Illus.). 1976. 21.95x (ISBN 0-7167-0521-4); resource bk. & instructor's manual 6.95x (ISBN 0-7167-0288-6). W H Freeman.
Universe World Stamp Album. Larry Grossman. (Illus.). 1980. 11.95 (ISBN 0-685-99699-9). Grossman Stamp.
Universities, Academics & the Great Schism. R. N. Swanson. LC 78-56764. (Cambridge Studies in Medieval Life & Thought: 3rd Ser., No. 12). 1979. 38.50 (ISBN 0-521-22127-7). Cambridge U Pr.
Universities & the International Distribution of Knowledge. Ed. by Irving J. Spitzberg, Jr. LC 80-16569. 222p. 1980. 21.95 (ISBN 0-03-056976-1). Praeger.
Universities & the Public: A History of Adult Higher Education in the United States. David N. Portman. LC 78-9333. 1979. text ed. 16.95 (ISBN 0-88229-116-5). Nelson-Hall.
Universities Facing the Future: An International Perspective. Ed. by W. Roy Niblett & R. Freeman Butts. LC 70-186577. (Higher Education Ser.). 1972. 16.95x o.p. (ISBN 0-87589-133-0). Jossey-Bass.
Universities for a Changing World: The Role of the University in the Later Twentieth Century. Ed. by M. D. Stephens & G. W. Roderick. LC 75-6567. 221p. 1975. 15.95 (ISBN 0-470-82209-0). Halsted Pr.
Universities Handbook: India. 20th ed. 1142p. 1979. 45.00x (ISBN 0-8002-1008-5). Intl Pubns Serv.
Universities in the Modern World. B. Fletcher. 1968. pap. 7.75 (ISBN 0-08-012762-2). Pergamon.
Universities in the Nineteenth Century. Michael Sanderson. 1975. 20.00x (ISBN 0-7100-8061-1). Routledge & Kegan.
University: An Organizational Analysis. Hugh Livingstone. 1974. 14.95x (ISBN 0-216-89705-X). Intl Ideas.
University & Government in Mexico: Autonomy in a Authoritarian System. Daniel C. Levy. LC 79-21134. 190p. 1980. 20.95 (ISBN 0-03-055276-1). Praeger.
University & Military Research: The Cayuga Lake Controversy. Dorothy Nelkin. LC 74-38285. 7.95 o.s.i. (ISBN 0-8076-0718-5, Orig. Pub. by Cornell U. Pr.); pap. 1.95 (ISBN 0-8076-0719-3). Braziller.
University & the City: Eight Cases of Involvement. Carnegie Commission on Higher Education. Ed. by George Nash. LC 72-14182. 176p. 1973. 10.50 o.p. (ISBN 0-07-010059-4, P&RB). McGraw.
University & the Man of Tomorrow. 1967. 10.00x (ISBN 0-8156-6008-1, Am U Beirut). Syracuse U Pr.
University & the Urban Crisis. Ed. by Howard Mitchell. LC 74-6113. (Community Psychology Ser: Vol. 2). 1974. text ed. 19.95 (ISBN 0-87705-139-9). Human Sci Pr.
University As an Organization. Carnegie Commission on Higher Education. Ed. by James A. Perkins. LC 72-8336. 352p. 1973. 14.50 o.p. (ISBN 0-07-010053-5, P&RB). McGraw.
University Authority & the Student: The Berkeley Experience. C. Michael Otten. LC 72-99485. (Illus.). 1970. 19.50x (ISBN 0-520-01607-6). U of Cal Pr.
University Chemistry, 3rd ed. Bruce H. Mahan. LC 74-19696. 1975. text ed. 21.95 (ISBN 0-201-04405-6). A-W.
University Connection. W. R. Niblett et al. (General Ser). 300p. (Orig.). 1975. pap. text ed. 20.75x (ISBN 0-85633-064-7, NFER). Humanities.
University Desk Encyclopedia. Herman Friedhoff & Ben Lenthall. 59.95 (ISBN 0-525-93001-9). Gaylord Prof Pubns.
University Desk Encyclopedia. 1977. 69.95 o.p. (ISBN 0-525-93001-9, Elsevier-Phaidon). Dutton.
University Economics: Elements of Inquiry. 3rd ed. Armen A. Alchian & William R. Allen. 1971. 21.95x (ISBN 0-534-00030-4); study guide 6.95x (ISBN 0-534-00184-X). Wadsworth Pub.
University in the American Future. Ed. by Thomas B. Stroup. LC 66-16232. 128p. 1966. 6.00x (ISBN 0-8131-1116-1). U Pr of Ky.
University Libraries for Developing Countries. Morris A. Gelfand. (Manuals for Libraries, Vol. 14). (Photos). 1971. pap. 7.00 (ISBN 92-3-100654-1, U708, UNESCO). Unipub.
University Library Administration. Rutherford D. Rogers & David C. Weber. (Illus.). 1971. 20.00 (ISBN 0-8242-0417-4). Wilson.
University of California: A Pictorial History. Albert G. Pickerell & May Dornin. (Illus.). 1968. 19.95 (ISBN 0-520-01010-8). U of Cal Pr.
University of California Library at Berkeley, 1900-1945. Kenneth G. Peterson. (U. C. Publ. in Librarianship: Vol. 8). 1970. pap. 10.00x (ISBN 0-520-09211-2). U of Cal Pr.
University of Illinois, Eighteen Sixty-Seven to Eighteen Ninety-Four: An Intellectual & Cultural History. Winton U. Solberg. LC 68-11030. (Illus.). 1968. 17.50 o.p. (ISBN 0-252-72424-0). U of Ill Pr.
University of Kentucky: The Maturing Years. Charles G. Talbert. LC 65-11827. (Illus.). 224p. 1965. 8.00 (ISBN 0-8131-1095-5). U Pr of Ky.
University of Montana: A Pictorial History. Stan B. Cohen & Don C. Miller. LC 80-53616. (Illus.). 96p. 1980. pap. 5.95 (ISBN 0-933126-12-3). Pictorial Hist.
University of Notre Dame: A Portrait of Its History & Campus. Thomas J. Schlereth. LC 74-27890. 1976. text ed. 25.00 o.p. (ISBN 0-268-01906-1); pap. text ed. 7.95x (ISBN 0-268-01905-3). U of Notre Dame Pr.
University of Oklahoma & World War II: A Personal Account, 1941-1946. George L. Cross. LC 80-16934. (Illus.). 320p. 1980. 15.95 (ISBN 0-8061-1662-5). U of Okla Pr.
University of Texas, Institute of Texan Cultures: Univ. of Texas, Institute of Texan Cultures. Ed. by Larry Whiting & David Rogers. (Illus.). 1978. pap. text ed. 6.95x (ISBN 0-8138-1875-3). Iowa St U Pr.
University of the Nations: The Story of the Geogorian University. Philip Caraman. (Illus.). 160p. (Orig.). 1981. pap. 6.95 (ISBN 0-8091-2355-X). Paulist Pr.
University Physics, 2 pts. 5th ed. Francis W. Sears et al. LC 75-20989. (Physics Ser.). (Illus.). 804p. 1976. Set. text ed. 24.95 (ISBN 0-201-06936-9); Pt. 1. text ed. 15.95 (ISBN 0-201-06937-7); Pt. 2. text ed. 15.95 (ISBN 0-201-06938-5). A-W.
University Physics for Science & Engineering. Donald E. Tilley. LC 75-14974. 1976. 21.95 (ISBN 0-8465-7536-1); instr's guide 3.75 (ISBN 0-8465-7537-X). Benjamin-Cummings.
University Professor John M. Dorsey. John M. Dorsey. (Illus.). 224p. 1980. 12.00 (ISBN 0-8143-1645-X). Wayne St U Pr.
University Records & Life in the Middle Ages. Tr. by Lynn Thorndike. (Columbia University Records of Civilization Ser.). 476p. 1975. pap. text ed. 6.95x (ISBN 0-393-09216-X). Norton.
University Science & Engineering Libraries. Ellis Mount. LC 74-34562. (Contributions in Librarianship & Information Science: No. 15). (Illus.). 214p. 1975. lib. bdg. 17.95 (ISBN 0-8371-7955-6, MSE/). Greenwood.
University Spanish-English & English-Spanish Dictionary. Gerd A. Gillhoff. (Apollo Eds.). (YA) (gr. 9-12). pap. 6.95 o.s.i. (ISBN 0-8152-0129-X, A129, TYC-T). T Y Crowell.
University Teacher & His World. Richard Startup. 1979. text ed. 34.00x (ISBN 0-566-00295-7, Pub. by Gower Pub Co England). Renouf.
University Teaching of Social Sciences: Statistics. Parasanta C. Mahalmobis. 1957. pap. 3.00 (ISBN 92-3-100424-7, U710, UNESCO). Unipub.
University Teaching of Social Sciences: International Law. Renee J. Dupry. 1967. pap. 6.00 (ISBN 92-3-100653-3, U707, UNESCO). Unipub.
Unkindest Cut: Life in the Backrooms of Medicine. Marcia Millman. LC 76-18726. 1977. 8.95 o.p. (ISBN 0-688-03120-X); pap. 4.95 o.p. (ISBN 0-688-08120-7). Morrow.
Unknown. Ed. by Donald R. Bensen. 1978. pap. 1.75 o.s.i. (ISBN 0-515-04820-8). Jove Pubns.
Unknown Avenues. Norman Borisoff. LC 72-77224. (Mystery & Adventure Ser.). (gr. 2-4). 1973. PLB 6.75 (ISBN 0-87191-205-8). Creative Ed.
Unknown Battle: Metz 1944. Anthony Kemp. LC 78-66240. (Illus.). 288p. 1980. 14.95 (ISBN 0-8128-2598-5). Stein & Day.
Unknown Earth: A Handbook of Geological Enigmas. William R. Corliss. LC 80-50159. (Illus.). 839p. 1980. 19.95 (ISBN 0-915554-06-2). Sourcebook.
Unknown England. Kenneth Scowen. Ian Niall. (Illus.). 128p. 1980. 24.00 (ISBN 0-7134-1843-5, Pub. by Batsford England). David & Charles.
Unknown Eric: A Selection of Documents for the General Library. Joseph G. Drazan. LC 80-25975. 239p. 1981. lib. bdg. 12.50 (ISBN 0-8108-1402-1). Scarecrow.
Unknown Five. Ed. by Donald R. Benson. 1978. pap. 1.75 o.s.i. (ISBN 0-515-04833-X). Jove Pubns.
Unknown Heart. Barbara Cartland. 1979. pap. 1.75 (ISBN 0-515-05859-9). Jove Pubns.
Unknown Heart. Barbara Cartland. (Barbara Cartland Ser.: No. 11). 176p. (Orig.). 1981. pap. 1.75 (ISBN 0-515-05859-9). Jove Pubns.
Unknown Oman. Wendell Phillips. (Arab Background Ser.). 1972. 14.00x (ISBN 0-685-77102-4). Intl Bk Ctr.
Unknown Philosophy of Sex. John A. Oates. (Intimate Life of Man Library Book). (Illus.). 1979. 51.45 (ISBN 0-89266-175-5). Am Classical Coll Pr.
Unknown Poe. Edgar A. Poe & Raymond Foye. LC 80-2431. 1980. 10.95x (ISBN 0-87286-119-8); pap. 5.95x (ISBN 0-87286-110-4). City Lights.
Unknown Powers. Brad Steiger. 1981. pap. 2.50 (ISBN 0-425-05005-X). Berkley Pub.
Unknown President: The Administration of President Millard Fillmore. Benson L. Grayson. LC 80-5962. 179p. 1981. lib. bdg. 17.75 (ISBN 0-8191-1456-1); pap. text ed. 8.75 (ISBN 0-8191-1457-X). U Pr of Amer.
Unknown Reality: Vol. One of a Seth Book. Jane Roberts. LC 77-1092. 308p. 1980. pap. 4.95 (ISBN 0-13-938779-X). P-H.
Unknown Virginia Woolf. Rogers Poole. LC 78-3458. 1978. 17.95 (ISBN 0-521-21987-6). Cambridge U Pr.
Unknown War: North China, 1937-1945. Michael Lindsay. LC 76-54567. (Illus.). 1977. 10.00 (ISBN 0-8467-0260-6). Hippocrene Bks.
Unknown War with Russia: Wilson's Siberian Intervention. Robert J. Maddox. LC 76-58761. (Illus.). 1977. 9.95 o.s.i. (ISBN 0-89141-013-9). Presidio Pr.
Unknown Warrior. James Leasor. 272p. 1981. 10.95 (ISBN 0-395-30228-5). HM.
Unleashed. Leon Orr. LC 79-13290. (Orion Ser.). 1979. pap. 2.95 (ISBN 0-8127-0230-1). Southern Pub.
Unless I See. John W. Bowman. LC 76-42859. (Illus.). 1977. pap. 4.00 (ISBN 0-89430-002-4). Morgan-Pacific.
Unless She Burn. Francine Mezo. 176p. 1981. pap. 2.25 (ISBN 0-380-76968-9, 76968). Avon.
Unlikely Legacy: The Story of John Ringling, the Circus & Sarasota. Kenneth Matthews & Robert McDevitt. (Illus.). 64p. 1979. pap. 3.95 (ISBN 0-936076-00-3). Aaron Pubs.
Unlikely Legacy, the Story of John Ringling: The Circus & Sarasota. 2nd rev. ed. Kenneth Matthews & Robert McDevitt. (Illus.). 64p. (Orig.). 1980. 5.95 (ISBN 0-936076-02-X); pap. 3.95 (ISBN 0-936076-00-3). Aaron Pubs.
Unlisted Legion. Jock Purves. 1978. pap. 3.45 (ISBN 0-85151-245-3). Banner of Truth.
Unlit Lamp. Radclyffe Hall. (Virago Modern Classic Ser.). 324p. 1981. pap. 5.95 (ISBN 0-8037-9171-2). Dial.
Unlocking Home Equity for the Elderly. Ed. by Kenneth Scholen & Yung-Ping Chen. 1980. 27.50 (ISBN 0-88410-595-4). Ballinger Pub.
Unlocking the Beauty of the Bible: A Study Guide by Alan D. Bennett. Ed. by Edith Samuel. Incl. Book of Praise: Dialogues Between Mark Van Doren & Maurice Samuel. 5.00 o.p. (ISBN 0-685-89266-2). UAHC.
Unlocking the Beauty of the Bible: A Study Guide. Alan D. Bennett. 5.00. UAHC.
Unmade Bed. Francoise Sagan. 1978. 9.95 o.s.i. (ISBN 0-440-09212-4, E Friede). Delacorte.
Unmaking of a President: Lyndon Johnson & Vietnam. Herbert Schandler. (Illus.). 1977. text ed. 22.00 (ISBN 0-691-07586-7). Princeton U Pr.
Unman-Kovrigin's Chronicles. Vadim Shefner. Tr. by Antonina Bouis et al from Rus. (Best of Soviet Science Fiction Ser.). 192p. 1981. 3.95 (ISBN 0-02-025230-7). Macmillan.
Unmarried Couples. Ian Pollock. (Illus., Orig.). 1978. pap. 3.95 (ISBN 0-8467-0521-4, Pub. by Two Continents). Hippocrene Bks.
Unmarried Mothers. Clark E. Vincent. LC 80-16580. x, 308p. 1980. Repr. of 1961 ed. lib. bdg. 25.00x (ISBN 0-313-22474-9, VIMO). Greenwood.
Unmasking of a King. Oscar Newman. 192p. 1981. 10.95 (ISBN 0-02-588890-0). Macmillan.
Unmasking: Ten Women in Metamorphosis. Ed. by Valerie H. Sheehan. LC 72-96163. 286p. 1973. 11.95 (ISBN 0-8040-0626-1). Swallow.
Unmentionable Vice. Michael Goodich. LC 78-13276. 179p. 1980. pap. 6.95 (ISBN 0-87436-300-4). Ross-Erikson.
Unmet Needs & the Delivery of Care. Paul Chapman. 110p. 1979. pap. text ed. 9.90x (ISBN 0-7199-0962-7, Pub. by Bedford England). Renouf.
Unmet Needs in Secondary Education. Ralph Walter. 144p. 1981. 5.00 (ISBN 0-8059-2773-5). Dorrance.
Unmusical New York: A Brief Criticism of Triumphs, Failures, & Abuses. Herman Klein. (Music Reprint Ser.). 1979. Repr. of 1910 ed. lib. bdg. 19.50 (ISBN 0-306-79517-5). Da Capo.
Unnatural Causes. P. D. James. 256p. 1975. pap. 2.25 (ISBN 0-445-00308-1). Popular Lib.
Unnderstanding Catholicism. Monika K. Hellwig. 192p. (Orig.). 1981. pap. 3.50 (ISBN 0-8091-2384-3). Paulist Pr.
Unnecessary Woman. Mollie Vesey. (Orig.). 1980. pap. 2.25 (ISBN 0-505-51503-2). Tower Bks.
Unnoticed Challenge: Soviet Maritime Strategy & the Global Choke Points. Robert J. Hanks. LC 80-83751. (Special Report Ser.). 68p. 1980. 6.50 (ISBN 0-89549-025-0). Inst Foreign Policy Anal.
U.N.O. & War Crimes. Frederic H. Maugham. LC 74-27728. 143p. 1975. Repr. of 1951 ed. lib. bdg. 12.75x (ISBN 0-8371-7911-4, MAUN). Greenwood.
Uno Corintios: Llamado a la Madurez. Marilyn Kunz & Catherine Schell. Tr. by Jose R. Velez from Eng. LC 76-1298. (Encuentros Biblicos). 77p. (Orig., Span.). 1976. pap. 1.25 (ISBN 0-89922-064-9). Edit Caribe.
Unofficial Art in the Soviet Union. Paul Sjeklocha & Igor Mead. (Illus.). 1967. 27.50x (ISBN 0-520-01181-3). U of Cal Pr.
Unofficial Hunting Rules. Jeff Danziger & Tom Davis. (Illus.). 64p. (Orig.). 1980. pap. 3.95 (ISBN 0-9603900-5-7). Lanser Pr.
Unordained Elders & Renewal Communities. Steven B. Clark. LC 75-35329. 1976. pap. 3.50 (ISBN 0-8091-1916-1). Paulist Pr.
Unpacking a Bundle. Helen Mack. 1977. 6.50 o.p. (ISBN 0-682-48921-2, Banner). Exposition.
Unplanned Parenthood: The Social Consequences of Teenage Childbearing. Frank F. Furstenberg, Jr. LC 76-8144. 1976. 15.95 (ISBN 0-02-911010-6). Free Pr.

Unplanned Parenthood: The Social Consequences of Teenage Childbearing. Frank F. Furstenberg, Jr. LC 76-8144. 1979. pap. text ed. 7.95 (ISBN 0-02-911030-0). Free Pr.
Unpleasantness at the Bellona Club. Dorothy L. Sayers. LC 56-8786. 1957. 12.95 o.p. (ISBN 0-06-013805-X, HarpT). Har-Row.
Unpredictable Bride, No. 6. Barbara Cartland. 1977. pap. 1.75 o.s.i. (ISBN 0-515-05567-0). Jove Pubns.
Unpriced Values: Decisions Without Market Prices. J. A. Sinden & Albert C. Worrell. LC 78-24183. 1979. 32.50 (ISBN 0-471-02742-1, Pub. by Wiley-Interscience). Wiley.
Unprovability of Consistency. G. Boolos. LC 77-85710. (Illus.). 1979. 26.95 (ISBN 0-521-21879-9). Cambridge U Pr.
Unpublished Coins of the Medieval Kingdom of Cyprus. Paul Lambros. Tr. by Michael Toumazou from Gr. (Illus.). 170p. (Eng., Fr., Gr.). 20.00 (ISBN 0-916710-76-9). Obol Intl.
Unpublished Plays of Thomas Holley Chivers. Thomas H. Chivers. LC 79-29747. 51.00x (ISBN 0-8201-1350-6). Schol Facsimiles.
Unpublished Writings of Edward Taylor, 3 vols. Thomas M. Davis & Virginia L. Davis. (American Literary Manuscripts Ser.). 1981. Set. lib. bdg. 90.00 (ISBN 0-8057-9655-X). Twayne.
Unquiet Landscape. Ed. by Denys Brunsden et al. LC 77-15583. (Geographical Magazine Ser.). 1978. Repr. of 1972 ed. 17.95 (ISBN 0-470-99345-6). Halsted Pr.
Unraveling the Special Education Maze: An Action Guide for Parents. Barbara C. Cutler. LC 80-54006. 260p. (Orig.). 1981. pap. text ed. 7.95 (ISBN 0-87822-224-3, 2243). Res Press.
Unraveling Zen's Red Thread: Ikkyu's Controversial Way. Jon Carter Covell & Abbot S. Yamada. LC 80-81040. (Illus.). 341p. 1980. 18.50 (ISBN 0-930878-19-1). Hollym Intl.
Unreachable Child: An Introduction to Early Childhood Autism. Sam B. Morgan. 208p. 1981. text ed. 15.95 (ISBN 0-87870-202-4); pap. text ed. 7.95 (ISBN 0-87870-201-6). Memphis St Univ.
Unreached Peoples, Eighty-One. C. Peter Wagner & Edward R. Dayton. (Orig.). 1981. pap. 8.95 (ISBN 0-89191-331-9). Cook.
Unreal Estate. Brian Swann. 48p. 1981. 25.00 (ISBN 0-915124-39-4, Bookslinger); pap. 6.00 (ISBN 0-915124-40-8). Toothpaste.
Unreal Past & Other Poems. K. R. Narayanaswamy. 6.75 (ISBN 0-89253-710-8); flexible cloth 3.00 (ISBN 0-89253-711-6). Ind-US Inc.
Unreal Reality: The Cinema of Harry Kumel. David Soren. LC 78-71774. (Illus.). 1979. pap. text ed. 9.50x (ISBN 0-87543-145-3). Lucas.
Unreasonable Summer. Dixie Browning. 192p. (Orig.). 1980. pap. 1.50 (ISBN 0-671-57012-9). S&S.
Unreliable Memoirs. Clive James. LC 80-24245. 176p. 1981. 10.00 (ISBN 0-394-51263-4). Knopf.
Unresponsive Bystander: Why Doesn't He Help? Bibb Latane & John M. Darley. LC 79-123548. (Psychology Ser). (Orig.). 1970. 10.95 (ISBN 0-13-938613-0). P-H.
Unromantic Agony: An Exhibition. Intro. by Dominique De Menil. (Illus.). 1965. pap. 2.50 (ISBN 0-914412-26-4). Inst for the Arts.
Unruly School: Disorders, Disruptions, & Crimes. Robert J. Rubel. LC 77-3837. (Illus.). 1977. 19.95 (ISBN 0-669-01668-3). Lexington Bks.
Unsafe As Houses: A Guide to Home Safety. Nei Ewart. (Illus.). 160p. 1981. 12.50 (ISBN 0-7137-1090-X, Pub. by Blandford Pr England). Sterling.
Unsaturated & Polyunsaturated Fatty Acid in Health & Disease. James F. Mead & Armand J. Fulco. (American Lectures in Living Chemistry Ser.). (Illus.). 208p. 1976. 22.75 (ISBN 0-398-03413-3). C C Thomas.
Unsaturated Fatty Acids in Atherosclerosis. 2nd ed. J. Enselme. 1969. 36.00 (ISBN 0-08-013060-7). Pergamon.
Unsearchable Wisdom of God: A Study of Providence in Richardson's Pamela. James L. Fortuna, Jr. LC 80-14919. (University of Florida Humanities Monograph: No. 49). vii, 130p. 1980. pap. 5.50 (ISBN 0-8130-0676-7). U Presses Fla.
Unseen Bird. S. C. Saha. 6.75 (ISBN 0-89253-727-2); flexible cloth 4.00 (ISBN 0-89253-728-0). Ind-US Inc.
Unseen Hand & Other Plays. Sam Shepard. LC 80-27628. 1981. 15.00 (ISBN 0-89396-040-3); pap. 7.95 (ISBN 0-89396-041-1). Urizen Bks.
Unsex'd Females: A Poem. Richard Polwhele. Ed. by Gina Luria. Bd. with Female Advocate; or, an Attempt to Recover the Rights of Women from Male Usurpation. Mary Ann Radcliffe. (Feminist Controversy in England, 1788-1810 Ser.). 1974. lib. bdg. 50.00 (ISBN 0-8240-0875-8). Garland Pub.
Unsolved Mysteries of the Past. Erich Daniken. 189p. 1981. 28.50 (ISBN 0-686-68311-0). Porter.
Unsolved Mysteries...with Sherlock Holmes & Dr. Watson. Judith Conaway. (gr. 7-9). 1976. 135.00 (ISBN 0-89290-113-6, CM-37). Soc for Visual.
Unsolved Problems of Co- & Graft Polymerization. O. Vogl & C. I. Simionescu. (Journal of Polymer Science Ser.: Polymer Symposium No. 64). 373p. 1979. 29.95 (ISBN 0-471-05696-0). Wiley.
Unsoundness of Mind in Relation to Criminal Acts. John C. Bucknill. Bd. with Care of the Insane & Their Legal Control; Factors of the Unsound Mind. W. A. Guy. (Contributions to the History of Psychology Ser., Vol. IV Pt. F: Insanity & Jurisprudence). 1980. Repr. of 1854 ed. 30.00 (ISBN 0-89093-329-4). U Pubns Amer.
Unspeakable Skipton. Pamela H. Johnson. 249p. 1981. 10.95 (ISBN 0-684-16336-5, ScribT). Scribner.
Unspiked Rail: Memoir of a Nevada Rebel. Sally S. Zanjani. LC 80-39920. (Lancehead Ser.). (Illus.). xv, 357p. 1981. price not set (ISBN 0-87417-064-8). U of Nev Pr.
Unspoken Dialogue: An Introduction to Nonverbal Communication. Judee K. Burgoon & Thomas Saine. (Illus., LC 77-078913). 1978. text ed. 13.95 (ISBN 0-395-25792-1); inst. manual 0.75 (ISBN 0-395-25793-X). HM.
Unspoken Motive: A Guide to Psychoanalytic Literary Criticism. Morton Kaplan & Robert Kloss. LC 79-163609. 1973. 10.00 o.s.i. (ISBN 0-02-916950-X). Free Pr.
Unstable Angina: Recognition & Management. Ed. by Allen G. Adelman & Bernard S. Goldman. LC 80-13211. 1980. 29.50 (ISBN 0-88416-271-0). PSG Pub.
Unstilled Voices. James Hefley & Marti Hefley. LC 80-70116. 224p. 1981. 8.95 (ISBN 0-915684-85-3). Christian Herald.
Unstress Yourself. Stuart Litvak. LC 79-89639. 172p. (Orig.). 1980. pap. 4.95 (ISBN 0-686-64397-6). Ross-Erikson.
Unstress Yourself! Stuart B. Litvak. (gr. 9 up). 1979. pap. 4.95x (ISBN 0-686-24982-8, Pub. by Mainstream). Ross-Erikson.
Unsuccessful Do-It-Yourselfer. Deryl Dunn. LC 80-51917. (Successful Ser.). (Illus.). 112p. 1980. pap. 3.95 (ISBN 0-89999-011-8). Structures Pub.
Unsuitable Job for a Woman. P. D. James. 288p. 1975. pap. 2.25 (ISBN 0-445-00297-2). Popular Lib.
Unsuitable Job for a Woman. P. D. James. 1980. lib. bdg. 13.95 (ISBN 0-8161-6788-5, Large Print Bks). G K Hall.
Unsung Heroes of Pro Basketball. Ray Hill. (Illus.). (gr. 5 up). 1973. 2.50 o.p. (ISBN 0-394-82415-6, BYR); PLB 3.69 (ISBN 0-394-92415-0). Random.
Unsung Heroes of the Major Leagues. Art Berke. LC 75-34909. (Illus.). 160p. (gr. 5 up). 1976. PLB 3.69 (ISBN 0-394-93096-7, BYR). Random.
Unsuspected. large type ed. Charlotte Armstrong. pap. 0.95 o.p. (ISBN 0-425-03070-9). Berkley Pub.
Unsuspected Eloquence: A History of the Relations Between Poetry & Music. James A. Winn. LC 80-27055. 384p. 1981. 18.95x (ISBN 0-300-02615-3). Yale U Pr.
Unsuspected Isle. Rebecca Rosse. (Orig.). 1980. pap. 1.95 (ISBN 0-532-23323-9). Manor Bks.
Untamed. Anne Crompton. 256p. (Orig.). 1981. pap. 2.50 (ISBN 0-523-41151-0). Pinnacle Bks.
Untamed Breed. Gordon D. Shirreffs. 352p. 1981. pap. 2.75 (ISBN 0-449-14387-2, GM). Fawcett.
Untamed Heart. Alexis Hill. 416p. (Orig.). 1980. pap. 2.75 (ISBN 0-515-04863-1). Jove Pubns.
Untapped Profits by Professionals in the Small Business Field. Luanna C. Blagrove. (Illus.). 169p. 1980. 29.95 (ISBN 0-9604466-2-1). Blagrove Pubns.
Untapped Resources of Aging People. Burgess Gordon. 1980. 5.50 (ISBN 0-682-49599-9). Exposition.
Untapped Sources & Research Opportunities in the Field of American Maritime History: A Symposium. 1968. pap. 3.00 o.p. (ISBN 0-913372-19-6). Mystic Seaport.
Unteraneid & Treuvorbehalt in Frankreich & England. Walther Kienast. LC 80-2022. 1981. Repr. of 1952 ed. 31.00 (ISBN 0-404-18572-X). AMS Pr.
Untersuchungen Zu Den Prosaschriften Henry Vaughans. Gunther Wiese. (Salburg Studies in English Literature, Elizabethan & Renaissance: No. 72). 1978. pap. text ed. 25.00x (ISBN 0-391-01568-0). Humanities.
Untersuchungen zu Gorgias' Schrift Ueber das Nichtseiende. Hans-Joachim Newiger. 1973. 44.75x (ISBN 3-11-003432-8). De Gruyter.
Untersuchungen Zur Genetik Des Fortpflanzungsverhaltens und der Fruchtkoerper- und Antibiotikabbildung Des Basidiomyceten Agrocybe Aegerita. F. Meinhardt. (Bibliotheca Mycologica: No. 75). (Illus.). 128p. (Ger.). 1981. pap. text ed. 20.00x (ISBN 3-7682-1275-0). Lubrecht & Cramer.
Unterwegs. David Shotter. 1974. pap. text ed. 7.95x o.p. (ISBN 0-435-38839-8); tchr's ed. 6.25x o.p. (ISBN 0-435-38840-1); four tapes 80.00 o.p. (ISBN 0-435-38841-X). Heinemann Ed.
Untie the Winds. Jean Clark. LC 75-31595. 340p. 1976. 9.95 o.s.i. (ISBN 0-02-525780-3, 52578). Macmillan.
Until My Last Breath. Francis M. Seeger. 1981. 5.95 (ISBN 0-932194-06-0). Green Hill.
Until the Colors Fade. Tim Jeal. 1976. 10.00 o.s.i. (ISBN 0-440-09299-X). Delacorte.
Until the Jaguar Sings. Tina Green. (YA) 1977. 4.95 o.p. (ISBN 0-685-71792-5, Avalon). Bouregy.
Until the Sun Dies. Robert Jastrow. 1980. pap. 4.95 (ISBN 0-446-97348-3). Warner Bks.
Untitled Biography of Tip N'Neill. Paul R. Clancy. 1980. 10.95 (ISBN 0-02-525700-5). Macmillan.
Untitled, Red, Blue, 2 vols. Louise Lawler. LC 78-59796. (Illus.). 1978. Set. pap. text ed. 7.95 (ISBN 0-931706-00-9). Vol. 1 (ISBN 0-931706-01-7). Vol. 2 (ISBN 0-931706-02-5). L Lawler.
Unto All Nations: A Guide to the Book of Acts & the Writings of Paul. Robert J. Matthews. 59p. (Orig.). 1975. pap. 1.50 o.p. (ISBN 0-87747-601-2). Deseret Bk.
Untold Facts About the Small Business Game. Luanna C. Blagrove. (Illus.). 171p. (Orig.). 1980. 24.95 (ISBN 0-9604466-1-3); pap. 19.95 (ISBN 0-9604466-0-5). Blagrove Pubns.
Untold Story: The Life of Isadora Duncan 1921-1927. Mary Desti. (Dance Ser.). (Illus.). 281p. 1981. Repr. of 1929 ed. lib. bdg. 25.00 (ISBN 0-306-76044-4). Da Capo.
Untouchable. Mulk R. Anand. 181p. 1974. pap. 2.75 (ISBN 0-88253-280-4). Ind-US Inc.
Untouchable: An Indian Life History. James M. Freeman. LC 78-55319. (Illus.). 1979. 19.50x (ISBN 0-8047-1001-5); pap. 8.95 (ISBN 0-8047-1103-8, SP40). Stanford U Pr.
Untouchables of India. Dilip Hiro. (Minority Rights Group: No. 26). 1975. pap. 2.50 (ISBN 0-89192-112-5). Interbk Inc.
Unused Power: The Work of the Senate Committee on Appropriations. Stephen Horn. 1970. 11.95 (ISBN 0-8157-3730-0). Brookings.
Unusual Animals. Kathleen Daly. (Look-Look Ser.). (Illus.). 1977. PLB 5.38 (ISBN 0-307-61834-X, Golden Pr); pap. 0.95 (ISBN 0-307-11834-7). Western Pub.
Unusual-by-Mail Catalog. Print Project. (Illus.). 192p. 1980. 14.95 (ISBN 0-312-83374-1); pap. 7.95 (ISBN 0-312-83375-X). St Martin.
Unusual Child. Joseph S. Roucek. LC 62-9772. 1962. 6.00 o.p. (ISBN 0-8022-1398-7). Philos Lib.
Unusual Sexual Behavior: The Standard Deviations. David Lester. 256p. 1976. 22.75 (ISBN 0-398-03343-9). C C Thomas.
Unveiled Faces: Men & Women of the Bible. Sr. Mary C. Barron. (Illus.). 120p. 1981. pap. 4.50 (ISBN 0-8146-1212-1). Liturgical Pr.
Unveiling of Arabia: The Story of Arabian Travel & Discovery. R. H. Kiernan. (Illus.). 360p. 1981. Repr. of 1937 ed. 27.50x (ISBN 0-7146-1990-6, F Cass Co). Biblio Dist.
Unveiling of Love. Sheikh Muzaffer. Tr. by Muhtar Holland from Turk. 1981. 10.95 (ISBN 0-89281-023-8); pap. 8.95 (ISBN 0-89281-017-3). Inner Tradit.
Unvote for a New America. Theodore L. Becker et al. 1976. pap. 8.50x o.p. (ISBN 0-205-05720-9). Allyn.
Unwanted Adventure of Harold Greenhouse. Wilkins. (gr. 3-5). pap. 0.95 o.p. (ISBN 0-590-05410-4, Schol Pap). Schol Bk Serv.
Unwanted Boy: The Autobiography of Governor Ben W. Hooper. Ben W. Hooper. Ed. by Everett R. Boyce. LC 63-14135. (Illus.). 1963. 12.50x (ISBN 0-87049-044-3). U of Tenn Pr.
Unwanted Pregnancy & Counselling. Juliet Cheetham. 1978. pap. 8.95 (ISBN 0-7100-0044-8). Routledge & Kegan.
Unwed Mother. rev. ed. Gloria Miklowitz. (Easy to Read Edition Ser.). (gr. 4 up). 1981. pap. 1.95 (ISBN 0-448-17248-8, Tempo). G&D.
Unwed Mother. Ed. by Robert W. Roberts. LC 80-20554. (Readers in Social Problems). viii, 270p. 1980. Repr. of 1966 ed. lib. bdg. 25.00x (ISBN 0-313-22677-6, ROUM). Greenwood.
Unwelcome Immigrant: The American Image of the Chinese, 1785-1882. Stuart C. Miller. 1969. 17.50x (ISBN 0-520-01380-8); pap. 3.25 (ISBN 0-520-02620-9). U of Cal Pr.
Unwilling Bride. Marnie Ellington. (Orig.). 1980. pap. 1.50 (ISBN 0-440-19743-0). Dell.
Unwilling Urbanites: The Life of Canadian Indians in a Prairie City. James N. Kerri. LC 78-63272. 1978. pap. text ed. 9.25 (ISBN 0-8191-0622-4). U Pr of Amer.
Unwillingly to School. 2nd ed. J. H. Kahn & J. P. Nursten. 1964. 12.25 (ISBN 0-08-013304-5); pap. 6.50 (ISBN 0-08-013295-2). Pergamon.
Unwillingly to School: School Phobia or School Refusal - a Psycho-Social Problem. 3rd ed. Jack H. Kahn et al. 250p. 1980. 29.00 (ISBN 0-08-025229-X); pap. 12.00 (ISBN 0-08-025230-3). Pergamon.
Unwordly Wise. Wei Wu-Wei. 88p. 1981. 6.50 (ISBN 0-85656-103-7). Great Eastern.
Unwritten Alliance: Rio-Banco & Brazilian-American Relations. E. Bradford Burns. LC 65-25661. (Illus.). 1966. 20.00x (ISBN 0-231-02855-5). Columbia U Pr.
Unwritten Law in Albania. Margaret M. Hasluck. LC 79-1607. 1981. Repr. of 1954 ed. 23.50 (ISBN 0-88355-910-2). Hyperion Conn.
Unwritten Philosophy & Other Essays. Francis M. Cornford. Ed. by William K. Guthrie. 1967. 23.95 (ISBN 0-521-04727-7); pap. 7.95x (ISBN 0-521-09444-5). Cambridge U Pr.
Up a Road Slowly. Irene Hunt. 192p. (YA) (gr. 8-12). 1980. pap. 1.95 (ISBN 0-448-16496-5, Tempo). G&D.
Up a Tall Tree. Anne Rockwell. LC 79-7695. (Reading-on-My-Own Bks.). (Illus.). 64p. (gr. 2). 1981. 4.95a (ISBN 0-385-15556-5); PLB (ISBN 0-385-15557-3). Doubleday.
Up Against Apartheid: The Role & the Plight of the Press in South Africa. Richard Pollak. LC 80-22363. (Science & International Affairs Ser.). 160p. 1981. price not set (ISBN 0-8093-1013-9). S Ill U Pr.
Up Against It. Joe Orton. LC 79-52099. 1979. pap. 4.95 (ISBN 0-394-17475-5, E736, Ever). Grove.
Up Against the Clock: Career Women Speak on the Choice to Have Children. Marilyn Fabe & Norma Wikler. 1980. pap. 2.75 (ISBN 0-446-95536-1). Warner Bks.
Up Against the Corporate Wall: Modern Corporations & Social Issues of the 80's. 4th ed. S. Seth. 1981. pap. 11.95 (ISBN 0-13-938308-5); 14.95 (ISBN 0-13-938316-6). P-H.
Up Against the Corporate Wall: Modern Corporations & Social Issues of the Seventies. 3rd ed. S. Prakash Sethi. (Illus.). 1977. pap. text ed. 12.95 (ISBN 0-13-938217-8). P-H.
Up Against the Wall, Mother: On Women's Liberation. Elsie Adams & Mary L. Briscoe. 1971. 8.95 (ISBN 0-02-470200-5, 47020). Macmillan.
Up & Down Book Starring Ernie & Bert. Street Sesame. (Tell-a-Tale Reader Ser.). (Illus.). (gr. k-3). PLB 4.77 (ISBN 0-307-68402-4, Golden Pr). Western Pub.
Up & Down California: The Journal of William H. Brewer. William H. Brewer. Ed. by Francis P. Farquhar. (California Library Reprint Ser: No. 59). (Illus.). 1974. 25.00x (ISBN 0-520-02803-1); pap. 5.95 (ISBN 0-520-02762-0). U of Cal Pr.
Up & Down on the Farm. James Riddell. (Illus.). 32p. (ps-4). 1981. 7.95 (ISBN 0-224-01709-8, Pub. by Chatto-Bodley-Jonathan). Merrimack Bk Serv.
Up & Down with Elvis Presley. Marge Crumbaker & Gabe Tucker. (Illus.). 320p. 1981. 12.95 (ISBN 0-399-12571-X). Putnam.
Up & Outer. Frederick Foster. 1980. pap. 4.95 (ISBN 0-8423-7799-9). Tyndale.
Up & Over. Doris B. Smith. 224p. (gr. 7 up). 1976. 7.92 (ISBN 0-688-22066-5); PLB 7.44 (ISBN 0-688-32066-X). Morrow.
Up Day, Down Day. Jacquie Hann. LC 77-15936. (Illus.). 32p. (gr. k-3). 1978. 6.95 (ISBN 0-590-07519-5, Four Winds). Schol Bk Serv.
Up for Grabs: Inquiries into Who Wants What. Daniel J. Chasan. LC 77-23881. 1977. 7.95 (ISBN 0-914842-18-8); pap. 4.95 (ISBN 0-914842-17-X). Madrona Pubs.
Up for Grabs: Inquiries into Who Wants What. Daniel Jack Chasen. (Illus.). 133p. 7.95 (ISBN 0-914842-18-8); pap. 4.95 (ISBN 0-914842-17-X). Madrona Pubs.
Up from Communism: Conservative Odysseys in American Intellectual History. John P. Diggins. LC 74-24505. (Illus.). 544p. 1975. 20.00 o.p. (ISBN 0-06-011042-2, HarpT). Har-Row.
Up from Grief: Patterns of Recovery. Bernadine Kreis & Alice Pattie. LC 69-13542. 1969. 6.95 (ISBN 0-8164-0198-5). Crossroad NY.
Up from Nigger. Dick Gregory. 1978. pap. 1.95 o.p. (ISBN 0-449-23416-9, Crest). Fawcett.
Up from Puerto Rico. Elena Padilla. LC 58-7171. 1958. 17.50x (ISBN 0-231-02213-1). Columbia U Pr.
Up from Seltzer. Peter Hockstein & Sandy Hoffman. LC 80-54617. (Illus.). 96p. 1981. pap. 3.95 (ISBN 0-89480-145-7). Workman Pub.
Up from Slavery. Booker T. Washington. LC 13-41242. 1933. 7.95 (ISBN 0-385-00003-0). Doubleday.

Up from the Depths. J. Warren Lowman. 183p. 1926. pap. 3.00 (ISBN 0-917714-28-8). Beinfeld Pub.

Up from the South: A Prospector in New Guinea, Nineteen Thirty-One to Nineteen Thirty-Seven. Jack O'Neill. Ed. by James Sinclair. (Illus.). 224p. 1979. text ed. 23.50x (ISBN 0-19-550567-0). Oxford U Pr.

Up from Underachievement. Gary S. Felton & Barbara E. Biggs. (Illus.). 208p. 1977. 14.75 (ISBN 0-398-03627-6); pap. 9.50 (ISBN 0-398-03639-X). C C Thomas.

Up Front with U. S. Day by Day in the Life of a Combat Infantryman in General Patton's Third Army. Walter L. Brown. LC 79-54035. (Illus.). 744p. 1979. 12.95x (ISBN 0-9604822-0-2); lib. bdg. write for info. (ISBN 0-9604822-0-2). Brown's Studio.

Up in a Balloon. Leonard Cottrell. LC 69-17423. (Illus.). (gr. 8 up). 1970. 10.95 (ISBN 0-87599-142-4). S G Phillips.

Up in the Air. Paul Picchiuti. (Hello World Ser.). 1967. pap. 1.65 (ISBN 0-8163-0305-3, 21620-0). Pacific Pr Pub Assn.

Up in the Clouds, Gentlemen Please. John Mills. LC 80-22002. (Illus.). 320p. 1981. 14.95 (ISBN 0-89919-024-3). Ticknor & Fields.

Up, Over, Under & Around: The New Explorers. Elaine Israel. LC 80-19618. (Illus.). 96p. (gr. 4 up). 1980. PLB 7.79 (ISBN 0-671-34002-6). Messner.

Up Sails. Mike Neigoff. LC 66-16080. (Pilot Book Ser). (Illus.). (gr. 3-5). 1966. 6.95g (ISBN 0-8075-8331-6). A Whitman.

Up the Alley with Jack & Joe. William Kotzwinkle. LC 74-2127. (Ready-to-Read Ser.). (Illus.). 64p. (gr. 1-3). 1974. 7.95g (ISBN 0-02-750940-0). Macmillan.

Up the Cockneys! Elizabeth Ring. 1974. 9.95 (ISBN 0-236-31081-X, Pub. by Paul Elek). Merrimack Bk Serv.

Up the Country. Emily Eden. 1980. Repr. 18.00x (ISBN 0-8364-0660-5, Pub. by Curzon Pr). South Asia Bks.

Up the Down Elevator. Norma Farber. LC 79-13199. (Illus.). (ps-3). 1979. 7.95 (ISBN 0-201-01924-8, 1924, A-W Childrens). A-W.

Up the Down Staircase. Bel Kaufman. 1972. pap. 2.50 (ISBN 0-380-01598-6, 48421). Avon.

Up the Line. 4th ed. Robert Silverberg. (Del Rey Bks). 256p. 1978. pap. 2.50 (ISBN 0-345-29696-6). Ballantine.

Up the Organization. Robert Townsend. 240p. 1978. pap. 2.50 (ISBN 0-449-23368-5, Crest). Fawcett.

Up the Pier. Helen Cresswell. LC 79-178598. (Illus.). 128p. (gr. 5-7). 1972. 7.95 (ISBN 0-02-725490-9). Macmillan.

Up the Trail from Texas. J. Frank Dobie. (Landmark Ser, No. 60). (Illus.). (gr. 7-9). 1955. PLB 4.39 o.p. (ISBN 0-394-90360-9). Random.

Up to Jerusalem. Richard E. Bauerle & Frederick W. Kemper. 1979. pap. 5.50 (ISBN 0-570-03795-6, 12-2777). Concordia.

Up to the Front of the Line: The Black Man in the American Political System. Robert P. Turner. 1975. 12.95 (ISBN 0-8046-9097-9, Natl U). Kennikat.

Up, Up, & Away. Margaret Hillert. (Just Beginning-to-Read Ser.). (Illus.). 32p. (gr. 1-6). 1981. PLB 4.39 (ISBN 0-695-41541-7); pap. 1.50 (ISBN 0-695-31541-2). Follett.

Up, up, & Away: All About Balloons, Blimps, & Dirigibles. Leroy Hayman. LC 79-27824. (Illus.). 192p. (gr. 7-12). 1980. PLB 8.29 (ISBN 0-671-33001-2). Messner.

Up Where I Used to Live. Max Schott. LC 78-11619. (Illinois Short Fiction Ser.). 1978. 10.00 (ISBN 0-252-00719-0); pap. 3.95 (ISBN 0-252-00720-4). U of Ill Pr.

Up with Jesus. Dick Eastman. 1971. pap. 0.95 (ISBN 0-8010-3327-6). Baker Bk.

Up Your Accountability: How to up Your Serviceability & Funding Credibility by Upping Your Accounting Ability. Paul Bennett. LC 73-89364. (Nonprofit-Ability Ser.). (Illus.). 1973. pap. 9.95 (ISBN 0-914756-02-8). Taft Corp.

Up Your Ante. Glen Chase. (Cherry Delight Ser.: No. 4). 1975. pap. 1.25 o.p. (ISBN 0-685-46896-8, LB4072K, Leisure Bks). Nordon Pubns.

Up Your Banners: A Novel. Donald Westlake. 1969. 16.95 (ISBN 0-02-626120-0). Macmillan.

Up Your Career. 3rd ed. Dean C. Dauw. (Illus.). 256p. 1980. pap. text ed. 8.95 (ISBN 0-917974-40-9). Waveland Pr.

Up Yours! Pierre Derriere. 1976. pap. 0.95 o.p. (ISBN 0-8439-0325-2, Leisure Bks). Nordon Pubns.

Upa Gurus. David G. Eberhart. 10.00 (ISBN 0-89253-679-9). Ind-US Inc.

Upanisads: The Selections from 108 Upanisads. T. M. P. Mahadevan. Tr. by T. M. P. Mahadevan from Sanskrit. 240p. (Orig.). 1975. pap. 3.20 (ISBN 0-88253-985-X). Ind-US Inc.

Upanishads, 2 vols. Tr. by F. Max Mueller. (Sacred Books of the East: Vols. 1, 15). 15.00x ea.; Vol. 1. (ISBN 0-8426-1437-0); Vol. 15. (ISBN 0-8426-1438-9). Verry.

Upanishads, 2 Vols. F. Max Muller. 1963. Repr. of 1890 ed. text ed. 5.00 ea. Vol. 1 (ISBN 0-486-20992-X) (ISBN 0-486-20993-8). Dover.

Upanishads, 4 Vols. Tr. by Swami Nikhilananda. LC 49-9558. Set. with notes 28.00 (ISBN 0-911206-14-0); 7.50 ea.; Vol. 1, 333p. (ISBN 0-911206-15-9); Vol. II, 400p. (ISBN 0-911206-16-7); Vol. III, 408p. (ISBN 0-911206-17-5); Vol. IV, 422p. (ISBN 0-911206-18-3). Ramakrishna.

Upanishads: Breath of the Eternal. Tr. by Swami Prabhavananda & Frederick Manchester. LC 48-5935. 6.95 (ISBN 0-87481-007-8). Vedanta Pr.

Upasaka Two & One. Buddhadharma. 1981. pap. 1.50 (ISBN 0-87881-078-1). Mojave Bks.

Upbuilders. Lincoln Steffens. LC 68-19419. (Americana Library Ser: No. 6). (Illus.). 373p. 1968. 10.50 (ISBN 0-295-73991-6, AL6); pap. 2.95 (ISBN 0-295-95036-6). U of Wash Pr.

Update -- Arab Emirates. Alison R. Lanier. (Country Orientation Ser.). 1980. pap. text ed. 25.00 (ISBN 0-933662-42-4). Intercult Network.

Update -- Bahrain-Qatar. Alison R. Lanier. (Country Orientation Ser.). 1980. pap. text ed. 25.00 (ISBN 0-933662-44-0). Intercult Network.

Update -- Belgium. Alison R. Lanier. (Country Orientation Ser.). 1980. pap. text ed. 25.00 (ISBN 0-933662-28-9). Intercult Network.

Update -- Brazil. Alison R. Lanier. (Country Orientation Ser.). 1980. pap. text ed. 25.00 (ISBN 0-933662-36-X). Intercult Network.

Update -- Britain. Alison R. Lanier. (Country Orientation Ser.). 1980. pap. text ed. 25.00 (ISBN 0-933662-35-1). Intercult Network.

Update -- Egypt. Alison R. Lanier. (Country Orientation Ser.). 1980. pap. text ed. 25.00 (ISBN 0-933662-32-7). Intercult Network.

Update -- France. Alison R. Lanier. (Country Orientation Ser.). 1980. pap. text ed. 25.00 (ISBN 0-933662-41-6). Intercult Pr.

Update -- Germany. Alison R. Lanier. (Country Orientation Ser.). 1980. pap. text ed. 25.00 (ISBN 0-933662-40-8). Intercult Network.

Update -- Hong Kong. Alison R. Lanier. (Country Orientation Ser.). 1980. pap. 25.00 (ISBN 0-933662-38-6). Intercult Pr.

Update -- Indonesia. Alison R. Lanier. (Counry Orientation Ser.). 1980. pap. text ed. 25.00 (ISBN 0-933662-37-8). Intercult Network.

Update -- Japan. Alison R. Lanier. (Country Orientation Ser.). 1980. pap. text ed. 25.00 (ISBN 0-933662-39-4). Intercult Network.

Update -- Kuwait. Alison R. Lanier. (Country Orientation Ser.). 1980. pap. text ed. 25.00 (ISBN 0-933662-29-7). Intercult Network.

Update -- Mexico. Alison R. Lanier. (Country Orientation Ser.). 150p. (Orig.). 1980. pap. text ed. 25.00 (ISBN 0-933662-25-4). Intercult Pr.

Update -- Nigeria. Alison R. Lanier. (Country Orientation Ser.). 1980. pap. text ed. 25.00 (ISBN 0-933662-27-0). Intercult Network.

Update -- Saudi Arabia. Alison R. Lanier. (Country Orientation Ser.). 150p. 1980. pap. text ed. 25.00 (ISBN 0-933662-26-2). Intercult Network.

Update -- Singapore. Alison R. Lanier. (Country Orientation Ser.). 1980. pap. text ed. 25.00 (ISBN 0-686-28735-5). Intercult Network.

Update -- South Korea. Alison R. Lanier. (Country Orientation Ser.). 1980. pap. text ed. 25.00 (ISBN 0-933662-33-5). Intercult Network.

Update -- Taiwan. Alison Lanier. (Country Orientation Ser.). 1980. pap. text ed. 25.00 (ISBN 0-933662-30-0). Intercult Network.

Update -- Venezuela. Alison R. Lanier. (Country Orientation Ser.). 1980. pap. text ed. 25.00 (ISBN 0-686-28736-3). Intercult Network.

Update IV: The Heart. J. Willis Hurst. (Updates Ser.). (Illus.). 224p. 1980. text ed. 30.00 (ISBN 0-07-031493-4, HP). McGraw.

Update on Space, Vol. 1. Ed. by B. J. Bluth & S. R. McNeal. (Illus., Orig.). 1981. pap. 7.95 (ISBN 0-937654-00-0). Natl Behavior.

Update: Peoples Republic of China. Alison R. Lanier. Ed. by Margaret D. Pusch. (Country Orientation Ser.). 150p. (Orig.). 1980. pap. 25.00 (ISBN 0-933662-44-0). Intercult Pr.

Update 1980. Ed. by Arleen Kaylin & Laurie Barnett. LC 80-21499. (The Great Contemporary Issues Ser.: Group Ii). (Illus.). 320p. 1980. 35.00 (ISBN 0-405-13781-8). Arno.

Upgrade Your Italian: A Review Grammar. Gifford Orwen. 1977. pap. 7.75 (ISBN 0-913298-12-3). S F Vanni.

Upgrading Coal Liquids. Ed. by Richard F. Sullivan. (ACS Symposium Ser.: No. 156). 1981. price not set (ISBN 0-8412-0629-5). Am Chemical.

Upgrading Lecture Rooms. Peter H. Smith. (Illus.). 1979. 38.90x (ISBN 0-85334-849-9, Pub. by Applied Science). Burgess-Intl Ideas.

Upgrading Residues & by-Products for Animals. J. T. Huber. 160p. 1981. 44.95 (ISBN 0-8493-5445-5). CRC Pr.

Upgrading Thermoplastics P-056: Materials, Economics. 1981. 950.00 (ISBN 0-89336-256-5). BCC.

Upgrading Water Treatment Plants to Improve Water Quality. American Water Works Association. (Handbooks-Proceedings). (Illus.). 132p. 1980. pap. text ed. 10.50 (ISBN 0-89867-245-7). Am Water Wks Assn.

Upholstering. James Brumbaugh. LC 72-83060. (Illus.). 400p. 1972. 9.95 (ISBN 0-672-23189-1). Audel.

Upholstering. Malcolm Flitman. LC 77-72396. 1977. pap. 4.95 o.p. (ISBN 0-8069-8756-1). Sterling.

Upholstering Methods. Fred W. Zimmernman. LC 80-25308. (Illus.). 196p. 1981. text ed. 12.00 (ISBN 0-87006-313-8). Goodheart.

Upjohn's Rural Architecture. Richard Upjohn. LC 74-16022. (Architecture & Decorative Art Ser). (Illus.). 14p. 1975. Repr. of 1852 ed. lib. bdg. 39.50 (ISBN 0-306-70639-3). Da Capo.

Upland Britain. R. Millward & A. Robinson. LC 79-56047. (Illus.). 192p. 1980. 25.00 (ISBN 0-7153-7823-6). David & Charles.

Upland Game Hunter's Bible. Dan Holland. LC 61-7604. pap. 3.50 o.p. (ISBN 0-385-01171-7). Doubleday.

Uplift: What People Themselves Can Do. Washington Consulting Group. LC 74-81131. (Illus.). 484p. 1974. pap. 7.95 o.p. (ISBN 0-913420-38-7). Olympus Pub Co.

Upon a Penny Loaf: The Wisdom of John Bunyan. John Bunyan. Compiled by Roger C. Palms. LC 78-12239. 1978. pap. 3.50 (ISBN 0-87123-573-0, 210573). Bethany Fell.

Upon the Objectives to Be Attained by the Establishment of a Public Library: Report of the Trustees of the Public Library of the City of Boston, 1852. Repr. 3.50. Boston Public Lib.

Upon the Objects to Be Attained by the Establishment of a Public Library: Report of the Trustees of the Public Library of the City of Boston. 1852. Repr. 3.50. Boston Public Lib.

Upon the Sweeping Flood. Joyce C. Oates. LC 66-16632. 10.95 (ISBN 0-8149-0172-7). Vanguard.

Upon the Willows & Other Stories. Rowena Tiemp-Torrevillas. 192p. 1980. pap. 5.75x (ISBN 0-686-28650-2). Cellar.

Upper Atmosphere & Magnetosphere. Geophysics Study Committee. 1977. pap. 10.00 (ISBN 0-309-02633-4). Natl Acad Pr.

Upper Cretaceous Belemnites from the Kristianstad Area. Walter K. Christensen. (Fossils & Strata: No. 7). 1975. pap. text ed. 15.00x (ISBN 8-200-09374-3, Dist. by Columbia U Pr). Universitet.

Upper Extremities Orthotics. Miles H. Anderson. (Illus.). 476p. 1979. 34.50 (ISBN 0-398-00044-1). C C Thomas.

Upper Limb on Tetraplegia. Moberg. 1979. 18.00. Thieme Stratton.

Upper Palaeolithic of Britain: A Study of Man & Nature in the Late Ice Age, Vols. I & II. John B. Campbell. (Illus.). 1978. 79.00 set (ISBN 0-19-813188-7). Oxford U Pr.

Upper Room. J. C. Ryle. 1977. 11.95 (ISBN 0-85151-017-5). Banner of Truth.

Upper Room Disciplines 1981. (Orig.). 1980. pap. 3.25x (ISBN 0-8358-0391-0). Upper Room.

Upper Secondary School. L. Spolton. 1967. 25.00 (ISBN 0-08-012497-6); pap. 13.75 (ISBN 0-08-012496-8). Pergamon.

Uprooted: The Appelberg Collection. Ed. by Harriet Feiner. LC 77-85136. 1977. pap. text ed. 3.50 o.p. (ISBN 0-87868-169-8). Child Welfare.

Uprooting & Development--Dilemmas of Coping with Modernization. Ed. by George V. Coelho et al. (Current Topics in Mental Health Ser.). 500p. 1980. 27.50 (ISBN 0-306-40509-1, Plenum Pr). Plenum Pub.

Uprooting & Social Change: The Role of Refugees in Development. Stephen L. Keller. LC 75-900452. 1975. 15.00x o.p. (ISBN 0-88386-586-6). South Asia Bks.

Ups & Downs of Jone Jenkins. Betty Bates. 1981. pap. 1.75 (ISBN 0-671-29950-6). Archway.

Upside & Down. Robert B. Ruddell et al. (Pathfinder - Allyn & Bacon Reading Program: Level 9). (gr. 1). 1978. text ed. 6.92 (ISBN 0-205-05114-6, 5451140); tchr's ed. 10.88 (ISBN 0-205-05129-4, 5451299). Allyn.

Upside Down & Inside Out: Poems for All Your Pockets. Bobbi Katz. LC 76-182294. (Illus.). 48p. (gr. 1-4). 1973. PLB 4.90 o.p. (ISBN 0-531-02621-3). Watts.

Upside-Down Cat. Elizabeth Parsons. LC 80-13507. (Illus.). 48p. (gr. 3-6). 1981. 9.95 (ISBN 0-689-50187-0, McElderry Bk). Atheneum.

Upside Down Creatures. Susan Harris. (Easy-Read Wildlife Books Ser.). (Illus.). (gr. 2-4). 1978. PLB 6.45 s&l (ISBN 0-531-02918-2). Watts.

Upstairs at the White House. J. B. West & Mary L. Kotz. (Illus.). 416p. 1974. pap. 2.95 (ISBN 0-446-93953-6). Warner Bks.

Upstart. Piers Paul Read. 352p. 1979. pap. 2.25 (ISBN 0-380-49023-4, 49023). Avon.

Upstate. Dugan Gilman. LC 79-142724. (Wesleyan Poetry Program: Vol. 55). 1971. 10.00x (ISBN 0-8195-2055-1, Pub. by Wesleyan U Pr); pap. 4.95 (ISBN 0-8195-1055-6). Columbia U Pr.

Upstate New York. Bradford B. Van Diver. (Geology Field Guide Ser.). (Illus.). 288p. 1980. pap. text ed. 10.95 (ISBN 0-8403-2214-3). Kendall-Hunt.

Upstream Christian in a Downstream World. Charles Dunn. 1979. pap. 3.50 (ISBN 0-88207-789-9). Victor Bks.

Uptake & Storage of Noradrenaline in Sympathic Nerves. Leslie L. Iversen. 1967. 35.50 (ISBN 0-521-05390-0). Cambridge U Pr.

Upton Sinclair. William Bloodworth, Jr. (United States Authors Ser.: No. 294). 1977. lib. bdg. 10.95 (ISBN 0-8057-7197-2). Twayne.

Upton Sinclair. Jon A. Yoder. LC 74-78450. (Modern Literature Ser.). 160p. 1975. 10.95 (ISBN 0-8044-2989-8). Ungar.

Uptown & Downtown. Fischler. pap. 6.50 (ISBN 0-8015-8196-6, Hawthorn). Dutton.

Upward Reach. Sterling W. Sill. LC 80-83863. 350p. 1980. 8.50 (ISBN 0-88290-167-2, 1060). Horizon Utah.

Ur-Drama: The Origins of Theatre. E. T. Kirby. LC 74-32656. 164p. 1975. 15.00x (ISBN 0-8147-4559-8); pap. 7.00x (ISBN 0-8147-4573-3). NYU Pr.

Urania: A Choice Collection of Psalm-Tunes, Anthems & Hymns. James Lyon. LC 69-11667. (Music Reprint Ser.). 198p. 1974. Repr. of 1761 ed. lib. bdg. 27.50 (ISBN 0-306-71198-2). Da Capo.

Uranium & Nuclear Energy. Mining Journal Books Ltd. 326p. 1980. 36.00x (ISBN 0-900117-20-6, Pub. by Mining Journal England). State Mutual Bk.

Uranium: Balance of Supply & Demand Nineteen Seventy Eight to Nineteen Ninety. Mining Journal Books Ltd. 60p. 1980. 20.00x1311 (ISBN 0-900117-19-2, Pub. by Mining Journal England). State Mutual Bk.

Uranium Deposits in Africa: Geology & Exploration. (Proceedings Ser.). 262p. 1980. pap. 33.00 (ISBN 92-0-041079-0, ISP 509, IAEA). Unipub.

Uranium Deposits of Arizona, California & Nevada. 1978. 40.30. Minobras.

Uranium Deposits of the Northern U. S. Region. 1977. 37.10. Minobras.

Uranium: Economic & Political Instability in a Strategic Commodity Market. Marian Radetzki. 1981. 30.00 (ISBN 0-312-83424-1). St Martin.

Uranium Enrichment & Public Policy. Thomas G. Moore. 1978. pap. 4.25 (ISBN 0-8447-3286-9). Am Enterprise.

Uranium Evaluation & Mining Techniques. 550p. 1981. pap. 69.50 (ISBN 92-0-040280-1, ISP 524, IAEA). Unipub.

Uranium Exploration Geology. (Illus., Orig.). 1971. pap. 25.25 (ISBN 92-0-041070-7, ISP 277, IAEA). Unipub.

Uranium Exploration Methods. (Illus.). 320p. (Orig.). 1974. pap. 29.00 (ISBN 92-0-041073-1, ISP 334, IAEA). Unipub.

Uranium Geology & Mines, South Texas. D. H. Eargle et al. (Illus.). 59p. 1971. 1.75 (GB 12). Bur Econ Geology.

Uranium Guidebook for Wyoming. 1976. xerox copy 40.00. Minobras.

Uranium in the Pine Creek Geosyncline: Proceedings. (Illus.). 759p. 1980. pap. 93.75 (ISBN 92-0-140080-2, ISP-555, IAEA). Unipub.

Uranium, Nonproliferation & Energy Security. Steven J. Warnecke. (Atlantic Papers Ser.: No. 37). 121p. 1980. write for info. 0.00 (ISBN 0-916672-77-8). Allanheld.

Uranium Ore Processing. (Panel Proceedings Ser). (Illus.). 1977. pap. 26.75 (ISBN 92-0-041176-2, ISP 453, IAEA). Unipub.

Uranium Production Technology. Charles D. Harrington. 584p. 1959. 27.50 (ISBN 0-442-03154-8, Pub. by Van Nos Reinhold). Krieger.

Uranium Resources of the Central & Southern Rockies. 1979. 33.80. Minobras.

Uranium Two Thirty-Four. V. V. Cherdyntsev. LC 73-184432. 1972. 23.95 o.p. (ISBN 0-470-15210-9). Halsted Pr.

Urashima Taro. Robert B. Goodman & Robert A. Spicer. Ed. by Ruth Tabrah. LC 73-79570. (Illus.). (gr. 1-7). 1973. 5.95 (ISBN 0-89610-013-8). Island Her.

Urashima, the Fisherman. (MacDonald Educational Ser.). (Illus., Arabic.). 3.50 (ISBN 0-686-53086-1). Intl Bk Ctr.

Urban Affair. Daniel Stern. 1980. 12.95 (ISBN 0-671-41226-4). S&S.

Urban Air Pollution Modeling. Michael M. Benarie. (Illus.). 1980. text ed. 45.00x (ISBN 0-262-02140-4). MIT Pr.

Urban America & Public Policies. 2nd ed. Marian L. Palley & Howard A. Palley. 336p. 1981. pap. text ed. 8.95 (ISBN 0-669-04004-5). Heath.

Urban America: From Downtown to No Town. David R. Goldfield & Blaine A. Brownell. LC 78-69562. (Illus.). 1979. pap. text ed. 11.50 (ISBN 0-395-27397-8). HM.

Urban America: The Policy Alternatives. David A. Caputo. LC 76-7351. (Illus.). 1976. text ed. 17.95x (ISBN 0-7167-0556-7); pap. text ed. 9.95x (ISBN 0-7167-0565-6). W H Freeman.

Urban American Indian. Alan L. Sorkin. LC 76-54459. (Illus.). 1978. 17.95 (ISBN 0-669-01296-3). Lexington Bks.

Urban Analysis. B. T. Robson. LC 68-25086. (Geographical Studies: No. 1). (Illus.). 1969. 47.50 (ISBN 0-521-07272-7); pap. 11.50 (ISBN 0-521-09989-7). Cambridge U Pr.

Urban Analysis for Branch Library System Planning. R. E. Coughlin et al. LC 71-133496. (Contributions in Librarianship & Information Science: No. 1). 1972. lib. bdg. 15.95 (ISBN 0-8371-5161-9, CLP/). Greenwood.

Urban & Regional Economics: A Guide to Information Sources. Ed. by Jean A. Shackelford. LC 74-11556. (Economics Information Guide Ser.: Vol. 14). 190p. 1980. 30.00 (ISBN 0-8103-1303-0). Gale.

Urban & Regional Economics: Structure & Change. M. Jarvin Emerson & F. Charles Lamphear. 375p. 1975. text ed. 15.95x o.p. (ISBN 0-205-04694-0). Allyn.

Urban & Regional Planning. J. Brian McLoughlin. (Orig.). 1978. pap. 9.95 (ISBN 0-571-09534-8, Pub. by Faber & Faber). Merrimack Bk Serv.

Urban & Regional Planning in an Age of Austerity. Ed. by Pierre Clavel & William W. Goldsmith. LC 79-21416. (Pergamon Policy Studies in Urban Affairs). 402p. 1980. 39.50 (ISBN 0-08-025539-6); pap. 7.50 (ISBN 0-08-025540-X). Pergamon.

Urban & Rural Development in Nigeria. H. I. Ajaegbu. 1976. text ed. 26.95 (ISBN 0-435-34030-1). Heinemann Ed.

Urban Anthropology: Cities in Their Cultural Setting. Richard G. Fox. (Illus.). 1977. pap. text ed. 9.95 (ISBN 0-13-939462-1). P-H.

Urban Areas, 4 pts. Incl. Pt. 1. Housing, 3 vols. Set. 234.00x (ISBN 0-686-01164-3); Pt. 2. Planning, 10 vols. Set. 819.00x (ISBN 0-686-01165-1); Pt. 3. Sanitation, 7 vols. Set. 630.00x (ISBN 0-686-01166-X); Pt. 4. Water Supply, 9 vols. Set. 810.00x (ISBN 0-686-01167-8). (British Parliamentary Papers Ser.). 1971 (Pub. by Irish Academic Pr Ireland). Biblio Dist.

Urban Atlanta: Redefining the Role of the City. Ed. by Andrew M. Hamer. LC 79-27699. (Research Monograph: No. 84). 256p. 1980. pap. 12.95 (ISBN 0-88406-125-6). Ga St U Busn Pub.

Urban Bosses, Machines, & Progressive Reformers. rev. ed. Bruce M. Stave & Sondra A. Stave. 178p. (Orig.). 1981. pap. 5.95 (ISBN 0-89874-119-X). Krieger.

Urban Business Profiles. LC 79-14909. (Small-Business Library: Vol. 1). 1979. 44.00 (ISBN 0-8103-1027-9). Gale.

Urban Capitalists: Entrepreneurs & City Growth in the Lackawanna & Lehigh Valleys, 1800-1920. Burton W. Folsom, Jr. LC 80-8864. (Studies in Industry & Society: No. 1). (Illus.). 208p. 1981. text ed. 16.50x (ISBN 0-8018-2520-2). Johns Hopkins.

Urban Challenge: Poverty & Race. Robert L. Green. 1978. pap. 7.95 o.p. (ISBN 0-695-81145-2). Follett.

Urban Change in China: Tsinan, Shantung, 1890-1949. David D. Buck. 1978. 21.50 (ISBN 0-299-07110-3). U of Wis Pr.

Urban Climate. Helmut Landsberg. (International Geophysics Ser.). 1981. write for info. (ISBN 0-12-435960-4). Acad Pr.

Urban Community: A Guide to Information Sources. Ed. by Anthony Filipovitch & Earl Reeves. LC 78-13171. (Urban Studies Information Guide Ser.: Vol. 4). 1978. 30.00 (ISBN 0-8103-1429-0). Gale.

Urban Costs of Climate Modification. Ed. by Terry A. Ferrar. LC 76-23288. (Environmental Science & Technology: a Wiley-Interscience Ser. of Texts & Monographs). 1976. 32.95 (ISBN 0-471-25767-2, Pub by Wiley-Interscience). Wiley.

Urban Crisis: A Symposium. J. V. Lindsay et al. LC 71-146555. (Symposia on Law & Society Ser). 1971. Repr. of 1969 ed. lib. bdg. 15.00 (ISBN 0-306-70115-4). Da Capo.

Urban Data Sources. J. R. Short. LC 79-42888. (Sources & Methods in Geography Ser.). 1980. pap. text ed. 7.50 (ISBN 0-408-10640-9). Butterworths.

Urban Decision Making...a Guide to Information Sources. Ed. by Mark Drucker. LC 80-19252. (Urban Studies Information Guide Ser. Part of the Gale Information Guide Library: Vol. 13). 200p. 1981. 30.00 (ISBN 0-8103-1481-9). Gale.

Urban Design: The Architecture of Towns & Cities. Paul D. Spreiregen. 1965. 29.50 o.p. (ISBN 0-07-060380-4, P&RB). McGraw.

Urban Development Action Grant Program: Papers & Conference Proceedings on Its First Two Years of Operation. Ed. by Richard P. Nathan & Jerry A. Webman. LC 80-84901. (Illus.). 124p. 1980. pap. 5.00 (ISBN 0-938882-00-7). PURRC.

Urban Development in Britain: Measurement of Consumer's Expenditure in the United Kingdom, 1920-38. P. A. Stone. Vol. 1. 42.00 (ISBN 0-521-06932-7); Vol. 2. 42.00 (ISBN 0-521-06558-5). Cambridge U Pr.

Urban Development in Modern China. Ed. by Laurence J. Ma & Edward W. Hanten. (Special Studies on China & East Asia). 250p. 1981. lib. bdg. 20.00x (ISBN 0-86531-120-X). Westview.

Urban Development in Nineteenth Century London: Lambeth, Battersea & Wandsworth 1838-1888. Janet Roebuck. (Illus.). 211p. 1979. 17.50x (ISBN 0-8476-3038-2). Rowman.

Urban Development in the Third World: Policy Guidelines. John D. Herbert. LC 78-19769. (Praeger Special Studies). 1979. 24.95 (ISBN 0-03-045731-9). Praeger.

Urban Development in the USA & Hungary. Ed. by Gyoergy Enyedi. (Illus.). 311p. 1978. 30.00x (ISBN 963-05-1514-8). Intl Pubns Serv.

Urban Development: The Process & the Problems. Wallace F. Smith. LC 74-79772. 320p. 1975. 20.00x (ISBN 0-520-02780-9); pap. 7.95x (ISBN 0-520-03956-4). U of Cal Pr.

Urban District Heating Using Nuclear Heat. (Panel Proceedings Ser). (Illus.). 1977. pap. text ed. 18.25 (ISBN 92-0-051077-9, IAEA). Unipub.

Urban Dynamics in Black Africa: An Interdisciplinary Approach. 2nd ed. Ed. by William J. Hanna & Judith L. Hanna. 1981. 15.95x (ISBN 0-202-24158-0). Aldine Pub.

Urban Ecology Through the Adaptive Use of Existing Buildings: A Selected Bibliography, Revising A-22 of Oct. 1978. George D. Hopkins, Jr. (Architecture Ser.: Bibliography a-281). 78p. 1980. pap. 8.50. Vance Biblios.

Urban Economics. W. H. Leahy et al. LC 75-88859. 1970. pap. text ed. 10.95 (ISBN 0-02-918280-8). Free Pr.

Urban Economics. Edwin S. Mills. 1972. 13.95x o.p. (ISBN 0-673-07716-0). Scott F.

Urban Economics. Richardson. 1978. 20.95 (ISBN 0-275-24430-X). Dryden Pr.

Urban Economics. David Segal. 1977. 18.95x (ISBN 0-256-00547-8). Irwin.

Urban Education: A Guide to Information Sources. Ed. by Donald W. Mocker & George E. Spear. LC 78-13627. (Urban Studies Information Guide Ser.: Vol. 3). 1978. 30.00 (ISBN 0-8103-1431-2). Gale.

Urban Education: An Annotated Bibliography. Arnold G. Parks. LC 80-69234. 135p. 1981. perfect bdg 9.50 (ISBN 0-86548-053-2). Century Twenty One.

Urban Education: Crisis or Opportunity. Sheldon Marcus & Philip D. Vairo. LC 72-5467. 1972. 10.00 (ISBN 0-8108-0531-6). Scarecrow.

Urban Education in America: Problems & Prospects. Raymond C. Hummel & John N. Nagle. (Illus.). 350p. 1973. 15.95 (ISBN 0-19-501656-4); pap. 5.95x (ISBN 0-19-501655-6). Oxford U Pr.

Urban Education in the 1970's: Reflections & a Look Ahead. Ed. by A. Harry Passow. LC 73-154693. 1971. text ed. 10.95x (ISBN 0-8077-1883-1); pap. 7.25x (ISBN 0-8077-1882-3). Tchrs Coll.

Urban Education: The City As a Living Curriculum. Ed. by Claude Mayberry, Jr. LC 80-67288. (Orig.). 1980. pap. text ed. 6.50 (ISBN 0-87120-100-3, 611-80206). Assn Supervision.

Urban Elderly: A Study of Life Satisfaction. Forrest J. Berghorn et al. LC 77-84407. 1978. text ed. 18.50x (ISBN 0-916672-98-0). Allanheld.

Urban Environment. Samuel E. Wallace. 1980. pap. 9.95 (ISBN 0-256-02218-6). Dorsey.

Urban Environmental Management: Planning for Pollution Control. Brian J. Berry & Frank E. Horton. (Illus.). 448p. 1974. 20.95 (ISBN 0-13-939611-X). P-H.

Urban Explosion. T. H. Elkins. (Studies in Contemporary Europe). 80p. (Orig.). 1973. pap. text ed. 2.75x (ISBN 0-333-12151-1). Humanities.

Urban Finance & Administration: A Guide to Information Sources. Ed. by Jerry McCaffery & John Mikesell. (Urban Studies Information Guide Ser.: Vol. 12). 200p. 1980. 30.00 (ISBN 0-8103-1464-9). Gale.

Urban Fiscal Stress: A Comparative Analysis of 66 U. S. Cities. James M. Howell & Charles F. Stamm. LC 79-3083. 176p. 1979. 19.95 (ISBN 0-669-03372-3). Lexington Bks.

Urban Forestry. Gene W. Grey & Frederick J. Deneke. LC 78-5275. 1978. text ed. 20.95 (ISBN 0-471-01515-6). Wiley.

Urban Future: A Choice Between Alternatives. John N. Jackson. (Urban & Regional Studies). 1972. text ed. 35.00x (ISBN 0-04-352034-0). Allen Unwin.

Urban Futures for Central Canada: Perspectives on Forecasting Urban Growth & Form. Ed. by L. S. Bourne et al. LC 73-92297. 1974. pap. 7.50x (ISBN 0-8020-6243-1). U of Toronto Pr.

Urban Futures Observed: In the Asian Third World. Richard L. Meier. LC 79-28624. (Pergamon Policy Studies on International Development). 256p. 1980. 29.50 (ISBN 0-08-025954-5). Pergamon.

Urban Geography. J. Beaujeu-Garnier & G. Chabot. (Geography for Advanced Study Ser.). 1967. 14.95 (ISBN 0-471-06115-8). Halsted Pr.

Urban Geography. 2nd ed. J. H. Johnson. 217p. 1973. text ed. 17.25 (ISBN 0-08-016927-9); pap. text ed. 7.00 (ISBN 0-08-016928-7). Pergamon.

Urban Governance & Minorities. Ed. by Herrington J. Bryce. LC 75-44875. (Illus.). 1976. text ed. 19.50 o.p. (ISBN 0-275-23500-9). Praeger.

Urban Government: Reader in Administration & Politics. 2nd ed. Ed. by Edward C. Banfield. LC 69-11169. 1969. text ed. 15.95 (ISBN 0-02-901690-8). Free Pr.

Urban Growth & City-Systems in the United States, 1840-1860. Allan Pred. LC 80-12098. (Studies in Urban History). 1980. text ed. 28.00x (ISBN 0-674-93091-6). Harvard U Pr.

Urban Growth & Land Development. Land Use Subcommittee. 1972. pap. 2.95 (ISBN 0-309-02044-1). Natl Acad Pr.

Urban Growth & Rural Stagnation: Studies in the Economy of an Indian Coalfield & Its Hinterland. Ed. by D. Rothermund et al. 1980. 36.00x (ISBN 0-8364-0662-1, Pub. by Manohar India). South Asia Bks.

Urban Growth Management Through Development Timing. David J. Brower et al. LC 75-19766. (Special Studies). 1976. text ed. 21.95 (ISBN 0-275-55530-5). Praeger.

Urban Guerilla: Studies on the Theory, Strategy & Practice of Political Violence in Modern Societies. Ed. by Johan Niezing. (Publications of the Polemological Centre of the Free University of Brussels: Vol. 4). 156p. 1974. pap. text ed. 17.75 (ISBN 90-237-6245-2, Pub. by Swets Pub Serv Holland). Swets North Am.

Urban Habitat: Past, Present & Future. Mary J. Huth. LC 77-7273. (Illus.). 1978. text ed. 17.95 (ISBN 0-88229-333-8). Nelson-Hall.

Urban Health Services: The Case of New York. Eli Ginzberg. LC 70-134987. 1970. 16.00x (ISBN 0-231-03515-2). Columbia U Pr.

Urban History: Reviews of Recent Research. Ed. by Patricia J. Rosof & William Zeisel. (Trends in History Ser.: Vol. 2, No. 1). 112p. 1980. write for info. (ISBN 0-917724-26-7). Haworth Pr.

Urban History Yearbook, 1978. Ed. by H. J. Dvos & H. J. Dyos. 255p. 1978. pap. 18.75x (ISBN 0-8476-3164-8). Rowman.

Urban History...a Guide to Information Sources. Ed. by John Buenker et al. LC 80-19643. (American Government & History Ser.,Part of the Gale Information Guide Library: Vol. 9). 400p. 1981. 30.00 (ISBN 0-8103-1479-7). Gale.

Urban Hydrological Modeling & Catchment Research: International Summary. (Technical Papers in Hydrology Ser.: No. 18). 48p. 1979. pap. 4.75 (ISBN 0-685-95367-X, U896, UNESCO). Unipub.

Urban Indicators: A Guide to Information Sources. Ed. by Thomas P. Murphy. LC 80-13333. (Urban Studies Information Guide Ser.: Vol. 10). 1980. 30.00 (ISBN 0-8103-1451-7). Gale.

Urban Inequality & Housing Policy in Tanzania: The Problem of Squatting. Richard E. Stren. LC 75-620118. (Research Ser.: No. 24). (Illus.). 128p. 1975. pap. 2.95x (ISBN 0-87725-124-X). U of Cal Intl St.

Urban Informal Sector in an Urban Economy: A Study in Ahmedabad. T. S. Papola. 156p. 1981. text ed. 15.95x (ISBN 0-7069-1133-4, Pub by Vikas India). Advent Bk.

Urban Information Thesaurus: A Vocabulary for Social Documentation. Ed. by Paul Rosenberg. LC 76-52604. 1977. lib. bdg. 27.50 (ISBN 0-8371-9483-0, UTH/). Greenwood.

Urban Institute Press. Laurie Stroblas. LC 79-20083. (Fun-to-Read Bk). (Illus.). (gr. 1-3). 1980. 6.95 (ISBN 0-688-41936-4); PLB 6.67 (ISBN 0-688-51936-9). Lothrop.

Urban Institutions & People of Indian Ancestry. Raymond Breton & Gail G. Akian. 52p. 1978. pap. text ed. 3.00x (ISBN 0-920380-14-X, Pub. by Inst Res Pub Canada). Renouf.

Urban Labor Market & Income Distribution in Peninsular Malaysia. Dipak Mazumdar. (World Bank Research Publications Ser.). (Illus.). 456p. 1981. 18.95 (ISBN 0-19-520213-9); pap. 7.95 (ISBN 0-19-520214-7). Oxford U Pr.

Urban Land Economics & Public Policy. Richard B. Andrews. LC 77-122281. 1971. 12.95 (ISBN 0-02-900710-0). Free Pr.

Urban Land Markets: Price Indices, Supply Measures, & Public Policy Effects. Ed. by J. Thomas Black & James E. Hoben. LC 80-53134. (ULI Research Report: No. 30). (Illus.). 238p. 1980. pap. 14.75 (ISBN 0-87420-593-X). Urban Land.

Urban Land Nexus & the State. A. J. Scott. 256p. 1980. 24.00 (ISBN 0-85086-079-2, 6390). Methuen Inc.

Urban Land Use Planning. 3rd ed. F. Stuart Chapin, Jr. & Edward J. Kaiser. LC 64-18666. (Illus.). 1979. 22.50 (ISBN 0-252-00580-5); wkbk 6.95 (ISBN 0-252-00791-3). U of Ill Pr.

Urban Land Use Planning in Hill Areas: A Case Study of Shillong. J. P. Singh. 192p. 1980. text ed. 18.00x (ISBN 0-391-02122-2). Humanities.

Urban Land Use Policy. Ed. by Richard B. Andrews. LC 70-169230. 1972. 15.95 (ISBN 0-02-900700-3). Free Pr.

Urban Landscapes: A New Jersey Portrait. George A. Tice. LC 75-30549. (Illus.). 112p. 1976. pap. 17.50 o.p. (ISBN 0-8135-0813-4). Rutgers U Pr.

Urban Law: A Guide to Information Sources. Ed. by Thomas P. Murphy & Robert D. Kline. (Urban Studies Information Guide Ser.: Vol. 11). 1980. 30.00 (ISBN 0-8103-1409-6). Gale.

Urban Life & Form. W. Z. Hirsch. 1963. 7.50 o.p. (ISBN 0-03-026525-8). HR&W.

Urban Life: The Sociology of Cities & Urban Society. Albert N. Cousins & Hans Nagpaul. LC 78-14427. 1979. text ed. 18.95 (ISBN 0-471-03026-0). Wiley.

Urban Management: A Guide to Information Sources. Ed. by Bernard H. Ross. LC 78-10310. (Urban Studies Information Guide Ser.: Vol. 8). 1979. 30.00 (ISBN 0-8103-1430-4). Gale.

Urban Modelling. M. Batty. (Cambridge Urban & Architectural Studies). (Illus.). 384p. 1976. 60.00 (ISBN 0-521-20881-5). Cambridge U Pr.

Urban Mosaic: Towards a Theory of Residential Differentiation. Duncan Timms. LC 70-123665. (Geographical Studies: No. 2). (Illus.). 1971. 39.50x (ISBN 0-521-07964-0); pap. 13.95x (ISBN 0-521-09988-9). Cambridge U Pr.

Urban Nation: Nineteen Twenty to Nineteen Eighty. George E. Mowry & Blaine E. Brownell. Ed. by David H. Donald. 1981. 12.50 (ISBN 0-8090-9541-6); pap. 5.95 (ISBN 0-8090-0148-9). Hill & Wang.

Urban Needs: A Bibliography & Directory for Community Resource Centers. Paula Kline. LC 78-9265. 1978. 13.50 (ISBN 0-8108-1148-0). Scarecrow.

Urban Neighborhood: A Sociological Perspective. Suzanne Keller. (Orig.). 1968. pap. text ed. 4.50 (ISBN 0-394-30773-9, RanC). Random.

Urban Nongrowth: City Planning for People. Earl Finkler et al. LC 75-23962. (Special Studies). 220p. 1976. text ed. 23.95 (ISBN 0-275-02230-7). Praeger.

Urban Open Spaces. Ed. by Lisa Taylor. (Illus.). 1981. pap. 9.95 (ISBN 0-8478-0304-X). Rizzoli Intl.

Urban Operations Research. R. Larson & A. Odoni. 1981. 32.00 (ISBN 0-13-939447-8). P-H.

Urban Origins of Rural Revolution: Elites & the Masses in Hunan Province, China, 1911-1927. Angus W. McDonald, Jr. 1978. 21.50x (ISBN 0-520-03228-4). U of Cal Pr.

Urban Outcomes: Schools, Streets, & Libraries. Frank S. Levy et al. (Oakland Project). 1974. 20.00x (ISBN 0-520-02546-6); pap. 6.95x (ISBN 0-520-03045-1). U of Cal Pr.

Urban Parks & Recreation: Challenges of the 1970's. Richard Kraus. 1972. pap. 1.50 (ISBN 0-86671-006-X). Comm Coun Great NY.

Urban Planning: A Guide to Information Sources. Anthony J. Catanese et al. LC 78-13462. (Urban Studies Information Guide Ser.: Vol. 2). 1979. 30.00 (ISBN 0-8103-1399-5). Gale.

Urban Planning Analysis: Methods & Models. Donald A. Krueckeberg & Arthur L. Silvers. LC 74-7087. 1974. text ed. 24.95 (ISBN 0-471-50858-6). Wiley.

Urban Planning Aspects of Water Pollution Control. Sigurd Grava. LC 72-87147. (Institute of Urban Environment Ser). (Illus.). 1969. text ed. 17.50x (ISBN 0-231-03280-3). Columbia U Pr.

Urban Planning Guide. Compiled by American Society of Civil Engineers. (Manual & Report on Engineering Practice Ser.: No. 49). 308p. 1969. pap. text ed. 8.00 (ISBN 0-87262-223-1). Am Soc Civil Eng.

Urban Policeman in Transition. J. R. Snibbe & H. M. Snibbe. (Illus.). 628p. 1973. 24.75 (ISBN 0-398-02661-0); pap. 16.75 (ISBN 0-398-02741-2). C C Thomas.

Urban Policy: A Guide to Information Sources. Ed. by Dennis Palumbo & George A. Taylor. LC 78-25957. (Urban Studies Information Guide Ser.: Vol. 6). 1979. 30.00 (ISBN 0-8103-1428-2). Gale.

Urban Policy & the Exterior City: Federal, State & Corporate Policies. H. V. Savitch. (Pergamon Policy Studies). 1979. 39.00 (ISBN 0-08-023390-2). Pergamon.

Urban Policy Game: A Simulation of Urban Politics. Thomas A. Henderson & John L. Foster. LC 78-17118. 1978. pap. text ed. 9.95x (ISBN 0-471-03398-7); tchr's manual avail. (ISBN 0-471-04219-6). Wiley.

Urban Policy Making. Ed. by Dale R. Marshall. LC 79-19162. (Sage Yearbooks in Politics & Public Policy: Vol. 7). (Illus.). 1979. 20.00x (ISBN 0-8039-1367-2); pap. 9.95x (ISBN 0-8039-1368-0). Sage.

Urban Political Analysis. David R. Morgan & Samuel A. Kirkpatrick. LC 74-156838. 1972. 15.95 (ISBN 0-02-922060-2). Free Pr.

Urban Political Analysis: The Politics of Collective Consumption. Patrick Dunleavy. 176p. 1980. text ed. 22.50x (ISBN 0-333-23948-2). Humanities.

Urban Political Movements: The Search for Power by Minority Groups in American Cities. Norman I. Fainstein & Susan S. Fainstein. LC 73-21876. 352p. 1974. ref. ed. 11.95 (ISBN 0-13-939330-7); pap. 9.95 ref. ed. (ISBN 0-13-939322-6). P-H.

Urban Political Systems: A Functional Analysis of Metro Toronto. Harold Kaplan. LC 67-29577. 1967. 20.00x (ISBN 0-231-02982-9). Columbia U Pr.

Urban Politics: A Guide to Information Sources. Ed. by Thomas P. Murphy. LC 78-54117. (Urban Studies Information Guide: Vol. 1). 1978. 30.00 (ISBN 0-8103-1395-2). Gale.

Urban Politics in Brazil: The Rise of Populism, 1925-1945. Michael L. Conniff. LC 80-54060. (Pitt Latin American Ser.). (Illus.). 280p. 1981. 19.95x (ISBN 0-8229-3438-8). U of Pittsburgh Pr.

Urban Politics in India: Area, Power, & Policy in a Penetrated System. Rodney W. Jones. 1974. 30.00x (ISBN 0-520-02545-8). U of Cal Pr.

Urban Politics in Nigeria: A Study of Port Harcourt. Howard Wolpe. 1975. 28.50x (ISBN 0-520-02451-6), U of Cal Pr.

Urban Politics in the Suburban Era. Thomas P. Murphy & John Rehfuss. 1976. pap. 10.95x (ISBN 0-256-01848-0). Dorsey.

Urban Politics in Victorian England: The Structure of Politics in Victorian Cities. Derek Fraser. 320p. 1976. text ed. 30.00x (ISBN 0-7185-1145-X, Leicester). Humanities.

Urban Poverty in a Cross-Cultural Context. Edwin Eames & Judith G. Goode. LC 72-90545. 1973. 14.95 (ISBN 0-02-908720-1). Free Pr.

Urban Poverty in Britain, Eighteen Thirty to Nineteen Sixty. J. H. Treble. 1979. 45.00 (ISBN 0-7134-1906-7, Pub. by Batsford England). David & Charles.

Urban Predicament. Ed. by William Gorham & Nathan Glazer. 363p. 1976. 12.50 (ISBN 0-87766-161-8, 14700); pap. 6.95 (ISBN 0-87766-160-X, 14500). Urban Inst.

Urban Problems & Public Policy. Ed. by Robert L. Linesberry & Louis H. Masotti. (Policy Studies Organization Ser.). 192p. 1975. 19.95 (ISBN 0-669-00017-5). Lexington Bks.

Urban Problems: Perspectives on Corporations, Governments, & Cities. Calvin J. Larson & Stan R. Nikkel. 1978. pap. text ed. 12.95 (ISBN 0-205-06530-9, 8165300); instr's man. o.p. avail. (ISBN 0-205-06547-3). Allyn.

Urban Problems: Psychological Inquiries. Ed. by Neil C. Kalt & Sheldon S. Zalkind. (Illus.). 464p. 1976. text ed. 14.95x (ISBN 0-19-502056-1); pap. text ed. 9.95x (ISBN 0-19-502059-6). Oxford U Pr.

Urban Process. Leonard Reissman. LC 64-20301. 1964. text ed. 7.50 (ISBN 0-02-926310-7); pap. text ed. 5.95 (ISBN 0-02-926300-X). Free Pr.

Urban Professionals & the Future of the Metropolis. Ed. by Paula J Dubeck & Zane L. Miller. (National University Publications, Interdisciplinary Urban Ser.). 134p. 1980. 12.50 (ISBN 0-8046-9261-0). Kennikat.

Urban Public Economics. Neenan. 1981. text ed. write for info. Duxbury Pr.

Urban Public Safety Systems: New Tools for Planners. Richard C. Larson. LC 77-9135. (IRP Ser.: Vol. 1). (Illus.). 1978. 23.95 (ISBN 0-669-01783-3). Lexington Bks.

Urban Public Safety Systems: Police Accountability Systems & Unionism. Richard C. Larson. LC 77-9136. (IRP Ser.: Vol. 2). 1978. 22.95 (ISBN 0-669-01785-X). Lexington Bks.

Urban Public Safety Systems Volume IV. Ed. by Thomas R. Willemain & Richard C. Larson. LC 77-80341. (Illus.). 1977. 21.95 (ISBN 0-669-01483-4). Lexington Bks.

Urban Public Transport: Evaluation of Performance. Ed. by OECD. (Road Research Ser.). (Illus.). 76p. 1980. pap. 5.50 (ISBN 9-2641-2127-7, 77-80-04-1). OECD.

Urban Public Transportation. Vukan Vuchic. (Illus.). 672p. 1981. text ed. 38.95 (ISBN 0-13-939496-6). P-H.

Urban Racial Violence in the Twentieth Century. Joseph Boskin. Ed. by Fred Krinsky. LC 78-75964. (Insight Ser: Studies in Contemporary Issues). (Orig.). 1969. pap. 3.95x (ISBN 0-02-473780-1). Macmillan.

Urban Racial Violence, in the Twentieth Century. 2nd ed. Joseph Boskin. 1976. pap. 4.95x (ISBN 0-02-470890-9). Macmillan.

Urban Reader. Susan Cahill & Michele Cooper. LC 75-137898. (Illus.). 1971. pap. text ed. 10.50 (ISBN 0-13-939041-3). P-H.

Urban, Regional & National Planning: Environmental Aspects: Proceedings. T. Hasegawa & IFAC Workshop, Kyoto Japan, Aug. 1978. Ed. by K. Inoue. LC 78-40573. 1978. text ed. 50.00 (ISBN 0-08-022013-4). Pergamon.

Urban Renegades: The Cultural Strategy of American Indians. new ed. Jeanne Guillemin. LC 74-30434. 240p. 1975. 17.50x (ISBN 0-231-03884-4). Columbia U Pr.

Urban Renewal & the Changing Residential Structure of the City. Michael J. White. (Illus.). 225p. (Orig.). 1980. pap. text ed. write for info. (ISBN 0-89836-029-3). Comm & Family.

Urban Renewal in Liverpool. David M. Muchnick. 120p. 1970. pap. text ed. 6.25x (Pub. by Bedford England). Renouf.

Urban Renewal Politics: Slum Clearance in Newark. Harold Kaplan. LC 63-19076. 1963. 20.00x (ISBN 0-231-02667-6). Columbia U Pr.

Urban Revitalization. Ed. by Donald B. Rosenthal. LC 79-27881. (Urban Affairs Annual Reviews: Vol. 18). (Illus.). 308p. 1980. 20.00 (ISBN 0-8039-1190-4); pap. 9.95 (ISBN 0-8039-1191-2). Sage.

Urban Runoff-Quantity & Quality. Compiled by American Society of Civil Engineers. 280p. 1975. pap. text ed. 14.00 (ISBN 0-87262-103-0). Am Soc Civil Eng.

Urban Scene: Myths & Realities. Joe R. Feagin. 1973. pap. text ed. 4.95 o.p. (ISBN 0-394-31647-9). Random.

Urban Sea: Long Island Sound. Lee E. Koppelman et al. LC 74-3161. (Illus.). 1976. text ed. 29.95 (ISBN 0-275-09010-8). Praeger.

Urban Service Problem: A Study of Housing Inspection. Pietro S. Nivola. LC 78-21444. 192p. 1979. 19.95 (ISBN 0-669-02801-0). Lexington Bks.

Urban Social Segregation. G. C. Peach. LC 74-80434. (Illus.). 450p. 1976. text ed. 23.00x (ISBN 0-582-48088-4). Longman.

Urban Social Structure. James M. Beshers. LC 80-27972. vii, 207p. 1981. Repr. of 1962 ed. lib. bdg. 19.75x (ISBN 0-313-22714-4, BEUR). Greenwood.

Urban Society: An Ecological Approach. 2nd ed. Amos H. Hawley. LC 80-17925. 350p. 1981. 14.95 (ISBN 0-471-05753-3). Wiley.

Urban Sociology. Mark Abrahamson. LC 75-25728. (Sociology Ser.). (Illus.). 320p. 1976. 17.95x (ISBN 0-13-939512-1). P-H.

Urban Sociology. 2nd ed. Mark Abrahamson. (Ser. in Sociology). (Illus.). 1980. text ed. 17.95 (ISBN 0-13-939587-3). P-H.

Urban Sociology. Robert A. Wilson & David A. Schulz. (P-H Ser. in Sociology). (Illus.). 1978. ref. ed. 17.95 (ISBN 0-13-939520-2). P-H.

Urban Sociology in an Urbanized Society. J. R. Mellor. (International Library of Sociology). 1977. 24.00 (ISBN 0-7100-8683-0). Routledge & Kegan.

Urban Space & Structures. Ed. by Leslie Martin & L. March. (Studies in Architecture: Vol. 1). 1972. 29.95 (ISBN 0-521-08414-8); pap. 9.95x (ISBN 0-521-09934-X). Cambridge U Pr.

Urban Storm Drainage. Ed. by P. R. Helliwell. LC 78-18235. 1978. 64.95 (ISBN 0-470-26461-6). Halsted Pr.

Urban Studies: An Introductory Reader. 2nd ed. Ed. by Louis K. Loewenstein. LC 76-19644. 1977. 19.95 (ISBN 0-02-919470-9); pap. text ed. 10.95 (ISBN 0-02-919440-7). Free Pr.

Urban Systems Models. Walter Helly. 1975. 25.00 (ISBN 0-12-339450-3). Acad Pr.

Urban Systems-Strategies for Regulation. L. S. Bourne. (Illus.). 284p. 1975. text ed. 29.95x (ISBN 0-19-874054-9); pap. text ed. 14.50x (ISBN 0-19-874055-7). Oxford U Pr.

Urban Transport & the Environment: Seminar OECD-ECMT, July 10-12, 1979, 4 pts. Organization for Economic Cooperation & Development & ECMT. (Orig.). 1980. pap. text ed. 12.00x set (ISBN 92-64-12001-7, 97 79 08 1). Pt. I, Background Reports (319 P.) Pt. II, Case Studies (283 P.) Pt. III, Overview (7 P.) Pt. IV, Conclusions (15 P.) OECD.

Urban Transport Economics. Ed. by D. A. Hensher. LC 76-11061. (Illus.). 1977. 45.00 (ISBN 0-521-21128-X); pap. 14.95x (ISBN 0-521-29140-2). Cambridge U Pr.

Urban Transportation Efficiency. Compiled by American Society of Civil Engineers. 448p. 1977. pap. text ed. 19.75 (ISBN 0-87262-174-X). Am Soc Civil Eng.

Urban Transportation Financing: Proceedings. ASCE Conference, Urban Transportation Division, 1979. LC 80-66290. 320p. 1980. pap. text ed. 25.50 (ISBN 0-87262-241-X). Am Soc Civil Eng.

Urban Transportation Innovation. Compiled by American Society of Civil Engineers. 432p. 1971. pap. text ed. 18.75 (ISBN 0-87262-044-1). Am Soc Civil Eng.

Urban Transportation Modeling & Planning. Peter R. Stopher. LC 74-21876. 224p. 1975. 24.95x (ISBN 0-669-96941-9). Lexington Bks.

Urban Transportation Policy & Management. Milton Pikarsky & Daphne Christensen. (Illus.). 1976. 22.95 (ISBN 0-669-00955-5). Lexington Bks.

Urban University in America. Maurice R. Berube. LC 77-87917. 1978. lib. bdg. 15.00 (ISBN 0-313-20031-9, BUU/). Greenwood.

Urban Villagers. Herbert J. Gans. LC 62-15362. 1965. pap. text ed. 7.95 (ISBN 0-02-911120-X). Free Pr.

Urban Waterfront Lands. Committee on Urban Waterfront Lands. xii, 243p. 1980. pap. text ed. 11.50 (ISBN 0-309-02940-6). Natl Acad Pr.

Urban Wilds. Ogden Tanner. (American Wilderness Ser.). (Illus.). 184p. 1975. 12.95 (ISBN 0-8094-1221-7). Time-Life.

Urban Wilds. Ogden Tanner. (American Wilderness). (Illus.). (gr. 6 up). 1975. PLB 11.97 (ISBN 0-8094-1335-3, Pub. by Time-Life). Silver.

Urban Workers on Relief, 2 Vols. in 1. Gladys L. Palmer & Katherine D. Wood. LC 75-165688. (FDR & the Era of the New Deal Ser.). 1971. Repr. of 1936 ed. Set. lib. bdg. 49.50 (ISBN 0-306-70336-X). Da Capo.

Urban World. 2nd ed. J. John Palen. Ed. by Eric M. Munson. 480p. 1981. text ed. 17.95 (ISBN 0-07-048107-5, C). McGraw.

Urbana Praise. Robert Fryling. (Orig.). 1979. pap. 2.95 o.p. (ISBN 0-87784-585-9). Inter-Varsity.

Urbane View: Life & Politics in Metropolitan America. Scott Greer. (Illus.). 352p. 1972. 14.95 (ISBN 0-19-501544-4). Oxford U Pr.

Urbane View: Life & Politics in Metropolitan America. Scott Greer. LC 71-182424. 364p. 1973. pap. 4.95 (ISBN 0-19-501728-5, 397, GB). Oxford U Pr.

Urbanism, Urbanization, & Change: Comparative Perspectives. 2nd ed. Paul Meadows & Ephraim H. Mizruchi. LC 75-28723. (Illus.). 448p. 1976. pap. text ed. 11.95 (ISBN 0-201-04616-4). A-W.

Urbanization & Cities: A Historical & Comparitive Perspective on Our Urbanizing World. Hilda Golden. 384p. 1981. text ed. 18.95 (ISBN 0-669-03175-5). Heath.

Urbanization & Counterurbanization. Ed. by Brian J. L. Berry. (Urban Affairs Annual Reviews: Vol. 11). (Illus.). 1976. 20.00x (ISBN 0-8039-0499-1); pap. 9.95x (ISBN 0-8039-0682-X). Sage.

Urbanization & Environmental Quality. T. R. Lakshmanan & Lata Chatterjee. Ed. by Salvatore Natoli. LC 76-57032. (Resource Papers for College Geography Ser.). 1977. pap. text ed. 4.00 (ISBN 0-89291-122-0). Assn Am Geographers.

Urbanization & Political Change: The Politics of Lagos, 1917-1967. Pauline H. Baker. 1975. 28.50x (ISBN 0-520-02066-9). U of Cal Pr.

Urbanization & Rural Development: A Spatial Policy for Equitable Growth. Dennis A. Rondinelli & Kenneth Ruddle. LC 78-17790. (Praeger Special Studies). 1978. 24.95 (ISBN 0-03-043111-5). Praeger.

Urbanization & Social Changes in West Africa. J. Gugler & W. Flanagan. LC 76-9175. (Urbanisation in Developing Countries Ser.). (Illus.). 1978. 24.95 (ISBN 0-521-21348-7); pap. 7.95x (ISBN 0-521-29118-6). Cambridge U Pr.

Urbanization & Urban Growth in the Caribbean. M. Cross. LC 78-67307. (Urbanization in Developing Countries Ser.). 1979. 23.95 (ISBN 0-521-22426-8); pap. 7.95x (ISBN 0-521-29491-6). Cambridge U Pr.

Urbanization & Urban India. N. V. Sovani. 7.50x (ISBN 0-210-22695-1). Asia.

Urbanization As a Social Process: An Essay on Movement & Change in Contemporary Africa. Kenneth Little. (Library of Man Ser.). 1974. 14.00x (ISBN 0-7100-7931-1). Routledge & Kegan.

Urbanization, Housing & the Development Process. David Drakakis-Smith. 256p. 1980. write for info. (ISBN 0-312-83519-1). St Martin.

Urbanization in Australia: The Post-War Experience. I. H. Burnley. LC 73-77261. (Illus.). 1973. 32.95 (ISBN 0-521-20250-7). Cambridge U Pr.

Urbanization in Latin America. UNESCO. Ed. by Philip M. Hauser. 1961. 20.00x (ISBN 0-231-03189-0). Columbia U Pr.

Urbanization in Latin America: Approaches & Issues. Ed. by Jorge E. Hardoy. LC 73-83594. 480p. 1975. pap. 4.50 o.p. (ISBN 0-385-08240-1, Anch). Doubleday.

Urbanization in Newly Developing Countries. Gerald Breese. (Illus., Orig.). 1966. pap. 8.95 ref. ed. (ISBN 0-13-939181-9). P-H.

Urbanization in Nigeria. Akin L. Mabogunje. LC 76-80853. 1969. 24.50x (ISBN 0-8419-0002-7, Africana); pap. 10.75 o.p. (ISBN 0-8419-0097-3, Africana). Holmes & Meier.

Urbanization in Papua New Guinea. H. B. Levine & Marlene Levine. LC 78-58795. (Urbanization in Developing Countries Ser.). 1979. 24.95 (ISBN 0-521-22230-3); pap. 9.95x (ISBN 0-521-29410-X). Cambridge U Pr.

Urbanization in Socialist Countries. George Musil. Orig. Title: Urbanizace v socialistickych zemich. (Illus.). 192p. 1980. 20.00 (ISBN 0-87332-180-4). M E Sharpe.

Urbanization in the Middle East. V. F. Costello. LC 76-11075. (Urbanization in Developing Countries Ser.). (Illus.). 1977. 19.95 (ISBN 0-521-21324-X); pap. 6.95x (ISBN 0-521-29110-0). Cambridge U Pr.

Urbanization in Tropical Africa, Nineteen Sixty to Nineteen Seventy-Nine: An Annotated Bibliography. A. M. O'Connor. (Reference Bks.). 1981. lib. bdg. 48.00 (ISBN 0-8161-8262-0). G K Hall.

Urbanization of America, 1860-1915. Blake McKelvey. 1963. 24.00 (ISBN 0-8135-0421-X). Rutgers U Pr.

Urbanization, Population Growth & Economic Deveopment in the Philippines. Ernesto D. Pernia. (Studies in Population & Urban Demography: No. 3). 1977. lib. bdg. 19.95 (ISBN 0-8371-9721-X, PEU/). Greenwood.

Urbanization Process of a Poor Mexican Neighborhood. Antonio Ugalde et al. LC 74-620102. 68p. 1974. pap. 3.95 (ISBN 0-292-78503-8). U of Tex Pr.

Urbanization Under Socialism: The Case of Czechslovakia. Karel J. Kansky. LC 75-44934. (Special Studies). (Illus.). 350p. 1976. text ed. 32.50 (ISBN 0-275-56770-2). Praeger.

Urbanman: The Psychology of Urban Survival. Ed. by John Helmer & Neil A. Eddington. LC 71-190152. 1973. 14.95 (ISBN 0-02-914480-9); pap. 3.95 (ISBN 0-02-914630-5). Free Pr.

Urdang Dictionary of Current Medical Terms. Urdang. 464p. 1981. 12.95 (ISBN 0-471-05853-X, Pub. by Wiley Med). Wiley.

Urdu Newspaper Reader. Muhammad Abd-al-Rahman Barker et al. LC 74-21940. (Spoken Language Ser.). (Illus.). 1974. Repr. of 1968 ed. 10.00x (ISBN 0-87950-337-8); cassettes 4 dual track 50.00x (ISBN 0-87950-338-6); cassettes with course-bk. 55.00x (ISBN 0-87950-339-4). Spoken Lang Serv.

Urea & Other Nonprotein Nitrogen Compounds in Animal Nutrition. Agriculture & Renewable Resources Board, National Research Council. LC 76-8240. 1976. pap. 5.50 (ISBN 0-309-02444-7). Natl Acad Pr.

Urea Cycle. Santiago Grisolia et al. LC 76-7382. 656p. 1976. 47.50 (ISBN 0-471-32791-3, Pub. by Wiley-Interscience). Wiley.

Uretheral Dynamics. Boyarsky & Labay. 503p. 1972. 23.00 o.p. (ISBN 0-683-00951-6, Pub. by Williams & Wilkins). Krieger.

Urewera Notebook. Katherine Mansfield. Intro. by Ian A. Gordon. (Illus.). 108p. 1978. pap. text ed. 12.95x (ISBN 0-19-558034-6). Oxford U Pr.

Urge to Die: Why Young People Commit Suicide. Peter Giovacchini. LC 80-24435. 256p. 1981. 12.95 (ISBN 0-02-543440-3). Macmillan.

Urgent Endoscopy of Digestive & Abdominal Diseases: New Fields of Gastrointestinal Endoscopy. International Symposium. (Illus.). 260p. 1972. 74.25 (ISBN 3-8055-1349-6). S Karger.

Urgent Future: People, Housing, City Region. Albert Mayer. 1967. 27.50 o.p. (ISBN 0-07-040991-9, P&RB). McGraw.

Uriah Phillips Levy. Harold W. Felton. LC 78-7726. (Illus.). (gr. 5 up). 1979. 5.95 (ISBN 0-396-07604-1). Dodd.

Urinary Concentrating Mechanism: Structure & Function. Rex L. Jamison & Wilhelm Kriz. (Illus.). 425p. 1981. text ed. 35.00x (ISBN 0-19-502801-5). Oxford U Pr.

Urinary Proteins. Ed. by L. Migone. (Contributions to Nephrology Ser.: Vol. 26). (Illus.). vi, 150p. 1981. pap. 54.00 (ISBN 3-8055-1848-X). S Karger.

Urinary System Basic Sciences. Ed. by Myron E. Tracht et al. 1973. spiral bdg. 10.00 o.p. (ISBN 0-87488-214-1). Med Exam.

Utah Two. Stan Welsh. (Illus.). 128p. 1981. 27.50 (ISBN 0-912856-65-3). Graphic Arts Ctr.

Utah's Heritage. S. George Ellsworth. LC 72-85712. (Illus.). 350p. (gr. 7-12). 1977. text ed. 15.00 (ISBN 0-87905-006-3). Peregrine Smith.

Ute Indians, Vol. 1. Incl. Analysis: Aboriginal Historical Groups of the Ute Indians of Utah. Julian H. Steward; Supplement: Native Components of the White River Ute Indians. Julian H. Steward. (American Indian Ethnohistory Ser: California & Basin Plateau Indians). (Illus.). lib. bdg. 42.00 (ISBN 0-8240-0736-0). Garland Pub.

Ute Indians, Vol. 2. Incl. Confederated Ute Indian Lands. Indian Claims Commission; Historical Summary of the Ute & the San Juan Mining Region. Leroy R. Hafen; Cultural Differences & Similarities Between Uintah & White River Indians. Anne M. Smith; Findings of Fact & Opinion. Indian Claims Commission. (American Indian Ethnohistory Ser: California & Basin Plateau Indians). (Illus.). lib. bdg. 42.00 (ISBN 0-8240-0737-9). Garland Pub.

Ute War: A History of the White River Massacre & the Privations & Hardships of the Captive White Women Among the Hostiles on Grand River. Thomas F. Dawson. Bd. with Ute Massacre! Brave Miss Meeker's Captivity. Josephine Meeker. LC 75-7119. (Indian Captivities Ser.: Vol. 93). 1976. Repr. of 1879 ed. lib. bdg. 44.00 (ISBN 0-8240-1717-X). Garland Pub.

Uthal. Etienne Mehul. Ed. by Philip Gossett & Charles Rosen. LC 76-49222. (Early Romantic Opera Ser.: Vol. 40). 1979. lib. bdg. 82.00 (ISBN 0-8240-2939-9). Garland Pub.

Utilice Su Casa Para Evangelizar. Lee Baggett. 1980. Repr. of 1979 ed. 1.10 (ISBN 0-311-13832-2). Casa Bautista.

Utilisation of the Social Sciences in Policy Making in the United States: Case Studies. 392p. (Orig.). 1980. pap. 20.00 (ISBN 9-2641-2128-5). OECD.

Utilitarianism. John S. Mill. Ed. by Samuel Gorovitz. LC 74-132935. (Text & Critical Essays Ser). (Orig.). 1971. pap. 10.95 (ISBN 0-672-61120-1, TC7). Bobbs.

Utilitarianism. John S. Mill. Ed. by Oskar Piest. 1957. pap. 2.95 (ISBN 0-672-60164-8, LLA1). Bobbs.

Utilitarianism & Cooperation. Donald Regan. 296p. 1980. text ed. 37.50x (ISBN 0-19-824609-9); pap. 15.95x. Oxford U Pr.

Utilitarianism: For & Against. J. J. Smart & B. Williams. LC 73-80487. 180p. 1973. 23.95 (ISBN 0-521-20297-3); pap. 6.95x (ISBN 0-521-09822-X). Cambridge U Pr.

Utilitarians. Jeremy Bentham & John S. Mill. Incl. Principles of Morals & Legislation. Bentham; Utilitarianism & on Liberty. John S. Mill. LC 62-2159. pap. 3.50 (ISBN 0-385-08256-8, C265, Anch). Doubleday.

Utility & Choice in Social Interaction. Lynne Ofshe & Richard Ofshe. LC 70-101539. (Illus.). 1970. 24.50x (ISBN 0-13-939645-4). Irvington.

Utilization & Recycle of Agricultural Wastes & Residues. Michael Schuler. 304p. 1980. 69.95 (ISBN 0-8493-5569-9). CRC Pr.

Utilization of Health Personnel: A Five Hospital Study. Harold M. Goldstein & Morris A. Horowitz. LC 78-12011. 1978. text ed. 22.00 (ISBN 0-89443-080-7). Aspen Systems.

Utilization of Short-Stay Hospitals: Annual Summary for the United States, 1975. Ed. by Audrey Shipp. (Series 13: No. 31). 1977. pap. 1.95 (ISBN 0-8406-0092-5). Natl Ctr Health Stats.

Utilization of Short-Stay Hospitals by Persons with Heart Disease & Malignant Neoplasms. Gloria J. Gardocki & Robert Pokras. Ed. by Audrey Shipp. (Ser. Thirteen: No. 52). 50p. 1981. pap. 1.75 (ISBN 0-8406-0214-6). Natl Ctr Health Stats.

Utilization of Solar Energy for Feedmill & Irrigation Operations. Texas Tech University. pap. cancelled (ISBN 0-930978-67-6). Solar Energy Info.

Utilization of Space Shuttle & Spacelab: Proceedings of an International Meeting Held in Bonn, 1976. Deutsche Gesellschaft Fur Luft und Raumfahrt. (Illus.). 1976. pap. 30.00x (ISBN 3-88135-034-9). Univelt Inc.

Utilization of Texas Serpentine. V. E. Barnes et al. (Illus.). 52p. 1950. 0.60 (PUB 5020). Bur Econ Geology.

Utilization of the Azolla-Anabaena Complex As a Nitrogen Fertilizer for Rice. (IRRI Research Paper Ser.: No. 11). 15p. 1977. pap. 5.00 (R051, IRRI). Unipub.

Utilization of Thorium in Power Reactors. (Technical Reports: No. 52). 1966. pap. 17.25 (ISBN 92-0-055066-5, IAEA). Unipub.

Utilization Patterns and Financial Characteristics of Nursing Homes in the United States: 1977 Nnhs. Barbara Bloom. Ed. by Audrey Shipp. (Series Thirteen: No. 53). 50p. 1981. pap. 1.75 (ISBN 0-8406-0215-4). Natl Ctr Health Stats.

Uto-Aztecan Cognate Sets. W. R. Miller. (U. C. Publ. in Linguistics: Vol. 48). 1967. pap. 4.50x o.p. (ISBN 0-520-09243-0). U of Cal Pr.

Utoli Moi Pechali. Lev Kopelev. (Rus.). 1981. 16.50 (ISBN 0-88233-483-2); pap. 9.00 (ISBN 0-88233-484-0). Ardis Pubs.

Utopia. Thomas More. Incl. Dialogue of Comfort Against Tribulation. 1955. 10.50x (ISBN 0-460-00461-1, Evman); pap. 2.95 (ISBN 0-460-01461-7, Evman). Dutton.

Utopia & Reality: A Collective Portrait of American Socialists. Betty G. Yorburg. LC 72-79573. 1969. 20.00x (ISBN 0-231-03268-4). Columbia U Pr.

Utopia & the Ideal Society. C. J. Davis. 410p. Date not set. price not set (ISBN 0-521-23396-8). Cambridge U Pr.

Utopia in Uruguay: Chapters in the Economic History of Uruguay. Simon G. Hanson. LC 79-1579. 1981. Repr. of 1938 ed. 19.75 (ISBN 0-88355-885-8). Hyperion Conn.

Utopian Flight from Unhappiness: Freud Against Marx on Social Progress. Martin G. Kalin. LC 73-80500. 1974. 14.95 (ISBN 0-911012-65-6). Nelson-Hall.

Utopian Literature: A Selection. James W. Johnson. 1968. pap. text ed. 1.95 (ISBN 0-394-30996-0, RanC). Random.

Utopianism & Education: Robert Owen & the Owenites. Ed. by John F. Harrison. LC 68-54675. (Orig.). 1969. pap. text ed. 5.25x (ISBN 0-8077-1498-4). Tchrs Coll.

Utrillo & the Painters of Montmartre. (Illus.). 1975. Repr. 5.95 o.p. (ISBN 0-88308-009-5). Lamplight Pub.

Utter Nonsense. Barney Saltzberg. (McGraw-Hill Paperbacks Ser.). (Illus.). 80p. (Orig.). 1980. pap. 3.95 (ISBN 0-07-054486-7). McGraw.

Utter Zoo. Edward Gorey. (Illus.). 1967. 4.95 (ISBN 0-8015-8268-7, Hawthorn). Dutton.

Utterly Irrational United States Monetary Policies & the Absolute Inevitability of a Major World Economic & Financial Crisis, 2 vols. in 1. Edmond C. Rossland. (Illus.). 1979. deluxe ed. 61.85 (ISBN 0-930008-37-5). Inst Econ Pol.

Uv-A: Biological Effects of Ultraviolet Radiation. John Parrish et al. LC 78-14968. (Illus.). 272p. 1978. 25.00 (ISBN 0-306-31121-6, Plenum Pr). Plenum Pub.

UV Curing in Screen Printing for Printed Circuits & the Graphic Arts. S. Wentink & S. Koch. 1980. 92.00 (ISBN 0-936840-00-5). Tech Marketing.

UV Curing: Science & Technology. Ed. by S. Peter Pappas. LC 78-56293. (Illus.). 1978. perfect bdg. 95.00 (ISBN 0-686-23773-0). Tech Marketing.

Uxpanapa: Agricultural Development in the Mexican Tropics. Peter T. Ewell & Thomas T. Poleman. LC 80-12208. (Pergamon Policy Studies). 220p. 1980. 25.00 (ISBN 0-08-025967-7). Pergamon.

Uzbeck-English Dictionary. Natalie Waterson. 240p. 1980. 55.00x (ISBN 0-19-713597-8). Oxford U Pr.

V

V. D. Venereal Disease and What You Should Do About It. new, rev ed. Eric W. Johnson. LC 78-8666. (Illus.). (YA) (gr. 5-12). 1978. 7.95 (ISBN 0-397-31811-1). Lippincott.

V-Discs: A History & Discography. Richard S. Sears. LC 80-1022. (Discographies: No. 5). (Illus.). xciii, 1166p. 1980. lib. bdg. 67.50 (ISBN 0-313-22207-X, SHD/). Greenwood.

V. K. Wellington Koo's Foreign Policy: Some Selected Documents. V. K. Wellington. Ed. by Wuncz King. (Studies in Chinese History & Civilization). 141p. 1977. Repr. of 1931 ed. 16.00 (ISBN 0-89093-071-6). U Pubns Amer.

V. S. Naipaul. Robert D. Hamner. (World Authors Ser.: West Indies: No. 258). 1973. lib. bdg. 10.95 (ISBN 0-8057-2647-0). Twayne.

V. Sackville-West. Sara R. Watson. (English Authors Ser.: No. 134). lib. bdg. 10.95 (ISBN 0-8057-1472-3). Twayne.

V. Sackville-West's Garden Book. V. Sackville-West. 1968. 13.95 o.p. (ISBN 0-7181-0536-2, Pub. by Michael Joseph). Merrimack Bk Serv.

V Was for Victory: Politics & American Culture During World War 2. John M. Blum. LC 75-38730. 384p. 1976. 12.95 o.p. (ISBN 0-15-194080-0). HarBraceJ.

V Was for Victory: Politics & American Culture During World War II. John M. Blum. LC 77-3426. 1977. pap. 5.95 (ISBN 0-15-693628-3, Harv). HarBraceJ.

Va De Cuento. R. Charran & B. Maharaj. (Illus.). 1977. pap. text ed. 2.50x (ISBN 0-582-76616-8). Longman.

Vacances Au Senegal. Roger J. Cazziol. (Illus.). 1971. text ed. 2.25x (ISBN 0-521-08180-7). Cambridge U Pr.

Vacation at Sea: A Travel Guide for Cruises. Else Daniels & Bennet Daniels. (Illus.). 1979. 12.95 (ISBN 0-671-18438-5); pap. 5.95 (ISBN 0-346-12423-9). Cornerstone.

Vacation Bible School Ideas. Eleanor Daniel. (Ideas Ser.). (Illus.). 1977. pap. text ed. 1.75 (ISBN 0-87239-128-0, 7971). Standard Pub.

Vacation Homes & Cabins: 16 Complete Plans. United States Dept. of Agriculture. 8.00 (ISBN 0-8446-5674-7). Peter Smith.

Vacation in Space. Leo P. Kelley. LC 78-68232. (Galaxy Five Ser.). (Illus.). 64p. (gr. 4 up). 1980. PLB 7.95 (ISBN 0-516-02255-5). Childrens.

Vacation Time, Leisure Time, Any Time You Choose. Calhoun. 1974. pap. 2.25 (ISBN 0-687-43596-X). Abingdon.

Vacationer's Guide to Orlando. Judi Grove. (Illus.). 150p. (Orig.). 1981. pap. 4.95x (ISBN 0-914788-39-6). East Woods.

Vaccine Preparation Techniques. Ed. by J. I. Duffy. LC 80-10174. 403p. 1980. 48.00 (ISBN 0-8155-0796-8). Noyes.

Vachel Lindsay: A Poet in America. Edgar L. Masters. LC 68-56452. (Illus.). 1969. Repr. of 1935 ed. 17.00x (ISBN 0-8196-0239-6). Biblo.

Vacuome de la Cellule Vegetale: Morphologie. P. Dangeard. Bd. with Vacuome Animal. R. Hovasse. (Illus.). 37p; Contractile Vacuoles of Protozoa; Food Vacuoles: Food Vacuoles. J. A. Kitching. (Protoplasmatologia: Vol. 3, Pt. D1, 2, 3a, 3b). (Illus.). iv, 41p. 1956. pap. 57.90 o.p. (ISBN 0-387-80423-4). Springer-Verlag.

Vacuum & Solid State Electronics. D. J. Harris & P. D. Robson. 1963. 23.00 (ISBN 0-08-009960-2); pap. 10.50 o.p. (ISBN 0-08-009959-9). Pergamon.

Vacuum & Thin Film Technology. Ed. by J. Yarwood. 1978. text ed. 40.00 (ISBN 0-08-022112-2). Pergamon.

Vacuum Arcs: Theory & Application. Ed. by J. M. Lafferty. LC 79-15654. 1980. 29.95 (ISBN 0-471-06506-4). Wiley.

Vacuum Sealing Techniques. A. Roth. 1966. 120.00 (ISBN 0-08-011587-X). Pergamon.

Vacuum Technology. Andrew Guthrie. LC 63-20631. 1963. 36.95 (ISBN 0-471-33722-6, Pub. by Wiley-Interscience). Wiley.

Vacuum Ultraviolet Radiation Physics: Proceedings of the 4th International Conference. Ed. by E. E. Koch et al. 848p. 1976. text ed. 125.00 (ISBN 0-08-018942-3). Pergamon.

Vadim Shershenevich. Anna Lawton. 1981. 15.00 (ISBN 0-88233-681-9). Ardis Pubs.

Vagabond. Colette. Tr. by Enid McLeod from Fr. LC 55-5832. 223p. 1975. 8.95 (ISBN 0-374-28233-1); pap. 4.95 (ISBN 0-374-51175-6). FS&G.

Vagabond Verse: Secular Latin Poems of the Middle Ages. Tr. by Edwin H. Zeydel. LC 66-13794. 1966. 9.95x o.p. (ISBN 0-8143-1288-8). Wayne St U Pr.

Vagabonding in the U S A. Ed Buryn. LC 80-10966. (Illus.). 448p. 1980. pap. 9.95 (ISBN 0-915904-50-0). And-Or Pr.

Vaginal Contraception. M. Jackson et al. 1980. lib. bdg. 29.95 (ISBN 0-8161-2211-3, Medical Publications). G K Hall.

Vaginal Contraception: New Developments. Gerald Zatuchni et al. (PARFR Series on Fertility Regulation). (Illus.). 384p. 1980. text ed. 17.50 (ISBN 0-06-142901-5, Harper Medical). Har-Row.

Vaginal Health. 1981. pap. 2.50 (ISBN 0-440-09368-6). Dell.

Vaginal Hysterectomy: Indications, Technique & Complications. 2nd ed. Laman A. Gray. (American Lectures in Gynecology & Obstetrics Ser.). (Illus.). 240p. 1963. 14.75 (ISBN 0-398-00721-7). C C Thomas.

Vagotomy & Pyloroplasty: Latest Advances, 1975-1980. Ed. by F. Holle & G. E. Holle. (Illus.). 160p. 1980. pap. 58.00 (ISBN 0-387-10083-0). Springer-Verlag.

Vail. Sandra Dallas. LC 78-94879. (Illus.). 1969. pap. 2.50 o.p. (ISBN 0-87108-005-2). Pruett.

Vail Epicure. Ed. by Victoria Hagar. (Epicure Ser.). 52p. (Orig.). 1979. pap. 2.50 (ISBN 0-89716-031-2). Peanut Butter.

Vain & the Vainglorious. Katrinka Blickle. LC 80-2324. 384p. 1981. 12.95 (ISBN 0-385-15182-9). Doubleday.

Vain Obliations. Katharine F. Gerould. 324p. 1980. Repr. of 1915 ed. lib. bdg. 25.00 (ISBN 0-89987-306-5). Century Bookbindery.

Vaisnavism & Society in Northern India. Urmila Bhagowalia. 1980. 22.00x (ISBN 0-8364-0664-8, Pub. by Intellectual India). South Asia Bks.

Vaisnavism, Saivism & Minor Religious Systems: Strassburg, 1913. R. G. Bhandakhar. LC 78-74263. (Oriental Religions Ser.: Vol. 1). 167p. 1980. lib. bdg. 22.00 (ISBN 0-8240-3900-9). Garland Pub.

Vaiyakarana Siddhanta Kaumudi of Bhattoji Diksita, Vol. I. P. V. Sastry. 1974. 11.50 (ISBN 0-8426-0582-7). Orient Bk Dist.

Vak: An Anthology of Australian, European & Indian Verse. Ed. by Sibnarayan Ray. 14.00 (ISBN 0-89253-623-3). Ind-US Inc.

Vakyapadiya of Bharthari-Chapter Three. K. A. Iyer. 1974. 15.00 (ISBN 0-8426-0617-3). Orient Bk Dist.

Val Verde. Judith Polley. 1974. 6.95 o.p. (ISBN 0-440-06092-3). Delacorte.

Valdepenas. Richard Lortz. LC 79-66114. 220p. 1980. 15.95 (ISBN 0-933256-06-X); pap. 7.95 (ISBN 0-933256-07-8). Second Chance.

Valencian Dramatists of Spain's Golden Age. John G. Weiger. LC 75-25558. (World Authors Ser.: Spain: No. 371). 1976. lib. bdg. 12.50 (ISBN 0-8057-6219-1). Twayne.

Valency & Molecular Structure. 4th ed. Cartmell & Fowles. 1977. 16.95 (ISBN 0-408-70809-3). Butterworths.

Valentina. Fern Michaels. 1981. pap. 2.75 (ISBN 0-345-29580-3). Ballantine.

Valentine Banquets. Ed. by Agnes D. Pylant. LC 63-21601. (Illus., Orig.). 1963. pap. 0.95 (ISBN 0-8054-9913-X). Broadman.

Valentine Estate. Stanley Ellin. LC 68-28541. 1968. 8.95 o.p. (ISBN 0-394-45033-7). Random.

Valentine Fantasy. Carolyn Haywood. LC 75-23083. (Illus.). 32p. (gr. k-3). 1976. 7.25 (ISBN 0-688-22055-X); PLB 6.96 (ISBN 0-688-32055-4). Morrow.

Valentine for Cousin Archie. Barbara Williams. LC 80-181. (Illus.). 32p. (gr. k-3). 1981. PLB 8.95 (ISBN 0-525-41930-6). Dutton.

Valentine for Fuzzboom. True Kelley. (gr. k-3). 1981. 5.95 (ISBN 0-395-30446-6). HM.

Valentine M'Clutchy, the Irish Agent: Chronicles of the Castle Cumber Property. William Carleton. Ed. by Robert L. Wolff. (Ireland Nineteenth Century Fiction - Ser. Two: Vol. 40). 480p. 1979. lib. bdg. 32.00 (ISBN 0-8240-3489-9). Garland Pub.

Valentine Mystery. Joan L. Nixon. Ed. by Kathleen Tucker. LC 79-7055. (First Read-Alone Mysteries). (Illus.). (gr. 1-3). 1979. 5.50g (ISBN 0-8075-8450-9). A Whitman.

Valentines & Vitrol. Rex Reed. 1977. 8.95 o.s.i. (ISBN 0-440-09336-8). Delacorte.

Valentine's Day. Nancy Reese. Ed. by Alton Jordan. (Holidays Ser.). (Illus.). (gr. k-3). 1977. PLB 3.50 (ISBN 0-89868-029-8, Read Res); pap. text ed. 1.75 (ISBN 0-89868-062-X). ARO Pub.

Valentine's Day. Cass R. Sandak. (gr. 2-4). 1980. PLB 7.90 (ISBN 0-531-04151-4). Watts.

Valentine's Day: Things to Make & Do. Robyn Supraner. LC 80-23780. (Illus.). 48p. (gr. 2-5). 1980. PLB 6.92 (ISBN 0-89375-424-2); pap. 1.75 (ISBN 0-89375-425-0). Troll Assocs.

Valery: Jeune Poete. Charles G. Whiting. (Yale Romantic Studies). 1960. pap. 27.50x (ISBN 0-685-69883-1). Elliots Bks.

Valhalla. Newton Thornberg. 372p. 1981. 10.95 (ISBN 0-316-84393-8). Little.

Valhalla Seven: Women's Fiction. Ed. by Rochelle H. Dubois. (Illus.). 55p. (Orig.). 1981. pap. 2.50 (ISBN 0-934536-05-8). Merging Media. Postponed.

Valiant Few: Crisis at the Alamo. Lon Tinkle. (gr. 5-9). 1964. 4.50g o.s.i. (ISBN 0-02-789380-4). Macmillan.

Valiant Little Tailor. Victor G. Ambrus. (Illus.). 24p. (ps-3). 1980. 9.95 (ISBN 0-19-279727-1). Oxford U Pr.

Valiant Sailor. C. Fox Smith. (Illus.). (gr. 6-10). 1957. 9.95 (ISBN 0-87599-105-X). S G Phillips.

Validity Issues in Evaluative Research. Ed. by Ilene N. Bernstein. LC 75-32373. (Sage Contemporary Social Science Issues: Vol. 23). 1976. 4.95x (ISBN 0-8039-0581-5). Sage.

Valis. Philip K. Dick. 240p. (Orig.). 1981. pap. 2.25 (ISBN 0-553-14156-2). Bantam.

Valium Papers. Henry L. Lennard. LC 80-84546. 150p. (Orig.). 1981. pap. 9.95 (ISBN 0-935824-02-2). Gondolier.

Valkyrie Encounter. Stephen Marlowe. 1978. pap. 1.95 (ISBN 0-515-04705-8). Jove Pubns.

Vallette Heritage. Louisa Bronte. 1978. pap. 2.25 (ISBN 0-515-04309-5). Jove Pubns.

Valley Forge. MacKinlay Kantor. 1976. pap. 1.95 o.p. (ISBN 0-345-25270-5). Ballantine.

Valley of Discord: Church & Society along the Connecticut River, 1636-1725. Paul R. Lucas. LC 75-22520. (Illus.). 288p. 1976. text ed. 15.00x (ISBN 0-87451-121-6). U Pr of New Eng.

Valley of Fear. Arthur C. Doyle. lib. bdg. 13.95x (ISBN 0-89966-232-3). Buccaneer Bks.

Valley of Fear. Arthur Conan Doyle. pap. 1.95 (ISBN 0-425-04911-6). Berkley Pub.

Valley of Romance. Jean Woodward. 192p. (YA) 1976. 5.95 (ISBN 0-685-66572-0, Avalon). Bouregy.

Valley of the Assassins. Ian MacAlister. 1978. pap. 1.50 o.p. (ISBN 0-449-13948-4, GM). Fawcett.

Valley of the Dolls. Jacqueline Susann. 1970. pap. 3.50 (ISBN 0-685-03305-8, 12772-1). Bantam.

Valley of the Giants. Peter Kyne. 1976. lib. bdg. 17.25x (ISBN 0-89968-056-9). Lightyear.

Valley of the Guns. Wayne D. Overholser. 1981. pap. 1.95 (ISBN 0-440-18825-3). Dell.

Valley of the Hawk. Margaret Mayo. (Harlequin Romances Ser.). 192p. 1980. pap. 1.25 o.p. (ISBN 0-373-02360-X, Pub. by Harlequin). PB.

Valley of the Kings: A Novel of Tutankhamun. Elizabeth E. Carter. LC 77-5157. 1977. 7.95 o.p. (ISBN 0-525-22777-6). Dutton.

Valley of the Lower Thames, 1640-1850. Fred C. Hamil. LC 73-86461. (Illus.). 1973. 17.50x o.p. (ISBN 0-8020-2109-3); pap. 7.50 (ISBN 0-8020-6220-2). U of Toronto Pr.

Valley of the Shadow. Janet Hickman. LC 73-10691. (Illus.). 288p. (gr. 4-8). 1974. 8.95 (ISBN 0-02-743750-7). Macmillan.

Valley of the Spirits: The Upper Skagit Indians of Western Washington. June M. Collins. LC 74-8719. (Illus.). 282p. 1974. pap. text ed. 8.50 (ISBN 0-295-95734-4). U of Wash Pr.

Valley of the Upper Yellowstone. Charles W. Cook et al. 1965. 6.95 (ISBN 0-8061-0664-6). U of Okla Pr.

Valley of Vision. Arthur Bennet. pap. 4.95 o.p. (ISBN 0-686-12544-4). Banner of Truth.

Valley of Vision: Discovering God Around the World. Winifred Walker. 64p. (Orig.). 1981. pap. write for info. Upper Room.

Valleys. Delia Goetz. LC 75-26980. (Illus.). 64p. (gr. 3-7). 1976. 6.25 (ISBN 0-688-22059-2); PLB 6.00 (ISBN 0-688-32059-7). Morrow.

Valleys of the Assassins. rev. ed. Freya Stark. (Illus.). 1972. 20.00 (ISBN 0-7195-2429-6). Transatlantic.

Valor of Francesco D'amini. Dominic N. Certo. (Orig.). 1979. pap. 2.25 (ISBN 0-532-23111-2). Manor Bks.

Valuable Nail: The Selected Poems of Gunter Eich. Tr. by Stuart Friebert et al from Ger. LC 80-85332. (Field Translation Ser.: No. 5). 150p. 1981. 9.95 (ISBN 0-932440-08-8); pap. 4.95 (ISBN 0-932440-09-6). Field-Oberlin.

Valuation of Real Estate. 2nd ed. Alfred A. Ring. 1970. ref. ed. 19.95 (ISBN 0-13-939892-9). P-H.

Valuation of Shopping Centers. Robert Garret et al. 1976. pap. 8.00 (ISBN 0-911780-38-6). Am Inst Real Estate Appraisers.

Value-Added Tax & Other Tax Reforms. Richard W. Lindholm. LC 76-24827. (Illus.). 332p. 1976. 21.95 (ISBN 0-911012-87-7). Nelson-Hall.

Value Added Tax in the Enlarged Common Market. Ed. by G. S. Wheatcroft. LC 73-2294. 140p. 1973. 15.95 (ISBN 0-470-93754-8). Halsted Pr.

Value Added Taxation in the ECC. D. A. Parkinson. 200p. 1980. 33.00x (ISBN 0-86010-190-8, Pub. by Graham & Trotman England). State Mutual Bk.

Value-Added Taxation: The Experience of the United Kingdom. A. R. Prest. 1980. pap. 4.25 (ISBN 0-8447-3404-7). Am Enterprise.

Value Analysis, Vol. 1. rev., 2nd ed. Carlos Fallon. LC 80-16194. (Illus.). 277p. 1980. text ed. 18.75 (ISBN 0-937144-00-2); pap. 10.75 (ISBN 0-937144-01-0). Triangle Pr.

Value & Crisis: Essays on Marxian Economics in Japan. Makoto Itoh. LC 80-8084. 192p. 1980. 13.50 (ISBN 0-85345-556-2); pap. 7.00 (ISBN 0-85345-557-0). Monthly Rev.

Value & Moral Development. Ed. by Thomas Hennessy. LC 76-18053. (Exploration Book). 1976. pap. 7.95 (ISBN 0-8091-1972-2). Paulist Pr.

Value & Price in the Labor-Surplus Economy. Stephen A. Marglin. (Illus.). 296p. 1976. 29.95x (ISBN 0-19-828194-3). Oxford U Pr.

Value & Valuation: Axiological Studies in Honor of Robert S. Hartman. Ed. by John W. Davis. LC 72-146661. 1972. 17.50x (ISBN 0-87049-130-X). U of Tenn Pr.

Value Areas & Their Development: Theory & Method of Self-Confrontation. Hubert J. Hermans. Tr. by Joseph A. Spiekerman from Dutch. 306p. 1975. text ed. 49.95 (ISBN 90-265-0225-7, Pub. by Swets Pub Serv Holland). Swets North Am.

Value Change in Chinese Society. Richard W. Wilson et al. LC 77-83479. (Praeger Special Studies). 1979. 26.95 (ISBN 0-03-023046-2). Praeger.

Value Clarification As Learning Process: A Handbook for Christian Educators. Brian Hall & Maury Smith. LC 73-81108. (Educator Formation Bks). (Orig.). 1974. pap. 8.95 (ISBN 0-8091-1797-5). Paulist Pr.

Value Conflicts & Curriculum Issues. Ed. by Jon Schaffarzick & Gary Sykes. LC 79-88125. 1980. 17.90 (ISBN 0-685-96793-X); in copies of ten 16.20 (ISBN 0-685-96794-8). McCutchan.

Value Engineering in Federal Construction Agencies. Building Research Advisory Board. LC 75-603933. (Orig.). 1969. pap. 4.75 (ISBN 0-309-01756-4). Natl Acad Pr.

Value-Freedom in Science & Technology: A Study of the Importance of Religious, Ethical, & Other Socio-Cultural Factors in Selected Medical Decisions Regarding Birth Control. Robert M. Veatch. LC 76-28192. (Harvard Dissertations in Religion). 1976. pap. 9.00 (ISBN 0-89130-080-5, 020108). Scholars Pr Ca.

Value in Social Theory: A Selection of Essays on Methodology. Gunnar Myrdal. (International Library of Sociology). 1968. Repr. of 1958 ed. 25.00x (ISBN 0-7100-3370-2). Routledge & Kegan.

Value Issues in Technology Assessment. Gordon A. Enk & William F. Hornick. (Special Studies in Science, Technology, & Public Policy). 180p. 1981. lib. bdg. 20.00x (ISBN 0-89158-973-2). Westview.

Value Moral Education. Ed. by Thomas Hennessy. LC 78-70814. 1979. pap. 9.95 (ISBN 0-8091-2150-6). Paulist Pr.

Value of Adventure: The Story of Sacajawea. Ann D. Johnson. LC 80-17623. (Value Tales Ser.). (Illus.). 66p. (gr. k-5). 1980. 6.95 (ISBN 0-916392-59-7, Dist. by Oak Tree Pubns). Value Comm.

Value of Agricultural Land. Colin Clark. (Illus.). 124p. 1973. text ed. 11.75 o.p. (ISBN 0-08-017070-6). Pergamon.

Value of Creativity: The Story of Thomas Edison. Ann D. Johnson. (Valuetales Ser.). (Illus.). 64p. (gr. k-6). 1981. 6.95 (ISBN 0-916392-72-4). Oak Tree Pubns.

Value of Fantasy: The Story of Hans Christian Andersen. Spencer Johnson. LC 79-18237. (ValueTales Ser.). (Illus.). (gr. k-6). 1979. 6.95 (ISBN 0-916392-43-0, Dist. by Oak Tree Pubns). Value Comm.

Value of Foresight: The Story of Thomas Jefferson. Ann D. Johnson. LC 79-19548. (Illus.). (gr. k-6). 1979. 6.95 (ISBN 0-916392-42-2, Dist. by Oak Tree Pubns.). Value Comm.

Value of Friendship: The Story of Jane Addams. Ann D. Johnson. LC 79-21643. (Value Tales Ser.). (Illus.). 1979. 6.95 (ISBN 0-916392-45-7). Value Comm.

Value of Giving: The Story of Beethovan. Ann D. Johnson. LC 78-31545. (ValueTales Ser.). (Illus.). (gr. k-6). 1979. 6.95 (ISBN 0-916392-34-1, Dist. by Oak Tree Pubns) Value Comm.

Value of Helping: The Story of Harriet Tubman. Ann D. Johnson. LC 79-21652. (Illus.). (gr. k-6). 1979. PLB 6.95g (ISBN 0-916392-41-4, Dist. by Oak Tree Pubns). Value Comm.

Value of Honesty: The Story of Confucius. Spencer Johnson. LC 78-4351. (ValueTales Ser.). (Illus.). (gr. k-6). 1979. 6.95 (ISBN 0-916392-36-8, Dist. by Oak Tree Pubns). Value Comm.

Value of Love: The Story of Johnny Appleseed. Ann D. Johnson. LC 79-31873. (ValueTales Ser.). (Illus.). (gr. k-6). 1979. 6.95 (ISBN 0-916392-35-X, Dist. by Oak Tree Pubns). Value Comm.

Value of Medicine. Philip Rhodes. 1977. text ed. 15.95x (ISBN 0-04-610004-0). Allen Unwin.

Value of Understanding: The Story of Margaret Mead. Spencer Johnson. LC 79-9800. (ValueTales Ser.). (Illus.). (gr. k-6). 1979. 6.95 (ISBN 0-916392-37-6, Dist. by Oak Tree Pubns). Value Comm.

Value-Philosophy of Alfred Edward Taylor: A Study in Theistic Implication. Charles W. Mason. LC 79-52512. 1979. pap. text ed. 13.75 (ISBN 0-8191-0772-7). U Pr of Amer.

Value, Price & Profit. Karl Marx. 1899. text ed. 2.95x o.p. (ISBN 0-04-331019-2). Allen Unwin.

Value Realms: Activities for Helping Students Develop Values. V. Presno & C. Presno. 1980. pap. text ed. 8.50x (ISBN 0-8077-2584-6). Tchrs Coll.

Value Tales Teacher's Manual. Sherri Butterfield. (Illus.). 120p. 1981. 9.95 (ISBN 0-916392-49-X, Dist. by Oak Tree Pubns). Value Comm.

Value to Agriculture of High-Quality Water from Nuclear Desalination. 1969. pap. 12.00 (ISBN 92-0-041069-3, IAEA). Unipub.

Values & Conduct. Joseph Margolis. (Orig.). 1971. text ed. 9.95x (ISBN 0-19-501327-1); pap. text ed. 4.95x (ISBN 0-19-501328-X). Oxford U Pr.

Values & Evaluation in Education. R. Straugham & J. Wrigley. 1980. text ed. 21.00 (ISBN 0-06-318137-1, IntlDept); pap. text ed. 11.20 (ISBN 0-06-318158-4). Har-Row.

Values & Moral Development in Higher Education. Ed. by G. Collier et al. LC 74-1599. 225p. 1974. 18.95 (ISBN 0-470-16549-9). Halsted Pr.

Values & Teaching. 2nd ed. Louis Raths et al. (Educational Foundations Ser.). 1978. pap. text ed. 9.95x (ISBN 0-675-08514-4). Merrill.

Values & the Credibility of the Professor. Louis W. Norris. LC 80-5501. 171p. 1980. lib. bdg. 16.75 (ISBN 0-8191-1114-7); pap. text ed. 8.75 (ISBN 0-8191-1115-5). U Pr of Amer.

Values & the Future. Kurt Baier & Nicholas Rescher. LC 68-14109. 1971. pap. text ed. 7.95 (ISBN 0-02-901190-6). Free Pr.

Values & the Quality of Life. Ed. by John King-Farlow & William R. Shea. LC 75-55511. 1976. pap. text ed. 4.95 o.p. (ISBN 0-88202-045-5). N Watson.

Values & Violence in Auschwitz: A Sociological Analysis. Anna Pawelczynska. 1979. 12.95 (ISBN 0-520-03210-1); pap. 4.95 (ISBN 0-520-04242-5, CAL-479). U of Cal Pr.

Values: Awareness, Significance & Action. Virginia Hash. 1975. pap. text ed. 7.95 (ISBN 0-8403-1286-5). Kendall Hunt.

Values Begin at Home. Ted Ward. 1979. pap. 3.95 (ISBN 0-88207-637-X). Victor Bks.

Values Clarification for Counselors: How Counselors, Social Workers, Psychologists, & Other Human Service Workers Can Use Available Techniques. Gordon M. Hart. (Illus.). 104p. 1978. 10.75 (ISBN 0-398-03847-3). C C Thomas.

Values, Curriculum & the Elementary School. Alexander Frazier. LC 79-87862. 1980. pap. text ed. 9.50 (ISBN 0-395-26739-0). HM.

Values, Education & the Adult. R. W. Paterson. (International Library of the Philosophy of Education). 1978. 20.00x (ISBN 0-7100-8968-6). Routledge & Kegan.

Values Guidance for Teens. Maureen Curley. (Children of the Kingdom Activities Ser.). (gr. 7-12). 1977. 7.95 (ISBN 0-686-13697-7). Pflaum Pr.

Values, Identities, & National Integration: Empirical Research in Africa. John N. Paden. 1980. 37.95 (ISBN 0-8101-0467-9). Northwestern U Pr.

Values in an American Government Textbook: Three Appraisals. Michael Novak et al. Ed. by Ernest W. Lefever. 57p. 1978. pap. 3.00. Ethics & Public Policy.

Values in Conflict: A Text Reader in Social Problems. Victor B. Ficker & James M. Rigterink. 512p. 1972. pap. text ed. 8.95x o.p. (ISBN 0-669-63487-5); instructor's manual free o.p. (ISBN 0-669-81067-3). Heath.

Values in Conflict: Blacks & the American Ambivalence Toward Violence. Charles A. Frye. LC 79-5516. 1980. pap. text ed. 9.00 (ISBN 0-8191-0899-5). U Pr of Amer.

Values in Conflict: Christianity, Marxism, Psychoanalysis & Existentialism. Ed. by Victor Comerchero. LC 74-111099. (Orig., Free booklet, "Suggestions for Instructors," available). 1970. pap. text ed. 12.95x (ISBN 0-89197-463-6). Irvington.

Values in Geography. Anne Buttimer. LC 74-76634. (CCG Resource Papers Ser.: No. 24). (Illus.). 1974. pap. text ed. 4.00 (ISBN 0-89291-071-2). Assn Am Geographers.

Values in Social Policy: Nine Contradictions. Jean Hardy. (Radical Social Policy Ser.). 132p. (Orig.). 1981. pap. price not set (ISBN 0-7100-0782-5). Routledge & Kegan.

Values in Social Work: A Re-Examination. Intro. by Morton Teicher. LC 65-15322. 107p. (Orig.). 1967. pap. text ed. 4.00x (ISBN 0-87101-345-2, CBO-345-I). Natl Assn Soc Wkrs.

Values of Growth. LC 75-44724. (Critical Choices for Americans Ser.: Vol. VI). 1976. 13.95 (ISBN 0-669-00418-9). Lexington Bks.

Values Orientation in School. Johnnie McFadden & Joseph C. Rotter. LC 80-69238. 90p. 1981. perfect bdg. 4.50 (ISBN 0-86548-045-1). Century Twenty One.

Valuing a Business: The Analysis & Appraisal of Closely Held Companies. Shannon Pratt. 500p. 1981. 42.50 (ISBN 0-87094-205-0). Dow Jones-Irwin.

Valuing a Company: Practices & Procedures. George D. McCarthy & Robert E. Healy. LC 74-166300. 521p. 1971. 38.95 (ISBN 0-8260-5825-6, Pub. by Wiley-Interscience). Wiley.

Valuing Common Stock: The Power of Prudence. George Lasry. 1979. 16.95 (ISBN 0-8144-5491-7). Am Mgmt.

Valuing the Timeshare Property. Kathleen Conroy. 97p. 1981. 15.00 (ISBN 0-911780-50-5). Am Inst Real Estate Appraisers.

Valvular Heart Disease. James E. Dalen & Joseph E. Alpert. 1981. text ed. price not set. Little.

Vamos a Ver. Helena Valenti. 1972. pap. 3.50 (ISBN 0-912022-31-0). EMC.

Vampire Jokes & Cartoons: A Comedy of Terrors. Ed. by Phil Hirsch. 1974. pap. 0.95 o.s.i. (ISBN 0-515-03498-3, N3498). Jove Pubns.

Vampire of Mons. Desmond Stewart. 1977. pap. 1.50 o.p. (ISBN 0-380-01681-8, 33522). Avon.

Vampire Tapestry. Suzy Charnas. 1980. 11.95 (ISBN 0-671-25415-4). S&S.

Vampirella, No. 1: Bloodstalk. Ron Goulart. (Orig.). 1975. pap. 1.25 o.s.i. (ISBN 0-446-76928-2). Warner Bks.

Vampirella, No. 3: Deadwalk. Ron Goulart. (Orig.). 1976. pap. 1.25 o.s.i. (ISBN 0-446-76930-4). Warner Bks.

Vampirella No. 6: Snakegod. Ron Goulart. 144p. (Orig.). 1976. pap. 1.25 o.s.i. (ISBN 0-446-86090-5). Warner Bks.

Vampires. Elwood D. Baumann. PLB 5.90 o.p. (ISBN 0-531-00128-8). Watts.

Vampires. Bernhardt J. Hurwood. (Illus.). 160p. 1981. pap. 7.95 (ISBN 0-8256-3202-1, Quick Fox). Music Sales.

Vampires of the Nightworld. David Bischoff. (Orig.). 1981. pap. 2.25 (ISBN 0-345-28763-0, Del Rey). Ballantine.

Vampires of the Slavs. Ed. by Jan L. Perkowski. 1976. soft cover 9.95 (ISBN 0-89357-026-5). Slavica.

Vampyre: A Bedside Companion. Ed. by Christopher Frayling. LC 78-53006. 1978. 9.95 o.p. (ISBN 0-684-15813-2, ScribT). Scribner.

Van Aaken Method. Ernst Van Aaken. Tr. by George Beinhorn from Ger. LC 75-20964. (Illus.). 135p. 1976. pap. 4.95 (ISBN 0-89037-070-2); handbk. 5.95 (ISBN 0-89037-071-0). Anderson World.

Van Alens: First Family of a Nation's First City. Samuel A. Schreiner, Jr. LC 80-70222. 448p. 1981. 12.95 (ISBN 0-87795-311-2). Arbor Hse.

Van der Waals Systems. Ed. by F. L. Boschke. (Topics in Current Chemistry: Vol. 93). (Illus.). 140p. 1980. 41.20 (ISBN 0-387-10058-X). Springer-Verlag.

Van Gogh. Meyer Shapiro. (Library of Great Painters Ser). (Illus.). 1950. 35.00 (ISBN 0-8109-0524-8). Abrams.

Van Gogh. Meyer Shapiro. LC 80-646. (Illus.). 160p. 1980. 14.95 (ISBN 0-385-17168-4). Doubleday.

Van Gogh. (Artists Ser.). (Illus.). 1977. pap. 5.95 (ISBN 0-8120-0717-6). Barron.

Van Goor's Concise Indonesian Dictionary: English-Indonesian Indonesian-English. A. L. Kramer, Sr. LC 66-21535. 1966. Repr. 8.95 (ISBN 0-8048-0611-X). C E Tuttle.

Van People: The Great American Rainbow Boogie. Douglas K. Hall. LC 77-451. (Illus.). 1977. 17.95 o.s.i. (ISBN 0-690-01418-X, TYC-T); pap. 8.95 o.s.i. (ISBN 0-690-01452-X, TYC-T). T Y Crowell.

Van Rhyne Heritage. Louisa Bronte. (Orig.). 1979. pap. 2.25 (ISBN 0-515-04310-9). Jove Pubns.

Van Sickle's Modern Airmanship. 5th ed. Ed. by John F. Welch. 896p. 1980. text ed. 24.95 (ISBN 0-442-25793-7). Van Nos Reinhold.

Van Til & the Use of Evidence. Thom Notaro. 1980. pap. 3.75 (ISBN 0-87552-353-6). Presby & Reformed.

Van Wyck Brooks. James R. Vitelli. (U. S. Authors Ser.: No. 134). 1969. lib. bdg. 10.95 (ISBN 0-8057-0096-X). Twayne.

Vanadium. Medical Sciences Division. LC 74-7131. (Medical & Biologic Effects of Environmental Pollutants Ser.). (Illus.). 128p. 1974. pap. 7.50 o.p. (ISBN 0-309-02218-5). Natl Acad Pr.

Vance & Nettie Palmer. Vivian Smith. LC 74-9791. (World Authors Ser.: Australia: No. 332). 168p. 1974. lib. bdg. 10.95 (ISBN 0-8057-2667-5). Twayne.

Vancouver, Explorer of the Pacific Coast. Ronald Syme. (Illus.). (gr. 3-7). 1970. 6.95 (ISBN 0-688-21807-5); PLB 5.71 o.p. (ISBN 0-686-66493-0). Morrow.

Vancouver Island Railroads. Robert Turner. LC 72-95484. (Illus.). 70p. 18.95 (ISBN 0-87095-046-0). Golden West.

Vancouver's First Century: A City Album, 1860-1960. Anne Kloppenborg et al. (Illus.). 172p. 1978. 25.00 (ISBN 0-295-95600-3). U of Wash Pr.

Vandalism: The Not-So-Senseless Crime. Arnold Madison. LC 70-125833. 1970. 5.50 (ISBN 0-395-28914-9, Clarion). HM.

Vandalism: The Not-So-Senseless Crime. Arnold Madison. 160p. (gr. 6 up). 1981. pap. 3.95 (ISBN 0-395-30069-6, Clarion). HM.

Vandals in the Bomb Factory: The History & Literature of the Students for a Democratic Society. G. Louis Heath. LC 75-40266. 1976. 21.00 (ISBN 0-8108-0890-0). Scarecrow.

Vanderbilt's Folly: History of Pennsylvania Turnpike. 6th ed. W. H. Shank. 1979. 3.00 (ISBN 0-933788-05-3). Am Canal & Transport.

Vanguards & Followers: Youth in the American Tradition. Louis Filler. LC 78-5893. 1978. 12.95 (ISBN 0-88229-459-8); pap. 7.95 (ISBN 0-88229-608-6). Nelson-Hall.

Vanguards of the Frontier: A Social History of the Northern Plains & Rocky Mountains from the Fur Traders to the Sod Busters. Everett Dick. LC 41-6157. (Illus.). 1965. pap. 9.95 (ISBN 0-8032-5048-7, BB 189, Bison). U of Nebr Pr.

Vanio & Zanda Zulan. Asaita Thakur. Tr. by Farley Richmond. (Translated from Gujarati). 8.00 (ISBN 0-89253-658-6); flexible cloth 4.80 (ISBN 0-89253-659-4). Ind-US Inc.

Vanished World of Jewry: Pictures by Eugene Rosow & Vivian Kleiman. Raphael Patai. (Illus.). 192p. 1981. 17.95 (ISBN 0-02-595120-3). Macmillan.

Vanished World: The Dinosaurs of Western Canada. Dale A. Russell. (Illus.). 1977. 15.00 (ISBN 0-660-00011-3, 56545-9, Pub. by Natl Mus Canada). U of Chicago Pr.

Vanishing Animals & Other Stories. Mary Morris. (Illus.). 192p. 1980. pap. 7.95 (ISBN 0-87923-388-5). Godine.

Vanishing Birds: Their Natural History & Conservation. Tim Halliday. LC 77-19010. (Illus.). 1978. 16.95 o.p. (ISBN 0-03-043561-7). HR&W.

Vanishing Britain. Roy Christian. 1977. 8.95 (ISBN 0-7153-7346-3). David & Charles.

Vanishing Creatures: Portraits of Endangered Species. Dugald Stermer. (Illus.). 80p. 1980. 15.95 (ISBN 0-89581-019-0); pap. 8.95 (ISBN 0-89581-021-2). Lancaster-Miller.

Vanishing Land. Hildegarde Flanner. 60p. (Orig.). 1980. pap. 6.00 (ISBN 0-931832-15-2). No Dead Lines.

Vanishing Landscapes: Land & Life in the Tulare Lake Basin. William L. Preston. (Illus.). 290p. 1981. 15.95 (ISBN 0-520-04053-8). U of Cal Pr.

Vanishing Old Castles in England. P. H. Ditchfield. (Philosophy of History Library Book). (Illus.). 109p. 1981. 49.75 (ISBN 0-86650-003-0). Gloucester Art.

Vanishing People: Fairy Lore & Legends. Katharine M. Briggs. 1979. pap. 3.95 (ISBN 0-394-73740-7). Pantheon.

Vanishing People: Fairy Lore & Legends. Katharine M Briggs. LC 78-53523. (Illus.). 1978. 8.95 (ISBN 0-394-50248-5). Pantheon.

Vanishing Sandwich. Mary B. Christian. (Goosehill Gang Ser.). (Illus.). 32p. (gr. 1-4). 1976. pap. 1.10 (ISBN 0-570-03609-7, 39-1034). Concordia.

Vanishing Street Furniture. Geoffrey Warren. 1978. 22.50 (ISBN 0-7153-7482-6). David & Charles.

Vanishing Thieves. Franklin W. Dixon. Ed. by Wendy Barish. (Hardy Boys Ser.). (Illus.). 192p. (Orig.). (gr. 2-7). 7.95 (ISBN 0-671-42292-8); pap. 1.95 (ISBN 0-671-42291-X). Wanderer Bks.

Vanishing Tower. Michael Moorcock. (Elric of Melnibone Ser.). (Illus.). 224p. 1980. 20.00slipcase (ISBN 0-915822-38-5). Archival Pr.

Vanishing Virgin. (Illus.). 4.95 (ISBN 0-910550-65-4). Centurion Pr.

Vanishing Wildlife of Latin America. Robert M. McClung. LC 80-25639. (Illus.). 160p. (gr. 7-9). 1981. 8.95 (ISBN 0-688-00378-8); PLB 8.59 (ISBN 0-688-00379-6). Morrow.

Vanishing Wings: A Tale of Three Birds of Prey. Griffing Bancroft. LC 77-182289. (Illus.). 160p. (gr. 9 up). 1972. PLB 5.88 o.p. (ISBN 0-531-02041-X). Watts.

Vanitie & Downe-Fall of Superstitious Popish Ceremonies. Peter Smart. LC 77-7428. (English Experience Ser.: No. 894). 1977. Repr. of 1628 ed. lib. bdg. 6.00 (ISBN 90-221-0894-5). Walter J Johnson.

Vanity Dies Hard. Ruth Rendell. 160p. Date not set. pap. 1.25 (ISBN 0-345-29286-3). Ballantine.

Vanity Fair. William M. Thackeray. 1957. 17.95x (ISBN 0-460-00298-8, Evman); pap. 4.95 (ISBN 0-460-01298-3). Dutton.

Vanity Fair. William M. Thackeray. (Literature Ser). (gr. 10-12). 1970. pap. text ed. 4.58 (ISBN 0-87720-741-0). AMSCO Sch.

Vanner's How-to Guide to Murals, Painting & Pinstriping. Keith Sessions. (Illus.). 1978. 8.95 (ISBN 0-8306-9888-4); pap. 5.95 (ISBN 0-8306-1032-4, 1032). TAB Bks.

Vannes & Its Region: A Study of Town & Country in Eighteenth-Century France. T. J. Le Goff. (Illus.). 496p. 1981. 69.00x (ISBN 0-19-822515-6). Oxford U Pr.

Vanya. Myrna Grant. LC 73-89729. 1974. pap. 2.45 (ISBN 0-88419-009-9). Creation Hse.

Vapheio Cups & Aegean Gold & Silver Ware. Ellen N. Davis. LC 76-23609. (Outstanding Dissertations in the Fine Arts). (Illus.). 1977. Repr. of 1973 ed. lib. bdg. 63.00 (ISBN 0-8240-2681-0). Garland Pub.

Vapor-Phase Organic Pollutants. Committee on Medical & Biologic Effects of Environmental Pollutants, Division of Medical Science, National Research Council. (Medical & Biologic Effects of Environmental Pollutants Ser.). 1976. pap. 13.00 (ISBN 0-309-02441-2). Natl Acad Pr.

Vaporizing Carburetors: One Hundred Miles per Gallon--the Real Facts. Brad Dennis & Al Rutan. (Illus.). 150p. (Orig.). 1981. pap. 14.95 (ISBN 0-936222-06-9). Rutan Pub.

Varangians of Byzantium. S. Blondal. Tr. by S. Benedikz. LC 77-82486. (Illus.). 1979. 49.95 (ISBN 0-521-21745-8). Cambridge U Pr.

Vardis Fisher. Joseph M. Flora. (U. S. Authors Ser.: No. 76). 1965. lib. bdg. 12.50 (ISBN 0-8057-0252-0). Twayne.

Vargas. Alberto Vargas & Reid Austin. 1981. pap. 8.95 (ISBN 0-517-53048-1, Harmony). Crown.

Vargas Regime. Robert M. Levine. LC 78-115222. 1970. 17.50x (ISBN 0-231-03370-2). Columbia U Pr.

Varia. John Ashton. LC 68-9573. (Illus.). 1968. Repr. of 1894 ed. 15.00 (ISBN 0-8103-3502-6). Gale.

Variability in Human Drug Response. S. E. Smith & M. D. Rawlins. 1976. 14.95 (ISBN 0-407-43301-5). Butterworths.

Variability of the Oceans. A. S. Monin et al. LC 77-826. 1977. 34.50 (ISBN 0-471-61328-2, Pub. by Wiley-Interscience). Wiley.

Variable Stars. W. Strohmeier. 287p. 1972. text ed. 42.00 (ISBN 0-08-016675-X). Pergamon.

Variable Syndrome. Don McGregor. 192p. 1981. Repr. lib. bdg. 16.95x (ISBN 0-89370-091-6). Borgo Pr.

Variable Syndrome: A Science Fiction Story. Don McGregor. (Also including: "Detectives, Inc." -- a memoir). 1981. pap. 10.00 (ISBN 0-934882-05-3). Fictioneer Bks.

Variable Winds at Jalna. Mazo De La Roche. 288p. 1975. pap. 1.50 o.p. (ISBN 0-449-22567-4, Q2567, Crest). Fawcett.

Variant English: An Introduction to Language Variation. Diane Bryen et al. (Elementary Education Ser.). 1978. pap. text ed. 8.50 (ISBN 0-675-08353-2); instr. manual 3.95 (ISBN 0-686-67995-4). Merrill.

Variant Versions of Targumic Traditions Within Codex Neofiti 1. Shirley Lund & Julia A. Foster. LC 77-5389. (Society of Biblical Literature. Aramaic Studies). 1977. pap. 7.50 (ISBN 0-89130-137-2, 061302). Scholars Pr Ca.

Variation & Adaptation in Plant Species. 2nd ed. David A. Jones & Dennis A. Wilkins. 1971. pap. text ed. 5.50x o.p. (ISBN 0-435-61480-0). Heinemann Ed.

Variation & Fixity in Nature. Frank Marsh. LC 75-36531. (Dimension Ser.). 1976. pap. 5.95 (ISBN 0-8163-0269-3, 22110-1). Pacific Pr Pub Assn.

Variation in the Polygonum Amphibium Complex & Its Taxonomic Significance. Richard S. Mitchell. (U. C. Publ. in Botany: Vol. 45). 1968. pap. 6.50x (ISBN 0-520-09018-7). U of Cal Pr.

Variation in Varietal Reaction to Rice Tungro Disease: Possible Causes. (IRRI Research Paper Ser.: No. 32). 8p. 1979. pap. 5.00 (R072, IRRI). Unipub.

Variation in Writing: Functional & Linguistic-Cultural Differences, Vol. 1. Ed. by Carl H. Fredericksen et al. 240p. 1981. prof. - refer. 16.50 (ISBN 0-89859-099-X). L Erlbaum Assocs.

Variation of Spotted & Spinner Porpoise (Genus Stennella) in the Eastern Pacific & Hawaii. William F. Perrin. LC 74-22939. (Scripps Institution of Oceanography Bulletin: Vol. 21). 1975. pap. 12.50x (ISBN 0-520-09527-8). U of Cal Pr.

Variational Analysis: Critical Extremals & Sturmian Extensions. Marston Morse. LC 72-8368. (Pure & Applied Mathematics Ser). 304p. 1973. 34.50 (ISBN 0-471-61700-8, Pub. by Wiley-Interscience). Wiley.

Variational Methods in Elasticity & Plasticity. 2nd ed. Kyuichiro Washizu. 1974. text ed. 64.00 (ISBN 0-08-017653-4). Pergamon.

Variational Methods in Optimization. Donald R. Smith. (Illus.). 464p. 1974. 22.95 (ISBN 0-13-940627-1). P-H.

Variational Methods in the Mechanics of Solids: Proceedings of the UUTAM Symposium, Sept. 11-13, 1978. S Nemat-Nasser. LC 80-41529. (Illus.). 426p. 1981. 100.00 (ISBN 0-08-024728-8). Pergamon.

Variational Principles in Dynamics & Quantum Theory. 3rd ed. Wolfgang Yourgrau & Stanley Mandelstam. LC 78-73521. 1979. pap. text ed. 4.00 (ISBN 0-486-63773-5). Dover.

Variational Principles of Mechanics. 4th ed. Cornelius Lanczos. LC 70-151376. 1970. 17.50x o.p. (ISBN 0-8020-1743-6). U of Toronto Pr.

Variations & Evolution in Plants. George L. Stebbins. LC 50-9426. (Columbia Biological Ser.: No. 16). (Illus.). 1950. 40.00x (ISBN 0-231-01733-2). Columbia U Pr.

Variations in Services for the Aged. Bleddyn P. Davies. 164p. 1971. pap. text ed. 6.25x (ISBN 0-7135-1621-6, Pub. by Bedford England). Renouf.

Variations on the Imperial Theme: Studies in Ceremonial Art & Collecting in the Age of Maximilian II & Rudolf II. Thomas D. Kaufmann. LC 77-94699. (Outstanding Dissertations in the Fine Arts Ser.). 1978. lib. bdg. 24.00x (ISBN 0-8240-3231-4). Garland Pub.

Variatons in Childrens Services Among Urban Authorities. Bleddyn Davies. 159p. 1972. pap. text ed. 6.25x (ISBN 0-7135-1676-3, Pub. by Bedford England). Renouf.

Varied Rhythms. Maharaja K. Singh. 3.75x o.p. (ISBN 0-210-33791-5). Asia.

Variedades del Espanol Actual. Lynn Ingamells & Standish Porter. (Illus.). 384p. (Span., Prog. Bk.). 1975. pap. text ed. 13.95x (ISBN 0-582-35026-3); tapes 45.00x (ISBN 0-582-37394-8); tapescript 4.00x (ISBN 0-582-35027-1). Longman.

Varietie of Lute-Lessons. Robert Dowland. LC 79-84102. (English Experience Ser.: No. 921). 76p. 1979. Repr. of 1610 ed. lib. bdg. 14.00 (ISBN 90-221-0921-6). Walter J Johnson.

Varieties & Problems of Twentieth Century Socialism. Jack R. Thomas & Louis Patsouras. LC 79-21450. 214p. 1981. text ed. 15.95 (ISBN 0-88229-444-X); pap. text ed. 8.95 (ISBN 0-88229-743-0). Nelson-Hall.

Varieties of Abnormality: A Phenomenological Analysis. Raymond J. McCall. (Illus.). 592p. 1975. 29.75 (ISBN 0-398-03280-7); pap. 21.75 (ISBN 0-398-03281-5). C C Thomas.

Varieties of Civil Religion. Robert N. Bellah & Phillip E. Hammond. LC 80-7742. 256p. 1981. 14.95 (ISBN 0-06-060776-9, HarpR). Har-Row.

Varieties of E. S. P. in the Edgar Cayce Readings. Doris T. Patterson. Orig. Title: Unfettered Mind. 77p. 1968. pap. 2.00 o.p. (ISBN 0-87604-036-9). ARE Pr.

Varieties of English. 2nd ed. G. L. Brook. 1977. text ed. 18.25x (ISBN 0-333-14284-5). Humanities.

Varieties of History: From Voltaire to the Present. Ed. by Fritz Stern. 1973. pap. 5.95 (ISBN 0-394-71962-X, Vin). Random.

Varieties of Human Value. Charles W. Morris. LC 56-6641. (Midway Reprint Ser). 1973. Repr. of 1956 ed. pap. 9.00x o.s.i. (ISBN 0-226-53883-4). U of Chicago Pr.

Varieties of Jewish Belief. Louis Barish & Rebecca Barish. 1979. Repr. 9.95 (ISBN 0-8246-0242-0). Jonathan David.

Varieties of Monetary Experience. Ed. by David M. Meiselman. LC 70-116027. (Economic Research Center Ser). 1971. 20.00x (ISBN 0-226-51930-9). U of Chicago Pr.

Varieties of Parable. Louis MacNeice. 1966. 28.50 (ISBN 0-521-05654-3). Cambridge U Pr.

Varieties of Political Conservatism. Ed. by Matthew Holden. LC 74-78561. (Sage Contemporary Social Science Issues: No. 16). 1974. 4.95x (ISBN 0-8039-0441-X). Sage.

Varieties of Psychotherapeutic Experience. David O. Orlinsky & Kenneth I. Howard. LC 74-22011. 1975. text ed. 15.70x (ISBN 0-8077-2458-0); pap. text ed. 11.95x (ISBN 0-8077-2478-5). Tchrs Coll.

Varieties of Religious Experience. William James. pap. 2.50 (ISBN 0-451-61603-0, ME1875, Ment). NAL.

Varieties of Religious Experience. William James. LC 77-76278. 1978. pap. 2.95 o.p. (ISBN 0-385-13267-0, Im). Doubleday.

Varieties of Travel. Ed. by Alan Hodge. LC 79-351286. (Selections from History Today Ser.: No. 8). (Illus.). 1969. 5.00 (ISBN 0-05-001535-4); pap. 3.95 (ISBN 0-685-09206-2). Dufour.

Varieties of Visual Experience. 3rd ed. Ed. by E. Feldman. 1981. pap. 15.95. P-H.

Varieties of Visual Experience. 2nd ed. Edmund B. Feldman. 536p. text ed. 17.95 (ISBN 0-13-940585-2). P-H.

Varieties of Work Experience: The Social Control of Occupational Groups & Roles. Ed. by Phyllis L. Stewart & Muriel Cantor. LC 74-6158. 1974. text ed. 13.95x (ISBN 0-470-82477-8); pap. text ed. 5.95x o.p. (ISBN 0-470-82478-6). Halsted Pr.

Variety, Equity, & Efficiency. Kelvin Lancaster. LC 78-24616. 1979. 25.00x (ISBN 0-231-04616-2). Columbia U Pr.

Variety in Contemporary English. W. R. O'Donnell & Loreto Todd. (Illus.). 176p. (Orig.). 1980. 25.00x (ISBN 0-04-421005-1, 2560); pap. 8.50 (ISBN 0-04-421006-X, 2561). Allen Unwin.

Variety in Your Preaching. Faris D. Whitesell & Lloyd M. Perry. 1954. 10.95 (ISBN 0-8007-0335-9). Revell.

Variety of Catholic Modernists. A. R. Vidler. (Sarum Lectures in the University of Oxford for the Year 1968-69). 1970. 36.00 (ISBN 0-521-07649-8). Cambridge U Pr.

Variety of Fiction: A Critical Anthology. Ed. by Edward A. Bloom & Lillian D. Bloom. LC 65-79102. 1969. pap. 7.50 (ISBN 0-672-63137-7). Odyssey Pr.

Variety of Poetry: An Anthology. Ed. by Edward A. Bloom et al. LC 64-13149. (Orig.). 1964. pap. 5.50 (ISBN 0-672-63138-5). Odyssey Pr.

Variety of Sex. (Illus.). pap. 5.00 (ISBN 0-910550-64-6). Centurion Pr.

Variety Photoplays. Edward Field. 1980. 3.50 (ISBN 0-917554-02-7). Maelstrom.

Variorum Commentary on the Poems of John Milton, Vol. 1. Ed. by Merritt Y. Hughes. LC 70-129962. 30.00x (ISBN 0-231-08879-5). Columbia U Pr.

Variorum Commentary on the Poems of John Milton, Vol. 2, 3 Pts. Ed. by Merritt Y. Hughes. LC 70-129962. 1972. 30.00x ea. Pt. 1 (ISBN 0-231-08880-9). Pt. 2 (ISBN 0-231-08881-7). Pt. 3 (ISBN 0-231-08882-5). Columbia U Pr.

Variorum Commentary on the Poems of John Milton, Vol. 4. Ed. by Walter MacKellar. 400p. 1975. 30.00 (ISBN 0-231-08883-3). Columbia U Pr.

Variorum Edition of Elizabeth Barrett Browning's Sonnets from the Portuguese. Ed. by Miroslava W. Dow. 201p. 1980. 12.50 (ISBN 0-87875-179-3). Whitston Pub.

Variorum Edition of Idylls of the King. John Pfordresher. 1088p. 1973. 30.00x (ISBN 0-231-03691-4). Columbia U Pr.

Variorum Edition of the Plays of W. B. Yeats. William B. Yeats. Ed. by R. K. Alspach. 1966. 40.00 (ISBN 0-02-501720-9). Macmillan.

Variorum Edition of the Poems of W. B. Yeats. William B. Yeats. Ed. by P. Allt. 1957. 19.95 (ISBN 0-02-501560-5). Macmillan.

Various Language: An Inquiry Approach to the Physical Sciences. Arnold Arons. (Illus.). 1977. 14.95x (ISBN 0-19-502147-9). Oxford U Pr.

Various Light. Alfred Corn. 1980. pap. 7.95 (ISBN 0-14-042284-6). Penguin.

Various Universe: A Study of the Journals & Memoirs of British Men & Women in the Indian Subcontinent Seventeen Sixty Five to Eighteen Fifty Six. Ketaki K. Dyson. 1979. 22.00x (ISBN 0-19-561074-1). Oxford U Pr.

Vark' Mastotsi: Life of Mastots. Koriwn. Ed. by Krikor Maksoudian. 1981. write for info. (ISBN 0-88206-030-9). Caravan Bks.

Varnishes of the Italian Violin-Makers of the Sixteenth, Seventeenth & Eighteenth Centuries & Their Influence on Tone. George Fry. (Illus.). 1977. Repr. of 1904 ed. text ed. 16.00 (ISBN 0-918624-02-9). Virtuoso.

Varoom. Ed. by Thomas Mooney. (Pal Paperbacks Kit A Ser.). (Illus., Orig.). (gr. 7-12). 1973. pap. text ed. 1.25 (ISBN 0-8374-3483-1). Xerox Ed Pubns.

Vasarely. Victor Vasarely. (Alpine Fine Arts Collection). (Illus.). 152p. 1980. 50.00 (ISBN 0-933516-01-0, Pub by Alpine Fine Arts). Hippocrene Bks.

Vasarely Four. Joray. 1980. 195.95 (ISBN 0-8120-5394-X). Barron.

Vasco Da Gama: Sailor Toward the Sunrise. Ronald Syme. (Illus.). (gr. 3-7). 1959. PLB 6.00 o.p. (ISBN 0-688-31588-7). Morrow.

Vascular Diseases: A Concise Guide to Diagnosis, Management, Pathogenesis, & Prevention. Sandor Friedman. 1981. write for info. (ISBN 0-88416-283-4). PSG Pub.

Vascular Emergencies. Henry Haimovici. 1981. 34.50 (ISBN 0-686-69607-7). ACC.

Vascular Flora of Georgia: An Annotated Checklist. Wilbur H. Duncan & John T. Kartesz. 149p. 1981. pap. 5.00 (ISBN 0-8203-0538-3). U of Ga Pr.

Vascular Neuroeffector Mechanisms. Ed. by John A. Bevan et al. 1979. 42.50 (ISBN 0-89004-302-7). Raven.

Vascular Plant Families. James P. Smith, Jr. (Illus.). 1977. pap. 9.10x (ISBN 0-916422-07-0). Mad River.

Vascular Plants of Continental Northwest Territories. William J. Cody & A. Erling Porsild. (Illus.). 676p. 1980. lib. bdg. 85.00x (ISBN 0-660-00119-5, 56546-7, Pub. by Natl Mus Canada). U of Chicago Pr.

Vascular Plants of San Luis Obispo County, California. Robert F. Hoover. LC 71-104883. 1970. 25.00x (ISBN 0-520-01663-7). U of Cal Pr.

Vascular Surgery. 3rd ed. Ed. by C. Rob. (Operative Surgery Ser.). 1976. 84.95 (ISBN 0-407-00644-3). Butterworths.

Vascular Surgery. C. R. Savage. (Pitman Nursing Books Ser.). (Illus.). 200p. 1970. 12.50x o.p. (ISBN 0-8464-0951-8). Beekman Pubs.

Vasculitides. Thomas R. Cupps & Anthony S. Fauci. 1981. pap. price not set. Saunders.

Vasculogenic Impotence. A. W. Zorgniotti & G. Rossi. (Illus.). 344p. 1980. 39.75 (ISBN 0-398-03982-8). C C Thomas.

Vasily I. Kelsiev: An Encounter Between the Russian Revolutionaries & the Old Believers. Paul Call. LC 78-78270. 350p. 1980. 33.50 (ISBN 0-913124-36-2). Nordland Pub.

Vasily Zhukovsky. Irina M. Semenko. LC 75-23419. (World Authors Ser.: Russia: No. 271). 1976. lib. bdg. 12.50 (ISBN 0-8057-2995-X). Twayne.

Vasn Vardanay Ew Hayots Paterazmin: On Vardan & the Armenian War. Eghihse. Ed. by Avedis K. Sanjian. 1981. write for info. (ISBN 0-88206-034-1). Caravan Bks.

Vasoactive Substances Relevant to Migraine. Ed. by Seymour Diamond et al. (Illus.). 112p. 1975. 14.50 (ISBN 0-398-03348-X). C C Thomas.

Vasodilatation. Ed. by Paul M. Vanhoutte & Isadore Leusen. 475p. 1981. 46.00 (ISBN 0-89004-602-6). Raven.

Vassouras: A Brazilian Coffee County, 1850-1900. Stanley J. Stein. LC 57-8627. (Studies in American Negro Life). 1970. pap. 5.95x (ISBN 0-689-70229-9, NL23). Atheneum.
Vast Venture: Hardy's Epic-Drama The Dynasts. Chester A. Garrison. (Salzburg Studies in English Literature, Poetic Drama & Poetic Theory: No. 18). 250p. 1973. pap. text ed. 25.00x (ISBN 0-391-01381-5). Humanities.
Vatican. Peter Hebblethwaite et al. LC 80-50854. (Illus.). 226p. 1980. 50.00 (ISBN 0-86565-002-0). Vendome.
Vatican Finances. Corrado Pallenberg. 1971. text ed. 10.50x (ISBN 0-391-00194-9). Humanities.
Vatican Frescoes of Michelangelo, 2 vols. Intro. by Andre Chastel. Tr. by Raymond Rosenthal from Fr. LC 80-66646. (Illus.). 528p. 1980. ltd. ed. 6000.00 (ISBN 0-89659-158-1). Abbeville Pr.
Vaudevillians. William Smith. LC 75-28477. (Illus.). 288p. 1976. 9.95 o.s.i. (ISBN 0-02-611890-4, 61189). Macmillan.
Vault of the Ages. Paul Anderson. 1978. pap. 1.95 (ISBN 0-425-04336-3, Medallion). Berkley Pub.
Vaulting: Gymnastics on Horseback. Paki Stedwell. LC 79-11556. (Illus.). 128p. (gr. 7-12). 1980. PLB 7.79 (ISBN 0-671-34023-9). Messner.
Vaya Con Dios. J. Benbow Bullock. (Illus.). 150p. 1981. pap. 6.95 (ISBN 0-937024-02-3). Gourmet Guides.
Vecellio's Renaissance Costume Book. Cesare Vecellio. LC 76-55952. (Pictorialarchive Ser.). (Illus.). 1977. pap. 5.00 (ISBN 0-486-23441-X). Dover.
Vector Analysis. N. Kemmer. LC 75-36025. (Illus.). 230p. 1977. 49.50 (ISBN 0-521-21158-1); pap. 15.95x (ISBN 0-521-29064-3). Cambridge U Pr.
Vector Analysis. L. Marder. (Unwin Studies in Physics & Applied Mathematics). 1970. text ed. 7.95x o.p. (ISBN 0-04-512010-2). Allen Unwin.
Vector Analysis for Mathematicians, Scientists & Engineers. 2nd ed. S. Simons. 1970. 15.00 (ISBN 0-08-006988-6); pap. 9.25 (ISBN 0-08-006895-2). Pergamon.
Vector & Tensor Analysis. George E. Hay. 1953. pap. text ed. 3.00 (ISBN 0-486-60109-9). Dover.
Vector & Tensor Analysis. Harry Lass. (International Ser. in Pure & Applied Mathematics). 1950. text ed. 19.95 o.p. (ISBN 0-07-036520-2, C). McGraw.
Vector & Tensor Methods. Frank Chorlton. LC 75-16460. 300p. 1976. 39.95x (ISBN 0-470-15604-X). Halsted Pr.
Vector Calculus. Jerold E. Marsden & Anthony J. Tromba. LC 75-17864. (Illus.). 1976. 22.95x (ISBN 0-7167-0462-5). W H Freeman.
Vector Calculus. 2nd ed. Jerrold E. Marsden & Anthony J. Tromba. LC 80-24663. (Illus.). 1981. text ed. 22.95x (ISBN 0-7167-1244-X). W H Freeman.
Vector Electrocardiography. Herman N. Uhley. (Illus.). 1962. 8.50 o.p. (ISBN 0-397-50086-6). Lippincott.
Vector Fields. J. A. Shercliff. LC 76-8153. (Illus.). 1977. 63.50 (ISBN 0-521-21306-1); pap. 12.95x (ISBN 0-521-29092-9). Cambridge U Pr.
Vector Measures. N. Dinculeanu. LC 68-6701. 1967. 36.30 o.p. (ISBN 0-08-012192-6). Pergamon.
Vector Spaces of Finite Dimension. G. C. Shephard. (University Mathematical Texts Ser.). 1966. 5.95 o.p. (ISBN 0-471-78324-2). Halsted Pr.
Vectorcardiography: A Programmed Introduction. 2nd ed. Lemberg. (Illus.). 1975. pap. 17.00 o.p. (ISBN 0-8385-9396-8). ACC.
Vectors & Matrices. Pamela Liebeck. 192p. 1971. 25.00 (ISBN 0-08-015823-4); pap. 12.75 (ISBN 0-08-015822-6). Pergamon.
Vectors & Tensors for Engineers & Scientists. F. A. Hinchey. LC 76-21725. 1976. 13.95 (ISBN 0-470-15194-3). Halsted Pr.
Vectors in Three-Dimensional Space. J. S. Chisholm. LC 77-82492. (Illus.). 1978. 63.50 (ISBN 0-521-21832-2); pap. 15.95 (ISBN 0-521-29289-1). Cambridge U Pr.
Vectors of Disease Agents: Interactions with Plants, Animals, & Men. Ed. by John J. McKelvey, Jr. et al. 350p. 1980. 34.95 (ISBN 0-03-056887-0). Praeger.
Vectors of Plant Pathogens. Ed. by K. Harris & K. Maramorosch. 1980. 48.00 (ISBN 0-12-326450-2). Acad Pr.
Vedanta: An Anthology of Hindu Scripture, Commentary, & Poetry. Ed. by Clive Johnson. LC 75-126033. 1971. 2.50 o.p. (ISBN 0-685-57296-X). Weiser.
Vedanta Explained: Samkara's Commentary on the Brahma-Sutrais, 2 vols. V. H. Date. 952p. 1974. text ed. 24.00x o.p. (ISBN 0-8426-0599-1). Verry.
Vedanta-Sara-Sangraha. Anantendra-Yati. Tr. by T. M. Mahadevan. 1974. pap. 2.00 (ISBN 0-89744-124-9, Pub. by Ganesh & Co. India). Auromere.
Vedanta-Sutras, Vols. 34 & 38. Ed. by F. Max Mueller. Tr. by Thibaut. (Sacred Books of the East Ser.). 15.00x ea.; Vol. 34. (ISBN 0-8426-1429-X); Vol. 38. (ISBN 0-8426-1430-3). Verry.
Vedanta Sutras, Vol. 48. Ed. by F. Max Mueller. (Sacred Books of the East Ser.). 15.00x (ISBN 0-8426-1431-1). Verry.
Vedantasara of Sadananda. Sadananda. pap. 1.95 o.s.i. (ISBN 0-87481-073-6). Vedanta Pr.
Vedantic Buddhism of the Buddha: A Collection of Historical Texts. Ed. by J. G. Jennings. 679p. 1975. text ed. 19.50x o.p. (ISBN 0-8426-0683-1). Verry.
Vedettes: A Collection of Stories. Edward Loomis. LC 64-16117. 112p. (Orig.). 1964. 5.95 (ISBN 0-8040-0309-2); pap. 2.75 (ISBN 0-8040-0310-6, 64). Swallow.
Vedic Hymns, Vols. 32 & 46. Ed. by F. Max Mueller. Tr. by Oldenburg. (Sacred Books of the East Ser.). 15.00x ea.; Vol. 32. (ISBN 0-8426-1432-X); Vol. 46. (ISBN 0-8426-1433-8). Verry.
Vedic India. G. S. Ghurye. 1979. 44.00x (ISBN 0-8364-0455-6). South Asia Bks.
Vedic Religion. Abel Bergaigne. Tr. by V. G. Paranjpe. 1978. 25.00 (ISBN 0-89684-006-9, Pub. by Motilal Banarsidass India). Orient Bk Dist.
Vega & Other Poems. Lawrence Durrell. LC 73-75122. 58p. 1973. 10.00 (ISBN 0-87951-009-9). Overlook Pr.
Vega Service, Repair Handbook 1971-1977 Models. 3rd ed. Jim Combs & Jeff Robinson. (Illus.). 1976. pap. 10.95 (ISBN 0-89287-130-X, A135). Clymer Pubns.
Vegas: A Memoir of a Dark Season. John G. Dunne. 1975. pap. 2.25 o.s.i. (ISBN 0-446-82931-5). Warner Bks.
Vegetable Cook Book. Sunset Editors. LC 72-92516. (Illus.). 96p. 1973. pap. 3.95 (ISBN 0-376-02903-X, Sunset Bks.). Sunset-Lane.
Vegetable Cookery. Phe Laws. 256p. 1980. pap. 6.95 (ISBN 0-8256-3828-3, Quick Fox). Music Sales.
Vegetable Farming. Hollis Lee. (Country Home & Small Farm Guides Ser.). (Illus.). 1978. pap. 2.95 (ISBN 0-88453-008-6). Barrington.
Vegetable Farming. (Country Home Ser.). 96p. 2.95 (ISBN 0-88453-008-6). Berkshire Traveller.
Vegetable Farming Systems in the People's Republica of China. Ed. by Donald L. Plucknett & Halsey Beemer. (Westview Special Studies in Agricultural Science). 350p. 1980. lib. bdg. 28.50x (ISBN 0-89158-999-6). Westview.
Vegetable Garden. M. M. Vilmorin-Andrieux. 620p. 1981. pap. 11.95 (ISBN 0-89815-041-8). Ten Speed Pr.
Vegetable Growers Primer. 2nd ed. J. Todd Miles. 58p. 1980. 11.95x (ISBN 0-9605070-0-0); soft cover 6.95x (ISBN 0-9605070-1-9). Foto Res.
Vegetable Growing for Southern Gardens. Bill Adams. LC 75-18204. 1976. write for info. (ISBN 0-88415-888-8); pap. 3.95 (ISBN 0-685-54016-2). Pacesetter Pr.
Vegetable Growing Handbook. Walter E. Splittstoesser. (Illus.). 1979. text ed. 14.00 (ISBN 0-87055-319-4). AVI.
Vegetable Parade. Susan Levan. LC 77-8078. (Orig.). 1979. pap. 10.00 (ISBN 0-914908-90-1). Street Fiction.
Vegetables. (Good Cook Ser.). (Illus.). 1979. lib. bdg. 11.97 (ISBN 0-8094-2859-8); kivar bdg. 9.96 (ISBN 0-8094-2860-1). Silver.
Vegetables & Fruits. James U. Crockett. (Encyclopedia of Gardening Ser.). (Illus.). 1972. 11.95 (ISBN 0-8094-1069-9); lib. bdg. avail. (ISBN 0-685-27455-1). Time-Life.
Vegetables & Fruits. James U. Crockett. LC 78-140420. (Time-Life Encyclopedia of Gardening). (Illus.). 1972. lib. bdg. 11.97 (ISBN 0-8094-1071-0, Pub. by Time-Life). Silver.
Vegetables & Fruits. James U. Crockett. LC 78-140420. (Time-Life Encyclopedia of Gardening Ser.). (Illus.). 1972. lib. bdg. 11.97 (ISBN 0-686-51064-X). Silver.
Vegetables & Herbs with a Difference. G. J. Binding. 1980. 19.50x (ISBN 0-85032-178-6, Pub. by Daniel Co England). State Mutual Bk.
Vegetables & Herbs with a Difference. G. J. Binding. 64p. 1972. pap. 3.00x (ISBN 0-8464-1059-1). Beekman Pubs.
Vegetables Cookbook. Lena Sturges. LC 74-18641. (Family Guidebooks Ser). (Illus.). 1975. pap. 1.95 (ISBN 0-8487-0365-0). Oxmoor Hse.
Vegetables for the Hot, Humid Tropics. Franklin W. Martin et al. (Studies in Tropical Agriculture). 1980. lib. bdg. 59.95 (ISBN 0-8490-3071-4). Gordon Pr.
Vegetables from Small Gardens. Joy Larkcom. 1977. 9.95 (ISBN 0-571-10644-7, Pub. by Faber & Faber). Merrimack Bk Serv.
Vegetables from Stems & Leaves. Millicent E. Selsam. (Illus.). 48p. (gr. 2-5). 1972. 7.44 o.p. (ISBN 0-688-30117-7). Morrow.
Vegetables: Growing & Cooking the Natural Way. W. E. Sherwell-Cooper. 1975. pap. 8.95 o.p. (ISBN 0-04-641027-9). Allen Unwin.
Vegetables in South-East Asia. G. A. C. Herklots. (Illus.). 1972. text ed. 20.00x (ISBN 0-04-635008-X). Allen Unwin.
Vegetarian Cooking. Sunset Editors. LC 80-53483. (Illus.). 96p. (Orig.). 1981. pap. 3.95 (ISBN 0-376-02910-2, Sunset Books). Sunset-Lane.
Vegetarian Feast. Barbara E. Echols. 1981. pap. text ed. 6.95 (ISBN 0-8120-2163-0). Barron.
Vegetarian Gourmet Cookery. Alan Hooker. LC 72-19332. (Illus., Orig.). 1970. pap. 5.95 (ISBN 0-912238-03-8). One Hund One Prods.
Vegetarian Medicines. Clarence Meyer. Ed. by David C. Meyer. (Illus.). 96p. (Orig.). 1981. pap. 5.95 (ISBN 0-916638-06-5). Meyerbooks.
Vegetarian Times Guide to Dining in the U. S. A. Vegetarian Times Magazine. 1980. pap. 8.95 (ISBN 0-689-10966-0). Atheneum.
Vegetarianism: A Way of Life. Dudley Giehl. 272p. 1981. pap. 3.95 (ISBN 0-06-464045-0, BN). Har-Row.
Vegetation Dynamics. Ed. by Wim G. Beeftink. 135p. 1980. pap. 31.60 (ISBN 90-6193-606-3). Kluwer Boston.
Vegetation Dynamics. J. Miles. LC 78-13070. (Outline Studies in Ecology). 80p. 1979. pap. text ed. 4.95x o.p. (ISBN 0-470-26504-3). Halsted Pr.
Vegetation Map of Papua New Guinea. (Land Research Ser.: No. 35). 24p. 1975. 13.50 (ISBN 0-643-00138-7, CSIRO). Unipub.
Vegetation Mapping. A. W. Kuchler. (Illus.). 1967. 27.00 (ISBN 0-8260-5150-2, Pub. by Wiley-Interscience). Wiley.
Vegetation of Wisconsin: An Ordination of Plant Communities. John T. Curtis. 1959. 19.50 (ISBN 0-299-01940-3). U of Wis Pr.
Vegetation Productivity. G. Jones. LC 78-40985. (Topics in Applied Geography Ser.). (Illus.). 1979. pap. text ed. 10.95 (ISBN 0-582-48577-0). Longman.
Vegetationsgeschichtliche und Pflanzensoziologische Untersuchungen Im Vicente Perez Nationalpark: Chile. M. C. Villagran. (Dissertationes Botanicae: No. 54). (Illus.). 166p. (Ger.). 1981. pap. text ed. 25.00x (ISBN 3-7682-1265-3). Lubrecht & Cramer.
Vehicle & Traffic Law (N.Y.) Gould Editorial Staff. 250p. (Supplemented annually). looseleaf 10.00 (ISBN 0-87526-130-2). Gould.
Vehicle Body Building: Pt. 1. Ed. by B. Coombes et al. (Engineering Craftsmen: Pt. 2). (Illus.). 1968. 26.50x (ISBN 0-686-65562-1). Intl Ideas.
Vehicle Body Building, Pt. 2, 2 vols. Ed. by B. Coombes. (Engineering Craftsmen: No. E22). (Illus.). 1969. Set. spiral bdg. 52.00x (ISBN 0-85083-063-X). Intl Ideas.
Vehicle Body Engineering. J. Pawlowski. Tr. by Guy Tidbury. (Illus.). 1970. 28.00x o.p. (ISBN 0-8464-0952-6). Beekman Pubs.
Vehicle Fitting. Ed. by R. Aylen et al. (Engineering Craftsmen; No. H8). (Illus.). 1978. spiral bdg. 21.00x (ISBN 0-685-90188-2). Intl Ideas.
Vehicle Laws of Pennsylvania. Gould Editorial Staff. Date not set. looseleaf 12.00 (ISBN 0-87526-233-3). Gould.
Vehicle Noise Regulation & Reduction. Society of Automotive Engineers. 1980. 22.50 (ISBN 0-89883-227-6). Soc Auto Engineers.
Vehicle Painting, Pt. 1. Ed. by F. Brown et al. (Engineering Craftsmen: No. E1). (Illus.). 1968. spiral bdg. 22.95x (ISBN 0-85083-032-X). Intl Ideas.
Vehicle Painting, Pt. 2. Ed. by F. Brown et al. (Engineering Craftsmen: No. E21). 1970. spiral bdg. 22.95x (ISBN 0-85083-116-4). Intl Ideas.
Vehicle Recovery: A Practical Manual for the Heavy-Vehicle Driver, Fleet Operator and Recovery Specialist. R. J. Grice. (Illus.). 1977. 25.00 (ISBN 0-685-75855-9). Transatlantic.
Vehicle Rescue. H. Grant. (Illus.). 1975. pap. 16.95 (ISBN 0-87618-137-X); instructor's guide 7.95 (ISBN 0-87618-611-8); systems chart 7.95 (ISBN 0-87618-610-X). R J Brady.
Vehicle Safety Inspection Systems: How Effective? W. Mark Crain. 1980. pap. 4.25 (ISBN 0-8447-3361-X). Am Enterprise.
Vehicle Structured Mechanics, 3rd International Proceedings. Society of Automotive Engineers. 1979. 30.00 (ISBN 0-89883-053-2). Soc Auto Engineers.
Vehicles at War. Dennis Bishop & Christopher Ellis. LC 75-20588. 1979. 25.00 (ISBN 0-498-01699-4). A S Barnes.
Veil of Sand. Ann Boyle. (YA) 1977. 5.95 (ISBN 0-685-81425-4, Avalon). Bouregy.
Veins & Their Control. John T. Shepherd & Paul M. Vanhoutte. LC 75-15353. (Illus.). 269p. 1975. text ed. 22.00 (ISBN 0-7216-8220-0). Saunders.
Veinte Cuentos Espanoles Del Siglo Veinte. Ed. by Enrique Anderson-Imbert & Lawrence B. Kiddle. (Orig., Span.). (gr. 10-12). 1961. pap. text ed. 9.50 (ISBN 0-13-941567-X). P-H.
Velazquez: A Catalogue Raissonne of His Oeuvre. Jose Lopez-Rey. 1963. 58.00 (ISBN 0-571-05465-X, Pub. by Faber & Faber). Merrimack Bk Serv.
Velga. Ivan Bunin. Tr. by Guy Daniels from Rus. LC 74-120786. (Illus.). (gr. 7 up). 1970. 6.95 (ISBN 0-87599-177-7). S G Phillips.
Velikovsky & Establishment Science. Velikovsky et al. Ed. by L. M. Greenberg et al. LC 77-93288. (Illus.). 1977. 12.95 (ISBN 0-917994-03-5); pap. 6.00 (ISBN 0-917994-04-3). Kronos Pr.
Velikovsky Reconsidered. Pensee (Editors of) LC 74-33637. 288p. 1976. 8.95 o.p. (ISBN 0-385-03118-1). Doubleday.
Velleius Paterculus, the Tiberian Narrative. Ed. by A. J. Woodman. LC 76-22985. (Classical Texts & Commentaries Ser: No. 19). 1977. 49.50 (ISBN 0-521-21397-5). Cambridge U Pr.
Velocidad. Harlan Wade. Tr. by Mamie M. Contreras from Eng. LC 78-26627. (Book About Ser.). Orig. Title: Speed. (Illus., Sp.). (gr. k-3). 1979. PLB 7.30 (ISBN 0-8172-1479-8). Raintree Pubs.
Velocity of Light. J. M. Sanders. 1965. 15.00 (ISBN 0-08-011315-X); pap. 7.50 (ISBN 0-08-011314-1). Pergamon.
Velvet Chancellors: A History of Post-War Germany. Terence Prittie. (Illus.). 286p. 1981. text ed. 26.00x (ISBN 0-8419-6750-4). Holmes & Meier.
Velvet Covered Brick. Howard Butt. LC 72-111352. 200p. 1973. 7.95 o.p. (ISBN 0-06-061258-4, HarpR). Har-Row.
Velvet Jungle, Vol. 3. Dan Chioco, Jr. & George Carpozi. LC 78-71442. 1979. pap. 2.25 o.p. (ISBN 0-87216-543-4). Playboy Pbks.
Velvet Monkey Wrench. rev. ed. John Muir. LC 72-96736. (Illus.). 247p. 1980. pap. 6.00 (ISBN 0-912528-02-8). John Muir.
Velvet Ribbons. Juliana Davison (Orig.). 1980. pap. 1.75 (ISBN 0-446-94271-5). Warner Bks.
Velvet Shadows. Andre Norton. 1978. pap. 1.95 (ISBN 0-449-23135-6, Crest). Fawcett.
Velvet Studies. C. V. Wedgwood. 159p. 1980. Repr. of 1946 ed. lib. bdg. 15.00 (ISBN 0-89987-861-X). Darby Bks.
Velveteen Rabbit. Margery Williams. (gr. 1-9). 1975. pap. 1.95 (ISBN 0-380-00255-8, 43257, Camelot). Avon.
Velveteen Rabbit. Margery Williams. (Illus.). 44p. 1981. pap. 2.25 (54148, Camelot). Avon.
Velveteen Rabbit: Or How Toys Become Real. Margery Williams. (Illus.). 50p. (Orig.). (gr. k-12). 1981. PLB 12.90 (ISBN 0-89471-127-X); pap. 3.95 (ISBN 0-89471-128-8). Running Pr.
Ven Francia. Lope F. Vega Capiro. LC 61-6615. 1963. 12.50x (ISBN 0-8122-7363-X). U of Pa Pr.
Vendee: A Sociological Analysis of the Counter-Revolution of 1973. Charles Tilly. LC 64-21247. (Illus.). 1976. 17.50x (ISBN 0-674-93300-1); pap. 7.95 (ISBN 0-674-93302-8). Harvard U Pr.
Veneering Simplified. Harry J. Hobbs. (Illus.). 126p. 1976. 6.95 o.p. (ISBN 0-684-14544-8, ScribT). Scribner.
Venereal Disease. new ed. Elizabeth S. Williams. Ed. by Alan J. Burnes. (Urban America Ser.). (Illus.). 64p. (Orig.). (gr. 6-10). 1969. pap. 0.95 o.p. (ISBN 0-88301-022-4). Pendulum Pr.
Venereal Disease. Eleanor R. Young. LC 73-8758. (Career Concise Guides Ser.). (gr. 7-12). 1973. text ed. 4.90 o.p. (ISBN 0-531-02642-6). Watts.
Venereal Diseases. 4th ed. A. King & C. Nicol. 1980. text ed. 45.00 (ISBN 0-02-858270-5). Macmillan.
Venetia. Georgette Heyer. 320p. 1981. pap. 1.95 (ISBN 0-515-05728-2). Jove Pubns.
Venetian. David Weiss. LC 76-18940. 1976. 9.95 o.p. (ISBN 0-688-03098-X). Morrow.
Venetian Empire. Jan Morris. LC 80-14046. (Helen & Kurt Wolff Bk). (Illus.). 208p. 1980. 19.95 (ISBN 0-15-193504-1). HarBraceJ.
Venetian Instrumental Music from Gabrieli to Vivaldi. Eleanor Selfridge-Field. 1975. 48.50x (ISBN 0-631-15440-X, Pub by Basil Blackwell England). Biblio Dist.
Venetian Moon. Clarissa Ross. (Original Historical Romance Ser.). 288p. 1980. pap. 2.75 (ISBN 0-515-04817-8, Jove). BJ Pub Group.
Venetian Opera in the Seventeenth Century. Simon T. Worsthorne. 1954. 36.00x (ISBN 0-19-816116-6). Oxford U Pr.
Venetian Painted Ceilings of the Renaissance. Juergen Schulz. (California Studies in the History of Art: No. VIII). (Illus.). 1968. 57.50x (ISBN 0-520-01154-6). U of Cal Pr.
Venetians. Colin Thubron. Ed. by Time-Life Books. (Seafarers Ser.). (Illus.). 176p. 1980. 14.95 (ISBN 0-8094-2681-1). Time-Life.
Veneto: Padua, Vicenza & Verona. Dorothy Daly. (Batsford Countries Ser.). (Illus.). 192p. 1975. 9.95 o.p. (ISBN 0-8038-7755-2). Hastings.

Venezuela in Pictures. Sterling Publishing Company Editors. LC 65-24381. (Visual Geography Ser.). (Illus., Orig.). (gr. 5 up). 1965. PLB 4.99 o.p. (ISBN 0-8069-1075-5); pap. 2.95 (ISBN 0-8069-1074-7). Sterling.

Venezuela: The Democratic Experience. Ed. by John D. Martz & David J. Myers. LC 77-7509. (Praeger Special Studies). 1977. text ed. 29.95 (ISBN 0-03-021841-1); pap. 11.95 (ISBN 0-03-023061-6). Praeger.

Venezuelan Foreign Policy: Its Organization & Beginning. Douglas H. Carlisle. LC 78-57979. 1978. pap. text ed. 9.50 (ISBN 0-8191-0317-9). U Pr of Amer.

Venganza De Tamar. Tirso De Molina. Ed. by A. K. Paterson. text ed. 27.00x (ISBN 0-521-07205-0). Cambridge U Pr.

Vengeance Hunt. Charles R. Pike. LC 80-69218. (Jubal Cade Westerns Ser.). 128p. 1980. pap. 2.95 (ISBN 0-87754-234-1). Chelsea Hse.

Vengeance Rides West. A. A. Baker. 192p. (YA) 1976. 4.95 o.p. (ISBN 0-685-67083-X, Avalon). Bouregy.

Vengenance of God. Lewis Arriola. 240p. 1981. 9.50 (ISBN 0-682-49687-1). Exposition.

Venice. Ed. by Toby Cole. 288p. (Orig.). 1980. pap. 6.95 (ISBN 0-88208-107-1). Lawrence Hill.

Venice. Aubrey Menen. (Great Cities Ser.). (Illus.). 1976. 14.95 (ISBN 0-8094-2262-X). Time-Life.

Venice. Aubrey Menen. (The Great Cities Ser.). (Illus.). (gr. 6 up). 1976. PLB 14.94 (ISBN 0-8094-2263-8, Pub by Time-Life). Silver.

Venice - Heart of the World. LC 78-670184. (Italia Artistica Ser.). (Illus.). 1976. pap. 10.00x (ISBN 0-8002-2135-4). Intl Pubns Serv.

Venice: A Thousand Years of Culture & Civilization. Peter Lauritzen. LC 78-2690. 1978. 12.95 (ISBN 0-689-10897-4); pap. 6.95 (ISBN 0-689-70603-0). Atheneum.

Venice & the Defense of Republican Liberty: Renaissance Values in the Age of the Counter Reformation. William J. Bouwsma. (Illus.). 1968. 30.00x (ISBN 0-520-00151-6). U of Cal Pr.

Venice for Pleasure. J. G. Links. (Illus.). 1968. 7.50 o.p. (ISBN 0-8023-1136-9). Dufour.

Venice Observed. Mary McCarthy. LC 64-49016. 1963. pap. 2.95 (ISBN 0-15-693521-X, HB61, Harv). HarBraceJ.

Venice Plot. Ray Rudorff. (YA) 1976. 7.95 o.p. (ISBN 0-399-11803-9, Dist. by Putnam). Berkley Pub.

Venice Preserved. Thomas Otway. Ed. by Malcolm Kelsall. LC 69-12902. (Regents Restoration Drama Ser.). 1969. 7.95x (ISBN 0-8032-0366-7); pap. 2.65x (ISBN 0-8032-5366-4, BB 271, Bison). U of Nebr Pr.

Venice: The Masque of Italy. Marcel Brion. 1962. 21.95 (ISBN 0-236-31030-5, Pub. by Paul Elek). Merrimack Bk Serv.

Venison Handbook. Brad Sagstetter. LC 80-84354. (Illus., Orig.). 1981. 5.95 (ISBN 0-89896-075-4). Larksdale.

Venn Diagrams. Robert Froman. LC 75-187937. (Young Math Ser). (Illus.). (gr. 1-5). 1972. 4.50 o.p. (ISBN 0-690-85996-1, TYC-J); PLB 7.89 (ISBN 0-690-85997-X). T Y Crowell.

Venom. Russell O'Neil. 1979. pap. 1.95 o.p. (ISBN 0-345-25419-8). Ballantine.

Venom Diseases. S. A. Minton. (American Lectures in Living Chemistry Ser.). (Illus.). 256p. 1974. 16.75 (ISBN 0-398-03051-0). C C Thomas.

Venomous Reptiles. rev. ed. Sherman A. Minton & Madge R. Minton. (Illus.). 320p. 1980. 12.95 (ISBN 0-684-16626-7, ScribT). Scribner.

Venomous Snakes of the World: A Checklist. Keith A. Harding & Kenneth R. Welch. 200p. 1980. 44.00 (ISBN 0-08-025495-0). Pergamon.

Venoms: Chemistry & Molecular Biology. Anthony T. Tu. LC 76-30751. 1977. 47.50 (ISBN 0-471-89229-7, Pub. by Wiley-Interscience). Wiley.

Venous Thrombosis & Pulmonary Embolism. Michael Hume et al. LC 70-122215. (Commonwealth Fund Publications Ser). 1970. 20.00x (ISBN 0-674-93320-6). Harvard U Pr.

Venous Trauma & Its Management. Ed. by Robert W. Hobson, II. Date not set. price not set (ISBN 0-87993-155-8). Futura Pub.

Ventana Cave: Stratigraphy & Archaeology. new ed. Emil W. Haury. LC 51-802. (Illus.). xxvii, 599p. 1975. text ed. 17.50x (ISBN 0-8165-0536-5). U of Ariz Pr.

Ventricles & Cisterns: Radiology of the Skull & Brain, Vol. 4. Thomas H. Newton & Gordon Potts. LC 78-173600. 1978. text ed. 67.50 (ISBN 0-8016-3661-2). Mosby.

Ventriloquism: How to Put on an Act, Use the Power of Suggestion, Write a Clever Accompanying Patter, & Make Your Own Dummy. Darryl Hutton. LC 75-14508. (Illus.). 96p. 1975. 7.95 (ISBN 0-8069-7022-7); lib. bdg. 7.49 (ISBN 0-8069-7023-5). Sterling.

Ventriloquism in a Nutshell. Kae H. Chung. (Illus.). 1974. pap. 3.00 (ISBN 0-686-20905-2, 065). Maher Ventril Studio.

Venture Capital. John R. Dominguez. LC 73-11667. (Illus.). 224p. 1974. 18.95 (ISBN 0-669-86918-X). Lexington Bks.

Venture Capital in Europe. Spiro A. Coutarelli. LC 76-2902. (Special Studies). 1977. text ed. 23.95 (ISBN 0-275-56680-3). Praeger.

Venture in History: The Production, Publication, & Sale of the Works of Hubert Howe Bancroft. Harry Clark. 1973. pap. 19.50x (ISBN 0-520-09417-4). U of Cal Pr.

Venture Management: The Business of the Inventor, Entrepreneur, Venture Capitalist, & Established Company. William H. Shames. LC 73-17642. (Illus.). 1974. 10.00 o.s.i. (ISBN 0-02-928400-7). Free Pr.

Venture of Form in the Novels of Virginia Woolf. Jean Alexander. LC 73-83260. 1974. 13.50 (ISBN 0-8046-9052-9). Kennikat.

Venture of Islam, 3 vols. Marshall G. Hodgson. Incl. Vol. 1. Classical Age of Islam. pap. 9.50 (ISBN 0-226-34683-8, P716); Vol. 2. Expansion of Islam in the Middle Period. pap. 9.50 (ISBN 0-226-34684-6, P717); Vol. 3. Gunpowder Empire & Modern Times. pap. 9.50 (ISBN 0-226-34685-4, P718). LC 73-87243. (Illus.). 1977 (Phoen). U of Chicago Pr.

Ventureno Confesionario of Jose Senan, O.F.M. Ed. by M. S. Beeler. (U. C. Publ. in Linguistics: Vol. 47). 1967. pap. 7.00x (ISBN 0-520-09242-2). U of Cal Pr.

Ventures in Education with Black Baptists in Tennessee. R. Powell. 5.95 o.p. (ISBN 0-8062-1142-3). Carlton.

Ventures in Song. Ed. by David J. Randolph & Bill Garrett. (Orig.). 1972. pap. 2.95 o.p. (ISBN 0-687-43682-6). Abingdon.

Ventures in Worship 3. Ed. by David J. Randolph. 224p. (Orig.). 1973. pap. 3.95 o.p. (ISBN 0-687-43689-3). Abingdon.

Venturi Analysis: Learning Better Golf from the Champions. Ken Venturi & Al Barkow. LC 80-69389. 1981. 14.95 (ISBN 0-689-11145-2). Atheneum.

Venturing Beyond the Campus: Students Who Leave College. C. Hess Haagen. LC 77-2541. 1977. pap. 10.00 (ISBN 0-8195-8027-9, Pub. by Wesleyan U Pr); pap. 5.00x o.p. (ISBN 0-685-79916-6). Columbia U Pr.

Venus & Mercury. Alan E. Nourse. LC 73-182900. (First Bks). (Illus.). 72p. (gr. 7 up). 1972. PLB 4.90 o.p. (ISBN 0-531-00765-0). Watts.

Venus Belt. L. Neil Smith. (Orig.). 1981. pap. 2.25 (ISBN 0-345-28721-5, Del Rey). Ballantine.

Venus, Near Neighbor of the Sun. Isaac Asimov. (Illus.). 224p. (gr. 5 up). 1981. 8.95 (ISBN 0-688-41976-3); PLB 8.59 (ISBN 0-688-51976-8). Morrow.

Venusian Health Magic. Michael X. 1972. pap. 12.95 (ISBN 0-685-37600-1). Saucerian.

Vera V. Slovo. Lev Z. Kopelev. (Illus., Rus.). 1977. 10.00 o.p. (ISBN 0-88233-301-1). Ardis Pubs.

Veracious Imagination: Essays on American History, Literature, & Biography. Cushing Strout. 328p. 1981. 17.50x (ISBN 0-8195-5048-5). Wesleyan U Pr.

Verano En Mexico. Robert Cabat & Louis Cabat. (Orig.). (gr. 7-12). 1975. pap. text ed. 4.58 (ISBN 0-87720-504-3). AMSCO Sch.

Verbal Aptitude Workbook for College Entrance Examinations. Mitchel Weiner. (gr. 10-12). 1979. pap. text ed. 3.75 (ISBN 0-8120-2074-X). Barron.

Verbal Behavior. B. F. Skinner. 1957. 21.00 (ISBN 0-13-941591-2). P-H.

Verbal Behavior: Adaption & Psychopathology. Walter Weintraub. LC 80-27021. 224p. 1981. text ed. price not set (ISBN 0-8261-2660-X); pap. text ed. price not set (ISBN 0-8261-2661-8). Springer Pub.

Verbal Behavior of the Deaf Child: Studies of Word Meanings & Associations. Joseph Rosenstein & Walter MacGinitie. LC 68-59116. 1969. pap. text ed. 4.75x (ISBN 0-8077-1720-7). Tchrs Coll.

Verbal Communication in Instructional Supervision. Richard H. Weller. LC 70-161300. (Illus.). 1971. text ed. 11.50x (ISBN 0-8077-2322-3). Tchrs Coll.

Verbal Conditioning & Behavior. J. P. Das. 1970. 25.00 (ISBN 0-08-012818-1). Pergamon.

Verbal Icon: Studies in the Meaning of Poetry. William K. Wimsatt. LC 54-7479. 320p. 1967. pap. 5.00x (ISBN 0-8131-0111-5). U Pr of Ky.

Verbal System of Southern Agaw. Robert Hetzron. (U. C. Publ. in Near Eastern Studies: Vol. 12). 1969. pap. 8.50x (ISBN 0-520-09306-2). U of Cal Pr.

Vercelli Book. Ed. by George P. Krapp. LC 32-10861. 1932. 17.50x (ISBN 0-231-08766-7). Columbia U Pr.

Vercelli Homilies Nine to Twenty-Three. Ed. by Paul E. Szarmach. (Toronto Old English Ser.). 192p. 1981. 25.00x (ISBN 0-8020-5528-1). U of Toronto Pr.

Verdacht. Friedrich Durrenmatt. Ed. by William Gillis. (gr. 9-12). 1964. pap. text ed. 7.20 (ISBN 0-395-04500-2). HM.

Verdi: His Life & Times. Peter Southwell-Sander. (Illustrated Lives & Times of the Composers). (Illus.). 1978. 16.95 (ISBN 0-8467-0421-8, Pub. by Two Continents); pap. 5.95 (ISBN 0-8467-0422-6). Hippocrene Bks.

Verdi, His Life & Times. expanded ed. Peter Southwell-Sander. (Illus.). 192p. Repr. of 1978 ed. 19.95 (ISBN 0-87666-639-X). Paganiniana Pubns.

Verdi, His Music, Life & Times. George Martin. (Music Reprint Ser.). 1979. Repr. of 1963 ed. 35.00 (ISBN 0-306-79549-3). Da Capo.

Verdi in the Age of Italian Romanticism. R. B. Kimbell. (Illus.). 800p. Date not set. price not set (ISBN 0-521-23052-7). Cambridge U Pr.

Verdict. Hildegard Knef. 1977. pap. 1.95 o.p. (ISBN 0-345-25401-5). Ballantine.

Verdict. Barry Reed. 1980. lib. bdg. 14.95 (ISBN 0-8161-3175-9, Large Print Bks). G K Hall.

Verdict. Lalit Sehgal. Tr. by Suresh Kohli. (Translated from Hindi). 8.00 (ISBN 0-89253-656-X); flexible cloth 3.00 (ISBN 0-89253-657-8). Ind-US Inc.

Verdicts on Lawyers. Ralph Nader & Mark Green. LC 75-23292. 1977. 10.00 o.p. (ISBN 0-690-01006-0, TYC-T); pap. 4.95 (ISBN 0-690-01667-0, TYC-T). T Y Crowell.

Vere e Nove Imagini de gli Dei delli Antichi. Ed. by Lorenzo Pignoria & Stephen Orgel. LC 78-68193. (Renaissance & the Gods: the Philosophy of Images Ser.). (Illus.). 1980. lib. bdg. 66.00 (ISBN 0-8240-3686-7). Garland Pub.

Verga's Milanese Tales. Olga Ragusa. 1964. 6.00 (ISBN 0-913298-33-6). S F Vanni.

Verhalten, Handeln und System. Wolfgang Schluchter. (Suhrkamp Taschenbuecher Wissenschaft: Vol. 310). 176p. (Orig.). 1980. pap. text ed. 6.50 (ISBN 3-518-07910-7, Pub. by Insel Verlag Germany). Suhrkamp.

Verification & SALT. Ed. by William C. Potter. (Westview Special Studies in National Security & Defense Policy). 200p. 1980. lib. bdg. 25.00x (ISBN 0-89158-886-8). Westview.

Verification of Mathematical & Physical Models in Hydraulic Engineering. Compiled by American Society of Civil Engineers. 904p. 1978. pap. text ed. 40.00 (ISBN 0-87262-131-6). Am Soc Civil Eng.

Veritable Years: 1949-1966. William Everson. 350p. 1978. 14.00 (ISBN 0-87685-379-3); pap. 7.50 (ISBN 0-87685-378-5). Black Sparrow.

Verity. Brenda Jagger. 1981. pap. 2.95 (ISBN 0-451-09718-1, E9718, Sig). NAL.

Verlaine. C. Chadwick. 1973. text ed. 16.25x (ISBN 0-485-14603-7, Athlone Pr); pap. text ed. 8.75x (ISBN 0-485-12203-0). Humanities.

Verlaine Crossing. Steven Otfinoski. LC 78-15460. (Pacesetters Ser.). (Illus.). (gr. 4 up). 1978. PLB 7.95 (ISBN 0-516-02161-3). Childrens.

Verliebtheit und Rollenspiel in Shakespeare's Verkleidungskomodien. Karlheinz Hoffmann. (Salzburg Studies in English Literature: Elizabethan & Renaissance Studies: No. 73). 1978. pap. text ed. 25.00x (ISBN 0-391-01411-0). Humanities.

Verlorene Koffer: Reader 1. Rita M. Walbruck. LC 80-22198. (Auf Heisser Spur Ser.). (gr. 9-12). 1981. pap. 1.95 (ISBN 0-88436-850-5). EMC.

Vermeer. rev. ed. Lawrence Gowing. LC 71-114356. (Icon Editions). (Illus.). 240p. 1975. pap. 5.95x o.s.i. (ISBN 0-06-430066-8, IN-66, HarpT). Har-Row.

Vermeer. (Painter & the Man Ser.). Date not set. price not set (ISBN 0-8120-5118-1). Barron.

Vermeer. Christopher Wright. (Illus.). 1977. 15.95 (ISBN 0-8467-0254-1, Pub. by Two Continents); pap. 9.95 (ISBN 0-8467-0253-3). Hippocrene Bks.

Vermilion. Nathan Aldyne. 1980. pap. 2.25 (ISBN 0-686-69261-6, 76596). Avon.

Vermilion Bird: T'ang Images of the South. Edward H. Schafer. 1967. 22.75x (ISBN 0-520-01145-7). U of Cal Pr.

Vermont. 23.00 (ISBN 0-89770-121-6). Curriculum Info Ctr.

Vermont: A Guide to the Green Mountain State. Federal Writers' Project. 1937. Repr. 45.00 (ISBN 0-403-02194-4). Somerset Pub.

Vermont Afternoons with Robert Frost. Vrest Orton. (Illus.). 63p. 1979. pap. 4.50 o.s.i. (ISBN 0-911570-17-9). Vermont Bks.

Vermont Atlas & Gazetteer. Ed. by William Hancock et al. (Illus.). 96p. (Orig.). 1978. pap. 6.95 (ISBN 0-89933-005-3). DeLorme Pub.

Vermont Blood. Barney Crosier. 128p. 1980. pap. 5.95 (ISBN 0-9603900-6-5). Lanser Pr.

Vermont Chronology & Factbook. R. I. Vexler. 1978. 8.50 (ISBN 0-379-16170-2). Oceana.

Vermont Folk-Songs & Ballads. Helen H. Flanders & George Brown. LC 68-20768. iv, 256p. 1968. Repr. of 1931 ed. 18.00 (ISBN 0-8103-5010-6). Gale.

Vermont for Every Season. George D. Aiken et al. (Illus.). 160p. 1980. 30.00 (ISBN 0-936896-00-0). VT Life Mag.

Vermont for Every Season. Ed. by Vt. Life Mag. Editors. (Illus.). 160p. 1980. 30.00. Greene.

Vermont Reflections. Marie T. Bonner. 62p. 1980. 3.95 (ISBN 0-8059-2740-9). Dorrance.

Vermont School Bus Ride. Montgomery. (Easy Reading Ser.: No. 1). 1974. 5.95 (ISBN 0-915248-00-X). Vermont Crossroads.

Vermont State Industrial Directory, Nineteen Eighty-One. State Industrial Directories Corp. Date not set. pap. price not set (ISBN 0-89910-043-0). State Indus D.

Vermont Stone Chambers: An Inquiry into Their Past. Giovanna Neudorfer. 1980. pap. 4.50 (ISBN 0-934720-22-3). VT Hist Soc.

Vermont Symphony Cookbook. Ed. by Angela Combes. (Illus.). 128p. 1981. pap. cancelled (ISBN 0-8397-8571-2). Eriksson.

Vermont: The State with the Storybook Past. Cora Cheney. LC 76-13804. (gr. 5-9). 1976. 9.95 o.p. (ISBN 0-8289-0283-6). Greene.

Vermont: The State with the Storybook Past. 2nd ed. Cora Cheney. (Illus.). 256p. (gr. 3-6). 1981. pap. 9.95 (ISBN 0-8289-0440-5). Greene.

Vermont: The States & the Nation. Charles T. Morrissey. (Illus.). 240p. 1981. 12.95 (ISBN 0-393-05625-2). Norton.

Vermont Woodfired Automobile. Jeff Danziger. 80p. 1980. pap. 3.95 (ISBN 0-9603900-2-2). Lanser Pr.

Vermonters. Dorman B. Kent. 187p. 1937. 3.00x o.p. (ISBN 0-934720-05-3). VT Hist Soc.

Vermont's First Settlers. Jay M. Holbrook. LC 76-151555. 1976. pap. 15.00 (ISBN 0-931248-03-5). Holbrook Res.

Verna Meyer's Menu Cookbook: Dining at Home in Style. Verna E. Meyer. LC 80-19120. 206p. 1980. 12.95 (ISBN 0-87518-199-6). Dillon.

Vernacular Architecture of the Lake Countries: A Field Handbook. R. W. Brunskill. (Illus.). 1978. pap. 8.95 (ISBN 0-571-09459-7, Pub. by Faber & Faber). Merrimack Bk Serv.

Vernacular Architecture of the Lake Countries. R. W. Brunskill. 1978. 16.95 (ISBN 0-571-09460-0, Pub. by Faber & Faber). Merrimack Bk Serv.

Vernal Walk; a Poem, Repr. Of 1801 Ed. Ebenezer Elliott. Bd. with Peter Faultless to His Brother Simon, Tales of Night, in Rhyme, & Other Poems. Repr. of 1820 ed. LC 75-31199. (Romantic Context Ser.: Poetry 1789-1830: Vol. 51). 1978. lib. bdg. 47.00 (ISBN 0-8240-2150-9). Garland Pub.

Vernon: An Anecdotal Novel. Osmond Beckwith. LC 81-65121. (Illus.). 204p. 1981. 10.00. Breaking Point.

Vernon Watkins & the Spring of Vision. Dora Polk. 1977. text ed. 14.50x (ISBN 0-7154-0349-4). Humanities.

Veronese. Richard Coche. (Oresko-Jupiter Art Bks). (Illus.). 1981. 17.95 (ISBN 0-933516-80-0, Pub. by Oresko-Jupiter England). Hippocrene Bks.

Veronica Ganz. Marilyn Sachs. (Illus.). (gr. 4-6). 1970. pap. 1.25 (ISBN 0-671-29774-0). PB.

Veronica My Daughter & Other Onitsha Plays & Stories. Ogali Ogali. Ed. by Reinhard W. Sander & Peter K. Ayers. LC 80-886. 376p. (Orig.). 1980. 18.00x (ISBN 0-914478-61-3); pap. 7.00x (ISBN 0-914478-62-1). Three Continents.

Verrazano, Explorer of the Atlantic Coast. Ronald Syme. LC 72-7130. (Illus.). 96p. (gr. 3-7). 1973. 6.75 o.p. (ISBN 0-688-21771-0); PLB 6.48 o.p. (ISBN 0-688-31771-5). Morrow.

Verres in Sicily. Cicero. Ed. by Humfrey Grose-Hodge & E. W. Davies. (Latin). text ed. 5.75x (ISBN 0-521-04653-X). Cambridge U Pr.

Verrier Elwin: A Pioneer Indian Anthropologist. Bhabagrahi Misra. 1974. lib. bdg. 8.95x (ISBN 0-210-40556-2). Asia.

Vers la Stature Parfaite De Jesus-Christ. Tr. by Gene Getz. (French Bks.). (Fr.). 1979. 1.95 (ISBN 0-8297-0820-0). Vida Pub.

Versailles Treaty. Harold C. Vaughan. LC 74-8865. (World Focus Bks). (Illus.). 72p. (gr. 6-9). 1975. PLB 4.47 o.p. (ISBN 0-531-02783-X). Watts.

Versatile Manager: A Grid Profile. Robert R. Blake & Jane S. Mouton. LC 80-68466. 215p. 1981. 13.95 (ISBN 0-87094-222-0). Dow Jones-Irwin.

Versatile Vegetables. Barbara Kyte & Kathy Greenberg. LC 80-83403. (Illus.). 1980. pap. 2.50 (ISBN 0-915942-16-X). Owlswood Prods.

Versatility of Kinship. Ed. by Linda S. Cordell & Stephen Beckerman. LC 80-525. (Studies in Anthropology). 1980. 40.00 (ISBN 0-12-188250-0). Acad Pr.

Verschwundene Miniatur. new ed. Erich Kaestner. Ed. by Otto P. Schinnerer. (Illus.). 1962. text ed. 6.95x o.p. (ISBN 0-669-29488-8). Heath.

Verse by the Side of the Road: Burma-Shave Signs & Jingles. Frank Rowsome, Jr. LC 65-24618. 1965. 6.95 (ISBN 0-8289-0038-8). Greene.

Verse of Royall Tyler. Royall Tyler. Ed. by Marius B. Peladeau. LC 68-14026. 1968. 10.95x (ISBN 0-8139-0235-5). U Pr of Va.

Verse That Is Fun. Ed. by Barbara Ireson. 1962. 6.95 (ISBN 0-571-05050-6, Pub. by Faber & Faber). Merrimack Bk Serv.

Verse with Prose. V. Balasubrahmanyam. 8.00 (ISBN 0-89253-559-8); flexible cloth 4.00 (ISBN 0-89253-560-1). Ind-US Inc.

Verse Writing. William H. Carruth. 123p. 1980. Repr. of 1925 ed. lib. bdg. 15.00 (ISBN 0-8482-3554-1). Norwood Edns.

Verse Writing in Schools. E. J. Bolton. 1966. 11.25 (ISBN 0-08-011993-X); pap. 5.75 (ISBN 0-08-011992-1). Pergamon.

Verses. V. Balasubrahmanyam. 8.00 (ISBN 0-89253-561-X); flexible cloth 4.00 (ISBN 0-89253-562-8). InterCulture.

Verses. Jack B. Yeats. 1981. pap. text ed. 6.00 (ISBN 0-391-01592-3). Humanities.

Verses for the Zodiac. Daisy Aldan. 7.95 (ISBN 0-913152-10-2). Green Hill.

Verses to the Memory of Joseph Warton DD, Repr. Of 1800. Richard Mant. Ed. by Donald H. Reiman. Bd. with Slave & Other Poetical Pieces: Being an Appendix to Poems. Repr. of 1807 ed; Poems. Repr. of 1806 ed; Simpliciad: a Satirico Didactic Poem (Dedicated to Wordsworth, Southey & Coleridge) Repr. of 1808 ed. LC 75-31229. (Romantic Context Ser: Poetry 1789-1830). 1979. lib. bdg. 47.00 (ISBN 0-8240-2178-9). Garland Pub.

Verses Vice Verses. R. L. Loughlin. LC 80-81692. 120p. 1981. 8.95 (ISBN 0-911906-18-5); pap. 5.95 (ISBN 0-911906-19-3). Harian Creative.

Versiculi: A Companion in Verse. Scottish Classics Group. 1976. pap. text ed. 2.50x (ISBN 0-05-002897-9); tchr's notes 1.50x (ISBN 0-05-002898-7). Longman.

Version & Themes Models. S. W. Segger. 1973. pap. text ed. 7.50x (ISBN 0-521-06276-4). Cambridge U Pr.

Versions of Medieval Comedy. Paul G. Ruggiers. LC 77-6384. 1977. pap. 5.95 (ISBN 0-8061-1438-X). U of Okla Pr.

Versos De Cada Dia: Estampas Numeradas. Marigloria Palma, pseud. LC 79-10463. (Coleccion UPREX, Ser. Poesia: No. 58). 100p. (Orig.). pap. 1.85 (ISBN 0-8477-0058-5). U of PR Pr.

Versprechen und Verlessen: Eine Psychologisch Linguistische Studie. Rudolf Meringer & Carl Mayer. (Classics in Psycholinguistics Ser.: No. 2). 1979. text ed. 40.00x (ISBN 90-272-0971-5). Humanities.

Verstandene Tod: Eine Untersuchung Zu Martin Heideggers Existenzialontologie. Adolf Sternberger. Ed. by Maurice Natanson. LC 78-66753. (Phenomenology Ser.: Vol. 14). 165p. 1979. lib. bdg. 17.00 (ISBN 0-8240-9556-1). Garland Pub.

Verstehen: Subjective Understanding in the Social Sciences. Marcello Truzzi. LC 73-1849. 1973. text ed. 5.95 (ISBN 0-201-07602-0). A-W.

Versty. Marina Tsvetaeva. (Rus.). 1972. pap. 3.50 (ISBN 0-88233-031-4). Ardis Pubs.

Versuch Einer Allegorie, Repr. Of 1766 Ed. J. J. Winckelmann. Bd. with De L'Allegorie. J. J. Winckelmann. Repr. of 1799 ed. LC 75-27890. (Renaissance & the Gods Ser.: Vol. 44). (Illus.). 1976. lib. bdg. 73.00 (ISBN 0-8240-2093-6). Garland Pub.

Vertebral Manipulation. 4th ed. G. D. Maitland. 1977. pap. 24.95 (ISBN 0-407-43505-0). Butterworths.

Vertebrate Ecology in the Northern Neotropics. Ed. by John F. Eisenberg. LC 79-9436. (Symposia of the National Zoological Park Ser.: No. 4). (Illus.). 271p. 1980. text ed. 25.00x (ISBN 0-87474-410-5); pap. text ed. 12.50x (ISBN 0-87474-409-1). Smithsonian.

Vertebrate Endocrinology. David O. Norris. LC 80-10332. (Illus.). 524p. 1980. text ed. 29.50 (ISBN 0-8121-0699-7). Lea & Febiger.

Vertebrate Hard Tissues. L. B. Halstead & R. Hill. (Wykeham Science Ser.: No. 30). 1974. 9.95x (ISBN 0-8448-1157-2). Crane Russak Co.

Vertebrate Limb & Somite Morphogenesis: The Third Symposium of the British Society for Developmental Biology. Ed. by D. A. Ede et al. LC 76-50312. (British Society for Developmenal Biology Symposium: No. 3). 1978. 75.00 (ISBN 0-521-21552-8). Cambridge U Pr.

Vertebrate Limb Regeneration. H. Wallace. 320p. 1981. price not set (ISBN 0-471-27877-7, Pub. by Wiley-Interscience). Wiley.

Vertebrate Retina: Principles of Structure & Function. R. W. Rodieck. LC 79-190434. (Biology Ser.). (Illus.). 1973. text ed. 65.00x (ISBN 0-7167-0696-2). W H Freeman.

Vertebrate Structures & Functions: Readings from Scientific American. Intro. by Norman K. Wessells. LC 73-17004. (Illus.). 1974. text ed. 19.95x (ISBN 0-7167-0890-6); pap. text ed. 9.95x (ISBN 0-7167-0889-2). W H Freeman.

Vertebrates: A Laboratory Text. Ed. by N. K. Wessels & Elizabeth M. Center. (Illus.). 250p. 1975. pap. 10.75 (ISBN 0-913232-26-2). W Kaufmann.

Vertebrates of Arizona: With Major Section on Arizona Habitats. Ed. by Charles H. Lowe, Jr. LC 63-11981. 1964. pap. 5.95x (ISBN 0-8165-0348-6). U of Ariz Pr.

Vertical Boring. 2nd ed. (Engineering Craftsmen: No. H28/1). (Illus.). 1976. spiral bdg. 16.50x (ISBN 0-85083-306-X). Intl Ideas.

Vertical Classification: A Study in Structuralism & the Sociology of Knowledge. Barry Schwartz. LC 80-24207. (Chicago Original Paperback Ser.). 232p. 1981. lib. bdg. 17.00x (ISBN 0-226-74208-3). U of Chicago Pr.

Vertical Coordination in the Pork Industry: Symposium. Ed. by Schneidau & Lawrence A. Duewer. (Illus.). 300p. 1972. text ed. 25.50 o.p. (ISBN 0-87055-114-0). AVI.

Vertical Farm Diversification. D. Howard Doane. (Illus.). 184p. 1950. 6.95 o.p. (ISBN 0-8061-0218-7). U of Okla Pr.

Vertical File & Its Satellites: A Handbook of Acquisition, Processing, & Organization. 2nd ed. Shirley Miller. LC 79-13773. (Library Science Text Ser.). 1979. lib. bdg. 17.50x (ISBN 0-87287-164-9). Libs Unl.

Vertical File Index. pap. 18.00 a year. Wilson.

Vertical Transportaion: Elevators & Escalators. G. R. Strakosch. 1967. 35.95 (ISBN 0-471-83167-0, Pub. by Wiley-Interscience). Wiley.

Vertical Turbulent Buoyant Jets: A Review of Experimental Data. C. J. Chen. (Heat & Mass Transfer: Vol. 4). (Illus.). 94p. 1979. 28.00 (ISBN 0-08-024772-5). Pergamon.

Vertical World of Yosemite. Ed. by Galen A. Rowell. LC 73-85908. (Illus.). 224p. 1974. 16.95 o.p. (ISBN 0-911824-28-6); pap. 11.95 (ISBN 0-911824-87-1). Wilderness.

Verts; or, the Three Creeds, 1876. Charles M. Davies. Ed. by Robert L. Wolff. LC 75-1506. (Victorian Fiction Ser.). 1975. lib. bdg. 66.00 (ISBN 0-8240-1580-0). Garland Pub.

Very Anxiously Engaged. Val C. Bagley. (Illus.). 96p. (Orig.). 1981. pap. 3.95 (ISBN 0-88290-157-5, 2042). Horizon Utah.

Very Close & Very Slow. Judith Hemschemeyer. LC 74-20951. (Wesleyan Poetry Program: Vol. 76). 69p. 1975. pap. 10.00x (ISBN 0-8195-2076-4, Pub. by Wesleyan U Pr); pap. 4.95 (ISBN 0-8195-1076-9). Columbia U Pr.

Very First Lady. Steve Dunleavy. 1980. 13.95 (ISBN 0-671-24691-7). S&S.

Very First Stories with Brian Badger & Friends. Shreck. 121p. Date not set. pap. 8.95 (ISBN 0-02-037120-9). Macmillan.

Very Funny, Charlie Brown: Selected Cartoons from "You're Out of Your Mind, Charlie Brown", Vol. 1. Charles M. Schulz. (Peanuts Ser.). (Illus.). 1978. pap. 1.50 (ISBN 0-449-23730-3, Crest). Fawcett.

Very Godly Defense, Defending the Mariage of Preists. Philip Melanchthon. Tr. by L. Beuchame. LC 76-25643. (English Experience Ser.: No. 199). 1969. Repr. of 1541 ed. 8.00 (ISBN 90-221-0199-1). Walter J Johnson.

Very Important Person's Workbook. Virginia A. Braxton. (Illus.). 16p. (gr. 1-5). 1980. pap. 1.75 (ISBN 0-935322-08-6). C J Frompovich.

Very Little Boy. Phyllis Krasilovsky. LC 62-7276. (gr. k-1). pap. 5.95a (ISBN 0-385-02756-7). Doubleday.

Very Little Boy. Phyllis Krasilovsky. LC 62-7276. (gr. k-1). pap. 1.95 (ISBN 0-385-00947-X, Zephyr). Doubleday.

Very Little Girl. Phyllis Krasilovsky. (gr. k-1). 1953. 5.95a (ISBN 0-385-07552-9); PLB (ISBN 0-385-07666-5). Doubleday.

Very Messy Room. Elizabeth Stanton & Henry Stanton. Ed. by Caroline Rubin. LC 78-1031. (Concept Bks.). (Illus.). 32p. (gr. 1-3). 1978. 6.95g (ISBN 0-8075-5077-9). A Whitman.

Very Nice Joke Book. Karen J. Gounaud. 1981. 6.95 (ISBN 0-395-30445-8); pap. text ed. 2.95 (ISBN 0-395-30442-3). HM.

Very Practical Meditation. Serene West. LC 79-20249. (Orig.). 1980. pap. 4.95 (ISBN 0-89865-006-2, Unilaw). Donning Co.

Very Private Affairs of Jason Smith. John S. McSwain. LC 77-83885. 1979. 8.00 o.p. (ISBN 0-89430-015-6). Morgan-Pacific.

Very Rich: A History of Wealth. Joseph J. Thorndike, Jr. LC 76-22578. (Illus.). 352p. 1976. deluxe ed. 345.00 (ISBN 0-8281-0334-8, Dist. by Scribner). Am Heritage.

Very Rich Book: America's Super-Millionaires & Their Money-Where They Got It, How They Spend It. Jacqueline Thompson. LC 80-21618. (Illus.). 454p. 1981. 13.95 (ISBN 0-688-00072-X). Morrow.

Very Rich Hours of Count von Stauffenberg. Paul West. LC 79-2662. 320p. 1980. 12.95 (ISBN 0-06-014593-5, HarpT). Har-Row.

Very Special Admiral. Patrick Beesly. (Illus.). 256p. 1981. 30.00 (ISBN 0-241-10383-5, Pub. by Hamish Hamilton England). David & Charles.

Very Special Intelligence. Patrick Beesly. LC 77-82615. 1978. 10.00 o.p. (ISBN 0-385-13206-9). Doubleday.

Very, Very Special Day. Frances U. De Armand. LC 63-8176. (Illus.). (gr. k-2). 1963. 5.95 o.s.i. (ISBN 0-8193-0042-X, Four Winds). Schol Bk Serv.

Very Worst Thing. Berthe Amoss. LC 77-174605. (Illus.). 48p. (gr. k-3). 1972. 5.95 o.s.i. (ISBN 0-8193-0559-6, Four Winds); PLB 5.41 o.s.i. (ISBN 0-8193-0560-X). Schol Bk Serv.

Very Young: Guiding Children from Infancy Through the Early Years. George Maxim. 576p. 1980. text ed. 17.95x (ISBN 0-534-00820-8). Wadsworth Pub.

Vesey Inheritance. Gwendoline Butler. 1977. pap. 1.50 o.p. (ISBN 0-449-23376-6, Crest). Fawcett.

Vespers at St. Mark's: Music of Alessandro Grandi, Giovanni Rovetta & Francesco Cavalli, 2 vols. James H. Moore. Ed. by George Buelow. (Studies in Musicology). 1981. Set. 59.95 (ISBN 0-8357-1143-9, Pub. by UMI Res Pr); Vol. 1. (ISBN 0-8357-1144-7); Vol. 2. (ISBN 0-8357-1145-5). Univ Microfilms.

Vespers of Palermo, 1823; The Forest Sanctuary; & Other Poems, 1825. Felicia D. Hemans. Ed. by Donald H. Reiman. LC 75-31217. (Romantic Context Ser.: Poetry 1789-1930). 1978. lib. bdg. 47.00 (ISBN 0-8240-2167-3). Garland Pub.

Vessel Voyage Data Analysis: A Comparative Study. Kim J. Loroch. LC 65-20766. (Illus.). 1966. 10.00x (ISBN 0-87033-131-0). Cornell Maritime.

Vessels Unto Honor. Connie Broome. LC 76-22242. 1977. pap. 3.25 (ISBN 0-87148-879-5). Pathway Pr.

Vestibular Function on Earth & in Space. J. Stahle. 1970. 55.00 (ISBN 0-08-015592-8). Pergamon.

Vestiges of the Natural History of Creation. Robert Chambers. (Victorian Library). 1969. Repr. of 1844 ed. text ed. 10.00x (ISBN 0-7185-5001-3, Leicester). Humanities.

Vestiges of Time. Richard C. Meredith. LC 77-76255. 1978. 6.95 o.p. (ISBN 0-385-13174-7). Doubleday.

Vestigia: Notes on the Life & Work of Janelle Viglini. Bern Porter. 1975. pap. 7.50 o.p. (ISBN 0-685-53396-4, 0-911156-15-3). Porter.

Vestryman's Guide. Van Bowen. pap. 1.95 (ISBN 0-8164-2136-6). Crossroad NY.

Veta Hispana: Panorama de la Civilizacion Espanola. Juan A. Calvo & Carlos Del Prado. LC 70-132804. (Illus.). 1972. 24.50 (ISBN 0-89197-494-6); pap. text ed. 14.95x (ISBN 0-89197-972-7). Irvington.

Veteran & Vintage Aircraft. Leslie Hunt. LC 74-29025. 1975. pap. 12.50 o.p. (ISBN 0-684-14895-1, SL 695, ScribT). Scribner.

Veteran Scales & Balances. Brian Jewell. 1979. pap. 7.50 (ISBN 0-85936-081-4, Pub. by Midas Bks England). Intl Schol Bk Serv.

Veterinarian's Limerick Book. Robert Gross. 1979. 4.50 o.p. (ISBN 0-8062-1213-6). Carlton.

Veterinary Aspect of Feline Behavior. Bonnie Beaver. LC 80-12085. (Illus.). 1980. text ed. 28.50 (ISBN 0-8016-0542-3). Mosby.

Veterinary Biology & Medicine of Captive Amphibians & Reptiles. Leonard C. Marcus. LC 80-24859. (Illus.). 236p. 1981. text ed. write for info. (ISBN 0-8121-0700-4). Lea & Febiger.

Veterinary Critical Care. Ed. by F. P. Sattler et al. LC 80-27880. (Illus.). 450p. 1981. text ed. write for info. (ISBN 0-8121-0702-0). Lea & Febiger.

Veterinary Drug Index. Benjamin Lewis & Leon O. Wilkin, Jr. LC 78-64717. 600p. 1981. text ed. write for info. (ISBN 0-7216-5764-8). Saunders.

Veterinary Endocrinology & Reproduction. 3rd ed. Ed. by L. E. McDonald. LC 79-22338. (Illus.). 560p. 1980. text ed. 39.50 (ISBN 0-8121-0712-8). Lea & Febiger.

Veterinary Gastroenterology. Ed. by Neil V. Anderson. LC 79-20234. (Illus.). 720p. 1980. text ed. 65.00 (ISBN 0-8121-0632-6). Lea & Febiger.

Veterinary Laboratory Manual. B. M. Bush. 1975. pap. text ed. 27.50x (ISBN 0-433-04910-3). Intl Ideas.

Veterinary Medicine & Animal Care Careers. Mary McHugh. (Illus.). 1977. lib. bdg. 6.45 (ISBN 0-531-01282-4). Watts.

Veterinary Medicine & Human Health. 2nd ed. Calvin W. Schwabe. (Illus.). 1969. 31.00 o.p. (ISBN 0-683-07595-0). Williams & Wilkins.

Veterinary Microbiology. K. C. Mahanta. 1966. pap. 7.25x (ISBN 0-210-26947-2). Asia.

Veterinary Multilingual Thesaurus, 4 vols. Ed. by Commission of the European Communities. 1122p. 1979. 4 vols. & index 325.00 (ISBN 3-598-07082-9, Pub. by K G Saur). Gale.

Veterinary Science. Boy Scouts of America. LC 19-600. (Illus.). 40p. (gr. 6-12). 1973. pap. 0.70x (ISBN 0-8395-3261-X, 3261). BSA.

Veterinary Surgery. 7th ed. Edward R. Frank. LC 59-12462. 1964. text ed. 34.95 (ISBN 0-8087-0606-3). Burgess.

Veterinary Toxicology. 2nd ed. R. D. Radeleff. LC 74-85846. (Illus.). 1970. text ed. 9.50 o.s.i. (ISBN 0-8121-0200-2). Lea & Febiger.

Vette (Corvette) Jay Schleifer. Ed. by Patricia McCarthy. (Pal Paperbacks Kit A Ser.). (Illus., Orig.). (gr. 7-12). 1974. pap. text ed. 1.25 (ISBN 0-8374-3470-X). Xerox Ed Pubns.

Vexed & Troubled Englishman 1590-1642. Carl Bridenbaugh. LC 68-17604. 512p. 1976. pap. 6.95 (ISBN 0-19-502020-0, GB453, GB). Oxford U Pr.

VFR Flight Review. Avram Goldstein. (Illus.). 1979. pap. 6.50 (ISBN 0-911721-67-3, Pub. by Airguide). Aviation.

VFR Pilot Exam-O-Grams. Federal Aviation Administration & Aviation Book Company Editors. (Illus.). 144p. 1980. pap. 3.50 (ISBN 0-911721-78-9). Aviation.

VHF Handbook for Radio Amateurs. Herbert S. Brier & William I. Orr. LC 74-75450. (Illus.). 336p. 1974. 6.95 (ISBN 0-93336-6-00-7). Radio Pubns.

Viaduct. Roy Brown. LC 68-23061. (gr. 5-7). 1968. 4.50g o.s.i. (ISBN 0-02-714890-4). Macmillan.

Viaje a la Luna. Julio Verne. (Span.). 7.95 (ISBN 84-241-5635-8). E Torres & Sons.

Viaje del "Aurora". C. S. Lewis. Tr. by Roberto Ingledew from Eng. LC 78-54297. (Cronicas de Narnia Ser.). 239p. (Orig., Span.). (gr. 4 up). 1978. pap. 2.95 (ISBN 0-89922-119-X). Edit Caribe.

Viaje Historico De un Pueblo. Mendez Fernandez. 24.95 (ISBN 0-87751-003-2, Pub by Troutman Press). E Torres & Sons.

Viajes de Gulliver. Jonathan Swift. (Span.). 7.95 (ISBN 84-241-5631-5). E Torres & Sons.

Viajes de Marco Polo. (Span.). 7.95 (ISBN 84-241-5627-7). E Torres & Sons.

Vibrating Gold Concentrators. Karl Von Mueller. 1980. pap. 4.00 (ISBN 0-89316-617-0); plastic bdg. 6.00 (ISBN 0-89316-618-9). Exanimo Pr.

Vibrating Systems. R. F. Chisnell. (Library of Mathematics). 1966. Repr. of 1960 ed. pap. 5.00 (ISBN 0-7100-4350-3). Routledge & Kegan.

Vibration. 2nd ed. R. E. Bishop. LC 79-11172. (Illus.). 1979. 29.50 (ISBN 0-521-22779-8); pap. 10.50 (ISBN 0-521-29639-0). Cambridge U Pr.

Vibration Analysis. Haberman. 1968. 23.95 (ISBN 0-675-09694-4). Merrill.

Vibration & Acoustic Measurement Handbook. Ed. by Michael P. Blake & William S. Mitchell. (Illus.). 1972. 34.50 (ISBN 0-8104-9195-8). Hayden.

Vibration & Shock in Damped Mechanical Systems. J. C. Snowdon. 1968. 39.95 (ISBN 0-471-81000-2, Pub. by Wiley-Interscience). Wiley.

Vibration & Waves in Physics. I. G. Main. LC 77-5546. (Illus.). 1978. 68.50 (ISBN 0-521-21662-1); pap. 15.95x (ISBN 0-521-29220-4). Cambridge U Pr.

Vibration Control. 2nd ed. J. N. Mac Duff & John R. Currey. 1981. write for info. (ISBN 0-89874-030-4). Krieger.

Vibration Engineering. W. Ker Wilson. 292p. 1959. 65.00x (ISBN 0-85264-023-4, Pub. by Griffin England). State Mutual Bk.

Vibrational & Rotational Relaxation in Gases. J. D. Lambert. (International Series of Monographs on Chemistry). (Illus.). 1978. 34.95x (ISBN 0-19-855605-5). Oxford U Pr.

Vibrational Spectra of Benzene Derivatives. G. Varsanyi. 1970. 59.50 (ISBN 0-12-714950-3). Acad Pr.

Vibrational Spectra of Organometallic Compounds. Edward Maslowsky, Jr. LC 76-18694. 1977. 35.00 o.p. (ISBN 0-471-58026-0, Pub. by Wiley-Interscience). Wiley.

Vibrational Spectroscopies for Absorbed Species. Ed. by Alexis T. Bell & Michael L. Hair. LC 80-21181. (ACS Symposium Ser.: No. 137). 1980. 31.00 (ISBN 0-8412-0585-X). Am Chemical.

Vibrational Spectroscopy of Adsorbates. Ed. by R. F. Willis. (Springer Series in Chemical Physics: Vol. 15). (Illus.). 200p. 1981. 29.50 (ISBN 0-387-10429-1). Springer-Verlag.

Vibrational Spectroscopy of Molecular Liquids & Solids. Ed. by S. Bratos & R. M. Pick. (NATO Advanced Study Institutes Ser., Ser. B: Physics: Vol. 56). 475p. 1980. 49.50 (ISBN 0-306-40445-1, Plenum Pr). Plenum Pub.

Vibrational Spectroscopy of Solids. P. M. Sherwood. LC 79-185566. (Cambridge Monographs in Physical Chemistry: No. 1). (Illus.). 256p. 1972. 45.00 (ISBN 0-521-08482-2). Cambridge U Pr.

Vibrations & Stability of Multiple Parameter System. K. Huseyin. (Mechanics of Elastic Stability: No. 3). 228p. 1978. 37.50x (ISBN 90-286-0136-8). Sijthoff & Noordhoff.

Vibrations from Blasting Rock. Lewis D. Leet. LC 60-10037. 1960. 7.95x (ISBN 0-674-93526-8). Harvard U Pr.

Viennese Porcelain. K. Tasnadi-Marik. (Illus.). 1975. 6.50 (ISBN 0-912728-05-1). Newbury Bks Inc.

Vient De Paraitre. Richard Martineau & Anne-Marie Girolami. 1975. pap. text ed. 3.75 (ISBN 0-88436-174-8). EMC.

Viento Sollozante. (Spanish Bks.). (Span.). 1979. 1.90 (ISBN 0-8297-0920-7). Vida Pub.

Viet Journal. James Jones. 272p. 1974. 7.95 o.s.i. (ISBN 0-440-08764-3). Delacorte.

Viet Nam: Land of Many Dragons. Hal Buell. LC 68-24027. (Illus.). (gr. 3 up). 1968. PLB 5.95 o.p. (ISBN 0-396-06466-3). Dodd.

Viet-Nam: Politics & Public Administration. Nghiem Dang. (Illus.). 1966. 15.00x (ISBN 0-8248-0049-4, Eastwest Ctr). U Pr of Hawaii.

Vietnam: a History in Documents. Gareth Porter. pap. write for info. (F553, Meridian Bks). NAL.

Vietnam, Beyond the War. Joseph S. Salzburg. LC 75-10622. 1975. 12.50 o.p. (ISBN 0-682-48258-7, Banner). Exposition.

Vietnam: Both Sides. Robert French. (Orig.). 1979. pap. 2.25 (ISBN 0-532-23177-5). Manor Bks.

Vietnam: Lotus in a Sea of Fire. Thich Nhat Hanh. (Orig.). 1967. pap. 1.65 o.p. (ISBN 0-8090-1334-7). Hill & Wang.

Vietnam on Film. Gilbert Adair. (Illus.). 208p. 1981. 12.95 (ISBN 0-906071-43-7). Proteus Pub NY.

Vietnam, Our Beloved Land. Nguyen C. Dam & Tran C. Linh. LC 68-21116. (Illus.). (gr. 5 up). 1968. pap. 3.85 o.p. (ISBN 0-8048-0614-4). C E Tuttle.

Vietnam Since the Fall of Saigon. William J. Duiker. LC 80-21166. (Southeast Asia Ser., Ohio University Papers in International Studies). (Illus.). 78p. (Orig.). 1981. pap. 9.00 (ISBN 0-89680-106-3). Ohio U Ctr Intl.

Vietnam: The Endless War. Leo Huberman et al. LC 77-127927. 1971. 5.95 o.p. (ISBN 0-85345-147-8, CL-1478); pap. 2.25 (ISBN 0-85345-196-6, PB-1966). Monthly Rev.

Vietnam: The View from Moscow, Peking, Washington. Daniel S. Papp. LC 80-20117. (Illus.). 263p. 1981. lib. bdg. 17.95x (ISBN 0-89950-010-2). McFarland & Co.

Vietnam Triangle: Moscow, Peking, Hanoi. Donald S. Zagoria. LC 67-25501. (Illus., Orig.). 1967. 8.95 (ISBN 0-672-53607-2). Pegasus.

Vietnam War. E. B. Fincher. (gr. 7 up). 1980. PLB 6.90 (ISBN 0-531-04112-3, C07). Watts.

Vietnam War Poems. Jocelyn Hollis. LC 80-65621. 48p. 1981. pap. 3.95 (ISBN 0-933486-14-6). Am Poetry Pr.

Vietnamese Americans: Patterns of Resettlement & Socioeconomic Adaption in the United States. Darell Montero & Marsha I. Weber. 1979. lib. bdg. 22.50x (ISBN 0-89158-264-9). Westview.

Vietnamese Anticolonialism, 1885-1925. David G. Marr. (Center for South & Southeast Asia Studies, UC Berkeley). 1971. 16.50 o.p. (ISBN 0-520-01813-3); pap. 9.95x o.p. (ISBN 0-520-02046-4, CAMPUS59). U of Cal Pr.

Vietnamese-English Phrase Book with Useful Word List: For English Speakers. William Gage & Duong Thanh Binh. LC 75-24857. (Vietnamese Refugee Education Ser.: No. 2). 1975. pap. text ed. 3.00x (ISBN 0-87281-044-5). Ctr Appl Ling.

Vietnamese Tradition on Trial, Nineteen Twenty to Nineteen Forty-Five. David G. Marr. (Illus.). 450p. 1981. 25.00 (ISBN 0-520-04180-1, CAMPUS 271); pap. 9.95 (ISBN 0-520-04277-8). U of Cal Pr.

View Beyond My Father. Mabel E. Allan. LC 78-7736. 1978. 5.95 (ISBN 0-396-07612-2). Dodd.

View from Another Shore. Franz Rottensteiner. 1978. pap. 1.75 o.s.i. (ISBN 0-515-04557-8). Jove Pubns.

View from Another Shore. Ed. by Franz Rottensteiner. LC 73-78082. 1976. pap. 3.95 o.p. (ISBN 0-8164-9273-5). Continuum.

View from Another Shore: European Science Fiction. Ed. by Franz Rottensteiner. LC 73-78082. 252p. (Translation from several languages). 1973. 6.95 o.p. (ISBN 0-8164-9151-8). Continuum.

View from Cold Mountain: Translations of Han-Shan. Tr. by Arthur Tobias & Jim Hardesty. 1976. 1.50 o.p. (ISBN 0-934834-16-4). White Pine.

View from Deacon Hill. Jack S. Scott. 192p. 1981. 9.95 (ISBN 0-89919-033-2). Ticknor & Fields.

View from Douglas Hill. Sue McConkey. 1958. 5.00 o.p. (ISBN 0-87482-051-0). Wake-Brook.

View from Eighty. Malcolm Cowley. 1981. lib. bdg. 9.95 (ISBN 0-8161-3156-2, Large Print Bks). G K Hall.

View from Hawk Mountain. Michael Harwood. LC 73-38905. 192p. 1973. pap. 2.95 o.p. (ISBN 0-684-16371-3, SL555, ScribT). Scribner.

View from Hill Cabin. Arnold Perrin. 1979. 10.95 (ISBN 0-89002-120-1); pap. 3.50 (ISBN 0-89002-119-8). Northwoods Pr.

View from Morningside: One Family's New York. Constance T. Colby. LC 78-4052. 1978. 8.95 o.s.i. (ISBN 0-397-01257-8). Lippincott.

View from Space: Photographic Exploration of the Planets. Merton Davies & Bruce C. Murray. LC 75-16887. 1971. 20.00x (ISBN 0-231-03557-8); pap. 7.50x (ISBN 0-231-08330-0). Columbia U Pr.

View from the Boys: A Sociology of Downtown Adolescents. Howard J. Parker. LC 74-76184. (People, Plans & Problems Ser.). 1974. 17.95 (ISBN 0-7153-6456-1). David & Charles.

View from the Bridge. Arthur Miller. (Plays Ser.). 1977. pap. 2.95 (ISBN 0-14-048135-4). Penguin.

View from the Earth, 1981. Guy Ottewell. (Illus.). 1980. pap. 4.00 (ISBN 0-934546-05-3). Astron Cal.

View from the Oak. Herbert Kohl & Judith Kohl. (Sierra Club-Scribner's Juvenile Ser.). 1977. 8.95 (ISBN 0-684-15016-6); pap. 4.95 (ISBN 0-684-15017-4). Sierra.

View from the Out House: The Joke's on the Bureaucrat. Pamela G. Wubben. 100p. 1980. pap. 3.33 (ISBN 0-935442-04-9). One Percent.

View from the Peacock's Tail: Poems. M. L. Rosenthal. 64p. 1972. 12.95 (ISBN 0-19-501593-2). Oxford U Pr.

View into a Modern, State-Operated Mental Health Facility: The Madden Zone Center. Ed. by Robert A. De Vito & Richard P. Tapley. 308p. 1975. 27.50 (ISBN 0-398-03207-6). C C Thomas.

View of Chinese Rugs: From the Seventeenth to the Twentieth Century. H. A. Lorentz. (Illus.). 216p. 1973. 95.00 (ISBN 0-7100-6912-X). Routledge & Kegan.

View of Greek Art. R. Ross Holloway. LC 72-187947. (Illus.). 213p. 1973. 15.00 (ISBN 0-87057-133-8, Pub. by Brown U Pr). Univ Pr of New England.

View of Lord Bolingbroke's Philosophy. William Warburton. Ed. by Rene Wellek. LC 75-11263. (British Philosophers & Theologians of the 17th & 18th Centuries Ser.). 1978. lib. bdg. 42.00 (ISBN 0-8240-1812-5). Garland Pub.

View of Programming Languages. Galler & Perlis. 1976. 18.95 (ISBN 0-201-02324-5). A-W.

View of the Constitution of the United States of America. William Rawle. LC 70-109548. (American Constitutional & Legal History Ser). 1970. Repr. of 1829 ed. lib. bdg. 35.00 (ISBN 0-306-71902-9). Da Capo.

View of the Court of Chancery. William L. Wellesley. 110p. 1980. Repr. of 1830 ed. lib. bdg. 15.00x (ISBN 0-8377-1303-X). Rothman.

View of Victorian Literature. Geoffrey Tillotson. 1978. 19.95 (ISBN 0-19-812044-3). Oxford U Pr.

Viewdata & Information Society. J. Martin. 1981. 29.95 (ISBN 0-13-941906-3). P-H.

Viewdata Revolution. Sam Fedida & Rex Malik. LC 79-23869. 186p. 1980. 34.95 (ISBN 0-470-26879-4). Wiley.

Viewer's Guide to Film Theory & Criticism. Robert T. Eberwein. LC 79-9380. 243p. 1979. 13.50 (ISBN 0-8108-1237-1). Scarecrow.

Viewer's Guide to Looking at Photographs. Jame T. Brooke. LC 77-74181. (Illus.). 1977. 7.95 o.p. (ISBN 0-918844-02-9); pap. 4.95 o.p. (ISBN 0-918844-01-0). Aurelian Pr.

Viewer's Television Book: A Personal Guide to Understanding Television & Its Influence. Stanley J. Baran. LC 80-81369. 109p. (Orig.). 1980. pap. 6.95 (ISBN 0-936522-00-3). Penrith.

Viewing Your Career. new ed. David Stone. Ed. by Morris Gall. LC 73-83977. (Consumer Education Ser). (Illus., Orig.). (gr. 7-12). 1973. pap. text ed. 1.45 o.p. (ISBN 0-88301-117-4). Pendulum Pr.

Viewpoint: Key to Fiction Writing. Francis L. Fugate. 1968. 8.95 (ISBN 0-87116-025-0). Writer.

Viewpoint on Nutrition. Arnold Pike. LC 80-24024. 221p. 1980. Repr. of 1973 ed. lib. bdg. 9.95x (ISBN 0-89370-621-3). Borgo Pr.

Viewpoints on English As a Second Language. Ed. by Burt et al. 1977. text ed. 7.95 (ISBN 0-88345-298-7). Regents Pub.

Views. Edward Dorn. Ed. by Donald Allen. LC 79-25498. (Writing 40 Ser.). 144p. 12.00 (ISBN 0-87704-050-8); pap. 5.95 (ISBN 0-87704-051-6). Four Seasons Foun.

Views from a Window: Conversations with Gore Vidal. Ed. by Robert J. Stanton & Gore Vidal. 320p. 1980. lib. bdg. 14.95 (ISBN 0-8184-0302-0). Lyle Stuart.

Views of a Nearsighted Cannoneer. Seymour Krim. 1968. pap. 1.95 o.p. (ISBN 0-525-47214-2). Dutton.

Views of Christian Nurture & Subjects Related Thereto. Horace Bushnell. LC 74-23297. 260p. 1975. Repr. of 1847 ed. lib. bdg. 26.00x (ISBN 0-8201-1147-3). Schol Facsimiles.

Views of Los Angeles. rev. ed. Ed. by William Burnett. (Illus.). 1979. 24.95 (ISBN 0-9602274-1-5); pap. 14.95 (ISBN 0-9602274-0-7). Portriga Pubns.

Views of Venice by Canaletto. Antonio Canaletto. (Illus.). pap. 6.00 (ISBN 0-486-22705-7). Dover.

Views on Capitalism. 2nd ed. Richard Romano & Melvin Leiman. 1975. pap. text ed. 6.95x (ISBN 0-02-477220-8, 47722). Macmillan.

Views on Science, Technology & Development. Ed. by V. Rabinowitch & E. Rabinowitch. LC 74-32201. 300p. 1975. text ed. 37.00 (ISBN 0-08-018241-0). Pergamon.

Vigil. LC 76-4400. 1976. 5.00 (ISBN 0-935490-07-8). Euclid Pub.

Vigil (a Novel) S. Bhaduri. 6.50x o.p. (ISBN 0-210-22621-8). Asia.

Vigilance: The Problem of Sustained Attention. C. M. Stroh. 1971. 22.00 (ISBN 0-08-016711-X). Pergamon.

Vigilante Days: Frontier Justice Along the Niobrara. Harold Hutton. LC 76-17742. (Illus.). 365p. 1978. 17.95 (ISBN 0-8040-0738-1, SB). Swallow.

Vigilante Politics. Ed. by H. Jon Rosenbaum & Peter C. Sederberg. LC 75-11168. 1976. 15.00x (ISBN 0-8122-7702-3). U of Pa Pr.

Vigilantes of Montana. Thomas J. Dimsdale. (Western Frontier Library: No. 1). 1978. Repr. of 1953 ed. 8.95 o.p. (ISBN 0-8061-0274-8, WFL 1); pap. 4.95 (ISBN 0-8061-1379-0). U of Okla Pr.

Vigilantism in America. Arnold Madison. LC 72-97771. (gr. 5 up). 6.95 (ISBN 0-395-28915-7, Clarion). HM.

Viglini Letters, Vol. 2. Janelle Viglini. 1976. 12.50 o.p. (ISBN 0-685-67144-5). Porter.

Viglini Letters: February 1973 - June 1974, Vol. 1. Bern Porter. 1975. pap. 7.50 o.p. (ISBN 0-685-53395-6, 0-911156-15-2). Porter.

Vignettes of Philosophy: Thirty-Five Vital Subjects. Homer T. Rosenberger. LC 77-71070. (Horizons of the Humanities Ser.: Vol. 3). 258p. 1977. lib. bdg. 9.00 (ISBN 0-917264-01-0). Rose Hill.

Viking Adventure. Clyde R. Bulla. LC 63-9208. (Illus.). (gr. 3-6). 1963. PLB 7.89 (ISBN 0-690-86015-3, TYC-J). T Y Crowell.

Viking & Cherokee. Arthur G. Peterson. LC 79-89769. (Illus.). 170p. 1980. pap. 8.75. A G Peterson.

Viking Process. Norman Hartley. 1976. pap. 1.95 (ISBN 0-380-00892-0, 31617). Avon.

Viking Process. Norman Hartley. 320p. 1980. pap. 2.75 (52993). Avon.

Viking Romance: Gongu-Hrolf's Saga. Illus. by Hermann Palsson & Paul Edwards. 144p. 1981. 10.00x (ISBN 0-8020-2392-4). U of Toronto Pr.

Viking Ships. I. Atkinson. LC 77-17510. (Introduction to the History of Mankind Ser.). 1979. 3.95 (ISBN 0-521-21951-5). Cambridge U Pr.

Viking Ships. W. W. Brogger & Hakon Shetelig. (Illus.). 196p. 1980. 27.50 (ISBN 0-906191-40-8, Pub. by Thule Pr England). Intl Schol Bk Serv.

Vikings. The British Museum & The Metropolitan Museum of Art. LC 79-25486. (Illus.). 192p. 1980. 22.95 (ISBN 0-688-03603-1). Morrow.

Vikings. Helen Clarke. (Civilization Library). (Illus.). (gr. 5 up). 1979. PLB 6.90 s&l (ISBN 0-531-03412-7). Watts.

Vikings. Michael Gibson & Harry Strongman. LC 77-86712. (Peoples of the Past Ser.). (Illus.). 1977. lib. bdg. 7.95 (ISBN 0-686-51161-1). Silver.

Vikings! Magnus Magnusson. (Illus.). 320p. 1980. 20.00 o.p. (ISBN 0-525-22892-6). Dutton.

Vikings. Sylvie Nickels. (Jackdaw Ser: No. 133). (gr. 7 up). 1976. 5.95 o.p. (ISBN 0-670-74683-5). Viking Pr.

Vikings. Place. (gr. 5 up). 1980. pap. 6.90 (ISBN 0-531-09170-8, G32). Watts.

Vikings. Robert Wernick. (Seafarers Ser.). (Illus.). 1979. lib. bdg. 14.94 (ISBN 0-686-50990-0). Silver.

Viking's Dawn. Henry Treece. LC 56-9962. (Illus.). (gr. 7-9). 1956. 9.95 (ISBN 0-87599-117-3). S G Phillips.

Vikings of the West-Expansion of Norway in Middle Ages. P. Andersen. (Tanum of Norway Tokens Ser). (Illus.). pap. 11.00x (ISBN 82-518-0026-9, N508). Vanous.

Vile Florentines. Timothy Holmes. 196p. 1981. 10.95 (ISBN 0-312-84677-0). St Martin.

Vilhelm Gronbech. P. M. Mitchell. (World Authors Ser.: No. 397). 1978. lib. bdg. 11.95 (ISBN 0-8057-6306-6). Twayne.

Villa Giustinian at Roncade. Carolyn K. Lewis. LC 76-23636. (Outstanding Dissertations in the Fine Arts). (Illus.). 643p. 1980. Repr. of 1973 ed. lib. bdg. 91.00 (ISBN 0-8240-2705-1). Garland Pub.

Villa Medici in Rome, 2 vols. Glenn M. Andres. LC 75-23778. (Outstanding Dissertations in the Fine Arts - Sixteenth Century). (Illus.). 1976. Set. lib. bdg. 121.00 (ISBN 0-8240-1975-X). Garland Pub.

Villa on the Palatine. Margot Arnold. 1978. pap. 1.75 o.p. (ISBN 0-425-03656-1, Medallion). Berkley Pub.

Village. Ivan Bunin. Tr. by I. Hapgood from Rus. 291p. 1975. Repr. of 1923 ed. 17.50 (ISBN 0-86527-320-0). Fertig.

Village: A History of Germantown, Ohio, 1804-1976. Carl M. Becker. LC 80-16683. (Historical Society of Germantown, Ohio Ser.). (Illus.). 209p. 1980. 15.00 (ISBN 0-8214-0550-0). Ohio U Pr.

Village & Family in Contemporary China. William L. Parish & Martin K. Whyte. LC 78-3411. xvi, 420p. 1980. pap. 8.95 (ISBN 0-226-64591-6, P899, Phoen). U of Chicago Pr.

Village & Seaport: Migration & Society in Eighteenth-Century Massachusetts. Douglas L. Jones. LC 80-54469. (Illus.). 240p. 1981. 15.00x (ISBN 0-87451-200-X). U Pr of New Eng.

Village Clusters & Rural Development. H. Ramachandran. 140p. 1980. text ed. 12.50 (ISBN 0-391-02138-9). Humanities.

Village Cricket. Gerald Howat. LC 79-56048. (Illus.). 1980. 17.95 (ISBN 0-7153-7727-2). David & Charles.

Village Economy: Land & People of Huecorio. Michael H. Belshaw. LC 66-28489. (Illus.). 1967. 22.50x (ISBN 0-231-02928-4). Columbia U Pr.

Village England. Ed. by Peter Crookston. 1980. 16.95 (ISBN 0-686-68275-0). Methuen Inc.

Village Gods of South India: 1921. Henry Whitehead. LC 78-74275. (Oriental Religions Ser.: Vol. 10). 188p. 1980. lib. bdg. 22.00 (ISBN 0-8240-3907-6). Garland Pub.

Village Had No Walls. V. Madgulkar. 1972. pap. 3.75x (ISBN 0-210-31153-3). Asia.

Village in Uhuru. Gabriel Ruhumbika. (Orig.). 1969. pap. text ed. 3.00x (ISBN 0-582-64011-3). Humanities.

Village Labourer. new ed. J. L. Hammond & B. Hammond. Ed. by Gordon E. Mingay. LC 77-21513. 1978. text ed. 22.00x (ISBN 0-582-48518-5); pap. text ed. 12.95x (ISBN 0-582-48082-5). Longman.

Village Life & Labour. Ed. by Raphael Samuel. (History Workshop Ser.). 1975. 22.50x (ISBN 0-7100-7499-9); pap. 9.95 (ISBN 0-7100-7500-6). Routledge & Kegan.

Village Life in South India: Cultural Design & Environmental Variation. Alan R. Beals. LC 74-76547. (Worlds of Man Ser). 1974. 11.00x (ISBN 0-88295-600-0); pap. 5.75x (ISBN 0-88295-601-9). AHM Pub.

Village London. Peter Crookston. 190p. 1979. pap. 4.95 (ISBN 0-500-27150-X). Thames Hudson.

Village of Curers & Assassins: On the Production of Fala Kpelle Cosmological Categories. Beryl L. Bellman. LC 73-76893. (Approaches to Semiotics: No. 39). 196p. 1975. text ed. 44.10x (ISBN 90-2793-042-2). Mouton.

Village of Outcasts. S. R. Van Iterson. LC 74-168478. 240p. (gr. 7 up). 1972. PLB 6.96 (ISBN 0-688-31988-2). Morrow.

Village of the Vampire Cat: A Novel. Lensey Namioka. LC 80-68737. 218p. (YA) (gr. 8-12). 1981. 8.95 (ISBN 0-440-09377-5). Delacorte.

Village Ordination. Thongyoy Worakwinto. Tr. by T. H. Silcock from Thai. (Scandinavian Inst. of Asian Studies Monographs: No. 25). (Illus.). 1976. pap. text ed. 9.25x (ISBN 0-7007-0092-7). Humanities.

Village Patriarch; a Poem, Repr. Of 1829 Ed. Ebenezer Elliott. Ed. by Donald H. Reiman. Bd. with Corn-Law Rhymes. Repr. of 1831 ed. LC 75-31202. (Romantic Context Ser.: Poetry 1789-1830). 1979. lib. bdg. 47.00 (ISBN 0-8240-2152-5). Garland Pub.

Village Planning in the Primitive World. Douglas Fraser. LC 68-24701. (Planning & Cities Ser). (Illus., Orig.). (YA) (gr. 9-12). 1968. pap. 5.95 o.p. (ISBN 0-8076-0468-2). Braziller.

Village That Slept. Monique P. De Ladebat. (Children's Literature Ser.). 1980. PLB 8.95 (ISBN 0-8398-2610-9). Gregg.

Village Viability in Contemporary Society. Ed. by Priscilla Reining & Barbara Lenkerd. (AAAS Selected Symposium: No. 34). 1979. lib. bdg. 23.50x (ISBN 0-89158-472-2). Westview.

Villagers at War: Some Papua New Guinea Experience in World War II. Neville K. Robinson. Ed. by E. K. Fisk. (Pacific Research Series Monograph: No. 2). 223p. 1980. pap. text ed. 12.95 (0475). Bks Australia.

Villagers (Huasipungo) A Novel. Jorge Icaza. Tr. by Bernard M. Dulsey from Span. LC 73-9551. (Arcturus Books Paperbacks). 238p. 1973. pap. 6.95 (ISBN 0-8093-0653-0). S Ill U Pr.

Villages. Richard Critchfield. LC 80-1721. (Illus.). 384p. 1981. 17.95 (ISBN 0-385-17212-5). Doubleday.

Villages pittoresques. (Beautes de la France). (Illus.). 1978. 24.25x (ISBN 2-03-013908-4, 3187). Larousse.

Villains. D. Houston. 1980. pap. 3.95 (ISBN 0-931064-21-X). Starlog Pr.

Villas & Cottages. 2nd ed. Calvert Vaux. LC 68-29858. (Architecture & Decorative Art Ser). (Illus.). 1968. Repr. of 1857 ed. lib. bdg. 29.50 (ISBN 0-306-71044-7). Da Capo.

Villas of Frascati, 1650-1750. Carl L. Franck. (Illus.). 1966. 20.00 (ISBN 0-85458-669-5). Transatlantic.

Villas on the Hudson: A Collection of Photo-Lithographs of Thirty-One Country Residences. LC 76-41854. (Architecture & Decorative Art Ser.). 1977. Repr. of 1860 ed. lib. bdg. 75.00 (ISBN 0-306-70800-0). Da Capo.

Ville Africaine, Famille Urbaine: Les Enseignants De Kinshasa. Guy Bernard. (Recherches Africaines: No. 6). 1968. pap. 23.50x (ISBN 90-2797-543-4). Mouton.

Ville Ouvriere au Temps du Socialisme Utopique: Toulon De 1815 a 1851. 2nd ed. Maurice Agulhon. (Civilisations et Societes: No. 18). 1977. pap. 24.70 (ISBN 90-2796-287-1). Mouton.

Villette. Charlotte Bronte. (World's Classics Ser.). 1954. 14.95 (ISBN 0-19-250047-3). Oxford U Pr.

Villiers De L'isle - Adam. William T. Conroy, Jr. (World Author Ser.: No. 491). 1978. 12.95 (ISBN 0-8057-6332-5). Twayne.

Villon: Un Testament ambique. new ed. P. Demarolle. (Collection themes et textes). (Orig., Fr.). 1973. pap. 6.75 (ISBN 2-03-035019-2, 2648). Larousse.

Vilyatpur 1848-1968: Social & Economic Change in a North Indian Village. Tom G. Kessinger. (Illus.). 1974. 20.00x (ISBN 0-520-02340-4). U of Cal Pr.

Vimalakirti Nirdesa Sutra. Charles Luk. LC 71-189851. 1975. pap. 3.95 o.p. (ISBN 0-394-73065-8). Random.

Vimalakirti Nirdesa Sutra. Tr. by Charles Luk from Chinese. LC 71-189851. 175p. 1981. pap. 5.95 (ISBN 0-87773-072-5). Great Eastern.

Vinaya Texts, Vols. 13, 17, & 20. Ed. by F. Max Mueller. Tr. by West. (Sacred Books of the East Ser.). 15.00x ea.; Vol. 13. (ISBN 0-8426-1434-6); Vol. 17. (ISBN 0-8426-1435-4); Vol. 20. (ISBN 0-8426-1436-2). Verry.

Vinca Dosimetry Experiment. (Technical Reports: No. 6). 1962. pap. 3.25 (ISBN 92-0-125062-2, IAEA). Unipub.

Vince Lombardi: The Immortal Coach. Julian May. LC 74-31947. (Sports Close-up Ser.). (gr. 3-9). 1975. PLB 5.95 o.p. (ISBN 0-913940-16-X); pap. 2.95 o.p. (ISBN 0-913940-23-2). Crestwood Hse.

Vincent Minelli & the Film Musical. Joseph A. Casper. LC 75-20614. (Illus.). 1977. 15.00 o.p. (ISBN 0-498-01784-2). A S Barnes.

Vincent Van Gogh. Ernest Raboff. LC 73-75362. 36p. (gr. 3-7). 1975. 6.95a o.p. (ISBN 0-385-05009-7); PLB (ISBN 0-385-06999-5). Doubleday.

Vincenzo Vela (Eighteen Twenty to Ninety-One) Nancy J. Scott. LC 78-74378. (Fine Arts Dissertations, Fourth Ser.). (Illus.). 1980. lib. bdg. 66.00 (ISBN 0-8240-3965-3). Garland Pub.

Vindication of the Rights of Brutes. Thomas Taylor. LC 66-10010. 1966. Repr. of 1792 ed. 20.00x (ISBN 0-8201-1045-0). Schol Facsimiles.

Vindication of the Rights of Woman: With Strictures on Political & Moral Subjects. Mary Wollstonecraft. (Feminist Controversy in England, 1788-1810 Ser.). 1974. lib. bdg. 50.00 (ISBN 0-8240-0891-X). Garland Pub.

Vines. James U. Crockett & Richard Cravens. (Time-Life Encyclopedia of Gardening Ser.). (Illus.). 1979. lib. bdg. 11.97 (ISBN 0-686-51067-4). Silver.

Vineyard Bible: A Central Narrative & Index. Ed. by Avery Brooke. 416p. 1980. 12.95 (ISBN 0-8164-0144-6). Seabury.

Vineyard Tales. Gale Huntington. LC 80-52793. 250p. (Orig.). (gr. 1-6). 1980. pap. 7.95 (ISBN 0-932384-13-7). Tashmoo.

Vinland the Good. H. Ingstad. (Tanum of Norway Tokens Ser). pap. 12.00x o.p. (ISBN 0-686-66670-4, N475). Vanous.

Vino: The Wine & Winemakers of Italy. Burton Anderson. (Illus.). 416p. 1980. 19.95 (ISBN 0-316-03948-9). Little.

Vintage. Anita Kornfeld. 1980. 13.95 (ISBN 0-671-25308-5). S&S.

Vintage Auto Almanac. 3rd, annual ed. Ed. by David W. Brownell. LC 76-649715. 1980. pap. 4.95 o.p. (ISBN 0-917808-03-7). Hemmings.

Vintage Auto Almanac. 4th ed. Ed. by David W. Brownell. LC 76-649715. 256p. 1981. pap. 8.95 (ISBN 0-917808-04-5). Hemmings.

Vintage Bradbury. Ray Bradbury. 1965. pap. 1.95 (ISBN 0-394-70294-8, Vin, V294). Random.

Vintage Bus Annual, No. 1. Ed. by Ken Blacker. (Illus.). 96p. 1979. 16.50x (ISBN 0-906116-09-0). Intl Pubns Serv.

Vintage Cameras & Images, Ident. & Value Guide. John Maloney. (Illus.). pap. 9.95 (ISBN 0-87069-342-5). Wallace-Homestead.

Vintage Cars. Phil Drackett. 4.50x (ISBN 0-392-06952-0, SpS). Soccer.

Vintage Lorry Annual. Ed. by Nick Baldwin. (Illus.). 96p. 1979. 16.50x (ISBN 0-906116-07-4). Intl Pubns Serv.

Vintage Murder. Ngaio Marsh. 1978. pap. 1.75 (ISBN 0-515-04534-9). Jove Pubns.

Vintage Nantucket. A. B. Whipple. LC 78-7107. (Illus.). 1978. 8.95 (ISBN 0-396-07517-7). Dodd.

Vintage: The Bold Survivors. Joan Dufault. (Illus.). 256p. 1978. 12.95 (ISBN 0-8298-0356-4). Pilgrim NY.

Vintage Wine Book. rev. ed. William S. Leedom. 1975. pap. 2.45 o.p. (ISBN 0-394-70230-1, Vin). Random.

Vinyl & Allied Polymers, Vol. 1. 1972. text ed. 27.50 (ISBN 0-592-05435-7). Butterworths.

Vinyl & Allied Polymers, Vol. 2. G. Mathews. 1972. text ed. 39.95 (ISBN 0-592-05443-8). Butterworths.

Viola Tricolor & Curator Carsten. Theodor Storm. LC 65-7498. 1956. 6.50 o.p. (ISBN 0-8044-2841-7); pap. 2.45 (ISBN 0-8044-6881-8). Ungar.

Violence. Festus Iyayi. 316p. (Orig.). 1979. 9.00 (ISBN 0-89410-105-6); pap. 5.00 (ISBN 0-89410-104-8). Three Continents.

Violence Against Children: Physical Child Abuse in the United States. David G. Gil. LC 77-130809. (Commonwealth Fund Publications Ser). (Illus.). 1970. 8.50x (ISBN 0-674-93941-7); pap. 3.50 (ISBN 0-674-93942-5). Harvard U Pr.

Violence & Aggression. Ronald Bailey. LC 76-1293. (Human Behavior). (Illus.). (gr. 5 up). 1976. PLB 9.99 o.p. (ISBN 0-8094-1951-3, Pub. by Time-Life). Silver.

Violence & Aggression. Ronald Bailey. (Human Behavior Ser.). 9.95 (ISBN 0-8094-1950-5). Time-Life.

Violence & Aggression in the History of Ideas. Ed. by Philip P. Wiener & John Fisher. 288p. 1974. pap. 4.95x o.p. (ISBN 0-8135-0772-3). Rutgers U Pr.

Violence & Crime in the Schools. Keith Baker & Tobert J. Rubel. LC 79-5325. 320p. 1980. 16.95 (ISBN 0-669-03389-8). Lexington Bks.

Violence & Criminal Justice. Ed. by Duncan Chappell & John Monahan. LC 74-31912. 1975. 16.95 (ISBN 0-669-98194-X). Lexington Bks.

Violence & Criminal Justice. Ed. by Duncan Chappell & John Monahan. 1977. pap. text ed. 6.95x o.p. (ISBN 0-669-01064-2). Heath.

Violence & Glory: Poems, Nineteen-Sixty-Two to Nineteen-Sixty-Eight. James Schevill. LC 76-75733. 1969. 7.95 o.p. (ISBN 0-8040-0313-0); pap. 5.95 (ISBN 0-8040-0314-9). Swallow.

Violence & Oppression. James C. Dick. LC 78-2235. 224p. 1979. 12.00x (ISBN 0-8203-0446-8). U of Ga Pr.

Violence & Repression in Latin America: A Quantitative & Historical Analysis. Ernest A. Duff & John F. McCamant. LC 75-16645. (Illus.). 1976. 19.95 (ISBN 0-02-907690-0). Free Pr.

Violence & the Family. Ed. by Maurice R. Green. (AAAS Selected Symposium: No. 47). 200p. 1980. lib. bdg. 17.50x (ISBN 0-89158-841-8); pap. text ed. 8.00 (ISBN 0-86531-141-2). Westview.

Violence & the Police: A Sociological Study of Law, Custom, & Morality. William A. Westley. 1970. 12.50x o.p. (ISBN 0-262-23042-9); pap. 4.95 (ISBN 0-262-73027-8, 187). MIT Pr.

Violence & the Violent Individual. Ed. by J. R. Hays et al. LC 80-24. (Illus.). 544p. 1981. text ed. 35.00 (ISBN 0-89335-116-4). Spectrum Pub.

Violence & Thought: Essays on Social Tensions in Africa. Ali A. Mazrui. (Orig.). 1969. text ed. 6.00x (ISBN 0-391-00207-4). Humanities.

Violence & Vandalism. John Ban & Lewis Ciminillo. LC 77-87607. text ed. 6.95x (ISBN 0-8134-1981-6, 1981). Interstate.

Violence As Protest: A Study of Riots & Ghettos. Robert M. Fogelson. LC 80-36808. xviii, 265p. 1980. Repr. of 1971 ed. lib. bdg. 22.50x (ISBN 0-313-22642-3, FOVP). Greenwood.

Violence, Conflict, & Politics in Colombia. Paul Oquist. LC 79-6778. (Studies in Social Discontinuity Ser.). 1980. 25.00 (ISBN 0-12-527750-4). Acad Pr.

Violence in America: Historical & Comparative Perspectives. rev., college ed. Ed. by Hugh D. Graham & Ted R. Gurr. LC 78-21934. (Illus.). 1979. 20.00x (ISBN 0-8039-0963-2); pap. 9.95x (ISBN 0-8039-0964-0). Sage.

Violence in Animal Human Societies. Arthur G. Neal et al. LC 76-21241. (Illus.). 1976. 17.95 (ISBN 0-88229-249-8). Nelson-Hall.

Violence in Modern Literature. James A. Gould & John J. Iorio. LC 71-182676. 208p. 1972. pap. 4.95x (ISBN 0-87835-037-3). Boyd & Fraser.

Violence in Our Schools: What to Know About It - What to Do About It. new ed. Staff of National Committee for Citizens in Education. 40p. (Orig.). 1975. pap. 3.50 (ISBN 0-934460-00-0). NCCE.

Violence in Our Time. Sandy Lesberg. (Illus.). 256p. 19.95x (ISBN 0-8464-0988-7). Beekman Pubs.

Violence in Schools: Perspectives, Programs & Positions. Ed. by James M. McPartland & Edward L. McDill. 1977. 17.95 (ISBN 0-669-01082-0). Lexington Bks.

Violence in the Arts. J. Fraser. LC 73-84319. 208p. 1976. 27.00 (ISBN 0-521-20331-7); pap. 7.95x (ISBN 0-521-29029-5). Cambridge U Pr.

Violence in the Communications Industry, 7 vols. Ed. by Canadian Royal Commission. 1977. Set. pap. text ed. 85.00x o.p. (ISBN 0-685-87415-X). Renouf.

Violence in the Family. Ed. by Marie Borland. 1976. text ed. 19.50x (ISBN 0-391-00610-X). Humanities.

Violence in the Home: A Socio-Legal Study. M. D. Freeman. 1979. 19.95 (ISBN 0-566-00129-2, 00407-3, Pub. by Saxon Hse England). Lexington Bks.

Violence Trail. George G. Gilman. (Edge Ser.: No. 25). 1978. pap. 1.75 (ISBN 0-523-41303-3). Pinnacle Bks.

Violencia y Criminalidad En Puerto Rico, 1898-1973: Apuntes para un Estudio De Historia Social. Blanca Silvestrini De Pacheco. LC 79-15801. Orig. Title: Analisis Historico De la Violencia en Puerto Rico. (Illus.). x, 237p. (Sp.). 1980. pap. text ed. write for info. (ISBN 0-8477-2488-3). U of PR Pr.

Violent Behavior: Social Learning Approaches to Prediction, Management & Treatment. Ed. by Richard B. Stuart. 400p. 1981. 20.00 (ISBN 0-87630-262-2). Brunner-Mazel.

Violent Crime. Richard Block. LC 76-40818. (Illus.). 1977. 15.95 (ISBN 0-669-01044-8). Lexington Bks.

Violent Crime: Historical & Contemporary Issues. Ed. by James A. Inciardi & Anne E. Pottieger. LC 78-14944. (Sage Research Progress Series in Criminology: Vol. 5). 1978. 12.95x (ISBN 0-8039-1107-6); pap. 6.50x (ISBN 0-8039-1108-4). Sage.

Violent Criminal Acts & Actors: A Symbolic Interactionist Study. Lonnie Athens. (International Library of Sociology). 1980. 14.00x (ISBN 0-7100-0342-0). Routledge & Kegan.

Violent Effigy. John Carey. LC 74-160359. 1979. pap. 4.95 (ISBN 0-571-11370-2, Pub. by Faber & Faber). Merrimack Bk Serv.

Violent Few. Donna Hamparian et al. LC 77-9128. (Dangerous Offender Project). 1978. 18.95 (ISBN 0-669-01779-5). Lexington Bks.

Violent Men. Hans Toch. 1981. text ed. 13.95x (ISBN 0-87073-888-7); pap. text ed. 7.95 (ISBN 0-685-99685-9). Schenkman.

Violent Season. Robert Goulet. 1961. 4.50 o.s.i. (ISBN 0-8076-0143-8). Braziller.

Violent Years. Patricia Jahns. 6.95 (ISBN 0-8038-7726-9). Hastings.

Violet Fairy Book. Andrew Lang. (Illus.). (gr. 6-8). 7.00 (ISBN 0-8446-0757-6). Peter Smith.

Violet in the Crucible: Shelley & Translation. Timothy Webb. 1977. 43.00x (ISBN 0-19-812059-1). Oxford U Pr.

Violets & Vinegar. Ed. by Jilly Cooper & Tom Hartman. LC 80-9059. 231p. 1981. 15.95 (ISBN 0-8128-2813-5). Stein & Day.

Violin: An Introduction to the Instrument. William Ballantine. LC 75-115772. (Keynote Bks). (Illus.). (gr. 7 up). 1971. PLB 4.90 o.p. (ISBN 0-531-01845-8). Watts.

Violin & Viola. Yehudi Menuhin. Ed. by William Primrose & Denis Stevens. LC 76-328. (Yehudi Menuhin Music Guide Ser). 1976. 12.95 (ISBN 0-02-871410-5); pap. 6.95 (ISBN 0-02-871350-8). Schirmer Bks.

Violin & Violoncello in Duo Without Accompaniment. Alexander Feinland & Oscar R. Iotti. LC 77-187707. (Detroit Studies in Music Bibliography Ser.: No. 25). (Based on the work of Alexander Feinland). 1973. 5.75 (ISBN 0-685-30615-1); pap. 4.25 (ISBN 0-911772-48-0). Info Coord.

Violin Close up. Peter Schaaf. LC 79-6337. (Illus.). 32p. (gr. 1 up). 1980. 6.95 (ISBN 0-590-07655-8, Four Winds). Schol Bk Serv.

Violin Concerto. Frederic B. Emery. LC 75-93979. (Music Ser). 1969. Repr. of 1928 ed. lib. bdg. 45.00 (ISBN 0-306-71822-7). Da Capo.

Violin Concerto. Benjamin Swalin. LC 72-8292. (Music Ser). 186p. 1973. Repr. of 1941 ed. lib. bdg. 19.50 (ISBN 0-306-70537-0). Da Capo.

Violin Fingering: It's Theory & Practice. Carl Flesch. (Music Reprint Ser.). Repr. of 1960 ed. lib. bdg. 35.00 (ISBN 0-306-79573-6). Da Capo.

Violin: Its Famous Makers & Players. Paul Stoeving. (Illus.). Repr. of 1928 ed. lib. bdg. 14.25x (ISBN 0-8371-4346-2, STVI). Greenwood.

Violin Makers: Portrait of a Living Craft. Mary A. Alburger. 1978. text ed. 26.25x (ISBN 0-575-02442-9). Humanities.

Violin Technique. Andre Mangeot. (Student's Music Library Ser). 1953. 6.95 (ISBN 0-234-77242-5). Dufour.

Violins of Saint-Jacques. Patrick L. Fermor. LC 76-29863. 1977. 7.95 o.p. (ISBN 0-312-84700-9). St Martin.

VIP with Psychiatric Impairment. Group for the Advancement of Psychiatry. LC 76-37208. 160p. 1973. 4.95 o.p. (ISBN 0-684-12778-4, ScribT). Scribner.

Viper Jazz. James Tate. LC 76-4943. (Wesleyan Poetry Program: Vol.82). 1976. lib. bdg. 10.00x (ISBN 0-8195-2082-9, Pub. by Wesleyan U Pr); pap. 4.95 (ISBN 0-8195-1082-3). Columbia U Pr.

Viral & Rickettsial Infections of Man. 4th ed. Frank L. Horsfall & Igor Tamm. (Illus., Span. & Ital. eds. avail). 1965. 15.50 o.p. (ISBN 0-397-52024-7). Lippincott.

Viral Cytopathology. H. H. Malherbe. 128p. 1980. 54.95 (ISBN 0-8493-5567-2). CRC Pr.

Viral Diseases of Cattle. Robert F. Kahrs. (Illus.). 224p. 1981. text ed. 15.00 (ISBN 0-8138-0860-X). Iowa St U Pr.

Viral Equation of State. E. A. Mason & T. H. Spurling. LC 69-17903. 1970. text ed. 44.00 (ISBN 0-08-013292-8); pap. text ed. 19.00 (ISBN 0-08-018988-1). Pergamon.

Viral Hepatitis. Raymond S. Koff. LC 78-17013. (Clinical Gastroenterology Monographs). 1978. 24.95 (ISBN 0-471-03695-1, Pub. by Wiley Medical). Wiley.

Viral Hepatitis: Etiology, Epidemiology, Pathogenesis & Prevention. Ed. by Girish N. Vyas et al. LC 78-882. (Clinical Ser). (Illus., Orig.). 1978. 64.50 (ISBN 0-89168-013-6). Franklin Inst Pr.

Viral Oncogenes, Vol. 44. Cold Spring Harbor Symposia on Quantitative Biology. LC 34-8174. (Illus.). 1322p. 1980. 2 book set 130.00 (ISBN 0-87969-043-7). Cold Spring Harbor.

Viral Oncology. Ed. by George Klein. 1980. text ed. 92.00 (ISBN 0-89004-390-6). Raven.

Viral Zoonoses. George Beran. (CRC Handbook in Zoonoses Sect B: Vol. 1). 480p. 1981. 64.95 (ISBN 0-8493-2911-6). CRC Pr.

Viral Zoonoses. Ed. by George Beran. (Handbook Series in Zoonoses Sect. B: Vol. 2). 464p. 1981. 64.95 (ISBN 0-8493-2912-4). CRC Pr.

Virgil: Selection from Aeneid Four Handbook. Ed. by J. V. Muir. LC 76-52324. (Cambridge Latin Texts Ser.). 1977. 6.95x (ISBN 0-521-21645-1). Cambridge U Pr.

Virgil: Selection from Aeneid Two Handbook. Ed. by C. Craddock. (Cambridge Latin Text Ser.). 80p. 1976. pap. 6.95x (ISBN 0-521-20858-0). Cambridge U Pr.

Virgil: Selections from Aeneid, Vol. 4. Ed. by J. Muir. (Latin Texts Ser.). 1977. limp bdg 3.25x (ISBN 0-521-21581-1). Cambridge U Pr.

Virgil: Selections from Aeneid II. Ed. by C. Craddock. (Latin Texts Ser). 1975. pap. 2.95x (ISBN 0-521-20827-0). Cambridge U Pr.

Virgil Selections from Aeneid VIII. Ed. by C. H. Craddock. (Latin Texts Ser.). 48p. 1973. pap. 2.95x (ISBN 0-521-20280-9). Cambridge U Pr.

Virgil's Aeneid: A Critical Description. Kenneth Quinn. LC 68-12248. 1968. 9.75x o.p. (ISBN 0-472-08739-8). U of Mich Pr.

Virgil's Georgics: A New Interpretation. Gary B. Miles. 1980. 17.50x (ISBN 0-520-03789-8). U of Cal Pr.

Virgil's Georgics: Selections. Ed. by D. A. John. (Illus., Orig.). 1973. pap. 4.50 (ISBN 0-571-09731-6, Pub. by Faber & Faber). Merrimack Bk Serv.

Virgin Archetype. John Layard. (Dunquin Ser.). (Orig.). 1973. pap. 6.50 o.p. (ISBN 0-88214-205-4). Spring Pubns.

Virgin Birth of Christ. Robert Gromacki. 200p. 1981. pap. 5.95 (ISBN 0-8010-3765-4). Baker Bk.

Virgin Birth of Christ. J. Gresham Machen. (Twin Brooks Ser). 1967. pap. 7.95 (ISBN 0-8010-5885-6). Baker Bk.

Virgin Birth of Christ. J. Gresham Machen. 1958. Repr. of 1930 ed. 12.95 (ISBN 0-227-67630-0). Attic Pr.

Virgin Diplomats. Elmer Bendiner. 1976. 10.00 o.p. (ISBN 0-394-48977-2). Knopf.

Virgin Fish of Babughat. Lokenath Bhattacharya. Tr. by Meenakshi Mukherjee from Bengali. (Indian Novels Ser.). 160p. 1975. 8.00 (ISBN 0-89253-016-2). Ind-US Inc.

Virgin in Paris. Barbara Cartland. (Barbara Cartland Ser.: No. 14). 208p. 1981. pap. 1.75 (ISBN 0-515-05571-9). Jove Pubns.

Virgin Islands National Park. Ruth Radlauer. LC 80-22457. (Parks for People Ser.). (Illus.). 48p. (gr. 3 up). 1981. PLB 9.25 (ISBN 0-516-07741-4). Childrens.

Virgin Islands National Park: The Story Behind the Scenery. Alan H. Robinson. Ed. by Gweneth R. DenDooven. LC 74-81560. (Illus.). 1974. 7.95 (ISBN 0-916122-39-5); pap. 3.50 (ISBN 0-916122-14-X). K C Pubns.

Virgin Islands: Pleasure Spots in the Caribbean. Bruce G. Lynn. LC 74-113992. 1975. 6.50 (ISBN 0-910294-34-8). Brown Bk.

Virgin Lands: Two Years in Kazakhstan Nineteen Fifty-Four to Nineteen Fifty-Five. Leonid I. Brezhnev. LC 79-42773. (Illus.). viii, 100p. 1979. 16.50 (ISBN 0-08-023584-0); pap. 6.75 (ISBN 0-08-023583-2). Pergamon.

Virgin of Chartres. Joseph F. Byrnes. LC 78-75174. 128p. 1981. 17.50 (ISBN 0-8386-2369-7). Fairleigh Dickinson.

Virgin Planet. Poul Anderson. 1973. pap. 1.50 o.s.i. (ISBN 0-446-88334-4). Warner Bks.

Virgin Queen. Maureen Peters. 1979. pap. 1.95 o.p. (ISBN 0-523-40510-3). Pinnacle Bks.

Virgin Seducer. John Clarke. Bd. with Batchelor-Keeper; Voyage to Cacklagallinia. Samuel Brunt; Account of the State of Learning in the Empire of Lilliput. (Foundations of the Novel Ser.: Vol. 49). lib. bdg. 50.00 (ISBN 0-8240-0561-9). Garland Pub.

Virgin Whiteness: The Poetry of Kamala Das. Devindra Kohli. (Greybird Ser.). 1975. 8.00 (ISBN 0-88253-668-0); pap. text ed. 4.00 (ISBN 0-88253-667-2). Ind-US Inc.

Virgin with Child. Tom McDonough. 1981. 11.95 (ISBN 0-670-74721-1). Viking Pr.

Virginal Conception & Bodily Resurrection of Jesus. Raymond Brown. LC 72-97399. 1973. pap. 2.95 (ISBN 0-8091-1768-1). Paulist Pr.

Virginia. 28.00 (ISBN 0-89770-122-4). Curriculum Info Ctr.

Virginia. James Wamsley. (Illus.). 128p. 1981. 27.50 (ISBN 0-912856-66-1). Graphic Arts Ctr.

Virginia: A History. Louis D. Rubin, Jr. (States & the Nation Ser.). (Illus.). 1977. 12.95 (ISBN 0-393-05630-9, Co-Pub. by AASLH). Norton.

Virginia & Truckee. Lucius Beebe & Charles Clegg. LC 63-14279. (Illus.). 64p. 1980. pap. 2.95 (ISBN 0-8310-6007-7). Howell-North.

Virginia & Truckee. Lucius Beefr. (Illus.). 68p. 1980. 2.95 o.p. (ISBN 0-89685-102-8). Chatham Pub CA.

Virginia & Truckee Locomotives. Karl R. Koenig. LC 80-67819. (Illus.). 88p. 1980. pap. 14.00 (ISBN 0-89685-102-8). Chatham Pub CA.

Virginia: Bourbonism to Byrd, 1870-1925. Allen W. Moger. LC 68-8538. (Illus.). 400p. 1968. 10.95 (ISBN 0-8139-0182-0). U Pr of Va.

Virginia Colony. Elswyth Thane. LC 69-16488. (Forge of Freedom Ser). (Illus.). (gr. 5-8). 1969. 8.95 (ISBN 0-02-789180-1, CCPr). Macmillan.

Virginia Constitutional Convention of 1901-1902. Ralph C. McDanel. LC 75-146556. (American Constitutional & Legal History Ser.). 1972. Repr. of 1928 ed. lib. bdg. 19.50 (ISBN 0-306-70204-5). Da Capo.

Virginia Convention of 1776. Hugh B. Grigsby. LC 75-75320. (American History, Politics & Law Ser). 1969. Repr. of 1855 ed. lib. bdg. 25.00 (ISBN 0-306-71281-4). Da Capo.

Virginia Convention of 1829-1830. Hugh B. Grigsby. LC 79-75321. (American History, Politics & Law Ser). 1969. Repr. of 1854 ed. lib. bdg. 19.50 (ISBN 0-306-71282-2). Da Capo.

Virginia Experiment. rev. ed. Alf J. Mapp, Jr. 1974. 22.50 (ISBN 0-87548-309-7); pap. 8.95 (ISBN 0-87548-308-9). Open Court.

Virginia Forms. W. Clyde Gouldman & Amy M. Hess. 1978. 60.00 (ISBN 0-87215-205-7). Michie.

Virginia Heritage Address Book. Eleanor L. Templeman. 1975. pap. 2.95x o.p. (ISBN 0-685-83284-8). Templeman.

Virginia in Our Century. Jean Gottmann. LC 68-8541. 1969. 9.95 (ISBN 0-8139-0109-X). U Pr of Va.

Virginia Life & Health. 1979. 15.00 (ISBN 0-930868-26-9). Merritt Co.

Virginia Papers of the Presidency, Vol. V: The White Burkett Miller Center Forums, 1981, Pt. 1. Ed. by Kenneth W. Thompson. 91p. 1981. lib. bdg. 11.75 (ISBN 0-8191-1502-9); pap. text ed. 5.50 (ISBN 0-8191-1503-7). U Pr of Amer.

Virginia Papers on the Presidency, Vol. 3: The White Burkett Miller Center Forums, Pt. 1. Ed. by Kenneth W. Thompson. LC 79-66241. 133p. 1980. lib. bdg. 13.25 o.p. (ISBN 0-8191-1120-1); pap. text ed. 6.25 o.p. (ISBN 0-8191-1121-X). U Pr of Amer.

Virginia Rules Annotated. Michie Staff. 470p. 1979. pap. 25.00 o.p. (ISBN 0-87215-317-7). Michie.

Virginia State Industrial Directory, Nineteen Eighty-One. State Industrial Directories Corp. Date not set. pap. price not set (ISBN 0-89910-044-9). State Indus D.

Virginia Tech Symposium on Applied Behavioral Science, Vol. I. Ed. by Joseph A. Sgro. LC 80-8614. 1981. 28.95 (ISBN 0-669-04332-X). Lexington Bks.

Virginia: The New Dominion, a History from 1607 to the Present. Virginius Dabney. LC 78-157580. (Illus.). 629p. 14.95 (ISBN 0-385-07150-7). U Pr of Va.

Virginia Title Examiners' Manual. rev. ed. Sydney F. Parham. 517p. 1973. 35.00 (ISBN 0-87215-151-4); 1977 suppl 15.00 (ISBN 0-87215-290-1). Michie.

Virginia Woolf. 2nd ed. Joan Bennett. 1945. 19.95 (ISBN 0-521-04160-0); pap. 7.95x (ISBN 0-521-09951-X). Cambridge U Pr.

Virginia Woolf. Bernard Blackstone. Ed. by Bonamy Dobree et al. Bd. with E. M. Forster. Rex Warner; Katherine Mansfield. Ian A. Gordon. LC 63-63095. (British Writers & Their Work Ser: Vol. 3). 1964. pap. 2.35x (ISBN 0-8032-5652-3, BB 452, Bison). U of Nebr Pr.

Virginia Woolf. Dorothy Brewster. LC 62-19050. (Gotham Library). 184p. (Orig.). 1962. 8.95x (ISBN 0-8147-0056-X); pap. 5.00 (ISBN 0-8147-0057-8). NYU Pr.

Virginia Woolf. Susan R. Gorsky. (English Authors Ser.: No. 243). 1978. 12.50 (ISBN 0-8057-6712-6). Twayne.

Virginia Woolf. Manly Johnson. LC 72-79944. (Modern Literature Ser.). 1973. 10.95 (ISBN 0-8044-2424-1). Ungar.

Virginia Woolf. Michael Rosenthal. LC 79-12161. 1979. 20.00x (ISBN 0-231-04848-3). Columbia U Pr.

Virginia Woolf. Carl Woodring. LC 66-19554. (Columbia Essays on Modern Writers Ser.: No. 18). (Orig.). 1966. pap. 2.00 (ISBN 0-231-02829-6, MW18). Columbia U Pr.

Virginia Woolf: A Study of Her Novels. T. E. Apter. LC 78-78175. (Gotham Library). 1979. Cusa. 17.50x (ISBN 0-8147-0568-5); Cusa. pap. 9.00x (ISBN 0-8147-0569-3). NYU Pr.

Virginia Woolf: The Critical Heritage. Ed. by Robin Majumader & Allen McLaurin. (Critical Heritage Ser.). 1975. 38.00x (ISBN 0-7100-8138-3). Routledge & Kegan.

Virginia Woolf: The Echoes Enslaved. A. McLaurin. LC 72-83589. 300p. 1973. 32.95 (ISBN 0-521-08704-X). Cambridge U Pr.

Virginia Woolf's "First Voyage" A Novel in the Making. Louise De Salvo. 202p. 1980. 19.50x (ISBN 0-8476-6199-7). Rowman.

Virginia Woolf's Mrs. Dalloway: A Study in Alienation. Jeremy Hawthorn. (Text & Context Ser.). 1975. text ed. 6.50x (ISBN 0-85621-046-3); pap. text ed. 2.75x (ISBN 0-85621-047-1). Humanities.

Virginia Woolf's Quarrel with Grieving. Mark Spilka. LC 80-11792. xii, 142p. 1980. 13.50x (ISBN 0-8032-4120-8). U of Nebr Pr.

Virginia Woolf's Vision of Life & Her Search for Significant Form: A Study in the Shaping Vision. Vijay Kapur. 195p. 1980. text ed. 15.50x (ISBN 0-391-01753-5). Humanities.

Virginian. Owen Wister. (Illus.). 1925. 12.95 (ISBN 0-02-630580-1); large print ed. 9.95 (ISBN 0-02-489480-X). Macmillan.

Virginian Germans. Klaus Wust. LC 69-17334. Repr. of 1975 ed. 10.95x (ISBN 0-8139-0256-8). U Pr of Va.

Virginius Affair. Richard H. Bradford. LC 20-520000. 1980. 12.50x (ISBN 0-87081-080-4). Colo Assoc.

Virgins, Vamps & Flappers: The American Silent Movie Heroine. Sumiko Higashi. LC 78-74106. 1979. 17.95 (ISBN 0-88831-028-5). EPWP.

Virgo. James A. Lely. (Sun Signs Ser.). (Illus.). (gr. 4-12). 1978. PLB 5.95 (ISBN 0-87191-646-0); pap. 2.95 (ISBN 0-89812-076-4). Creative Ed.

Virgo. Julia Parker. (Pocket Guides to Astrology Ser.). (Orig.). 1980. pap. write for info. (ISBN 0-671-25549-5, Fireside). S&S.

Virial Coefficients of Gases: A Critical Compilation. J. H. Dymond & E. B. Smith. (Oxford Science Research Papers Ser). 1969. pap. 18.95x o.p. (ISBN 0-19-855345-5). Oxford U Pr.

Viridian's Trail. J. T. Edson. (J. T. Edson Ser.). 1978. pap. 1.50 o.p. (ISBN 0-425-03847-5, Medallion). Berkley Pub.

Virological Procedures. J. M. Hoskins. 1967. 19.95 (ISBN 0-407-79000-4). Butterworths.

Virology. Renato Dulbecco & Harold Ginsberg. (Illus.). 408p. 1980. 20.00 (ISBN 0-06-140725-9, Harper Medical). Har-Row.

Virology in Agriculture. Ed. by T. O. Diener & J. A. Romberger. (Landmark Studies Ser). 1977. 23.50x o.p. (ISBN 0-87663-805-1). Universe.

Virology in Agriculture. John A. Romberger. LC 76-42139. (Beltsville Symposia in Agricultural Reasearch Ser.: No. 1). 320p. 1977. text ed. 23.50 (ISBN 0-916672-14-X). Allanheld.

Virtues. P. T. Geach. LC 76-19627. 1977. 20.50 (ISBN 0-521-21350-9). Cambridge U Pr.

Virtues & Vices. Grania Beckford. 304p. 1981. 13.95 (ISBN 0-312-84954-0); pap. 5.95 (ISBN 0-312-84955-9). St Martin.

Virtues & Vices & Other Essays in Moral Philosophy. Philippa Foot. 1981. pap. 5.95 (ISBN 0-520-04396-0, CAL 494). U of Cal Pr.

Virtues & Vices & Other Essays in Moral Philosophy. Philippa R. Foot. 1979. 20.00x (ISBN 0-520-03686-7). U of Cal Pr.

Virtues: Die Tugenden. Herbert Witzenmann. Tr. by Daisy Aldan. 1975. 3.95 (ISBN 0-913152-17-X). PLB 5.95 (ISBN 0-685-52245-8). Folder Edns.

Virtues of Hell. Pierre Boulle. Tr. by Patricia Wolf from Fr. LC 74-81811. 224p. 1974. 8.95 (ISBN 0-8149-0744-X). Vanguard.

Virtuoso. Thomas Shadwell. Ed. by Marjorie H. Nicolson & David S. Rodes. LC 65-19466. (Regents Restoration Drama Ser). 1966. 9.75x (ISBN 0-8032-0368-3); pap. 2.65x (ISBN 0-8032-5368-0, BB 254, Bison). U of Nebr Pr.

Virtuous Orphan; or, the Life of Marianne, Countess of ---, 4 vols. Mary Collyer. Ed. by Ronald Paulson. LC 78-60843. (Novel 1720-1805 Ser.). 1979. lib. bdg. 31.00 ea. Garland Pub.

Virtuous Villager; or, Virgin's Victory, 1742, 2 vols. in 1. Charles Mouhy. Ed. by Michael F. Shugrue. Tr. by Eliza Haywood from Fr. (Flowering of the Novel, 1740-1775 Ser: Vol. 7). 1974. lib. bdg. 50.00 (ISBN 0-8240-1106-6). Garland Pub.

Virus. OAS General Secretariat. (Serie De Biologia: No. 8). 72p. (Orig.). 1980. pap. text ed. 2.00 (ISBN 0-8270-1169-5). OAS.

Virus Chemotherapy. Ed. by F. E. Hahn. (Antibiotics & Chemotherapy Ser.: Vol. 27). (Illus.). vi, 310p. 1980. 114.00 (ISBN 3-8055-0263-X). S Karger.

Virus-Induced Enzymes. Seymour S. Cohen. LC 68-55418. (Biology Ser.: No. 24). (Illus.). 1968. 22.50x (ISBN 0-231-03053-3). Columbia U Pr.

Virus-Induced Immunopathology. Ed. by Morris Pollard. (Perspectives in Virology: Vol. 6). 1969. 37.50 (ISBN 0-12-560556-0). Acad Pr.

Virus-Insect Relationships. Kenneth M. Smith. (Illus.). 1977. text ed. 30.00x (ISBN 0-582-46612-1). Longman.

Virus That Ate Cannibals: And Other True Stories. Carol Eron. 256p. 1981. 12.95 (ISBN 0-02-536250-X). Macmillan.

Viruses. Alan E. Nourse. LC 75-19142. (First Bks.). (Illus.). 72p. (gr. 5 up). 1976. PLB 6.45 (ISBN 0-531-00839-8). Watts.

Viruses. Kenneth M. Smith. 1962. pap. 8.50 (ISBN 0-521-06496-1). Cambridge U Pr.

Viruses in Naturally Occurring Cancers. Ed. by Myron Essex et al. LC 80-67166. (Cold Spring Harbor Conferences on Cell Proliferation Ser.: Vol. 7). (Illus.). 1284p. 1980. 2 book set 125.00 (ISBN 0-87969-131-X). Cold Spring Harbor.

Viruses in Plant Hosts: Form, Distribution, & Pathologic Effects. Katherine Esau. LC 68-9831. (Illus.). 1968. 25.00x (ISBN 0-299-05110-2). U of Wis Pr.

Vis & Ramin. Ed. & tr. by George Morrison. LC 70-169960. (Persian Heritage Ser). 492p. 1972. 22.50x (ISBN 0-231-03408-3). Columbia U Pr.

Visa Qualifying Examination Review, Vol. 1: Basic Sciences. Majid Ali et al. LC 78-61617. 1978. pap. 11.75 (ISBN 0-87488-124-2). Med Exam.

Visa Qualifying Examination Review, Vol. 2: Clinical Sciences. Michael A. Baker. LC 78-61618. 1978. pap. 11.75 (ISBN 0-87488-125-0). Med Exam.

Visaladeuarasa: A Restoration of the Text. J. D. Smith. LC 75-30441. (Cambridge Oriental Publications Ser.: No. 26). 260p. 1977. 64.00 (ISBN 0-521-20815-7). Cambridge U Pr.

Viscera of the Domestic Mammals. R. Nickel et al. LC 72-95370. (Illus.). 1973. 54.60 o.p. (ISBN 0-387-91107-3). Springer-Verlag.

Visceral Muscle: Its Structure & Function. Henry Huddart & Stephen Hunt. LC 75-42464. (Tertiary Level Biology Ser.). 1975. 18.95 (ISBN 0-470-15221-4). Halsted Pr.

Viscoelastic Properties of Polymers. 3rd ed. John D. Ferry. LC 79-2866. 1980. 48.00 (ISBN 0-471-04894-1, Pub. by Wiley Interscience). Wiley.

Visconti Hours. Intro. by Millard Meiss. LC 75-75371. (Illus.). 264p. 1972. slipcase 70.00 (ISBN 0-8076-0651-0). Braziller.

Viscosity of Protoplasm. L. V. Heilbrunn. (Protoplasmatologia: Vol. 2, Pt. C1). (Illus.). 1958. pap. 32.50 o.p. (ISBN 0-387-80485-4). Springer-Verlag.

Viscount Dundee. Louis A. Barbe. 159p. 1980. Repr. lib. bdg. 20.00 (ISBN 0-89987-053-8). Darby Bks.

Viscount Maua & the Empire of Brazil: A Biography of Irineu Evangelista De Sousa. Anyda Marchant. 1965. 22.75x (ISBN 0-520-00807-3). U of Cal Pr.

Vishishadvaita: Philosophy & Religion. Ramanuja Research Society. 273p. 1975. 10.75 (ISBN 0-88253-683-4). Ind-US Inc.

Vishnu Purana, 2 vols. Tr. by H. H. Wilson from Sanskrit. 965p. 1980. 36.00 (ISBN 0-89744-995-9, Pub. by Orient Reprint India). Auromere.

Visible & Invisible Group: Two Perspectives on Group Psychotherapy & Group Process. Yvonne Agazarian & Richard Peters. (Illus.). 304p. 1981. 27.50 (ISBN 0-7100-0692-6). Routledge & Kegan.

Visible Hand: The Managerial Revolution in American Business. Alfred D. Chandler, Jr. 1980. pap. 8.95 (ISBN 0-674-94052-0). Harvard U Pr.

Visible Heritage, Columbia County, New York: A History in Art & Architecture. Ruth Piwonka & Roderic H. Blackburn. LC 77-9093. 160p. 1977. 14.95 (ISBN 0-89062-053-9, Pub. by Columbia County); pap. 10.95 (ISBN 0-89062-028-8). Pub Ctr Cult Res.

Visible Words: A Study of Inscriptions in Books As Works of Art. John Sparrow. LC 68-10027. (Illus.). 1969. 75.00 (ISBN 0-521-06534-8). Cambridge U Pr.

Vision. David Wilkerson. (Orig.). 1974. pap. 1.75 o.s.i. (ISBN 0-515-05294-9). Jove Pubns.

Vision. Tr. by David Wilkerson. (Spanish Bks.). (Span.). 1979. 1.65 (ISBN 0-8297-0608-9). Vida Pub.

Vision. Tr. by David Wilkerson. (French Bks.). (Fr.). 1979. 1.95 (ISBN 0-686-28823-8). Vida Pub.

Vision & Acquisition. Ian Overington. LC 75-45872. 1976. 44.50x (ISBN 0-8448-0917-9). Crane-Russak Co.

Vision & Aftermath. 1980. pap. 6.95 (ISBN 0-7145-0599-4). Riverrun NY.

Vision & Design. Roger Fry. (Illus.). pap. 3.95 o.p. (ISBN 0-452-00033-5, FM33, Mer). NAL.

Vision & Invention: A Course in Art Foundamentals. Calvin Harlan. 1969. ref. ed. 18.95 (ISBN 0-13-942243-9). P-H.

Vision & Resonance: Two Senses of Poetic Form. John Hollander. 325p. 1975. 16.95 (ISBN 0-19-501898-2). Oxford U Pr.

Vision & the Need. Richard Faber. (Illus.). 1966. 5.95 (ISBN 0-571-06595-3, Pub. by Faber & Faber). Merrimack Bk Serv.

Vision & the Voice. Aleister Crowley. 7.50 (ISBN 0-685-47278-7). Weiser.

Vision & Victory: A Collection of Addresses 1942-1948. Abba H. Silver. (Return to Zion Ser.). (Illus.). 232p. 1980. Repr. of 1949 ed. lib. bdg. 17.50x (ISBN 0-87991-124-7). Porcupine Pr.

Vision & Visual Perception. Ed. by Clarence H. Graham et al. LC 65-12711. 1965. 54.95 (ISBN 0-471-32170-2). Wiley.

Vision for America. Gerald R. Ford. (YA) 1981. limited signed ed. 50.00 (ISBN 0-935716-08-4). Lord John.

Vision of a Contemporary University: A Case Study of Expansion & Development in American Higher Education, 1950-75. Russell M. Cooper & Margaret B. Fisher. LC 80-29022. (Illus.). iv, 380p. 1981. 12.95 (ISBN 0-8130-0702-X). U Presses Fla.

Vision of an Artist & Writer. James J. Davidson. 1981. 6.95 (ISBN 0-533-04806-0). Vantage.

Vision of God & Man. Inayat Khan. (Sufi Message of Hazrat Inayat Khan Ser.: Vol. 12). 1979. 6.95 (ISBN 90-6325-100-9, Pub. by Servire BV Netherlands). Hunter Hse.

Vision of God: The Christian Doctrine of the Summum Bonum. abr. ed. Kenneth E. Kirk. Ed. by G. R. Dunstan. 1978. Repr. of 1934 ed. 13.95 (ISBN 0-227-67830-3). Attic Pr.

Vision of History in Early Britain: From Gildas to Geoffrey of Monmouth. Robert W. Hanning. LC 66-17856. 1966. 20.00x (ISBN 0-231-02826-1). Columbia U Pr.

Vision of Landscape in Renaissance Italy. Richard A. Turner. LC 66-11977. (Illus.). 336p. 1974. 26.50x (ISBN 0-691-03849-X, 319); pap. 7.95 (ISBN 0-691-00307-6, 319). Princeton U Pr.

Vision of Matthew: Christ, Church & Morality in the First Gospel. John P. Meier. LC 78-70820. 1979. pap. 5.95 (ISBN 0-8091-2171-9). Paulist Pr.

Vision of Melville & Conrad. Leon F. Seltzer. LC 78-108735. 1970. 10.00x (ISBN 0-8214-0065-7). Ohio U Pr.

Vision of Piers Plowman. Langland. 1979. 14.00x (ISBN 0-460-10571-X, Everyman); pap. 8.95 (ISBN 0-460-11571-5, Everyman). Dutton.

Vision of Stephen. Lolah Burford. LC 77-185142. 192p. 1972. 5.95 o.s.i. (ISBN 0-02-518120-3). Macmillan.

Vision of the Disinherited: The Making of American Pentecostalism. Robert M. Anderson. 1979. 16.95 (ISBN 0-19-502502-4). Oxford U Pr.

Vision of the Eagle: A Novel. Kay L. McDonald. LC 77-2579. 1977. 9.95 o.s.i. (ISBN 0-690-01491-0, TYC-T). T Y Crowell.

Vision of the Trinity. George H. Tavard. LC 80-5845. 166p. (Orig.). 1981. lib. bdg. 17.75 (ISBN 0-8191-1412-X); pap. text ed. 8.75 (ISBN 0-8191-1413-8). U Pr of Amer.

Vision of the Void: Theological Reflections on the Works of Elie Wiesel. Michael Berenbaum. LC 78-27321. 1979. 15.00 (ISBN 0-8195-5030-2, Pub. by Wesleyan U Pr). Columbia U Pr.

Vision Shared: The Words & Pictures of the Fsa Photographers, 1935-1943. Arthur Rothstein et al. LC 76-5381. (Illus.). 1976. 39.95 o.p. (ISBN 0-312-85015-8); prepub. 35.00 o.p. (ISBN 0-685-67163-1). St Martin.

Vision Training for Better Learning. Donald J. Getz & Lora McGraw. 1981. spiral bound 12.95 (ISBN 0-87804-430-2). Mafex.

Visionary Architects: Boullee, Ledoux, Lequeu. Intro. by J. C. Lemagny & Dominique De Menil. (Illus.). 1968. pap. 8.00 (ISBN 0-914412-21-3). Inst for the Arts.

Visionary Love: A Spirit Book of Gay Mythology & Transmutational Faerie. Mitch Walker. LC 80-51514. (Illus.). 120p. (Orig.). 1980. pap. 4.95 (ISBN 0-9604450-0-5). Treeroots.

Visiones de Hoy. Robert B. Brown & Barry J. Luby. 228p. 1971. pap. text ed. 8.95 (ISBN 0-15-594930-6, HC); tapes 60.00 (ISBN 0-15-594931-4). HarBraceJ.

Visiones De Latinoamerica: A Cultural Reader. 2nd ed. Robert Phillips & Olga Marquez. (Illus.). 224p. 1980. pap. text ed. 10.50 scp (ISBN 0-06-045223-4, HarpC). Har-Row.

Visionetics: The Holistic Way to Better Eyesight. Lisette Scholl. LC 77-12882. 1978. pap. 4.95 (ISBN 0-385-13279-4, Dolp). Doubleday.

Visioning. Strange De Jim. LC 79-66208. (Illus., Orig.). 1979. pap. 5.95 (ISBN 0-9605308-0-0). Ash-Kar Pr.

Visions. Martin A. Grove. 496p. (Orig.). 1980. pap. 2.75 (ISBN 0-89083-695-7). Zebra.

Visions & Chimeras. Prosser H. Frye. LC 66-23517. 1929. 9.00x (ISBN 0-8196-0179-9). Biblo.

Visions & Venturers. Theodore Sturgeon. 1978. pap. 1.75 o.s.i. (ISBN 0-440-12648-7). Dell.

Visions from Piers Plowman. William Langland. Tr. by Nevill Coghill. 1953. 3.50x o.p. (ISBN 0-19-519578-7). Oxford U Pr.

Visions of America: By the Poets of Our Time. Ed. by David Kherdian. LC 72-81067. (Illus.). 96p. (gr. 7 up). 1973. 8.95 (ISBN 0-02-750250-3). Macmillan.

Visions of China: Photographs by Marc Riboud, 1957-1980. Marc Riboud. (Illus.). 1981. 30.00 (ISBN 0-394-51535-8); pap. 14.95 (ISBN 0-394-74840-9). Pantheon.

Visions of Handy Hopper, 7 vols. William Hull. 1975. Set. 100.00 (ISBN 0-88253-813-6); Set. pap. 50.00 (ISBN 0-88253-812-8). Ind-US Inc.

Visions of Isabelle. William Bayer. 1976. 7.95 o.s.i. (ISBN 0-440-09315-5). Delacorte.

Visions of Jesus. Compiled by Chester Huyssen & Lucille Huyssen. 1977. pap. 2.95 (ISBN 0-88270-223-8). Logos.

Visions of Sugar Plums. Betsy Fox. 1980. 6.95 (ISBN 0-935746-00-5). Green Hill.

Visions of the End. Bernard McGinn. LC 79-4303. (Records of Civilization XCVI). 1979. 27.50x (ISBN 0-231-04594-8). Columbia U Pr.

Visions of the Future: Magic Boards. Saul Stadtmauer. LC 77-10735. (Myth, Magic & Superstition Ser.). (Illus.). (gr. 4-5). 1977. PLB 9.65 (ISBN 0-8172-1040-7). Raintree Pubs.

Visions of the Future: Magic Numbers & Cards. Stephanie A. Reiff. LC 77-22801. (Myth, Magic & Superstition Ser.). (Illus.). (gr. 4-5). 1977. PLB 9.65 (ISBN 0-8172-1027-X). Raintree Pubs.

Visions of the Future: Palm Reading. Elizabeth Hoffman. LC 77-22207. (Myth, Magic & Superstition Ser.). (Illus.). (gr. 4-5). 1977. PLB 9.65 (ISBN 0-8172-1029-6). Raintree Pubs.

Visions of Yesterday. Jeffrey Richards. (Illus.). 1974. 23.50 (ISBN 0-7100-7576-6). Routledge & Kegan.

Visions Seminars. Carl G. Jung. 1976. pap. 25.00 set (ISBN 0-88214-111-2). Spring Pubns.

Visit. Ian Hamilton. 45p. 1970. 5.95 (ISBN 0-571-09369-8, Pub. by Faber & Faber). Merrimack Bk Serv.

Visit from a Turtle. Gene Deitch. LC 74-469. (ps-3). 1974. 2.95 o.p. (ISBN 0-531-02727-9); PLB 4.90 o.p. (ISBN 0-531-02726-0). Watts.

Visit from St. Alphabet. Dave Morice. (Illus.). 20p. (Orig.). (gr. 3 up). 1980. pap. 5.00 (ISBN 0-915124-47-5). Toothpaste.

Visit from St. Nicholas. Clement C. Moore. (Illus.). 1980. pap. 1.95 (ISBN 0-671-95528-4). Wanderer Bks.

Visit to the Eagles' Nest. Tina Jordan. (Illus.). 20p. (gr. 3-5). 1980. PLB 1.85 (ISBN 0-938574-00-0). Cherubim.

Visit to the Factory. Althea. (Illus.). 24p. 1980. pap. 1.45 ea.; pap. in 5 pk. avail. (ISBN 0-85122-192-0, Pub. by Dinosaur Pubns). Merrimack Bk Serv.

Visit to the Mountains. Barbara B. Simons. LC 78-13562. (Adventures in Nature Ser). (Illus.). (gr. 2-6). 1980. PLB 6.95 (ISBN 0-916392-31-7); pap. 3.95 (ISBN 0-916392-30-9). Oak Tree Pubns.

Visit to the Prairies. Barbara B. Simons. LC 78-13738. (Adventures in Nature Ser). (Illus.). (gr. 2-6). 1978. PLB 6.95 (ISBN 0-916392-33-3); pap. 3.95 (ISBN 0-916392-32-5). Oak Tree Pubns.

Visitants: A Novel. Randolph Stow. LC 80-53710. 192p. 1981. 9.95 (ISBN 0-8008-8018-8). Taplinger.

Visites Chez les Francais. Muriel Reed. Ed. by Jeffrey J. Carre & Marie-Rose Carre. (Illus., Orig., Fr.). 1966. pap. text ed. 8.50 (ISBN 0-13-942250-1). P-H.

Visiting Museums. Anne White. 1968. 6.50 (ISBN 0-571-08741-8, Pub. by Faber & Faber). Merrimack Bk Serv.

Visitor. Chauncey G. Parker, 3rd. 1981. pap. 2.50 (ISBN 0-451-09562-6, E9562, Sig). NAL.

Visitor: Jack Kerouac in Old Saybrook. John C. Holmes. 1980. limited edition, numbered & signed by the author 8.00 (ISBN 0-934660-04-2). TUVOTI.

Visitor's Guide to L.A. Marjorie Stokell. Ed. by Susan Harper. LC 80-67475. (Illus.). 224p. (Orig.). 1981. pap. 6.95 (ISBN 0-89395-061-0). Cal Living Bks.

Visitor's London. 1978. pap. 1.95 o.p. (ISBN 0-905522-06-0, 8076, Dist. by Arco). Barrie & Jenkins.

Visits to Monasteries in the Levant. Robert C. Zouche. LC 80-2200. 1981. Repr. of 1916 ed. 45.00 (ISBN 0-404-18989-X). AMS Pr.

Visits to the Juvenile Library, Repr. Of 1805 Ed. Eliza Fenwick. Bd. with Adventures of Ulysses. Charles Lamb. Repr. of 1808 ed. LC 75-32152. (Classics of Children's Literature, 1621-1932: Vol. 18). 1976. PLB 38.00 (ISBN 0-8240-2266-1). Garland Pub.

Visnuism & Sivaism: A Comparison. J. Gonda. 1970. text ed. 13.50x (ISBN 0-485-17409-X, Athlone Pr). Humanities.

Vista Hispanica. Ruth R. Ginsburg et al. (gr. 9-12). 1978. text ed. 15.40 (ISBN 0-205-05875-2, 4258754); tchr's ed. 4.40 (ISBN 0-205-05870-1, 4258770). Allyn.

Vistas in Astronomy, Vol. 23 Complete. P. Beer & A. Beer. 1980. 112.50 (ISBN 0-08-026046-2). Pergamon.

Vistula Voyage. Marion M. Coleman. LC 73-82795. (Pocket Folklore Ser.: No. 3). (Illus.). 95p. (Orig.). 1974. pap. 3.00 o.p. (ISBN 0-910366-16-0). Alliance Coll.

Visual Aesthetics. J. De Lucio-Meyer. LC 74-120. (Icon Editions). (Illus.). 240p. 1974. pap. 7.95x o.s.i. (ISBN 0-06-430052-8, IN-52, HarpT). Har-Row.

Visual Aids for Paramedical Vocabulary. J. E. Schmidt. (Illus.). 196p. 1973. 10.75 (ISBN 0-398-02609-2). C C Thomas.

Visual Anatomy, Vol. 1: Head & Neck. Sydney M. Friedman. (Illus.). 1970. 20.50x o.p. (ISBN 0-06-140836-0, Harper Medical). Har-Row.

Visual Anatomy, Vol. 3: Back & Limbs. Sydney M. Friedman. (Illus.). 1972. 21.50x o.p. (ISBN 0-06-140835-2, Harper Medical). Har-Row.

Visual & Auditory Perception. Gerald M. Murch. LC 74-172349. (Illus.). 1973. pap. 14.95 (ISBN 0-672-60779-4). Bobbs.

Visual & Transfer Skill Mastery, 2 levels. Kitty Wehrli. (Michigan Arithmetic Program Ser.). 1976. wkbk. 7.00x ea.; Levels 1 & 2. (ISBN 0-89039-948-4). Ann Arbor Pubs.

Visual Approach to Park Design. Albert J. Rutledge. 1981. lib. bdg. 21.50 (ISBN 0-8240-7258-8). Garland Pub.

Visual Art, Mathematics & Computers: Selections from the Journal Leonardo. Ed. by Frank J. Malina. 1979. text ed. 64.00 (ISBN 0-08-021854-7); pap. text ed. 20.00 o.p. (ISBN 0-08-021853-9). Pergamon.

Visual Artist's Guide to the New Copyright Law. Tad Crawford. 1978. pap. 5.50 o.s.i. (ISBN 0-8038-7763-3). Hastings.

Visual Aural Discriminations: A Self-Instructional Workbook for Initial Two-Letter Blends, 5 bks. reusable ed. Elizabeth M. Henzl. (gr. 1-12). 1973. wkbk. 5.00 ea.; Bk. 1. (ISBN 0-89039-035-5); Bk. 2. (ISBN 0-89039-037-1); Bk. 3. (ISBN 0-89039-039-8); Bk. 4. (ISBN 0-89039-041-X); Bk. 5. (ISBN 0-89039-043-6). Ann Arbor Pubs.

Visual Awareness & Design: An Introductory Program in Perceptual Sensitivity, Conceptual Awareness, & Basic Design Skills. Philip Thiel. LC 80-51079. (Illus.). 272p. 1981. 35.00 (ISBN 0-295-95712-3); pap. 19.50 (ISBN 0-295-95786-7). U of Wash Pr.

Visual Blight in America. P. Lewis et al. LC 73-88850. (CCG Resource Papers Ser.: No. 23). (Illus.). 1973. pap. text ed. 4.00 (ISBN 0-89291-070-4). Assn Am Geographers.

Visual Coding & Adaptability. Ed. by Charles S. Harris. LC 79-26604. (Illus.). 400p. 1980. 24.95 (ISBN 0-89859-016-7). L Erlbaum Assocs.

Visual Communication for the Hard of Hearing: History, Research & Methods. 2nd ed. John J. O'Neill & Herbert J. Oyer. (Illus.). 224p. 1981. text ed. 14.95 (ISBN 0-13-942466-0). P-H.

Visual Data. Roger E. Kranich & Jerry L. Messec. 1979. pap. 2.50 (ISBN 0-88323-153-0, 243); free answer key 1.00 (ISBN 0-88323-157-3). Richards Pub.

Visual Defects. Diane L. Docs. (Illus.). 1978. 20.00 (ISBN 0-685-89697-8). Dayton Labs.

Visual Design in Dress. M. Davis. 1979. 16.95 (ISBN 0-13-942409-1). P-H.

Visual Dictionary of Art. Ed. by Ann Hill. LC 73-76181. (Illus.). 1980. pap. 14.95 (ISBN 0-8212-1094-7, 903825PB). NYGS.

Visual Disorders in Cerebral Palsy. Ed. by Vernon H. Smith. (Clinics in Developmental Medicine Ser. No. 9). 62p. 1963. 3.25 o.p. (ISBN 0-685-24715-5). Lippincott.

Visual Display Terminals: A Manual Covering Ergonomics, Workplace Design, Health & Safety, Task Organization. A. Cakir et al. LC 80-40070. 328p. 1980. 49.00 (ISBN 0-471-27793-2, Pub. by Wiley-Interscience). Wiley.

Visual Electrodiagnosis in Systematic Diseases. Ed. by E. Schmoger & J. H. Kelsey. (Documenta Opthalmologica Ser.: No. 23). 290p. 1980. lib. bdg. 68.50 (ISBN 90-6193-163-0, Pub by Dr. W. Junk). Kluwer Boston.

Visual Evoked Potentials in Central Disorders of the Visual System. Kenneth A. Kooi & Robert E. Marshall. (Illus.). 1979. text ed. 25.00 (ISBN 0-06-141477-8, Harper Medical). Har-Row.

Visual Experience. B. Lowry. 1975. pap. 13.95 (ISBN 0-13-942490-3). P-H.

Visual Illusions: Their Causes, Characteristics & Applications. M. Luckiesh. (Illus.). 8.50 (ISBN 0-8446-0780-0). Peter Smith.

Visual Imagery & Its Relations to Problem Solving. Geir Kaufmann. 1980. pap. 13.00x (ISBN 82-00-01788-5, Dist. by Columbia U Pr.). Universitet.

Visual Impairment in the Schools. Randall K. Harley & G. Allen Lawrence. (Illus.). 168p. 1977. 14.75 (ISBN 0-398-03587-3). C C Thomas.

Visual Language Cookbook. new ed. Gayle Joyce & Laurene Gallimore. (Illus.). 60p. (gr. 6-12). 1979. 14.95 (ISBN 0-917002-41-5). Joyce Media.

Visual Marketing: A Program for the Design Profession. Ed. by Eastman Kodak Company. (Illus.). 92p. (Orig.). 1978. pap. 6.25 (ISBN 0-87985-249-6, V1-36). Eastman Kodak.

Visual Materials for the Language Teacher. Andrew Wright. (Handbooks for Language Teachers Ser.). (Illus.). 192p. 1975. pap. text ed. 7.50x (ISBN 0-582-52267-6). Longman.

Visual Optics, 2 vols. 5th ed. Emsley. (Illus.). 1976. Vol. 1. 34.95 (ISBN 0-407-93415-4); Vol. 2. 34.95 (ISBN 0-407-93414-6). Butterworths.

Visual Optics & Refraction: A Clinical Approach. David D. Michaels. (Illus.). 518p. 1975. 29.50 o.p. (ISBN 0-8016-3424-5). Mosby.

Visual Optics & Refraction: A Clinical Approach. 2nd ed. David D. Michaels. LC 80-15472. (Illus.). 748p. 1980. text ed. 59.50 (ISBN 0-8016-3414-8). Mosby.

Visual Perception. Tom N. Cornsweet. 1970. text ed. 22.95 (ISBN 0-12-189750-8). Acad Pr.

Visual Perceptual Skillsbook. Jerome Rosner. (gr. k-3). 1981. 11.70 (ISBN 0-8027-9126-3). Walker & Co.

Visual Scripting. Ed. by John Halas. (Library of Animation Technology). Date not set. 30.00 o.p. (ISBN 0-8038-7757-9). Hastings.

Visual Search. Committee on Vision. (Illus.). 152p. 1973. pap. 8.20 (ISBN 0-309-02103-0). Natl Acad Pr.

Visual Thinking. Rudolf Arnheim. (Illus.). 1980. 13.95x (ISBN 0-686-64912-5, CAL229); pap. 6.95 (ISBN 0-520-01871-0). U of Cal Pr.

Visualization of Climate. Joe R. Eagleman. LC 75-36988. (Illus.). 1976. 19.95 (ISBN 0-669-00408-1). Lexington Bks.

Visualization: The Uses of Imagery in the Health Professions. Errol R. Korn & Karen Johnson. 1981. write for info. (ISBN 0-88416-300-8). PSG Pub.

Visualizing Business Finance. W. R. Purcell, Jr. Date not set. 25.00 (ISBN 0-8436-0760-2). CBI Pub. Postponed.

Visualizing Change: Model Building & the Change Process. Gordon L. Lippitt. LC 73-81361. (Illus.). 370p. 1973. pap. 14.50 (ISBN 0-88390-125-0). Univ Assocs.

Visually & Transfer Skill Mastery, 2 levels. W. Edward. Incl. Level 1. Addition & Multiplication (ISBN 0-89039-948-4); Level 2. Subtraction & Division (ISBN 0-89039-850-X). pap. 7.00 ea. Ann Arbor FL.

Visually Handicapped Child in School. Ed. by Berthold Lowenfeld. LC 72-12303. (John Day Bk.). 448p. 1973. 16.00 o.s.i. (ISBN 0-381-97097-3, TYC-T). T Y Crowell.

Visually Handicapped Children & Young People. Elizabeth K. Chapman. (Special Needs in Education Ser.). 1978. 16.00 (ISBN 0-7100-8878-7). Routledge & Kegan.

Vita Haroldi: The Romance of the Life of Harold, King of England. Ed. by William D. Birch. Tr. by William D. Birch. LC 80-2232. 1981. Repr. of 1885 ed. 32.50 (ISBN 0-404-18753-6). AMS Pr.

Vita Sexualis. Ogai Mori. Tr. by Kazuji Ninomiya & Sanford Goldstein. LC 72-79020. 1972. pap. 4.95 (ISBN 0-8048-1048-6). C E Tuttle.

Vitae. Cornelius Nepos. Ed. by E. O. Winstedt. (Oxford Classical Texts Ser). 1904. 14.95x (ISBN 0-19-814617-5). Oxford U Pr.

Vitae Sanctorum Hiberniae, 2 Vols. Charles Plummer. 1910. 48.00x set (ISBN 0-19-821390-5). Oxford U Pr.

Vital Few: American Economic Progress & Its Protagonists. Jonathan Hughes. LC 65-23202. 520p. 1973. pap. 6.95 (ISBN 0-19-519743-7, GB393, GB). Oxford U Pr.

Vital Karate. Masutatsu Oyama. LC 67-19867. (Illus.). pap. 5.95 (ISBN 0-87040-143-2). Japan Pubns.

Vital Maturity: Living Longer & Better. Morton Puner. 1979. 12.50x (ISBN 0-87663-232-0); pap. 6.95 (ISBN 0-87663-994-5). Universe.

Vital Problems of Religion. J. R. Cohu. 304p. Repr. of 1914 ed. text ed. 2.95 (ISBN 0-567-02077-0). Attic Pr.

Vital Records of Falmouth, Mass. to Eighteen Fifty. Oliver B. Brown. LC 76-3955. 1976. 8.00x (ISBN 0-930272-01-3). RI Mayflower.

Vital Records of Georgetown, Massachusetts to 1850. Repr. of 1928 ed. 7.50 o.p. (ISBN 0-88389-073-9). Essex Inst.

Vital Records of Gloucester, Massachusetts: Marriages, Vol. 2. Repr. of 1923 ed. 15.00 o.p. (ISBN 0-88389-074-7). Essex Inst.

Vital Records of Lawrence, Massachusetts to 1850. Repr. of 1926 ed. 7.50 o.p. (ISBN 0-88389-076-3). Essex Inst.

Vital Records of Marshfield, Massachusetts to the Year 1850. Robert M. Sherman & Ruth W. Sherman. LC 73-85851. 491p. 1969. Repr. of 1969 ed. 13.00x (ISBN 0-930272-04-8). RI Mayflower.

Vital Records of Newburyport, Massachusetts, to the End of the Year 1849, 2 vols. Incl. Vol. 1, Births. 428p. 1911; Vol. 2, Marriages & Deaths. 845p. 1911. LC 11-7325. 15.00 ea. o.p. (ISBN 0-88389-038-0). Essex Inst.

Vital Records of Shelburne, Massachusetts, to the End of the Year 1849. LC 31-30067. 190p. 1931. 5.00 o.p. (ISBN 0-88389-041-0, Dist. by U Pr of New Eng). Essex Inst.

Vital Records of Tewksbury, Massachusetts, to the End of the Year 1849. LC 13-5097. 246p. 1912. 7.50 o.p. (ISBN 0-88389-043-7, Dist. by U Pr of New Eng). Essex Inst.

Vital Records of Tyngsboro, Massachusetts, to the End of the Year 1849. LC 13-5098. 119p. 1912. 5.00 o.p. (ISBN 0-88389-044-5, Dist. by U Pr of New Eng). Essex Inst.

Vital Records of Yarmouth, Mass. to Eighteen Fifty, 2 vols. Robert M. Sherman & Ruth W. Sherman. LC 79-189435. 1975. Set. 20.00x (ISBN 0-930272-00-5). RI Mayflower.

Vital Resources, Vol. I. Commission on Critical Choices. LC 75-44718. (Critical Choices for Americans Ser.). 1976. 17.95 (ISBN 0-669-00413-8). Lexington Bks.

Vital Signs: A Doctor Diagnoses the Medical Profession. Jean Bernard. LC 75-8715. 322p. 1975. 9.95 o.s.i. (ISBN 0-02-510150-1). Macmillan.

Vital Signs: New and Selected Poems. David R. Slavitt. LC 74-18833. 6.95 o.p. (ISBN 0-385-01365-5). Doubleday.

Vital Signs with Related Clinical Measurement. 3rd ed. Betty McInnes. (Illus.). 1979. pap. 9.50 (ISBN 0-8016-3333-8). Mosby.

Vital Spark. John P. Wright. 1974. text ed. 9.95x o.p. (ISBN 0-435-68945-2). Heinemann Ed.

Vital Statistics of the United States, 1937-1956, 43 vols. U. S. National Office of Vital Statistics. Incl. 1937, 2 vols. Vol. 1. 23.50 (ISBN 0-8371-1670-8, VITA); Vol. 2. 23.50 (ISBN 0-8371-1671-6, VITB); 1938, 2 vols. Vol. 1. 23.50 (ISBN 0-8371-1672-4, VITC); Vol. 2. 23.50 (ISBN 0-8371-1673-2, VITD); 1939, 2 vols. Vol. 1. 23.50 (ISBN 0-8371-1674-0, VITE); Vol. 2. 23.50 (ISBN 0-8371-1675-9, VITF); 1940, 3 vols. Vol. 1. 26.50 (ISBN 0-8371-1676-7, VITG); Vol. 2. 26.50 (ISBN 0-8371-1677-5, VITH); Vol. 3. 26.50 (ISBN 0-8371-1678-3, VITI); 1941, 2 vols. Vol. 1. 19.50 (ISBN 0-8371-1679-1, VITJ); Vol. 2. 19.50 (ISBN 0-8371-1680-5, VITK); 1942, 2 vols. Vol. 1. 21.75 (ISBN 0-8371-1681-3, VITL); Vol. 2. 21.75 (ISBN 0-8371-1682-1, VITM); 1943, 2 vols. Vol. 1. 24.00 (ISBN 0-8371-1683-X, VITN); Vol. 2. 24.00 (ISBN 0-8371-1684-8, VITO); 1944, 2 vols. Vol. 1. 25.00 (ISBN 0-8371-1685-6, VITP); Vol. 2. 25.00 (ISBN 0-8371-1686-4, VITQ); 1945, 2 vols. Vol. 1. 24.00 (ISBN 0-8371-1687-2, VITR); Vol. 2. 24.00 (ISBN 0-8371-1688-0, VITS); 1946, 2 vols. Vol. 1. 25.75 (ISBN 0-8371-1689-9, VITT); Vol. 2. 25.75 (ISBN 0-8371-1690-2, VITU); 1947, 2 vols. Vol. 1. 25.75 (ISBN 0-8371-1691-0, VITW); Vol. 2. 25.75 (ISBN 0-8371-1692-9, VITX); 1948, 2 vols. Vol. 1. 25.50 (ISBN 0-8371-1693-7, VITY); Vol. 2. 25.50 (ISBN 0-8371-1694-5, VITZ); 1949, 2 vols. Vol. 1. 28.00 (ISBN 0-8371-1695-3, VIUA); Vol. 2. 28.00 (ISBN 0-8371-1696-1, VIUB); 1950, 3 vols. Vol. 1. 28.00 (ISBN 0-8371-1697-X, VIUC); Vol. 2. 28.00 (ISBN 0-8371-1698-8, VIUD); Vol. 3. 28.00 (ISBN 0-8371-1699-6, VIUE); 1951, 2 vols. Vol. 1. 27.00 (ISBN 0-8371-1700-3, VIUF); Vol. 2. 27.00 (ISBN 0-8371-1701-1, VIUG); 1952, 2 vols. Vol. 1. 26.00 (ISBN 0-8371-1702-X, VIUH); Vol. 2. 26.00 (ISBN 0-8371-1703-8, VIUI); 1953, 2 vols. Vol. 1. 27.00 (ISBN 0-8371-1704-6, VIUJ); Vol. 2. 27.00 (ISBN 0-8371-1705-4, VIUK); 1954, 2 vols. Vol. 1. 26.00 (ISBN 0-8371-1707-0, VIUL); Vol. 2. 26.00 (ISBN 0-686-66669-0, VIUM); 1955, 3 vols. Vol. 1. 26.00 (ISBN 0-8371-1708-9, VIUN); Vol. 2. 26.00 (ISBN 0-8371-1709-7, VIUO); Vol. 3. 26.00 (ISBN 0-8371-1710-0, VIUP); 1956, 2 vols. Vol. 1. 28.00 (ISBN 0-8371-1711-9, VIUQ); Vol. 2. 28.00 (ISBN 0-8371-1712-7, VIUR). (Illus.). 1968. Repr. of 1956 ed. Set. lib. bdg. 990.00x (ISBN 0-8371-2512-X, VISU); single years avail. (ISBN 0-685-24752-X). Greenwood.

Vital Statistics on Congress Nineteen Eighty. John F. Bibby et al. 1980. 12.25 (ISBN 0-8447-3408-X); pap. 5.25 (ISBN 0-8447-3401-2). Am Enterprise.

Vitality & Aging: Implications of the Rectangular Curve. James F. Fries & Lawrence M. Crapo. 1981. text ed. price not set (ISBN 0-7167-1308-X); pap. text ed. price not set (ISBN 0-7167-1309-8). W H Freeman.

Vitality of the Individual in the Thought of Ancient Israel. 2nd ed. Aubrey R. Johnson. 1964. 12.50x (ISBN 0-7083-0349-8). Verry.

Vitalizing Intimacy in Marriage. Patricia Y. Travis & Robert P. Travis. LC 79-4374. 1979. 11.95 (ISBN 0-88229-398-2). Nelson-Hall.

Vitamin - Trace Mineral - Protein Interactions, Vol. 2. N. W. Flodin. Ed. by D. F. Horrobin. (Annual Research Reviews). 1980. 30.00 (ISBN 0-88831-062-5, Dist. by Pergamon). Eden Med Res.

Vitamin B-Six Book. Ruth Adams & Frank Murray. 176p. (Orig.). 1980. pap. 1.75 (ISBN 0-915962-30-6). Larchmont Bks.

Vitamin B-Twelve, Vols. 1 & 2. David Dolphin. 1070p. 1981. Set. 95.00 (ISBN 0-471-03655-2, Pub. by Wiley-Interscience). Wiley.

Vitamin C Against Cancer. H. L. Newbold. LC 79-5301. (Illus.). 384p. 1981. pap. 7.95 (ISBN 0-8128-6098-5). Stein & Day.

Vitamin C: Recent Aspects of Its Physiological & Technological Importance. Ed. by G. G. Birch & K. J. Parker. LC 74-16050. 259p. 1974. 44.95 (ISBN 0-470-07325-X). Halsted Pr.

Vitamin C, the Common Cold, & the Flu. Linus Pauling. LC 76-28516. (Illus.). 1976. pap. 6.95x (ISBN 0-7167-0361-0). W H Freeman.

Vitamin C, the Common Cold & the Flu. rev. ed. 224p. 1981. pap. 2.75 (ISBN 0-425-04853-5). Berkley Pub.

Vitamin Co-Factors of Enzyme Systems. F. A. Robinson. 1966. 54.45 o.p. (ISBN 0-08-011319-2). Pergamon.

Vitamin D: Biochemical & Clinical Aspects Related to Calcium Metabolism. Ed. by A. W. Norman et al. 973p. 1977. text ed. 109.50x (ISBN 3-11006-918-0). De Gruyter.

Vitamin D. Molecular Biology & Clinical Nutrition. Norman. 760p. 1980. 85.00 (ISBN 0-8247-6891-4). Dekker.

Vitamin E & Aging. Erwin DiCyan. pap. 1.95 o.s.i. (ISBN 0-685-30713-1, V2761). Jove Pubns.

Vitamin E for Ailing & Healthy Hearts. Wilfrid E. Shute & Harald Taub. 1972. pap. 2.50 (ISBN 0-515-05724-X). Jove Pubns.

Vitamin E: The Rejuvenation Vitamin. Carlson Wade. 1979. pap. 1.95 (ISBN 0-441-71231-2). Charter Bks.

Vitamin Pioneers. Herbert Bailey. 1970. pap. 0.95 (ISBN 0-515-02239-X). Jove Pubns.

Vitamin, Trace Mineral, Protein Interactions, Vol. 1. N. W. Flodin. Ed. by D. F. Horrobin. (Annual Research Reviews). 1979. 26.40 (ISBN 0-88831-042-0). Eden Med Res.

Vitamin-Trace Mineral-Protein Interactions, Vol. 3. Nestor W. Flodin. Ed. by David F. Horribin. (Annual Research Reviews). 362p. 1980. 38.00 (ISBN 0-88831-085-4). Eden Med Res.

Vitamins. Alan E. Nourse. (Career Concise Guides Ser.). (Illus.). (gr. 6 up). 1977. PLB 6.45 (ISBN 0-531-00096-6). Watts.

Vitamins & Food Supplements, GA-036. BCC Staff. 1980. 975.00 (ISBN 0-89336-090-2). BCC.

Vitamins & Hormones, Vol. 38. Ed. by P. L. Munson et al. (Serial Publication Ser.). 1981. write for info. (ISBN 0-12-709838-0). Acad Pr.

Vitamins & Hormones: Advances in Research & Applications. Ed. by Robert S. Harris et al. Incl. Vols. 1-8. 1943-50. 42.00 ea. Vol. 1 (ISBN 0-12-709801-1). Vol. 2 (ISBN 0-12-709802-X). Vol. 3 (ISBN 0-12-709803-8). Vol. 4 (ISBN 0-12-709804-6). Vol. 5 (ISBN 0-12-709805-4). Vol. 6 (ISBN 0-12-709806-2). Vol. 7 (ISBN 0-12-709807-0). Vol. 8 (ISBN 0-12-709808-9); Vol. 9. 1951. 42.00 (ISBN 0-12-709809-7); Vol. 10. 1952. 42.00 (ISBN 0-12-709810-0); Vols. 11-16. 1953-58. Vols. 11-12. 42.00 ea.; Vol. 11. (ISBN 0-12-709811-9); Vol. 12. (ISBN 0-12-709812-7); Vols. 13-16. 42.00 ea.; Vol. 13. (ISBN 0-12-709813-5); Vol. 14. (ISBN 0-12-709814-3); Vol. 15. (ISBN 0-12-709815-1); Vol. 16. (ISBN 0-12-709816-X); Vol. 17. Ed. by Robert S. Harris. 1959. 42.00 ea. (ISBN 0-12-709817-8); Vol. 18. 1960. 42.00 (ISBN 0-12-709818-6); Vol. 19. 1961. 42.00 (ISBN 0-12-709819-4); Vol. 20. Incl. International Symposium on Vitamin E & Metabolism. I. G. Wool. 1962. 42.00 (ISBN 0-12-709820-8); Vol. 21. 1963. 42.00 (ISBN 0-12-709821-6); Vol. 22. Incl. International Symposium on Vitamin B6. 1964. 42.00 (ISBN 0-12-709822-4); Vol. 23. 1965. 42.00 (ISBN 0-12-709823-2); Vol. 24. 1966. 42.00 (ISBN 0-12-709824-0); Vol. 25. 1967. 42.00 (ISBN 0-12-709825-9); Vol. 26. 1968. 42.00 (ISBN 0-12-709826-7); Vol. 27. 1970. 42.00 (ISBN 0-12-709827-5); Vol. 28. Ed. by Paul L. Munson. 1971. 42.00 (ISBN 0-12-709828-3); Vol. 29. 1971. 42.00 (ISBN 0-12-709829-1); Vol. 30. 1972. 42.00 (ISBN 0-12-709830-5); Vol. 35. Ed. by Paul L. Munson et al. 1978. 42.00 (ISBN 0-12-709835-6); Vol. 36. Ed. by Paul L. Munson et al. 1979. 51.50 (ISBN 0-12-709836-4). Acad Pr.

Vitamins & Hormones: Advances in Research & Applications, Vol. 37. Ed. by Paul L. Munson et al. LC 43-10535. 1980. 35.00 (ISBN 0-12-709837-2). Acad Pr.

Vitamins: Chemistry, Physiology, Pathology, Methods. Ed. by W. H. Sebrell, Jr. & Robert S. Harris. Incl. Vol. 1. 2nd ed. 1967. 55.25 (ISBN 0-12-633761-6); Vol. 2. 1968. 52.25 (ISBN 0-12-633762-4); Vol. 3. 1971. 62.50 (ISBN 0-12-633763-2); Vol. 5. 1972. 48.50 (ISBN 0-12-633765-9); Vols. 6-7. Ed. by Paul Gyorgy & W. N. Pearson. 1968. Vol. 6. 36.00 (ISBN 0-12-633706-3); Vol. 7. 37.50 (ISBN 0-12-633707-1). Acad Pr.

Vitamins in Human Biology & Medicine. M. H. Briggs. 304p. 1981. 69.95 (ISBN 0-8493-5673-3). CRC Pr.

Vitamins: What They Are. Henry Borsook. (Orig.). pap. 1.75 (ISBN 0-515-05132-2). Jove Pubns.

Vitas Patrum: The Lyff of the Olde Auncyent Fathers Hermytes. Saint Jerome. Tr. by W. Caxton. LC 77-7409. (English Experience Ser.: No. 874). 1977. Repr. of 1495 ed. lib. bdg. 99.00 (ISBN 90-221-0874-0). Walter J Johnson.

Vitede 'piu Eccellenti Architetti, Pittori,et Scultori, 2 vols. Giorgio Vasari. (Documents of Art & Architectural History, Ser. 1: Vol. 1). (Ital.). 1980. Repr. of 1550 ed. Set. 85.00x (ISBN 0-89371-101-2). Broude Intl Edns.

Vitesse. Harlan Wade. Tr. by Claude Potvin & Rose-Ella Potvin. (Book About Ser.). Orig. Title: Speed. (Illus., Fr.). (gr. k-3). 1979. PLB 7.30 (ISBN 0-8172-1454-2). Raintree Pubns.

Vitreoretinal Disorders: Diagnosis & Management. Felipe L. Tolentino et al. LC 73-81838. (Illus.). 1976. text ed. 65.00 o.p. (ISBN 0-7216-8870-5). Saunders.

Vitreous Surgery & Advances in Fundus Diagnosis & Management. Freeman. (Illus.). 1976. 65.00 o.p. (ISBN 0-8385-9485-9). ACC.

Vitruvius & Later Roman Building Manuals. Ed. by W. H. Plommer. LC 72-90487. (Classical Studies). (Illus.). 128p. 1973. 16.95 (ISBN 0-521-20141-1). Cambridge U Pr.

Vittorino Da Feltre & Other Humanist Educators. William H. Woodward. LC 63-22510. (Orig.). 1964. text ed. 9.75 (ISBN 0-8077-2359-2); pap. text ed. 5.50x (ISBN 0-8077-2356-8). Tchrs Coll.

Viva Cristo Rey: The Cristero Rebellion & the Church-State Conflict in Mexico. David C. Bailey. (Illus.). 358p. 1974. 17.50x (ISBN 0-292-78700-6). U of Tex Pr.

Viva la Difference. Penelope Ashe. 304p. 1976. pap. 1.95 o.p. (ISBN 0-345-24126-6). Ballantine.

Vivaldi in Early Fall. John Engels. LC 80-24571. (Contemporary Poetry Ser.). 88p. 1981. 8.50 (ISBN 0-8203-0543-X); pap. 4.50 (ISBN 0-8203-0552-9). U of Ga Pr.

Vivaldi Violin Concertos: A Handbook. Arlan S. Martin. LC 76-169698. 1972. 10.00 (ISBN 0-8108-0432-8). Scarecrow.

Vivamos En el Espiritu Cada Dia. Pat H. Carter. 160p. 1979. pap. 2.60 (ISBN 0-311-09089-3). Casa Bautista.

Vivekachudamani of Shri Shankaracharya. Shankara. Tr. by Swami Madhavananda. (Sanskrit & Eng). pap. 3.25 o.s.i. (ISBN 0-87481-147-3). Vedanta Pr.

Vivekananda: The Yogas & Other Works. Compiled by Swami Nikhilananda. LC 53-7534. (Illus.). 1018p. includes biography 14.95 (ISBN 0-911206-04-3). Ramakrishna.

Vives' Introduction to Wisdom: A Renaissance Textbook. Marian L. Tobriner. LC 68-54677. 1968. text ed. 8.75 (ISBN 0-8077-2278-2); pap. text ed. 4.00x (ISBN 0-8077-2275-8). Tchrs Coll.

Vivid Air: The Lafayette Escadrille. Philip M. Flammer. LC 80-22059. (Illus.). 288p. 1981. 17.50 (ISBN 0-8203-0537-5). U of Ga Pr.

Vivisection & the True Aims of Education in Biology. 3rd ed. George K. Russell. 11p. (gr. 8-12). pap. 0.75 (ISBN 0-913098-30-2). Myrin Institute.

Vivitar Guide. John Wolf. (Illus.). 144p. 1980. 12.95 (ISBN 0-87165-065-7); pap. 7.95 (ISBN 0-87165-066-5). Ziff-Davis Pub.

Vixen in Velvet. Fern Michaels. 224p. Date not set. pap. 2.25 (ISBN 0-345-29611-7). Ballantine.

Vixen O-Three. Clive Cussler. 1978. 9.95 o.p. (ISBN 0-670-74741-6). Viking Pr.

Vixens. James Brough. 1981. 12.95 (ISBN 0-671-22688-6). S&S.

Vladimir Nabokov. L. L. Lee. (U. S. Authors Ser.: No. 266). 1976. lib. bdg. 12.50 (ISBN 0-8057-7166-2). Twayne.

Vladimir Nabokov. Donald E. Morton. LC 74-76128. (Modern Literature Ser.). 176p. 1974. 10.95 (ISBN 0-8044-2638-4). Ungar.

Vladimir Nabokov: A Tribute. Ed. by Peter Quennell. (Illus.). 150p. 1981. pap. 5.95. Morrow.

Vladimir Nabokov: America's Russian Novelist. George Hyde. (Critical Appraisals Ser.). 1977. text ed. 18.25x (ISBN 0-391-00763-7). Humanities.

Vladimir Soloviev & His Messianic Work. D. Stremooukhoff. Tr. by Elizabeth Meyendorff from Fr. LC 78-78264. 375p. (Orig.). 1980. pap. 37.50 (ISBN 0-913124-37-0). Nordland Pub.

Vladimir Soloviev: Russian Mystic. Paul M. Allen. (Illus.). 512p. 1978. pap. 9.95 (ISBN 0-8334-1750-9). Steinerbks.

VNR Dictionary of Ships & the Sea. John V. Noel, Jr. 400p. 1980. text ed. 19.95 (ISBN 0-442-25631-0). Van Nos Reinhold.

Vocabulaire Des Sciences Sociales: Concepts et Indices. Raymond Boudon & Paul Lazarsfeld. (Methodes De la Sociologie: No. 1). 1971. pap. text ed. 20.50x (ISBN 90-2796-891-8). Mouton.

Vocabulaire politique et social en France de 1869 a 1872. Jean Dubois. (Fr). pap. 11.95x (ISBN 0-685-14095-4). Larousse.

Vocabulario Puertorriqueno. De Rosario. 1966. 10.95 (ISBN 0-87751-010-5, Pub by Troutman Press). E Torres & Sons.

Vocabulary & Composition Through Pleasurable Reading, Bk. 3. Harold Levine. (Orig.). (gr. 10-12). 1976. wkbk. 6.75 (ISBN 0-87720-306-7); pap. text ed. 5.92 (ISBN 0-87720-377-6). AMSCO Sch.

Vocabulary & Composition: Through Pleasurable Reading, Book 4. Harold Levine. (gr. 11-12). 1978. wkbk 6.75 (ISBN 0-87720-376-8); pap. text ed. 5.92 (ISBN 0-87720-378-4). AMSCO Sch.

Vocabulary & Composition Through Pleasurable Reading, Bk. 5. Harold Levine. (gr. 10-12). 1979. pap. text ed. 5.92 (ISBN 0-87720-385-7); wkbk 6.75 (ISBN 0-87720-379-2). AMSCO Sch.

Vocabulary & Composition Through Pleasurable Reading, Bk. 6. Harold Levine. (gr. 11-12). 1979. pap. text ed. 5.92 (ISBN 0-87720-388-1); wkbk. 6.75 (ISBN 0-87720-387-3). AMSCO Sch.

Vocabulary Builder & Guide to Verbal Tests. 5th ed. David R. Turner. LC 73-77242. 1973. pap. 5.00 (ISBN 0-668-00535-1). Arco.

Vocabulary Building & Word Study. Mary Lewick-Wallace. Ed. by Alton Raygor. (Communication Skills Ser.). 240p. (Orig.). 1981. pap. text ed. 8.95 (ISBN 0-07-067902-9, C). McGraw.

Vocabulary Building: Syllabus, Level III. Diana C. Watson & Hernan Hurtado. 1973. pap. text ed. 5.25 (ISBN 0-89420-007-0, 270043); cassette recordings 69.20 (ISBN 0-89420-194-8, 270000). Natl Book.

Vocabulary Building: Syllabus, Level IV. Diana C. Watson & Malcom Watson. 1975. pap. text ed. 5.35 (ISBN 0-89420-039-9, 270053); cassette recordings 68.90 (ISBN 0-89420-195-6, 270200). Natl Book.

Vocabulary Control for Information Retrieval. F. Wilfrid Lancaster. LC 78-186528. (Illus.). xiv, 233p. 1972. text ed. 25.00 (ISBN 0-87815-006-4). Info Resources.

Vocabulary Development in the Classroom. Lee C. Deighton. LC 59-8372. 1959. pap. text ed. 3.75 (ISBN 0-8077-1236-1). Tchrs Coll.

Vocabulary for the College-Bound Student. Harold Levine. (Orig.). (gr. 9-12). 1964. text ed. 8.83 (ISBN 0-87720-367-9); pap. text ed. 4.92 (ISBN 0-87720-366-0); wkbk. 5.58 (ISBN 0-87720-312-1); with answers 3.25 (ISBN 0-87720-313-X). AMSCO Sch.

Vocabulary for the High School Student. Harold Levine. (Orig.). (gr. 9-12). 1967. text ed. 8.83 (ISBN 0-87720-365-2); pap. text ed. 4.92 (ISBN 0-87720-364-4); wkbk. 5.58 (ISBN 0-87720-310-5); with answer 3.25 (ISBN 0-87720-311-3). AMSCO Sch.

Vocabulary Foundations for the College Student. Harold Levine & Robert T. Levine. (Orig.). 1980. pap. text ed. 7.50 (ISBN 0-87720-962-6). AMSCO Sch.

Vocabulary Improvement. 3rd ed. Nancy Davis. 1978. pap. text ed. 10.50x (ISBN 0-07-015543-7, C). McGraw.

Vocabulary Improvement: A Program for Self-Instruction. rev. 2nd ed. Nancy B. Davis. 192p. 1973. pap. text ed. 7.95 (ISBN 0-07-015513-5, C); instructor's manual 5.95 (ISBN 0-07-015543-7). McGraw.

Vocabulary in Context: Getting the Precise Meaning. Walter Pauk. (Skill at a Time Ser). 64p. (gr. 9 up). 1975. pap. text ed. 2.40x (ISBN 0-89061-021-5). Jamestown Pubs.

Vocabulary of Organic Chemistry. Milton Orchin et al. LC 79-25930. 1980. 35.00 (ISBN 0-471-04491-1, Pub. by Wiley-Interscience). Wiley.

Vocabulary Through Pleasurable Reading, Bk. 1. Harold Levine. (Orig.). (gr. 7-10). 1974. pap. text ed. 5.92 (ISBN 0-87720-373-3); wkbk. 6.75 (ISBN 0-87720-368-7). AMSCO Sch.

Vocabulary Through Pleasurable Reading Book, Bk. 2. Harold Levine. (gr. 7-12). 1974. wkbk 6.75 (ISBN 0-87720-369-5); pap. text ed. 5.92 (ISBN 0-87720-374-1). AMSCO Sch.

Vocal Gymnastics for the Pop Singer. Al Berkman. 1976. 8.00 (ISBN 0-934972-07-9). Melrose Pub Co.

Vocal Music. David Ewen. LC 74-34115. (Illus.). 272p. (YA) (gr. 7-12). 1975. 10.95 o.p. (ISBN 0-531-02829-1). Watts.

Vocation & Spirituality of the DRE: An NPCD Publication. Pref. by Francis D. Kelley. 3.50. Natl Cath Educ.

Vocation As the Core of American Social Philosophy. Harold H. Punke. LC 75-3521. 1975. text ed. 9.50x (ISBN 0-8134-1718-X, 1718). Interstate.

Vocation of Man. Johann G. Fichte. Tr. by William Smith. LC 56-44104. 1956. pap. 3.95 (ISBN 0-672-60220-2, LLA50). Bobbs.

Vocational & Career Education. Calfrey C. Calhoun & Alton V. Finch. text ed. 17.95x (ISBN 0-534-00437-7). Wadsworth Pub.

Vocational & Personal Adjustments in Practical Nursing. 3rd ed. Betty G. Becker & Dolores T. Fendler. LC 77-10153. (Illus.). 1978. pap. text ed. 9.50 (ISBN 0-8016-0565-2). Mosby.

Vocational & Technical Mathematics in Action. Samuel Levine. (Illus., Orig.). 1969. pap. 11.95x (ISBN 0-8104-5717-2); inst. guide & ans. bk. 1.95x (ISBN 0-8104-5719-9); transparencies 102.15 (ISBN 0-8104-8851-5). Hayden.

Vocational Development. Donald E. Super et al. LC 57-11370. 1957. text ed. 7.50x (ISBN 0-8077-2233-2). Tchrs Coll.

Vocational Maturity During the High School Years. Jean-Pierre Jordaan & Martha B. Hyde. LC 78-23973. 1979. text ed. 22.50 (ISBN 0-8077-2453-X). Tchrs Coll.

Vocational Maturity of Ninth-Grade Boys. Donald E. Super & Phoebe L. Overstreet. LC 60-12516. 1960. text ed. 7.25x (ISBN 0-8077-2236-7). Tchrs Coll.

Vocational Preparation of Retarded Citizens. Don E. Brolin. (Illus.). 320p. 1976. text ed. 18.95 (ISBN 0-675-08667-1). Merrill.

Vocational Rehabilitation of the Disabled: An Overview. Ed. by David Malikin & Herbert Rusalem. LC 69-19258. 1969. 15.00x (ISBN 0-8147-0283-X). NYU Pr.

Vocational Rehabilitation of the Mentally Retarded: A Book of Readings. Ed. by Lloyd K. Daniels. (Illus.). 648p. 1974. text ed. 37.75 (ISBN 0-398-02582-7). C C Thomas.

Vocational Rehabilitation: Profession & Process. Ed. by John G. Cull & Richard E. Hardy. (Amer. Lec. in Social & Rehabilitation Psychology Ser.). (Illus.). 576p. 1977. 29.75 (ISBN 0-398-02266-6). C C Thomas.

Vocational-Technical Core Collection: Vol. I, Books. Jack Hall & Victoria C. Lessard. 400p. 1980. 35.00 (ISBN 0-918212-46-4). Neal-Schuman.

Vocational-Technical Core Collection: Vol. II, Media. Jack Hall & Victoria C. Lessard. 400p. 1981. 35.00 (ISBN 0-918212-47-2). Neal-Schuman.

Vocational Training & Employment of Youth. Selden C. Menefee. LC 70-166953. (FDR & the Era of the New Deal Ser). 1971. Repr. of 1942 ed. lib. bdg. 17.50 (ISBN 0-306-70357-2). Da Capo.

Vocations for Boys. rev. ed. Harry D. Kitson & Edgar M. Stover. LC 55-8677. (gr. 9 up). 1955. 5.95 o.p. (ISBN 0-15-293917-2, HJ). HarBraceJ.

Vocations for Girls. rev. ed. Mary R. Lingenfelter & Harry D. Kitson. LC 39-22231. (gr. 7 up). 1951. 5.95 o.p. (ISBN 0-15-294096-0, HJ). HarBraceJ.

Voces de juventud. Joseph M. Vocolo et al. (gr. 9-12). 1978. pap. text ed. 4.80 (ISBN 0-205-05816-7, 4258169). Allyn.

Voces: Eine Bibliofraphie zu Woetern und Begriffen aus der Patristik (1918-1978) Hermann J. Sieben. (Bibliographia Patristica). 461p. 1979. text ed. 81.25x (ISBN 3-11-007966-6). De Gruyter.

Vogel's Elementary Practical Organic Chemistry: Small Scale Preparations, Pt. 1. 3rd ed. A. I. Vogel. Ed. by Smith & Waldron. 1979. text ed. 24.00 (ISBN 0-582-47009-9). Longman.

Vogel's Textbook of Macro & Semimicro Qualitative Inorganic Analysis. 5th ed. Ed. by A. I. Vogel & G. Svehla. LC 77-8290. 1979. 40.00x (ISBN 0-582-44367-9). Longman.

Vogel's Textbook of Quantitative Inorganic Analysis. 4th ed. A. I. Vogel. Ed. by J. Bassett et al. LC 77-5545. (Illus.). 1978. text ed. 42.00x (ISBN 0-582-46321-1). Longman.

Vogue Body & Beauty Book. Bronwen Meredith. (Illus.). 360p. 1981. pap. 6.95 (ISBN 0-89104-199-0). A & W Pubs.

Voice. Gabriel Okara. LC 76-90298. 1970. pap. text ed. 3.50x o.p. (ISBN 0-8419-0015-9, Africana). Holmes & Meier.

Voice. Gabriel Okara. 96p. 1964. pap. 2.25 o.p. (ISBN 0-531-06048-9, Fontana Pap). Watts.

Voice & Its Disorders. 4th ed. Margaret Greene. 446p. 1980. 47.50. Lippincott.

Voice & Its Disorders. 3rd ed. Margaret C. Greene. LC 72-560. (Illus.). 512p. 1972. 22.50 o.p. (ISBN 0-397-50300-8). Lippincott.

Voice & the Actor. Cicely Berry. (Illus.). 144p. 1974. 11.95 (ISBN 0-02-510370-9). Macmillan.

Voice & the Eye: The Analysis of Social Movements. Alain Touraine. Tr. by Alan Duff from Fr. Orig. Title: Voix et le Regard. Date not set. 37.59 (ISBN 0-521-23874-9); pap. 12.95 (ISBN 0-521-28271-3). Cambridge U Pr.

Voice & Voice Therapy. 2nd ed. Daniel R. Boone. (Illus.). 1977. 18.95 (ISBN 0-13-943100-4). P-H.

Voice As an Instrument. 2nd ed. Raymond Rizzo. LC 77-9433. 1977. pap. text ed. 8.50 (ISBN 0-672-61407-3) Bobbs.

Voice Audience Content. Susan Gibson. 1979. pap. text ed. 8.95 (ISBN 0-582-28108-3); instrs.' manual free (ISBN 0-582-28133-4). Longman.

Voice Celestial. Ernest Holmes & Fenwicke Holmes. (Illus.). 1978. pap. 8.95 (ISBN 0-911336-71-0). Sci of Mind.

Voice Crying in the Wilderness: Essays on the Problem of Science & World Affairs. Bernard T. Feld. (Illus.). 1979. 35.00 (ISBN 0-08-023106-3). Pergamon.

Voice from the Chorus. Abram Tertz, pseud. LC 76-7526. 352p. 1976. pap. 10.00 (ISBN 0-374-28500-4). FS&G.

Voice from the Cross. Andrew W. Blackwood, Jr. (Minister's Paperback Library Ser.). 1978. pap. 1.95 (ISBN 0-8010-0742-9). Baker Bk.

Voice from the Living. Marc Lovell. LC 77-92221. 1978. 7.95 o.p. (ISBN 0-385-14104-1). Doubleday.

Voice in Her Tribe: A Navajo Woman's Own Story. Irene Stewart. (Ballena Press Anthropological Papers: No. 17). (Illus.). 91p. 1980. pap. 5.95 o.p. (ISBN 0-87919-088-4). Ballena Pr.

Voice in the Wilderness. Allan May. LC 77-28519. (Illus.). 1978. 12.95 (ISBN 0-88229-309-5); pap. 6.95 (ISBN 0-88229-605-1). Nelson-Hall.

Voice in the Wilderness: Collected Essays of Corliss Lamont. new ed. Corliss Lamont. LC 74-75351. 327p. 1974. 10.00 (ISBN 0-87975-044-8); pap. 5.95 (ISBN 0-87975-060-X). Prometheus Bks.

Voice of Armageddon. David Lippincott. 1975. pap. 1.75 o.p. (ISBN 0-451-06949-8, E6949, Sig). NAL.

Voice of Bugle Ann & the Daughter of Bugle Ann. MacKinlay Kantor. 192p. 1980. pap. 1.95 (ISBN 0-515-05458-5). Jove Pubns.

Voice of Illness. Aarne Siirala. (A Study in Therapy & Prophecy). 1981. Repr. of 1964 ed. soft cover 19.95 (ISBN 0-88946-995-4). E Mellen.

Voice of Maine. William Pohl. (Illus.). 176p. Date not set. 18.95 (ISBN 0-8159-7104-4). Devin. Postponed.

Voice of Our Fathers. Homer C. Hoeksma. LC 80-8082. 1980. 18.95 (ISBN 0-8254-2841-6). Kregel.

Voice of Terror: A Biography of Johann Most. Frederic Trautmann. LC 79-8279. (Contributions in Political Science: No. 42). (Illus.). xxv, 288p. 1980. lib. bdg. 25.00 (ISBN 0-313-22053-0, TVT/). Greenwood.

Voice of the Coyote. J. Frank Dobie. LC 49-8879. (Illus.). 1961. pap. 3.95 (ISBN 0-8032-5050-9, BB 109, Bison). U of Nebr Pr.

Voice of the Devil. G. Campbell Morgan. (Morgan Library). 1978. pap. 2.45 (ISBN 0-8010-6058-3). Baker Bk.

Voice of the Lord: A Biography of George Fox. Harry E. Wildes. LC 64-10896. 1964. 11.50x o.p. (ISBN 0-8122-7431-8). U of Pa Pr.

Voice of the Night. Brian Coffey. LC 79-7327. 1980. 10.95 (ISBN 0-385-15258-2). Doubleday.

Voice of the Silence. Helena P. Blavatsky. LC 73-7619. 1970. pap. 2.50 (ISBN 0-8356-0380-6, Quest). Theos Pub Hse.

Voice of the Silence: Chosen Fragments from the Book of the Golden Precepts. Tr. & intro. by Helena P. Blavatsky. iv, 110p. 1928. Repr. of 1889 ed. 3.00 (ISBN 0-938998-06-4). Theosophy.

Voice of the Silence: Verbatim with 1889 Original Ed. Helena P. Blavatsky. LC 76-25345. 1976. 4.00 (ISBN 0-911500-04-9); pap. 2.25 (ISBN 0-911500-05-7). Theos U Pr.

Voice of the Tambaran: Truth & Illusion in Ilahita Arapesh Religion. Donald F. Tuzin. 350p. 1980. 20.00x (ISBN 0-520-03964-5). U of Cal Pr.

Voice of the Third World: Dom Helder Camara. Bernhard Moosbrugger & Gladys Weigner. LC 80-82008. (Illus.). 1972. pap. 1.95 (ISBN 0-8091-1738-X). Paulist Pr.

Voice on the CB. Jay Schleifer. Ed. by Thomas J. Mooney. (Beginning Pal Paperbacks Ser.). (Illus., Orig.). (gr. 7-12). 1977. pap. text ed. 1.25 (ISBN 0-8374-3463-7). Xerox Ed Pubns.

Voice Quality: A Classified Bibliography of Research. John Laver. (Library & Information Sources in Linguistics: No. 5). 1978. text ed. 30.25x (ISBN 90-272-0996-0). Humanities.

Voice-Speech-Language: Clinical Communicology - Its Physiology & Pathology. Richard Luchsinger & Godfrey E. Arnold. 1965. 34.95x (ISBN 0-534-00680-9). Wadsworth Pub.

Voice Still Speaks. Morris Adler. Ed. by Jacob Chinitz. LC 68-57433. 1969. 10.00x (ISBN 0-8197-0052-5). Bloch.

Voice Therapy & Voice Improvement: A Simple & Practical Approach Through Correct Muscle Usage. Walter Schumacher. (Illus.). 144p. 1974. 11.75 (ISBN 0-398-02920-2). C C Thomas.

Voice Through a Cloud. Denton Welch. 1981. Repr. of 1950 ed. 12.95 (ISBN 0-8290-0357-6). Irvington.

Voiceless University: An Argument for Intellectual Autonomy. Harold Zyskind & Robert Sternfeld. LC 78-132822. (Higher Education Ser.). 1971. 11.95x o.p. (ISBN 0-87589-103-9). Jossey-Bass.

Voices. Beatrice Sparks. 1980. pap. 1.95 o.s.i. (ISBN 0-440-19024-X). Dell.

Voices & Words of Women & Men. Ed. by Cheris Kramarae. 195p. 1981. 28.80 (ISBN 0-08-026106-X). Pergamon.

Voices from the Bottom Brown Book. Ed. by Edward Spargo et al. (College Reading Skills Ser). (Illus.). 176p. (gr. 12 up). 1972. pap. text ed. 4.80x (ISBN 0-89061-004-5). Jamestown Pubs.

Voices from the Bottom Olive Book. Ed. by Edward Spargo et al. (College Reading Skills Ser). (Illus.). 176p. (gr. 12 up). 1972. pap. text ed. 4.80x (ISBN 0-89061-003-7). Jamestown Pubs.

Voices from the Bottom Purple Book. Ed. by Edward Spargo et al. (College Reading Skills Ser). (Illus.). 176p. (gr. 12 up). 1972. pap. text ed. 4.80x (ISBN 0-89061-005-3). Jamestown Pubs.

Voices from the Great Black Baseball Leagues. John Holway. LC 75-11931. (Illus.). 384p. 1975. 9.95 (ISBN 0-396-07124-4). Dodd.

Voices from the Holocaust. Ed. by Sylvia Rothchild. 1981. 14.95 (ISBN 0-453-00396-6, H396). NAL.

Voices from Three-Mile Island: The People Speak Out. Robert Leppzer. LC 80-20933. (Illus.). 1980. 8.95 (ISBN 0-89594-041-8); pap. 3.95 (ISBN 0-89594-042-6). Crossing Pr.

Voices in Stone. W. Doblhofer. 1971. pap. 2.95 o.s.i. (ISBN 0-02-046150-X, Collier). Macmillan.

Voices in the Fog. Kate Cameron. (Holderly Hall Ser: No. 3). 1975. pap. 0.95 o.p. (ISBN 0-685-51410-2, LB230NK, Leisure Bks). Nordon Pubns.

Voices in the Whirlwind & Other Essays. Ezekiel Mphahlele. LC 70-163568. 1972. 6.95 o.p. (ISBN 0-8090-9627-7); pap. 2.65 o.p. (ISBN 0-8090-1361-4). Hill & Wang.

Voices: Interviews with Handicapped People. Michael D. Orlansky & William L. Heward. (Special Education Ser.). (Illus.). 352p. (Orig.). Date not set. pap. text ed. price not set (ISBN 0-675-08024-X). Merrill.

Voices Long Silent: An Oral Inquiry into the Japanese American Evacuation. Ed. by Arthur A. Hansen & Betty E. Mitson. 1974. 7.95 (ISBN 0-930046-04-8). CSUF Oral Hist.

Voices of America: The Nation's Story in Slogans, Sayings, & Songs. Thomas A. Bailey. LC 76-8143. 1976. 17.95 (ISBN 0-02-901260-0). Free Pr.

Voices of Change in the Spanish American Theater: An Anthology. Ed. & tr. by William I. Oliver. (Texas Pan American Ser). 294p. 1971. 15.00 (ISBN 0-292-70123-3). U of Tex Pr.

Voices of Change: Southern Pulitzer Winners. Maurine H. Beasley & Richard R. Harlow. LC 79-52511. 1979. pap. text ed. 8.50 (ISBN 0-8191-0771-9). U Pr of Amer.

Voices of Children 1700-1914. Irina Strickland. 1973. 12.50x o.p. (ISBN 0-631-11780-6, Pub. by Basil Blackwell England). Biblio Dist.

Voices of Czechoslovak Socialists. Ed. by Committee to Defend Czech Socialists. 1977. pap. 3.95 (ISBN 0-686-23504-5, Merlin Pr). Carrier Pigeon.

Voices of Film Experience, 1894 to the Present. Jay Leyda. 1977. 24.95 (ISBN 0-02-571600-X, 57160). Macmillan.

Voices of French Pacifism. Incl. La Paix et l'Enseignement Pacifiste, Lecons Professees a l'Ecole des Hautes Etudes Sociales. Estournelles De Constant et al; International Peace: Speeches. Estournelles De Constant et al; Le Mensonge du Pacifisme. Ferdinand Brunetiere; A Propos du Pacifisme. Frederic Passy et al. LC 71-147705. (Library of War & Peace; Problems of the Organized Peace Movement: Selected Documents). lib. bdg. 38.00 (ISBN 0-8240-0239-3). Garland Pub.

Voices of German Expressionism. Ed. by Victor H. Miesel. LC 71-90968. 1974. 5.95 o.s.i. (ISBN 0-13-943712-6). Brown Bk.

Voices of German Pacifism. Incl. Das Personliche Wirken und Werben. Arthur Muller; German Pacifism During the War. Caroline E. Playne; Die Fuhrer der Deutschen Friedensbewegung, 1890-1923. Hans Wehberg; Hans Wehberg Als Pazifist in Weltkrieg. Hans Wehberg. LC 71-147710. (Library of War & Peace; Problems of the Organized Peace Movement: Selected Documents). lib. bdg. 38.00 (ISBN 0-8240-0241-5). Garland Pub.

Voices of India. Govinda V. Ramroop. 1980. 4.95 (ISBN 0-533-03273-3). Vantage.

Voices of Loving. Anne Neville. (Starlight Romance Ser.). 144p. 1981. pap. 1.75 (ISBN 0-553-14363-8). Bantam.

Voices of Melancholy. Bridget G. Lyons. (Ideas & Forms in English Literature). 1971. 15.00 (ISBN 0-7100-7001-2). Routledge & Kegan.

Voices of Negro Protest in Amercia. William H. Burns. LC 80-21197. 88p. 1980. Repr. of 1963 ed. lib. bdg. 17.50x (ISBN 0-313-22219-3, BUVN). Greenwood.

Voices of Seventeen Seventy Six. Richard Wheeler. LC 72-78277. (Illus.). 384p. 1972. 12.95 o.s.i. (ISBN 0-690-86422-1, TYC-T). T Y Crowell.

Voices of Seventeen Seventy-Six. Richard Wheeler. 1975. pap. 1.95 (ISBN 0-449-30742-5, C742, Prem). Fawcett.

Voices of Spirit. Charles H. Hapgood. 1975. 8.95 o.p. (ISBN 0-440-05983-6, Sey Lawr). Delacorte.

Voices of Spirit. Charles H. Hapgood. 1976. pap. 1.75 o.p. (ISBN 0-685-73462-5, LB404, Leisure Bks). Nordon Pubns.

Voices of the Civil War. Richard Wheeler. LC 75-33705. (Illus.). 416p. 1976. 15.95 o.s.i. (ISBN 0-690-01090-7, TYC-T). T Y Crowell.

Voices of the Industrial Revolution: Selected Readings from the Liberal Economists & Their Critics. Ed. by John Bowditch & Clement Ramsland. 1961. pap. 4.50 (ISBN 0-472-06053-8, 53, AA). U of Mich Pr.

Voices of the Rainbow. Kenneth Rosen. LC 80-52071. 232p. 1980. pap. 4.95 (ISBN 0-394-17747-9). Seaver Bks.

Voices of the Rainbow. Ed. by Kenneth Rosen. (Seaver-Grove Bk.). 1980. pap. 4.95 o.p. (ISBN 0-394-17747-9). Grove.

Voices of Time. Ed. by J. T. Fraser. 12.50 o.s.i. (ISBN 0-8076-0318-X). Braziller.

Voices of Women: Three Critics on Three Poets on Three Heroines. Ed. by Cynthia Navaretta. LC 80-80281. (Illus.). 1980. pap. 4.50. Midmarch Assocs.

Voices Under the Ground: Themes & Images in the Early Poetry of Gunnar Ekelof. Ross Shideler. (U. C. Publ. in Modern Philology: Vol. 104). 1973. pap. 8.00x (ISBN 0-520-09415-8). U of Cal Pr.

Voices, Voices. Stefan Grunwald. (Orig.). 1980. pap. 4.95 (ISBN 0-89865-040-2). Donning Co.

Voices Within the Ark. Ed. by Howard Schwartz & Anthony Rudolf. 1980. pap. 14.95 (ISBN 0-380-76109-2, 76109). Avon.

Voices Within the Ark: The Modern Jewish Poets. Ed. by Howard Schwartz & Anthony Rudolf. 1980. 39.50 (ISBN 0-916366-11-1); slipcased ed. 50.00. Pushcart Pr.

Voici les Desmarets! Victor H. Taylor. 1958. pap. text ed. 1.95x o.p. (ISBN 0-435-37881-3). Heinemann Ed.

Voila Careme! The Gastronomic Adventures of History's Greatest Chef. Adam Gopnik & Jack Huberman. 1980. pap. 4.95 (ISBN 0-312-85098-0). St Martin.

Voiles in Time. Hugh MacLennan. 320p. 1980. 12.95 (ISBN 0-312-59590-5). St Martin.

Voix d'Afrique. Joyce Hutchinson. 4.95x (ISBN 0-521-05356-0). Cambridge U Pr.

Voix et silences: Les Meilleures pieces radiophoniques francaises. Ed. by Anna Otten. Incl. Silences de Paris. Albert Camus & V. Vedres; Une L'arme. Jean Forest & Rene Clair; C'est vrai mais il ne faut pas le croire. Claude Aveline; Frederic General. Jacques Constant; Interview. Robert Pinget. LC 68-11212. (Illus., Fr.). 1968. pap. text ed. 5.95x (ISBN 0-89197-466-0). Irvington.

Volcano. Susan Heller & Douglas Wallin. (Orig.). 1981. pap. 3.25 (ISBN 0-440-19319-2). Dell.

Volcano!! Scott C. Stone. (Illus.). 1978. pap. 4.95 (ISBN 0-89610-064-2). Island Her.

Volcano: Mt. St. Helens. Ed. by Robert D. Shangle. (Illus.). 48p. 1980. pap. 4.95 (ISBN 0-89802-178-2). Beautiful Am.

Volcanoes. Peter Francis. 1976. pap. 5.95 (ISBN 0-14-021897-1, Pelican). Penguin.

Volcanoes. Susan Harris. (Easy-Read Fact Bks.). (Illus.). (gr. 2-4). 1979. PLB 6.45 s&l (ISBN 0-531-02277-3). Watts.

Volcanoes. Greg Jefferies. (Jackdaw Ser: No. 76). 1970. 5.95 o.p. (ISBN 0-670-74762-9, Grossman). Viking Pr.

Volcanoes. M. B. Lambert. LC 78-64573. (Illus.). 70p. 1979. pap. 7.95 (ISBN 0-295-95783-2). U of Wash Pr.

Volcanoes. Ruth Radlauer. LC 80-25464. (Illus.). 48p. (gr. 3 up). 1981. PLB 9.25g (ISBN 0-516-07835-6, Elk Grove Bks). Childrens.

Volcanoes: A Primer. Robert Decker & Barbara Decker. LC 80-20126. (Geology Ser.). (Illus.). 1981. text ed. 17.95x (ISBN 0-7167-1241-5); pap. text ed. 8.95x (ISBN 0-7167-1242-3). W H Freeman.

Volcanoes As Landscape Forms. 2nd ed. C. A. Cotton. (Illus.). 1969. Repr. of 1944 ed. 21.75 o.s.i. (ISBN 0-02-843210-X). Hafner.

Volcanoes from Puebla. Kenneth Gangemi. 192p. 1979. 11.95 (ISBN 0-7145-2577-4, Pub. by M Boyars). Merrimack Bk Serv.

Volcanoes: Mountains of Fire. Barbara B. Simons. LC 76-15550. (Science Information Ser.). (Illus.). (gr. 4). 1976. PLB 8.65 (ISBN 0-8172-0350-8). Raintree Pubs.

Volcanoes: Nature's Fireworks. Hershell H. Nixon & Joan L. Nixon. LC 77-16873. (Illus.). (gr. 2-5). 1978. 4.95 (ISBN 0-396-07559-2). Dodd.

Volcanoes of the Earth. rev. ed. Fred M. Bullard. LC 76-2560. (Illus.). 544p. 1976. 40.00 (ISBN 0-292-78701-4). U of Tex Pr.

Voleur de'Enfants. Supervielle. (Easy Reader, A). pap. 2.90 (ISBN 0-88436-111-X, FRA110052). EMC.

Volga Germans: Pioneers in the Pacific Northwest. Richard Scheuerman & Clifford Trafzer. LC 80-52314. (GEM Books-Historical Ser.). (Illus.). 240p. (Orig.). 1981. 18.95; pap. 7.95 (ISBN 0-89301-073-1). U Pr of Idaho.

Volia: Izbrannoe. Semen Lipkin. (Rus.). 1981. 14.00 (ISBN 0-88233-674-6). Ardis Pubs.

Volkhavaar. Tanith Lee. (Science Fiction Ser). 1977. pap. 1.75 (ISBN 0-87997-312-9, UE1539). DAW Bks.

Volkisch Ideology & the Roots of Nazism: The Early Writings of Arthur Moeller van den Bruck. Paul Harrison Silfen. LC 73-86549. 1973. 5.00 o.p. (ISBN 0-682-47786-9, University). Exposition.
Volkswagen Dasher Service Manual Model Years 1974-1981. Robert Bentley, Inc. (Illus.). 1980. pap. 19.95 (ISBN 0-8376-0083-9). Bentley.
Volkswagen, Nineteen Seventy to Nineteeen Seventy-Nine. Chilton's Automotive Editorial Dept. LC 78-20249. (Chilton's Repair & Tune-up Guides). (Illus.). 1979. pap. 8.95 (ISBN 0-8019-6837-2). Chilton.
Volkswagen Nineteen Seventy to Seventy-Nine. (Illus.). 288p. (Spanish.). 1980. pap. 8.95. Chilton.
Volkswagen Official Service Manual Type 1. Beetle, Super Beetle, & Karmann Ghia, 1970-1979. Volkswagen of America Inc. LC 78-75039. (Illus.). 448p. 1979. pap. 18.50 (ISBN 0-8376-0096-0). Bentley.
Volkswagen Official Service Manual Type 2, Station Wagon-Bus, 1968-1979. 4th rev. ed. Volkswagen of America Inc. LC 78-75038. (Illus.). 464p. 1979. pap. 18.50 (ISBN 0-8376-0094-4). Bentley.
Volkswagen Performance Tuning: 1200-2000cc Engines, All Years. 2nd ed. Eric Jorgensen. Ed. by Jeff Robinson. (Illus.). 200p. 1978. pap. text ed. 10.95 (ISBN 0-89287-223-3, A128). Clymer Pubns.
Volkswagen Rabbit Diesel Service Manual, 1977-1981. Robert Bentley, Inc. (Illus.). 432p. (Orig.). 1980. pap. 18.50 (ISBN 0-8376-0104-5). Bentley.
Volkswagen Rabbit Diesel Service Manual 1977-1981, Including Pickup Truck. rev. ed. Robert Bentley, Inc. (Illus.). 480p. (Orig.). 1981. pap. 18.50 (ISBN 0-8376-0104-5). Bentley.
Volkswagen Rabbit-Scirocco Service Manual, Gasoline Models, 1975, 1976, 1977, 1978, 1979. rev. ed. Robert Bentley, Inc. LC 79-57170. (Illus.). 628p. (Orig.). 1980. pap. 18.50 (ISBN 0-8376-0098-7). Bentley.
Volkswagen Rabbit-Scirocco Service Manual 1980-1981, Gasoline Models, Including Pickup Truck. rev. ed. Robert Bentley, Inc. (Illus.). 600p. (Orig.). 1981. pap. 18.50 (ISBN 0-8376-0099-5). Bentley.
Volkswagen Service - Repair Handbook: 411 & 412, 1968-1974. 2nd ed. Eric Jorgensen. Ed. by Jeff Robinson. (Illus.). 248p. 1975. pap. text ed. 10.95 (ISBN 0-89287-041-9, A125). Clymer Pubns.
Volkswagen Service--Repair Handbook: Beetle, Super Beetle, Karmann Ghia, 1961-1979. Eric Jorgensen. Ed. by Jeff Robinson. (Illus.). 1977. pap. 11.95 (ISBN 0-89287-144-X, A104). Clymer Pubns.
Volkswagen Service--Repair Handbook: Dasher, 1974-1980. Eric Jorgensen. Ed. by Jeff Robinson. (Illus.). 1977. pap. 10.95 (ISBN 0-89287-154-7, A121). Clymer Pubns.
Volkswagen Service--Repair Handbook: Rabbit, Scirocco-1975-1979. Eric Jorgensen. Ed. by Jeff Robinson. (Illus.). 1978. pap. 10.95 (ISBN 0-89287-157-1, A122). Clymer Pubns.
Volkswagen Service-Repair Handbook: Squareback & Fastback, 1962-1973. Eric Jorgensen. Ed. by Jeff Robinson. (Illus.). 304p. 1974. pap. text ed. 10.95 (ISBN 0-89287-039-7, A120). Clymer Pubns.
Volkswagen Transporter: 1961-1979, Service, Repair Handbok. Eric Jorgensen. Ed. by Jeff Robinson. (Illus.). 1978. pap. 10.95 (ISBN 0-89287-277-2, A110). Clymer Pubns.
Volleyball. Linda Fernandez & Walt Evans. (Burns Sports Ser.). 156p. Date not set. pap. cancelled (ISBN 0-695-81570-9). Follett.
Volleyball. Barrie MacGregor. (EP Sport Ser.). (Illus.). 1979. 12.95 (ISBN 0-8069-9160-7, Pub. by EP Publishing England). Sterling.
Volleyball. Wilbur Peck. (Orig.). 1970. pap. 3.95 o.s.i. (ISBN 0-02-029570-7, Collier). Macmillan.
Volleyball. 2nd ed. Allen Scates & Jane Ward. 1975. 6.50x (ISBN 0-205-04817-X). Allyn.
Volleyball Is for Me. Art Thomas. LC 80-12925. (Sports for Me Books). (Illus.). (gr. 2-5). 1980. PLB 5.95g (ISBN 0-8225-1094-4). Lerner Pubns.
Volleyball Jinx. Bobbi Katz. Ed. by Caroline Rubin. (Springboard Books Ser.). (Illus.). (gr. 3-7). 1977. 5.75g (ISBN 0-8075-8512-2). A Whitman.
Vollstandigste Naturgeschicte der affen. Heinrich G. Reichenbach. LC 78-72725. Repr. of 1863 ed. 72.50 (ISBN 0-404-18298-4). AMS Pr.
Volpone Notes & Alchemist Notes. James P. McGlone & A. M. Fiskin. (Orig.). 1967. pap. 1.95 o.s.i. (ISBN 0-8220-1349-5). Cliffs.
Voltaire. Wayne Andrews. (Illus.). 13.95 (ISBN 0-8112-0800-1); pap. 5.95 (ISBN 0-8112-0802-8, NDP519). New Directions.
Voltaire. Wayne Andrews. LC 80-29565. (Illus.). 1981. 13.95 (ISBN 0-8112-0800-1); pap. 5.95 (ISBN 0-8112-0802-8, NDP519). New Directions.
Voltaire. (Twayne's World Authors Ser.: No. 583). Date not set. cloth 10.95 (ISBN 0-8057-6425-9). Twayne.
Voltaire: The Age of Louis XIV & Other Selected Writings. Voltaire. Ed. & intro. by J. H. Brumfit. 1963. text ed. 20.00x (ISBN 0-8290-0219-7). Irvington.
Volterra & Weiner Theories of Nonlinear Systems. Martin Schetzen. LC 79-13421. 1980. 32.50 (ISBN 0-471-04455-5, Pub. by Wiley-Interscience). Wiley.
Volterra Integral Equations & Topological Dynamics. Richard K. Miller & George R. Sell. LC 52-42839. (Memoirs: No. 102). 1979. pap. 7.60 (ISBN 0-8218-1802-3, MEMO-102). Am Math.
Volume & Integral. W. W. Rogosinski. (University Mathematical Texts Ser.). 1952. 7.95 (ISBN 0-471-73128-5). Halsted Pr.
Volume Feeding Menu Selector. Alta Atkinson. Ed. by Eulalia Blair. LC 78-145861. 1971. 16.95 (ISBN 0-8436-0528-6). CBI Pub.
Volume Reduction of Low-Activity Solid Wastes. (Technical Reports: No. 106). (Illus., Orig.). 1970. pap. 3.25 (ISBN 92-0-125170-X, IAEA). Unipub.
Voluntary Action in a Changing World. F. J. Gladstone. 137p. 1979. pap. text ed. 9.90x (ISBN 0-7199-1033-1, Pub. by Bedford England). Renouf.
Voluntary Agencies in the Welfare State. Ralph M. Kramer. 400p. 1981. 24.95x (ISBN 0-520-04290-5). U of Cal Pr.
Voluntary Associations & Nordic Party Systems. Victor A. Pestoff. 210p. 1982. 24.95 (ISBN 0-87855-354-1). Transaction Bks. Postponed.
Voluntary Non-Profit Sector: An Economic Analysis. Burton A. Weisbrod. LC 77-9132. 1977. 21.00 (ISBN 0-669-01772-8). Lexington Bks.
Voluntary Service Overseas. Michael Adams. (Illus., Orig.). 1968. pap. 6.95 (ISBN 0-571-08337-4, Pub. by Faber & Faber). Merrimack Bk Serv.
Voluntary Standard for the Electronic Purchase Order and Invoice. Ed. by National Retail Merchants Association. 1980. 18.75. Natl Ret Merch.
Voluntary Tax: New Perspectives on Sophisticated Estate Tax Avoidance. George Cooper. LC 78-20853. (Studies of Government Finance). 1979. 9.95 (ISBN 0-8157-1552-8); pap. 3.95 (ISBN 0-8157-1551-X). Brookings.
Volunteer Community: Creative Uses of Human Resources. 2nd ed. Eva Schindler-Rainman & Ronald Lippitt. LC 75-18516. 176p. 1975. pap. 9.50 (ISBN 0-88390-140-4). Univ Assocs.
Volunteer Fire Company. Ernest Earnest. LC 78-8785. (Illus.). 224p. 1980. pap. 6.95 (ISBN 0-8128-6094-2). Stein & Day.
Volunteer Spring. Judy Long. LC 75-38365. (gr. 5). 1976. 5.95 (ISBN 0-396-07304-2). Dodd.
Volunteer Spring. Judy Long. (YA) (gr. 7-9). 1977. pap. 1.50 (ISBN 0-671-56002-6). PB.
Volunteer Subject. Robert Rosenthal & Ralph L. Rosnow. LC 74-16378. (Personality Processes Ser). 288p. 1975. 23.95 (ISBN 0-471-73670-8, Pub. by Wiley-Interscience). Wiley.
Volunteerism: An Emerging Profession. Ed. by John G. Cull & Richard E. Hardy. (Amer. Lec. Social & Rehabilitation Psychology Ser.). (Illus.). 220p. 1974. 16.75 (ISBN 0-398-02788-9). C C Thomas.
Volunteers. Armand Lauffer & Sarah Gorodezky. LC 77-9003. (Sage Human Services Guides: Vol. 5). 1977. pap. 6.00x (ISBN 0-8039-0884-9). Sage.
Volunteers & the Making of Presidents. Jane Dick. LC 79-27734. (Illus.). 250p. 1980. 10.95 (ISBN 0-396-07839-7); pap. 6.95 (ISBN 0-396-07840-0). Dodd.
Volvo Nineteen Seventy to Eighty-One. (Illus.). 288p. 1980. pap. 8.95. Chilton.
Volvo Penta Aquamatic Boat Engine. Keith Beardow. (Illus.). 224p. 1980. 27.00 (ISBN 0-7153-8000-1). David & Charles.
Volvo Service-Repair Handbook: 122s Series & P 1800, All Years. Clymer Publications Staff. (Illus.). 224p. 1972. pap. text ed. 10.95 (ISBN 0-89287-066-4, A220). Clymer Pubns.
Volvo Service Repair Handbook: 140 Series, 1967-1974. Eric Jorgensen. Ed. by Jeff Robinson. (Illus.). 1978. pap. 10.95 (ISBN 0-89287-227-6, A222). Clymer Pubns.
Volvo: 240 Series 1975-1979--Service, Repair Handbook. Ray Hoy. Ed. by Eric Jorgensen. (Illus.). 1978. pap. 10.95 (ISBN 0-89287-278-0, A223). Clymer Pubns.
Von Den Trobadors Genannten Oder Gefeierten Damen. Fritz Bergert. LC 80-2164. 1981. Repr. of 1913 ed. 26.50 (ISBN 0-404-19028-6). AMS Pr.
Von der Energiekonzeption Zur Energie-Politik. 1976. pap. 8.00 o.p. (ISBN 0-89192-186-9). Interbk Inc.
Von der Hintergehbarkeit der Sprache. Elmar Holenstein. (Suhrkamp Taschenbuecher Wissenschaft: No. 316). 216p. (Orig.). 1980. pap. text ed. 7.15 (ISBN 3-518-07916-6, Pub. by Insel Verlag Germany). Suhrkamp.
Von Nun an Neue Deutsche Erzaehler. Hans-Ulrich Mueller-Schwefe. (Edition Suhrkamp). 300p. (Orig.). 1980. pap. text ed. 5.20 (ISBN 3-518-11003-9, Pub. by Insel Verlag Germany). Suhrkamp.
Von Ryan's Return. David Westheimer. LC 80-24232. 481p. 1980. Repr. of 1980 ed. large print ed. 12.95 (ISBN 0-89621-253-X). Thorndike Pr.
Von Stroheim. Thomas Q. Curtiss. LC 78-143300. (Illus.). xxii, 357p. 1971. 10.00 o.p. (ISBN 0-374-28520-9). FS&G.
Vonnegut: A Preface to His Novels. Richard Giannone. LC 76-54943. (National University Pubns. Literary Criticism Ser.). 1977. 11.50 (ISBN 0-8046-9167-3). Kennikat.
Voodoo. Kyle Kristos. LC 76-18989. (gr. 4-8). 1976. 7.95 (ISBN 0-397-31706-9); pap. 2.95 (ISBN 0-397-31707-7). Lippincott.
Voodoo. Gauri Pant. 1972. 8.00 (ISBN 0-88253-707-5); pap. text ed. 4.00 (ISBN 0-88253-845-4). Ind-US Inc.
Voodoo & Hoodoo. Jim Haskins. LC 77-17213. (Illus.). 226p. 1981. pap. 6.95 (ISBN 0-8128-6085-3). Stein & Day.
Voodoo & Magic Practices. Jean Kerboull. 1978. 9.50 o.p. (ISBN 0-214-20524-X, 8063, Dist. by Arco). Barrie & Jenkins.
Voodoo Die. Warren Murphy. (Destroyer Ser.: No. 33). (Orig.). 1978. pap. 1.75 (ISBN 0-523-40909-5). Pinnacle Bks.
Voodoo Heritage. Michel S. Laguerre. LC 79-25318. (Sage Library of Social Research: No. 98). (Illus.). 231p. 1980. 18.00x (ISBN 0-8039-1402-4); pap. 8.95x (ISBN 0-8039-1403-2). Sage.
Voodoo: Its Origins & Practices. Henry Gilfond. (Illus.). 160p. (gr. 6 up). 1976. PLB 5.90 o.p. (ISBN 0-531-00347-7). Watts.
Vorlesungen Uber Partielle und Pfaffsche Diggerentialgleichungen. W. Haack & W. Wendland. (Mathematische Reihe Ser.: No. 39). (Illus.). 555p. (Ger.). 1969. 73.50 (ISBN 3-7643-0159-7). Birkhauser.
Vorlesungen Ueber Variationsrechnung. Oskar Bolza. LC 62-8228. 19.95 (ISBN 0-8284-0160-8). Chelsea Pub.
Vorlesungen Ueber Zahlentheorie, 3 Vols. in One. Edmund Landau. LC 49-235. (Ger). 29.95 (ISBN 0-8284-0032-6). Chelsea Pub.
Vorlesungen Ueberdie Altrussische Literatur (Mitteinem Nachwort Von R.O. Jakobson) N. S. Trubetzkoy. 167p. 1973. pap. 10.95x o.p. (ISBN 0-685-47487-9). Schoenhof.
Vortex. David Heller. 1978. pap. 1.95 (ISBN 0-380-42762-1, 42762). Avon.
Vortex Flows. Ed. by Walter L. Swift et al. 171p. 1980. 28.00 (G00181). ASME.
Vortex: Pound, Eliot, & Lewis. Timothy Materer. LC 79-13009. (Illus.). 1979. 14.50x (ISBN 0-8014-1225-0). Cornell U Pr.
Voter Education Curriculum Guide. NASSP. Ed. by Carol Bruce. 78p. (Orig.). 1980. pap. text ed. 10.00 (ISBN 0-88210-114-5). Natl Assn Principals.
Voters, Parties & Elections: Quantitative Essays in the History of Popular American Voting Behaviour. J. Silbey & S. McSeveney. 434p. 1972. pap. 9.95 o.p. (ISBN 0-471-00684-X). Krieger.
Voting & the Handling of Disputes in the Security Council. Eduardo Jimenez de Arechaga. LC 78-3780. (Carnegie Endowment for International Peace, United Nations: No. 5). 1978. Repr. of 1950 ed. lib. bdg. 17.75x (ISBN 0-313-20332-6, ARVH). Greenwood.
Voting Behavior in Nevada. Elmer Rusco. LC 66-63499. (History & Political Science Ser.: No. 9). ix, 78p. 1966. pap. 1.75x (ISBN 0-87417-014-1). U of Nev Pr.
Voting for President: The Electoral College & the American Political System. Wallace S. Sayre & Judith H. Parris. (Studies in Presidential Selection). 169p. 1970. pap. 4.95 (ISBN 0-8157-7719-1). Brookings.
Voting in Provincial America: A Study of Elections in the Thirteen Colonies, 1689-1776. Robert J. Dinkin. LC 77-71861. (Contributions in American History: No. 64). (Illus.). 1977. lib. bdg. 18.95 (ISBN 0-8371-9543-8, DIV/). Greenwood.
Voting Patterns of the United States Supreme Court: Cases in Federalism, 1889-1959. John D. Sprague. LC 68-18392. 1968. 22.50x (ISBN 0-672-51175-4). Irvington.
Voting Patterns of the United States Supreme Court: Cases in Federalism, 1889-1959. LC 68-18392. 1968. 8.50 (ISBN 0-672-51175-4). Bobbs.
Vought F4U-1, 7 Corsair. LC 70-113959. (Arco-Aircam Aviation Ser., No. 28). 1971. pap. 3.25 o.p. (ISBN 0-668-02314-7). Arco.
Vow. Maria B. Fogelin. 272p. (Orig.). 1980. pap. 2.50 (ISBN 0-89083-653-1). Zebra.
Vowel & Dipthong Tones. 1977. pap. 1.95. Primary Pr.
Vowel Sounds & Silent Letters: Syllabus. Joanne Piper. 1975. pap. text ed. 4.85 (ISBN 0-89420-023-2, 240008); cassette recordings 22.05 (ISBN 0-89420-196-4, 240000). Natl Book.
Vox Civitatis, or Londons Complaint Against Her Children in the Countrey. Benjamin Spenser. LC 79-84137. (English Experience Ser.: No. 954). 52p. (Eng.). 1979. Repr. of 1625 ed. lib. bdg. 8.00 (ISBN 90-221-0954-2). Walter J Johnson.
Vox Graeca. 2nd ed. W. Sidney Allen. (Illus.). 1968. 15.95x (ISBN 0-521-20626-X). Cambridge U Pr.
Vox Latina. 2nd ed. W. S. Allen. LC 78-1153. (Illus.). 1978. 15.95 (ISBN 0-521-22049-1). Cambridge U Pr.
Voyage: A Novel of 1896. Sterling Hayden. 1977. pap. 2.50 (ISBN 0-380-01780-6, 37200). Avon.
Voyage into Danger. Clara L. Brown. (Illus.). 150p. 1972. 4.95 o.p. (ISBN 0-8158-0291-9). Chris Mass.
Voyage of a Lifetime: A Journal. Hap Barhydt. (Illus.). 75p. (Orig.). 1980. pap. 4.95 (ISBN 0-9605346-0-1). Remarkable Pubns.
Voyage of Discovery: George Deacon 70th Anniversary Volume. new ed. Ed. by Martin V. Angel. LC 76-57958. 1977. 120.00 (ISBN 0-08-021380-4). Pergamon.
Voyage of Pleasure: The Log of Bernard Gilboy's Transpacific Cruise in the Boat "Pacific" 1882-1883. John B. Tompkins. LC 56-12045. (Illus.). 1956. pap. 6.00 (ISBN 0-87033-004-7). Cornell Maritime.
Voyage of Prudence: The World View of Alan of Lille. John M. Trout. LC 79-66473. 1979. pap. text ed. 9.00 (ISBN 0-8191-0840-5). U Pr of Amer.
Voyage of Saint Brendan: Journey to the Promised Land. John J. O'Meara. (Dolmen Texts: No. 1). (Illus.). 1978. text ed. 9.00x (ISBN 0-391-00710-6, Dolmen Pr). Humanities.
Voyage of the Beagle. Charles Darwin. 1955. 15.00x (ISBN 0-460-00104-3, Evman); pap. 7.95 (ISBN 0-460-01104-9). Dutton.
Voyage of the Dawn Treader. C. S. Lewis. (Illus.). (gr. 4-6). 1952. 8.95 (ISBN 0-02-758800-9). Macmillan.
Voyage of the Flying Bird. Margaret Titcomb. LC 74-94023. (Illus.). (gr. 7-9). 1970. 3.95 o.s.i. (ISBN 0-8048-0723-X). C E Tuttle.
Voyage of the Kon-Tiki. Dolores Engel. LC 78-26766. (Raintree Great Adventures). (Illus.). (gr. 3-6). 1979. PLB 8.95 (ISBN 0-8393-0151-0). Raintree Child.
Voyage of the Secret Duchess. Florence Hurd. (Orig.). 1975. pap. 0.95 o.s.i. (ISBN 0-380-00353-8, 24554). Avon.
Voyage of the Wanderer. Samantha Gardner. 1977. 6.50 o.p. (ISBN 0-533-03045-5). Vantage.
Voyage of Torres: The Discovery of the Southern Coastline of New Guinea & Torres Strait by Captain Luis Baez De Torres in 1606. Brett Hilder. (Illus.). 194p. 1981. 21.75x (ISBN 0-7022-1275-X). U of Queensland Pr.
Voyage Through Childhood to the Adult World. E. A. Frommer. 1969. 22.00 (ISBN 0-08-006496-5); pap. 10.75 (ISBN 0-08-006495-7). Pergamon.
Voyage to America, 1783-1786, Rus. Grigorii I. Shelikhov. Ed. by Richard A. Pierce. Tr. by Marina Ramsey. (Materials for the Study of Alaska History Ser.: No. 19). (Illus.). 1981. 15.50x (ISBN 0-919642-67-5). Limestone Pr.
Voyage to Dauphin Island in 1720: The Journal of Bertet De la Clue. Ed. by Francis Escoffier & Jay Higginbotham. Tr. by Francis Escoffier & Jay Higginbotham. LC 73-91909. (Illus., Fr.). 1974. 7.95 (ISBN 0-914224-02-6). Museum Mobile.
Voyage to Santa Fe. Janice H. Giles. 1977. pap. 1.75 (ISBN 0-380-00965-X, 32417). Avon.
Voyage to the Bottom of the Sea. Norman Habel. (Purple Puzzle Tree Bk). (Illus.). (ps-5). 1972. pap. 0.85 (ISBN 0-570-06524-0, 56-1228). Concordia.
Voyager: The Story of a Space Mission. Margaret Poynter & Arthur Lane. LC 80-18723. (Illus.). 160p. 1981. 9.95 (ISBN 0-689-30827-2). Atheneum.
Voyagers. Vivian Lord. 1980. pap. 2.75 (ISBN 0-449-14358-9, GM). Fawcett.
Voyages, 8 vols. Richard Hakluyt. 1962. 6.00x ea. (Evman). Vol. 1 (ISBN 0-460-00264-3). Vol. 2 (ISBN 0-460-00265-1). Vol. 3 (ISBN 0-460-00313-5). Vol. 4. o.p. (ISBN 0-460-00314-3). Vol. 5 (ISBN 0-460-00338-0). Vol. 6. o.p. (ISBN 0-460-00339-9). Vol. 7 (ISBN 0-460-00388-7). Vol. 8. o.p. (ISBN 0-460-00389-5). Dutton.
Voyages, & Adventures of Captain Robert Boyle. William R. Chetwood. LC 79-170565. (Foundations of the Novel Ser.: Vol. 46). lib. bdg. 50.00- (ISBN 0-8240-0558-9). Garland Pub.
Voyages, Dangerous Adventures & Imminent Escapes of Captain Richard Falconer. William R. Chetwood. LC 77-170543. (Foundations of the Novel Ser.: Vol. 32). lib. bdg. 50.00 (ISBN 0-8240-0544-9). Garland Pub.

Voyages of de la Perouse. De la Perouse. Ed. by Michael S. Gant. Orig. Title: Voyage Round the World. (Illus.). 265p. pap. 6.95 o.s.i. (ISBN 0-934136-02-5). Western Tanager. Postponed.

Voyages of Enlightenment: Malaspina on the Northwest Coast, 1791-1792. Thomas Vaughan et al. LC 77-88147. (North Pacific Studies Ser.: No. 3). (Illus.). 72p. 1977. pap. 3.95 (ISBN 0-87595-058-2). Oreg Hist Soc.

Voyages to Paradise: In the Wake of Captain Cook, No. XV. William R. Gray. LC 78-21187. (Illus.). 1981. 6.95 (ISBN 0-87044-284-8); lib. bdg. 8.50 (ISBN 0-87044-289-9). Natl Geog.

Voyages to the Inland Sea, Vol 3. Ed. by John Judson. Thomas McGrath & Robert Dana. LC 73-78705. 83p. 1973. 6.00x (ISBN 0-917540-03-4); pap. 3.50x (ISBN 0-917540-12-3). Ctr Cont Poetry.

Voyages, Travels & Adventures of William Owen Gwin Vaughan, Esq, Pt. 1. William R. Chetwood. LC 76-170591. (Foundations of the Novel Ser.: Vol. 61). lib. bdg. 50.00 (ISBN 0-8240-0573-2). Garland Pub.

Voyages, Travels & Adventures of William Owen Gwin Vaughan, Esq, Pt. 2. William R. Chetwood. LC 76-170591. (Foundations of the Novel Ser.: Vol. 62). lib. bdg. 50.00 (ISBN 0-8240-0574-0). Garland Pub.

Voyce from the Watch Tower: Part Five, 1660-1662. Edmund Ludlow. Ed. by A. B. Worden. (Royal Historical Society: Camden Society Fourth Ser.: Vol. 21). 370p. 1980. 20.00x (ISBN 0-8476-3308-X). Rowman.

Voyeur. (Illus.). pap. 5.00 (ISBN 0-910550-63-8). Centurion Pr.

Voz Folklorica De Puerto Rico. Rosa-Nieves. 1967. 16.95 (ISBN 0-87751-009-1, Pub by Troutman Press). E Torres & Sons.

Vozdushnye Puti. Boris Pasternak. 1976. 12.00 (ISBN 0-88233-229-5); pap. 4.50 (ISBN 0-88233-230-9). Ardis Pubs.

Vozvrashchenie Chorba. Vladimir Nabokov. (Sobranie Rasskazov I Povestei: Vol. 1). (Rus.). 1976. pap. 7.00 (ISBN 0-88233-226-0). Ardis Pubs.

Vrais Createurs De l'Opera Francais: Perrin et Cambert. Arthur Pougin. LC 80-2296. 1981. Repr. of 1881 ed. 33.50 (ISBN 0-404-18862-1). AMS Pr.

VS Basic for Business: For the IBM 360-370. A. J. Parker. 1982. pap. text ed. 12.95 (ISBN 0-8359-8439-7). Reston.

Vues D'un Citoyen. C. - H. Piarron De Chamousset. 535p. (Fr.). 1977. Repr. of 1757 ed. lib. bdg. 47.50x o.p. (ISBN 0-8287-0690-5). Clearwater Pub.

Vuillard. Stuart Preston. LC 74-142739. (Library of Great Painters). (Illus.). 1971. 35.00 (ISBN 0-8109-0538-8). Abrams.

Vuillard: Drawings 1855-1930. Intro. by John Russell. LC 78-65873. (Illus.). 1978. pap. 9.60 (ISBN 0-917418-59-X). Am Fed Arts.

Vulcanization of Elastomers: Principles & Practice of Vulcanization of Commercial Rubbers. Ed. by G. Alliger & I. J. Sjothun. 1978. Repr. of 1964 ed. lib. bdg. 21.50 (ISBN 0-88275-686-9). Krieger.

Vulgaria Uiri Doctissimi Guil. Hormani Caesarisburgensis. William Horman. LC 74-28865. (English Experience Ser.: No. 745). 1975. Repr. of 1519 ed. 46.00 (ISBN 90-221-0745-0). Walter J Johnson.

Vulnerable Teacher. Ken Macrorie. 192p. (Orig.). 1974. 6.95 (ISBN 0-8104-5936-1). Hayden.

Vultures. Robert E. Howard. (Illus.). 1973. 8.50 (ISBN 0-87707-115-2). Fictioneer Bks.

Vultures. Vijay Tendulkar. Tr. by Priya Adarkar from Marathi. 140p. 1975. pap. 2.40 (ISBN 0-88253-682-6). Ind-US Inc.

Vunamami: Economic Transformation in a Traditional Society. Richard F. Salisbury. LC 70-79062. 1970. 22.75x (ISBN 0-520-01647-5). U of Cal Pr.

VW Beetle. Robin Fry. LC 80-67583. (Illus.). 160p. 1980. 22.50 (ISBN 0-7153-7859-7). David & Charles.

VW Bodywork. Dave Tabler. Ed. by Eric Jorgensen. (Illus.). 1978. pap. 7.95 (ISBN 0-89287-228-4, A109). Clymer Pubns.

VW Connection. Mary W. Sullivan. 128p. (gr. 5 up). 1981. 8.95 (ISBN 0-525-66701-6). Elsevier-Nelson.

VW Nineteen Seventy to Nineteen Eighty-One. LC 80-70339. (Illus.). 288p. 1980. pap. 8.95. Chilton.

VW Rabbit. LC 80-80764. (Saturday Mechanic Car Care Guides). (Illus.). 176p. 12.95 (ISBN 0-87851-932-7); pap. 6.95 (ISBN 0-87851-924-6). Hearst Bks.

VW Story. Jerry Sloniger. (Illus.). 216p. 1981. 37.95 (ISBN 0-85059-441-3). Aztex.

W

W. A. Mozart: Don Giovanni. Julian Rushton. (Cambridge Opera Handbooks Ser.). (Illus.). Date not set. price not set (ISBN 0-521-22826-3); pap. price not set (ISBN 0-521-29663-3). Cambridge U Pr.

W. B. Yeats. Raymond Cowell. LC 76-101771. (Literary Critiques Ser). (Illus., Orig.). 1970. PLB 4.95 o.p. (ISBN 0-668-02180-2). Arco.

W. B. Yeats. Frank Tuohy. (Illus.). 1976. 17.95 o.s.i. (ISBN 0-02-620450-9). Macmillan.

W. B. Yeats. William B. Yeats. 49p. 1980. Repr. of 1927 ed. lib. bdg. 6.50 (ISBN 0-8495-6126-4). Arden Lib.

W. B. Yeats: A Literary Study. Charles L. Wrenn. 50p. 1980. Repr. of 1920 ed. lib. bdg. 10.00 (ISBN 0-8492-2998-7). R West.

W. B. Yeats & His World. Micheal MacLiammoir & Eavan Boland. LC 77-90492. (Illus.). 1978. 10.95 o.p. (ISBN 0-684-15573-7, ScribT). Scribner.

W. B. Yeats & Irish Folklore. Mary W. Thuente. 286p. 1981. 26.50x (ISBN 0-389-20161-8). B&N.

W. B. Yeats & the Designing of Ireland's Coinage. William B. Yeats et al. Ed. by Brian Cleeve. (New Yeats Papers Ser.: No. 3). 1972. pap. text ed. 3.75x (ISBN 0-85105-221-5, Dolmen Pr). Humanities.

W. B. Yeats & the Emergence of the Irish Free State, 1918-1939: Living in the Explosion. Bernard G. Krimm. 324p. 1981. 20.00x (ISBN 0-87875-200-5). Whitston Pub.

W. B. Yeats & W. T. Horton: The Record of an Occult Friendship. George M. Harper. 224p. text ed. 23.25x (ISBN 0-391-01907-4). Humanities.

W. B. Yeats, Manuscripts & Printed Books, Exhibited in the Library of Trinity College, Dublin. R. O. Dougan. 50p. 1980. Repr. of 1956 ed. lib. bdg. 10.00 (ISBN 0-8492-4216-9). R West.

W. D. Snodgrass. Paul L. Gaston. (United States Authors Ser.: No. 316). 1978. lib. bdg. 12.50 (ISBN 0-8057-7242-1). Twayne.

W. E. B. Du Bois: A Bibliography of His Published Writings. rev. ed. Paul G. Partington. LC 79-17920. 1979. lib. bdg. 15.00 (ISBN 0-9602538-1-5). P G Partington.

W. E. B. DuBois: Negro Leader in a Time of Crisis. Francis L. Broderick. 1959. 10.00x (ISBN 0-8047-0558-5); pap. 2.95 o.p. (ISBN 0-8047-0559-3). Stanford U Pr.

W. E. B. DuBois Reader. Ed. by Andrew G. Paschal. LC 70-150672. 1971. 8.95 o.s.i. (ISBN 0-02-595100-9). Macmillan.

W. E. B. DuBois Reader. Andrew G. Paschall. 1971. pap. 2.45 o.s.i. (ISBN 0-02-035950-0, Collier). Macmillan.

W. Eugene Smith: His Photographs & Notes. LC 70-99254. (Illus.). 22.50 (ISBN 0-912334-09-6); pap. 14.95 (ISBN 0-912334-08-8). Aperture.

W. Eugene Smith: Master of the Photographic Essay. Commentary by William S. Johnson. LC 80-68723. (Illus.). 1981. 35.00 (ISBN 0-89381-070-3). Aperture.

W. H. Auden. James P. Brophy. LC 70-126545. (Columbia Essays in Modern Writers Ser.: No. 54). (Orig.). 1970. pap. 2.00 (ISBN 0-231-03265-X, MW54). Columbia U Pr.

W. H. Auden. George T. Wright. LC 68-24302. (U. S. Authors Ser.: No. 144). 1969. lib. bdg. 10.95 (ISBN 0-8057-0028-5). Twayne.

W. H. Auden: Nineteen Hundred Seven to Nineteen Hundred Seventy-Three. Edward Mendelson. (Illus.). 64p. 1980. 11.00 (ISBN 0-87104-264-9). NY Pub Lib.

W. H. Davies: A Critical Biography. Richard J. Stonesifer. 1965. 17.50x (ISBN 0-8195-3056-5, Pub. by Wesleyan U Pr). Columbia U Pr.

W. H. R. Rivers. Richard Slobodin. LC 78-6393. (Leaders of Modern Anthropology Ser.). (Illus.). 1978. 22.50x (ISBN 0-231-03582-9). Columbia U Pr.

(W) Hole of the Doughnut. S. Y. Kuroda. (Studies in Generative Linguistic Analysis: No. 1). 258p. 1980. text ed. 62.25x (ISBN 90-6439-161-0). Humanities.

W-O-T Position or Self-Actualization for Women. Mae A. Junod. 280p. 12.95 (ISBN 0-938968-00-9). Impact MI.

W. P. A. Historical Records Survey: A Guide to the Unpublished Inventories, Indexes, & Transcripts. Compiled by Loretta L. Hefner. LC 80-51489. 1980. pap. text ed. 6.00 (ISBN 0-931828-25-2). Soc Am Archivists.

W. R. Matthews: Philosopher & Theologian. H. P. Owen. 80p. 1976. pap. text ed. 7.00x (ISBN 0-485-12027-5, Athlone Pr). Humanities.

W. S. Gilbert. Max K. Sutton. (English Authors Ser.: No. 178). 1975. lib. bdg. 10.95 (ISBN 0-8057-1217-8). Twayne.

W. S. Gilbert: An Anniversary Survey & Exhibition Checklist. Reginald Allen. (Illus.). 1963. 5.50x o.p. (ISBN 0-8139-0002-6, Bibliographical Soc., U of Va). U Pr of Va.

W. S. Gilbert, His Life & Letters. Sidney Dark & Rowland Grey. LC 71-164210. 1971. Repr. of 1923 ed. 18.00 (ISBN 0-8103-3789-4). Gale.

W. S. Merwin. Cheri Davis. (United States Authors Ser.: No. 360). 1981. lib. bdg. 11.95 (ISBN 0-8057-7301-0). Twayne.

W. Somerset Maugham & His World. Frederick Raphael. LC 76-19742. (Encore Edition). (Illus.). 1977. 3.95 (ISBN 0-684-16552-X, ScribT). Scribner.

Wacky World of Skiing. Craig Peterson. (Illus.). 128p. 1980. 9.95 (ISBN 0-913276-31-6). Stone Wall Pr.

Wad of Poems. Gopal Honnalgere. (Redbird Ser.). 1975. 6.75 (ISBN 0-88253-670-2); pap. text ed. 4.00 (ISBN 0-88253-669-9). Ind-US Inc.

Wade & Phillips Constitutional & Administrative Law. 9th ed. Ed. by A. W. Bradley & E. C. S. Wade. LC 77-5941. 1978. text ed. 34.00x (ISBN 0-582-48826-5); pap. text ed. 19.95x (ISBN 0-582-48827-3). Longman.

Wadsworth Anaerobic Bacteriology Manual. Vera Sutter et al. LC 79-29670. (Illus.). 1980. pap. text ed. 9.50 (ISBN 0-8016-4848-3). Mosby.

Wadsworth & the Human Heart. John Beer. 1979. 20.00x (ISBN 0-231-04646-4). Columbia U Pr.

Wadsworth English Workbook. Hans P. Guth. 160p. 1980. pap. text ed. 5.95x (ISBN 0-534-00848-8). Wadsworth Pub.

Waffen-SS in Russia. Bruce Quarrie. (World War Two Photo Album: No. 3). (Illus.). 96p. 1981. pap. 5.95 (ISBN 0-89404-043-X). Aztex.

Wage & Hour Handbook for Hotels, Restaurants, & Institutions. Arch Stokes. LC 78-9278. 1978. 14.95 (ISBN 0-8436-2133-8). CBI Pub.

Wage Bargain & the Labor Market. H. M. Douty. 160p. 1980. 12.00 (ISBN 0-8018-2393-5); pap. 4.95 (ISBN 0-8018-2394-3). Johns Hopkins.

Wage Control & Inflation in the Soviet Bloc Countries. Ed. by Jan Adam. 266p. 1980. 22.95 (ISBN 0-03-057007-7). Praeger.

Wage Controls in Canada, 1975-78. A. Maslove & G. Swimmer. 182p. 1980. pap. text ed. 11.95x (ISBN 0-920380-50-6, Pub. by Inst Res Pub Canada). Renouf.

Wage Determination in Asia & the Pacific: The Views of Employers' Organisations-Reports & Documents Submitted to an ILO-DANIDA Regional Seminar (Singapore, October 8-12, 1979) International Labour Office. (Labour-Management Relations Ser.: No. 58). ii, 169p. (Orig.). 1980. pap. 11.40 (ISBN 92-2-102492-X). Intl Labour Office.

Wage Differentials & Economic Growth. Pasquale M. Sgro. 147p. 1980. 28.50x (ISBN 0-389-20002-6). B&N.

Wage-Earning Women: Industrial Work & Family Life in the U. S., 1900-1930. Leslie Tentler. 1979. 16.95x (ISBN 0-19-502627-6). Oxford U Pr.

Wage Formation & the Economy. Gosta Edgren et al. Tr. by Margareta Eklof. (Illus.). 1973. text ed. 32.50x (ISBN 0-04-330232-7). Allen Unwin.

Wage Increases & Labour Productivity in Japanese Smaller Business. 34p. 1972. 2.75 (APO11, APO). Unipub.

Wage, Labour & Capital. Karl Marx. 1978. pap. 1.25 (ISBN 0-8351-0547-4). China Bks.

Wage Patterns & Wage Policy in Modern China, 1919-1972. Christopher Howe. (Studies in Chinese History, Literature & Institutions). (Illus.). 180p. 1973. 39.95 (ISBN 0-521-20199-3). Cambridge U Pr.

Wage Policy in the British Coalmining Industry. L. J. Handy. LC 80-40229. (Department of Applied Economics Monograph: No. 27). 312p. Date not set. price not set (ISBN 0-521-23535-9). Cambridge U Pr.

Wage-Price Guideposts. John Sheahan. (Studies in Wage-Price Policy). 1967. 11.95 (ISBN 0-8157-7842-2); pap. 4.95 (ISBN 0-8157-7841-4). Brookings.

Wage Survey of Foreign Capital Affiliated Enterprises in Japan. 1978. 160.00 (ISBN 0-686-19035-1). A M Newman.

Wage War on Silence. Vassar Miller. LC 63-17793. (Wesleyan Poetry Program: Vol. 8). (Orig.). 1963. 10.00x (ISBN 0-8195-2008-X, Pub. by Wesleyan U Pr); pap. 2.45 o.p. (ISBN 0-8195-1008-4). Columbia U Pr.

Wagered Weekend. Jayne Castle. (Candlelight Romance Ser.). (Orig.). Date not set. pap. 1.50 (ISBN 0-440-19413-X). Dell.

Wages & Earnings. Andrew Dean. (Reviews of United Kingdom Statistical Sources Ser.: Vol. XIII). 1980. 45.00 (ISBN 0-08-024060-7). Pergamon.

Wages & Earnings of the Working Class. Leone Levi. 151p. 1971. Repr. of 1885 ed. 23.00x (ISBN 0-686-28331-7, Pub. by Irish Academic Pr). Biblio Dist.

Wages of Expectation: A Biography of Edward Dahlberg. Charles L. DeFanti, Jr. LC 77-94390. (Gotham Library). 1978. 15.00x (ISBN 0-8147-1763-2); pap. 7.00x (ISBN 0-8147-1764-0). NYU Pr.

Wages of Sin. Gerald Haslam. Ed. by Kirk Robertson. (Illus.). 88p. (Orig.). 1980. pap. 4.00 (ISBN 0-916918-11-4). Duck Down.

Wages of War, Eighteen Sixteen to Nineteen Sixty-Five. J. David Singer & Melvin Small. 1974. codebk 8.00 (ISBN 0-89138-068-X). ICPSR.

Wages, Price & Profit. Karl Marx. 1965. pap. 1.25 (ISBN 0-8351-0422-2). China Bks.

Waging Peace: The Swiss Experience. William B. Lloyd, Jr. LC 80-15577. (Illus.). xii, 101p. 1980. Repr. of 1958 ed. lib. bdg. 16.75x (ISBN 0-313-22506-0, LLWP). Greenwood.

Wagner: A Bibliography, 2 vols. C. Von Westernhagen. LC 77-88680. (Illus.). 1979. Vol. 1 (1813-64) 27.50 (ISBN 0-521-21930-2); Vol. 2 (1864-83) 27.50 (ISBN 0-521-21932-9); 49.50 set (ISBN 0-521-08774-0). Cambridge U Pr.

Wagner Companion. Ed. by Peter Burbidge & Richard Sutton. LC 79-50099. 1979. 39.50 (ISBN 0-521-22787-9); pap. 9.95 (ISBN 0-521-29657-9). Cambridge U Pr.

Wagner Companion. Raymond Mander & Joe Mitchenson. LC 78-52877. (Illus.). 1978. 12.95 o.p. (ISBN 0-8015-8356-X). Dutton.

Wagner Report: Readings for Teachers & Parents. Hilmar Wagner. 1976. pap. text ed. 7.00x (ISBN 0-8191-0032-3). U Pr of Amer.

Wagon Roads West: A Study of Federal Road Surveys and Construction in the Trans-Mississippi West, 1846-1869. W. Turrentine Jackson. LC 79-13959. (Illus.). 1979. 19.95x (ISBN 0-8032-4405-3); pap. 6.50 (ISBN 0-8032-9402-6, BB 712, Bison). U of Nebr Pr.

Wagon Train Nineteen Fifty-Eight. Joy Cowgill. (Illus.). 78p. 1980. pap. 12.95 (ISBN 0-916552-21-7). Acoma Bks.

Wagons & Rails. Jane V. Barker & Sybil Downing. (Colorado Heritage Ser.: Bk. 9). (Illus.). 44p. (gr. 3-4). 1980. pap. 3.00x (ISBN 0-87108-225-X). Pruett.

Wags to Witches: More Jokes, Riddles, & Puns. Victoria Gomez. LC 80-17405. (Illus.). 64p. (gr. 2-6). 1981. 6.95 (ISBN 0-688-41954-2); PLB 6.67 (ISBN 0-688-51954-7). Morrow.

Wah-To-Yah and the Taos Trail. Lewis H. Garrard. (Western Frontier Library: No. 5). 1966. 6.95 (ISBN 0-8061-0322-1); pap. 7.95 (ISBN 0-8061-1016-3). U of Okla Pr.

Wahington, D. C. Review of Art. Leslie J. Krantz. LC 79-56026. (Illus.). 124p. 1980. pap. 8.95 (ISBN 0-8149-0832-2). Vanguard.

Wahrheit Ist eine Nachbarschaft, Die Nichts Trennt. Francis Schwanauer. 196p. (Ger.). 1980. pap. text ed. 9.50 (ISBN 0-8191-0995-9). U Pr of Amer.

Waikiki Nurse. Laura C. Raef. 192p. (YA) 1976. 4.95 o.p. (ISBN 0-685-62027-1, Avalon). Bouregy.

Waikna, or, Adventures on the Mosquito Shore. Samuel A. Bard, pseud. Ed. by Daniel E. Alleger. LC 65-28697. (Latin American Gateway Ser.). (Illus.). 1965. Repr. of 1855 ed. 9.00 (ISBN 0-8130-0217-6). U Presses Fla.

Wait-for-Me Kitten. Patricia Scarry. (Illus.). (ps-2). 1962. PLB 4.57 o.p. (ISBN 0-307-60643-0, Golden Pr). Western Pub.

Wait for Me, Watch for Me, Eula Bee. Patricia Beatty. (gr. 7-9). 1978. 8.95 (ISBN 0-688-22151-3); PLB 8.59 (ISBN 0-688-32151-8). Morrow.

Wait for What Will Come. Barbara Michaels. LC 78-18319. 1978. 8.95 o.p. (ISBN 0-396-07577-0). Dodd.

Wait Until Tomorrow. Harriet M. Savitz. (Orig.). 1981. pap. 1.75 (ISBN 0-451-09780-7, E9780, Sig). NAL.

Wait Without Hope. Krishna N. Sinha. (Greenbird Bk.). 1976. flexible bdg. 6.75 (ISBN 0-89253-149-5); flexible bdg. 6.50 (ISBN 0-685-69684-7). Ind-US Inc.

Wait Without Idols. Gabriel Vahanian. LC 64-11429. 1964. 6.95 o.s.i. (ISBN 0-8076-0255-8); pap. 2.95 o.s.i. (ISBN 0-8076-0374-0). Braziller.

Waiter & Waitress Training Manual. Sondra Dahmer & Kurt Kahl. LC 73-83574. 1974. pap. 7.95 (ISBN 0-8436-0575-8). CBI Pub.

Waiter-Waitress. Ser-Vo-Tel Institute. (Foodservice Career Education Ser.). 1974. pap. text ed. 4.95 (ISBN 0-8436-2022-6). CBI Pub.

Waiters on the Dance. Julian J. Savarin. LC 78-2997. 1978. 8.95 o.p. (ISBN 0-312-85416-1). St Martin.

Waiting. Mary Napier. 240p. (Orig.). 1980. pap. 2.25 (ISBN 0-553-13477-9). Bantam.

Waiting Father. Helmot Thielicke. LC 75-12284. (Jubilee Bks.). 192p. 1975. pap. 1.95 (ISBN 0-06-068011-3, HJ-3, HarpR). Har-Row.

Waiting for a "Pearl Harbor" Japan Debates Defense. Tetsuya Kataoka. (Publication Ser.: No. 232). 90p. (Orig.). 1981. pap. 7.95 (ISBN 0-8179-7322-2). Hoover Inst Pr.

Waiting for Godot. Samuel Beckett. Tr. by Samuel Beckett from Fr. 1954. pap. 2.95 (ISBN 0-394-17204-3, E33, Ever). Grove.

Waiting for Johnny Miracle. Alice Bach. LC 79-2813. 256p. (YA) (gr. 7-12). 1980. 8.95 (ISBN 0-06-020348-X, HarpJ); PLB 8.79 (ISBN 0-06-020349-8). Har-Row.

Waiting for Me Waiting for the Train Hilda Dearwater. Jack Libert. (Illus.). 1972. pap. 2.00 (ISBN 0-911732-59-4). Irego.

Waiting for My Life, Poems. Linda Paston. 1981. 14.95 (ISBN 0-393-01441-X); pap. 4.95 (ISBN 0-393-00049-4). Norton.

Waiting for Thursday. Hamilton Jobson. LC 77-10284. 1978. 7.95 o.p. (ISBN 0-312-85426-9). St Martin.

Waiting for Willa. Dorothy Eden. 1977. pap. 1.95 (ISBN 0-449-23187-9, Crest). Fawcett.

Waiting Land: A Spell in Nepal. Dervla Murphy. (Illus.). 1969. 8.95 (ISBN 0-7195-1745-1). Transatlantic.

Waiting on God. Andrew Murray. 160p. 1981. pap. 2.50 (ISBN 0-88368-101-3). Whitaker Hse.

Waiting with Abstain. Alistair Sampson. (Illus.). 172p. 1978. 9.95 (ISBN 0-916838-14-5). Schiffer.

Waiting Years. Fumiko Enchi. Tr. by John Bester from Jap. LC 72-15864. 203p. 1980. pap. 4.95 (ISBN 0-87011-424-7). Kodansha.

Wake up, It's a Crash: A Survivor's Account. Earl Moorhouse. (Illus.). 184p. 1981. 17.95 (ISBN 0-7153-8093-1). David & Charles.

Wake up It's Night. Reiget. (ps-3). pap. 1.25 (ISBN 0-590-05404-X, Schol Pap). Schol Bk Serv.

Wakefield's Passion. Catherine Linden. 208p. 1981. pap. 2.25 (ISBN 0-380-77626-X). Avon.

Waking Brain. 2nd ed. Horace W. Magoun. (A Salmon Lecture Ser). (Illus.). 196p. 1969. 111.75 (ISBN 0-398-01201-6). C C Thomas.

Waldara Answers: Lecture Questions, Bk. 2. 1975. pap. 1.95 (ISBN 0-934258-09-0). W A Reilly.

Walden. Henry D. Thoreau. (Literature Ser). (gr. 7-12). 1969. pap. text ed. 3.67 (ISBN 0-87720-719-4). AMSCO Sch.

Walden, 2vols. Henry D. Thoreau. Ed. by F. B. Sanborn. LC 80-2685. 1981. Repr. of 1909 ed. 58.50 (ISBN 0-404-19080-4). AMS Pr.

Walden. Henry David Thoreau. pap. 2.95 (ISBN 0-385-09503-1, C10, Anch). Doubleday.

Walden & Civil Disobedience. Henry D. Thoreau. Ed. by Owen Thomas. (Critical Editions). (Annotated). (gr. 9-12). 1966. pap. text ed. 4.95x (ISBN 0-393-09665-3, Nortonc). Norton.

Walden & Civil Disobedience. Henry D. Thoreau. 1973. pap. 1.75 (ISBN 0-451-51339-8, CE1339, Sig Classics). NAL.

Walden & Other Writings. Henry D. Thoreau. pap. 1.75. Bantam.

Walden: Selected Essays. Henry D. Thoreau. Ed. by George F. Whicher. 1973. pap. 3.45 (ISBN 0-87532-109-7). Hendricks House.

Walden with Reader's Guide. Henry D. Thoreau. (Literature Program Ser.). (Orig.). (gr. 7-12). 1973. pap. text ed. 4.33 (ISBN 0-87720-818-2); tchr's ed. s.p. 2.80 (ISBN 0-87720-918-9). AMSCO Sch.

Waldorf Education for Adolescence. Rudolf Steiner. 1980. pap. 9.50x (ISBN 0-906492-37-8, Pub. by Kolisko Archives). St George Bk Serv.

Waldorf; or, the Dangers of Philosophy: A Philosophical Tale, 2 vols. Sophia King. Ed. by Gina Luria. (Feminist Controversy in England, 1788-1810 Ser.). 1974. Set. lib. bdg. 76.00 (ISBN 0-8240-0871-5); lib. bdg. 50.00 ea. Garland Pub.

Waldorf: The Story Behind America's Grandest Hotel. Ward Morehouse, III. (Illus.). 320p. 1981. 11.95 (ISBN 0-399-12541-8). Putnam.

Waldstein Woolen Mill. Herman Freudenberger. (Kress Library of Business & Economics: No. 18). (Illus.). 1963. pap. 5.00x (ISBN 0-678-09912-X, Baker Lib). Kelley.

Wales: A New Study. Ed. by David Thomas. 1977. 32.00 (ISBN 0-7153-7302-1). David & Charles.

Wales: A Study from the Air. Michael Williams. 1975. pap. text ed. 6.95x o.p. (ISBN 0-435-34921-X). Heinemann Ed.

Wales: Going Places. Wales Tourist Board. (Illus.). 72p. 1980. pap. write for info. (ISBN 0-900784-76-8, Pub. by Auto Assn-British Tourist Authority England). Merrimack Bk Serv.

Wales in History: The Adventurers, 1485-1760, 3 vols, Bk. 3. D. Fraser. 1976. 12.50 (ISBN 0-7083-0610-1). Verry.

Wales: South & West. John B. Hilling. 1976. 17.95 (ISBN 0-7134-3057-5, Pub. by Batsford England). David & Charles.

Wales: Where to Stay. rev. ed. Wales Tourist Board. (Illus.). 380p. 1981. pap. price not set (ISBN 0-900784-79-2, Pub. by Auto Assn-British Tourist Authority England). Merrimack Bk Serv.

Walk, Conversation, & Character of Christ. Alexander Whyte. (Religious Heritage Reprint Library). 339p. 1975. Repr. of 1905 ed. 7.95 o.p. (ISBN 0-8010-9568-9). Baker Bk.

Walk Easy on the Earth. James Kavanaugh. (Illus.). 1979. 8.95 (ISBN 0-525-93078-7). Dutton.

Walk Home from the Ice-House. Vern Rutsala. LC 80-70566. (Poetry Ser.). 1980. 9.95 (ISBN 0-915604-47-7); pap. 4.95 (ISBN 0-915604-48-5). Carnegie-Mellon.

Walk in Space: The Story of Project Gemini. Gene Gurney. (gr. 5 up). 1967. PLB 5.99 (ISBN 0-394-90417-6, BYR). Random.

Walk in the Snow. Phyllis S. Busch. (Illus.). 40p. (gr. k-3). 1971. 8.95 (ISBN 0-397-31233-4). Lippincott.

Walk in the Spirit: Seeking & Understanding the Baptism in the Holy Spirit. Michael Harper. LC 78-135047. 98p. 1968. pap. 2.50 o.p. (ISBN 0-912106-70-0). Logos.

Walk in the World of the Strong. Robert L. Rothstein. 378p. 1980. pap. 8.50x (ISBN 0-231-04339-2). Columbia U Pr.

Walk on the Supply Side: Economic Policies for the Eighties & Beyond. Bruce R. Bartlett. 256p. 1981. 14.95 (ISBN 0-87000-505-7). Arlington Hse.

Walk on the West Side: California on the Brink. Herbert Gold. LC 80-70216. 208p. 1981. 10.95 (ISBN 0-87795-305-8); pap. 4.95 (ISBN 0-87795-322-8). Arbor Hse.

Walk Out with Me. Jack McDuffie. 1979. 1.80 (ISBN 0-686-28798-3). Forward Movement.

Walk, Run, or Retreat: The Modern School Administrator. Neil V. Sullivan et al. LC 71-135013. 192p. 1971. 8.95x (ISBN 0-253-36305-5). Ind U Pr.

Walk Softly on the Green. Jack Cole. LC 80-52463. 288p. 1981. 8.95 (ISBN 0-938556-00-2). Taugus Hse.

Walk Straight Through the Square: Walking Tours of Europe's Most Picturesque Cities. Juliann V. Skurdenis & Lawrence J. Smircich. LC 76-3516. (Illus.). 1976. 8.95 o.p. (ISBN 0-679-50572-5); pap. 5.95 o.p. (ISBN 0-679-50628-4). McKay.

Walk the World Proudly. Helen Lowrie Marshall. LC 69-15210. 1969. 2.95 o.p. (ISBN 0-385-08253-3). Doubleday.

Walk Through Leicester. Watts. 1967. Repr. of 1804 ed. text ed. 5.00x (ISBN 0-7185-1073-9, Leicester). Humanities.

Walk Through the Shire: Wherin We Discover Some Rare Drawings of Hobbit Life. Michael Green. (Illus., Orig.). 1980. lib. bdg. 12.90 (ISBN 0-89471-114-8); pap. 4.95 (ISBN 0-89471-115-6). Running Pr.

Walk Through the Year. Edwin W. Teale. LC 78-9786. (Illus.). 1978. 15.00 (ISBN 0-396-07621-1). Dodd.

Walk to the End of the World. Suzy M. Charnas. Date not set. pap. 2.50 (ISBN 0-345-27946-8). Ballantine.

Walk Together Children. Ashley Bryan. (gr. 2 up). pap. 2.95 (ISBN 0-689-70485-2, A-112, Aladdin). Atheneum.

Walk Toward Peace. Johanna Schaefer. 1977. 4.50 o.p. (ISBN 0-682-48798-8). Exposition.

Walk with Christ Through the Resurrection. Dawson McAllister. (Discussion Manual Ser.). 150p. 1981. pap. 7.95 (ISBN 0-8024-9192-8). Moody.

Walk with Christ to the Cross. Dawson McAllister. (Discussion Manual Ser.). 150p. 1981. pap. 7.95 (ISBN 0-8024-9193-6). Moody.

Walk with Your Eyes. Marcia Brown. (Marcia Brown Concept Library). (Illus.). (gr. 1-4). 1979. 4.95 (ISBN 0-531-02385-0); PLB 7.90 s&l (ISBN 0-531-02925-5). Watts.

Walkabout Long Canoe. Dennis Steley. LC 78-59309. (Destiny Ser.). 1979. pap. 4.95 (ISBN 0-8163-0248-0). Pacific Pr Pub Assn.

Walker Evans & Robert Frank: A Study of Experience. Ed. by Tod Papageorge. (Illus.). 72p. 1981. pap. write for info. (ISBN 0-89467-015-8). Yale Art Gallery.

Walker Washington Guide. rev. ed. John Walker & Katharine Walker. LC 75-4256. Orig. Title: Washington Guidebook. (Illus.). 288p. (Orig.). 1981. pap. 4.95 (ISBN 0-915472-02-3). Guide Pr.

Walker's Handbook. Hugh D. Westacott. (Illus., Orig.). 1979. pap. 5.95 (ISBN 0-14-046267-8). Penguin.

Walker's Manual of Western Corporations: 72nd Annual Edition, 2 vols. Walker's Manual Inc. LC 10-19951. 1650p. 1981. Set. 182.00 (ISBN 0-916234-05-3). Walkers Manual.

Walkie-Talkie Patrol. Norman Borisoff. LC 72-75122. (Mystery & Adventure Ser.). (gr. 2-4). 1973. PLB 6.75 (ISBN 0-87191-097-7). Creative Ed.

Walking! John T. Davis. 1979. 12.95 o.p. (ISBN 0-8362-2403-5); pap. 5.95 o.p. (ISBN 0-8362-2404-3). Andrews & McMeel.

Walking Book. Gerald Donaldson. LC 78-14161. (Illus.). 1979. 8.95 o.p. (ISBN 0-03-049361-7); pap. 5.95 o.p. (ISBN 0-03-049356-0). HR&W.

Walking Dead. Peter Dickinson. LC 77-5299. 1978. 6.95 o.p. (ISBN 0-394-42010-1). Pantheon.

Walking Down the Stairs. Galway Kinnell. Ed. by Donald Hall. LC 77-23752. (Poets on Poetry Ser.). pap. 5.95 (ISBN 0-472-52530-1). U of Mich Pr.

Walking Home Dead. Stephen Dunning. (Poetry Ser.: No. 12). 40p. (Orig.). 1981. pap. 4.50 (ISBN 0-930020-11-1). Stone Country.

Walking in the Countryside. David Sharp. LC 77-85013. 1978. 14.95 (ISBN 0-7153-7495-8). David & Charles.

Walking into Time. William Monaghan & Louise Louis. (Illus.). 1971. Repr. of 1969 ed. text ed. 3.98. Pen-Art.

Walking Old Railways. Christopher Somerville. LC 78-74078. 1979. 14.95 (ISBN 0-7153-7681-0). David & Charles.

Walking on the Wings of the Wind. Rembert Weakland. 144p. (Orig.). 1980. pap. 2.95 (ISBN 0-8091-2334-7). Paulist Pr.

Walking on Water. Madeleine L'Engle. LC 80-21066. (Wheaton Liteary Ser.). 200p. 1980. text ed. 7.95 (ISBN 0-87788-918-X). Shaw Pubs.

Walking Out. Ann Elwood & John Raht. Ed. by Mark Becker. 176p. (gr. 7 up). 1979. pap. 1.50 (ISBN 0-448-17080-9, Tempo). G&D.

Walking Shoes. Anne Rockwell. LC 79-7696. (Reading on My Own Ser.). (Illus.). (ps-3). 1980. 4.95a (ISBN 0-385-14730-9); PLB (ISBN 0-385-14731-7). Doubleday.

Walking Through Scotland. David MacInnes & Kathleen MacInnes. LC 80-68895. (Illus.). 192p. 1981. 19.95 (ISBN 0-7153-8090-7). David & Charles.

Walking Through the Fire: A Hospital Journal. Laurel Lee. 1977. 6.95 o.p. (ISBN 0-525-22955-8). Dutton.

Walking to Where the River Ends. Wang Fang-Yu et al. (Illus.). 96p. 1980. pap. 12.50x (ISBN 0-208-01882-4, Archon). Shoe String.

Walking with God. W. Phillip Keller. 1980. 7.95 (ISBN 0-8007-1140-8). Revell.

Walks in the Catskills. John Bennet & Seth Masia. LC 74-81304. (Illus.). 204p. 1974. lib. bdg. 10.25 o.p. (ISBN 0-914788-00-0); pap. 6.95 (ISBN 0-914788-00-0). East Woods.

Walks in the Great Smokies. Rod Albright & Priscilla Albright. LC 79-4898. (Illus.). 192p. 1979. lib. bdg. 10.25 o.p. (ISBN 0-914788-14-0). East Woods.

Walks of Jesus. Bessie Lewis. 1976. 1.25 o.p. (ISBN 0-8042-3598-8). John Knox.

Walks, Walls & Fences. James E. Russell. Ed. by Shirley M. Horowitz & Marilyn M. Auer. (Illus., Orig.). 1981. pap. 6.95 (ISBN 0-932944-36-1). Creative Homeowner.

Walks with Nature in Rocky Mountain National Park. Donna Dannen & Kent Dannen. LC 80-26665. (Illus.). 64p. 1981. pap. 3.95 (ISBN 0-914788-38-8). East Woods.

Wall Around the World. Theodore Cogswell. 1973. pap. 1.25 (ISBN 0-515-03278-6, N3278). Jove Pubns.

Wall Coverings & Decoration. Abel Banov & Marie-Jeanne Lytle. LC 76-28710. (Illus.). 1976. 13.95 (ISBN 0-912336-24-2); pap. 6.95 (ISBN 0-912336-25-0). Structures Pub.

Wall: Intimacy. 3rd ed. Jean-Paul Sartre. Tr. by Lloyd Alexander. LC 73-88731. 1969. pap. 3.75 (ISBN 0-8112-0190-2, NDP272). New Directions.

Wall of Years. Andrew M. Stephenson. (Orig.). 1980. pap. 2.75 (ISBN 0-440-19431-8). Dell.

Wall Street & FDR. Antony C. Sutton. 1975. 7.95 o.p. (ISBN 0-87000-328-3). Arlington Hse.

Wall Street & the Bolshevik Revolution. Antony C. Sutton. 1974. 7.95 o.p. (ISBN 0-87000-276-7). Arlington Hse.

Wall Street Gospel. Joe Magliato. LC 80-84629. (Orig.). 1981. pap. 4.95 (ISBN 0-89081-279-9). Harvest Hse.

Wall Street in the American Novel. Wayne W. Westbrook. LC 79-47997. (Gotham Library Ser.). 224p. 1980. 20.00x (ISBN 0-8147-9194-8); pap. 8.00x (ISBN 0-8147-9195-6). NYU Pr.

Wall Street in Transition: The Emerging System & Its Impact on the Economy. Henry G. Manne et al. LC 74-15255. (Moskowitz Lectures). 206p. 1974. 10.00x (ISBN 0-8147-5369-8). NYU Pr.

Wall Street Journal Book of Wit. Ed. by Charles Preston. 160p. (Orig.). 1981. pap. 7.95 (ISBN 0-87094-227-1). Dow Jones-Irwin.

Wall Street Journal Cartoon Portfolio. Ed. by Charles Preston. LC 79-20777. (Illus.). 1979. 12.95 o.p. (ISBN 0-87128-584-3, Pub. by Dow Jones); pap. 7.95 (ISBN 0-87128-581-9). Dow Jones-Irwin.

Wall Street Journal Views America Tomorrow. Ed. by Donald Moffitt. LC 76-52501. 1977. 11.95 (ISBN 0-8144-5438-0). Am Mgmt.

Wall Street Manual for Teenagers. C. M. Flumiani. (Illus.). 80p. (gr. 7-12). 1973. 19.75 (ISBN 0-913314-24-2). Am Classical Coll Pr.

Wall Street Manual for Teenagers. C. M. Flumiani. (Illus.). 99p. 1981. 13.75 (ISBN 0-89266-287-5). Am Classical Coll Pr.

Wallace & Bates in the Tropics: An Introduction to the Theory of Natural Selection. Ed. by Barbara G. Beddall. LC 69-12174. (Illus.). (gr. 7 up). 1969. 5.95g o.s.i. (ISBN 0-02-708680-1). Macmillan.

Wallace-Homestead Price Guide to American Country Antiques. Don Raycraft & Carol Raycraft. (Illus.). 1978. sofbound 8.95 o.p. (ISBN 0-87069-230-5). Wallace-Homestead.

Wallace-Homestead Price Guide to Antiques & Pattern Glass. 7th ed. Ed. by Robert W. Miller. (Illus.). 592p. 1980. pap. 10.95 (ISBN 0-87069-305-0). Wallace-Homestead.

Wallace-Homestead Price Guide to Oriental Antiques. Sandra Andancht et al. (Illus.). 308p. 1980. pap. 17.95 (ISBN 0-87069-295-X). Wallace-Homestead.

Wallace Stegner. Forrest G. Robinson & Margaret G. Robinson. (U.S. Authors Ser.: No. 282). 1977. lib. bdg. 10.95 (ISBN 0-8057-7182-4). Twayne.

Wallace Stevens. Lucy Beekett. 208p. 1974. 36.00 (ISBN 0-521-20278-7); pap. 10.50x (ISBN 0-521-29194-1). Cambridge U Pr.

Wallace Stevens. William Burney. (U. S. Authors Ser.: No. 127). 1968. lib. bdg. 10.95 (ISBN 0-8057-0696-8). Twayne.

Wallace Stevens: An Introduction to the Poetry. Susan B. Weston. LC 77-1594. (Twentieth Century American Poets Ser.). 1977. 15.00x (ISBN 0-231-03990-5). Columbia U Pr.

Wallace Stevens Checklist & Bibliography of Stevens Criticism. Samuel F. Morse et al. LC 63-21871. 98p. 1963. 7.95x (ISBN 0-8040-0316-5). Swallow.

Wallace Stevens: The Poems of Our Climate. Harold Bloom. 416p. 1980. pap. 8.95 (ISBN 0-8014-9185-1). Cornell U Pr.

Wallace-Vaughn Debate. G. K. Wallace & Ray Vaughn. 4.95 (ISBN 0-89315-350-8). Lambert Bk.

Wallaces of Iowa. Russell Lord. LC 76-167843. (FDR & the Era of the New Deal Ser.). (Illus.). 615p. 1972. Repr. of 1947 ed. lib. bdg. 49.50 (ISBN 0-306-70325-4). Da Capo.

Walled Garden of Truth. Tr. by David Pendlebury. 1976. pap. 2.95 o.p. (ISBN 0-525-47414-5). Dutton.

Walled Garden: The Saga of Jewish Family Life & Tradition. Chaim Bermant. (Illus.). 272p. 1975. 12.95 o.s.i. (ISBN 0-02-510100-5). Macmillan.

Walled-in: The True Story of a Cult. Robert Connor. 1979. pap. 2.25 o.p. (ISBN 0-451-08662-7, E8662, Sig). NAL.

Walleyes & Walleye Fishing. Joe Fellegy, Jr. LC 72-89440. (Illus.). 210p. 1973. 8.95 (ISBN 0-87518-054-X). Dillon.

Wallpaper. Brenda Greysmith. (Illus.). 1976. 12.95 o.s.i. (ISBN 0-02-545610-5). Macmillan.

Wallpaper Fox. Morris Philipson. 1978. pap. 1.95 (ISBN 0-515-04436-9). Jove Pubns.

Wallpaper in America: From the Seventeenth Century to World War I. Catherine Lynn. (Illus.). 1980. 45.00 (ISBN 0-393-01448-7, A Barra Foundation - Cooper-Hewitt Bk). Norton.

Walls & Ceilings. Ed. by Time-Life Bks. (Home Repair & Improvement Ser.). (Illus.). 128p. 1980. 10.95 (ISBN 0-8094-3450-4). Time-Life.

Walls Are to Be Walked. Nathan Zimelman. (gr. k-3). 1977. PLB 6.95 o.p. (ISBN 0-525-42175-0). Dutton.

Walls, Floors, Ceilings. Jackson Hand. LC 75-29778. (Popular Science Bk.). (Illus.). 384p. 1976. 9.95 o.p. (ISBN 0-06-011772-9, HarpT). Har-Row.

Wall's History of Three Color Photography. E. J. Wall. Date not set. 46.95 o.p. (ISBN 0-8038-8954-2). Hastings.

Wally the Whale Who Loved Balloons. Yuichi Watanabe. Tr. by Diane Ooka from Japanese. (Illus.). Date not set. 8.95 (ISBN 0-89346-150-4). Heian Intl. Postponed.

Walras's Economics. M. Morishima. LC 76-40833. 1977. 29.95 (ISBN 0-521-21487-4). Cambridge U Pr.

Walsh Colville; or, a Young Man's First Entrance into Life: A Novel. Anna Maria Porter. Ed. by Gina Luria. (Feminist Controversy in England, 1788-1810 Ser.). 1974. lib. bdg. 50.00 (ISBN 0-8240-0876-6). Garland Pub.

Walsingham; or, the Pupil of Nature: A Domestic Story, 4 vols. Mary Robinson. Ed. by Gina Luria. (Feminist Controversy in England, 1788-1810 Ser.). 1974. Set. lib. bdg. 152.00 (ISBN 0-8240-0878-2); lib. bdg. 50.00 ea. Garland Pub.

Walt & Pepper. Lisl Weil. LC 73-22183. (Illus.). 40p. (ps-3). 1974. 5.95 o.s.i. (ISBN 0-8193-0758-0, Four Winds). Schol Bk Serv.

Walt Disney. Norita Larson. LC 74-14925. 40p. (gr. 4-8). 1975. PLB 5.75 o.p. (ISBN 0-87191-407-7). Creative Ed.

Walt Disney Character Tubby Book. Illus. by Walt Disney Productions. (Tubby Bks.). (Illus.). 10p. (ps). 1980. vinyl book 2.95 (ISBN 0-671-41334-1, Pub. by Windmill). S&S.

Walt Disney Productions Presents Goofy's Gags. Walt Disney Productions. LC 74-2043. (Disney's Wonderful World of Reading Ser: No. 19). (Illus.). 48p. (ps-3). 1974. 3.95 (ISBN 0-394-82558-6, BYR); PLB 4.99 (ISBN 0-394-92558-0). Random.

Walt Disney Productions Presents "the Rescuers". Walt Disney Productions. LC 76-54412. (Disney's Wonderful World of Reading: No. 37). (Illus.). (ps-2). 1977. 3.95 (ISBN 0-394-83456-9, BYR); PLB 4.99 (ISBN 0-394-93456-3). Random.

Walt Disney Productions Presents The Haunted House. Walt Disney Productions. LC 75-16430. (Disney's Wonderful World of Reading Ser.: No. 33). (Illus.). 48p. (ps-3). 1976. 3.95 (ISBN 0-394-82570-5, BYR); PLB 4.99 (ISBN 0-394-92570-X). Random.

Walt Disney Productions Presents The Mystery of the Missing Peanuts. Walt Disney Productions. LC 75-1088. (Disney's Wonderful World of Reading Ser: No. 30). (Illus.). 48p. (gr. 1-2). 1975. 3.95 (ISBN 0-394-82572-1, BYR); PLB 4.99 (ISBN 0-394-92572-6). Random.

Walt Disney's Alice in Wonderland. Walt Disney Studio. (Illus.). 1951. 1.95 (ISBN 0-307-10426-5, Golden Pr); PLB 7.62 (ISBN 0-307-60426-8). Western Pub.

Walt Disney's Bambi. Walt Disney Studio. (Illus.). (gr. k-3). 1941. 1.95 (ISBN 0-307-10450-8, Golden Pr); PLB 7.62 (ISBN 0-307-60450-0). Western Pub.

Walt Disney's Christmas Parade. Walt Disney Studios. 1977. pap. 1.95 o.p. (ISBN 0-307-11191-1, Golden Pr). Western Pub.

Walt Disney's Cinderella. Walt Disney Productions. LC 74-22325. (Disney's Wonderful World of Reading Ser.: No. 16). (Illus.). 48p. (ps-3). 1974. 3.95 (ISBN 0-394-82552-7, BYR); PLB 4.99 (ISBN 0-394-92552-1). Random.

Walt Disney's Cinderella. Walt Disney Studio. (Illus.). (ps-2). 1950. PLB 5.00 (ISBN 0-307-60114-5, Golden Pr). Western Pub.

Walt Disney's Cinderella. (Illus.). (gr. k-3). 1950. 1.95 (ISBN 0-307-10425-7, Golden Pr); PLB 7.62 (ISBN 0-307-60425-X). Western Pub.

Walt Disney's Dumbo: On Land, on Sea, in the Air. Jerry Walters. (Disney's Wonderful World of Reading Ser.: No. 1). (Illus.). (ps-3). 1973. 3.95 (ISBN 0-394-82518-7, BYR); PLB 4.99 (ISBN 0-394-92518-1). Random.

Walt Disney's Gulliver Mickey. Walt Disney Productions. LC 74-23399. (Disney's Wonderful World of Reading Ser: No. 27). (Illus.). 48p. (gr. 1-2). 1975. 3.95 (ISBN 0-394-82561-6, BYR); PLB 4.99 (ISBN 0-394-92561-0). Random.

Walt Disney's Mary Poppins. Ed. by Anne Bedford. (Illus.). (ps-3). 1976. PLB 7.62 (ISBN 0-307-60850-6, Golden Pr). Western Pub.

Walt Disney's Mickey & His Friends. Illus. by Walt Disney Studios. (Kids Paperbacks). (Illus.). (ps-4). 1977. PLB 7.62 (ISBN 0-307-62364-5, Golden Pr); pap. 1.95 (ISBN 0-307-12364-2). Western Pub.

Walt Disney's Mickey Mouse & Donald Duck at the Circus. Walt Disney Productions. (Colorforms Bks.). (Illus.). (ps-2). 1973. 2.95 o.p. (ISBN 0-394-82656-6, BYR). Random.

Walt Disney's Mother Goose. Ed. by Al Dempster. (ps-1). 1952. PLB 5.00 (ISBN 0-307-60079-3, Golden Pr). Western Pub.

Walt Disney's Mother Goose. Illus. by Walt Disney Studio. (Illus.). (gr. k-2). 1970. 1.95 (ISBN 0-307-10878-3, Golden Pr); PLB 7.62 (ISBN 0-307-60878-6). Western Pub.

Walt Disney's Nursery Tales. Illus. by Walt Disley Studio. 1971. 4.95 (ISBN 0-307-12068-6, Golden Pr); PLB 9.15 o.p. (ISBN 0-307-62068-9). Western Pub.

Walt Disney's One Hundred One Dalmations. Walt Disney Productions. LC 74-10829. (Disney's Wonderful World of Reading: No. 23). (Illus.). 48p. (ps-3). 1975. 3.95 (ISBN 0-394-82571-3, BYR); PLB 4.99 (ISBN 0-394-92571-8). Random.

Walt Disney's Peter & the Wolf. Walt Disney Productions. LC 74-6423. (Disney's Wonderful World of Reading Ser.: No. 20). (Illus.). 48p. (ps-3). 1974. 3.95 (ISBN 0-394-82563-2, BYR); PLB 4.99 (ISBN 0-394-92563-7). Random.

Walt Disney's Peter & the Wolf. Walt Disney Studio. (Illus.). (gr. k-3). 1976. PLB 5.00 (ISBN 0-307-60056-4, Golden Pr). Western Pub.

Walt Disney's Peter Pan. (gr. 3-6). 1975. 1.95 (ISBN 0-307-10453-2, Golden Pr); PLB 7.62 (ISBN 0-307-60453-5). Western Pub.

Walt Disney's Peter Pan & Captain Hook. Mary Carey. (Disney's Wonderful World of Reading Ser.: No. 4). (Illus.). (ps-3). 1973. 3.95 (ISBN 0-394-82517-9, BYR); PLB 4.99 (ISBN 0-394-92517-3). Random.

Walt Disney's Peter Pan & Wendy. Annie N. Bedford. (Illus.). 24p. (gr. k-3). 1976. PLB 5.00 (ISBN 0-307-60110-2, Golden Pr). Western Pub.

Walt Disney's Pinocchio. Walt Disney Studio. (Illus.). (gr. k-3). 1953. 1.95 (ISBN 0-307-10580-6, Golden Pr); PLB 7.62 (ISBN 0-307-60580-9). Western Pub.

Walt Disney's Snow White & the Seven Dwarfs. Walt Disney Productions. (Disney's Wonderful World of Reading Ser.: No. 8). (Illus.). (ps-3). 1973. 3.95 (ISBN 0-394-82625-6, BYR); PLB 4.99 (ISBN 0-394-92625-0). Random.

Walt Disney's Snow White & the Seven Dwarfs. Walt Disney Studio. (Illus.). (gr. 1-4). 1952. 1.95 (ISBN 0-307-10451-6, Golden Pr); PLB 7.62 (ISBN 0-307-60451-9). Western Pub.

Walt Disney's Story Land. Walt Disney Studio. (Illus.). (gr. 1-5). 1962. 6.95 (ISBN 0-307-16547-7, Golden Pr); PLB 13.77 (ISBN 0-307-66547-X). Western Pub.

Walt Disney's Storybook Friends. (Illus.). 1976. 2.95 (ISBN 0-307-13767-8, Golden Pr); PLB 9.15 o.p. (ISBN 0-307-63767-0). Western Pub.

Walt Disney's Storytime Play Set, 6 bks. (ps). Date not set. pap. 5.50 boxed set (ISBN 0-307-13648-5, Golden Pr). Western Pub.

Walt Disney's the Brave Little Tailor. Walt Disney Productions. LC 74-1253. (Disney's Wonderful World of Reading Ser.: No. 18). (Illus.). 48p. (ps-3). 1974. 3.95 (ISBN 0-394-82559-4, BYR); PLB 4.99 (ISBN 0-394-92559-9). Random.

Walt Disney's the Jungle Book. Kipling. (Illus.). 128p. 1980. 9.95 (ISBN 0-517-54324-9, Harmony); pap. 5.95 (ISBN 0-517-54328-1, Harmony); 24-copy prepak 142.80 (ISBN 0-686-68778-7). Crown.

Walt Disney's the Penguin That Hated the Cold. Barbara Brenner. (Disney's Wonderful World of Reading Ser.: No. 7). (Illus.). (ps-3). 1973. 3.95 (ISBN 0-394-82628-0, BYR); PLB 4.99 (ISBN 0-394-92628-5). Random.

Walt Disney's the Three Little Pigs. Barbara Brenner. (Disney's Wonderful World of Reading Ser.: No. 6). (Illus.). (ps-3). 1974. 3.95 (ISBN 0-394-82522-5, BYR); PLB 4.99 (ISBN 0-394-92522-X). Random.

Walt Disney's Winnie-the-Pooh: A Tight Squeeze. A. A. Milne. (Illus.). (ps-3). 1962. 1.95 (ISBN 0-307-10859-7, Golden Pr); PLB 7.62 (ISBN 0-307-60859-X). Western Pub.

Walt Disney's Winnie-the-Pooh & Eeyore's Birthday. A. A. Milne. 1964. 1.95 (ISBN 0-307-10861-9, Golden Pr); PLB 7.62 (ISBN 0-307-60861-1). Western Pub.

Walt Disney's Winnie the Pooh & Tigger Too. Walt Disney Productions. LC 75-20349. (Disney's Wonderful World of Reading Ser: No. 35). (Illus.). 48p. (ps-3). 1976. 3.95 (ISBN 0-394-82569-1, BYR); PLB 4.99 (ISBN 0-394-92569-6). Random.

Walt Disney's Winnie-the-Pooh Meets Tigger. Walt Disney Studios. (Illus.). 1973. 1.95 (ISBN 0-307-10869-4, Golden Pr); PLB 7.62 (ISBN 0-307-60869-7). Western Pub.

Walt Disney's Winnie-the-Pooh's Blanket Book. Walt Disney. (Illus.). (ps). 1980. 5.95 (ISBN 0-525-69517-6, Gingerbread). Dutton.

Walt Frazier. Larry Batson. LC 74-2013. (Creative Superstars Ser.). 32p. 1974. PLB 5.95 (ISBN 0-87191-348-8); pap. 2.95 (ISBN 0-89812-179-5). Creative Ed.

Walt Kuhn: An Imaginary History of the West. Frwd. by Fred S. Bartlett. LC 64-+012. (Illus.). 52p. 1964. pap. 2.50 (ISBN 0-88360-008-0). Amon Carter.

Walt Whitman. James E. Miller, Jr. (U. S. Authors Ser.: No. 20). lib. bdg. 9.95 (ISBN 0-8057-0792-1). Twayne.

Walt Whitman. Bliss Perry. LC 80-25319. (American Men & Women of Letters Ser.). 346p. 1981. pap. 5.95 (ISBN 0-87754-151-5). Chelsea Hse.

Walt Whitman: A Life. Justin D. Kaplan. (Illus.). 1980. 15.00 (ISBN 0-671-22542-1). S&S.

Walt Whitman Among the French: Poet & Myth. Besty Erkkila. LC 79-3204. 1980. 16.50x (ISBN 0-691-06426-1). Princeton U Pr.

Walt Whitman & the Body Beautiful. Harold Aspiz. LC 79-28280. 288p. 1980. 19.95 (ISBN 0-252-00799-9). U of Ill Pr.

Walt Whitman & the Critics: A Checklist of Criticism, 1900-1978. Jeanetta Boswell. LC 80-20528. (Scarecrow Author Bibliographies Ser.: No. 51). 270p. 1980. 14.50 (ISBN 0-8108-1355-6). Scarecrow.

Walt Whitman & the Springs of Courage. Haniel Long. LC 38-27504. (National University Publications Literary Criticism Ser.). 1977. 7.50 (ISBN 0-8046-9190-8). Kennikat.

Walt Whitman: Leaves of Grass: A Textual Variorum of the Printed Poems, 1855-1892, 3 Vols. Walt Whitman. Ed. by Sculley Bradley et al. LC 78-65727. (Collected Writings of Walt Whitman Ser.). 944p. 1980. 125.00x set (ISBN 0-8147-1024-7); Vol. 1 (ISBN 0-8147-1014-X); Vol. 2 (ISBN 0-8147-1015-8); Vol. 3 (ISBN 0-8147-1016-6). NYU Pr.

Walt Whitman on Long Island. Bertha Funnell. LC 78-134275. (Empire State Historical Publications Ser). 1971. 8.50 (ISBN 0-8046-8091-4). Friedman.

Walt Whitman: The Critical Heritage. Ed. by Milton Hindus. 1971. 27.00x (ISBN 0-7100-7087-X). Routledge & Kegan.

Walt Whitman: The Measure of His Song. 1st ed. Bly et al. Ed. by Jim Perlman & Dan Campion. LC 80-85268. (Illus.). 288p. (Orig.). 1981. 13.95 (ISBN 0-930100-09-3); pap. 7.95 (ISBN 0-930100-08-5). Holy Cow.

Walt Whitman's Champion: William Douglas O'Connor. Jerome Loving. LC 77-89511. 248p. 1978. 13.50 (ISBN 0-89096-039-9). Tex A&M Univ Pr.

Walt Whitman's Poetry & the Evolution of Rhythmic Forms & Walt Whitman's Thought & Art. Pasquale Jannacone. Tr. by Peter Militineos. LC 72-90791. 1973. 19.00 o.s.i. (ISBN 0-910972-31-1). IHS-PDS.

Walt Whitman's Western Jaunt. Walter H. Eitner. LC 80-29336. (Illus.). 144p. 1981. text ed. 18.00 (ISBN 0-7006-0212-7). Regents Pr KS.

Walter Anderson's Illustrations of Epic & Voyage. Ed. by Redding S. Sugg, Jr. LC 80-12239. (Illus.). 160p. 1980. 18.95 (ISBN 0-8093-0973-4). S Ill U Pr.

Walter Bagehot. Harry R. Sullivan. LC 74-32309. (English Authors Ser.: No. 182). 1975. lib. bdg. 12.50 (ISBN 0-8057-1018-3). Twayne.

Walter Benjamin: Or Toward a Revolutionary Criticism. Terry Eagleton. 224p. 1981. 19.50 (ISBN 0-8052-7100-7, Pub. by NLB England); pap. 8.50 (ISBN 0-8052-7099-X). Schocken.

Walter Crane. Isobel Spencer. LC 75-18567. (Illus.). 208p. 1976. 25.00 o.s.i. (ISBN 0-02-612930-2). Macmillan.

Walter Cronkite. Nathan Aaseng. (Achievers Ser.). (Illus.). (gr. 4-9). 1981. PLB 5.95 (ISBN 0-8225-0486-3). Lerner Pubns.

Walter Cronkite. Norita Larson & Paula Taylor. LC 75-2103. (Creative Education Closeup Bks.). (Illus.). 32p. (gr. 3-6). 1975. PLB 5.75 o.p. (ISBN 0-87191-424-7). Creative Ed.

Walter Durbin: Texas Ranger & Sheriff. Robert W. Stephens. 8.95 (ISBN 0-685-48823-3). Nortex Pr.

Walter F. Isaacs: An Artist in America, Eighteen Eighty-Six to Nineteen Sixty-Four. Spencer Moseley & Gervais Reed. (Index of Art in the Pacific Northwest Ser: No. 8). (Illus.). Date not set. price not set o.p. (ISBN 0-295-95389-6); pap. price not set o.p. (ISBN 0-295-95396-9). U of Wash Pr. Postponed.

Walter Farley's Black Stallion Books, 4 bks. Walter Farley. Incl. Black Stallion. LC 41-21882; Black Stallion Returns. LC 45-8763; Black Stallion & Satan. LC 49-6117; Black Stallion Mystery. LC 57-7527. (gr. 4-9). 1979. Boxed Set. pap. 7.75 (ISBN 0-394-84176-X, BYR). Random.

Walter Farley's How to Stay Out of Trouble with Your Horse: Some Basic Safety Rules to Help You Enjoy Riding. Walter Farley. LC 79-8922. (Illus.). 80p. (gr. 4-8). 1981. 7.95a (ISBN 0-385-15480-1); lib. bdg. (ISBN 0-385-15481-X). Doubleday.

Walter Gibson's Big Book of Magic for All Ages. Walter B. Gibson. LC 80-496. (Illus.). 240p. 1980. 12.95 (ISBN 0-385-14808-9). Doubleday.

Walter Gropius. James M. Fitch. LC 60-13308. (Masters of World Architecture Ser). (Illus.). 1960. 7.95 o.s.i. (ISBN 0-8076-0130-6); pap. 3.95 o.s.i. (ISBN 0-8076-0228-0). Braziller.

Walter Hines Page: Ambassador to the Court of St. James's. Ross Gregory. LC 78-94067. (Illus.). 252p. 1970. 12.00x (ISBN 0-8131-1198-6). U Pr of Ky.

Walter Kerr: An Analysis of His Criticism. Roderick Bladel. LC 76-3721. 216p. 1976. 10.00 (ISBN 0-8108-0917-6). Scarecrow.

Walter Lippmann. Larry L. Adams. (World Leaders Ser.: No. 58). 1977. lib. bdg. 10.95 (ISBN 0-8057-7709-1). Twayne.

Walter Lippmann & the American Century. Ronald Steel. (Illus.). 640p. 1980. 19.95 (ISBN 0-316-81190-4). Little.

Walter Pater. Arthur C. Benson. LC 67-23876. (Library of Lives & Letters: British Writers Ser.). 1968. Repr. of 1906 ed. 15.00 (ISBN 0-8103-3054-7). Gale.

Walter Pater. Gerald Monsman. (English Authors Ser.: No. 207). 1977. lib. bdg. 10.95 (ISBN 0-8057-6676-6). Twayne.

Walter Pater: Humanist. Richmond Crinkley. LC 70-119811. 200p. 1970. 10.00x (ISBN 0-8131-1221-4). U Pr of Ky.

Walter Pater's Reading: A Bibliography of His Library Borrowings & Literary References, 1858 to 1873. Billie A. Inman. LC 78-68284. 390p. 1981. lib. bdg. 40.00 (ISBN 0-8240-9790-4). Garland Pub.

Walter Payton. Joe Soucheray. (Sports Superstars Ser.). (Illus.). (gr. 3-9). 1979. PLB 5.95 (ISBN 0-87191-722-X); pap. 2.95 (ISBN 0-89812-160-4). Creative Ed.

Walter Raleigh: Man of Two Worlds. Henrietta Buckmaster. (World Landmark Ser, No. 58). (Illus.). (gr. 5-8). 1964. PLB 4.39 o.p. (ISBN 0-394-90558-X, BYR). Random.

Walter Reuther: Labour's Rugged Individualist. Jean Gould & Hickok Lorena. LC 71-39225. 1972. 8.95 (ISBN 0-396-06409-4). Dodd.

Walter Scott. Robin Mayhead. LC 72-88622. (British Authors Ser.). 128p. 1973. 27.50 (ISBN 0-521-20115-2); pap. 7.95x (ISBN 0-521-09781-9). Cambridge U Pr.

Walter Scott & the Historical Imagination. David Brown. 1979. 26.00x (ISBN 0-7100-0301-3). Routledge & Kegan.

Walter, the Homing Pigeon. Nathaniel Benchley. LC 79-2696. (Illus.). 32p. (gr. 1-4). 1981. 7.95 (ISBN 0-06-020507-5, HarpJ); PLB 7.89g (ISBN 0-06-020508-3). Har-Row.

Walter Van Tilburg Clark. Max Westbrook. (U. S. Authors Ser.: No. 155). 1970. lib. bdg. 10.95 (ISBN 0-8057-0148-6). Twayne.

Walther Von der Vogelweide: Gedichte (Mittelhochdeutscher Text und Uebertragung) Walther Von Der Vogelweide. 291p. 1965. pap. 2.60x o.p. (ISBN 0-685-47486-0). Schoenhof.

Walton War & Tales of the Great Smoky Mts. Cal Carpenter. 4.95 (ISBN 0-932298-03-6). Green Hill.

Waltz Across Texas. Max Crawford. 1977. pap. 1.95 (ISBN 0-380-01856-X, 36533). Avon.

Waltz of Hearts, No. 139. Barbara Cartland. 160p. (Orig.). 1981. pap. 1.95 (ISBN 0-553-14586-X). Bantam.

Waltzes for Piano. Frederic Chopin. (Carl Fischer Music Library: No. 309). 80p. (gr. 9-12). 1902. pap. 3.00 (ISBN 0-686-64064-0, L 309). Fischer Inc NY.

Wampum. Anne Molloy. (Illus.). (gr. 3 up). 1977. 7.95 (ISBN 0-8038-8079-0). Hastings.

Wanda Hickey's Night of Golden Memories & Other Diasters. Jean Shepherd. LC 72-161317. (Illus.). 1971. 6.95 o.p. (ISBN 0-385-04870-X). Doubleday.

Wanderer. Alain-Fournier. Tr. by Lowell Bair. 1971. pap. 1.25 o.p. (ISBN 0-451-50538-7, CY538, Sig Classics). NAL.

Wanderer. Fritz Lieber. (Science Fiction Ser.). 1980. lib. bdg. 15.95 (ISBN 0-8398-2642-7). Gregg.

Wanderer: A Reissue with a New Introduction & Illustrations. Sterling Hayden. (Illus.). 1977. 10.95 (ISBN 0-393-07521-4). Norton.

Wanderer; or, Memoirs of Charles Searle, Esq., 1766: Containing His Adventures by Sea and Land, 2 vols. in 1. Ed. by Michael F. Shugrue. (Flowering of the Novel, 1740-1775 Ser: Vol. 74). 1974. lib. bdg. 50.00 (ISBN 0-8240-1173-2). Garland Pub.

Wanderers All: An American Pilgrimage. Gregory Armstrong. LC 76-26210. 1977. 6.95 o.p. (ISBN 0-06-010139-3, HarpT). Har-Row.

Wanderers Twain: Exploratory Memoir on Helen Modjeska & Henryk Sienkiewicz. Arthur P. Coleman & Marion M. Coleman. LC 63-20948. (Illus.). 1964. 5.00 (ISBN 0-910366-23-3). Alliance Coll.

Wandering Aramean: Collected Aramaic Essays. Joseph A. Fitzmyer. LC 77-21379. (Society of Biblical Literature. Monograph: No. 25). 1979. 15.00 (ISBN 0-89130-150-X); pap. 12.00 (ISBN 0-89130-152-6, 060025). Scholars Pr Ca.

Wandering in Eden: Three Ways to the East Within Us. Michael Adam. 1976. 10.00 o.p. (ISBN 0-394-49980-8); pap. 4.95 (ISBN 0-394-73141-7). Knopf.

Wandering Patentee, 4 vols. in 2 vols. facsimile ed. Tate Wilkinson. 1973. Repr. of 1795 ed. Set. 20.00x o.p. (ISBN 0-85967-123-2, Pub. by Scolar Pr England). Biblio Dist.

Wandering Showman I. David Lano. viii, 290p. 1957. 5.75 o.p. (ISBN 0-87013-027-7). Mich St U Pr.

Wandering Stars: Anthology of Jewish Fantasy & Science Fiction. Ed. by Jack Dann. LC 73-4146. 252p. 1974. 8.95 o.s.i. (ISBN 0-06-010944-0, HarpT). Har-Row.

Wanderings: Chaim Potok's History of the Jews. Chaim Potok. LC 78-54915. 1978. 20.00 (ISBN 0-394-50110-1). Knopf.

Wanderings in South America. Charles Waterton. Intro. by Gilbert Phelps. (Illus.). 257p. 1974. 15.00x (ISBN 0-85314-155-X). Transatlantic.

Wanderings of the Little Blue Butterfly in Fairyland. Anna Lesznai. Tr. by Caroline Bodoczky from Hungarian. (Illus.). 23p. 1978. 7.50x (ISBN 963-13-0618-6). Intl Pubns Serv.

Wang Kuo-wei's "Jen-Chien Tz'u-Hua" A Study in Chinese Literary Criticism. Kuo-Wei Wang. Tr. by Adele A. Rickett from Chinese. LC 78-21212. 150p. 1979. 10.00 (ISBN 0-295-95657-7). U of Wash Pr.

Wang Shou-Jen As a Statesman. Yu-Chuan Chang. (Studies in Chinese History & Civilization). 517p. 1977. Repr. of 1940 ed. 21.00 (ISBN 0-89093-094-5). U Pubns Amer.

Waning of the Middle Ages. J. Huizinga. LC 54-4529. pap. 3.95 (ISBN 0-385-09288-1, A42, Anch). Doubleday.

Wankel RC Engine. R. F. Ansdale. LC 69-18692. (Illus.). 1969. 15.00 o.p. (ISBN 0-498-07410-2). A S Barnes.

Wankel Rotary Engine: Introduction & Guide. Harris E. Dark. LC 73-16676. (Illus.). 160p. 1974. 8.50x (ISBN 0-253-19021-5). Ind U Pr.
Wanted! Ed. by Eric Seidman. 1980. pap. 8.95 (ISBN 0-553-01224-X). Bantam.
Wanting, Becoming, Believing. William L. Joiner. 152p. 1981. pap. 5.95 (ISBN 0-8170-0884-5). Judson.
Wanting of Levine. Michael Halberstam. 1979. pap. 2.25 o.p. (ISBN 0-425-04088-7). Berkley Pub.
Wants, Decisions & Human Action: A Praxeological Investigation. Andrew B. Schoedinger. LC 78-62705. 1978. pap. text ed. 9.50 (ISBN 0-8191-0591-0). U Pr of Amer.
War - Patriotism - Peace. Leo Tolstoy. LC 77-147488. (Library of War & Peace; the Character & Causes of War). lib. bdg. 38.00 (ISBN 0-8240-0281-4). Garland Pub.
War - What for? George Kirkpatrick. LC 78-147519. (Library of War & Peace; Labor, Socialism & War). lib. bdg. 38.00 (ISBN 0-8240-0307-1). Garland Pub.
War Album Five. Ed. by Heinz Birkholz. (Illus.). 96p. (Orig.). 1979. pap. 10.00x (ISBN 0-85242-667-4). Intl Pubns Serv.
War: An Anthology. Ed. by Edward Huberman & Elizabeth Huberman. (Orig.). 1969. pap. 1.50 o.s.i. (ISBN 0-671-48109-6). WSP.
War, An Essay. Jonathan Dymond. LC 72-147433. (Library of War & Peace; Proposals for Peace: a History). lib. bdg. 38.00 (ISBN 0-8240-0480-9). Garland Pub.
War & Domestic Political Violence: The American Capacity for Repression & Reaction. Michael Stohl. LC 76-22799. (Sage Library of Social Research: Vol. 30). 1976. 18.00x (ISBN 0-8039-0575-9); pap. 8.95x (ISBN 0-8039-0576-9). Sage.
War & Economic Development. Ed. by J. M. Winter. LC 74-82219. (Illus.). 320p. 1975. 41.00 (ISBN 0-521-20535-2). Cambridge U Pr.
War & Government in Habsburg Spain 1560-1620. I. A. Thompson. 1976. text ed. 36.50x (ISBN 0-485-11166-7, Athlone Pr). Humanities.
War & Imperialism in Republican Rome, 327-70 B.C. William V. Harris. 1979. 45.00x (ISBN 0-19-814827-5). Oxford U Pr.
War & Its Alleged Benefits. Jacques Novicow. LC 75-147482. (Library of War & Peace; the Character & Causes of War). lib. bdg. 38.00 (ISBN 0-8240-0274-1). Garland Pub.
War & Its Causes. Luther L. Bernard. LC 71-147465. (Library of War & Peace; the Character & Causes of War). lib. bdg. 38.00 (ISBN 0-8240-0256-3). Garland Pub.
War & Military Courts: Judicial Interpretation of Its Meaning. Dorothy Schaffter. 1980. 20.00 (ISBN 0-682-49570-0, Universtiy). Exposition.
War & Morality. Richard Wasserstrom. 1970. pap. 7.95x (ISBN 0-534-00681-7). Wadsworth Pub.
War & Passion. Leslie Arlen. (Borodins Ser.: No. 2). 368p. (Orig.). 1981. pap. 2.75 (ISBN 0-515-05481-X). Jove Pubns.
War & Peace. Leo Tolstoy. Tr. by Constance Garnett. LC 76-6103. 1320p. 1976. 12.50 o.s.i. (ISBN 0-690-01108-3, TYC-T). T Y Crowell.
War & Peace from Genesis to Revelation. Vernard Eller. 232p. 1981. pap. 8.95 (ISBN 0-8361-1947-9). Herald Pr.
War & Peace in Contemporary Social & Philosophical Theory. Irving L. Horowitz. Orig. Title: Idea of War & Peace in Contemporary Philosophy. 218p. 1973. Repr. of 1957 ed. text ed. 9.50x (ISBN 0-391-00284-8). Humanities.
War & Peace in the Middle East: The Experiences & Views of a U. N. Observer. Odd Bull. (Illus., Stickered only). 1977. lib. bdg. 19.25x (ISBN 0-89158-706-3). Westview.
War & Peace in the World's Religions. John Ferguson. 1978. 10.95 (ISBN 0-19-520073-X); pap. 3.95 (ISBN 0-19-520074-8). Oxford U Pr.
War & Peas. Michael Foreman. LC 74-10368. (Illus.). (ps-3). 1974. 7.95 (ISBN 0-690-00628-4, TYC-J); PLB 8.74 (ISBN 0-690-00629-2). T Y Crowell.
War & Rural Life in the Early Modern Low Countries. Myron P. Gutmann. 322p. 1980. text ed. 34.25 (ISBN 90-232-1740-3). Humanities.
War & Society in Africa. Ed. by Bethwell A. Ogot. 276p. 1972. 28.50x (ISBN 0-7146-2129-3, F Cass Co). Biblio Dist.
War & Society in East Central Europe During the Eighteenth & Nineteenth Centuries: Special Topics & Generalizations, Vol. 1. Ed. by Bela K. Kiraly & Gunther E. Rothenberg. (Studies on Society in Change: No. 10). 1979. 22.50 (ISBN 0-930888-04-9). Brooklyn Coll Pr.
War & Society in Europe, 1618-1648. J. V. Polisensky. LC 77-71423. (Illus.). 1978. 35.50 (ISBN 0-521-21659-1). Cambridge U Pr.
War & Society in Renaissance Florence: The De Militia of Leonardo Bruni. C. C. Bayley. LC 62-3048. 1961. 30.00x o.p. (ISBN 0-8020-7047-7). U of Toronto Pr.
War & the Christian. Charles E. Raven. LC 75-147675. (Library of War & Peace; Relig. & Ethical Positions on War). lib. bdg. 38.00 (ISBN 0-8240-0432-9). Garland Pub.
War & the Liberal Conscience. Michael Howard. 1978. 9.50 (ISBN 0-8135-0866-5). Rutgers U Pr.
War & the Russian Government. Paul P. Gronsky & Nicholas J. Astrov. 17.50 (ISBN 0-86527-207-7). Fertig.
War & the Workers. Norman Angell. LC 74-147518. (Library of War & Peace; Labor, Socialism & War). lib. bdg. 38.00 (ISBN 0-8240-0455-8). Garland Pub.
War & Trade in the Northern Seas: Anglo-Scandinavian Economic Relations in the Mid-Eighteenth Century. H. S. Kent. LC 72-75304. (Studies in Economic History). (Illus.). 288p. 1973. 40.95 (ISBN 0-521-08579-9). Cambridge U Pr.
War & Waste: A Series of Discussions of War & War Accessories. David S. Jordan. LC 71-147473. (Library of War & Peace; the Character & Causes of War). lib. bdg. 38.00 (ISBN 0-8240-0265-2). Garland Pub.
War & Welfare: Social Engineering in America, 1890-1925. John F. McClymer. LC 79-54060. (Contributions in American History: No. 84). xvi, 248p. 1980. lib. bdg. 22.95 (ISBN 0-313-21129-9, MWW/). Greenwood.
War at Sea, 4 vols. John Van Duyn & Southworth. Incl. Bk. 1. Ancient Fleets: The Story of Naval Warfare Under Oars, 2600 B.C. - 1597 A.D. LC 67-16200. 370p. o.p. (ISBN 0-685-59135-2, H-588); Bk. 2. Age of Sails: The Story of Naval Warfare Under Sail, 1213 A.D. - 1853 A.D. LC 68-17224. 468p (H-589); Bk. 3. Age of Steam, Pt. 1: 1783-1936 (H-590); Bk. 4. Age of Steam, Pt. 2: The Story of Engine-Powered Naval Warfare, 1936-1972. LC 67-16200. 443p (H-591). (Illus.). 7.50 ea. Hippocrene Bks.
War Between the Generals. David Irving. (Illus.). 480p. 1981. 17.95 (ISBN 0-312-92920-X). St Martin.
War Between the Generals: Inside the Allied High Command. David Irving. (Illus.). 384p. 1981. 17.95 (ISBN 0-312-92920-X). Congdon & Lattes.
War Between the Pitiful Teachers & the Splendid Kids. Stanley Kiesel. LC 80-13450. 256p. (gr. 6 up). 1980. 9.95 (ISBN 0-525-42201-3). Dutton.
War Beyond the Stars. Joel French & Jane French. LC 79-90267. 1979. pap. 3.50 (ISBN 0-89221-067-2). New Leaf.
War Bonnet. Clay Fisher. 1979. pap. 1.50 o.p. (ISBN 0-685-94372-0, 12978-3). Bantam.
War, Business, & World Military-Industrial Complexes. Ed. by Benjamin F. Cooling. (National University Publications, Political Science Ser.). 1981. 19.50 (ISBN 0-8046-9276-9). Kennikat.
War Chief. Edgar R. Burroughs. 1976. Repr. of 1927 ed. lib. bdg. 15.95x (ISBN 0-89966-044-4). Buccaneer Bks.
War Chief. Donald C. Porter. (Colonization of America Ser.). 384p. (Orig.). 1980. pap. 2.75 (ISBN 0-553-13803-0). Bantam.
War Comes to Castle Rising. Fanny Cradock. 1978. 9.95 o.p. (ISBN 0-525-23009-2). Dutton.
War Comes to Long An: Revolutionary Conflict in a Vietnamese Province. Jeffrey Race. LC 79-145793. 1971. 22.75x (ISBN 0-520-01914-8); pap. 5.95x (ISBN 0-520-02361-7, CAL254). U of Cal Pr.
War Correspondence of Leon Trotsky: The Balkan Wars (1912-13, Pt. 1. Leon Trotsky. 1981. lib. bdg. 30.00 (ISBN 0-913460-67-2); pap. 8.95 (ISBN 0-913460-68-0). Monad Pr.
War Dance: A Study of the Psychology of War. Eric G. Howe. LC 74-147471. (Library of War & Peace; the Character & Causes of War). lib. bdg. 38.00 (ISBN 0-8240-0263-6). Garland Pub.
War, Diplomacy, & History: Papers & Reviews. Raymond G. O'Connor. LC 79-88951. 1979. pap. text ed. 11.25 (ISBN 0-8191-0790-5). U Pr of Amer.
War, Economy & Society: 1939-1945. Alan S. Milward. 1977. 21.50x (ISBN 0-520-03338-8, CAL432); pap. 6.95 (ISBN 0-520-03942-4). U of Cal Pr.
War, Economy & the Military Mind. Ed. by Geoffrey Best & Andrew Wheatcroft. 136p. 1976. 12.50x (ISBN 0-87471-757-4). Rowman.
War Eighteen Twelve. George May. (Illus.). 43p. (Orig.). 1962. pap. 1.50 (ISBN 0-911872-28-0). Mackinac Island.
War Film. Ivan Butler. LC 73-3765. (Illus.). 192p. 1973. 10.00 o.p. (ISBN 0-498-01395-2). A S Barnes.
War Flying in France. George A. Vaughn, Jr. 1980. pap. 23.00 (ISBN 0-89126-082-X). Military Aff Aero.
War for Peace. Leonard Woolf. LC 75-148376. (Library of War & Peace; the Character & Causes of War). lib. bdg. 38.00 (ISBN 0-8240-0465-5). Garland Pub.
War: Four Christian Views. Ed. by Robert G. Clouse. 220p. 1981. pap. 5.95 (ISBN 0-87784-801-7). Inter Varsity.
War Games. Karl Hansen. LC 80-85104. 288p. (Orig.). 1981. pap. 2.50 (ISBN 0-87216-837-9). Playboy Pbks.
War God. Frederick E. Smith. 336p. (Orig.). 1981. pap. 2.75 (ISBN 0-553-13663-1). Bantam.
War Government, Federal & State, 1861-65. William B. Weeden. LC 75-87685. (Law, Politics & History Ser.). 1972. Repr. of 1906 ed. lib. bdg. 39.50 (ISBN 0-306-71707-7). Da Capo.
War Horses. Bill Bragg. (Orig.). 1980. pap. 1.75 (ISBN 0-505-51511-3). Tower Bks.
War in Clare Nineteen Eleven-Nineteen Twenty-One: Personal Memoirs of the Irish War of Independence. Michael Brennan. 112p. 1981. 12.50x (ISBN 0-906127-26-2, Pub. by Irish Academic Pr Ireland). Biblio Dist.
War in Deep Heaven: The Space Trilogy of C. S. Lewis. Walter Hooper. 1981. pap. 2.95 (ISBN 0-686-62903-5, Collier). Macmillan.
War in Heaven. Stella P. Revard. LC 79-23297. (Illus.). 1980. 18.50x (ISBN 0-8014-1138-6). Cornell U Pr.
War in Its Effect Upon Women. Helena M. Swanwick. LC 74-147727. (Library of War & Peace; the Character & Causes of War). lib. bdg. 38.00 (ISBN 0-8240-0280-6). Garland Pub.
War in Melville's Imagination. Joyce S. Adler. (Gotham Library). 208p. 1981. 17.50x (ISBN 0-8147-0574-X); pap. 7.95x (ISBN 0-8147-0575-8). NYU Pr.
War in South Africa: Its Causes & Effects. J. A. Hobson. LC 68-9620. 1970. Repr. of 1900 ed. 16.50 (ISBN 0-86527-208-5). Fertig.
War in South Africa: Its Causes & Effects. John A. Hobson. Bd. with War & Its Causes. George P. Gooch. (Library of War & Peace; the Political Economy of War). lib. bdg. 38.00 (ISBN 0-8240-0290-3). Garland Pub.
War in the Desert. Richard Collier. (World War II Ser.). 1977. 12.95 (ISBN 0-8094-2474-6). Time-Life.
War in the Desert. Richard Collier. LC 77-81945. (World War 11 Ser.). (gr. 6 up). 1977. PLB 11.97 (ISBN 0-8094-2475-4). Silver.
War in the Desert: An R. A. F. Frontier Campaign. John B. Glubb. LC 80-1929. 1981. Repr. of 1961 ed. 38.00 (ISBN 0-404-18964-4). AMS Pr.
War in the East. new ed. Strategy & Tactics Staff. Ed. by James F. Dunnigan. (Illus.). 9.95 o.p. (ISBN 0-917852-00-1). Simul Pubns.
War in the Modern World. rev. ed. Theodore Ropp. 1962. pap. 3.95 (ISBN 0-02-036400-8, Collier). Macmillan.
War in the Next Decade. Ed. by Roger A. Beaumont & Martin Edmonds. LC 73-77251. 1974. 14.00x (ISBN 0-8131-1291-5). U Pr of Ky.
War in the Outposts. Simon Rigge. Ed. by Editors of Time-Life Books. (World War II Ser.). (Illus.). 208p. 1981. 13.95 (ISBN 0-8094-3379-6). Time-Life.
War in the Shadows: The Guerrilla in History, 2 vols. Robert B. Asprey. LC 72-92400. 1632p. 1975. Set. Two-volumes, slipcased 35.00 o.p. (ISBN 0-385-03470-9). Doubleday.
War Is Over. Phil Ochs. 1971. pap. 3.95 o.s.i. (ISBN 0-02-074570-2, Collier). Macmillan.
War Lords. A. G. Gardiner. (Wayfarer's Library). 328p. lib. bdg. 20.00 (ISBN 0-89984-232-1). Century Bookbindery.
War Lords. A. J. Taylor. LC 77-13962. 1978. 10.00 o.p. (ISBN 0-689-10840-0). Atheneum.
War: No Glory, No Profit, No Need. Norman Thomas. Ed. by Bernard K. Johnpoll. Bd. with Challenge of War: An Economic Interpretation. Norman Thomas. LC 70-147530. (Library of War & Peace; Labor, Socialism & War). lib. bdg. 38.00 (ISBN 0-8240-0313-6). Garland Pub.
War of American Independence. R. E. Evans. (Cambridge Introduction to the History of Mankind Ser.). (Illus.). 48p. (gr. 6-9). 1976. pap. 3.95 (ISBN 0-521-20903-X). Cambridge U Pr.
War of American Independence: Military Attitudes, Policies & Practice,1763-1789. Don Higginbotham. LC 77-74433. (Wars of the United States Ser.). (Illus.). 524p. 1977. pap. 6.95x (ISBN 0-253-28910-6). Ind U Pr.
War of Eighteen Twelve. Richard Howard. (Jackdaw Ser: No. C25). 1972. 5.95 o.s.i. (ISBN 0-670-74967-2, Grossman). Viking Pr.
War of Ideas: The U. S. Propaganda Campaign in Vietnam. Robert W. Chandler. (Westview Special Studies in National Defense & Security Ser.). 301p. 1981. lib. bdg. 25.00x (ISBN 0-86531-082-3). Westview.
War of Steel & Gold: A Study of the Armed Peace. 3rd ed. Henry N. Brailsford. (Development of the Industrial Society Ser.). 340p. 1980. Repr. 25.00x (ISBN 0-7165-1767-1, Pub. by Irish Academic Pr). Biblio Dist.
War of Steel & Gold: Study of the Armed Peace. Henry N. Brailsford. LC 75-147545. (Library of War & Peace; Control & Limitation of Arms). lib. bdg. 38.00 (ISBN 0-8240-0326-8). Garland Pub.
War of the Polish Sucession John L. Sutton. LC 80-51021. 256p. 1980. 19.50x (ISBN 0-8131-1417-9). U Pr of Ky.
War of the Roses. Warren Adler. (Orig.). 1981. 10.95 (ISBN 0-446-51220-6). Warner Bks.
War of the Running Fox. Bob Langley. LC 78-15445. 1979. 6.95 o.p. (ISBN 0-684-15918-X, ScribT). Scribner.
War of the Worlds. H. G. Wells. (Literature Ser). (gr. 7-12). 1970. pap. text ed. 3.33 (ISBN 0-87720-742-9). AMSCO Sch.
War of the Worlds & the Time Machine. H. G. Wells. pap. 1.95 (ISBN 0-385-08274-6, Dolphin). Doubleday.
War of Wizards. Margaret Storey. (Illus.). (ps-5). 1976. 8.95 (ISBN 0-686-24629-2, Pub. by Faber & Faber). Merrimack Bk Serv.
War of 1812. John K. Mahon. LC 79-137856. (Illus.). 391p. 1972. 12.50 o.p. (ISBN 0-8130-0318-0). U Presses Fla.
War on Charity Ross. Jack M. Bickham. 1976. pap. 1.75 (ISBN 0-441-87262-X). Ace Bks.
War on Films: The American Cinema & World War I, 1914-1941. Michael T. Isenberg. LC 76-19835. 400p. 1981. 20.00 (ISBN 0-8386-2004-3). Fairleigh Dickinson.
War on Pollution. Mike Lyth. LC 76-52304. 1977. 9.95x (ISBN 0-8448-1137-8). Crane- Russak Co.
War on Powder River. Helena H. Smith. LC 65-28734. (Illus.). 1967. pap. 5.25 (ISBN 0-8032-5188-2, BB 375, Bison). U of Nebr Pr.
War on Villa Street: A Novel. Harry Mazer. LC 78-50454. (gr. 7 up). 1978. 7.95 (ISBN 0-440-09349-X). Delacorte.
War on Want. Ed. by G. Evans. 1962. pap. 4.20 (ISBN 0-08-009667-0). Pergamon.
War Party. John Benteen. (Sundance Ser.: No. 14). 1974. pap. 1.50 (Leisure Bks). Nordon Pubns.
War Party. Max Brand. 1975. pap. 1.50 (ISBN 0-446-88933-4). Warner Bks.
War Party. John S. Daniels. Bd. with The Crossing. 1979. pap. 1.95 (ISBN 0-451-08761-5, J8761, Sig). Norton.
War-Path & Bivouac: The Big Horn & Yellowstone Expedition. John F. Finerty. Ed. by Milo M. Quaife. LC 67-89221. (Illus.). 1966. pap. 7.50 (ISBN 0-8032-5059-2, BB 329, Bison). U of Nebr Pr.
War, Peace & International Relations. 2nd ed. Ziegler. 1981. pap. text ed. 8.95 (ISBN 0-316-98493-0). Little.
War, Peace & Nonresistance. rev. ed. Guy F. Hershberger. LC 53-7586. 1969. 12.95 (ISBN 0-8361-1449-3). Herald Pr.
War, Peace, & the Future. Ellen Key. LC 78-147728. (Library of War & Peace; the Character & Causes of War). lib. bdg. 38.00 (ISBN 0-8240-0507-4). Garland Pub.
War, Politics, & Revolution in Provincial Massachusetts. William Pencak. (Illus.). 276p. 1980. write for info. (ISBN 0-930350-10-3). NE U Pr.
War Powers Resolution: The Role of Congress in U. S. Armed Intervention. Pat M. Holt. 1978. pap. 4.25 (ISBN 0-8447-3299-0). Am Enterprise.
War Powers Under the Constitution of the United States. William Whiting. LC 70-169640. (American Constitutional & Legal History Ser). 1972. Repr. of 1871 ed. lib. bdg. 59.50 (ISBN 0-306-70361-0). Da Capo.
War, Presidents & Public Opinion. John E. Mueller. LC 72-8072. 288p. 1973. pap. text ed. 11.95x (ISBN 0-471-62300-8). Wiley.
War Propaganda & the United States. Harold Lavine & James Wechsler. 1940. 18.50x (ISBN 0-686-50035-0). Elliots Bks.
War Propoganda & the United States. James Wechsler & Harold Lavine. LC 72-147476. (Library of War & Peace; the Character & Causes of War). lib. bdg. 38.00 (ISBN 0-8240-0268-7). Garland Pub.
War Stories. Bill Costley. 30p. 1981. write for info. (ISBN 0-933292-03-1); pap. write for info. (ISBN 0-933292-02-3). Arts End.
War Story. Gordon McGill. 1981. pap. 2.75 (ISBN 0-440-19416-4). Dell.
War, Strategy & Maritime Power. B. Mitchell Simpson, 3rd. 1977. 25.00 (ISBN 0-8135-0842-8). Rutgers U Pr.
War System: An Interdisciplinary Approach. Ed. by Richard A. Falk & Samuel S. Kim. LC 79-19566. (Westview Special Studies in Peace, Conflict, & Conflict Resolution). 500p. 1980. lib. bdg. 35.00x (ISBN 0-89158-569-9); pap. text ed. 15.00x (ISBN 0-86531-042-4). Westview.
War, Technology, & Society in the Middle East. V. J. Parry & M. E. Yapp. (Illus.). 464p. 1975. 33.00x (ISBN 0-19-713581-1). Oxford U Pr.

War That Never Ended: The American Civil War. R. Cruden. 1973. pap. text ed. 9.95 o.p. (ISBN 0-13-944355-X). P-H.

War Through the Ages. new & enl. ed. Lynn Montross. LC 60-7533. (Illus.). 1960. 22.95 o.s.i. (ISBN 0-06-013000-8, HarpT). Har-Row.

War Through the Children's Eyes: The Soviet Occupation of Poland & the Deportations, 1939-1941. Ed. by Jan Gross & Irena Gross. LC 80-83832. (Publications Ser.: No.247). 300p. 1981. 21.95. Hoover Inst Pr.

War to End War. Mollie Hardwick. (Upstairs, Downstairs). 244p. 1975. pap. 1.50 o.s.i. (ISBN 0-440-15987-3). Dell.

War to the Death: The Sieges of Saragossa, 1808-1809. Raymond Rudorff. LC 73-21293. 304p. 1974. 8.95 o.s.i. (ISBN 0-02-605940-1). Macmillan.

War Trail. John Benteen. (Sundance Ser. No. 19: No. 19). 1976. pap. 1.50 (ISBN 0-8439-0373-2, Leisure Bks). Nordon Pubns.

War Train. Brown Meggs. LC 79-55612. 1981. 13.95 (ISBN 0-689-11052-9). Atheneum.

War Under the Pacific. Keith Wheeler. Ed. by Time-Life Books Editors. (World War Two Ser.). (Illus.). 208p. 1980. 13.95 (ISBN 0-8094-3375-3). Time-Life.

War Vehicles. Christopher Maynard. (Question & Answer Books Ser.). (Illus.). 36p. (gr. 3-8). 1980. PLB 5.95 (ISBN 0-8225-1185-1). Lerner Pubns.

War with Hannibal. Livy. Tr. by Aubrey De Selincourt. (Classics Ser.). (Orig.). 1965. pap. 5.95 (ISBN 0-14-044145-X). Penguin.

War with the Seminoles, 1835-1842: The Florida Indians Fight for Their Freedom & Homeland. Kenneth M. Jones. LC 74-8811. (Focus Bks). (Illus.). 96p. (gr. 8 up). 1975. PLB 4.47 o.p. (ISBN 0-531-02781-3). Watts.

War with the Spain in Eighteen Ninety-Eight. David F. Trask. Ed. by Louis Morton. LC 80-2314. (Macmillan Wars of the United States Ser.). (Illus.). 775p. 1981. 29.95 (ISBN 0-02-932950-7). Macmillan.

War Within & Without: Diaries & Letters, Nineteen Thirty-Nine to Nineteen Forty-Four. Anne M. Lindbergh. 1980. 14.95 (ISBN 0-15-194661-2). HarBraceJ.

War Without Violence. Krishnalal Shiridharani. LC 79-147633. (Library of War & Peace; Non-Resis. & Non-Vio.). lib. bdg. 38.00 (ISBN 0-8240-0409-4). Garland Pub.

Ward of the Generations: The Revolt of 1173-4. Thomas M. Jones. LC 80-18411. (Sponsor Ser.). 242p. (Orig.). 1980. pap. 18.50 (ISBN 0-8357-0528-5, SS-00141). Univ Microfilms.

Ward Sister. Sue Pembrey. (RCN Research Monograph). 184p. 1981. pap. text ed. 10.00 (ISBN 0-443-02411-1). Churchill.

Warden. Anthony Trollope. (Zodiac Press Ser.). 1978. 9.95 (ISBN 0-7011-1255-7, Pub. by Chatto Bodley Jonathan). Merrimack Bk Serv.

Warden. Anthony Trollope. Ed. by N. L. Clay. (Guide Novel Ser.). pap. text ed. 3.95x o.p. (ISBN 0-435-16880-0). Heinemann Ed.

Ward's Automotive Yearbook. Ed. by Harry A. Stark. 1980. 60.00 (ISBN 0-686-18833-0). Wards Comm.

Warehousing: Analysis for Effective Operations. Victor G. Powell. 240p. 1976. text ed. 29.50x (ISBN 0-220-66301-7, Pub. by Busn Bks England). Renouf.

Warfare in Feudal Europe, 730-1200. John Beeler. LC 74-148018. (Illus.). 288p. 1971. 19.50x (ISBN 0-8014-0638-2); pap. 4.95 (ISBN 0-8014-9120-7, CP120). Cornell U Pr.

Warfare in Primitive Societies: A Bibliography. rev. ed. William T. Divale. LC 73-81978. (War-Peace Bibliography Ser.: No. 2). 123p. 1973. pap. text ed. 2.50 (ISBN 0-87436-122-2). ABC-Clio.

Warfare State. Fred J. Cook. 1964. pap. 1.50 o.s.i. (ISBN 0-02-072770-4, Collier). Macmillan.

Warfield Syndrome. Henry Denker. 324p. 1981. 12.95 (ISBN 0-399-12612-0). Putnam.

Warhead. F. Robert Baker. 304p. (Orig.). 1981. pap. 2.50 (ISBN 0-553-14790-0). Bantam.

Warhol. Richard Morphet. (Tate Gallery Art Ser.). (Illus.). 1977. 6.95 o.p. (ISBN 0-8120-5140-8). Barron.

Waring Papers: The Collected Works of Antonio J. Waring. Ed. by Stephen Williams. LC 67-27476. (Papers of the Peabody Museum Ser.). 1977. pap. 20.00 (ISBN 0-87365-169-3). Peabody Harvard.

Warlord of Mars. Edgar R. Burroughs. 1976. Repr. of 1919 ed. lib. bdg. 13.95x (ISBN 0-89966-045-2). Buccaneer Bks.

Warlords. Bob Langley. LC 80-20572. 223p. 1981. 9.95 (ISBN 0-688-00069-X). Morrow.

Warlords, Artists, & Commoners: Japan in the Sixteenth Century. Ed. by George Elison & Bardwell Z. Smith. LC 80-24128. (Illus.). 372p. 1981. 20.00x (ISBN 0-8248-0692-1). U Pr of Hawaii.

Warlord's World. Christopher Anuil. (Science Fiction Ser). pap. 1.25 o.p. (ISBN 0-87997-201-7, UY1201). DAW Bks.

Warm Air Heating. D. Kut. LC 71-122009. 1971. 42.00 (ISBN 0-08-015853-6); pap. 21.00 (ISBN 0-08-019006-5). Pergamon.

Warm As Wool, Cool As Cotton: The Story of Natural Fibers & Fabrics & How to Work with Them. Carter Houck. LC 74-18089. (Illus.). 96p. (gr. 3-6). 1975. 6.95 (ISBN 0-395-28861-4, Clarion). HM.

Warm Desert Environment. A. Goudie & J. Wilkinson. LC 76-9731. (Topics in Geography Ser). (Illus.). 1977. 14.50 (ISBN 0-521-21330-4); pap. 7.95 (ISBN 0-521-29105-4); 26.50x (ISBN 0-521-21912-4). Cambridge U Pr.

Warm Rooms & Cold. Lars Gustafsson. Tr. by Yvonne Sandstroem. (Orig.). 1975. pap. 3.50 (ISBN 0-914278-05-3). Copper Beech.

Warm Smiles, Happy Faces. Charlie Daniel & Becky Daniel. (gr. k-4). 1978. 4.95 (ISBN 0-916456-24-2, GA79). Good Apple.

Warm Snuggles & Cold Ouchies: A Parable for Children Over & Under 21. Jim Ballard. LC 75-25393. (Mandala Ser. in Education). 1975. pap. 2.50 (ISBN 0-916250-05-9). Irvington.

Warm Summer. Craig Massey. (Hearth Classic Ser.). 192p. 1980. pap. 2.50 (ISBN 0-310-41772-4). Zondervan.

Warm Up for Little League Baseball. Morris Shirts. LC 70-151708. (Illus.). 176p. (gr. 2 up). 1976. 7.95 (ISBN 0-8069-4044-1); PLB 7.49 (ISBN 0-8069-4045-X). Sterling.

Warm up for Little League Baseball. Morris A. Shirts. Date not set. pap. 1.95 (ISBN 0-671-42422-X). Archway.

Warm up for Little League Baseball. Morris A. Shirts. (Illus.). (gr. 3-6). 1977. pap. 1.75 (ISBN 0-671-41135-7). PB.

Warm up for Soccer. G. Lammich & H. Kadow. LC 74-31697. (Illus.). 128p. (gr. 5 up). 1975. 8.95 (ISBN 0-8069-4090-5); PLB 8.29 (ISBN 0-8069-4091-3). Sterling.

Warming Fires: The Quest for Community in America. James Sellers. 224p. 1975. 7.95 (ISBN 0-8164-0273-6). Crossroad NY.

Warmint. Walter De La Mare. LC 76-454. (Illus.). 32p. (gr. k-2). 1976. 4.95 (ISBN 0-684-14663-0, ScribJ). Scribner.

Warmongers. Howard S. Katz. Ed. by Stephen A. Zarlenga. LC 78-73738. (Illus.). 1979. 14.95 (ISBN 0-916728-06-4). Bks in Focus.

Warner Collector' Guide to American Clocks: Anita Schorsch. (Orig.). 1981. pap. 9.95 (ISBN 0-446-97633-4). Warner Bks.

Warner Collector's Guide to American Long Arms. H. Michael Madaus. (Orig.). 1981. pap. 9.95 (ISBN 0-446-97628-8). Warner Bks.

Warner Collectors' Guide to American Quilts. Phyllis Haders. (Orig.). 1981. pap. 9.95 (ISBN 0-446-97636-9). Warner Bks.

Warner Collectors' Guide to American Toys. William Ayres. (Orig.). 1981. pap. 9.95 (ISBN 0-446-97632-6). Warner Bks.

Warning: Anthology of Poetry from Prisoners of Oklahoma. Ed. by Mary McAnally. 1980. pap. 5.00 (ISBN 0-931350-03-4). Moonlight Pubns.

Warning Call. Robert G. Keller. 1981. pap. 1.95 (ISBN 0-8439-0890-4, Leisure Bks). Nordon Pubns.

Warranties in the Sale of Goods 1980. (Commercial Law & Practice Course Handbook Series 1980-81: Vol. 244 & 245). 1980. pap. 25.00 (ISBN 0-685-90295-1, A6-3091). PLI.

Warranties in the Sale of Goods 1980: Course Handbook, 2 vols. Ed. by Barkley Clark. LC 78-643376. (Nineteen Eighty to Nineteen Eighty-One Commercial Law & Practice Course Handbook Ser.). 1131p. 1980. pap. text ed. 25.00 (ISBN 0-686-69173-3, A6-3091). PLI.

Warren Akin Candler: The Conservative As Idealist. Mark K. Bauman. LC 80-22230. 290p. 1981. 16.00 (ISBN 0-8108-1368-8). Scarecrow.

Warren-Ballard Debate. Thomas B. Warren & L. S. Ballard. 1979. 7.95 (ISBN 0-934916-39-X). Natl Christian Pr.

Warren-Flew Debate on the Existence of God. Ed. by Thomas B. Warren & A. G. Noflew. 1977. 12.95 (ISBN 0-934916-40-3). Natl Christian Pr.

Warren Hastings. Lionel J. Trotter. (Rulers of India Ser). 1962. 3.50x o.p. (ISBN 0-8426-1572-5). Verry.

Warren-Matson Debate on the Existence of God. Thomas B. Warren & Wallace I. Matson. LC 78-64546. 1979. 12.95 (ISBN 0-934916-41-1); pap. 9.95 (ISBN 0-934916-45-4). Natl Christian Pr.

Warrior. Wade Everett. 160p. 1981. pap. 1.75 (ISBN 0-345-29432-7). Ballantine.

Warrior Flame. Cody Kennedy, Jr. 1980. pap. 2.50 (ISBN 0-446-81676-0). Warner Bks.

Warrior Queen. James Sinclair. 1979. pap. 2.25 o.p. (ISBN 0-425-03947-1). Berkley Pub.

Warrior Tradition in Modern Africa. Ed. by Ali A. Mazrui. (International Studies in Sociology & Social Anthropology Ser.: No. XXIII). 1977. text ed. 34.25x (ISBN 90-04-05646-7). Humanities.

Warriors. John Jakes. (Kent Family Chronicles: No. 6). (Orig.). 1977. pap. 2.95 (ISBN 0-515-05893-9). Jove Pubns.

Warriors: A Parris Island Journal. Richard Stack. (Illus.). 128p. (Orig.). 1975. pap. 4.95 o.p. (ISBN 0-06-090319-8, CN319, CN). Har-Row.

Warriors & Weapons of Early Times in Color. Niels Saxtorph. (Illus.). 260p. 1980. 9.95 (ISBN 0-7137-0735-6, Pub. by Blandford Pr England). Sterling.

Warriors at Work: The Volunteer Armed Force. Sar A. Levitan & Karen C. Alderman. LC 77-21234. (Sage Library of Social Research: Vol. 58). 1977. 18.00x (ISBN 0-8039-0932-2); pap. 8.95x (ISBN 0-8039-0933-0). Sage.

Warrior's Looking Glass: Wherein Is Shewn from Many High Authorities the Trivial Causes, Cruel Nature, Direful Effects & Anti-Christian Spirit & Practice of War. George Beaumont. LC 76-147426. (Library of War & Peace; Proposals for Peace: a History). lib. bdg. 38.00 (ISBN 0-8240-0218-0). Garland Pub.

Warrior's Path. Louis L'Amour. 1981. lib. bdg. 13.95 (ISBN 0-8161-3145-7, Large Print Bks). G K Hall.

Warrior's Path. Louis L'Amour. 240p. (Orig.). 1980. pap. 1.95 (ISBN 0-553-14207-0). Bantam.

Warriors to Managers: The French Military Establishment Since 1945. Michel L. Martin. LC 79-28114. (Illus.). 424p. 1981. 21.00x (ISBN 0-8078-1421-0). U of NC Pr.

Warriors with Wings. W. H. Fear. pap. 2.00x (ISBN 0-392-07289-0, SpS). Soccer.

Warrior's Woman. Phyllis Leonard. 1978. pap. 2.25 (ISBN 0-515-04620-5). Jove Pubns.

Wars. Timothy Findley. 1977. 8.95 o.s.i. (ISBN 0-440-09397-X, Sey Lawr). Delacorte.

Wars of America. rev. ed. Robert Leckie. LC 78-4735. (Illus.). 1981. 20.00 (ISBN 0-06-012571-3, HarpT). Har-Row.

Wars of the Crusades. Terence Wise. 1980. text ed. 19.50x (ISBN 0-85045-300-3). Humanities.

Wars of the Iroquois: A Study in Intertribal Trade Relations. George T. Hunt. 1960. pap. 7.95x (ISBN 0-299-00164-4). U of Wis Pr.

Wars, Plots & Scandals in Post-War France. Philip Williams. LC 77-96105. 1970. 31.95 (ISBN 0-521-07741-9). Cambridge U Pr.

Warsaw: A Portrait of the City. Stanislaw Jankowski & Piotr Rafalski. Tr. by Miroslan Lubon from Pol. LC 80-460054. Orig. Title: Warszawa - Portret Miasta. (Illus.). 1979. 25.00x (ISBN 0-8002-2289-X). Intl Pubns Serv.

Warsaw Diary of Chaim A. Kaplan. Ed. by Abraham I. Katsh. C. A. Kaplan. LC 72-90277. (Illus.). 400p. 1973. pap. 2.95 o.s.i. (ISBN 0-02-034000-1, Collier). Macmillan.

Warsaw Ghetto Memoirs of Janusz Korczak. E. P. Kulawiec. LC 78-63065. 1978. pap. text ed. 8.00 (ISBN 0-8191-0611-9). U Pr of Amer.

Warsaw Rising of Nineteen Forty Four. J. M. Ciechanowski. LC 73-79315. (Soviet & East European Studies). 348p. 1974. 38.50 (ISBN 0-521-20203-5). Cambridge U Pr.

Warships. Hugh Gregor. LC 78-64660. (Fact Finders Ser.). (Illus.). 1979. lib. bdg. 3.96 (ISBN 0-686-51132-8). Silver.

Warships of the World. Antony Preston. (Illus.). 1979. 19.95 o.s.i. (ISBN 0-8464-0962-3). Beekman Pubs.

Wartime. Milovan Djilas. LC 80-16174. 1980. 7.95 (ISBN 0-15-694712-9, Harv). HarBraceJ.

Wartime Alliance & the Zonal Division of Germany. Tony Sharp. (Illus.). 232p. 1975. 29.95x (ISBN 0-19-822521-0). Oxford U Pr.

Wartime Chrildren, 1939-1945. Eleanor Allen. (Junior Reference Ser.). (Illus.). 64p. (gr. 7 up). 7.95 (ISBN 0-7136-1503-6). Dufour.

Wartime Economic Development in China: New York, 1939. Ch'Ao-Ting Chi. LC 78-74328. (Modern Chinese Economy Ser.: Vol. 36). 199p. 1980 (ISBN 0-8240-4284-0). lib. bdg. 22.00 (ISBN 0-686-62489-0). Garland Pub.

Wartime Mission in Spain. Carlton Hayes. LC 76-18191. (Politics & Strategy of World War II Ser.). 1976. Repr. of 1945 ed. lib. bdg. 27.50 (ISBN 0-306-70771-3). Da Capo.

Wartime Production Controls. David Novick et al. LC 76-5795. (FDR & the Era of the New Deal Ser). 1976. Repr. of 1949 ed. lib. bdg. 35.00 (ISBN 0-306-70818-3). Da Capo.

Wartime Shipyard: A Study in Social Disunity. Katherine Archibald. LC 76-7621. (FDR & the Era of the New Deal Ser.). 1976. Repr. of 1947 ed. 22.50 (ISBN 0-306-70802-7). Da Capo.

Wartime Women: Sex Roles, Family Relations, & the Status of Women During World War II. Karen Anderson. LC 80-1703. (Contributions in Women's Studies Ser.: No. 20). 224p. 1981. lib. bdg. 22.95 (ISBN 0-313-20884-0, AWW/). Greenwood.

Warton & Morton. Russell E. Erickson. 1977. pap. 1.25 (ISBN 0-440-49522-9, YB). Dell.

Warwick's Choice. Rosalind Laker. 1981. pap. 2.50 (ISBN 0-451-09664-9, E9664, Sig). NAL.

Warwickshire: A Shell Guide. Douglas Hickman. (Illus.). 1979. 15.95 (ISBN 0-571-10831-8, Pub. by Faber & Faber). Merrimack Bk Serv.

Was It Incest or Child Abuse? R. S. Hart, pseud. 95p. (Orig.). 1981. pap. 5.95 (ISBN 0-9604226-0-9). R S Hart.

Was It Murder? James Hilton. LC 75-44984. (Crime Fiction Ser). 1976. Repr. of 1935 ed. lib. bdg. 17.50 (ISBN 0-8240-2376-5). Garland Pub.

Was There a Resurrection? The Challenge to Reason & Belief. Intro. by Kessler. 1977. 6.95 o.p. (ISBN 0-533-02987-2). Vantage.

Was War Necessary? National Security & U. S. Entry into War. Melvin Small. LC 80-13536. (Sage Library of Social Research: Vol. 105). (Illus.). 311p. 1980. 18.00 (ISBN 0-8039-1486-5); pap. 8.95 (ISBN 0-8039-1487-3). Sage.

Wash & Brush up. Eleanor Allen. (Junior Reference Ser.). (Illus.). 64p. (gr. 7 up). 7.95 (ISBN 0-7136-1639-3). Dufour.

Wash & Gouache: A Study of the Development of the Materials of Watercolor. Marjorie B. Cohn. LC 77-176. 120p. 1980. pap. 7.50 (ISBN 0-916724-06-9). Fogg Art.

Washburn College Bible. Ed. by Bradbury Thompson. 1808p. 1980. 65.00 (ISBN 0-19-502786-8). Oxford U Pr.

Washday. Susan Merrill. LC 77-12621. (Illus.). (ps-4). 1978. 6.95 (ISBN 0-395-28817-7, Clarion). HM.

Washi: The World of Japanese Paper. Sukey Hughes. LC 78-55094. (Illus.). 1978. 50.00 (ISBN 0-87011-318-6); deluxe ed. 250.00 (ISBN 0-87011-350-X). Kodansha.

Washing on the Line. Beauton Riley. 4.95 o.p. (ISBN 0-685-48820-9). Nortex Pr.

Washington. Norman H. Clark. (States & the Nation Ser). (Illus.). 1976. 12.95 (ISBN 0-393-05587-6, Co-Pub by AASLH). Norton.

Washington. 28.00 (ISBN 0-89770-123-2). Curriculum Info Ctr.

Washington: A Guide to the Evergreen State. Federal Writers' Project. 688p. 1941. Repr. 49.00 (ISBN 0-403-02196-0). Somerset Pub.

Washington: a History of the Capital. Constance M. Green. 1976. pap. 7.50 (ISBN 0-691-00585-0). Princeton U Pr.

Washington & Lee at Monmouth: The Making of a Scapegoat. Theodore Thayer. 1976. 9.95 (ISBN 0-8046-9139-8, Natl U). Kennikat.

Washington Chronology & Factbook, Vol. 47. R. I. Vexler. 1978. 8.50 (ISBN 0-379-16172-9). Oceana.

Washington: City & Capital. Federal Writers' Project. 528p. 1942. Repr. 54.00 (ISBN 0-403-02237-1). Somerset Pub.

Washington Community: Eighteen Hundred - Eighteen Twenty-Eight. James S. Young. LC 66-14080. 1966. 17.50x (ISBN 0-231-02901-2). Columbia U Pr.

Washington, D. C. Gore Vidal. Date not set. pap. 2.50 (ISBN 0-345-27946-8). Ballantine.

Washington, D. C. on Twenty-Five Dollars a Day: 1980-81 Edition. 1981. pap. 4.95 (ISBN 0-671-25493-6). Frommer-Pasmantier.

Washington, D.C. A Guide to the Nation's Capital. rev. ed. Ed. by Randle B. Truett & Federal Writers' Project. LC 67-25608. (American Guide Ser.). (Illus.). 1968. 12.95 (ISBN 0-8038-8010-3). Hastings.

Washington, D.C. in Color. Barbara J. Stewart. (Profiles of America Ser.). (Illus.). 1977. 6.95 (ISBN 0-8038-8083-9). Hastings.

Washington: Design for the Federal City. National Archives of the United States Office of Education. 1981. pap. 9.95 (ISBN 0-87491-417-5). Acropolis.

Washington Embrace of Business. Roger M. Blough. 160p. 1975. 12.50x (ISBN 0-915604-03-5). Columbia U Pr.

Washington in Pieces. John Nollson. LC 80-713. 264p. 1981. 11.95 (ISBN 0-385-15413-5). Doubleday.

Washington Information Directory Nineteen Eighty to Eighty One. Congressional Quarterly Inc. Ed. by Congressional Quarterly Inc. 931p. 1980. pap. text ed. 25.00 (ISBN 0-87187-152-1). Congr Quarterly.

Washington Information Workbook. 5th ed. Ed. by Micheal Glennon. LC 79-63792. 1981. pap. 45.00 (ISBN 0-686-25747-2). Wash Res.

Washington Irving. Mary W. Bowden. (United States Authors Ser.: No. 397). 1981. lib. bdg. 9.95 (ISBN 0-8057-7314-2). Twayne.

Washington Irving. Charles D. Warner. LC 80-23548. (American Men & Women of Letters Ser.). 310p. 1981. pap. 4.95 (ISBN 0-87754-153-1). Chelsea Hse.

Washington Irving: An American Study, 1802-1832. William L. Hedges. LC 80-23564. (Goucher College Ser.). xiv, 274p. 1980. Repr. of 1965 ed. lib. bdg. 27.50x (ISBN 0-313-21159-0, HEWI). Greenwood.

Washington Irving & the House of Murray: Geoffrey Crayon Charms the British, 1817-1856. Ed. by Ben H. McClary. LC 73-77843. (Illus.). 1969. 14.50x (ISBN 0-87049-094-X). U of Tenn Pr.

Washington Irving Journals & Notebooks, 1807-1822, Vol. 2. Ed. by Walter A. Reichart & Lillian Schlissel. (Critical Editions Program Ser.). 1981. lib. bdg. 32.00 (ISBN 0-8057-8501-9). Twayne.

Washington Irving Miscellaneous Writings, 1803-1859. Wayne Kime. (Critical Editions Program). 1981. lib. bdg. 75.00 (ISBN 0-8057-8520-5). Twayne.

Washington Irving's Tales of the Supernatural. Washington Irving. Ed. by Edward Wagenknecht. (Illus.). 288p. 1981. 14.95 (ISBN 0-916144-64-X); pap. 7.95 (ISBN 0-916144-65-8). Stemmer Hse.

Washington Is Leaking. Art Buchwald. 1977. pap. 2.50 (ISBN 0-449-23294-8, Crest). Fawcett.

Washington Lobby. 3rd ed. Congressional Quarterly. 1979. pap. text ed. 6.95 (ISBN 0-87187-178-5). Congr Quarterly.

Washington Merry-Go-Round of Libel Actions. Douglas A. Anderson. LC 79-18126. 1980. 19.95x; pap. 9.95 (ISBN 0-88229-746-5). Nelson-Hall.

Washington on Foot. 2nd ed. Allan Hodges & Carol Hodges. LC 80-15844. (Illus.). 202p. 1980. pap. 4.25 (ISBN 0-87474-527-6). Smithsonian.

Washington on Foot: A City Planner's Guide to the Nation's Capital. 2nd. ed. Ed. by Allan A. Hodges & Carol Hodges. LC 76-1355. (Illus.). 208p. 1980. pap. 4.25 o.p. (ISBN 0-87474-525-X). Smithsonian.

Washington Playland. Edmund Griffen & Daniel Dodge. 1976. pap. 1.95 o.p. (ISBN 0-685-73463-3, LB403, Leisure Bks). Nordon Pubns.

Washington Politics: Published Under the Auspices of the Citizenship Clearing House. Daniel M. Ogden, Jr. & Hugh A. Bone. LC 80-25647. (Illus.). vi, 77p. 1981. Repr. of 1960 ed. lib. bdg. 19.75x (ISBN 0-313-22803-5, OGWP). Greenwood.

Washington Redskins. Julian May. (NFL Today). (Illus.). (gr. 3-6). 1977. PLB 6.45 (ISBN 0-87191-597-9); pap. 2.95 (ISBN 0-686-67472-3). Creative Ed.

Washington Reporters. Stephen Hess. LC 80-70077. 275p. 1981. 17.95 (ISBN 0-8157-3594-4); pap. 6.95 (ISBN 0-8157-3593-6). Brookings.

Washington Representatives. 5th ed. Ed. by Arthur C. Close & Craig Colgate, Jr. LC 76-21152. 1981. pap. 35.00 (ISBN 0-910416-35-4). Columbia Bks.

Washington Representatives. 4th ed. Ed. by Arthur C. Close & Craig Colgate, Jr. LC 76-21152. 1980. pap. 30.00x o.p. (ISBN 0-910416-33-8). Columbia Bks.

Washington Shores. Spencer Gill. (Illus.). 128p. 1981. 27.50 (ISBN 0-912856-68-8). Graphic Arts Ctr.

Washington Square. Henry James. (Literature Ser). (gr. 10-12). 1970. pap. text ed. 3.33 (ISBN 0-87720-743-7). AMSCO Sch.

Washington Square. Henry James. 1963. pap. 1.95 (ISBN 0-14-001920-0). Penguin.

Washington State Industrial Directory, 1981. State Industrial Directories Corp. Date not set. pap. price not set (ISBN 0-89910-007-4). State Indus Dir.

Washington State Place Names. rev. ed. James W. Phillips. LC 73-159435. (Illus.). 186p. 1971. 11.50 (ISBN 0-295-95158-3); pap. 6.95 (ISBN 0-295-95498-1). U of Wash Pr.

Washington the Open City. Guy Friddell & Franz Burda. 250p. 1974. 14.95 o.p. (ISBN 0-914962-01-9). Burda Pubns.

Washington University Papyri I: Non-Literary Texts, Nos. 1-16. Verne B. Schuman. LC 79-14199. (American Society of Papyrologists Ser.: No. 17). 15.00 (ISBN 0-89130-286-7). Scholars Pr CA.

Washington's Birthday. Clyde R. Bulla. LC 66-10504. (Holiday Ser.). (Illus.). (gr. 1-3). 1967. PLB 7.89 (ISBN 0-690-86796-4, TYC-J). T Y Crowell.

Washington's Yesterdays. Lucile McDonald. (Illus.). 192p. 1975. pap. 3.95 o.p. (ISBN 0-8323-0258-9). Binford.

Washout. Carol Carrick. LC 78-8135. (Illus.). (gr. 1-4). 1978. 6.95 (ISBN 0-395-28781-2, Clarion). HM.

Washout at Liberty Valley. F. A. Jaroch et al. (Adventures of the Sneeky Sneekers Ser.). (Illus.). 32p. (gr. 1-4). 1978. PLB 7.95 (ISBN 0-516-03407-3). Childrens.

Wasp, Where Is Thy Sting? Florence King. pap. 4.95 (ISBN 0-8128-6025-X). Stein & Day.

Wasps. Aristophanes. Ed. by Douglas M. MacDowell. 1971. text ed. 22.50x (ISBN 0-19-814182-3). Oxford U Pr.

Wasps. Howard E. Evans & Mary J. Eberhard. LC 78-12448. (Ann Arbor Science Library). 1970. pap. 3.45 o.p. (ISBN 0-472-05018-4, 518, AA). U of Mich Pr.

Wasps. Howard E. Evans & Mary J. Eberhard. LC 71-124448. (Ann Arbor Science Library Ser.). 272p. 1970. 7.95 (ISBN 0-472-00118-3); pap. 3.45 (ISBN 0-472-05018-4). U of Mich Pr.

Wasps: An Account of the Biology & Natural History of Social & Solitary Wasps. J. Philip Spradbery. LC 73-7872. (Biology Ser). (Illus.). 424p. 1973. 22.50 (ISBN 0-295-95287-3). U of Wash Pr.

Waste & Water Renovation & Conservation. L. T. Kardos et al. (Penn State Studies: No. 23). (Illus.). 72p. 1967. pap. 3.95x o.p. (ISBN 0-271-00272-7). Pa Hist & Mus.

Waste Discharge into the Marine Environment: Principles & Guidelines. World Health Organization. LC 80-40899. (Illus.). 544p. 1980. 75.00 (ISBN 0-08-026194-9). Pergamon.

Waste Disposal Effects on Ground Water. David W. Miller. LC 78-65680. (Illus.). 512p. 1980. pap. 16.00x (ISBN 0-912722-01-0). Prem Press.

Waste Energy Utilization Technology. Kiang. 264p. 1981. 29.75 (ISBN 0-8247-1173-4). Dekker.

Waste Land. T. S. Eliot. Ed. by C. B. Cox & A. P. Hinchiffe. LC 70-127569. (Casebook Ser). 1970. pap. text ed. 2.50 o.s.i. (ISBN 0-87695-040-3). Aurora Pubs.

Waste Land As Grail Romance: Eliot's Use of the Medieval Grail Legends. Everett A. Gillis. (Graduate Studies: No. 6). 26p. 1974. pap. 2.00 (ISBN 0-89672-013-6). Tex Tech Pr.

Waste Management & Control. Committee On Pollution. 1966. pap. 6.25 o.p. (ISBN 0-309-01400-X). Natl Acad Pr.

Waste Management & Resources Recovery Information Database. Randall L. Voight. 1979. 400.00 (ISBN 0-930318-07-2); quarterly updates 125.00. Intl Res Eval.

Waste of Nations: The Economic Utilization of Human Waste in Agriculture. L. A. Fahm. LC 79-88260. (LandMark Studies). (Illus.). 188p. 1980. text ed. 24.50 (ISBN 0-916672-28-X). Allanheld.

Waste of Timelessness & Other Early Stories. Anais Nin. 1977. 7.95 o.s.i. (ISBN 0-8027-0569-3). Walker & Co.

Waste of Timelessness: And Other Early Stories. Anais Nin. LC 74-28648. 105p. 1980. 7.95 (ISBN 0-8027-0569-3). Ohio U Pr.

Waste Treatment in Agriculture. P. N. Hobson & A. M. Robertson. (Illus.). 1977. 43.50x (ISBN 0-85334-736-0, Pub. by Applied Science). Burgess-Intl Ideas.

Waste Watchers: A Citizen's Handbook for Conserving Energy & Resources. Arthur H. Purcell. LC 79-8438. (Illus.). 1980. pap. 4.50 (ISBN 0-385-14220-X, Anch). Doubleday.

Wasted Manpower. Corrington Gill. LC 72-2371. (FDR & the Era of the New Deal Ser). 316p. 1973. Repr. of 1939 ed. lib. bdg. 32.50 (ISBN 0-306-70467-6). Da Capo.

Wastes Management Concepts for the Coastal Zone. Committee On Oceanography & Committee on Ocean Engineering. (Orig.). 1970. pap. 4.25 (ISBN 0-309-01855-2). Natl Acad Pr.

Wastewater Engineering Design for Unsewered Areas. Rein Laak. LC 80-65509. (Illus.). 172p. 1980. 28.00 (ISBN 0-250-40373-0). Ann Arbor Science.

Wastewater Management: A Guide to Information Sources. Ed. by George Tchobanoglous et al. LC 74-11570. (Man & the Environment Information Guide Ser.: Vol. 2). 260p. 1976. 30.00 (ISBN 0-8103-1338-3). Gale.

Wastewater Reuse & Recycling Technology. Gordon Culp et al. LC 80-21778. (Pollution Technology Review Ser.: 72). (Illus.). 838p. 1981. 49.00 (ISBN 0-8155-0829-8). Noyes.

Wastewater Systems Engineering. Homer Parker. (Illus.). 464p. 1975. 27.95 (ISBN 0-13-945758-5). P-H.

Wastewater Treatment. Donald W. Sundstrom & Herbert E. Klei. LC 78-13058. (Illus.). 1979. 27.95 (ISBN 0-13-945832-8). P-H.

Wastewater Treatment & Resource Recovery. 47p. 1980. pap. 5.00 (ISBN 0-88936-260-2, IDRC154, IDRC). Unipub.

Wastewater Treatment Plant Design. Compiled by American Society of Civil Engineers. (Manual & Report on Engineering Practice Ser.: No. 36). 550p. 1977. text ed. 20.00 (ISBN 0-87262-213-4). Am Soc Civil Eng.

Wat Haripunjaya: A Study of the Royal Temple of the Buddha's Relic, Lamphun, Thailand. Donald K. Swearer. LC 75-33802. (American Academy of Religion. Studies in Religion). 1976. pap. 7.50 (ISBN 0-89130-052-X, 010010). Scholars Pr Ca.

Watch & Pray with Me: The Seven Last Words. Karl Rahner. 1977. pap. 4.95 (ISBN 0-8164-2126-9). Crossroad NY.

Watch for the Morning. Elisabeth Macdonald. LC 77-13662. 1978. 9.95 o.p. (ISBN 0-684-15358-0, ScribT). Scribner.

Watch Honeybees with Me. Judy Hawes. LC 64-19169. (Let's-Read-&-Find-Out Science Bk). (Illus.). (gr. k-3). 1964. bds. 7.95 (ISBN 0-690-86937-1, TYC-J). T Y Crowell.

Watch House. Robert Westall. LC 77-19088. (gr. 5-9). 1978. 7.95 (ISBN 0-688-80149-8); PLB 7.63 (ISBN 0-688-84149-X). Greenwillow.

Watch It Come Down. John Osborne. 1975. 8.50 (ISBN 0-571-10854-7, Pub. by Faber & Faber); pap. 3.95 o.p. (ISBN 0-571-10855-5). Merrimack Bk Serv.

Watch Out for the Chicken Feet in Your Soup. Tomie De Paola. LC 74-8201. (Illus.). (ps-3). 1974. PLB 6.95 (ISBN 0-13-945782-8); pap. 1.95 (ISBN 0-13-945766-6). P-H.

Watch Out for the Foreign Guests! China Encounters the West. Orville Schell. 1981. 8.95 (ISBN 0-394-51331-2). Pantheon.

Watch Out for the Wind. C. J. Mize. (Orig.). 1980. pap. 2.25 (ISBN 0-505-51555-5). Tower Bks.

Watch That Watch. Hila Colman. (Illus.). (gr. k-3). 1962. PLB 6.48 o.p (ISBN 0-688-31623-9). Morrow.

Watch Those Red Wheels Roll. Marion Renick. LC 65-14766. (Illus.). 128p. (gr. 2-6). 1965. 5.95 (ISBN 0-684-13172-2, ScribJ). Scribner.

Watch Your Teaching: Home Study. Garver. pap. 3.95 (ISBN 0-686-12324-7). Christs Mission.

Watchboy, What of the Night? Turner Cassity. LC 66-23920. (Wesleyan Poetry Program: Vol. 31). (Orig.). 1966. 10.00x (ISBN 0-8195-2031-4, Pub. by Wesleyan U Pr); pap. 4.95x (ISBN 0-8195-1031-9). Columbia U Pr.

Watchdog on the Potomac: A Study of the Comptroller General of the United States. Joseph Pois. LC 78-66276. 1979. pap. text ed. 12.00 (ISBN 0-8191-0691-7). U Pr of Amer.

Watcher. Isaac E. Mozeson. 48p. (Orig.). 1980. pap. 2.50 (ISBN 0-917402-17-0). Downtown Poets.

Watcher & Other Stories. Italo Calvino. Tr. by William Weaver & Archibald Colquhoun. LC 75-9829. 181p. 1975. pap. 2.95 (ISBN 0-15-694952-0, HPL65, HPL). HarBraceJ.

Watcher in the Dark. Dorothy Daniels. (Orig.). 1973. pap. 0.95 o.p. (ISBN 0-685-32391-9, 345-26509-2-095). Ballantine.

Watchers at the Pond. Franklin Russell. 1981. pap. 8.95 (ISBN 0-87923-390-7). Godine.

Watchers of Space. Nancy Etchemendy. (Illus.). (gr. 3-7). 1980. pap. 1.50 (ISBN 0-380-75374-X, 75347, Camelot). Avon.

Watchers of the Dark. Lloyd Biggle, Jr. 1975. pap. 0.95 o.p. (ISBN 0-685-53128-7, LB275NK, Leisure Bks). Nordon Pubns.

Watches: A Complete History of the Technical & Decorative Development of the Watch. 3rd rev. & enlarg. ed. Cecil Clutton & George Daniels. (Illus.). 312p. 1979. 92.50 (ISBN 0-85667-058-8, Pub by Sotheby Parke Bernet England). Biblio Dist.

Watches & Clocks in the Sir David Salomons Collection. George Daniels & Ohannes Markarian. (Illus.). 320p. 1981. 80.00x (ISBN 0-85667-074-X, Pub. by Sotheby Parke Bernet England). Biblio Dist.

Watches in Color. Richard Good. (Illus.). 1979. 12.95 (ISBN 0-7137-0831-X, Pub. by Blandford Pr England). Sterling.

Watches in Color. Richard Good. (Illus.). 218p. 1981. pap. 6.95 (Pub. by Blandford Pr England). Sterling.

Watching American Politics. Ed. by Dan Nimmo & William L. Rivers. LC 80-23788. (Illus.). 336p. (Orig.). 1981. pap. text ed. 9.95 (ISBN 0-582-28197-0). Longman.

Watching the World. Raymond Clapper. (FDR & the Era of the New Deal Ser.). 1975. Repr. of 1944 ed. 35.00 (ISBN 0-306-70730-6). Da Capo.

Watchmakers & Clockmakers of the World, 2 vols. 3rd ed. G. H. Baillie & Brian Loomes. (Illus.). 1976. 29.95x set (ISBN 0-686-65563-X). Vol. 1 (ISBN 0-7198-0040-4). Vol. 2 (ISBN 0-7198-0080-3). Intl Ideas.

Watchman's Stone. Rona Randall. 240p. 1976. pap. 1.75 o.p. (ISBN 0-345-25107-5). Ballantine.

Watchmen in the Night: Presidential Accountability After Watergate. Theodore Sorensen. LC 75-1273. 1975. 12.00x (ISBN 0-262-19133-4); pap. 5.95 (ISBN 0-262-69055-1). MIT Pr.

Water. Kenneth S. Davis & Luna Leopold. LC 66-18677. (Life Science Library). (Illus.). (gr. 5 up). 1970. PLB 8.97 o.p. (ISBN 0-8094-0473-7, Pub. by Time-Life). Silver.

Water. rev. ed. Harlan Wade. LC 78-21290. (Book About Ser.). (Illus.). (gr. k-3). 1979. PLB 7.30 (ISBN 0-8172-1539-5). Raintree Pubs.

Water: A Primer. Luna B. Leopold. LC 73-19844. (Geology Ser.). (Illus.). 1974. text ed. 16.95x (ISBN 0-7167-0264-9); pap. text ed. 8.95x (ISBN 0-7167-0263-0). W H Freeman.

Water: A Scarce Resource. Henry Gilfond. LC 78-3563. (Impact Bks.). (Illus.). 1978. lib. bdg. 6.90 s&l (ISBN 0-531-02205-6). Watts.

Water Activity: Influences on Food Quality: Proceedings of Second International Symposium on Properties of Water Affecting Food Quality. Ed. by Louis B. Rockland & George F. Stewart. LC 79-26632. 1980. 60.00 (ISBN 0-12-591350-8). Acad Pr.

Water & Energy in Colorado's Future. Colorado Energy Research Institute, Colorado School of Mines. 330p. 1981. lib. bdg. 25.00x (ISBN 0-86531-118-8). Westview.

Water & Life. Adolph Caso. 94p. (Eng. & It.). 1976. pap. 5.00 (ISBN 0-8283-1682-1). Dante U Am.

Water & Metropolitan Man. Compiled by American Society of Civil Engineers. 96p. 1969. pap. text ed. 7.75 (ISBN 0-87262-011-5). Am Soc Civil Eng.

Water & Piping Problems: A Troubleshooter's Guide for Large & Small Buildings. Henry L. Shuldener & James B. Fullman. 275p. 1981. 19.95 (ISBN 0-471-08082-9, Pub. by Wiley-Interscience). Wiley.

Water & Plant Life. Michael Baron. 1967. pap. text ed. 5.95x (ISBN 0-435-61054-6). Heinemann Ed.

Water & Plants. Hans Meidner & D. W. Sheriff. LC 75-41425. (Tertiary Level Biology Ser). 148p. 1976. pap. 13.95 (ISBN 0-470-14996-5). Halsted Pr.

Water & Related Land Resource Systems: Proceedings of the IFAC Symposium, Cleveland, Ohio, U. S. A., 28-31 May 1980. Ed. by Y. Haimes & J. Kindler. LC 80-41690. (IFAC Proceedings Ser.). (Illus.). 550p. 1981. 120.00 (ISBN 0-08-027307-6). Pergamon.

Water & Shore Birds. Walter Thiede. (Illus.). 144p. 1981. pap. 5.95 (ISBN 0-7011-2527-6, Pub. by Chatto-Bodley-Jonathan). Merrimack Bk Serv.

Water & Steam: Their Properties & Current Industrial Applications: Proceedings. International Conference on the Properties of Steam, 9th, Munich, West Germany, Sep. 10-14, 1979. (Illus.). 704p. 1980. 115.00 (ISBN 0-08-025431-4). Pergamon.

Water & the West: The Colorado River Compact & the Politics of Water in the American West. Norris Hundley, Jr. (Illus.). 432p. 1975. 30.00x (ISBN 0-520-02700-0). U of Cal Pr.

Water & Tribal Settlements in South-East Arabia: A Study of Aflaj of Oman. J. C. Wilkinson. (Oxford Research Studies in Geography). (Illus.). 1977. 37.50x (ISBN 0-19-823217-9). Oxford U Pr.

Water & Waste Water Technology. Mark J. Hammer. LC 75-2000. 502p. 1975. text ed. 21.95 (ISBN 0-471-34726-4); solutions manual avail. (ISBN 0-471-34727-2). Wiley.

Water & Waste-Water Technology, SI Version. Mark J. Hammer. LC 77-9243. 1977. text ed. 22.95 (ISBN 0-471-03787-7); solutions manual avail. (ISBN 0-471-03819-9). Wiley.

Water & Wastewater Control Engineering: Glossary. Compiled by American Society of Civil Engineers. 400p. 1969. text ed. 15.00 o.p. (ISBN 0-87262-014-X). Am Soc Civil Eng.

Water As a Productive Environment. C. F. Hickling. 250p. 1980. 29.00x (ISBN 0-85664-062-X, Pub. by Croom Helm England). State Mutual Bk.

Water Babies. Charles Kingsley. (Childrens Illustrated Classics Ser). (Illus.). 1975. Repr. of 1957 ed. 11.00x o.p. (ISBN 0-460-05037-0, Pub. by J. M. Dent England). Biblio Dist.

Water Babies. Charles Kingsley. LC 75-32190. (Classics of Children's Literature, 1621-1932: Vol. 52). (Illus.). 1976. Repr. of 1885 ed. PLB 38.00 (ISBN 0-8240-2301-3). Garland Pub.

Water-Based Industrial Finishes: Recent Developments. Ed. by M. T. Gillis. LC 80-17520. (Chemical Technology Review: No. 167). 435p. 1980. 48.00 (ISBN 0-8155-0812-3). Noyes.

Water-Based Paint Formulations. E. W. Flick. LC 75-2939. 396p. (Index of chemicals & suppliers). 1975. 28.00 o.p. (ISBN 0-8155-0571-X). Noyes.

Water Chemistry. Vernon L. Snoeyink & David Jenkins. (SPE Monographs). 1980. text ed. 27.95 (ISBN 0-471-05196-9); lab manual avail. (ISBN 0-471-06272-3). Wiley.

Water Child. Judith Bolinger & Jane English. LC 80-80650. (Orig.). 1980. pap. 6.95 (ISBN 0-89793-023-1). Hunter Hse.

Water Chlorination: Environmental Impact & Health Effects, Vol. 3. Ed. by Robert L. Jolley et al. LC 77-92588. (Illus.). 1200p. 1980. 37.50 (ISBN 0-250-40342-0). Ann Arbor Science.

Water Circle. James Broughton. 1977. pap. 1.50 (ISBN 0-686-28712-6). Man-Root.

Water-Colour Painting in Britain: Vol. III The Victorian Period. Martin Hardle. 1968. 120.00 (ISBN 0-7134-0718-2, Pub. by Batsford England). David & Charles.

Water Conservation-Needs & Implementing Strategies. Compiled by American Society of Civil Engineers. 280p. 1979. pap. text ed. 19.50 (ISBN 0-87262-198-7). Am Soc Civil Eng.

Water Crisis. Ed. by George A. Nikolaieff. (Reference Shelf Ser: Vol. 38, No. 6). 1967. 6.25 (ISBN 0-8242-0093-4). Wilson.

Water Customer Information: Proceedings. American Water Works Association. (AWWA Handbooks Proceedings Ser.). (Illus.). 56p. 1979. pap. text ed. 6.00 (ISBN 0-89867-222-8). Am Water Wks Assn.

Water Deficits & Plant Growth, 5 vols. Ed. by Theodore T. Kozlowski. LC 68-14658. Vol. 1 1968. 48.00 (ISBN 0-12-424150-6); Vol. 2 1968. 40.50 (ISBN 0-12-424152-2); Vol. 3 1972. 40.50 (ISBN 0-12-424153-0); Vol. 4 1976. 48.50 (ISBN 0-12-424154-9); Vol. 5, 1978. 39.50 (ISBN 0-12-424155-7); Set. 176.50. Acad Pr.

Water Deficits & Plant Growth: Woody Plant Communities, Vol. 6. T. T. Kozlowski. 1981. write for info. (ISBN 0-12-424156-5). Acad Pr.

Water Disinfection with Ozone, Chloramines, or Chlorine Dioxide. American Water Works Association. (Handbooks-Proceedings Ser.). (Illus.). 224p. 1980. pap. text ed. 10.00 (ISBN 0-89867-244-9). Am Water Wks Assn.

Water Dog. Richard A. Wolters. 1964. 11.95 (ISBN 0-525-23021-1). Dutton.

Water Encyclopedia. Ed. by David K. Todd. LC 76-140311. 1970. 40.00 o.s.i. (ISBN 0-912394-01-3). Water Info.

Water: Experiments to Understand It. Boris Arnov. (gr. 5 up). 1980. 6.95 (ISBN 0-688-41927-5); lib. bdg. 6.67 (ISBN 0-688-51927-X). Morrow.

Water Flow in Plants. J. A. Milburn. LC 77-30743. (Integrated Themes in Biology Ser.). (Illus.). 1979. pap. text ed. 17.50 (ISBN 0-582-44387-3). Longman.

Water Flying. Franklin T. Kurt. LC 73-13362. (Illus.). 288p. 1974. 12.95 (ISBN 0-02-567130-8). Macmillan.

Water for a Starving World. Malin Falkenmark & Gunnar Lindh. LC 76-45475. 1977. 19.75 o.p. (ISBN 0-89158-211-8); pap. text ed. 6.95x o.p. (ISBN 0-89158-212-6). Westview.

Water for Dinosaurs & You. Roma Gans. LC 78-158691. (Let's-Read-&-Find-Out Science Bk). (Illus.). (gr. k-3). 1972. PLB 7.89 (ISBN 0-690-87027-2, TYC-J); pap. 2.95 crocodile paperback ser. (ISBN 0-690-00202-5, TYC-J). T Y Crowell.

Water for New York: A Study in State Administration of Water Resources. Roscoe C. Martin. LC 60-9946. 1960. 7.95x (ISBN 0-8156-2028-4). Syracuse U Pr.

Water for the Southwest: Historical Survey & Guide to Historic Sites. Compiled by American Society of Civil Engineers. 224p. 1973. pap. text ed. 13.00 (ISBN 0-87262-056-5). Am Soc Civil Eng.

Water for the West: The Bureau of Reclamation, 1902-1977. Michael C. Robinson. (Illus.). 1979. pap. text ed. 6.00 o.p. (ISBN 0-917084-30-6). Am Public Works.

Water Gators in Hell. Douglas F. MacKenzie. 1977. 4.50 o.p. (ISBN 0-533-02936-8). Vantage.

Water Hammer. Goldman. 7.00 o.p. (ISBN 0-686-00162-1). Columbia Graphs.

Water in a Developing World: The Management of a Critical Resource. Ed. by Albert E. Utton & Ludwik A. Teclaff. (Special Studies in Natural Resources & Energy Management). 1978. lib. bdg. 25.50x (ISBN 0-89158-050-6). Westview.

Water in Environmental Planning. Thomas Dunne & Luna B. Leopold. LC 78-8013. (Illus.). 1978. text ed. 33.95x (ISBN 0-7167-0079-4). W H Freeman.

Water in Polymers. Ed. by Stanley P. Rowland. LC 80-13860. (ACS Symposium Ser.: No. 127). 1980. 48.00 (ISBN 0-8412-0559-0). Am Chemical.

Water in the Garden. Douglas Bartrum. 1968. 5.95 o.p. (ISBN 0-8231-6025-4). Branford.

Water Is Wide. Pat Conroy. 1979. pap. 2.25 (ISBN 0-380-46037-8, 46037). Avon.

Water Jump: The Story of Transatlantic Flight. David Beaty. LC 76-5116. (Illus.). 288p. (YA) 1977. 10.00 o.p. (ISBN 0-06-010296-9, HarpT). Har-Row.

Water Level Route. Charles M. Knoll. (Illus.). 64p. (Orig.). 1977. pap. 5.95 (ISBN 0-686-61272-8). Natl Rail Rochester.

Water Level Route. 2nd ed. Charles M. Knoll. 1981. pap. 5.95 (ISBN 0-686-64650-9). Natl Rail Rochester.

Water Management & Environment in Latin America: Analysis & Case Studies of Water Management, Including New Approaches Through Simulation Modelling & the Environmental Consequences of Past & Potential Trends in Water Use. United Nations Economic Commission for Latin America. (Environmental Sciences & Applications Ser.: Vol. 12). 1979. 68.00 (ISBN 0-08-023580-8); pap. 23.00 (ISBN 0-08-024457-2). Pergamon.

Water Management for Arid Lands: Proceedings. Training Workshop on Water Management for Arid Regions, Ministry of Irrigation, Government of Egypt, in Cooperation with the United Nations Environment Programme, Cairo, Egypt. Ed. by M. A. Samaha et al. LC 79-40504. (Water Development, Supply & Management: Vol. 13). (Illus.). 280p. 1980. 40.00 (ISBN 0-08-022431-8). Pergamon.

Water Management for Irrigation & Drainage. Compiled by American Society of Civil Engineers. 640p. 1977. pap. text ed. 46.00 (ISBN 0-87262-097-2). Am Soc Civil Eng.

Water Management in England & Wales. Elizabeth Porter. LC 77-83998. (Cambridge Geographical Studies: No. 10). (Illus.). 1979. 40.50 (ISBN 0-521-21865-9). Cambridge U Pr.

Water Management Organization in China. Ed. by James E. Nickum. 1981. 22.50 (ISBN 0-87332-140-5). M E Sharpe.

Water Mite Genera & Subgenera. David Cook. (Memoris Ser: No. 21). (Illus.). 860p. 1974. 55.00 (ISBN 0-686-08749-6). Am Entom Inst.

Water Mites from India. David R. Cook. (Memoirs Ser: No. 9). (Illus.). 411p. 1967. 25.00 (ISBN 0-686-17145-4). Am Entom Inst.

Water Mites of Liberia. David R. Cook. (Memoirs Ser: No. 6). (Illus.). 418p. 1966. 25.00 (ISBN 0-686-17144-6). Am Entom Inst.

Water of Kane. O. A. Bushnell. LC 80-5463. 472p. 1980. 12.95 (ISBN 0-8248-0714-6). U Pr of Hawaii.

Water of Life. John W. Armstrong. 136p. 1971. pap. 4.75x (ISBN 0-8464-1060-5). Beekman Pubs.

Water of Life. Jay Williams. LC 79-19438. (Illus.). 40p. (gr. k-3). 1980. 8.95 (ISBN 0-590-07530-6, Four Winds). Schol Bk Serv.

Water Planning in Britain. Dennis J. Parker & Edmund C. Penning-Rowsell. (Resource Management Ser.: No. 1). (Illus.). 288p. (Orig.). 1980. text ed. 34.00x (ISBN 0-04-711006-6); pap. text ed. 17.95x (ISBN 0-04-711007-4). Allen Unwin.

Water Plants. Laurence Pringle. LC 74-23942. (Let's-Read & Find-Out Science Bk). (Illus.). 40p. (gr. k-3). 1975. 6.95 o.p. (ISBN 0-690-00737-X, TYC-J); PLB 7.89 (ISBN 0-690-00738-8). T Y Crowell.

Water Pollution: A Guide to Information Sources. Ed. by Allen W. Knight & Mary Ann Simmons. LC 73-17537. (Man & the Environment Information Guide Ser.: Vol. 9). 1980. 30.00 (ISBN 0-8103-1346-4). Gale.

Water Pollution: Causes & Effects in Australia. D. W. Connell. 1974. 9.00x (ISBN 0-7022-0880-9); pap. 5.50x o.s.i. (ISBN 0-7022-0881-7). U of Queensland Pr.

Water Pollution Control. W. W. Eckenfelder & D. Ford. (Illus.). 17.50 (ISBN 0-8363-0099-8). Jenkins.

Water Pollution Control Technology. J. K. Bewtra. (Theoretical & Applied Environmental Reviews: Vol. 1). 200p. 1981. 25.00 (ISBN 3-7186-0027-7). Harwood Academic.

Water Pollution Microbiology. Ed. by Ralph Mitchell. LC 73-168641. 1972. Vol. 1. 20.50 (ISBN 0-471-61100-X, Pub. by Wiley-Interscience); Vol. 2 1978. 33.00 (ISBN 0-471-01902-X). Wiley.

Water Pollution Technology. John A. Black. (Illus.). 1977. ref. ed. 16.95 o.p. (ISBN 0-87909-875-9). Reston.

Water Polo. David Barr & Andrew Gordon. (Illus.). 112p. (YA) 1981. 12.95 (Pub. by EP Publishing England). Sterling.

Water Power Engineering. M. M. Dandekar & N. K. Sharma. 1980. pap. text ed. 12.50x (ISBN 0-7069-0700-0, Pub. by Vikas India). Advent Bk.

Water Problems in Oil Production: An Operator's Manual. 2nd ed. L. C. Case. LC 75-118940. 1977. 23.00 (ISBN 0-87814-001-8). Pennwell Pub.

Water Problems of Urbanizing Areas. Compiled by American Society of Civil Engineers. 360p. 1979. pap. text ed. 20.00 (ISBN 0-87262-145-6). Am Soc Civil Eng.

Water Purification Processes, GB-053: A Technical Market Analysis. Ed. by Business Communications Co. 1979. 750.00 (ISBN 0-89336-231-X). BCC.

Water Quality Criteria for Fresh Water Fish. Ed. by Richard Lloyd & J. S. Alabaster. LC 79-41350. 1980. text ed. 52.50 (ISBN 0-408-10673-5). Butterworths.

Water Quality in Catchment Ecosystems. A. M. Gower. LC 79-42907. (Institution of Environmental Sciences Ser.). 335p. 1980. 50.00 (ISBN 0-471-27692-8, Pub. by Wiley-Interscience). Wiley.

Water Quality in Warmwater Fish Ponds. Claude E. Boyd. (Illus.). 366p. 1979. pap. 9.95x (ISBN 0-8173-0055-4, Pub. by Ag Experiment). U of Ala Pr.

Water Quality Management. Peter A. Krenkel & Vladimir Novotny. LC 80-516. 1980. 65.00 (ISBN 0-12-426150-7). Acad Pr.

Water Quality Technology Conference - Nineteen Seventy-Nine. American Water Works Association. (AWWA Handbooks Proceedings Ser.). (Illus.). 350p. 1980. pap. text ed. 10.00 (ISBN 0-89867-231-7). Am Water Wks Assn.

Water Quality Technology Conference: 1978-New Laboratory Tools for Quality Control in Water Treatment & Distribution. (AWWA Handbooks-Proceedings Ser.). (Illus.). 1979. pap. text ed. 10.00 (ISBN 0-89867-175-2). Am Water Wks Assn.

Water Resistance in Paper Coatings: A Panel Discussion. Robert D. Athey, Jr. et al. (TAPPI PRESS Reports). 1979. pap. 33.95 (ISBN 0-89852-382-6, 01-01-R082). TAPPI.

Water-Resource Development: The Economics of Project Evaluation. Otto Eckstein. LC 58-7501. (Economic Studies: No. 104). (Illus.). 1958. 16.50x (ISBN 0-674-94785-1). Harvard U Pr.

Water Resources for Our Cities. Duane Baumann & Daniel Dworkin. Ed. by Salvatore J. Natoli. LC 78-59100. (Resource Papers for College Geography Ser.). (Illus.). 1978. pap. text ed. 4.00 (ISBN 0-89291-130-1). Assn Am Geographers.

Water Resources in the Arab Middle East & North Africa. Christian Gischler. (Illus.). 1979. lib. bdg. 23.00x (ISBN 0-906559-00-6). Westview.

Water Resources Planning in New England. Stuart G. Koch. LC 79-66453. (Illus.). 200p. 1980. 12.00x (ISBN 0-87451-176-3). U Pr of New Eng.

Water Reuse: State-of-the-Art. E. Joe Middlebrooks. 1981. text ed. 40.00 (ISBN 0-250-40359-5). Ann Arbor Science.

Water Rights & Irrigation Practices in Lahj: A Study of the Application of Customary & Shri'ah Law in South-West Arabia. A. M. Maktari. LC 76-145606. (Oriental Publications: No. 21). (Illus.). 1972. 44.50 (ISBN 0-521-07930-6). Cambridge U Pr.

Water, Rock & Sand: Poems. Peter S. Levi. 1962. 5.95 (ISBN 0-8023-1071-0). Dufour.

Water, Sanitary & Waste Services for Buildings. Alan F. Wise. (Mitchell's Building Construction Ser.). 156p. 1979. pap. 13.95x (ISBN 0-470-26888-3). Halsted Pr.

Water Skiing. Boy Scouts Of America. LC 19-600. (Illus.). 48p. (gr. 6-12). 1969. pap. 0.70x (ISBN 0-8395-3357-8, 3357). BSA.

Water Skiing Skill. Glen E. Anderson. (Quick & Easy Ser). (gr. 7-12). 1968. pap. 1.95 o.s.i. (ISBN 0-02-079080-5, Collier). Macmillan.

Water-Soluble Polymers: Developments Since 1978. Yale L. Meltzer. LC 80-26174. (Chemical Technology Rev. Ser.: 181). (Illus.). 608p. 1981. 54.00 (ISBN 0-8155-0834-4). Noyes.

Water-Soluble Polymers: Recent Developments. Y. Meltzer. LC 78-68940. (Chemical Technology Review Ser.: No. 126). (Illus.). 1979. 48.00 o.p. (ISBN 0-8155-0742-9). Noyes.

Water Sports. Charles Coombs. (Young Readers Bookshelf). (Illus.). (gr. 4-7). 4.25 o.p. (ISBN 0-8313-0022-1); PLB 6.19 (ISBN 0-685-23444-4). Lantern.

Water Supplies for Fire Protection. IFSTA Committee. Ed. by Jerry Laughlin & Connie E. Williams. LC 78-58881. (IFSTA Ser.: No. 205). (Illus.). 1978. pap. text ed. 7.00 (ISBN 0-87939-029-8). Intl Fire Serv.

Water Supply Engineering. N. S. Shah. 1972. 4.50x (ISBN 0-210-31171-1). Asia.

Water Systems Nineteen Seventy-Nine. Compiled by American Society of Civil Engineers. 240p. 1979. pap. text ed. 17.75 (ISBN 0-87262-143-X). Am Soc Civil Eng.

Water Tables. James Seay. LC 73-15014. (Wesleyan Poetry Program: Vol. 72). 72p. 1974. pap. 4.95 (ISBN 0-8195-1072-6, Pub. by Wesleyan U Pr). Columbia U Pr.

Water Trails West. Western Writers of America. LC 77-82973. 1978. 12.95 o.p. (ISBN 0-385-12709-X). Doubleday.

Water Trails West. Western Writers of America. 1979. pap. 3.50 (ISBN 0-380-47688-6, 47688, Discus). Avon.

Water Transport in Cells & Tissue. C. R. House. 562p. 1974. 39.75 o.p. (ISBN 0-685-90285-4, Pub. by W & W). Krieger.

Water Travel from the Beginning. Alma Gilleo. LC 77-22822. (From the Beginning Ser.). (Illus.). (gr. 1-4). 1977. PLB 5.50 (ISBN 0-89565-001-0). Childs World.

Water Treatment: A Survey of Current Methods of Purifying Domestic Supplies & Treating Industrial Effluents & Sewage. 4th ed. G. V. James. (Illus.). 1971. 28.95x (ISBN 0-291-39360-8). Intl Ideas.

Water Treatment Handbook. 5th ed. Degremont. LC 79-87503. 1186p. 1979. 73.95x (ISBN 0-470-26749-6). Halsted Pr.

Water Treatment Plant Design. Compiled by American Society of Civil Engineers. 364p. 1969. text ed. 15.00 (ISBN 0-87262-012-3). Am Soc Civil Eng.

Water Under the Bridge. Sumner L. Elliot. 1978. pap. 1.95 o.p. (ISBN 0-685-54639-X, 04722-8). Jove Pubns.

Water Utility Accounting. 2nd ed. American Water Works Association. (General References Ser.). (Illus.). 288p. 1980. text ed. 28.00 (ISBN 0-89867-237-6). Am Water Wks Assn.

Water: What's in It for You? A Concise Discussion of the Vital Role of Water in Your Health. Allen McDaniels. 1972. pap. 1.50 o.p. (ISBN 0-9600300-2-6). Heather Foun.

Watercolor by Design. Mario Cooper. (Illus.). 176p. 1980. 21.95 (ISBN 0-8230-5655-4). Watson-Guptill.

Watercolor, Wax & Wool: The Art of Janet Shook Lacoste. Intro. by Amy F. Lee & Al Lowman. LC 80-82780. (Illus.). 88p. (Orig.). 1980. pap. 10.00 (ISBN 0-933164-81-5). U of Tex Inst Tex Culture.

Watercolors. J. M. Parramon & G. Fresquet. (Art Ser.). (Orig.). 1980. pap. 4.95 (ISBN 0-89586-074-0). H P Bks.

Watercolour Painting: A Beginner's Guide. Joan M. Catchpole. (Illus.). 1975. 15.95x (ISBN 0-7188-2162-9). Intl Ideas.

Waterfall. Margaret Drabble. 1977. pap. 2.50 (ISBN 0-445-04118-8). Popular Lib.

Waterflood Calculations for Hand-Held Computers. Forrest A. Garb. (Illus.). 200p. 1981. 19.95 (ISBN 0-87201-895-4). Gulf Pub.

Waterford & Tramore Railway. H. Fayle & A. T. Newham. (Illus.). 56p. 1972. 5.95 (ISBN 0-7153-5518-X). David & Charles.

Waterfowl in the Marshes. A. C. Becker, Jr. LC 69-13030. (Illus.). 1969. 9.95 o.p. (ISBN 0-498-06948-6). A S Barnes.

Waterfowl of the World, 4 vols. Jean Delacour. LC 73-76659. (Illus.). 284p. 1974. slipcased 150.00 o.p. (ISBN 0-668-02970-6). Arco.

Waterfront Cookbook: Secrets of San Francisco Restaurant Chefs. rev. ed. Joseph Orlando. Ed. by Gail Larrick. LC 80-66582. (Illus.). 144p. 1980. pap. 5.95 (ISBN 0-89395-045-9); spiral binding 8.95 (ISBN 0-89395-063-7). Cal Living Bks.

Waterfront Development: A Bibliography. Charles W. Barr. (Public Administration Ser.: Bibliography P-462). 51p. 1980. pap. 5.50. Vance Biblios.

Waterfront Living: How to Buy Real Estate on the Water. George W. DeLong. LC 79-57321. (Illus., Orig.). 1981. pap. 10.00 (ISBN 0-9603414-0-4). DeLong & Assoc.

Watergate: An Annotated Bibliography. Kenyon C. Rosenberg & Judith K. Rosenberg. LC 75-6880. 141p. 1975. lib. bdg. 11.50x o.p. (ISBN 0-87287-116-9). Libs Unl.

Watergate Hearings: Index to the Senate Select Committee Reports. Compiled by Hedda Garza. LC 80-53886. 625p. 1981. lib. bdg. price not set (ISBN 0-8420-2175-2). Scholarly Res Inc.

Waterhouses, the Romantic Alternative. Ferenc Mate. (Illus.). 1978. 14.95 o.p. (ISBN 0-920256-01-5, ScribT). Scribner.

Watering Hole: A User's Guide to Montana Bars. Joan Melcher. 128p. 1980. pap. text ed. 6.95 (ISBN 0-938314-00-9). MT Mag.

Waterloo. Ed. by Lord Chalfont. LC 79-3499. (Illus.). 1980. 17.95 o.p. (ISBN 0-394-51119-0). Knopf.

Waterloo Directory of Victorian Periodicals. Ed. by Michael Wolff et al. 1203p. 1980. 215.00 (ISBN 0-08-026079-9). Pergamon.

Waterloo: The Hundred Days. David Chandler. LC 80-36696. 224p. 1981. 18.95. Macmillan.

Watermelon Wine: The Spirit of Country Music. Frye Gaillard. LC 76-62766. (Illus.). 240p. 1977. 10.00 o.p. (ISBN 0-312-85697-0). St Martin.

Watermills of Britain. Leslie Syson. LC 80-66088. (Illus.). 192p. 1980. 24.00 (ISBN 0-7153-7824-4). David & Charles.

Waterrape: The Conspiracy That Succeeded. A. W. Bell. 1977. 5.95 o.p. (ISBN 0-533-02982-1). Vantage.

Waters Above. Joseph Dillow. 1980. 12.95 (ISBN 0-8024-9198-7). Moody.

Waters Dark & Deep. J. Farragut Jones. (Orig.). 1981. pap. 2.75 (ISBN 0-440-19470-9). Dell.

Water's Edge & Other Stories. Krishnan Srinivasan. 120p. 1981. text ed. 10.50x (ISBN 0-86590-009-4, Pub. by Writers Workshop India). Apt Bks.

Waters of the Wilderness. Shirley Seifert. 1976. Repr. of 1941 ed. lib. bdg. 9.95 (ISBN 0-89190-142-6). Am Repr-Rivercity Pr.

Watershed Development. (FAO Soils Bulletin: No. 44). 266p. 1980. pap. 14.25 (ISBN 92-5-100859-0, F1966, FAO). Unipub.

Watershed in India 1914-1922. Algernon Rumbold. 1979. text ed. 40.00x (ISBN 0-485-11182-9, Athlone Pr). Humanities.

Watershed Management. Compiled by American Society of Civil Engineers. 792p. 1975. pap. text ed. 29.50 (ISBN 0-87262-122-7). Am Soc Civil Eng.

Watershed of Two Eras: Europe in 1900. Jan Romein. Tr. by Arnold Pomerans from Dutch. LC 77-14841. 1978. 30.00x (ISBN 0-8195-5026-4, Pub. by Wesleyan U Pr). Columbia U Pr.

Watership Down. deluxe ed. Richard Adams. LC 73-6044. 448p. 1975. 12.95 (ISBN 0-02-700030-3, 70003). Macmillan.

Watership Down. Richard Adams. 1975. pap. 2.50 (ISBN 0-380-00293-0, 39586). Avon.

Waterside Pubs: Pubs of the (British) Inland Waterways. Ronald Russell. LC 74-81057. 1975. 10.50 (ISBN 0-7153-6743-9). David & Charles.

Waterskiing. George Athans, Jr. & Clint Ward. LC 75-7706. (Illus.). 120p. 1975. pap. 4.95 o.p. (ISBN 0-312-85715-2). St Martin.

Waterskiing. Paul Seaton & David Emery. 1979. 10.95 (ISBN 0-571-11325-7, Pub. by Faber & Faber); pap. 6.95 (ISBN 0-571-11222-6). Merrimack Bk Serv.

Waterway Industrial Sites: A Chicago Case Study. David M. Solzman. LC 66-29231. (Research Papers Ser.: No. 107). 138p. 1967. pap. 8.00 (ISBN 0-89065-016-0). U Chicago Dept Geog.

Waterway West: The Story of the Erie Canal. Mary K. Phelan. LC 77-1787. (Illus.). (gr. 5-9). 1977. 8.95 (ISBN 0-690-01333-7, TYC-J). T Y Crowell.

Waterways of Britain: A Social Panorama. D. D. Gladwin. 1976. 22.50 (ISBN 0-7134-3159-8). David & Charles.

WATFIV. J. Moore. 1975. pap. 13.95 (ISBN 0-87909-876-7). Reston.

Wathen's Law. Richard B. Wathen. LC 80-51730. 306p. (Orig.). 1980. pap. 5.95 (ISBN 0-89526-891-4). Regnery-Gateway.

Watson Drawing Book. Ernest W. Watson & Aldren A. Watson. 1981. pap. 9.95 (ISBN 0-442-20054-4). Van Nos Reinhold.

Watsons. Jane Austen. LC 72-9808. 318p. 1973. Repr. of 1958 ed. lib. bdg. 24.75x (ISBN 0-8371-6598-9, AUTW). Greenwood.

Watsons Advanced Textile Design. 4th ed. Grosicki. Ed. by Watson. 1977. 42.95 (ISBN 0-408-00250-6). Butterworths.

Watson's Choice. Gladys Mitchell. 1981. pap. 2.25 o.s.i. (ISBN 0-440-19501-2). Dell.

Watson's Classic Book on the Play of the Hand at Bridge. Louis H. Watson. Ed. by Sam Fry, Jr. 1959. pap. 3.95 (ISBN 0-06-463209-1, EH 209, EH). Har-Row.

Watson's Revenge. Richard Mallett. (Illus.). 36p. 1974. pap. 4.00 o.p. (ISBN 0-915230-01-1). Rue Morgue.

Watson's Textile Design & Color. 7th ed. William Watson. Ed. by Z. J. Grosicki. 1977. text ed. 35.95 (ISBN 0-408-70515-9). Butterworths.

Watsonville: Memories That Linger. Betty Lewis. LC 76-41500. (Illus.). 1976. 10.00 o.p. (ISBN 0-913548-37-5, Valley Calif). Western Tanager.

Watsonville: More Memories That Linger, Vol. 2. Betty Lewis. LC 76-41500. (Illus.). 168p. 1980. 11.95 (ISBN 0-934136-08-4, Valley Calif). Western Tanager.

Watteau. Rene Huyghe. LC 75-97899. (Great Draughtsmen Ser.). 1970. 7.95 o.p. (ISBN 0-8076-0545-X). Braziller.

Watteau. (Selected Artist Art Ser.). 1977. pap. 5.95 (ISBN 0-8120-0813-8). Barron.

Watteau & the North Studies in the Dutch & Flemish Baroque Influence on French Rocco Painting. Oliver Banks. LC 76-23602. (Outstanding Dissertations in the Fine Arts Ser.). 1977. lib. bdg. 63.00x (ISBN 0-8240-2676-4). Garland Pub.

Watteau's Drawings: Their Use & Significance. Martin Eidelberg. LC 76-23616. (Outstanding Dissertations in the Fine Arts - 18th Century). (Illus.). 1977. Repr. of 1965 ed. lib. bdg. 56.00 (ISBN 0-8240-2687-X). Garland Pub.

Wau-Bun, the "Early" Days in the Northwest. Juliette Kinzie. LC 75-7095. (Indian Captivities Ser.: Vol. 70). 1976. Repr. of 1856 ed. lib. bdg. 44.00 (ISBN 0-8240-1694-7). Garland Pub.

Wave. Christopher Hyde. LC 81-80090. 272p. 1981. pap. 2.95 (ISBN 0-87216-848-4). Playboy Pbks.

Wave Equation on a Curved Space-Time. F. G. Friedlander. LC 74-14435. (Cambridge Monographs on Mathematical Physics). (Illus.). 328p. 1976. 65.50 (ISBN 0-521-20567-0). Cambridge U Pr.

Wave Mechanics. G. Ludwig. 1968. 28.00 (ISBN 0-08-012302-3); pap. 10.75 (ISBN 0-08-012303-1). Pergamon.

Wave Mechanics & Its Applications. P. Gombas & D. Kisdi. LC 73-5789. 250p. 1974. text ed. 23.00 (ISBN 0-08-016979-1). Pergamon.

Wave of Fear: A Classic Horror Anthology. Ed. by Hugh Lamd. LC 74-1963. 1974. 7.95 o.p. (ISBN 0-8008-8063-3). Taplinger.

Wave Principle. Ralph N. Elliott. (Illus.). 1979. deluxe ed. 79.75 (ISBN 0-918968-33-X). Inst Econ Pol.

Wave Propagation Theory. James R. Wait. LC 80-23286. 400p. 1981. 40.01 (ISBN 0-08-026345-3); pap. 20.01 (ISBN 0-08-026344-5). Pergamon.

Wave Scattering from Statistically Rough Surfaces. F. G. Bass & M. Fuchs. 1978. text ed. 105.00 (ISBN 0-08-019896-1). Pergamon.

Wave Transmission. F. R. Connor. (Introductory Topics in Electronics & Telecommunications Ser.). (Illus.). 1972. pap. text ed. 11.00x (ISBN 0-7131-3278-7). Intl Ideas.

Wavelengths of X-Ray Emission Lines & Absorption Edges. Ed. by Y. Cauchois et al. LC 78-40419. 1978. text ed. 150.00 (ISBN 0-08-022448-2); pap. text ed. 80.00 (ISBN 0-08-023392-9). Pergamon.

Waverley: Or 'Tis Sixty Years Since. Sir Walter Scott. Ed. by Claire Lamont. 512p. 1981. 58.00 (ISBN 0-19-812643-3). Oxford U Pr.

Waverly. Walter Scott. 1969. 15.50x (ISBN 0-460-00075-6, Evman); pap. 8.95 (ISBN 0-460-01075-1). Dutton.

Waverly Dictionary. 2nd ed. May Rogers. LC 66-27850. 1967. Repr. of 1885 ed. 20.00 (ISBN 0-8103-3222-1). Gale.

Waves. Herbert S. Zim. (Illus.). (gr. 3-7). 1967. PLB 6.48 (ISBN 0-688-31479-1). Morrow.

Waves: A Mathematical Approach to the Common Types of Wave Motion. 2nd ed. C. A. Coulson & A. Jeffrey. (Illus.). 1978. pap. text ed. 12.95x (ISBN 0-582-44954-5). Longman.

Waves & Beaches: The Dynamics of the Ocean Surface. rev. updated ed. Willard Bascom. LC 79-7038. (Illus.). 1980. 12.00 (ISBN 0-385-14845-3, Anchor Pr); pap. 6.95 (ISBN 0-385-14844-5, Anchor Pr). Doubleday.

Waves & Interactions in Solid State Plasmas. P. M. Platzman & P. A. Wolff. (Solid State Physics: Suppl. 13). 1973. 26.50 (ISBN 0-12-607773-8). Acad Pr.

Waves, Atoms, & Solids. D. A. Davies. LC 77-2192. (Illus.). 1978. pap. text ed. 19.50x (ISBN 0-582-44174-9). Longman.

Waves in Fluids. J. Lighthill. LC 77-8174. (Illus.). 1978. 56.50 (ISBN 0-521-21689-3); pap. 22.95x (ISBN 0-521-29233-6). Cambridge U Pr.

Waves, Rays & Oscillations, Bk. 6. W. Bolton. LC 80-41396. (Study Topics in Physics). 96p. 1980. pap. text ed. write for info. (ISBN 0-408-10657-3). Butterworths.

Wax & Casting: A Notebook of Process & Technique. Roger Armstrong. (Illus.). 160p. 1981. pap. write for info. (ISBN 0-89863-038-X). Star Pub CA.

Wax Portraits & Silhouettes. Ethel S. Bolton. LC 71-164115. 88p. 1974. Repr. of 1914 ed. 18.00 (ISBN 0-8103-3168-3). Gale.

Way. A. L. Anderson. 1978. pap. 1.75 (ISBN 0-8100-0006-7, 12N1715). Northwest Pub.

Way. Josemaria E. de Balaguer. 228p. 1979. pap. 2.95 (ISBN 0-933932-35-9). Scepter Pubs.

Way Back: Toward Accountability in America's Cities. Peter F. Rousmaniere. (Municipal Securities Regulation Ser.). 231p. 1979. pap. 25.00x (ISBN 0-916450-21-X). Coun on Municipal.

Way Down South, Up North. E. Frederic Morrow. LC 72-13451. 1973. 6.95 (ISBN 0-8298-0246-0). Pilgrim NY.

Way Home. Theodore Sturgeon. 1978. pap. 1.50 o.p. (ISBN 0-515-04467-9). Jove Pubns.

Way It Is. Ed. by John Holland. LC 69-11495. (Curriculum Related Bks). (Illus.). (gr. 7 up). 1969. 6.75 o.p. (ISBN 0-15-294830-9, HJ). HarBraceJ.

Way Life Is. Genevieve Dormann. LC 66-12903. 1966. 5.00 o.s.i. (ISBN 0-8076-0345-7). Braziller.

Way Mothers Are. Miriam Schlein. LC 63-13332. (Concept Bks.). (Illus.). (ps-2). 1963. 6.95g (ISBN 0-8075-8692-7). A Whitman.

Way of a Pilgrim. Tr. by Reginald M. French from Rus. (Illus.). 242p. 1974. 7.50 (ISBN 0-8164-0259-0); pap. 3.95 (ISBN 0-8164-2069-6, SP18). Crossroad NY.

Way of a Pilgrim-& the Pilgrim Continues His Way. Tr. by Helen Bacovcin. LC 76-52000. 1978. pap. 2.45 (ISBN 0-385-12400-7, Im). Doubleday.

Way of a Trout. G. P. Van Gytenbeek. (Illus.). 1972. 8.95 o.p. (ISBN 0-397-00872-4). Lippincott.

Way of All Flesh. Samuel Butler. 1954. 12.95x (ISBN 0-460-00895-1, Evman). Dutton.

Way of All Flesh. Samuel Butler. Ed. by Robert L. Wolff. LC 75-1540. (Victorian Fiction Ser.). 1975. Repr. of 1903 ed. lib. bdg. 66.00 (ISBN 0-8240-1611-4). Garland Pub.

Way of All the Earth. Anna Akhmatova. Tr. by D. M. Thomas from Rus. LC 79-1953. 96p. 1980. 9.00 (ISBN 0-8214-0429-6); pap. 5.95 (ISBN 0-8214-0430-X). Ohio U Pr.

Way of an Ant. Kazue Mizumura. LC 72-87155. (Illus.). (gr. 1-5). 1970. 7.95 (ISBN 0-690-87044-2, TYC-J); PLB 8.79 (ISBN 0-690-87045-0). T Y Crowell.

Way of an Eagle. Ethel M. Dell. (Barbara Cartland's Library of Love: Vol. 7). 193p. 1979. 12.95x (ISBN 0-7156-1383-9, Pub. by Duckworth England). Biblio Dist.

Way of Being. Carl R. Rogers. 288p. 1980. 14.95 (ISBN 0-395-29915-2). HM.

Way of Being. Carl R. Rogers. LC 80-82291. 288p. 1981. pap. text ed. 6.95 (ISBN 0-395-29735-4). HM.

Way of Contentment. Ekiken Kaibara. Bd. with Greater Learning for Women. (Studies in Japanese History & Civilization). 1979. Repr. of 1913 ed. 19.00 (ISBN 0-89093-253-0). U Pubns Amer.

Way of Discipleship to Christ. Stephen Isaac. LC 76-57021. 1976. pap. 3.50 (ISBN 0-910378-12-6). Christward.

Way of Discovery: An Introduction to the Thought of Michael Polanyi. Richard Gelwick. LC 76-47429. 1977. 14.95 (ISBN 0-19-502192-4). Oxford U Pr.

Way of Discovery: An Introduction to the Thought of Michael Polanyi. Richard Gelwick. 1977. pap. 4.95 (ISBN 0-19-502193-2, GB492, GB). Oxford U Pr.

Way of Divine Love. Josefa Menendez. LC 79-112493. 1977. pap. 7.50 (ISBN 0-89555-030-X, 104). TAN Bks Pubs.

Way of Education. Sohan Singh. 1968. 5.25x o.p. (ISBN 0-210-27171-X). Asia.

Way of Herbs. Michael Tierra. (Illus., Orig.). 1980. pap. 6.95 (ISBN 0-913300-43-8). Unity Pr.

Way of His Own. T. A. Dyer. (gr. 5-8). 1981. 7.95 (ISBN 0-395-30443-1). HM.

Way of Holiness. Samuel L. Brengle. 1966. Repr. of 1902 ed. 3.25 (ISBN 0-86544-008-5). Salvation Army.

Way of Karate: Beyond Technique. Shigeru Egami. LC 75-12069. (Illus.). 190p. 1976. 12.95 o.p. (ISBN 0-87011-254-6). Kodansha.

Way of Lao Tzu: Tao-Te Chins. Lao Tzu. Tr. by Wing-Tsit Chan. LC 62-21266. (Orig.). 1963. 5.95 (ISBN 0-672-60350-0, LLA139). Bobbs.

Way of Life. Charles Hodge. 1978. pap. 3.95 (ISBN 0-85151-273-9). Banner of Truth.

Way of Life. M. L. Sexton. (Ser. Outlines). 2.95 (ISBN 0-89315-352-4). Lambert Bk.

Way of Life: An Address Delivered to Yale Students Sunday Evening, April 20, 1913. William Osler. (Illus.). 56p. 1969. 6.75 (ISBN 0-398-01433-7). C C Thomas.

Way of Life at the Heart of the Tao Te Ching. Tr. by Benjamin Hoff. 1980. 16.95 (ISBN 0-8348-0156-6, Pub. by John Weatherhill Inc Japan). C E Tuttle.

Way of Love. John B. Glubb. LC 75-44945. 1976. 7.95 (ISBN 0-916624-01-3). TSU Pr.

Way of Love. George H. Tavard. LC 76-22542. 1977. 6.95x o.p. (ISBN 0-88344-700-2). Orbis Bks.

Way of Perfection. St. Teresa of Avila. pap. 2.95 (ISBN 0-385-06539-6, D176, Im). Doubleday.

Way of Phenomenology: Criticism As a Philosophical Discipline. Richard M. Zaner. LC 77-114178. (Traditions in Philosophy Ser). 1970. pap. 5.50 (ISBN 0-672-63611-5). Pegasus.

Way of Phenomenology: Criticism As a Philosophical Discipline. Richard M. Zaner. LC 77-114178. 1970. 18.95x (ISBN 0-672-53611-0). Irvington.

Way of Philosophy. rev. ed. Ed. by Philip Wheelwright. 1960. 13.20 o.p. (ISBN 0-672-63217-9). Odyssey Pr.

Way of St. Francis. Robert H. Garner. 1981. 6.95 (ISBN 0-8062-1605-0). Carlton.

Way of Seeing. Phil Rusten. 1978. 19.00. Way of Seeing.

Way of Tao, Pt. I. Bhagwan S. Rajneesh. Tr. by Dolli Didi. 1978. 24.00 (ISBN 0-89684-025-5, Pub. by Motilal Barnarsidass). Orient Bk Dist.

Way of Tenderness. Kevin O'Shea. LC 78-61728. (Orig.). 1978. pap. 2.45 (ISBN 0-8091-2166-2). Paulist Pr.

Way of the Immortal Threefold Self: The Straight Path. Robert E. Birdsong. (Aquarian Academy Monograph: Ser. E, No. 4). 1980. pap. 1.45 (ISBN 0-917108-29-9). Sirius Bks.

Way of the Lawless. Max Brand. 1980. pap. 1.75 (ISBN 0-446-94301-0). Warner Bks.

Way of the Lawless. Max Brand. (gr. 7-12). 1979. lib. bdg. 12.95 (ISBN 0-8161-6747-8). G K Hall.

Way of the Mystics: The Early Christian Mystics & the Rise of the Sufis. Margaret Smith. 1979. 14.95 (ISBN 0-19-520039-X). Oxford U Pr.

Way of the New World: The Black Novel in America. Addison Gayle, Jr. LC 74-9449. 336p. 1975. 10.00 o.p. (ISBN 0-385-04103-9, Anchor Pr). Doubleday.

Way of the New World: The Black Novel in America. Addison Gayle, Jr. LC 74-9449. 440p. 1976. pap. 3.95 (ISBN 0-385-04135-7, Anch). Doubleday.

Way of the Peaceful Warrior: A Basically True Story. Dan Millman. LC 79-66725. 210p. 1980. 8.95 (ISBN 0-87477-121-8). J P Tarcher.

Way of the River: A Book of Scriptural Meditations. Ernest Ferlita. LC 76-45675. 1977. pap. 1.95 (ISBN 0-8091-2009-7). Paulist Pr.

Way of the Shaman: A Guide to Power & Healing. Michael Harner. LC 79-2995. 192p. 1980. 9.95 (ISBN 0-06-063710-2, HarpR). Har-Row.

Way of the Sufi. Idries Shah. 1970. pap. 3.95 (ISBN 0-525-47261-4). Dutton.

Way of the Tamarisk. Anne Worboys. 216p. 1975. 6.95 o.s.i. (ISBN 0-440-05990-9). Delacorte.

Way of the Upright: A Jewish View of Economic Justice. Richard G. Hirsch. (Issues of Conscience Ser.). 128p. (Orig.). 1973. pap. 0.50 (ISBN 0-8074-0094-7, 180205). UAHC.

Way of the Weather. Jerome Spar. LC 66-30641. (Creative Science Ser). (gr. 4-9). 1967. PLB 7.95 (ISBN 0-87191-013-6). Creative Ed.

Way of the West, 5 vols. Arthur J. Slavin. 1973-1975. Vols. A & 1-3. pap. text ed. 14.95x ea. Vol. A (ISBN 0-471-00907-5). Vol. B. pap. text ed. 14.50x (ISBN 0-471-00908-3). Vol. 1 (ISBN 0-471-00788-9). Vol. 2 (ISBN 0-471-00789-7). Vol. 3 (ISBN 0-471-00891-5). Wiley.

Way of the White Clouds. Lama A. Govinda. (Clear Light Ser). (Illus.). 1970. pap. 8.95 (ISBN 0-394-73005-4). Shambhala Pubns.

Way of the Wilderness. G. I. Davies. LC 77-95442. (Society for Old Testament Monographs). (Illus.). 1979. 22.50 (ISBN 0-521-22057-2). Cambridge U Pr.

Way of the Wolf: The Gospel in New Images. Martin Bell. LC 77-120366. (Illus.). 1970. 6.95 (ISBN 0-8164-0202-7); 2 records 7.95 ea. Crossroad NY.

Way of the Word. John Meagher. 250p. 1975. 9.50 (ISBN 0-8164-0270-1). Crossroad NY.

Way of the World. William Congreve. Ed. by Kathleen M. Lynch. LC 65-10543. (Regents Restoration Drama Ser). 1965. 8.95x (ISBN 0-8032-0354-3); pap. 2.75x (ISBN 0-8032-5354-0, BB 251, Bison). U of Nebr Pr.

Way of Words: An Informal Logic. Ronald Munson. LC 75-31028. (Illus.). 448p. 1976. 15.75 (ISBN 0-395-20625-1); answer bk. 2.00 (ISBN 0-395-24229-0). HM.

Way of Working. Ed. by D. M. Dooling. LC 78-68366. 1979. pap. 3.50 (ISBN 0-385-14163-7, Anch). Doubleday.

Way Out. William Sheldon & Warren H. Wheelock. (Orig.). (RL 3). 1972. pap. text ed. 4.96 (ISBN 0-205-03337-7, 5233372); tchrs'. guide 2.40 (ISBN 0-205-03338-5, 5233380); activities 20.00 (ISBN 0-205-03339-3, 5233399). Allyn.

Way Out: A Story of the Cumberland Today. Emerson Hough. 1976. lib. bdg. 14.75x (ISBN 0-89968-048-8). Lightyear.

Way Out Must Lead in: Life Histories of the Civil Rights Movement. rev. ed. William R. Beardsley. 187p. 1981. pap. 4.95 (ISBN 0-88208-120-9). Lawrence Hill.

Way People Pray: An Introduction to the History of Religions. John T. Catoir. LC 73-91369. (Orig.). 1974. pap. 1.95 (ISBN 0-8091-1805-X). Paulist Pr.

Way Station. Clifford Simak. LC 79-20182. 1980. Repr. of 1963 ed. lib. bdg. 10.00x (ISBN 0-8376-0440-0). Bentley.

Way They Play, Bk. 2. Samuel Applebaum & Sada Applebaum. (Illus.). 384p. 1973. 9.95 (ISBN 0-87666-438-9, Z-4). Paganiniana Pubns.

Way They Play, Bk. 7. Samuel Applebaum & Henry Roth. (Illus.). 288p. 1980. 9.95 (ISBN 0-87666-619-5, Z-33). Paganiniana Pubns.

Way They Play, Bk. 8. Samuel Applebaum & Henry Roth. (Illus.). 288p. 1980. 9.95 (ISBN 0-87666-622-5, Z-34). Paganiniana Pubns.

Way Things Work Book of Nature. 1980. 17.50 (ISBN 0-671-22455-7). S&S.

Way to Be Free. J. F. Bennett. 1980. pap. 6.95 (ISBN 0-87728-491-1). Weiser.

Way to Beauty: Planting & Landscaping in the Rocky Mountains. George W. Kelly. (Illus.). 176p. 1976. pap. 2.95 o.p. (ISBN 0-87108-096-6). Pruett.

Way to Chinese Painting. Sze Mai-Mai. (Illus.). 1959. pap. 3.95 (ISBN 0-394-70166-6, Vin). Random.

Way to Christianity: The Pilgrim. Richard Chilson. 1980. pap. 8.95 (ISBN 0-03-053426-7). Winston Pr.

Way to End Inflation. John Davidson. 1980. 7.95 (ISBN 0-533-04736-6). Vantage.

Way to Go Home. Eric Pendry. 1978. 8.95 (ISBN 0-393-08834-0). Norton.

Way to Happiness. Iverna Tompkins. 1978. pap. 1.95 pocketsize o.p. (ISBN 0-88270-292-0). Logos.

Way to Health. Robert R. Leichtman & Carl Japikse. (Art of Living). 90p. Date not set. pap. 3.00 (ISBN 0-89804-037-X). Ariel Pr.

Way to Natural Beauty. Cheryl Tiegs. (Illus.). 1980. 12.95 (ISBN 0-686-68753-1, 24894). S&S.

Way to Remember. Susan Davis. Ed. by Tom Davis. 32p. (ps up). 1980. pap. write for info. (ISBN 0-8280-0023-9). Review & Herald.

Way to Sketch: With Special Reference to Water Color. Vernon Blake. (Illus.). 144p. (Unabridged replication of 2nd ed.). 1981. pap. price not set (ISBN 0-486-24119-X). Dover.

Way to the Old Sailors Home. Thomas Baird. LC 76-26260. 1977. 8.95 o.s.i. (ISBN 0-06-010173-3, HarpT). Har-Row.

Way to Wealth, Wherein Is Plainly Taught a Remedy for Sedicion. Richard Crowley. LC 74-28843. (English Experience Ser.: No. 724). 1975. Repr. of 1550 ed. 3.50 (ISBN 90-221-0724-8). Walter J Johnson.

Way We Die. David Dempsey. Orig. Title: Dying in America. 288p. 1975. 12.95 (ISBN 0-02-530750-9). Macmillan.

Way We Die Now. Michael Z. Lewin. 1979. pap. 1.95 o.p. (ISBN 0-425-04028-3). Berkley Pub.

Way We Live Now. Anthony Trollope. Ed. by Robert Tracy. LC 74-132935. (Library of Literature Ser.). 1974. pap. 13.95 (ISBN 0-672-61016-7, LL32). Bobbs.

Way We Wore: Fashion Illustrations of Children's Wear 1870-1970. Linda Martin. LC 78-17243. (Illus.). 1978. 17.50 (ISBN 0-684-15655-5, ScribT). Scribner.

Way We Work. Andrew Hepworth & Michael Osbaldeston. 1979. text ed. 26.50x (ISBN 0-566-00212-4, Pub. by Gower Pub Co England). Renouf.

Way Women Write: Sex & Style in Contemporary Prose. Mary P. Hiatt. LC 77-14122. 1977. pap. 7.75x (ISBN 0-8077-2542-0). Tchrs Coll.

Wayfarers. Knut Hamsun. Tr. by James McFarlane. 1981. pap. 7.95 (ISBN 0-374-51635-9). FS&G.

Wayfarers. Knut Hamsun. Tr. by James McFarlane from Norwegian. 460p. 1980. 15.95 (ISBN 0-374-28672-8). FS&G.

Wayfarers All. Kenneth Grahame. (Illus.). 32p. (gr. 1 up). 1981. 10.95 (ISBN 0-684-16876-6). Scribner.

Wayne County: The Aesthetic Heritage of a Rural Area. Stephen W. Jacobs. LC 79-64132. (Architecture Worth Saving Ser.). (Illus.). 288p. 1979. 22.50 (ISBN 0-89062-044-X, Pub. by Wayne County Hist Soc); pap. 10.00 (ISBN 0-89062-041-5). Pub Ctr Cult Res.

Ways & Means. Margaret Collis. LC 77-83015. (Using the Environment Ser.). (Illus.). 1977. pap. text ed. 9.30 (ISBN 0-356-05001-7). Raintree Child.

Ways of a Judge: Reflections from the Federal Apellate Bench. Frank Coffin. 288p. 1980. 10.95 (ISBN 0-395-29461-4). HM.

Ways of Animals, 10 bks. Aileen Fisher. (Nature Ser). (ps-6). 1973. Set. 69.60 (ISBN 0-8372-0880-7); 252.24 set, tchrs. guide, 10 filmstrips, record ed. (ISBN 0-8372-0883-1, 883); 252.24 set, tchrs. guide, 10 filmstrips, cassette ed (ISBN 0-8372-2884-0); tchrs. guide by sue beauregard 3.00 (ISBN 0-8372-0869-6). Bowmar-Noble.

Ways of Aquitaine. Freda White. (Illus.). 172p. 1980. 8.95 o.p. (ISBN 0-571-08445-1, Pub by Faber & Faber). Merrimack Bk Serv.

Ways of Being Religious: Readings for a New Approach to Religion. Frederick J. Streng et al. (Illus.). 608p. 1973. 17.95 (ISBN 0-13-946277-5). P-H.

Ways of Escape. Graham Greene. Date not set. 12.95 (ISBN 0-671-41219-1). S&S.

Ways of Friendship. Ignace Lepp. 1968. 8.95 (ISBN 0-02-570410-9); pap. 1.25 (ISBN 0-02-086650-X). Macmillan.

Ways of Health: Holistic Approaches to Ancient & Contemporary Medicine. David J. Sobel. LC 78-14081. 1979. pap. 7.95 (ISBN 0-15-694992-X, Harv). HarBraceJ.

Ways of Meaning: An Introduction to a Philosophy of Language. Mark Platts. 1978. 22.00x (ISBN 0-7100-0000-6); pap. 11.00 (ISBN 0-7100-0001-4). Routledge & Kegan.

Ways of Medieval Life & Thought. Frederick M. Powicke. LC 64-13394. (Illus.). 1949. 9.50x (ISBN 0-8196-0137-3). Biblo.

Ways of My Grandmothers. Beverly H. Wolf. 224p. 1981. pap. 5.95. Morrow.

Ways of My Grandmothers. Beverly H. Wolf. LC 79-91645. 224p. 1980. 9.95 (ISBN 0-688-03665-1). Morrow.

Ways of Paradox & Other Essays. W. V. Quine. (Orig.). 1966. pap. text ed. 4.95 o.p. (ISBN 0-394-30449-7). Random.

Ways of Plants. Aileen Fisher. Incl. Plant Magic (ISBN 0-8372-2391-1); Mysteries in the Garden; Swords & Daggers (ISBN 0-8372-2393-8); And a Sunflower Grew (ISBN 0-8372-2394-6); Petals Yellow & Petals Red (ISBN 0-8372-2395-4); Now That Spring Is Here (ISBN 0-8372-2396-2); As the Leaves Fall Down (ISBN 0-8372-2397-0); Prize Performances (ISBN 0-8372-2398-9); Tree with a Thousand Uses (ISBN 0-8372-2399-7); Seeds on the Go (ISBN 0-8372-2400-4). (Illus.). 1977. 6.96 ea.; tchr's. guide 3.00 (ISBN 0-685-80031-8); 10 bks., 10 filmstrips, tchr's guide record ed. 252.24 (ISBN 0-8372-3318-6); cassette ed. 252.24 (ISBN 0-8372-3317-8). Bowmar-Noble.

Ways of Reading the Bible. Ed. by Michael Wadsworth. 225p. 1981. 27.50x (ISBN 0-389-20162-6). B&N.

Ways of Russian Theology: Pt. 2. Georges Florvosky. Ed. by Richard S. Haugh et al. (Collected Works of Georges Florovsky). 400p. (Orig.). 1980. pap. 27.50 (ISBN 0-913124-24-9). Nordland Pub.

Ways of Studying Children: An Observational Manual for Early Childhood Teachers. 2nd ed. Millie Almy & Celia Genishi. LC 79-13881. 1979. pap. text ed. 8.50x (ISBN 0-8077-2551-X). Tchrs Coll.

Ways of Sunlight. Samuel Selvon. 188p. (Orig.). 1979. 9.00 (ISBN 0-89410-109-9); pap. 5.00 (ISBN 0-89410-108-0). Three Continents.

Ways of the Poem. rev. ed. Josephine Miles. LC 78-146676. (English Literature Ser). 448p. 1972. pap. text ed. 9.50x (ISBN 0-13-946319-4). P-H.

Ways of the Six Footed. rev. ed. Anna B. Comstock. (Illus.). 176p. 1977. 7.95 (ISBN 0-8014-1081-9). Comstock.

Ways of the Spirit. Leon J. Suenens. Ed. by Elizabeth Hamilton. 1976. 5.95 (ISBN 0-8164-1218-9). Crossroad NY.

Ways of Thinking of Eastern Peoples: India, China, Tibet, Japan. rev. ed. Hajime Nakamura. Ed. by Philip P. Wiener. 1964. 15.00x o.p. (ISBN 0-8248-0010-9, Eastwest Ctr); pap. text ed. 7.95x (ISBN 0-8248-0078-8). U Pr of Hawaii.

Ways of Wildlife. Ed. by Eleanor Horwitz. LC 77-2208. 172p. 1977. text ed. 7.95 (ISBN 0-590-07527-6, Citations); pap. 2.95 (ISBN 0-590-09617-6). Schol Bk Serv.

Ways of Wildlife. Ed. by Eleanor Horwitz & Wildlife Society Elementary Education Committee. LC 77-2208. (Illus.). 159p. (gr. 1-6). 1977. 7.95 (ISBN 0-590-07527-6, Citation); pap. 2.95 (ISBN 0-590-09617-6). Schol Bk Serv.

Ways Out: Utopian Communal Groups in an Age of Babylon. John R. Hall. (International Library of Sociology Ser.). 1978. 22.50 (ISBN 0-7100-8807-8). Routledge & Kegan.

Ways Through Bracken. Thomas A. Clark. 1980. signed ltd. ed. 20.00 (ISBN 0-912330-44-9); pap. 7.50 (ISBN 0-912330-44-9). Jargon Soc.

Ways to High Consciousness. Meredith Murray. 136p. 1978. pap. 2.50 (ISBN 0-8334-1706-1). Multimedia.

Ways to Move. R. Robinson. (Topics in Geography Ser.). (Illus.). 1977. 16.95 (ISBN 0-521-21271-5); pap. 8.95 (ISBN 0-521-29081-3). Cambridge U Pr.

Ways to Shiva: Life & Ritual in Hindu India. Joseph M. Dye. LC 80-25113. (Illus.). 94p. (Orig.). 1980. pap. 4.95 (ISBN 0-87633-038-3). Phila Mus Art.

Ways to Teach Children. Iris V. Cully. LC 66-24201. 1966. 1.00x o.p. (ISBN 0-8006-0076-2). Fortress.

Wayside Tavern. Norah Lofts. LC 80-954. 384p. 1980. 11.95 (ISBN 0-385-17201-X). Doubleday.

Waystage English. J. Van Ek. (Council of Europe Language Learning Ser.). 1980. pap. 5.95 (ISBN 0-08-024590-0). Pergamon.

Wayward Liberal: A Political Biography of Donald Richberg. Thomas E. Vadney. LC 75-132832. 1970. 12.50x (ISBN 0-8131-1243-5). U Pr of Ky.

Wayward Servants: The Two Worlds of the African Pygmies. Colin M. Turnbull. LC 75-5002. (Illus.). 1976. Repr. of 1965 ed. lib. bdg. 37.00x (ISBN 0-8371-7927-0, TUWS). Greenwood.

Wayward Welfare State. Roger Freeman. (Publications Ser.: No. 249). (Illus.). 415p. 1981. price not set. Hoover Inst Pr.

Wayward Winds. Evelyn Kahn. (Orig.). 1980. pap. write for info. (ISBN 0-671-83128-3). PB.

Wayward Winds. Roger SeLegue. LC 80-52064. 464p. (Orig.). 1980. pap. 3.95x (ISBN 0-9604600-0-4). Rooney Pubns.

Wayzgoose: A Symposium for Contemporary Bookmaking. 1980. 12.50 (ISBN 0-686-65300-9). Moretus Pr.

W.B. Yeats: The Critical Heritage. Ed. by A. Norman Jeffares. (Critical Heritage Ser.). 1977. 34.00 (ISBN 0-7100-8480-3). Routledge & Kegan.

We Agnostics: On the Tight Rope to Eternity. Basset, Bernard, S.J. 1968. pap. 0.95 (ISBN 0-385-08106-5, Im). Doubleday.

We All Share. Dorothy Corey. Ed. by Ann Fay. LC 80-18988. (Self-Starter Bks.). (Illus.). 32p. (ps-1). 1980. 6.50 (ISBN 0-8075-8696-X). A Whitman.

We Almost Lost Detroit. John G. Fuller. 1976. pap. 1.95 o.p. (ISBN 0-345-25266-7). Ballantine.

We Americans: A Topical History of the United States. Leonard Pitt. (Single volume edition). 1976. 16.95x o.p. (ISBN 0-673-05974-X). Scott F.

We & the Other. Eda Howink. 1980. 5.50 (ISBN 0-8233-0315-2). Golden Quill.

We Are Aging. Jack Botwinick. 1981. text ed. cancelled (ISBN 0-8261-3380-0); pap. text ed. 11.95 (ISBN 0-8261-3381-9). Springer Pub.

We Are All Brothers. Louis Evely. 120p. 1975. pap. 1.45 (ISBN 0-385-04830-0, Im). Doubleday.

We Are Amused: The Cartoonist's View of Royalty. Ed. by Peter Grosvenor. 1979. 9.95 (ISBN 0-370-30139-0, Pub. by Chatto Bodley Jonathan). Merrimack Bk Serv.

We Are but a Moment's Sunlight: Understanding Death. Charles S. Adler. 1976. pap. 1.95 (ISBN 0-671-48772-8). WSP.

We Are Everywhere: A Celebration of Lavender Culture. Karla Jay & Allen Young. (Orig.). 1978. pap. 1.95 o.p. (ISBN 0-685-87092-8). Jove Pubns.

We Are Mesquakie, We Are One. Hadley Irwin. 128p. (gr. 5 up). 1980. 7.95 (ISBN 0-912670-85-1). Feminist Pr.

We Are One-American Jewry & Israel. Melvin I. Urofsky. LC 77-12878. 1978. 10.95 o.p. (ISBN 0-385-07580-4, Anchor Pr). Doubleday.

We Are the Earthquake Generation. Jeffrey Goodman. 1980. pap. 2.75 (ISBN 0-425-04991-4). Berkley Pub.

We Became Wives of Happy Husbands. Darien B. Cooper & Anne K. Carroll. 168p. 1976. pap. 3.50 (ISBN 0-88207-731-7). Victor Bks.

We Believe. Sr. Mary D. Bothwell. (Christ Our Life Ser.). (Illus.). (gr. 4). 1981. pap. text ed. 3.80 (ISBN 0-8294-0367-1); tchr's ed. 6.95 (ISBN 0-8294-0368-X). Loyola.

We Believe. Ralph M. Riggs. 1954. 2.95 (ISBN 0-88243-780-1, 02-0780). Gospel Pub.

We Believe in Biblical Innerancy. Charles Ryrie. 61p. 1981. pap. 0.35 (ISBN 0-937396-53-2). Walterick Pubs.

We Believe in Creation. Charles Ryrie. 62p. 1981. pap. 0.35 (ISBN 0-937396-54-0). Walterick Pubs.

We Buy Junque - We Sell Antiques. Clarissa Start. 158p. (Orig.). 1979. pap. 5.95 (ISBN 0-86629-012-5). Sunrise MO.

We Came a-Marching... One, Two, Three. Mildred Hobzek. LC 78-7793. (Illus.). 40p. (ps-3). 1978. PLB 5.95 (ISBN 0-590-07720-1, Four Winds). Schol Bk Serv.

We Came to Help. Monika Schwinn & Bernhard Diehl. LC 76-13882. (Helen & Kurt Wolff Bk.). (Illus.). 1976. 8.95 o.p. (ISBN 0-15-195595-6). HarBraceJ.

We Can, Vol. 1. Robin R. Star. 88p. (gr. 4 up). 1980. PLB 5.00 (ISBN 0-88200-135-3, C2670). Alexander Graham.

We Can, Vol. 2. Robin R. Star. 98p. (gr. 4 up). 1980. PLB 5.00 (ISBN 0-88200-136-1, C2786). Alexander Graham.

We Can Teach You to Play Soccer. Bill Muse & Dan White. 160p. 1976. pap. 3.95 o.p. (ISBN 0-8015-6911-7). Dutton.

We Can Win Others. Theron B. Chastain. 1953. pap. 1.75 o.p. (ISBN 0-8170-0194-8). Judson.

We Can't Afford It. Sandy Hintz & Martin Hintz. LC 76-46433. (Interaction 2 Ser). (Illus.). (gr. k-3). 1977. PLB 7.95 o.p. (ISBN 0-8172-0066-5, Raintree Editions). Raintree Pubs.

We Could Be Happy Together. Vivek Adarkar. 105p. 1973. 4.00x (ISBN 0-210-22370-7). Asia.

We Dare to Say Our Father. Louis Evely. 120p. 1975. pap. 1.45 (ISBN 0-385-06274-5, Im). Doubleday.

We Didn't Have Much but We Sure Had Plenty: Stories of Rural Women. Sherry Thomas. LC 80-956. (Illus.). 208p. 1981. pap. 7.95 (ISBN 0-385-14951-4, Anch). Doubleday.

We Didn't Mean to. Sharon Addy. LC 80-24976. (Life & Living from a Child's Point of View Ser.). (Illus.). 32p. (gr. k-5). 1981. PLB 9.65 (ISBN 0-8172-1370-8). Raintree Child.

We Didn't Mean to Go to Sea. Arthur Ransome. (Children's Literature Ser.). 1981. PLB 11.98 (ISBN 0-8398-2698-2). Gregg.

We Die Before We Live: Talking with the Very Ill. Daniel Berrigan. 160p. 1980. 9.95 (ISBN 0-8164-0462-3). Seabury.

We Don't Live in Snow Houses Now. Ed. by Susan Cowan. (Illus.). 194p. (Inuktitut, Eng.). 1981. pap. 11.95 (ISBN 0-920234-00-3, 08912-6, Pub. by Canadian Artic Producers Ltd). U of Chicago Pr.

We Eat the Mines & the Mines Eat Us: Dependency & Exploitation in Bolivian Tin Mines. June Nash. LC 79-11623. 1979. 25.00 (ISBN 0-231-04710-X). Columbia U Pr.

We Fed Them Cactus. Fabiola Cabeza De Baca. LC 54-12881. (Zia Books). 208p. 1979. pap. 4.95 (ISBN 0-8263-0517-2). U of NM Pr.

We Have Always Lived in the Castle. Shirley Jackson. 1974. pap. 2.25 (ISBN 0-445-08321-2). Popular Lib.

We Have but Faith. Ed. by Tom E. Kakonis & John Scally. LC 74-20434. 152p. 1975. 6.95 (ISBN 0-88498-023-5); text ed. 6.25 o.p. (ISBN 0-685-52606-2). Brevet Pr.

We Have Eaten the Forest: The Story of a Montagnard Village in the Central Highlands of Vietnam. Georges Condominas. Tr. by Adrienne Foulke. 1977. 17.50 o.p. (ISBN 0-686-63835-2); pap. 10.95 (ISBN 0-8090-1386-X). Hill & Wang.

We Have Not Vanished: Eastern Indians of the United States. Alfred Tamarin. (Illus.). 128p. (gr. 3-6). 1974. lib. ed. 5.97 o.p. (ISBN 0-695-40332-X). Follett.

We Hide, You Seek. Jose Aruego & Ariane Dewey. LC 78-13638. (Illus.). (gr. k-3). 1979. 7.95 (ISBN 0-688-80201-X); PLB 7.63 (ISBN 0-688-84201-1). Greenwillow.

We Italian Americans: A Pictorial History. Commentaries by Betty B. Caroli. (Illus.). 300p. Date not set. 25.00x (ISBN 0-913256-38-2). Ctr Migration.

We Jews: Invitation to a Dialogue. Efraim M. Rosenweig. LC 77-81359. 1978. 7.95 (ISBN 0-8015-8428-0, Hawthorn). Dutton.

We Knew Stonewall Jackson. Richard Wheeler. LC 76-58009. (Illus.). 1977. 9.95 (ISBN 0-690-01289-6, TYC-T). T Y Crowell.

We Knew William Tecumseh Sherman. Richard Wheeler. LC 77-4334. (Illus.). 1977. 8.95 o.p. (ISBN 0-690-01426-0, TYC-T). T Y Crowell.

We Led the Way: Darby's Rangers. William O. Darby & William H. Baumer. LC 80-10431. (Illus.). 1980. 14.95 (ISBN 0-89141-082-1). Presidio Pr.

We Like Kindergarten. Clara Cassidy. (Illus.). 24p. (ps-k). 1965. PLB 4.57 o.p. (ISBN 0-307-60552-3, Golden Pr). Western Pub.

We Live in the City: Short Stories. Lois Lenski. (Roundabout America Stories Ser). (Illus.). (gr. k-3). 1954. PLB 4.82 o.p. (ISBN 0-397-30291-6). Lippincott.

We Live in the Country, Vol. 8. (Vegetable Puppets Ser.). (Illus.). 10p. (ps). 1979. 2.50 o.p. (ISBN 0-89346-123-7, Pub. by Froebel-Kan Japan). Heian Intl.

We Love You, Snoopy: Selected Cartoons from "Snoopy, Come Home". Charles M. Schulz. (Peanuts Ser.). (Illus.). 1979. pap. 1.50 (ISBN 0-449-23958-6, Crest). Fawcett.

We Love Your Body. Lani Miller & Diane Rodgers. LC 80-81842. 1980. pap. 9.95 (ISBN 0-933350-32-5). Morse Pr.

We Made a Garden. Margery Fish. (Illus.). 120p. 1970. 10.50 (ISBN 0-7153-4876-0). David & Charles.

We Mind If You Smoke. Don C. Matchan. 1977. pap. 1.95 (ISBN 0-515-03680-3). Jove Pubns.

We Need a Creed. Clyde Farrar. 100p. 1981. 7.95 (ISBN 0-9605588-0-2). Farrar Pub.

We Never Make Mistakes. Aleksandr Solzhenitsyn. Tr. by Paul W. Blackstock from Rus. 1971. pap. 3.95 (ISBN 0-393-00598-4, Norton Lib). Norton.

We Own It: Starting & Managing Co-Ops, Collectives & Employee Owned Ventures. Jim Beatty et al. 1981. 14.00 (ISBN 0-917510-02-X); pap. 9.00 (ISBN 0-917510-03-8). Bell Springs Pub.

We Really Do Need to Listen. Reuben Welch. LC 78-50098. (Illus.). 1978. 5.95 (ISBN 0-914850-30-X); pap. 2.50 (ISBN 0-914850-69-5); pap. text ed. 1.50 study guide (ISBN 0-686-67968-7). Impact Tenn.

We Remember, Elvis! Wanda J. Hill. LC 78-59596. (Illus.). 1978. 17.50 (ISBN 0-89430-028-8). Morgan-Pacific.

We Remember Philip. Norma Simon. Ed. by Caroline Rubin. LC 78-11691. (Concept Bks). (Illus.). (gr. 2-4). 1978. 6.50g (ISBN 0-8075-8709-5). A Whitman.

We Shall Not Overcome: Populism & Southern Blue-Collar Workers. Robert E. Botsch. LC 80-11567. 312p. 1981. 19.50x (ISBN 0-8078-1444-X). U of NC Pr.

We Should Be Thankful. Mrs. James Swartzentruber. (God Is Good Ser.). 1976. 2.00 (ISBN 0-686-18188-3). Rod & Staff.

We, the American Women. Beth Millstein & Jeanne Bodin. (Illus.). 331p. 1977. lib. bdg. 17.20 (ISBN 0-574-42003-7, 11-1003); pap. text ed. 10.00 (ISBN 0-574-42000-2, 11-1002); tchrs'. guide 2.14 (ISBN 0-574-42001-0, 11-1001); student activity bk. 2.73 (ISBN 0-686-67300-X, 11-1002). SRA.

We, the People. Lonnelle Aikman. LC 78-57740. 1978. text ed. 2.95 (ISBN 0-916200-13-2); pap. 2.00 (ISBN 0-916200-14-0). US Capitol Hist Soc.

We, the People. Elizabeth Yates. (Bicentennial Historiettes). (Illus.). 64p. (gr. 7-8). 1976. text ed. 4.95x (ISBN 0-914378-06-6); pap. text ed. 0.95x (ISBN 0-915892-18-9). Regional Ctr Educ.

We the People: A History of the U. S., Combined. James I. Clark & Robert Remini. 1975. pap. text ed. 11.95 (ISBN 0-02-471730-4, 47173); tchrs' manual free (ISBN 0-02-471740-1). Macmillan.

We the People: A History of U. S, 2 vols. James I. Clark & Robert Remini. 1975. Vol. 1. pap. text ed. 8.95x (ISBN 0-02-471710-X, 47171); Vol. 2. pap. text ed. 8.95x (ISBN 0-02-471720-7, 47172). Macmillan.

We, the People: American Character & Social Change. Ed. by Gordon J. DiRenzo. LC 76-51926. (Contributions in Sociology: No. 24). (Illus.). 1977. lib. bdg. 25.00 (ISBN 0-8371-9481-4, DWP/). Greenwood.

We the Russians: Voices from Russia. Ed. by Colette Shulman. LC 78-83345. (Illus.). 320p. (gr. 9 up). 1971. pap. 2.95 o.p. (ISBN 0-275-88550-X). Praeger.

We the Unreconciled. Sujatha Modayil. (Redbird Ser.). 52p. 1975. 10.00 (ISBN 0-88253-672-9); pap. text ed. 4.80 (ISBN 0-88253-671-0). Ind-US Inc.

We Think the World of You. J. R. Ackerley. 180p. 1981. pap. 5.95 (ISBN 0-916870-36-7). Creative Arts Bk.

We Too Are the People. Louise V. Armstrong. LC 74-168679. (FDR & the Era of the New Deal Ser.). Repr. of 1938 ed. lib. bdg. 42.50 (ISBN 0-306-70367-X). Da Capo.

We Took to Cruising: From Maine to Florida Afloat. Talbot Hamlin & Jessica Hamlin. (Illus.). 1951. 8.95 o.p. (ISBN 0-911378-27-8). Sheridan.

We Walked to Moscow. Jerry Lehmann. (Illus.). 1966. pap. 3.00 (ISBN 0-934676-07-0). Greenlf Bks.

We Want You - Is Hitler Alive? Michael X. 1969. pap. 5.95 (ISBN 0-685-20205-4). Saucerian.

We Went Looking. Aileen Fisher. LC 68-13568. (Illus.). (gr. k-3). 1968. 7.95 o.p. (ISBN 0-690-87150-3, TYC-J). T Y Crowell.

We Were Children Then: Ninety Wisconsin Writers, Age Sixty to Ninety-Six. Ed. by Robert E. Gard et al. LC 76-22967. 1976. pap. 8.95 (ISBN 0-88361-041-8). Stanton & Lee.

We Will Suffer & Die If We Have To. Colin Hodgetts. 1971. pap. 1.95 o.p. (ISBN 0-8170-0527-7). Judson.

We Work with Horses. Patrice Clay. (Illus.). 160p. (YA) (gr. 7-12). 1980. 8.95 (ISBN 0-399-20735-X). Putnam.

We Would Not Kill. Hobart Mitchell. 1980. write for info (ISBN 0-913408-63-8). Friends United.

Weak in the World of the Strong: The Third World in the International System. Robert L. Rothstein. LC 77-7889. (Institute of War & Peace Studies). 1977. 18.00x (ISBN 0-231-04338-4). Columbia U Pr.

Weak Interaction of Elementary Particles. L. B. Okun. 1965. text ed. 30.00 (ISBN 0-08-011122-X); pap. text ed. 19.50 (ISBN 0-08-013702-4). Pergamon.

Weak States in a World of Power: The Dynamics of International Relationships. Marshall Singer. LC 70-158070. 1972. 16.95 (ISBN 0-02-928900-9). Free Pr.

Weak States in the International System. Michael Handel. 144p. 1980. 27.50x (ISBN 0-7146-3117-5, F Cass Co). Biblio Dist.

Wealth: A Brief Explanation of the Causes of Economic Welfare. Edwin Cannan. LC 79-1575. 1981. Repr. of 1928 ed. 22.50 (ISBN 0-88355-881-5). Hyperion Conn.

Wealth & Personal Incomes. A. B. Atkinson et al. LC 77-30556. 1978. text ed. 37.00 (ISBN 0-08-022450-4). Pergamon.

Wealth & Poverty. George Gilder. LC 80-50556. 1981. 16.95 (ISBN 0-465-09105-9). Basic.

Wealth & Power in America: An Analysis of Social Class & Income Distribution. Gabriel Kolko. LC 62-11584. 178p. 1962. pap. text ed. 4.95x (ISBN 0-03-037491-X). Praeger.

Wealth & Power in Tudor England: Essays Pressented to S. T. Bindoff. Ed. by E. W. Ives et al. (Illus.). 1978. text ed. 43.00x (ISBN 0-485-11176-4, Athlone Pr). Humanities.

Wealth & Want. D. Urquhart. 116p. 1971. Repr. of 1845 ed. 21.00x (ISBN 0-7165-1787-6, Pub. by Irish Academic Pr Ireland). Biblio Dist.

Wealth from Knowledge. J. Langrish et al. 1972. 24.95 (ISBN 0-470-51721-2). Halsted Pr.

Wealth, Income, & Inequality. 2nd ed. Ed. by A. B. Atkinson. (Illus.). 450p. 1981. 42.00x (ISBN 0-19-877143-6); pap. 21.00x (ISBN 0-19-877144-4). Oxford U Pr.

Wealth of Japan. Edmund O'Connor. Ed. by Malcolm Yapp et al. (World History Ser.). (Illus.). 32p. (gr. 10). 1980. Repr. of 1977 ed. lib. bdg. 5.95 (ISBN 0-89908-237-8); pap. text ed. 1.95 (ISBN 0-89908-212-2). Greenhaven.

Wealth of Nations: Representative Selections. Adam Smith. Ed. by Bruce Mazlish. LC 60-12945. 1961. pap. 6.95 (ISBN 0-672-60327-6, LLA125). Bobbs.

Wealth of Nations: Selections. Adam Smith. Ed. by George J. Stigler. LC 57-12307. (Crofts Classics Ser.). 1957. pap. text ed. 2.75x (ISBN 0-88295-093-2). AHM Pub.

Wealth of Some Nations. Malcolm Caldwell. 192p. 1977. 10.00 (ISBN 0-905762-01-0); pap. 6.00. Lawrence Hill.

Wealth Redistribution & the Income Tax. Ed. by Arleen A. Leibowitz. LC 77-18652. 1978. 15.95 (ISBN 0-669-01506-7). Lexington Bks.

Wealth Seeker: Shadow No. 21. Maxwell Grant. 1978. pap. 1.25 o.p. (ISBN 0-515-04283-8). Jove Pubns.

Weapon of the Night. (Nick Carter Ser.). 1979. pap. 1.95 (ISBN 0-441-87635-8). Charter Bks.

Weapon Retention Techniques for Officer Survival. Robert J. Downey. (Illus.). 128p. 1980. write for info. o.p. (ISBN 0-398-04108-3). C C Thomas.

Weapon Retention Techniques for Officer Survival. Robert J. Downey & Jordon T. Roth. (Illus.). 128p. 1980. text ed. 14.75 (ISBN 0-398-04108-3). C C Thomas.

Weapon Systems Nineteen Eighty to Nineteen Eighty-One. Pretty. 1980. 135.00 (ISBN 0-531-03935-8). Watts.

Weapon Systems Nineteen Seventy-Nine to Nineteen Eighty. Pretty. 1980. 84.50 (ISBN 0-531-03299-X). Watts.

Weaponless Defense: A Law Enforcement Guide to Non-Violent Control. Jack Hibbard & Bryan A. Fried. (Illus.). 184p. 1980. pap. text ed. 15.75 spiral vinyl bdg. (ISBN 0-398-03936-4). C C Thomas.

Weaponless Warriors. Richard Kim. Ed. by John Scurra. LC 74-21218. (Ser. 313). (Illus.). 1974. pap. text ed. 5.95 (ISBN 0-89750-041-5). Ohara Pubns.

Weapons. The Diagram Group. (Illus.). 320p. 1980. 25.00 (ISBN 0-312-85946-5). St Martin.

Weapons. Robin Snelson. 1979. pap. 3.95 (ISBN 0-931064-13-9). Starlog.

Weapons: A Pictorial History. Edwin Tunis. LC 76-29699. (Illus.). (gr. 6 up). 1977. 14.95 (ISBN 0-690-01340-X, TYC-J). T Y Crowell.

Weapons & Equipment of the Marlborough Wars. Anthony Kemp. (Illus.). 192p. 1981. 24.95 (ISBN 0-7137-1013-6, Pub. by Blandford Pr England). Sterling.

Weapons & Equipment of the Napoleonic Wars. Philip Haythornthwaite. (Illus.). 1979. 24.95 (ISBN 0-7137-0906-5, Pub by Blandford Pr England). Sterling.

Weapons & Equipment of the Victorian Soldier. Donald Featherstone. (Illus.). 1978. 19.95 (ISBN 0-7137-0847-6, Pub. by Blandford Pr England). Sterling.

Weapons: The International Game of Arms, Money & Diplomacy. Russell W. Howe. LC 79-7494. 1980. 19.95 (ISBN 0-385-12809-6). Doubleday.

Wear in Slurry Pipelines. Lavinia Gittins. (BHRA Information Ser.). (Illus.). 173p. (Orig.). Date not set. pap. 45.00 (ISBN 0-906085-45-4). BHRA Fluid.

Wear of Metals. A. D. Sarkar. 1976. 23.00 (ISBN 0-08-019738-8); pap. 11.25 (ISBN 0-08-019737-X). Pergamon.

Weather. Boy Scouts Of America. LC 19-600. 60p. (gr. 6-12). 1963. pap. 0.70x (ISBN 0-8395-3274-1, 3274). BSA.

Weather. Herta S. Breiter. LC 77-27239. (Read About Science Ser.). (Illus.). (gr. k-3). 1978. PLB 9.95 (ISBN 0-8393-0079-4). Raintree Child.

Weather. Julian May. (Beginning Science Ser.). (Illus.). (gr. 2-4). 1966. PLB 5.97 o.p. (ISBN 0-695-89210-X). Follett.

Weather. Martha Ryan. (Easy-Read Fact Bks.). (Illus.). 48p. (gr. 2-4). 1976. PLB 4.47 o.p. (ISBN 0-531-00361-2). Watts.

Weather. Graham Sutton. (Teach Yourself Ser.). 1975. pap. 3.95 o.p. (ISBN 0-679-10410-0). McKay.

Weather. Philip D. Thompson & Robert O'Brien. LC 65-14589. (Life Science Library). (Illus.). (gr. 5 up). 1968. PLB 8.97 o.p. (ISBN 0-8094-0467-2, Pub. by Time-Life). Silver.

Weather Almanac: A Reference Guide to Weather & Climate of the U.S. & Its Key Cities. 2nd ed. Ed. by James Ruffner & Frank Bair. LC 73-9342. 1977. 42.00 (ISBN 0-8103-1043-0). Gale.

Weather Almanac: A Reference Guide to Weather & Climate of the United States & Its Key Cities. Ed. by James Ruffner & Frank Bair. (Illus.). 700p. 1981. 42.00 (ISBN 0-8103-1053-8). Gale.

Weather & Climate. Svante Bodin. (Illus.). 1978. 13.95 (ISBN 0-7137-0858-1, Pub. by Blandford Pr England). Sterling.

Weather & Climate. Julius London. LC 59-13618. (Illus.). (gr. 4-6). 1960. PLB 6.95 (ISBN 0-87396-012-2). Stravon.

Weather & Climate. Seymour Simon. (Science Library: No. 7). (gr. 4-6). 1969. PLB 4.99 (ISBN 0-394-80805-3); pap. 1.50 (ISBN 0-394-80805-3). Random.

Weather & Climate Data for Philippine Rice Research. (IRRI Research Paper Ser.: No. 41). 14p. 1979. pap. 5.00 (R081, IRRI). Unipub.

Weather & Climate Modification. Committee on Atmospheric Sciences. (Illus.). 256p. 1973. pap. 8.75 (ISBN 0-309-02121-9). Natl Acad Pr.

Weather & Climate Modification: Problems & Progress. Intro. by Thomas F. Malone. LC 79-22479. 1980. Repr. of 1973 ed. 28.00 (ISBN 0-8103-1017-1). Gale.

Weather & Life: An Introduction to Biometeorology. William P. Lowry. 1969. text ed. 17.95 (ISBN 0-12-457750-4); ans. bklet. 3.00 (ISBN 0-12-457756-3). Acad Pr.

Weather & the Animal World. J. H. Prince. 1975. 6.95 (ISBN 0-525-66416-5). Elsevier-Nelson.

Weather Atlas of the United States. U. S. Environmental Data Service. LC 74-11931. 1975. 40.00 (ISBN 0-8103-1048-1). Gale.

Weather Book for Pilots. Leo Goldfarb. (Illus.). Date not set. spiral bdg. 8.95 (ISBN 0-911721-72-X, Pub. by Weather Book). Aviation.

Weather Elements: Text in Elementary Meteorology. 5th ed. T. Blair & R. Fite. 1965. ref. ed. 17.95 (ISBN 0-13-947721-7). P-H.

Weather for Outdoormen. Walter Dabberdt. (Illus.). 224p. 1981. 12.95 (ISBN 0-684-16865-0, ScribT). Scribner.

Weather in Africa. Martha Gellhorn. LC 79-23763. 236p. 1980. 8.95 (ISBN 0-396-07781-1). Dodd.

Weather Made to Whose Order? American Sunbeam Staff. (Illus.). 56p. Date not set. self cover 2.00 (ISBN 0-918700-04-3). Duverus Pub. Postponed.

Weather Matrix & Human Behavior. Michael A. Persinger. LC 80-18422. 300p. 1980. 27.95 (ISBN 0-03-057731-4). Praeger.

Weather Modification, Prospect & Problems. Georg Breuer. Tr. by H. T. Morth from Ger. LC 79-73236. (Illus.). 1980. 29.95 (ISBN 0-521-22453-5); pap. 8.95 (ISBN 0-521-29577-7). Cambridge U Pr.

Weather Modification: Technology & Law. Ed. by Ray J. Davis & Lewis Grant. LC 78-55519. (AAAS Selected Symposia Ser.). 1978. lib. bdg. 17.50x (ISBN 0-89158-153-7). Westview.

Weather of Six Mornings: Poems. Jane Cooper. LC 68-29507. 1969. 9.95 (ISBN 0-02-528070-8). Macmillan.

Weather of the San Francisco Bay Region. Harold Gilliam. (California Natural History Guides: No. 6). (Illus., Orig.). 1962. 12.95x (ISBN 0-520-03425-2); pap. 3.95 (ISBN 0-520-00469-8). U of Cal Pr.

Weather or Not: A Study of Weather Control. Sam Birdsong. pap. 1.75 (ISBN 0-918700-09-4). Duverus Pub.

Weather War. Leonard Leokum & Paul Posnick. 1978. pap. 2.25 o.p. (ISBN 0-523-40229-5). Pinnacle Bks.

Weathering. rev. ed. C. D. Ollier. LC 75-320198. (Geomorphology Text). (Illus.). 304p. 1975. pap. text ed. 18.95x (ISBN 0-582-48180-5). Longman.

Weathering. Ray Smith. 1980. pap. 2.50 (ISBN 0-930600-13-4). Uzzano Pr.

Weathering the Storm: Women of the American Revolution. Elizabeth Evans. LC 74-10524. (Encore Edition). 1975. 4.95 o.p. (ISBN 0-684-15673-3, ScribT). Scribner.

Weathering the Wilderness: The Sierra Club Guide to Practical Meteorology. William E. Reifsnyder. LC 79-20859. (Outdoor Guides Ser.). (Illus.). 272p. 1980. pap. 8.95 (ISBN 0-87156-266-9). Sierra.

Weatherizing Your Home. George R. Drake. (Illus.). 1978. ref. ed 13.95 (ISBN 0-8359-8592-X). Reston.

Weatherproofing. Ed. by Time Life Books. LC 76-55869. (Home Repair & Improvement Ser.). (Illus.). (gr. 7 up). 1977. lib. bdg. 11.97 (ISBN 0-685-77685-9, Pub. by Time-Life). Silver.

Weatherproofing. Ed. by Time-Life Books. (Home Repair Ser.). (Illus.). 1977. 10.95 (ISBN 0-8094-2370-7). Time-Life.

Weathers. Rhodri Jones. 1971. pap. text ed. 2.50x o.p. (ISBN 0-435-14504-5). Heinemann Ed.

Weavers. Leonard E. Fisher. LC 66-10581. (Colonial Americans Ser). (Illus.). (gr. 4-6). 1966. PLB 4.90 o.p. (ISBN 0-531-01037-6). Watts.

Weaver's Gift. Kathryn Lasky. LC 80-12042. (Illus.). 64p. (gr. 3-7). 1981. 8.95g (ISBN 0-7232-6191-1). Warne.

Weaves of the Incas. Ulla Nass. (Illus.). 108p. soft cover 16.95. Nass.

Weaving & Other Pleasant Occupations. Ruby K. Polkinghorne. LC 71-143640. 1971. Repr. of 1940 ed. 18.00 (ISBN 0-8103-3659-6). Gale.

Weaving Arts of the North American Indian. Frederick J. Dockstader. LC 78-381. (Illus.). 1978. 25.00 (ISBN 0-690-01739-1, TYC-T). T Y Crowell.

Weaving As a Hobby. Marguerite Ickis. (Illus.). (gr. 9 up). 1968. 6.95 o.p. (ISBN 0-8069-5110-9); PLB 6.69 o.p. (ISBN 0-8069-5111-7). Sterling.

Weaving Book: Patterns & Ideas. Helene Bress. (Illus.). Date not set. 40.00 (ISBN 0-684-15664-4, ScribT). Scribner. Postponed.

Weaving in Miniature. Carol Strickler & Barbara Taggart. Ed. by Linda Ligon. LC 80-80935. (Illus.). 86p. 1980. 6.95 (ISBN 0-934026-02-5). Interweave.

Weaving Life's Story. Jackie Larsen. (Illus.). 1978. soft cover 4.95x (ISBN 0-686-14922-X). J Larsen.

Weaving on a Backstrap Loom: Pattern Design from Guatemala. Judy Z. De Rodriquez & Nona M. Ziek. (Illus.). 1978. 14.95 o.p. (ISBN 0-8015-3187-X). Dutton.

Weaving, Spinning, and Dyeing. Lavonne Axford. LC 75-16436. (Spare Time Guides Ser.: No. 7). 148p. 1975. lib. bdg. 11.50x o.p. (ISBN 0-87287-080-4). Libs Unl.

Weaving, Step by Step. Nell Znamierowski. (Step by Step Craft Ser). 1967. PLB 9.15 o.p. (ISBN 0-307-62002-6, Golden Pr); pap. 2.95 (ISBN 0-307-42002-7). Western Pub.

Weaving Tricks. Susan Gilmurray. 128p. 1981. 12.95 (ISBN 0-442-26132-2). Van Nos Reinhold.

Weaving with Reeds & Fibers. Osma G. Tod & Oscar H. Benson. Orig. Title: Hand Weaving with Reeds & Fibers. (Illus.). 224p. 1975. pap. 3.00 (ISBN 0-486-23143-7). Dover.

Web of Darkness. Marion Z. Bradley. 1981. pap. 4.95 (ISBN 0-89865-032-1, Starblaze). Donning Co.

Web of Honey. Cecile Gilmore. (YA) 1970. 5.95 (ISBN 0-685-07463-3, Avalon). Bouregy.

Web of Life. Robert Herrick. 321p. 1980. Repr. of 1900 ed. lib. bdg. 15.95x (ISBN 0-89968-189-1). Lightyear.

Web of Life. John H. Storer. LC 53-12063. (Illus.). 142p. 1981. pap. 5.95 (ISBN 0-8159-7203-2). Devin.

Web of Modern Greek Politics. Jane P. Carey & Andrew G. Carey. LC 68-28394. (Illus.). 1968. 18.00x (ISBN 0-231-03170-X). Columbia U Pr.

Web of the Universe. 2nd ed. E. L. Gardner. 1960. 3.00 o.p. (ISBN 0-7229-5086-1). Theos Pub Hse.

Web of the Witch World. Andre Norton. 192p. 1976. pap. 1.95 (ISBN 0-441-87875-X). Ace Bks.

Web of Traitors. Geoffrey Trease. LC 52-11124. (gr. 6 up). 6.95 (ISBN 0-8149-0433-5). Vanguard.

Web of Urban Housing. Frank de Leeuw et al. 240p. 1975. 10.00 (ISBN 0-87766-151-0, 12900); pap. 4.95 (ISBN 0-87766-151-0, 12700). Urban Inst.

Web of Violence: A Study of Violence in the Family. Jean Renvoizie. 1978. 16.00 (ISBN 0-7100-8804-3). Routledge & Kegan.

Web That Has No Weaver. Ted Kaptchuk. (Illus.). 304p. 1981. 15.00 (ISBN 0-312-92932-3). St Martin.

Web That Has No Weaver: Understanding Chinese Medicine. Ted J. Kaptchuk. (Illus.). 304p. 1981. 15.00 (ISBN 0-312-92932-3). Congdon & Lattes.

Webb Society Deep-Sky Oberver's Handbook: Galaxies, Vol. 4. Ed. by Kenneth G. Jones. 296p. 1981. pap. 14.95 (ISBN 0-89490-050-1). Enslow Pubs.

Webb Society Deep-Sky Observer's Handbook: Vol. III: Open & Globular Clusters. Webb Society. Ed. by Kenneth G. Jones. LC 78-31260. (Illus.). 224p. 1980. pap. 8.95 (ISBN 0-89490-034-X). Enslow Pubs.

Webelos Den Activities. Boy Scouts Of America. (Illus.). 1969. pap. 0.85x (ISBN 0-8395-3853-7, 3853). BSA.

Webelos Den Leader's Book. Boy Scouts Of America. LC 67-23387. (Illus.). 1967. pap. 1.75x (ISBN 0-8395-3217-2, 3217). BSA.

Webelos Scout Book. Boy Scouts Of America. LC 67-14536. (Illus.). (gr. 5). 1973. flexible bdg. 1.75x (ISBN 0-8395-3232-6, 3232). BSA.

Weber & Islam. Bryan S. Turner. (International Library of Sociology). 1974. 22.00x (ISBN 0-7100-7848-X). Routledge & Kegan.

Weber & Islam: A Critical Study. Bryan S. Turner. 1978. pap. 8.95 (ISBN 0-7100-8942-2). Routledge & Kegan.

Weber on Bowling: The Complete Guide to Getting Your Game Together. Dick Weber & Roland Alexander. LC 80-23649. 1981. 12.95 (ISBN 0-13-947937-6). P-H.

Webster's American Military Biographies. Merriam-Webster Editorial Staff. 1978. 12.95 o.p. (ISBN 0-87779-063-9). Merriam.

Webster's Big Seven Collegiate Dictionary. rev. ed. Ed. by Merriam Company. 1976. 14.95 (ISBN 0-87779-314-X). Merriam.

Webster's Biographical Dictionary. Merriam Company. 1976. 15.00 (ISBN 0-87779-443-X). Merriam.

Webster's Collegiate Thesaurus. Ed. by Merriam Webster Editorial Staff. 1976. 10.95 (ISBN 0-87779-069-8); brown skivertex 11.95 (ISBN 0-87779-070-1). Merriam.

Webster's Dictionary for Everyday Use. Ed. by John G. Alee. 445p. 1971. pap. 2.50 (ISBN 0-06-463330-6, E*H 330, EH). Har-Row.

Webster's Elementary Spelling Book: Blue-Back Speller. 1969. pap. 3.50 o.s.i. (ISBN 0-917420-04-7). Buck Hill.

Webster's Instant Word Guide. Ed. by Merriam-Webster Reference Editor. 384p. 1972. 2.95 (ISBN 0-87779-273-9). Merriam.

Webster's New Collegiate Dictionary. 8th ed. Merriam-Webster Editorial Staff. 1568p. 1980. gray lexotone 11.95 (ISBN 0-87779-398-0); thumb-indexed red linen 12.95 (ISBN 0-87779-399-9); thumb-indexed brown skivertex 13.95 (ISBN 0-87779-400-6). Merriam.

Webster's New Geographical Dictionary. rev. ed. Merriam-Webster Editorial Staff. (Illus.). 1568p. 1977. 14.95 (ISBN 0-87779-446-4). Merriam.

Webster's New World Crossword Treasury, Vol. 1. Maynard Nichols. LC 75-13672. (Funk & W Bk.). 1974. pap. 2.50 o.s.i. (ISBN 0-308-10216-9, TYC-T). T Y Crowell.

Webster's New World Crossword Treasury, Vols. 2-3. Ed. by C. Maynard Nichols. 1972. pap. 2.50 ea. o.s.i. (TYC-T); Vol. 2. pap. (ISBN 0-690-00374-9); Vol. 3. pap. (ISBN 0-690-00375-7). T Y Crowell.

Webster's New World Crossword Treasury, Vol. 4. Maynard Nichols. LC 75-785. (Funk & W Bk.). 64p. 1974. pap. 2.50 o.s.i. (ISBN 0-308-10106-5, F89, TYC-T). T Y Crowell.

Webster's New World Dictionary: Of the American Language. 704p. 1976. pap. 2.50 (ISBN 0-445-08500-2). Popular Lib.

Webster's New World Thesaurus. Ed. by Charlton Laird. pap. 5.95 (ISBN 0-452-00535-3, F535, Mer). NAL.

Webster's Scholastic Dictionary. (gr. 9 up). pap. 1.95 (ISBN 0-8049-2001-X, D1). Airmont.

Webster's School Thesaurus. Merriam-Webster Editorial Staff. 1978. 7.95 (ISBN 0-87779-178-3). Merriam.

Webster's Secretarial Handbook. Merriam-Webster Editorial Staff. 1976. 9.95 (ISBN 0-87779-036-1). Merriam.

Webster's Travelers Phrase Books. Incl. English-French. pap. 3.95 (ISBN 0-528-84180-7); English-German. pap. 3.95 (ISBN 0-528-84181-5); English-Italian. pap. 3.95 (ISBN 0-528-84182-3); English-Spanish. pap. 3.95 (ISBN 0-528-84183-1). 1976. Rand.

Weddell Seal, Consummate Diver. Gerald L. Kooyman. LC 80-18794. (Illus.). 176p. Date not set. price not set (ISBN 0-521-23657-6). Cambridge U Pr.

Wedding. James Shirley. Ed. by Martin Flavin & Stephen Orgel. LC 79-54338. (Renaissance Drama Second Ser.). 330p. 1980. lib. bdg. 36.00 (ISBN 0-8240-4456-8). Garland Pub.

Wedding Album: Custom & Lore Through the Ages. Alice Lea & Nast Tasman. (Illus.). 96p. cancelled o.s.i. (ISBN 0-8027-0653-3); pap. cancelled o.s.i. (ISBN 0-8027-7159-9). Walker & Co. Postponed.

Wedding Book: Alternative Ways to Celebrate Marriage. Howard Kirschenbaum & Rockwell Stensrud. LC 73-17901. 1974. pap. 4.50 (ISBN 0-8164-2090-4). Crossroad NY.

Wedding Day in Literature & Art: A Collection of the Best Descriptions of Wedding from the Works of the World's Leading Novelists & Poets. Charles F. Carter. LC 74-86598. 1969. Repr. of 1900 ed. 15.00 (ISBN 0-8103-0154-7). Gale.

Wedding Feast & Two Novellas. Michael Brodsky. 1981. 15.00 (ISBN 0-916354-81-4); pap. 6.95 (ISBN 0-89396-002-0). Urizen Bks.

Wedding in the Family. Rosamond Du Jardin. LC 58-10145. (gr. 4-9). 1958. 7.95 o.p. (ISBN 0-397-30441-2). Lippincott.

Wedding Is Destiny. Cecile Gilmore. 256p. (YA) 1973. 5.95 (ISBN 0-685-30371-3, Avalon). Bouregy.

Wedding of Zein. Tayeb Salih. Tr. by Denys Johnson-Davies from Arabic. 120p. (Orig.). 1978. 9.00 (ISBN 0-89410-200-1); pap. 5.00 (ISBN 0-89410-201-X). Three Continents.

Wedding Party (at Cana) Scripture Union. 1978. pap. 0.49 (ISBN 0-87508-931-3). Chr Lit.

Wedding Photography for Today. Greg Lewis. (Illus.). 136p. 1980. 19.95 (ISBN 0-8174-6410-7); pap. 9.95 (ISBN 0-8174-6411-5). Amphoto.

Wedding Troika. Jovan V. Vukcevich. 1980. pap. 4.95 (ISBN 0-910286-76-0). Boxwood.

Weddings at Nether Powers & Other New Poems. Peter Redgrove. 1979. pap. 7.95 (ISBN 0-7100-0255-6). Routledge & Kegan.

Wedge. Doug Ford. 160p. 1965. pap. 2.95 (ISBN 0-346-12357-7). Cornerstone.

Wedgwood Circle: 1730-1897; Four Generations of Wedgwoods & Their Friends. Barbara Wedgwood & Hensleigh Wedgwood. LC 80-65213. (Illus.). 408p. 1980. 22.50 (ISBN 0-89860-038-3). Eastview.

Wednesday's Wrath. Don Pendleton. (Executioner Ser.: No. 35). 1979. pap. 1.95 (ISBN 0-523-41099-9). Pinnacle Bks.

Wee Green Witch. Mary Leister. LC 78-12380. (Illus.). (ps up). 1978. 9.95 (ISBN 0-916144-30-5); pap. 3.95 (ISBN 0-916144-31-3). Stemmer Hse.

Wee Little Man. Jean Berg. (Beginning-to-Read Ser.). (ps-3). 1963. 3.95 o.p. (ISBN 0-695-89220-7); lib. ed. 2.97 o.p. (ISBN 0-695-49220-9); pap. 1.50 o.p. (ISBN 0-695-39220-4). Follett.

Wee Sing & Play. Pamela Beall & Susan Nipp. (Illus.). 64p. (Orig.). 1981. pap. 2.25 (ISBN 0-8431-0391-4). Price Stern.

Weed Control Handbook, Vol. II. Fryer. (Illus.). 1978. Vol. 2. 36.50 (ISBN 0-8016-1716-2, Blackwell). Mosby.

Weed Science: Principles & Practices. Glenn C. Klingman & Floyd M. Ashton. LC 75-8908. 431p. 1975. 22.50 (ISBN 0-471-49171-3, Pub. by Wiley-Interscience). Wiley.

Weeding Library Collections. Stanley J. Slote. LC 74-23062. (Research Studies in Library Science: No. 14). 1975. lib. bdg. 20.00x (ISBN 0-87287-105-3). Libs Unl.

Weeding of Covent Garden & the Sparagus Garden. Richard Brome. Ed. by Donald S. McClure & Stephen Orgel. LC 79-54351. (Renaissance Drama Second Ser.). 438p. 1980. lib. bdg. 50.00 (ISBN 0-8240-4468-1). Garland Pub.

Weeding the Duchess. Sarah Maclay. 1979. 25.00; pap. 5.00. Black Stone.

Weeds. Mea Allan. (Illus.). 1978. 14.95 o.p. (ISBN 0-670-75657-1). Viking Pr.

Weeds. 2nd ed. Walter C. Muenscher. LC 79-48017. (Illus.). 560p. 1980. 29.50x (ISBN 0-8014-1266-8). Comstock.

Weeds & Wildflowers of Eastern North America. T. Merrill Prentice & Elizabeth O. Sargent. 1973. 25.00 (ISBN 0-87577-063-0). Peabody Mus Salem.

Weeds, Wood, Stone & Mettle. Marilyn Kitchell. (Orig.). 1980. limited signed ed. 20.00x (ISBN 0-915316-77-3); pap. 7.50x (ISBN 0-915316-76-5). Pentagram.

Weegee. Alene Talmey. LC 77-80020. (Aperture History of Photography Ser.: No. 8). (Illus.). 1978. 8.95 (ISBN 0-89381-021-5). Aperture.

Week Down in Devon: A History of the Devon Horse Show. Christopher Hyde. LC 76-3102. (Illus.). 160p. 1976. 15.00 o.p. (ISBN 0-685-62924-4). Chilton.

Week in Agata's World: Poland. Eliot Elisofon. (Face to Face Bks). (Illus.). (gr. k-3). 1970. 4.50 o.p. (ISBN 0-02-733370-1, CCPr); text ed. 1.36 (ISBN 0-02-733380-9, CCPr). Macmillan.

Week in Amy's World: New England. Inger McCabe. (Face to Face Bks). (Illus.). (gr. k-3). 1970. 4.50 o.p. (ISBN 0-685-04412-2, CCPr); text ed. 1.36 o.p. (ISBN 0-685-04413-0, CCPr). Macmillan.

Week in Aya's World: The Ivory Coast. Marc Bernheim & Evelyne Bernheim. LC 70-75391. (Face to Face Books Ser). (Illus.). (gr. k-3). 1969. 4.50g (ISBN 0-02-709050-7, CCPr); text ed. 1.36 o.p. (ISBN 0-02-709070-1, CCPr). Macmillan.

Week in Bico's World: Brazil. Claudia Andujar & Seymour Reit. (Face to Face Bks). (Illus.). (gr. k-3). 1970. 6.95 (ISBN 0-02-705550-7, CCPr). Macmillan.

Week in Daniel's World: France. Hugh Weiss. LC 69-18809. (Face to Face Books Ser). (Illus.). (gr. k-3). 1969. 4.95g (ISBN 0-685-16355-5, CCPr); text ed. 1.36 o.p. (ISBN 0-02-792610-9, CCPr). Macmillan.

Week in Henry's World: El Barrio. Inger McCabe. LC 78-146609. (Face to Face Bks). (Illus.). (gr. k-2). 1971. 4.95g (ISBN 0-685-00338-8, CCPr); pap. text ed. 1.36 o.p. (ISBN 0-02-765380-3, CCPr). Macmillan.

Week in Lateef's World: India. Ray Shaw & Charlotte Zolotow. (Face to Face Bks.). (gr. k-3). 1970. 7.95 (ISBN 0-02-782380-6, CCpr); text ed. 1.36 o.p. (ISBN 0-02-782360-1). Macmillan.

Week in Leonora's World: Puerto Rico. Eliot Elisofon. LC 72-146610. (Face to Face Ser). (Illus.). (gr. k-2). 1971. 4.50g o.s.i. (ISBN 0-02-733350-7, CCPr); pap. text ed. 1.36 o.s.i. (ISBN 0-02-733420-1, CCPr). Macmillan.

Week in Robert's World: The South. Nancy Roberts. LC 69-16211. (Face to Face Books Ser). (Illus.). (gr. k-3). 1969. 4.50g o.s.i. (ISBN 0-685-16359-8, CCPr); text ed. 1.36 o.s.i. (ISBN 0-685-16360-1, CCPr). Macmillan.

Week in-Week Out: A New Look at Liturgical Preaching. David E. Babin. 1976. 7.95 (ISBN 0-8164-0287-6). Crossroad NY.

Week Mom Unplugged the TVs. Terry W. Phelan. LC 78-12180. (Illus.). 48p. (gr. 2-6). 1979. 5.95 (ISBN 0-590-07561-6, Four Winds). Schol Bk Serv.

Weekend. Tania Grossinger. Date not set. pap. 2.95 (ISBN 0-440-19375-3). Dell.

Weekend. Bill Powers. (Triumph Books). (Illus.). (gr. 6 up). 1978. PLB 6.90 s&l (ISBN 0-531-01467-3). Watts.

Weekend a Paris. Mary Glasgow. (Choucas (Jackdaw in French) Ser: No. CH2). 1973. 5.95 o.p. (ISBN 0-670-75625-3, Grossman). Viking Pr.

Weekend Adventures for City-Weary People: A Guide to Overnight Trips in Northern California. rev. ed. Carole T. Meyers. LC 80-24121. (Weekend Adventures for City-Weary People, a Guide to Overnight Trips in the U.S.A. Ser.). Orig. Title: Weekend Adventures for City-Weary Families, a Guide to Overnight Trips in Northern California, 1976. (Illus.). 1980. pap. 5.95 (ISBN 0-917120-06-X). Carousel Pr.

Weekend Man. Richard B. Wright. 1971. 6.95 o.p. (ISBN 0-374-28740-6). FS&G.

Weekend Man. Richard B. Wright. 1972. pap. 1.75 o.p. (ISBN 0-451-08245-1, E8245, Sig). NAL.

Weekly Summary: April Twentieth to August Third, Nineteen Eighteen. Ed. by Richard D. Challener. LC 77-17413. (United Ststes Military Intelligence 1917-1927 Ser.). 1978. lib. bdg. 60.50 (ISBN 0-8240-3003-6). Garland Pub.

Weekly Summary: December Thirteenth, Nineteen Nineteen to January Thirty-First, Nineteen Twenty. Ed. by Richard D. Challener. LC 77-17413. (United States Military Intelligence 1917-1927 Ser.). 1978. lib. bdg. 60.50 (ISBN 0-8240-3010-9). Garland Pub.

Weekly Summary: February Eighth to May Seventeenth, Nineteen Nineteen. Ed. by Richard D. Challener. LC 77-17413. (United States Military Intelligence 1917-1927 Ser.). 1978. lib. bdg. 60.50 (ISBN 0-8240-3006-0). Garland Pub.

Weekly Summary: January Twenty-Sixth to April Thirteenth, Nineteen Eighteen. Ed. by Richard D. Challener. LC 77-17413. (United States Military Intellegence 1917-1927 Ser.). 1978. lib. bdg. 60.50 (ISBN 0-8240-3002-8). Garland Pub.

Weekly Summary: July Ninth to September Twenty-Seventh, Nineteen Nineteen. Ed. by Richard D. Challener. LC 77-17413. (United States Military Intelligence 1917-1927 Ser.). 1978. lib. bdg. 60.50 (ISBN 0-8240-3008-7). Garland Pub.

Weekly Summary: May Twenty-Fourth to July Second, Nineteen Nineteen. Ed. by Richard D. Challener. LC 77-17413. (United States Military Intelligence 1917-1927 Ser.). 1978. lib. bdg. 60.50 (ISBN 0-8240-3007-9). Garland Pub.

Weekly Summary: November Second, Nineteen Eighteen to February First, Nineteen Nineteen. Ed. by Richard D. Challener. LC 77-17413. (United States Military Intelligence 1917-1927 Ser.). 1978. lib. bdg. 60.50 (ISBN 0-8240-3005-2). Garland Pub.

Weekly Summary: October Fourth to December Sixth, Nineteen Nineteen. Ed. by Richard D. Challener. LC 77-17413. (United States Military Intelligence 1917-1927 Ser.). 1978. lib. bdg. 60.50 (ISBN 0-8240-3009-5). Garland Pub.

Weekly Torah Reader: Book of Genesis. rev. ed. Sidney M. Fish. 1977. pap. 3.45x (ISBN 0-8197-0036-3). Bloch.

Weep for Her. Sara Woods. 224p. 1981. 9.95 (ISBN 0-312-86019-6). St Martin.

Weep Some More, My Lady. Sigmund Spaeth. (Music Reprint 1980 Ser.). (Illus.). xv, 268p. 1980. Repr. of 1927 ed. lib. bdg. 22.50 (ISBN 0-306-76003-7). Da Capo.

Weeping May Tarry: My Long Night with Cancer. Hazel Lin. LC 79-55554. 1980. 9.95 (ISBN 0-8283-1738-0). Branden.

Weeping Season. Gauri Pant. (Redbird Book). 36p. 1975. 4.80 (ISBN 0-88253-717-2); pap. 4.00 (ISBN 0-88253-847-0). Ind-US Inc.

Wehrmacht & German Rearmament. Wilhelm Deist. 230p. 1981. 30.00x (ISBN 0-8020-2423-8). U of Toronto Pr.

Weighing & Balancing. Jane J. Srivastava. LC 73-106579. (Young Math Ser.). (Illus.). (gr. 1-4). 1970. 7.95 (ISBN 0-690-87114-7, TYC-J); filmstrip with record 12.85 (ISBN 0-690-87116-3); filmstrip with cassette 15.85 (ISBN 0-690-87118-X). T Y Crowell.

Weighing Machines: Application of Electricity & Electronics to Weighting Machines, Vol. 3. E. H. Griffiths. 248p. 1970. 49.75x (ISBN 0-85264-160-5, Pub. by Griffin England). State Mutual Bk.

Weighing Machines: Non-Self-Indicating Mechanisms, Vol. 1. T. J. Metcalfe. 192p. 1969. 42.50x (ISBN 0-85264-095-1, Pub. by Griffin England). State Mutual Bk.

Weighing Machines: Semi-Self-Indicating & Self-Indicating Mechanisms, Vol. 2. T. J. Metcalfe. 178p. 1969. 44.95x (ISBN 0-686-68843-0, Pub. by Griffin England). State Mutual Bk.

Weight! A Better Way to Lose. Roger Campbell. 128p. 1976. pap. 2.95 (ISBN 0-88207-735-X). Victor Bks.

Weight & Weightlessness. Franklyn M. Branley. LC 70-132292. (Let's-Read-and-Find-Out Science Bk). (Illus.). (gr. k-3). 1972. PLB 7.89 (ISBN 0-690-87329-8, TYC-J). T Y Crowell.

Weight Control: The Behavioural Strategies. Ed. by Michael D. LeBow. LC 79-41728. 352p. 1981. 35.75 (ISBN 0-471-27745-2, Pub. by Wiley-Interscience). Wiley.

Weight Lifting & Progressive Resistance Exercise. Jim Murray. (Illus.). 1954. 11.50 (ISBN 0-8260-6560-0). Ronald Pr.

Weight No Longer. William G. Johnson & Peter Stalonas. 188p. 1981. 19.95 (ISBN 0-88289-261-4). Pelican.

Weight of the Historical Inevitabilities at the End of the 20th Century & the Future of Humanity. Lorenzo G. Grant. (Illus.). 141p. 1981. 41.75 (ISBN 0-930008-76-6). Inst Econ Finan.

Weight on the Thoroughbred Racehorse. Irene McCanliss. 1967. lib. bdg. 7.50 o.p. (ISBN 0-686-28404-6). Thoroughbred Own and Breed.

Weight Training. Stacy Bentley. (Burns Sports Ser.). 156p. Date not set. pap. 4.95 (ISBN 0-695-81572-5). Follett. Postponed.

Weight Training in Athletics. J. Murray & P. Karpovick. 1956. 8.95 (ISBN 0-13-947986-4). P-H.

Weight Training in Athletics & Physical Education. Gene Hooks. (Illus.). 272p. 1974. 15.50 (ISBN 0-13-947994-5). P-H.

Weight Watchers Holiday & Party Cookbook. Weight Watchers International. 1980. 12.95 (ISBN 0-453-01005-9, TE-5). NAL.

Weight Watchers New Program Cookbook. Jean Nidetch. 1979. 9.95 o.p. (ISBN 0-453-01003-2, TE3, Sig). NAL.

Weighting for Baudot & Other Problems for You & Your Computer. Francis Federighi & Edward D. Reilly. (Illus.). 1978. 9.95 (ISBN 0-89529-061-8). Avery Pub.

Weil Representation I: Intertwining Distributions & Discrete Spectrum. Stephen Rallis & Gerard Schiffmann. LC 80-12191. (Memoirs of the American Mathematical Society Ser.). 1980. 6.40 (ISBN 0-8218-2231-4, MEMO-231). Am Math.

Weimar Germany's Left-Wing Intellectuals: A Political History of the Weltbuhne & Its Circle. Istvan Deak. (Illus.). 1968. 23.75x (ISBN 0-520-00309-8). U of Cal Pr.

Weimar, the German Naval Officer Corps & the Rise of National Socialism. Keith W. Bird. 1977. pap. text ed. 34.25x (ISBN 90-6032-094-8). Humanities.

Weinberg der Freiheit. Ed. by Will Schaber. Date not set. 10.50 (ISBN 0-8044-2763-1). Ungar.

Weird & the Beautiful. Richard Headstrom. LC 78-75309. (Illus.). 132p. Date not set. 12.00 o.p. (ISBN 0-498-02394-X). A S Barnes. Postponed.

Weird Gardens. Ed. by Yerian & Cameron. (gr. 4-6). Date not set. pap. cancelled (ISBN 0-590-30025-3, Schol Pap). Schol Bk Serv.

Weird Henry Bird. Sarah Sargent. 128p. (gr. 4-6). 1980. 7.95 (ISBN 0-517-54137-8). Crown.

Weird Heroes. Byron Preiss. 1975. pap. 1.50 o.p. (ISBN 0-515-03746-X). Jove Pubns.

Weird Heroes, Vol. 8. Ed. by Byron Preiss. (Orig.). 1977. pap. 1.75 o.p. (ISBN 0-515-04257-9). Jove Pubns.

Weird Heroes, Vol. 7, Bk. 2: Eye of the Vulture. Byron Preiss & Ron Goulart. (Orig.). 1977. pap. 1.50 o.p. (ISBN 0-515-04293-5). Jove Pubns.

Weird Tales, No. 1. Ed. by Lin Carter. 288p. (Orig.). 1981. pap. 2.50 (ISBN 0-89083-714-7). Zebra.

Weird Tales, No. 2. Ed. by Lin Carter. 288p. (Orig.). 1981. pap. 2.50 (ISBN 0-89083-715-5). Zebra.

Weird Tales Story. Ed. by Robert Weinberg. LC 77-73602. 1977. 17.50 (ISBN 0-913960-16-0). Fax Collect.

Weird Witch's Spell. Ed. by Robert Vitarelli. (Pal Paperbacks Kit A Ser.). (Illus., Orig.). (gr. 7-12). 1972. pap. text ed. 1.25 (ISBN 0-8374-3480-7). Xerox Ed Pubns.

Weird Worlds, No. 3. Ed. by Stine. (gr. 7-12). 1980. pap. 1.50 (ISBN 0-590-30036-9, Schol Pap). Schol Bk Serv.

Weirdest People in the World. C. B. Colby. (Illus.). 192p. (gr. 8 up). 1973. 5.95 o.p. (ISBN 0-8069-3922-2); PLB 5.89 o.p. (ISBN 0-8069-3923-0). Sterling.

Weirdies, Weirdies, Weirdies. Ed. by Helen Hoke. LC 73-14010. (Terrific Triple Titles Ser). (Illus.). 244p. (gr. 6 up). 1975. PLB 7.90 (ISBN 0-531-02683-3). Watts.

Weland: Smith of the Gods. Ursula Synge. LC 73-5945. (Illus.). 94p. (gr. 7 up). 1973. 9.95 (ISBN 0-87599-200-5). S G Phillips.

Welcome: Christian Parenting. Judith Tate-O'Brien. 68p. (Orig.). 1980. pap. 4.00 (ISBN 0-936098-15-5); instrs.' guide 3.00 (ISBN 0-686-68853-8). Natl Marriage.

Welcome Christian: What Baptism Means Today. Joseph T. Nolan. (Illus.). 40p. 1977. pap. 1.50 o.p. (ISBN 0-89570-105-7). Claretian Pubns.
Welcome Home, Charlie. Louise Kantenwein. (Illus.). 64p. 1981. 5.00 (ISBN 0-682-49681-2). Exposition.
Welcome Home, Jellybean. Shyer. (gr. 3-5). 1980. pap. 1.25 (ISBN 0-590-30902-1, Schol Pap). Schol Bk Serv.
Welcome Home, Jellybean. Marlene F. Shyer. LC 77-17970. 160p. (gr. 6-8). 1978. reinforced bdg. 8.95 (ISBN 0-684-15519-2, ScribJ). Scribner.
Welcome of Tears: The Tapirape Indians of Central Brazil. Charles Wagley. LC 76-42665. (Illus.). 1978. pap. 7.95x (ISBN 0-19-502208-4). Oxford U Pr.
Welcome the Birds. Stewart. 7.95 (ISBN 0-392-07518-0, LTB). Soccer.
Welcome the Birds to Your Home. Jane Curtis & Will Curtis. LC 79-20819. (Illus.). 1980. 9.95 (ISBN 0-8289-0353-0); pap. 5.95 (ISBN 0-8289-0354-9). Greene.
Welcome to a New Life. Oscar J. Klinkerman. LC 75-31786. 32p. 1976. pap. 1.50 (ISBN 0-570-03720-4, 12-2622). Concordia.
Welcome to English, 5 bks. rev. ed. Thomas Lismore. Incl. Bk. 1. pap. text ed. 2.75 (ISBN 0-88345-190-5, 18073); cassettes 25.00 (ISBN 0-685-48094-1); Bk. 2. pap. text ed. 2.75 (ISBN 0-88345-191-3, 18074); cassettes 40.00 (ISBN 0-685-48095-X); Bk. 3. pap. text ed. 3.25 (ISBN 0-88345-192-1, 18075); cassettes 40.00 (ISBN 0-685-48096-8); Bk. 4. pap. text ed. 3.25 (ISBN 0-88345-193-X, 18076); cassettes 40.00 (ISBN 0-685-48097-6); Bk. 5. pap. text ed. 3.25 (ISBN 0-88345-194-8, 18077); cassettes 40.00 (ISBN 0-685-48098-4). (gr. 1-6). 1973-74. tchr's manual, bks. 4 & 5 4.95. Regents Pub.
Welcome to English: Introductory Teacher's Manual. Willard D. Sheeler. (Illus.). 1977. pap. text ed. 2.50x (ISBN 0-19-502219-X). Oxford U Pr.
Welcome to English: Let's Begin. new ed. John Chapman. (Welcome to English Ser.). (Illus.). 48p. 1980. pap. 2.50 (ISBN 0-88345-379-7); tchr's manual 1.95 (ISBN 0-88345-448-3). Regents Pub.
Welcome to English: Let's Begin - A. John Chapman. (gr. 3-6). 1978. pap. text ed. 1.25 o.p. (ISBN 0-88345-354-1); tchr's manual, 1-3 4.95 (ISBN 0-88345-355-X). Regents Pub.
Welcome to English Teacher's Guide. Willard D. Sheeler. (Welcome to English Ser.). 1978. pap. text ed. 4.50x ea. Bks 1 & 2 (ISBN 0-19-520020-9). Bks 3 & 4 (ISBN 0-19-520021-7). Bks 5 & 6 (ISBN 0-19-520022-5). Oxford U Pr.
Welcome to English: Teacher's Manual 4-5. John Chapmann. (Welcome to English Ser.). 134p. 1980. pap. text ed. 4.95 (ISBN 0-88345-368-1, 18499). Regents Pub.
Welcome to God's Family. Geneal Kramer. (Illus.). 40p. (gr. k-5). 1980. pap. 1.25 (ISBN 0-912228-66-0). St Anthony Mess Pr.
Welcome to Hard Times. E. L. Doctorow. 224p. 1975. 8.95 (ISBN 0-394-49833-X); pap. 3.95 (ISBN 0-394-73107-7). Random.
Welcome to the Barbecue. Ronald A. Kolm. 65p. (Orig.). 1981. pap. 2.95 (ISBN 0-9605626-0-5). Low-Tech.
Welcome to the Monkey House. Kurt Vonnegut, Jr. pap. 2.75 (ISBN 0-440-19478-4). Dell.
Welcome to the Planet Earth: A Five Year Baby Journal. Sally Green & Michael Green. (Illus.). 96p. (Orig.). 1981. lib. bdg. 12.90 (ISBN 0-89471-125-3); pap. 6.95 (ISBN 0-89471-126-1). Running Pr.
Welcome to the Stork Club. Mearle L. Allen. LC 79-5424. 300p. Date not set. 14.95 (ISBN 0-498-02395-8). A S Barnes. Postponed.
Welcome to the Tax Revolt. Bill Green. (Illus.). 192p. 1981. 11.95 (ISBN 0-936602-10-4). Harbor Pub CA.
Welcoming God's Forgiveness. Carol C. Castro. 30p. (Orig.). 1978. pap. 1.05 adult resource bk.; pap. 10.25 (ISBN 0-697-01737-0). Wm C Brown.
Welcoming God's Forgiveness. Carol C. Castro. 120p. 1978. pap. text ed. 3.50 (ISBN 0-697-01681-1); 4.50 (ISBN 0-697-01682-X); classroom tchr's guide .75; adult resource book, pack/10,10.25 1.05 (ISBN 0-697-01685-4). Wm C Brown.
Welcoming Jesus. Carol C. Castro. 120p. 1979. pap. 3.50 (ISBN 0-697-01702-8); leader's guide 4.50 (ISBN 0-697-01703-6); classroom teacher's guide .75 (ISBN 0-697-01738-9); adult resource book, pack/10, 10.25 1.05 (ISBN 0-697-01704-4). Wm C Brown.
Welcoming Jesus: Adult Resource Book. Carol C. Castro. 30p. (Orig.). 1979. pap. 1.05 adult resource bk.; Set. tchr's manual 0.75 (ISBN 0-697-01738-9). Wm C Brown.
Welded Joint Design. John G. Hicks. LC 78-32047. 82p. 1979. 19.95 (ISBN 0-470-26686-4). Halsted Pr.
Welder's Bible. Don Geary. (Illus.). 420p. 1980. 16.95 (ISBN 0-8306-9938-4); pap. 10.95 (ISBN 0-8306-1244-0, 1244). Tab Bks.
Welders-Fitters Guide. John P. Stewart. LC 78-64873. 1979. pap. 7.95 (ISBN 0-672-23325-8). Audel.
Welders Guide. 2nd ed. James Brumbaugh. LC 72-97632. 736p. 1973. 12.95 (ISBN 0-672-23202-2). Audel.
Welder's Handbook. John P. Stewart. 1981. 25.95 (ISBN 0-8359-8605-5). Reston.
Welding. C. Bainbridge. (Teach Yourself Ser.). 1974. pap. 3.95 o.p. (ISBN 0-679-10495-X). McKay.
Welding & Metal Fabrication. Charles R. Flood. 1981. text ed. price not set (ISBN 0-408-00448-7). Butterworths.
Welding & Other Joining Processes. Roy A. Lindberg & Norman R. Braton. 544p. 1976. text ed. 26.95x (ISBN 0-205-05000-X, 3250008). Allyn.
Welding, Brazing & Soldering. E. F. Lindsley. LC 77-26479. (Illus.). 1980. pap. 4.95 (ISBN 0-06-090723-1, CN 723, CN). Har-Row.
Welding Craft Practice, Pt. 1, Vols. 1-2. N. Parkin & C. R. Flood. 1969. Pt. 1. pap. 4.40 (ISBN 0-08-012980-3); Pt. 2. pap. 5.25 (ISBN 0-08-013000-3). Pergamon.
Welding Encyclopedia. 18th ed. Ed. by T. B. Jefferson & D. T. Jefferson. (Monticello Bks). 1981. 20.00 (ISBN 0-686-28906-4). Jefferson Pubns.
Welding Guidelines with Aircraft Supplement. William Kielhorn. (Aviation Maintenance Training Course Ser.). (Illus.). 187p. 1978. text ed. 10.95 (ISBN 0-89100-136-0, E*A-W*B-2). Aviation Maintenance.
Welding Metallurgy of Stainless & Heat-Resisting Steels. R. Castro & J. J. De Cadenet. Tr. by R. C. Jain from Fr. LC 74-76582. (Illus.). 200p. 1975. 29.95 (ISBN 0-521-20431-3). Cambridge U Pr.
Welding: Methods & Metallurgy. M. D. Jackson. 422p. 1967. 37.50x (ISBN 0-85264-003-X, Pub. by Griffin England). State Mutual Bk.
Welding of HSLA (Microalloyed) Structural Steels. Ed. by A. B. Rothwell & J. Malcolm Gray. 1978. 42.00 (ISBN 0-87170-005-0). ASM.
Welding Practices, 6 vols. Ed. by J. Bell et al. Incl. Vol. 1. General Welding & Cutting; Vol. 2. Advanced Pipe & Tube Welding; Vol. 3. Tungsten Arc Gas Shielded Welding; Vol. 4. Metal Arc Gas Shielded Welding; Vol. 5. Manual Metal Arc Welding; Vol. 6. Oxy-Acetlene Welding. 1977. Set. 115.00x (ISBN 0-685-91105-5). Intl Ideas.
Welding: Principles & Practice. Henry Horwitz. LC 77-76341. (Illus.). 1978. text ed. 19.50 (ISBN 0-395-24473-0); instr's. manual 1.15 (ISBN 0-395-24474-9). HM.
Welding: Principles & Practice. Raymond Sacks. (gr. 10-12). 1976. text ed. 23.32 (ISBN 0-87002-073-0); student guide 4.40 (ISBN 0-87002-193-1); tchr's guide 3.60 (ISBN 0-87002-198-2). Bennett IL.
Welding: Principles & Practices. rev. ed. Sacks. (gr. 10-12). 1981. text ed. 24.40 (ISBN 0-87002-321-7). Bennett IL.
Welding Procedures: Electric Arc. Frank R. Schell. LC 76-14084. (gr. 10-12). 1977. pap. text ed. 5.00 (ISBN 0-8273-1603-8); instr's manual 1.60 (ISBN 0-8273-1697-6). Delmar.
Welding Procedures: MIG & TIG. Frank R. Schell & Bill J. Matlock. LC 76-62715. 1978. pap. text ed. 8.80 (ISBN 0-8273-1646-1); instr's manual 1.60 (ISBN 0-8273-1697-6). Delmar.
Welding Procedures:Oxyacetylene. Frank R. Schell. LC 76-4306. 1977. pap. text ed. 5.00 (ISBN 0-8273-1600-3); instr's manual 1.60 (ISBN 0-8273-1697-6). Delmar.
Welding Process Technology. Peter Thomas Houldcroft. LC 76-47408. (Illus.). 1977. 35.50 (ISBN 0-521-21530-7). Cambridge U Pr.
Welding Processes. Griffin et al. LC 76-28745. (gr. 9-12). 1978. 15.00 (ISBN 0-8273-1257-1); instructor's guide 1.60 (ISBN 0-8273-1259-8). Delmar.
Welding Processes. P. T. Houldcroft. (Engineering Design Guides). (Illus.). 30p. 1975. pap. 9.95x (ISBN 0-19-859137-3). Oxford U Pr.
Welding Technology Student's Manual. Gower A. Kennedy. LC 77-4673. (gr. 11-12). 1977. pap. text ed. 7.50 (ISBN 0-672-97109-7); tchr's manual 6.67 (ISBN 0-672-97158-5). Bobbs.
Welding's Engineering Data Sheets. 8th ed. (Monticello Bks). 176p. 1978. soft cover 7.25 (ISBN 0-686-12001-9). Jefferson Pubns.
Welfare Analysis of Policies Affecting Prices & Products. Robert D. Willig. LC 78-75051. (Outstanding Dissertations in Economics). 1980. lib. bdg. 20.00 (ISBN 0-8240-4129-1). Garland Pub.
Welfare & Efficiency: Their Interactions in Western Europe & Implications for International Economic Relations. Theodore Geiger & F. M. Geiger. (Illus.). 1979. text ed. 31.25x (ISBN 0-333-26864-4). Humanities.
Welfare Bind. Naomi Gottlieb. LC 73-17259. 240p. 1974. 17.50x (ISBN 0-231-03762-7). Columbia U Pr.
Welfare Economics: A Liberal Restatement. C. K. Rowley & A. T. Peacock. LC 75-22430. 198p. 1975. 24.95 (ISBN 0-470-74362-X). Halsted Pr.
Welfare Economics & the Elements of Socialism. Maurice Dobb. LC 69-16280. (Illus.). 1969. 41.50 (ISBN 0-521-07462-2); pap. 13.95x (ISBN 0-521-09937-4). Cambridge U Pr.
Welfare Economics: Introduction & Development of Basic Concepts. Yew-Kwang Ng. LC 79-22797. 332p. 1980. text ed. 24.95x (ISBN 0-470-26886-7). Halsted Pr.
Welfare in America: Controlling the "Dangerous Classes". Ed. by Betty R. Mandell. 192p. 1975. pap. 3.95 o.p. (ISBN 0-13-949305-0, Spec). P-H.
Welfare in Rural Areas: The North Carolina-Iowa Income Maintenance Experiment. Ed. by John L. Palmer. Joseph A. L. Pechman. (Studies in Social Experimentation). 1978. 14.95 (ISBN 0-8157-6896-6); pap. 5.95 (ISBN 0-8157-6895-8). Brookings.
Welfare Industry: Functionaries & Recipients in Public Aid. David Street et al. LC 79-1167. (City & Society: Vol. 4). 199p. 1979. 18.00x (ISBN 0-8039-1227-7); pap. 8.95x (ISBN 0-8039-1228-5). Sage.
Welfare, Justice, & Freedom. Scott Gordon. LC 80-14571. 256p. 1980. 17.50x (ISBN 0-231-04976-5). Columbia U Pr.
Welfare Law & Policy: Studies in Teaching, Practice & Research. Ed. by Martin Partington & J. L. Jowell. 1979. 37.50x (ISBN 0-89397-051-4). Nichols Pub.
Welfare Medicine in America: A Case Study of Medicaid. Robert Stevens & Rosemary Stevens. LC 74-2870. 1974. 16.95 (ISBN 0-02-931520-4). Free Pr.
Welfare Rights- the Local Authorities Role. Anne Howard. 52p. 1978. pap. text ed. 4.40x (ISBN 0-7199-0946-5, Pub. by Bedford England). Renouf.
Welfare State. Christopher Wright. (Illus.). 72p. (gr. 9-12). 1981. 14.95 (ISBN 0-7134-2375-7, Pub. by Batsford England). David & Charles.
Welfare State & Equality: Structural & Ideological Roots of Public Expenditures. Harold L. Wilensky. 1975. pap. 5.95x (ISBN 0-520-02908-9). U of Cal Pr.
Welfare State: Its Aims, Benefits & Costs. J. F. Sleeman. 1973. pap. text ed. 7.95x o.p. (ISBN 0-04-360029-8). Allen Unwin.
Welfare State: Who Is My Brother's Keeper. Fred Krinsky & Joseph Boskin. (Insight Ser). 144p. (Orig.). 1968. pap. text ed. 4.95x (ISBN 0-02-476040-4, 47604). Macmillan.
Welfare System & Mental Health, Vol. 8. GAP Committee on Psychiatry & Social Work. LC 73-178268. (Report No. 85). 1973. pap. 2.00 (ISBN 0-87318-119-0). Adv Psychiatry.
Welfare the Elusive Consensus: Where We Are, How We Got There, & What's Ahead. Lester M. Salamon. LC 78-12163. (Praeger Special Studies). 1978. 24.95 (ISBN 0-03-045601-0). Praeger.
Welfare: The Political Economy of Welfare Reform in the United States. Martin Anderson. LC 77-20644. (Publications 181). 276p. 1978. 12.95 (ISBN 0-8179-6811-3). Hoover Inst Pr.
Well. Jack Cady. 1981. 11.95 (ISBN 0-87795-287-6). Arbor Hse.
Well & the Cathedral: With an Introduction on Its Use in the Practice of Meditation. 2nd ed. Ira Progoff. LC 76-20823. (Entrance Meditation Ser.). 1977. 8.95 (ISBN 0-87941-004-3); pap. 3.95 1980 (ISBN 0-87941-005-1). Dialogue Hse.
Well-Being. Ed. by Barbara Salat & David Copperfield. LC 78-1219. 1979. pap. 5.95 (ISBN 0-385-14221-8, Anch). Doubleday.
Well-Body Book. Hal Bennett & Michael Samuels. (YA) 1973. pap. 7.95 (ISBN 0-394-70969-1). Random.
Well-Bound Words: A Rhetoric. John J. Ruszkiewicz. 1981. text ed. 11.95x (ISBN 0-673-15355-X). Scott F.
Well Church Book. Browne Barr. 1976. 7.95 (ISBN 0-8164-0304-X). Crossroad NY.
Well Design: Drilling & Production. Benjamin C. Craft et al. 1962. ref. ed. 31.95x (ISBN 0-13-950022-7). P-H.
Well... Excuse Me. Dennis Roberts. LC 80-84233. 64p. (Orig.). 1981. pap. 1.25 (ISBN 0-89081-265-9). Harvest Hse.
We'll Have a Friend for Lunch. Jane Flory. (gr. k-3). 1981. pap. 3.45x (ISBN 0-395-31126-8). HM.
Well, I Don't Know. Terry T. Schulte. 167p. (Orig.). 1980. pap. 4.95. Schulte.
Well of Days. Ivan Bunin. Tr. by G. Struve & H. Miles. 351p. 1976. Repr. of 1933 ed. 17.50 (ISBN 0-86527-326-X). Fertig.
Well of Loneliness. Radclyffe Hall. 448p. 1981. pap. 3.95 (ISBN 0-380-54247-1, Bard). Avon.
Well-Tempered Clavier by Johann Sebastian Bach. Hermann Keller. Tr. by Leigh Gerdine. 1977. 18.50 (ISBN 0-393-02187-4). Norton.
Well Tun'd Word: Musical Interpretations of English Poetry, 1597-1651. Elise B. Jorgens. (Illus.). 320p. 1981. 25.00x (ISBN 0-8166-1029-0). U of Minn Pr.
Well-Weighed Syllables. D. Attridge. LC 74-80362. (Illus.). 280p. 1975. 42.50 (ISBN 0-521-20530-1); pap. 12.95 (ISBN 0-521-29722-2). Cambridge U Pr.
Well, Why Didn't You Say So? Jo A. Wold. LC 75-8584. (Self Starter Bks.). 32p. (gr. k-2). 1975. 6.50g (ISBN 0-8075-8724-9). A Whitman.
Wellesley Affair: Richard Marquess Wellesley & the Conduct of Anglo-Spanish Diplomacy, 1809-1812. John K. Severn. LC 80-25416. x, 294p. 1980. 21.50 (ISBN 0-8130-0684-8). U Presses Fla.
Wellesley Index to Victorian Periodicals, 1824-1900, 3 vols. Ed. by Walter E. Houghton. Incl. Vol. 1. 1966. 115.00x (ISBN 0-8020-1393-7); Vol. 2. 1972. 125.00x (ISBN 0-8020-1910-2); Vol. 3. 1978. 125.00x (ISBN 0-8020-2253-7). LC 66-5405. Set. 300.00x (ISBN 0-8020-2343-6). U of Toronto Pr.
Wellness: An Arthritis Reality. Beth Ziebell. LC 80-84001. 144p. 1981. pap. text ed. 6.95 (ISBN 0-8403-2329-8). Kendall-Hunt.
Wellness R. S. V. P. Your Personal Invitation. Stafford G. Cox et al. 1980. pap. 3.95 (ISBN 0-8053-2304-X, 800100). Benjamin Cummings.
Wellness Workbook: A Guide to Attaining High Level Wellness. Regina S. Ryan & John W. Travis. 15.95 (ISBN 0-89815-033-7); pap. 9.95 (ISBN 0-89815-032-9). Ten Speed Pr.
Wellness: Your Invitation to Full Life. John J. Pilch. Ed. by Miriam Frost. Orig. Title: Wellness. 128p. (Orig.). 1981. pap. text ed. 5.95 (ISBN 0-03-059062-0). Winston Pr.
Wells Fargo in Arizona Territory. John Theobald & Lillian Theobald. Ed. by Bert M. Fireman. LC 78-67555. 1978. 12.50 (ISBN 0-685-67972-1); pap. 10.00 (ISBN 0-685-67973-X). AZ Hist Foun.
Wells of Power: The Oil Fields of South-Western Asia. Olaf Caroe. (Middle East in the 20th Century Ser.). 1976. Repr. of 1951 ed. lib. bdg. 22.50 (ISBN 0-306-70825-6). Da Capo.
Wellspring of Guidance: Messages 1963-1968. rev. ed. The Universal House of Justice. LC 76-129996. 1976. 9.00 (ISBN 0-87743-032-2, 7-25-05); pap. 5.00 (ISBN 0-87743-033-0, 7-25-06). Baha'i.
Wellspring: On the Myth & Source of Culture. Robert P. Armstrong. LC 73-85781. (Illus.). 100p. 1975. 15.50x (ISBN 0-520-02571-7). U of Cal Pr.
Wellsprings of the American Spirit. Ed. by F. Ernest Johnson. (Religion & Civilization Series of the Institute for Religious & Social Studies). 1964. Repr. of 1948 ed. 22.50x (ISBN 0-8154-0121-3). Cooper Sq.
Wellsprings of Torah. Alexander Z. Friedman. Tr. by Gertrude Hirchter from Yiddish. 584p. 1980. 13.95 (ISBN 0-910818-04-5); pap. 10.95 (ISBN 0-910818-20-7). Judaica Pr.
Welsh Country Parson. D. Parry Jones. 1975. 19.95 (ISBN 0-7134-2916-X, Pub. by Batsford England). David & Charles.
Welsh Dylan: Dylan Thomas's Life, Writing & His Wales. John Ackerman. 1981. pap. text ed. 5.25x (ISBN 0-586-08350-2). Humanities.
Welsh Grammar. Stephen J. Williams. 184p. 1980. pap. text ed. 20.00 (ISBN 0-7083-0737-X). Verry.
Welsh Language: Studies in Its Syntax & Semantics. Morris Jones & A. R. Thomas. 1978. pap. text ed. 32.50x (ISBN 0-7083-0671-3). Verry.
Welsh Law of Women: Studies Presented to Professor Daniel A. Binchy-1980. Ed. by D. Jenkins & M. E. Owen. 1980. write for info. (ISBN 0-7083-0771-X). Verry.
Welsh Narrow Gauge Railway. J. D. Prideaux. (Illus.). 1976. 11.95 (ISBN 0-7153-7184-3). David & Charles.
Welsh Poems: Sixth Century to 1600. Ed. & tr. by Gwyn Williams. 1974. 11.95x (ISBN 0-520-02603-9). U of Cal Pr.
Welsh Poems: Sixth Century to 1600. Ed. by Gwyn Williams. 1973. pap. 2.95 o.p. (ISBN 0-571-10379-0, Pub. by Faber & Faber). Merrimack Bk Serv.
Welsh Proverbs with English Translations. Henry H. Vaughan. LC 68-17945. (Eng. & Welsh.). 1969. Repr. of 1889 ed. 20.00 (ISBN 0-8103-3205-1). Gale.
Welsh Wars of Edward First. John E. Morris. 1901. 15.95x o.p. (ISBN 0-19-822304-8). Oxford U Pr.
Welshpool & Lanfair Light Railway. Ralph Cartwright & R. T. Russell. LC 80-70290. (Illus.). 208p. 1981. 19.95 (ISBN 0-7153-8151-2). David & Charles.
Wendell Castle Book of Wood Lamination. Wendell Castle & David Edman. 192p. 1980. 18.95 (ISBN 0-442-21478-2). Van Nos Reinhold.

Wendell Wilkie, Eighteen Ninety Two to Nineteen Fourty Four. Mary Earhart Dillon. LC 71-39040. (FDR & the Era of the New Deal Ser). 378p. 1972. Repr. of 1952 ed. lib. bdg. 35.00 (ISBN 0-306-70456-0). Da Capo.

Wenlockian & Ludlovian Ages Brachiopods from the Roberts Mountain Formation of Central Nevada. J. G. Johnson et al. (Publications in Geological Sciences: Vol. 115). 1976. pap. 13.75x (ISBN 0-520-09542-1). U of Cal Pr.

Went Missing: 15 Vessels That Disappeared on Lake Superior. 3rd ed. (Illus.). write for info. o.s.i. (ISBN 0-932212-09-3). Avery Color.

Went South. Marianne Wiggins. 1980. 9.95 (ISBN 0-440-09420-8). Delacorte.

Wentletrap Trap. Jean C. George. (Illus.). (ps-3). 1978. PLB 7.95 o.p. (ISBN 0-525-42310-9). Dutton.

Wenzel's Menu Maker. 2nd ed. William Wenzel, Jr. LC 79-13732. 1979. 99.95 (ISBN 0-8436-2135-4). CBI Pub.

We're All Kin: A Cultural Study of a Mountain Neighborhood. Carlene F. Bryant. LC 81-473. 160p. 1981. 9.50x (ISBN 0-87049-312-4). U of Tenn Pr.

Were Ancient Heresies Disguised Social Movements? A. H. Jones. Ed. by Clarence L. Lee. LC 66-11534. (Facet Bks.). 1966. pap. 1.00 (ISBN 0-8006-3023-8, 1-3023). Fortress.

We're Building a New School! Diary of a Teacher in Mozambique, 1977-1978. Chris Searle. (Illus.). 240p. (Orig.). 1981. 16.95 (ISBN 0-905762-87-8, Pub. by Zed Pr); pap. cancelled (ISBN 0-905762-88-6). Lawrence Hill.

Were He a Stranger? Mary Craig. LC 78-19073. 1978. 6.95 (ISBN 0-396-07590-8). Dodd.

We're in the Money. Andrew Bergman. 1975. pap. 3.95 (ISBN 0-06-131948-1, TB1948, Torch). Har-Row.

We're in the Money: Depression America & Its Films. Andrew Bergman. LC 74-159533. (Illus.). 1971. 12.00x, cusa (ISBN 0-8147-0964-8). NYU Pr.

We're Number One: State--Ole Miss Jokes. rev. ed. Sally Walton & Faye Wilkinson. (Illus.). 72p. 1980. pap. 3.95 (ISBN 0-937552-04-6). Quail Ridge.

We're off to See the Lizard. Barbara Brenner. LC 76-10350. (Read to Myself Ser.). (Illus.). 32p. (gr. k-2). 1977. PLB 7.75 (ISBN 0-8172-0151-3). Raintree Pubs.

Were Those the Days? H. C. Barnard. 1969. 16.00 (ISBN 0-08-007107-4). Pergamon.

Were-Wolves & Will-O-the-Wisps: French Tales of Mackinac Retold. Dirk Gringhuis. (Illus., Orig.). 1974. pap. 2.50 (ISBN 0-911872-14-0). Mackinac Island.

Werewolf. Bruce Lowery. LC 72-139981. 1969. 7.95 (ISBN 0-8149-0669-9). Vanguard.

Werewolf of London. Carl Dreadstone. (Orig.). 1977. pap. 1.25 o.p. (ISBN 0-425-03413-5, Medallion). Berkley Pub.

Werke, 5 vols. Leopold Kronecker. LC 66-20394. 1969. Repr. Set. 99.50 (ISBN 0-8284-0224-8). Chelsea Pub.

Werner Herzog: Images at the Horizon. Ed. by Gene Walsh. Roger Eberto. (Facets Multimedia Ser.). (Illus., Orig.). 1980. pap. 4.00 (ISBN 0-918432-26-X). NY Zoetrope.

Wes Weatherby, Gunfighter. Merle M. Funk. (YA) 1979. 5.95 (ISBN 0-685-93883-2, Avalon). Bouregy.

Wes Wyatt System of Seminar Selling. Wes Wyatt. LC 80-67857. 1980. 19.95 (ISBN 0-87863-018-X). Farnswth Pub.

Wesley's New Testament Notes. 12.95 (ISBN 0-686-12927-X). Schmul Pub Co.

Wesley's Veterans, 7 vols. pap. 5.95 ea. Schmul Pub Co.

Wesley's Works, 14 vols. 175.00 set (ISBN 0-686-23581-9). Schmul Pub Co.

Wessex Dialect. Norman Rogers. 1979. text ed. 9.25x (ISBN 0-239-00182-6). Humanities.

Wessex: Regional Archaeology. Peter Fowler. 1967. 3.95x o.p. (ISBN 0-435-32965-0). Heinemann Ed.

West. rev ed. Jerry E. Jennings. LC 78-54256. (United States Ser). (Illus.). (gr. 5 up). 1979. text ed. 9.93 1-4 copies & 5 or more 7.94 (ISBN 0-88296-077-6); tchrs' annotated ed. 13.68 (ISBN 0-88296-347-3). Fideler.

West Africa. 8th ed. R. J. Church. (Geographies for Advanced Study Ser.). (Illus.). 560p. 1980. pap. 28.00 (ISBN 0-582-30020-7). Longman.

West Africa Partitioned, Vol. 1: The Loaded Pause, 1885-1889. John D. Hargreaves. (Illus.). 288p. 1974. 19.50x (ISBN 0-299-06720-3). U of Wis Pr.

West Africa Portraits: A Biographical Dictionary of West African Personalities, 1947-1977. Ed. by A. H. Kirk-Greene. 1981. 25.00x (ISBN 0-7146-3112-4, F Cass Co). Biblio Dist.

West Africa Today. Ed. by Nancy Hoepli. (Reference Shelf Ser.). 1970. 6.25 (ISBN 0-8242-0414-X). Wilson.

West African Freshwater Fish. Michael Holden & William Reed. LC 74-170516. (West African Nature Handbooks). (Illus.). 68p. (Orig.). 1972. pap. 5.00x (ISBN 0-582-60426-5). Intl Pubns Serv.

West African Trade & Coast Society: A Family Study. Margaret Priestley. (West African History Ser.). 1969. 9.50x o.p. (ISBN 0-19-215638-1). Oxford U Pr.

West African Verse: An Anthology. Ed. by Donatus I. Nwoga. (Orig.). 1967. pap. text ed. 3.00x (ISBN 0-582-60100-2). Humanities.

West African Wager: Houphouet Versus Nkrumah. Jon Woronoff. LC 72-5155. 1972. 13.00 (ISBN 0-8108-0523-5). Scarecrow.

West & by North. Ed. by Louis B. Wright & Elaine Fowler. 1971. 10.00 o.s.i. (ISBN 0-440-09490-9). Delacorte.

West Arms Library of Big-5, U. S. Arms Manufacturers, 5 vols. Bill West. (Illus.). 1977. Set. 149.00 (ISBN 0-685-27896-4). Vol. 1 (ISBN 0-911614-12-5). Vol. 2 (ISBN 0-911614-07-9). Vol. 3 (ISBN 0-911614-08-7). Vol. 4 (ISBN 0-911614-10-9). Vol. 5 (ISBN 0-911614-05-2). B West.

West Bank & Gaza: Toward the Making of a Palestinian State. Emile A. Nakhleh. 1979. pap. 4.25 (ISBN 0-8447-3335-0). Am Enterprise.

West Berlin: History of the Nineteen Seventy-One Agreement. V. Vysotsky. (Illus.). 355p. 1975. 12.50x (ISBN 0-8464-0964-X). Beekman Pubs.

West Coast Beaches: A Complete Guide from Baha to Canada. Sarah Dixon & Peter Dixon. 1979. pap. 8.95 o.p. (ISBN 0-87690-285-9). Dutton.

West Coast Lighthouses. James A. Gibbs. Ed. by Douglas A. Pfeiffer. (Illus.). 96p. (Orig.). 1981. pap. 5.95 (ISBN 0-912856-72-6). Graphic Arts Ctr.

West Coast Plays, No. 6. Ed. by Rick Foster. Incl. Dinosauer. Glenn Hopkins & Wayne Lindberg; Jacob's Ladder. Barbara Graham; Pizza. Michele Linfante; Sylvester the Cat vs. Galloping Billy Bronco. Michael Lynch. 1980. pap. 5.00. West Coast Plays.

West Coast Route to Scotland. Geoffrey Kichenside. LC 75-35925. 1976. 11.95 (ISBN 0-7153-7157-6). David & Charles.

West Country. rev. ed. British Tourist Authority. (Illus.). 274p. 1981. pap. write for info. (ISBN 0-86143-046-8, Pub. by Auto Assn-British Tourist Authority England). Merrimack Bk Serv.

West Country Cookery. Kathleen Thomas. 1979. 24.00 (ISBN 0-7134-0041-2, Pub. by Batsford England). David & Charles.

West Country (Cornwall, Devon, Dorset, Somerset) Colourmaster. (Travel in England Ser.). (Illus.). 96p. 1975. 7.95 (ISBN 0-685-51761-6). Transatlantic.

West Country Historic Houses & Their Families: The Cotswolds Area, Vol. 3. Eric R. Delderfield. (Illus.). 1973. 13.50 (ISBN 0-7153-6089-2). David & Charles.

West Country Historic Houses & Their Families, Vol. 2: Dorset, Wiltshire & N. Somerset. Eric R. Delderfield. 13.50 (ISBN 0-7153-4910-4). David & Charles.

West Country Shipwrecks (England) A Pictorial Record, 1866-1973. John Behenna. LC 74-76205. 1975. 10.50 (ISBN 0-7153-6569-X). David & Charles.

West Country Weather Guide. Craig Rich. 1980. pap. 4.50 (ISBN 0-7153-8052-4). David & Charles.

West End Horror. Nicholas Meyer. Date not set. pap. 2.50 (ISBN 0-345-28481-X). Ballantine.

West German Foreign Aid, 1956-1966. Karel Holbik & Henry Allen Myers. LC 68-58498. 1968. 7.95x (ISBN 0-8419-8716-5, Pub. by Boston U Pr). Holmes & Meier.

West German Mark & the New Monetary World Leadership. Peter U. Hogenmiller. (Illus.). 1980. deluxe ed. 59.75 (ISBN 0-930008-56-1). Inst Econ Pol.

West German Poets on Society & Politics. Karl H. Van D'Elden. LC 78-20793. 1979. 14.95x (ISBN 0-8143-1628-X). Wayne St U Pr.

West German Reparations to Israel. Nicholas Balabkins. LC 70-152724. 1971. 25.00 (ISBN 0-8135-0691-3). Rutgers U Pr.

West Germany. Walter Marsden. 1978. 22.50 (ISBN 0-7134-1087-6). David & Charles.

West Germany. George Morey. LC 75-44866. (Macdonald Countries). (Illus.). (gr. 7 up). 1976. lib. bdg. 7.95 (ISBN 0-685-73288-6, Pub. by Macdonald Ed). Silver.

West Germany: An Introduction. Gunther Kloss. LC 75-25564. 180p. 1976. text ed. 28.95 (ISBN 0-470-49357-7). Halsted Pr.

West Germany in Pictures. Sterling Publishing Company Editors. LC 67-16018. (Visual Geography Ser). (Illus., Orig.). (gr. 6 up). 1967. PLB 4.99 (ISBN 0-8069-1095-X); pap. 2.95 (ISBN 0-8069-1094-1). Sterling.

West Germany: Politics & Society. David Childs & Jeffrey Johnson. 1980. write for info. (ISBN 0-312-86300-4). St Martin.

West Germany's Foreign Policy: Nineteen Forty-Nine to Nineteen Seventy-Nine. Ed. by Wolfram F. Hanrieder. (Special Study in West European Politics & Society). 1979. lib. bdg. 24.50x (ISBN 0-89158-579-6). Westview.

West Ham: A Study in Social & Industrial Problems, London, 1907. Edward G. Howarth & Mona Wilson. LC 79-56958. (English Working Class Ser.). 1980. lib. bdg. 35.00 (ISBN 0-8240-0111-7). Garland Pub.

West Highland Railway. John Thomas. LC 76-26734. (Illus.). 1976. 10.50 (ISBN 0-7153-7281-5). David & Charles.

West Highland White Terriers. May Pacey. (Foyle's Handbks). 1973. 3.95 (ISBN 0-685-55803-7). Palmetto Pub.

West in the Life of the Nation. Arrell Gibson. 1976. 15.95x (ISBN 0-669-61515-3). Heath.

West in the Middle Ages. Anne Bailey & Seymour Reit. Ed. by Irwin Shapiro. (Universal History Ser.). (Illus.). (gr. 7-10). 1966. PLB 6.08 o.p. (ISBN 0-307-60986-3, Golden Pr). Western Pub.

West Indian Literature: An Index to Criticism, 1930-1975. Jeannette B. Allis. (Reference Bks.). 1981. lib. bdg. 30.00 (ISBN 0-8161-8266-3). G K Hall.

West Indian Migration: The Montserrat Case. Stuart Philpott. (Monographs on Social Anthropology). (Illus.). 228p. 1973. text ed. 19.50x (ISBN 0-391-00287-2, Athlone Pr). Humanities.

West Indian Narrative: An Introductory Anthology. Kenneth Ramchand. 1966. pap. text ed. 3.75x (ISBN 0-17-566009-3). Humanities.

West Indian Poetry. Lloyd W. Brown. (World Authors Ser.: No. 422). 1978. lib. bdg. 12.50 (ISBN 0-8057-6262-0). Twayne.

West Indian Science Curriculum, 3 wkbks. University of the West Indies - British Council. (gr. 7-10). 1974-75. pap. text ed. 1.95x ea. o.p.; Bk. 1. pap. (ISBN 0-435-57100-1); Bk. 2. pap. (ISBN 0-435-57101-X); Bk. 3. pap. (ISBN 0-435-57102-8); Bk. 1. tchr's guide 12.95x o.p. (ISBN 0-435-57103-6); Bk. 2. tchr's guide 14.75x o.p. (ISBN 0-435-57104-4); Bk. 3. tchr's guide 13.95x o.p. (ISBN 0-435-57105-2). Heinemann Ed.

West Indies, Repr. Of 1810 Ed. James Montgomery. Ed. by Donald H. Reiman. Bd. with World Before the Flood; a Poem, in Ten Cantos. with Other Occasional Pieces. Repr. of 1813 ed. LC 75-31239. (Romantic Context Ser.: Poetry 1789-1830). 1979. lib. bdg. 47.00 (ISBN 0-8240-2187-8). Garland Pub.

West Indies & Their Future. Daniel Guerin. 1961. text ed. 8.50x (ISBN 0-391-02067-6). Humanities.

West Indies at the Crossroads. Earl Gooding. 256p. 1981. text ed. 12.95x (ISBN 0-87073-052-5); pap. text ed. 6.95x (ISBN 0-87073-053-3). Schenkman.

West: Manhattan to Oregon. Conrad Pendleton. LC 66-20103. 72p. 1966. 4.75 (ISBN 0-8040-0318-1). Swallow.

West Midland Underground. Michael Wilding. 1975. 7.95x; pap. 4.25x (ISBN 0-7022-0991-0). U of Queensland Pr.

West Midlands. C. Pritchard. (Geography of the British Isles Ser). (Illus.). 116p. 1975. 6.95x (ISBN 0-521-20029-6). Cambridge U Pr.

West of Alfred Jacob Miller. rev. & enl. ed. Alfred J. Miller. Ed. by Marvin C. Ross. (Illus.). 1968. 37.50 o.p. (ISBN 0-8061-0229-2). U of Okla Pr.

West of Owen Wister: Selected Short Stories. Owen Wister. LC 74-175805. 1972. 9.95x (ISBN 0-8032-0808-1); pap. 1.95 (ISBN 0-8032-5760-0, BB 546, Bison). U of Nebr Pr.

West of the American Dream. Neil Claremon. 1973. pap. 1.95 (ISBN 0-688-05164-2). Morrow.

West of the Moon. Edith St. George. 192p. 1981. pap. 1.50 (ISBN 0-671-57069-2). S&S.

West of the Rimrock. Wayne D. Overholser. 1981. pap. 1.95 o.s.i. (ISBN 0-440-19586-1). Dell.

West of the Texas Kid, Eighteen Eighty-One to Nineteen Ten: Recollections of Thomas Edgar Crawford, Cowboy, Gun Fighter, Rancher, Hunter, Miner. Thomas E. Crawford. Ed. by Jeff C. Dykes. (Western Frontier Library: No. 20). (Illus.). 1962. bds. 5.95 (ISBN 0-8061-0513-5); pap. 3.95 (ISBN 0-8061-1117-8). U of Okla Pr.

West Over Sea. Jon Leirfall. 160p. 1980. 14.95 (ISBN 0-906191-15-7, Pub. by Thule Pr England). Intl Schol Bk Serv.

West Point. 7.50 (ISBN 0-88427-031-9); pap. 3.95 (ISBN 0-88427-032-7). Green Hill.

West Point Fitness & Diet Book. James L. Anderson & Martin Cohen. 256p. 1981. pap. 2.95 (ISBN 0-380-54205-6, 54205). Avon.

West Point Fitness & Diet Book. James L. Anderson & Martin Cohen. 1978. pap. 3.95 (ISBN 0-380-01894-2, 37342). Avon.

West Point Story. Nardi R. Campion & Red Reeder. (Landmark Ser, No. 70). (Illus.). (gr. 4-6). 1956. PLB 4.39 o.p. (ISBN 0-394-90370-6, BYR). Random.

West Portals of Chartres Cathedral, I: The Iconology of the Creation. Jan Van der Meulen & Nancy W. Price. LC 80-5586. 1981. lib. bdg. 19.75 (ISBN 0-8191-1402-2); pap. text ed. 10.50 (ISBN 0-8191-1403-0). U Pr of Amer.

West Semitic Personal Names in the Murasu Documents. Michael D. Coogan. LC 75-23246. (Harvard Semitic Monographs). 1976. 7.50 (ISBN 0-89130-019-8, 040007). Scholars Pr Ca.

West Somerset Mineral Railway: And the Story of the Brendon Hills Iron. 2nd ed. Roger Sellick. (Illus.). 126p. 1970. 10.50 (ISBN 0-7153-4662-8). David & Charles.

West Tennessee Rebel: The Diary of Robert H. Cartmell, 1853-1866. Ed. by Emma I. Williams. (Illus.). 1981. 16.95x (ISBN 0-87870-096-X). Memphis St Univ. Postponed.

West Texas After the Discovery of Oil: A Modern Interpretation. Richard R. Moore. (Illus.). 1971. 8.50 o.p. (ISBN 0-8363-0100-5). Jenkins.

West That Was: From Texas to Montana. John Leakey & Nellie S. Yost. LC 58-14110. (Illus.). 1965. pap. 2.95 (ISBN 0-8032-5117-3, BB 304, Bison). U of Nebr Pr.

West Virginia. Arnout Hyde, Jr. LC 80-82049. (Illus.). 128p. 1980. 25.00 (ISBN 0-9604590-0-6); lea. bdg. 125.00 (ISBN 0-9604590-1-4). A Hyde.

West Virginia. 23.00 (ISBN 0-89770-124-0). Curriculum Info Ctr.

West Virginia. John A. Williams. (States & the Nation Ser). (Illus.). 1976. 12.95 (ISBN 0-393-05590-6, Co-Pub by AASLH). Norton.

West Virginia: A Guide to the Mountain State. LC 72-84516. 1941. 54.00 (ISBN 0-403-02197-9). Somerset Pub.

West Virginia Chronology & Factbook, Vol. 48. R. I. Vexler. 1978. 8.50 (ISBN 0-379-16173-7). Oceana.

West Virginia Code Annotated, 20 vols. write for info. incl. 1980 suppl. & index (ISBN 0-87215-138-7); write for info. 1980 suppl. (ISBN 0-87215-346-0). Michie.

West Virginia Pilgrim. James Lewis. 228p. 1976. 8.95 (ISBN 0-8164-0297-3). Crossroad NY.

West Virginia State Industrial Directory, 1980-81. State Industrial Directories Corp. 1980. pap. 25.00 (ISBN 0-89910-022-8). State Indus Dir.

West Virginia: The Mountain State. 2nd ed. Festus P. Summers & C. H. Ambler. 1958. text ed. 19.95 (ISBN 0-13-951699-9). P-H.

Western. Stanley Noyes. 32p. (Orig.). 1980. pap. 3.00 (ISBN 0-88235-044-7). San Marcos.

Western Adventure. Irene Fortner. Date not set. 4.95 (ISBN 0-8062-1647-6). Carlton.

Western American Indian: Case Studies in Tribal History. Ed. by Richard N. Ellis. LC 70-181597. xiv, 203p. 1972. 11.95x (ISBN 0-8032-0804-9); pap. 3.95x (ISBN 0-8032-5754-6, BB 548, Bison). U of Nebr Pr.

Western & Eastern Rambles: Travel Sketches of Nova Scotia. Joseph Howe. Ed. by M. G. Parks. LC 72-97424. (Illus.). 1973. pap. 4.50 (ISBN 0-8020-6183-4). U of Toronto Pr.

Western Approaches to Eastern Philosophy. Troy W. Organ. LC 75-14554. 282p. 1975. 13.95x (ISBN 0-8214-0194-7). Ohio U Pr.

Western Aristocracies & Imperial Court A.D. Three Hundred Sixty-Four - Four Hundred Twenty-Five. John Matthews. 442p. 1975. 45.00x (ISBN 0-19-814817-8). Oxford U Pr.

Western Art of Frederic Remington. Matthew Baigell. Date not set. pap. 9.95 (ISBN 0-345-29026-7). Ballantine.

Western Church in the Later Middle Ages. Francis Oakley. LC 79-7621. 1979. 19.50x (ISBN 0-8014-1208-0). Cornell U Pr.

Western Civilization, 2 vols. Robert E. Herzstein. Incl. Vol. 1. From the Origins Through the Seventeenth Century. 11.95 (ISBN 0-395-19370-2); Vol. 2. From the Seventeenth Century to the Present. 11.95 (ISBN 0-395-19371-0); instructor's manual pap. 2.50 (ISBN 0-395-14043-9). 1975. Set. 20.50 (ISBN 0-395-14042-0). HM.

Western Civilization, 2 vols. 2nd ed. William L. Langer et al. Incl. Vol. 1. Prehistory to the Peace of Utrecht. 526p (ISBN 0-06-043844-4); Vol. 2. The Expansion of Empire to Europe in the Modern World. 485p (ISBN 0-06-043846-0). 1975. pap. text ed. 15.50 scp ea. (ISBN 0-686-67088-4, HarpC); test item to accompany vol. 1 avail. (ISBN 0-06-363843-6); test item to accompany vol. 2 avail. (ISBN 0-06-363844-4). Har-Row.

Western Civilization: A Concise History. Marvin Perry et al. (Illus.). 704p. 1981. pap. text ed. 14.95 (ISBN 0-395-29313-8); write for info. instr's manual. HM.

Western Civilization: A Concise History. Ed. by Marvin Perry et al. Incl. Vol. 1. To 1789. pap. text ed. 9.95 (ISBN 0-395-29314-6); Vol. 2. From the 1600s. pap. text ed. 9.95 (ISBN 0-395-29315-4). (Illus.). 400p. 1981. price not set instrs. manual (ISBN 0-395-29316-2). HM.

Western Civilization, an Urban Perspective, 3 vols. F. Roy Willis. Incl. Vol. 1. From the Rise of Athens Through the Late Middle Ages (ISBN 0-669-89235-1); Vol. 2. From 1300 Through 1815 (ISBN 0-669-89243-2); Vol. 3. From 1815 to the Contemporary Age. o.p. (ISBN 0-669-89250-5). 1973. pap. text ed. 7.95x ea. o.p.; instructors' manual free o.p. (ISBN 0-669-84913-8). Heath.

Western Civilization: An Urban Perspective, 2 vols. 2nd ed. F. Roy Willis. 1977. pap. text ed. 12.95x ea. o.p.; Vol. 1. (ISBN 0-669-00455-3); Vol. 2. (ISBN 0-669-00463-4); instructor's manual free o.p. (ISBN 0-669-00471-5). Heath.

Western Civilization: An Urban Perspective, 2 vols. 3rd ed. F. Roy Willis. (Vol. 1, 688 pp.:vol. 2, 560 pp.). 1981. Vol. 1. pap. text ed. 12.95 (ISBN 0-669-03364-2); Vol. 2. pap. text ed. 12.95 (ISBN 0-669-03365-0); instructor's guide (ISBN 0-669-03366-9). Heath.

Western Civilization & the Natives of South Africa: Studies in Culture Contact. Ed. by Isaac Schapera. 1967. text ed. 14.00x (ISBN 0-7100-2083-X). Humanities.

Western Civilization: People & Progress, 2 vols. T. Walter Wallbank et al. Incl. Vol. 1. Ancient World to 1750 (ISBN 0-673-15082-8); Vol. 2. 1650 to the Present (ISBN 0-673-15083-6). 1977. pap. 8.95x ea. Scott F.

Western Civilization: People & Progress. T. Walter Wallbank et al. 1977. pap. 13.95x (ISBN 0-673-15081-X). Scott F.

Western Civilization Since Fifteen Hundred. 2 nd ed. Walther Kirchner. (gr. 9-12). 1975. pap. 4.95 (ISBN 0-06-460111-0, CO 111, COS). Har-Row.

Western Civilization to Fifteen Hundred. Walther Kirchner. (gr. 9-12). 1960. pap. text ed. 3.95 (ISBN 0-06-460110-2, CO 110, COS). Har-Row.

Western Civilization Vol. II, Since 1715. Michael Cheilik. LC 80-66627. (Cliffs Rapid Review Ser.). 112p. (Orig.). (gr. 10-12). 1980. pap. text ed. 3.95 (ISBN 0-8220-1742-3). Cliffs.

Western Coal: Promise or Problem? Wallace E. Tyner et al. LC 78-3005. (Illus.). 1978. 19.95 (ISBN 0-669-02320-5). Lexington Bks.

Western Coinages of Nero. David W. MacDowall. LC 74-82869. (Numismatic Notes & Monographs: No. 161). (Illus.). xvii, 256p. (Orig.). 1979. pap. 40.00 (ISBN 0-89722-176-1). Am Numismatic.

Western Collector: Handbook & Price Guide to Avon Bottles, 1977-78. 320p. 14.95. Avons Res.

Western Collector: Handbook & Price Guide to Avon Bottles, 1975-76. 224p. 12.95. Avons Res.

Western Cooking. Lois McBride. (Illus.). 288p. 1976. 10.95 o.p. (ISBN 0-679-50598-9); pap. 5.95 o.p. (ISBN 0-679-50635-7). McKay.

Western Europe. Robert Clayton. LC 71-135281. (Finding Out About Geography Ser). (Illus.). (gr. 3-6). 1972. 4.50 o.p. (ISBN 0-381-99847-9, A86820, JD-J). John Day.

Western Europe & the Development of the Law of the Sea. F. Durante. 1980. 75.00 (ISBN 0-379-20288-3). Oceana.

Western Europe & the New International Economic Order: Representative Samples of European Perspectives. Ed. by Ervin Laszlo & Joel Kurtzman. LC 80-16620. (Pergamon Policy Studies). 120p. 1980. 16.50 (ISBN 0-08-025114-5). Pergamon.

Western Europe: Geographical Analysis. Aubrey Diem. LC 77-24617. 1979. text ed. 27.95 (ISBN 0-471-21400-0). Wiley.

Western Europe in Color. Alice F. Mutton. (Illus.). 279p. 1972. 12.75 (ISBN 0-7137-0546-9); pap. 7.50 (ISBN 0-7137-0555-8). Transatlantic.

Western Europe: The Trials of Partnership. Commission on Critical Choices. LC 75-44726. (Critical Choices of Americans Ser.: Vol. 8). 1976. 22.95 (ISBN 0-669-00423-5). Lexington Bks.

Western European Cities in Crisis. Ed. by Michael C. Romanos. LC 78-21445. (Illus.). 1979. 24.95 (ISBN 0-669-02800-2). Lexington Bks.

Western European Idea in Education. V. Mallinson. (Illus.). 34.00 (ISBN 0-08-025208-7). Pergamon.

Western Europe's Global Reach: Regional Cooperation & Worldwide Aspirations. Ed. by Werner J. Feld. (Policy Studies). 1980. 30.00 (ISBN 0-08-025130-7). Pergamon.

Western Europe's Migrant Workers. Jonathan Power. (Minority Rights Group: No. 28). 1976. pap. 2.50 (ISBN 0-89192-085-4). Interbk Inc.

Western Fertilizer Handbook. 6th ed. California Fertilizer Association. 252p. 1980. pap. text ed. 5.50 (ISBN 0-8134-2122-5). Interstate.

Western Fertilizer Handbook. 6th ed. perfect bdg. 9.00 (ISBN 0-8134-2122-5). Thomson Pub CA.

Western: Focus on. J. Nachbar. 7.95 (ISBN 0-13-950634-9); pap. 3.25 (ISBN 0-13-950626-8). P-H.

Western Garden Book: Sunset New. 4th rev. ed. Sunset Editors. LC 78-70266. (Illus.). 512p. 1979. pap. 11.95 (ISBN 0-376-03889-6, Sunset Bks). Sunset-Lane.

Western Greek Land: Use & City-Planning in the Archaic Period. Guy P. Metraux. LC 77-94709. (Outstanding Dissertations in the Fine Arts Ser.). 1978. lib. bdg. 21.00x (ISBN 0-8240-3241-1). Garland Pub.

Western Hemisphere. Drummond. (Our World Today Ser.). (gr. 5-8). 1978. text ed. 15.80 (ISBN 0-205-05856-6, 7758561); tchr's guide 9.60 (ISBN 0-205-05857-4, 77857X). Allyn.

Western Hemisphere: Its Influence on United States Policies to the End of World War Two. Wilfrid H. Callcott. 1968. 25.00x (ISBN 0-292-78390-6). U of Tex Pr.

Western Heritage of Faith & Reason. J. Calvin Keene. LC 63-9052. 1963. 13.95 (ISBN 0-9603084-0-7). J Calvin Keene.

Western Home Landscaping. Ken Smith. LC 78-51897. (Illus.). 1978. pap. 5.95 (ISBN 0-89586-012-0). H P Bks.

Western Horse. John A. Gorman. LC 66-12997. (Illus.). (gr. 9-12). 1967. 14.60 (ISBN 0-8134-0126-7); text ed. 10.95 (ISBN 0-685-03940-4). Interstate.

Western Horse Behavior & Training. Robert W. Miller. 336p. 1975. 6.95 (ISBN 0-385-08181-2, Dolp). Doubleday.

Western Horsemanship. Charles R. Self. (Illus.). 1979. 11.95 (ISBN 0-87691-291-9). Winchester Pr.

Western Impressions. Ray Atkeson. Ed. by Robert D. Shangle. LC 78-102327. 1976. 27.50 (ISBN 0-915796-11-2). Beautiful Am.

Western Influences on Political Parties to 1825. H. C. Hockett. LC 75-87650. (American Scene Ser.). 1970. Repr. of 1917 ed. lib. bdg. 19.50 (ISBN 0-306-71777-8). Da Capo.

Western Intellectual Tradition: Greece Through the Middle Ages, Vol. 1. David C. Riede & J. Wayne Baker. 208p. 1980. pap. text ed. 8.50 (ISBN 0-8403-2259-3). Kendall-Hunt.

Western Invasions of the Pacific & Its Continents: A Study of Moving Frontiers & Changing Landscapes, 1513-1958. Archibald G. Price. LC 80-14037. (Illus.). xi, 236p. 1980. Repr. of 1963 ed. lib. bdg. 20.75x (ISBN 0-313-22433-1, PRWE). Greenwood.

Western Islamic Architecture. John D. Hoag. LC 63-7516. (Great Ages of World Architecture Ser). (Illus.). 1963. 7.95 o.s.i. (ISBN 0-8076-0212-4); pap. 5.95 o.s.i. (ISBN 0-8076-0341-4). Braziller.

Western Liberalism: A History in Documents from Locke to Croce. Ed. by E. K. Bramsted & K. J. Melhuish. 1978. text ed. 31.00x (ISBN 0-582-48830-3); pap. text ed. 16.95x (ISBN 0-582-48831-1). Longman.

Western Man & Environmental Ethics. Ed. by Ian G. Barbour. LC 72-1936. 1973. pap. text ed. 6.50 (ISBN 0-201-00387-2). A-W.

Western Man: Photographs from the National Western Stock Show. Sandy Hume. 1980. 18.95 (ISBN 0-933472-48-X); pap. 12.95 (ISBN 0-933472-49-8). Johnson Colo.

Western Maryland Railroad. Roger Cook & Karl Zimmerman. (Illus.). 320p. 1981. 25.00 (ISBN 0-8310-7139-7). Howell-North.

Western Medieval Civilization. Deno J. Geanakoplos. 1978. text ed. 16.95x (ISBN 0-669-00868-0). Heath.

Western Memorabilia: Collectibles of the Old West. William C. Ketchum, Jr. (Illus.). 256p. 1980. 30.00 (ISBN 0-8437-3357-8). Hammond Inc.

Western Movies. Ed. by William T Pilkington & Don Graham. LC 78-21427. (Illus.). 184p. 1979. 13.95 o.p. (ISBN 0-8263-0496-6); pap. 6.95 (ISBN 0-8263-0497-4). U of NM Pr.

Western Outlaws. Vincent P. Rennert. LC 68-11268. (America in the Making Ser). (Illus.). (gr. 7 up). 1968. 4.95g o.s.i. (ISBN 0-02-775740-4, CCPr). Macmillan.

Western Peace Officer: A Legacy of Law & Order. Frank R. Prassel. 330p. 1980. pap. 7.95 (ISBN 0-8061-1694-3). U of Okla Pr.

Western Philosophy. Charles H. Patterson. Incl. Vol. 1. 600 B.C.-1600 A.D (ISBN 0-8220-1550-1); Vol. 2. Since 1600. pap. text ed. o.p. (ISBN 0-8220-1552-8). (Cliffs Course Outlines Ser.). 1971. pap. text ed. 2.95 o.p. (ISBN 0-685-41966-5). Cliffs.

Western Philosophy: An Introduction. R. J. Hollingdale. 1966. text ed. 5.00x (ISBN 0-900707-02-X). Humanities.

Western Political Theory in the Face of the Future. J. Dunn. LC 78-25625. (Themes in the Social Sciences Ser.). 1979. 24.95 (ISBN 0-521-22619-8); pap. 5.95x (ISBN 0-521-29578-5). Cambridge U Pr.

Western Portal of Saint-Loup-De-Naud. Clark Maines. LC 78-74373. (Fine Arts Dissertations, Fourth Ser.). (Illus.). 1980. lib. bdg. 44.00 (ISBN 0-8240-3960-2). Garland Pub.

Western Question in Greece & Turkey: A Study in the Contrast of Civilizations. 2nd ed. Arnold J. Toynbee. LC 68-9598. (Illus., Maps). 1970. Repr. of 1922 ed. 18.00 (ISBN 0-86527-209-3). Fertig.

Western Reaches. Leonard Nathan. 1963. 2.25 o.p. (ISBN 0-934612-06-4). Talisman.

Western Reserve & the Fugitive Slave Law: A Prelude to the Civil War. William C. Cochran. LC 71-127273. 1972. Repr. of 1920 ed. 22.50 (ISBN 0-306-71212-1). Da Capo.

Western Riding: Your Self-Teaching Guide. Don Zoll. 1979. 9.95 o.p. (ISBN 0-679-51452-X). McKay.

Western Saharans: Background to Conflict. Virginia Thompson & Richard Adloff. 348p. 1980. 27.50 (ISBN 0-389-20148-0). B&N.

Western Septet: Seven Stories of the American West. new ed. Henryk Sienkiewicz. Ed. by Marion M. Coleman. LC 72-96321. (Illus.). 175p. 1973. pap. 5.00 (ISBN 0-910366-15-2). Alliance Coll.

Western Spirituality: Historical Roots & Ecumenical Routes. Ed. by Matthew Fox. 1979. 9.95 o.p. (ISBN 0-8190-0635-1). Fides Claretian.

Western States Life & Health. 1979. 15.00 (ISBN 0-930868-30-7). Merritt Co.

Western States Property & Causalty. 1980. 15.00 (ISBN 0-930868-31-5). Merritt Co.

Western Story: The Recollections of Charley O'Kieffe 1884-1898. Charley O'Kieffe. LC 60-5381. (Pioneer Heritage Ser: Vol. 2). (Illus.). xvi, 223p. 1960. 11.95x (ISBN 0-8032-0134-6); pap. 2.95 (ISBN 0-8032-5796-1, BB 585, Bison). U of Nebr Pr.

Western Towns & Buildings. John White & Margaret P. Morison. 364p. 1980. 22.50x (ISBN 0-85564-156-8, Pub. by U of West Australia). Intl Schol Bk Serv.

Western Trips & Trails. E. M. Sterling. (Illus.). 350p. (Orig.). 1981. pap. 6.95 (ISBN 0-87108-584-4). Pruett.

Western Water Resources: Coming Problems & the Policy Alternatives. Federal Reserve Bank of Kansas City. LC 80-14142. 376p. 1980. lib. bdg. 25.00x (ISBN 0-86531-036-X). Westview.

Western Wind. John Frederick Nims. 1974. pap. text ed. 8.85 (ISBN 0-394-31231-7). Random.

Western Wind. Oliver B. Patton. 384p. 1981. pap. 2.95 (ISBN 0-445-04634-1). Popular Lib.

Western Words: A Dictionary of the American West. Ramon F. Adams. LC 68-31369. 355p. 1981. pap. 9.95 (ISBN 0-8061-1173-9). U of Okla Pr.

Western World in the Twentieth Century. Ed. by Bernard W. Wishy. LC 61-8987. (gr. 9 up). 1961. 20.00x (ISBN 0-231-02489-4). Columbia U Pr.

Westerner. Zane Grey. (Large Print Bks.). 1980. lib. bdg. 10.95 (ISBN 0-8161-3125-2). G K Hall.

Westghosts: The Psychic World of California. Hans Holzer. LC 77-88693. 253p. 1980. pap. 5.95 (ISBN 0-8040-0759-4). Swallow.

Westing Game. Ellen Raskin. 1980. pap. 1.75 (ISBN 0-380-49346-2, 49346, Camelot). Avon.

Westmark. Lloyd Alexander. LC 80-22242. (gr. 5 up). 1981. 9.95 (ISBN 0-525-42335-4). Dutton.

Westminster Abbey & Its Estates in the Middle Ages. Barbara Harvey. (Illus.). 1977. text ed. 57.00x (ISBN 0-19-822449-4). Oxford U Pr.

Westminster Concise Bible Dictionary. Barbara Smith. LC 80-25771. 1981. pap. 5.95 (ISBN 0-664-24363-0). Westminster.

Westminster Confession of Faith. J. McPherson. (Handbooks for Bible Classes). 175p. pap. text ed. 8.95 (ISBN 0-567-28143-4). Attic Pr.

Westminster Confession of Faith: A New Edition. Douglas Kelly et al. 102p. 1980. pap. 5.95 (ISBN 0-87921-060-5). Attic Pr.

Westminster Confession of Faith: A Study Manual. G. I. Williamson. 5.50 (ISBN 0-87552-538-5). Presby & Reformed.

Westminster Workshop: A Student's Guide to the British Government. 4th ed. R. K. Mosley. LC 78-41284. (Illus.). 1979. pap. 9.50 (ISBN 0-08-020636-0); pap. 9.50 (ISBN 0-08-020635-2); pap. 6.75 (ISBN 0-08-024316-9). Pergamon.

Westmoreland Davis: Virginia Planter - Politician 1859-1942. Jack T. Kirby. LC 68-22730. (Illus.). 232p. 1968. 9.95 (ISBN 0-8139-0158-8). U Pr of Va.

Westphal Empire. Al Fosbenner. (Orig.). 1980. pap. 2.75 (ISBN 0-440-19492-X). Dell.

West's Book of Legal Forms. Robert D. McNutt. 200p. 1981. pap. text ed. 3.96 (ISBN 0-8299-0516-2). West Pub.

West's Business Law: Alternate UCC Comprehensive Edition. Kenneth W. Clarkson et al. 750p. 1981. text ed. 13.95 (ISBN 0-8299-0366-6). West Pub.

West's Business Law: Alternate UCC Comprehensive Edition. Kenneth W. Clarkson et al. write for info. alt. test items (ISBN 0-8299-0526-X). West Pub.

West's Business Law: Text & Cases. Kenneth Clarkson et al. (Illus.). 1980. text ed. 20.95 (ISBN 0-8299-0295-3); study guide 5.95 (ISBN-0-8299-0305-4); instrs.' manual avail. (ISBN 0-8299-0466-2). West Pub.

West's Federal Taxation: 1979 Annual: Individual Incomes Taxes. new rev. ed. Lawrence C. Phillips & William H. Hoffman. 1978. text ed. 17.95 (ISBN 0-8299-0178-7); solutions manual avail. (ISBN 0-8299-0567-7). West Pub.

West's Review Covering Multistate Subjects. LC 79-24976. 448p. 1979. pap. text ed. 23.95 (ISBN 0-8299-2081-1). West Pub.

West's Textbook of Cosmetology. Jerry J. Ahern. (Illus.). 500p. 1980. text ed. 15.95 (ISBN 0-8299-0343-7). West Pub.

Westview Environmental Studies, 3 vols. Ed. by J. Rose & E. W. Weidener. Incl. Vol. 1. Pesticides: Boon or Bane? M. B. Green. LC 76-5881. 18.00x (ISBN 0-89158-610-5); Vol. 2. Climate & the Environment: The Atmospheric Impact on Man. John F. Griffiths. LC 76-5801. pap. text ed. 11.00x (ISBN 0-236-40022-3); Vol. 3. Electromagnetism, Man & the Environment. Joseph H. Battocletti. LC 76-7905. 17.50x (ISBN 0-89158-612-1). 1976. Westview.

Westward by Canal. Ruth Franchere. LC 71-185217. (Illus.). (gr. 5-9). 1972. 8.95 (ISBN 0-02-735700-7). Macmillan.

Westward of Ye Laurall Hills, 1750-1850: 1750-1850. Helen E. Vogt. LC 75-21087. (Illus.). 1976. 15.00 (ISBN 0-87012-226-6). H Vogt.

Westward to Laughter. Colin MacInnes. LC 76-95637. 1970. 5.95 o.p. (ISBN 0-374-28764-3). FS&G.

Westward to Vinland. Henry Treece. LC 67-22812. (gr. 7-9). 1967. 9.95 (ISBN 0-87599-136-X). S. G. Phillips.

Wet Fire. W. H. Wheeler. (Pacesetter Ser.). (Illus.). 64p. (gr. 4 up). 1978. PLB 7.95 (ISBN 0-516-02174-5). Childrens.

Wet Landing-Dry Landing. Margaret Nesheim. (Illus.). 192p. 1981. 10.00 (ISBN 0-682-49673-1). Exposition.

Wet Plates & Dry Gulches. Gilbert L. Campbell. LC 71-41602. (Wild & Woolly West Ser., No. 8). (Illus., Orig.). 1973. 7.00 (ISBN 0-910584-94-X); pap. 2.00 (ISBN 0-910584-11-7). Filter.

Wetlands: Bogs, Marshes & Swamps. Lewis A. Buck. LC 73-5711. (Finding-Out Books for Science & Social Studies, Grades 1-4). 64p. (gr. 2-4). 1974. PLB 6.95 (ISBN 0-8193-0702-5, Pub. by Parents). Enslow Pubs.

We've Been Robbed: A Baptist Minister Explores the Fundamentalist's Dilemma. Will Meloon. LC 70-166500. 87p. 1971. pap. 2.95 o.p. (ISBN 0-912106-19-0). Logos.

Weyer's Warships of the World: 1979-81 Flottentaschenbuch. 55th ed. Ed. by G. Albrecht. LC 46-43961. (Illus.). 680p. (Eng. & Ger.). 1979. 48.95x (ISBN 0-933852-20-7). Nautical & Aviation.

Whack Your Porcupine & Other Drawings. B. Kliban. LC 76-52861. (Illus.). 1977. pap. 3.50 (ISBN 0-911104-92-5). Workman Pub.

Whale Called Killer. Erich Hoyt. (Illus.). 28p. 1981. 15.95 (ISBN 0-525-22970-1). Dutton.

Whale for the Killing. Farley Mowat. 224p. 1981. pap. 2.25 (ISBN 0-553-14702-1). Bantam.

Whale in Darkness. R. F. Brissenden. LC 79-56757. 71p. 1980. 14.95 (ISBN 0-7081-1033-5, 0576). Bks Australia.

Whale: Mighty Monarch of the Sea. Jacques-Yves Cousteau & Philippe Diole. LC 71-180052. (Undersea Discoveries of Jacques-Yves Cousteau). (Illus.). 1977. pap. 8.95 (ISBN 0-89104-077-3). A & W Pubs.

Whale Sound. Ed. by Greg Gatenby. (Illus.). 1977. pap. 6.95 (ISBN 0-88894-135-8, Pub. by Douglas & McIntyre). Madrona Pubs.

Whalers. Cal Whipple. (Seafarers Ser.). (Illus.). 1979. lib. bdg. 11.97 (ISBN 0-686-50991-5). Silver.

Whalers & Whaling: The Story of the Whaling Ships up to the Present Day. E. Keble Chatterton. LC 79-178626. (Illus.). 248p. 1975. Repr. of 1925 ed. 18.00 (ISBN 0-8103-4028-3). Gale.

Whales. Nigel Bonner. (Illus.). 248p. 1980. 24.95 (ISBN 0-7137-0887-5, Pub. by Blandford Pr England). Sterling.

Whales. Susan Harris. (gr. 2-4). PLB 6.45 (ISBN 0-531-00444-9). Watts.

Whales. Helen Hoke & Valerie Pitt. LC 72-11769. (First Bks). (Illus.). 72p. (gr. 4 up). 1973. PLB 6.45 (ISBN 0-531-00779-0). Watts.

Whales. George Shea. LC 80-18413. (Creatures Wild & Free Ser.). (gr. 1-6). 1981. 5.95 (ISBN 0-88436-768-1). EMC.

Whales. E. J. Slijper. LC 78-74217. (Illus.). 1979. Repr. 32.50x (ISBN 0-8014-1161-0). Cornell U Pr.
Whales. Jane W. Watson. (Big Picture Bk.). (Illus.). (ps-k). 1979. PLB 7.62 (ISBN 0-307-60824-7, Golden Pr); pap. 1.95 (ISBN 0-307-10824-4). Western Pub.
Whales & Other Sea Animals. Ed. by Time-Life Television. (Wild Wild World of Animal Ser.). 1977. 10.95 (ISBN 0-913948-10-1). Time-Life.
Whales & Other Sea Mammals. LC 76-45496. (Wild, Wild World of Animals Ser.). (Illus.). (gr. 5 up). 1976. PLB 11.97 (ISBN 0-685-77686-7, Pub. by Time-Life). Silver.
Whales, Dolphins, & Porpoises. Ronald M. Lockley. LC 79-88317. (Illus.). 1979. 15.95 (ISBN 0-393-01283-2). Norton.
Whales, Dolphins, & Porpoises. Ed. by Kenneth S. Norris. (Library Reprint Ser.). 1978. 42.50x (ISBN 0-520-03283-7). U of Cal Pr.
Whalesongs. 2nd ed. Robert Gibb. 42p. 1979. 30.00 o.p. (ISBN 0-918824-17-6); pap. cancelled o.p. (ISBN 0-918824-16-8). Turkey Pr.
Whaling City, a History of New London. Robert O. Decker. LC 74-30794. (Illus.). 413p. 1976. 15.00 (ISBN 0-87106-053-1). New London County.
Whaling Issue in U.S.-Japan Relations. Ed. by John R. Schmidhauser & George O. Totten, III. 1978. lib. bdg. 26.50x (ISBN 0-89158-176-6). Westview.
Wharton's Criminal Evidence: 1972-73, 4 vols. 13th ed. Charles E. Torcia. LC 72-84859. 1972. 170.00 (ISBN 0-686-14501-1). Lawyers Co-Op.
Wharton's Criminal Procedure, 4 vols. 12th ed. Charles E. Torcia. LC 74-84181. 1976. 170.00 (ISBN 0-686-14562-3). Lawyers Co-Op.
What a Dog. Sharon Gordon. (Illus.). 32p. (gr. k-2). 1980. PLB 2.96 (ISBN 0-89375-393-9); pap. 0.95 (ISBN 0-89375-293-2). Troll Assocs.
What a Fine Day For. Ruth Krauss. LC 67-18464. (gr. k-2). 1967. 5.95 o.s.i. (ISBN 0-8193-0197-3, Four Winds). Schol Bk Serv.
What a Life. Lamar Vest. 1974. pap. 1.75 (ISBN 0-87148-904-X). Pathway Pr.
What a Married Couple Should Know About Sex. John F. Knight. LC 78-71469. 1979. pap. 5.95 (ISBN 0-8163-0388-6, 23104-3). Pacific Pr Pub Assn.
What a Modern Catholic Believes About Eucharist. John Krump. 96p. (Orig.). 1974. pap. 4.95 (ISBN 0-88347-040-3). Thomas More.
What a Modern Catholic Believes About Worship. C. J. McNaspy. 91p. (Orig.). 1972. pap. 4.95 (ISBN 0-88347-031-4). Thomas More.
What a Nightmare, Charlie Brown. Shulz. pap. 1.95 (ISBN 0-590-12114-6, Schol Pap). Schol Bk Serv.
What a Teenager Ought to Know About Sex & God. Jack D. Pierson. (Teenager's Essential Education Library). (Illus.). 147p. 1981. 21.75 (ISBN 0-89266-288-3). Am Classical Coll Pr.
What a United States Senator Does. Roy Hoopes. LC 75-11772. (gr. 4 up). 1975. PLB 8.79 (ISBN 0-381-99621-2, JD-J). John Day.
What a Way to Go. Glen Chase. (Cherry Delight Ser.: No. 15). 1974. pap. 1.25 o.p. (ISBN 0-685-47978-1, LB208ZK, Leisure Bks). Nordon Pubns.
What a Way to Go. Joe Lake. 1980. 6.95 (ISBN 0-533-04440-5). Vantage.
What a Way to See. Joan Hodgkin & Norman Hodgkin. (Illus.). (gr. k-2). 1974. 2.25x (ISBN 0-933892-12-8). Child Focus Co.
What a Young Man Should Know About Sex. John F. Knight. LC 76-48572. 1977. pap. 5.95 (ISBN 0-8163-0312-6, 23111-8). Pacific Pr Pub Assn.
What a Young Woman Should Know About Sex. John F. Knight. LC 76-48571. 1977. pap. 5.95 (ISBN 0-8163-0311-8, 23112-6). Pacific Pr Pub Assn.
What About Me. Carl Fischer. (Dimensions of Personality Ser.). (gr. 3). 2.65x (ISBN 0-8278-0124-6); tchr's ed. 5.95x (ISBN 0-8278-0106-8); group activity sheets 5.95x (ISBN 0-8278-0195-5, 01955). Pflaum-Standard.
What About Me. Colby F. Rodowski. 160p. (gr. 6 up). 1976. PLB 7.90 (ISBN 0-531-01209-3). Watts.
What About Me? Francine S. Spilke. (Divorced Family Ser.). (Illus.). 80p. (gr. 3-9). 1979. 6.95 (ISBN 0-517-53784-2, Michelman Bks). Crown.
What About the Wankel Engine? Scott Corbett. LC 74-8593. (Illus.). 80p. (gr. 3-7). 1974. 6.95 (ISBN 0-590-07369-9, Four Winds). Schol Bk Serv.
What About VD? Phyllis S. Busch. LC 75-45147. 128p. (gr. 7 up). 1976. 6.95 (ISBN 0-685-62043-3, Four Winds). Schol Bk Serv.
What Am I? Joan W. German. LC 78-73531. (Illus.). (ps-2). Date not set. price not set (ISBN 0-89799-163-X); pap. price not set (ISBN 0-89799-081-1). Dandelion Pr. Postponed.
What Am I? A Picture Quiz Book. Ruth Leon. (Illus.). (ps-2). 1949. PLB 4.57 o.p. (ISBN 0-307-60509-4, Golden Pr). Western Pub.
What Am I Doing Here? Wanden M. Kane. Tr. by Marlice Dotson. (Illus.). 122p. (Orig.). 1979. pap. 4.50 (ISBN 0-910584-54-0). Filter.
What Amanda Saw. Naomi Lazard. LC 80-14516. (Illus.). 32p. (gr. k-3). 1981. 7.95 (ISBN 0-688-80272-9); PLB 7.63 (ISBN 0-688-84272-0). Greenwillow.
What Americans Should to Do About Crime. L. Harold DeWolf. LC 75-36728. (Illus.). 160p. (Orig.). 1976. pap. 4.95 (ISBN 0-06-061912-0, RD138, HarpR). Har-Row.
What an Altar Guild Should Know. Paul H. Lang. 1964. ring bdg. 5.95 (ISBN 0-570-03501-5, 14-1528). Concordia.
What & How of Reading Instruction. J. David Cooper et al. 1979. pap. text ed. 13.50 (ISBN 0-675-08287-0); instructor's manual 3.95 (ISBN 0-686-67294-1). Merrill.
What Anglican (Episcopalians) Believe. David L. Edwards. 1975. 1.00 (ISBN 0-686-28799-1). Forward Movement.
What Are Faces for? Jack Winder. Ed. by Alton Jordan. (Buppet Series). (Illus.). (gr. k-3). 1981. PLB 4.50 (ISBN 0-89868-096-4, Read Res); pap. text ed. 1.95 (ISBN 0-89868-107-3). ARO Pub.
What Are Friends for? Ed. by Mary Verdick. (Pal Paperbacks - Pal Skills Ser.). (Illus., Orig.). (gr. 7-12). 1978. pap. text ed. 1.25 (ISBN 0-8374-6703-9). Xerox Ed Pubns.
What Are My Chances? Ben Eiseman. LC 79-67118. (Illus.). 1980. text ed. 14.95 (ISBN 0-7216-3344-7). Saunders.
What Are Street Games? Anthony Ravielli. LC 80-22657. 1981. 10.95 (ISBN 0-689-30838-8). Atheneum.
What Are the Questions? & Other Essays: Further Contributions to Economics. Joan Robinson. 214p. 1981. 17.50x (ISBN 0-87332-199-5); pap. 8.95x (ISBN 0-87332-200-2). M E Sharpe.
What Are They Saying About Christian-Jewish Relations? John T. Pawlikowski. LC 79-56135. 144p. (Orig.). 1980. pap. 2.95 (ISBN 0-8091-2239-1). Paulist Pr.
What Are They Saying About Creation? Zachary Hayes. LC 80-80870. 128p. 1980. pap. 2.95 (ISBN 0-8091-2286-3). Paulist Pr.
What Are They Saying About Death & Christian Hope? Monika K. Hellwig. LC 78-61726. 1978. pap. 2.45 (ISBN 0-8091-2165-4). Paulist Pr.
What Are They Saying About Dogma? William E. Reiser. LC 78-58955. 1978. pap. 2.45 (ISBN 0-8091-2127-1). Paulist Pr.
What Are They Saying About Jesus? Gerald O'Collins. LC 77-70640. 1977. pap. 2.45 (ISBN 0-8091-2017-8). Paulist Pr.
What Are They Saying About Luke & Acts? A Theology of the Faithful God. Robert J. Karris. LC 79-83899. (Orig.). 1979. pap. 2.45 (ISBN 0-8091-2191-3). Paulist Pr.
What Are They Saying About the Book of Revelation? John J. Pilch. LC 78-51594. 1978. pap. 2.45 (ISBN 0-8091-2126-3). Paulist Pr.
What Are They Saying About the Prophets? David P. Reid. LC 80-80869. (Orig.). 1980. pap. 2.95 (ISBN 0-8091-2304-5). Paulist Pr.
What Are They Saying About the Resurrection? Gerald O'Collins. LC 78-51594. 1978. pap. 2.45 (ISBN 0-8091-2109-3). Paulist Pr.
What Are They Saying About the Trinity? Joseph A. Bracken. LC 78-70819. 1979. pap. 2.45 (ISBN 0-8091-2179-4). Paulist Pr.
What Are We Doing Here? Associated Women's Organization, Mars Hill Bible School. 1972. pap. 3.75 (ISBN 0-89137-404-3). Quality Pubns.
What Are We Going to Do, Michael? Nellie Burchardt. LC 73-5743. (gr. 4-6). 1973. PLB 4.90 o.p. (ISBN 0-531-02637-X). Watts.
What Are We Going To Do With All These Rotting Fish? & Seven Other Short Plays for Church & Community. Ed. by Norman C. Habel. LC 79-119766. (Open Bks). (Illus.). 160p. (Orig.). 1970. pap. 3.25 (ISBN 0-8006-0147-5, 1-147). Fortress.
What Are You Afraid of? An Illustrated Dictionary of Fearful Words Ending in Phobia. Sam Goldstein. (Weirdictionaries Ser.). (Illus.). 72p. (Orig.). 1981. pap. 3.95 (ISBN 0-938338-05-6). Winds World Pr.
What Black Librarians Are Saying. E. J. Josey. LC 72-5372. 1972. 10.00 (ISBN 0-8108-0530-8). Scarecrow.
What Can a Hippopotamus Be? Mike Thaler. LC 74-30104. (Illus.). (gr. k-3). 1975. 5.95 o.s.i. (ISBN 0-8193-0809-9, Four Winds); PLB 5.41 o.s.i. (ISBN 0-8193-0810-2). Schol Bk Serv.
What Can a Police Officer Do: A Comparative Study: USA - German Federal Republic - Israel - Italy. LC 74-77522. (New York University Criminal Law Education & Research Center Monograph: Vol. 7). (Illus.). xiii, 272p. (Orig.). 1974. pap. text ed. 12.50x (ISBN 0-8377-0417-0). Rothman.
What Can Be Automated? The Computer Science & Engineering Research Study (COSERS) Ed. by Bruce W. Arden. 920p. 1980. text ed. 29.95x (ISBN 0-262-01060-7). MIT Pr.
What Can She Be? A Computer Scientist. Gloria Goldreich & Esther Goldreich. LC 78-31988. (What Can She Be Ser.). (Illus.). (gr. 2-5). 1979. 7.50 (ISBN 0-688-41887-2); PLB 7.20 (ISBN 0-688-51887-7). Lothrop.
What Can She Be? A Farmer. Gloria Goldreich & Esther Goldreich. LC 76-12474. (What Can She Be? Ser.). (Illus.). 48p. (gr. k-5). 1976. PLB 7.20 (ISBN 0-688-51768-4). Lothrop.
What Can She Be? A Film Producer. Gloria Goldreich & Esther Goldreich. LC 77-8889. (What Can She Be? Ser.). (Illus.). (gr. 1-5). 1977. 6.25 o.p. (ISBN 0-688-41815-5); PLB 7.20 (ISBN 0-688-51815-X). Lothrop.
What Can She Be? A Geologist. Gloria Goldreich & Esther Goldreich. LC 76-10316. (What Can She Be? Ser.). (Illus.). 48p. (gr. 1-5). 1976. 7.20 (ISBN 0-688-51767-6). Lothrop.
What Can She Be? A Lawyer. Gloria Goldreich & Esther Goldreich. LC 72-10587. (What Can She Be? Ser.). (Illus.). 40p. (gr. k-5). 1973. PLB 7.20 (ISBN 0-688-51521-5). Lothrop.
What Can She Be? A Legislator. Gloria Goldreich & Esther Goldreich. (What Can She Be? Ser). (Illus.). (gr. 1-5). 1978. 7.50 (ISBN 0-688-41865-1); PLB 7.20 (ISBN 0-688-51865-6). Lothrop.
What Can She Be? A Musician. Gloria Goldreich & Esther Goldreich. LC 74-28461. (What Can She Be? Ser.). (Illus.). 48p. (gr. k-5). 1975. 7.50 (ISBN 0-688-41701-9); PLB 7.20 (ISBN 0-688-51701-3). Lothrop.
What Can She Be? A Newscaster. Gloria Goldreich & Esther Goldreich. LC 73-4940. (What Can She Be? Ser.). (Illus.). 48p. (gr. k-5). 1973. PLB 7.20 (ISBN 0-688-51540-1). Lothrop.
What Can She Be? A Police Officer. Gloria Goldreich & Esther Goldreich. LC 75-7442. (What Can She Be? Ser.). (Illus.). 48p. (gr. k-5). 1975. PLB 7.20 (ISBN 0-688-51706-4). Lothrop.
What Can She Be? A Scientist. Gloria Goldreich & Esther Goldreich. LC 80-25011. (What Can She Be Ser.). (Illus.). 32p. (gr. 3-6). 1981. 7.95 (ISBN 0-03-055671-6). HR&W.
What Can She Be? a Veterinarian. Gloria Goldreich & Esther Goldreich. LC 76-177324. (What Can She Be? Ser.). (Illus.). 48p. (gr. k-5). 1972. PLB 7.20 (ISBN 0-688-51501-0). Lothrop.
What Can She Be? An Architect. Gloria Goldreich & Esther Goldreich. LC 73-17710. (What Can She Be? Ser.). (Illus.). 48p. (gr. k-5). 1974. PLB 7.20 (ISBN 0-688-51579-7). Lothrop.
What Can We Do? A Food, Land, Hunger Action Guide. William Valentine. (Illus., Orig.). 1980. pap. 2.45 (ISBN 0-935028-06-4). Inst Food & Develp.
What Can We Do Today, Mommy. Kathy Farrell & Mary Sweeney. (Illus.). 127p. (Orig.). 1980. 6.95 (ISBN 0-9604118-0-1). Growing Together.
What Can You Say About God? Except God. William A. Luijpen. LC 76-171103. 1971. pap. 1.95 (ISBN 0-8091-1713-4). Paulist Pr.
What Catholics Should Know About Jews: And Other Christians. Edward Zeron. 1980. pap. 3.25 (ISBN 0-697-01739-7). Wm C Brown.
What Christians Stand For in the Secular World. William Temple. Ed. by Franklin Sherman. LC 65-21081. (Facet Bks.). (Orig). 1965. pap. 1.00 (ISBN 0-8006-3021-1, 1-3021). Fortress.
What Coleridge Thought. Owen Barfield. LC 73-153100. 1971. 17.50 (ISBN 0-8195-4040-4, Pub. by Wesleyan U Pr). Columbia U Pr.
What College Students Know. Educational Testing Service & The Council on Learning. LC 80-69767. 200p. (Orig.). 1980. pap. 10.95 (ISBN 0-915390-31-0). Change Mag.
What College Students Know About Their World. Council on Learning's National Task Force. LC 80-69768. 56p. (Orig.). 1980. pap. 5.95 (ISBN 0-915390-30-2). Change Mag.
What Color Is It? Deborah Manley. LC 78-26525. (Ready, Set, Look Ser.). (Illus.). (gr. k-3). 1979. PLB 9.65 (ISBN 0-8172-1300-7). Raintree Pubs.
What Color Is Your Parachute? 5th.rev. ed. Richard N. Bolles. (Illus.). 1979. 11.95 o.p. (ISBN 0-89815-002-7); pap. 5.95 o.p. (ISBN 0-687-01211-2). Ten Speed Pr.
What Color Is Your Parachute? rev. ed. Richard N. Bolles. 352p. 1981. 14.95 (ISBN 0-89815-047-7); pap. 6.95 (ISBN 0-89815-046-9). Ten Speed Pr.
What Color Is Your Parachute? 1981 Ed. R. N. Bolles. (Illus.). 1981. 14.95 (ISBN 0-89815-047-7); pap. 6.95 (ISBN 0-89815-046-9). Ten Speed Pr.
What Comes Out of an Egg. Ernest Prescott. (Easy-Read Wildlife Ser.). (Illus.). 32p. (gr. 2-4). 1976. PLB 4.90 o.p. (ISBN 0-531-00362-0). Watts.
What Computers Can Do. Donald D. Spencer. LC 76-21227. 1977. pap. 5.95 (ISBN 0-89218-029-3). Camelot Pub.
What Computers Can't Do: A Critique of Artificial Reason. Hubert L. Dreyfus. LC 67-22524. (Illus.). 1972. 12.95 o.p. (ISBN 0-06-011082-1, HarpT). Har-Row.
What Dentists Do: A Patient's Guide to Modern Dentistry. S. Sigmund Stahl et al. (Appleton Consumer Health Guides). (Illus.). 226p. 1980. 12.95 (ISBN 0-8385-9712-2); pap. 5.95 (ISBN 0-8385-9711-4). ACC.
What Did Jesus Say About That? Stanley C. Baldwin. 156p. 1975. pap. 3.50 (ISBN 0-88207-718-X). Victor Bks.
What Did They Do to Miss Lily. Sonia Wolff. 288p. 1981. 12.95 (ISBN 0-06-014851-6, HarpT). Har-Row.
What Did You Bring? Daisy Ellsworth. (Sesame Street Early Bird Bk). (Illus.). 32p. (ps). 1981. 3.50 (ISBN 0-307-11603-4, Golden Pr). Western Pub.
What Did You Say? A Book of Homophones. Sylvia R. Tester. LC 77-9494. (Using Words Ser.). (Illus.). (gr. k-3). 1977. PLB 5.50 (ISBN 0-913778-91-5). Childs World.
What Difference Does It Make, Danny? Helen Young. LC 80-65665. (Illus.). 96p. (gr. 1-6). 1980. 7.95 (ISBN 0-233-97248-X). Andre Deutsch.
What Do Colleges Really Want for Admissions? Ed. by Donald L. Halsted. 1977. pap. 9.00 o.p. (ISBN 0-686-00916-9, D-110). Essence Pubns.
What Do I Do: English - Spanish Edition. Norma Simon. LC 74-79544. (Concept Bks.). (Illus.). (ps-2). 1969. 6.95g (ISBN 0-8075-8823-7). A Whitman.
What Do I Do Next? A Manual for People Just Entering Government Service. Warren W. Jones & Albert Solnit. LC 80-67754. (Illus.). 116p. (Orig.). 1980. pap. 9.95 (ISBN 0-918286-20-4). Planners Pr.
What Do I Do Now, Mom? Jean D. Crowther. LC 80-82257. (Illus.). 86p. (gr. 9-12). 1980. 5.50 (ISBN 0-88290-134-6). Horizon Utah.
What Do I Say. Norma Simon. LC 67-17420. (Concept Bks.). (Illus.). (ps-2). 1967. 6.95g (ISBN 0-8075-8826-1). A Whitman.
What Do I Say? English-Spanish Edition. Norma Simon. LC 67-17420. (Concept Bks.). (Illus.). (ps-2). 6.95g (ISBN 0-8075-8828-8). A Whitman.
What Do I Say? Protecting Your Child from Sexual Assault. Jennifer Fay & Caren Adams. (Illus.). 96p. (Orig.). 1981. pap. 3.95 (ISBN 0-915166-24-0). Impact Pubs Cal.
What Do the Animals Do in the Zoo. Jane B. Moncure. LC 75-33954. (Illus.). (ps-4). 1976. 5.50 (ISBN 0-913778-31-1). Childs World.
What Do TV Producers Know About Their Young Viewers. Ed. by Steftung P. Jeunesse. 1979. text ed. 12.00 (ISBN 3-598-10092-2). K G Saur.
What Do We Do When We're Asleep? Patricia M. Eldred. (Creative's Questions & Answers Ser.). (Illus.). 32p. (gr. 3-4). Date not set. lib. bdg. 5.65 (ISBN 0-87191-752-1); pap. 2.75 (ISBN 0-89812-221-X). Creative Ed. Postponed.
What Do You Do in Quicksand? Lois Ruby. 224p. 1981. pap. 1.95 (ISBN 0-449-70004-6, Juniper). Fawcett.
What Do You Do When Your Mouth Won't Open? Susan B. Pfeffer. LC 80-68731. (Illus.). 128p. (gr. 4-7). 1981. 7.95 (ISBN 0-440-09471-2); PLB 7.44 (ISBN 0-440-09475-5). Delacorte.
What Do You Do with a Kangaroo? Mercer Mayer. LC 72-87073. (Illus.). 48p. (gr. k-3). 1974. 6.95 (ISBN 0-590-07286-2, Four Winds). Schol Bk Serv.
What Do You Do with a Kangaroo? Mercer Mayer. (Illus.). (gr. k-3). 1975. pap. 1.95 (ISBN 0-590-10007-6, Schol Pap); pap. 3.50 bk. & record (ISBN 0-590-20791-1). Schol Bk Serv.
What Do You Do with a Kinkajou? Alice Gilborn. LC 75-29195. 1976. 8.95 o.s.i. (ISBN 0-397-01109-1). Lippincott.
What Do You Do with Joe? Problem Pupils & Tactful Teachers. Elizabeth Crisci. (Illus.). 64p. (Orig.). 1981. pap. 3.50 (ISBN 0-87239-414-X, 3650). Standard Pub.
What Do You Expect? An Inquiry into Self-Fulfilling Prophecies. Paul M. Insel & Lenore F. Jacobson. LC 75-2529. (Education Ser.). 246p. 1975. pap. text ed. 8.95 (ISBN 0-8465-2670-0, 52670). Benjamin-Cummings.
What Do You Mean, I Still Don't Have Equal Rights? Cathy Guisewite. 128p. pap. 3.95 (ISBN 0-8362-1158-8). Andrews & McMeel.
What Do You Play on a Summer Day? Ethel Kessler & Leonard Kessler. LC 76-18095. (Illus.). (ps-3). 1977. 5.95 o.s.i. (ISBN 0-8193-0866-8, Four Winds); PLB 5.41 o.s.i. (ISBN 0-8193-0867-6). Schol Bk Serv.
What Do You Say, Dear? Joslin. (ps-3). 1980. pap. 1.50 (ISBN 0-590-01625-3, Schol Pap). Schol Bk Serv.

What Do You See? Janina Domanska. LC 73-6052. (Illus.). 32p. (gr. k-2). 1974. 8.95 (ISBN 0-02-732830-9, 73283). Macmillan.

What Do You Think? D. Byrne & A. Wright. (Illus.). 1974. pap. text ed. 2.75x student bk. 1 (ISBN 0-582-52269-2); pap. text ed. 2.50x tchr's bk. 1 (ISBN 0-582-52270-6); pap. text ed. 2.75x student bk. 2 (ISBN 0-582-52271-4); pap. text ed. 2.50x tchr's bk. 2 (ISBN 0-582-52272-2). Longman.

What Do You Think, Vol. 4. (Vegetable Puppets Ser.). (Illus.). 10p. (ps). 1979. 2.50 o.p. (ISBN 0-89346-119-9, Pub. by Froebel-Kan Japan). Heian Intl.

What Do You Think of Jesus? David P. Scaer. LC 72-97341. 144p. 1973. pap. 3.75 (ISBN 0-570-03153-2, 12-2538). Concordia.

What Do You Want to Know About Guppies? Seymour Simon. LC 77-5930. (Illus.). 80p. (gr. 2-5). 1977. 7.95 (ISBN 0-590-07412-1, Four Winds). Schol Bk Serv.

What Does a Koala Bear Need? Jane B. Moncure. LC 75-33956. (Illus.). (ps-3). 1976. 5.50 (ISBN 0-913778-34-6). Childs World.

What Does a Lifeguard Do? Kathy Pelta. LC 76-53440. (What Do They Do Ser.). (gr. 4 up). 1977. 5.95 (ISBN 0-396-07406-5). Dodd.

What Does a Meteorologist Do? Grant Compton. (What Do They Do Ser.). (Illus.). 80p. (gr. 5 up). 1981. PLB 5.95 (ISBN 0-396-07931-8). Dodd.

What Does an Airplane Pilot Do? Kathy Pelta. LC 80-23530. (What Do They Do Ser.). (Illus.). 80p. (gr. 5 up). 1981. PLB 5.95 (ISBN 0-396-07910-5). Dodd.

What Does It Mean to Be Born Again? John W. White. (Orig.). 1977. pap. 1.95 (ISBN 0-87123-641-9, 200641). Bethany Fell.

What Does the Charpy Test Really Tell Us? Ed. by A. R. Rosenfield et al. 1978. 32.00 (ISBN 0-87170-027-1). ASM.

What Does the Rooster Say, Yoshio? Edith Battles. Ed. by Kathy Pacini. LC 78-12824. (Self-Starter Bks). (Illus.). (ps-2). 1978. 6.50g (ISBN 0-8075-8833-4). A Whitman.

What Economics Is About. Michael B. Brown. 368p. 1970. pap. 7.95x o.p. (ISBN 0-8464-0966-6). Beekman Pubs.

What Ever Became of the Bonner Boys. Campbell Geeslin. 1981. 10.95 (ISBN 0-671-42430-0). S&S.

What Ever Happened to Amelia Earhart? Melinda Blau. LC 77-22173. (Great Unsolved Mysteries Ser.). (Illus.). (gr. 4-5). 1977. PLB 9.65 (ISBN 0-8172-1057-1). Raintree Pubs.

What Every Child Would Like His Parents to Know. Lee Salk. 224p. 1973. pap. 2.50 (ISBN 0-446-91705-2). Warner Bks.

What Every Christian Should Know About Growing. LeRoy Eims. 168p. 1976. pap. 3.95 (ISBN 0-88207-727-9). Victor Bks.

What Every Conservative Should Know About Communism. Lyndon H. LaRouche, Jr. LC 80-20325. (Illus.). 149p. (Orig.). 1980. pap. 3.95 (ISBN 0-933488-06-8). New Benjamin.

What Every Credit Executive Should Know About Chapter Eleven of the Bankruptcy Code. Benjamin Weintraub. LC 80-82081. 133p. 1980. pap. 9.50 (ISBN 0-934914-32-X). NACM.

What Every Engineer Should Know About Economic Decision Making. Shupe. 224p. 1980. 12.50 (ISBN 0-8247-1019-3). Dekker.

What Every Family Needs or Whatever Happened to Mom, Dad, & the Kids. Carl Brecheen & Paul Faulkner. LC 78-68726. (Journey Bks.). 1979. pap. 2.60 (ISBN 0-8344-0104-5). Sweet.

What Every Family Should Know About Strokes. Lucille Hess & Robert Bahr. (Appleton Consumer Health Guides). 128p. 1981. 12.95 (ISBN 0-8385-9717-3); pap. 5.95 (ISBN 0-8385-9716-5). ACC.

What Every Girl Should Know. Margaret Sanger. LC 80-16988. 96p. 1980. pap. 3.95 (ISBN 0-87754-219-8). Chelsea Hse.

What Every Husband Should Know About Having a Baby: The Psychoprophlactic Way. Jeannette L. Sasmor. LC 72-75633. 1972. 14.95 (ISBN 0-911012-18-4); pap. 7.95 (ISBN 0-88229-496-2). Nelson-Hall.

What Every Supervisor Should Know, the Basics of Supervisory Management. 4th ed. Lester R. Bittel. LC 79-16387. 1980. 18.95x (ISBN 0-07-005573-4); text ed. 16.75x (ISBN 0-07-005561-0); Skills Development portfolio 5.95 (ISBN 0-07-005562-9); Course & Management key 4.50 (ISBN 0-07-005563-7). McGraw.

What Every Woman Needs to Know About the Law. Martha Pomroy. LC 80-85109. 432p. 1981. pap. 3.95 (ISBN 0-87216-835-2). Playboy Pbks.

What Every Woman Should Know About Finances. Fred A. Lumb. LC 77-93504. 1978. 8.95 (ISBN 0-87863-148-8). Farnswth Pub.

What Every Woman Should Know About Hysterectomy. W. Gifford-Jones. LC 76-45747. (Funk & W Bk.). 1977. 8.95 o.p. (ISBN 0-308-10275-4, TYC-T). T Y Crowell.

What Everyone Should Know About Transcendential Meditation. (Orig.). pap. 1.50 (ISBN 0-89129-234-9). Jove Pubns.

What Floats? Mary Brewer. LC 75-34107. (Illus.). (ps-3). 1976. PLB 5.50 (ISBN 0-913778-25-7); pap. 2.75 (ISBN 0-89565-065-7). Childs World.

What God Did for ZEKE the Fuzzy Caterpillar. Robert O'Rourke. Ed. by Judith Sparks. (Happy Day Book). (Illus.). 24p. (gr. 1-3). 1980. 0.98 (ISBN 0-87239-406-9, 3638). Standard Pub.

What Great Men Have Said About Great Men. Ed. by William Wale. LC 68-17944. 1968. Repr. of 1902 ed. 18.00 (ISBN 0-8103-3195-0). Gale.

What Handwriting Tells You: About Yourself, Your Friends, & Famous People. M. N. Bunker. 12.95 (ISBN 0-911012-02-8). Nelson-Hall.

What Happened in the Mooney Case. Ernest J. Hopkins. LC 73-107411. (Civil Liberties in American History Ser). 1970. Repr. of 1932 ed. lib. bdg. 27.50 (ISBN 0-306-71891-X). Da Capo.

What Happened on Lexington Green: An Inquiry into the Nature & Methods of History. P. Bennett. Ed. by Richard H. Brown & Van R. Halsey. (Amherst Ser.). (gr. 9-12). 1970. pap. text ed. 4.52 (ISBN 0-201-00461-5, Sch Div); tchr's. manual 1.92 (ISBN 0-201-00463-1). A-W.

What Happened to Fairbanks? The Effects of the Trans-Alaska Oil Pipeline on the Community of Fairbanks, Alaska. Mim Dixon. (Social Impact Assessment Ser.: No. 1). (Illus.). 337p. 1980. pap. text ed. 9.50x (ISBN 0-89158-961-9). Westview.

What Happened to My Bread. Pat Workman. 1981. 3.95 (ISBN 0-932298-12-5). Green Hill.

What Happens at a Newspaper. Arthur Shay. LC 76-183835. (What Happens Ser.). (Illus.). 32p. (gr. 2-4). 1972. 5.95 o.p. (ISBN 0-8092-8612-2); PLB avail o.p. (ISBN 0-685-23702-8). Contemp Bks.

What Happens If... ? Rose Wyler. (gr. k-3). 1976. pap. 1.25 o.p. (ISBN 0-590-09845-4, Schol Pap). Schol Bk Serv.

What Happens in Art. Matthew Lipman. LC 66-27473. (Century Philosophy Ser.). (Orig.). 1967. pap. text ed. 8.95x (ISBN 0-89197-470-9). Irvington.

What Happens in Book Publishing. 2nd ed. Ed. by Chandler B. Grannis. LC 67-19875. 1967. 22.50x (ISBN 0-231-02948-9). Columbia U Pr.

What Happens in Hamlet. 3rd ed. John D. Wilson. 1951. 49.50 (ISBN 0-521-06835-5); pap. 10.50x (ISBN 0-521-09109-8, 109). Cambridge U Pr.

What Happens in Indian Music: A Practical Introduction. Neil Sorrell. (Illus.). 1980. pap. 27.50x (ISBN 0-8147-7815-1). NYU Pr.

What Happens in Public Relations. Ed. by Gerald J. Voros & Paul Alvarez. 275p. 1981. 17.95 (ISBN 0-8144-5652-9). Am Mgmt.

What Happens Next. Sesame Street. (Sesame Street Pop-up Ser: No. 4). (Illus.). (ps-2). 1971. 4.95 o.p. (ISBN 0-394-82336-2). Random.

What Happens Next? Stories to Finish for Intermediate Writers. Andrew D. Washton. 1978. pap. text ed. 5.95x (ISBN 0-8077-2454-8). Tchrs Coll.

What Happens to a Hamburger. Paul Showers. LC 70-106578. (Let's Read & Find Out Science Bk). (Illus.). (gr. k-3). 1970. bds. 7.95 (ISBN 0-690-87540-1, TYC-J); PLB 7.89 (ISBN 0-690-87541-X); filmstrip with record 11.95 (ISBN 0-690-87542-8); filmstrip with cassette 14.95 (ISBN 0-690-87544-4). T Y Crowell.

What Happens When Children Grow. Margret B. Jacobsen. 1977. pap. 2.50 o.p. (ISBN 0-88207-736-8). Victor Bks.

What Happens When Women Pray. Evelyn Christenson & Viola Blake. 144p. 1975. pap. 2.95 (ISBN 0-88207-715-5). Victor Bks.

What Helped Me: When My Loved One Died. Ed. by Earl A. Grollman. LC 80-68166. 160p. 1981. 9.95 (ISBN 0-8070-3228-X). Beacon Pr.

What Henry Miller Said & Why It Is Important. 2nd ed. Bernard H. Porter. (Illus.). 1972. 8.50 o.p. (ISBN 0-685-19458-2). Porter.

What Herbs Are All About. Jack Challem & Renate Challem. LC 80-82913. 150p. (Orig.). 1980. pap. 2.95 (ISBN 0-87983-242-8). Keats.

What Husbands Wish Their Wives Knew About Money. Larry Burkett. 1977. pap. 2.95 (ISBN 0-88207-758-9). Victor Bks.

What I Like About Toads. Judy Hawes. LC 76-78262. (Let's Read & Find Out Science Bk). (Illus.). (gr. k-3). 1969. PLB 7.89 (ISBN 0-690-87577-0, TYC-J); filmstrip with record 11.95 (ISBN 0-690-87578-9); filmstrip with cassette 14.95 (ISBN 0-690-87580-0). T Y Crowell.

What I Like About Toads. Judy Hawes. LC 76-78262. (Crocodile Paperbacks Ser.). (Illus.). 33p. (gr. k-3). 1972. pap. 2.95 (ISBN 0-690-87582-7, TYC-J). T Y Crowell.

What I Saw in America. 2nd ed. G. K. Chesterton. LC 68-16226. (American Scene Ser). 1968. Repr. of 1922 ed. 29.50 (ISBN 0-306-71009-9). Da Capo.

What If.... Gale Brennan. (Illus.). 32p. (Orig.). (ps-2). 1980. pap. 1.95 (ISBN 0-89542-932-2). Ideals.

What If? Gale Brennan & Tom LaFleur. (Illus.). 1980. 7.35g (ISBN 0-516-09154-9). Childrens.

What If, Vol. 1. Richard A. Lupoff. (Orig.). 1980. pap. write for info. (ISBN 0-671-83189-5). PB.

What If I Don't Go Overseas. Charles Smith. 1981. pap. 0.50 (ISBN 0-87784-182-9). Inter-Varsity.

What in the World Has Gotten into the Church? David Hesselgrave & Ronald Hesselgrave. 128p. 1981. pap. 3.95 (ISBN 0-8024-9386-6). Moody.

What in the World Is Happening? Ray Brubaker. 1981. pap. 3.95 (ISBN 0-8407-5767-0). Nelson.

What Is a Bird? Jenifer W. Day. (Child's Golden Science Bks). (Illus.). 32p. (gr. k-4). 1975. PLB 6.92 (ISBN 0-307-61805-6, Golden Pr). Western Pub.

What Is a Doctor? Alex Comfort. LC 80-51834. 240p. 1980. text ed. 10.95 (ISBN 0-89313-022-2). G F Stickley Co.

What Is a Flower? Jenifer W. Day. (Child's Golden Science Bks). (Illus.). 32p. (gr. k-4). 1975. PLB 6.92 (ISBN 0-307-61800-5, Golden Pr). Western Pub.

What Is a Fruit? Jenifer W. Day. (Child's Golden Science Bks.). (Illus.). (gr. k-4). 1976. PLB 6.92 (ISBN 0-307-61801-3, Golden Pr). Western Pub.

What Is a Girl? What Is a Boy? Stephanie Waxman. LC 76-42451. (Illus.). 48p. (ps-12). 1976. 6.95 (ISBN 0-915238-11-X); pap. 4.95 (ISBN 0-915238-10-1). Peace Pr.

What Is a Jew? Israel Ministry. 1975. 30.00 (ISBN 0-379-13904-9). Oceana.

What Is a Jew? Morris N. Kertzer. 1978. pap. 2.95 (ISBN 0-02-086350-0, Collier). Macmillan.

What Is a Laser? Bruce Lewis. LC 78-11100. (Skylight Bks.). (Illus.). (gr. 3-5). 1979. 5.95 (ISBN 0-396-07646-7). Dodd.

What Is a Mammal? Jenifer W. Day. (Child's Golden Science Bks). (Illus.). 32p. (gr. k-4). 1975. PLB 6.92 (ISBN 0-307-61802-1, Golden Pr). Western Pub.

What Is a Masterpiece? Kenneth Clark. (Illus.). pap. 2.95 (ISBN 0-500-27206-9). Thames Hudson.

What Is a Shadow? Experiences with Gravity, Shadows, Mirrors & Electricity. Bob Ridiman. LC 73-4368. (Humpty Dumpty Bk.). (Illus.). 52p. (gr. k-3). 1973. 5.95 o.s.i. (ISBN 0-8193-0688-6, Four Winds); PLB 5.41 o.s.i. (ISBN 0-8193-0689-4). Schol Bk Serv.

What Is a Tree? Jenifer W. Day. (Child's Golden Science Bks). (Illus.). 32p. (gr. k-4). 1975. PLB 6.92 (ISBN 0-307-61804-8, Golden Pr). Western Pub.

What Is a Woman. 2nd ed. William H. Graham. (Illus.). 1967. 12.50 (ISBN 0-910550-16-6). Elysium.

What Is Acuncture? How Does It Work? Eric H. Stievater. 48p. 1971. pap. 3.00x (ISBN 0-8464-1061-3). Beekman Pubs.

What Is Allergy? A Guide for the Allergic Person. Raymond T. Benack. (Illus.). 172p. 1967. 17.50 (ISBN 0-398-00128-6). C C Thomas.

What Is an Insect? Jenifer W. Day. (Child's Golden Science Bks.). (Illus.). (gr. k-4). 1976. PLB 6.92 (ISBN 0-307-61803-X, Golden Pr). Western Pub.

What Is Art. Leo Tolstoy. Tr. by Aylmer Maude. LC 60-9557. 1960. pap. 5.50 (ISBN 0-672-60221-0, LLA51). Bobbs.

What Is B. F. Skinner Really Saying? Robert D. Nye. 1979. 11.95 (ISBN 0-13-952192-5, Spec); pap. 4.95 (ISBN 0-13-952184-4). P-H.

What Is Cinema? Andre Bazin. Tr. by Hugh Gray. LC 67-18899. 1967. 12.95x (ISBN 0-520-00091-9); pap. 3.45 (ISBN 0-520-00092-7, CAL151). U of Cal Pr.

What Is Cinema, Vol. 2. Andre Bazin. Tr. & compiled by Hugh Gray. 1971. 12.95x (ISBN 0-520-02034-0); pap. 4.50 (ISBN 0-520-02255-6, CAL250). U of Cal Pr.

What Is Cinema Verite? M. Ali Issari & Doris A. Paul. LC 79-20110. 216p. 1979. 11.50 (ISBN 0-8108-1253-3). Scarecrow.

What Is Economics? 2nd ed. Jim Eggert. LC 77-5781. (Illus.). 176p. 1977. 8.95 (ISBN 0-913232-49-1); pap. 4.95 (ISBN 0-913232-48-3). W Kaufmann.

What Is Educational Planning? Philip H. Coombs. (Fundamentals of Educational Planning Ser). (Orig.). 1971. pap. 6.00 (ISBN 92-803-1037-2, U715, UNESCO). Unipub.

What Is Governing? Purpose & Policy in Washington. Richard Rose. LC 77-13476. (Illus.). 1978. pap. 9.95x ref. ed. (ISBN 0-13-952127-5). P-H.

What Is Hypnosis? Andrew Salter. 106p. 1973. pap. 3.95 (ISBN 0-374-51038-5, N439). FS&G.

What Is I.Q.? Karl Liungman. 1975. pap. 5.95 (ISBN 0-86033-040-0). Gordon-Cremonesi.

What Is It? Joan Loss. LC 73-9038. 48p. (gr. 5-7). 1974. 4.95 o.p. (ISBN 0-385-06703-8). Doubleday.

What Is Karate? Masutatsu Oyama. LC 66-21210. (Illus.). 176p. 1974. 22.00 (ISBN 0-87040-147-5). Japan Pubns.

What Is Life? Erwin Schrodinger. Bd. with Mind & Matter. pap. 8.95x (ISBN 0-521-09397-X). Cambridge U Pr.

What is Literature? Ed. by Paul Hernadi. LC 77-23640. 288p. 1978. 12.50x (ISBN 0-253-36505-8). Ind U Pr.

What Is Literature. Jean-Paul Sartre. 7.50 (ISBN 0-8446-2867-0). Peter Smith.

What Is Love. Alan Willoughby. Ed. by Alton Jordan. (Elephant Ser.). (Illus.). (gr. k-3). 1975. PLB 3.50 (ISBN 0-89868-018-2, Read Res); pap. text ed. 1.75 (ISBN 0-89868-051-4). ARO Pub.

What Is Man? David Jenkins. LC 79-132998. 1971. pap. 1.95 o.p. (ISBN 0-8170-0516-1). Judson.

What Is Man? B. L. Smith. 1977. 4.00 o.p. (ISBN 0-682-48831-3). Exposition.

What Is Man: Contemporary Anthropology in Theological Perepective. Wolfhart Pannenberg. Tr. by Duane A. Priebe from Ger. LC 74-101429. 168p. 1972. pap. 3.75 (ISBN 0-8006-1252-3, 1-1252). Fortress.

What Is Mathematics? An Elementary Approach to Ideas & Methods. Richard Courant & Herbert Robbins. (Illus.). 1979. pap. 8.95 (ISBN 0-19-502517-2, GB576, GB). Oxford U Pr.

What Is Meditation? Ed. by John White. LC 73-81126. 280p. 1974. pap. 2.95 (ISBN 0-385-07638-X, Anch). Doubleday.

What Is Money? Elizabeth James & Carol Barkin. LC 76-46589. (Money Ser.). (Illus.). (gr. k-1). 1977. PLB 8.65 (ISBN 0-8172-0275-7). Raintree Pubs.

What Is New? What Is Missing? What Is Different? Patricia Ruben. LC 78-8109. (Illus.). (gr. k-2). 1978. 8.95 (ISBN 0-397-31816-2). Lippincott.

What Is Pink. Christina Rossetti. LC 71-152289. (Illus.). (ps-3). 1971. 6.95 (ISBN 0-685-00251-9). Macmillan.

What Is Political Philosophy? Leo Strauss. LC 73-1408. 315p. 1973. Repr. of 1959 ed. lib. bdg. 22.50x (ISBN 0-8371-6802-3, STPP). Greenwood.

What Is Process Theology? Robert B. Mellert. LC 74-28933. 1975. pap. 2.95 (ISBN 0-8091-1867-X). Paulist Pr.

What Is Redaction Criticism? Norman Perrin. Ed. by Dan O. Via, Jr. LC 72-81529. (Guides to Biblical Scholarship). 96p. (Orig.). 1969. pap. 2.75 (ISBN 0-8006-0181-5, 1-181). Fortress.

What Is Religion. Paul Tillich. 1973. pap. 4.95x (ISBN 0-06-131732-2, TB1732, Torch). Har-Row.

What Is Religion? An Inquiry for Christian Theology, Concilium 136. Ed. by Mircea Eliade & David Tracy. (New Concilium 1980). 128p. 1980. pap. 5.95 (ISBN 0-8245-4769-1). Crossroad NY.

What Is Science? John M. Scott. LC 70-179362. (Finding-Out Books for Science & Social Studies, Grades 1-4). (Illus.). 64p. (gr. 2-4). 1972. PLB 6.95 (ISBN 0-8193-0539-1, Pub. by Parents). Enslow Pubs.

What Is Sexuality? Wilhelm Reich. 1981. 10.95 (ISBN 0-374-28843-7). FS&G.

What Is Sociology? Norbert Elias. 1978. 15.00x (ISBN 0-231-04550-6). Columbia U Pr.

What Is Symbolism? Henri Peyre. Tr. by Emmett Parker from Fr. LC 79-4686. 176p. 1980. 15.75 (ISBN 0-8173-7004-8). U of Ala Pr.

What Is the Church? Victor De Waal. LC 70-121057. (Orig.). 1970. pap. 1.95 o.p. (ISBN 0-8170-0492-0). Judson.

What Is the Reason? Chaim Press. Repr. of 1975 ed. Vols 1,2,3, except where noted 5.95x ea.; Vol. 6. 5.95 o.p. (ISBN 0-8197-0377-X). Bloch.

What Is the Revolution? Friedrich Julius Stahl. Tr. by Timothy D. Taylor from Ger. Orig. Title: Was Ist Die Revolution? 1977. pap. 3.55 limited ed. o.p. (ISBN 0-918288-06-1). Slavia Lib.

What Is Theology? M. F. Wiles. 1977. 7.95x (ISBN 0-19-213525-2); pap. 4.50x (ISBN 0-19-289066-2). Oxford U Pr.

What Is This Thing Called Love. Nelson M. Smith. 1970. 6.65 (ISBN 0-89137-505-8); pap. 3.10 (ISBN 0-89137-504-X). Quality Pubns.

What Is This Thing Called Science? An Assessment of the Nature & Status of Science & Its Methods. A. F. Chalmers. 1976. pap. text ed. 10.50x (ISBN 0-7022-1341-1). Humanities.

What Is Truth. C. J. Williams. LC 75-23533. 120p. 1976. 21.50 (ISBN 0-521-20967-6). Cambridge U Pr.

What Is Value? Everett W. Hall. (International Library of Psychology, Philosophy & Scientific Method). 1961. Repr. of 1952 ed. text ed. 10.00x (ISBN 0-391-00452-2). Humanities.

What Is Your Name: A Popular Account of the Meaning & Derivations of Christian Names. Sophy Moody. LC 73-5523. 1975. Repr. of 1863 ed. 26.00 (ISBN 0-8103-4250-2). Gale.

What It Means to Be a Christian. Robert W. Youngs. 1977. pap. 3.50 o.p. (ISBN 0-8015-8520-1). Dutton.

What It Takes: Developing Skills for Contemporary Living. Thompson Clayton. LC 70-186590. (Illus., Orig., Special education ser. for slow learners). (gr. 4-9). 1972. pap. 3.20 (ISBN 0-8224-7400-X); tchrs' manual free (ISBN 0-8224-7401-8). Pitman Learning.

What It Takes to Feel Good: The Nickolaus Technique. Benno Isaacs & Jay Kobler. (Illus.). 1978. 12.95 o.p. (ISBN 0-670-75824-8). Viking Pr.

What It's All About. Norma Klein. (YA) (gr. 7-10). 1978. pap. 1.75 (ISBN 0-671-29997-2). PB.

What It's Like to Be a Flight Attendant. Elizabeth Rich. LC 80-6152. 192p. 1981. 12.95 (ISBN 0-8128-2785-6). Stein & Day.

What Jesus Means to Me. Herman W. Gockel. 1956. 4.50 (ISBN 0-570-03021-8, 6-1008). Concordia.

What Jesus Said About It. K. Henry Koestline. pap. 1.50 (ISBN 0-451-07763-6, W7763, Sig). NAL.

What Katy Did. Sarah C. Woolsey. LC 75-32177. (Classics of Children's Literature, 1621-1932: Vol. 40). (Illus.). 1976. Repr. of 1873 ed. PLB 38.00 (ISBN 0-8240-2289-0). Garland Pub.

What Kind of a House Is That? Harry Devlin. LC 78-77792. (Illus.). (gr. 5 up). 1969. 5.95 o.s.i. (ISBN 0-8193-0315-1, Four Winds); PLB 5.41 o.s.i. (ISBN 0-8193-0316-X). Schol Bk Serv.

What Kind of Guy Do You Think I Am? Sidney Offit. (YA) (gr. 8 up). 1979. pap. 1.50 (ISBN 0-440-99455-1, LFL). Dell.

What Lily Goose Found. Annabelle Sumera. (Young Reader Ser.). (Illus.). (gr. k-3). 1979. PLB 5.00 (ISBN 0-307-60163-3, Golden Pr). Western Pub.

What Little I Remember. Otto R. Frisch. LC 78-18096. (Illus.). 227p. 1980. pap. 9.95 (ISBN 0-521-28010-9). Cambridge U Pr.

What Maisie Knew. Henry James. pap. 2.50 o.p. (ISBN 0-385-09289-X, A43, Anch). Doubleday.

What Makes a Lemon Sour? Gail K. Haines. LC 76-28687. (Illus.). (gr. 1-5). 1978. 6.25 o.p. (ISBN 0-688-22093-2); PLB 6.96 (ISBN 0-688-32093-7). Morrow.

What Makes a Nuclear Power Plant Work? Erich Fuchs. Tr. by Kroll Edite from Ger. LC 73-182237. (Illus.). 32p. (gr. 3-7). 1972. 5.95 o.s.i. (ISBN 0-440-09723-1, Sey Lawr). Delacorte.

What Makes a Shadow? Clyde Bulla. (Illus.). (gr. k-3). 1971. pap. 1.25 o.p. (ISBN 0-590-03427-8, Schol Pap). Schol Bk Serv.

What Makes a Shadow. Clyde R. Bulla. LC 62-11001. (Let's-Read-&-Find-Out Science Bk). (Illus.). (gr. k-3). 1962. PLB 7.89 (ISBN 0-690-87648-3, TYC-J). T Y Crowell.

What Makes Day & Night. Franklyn M. Branley. LC 60-8258. (Let's-Read-&-Find-Out Science Bk). (Illus.). (gr. k-3). 1961. PLB 7.89 (ISBN 0-690-87790-0, TYC-J). T Y Crowell.

What Makes It Work. George Papallo. LC 76-14838. 1976. 9.95 (ISBN 0-668-03962-0); pap. 4.95 (ISBN 0-668-03963-9). Arco.

What Makes Music Work? Philip Seyer & Paul Harmon. Ed. by Allan Novick. (Wiley Self-Teaching Guide Ser.). 300p. 1981. pap. text ed. 9.85 (ISBN 0-471-35192-X). Wiley.

What Mary Jo Shared. Janice M. Udry. LC 66-16082. (Illus.). 40p. (gr. k-2). 1966. 6.95g (ISBN 0-8075-8842-3). A Whitman.

What Mary Jo Wanted. Janice M. Udry. LC 68-9123. (Illus.). 40p. (gr. k-3). 1968. 5.95g o.p. (ISBN 0-8075-8848-2). A Whitman.

What Mothers Are Good for. LC 78-74576. (Illus.). 1979. 3.95 o.p. (ISBN 0-932212-13-1). Avery Color.

What Moves Is Not the Wind. James Nolan. 72p. 1980. 10.00 (ISBN 0-8195-2099-3, Pub. by Wesleyan U Pr); pap. 4.95 (ISBN 0-8195-1099-8). Columbia U Pr.

What Must Humanity Do? Javed Husain. 39p. 1980. 3.95 (ISBN 0-8059-2729-8). Dorrance.

What My Heart Wants to Tell. Verna M. Slone. LC 78-31688. (Illus.). 1979. 8.95 o.p. (ISBN 0-915220-47-4). New Republic.

What No One, but Absolutely No One Knows About Money. Charles D. Radford. (Illus.). 127p. 1981. 31.25 (ISBN 0-89266-284-0). Am Classical Coll Pr.

What Nobody, but Absolutely Nobody Knows About Sex, or New Discoveries into the Metaphysics of Sex. Robert C. Rimbaud. (Illus.). 113p. 1981. 18.25 (ISBN 0-89266-286-7). Am Classical Coll Pr.

What Odd Expedients & Other Poems by Robinson Jeffers. Robert I. Scott. 1981. 14.50 (ISBN 0-208-01885-9, Archon). Shoe String.

What on Earth's Going to Happen? Ray C. Stedman. LC 73-104085. 1970. pap. 2.25 o.p. (ISBN 0-8307-0532-5, 5016002). Regal.

What Pet Will I Get? Susan M. Drawbaugh. LC 77-83881. 1977. 5.95 (ISBN 0-89430-017-2). Morgan-Pacific.

What Poetry Is. Harry Mulisch. Ed. by Stanley H. Barkan. Tr. by Claire Nicolas White. (Cross-Cultural Review Chapbook 9). 40p. (Dutch & Eng.). 1980. pap. 3.50 (ISBN 0-89304-808-9). Cross Cult.

What Price Defense? Edmund S. Muskie & Bill Brock. LC 74-21550. 1974. 5.75 (ISBN 0-8447-2054-2); pap. text ed. 2.50 o. p. (ISBN 0-8447-2053-4). Am Enterprise.

What Psychology Can We Trust. Goodwin B. Watson. LC 61-15927. 1961. pap. 2.25x (ISBN 0-8077-2308-8). Tchrs Coll.

What Really Happened to the Dinosaurs? Daniel Cohen. (gr. 3-5). 1977. PLB 8.95 (ISBN 0-525-42472-5). Dutton.

What Research Has to Say About Reading Instruction. Ed. by S. Jay Samuels. 1978. pap. text ed. 6.25 (ISBN 0-685-59434-3). Intl Reading.

What Research Says to the Science Teacher. Ed. by Mary B. Rowe. 1978. pap. 3.50 (ISBN 0-87355-009-9). Natl Sci Tchrs.

What Research Says to the Science Teacher, Vol. 2. Ed. by Mary B. Rowe. (Orig.). 1979. pap. 4.00 (ISBN 0-87355-013-7). Natl Sci Tchrs.

What Schools Are For. John I. Goodlad. LC 79-54644. (Foundation Monograph Ser.). 136p. 1979. pap. 5.50 (ISBN 0-87367-422-7). Phi Delta Kappa.

What Shall I Film? Ivan Watson. 1975. 9.95 o.p. (ISBN 0-85242-432-9, Pub. by Fountain). Morgan.

What Shall I Read? 2nd ed. 1978. 12.95x (ISBN 0-85365-560-X, Pub. by Lib Assn England). Oryx Pr.

What Shall We Do with the Bible? Rubel Shelly. 1975. 6.95 (ISBN 0-934916-42-X). Natl Christian Pr.

What So Proudly We Hail: All About Our American Flag, Monuments & Symbols. Maymie R. Krythe. LC 68-15993. (YA) 1968. 9.95 o.s.i. (ISBN 0-06-003157-3, HarpT); lib. bdg. 8.97 (ISBN 0-06-012464-4). Har-Row.

What Sort of Life? Patricia Rowan. 138p. 1981. pap. text ed. 15.25x (ISBN 0-85633-200-3, NFER). Humanities.

What Style Is It? John Poppeliers et al. (Illus.). 1977. text ed. 4.95 (ISBN 0-89133-065-8). Preservation Pr.

What Susan Wanted. Sally Scott. LC 56-5235. (Illus.). (gr. 1-4). 1956. 3.95 o.p. (ISBN 0-15-295528-3, HJ). HarBraceJ.

What Teenagers Want to Know. Shideler Harpe & Wesley W. Hall. (Illus.). 1979. pap. 2.50 (ISBN 0-910304-11-4). Budlong.

What the Animals Tell Me. Beatrice Lydecker. LC 76-9997. (Illus.). 1977. 8.95 (ISBN 0-06-065316-7, HarpR). Har-Row.

What the Author Meant. George R. Foss. 196p. 1980. Repr. of 1932 ed. lib. bdg. 25.00 (ISBN 0-89984-204-6). Century Bookbindery.

What the Bible Does Not Say. John L. Stout. LC 80-84340. (Illus.). 208p. 1981. 10.95 (ISBN 0-8187-0042-4). Harlo Pr.

What the Bible Is All About. Henrietta C. Mears. LC 79-92452. 12.95 (ISBN 0-8307-0512-0, 5102421); pap. 7.95 (ISBN 0-8307-0473-6, 54-047-03). Regal.

What the Bible Is All About. Henrietta C. Mears. 698p. 1980. pap. 7.95 (ISBN 0-89066-024-7). World Wide Pubs.

What the Bible Says About Faith & Opinion. W. Robert Palmer. LC 79-57088. (What the Bible Says Ser.). 1980. 13.50 (ISBN 0-89900-076-2). College Pr Pub.

What the Bible Says About Fasting & Prayer. Don DeWelt. LC 79-57087. (What the Bible Says Ser.). 1981. 13.50 (ISBN 0-89900-077-0). College Pr Pub. Postponed.

What the Bible Says About Goodness. Georgaan Bennett. LC 80-69626. (What the Bible Says Ser.). 350p. 1981. 13.50 (ISBN 0-89900-080-0). College Pr Pub.

What the Bible Says About Heaven & Hell. Fred Thompson, Jr. (What the Bible Says Ser.). 400p. 1981. 13.50 (ISBN 0-89900-081-9). College Pr Pub.

What the Bible Says About Praise & Promise. James Van Buren & Don Dewett. LC 80-66127. (What the Bible Says Ser.). 450p. 1980. 13.50 (ISBN 0-89900-078-9). College Pr Pub.

What the Bible Says About the Bible. Owen Crouch. (What the Bible Says Ser.). 400p. 1981. 13.50 (ISBN 0-89900-082-7). College Pr Pub.

What the Bible Says About the Covenant. Mont Smith. (What the Bible Says Ser.). 400p. 1981. 13.50 (ISBN 0-89900-083-5). College Pr Pub.

What the Bible Says About the Second Coming. Ralph Earle. (Direction Bks). 1973. pap. 1.95 (ISBN 0-8010-3307-1). Baker Bk.

What the Bible Says About Women. Julia Staton. LC 80-66128. (What the Bible Says Ser.). 400p. 1980. 13.50 (ISBN 0-89900-079-7). College Pr Pub.

What the Bible Says About Your Personality. David O. Yates. LC 80-7759. 192p. (Orig.). 1980. pap. 5.95 (ISBN 0-06-069711-3, RD 333, HarpR). Har-Row.

What the Bible Teaches. F. G. Smith. 576p. Repr. of 1914 ed. 5.50. Faith Pub Hse.

What the Buddha Taught. rev. ed. Walpola Rahula. (Illus.). 168p. 1974. pap. 4.95 (ISBN 0-394-17827-0, E641, Ever). Grove.

What the Buddha Taught. Walpola Rahula. (Illus.). 1967. pap. 6.95 (ISBN 0-900406-02-X). Dufour.

What the Catholic Bible Teaches: Home Study. B. I. Moody. pap. 3.00x o.p. (ISBN 0-686-12325-5). Christs Mission.

What the Church Is Doing for Divorced & Remarried Catholics. James Castelli. (Illus.). 1978. pap. 1.95 (ISBN 0-89570-155-3). Claretian Pubns.

What the "Friends of the People" Are & How They Fight the Social-Democrats. Lenin. 1978. 3.95 (ISBN 0-8351-0524-5); pap. 1.95 (ISBN 0-8351-0491-5). China Bks.

What the Gospels Say About Jesus. LC 78-53636. (Journeys Ser). 1978. pap. text ed. 4.20x (ISBN 0-88489-103-8); tchrs' guide 2.60x (ISBN 0-88489-105-4). St Marys.

What the Liberty Bell Proclaimed. Leon Spitz. 1975. Repr. of 1951 ed. 4.95x (ISBN 0-8197-0033-9). Bloch.

What the Moon Astronauts Do. Robert W. Hill. LC 75-143416. (Illus.). (gr. 3 up). 1971. PLB 7.89 (ISBN 0-381-99795-2, A87120, JD-J). John Day.

What the New Testament Is All About. Henrietta C. Mears. pap. 3.95 (ISBN 0-8307-0525-2, 5015618). Regal.

What the Old Testament Is All About. Henrietta C. Mears. LC 76-51196. (Illus.). 1977. pap. 1.95 (ISBN 0-8307-0466-3, S111-1-28). Regal.

What the President of the U. S. Does. Roy Hoopes. LC 74-5067. (Illus.). (gr. 4-10). 1974. 7.95 (ISBN 0-381-99628-X, JD-J); PLB 8.79 (ISBN 0-381-99628-X); pap. 2.50 (ISBN 0-381-99601-8). John Day.

What the Sophisticated Man of the World Ought to Know About Women. David D'Avenant. (Illus.). 1980. 41.45 (ISBN 0-89266-213-1). Am Classical Coll Pr.

What the Wind Told. Betty Boegehold. LC 73-22184. (Illus.). 48p. (ps-3). 1974. 5.95 o.s.i. (ISBN 0-8193-0756-4, Four Winds); PLB 5.41 o.s.i. (ISBN 0-8193-0757-2). Schol Bk Serv.

What the Worms Ignore the Birds Are Wild About. Howard Aaron. 1979. 2.50 (ISBN 0-918116-15-5). Jawbone Pr.

What, Then, Is Man? A Symposium. 356p. 1971. 8.95 (ISBN 0-570-03125-7, 12-2361). Concordia.

What They Did to Miss Lily. Sonia Wolff. LC 80-8709. 288p. 1981. 12.95 (ISBN 0-06-014861-6, HarpT). Har-Row.

What Think Ye of Christ's Church? James D. Bales. pap. 0.50 o.p. (ISBN 0-89315-353-2). Lambert Bk.

What Time Is It? Illus. by T. Izawa & S. Hijkata. (Puppet Storybooks). (Illus.). 18p. (gr. k-2). 1981. 3.50 (ISBN 0-448-09753-2). G&D.

What Time Is It? Zokeisha. (Puppet Story Board Bks.). (Illus.). 12p. (ps-k). Date not set. boards 2.95 (ISBN 0-671-42646-X, Little Simon). S&S.

What Time of Night Is It. Mary Stolz. LC 80-7917. (Ursula Nordstrom Bk.). 224p. (gr. 6 up). 1981. 9.95 (ISBN 0-06-026061-0, HarpJ); PLB 9.89g (ISBN 0-06-026062-9). Har-Row.

What to Do - When & Why: At School, at Parties, at Home, in Your Growing World. Marjabelle Y. Stewart & Ann Buchwald. LC 75-31840. (gr. 7 up). 1975. 7.95 (ISBN 0-679-50566-0). McKay.

What to Do About Bites & Stings of Venomous Animals. Robert E. Arnold. 128p. 1973. 9.95 (ISBN 0-02-503250-X). Macmillan.

What to Do About Your Brain Injured Child. Glenn Doman. LC 72-92202. 312p. 1974. 9.95 (ISBN 0-385-02139-9). Doubleday.

What to Do After You Hit Return. Peoples Computer Company. 180p. 1980. 14.95 (ISBN 0-8104-5476-9). Hayden.

What to Do Between Here & There: Activities for Families on the Go. Susan Kirsch. (Illus.). 128p. 1980. 10.95 (ISBN 0-13-955112-3, Spec); pap. 3.95 (ISBN 0-13-955104-2). P-H.

What to Do Until the Counselor Comes. S. Norman Feingold & Shirley Levin. (Careers in Depth Ser.). 128p. 1980. lib. bdg. 7.97 (ISBN 0-8239-0506-3). Rosen Pr.

What to Do Until the Lawyer Comes. Stephen Landsman et al. LC 76-2802. 1977. pap. 2.95 (ISBN 0-385-11163-0, Anch). Doubleday.

What to Do When There's Nothing to Do: A Mother's Handbook. Ed. by Elizabeth M. Gregg & Boston Children'S Medical Center Staff. 1968. 5.95 o.s.i. (ISBN 0-440-09466-6, Sey Lawr). Delacorte.

What to Do When You Pray. Lucille Walker. 1978. 3.95 o.p. (ISBN 0-88270-279-3). Logos.

What to Do When You Think You Can't Have a Baby. Karol White. LC 80-1730. (Illus.). 216p. 1981. 11.95 (ISBN 0-385-15446-1). Doubleday.

What to Do with Doubt. Ellen G. White. 31p. 1970. pap. 0.75 (ISBN 0-8163-0079-8, 23265-2). Pacific Pr Pub Assn.

What to Do with the Rocks in Your Head. Michael Scheier. (gr. 5 up). 1980. pap. 7.90 (ISBN 0-531-04174-3, G34). Watts.

What to Do with Your Pictures. Clarence Inman. (Orig.). 1980. pap. cancelled (ISBN 0-89586-058-9). H P Bks.

What to Eat & Why: The Science of Nutrition. Ronald V. Fodor. LC 78-24086. (Illus.). (gr. 4-6). 1979. 6.50 (ISBN 0-688-22189-0); PLB 6.24 (ISBN 0-688-32189-5). Morrow.

What to Listen for in Music. rev. ed. Aaron Copland. (RL 9). 1964. pap. 1.95 (ISBN 0-451-61882-3, MJ1882, Ment). NAL.

What to Name the Baby. 1980. pap. 2.50 (ISBN 0-671-82739-1). PB.

What to Remember to Be Happy. John Da Free. (Illus.). pap. 4.95 (ISBN 0-913922-36-6). Dawn Horse Pr.

What to Tell Your Child About Sex. rev. ed. Child Study Association Of America. (Illus.). 1968. 3.95 o.p. (ISBN 0-8015-8550-3). Dutton.

What to Tell Your Child About Sex. rev. ed. CSAAT. 1974. 4.95 (ISBN 0-686-12277-1). Jewish Bd Family.

What Was Naturalism? Materials for an Answer. Ed. by Edward Stone. (Orig.). 1959. pap. text ed. 8.95 o.p. (ISBN 0-13-955179-4). P-H.

What We Can Do for Each Other: An Interdisciplinary Approach to Development Anthropology. Ed. by Glynn Cochrane. 1976. pap. text ed. 7.00x (ISBN 90-6032-069-7). Humanities.

What We Know About Cancer. Ed. by R. C. Harris. 1970. pap. 4.95 o.p. (ISBN 0-04-616009-4). Allen Unwin.

What We Talk About When We Talk About Love. Raymond Carver. LC 80-21752. 176p. 1981. 9.95 (ISBN 0-394-51684-2). Knopf.

What Were the Crusades? Jonathan Riley-Smith. 1977. 12.50 o.p. (ISBN 0-87471-944-5). Rowman.

What, When, & Where Guide to Northern California. Basil Charles Wood. LC 75-2858. 144p. 1977. pap. 4.95 (ISBN 0-385-05052-6). Doubleday.

What, When & Where Guide to Southern California. rev. ed. Basil Charles Wood. LC 78-3264. 1979. pap. 3.95 (ISBN 0-385-14043-6). Doubleday.

What Will Happen to You When the Soviets Take Over. Ed. by Ingo Swann. LC 80-25438. 244p. (Orig.). 1980. write for info. (ISBN 0-9604946-6-9). Starform.

What Will I Be? Kathleen Cowles. (Young Reader Ser.). (gr. k-3). 1979. PLB 5.00 (ISBN 0-307-60174-9, Golden Pr). Western Pub.

What Will It Be? Jane B. Moncure. LC 75-35542. (Illus.). (ps-3). 1976. PLB 5.50 (ISBN 0-913778-24-9); pap. 2.75 (ISBN 0-89565-066-5). Childs World.

What Will It Rain? A Book About Fall. Jane B. Moncure. LC 76-46295. (Illus.). (ps-3). 1977. 5.50 (ISBN 0-913778-69-9). Childs World.

What Will Simon Say? Lila McGinnis. LC 73-89291. 236p. 1974. 4.95 o.p. (ISBN 0-88270-074-X); pap. 2.95 o.p. (ISBN 0-88270-075-8). Logos.

What Will We Do in the Morning? The Exceptional Student in the Regular Classroom. Michael L. Hardman et al. 450p. 1981. pap. text ed. write for info. (ISBN 0-697-06056-X); instr's manual avail. (ISBN 0-697-06057-8). Wm C Brown.

What Women Should Know About the Breast Cancer Controversy. George Crile, Jr. 128p. 1973. 4.95 o.s.i. (ISBN 0-02-528800-8). Macmillan.

What Women Want: The Ideologies of the Movement. Gayle G. Yates. 224p. 1975. 12.50x (ISBN 0-674-95077-1); pap. 3.95 (ISBN 0-674-95079-8). Harvard U Pr.

What Words Can Wield. Nathalie Sarraute. LC 80-19957. 144p. 1980. 10.00 (ISBN 0-8076-0978-1); pap. 5.95 (ISBN 0-8076-0979-X). Braziller.

What Works When Life Doesn't. D. Stuart Briscoe. 144p. 1976. pap. 3.50 (ISBN 0-88207-725-2). Victor Bks.

What Would Happen If... Linda P. Silbert & Alvin J. Silbert. (Little Twirps, TM Creative Thinking Wkbks.). (Illus.). (gr. 3-9). 1976. wkbk. 2.25 (ISBN 0-89544-018-0, 018). Silbert Bress.

What You Always Wanted to Know About Operating a Small Business but Didn't Know Who to Ask. Kathryn A. Erskine. (Illus.). 69p. (Orig.). 1980. pap. 9.95 (ISBN 0-9605058-0-6). Erskine.

What You Know with No Name for It. Keith Abbott. 1976. signed ed. o.p. 7.00 (ISBN 0-912652-34-9); pap. 3.00 (ISBN 0-912652-33-0). Blue Wind.

What You Need to Know About Your Gold & Silver. Oscar T. Branson. (Illus.). 56p. (Orig.). 1980. pap. 4.95 (ISBN 0-918080-44-4). Treasure Chest.

What You Need to Know to Own & Operate a Small Business: Youth Entrepreneurship. Edgar Persons. (Orig.). 1981. pap. write for info. (ISBN 0-89514-031-4). Am Voc Assn.

What You Say Is What You Get. Don Gossett. 192p. 1976. pap. 2.50 (ISBN 0-88368-066-1). Whitaker Hse.

What You Should Know About Contracts. Robert A. Farmer. LC 69-11145. (Know Your Law Ser). (Illus.). 1969. lib. bdg. 4.95 o.p. (ISBN 0-668-01826-7). Arco.

What You Should Know About Homosexuality. Ed. by Charles W. Keysor. pap. 6.95 (ISBN 0-310-38231-9). Zondervan.

What You Should Know About Individual Retirement Accounts. L. L. Unthank & Harry M. Behrendt. LC 77-90480. 1978. 12.95 o.p. (ISBN 0-87094-156-9). Dow Jones-Irwin.

What You Should Know About Medical Lab Tests. Ernest Kolowrat et al. LC 79-7092. (Illus.). 1979. 10.95 (ISBN 0-690-01831-2, TYC-T). T Y Crowell.

What You Should Know About Prophecy. C. M. Ward. (Radiant Life Ser.). 1976. pap. 1.95 (ISBN 0-88243-890-5, 02-0890, Radiant Books); teacher's ed. 2.50 (ISBN 0-88243-164-1, 32-0164). Gospel Pub.

What You Should Know About the Holy Spirit. J. W. Jepson. pap. 2.95 (ISBN 0-89728-062-8, 669313). Omega Pubns OR.

What You Should Know About the Rapture. Charles C. Ryrie. (What You Know Ser.). 128p. 1981. pap. 2.95 (ISBN 0-8024-9416-1). Moody.

What You Should Know About Your Husband's Money... Before the Divorce. Shelley Aspaklaria & Gerson Geltner. LC 80-52403. Orig. Title: Everything You Want to Know About Your Husband's Money... & Need to Know Before the Divorce. 256p. 1981. pap. 5.95 (ISBN 0-87223-646-3). Wideview Bks.

What You Still Don't Know About Male Sexuality. Barry McCarthy. LC 77-4239. 1977. 8.95 o.s.i. (ISBN 0-690-01443-0, TYC-T). T Y Crowell.

What You Think of Me Is None of My Business. Terry Cole-Whittaker. LC 79-21739. 1979. 9.95 (ISBN 0-916392-39-2). Oak Tree Pubns.

What You Want to Know About Childbirth. rev. ed. Millicent James. (Illus.). 1971. pap. 2.95 (ISBN 0-589-00619-3, Dist. by C E Tuttle). Reed.

What Your Handwriting Tells About You. Joan H. Robie. LC 77-91726. 1978. 5.95 (ISBN 0-8054-6922-2). Broadman.

What You've Got Coming in Social Security & Medicare. Bill Steif. 101p. (Orig.). 1980. pap. 1.50 o.s.i. (ISBN 0-915106-16-7). Newspaper Ent.

What You've Got Coming in Social Security & Medicare. William Steif. LC 79-87560. 1979. pap. 1.50 o.p. (ISBN 0-915106-15-9, Enterprise Pubns). Newspaper Ent.

Whatcom Seascapes: The Influence of the Sea on Whatcom County. Whatcom Museum of History & Art. LC 77-140515. (Whatcom Museum Ser.). (Illus.). 80p. 1970. pap. 5.00 (ISBN 0-295-95578-3). U of Wash Pr.

Whatever Became of Sin? Karl Menninger. 1973. 8.95 (ISBN 0-8015-8556-2, Hawthorn); pap. 4.95 (ISBN 0-8015-8554-6, Hawthorn). Dutton.

Whatever Happened to Eden? John R. Sheaffer & Raymond H. Brand. 1980. pap. 4.95 (ISBN 0-8423-7871-5). Tyndale.

Whatever Happened to Friday? and Other Questions Catholics Ask. Joseph C. Gibbons. LC 79-91275. (Orig.). 1980. pap. 2.95 (ISBN 0-8091-2278-2). Paulist Pr.

Whatever Happened to Shell's New Philosophy of Management? F. H. Blackler & C. A. Brown. 184p. 1980. text ed. 29.00x (ISBN 0-566-00306-6, Pub. by Gower Pub Co England). Renouf.

Whatever Happened to...? The Great Pop & Rock Music Nostalgia Book. Steve Fisher. (Illus.). 192p. 1981. pap. 8.95 (ISBN 0-906071-40-2). Proteus Pub NY. Postponed.

What's a Body to Do? Ruth Odor. Ed. by Jane Buerger. (Illus.). 1980. 5.95 (ISBN 0-89565-176-9, 4933). Standard Pub.

What's a Body to Do? (Choose-a-Card Ser). (gr. 2-6). 1979. pap. text ed. 5.95 (ISBN 0-913916-87-0, 1P87-0). Incentive Pubns.

What's a Nice Girl Like You Doing with a Double Bed. Cathy Guisewite. 160p. 1981. pap. 4.95 (ISBN 0-553-01316-5). Bantam.

What's a Wilderness Worth? Anne Stewart. LC 79-13781. (Story of Environmental Action Ser.). (Illus.). (gr. 7 up). 1979. PLB 8.95 (ISBN 0-87518-182-1). Dillon.

What's Ahead? Charles Harris. (Radiant Life Ser.). 128p. (Orig.). 1981. pap. price not set. Gospel Pub.

What's Best for You. Judie Angell. 192p. (gr. 6 up). 1981. 8.95 (ISBN 0-87888-181-6). Bradbury Pr.

What's Cooking in Kentucky. Irene Hayes. 1979. 12.95 o.p. (ISBN 0-397-01357-4); pap. 7.95 o.p. (ISBN 0-397-01356-6). Lippincott.

What's Cooking in Kentucky, 2 vols. Irene Hayes. Date not set. spiral bdg. 6.95x ea. Vol. 1, 204pp (ISBN 0-938402-02-1). Vol. 2, 196pp (ISBN 0-938402-03-X). Hayes Bk Co.

What's Cooking in Kentucky. rev. ed. Irene Hayes. (Illus.). 1979. laminated cover 12.95 (ISBN 0-938402-01-3). Hayes Bk Co.

What's Cooking in Towne & Country USA, Vol. I. Lois A. Weist. (Special Collectors' Keepsake Ser.). (Illus.). 240p. 1979. 14.99 (ISBN 0-938166-00-X). Weist Pub OH.

What's Cooking in Towne & Country USA, Vol. II. Lois A. Weist. (Special Collectors' Keepsake Ser.). (Illus.). 250p. 1979. 14.99 (ISBN 0-938166-01-8). Weist Pub OH.

What's Creative About Creative Writing? John E. Westburg. pap. 3.00 (ISBN 0-87423-018-7). Westburg.

Whats Down That Road? Harriet U. Fish. (Illus.). 100p. (Orig.). 1979. pap. 6.95 (ISBN 0-918146-41-0). Peninsula WA.

What's for Dinner Tomorrow? Corporate Views of New Food Products. Gino Crochetti & Frank Stella. LC 79-93419. 1979. pap. 5.00 (ISBN 0-918780-15-2). Inform.

What's Going to Happen to Me? When Parents Separate or Divorce. Eda LeShan. LC 78-4340. (Illus.). 144p. (gr. 3 up). 1978. 7.95 (ISBN 0-590-07535-7, Four Winds). Schol Bk Serv.

What's Gone Wrong with the Harvest? James F. Engel & Wilbert H. Norton. 192p. 1975. pap. 4.95 kivar (ISBN 0-310-24161-8). Zondervan.

What's in a Name. Ed. by Favius Friedman. (gr. 7-12). 1976. pap. 1.25 (ISBN 0-590-00090-X, Schol Pap). Schol Bk Serv.

What's in a Name: Famous Brand Names. Oren Arnold. LC 79-15555. 128p. (gr. 7 up). 1979. PLB 7.79 (ISBN 0-671-32932-4). Messner.

What's in a Name? Surnames of America. La Reina Rule & William K. Hammond. 1977. pap. 1.95 o.s.i. (ISBN 0-515-04460-1). Jove Pubns.

What's in It for You? The Shoppers' Complete Guide to Health Store Products. rev. ed. Carlson Wade. LC 80-84443. (Pivet Original Health Bk.). 144p. (Orig.). 1981. pap. 1.95 (ISBN 0-87983-244-4). Keats.

What's Inside of Animals. Herbert S. Zim. (Illus.). (gr. 11 up). 1953. PLB 6.96 (ISBN 0-688-26518-9). Morrow.

What's Inside of Engines. Herbert S. Zim. (Illus.). (gr. 1 up). 1953. PLB 6.96 (ISBN 0-688-31554-2). Morrow.

What's Inside of Me. Herbert S. Zim. (Illus.). (ps-3). 1952. PLB 6.96 (ISBN 0-688-21551-3). Morrow.

What's Inside of Plants. Herbert S. Zim. (Illus.). (ps-3). 1952. PLB 6.96 (ISBN 0-688-31490-2). Morrow.

What's Inside the Box? Kessler. (gr. 2-3). 1980. pap. 3.50 incl. record (ISBN 0-590-24007-2, Schol Pap). Schol Bk Serv.

What's Inside the Earth. Herbert S. Zim. (Illus.). (gr. 1 up). 1953. PLB 6.96 (ISBN 0-688-31475-9). Morrow.

What's Inside: The Story of an Egg That Hatched. May Garelick. (Illus.). (gr. k-3). 1970. pap. 1.25 (ISBN 0-590-02947-9, Schol Pap). Schol Bk Serv.

What's It Worth? Probing Our Values with Questions Jesus Asked. Margaret Ragland. 1977. pap. 3.75 (ISBN 0-89137-409-4). Quality Pubns.

What's Just Ahead. Robert Pierson. LC 78-14219. (Flame Ser.). 1978. pap. 0.95 (ISBN 0-8127-0203-4). Southern Pub.

What's Next? Ernest Gordon & Peter Funk. 1978. pap. 3.95 o.p. (ISBN 0-88270-282-3). Logos.

What's Next? New Life in Christ Guidebook for Children. Ralph W. Harris. 1972. pap. 0.35 (ISBN 0-88243-559-0, 02-0559). Gospel Pub.

What's Right. Eugene Baker. Ed. by Jane Buerger. (Illus.). 1980. 5.95 (ISBN 0-89565-175-0, 4932). Standard Pub.

What's Skin for? Pat Blakely. (Creative Question & Answer Library). 32p. (gr. 3-4). Date not set. PLB 5.75 (ISBN 0-87191-745-9); pap. 2.75 (ISBN 0-89812-214-7). Creative Ed. Postponed.

What's the Big Idea? And Thirty-Five Other Unusual Puzzles. Don Rubin. 1979. pap. 3.95 (ISBN 0-685-93958-8). Lippincott.

What's the Matter, Sylvie, Can't You Ride? Karen B. Andersen. LC 80-12514. (Illus.). 32p. (ps-3). 1981. 8.95 (ISBN 0-8037-9607-2); PLB 8.44 (ISBN 0-8037-9621-8). Dial.

What's the Matter with Carruthers? James Marshall. LC 72-75607. (Illus.). 32p. (gr. k-3). 1972. reinforced bdg. 6.95 (ISBN 0-395-13895-7). HM.

What's the Matter with Me? Eda LeShan. (gr. 7-12). 1976. pap. 1.25 o.p. (ISBN 0-590-10162-5, Schol Pap). Schol Bk Serv.

What's the Time, Starling? A First Look at Nature's Clocks. Solveig P. Russell. (Illus.). (gr. 2-5). 1977. 6.95 o.p. (ISBN 0-679-20420-2). McKay.

What's to Eat. Edith Down. 1981. text ed. 11.96 (ISBN 0-87002-333-0). Bennett Co.

What's up Duck. Mike Thaler. (Illus.). (gr. 4 up). 1978. PLB 6.90 s&l (ISBN 0-531-01479-7). Watts.

What's up There? Diane L. Moche. (gr. 4-6). 1976. pap. 1.25 (ISBN 0-590-04850-3, Schol Pap). Schol Bk Serv.

What's Worrying You, Timothy Joe. Sally L. Eaton. 1979. 4.50 o.p. (ISBN 0-8062-1209-8). Carlton.

What's Wrong with Being a Skunk? Miriam Schlein. LC 73-88078. (Illus.). 40p. (gr. k-3). 1974. 6.95 (ISBN 0-590-07305-2, Four Winds). Schol Bk Serv.

What's Wrong with Our Weather? The Climatic Threat of the 21st Century. John Gribbin. 1979. 9.95 o.p. (ISBN 0-684-15807-8, ScribT). Scribner.

What's Wrong with the Mental Health Movement. K. Edward Renner. LC 74-26831. 272p. 1975. 15.95 (ISBN 0-88229-180-7). Nelson-Hall.

What's Wrong with the Modern World? Agenda for a New Society. Michael Shanks. 1979. 9.95 (ISBN 0-370-30101-3, Pub. by Chatto Bodley Jonathan). Merrimack Bk Serv.

Wheat: A Bibliography of the World Literature, 3 Vols. International Maize & Wheat Improvement Center. LC 71-154563. 1971. Set. 77.50 (ISBN 0-8108-0393-3). Scarecrow.

Wheat & the AAA. Joseph S. Davis. LC 76-172868. (FDR & the Era of the New Deal Ser.). 468p. 1973. Repr. of 1935 ed. 49.50 (ISBN 0-306-70375-0). Da Capo.

Wheat Economy. G. E. Britnell. LC 39-25982. 1974. 19.50x o.p. (ISBN 0-8020-7034-5). U of Toronto Pr.

Wheat Killing. Peter Tanous & Paul Rubinstein. LC 77-27682. 1979. 10.00 (ISBN 0-385-14233-1). Doubleday.

Wheat Plant: Its Origin, Culture, Growth, Development, Composition, Varieties Together with Information on Corn & Its Culture, 2 vols. John H. Klippart. 1980. Set. lib. bdg. 200.00 (ISBN 0-8490-3119-2). Gordon Pr.

Wheat: Production & Utilization. George E. Inglett. (Illus.). 1974. text ed. 35.00 (ISBN 0-87055-154-X). AVI.

Wheat Studies in the People's Republic of China. Commission on International Relations. 1977. pap. 10.00 (ISBN 0-309-02637-7). Natl Acad Pr.

Wheaten Years: The History of Ireland's Soft Coated Wheaten Terrier. Maureen Holmes. LC 77-88422. 14.95. B P Reynolds.

Whedon's Commentary on First Corinthians, Vol. 4. 11.95 (ISBN 0-686-13331-5). Schmul Pub Co.

Whedon's Commentary on Luke, Vol. 2. 11.95 (ISBN 0-686-13330-7). Schmul Pub Co.

Whedon's Commentary on Matthew, Vol. 1. 11.95 (ISBN 0-686-13329-3). Schmul Pub Co.

Whedon's Commentary on Titus & Revelations, Vol. 5. 11.95 (ISBN 0-686-13332-3). Schmul Pub Co.

Wheedle on the Needle. Steve Cosgrove. (Serendipity Bks). (Illus.). (gr. k-4). 1978. PLB 6.95 (ISBN 0-87191-663-0). Creative Ed.

Wheel. rev. ed. Harlan Wade. LC 78-21128. (Book About Ser.). (Illus.). (gr. k-3). 1979. PLB 7.30 (ISBN 0-8172-1531-X). Raintree Pubs.

Wheel of Love & Other Stories. Joyce C. Oates. LC 79-134661. 1970. 10.95 (ISBN 0-8149-0676-1). Vanguard.

Wheel of Servitude: Black Forced Labor After Slavery. Daniel A. Novak. LC 77-76334. 144p. 1978. 10.50x (ISBN 0-8131-1371-7). U Pr of Ky.

Wheel of Truth: An Ancestral Saga. Gertrude S. Lowry. (Illus.). 1977. 15.00 o.p. (ISBN 0-682-48886-0, University). Exposition.

Wheel on the Chimney. Margaret Brown. (Illus.). (gr. k-3). 1954. 9.95 (ISBN 0-397-30288-6). Lippincott.

Wheelchair Book: Mobility for the Disabled. Herman L. Kamenetez. (Illus.). 288p. 1969. pap. 18.75 photocopy ed., spiral (ISBN 0-398-00965-1). C C Thomas.

Wheelchair Bowling: A Complete Guide to Bowling for the Handicapped. Jim Lane & Dick Schaaf. LC 78-24103. (Illus.). 96p. (Orig.). 1980. pap. 7.95 (ISBN 0-9605306-0-6). Wheelchair Bowlers.

Wheelchair Recipes from the Collection of Momma Wheels. Maxine Smolen. Ed. by Debbie Hammond. 1980. 9.95 (ISBN 0-87949-171-X). Ashley Bks.

Wheelchair Willie & Other Plays. Alan Brown. 1980. pap. 4.95 (ISBN 0-7145-3655-5). Riverrun NY.

Wheeler & Goldhor's Practical Administration of Public Libraries. rev. ed. Ed. by Carlton Rochell. LC 79-3401. (Illus.). 480p. 1981. 27.50 (ISBN 0-06-013601-4, HarpT). Harrow.

Wheeler's RV Resort & Campground Guide: Nineteen Eighty-One. (Illus.). 1981. pap. 6.95 (ISBN 0-670-75955-4). Viking Pr.

Wheels. Byron Barton. LC 78-20541. (Illus.). (ps-3). 1979. 7.95 (ISBN 0-690-03951-4, TYC-J); PLB 6.89 (ISBN 0-690-03952-2). T Y Crowell.

Wheels. William Stobbs. (Illus.). (ps). 1979. 1.25 (ISBN 0-370-02005-7, Pub. by Chatto Bodley Jonathan). Merrimack Bk Serv.

Wheels: A Pictorial History. Edwin Tunis. LC 76-25809. (Illus.). (gr. 6 up). 1977. 12.95 (ISBN 0-690-01341-8, TYC-J). T Y Crowell.

Wheels & Grindstones. Sue Turner. 1980. pap. 4.95 (ISBN 0-87397-180-9). Strode.

Wheels for Kids. John Gabriel Navarra. LC 73-76448. 64p. (gr. k-3). 1973. 5.95 o.p. (ISBN 0-385-02693-5); PLB write for info. o.p. (ISBN 0-385-04630-8). Doubleday.

Wheels of Fortune. Francis A. Seufert. Ed. by Thomas Vaughan. LC 80-81719. (Illus.). 304p. 1981. 19.95 (ISBN 0-87595-083-3); pap. 12.95 (ISBN 0-87595-069-8). Oreg Hist Soc.

Wheels Within Wheels. Dervla Murphy. LC 79-27095. 240p. 1980. 10.95 (ISBN 0-89919-006-5). Ticknor & Fields.

Wheelworld. Harry Harrison. 192p. 1981. pap. 2.25 (ISBN 0-553-14339-5). Bantam.

Wheelwright's Shop. George Sturt. 32.50 (ISBN 0-521-06570-4); pap. 9.95 (ISBN 0-521-09195-0). Cambridge U Pr.

Wheldon Costing Simplified. 5th ed. L. W. Owler & J. L. Brown. (Illus.). 336p. 1978. pap. text ed. 11.95x (ISBN 0-7121-2309-1, Pub. by Macdonald & Evans England). Intl Ideas.

Wheldon's Business Statistics. 8th ed. G. L. Thirkettle. (Illus.). 256p. 1976. pap. text ed. 11.95x (ISBN 0-7121-2331-8, Pub. by Macdonald & Evans England). Intl Ideas.

Wheldon's Cost Accounting & Costing Methods. 14th ed. L. W. Owler & J. L. Brown. (Illus.). 784p. 1978. text ed. 21.00x (ISBN 0-7121-2334-2, Pub. by Macdonald & Evans England). Intl Ideas.

When a Christian & a Jew Marry. Ronald Luka & Bernard Zlotowitz. LC 73-77393. 96p. (Orig.). 1973. pap. 1.95 (ISBN 0-8091-1748-7). Paulist Pr.

When a Christian Sins. John R. Rice. 1954. pap. 1.50 (ISBN 0-8024-9434-X). Moody.

When a Lady: Prose-1981. Mark Esingel et al. 70p. 1981. 8.95 (ISBN 0-87376-038-7). Red Dust.

When a Parent Is Mentally Ill: What to Say to Your Child. Helene S. Arnstein. 36p. 1974. pap. 1.25 (ISBN 0-686-12282-8). Jewish Bd Family.

When All Is Said & Done. David Bergelson. Tr. by Bernard Martin from Yiddish. LC 76-25614. xxi, 310p. 1978. 15.00 (ISBN 0-8214-0360-5); pap. 7.25 (ISBN 0-8214-0392-3). Ohio U Pr.

When Are We Ever Gonna Have to Use This? Hal M. Saunders. (Illus.). viii, 88p. (Orig.). (gr. 5-12). 1980. pap. text ed. 6.95 (ISBN 0-9604812-0-6). HMS Pubns.

When Birds Change Their Feathers. Roma Gans. LC 78-20627. (Let's-Read-&-Find-Out Science Books). (Illus.). 40p. (gr. k-3). 1980. 7.95 (ISBN 0-690-03947-6, TYC-J); PLB 7.89 (ISBN 0-690-03948-4). T Y Crowell.

When Buffalo Free the Mountains. Nancy Wood. LC 76-42412. (Illus.). 256p. (gr. 10-12). 1980. 14.95 (ISBN 0-385-01474-0). Doubleday.

When Buffalo Ran. George B. Grinnell. (Western Frontier Library: No. 31). (Illus.). 1966. 6.95 (ISBN 0-8061-0715-4); pap. 2.95 (ISBN 0-8061-1271-9). U of Okla Pr.

When Children Move. Ed. by Monroe D. Cohen. LC 72-83410. (Illus.). 47p. 1972. 1.50x o.p. (ISBN 0-87173-045-6). ACEI.

When Children Need Special Help with Emotional Problems. Greta Mayer & Mary Hoover. 55p. 1974. pap. 1.25 (ISBN 0-686-12281-X). Jewish Bd Family.

When Children Think: Using Journals to Encourage Creative Thinking. Gabriel Jacobs. LC 71-78837. 1970. pap. text ed. 4.75 (ISBN 0-8077-1558-1). Tchrs Coll.

When Clay Sings. Byrd Baylor. (Illus.). 32p. (gr. 1-5). pap. 2.95 (ISBN 0-689-70482-8, A-109, Aladdin). Atheneum.

When Compassion Was a Crime: Germany's Silent Heroes, 1933-1945. H. D. Leuner. 1978. pap. 12.95 (ISBN 0-85496-138-0). Dufour.

When Consumers Complain. Arthur Best. LC 80-21789. 256p. 1981. 16.95 (ISBN 0-231-05124-7). Columbia U Pr.

When Couples Part: How the Legal System Can Work for You. Lawrence E. Kahn. 192p. 1981. 10.95 (ISBN 0-531-09944-X). Watts.

When Dreams & Heroes Died: A Portrait of Today's College Student. Arthur Levine. LC 80-8005. (Carnegie Council Ser.). 1980. text ed. 13.95x (ISBN 0-87589-481-X). Jossey-Bass.

When Dust Shall Sing. George L. Britt. 1958. 4.95 (ISBN 0-87148-901-5). Pathway Pr.

When Eight Bells Toll. Alistair MacLean. 1978. pap. 2.50 (ISBN 0-449-23893-8, Crest). Fawcett.

When Elvis Died. Neal Gregory & Janice Gregory. LC 80-19862. (Illus.). 300p. 1980. 13.95 (ISBN 0-89461-032-5). Comm Pr Inc.

When Farmers Voted Red: The Gospel of Socialism in the Oklahoma Countryside, 1910-1924. Garin Burbank. LC 76-5259. (Contributions in American History Ser.: No. 53). (Illus.). 1976. lib. bdg. 15.00 (ISBN 0-8371-8903-9, BSO/). Greenwood.

When France Was De Gaulle. Roby Eunson. LC 71-161838. (Illus.). (gr. 7 up). 1971. PLB 6.90 (ISBN 0-531-02005-3). Watts.

When Fresno Rode the Rails. Edward Hamm, Jr. Ed. by Mac Sebree. (Special Ser.: No. 73). (Illus.). 1979. pap. 9.50 (ISBN 0-916374-37-8). Interurban.

When from Viet Nam. James Spencer. 1981. 6.00 (ISBN 0-8062-1681-6). Carlton.

When God & I Talk. Clyde L. Herring. (gr. 7-12). 1981. pap. 3.50 (ISBN 0-8054-5334-2). Broadman.

When God Intrudes. Michael Scrogin. 112p. 1981. pap. 4.95 (ISBN 0-8170-0903-5). Judson.

When God Laid Down the Law. Evelyn Marxhausen. LC 59-1259. (Arch Bk.). 1981. pap. 0.79 (ISBN 0-570-06142-3). Concordia.

When God Told Us His Name: Moses & the Burning Bush. Norman Habel. (Purple Puzzle Tree Ser). (Illus., Orig.). (ps-4). 1971. pap. 0.85 (ISBN 0-570-06509-7, 56-1209). Concordia.

When God Was All Alone. Norman Habel. (Purple Puzzle Tree Ser). (Illus., Orig.). (ps-4). 1971. pap. 0.85 (ISBN 0-570-06500-3, 56-1200). Concordia.

When God's Children Suffer. Horatius Bonar. LC 80-84441. (Shepherd Classics Ser.). 144p. 1981. pap. 5.95 (ISBN 0-87983-245-2). Keats.

When Governments Collide: Coercion & Diplomacy in the Vietnam Conflict, 1964-1968. Wallace J. Thies. 500p. 1980. 20.00x (ISBN 0-520-03962-9). U of Cal Pr.

When Governments Come to Washington: Governors, Mayors, & Intergovernmental Lobbying. Donald H. Haider. LC 73-17643. (Illus.). 1974. 15.95 (ISBN 0-02-913370-X). Free Pr.

When Harlem Was in Vogue. David L. Lewis. LC 80-2704. (Illus.). 400p. 1981. 17.95 (ISBN 0-394-49572-1). Knopf.

When Harlem Was Jewish, Eighteen Seventy to Nineteen Thirty. Jeffrey Gurock. 1979. 17.50x (ISBN 0-231-04666-9). Columbia U Pr.

When Harlie Was One. David Gerrold. 288p. 1975. pap. 1.50 o.p. (ISBN 0-345-24390-0). Ballantine.

When Hitler Stole Pink Rabbit. Judith Kerr. (gr. 3 up). 1973. pap. 1.50 (ISBN 0-440-49017-0, YB). Dell.

When I Do, I Learn: A Guide to Creative Planning for Teachers & Parents of Preschool Children. rev. ed. Barbara J. Taylor. LC 74-2122. (Illus.). 250p. 1977. text ed. 12.95x o.p. (ISBN 0-8425-0954-2); pap. 7.95x (ISBN 0-8425-1023-0). Brigham.

When I Fall in Love. Bill Adler & Gary Wagner. LC 78-78051. 1979. pap. 1.95 o.p. (ISBN 0-87216-385-7). Playboy Pbks.

When I Survey. Herman Hoeksema. LC 76-57122. 1977. 9.95 (ISBN 0-8254-2817-3). Kregel.

When I Was a Boy, Vol. II. Jim Hausman. (Illus., Orig.). 1978. pap. 1.95 o.s.i. (ISBN 0-8220-1625-7). Centennial.

When I Was a Boy, 2 vols. Tim Hausman. (Illus., Orig.). pap. 1.95 ea. o.s.i. Vol. 1 (ISBN 0-8220-1624-9). Vol. 2 (ISBN 0-8220-1625-7). Cliffs.

When I Was Old. Georges Simenon. LC 70-153690. (Helen & Kurt Wolff Bk). (Illus.). 343p. 1971. 8.50 o.p. (ISBN 0-15-195950-1). HarBraceJ.

When I Was Your Age... Stop. Edmond C. Hallberg & William G. Thomas. LC 73-6061. 1973. 5.95 o.s.i. (ISBN 0-02-913490-0). Free Pr.

When in Doubt...Faith It. David Wilkerson. LC 72-83844. (Illus.). 64p. (Orig.). 1972. pap. 0.95 o.p. (ISBN 0-8307-0168-0, 50-066-00). Regal.

When in Rome. Ngaio Marsh. 224p. 1980. pap. 1.95 (ISBN 0-515-05627-8). Jove Pubns.

When Is an Example Binding? Biblical Hermeneutics. Thomas B. Warren. 1975. pap. 4.95 (ISBN 0-934916-43-8). Natl Christian Pr.

When Is Now: Experiments with Time & Timekeeping Devices. Henry Humphrey & Deirdre Humphrey. (Illus.). 80p. (gr. 6-7). 1981. 7.95a (ISBN 0-385-13215-8); PLB (ISBN 0-385-13216-6). Doubleday.

When Isaiah Saw the Sizzling Seraphim. Norman Habel. (Purple Puzzle Tree Bk). (ps-5). 1972. pap. 0.85 (ISBN 0-570-06523-2, 56-1227). Concordia.

When It's Your Turn to Speak. new & enl. ed. Orvin Larson. LC 70-108942. 1971. 9.95 o.s.i. (ISBN 0-06-012526-8, HarpT). Har-Row.

When Jacob Buried His Treasure. Norman C. Habel. (Purple Puzzle Tree Ser). (Illus., Orig.). (ps-4). 1971. pap. 0.85 (ISBN 0-570-06508-9, 56-1208). Concordia.

When Jeremiah Learned a Secret from God. Norman Habel. (Purple Puzzle Tree Bk). (Illus.). (ps-5). 1972. pap. 0.85 (ISBN 0-570-06525-9, 56-1229). Concordia.

When Jesus Did His Miracles of Love. Norman C. Habel. (Purple Puzzle Tree Bk.). 1972. pap. 0.85 (ISBN 0-570-06541-0, 56-1245). Concordia.

When Jesus' Friends Betrayed Him. Norman C. Habel. (Purple Puzzle Tree Bk.). 1972. pap. 0.85 (ISBN 0-570-06547-X, 56-1251). Concordia.

When Jesus Prayed. Brenda Poinsett. LC 80-67896. 1981. pap. 3.25 (ISBN 0-8054-5179-X). Broadman.

When Jesus Rode in the Purple Puzzle Parade. Norman C. Habel. (Purple Puzzle Tree Bk.). 1972. pap. 0.85 (ISBN 0-570-06546-1, 56-1250). Concordia.

When Jesus Told His Parables. Norman C. Habel. (Purple Puzzle Tree Bk). 1972. pap. 0.85 (ISBN 0-570-06542-9, 56-1246). Concordia.

When Jesus Was Born. Maryann J. Dotts. LC 79-3958. (Illus.). (ps-3). 1979. 5.95g (ISBN 0-687-45020-9). Abingdon.

When Laughing Boy Was Born. Norman C. Habel. (Purple Puzzle Tree Ser). (Illus., Orig.). (ps-4). 1971. pap. 0.85 (ISBN 0-570-06505-4, 56-1205). Concordia.

When Life Calls. Estle H. Bedell. 1979. 6.95 o.p. (ISBN 0-8062-1191-1). Carlton.

When Life Tumbles in. Batsell B. Baxter. (Direction Books). 136p. 1976. pap. 2.25 (ISBN 0-8010-0668-6). Baker Bk.

When Love Is Not Enough. Marian Wells. LC 79-4534. 1979. pap. 3.50 (ISBN 0-87123-646-X, 210646). Bethany Fell.

When Love Was Not Enough. Clifford Mason. LC 80-82853. 272p. (Orig.). 1981. pap. 2.50 (ISBN 0-87216-779-8). Playboy Pbks.

When Loved Ones Are Called Home. Herbert Wernecke. (Ultra Bks Ser). 3.95 (ISBN 0-8010-9504-2); pap. 1.50 (ISBN 0-8010-9513-1). Baker Bk.

When Mama Was a Little Girl: Memories of a Georgia Childhood. Eleanor D. Clark. (Illus.). 64p. 1980. 6.00 (ISBN 0-682-49663-4). Exposition.

When Marriage Ends. Russell J. Becker. Ed. by Willam E. Julme. LC 74-152366. (Pocket Counsel Bks). 64p. (Orig.). 1971. pap. 1.75 (ISBN 0-8006-1102-0, 1-1102). Fortress.

When Marriage Ends: A Study in Status Passage. Nicky Hart. 277p. 1976. pap. 11.95 (ISBN 0-422-74690-8, 6371). Methuen Inc.

When Megan Went Away. Jane Severance. LC 79-90437. 32p. (gr. k-2). 1979. pap. 2.50 (ISBN 0-914996-22-3). Lollipop Power.

When Memory Comes. Saul Friedlander. 1980. pap. 2.75 (ISBN 0-686-69240-3, 50807, Discus). Avon.

When Men & Mountains Meet: Explorers of the Western Himalayas 1820-75. John Keay. (Illus.). 1978. 18.50 (ISBN 0-7195-3334-1). Transatlantic.

When Men Revolt & Why. J. C. Davies. LC 74-142361. 1971. 12.95 (ISBN 0-02-907310-3); pap. text ed. 9.95 (ISBN 0-02-907000-7). Free Pr.

When Michael Calls. John Farris. 1981. pap. price not set (ISBN 0-671-43118-8). PB.

When My Mommy Died: A Child's View of Death. Janice M. Hammond. (Illus.). 27p. (Orig.). (ps-5). 1980. pap. 3.95 (ISBN 0-9604690-0-1). Cranbrook Pub.

When My Ship Comes in. C. L. Paddock. (Uplook Ser.). 32p. 1962. pap. 0.75 (ISBN 0-8163-0080-1, 23345-2). Pacific Pr Pub Assn.

When Nature Runs Wild. Thomas P. Johnson. LC 67-31553. (Illus.). (gr. 5-9). 1969. PLB 7.50 o.p. (ISBN 0-87191-005-5). Creative Ed.

When Nature Speaks; The Life of Dr. Forrest Shaklee. Georges Spunt. LC 77-9916. 1977. 8.95 (ISBN 0-8119-0279-X). Fell.

When Nomads Settle. Philip C. Salzman. (Praeger Special Studies Ser.). 192p. 1980. 18.95 (ISBN 0-03-052501-2). Praeger.

When Oklahoma Took the Trolley. Allison Chandler. Ed. by Mac Sebree. LC 79-92539. (Special Ser.: No. 71). 1980. 21.95 (ISBN 0-916374-35-1). Interurban.

When People Use Computers: An Approach to Developing an Interface. Marilyn Mehlmann. (Ser. in Software). (Illus.). 160p. 1981. text ed. 15.00 (ISBN 0-13-956219-2). P-H.

When Pregnancy Fails: Families Coping with Miscarriage, Stillbirth & Infant Death. Susan O. Borg & Judith Lasker. LC 80-68167. 224p. 1981. 12.95 (ISBN 0-8070-3226-3, BP 613); pap. 6.95 (ISBN 0-8070-3227-1). Beacon Pr.

When Prophecy Fails: A Social & Psychological Study of a Modern Group That Predicted the Destruction of the World. Leon Festinger et al. pap. 4.95x (ISBN 0-06-131132-4, TB1132, Torch). Har-Row.

When Revival Comes. Jack R. Taylor & C. S. Hawkins. LC 80-66956. 1980. pap. 4.25 (ISBN 0-8054-6226-0). Broadman.

When Rock Was Young: A Nostalgic Review of the Top Forty Era. Bruce Pollock. LC 80-23460. (Illus.). 224p. 1981. 13.95 (ISBN 0-03-049836-8, Owl Books); pap. 6.95 (ISBN 0-03-049841-4). HR&W.

When Schools Are Desegregated: Problems & Possibilities for Students, Educators, Parents & the Community. Ed. by Murray L. Wax. 300p. 1982. 19.95 (ISBN 0-87855-376-2). Transaction Bks. Postponed.

When Shadows Fall. William A. Lauterbach. 1945. pap. 0.85 (ISBN 0-570-03537-6, 14-1573). Concordia.

When Should I Water. K. A. Handreck. 1980. 10.00x (ISBN 0-643-02522-7, Pub. by CSJRO Australia). State Mutual Bk.

When Sirens Scream. Robert E. Rubinstein. LC 80-2788. 160p. (gr. 6 up). 1981. PLB 7.95 (ISBN 0-396-07937-7). Dodd.

When Someone Dies. Edgar N. Jackson. Ed. by William E. Hulme. LC 76-154488. (Pocket Counsel Bks). 64p. (Orig.). 1971. pap. 1.75 (ISBN 0-8006-1103-9, 1-1103). Fortress.

When Sorrow-Song Descends on You. Vinoko Akpalu. Tr. by Kofi Awoonor. (Cross-Cultural Review Chapbook 14). 16p. (Ewe & Eng.). 1980. pap. 2.00 (ISBN 0-89304-813-5). Cross Cult.

When T V Began: The First TV Shows. Sally Berke. LC 78-15168. (Famous Firsts Ser.). (Illus.). 1978. lib. bdg. 7.35 (ISBN 0-686-50003-2). Silver.

When Teachers Face Themselves. Arthur T. Jersild. LC 55-12176. (Horace Mann Lincoln Institute Ser). 1955. pap. text ed. 6.95x (ISBN 0-8077-1575-1). Tchrs Coll.

When the Angels Laughed. Eddy Swieson & Howard Norton. 1978. pap. 3.95 o.p. (ISBN 0-88270-264-5). Logos.

When the Birds Fly South. Stanton A. Coblentz. Ed. by R. Reginald & Douglas Menville. LC 80-23935. (Newcastle Forgotten Fantasy Library Ser.: Vol. 23). 223p. 1980. Repr. lib. bdg. 11.95x (ISBN 0-89370-522-5). Borgo Pr.

When the Birds Fly South. Stanton A. Coblentz. (Newcastle Forgotten Fantasy Library: Vol. 23). 1980. lib. bdg. 10.95x o.p. (ISBN 0-87877-522-6); pap. 4.95 (ISBN 0-87877-122-0). Newcastle Pub.

When the Clock Strikes Thirteen. David Hanna. 1976. pap. 1.50 o.p. (ISBN 0-685-73464-1, LB387, Leisure Bks). Nordon Pubns.

When the Cook Can't Look: A Cooking Handbook for the Blind & Visually Impaired. Ralph Read. 144p. 1981. 9.95 (ISBN 0-8264-0034-5). Continuum.

When the Dream Dies. A. Bertram Chandler. 160p. 1981. 12.95 (ISBN 0-8052-8089-8, Pub. by Allison & Busby, England). Schocken.

When the Eagle Screamed: The Romantic Horizon in American Diplomacy, 1800-1860. William H. Goetzmann. (Illus., Orig.). 1966. pap. 7.95x (ISBN 0-471-31001-8). Wiley.

When the Earth Was Young. David Yeadon. LC 76-42430. 1978. pap. 5.95 o.p. (ISBN 0-385-12466-X). Doubleday.

When the First Man Came. Norman C. Habel. (Purple Puzzle Tree Ser). (Illus., Orig.). (ps-4). 1971. pap. 0.85 (ISBN 0-570-06501-1, 56-1201). Concordia.

When the Legends Die. Hal G. Borland. LC 63-11753. (gr. 10 up). 1963. 9.95 (ISBN 0-397-00303-X). Lippincott.

When the Movies Began: First Film Stars. Edgar Marvin. LC 78-15167. (Famous Firsts Ser.). (Illus.). 1978. lib. bdg. 7.35 (ISBN 0-686-51118-2). Silver.

When the Music Changed. Marie R. Reno. 1980. pap. 12.95 (ISBN 0-453-00384-2, H384). NAL.

When the Owl Called. Mary Kennedy. LC 78-73530. (Illus.). (gr. 2-5). Date not set. price not set (ISBN 0-89799-164-8); pap. price not set (ISBN 0-89799-082-X). Dandelion Pr. Postponed.

When the Purple Waters Came Again. Norman C. Habel. (Purple Puzzle Tree Ser). (Illus., Orig.). (ps-4). 1971. pap. 0.85 (ISBN 0-570-06503-8, 56-1203). Concordia.

When the Red King Woke. Joseph E. Kelleam. (YA) 4.95 o.p. (ISBN 0-685-07464-1, Avalon). Bouregy.

When the Roses Fade. Janet E. Pruet. 1981. 4.95 (ISBN 0-8062-1644-1). Carlton.

When the Santos Talked. Angelico Chavez. LC 76-53086. 1977. Repr. of 1957 ed. 15.00 o.p. (ISBN 0-88307-528-8). Gannon.

When the Shooting Stops...the Cutting Begins: A Film Editor's Story. Ralph Rosenblum & Robert Karen. 1980. pap. 4.95 (ISBN 0-14-005698-X). Penguin.

When the Sky Fell Down. Keith Willey. 231p. 1980. 13.95x (ISBN 0-00-216434-5, Pub. by W Collins Australia). Intl Schol Bk Serv.

When the Sky Is Like Lace. Elinor L. Horwitz. LC 75-9664. 32p. (gr. k-2). 1975. 8.95 (ISBN 0-397-31550-3). Lippincott.

When the Spirit Comes. Colin Urquhart. LC 75-21165. 128p. 1974. pap. 1.95 (ISBN 0-87123-645-1, 200645). Bethany Fell.

When the Tree Flowered: The Fictional Autobiography of Eagle Voice, a Sioux Indian. John G. Neihardt. LC 75-116055. 1970. pap. 4.95 (ISBN 0-8032-5724-4, BB 526, Bison). U of Nebr Pr.

When the Tree Sings. Stratis Hayiaras. 192p. 1981. pap. 2.95. Ballantine.

When the Twain Meet: The Rise of Western Medicine in Japan. John Z. Bowers. LC 80-22356. (Henry E. Sigerist Supplement to the Bulletin of the History of Medicine Ser.: No. 5). 192p. 1981. text ed. 14.00x (ISBN 0-8018-2432-X). Johns Hopkins.

When the Union Organizer Knocks. new ed. Tom Rose. (Illus.). 150p. 1972. pap. 7.95 (ISBN 0-686-05611-6). American Ent Texas.

When the West Was Wild. Robert Hoare. (Junior Reference Ser.). (Illus.). 64p. (gr. 7 up). 1976. 7.95 (ISBN 0-7136-1619-9). Dufour.

When the Whippoorwill. Marjorie K. Rawlings. pap. 1.75 o.p. (ISBN 0-89176-522-0, 6522). Mockingbird Bks.

When the Whippoorwill. Marjorie K. Rawlings. 1980. pap. 2.25 (ISBN 0-89176-035-0). Mockingbird Bks.

When the Wind Blows. Cyril Hare. LC 75-44980. (Crime Fiction Ser). 1976. Repr. of 1949 ed. lib. bdg. 17.50 (ISBN 0-8240-2373-0). Garland Pub.

When the Wind Changed. Ruth Park. (Illus.). 32p. (Orig.). (ps-3). 1981. 8.95 (ISBN 0-698-20525-1, Peppercorn); pap. 4.95 (ISBN 0-698-20526-X). Coward.

When the Winds Blow. Derek Tangye. (Illus.). 1981. write for info. (ISBN 0-7181-1932-0). Merrimack Bk Serv.

When Timber Stood Tall. Joseph H. Pierre. LC 79-21006. (Illus.). 192p. 1980. 19.95 (ISBN 0-87564-909-2). Superior Pub.

When Time Was Born. James T. Farrell. 1966. 3.50 (ISBN 0-912292-04-0); signed ltd. ed. 25.00 (ISBN 0-912292-05-9). The Smith.

When to Duck–When to Win in Bridge. Terence Reese & Roger Trezel. LC 77-23677. 1978. pap. 3.95 (ISBN 0-8119-0401-6). Fell.

When Trees Are Green & Daisies Dance. Rebecca J. Lunney. 1981. 4.75 (ISBN 0-8062-1622-0). Carlton.

When Trees Were Green: The Story of Robin Heron. Inez Heron. LC 78-53879. 1978. 10.00 o.p. (ISBN 0-312-86673-9). St Martin.

When Walls Are High. Elizabeth V. Hamilton. LC 72-93195. 1973. 6.00 (ISBN 0-937684-09-0). Tradd St Pr.

When We Grow up. Bahiyyih Nakhjavani. 1979. 6.50 (ISBN 0-85398-085-3, 7-32-38, Pub. by G Ronald England); pap. 2.25 (ISBN 0-85398-086-1, 7-32-39, Pub. by G Ronald England). Baha'i.

When We Grow Up. Anne Rockwell. LC 80-21768. (Illus.). (ps-1). 1981. PLB 10.95 (ISBN 0-525-42575-6). Dutton.

When We Were Boys. William O'Brien. (Nineteenth Century Fiction Ser.: Ireland: Vol. 76). 556p. 1979. lib. bdg. 46.00 (ISBN 0-8240-3525-9). Garland Pub.

When We Were Very Young. A. A. Milne. (gr. 1-5). 1961. 6.95 (ISBN 0-525-42580-2). Dutton.

When We Were Young: An Album of Stars. P. Fortunato. 1980. 8.95 (ISBN 0-13-956482-9); pap. 2.50 (ISBN 0-13-956474-8). P-H.

When Wilderness Was King. Randall Parrish. 1976. lib. bdg. 17.25x (ISBN 0-89968-088-7). Lightyear.

When Will I Read? Miriam Cohen. LC 76-28320. (ps-3). 1977. 8.25 (ISBN 0-688-80073-4); PLB 7.92 (ISBN 0-688-84073-6). Greenwillow.

When William Fourth Was King. John Ashton. LC 67-23943. (Social History Reference Ser). 1968. Repr. of 1896 ed. 15.00 (ISBN 0-8103-3255-8). Gale.

When Willy Went to the Wedding. Judith Kerr. LC 72-8027. (Illus.). (gr. k-3). 1973. 5.95 o.p. (ISBN 0-8193-0658-4, Four Winds); PLB 5.41 o.p. (ISBN 0-8193-0659-2). Schol Bk Serv.

When Winter Comes. Russell Freedman. LC 80-22831. (Illus.). (gr. 1-3). 1981. PLB 7.95 (ISBN 0-525-42583-7). Dutton.

When Workers Fight: The Politics of Industrial Relations in the Progressive Era, 1898-1916. Bruno Ramirez. LC 77-83895. (Contributions in Labor History: No. 2). 1978. lib. bdg. 18.95 (ISBN 0-8371-9826-7, RAW/). Greenwood.

When Worlds Collide. Philip Balmer & Edwin Wylie. 192p. 1975. pap. 2.25 (ISBN 0-446-92812-7). Warner Bks.

When You Find a Rock: A Field Guide. Barrie Klaits. LC 75-38519. (Illus.). 64p. (gr. 3-7). 1976. 8.95 (ISBN 0-02-750790-4, 75079). Macmillan.

When You Least Expect Love. Diane Jones. (YA) 1978. 5.95 (ISBN 0-685-84750-0, Avalon). Bouregy.

When You Open Your Bible. Paul Ricchiuti. LC 67-18008. (Hello World Ser.). 1967. pap. 1.65 (ISBN 0-8163-0307-X, 23380-9). Pacific Pr Pub Assn.

When You Run Out of Fantastic-Persevere. Reuben Welch. LC 76-20999. 1976. pap. text ed. 1.50 study guide (ISBN 0-914850-30-X); pap. text ed. 1.50 study guide (ISBN 0-686-67577-0); pap. text ed. 1.50 study guide (ISBN 0-686-67578-9). Impact Tenn.

When Your Child Is Ill. rev. ed. Samuel Karelitz. LC 69-16463. 1969. 7.95 o.p. (ISBN 0-394-45168-6). Random.

When Your Name Is on the Door: The Independent Businessowner's Guide to Survival, Profits & Happiness. Eugene D. Brodie. LC 80-66756. 225p. 1981. 24.95 (ISBN 0-916728-45-5). Bks in Focus.

When Your Parents Grow Old. Jane Otten & Florence D. Shelley. LC 76-10697. (Funk & W Bk.). 1976. 9.95 o.s.i. (ISBN 0-308-10256-8, TYC-T). T Y Crowell.

When You're a Widow. Clarissa Start. LC 73-78880. (Illus.). 1973. 4.95 (ISBN 0-570-03288-1, 15-2084). Concordia.

When You're Married. William B. Ward. (Orig.). 1947. pap. 1.50 (ISBN 0-8042-2604-0). John Knox.

Whence & Wherefore: The Cosmological Destiny of Man Scientifically & Philosophically Considered. Zev Zahavy. LC 77-84786. 1978. 7.50 o.p. (ISBN 0-498-02190-4). A S Barnes.

When's Later, Daddy? Bil Keane. (Family Circus Ser.). (Illus.). 1979. pap. 1.50 (ISBN 0-449-14124-1, GM). Fawcett.

Where Animals Live. R. A. Marchant. LC 69-18240. (Illus.). (gr. 5-8). 1970. 7.95g (ISBN 0-02-762420-X). Macmillan.

Where Are My Legions. Gene Smith. LC 79-28277. 320p. 1980. 12.95 (ISBN 0-688-03645-7). Morrow.

Where Are the Children? Betty R. Mandell. 128p. 1973. 17.95 (ISBN 0-669-88963-6). Lexington Bks.

Where Are We Going? Deborah Manley. LC 78-31860. (Ready, Set, Look Ser.). (Illus.). (gr. k-3). 1979. PLB 9.65 (ISBN 0-8172-1305-8). Raintree Pubs.

Where Are We Running? June Strong. LC 78-26271. (Orion Ser.). 1979. pap. 1.95 (ISBN 0-8127-0207-7). Southern Pub.

Where Are You Going with That Coal? Roy Doty & Len Maar. LC 75-36586. (gr. 4-7). 1978. 5.95a (ISBN 0-385-11515-6); PLB (ISBN 0-385-11516-4). Doubleday.

Where Are You Going with That Energy? Roy Doty & Len Maar. LC 75-36587. (gr. 2-5). 1978. 5.95a (ISBN 0-385-11519-9); PLB (ISBN 0-385-11520-2). Doubleday.

Where Artists Live: 1970, Report No. 5. (National Endowment for the Arts Research Division Reports). 80p. (Orig.). 1977. pap. 3.00x (ISBN 0-89062-095-4, Pub. by Natl Endow Arts). Put Ctr Cultures.

Where Beauty Dwells. Emilie Loring. 1976. Repr. of 1941 ed. lib. bdg. 13.20 (ISBN 0-88411-364-7). Amereon Ltd.

Where Black Rules White: A Journey Across & About Hayti. Hesketh Prichard. 298p. 1971. Repr. of 1900 ed. 24.00x (ISBN 0-7165-1819-8, Pub. by Irish Academic Pr Ireland). Biblio Dist.

Where Can the Animals Go. Ron Wegen. LC 77-15001. (Illus.). (gr. k-3). 1978. 7.95 (ISBN 0-688-80137-4); PLB 7.63 (ISBN 0-688-84137-6). Greenwillow.

Where Colleges Are & Who Attends: Effects of Accessability on College Attendance. Carnegie Commission on Higher Education & C. Arnold Anderson. LC 72-2009. (Illus.). 352p. 1972. 10.95 o.p. (ISBN 0-07-010046-2, P&RB). McGraw.

Where Colleges Fail: A Study of the Student As a Person. Nevitt Sanford. LC 67-13279. (Higher Education Ser.). 1967. 12.95x o.p. (ISBN 0-87589-003-2). Jossey-Bass.

Where Cross the Crowded Ways: Prayers of a City Pastor. Ernest T. Campbell. 1973. pap. 2.95 o.p. (ISBN 0-8096-1861-3, Assn Pr). Follett.

Where Did Everybody Go? Paul Molloy. LC 79-6605. 192p. 1981. 11.95 (ISBN 0-385-04997-8). Doubleday.

Where Did My Mother Go? Edna M. Preston. LC 77-15064. (Illus.). 32p. (gr. k-3). 1978. 7.95 (ISBN 0-590-07347-8, Four Winds). Schol Bk Serv.

Where Did That Word Come from. Albert G. Miller. (ABC Serendipity Ser). (Illus.). (gr. 2-6). 1973. 6.57 o.p. (ISBN 0-8372-1815-2); pap. 4.35 o.p. (ISBN 0-8372-0823-8). Bowmar-Noble.

Where Do Bastards Go to Die. Verne Benedict. 1981. 9.95 (ISBN 0-533-04879-6). Vantage.

Where Do I Fit In? June Noble. LC 79-1073. (Illus.). 32p. (gr. k-2). 1981. 6.95 (ISBN 0-03-046181-2). HR&W.

Where Do I Go from Here with My Life. R. N. Bolles & John Crystal. LC 78-61867. (Illus.). 1980. pap. 9.95 (ISBN 0-89815-028-0). Ten Speed Pr.

Where Do I Stand? Living Theological Options for Contemporary Christians. 3rd ed. W. Widick Schroeder & Keith A. Davis. LC 78-59809. (Studies in Ministry & Parish Life). 1978. 13.50x (ISBN 0-913552-12-7); pap. 6.00x (ISBN 0-913552-13-5). Exploration Pr.

Where Do We Go from Here: Conditions of Women in Blue-Collar Jobs. Pamela Roby. 258p. 1981. text ed. 15.50x (ISBN 0-87073-172-6); pap. text ed. 8.95x (ISBN 0-87073-173-4). Schenkman.

Where Does a Mother Go to Resign? Barbara Johnson. LC 79-12686. 1979. pap. 3.50 (ISBN 0-87123-606-0, 210606). Bethany Fell.

Where Does All That Smoke Come from? Inger Sandberg. LC 72-1445. (Illus.). 32p. (ps-3). 1972. 4.95 o.s.i. (ISBN 0-440-09651-0, Sey Lawr); PLB 4.58 (ISBN 0-440-09652-9, 9652, Sey Lawr). Delacorte.

Where Does It Come from? That's a Good Question. Tobi Tobias. (Illus.). (gr. k-3). 1977. PLB 7.95 o.p. (ISBN 0-516-03667-X). Childrens.

Where Does the Garbage Go? Paul Showers. LC 73-14881. (Let's-Read-&-Find-Out Science Bk). (Illus.). (ps-3). 1974. 7.95 (ISBN 0-690-00392-7, TYC-J); PLB 7.89 (ISBN 0-690-00402-8). T Y Crowell.

Where Does the Marine Corps Go from Here? Martin Binkin & Jeffrey Record. (Studies in Defense Policy). 1976. pap. 3.95 (ISBN 0-8157-0963-3). Brookings.

Where Does Your Garden Grow? Augusta Goldin. (Let's-Read-&-Find-Out Science Bk). (Illus.). (gr. k-3). 1967. bds. 7.95 (ISBN 0-690-88357-9, TYC-J); PLB 7.89 (ISBN 0-690-88358-7). T Y Crowell.

Where Eagles Dare. Alistair MacLean. 1979. pap. 2.50 (ISBN 0-449-24121-1, Crest). Fawcett.

Where Eagles Nest. Anne Hampson. 192p. (Orig.). 1980. pap. 1.50 (ISBN 0-671-57040-4). S&S.

Where Faith Begins. C. Ellis Nelson. LC 67-22004. 1967. pap. 4.50 o.s.i. (ISBN 0-8042-1471-9). John Knox.

Where Flies Don't Land. Jerry Graham & M. L. Johnson. (Illus.). 1977. pap. 3.95 o.p. (ISBN 0-88270-222-X). Logos.

Where Have All the Robots Gone? Worker Dissatisfaction in the Seventies. Harold L. Sheppard & Neal Q. Herrick. LC 72-77285. 1972. 7.95 (ISBN 0-02-928600-X); pap. text ed. 3.95 (ISBN 0-02-928590-9). Free Pr.

Where Have All the Sardines Gone? Randall A. Reinstedt. LC 79-101716. (Illus.). 1978. pap. 5.95 (ISBN 0-933818-05-X). Ghost Town.

Where Have You Been? Margaret W. Brown. (Illus.). (gr. k-2). 1963. 3.50 o.s.i. (ISBN 0-8038-8018-9). Hastings.

Where Have You Gone, Joe DiMaggio? The Story of America's Last Hero. Maury Allen. (RL 9). 1976. pap. 1.50 o.p. (ISBN 0-451-06986-2, W6986, Sig). NAL.

Where He Leads. Dale E. Rogers. (Illus.). 1974. deluxe ed. 5.95 (ISBN 0-8007-0723-0); pap. 1.50 o.p. (ISBN 0-8007-8194-5, Spire Bks). Revell.

Where He Leads. Dale E. Rogers. 1975. pap. 1.50 (ISBN 0-89129-002-8). Jove Pubns.

Where Helen Lies. Rae Foley. 1978. pap. 1.75 o.s.i. (ISBN 0-515-04490-3). Jove Pubns.

Where I Hang My Hat. Dick Gallup. LC 70-123977. (Full Court Rebound Bk.). 1978. 14.95 (ISBN 0-685-60029-7). Full Court NY.

Where in the World Is Henry? Lorna Ballan. LC 79-10391. (Illus.). (gr. k-11). 1980. Repr. 5.95g (ISBN 0-687-45092-6). Abingdon.

Where Is Bone? Palmer & Weinert. 1980. pap. 1.50 (ISBN 0-380-75242-5, 75242, Camelot). Avon.

Where Is God When It Hurts. Philip Yancey. 1977. 6.95 (ISBN 0-310-35410-2); pap. 4.95 (ISBN 0-310-35411-0). Zondervan.

Where Is God When It Hurts? A Study Guide. Philip Yancey. (Orig.). 1978. pap. 1.95 (ISBN 0-310-35431-5). Zondervan.

Where Is He Now? Sports Heroes of Yesterday Revisited. Jack Drees & James C. Mullen. LC 71-188243. (Illus.). 1973. 7.95 o.p. (ISBN 0-8246-0145-9). Jonathan David.

Where Is History Going? John W. Montgomery. LC 69-11659. 1969. 5.95 (ISBN 0-87123-640-0, 210640). Bethany Fell.

Where Is It? Tana Hoban. LC 73-8573. (Illus.). 32p. (ps-2). 1974. 7.95 (ISBN 0-02-744070-2). Macmillan.

Where Is Jesus? Joyce Morse. (Books I Can Read). 32p. (gr. 2). 1980. pap. 1.25 (ISBN 0-8127-0280-8). Southern Pub.

Where Is Love, No. 71. Barbara Cartland. 1978. pap. 1.50 o.s.i. (ISBN 0-515-04476-8). Jove Pubns.

Where Is the Ark of the Covenant? Arthur E. Bloomfield. LC 76-2257. 1976. pap. 1.75 (ISBN 0-87123-004-6, 200004). Bethany Fell.

Where Is the Bear? Betty Hubka. (Young Reader Ser.). (gr. k-3). 1979. PLB 5.00 (ISBN 0-307-60204-4, Golden Pr). Western Pub.

Where Is the Eagle? William E. Coffer. 288p. 1981. 16.95 (ISBN 0-442-26163-2). Van Nos Reinhold.

Where Is the Keeper? Mabel Watts. 1979. PLB 4.77 (ISBN 0-307-68469-5, Whitman). Western Pub.

Where Is the Lord God of Elijah? E. K. Cox. pap. 2.95 o.p. (ISBN 0-686-12926-1). Schmul Pub Co.

Where It's At. William Sheldon & Warren H. Wheelock. (Orig.). (RL 4). 1973. pap. text ed. 4.96 (ISBN 0-205-03344-X, 5233445); tchrs'. guide 2.40 (ISBN 0-205-03342-3, 5233429); Allyn.

Where Late the Sweet Birds Sang. Kate Wilhelm. LC 75-6379. 260p. (YA) 1976. 10.00 o.p. (ISBN 0-06-014654-0, HarpT). Har-Row.

Where Living Waters Flow. Claire Lynn. 99p. 1979. pap. 2.00 (ISBN 0-89323-002-2). BMA Pr.

Where Love Has Gone. Harold Robbins. 1977. pap. 3.50 (ISBN 0-671-82676-X). PB.

Where Monsters Walk. Michael Avallone. (gr. 7 up). 1978. pap. 1.25 (ISBN 0-590-11914-1, Schol Pap). Schol Bk Serv.

Where Mountains Wait. Fran Wilson. 192p. (Orig.). 1980. pap. 1.50 (ISBN 0-671-57009-9). S&S.

Where My Money Is Going: Income & Expense Budget. Ed. by Roger Huber. (Orig.). 1980. pap. 10.00x (ISBN 0-918300-00-2); wkbk. 10.00. Lankey.

Where No Sun Shines. Leo P. Kelley. LC 78-68229. (Galaxy Five Ser.). (Illus.). 64p. (gr. 4 up). 1980. PLB 7.95 (ISBN 0-516-02256-3). Childrens.

Where Peoples Meet: Racial & Ethnic Frontiers. Everett C. Hughes & Helen M. Hughes. LC 80-27901. 204p. 1981. Repr. of 1952 ed. lib. bdg. 19.75x (ISBN 0-313-22785-3, HUWP). Greenwood.

Where Peter Is: A Survey of Ecclesiology. Edward J. Gratsch. LC 74-34578. 290p. 1975. pap. 5.95 (ISBN 0-8189-0302-3). Alba.

Where the Action Is. Ralph P. Martin. LC 75-23515. 1976. pap. 2.25 (ISBN 0-8307-0361-6, S303-1-08). Regal.

Where the Air Is Clear. Carlos Fuentes. Tr. by Sam Hileman. 1971. pap. 7.95 (ISBN 0-374-50919-0, N405). FS&G.

Where the Birds Are. Mabel Gillespie. LC 76-55062. (Illus., Orig.). 1976. pap. 4.95 (ISBN 0-932384-03-X). Tashmoo.

Where the Bright Lights Shine. Anne N. Stallworth. LC 75-25145. 1978. 7.95 (ISBN 0-8149-0770-9). Vanguard.

Where the Brook Begins. Margaret F. Bartlett. LC 60-9773. (Let's-Read-&-Find-Out Science Bk). (Illus.). (gr. k-3). 1961. 7.95 (ISBN 0-690-88428-1, TYC-J). T Y Crowell.

Where the Buffaloes Begin. Olaf Baker. LC 80-23319. (Illus.). 48p. (gr. 1-4). 1981. 9.95g (ISBN 0-7232-6195-4). Warne.

Where the Deer & the Cantaloupe Play. T. Ernesto Bethancourt. 90p. 1980. write for info. (ISBN 0-916392-69-4). Oak Tree Pubns.

Where the Elf King Sings. Judie Wolkoff. LC 80-15298. 160p. (gr. 5-7). 8.95 (ISBN 0-87888-169-7). Bradbury Pr.

Where the Field Goes. Jeanne Lohmann. 1976. pap. 3.00 (ISBN 0-686-17445-3). J A Lohmann.

Where the Highway Ends. Geneva Hamilton. LC 74-77228. (Illus.). 1977. 9.95 (ISBN 0-914598-26-0); pap. 4.95 (ISBN 0-914598-25-2). Padre Prods.

Where the Jackals Howl & Other Stories. Amos Oz. Tr. by Nicholas De Lange & Philip Simpson. (Helen & Kurt-Wolff Bk.). 1981. 12.95 (ISBN 0-15-196038-0). HarBraceJ.

Where the Jobs Are. William J. McBurney, Jr. 320p. Date not set. pap. 6.95 (ISBN 0-8019-7025-3). Chilton.

Where the Light Was Burning. Ron Grant. 192p. 1981. 8.95 (ISBN 0-89962-044-2). Todd & Honeywell.

Where the Money Grows. Garet Garrett. 1966. Repr. of 1911 ed. flexible cover 2.50 (ISBN 0-87034-024-7). Fraser Pub Co.

Where the Money Was. Willie Sutton & Edward Linn. 1977. pap. 1.95 (ISBN 0-345-28122-5). Ballantine.

Where the Red Fern Grows. Wilson Rawls. LC 61-9201. 7.95a (ISBN 0-385-02059-7); PLB (ISBN 0-385-05619-2). Doubleday.

Where the Wasteland Ends: Politics & Transcendence in Post-Industrial Society. Theodore Roszak. 480p. 1973. pap. 2.95 (ISBN 0-385-02738-9, Anch). Doubleday.

Where the Wolf Leads. Jane Arbor. (Harlequin Romances). 192p. 1981. pap. 1.25 (ISBN 0-373-02396-0, Pub. by Harlequin). PB.

Where the World Is, Teaching Basic Skills Outdoors. John Dacey. (Illus.). 192p. (Orig.). 1981. pap. 10.95 (ISBN 0-8302-9605-0). Goodyear.

Where There's Smoke. Ed McBain. 1975. 6.95 o.p. (ISBN 0-394-49670-1). Random.

Where They Go to Die. Richard M. Garvin & Robert E. Burger. 1968. 4.95 o.p. (ISBN 0-440-09511-5). Delacorte.

Where Time Stood Still: A Portrait of Appalachia. Bruce Roberts & Nancy Roberts. (gr. 5-9). 1970. 6.95 o.s.i. (ISBN 0-02-777440-6, CCPr). Macmillan.

Where to Camp in France. (Illus.). 1979. pap. 3.95 o.p. (ISBN 0-905136-08-X, ADON 8108-2, Pub. by Nicholson). Barrie & Jenkins.

Where to Camp in Great Britain. (Illus.). 1979. pap. 4.95 o.p. (ISBN 0-905522-19-2, ADON 8106-6, Pub. by Nicholson). Barrie & Jenkins.

Where to Camp in Spain. Camping Club. (Nicholson Leisure Guides). (Illus.). 1979. pap. 3.95 o.p. (ISBN 0-905522-38-9, ADON 8110-4, Pub. by R Nicholson). Barrie & Jenkins.

Where to Eat in America. William Rice & Burton Wolf. 1977. pap. 5.95 o.p. (ISBN 0-394-73438-6). Random.

Where to Find More: A Handbook to Reference Service. James M. Hillard. LC 77-6406. 1977. 10.00 (ISBN 0-8108-1039-5). Scarecrow.

Where to Find What: A Handbook to Reference Service. James M. Hillard. LC 75-6723. 281p. 1975. 12.00 (ISBN 0-8108-0813-7). Scarecrow.

Where to Go for What: How to Research, Organize & Present Your Information. Mara Miller. (Illus.). 240p. 1981. 11.95 (ISBN 0-13-957217-1, Spec); pap. 5.95 (ISBN 0-13-957209-0). P-H.

Where to Now, Blue? Adrien Stoutenburg. LC 78-4336. 192p. (gr. 3-7). 1978. 7.95 (ISBN 0-590-07518-7, Four Winds). Schol Bk Serv.

Where to Stay: East Anglia. Automobile Association - British Tourist Authority. 1979. pap. 2.95 o.p. (ISBN 0-86143-005-0, Pub. by B T a). Merrimack Bk Serv.

Where to Stay: East Midlands. Automobile Association - British Tourist Authority. 1979. pap. 2.95 o.p. (ISBN 0-86143-003-4, Pub. by B T a). Merrimack Bk Serv.

Where to Stay: English Lakeland. Automobile Association -British Tourist Authority. 1979. pap. 2.95 o.p. (ISBN 0-903265-98-2, Pub. by B T a). Merrimack Bk Serv.

Where to Stay: Heart of England. Automobile Association - British Tourist Authority. 1979. pap. 2.95 o.p. (ISBN 0-86143-002-6, Pub. by B T a). Merrimack Bk Serv.

Where to Stay in Wales. Automobile Association - British Tourist Authority. (Illus.). 1979. pap. 4.50 o.p. (ISBN 0-900784-70-9, Pub. by B T a). Merrimack Bk Serv.

Where to Stay: North West England. Automobile Association - British Tourist Authority. 1979. pap. 2.95 o.p. (ISBN 0-86143-000-X, Pub. by B T a). Merrimack Bk Serv.

Where to Stay: Northumbria. Automobile Association - British Tourist Authority. 1979. pap. 2.95 o.p. (ISBN 0-903265-99-0, Pub. by B T a). Merrimack Bk Serv.

Where to Stay: South East England. Automobile Association - British Tourist Authority. 1979. pap. 2.95 o.p. (ISBN 0-86143-009-3, Pub. by B T a). Merrimack Bk Serv.

Where to Stay: South of England. Automobile Association - British Tourist Authority. 1979. pap. 2.95 o.p. (ISBN 0-86143-008-5, Pub. by B T a). Merrimack Bk Serv.

Where to Stay: Thames & Chilterns. Automobile Association - British Tourist Authority. 1979. pap. 2.95 o.p. (ISBN 0-86143-004-2, Pub. by B T a). Merrimack Bk Serv.

Where to Stay USA. Council on International Educational Exchange. (Illus.). 368p. 1980-81. pap. 4.95 (ISBN 0-671-25496-0). Frommer-Pasmantier.

Where to Stay: West Country. Automobile Association - British Tourist Authority. 1979. pap. 2.95 o.p. (ISBN 0-86143-007-7, Pub. by B T a). Merrimack Bk Serv.

Where to Stay: Yorkshire & Humberside. Automobile Association - British Tourist Authority. 1979. pap. 2.95 o.p. (ISBN 0-86143-001-8, Pub. by B T a). Merrimack Bk Serv.

Where to, Tarapada-Babu? Tarapada Roy. Tr. by Shyamasree Devi & P. Lal. (Saffronbird Bk.). 51p. 1975. 10.00 (ISBN 0-88253-839-X); pap. 4.80 (ISBN 0-88253-840-3). Ind-US Inc.

Where Tomorrow? Bob Young & Jan Young. (YA) (gr. 7-9). 1969. pap. 0.75 (ISBN 0-671-29535-7). PB.

Where Was Everyone When Sabrina Screamed? Amelia Walden. (gr. 7-12). 1975. pap. 1.25 (ISBN 0-590-00091-8, Schol Pap). Schol Bk Serv.
Where Water Flows: The Rivers of Arizona. Lawrence C. Powell. (Illus.). 120p. 1980. 25.00 (ISBN 0-87358-222-5). Northland.
Where We Are: A Hard Look at Family & Society. Buder et al. 1970. pap. 3.50 (ISBN 0-686-12284-4). Jewish Bd Family.
Where We Used to Work. Kenneth Hudson. 1980. text ed. 20.75x (ISBN 0-212-97025-9). Humanities.
Where Will All the Animals Go? Sharon Holaves. (Illus.). (gr. k-2). 1978. PLB 5.00 (ISBN 0-307-60175-7, Golden Pr). Western Pub.
Where You Live May Be Hazardous to Your Health. Robert Shakman. 1978. 14.95 (ISBN 0-8128-2506-3); pap. 5.95 (ISBN 0-8128-6001-2). Stein & Day.
Whereby We Thrive: A History of American Farming 1607-1972. John T. Schlebecker. 342p. 1975. 15.50 (ISBN 0-8138-0090-0). Iowa St U Pr.
Where's Al. Byron Barton. LC 78-171866. (Illus.). 32p. (ps-2). 1972. 7.95 (ISBN 0-395-28765-0, Clarion). HM.
Where's Hodgey? Karen Sadowski & Robert Gadbois. LC 77-1999. (Books by Children for Children). (gr. 2-5). 1977. PLB 6.45 (ISBN 0-87191-610-X). Creative Ed.
Where's It At? Gary Richardson. 1978. pap. 3.50 (ISBN 0-88207-182-3). Victor Bks.
Where's Jim Now. Bianca Bradbury. (gr. 5-9). 1978. 7.95 (ISBN 0-395-27160-6). HM.
Where's Mark? Jacquie Hann. LC 76-54869. (Illus.). 40p. (gr. k-3). 1977. 5.95 (ISBN 0-590-07499-7, Four Winds). Schol Bk Serv.
Where's PJ? Bil Keane. (Family Circus Ser.). (Illus.). 1978. pap. 1.50 (ISBN 0-449-13982-4, GM). Fawcett.
Where's Spot? Hill. 6.95 (ISBN 0-399-20758-9). Putnam.
Where's That Poem? rev & enl ed. Helen Morris. 287p. 1980. pap. 10.50x (ISBN 0-631-11791-1, Pub. by Basil Blackwell). Biblio Dist.
Where's the Kids, Herman? Jim Unger. 1978. pap. 2.50 (ISBN 0-8362-1105-7). Andrews & McMeel.
Where's Your Head? Dale Bick Carlson. LC 77-2292. (Illus.). (gr. 6-12). 1977. 8.95 (ISBN 0-689-30578-8). Atheneum.
Wherever They May Be: One Woman's Battle Against Nazism. Beate Klarsfeld. LC 74-81809. 352p. 1975. 10.00 (ISBN 0-8149-0748-2). Vanguard.
Wherewithal: A Guide to Resources for Museums & Historical Societies. Tema Harnik. 120p. (Orig.). 1981. pap. write for info. (ISBN 0-935654-01-1, Pub. by Ctr for Arts Info). Pub Ctr Cult Res.
Wheston's Commentaries on Acts, Romans, Vol. 3. 11.95 (ISBN 0-686-13906-2). Schmul Pub Co.
Which Church. Carl Ketcherside. pap. 0.50. Reiner.
Which Is Biggest? Mary Brewer. LC 75-35970. (Illus.). (ps-3). 1976. PLB 5.50 (ISBN 0-913778-26-5); pap. 2.75 (ISBN 0-89565-067-3). Childs World.
Which Is the Best Place: Adapted from the Russian of Pyotr Dudochkin. Mirra Ginsburg. LC 75-31946. (Illus.). 32p. (ps-1). 1976. 8.95 (ISBN 0-02-735980-8, 73598). Macmillan.
Which Is the Witch? W. K. Jasner. LC 78-11757. (I Am Reading Bks.). (Illus.). (gr. 2-4). 1979. 4.95 (ISBN 0-394-83978-1); PLB 5.99 (ISBN 0-394-93978-6). Pantheon.
Which One Is Different? Joel Rothman. LC 74-5. 32p. (ps-1). 1975. PLB 6.95 (ISBN 0-385-11017-0). Doubleday.
Which Tribe Do You Belong to? Alberto Moravia. Tr. by Angus Davidson from Ital. 1974. 7.95 o.p. (ISBN 0-374-28922-0). FS&G.
Which Way, Black Cat? Lattimore. (gr. 3-5). 1980. pap. 1.25 (ISBN 0-590-30040-7, Schol Pap). Schol Bk Serv.
Which Way Courage. Eiveen Weiman. LC 80-36725. 144p. (gr. 4-7). 1981. PLB 8.95 (ISBN 0-689-30835-3). Atheneum.
Which Way Is South Africa Going? Gwendolen M. Carter. LC 79-3658. 256p. 1980. 12.95 (ISBN 0-253-10874-8). Ind U Pr.
Which Way the Family? Larry Christenson. 1973. pap. 0.75 (ISBN 0-87123-643-5, 260643). Bethany Fell.
Which Way the Wind. Hans Herlin. Tr. by Richard Winston & Clara Winston. LC 78-4013. 1978. 10.00 o.p. (ISBN 0-312-86709-3). St Martin.
Which Way to Happiness. Dan Baumann. 160p. 1981. pap. price not set (ISBN 0-8307-0773-5). Regal.
Which Way to Nineveh. Ethel Barrett. LC 79-96703. (Venture Bks.). (gr. 4-8). pap. 1.95 (ISBN 0-8307-0006-4, S062100). Regal.
Which Way Western Man? William G. Simpson. LC 79-91738. 758p. 1980. pap. 7.00 (ISBN 0-937944-01-7). Natl Alliance.
Which Wine? rev. ed. Peter M. Sichel & Judy L. Allen. LC 77-71723. 1977. pap. 5.95 o.p. (ISBN 0-89104-075-7). A & W Pubs.
Whiff of Burnt Boats. Geoffrey Trease. (Autobiography). 1971. 7.95 o.p. (ISBN 0-312-86730-1). St Martin.
Whiff of Death. Isaac Asimov. 1979. pap. 1.95 (ISBN 0-449-23660-9, Crest). Fawcett.
Whig Organization in the General Election of 1790: Selections from the Blair Adam Papers. Ed. by Donald E. Ginter. 1967. 20.00x (ISBN 0-520-00477-9). U of Cal Pr.
Whig Party in the South. Arthur C. Cole. 1959. 7.50 (ISBN 0-685-24467-9). Peter Smith.
Whig Supremacy, 1714-1760. 2nd ed. Basil Williams. Ed. by C. H. Stuart. (Oxford History of England Ser.). 1962. 33.00x (ISBN 0-19-821710-2). Oxford U Pr.
While My Guitar Gently Weeps: A Novel. Paul Breeze. LC 80-22065. 222p. 1981. 9.95 (ISBN 0-8008-8247-4). Taplinger.
While Still We Live. Helen MacInnes. 448p. 1981. pap. 2.75 (ISBN 0-449-24054-1, Crest). Fawcett.
While the Horses Galloped to London. Mabel Watts. LC 72-8096. (Illus.). 48p. (gr. k-3). 1971. 5.95 o.s.i. (ISBN 0-8193-0652-5, Four Winds); PLB 5.41 o.s.i. (ISBN 0-8193-0653-3). Schol Bk Serv.
While Waiting for the Bell to Ring. Ruth Beechick. LC 79-53445. (Orig.). 1981. pap. 3.25 (ISBN 0-89636-032-6). Accent Bks.
While You Were Gone: A Report on Wartime Life in the United States. Ed. by Jack Goodman. LC 73-19969. (FDR & the Era of the New Deal Ser). 625p. 1974. Repr. of 1946 ed. lib. bdg. 49.50 (ISBN 0-306-70605-9). Da Capo.
Whiltshire: A Shell Guide. J. H. Cheetham & John Piper. (Illus.). 1968. 12.95 (ISBN 0-571-04633-9, Pub. by Faber & Faber). Merrimack Bk Serv.
Whim-Wham Book. Duncan Emrich. LC 75-9872. (Illus.). 352p. 1975. 8.95 (ISBN 0-590-07315-X, Four Winds). Schol Bk Serv.
Whimsical Christian: Eighteen Essays. Dorothy L. Sayers. 1978. 10.95 (ISBN 0-02-606930-X). Macmillan.
Whip Hand. Dick Francis. 336p. 1981. pap. 2.75 (ISBN 0-671-41903-X). PB.
Whipping Boy. Beth Holmes. 1979. pap. 2.50 (ISBN 0-515-04698-1). Jove Pubns.
Whipping Star. Frank Herbert. (Science Fiction Ser.). 1980. pap. 13.95 (ISBN 0-8398-2648-6). Gregg.
Whipple's Castle. Thomas Williams. LC 68-58852. 1969. 8.95 o.p. (ISBN 0-394-45170-8). Random.
Whips & Whipmaking: With a Practical Introduction to Braiding. D. W. Morgan. LC 72-78240. (Illus.). 1972. pap. 6.00 (ISBN 0-87033-270-8). Cornell Maritime.
Whirling Dervishes. Ira Friedlander. LC 74-30416. (Illus.). 1975. 15.00 o.s.i. (ISBN 0-02-541540-9). Macmillan.
Whirlwinds in the Plain: Ludwig Leichardt - Friends, Foes & History. E. M. Webster. 484p. 1980. 40.00x (ISBN 0-522-84181-3, Pub. by Melbourne U Pr Australia). Intl Schol Bk Serv.
Whisker of Hercules No. 103: The Man Who Was Scared No. 104. Kenneth Robeson. 208p. 1981. pap. 1.95 (ISBN 0-553-14616-5). Bantam.
Whiskers, the Bank Mouse. Claudia E. Wells. LC 77-10823. (Illus.). (gr. 1-4). 1981. pap. write for info. (ISBN 0-930506-01-4). Popcorn Pubs.
Whiskey Jim & a Kid Named Billie. W. H. Hutchinson & R. N. Mullins. 5.00 o.p. (ISBN 0-685-48822-5). Nortex Pr.
Whiskey Man. Howell Raines. 1980. pap. 2.50 (ISBN 0-449-24335-4, Crest). Fawcett.
Whisky. James Ross. (Illus.). 1970. 12.00 (ISBN 0-7100-6685-6). Routledge & Kegan.
Whisper My Name. Fern Michaels. 192p. 1981. pap. 1.50 (ISBN 0-671-57061-7). S&S.
Whisper of Darkness. Anne Mather. (Harlequin Presents Ser.). 192p. 1980. pap. 1.50 (ISBN 0-373-10376-X, Pub. by Harlequin). PB.
Whisper of the Axe. Richard Condon. Date not set. pap. 2.25 (ISBN 0-345-28296-5). Ballantine.
Whispering Mezuzah. Carol K. Hubner. (Judaica Youth Series: Devorah Doresh Mysteries). (Illus.). 1979. 5.95 (ISBN 0-910818-18-5); pap. 4.95 (ISBN 0-686-64802-1). Judaica Pr.
Whispering Range. Ernest Haycox. 231p. 1975. Repr. of 1931 ed. lib. bdg. 9.95 o.p. (ISBN 0-89190-979-6). Am Repr-Rivercity Pr.
Whisperings Within. David Barash. 288p. 1981. pap. 4.95 (ISBN 0-14-005699-8). Penguin.
Whispers. Dorothy Fletcher. 432p. (Orig.). 1980. pap. 2.50 (ISBN 0-89083-675-2). Zebra.
Whispers. Dean R. Koontz. 1981. pap. 2.95 (ISBN 0-425-04707-5). Berkley Pub.
Whispers Near Niagara. S. Santhi. 5.00 (ISBN 0-89253-731-0); flexible cloth 4.00 (ISBN 0-89253-732-9). Ind-US Inc.
Whispers of the Angel (Nawa-E-Sarosh) Mirza A. Ghalib. (Illus.). 56p. 1969. 3.00 (ISBN 0-88253-384-3). Ind-US Inc.
Whistle. James Jones. 1979. pap. 2.75 o.s.i. (ISBN 0-440-19262-5). Dell.
Whistle-Blowing! Loyalty & Dissent in the Corporation. Ed. by Alan F. Westin. LC 80-15800. 192p. 1980. 12.50 (ISBN 0-07-069483-4, P&RB). McGraw.
Whistle for Willie. Ezra J. Keats. (Illus.). (ps-1). 1964. PLB 7.95 (ISBN 0-670-76240-7). Viking Pr.
Whistle in the Graveyard: Folktales to Chill Your Bones. Maria Leach. 128p. (gr. 4-6). 1974. 7.95 (ISBN 0-670-76245-8). Viking Pr.
Whistler. rev. ed. Jean N. Dale & Williard D. Sheeler. (Reading & Excercise Ser.: No. 1). 1976. pap. 2.50 (ISBN 0-89285-050-7); cassette tapes 29.50 (ISBN 0-89285-068-X). ELS Intl.
Whistler. Ed. by Jean N. Dale & Willard D. Sheeler. (Reading & Exercise Ser.). (gr. k-6). 1973. pap. text ed. 2.50x (ISBN 0-19-433619-0). Oxford U Pr.
Whistler. Bernhard Sickert. 175p. 1980. Repr. lib. bdg. 25.00 (ISBN 0-8495-5039-4). Arden Lib.
Whistler in the Mist. Rosalie K. Fry. LC 68-29467. (Illus.). 144p. (gr. 4 up). 1968. 3.75 (ISBN 0-374-38382-0). FS&G.
Whistler Landscapes & Seascapes. Donald Holden. (Illus.). 1976. pap. 8.95 o.p. (ISBN 0-8230-5726-7). Watson-Guptill.
Whistler Peacock Room. rev. ed. Susan Hobbs. LC 80-20516. (Illus.). 1980. pap. 1.50 (ISBN 0-934686-34-3). Freer.
Whitaker's Almanac, 1981. 113th ed. (Illus.). 2000p. 1981. 32.00 (ISBN 0-8103-0947-5). Gale.
White African. L. S. Leakey. (Walden Editions). 1973. pap. 1.50 o.p. (ISBN 0-685-32481-8, 345-23566-5-150). Ballantine.
White Among the Reds. Masha Williams. 224p. 1980. 25.00x (ISBN 0-85683-044-5, Pub. by Shepheard-Walwyn England). State Mutual Bk.
White & Negro Spirituals, Their Life Span & Kinship. George P. Jackson. (Music Reprint Ser). (Illus.). xii, 349p. 1975. Repr. of 1944 ed. lib. bdg. 32.50 (ISBN 0-306-70667-9). Da Capo.
White & the Gold. Thomas B. Costain. 5.95 (ISBN 0-385-04526-3); limited edition o.p. 35.00. Doubleday.
White Archer: An Eskimo Legend. James Houston. LC 67-17154. (gr. 8-12). 1979. Repr. of 1967 ed. 2.95 (ISBN 0-15-696224-1, HJ). HarBraceJ.
White Army. Anton I. Denikin. Tr. by Catherine Zvegintzov from Rus. LC 72-97041. (Russian Ser.: Vol. 45). (Illus.). 368p. 1973. Repr. of 1930 ed. lib. bdg. 15.00 (ISBN 0-87569-052-1). Academic Intl.
White Attitudes Toward Black People. Angus Campbell. LC 74-161548. 177p. 1971. cloth 10.00 (ISBN 0-87944-007-4); pap. 6.00 (ISBN 0-87944-006-6). U of Mich Soc Res.
White Awareness: A Handbook for Anti-Racism Training. Judy H. Katz. LC 77-18610. 1978. pap. 5.95 (ISBN 0-8061-1466-5). U of Okla Pr.
White Bird. Clyde R. Bulla. LC 66-10505. (Illus.). (gr. 2-5). 1966. 7.95 (ISBN 0-690-88499-0, TYC-J). T Y Crowell.
White Buses Can Fly. Robert T. Smith. 32p. (gr. 5-12). 1973. PLB 4.95 (ISBN 0-87191-225-2). Creative Ed.
White Cells in Inflammation. Ed. by C. Gordon Van Arman. (Illus.). 160p. 1974. text ed. 19.00 (ISBN 0-398-03120-7). C C Thomas.
White Coat, Clenched Fist: The Political Education of an American Physician. Fitzhugh Mullan. 1976. 12.95 (ISBN 0-02-587910-3). Macmillan.
White Collar: American Middle Classes. C. Wright Mills. 1956. pap. 6.95 (ISBN 0-19-500677-1, GB). Oxford U Pr.
White-Collar Challenge to Nuclear Safeguards. Herbert Edelhertz & Marilyn Walsh. LC 77-15816. (Human Affairs Research Center Ser.). (Illus.). 1978. 13.95 (ISBN 0-669-02058-3). Lexington Bks.
White-Collar Crime. August Bequai. LC 77-11242. (Illus.). 1978. 16.95 (ISBN 0-669-01900-3). Lexington Bks.
White Collar Crime. Carroll. 1981. text ed. 18.95. Butterworth.
White-Collar Crime: Offenses in Business, Politics, & Professions. rev. ed. Gilbert Geis & Robert S. Meier. LC 76-27223. 1977. pap. text ed. 8.95 (ISBN 0-02-911600-7). Free Pr.
White-Collar Crime: Theory & Research. Ed. by Gilbert Geis & Ezra Stotland. LC 79-26672. (Sage Criminal Justice System Annuals: Vol. 13). (Illus.). 320p. 1980. 20.00x (ISBN 0-8039-1404-0); pap. 9.95x (ISBN 0-8039-1405-9). Sage.
White Collar Crimes. 389p. 1980. 50.00 (ISBN 0-686-28718-5, C168). ALI-ABA.
White Collar Power: A History of the ACOA. Bruce Juddery. 320p. 1981. text ed. 27.50x (ISBN 0-86861-138-7, 2519); pap. text ed. 12.50x (ISBN 0-86861-146-8, 2520). Allen Unwin.
White-Collar Proletariat: The Industrial Behaviour of British Civil Servants. Mike Kelley. 208p. (Orig.). 1980. pap. 21.75 (ISBN 0-7100-0623-3). Routledge & Kegan.
White-Collar Unionism: The Rebellious Salariat. Clive Jenkins & Barry Sherman. 1979. 20.00x (ISBN 0-7100-0216-5); pap. 8.75 (ISBN 0-7100-0237-8). Routledge & Kegan.
White Collar Workers in America Eighteen Ninety to Nineteen Forty: A Social-Political History in International Perspective. Jurgen Kocka. LC 80-40572. (Sage Studies in 20th Century History: Vol. 10). (Illus.). 1980. 25.00x (ISBN 0-8039-9844-9); pap. 12.50x (ISBN 0-8039-9845-7). Sage.
White Colors. F. D. Reeve. 1973. 7.95 o.p. (ISBN 0-374-28927-1). FS&G.
White Columns. Cynthia Van Hazinga. (Orig.). 1980. pap. 2.75 (ISBN 0-440-19419-9). Dell.
White Continent. D. C. Poyer. (Orig.). pap. 2.50 (ISBN 0-515-05479-8). Jove Pubns.
White Coverlet. Mark Halperin. 1979. 2.50 (ISBN 0-918116-14-7). Jawbone Pr.
White Dawn: A Eskimo Saga. James Houston. LC 72-134575. 1971. 8.50 o.p. (ISBN 0-15-196115-8, HJ). HarBraceJ.
White Devil. John Webster. Ed. by J. R. Mulryne. LC 68-20771. (Regents Renaissance Drama Ser). 1969. 9.95x (ISBN 0-8032-0287-3); pap. 2.95x (ISBN 0-8032-5288-9, BB 233, Bison). U of Nebr Pr.
White Dial Clock. Brian Loomes. LC 74-13515. (Illus.). 172p. 1975. 10.95 (ISBN 0-8069-8772-3). Sterling.
White Dial Clocks: The Complete Guide. Brian Loomes. (Illus.). 192p. 1981. price not set (ISBN 0-7153-8073-7). David & Charles.
White Dragon. Anne McCaffrey. Date not set. pap. 2.50 (ISBN 0-345-29525-0, Del Rey Bks). Ballantine.
White Eagles Over Serbia. Lawrence Durrell. LC 58-7779. 1958. 9.95 (ISBN 0-87599-030-4). S G Phillips.
White Earth Snowshoe Guidebook. Tom Hollatz. LC 72-89554. (Illus.). 128p. 1973. 5.00 (ISBN 0-87839-014-6); pap. 3.50 (ISBN 0-87839-010-3). North Star.
White Fang. Jack London. (gr. 7 up). 1935. 10.95 (ISBN 0-02-574750-9). Macmillan.
White Fang. Jack London. (gr. 7-12). 1972. pap. 1.50 (ISBN 0-590-03130-9, Schol Pap). Schol Bk Serv.
White Fang: Student Activity Book. Marcia Sohl & Gerald Dackerman. (Now Age Illustrated Ser.). (Illus.). (gr. 4-12). 1976. wkbk. 0.95 (ISBN 0-88301-295-2). Pendulum Pr.
White Fire. Jan MacLean. (Harlequin Romances Ser.). 192p. 1980. pap. 1.25 (ISBN 0-373-02348-0, Pub. by Harlequin). PB.
White Fires Burning. Catherine Dillon. 1977. pap. 1.95 o.p. (ISBN 0-451-08281-8, J8281, Sig). NAL.
White Front Cars of San Francisco. Charles A. Smallwood. Ed. by Jim Walker. LC 78-71892. (Special Ser.: No. 44). 1978. 35.00 (ISBN 0-916374-32-7). Interurban.
White Goddess: A Historical Grammar of Poetic Myth. rev. & enl. ed. Robert Graves. 511p. 1966. pap. 7.95 (ISBN 0-374-50493-8, N295). FS&G.
White Hell. Jake Logan. LC 76-49402. (Slocum Ser: No. 10). 1977. pap. 1.50 (ISBN 0-87216-648-1). Playboy Pbks.
White Hell. Jake Logan. LC 76-49402. (Jake Logan Ser.). 192p. (Orig.). 1981. pap. 1.95 (ISBN 0-87216-864-6). Playboy Pbks.
White Horse with Wings. Anthea Davies. (gr. 5-8). 1970. 4.95g o.s.i. (ISBN 0-02-726230-8). Macmillan.
White Hotel. D. M. Thomas. LC 80-52004. 256p. 1981. 11.95 (ISBN 0-670-76292-X). Viking Pr.
White House Mystique. Wallace Henley. 1977. pap. 1.50 (ISBN 0-89129-253-5). Jove Pubns.
White into Red: A Study of the Assimilation of White Persons Captured by Indians. J. Norman Heard. LC 72-13133. (Illus.). 1973. 10.00 (ISBN 0-8108-0581-2). Scarecrow.
White Jade Fox. Andre Norton. 1979. pap. 1.95 (ISBN 0-449-24005-3, Crest). Fawcett.
White Labyrinth: Understanding the Organization of Health Care. David B. Smith & Arnold D. Kaluzny. LC 75-7012. 250p. 1975. 23.50x (ISBN 0-8211-1854-4); text ed. 21.00x (ISBN 0-685-53678-5). McCutchan.
White Latern. Evan S. Connell. 1981. pap. 5.95 (ISBN 0-686-69130-X). HR&W.
White Leopard. Inglis Fletcher. 304p. 1976. Repr. of 1931 ed. lib. bdg. 14.95x (ISBN 0-89244-013-9). Queens Hse.
White Lie Assignment. Peter Driscoll. LC 72-688. 216p. 1975. 7.50 o.p. (ISBN 0-397-00904-6). Lippincott.
White Majority: Between Poverty & Affluence. Ed. by Louise K. Howe. 1971. pap. 1.95 o.p. (ISBN 0-394-71666-3, V666, Vin). Random.

White Man, Listen! Richard Wright. LC 78-17905. 1978. Repr. of 1957 ed. lib. bdg. 17.75x (ISBN 0-313-20533-7, WRWM). Greenwood.

White Man, Think Again. Anthony Jacob. pap. 4.00x (ISBN 0-911038-09-4). Noontide.

White Man's Burden: Historical Origins of Racism in the United States. Winthrop D. Jordan. 1974. pap. 4.95 (ISBN 0-19-501743-9, GB402, GB). Oxford U Pr.

White Man's Indian: Images of the American Indian from Columbus to the Present. Robert F. Berkhofer, Jr. LC 78-11047. (Illus.). 1979. pap. 4.95 (ISBN 0-394-72794-0, V-794, Vin). Random.

White Man's Road. Benjamin Capps. LC 78-85926. 1969. 8.95 o.s.i. (ISBN 0-06-010602-6, HarpT). Har-Row.

White Monkeys. Bin Ramke. LC 80-24582. (Contemporary Poetry Ser.). 85p. 1981. 8.50 (ISBN 0-8203-0544-8); pap. 4.50 (ISBN 0-8203-0551-0). U of Ga Pr.

White Mountains. John Christopher. (gr. 7 up). 1967. 9.95 (ISBN 0-02-718360-2). Macmillan.

White Mountains - East. Philip Preston. (Illus.). 270p. (Orig.). 1981. pap. 8.50 (ISBN 0-9603106-1-4). Waumbek.

White Mountains: Place & Perceptions. LC 80-68935. (Illus.). 200p. pap. 10.00 (ISBN 0-87451-190-9). U Pr of New Eng.

White Mutiny. Edwin Hirschmann. 1980. 24.00x (ISBN 0-8364-0639-7). South Asia Bks.

White Nights of St. Petersburg. Geoffrey Trease. LC 67-29447. (gr. 7 up). 1968. 6.95 (ISBN 0-8149-0423-8). Vanguard.

White Nights, Red Dawn. Frederick Nolan. 416p. 1980. 13.95 (ISBN 0-02-589850-7). Macmillan.

White Nights: The Story of a Prisoner in Russia. Menachem Begin. LC 78-69610. 1979. 8.95 o.s.i. (ISBN 0-06-010289-6, HarpT). Har-Row.

White Nile. Alan Moorehead. LC 78-160663. (Illus.). 1971. deluxe ed. 20.00 o.s.i. (ISBN 0-06-013049-0, HarpT). Har-Row.

White Nile Arabs: Political Leadership & Economic Change. Abbas Ahmed Mohammed. (Monographs on Social Anthropology: No. 53). 1980. text ed. 37.50x (ISBN 0-391-00969-9, Athlone Pr). Humanities.

White on Red: Images of the American Indian. Ed. by Nancy B. Black & Bette S. Weidman. 1976. 17.50 (ISBN 0-8046-9084-7, Natl U). Kennikat.

White Paper on Science Museums. Howard Learner. (Orig.). 1979. pap. 4.00 (ISBN 0-89329-095-5). Ctr Sci Public.

White Papers of Japan: Annual Abstract of Official Reports & Statistics of the Japanese Government 1978-79. Ed. by The Japan Institute of International Affairs. LC 72-620531. (Illus.). 228p. (Orig.). 1980. pap. 37.50x (ISBN 0-8002-2734-4). Intl Pubns Serv.

White Pony. Mary Oldham. (Books for Young Readers). 128p. (gr. 4-9). 1981. 7.95g (ISBN 0-8038-0800-3). Hastings.

White, Red, & Black: The Seventeenth Century Virginian. Wesley F. Craven. LC 79-163980. (Richard Lecture Ser). 1971. 9.95x (ISBN 0-8139-0372-6). U Pr of Va.

White Rising. Zane Kotker. LC 80-20011. 288p. 1981. 11.95 (ISBN 0-394-40776-8). Knopf.

White Road. Claude Esteban. Tr. by David Cloutier. LC 78-64433. 1979. 7.50 (ISBN 0-685-39466-2). Charioteer.

White Robin. Miss Read. 1980. 8.95 (ISBN 0-395-29452-5); pap. write for info. HM.

White Rose. Clare Rossiter. LC 77-12260. 1978. 7.95 o.p. (ISBN 0-312-86789-1). St Martin.

White Rose & the Black. Lorna Baxter. 147p. (gr. 3-7). 1981. 10.95 (ISBN 0-571-11413-X, Pub. by Faber & Faber). Merrimack Bk Serv.

White Sails to China. Clyde R. Bulla. LC 55-9207. (Illus.). (gr. 2-5). 1955. 8.95 (ISBN 0-690-88712-4, TYC-J); PLB 7.89 (ISBN 0-690-88713-2). T Y Crowell.

White Sands Incident. Daniel W. Fry. 120p. 1967. 3.95 o.s.i. (ISBN 0-910228-05-1). Best Bks.

White Savannahs. W. E. Collin. LC 73-92516. (Literature of Canada Ser.). 1975. pap. 5.95 (ISBN 0-8020-6241-5). U of Toronto Pr.

White Serpent: Hon-Chew Hee's Serigraph. Hon-Chew Hee. (Illus.). 60p. 1979. pap. 10.50 (ISBN 0-89955-004-5, Pub. by Art Book Co). Intl Schol Bk Serv.

White Slave Trade & the Immigrants: A Chapter in American Social History. Francesco Cordasco & Thomas M. Pitkin. LC 80-25556. 1981. write for info. (ISBN 0-87917-077-8); pap. write for info. (ISBN 0-87917-076-X). Blaine Ethridge.

White Slaves of England. J. C. Cobden. 498p. 1971. Repr. of 1860 ed. 31.00x (ISBN 0-686-28327-9, Pub. by Irish Academic Pr). Biblio Dist.

White Spaces in Shakespeare. Paul Bertram. 112p. 1981. 12.50x (ISBN 0-934958-01-7); pap. 8.00x (ISBN 0-934958-02-5). Arete Pr.

White Sparrow. Roy Brown. LC 74-19352. 192p. (gr. 6 up). 1975. 6.95 (ISBN 0-395-28897-5, Clarion). HM.

White-Tailed Deer. Anne LaBastille. Ed. by Russell Bourne & Bonnie S. Lawrence. (Ranger Rick's Best Friends Ser.: No. 1). (Illus.). (gr. 1-6). 1973. 2.50 o.p. (ISBN 0-912186-00-3). Natl Wildlife.

White Town, U.S.A. Peter Binzen. LC 70-85565. 1971. pap. 2.45 (ISBN 0-394-71077-0, V-77, Vin). Random.

White Trash: An Anthology of Contemporary Southern Poets. nd ed. Ed. by Nancy Stone & Robert W. Grey. 135p. 1981. pap. 7.50 (ISBN 0-917990-06-4). New South Co.

White Water, Still Water. J. Allan Bosworth. (gr. 5-7). pap. 1.25 (ISBN 0-671-29923-9). Archway.

White Wave: A Chinese Tale. Diane Wolkstein. LC 78-4781. (Illus.). (gr. 2 up). 1979. 6.95 (ISBN 0-690-03893-3, TYC-J); PLB 6.89 (ISBN 0-690-03894-1). T Y Crowell.

White Wealth & Black Poverty: American Investments in Southern Africa. Barbara Rogers. LC 75-35353. (Studies in Human Rights: No. 2). 288p. 1976. lib. bdg. 17.50 (ISBN 0-8371-8277-8, RWW/). Greenwood.

White Wolf. Max Brand. 1975. pap. 1.75 (ISBN 0-446-94605-2). Warner Bks.

White Workers & Black Trainees: An Outline of Some of the Issues Raised by Special Training Programs for the Disadvantaged. Joe Shedd. (Key Issues Ser.: No. 13). 1973. pap. 2.00. NY Sch Indus Rel.

Whiteboy: A Story of Ireland. Anna M. Hall. (Nineteenth Century Fiction Ser.: Ireland: Vol. 48). 634p. 1979. lib. bdg. 46.00 (ISBN 0-8240-3497-X). Garland Pub.

Whitefield's Sermon Outlines. Sheldon B. Quincer. pap. 3.95 (ISBN 0-8028-1157-4). Eerdmans.

Whitehall & the Wilderness: The Middle West in British Colonial Policy, 1760 to 1775. Jack M. Sosin. LC 80-21061. (Illus.). xi, 307p. 1981. Repr. of 1961 ed. lib. bdg. 35.00x (ISBN 0-313-22678-4, SOWW). Greenwood.

Whitehead Vs. Hartshorne: Basic Metaphysical Issues. R. J. Connelly. LC 80-69053. 172p. (Orig.). 1981. lib. bdg. 17.75 (ISBN 0-8191-1420-0); pap. text ed. 9.00 (ISBN 0-8191-1421-9). U Pr of Amer.

Whitehead's Metaphysics. Ivor Leclerc. 1978. Repr. of 1958 ed. text ed. 15.00x (ISBN 0-391-00570-7). Humanities.

Whitehead's Philosophy: Selected Essays, 1935-1970. Charles Hartshorne. LC 72-75343. (Landmark Ed.). 1972. 19.50x (ISBN 0-8032-0806-5). U of Nebr Pr.

Whitehead's View of Reality. Charles Hartshorne & Creighton Peden. 96p. (Orig.). Date not set. pap. 6.95 (ISBN 0-8298-0381-5). Pilgrim NY.

Whiteoaks of Jalna. Mazo De La Roche. (Jaina Ser.). 1977. pap. 2.25 (ISBN 0-449-23510-6, Crest). Fawcett.

Whites in Desegregated Schools. Center for Equal Education. LC 76-24186. 1976. 4.50 (ISBN 0-685-84406-4). Integrated Ed Assoc.

Whiteside Island Story-Merald Isle of St. Louis Bay. Claire W. Schumacher. LC 74-29021. 65p. 1980. 2.50 (ISBN 0-917378-04-0). Schumacher Pubns.

Whitetail Deer Hunter's Handbook. John Weiss. (Illus.). 1979. 12.95 (ISBN 0-87691-279-X). Winchester Pr.

Whitetail: Fundamentals & Fine Points for the Hunter. rev. ed. George Mattis. 290p. 1980. 15.95 (ISBN 0-442-23355-8). Van Nos Reinhold.

Whitewater. Paul Horgan. 1971. pap. 1.50 o.s.i. (ISBN 0-446-68625-5). Warner Bks.

Whitewater! Norman Strung et al. LC 75-26912. (Illus.). 256p. 1976. 14.95 o.s.i. (ISBN 0-02-615110-3, 61511). Macmillan.

Whitewater Canoeing. William O. Sandreuter. 1976. 10.95 (ISBN 0-87691-223-4). Winchester Pr.

Whitework & Cutwork. Ed. by Burda. (Burda Bks.). Date not set. 3.00x (ISBN 0-686-64667-3, B803). Toggitt.

Whitfield's University Rhyming Dictionary. Jane S. Whitfield. Ed. by Frances Stillman. (Apollo Eds.). pap. 3.95 (ISBN 0-8152-0080-3, A80, TYC-T). T Y Crowell.

Whither Civilization? Frank A. Parker. 1981. 10.00 (ISBN 0-533-04882-6). Vantage.

Whitman. Edgar L. Masters. LC 68-22695. 1968. Repr. of 1937 ed. 15.00x (ISBN 0-8196-0210-8). Biblo.

Whitman: An Interpretation in Narrative. Emory Holloway. LC 70-79953. (Illus.). 1969. Repr. of 1926 ed. 16.00x (ISBN 0-8196-0236-1). Biblo.

Whitman Massacre. Mary Saunders. 1978. 5.50 (ISBN 0-87770-188-1); pap. 2.95 (ISBN 0-685-87578-4). Ye Galleon.

Whitman's off Season Travel Guide to Europe: Europe at Its Best from September to May. John Whitman. LC 73-91600. 352p. 1975. 17.50 o.p. (ISBN 0-312-86905-3); pap. 6.95 o.p. (ISBN 0-312-86940-1). St Martin.

Whitman's Restaurant Guide to Minnesota. John Whitman. (Illus.). 1976. pap. 1.00 (ISBN 0-685-78748-6). Nodin Pr.

Whitman's Travel Guide to Minnesota. John Whitman. (Illus.). 1977. pap. 1.00 (ISBN 0-685-88678-6). Nodin Pr.

Whitney's New Glasses. Linda P. Silbert & Alvin J. Silbert. (Little Twirps, TM Understanding People Book). (Illus.). (gr. k-4). 1978. pap. 2.25 (ISBN 0-89544-052-0). Silbert Bress.

Whitsun Weddings. Philip Larkin. 46p. 1964. 8.95 (ISBN 0-571-05750-0, Pub. by Faber & Faber). Merrimack Bk Serv.

Whitsun Weddings. Philip Larkin. 46p. 1971. pap. 3.95 (ISBN 0-571-09710-3, Pub. by Faber & Faber). Merrimack Bk Serv.

Whitten-Lanier Debate. D. J. Whitten & Roy H. Lanier. pap. 4.95 (ISBN 0-89315-356-7). Lambert Bk.

Whittington's Dictionary of Plastics. 2nd rev. ed. Lloyd R. Whittington. LC 78-73776. 1978. 25.00 (ISBN 0-87762-267-1). Technomic.

Whittling & Wood Carving. H. Hoppe. LC 69-19488. (Little Craft Book Ser.). (gr. 4 up). 1969. 5.95 (ISBN 0-8069-5126-5); PLB 6.69 (ISBN 0-8069-5127-3). Sterling.

Whiz, the Elf Who Made Christmas Special. Jim Duff. (Story Book Ser.). (Illus.). (ps-5). 1980. 5.95 (ISBN 0-89305-030-X); pap. 0.89 coloring book (ISBN 0-89305-031-8). Anna Pub.

Who. G. Herman. 1972. 5.95 o.s.i. (ISBN 0-02-551180-7). Macmillan.

Who. G. Herman. 1972. pap. 1.95 o.s.i. (ISBN 0-02-060730-X, Collier). Macmillan.

Who Am I in the Lives of Children? An Introduction to Early Childhood Education. Stephanie Feeney & Doris Christensen. (Early Childhood Education Ser.). 1978. text ed. 14.95 (ISBN 0-675-08391-5); instructor's manual 3.95 (ISBN 0-685-86845-1). Merrill.

Who & What & Where in the Bible. Donald M. McFarlan. LC 74-3709. (Illus.). 216p. (Orig.). 1974. pap. 4.50 o.p. (ISBN 0-8042-0001-7). John Knox.

Who Are the Chinese Texans? Marian Martinello & William T. Field. (Young Readers Ser.). (Illus.). 81p. (Orig.). (gr. 3-6). 8.95x (ISBN 0-933164-36-X); pap. 5.95 (ISBN 0-933164-46-7). U. of Tex Inst Tex Culture.

Who Are the Handicapped? James S. Haskins. LC 76-2777. (gr. 4-7). 1978. 6.95a (ISBN 0-385-09609-7); PLB (ISBN 0-385-09610-0). Doubleday.

Who Are We & Where Are We Going: A Parish Planning Guide. William C. Harms. 96p. (Orig.). 1981. pap. 9.00 (ISBN 0-8215-9806-6). Sadlier.

Who Are You? A Teen-Ager's Guide to Self-Understanding. Elizabeth McGough. (Illus.). (gr. 7-9). 1976. 8.25 (ISBN 0-688-22091-6); PLB 7.92 (ISBN 0-688-32091-0). Morrow.

Who Are You Monsieur Gurdjieff? Rene Zuber. Tr. by Jenny Koralek. 80p. 1980. pap. 7.50 (ISBN 0-7100-0674-8). Routledge & Kegan.

Who Bears the Tax Burden? Joseph A. B. Pechman & Benjamin A. Okner. LC 74-280. (Studies of Government Finance). 120p. 1974. 9.95 (ISBN 0-8157-6968-7); pap. 3.95 (ISBN 0-8157-6967-9). Brookings.

Who Benefits from Government Expenditure? A Case Study of Columbia. Marcello Selowsky. (World Bank Research Publication Ser.). 1979. 14.95x (ISBN 0-19-520098-5); pap. 5.95x (ISBN 0-19-520099-3). Oxford U Pr.

Who Built the Bridge. Norman Bate. (Encore Edition). (Illus.). (gr. k-5). 1954. 1.49 o.p. (ISBN 0-684-15828-0, ScribT). Scribner.

Who Can Deny Love. Barbara Cartland. LC 79-28822. 1979. 6.95 (ISBN 0-87272-086-1, Duron Bks). Brodart.

Who Cares? Bernard Palmer & Marjorie Palmer. (Who Books Ser.). (Illus.). 1979. pap. 1.25 (ISBN 0-87123-713-X, 260713). Bethany Fell.

Who Cares About an Alcoholism Program in the General Hospital? American Hospital Association. 56p. 1972. pap. 6.25 (ISBN 0-87258-088-1, 1245). Am Hospital.

Who Cares? I Do. Munro Leaf. LC 74-15172. 48p. (ps-3). 1971. 7.89 (ISBN 0-397-31521-X); pap. 2.25 (ISBN 0-397-31276-8). Lippincott.

Who Comes to Your House? Margaret Hillert. (Illus.). (ps-2). 1973. PLB 4.57 o.p. (ISBN 0-307-60575-2, Golden Pr). Western Pub.

Who Controls the Controllers? A Case Study of Political Behavior. James S. Eckenrod. Ed. by Jack R. Fraenkel. (Crucial Issues in American Government Ser.). (gr. 9-12). 1976. pap. text ed. 4.96 (ISBN 0-205-04908-7, 7649088). Allyn.

Who Controls the Schools. NCCE & Carl Marburger. 1978. pap. 3.50 (ISBN 0-934460-06-X). NCCE.

Who Controls Your Child? Orley Herron. 176p. 1980. pap. 8.95 (ISBN 0-8407-5221-0). Nelson.

Who Crucified Jesus? Solomon Zeitlin. 1976. pap. 4.95 (ISBN 0-8197-0013-4). Bloch.

Who Decides What in Europe. Klaus Boehm & Brian Morris. 256p. 1981. lib. bdg. 27.50 (ISBN 0-87196-388-4). Facts on File.

Who Discriminates Against Women. Ed. by Florence Denmark. LC 74-78560. (Sage Contemporary Social Science Issues: Vol. 15). 1974. 4.95x (ISBN 0-8039-0440-1). Sage.

Who Distributes What & Where. 2nd ed. 1981. 39.00 (ISBN 0-8352-1373-0). Bowker.

Who Distributes What & Where: An International Directory of Publishers, Imprints, Agents, & Distributors. 500p. 1980. pap. 35.00 (ISBN 0-8352-1230-0). Bowker.

Who Divorces? Barbara Thornes & Jean Collard. (Orig.). 1979. pap. 14.50 (ISBN 0-685-67323-5). Routledge & Kegan.

Who Do You Think You Are, Charlie Brown: Selected Cartoons from "Peanuts Every Sunday", Vol. 1. Charles M. Schulz. (Peanuts Ser.). (Illus.). 1978. pap. 1.50 (ISBN 0-449-23948-9, Crest). Fawcett.

Who Educates Your Child? D. Bruce Lockerbie. 216p. (Orig.). 1981. pap. 5.95 (ISBN 0-310-44001-7). Zondervan.

Who Goes Home? John R. Butler. 75p. 1970. pap. text ed. 5.00x (ISBN 0-7135-1593-7, Pub. by Bedford England). Renouf.

Who Goes There. Dorothy P. Lathrop. (Illus.). (gr. 1-3). 1963. 4.95g o.s.i. (ISBN 0-02-754350-1). Macmillan.

Who Goes to Bed. Cynthia Watts. (Hello World Ser.). 1977. pap. 1.65 (ISBN 0-8163-0291-X). Pacific Pr Pub Assn.

Who Goes to School? Margaret Hillert. (Just Beginning-to-Read Ser.). 1980. PLB 4.39 (ISBN 0-695-41458-5); pap. 1.50 (ISBN 0-695-31458-0). Follett.

Who Is Bruce Simonds. Virginia Gaburo. 44p. 1978. saddle-sticed 13.95, soft cover, lP recording. Lingua Pr.

Who Is God??? God Is Love!!! Walter E. Adams. 115p. (Orig.). 1981. pap. 2.95 (ISBN 0-937408-02-6). Gospel Pubns Fl.

Who Is That? Warren B. Meyers. (Illus.). 1976. pap. 3.95 (ISBN 0-8065-0535-4). Citadel Pr.

Who Is the Client? The Ethics of Psychological Intervention in the Criminal Justice System. Ed. by John Monahan. LC 80-14101. 1980. 7.50 (ISBN 0-912704-14-4). Am Psychol.

Who Is the Greatest. Arthur W. Spalding. LC 41-11607. (Harvest Ser.). 1976. pap. 3.95 (ISBN 0-8163-0271-5, 23568-9). Pacific Pr Pub Assn.

Who Is the Next. Henry K. Webster. LC 75-46005. (Crime Fiction Ser). 1976. Repr. of 1931 ed. lib. bdg. 17.50 (ISBN 0-8240-2397-8). Garland Pub.

Who Is the Next? Henry K. Webster. LC 80-8720. 320p. 1981. pap. 2.25 (ISBN 0-06-080539-0, P/539, PL). Har-Row.

Who Is Victoria? Betty K. Erwin. (Illus.). (gr. 4-6). 1976. pap. 1.25 (ISBN 0-671-29752-X). PB.

Who Is Your Doctor & Why? Alonzo J. Shadman. LC 80-82320. 446p. 1980. pap. 3.95 (ISBN 0-87983-227-4). Keats.

Who Killed Adam? A Look at the Major Types of Fossil Man. Edward Lugenbeal. LC 78-8513. (Flame Ser.). 1978. pap. 0.95 (ISBN 0-8127-0186-0). Southern Pub.

Who Killed Daddy? Woolfolk. (gr. 7-12). 1980. pap. 1.25 (ISBN 0-590-30032-6, Schol Pap). Schol Bk Serv.

Who Killed George Jackson? Fantasies, Paranoia, & the Revolution. Jo Durden-Smith. 1976. 10.00 o.p. (ISBN 0-394-48291-3). Knopf.

Who Killed Harlowe Thrombey, No. 9. Edward Packard. (Choose Your Own Adventure Ser.). 128p. (Orig.). (gr. 3-8). 1981. pap. 1.50 (ISBN 0-553-14357-3). Bantam.

Who Killed Robert Prentice? Dennis Wheatley & Jay Links. 117p. 1980. 17.95 (ISBN 0-686-64567-7). Mayflower Bks.

Who Knows Ten: Children's Tales of the Ten Commandments. Molly Cone. LC 65-24639. (Illus.). (gr. 3-5). 1968. text ed. 5.00 (ISBN 0-8074-0080-7, 102551); record 5.95 (ISBN 0-8074-0081-5, 102552). UAHC.

Who Knows the Little Man? Walburga Attenberger. (Illus.). (ps-1). 1972. PLB 3.39 o.p. (ISBN 0-394-92427-4). Random.

Who Likes the Sun. Beatrice S. De Regniers & Leona Pierce. LC 61-6112. (Illus.). (gr. k-2). 1961. 3.95 o.p. (ISBN 0-15-296065-1, HJ). HarBraceJ.

Who Lives Here? Pat Witte & Eve Witte. (Golden Touch & Feel Bk). (Illus.). 1961. 3.95 (ISBN 0-307-12147-X, Golden Pr). Western Pub.

Who Lives in the Zoo? Illus. by Jan Palmer. (Golden Storytime Bks.). (Illus.). 24p. (ps). 1981. 1.95 (ISBN 0-307-11958-0, Golden Pr); PLB 1.56 (ISBN 0-686-69208-X). Western Pub.

Who Lives on the Farm? (Illus.). (ps). 1980. 1.50 (ISBN 0-307-11985-8, Golden Pr); PLB 6.08 (ISBN 0-307-61985-0). Western Pub.

Who Loves? Bernard Palmer & Marjorie Palmer. (Who Books Ser.). (Illus.). 1979. pap. 1.25 (ISBN 0-87123-711-3, 260711). Bethany Fell.

Who Made. Bernard Palmer & Marjorie Palmer. (Who Books Ser.). (Illus.). 1979. pap. 1.25 (ISBN 0-87123-714-8, 260714). Bethany Fell.
Who Makes Machinery Nineteen Seventy-Eight (West Germany) 40th ed. Ed. by Hoppenstedt Wirtschaftsverlag. 1978. pap. 15.00x o.p. (ISBN 3-87362-001-4). Intl Pubns Serv.
Who Makes Machinery? West Germany 1980. 42nd ed. LC 53-30391. 844p. (Orig.). pap. 15.00x (ISBN 3-87362-010-3). Intl Pubns Serv.
Who Might Have Said What. Paul T. Manchester. 1981. 4.75 (ISBN 0-8062-1575-5). Carlton.
Who Named the Daisy? Who Named the Rose? Mary Durant. LC 76-22513. (Illus.). 1977. 7.95 (ISBN 0-396-07332-8). Dodd.
Who Needs the Family? O. R. Johnston. LC 80-7780. 152p. (Orig.). 1980. pap. 5.95 (ISBN 0-87784-588-3). Inter-Varsity.
Who Offers Part-Time Degree Programs? A National Survey of Postsecondary Institutions Offering Daytime, Evening, Weekend, Summer & External Degree Programs-1981 Edition. Ed. by Peterson's Guides Editors. 250p. 1981. pap. 6.00 (ISBN 0-87866-121-2). Petersons Guid.
Who Owns a River? Wendy W. Adamson. LC 76-53011. (Story of Environmental Action Ser.). (Illus.). (gr. 7 up). 1977. PLB 7.95 (ISBN 0-87518-140-6). Dillon.
Who Owns the Media? Concentration of Ownership in the Mass Communications Industry. Ed. by Benjamin M. Compaine. LC 79-15891. (Communications Library). 1979. 24.95x (ISBN 0-914236-36-9). Knowledge Indus.
Who Owns the Unicorn. Katherine Lucas & Louse Lucas. (Illus., Orig.). (gr. 4-12). 1980. pap. text ed. 3.95 (ISBN 0-914634-69-0, 7918). DOK Pubs.
Who Owns the Wildlife? The Political Economy of Conservation in Nineteenth Century America. James Tober. LC 80-23482. (Contributions in Economics & Economic History Ser.: No. 37). (Illus.). 300p. 1981. lib. bdg. 29.95 (ISBN 0-313-22597-4, TOW/). Greenwood.
Who Owns Whom: Australasia & Far East 1979-1980. 9th ed. LC 72-62467. 1190p. 1979. 175.00x (ISBN 0-8002-2415-9). Intl Pubns Serv.
Who Owns Whom: Australasia & the Far East 1978-79. 8th ed. LC 72-624679. 1979. 115.00x o.p. (ISBN 0-8002-2199-0). Intl Pubns Serv.
Who Owns Whom: Continental Europe 1979, 2 vols. 18th ed. LC 63-24027. 1979. Set. 162.50x o.p. (ISBN 0-8002-2196-6). Intl Pubns Serv.
Who Owns Whom: Continental Europe 1980, 2 vols. 19th ed. LC 63-24027. 2518p. 1980. 190.00x (ISBN 0-8002-2416-7). Intl Pubns Serv.
Who Owns Whom: North America 1979-1980. 11th ed. LC 74-646353. 1979. 310.00x o.p. (ISBN 0-8002-2197-4). Intl Pubns Serv.
Who Owns Whom: North America, 1980-81. 12th ed. LC 74-646353. 1100p. 1980. 225.00x (ISBN 0-8002-2417-5). Intl Pubns Serv.
Who Owns Whom: United Kingdom & Republic of Ireland 1980-1981, 2 vols. 23rd ed. LC 59-52911. 2200p. 1980. 190.00x (ISBN 0-8002-2418-3). Intl Pubns Serv.
Who Owns Whom: United Kingdom & Republic of Ireland 1979-80, 2 vols. 22nd ed. LC 59-52911. 1979. Set. 162.50x o.p. (ISBN 0-8002-2198-2). Intl Pubns Serv.
Who Owns Whom: United Kingdom & the Republic of Ireland 1980-81, 2 vols. 23rd ed. LC 59-52911. 2200p. 1980. 190.00x (ISBN 0-8002-2418-3). Intl Pubns Serv.
Who Pays for Clean Water? Elizabeth Lake et al. (Westview Replica Edition Ser.). (An Urban systems research report). 1979. lib. bdg. 24.00x (ISBN 0-89158-586-9). Westview.
Who Pays the Property Tax? A New View. Henry J. Aaron. (Studies of Government Finance). 1975. 9.95 (ISBN 0-8157-0022-9); pap. 3.95 (ISBN 0-8157-0021-0). Brookings.
Who Played Who in the Movies. Roy Pickard. LC 80-26546. 304p. 1981. 14.95 (ISBN 0-8052-3766-6); pap. 5.95 (ISBN 0-8052-0676-0). Schocken.
Who Rules the Police? Ed. by Leonard Ruchelman. LC 72-96430. 288p. 1973. 15.00x (ISBN 0-8147-7354-0). NYU Pr.
Who Rules the Universities? An Essay in Class Analysis. David M. Smith. LC 73-90075. 224p. 1974. 7.95 o.p. (ISBN 0-85345-320-9, CL-3209). Monthly Rev.
Who Rules Your Life? Prentice A. Meador, Jr. LC 79-64089. (Journey Bks.). 1979. pap. 2.60 (ISBN 0-8344-0107-X). Sweet.
Who Runs the Computer? Strategies for the Management of Computers in Higher Education. Martin D. Robbins et al. LC 75-19416. 102p. 1975. 19.75x (ISBN 0-89158-000-X). Westview.
Who Says? Ed. by Fritz Ridenour et al. LC 68-16268. (Illus., Orig.). (YA) 1968. pap. 1.85 o.p. (ISBN 0-8307-0002-1, S123118). Regal.
Who Says? A Black Perspective on the Authority of New Testament Exegesis Highlighting the Foundation for Its Interpretations & Applications. Walter A. McCray. Ed. by William H. Bentley. 75p. (Orig.). 1981. pap. 3.00 (ISBN 0-933176-35-X). Black Light Fellow.
Who Says So? Paula Hendrich. LC 73-177318. (Illus.). 128p. (gr. 4 up). 1972. PLB 6.96 o.p. (ISBN 0-688-51481-2). Lothrop.
Who Shall Be the Sun?: Poems Based on the Lore, Legends, & Myths of Northwest Coast & Plateau Indians. David Wagoner. LC 78-1836. (Illus.). 144p. 1978. 9.95x (ISBN 0-253-36527-9). Ind U Pr.
Who Shaped Our Time. Lynn Gilbert & Gaylen Moore. Ed. by Carol Southern. 1981. 17.95 (ISBN 0-517-54371-0). Potter.
Who Should Play God ? Jeremy Rifkin & Ted Howard. 1977. pap. 2.25 o.s.i. (ISBN 0-440-19504-7). Dell.
Who Should Play God? Jeremy Rifkin & Ted Howard. 1977. 8.95 o.p. (ISBN 0-440-09552-2). Delacorte.
Who Should Support Children? Citizen Monitoring of New York City's Parent Locator & Support Program. 1977. 3.00 (ISBN 0-86671-038-8). Comm Coun Great NY.
Who Should Survive the Purge in American Education & Why. Daniel T. Grant. (Illus.). 1978. 7.50 o.p. (ISBN 0-682-48659-0). Exposition.
Who Slept There? Louise Harle. 1979. 9.75 o.p. (ISBN 0-8062-1165-2). Carlton.
Who Speaks for Earth? Ed. by Maurice Strong. 160p. 1973. 6.95 (ISBN 0-393-06392-5); pap. 2.95x (ISBN 0-393-09341-7). Norton.
Who Speaks for the Child? Ed. by Norman E. Silberberg & Margaret C. Silberberg. (Illus.). 226p. 1974. 16.75 (ISBN 0-398-03014-6); pap. 12.50 (ISBN 0-398-03015-4). C C Thomas.
Who Stole Kathy Young? Margaret G. Clark. LC 80-1013. (gr. 5 up). 1980. 6.95g (ISBN 0-396-07888-5). Dodd.
Who Supplies What? 1652p. 1978. 42.50x o.p. (ISBN 0-8002-1302-5). Intl Pubns Serv.
Who Taught Me. Florence P. Heide. (Concept Ser. II). (Illus.). (gr. 1-4). 1978. pap. 3.50 (ISBN 0-570-07786-9, 56-1309). Concordia.
Who Tells? Bernard Palmer & Marjorie Palmer. (Who Books Ser.). (Illus.). 1979. pap. 1.25 (ISBN 0-87123-712-1, 260712). Bethany Fell.
Who Tempers the Wind. Mary E. Osborn. LC 63-117821. 115p. 1963. pap. 2.75 (ISBN 0-8040-0320-3). Swallow.
Who Then Is Paul? Hubert R. Johnson. Ed. by Chevy Chase Manuscripts. LC 80-1406. 272p. 1981. lib. bdg. 19.75 (ISBN 0-8191-1364-6); pap. text ed. 10.75 (ISBN 0-8191-1365-4). U Pr of Amer.
Who Threw That Pie? The Birth of Movie Comedy. Robert Quackenbush. Ed. by Kathy Pacini. LC 78-27047. (Illus.). (gr. 3 up). 1979. 6.50g (ISBN 0-8075-9058-4). A Whitman.
Who Took the Farmer's Hat? Joan L. Nodset & Fritz Siebel. (gr. k-3). 1970. pap. 1.50 (ISBN 0-590-02950-9, Schol Pap). Schol Bk Serv.
Who Took the Top Hat Trick. Joan Bowden. (Eager Readers Ser.). (Illus.). (gr. k-3). 1975. PLB 5.00 (ISBN 0-307-60805-0, Golden Pr). Western Pub.
Who Walks the Attic. Laura Bannon. LC 62-20174. (Pilot Book Ser). (Illus.). (gr. 3-5). 1967. 6.95g (ISBN 0-8075-9064-9). A Whitman.
Who Wants to Cook? Mary Philip. 1977. pap. text ed. 4.95x o.p. (ISBN 0-435-42650-8). Heinemann Ed.
Who Was That Masked Man? The Story of the Lone Ranger. rev. ed. David Rothel. LC 80-27237. (Illus.). 290p. 1981. 19.90 (ISBN 0-498-02538-1). A S Barnes.
Who Was That Masked Woman? Noretta Koertge. 266p. 1981. 11.95 (ISBN 0-312-87032-9). St Martin.
Who Was When? 3rd ed. Ed. by Miriam A. De Ford & Joan S. Jackson. 1976. 30.00 (ISBN 0-8242-0532-4). Wilson.
Who Was Who Among English & European Authors, 1931-1949, 3 vols. LC 77-280. (Gale Composite Biographical Dictionary Ser.: No. 2). Orig. Title: Writers & Author's Who's Who, Who's Who Among Living Authors of Older Nations. 1978. 125.00 set (ISBN 0-8103-0400-7). Gale.
Who Was Who Among North American Authors: A Composite Bio-Bibliography of Authors, Poets & Journalists Active in the Period 1921-39, Based on Entries Which Originally Appeared in "Who's Who Among North American Authors", As Originally Compiled by Alberta Lawrence, 2 vols. LC 76-23545. (Gale Composite Biographical Dictionary Ser.: No. 1). 1976. Set. 78.00 (ISBN 0-8103-1041-4). Gale.
Who Was Who in Journalism, Nineteen Twenty-Five-Nineteen Twenty-Eight. LC 78-13580. (Composite Biographical Dictionary Ser.: No. 4). 1978. 62.00 (ISBN 0-8103-0401-5). Gale.
Who Was Who in the Roman World. Ed. by Diana Bowder. LC 80-67821. (Illus.). 256p. 1980. 25.00 (ISBN 0-8014-1358-3). Cornell U Pr.
Who Was Who in the Theatre: Nineteen Twelve-Nineteen Seventy-Six, 4 vols. Incl. Vol. 1-4. Biographical Dictionary of Actors, Actresses, Directors, Playwrights, & Producers of the English Speaking Theatre. LC 78-9634. (Composite Biographical Dictionary Ser.: No. 3). 1978. 210.00 set (ISBN 0-8103-0406-6). Gale.
Who Was Who in the U. S. S. R. A Biographic Directory Containing Five Thousand & Fifteen Biographies of Prominent Soviet Historical Personalities. Institute for the Study of the U. S. S. R. Ed. by Heinrich E. Schulz et al. LC 70-161563. 1972. 50.00 (ISBN 0-8108-0441-7). Scarecrow.
Who Was Who in World War II. John Keegan. LC 77-95149. (Illus.). 1978. 14.95 o.p. (ISBN 0-690-01753-7, TYC-T). T Y Crowell.
Who Were the Fascists? Social Roots of European Fascism. Ed. by Stein U. Larsen. 800p. 1981. 44.00x (ISBN 8-20005-331-8). Universitet.
Who? What? Where? Bible Quizzes. Max Stilson. (Quiz & Puzzle Bks.). 96p. 1980. pap. 1.95 (ISBN 0-8010-8012-6). Baker Bk.
Who Will Raise the Children? New Options for Fathers (Mothers) James Levine. LC 76-18743. 1976. 8.95 o.p. (ISBN 0-397-01120-2). Lippincott.
Who Would Want to Kill Hallie Panky's Cat? new ed. Gary Majors. 160p. 1980. 6.95 (ISBN 0-8038-8094-4). Hastings.
Who Would You Like to Be. Ron Hosen. 200p. (Orig.). 1980. pap. 4.95 (ISBN 0-89260-195-7). Hwong Pub.
Who Writes What: Nineteen Eighty-One Edition. Ed. by Price Gaines. LC 76-6787. 498p. 1980. pap. 10.50 (ISBN 0-87218-013-1). Natl Underwriter.
Who Wrote It. William A. Wheeler. LC 68-30667. 1968. Repr. of 1881 ed. 15.00 (ISBN 0-8103-3228-0). Gale.
Whoa! I Yelled Whoa! Loren L. Fenton. LC 78-50460. (Destiny Ser.). 1979. pap. 4.95 (ISBN 0-8163-0249-9). Pacific Pr Pub Assn.
Who'd Hire John Brett. John Brett. 176p. 1981. 9.95 (ISBN 0-312-87038-8). St Martin.
Whodunits, Farces, & Fantasies: Ten Short Plays. Robert F. Boynton & Maynard Mack. (Literature Ser.). 192p. 1976. pap. 5.95x (ISBN 0-8104-5503-X). Hayden.
Whole Air Weather Guide. Walter F. Dabberdt. (Illus.). 1976. pap. 3.50 (Pub. by Solstice). Aviation.
Whole Armor & the Secret Ladder. Wilson Harris. 1973. pap. 5.95 (ISBN 0-571-10231-X, Pub. by Faber & Faber). Merrimack Bk Serv.
Whole Bath Catalog. Consumer Guide Editors. 1979. 14.95 (ISBN 0-671-25200-3, Fireside); pap. 7.95 (ISBN 0-671-24768-9). S&S.
Whole Body Tone-up Book. Valerie Hockert. LC 80-53499. (Orig.). 1980. pap. 5.95 (ISBN 0-935698-01-9). Tasa Pub Co.
Whole Child: A Sourcebook. Stevanne Auerbach. (Illus.). 320p. 1981. 17.95 (ISBN 0-399-12364-4). Putnam.
Whole Child: New Trends in Early Education. 2nd ed. Hendrick. LC 79-9135. 1980. 18.95 (ISBN 0-8016-2145-3). Mosby.
Whole Comical Works of Monsr. Scarron, Part One. Paul Scarron. LC 78-170503. (Foundations of the Novel Ser.: Vol. 2). lib. bdg. 50.00 (ISBN 0-8240-0514-7). Garland Pub.
Whole Comical Works of Monsr. Scarron, Parts Two & Three. Paul Scarron. LC 78-170503. (Foundations of the Novel Ser.: Vol. 3). lib. bdg. 50.00 (ISBN 0-8240-0515-5). Garland Pub.
Whole Craft of Spinning from the Raw Material to the Finished Yarn. Carol Kroll. 1980. pap. 1.75 (ISBN 0-486-23968-3). Dover.
Whole Days in the Trees. Marguerite Duras. Tr. by Anita Barrows. 1981. 10.95 (ISBN 0-7145-3820-5); pap. 5.95 (ISBN 0-7145-3854-X). Riverrun NY.
Whole Earth Catalog. 16th ed. 75. pap. 8.00 o.p. (ISBN 0-14-003544-3). Penguin.
Whole Earth Cooking for the Eighties. Sharon Cadwallader. (Illus.). 128p. 1981. 9.95 (ISBN 0-312-87050-7); pap. 5.95 (ISBN 0-312-87051-5). St Martin.
Whole Garden Catalog. Marliss Johnston. (Illus.). 1980. lib. bdg. 17.50 (ISBN 0-933474-13-X, Gabriel Bks); pap. 12.95 (ISBN 0-933474-17-2, Gabriel Bks). Minn Scholarly.
Whole Hiker's Handbook. Ed. by William Kemsley. LC 79-88627. (Illus.). 1979. 12.95 (ISBN 0-688-03476-4, Quill); pap. 9.95 (ISBN 0-688-08476-1). Morrow.
Whole Home Electronics Catalog. LC 9-21581. (Illus.). 1979. 12.95 o.p. (ISBN 0-8092-7093-5); pap. 6.95 o.p. (ISBN 0-8092-7092-7). Contemp Bks.
Whole Internist Catalog: A Compendium of Clues to Diagnosis & Management. Arlan J. Gottlieb et al. LC 79-66034. (Illus.). 509p. 1980. pap. text ed. 19.50 (ISBN 0-7216-4179-2). Saunders.
Whole Language, Language. Kenneth Gaburo. (Illus.). 41p. 1981. softcover 9.75. Lingua Pr.
Whole Lay Ministry Catalog. Barbara Kuhn. (Orig.). 1979. pap. 8.95 (ISBN 0-8164-2187-0). Crossroad NY.
Whole Loaf: Stories from Israel. Ed. by Sholem J. Kahn. 1962. 7.95 o.s.i. (ISBN 0-8149-0559-5). Vanguard.
Whole Lotta Shakin' Goin' on: Jerry Lee Lewis. Robert Cain. (Illus.). 1981. pap. 9.95. Dial.
Whole New Ball Game. Steve Sloan. LC 75-24737. (Illus.). 168p. 1975. 5.95 (ISBN 0-8054-5559-0). Broadman.
Whole Numbers. P. Driscoll et al. Ed. by K. West & D. Johnston. (Math Skills for Daily Living Ser.). (Illus.). 32p. (gr. 7-12). 1979. pap. text ed. 3.95x (ISBN 0-87453-091-1, 82091). Denoyer.
Whole Person Health Care. rev. ed. Mark Tager & Charles Jennings. LC 78-10103. (Illus.). 1979. pap. 9.95 o.p. (ISBN 0-918480-08-6). Victoria Hse.
Whole School Book: Teaching & Learning Late in the Twentieth Century. Robert E. Samples et al. 1977. pap. text ed. 8.95 (ISBN 0-201-06699-8). A-W.
Whole Truth. pap. 1.00 (ISBN 0-686-00183-4). McNally.
Whole Wheat Harvest-Recipes for Unground Wheat. Michael Collings & Judith Collings. pap. 2.95 (ISBN 0-89036-143-6). Hawkes Pub Inc.
Whole World Cookbook. Killeen. 1979. text ed. 15.95 (ISBN 0-87002-913-4). Bennett IL.
Whole World Handbook: A Guide to Study, Travel, & Work Abroad. Council on International Educational Exchange. 352p. 1981. pap. 5.95 (ISBN 0-525-93171-6). Dutton.
Whole World in His Hands: A Pictoral Biography of Paul Robeson. Susan Robeson. (Illus.). 256p. 1981. 17.95 (ISBN 0-8065-0754-3). Citadel Pr.
Whole World Is Watching: Mass Media in the Making & Unmaking of the New Left. Todd Gitlin. 1980. 12.95 (ISBN 0-520-03889-4). U of Cal Pr.
Whole World Oil Directory, 2 vols. 920p. 1979. 60.00 set (ISBN 0-686-62484-X). B Klein Pubns.
Wholefood Cookery Book. Ursula M. Cavanagh. (Orig.). 1971. 10.95 (ISBN 0-571-08871-6, Pub. by Faber & Faber); pap. 6.50 (ISBN 0-571-10617-X). Merrimack Bk Serv.
Wholeness from God. (Aglow Bible Study Bk. E-1). 64p. 1.95 (ISBN 0-930756-45-2, 4220-E1). Women's Aglow.
Wholesaling. 3rd ed. Theodore N. Beckman et al. (Illus.). (gr. 9-12). 1959. text ed. 22.50 (ISBN 0-471-06585-4, Pub. by Ronald Pr). Wiley.
Wholistic Health: A Whole Person Approach to Primary Health Care. Donald A. Tubesing. LC 78-3466. 1978. 19.95 (ISBN 0-87705-370-7). Human Sci Pr.
Wholley Man. Bernard Gunther et al. (Essence Books Ser.). (Illus.). (YA) 1973. pap. 0.50 o.s.i. (ISBN 0-02-080230-7, Collier). Macmillan.
Wholly for God. William Law. Ed. by Andrew Murray. LC 76-6622. 336p. 1976. pap. 3.50 (ISBN 0-87123-602-8, 200602). Bethany Fell.
Wholly Living. John A. Huffman, Jr. 132p. 1981. pap. 3.95 (ISBN 0-89693-005-X). Victor Bks.
Whom God Hath Joined. Rubel Shelly. 3.50 (ISBN 0-89315-354-0). Lambert Bk.
Whom We Shall Welcome. President's Commission On Immigration & Naturalization. LC 73-146270. (Civil Liberties in American History Ser.). 1971. Repr. of 1953 ed. lib. bdg. 35.00 (ISBN 0-306-70145-6). Da Capo.
Whoop-up Country: The Canadian-American West, 1865-1885. Paul F. Sharp. LC 73-3166. (Illus.). 368p. 1978. pap. 7.95 (ISBN 0-8061-1484-3). U of Okla Pr.
Whoppers: Tall Tales & Other Lies. Alvin Schwartz. LC 74-32024. (gr. 4-7). 1975. 8.95 (ISBN 0-397-31575-9); pap. 2.95 (ISBN 0-397-31612-7). Lippincott.
Whores Before Descartes: Assorted Poetry & Sordid Prose. Stuart L. Burns. LC 80-54381. 96p. (Orig.). 1980. pap. 4.50 (ISBN 0-9605326-0-9). Wash Launderan.
Whores Rhetorick, Calculated to the Meridian of London, & Conformed to the Rules of Art. LC 79-17643. 1979. 27.00 (ISBN 0-8201-1338-7). Schol Facsimiles.
Who's a Silly Egg? Bob Reese. Ed. by Alton Jordan. (Buppet Series). (Illus.). (gr. k-3). 1981. PLB 4.50 (ISBN 0-89868-092-1, Read Res); pap. text ed. 1.95 (ISBN 0-89868-103-0). ARO Pub.
Who's Afraid? Bernice Rabe. LC 79-23289. (Illus.). (gr. 7 up). 1980. PLB 7.95 (ISBN 0-525-42708-2, Skinny Book); pap. 2.50 (ISBN 0-525-45051-3, Skinny Book). Dutton.

Who's Afraid of Elizabeth Taylor. Brenda Maddox. 1978. pap. 1.95 o.s.i. (ISBN 0-515-04583-7). Jove Pubns.
Who's Afraid of the Dark? Muriel Stanek. Ed. by Kathleen Tucker. LC 80-19074. (Concept Bks.). (Illus.). 32p. (gr. 1-3). 1980. 6.50g (ISBN 0-8075-9011-8). A Whitman.
Who's Calling My Name. Jerreal Buchanan. LC 76-58063. 1977. pap. 3.50 (ISBN 0-8054-5418-7). Broadman.
Who's Cooking What in Illinois. Ed. by Who's Cooking What Editors. 1978. 10.00 o.p. (ISBN 0-533-03440-X). Vantage.
Who's Hu? Lensey Namioka. LC 80-20062. 124p. (gr. 4 up). 1981. 8.95 (ISBN 0-8149-0843-8). Vanguard.
Who's New at the Zoo. Bob Reese. Ed. by Dan Wasserman. (Ten Word Bks.). (Illus.). (gr. k-1). 1979. PLB 4.50 (ISBN 0-89868-074-3); pap. 1.95 (ISBN 0-89868-085-9). Aro Pub.
Who's New Wave in Music, 1976 to 1980: A Catalog & Directory. Compiled by David Bianco. LC 80-21534. 300p. (Orig.). 1981. pap. 5.50 (ISBN 0-938136-00-3). Lunchroom Pr.
Who's on First. William Buckley, Jr. 288p. 1981. pap. 2.75 (ISBN 0-380-52555-0, 52555). Avon.
Who's on Time? Donald J. Lehnus. LC 79-17330. 177p. 1980. lib. bdg. 17.50 (ISBN 0-379-20684-6). Oceana.
Who's Poisoning America: Corporate Polluters & Their Victims in the Chemical Age. Ed. by Ralph Nader et al. 320p. 1981. 12.95 (ISBN 0-87156-276-6). Sierra.
Who's Running Your Life: A Look at Young People's Rights. Jules Archer. (Illus.). (gr. 7 up). 1979. PLB 7.95 (ISBN 0-15-296058-9, HJ). HarBraceJ.
Who's That Pushy Bitch? Java Harris. 1981. 6.50. Jungle Garden.
Who's There. Norman Borisoff. LC 72-75123. (Mystery & Adventure Ser.). (gr. 2-4). 1973. PLB 6.75 (ISBN 0-87191-098-5). Creative Ed.
Who's What in Canadian Who's Who. 15th ed. Ed. by Kieran Simpson. 1980. pap. 15.00 (ISBN 0-8020-4584-7). U of Toronto Pr.
Who's Who Among Black Americans, 1980-1981. 3rd ed. Ed. by William C. Matney. LC 76-643293. 1981. 49.95 (ISBN 0-915130-33-5). Who's Who Black Am.
Who's Who Among Black Americans 1980-81. 3rd ed. (Published once every 3 yrs.). 1980. 49.95 (ISBN 0-915130-33-5). Educ Comm.
Who's Who Among Living Authors of Older Nations. LC 28-28492. 1966. Repr. of 1931 ed. 28.00 (ISBN 0-8103-3022-9). Gale.
Who's Who in America 1974-75, 2 vols. 38th ed. LC 4-16934. 1974. 69.50 set (ISBN 0-8379-0138-3). Marquis.
Who's Who in America 1976-77, 2 vols. 39th ed. LC 4-16934. 3424p. 1976. Set. 72.50 (ISBN 0-8379-0139-1). Marquis.
Who's Who in America: 1978-79, 2 vols. 40th ed. LC 4-16934. 1978. 79.50 (ISBN 0-8379-0140-5). Marquis.
Who's Who in Art. 19th ed. LC 27-104051. 1979. 48.00x (ISBN 0-900083-07-7). Intl Pubns Serv.
Who's Who in Art. 19th ed. (Illus.). 1980. 55.00 (ISBN 0-8103-0932-7). Gale.
Who's Who in Canada 1980-81. 70th ed. Ed. by Herbert E. Barnett & Hugh Fraser. (Illus.). 1496p. 1980. 75.00x (ISBN 0-8002-2744-1). Intl Pubns Serv.
Who's Who in Chiropractic, International 1976-78. Ed. by Fern L. Dzaman et al. LC 77-79754. (Illus.). 1977. 49.50 (ISBN 0-918336-01-5); (ISBN 0-685-93606-6). Chiropractic.
Who's Who in Computer Education & Research: International Edition. Ed. by T. C. Hsiao. LC 75-16506. 300p. cancelled (ISBN 0-686-11153-2). Sci & Tech Pr.
Who's Who in Consulting: A Reference Guide to Professional Personnel Engaged in Consultation for Business, Industry & Government. 2nd ed. Ed. by Paul Wasserman & Janice McLean. LC 73-16373. 1973. 90.00 (ISBN 0-8103-0360-4). Gale.
Who's Who in Continuing Education. Compiled by Clene, Inc. 304p. 1979. 40.00 (ISBN 0-89664-024-8, Pub. by K G Saur). Gale.
Who's Who in Dickens. Thomas A. Fyfe. LC 73-142011. 1971. Repr. of 1912 ed. 24.00 (ISBN 0-8103-3630-8). Gale.
Who's Who in Dickens. Thomas A. Fyfe. 352p. Repr. of 1913 ed. lib. bdg. 30.00 (ISBN 0-8495-1713-3). Arden Lib.
Who's Who in Education. 926p. 1981. 28.50x (ISBN 0-686-15410-X, Pub by Intl Biog). Biblio Dist.
Who's Who in Electronics. rev. ed. Ed. by Jeanne Ring. (Annual). 1981. 62.95 (ISBN 0-916512-66-5). Harris Pub.
Who's Who in Engineering. Engineers Joint Council Editors. 1976. 50.00 o.p. (ISBN 0-685-41717-4, 107-76). AAES.
Who's Who in Engineering. 3rd ed. 605p. 50.00 o.p. (ISBN 0-686-27573-X, 107-77). AAES.
Who's Who in Engineering. 4th ed. 1980. 75.00 (ISBN 0-686-63168-4, 107-80). AAES.
Who's Who in Europe 1980-81. 4th ed. LC 65-73851. 3500p. 1980. 190.00 (ISBN 2-87061-001-7). Intl Pubns Serv.
Who's Who in Fashion. Ann Stegemayer. (Illus.). 1980. text ed. 13.50 (ISBN 0-87005-257-8). Fairchild.
Who's Who in Fiction: A Dictionary of Noted Names in Novels, Tales, Romances, Poetry & Drama. Ed. by Helena Swan. LC 73-167218. 1975. Repr. of 1906 ed. 24.00 (ISBN 0-8103-4114-X). Gale.
Who's Who in Germany, 2 vols. 7th ed. Ed. by Otto J. Groeg. (Who's Who Ser.). 1600p. 1980. 147.00x (ISBN 3-921220-28-9, Pub. by Who's Who Germany). Standing Orders.
Who's Who in Germany, 1980, 2 vols. 7th ed. Ed. by Otto J. Groeg. LC 56-3621. 1500p. 1980. Set. 175.00 (ISBN 3-921220-28-9). Intl Pubns Serv.
Who's Who in Government 1975-76. 2nd ed. LC 72-623344. 772p. 1975. 52.50 (ISBN 0-8379-1202-4). Marquis.
Who's Who in H. G. Wells. Brian Ash. 1979. 22.50 (ISBN 0-241-89597-9, Pub. by Hamish Hamilton). David & Charles.
Who's Who in Health Care. Ed. by Andrew A. Hyman & Elliot A. Sainer. LC 77-79993. 1977. text ed. 60.00 (ISBN 0-89443-074-2). Aspen Systems.
Who's Who in Lebanon 1980-1981. 821p. 1980. 60.00 (ISBN 2-903188-01-7, PUB5, Publitec). Unipub.
Who's Who in Malaysia & Singapore 1979-80. 13th ed. Ed. by J. Victor Morais. (Illus.). 761p. 1980. 60.00x (ISBN 0-8002-2469-8). Intl Pubns Serv.
Who's Who in Malaysia: 1978-79. 12th ed. Ed. by Victor J. Morais. LC 72-940164. (Illus.). 1978. 50.00x o.p. (ISBN 0-8002-0411-5). Intl Pubns Serv.
Who's Who in Military History. John Keegan & Andrew Wheatcroft. LC 76-13284. 1976. 25.00 o.p. (ISBN 0-688-02956-6). Morrow.
Who's Who in Powder Metallurgy 1979. rev. ed. LC 77-14732. 1978. pap. 25.00 o.p. (ISBN 0-918404-45-2). Am Powder Metal.
Who's Who in Public Relations. 5th ed. LC 62-4348. 1976. 35.00 (ISBN 0-914016-25-3). P R Pub Co.
Who's Who in Religion 1975-76. 1st ed. LC 75-21777. 616p. 1975. 52.50 (ISBN 0-8379-1601-1). Marquis.
Who's Who in Science Fiction. Brian Ash. LC 76-11667. (YA) (gr. 9 up). 1976. 10.95 (ISBN 0-8008-8274-1). Taplinger.
Who's Who in Scottish History. Gordon Donaldson & Robert S. Morpeth. (Comparative Literature Ser.). (Illus.). 254p. 1973. 18.00x o.p. (ISBN 0-686-63951-0). B&N.
Who's Who in Sherlock Holmes. Scott R. Bullard & Michael Collins. LC 79-66638. 1980. 14.95 (ISBN 0-8008-8281-4); pap. 7.95 (ISBN 0-8008-8282-2). Taplinger.
Who's Who in Switzerland. 146.20 o.p. (ISBN 0-685-55055-9). Adler.
Who's Who in Switzerland, 1978-79. 11th ed. LC 52-39693. 1978. 95.00x o.p. (ISBN 2-8263-0638-3). Intl Pubns Serv.
Who's Who in Technology: Austria, Germany, Switzerland, 2 vols. Ed. by Otto J. Groeg. 1055p. 1979. Set. 195.00x (ISBN 3-921220-24-6). Intl Pubns Serv.
Who's Who in the Arts: Germany, Vols. 2. 1975. 160.00 set (ISBN 3-921220-22-X). Adler.
Who's Who in the Bible. George Barr. LC 74-6570. 1974. 8.95 o.p. (ISBN 0-685-50512-X). Jonathan David.
Who's Who in the Bible: From Historic Sources. Richard Coggins. (Illus.). 232p. 1981. 16.50x (ISBN 0-686-69582-8). B&N.
Who's Who in the East. 18th ed. 944p. 1981. 62.50 (ISBN 0-8379-0618-0). Marquis.
Who's Who in the East 1975-76. 15th ed. LC 43-18522. 816p. 1975. 47.50 (ISBN 0-8379-0615-6). Marquis.
Who's Who in the Midwest. 17th ed. LC 50-289. 824p. 1980. 57.50 (ISBN 0-8379-0717-9, 030234). Marquis.
Who's Who in the New Testament. Ronald Brownrigg. 1971. 18.95 o.p. (ISBN 0-03-086262-0). HR&W.
Who's Who in the People's Republic of China. Wolfgang Bartke. (Illus.). 750p. 1981. 100.00 (ISBN 0-87332-183-9). M E Sharpe.
Who's Who in the Socialist Countries. new ed. Borys Lewytzkyi & Julius Stroynowskj. 736p. 1978. 140.00 (ISBN 0-89664-011-6, Pub. by K G Saur). Gale.
Who's Who in the South & Southwest. 17th ed. LC 50-58231. 880p. 1980. 57.50 (ISBN 0-8379-0817-5, 030242). Marquis.
Who's Who in the Theatre, 2 vols. 17th ed. Ed. by Ian Herbert. 1500p. 1981. Set. 150.00 (ISBN 0-8103-0234-9). Gale.
Who's Who in the World. 5th ed. LC 79-139215. 992p. 1980. 59.50 (ISBN 0-8379-1105-2, 030244). Marquis.
Who's Who in the Zoo. Linell Smith. (Illus.). 48p. (gr. k-1). 1981. pap. 5.95 (ISBN 0-916392-78-3). Oak Tree Pubns.
Who's Who in Twentieth Century Literature. Martin Seymour-Smith. LC 75-21470. 1976. 12.95 o.p. (ISBN 0-03-013926-0). HR&W.
Who's Who of American Women. 12th ed. LC 58-12364. 920p. 1981. 62.50 (ISBN 0-8379-0412-9). Marquis.
Who's Who of American Women 1975-76. 9th ed. LC 58-13264. 976p. 1975. 47.50 (ISBN 0-8379-0409-9). Marquis.
Who's Who of British Members of Parliament: 1946-1978, Vol. 4. Michael Stenton. 1981. text ed. 86.50x (ISBN 0-391-01087-5). Humanities.
Who's Who of Flapland. David Halliwell. 1971. pap. 4.95 (ISBN 0-571-09678-6, Pub. by Faber & Faber). Merrimack Bk Serv.
Who's Who of Horrors. David J. Hogan. LC 79-17606. 1980. 19.95 (ISBN 0-498-02475-X). A S Barnes.
Who's Who of Southern Africa 1979: Including Mauritius & Incorporating South African Who's Who & the Central African Who's Who. 62nd ed. LC 15-10690. 1978. 50.00x o.p. (ISBN 0-8002-1324-6). Intl Pubns Serv.
Who's Who of the Colored Race. Ed. by Frank L. Mather. LC 79-178669. 1976. Repr. of 1915 ed. 42.00 (ISBN 0-8103-4247-2). Gale.
Who's Who on the Postage Stamps of Eastern Europe. Paul G. Partington. LC 79-22183. (Illus.). viii, 498p. 1979. lib. bdg. 31.50 (ISBN 0-8108-1266-5). Scarecrow.
Who's Who 1981-82. 133rd ed. 2700p. 1981. 99.50x (ISBN 0-686-69393-0). St Martin.
Who's Zoo: Animal Jokes & Riddles. Gary Poole. (Orig.). (gr. 3 up). pap. 1.25 (ISBN 0-448-17279-8, Tempo). G&D.
Whose Birthday Is It? Bill Woodman. Ed. by Jennifer Anderson. LC 79-2776. (Illus.). 48p. 1980. 7.95 (ISBN 0-690-04005-9, TYC-J); PLB 7.89 (ISBN 0-690-04006-7). T Y Crowell.
Whose Body? Dorothy L. Sayers. 1961. pap. 1.95 (ISBN 0-380-00897-1, 51888). Avon.
Whose Cat Is That? Virginia Kahl. (Illus.). 32p. (gr. k-2). 1979. 7.95 (ISBN 0-684-16097-8). Scribner.
Whose Child?: Children's Rights, Parental Authority, & State Power. Ed. by William Aiken & Hugh LaFollette. 310p. 1980. 22.50x (ISBN 0-8476-6282-9). Rowman.
Whose House Is It? Alice L. Hopf. LC 80-13852. (Illus.). 64p. (gr. 3-5). 1980. 7.95 (ISBN 0-396-07847-8). Dodd.
Whose House Is It? Paul Ricchiuti. (Hello World Ser.). 1967. pap. 1.40 o.p. (ISBN 0-8163-0308-8, 23610-9). Pacific Pr Pub Assn.
Whose Law? What Order? A Conflict Approach to Criminology. William J. Chambliss & Milton Mankoff. LC 75-23220. 256p. 1976. pap. text ed. 11.95x (ISBN 0-471-14476-2). Wiley.
Whose Life Is It Anyway? Brian Clark. 160p. 1980. pap. 2.50 (ISBN 0-380-52407-4, 52407). Avon.
Whose Town? Lorenz Graham. LC 69-13639. (gr. 5 up). 1969. 8.95 (ISBN 0-690-88783-3, TYC-J). T Y Crowell.
Whosoever Will. Herman Hoeksema. LC 77-189070. 1973. pap. 2.95 (ISBN 0-8254-2819-X). Kregel.
Why A B M? Policy Issues in the Missile Defense Controversy. Ed. by J. J. Holst & W. Schneider, Jr. 1969. 12.75 (ISBN 0-08-015625-8). Pergamon.
Why: A Book of Reasons. Irving Adler & Ruth Adler. LC 61-13113. (Reason Why Ser). (Illus.). (gr. 3-6). 1961. PLB 4.79 o.p. (ISBN 0-381-99950-5, A88600, JD-J). John Day.
Why a Duck. Ed. by Richard Anobile. (Illus.). 288p. 1974. pap. 5.95 large-format (ISBN 0-380-00452-6, 40774). Avon.
Why Am I...? A New Thought on Genetics. Josef Esser. 122p. 1980. 5.95 (ISBN 0-8059-2716-6). Dorrance.
Why Am I Different? Norma Simon. Ed. by Caroline Rubin. LC 76-41172. (Concept Books). (Illus.). 32p. 1976. 6.50g (ISBN 0-8075-9074-6). A Whitman.
Why Am I So Miserable If These Are the Best Years of My Life? Andrea B. Eagan. LC 75-43726. (gr. 8 up). 1976. 8.95 (ISBN 0-397-31655-0). Lippincott.
Why Am I So Miserable If These Are the Best Years of My Life? Andrea B. Eagan. 1979. pap. 2.25 (ISBN 0-380-46136-6, 46136). Avon.
Why & How of Home Horticulture. D. R. Bienz. LC 79-19915. (Illus.). 1980. text ed. 17.95x (ISBN 0-7167-1078-1). W H Freeman.
Why & How: Some Problems & Methods in Historical Biology. George G. Simpson. LC 79-42774. (Illus.). 270p. 1980. 44.00 (ISBN 0-08-025785-2); pap. 22.00 (ISBN 0-08-025784-4). Pergamon.
Why Animals Behave the Way They Do. Eugene J. Walter, Jr. (Illus.). 64p. (gr. 5 up). 1981. 9.95 (ISBN 0-684-16879-0). Scribner.
Why Architecture? William Muschenheim. 13.50 (ISBN 0-89720-033-0). Green Hill.
Why Are Some People Left-Handed? Barbara Haislet. (Creative's Questions & Answers Ser.). (Illus.). 32p. (gr. 3-4). Date not set. PLB 5.65 (ISBN 0-87191-753-X); pap. 2.75 (ISBN 0-89812-222-8). Creative Ed. Postponed.
Why Are You Afraid. Michael Buckley. pap. 5.95 (ISBN 0-87061-060-0). Chr Classics.
Why Are You Not a Criminal. Joseph W. Rogers. LC 77-2005. 192p. 1977. 10.95 (ISBN 0-13-957811-0, Spec); pap. 3.95 (ISBN 0-13-957803-X). P-H.
Why Art? Florence M. Daniels. LC 77-28084. (Illus.). 1978. 14.95 (ISBN 0-88229-173-4); pap. 8.95 (ISBN 0-88229-604-3). Nelson-Hall.
Why Be a Catholic? Ed. by Brennan Hill & Mary R. Newland. 108p. (Orig.). 1979. pap. 2.00 (ISBN 0-697-01713-3). Wm C Brown.
Why Be a Christian? Ellen G. White. 32p. 1970. pap. 0.75 (ISBN 0-8163-0081-X, 23615-8). Pacific Pr Pub Assn.
Why Believe? Richard Koffarnus. LC 80-53673. 96p. (Orig.). 1981. pap. 2.25 (ISBN 0-87239-425-5, 40090). Standard Pub.
Why Brownlee Left. Paul Mulcoon. LC 80-50846. 48p. 1981. pap. 4.95 (ISBN 0-916390-13-6). Wake Forest.
Why Buildings Stand Up: The Strength of Architecture from the Pyramid to the Skyscraper. Mario Salvadori. (Illus.). 1980. cancelled (ISBN 0-393-01401-0). Norton.
Why Can't a Woman Be More Like a Man? Celia Halas. 288p. 1981. 10.95 (ISBN 0-02-547430-8). Macmillan.
Why Can't I Fly? Rita Gelman. (gr. k-3). 1977. pap. 1.50 (ISBN 0-590-10331-8, Schol Pap). Schol Bk Serv.
Why Can't They Be Like Us? Facts & Fallacies About Ethnic Differences & Group Conflicts in America. Andrew M. Greeley. LC 73-81091. (Institute of Human Relations Press Paperback Ser). x, 76p. (Orig.). 1980. pap. 1.50 (ISBN 0-87495-009-0). Am Jewish Comm.
Why Capitalism Means War. Henry N. Brailsford. LC 70-147494. (Library of War & Peace; the Political Economy of War). lib. bdg. 38.00 (ISBN 0-8240-0287-3). Garland Pub.
Why Children Misbehave. Bruce Narramore. 176p. 1980. 8.95 (ISBN 0-310-30360-5). Zondervan.
Why Choose the Episcopal Church? John W. Krumm. 1974. 1.35 (ISBN 0-686-28800-9). Forward Movement.
Why Churches Die. Hollis Green. 224p. (Orig.). 1972. pap. 3.95 (ISBN 0-87123-642-7, 210642). Bethany Fell.
Why Churches Should Not Pay Taxes. Dean M. Kelley. LC 76-62944. 1977. 6.95 o.p. (ISBN 0-06-064302-1, HarpR). Har-Row.
Why Conform? Martyn Goff. (Liberal Studies Ser.). 1968. pap. text ed. 1.75x o.p. (ISBN 0-435-46538-4). Heinemann Ed.
Why Daddy Loves to Come Home. Al Fabrizio & Mrs. Al Fabrizio. 0.50 (ISBN 0-89985-108-8). Christ Nations.
Why David Can. Loyd Littlepage. (Illus.). (ps-3). 1977. 2.50 (ISBN 0-911336-67-2). Sci of Mind.
Why Deflation Is Coming in the Nineteen Eighties. James A. McCune. (Illus.). 1981. 8.95 (ISBN 0-686-69292-6). Yorkshire Pub.
Why did God let Grandpa Die? Phoebe Cranor. LC 76-17737. 1976. pap. 1.95 (ISBN 0-87123-603-6, 200603). Bethany Fell.
Why Did God Make Me? Concilium, Vol. 108. Ed. by Hans Kung & Jurgen Moltmann. 1978. pap. 4.95 (ISBN 0-8164-2167-6). Crossroad NY.
Why Did Grandma Die? Trudy Madler. LC 79-23892. (Life & Living from a Child's Point of View Ser.). (Illus.). (gr. k-5). 1980. PLB 9.65 (ISBN 0-8172-1354-6). Raintree Child.
Why Did This Happen to Me? Leslie Brandt. 1978. pap. 2.25 (ISBN 0-570-03777-8, 12-2724). Concordia.
Why Didn't I Say That? The Art of Verbal Self-Defense. Donald Carroll. 1980. 7.95 (ISBN 0-531-09923-7, C37). Watts.
Why Didn't I Think of That. Randy Cohen & Alexandra Anderson. (Illus.). 1980. pap. 5.95 (ISBN 0-449-90037-1, Columbine). Fawcett.
Why Didn't They Ask Evans. Agatha Christie. 1981. pap. 2.25 (ISBN 0-440-10704-0). Dell.
Why Distributed Computing? An NCC Review of Potential & Experience in UK. P. J. Down & F. E. Taylor. LC 77-363488. 168p. 1976. pap. 25.00x (ISBN 0-85012-170-1). Intl Pubns Serv.
Why Do I Daydream? Betty R. Wright. LC 80-25561. (Life & Living from a Child's Point of View Ser.). (Illus.). 32p. (gr. k-5). 1981. PLB 9.65 (ISBN 0-8172-1371-6). Raintree Child.
Why Do I Shout at My Wife? Dick Jewett. (Uplook Ser.). 1978. pap. 0.75 (ISBN 0-8163-0300-2, 23617-4). Pacific Pr Pub Assn.
Why Do Some Urban Schools Succeed? The Phi Delta Kappa Study of Exceptional Urban Elementary Schools. LC 80-81869. 225p. (Orig.). 1980. pap. 7.00 (ISBN 0-87367-773-0). Phi Delta Kappa.

Why Do We Eat? Pamela Espeland. (Creative's Questions & Answers Library). (Illus.). 32p. (gr. 3-4). Date not set. PLB 5.75 (ISBN 0-87191-747-5); pap. 2.75 (ISBN 0-89812-216-3). Creative Ed. Postponed.

Why Do We Have Skeletons? Paul D. Schneck. (Creative Questions & Answers Ser.). (Illus.). 32p. (gr. 3-4). Date not set. PLB 5.65 (ISBN 0-87191-750-5); pap. 2.75 (ISBN 0-89812-219-8). Creative Ed. Postponed.

Why Do We Laugh? A. A. Redpath. (Creative's Questions & Answers Ser.). (Illus.). 32p. (gr. 3-4). Date not set. PLB 5.65 (ISBN 0-87191-751-3); pap. 2.75 (ISBN 0-89812-220-1). Creative Ed. Postponed.

Why Do You Need a Personal Computer. Lance A. Leventhal & Irving Stafford. LC 80-2391. (Self-Teaching Guide Ser.). 320p. 1980. pap. text ed. 8.95 (ISBN 0-471-04784-8). Wiley.

Why Does Language Matter to Philosophy. I. Hacking. LC 75-19432. 180p. 1975. 26.95 (ISBN 0-521-20923-4); pap. 7.95x (ISBN 0-521-09998-6). Cambridge U Pr.

Why Does the Weather Change? Patricia Frevert. (Creative's Questions & Answer Library). (Illus.). (gr. 3-4). Date not set. PLB 5.75 (ISBN 0-87191-748-3); pap. 2.75 (ISBN 0-89812-214-7). Creative Ed. Postponed.

Why Doesn't God Do Something? Phoebe Cranor. LC 78-118. (YA) 1978. pap. 1.95 (ISBN 0-87123-605-2, 200605). Bethany Fell.

Why Families Move. 2nd ed. Peter H. Rossi. LC 79-25370. (Illus.). 243p. 1980. 18.00 (ISBN 0-8039-1348-6); pap. 8.95x (ISBN 0-8039-1349-4). Sage.

Why God Allows Trials & Disappointments. Gerald R. Nash. (Uplook Ser.). 31p. 1972. pap. 0.75 (ISBN 0-8163-0082-8, 23618-2). Pacific Pr Pub Assn.

Why God Permits Evil. Miller Williams. LC 77-8711. 1977. 9.95 (ISBN 0-8071-0377-2); pap. 4.95 (ISBN 0-8071-0378-0). La State U Pr.

Why Gone Those Times? James W. Schultz. Ed. by Lee Silliman. LC 72-9262. (Civilization of the American Indian Ser.: Vol. 127). 271p. 1974. 12.95 (ISBN 0-8061-1068-6). U of Okla Pr.

Why Government Programs Fail: Improving Policy Implementation. James S. Larson. LC 79-26917. 140p. 1980. 18.95 (ISBN 0-03-053956-0). Praeger.

Why Growth Rates Differ: Postwar Experience in Nine Western Countries. Edward F. Denison. 1967. 18.95 (ISBN 0-8157-1806-3); pap. 7.95 (ISBN 0-8157-1805-5). Brookings.

Why Has Development Neglected Rural Women? A Review of the South Asian Literature. Nici Nelson. LC 79-40235. (Women in Development Ser.: Vol. 1). (Illus.). 1979. 28.00 (ISBN 0-08-023377-5); pap. 10.50 (ISBN 0-08-023376-7). Pergamon.

Why Have the Birds Stopped Singing? Zoa Sherburne. 192p. (gr. 7 up). 1974. PLB 6.96 (ISBN 0-688-30111-8). Morrow.

Why Have They Taken Our Children? Jack W. Baugh & Jefferson Morgan. 1978. 8.95 o.s.i. (ISBN 0-440-09463-1). Delacorte.

Why Heart Attack? Sam Mo. 1981. 6.95 (ISBN 0-8062-1546-1). Carlton.

Why I Am a Catholic Charismatic: A Catholic Explains. Ronda Chervin. 1978. pap. 2.95 (ISBN 0-89243-089-3). Liguori Pubns.

Why I Can Say I Am God. Herbert L. Beierle. 1978. 1.00 (ISBN 0-686-23898-2). God Unltd U of Healing.

Why I Left the Convent. Bridget Keating. 1979. 4.50 o.p. (ISBN 0-8062-1062-1). Carlton.

Why I Left the Roman Catholic Church. Charles Davis. 1976. pap. 3.00. Am Atheist.

Why I Live in the Forest. James Nolan. LC 74-5967. (Wesleyan Poetry Program: Vol. 74). 1974. 10.00x (ISBN 0-8195-2074-8, Pub. by Wesleyan U Pr); pap. 4.95 (ISBN 0-8195-1074-2). Columbia U Pr.

Why Information Systems Fail. Henry C. Lucas, Jr. LC 74-18395. 144p. 1975. 12.50x (ISBN 0-231-03792-9). Columbia U Pr.

Why Is Everyone Growing up & I'm Still in the 8th Grade? Poems About School Life Today. Paula B. Rehr. (Illus.). 48p. pap. 3.50 (ISBN 0-686-63982-0). Garrett Pk.

Why Is the Third World Poor? Pierro Gheddo. Tr. by Kathryn Sullivan from It. LC 72-85793. 196p. 1973. pap. 4.95x o.p. (ISBN 0-88344-757-6). Orbis Bks.

Why Is Welfare So Hard to Reform? Henry J. Aaron. (Studies in Social Economics). 71p. 1973. 3.95 (ISBN 0-8157-0019-9). Brookings.

Why Jesus? F. J. Huegel. 1970. pap. 1.50 (ISBN 0-87123-635-4, 200635). Bethany Fell.

Why Jobs Die & What to Do About It: Job Redesign & Future Productivity. Robert N. Ford. 1979. 15.95 (ISBN 0-8144-5502-6). Am Mgmt.

Why Johnny Can't Add: The Failure of the New Math. Morris Kline. LC 72-80894. 256p. 1973. 7.95 o.p. (ISBN 0-312-87780-3, W3500). St Martin.

Why Johnny Can't Read & What You Can Do About It. Rudolf Flesch. 1966. pap. 1.95 (ISBN 0-06-080088-7, P88, PL). Har-Row.

Why Johnny Still Can't Read: A New Look at the Scandal of Our Schools. Rudolf Flesch. LC 80-8686. 192p. 1981. 10.95 (ISBN 0-06-014842-X, HarpT). Har-Row.

Why Judaism? A Search for Meaning in Jewish Identity. Henry Cohen. 192p. 1973. pap. 5.00 (ISBN 0-8074-0077-7, 161901). UAHC.

Why Lenin? Why Stalin? a Reappraisal of the Russian Revolution, 1900-1930. 2nd ed. Theodore H. Von Laue. LC 79-152063. 1971. pap. text ed. 6.50 scp (ISBN 0-397-47200-5, HarpC). Har-Row.

Why Listen? The Difficult Sayings of Jesus. William Neil. (Orig.). pap. 1.50 (ISBN 0-89129-227-6). Jove Pubns.

Why Males Exist: An Inquiry into the Evolution of Sex. Fred Hapgood. 1980. pap. 2.95 (ISBN 0-451-61908-0, ME1908, Mentor). NAL.

Why Me? Nancy Mack. LC 76-13175. (Moods & Emotions Ser.). (Illus.). 32p. (gr. k-3). 1976. PLB 8.95 (ISBN 0-8172-0012-6). Raintree Pubs.

Why Me, God? 2nd ed. Robert N. Schaper. LC 73-82763. 1977. pap. 3.50 (ISBN 0-8307-0452-3, S273-1-28). Regal.

Why Me, Lord? Paul W. Powell. 120p. 1981. pap. 3.95 (ISBN 0-89693-007-6). Victor Bks.

Why Me? The Story of Jenny. Patricia Dizeno. (gr. 7 up). 1976. pap. 1.50 (ISBN 0-380-00563-8, 41269). Avon.

Why Men Confess. O. John Rogge. LC 78-140376. (Civil Liberties in American History Ser). 1971. Repr. of 1959 ed. lib. bdg. 27.50 (ISBN 0-306-70088-3). Da Capo.

Why Men Go Back. Charles W. Conn. 1966. 5.95 (ISBN 0-87148-902-3). Pathway Pr.

Why Men Rebel. Ted R. Gurr. LC 74-84865. (Center of International Studies). 1970. 21.00x (ISBN 0-691-07528-X); pap. 5.95 (ISBN 0-691-02167-8). Princeton U Pr.

Why Nations Act: Theoretical Perspectives for Comparative Foreign Policy Studies. Ed. by Maurice A. East et al. Stephen A. Salmore & Charles F. Hermann. LC 77-22119. (Sage Focus Editions: Vol. 2). 1978. 18.95x (ISBN 0-8039-0718-4); pap. 9.95x (ISBN 0-8039-0719-2). Sage.

Why Not Be for Real? Stephen Pileggi. LC 80-17814. (Open Mind Bk.). 64p. (Orig.). 1980. pap. 4.95 (ISBN 0-916392-57-0). Oak Tree Pubns.

Why on Earth. rev. ed. Joan Hodgson. 144p. 1979. pap. 4.95 (ISBN 0-85487-043-1). De Vorss.

Why Organizers Fail: The Story of a Rent Strike. Harry Brill. LC 76-104103. 1971. 14.50x (ISBN 0-520-01672-6). U of Cal Pr.

Why Our Universities Are Turning Out Ordinary Barbarians. Sylvester Moravisin. (American Culture Library). (Illus.). 105p. 1981. 47.85 (ISBN 0-89266-299-9). Am Classical Coll Pr.

Why Pacifists Should Be Socialists. George Lansbury. LC 72-147520. (Library of War & Peace; Labor, Socialism & War). lib. bdg. 38.00 (ISBN 0-8240-0454-X). Garland Pub.

Why Packet Switching. G. B. Bleazard. (Illus.). 174p. (Orig.). 1979. pap. 32.50 (ISBN 0-85012-194-9). Intl Pubns Serv.

Why People Join the Church. Edward A. Rauff. LC 79-90741. (Orig.). 1980. pap. 5.95 (ISBN 0-8298-0387-4). Pilgrim NY.

Why Policies Succeed or Fail. Ed. by Helen M. Ingram & Dean E. Mann. LC 79-26317. (Sage Yearbooks in Politics & Public Policy: Vol. 8). (Illus.). 312p. 1980. 20.00 (ISBN 0-8039-1416-4); pap. 9.95 (ISBN 0-8039-1417-2). Sage.

Why Psychology Has Failed. Thomas R. Sutherland. (Illus.). 125p. 1980. deluxe ed. 32.50 (ISBN 0-89920-010-9). Am Inst Psych.

Why Pursue the Buddha? Gibun Kimura. Tr. by Ken'Ichi Yokogawa from Japanese. LC 75-14981. Orig. Title: Kagerinaki Daihi. (Illus.). 160p. 1976. 5.95 o.p. (ISBN 0-912624-00-0). Nembutsu Pr.

Why Raise Ugly Kids? How You Can Fulfill Your Child's Health & Happiness Potential. Hal A. Huggins. (Illus.). 256p. 1981. 12.95 (ISBN 0-87000-507-3). Arlington Hse.

Why Revival of "SALT" Won't Stop War. Lyndon H. LaRouche, Jr. 116p. (Orig.). 1980. pap. 3.95 (ISBN 0-933488-08-4). New Benjamin.

Why Seek Ye the Dead Among the Living? A Guide for Widows. Alan C. Tibbetts. LC 80-68057. 108p. 1980. 5.95 (ISBN 0-8059-2754-9). Dorrance.

Why Sermon Outlines. Russell E. Spray. (Sermon Outline Ser.). 48p. (Orig.). 1980. pap. 1.95 (ISBN 0-8010-8188-2). Baker Bk.

Why Should the Devil Have All the Good Music: Jesus Music, Where It Began, Where It Is, & Where It Is Going. Paul Baker. 1979. 7.95 (ISBN 0-8499-2858-3). Word Bks.

Why South Africa Will Survive. L. H. Gann & Peter Duignan. 329p. 1980. write for info. St Martin.

Why Suffer? Ann Wigmore. (Illus.). 173p. pap. text ed. 2.95. Hippocrates.

Why Switzerland? J. Steinberg. LC 75-36024. (Illus.). 224p. 1976. 23.50 (ISBN 0-521-21139-5). Cambridge U Pr.

Why Switzerland? J. Steinberg. LC 75-36024. (Illus.). 225p. 1981. pap. 9.50 (ISBN 0-521-28144-X). Cambridge U Pr.

Why the Cake Won't Rise & the Jelly Won't Set: A Complete Guide to Avoiding Kitchen Failures. Kathleen Thorne-Thomsen & Linda Brownridge. LC 78-6997. (Illus.). 1979. 10.95 (ISBN 0-89479-036-6). A & W Pubs.

Why the Church. Ed. by Walter Burghardt. LC 77-74583. 1977. pap. 4.95 (ISBN 0-8091-2028-3). Paulist Pr.

Why the Jackal Won't Speak to the Hedgehog. Harold Berson. LC 69-13439. (Illus.). (ps-2). 1969. 6.95 (ISBN 0-395-28768-5, Clarion). HM.

Why the Japanese Have Been So Successful in Business. Friedrich Furstenberg. LC 73-77702. 110p. 1974. 15.00 (ISBN 0-900537-11-6). Hippocrene Bks.

Why the Lyrical Ballads? John E. Jordan. LC 75-27926. 1976. 15.75x (ISBN 0-520-03124-5). U of Cal Pr.

Why the North Star Stands Still: And Other Indian Legends. William R. Palmer. (Illus.). 118p. 1978. 2.50. Zion.

Why the Poor Get Richer & the Rich Slow Down. W. W. Rostow. (Illus.). 456p. 1980. text ed. 19.95 (ISBN 0-292-73012-8). U of Tex Pr.

Why the Poor Pay More. Ed. by Frances Williams. (Illus.). 1977. text ed. 16.00x (ISBN 0-333-23643-2); pap. text ed. 7.75x (ISBN 0-333-23644-0). Humanities.

Why the Sun & the Moon Live in the Sky. Elphinstone Dayrell. (Illus.). (gr. k-3). 1977. 3.75 (ISBN 0-395-25381-0, Sandpiper); pap. 1.95 (ISBN 0-686-68009-X). HM.

Why the Tides Ebb & Flow. Joan Bowden. (gr. k-3). 1979. PLB 7.95 (ISBN 0-395-28378-7). HM.

Why They Call Him The Buffalo Doctor. Jean Cummings. LC 73-147172. 309p. 1980. Repr. of 1971 ed. 10.95 (ISBN 0-8187-0035-1). Swallow.

Why They Give: American Jews & Their Philanthropies. Milton Goldin. LC 75-17655. 1976. 10.95 o.s.i. (ISBN 0-02-544560-X, 54456). Macmillan.

Why Trade It In? Your Mechanic Can Save You Money. George Fremon & Suzanne Fremon. LC 76-42603. (Illus.). 1980. pap. 5.95 (ISBN 0-89709-016-0). Liberty Pub.

Why Vietnam: Prelude to America's Albatross. Archimedes L. Patti. (Illus.). 700p. 1981. 19.50 (ISBN 0-520-04156-9). U of Cal Pr.

Why War? Frederick Howe. LC 70-147497. (Library of War & Peace; the Political Economy of War). lib. bdg. 38.00 (ISBN 0-8240-0291-1). Garland Pub.

Why We Can't Wait. Martin L. King, Jr. (Illus.). (RL 7). pap. 1.50 (ISBN 0-451-61887-4, MW1887, Ment). NAL.

Why We Fought. C. H. Grattan. Ed. by Keith Nelson. LC 70-84163. 1969. 24.50x (ISBN 0-672-60944-4). Irvington.

Why We Have Thanksgiving. Margaret Hillert. (Just Beginning-to-Read Ser.). (Illus.). 32p. (gr. 1-6). 1981. PLB 4.39 o.p. (ISBN 0-695-41550-6); pap. 1.50 o.p. (ISBN 0-695-31550-1). Follett.

Why We Think As We Do. Robert A. Liston. (gr. 7 up). 1977. PLB 6.90 s&l o.p. (ISBN 0-531-00390-6). Watts.

Why, What & How of Interest Development Centers. Berdine Stoltz & Pamela Saloom. 1978. pap. text ed. 3.95 (ISBN 0-936386-02-9). Creative Learning.

Why Wild Edibles? The Joys of Finding, Fixing, & Tasting - West of the Rockies. Russ Mohney. LC 75-12071. (Illus.). 320p. 1975. pap. 7.95 o.s.i. (ISBN 0-914718-07-X). Pacific Search.

Why Winners Win. Art Garner. 128p. 1981. 6.95 (ISBN 0-88289-267-3). Pelican.

Why Would I Lie? Hollis Hodges. 1980. pap. 2.25 (ISBN 0-686-69259-4, 50732). Avon.

Why You Get Sick & How You Get Well. Ilse Goldsmith. LC 70-115448. (Illus.). (gr. 4-6). 1970. 7.95 (ISBN 0-8069-3036-5); PLB 7.49 (ISBN 0-8069-3037-3). Sterling.

Why You Lose at Tennis. Vincent Fotre. 128p. pap. 1.95 o.p. (ISBN 0-06-463326-8, 326, EH). Har-Row.

Why Your House May Be Hazardous to Your Health. Alfred Zamm. 1980. 9.95 (ISBN 0-671-24128-1). S&S.

Why Your Stomach Hurts. Gary Null & Steve Null. LC 78-23507. 1979. 8.95 (ISBN 0-396-07630-0). Dodd.

Whys & Wherefores of Corporate Practice. 3rd ed. S. Gorlick. 1978. 14.50 (ISBN 0-87489-209-0). Med Economics.

Whyte's Bible Characters. Alexander Whyte. (Illus.). 1968. 16.95 (ISBN 0-310-34410-7). Zondervan.

Wi the Haill Voice. Vladimir Mayakovsky. Tr. by Edwin Morgan from Rus. (Translation Ser.). (Scots.). 1979. 6.95 o.s.i. (ISBN 0-902145-41-X, Pub. by Carcanet New Pr England). Persea Bks.

Wichita Grammar. David S. Rood. LC 75-25122. (American Indian Linguistics Ser.). 1976. lib. bdg. 42.00 (ISBN 0-8240-1972-5). Garland Pub.

Wichita Indians: Wichita Indian Archaeology & Ethnology: a Pilot Study. Robert E. Bell. Ed. by David A. Horr. (Plains Indians - American Indian Ethnohistory Ser.). 1974. lib. bdg. 42.00 (ISBN 0-8240-0770-0). Garland Pub.

Wicked Cousin. Zabrina Faire. (Orig.). 1980. pap. 1.75 (ISBN 0-446-94104-2). Warner Bks.

Wicked Guardian. Elsie Lee. 1979. pap. 1.95 o.s.i. (ISBN 0-440-19801-1). Dell.

Wicked Pack of Cards. 2nd ed. Rosemary Harris. (gr. 5 up). 1973. 6.50 (ISBN 0-571-10530-5, Pub. by Faber & Faber). Merrimack Bk Serv.

Wicked Tricks of Tyl Uilenspiegel. Jay Williams. LC 77-7884. (Illus.). 64p. (gr. 1-5). 1978. 8.95 (ISBN 0-590-07478-4, Four Winds). Schol Bk Serv.

Wicked Way to Die. J. G. Jefferys. (Jeremy Sturrock Ser). 256p. 1973. 5.95 o.s.i. (ISBN 0-8027-5284-5). Walker & Co.

Wicked Witch of Troll Cave. Don A. Torgersen. LC 80-12043. (Troll Stories Ser.). (Illus.). 32p. (gr. k-4). 1980. PLB 7.95 (ISBN 0-516-03672-6). Childrens.

Wickiser Annals. Mary A. Burgess. LC 80-11075. 64p. 1981. lib. bdg. 8.95x (ISBN 0-89370-802-X); pap. 2.95x (ISBN 0-89370-902-6). Borgo Pr.

Widdecombe Fair. George Adamson. (Illus.). (ps-5). 1966. 6.50 (ISBN 0-571-06559-7, Pub. by Faber & Faber). Merrimack Bk Serv.

Wide-Angle Lens: Stories of Time & Space. Ed. by Phyllis R. Fenner. LC 80-16992. (Illus.). 224p. (gr. 7-9). 1980. 7.95 (ISBN 0-688-22241-2); PLB 7.63 (ISBN 0-688-32241-7). Morrow.

Wide Awake Jake. Helen Young. LC 74-19424. (Illus.). 32p. (gr. k-3). 1975. 6.75 o.p. (ISBN 0-688-22024-X); PLB 6.48 o.p. (ISBN 0-688-32024-4). Morrow.

Wide Awake Owl. Louis Slobodkin. (gr. 1-2). 1958. 4.50g o.s.i. (ISBN 0-02-785890-1). Macmillan.

Wide-Awake Timothy. Joyce Wakefield. LC 80-21843. (Illus.). 32p. (gr. k-4). 1981. PLB 7.95 (ISBN 0-516-03658-0). Childrens.

Wide Doors Open. Theodore L. Harris et al. (Keys to Independence in Reading Ser.). (Illus., Orig.). (gr. 3). 1973. text ed. 2.70 (ISBN 0-87892-038-2); tchrs' manual 3.96 (ISBN 0-87892-039-0); avail. wkbk. 2.64 (ISBN 0-87892-040-4). Economy Co.

Wide Horizon Reading Scheme. Ronald Ridout & Ian Serraillier. Incl. Introductory Stage. Look Alive (ISBN 0-435-11771-8); Introductory Stage. Making Good (ISBN 0-435-11772-6); Introductory Stage. Cave of Death (ISBN 0-435-11773-4); Stage One. I Dare You (ISBN 0-435-11774-2); Stage One. Jungle Adventure (ISBN 0-435-11775-0); Stage One. Katy at Home (ISBN 0-435-11770-X); Stage Two. Read to Enjoy (ISBN 0-435-11776-9); Stage Two. Adventure of Dick Varley (ISBN 0-435-11777-7); Stage Two. Guns in the Wild (ISBN 0-435-11778-5); Stage Two. Katy at School (ISBN 0-435-11779-3); Stage Three. To Please You (ISBN 0-435-11780-7); Stage Three. Treasure Ahead (ISBN 0-435-11781-5); Stage Four. Whatever the Odds (ISBN 0-435-11782-3); Stage Four. Mountain Rescue (ISBN 0-435-11783-1); Stage Four. Fight for Freedom (ISBN 0-435-11784-X). (gr. 6-9). pap. text ed. 3.25x ea. o.p. Heinemann Ed.

Wide House. Taylor Caldwell. 1974. Repr. of 1945 ed. lib. bdg. 19.55 (ISBN 0-88411-156-3). Amereon Ltd.

Wide House. Taylor Caldwell. 1979. pap. 2.75 (ISBN 0-515-05620-0). Jove Pubns.

Wide-Mouthed Frog. Rex Schneider. LC 80-13449. (Illus.). 32p. (gr. k up). 1980. 9.95 (ISBN 0-916144-58-5); pap. 5.95 (ISBN 0-916144-59-3). Stemmer Hse.

Wide Neighborhoods: A Story of the Frontier Nursing Service. Mary Breckinridge. (Illus.). 400p. 1981. 18.50 (ISBN 0-8131-1453-5); pap. 8.50 (ISBN 0-8131-0149-2). U Pr of Ky.

Wide World of John Steinbeck. Peter Lisca. 332p. 1981. Repr. of 1958 ed. 15.00 (ISBN 0-87752-217-0). Gordian.

Wide World of Words. Joan D. Berbrich. (Orig.). (gr. 7-10). 1975. 7.17 (ISBN 0-87720-340-7). AMSCO Sch.

Wideband Voltage Amplifiers. C. W. Davidson. 1974. pap. text ed. 12.00x (ISBN 0-7002-0235-8). Intl Ideas.

Widening Circle: Essays on the Circulation of Literature in Eighteenth-Century Europe. Ed. by Paul J. Korshin et al. 1976. 17.50x (ISBN 0-8122-7717-1). U of Pa Pr.

Widening Gap: Development in the 1970's. Ed. by Barbara Ward et al. LC 75-151617. 1971. 30.00x (ISBN 0-231-03538-1). Columbia U Pr.

Widening Gulf: Asian Nationalism & American Policy. Selig S. Harrison. LC 76-57881. (Illus.). 1978. 17.95 (ISBN 0-02-914080-3). Free Pr.

Widening Path. Robert B. Ruddell et al. (Pathfinder - Allyn & Bacon Reading Program: Level 19). (gr. 6). 1978. text ed. 9.56 (ISBN 0-205-05229-0, 5452295); tchr's ed. 14.60 (ISBN 0-205-05231-2, 5452317). Allyn.

Widow. Pierre Rey. 1978. pap. 2.50 o.p. (ISBN 0-425-04010-0, Dist. by Putnam). Berkley Pub.

Widow: A Critical Edition. Thomas Middleton. Ed. by Robert T. Levine. (Salzburg Studies in English Literature, Jacobean Studies Drama Ser.: No. 56). 260p. 1975. pap. text ed. 25.00x (ISBN 0-391-01482-X). Humanities.

Widow LeRouge. Emile Gaboriau. 293p. 1980. Repr. of 1900 ed. lib. bdg. 12.50x (ISBN 0-89968-184-0). Lightyear.

Widowers' Houses. George B. Shaw. Ed. by Jerald Bringle. LC 79-56699. (Bernard Shaw Early Texts: Play Manuscripts in Facsimile). 1981. lib. bdg. 50.00 (ISBN 0-8240-4575-0). Garland Pub.

Widower's Son. Alan Sillitoe. 1978. pap. 1.95 (ISBN 0-06-080465-3, P 465, PL). Har-Row.

Widower's Son. Alan Sillitoe. LC 76-52776. 1977. 8.95 o.s.i. (ISBN 0-06-013892-0, HarpT). Har-Row.

Widowhood. Henry P. Brehm & Helena Z. Lopata. LC 78-19789. 200p. 1981. price not set (ISBN 0-03-046301-7). Praeger.

Widowhood. Helena Z. Lopata & Henry P. Brehm. LC 78-19789. 1979. 18.95 (ISBN 0-03-046301-7). Praeger.

Widow's Children. Paula Fox. 1977. pap. 1.75 (ISBN 0-380-01791-1, 35352). Avon.

Widow's Guide. Isabella Taves. LC 80-6219. 256p. 1981. 9.95 (ISBN 0-8052-3769-0). Schocken.

Widow's Guide to Life: How to Adjust-How to Grow. Ida Fisher & Byron Lane. 224p. 1981. 13.95 (ISBN 0-13-959452-3, Spec); pap. 6.95 (ISBN 0-13-959445-0). P-H.

Widow's Tears. George Chapman. Ed. by Ethel M. Smeak. LC 65-24305. (Regents Renaissance Drama Ser). 1966. 8.50x (ISBN 0-8032-0257-1); pap. 1.65x (ISBN 0-8032-5258-7, BB 217, Bison). U of Nebr Pr.

Widow's Walk. Pamela Comings. Ed. by Carole Baron. 1981. 12.95 (ISBN 0-686-68920-8). Crown.

Wie Spare Ich Energie Im Betrieb. 1976. pap. 6.00 o.p. (ISBN 0-89192-171-0). Interbk Inc.

Wieland: Or, the Transformation. Charles Brockden Brown. pap. 2.50 (ISBN 0-385-03100-9, C320, Anch). Doubleday.

Wielka Encyklopedia Powszechna, 12 vols. (Polish., Including 1 supplement). 1968-1969. 685.00 (ISBN 0-8277-3104-3). Maxwell Sci Intl.

Wife. Judith Burnley. 1978. pap. 1.50 o.s.i. (ISBN 0-515-04568-3). Jove Pubns.

Wife Beating: The Silent Crisis. Roger Langley & Richard C. Levy. 1977. 9.95 (ISBN 0-87690-231-X). Dutton.

Wife by Contract. Flora Kidd. (Harlequin Presents Ser.). 192p. 1980. pap. 1.50 (ISBN 0-373-10400-6, Pub. by Harlequin). PB.

Wife Called Tommie. Thelma Norman. LC 74-78317. (Destiny Ser.). 1975. pap. 4.95 (ISBN 0-8163-0170-0, 23680-2). Pacific Pr Pub Assn.

Wife for a Year. Rachel Lindsay. (Harlequin Presents Ser.). 192p. (Orig.). 1981. pap. 1.50 (ISBN 0-373-10413-8, Pub. by Harlequin). PB.

Wife of Bath's Prologue & Tale. Geoffrey Chaucer. Ed. by J. Winny. (Selected Tales from Chaucer). 1966. text ed. 5.75x (ISBN 0-521-04630-0). Cambridge U Pr.

Wife of Heracles. Sophocles. Tr. by Gilbert Murray. 1947. pap. text ed. 3.95x (ISBN 0-04-882054-7). Allen Unwin.

Wife of His Youth & Other Stories. Charles W. Chesnutt. (Illus.). 1968. pap. 5.95 (ISBN 0-472-06134-8, 134, AA). U of Mich Pr.

Wife of Martin Guerre. Janet Lewis. LC 70-135357. 109p. 1941. 5.00 o.s.i. (ISBN 0-8040-0079-4); pap. 3.95 (ISBN 0-8040-0321-1). Swallow.

Wife of Rossetti. Violet Hunt. 338p. 1980. Repr. of 1932 ed. lib. bdg. 30.00 (ISBN 0-8492-5283-0). R West.

Wife or Death & the Golden Goose. Ellery Queen. 1978. pap. 1.75 (ISBN 0-451-08087-4, E8087, Sig). NAL.

Wife to Order. Lucy Walker. Date not set. pap. 1.75 (ISBN 0-345-29275-8). Ballantine.

Wife's Trials; or, Lilian Grey, Repr. Of 1858 Ed. Emma J. W. Guyton. Ed. by Robert L. Wolff. Bd. with Married Life. Repr. of 1863 ed; Husbands & Wives. Repr. of 1873 ed. LC 75-492. (Victorian Fiction Ser.). 1975. lib. bdg. 66.00 (ISBN 0-8240-1568-1). Garland Pub.

Wigmakers. Leonard E. Fisher. LC 65-21628. (Colonial Americans Ser). (Illus.). (gr. 4-6). 1965. PLB 4.90 o.p. (ISBN 0-531-01039-2). Watts.

Wikchamni Grammar. Geoffrey Gamble. LC 77-8566. (Publications in Linguistics Ser.: Vol. 89). 1978. 11.00x (ISBN 0-520-09589-8). U of Cal Pr.

Wilbur D. Steele. Martin Bucco. (U. S. Authors Ser. 198). lib. bdg. 10.95 (ISBN 0-8057-0688-7). Twayne.

Wilbur the Warrior. Louis Slobodkin. LC 79-175537. (Illus.). (gr. 1-3). 5.95 (ISBN 0-8149-0713-X). Vanguard.

Wilbye. David Brown. (Oxford Studies of Composers). 72p. 1974. pap. 7.95x (ISBN 0-19-315220-7). Oxford U Pr.

Wild Alaska. Dale Brown. (American Wilderness Ser.). (Illus.). 1972. 12.95 (ISBN 0-8094-1152-0). Time-Life.

Wild Alaska. Dale Brown. LC 74-190658. (American Wilderness Ser). (Illus.). (gr. 6 up). 1972. lib. bdg. 11.97 (ISBN 0-8094-1153-9, Pub. by Time-Life). Silver.

Wild & Wonderful. Janet Dailey. (Harlequin Presents Ser.). 192p. 1981. pap. 1.50 (ISBN 0-373-10416-2, Pub. by Harlequin). PB.

Wild & Woolly Animal Book. Nita Jonas. (Illus.). (gr. k-2). 1961. PLB 3.69 o.p. (ISBN 0-394-90688-8, BYR). Random.

Wild & Woolly Mammoths. Aliki. LC 76-18082. (Let's-Read-&-Find-Out Science Bk). (Illus.). (gr. k-3). 1977. PLB 7.89 (ISBN 0-690-01276-4, TYC-J). T Y Crowell.

Wild Angel. E. C. Spykman. (Children's Literature Ser.). 1981. PLB 9.95 (ISBN 0-8398-2624-9). Gregg.

Wild Animal Babies. Kathleen Daly. (Illus.). (ps-1). 1958. PLB 5.00 (ISBN 0-307-60332-6, Golden Pr). Western Pub.

Wild Animal Shelter. Esther Kellner. (gr. 4-6). 1978. pap. 1.25 (ISBN 0-590-11915-X, Schol Pap). Schol Bk Serv.

Wild Animal, White Man. Bernhard Grzimek. Tr. by Michael Glenny. (Illus.). 1966. 8.95 o.p. (ISBN 0-8090-9725-7). Hill & Wang.

Wild Animals. Illus. by Tony Chen. LC 80-53105. (Board Bks.). (Illus.). 14p. (ps). 1981. boards 2.95 (ISBN 0-394-84748-2). Random.

Wild Animals. Stella Nathan. (Word Bird Bks.). (Illus.). 24p. (ps-2). 1977. PLB 5.22 o.p. (ISBN 0-307-66252-7, Golden Pr). Western Pub.

Wild Animals. William Stobbs. (Illus.). (ps). 1979. 1.25 (ISBN 0-370-10735-7, Pub. by Chatto Bodley Jonathan). Merrimack Bk Serv.

Wild Animals Around Your Home. Paul Villiard. (Illus.). 192p. 1975. 9.95 (ISBN 0-87691-170-X). Winchester Pr.

Wild Animals Around Your Home. Paul Villiard. LC 74-16877. (Encore Edition). (Illus.). (gr. 2-7). 1975. pap. 0.95 (ISBN 0-684-15776-4, SL615, ScribT). Scribner.

Wild Animals I Have Known. Ernest T. Seton. LC 77-7918. (Illus.). (gr. 5 up). 1977. pap. 4.95 o.s.i. (ISBN 0-87905-033-0). Peregrine Smith.

Wild Animals in Captivity: An Outline of the Biology of Zoological Gardens. H. Hediger. Tr. by Geoffrey Sircom. Orig. Title: Wildtiere -in Gefaengschaft: ein Grundriss -Des Tiergartenbiologie. 1950. pap. text ed. 3.50 (ISBN 0-486-21260-2). Dover.

Wild Animals of Nepal. Hemant R. Mishra & Dorothy Mierow. (Illus.). 6.95x (ISBN 0-685-89511-4). Himalaya Hse.

Wild Animals That Help People. Michael J. Walker. (gr. 4-7). 1977. 7.95 o.p. (ISBN 0-679-20396-6). McKay.

Wild Australia. Douglas Dorward. (Illus.). 128p. 1980. 20.95x (ISBN 0-00-211446-1, Pub. by W Collins Australia). Intl Schol Bk Serv.

Wild Bill Hiccup's Riddle Book. Ann Bishop. Ed. by Caroline Rubin. LC 75-33161. (Riddle Bk.). (Illus.). 1975. 5.75g (ISBN 0-8075-9097-5). A Whitman.

Wild Bill Sullivan: King of the Hollow. Ann R. Hammons. LC 80-19625. 1980. 9.95 (ISBN 0-87805-127-9). U Pr of Miss.

Wild Blue U. E. Miller & P. Coffey. 1972. 7.95 o.s.i. (ISBN 0-02-584840-2). Macmillan.

Wild Blue U: The Story of the United States Air Force Academy. E. Miller & P. Coffey. 192p. 1972. pap. 3.95 o.s.i. (ISBN 0-02-035100-3, Collier). Macmillan.

Wild Boar Forest. L. S. Chwun. LC 75-13303. pap. 4.95 o.p. (ISBN 0-87359-008-2). Northwood Inst.

Wild Bobcats. Anne LaBastille. Ed. by Russell Bourne & Bonnie S. Lawrence. LC 73-89875. (Ranger Rick's Best Friends Ser.: No. 2). (Illus.). 32p. (gr. 1-6). 1973. 2.50 (ISBN 0-912186-07-0). Natl Wildlife.

Wild Branch on the Olive Tree. William Treacy & Raphael Levine. LC 74-24492. (Illus.). 200p. 1975. 6.95 o.p. (ISBN 0-8323-0240-6). Binford.

Wild Bunch. Ernest Haycox. 245p. 1975. Repr. of 1943 ed. lib. bdg. 9.95 o.p. (ISBN 0-89190-973-7). Am Repr-Rivercity Pr.

Wild Canids: Their Systematics, Behavioral Ecology & Evolution. Ed. by M. W. Fox. 508p. 1975. 22.50 (ISBN 0-442-22430-3). Krieger.

Wild Cat. Laura Black. 416p. 1981. pap. 2.75 (ISBN 0-446-95754-2). Warner Bks.

Wild Dogs of the World. Lois E. Bueler. LC 72-96435. (Illus.). 274p. (Orig.). 1980. pap. 6.95 (ISBN 0-8128-6075-6). Stein & Day.

Wild Duck. Henrik Ibsen. Ed. by Kai Jurgensen & Robert Schenkkan. Tr. by Kai Jurgensen & Robert Schenkkan. LC 66-21588. 1966. pap. text ed. 2.95x (ISBN 0-88295-046-0). AHM Pub.

Wild Duck. Henrik Ibsen. Ed. by Dounia B. Christiani. (Critcal Editions). (gr. 9-12). 1969. 5.00 (ISBN 0-393-04187-5, NortonC); pap. text ed. 5.00 (ISBN 0-393-09825-7). Norton.

Wild Duck. Henrik Ibsen. Tr. by Christopher Hampton. 120p. 1981. pap. 7.50 (ISBN 0-571-11601-9, Pub. by Faber & Faber). Merrimack Bk Serv.

Wild Edge: Life & Lore of the Great Atlantic Beaches. Philip Kopper. 288p. 1981. pap. 6.95 (ISBN 0-14-004497-2). Penguin.

Wild Edible Plants of New England: A Field Guide, Including Poisonous Plants Often Encountered. Joan Richardson. (Illus.). 256p. (Orig.). 1981. pap. 9.95 (ISBN 0-89933-009-6). DeLorme Pub. Postponed.

Wild Edibles of the Northeast. E. Barrie Kavasch. (Northeast Color Ser.). (Illus.). 64p. (Orig.). 1981. pap. 4.95 (ISBN 0-686-69148-2). Hancock Hse.

Wild Fire. Barbara Riefe. LC 80-83569. 384p. (Orig.). 1981. pap. 2.95 (ISBN 0-87216-798-4). Playboy Pbks.

Wild-Flower Gardening. Ed. by Time-Life Books. (Time-Life Encyclopedia of Gardening Ser.). 1977. 11.95 (ISBN 0-8094-2554-8). Time-Life.

Wild Flowers. Homer D. House. (Illus.). 626p. 1974. 19.95 (ISBN 0-02-554560-4). Macmillan.

Wild Flowers. Helen L. Pursey. (Hamlyn Nature Guide Ser.). (Illus.). 1978. 8.95 (ISBN 0-600-39381-X). Transatlantic.

Wild Flowers: A Photographic Guide. Desmond Parish & Marjorie Parish. (Illus.). 1979. 12.95 (ISBN 0-7137-0947-2, Pub by Blandford Pr England). Sterling.

Wild Flowers in South Carolina. Wade T. Batson. LC 64-23760. (Illus.). 146p. 1980. pap. 5.95 (ISBN 0-87249-257-5). U of SC Pr.

Wild Flowers of Britain. Roger Phillips. LC 78-303430. (Illus.). 1977. Repr of 1977 ed. 27.50x (ISBN 0-7063-5580-6). Intl Pubns Serv.

Wild Flowers of Britain & Northern Europe. Richard Fitter & Alastair Fitter. LC 74-3756. (Encore Edition). (Illus.). 1974. 3.95 o.p. (ISBN 0-684-15246-0, ScribT). Scribner.

Wild Flowers of the Pacific Coast. 3rd ed. Leslie L. Haskin. LC 66-28384. (Illus.). 1981. pap. 8.95 (ISBN 0-8323-0385-2). Binford.

Wild Flowers of Wilson's Promontory National Park. J. Ros Garnet. (Illus.). 1979. 7.95x (ISBN 0-85091-111-7, Pub. by Lothian). Intl Schol Bk Serv.

Wild Food in Australia. A. B. Cribb & J. W. Cribb. 1980. pap. 5.95x (ISBN 0-00-634436-4, Pub. by W Collins Australia). Intl Schol Bk Serv.

Wild Food Plants of Indiana & Adjacent States. Alan McPherson & Sue McPherson. LC 76-48528. (Illus.). 192p. 1977. 12.50x (ISBN 0-253-19039-8); pap. 4.95x (ISBN 0-253-28925-4). Ind U Pr.

Wild Foods: A Beginner's Guide to Identifying, Harvesting & Preparing Safe & Tasty Plants from the Outdoors. Laurence Pringle. LC 78-1910. (Illus.). 192p. (gr. 7 up). 1978. 10.95 (ISBN 0-590-07511-X, Four Winds). Schol Bk Serv.

Wild Foods: Treats for Your Table. Charlotte Bull. (Illus.). 1981. 9.95 (ISBN 0-689-11031-6). Atheneum.

Wild Game Cook Book. Martin Rywell. 74p. 1952. pap. 3.95 (ISBN 0-917420-05-5). Buck Hill.

Wild Garden. Judith Berrisford. 1973. 8.95 (ISBN 0-571-04821-8, Pub. by Faber & Faber). Merrimack Bk Serv.

Wild Garden or Speaking of Writing. Angus Wilson. 1963. 12.95x (ISBN 0-520-01346-8); pap. 1.25 (ISBN 0-520-01347-6, CAL112). U of Cal Pr.

Wild Geese. Eilis Dillon. 1981. 12.95 (ISBN 0-671-22852-8). S&S.

Wild Geese of the World. Myrfyn Owen. (Illus.). 236p. 1981. 45.00 (ISBN 0-686-69428-7, Pub. by Batsford England). David & Charles.

Wild-Goose Chase: A Modern Critical Edition with Commentary and Notes Based on the 1652 Folio. John Fletcher. Ed. by Rota H. Lister & Stephen Orgel. LC 79-54349. (Renaissance Drama Second Ser.). 200p. 1980. lib. bdg. 22.00 (ISBN 0-8240-4466-5). Garland Pub.

Wild Grass. Lu Hsun. 1974. pap. 1.95 (ISBN 0-8351-0435-4). China Bks.

Wild Green Things in the City: A Book of Weeds. Anne O. Dowden. LC 72-158687. (Illus.). (gr. 5-8). 1972. 8.95 o.p. (ISBN 0-690-89067-2, TYC-J). T Y Crowell.

Wild Gypsy Love. Corinne Johnston. (Orig.). 1976. pap. 1.75 o.s.i. (ISBN 0-515-04014-2). Jove Pubns.

Wild Heart. Dale Carlson. (Triumph Bks.). 1977. PLB 6.90 (ISBN 0-531-01326-X). Watts.

Wild Herds. Time-Life Television. (Wild, Wild World of Animals Ser.). (Illus.). 1977. 10.95 (ISBN 0-913948-11-X). Time-Life.

Wild Herds. (Wild, Wild World of Animals). (Illus.). (gr. 5 up). 1977. lib. bdg. 11.97 (ISBN 0-685-77697-2). Silver.

Wild Horse Gatherers. Alden Robertson. (Illus.). (gr. 7 up). 1978. pap. 10.95 (ISBN 0-684-15591-5, ScribJ, ScribJ). Scribner.

Wild Horse Gatherers. Alden Robertson. LC 77-17512. (Sierra Club-Scribner Juvenile Ser.). (Illus.). (gr. 7 up). 1978. 10.95 o.p. (ISBN 0-684-15589-3); pap. 6.95 (ISBN 0-684-15591-5). Sierra.

Wild Horse of the West. Walker D. Wyman. LC 66-17457. (Illus.). 1962. pap. 2.45 (ISBN 0-8032-5223-4, B*B 144, Bison). U of Nebr Pr.

Wild Horse Running. Sam Savitt. (Illus.). (gr. 4-6). 1976. pap. 1.50 (ISBN 0-590-00092-6, Schol Pap). Schol Bk Serv.

Wild Horses. Evelyn Bolton. LC 74-9530. (Evelyn Bolton's Horse Stories Ser). (Illus.). 32p. (gr. 3-7). 1974. PLB 5.95 (ISBN 0-87191-374-7); pap. 2.95 (ISBN 0-89812-126-4). Creative Ed.

Wild Hunt. Jill Tattersall. 1977. pap. 1.75 o.p. (ISBN 0-449-23380-4, Crest). Fawcett.

Wild Irish Boy. Charles R. Maturin. Ed. by Robert L. Wolff. (Ireland-Nineteenth Century Fiction, Ser. Two: Vol. 11). 1979. lib. bdg. 126.00 (ISBN 0-8240-3460-0); lib. bdg. 46.00 ea. Garland Pub.

Wild Irish Girl. Lady Morgan S. Owenson. Ed. by Robert L. Wolff. (Ireland-Nineteenth Century Fiction, Ser. Two: Vol. 6). 1979. lib. bdg. 126.00 (ISBN 0-8240-3455-4); lib. bdg. 46.00 ea. Garland Pub.

Wild Ivory. Horace S. Mazet. 1971. 6.95 o.p. (ISBN 0-87874-003-1, Nautilus). Galloway.

Wild Jack. John Christopher. 192p. (gr. 5-9). 1974. 8.95 (ISBN 0-02-718300-9, 71830). Macmillan.

Wild Jack. John Christopher. LC 77-16437. (gr. 5-9). 1978. pap. 1.95 o.s.i. (ISBN 0-02-042410-8, 04241, Collier). Macmillan.

Wild Life in the Far West...Comprising Hunting & Trapping Adventures with Kit Carson & Others: Captivity & Life Among the Comanches. James Hobbs. LC 75-7113. (Indian Captivities Ser.: Vol. 87). 1977. Repr. of 1872 ed. 44.00 (ISBN 0-8240-1711-0). Garland Pub.

Wild Mammals of Hong Kong. Patricia Marshall. (Illus.). 1967. pap. 1.40x o.p. (ISBN 0-19-638060-X). Oxford U Pr.

Wild Mammals of Missouri. Charles W. Schwartz & E. R. Schwartz. (Illus.). 1959. 15.00x o.p. (ISBN 0-8262-0001-X). U of Mo Pr.

Wild Mammals of Missouri. rev. ed. Charles W. Schwartz & Elizabeth R. Schwartz. 384p. 1981. text ed. 35.00 (ISBN 0-8262-0324-8). U of Mo Pr.

Wild Mammals of New England: Field Guide Edition. rev. ed. Alfred J. Godin. Ed. by Harry Vanderweide. (Illus.). 200p. 1981. pap. 6.95 (ISBN 0-89933-012-6). DeLorme Pub.

Wild Martin & the Crow. Joan Tate. pap. text ed. 1.95x o.p. (ISBN 0-435-11888-9). Heinemann Ed.

Wild Mushroom Recipes. Carole Eberly. (Illus.). 64p. (Orig.). 1979. pap. 1.50 (ISBN 0-932296-05-X). Eberly Pr.

Wild Mushrooms Worth Knowing. Ansel H. Stubbs. LC 76-107330. Orig. Title: Wild Mushrooms of the Central Midwest. (Illus.). 160p. 1980. pap. 7.95 (ISBN 0-913504-58-0). Lowell Pr.

Wild Nights. Emma Tennant. LC 79-3365. 132p. 1980. 9.95 (ISBN 0-15-196725-3). HarBraceJ.

Wild Oats. Jacob Epstein. 1980. pap. 2.75 (ISBN 0-671-83393-6). PB.

Wild Oats. John O'Keeffe. 1977. pap. 3.25x (ISBN 0-87830-556-4). Theatre Arts.

Wild Oats of Han. Katharine S. Prichard. (Illus.). 160p. (gr. 4-7). 1973. 4.95g o.s.i. (ISBN 0-02-775200-3). Macmillan.

Wild One. Marianne Harvey. (Orig.). 1981. pap. 2.95 (ISBN 0-440-19207-2). Dell.

Wild One. John Reese. 1978. pap. 1.25 o.p. (ISBN 0-449-13953-0, GM). Fawcett.

Wild Orphan. Glen Rounds. (Illus.). (gr. 4-6). 1961. 7.95 (ISBN 0-8234-0147-2). Holiday.

Wild Orphan Friends. William J. Weber. LC 76-11738. (Illus.). 160p. (gr. 5 up). 1976. 6.95 o.p. (ISBN 0-03-017536-4). HR&W.

Wild Orphan Friends. William J. Weber. LC 76-11738. (Illus.). 160p. (gr. 5 up). 1980. pap. 3.50 (ISBN 0-03-056822-6). HR&W.

Wild Party, A Certain Wilderness, The Set-Up. Joseph M. March. LC 68-27623. (Illus.). 310p. 1968. ltd. autographed ed. 25.00 (ISBN 0-87027-104-0); 10.95 (ISBN 0-87027-103-2). Wheelwright.

Wild Pigeons & Doves. rev. ed. Jean Delacour. (Illus.). 189p. 1980. 9.95 (ISBN 0-87666-968-2, AP-6810). TFH Pubns.
Wild Places of the South. Steve Price. LC 79-26290. (Illus.). 200p. 1980. lib. bdg. 11.25 o.p. (ISBN 0-914788-22-1). East Woods.
Wild River Wilderness. 1976. pap. 3.95 (ISBN 0-89272-039-5). Down East.
Wild Stallions. John Benteen. (Sundance: No. 7). 1979. pap. 1.75 (ISBN 0-8439-0705-3, Leisure Bks). Nordon Pubns.
Wild Strawberries. Angela Thirkell. LC 80-7834. (Barsetshire Ser.). 280p. 1980. pap. 2.25 (ISBN 0-06-080526-9, P526, PL). Har-Row.
Wild Tales. Howard Schwach. Ed. by Patricia McCarthy. (Pal Paperbacks Kit A Ser.). (Illus., Orig.). (gr. 7-12). 1974. pap. text ed. 1.25 (ISBN 0-8374-3473-4). Xerox Ed Pubns.
Wild Teas, Coffees, & Cordials. Hilary Stewart. (Illus.). 128p. 1981. 7.95 (ISBN 0-295-95804-9). U of Wash Pr.
Wild Times. Brian Garfield. 1980. pap. 2.50 o.s.i. (ISBN 0-440-19457-1). Dell.
Wild Violets. Phyllis Green. (gr. k-6). 1980. pap. 1.25 (ISBN 0-440-49671-3, YB). Dell.
Wild Washerwoman. John Yeoman. LC 78-32147. (Illus.). (gr. k-3). 1979. 8.95 (ISBN 0-688-80219-2); PLB 8.59 (ISBN 0-688-84219-4). Greenwillow.
Wild Winds of Mayaland. Lucy Fuchs. (YA) 1978. 5.95 (ISBN 0-685-85784-0, Avalon). Bouregy.
Wild, Wonderful World of Parachutes & Parachuting. Bud Sellick. LC 80-20506. 1981. 17.95 (ISBN 0-13-959577-5). P-H.
Wild Young Desert. Ann Atwood. LC 73-106536. (Illus.). (gr. 6 up). 1970. 5.95 o.p. (ISBN 0-684-12625-7, ScribJ). Scribner.
Wild Young Man Called John. Norman C. Habel. 1972. pap. 0.85 (ISBN 0-570-06539-9, 56-1243). Concordia.
Wildcat. Irene Makin. (gr. 4-6). 1969. PLB 6.00 o.p. (ISBN 0-688-51093-0). Lothrop.
Wildcats. J. T. Edson. 192p. (Orig.). 1981. pap. 1.95 (ISBN 0-425-04755-5). Berkley Pub.
Wildeaters. Sally Helgesen. LC 79-7867. 168p. 1981. 9.95 (ISBN 0-385-14637-X). Doubleday.
Wilder Musings. Anne Wilder. 64p. 1981. 5.00 (ISBN 0-682-49725-8). Exposition.
Wilder Shore. Daphne Clair. (Harlequin Presents Ser.). 192p. 1980. pap. 1.50 (ISBN 0-373-10385-9, Pub. by Harlequin). PB.
Wilderness & Gardens: An American Lady's Prospect. Margaret L. Been. (Illus.). 1974. pap. 5.00 (ISBN 0-87423-011-X). Westburg.
Wilderness Areas of North America. Ann Sutton & Myron Sutton. LC 74-8860. (Funk & W Bk.). (Illus.). 428p. 1974. 10.95 o.s.i. (ISBN 0-308-10124-3, TYC-T). T Y Crowell.
Wilderness Areas of North America. Ann Sutton & Myron Sutton. LC 74-8860. (Funk & W Bk.). (Illus.). 1975. pap. 4.95 o.s.i. (ISBN 0-308-10125-1, F117, TYC-T). T Y Crowell.
Wilderness Canoeing. John W. Malo. LC 71-140902. (Illus.). 1971. 7.95 o.s.i. (ISBN 0-02-579270-9). Macmillan.
Wilderness Canpeina & Campina. Clifford. Jacobson. (Illus.). 1977. 13.95 (ISBN 0-87690-228-X); pap. 6.95 (ISBN 0-87690-229-8). Dutton.
Wilderness Champion: The Story of a Great Hound. Joseph W. Lippincott. (Illus.). (gr. 7-9). 1944. 9.95 (ISBN 0-397-30099-9). Lippincott.
Wilderness Cookbook. Berndt Berglund & Clare Bolsby. LC 72-12158. 192p. 1973. 4.95 (ISBN 0-684-14661-4, ScribT); pap. 3.95 (ISBN 0-684-14715-7, ScribT). Scribner.
Wilderness Economics & Policy. Lloyd C. Irland. LC 78-24791. 256p. 1979. 19.95 (ISBN 0-669-02821-5). Lexington Bks.
Wilderness Europe. Douglas Botting. (World's Wild Places Ser.). (Illus.). 1976. lib. bdg. 11.97 (ISBN 0-686-51025-9). Silver.
Wilderness Europe. Douglas Botting. (World's Wild Places). (Illus.). 1976. 12.95 (ISBN 0-8094-2062-7). Time-Life.
Wilderness Family Pt. 2. Crome. (gr. 3-5). pap. 1.50 (ISBN 0-590-12113-8, Schol Pap). Schol Bk Serv.
Wilderness Journey. Dorothy B. Kidney. (Illus.). 200p. (Orig.). 1980. pap. 7.95 (ISBN 0-930096-10-X). G Gannett.
Wilderness Journey. William O. Steele. LC 55-9006. (Illus.). (gr. 4-6). 6.75 o.p. (ISBN 0-15-297318-4, HJ). HarBraceJ.
Wilderness Life. Calvin Rutstrum. 256p. 1975. 10.95 (ISBN 0-02-606390-5). Macmillan.
Wilderness Manhunt: The Spanish Search for La Salle. Robert S. Weddle. LC 72-1579. (Illus.). 286p. 1973. 14.95 (ISBN 0-292-79000-7). U of Tex Pr.
Wilderness Neighbors. Bradford Angier. LC 76-26303. 228p. 1981. pap. 5.95 (ISBN 0-8128-6100-0). Stein & Day.
Wilderness of Miseries: War & Warriors in Early America. John E. Ferling. LC 79-8951. (Contributions in Military History: No. 22). (Illus.). xiv, 227p. 1980. lib. bdg. 25.00 (ISBN 0-313-22093-X, FWW/). Greenwood.
Wilderness Politics & Indian Gifts: The Northern Colonial Frontier, 1748-1763. Wilbur R. Jacobs. LC 51-2149. Orig. Title: Anglo-French Rivalry Along the Ohio & Northwest Frontier-1748-1763. (Illus.). 1966. pap. 1.65 (ISBN 0-8032-5100-9, BB 351, Bison). U of Nebr Pr.
Wilderness Reader. Frank Bergon. (Orig.). 1980. pap. 3.50 (ISBN 0-451-61902-1, ME1902, Ment). NAL.
Wilderness Search & Rescue: A Complete Handbook. Timothy J. Setnicka. Ed. by Kenneth Andrasko. (Illus., Orig.). 1981. pap. 12.95 (ISBN 0-910146-21-7). Appalach Mtn.
Wilderness Survival. Boy Scouts of America. LC 19-600. (Illus.). 40p. (gr. 6-12). 1974. pap. 0.70x (ISBN 0-8395-3265-2, 3265). BSA.
Wilderness Survival. Bernard Shanks. LC 80-17508. (Illus.). 224p. 1980. text ed. 15.00x (ISBN 0-87663-343-2); pap. 5.95 (ISBN 0-87663-998-8). Universe.
Wilderness Track. Owen G. Irons. 224p. (Orig.). 1980. pap. 1.95 (ISBN 0-89083-659-0). Zebra.
Wilderness Venture. Elizabeth Howard. LC 72-12945. (gr. 7 up). 1973. 6.75 o.p. (ISBN 0-688-20074-5). Morrow.
Wilderness Visions: Science Fiction Westerns, Vol. 1. David Mogen. LC 80-8673. (I. O. Evans Studies in the Philosophy & Criticism of Literature: No. 1). 64p. 1981. lib. bdg. 8.95x (ISBN 0-89370-152-1); pap. text ed. 2.95x (ISBN 0-89370-252-8). Borgo Pr.
Wilderness Waterways: A Guide to Information Sources. Ed. by Ronald Ziegler. LC 78-10410. (Sports, Games, & Pastimes Information Guide Ser.: Vol. 1). 1979. 30.00 (ISBN 0-8103-1434-7). Gale.
Wilderness (Yuan-yeh) Ts'ao Yu. Tr. by Christopher C. Rand & Joseph S. Lau. LC 78-65981. (Chinese Literature in Translation Ser.). 160p. 1980. 12.50x (ISBN 0-253-17297-7). Ind U Pr.
Wildfire. Mavis T. Clark. LC 73-19049. 224p. (gr. 6-9). 1974. 5.95g o.s.i. (ISBN 0-02-718970-8, 71897). Macmillan.
Wildfire. Zane Grey. 1981. pap. price not set (ISBN 0-671-43194-3). PB.
Wildflower Gardening. O. Allen. LC 77-73630. (Encyclopedia of Gardening Ser.). (Illus.). (gr. 6 up). 1977. PLB 11.97 (ISBN 0-8094-2555-6, Pub. by Time-Life). Silver.
Wildflowers & the Stories Behind Their Names. Phillis S. Busch. LC 73-1351. (Illus.). (gr. 3up). 1977. 10.00 (ISBN 0-684-14820-X, ScribT). Scribner.
Wildflowers in Britain. Allison Rose. 7.50x (ISBN 0-392-07390-0, LTB). Soccer.
Wildflowers of the Northeastern United States. LC 77-18598. (Illus.). 1980. 8.95 (ISBN 0-8120-0937-1). Barron.
Wildflowers of the Outer Banks: Kitty Hawk to Hatteras. Dunes of Dare Garden Club. LC 79-18927. (Illus.). 1980. pap. 6.95 (ISBN 0-8078-4061-0, 4061). U of NC Pr.
Wildflowers of Western America. John E. Klimas. 1974. write for info. o.p. Knopf.
Wildflowers 1, the Cascades. Elizabeth Horn. (Illus.). 1977. pap. 8.95 (ISBN 0-911518-07-X). Touchstone Pr Ore.
Wildfowler's Heritage. Ed. by James M. Jordan & George T. Alcorn. LC 80-85152. (Illus.). 120p. 1981. 46.50 (ISBN 0-938694-03-0); deluxe ed. 125.00; deluxe ed. with remarque 175.00. Jordan & Co.
Wildkeepers' Guest. Nigel Grimshaw. (gr. 5-7). 1978. 9.95 (ISBN 0-571-10899-7, Pub. by Faber & Faber). Merrimack Bk Serv.
Wildlife. Photos by Robert Smith. LC 76-5667. (Illus.). 120p. (Text by Robert Storm). 1976. pap. 10.95 (ISBN 0-912856-27-0); 20.00 o.p. (ISBN 0-686-67420-0). Graphic Arts Ctr.
Wildlife Adventure Ser, 8 vols. W. S. Briscoe & Leonard R. Briscoe. (gr. 3-7). 1966. pap. text ed. 6.52 ea. (Sch Div); tchr's. manual 3.72 (ISBN 0-201-40712-4). A-W.
Wildlife & Protected Areas: An Overview. (UNEP Report Ser.: No. 6). 50p. 1981. pap. 7.00 (ISBN 0-686-69543-7, UNEP 38, UNEP). Unipub.
Wildlife Begins at Home. Tony Soper. LC 75-10700. 1975. 11.95 (ISBN 0-7153-7111-8). David & Charles.
Wildlife Biology. Raymond F. Dasmann. 256p. 1981. text ed. 17.95 (ISBN 0-471-08042-X). Wiley.
Wildlife Biotelemetry. Ed. by H. P. Kimmich. (Journal: Biotelemetry & Patient Monitoring: Vol. 7, No. 3-4). (Illus.). 116p. 1980. pap. write for info. (ISBN 3-8055-2093-X). S Karger.
Wildlife Conservation Principles & Practices. rev. ed. Ed. by Richard D. Teague & Eugene Decker. LC 79-2960. (Illus.). 280p. 1979. pap. 7.50 (ISBN 0-933564-06-6). Wildlife Soc.
Wildlife Ecology: An Analytical Approach. Aaron N. Moen. LC 73-6833. (Animal Science Ser.). (Illus.). 1973. text ed. 35.95x (ISBN 0-7167-0826-4). W H Freeman.
Wildlife in Britain & Ireland. Richard Perry. (Illus.). 253p. 1978. 16.00x (ISBN 0-85664-306-8, Pub. by Croom Helm Ltd England). Biblio Dist.
Wildlife in Papua New Guinea. Eric Lindgren. (Illus.). 1976. 12.50 o.p. (ISBN 0-584-97052-8). R Curtis Bks.
Wildlife in Tanzanian Settlement Policy: The Case of the Selous. Gordon Matzke. LC 77-18175. (Africa Ser.: No. 28). 1978. pap. 6.50x (ISBN 0-915984-50-4). Syracuse U Foreign Comp.
Wildlife in Wood. Richard Le Master. 1978. 19.95 (ISBN 0-9601840-1-5, Pub. by Model Tech). Contemp Bks.
Wildlife Management. Robert H. Giles, Jr. LC 78-15700. (Animal Science Ser.). (Illus.). 1978. text ed. 23.95x (ISBN 0-7167-0082-4). W H Freeman.
Wildlife Management Techniques Manual. 4th ed. The Wildlife Society. Ed. by Sanford D. Schemnitz. LC 80-19970. (Illus.). 722p. 1980. 20.00 (ISBN 0-933564-08-2). Wildlife Soc.
Wildlife of Mexico: The Game Birds & Mammals. A. Starker Leopold. LC 59-6865. (Illus.). 568p. 1959. 35.00 (ISBN 0-520-00724-7). U of Cal Pr.
Wildlife Sounds & Their Recording. Eric Simms. (Illus.). 1980. 13.95 (ISBN 0-236-40134-3, Pub. by Paul Elek). Merrimack Bk Serv.
Wildlife Stories of Faith McNulty: A Reporter at Large in the Natural World. Faith McNulty. LC 79-7400. (Illus.). 480p. 1980. 17.95 (ISBN 0-385-14300-1). Doubleday.
Wildlings. Mary Leister. LC 76-2063. (Illus.). 192p. 1976. 8.95 (ISBN 0-916144-06-2). Stemmer Hse.
Wildly Successful Plants: Handbook of North American Weeds. Lawrence J. Crockett. (Illus.). 1977. 12.95 o.s.i. (ISBN 0-02-528850-4, 52885). Macmillan.
Wildness Is All Around Us. Eugene Kinkead. (Illus.). 178p. 1978. pap. 10.00x (ISBN 0-87690-277-8). E Kinkead.
Wildtrack, Reminiscences of a Nature Detective. Hugh Falkus. LC 78-16537. 1979. 14.95 o.p. (ISBN 0-03-046506-0). HR&W.
Wildwaters. Buddy Mays. LC 76-58033. (Illus.). 1977. pap. 6.95 o.p. (ISBN 0-87701-089-7). Chronicle Bks.
Wildwood Wisdom. Ellsworth Jaeger. (Illus.). (gr. 7 up). 1966. 12.95 (ISBN 0-02-558890-7). Macmillan.
Wiley & the Hairy Man: Adapted from an American Folk Tale. Molly G. Bang. LC 75-38581. (Ready-to-Read Ser). (Illus.). 64p. (gr. 1-4). 1976. 8.95 (ISBN 0-02-708370-5, 70837). Macmillan.
Wiley Metric Guide. P. J. O'Neill. 1976. 7.95 o.p. (ISBN 0-471-02142-3). Wiley.
Wiley Reader: Designs for Writing. brief ed. Caroline D. Eckhardt & David H. Stewart. LC 78-15326. 1979. pap. 8.95 (ISBN 0-471-03499-1); tchrs. manual avail. (ISBN 0-471-04877-1). Wiley.
Wiley Reader: Designs for Writing. Caroline D. Eckhardt et al. LC 75-29499. 592p. 1976. 9.95 (ISBN 0-471-22970-9); instructor's manual avail. (ISBN 0-471-01458-3). Wiley.
Wilfred Pickles Invites You to Have Another Go. Wilfred Pickles. LC 77-85030. 1978. 14.95 (ISBN 0-7153-7393-5). David & Charles.
Wilfred the Rat. James Stevenson. LC 77-1091. (Illus.). (ps-3). 1977. 7.25 (ISBN 0-688-80103-X); PLB 6.96 (ISBN 0-688-84103-1). Greenwillow.
Wilhelm Busch. Dieter P. Lotze. (World Authors Ser.: No. 525). 1979. lib. bdg. 14.50 (ISBN 0-8057-6365-1). Twayne.
Wilhelm Dilthey: A Hermeneutic Approach to the Study of History & Culture. Ilse N. Bulhof. (Martinus Nijhoff Philosophy Library: No. 2). 225p. 1980. lib. bdg. 37.00 (ISBN 90-247-2360-4, Pub. by Martinus Nijhoff). Kluwer Boston.
Wilhelm Dilthey: An Introduction. Herbert A. Hodges. 1969. Repr. of 1944 ed. 13.00 (ISBN 0-86527-211-5). Fertig.
Wilhelm Dilthey: Pioneer of the Human Sciences. H. P. Rickman. 1980. 16.50x (ISBN 0-520-03879-7). U of Cal Pr.
Wilhelm Dilthey: The Critique of Historical Reason. Michael Ermarth. write for info. (ISBN 0-226-21743-4). U of Chicago Pr.
Wilhelm Meister: The Years of Apprenticeship. Johann W. Von Goethe. Tr. by H. M. Waidson. 1980. 11.95 ea.; Vol. I. (ISBN 0-7145-3675-X); Vol. II. (ISBN 0-7145-3699-7); Vol. 3. (ISBN 0-7145-3702-0). Riverrun NY.
Wilhelm Muller: The Poet of the Schubert Song Cycles. Cecilia C. Baumann. LC 80-12806. (Studies in German Literature). (Illus.). 208p. 1981. 17.50x (ISBN 0-271-00266-2). Pa St U Pr.
Wilhelm Raabe. Horst S. Daemmrich. (World Authors Ser.: No. 594). 1981. lib. bdg. 13.95 (ISBN 0-8057-6436-4). Twayne.
Wilhelm Tell. Friedrich Von Schiller. Tr. by Gilbert Jordan. LC 63-12200. (Orig.). 1964. pap. 4.90 o.p. (ISBN 0-672-60416-7). Bobbs.
Wilhelm Von Humboldt's Conception of Linguistic Relativity. Roger L. Brown. LC 67-30542. (Janua Linguarum, Ser. Minor: No. 65). (Orig.). 1967. pap. text ed. 20.00x (ISBN 90-2790-593-2). Mouton.
Wilhelm Wundt & the Making of a Scientific Psychology. Ed. by Robert W. Rieber. 260p. 1980. 24.50 (ISBN 0-306-40483-4, Plenum Pr). Plenum Pub.
Wilhemina Jones, Future Star. Dingda McCannon. LC 79-53602. (YA) (gr. 8-12). 1980. 8.95 (ISBN 0-440-04572-X). Delacorte.
Wilhite-Dew Debate. J. Portert Wilhite & James F. Dew. pap. 2.50 (ISBN 0-89315-355-9). Lambert Bk.
Wilkie Collins, a Critical Survey of His Prose Fiction with a Bibliography. R. V. Andrews. Ed. by E. F. Bleiler. LC 78-60801. (The Fiction of Popular Culture Ser.: Vol. 1). 367p. 1979. lib. bdg. 35.00 (ISBN 0-8240-9667-3). Garland Pub.
Wilkie Collins: An Annotated Bibliography 1889-1976. Kirk H. Beetz. LC 77-26609. (Author Bibliographies Ser.: No. 35). 1978. 10.00 (ISBN 0-8108-1103-0). Scarecrow.
Wilkie Collins: The Critical Heritage. Ed. by Norman Page. (Critical Heritage Ser.). 1974. 27.00x (ISBN 0-7100-7843-9). Routledge & Kegan.
Will. G. Gordon Liddy. 1981. pap. 3.50 (ISBN 0-440-09666-9). Dell.
Will, 2 vols. Brian O'Shaughnessy. LC 79-13524. 1980. Vol. 1, 240 P. 57.50 (ISBN 0-521-22679-1); Vol. 2, 360 P. 62.50 (ISBN 0-521-22680-5). Cambridge U Pr.
Will. Richard M. Stern. 1977. pap. 1.95 o.p. (ISBN 0-345-25763-4). Ballantine.
Will All the King's Men. J. H. Olthuis et al. 1972. pap. 3.95 o.p. (ISBN 0-686-11987-8). Wedge Pub.
Will & Destiny: Morality & Tragedy in George Eliot's Novels. Felicia Bonaparte. LC 74-16832. 221p. 1975. 15.00x (ISBN 0-8147-0983-4); pap. 7.00x (ISBN 0-8147-1030-1). NYU Pr.
Will Capitalism Survive? A Challenge by Paul Johnson with Twelve Responses. Ed. by Ernest Lefever. 79p. 1979. pap. 3.00 (ISBN 0-89633-026-5). Ethics & Public Policy.
Will Dad Ever Move Back Home? Paula Z. Hogan. LC 79-24058. (Life & Living from a Child's Point of View Ser.). (Illus.). (gr. k-5). 1980. PLB 9.65 (ISBN 0-8172-1356-2). Raintree Child.
Will-God's Way: The True Autobiography of an Orphan. Macye Ross. 1981. 8.95 (ISBN 0-533-04846-X). Vantage.
Will I Ever Be Good Enough? Judith Conaway. LC 76-45854. (Moods & Emotions Ser.). (Illus.). (gr. k-3). 1977. PLB 8.95 (ISBN 0-8172-0059-2). Raintree Pubs.
Will I Ever Be Older? Eva Grant. LC 80-24782. (Life & Living from a Child's Point of View Ser.). (Illus.). (gr. k-5). 1981. PLB 9.65 (ISBN 0-8172-1363-5). Raintree Child.
Will I Have a Friend. Miriam Cohen. (Illus.). (gr. k-1). 1967. 7.95 (ISBN 0-02-722790-1). Macmillan.
Will in Love. Rosemary A. Sisson. (gr. 7 up). 1977. 9.25 (ISBN 0-688-22107-6); lib. bdg. 8.88 (ISBN 0-688-32107-0). Morrow.
Will James: The Last Cowboy Legend. rev. ed. Anthony A. Amaral. LC 80-155. (Lancehead Ser.). (Illus.). xiv, 175p. 1980. 12.00 (ISBN 0-87417-058-3). U of Nev Pr.
Will N. Harben. James K. Murphy. (United States Authors Ser.: No. 330). 1979. lib. bdg. 13.50 (ISBN 0-8057-7245-6). Twayne.
Will of God. Morris Ashcraft. LC 80-65714. 1980. pap. 4.25 (ISBN 0-8054-1620-X). Broadman.
Will of God. Leslie Weatherhead. 1976. pap. 1.25 (ISBN 0-89129-165-2). Jove Pubns.
Will of God. Leslie D. Weatherhead. 56p. 1974. Repr. large print 6.95 o.p. (ISBN 0-687-45575-8); gift ed. 4.95 o.p. (ISBN 0-687-45573-1). Abingdon.
Will of the People: Education in Nevada. Anthony Saville & George Kavina. 1977. pap. text ed. 10.00x (ISBN 0-8191-0162-1). U Pr of Amer.
Will Our Children Have Faith? John H. Westerhoff. 1976. 6.95 (ISBN 0-8164-0319-8). Crossroad NY.
Will Our President Die in Office? Gordon Lindsay. (Prophecy Ser.). 1980. 2.25 (ISBN 0-89985-984-4). Christ Nations.
Will Rogers. E. Paul Alworth. (U. S. Authors Ser.: No. 236). 1974. lib. bdg. 10.95 (ISBN 0-8057-0634-8). Twayne.
Will Rogers. Betty Rogers. LC 79-4743. (Illus.). 1979. pap. 5.95 (ISBN 0-8061-1600-5). U of Okla Pr.
Will Rogers: His Life & Times. Richard M. Ketchum. LC 73-8713. (Illus.). 416p. 1973. 15.00 (ISBN 0-8281-0262-7, Dist. by Scribner); deluxe ed. 17.50 slipcased (ISBN 0-8281-0263-5, Dist. by Scribner). Am Heritage.
Will Shakespeare. John Mortimer. 1978. 8.95 o.s.i. (ISBN 0-440-09792-4). Delacorte.

Will She Be Right? The Future of Australia. Herman Kahn & Thomas Pepper. (Illus.). 199p. 1981. text ed. 18.75 (ISBN 0-7022-1568-6); pap. 7.25 (ISBN 0-7022-1569-4). U of Queensland Pr.

Will the Corporation Survive? John L Paluszek. LC 77-5730. (Illus.). 1977. 11.95 o.p. (ISBN 0-87909-894-5); pap. 7.95 (ISBN 0-87909-893-7). Reston.

Will the Real Monday Please Stand up. Pamela Reynolds. (gr. 7-9). 1976. pap. 1.75 (ISBN 0-671-42067-4). Archway.

Will the Real Monday Please Stand up? Pamela Reynolds. (YA) (gr. 7-9). 1976. pap. 1.25 (ISBN 0-671-29789-9). PB.

Will the Real Norman Mailer Please Stand up. Ed. by Laura Adams. LC 73-83259. 288p. 1974. 16.00 (ISBN 0-8046-9066-9). Kennikat.

Will the Real Renie Lake Please Stand up. Barbara Morgenroth. LC 80-21904. 168p. (gr. 6 up). 1981. PLB 9.95 (ISBN 0-689-30820-5). Atheneum.

Will to Believe. Marcus Bach. 1973. pap. 6.50 (ISBN 0-911336-46-X). Sci of Mind.

Will to Go on. Bernard Brodsky. 64p. (Orig.). 1981. pap. 3.75 (ISBN 0-931896-01-0). Cove View.

Will to Live. Thamsanqa E. Bham. LC 79-66395. 115p. 1980. 6.95 (ISBN 0-533-04383-2). Vantage.

Will to Live. Hugh Franks. 1979. 14.00 (ISBN 0-7100-0181-9). Routledge & Kegan.

Will to Live: Five Steps to Officer Survival. G. W. Boyd. 144p. 1980. 12.50 (ISBN 0-398-04020-6). C C Thomas.

Will to Live: Selected Writings of Arthur Schopenhauer. Arthur Schopenhauer. Ed. by Richard Taylor. LC 67-17822. pap. 4.95 (ISBN 0-8044-6847-8). Ungar.

Will We Meet Each Other's Needs? James R. Hine. 1979. pap. text ed. 7.50 (ISBN 0-8134-2052-0, 2052). Interstate.

Will Weng's Crossword Puzzles: Fifty Original Sunday-Sized Crossword Puzzles, Vol. 7. Will Weng. 64p. 1980. 3.95 (ISBN 0-8129-0933-X). Times Bks.

Will Weng's Crossword Puzzles, No. 5. Ed. by Will Weng. Date not set. pap. cancelled (ISBN 0-8129-0812-0). Times Bks. Postponed.

Will Weng's Holiday Puzzles: Fifty Original Sunday-Size Crossword Puzzles with Holiday Themes. Will Weng. 64p. 1980. 3.95 (ISBN 0-8129-0934-8). Times Bks.

Will You Be My Friend? James Kavanaugh. 1971. 6.95 (ISBN 0-87690-166-6). Dutton.

Will You Count the Stars Without Me? Jane B. Zalben. (Illus.). 32p. 1979. 8.95 (ISBN 0-374-38433-9). FS&G.

Will You Die for Me? Tex Watson. 1978. 7.95 o.p. (ISBN 0-8007-0912-8); 2.50 o.p. (ISBN 0-8007-8361-1, Spire Bks). Revell.

Will You Love Me in September. Philippa Carr. 324p. 1981. 11.95 (ISBN 0-399-12590-6). Putnam.

Willa Cather. Edward K. Brown & Leon Edel. (YA) 1953. 6.95 o.p. (ISBN 0-394-45196-1). Knopf.

Willa Cather. Philip L. Gerber. LC 75-2287. (U. S. Authors Ser.: No. 258). 1975. lib. bdg. 9.95 (ISBN 0-8057-7155-7). Twayne.

Willa Cather. Ed. by Phillip L. Gerber. LC 75-2287. (Twayne's U. S. Authors Ser.). 187p. 1975. pap. text ed. 4.95 (ISBN 0-672-61508-8). Bobbs.

Willa Cather. Dorothy T. McFarland. LC 74-190351. (Modern Literature Ser.). 1972. 10.95 (ISBN 0-8044-2610-4). Ungar.

Willa Cather. Rene Rapin. 115p. 1980. Repr. of 1930 ed. lib. bdg. 12.50 (ISBN 0-8492-7730-2). R West.

Willa Cather: A Critical Biography. E. K. Brown & Leon Edel. 304p. 1980. pap. 2.95 (ISBN 0-380-49676-3, 49676, Discus). Avon.

Willa Cather: A Memoir. Elizabeth S. Sergeant. LC 52-13732. (Illus.). 1963. pap. 1.95 (ISBN 0-8032-5179-3, BB 159, Bison). U of Nebr Pr.

Willa Cather: Her Life & Art. James Woodress. LC 71-124673. (Illus.). 228p. 1975. pap. 3.50 (ISBN 0-8032-5815-1, BB 600, Bison). U of Nebr Pr.

Willa Cather Living: A Personal Record. Edith Lewis. LC 76-17551. 1976. pap. 2.95 (ISBN 0-8032-5849-6, BB 623, Bison). U of Nebr Pr.

Willa Cather's Collected Short Fiction, 1892-1912. rev. ed. Willa Cather. Ed. by Virginia Faulkner. LC 73-126046. 1970. 19.50x (ISBN 0-8032-0770-0). U of Nebr Pr.

Willaby. Rachel Isadora. LC 77-4469. (Illus.). (gr. k-3). 1977. 8.95 (ISBN 0-02-747460-7, 74746). Macmillan.

Willamette Landings: Ghost Towns of the River. 2nd ed. Howard M. Corning. LC 73-81023. 272p. 1973. 8.95 (ISBN 0-87595-093-0); pap. 6.95 (ISBN 0-87595-042-6). Oreg Hist Soc.

Willard Motley. Robert E. Fleming. (United States Authors Ser.: No. 302). 1978. lib. bdg. 12.50 (ISBN 0-8057-7207-3). Twayne.

Willard V. O. Quine. Alex Orenstein. (World Leaders Ser.: No. 15). 1977. lib. bdg. 12.50 (ISBN 0-8057-7716-4). Twayne.

William Allen White's America. Walter Johnson. Ed. by Frank Freidel. LC 78-66541. (The History of the United States Ser.: Vol. 10). 630p. 1979. lib. bdg. 50.00 (ISBN 0-8240-9702-5). Garland Pub.

William & John Linnel: 18th Century London Furniture-Makers, 2 vols. Helena Hayward & Pat Kirkham. LC 80-51404. (Illus.). 400p. 1980. slipcased 125.00 (ISBN 0-8478-0325-2). Rizzoli Intl.

William & Mary & Their House. Charles Ryskamp & A. W. Vliegenthart. (Illus.). 266p. 1980. 59.00x (ISBN 0-19-520185-X). Oxford U Pr.

William Balston, Paper Maker, 1759-1849. Thomas Balston. Ed. by John Bidwell. LC 78-74387. (Nineteenth-Century Book Arts & Printing History Ser.: Vol. 2). (Illus.). 1979. lib. bdg. 22.00 (ISBN 0-8240-3876-2). Garland Pub.

William Beckford. Robert J. Gemmett. (English Authors Ser.: No. 204). 1977. lib. bdg. 12.50 (ISBN 0-8057-6674-X). Twayne.

William Beveridge: A Biography. Jose Harris. 1977. 37.50x (ISBN 0-19-822459-1). Oxford U Pr.

William Blake. Martin Butlin. (Tate Gallery: Little Art Book Ser.). (Illus.). 1977. pap. 1.95 (ISBN 0-8120-0855-3). Barron.

William Blake. David G. Gillham. LC 72-80296. (British Authors Ser). (Illus.). 224p. 1973. 32.50 (ISBN 0-521-08680-9); pap. 8.95x (ISBN 0-521-09735-5). Cambridge U Pr.

William Blake. Victor Paananen. (English Authors Ser.: No. 202). 1977. lib. bdg. 10.95 (ISBN 0-8057-6672-3). Twayne.

William Blake. Kathleen Raine. (World of Art Ser). (Illus.). 1970. pap. 9.95 (ISBN 0-19-519931-6). Oxford U Pr.

William Blake: A Critical Essay. Algernon C. Swinburne, Jr. Ed. by Hugh J. Luke. LC 70-81397. 1970. pap. 4.75x (ISBN 0-8032-5707-4, BB 504, Bison). U of Nebr Pr.

William Blake; or, the English Farmer, 1848. William E. Heygate. Ed. by Robert L. Wolff. LC 75-473. (Victorian Fiction Ser.). 1975. lib. bdg. 66.00 (ISBN 0-8240-1551-7). Garland Pub.

William Blake: Songs of Innocence & Experience. Ed. by Margaret Bottrall. (Casebook Ser.). 1970. 2.50 o.s.i. (ISBN 0-87695-037-3). Aurora Pubs.

William Blake's Writings, 2 vols. William Blake. Ed. by G. E. Bentley. (Oxford English Texts Ser.). (Illus.). 1979. 185.00x (ISBN 0-19-811885-6). Oxford U Pr.

William Blathwayt. Gertrude A. Jacobsen. (Yale Historical Studies, Miscellany: No. XXI). 1932. 47.50x (ISBN 0-685-69829-7). Elliots Bks.

William Booth & His Army. Virgil Robinson. LC 75-25226. (Panda Ser). 1976. pap. 4.95 (ISBN 0-8163-0272-3, 23685-1). Pacific Pr Pub Assn.

William Bradford. Perry D. Westbrook. (United States Authors Ser.). 1978. lib. bdg. 12.50 (ISBN 0-8057-7243-X). Twayne.

William Bradford of Plymouth Colony. William J. Jacobs. LC 74-870. (Visual Biography Ser.). (Illus.). 64p. (gr. 4-6). 1974. PLB 4.90 o.p. (ISBN 0-531-02724-4). Watts.

William Byrd. 2nd ed. Edmund H. Fellowes. 1948. 11.25x o.p. (ISBN 0-19-315204-5). Oxford U Pr.

William Byrd of Westover, 1674-1744. Pierre L. Marambaud. LC 70-151251. (Illus.). 300p. 1971. 17.50x (ISBN 0-8139-0346-7). U Pr of Va.

William Callow. Jan Reynolds. LC 79-56444. (Illus.). 272p. 1980. 150.00 (ISBN 0-7134-1438-3, Pub. by Batsford England). David & Charles.

William Carleton, Irish Peasant Novelist: A Preface to His Fiction. Robert L. Wolff. LC 79-4399. 200p. 1980. lib. bdg. 18.00 (ISBN 0-8240-3527-5). Garland Pub.

William Carlos Williams. M. Weaver. LC 77-149431. (Illus.). 1977. 38.00 (ISBN 0-521-08072-X); pap. 8.50x (ISBN 0-521-29195-X). Cambridge U Pr.

William Carlos Williams. Thomas R. Whitaker. LC 68-24297. (U. S. Authors Ser.: No. 139). 1968. lib. bdg. 10.95 (ISBN 0-8057-0816-2). Twayne.

William Carlos Williams & the American Scene, 1920-1940. Dickran Tashjian. LC 78-20657. (Cal. Ser.: No. 420). (Illus.). 1979. 34.50 (ISBN 0-520-03854-1); pap. 10.95 (ISBN 0-520-03878-9). U of Cal Pr.

William Carlos Williams' Paterson: Language & Landscape. Joel Conarroe. LC 73-92854. 1974. pap. 4.95x (ISBN 0-8122-1046-8). U of Pa Pr.

William Caxton. Frieda E. Penninger. (English Authors Ser.: No. 263). 1979. lib. bdg. 12.95 (ISBN 0-8057-6759-2). Twayne.

William Caxton & Charles Knight. Kenneth Day. (Illus.). 240p. pap. 9.50 (ISBN 0-913720-06-2). Sandstone.

William Chapple: Eighteen Seventy-Six Revised Price List Planes. 1980. pap. 2.50 (ISBN 0-913602-35-3). K Roberts.

William Charles Scully. John R. Doyle, Jr. (World Authors Ser.: No. 490). 1978. lib. bdg. 13.50 (ISBN 0-8057-6331-7). Twayne.

William Cobbett. James Sambrook. (Routledge Author Guides Ser). 236p. 1973. 13.50x (ISBN 0-7100-7560-X); pap. 8.95 (ISBN 0-7100-7561-8). Routledge & Kegan.

William Cobbett & the Politics of Earth. Gerald Duff. (Salzburg Studies in English Literature, Romantic Reassessment: No. 24). 143p. 1972. pap. text ed. 25.00x (ISBN 0-391-01366-1). Humanities.

William Cobbett & the United States, 1792-1835: Bibliographies with Notes & Extracts. Pierce W. Gaines. LC 79-168901. 1971. 15.95x (ISBN 0-912296-00-3, Dist. by U Pr of Va). Am Antiquarian.

William Cobbett: His Thoughts & His Times. J. W. Osborne. LC 66-18874. 10.00 (ISBN 0-910294-35-6). Brown Bk.

William Cowper. Norman Nicholson. 167p. 1980. Repr. of 1951 ed. text ed. 25.00 (ISBN 0-8492-1973-6). R West.

William Crawford Gorgas: Warrior in White. Edward F. Dolan, Jr. & H. T. Silver. LC 68-14243. (Illus.). (gr. 8 up). 1968. 4.50 (ISBN 0-396-05708-X). Dodd.

William Cullen Bryant. John Bigelow. LC 79-78114. (Library of Lives & Letters). 1970. Repr. of 1890 ed. 18.00 (ISBN 0-8103-3369-4). Gale.

William Cullen Bryant. John Bigelow. LC 80-19850. (American Men & Women of Letters Ser.). 360p. 1980. pap. 5.95 (ISBN 0-87754-160-4). Chelsea Hse.

William Cullen Bryant. Albert F. McLean, Jr. (U. S. Authors Ser.: No. 59). 1964. lib. bdg. 10.95 (ISBN 0-8057-0108-7). Twayne.

William Dean Howells: A Bibliography. Vito J. Brenni. LC 73-4855. (Author Bibliographies Ser.: No. 9). 1973. 10.00 (ISBN 0-8108-0620-7). Scarecrow.

William Dunbar. Edmund Reiss. (English Authors Ser.: No. 257). 1979. lib. bdg. 12.95 (ISBN 0-8057-6750-9). Twayne.

William E. Donoghue's Complete Money Market Guide. William E. Donoghue & Thomas Tilling. LC 80-8200. (Illus.). 256p. 1981. 12.95 (ISBN 0-690-02008-2, HarpT). Har-Row.

William Ellery: A Rhode Island Politico & Lord of Admiralty. William M. Fowler, Jr. LC 72-12673. (Illus.). 1973. 10.00 (ISBN 0-8108-0576-6). Scarecrow.

William Ellery Channing & L'Academie Des Sciences Morales et Politques 1870: L'Etude Sur Channing & the Lost Prize Essay. Hester Hastings. LC 59-10107. (Illus.). 61p. 1959. pap. 2.00 (ISBN 0-87057-055-2, Pub. by Brown U Pr). Univ Pr of New England.

William Empson. J. R. Willis. LC 74-76254. (Columbia Essays on Modern Writers Ser.: No. 39). 1969. pap. 2.00 (ISBN 0-231-03131-9, MW39). Columbia U Pr.

William Empson & the Philosophy of Literary Criticism. Christopher Norris. 1978. text ed. 25.75x (ISBN 0-485-11175-6, Athlone Pr). Humanities.

William Everson: A Descriptive Bibliography, 1934-1976. Lee Bartlett & Allan Campo. LC 77-5397. (Author Bibliographies Ser.: No. 33). 1977. 10.00 (ISBN 0-8108-1037-9). Scarecrow.

William Faulkner. Frederick J. Hoffman. (U. S. Authors Ser.: No. 1). lib. bdg. 9.95 (ISBN 0-8057-0244-X). Twayne.

William Faulkner. Joachim Seyppel. LC 74-134826. (Modern Literature Ser.). 120p. 10.95 (ISBN 0-8044-2820-4); pap. 3.45 (ISBN 0-8044-6858-3). Ungar.

William Faulkner: His Life & Work. David Minter. LC 80-13089. 325p. 1980. text ed. 16.95x (ISBN 0-8018-2347-1). Johns Hopkins.

William Faulkner: The Abstract & the Actual. Panthea R. Broughton. LC 74-77324. 222p. 1974. 12.50 (ISBN 0-8071-0083-8). La State U Pr.

William Faulkner: The Critical Heritage. Ed. by John Bassett. (Critical Heritage Ser.). 1975. 36.00 (ISBN 0-7100-8124-3). Routledge & Kegan.

William Faulkner, the William B. Wisdom Collection: A Descriptive Catalog. Thomas Bonner, Jr. & Guillermo N. Falcon. LC 79-26556. (Illus.). 1980. pap. 13.00 (ISBN 0-9603212-2-5). Tulane Univ.

William G. Brownlow: Fighting Parson of the Southern Highlands. E. Merton Coulter. LC 71-136309. (Tennesseana Editions Ser.). (Illus.). 458p. 1971. 10.50x o.p. (ISBN 0-87049-118-0). U of Tenn Pr.

William Gibbs McAdoo: A Passion for Change, 1863-1917. John J. Broesamle. LC 73-83261. 320p. 1974. 12.50 (ISBN 0-8046-9043-X). Kennikat.

William Gilpin: Western Nationalist. Thomas L. Karnes. (Illus.). 1969. 19.95x (ISBN 0-292-70003-2). U of Tex Pr.

William Golding. Bernard F. Dick. (English Authors Ser.: No. 57). 1968. lib. bdg. 10.95 (ISBN 0-8057-1224-0). Twayne.

William Golding: Some Critical Considerations. Ed. by Jack I. Biles & Robert O. Evans. LC 77-73705. 296p. 1978. 18.00x (ISBN 0-8131-1362-8). U Pr of Ky.

William Goldman. Richard Andersen. (United States Authors Ser.: No. 326). 1979. lib. bdg. 10.95 (ISBN 0-8057-7259-6). Twayne.

William Goyen. Robert Phillips. (United States Authors Ser.: No. 329). 1979. lib. bdg. 12.50 (ISBN 0-8057-7269-3). Twayne.

William Gropper. Louis Lozowick. (Illus.). 200p. 1981. 40.00 (ISBN 0-87982-033-0). Art Alliance.

William H. Crawford, 1772-1834. Chase C. Mooney. LC 70-147853. 376p. 1974. 18.00x (ISBN 0-8131-1246-X). U Pr of Ky.

William H. Fox Talbot. Andre Jammes. 1974. pap. 5.95 o.s.i. (ISBN 0-02-000450-8, Collier). Macmillan.

William H. Fox Talbot: Inventor of the Positive-Negative Process. Andre Jammes. Tr. by Maureen Oberli-Turner. (Men & Movements Ser.: Vol. 2). (Illus.). 96p. 1974. 10.95 o.s.i. (ISBN 0-02-558900-8). Macmillan.

William H. Jackson. Beaumont Newhall & Diana Edkins. LC 73-89076. (Morgan & Morgan Monograph). 160p. 1974. 14.00 o.p. (ISBN 0-87100-045-8). Morgan.

William Harborne & the Trade with Turkey: Secret Agent, 1578-1581. Susan Skilliter. (Illus.). 1978. 49.00x (ISBN 0-19-725971-5). Oxford U Pr.

William Harper Wright: His Ancestry & Descendants & Allied Lines of Stone's River, Tennessee. Mildred S. Wright. LC 80-52849. (Illus.). 183p. 1980. 35.00 (ISBN 0-917016-16-5); accopress 25.00 (ISBN 0-917016-17-3). M S Wright.

William Harrison Ainsworth & His Friends, 2 vols. Arthur Conan Doyle. Ed. by E. F. Bleiler. LC 78-60905. (Fiction of Popular Culture Ser.: Vol. 5). 1979. Set. lib. bdg. 88.00 (ISBN 0-8240-9663-0). Garland Pub.

William Harvey & His Age: The Professional & Social Context of the Discovery of Circulation. Charles Webster et al. LC 78-20526. 1979. 12.50x (ISBN 0-8018-2213-0). Johns Hopkins.

William Harvey: Trailblazer of Scientific Medicine. Rebecca Markus. (Biography Ser). (gr. 7 up). 1962. PLB 5.90 o.p. (ISBN 0-531-00882-7). Watts.

William Hazlitt, Critic of Power. John Kinnaird. (Illus.). 1978. 25.00x (ISBN 0-231-04600-6). Columbia U Pr.

William Heinesen. W. Glyn Jones. (World Authors Ser.: Denmark: No. 282). 1974. lib. bdg. 12.50 (ISBN 0-8057-2418-4). Twayne.

William Henry Bragg, Eighteen Sixty-Two to Nineteen Forty-Two. Gwendolen M. Caroe. LC 77-84799. (Illus.). 1978. 29.95 (ISBN 0-521-21839-X). Cambridge U Pr.

William Henry Fry. William T. Upton. LC 73-20224. (Music Ser.). 346p. 1974. Repr. of 1954 ed. lib. bdg. 25.00 (ISBN 0-306-70625-3). Da Capo.

William Henry Holtzclaw: Scholar in Ebony. Robert F. Holtzclaw. LC 76-29278. (Illus.). 252p. 1977. 8.92 (ISBN 0-913228-19-2). Keeble Pr.

William Henry Hudson. John T. Frederick. (English Authors Ser.: No. 130). 10.95 (ISBN 0-8057-1276-3). Twayne.

William Henry Jackson's Colorado. William C. Jones & Elizabeth B. Jones. (Illus.). 192p. 1976. 27.95 (ISBN 0-87108-092-3); deluxe limited edition o.p. 76.00 (ISBN 0-87108-093-1). Pruett.

William Henry Jackson's Rocky Mountain Railroad Album: Steel & Steam Across the Great Divide. Ed. by Jackson C. Thode. (Illus.). 1977. 195.00 (ISBN 0-913582-14-X). Sundance.

William Herschel & His Work. James Sime. 272p. 1900. text ed. 3.50 (ISBN 0-567-04521-8). Attic Pr.

William Heytesbury: Medieval Logic & the Rise of Mathematical Physics. Curtis Wilson. (Medieval Science Pubns., No. 3). 1956. 20.00x (ISBN 0-299-01350-2). U of Wis Pr.

William Hickling Prescott. Donald G. Darnell. LC 74-26789. (U. S. Authors Ser.: No. 251). 1975. lib. bdg. 10.95 (ISBN 0-8057-0598-8). Twayne.

William Holman Hunt & Typological Symbolism. George Landow. LC 77-91017. 1979. 30.00x (ISBN 0-300-02196-8). Yale U Pr.

William James. Bernard P. Brennan. (U. S. Authors Ser.: No. 131). 1968. lib. bdg. 10.95 (ISBN 0-8057-0408-6). Twayne.

William Jennings Bryan & the Campaign of 1896. Ed. by George F. Whicher. (Problems in American Civilization Ser.). 1953. pap. text ed. 4.95x o.p. (ISBN 0-669-24000-1). Heath.

William Jessop, Engineer. Charles Hadfield & A. W. Skempton. 1979. 28.00 (ISBN 0-7153-7603-9). David & Charles.

William King (Sixteen Fifty to Seventeen Twenty-Nine) William King. LC 75-11228. (British Philosophers & Theologians of the 17th & 18th Centuries Ser.). 1978. lib. bdg. 42.00 (ISBN 0-8240-1782-X). Garland Pub.
William Klein: Photographs. William Klein. Ed. by John Heilpern. (Monograph). (Illus.). 1980. 40.00 (ISBN 0-89381-049-5); ltd. ed. 300.00 (ISBN 0-89381-053-3). Aperture.
William Law. Erwin P. Randolph. (English Author Ser.: No. 282). 1980. lib. bdg. 10.95 (ISBN 0-8057-6765-7). Twayne.
William Law on Christian Perfection. William Law. 144p. 1981. pap. 2.95 (ISBN 0-87123-117-4, 210117). Bethany Fell.
William Lisle Bowles. William L. Bowles. Ed. by Donald H. Reiman. LC 75-31166. (Romantic Context Ser.: Poetry 1789-1830). 1978. lib. bdg. 47.00 (ISBN 0-8240-2119-3). Garland Pub.
William Lisle Bowles: Poems, Never Before Published. 1815. William L. Bowles. Ed. by Donald H. Reiman. LC 75-31168. (Romantic Context Ser.: Poetry 1789-1830). 1978. lib. bdg. 47.00 (ISBN 0-8240-2121-5). Garland Pub.
William Lloyd Garrison. John J. Chapman. (American Newspapermen 1790-1933 Ser.). 1974. Repr. 17.50x (ISBN 0-8464-0027-8). Beekman Pubs.
William Lobb, Plant Hunter for Veitch & Messenger of the Big Tree. Joseph Ewan. (Publications in Botany, Vol. 67). 1974. pap. 6.75x (ISBN 0-520-09501-4). U of Cal Pr.
William McDougall, Explorer of the Mind: Studies in Psychical Research. Ed. by Raymond Van Over & Laura Oteri. LC 67-23366. 1967. 8.50 o.p. (ISBN 0-912326-20-4). Garrett-Helix.
William Marples & Sons Price List of American Tools & Hardware, Nineteen Hundred Nine. 1980. pap. 4.50 (ISBN 0-913602-41-8). K Roberts.
William Mawdesley Best: Treatise on the Principles of Evidence & Practice As to Proofs in Courts of Common Law, Repr. Of 1849 Ed. William M. Best. Ed. by David Berkowitz & Samuel Thorne. Bd. with Sir James Fitzjames Stephen: Digest of the Law of Evidence. Sir James F. Stephen. Repr. of 1876 ed. LC 77-86653. (Classics of English Legal History in the Modern Era Ser.). 1979. lib. bdg. 55.00 (ISBN 0-8240-3086-9). Garland Pub.
William Maxwell to Robert Burns. Robert Thornton. 269p. 1980. text ed. 26.00x (ISBN 0-85976-052-9). Humanities.
William Morris. Frederick Kirchhoff. (English Authors Ser.: No. 262). 1979. lib. bdg. 14.50 (ISBN 0-8057-6723-1). Twayne.
William Morris & His Earthly Paradises. Roderick Marshall. (Illus.). 317p. 1980. 29.50x (ISBN 0-389-20085-9). B&N.
William Morris: Prose, Verse, Lectures, & Essays. Ed. by G. D. Cole. (Nonesuch Library). 1978. 11.95 (ISBN 0-370-00514-7, Pub. by Chatto Bodley Jonathan). Merrimack Bk Serv.
William Morris: The Critical Heritage. Ed. by Peter Faulkner. (Critical Heritage Ser.). 480p. 1973. 38.50 (ISBN 0-7100-7520-0). Routledge & Kegan.
William Morris's "the Defence of Guenevere", & Other Poems. Ed. by Margaret A. Lourie. LC 80-83223. 275p. 1981. lib. bdg. 33.00 (ISBN 0-8240-9452-2). Garland Pub.
William Nicholson. Lillian Browse. (Illus.). 1956. 15.00 o.p. (ISBN 0-246-63804-4). Dufour.
William O. Douglas Inquiry into the State of Individual Freedom. Ed. by Harry W. Ashmore. 1979. lib. bdg. 23.50x (ISBN 0-89158-371-8). Westview.
William O'Brien & the Course of Irish Politics, 1881-1918. Joseph V. O'Brien. LC 74-22970. 350p. 1976. 22.75x (ISBN 0-520-02886-4). U of Cal Pr.
William of St. Thierry: Exposition on the Song of Songs. (Cistercian Fathers Ser.: No. 6). 1970. 7.95 (ISBN 0-7165-1006-5). Cistercian Pubns.
William of St. Thierry: On Contemplating God, Prayer, Meditations. Tr. by Sr. Penelope. (Cistercian Fathers Ser.: No. 3). 1970. pap. 4.00 (ISBN 0-87907-903-7). Cistercian Pubns.
William Orlando Darby: A Military Biography. Michael J. King. Date not set. 19.50 (ISBN 0-208-01867-0, Archon). Shoe String. Postponed.
William Paca: A Biography. Gregory A. Stiverson & Phebe R. Jacobsen. LC 76-17519. (Illus.). 1976. 7.95 (ISBN 0-938420-18-6); pap. 4.95 (ISBN 0-686-23680-7). Md Hist.
William Paterson: Lawyer & Statesman, 1745-1806. John E. O'Connor. 1979. 23.50 (ISBN 0-8135-0880-0). Rutgers U Pr.
William Penn. Harry E. Wildes. LC 73-1857. 512p. 1974. 14.95 o.s.i. (ISBN 0-02-628570-3). Macmillan.
William Penn, Architect of a Nation. John B. Trussell, Jr. (Illus.). 79p. (Orig.). 1980. pap. 2.25 (ISBN 0-89271-008-X). Pa Hist & Mus.
William Penn's Own Account of the Lenni Lenape or Delaware Indians. rev. ed. William Penn & Albert C. Myers. (Illus.). 96p. 1981. pap. 4.95 (ISBN 0-912608-13-7). Mid Atlantic.
William Plumer's Memorandum of Proceedings in the United States Senate 1803-1807. Ed. by Everett S. Brown. LC 74-94626. (Law, Politics & History Ser). 1969. Repr. of 1923 ed. 65.00 (ISBN 0-306-71823-5). Da Capo.
William Prynne. Wiliam Prynne et al. Ed. by David S. Berkowitz & Samuel E. Thorne. (English Legal History Ser.: Vol. 124). 589p. 1979. lib. bdg. 55.00 (ISBN 0-8240-3161-X). Garland Pub.
William Randolph Hearst: His Role in American Progressivism. Roy E. Littlefield, III. LC 80-5729. 405p. 1980. lib. bdg. 22.75 (ISBN 0-8191-1320-4); pap. text ed. 13.75 (ISBN 0-8191-1321-2). U Pr of Amer.
William Rockhill Nelson: A Story of a Man, a Newspaper, & a City. The Kansas City Star Staff. (American Newspapermen 1790-1933 Ser.). (Illus.). 274p. 1974. Repr. of 1915 ed. 17.50x o.s.i. (ISBN 0-8464-0017-0). Beekman Pubs.
William S. Culbertson: In Search of a Rendezvous. J. Richard Snyder. LC 79-6025. 156p. 1980. text ed. 16.75 (ISBN 0-8191-0972-X); pap. text ed. 8.75 (ISBN 0-8191-0973-8). U Pr of Amer.
William Saroyan. Howard R. Floan. (U. S. Authors Ser.: No. 100). 1966. lib. bdg. 10.95 (ISBN 0-8057-0652-6). Twayne.
William Shakespeare: A Reader's Guide. Alfred Harbage. 498p. 1963. pap. 7.95 (ISBN 0-374-50288-9, N243). FS&G.
William Shakespeare: Records & Images. S. Schoenbaum. (Illus.). 316p. 1981. 98.00 (ISBN 0-19-520234-1). Oxford U Pr.
William Shakespeare: Spacious in the Possession of Dirt. John McCall. 1978. pap. text ed. 12.00x (ISBN 0-8191-0378-0). U Pr of Amer.
William Shipley: Founder of the Royal Society of Arts--A Biography with Documents. D. G. Allan. (Illus.). 240p. 1979. 22.50x (ISBN 0-85967-483-5, Pub. by Scolar Pr England); pap. 9.95x (ISBN 0-85967-484-3). Biblio Dist.
William Sidney Walker (Seventeen Ninety-Five to Eighteen Forty-Six) William S. Walker. Ed. by Donald H. Reiman. LC 75-31269. (Romantic Context Ser.: Poetry 1789-1830). 1977. lib. bdg. 47.00 (ISBN 0-8240-2215-7). Garland Pub.
William Sotheby (Seventeen Fifty-Seven to Eighteen Thirty-Three) Oberon & Orestes. William Sotheby. Ed. by Donald H. Reiman. LC 75-31259. (Romantic Context Ser.: Poetry 1789-1830). 1978. Repr. of 1802 ed. lib. bdg. 47.00 (ISBN 0-8240-2206-8). Garland Pub.
William Sotheby (Seventeen Fifty-Seven to Eighteen Thirty-Three) Poems 1790-1818. William Sotheby. Ed. by Donald H. Reiman. LC 75-31256. (Romantic Context Ser.: Poetry 1789-1830). 1978. lib. bdg. 47.00 (ISBN 0-8240-2203-3). Garland Pub.
William Sotheby (Seventeen Fifty-Seven to Eighteen Thirty-Three) Saul. William Sotheby. Ed. by Donald H. Reiman. LC 75-31257. (Romantic Context Ser.: Poetry 1789-1830). 1978. Repr. of 1807 ed. lib. bdg. 47.00 (ISBN 0-8240-2204-1). Garland Pub.
William Starbuck Mayo. Gerald C. VanDusen. (United States Authors Ser.: No. 345). 1979. lib. bdg. 13.50 (ISBN 0-8057-7278-2). Twayne.
William Strickland-Architect & Engineer 1788-1854. enl. ed. Agnes A. Gilchrist. LC 69-13714. (Architecture & Decorative Art Ser). (Illus.). 1969. Repr. of 1950 ed. lib. bdg. 29.50 (ISBN 0-306-71235-0). Da Capo.
William Styron. Marc L. Ratner. (U. S. Authors Ser.: No. 196). lib. bdg. 10.95 (ISBN 0-8057-0708-5). Twayne.
William Styron's Nat Turner: Ten Black Writers Respond. Ed. by John H. Clarke. 1968. 4.95 o.p. (ISBN 0-8070-6426-2); pap. 1.95 o.p. (ISBN 0-8070-6427-0, BP304). Beacon Pr.
William the Conqueror. Thomas B. Costain. (Landmark Ser.: No. 41). (Illus.). (gr. 7-10). 1959. PLB 4.39 o.p. (ISBN 0-394-90541-5, BYR). Random.
William the Conqueror: The Norman Impact Upon England. David C. Douglas. (English Monarchs Ser.). 1964. 20.00x (ISBN 0-520-00348-9); pap. 5.95 (ISBN 0-520-00350-0, CAL131). U of Cal Pr.
William Third. David Ogg. 1968. pap. 1.25 o.s.i. (ISBN 0-02-053160-2, Collier). Macmillan.
William Trost Richards (Eighteen Thirty-Three to Nineteen Hundred Five: American Landscape & Marine Painter. Linda S. Ferber. LC 78-74367. (Outstanding Dissertations in the Fine Arts Ser.). (Illus.). 525p. 1979. lib. bdg. 50.00 (ISBN 0-8240-3955-6). Garland Pub.
William Troy: Selected Essays. Ed. by Stanley Hyman. 1967. 19.00 (ISBN 0-8135-0553-4). Rutgers U Pr.
William Wantling: A Biography & Selected Writings. John Pryos. 80p. (Orig.). 1981. pap. 4.50 (ISBN 0-933180-09-8). Spoon Riv Poetry.
William Warren Scranton: Pennsylvania Statesman. George D. Wolf. LC 80-21736. (Illus.). 160p. 1981. 16.50x (ISBN 0-271-00278-6, Keystone Bks). Pa St U Pr.
William Wetmore Story & His Friends, 2 vols. in one. Henry James. LC 69-18460. (Library of American Art Ser). 1969. Repr. of 1903 ed. lib. bdg. 49.50 (ISBN 0-306-71249-0). Da Capo.
William Wilkins, Seventeen Seventy-Eight to Eighteen Thirty-Nine. R. W. Liscombe. LC 78-73247. 320p. 1980. 49.50 (ISBN 0-521-22528-0). Cambridge U Pr.
William Wordsworth. Geoffrey H. Durrant. (British Authors Ser). 28.50 (ISBN 0-521-07608-0); pap. 7.95 (ISBN 0-521-09584-0). Cambridge U Pr.
William Wordsworth. Russell Noyes. (English Authors Ser.: No. 118). lib. bdg. 9.95 (ISBN 0-8057-1580-0). Twayne.
William Wordsworth: A Biography. Hunter Davies. LC 80-66004. (Illus.). 1980. 17.95 (ISBN 0-689-11087-1). Atheneum.
William Wordsworth: A Biography, 2 vols. Mary Moorman. (Vol. 1, Early Years, 1770-1803; vol. 2, Later Years, 1803-1850). Vol. 1. 39.00x (ISBN 0-19-811565-2); Vol. 2. pap. 5.95x (ISBN 0-19-881146-2, OPB). Oxford U Pr.
William Wordsworth und Die Romantische Paradieseskonzeption. Dorothea Steiner. (Salzburg Studies in English Literature, Romantic Reassessment: No.31). 1973. pap. text ed. 25.00x (ISBN 0-391-01532-X). Humanities.
William Wyler. Michael Anderegg. (Theatrical Arts Ser.). 1979. lib. bdg. 10.95 (ISBN 0-8057-9268-6). Twayne.
Williams Holmes McGuffey & His Readers. Harvey C. Minnich. LC 74-19214. (Illus.). xii, 203p. 1975. Repr. of 1936 ed. 18.00 (ISBN 0-8103-4104-2). Gale.
Williams Site: A Frontier Mongollon Village in West-Central New Mexico. Watson Smith. LC 73-86928. (Peabody Museum Papers: Vol. 39, No. 2). 1973. pap. text ed. 10.00 (ISBN 0-87365-190-1). Peabody Harvard.
Williamsburg Christmas. Donna C. Sheppard. LC 80-7487. (Illus.). 84p. (Orig.). 1980. 9.95 (ISBN 0-87935-053-9); pap. 4.95 (ISBN 0-87935-054-7). Williamsburg.
Williamsburg Galaxy. Burke Davis. LC 68-12135. 1968. 4.95 o.p. (ISBN 0-03-068690-3, Pub. by Williamsburg). HR&W.
Williamsburg Hornbook. Felicity Wise. LC 73-16301. (Illus.). 128p. 1973. op (ISBN 0-8117-1896-4); pap. 3.95 (ISBN 0-8117-1203-6). Stackpole.
Williamsburg Novels, 7 vols. Elswyth Thane. 1981. Set. lib. bdg. 105.00 (ISBN 0-8161-3177-5, Large Print Bks). G K Hall.
Williamsburg Trilogy. Daniel Fuchs. 1977. pap. 4.95 (ISBN 0-380-01468-8, 13672). Avon.
Williamson Reports: A Study. Sarah K. Vann. LC 75-149992. 1971. 10.00 (ISBN 0-8108-0375-5). Scarecrow.
Williamson Reports of Nineteen Twenty-One & Nineteen Twenty-Three: Including Training for Library Work & Training for Library Service. Charles C. Williamson. LC 78-25204. 1971. 13.50 (ISBN 0-8108-0417-4). Scarecrow.
Willie & Billie & Other Tales for Children. Cissy Rose. 1980. 4.50 (ISBN 0-8062-1343-4). Carlton.
Willie & Phil. Joyce Thompson. 1980. pap. 1.95 (ISBN 0-686-69243-8, 75804). Avon.
Willie & the Wildcat Well. Alberta W. Constant. LC 62-7741. (Illus.). (gr. 5-9). 1962. 8.95 o.p. (ISBN 0-690-89351-5, TYC-J). T Y Crowell.
Willie Blows a Mean Horn. Ianthe Thomas. LC 74-2637. (Illus.). 24p. (gr. k-3). 1981. 7.95 (ISBN 0-06-026106-4, HarpJ); PLB 7.89 (ISBN 0-06-026107-2). Har-Row.
Willie Mays, "Play Ball!". Willie Mays & Maxine Berger. LC 80-13352. (Illus.). 160p. (gr. 7 up). 1980. PLB 8.29 (ISBN 0-671-41314-7). Messner.
Willie the Slowpoke. Rose Greydanus. (Illus.). 32p. (gr. k-2). 1980. PLB 2.96 (ISBN 0-89375-394-7); pap. 0.95 (ISBN 0-89375-294-0). Troll Assocs.
Willie the Squowse. Ted Allan. (Illus.). (gr. 2 up). 1978. 6.95 (ISBN 0-8038-8086-3). Hastings.
Willie's Fire Engine. Charles Keeping. (Illus.). 32p. (ps-3). 1980. 10.95 (ISBN 0-19-279728-X). Oxford U Pr.
Willie's Time. Charles Einstein. 1979. 12.95 (ISBN 0-397-01329-9). Lippincott.
Willie's Time: A Memoir. Einstein. pap. 2.50 (ISBN 0-425-04658-3). Berkley Pub.
Willing Hostage. Marlys Millhiser. 1977. pap. 1.50 o.p. (ISBN 0-449-23226-3, Crest). Fawcett.
Williston on Contracts: 1957-1977, 22 vols. 3rd ed. Walter H. Jaeger. LC 59-558. 1957. Vols. 1-16. 803.00 (ISBN 0-686-14488-0). Lawyers Co-Op.
Williston on Sales: 1973-74, 3 vols. 4th ed. Alphonse M. Squillante & John R. Fonseca. LC 73-88236. 1973. 150.00 (ISBN 0-686-14489-9). Lawyers Co-Op.
Willmoore Kendall Contra Mundum. Willmoore Kendall. 1971. 11.95 o.s.i. (ISBN 0-87000-101-9). Arlington Hse.
Willo. Karen Snow. 288p. 1981. pap. 2.95 (ISBN 0-523-41189-8). Pinnacle Bks.
Willow Farm. Alison Prince. 224p. (gr. 7 up). 1981. pap. 1.95 (ISBN 0-448-17270-4, Tempo). G&D.
Willow Herb. Rona Randall. 160p. (Orig.). Date not set. pap. 1.75 (ISBN 0-345-28586-7). Ballantine.
Willow Pattern China: With Separate Price Guide. 2nd ed. Veryl M. Worth. (Illus.). 1981. pap. 9.95. Worth Co.
Willow Whistle. Cornelia Meigs. (Illus.). (gr. 4-6). 1931. 4.95g o.s.i. (ISBN 0-02-766470-8). Macmillan.
Willow Wind Farm: Betsy's Story. Anne Pellowski. (Illus.). 176p. (gr. 9-12). 1981. 8.95 (ISBN 0-399-20781-3). Philomel.
Willow Wood. Elizabeth Savage. 1979. pap. 2.25 o.p. (ISBN 0-425-04166-2). Berkley Pub.
Willowcat & the Chimney Sweep. Sara G. Harrell. LC 80-81702. (Illus.). 1980. 6.95 (ISBN 0-931948-07-X). Peachtree Pubs.
Willowcat & the Chimney Sweep. Sara G. Harrell. (Illus.). 32p. 1980. 6.95 (ISBN 0-931948-07-X). Peachtree Pubs.
Willowdale Handcar. Edward Gorey. LC 62-17515. (Illus.). 1979. 5.95 (ISBN 0-396-07767-6). Dodd.
Willowwood. Mollie Hardwick. 1981. lib. bdg. 16.95 (ISBN 0-8161-3154-6, Large Print Bks). G K Hall.
Wills & Intestacies. J. Comyn & R. Johnson. LC 78-92109. 1970. 13.75 (ISBN 0-08-006691-7); pap. 6.25 (ISBN 0-08-006690-9). Pergamon.
Will's Boy: A Memoir. Wright Morris. LC 80-8708. 192p. 1981. 11.95 (ISBN 0-06-014856-X, HarpT). Har-Row.
Wills Commentary on Matthew & Mark. 6.45 ea. o.p. Schmul Pub Co.
Wills, Death & Taxes: Basic Principles for Protecting Estates. Lawrence W. Dixon. (Quality Paperback: No. 228). (Orig.). 1977. pap. 2.95 (ISBN 0-8226-0228-8). Littlefield.
Wills Laws of the U.S. 1979 ed. 200p. 1978. 6.00 (ISBN 0-87526-213-9). Gould.
Will's Quill. Don Freeman. (Illus.). 32p. (gr. k-3). 1975. PLB 7.95 (ISBN 0-670-76922-3). Viking Pr.
Willy Bear. Mildred Kantrowitz. LC 80-15295. (Illus.). 40p. (ps-1). 1980. Repr. of 1976 ed. 7.95 (ISBN 0-590-07781-3, Four Winds). Schol Bk Serv.
Willy Wong: American. Oakes. (gr. 4-6). pap. 0.95 o.s.i. (ISBN 0-686-68478-8, 29725). Archway.
Wilma & the Water Pistol That Wouldn't Shoot Straight. Nancy R. Bjorkman. (Illus.). (gr. k-4). 1976. PLB 7.62 o.p. (ISBN 0-307-65695-0, Golden Pr). Western Pub.
Wilma Rudolph on Track. Wilma Rudolph. (gr. 4-9). Date not set. pap. cancelled (ISBN 0-671-33064-0). Wanderer Bks.
Wilmington: A Pictorial History. Carol E. Hoffecker. Ed. by Donna R. Friedman. (Illus.). 208p. 1981. pap. write for info. (ISBN 0-89865-057-7). Donning Co.
Wilsonian Maritime Diplomacy: 1913-1921. Jeffrey J. Safford. 1978. 20.00 (ISBN 0-8135-0850-9). Rutgers U Pr.
Wilson's Choice. Giles Tippette. (Orig.). 1981. pap. 1.95 (ISBN 0-440-19518-7). Dell.
Wilt. Wilt Chamberlain & David Shaw. (Illus.). 368p. 1975. pap. 1.95 o.s.i. (ISBN 0-446-79621-2). Warner Bks.
Wilt Chamberlain. George Heaslip. LC 73-13894. (Creative Superstars Ser.). 1974. PLB 5.95 (ISBN 0-87191-288-0); pap. 2.95 (ISBN 0-685-47498-4). Creative Ed.
Wilt Chamberlain. Kenneth Rudeen. LC 74-94800. (Biography Ser.). (Illus.). (gr. 2-5). 1970. 7.95 (ISBN 0-690-89458-9, TYC-J); PLB 7.89 (ISBN 0-690-01134-2). T Y Crowell.
Wilt: Just Like Any Other 7-Foot Black Millionaire Who Lives Next Door. Wilt Chamberlain & David Shaw. (Illus.). 362p. 1973. 6.95 o.s.i. (ISBN 0-02-523360-2). Macmillan.
Wilt Thou Go with This Man? Brownlow North. 1966. pap. 1.95 (ISBN 0-686-12545-2). Banner of Truth.
Wilt! Wilton Chamberlain. James Hahn & Lynn Hahn. Ed. by Howard Schroeder. (Sports Legends Ser.). (Illus.). 48p. (Orig.). (gr. 3-5). 1981. PLB 5.95 (ISBN 0-89686-124-4); pap. text ed. 2.95 (ISBN 0-89686-139-2). Crestwood Hse.

Wilton Book of Classic Deserts. Ed. by Eugene T. Sullivan & Marilynn C. Sullivan. LC 78-140191. 1970. 10.95 (ISBN 0-912696-02-8). Wilton.
Wilton Book of Wedding Cakes. Ed. by Eugene T. Sullivan & Marilynn C. Sullivan. LC 75-175098. 1971. 10.95 (ISBN 0-912696-03-6). Wilton.
Wiltons. Eden Hughes. (Orig.). 1980. pap. 2.95 (ISBN 0-451-09520-0, E9520, Sig). NAL.
Wilton's Wonderland of Cake Decorating. Ed. by McKinley Wilton & Norman Wilton. 1960. 12.95 (ISBN 0-912696-00-1). Wilton.
Wily Witch & All the Other Fairy Tales & Fables. Godfried Bomans. Tr. by Patricia Crampton from Dutch. LC 76-54196. (Illus.). 208p. (gr. 3 up). 1977. 9.95 (ISBN 0-916144-09-7). Stemmer Hse.
Wimbledon 1877-1977. Max Robertson. LC 77-365693. (Illus.). 1979. 12.50x (ISBN 0-905418-50-6). Intl Pubns Serv.
Wimpy in What's Good to Eat? Bill Pearson. Ed. by Philip Mann. (Shape Board Play Book). (Illus.). 14p. (gr. k-3). 1980. bds. 2.95 comb bdg. (ISBN 0-89828-127-X, 6009). Tuffy Bks.
Wimsey Family. C. W. Scott-Giles. LC 78-2074. (Illus.). 1978. 6.95 o.s.i. (ISBN 0-06-014001-1, HarpT). Har-Row.
Wimsey Set II, 4 bks. Dorothy L. Sayers. Incl. Have His Carcase; Strong Poison; Five Red Herrings; Murder Must Advertise. (Large Print Bks.). 1980. lib. bdg. 60.00 set (ISBN 0-8161-3136-8). G K Hall.
Win at Chess. Fred Reinfeld. Orig. Title: Chess Quiz. 1945. pap. 2.50 (ISBN 0-486-20438-3). Dover.
Win Your Personal Tax Revolt. Bill Greene. (Illus.). 192p. 1981. 11.95 (ISBN 0-936602-10-4). Harbor Pub CA.
Winchester in the Early Middle Ages: An Edition & Discussion of the Winton Domesday. Frank Barlow. (Winchester Studios). (Illus.). 1977. 98.00x (ISBN 0-19-813169-0). Oxford U Pr.
Winchester Yields: A Study in Medieval Agricultural Productivity. J. Z. Titow. LC 72-171685. (Cambridge Studies in Economic History). 1972. 89.50 (ISBN 0-521-08349-4). Cambridge U Pr.
Wind & Snow Load, Vol. 7. Building Research Establishment. 1978. 38.00x (ISBN 0-86095-802-7). Longman.
Wind Birds. Peter Matthiessen. (Illus.). 192p. 1973. 9.95 o.p. (ISBN 0-670-77096-5, Studio). Viking Pr.
Wind Blew. Pat Hutchins. LC 73-11691. (Illus.). 32p. (ps-2). 1974. 10.95 (ISBN 0-02-745910-1). Macmillan.
Wind Brings up the Rain. Eric Malpass. 266p. 1981. 10.95 (ISBN 0-312-88215-7). St Martin.
Wind-Catchers: American Windmills of Yesterday & Tomorrow. Volta Torrey. (Illus.). 240p. (Orig.). 1981. pap. 9.95 (ISBN 0-8289-0438-3). Greene.
Wind Chill Factor. Thomas Gifford. 384p. 1976. pap. 2.75 (ISBN 0-345-29728-8). Ballantine.
Wind Dancers. R. M. Meluch. (Orig.). 1981. pap. 1.95 (ISBN 0-451-09786-6, J9786, Sig). NAL.
Wind Effects on Buildings: Vol. 1, Design Applicatons. T. V. Lawson. (Illus.). xii, 344p. 1980. 55.00x (ISBN 0-85334-887-1). Burgess-Intl Ideas.
Wind Effects on Buildings: Volume 2--Statistics & Meteorology. T. V. Lawson. (Illus.). xii, 160p. 1980. 30.00x (ISBN 0-85334-893-6). Burgess-Intl Ideas.
Wind Energy. L. Jarass et al. (Illus.). 230p. 1981. 43.70 (ISBN 0-387-10362-7). Springer-Verlag.
Wind Energy Systems Program Summary Nineteen Eighty. Raytheon Service Co. 230p. 1981. pap. 19.50 (ISBN 0-89934-108-X). Solar Energy Info.
Wind Engineering: Proceedings of the 5th International Conference, Colorado State University, USA, July 8-14, 1979, 2 vols. Ed. by J. E. Cermak. LC 80-40753. (Illus.). 1400p. 1981. Set. 200.00 (ISBN 0-08-024745-8). Pergamon.
Wind Eye. Robert Westall. LC 77-5162. (gr. 5-9). 1977. 8.25 (ISBN 0-688-80114-5); PLB 7.92 (ISBN 0-688-84114-7). Greenwillow.
Wind Forces on Buildings & Structures: An Introduction. E. L. Houghton & N. B. Carruthers. 1976. 22.95 (ISBN 0-470-15147-1). Halsted Pr.
Wind from Hastings. Morgan Llywelyn. 1979. pap. 2.50 (ISBN 0-446-82969-2). Warner Bks.
Wind from the Abyss. Janet E. Morris. (New Age Ser.). 352p. (Orig.). 1981. pap. 2.50 (ISBN 0-553-14343-3). Bantam.
Wind in the Cypress. Ruth M. Sears. 1975. pap. 1.25 o.p. (ISBN 0-685-57554-3, LB302ZK, Leisure Bks). Nordon Pubns.
Wind in the Leaves. Virginia MacKenzie. 89p. 1980. 5.95 (ISBN 0-8059-2743-3). Dorrance.
Wind in the Willows. Kenneth Graham. (gr. k-6). 1981. pap. 1.50 (ISBN 0-440-49555-5, YB). Dell.
Wind in the Willows. Kenneth Grahame. LC 80-197. (Illus.). 216p. (gr. 2-7). 1980. 16.95 (ISBN 0-03-056294-5). HR&W.
Wind in the Willows. Kenneth Grahame. 253p. Repr. of 1908 ed. lib. bdg. 11.60x (ISBN 0-88411-877-0). Amereon Ltd.
Wind in the Willows. (Illustrated Junior Library). (Illus.). 224p. 1981. pap. 4.95 (ISBN 0-448-11028-8). G&D.
Wind Is Air. Mary Brewer. LC 75-34141. (Illus.). (ps-3). 1976. PLB 5.50 (ISBN 0-913778-27-3); pap. 2.75 (ISBN 0-89565-068-1). Childs World.
Wind Is Not a River. Arnold A. Griese. LC 77-5082. (Illus.). (gr. 4-7). 1978. 8.95 (ISBN 0-690-03807-0, TYC-J); PLB 8.79 (ISBN 0-690-03842-9). T Y Crowell.
Wind Loading on Buildings. Angus J. Macdonald. LC 75-11988. 219p. 1975. 29.95 (ISBN 0-470-55976-4). Halsted Pr.
Wind Machines. F. P. Eldridge. 1975. pap. 7.50 (ISBN 0-930978-98-6). Solar Energy Info.
Wind Machines: Guide to Manufacturers, Products & Research Activities. Rockwell International et al. Ed. by J. A. Bereny. LC 78-68748. cancelled (ISBN 0-930978-63-3); pap. 15.95 (ISBN 0-930978-28-5). Solar Energy Info.
Wind of Morning. Hugh Boustead. (Illus.). 1979. 9.95 (ISBN 0-7011-1314-6, Pub. by Chatto Bodley Jonathan). Merrimack Bk Serv.
Wind on the Buffalo Grass. Ed. by Leslie Tillett. LC 76-6098. (Illus.). 1976. 35.00 o.s.i. (ISBN 0-690-01155-5, TYC-T). T Y Crowell.
Wind Over Stonehenge. Pamela Dorre. (Pacesetters Ser.). (Illus.). 64p. (gr. 4 up). 1978. PLB 7.95 (ISBN 0-516-02175-3). Childrens.
Wind Power & Other Energy Options. David R. Inglis. LC 78-9102. (Illus.). 1978. 16.00 (ISBN 0-472-09303-7); pap. 8.50 (ISBN 0-472-06303-0). U of Mich Pr.
Wind Power Book. Jack Park. (Illus.). 1981. 19.95 (ISBN 0-917352-05-X); pap. 11.95 (ISBN 0-917352-06-8). Cheshire.
Wind Power for the Homeowner: A Guide to Selecting, Siting, & Installing an Electricity-Generating Wind Power System. Donald Marier & Dan Wallace. (Illus.). 320p. 1981. 14.95 (ISBN 0-87857-334-8); pap. 10.95 (ISBN 0-87857-350-X). Rodale Pr Inc.
Wind Power: Who's Doing What, Why & Where. BCC Staff. 1981. 750.00 (ISBN 0-89336-240-9, E-040). BCC.
Wind, Sand & Sky. Rebecca Caudill. (Illus.). 32p. (gr. k-6). 1976. PLB 7.95 (ISBN 0-525-42899-2). Dutton.
Wind, Sand & Stars. Antoine De Saint-Exupery. LC 65-35872. 1967. pap. 2.75 (ISBN 0-15-697090-2, HPL14, HPL). HarBraceJ.
Wind Shifting West. Shirley A. Grau. 1977. pap. 1.95 o.p. (ISBN 0-449-23349-9, Crest). Fawcett.
Wind Song: Our Ten Years in the Yacht Delivery Business. Patrick Ellam & June Ellam. LC 75-37353. (Illus.). 256p. 1976. 10.95 (ISBN 0-87742-061-0). Intl Marine.
Wind That Swept Mexico: The History of the Mexican Revolution of 1910-1942. new ed. Anita Brenner. (Texas Pan American Ser). (Illus.). 310p. 1971. 17.95 (ISBN 0-292-70106-3). U of Tex Pr.
Wind up the Willow. Alan Brown. 1981. 9.95 (ISBN 0-7145-3808-6); pap. 4.95 (ISBN 0-686-68791-4). Riverrun NY.
Wind Whales of Ishmael. Philip J. Farmer. (Orig.). 1977. pap. 1.95 (ISBN 0-441-89240-X). Ace Bks.
Wind Will Not Subside: Years in Revolutionary China,1964-1969. David Milton & Nancy D. Milton. LC 75-10370. 1976. pap. 7.95 (ISBN 0-394-70936-5). Pantheon.
Wind Without Rain. Herbert Krause. LC 76-28868. 1976. Repr. of 1939 ed. 9.95 (ISBN 0-88498-045-6); text ed. 9.95 o.p. (ISBN 0-685-71797-6); leatherette 12.95 (ISBN 0-685-71798-4). Brevet Pr.
Windchange. rev. ed. Theodore L. Harris et al. (Keys to Reading Ser.). (Illus.). 192p. (gr. 8). 1975. pap. text ed. 3.48 (ISBN 0-87892-465-5); resource bk. 9.90 (ISBN 0-87892-467-1); catalog student guide 3.96 (ISBN 0-87892-468-X); tchr's ed. 3.96 (ISBN 0-87892-469-8); duplicating masters 19.53 (ISBN 0-87892-499-X). Economy Co.
Windchime Legacy. Mykel. 419p. 1980. 12.95 (ISBN 0-312-88219-X). St Martin.
Windell & Ann Phillips: The Community of Reform 1840-1880. Irving H. Bartlett. (Illus.). 1981. 17.95 (ISBN 0-393-01426-6). Norton.
Windfall. Andrea Harris. LC 78-78053. 1979. pap. 1.75 o.p. (ISBN 0-87216-544-2). Playboy Pbks.
Windfalls. Aidan C. Mathews. 48p. 1978. pap. text ed. 5.00x (ISBN 0-85105-325-4, Dolmen Pr). Humanities.
Windfalls. Frances B. Richman. 1980. 5.50 (ISBN 0-8233-0313-6). Golden Quill.
Windfalls of Kent. Jerry West. 128p. 1980. 24.75x (ISBN 0-7050-0065-6, Pub. by Skilton & Shaw England). State Mutual Bk.
Windhaven Plantation. Marie De Jourlet. (Orig.). 1977. pap. 2.75 (ISBN 0-523-41472-2). Pinnacle Bks.
Windhaven's Peril. Marie De Jourlet. (Windhaven Ser.). 1979. pap. 2.75 (ISBN 0-523-41258-4). Pinnacle Bks.
Winding Passage: Essays & Sociological Journeys, 1960-1980. Daniel Bell. LC 79-57350. (Illus.). 446p. 1980. 25.00 (ISBN 0-89011-545-1). Abt Assoc.
Winding Sheet. Robert Cassilis. 222p. 1980. 16.95 (ISBN 0-241-89863-3, Pub. by Hamish Hamilton England). David & Charles.
Winding Stair. Daphne Du Maurier. 1972. pap. 2.25 (ISBN 0-380-01848-9, 35459). Avon.
Winding Stair. Jane A. Hodge. 1978. pap. 2.25 (ISBN 0-449-23590-4, Crest). Fawcett.
Windjammers. Oliver E. Allen. (Seafarers Ser.). (Illus.). 1979. lib. bdg. 11.97 (ISBN 0-686-50989-7). Silver.
Windmill Years. Vicky Martin. LC 77-10290. 1978. 8.95 o.p. (ISBN 0-312-88222-X). St Martin.
Windmills. Frank Brangwyn & Hayter Preston. LC 70-176821. (Illus.). 126p. 1975. Repr. of 1923 ed. 20.00 (ISBN 0-8103-4077-1). Gale.
Windmills: An Old-New Energy Source. Lucile McDonald. (Illus.). (gr. 4 up). 1981. 10.95 (ISBN 0-525-66708-3). Elsevier-Nelson.
Window. Vern Rutsala. LC 64-22374. (Wesleyan Poetry Program: Vol. 24). (Orig.). 1964. 10.00x (ISBN 0-686-66568-6, Pub. by Wesleyan U Pr); pap. 4.95x (ISBN 0-8195-1024-6). Columbia U Pr.
Window Box Gardening. Xenia Field. (Illus.). 139p. 1975. 8.95 (ISBN 0-7137-0656-2). Transatlantic.
Window-Box Gardening. Henry Teuscher. (Illus.). 1956. 4.95 o.s.i. (ISBN 0-02-617000-0). Macmillan.
Window in the Sky. A. T. Lawton. 1979. 19.25 (ISBN 0-08-024663-X). Pergamon.
Window on the Sea. Herbert L. Minshall. Ed. by Richard F. Pourade. LC 80-52787. (Illus.). 190p. 1980. 18.50 (ISBN 0-913938-22-X). Copley Bks.
Window on the Unknown: A History of the Microscope. Corinne Jacker. LC 66-24490. (Illus.). (gr. 6 up). 1966. 5.95 o.p. (ISBN 0-684-20857-1, ScribJ). Scribner.
Window on the Wild. Scott. 8.95 (ISBN 0-399-20722-8). Putnam.
Window Over the Sink: A Mainly Affectionate Memoir. Peg Bracken. 1981. 10.95 (ISBN 0-15-196986-8). HarBraceJ.
Window Selection: A Guide for Architects & Designers. Ian D. Collins & Eric J. Collins. (Illus.). 1977. text ed. 16.95 (ISBN 0-408-00285-9). Butterworths.
Windows. Val Clery. (Illus.). 168p. 1979. 14.95 o.p. (ISBN 0-670-77180-5, Studio). Viking Pr.
Windows. D. G. Compton. 1979. 9.95 o.p. (ISBN 0-399-12378-4). Berkley Pub.
Windows. D. G. Compton. LC 79-921. 1979. 10.95 o.p. (ISBN 0-399-12378-4). Berkley Pub.
Windows & Walls: Designs-Patterns-Projects. Alexandra Eames. LC 80-80753. 160p. 1980. 17.95 (ISBN 0-8487-0507-6). Oxmoor Hse.
Windows at Tiffany's: The Art of Gene Moore. Judith Goldman. (Illus.). 280p. 1980. 50.00 (ISBN 0-686-62688-5, 1655-X). Abrams.
Windows for the Crown Prince: An American Woman's Four Years As Private Tutor to the Crown Prince of Japan. Elizabeth G. Vining. (Illus.). (gr. 7-9). 1952. 9.95 (ISBN 0-397-00037-5). Lippincott.
Windows of Nature. Maitreya Stillwater. (Illus., Orig.). (gr. 1-12). 1978. pap. 2.25 (ISBN 0-912300-90-6, 90-6). Troubador Pr.
Windows of Saint Justin Martyr. Louis P. Giorgi. LC 80-67119. (Illus.). 128p. 1981. 25.00 (ISBN 0-87982-034-9). Art Alliance.
Windows of Tarot. F. Graves. LC 73-85990. 1973. pap. 4.95 (ISBN 0-87100-027-X). Morgan.
Windows on Africa: A Symposium. Ed. by Robert T. Parsons. 1972. text ed. 27.50x (ISBN 9-0040-1705-4). Humanities.
Windows on the Holy Land. J. C. Pedlow. 150p. pap. text ed. 8.95 (ISBN 0-227-67839-7). Attic Pr.
Windows on the Past: Portraits at the Essex Institute. Andrew Oliver & Eryant F. Tolles, Jr. (E. I. Museum Booklet Ser.). (Illus.). 60p. (Orig.). 1981. pap. 4.95 (ISBN 0-88389-080-1). Essex Inst.
Windows on the World: World News Reporting Nineteen Hundred to Nineteen Twenty. Robert Desmond. LC 80-19397. 565p. 1980. text ed. 28.50 (ISBN 0-87745-104-4). U of Iowa Pr.
Windpower: Handbook of Wind Energy Conversion. V. Daniel Hunt. 640p. 1981. text ed. 39.50 (ISBN 0-442-27389-4). Van Nos Reinhold.
Windpower Principles: Their Applications on the Small Scale. N. G. Calvert. LC 79-19706. 1980. 26.95x (ISBN 0-470-26867-0). Halsted Pr.
Windrose. Brewster Ghiselin. (University of Utah Press Poetry Series). 252p. 1980. 15.00 (ISBN 0-87480-167-2). U of Utah Pr.
Winds of Change. Marie Nowinson. 1979. pap. 2.25 o.p. (ISBN 0-345-27587-X). Ballantine.
Winds of Change: Report of a Conference on Activity Programs in Long-Term Care Institutions. American Hospital Association. 48p. 1971. pap. 5.00 o.p. (ISBN 0-87258-081-4, 1890). Am Hospital.
Winds of Change, 1914-1939. Harold MacMillan. LC 66-21710. (Illus.). 1966. 20.00 o.p. (ISBN 0-06-012753-8, HarpT). Har-Row.
Winds of Darkover. Marion Z. Bradley. 1977. pap. 1.95 (ISBN 0-441-89253-1). Ace Bks.
Winds of Desire. Marilyn Granbeck. (Orig.). pap. 1.95 (ISBN 0-515-04337-0). Jove Pubns.
Winds of Doctrine & Platoism & the Spiritual Life. George Santayana. 1958. 8.25 (ISBN 0-8446-0242-6). Peter Smith.
Winds of Fire. Vyankatesh Madgulkar. Tr. by Pramod Kale from Marathi. 113p. 1975. pap. 1.95 (ISBN 0-88253-693-1). Ind-US Inc.
Winds of Gold. Gary McCarthy. 1980. pap. write for info. (ISBN 0-671-82730-8). PB.
Winds of Kabul. Paula Favage. LC 80-83562. 288p. (Orig.). 1981. pap. 2.75 (ISBN 0-87216-807-7). Playboy Pbks.
Winds of Summer. Arlene Hale. 1980. lib. bdg. 13.50 (ISBN 0-8161-3168-6, Large Print Bks). G K Hall.
Winds of the Old Days. Betsy Aswad. 288p. 1980. 9.95 (ISBN 0-8037-9638-2). Dial.
Winds of Virtue. rev. ed. Jean N. Dale & Willard D. Sheeler. (Reading & Exercise Ser.: No. 3). 1975. pap. 2.50 (ISBN 0-89285-052-3); cassette tapes 29.50 (ISBN 0-89285-070-1). ELS Intl.
Winds of Virtue. Ed. by Jean N. Dale & Willard D. Sheeler. (Reading & Exercise Ser.). (gr. k-6). 1974. pap. text ed. 2.50x (ISBN 0-19-433621-2). Oxford U Pr.
Winds of Winter. Sandra Field. (Harlequin Romances). 192p. 1981. pap. 1.25 (ISBN 0-373-02398-7, Pub. by Harlequin). PB.
Winds, Waves & Maritime Structures. R. R. Minikin. 295p. 1963. 29.75x (ISBN 0-85264-091-9, Pub. by Griffin England). State Mutual Bk.
Windsinger. Frances Gillmor. LC 75-17380. (Zia Bks). 226p. 1976. pap. 3.95 o.p. (ISBN 0-8263-0397-8). U of NM Pr.
Windsinger. Gary Smith. (Illus.). 176p. 1978. pap. 5.95 (ISBN 0-345-25677-8). Ballantine.
Windsinger. Gary Smith. (Illus.). 176p. 1976. 7.95 (ISBN 0-87156-192-1). Windsinger.
Windsong Summer. Patricia C. Hass. LC 77-16878. (gr. 5 up). 1978. 5.95 (ISBN 0-396-07561-4). Dodd.
Windsor Handbook. Wallace Nutting. LC 73-77579. (Illus.). 1973. pap. 4.95 (ISBN 0-8048-1105-9). C E Tuttle.
Windsor Story. James Bryan & Charles Murphy. 1981. pap. 3.95 (ISBN 0-440-19346-X). Dell.
Windsound. Doris Vallejo. (Orig.). 1981. pap. 2.25 (ISBN 0-425-04803-9). Berkley Pub.
Windsurfing. Ernstfried Prade. (EP Sport Ser.). (Illus.). 1979. 12.95 (ISBN 0-8069-9166-6, Pub. by EP Publishing England). Sterling.
Windsurfing: The Complete Guide. Glenn Taylor. 288p. 1980. pap. 7.95 (ISBN 0-07-063154-9, GB). McGraw.
Windsurfing with Ken Winner: A Complete Illustrated Guide to a Fast-Growing Sport. Ken Winner & Roger Jones. LC 80-8399. (Illus.). 136p. (Orig.). 1981. pap. 8.95 (ISBN 0-06-250971-3, CN 4007, CN). Har-Row.
Windswept. Mary E. Chase. 1941. 10.95 (ISBN 0-02-524510-4). Macmillan.
Windswept. Athena Dallas-Damis. LC 78-75130. Date not set. write for info. (ISBN 0-89241-087-6). Caratzas Bros. Postponed.
Windswept. Athena Dallas-Damis. (Orig.). 1981. pap. 2.25 (ISBN 0-451-09666-5, E9666, Sig). NAL.
Windswept. Kristen James. (Orig.). 1981. pap. 2.75 (ISBN 0-671-42773-3). PB.
Windy Lindy. Peggy Byrd. (Illus.). 1981. pap. 4.50 (ISBN 0-8062-1702-2). Carlton.
Wine & Bitters. Isabelle K. Savell. (Illus.). 1975. pap. 2.45 (ISBN 0-89062-008-3). Rockland County Hist.
Wine, Beer, and Spirits. Dean Tudor. LC 74-80964. (Spare Time Guides Ser.: No. 6). 200p. 1975. lib. bdg. 11.50x o.p. (ISBN 0-87287-081-2). Libs Unl.
Wine Bibber's Bible. rev. ed. James N. Pratt. (Illus.). 192p. 1981. pap. 6.95 (ISBN 0-89286-182-7). One Hurd One Prods.
Wine Buyers Guide. Clifton Fadiman & Sam Aaron. LC 76-47678. (Illus.). 1977. 17.50 o.p. (ISBN 0-8109-1754-8); pap. 8.95 (ISBN 0-8109-2063-8). Abrams.
Wine Country. Sunset Editors. LC 79-88017. (Illus.). 128p. 1979. pap. 4.95 o.p. (ISBN 0-376-06943-0, Sunset Bks). Sunset-Lane.

Wine Country: California. Sunset Editors. LC 79-88017. (Illus.). 128p. 1979. pap. 4.95 (Sunset Bks.). Sunset-Lane.
Wine Country USA- Canada. 1975. pap. 2.00 (ISBN 0-918734-26-6). Reymont.
Wine Family in America, Section 3. Jacob D. Wine & J. Floyd Wine. LC 53-4352. (Illus.). 1971. 16.00 (ISBN 0-9604350-0-X). J F Wine.
Wine Grape Varieties in the San Joaquin Valley. A. N. Kasimatis et al. 1972. pap. 5.00x (ISBN 0-931876-23-0, 4009). Ag Sci Pubns.
Wine: How to Develop Your Taste & Get Your Money's Worth. William J. Sharp & Joseph Martin. (Illus.). 192p. 1976. text ed. 9.95 (ISBN 0-13-957746-7, Spec); pap. 3.95 (ISBN 0-13-957738-6). P-H.
Wine Log. Irene J. Kleinsinger. (Illus.). 96p. 1980. 9.95 (ISBN 0-9605146-1-9); pap. 4.95 (ISBN 0-9605146-0-0). Kleinsinger.
Wine Making for All. James MacGregor. 1966. 3.95 o.p. (ISBN 0-571-06646-1, Pub. by Faber & Faber). Merrimack Bk Serv.
Wine Merchandising. J. J. Haszonics & S. Barratt. (Illus.). 12.95x (ISBN 0-685-01585-8). Radio City.
Wine Merchants. S. W. Karl. (Orig.). 1979. pap. 1.95 (ISBN 0-532-23271-2). Manor Bks.
Wine of Astonishment. William Sears. 1963. pap. 1.95 o.s.i. (ISBN 0-85398-009-8, 7-31-64, Pub. by George Ronald England). Baha'i.
Wine of God. Kurt E. Koch. LC 74-81561. 1974. pap. 2.95 (ISBN 0-8254-3017-8). Kregel.
Wine of Life & Other Essays on Societies, Energy & Living Things. Harold J. Morowitz. 240p. 1981. pap. 2.95 (ISBN 0-553-14353-0). Bantam.
Wine of the Generals. R. Page Jones. 1978. pap. 1.95 o.s.i. (ISBN 0-515-04547-0). Jove Pubns.
Wine Production Technology in the United States. Ed. by Maynard A. Amerine. LC 80-28041. (Symposium Ser.: No. 145). 1981. price not set (ISBN 0-8412-0596-5); pap. price not set (ISBN 0-8412-0602-3). Am Chemical.
Wine Service Procedures. Tourism Education Corporation. 1976. 13.95 (ISBN 0-8436-2088-9). CBI Pub.
Wine Tasting. 5th ed. Michael Broadbent. (Christie Wine Publications). 68p. 1977. 8.50x o.p. (ISBN 0-903432-11-0). Intl Pubns Serv.
Wine-Tasting Course: The Practical Way to Know & Enjoy Wine. John Gottfried & Patricia Gottfried. (Illus.). 1978. 14.95 o.p. (ISBN 0-679-51451-1); pap. 6.95 o.p. (ISBN 0-679-50810-4). McKay.
Wine Tour of France. Frederick S. Wildman, Jr. (Illus.). 320p. 1972. 9.95 o.p. (ISBN 0-688-00088-6). Morrow.
Wine Trade. A. D. Francis. (Merchant Adventurers). (Illus.). 1972. text ed. 11.25x (ISBN 0-7136-1308-4). Humanities.
Winemaking & Brewing. Ben Turner. (Illus.). 1976. 12.95 (ISBN 0-7207-0924-5, Pub. by Michael Joseph). Merrimack Bk Serv.
Winemasters: The Story Behind the Glory & the Scandal of Bordeaux. Nicholas Faith. LC 77-11812. (Illus.). 1978. 12.95 o.p. (ISBN 0-06-011264-6, HarpT). Har-Row.
Wines & Spirits. Alec Waugh. LC 68-55300. (Foods of the World Ser). (Illus.). (gr. 6 up). 1968. PLB 14.94 (ISBN 0-8094-0061-8, Time-Life). Silver.
Wines & Spirits. Alec Waugh. (Foods of the World Ser). (Illus.). 1968. 14.95 (ISBN 0-8094-0034-0). Time-Life.
Wines & Wineries of New South Wales. James Halliday. 165p. 1981. text ed. 10.95x (ISBN 0-7022-1570-8). U of Queensland Pr.
Wines from Jams & Preserved Fruits. T. Edwin Belt. 1973. pap. 2.50 (ISBN 0-263-51655-5). Transatlantic.
Wines of Burgundy: The International Wire & Food Society's Guide. H. W. Yoxall. LC 78-57582. (Illus.). 192p. 1980. pap. 5.95 (ISBN 0-8128-6091-8). Stein & Day.
Wines of Spain & Portugal. Jan Read. (Illus.). 1980. 13.95 (ISBN 0-571-10266-2, Pub. by Faber & Faber). Merrimack Bk Serv.
Wines of the Midwest. Ruth E. Church. LC 77-83753. (Illus.). 207p. 1981. 14.95 (ISBN 0-8040-0779-9). Swallow.
Wines: Their Sensory Evaluation. Maynard A. Amerine & Edward B. Roessler. LC 76-13441. (Illus.). 1976. text ed. 13.95x (ISBN 0-7167-0553-2). W H Freeman.
Winetaster's Guide to Europe: How to Visit Over 300 Vineyards & Cellars on Your European Vacation. Anthony Hogg. (Illus.). 1980. 17.50 (ISBN 0-525-93071-X); pap. 8.95 (ISBN 0-525-93084-1). Dutton.
Wing & the Flame. Emily Hanlon. LC 80-15082. 192p. (gr. 7up). 9.95 (ISBN 0-87888-168-9). Bradbury Pr.
Wing Beat: A Collection of Eagle Woodcuts. G. E. Pogony. Tr. by Douglas J. Graham from Hungarian. LC 76-22176. (Illus.). 1976. 20.00x (ISBN 0-933652-10-0). Domjan Studio.
Wing Chun Kung-Fu. J. Yimm Lee. LC 72-87863. (Ser. 309). (Illus.). 1972. pap. 7.95 (ISBN 0-89750-037-7). Ohara Pubns.
Wing of the Dove. Henry James. 1978. 17.50 (ISBN 0-393-04478-5). Norton.
Wing Theory in Supersonic Flow. E. Carafoli. 1969. 90.00 (ISBN 0-08-012330-9). Pergamon.
Winged Warfare. William A. Bishop. (Air Combat Classics Ser.). (Illus.). 288p. 1981. 11.95 (ISBN 0-668-05162-0); pap. 5.95 (ISBN 0-668-05164-7). Arco.
Wings. Arthur L. Kopit. 78p. 1978. 8.95 (ISBN 0-8090-9756-7, Mermaid); pap. 3.95 (ISBN 0-8090-1239-1). Hill & Wang.
Wings Against the Sky. Richard Hough. 1981. pap. 2.50 (ISBN 0-440-19591-8). Dell.
Wings & Wishes. (Reading Basics Plus Ser.). (gr. 2). 1976. 8.36 (ISBN 0-06-517013-X, SchDept); tchr's ed. 15.92 (ISBN 0-06-517211-6); wkbk. 3.32 (ISBN 0-06-517308-2); tchr's wkbk. 6.60 (ISBN 0-06-517408-9). Har-Row.
Wings for Nurse Karen. Annie L. Gelsthorpe. (YA) 1978. 5.95 (ISBN 0-685-86417-0, Avalon). Bouregy.
Wings for Words: The Story of Johann Gutenberg & His Invention of Printing. Douglas C. McMurtrie. LC 78-167061. (Tower Bks). (Illus.). 175p. 1972. Repr. of 1940 ed. 20.00 (ISBN 0-8103-3936-6). Gale.
Wings from the Wind: An Anthology of Poetry. Ed. & illus. by Tasha Tudor. LC 64-19059. (gr. k-6). 1964. PLB 7.89 (ISBN 0-397-30789-6). Lippincott.
Wings in Your Future: Aviation for Young People. rev. ed. Leo Schneider & Maurice U. Ames. LC 55-5966. (Illus.). (gr. 7-9). 1955. 4.95 o.p. (ISBN 0-15-297855-0, HJ). HarBraceJ.
Wings O'er the Sea. Grace Blakeslee. 1980. 5.50 (ISBN 0-8233-0323-3). Golden Quill.
Wings of Desire. Paula Dion. 1978. pap. 2.25 o.p. (ISBN 0-685-66223-3). Ballantine.
Wings of Ecstasy. Barbara Cartland. (Barbara Cartland Ser.: No. 16). (Orig.). 1981. pap. 1.75 (ISBN 0-515-05955-2). Jove Pubns.
Wings of Mystery: True Stories of Aviation History. rev. ed. Dale Titler. (Illus.). 1981. 8.95 (ISBN 0-396-07826-5). Dodd.
Wings of Peace. John Creasey. 1978. 7.95 o.s.i. (ISBN 0-8027-5388-4). Walker & Co.
Wings of the Dove. Henry James. Ed. by J. Donald Crowley & Richard A. Hocks. (Norton Critical Edition Ser.). 1978. 17.50x (ISBN 0-393-04478-5); pap. 7.95 (ISBN 0-393-09088-4). Norton.
Wings of the Eagle. Nancy Dorer & Frances Dorer. (Orig.). 1979. pap. 1.95 (ISBN 0-532-23287-9). Manor Bks.
Wings of the Falcon. Barbara Michaels. LC 77-24927. 1977. 8.95 (ISBN 0-396-07458-8). Dodd.
Wings of the Hawk. Leigh F. James. (Colonization of America Ser.). 408p. (Orig.). 1981. pap. 2.95 (ISBN 0-553-14276-3). Bantam.
Wings of the Luftwaffe. Eric Brown. LC 77-14891. 1978. 10.95 o.p. (ISBN 0-385-13521-1). Doubleday.
Wings of the Morning: Little Lower Than the Angels. rev. ed. Roland B. Gittelsohn. (Illus.). (gr. 10). 1969. text ed. 7.00 (ISBN 0-8074-0194-3, 161850). wkbk. 2.25 (ISBN 0-8074-0196-X, 161852). UAHC.
Wings of Victory. Richard Hough. LC 80-24111. Orig. Title: Fight to the Finish. 224p. 1980. 8.95 (ISBN 0-688-03758-5). Morrow.
Wings on the Screen. Bertil Skogsberg. Tr. by George Bisset from Swedish. (Illus.). 192p. 1981. 25.00 (ISBN 0-498-02495-4). A S Barnes.
Wings Over the Seven Seas. Wilbur H. Morrison. LC 73-22597. (Illus.). 1976. 20.00 o.p. (ISBN 0-498-01485-1). A S Barnes.
Wings: The Early Years of Aviation. Richard Rosenblum. LC 79-26363. (Illus.). 64p. (gr. 3-7). 1980. 7.95 (ISBN 0-590-07576-4, Four Winds). Schol Bk Serv.
Wink of the Word: A Study of James Joyce's Phatic Communication. A. M. Knuth. 1976. pap. text ed. 17.25x (ISBN 0-391-02068-4). Humanities.
Winking at the Brim. Gladys Mitchell. 1981. pap. 2.25 (ISBN 0-440-19326-5). Dell.
Winnebago Indians. Incl. Winnebago Ethnology. J. A. Jones; Economic & Historical Background for the Winnebago Indian Claims. Alice E. Smith & Vernon Carstensen; Findings of Fact, & Opinion. Indian Claims Commission. (American Indian Ethnohistory Ser: North Central & Northeastern Indians). (Illus.). lib. bdg. 42.00 (ISBN 0-8240-0761-1). Garland Pub.
Winnebago Mysteries & Other Stories. Moira Crone. Date not set. pap. cancelled (ISBN 0-916300-17-X). Gallimaufry.
Winnebago Tribe. Paul Radin. LC 64-63594. (Illus.). 1970. pap. 8.50 (ISBN 0-8032-5710-4, BB 512, Bison). U of Nebr Pr.
Winner Got Scars Too: The Life & Legends of Johnny Cash. Christopher S. Wren. 1974. pap. 1.25 o.p. (ISBN 0-345-23731-5). Ballantine.
Winner Take All: From Trial to Triumph, Vol. 1. S. J. Freebairen-Smith & G. N. Littlejohn. 1977. pap. text ed. 5.25x (ISBN 0-435-36320-4). Heinemann Ed.
Winners. Judith Green. 240p. 1981. pap. 2.75. Ballantine.
Winners & Losers. Ed. by L. M. Schulman. LC 68-24106. (gr. 7 up). 1968. 5.95 o.s.i. (ISBN 0-02-781380-0). Macmillan.
Winners & Losers: Styles of Development & Change in an Indian Region. Ed. by S. Devadas Pillai. C. Baks. 407p. 1979. text ed. 36.00 (ISBN 0-8426-1679-9). Verry.
Winner's Circle. Joseph Hayes. 1981. pap. 3.50 (ISBN 0-440-19532-2). Dell.
Winner's Edge. Bob Oates, Jr. Date not set. 12.95 (ISBN 0-686-68762-0). Mayflower Bks.
Winner's Edge: How to Develop the Critical Attitude of Success. Denis Waitly. 256p. 1980. 9.95 (ISBN 0-8129-0897-X). Times Bks.
Winners in Gymnastics. Frank Litsky. (Picture Life Books Ser.). (Illus.). (gr. 2 up). 1978. PLB 6.45 s&l (ISBN 0-531-02887-9). Watts.
Winners on Ice. Frank Litsky. (Picture Life Bks.). (Illus.). (gr. k-3). 1979. PLB 6.45 s&l (ISBN 0-531-02291-9). Watts.
Winners on the Ski Slopes. John Fry. LC 78-16443. (Picture Life Bks.). (Illus.). (gr. k-3). 1979. PLB 6.45 s&l (ISBN 0-531-02292-7). Watts.
Winners on the Tennis Court. William G. Glickman. (Picture Life Books Ser.). (Illus.). (gr. 2 up). 1978. PLB 6.45 s&l (ISBN 0-531-02912-3). Watts.
Winner's: Recipes That Won the Contests & How You Can Be a Winner Too! Karen Green. LC 79-24003. 256p. 1980. 12.95 (ISBN 0-688-03566-3). Morrow.
Winnie Ille Pu: A Latin Edition of Winnie-the-Pooh. A. A. Milne. Tr. by Alexander Lenard. (Illus.). (gr. 7 up). 1962. 6.95 o.p. (ISBN 0-525-43007-5). Dutton.
Winnie Puh. Walt Disney. Tr. by Rene Sanchez from Eng. Orig. Title: Winnie-the-Pooh Book. (Illus.). 24p. (Span.). (ps-3). 1977. PLB 5.92 o.p. (ISBN 0-307-68827-5, Golden Pr). Western Pub.
Winnie the Pooh. A. A. Milne. (Illus.). (gr. 1-5). 6.95 (ISBN 0-525-43035-0). Dutton.
Winnie the Pooh All Year Long. Illus. by Bill Williams. (Golden Sturdy Shape Bks.). (Illus.). 14p. 1981. 2.95 (ISBN 0-307-12260-3, Golden Pr). Western Pub.
Winnie-the-Pooh & Eeyore's House. A. A. Milne. (Tell-a-Tale Reader). (Illus.). (gr. k-3). 1976. PLB 4.77 (ISBN 0-307-68620-5, Whitman). Western Pub.
Winnie-the-Pooh & His Friends. Walt Disney. (Illus.). (ps-3). 1976. PLB 5.38 (ISBN 0-307-68957-3, Golden Pr). Western Pub.
Winnie-the-Pooh & the Blustery Day. A. A. Milne. (Tell-a-Tale Readers). (Illus.). (gr. k-3). 1979. PLB 4.77 (ISBN 0-307-68577-2, Whitman). Western Pub.
Winnie-the-Pooh & the Unbouncing of Tigger. (ps-2). 1977. 1.95 (ISBN 0-307-10504-0, Golden Pr); PLB 7.62 (ISBN 0-307-60504-3). Western Pub.
Winnie-the-Pooh & Tigger. A. A. Milne. (Illus.). (gr. k-3). 1976. PLB 5.00 (ISBN 0-307-60121-8, Golden Pr). Western Pub.
Winnie-the-Pooh Book. Al White. (Illus.). (ps-1). 1965. PLB 5.38 (ISBN 0-307-68927-1, Golden Pr). Western Pub.
Winnie-the-Pooh Do-It-Yourself Counting Book. (Golden Play & Learn Bk.). 14p. (ps). Date not set. pap. 2.95 (ISBN 0-307-10727-2, Golden Pr). Western Pub.
Winnie-the-Pooh Every Day Is Special. (Wipe-off Bks.). 9p. (ps). 2.39 (ISBN 0-307-01845-8, Golden Pr). Western Pub.
Winnie-the-Pooh Meets Gopher. A. A Milne. (Illus.). 24p. (gr. k-3). 1976. PLB 5.00 (ISBN 0-307-60017-3, Golden Pr). Western Pub.
Winnie-the-Pooh: Unbouncing of Tigger. A. A. Milne. (Tell-a-Tale Readers). (Illus.). (gr. k-3). 1978. PLB 4.77 (ISBN 0-307-10504-0, Whitman); pap. 1.95 (ISBN 0-307-10504-0). Western Pub.
Winnie the Pooh's Calendar Book: 1981. A. A. Milne. (Illus.). 1980. 3.95 o.p. (ISBN 0-525-43049-0). Dutton.
Winnie-the-Pooh's Calendar Book 1982. A. A. Milne. 32p. (ps up). 1981. spiral 4.50 (ISBN 0-525-43050-4). Dutton.
Winning at Casino Gambling. Terence Reese. 1979. pap. 1.75 (ISBN 0-451-08617-1, E8617, Sig). NAL.
Winning at Casino Gambling: An International Guide. Terence Reese. LC 78-62195. 1978. 9.95 (ISBN 0-8069-0138-1); lib. bdg. 9.29 (ISBN 0-8069-0139-X). Sterling.
Winning at Office Politics. Andrew J. DuBrin. Date not set. pap. 2.95 (ISBN 0-345-29532-3). Ballantine.
Winning at Work. Florence Seaman & Anne Lorimer. 192p. 1980. pap. 2.95 (ISBN 0-553-14244-5). Bantam.
Winning Basketball Plays: By America's Foremost Coaches. 2nd ed. Ed. by Clair Bee. (Illus.). 1963. 18.50 o.p. (ISBN 0-8260-0875-5). Ronald Pr.
Winning Bowling. Earl Anthony & Dawson Taylor. LC 77-75718. (Winning Ser.). (Illus.). 1977. 8.95 o.p. (ISBN 0-8092-7792-1); pap. 5.95 (ISBN 0-8092-7791-3). Contemp Bks.
Winning by Negotiation. Tessa A. Warschaw. LC 80-14535. 264p. 1980. 10.95 (ISBN 0-07-000780-2, GB). McGraw.
Winning Chess Combinations. H. Bouwmeester. 1977. 15.95 (ISBN 0-7134-0419-1, Pub. by Batsford England); pap. 12.50 (ISBN 0-7134-0420-5). David & Charles.
Winning Chess Tactics. I. A. Horowitz. LC 73-81634. (Illus.). 3.95 o.s.i. (ISBN 0-88365-060-6). Brown Bk.
Winning Combination. Julie Anthony & Nick Bollitieri. (Illus.). 224p. 1980. 12.50 (ISBN 0-684-16710-7, ScribT). Scribner.
Winning Elections: A Handbook in Participatory Politics. Dick Simpson. LC 78-171874. 1971. 10.00x o.p. (ISBN 0-8040-0541-9); pap. 4.95x o.p. (ISBN 0-8040-0542-7). Swallow.
Winning Elections: A Handbook in Participatory Politics. rev. & enl. ed. Dick Simpson. (Illus.). 240p. 1981. 13.95x (ISBN 0-8040-0365-3); text ed. 7.95x (ISBN 0-8040-0366-1). Swallow.
Winning Hearts & Minds: War Poems by Vietnam Veterans. LC 72-12486. 1972. pap. 3.50. Packrat Pr.
Winning Ideas in the Social Studies. Steven L. Jantzen. LC 77-9530. (Illus.). 1977. pap. text ed. 5.50x (ISBN 0-8077-2541-2). Tchrs Coll.
Winning Images. Robert L. Shook. 1977. 9.95 (ISBN 0-02-610540-3, 61054). Macmillan.
Winning in the Commodities Market: A Money-Making Guide to Commodity Futures Trading. George Angell. LC 78-18129. 1979. 12.95 (ISBN 0-385-14208-0). Doubleday.
Winning Is Everything--Losing Is Nothing! C. E. Feltner, Jr. LC 80-68579. 200p. 1981. 9.95 (ISBN 0-87754-066-7). Chelsea Hse.
Winning Is Everything & Other American Myths. Thomas Tutko & William Bruns. 224p. 1976. 8.95 o.s.i. (ISBN 0-02-620770-2). Macmillan.
Winning Kicker. Thomas J. Dygard. LC 77-17727. (gr. 7 up). 1978. PLB 7.20 (ISBN 0-688-32140-2). Morrow.
Winning Men of Tennis. Nathan Aaseng. LC 80-28598. (Sports Heroes Library). (Illus.). (gr. 4 up). 1981. PLB 5.95 (ISBN 0-8225-1068-5). Lerner Pubns.
Winning Methods of Bluffing & Betting in Poker. Lyn Taetzsch. LC 75-36140. (Illus.). 138p. (Orig.). 1981. pap. 6.95. Sterling.
Winning of the World. Ben Hansen. 176p. (Orig.). 1980. pap. 4.95 (ISBN 0-931590-04-3). Antietam Pr.
Winning on the Wind: Championship Soaring Techniques, Sailplanes & History. George B. Moffat. LC 74-82783. (Illus.). 244p. 1974. pap. 5.95 (ISBN 0-930514-00-9, Pub. by Soaring). Aviation.
Winning Option. Ralph T. Dames. LC 79-23369. 128p. 1981. 14.95 (ISBN 0-88229-527-6). Nelson-Hall.
Winning Plays in Pro Football. George Sullivan. LC 75-6821. (Illus.). 128p. (gr. 5 up). 1975. PLB 4.95 (ISBN 0-396-07148-1). Dodd.
Winning Poker Systems. Norman Zadeh. LC 74-5234. (Illus.). 228p. 1974. 8.95 o.p. (ISBN 0-13-961292-0); pap. 3.95 o.p. (ISBN 0-13-961284-X). P-H.
Winning Proposal: How to Write It. Herman R. Holtz & Terry D. Schmidt. (Business Communication Ser.). (Illus.). 384p. 1981. text ed. 18.95x (ISBN 0-07-029649-9). McGraw.
Winning Sandwiches for Menu Makers. Wheat Flour Institute. Ed. by Kathleen M. Thomas. LC 76-45621. (Illus.). 1976. 18.95 (ISBN 0-8436-2123-0). CBI Pub.
Winning Squash Racquets. new ed. Jack Barnaby. 1979. 17.95 (ISBN 0-205-06175-3). Allyn.
Winning Supply & Service Business in Offshore Oil & Gas Markets. Shell UK Exploration & Production Ltd. 112p. 1976. 77.00x (ISBN 0-86010-025-1, Pub. by Graham & Trotman England). State Mutual Bk.
Winning the Age Game. Gloria Heidi. 1977. pap. 6.95 (ISBN 0-89104-061-7). A & W Pubs.
Winning the Diet Wars. Meridee Merzer. LC 79-2765. 1980. 9.95 (ISBN 0-15-196378-9). HarBraceJ.
Winning the Losing Battle. Eda LeShan. 176p. (Orig.). 1981. pap. 2.50 (ISBN 0-553-14147-3). Bantam.
Winning the Salary Game: Salary Negotiation for Women. Sherry Chastain. 192p. 1980. text ed. 9.95 (ISBN 0-471-08433-6); pap. text ed. 6.95 (ISBN 0-471-08023-3). Wiley.
Winning the Two-Dollar Bet. Walter B. Gibson. (Gambler's Book Shelf). 1975. pap. 2.95 (ISBN 0-89650-556-1). Gamblers.
Winning Through Enlightenment. Ron Smothermon. 1980. pap. 5.95 (ISBN 0-932654-01-0). Context Pubns.

Winning Tournament Karate. Chuck Norris. Ed. by John Cocoran. LC 75-5497. (Ser. 121). (Illus.). 1975. pap. text ed. 5.95 (ISBN 0-89750-016-4). Ohara Pubns.

Winning Volleyball. 2nd ed. Allen E. Scates. 304p. 1976. text ed. 18.95x (ISBN 0-205-04875-7). Allyn.

Winning Ways. Ray Bard & Larry Davis. LC 79-20395. 1979. write for info 3 ring notebk. (ISBN 0-89384-043-2). Learning Concepts.

Winning Ways. LeRoy Eims. LC 74-77319. 160p. 1974. pap. 2.95 (ISBN 0-88207-707-4). Victor Bks.

Winning Ways in Health Care: Transactional Analysis for Effective Communication. Dorothy Jongeward & Muriel James. 1981. pap. text ed. 7.95 (ISBN 0-201-00451-8). A-W.

Winning Weapon: The Atomic Bomb in the Cold War Nineteen Forty-Five to Nineteen Fifty. Gregg F. Herken. LC 80-7643. 416p. 1981. 15.00 (ISBN 0-394-50394-5). Knopf.

Winning with Money. Beryl W. Sprinkel & Robert J. Genetski. LC 76-47751. 1977. 10.95 o.p. (ISBN 0-87094-135-6). Dow Jones-Irwin.

Winning with People for Health Care Professionals. M. James & D. Jongeward. 1980. pap. cancelled (ISBN 0-201-00451-8). A-W.

Winning with Science: Source Book of Grants, Prizes & Awards for Science Competition. William S. Loiry. (Illus.). 224p. 1981. 11.95 (ISBN 0-87460-355-2). Lion.

Winning with Statistics: A Painless First Look at Numbers, Ratios, Percentages, Means & Inference. Richard P. Runyon. (Statistics Ser.). (Illus.). 1977. pap. text ed. 8.95 (ISBN 0-201-06654-8). A-W.

Winning with Your Lawyer. Burton Marks & Gerald Golfarb. (McGraw-Hill Paperbacks Ser.). 224p. (Orig.). 1980. pap. 6.95 (ISBN 0-07-040390-2, SB). McGraw.

Winning Without Counting. Stanford Wong. LC 80-10723. (Illus.). 237p. 1980. 50.00 (ISBN 0-935926-01-1). Pi Yee Pr.

Winning Women of Tennis. Nathan Aaseng. (Sports Heroes Library). (Illus.). (gr. 4 up). 1981. PLB 5.95 (ISBN 0-8225-1067-7). Lerner Pubns.

Winning Your Personal Injury Suit. John Guinther. LC 79-6575. 312p. (Orig.). 1980. pap. 6.95 (ISBN 0-385-15005-9, Anch). Doubleday.

Winnipeg General Strike. Donald C. Masters. LC 51-5058. (Illus.). xv, 159p. 1950. 11.50 o.p. (ISBN 0-8020-7018-3); pap. 4.00 o.p. (ISBN 0-8020-6217-2). U of Toronto Pr.

Winnowing Winds. Ann Marlowe. LC 77-3881. 1977. 7.95 (ISBN 0-396-07445-6). Dodd.

Winslow Homer. Lloyd Goodrich. (Illus.). 144p. 1976. pap. 6.95 o.p. (ISBN 0-89104-017-X). A & W Pubs.

Winslow Homer. Stephanie Stepanek. 1977. pap. 2.00 (ISBN 0-87846-115-9). Mus Fine Arts Boston.

Winslow Homer: An Annotated Bibliography of Periodical Literature. Melinda D. Davis. LC 75-29243. 1975. 10.00 (ISBN 0-8108-0876-5). Scarecrow.

Winston Churchill. Manfred Weidhorn. (English Authors Ser.: No. 264). 1979. lib. bdg. 12.50 (ISBN 0-8057-6760-6). Twayne.

Winston Churchill: A Political Biography. V. Trukhanovsky. 1978. 9.00 (ISBN 0-8285-9151-2). Progress Pubs.

Winston Churchill & His Inner Circle. John Colville. 1981. 13.95 (ISBN 0-671-42583-8, Wyndham Bks). S&S.

Winston S. Churchill: His Complete Speeches, 1897-1963, 8 vols. Ed. by Robert R. James. LC 74-505. 1981. pap. 97.50 (ISBN 0-87754-128-0). Chelsea Hse.

Winter. Richard L. Allington & Kathleen Krull. LC 80-25115. (Beginning to Learn About Ser.). (Illus.). 32p. (ps-2). 1981. PLB 9.65 (ISBN 0-8172-1340-6). Raintree Child.

Winter Always Comes. Donald Honig. LC 76-54874. 144p. (gr. 7-11). 1977. 5.95 (ISBN 0-590-07452-0, Four Winds). Schol Bk Serv.

Winter at Valley Forge. Van Wyck Mason. (Landmark Ser: No. 33). (Illus.). (gr. 10-12). 1953. PLB 5.99 (ISBN 0-394-90333-1, BYR). Random.

Winter Count. Barry Lopez. (Illus.). 96p. 1981. 9.95 (ISBN 0-684-16817-0, ScribT). Scribner.

Winter Donkey. Lois Lamplugh. (gr. 3-7). 1980. 8.95 (ISBN 0-233-97198-X). Andre Deutsch.

Winter Evening. Shrikant Varma. Tr. by Jai Ratan & K. B. Vaid. 100p. (Eng.). 1975. 14.00 (ISBN 0-88253-674-5); pap. 4.80 (ISBN 0-88253-673-7). Ind-US Inc.

Winter Folk. G. Walton Williams. 3.95 (ISBN 0-932298-11-7). Green Hill.

Winter Garden. Beryl Bainbridge. 1981. 8.95 (ISBN 0-8076-1011-9). Braziller.

Winter Harvest. Norah Lofts. 1976. pap. 1.75 o.p. (ISBN 0-449-22855-X, X2855, Crest). Fawcett.

Winter Has Lasted Too Long. James Kavanaugh. 1977. 6.95 (ISBN 0-87690-248-4). Dutton.

Winter Hell. Jory Sherman. (Gunn Ser.: No. 5). 256p. (Orig.). 1981. pap. 1.95 (ISBN 0-89083-708-2). Zebra.

Winter Hero. James L. Collier & Christopher Collier. LC 78-7609. 160p. (gr. 7 up). 1978. 7.95 (ISBN 0-590-07529-2, Four Winds). Schol Bk Serv.

Winter Hiking & Camping. 2nd ed. John Danielsen. (Illus.). 1977. 6.95 (ISBN 0-935272-04-6). ADK Mtn Club.

Winter in the Blood. James Welch. LC 74-5985. 192p. 1981. pap. 2.25 (ISBN 0-06-080537-4, P 537, PL). Har-Row.

Winter Is Here! Jane B. Moncure. LC 75-14201. (ps-2). 1975. 5.50 (ISBN 0-913778-10-9). Childs World.

Winter Journey. T. A. Broughton. 1980. 10.95 (ISBN 0-525-23515-9). Dutton.

Winter Journey. T. Alan Broughton. 320p. 1981. pap. 2.95 (ISBN 0-449-24369-9, Crest). Fawcett.

Winter Love Song. Meredith Kingston. (Second Chance at Love, Contemporary Ser.: No. 2). 192p. (Orig.). 1981. pap. 1.75 (ISBN 0-515-05637-5). Jove Pubns.

Winter News. John Haines. LC 66-14660. (Wesleyan Poetry Program: Vol. 29). (Orig.). 1966. 10.00x (ISBN 0-8195-2029-2, Pub. by Wesleyan U Pr); pap. 4.95 (ISBN 0-8195-1029-7). Columbia U Pr.

Winter of Artifice. Anais Nin. LC 61-17530. 175p. (Orig.). 1961. pap. 5.95 (ISBN 0-8040-0322-X, 29). Swallow.

Winter of the Birds. Helen Cresswell. LC 75-34278. 192p. (gr. 7 up). 1976. 9.95 (ISBN 0-02-725510-7, 72551). Macmillan.

Winter of the Owl. June A. Hanson. LC 80-15966. (Illus.). 144p. (gr. 5-9). 1980. 8.95 (ISBN 0-02-742530-4). Macmillan.

Winter of the Wolf. G. Clifton Wisler. (gr. 6 up). 1980. 7.95 (ISBN 0-525-66716-4). Elsevier-Nelson.

Winter Olympics. Frank Litsky. (First Bks.). (Illus.). (gr. 4 up). 1979. PLB 6.45 s&l (ISBN 0-531-02946-8). Watts.

Winter Olympics. Julian May. LC 76-4860. (Sports Classics Ser.). (Illus.). (gr. 4-12). 1976. PLB 8.95 o.p. (ISBN 0-87191-504-9). Creative Ed.

Winter on Her Own. Elizabeth Howard. LC 68-16625. (gr. 7 up). 1968. 7.75 (ISBN 0-688-21710-9). Morrow.

Winter Outdoor Living. Merlin Gode. 1978. pap. text ed. 2.75 (ISBN 0-89832-008-9). Brighton Pub.

Winter People. Phyllis A. Whitney. 1978. pap. 1.95 (ISBN 0-449-23681-1, Crest). Fawcett.

Winter Picnic. Robert Welber. LC 77-77418. (Illus.). (gr. 7 up). 1970. PLB 5.99 o.s.i. (ISBN 0-394-90444-3). Pantheon.

Winter Pony. Jean S. Doty. (Illus.). 112p. (gr. 4-6). 1975. 7.95 (ISBN 0-02-732760-4). Macmillan.

Winter Queen: A Biography of Elizabeth of Bohemia. Josephine Ross. 1979. 16.95x (ISBN 0-312-88232-7). St Martin.

Winter War: The Russo-Finnish Conflict, 1939-1940. Eloise Engle & Lauri A. Paananen. LC 72-1217. (Illus.). 250p. 1973. 7.95 o.p. (ISBN 0-684-13047-5, ScribT). Scribner.

Winter Wedding. Betty Neels. (Harlequin Romances Ser.). (Orig.). 1980. pap. text ed. 1.25 o.p. (ISBN 0-373-02338-3, Pub. by Harlequin). PB.

Winter When Time Was Frozen. Els Pelgrom. Tr. by Maryka Rudnik & Raphael Rudnik. LC 80-21224. Orig. Title: De Kinderen Van Het Achtste Woud. 224p. (gr. 4-6). 1980. 8.95 (ISBN 0-688-22247-1); PLB 8.59 (ISBN 0-688-32247-6). Morrow.

Winter Wonders. Toni Bauman & June Zinkgraf. (gr. k-6). 1978. 12.95 (ISBN 0-916456-29-3, GA89). Good Apple.

Wintering Out. Seamus Heaney. 1972. pap. 5.95x (ISBN 0-19-519820-4). Oxford U Pr.

Winterize Your Yard & Garden. George Taloumis. LC 76-18862. (Illus.). 1976. 9.95 o.p. (ISBN 0-397-01178-4). Lippincott.

Winter's Crimes Eleven. George Hardinge. 1980. 9.95 (ISBN 0-312-88238-6). St Martin.

Winters Heart. Cathryn Ladame. 192p. 1981. pap. 1.50 (ISBN 0-671-57055-2). S&S.

Winter's Love. Felicia Bryce. 192p. (YA) 1976. 4.95 o.p. (ISBN 0-685-59254-5, Avalon). Bouregy.

Winters of the World: Earth Under the Ice Ages. Brian John. 256p. 1979. 24.95x (ISBN 0-470-26844-1). Halsted Pr.

Winter's Tale. William Shakespeare. Ed. by Arthur Quiller-Couch et al. (New Shakespeare Ser). 1968. 23.95 (ISBN 0-521-07563-7); pap. 4.50x (ISBN 0-521-09506-9). Cambridge U Pr.

Winter's Tales. Ed. by Caroline Hobhouse. 1980. 9.95 (ISBN 0-312-88375-7). St Martin.

Winter's Tales 26. A. D. Maclean. 224p. 1981. 11.95 (ISBN 0-312-88414-1). St Martin.

Winter's Task. Robert Wells. 63p. (Orig.). 1980. pap. 7.95 (ISBN 0-85635-210-1, Pub. by Carcanet New England Pr). Persea Bks.

Winters Without Snow. new ed. Colleen McElroy. LC 79-92501. 81p. 1980. pap. 5.95 (ISBN 0-918408-17-2). Reed & Cannon.

Winterspelt. Alfred Andersch. LC 76-56262. 1978. 10.00 o.p. (ISBN 0-385-01368-X). Doubleday.

Winterthur Bk, No. 7. Ed. by Ian M. Quimby. (Winterthur Bk.). (Illus.). 1972. 15.00 (ISBN 0-8139-0370-X). U of Chicago Pr.

Winterthur Coloring Book. Joyce F. Halbrook. (Illus.). 1979. pap. 2.95 (ISBN 0-912724-06-4). Winterthur.

Winterthur Museum & Gardens. 3rd ed. (Illus.). 1980. pap. 3.00 (ISBN 0-912724-04-8). Winterthur.

Winthrop Covenant. Louis Auchincloss. 1977. pap. 1.95 o.p. (ISBN 0-345-25668-9). Ballantine.

Winthrop Woman. Anya Seton. 1975. pap. 1.75 o.s.i. (ISBN 0-515-03442-8). Jove Pubns.

Wipeoff Multiplication Table Quiz Book. Nancy Salloway. 12p. (gr. 3 up). 1980. pap. 1.50 (ISBN 0-937518-05-0). Hartley Hse.

Wipeout! Pete Pomeroy. (gr. 7-12). 1972. pap. 0.95 o.p. (ISBN 0-590-08769-X, Schol Pap). Schol Bk Serv.

WIPO Glossary of the Terms of the Law of Copyright & Neighboring Rights. 281p. 1980. pap. 39.50 (ISBN 92-805-0016-3, WIPO63, WIPO). Unipub.

Wire Fox Terriers. Linda Beak. Ed. by Christina Foyle. (Foyle's Handbks). 1973. 3.95 (ISBN 0-685-55789-8). Palmetto Pub.

Wire Tappers. Arthur Stringer. 1976. lib. bdg. 15.30x (ISBN 0-89968-121-2). Lightyear.

Wire Womb: Life in a Girls' Penal Institution. Henry P. Lampman. LC 72-90555. 1973. 12.95 (ISBN 0-911012-23-0). Nelson-Hall.

Wireless Telegraphy. Ed. by Eric Eastwood. LC 73-22705. 391p. 1974. 42.95 (ISBN 0-470-22950-0). Halsted Pr.

Wires & Watts: Understanding & Using Electricity. Irwin Math. (Illus.). 96p. (gr. 7 up). 1981. 8.95 (ISBN 0-686-69287-X). Scribner.

Wiretapping & Eavesdropping, Vol. 1. Clifford Fishman. LC 78-18629. 1978. 47.50. Lawyers Co-Op.

Wiretapping & Electronic Eavesdropping, the Law & Its Implications: A Comparative Study. Juris Cederbaums. (New York University Criminal Law Education & Research Center Monograph: No. 2). 77p. (Orig.). 1969. pap. text ed. 8.50x (ISBN 0-8377-0402-2). Rothman.

Wiring Simplified. 33rd ed. Ed. by H. P. Richter & W. C. Schwan. LC 33-7980. 160p. 1981. 3.50 (ISBN 0-9603294-1-2). Park Pub.

Wirral. Alan Brack. LC 79-56465. (Illus.). 176p. 1980. 30.00 (ISBN 0-7134-1378-6, Pub. by Batsford England). David & Charles.

Wirriyamu. Williams Sassine. Tr. by John Reed & Clive Wake. (African Writers Ser.). 148p. 1980. pap. 5.50 (ISBN 0-435-90199-0). Heinemann Ed.

Wisconsin. Justin Isherwood. (Illus.). 128p. 1981. 27.50 (ISBN 0-912856-67-X). Graphic Arts Ctr.

Wisconsin. 28.00 (ISBN 0-89770-125-9). Curriculum Info Ctr.

Wisconsin: A History. Richard N. Current. LC 77-2176. (States & the Nation Ser.). (Illus.). 1977. 12.95 (ISBN 0-393-05624-4, Co-Pub by AASLH). Norton.

Wisconsin: A History. Robert C. Nesbit. LC 72-9990. (Illus.). 620p. 1973. 15.004 (ISBN 0-299-06370-4). U of Wis Pr.

Wisconsin: A State Guide. Federal Writers' Project. 49.00 (ISBN 0-403-02198-7). Somerset Pub.

Wisconsin Chronology & Factbook, Vol. 49. R. I. Vexler. 1978. 8.50 (ISBN 0-379-16174-5). Oceana.

Wisconsin Indians. Nancy O. Lurie. LC 80-10758. (Illus.). 66p. (Orig.). 1980. pap. 2.00 (ISBN 0-87020-195-6). State Hist Soc Wis.

Wisconsin My Home. Erna O. Xan. 232p. 1976. 15.00 (ISBN 0-299-00711-1); pap. 5.25 (ISBN 0-299-00714-6). U of Wis Pr.

Wisconsin Quantity Cuisine: The Foods That Make Wisconsin Famous. Charles F. Church. LC 76-45274. 1976. 14.95 (ISBN 0-685-74394-2). CBI Pub.

Wisconsin State Industrial Directory, 1980. State Industrial Directories Corp. 1979. pap. 50.00 (ISBN 0-89910-010-4). State Indus Dir.

Wisconsin Story. rev. ed. H. Russell Austin. (Illus.). 650p. (gr. 6 up). 1948. pap. 6.00 (ISBN 0-686-27878-X). Milwaukee Journal.

Wisconsin Supplement for Real Estate Principles & Practices. Garfield R. Stock. (Business Ser.). 1977. pap. text ed. 4.95 (ISBN 0-675-08508-X). Merrill.

Wisconsin Writers. William A. Titus. LC 77-145704. 1974. Repr. of 1930 ed. 24.00 (ISBN 0-8103-3658-8). Gale.

Wisconsin's Champion Trees. Ed. by R. Bruce Allison. (Illus.). 128p. (Orig.). 1980. lib. bdg. 15.00 (ISBN 0-913370-09-6); pap. 6.95 (ISBN 0-686-27407-5). Wisconsin Bks.

Wisdom & Cult: A Critical Analysis of the Views of Cult in the Wisdom Literatures of Israel & the Ancient Near East. Leo G. Perdue. LC 76-47453. (Society of Biblical Literature. Dissertation Ser.: No. 30). 1977. pap. 9.00 (ISBN 0-89130-094-5, 060130). Scholars Pr Ca.

Wisdom & Education. Douglas E. Lawson. LC 61-11660. 168p. 1961. 4.95x (ISBN 0-8093-0048-6). S Ill U Pr.

Wisdom Community. Edward K. Braxton. LC 80-81053. 224p. (Orig.). 1980. pap. 7.95 (ISBN 0-8091-2307-X). Paulist Pr.

Wisdom from Above. LeRoy Eims. 1978. pap. 3.50 (ISBN 0-88207-761-9). Victor Bks.

Wisdom from the East: Meditations, Reflections, Proverbs & Chants. Ellen K. Hua. LC 73-21886. (Illus.). 128p. (Orig.). 1974. pap. 2.25 (ISBN 0-87407-202-6, FP2). Thor.

Wisdom from the Nile: A Collection of Folk-Stories from Northern & Central Sudan. Ed. by Ahmed Al Shahi & F. C. Moore. (Illus.). 270p. 1978. text ed. 37.50x (ISBN 0-19-815147-0). Oxford U Pr.

Wisdom from White Eagle. White Eagle. 5.95 (ISBN 0-85487-004-0). De Vorss.

Wisdom in Israel. Gerhard Von Rad. Tr. by James D. Martin from Ger. Orig. Title: Weisheit in Israel. 336p. 1973. 15.95 o.p. (ISBN 0-687-45756-4). Abingdon.

Wisdom in the Old Testament Tradition. Donn F. Morgan. LC 80-84653. 17.50 (ISBN 0-8042-0188-9); pap. 8.95 (ISBN 0-8042-0189-7). John Knox.

Wisdom Literature of the Bible: Proverbs, Job, Ecclesiastes. Leon H. Spotts. 1967. pap. 1.25 (ISBN 0-8074-0198-6, 247310). UAHC.

Wisdom Literature: Ruth, Esther, Job, Proverbs, Ecclesiastes, Canticles. Roland E. Murphy. (The Forms of the Old Testament Literature Ser.). (Orig.). 1981. pap. write for info. (ISBN 0-8028-1877-3). Eerdmans.

Wisdom of Buddhism. new ed. Ed. by Christmas Humphreys. 1979. text ed. 13.50x (ISBN 0-391-00950-8). Humanities.

Wisdom of John Woolman: With a Selection from His Writings As a Guide to the Seekers of Today. Reginald Reynolds. LC 79-8724. xii, 178p. 1981. Repr. of 1948 ed. lib. bdg. 22.50x (ISBN 0-313-22190-1, REJW). Greenwood.

Wisdom of Man: Selected Discourses. M. R. Bawa Muhaiyaddeen. LC 80-20541. (Illus.). 168p. 1980. 10.00 (ISBN 0-914390-16-3). Fellowship Pr PA.

Wisdom of Plato: An Attempt at an Outline, 2 vols. Nehemiah Jordan. LC 80-1409. (Orig.). 1981. Set. lib. bdg. 47.50 (ISBN 0-8191-1408-1); Set. pap. text ed. 33.00 (ISBN 0-8191-1409-X). Vol. I, 544p. Vol. 2, 536p. U Pr of Amer.

Wisdom of the Ancients. T. Lobsang Rampa. 1975. pap. 2.50 (ISBN 0-685-70568-4). Weiser.

Wisdom of the Desert. Thomas Merton. LC 59-15021. 1970. 6.50 (ISBN 0-8112-0313-1); pap. 2.95 (ISBN 0-8112-0102-3, NDP295). New Directions.

Wisdom of the Overself. Paul Brunton. 1970. pap. 7.50 (ISBN 0-87728-062-2). Weiser.

Wisdom of the Sasanian Sages: Denkard Book Six. Tr. by Shaul Shaked. (Bibliotheca Persica: Persian Heritage Ser.: No. 36). 1979. lib. bdg. 50.00x (ISBN 0-89158-376-9). Westview.

Wisdom of the Serpent. Joseph L. Henderson & Maud Oakes. 1971. pap. 1.95 o.s.i. (ISBN 0-02-065370-0, Collier). Macmillan.

Wisdom of the Soul. 3rd ed. H. C. Randall-Stevens. (Illus.). 1974. 10.00 (ISBN 0-685-27228-1). Weiser.

Wisdom of the Taoists. D. Howard Smith. LC 80-15629. (Wisdom Ser.). 96p. 1980. 4.95 (ISBN 0-8112-0777-3, NDP509). New Directions.

Wisdom of the Vedas. J. C. Chatterji. LC 80-51550. 100p. 1980. pap. 3.95 (ISBN 0-8356-0538-8, Quest). Theos Pub Hse.

Wisdom of the Vedas. Jagadish C. Chatterji. LC 73-8889. Orig. Title: India's Outlook on Life. 100p. 1973. Repr. of 1931 ed. 3.95 o.p. (ISBN 0-8356-0214-1). Theos Pub Hse.

Wisdom of Unity (Manisa-Pancakam) Shankara. Tr. by T. M. Mahadevan. (Orig., Sanskrit & Eng.). pap. 1.25 o.p. (ISBN 0-89744-125-7, Pub. by Ganesh & Co. India). Auromere.

Wisdom of William Earnest Hocking. Ed. by John Howie & Leroy Rouner. LC 78-61397. 1978. pap. text ed. 6.75 (ISBN 0-8191-0595-3). U Pr of Amer.

Wisdom of Words: Language, Theology, & Literature in the New England Renaissance. Philip F. Gura. 192p. 1981. 17.50 (ISBN 0-8195-5053-1). Wesleyan U Pr.

Wise Blood. Flannery O'Connor. 232p. 1962. 10.95 (ISBN 0-374-29128-4); pap. 5.95 (ISBN 0-374-50584-5). FS&G.

Wise King & the Baby. Yvonne Patterson. LC 59-1258. (Arch Bk.: No. 18). (Illus.). (gr. k-4). 1981. pap. 0.79 (ISBN 0-686-69321-3). Concordia.

Wise Man's Guide to Fine Spirits Through the Coming Financial Hard Times. rev. ed. Sandy I. Niehaus. Ed. by Toni Stollo. (Illus.). 56p. 1980. 3.85 (ISBN 0-938452-00-2). Santam.
Wise Men of the Wires: The History of Farady House. F. W. Lipscomb. (Illus.). 1973. text ed. 9.25x (ISBN 0-09-117060-5). Humanities.
Wise Men Visit Jesus. (Tell-a-Bible Story Ser.). (Illus.). 28p. bds. 0.69 (ISBN 0-686-68643-8, 3687). Standard Pub.
Wise Robin. (Ladybird Stories Ser.). (Illus., Arabic.). 2.50x (ISBN 0-686-53065-9). Intl Bk Ctr.
Wise up & Live. 2nd ed. Paul E. Larsen. LC 73-86222. pap. 2.75 (ISBN 0-8307-0453-1, S274-1-24). Regal.
Wise Woman. Joyce Rogers. LC 80-68538. 1981. 6.95 (ISBN 0-8054-5289-3). Broadman.
Wise Woman & Other Fantasy Stories. George MacDonald. Ed. by Glenn G. Sadler. (Fantasy Stories of George MacDonald Ser.). 176p. 1980. pap. 2.95 (ISBN 0-8028-1860-9). Eerdmans.
Wise Woman Builds Her House. Bessie Patterson. 1979. pap. 3.75 (ISBN 0-89137-413-2). Quality Pubns.
Wise Woman, or the Lost Princess. George MacDonald. LC 75-32187. (Classics of Children's Literature, 1621-1932: Vol. 50). (Illus.). 1976. Repr. of 1882 ed. PLB 38.00 (ISBN 0-8240-2299-8). Garland Pub.
Wisedome of the Ancients. Frances Bacon. Tr. by A. Gorges. LC 68-54614. (English Experince Ser.: No. 1). 176p. 1968. Repr. of 1619 ed. 13.00 (ISBN 90-221-0001-4). Walter J Johnson.
Wiseguys. Vincent Teresa. 1978. 7.95 o.p. (ISBN 0-525-23560-4). Dutton.
Wisely Train the Younger Women. Mrs. Elmer Patterson. 1973. pap. 3.45 (ISBN 0-89137-406-X). Quality Pubns.
Wiser Than Winter. Dorothy Pitkin. (gr. 7-9). 1960. PLB 5.69 o.p. (ISBN 0-394-91828-2). Pantheon.
Wish Again, Big Bear. Richard Margolis. LC 75-160070. (gr. k-2). 1972. 7.95g (ISBN 0-02-762410-2). Macmillan.
Wish Card Ran Out! James Stevenson. (Illus.). 32p. (gr. k-4). 1981. 7.95 (ISBN 0-688-80305-9); PLB 7.63 (ISBN 0-688-84305-0). Greenwillow.
Wish, Come True. Mary Q. Steele. LC 79-10321. (Illus.). (gr. 4-6). 1979. 7.95 (ISBN 0-688-80230-3); PLB 7.63 (ISBN 0-688-84230-5). Greenwillow.
Wish To Be Free: Society, Psyche, & Value Change. Fred Weinstein & Gerald M. Platt. LC 71-83291. 1969. 18.50x (ISBN 0-520-01398-0); pap. 0.85x o.p. (ISBN 0-520-02493-1). U of Cal Pr.
Wish You Were Here. Pasadena Art Alliance. 1979. pap. 4.50 (ISBN 0-937042-02-1). Pasadena Art.
Wishes Fall Out As They're Willed: Shakespeare & the Tragicomic Archetype. William Babula. (Salzburg Studies in English Literature, Elizabethan & Renaissance Studies Ser.: No. 48). 133p. 1975. pap. text ed. 25.00x (ISBN 0-391-01305-X). Humanities.
Wishes, Whispers & Secrets. Jane B. Moncure. LC 78-31295. (Illus.). (ps-3). 1979. PLB 5.95 (ISBN 0-89565-024-X). Childs World.
Wishful Lying. Rose Blue. LC 79-21806. (Children's Ser.). 32p. 1980. 8.95 (ISBN 0-87705-473-8). Human Sci Pr.
Wishful Thinking: A Theological ABC. Frederick Buechner. LC 72-9872. 128p. 1973. 7.95 (ISBN 0-06-061155-3, HarpR). Har-Row.
Wishing Bone. David Severn. (Illus.). (gr. 3-6). 1977. 10.95 (ISBN 0-04-823141-X). Allen Unwin.
Wishing Bone Cycle: Narrative Poems from the Swampy Cree Indians. Ed. & tr. by Howard Norman. 192p. 1976. 9.95 (ISBN 0-88373-045-6); pap. 3.45 (ISBN 0-88373-046-4). Stonehill Pub Co.
Wishing Hat. Annegert Fuchshuber. Tr. by Elizabeth D. Crawford. (ps-3). 1977. 7.25 (ISBN 0-688-22100-9); PLB 6.96 (ISBN 0-688-32100-3). Morrow.
Wishing Night. Carole Vetter. (Illus.). (gr. k-3). 1966. 4.50g o.s.i. (ISBN 0-02-791700-2). Macmillan.
Wishing Tree. Sandra Paretti. 1978. pap. 1.95 o.p. (ISBN 0-449-23604-8, Crest). Fawcett.
Wising up. Jo Foxworth. 1980. 9.95 (ISBN 0-440-09605-7). Delacorte.
Wisps of Wit & Wisdom, or Knowledge in a Nutshell. Albert P. Southwick. LC 68-30582. 1968. Repr. of 1892 ed. 15.00 (ISBN 0-8103-3095-4). Gale.
Wispy, the Littlest Witch. Rosemary Varney. LC 76-48097. (Illus.). (ps-3). 1977. 5.50 (ISBN 0-913778-70-2). Childs World.
Wissenschaft und Methode: Interpreationen Zur aristotelischen Theorie der Naturwissenschaft. Wolfgang Kullmann. (Ger.). 1974. 85.30x (ISBN 3-11-004481-1). De Gruyter.
Wissenschaftliche Abhandlungen, 3 Vols. Ludwig Boltzmann. Ed. by Fritz Hasenohrl. LC 66-26524. (Ger). 1969. Set. 89.50 (ISBN 0-8284-0215-9). Chelsea Pub.
Wit & Humor of Colonial Days 1607-1800. Carl Holliday. LC 71-148586. 1970. Repr. of 1912 ed. 15.00 (ISBN 0-8103-3592-1). Gale.
Wit & Humor of Oscar Wilde. Oscar Wilde. Ed. by Alvin Redman. 1959. pap. 3.50 (ISBN 0-486-20602-5). Dover.
Wit & Humor of Well-Known Quotations. Marshall Brown. LC 70-146919. 1971. Repr. of 1905 ed. 20.00 (ISBN 0-8103-3644-8). Gale.
Wit & Whiggery: The Rev. Sydney Smith (1771-1845) Howard Mackey. LC 79-64194. 1979. pap. text ed. 16.25 (ISBN 0-8191-0756-5). U Pr of Amer.
Wit & Wisdom from West Africa: A Book of Proverbial Philosophy, Idioms, Enigmas, & Laconisms. Richard F. Burton. LC 77-79952. 1969. Repr. of 1865 ed. 16.00x (ISBN 0-8196-0243-4). Biblo.
Wit & Wisdom of Billy Graham. Ed. by Bill Adler. LC 80-65430. 256p. Date not set. 8.95 (ISBN 0-915684-61-6). Christian Herald. Postponed.
Wit & Wisdom of Bishop Fulton J. Sheen. Ed. by Bill Adler. LC 78-82959. 1969. pap. 2.45 (ISBN 0-385-02691-9, D268, Im). Doubleday.
Wit & Wisdom of Charles Lamb. Ernest D. North. 267p. 1980. Repr. of 1892 ed. lib. bdg. 25.00 (ISBN 0-8495-4109-3). Arden Lib.
Wit & Wisdom of the Christian Fathers of Egypt: The Syrian Version of the Apophthegmata Patrum. Compiled by Anan Isho. Tr. by Ernest A. Wallis Budge. LC 80-2354. 1981. Repr. of 1934 ed. 53.50 (ISBN 0-404-18900-8). AMS Pr.
Wit & Wisdom of the Italian Renaissance. Charles Speroni. 1964. 20.00x (ISBN 0-520-01199-6). U of Cal Pr.
Wit of the West. Oren Arnold. 1975. 2.95 (ISBN 0-685-59275-8). Nortex Pr.
Wit, Wisdom & Foibles of the Great. Charles A. Shriner. LC 68-30617. 1969. Repr. of 1918 ed. 22.00 (ISBN 0-8103-3297-3). Gale.
Wit Without Money: A Comedy. Francis Beaumont & John Fletcher. LC 73-25968. (English Experience Ser.: No. 264). 66p. Repr. of 1639 ed. 11.50 (ISBN 90-221-0264-5). Walter J Johnson.
Witch & the Owl. Terry Riley & Rosemary Day. (Illus.). 1981. 10.95x (ISBN 0-460-06886-5, Pub. by J. M. Dent England). Biblio Dist.
Witch Can Fly. Dave L. Obanda. Date not set. 6.95 (ISBN 0-533-04836-2). Vantage.
Witch Doctor's Apprentice. Nicole Maxwell. (Illus.). 288p. 1975. pap. 1.95 o.s.i. (ISBN 0-02-096020-4, Collier). Macmillan.
Witch Dog. John Beatty & Patricia Beatty. LC 68-11213. (gr. 7 up). 1968. 7.75 o.p. (ISBN 0-688-21433-9). Morrow.
Witch Family. Eleanor Estes. LC 60-11250. (Illus.). (gr. 3-7). 1960. 7.50 o.p. (ISBN 0-15-298571-9, HJ). HarBraceJ.
Witch, Goblin & Ghost in the Haunted Woods. Sue Alexander. LC 80-20863. (I Am Reading Ser.). (Illus.). 48p. (gr. 1-3). 1981. 4.95 (ISBN 0-394-84443-2); PLB 5.95 (ISBN 0-394-94443-7). Pantheon.
Witch, Goblin & Ghost in the Haunted Woods. Sue Alexander. LC 80-20863. (I Am Reading Bk.). (Illus.). 72p. (gr. 1-4). 1981. 4.95 (ISBN 0-394-84443-2); PLB 5.99 (ISBN 0-394-94443-7). Pantheon.
Witch Grows up. Bridwell. (ps-3). 1980. pap. 1.25 (ISBN 0-590-30045-8, Schol Pap). Schol Bk Serv.
Witch House & Other Tales Our Settlers Told. H. Joseph Raskin & Edith Raskin. (gr. 4-6). 1978. pap. 1.25 (ISBN 0-590-11916-8, Schol Pap). Schol Bk Serv.
Witch Hunting, Magic & the New Philosophy. Brian Easlea. (Harvester Studies in Philosophy Ser.: No. 14). 280p. 1980. text ed. 42.50x (ISBN 0-391-01807-8); pap. text ed. 16.50x (ISBN 0-391-01808-6). Humanities.
Witch in the Cherry Tree. Margaret Mahy. LC 73-6738. (Illus.). 32p. (gr. k-3). 1974. 5.95 o.s.i. (ISBN 0-8193-0646-0, Four Winds); PLB 5.41 o.s.i. (ISBN 0-8193-0647-9). Schol Bk Serv.
Witch in the House. Ruth Chew. (Illus.). (gr. 2-3). 1976. pap. 1.50 (ISBN 0-590-00093-4, Schol Pap). Schol Bk Serv.
Witch in the Shrouds: A Voyage in Miniature. Bess Taylor. 148p. (gr. 4-6). 1980. 6.95 (ISBN 0-8059-2720-4). Dorrance.
Witch Lady Mystery. Carol B. York. (gr. 4-6). 1977. pap. 1.25 (ISBN 0-590-11917-6, Schol Pap). Schol Bk Serv.
Witch Next Door. Norman Bridwell. (Illus.). (gr. k-3). 1971. pap. 1.25 (ISBN 0-590-00342-9, Schol Pap); pap. 3.95 witch next door & indian two feet (2 bks.) & 1 record (ISBN 0-590-04394-3). Schol Bk Serv.
Witch of Blackbird Pond. Elizabeth Speare. 256p. (gr. 5-8). 1972. pap. 1.75 (ISBN 0-440-49569-5, YB). Dell.
Witch of Edmonton by Thomas Dekker: A Critical Edition. Ed. by Etta S. Onat & Stephen Orgel. LC 79-54355. (Renaissance Drama Second Ser.). 400p. 1980. lib. bdg. 44.00 (ISBN 0-8240-4472-X). Garland Pub.
Witch of Glen Gowrie. William MacKellar. LC 77-16864. (gr. 5-8). 1978. 5.95 (ISBN 0-396-07531-2). Dodd.
Witch of Hissing Hill. Mary Calhoun. (Illus.). (gr. k-3). 1964. PLB 7.44 (ISBN 0-688-31762-6). Morrow.
Witch of the Cumberlands. Mary Jo Stephens. LC 73-22062. (Illus.). 240p. (gr. 4-9). 1974. 8.95 (ISBN 0-395-18509-2). HM.
Witch, Warlock, & Magician. William H. D. Adams. LC 73-5621. 1971. Repr. of 1889 ed. 30.00 (ISBN 0-8103-3619-7). Gale.
Witch Who Saved Halloween. Marion T. Price. 1980. pap. 1.75 (ISBN 0-380-00097-0, 51417, Camelot). Avon.
Witch Who Wasn't. Jane H. Yolen. (Illus.). (gr. k-3). 1964. 4.95g o.s.i. (ISBN 0-02-793650-3). Macmillan.
Witch Who Went for a Walk. Margaret Hillert. (Illus.). (gr. 1-6). 1981. PLB 4.39 (ISBN 0-695-41549-2); pap. 1.50 (ISBN 0-695-31549-8). Follett.
Witch World. Andre Norton. 224p. 1977. pap. 1.95 (ISBN 0-441-89705-3). Ace Bks.
Witchcraft. Emma L. Byars. 1981. 4.50 (ISBN 0-8062-1580-1). Carlton.
Witchcraft. Charles A. Hoyt. 1981. price not set (ISBN 0-8093-0964-5); pap. price not set (ISBN 0-8093-1015-5). S Ill U Pr.
Witchcraft. Charles Williams. (Orig.). pap. 3.95 o.p. (ISBN 0-452-00400-4, F400, Mer). NAL.
Witchcraft & Black Magic. Montague Summers. LC 70-174114. (Illus.). 1971. Repr. of 1916 ed. 22.00 (ISBN 0-685-02995-6). Gale.
Witchcraft & Magic: The Supernatural World of Primitive Man. Arthur S. Gregor. LC 72-1166. (Illus.). 160p. (gr. 5-9). 1972. pap. 2.45 o.p. (ISBN 0-684-14537-5, SL 619, ScribT). Scribner.
Witchcraft & Sorcery: An Anthropological Perspective of the Occult. John A. Rush. (Illus.). 176p. 1974. 14.75 (ISBN 0-398-02981-4); pap. 11.25 (ISBN 0-398-03019-7). C C Thomas.
Witchcraft & the Black Art: A Book Dealing with the Psychology & Folklore of the Witches. J. W. Wickwar. LC 71-151817. 1971. Repr. of 1925 ed. 26.00 (ISBN 0-8103-3692-8). Gale.
Witchcraft at Salem. Chadwick Hansen. LC 69-15825. (Illus.). 1969. 10.00 o.s.i. (ISBN 0-8076-0492-5). Braziller.
Witchcraft in England. Christina Hole. 1966. pap. 1.50 o.s.i. (ISBN 0-02-028860-3, Collier). Macmillan.
Witchcraft in Europe, 1100-1700: A Documentary History. Ed. by Alan C. Kors & Edward Peters. LC 71-170267. (Illus.). 1973. 17.50x (ISBN 0-8122-7645-0); pap. 9.95x (ISBN 0-8122-1063-8, Pa Paperbks). U of Pa pr.
Witchcraft in History. Ronald Holmes. 1977. pap. 5.95 (ISBN 0-8065-0575-3). Citadel Pr.
Witchcraft in Ireland. Patrick Byrne. 76p. 1967. pap. 3.25 o.p. (ISBN 0-85342-038-6). Irish Bk Ctr.
Witchcraft in Tudor & Stuart England: A Regional & Comparative Study. Alan MacFarlane. 1970. 25.00 (ISBN 0-7100-6403-9). Routledge & Kegan.
Witchcraft, Magic & Alchemy. Grillot De Givry. Tr. by J. Courtney Locke from Fr. (Illus.). 395p. 1971. pap. 6.50 (ISBN 0-486-22493-7). Dover.
Witchcraft of Salem Village. Shirley Jackson. (gr. 4-6). 1956. 2.95 o.p. (ISBN 0-394-80369-8, BYR). Random.
Witchcraft, Oracles & Magic Among the Azande. Edward E. Evans-Pritchard. 1937. 45.00x (ISBN 0-19-823103-2). Oxford U Pr.
Witches. Francoise Mallet-Joris. Tr. by Herma Briffault from Fr. 1969. 6.95 o.p. (ISBN 0-374-29157-8). FS&G.
Witches. Therese R. Revesz. LC 77-10626. (Myth, Magic & Superstition Ser.). (Illus.). (gr. 4-5). 1977. PLB 9.65 (ISBN 0-8172-1034-2). Raintree Pubs.
Witches' Advocate: Basque Witchcraft & the Spanish Inquisition, 1609-1614. Gustav Henningsen. LC 79-23102. (Basque Book Ser.). (Illus.). xxxii, 607p. 1980. 24.00 (ISBN 0-87417-056-7). U of Nev Pr.
Witches & Demons in History & Folklore. F. Roy Johnson. (Illus.). 1978. Repr. 8.50 (ISBN 0-930230-31-0). Johnson NC.
Witches & Warlocks. Philip W. Sergeant. LC 72-164055. (Illus.). 290p. 1975. Repr. of 1936 ed. 20.00 (ISBN 0-8103-3979-X). Gale.
Witches Four. Marc Brown. LC 79-5263. (Illus.). 48p. (ps-3). 1980. 4.95 (ISBN 0-8193-1013-1); PLB 5.95 (ISBN 0-8193-1014-X). Parents.
Witches of All Saints. Jill Tattersall. 240p. 1976. pap. 1.50 o.p. (ISBN 0-449-22776-6, Q2776, Crest). Fawcett.
Witches, Pumpkins & Grinning Ghosts: The Story of the Halloween Symbols. Edna Barth. LC 72-75705. (Illus.). 96p. (gr. 2-6). 1972. 8.95 (ISBN 0-395-28847-9, Clarion). HM.
Witches, Whales, Petticoats, & Sails. Barbara M. Marhoefer. LC 74-151807. (Empire State Historical Publications Ser). (Illus.). 1971. 12.95 (ISBN 0-8046-8092-2). Friedman.
Witches, Wit & a Werewolf. Ed. by Jeanne B. Hardendorff. LC 75-153516. (Illus.). 128p. (gr. 4-6). 1971. 7.89 (ISBN 0-397-31542-2). Lippincott.
Witchfinder. Mary Rayner. LC 76-22600. (Illus.). (gr. 5-9). 1976. 7.25 (ISBN 0-688-22082-7); PLB 6.96 (ISBN 0-688-32082-1). Morrow.
Witch's Broom. Ruth Chew. (gr. k-3). 1978. pap. 1.50 (ISBN 0-590-05407-4, Schol Pap). Schol Bk Serv.
Witch's Broom. Ruth Chew. LC 77-6090. (Illus.). (gr. 2-5). 1977. 5.95 (ISBN 0-396-07486-3). Dodd.
Witch's Buttons. (ps-3). pap. 1.50 (ISBN 0-590-09840-3, Schol Pap). Schol Bk Serv.
Witch's Christmas. Norman Bridwell. (Illus.). (gr. k-3). 1972. pap. 1.25 (ISBN 0-590-09216-2, Schol Pap); pap. 3.95 witch's christmas & clifford the big red dog (2 bks.) & 1 record (ISBN 0-590-04385-4). Schol Bk Serv.
Witchs Daughter. Nina Bawden. (gr. 4-6). 1974. pap. 0.95 o.s.i. (ISBN 0-671-29720-1). Archway.
Witch's Daughter. Nina Bawden. (gr. 4-6). 1973. pap. 0.95 (ISBN 0-671-29720-1). PB.
Witch's Egg. Madeleine Edmondson. LC 72-97769. (Illus.). (gr. 1-4). 1974. 5.95 (ISBN 0-395-28790-1, Clarion). HM.
Witch's Garden. Ruth Chew. (gr. k-3). 1979. pap. 1.50 (ISBN 0-590-12107-3, Schol Pap). Schol Bk Serv.
Witch's Garden. Harold A. Hansen. Tr. by Muriel Crofts from Danish. LC 78-5469. (Illus.). 1978. pap. 4.95 o.p. (ISBN 0-913300-47-0). Unity Pr.
Witch's House. Charlotte Armstrong. 1975. pap. 0.95 o.p. (ISBN 0-425-02797-X, Medallion). Berkley Pub.
Witchs Lamp. Edith S. Pederson. (Childrens Bk). Orig. Title: Teddy & the Witchs Lamp. (Illus.). 128p. (gr. 1-5). 1970. pap. 1.50 (ISBN 0-8024-1960-7). Moody.
Witch's Magic Cloth. Miyoko Matsutani. Tr. by Alvin Tresselt. LC 79-77787. Orig. Title: Yamanbano Nishiki. (gr. k-3). 1969. 5.95 o.s.i. (ISBN 0-8193-0319-4, Four Winds); PLB 5.41 o.s.i. (ISBN 0-8193-0320-8). Schol Bk Serv.
Witch's Pig: A Cornish Folktale. (gr. k-3). 1977. 7.25 o.p. (ISBN 0-688-22092-4); PLB 7.92. (ISBN 0-688-32092-9). Morrow.
Witch's Sister. Phyllis R. Naylor. 1980. pap. 1.95 (ISBN 0-689-70471-2, Aladdin). Atheneum.
Witch's Tales. new ed. Corinne Denan. LC 79-66328. (Illus.). 48p. (gr. 2-6). 1980. lib. bdg. 4.89 (ISBN 0-89375-324-6). pap. 1.50 (ISBN 0-89375-323-8). Troll Assocs.
Witch's Vacation. Norman Bridwell. (Illus.). (gr. k-3). 1975. pap. 1.25 (ISBN 0-590-09839-X, Schol Pap); pap. 3.50 bk & record (ISBN 0-590-20697-4). Schol Bk Serv.
Witcracks: Jokes & Jests from American Folklore. Alvin Schwartz. LC 73-7630. (Illus.). (gr. 4 up). 1973. 8.95 (ISBN 0-397-31475-2); pap. 2.50 (ISBN 0-397-31476-0). Lippincott.
Witenagemot in the Reign of Edward the Confessor: A Study in the Constitutional History of Eleventh-Century England. Trygovi J. Oleson. LC 80-2217. 1981. Repr. of 1955 ed. 29.50 (ISBN 0-404-18769-2). AMS Pr.
With a Face Like Mine. Sharon L. Berman. 160p. 1981. 8.95 (ISBN 0-87777-062-X, Pub. by R W Baron). Dutton.
With Akhmatova at the Black Gates. Stephen Berg. LC 80-14469. 1981. 10.00 (ISBN 0-252-00833-2); pap. 3.95 (ISBN 0-252-00834-0). U of Ill Pr.
With All the Views: Collected Poems. Adrian Stokes. Ed. by Peter Robinson. 160p. 1981. 17.50x (ISBN 0-933806-04-3). Black Swan CT.
With All Your Heart: Bechol Levavcha, 2 vols. Harvey J. Fields. (Illus.). (gr. 7-9). 1977. 8.00 (ISBN 0-8074-0197-8, 142611). UAHC.
With All Your Mind. Yandall Woodfin. 272p. 1980. pap. 8.95 (ISBN 0-687-45839-0). Abingdon.
With an Holy Calling. Josephine C. Edwards. LC 78-5367. (Destiny Ser.). 1979. pap. 4.95 (ISBN 0-8163-0250-2). Pacific Pr Pub Assn.
With Anger-with Love. Susan Sherman. pap. 3.50 (ISBN 0-913142-05-0). Out & Out.
With Beauregard in Mexico. Ed. by T. Harry Williams. LC 69-19760. (American Scene Ser.). 1969. Repr. of 1956 ed. lib. bdg. 17.50 (ISBN 0-306-71255-5). Da Capo.
With Bright Wings: A Book of the Spirit. Mary G. Swift. LC 75-44806. 1976. pap. 5.95 (ISBN 0-8091-1936-6). Paulist Pr.
With Caesar's Legions. Reuben F. Wells. LC 60-16709. (Illus.). (gr. 7-11). 1951. 8.50x (ISBN 0-8196-0110-1). Biblo.

With Child. Phyllis Chesler. 1981. pap. 2.95 (ISBN 0-425-04834-9). Berkley Pub.
With Christ in the School of Prayer. Andrew Murray. (Spire Bk). pap. 1.95 (ISBN 0-8007-8046-9). Revell.
With Dersu the Hunter. Vladimir Arsenyev. LC 65-25971. (gr. 6-9). 3.95 o.p. (ISBN 0-8076-0325-2). Braziller.
With Essex in Ireland. Emily Lawless. Ed. by Robert L. Wolff. (Ireland Nineteenth Century Fiction - Ser. Two: Vol. 72). 348p. 1979. lib. bdg. 32.00 (ISBN 0-8240-3521-6). Garland Pub.
With Eyes Wide Open. Peter Steinke. LC 74-3735. 1974. pap. 2.50 (ISBN 0-570-03180-X, 12-2583). Concordia.
With Face to the Wall. Miltos Sahtouris. Tr. by Kimon Friar. 1980. 7.50 (ISBN 0-685-54466-4). Charioteer.
With Fidel: A Portrait of Castro & Cuba. Ed. by Frank Mankiewicz & Kirby Jones. (Illus.). 240p. Date not set. pap. 1.95 (ISBN 0-345-28242-6). Ballantine.
With Friends Like That. Michael Fairley. 1981. 12.95 (ISBN 0-87949-194-9). Ashley Bks.
With God in Red China. Mary Wang. LC 77-78610. 1977. pap. 1.95 (ISBN 0-87123-186-7, 200186). Bethany Fell.
With God in Russia. Ciszek, Walter J., Fr., S.J. & Flaherty, Daniel L., Fr., S.J. pap. 2.45 (ISBN 0-385-03954-9, D200, Im). Doubleday.
With God We Can. Roy E. Davis. 1978. pap. 4.95 (ISBN 0-87707-211-6). CSA Pr.
With God's Help Flowers Bloom. Elaine Anderson. 1978. pap. 3.75 (ISBN 0-89137-411-6); study guide 2.45 (ISBN 0-89137-412-4). Quality Pubns.
With It. William D. Sheldon et al. (Breakthrough Ser). (gr. 7-12). 1972. pap. text ed. 3.80 (ISBN 0-205-03092-0, 5230926); tchrs'. guide 2.40 (ISBN 0-205-02920-5, 5229200). Allyn.
With Joy: Poems for Children. rev. ed. Ed. by T. E. Wade et al. (Illus.). 48p. (gr. 1-6). 1980. pap. 0.95 (ISBN 0-930192-08-7). Gazelle Pubns.
With Justice for All. John Perkins. LC 80-50262. 192p. 1981. text ed. 7.95 (ISBN 0-8307-0754-9, 5108802). Regal. Postponed.
With Long Life. Penny E. Wheeler. LC 78-13748. (Crown Ser.). 1978. pap. 4.50 (ISBN 0-8127-0192-5). Southern Pub.
With Love, from Jo. Jossy Ann Bolivar. Ed. by Josefa V. Bolivar. LC 80-13999. (Illus.). 120p. (Orig.). 1980. pap. 5.95 (ISBN 0-914598-01-5). Padre Prods.
With Love from Karen. Marie Killilea. 1964. pap. 1.75 o.s.i. (ISBN 0-440-19615-9). Dell.
With Love from Karen. Marie Killilea. (gr. 7-12). 1980. pap. 1.95 (ISBN 0-440-99615-5, LE). Dell.
With Love, Mother. Emma L. Thayne. 31p. 1975. 0.75 o.p. (ISBN 0-87747-551-2). Deseret Bk.
With Malice Toward None: A War Diary by Cecil King. Cecil King. Ed. by William Armstrong. LC 70-175619. 343p. 1971. 28.50 (ISBN 0-8386-1067-6). Fairleigh Dickinson.
With Merrill's Cavalry. Samuel E. Baird. Ed. by Charles Annegan. LC 80-69601. (Illus.). 64p. 1981. 15.95 (ISBN 0-9605200-0-7). Bk Habit.
With Mini & Maxi in Muffkinland. V. Gilbert Beers. (Muffin Family Adventure Ser.). 79p. (gr. k-4). 1981. text ed. 8.95 (ISBN 0-8024-4063-0). Moody.
With Objectives in Mind. Len Ennever & Wynne Harlen. LC 77-82993. (Science 5-13 Ser.). (Illus.). 1977. pap. text ed. 9.30 (ISBN 0-356-04009-7). Raintree Child.
With Paper, About Paper. Ed. by Charlotta Kotik. LC 80-69318. (Illus.). 1980. pap. 7.50 (ISBN 0-914782-35-5). Buffalo Acad.
With Pen & Tongue. Ursula M. Bygott. 444p. 1980. 37.50x (ISBN 0-522-84150-3, Pub. by Melbourne U Pr Australia). Intl Schol Bk Serv.
With Perfect Faith: The Foundations of Jewish Belief. J. David Bleich. 1980. write for info. (ISBN 0-88482-924-3). Hebrew Pub.
With Secret Friends. Cooper Edens. (Illus.). 44p. (Orig.). 1981. pap. 8.95 (ISBN 0-914676-57-1). Green Tiger.
With Shuddering Fall. Joyce C. Oates. LC 64-23317. 1964. 10.95 (ISBN 0-8149-0173-5). Vanguard.
With Shuddering Fall. Joyce C. Oates. 1976. pap. 1.75 (ISBN 0-449-24930-1, X2930, Crest). Fawcett.
With Six You Get Eggroll. Gwen Bagni & Paul Dubov. (Willow Bks). (gr. 7-8). 1971. pap. 0.75 o.s.i. (ISBN 0-515-00055-8, JT55). Jove Pubns.
With Sound & Color: An Intermediate Chinese-English Reader. Florence C. Chang. LC 80-68257. (Chinese Can Be Fun Ser.: Bk. 2). (Illus.). 71p. (Orig.). (gr. 6-9). 1980. pap. text ed. 3.50 (ISBN 0-936620-01-3). Ginkgo Hut.
With Stethoscope in Asia: Korea. Sherwood Hall. LC 77-81765. 1978. 15.95 (ISBN 0-930696-01-8). MCL Assocs.
With Strings Attached: Reminiscences & Reflections. Joseph Szigeti. (Music Reprint Ser.). 1979. Repr. of 1947 ed. lib. bdg. 29.50 (ISBN 0-306-79567-1). Da Capo.
With the Eagles. Paul L. Anderson. LC 57-9447. (Illus.). (gr. 7-11). 1929. 8.50x (ISBN 0-8196-0100-4). Biblo.
With Their Ears Pricked Forward: Tales of Mules I've Known. Joshua A. Lee. 1980. 8.95 (ISBN 0-89587-018-5). Blair.
With Their Whole Strength. William Wilson. LC 80-2084. 128p. (gr. 6 up). 1981. pap. 2.75 (ISBN 0-385-17435-7, Im). Doubleday.
With These Hands: Women Working on the Land. Ed. by Florence Howe & John A. Rothermich. (Women's Lives - Women's Work). (Orig.). pap. text ed. 6.45 (ISBN 0-07-020441-1). Webster-McGraw.
With These Hands: Women Working on the Land. Joan M. Jensen. (Women's Lives - Women's Work Ser.). (Illus.). 336p. 1981. 17.95 (ISBN 0-912670-90-8); pap. 6.95 (ISBN 0-912670-71-1). Feminist Pr.
With This Gift: The Story of Edgar Cayce. Anne Neimark. (Illus.). (gr. 7 up). 1978. 7.95 (ISBN 0-688-22147-5); PLB 7.63 (ISBN 0-688-32147-X). Morrow.
With This Ring... One Hundred Years of Marriage. Elizabeth Laverack. (Illus.). 138p. 1980. pap. 17.95 (ISBN 0-241-89895-1, Pub. by Hamish Hamilton England). David & Charles.
With Tigers in the Wild: An Experience in an Indian Forest. Fateh S. Rathmore et al. (Illus.). 196p. 1981. text ed. 75.00 (ISBN 0-7069-1023-0, Pub. by Vikas India). Advent Bk.
With William Burroughs. Victor Bockris. 288p. 1981. 14.95 (ISBN 0-394-51809-8); pap. 7.95 (ISBN 0-394-17828-9). Seaver Bks.
With Wings As Eagles. Perry D. Gresham. LC 80-66183. 1980. 10.95 (ISBN 0-89305-025-3); pap. 5.95 (ISBN 0-89305-026-1). Anna Pub.
Wither the State? Politics & Public Enterprise in Three Countries. Ira Sharkansky. 9.95 (ISBN 0-934540-01-2); pap. 7.95 (ISBN 0-934540-00-4). Chatham Hse Pubs.
Withering Away of the City. York Willbern. LC 63-19642. 136p. 1964. 7.00 o.p. (ISBN 0-8173-4709-7). U of Ala Pr.
Witherwing. David Jarrett. (Orig.). 1979. pap. 1.95 o.s.i. (ISBN 0-446-90115-6). Warner Bks.
Within the Barbed Wire Fence: A Japanese Man's Account of His Internment in Canada. Takeo U. Nakano & Leatrice Nakano. (Illus.). 136p. 1981. 10.00 (ISBN 0-295-95789-1). U of Wash Pr.
Within the Sound of These Waves: The Story of the Kings of Hawaii Island, Containing a Full Account of the Death of Captain Cook, Together with the Hawaiian Adventures of George Vancouver & Sundry Other Mariners. William H. Chickering. LC 70-138584. (Illus.). 1971. Repr. of 1941 ed. lib. bdg. 21.75x (ISBN 0-8371-5783-8, CHSW). Greenwood.
Within the Whirlwind. Eugenia Ginzburg. Tr. by Ian Boland. (Helen & Kurt Wolff Bk.). 1981. 14.95 (ISBN 0-15-197517-5). HarBraceJ.
Without a Lawyer. Steve Sarshik & Walter Szykitka. (Orig.). 1980. pap. 5.95 (ISBN 0-452-25226-1, Z5226, Plume). NAL.
Without a Man of Her Own. Linda Dubreuil. (Orig.). 1975. pap. 1.50 o.p. (ISBN 0-685-53906-7, LB282DK, Leisure Bks). Nordon Pubns.
Without a Trace. Background GmbH. Ed. by Partisan Press Staff. (Illus.). 128p. (Orig.). 1980. pap. 4.95 (ISBN 0-935150-00-5). Partisan Pr.
Without a Trace: New Information from the Triangle. Charles Berlitz. LC 76-41438. 1977. 7.95 o.p. (ISBN 0-385-11139-8). Doubleday.
Without Bombast & Blunders: An Executive's Guide to Effective Writing. Frances D. Naczi. LC 80-17857. 1980. 5.95 (ISBN 0-87863-007-4). Farnswth Pub.
Without Fear or Favor: An Uncompromising Look at the New York Times. Harrison Salisbury. 640p. 1981. pap. 8.95 (ISBN 0-345-29711-3). Ballantine.
Without Feathers. Woody Allen. LC 74-29597. 1975. PLB 7.95 (ISBN 0-394-49743-0). Random.
Without Me You're Nothing: The Essential Guide to Home Computers. Frank Herbert & Max Barnard. 1981. 12.95 (ISBN 0-671-41287-6). S&S.
Without Roof. Kinereth Gensler. LC 80-70829. 64p. (Orig.). 1981. pap. 4.95 (ISBN 0-914086-32-4). Alicejamesbooks.
Without Spanking or Spoiling: A Practical Approach to Toddler & Preschool Guidance. Elizabeth Crary. LC 79-18253. (Illus.). 104p. (Orig.). 1979. pap. 6.95 (ISBN 0-9602862-0-9); write for info leaders' guide (ISBN 0-9602862-1-7). Parenting Pr.
Without Words: An Introduction to Nonverbal Communication. M. Van Schaack. 1977. 550.00 (ISBN 0-13-961417-6). P-H.
Witkacy: A Critical Study of Stanislaw Ignacy Witkiewicz As an Imaginative Writer. Daniel Gerould. LC 79-3872. (Illus.). 400p. 1981. 25.00 (ISBN 0-295-95714-X). U of Wash Pr.
Witness & I. O. Edmund Clubb. LC 74-11385. 240p. 1975. 16.00x (ISBN 0-231-03859-3). Columbia U Pr.
Witness Before the Fact. E. X. Ferrars. (Large Print Bks.). 1980. lib. bdg. 11.95 (ISBN 0-8161-3126-0). G K Hall.
Witness Cooperation: With a Handbook of Witness Management. Frank J. Cannavale, Jr. & William Falcon. LC 75-28939. 1976. 21.95 (ISBN 0-669-00329-8). Lexington Bks.
Witness of Edith Barfoot: The Joyful Vocation to Suffering. Edith Barfoot. 1977. 4.25x (ISBN 0-631-17910-0, Pub by Basil Blackwell England). Biblio Dist.
Witness to History. Charles E. Bohlen. 1973. pap. 6.95x (ISBN 0-393-09287-9, 9287). Norton.
Witness to Our Time. rev. ed. Alfred Eisenstaedt. 352p. 1980. 25.00 (ISBN 0-670-77702-1, Studio). Viking Pr.
Witness to the Holocaust. Azriel Eisenberg. 649p. 1981. 17.95 (ISBN 0-8298-0432-3). Pilgrim NY.
Witnesses. Edgar Bowers. 22p. (Orig.). 1981. pap. 22.50 (ISBN 0-936576-05-7). Symposium Pr.
Witnesses. Marcy M. Heidish. 1981. lib. bdg. 13.95 (ISBN 0-8161-3159-7, Large Print Bks). G K Hall.
Witnesses. Arthur Markve. Orig. Title: New Harmony of the Gospels. 416p. 1957. kivar 5.95 (ISBN 0-87123-393-2, 210393). Bethany Fell.
Witnesses Through Trial. Marvin L. Moore. LC 78-24294. (Orion Ser). 1979. pap. 1.95 (ISBN 0-8127-0216-6). Southern Pub.
Witnesses to a Vanishing America: The Nineteenth-Century Response. Lee C. Mitchell. LC 80-8567. (Illus.). 288p. 1981. 16.50x (ISBN 0-691-06461-X). Princeton U Pr.
Witnessing Made Easy. C. S. Lovett. 1971. pap. 4.95 (ISBN 0-938148-01-X). Personal Christianity.
Witold Gombrowicz. Ewa M. Thompson. (World Authors Ser.: No. 510). 1979. lib. bdg. 14.50 (ISBN 0-8057-6351-1). Twayne.
Wits Theatre of the World. Robert Allot. LC 70-17131. (English Experience Ser.: No. 359). 560p. Repr. of 1599 ed. 51.00 (ISBN 90-221-0359-5). Walter J Johnson.
Wittes Pilgrimage, (by Poeticall Essaies) Through a World of Amorous Sonnets, Etc. John Davies. LC 79-84099. (English Experience Ser.: No. 919). 172p. 1979. Repr. of 1605 ed. lib. bdg. 17.00 (ISBN 90-221-0919-4). Walter J Johnson.
Wittgenstein. Robert J. Fogelin. (Arguments of the Philosophers Ser.). 1976. 16.00x (ISBN 0-7100-8426-9). Routledge & Kegan.
Wittgenstein & Historical Understanding. Aryeh Botwinick. LC 80-5968. 65p. (Orig.). 1981. pap. text ed. 5.00 (ISBN 0-8191-1431-6). U Pr of Amer.
Wittgenstein & Justice: On the Significance of Ludwig Wittgenstein for Social & Political Thought. Hanna F. Pitkin. LC 76-138508. 1972. 20.00x (ISBN 0-520-01841-9); pap. 7.95x (ISBN 0-520-02329-3). U of Cal Pr.
Wittgenstein & Political Philosophy: A Reexamination of the Foundations of Social Science. John W. Danford. LC 78-6716. xiv, 166p. 1981. pap. 6.95 (ISBN 0-226-13594-2). U of Chicago Pr.
Wittgenstein for Preaching: A Model for Communication. Thomas D. Peterson. LC 80-5802. 192p. 1980. lib. bdg. 17.00 (ISBN 0-8191-1342-5); pap. text ed. 8.75 (ISBN 0-8191-1343-3). U Pr of Amer.
Wittgenstein: Language & World. John V. Canfield. 256p. 1981. lib. bdg. 17.50x (ISBN 0-87023-318-1); pap. text ed. 7.50x (ISBN 0-87023-319-X). U of Mass Pr.
Wittgenstein, the Early Philosophy: An Exposition of the Tractatus. Henry L. Finch. LC 73-135985. 1971. text ed. 10.00x o.p. (ISBN 0-391-00123-X). Humanities.
Wittgenstein Workbook. Christopher Coope et al. LC 79-135161. 1970. pap. 3.50x (ISBN 0-520-01840-0, CAMPUS48). U of Cal Pr.
Wittgenstein's Conception of Philosophy. K. T. Fann. 1969. 14.50x (ISBN 0-520-01615-7); pap. 4.75x (ISBN 0-520-01837-0, CAMPUS 171). U of Cal Pr.
Wittgenstein's Philosophy of Language: Some Aspects of Its Development. James Bogen. (International Library of Philosophy & Scientific Method). 1972. text ed. 15.00x (ISBN 0-391-00227-9). Humanities.
Wiz Book. L. Frank Baum. 1978. pap. 1.95 o.p. (ISBN 0-425-03959-5, Medallion). Berkley Pub.
Wiz Scrapbook. Richard J. Anobile. 1978. pap. 7.95 o.p. (ISBN 0-425-03963-3, Medallion). Berkley Pub.
Wizard. John Varley. 1980. pap. 2.50. Berkley Pub.
Wizard & His Magic Spells. Kent. (Illus.). (gr. 2-3). 1980. pap. 3.50 incl. record (ISBN 0-590-24008-0, Schol Pap). Schol Bk Serv.
Wizard Book of Magic. Norman Hunter. LC 78-52333. (gr. 4-8). 1978. 6.95 (ISBN 0-8069-4586-9); PLB 6.69 (ISBN 0-8069-4587-7). Sterling.
Wizard Children of Finn. Tannen. LC 80-20955. (Illus.). 256p. (gr. 3 up). 1981. 8.95 (ISBN 0-394-84744-X); PLB 8.99 (ISBN 0-394-94744-4). Knopf.
Wizard in the Tree. Lloyd Alexander. (gr. k-6). 1981. pap. 1.50 (ISBN 0-440-49556-3, YB). Dell.
Wizard McBean & His Flying Machine. Dennis Nolan. LC 77-3472. (Illus.). (ps-2). 1977. PLB 7.95 (ISBN 0-13-961607-1); pap. 2.50 (ISBN 0-13-961599-7). P-H.
Wizard of Oz. L. Frank Baum. (Illus.). (gr. 3-6). 1970. 5.95g o.s.i. (ISBN 0-02-708520-1). Macmillan.
Wizard of Oz. L. Frank Baum. Ed. by Allen Chaffee. (Illus.). (gr. k-3). 1950. 4.95 (ISBN 0-394-80689-1, BYR); PLB 5.99 (ISBN 0-394-90689-6). Random.
Wizard of Oz. L. Frank Baum. (gr. 4-6). 1967. pap. 1.50 (ISBN 0-590-08604-9, Schol Pap). Schol Bk Serv.
Wizard of Oz. L. Frank Baum. (Tempo Classic Ser.). 1980. pap. 1.50 (ISBN 0-448-17134-1, Tempo). G&D.
Wizard of Oz. Adapted by Mary Carey. (Illus.). (gr. k-3). 1976. PLB 5.00 (ISBN 0-307-60119-6, Golden Pr). Western Pub.
Wizard of Oz. Donna Kelly. (Illus.). (gr. k-2). 1976. PLB 5.38 (ISBN 0-307-68906-9, Golden Pr). Western Pub.
Wizard of Oz. (Illustrated Junior Library). (Illus.). 224p. 1981. pap. 4.95 (ISBN 0-448-11026-1). G&D.
Wizard of Wallaby Wallow. Jack Kent. LC 79-153785. (Illus.). (gr. k-3). 1971. 5.95 o.s.i. (ISBN 0-8193-0513-8, Four Winds); PLB 5.41 o.s.i. (ISBN 0-8193-0514-6). Schol Bk Serv.
Wizard Tales. new ed. Corinne Denan. LC 79-66331. (Illus.). 48p. (gr. 2-6). 1980. lib. bdg. 4.89 (ISBN 0-89375-330-0); pap. 1.50 (ISBN 0-89375-329-7). Troll Assocs.
Wizard's Daughter. Barbara Michaels. LC 80-15157. 352p. 1980. 9.95 (ISBN 0-396-07899-0). Dodd.
Wizard's Eye. Charles Milligan & Jim Higgs. Ed. by Jane Vandenburgh. LC 78-13507. (Illus.). 1978. pap. 8.95 o.p. (ISBN 0-87701-119-2, Prism Editions). Chronicle Bks.
Wizards That Peep. Siegbert Becker. Ed. by Mentor Kujath. 1978. pap. 5.95 (ISBN 0-8100-0054-7, 15N0366). Northwest Pub.
Wladyslaw Stanislaw Reymont. Jerzy Krzyzanowski. (World Authors Ser.: Poland: No. 248). lib. bdg. 10.95 (ISBN 0-8057-2758-2). Twayne.
Wobble the Witch Cat. Mary Calhoun. (Illus.). (gr. k-3). 1958. PLB 6.48 (ISBN 0-688-31621-2). Morrow.
Wobbly. Ralph Chaplin. LC 70-166089. (Civil Liberties in American History Ser). 1972. Repr. of 1948 ed. lib. bdg. 37.50 (ISBN 0-306-70212-6). Da Capo.
Wobbly Tooth. Nancy E. Cooney. (Illus.). 32p. (Orig.). (gr. k-3). 1981. pap. 2.95 (ISBN 0-399-20776-7, Peppercorn). Putnam.
Wodwo. Ted Hughes. LC 67-28808. 1967. 6.95 o.p. (ISBN 0-06-011992-6, HarpT). Har-Row.
Wodwo. Ted Hughes. 1971. pap. 5.95 (ISBN 0-571-09714-6, Pub. by Faber & Faber). Merrimack Bk Serv.
Woe or Wonder: The Emotional Effect of Shakespearean Tragedy. J. V. Cunningham. 134p. 1964. pap. 4.50x (ISBN 0-8040-0323-8, 67). Swallow.
Woe Shirt. Paule Barton. Tr. by Howard Norman from Creole. LC 80-81728. (Illus.). 64p. 12.50 (ISBN 0-915778-37-8); deluxe ed. 40.00x (ISBN 0-915778-36-X). Penmaen Pr.
Woerterbuch Des Juedischen Rechts. M. Cohn. (Illus.). xii, 196p. 1981. 57.00 (ISBN 3-8055-2062-X). S Karger.
Wok Cookery. Ceil Dyer. LC 77-83279. (Illus.). 1977. pap. 5.95 (ISBN 0-912656-75-1). H P Bks.
Wok, Fondue, & Chafing Dish. Culinary Arts Institute Staff. LC 78-54625. (Adventures in Cooking Ser.). (Illus.). 1980. cancelled (ISBN 0-8326-0606-5, 1518); pap. 3.95 (ISBN 0-8326-0605-7, 2518). Delair.
Wole Soyinka. Eldred D. Jones. (World Authors Ser.: Nigeria: No. 256). 1971. lib. bdg. 10.95 (ISBN 0-8057-2852-X). Twayne.
Wolf. Richard Rose. 288p. (Orig.). 1980. pap. 2.50 (ISBN 0-89083-657-4). Zebra.
Wolf: A Species in Danger. Erik Zimen. 1981. 13.95 (ISBN 0-440-09619-7). Delacorte.
Wolf & the Seven Little Kids. Felix Hoffman. LC 59-16357. (Illus.). 32p. (ps-3). 1959. 6.95 (ISBN 0-15-299108-5, HJ). HarBraceJ.

Wolf by the Ears: Thomas Jefferson & Slavery. John C. Miller. LC 76-51590. 1977. 15.95 (ISBN 0-02-921500-5). Free Pr.
Wolf Country. (Trailsman: No. 7). (Orig.). 1981. pap. price not set (ISBN 0-451-09905-2, Sig). NAL.
Wolf Cub Scout Book. rev. ed. Boy Scouts Of America. LC 67-14539. (Illus.). 192p. (gr. 3). 1973. flexible bdg. 1.75x (ISBN 0-8395-3207-5, 3207). BSA.
Wolf Huber Studies: Aspects of Renaissance Thought & Practice in Danube School Painting. Patricia Rose. LC 76-23711. (Outstanding Dissertations in the Fine Arts - 16th Century). (Illus.). 1977. Repr. of 1973 ed. lib. bdg. 63.00 (ISBN 0-8240-2725-6). Garland Pub.
Wolf Hunt. Mark Elder. (Orig.). 1976. pap. 1.50 o.p. (ISBN 0-345-25264-0). Ballantine.
Wolf King. J. A. Senn. Ed. by Mary Verdick. (Pal Paperbacks - Pal Skills Ser.). (Illus., Orig.). (gr. 7-12). 1978. pap. text ed. 1.25 (ISBN 0-8374-6707-1). Xerox Ed Pubns.
Wolf King. Ann Turnbull. LC 75-25513. (gr. 4-8). 1976. 5.95 (ISBN 0-395-28927-0, Clarion). HM.
Wolf Masks: Violence in Contemporary Poetry. Lawrence R Ries. LC 76-30540. (National University Pubns. Literary Criticism Ser.). 1977. 12.95 (ISBN 0-8046-9168-1). Kennikat.
Wolf Moon. Jean Pedrick. LC 73-94067. 72p. 1974. pap. 4.95 (ISBN 0-914086-03-0). Alicejamesbooks.
Wolf of Masada. John Fredman. 416p. 1979. pap. 2.50 (ISBN 0-380-49049-8, 49049). Avon.
Wolf of My Own. Jan Wahl. LC 69-10501. (Illus.). (gr. k-2). 1969. 5.95g o.s.i. (ISBN 0-02-792330-4). Macmillan.
Wolf Story. David McPhail. (Illus.). 32p. (gr. 1-5). 1981. 8.95 (ISBN 0-684-16713-1). Scribner.
Wolf: The Ecology & Behavior of an Endangered Species. L. David Mech. LC 80-27364. (Illus.). 385p. 1981. pap. 8.95 (ISBN 0-8166-1026-6). U of Minn Pr.
Wolf to the Slaughter. Ruth Rendell. 192p. Date not set. pap. 1.95 (ISBN 0-345-29284-7). Ballantine.
Wolf Tracks. David Case. (Orig.). 1980. pap. 1.95 (ISBN 0-505-51485-0). Tower Bks.
Wolf! Wolf! Gerald Rose & Elizabeth Rose. (Illus.). (ps-5). 1974. 6.95 (ISBN 0-571-10405-3, Pub. by Faber & Faber). Merrimack Bk Serv.
Wolfenbuettel Lithuanian Postile Manuscript of the Year 1573, 3 vols. Ed. by Gordon B. Ford, Jr. LC 66-4719. 1966. 200.00 ea. o.p. Vol. 1 (ISBN 0-910198-14-4). Vol. 2 (ISBN 0-910198-15-2). Vol. 3 (ISBN 0-910198-16-0). Baltica Pr.
Wolfer. James B. Chaffin. 1980. pap. 1.50 (ISBN 0-505-51461-3). Tower Bks.
Wolff's Headache & Other Head Pain. 4th ed. Ed. by Donald J. Dalessio. (Illus.). 750p. 1980. text ed. 35.00x o.p. (ISBN 0-19-502624-1). Oxford U Pr.
Wolfgang Amadeus Mozart, Master of Pure Music. Monroe Stearns. (Biography Ser). (Illus.). (gr. 7 up). 1968. PLB 6.90 (ISBN 0-531-00906-8). Watts.
Wolfgang Paalen. Jose Pierre. (Filipacchi Art Ser.). (Illus.). 76p. 1980. 25.00 (ISBN 2-8501-8106-4); pap. cancelled (ISBN 2-85018-095-5). Hippocrene Bks.
Wolfhart Pannenberg & Religious Philosophy. David McKenzie. LC 80-8171. 169p. 1980. lib. bdg. 17.50 (ISBN 0-8191-1314-X); pap. text ed. 9.00 (ISBN 0-8191-1315-8). U Pr of Amer.
Wolfman. Carl Dreadstone. (Universal Horror Library). 1977. pap. 1.25 o.p. (ISBN 0-425-03446-1, Medallion). Berkley Pub.
Wolfman Cometh. R. W. Lambert. 4.00 o.p. (ISBN 0-8062-1057-5). Carlton.
Wolfram Von Eschenbach. James F. Poag. (World Authors Ser.: Germany: No. 233). lib. bdg. 10.95 (ISBN 0-8057-2304-8). Twayne.
Wolfson Geochemical Atlas of England & Wales. Applied Geochemistry Research Group. (Illus.). 1978. 98.00x (ISBN 0-19-891113-0). Oxford U Pr.
Wollstonecraft Anthology. Ed. by Janet M. Todd. LC 77-72192. (Illus.). 288p. 1977. 16.50x (ISBN 0-253-36605-4). Ind U Pr.
Wolves. Jane Rockwell. LC 77-1551. (First Bks.). (Illus.). (gr. 4-6). 1977. PLB 6.45 s&l (ISBN 0-531-02910-7). Watts.
Wolves, Bears & Bighorns: Wilderness Observations & Experiences of a Professional Outdoorsman. John S. Crawford. (Illus.). 192p. 1980. 19.95 (ISBN 0-88240-146-7); pap. 12.95 (ISBN 0-686-63422-5). Alaska Northwest.
Wolves of Aam. Jane L. Curry. LC 80-24370. 204p. (gr. 7 up). 1981. 9.95 (ISBN 0-689-50173-0, McElderry Book). Atheneum.
Wolves of Willoughby Chase. Joan Aiken. (gr. 7-12). 1981. pap. 1.75 (ISBN 0-440-99629-5, LE). Dell.
Woman. Sibilla Aleramo. Tr. by Rosalind Delmar from Italian. (Illus.). 200p. 1980. 10.95 (ISBN 0-520-04108-9). U of Cal Pr.
Woman. Edward Boubat. LC 72-86679. (Illus.). 143p. 1973. 15.00 (ISBN 0-8076-0664-2). Braziller.
Woman Ahead of Her Time. Rose Safran. 1981. pap. 5.95 (ISBN 0-9602786-2-1). Tide Bk Pub Co.
Woman: An Affirmation. Alice Fannin et al. 1978. pap. text ed. 9.95x (ISBN 0-669-01991-7); instructor's manual free (ISBN 0-669-01992-5). Heath.
Woman & Colonization: Anthropological Perspectives. Ed. by Mona Etienne & Eleanor Leacock. LC 79-15318. 352p. 1980. 26.95 (ISBN 0-03-052586-1); pap. 9.95 (ISBN 0-03-052581-0). Praeger.
Woman & Medieval England. Darlene Templeton et al. LC 79-19011. (Woman in History Ser.: Vol. 13). (Illus.). 80p. 1980. 15.95 (ISBN 0-86663-057-0); pap. 9.00 (ISBN 0-86663-058-9). Ide Hse.
Woman & Nature: The Roaring Inside Her. Susan Griffin. LC 77-3752. 1978. 9.95 o.s.i. (ISBN 0-06-011511-4, HarpT). Har-Row.
Woman & Society in Eighteenth Century France: Essays in Honour of John Stephenson Spink. Ed. by Eva Jacobs et al. 1979. text ed. 37.50x (ISBN 0-485-11184-5, Athlone Pr). Humanities.
Woman & Society in the Spanish Drama of the Golden Age. Melveena McKendrick. LC 73-82457. 384p. 1974. 56.00 (ISBN 0-521-20294-9). Cambridge U Pr.
Woman & Temperance: The Quest for Power & Liberty, 1873 to 1900. Ruth Bordin. Ed. by Allen F. Davis. (American Civilization Ser.). 220p. 1980. 17.50 (ISBN 0-87722-157-X). Temple U Pr.
Woman & the Sea. Richard Tregaskis. (Illus.). 6.50 (ISBN 0-910550-17-4). Elysium.
Woman As Writer. Jeanette Webber & Joan Grumman. (Illus., LC 77-074379). 1978. pap. text ed. 10.50 (ISBN 0-395-26438-3). HM.
Woman at Home. Arlene R. Cardozo. 1978. pap. 1.95 o.s.i. (ISBN 0-515-04501-2). Jove Pubns.
Woman at Otowi Crossing: A Novel. Frank Waters. LC 66-25961. 300p. 1981. pap. 6.95 (ISBN 0-8040-0415-3, SB). Swallow.
Woman at the End of the Mattress. Michael Knoll. Ed. by Joan H. Lee. 64p. 1981. pap. 4.95 (ISBN 0-932220-12-6). Broken Whisker.
Woman at the Well. Dale E. Rogers. 1970. 6.95 (ISBN 0-8007-0385-5); pap. 1.95 (ISBN 0-8007-8090-6, Spire Bks). Revell.
Woman Between. Jaroldeen Edwards. 1980. 2.25 (ISBN 0-380-75846-6, 75846). Avon.
Woman Beyond Roleplay. Elizabeth Skoglund. LC 75-893. 1975. pap. 1.25 o.p. (ISBN 0-912692-62-6). Cook.
Woman Called Scylla. David Gurr. LC 80-51998. 324p. 1981. 13.95 (ISBN 0-670-77775-7). Viking Pr.
Woman, Church & State. Matilda J. Gage. LC 80-13639. 336p. 1980. pap. 7.95 (ISBN 0-930436-04-0). Persephone.
Woman Citizen: Social Feminism in the 1920's. J. Stanley Lemons. LC 72-75488. 280p. 1975. pap. 3.45 (ISBN 0-252-00563-5). U of Ill Pr.
Woman Clothed with the Sun. Ed. by John J. Delaney. LC 60-5922. pap. 3.50 (ISBN 0-385-08019-0, D118, Im). Doubleday.
Woman Doctor's Diet for Teenage Girls. Barbara Edelstein. 288p. 1981. pap. 2.50 (ISBN 0-345-28879-3). Ballantine.
Woman Doctor's Diet for Women. Barbara Edelstein. Date not set. pap. 2.50 (ISBN 0-345-28015-6). Ballantine.
Woman Doctor's Diet for Women. Barbara Edelstein. 199p. 1981. pap. 2.50 (ISBN 0-345-29488-2). Ballantine.
Woman for All Seasons. Jeanne Hendricks. LC 77-23045. 1977. pap. 3.95 (ISBN 0-8407-5630-5). Nelson.
Woman for President, Foundation of the Federation of the Goths, Stretching from Iran to Norway. H. Winky-Lotz. (Historical Novel, Europe About 175 B. C. to 95 B. C. Ser.: Vol. I). (Illus.). 312p. 1980. 14.55 (ISBN 0-936112-02-6); pap. 11.25 (ISBN 0-936112-09-3). Willyshe Pub.
Woman for President, the Roots of "Cinderella" of Our Fairy Tale. H. Winky-Lotz. (Historical Novel, Europe About 95 B. C. to 57 B. C. Ser.: Vol. II). (Illus.). 245p. 1980. 14.55 (ISBN 0-936112-08-5); pap. 11.25 (ISBN 0-936112-03-4). Willyshe Pub.
Woman Golfer's Catalogue. Jolee Edmondson. LC 79-65116. (Illus.). 1980. 18.95 (ISBN 0-8128-2685-X); pap. 10.95 (ISBN 0-8128-6041-1). Stein & Day.
Woman in a Man's Church. Arleen Swidler. LC 72-86596. 96p. (Orig.). 1972. pap. 1.95 (ISBN 0-8091-1740-1, Deus). Paulist Pr.
Woman in America: A Guide to Information Sources. Ed. by Virginia R. Terris. LC 73-17564. (American Studies Information Guide Ser.: Vol. 7). 1980. 30.00 (ISBN 0-8103-1268-9). Gale.
Woman in Ancient Greece. Arthur F. Ide. LC 79-19011. (Woman in History Ser.: Vol. 7). (Illus.). 51p. 1980. 9.00 (ISBN 0-86663-012-0); pap. 6.00 (ISBN 0-86663-013-9). Ide Hse.
Woman in Ancient Rome. Frederick Ide. LC 79-19011. (Woman in History Ser.: Vol. 6). (Illus.). 54p. 1980. 9.00 (ISBN 0-86663-010-4); pap. 7.00 (ISBN 0-86663-011-2). Ide Hse.
Woman in Biblical Israel. Arthur F. Ide. LC 79-19011. (Woman in History Ser.: Vol. 5). (Illus.). 50p. 1980. 9.00 (ISBN 0-86663-008-2); pap. 6.00 (ISBN 0-86663-009-0). Ide Hse.
Woman in Black. E. C. Bentley. 1976. lib. bdg. 13.95x (ISBN 0-89968-166-2). Lightyear.
Woman in Business. Callie F. Struggs. Ed. by Arthur F. Ide. LC 79-19011. (Woman in History Ser.: Vol. 56). (Illus.). 80p. (Orig.). 1981. 8.95 (ISBN 0-86663-020-1); pap. 6.95 (ISBN 0-86663-021-X). Ide Hse.
Woman in Contemporary Education. Callie F. Struggs. Ed. by Arthur F. Ide. LC 79-19011. (Woman in History Ser.: Vol. 61). (Illus.). 82p. (Orig.). 1981. 12.95 (ISBN 0-86663-022-8); pap. 9.00 (ISBN 0-86663-023-6). Ide Hse.
Woman in Early Christianity & Christian Society. Arthur F. Ide. LC 79-19011. (Woman in History Ser.: Vol. 9). (Illus.). 53p. 1980. 9.00 (ISBN 0-86663-016-3); pap. 6.95 (ISBN 0-86663-017-1). Ide Hse.
Woman in India. Mary F. Billington. (Illus.). 269p. 1973. 17.50x (ISBN 0-8002-0978-8). Intl Pubns Serv.
Woman in Islam. B. Aisha Lemu & Gatima Heeren. 51p. 1980. pap. 2.95x (ISBN 0-86037-004-6, Pub. by Islamic Council of Europe England). Intl Schol Bk Serv.
Woman in Italy: From the Introduction of the Chivalrous Service of Love to the Appearance of the Professional Actress. William Boulting. LC 79-2932. (Illus.). 356p. 1981. Repr. of 1910 ed. 27.50 (ISBN 0-8305-0099-5). Hyperion Conn.
Woman in Judaism. Denese B. Mann. 1979. pap. 4.50 (ISBN 0-9603348-0-7). Jonathan Pubns.
Woman in Reformation Europe. Marisa SorBello. Ed. by Arthur F. Ide. LC 79-19011. (Woman in History Ser.: Vol. 19). (Illus.). 80p. (Orig.). 1981. 16.95 (ISBN 0-86663-053-8); pap. 10.95 (ISBN 0-86663-054-6). Ide Hse.
Woman in Sexist Society. Vivian Gornick & Barbara K. Moran. 1972. pap. 2.50 (ISBN 0-451-61351-1, ME1883, Ment). NAL.
Woman in the Age of Christian Martyrs. Arthur F. Ide & Charles A. Ide. LC 79-19011. (Woman in History Ser.: Vol. 10). (Illus.). ix, 98p. 1980. 9.00 (ISBN 0-86663-000-7); pap. 8.00 (ISBN 0-86663-001-5). Ide Hse.
Woman in the American Colonial South. Arthur F. Ide. LC 79-19011. (Woman in History Ser.: Vol. 30). 88p. (Orig.). 1980. 12.00 (ISBN 0-86663-018-X); pap. 8.00 (ISBN 0-86663-019-8). Ide Hse.
Woman in the Church. Louis Bouyer. Tr. by Marilyn Teichert from Fr. LC 79-84878. Orig. Title: Mystere et Ministeres De la Femme Dans L'eglise. 132p. (Orig.). 1979. pap. 4.95 (ISBN 0-89870-002-7). Ignatius Pr.
Woman in the Civilization of the Ancient Near East. Arthur F. Ide. LC 79-19011. (Woman in History Ser.: Vol. 2). (Illus.). 82p. (Orig.). 1981. 8.00 (ISBN 0-86663-006-6); pap. 6.00 (ISBN 0-86663-007-4). Ide Hse.
Woman in the House: A Study of Women Members of Parliament. Elizabeth Vallance. 1979. text ed. 23.75x (ISBN 0-485-11186-1, Athlone Pr). Humanities.
Woman in the Woods. Kathleen Farmer. LC 80-22021. (Illus.). 1980. pap. 5.95 (ISBN 0-934802-08-4). Ind Camp Supply.
Woman in the Year Two Thousand. Ed. by Maggie Trip. LC 74-80707. 1981. pap. 6.00 (ISBN 0-686-68893-7). Arbor Hse.
Woman in Yorkist England. Darlene Tempelton. Ed. by Arthur F. Ide. LC 79-19011. (Woman in History Ser.: Vol. 16). (Illus.). 80p. 12.95 (ISBN 0-86663-051-1); pap. 9.95. Ide Hse.
Woman: New Dimensions. Ed. by Walter J. Burghardt. LC 76-50965. 1977. pap. 5.95 (ISBN 0-8091-2011-9). Paulist Pr.
Woman of Fifty. Rheta C. Dorr. Ed. by Annette K. Baxter. LC 79-8787. (Signal Lives Ser.). 1980. Repr. of 1924 ed. lib. bdg. 40.00x (ISBN 0-405-12835-5). Arno.
Woman of Justice. Georgia Di Donato. (Large Print Bks.). 1980. lib. bdg. 15.95 (ISBN 0-8161-3132-5). G K Hall.
Woman of Substance. Barbara T. Bradford. 1980. pap. 2.95 (ISBN 0-380-49163-X, 49163). Avon.
Woman of Texas. R. T. Stevens. 1981. pap. 2.95 (ISBN 0-440-19555-1). Dell.
Woman of the Eighteenth Century: Her Life, from Birth to Death, Her Love & Her Philosophy in the Worlds of Salon, Shop & Street. Edmond L. Goncourt. Tr. by Jacques Le Clercq & Ralph Roeder. LC 79-2937. (Illus.). 347p. 1981. Repr. of 1927 ed. 26.50 (ISBN 0-8305-0103-7). Hyperion Conn.
Woman of the Maya. Stella G. Zarate. 1978. 7.50 o.p. (ISBN 0-682-49053-9). Exposition.
Woman Offender: A Bibiliographic Sourcebook. S. Sturgeon & L. Rans. vi, 63p. 1975. pap. 5.00 (ISBN 0-686-28749-5). Entropy Ltd.
Woman on the American Frontier. William W. Fowler. LC 73-12867. 1974. Repr. of 1878 ed. 30.00 (ISBN 0-8103-3702-9). Gale.
Woman Once Loved. Amanda Russell. (Orig.). 1979. pap. 2.50 (ISBN 0-515-04598-5). Jove Pubns.
Woman Poet - the Midwest. 1981. pap. 12.95 (ISBN 0-935634-05-3); pap. text ed. 6.00 (ISBN 0-935634-04-5). Women-in-Lit.
Woman Poet - the Northeast. Ed. by Elaine Dallman et al. (Woman Poet Ser.). 140p. (Orig.). 1981. 12.95 (ISBN 0-935634-03-7); pap. text ed. 6.00 (ISBN 0-935634-02-9). Women-in-Lit.
Woman Poet - the West. Ed. by Elaine Dallman et al. LC 79-55988. (Woman Poet Ser.). 100p. (Orig.). 1980. 12.95 (ISBN 0-935634-01-0); pap. 6.00 (ISBN 0-935634-00-2). Women-in-Lit.
Woman Poet: The South. 1981. pap. 12.95 (ISBN 0-935634-07-X); pap. text ed. 6.00 (ISBN 0-935634-06-1). Women-in-Lit.
Woman Power! Mary L. Brady et al. (Illus.). 156p. 1981. pap. 4.95. J P Tarcher.
Woman Power in Textile & Apparel Sales. Eric Hertz & Jerry Sherman. LC 78-61155. 1979. 8.95 (ISBN 0-87005-199-7). Fairchild.
Woman: Roles & Status in Eight Countries. Janet Z. Giele & Audrey C. Smock. LC 76-39950. 1977. 26.50 (ISBN 0-471-01504-0, Pub. by Wiley-Interscience). Wiley.
Woman Space: Future & Fantasy Stories by Women. Ed. by Claudia M. Lamperti. 60p. (Orig.). 1981. pap. 3.95. New Victoria Pubs.
Woman Speaks: The Lectures, Seminars, & Interviews of Anais Nin. Ed. by Evelyn Hinz. LC 75-15111. 270p. 1975. 13.95x (ISBN 0-8040-0693-8); pap. 6.95x (ISBN 0-8040-0694-6). Swallow.
Woman the Gatherer. Ed. by Francis Dahlberg. LC 80-25262. (Illus.). 288p. 1981. text ed. 15.00x (ISBN 0-300-02572-6). Yale U Pr.
Woman to Deliver Her People: Joanna Southcott & English Millenarianism in an Era of Revolution. James K. Hopkins. (Illus.). 320p. 1981. text ed. 22.50x (ISBN 0-292-79017-1). U of Tex Pr.
Woman to Woman. Eugenia Price. pap. 2.95 (ISBN 0-310-31392-9). Zondervan.
Woman Triumphant: Feminism in French Literature 1610-1652. Ian MacLean. (Illus.). 1977. 45.00x (ISBN 0-19-815741-X). Oxford U Pr.
Woman Unliberated: Difficulties & Limitations in Changing Self. new ed. C. M. Hall. LC 78-21874. 1979. pap. text ed. 14.95 (ISBN 0-89116-097-3). Hemisphere Pub.
Woman Wants God. Mary L. Lacy. 1959. pap. 1.25 o.p. (ISBN 0-8042-3596-1). John Knox.
Woman Warrior: Memoirs of a Girlhood Among Ghosts. Maxine H. Kingston. LC 77-3246. 1977. pap. 2.45 (ISBN 0-394-72392-9, Vin). Random.
Woman Who Dared. Richard Erdoes. 1978. pap. 1.95 o.p. (ISBN 0-449-13975-1, GM). Fawcett.
Woman Who Got on at Jaspar Station & Other Stories. O'Hagan. 1963. 1.65 o.p. (ISBN 0-8040-0326-2). Swallow.
Woman Who Lived in a Prologue. Nina Schneider. 1980. 13.95 (ISBN 0-395-28211-X). HM.
Woman Who Lived in a Prologue. Nina Schneider. 384p. 1981. pap. 2.75 (ISBN 0-445-04631-7). Popular Lib.
Woman Who Loved John Wilkes Booth. Pamela R. Russell. 1979. pap. 2.25 (ISBN 0-515-04869-0). Jove Pubns.
Woman Who Murdered Black Satin: The Bermondsey Horror. Albert I. Borowitz. 347p. 1981. 17.50 (ISBN 0-8142-0320-5). Ohio St U Pr.
Woman Who Slept with Men to Take the War Out of Them & Tree. Deena Metzger. LC 80-83933. 192p. 1981. 12.95 (ISBN 0-915238-42-X); pap. 8.95 (ISBN 0-915238-43-8). Peace Pr.
Woman with a Purpose: The Diaries of Elizabeth Smith 1872-1884. Ed. by Veronica Strong-Boag. (Social History of Canada Ser.). 320p. 1980. 25.00x (ISBN 0-8020-2360-6); pap. 10.00x (ISBN 0-8020-6397-7). U of Toronto Pr.
Woman-Work: Women & the Party in Revolutionary China. Delia Davin. (Illus.). 1979. pap. 4.50 (ISBN 0-19-285080-6, GB 566, GB). Oxford U Pr.
Woman Wrapped in Silence. John W. Lynch. 1976. pap. 3.45 (ISBN 0-8091-1905-6). Paulist Pr.
Womanblood: Portraits of Women in Poetry & Prose. Ed. by Aline O'Brien & Chrys Rasmussen. LC 80-69814. 200p. (Orig.). 1981. pap. 5.95 (ISBN 0-939140-00-4). Continuing SAGA.
Womanhood in America: From Colonial Times to the Present. Mary P. Ryan. 1975. 15.00 o.p. (ISBN 0-531-05365-2); pap. 5.95 o.p. (ISBN 0-531-05568-X). Watts.

Womanhood in Radical Protestantism: 1525-1675. Joyce L. Irwin. (Studies in Women & Religion: Vol. 1). 1979. soft cover 24.95x (ISBN 0-88946-547-9). E Mellen.

Womanhood Media: Current Resources About Women. Helen Wheeler. LC 72-7396. 1972. 10.00 (ISBN 0-8108-0549-9). Scarecrow.

Womanhood Media Supplement: Additional Current Resources About Women. Helen Wheeler. LC 72-7396. 1975. 18.00 (ISBN 0-8108-0858-7). Scarecrow.

Womaning: Overcoming Male Dominance of Executive Row. Dean B. Peskin. Ed. by Sylvia Ashton. 1980. 15.95 (ISBN 0-87949-165-5). Ashley Bks.

Womanist Therapy. Carolyn H. Warmsun et al. (Pergamon General Psychology Ser.). 30.01 o.p. (ISBN 0-08-022274-9). Pergamon.

Womankind: A Celebration. Michael Adam. LC 78-20623. (Illus.). 1979. 15.95 (ISBN 0-06-010032-X, HarpT). Har-Row.

Womanlist. Marjorie P. Weiser & Jean S. Arbeiter. LC 80-65983. (Illus.). 512p. 1981. 19.95 (ISBN 0-689-11083-9); pap. 10.95 (ISBN 0-689-11113-4). Atheneum.

Womanpower & Health Care. Marlene Grissum & Carol Spengler. LC 75-41571. 1976. pap. 8.95 (ISBN 0-316-32895-2). Little.

Womanrise (Anthology) Rashidah Ismaili et al. Ed. by Louis R. Rivera. (Illus.). 128p. (Orig.). 1978. pap. 4.25 (ISBN 0-917886-05-4). Shamal Bks.

Woman's Age. Rachel Billington. LC 79-23723. 469p. 1980. 12.95 (ISBN 0-671-40115-7). Summit Bks.

Woman's Age. Rachel Billington. 528p. 1981. pap. 2.95 (ISBN 0-553-14142-2). Bantam.

Woman's Almanac. Ed. by Hana Umlauf & Barbara McDowell. LC 77-75353. 1977. pap. 3.95x o.p. (ISBN 0-911818-07-3). World Almanac.

Woman's Almanac: Twelve How to Handbooks in One. Compiled by Kathryn Paulsen & Ryan A. Kuhn. LC 76-2055. (Illus.). 1976. 12.50 o.p. (ISBN 0-397-01113-X); pap. 8.95 (ISBN 0-397-01138-5). Lippincott.

Woman's Book of Money-a Guide to Financial Independence. Sylvia Auerbach. LC 75-44952. 220p. 1976. pap. 4.95 (ISBN 0-385-09883-9, Dolp). Doubleday.

Woman's Carpentry Book: Building Your Home from the Ground up. Jeanne Tetrault. LC 78-22801. (Illus.). 400p. 1980. 19.95 (ISBN 0-385-17183-8, Anchor Pr); pap. 10.95 (ISBN 0-385-14269-2). Doubleday.

Woman's Choice. Eugenia Price. pap. 2.95 (ISBN 0-310-31382-1). Zondervan.

Woman's Choice: The Best Modern Guide to Unplanned Pregnancy. Samuel J. Barr & Dan Abelow. pap. 4.95 (ISBN 0-934954-11-9). Public Info Pr.

Woman's Day Book of Antique Collectibles. Dorothy Jenkins. (Illus.). 240p. 1981. 19.95 (ISBN 0-312-88647-0). St Martin.

Woman's Day Book of Beauty, Health & Fitness Hints. Sharon Gold. LC 80-12022. (Illus.). 166p. 1980. pap. 5.95 (ISBN 0-688-08611-X, Quill). Morrow.

Woman's Day Book of No-Pattern Sewing. Lorraine Ruggieri. 128p. (Orig.). 1981. pap. 6.95 (ISBN 0-449-90053-3, Columbine). Fawcett.

Woman's Day Decorative Needlework for the Home. Ed. by Nancy Schraffenberger. (Illus.). 176p. 1981. 15.95 (ISBN 0-8069-5442-6, Columbia Hse). Sterling.

Woman's Day Dictionary of Antique Furniture. Edith Gaines & Dorothy H. Jenkins. (Illus.). 1979. pap. 4.95 (ISBN 0-8015-8792-1, Hawthorn). Dutton.

Woman's Day Old-Fashioned Desserts. Barbara Myers. 1978. 10.95 o.s.i. (ISBN 0-397-01314-0). Lippincott.

Woman's Day Plain & Fancy Ground Beef Cookbook. Jeri Laber. 1978. 8.95 (ISBN 0-394-41372-5). Random.

Woman's Dress for Success Book. John T. Molloy. (Illus.). 1978. pap. 4.95 (ISBN 0-446-97572-9). Warner Bks.

Woman's Eyes. Gus Weill. 208p. 1976. pap. 1.50 o.p. (ISBN 0-345-24774-4). Ballantine.

Woman's Fiction: A Guide to Novels by & About Women in America, 1820-1870. Nina Baym. 1980. 17.50 (ISBN 0-8014-1128-9); pap. 4.95. Cornell U Pr.

Woman's Guide. Phyllis Butler. Ed. by Jan Leonard. LC 80-66585. (Savvy San Francisco Ser.). (Illus.). 64p. (Orig.). 1980. pap. 2.50 (ISBN 0-89395-047-5). Cal Living Bks.

Woman's Guide to Business Travel. Penelope Naylor. 288p. (Orig.). Date not set. pap. 4.95 (ISBN 0-346-12441-7). Cornerstone. Postponed.

Woman's Guide to Financial Savvy. Judith Briles. 192p. 1981. 10.95 (ISBN 0-312-88649-7). St Martin.

Woman's Guide to Fixing the Car. Arlene Weissler & Paul Weissler. (Illus.). 128p. 1973. 6.95 o.s.i. (ISBN 0-8027-0416-6); pap. 3.95 (ISBN 0-8027-7091-6). Walker & Co.

Woman's Guide to Starting a Business. Claudia Jessup. LC 75-21463. 1976. 8.95 o.p. (ISBN 0-03-014606-2); pap. 4.95 o.p. (ISBN 0-03-017611-5). HR&W.

Woman's Guide to Starting a Small Business. Mary Lester. LC 80-24298. pap. 2.50 (ISBN 0-87576-093-7). Pilot Bks.

Woman's Guide to Wall Street. N. L. Jarvis. 195p. 1981. 28.50 (ISBN 0-686-68312-9). Porter.

Woman's Health. Gillian Strube. 164p. 1980. 29.00x (ISBN 0-85664-940-6, Pub. by Croom Helm Ltd England). Biblio Dist.

Woman's Health & Medical Guide. Ed. by Better Homes & Gardens Books Editors. (Illus.). 96p. 1981. 24.95 (ISBN 0-696-00275-2). Meredith Corp.

Woman's I View. Anne W. Schaef. Orig. Title: Another Reality: the Female System & White Male System. 180p. (Orig.). 1981. 12.95 (ISBN 0-03-059061-2); pap. 6.95 (ISBN 0-03-059061-2). Winston Pr.

Woman's Index. Compiled by Frieda Carrol. LC 80-70675. 200p. 1981. 12.95 (ISBN 0-9605246-6-5); pap. 9.95. Biblio Pr Ga.

Woman's Journey, Vol. I. Louise Eberhardt. 1976. pap. 6.50 (ISBN 0-686-15678-1). New Comm Pr.

Woman's Journey, Vol. II. Louise Eberhardt. 1978. pap. 6.50 (ISBN 0-686-15679-X). New Comm Pr.

Woman's Life in Colonial Days. Carl Holliday. LC 72-140408. 1970. Repr. of 1922 ed. 18.00 (ISBN 0-8103-3593-X). Gale.

Woman's Mission to Humanity. Wilmon H. Sheldon. LC 68-8815. 1968. 3.95 o.p. (ISBN 0-8158-0008-8). Chris Mass.

Woman's Money Book. Gene Mackevich. 224p. 1981. pap. 2.95 (ISBN 0-553-14711-0). Bantam.

Woman's Notebook: Being a Book of Women's Quotes with Space for Notes. Ed. by Amy Shapiro. (Illus.). 96p. (Orig.). 1980. lib. bdg. 12.90 (ISBN 0-89471-094-X); pap. 4.95 (ISBN 0-89471-095-8). Running Pr.

Woman's Orgasm. Georgia Kline-Graber & Benjamin Graber. 1976. pap. 2.25 (ISBN 0-445-08537-1). Popular Lib.

Woman's Own Pot Plant Doctor - a Guide to Coping with Pot Plant Ailments. Hazel Evans & Alan Kumm. (Illus.). 1978. pap. 4.95 (ISBN 0-600-37150-6). Transatlantic.

Woman's Philosophy of Woman: Or, Woman Affranchised. an Answer to Michelet, Proudhon, Girardin, Legouve, Comte, & Other Modern Innovators. Jenny P. Hericourt. LC 79-2940. 317p. 1981. Repr. of 1864 ed. 23.50 (ISBN 0-8305-0105-3). Hyperion Conn.

Woman's Place. Anne E. Crompton. (Illus.). 224p. 1980. pap. 2.25 (ISBN 0-345-28790-8). Ballantine.

Woman's Place: Options & Limits in Professional Careers. Cynthia F. Epstein. 1970. 14.00x (ISBN 0-520-01581-9); pap. 3.95 (ISBN 0-520-01870-2, CAL227). U of Cal Pr.

Woman's Quest for Serenity. Gigi Tchividjian. 1981. 7.95 (ISBN 0-8007-1183-1). Revell.

Woman's Role in the Church. John M. Jicks & Bruce L. Morton. pap. 2.95 (ISBN 0-89315-362-1). Lambert Bk.

Woman's Selling Game: How to Sell Yourself & Anything Else. Carole Hyatt. 1980. pap. 4.95 (ISBN 0-446-97195-2). Warner Bks.

Woman's Tale: A Journal of Inner Exploration. Ronda Chervin & Mary Neill. 160p. (Orig.). 1980. pap. 7.95 (ISBN 0-8164-2016-5). Crossroad NY.

Woman's Total Reshape Program: Have the Figure You Always Wanted. Vera Abriel. (Illus.). 256p. 1981. 12.95 (ISBN 0-525-93148-1). Dutton.

Woman's "True" Profession: Voices from the History of Teaching. Nancy Hoffman. (Women's Lives - Women's Work Ser.). (Illus.). 352p. (Orig.). (gr. 11-12). 1981. 17.95 (ISBN 0-912670-93-2); pap. 6.95 (ISBN 0-912670-72-X). Feminist Pr.

Woman's Voice. Dorothy Uris. 1978. pap. 2.95 (ISBN 0-06-463471-X, EH 471, EH). Har-Row.

Woman's Who's Who of America: A Biographical Dictionary of Contemporary Women of the United States & Canada, 1914-1915. LC 74-6280. 1976. Repr. of 1914 ed. 64.00 (ISBN 0-8103-4018-6). Gale.

Woman's Work Book. Karin Abarbanel & Gonnie M. Siegel. 1977. pap. 2.50 (ISBN 0-446-81353-2). Warner Bks.

Woman's Work Book. Karin Abarbanol & Gonnie M. Siegel. 352p. 1981. pap. 3.50 (ISBN 0-446-91658-7). Warner Bks.

Woman's Workshop on Faith. Martha Hook. 1977. 2.50 (ISBN 0-310-26231-3); study guide 1.95 (ISBN 0-310-26241-0). Zondervan.

Woman's Workshop on Motherhood. Barbara Bush. (Women's Workshop Ser.). 144p. 1981. pap. 3.95 (ISBN 0-310-43031-3, 12013P). Zondervan.

Woman's Workshop on Romans-Leader's Manual. Carolyn Nystrom. 112p. (Orig.). 1981. pap. 1.95 (ISBN 0-310-41911-5). Zondervan.

Woman's Workshop on Romans-Student's Manual. Carolyn Nystrom. 144p. (Orig.). 1981. pap. 2.95 (ISBN 0-310-41921-2). Zondervan.

Woman's World. Clyde M. Narramore. pap. 2.95 (ISBN 0-310-29962-4). Zondervan.

Womanspirit Rising: A Feminist Reader in Religion. Carol P. Christ & Judith Plaskow. LC 78-3363. (Orig.). 1979. pap. 6.95 (ISBN 0-06-061385-8, RD 275, HarpR). Har-Row.

Women. J. Reiter. LC 78-1346. (Old West Ser.). (Illus.). 1978. lib. bdg. 12.96 (ISBN 0-686-51082-8). Silver.

Women. Joan Reiter & Time-Life Books Editors. (Old West Ser.). (Illus.). 1978. 12.95 (ISBN 0-8094-1512-7). Time-Life.

Women: A Pictorial Archive from 19th Century Sources. Ed. by Jim Harter. (Pictorial Achive Ser.). 1978. pap. 4.50 (ISBN 0-486-23703-6). Dover.

Women & Achievement: Social & Motivational Analyses. Ed. by M. S. Mednick et al. LC 75-22047. 447p. 1975. 19.95 (ISBN 0-470-59025-4); pap. 11.95 (ISBN 0-470-99150-X). Halsted Pr.

Women & Alcohol. Camberwell Council on Alcoholism. LC 80-40370. 207p. 1980. 22.00 (ISBN 0-422-76960-6, 2007); pap. 10.95 (2007). Methuen Inc.

Women & Ambition: A Bibliography. Patricia S. Faunce. LC 79-18347. 724p. 1980. lib. bdg. 32.50 (ISBN 0-8108-1242-8). Scarecrow.

Women & American Trade Unions. James J. Kenneally. LC 77-9240. 1978. 17.95 (ISBN 0-88831-026-9). EPWP.

Women & Atheism: The Ultimate Liberation. Madalyn M. O'Hair. 1979. pap. 3.00. Am Atheist.

Women & Catholic Priesthood: An Expanded Vision. Anne M. Gardiner. LC 76-12357. 1976. pap. 5.95 (ISBN 0-8091-1955-2). Paulist Pr.

Women & Colonization. Ed. by Mona Etienne. Eleanor Leacock. 1979. 26.95 (ISBN 0-03-052586-1); pap. 9.95 (ISBN 0-03-052581-0). Praeger.

Women & Crime. Rita J. Simon. LC 74-25067. 128p. 1975. 15.95 (ISBN 0-669-97428-5). Lexington Bks.

Women & Development: Perspectives from South & Southeast Asia. Ed. by Rounaq Jahan & H. Papanek. 439p. 1979. text ed. 27.00 (ISBN 0-8426-1657-8). Verry.

Women & Development: Perspectives from South & Southeast Asia. Ed. by Rounaq Jahan & Hanna Papanek. 1980. 16.00x (ISBN 0-8364-0596-X, Pub. by Bangladesh Inst Law India). South Asia Bks.

Women & Dualism. Lynda M. Glennon. 1979. pap. text ed. 9.95 (ISBN 0-582-28076-1). Longman.

Women & Educational Leadership. Sari K. Biklen & Marilyn Branningan. LC 79-7748. 288p. 1980. 23.95 (ISBN 0-669-03216-6). Lexington Bks.

Women & Feminism: A Guide to Information Sources. Ed. by Elizabeth Tingley & Donald F. Tingley. (American Government & History Information Guide Ser.: Vol. 12). 325p. 1981. 30.00 (ISBN 0-8103-1492-4). Gale.

Women & Film: A Bibliography. Rosemary R. Kowalski. LC 76-25051. 1976. 13.50 (ISBN 0-8108-0974-5). Scarecrow.

Women & Horses. Ron Davis. (Illus., Orig.). 1981. pap. 2.50 (ISBN 0-914140-11-6). Carpenter Pr.

Women & Household Labor. Ed. by Sarah F. Berk. LC 79-23003. (Sage Yearbooks in Women's Policy Studies: Vol. 5). (Illus.). 295p. 1980. 20.00 (ISBN 0-8039-1211-0); pap. 9.95 (ISBN 0-8039-1212-9). Sage.

Women & Language in Literature & Society. Ed. by Sally McConnell-Ginet et al. (Praeger Special Studies). 470p. 1980. 25.95 (ISBN 0-03-057892-2); pap. 11.95 (ISBN 0-03-057893-0). Praeger.

Women & Low Pay. Ed. by Peter Sloane. 1980. text ed. 30.00x (ISBN 0-333-26817-2). Humanities.

Women & Marriage in Kpelle Society. Caroline H. Bledsoe. LC 78-66170. (Illus.). 233p. 1980. 16.50x (ISBN 0-8047-1019-8). Stanford U Pr.

Women & Media. Ed. by Helen Baehr. LC 80-41424. (Illus.). 150p. 1980. 14.25 (ISBN 0-08-026061-6). Pergamon.

Women & Medicine. Beatrice S. Levin. LC 80-12705. 272p. 1980. 13.50 (ISBN 0-8108-1296-7). Scarecrow.

Women & Men. Ed. by Suzanne Fremon. (Reference Shelf Ser.). 1977. 6.25 (ISBN 0-8242-0607-X). Wilson.

Women & Men: Changing Roles, Relationships, & Perceptions. Libby A. Cater et al. LC 76-14472. (Special Studies). 1977. text ed. 19.95 o.p. (ISBN 0-03-021476-9). Praeger.

Women & Men Speaking. Cheris Kramerae. (Orig.). 1981. pap. text ed. 11.95 (ISBN 0-88377-179-9). Newbury Hse.

Women & Men Together: An Anthology of Short Fiction. Dawson Gaillard & John Mosier. (Illus., LC 77-078566). 1977. pap. text ed. 9.75 (ISBN 0-395-25032-3); inst. manual 0.50 (ISBN 0-395-25033-1). HM.

Women & Ministry in the New Testament. Elizabeth N. Tetlow. LC 79-57398. 256p. (Orig.). 1980. pap. 6.95 (ISBN 0-8091-2249-9). Paulist Pr.

Women & Minorities in Banking: Shortchanged-Update. Council on Economic Priorities & Tina L. Simcich. LC 76-50522. (Praeger Special Studies). 1977. 20.95 (ISBN 0-03-040336-7). Praeger.

Women & Money. Mary Rogers & Nancy Joyce. 1979. pap. 2.25 (ISBN 0-686-68425-7, 46003). Avon.

Women & Philanthropy in Nineteenth-Century England. F. K. Prochaska. (Illus.). 312p. 1980. 36.00 (ISBN 0-19-822627-6); pap. 21.00 (ISBN 0-19-822628-4). Oxford U Pr.

Women & Property in Morocco. Vanessa Maher. LC 74-80351. (Studies in Social Anthropology: No. 10). (Illus.). 164p. 1975. 27.50 (ISBN 0-521-20548-4). Cambridge U Pr.

Women & Psychotherapy. Ed. by Annette M. Brodsky & Rachel Hare-Mustin. 428p. 1980. 22.50 (ISBN 0-89862-605-6). Guilford Pr.

Women & Religion in America: Vol 1, the Nineteenth Century. Rosemary Ruether & Rosemary Keller. LC 80-8346. (Illus.). 352p. 1981. 15.00 (ISBN 0-06-066829-6, HarpR). Har-Row.

Women & Religion: Proceedings. rev. ed. American Academy of Religion, 1972 & 1973. Ed. by Joan Arnold & Joan A. Romero. LC 74-83126. (American Academy of Religion. Aids for the Study of Religion). 1974. pap. 9.00 (ISBN 0-89130-224-7, 010301). Scholars Pr Ca.

Women & Religion: Readings in the Western Tradition from Aeschylus to Mary Daly. Ed. by Elizabeth Clark & Herbert W. Richardson. LC 76-9975. 1976. pap. 6.95 (ISBN 0-06-061398-X, RD-178, HarpR). Har-Row.

Women & Schooling. Rosemary Deem. (Education Bks). 1978. 16.00x (ISBN 0-7100-8957-0); pap. 7.95 (ISBN 0-7100-8958-9). Routledge & Kegan.

Women & Social Policy. Constantina Safilios-Rothschild. (P-H Series in Social Policy). 224p. 1974. pap. 8.95 ref. ed. (ISBN 0-13-961680-2). P-H.

Women & Society: A Critical Review of the Literature with a Selected Annotated Bibliography. Ed. by Marie E. Rosenberg. Len V. Bergstrom. LC 73-77874. 1975. 20.00x (ISBN 0-8039-0248-4). Sage.

Women & Society: An Anthropological Reader. Ed. by Sharon W. Tiffany. 1979. 20.95 (ISBN 0-920792-01-4). EPWP.

Women & Society: Citations 3601 to 6000, an Annotated Bibliography. Ed. by Jo Ann D. Een & Marie B. Rosenberg-Dishman. LC 77-18985. 1978. 20.00x (ISBN 0-8039-0856-3). Sage.

Women & Support Networks. Blanche Wiesen-Cooke. (Out & Out Pamphlet Ser.). pap. 2.00 (ISBN 0-918314-10-0). Out & Out.

Women & Technological Change in Developing Countries. Ed. by Roslyn Dauber & Melinda Cain. (AAAS Selected Symposium: No. 53). 250p. 1980. lib. bdg. 21.50x (ISBN 0-89158-791-8). Westview.

Women & the American City. Ed. by Catherine Stimpson et al. LC 80-53136. 280p. 1981. lib. bdg. 16.00x (ISBN 0-226-77478-3); pap. 5.95 (ISBN 0-226-77479-1). U of Chicago Pr.

Women and the American Economy: A Look to the 1980's. Juanita M. Kreps. LC 76-4105. (American Assembly Ser.). (Illus.). 192p. 1976. pap. 4.00 (ISBN 0-13-962316-7, Spec). P-H.

Women & the American Labor Movement: From World War I to the Present. Philip S. Foner. LC 80-753. (Illus.). 1980. 22.50 (ISBN 0-02-910380-0). Free Pr.

Women & the Future: Changing Sex Roles in Modern America. Janet Z. Giele. LC 77-2472. 1979. pap. text ed. 7.95 (ISBN 0-02-911690-2). Free Pr.

Women & the Law in Washington State. Washington State Women's Council. LC 77-6374. 1977. pap. 2.95 (ISBN 0-914842-19-6). Madrona Pubs.

Women & the Law: The Social Historical Perspective. D. Kelly Weisberg. 600p. 1981. text ed. 24.95x (ISBN 0-87073-586-1); pap. text ed. 9.95x (ISBN 0-87073-587-X). Schenkman.

Women & the Making of the Working Class: Lyon 1830-1870. Laura S. Strumingher. LC 78-74841. 1979. 14.95 (ISBN 0-88831-027-7). EPWP.

Women & the Mass Media: Sourcebook for Research & Action. Matilda Butler & William Paisley. 432p. 1979. text ed. 26.95 (ISBN 0-87705-409-6); pap. text ed. 9.95x (ISBN 0-87705-419-3). Human Sci Pr.

Women & the Military. Martin Binkin & Shirley J. Bach. (Studies in Defense Policy). 1980. 9.95 (ISBN 0-8157-0966-8); pap. 3.95 (ISBN 0-8157-0965-X). Brookings.

Women & the Power to Change. Carnegie Commission on Higher Education. 224p. 1975. 10.95 o.p. (ISBN 0-07-010124-8, P&RB). McGraw.

Women & the Word of God. Susan Foh. 6.95 (ISBN 0-87552-268-8). Presby & Reformed.

Women & the Word of God: A Response to Biblical Feminism. Susan T. Foh. 280p. 1981. pap. 6.95. Baker Bk.

Women & the Word: Sermons. Ed. by Helen G. Crotwell. LC 77-78627. 144p. (Orig.). 1978. pap. 4.25 (ISBN 0-8006-1318-X, 1-1318). Fortress.

Women & Urban Society: A Guide to Information Sources. Ed. by Hasia R. Diner. LC 78-13109. (Urban Studies Information Guide Ser.: Vol. 7). 1979. 30.00 (ISBN 0-8103-1425-8). Gale.

Women & Violence. Miriam F. Hirsch. 416p. 1980. text ed. 17.95. Van Nos Reinhold.

Women & Wilderness: Women in Wilderness Professions & Lifestyles. Anne LaBastille. LC 80-14369. (Illus.). 320p. 1980. 12.95 (ISBN 0-87156-234-0). Sierra.

Women & Work: Honest Answers to Real Questions. Carole Hyatt. 400p. 1980. 14.95 (ISBN 0-87131-324-3). M Evans.

Women & World Developmemt, 2 vols, Vol.1. Ed. by Irene Tinker & Michelle B. Bramsen. Incl. Vol. 2. An Annotated Bibliography. Mayra Buvinic. 416p. Set. pap. 6.95. Overseas Dev Council.

Women & World Development. Ed. by Irene Tinker et al. LC 76-20602. 1976. 29.95 (ISBN 0-275-56520-3). Praeger.

Women & World Development with an Annotated Bibliography, 2 vols. Ed. by Irene Tinker et al. 416p. 1976. pap. 6.95. Overseas Dev Council.

Women Artists: An Historical, Contemporary & Feminist Bibliography. Donna G. Bachmann & Sherry Piland. LC 78-19182. 1978. 16.50 (ISBN 0-8108-1149-9). Scarecrow.

Women Artists in America: Eighteenth Century to Present. rev. ed. J. L. Collins & Glenn Opitz. (Illus.). 1981. 60.00 (ISBN 0-938290-00-2). Apollo.

Women Artists: Recognition & Reappraisal from the Early Middle Ages to the Twentieth Century. Karen Petersen & J. J. Wilson. (Illus., Orig.). 1976. pap. 6.95 (ISBN 0-06-090387-2, CN387, CN). Har-Row.

Women Artists: Recognition & Reappraisal From the Early Middle Ages to the Twentieth Century. Karen Petersen & J. J. Wilson. LC 76-23505. 212p. 1976. 15.00x (ISBN 0-8147-6567-X). NYU Pr.

Women As Interpreters of the Visual Arts, 1820-1979. Ed. by Claire R. Sherman & Adele M. Holcomb. LC 80-785. (Contributions in Women's Studies: No. 18). (Illus.). 512p. 1981. lib. bdg. 35.00 (ISBN 0-313-22056-5, SWS/). Greenwood.

Women at Point Sur. Robinson Jeffers. 1975. 12.00 o.p. (ISBN 0-912950-23-4). Blue Oak.

Women at the Hague: The International Congress of Women & Its Results. Jane Addams et al. LC 73-147452. (Library of War & Peace; Peace Leaders: Biographies & Memoirs). lib. bdg. 38.00 (ISBN 0-8240-0246-6). Garland Pub.

Women at Work. Sarah Harris. (History in Focus Ser.). (Illus.). 72p. (gr. 6-9). 1981. 14.95 (ISBN 0-7134-3551-8, Pub. by Batsford England). David & Charles.

Women at Work. Betty Medsger. (Illus.). 224p. 1975. 14.95 o.p. (ISBN 0-685-52958-4); pap. 7.95 o.p. (ISBN 0-8362-0614-2). Andrews & McMeel.

Women at Work: One Hundred Fifty Photographs by Lewis Hine. Lewis Hine. (Illus.). 128p. (Orig.). 1981. pap. price not set (ISBN 0-486-24154-8). Dover.

Women at Work: The Transformation of Work & Community in Lowell, Massachusetts, 1826-1860. Thomas Dublin. 360p. 1981. pap. 7.50x (ISBN 0-231-04167-5). Columbia U Pr.

Women Can Wait: The Pleasures of Motherhood After Thirty. Terri Schultz. 1979. pap. 4.95 (ISBN 0-385-14040-1, Dolp). Doubleday.

Women Composers: A Handbook. Susan Stern. LC 78-5505. 1978. 10.00 (ISBN 0-8108-1138-3). Scarecrow.

Women, Crime & Criminology: A Feminist Critique. Carol Smart. 1976. 15.00 (ISBN 0-7100-8449-8). Routledge & Kegan.

Women, Crime & Criminology: A Feminist Critique. Carol Smart. 1978. pap. 7.95 (ISBN 0-7100-8833-7). Routledge & Kegan.

Women, Crime & Justice. Ed. by Susan K. Datesman. Frank R. Scarpitti. (Illus., Orig.). 1980. pap. text ed. 5.95x (ISBN 0-19-502676-4). Oxford U Pr.

Women, Crime, & the Criminal Justice System. Lee H. Bowker. LC 78-57180. (Illus.). 1978. 23.95 (ISBN 0-669-02374-4). Lexington Bks.

Women, Design, & the Cambridge School. Dorothy M. Anderson. LC 80-81341. (Illus.). 246p. 1980. 15.95 (ISBN 0-914886-10-X). PDA Pubs.

Women: From the Greeks to the French Revolution. Susan Bell. 1972. pap. 6.95 o.p. (ISBN 0-534-00284-6). Wadsworth Pub.

Women: From the Greeks to the French Revolution. Ed. by Susan G. Bell. LC 80-51750. xiv, 313p. 1980. 17.50x (ISBN 0-8047-1094-5); pap. 5.95x (ISBN 0-8047-1082-1). Stanford U Pr.

Women Have Always Worked: An Historical Overview. Ed. by Florence Howe & John A. Rothermich. (Women's Lives - Women's Work Ser.). 208p. (Orig.). 1980. pap. text ed. 4.71 (ISBN 0-07-020435-7). Webster-McGraw.

Women Have Always Worked: An Historical Overview. Alice Kessler-Harris. (Women's Lives - Women's Work Ser.). (Illus.). 165p. (Orig.). (gr. 11-12). 1980. 14.95 (ISBN 0-912670-86-X); pap. 5.95 (ISBN 0-912670-67-3). Feminist Pr.

Women, Health, & Choice. Margarete Dandelowski. (Illus.). 288p. 1981. pap. text ed. 11.95 (ISBN 0-13-962183-0). P-H.

Women, Health & Reproduction. Helen Roberts. 208p. (Orig.). 1981. pap. 11.95 (ISBN 0-7100-0703-5). Routledge & Kegan.

Women in a Man's Church, Concilium 134. Ed. by Virgil Elizondo & Norbert Greinacher. (New Concilium 1980: Vol. 134). 128p. 1980. pap. 5.95 (ISBN 0-8164-4767-5). Crossroad NY.

Women in Academia: Evolving Policies Toward Equal Opportunities. Ed. by Elga Wasserman et al. LC 74-1734. (Special Studies). (Illus.). 188p. 1975. text ed. 22.95 (ISBN 0-275-09530-4). Praeger.

Women in Administration: A Book of Readings. National Association for Women Deans, Administration & Counselors. 1979. pap. 8.50 (ISBN 0-686-27727-9). Natl Assn Women.

Women in America: A Guide to Books, 1963-1975, with an Appendix on Books Published 1976-1979. Barbara Haber. 360p. 1981. pap. 6.95 (ISBN 0-252-00826-X). U of Ill Pr.

Women in American Music: A Bibliography. JoAnn Skowronski. LC 77-26611. 1978. 10.00 (ISBN 0-8108-1105-7). Scarecrow.

Women in American Religion. Ed. by Janet W. James. LC 79-5261. 288p. 1980. 21.95x (ISBN 0-8122-7780-5); pap. 9.95x (ISBN 0-8122-1104-9). U of Pa Pr.

Women in American Theatre. Helen K. Chinoy & Linda W. Jenkins. Ed. by Herber Michelman. (Illus.). 384p. 1981. 15.95 (ISBN 0-517-53729-X, Michaelman Books). Crown.

Women in Antiquity. Charles T. Seltman. LC 78-20490. 1981. Repr. of 1956 ed. 23.50 (ISBN 0-88355-867-X). Hyperion Conn.

Women in Antiquity: An Annotated Bibliography. Leanna Goodwater. LC 75-23229. 1975. 10.00 (ISBN 0-8108-0837-4). Scarecrow.

Women in Archaeology. Barbara Williams. 174p. 1981. 9.95. Walker & Co.

Women in Buddhism. Diana Paul. 1980. 19.00 (ISBN 0-89581-456-0, Asian Humanities). Lancaster-Miller.

Women in Business: How to Make Yourself Marketable. Leslie S. Douglass. (Illus.). 192p. 1980. 9.95 (Spec); pap. 4.95. P-H.

Women in Business: How to Make Yourself Marketable. Leslie S. Douglass. (Illus.). 192p. 1980. 10.95 (ISBN 0-13-962019-2, Spec); pap. 4.95 (ISBN 0-13-962001-X). P-H.

Women in Changing Japan. Ed. by Joyce Lebra et al. LC 75-33663. (Special Studies on China & East Asia Ser). 250p. 1976. 26.50x (ISBN 0-89158-019-0). Westview.

Women in Class Struggle. 2nd ed. Marlene Dixon. LC 79-67272. (Orig.). 1980. pap. 4.00 (ISBN 0-89935-005-4). Synthesis Pubns.

Women in Cuba--Twenty Years Later. Margaret Randall. (Illus.). 182p. 1981. 15.95 (ISBN 0-918266-15-7); pap. 6.95 (ISBN 0-918266-14-9). Smyrna.

Women in Cultures of the World. new ed. Dorothy Hammond & Alta Jablow. LC 75-32850. (Cummings Modular Program in Anthropology). 1976. text ed. 8.95 o.p. (ISBN 0-8465-2610-7); pap. text ed. 4.95 o.p. (ISBN 0-8465-2611-5). Benjamin-Cummings.

Women in Divorce. William J. Goode. LC 78-14243. 1978. Repr. of 1965 ed. lib. bdg. 27.50x (ISBN 0-313-21026-8, GOWD). Greenwood.

Women in Eastern Europe & the Soviet Union. Ed. by T. Yedlin. 250p. 27.50 (ISBN 0-03-055311-3). Praeger.

Women in Federal Employment Programs. Lorraine A. Underwood. (Institute Paper). 53p. 1979. pap. 4.00 (ISBN 0-87766-242-8, 24400). Urban Inst.

Women in Film Noir. Ann Kaplan. (BFI Ser.). 1979. pap. 5.75 o.p. (ISBN 0-85170-083-7). NY Zoetrope.

Women in Food Production, Food Handling & Nutrition. (Food & Nutrition Paper: No. 8). 232p. 1980. pap. 12.50 (ISBN 92-5-100691-1, F1857, FAO). Unipub.

Women in History. Susan Raven & Alison Weir. (Illus.). 288p. 1981. 19.95 (ISBN 0-517-53982-9, Harmony). Crown.

Women in India: Two Perspectives. Doranne Jacobson & Susan Wadley. 1977. 7.00x (ISBN 0-8364-0012-7); pap. text ed. 5.00x (ISBN 0-8364-0013-5). South Asia Bks.

Women in Islam. Naila Minai. LC 80-52405. 320p. 1981. 11.95 (ISBN 0-87223-666-8). Seaview Bks.

Women in Judaism: The Status of Women in Formative Judaism. Leonard Swidler. LC 75-46561. 248p. 1976. 11.50 (ISBN 0-8108-0904-4). Scarecrow.

Women in Latin American History: Their Lives & Views. Ed. by June E. Hahner. LC 75-620131. (Latin American Studies Ser.: Vol. 34). 1976. pap. text ed. 5.00 o.p. (ISBN 0-87903-034-8). UCLA Lat Am Ctr.

Women in Latin American History: Their Lives & Views. rev. ed. Ed. by June E. Hahner. LC 80-620044. (Latin American Studies: Vol. 51). 1981. pap. text ed. price not set (ISBN 0-87903-051-8). UCLA Lat Am Ctr.

Women in Law Enforcement. 2nd ed. P. Horne. (Illus.). 288p. 1980. 15.50 (ISBN 0-398-04029-X); pap. 10.50 (ISBN 0-398-04030-3). C C Thomas.

Women in Literature: Criticism of the Seventies. Carol F. Myers. LC 75-35757. 1976. 12.00 (ISBN 0-8108-0885-4). Scarecrow.

Women in Management. Laurie Larwood & Marion M. Wood. LC 76-27033. 1977. 19.95 (ISBN 0-669-00973-3). Lexington Bks.

Women in Management. Betty A. Stead. (Illus.). 1978. 15.95 (ISBN 0-13-961730-2); pap. text ed. 9.95 (ISBN 0-13-961722-1). P-H.

Women in Medicine: An Annotated Bibliography of the Literature on Women Physicians. Sandra L. Chaff et al. LC 77-24914. 1977. 40.00 (ISBN 0-8108-1056-5). Scarecrow.

Women in Medieval Society. Ed. by Susan M. Stuard. LC 75-41617. (Middle Ages Ser). 220p. 1976. 16.00x (ISBN 0-8122-7708-2); pap. 5.95x (ISBN 0-8122-1088-3). U of Pa Pr.

Women in Modern Industry: London Nineteen Fifteen. B. L. Hutchins. LC 79-56959. (English Working Class Ser.). 1980. lib. bdg. 28.00 (ISBN 0-8240-0112-5). Garland Pub.

Women in Music: A Biobibliography. Don L. Hixon & Don Hennessee. LC 75-23075. 358p. 1975. 15.00 (ISBN 0-8108-0869-2). Scarecrow.

Women in Muslim History. Charis Waddy. (Illus.). 1980. lib. bdg. 23.00 (ISBN 0-582-78084-5). Longman.

Women in New Zealand Society. Ed. by Beryl Hughes & Phillida Bunkle. 304p. 1980. text ed. 21.00x (ISBN 0-86861-026-7, 2521); pap. text ed. 11.50x (ISBN 0-86861-034-8, 2522). Allen Unwin.

Women in Politics. Ed. by Jane S. Jaquette. LC 74-1037. 384p. 1974. 26.50 (ISBN 0-471-44022-1, Pub. by Wiley-Interscience). Wiley.

Women in Prison. Edna W. Chandler. LC 72-88765. (gr. 9 up). 7.95 o.p. (ISBN 0-672-51702-7). Bobbs.

Women in Psychiatry. 1973. 1.25 o.p. (ISBN 0-685-77449-X, 231). Am Psychiatric.

Women in Public Office: A Biographical Directory & Statistical Analysis. 2nd ed. Compiled by Center for the American Woman & Politics. LC 78-7463. 1978. 35.00 (ISBN 0-8108-1142-1). Scarecrow.

Women in Public: The Women's Movement 1850-1900. Patricia Hollis. 1979. text ed. 25.00x (ISBN 0-04-900033-0). Allen Unwin.

Women in Revolutionary Paris, Seventeen Eighty-Nine to Seventeen Ninety-Five. Ed. by Darline G. Levy et al. LC 79-4102. 1979. text ed. 22.50 (ISBN 0-252-00409-4); pap. 10.00 (ISBN 0-252-00855-3). U of Ill Pr.

Women in Rural Development: Critical Issues. (a WEP Study) International Labour Office, Geneva. x, 214p. (Orig.). 1980. pap. 7.15 (ISBN 92-2-102388-5). Intl Labour Office.

Women in Science. H. J. Mozans. 1974. 17.50x o.p. (ISBN 0-262-13113-7); pap. 5.95 (ISBN 0-262-63054-0). MIT Pr.

Women in Social Work. Ronald G. Walton. 1975. 25.00x (ISBN 0-7100-8041-7). Routledge & Kegan.

Women in Socialist Society. Marlis Allendorf. LC 75-17597. (Illus.). 223p. 1976. 12.95 o.p. (ISBN 0-7178-0442-9). Intl Pub Co.

Women in Sport: A Guide to Information Sources. Ed. by Mary L. Remley. LC 80-14773. (Sports, Games, & Pastimes Information Guide Ser.: Vol. 10). 140p. 1980. 30.00 (ISBN 0-8103-1461-4). Gale.

Women in Stuart England & America: A Comparative Study. Roger Thompson. 1978. pap. 8.95 (ISBN 0-7100-8900-7). Routledge & Kegan.

Women in Television News. Judith S. Gelfman. LC 75-33167. (Illus.). 213p. 1976. 15.00x (ISBN 0-231-03994-8). Columbia U Pr.

Women in the Comics. Maurice Horn. LC 77-24317. (Illus.). 240p. 1981. pap. 9.95 (ISBN 0-87754-205-8). Chelsea Hse.

Women in the Criminal Justice System. Clarice Feinman. LC 80-12539. (Illus.). 1980. 19.95 (ISBN 0-03-052561-6); pap. 8.95 (ISBN 0-03-052566-7). Praeger.

Women in the Development Process: A Select Bibliography on Women in Sub-Saharan Africa & Latin America. Suzanne S. Saulniers & Cathy A. Rakowski. 1978. pap. 6.95x (ISBN 0-292-79010-4). U of Tex Pr.

Women in the Health System: Patients, Providers & Programs. Helen T. Marieskind. LC 80-19961. (Illus.). 330p. 1980. pap. text ed. 13.95 (ISBN 0-8016-3106-8). Mosby.

Women in the Labor Force in Nineteen Ninety. Ralph E. Smith. (Institute Paper). 176p. 1979. pap. 7.00 (ISBN 0-685-99692-1, 24600). Urban Inst.

Women in the Labor Market. Ed. by Cynthia Lloyd et al. LC 79-15547. 1977. 27.50x (ISBN 0-231-04638-3). Columbia U Pr.

Women in the Media. 119p. 1980. pap. 7.00 (ISBN 92-3-101687-3, U1027, UNESCO). Unipub.

Women in the Middle Ages. Frances Gies & Joseph Gies. LC 77-25832. (Illus.). 1978. 10.95 o.s.i. (ISBN 0-690-01724-3, TYC-T). T Y Crowell.

Women in the Modern World. Mirra Komarovsky. (Reprints in Sociology Ser). 1971. lib. bdg. 28.50x (ISBN 0-697-00213-6); pap. text ed. 8.95x (ISBN 0-89197-979-4). Irvington.

Women in the Organization. Harold H. Frank. LC 76-20167. 1977. 13.50x (ISBN 0-8122-7715-5). U of Pa Pr.

Women in the Printing Trades: A Sociological Study, London Nineteen Four. Ed. by J. Ransay Macdonald. LC 79-56961. (English Working Class Ser.). 1980. lib. bdg. 18.00 (ISBN 0-8240-0114-1). Garland Pub.

Women in the Professions. Laurily K. Epstein. LC 75-18051. (Illus.). 160p. 1975. 18.95 (ISBN 0-669-00130-9). Lexington Bks.

Women in the Professions: What's All the Fuss About? Ed. by Linda S. Fidell & John De Lamater. LC 73-89940. (Sage Contemporary Social Science Issues Ser.: Vol. 8). 1974. 4.95x (ISBN 0-8039-0337-5). Sage.

Women in the Two Germanies: A Comparative Study of a Socialist & a Non-Socialist Society. Harry G. Shaffer. (Pergamon Policy Studies on Social Policy). (Illus.). 256p. 1981. 26.00 (ISBN 0-08-023862-9). Pergamon.

Women in the U. S. Labor Force. Ed. by Ann F. Cahn. LC 78-22130. (Praeger Special Studies). 1979. 29.95 (ISBN 0-03-045646-0). Praeger.

Women in the Wilderness. China Galland. LC 80-7830. (Illus.). 256p. (Orig.). 1980. pap. 7.95 (ISBN 0-06-090817-3, CN 817, CN). Har-Row.

Women in the World: A Comparative Study. new ed. Ed. by Lynne B. Iglitzin & Ruth Ross. LC 74-14197. (Studies in International & Comparative Politics: No. 6). 427p. 1976. text ed. 26.50 (ISBN 0-87436-200-8); pap. text ed. 8.25 (ISBN 0-87436-201-6). ABC-Clio.

Women in Theatre: Compassion & Hope. Ed. by Karen Malpede. 1981. 15.00 (ISBN 0-89676-054-5); pap. 10.00 (ISBN 0-89676-055-3). Drama Bk.

Women in Top Jobs: Four Studies in Achievement. Patricia Walters et al. (Political & Economic Planning Ser.). 1971. text ed. 35.00x (ISBN 0-04-331046-X). Allen Unwin.

Women in Transition. Andrew J. DuBrin. (Illus.). 196p. 1972. 13.75 o.p. (ISBN 0-398-02273-9). C C Thomas.

Women in Transition: A Feminist Handbook on Separation & Divorce. Women in Transition, Inc. LC 75-15728. (Illus.). 1975. pap. 8.95 o.p. (ISBN 0-684-14257-0, SL591, ScribT). Scribner.

Women in White. Geoffrey Marks & William K. Beatty. LC 70-38381. (Illus.). 288p. 6.95 o.p. (ISBN 0-684-12843-8, ScribT). Scribner.

Women, Law, & the Genesis Tradition. C. Carmichael. 130p. 1979. 12.50x (ISBN 0-85224-364-2, Pub. by Edinburgh U Pr Scotland). Columbia U Pr.

Women Make Movies. Alexa Foreman. (Illus.). 1981. 20.00 (ISBN 0-685-94786-6); pap. 10.00 (ISBN 0-685-94787-4). Bocklegger Pr.

Women Making It. Ruth Halcomb. 288p. 1981. pap. 2.95 (ISBN 0-345-29348-7). Ballantine.

Women Making It. Ruth Halcomb. LC 79-51129. 1979. 13.95 (ISBN 0-689-10995-4). Atheneum.

Women, Men & the Division of Labor. Kathleen Newland. LC 80-51662. (Worldwatch Papers). 1980. pap. 2.00 (ISBN 0-916468-36-4). Worldwatch Inst.

Women Ministers: How Women Are Redifining Traditional Roles. Ed. by Judith L. Weidman. LC 80-8345. 192p. (Orig.). 1981. pap. 5.95 (ISBN 0-06-069291-X, RD 345, HarpR). Har-Row.

Women, Minorities, & Discrimination. Ed. by Phyllis A. Wallace & Annette M. LaMond. LC 76-53903. (Illus.). 1977. 21.50 (ISBN 0-669-01282-3). Lexington Bks.

Women Next Door. Ed. by Christopher D'Amanda & Milan Korcok. 1981. 5.95 (ISBN 0-932194-07-9). Green Hill.

Women Novelists in Spain & Spanish America. Lucia Fox-Lockert. LC 79-23727. 356p. 1979. 19.00 (ISBN 0-8108-1270-3). Scarecrow.

Women of a Certain Age: The Midlife Search for Self. Lillian Rubin. LC 79-1681. 320p. 1981. pap. 4.95 (ISBN 0-06-090833-5, CN 833, CN). Har-Row.

Women of America: A History. Carol Berkin & Mary B. Norton. LC 78-69589. (Illus.). 1979. pap. text ed. 10.95 (ISBN 0-395-27067-7). HM.

Women of China in Struggle. Bobby Siu. 240p. 1981. text ed. 18.95 (ISBN 0-905762-58-4, Pub. by Zed Pr); pap. text ed. 8.50 (ISBN 0-905762-63-0). Lawrence Hill.

Women of Courage. Dorothy Nathan. (Landmark Ser: No. 107). (Illus.). (gr. 5-9). 1964. PLB 5.99 (ISBN 0-394-90407-9, BYR); pap. 0.75 (ISBN 0-394-82186-6). Random.

Women of Dallas. Burt Hirschfeld. (Dallas Ser.: Vol. 2). 288p. (Orig.). 1981. pap. 2.75 (ISBN 0-553-14497-9). Bantam.

Women of Eden. Marilyn Harris. 608p. 1981. pap. 2.95 (ISBN 0-345-28965-X). Ballantine.

Women of Egypt. Elizabeth Cooper. LC 79-2934. (Illus.). 380p. 1981. Repr. of 1914 ed. 26.50 (ISBN 0-8305-0102-9). Hyperion Conn.

Women of Grace. Betty J. Grams. LC 77-93409. 1978. pap. 1.95 (ISBN 0-88243-751-8, 02-0751, Radiant Books); teacher's ed 2.50 (ISBN 0-88243-226-5, 32-0226). Gospel Pub.

Women of Minnesota: Selected Biographical Essays. Ed. by Barbara Stuhler & Gretchen Kreuter. LC 77-3361. (Illus.). 402p. 1977. 12.00 (ISBN 0-87351-112-3). Minn Hist.

Women of Seventy-Six. Sally S. Booth. (gr. 4 up). 1974. 9.95g (ISBN 0-8038-8066-9). Hastings.

Women of the Caesars. Guglielmo Ferrero. (Illus.). 1977. 47.15 (ISBN 0-930582-05-5). Am Classical Coll Pr.

Women of the Forest. Robert Murphy et al. (Illus.). 256p. 1974. 12.50x (ISBN 0-231-03682-5); pap. 5.00x (ISBN 0-231-03881-X). Columbia U Pr.

Women of the Mayflower & Women of Plymouth Colony. Ethel J. Noyes. LC 73-12780. Repr. of 1921 ed. 18.00 (ISBN 0-8103-3668-5). Gale.

Women of the Renaissance. Maude la Claviere & Marie Alphonse Rene de. 510p. 1980. Repr. of 1905 ed. lib. bdg. 50.00 (ISBN 0-8482-5077-X). Norwood Edns.

Women of the West. Dorothy Levenson. LC 72-10441. (First Bks). (Illus.). 96p. (gr. 4-7). 1973. PLB 4.90 o.p. (ISBN 0-531-00793-6). Watts.

Women of Trachis. Sophocles. Tr. by C. K. Williams & Gregory W. Dickerson. (Greek Texts in New Translations Ser.). 1978. text ed. 10.95x (ISBN 0-19-502050-2). Oxford U Pr.

Women on the Hollywood Screen. Frank Manchel. (Illus.). (gr. 7 up). 1977. PLB 6.90 s&l o.p. (ISBN 0-531-00389-2). Watts.

Women on the Job: The Attitudes of Women to Their Work. Judity B. Agassi. LC 78-24789. (Illus.). 272p. 1979. 25.95 (ISBN 0-669-02815-0). Lexington Bks.

Women on the Wall. Wallace Stegner. LC 80-22461. x, 277p. 1981. 16.50x (ISBN 0-8032-4111-9); pap. 5.50 (ISBN 0-8032-9110-8, BB-710, Bison). U of Nebr Pr.

Women; or, Pour et Contre: A Tale, 3 vols. Charles R. Maturin. Ed. by Robert L. Wolff. (Ireland Nineteenth Century Fiction, Ser. Two: Vol. 13). 1979. Set. lib. bdg. write for info. (ISBN 0-8240-3462-7); lib. bdg. 46.00 ea. Garland Pub.

Women Organizing: An Anthology. Bernice Cummings & Victoria Schuck. LC 79-18956. 422p. 1979. 21.50 (ISBN 0-8108-1245-2). Scarecrow.

Women Out of Bondage & in Love. Beatrice B. Kennedy. 1978. 4.00 o.p. (ISBN 0-682-49152-7). Exposition.

Women Over Forty: Visions & Realities. Marilyn Block. LC 80-20774. (Focus on Women Ser.: No. 4). 176p. 1980. text ed. 19.95 (ISBN 0-8261-3000-3); pap. text ed. 11.95 (ISBN 0-8261-3001-1). Springer Pub.

Women Pastors. O. John Eldred. 128p. 1981. pap. 4.95 (ISBN 0-8170-0901-9). Judson.

Women Playwrights in England: 1363-1750. Nancy Cotton. LC 78-73155. 256p. 1980. 15.00 (ISBN 0-8387-2381-0). Bucknell U Pr.

Women Poets in Pre-Revolutionary America, 1650-1775. Pattie Cowell. LC 80-50492. (Illus.). 400p. 1981. 25.00x (ISBN 0-87875-192-0). Whitston Pub.

Women, Politics, & Change: The Kaum Ibu UMNO Malaysia, 1945-1972. Lenore Manderson. (East Asian Social Science Monographs). (Illus.). 260p. 1981. 34.50 (ISBN 0-19-580437-6). Oxford U Pr.

Women Priests: Yes or No? Emily C. Hewitt & Suzanne R. Hiatt. LC 72-81027. 128p. 1973. pap. 2.95 (ISBN 0-8164-2076-9, SP77). Crossroad NY.

Women Returning to Work: Policies & Progress in Five Countries. Alice M. Yohalem. LC 79-55819. (LandMark Studies). (Illus.). 304p. 1980. text ed. 25.00 (ISBN 0-916672-51-4). Allanheld.

Women Say, the Men Say. Evelyn Shapiro & Barry Shapiro. 1979. postponed 14.95 (ISBN 0-440-09626-X). Delacorte.

Women Scientists in Industry & Government: How Much Progress in the 1970's. Committee on the Education & Employment of Women in Science & Engineering. LC 80-80079. vii, 56p. 1980. pap. text ed. 5.00 (ISBN 0-309-03023-4). Natl Acad Pr.

Women Scientists Roster. Compiled by Iris R. Weiss & Carol Place. 143p. (Orig.). 1979. pap. 3.50 (ISBN 0-87355-015-3). Natl Sci Tchrs.

Women See Women. Ed. by Cheryl Wiesenfeld et al. (Illus.). 176p. 1976. 12.50 o.s.i. (ISBN 0-690-00965-8, TYC-T); pap. 6.95 o.s.i. (ISBN 0-690-00972-0, TYC-T). T Y Crowell.

Women, Sex & Pornography: A Controversial Study. Beatrice Faust. (Illus.). 256p. 1981. 11.95 (ISBN 0-02-537050-2). Macmillan.

Women, Sex, & Race: A Realistic View of Sexism & Racism. Bernard Braxton. LC 72-91049. 228p. 1973. 7.95 (ISBN 0-930876-01-6); pap. 3.95 (ISBN 0-930876-02-4). Verta Pr.

Women-Sex & Sexuality. Ed. by Catherine Stimpson & Ethel S. Person. 384p. 1981. lib. bdg. 14.50x (ISBN 0-226-77476-7); pap. 5.95 (ISBN 0-226-77477-5, P 914, Phoen). U of Chicago Pr.

Women Still Weep: A Sequel to Women Must Weep. Mary Orr. 1980. pap. 1.25 (ISBN 0-686-68851-1). Dramatists Play.

Women Students in India. Savitri Sharma. 1979. text ed. 12.50x (ISBN 0-391-01831-0). Humanities.

Women Take Issue: Aspects of Women's Subordination. Women's Studies Group Centre for Contemporary Cultural Studies. (Illus.). 1979. text ed. 17.00x (ISBN 0-09-133600-7, Hutchinson U Lib); pap. text ed. 8.50x (ISBN 0-09-133601-5, Hutchinson U Lib). Humanities.

Women Talking. (Illus.). 1976. 12.95 (ISBN 0-910550-18-2, Co-Pub. & Dist. by Lyle Stuart). Elysium.

Women Teachers in the Twentieth Century in England & Wales. Geoffrey Partington. (General Ser.). (Orig.). 1976. pap. text ed. 10.75x (ISBN 0-85633-100-7, NFER). Humanities.

Women: The Fifth World. Elise Boulding. LC 80-65602. (Headline Ser.: No. 248). (Illus.). 64p. (Orig.). 1980. pap. 2.00 (ISBN 0-87124-059-9). Foreign Policy.

Women View Librarianship: Nine Perspectives. Kathryn R. Lundy. LC 80-23611. (ACRL Publications in Librarianship: No. 41). 108p. 1980. pap. 7.00 (ISBN 0-8389-3251-7). ALA.

Women, War & Revolution. Ed. by Carol R. Berkin & Clara M. Lovett. LC 79-26450. 1980. text ed. 27.50x (ISBN 0-8419-0502-9); pap. text ed. 9.75x (ISBN 0-8419-0545-2). Holmes & Meier.

Women, War, & Work: The Impact of World War I on Women Workers in the United States. Maurine W. Greenwald. LC 80-540. (Contributions in Women's Studies: No. 12). (Illus.). xxvii, 309p. 1980. lib. bdg. 27.50 (ISBN 0-313-21355-0, GWW/). Greenwood.

Women We Wanted to Look Like. Brigid Keenan. LC 78-4014. (Illus.). 1978. 14.95 o.p. (ISBN 0-312-88783-3). St Martin.

Women Who Made Bible History. Harold J. Ockenga. 1971. pap. 5.95 (ISBN 0-310-30461-X). Zondervan.

Women Who Made the West. Western Writers of America. LC 79-8442. (Illus.). 1980. 10.95 (ISBN 0-385-15801-7). Doubleday.

Women Who Shaped History. Henrietta Buckmaster. (gr. 7 up). 1968. 8.95 (ISBN 0-02-715210-3, CCPr). Macmillan.

Women Who Win: Exercising Your Rights in Sports. Bonnie L. Parkhouse & Jackie Lapin. (Illus.). 272p. 1980. 11.95 (ISBN 0-13-962365-5, Spec); pap. 5.95 (ISBN 0-13-962357-4). P-H.

Women Winning: A Handbook for Action Against Sex Discrimination. Ed. by Virginia E. Pendergrass. LC 78-27379. 1979. 16.95 (ISBN 0-88229-450-4); pap. 8.95 (ISBN 0-88229-699-X). Nelson-Hall.

Women, Work, & Family. Frank L. Mott. LC 77-18329. (Illus.). 1978. 16.95 (ISBN 0-669-02092-3). Lexington Bks.

Women, Work, & Health: Challenge to Corporate Policy. Ed. by D. C. Walsh & R. H. Egdahl. (Springer Ser. on Industry & Health: Vol. 8). 259p. 1980. pap. 12.00 (ISBN 0-387-90478-6). Springer-Verlag.

Women Workers & the Industrial Revolution, 1750-1850. Ivy Pinchbeck. LC 75-96378. Repr. of 1930 ed. 25.00x (ISBN 0-678-05106-2). Kelley.

Women Workers in the First World War: The British Experience. Gail Braybon. 224p. 1981. 24.50x (ISBN 0-389-20100-6). B&N.

Women Working: An Anthology of Stories & Poems. Ed. by Nancy Hoffman & Florence Howe. (Women's Lives-Women's Work Ser). (Illus.). 1979. pap. 5.95 (ISBN 0-912670-57-6, Co-Pub. by McGraw). Feminist Pr.

Women Writers & Poetic Identity: Dorothy Wordsworth, Emily Bronte & Emily Dickinson. Margaret Homans. LC 80-7527. 244p. 1980. 14.75x (ISBN 0-691-06440-7). Princeton U Pr.

Women Writers in Black Africa. Lloyd W. Brown. LC 80-1710. (Contributions in Women's Studies: No. 21). 256p. 1981. lib. bdg. 23.95 (ISBN 0-313-22540-0, BRW/). Greenwood.

Women Writers in France: Variations on a Theme. Germaine Bree. 104p. 1973. 7.00 (ISBN 0-8135-0771-5). Rutgers U Pr.

Women's Basketball. Mildred J. Barnes. (Illus.). 250p. 1972. text ed. 13.95x o.s.i. (ISBN 0-686-66634-8, 623450X). Allyn.

Women's Basketball. 2nd ed. Mildred J. Barnes. (Illus.). 1980. text ed. 18.95x (ISBN 0-205-06604-6, 6266045). Allyn.

Women's Basketball. Cathy Rush & Lawrie Mifflin. 1976. pap. 4.95 (ISBN 0-8015-8794-8, Hawthorn). Dutton.

Women's Coats, Suits, Rainwear, Furs. Fairchild Market Research Division. (Fairchild Fact File Ser.). 1980. pap. 10.00 (ISBN 0-87005-328-0). Fairchild.

Women's Dresses. Fairchild Market Research Division. (Fact File Ser). 1978. pap. 10.00 (ISBN 0-87005-256-X). Fairchild.

Women's Dresses. Fairchild Market Research Division. (Fairchild Fact Files). (Illus.). 50p. 1981. pap. 10.00 (ISBN 0-87005-356-6). Fairchild.

Women's Education in the United States: A Guide to Information Sources. Ed. by Kay S. Wilkins. LC 79-54691. (Education Information Guide Ser.: Vol. 4). 1979. 30.00 (ISBN 0-8103-1410-X). Gale.

Women's Gun. (Illus.). 1975. pap. 1.50 (ISBN 0-88447-030-X). Diana Pr.

Women's Gymnastics. Jill Coulton. (EP Sport Ser.). (Illus.). 116p. 1979. 12.95 (ISBN 0-8069-9168-2, Pub. by EP Publishing England); pap. 6.95 (ISBN 0-8069-9170-4, Pub. by EP Publishing England). Sterling.

Women's Gymnastics. 2nd ed. Kitty Kjeldsen. 100p. 1975. pap. text ed. 3.95x o.p. (ISBN 0-205-04841-2, 6248411). Allyn.

Women's Gymnastics. Jack Wiley. LC 79-64732. (Illus.). 176p. (Orig.). 1980. pap. 7.95 (ISBN 0-89037-223-3). Anderson World.

Women's Gymnastics: Coach, Participant, Spectator. Mimi Murray. 1979. text ed. 18.95x (ISBN 0-205-06162-1, 6261620). Allyn.

Women's Health Movement: Feminist Alternatives to Medical Control. Sheryl B. Ruzek. LC 78-15483. (Praeger Special Studies). 1978. 29.95 (ISBN 0-03-041436-9); pap. 10.95 (ISBN 0-03-056236-8). Praeger.

Women's History: A Literature of Struggle Program Guide. Ed. by Virginia Drachman & Zena Harvey-Felder. (MicroSources: Social Science Skills Development Program Ser.). 67p. (gr. 9-12). 1980. pap. text ed. 7.95 (ISBN 0-667-00618-4). Microfilming Corp.

Women's History: Resources at the State Historical Society of Wisconsin. 4th, rev., enl. ed. James P. Danky et al. LC 79-17522. 1981. pap. 3.00 (ISBN 0-87020-189-1). State Hist Soc Wis.

Women's Inner Fashions: Nightwear & Daywear. Fairchild Market Research Division. (Fairchild Fact File Ser.). 1979. pap. 10.00 (ISBN 0-87005-323-X). Fairchild.

Women's Issues & Social Work Practice. Ed. by Elaine Norman & Arlene Mancuso. LC 79-91106. 276p. 1980. pap. text ed. 7.95 (ISBN 0-87581-249-X). Peacock Pubs.

Women's Legacy: Interpretive Essays in U. S. History. Bettina Aptheker. (Orig.). Date not set. 10.00 (ISBN 0-7178-0572-7); pap. 3.50 (ISBN 0-7178-0566-2). Intl Pub Co. Postponed.

Women's Liberation Ideology & Union Participation: A Study. Marilyn S. Boyd. LC 79-65257. 135p. 1981. perfect bdg. 10.95 (ISBN 0-86548-024-9). Century Twenty One.

Women's Movement in the Seventies: An International English-Language Bibliography. Albert Krichmar et al. LC 77-21416. 1977. 35.00 (ISBN 0-8108-1063-8). Scarecrow.

Women's Networks. Carol Kleinman. 1981. pap. 2.95 (ISBN 0-345-29355-X). Ballantine.

Women's Oppression Today: Problems in Marxist Feminst Analysis. Michele Barrett. 280p. 1981. 19.50x (ISBN 0-8052-7091-4, Pub. by NLB England); pap. 8.50 (ISBN 0-8052-7090-6). Schocken.

Women's Rights. Janet Stevenson. LC 74-182299. (First Bks). (Illus.). 96p. (gr. 5-7). 1972. PLB 4.90 o.p. (ISBN 0-531-00763-4). Watts.

Women's Rights & the Law: The Impact of the ERA on State Laws. Barbara A. Brown et al. LC 77-9961. (Praeger Special Studies). 1977. text ed. 39.95 (ISBN 0-03-022316-4); pap. 11.95 (ISBN 0-03-022311-3). Praeger.

Women's Rights Movement in the United States 1848-1970: A Bibliography & Sourcebook. Albert Krichmar et al. LC 72-4702. 1972. 15.00 o.p. (ISBN 0-8108-0528-6). Scarecrow.

Women's Room. Marilyn French. 1980. pap. 3.50 (ISBN 0-515-05933-1). Jove Pubns.

Women's Running. Joan Ullyot. LC 75-20962. (Illus.). 1976. pap. 4.95 (ISBN 0-89037-074-5); handbk. 5.95 (ISBN 0-89037-100-8). Anderson World.

Women's Sexual Development: Outer Form & Inner Space. Ed. by Martha Kirkpatrick. (Women in Context Ser.). (Illus.). 290p. 1980. 25.00 (ISBN 0-306-40375-7, Plenum Pr). Plenum Pub.

Women's Soccer Guide. Valerie Tucker. LC 79-64301. (Illus.). 140p. (Orig.). 1981. pap. 4.95 (ISBN 0-89037-221-7). Anderson World.

Women's Sportswear, Seperates, Jeans & Active Wear. Fairchild Market Research Division. (Fact File Ser.). (Illus.). 100p. 1980. pap. 10.00 (ISBN 0-87005-352-3). Fairchild.

Women's Sportwear & Casual Wear. Fairchild Market Research Division. (Fact File Ser). 1978. pap. 10.00 (ISBN 0-87005-252-7). Fairchild.

Women's Status & Fertility in the Muslim World. Ed. by James Allman. LC 78-5897. 1978. 29.95 (ISBN 0-03-042926-9). Praeger.

Women's Studies: A Recommended Core Bibliography. Esther Stineman & Catherine Loeb. LC 79-13679. 1979. lib. bdg. 35.00x (ISBN 0-87287-196-7). Libs Unl.

Women's Tennis: A Historical Documentary. Angela Lumpkin. 200p. 1981. 15.00 (ISBN 0-87875-189-0). Whitston Pub.

Women's Track & Field. Betty Costanza & Alfred Glossbrenner. LC 77-70120. 1978. pap. 5.95 (ISBN 0-8015-8795-6, Hawthorn). Dutton.

Women's "True" Profession: Voices from the History of Teaching. Ed. by Florence Howe & John A. Rothermich. (Women's Lives-Women's Work Ser.). 352p. (Orig.). 1981. pap. text ed. 6.45 (ISBN 0-07-020437-3). McGraw.

Women's Two Roles: At Home & Work. rev. ed. Alva Myrdal & Viola Klein. (International Library of Sociology & Social Reconstruction). (Illus.). 1970. pap. text ed. 6.50x (ISBN 0-7100-2894-6). Humanities.

Women's Work & Wages in the Soviet Union. Alastair McAulay. 248p. 1981. text ed. 28.50x (ISBN 0-04-339020-X, 2605). Allen Unwin.

Women's Work & Wages: London, Nineteen Nine. Edward Cadbury et al. LC 79-56954. (English Working Class). 1980. lib. bdg. 30.00 (ISBN 0-8240-0108-7). Garland Pub.

Women's Work & Women's Studies 1971. Kirsten Drake et al. (Annual). 1972. pap. 4.50x o.p. (ISBN 0-912786-18-3). Know Inc.

Women's Work in Soviet Russia: Continuity in the Midst of Change. Michael P. Sacks. LC 75-19813. (Special Studies). 1976. 19.95 o.p. (ISBN 0-275-55790-1). Praeger.

Wonder Aces of the Air. A. J. Smithers. 1980. 19.95 (ISBN 0-86033-077-X). Gordon-Cremonesi.

Wonder & Worship. James Carroll. LC 70-133469. 1970. pap. 1.95 (ISBN 0-8091-1871-8). Paulist Pr.

Wonder Book. Nathaniel Hawthorne. (Classics Ser). (gr. 5 up). pap. 1.25 (ISBN 0-8049-0118-X, CL-118). Airmont.

Wonder Bread from a Boy's Lunch. Norman C. Habel. 1972. pap. 0.85 (ISBN 0-570-06545-3, 56-1249). Concordia.

Wonder-Dog. Richard A. Hughes. LC 77-1977. (gr. 3up). 1977. 9.25 (ISBN 0-688-80099-8); PLB 8.88 (ISBN 0-688-84099-X). Greenwillow.

Wonder-Fish from the Sea. Josef Guggenmos. Tr. by Alvin Tresselt. LC 78-148165. (Illus.). (gr. k-3). 1971. 5.95 o.s.i. (ISBN 0-8193-0483-2, Four Winds); PLB 5.41 o.s.i. (ISBN 0-8193-0484-0). Schol Bk Serv.

Wonder of Animals. (Illus.). 1976. 5.95 (ISBN 0-307-16807-7, Golden Pr); PLB 10.69 o.p. (ISBN 0-307-66807-X). Western Pub.

Wonder of Hands. Edith Baer. LC 77-93852. (gr. k-3). 1970. 5.95 o.s.i. (ISBN 0-8193-0420-4, Four Winds); PLB 5.41 o.s.i. (ISBN 0-8193-0421-2). Schol Bk Serv.

Wonder of Intelligence. Francis J. Klauder. LC 73-79083. (Illus.). 144p. 1973. 6.95 (ISBN 0-8158-0307-9). Chris Mass.

Wonder of Life. John A. Moore. (Illus.). (gr. 4-6). 1960. PLB 6.95 (ISBN 0-87396-016-5). Stravon.

Wonder of Man. Joseph Krimsky. 1968. pap. 3.95 (ISBN 0-911336-21-4). Sci of Mind.

Wonder of the Word of God. Robert L. Sumner. 1969. pap. 0.95 (ISBN 0-87398-933-3, Pub. by Bibl Evang Pr). Sword of Lord.

Wonder of Words: An Introduction to Language for Every Man. Isaac Goldberg. LC 74-164294. 1971. Repr. of 1938 ed. 22.00 (ISBN 0-8103-3777-0). Gale.

Wonder Wheels. Lee B. Hopkins. (YA) (gr. 7-12). 1980. pap. 1.50 (ISBN 0-440-99511-6, LFL). Dell.

Wonder Women of Sports. Betty M. Jones. LC 80-20232. (Step-up Book Ser.: No. 33). (Illus.). 72p. (gr. 2-5). 1981. PLB 4.99 (ISBN 0-394-94475-5); pap. 3.95 boards (ISBN 0-394-84475-0). Random.

Wonder World of Ants. Wilfrid S. Bronson. LC 37-27454. (Illus.). (gr. 3-7). 1937. 5.25 o.p. (ISBN 0-15-299287-1, HJ). HarBraceJ.

Wonderful Adventures of Phra the Phoenician. Edwin L. Arnold. Ed. by R. Reginald & Douglas Menville. LC 80-19173. (Newcastle Forgotten Fantasy Library Ser.: Vol. 11). 329p. 1980. Repr. of 1977 ed. lib. bdg. 10.95x (ISBN 0-89370-510-1). Borgo Pr.

Wonderful Crisis of Middle Age. Eda LeShan. 320p. 1974. pap. 2.95 (ISBN 0-446-93746-0). Warner Bks.

Wonderful Little Boy. Helen E. Buckley. LC 73-101469. (Illus.). (gr. k-3). 1970. 8.25 o.p. (ISBN 0-688-41150-9); PLB 6.96 o.p. (ISBN 0-688-51150-3). Lothrop.

Wonderful Money Making Opportunity for Everyone: Roadside Marketing for Maximal Profits. Lawrence Watts. (Illus.). 1980. 39.75 (ISBN 0-89266-214-X). Am Classical Coll Pr.

Wonderful Story of How You Were Born. rev. ed. Sidonie M. Gruenberg. LC 71-92055. (Illus.). (gr. 3-5). 1970. 6.95a (ISBN 0-385-03674-4); PLB (ISBN 0-385-03680-9); pap. 1.49 o.p. (ISBN 0-385-05383-5). Doubleday.

Wonderful Story of Jesus. David R. Collins. 1980. 5.95 (ISBN 0-570-03490-6, 56-1344); pap. 1.50 (ISBN 0-570-03491-4, 56-1345). Concordia.

Wonderful Storybook. Margaret W. Brown. 1974. PLB 10.69 o.p. (ISBN 0-307-65777-9, Golden Pr). Western Pub.

Wonderful Webbers. June Lange. (Illus.). 1967. 12.95 (ISBN 0-910550-19-0). Elysium.

Wonderful Window Word Book. H. L. Ross. LC 79-1910. (Illus.). (ps-k). 1979. 1.95 (ISBN 0-525-69018-2, Gingerbread Bks); PLB 5.95 o.p. (ISBN 0-525-69019-0). Dutton.

Wonderful Winter. Marchette Chute. (gr. 5-9). 1954. PLB 5.95 o.p. (ISBN 0-525-43208-6). Dutton.

Wonderful Wizard of Oz. L. Frank Baum. (gr. 3 up). 1979. pap. 1.25 (ISBN 0-307-21620-9, Golden Pr). Western Pub.

Wonderful Works of God. Paul E. Eickmann. (Orig.). 1970. pap. 3.25 (ISBN 0-8100-0015-6, 7-N38); pap. wkbk. avail. (ISBN 0-685-04632-X). Northwest Pub.

Wonderful World of Checkers & Draughts. Tom Wiswell & Jules Leopold. LC 78-69631. (Illus.). 1981. 9.95 (ISBN 0-498-02258-7). A S Barnes.

Wonderful World of Ellwood Patterson Cubberley: An Essay on the Historiography of American Education. Lawrence A. Cremin. LC 65-20759. (Orig.). 1965. text ed. 4.25x (ISBN 0-8077-1215-9); pap. text ed. 2.25x (ISBN 0-8077-1212-4). Tchrs Coll.

Wonderful World of Freezer Cooking. Helen Quat. (Illus.). 1969. pap. 1.50 o.p. (ISBN 0-451-06788-6, W6788, Sig). NAL.

Wonderful World of Honey. Joe Parkhill. 6.95 (ISBN 0-936744-01-4). Green Hill.

Wonderful World of Horses Coloring Album. Rita Warner. (Illus.). 32p. (Orig.). (gr. 3 up). 1976. pap. 3.50 (ISBN 0-912300-69-8, 69-8). Troubador Pr.

Wonderful World of J. Wesley Smith. Burr Shafer. LC 60-15077. (Illus.). 1960. 5.95 (ISBN 0-8149-0199-9). Vanguard.

Wonderful World of Penthouse Sex. 1976. pap. 2.50 o.s.i. (ISBN 0-446-91151-8). Warner Bks.

Wonderful World of Puppets. Gunter Bohmer. LC 76-107968. (Illus.). 1971. 9.95 (ISBN 0-8238-0084-9). Plays.

Wonderfully Made. Ruth S. Hummell. LC 67-24878. (Concordia Sex Education Ser). (gr. 4-6). 1967. 4.50 (ISBN 0-570-06602-6, 14-1502); color film & 33 1 10.00 (ISBN 0-685-08655-0, 79-3101). Concordia.

Wonderlamp. Don Stevenson & Hugh Blyth. (Illus.). 49p. 1981. text ed. price not set (ISBN 0-933770-19-7). Kalimat.

Wonderland. Joyce C. Oates. LC 72-155669. 10.95 (ISBN 0-8149-0659-1). Vanguard.

Wonderland. Joyce C. Oates. 1979. pap. 1.95 o.p. (ISBN 0-449-22951-3, Crest). Fawcett.

Wonderland Frieze. John Burningham. (Illus.). (ps-3). 1981. 4.95 (ISBN 0-224-61537-8). Merrimack Bk Serv.

Wonderous Mushroom: Mycolatry in Mesoamerica. R. Gordon Wasson. LC 79-26895. (Illus.). 178p. 1980. 14.95 (ISBN 0-07-068441-3); deluxe ed. 435.00 (ISBN 0-07-068442-1); pap. 10.95 (ISBN 0-07-068443-X). McGraw.

Wonders in Weeds. William Smith. 187p. 1977. 13.00x (ISBN 0-8464-1062-1). Beekman Pubs.

Wonders of Alligators & Crocodiles. Wyatt Blassingame. (Illus.). (gr. 4-6). 1974. pap. 1.25 (ISBN 0-590-04842-2, Schol Pap). Schol Bk Serv.

Wonders of Camels. Sigmund A. Lavine. LC 78-22436. (Wonder Ser.). (Illus.). (gr. 4 up). 1979. 5.95 (ISBN 0-396-07670-X). Dodd.

Wonders of Cattle. Vincent Scuro. LC 80-1019. (Wonders Ser.). (Illus.). 64p. (gr. 4 up). 1980. PLB 6.95 (ISBN 0-396-07892-3). Dodd.

Wonders of Coral & Coral Reefs. Morris K. Jacobson & David R. Franz. LC 78-22437. (Wonder Ser.). (Illus.). (gr. 5 up). 1979. 5.95 (ISBN 0-396-07679-3). Dodd.

Wonders of Creation. Alfred M. Rehwinkel. LC 74-8416. 288p. 1973. pap. 6.95 (ISBN 0-87123-649-4, 210649). Bethany Fell.

Wonders of Donkeys. Sigmund A. Lavine & Vincent Scuro. LC 78-7737. (Wonders Ser.). (Illus.). (gr. 4 up). 1979. 5.95 (ISBN 0-396-07592-4). Dodd.

Wonders of Dust. Christie McFall. LC 80-14285. (Wonders Ser.). (Illus.). 80p. (gr. 5 up). 1980. PLB 6.95 (ISBN 0-396-07850-8). Dodd.

Wonders of Fungi. Lucy Kavaler. LC 64-10450. (Illus.). (gr. 6-8). 1964. PLB 7.89 (ISBN 0-381-99770-7, A90800, JD-J). John Day.

Wonders of Geese & Swans. Thomas D. Fegely. LC 75-38360. (Wonder Ser.). 1976. 5.95 (ISBN 0-396-07307-7). Dodd.

Wonders of Herbs. Sigmund A. Lavine. LC 75-38356. (Wonders Ser.). (gr. 5 up). 1976. 5.95 (ISBN 0-396-07294-1). Dodd.

Wonders of Inventions. Mary G. Bonner. (Illus.). (gr. 4-9). 1961. 4.25 o.p. (ISBN 0-8313-0007-8); PLB 6.19 o.p. (ISBN 0-685-13790-2). Lantern.

Wonders of Jellyfish. Morris Jacobson & David R. Franz. LC 77-92326. (Wonders Ser.). (Illus.). (gr. 5 up). 1978. 5.95 (ISBN 0-396-07560-6). Dodd.

Wonders of Llamas. Roger Perry. LC 77-6492. (Wonders Ser.). (Illus.). (gr. 5 up). 1977. 5.95 (ISBN 0-396-07460-X). Dodd.

Wonders of Mice. Sigmund A. Lavine. LC 80-1018. (Wonders Ser.). (Illus.). 80p. (gr. 4 up). 1980. PLB 5.95 (ISBN 0-396-07891-5). Dodd.

Wonders of Nature. Macmillan. (Illus.). 240p. 1981. 24.95 (ISBN 0-02-619550-X). Macmillan.

Wonders of Parasites. Philip Goldstein. LC 69-15171. (Illus.). (gr. 5-10). 1969. 4.25 o.p. (ISBN 0-8313-0064-7); PLB 6.19 (ISBN 0-685-13791-0). Lantern.

Wonders of Pigs. Sigmund A Lavine & Vincent Scuro. (Wonders Ser.). (Illus.). 80p. (gr. 4 up). 1981. PLB 6.95 (ISBN 0-396-07943-1). Dodd.

Wonders of Prairie Dogs. G. Earl Chace. LC 76-12510. (Wonders Ser.). (gr. 5 up). 1976. 5.95 o.p. (ISBN 0-396-07366-2). Dodd.

Wonders of Sea Horses. Anne E. Brown. LC 78-22439. (Wonder Ser.). (Illus.). (gr. 5 up). 1979. 5.95 (ISBN 0-396-07664-5). Dodd.

Wonders of Sponges. Morris Jacobson & Rosemary Pang. LC 75-38363. (Wonder Ser.). 1976. 5.95 (ISBN 0-396-07300-X). Dodd.

Wonders of Terns. Elizabeth A. Schreiber. LC 77-16862. (Wonders Ser.). (Illus.). (gr. 5 up). 1978. 5.95 (ISBN 0-396-07549-5). Dodd.

Wonders of Terrariums. Sigmund A. Lavine. LC 77-6493. (Wonders Se). (Illus.). (gr. 5 up). 1977. PLB 5.95g. (ISBN 0-396-07488-X). Dodd.

Wonders of the Age: Masterpieces of Early Safavid Painting, 1501-1576. Stuart C. Welch. LC 79-2480. 223p. 1979. pap. 12.95 (ISBN 0-916724-38-7). Fogg Art.

Wonders of the Owl World. Sigmund A. Lavine. LC 77-143288. (gr. 3-7). 1971. PLB 5.95 (ISBN 0-396-06321-7). Dodd.

Wonders of the Seasons. Bertha M. Parker. (gr. 3-6). 1974. PLB 7.15 o.p. (ISBN 0-307-60477-2, Golden Pr). Western Pub.

Wonders of the World. Ronald Clark. LC 79-27835. (Illus.). 96p. 1980. 11.95 (ISBN 0-668-04932-4, 4932-4). Arco.

Wonders of Wild Ducks. Thomas D. Fegely. LC 75-11443. (Wonders Ser.). (Illus.). 80p. (gr. 3-7). 1975. PLB 5.95 (ISBN 0-396-07226-7). Dodd.

Wonders: Writings & Drawings for the Child in Us All. Ed. by Jonathan Cott & Mary Gimbel. LC 80-17146. (Rolling Stone Press Book). (Illus.). 1980. 17.95 (ISBN 0-671-40053-3). Summit Bks.

Wonderworks: Science Fiction & Fantasy Art. Michael Whelan. Ed. by Polly Freas & Kelly Freas. LC 79-12575. (Illus.). 1979. 13.95 (ISBN 0-915442-75-2, Starblaze); pap. 7.95 (ISBN 0-915442-74-4, Starblaze); collector's edition 30.00 (ISBN 0-915442-83-3). Donning Co.

Wondrous Cross. Mary M. Kasapor. 1980. 6.95 (ISBN 0-533-04596-7). Vantage.

Wood. Robert Summitt & Alan Sliker. (CRC Handbook of Materials Science: Vol. IV). 464p. 1980. 59.95 (ISBN 0-8493-0234-X). CRC Pr.

Wood: An Ancient Fuel with a New Future. Nigel Smith. LC 80-54881. (Worlwatch Papers). 1981. pap. 2.00 (ISBN 0-916468-41-0). Worldwatch Inst.

Wood & Cellulose Science. A. J. Stamm. (Illus.). 1964. 30.50 (ISBN 0-8260-8495-8, Pub. by Wiley-Interscience). Wiley.

Wood & Wood Grains: A Photographic Album for Artists & Designers. Phil Brodatz. (Illus.). 8.75 (ISBN 0-8446-0040-7). Peter Smith.

Wood As a Raw Material. G. Tsoumis. 1968. 19.00 o.p. (ISBN 0-08-012378-3). Pergamon.

Wood As an Industrial Arts Material. Wayne K. Murphey & Richard Jorgensen. 1974. text ed. 21.00 (ISBN 0-08-017906-1); pap. text ed. 12.75 (ISBN 0-08-017907-X). Pergamon.

Wood As Building & Hobby Material: How to Use Lumber & Wood-Base Panels & Wood Wisely in Construction, for Furniture, & As Fuel. Hans Kubler. LC 80-13380. 256p. 1980. 19.95 (ISBN 0-471-05390-2, Pub. by Wiley-Interscience). Wiley.

Wood Beyond the World. William Morris. (Facsimile of the Kelmscott Press Edition). Repr. of 1894 ed. 9.00 (ISBN 0-8446-4589-3). Peter Smith.

Wood Book: An Entertaining, Interesting, & Even Useful Compendium of Facts, Notions, Opinions, & Sentiments About Wood... & Its Growing, Cutting, Woodworking & Burning. Jan Adkins. 1980. pap. 9.95 (ISBN 0-316-01082-0). Little.

Wood Burning for Power. Ed. by Ellen M. Leonard. 135p. 1980. pap. 14.95 (ISBN 0-89934-048-2, B048-PP). Solar Energy Info.

Wood-Burning Stove Book. Geri Harrington. LC 77-7401. (Illus.). 1977. pap. 9.95 (ISBN 0-02-080250-1, Collier). Macmillan.

Wood Carvers of Cordova, New Mexico: Social Dimensions of an Artistic "Revival". Charles L. Briggs. LC 79-20883. 1980. 19.95 (ISBN 0-87049-275-6). U of Tenn Pr.

Wood Carving. Boy Scouts Of America. LC 19-600. (Illus.). 48p. (gr. 6-12). 1966. pap. 0.70x (ISBN 0-8395-3315-2, 3315). BSA.

Wood Carving. rev. ed. William Wheeler & Charles H. Hayward. (Illus.). 1979. pap. 5.95 (ISBN 0-8069-8790-1). Sterling.

Wood Carving & Whittling for Everyone. Franklin H. Gottshall. LC 77-23224. (Illus.). 1977. 12.95 o.p. (ISBN 0-684-14886-2, ScribT). Scribner.

Wood Carving & Whittling for Everyone. Franklin H. Gottshall. LC 77-23224. (Illus.). 1980. pap. 9.95 (SL 921, ScribT). Scribner.

Wood Carving & Whittling Made Easy. Franklin H. Gottshall. 1963. 9.95 (ISBN 0-02-544860-9). Macmillan.

Wood Construction. B. A. Richardson. 1978. text ed. 30.00x (ISBN 0-904406-14-8, Construction Pr). Longman.

Wood Engravings of Joan Hassall. Ruari McLean. LC 80-6193. (Illus.). 120p. 1981. pap. 7.95 (ISBN 0-8052-0675-2). Schocken.

Wood Finishing. J. W. Collier. 1967. 13.75 (ISBN 0-08-011242-0). Pergamon.

Wood Finishing. Harry R. Jeffrey. (gr. 9-12). 1957. pap. text ed. 6.56 (ISBN 0-87002-012-9). Bennett IL.

Wood Finishing. rev. ed. F. N. Vanderwalker. LC 76-21190. (Illus.). 408p. 1980. pap. 6.95 (ISBN 0-8069-8798-7). Sterling.

Wood Finishing-Plain & Decorative. F. N. Vanderwalker. LC 76-21190. (Illus.). 1970. 9.95 o.p. (ISBN 0-87749-024-4); pap. 6.95 o.p. (ISBN 0-8069-8798-7). Sterling.

Wood for Wood-carvers & Craftsmen. Robert L. Butler. LC 73-10513. (Illus.). 192p. 1975. 12.00 (ISBN 0-498-01376-6); pap. 4.95 o.p. (ISBN 0-498-02048-7). A S Barnes.

Wood Furniture: Finishing, Refinishing, Repairing. James E. Brumbaugh. LC 73-91640. (Illus.). 352p. 1974. 9.95 (ISBN 0-672-23216-2). Audel.

Wood Heat Is Yours for the Axing. Harold O. Fichter. (Illus.). 1980. pap. 4.00 (ISBN 0-918424-02-X). Menaid.

Wood Houses for Country Living. L. O. Anderson. LC 77-6213. (Illus.). 1977. pap. 5.95 o.p. (ISBN 0-8069-8800-2). Sterling.

Wood Houses: Form in Rural Architecture. Werner Blaser. (Illus.). 216p. (Eng., Fr. & Ger.). 1980. text ed. 19.00 (ISBN 0-89192-300-4). Interbk Inc.

Wood Laminating. rev. ed. J. Hugh Capron. (gr. 11-12). 1972. 14.00 (ISBN 0-87345-046-9). McKnight.

Wood: Materials & Processes. rev. ed. John L. Feirer. (gr. 7-12). 1980. text ed. 17.28 (ISBN 0-87002-307-1); student guide 4.44 (ISBN 0-87002-179-6). Bennett IL.

Wood: Materials & Processes. John L. Feirer. 587p. (gr. 7-12). 1975. text ed. 15.96 o.p. (ISBN 0-87002-126-5); wkbk. 4.44 o.p. (ISBN 0-87002-179-6). Bennett IL.

Wood Materials & Processes. John L. Feirer. (Illus.). 592p. 1976. 27.50 (ISBN 0-684-14803-X, ScribT). Scribner.

Wood, Metal & Plastic: A Creative Introduction to Methods & Materials. Ed. by Saul Lapidus. (Illus.). 1978. 12.50 o.p. (ISBN 0-679-50757-4); pap. 6.95 o.p. (ISBN 0-679-50808-2). McKay.

Wood Projects for the Garden. LC 76-29251. (Illus.). 1977. 4.95 (ISBN 0-917102-31-2). Ortho.

Wood Projects for the Home. Ron Hildebrand. Ed. by Ortho Books Editorial Staff. LC 80-66343. (Illus.). 96p. (Orig.). 1981. pap. 4.95 (ISBN 0-917102-85-1). Ortho.

Wood Shed. Rayner Heppenstall. 1980. pap. 4.95 (ISBN 0-7145-0616-8). Riverrun NY.

Wood Stove Cookery. Pamela G. Wubben. 50p. 1981. pap. 3.75 (ISBN 0-935442-05-7). One Percent.

Wood Stove Handbook. Wilburn W. Newcomb. LC 78-57170. 1978. pap. 7.95 (ISBN 0-672-23319-3). Audel.

Wood Stoves. Sunset Editors. LC 79-88160. (Illus.). 96p. 1979. pap. 4.95 (ISBN 0-376-01882-8, Sunset Bks). Sunset-Lane.

Wood Technology. Glenn E. Baker & L. Dayle Yeager. LC 72-83817. 1974. 20.95 (ISBN 0-672-20917-9); student's manual 6.95 (ISBN 0-672-97107-0). Bobbs.

Wood Technology Student's Manual. L. Dayle Yeager & Glenn E. Baker. 176p. 1977. pap. text ed. 6.95 (ISBN 0-672-97107-0). Bobbs.

Woodall's Nineteen Eighty-One Sunbelt Retirement Directory. 1981. pap. 6.95 (ISBN 0-671-41536-0). Woodall.

Woodall's RV How to Guide. Date not set. pap. 4.95 (ISBN 0-671-25520-7). Woodall.

Woodall's RV Owner's Handbook, Vol. 1. 4.95 (ISBN 0-671-24614-3). Woodall.

Woodall's RV Owner's Handbook, Vol. 2. 4.95 (ISBN 0-671-25163-5). Woodall.

Woodblock Cutting & Printing. Manly Banister. LC 76-19813. (Illus.). (YA) 1976. 7.95 o.p. (ISBN 0-8069-5374-8); PLB 7.49 o.p. (ISBN 0-8069-5375-6). Sterling.

Woodburn Grange. William Howitt. Ed. by Robert L. Wolff. LC 75-1511. (Victorian Fiction Ser.). 1975. Repr. of 1867 ed. lib. bdg. 66.00 (ISBN 0-8240-1585-1). Garland Pub.

Woodburner's Encyclopedia. Jay Shelton. (Orig.). 1980. pap. write for info. (ISBN 0-440-59652-1). Dell.

Woodburning Stove Book. Geri Harrington. 1977. 14.95 (ISBN 0-02-548440-0). Macmillan.

Woodcarver's Primer. John Upton. LC 73-4345. (Illus.). 210p. 1979. 9.95 o.p. (ISBN 0-8069-8786-3); pap. 6.95 (ISBN 0-8069-8788-X). Sterling.

Woodcarving. William Wheeler & Charles Hayward. LC 74-6469. (Drake Home Craftsman Ser.). (Illus.). 124p. 1972. 8.95 o.p. (ISBN 0-8069-8793-6); pap. 5.95 (ISBN 0-8069-8790-1). Sterling.

Woodcolliers & Charcoal Burning. Lyn Armstrong. 96p. 1980. pap. 6.95x (ISBN 0-905259-05-X, Pub. by Coach Pub Hse England). Intl Schol Bk Serv.

Woodcutter's Companion: A Guide to Locating, Cutting, Transporting & Storing Your Own Firewood. Maurice Cohen. Ed. by Amy Rowland. (Illus.). 160p. (Orig.). 1981. 11.95 (ISBN 0-87857-328-3); pap. 7.95 (ISBN 0-87857-329-1). Rodale Pr Inc.

Woodcutter's Duck. Krystyna Turska. LC 72-85763. (Illus.). 32p. (gr. k-3). 1973. 5.95g o.s.i. (ISBN 0-02-789540-8). Macmillan.

Woodcutters of the Netherlands in the Fifteenth Century. William M. Conway. 1970. Repr. of 1884 ed. text ed. 31.50x (ISBN 90-6004-034-1). Humanities.

Wooden & Brick Buildings with Details. A. J. Bicknell. (Architecture & Decorative Art Ser.). 1977. Repr. of 1875 ed. 75.00 (ISBN 0-306-70832-9). Da Capo.

Wooden Boat Construction. Ron Jurd. (Questions & Answers Ser.). (Illus.). 92p. (Orig.). 1979. pap. 7.50 (ISBN 0-408-00315-4). Transatlantic.

Wooden Gong: A Novel. Ntieyong U. Akpan. (Orig.). 1965. pap. text ed. 2.00x (ISBN 0-582-64012-1). Humanities.

Wooden Leg: A Warrior Who Fought Custer. Tr. by Thomas B. Marquis. LC 31-10067. (Illus.). 1962. pap. 3.50 (ISBN 0-8032-5124-6, BB 126, Bison). U of Nebr Pr.

Wooden Man. Max Bollinger. LC 74-1141. (Illus.). 24p. (ps-3). 1974. 6.95 (ISBN 0-395-28769-3, Clarion). HM.

Wooden Planes in 19th Century America. 2nd ed. (Illus.). 1978. 28.00 o.p. (ISBN 0-913602-26-4). K Roberts.

Wooden-Sharman Method: A Guide to Winning Basketball. John Wooden et al. (Illus.). 128p. 1975. 9.95 o.s.i. (ISBN 0-02-631300-6). Macmillan.

Wooden Shepherdess: The Human Predicament, 2. Richard Hughes. LC 76-181656. 400p. 1973. 10.00 o.s.i. (ISBN 0-06-011986-1, HarpT). Har-Row.

Wooden Toys. Ed. by Xenia L. Parker. LC 77-92312. (Illus.). 1978. 12.95 o.p. (ISBN 0-8015-4809-8, Hawthorn); pap. 7.95 (ISBN 0-8015-8817-0, Hawthorn). Dutton.

Woodframe Houses: Construction & Maintenance. (Illus.). 223p. 1981. pap. 7.95 (ISBN 0-8069-7512-1). Sterling.

Woodland Crafts in Britain: An Account of the Traditional Uses of Trees & Timbers in the British Countryside. new ed. Herbert L. Edlin. (Illus.). 182p. 1973. 14.95 (ISBN 0-7153-5852-9). David & Charles.

Woodland Life. G. Mandahl-Barth. (European Ecology Ser.). (Illus.). 1966. 9.95 (ISBN 0-7137-0417-9, Pub by Blandford Pr England). Sterling.

Woodlanders. Thomas Hardy. 1981. pap. 4.95 (ISBN 0-14-043153-5). Penguin.

Woodlands Around the World. Corinne J. Naden. LC 72-12712. (First Bks). (Illus.). 72p. (gr. 4-8). 1973. PLB 6.45 (ISBN 0-531-00802-9). Watts.

Woodlice. S. Sutton. (Illus.). 144p. 1980. 12.00 (ISBN 0-08-025942-1). Pergamon.

Woodrow Wilson. 3rd ed. Arthur Walworth. 1978. 19.95x (ISBN 0-393-07533-8); pap. 10.95x (ISBN 0-393-09012-4). Norton.

Woodrow Wilson: A Selected Bibliography. Laura S. Turnbull. LC 70-159106. 1971. Repr. of 1948 ed. 11.50 (ISBN 0-8046-1650-7). Kennikat.

Woodrow Wilson & the Far East: The Diplomacy of the Shantung Question. Russell H. Fifield. (Illus.). 1965. Repr. of 1952 ed. 17.50 (ISBN 0-208-00601-X, Archon). Shoe String.

Woodrow Wilson & the War Congress, 1916-18. Seward W. Livermore. LC 66-14666. Orig. Title: Politics Is Adjourned. 335p. 1968. pap. 2.95 (ISBN 0-295-78564-0, WP42). U of Wash Pr.

Woodrow Wilson, Champion of Peace. Ira Mothner. LC 69-10888. (Biography Ser). (Illus.). (gr. 7 up). 1969. PLB 5.90 o.p. (ISBN 0-531-00932-7). Watts.

Woods Practical Guide to Noise Control. 3rd ed. Ian Sharland. LC 74-181675. (Illus.). 1979. 10.00x (ISBN 0-8002-0030-6). Intl Pubns Serv.

Woodshed. Rayner Heppenstall. 1967. pap. 4.95 (ISBN 0-214-15817-9). Dufour.

Woodshed Mystery. Gertrude C. Warner. LC 62-19726. (Boxcar Children Mysteries-Pilot Bk.). (Illus.). 128p. (gr. 3-7). 6.95g (ISBN 0-8075-9206-4). A Whitman.

Woodshop Tool Maintenance. rev. ed. Beryl M. Cunningham & Wm. Holtrop. (Illus.). 296p. 1974. text ed. 18.40 (ISBN 0-87002-145-1). Bennett IL.

Woodstock. Walter Scott. 1969. 11.50x (ISBN 0-460-00072-1, Evman). Dutton.

Woodswoman. Anne Labastille. LC 75-34071. 1976. 10.95 (ISBN 0-525-23715-1); pap. 4.50 (ISBN 0-525-47504-4). Dutton.

Woodsy Owl & the Trail Bikers. Graham Kennon. (Illus.). 24p. (gr. k-3). 1976. PLB 5.00 (ISBN 0-307-60107-2, Golden Pr). Western Pub.

Woodturner's Bible. Percy Blandford. (Illus.). 1979. 15.95 (ISBN 0-8306-9820-5); pap. 9.95 (ISBN 0-8306-1044-8, 1044). TAB Bks.

Woodturning. Eldon Rebhorn. (gr. 9-12). 1970. text ed. 13.28 (ISBN 0-87345-047-7). McKnight.

Woodturning for Pleasure. Gordon Stokes. (Illus.). 128p. 1980. 12.95 (ISBN 0-13-962563-1, Spec); pap. 4.95 (ISBN 0-13-962555-0). P-H.

Woodwind Anthology. (Illus.). 1980. 37.00 (ISBN 0-686-15891-1). Instrumentalist Co.

Woodwind Ensemble. Himie Voxman & Lyle Merriman. 18.00 (ISBN 0-686-15887-3). Instrumentalist Co.

Woodwind Solo. Himie Voxman & Lyle Merriman. 18.00 (ISBN 0-686-15888-1). Instrumentalist Co.

Woodwinds: Fundamental Performance Techniques. Gene A. Saucier. LC 80-5223. (Illus.). 300p. 1981. pap. text ed. 12.95 (ISBN 0-02-872300-7). Schirmer Bks.

Woodwork. Boy Scouts Of America. LC 19-600. (Illus.). 48p. (gr. 6-12). 1970. pap. 0.70x (ISBN 0-8395-3316-0, 3316). BSA.

Woodwork of Greek Roofs. A. Trevor Hodge. (Cambridge Classical Studies). 1960. 17.95 (ISBN 0-521-05280-7). Cambridge U Pr.

Woodwork Projects & Design. Ian Punter. (Illus.). 96p. 1981. 14.95 (ISBN 0-7134-3549-6, Pub. by Batsford England). David & Charles.

Woodworker Annual, Vol. 83. (Illus.). 772p. 1979. 25.00x (ISBN 0-85242-713-1). Intl Pubns Serv.

Woodworking. Frank Jackson. LC 68-121944. (Pegasus Books: No. 7). (Illus.). 1966. 10.50x (ISBN 0-234-77878-4). Intl Pubns Serv.

Woodworking. Los Angeles Unified School District. Ed. by Richard A. Vorndran. LC 77-73286. 96p. (gr. 7-9). 1978. pap. text ed. 4.40 (ISBN 0-02-820400-X). Glencoe.

Woodworking. McKnight Staff Members & Wilbur R. Miller. LC 78-53386. (Basic Industrial Arts Ser.). (Illus.). 1978. 6.00 (ISBN 0-87345-791-9); softbound 4.48 (ISBN 0-87345-783-8). McKnight.

Woodworking. Willis H. Wagner. LC 77-89985. (Illus.). 1978. text ed. 4.80 (ISBN 0-87006-257-3). Goodheart.

Woodworking & Furniture Making. G. W. Endacott. (Drake Home Craftman Ser.). (Illus.). 1976. pap. 5.95 (ISBN 0-8069-8804-5). Sterling.

Woodworking Basics. J. H. Douglass. 320p. 1980. 14.95 (ISBN 0-442-23152-0). Van Nos Reinhold.

Woodworking for Cave Dwellers. Charles C. Burke. (Illus.). 1978. pap. 6.95 (ISBN 0-8306-1022-7, 1022). TAB Bks.

Woodworking for Industry. Feirer. 1979. text ed. 19.28 (ISBN 0-87002-242-3); wkbk. 5.28 (ISBN 0-87002-300-4). Bennett IL.

Woodworking Projects. 2nd ed. Sunset Editors. LC 75-6222. (Illus.). 96p. 1975. pap. 3.95 (ISBN 0-376-04884-0, Sunset Bks.). Sunset-Lane.

Woodworking Projects for the Home. Popular Science Authors. LC 73-86629. (Popular Science Ser). (Illus.). 312p. 1974. 12.95 o.s.i. (ISBN 0-06-013394-5, HarpT). Har-Row.

Woodworking Projects You Can Build. Better Homes & Gardens. 1980. 4.95 (ISBN 0-696-00325-2). BH&G.

Woodworking Techniques: Joints & Their Applications. R. J. DeChristoforo. (Illus.). 1979. ref.ed. 16.95 (ISBN 0-8359-8785-X). Reston.

Woodworking Technology. rev. ed. James J. Hammond et al. (Illus.). (gr. 10-12). 1980. text ed. 17.28 (ISBN 0-87345-893-1); study guide 5.20 (ISBN 0-87345-894-X); ans. key avail. (ISBN 0-87345-895-8). McKnight.

Woodworking Workbook. rev. ed. Talmage Nichols & Harold Stiles. (gr. 9-12). 1971. pap. 3.40 (ISBN 0-87002-105-2); ans sheet avail. (ISBN 0-685-00121-0). Bennett IL.

Woody Allen. Myles Palmer. (Illus.). 128p. 1980. pap. 6.95 (ISBN 0-906071-39-9). Proteus Pub NY.

Woody Allen: Clown Prince of American Humor. Bill Adler & Jeffrey Feinman. (Illus.). 192p. (Orig.). 1975. pap. 1.75 o.p. (ISBN 0-523-00786-8). Pinnacle Bks.

Woody Guthrie & Me: An Intimate Reminiscence. Ed Robbin. (Illus.). 1980. pap. 6.95 (ISBN 0-89581-015-8). Lancaster-Miller.

Woody Plants of Ohio. E. L. Braun. 1969. 35.00 (ISBN 0-02-841890-5). Hafner.

Woody Woodpecker Takes a Trip. Ann McGovern. (Illus.). (gr. k-3). 1976. PLB 5.00 (ISBN 0-307-60445-4, Golden Pr). Western Pub.

Woody Woodpecker: The Pirate Treasure. 24p. (ps-2). 1977. 1.95 (ISBN 0-307-10505-9, Golden Pr); PLB 7.15 o.p. (ISBN 0-307-60550-7). Western Pub.

Woof! Danae Dobson. 1979. 4.95 (ISBN 0-8499-0142-1). Word Bks.

Wool & String. (MacDonald Educational Ser.). (Illus., Arabic.). 3.50 (ISBN 0-686-53100-0). Intl Bk Ctr.

Wool-Bag Book. Margaret Hutchings. (Make & Play Ser.). (Illus.). 48p. (gr. 5-6). 1976. pap. 1.50 (ISBN 0-263-05911-1). Transatlantic.

Wool Handbook. 3rd ed. Ed. by Werner Von Bergen. LC 63-11600. (Illus.). 1963-70. 77.50 ea. Vol. 2, Pt. 1 (ISBN 0-471-91015-5). Vol. 2, Pt. 2 (ISBN 0-471-91016-3, Pub. by Wiley-Interscience). Wiley.

Woolen Industry of the Midwest. Norman L. Crockett. LC 75-111505. (Illus.). 176p. 1970. 10.50x (ISBN 0-8131-1195-1). U Pr of Ky.

Worcester Porcelain & Lund's Bristol. 2nd ed. Franklin A. Barrett. 1966. 25.00 (ISBN 0-571-06739-5, Pub. by Faber & Faber). Merrimack Bk Serv.

Worchestershire. Canon Leatherbarrow. (Batsford Britain Ser.). (Illus.). 1974. 8.95 o.p. (ISBN 0-8038-8068-5). Hastings.

Worchestershire: A Shell Guide. J. Lees-Milne. (Illus.). 1964. 12.95 (ISBN 0-571-05936-8, Pub. by Faber & Faber). Merrimack Bk Serv.

Word. Agnes Lawless & Eadie Goodboy. (Aglow Bible Study Bk.: No. E-4). (Illus.). 64p. (Orig.). 1980. pap. 1.95 (ISBN 0-930756-59-2, 4220-E4). Women's Aglow.

Word! Ed. by Mark Soppeland. (Illus.). 120p. (Orig.). 1980. pap. 6.95 (ISBN 0-913232-60-2). W Kaufmann.

Word. (Aglow Bible Study: Bk. E-4). 64p. 1980. pap. 1.95 (ISBN 0-930756-59-2, 4220-E4). Women's Aglow.

Word at World's End. Francis Brabazon. 88p. 1971. 5.95 (ISBN 0-686-05767-8); pap. 2.95 (ISBN 0-686-05768-6). Meher Baba Info.

Word Attack & Spelling: An Audio Tutorial. A. Raygor & R. Scnmelzer. 1981. 250.00 (ISBN 0-13-963215-8); student wkbk. 7.95 (ISBN 0-13-963223-9). P-H.

Word Attack Skills. John Ireland. LC 77-82988. (Teaching 5 to 13 Reading Ser.). (Illus.). 1977. pap. text ed. 6.95 (ISBN 0-356-05055-6). Raintree Child.

Word Becoming Flesh. Horace Hummel. 1979. 20.95 (ISBN 0-570-03273-3, 15-2718). Concordia.

Word Bird's Circus Surprise. Jane B. Moncure. LC 80-29528. (Word Birds for Early Birds Ser.). (Illus.). 32p. (gr. k-2). 1981. PLB 5.50 (ISBN 0-89565-162-9). Childs World.

Word-by-Word Translations of Songs & Arias, Pt. 1: German & French. Berton Coffin et al. LC 66-13746. 1966. 17.50 (ISBN 0-8108-0149-3). Scarecrow.

Word-by-Word Translations of Songs & Arias, Pt. 2: Italian. Arthur Schoep & Daniel Harris. LC 66-13746. (A Companion to The Singer's Repertoire). 1972. 21.00 (ISBN 0-8108-0463-8). Scarecrow.

Word Clowns & Sentence Circuses. James N. Blake. (Illus.). 48p. 1973. pap. 5.75 (ISBN 0-398-02790-0). C C Thomas.

Word Clues. Amsel Greene. (Honor Groups). (gr. 11-12). 1962. text ed. 6.32 (ISBN 0-06-538011-8, SchDept); study guide 1.44 (ISBN 0-06-538203-X). Har-Row.

Word Comprehension & Paragraph Exercises C. (gr. 1-3). 1972. pap. text ed. 0.50 incl. tchrs' manual (ISBN 0-8449-1972-1). Learning Line.

Word Comprehension & Paragraph Exercises F. (gr. 4-6). 1972. pap. text ed. 1.00 incl. tchrs' manual (ISBN 0-8449-1974-8). Learning Line.

Word Controlled Humans. John Harland. LC 80-52563. 120p. 1981. 8.95 (ISBN 0-914752-13-8); pap. 5.00 (ISBN 0-914752-12-X). Sovereign Pr.

Word Fitly Spoken. Kenneth G. Mills. 1980. 14.95 (ISBN 0-686-64679-7); pap. 7.95 (ISBN 0-919842-05-4). Sun-Scape Pubns.

Word for Word. Edward C. Pinkerton. LC 77-20391. Date not set. price not set (ISBN 0-930454-06-5, Dist. by Stein & Day). Verbatim. Postponed.

Word for Word: The Rewriting of Fiction. Wallace Hildick. 1966. pap. 2.95x (ISBN 0-393-09674-2, NortonC). Norton.

Word for World Is Forest. Ursula K. Le Guin. LC 75-37085. (YA) 1976. 6.95 o.p. (ISBN 0-399-11716-4, Dist. by Putnam). Berkley Pub.

Word Frequencies of Spoken American English. Hartvig Dahl. LC 80-116646. 1980. 60.00 (ISBN 0-930454-07-3). Verbatim.

Word Frequency in Newspaper Bengali. Jack A. Dabbs. LC 66-64723. 1966. 3.00 (ISBN 0-911494-04-9). Dabbs.

Word from Our Sponsor. Judie Angell. (gr. 7 up). 1981. pap. 1.75 (ISBN 0-440-99525-6, LE). Dell.

Word from Our Sponsor: Or My Friend Alfred. Judie Angell. LC 78-25716. (gr. 5-7). 1979. 8.95 (ISBN 0-87888-142-5). Bradbury Pr.

Word Geography of California & Nevada. Elizabeth S. Bright. (U. C. Publ. in Linguistics: Vol. 69). 1971. pap. 8.50x (ISBN 0-520-09367-4). U of Cal Pr.

Word Geography of the Eastern United States. Hans Kurath. 1949. pap. 7.95x (ISBN 0-472-08532-8). U of Mich Pr.

Word in Stone: The Role of Architecture in the Nationalist Socialist Ideology. Robert R. Taylor. (Illus.). 1974. 25.00x (ISBN 0-520-02193-2). U of Cal Pr.

Word in Worship. William Skudlarek. LC 80-25525. (Abingdon Preacher's Library). 128p. (Orig.). 1981. pap. 4.95 (ISBN 0-687-46131-6). Abingdon.

Word-Index to a Week on the Concord & Merrimack Rivers. James Karabatsos. LC 80-2510. 1981. Repr. of 1971 ed. 18.50 (ISBN 0-404-19058-8). AMS Pr.

Word Index to Walden, Turth Textual Notes. J. Stephen Sherwin. LC 80-2517. 1981. Repr. of 1960 ed. 24.50 (ISBN 0-404-19065-0). AMS Pr.

Word Information Processing Concepts: Careers Technology, & Applications. Marly Bergerud & Jean Gonzalez. 512p. 1981. text ed. 16.95 (ISBN 0-471-08499-9). Wiley.

Word into Silence. John Main. 96p. 1981. pap. 3.95 (ISBN 0-8091-2369-X). Paulist Pr.

Word Irony & Its Context: 1500-1755. Norman D. Knox. LC 60-13606. 1961. 14.75 o.p. (ISBN 0-8223-0100-8). Duke.

Word List to James Joyce's "Exiles". Ruth Bauerle. LC 80-8487. 240p. 1981. lib. bdg. 40.00 (ISBN 0-8240-9500-6). Garland Pub.

Word Machine, 3 vols. Joyce M. Burkes. LC 79-67050. 1979. Set. 4.95. Bk. I (ISBN 0-931218-02-0). Bk. II (ISBN 0-931218-03-9). Bk. III (ISBN 0-931218-04-7). Liberty Pub.

Word Machine, Bk. 1. rev ed. Joyce M. Burkes. LC 79-67050. (Illus.). (gr. k-1). 1978. pap. 4.95 (ISBN 0-931218-02-0, 1001). Joybug.

Word Machine, Bk. 2. Joyce M. Burkes. LC 79-67050. (Illus.). (gr. 2-4). 1979. pap. 4.95 (ISBN 0-931218-03-9, 1002). Joybug.

Word Machine, Bk. 3. Joyce M. Burkes. LC 79-67050. (Illus., Orig.). (gr. 2-6). 1979. pap. 4.95 (ISBN 0-931218-04-7, 1003). Joybug.

Word Mastery Made Simple. Arthur Waldhorn & Arthur Zeiger. pap. 3.50 (ISBN 0-385-01213-6, Made). Doubleday.

Word Music & Word Magic: Children's Literature Methods. James A. Smith & Dorothy M. Park. 1977. text ed. 17.80 (ISBN 0-205-05587-7, 2255871). Allyn.

Word of the Lord Grows. Martin H. Franzmann. 1961. 10.95 (ISBN 0-570-03222-9, 15-1861). Concordia.

Word of Truth. Dale Moody. 624p. 1981. 24.95 (ISBN 0-8028-3533-3). Eerdmans.

Word Origins & Their Romantic Stories. Wilfred Funk. LC 50-42316. (Funk & W Bk.). (gr. 9-12). 1950. text ed. 6.95 o.s.i. (ISBN 0-308-40069-0, TYC-T); pap. 4.75 o.s.i. (ISBN 0-308-90048-0, F39, TYC-T). T Y Crowell.

Word Perception for Teachers. 3rd ed. Sterl Artley. (Lucas Text Ser). 1978. text ed. 2.75x saddle stitched (ISBN 0-87543-141-0). Lucas.

Word Politics: Verbal Strategy Among the Superpowers. Thomas M. Franck & Edward Weisband. 1971. 12.95 (ISBN 0-19-501460-X); pap. 4.95x (ISBN 0-19-501459-6). Oxford U Pr.

Word Power. 1980. pap. 2.50 (ISBN 0-425-04721-0). Berkley Pub.

Word Power Made Easy. Norman Lewis. pap. 2.95 (ISBN 0-671-42416-5). PB.

Word Power Made Easy: The Complete Handbook for Building a Bigger & Better Vocabulary. Norman Lewis. LC 77-14894. 1978. 10.95 o.p. (ISBN 0-385-14085-1). Doubleday.

Word Processing. Bettie H. Ellis. (Concepts & Applications). (Illus.). 48p. 1980. 7.48 (ISBN 0-07-019242-1, G). McGraw.

Word Processing. 2nd ed. A. Rosen & R. Freiden. 1981. 15.95 (ISBN 0-13-963488-6). P-H.

Word Processing. A. Rosen & R. Freiden. 1977. text ed. 16.95 (ISBN 0-13-963504-1). P-H.

Word Processing: A Guide to Typography, Taste & in-House Graphics. Rod Van Uchelen. 128p. 1980. 14.95 (ISBN 0-442-28647-3); pap. 7.95 (ISBN 0-442-28646-5). Van Nos Reinhold.

Word Processing & Text Editing. John Zarrella. LC 80-114189. (Microprocessor Software Engineering Concepts Ser.). (Illus.). 1980. pap. 7.95 (ISBN 0-935230-01-7). Microcomputer Appns.

Word Processing: Concepts & Careers. Marly Bergerud & Jean Gonzalez. LC 77-15794. (Word Processing Ser.). 1978. pap. text ed. 13.95 (ISBN 0-471-02748-0); tchrs. manual 2.95 (ISBN 0-471-03778-8). Wiley.

Word Processing: Concepts & Careers. 2nd ed. Marly Bergerud & Jean Gonzalez. (Wiley Word Processing Ser.). 256p. 1981. text ed. 14.95 (ISBN 0-471-06010-0); write for info. tchrs'. ed. (ISBN 0-471-09093-X); write for info. resource manual (ISBN 0-471-09093-X). Wiley.

Word Processing: Current Practices & Future Developments. 300p. (Orig.). 1980. pap. text ed. 80.00x (ISBN 0-903796-55-4, Pub. by Online Conferences England). Renouf.

Word Processing Equipment Survey. Derek Skelcher. 222p. (Orig.). 1980. pap. 125.00x (ISBN 0-903796-56-2, Pub. by Online Conferences England). Renouf.

Word Processing in the Modern Office. 2nd ed. P. B. Cecil. 1980. pap. 10.95 (ISBN 0-8053-1758-9); instrs manual 3.95 (ISBN 0-8053-1760-0); student wkbk 3.95 (ISBN 0-8053-1761-9). A-W.

Word Processing in the Modern Office: Student Workbook. Paula B. Cecil. 1980. 3.95 o.p. (ISBN 0-8053-1761-9). Benjamin Cummings.

Word Processing Markets, Where? Why?, G-050. Ed. by Business Communications. 1979. 650.00 (ISBN 0-89336-216-6). BCC.

Word Processing: Operations, Applications, & Administration. Walter Kleinschrod et al. LC 79-13613. 1980. 19.95 (ISBN 0-672-97270-0); tchrs. manual 3.33 (ISBN 0-672-97271-9). Bobbs.

Word Processing: Selection, Implementation & Uses. Ed. by Online Conference, Ltd. 1979. text ed. 63.50x (ISBN 0-903796-32-5). Renouf.

Word Processing Systems Manual for Support Staff. Gladys O. Hansen. (Illus.). 1980. pap. text ed. 22.50 (ISBN 0-936512-01-6). Telecom Lib.

Word Processing Systems Manual (1) for Originators & Support Staff. & for Support Staff. Gladys O. Hansen. (Illus., Orig.). 1980. pap. text ed. 40.00 set (ISBN 0-936512-02-4). Telecom Lib.

Word Processing Users' Manual. Thomas J. Anderson & William R. Trotter. LC 73-94097. 1976. pap. 10.95 (ISBN 0-8144-5424-0). Am Mgmt.

Word Processors: A Programmed Training Guide with Practical Applications. N. Kathryn Layman & Adrienne G. Renner. (Illus.). 352p. 1981. text ed. 19.95 (ISBN 0-13-963520-3). P-H.

Word Shadows of the Great: The Lure of Autograph Collecting. Thomas F. Madigan. LC 70-145705. (Illus.). 1971. Repr. of 1930 ed. 20.00 (ISBN 0-8103-3378-3). Gale.

Word Studies in the Greek New Testament, for the English Reader, 16 bks. Kenneth S. Wuest. Incl. Bk. 1. Golden Nuggets. pap. 2.25 (ISBN 0-8028-1242-2); Bk. 2. Bypaths. pap. 2.95 (ISBN 0-8028-1318-6); Bk. 3. Treasures. pap. 2.95 (ISBN 0-8028-1243-0); Bk. 4. Untranslatable Riches. pap. 2.25 (ISBN 0-8028-1241-4); Bk. 5. Studies in Vocabulary. pap. 2.45 (ISBN 0-8028-1240-6); Bk. 6. Great Truths to Live by. pap. 3.45 (ISBN 0-8028-1246-5); Bk. 7. Mark. pap. 3.95 (ISBN 0-8028-1230-9); Bk. 8. Romans. pap. 3.95 (ISBN 0-8028-1231-7); Bk. 9. Galatians. pap. 2.95 (ISBN 0-8028-1232-5); Bk. 10. Ephesians & Colossians. pap. 3.95 (ISBN 0-8028-1233-3); Bk. 11. Philippians. pap. 2.25 (ISBN 0-8028-1234-1); Bk. 12. Pastoral Epistles. pap. 3.95 (ISBN 0-8028-1236-8); Bk. 13. Hebrews. pap. 2.95 (ISBN 0-8028-1235-X); Bk. 14. First Peter. pap. 2.45 (ISBN 0-8028-1237-6); Bk. 15. In These Last Days. pap. 3.95 (ISBN 0-8028-1238-4); Bk. 16. Prophetic Light in the Present Darkness. pap. 2.95 (ISBN 0-8028-1239-2). Set. 50.00 (ISBN 0-8028-2280-0). Eerdmans.

Word Studies in the New Testament, 4 Vols. Marvin Vincent. 1957. 42.50 (ISBN 0-8028-8083-5). Eerdmans.

Word to the Wise. Hudson T. Armerding. 1980. pap. 3.95 (ISBN 0-8423-0099-6). Tyndale.

Word Watchers' Handbook: A Deletionary of the Most Abused & Misused Words. Phyllis Martin. LC 76-12741. 1976. 7.95 o.p. (ISBN 0-679-20354-0); pap. 3.95 o.p. (ISBN 0-679-20369-9). McKay.

Wordarrows: Indians & Whites in the New Fur Trade. Gerald Vizenor. LC 78-3202. xiv, 164p. 1981. pap. 6.95 (ISBN 0-8166-0862-8). U of Minn Pr.

Wordplay & Poetry. Ernest C. Tate. LC 80-52182. 1981. 5.95 (ISBN 0-533-04746-3). Vantage.

Words. Selma Chambers. (Illus.). (ps-3). 1948. PLB 5.00 (ISBN 0-307-60045-9, Golden Pr). Western Pub.

Words. Robert Creeley. LC 67-12213. (Orig.). 1967. 7.95 o.p. (ISBN 0-684-10090-8, ScribT). Scribner.

Words. Kenneth E. Hagin. 1979. mini bk. .50 (ISBN 0-89276-057-5). Hagin Ministries.

Words. Jean-Paul Sartre. 160p. 1977. pap. 1.50 o.p. (ISBN 0-449-30803-0, Prem). Fawcett.

Words - From Print to Meaning: Classroom Activities. Lou E. Burmeister. LC 74-20488. 176p. 1975. pap. text ed. 7.50 (ISBN 0-201-00770-3). A-W.

Words?! A Book About the Origins of Everyday Words & Phrases. Jane Sarnoff. (Illus.). 48p. (gr. 4-7). 1981. 8.95 (ISBN 0-686-69286-1). Scribner.

Words & Arms: A Dictionary of Security & Defense Terms with Supplementary Data. Ed. by Wolfram F. Hanrieder & Larry V. Buel. 1979. lib. bdg. 27.50x (ISBN 0-89158-383-1). Westview.

Words & Buildings. Jock Kinneir. 192p. 1981. 32.50 (ISBN 0-8230-7487-0, Whitney Lib). Watson-Guptill.

Words & Ideas. 5th ed. Hans P. Guth. 528p. 1980. text ed. 11.95x (ISBN 0-534-00815-1). Wadsworth Pub.

Words & Ideas: A Handbook for College Writing. 4th ed. Hans P. Guth. 1975. 10.95x o.p. (ISBN 0-534-00371-0). Wadsworth Pub.

Words & Idioms. Logan P. Smith. LC 77-148923. 1971. Repr. of 1925 ed. 22.00 (ISBN 0-8103-3651-0). Gale.

Words & Meanings: Essays Presented to David Winton Thomas. Ed. by Peter R. Ackroyd & Barnabas Lindars. LC 68-29649. 1968. 36.00 (ISBN 0-521-07270-0). Cambridge U Pr.

Words & Phrases Index, Vols. 1 & 3. C. Edward Wall & Edward Przebienda. LC 68-58894. 1969. 25.00 ea. Pierian.

Words & Places, or Etymological Illustrations of History, Ethnology, & Geography. 4th ed. Isaac Taylor. 1968. Repr. of 1909 ed. 20.00 (ISBN 0-8103-3240-X). Gale.

Words & Things. Roger Brown. LC 58-9395. 1968. 15.95 (ISBN 0-02-904800-1); pap. text ed. 7.95 (ISBN 0-02-904810-9). Free Pr.

Words & Things: An Examination of, & an Attack on, Linguistic Philosophy. Ernest Gellner. 1979. 24.00 (ISBN 0-7100-0260-2); pap. 12.50 (ISBN 0-7100-0285-8). Routledge & Kegan.

Words & What They Do to You: Beginning Lessons in General Semantics for Junior & Senior High School. Catherine Minteer. (gr. 7-12). text ed. 4.00x (ISBN 0-910780-06-4). Inst Gen Semantics.

Words & Works of Jesus Christ. J. Dwight Pentecost. 576p. 1981. 16.95 (ISBN 0-310-30940-9, 17015). Zondervan.

Words Are Important: Primary Level (Tan) Bk. E. H. Schuster. (gr. 4). 1975. pap. 1.48x (ISBN 0-8437-7983-7). Hammond Inc.

Words Are Important Series. E. H. Schuster. Incl. Level A (Blue) Bk. (gr. 5) (ISBN 0-8437-7985-3); Level B (Red) Bk. (gr. 6) (ISBN 0-8437-7991-8); Level C (Green) Bk. (gr. 7) (ISBN 0-8437-7980-2); Level D (Orange) Bk. (gr. 8) (ISBN 0-8437-7950-0); Level E (Purple) Bk. (gr. 9) (ISBN 0-8437-7955-1); Level F (Brown) Bk. (gr. 10) (ISBN 0-8437-7960-8); Level G (Pink) Bk. (gr. 11) (ISBN 0-8437-7965-9); Level H (Grey) Bk. (gr. 12) (ISBN 0-8437-7970-5). 1979. pap. 1.48x ea. Hammond Inc.

Words at Work. 2nd ed. Joseph Bellafiore. (gr. 10-12). 1968. pap. text ed. 4.42 (ISBN 0-87720-320-2). AMSCO Sch.

Words Every College Student Should Know. Kenneth A. Oliver. 465p. (Orig.). 1981. pap. 12.95 (ISBN 0-913244-50-3). Hapi Pr.

Words, Facts & Phrases: A Dictionary of Curious, Quaint, & Out-of-the-Way Matters. Eliezer E. Edwards. LC 68-21768. 1968. Repr. of 1881 ed. 24.00 (ISBN 0-8103-3087-3). Gale.

Words Fail Me. Philip Howard. 1981. 13.95 (ISBN 0-19-520237-6). Oxford U Pr.

Words Fitly Spoken: Reflections & Prayers. Robert H. Klenck. LC 79-13449. 1979. 7.95 (ISBN 0-396-07764-1, 07764-1, Dist. by W.W. Norton). Dembner Bks.

Words for the Wind. T. K. Doraiswamy. (Greenbird Book). 76p. 1975. 14.00 (ISBN 0-88253-676-1); pap. 6.75 (ISBN 0-88253-675-3). Ind-US Inc.

Words for Work: Writing Fundamentals for Technical-Vocational Students. Alec Ross. (Illus., Orig.). 1970. pap. text ed. 8.50 (ISBN 0-395-05333-1). HM.

Words for Writing. Hubert Thomas. (gr. 2-5). 1977. 1.75x (ISBN 0-933892-13-6). Child Focus Co.

Words from the Romance Languages. Horace C. Danner. LC 80-82095. (Clavis Ser.). (Illus.). 232p. 1980. pap. 7.00 (ISBN 0-937600-00-8). Imprimis.

Words in a Corner: Studies in Montaigne's Latin Quotations. Mary B. McKinley. (French Forum Monograraphs: No. 26). 120p. (Orig.). 1981. pap. 9.50 (ISBN 0-917058-25-9). French Forum.

Words in Our Hands. Ada B. Litchfield. Ed. by Kathleen Tucker. LC 79-28402. (Concept Bk.: Level 2). (Illus.). (gr. 2-6). 1980. 6.95g (ISBN 0-8075-9212-9). A Whitman.

Words into Rhythm. D. W. Harding. LC 76-7805. 1976. 27.50 (ISBN 0-521-21267-7). Cambridge U Pr.

Words Like Fire: Discourses on Jesus. Bhagwan S. Rajneesh. LC 80-8343. 288p. (Orig.). 1981. pap. 5.95 (ISBN 0-06-066787-7, RD 347, HarpR). Har-Row.

Words of a Believer & the Past & Future of the People. Hughes F. Lamennais. vi, 208p. 1972. Repr. of 1891 ed. 15.00 (ISBN 0-86527-212-3). Fertig.

Words of Certitude: Excerpts from His Talks & Writings As Bishop & Pope. Pope John Paul II. Tr. by Anthon Buono from It. LC 80-81440. 136p. 1980. pap. 2.95 (ISBN 0-8091-2302-9). Paulist Pr.

Words of Cheer for Daily Life. C. H. Spurgeon. pap. 2.25 (ISBN 0-686-09101-9). Pilgrim Pubns.

Words of Comfort & Cheer. Mrs. Charles E. Cowman. kivar bdg. o. p. 6.95 (ISBN 0-310-22550-7); pap. 4.95 (ISBN 0-310-22551-5). Zondervan.

Words of Jesus in Our Gospel. Stanley B. Marrow. LC 79-52105. 1979. pap. 4.95 (ISBN 0-8091-2215-4). Paulist Pr.

Words of Kukumlima. Daniel Pinkwater. LC 80-24713. (gr. 4-7). 1981. 9.95 (ISBN 0-525-43380-5). Dutton.

Words of Mercury: Shakespeare & English Mythography, of the Renaissance. Noel Purdon. (Salzburg Studies in English Literature, Elizabethan & Renaissance Studies: No. 39). (Illus.). 246p. 1974. pap. text ed. 25.00x (ISBN 0-391-01503-6). Humanities.

Words of the Lagoon: Fishing & Marine Lore in the Palau District of Micronesia. R. E. Johannes. (Illus.). 320p. 1981. 14.95x (ISBN 0-520-03929-7). U of Cal Pr.

Words of the World's Religion. Robert S. Ellwood, Jr. 1977. pap. text ed. 11.95x (ISBN 0-13-965004-0). P-H.

Words of Warning for Daily Life. C. H. Spurgeon. pap. 2.25 (ISBN 0-686-09100-0). Pilgrim Pubns.

Words of Welcome. Amy Bolding. (Preaching Helps Ser). (Orig.). 1965. pap. 2.95 (ISBN 0-8010-0550-7). Baker Bk.

Words of Wisdom for Daily Life. C. H. Spurgeon. pap. 2.25 (ISBN 0-686-09099-3). Pilgrim Pubns.

Words on Mime. Etienne Decroux. 208p. 1981. 12.00x (ISBN 0-89676-045-6). Drama Bk.

Words on Target: For Better Christian Communication. Sue Nichols. LC 63-16410. (Illus., Orig.). 1963. pap. 3.95 (ISBN 0-8042-1476-X). John Knox.

Words, Phrases, Clauses. 3rd ed. Edward J. Fox, Jr. & Malcolm T. Moore. 120p. (gr. 6-10). 1980. pap. text ed. 3.50x (ISBN 0-686-67158-9). Ind Sch Pr.

Words, Phrases, Clauses: Exercises in English Grammar. 3rd ed. Edward J. Fox & Malcolm T. Moore. 120p. (gr. 6-12). 1980. pap. text ed. 3.50 (ISBN 0-88334-128-X). Ind Sch Pr.

Words, Pictures, Media: Communication in Educational Politics. Lloyd Prentice. 91p. 1976. pap. text ed. 4.00 (ISBN 0-917754-01-8). Inst Responsive.

Words, Sounds & Thoughts: More Activities to Enrich Children's Communication Skills. Dorothy G. Hennings. LC 76-57242. 352p. 1977. text ed. 11.95 (ISBN 0-590-07522-5, Citation); pap. 5.95 (ISBN 0-590-09616-8). Schol Bk Serv.

Words to Live By. Chiara Lubich. Ed. by Hugh Moran. Tr. by Raymond Dauphinais from Fr. & Ital. LC 80-82419. Orig. Title: Paroles Pour Vivre. 160p. (Orig.). 1980. pap. 4.50 (ISBN 0-911782-08-7). New City.

Words to Live by: Chiara Lubich & Christians from All Over the World. Ed. by Hugh Moran. Tr. by Raymond Dauphinais & Hugh Moran. LC 80-82419. 1980. pap. 4.50 (ISBN 0-911782-08-7). New City.

Words to Winners of Souls. Horatius Bonar. (Summit Bks.). 1979. pap. 1.65 (ISBN 0-8010-0773-9). Baker Bk.

Words with Music: The Broadway Musical Libretto. Lehman Engel. LC 80-15412. 1981. pap. 6.95 (ISBN 0-02-870370-7). Schirmer Bks.

Words, Words, Words, Bk. 1. W. D. Sheeler & R. W. Markley. 128p. (gr. 9-12). 1981. pap. text ed. 6.95 (ISBN 0-88345-419-X, 18829). Regents Pub.

Words, Words, Words, Bk 2. W. D. Sheeler & R. W. Markley. (Words, Words, Words). 128p. (gr. 9-12). 1981. pap. text ed. 6.95 (ISBN 0-88345-449-1). Regents Pub.

Words You Need. Paul F. Fletcher & Milton Elson. 288p. (Orig.). 1981. pap. 6.00 (ISBN 0-8215-9821-X). Sadlier.

Wordsworth. Oliver Elton. 96p. 1980. Repr. of 1924 ed. 15.00 (ISBN 0-8492-0788-6). R West.

Wordsworth & Coleridge - Lyrical Ballads 1805. 2nd ed. Derek Roper. 432p. 1976. pap. 12.95 (ISBN 0-7121-0140-3, Pub. by Macdonald & Evans England). Intl Ideas.

Wordsworth & Coleridge in Their Time. A. S. Byatt. LC 73-82999. (Illus.). 288p. 1973. 19.50x (ISBN 0-8448-0040-6). Crane-Russak Co.

Wordsworth & the Great System: A Study of Wordsworth's Poetic Universe. Geoffrey H. Durrant. LC 78-92247. 1970. 34.00 (ISBN 0-521-07704-4). Cambridge U Pr.

Wordsworth Criticism Since 1952: A Bibliography. Ronald B. Hearn. (Salzburg Studies in English Literature Romantic Reassessment: No. 83). 1978. pap. text ed. 25.00x (ISBN 0-391-01402-1). Humanities.

Wordsworth Selection. Ed. by Edith C. Batho. 1962. pap. text ed. 1.75x (ISBN 0-485-61004-3, Athlone Pr). Humanities.

Wordsworth's Dirge & Promise: Napoleon, Wellington, & the Convention of Cintra. Gordon K. Thomas. LC 77-125102. 190p. 1971. 7.95x o.p. (ISBN 0-8032-0777-8). U of Nebr Pr.

Wordsworth's Philosophical Poetry, 1797-1814. John A. Hodgson. LC 79-24921. xxii, 216p. 1980. 17.50x (ISBN 0-8032-2310-2). U of Nebr Pr.

Wordtree: A Transitive Taxonomy for Solving Problems. Henry G. Burger. 360p. 1981. 87.00 (ISBN 0-936312-00-9). Wordtree.

Wordworld. Wilson H. Lane et al. (Illus.). (gr. k-3). 1976. pap. 6.99 pupil's materials (ISBN 0-87892-880-4); tchr's handbook 3.99 (ISBN 0-87892-881-2); tapes 144.30 (ISBN 0-87892-878-2); duplicating masters 4.59 (ISBN 0-87892-882-0). Economy Co.

Wordworth & the Poetry of Epitaphs. D. D. Devlin. 143p. 1980. 26.00x (ISBN 0-389-20040-9). B&N.

Work-a-Day: Your Classrookm Employment Agency. Elizabeth Marten. 59p. 1979. pap. 4.95 (ISBN 0-914634-73-9, 7919). DOK Pubs.

Work Accomplished by the Inter-American Juridical Committee During Its Regular Meeting: Held from January 14 to February 9, 1980. OAS General Secretariat. 127p. 1980. pap. text ed. 11.00 (ISBN 0-8270-1223-3). OAS.

Work, Aging, & Social Change: Professionals & the One Life-One Career Imperative. Seymour B. Sarason. LC 76-27224. 1979. pap. text ed. 7.95 (ISBN 0-02-927930-5). Free Pr.

Work Analysis & Design for Hotels, Restaurants & Institutions. 2nd ed. Edward A. Kazarian. (Illus.). 1979. text ed. 19.50 (ISBN 0-87055-317-8). AVI.

Work & Authority in Industry: Ideologies of Management in the Course of Industrialization. Reinhard Bendix. 1974. pap. 6.95x (ISBN 0-520-02628-4). U of Cal Pr.

Work & Family Life: The Role of the Social Infrastructure in Eastern European Countries. International Labour Office, Geneva. (Illus.). vi, 77p. (Orig.). 1980. pap. 8.55 (ISBN 92-2-102167-X). Intl Labour Office.

Work and Leisure: An Inter-Disciplinary Study in Theory, Education, and Planning. Ed. by J. T. Haworth & M. A. Smith. 216p. 1976. pap. text ed. 4.95x o.p. (ISBN 0-86019-009-9). Princeton Bk Co.

Work & Leisure in the Soviet Union: A Time-Budget Analysis. Jiri Zuzanek. 1980. 29.95 (ISBN 0-03-056292-9). Praeger.

Work & Love: The Crucial Balance. Jay B. Rohrlich. LC 80-14727. 254p. 1980. 10.95 (ISBN 0-671-40087-8). Summit Bks.

Work & Motivation. Victor H. Vroom. LC 64-17155. 1964. 24.95 (ISBN 0-471-91205-0). Wiley.

Work & Non-Work in the Year 2001. Marvin D. Dunnette. LC 72-94643. 1973. pap. text ed. 7.95 o.p. (ISBN 0-8185-0080-8). Brooks-Cole.

Work & Organization in Kibbutz Industry. Ed. by Uri Leviatan. Tr. by Menachem Rosner. 204p. 1980. lib. bdg. 20.00 (ISBN 0-3482-1640-7). Norwood Edns.

Work & Play. Rhodri Jones. 1971. pap. text ed. 2.50x o.p. (ISBN 0-435-14502-9). Heinemann Ed.

Work & Religion, Concilium 131. Ed. by Gregory Baum. (New Concilium 1980). 128p. 1980. pap. 5.95 (ISBN 0-8164-4764-0). Crossroad NY.

Work & Retirement: Policy Issues. Ed. by Pauline K. Ragan. LC 79-91688. 178p. 1980. pap. 6.00 (ISBN 0-88474-094-3). USC Andrus Geron.

Work & Revolution in France. W. H. Sewell, Jr. LC 80-12103. (Illus.). 336p. 1980. 35.95 (ISBN 0-521-23442-5); pap. 8.95 (ISBN 0-521-29951-9). Cambridge U Pr.

Work & the Nature of Man. Frederick Herzberg. (Illus.). 224p. 1973. pap. 1.50 o.p. (ISBN 0-451-61239-6, MW1239, Ment). NAL.

Work & the Nature of Man. Frederick Herzberg. LC 65-27422. 1966. 9.95 (ISBN 0-690-00371-4, TYC-T). T Y Crowell.

Work & Welfare in Britain & the U. S. A. Bruno Stein. LC 75-44186. 1976. 14.95 (ISBN 0-470-15007-6). Halsted Pr.

Work & Workers: A Sociological Analysis. rev. ed. Lee Braude. LC 79-20996. 240p. 1981. Repr. of 1975 ed. lib. bdg. write for info. (ISBN 0-89874-017-7). Krieger.

Work at Writing: A Workbook to Accompany Writing at Work. Ernst Jacobi. 112p. 1980. pap. text ed. 5.50x (ISBN 0-8104-6117-X). Hayden.

Work Attitudes & Labor Market Experience: Evidence from the National Longitudinal Surveys. Paul J. Andrisani et al. LC 78-2520. 1978. 24.95 (ISBN 0-03-041586-1). Praeger.

Work Book: A Guide to Skilled Jobs. Joyce S. Mitchell. LC 78-62196. (Illus.). 1978. 9.95 (ISBN 0-8069-3108-6); lib. bdg. 9.29 (ISBN 0-8069-3109-4). Sterling.

Work Design. Stephan Konz. LC 78-50042. (Industrial Engineering Ser.). 1979. text ed. 22.50 (ISBN 0-88244-162-0). Grid Pub.

Work, Distances: Poems. Ken Smith. LC 75-189189. 98p. 1972. pap. 5.00 o.s.i. (ISBN 0-8040-0588-5); pap. 5.00 (ISBN 0-8040-0589-3). Swallow.

Work Effectiveness. General Electric Company. 94p. 1973. pap. 7.00 (ISBN 0-932078-01-X). GE Tech Prom & Train.

Work Ethic in Business: Proceedings of the Third National Conference on Business Ethics. Ed. by W. Michael Hoffman & Thomas J. Wyly. LC 80-22708. (Ethics Resource Center Ser.). 320p. 1981. lib. bdg. 22.50 (ISBN 0-89946-068-2). Oelgeschlager.

Work-Factor Time Standards: Measurement of Manual & Mental Work. Joseph H. Quick et al. (Illus.). 1962. 24.50 o.p. (ISBN 0-07-051061-X). McGraw.

Work, Family & the Career: New Frontiers in Theory & Research. Ed. by C. Brooklyn Derr. LC 80-13598. 320p. 1980. 25.95 (ISBN 0-03-056717-3). Praeger.

Work for Being in the Machine Age. Donald Petacchi. LC 80-82646. 1980. 12.50 (ISBN 0-8022-2376-1). Philos Lib.

Work, for the Night Is Coming. Jared Carter. 64p. 1981. 12.95 (ISBN 0-02-522090-X); pap. 5.95 (ISBN 0-02-069290-0). Macmillan.

Work Furlough & the County Jail. Alvin Rudoff. 212p. 1975. 17.25 (ISBN 0-398-03437-0). C C Thomas.

Work Hazards & Industrial Conflict. Carl Gersuny. LC 80-51506. (Illus.). 200p. 1981. 12.00 (ISBN 0-87451-189-5). U Pr of New Eng.
Work Improvement. Guy C. Close, Jr. LC 60-9616. (Illus.). 1960. text ed. 21.95 (ISBN 0-471-16071-7). Wiley.
Work in America: Report of a Special Task Force to the Secretary of Health, Education, & Welfare. U. S. Department of Health, Education, & Welfare. 262p. 1973. pap. 4.95 (ISBN 0-262-58023-3). MIT Pr.
Work in the Home. Rose E. Steidl & Esther C. Bratton. LC 67-29007. 1968. 21.95 (ISBN 0-471-82085-7). Wiley.
Work in the Hood: The First Entertaining Organic Chemistry Laboratory Guide. James W. Zubrick. LC 80-69113. (Illus.). 120p. (Orig.). 1980. pap. 4.50 (ISBN 0-937926-00-0). Scienspot.
Work Incentive Experience. Charles Garvin et al. LC 77-83926. 243p. 1978. text ed. 19.50x (ISBN 0-916672-99-9). Allanheld.
Work Incentives & Income Guarantees: The New Jersey Negative Income Tax Experiment. Joseph A. K. Pechman. Ed. by P. Michael Timpane. (Studies in Social Experimentation). 232p. 1975. 11.95 (ISBN 0-8157-6976-8); pap. 4.95 (ISBN 0-8157-6975-X). Brookings.
Work Measurement: A Guidebook to Word Processing Management. rev. ed. Arthur Thursland. 1980. text ed. 45.00 (ISBN 0-935220-01-1). Intl Word Process.
Work Measurement in the Office. B. J. Hamill & P. M. Steele. (Illus.). 268p. 1974. 25.00 o.s.i. (ISBN 0-7161-0147-5). Herman Pub.
Work, Mobility, & Participation: A Comparative Study of American & Japanese Industry. Robert E. Cole. LC 77-80468. 1979. 22.50x (ISBN 0-520-03542-9); pap. 6.95x (ISBN 0-520-04204-2). U of Cal Pr.
Work Nexus. Eli Ginzberg. LC 80-82882. (Foundation Monograph Ser.). 100p. (Orig.). 1981. pap. 5.00 (ISBN 0-87367-425-1). Phi Delta Kappa.
Work of Adalbert Johann Volck, 1828-1912: Who Chose for His Name the Anagram, V. Blada, 1861-1865. George M. Anderson. (Illus.). 1970. 35.00 (ISBN 0-938420-19-4). Md Hist.
Work of Administration in Nigeria: Case Studies. D. J. Murray. (Illus.). 1970. text ed. 6.75x (ISBN 0-09-099610-0, Hutchinson U Lib); pap. text ed. 3.25x (ISBN 0-09-099611-9, Hutchinson U Lib). Humanities.
Work of Ben Jonson. Ben Jonson. Ed. by C. H. Herford et al. Incl. Vol. 1. 42.00x (ISBN 0-19-811352-8); Vol. 2. 42.00x (ISBN 0-19-811353-6); Vol. 5. 46.50x (ISBN 0-19-811356-0); Vol. 7. 49.00x (ISBN 0-19-811358-7); Vol. 8. 49.00x (ISBN 0-19-811359-5); Vol. 10. 49.00x (ISBN 0-19-811361-7); Vol. 11. 49.00x (ISBN 0-19-811362-5). 1925-52. Oxford U Pr.
Work of Charles Abrams: Housing & Urban Renewal in the U. S. A. & the Third World. Ed. by O. H. Koenigsberger et al. (Illus.). 264p. 1980. 55.00 (ISBN 0-08-026111-6). Pergamon.
Work of Hartford's First Printer. Albert C. Bates. 1925. pap. 0.50 (ISBN 0-686-26791-5). Conn Hist Soc.
Work of Sartre: Vol. 1 Search for Freedom, Vol. 1. LC 78-31525. (Philosophy Now Ser.). 279p. 1979. 30.00x (ISBN 0-391-00546-4); pap. 13.00x (ISBN 0-686-63227-3). Humanities.
Work of the Church Treasurer. Thomas E. McLeod. 80p. 1981. pap. 6.95 (ISBN 0-8170-0908-6). Judson.
Work of the Church Trustee. Orlando L. Tibbetts. 1979. pap. 4.50 (ISBN 0-8170-0825-X). Judson.
Work of the Counselor. 3rd ed. Leona E. Tyler. 1969. 17.95x (ISBN 0-13-965087-3). P-H.
Work of the Deacon & Deaconess. Harold Nichols. (Orig.). pap. 2.95 (ISBN 0-8170-0328-2). Judson.
Work of the Gods in Tikopia, 2 vols. in 1. 2nd ed. Raymond Firth. (Monographs on Social Anthropology 1 & 2). 1967. text ed. 25.00x (ISBN 0-485-19501-1, Athlone Pr). Humanities.
Work of the Holy Spirit. Octavius Winslow. pap. 12.95 o.p. (ISBN 0-85151-279-8). Banner of Truth.
Work of the Industrial Film Maker. John Burder. (Library of Film & Television Practice). Date not set. 16.95 (ISBN 0-8038-8053-7). Hastings.
Work of the International Law Commission. 325p. 1980. pap. 16.00 (UN80-5-11, UN). Unipub.
Work of the Motion Picture Cameraman. Freddie Young & Paul Petzold. (Library of Film & Television Practice). Date not set. 16.50 (ISBN 0-8038-8061-8). Hastings.
Work of the Science Film Maker. Alex Strasser. (Library of Film & Television Practice). Date not set. 18.95 (ISBN 0-8038-8051-0). Hastings.
Work of the Television Journalist. 2nd ed. Robert Tyrrell. LC 80-41970. 200p. 1981. 22.95 (ISBN 0-240-51051-8). Focal Pr.
Work of the Usher. Alvin D. Johnson. (Orig.). pap. 2.75 (ISBN 0-8170-0356-8). Judson.
Work, Productivity & Job Satisfaction: An Evaluation of Policy-Related Research. Raymond A. Katzell et al. LC 75-21726. (Illus.). 445p. (Orig.). 1975. pap. text ed. 7.00 (ISBN 0-15-003082-7, Psych Corp). HarBraceJ.
Work Redesign. J. Richard Hackman & Greg R. Oldham. LC 79-8918. 1980. pap. text ed. 7.95 (ISBN 0-201-02779-8). A-W.
Work Simplification: Creative Thinking About Work Problems. Robert N. Lehrer. 1957. ref. ed. 16.95x o.p. (ISBN 0-13-965319-8). P-H.
Work, Society & Politics: The Factory North of England in the Second Half of the Nineteenth Century. Patrick Joyce. 1980. text ed. write for info. (ISBN 0-391-02215-6). Humanities.
Work Stress & Social Support. James S. House. LC 80-82234. 200p. 1981. pap. text ed. cancelled (ISBN 0-201-03101-9). A-W.
Work-Stress Connection: How to Cope with Job Burnout. Robert L. Veninga & James P. Spradley. 348p. 1981. 12.95 (ISBN 0-316-80747-8). Little.
Work Study & Related Management Services. 3rd ed. Dennis A. Whitmore. LC 68-135711. (Illus.). 336p. 1968. 12.50x (ISBN 0-434-92253-6). Intl Pubns Serv.
Work This One Out. L. H. Longley-Cook. 1978. pap. 1.25 o.p. (ISBN 0-449-13933-6, GM). Fawcett.
Work Trap. Martin Helldorfer. LC 80-53205. (Illus.). 140p. 1981. pap. 4.95 (ISBN 0-88489-127-5). St Mary's.
Work Values Inventory: MRC Machine-Scorable Test Booklets. Donald E. Super. 41.24 (ISBN 0-395-09529-8); directions manual 2.51 (ISBN 0-395-09530-1); specimen set. pap. 2.16 (ISBN 0-395-09531-X). HM.
Work-Wise: Learning Bout the World from Books--Critical Guide to Bool Selection & Usage. Diane Gersoni-Edelman. LC 79-11920. (Selection Guide Ser.: No. 3). 258p. 1980. 16.50 (ISBN 0-87436-264-4, Co-Pub. by Neal-Schuman). ABC-Clio.
Workaholic & His Family: An Inside Look. Frank Minirth et al. 144p. (Orig.). 1981. 8.95 (ISBN 0-8010-6111-3). Baker Bk.
Workaholics: Living with Them, Working with Them. Marilyn Macholoitz. 1981. pap. 2.95 (ISBN 0-451-61971-4, ME1971, Mentor Bks). NAL.
Workaholics: Make Laziness Work for You. Wayne E. Oates. LC 77-80906. 1978. 5.95 o.p. (ISBN 0-385-12977-7). Doubleday.
Workboats. Troup. 1980. write for info. (ISBN 0-85501-212-9). Heyden.
Workbook & Laboratory Manual for Progress in Spanish. 2nd ed. Ruth K. Crispin & John Crispin. 1978. pap. 4.95x (ISBN 0-673-15148-4). Scott F.
Workbook & Laboratory Manual in Chemistry. rev. ed. Walter L. Ahner. (Illus.). (gr. 11-12). 1964. pap. 6.92 (ISBN 0-87720-125-0). AMSCO Sch.
Workbook & Laboratory Manual in Physics. 2nd ed. Walter L. Ahner & Sheldon R. Diamond. (Illus., Orig.). (gr. 11-12). 1967. wkbk. 7.33 (ISBN 0-87720-176-5). AMSCO Sch.
Workbook for a Beginning-Intermediate Grammar of Hellenistic Greek. Lane C. McGaughy. LC 76-44351. (Society of Biblical Literature. Sources for Biblical Study). 1976. pap. text ed. 6.00 (ISBN 0-89130-093-7, 060306). Scholars Pr Ca.
Workbook for Aphasia: Exercises for the Redevelopment of Higher Level Language Functioning. Susan H. Brubaker. LC 78-5305. 1978. 9.95 (ISBN 0-8143-1595-X). Wayne St U Pr.
Workbook for Automotive Engines. 6th ed. William H. Crouse & Donald L. Anglin. (Automotive Technology Ser.). (Illus.). 96p. 1981. pap. 6.95 (ISBN 0-07-014826-0, G). McGraw.
Workbook for Basic Verbal Skills. 2nd ed. Philip Burnham & Richard Lederer. 74p. (gr. 9-12). 1980. 2.50 (ISBN 0-88334-130-1). Ind Sch Pr.
Workbook for Learning Medical Terminology Step by Step. Clara G. Young. LC 79-11068. (Illus.). 1979. 10.50 (ISBN 0-8016-5658-3). Mosby.
Workbook for Medical Assistants. Miriam G. Austrin et al. (Illus.). 198p. 1980. pap. text ed. 10.95 (ISBN 0-8016-0409-5). Mosby.
Workbook for Short Term Planning. Birchfield Keaton & Henry F. Keaton. 58p. 1973. 15.00 (ISBN 0-686-68579-2, 14913). Hospital Finan.
Workbook for Speech Fundamentals. David H. Dobkins & Richard Kneller. 128p. 1980. pap. text ed. 5.25 (ISBN 0-8403-2257-7). Kendall-Hunt.
Workbook for the Economics of Taxation. Simon James & Christopher Nobes. 72p. 1978. pap. 3.00x (ISBN 0-86003-608-1, Pub. by Allan Pubs England). State Mutual Bk.
Workbook in Accounting. 3rd ed. Langley. 1981. text ed. price not set (ISBN 0-408-10680-8). Butterworth.
Workbook in Basic Computer Programming (Fortran 4) Elwood W. Guernsey. (Illus.). 192p. 1973. pap. 17.75 (ISBN 0-398-02592-4). C C Thomas.
Workbook in Everyday French, 2 bks. rev. ed. Gerard Charbonneau & Hubert Seguin. 213p. (gr. 9-11). 1971. Bk. 1. pap. text ed. 3.75 (ISBN 0-88345-167-0, 17479); Bk. 2. pap. text ed. 3.75 (ISBN 0-88345-168-9, 17480); answer key 2.75 (ISBN 0-685-38985-5). Regents Pub.
Workbook in Everyday German. Ursula Meyer & Alice Wolfson. (gr. 9-10). 1976. pap. text ed. 3.75 (ISBN 0-88345-277-4). Regents Pub.
Workbook in French First Year. 2nd ed. Eli Blume. (Illus., Orig.). (gr. 8-11). 1967. wkbk. 6.00 (ISBN 0-87720-452-7). AMSCO Sch.
Workbook in French Three Years. 2nd. ed. Eli Blume. (Illus., Orig.). (gr. 10-12). 1978. wkbk. 6.75 (ISBN 0-87720-459-4). AMSCO Sch.
Workbook in French Two Years. 3rd ed. Eli Blume. (Orig.). (gr. 10-11). 1979. pap. text ed. 7.92 (ISBN 0-87720-470-5). AMSCO Sch.
Workbook in French Two Years. Eli Blume. (Illus., Orig.). (gr. 9-12). 1966. wkbk 5.83 o.p. (ISBN 0-87720-455-1). AMSCO Sch.
Workbook in Latin First Year. Charles I. Freundlich. (Illus., Orig.). (gr. 8-11). 1963. wkbk 6.75 (ISBN 0-87720-553-1). AMSCO Sch.
Workbook in Latin Two Years. Charles I. Freundlich. (Illus., Orig.). (gr. 9-12). 1965. wkbk 6.75 (ISBN 0-87720-556-6). AMSCO Sch.
Workbook in Organic Chemistry: Exercises in the Properties, Behavior, & Synthesis of Organic Compounds. T. A. Geissman. (Illus.). 1972. pap. text ed. 9.95x (ISBN 0-7167-0167-7). W H Freeman.
Workbook in Spanish First Year. Robert J. Nassi. (Illus., Orig.). (gr. 8-11). 1964. wkbk 5.58 (ISBN 0-87720-503-5). AMSCO Sch.
Workbook in Spanish First Year. 2nd ed. Robert J. Nassi & Bernard Bernstein. (gr. 9-12). 1973. wkbk 6.25 (ISBN 0-87720-519-1). AMSCO Sch.
Workbook in Spanish Three Years. Robert J. Nassi et al. (Orig.). (gr. 10-12). 1966. wkbk 6.25 (ISBN 0-87720-509-4). AMSCO Sch.
Workbook in Spanish Two Years. 2nd ed. Robert J. Nassi & Bernard Bernstein. (Illus., Orig.). (gr. 9-12). 1969. wkbk 6.25 (ISBN 0-87720-506-X). AMSCO Sch.
Workbook of Current English. 2nd ed. William E. Mahaney. 1981. pap. text ed. 6.95x (ISBN 0-673-15405-X). Scott F.
Workbook of Solutions & Dosage of Drugs, Including Arithmetic. 10th ed. Ellen M. Anderson & Thora M. Vervoren. (Illus.). 168p. 1976. pap. 7.95 o.p. (ISBN 0-8016-0235-1). Mosby.
Workbook of Solutions & Dosage of Drugs, Including Arithmetic. 11th ed. Thora Vervoren & Joan Oppenger. (Illus.). 1980. pap. text ed. 9.50 (ISBN 0-8016-0236-X). Mosby.
Workbook to Accompany Weimer Introduction to Business. 5th ed. John H. Porter et al. 1974. pap. text ed. 6.50x o.p. (ISBN 0-256-01618-6). Irwin.
Worked Examples & Problems in Ordinary Chemistry. A. Holderness & J. Lambert. 1971. pap. text ed. 3.95x o.p. (ISBN 0-435-64422-X). Heinemann Ed.
Worked Examples in Basic Electronics. P. W. Crane. 1967. 18.00 (ISBN 0-08-012217-5); pap. 7.00 (ISBN 0-08-012216-7). Pergamon.
Worked Examples in Engineering Field Theory. Ed. by A. J. Baden-Fuller. 1977. text ed. 42.00 (ISBN 0-08-018143-0); pap. text ed. 15.00 (ISBN 0-08-018142-2). Pergamon.
Worked Examples in Engineering in Si Units: Vol. 1 Engineering Science. Matthew Bates. 1974. pap. text ed. 7.95x o.p. (ISBN 0-04-620003-7). Allen Unwin.
Worked Examples in Engineering in Si Units: Vol. 2 Electrical Science. Matthew Bates. 1974. pap. text ed. 7.95x o.p. (ISBN 0-04-620005-3). Allen Unwin.
Worked Examples in Engineering in Si Units: Vol. 3 Electrical Engineering. Matthew Bates. 1974. pap. text ed. 7.95x o.p. (ISBN 0-04-620007-X). Allen Unwin.
Worked Examples in Physical Electronics. P Lynch & A. Nicolaides. (Illus.). 1972. pap. text ed. 15.95x (ISBN 0-245-50530-X). Intl Ideas.
Worked Examples in Turbomachinery: Fluid Mechanics & Thermodynamics. S. L. Dixon. LC 75-9757. 116p. 1975. text ed. 18.75 (ISBN 0-08-019797-3); pap. text ed. 9.00 (ISBN 0-08-019700-0). Pergamon.
Worked Problems in Heat, Thermodynamics & Kinetic Theory. L. Pincherle. 1966. 22.00 (ISBN 0-08-012016-4); pap. 10.75 (ISBN 0-08-012015-6). Pergamon.
Worker & the Job: Coping with Change. Ed. by Jerome M. Rosow. LC 74-765. (American Assembly Bk.). (Illus.). 224p. 1974. 7.95 (ISBN 0-13-965350-3, Spec); pap. 2.95 (ISBN 0-13-965350-3, Spec). P-H.
Worker Burnout Phenomenon: Implications of Current Research for the Child Protective System. 1978. 1.00. Comm Coun Great NY.
Worker in Australia: A Behavioral Science Perspective. Ed. by Allan Bordow. (Illus.). 1978. text ed. 21.75x (ISBN 0-7022-1473-6); pap. text ed. 12.75x (ISBN 0-7022-1474-4). U of Queensland Pr.
Worker in Post-Industrial Capitalism: Liberal & Radical Responses. Bertram Silverman & Murray Yanowitch. LC 73-14431. (Illus.). 1974. pap. text ed. 8.95 (ISBN 0-02-928770-7). Free Pr.
Worker Militancy & Its Consequences, 1965-75: New Directions in Western Industrial Relations. Ed. by Solomon Barkin. LC 75-3745. (Special Studies). (Illus.). 448p. 1975. text ed. 31.95 (ISBN 0-275-07410-2); pap. 11.95 (ISBN 0-275-89440-1). Praeger.
Worker Participation & the Crisis of Liberal Democracy. Sherri Dewitt. (Westview Replica Edition Ser.). 150p. 1980. lib. bdg. 18.00x (ISBN 0-89158-922-8). Westview.
Worker Participation: Individual Control & Performance. David Guest. 252p. 1974. 15.00x (ISBN 0-85292-097-0). Intl Pubns Serv.
Worker Participation: Success & Problems. Ed. by Hem C. Jain. LC 80-57. (Praeger Special Studies). 1980. 24.95 (ISBN 0-03-052451-2). Praeger.
Worker Self-Management in Industry: The West European Experience. Ed. by G. David Garson. LC 77-2774. (Praeger Special Studies). 1977. text ed. 29.95 (ISBN 0-03-022406-3). Praeger.
Worker Views His Union. Joel Seidman et al. LC 58-5686. 1958. 10.50x o.s.i. (ISBN 0-226-74529-5). U of Chicago Pr.
Workers & Employers: Documents on Trade Union & Industrial Relations in Britain Since the Eighteenth Century. J. T. Ward & Hamish Fraser. 384p. 1980. 35.00 (ISBN 0-208-01878-6, Archon). Shoe String.
Workers & Employers in Japan: The Japanese Employment Relations System. Ed. by Kazuo Okochi & Bernard Karsh. 548p. 1974. 25.00x o.p. (ISBN 0-691-03097-9). Princeton U Pr.
Workers & Managers in Latin America. Ed. by Stanley M. Davis & Louis W. Goodman. LC 72-3745. 192p. 1972. o. p. 12.50 o.p. (ISBN 0-669-74658-4); pap. 6.95 o.p. (ISBN 0-686-66688-7). Heath.
Workers & Wages in an Urban Labor Market. Albert Rees & George P. Shultz. LC 75-110114. (Studies in Business & Society Ser). 1970. 12.50x (ISBN 0-226-70705-9). U of Chicago Pr.
Worker's Control. Ernie Roberts. (Ruskin House Ser. in Trade Union Studies). 1973. text ed. 12.50x o.p. (ISBN 0-04-321013-9); pap. text ed. 6.95x (ISBN 0-04-321014-7). Allen Unwin.
Workers' Control in America. David Montgomery. LC 78-32001. (Illus.). 1979. 16.95 (ISBN 0-521-22580-9). Cambridge U Pr.
Workers' Control in America: Studies in History of Work, Technology, & Labor Struggles. David Montgomery. 1980. 5.95 (ISBN 0-521-28006-0). Cambridge U Pr.
Workers in a Labyrinth: Jobs & Survival in a Bank Bureaucracy. Robert Jackall. LC 77-84347. 202p. 1978. text ed. 18.00x (ISBN 0-916672-09-3). Allanheld.
Workers in Industrial America: Essays on the 20th Century Struggle. David Brody. 1979. text ed. 14.95x (ISBN 0-19-502490-7); pap. text ed. 3.95x (ISBN 0-19-502491-5). Oxford U Pr.
Workers in the Dawn. George Gissing. Ed. by Robert L. Wolff. LC 75-1527. (Victorian Fiction Ser.). 1975. Repr. of 1880 ed. lib. bdg. 66.00 (ISBN 0-8240-1599-1). Garland Pub.
Workers Under Stress: The Impact of Work Pressure on Group Cohesion. Stuart M. Klein. LC 75-160046. (Illus.). 136p. 1971. 9.50x (ISBN 0-8131-1253-2). U Pr of Ky.
Workers Who Drink. Carl J. Schramm et al. LC 76-58248. 1978. 18.95 (ISBN 0-669-01342-0). Lexington Bks.
Workes. facsimile ed. Ben Jonson. 1976. Repr. of 1616 ed. 110.00x o.p. (ISBN 0-85967-240-9, Pub. by Scolar Pr England). Biblio Dist.
Workhorse of the Western Front: The Story of the 30th Infantry Division. Robert L. Hewitt. LC 80-68981. (Divisional Ser.: No. 16). (Illus.). 404p. 1980. Repr. of 1946 ed. 25.00 (ISBN 0-89839-036-2). Battery Pr.
Working. Helen Oxenbury. (Baby Board Bks.). (Illus.). 12p. (ps-k). Date not set. boards 3.50 (ISBN 0-671-42112-3, Little Simon). S&S.
Working Approach to Human Relations in Organizations. Janis K. Day. LC 79-24589. 1980. pap. text ed. 15.95 (ISBN 0-8185-0347-5). Brooks-Cole.

Working at Home for Profit. Joanna Johnson. 243p. 1980. 25.00x (ISBN 0-631-12771-2, Pub. by Basil Blackwell); pap. 9.95x (ISBN 0-631-12583-3). Biblio Dist.

Working Bibliography of Greek Law. G. M Calhoun & C. Delamere. 1968. Repr. of 1927 ed. text ed. 23.00x (ISBN 90-6032-051-4). Humanities.

Working Class Autonomy & the Crisis. Ed. by Mario Tronti et al. 1981. text ed. 33.75x (ISBN 0-391-01811-6); pap. text ed. write for info. (ISBN 0-391-01812-4). Humanities.

Working Class Giant: The Life of William Z. Foster. Arthur Zipser. (Orig.). 1981. 11.00 (ISBN 0-7178-0590-5); pap. 4.25 (ISBN 0-7178-0582-4). Intl Pub Co.

Working Class in Welfare Capitalism. Walter Korpi. (International Library of Sociology). 1978. 28.00x (ISBN 0-7100-8848-5). Routledge & Kegan.

Working Class Manager. S. G. Reddding. 1979. text ed. 23.00x (ISBN 0-566-00291-4, Pub. by Gower Pub Co England). Renouf.

Working Class Radicalism in Mid-Victorian England. Trygve Tholfsen. LC 76-43323. 1977. 22.50x (ISBN 0-231-04234-5). Columbia U Pr.

Working Class Youth Culture. Ed. by Geoff Mungham & Geoff Pearson. (Routledge Direct Editions Ser.). (Orig.). 1976. pap. 9.95 (ISBN 0-7100-8374-2). Routledge & Kegan.

Working Classes in Victorian Fiction. P. J. Keating. (Illus.). 1979. pap. 8.95 (ISBN 0-7100-0196-7). Routledge & Kegan.

Working Classes in Victorian Fiction. P. J. Keating. (Illus.). 1971. 22.50 (ISBN 0-7100-6991-X). Routledge & Kegan.

Working Daughters of Hong Kong: Female Piety or Power in the Family? Janet W. Salaff. LC 80-23909. (ASA Rose Monographs). (Illus.). 304p. Date not set. price not set (ISBN 0-521-23679-7); pap. price not set (ISBN 0-521-28148-2). Cambridge U Pr.

Working Dogs. George S. Fichter. (First Bks.). (Illus.). (gr. 4-6). 1979. PLB 6.45 s&l (ISBN 0-531-02887-9). Watts.

Working Effectively with Task Force Oriented Groups. Donald Seaman. Ed. by Alan Pardoen. (Adult Education Association Professional Development Ser.). (Illus.). 144p. 1981. text ed. 12.95x (ISBN 0-07-000554-0, C). McGraw.

Working for a Healthier America. Ed. by Walter J. McNerney. 304p. 1980. 25.00 (ISBN 0-88410-718-3). Ballinger Pub.

Working for Capitalism. Richard Pfeffer. 1979. 22.50 (ISBN 0-231-04426-7); pap. 8.00 (ISBN 0-231-04427-5). Columbia U Pr.

Working Girl in a Man's World. Jan Manette. LC 66-22896. 223p. 1966. 6.00 (ISBN 0-915988-01-1, Pub. by Hawthorne Books). Reading Gems.

Working Green Wood with Peg. Patrick Spielman. LC 79-91406. (Illus.). 160p. 1980. 14.95 (ISBN 0-8069-5416-7); lib. bdg. 13.29 (ISBN 0-8069-5417-5); pap. 7.95 (ISBN 0-8069-8924-6). Sterling.

Working Hours: An Economic Analysis. Owen. LC 78-22287. (Illus.). 1979. 21.95 (ISBN 0-669-02740-5). Lexington Bks.

Working in Hair-Dressing. Marina Thaine & Robert Griffin. 1980. 16.95 (ISBN 0-7134-3323-X). David & Charles.

Working in Precious Metals. Ernest A. Smith. (Illus.). 1978. 24.00x (ISBN 0-7198-0032-3). Intl Ideas.

Working in Wood. Ernest Scott. 1980. 25.00 (ISBN 0-686-63362-5). Putnam.

Working in Wood: An Illustrated Encyclopedia. Ernest Scott. (Illus.). 272p. 1980. 25.00 (ISBN 0-399-12550-7). Putnam.

Working It Out: 23 Women Writers, Artists, Scientists, & Scholars Talk About Their Lives & Work. Ed. by Sara Ruddick & Pamela Daniels. LC 76-54624. 1978. pap. 5.95 (ISBN 0-394-73557-9). Pantheon.

Working Kids on Working. Sheila Cole. (gr. 5 up). 1980. 8.95 (ISBN 0-688-41959-3); PLB 8.59 (ISBN 0-688-51959-8). Morrow.

Working Life: A Social Science Contribution to Work Reform. Bertil Gardell & Gunn Johansson. LC 80-40289. 352p. 1981. 46.95 (ISBN 0-471-27801-7, Pub. by Wiley-Interscience). Wiley.

Working Life: Social Science Contribution to Work Reform. Bertil Gardell & Bunn Johansson. 352p. 1981. write for info. (ISBN 0-471-27801-7, Pub. by Wiley-Interscience). Wiley.

Working Lives: The "Southern Exposure" History of Labor in the South. Ed. by Marc S. Miller. (Illus.). 1981. 17.95 (ISBN 0-394-50912-9); pap. 7.95 (ISBN 0-394-73965-5). Pantheon.

Working Makes Sense. Charles H. Kahn & J. Bradley Hanna. 1973. pap. 3.96 (ISBN 0-8224-7490-5); tchrs. manual free (ISBN 0-8224-5212-X). Pitman Learning.

Working Men's Social Clubs & Educational Institutes: London Nineteen Four. Henry Solly. LC 79-56943. (English Working Class Ser.). 1980. lib. bdg. 22.00 (ISBN 0-8240-0124-9). Garland Pub.

Working of Christ in Man: The Thousand-Year Old Frescoes in the Church of St. George on the Island of Reichenau. Karl Hublow. 1979. 15.75 (ISBN 0-903540-28-2, Pub. by Floris Books). St George Bk Serv.

Working of Econometric Models. M. Morishima et al. LC 79-184901. (Illus.). 300p. 1972. 44.50 (ISBN 0-521-08502-0). Cambridge U Pr.

Working of the Holy Spirit in Daily Life. Sr. Eva Of Friedenshort. 1974. pap. 1.25 (ISBN 0-87123-647-8, 200647). Bethany Fell.

Working on Words. John Canney et al. vi, 250p. (Orig.). 1981. pap. text ed. 6.95 (ISBN 0-913580-72-4). Gallaudet Coll.

Working Papers: Group A, Chapters 1-12. pap. 7.95 (ISBN 0-13-002816-9). P-H.

Working Papers: Group A, Chapters 12-24. pap. 7.95 (ISBN 0-13-002824-X). P-H.

Working Papers: Group B, Chapters 1-12. pap. 7.95 (ISBN 0-13-002832-0). P-H.

Working Papers: Group B, Chapters 12-24. pap. 7.95 (ISBN 0-13-002840-1); student guide 8.95 (ISBN 0-13-002782-0). P-H.

Working Papers in the Matter of Training the Legal Secretary. rev. ed. LC 79-90998. 1979. 15.00 (ISBN 0-915362-16-3). M K Heller.

Working Papers in the Theory of Action. Talcott Parsons et al. LC 80-24475. 269p. 1981. Repr. of 1953 ed. lib. bdg. 25.00x (ISBN 0-313-22468-4, PAWP). Greenwood.

Working Papers of the 1975 Conference on Education of Psychiatrists. Ed. by Ewald Busse & James N. Sussex. 432p. 1976. 12.50 (ISBN 0-685-83185-X, P236-0). Am Psychiatric.

Working Parent Food Book. Adeline G. Shell & Kay Reynolds. 1979. 9.95 (ISBN 0-671-18439-3); pap. 4.95 (ISBN 0-346-12421-2). Cornerstone.

Working Plans for Working Decoys. Charles F. Murphy. (Illus.). 1979. 14.95 (ISBN 0-87691-286-2). Winchester Pr.

Working Smart: How to Accomplish More in Half the Time. Michael LeBoeuf. 1980. pap. 2.50 (ISBN 0-446-91273-5). Warner Bks.

Working the Street: Police Discretion & the Dilemmas of Reform. Michael Brown. LC 80-69175. 380p. 1981. text ed. 15.00 (ISBN 0-87154-190-4). Russell Sage.

Working Through Grief. Marcelle Chenard. (Thantology Service Ser.). 70p. 1980. 6.95 (ISBN 0-930194-05-5). Highly Specialized.

Working Together: Improving Communication on Your Job. Sherod Miller et al. (Illus.). 200p. 1980. pap. 49.95 (ISBN 0-917340-11-6). Interpersonal Comm.

Working Together on Rudolf Stein's Mystery Dramas: Steiner's Mystery Dramas. Hans Pusch. LC 80-67024. (Illus.). 144p. (Orig.). 1980. pap. text ed. 9.95 (ISBN 0-910142-91-2). Anthroposophic.

Working Wardrobe: An Easy, Affordable Approach to Successful Dressing. Janet Wallach. 1981. 14.95 (ISBN 0-87491-072-2). Acropolis.

Working When You Want to Work. John Fanning. 1969. pap. 1.25 o.s.i. (ISBN 0-02-008200-2, Collier). Macmillan.

Working with a Language. T. W. Haggitt. (Illus.). 9.50x (ISBN 0-392-01959-0, Sps). Soccer.

Working with Kazan. Ed. by Jeanine Basinger. (Illus.). 1973. pap. 4.00 (ISBN 0-8195-8016-3, Pub. by Wesleyan U Pr). Columbia U Pr.

Working with Leather. Guy R. Williams. (Illus.). 1967. 7.95 o.s.i. (ISBN 0-87523-161-6). Emerson.

Working with Men's Groups, Vol. 1. new ed. Roger Karsk & Bill Thomas. 1979. pap. 6.50 (ISBN 0-686-25093-1). New Comm Pr.

Working with Nature: A Practical Guide. John W. Brainerd. (Illus.). 550p. 1973. 24.95x (ISBN 0-19-501667-X). Oxford U Pr.

Working with Oils. Norman Battershill. (Leisure Arts Painting Ser.). (Illus.). 32p. 1980. pap. 2.50 (ISBN 0-8008-8542-2, Pentalic). Taplinger.

Working with Parents: Guidelines for Early Childhood & Elementary Teachers. Shari Nedler & Oralie McAfee. 1979. pap. text ed. 9.95x (ISBN 0-534-00622-1). Wadsworth Pub.

Working with People: Human Resource Management in Action. Donald B. Miller. LC 79-16914. 1979. pap. 11.95 (ISBN 0-8436-0776-9). CBI Pub.

Working with People in Crisis: Theory & Practice. Samuel L. Dixon. LC 78-31227. (Illus.). 1979. pap. text ed. 9.95 (ISBN 0-8016-1320-5). Mosby.

Working with Photography. Leila Jeffries & Anna Illot. 1980. 16.95 (ISBN 0-7134-3311-6). David & Charles.

Working with Roosevelt. Samuel I. Rosenman. LC 75-168391. (FDR & the Era of the New Deal Ser.). (Illus.). 1972. Repr. of 1952 ed. lib. bdg. 49.50 (ISBN 0-306-70328-9). Da Capo.

Working with Stained Glass. Paul W. Wood. LC 80-54350. (Illus.). 104p. 1981. 9.95; lib. bdg. 9.29 (ISBN 0-8069-5441-8); pap. 5.95 (ISBN 0-8069-8966-1). Sterling.

Working with Stained Glass: Fundamental Techniques & Applications. Jean-Jacques Duval. LC 74-184975. (Illus.). 1972. 10.95 o.s.i. (ISBN 0-690-89706-5, TYC-T). T Y Crowell.

Working with Stained Glass: Fundamental Techniques & Applications. Jean-Jacques Duval. LC 74-184975. (Funk & W Bk.). (Illus.). 144p. 1975. pap. 5.95 (ISBN 0-308-10153-7, F112, TYC-T). T Y Crowell.

Working with Structuralism: Essays & Reviews on Nineteenth & Twentieth-Century Literature. David Lodge. 240p. 1981. 30.00 (ISBN 0-7100-0658-6). Routledge & Kegan.

Working with Student Teachers. Florence B. Stratemeyer & M. Lindsey. LC 58-8555. 1958. pap. text ed. 9.50x (ISBN 0-8077-2222-7). Tchrs Coll.

Working with the Aged. Marcella B. Weiner et al. (Illus.). 1978. pap. 10.95 ref. ed. (ISBN 0-13-967570-1). P-H.

Working with the Bilingual Community. Maria E. Brisk et al. LC 79-84372. 90p. (Orig.). 1979. pap. 4.50 (ISBN 0-89763-013-0). Natl Clearinghse Bilingual Ed.

Working with the Computer. Gilbert Mansell. 156p. 1972. pap. text ed. 9.75 (ISBN 0-08-016014-X). Pergamon.

Working with the Oscilloscope. Albert C. Saunders. LC 68-29175. (Illus., Orig.). 1968. 8.95 o.p. (ISBN 0-8063-8472-7); pap. 5.95 (ISBN 0-8306-7472-1, 472). TAB Bks.

Working with the Revenue Code-1979. 1978. pap. 14.00 o.p. (ISBN 0-685-79157-2). Am Inst CPA.

Working with the Young Child: A Text of Readings-II. Ed. by John R. Hranitz & Ann M. Noakes. LC 78-56266. 1978. pap. text ed. 18.75 (ISBN 0-8191-0520-1). U Pr of Amer.

Working with Watercolour. Leslie Worth. (Leisure Arts Painting Ser.). (Illus.). 32p. 1980. pap. 2.50 (ISBN 0-8008-8546-5, Pentalic). Taplinger.

Working with Wood. Michael Lawrence. LC 78-65631. (Illus.). 1979. 11.95 (ISBN 0-690-01810-X, TYC-T); pap. 5.95 (ISBN 0-690-01820-7, TYC-T). T Y Crowell.

Working with Wood. (Home Repair & Improvement Ser.). (Illus.). 1979. lib. bdg. 11.97 (ISBN 0-8094-2427-4); kivar bdg. 7.95 (ISBN 0-686-66219-9). Silver.

Working with Wood: Background Information. Sheila Parker. LC 77-82995. (Science 5-13 Ser.). (Illus.). 1977. pap. text ed. 8.25 (ISBN 0-356-04010-0). Raintree Child.

Working with Wood: Stages 1 & 2. Sheila Parker. LC 77-82995. (Science 5-13 Ser.). (Illus.). 1977. pap. text ed. 8.25 (ISBN 0-356-04011-9). Raintree Child.

Working Woman's Beauty Book. Sharron Hannon. LC 78-19959. 220p. 1981. pap. 7.95. Stein & Day.

Working Your Way Through College. R. Winston. 1979. pap. 7.95 (ISBN 0-930204-04-2). Lord Pub.

Workingman's Paradise. John Miller. Ed. by Michael Wilding. 272p. 1980. 18.50x (ISBN 0-424-00057-1, Pub.by Sydney U Pr Australia). Intl Schol Bk Serv.

Workjobs: Activity-Centered Learning for Early Childhood Education. Mary B. Baratta-Lorton. 1972. text ed. 11.95 (ISBN 0-201-04311-4, Sch Div). A-W.

Workjobs for Parents. new ed. Baratta & Mary B. Lorton. (gr. k-3). 1975. 5.50 (ISBN 0-201-04303-3). A-W.

Workless State: A Study of Unemployment. Brian Showler & Adrian Sinfield. 252p. 1981. 20.00x (ISBN 0-85520-327-7, Pub. by Martin Robertson England); pap. 9.95x (ISBN 0-85520-340-4). Biblio Dist.

Workload Measures in the Court. National Center for State Courts. 1980. pap. 8.00 (ISBN 0-89656-043-0, R0051). Natl Ctr St Courts.

WORKMAC: A Bibliographic Format for Works in Analytic On-Line Library Union Catalogs. Herbert H. Hoffman. 1980. pap. 5.00x (ISBN 0-89537-016-6). Headway Pubns.

Workmen's Compensation Law of Indiana. Benjamin F. Small. 1950. with suppl. 35.00 o.p. (ISBN 0-672-82540-6, Bobbs-Merrill Law). Michie.

Workmen's Compensation New York. 1981 ed. Joseph A. Clifford. 75p. 1978. 5.00 (ISBN 0-87526-214-7). Gould.

Workover Well Control. Neal Adams. 320p. 1981. 27.50 (ISBN 0-87814-142-1). Pennwell Pub.

Workplace & Union. Ian Boraston et al. 1975. text ed. 11.95x o.p. (ISBN 0-435-85090-3). Heinemann Ed.

Workplace Democracy. Daniel Zwerdling. LC 79-2025. 1979. pap. 5.95 (ISBN 0-06-090733-9, CN-733, CN). Har-Row.

Workplace Perspectives on Education & Training. Ed. by Peter B. Doeringer. (Boston Studies in Applied Economics). 184p. 1981. lib. bdg. 17.50 (ISBN 0-89838-054-5, Pub. by Martinus Nijhoff). Kluwer Boston.

Works, 13 vols. George G. Byron. Ed. by E. H. Coleridge & R. E. Prothero. 1967. lib. bdg. 450.00 (ISBN 0-374-91140-1). Octagon.

Works, 4 vols. Samuel Clarke. LC 75-11207. (British Philosophers & Theologians of the 17th & 18th Centuries: Vol. 12). 1976. Repr. of 1742 ed. Set. lib. bdg. write for info. (ISBN 0-8240-1762-5); lib. bdg. 42.00 ea. Garland Pub.

Works, 8 vols. Margaret Sanger. Incl. Vol. 1. Margaret Sanger, an Autobiography. Intro. by A. Guttmacher. 33.00 (ISBN 0-08-018730-7); Vol. 2. Happiness in Marriage. 18.00 (ISBN 0-08-018731-5); Vol. 3. Motherhood in Bondage. 33.00 (ISBN 0-08-018732-3); Vol. 4. My Fight for Birth Control. 24.00 (ISBN 0-08-018733-1); Vol. 5. The New Motherhood. 18.00 (ISBN 0-08-018734-X); Vol. 6. Pivot of Civilization. 21.00 (ISBN 0-08-018735-8); Vol. 7. What Every Boy & Girl Should Know. 13.50 (ISBN 0-08-018736-6); Vol. 8. Woman & the New Race. 18.00 (ISBN 0-08-018737-4). Repr. 200.00 set (ISBN 0-08-020244-6). Pergamon.

Works, 4 vols. Benjamin Whichcote. LC 75-11265. (British Philosophers & Theologians of the 17th & 18th Centuries: Vol. 64). 1977. Repr. of 1751 ed. Set. lib. bdg. write for info. (ISBN 0-8240-1814-1); lib. bdg. 42.00 ea. Garland Pub.

Works. Charles Williams. Incl. War in Heaven. pap. 3.95 (ISBN 0-8028-1219-8); Many Dimensions. pap. 3.95 (ISBN 0-8028-1221-X); Place of the Lion. pap. 2.95 (ISBN 0-8028-1222-8); Shadows of Ecstacy. pap. 3.95 (ISBN 0-8028-1223-6); Descent into Hell. pap. 3.95 (ISBN 0-8028-1220-1). 1965. pap. 24.50 boxed set (ISBN 0-8028-1215-5). Eerdmans.

Works & Correspondence, 11 vols. David Ricardo. Ed. by P. Sraffa. 1951. Vols. 1-2, 4, 6 & 8-11. 49.50 ea.; Vols. 3, 5 & 7. 50.50 ea. Cambridge U Pr.

Works & Days. Lewis Mumford. LC 78-14077. 545p. 1979. 13.95 (ISBN 0-15-164087-4). HarBraceJ.

Works & Doctrine of Jacques Hittorff (1792-1867) Donald D. Schneider. LC 76-23721. (Outstanding Dissertations in the Fine Arts Ser.). 1977. lib. bdg. 133.00x (ISBN 0-8240-2727-2). Garland Pub.

Works by J. A. D. Ingres in the Collection of the Fogg Art Museum, Vol. III. Marjorie B. Cohn & Susan L. Siegfried. Ed. by Peter Walsh & Andrea Kaliski. (Fogg Art Museum Handbooks). (Illus.). 190p. pap. write for info. Fogg Art.

Works in Architecture of Robert & James Adam. Robert Adam & James Adam. LC 78-62405. (Illus.). 144p. 1980. 50.00 o.p. (ISBN 0-486-23810-5). Dover.

Works of Asher Benjamin: Boston, 1806-1843, 7 vols. Asher Benjamin. Incl. Country Builder's Assistant: 1797. 84p. (ISBN 0-306-71027-7); American Builder's Companion: 1806. 158p. (ISBN 0-306-71026-9); Rudiments of Architecture: 1814. 162p. (ISBN 0-306-71031-5); Practical House Carpenter: 1830. 248p. (ISBN 0-306-71029-3); Practice of Architecture: 1833. 236p. (ISBN 0-306-71030-7); Builder's Guide: 1839. 174p. 40.00 (ISBN 0-306-70971-6); Elements of Architecture: 1843. 290p. 35.00 (ISBN 0-306-71028-5). (Architecture & Decorative Art Ser.). 1974. 37.50 ea.; Set. 225.00 (ISBN 0-306-71032-3). Da Capo.

Works of Benjamin B. Warfield, 10 vols. Benjamin B. Warfield. 1981. Repr. of 1932 ed. 149.50 (ISBN 0-8010-9645-6). Baker Bk.

Works of Brooks, 6 vols. Thomas Brooks. 1980. Set. 90.00. Banner of Truth.

Works of Fisher Ames, 2 Vols. Ed. by Seth Ames. LC 69-14409. (American Scene Ser). 1969. Repr. of 1854 ed. Set. lib. bdg. 69.50 (ISBN 0-306-71122-2). Da Capo.

Works of Francis Lodwick: A Study of His Writings in the Intellectual Context of the Seventeenth Century. Vivian Salmon. (Classics of Linguistics Ser.). (Illus.). 263p. 1972. text ed. 24.00x (ISBN 0-582-52494-6). Longman.

Works of Geber. Ibn H. Jabir. LC 79-8615. Repr. of 1928 ed. 32.50 (ISBN 0-404-18479-0). AMS Pr.

Works of Genius: A Catalogue & a Commentary, Pt. 1, A-c. John H. Jenkins. (Illus.). 9.50 (ISBN 0-8363-0151-X). Jenkins.

Works of Geoffrey Chaucer. 2nd ed. Geoffrey Chaucer. Ed. by F. N. Robinson. (New Cambridge Editions). xliv, 1002p. 1957. text ed. 15.50 (ISBN 0-395-05568-7). HM.

Works of Isambard Kingdom Brunel - an Engineering Appreciation. Ed. by Alfred Pugsley. 232p. 1980. 40.00x (ISBN 0-7277-0030-8, Pub. by Telford England). State Mutual Bk.

Works of Isambard Kingdom Brunel: An Engineering Appreciation. Ed. by Alfred Pugsley. LC 79-41470. (Illus.). 232p. 1980. 29.95 (ISBN 0-521-23239-2). Cambridge U Pr.

Works of Jane Austen. Jane Austen. (Spring Books Ser. of Classics). 1979. 14.00 (ISBN 0-600-00603-4). Transatlantic.

Works of John Dryden. John Dryden. Incl. Vol. I, Poems, 1649-1680. Ed. by Edward N. Hooker & H. T. Swedenberg. 1956. 34.00x (ISBN 0-686-60761-9); Vol. II, Poems, 1681-1684. Ed. by H. T. Swedenberg. 1973. 34.00x (ISBN 0-686-60762-7); Vol. III, Poems, 1684-1692. Ed. by Earl Miner & Vinton A. Dearing. 1970. 34.00 (ISBN 0-520-01625-4); Vol. IV, Poems, 1693-1699. Ed. by A. B. Chambers et al. 1974. 39.50x (ISBN 0-686-60763-5); Vol. VIII, Plays, The Wild Gallant, The Rival Ladies, The Indian Ladies. Ed. by John H. Smith et al. 1962. 34.00x (ISBN 0-520-00359-4); Vol. IX, Plays; The Indian Emporour, Secret Love, Sir Martin Mar-All. Ed. by John Loftis & Vinton A. Dearing. 1966. 34.00x (ISBN 0-520-00360-8); Vol. X, Plays; The Tempest, Tyrannick Love, An Evenings Love. Ed. by Maximillan E. Novak & George R. Guiffey. 1970. 34.00x (ISBN 0-520-01589-4); Vol. XI, Plays; The Conquest of Granada, Part I & II, Marriage-a-la Mode, & The Assignation-or, Love in a Nunnery. Ed. by John Loftis et al. 1978. 40.00x (ISBN 0-520-02125-8); Vol. XV, Plays; Albion & Albanios, Don Sebastion, Anphitryon. Ed. by Earl Miner. 1976. 42.50x (ISBN 0-520-02129-0); Vol. XVII, Prose, 1668-1691, an Essay of Dramatic Poesie & Shorter Works. Ed. by Samuel A. Monk & A. E. Maurer. 1972. 35.00x (ISBN 0-520-01814-1); Vol. XVIII, The History of the League, 1684. Ed. by Alan Roper & Dearing Vinton. 1974. 36.50x (ISBN 0-686-60764-3); Vol. XIX, Prose, The Life of St. Francis Xavier. Ed. by Alan Roper & Dearing A. Vinton. 1979. 42.00x (ISBN 0-520-02132-0). U of Cal Pr.

Works of John Owen, 16 vols. John Owen. 14.95 ea. Banner of Truth.

Works of Jonathan Edwards, 2 vols. Jonathan Edwards. 1979. Set. 56.95 (ISBN 0-686-12492-8); Vol. 1. 29.95 (ISBN 0-85151-216-X); Vol. 2. 29.95 (ISBN 0-85151-217-8). Banner of Truth.

Works of Love. Wright Morris. LC 51-11978. x, 269p. 1972. pap. 2.45 (ISBN 0-8032-5767-8, BB 558, Bison). U of Nebr Pr.

Works of Mariotto Abertinelli. Ludovico Borgo. LC 75-23781. (Outstanding Dissertations in the Fine Arts - 16th Century). (Illus.). 1976. lib. bdg. 60.50 (ISBN 0-8240-1978-4). Garland Pub.

Works of Mather Byles. Mather Byles. LC 78-6439. 1978. 56.00x (ISBN 0-8201-1309-3). Schol Facsimiles.

Works of Mr. John Oldham. John Oldham. LC 79-26304. 1980. Repr. of 1686 ed. 72.00x (ISBN 0-8201-1337-9). Schol Facsimiles.

Works of Nathaniel Lee, 2 vols. Thomas B. Stroup. Ed. by Arthur L. Cooke. LC 54-14766. 1954. Set. 27.50 (ISBN 0-8108-0236-8). Scarecrow.

Works of Robert Traill, 2 vols. Robert Traill. 1975. Set. 27.95 (ISBN 0-686-12488-X). Vol. 1 (ISBN 0-85151-229-1). Vol. 2 (ISBN 0-85151-230-5). Banner of Truth.

Works of Robert Whytt. Robert Whytt. Bd. with Memoirs on the Nervous System. Marshall Hall; Memoirs. Pierre J. Cabanis; Two Essays. G. S. Hall & E. DuBois-Reymond. (Contributions to the History of Psychology Ser., Vol. I, Pt. E: Physiological Psychology). 1978. Repr. of 1768 ed. 30.00 (ISBN 0-89093-174-7). U Pubns Amer.

Works of Sir David Lindsay of the Mount, 1490-1555, 4 vols. Ed. by Douglas Hamer. 1931-1936. 126.00 (ISBN 0-384-32819-9). Johnson Repr.

Works of Ta'unga: Records of a Polynesian Traveller in the South Seas, 1833-1896. Ta'unga. Ed. by Ron Crocombe. (Pacific History Ser.: No. 2). (Illus.). 1968. 7.50x (ISBN 0-87022-165-5). U Pr of Hawaii.

Works of Tomioka Tessai. Illus. by Tomioka Tessai. (Illus.). 152p. (Orig.). 1968. pap. 5.00 (ISBN 0-88397-015-5). Intl Exhibit Foun.

Works of Wordsworth. rev. new ed. William Wordsworth. (Cambridge Editions Ser.). Date not set. 15.00 (ISBN 0-395-18496-7). HM. Postponed.

Works on Sibbes, Vol. 1. Richard Sibbes. 1979. 14.95 (ISBN 0-85151-169-4). Banner of Truth.

Works: The Oceana & Other Works with an Account of His Life by John Toland. James Harrington. LC 34-35411. (Illus.). 654p. 1980. Repr. of 1771 ed. 110.00x (ISBN 3-511-00042-4). Intl Pubns Serv.

Works, 1857-74, 15 Vols. Francis Bacon. Ed. by James Spedding et al. 1951. Set. 595.00 (ISBN 0-403-00003-3). Scholarly.

Works: 1884-1917, 21 vols. Herbert Spencer. LC 68-109116. 1966. Repr. Set. 999.00x (ISBN 3-535-00480-2). Intl Pubns Serv.

Works 2 Vols: Vol. 1. Prose, Vol. 2. Poetry. Joel Barlow. LC 68-17012. 1970. Set. 120.00x (ISBN 0-8201-1062-0). Schol Facsimiles.

Workshop Crafts. Linda Hetzer. LC 77-28707. (Illustrated Crafts for Beginners). (Illus.). (gr. 3-7). 1978. PLB 9.95 (ISBN 0-8172-1184-5). Raintree Pubs.

Workshop Ideas. John Capotosto et al. LC 72-95384. (Illus.). 1977. 5.95 o.p. (ISBN 0-668-02940-4); pap. 2.95 o.p. (ISBN 0-668-04099-8). Arco.

Workshop Management: A Behavorial & Systems Approach. Douglas B. Simpson & Philip M. Podsakoff. (Illus.). 152p. 1975. 17.50 (ISBN 0-398-03364-1). C C Thomas.

Workshop of Problems in Today's Pennsylvania. Millard Altland & John Wildasin. (gr. 8-12). 1968. pap. 1.85 o.p. (ISBN 0-931992-23-0). Penns Valley.

Workshop on Fertility Control. J. R. Newton et al. (Royal Society of Medicine International Congress & Symposium Ser.: No. 31). 1980. 17.50 (ISBN 0-8089-1297-6). Grune.

Workshop Processes, Practices & Materials. Bruce J. Black. (Illus.). 282p. 1979. pap. 13.95x (ISBN 0-7131-3409-7). Intl Ideas.

Workshop Technology, Pt. 1. 5th ed. W. A. Chapman. (Illus.). 1976. pap. 14.95x (ISBN 0-7131-3269-8). Intl Ideas.

Workshop Technology, Pt. 2. 4th ed. W. A. Chapman. (Illus.). 1972. pap. 14.95x (ISBN 0-7131-3272-8). Intl Ideas.

Workshops for Parents & Teachers. Catharine S. Bush. (Language Remediation & Expansion Ser.). 1981. spiral 15.00 (ISBN 0-88450-738-6). Communication Skill.

Workshops for the Handicapped in the United States: An Historical & Developmental Perspective. Nathan Nelson. 480p. 1971. pap. 20.25 spiral (ISBN 0-398-02168-6). C C Thomas.

Workshops in Cognitive Processes. Ed. by A. Bennett et al. (Illus.). 120p. 1980. write for info. (ISBN 0-7100-0579-2); pap. 9.75 (ISBN 0-7100-0580-6). Routledge & Kegan.

Workshops on Chromosomal Aspects of the Male Sterility in Mammals: Abstracts. Ed. by A. G. Searle & P. De Boer. (Journal; Cytogenetics & Cell Genetics: Vol. 27; No. 4). (Illus.). 84p. 1980. pap. 6.75 (ISBN 3-8055-1610-X). S Karger.

Worksteads. Jeremy J. Hewes. LC 80-941. 1981. pap. 9.95 (ISBN 0-385-15995-1, Dolp). Doubleday.

Workweek Revolution: A Guide to the Changing Workweek. D. L. Fleuter. 1975. 9.95 o.p. (ISBN 0-201-03571-5). A-W.

Workyards-Playgrounds Planned for Adventure. Nancy Rudolph. LC 74-5187. (Illus.). 1974. pap. 7.50x (ISBN 0-8077-2423-8). Tchrs Coll.

World Aircraft: Military, 1945-1960. Enzo Angelucci & Paolo Matricardi. (Illus.). 1980. pap. 7.95 (ISBN 0-528-88205-8). Rand.

World Almanac & Book of Facts Nineteen Eighty-One. Ed. by Hana U. Lane. 976p. 1980. 8.95 (ISBN 0-911818-17-0); pap. 4.50 (ISBN 0-911818-09-X). World Almanac.

World Almanac & Book of Facts, 1980. Ed. by Newspaper Enterprise Inc. 1979. 7.95 (ISBN 0-385-15711-8). Doubleday.

World Almanac & Book of Facts 1981. Hana Umlauf Lane. 1980. 8.95 o.p. (ISBN 0-911818-18-9); pap. 4.50 o.p. (ISBN 0-911818-17-0). Newspaper Ent.

World Almanac Book of Buffs, Masters, Mavens & Uncommon Experts. Ed. by Henry Doering. LC 80-81179. 352p. (Orig.). 1980. pap. 6.95 (ISBN 0-911818-13-8). World Almanac.

World Almanac Book of Buffs, Masters, Mavens & Uncommon Experts. World Almanac Editors. LC 80-8179. 1980. 12.50 (ISBN 0-13-967836-0). P-H.

World Almanac Book of Who. Ed. by Hana Umlauf Lane. 352p. (Orig.). 1980. pap. 5.95 (ISBN 0-911818-11-1). World Almanac.

World Almanac Book of Who. World Almanac Editors. LC 80-81180. 1980. 12.50 (ISBN 0-13-967844-1). P-H.

World Almanac Guide to Metrics. Newspaper Enterprise Assoc. 1977. pap. 1.75 o.p. (ISBN 0-449-13828-3, GM). Fawcett.

World Aluminum-Bauxite Market. Douglas Woods & James C. Burrows. LC 78-19455. 1980. 24.50 (ISBN 0-03-044356-3). Praeger.

World & Africa: Inquiry into the Part Which Africa Has Played in World History. rev. ed. William E. Du Bois. LC 65-16392. (Illus., Orig.). 1965. 8.95 (ISBN 0-7178-0222-1); pap. 4.25 (ISBN 0-7178-0221-3). Intl Pub Co.

World & Its Streets, Places. Larry Eigner. 180p. (Orig.). 1977. ltd. signed o.p. 15.00 (ISBN 0-87685-269-X); pap. 5.00 (ISBN 0-87685-268-1). Black Sparrow.

World Anthropology Ser. Ed. by Florencio Sanchez-Camara & Felipe Ayala. (World Antropology Ser.). 1979. text ed. 24.75x (ISBN 90-279-7860-3). Mouton.

World Armaments & Disarmament: SIPRI Yearbook 1980. SIPRI. 1980. 49.50x (ISBN 0-8448-1375-3). Crane-Russak Co.

World Armaments & Disarmament: SIPRI Yearbooks 1968-1979 Cumulative Index. SIPRI. LC 80-65479. 90p. 1980. 16.50x (ISBN 0-8448-1348-6). Crane-Russak Co.

World Armies. John Keegan. 1980. 40.00 (ISBN 0-87196-407-4). Facts on File.

World Army Uniforms: Nineteen Thirty-Nine to the Present. Andrew Mollo et al. (Illus.). 360p. 1981. 24.95 (ISBN 0-7137-1189-2, Pub. by Blandford Pr England). Sterling.

World Around the Corner. Maurice Gee. (Illus.). 80p. (gr. 4-6). 1981. 9.95 (ISBN 0-19-558061-3). Oxford U Pr.

World As It Was: A Photographic Portrait 1865 to 1921. Margarett Loke. LC 80-13031. (Illus.). 220p. 1980. 24.95 (ISBN 0-671-25376-X). Summit Bks.

World As Power. new ed. John Woodroffe. Bd. with Mahamaya: Power As Consciousness. John Woodroffe & Pramatha N. Mukhyopadhyaya. 1974. 13.95 (ISBN 0-89744-119-2, Pub. by Ganesh & Co. India). Auromere.

World As Will & Representation, 2 vols. Arthur Schopenhauer. Tr. by E. F. Payne. Set. 22.00 (ISBN 0-8446-2885-9). Peter Smith.

World As Will & Representation, 2 Vols. Arthur Schopenhauer. Tr. by E. F. Payne. 1966. pap. text ed. 6.50 ea.; Vol. 1. pap. text ed. (ISBN 0-486-21761-2); Vol. 2. pap. text ed. (ISBN 0-486-21762-0). Dover.

World at Large. Christine Zawadiwsky. 1978. pap. 24.00 o.p. (ISBN 0-931460-06-9). Bieler.

World at War. Mark Arnold-Foster. (RL 8). 1974. pap. 1.95 (ISBN 0-451-05775-9, J5775, Sig). NAL.

World Atlas of Geomorphic Features. R. E. Snead. LC 77-28009. 300p. 1980. 39.50 (ISBN 0-88275-272-3). Krieger.

World Atlas of Golf. Pat Ward-Thomas et al. 1976. 25.00 o.p. (ISBN 0-394-40814-4). Random.

World Authors: Nineteen Seventy to Nineteen Seventy-Five. Ed. by John Wakeman. 1979. 40.00 (ISBN 0-8242-0641-X). Wilson.

World Automotive Industry. Gerald Bloomfield. LC 77-91774. 1978. 38.00 (ISBN 0-7153-7539-3). David & Charles.

World A.V. Programme Directory: The International Selection & Buying Guide to A.V. Software, with Full Programmed Descriptions & Regular Updating Service. Incl. Part One: Science & Technology. One Year. 150.00 o.p. (ISBN 0-686-64941-9); Two Years. 285.00 o.p. (ISBN 0-686-64942-7); Three Years. 405.00 o.p. (ISBN 0-686-64943-5); Part Two: Arts & Humanities. One Year. 150.00 o.p. (ISBN 0-8352-1195-9); Two Years. 285.00 o.p. (ISBN 0-686-64944-3); Three Years. 405.00 o.p. (ISBN 0-686-64945-1); Part Three: Training & Self-Development. One Year. 150.00 o.p. (ISBN 0-8352-1196-7); Two Years. 285.00 o.p. (ISBN 0-686-64946-X); Three Years. 405.00 o.p. (ISBN 0-686-64947-8); Part Four: Entertainment & Leisure. One Year. 150.00 o.p. (ISBN 0-8352-1197-5); Two Years. 285.00 o.p. (ISBN 0-686-64948-6); Three Years. 405.00 o.p. (ISBN 0-686-64949-4). One Year. complete directory all parts 360.00 o.p. (ISBN 0-8352-1193-2); Two Years. 684.00 o.p. (ISBN 0-686-64939-7); Three Years. 972.00 o.p. (ISBN 0-686-64940-0); 1,080.00 3 year subscription plus microfiche o.p. Bowker.

World Bank Since Bretton Woods. Edward S. Mason & Robert E. Asher. LC 73-1089. 1973. 21.95 (ISBN 0-8157-5492-2). Brookings.

World Before Us: Poems 1950-1970. Theodore Weiss. LC 71-119143. 1970. 9.95 (ISBN 0-02-625720-3). Macmillan.

World Beneath the Sea. Susan Harris. LC 78-10880. (Easy-Read Fact Bks.). (Illus.). (gr. 2-4). 1979. PLB 6.45 s&l (ISBN 0-531-02854-2). Watts.

World Between. Norman Spinrad. (Orig.). 1979. pap. 1.75 o.p. (ISBN 0-685-67757-5). Jove Pubns.

World Beyond. Ruth Montgomery. 1978. pap. 2.25 (ISBN 0-449-24085-1, Crest). Fawcett.

World Blacks: Self Help & Achievement. James H. Boykin. LC 19-53631. ix, 193p. 1980. pap. 6.25 (ISBN 0-9603342-0-3). Boykin.

World Blindness & Its Prevention. John Wilson & International Agency for the Prevention of Blindness. 104p. 1980. text ed. 17.95x (ISBN 0-19-261249-2). Oxford U Pr.

World Book Atlas. Ed. by Edward B. Espenshade, Jr. & Joel L. Morrison. LC 76-57897. (Illus.). 1977. text ed. 15.95 o.p. (ISBN 0-7166-2026-X). World Bk-Chilcraft.

World Book Dictionary, 2 vols. rev. ed. Ed. by Clarence L. Barnhart. Robert K. Barnhart. LC 79-53618. (Illus.). (gr. 4-12). 1980. Set. PLB write for info. (ISBN 0-7166-0280-6). World Bk-Childcraft.

World Book Encyclopedia, 22 vols. rev. ed. World Book-Childcraft International. LC 79-84167. (Illus.). (gr. 4-12). 1980. Set. PLB write for info. (ISBN 0-7166-0080-3). World Bk-Childcraft.

World Book Illustrated Home Medical Encyclopedia, 4 vols. World Book-Childcraft International, Inc. LC 79-56907. (Illus.). 1038p. 1980. write for info. (ISBN 0-7166-2060-X). World Bk-Childcraft.

World Book of Children's Games. Arnold, 1977. pap. 1.75 o.p. (ISBN 0-449-23044-9, Crest). Fawcett.

World Book of Children's Games. Arnold Arnold. LC 77-142134. (Illus.). 1972. 9.95 o.s.i. (ISBN 0-690-00372-2, TYC-T). T Y Crowell.

World Book of House Plants. rev. ed. Elvin McDonald. LC 74-23165. (Funk & W Bk.). (Illus.). 320p. 1975. 9.95 o.s.i. (ISBN 0-308-10087-5, TYC-T). T Y Crowell.

World Book of Soups. Nina Froud. 224p. 1975. pap. 1.50 o.p. (ISBN 0-345-24357-9). Ballantine.

World Book Student Handbook, 2 vols. LC 77-95232. 1977. Set. 19.95 o.p. (ISBN 0-685-88170-9); Vol. 1. (ISBN 0-7166-2053-7); Vol. 2. (ISBN 0-7166-2054-5). World Bk-Chilcraft.

World Book Student Handbook, 2 vols. rev. ed. LC 77-95232. 1979. Repr. of 1978 ed. 27.00 (ISBN 0-685-88170-9). Vol. 1 (ISBN 0-7166-2053-7). Vol. 2 (ISBN 0-7166-2054-5). World Bk-Childcraft.

World Book Year Book. Pref. by Wayne Wille. LC 62-4818. (Illus.). 608p. (gr. 6-12). 1980. PLB write for info. (ISBN 0-7166-0481-7). World Bk-Childcraft.

World Bread Cup. Consultation on Church Union. 1978. 0.85 (ISBN 0-686-28801-7). Forward Movement.

World Budget Guide to Austria. pap. 1.95 o.p. (ISBN 0-452-00374-1, FM374, Mer). NAL.

World Budget Guide to France. 1972. pap. 1.95 o.p. (ISBN 0-452-00371-7, FM371, Mer). NAL.

World Budget Guide to Portugal. 1972. pap. 1.95 o.p. (ISBN 0-452-00372-5, FM372, Mer). NAL.

World Budget Guide to Switzerland. 1972. pap. 1.95 o.p. (ISBN 0-452-00373-3, FM373, Mer). NAL.

World by Itself: Tradition & Change in the Venetian Lagoon. Shirley Guiton. (Illus.). 1978. 17.95 (ISBN 0-241-89434-4, Pub. by Hamish Hamilton). David & Charles.

World Calendar: Addresses & Occasional Papers Chronologically Arranged on the Progress of Calendar Reform Since 1930. Elisabeth Achelis. LC 73-102214. Repr. of 1937 ed. 18.00 (ISBN 0-8103-3784-3). Gale.

World Called Solitude. Stephen Goldin. LC 78-22611. (Science Fiction Ser.). 192p. 1981. 9.95 (ISBN 0-385-14375-3). Doubleday.

World Capital Shortage. Alan Heslop. (Key Issues Lecture Ser). 1978. 8.50 (ISBN 0-672-97208-5); pap. 5.50 (ISBN 0-686-68026-X). Bobbs.

World Cars Nineteen Hundred Eighty. 19th ed. 1980. 33.95 o.p. (ISBN 0-531-03940-4). Watts.

World Cars 1977. Ed. by Automobile Club of Italy. LC 7-643381. (Illus.). 1977. 33.95 (ISBN 0-910714-09-6). Herald Bks.

World Cars 1979. Ed. by Automobile Club of Italy. LC 7-643381. (Illus.). 1979. 33.95 (ISBN 0-910714-11-8). Herald Bks.

World Cattle, 2 Vols. John E. Rouse. LC 69-10620. (Illus.). 1970. Set. 42.50 (ISBN 0-8061-0864-9). U of Okla Pr.

World Challenge. Jean-Jacques Servan-Schreiber. 1981. 14.95 (ISBN 0-671-42524-2). S&S.

World Champions. Anthony Pritchard. LC 73-15147. (Illus.). 1974. 7.95 o.s.i. (ISBN 0-02-599210-4). Macmillan.

World Champions: The Oakland Raiders. (Illus.). 1977. pap. 3.00 o.p. (ISBN 0-916290-08-5). Squarebooks.

World Chess Champions. E. G. Winter. (Illus.). 208p. 1981. 14.51 (ISBN 0-08-024094-1); pap. 8.51 (ISBN 0-08-024117-4). Pergamon.

World Chess Championship - a History. Al Horowitz. (Illus.). 288p. 1973. 9.95 o.s.i. (ISBN 0-02-554150-1). Macmillan.

World Christianity: Eastern Asia. Ed. by David C. Liao. 198p. 1979. pap. 9.00 (ISBN 0-912552-31-X). MARC.

World Christianity: Eastern Asia. 1979. 8.00 (ISBN 0-912552-31-X). MARC.

World Christianity: Middle East. Ed. by Don M. McCurry. 1979. pap. text ed. 9.00 (ISBN 0-912552-27-1). MARC.

World Christianity: Middle East. 1979. 8.00 (ISBN 0-912552-27-1). MARC.

World Christianity: South Asia. Ed. by Roger E. Hedlund. 320p. 1980. 12.00 (ISBN 0-912552-33-6). MARC.

World Christianity: South Asia. 1980. 10.00 (ISBN 0-912552-33-6). MARC.

World Civil Aircraft Since Nineteen Forty-Five. Michael Hardy. (Illus.). 1980. 10.95 (ISBN 0-684-16266-0, ScribT). Scribner.

World Civilization, 2 vols. Joseph M. Leon. Incl. Vol. 1. To 1715. 1970. pap. text ed. 4.95 (ISBN 0-8220-1509-9); Vol. 2. Since 1650. 1969. pap. text ed. 4.95 (ISBN 0-8220-1510-2). (Cliffs Course Outlines Ser.). Cliffs.

World Civilizations, 2 vols. 5th ed. Edward M. Burns & Philip L. Ralph. (Illus.). 1974. 19.95x (ISBN 0-393-09276-3); Vol. 1. pap. text ed. 13.95x (ISBN 0-393-09266-6); Vol. 2. pap. text ed. 13.95x (ISBN 0-393-09272-0); Vol. 1. study guide 4.95x (ISBN 0-393-09277-1); Vol. 2. study guide 2.50x (ISBN 0-393-09285-2). Norton.

World Civilizations. 6th ed. Edward M. Burns & Philip L. Ralph. (Illus.). 1981. Two Vols. In 1. price not set (ISBN 0-393-95077-8); Vol. 1. pap. price not set (ISBN 0-393-95083-2); Vol. 2. pap. price not set (ISBN 0-393-95095-6). Norton. Postponed.

World Class. Jane Boyar & Burt Boyar. LC 75-10257. 512p. 1975. 10.00 o.p. (ISBN 0-394-46053-7). Random.

World Coal Resources. G. B. Fettweis. (Developments in Economic Geology Ser.). 425p. 1979. 80.50 (ISBN 0-444-99779-2). Elsevier.

World Coins & Their Values. Richard Thompson. 224p. (gr. 8 up). Date not set. 3.95 (ISBN 0-307-24408-3, Golden Pr). Western Pub.

World Collectors Annuary, 31 vols. A. M. Van Voorthuijsen. write for info. vols. 1-30, 1943-78; Vol. 30. vol. 31, 1979 100.00 (ISBN 0-685-52513-9). Heinman.

World Communications: A Two Hundred Country Survey of Press, Radio, Television, Film. 550p. 1975. 23.25 (ISBN 0-89059-001-X). Bowker.

World Communications: Threat or Promise - A Socio-Technical Approach. rev. ed. Colin Cherry. LC 78-3761. 1978. 30.25 (ISBN 0-471-99616-5); pap. 13.00 (ISBN 0-471-99660-2, Pub. by Wiley-Interscience). Wiley.

World Communism: A History of the Communist International. Franz Borkenau. 1962. pap. 6.50 (ISBN 0-472-06067-8, 67, AA). U of Mich Pr.

World Conqueror & World Renouncer. J. Tambiah. LC 76-8290. (Cambridge Studies in Social Anthropology: No. 15). 1976. 49.95 (ISBN 0-521-21140-9); pap. 14.95x (ISBN 0-521-29290-5). Cambridge U Pr.

World Copper Industry: Structure & Economic Analysis. Raymond Mikesell. LC 79-4581. (Resources for the Future Ser.). 1979. 25.00x (ISBN 0-8018-2257-2); pap. 10.95 (ISBN 0-8018-2270-X). Johns Hopkins.

World Design Sources Directory 1980: An ICOGRADA ICSID Publication. Ed. by Centre De Creation Industrielle, Paris, France. LC 79-41455. 192p. 1980. 29.00 (ISBN 0-08-025676-7). Pergamon.

World Dictionary of Awards & Prizes. 1979. 58.00 (ISBN 0-905118-32-4, Europa). Gale.

World Directory of Engineering Schools. 2nd ed. Geographics Editors. LC 80-66864. 1980. pap. 28.95 (ISBN 0-930722-02-7). Geographics.

World Directory of Multinational Enterprises, 2 vols. John Dunning & John Stepford. 1500p. 1980. 195.00 set (ISBN 0-686-65762-4); Vol. 1. (ISBN 0-87196-440-6); Vol. 2. (ISBN 0-87196-441-4). Facts on File.

World Directory of Stockshot & Film Production Libraries. J. Chittock. 1969. 32.00 (ISBN 0-08-013246-4). Pergamon.

World Divided. Ed. by G. K. Helleiner. LC 75-16606. (Perspectives on Development Ser.: No. 5). 1976. 47.50 (ISBN 0-521-20948-X); pap. 15.95x (ISBN 0-521-29006-6). Cambridge U Pr.

World Dynamics. 2nd ed. Jay Forrester. 1979. text ed. 15.00x (ISBN 0-262-06066-3); pap. 7.95 (ISBN 0-262-56018-6). MIT Pr.

World Economic Development. Herman Kahn. 1979. lib. bdg. 27.50 (ISBN 0-89158-392-0). Westview.

World Economic Survey: Niniteen Seventy-Nine to Nineteen Eighty. 116p. 1980. pap. 10.00 (UN80-2C2, UN). Unipub.

World Economic Survey 1978 - Current Trends in the World Economy. 125p. 1980. pap. 10.00 (ISBN 0-686-68980-1, UN80/2C1, UN). Unipub.

World Economic Survey, 1979-80. United Nations. LC 48-1401. 116p. (Orig.). 1980. pap. 10.00x (ISBN 0-8002-1108-1). Intl Pubns Serv.

World Economy. David Killingray. Ed. by Malcolm Yapp et al. (World History Ser.). (Illus.). 32p. (gr. 10). 1980. Repr. of 1977 ed. lib. bdg. 5.95 (ISBN 0-89908-143-6); pap. text ed. 1.95 (ISBN 0-89908-118-5). Greenhaven.

World Economy: History & Prospect. W. W. Rostow. 877p. 1980. pap. text ed. 20.00 (ISBN 0-292-79016-3). U of Tex Pr.

World Electric Power Industry. N. B. Guyol. 1969. 60.00x (ISBN 0-520-01484-7). U of Cal Pr.

World Elsewhere: The Place of Style in American Literature. Richard Poirier. 1966. 12.95 (ISBN 0-19-500061-7). Oxford U Pr.

World Elsewhere: The Place of Style in American Literature. Richard Poirier. 270p. 1966. pap. 4.95 (ISBN 0-19-500778-6, 264, GB). Oxford U Pr.

World Employment Programme, Seventh Progress Report on Income Distribution & Employment: A Progress Report on WEP Research Undertaken Within the Framework of the Income Distribution & Employment Programme. International Labour Office, Geneva. 80p. (Orig.). 1979. pap. 5.70 (ISBN 9-22-102294-3). Intl Labour Office.

World Encompassed: Francis Drake & His Great Voyage. Derek Wilson. LC 77-3782. (Illus.). 1978. 12.95 o.s.i. (ISBN 0-06-014679-6, HarpT). Har-Row.

World Encyclopedia of Black Peoples, Vols. 1 & 2. Ed. by Harry Waldman. LC 74-28076. 1974-81. lib. bdg. 59.00 ea. Scholarly.

World Encyclopedia of Cartoons, 6 vols. Ed. by Maurice Horn & Richard E. Marschall. LC 79-26071. (Illus.). 1981. pap. 70.00 (ISBN 0-87754-121-3). Chelsea Hse.

World Encyclopedia of Comics. Ed. by Maurice Horn. 1977. pap. 10.00 (ISBN 0-380-01735-0, 34249). Avon.

World Energy Book: A-Z Atlas & Statistical Source Book. Ed. by Ray Oddy et al. LC 78-50805. 1978. 27.50x (ISBN 0-89397-032-8). Nichols Pub.

World Energy; Issues & Policies: Proceedings. Oxford Energy Seminar, First & Robert Mabro. 384p. 1980. 44.00x (ISBN 0-19-920119-6). Oxford U Pr.

World Energy Markets & OPEC Stability. Ali Ezzati. LC 77-14615. 1978. 21.00 (ISBN 0-669-01950-X). Lexington Bks.

World Energy Problems: An Economic Analysis. Richard Gordon. (Illus.). 320p. 1981. text ed. 30.00x (ISBN 0-262-07080-4). MIT Pr.

World Energy Triangle: A Strategy for Cooperation. Thomas R. Hoffmann & Brian Johnson. 1981. 20.00 (ISBN 0-905347-15-3). Ballinger Pub.

World Evangelism & the Word of God. Arthur Johnston. LC 74-13788. 304p. 1974. pap. 3.95 (ISBN 0-87123-600-1, 210600). Bethany Fell.

World Faiths in Education. W. Owen Cole. (Unwin Education Books). (Illus.). 1978. text ed. 22.50x (ISBN 0-04-371054-9); pap. text ed. 8.95x (ISBN 0-04-371055-7). Allen Unwin.

World Fish Farming Cultivation & Economics. E. Evan Brown. (Illus.). 1977. lib. bdg. 20.50 (ISBN 0-87055-234-1). AVI.

World Food & Nutrition Study: Interim Report. Commission on International Relations, National Research Council. LC 75-37120. xix, 82p. 1975. pap. 5.50 (ISBN 0-309-02436-6). Natl Acad Pr.

World Food & Nutrition Study: Potential Contributions of Research, Commission on International Relations. National Research Council. 1977. pap. 10.50 (ISBN 0-309-02628-8). Natl Acad Pr.

World Food & Nutrition Study: Supporting Papers, 5 vols. Commission on International Relations. 1977. Vol. I. pap. 6.75 (ISBN 0-309-02647-4); Vol. II. pap. 6.75 (ISBN 0-309-02726-8); Vol. III. pap. 7.00 (ISBN 0-309-02730-6); Vol. IV. pap. 6.00 (ISBN 0-309-02727-6); Vol. V. pap. 6.00 (ISBN 0-309-02646-6). Natl Acad Pr.

World Food Conference & Global Problem Solving. Thomas G. Weiss & Robert S. Jordan. LC 75-19830. (Special Studies). 1976. text ed. 19.50 o.p. (ISBN 0-275-55840-1). Praeger.

World Food Crisis. Ed. by Herbert L. Marx, Jr. (Reference Shelf Ser: Vol. 47, No. 6). 1975. 6.25 (ISBN 0-8242-0574-X). Wilson.

World Food, Pest Losses & the Environment. Ed. by David Pimentel. LC 77-90418. (AAAS Selected Symposium Ser.: No. 13). (Illus.). 1978. lib. bdg. 22.00x (ISBN 0-89158-441-2). Westview.

World Food Problem & U. S. Food Politics & Policies: 1977. Ed. by Ross B. Talbot. 1978. pap. text ed. 7.50 (ISBN 0-8138-0970-3). Iowa St U Pr.

World Food Problem: Consensus & Conflict. Ed. by Radha Sinha & Gordon Drabek. 1978. text ed. 32.00 (ISBN 0-08-022229-3); pap. text ed. 22.00 (ISBN 0-08-024318-5). Pergamon.

World Food Production--Environment--Pesticides: Plenary Lectures. International Congress of Pesticides Chemistry, 4th, Zurich, July 1978. Ed. by H. Geissbuehler et al. (IUPAC Symposia). 1978. text ed. 30.00 (ISBN 0-08-022374-5); pap. text ed. 10.00 o.p. (ISBN 0-08-022375-3). Pergamon.

World Food Programme: Report of the Eighth Session of the UN - FAO Committee on Food Aid Policies & Programmes. 55p. 1980. pap. 7.50 (ISBN 92-5-100895-7, F1967, FAO). Unipub.

World Food Programme: Report of the Ninth Session. 53p. 1981. pap. 6.00 (ISBN 92-5-100953-8, F2092, FAO). Unipub.

World Food Prospects & Agriculture Potential. Marilyn Chou et al. LC 76-24346. 1977. text ed. 28.95 (ISBN 0-275-23770-2). Praeger.

World Food Resources: Actual & Potential. M. Allaby. (Illus.). 1977. 52.90x (ISBN 0-85334-731-X, Pub. by Applied Science). Burgess-Intl Ideas.

World Food Situation: Problems & Prospects to 1985, Vol. 2. United States Department of Agriculture. 1976. 37.50 (ISBN 0-379-00573-5). Oceana.

World for a Marketplace: Episodes in the History of European Expansion. John Parker. LC 78-71068. (Illus.). 1978. 15.00 (ISBN 0-9601798-0-1). Assocs James Bell.

World Free Flight Review. Ed. by William R. Hartill. (Illus.). 1978. 30.00 (ISBN 0-933066-01-5). World Free Flight.

World Furniture. P. Philip & P. Atterbury. (Illus.). Date not set. 30.00 (ISBN 0-686-68700-0). Mayflower Bks.

World Gold Coin Value Guide. Lorraine S. Durst & Sanford J. Durst. LC 80-51832. 1980. softcover 9.00 (ISBN 0-686-64442-5); lib. bdg. 12.00 (ISBN 0-915262-54-1). S J Durst.

World Guide to Abbreviations of Organizations. 6th ed. Ed. by F. A. Buttress. 500p. 1980. write for info. (ISBN 0-8103-2024-X). Gale.

World Guide to Libraries. 5th rev. ed. 1500p. 1980. 225.00 (ISBN 0-89664-043-4, Pub. by K G Saur). Gale.

World Guide to Scientific Associations & Learned Societies. 3rd ed. Ed. by Michael Zils. (Handbook of International Documentation & Information Ser.: Vol. 13). 400p. 1981. 150.00 (ISBN 3-598-20517-1, Dist. by Gale Research). K G Saur.

World Guide to Terminological Activities. Magdalena Krommer-Benz. (Infoterm Ser.: Vol. 4). 311p. 1977. pap. text ed. 45.00 (ISBN 3-7940-5504-7, Pub. by K G Saur). Gale.

World Guide to Trade Associations. 2nd ed. Ed. by Michael Zils. (Handbook of International Documentation & Information Ser.: Vol. 12). 845p. 1980. 180.00 (ISBN 3-598-20513-9, Dist by Gale Research Co.). K G Saur.

World Handbook of Political & Social Indicators. 2nd ed. Charles L. Taylor & Michael C. Hudson. LC 70-179479. (Illus.). 464p. 1972. 28.00x o.p. (ISBN 0-300-01555-0); pap. 8.95x (ISBN 0-300-01871-1). Yale U Pr.

World Historical Fiction Guide: Annotated Chronological, Geographical & Topical List of Selected Historical Novels. 2nd ed. Daniel D. McGarry & Sarah H. White. LC 73-4357. 1973. 20.50 (ISBN 0-8108-0616-9). Scarecrow.

World History. Edwin Dunbaugh. (Quick & Easy Ser). (Orig.). 1963. pap. 1.95 o.s.i. (ISBN 0-02-079950-0, Collier). Macmillan.

World History. 3rd ed. William H. McNeill. (Illus.). 1979. 24.95 (ISBN 0-19-502554-7); pap. text ed. 11.95x (ISBN 0-19-502555-5). Oxford U Pr.

World History: A Brief Introduction. new rev. ed. Joseph Reither. LC 65-17275. Orig. Title: World History at a Glance. (Illus.). 512p. 1973. pap. 5.95 (ISBN 0-07-051875-0, SP). McGraw.

World History in the Light of Anthroposophy. new ed. Rudolf Steiner. Tr. by George Adams & Mary Adams. 1978. pap. 5.50 o.p. (ISBN 0-85440-316-7). Anthroposophic.

World History Made Simple. rev. ed. Jack C. Estrin. 1957. pap. 3.50 (ISBN 0-385-01220-9, Made). Doubleday.

World History of Physical Education: Cultural, Philosophical & Comparative. 2nd ed. Deobold B. Van Dalen & Bruce Bennett. 1971. ref. ed. 20.95x (ISBN 0-13-967919-7). P-H.

World History of Rashid Al-Din. Basil Gray. (Illus.). 1979. 42.00 (ISBN 0-571-10918-7, Pub. by Faber & Faber). Merrimack Bk Serv.

World History of the Twentieth Century: Western Dominance 1900-45, Vol. 1. J. A. Grenville. (Illus.). 605p. 1981. 32.50x (ISBN 0-389-20171-5). B&N.

World History Review Text. 2nd ed. Irving Gordon. (gr. 10-12). 1979. text ed. 14.75 (ISBN 0-87720-625-2); pap. text ed. 8.92 (ISBN 0-87720-624-4). AMSCO Sch.

World History: Special Issue 17. pap. 1.00 o.p. (ISBN 0-685-78420-7). The Smith.

World Hoax. Ernest F. Elmhurst. 233p. 1976. pap. 4.50x (ISBN 0-911038-81-7). Noontide.

World Hunger: A Guide to the Economic & Political Dimensions. Nicole Ball. Ed. by Richard D. Burns. (War-Peace Bibliography Ser.: No. 15). (Illus.). 1981. lib. bdg. price not set (ISBN 0-87436-308-X). ABC-Clio.

World Hypotheses: A Study in Evidence. Stephen C. Pepper. 1970. pap. 6.95x (ISBN 0-520-00994-0, CAMPUS31). U of Cal Pr.

World in a Frame: What We See in Films. Leo Braudy. LC 75-6151. 1977. pap. 3.95 (ISBN 0-385-03605-1, Anchor Pr). Doubleday.

World in Crisis. A. Roman. 1981. 11.95 (ISBN 0-533-04903-2). Vantage.

World in Depression, 1929-1939. Charles P. Kindleberger. (Library Reprint Ser: No. 64). 1975. 15.75 o.p. (ISBN 0-520-02912-7); pap. 4.95x (ISBN 0-520-02514-8). U of Cal Pr.

World in Nineteen Seventy-Five: History As We Lived It. Associated Press. (Illus.). 300p. (gr. 7 up). 1976. PLB 9.85 o.p. (ISBN 0-531-00331-0). Watts.

World in Nineteen-Seventy Seven. Associated Press. (Illus.). 1978. lib. bdg. 11.90 s&l o.p. (ISBN 0-531-01414-2). Watts.

World in the Attic. Wright Morris. LC 49-5058. 1971. 10.95x (ISBN 0-8032-3053-2); pap. 3.50 (ISBN 0-8032-5729-5, BB 528, Bison). U of Nebr Pr.

World in the Curriculum: Curricular Strategies for the 21st Century. Humphrey Tonkin. LC 80-69765. 200p. (Orig.). 1980. pap. 6.95 (ISBN 0-915390-28-0). Change Mag.

World in Their Web: The Textile Multi-Nationals To-Day. F. Clairmonte & J. Cavanagh. 300p. (Orig.). 1981. 22.95 (ISBN 0-905762-95-9, Pub. by Zed Pr); pap. cancelled (ISBN 0-905762-96-7). Lawrence Hill.

World in Transition: Challenges to Human Rights, Development & World Order. Ed. by Henry H. Han. LC 79-66422. 1979. pap. text ed. 17.75 (ISBN 0-8191-0824-3). U Pr of Amer.

World Index of Economic Forecasts. Ed. by George Cyriax. LC 78-56982. (Praeger Special Studies). 1978. 175.00 (ISBN 0-03-046216-9). Praeger.

World Industrial Archaeology. K. Hudson. LC 77-94225. (New Studies in Archaeology). 1979. 49.50 (ISBN 0-521-21991-4); pap. 14.50x (ISBN 0-521-29330-8). Cambridge U Pr.

World Inflation & the Less-Developed Countries. Cline, William R. & Assocs. 300p. 1981. 19.95 (ISBN 0-8157-1468-8); pap. 7.95 (ISBN 0-8157-1467-X). Brookings.

World Insurance Trends: Proceedings of the 1st International Insurance Conference. Ed. by Davis W. Gregg & Dan M. McGill. LC 58-11409. 1960. 22.00 o.p. (ISBN 0-8122-7220-X). U of Pa Pr.

World Is Full of Divorced Women. Jackie Collins. 416p. (Orig.). 1981. pap. 2.95 (ISBN 0-446-83183-2). Warner Bks.

World Is New. Joel S. Goldsmith. LC 62-7953. 1978. 8.95 (ISBN 0-06-063291-7, HarpR). Har-Row.

World Is Round. Tony Rothman. (Del Rey Bks.). 1978. pap. 1.95 o.p. (ISBN 0-345-27213-7). Ballantine.

World Is Split. N. K. Sethi. 8.00 (ISBN 0-89253-736-1). Ind-US Inc.

World Leaders. Jean Blondel. LC 79-63826. (Illus.). 1980. 20.00x o.p. (ISBN 0-8039-9830-9); pap. 9.95x o.p. (ISBN 0-8039-9831-7). Sage.

World List Annual 1979. Gascoigne. (World List Ser.). 1980. text ed. 29.95 (ISBN 0-408-70858-1). Butterworths.

World List of Aquatic Sciences & Fisheries Serial Titles. (FAO Fisheries Technical Paper: No. 147). 128p. 1980. pap. 7.00 (ISBN 92-5-100904-X, F1946, FAO). Unipub.

World List of Aquatic Sciences & Fisheries Serial Titles. (FAO Fisheries Technical Paper: No. 148). 128p. 1980. pap. 6.00 (ISBN 92-5-000882-1, F1947, FAO). Unipub.

World List of Universities, Other Institutions of Higher Education & University Organizations 1979-1981. Ed. by D. J. Aitken. 693p. 1979. text ed. 57.64x (ISBN 3-11008-077-X). De Gruyter.

World Markets for Construction. John Bunton. (Illus.). 1979. 33.50x (ISBN 0-7198-2720-5). Intl Ideas.

World Military Aircraft Since Nineteen Forty-Five. Robert Jackson. (Illus.). 1980. 10.95 (ISBN 0-684-16265-2, ScribT). Scribner.

World Military Order. Mary Kaldor & Ashborn Eide. LC 78-87885. 1979. 28.95 (ISBN 0-03-053371-6). Praeger.

World Mineral Trends & U. S. Supply Problems. Leonard L. Fischman. LC 80-8025. (Resources for the Future, Inc. Research Paper R-20). (Illus.). 576p. (Orig.). 1981. pap. text ed. 15.00x (ISBN 0-8018-2491-5). Johns Hopkins.

World News Prism: Changing Media, Clashing Ideologies. William A. Hachten. 120p. 1981. pap. text ed. 6.50 (ISBN 0-8138-1580-0). Iowa St U Pr.

World Nutrition & Nutrition Education. Ed. by H. M. Sinclair & G. R. Howat. (Illus.). 272p. 1980. text ed. 42.50x (ISBN 0-19-261176-3). Oxford U Pr.

World Nutrition & Nutrition Education. 226p. 1981. 50.50 (ISBN 92-3-101736-5, U1057, UNESCO). Unipub.

World Ocean. 2nd ed. William Anikouchine & Richard Sternberg. (Illus.). 512p. 1981. 19.95 (ISBN 0-13-967778-X). P-H.

World Ocean: An Introduction to Oceanography. W. Anikouchine & R. Sternberg. 1973. 18.95 (ISBN 0-13-967752-6). P-H.

World Ocean Atlas, Vol. 2: Atlantic & Indian Oceans. S. G. Gorshkov. 3504p. 1979. 400.00 (ISBN 0-08-021953-5). Pergamon.

World of a Tree. Arnold Darlington. 1972. 6.95 (ISBN 0-571-09624-7, Pub. by Faber & Faber). Merrimack Bk Serv.

World of Aldus Manutius: Business & Scholarship in Renaissance Venice. M. J. Lowry. LC 78-58631. (Illus.). 1979. 36.50x (ISBN 0-8014-1214-5). Cornell U Pr.
World of an Estuary. Heather Angel. (Illus.). 1974. 7.95 (ISBN 0-571-10378-2, Pub. by Faber & Faber). Merrimack Bk Serv.
World of Ancient Times. Carl Roebuck. (Illus.). 1966. pap. text ed. 13.95x (ISBN 0-684-13726-7, ScribC). Scribner.
World of Animals. Mary Verdick. Ed. by Thomas J. Mooney. (Beginning Pal Paperbacks Ser.). (Illus., Orig.). (gr. 7-12). 1977. pap. text ed. 1.25 (ISBN 0-8374-3457-2). Xerox Ed Pubns.
World of Art. Paul Weiss. LC 61-5168. (Arcturus Books Paperbacks). 204p. 1964. pap. 5.95 (ISBN 0-8093-0112-1). S Ill U Pr.
World of Asif Currimbhoy. Faubion Bowers. 4.80 (ISBN 0-89253-664-0); flexible cloth 3.00 (ISBN 0-89253-665-9). Ind-US Inc.
World of Baroque & Classical Musical Instruments. Jeremy Montagu. LC 78-65227. (Instrument Ser.). (Illus.). 1979. 23.95 (ISBN 0-87951-089-7). Overlook Pr.
World of Bernini. Robert Wallace. (Library of Art). (Illus.). 1970. 15.95 (ISBN 0-8094-0257-2). Time-Life.
World of Bernini. Robert Wallace. LC 70-122329. (Library of Art Ser.). (Illus.). (gr. 6 up). 1970. 12.96 (ISBN 0-8094-0286-6, Pub. by Time-Life). Silver.
World of Black Singles: Changing Patterns of Male-Female Relations. Robert Staples. LC 80-1025. (Contributions in Afro-American & African Studies: No. 57). 288p. 1981. lib. bdg. 25.00 (ISBN 0-313-22478-1, SBS/). Greenwood.
World of Bruegel. Timothy Foote. (Library of Art). (Illus.). 1968. 15.95 (ISBN 0-8094-0246-7). Time-Life.
World of Bruegel. Timothy Foote. LC 68-31677. (Library of Art Ser.). (Illus.). (gr. 6 up). 1968. 12.96 (ISBN 0-8094-0275-0, Pub. by Time-Life). Silver.
World of Butterflies. Michael Dickens & Eric Storey. (Illus.). 128p. 1973. 5.95 o.s.i. (ISBN 0-02-531400-9). Macmillan.
World of Cactus & Succulents. Ed. by Staff of Ortho Books. LC 77-89689. (Illus.). 1978. pap. 4.95 (ISBN 0-917102-59-2). Ortho.
World of Canadian Writing: Critiques & Recollections. George Woodcock. LC 80-15497. 312p. 1981. pap. price not set (ISBN 0-295-95808-1). U of Wash Pr.
World of Cats in Color. rev. ed. Ted Allen. (Illus.). 96p. 1974. 4.95 o.p. (ISBN 0-668-03416-5). Arco.
World of Cezanne. Richard W. Murphy. (Library of Art). (Illus.). 1968. 15.95 (ISBN 0-8094-0243-2). Time-Life.
World of Cezanne. Richard W. Murphy. LC 68-17688. (Library of Art Ser.). (Illus.). (gr. 6 up). 1968. 12.96 (ISBN 0-8094-0272-6, Pub. by Time-Life). Silver.
World of Charlemagne. Friedrich Heer. LC 74-22219. (Illus.). 272p. 1975. 19.95 (ISBN 0-02-550450-9, 55045). Macmillan.
World of Choice: Careers and You- Student Workbook. Ralp Ressler. LC 77-4182. (Illus.). 1978. pap. 7.95 (ISBN 0-88280-050-7); tchr's guide 9.95 (ISBN 0-88280-051-5). ETC Pubns.
World of Communications: Audiovisual Media. Hauenstein & Bachmeyer. (gr. 9-12). 1975. text ed. 14.64 (ISBN 0-87345-662-9); teacher's guide 29.33 (ISBN 0-87345-663-7); activity manuals 4.67 ea.; filmstrip set 200.00 (ISBN 0-685-63840-5); 2 films 180.00 (ISBN 0-685-63841-3); transparency package 260.00 (ISBN 0-685-63842-1). McKnight.
World of Communications: Visual Media. A. Dean Hauenstein & Steven A. Bachmeyer. (gr. 9-12). 1974. text ed. 14.64 (ISBN 0-87345-675-0); teacher's guide 29.33 (ISBN 0-87345-677-7); lab manual 6.33 (ISBN 0-87345-676-9); filmstrip set 200.00 (ISBN 0-685-42203-8); 2 films 170.00 (ISBN 0-685-42204-6); transparency set 325.00 (ISBN 0-685-42205-4). McKnight.
World of Construction. Industrial Arts Curriculum Project Staff. (gr. 7-9). text ed. 14.64 (ISBN 0-87345-462-6); tchrs' guide 32.00 (ISBN 0-87345-465-0); lab. manual 5.28 (ISBN 0-87345-463-4); big builder game 14.00 (ISBN 0-685-28871-4); filmstrip set 90.00 (ISBN 0-685-28872-2); transparency set 390.00 (ISBN 0-685-28873-0). McKnight.
World of Copernicus. Angus Armitage. 1972. pap. 5.95x (ISBN 0-8464-0979-8). Beekman Pubs.
World of Copley. Alfred Frankenstein. LC 74-113381. (Library of Art Ser.). (Illus.). (gr. 6 up). 1970. 12.96 (ISBN 0-8094-0284-X, Pub. by Time-Life). Silver.
World of Cosmetology: A Professional Text. Sylvia Franco et al. LC 79-20678. (Illus.). 512p. 1980. text ed. 14.96 (ISBN 0-07-021791-2). McGraw.
World of Cosmetology, A Professional Text: Student Activities Manual. Sylvia Franco et al. (Illus.). 352p. 1980. 7.96 (ISBN 0-07-021792-0, G); instructor's planning manual 17.00 (ISBN 0-07-021793-9). McGraw.
World of Dahlias. Keith Hammett. (Illus.). 144p. 1980. 17.50 (ISBN 0-589-01265-7, Pub. by Reed Bks Australia). C E Tuttle.
World of Dance. Melvin Berger. LC 78-14498. (Illus.). (gr. 5 up). 1978. 9.95 (ISBN 0-87599-221-8). S G Phillips.
World of Dante: Essays on Dante & His Times. Cecil Grayson. (Illus.). 204p. 1980. text ed. 36.00x. Oxford U Pr.
World of Delacroix. Tom Prideaux. (Library of Art). (Illus.). 1966. 15.95 (ISBN 0-8094-0233-5). Time-Life.
World of Delacroix. Tom Prideaux. LC 66-21130. (Library of Art Ser.). (Illus.). (gr. 6 up). 1966. 12.96 (ISBN 0-8094-0262-9, Pub. by Time-Life). Silver.
World of Diamonds. Timothy S. Green. LC 80-26196. (Illus.). 1981. price not set (ISBN 0-688-03731-3). Morrow.
World of Difference. Heather McHugh. 1981. 8.95 (ISBN 0-395-30231-5); pap. 4.95 (ISBN 0-395-30232-3). HM.
World of Don Quixote. Richard L. Predmore. LC 67-20879. 1967. 7.50x (ISBN 0-674-96090-4). Harvard U Pr.
World of Drafting. Stan Ross. (gr. 7-9). 1971. text ed. 15.16 (ISBN 0-87345-078-7). McKnight.
World of Dreams. Havelock Ellis. LC 75-43879. (Illus.). 1976. Repr. of 1922 ed. 24.00 (ISBN 0-8103-3780-0). Gale.
World of Duke Ellington. Stanley Dance. (Da Capo Quality Paperbacks Ser.). xii, 311p. pap. 7.95 (ISBN 0-306-80136-1). Da Capo.
World of Durer. Francis Russell. (Library of Art). (Illus.). 1967. 15.95 (ISBN 0-8094-0241-6). Time-Life.
World of Durer. Francis Russell. LC 67-29856. (Library of Art Ser.). (Illus.). (gr. 6 up). 1967. 12.96 (ISBN 0-8094-0270-X, Pub. by Time-Life). Silver.
World of Earl Hines. Stanley Dance. LC 77-2269. (Illus.). 1977. pap. 5.95 encored. o.p. (ISBN 0-684-16351-9, ScribT, ScribT). Scribner.
World of Elia: Charles Lamb's Essayistic Romanticism. Fred V. Randel. (National University Publications Literary Criticism Ser.). 1975. 12.95 (ISBN 0-8046-9118-5, Natl U). Kennikat.
World of Ellen March. Jeannette Eyerly. LC 64-19039. (gr. 7-9). 1964. 9.95 (ISBN 0-397-30793-4). Lippincott.
World of Flo Ziegfeld. Randolph Carter. 1974. 9.95 o.p. (ISBN 0-236-31053-4, Pub. by Paul Elek). Merrimack Bk Serv.
World of Freshwater Fish. Thomas D. Fegely. LC 77-16879. (Illus.). (gr. 5 up). 1978. 6.95 (ISBN 0-396-07562-2). Dodd.
World of Gainsborough. Jonathan N. Leonard. (Library of Art). (Illus.). 1969. 15.95 (ISBN 0-8094-0253-X). Time-Life.
World of Gainsborough. Jonathan N. Leonard. LC 73-84574. (Library of Art Ser.). (Illus.). (gr. 6 up). 1969. 12.96 (ISBN 0-8094-0282-3, Pub. by Time-Life). Silver.
World of Ghosts. Alan C. Jenkins. (Illus.). 1978. 6.95 (ISBN 0-7011-5087-4, Pub. by Chatto Bodley Jonathan). Merrimack Bk Serv.
World of Giotto. Sarel Eimerl. (Library of Art). (Illus.). 1967. 15.95 (ISBN 0-8094-0239-4). Time-Life.
World of Giotto. Sarel Eimerl. LC 67-23024. (Library of Art Ser.). (Illus.). (gr. 6 up). 1967. 12.96 (ISBN 0-8094-0268-8, Pub. by Time-Life). Silver.
World of Golf & the Game of Life. Charles F. Kemp. (Illus.). 1978. pap. 2.95 (ISBN 0-8272-4212-3). Bethany Pr.
World of Goya. Richard Schickel. (Library of Art). (Illus.). 1968. 15.95 (ISBN 0-8094-0247-5). Time-Life.
World of Goya. Richard Schickel. LC 68-56432. (Library of Art Ser.). (Illus.). (gr. 6 up). 1968. 12.96 (ISBN 0-8094-0276-9, Pub. by Time-Life). Silver.
World of Grace. L. J. O'Donovan. 1980. 14.95 (ISBN 0-8164-0212-4); pap. 7.95 (ISBN 0-8164-2006-3). Crossroad NY.
World of Gwendolyn Brooks. Gwendolyn Brooks. LC 74-160646. 1971. 15.00 (ISBN 0-06-010538-0, HarpT). Har-Row.
World of Harlequin. A. Nicoll. LC 76-18411. (Illus.). 1976. 58.00 (ISBN 0-521-05834-1); pap. 18.95 (ISBN 0-521-29132-1). Cambridge U Pr.
World of Her Own. Nancy Levinson. LC 80-81791. (Illus.). 128p. (gr. 5 up). 1981. PLB 6.59 (ISBN 0-8178-0014-X). Harvey.
World of Herbs & Spices. Ortho Books Editorial Staff. LC 78-57892. (Illus.). 1979. pap. 4.95 (ISBN 0-917102-72-X). Ortho.
World of Heroes: Selections from Homer, Herodotus & Sophocles. Joint Association of Classical Teachers' Greek Course. LC 79-10740. (Illus.). 1979. pap. 9.95x (ISBN 0-521-22462-4). Cambridge U Pr.
World of Horses. Margaret C. Self. 1961. 8.95 o.p. (ISBN 0-07-056108-7, GB). McGraw.
World of Hurt: A Novel. Bo Hathaway. LC 80-18147. 272p. 1981. 11.95 (ISBN 0-8008-8586-4). Taplinger.
World of Ideas: A Guide to Effective Reading. H. A. Bamman et al. LC 74-84819. 1970. text ed. 8.95 (ISBN 0-8464-3003-7). Benjamin-Cummings.
World of Ideas: A Guide to Effective Reading. H. A. Bamman et al. 1970. 8.95 (ISBN 0-201-43003-7); tchr's guide 4.50 (ISBN 0-201-43004-5). A-W.
World of Indonesian Textiles. Michael E. Gaworski & Wanda Warming. LC 80-82526. (Illus.). 280p. 1981. 50.00 (ISBN 0-87011-432-8). Kodansha.
World of Islam. Richard Tames. (Jackdaw Ser: No. 143). (gr. 7 up). 1976. 5.95 o.p. (ISBN 0-670-78671-3). Viking Pr.
World of J. B. Priestley. Ed. by Donald Macrae. 1967. text ed. 5.95x o.p. (ISBN 0-435-82725-1). Heinemann Ed.
World of Japanese Business. T. F. M. Adams & N. Kobayashi. LC 71-82661. (Illus.). 326p. 1969. 14.95x (ISBN 0-87011-091-8). Kodansha.
World of Japanese Ceramics. Herbert H. Sanders & Kenkichi Tomimoto. LC 67-16771. (Illus.). 267p. 1981. 27.50 (ISBN 0-87011-042-X). Kodansha.
World of Jimmy Connors. Jim Burke. (Illus., Orig.). 1976. pap. 1.50 o.p. (ISBN 0-685-64019-1, LB330DK, Leisure Bks). Nordon Pubns.
World of John Singleton Copley. Alfred Frankenstein. (Library of Art). (Illus.). 1969. 15.95 (ISBN 0-8094-0255-6). Time-Life.
World of Kafka. J. P Stern. (Illus.). 256p. 1980. 18.95 (ISBN 0-03-051366-9). HR&W.
World of Lady Jane Grey. Gladys Malvern. LC 64-23320. (Illus.). (gr. 9 up). 1964. 7.95 (ISBN 0-8149-0357-6). Vanguard.
World of Language for Deaf Children: Basic Principles, a Maternal Reflective Method, Pt. 1. 3rd ed. A. Van Uden. (Modern Approaches to the Diagnosis & Instruction of Multi-Handicapped Children: Vol. 4). 348p. 1977. text ed. 36.00 (ISBN 90-265-0253-2, Pub. by Swets Pub Serv Holland). Swets North Am.
World of Learning 1979-1980, 2 vols. 30th ed. LC 47-30172. 2100p. 1980. Set. 105.00x o.p. (ISBN 0-905118-40-5). Intl Pubns Serv.
World of Learning 1980-81. 2000p. 1981. 125.00 (ISBN 0-905118-52-9, EUR 25, Europa). Unipub.
World of Learning 1980-81, 2 vols. 31st ed. LC 47-30172. 1981. Set. 125.00x (ISBN 0-905118-52-9). Intl Pubns Serv.
World of Learning 1980-81, 2 vols. 31st ed. LC 47-30172. 2000p. 1981. 130.00 (Pub. by Europa England). Gale.
World of Leonardo. Robert Wallace. (Library of Art). (Illus.). 1966. 15.95 (ISBN 0-8094-0234-3). Time-Life.
World of Leonardo. Robert Wallace. LC 66-24104. (Library of Art Ser.). (Illus.). (gr. 6 up). 1966. 12.96 (ISBN 0-8094-0263-7, Pub. by Time-Life). Silver.
World of Mammals. Augusto V. Taglianti. Tr. by John Gilbert. LC 80-69173. (Abbeville Press Encyclopedia of Natural Science). (Illus.). 256p. 1980. 13.95 (ISBN 0-89659-183-2); pap. 7.95 (ISBN 0-89659-184-0). Abbeville Pr.
World of Man. Georg W. Groddeck. LC 51-13247. (Illus.). 272p. 1951. 12.50x o.p. (ISBN 0-85478-030-0). Intl Pubns Serv.
World of Manet. Pierre Schneider. (Library of Art). (Illus.). 1968. 15.95 (ISBN 0-8094-0248-3). Time-Life.
World of Manet. Pierre Schneider. LC 68-58484. (Library of Art Ser.). (Illus.). (gr. 6 up). 1968. 12.96 (ISBN 0-8094-0277-7, Pub. by Time-Life). Silver.
World of Manufacturing. (gr. 7-9). text ed. 15.96 (ISBN 0-87345-550-9); tchr's guide 32.00 (ISBN 0-87345-552-5); lab. manual 5.00 (ISBN 0-87345-551-7); game 15.00 (ISBN 0-685-28865-X); filmstrip set 306.00 (ISBN 0-685-28866-8); transparency set 390.00 (ISBN 0-685-28867-6). McKnight.
World of Marcel Duchamp. Calvin Tomkins. (Library of Art). (Illus.). 1966. 15.95 (ISBN 0-8094-0236-X). Time-Life.
World of Marcel Duchamp. Calvin Tomkins. LC 66-28544. (Library of Art Ser.). (Illus.). (gr. 6 up). 1966. 12.96 (ISBN 0-8094-0265-3, Pub. by Time-Life). Silver.
World of Matisse. John Russell. (Library of Art). (Illus.). 1969. 15.95 (ISBN 0-8094-0249-1). Time-Life.
World of Matisse. John Russell. LC 69-19503. (Library of Art Ser.). (Illus.). (gr. 6 up). 1969. 12.96 (ISBN 0-8094-0278-5, Pub. by Time-Life). Silver.
World of Medieval & Renaissance Musical Instruments. Jeremy Montagu. LC 76-5987. (Illus.). 1976. 27.95 (ISBN 0-87951-045-5). Overlook Pr.
World of Medieval Learning. Anders Piltz. Tr. by Davis Jones. (Illus.). 1981. 30.00x (ISBN 0-389-20206-1). B&N.
World of Michelangelo. Robert Coughlan. (Library of Art). (Illus.). 1966. 15.95 (ISBN 0-8094-0232-7). Time-Life.
World of Michelangelo. Robert Coughlan. LC 66-16540. (Library of Art Ser.). (Illus.). (gr. 6 up). 1966. 12.96 (ISBN 0-8094-0261-0, Pub. by Time-Life). Silver.
World of Moses. Paul F. Bork. LC 78-5022. (Horizon Ser.). 1978. pap. 4.95 (ISBN 0-8127-0166-6). Southern Pub.
World of Moths. Michael Dickens & Eric Storey. (Illus.). 128p. 1974. 6.95 o.s.i. (ISBN 0-02-531390-8). Macmillan.
World of Movies: Seventy Years of Film History. Richard Lawton. (Illus.). 384p. 1974. 25.00 o.s.i. (ISBN 0-440-08586-1). Delacorte.
World of Musical Comedy. 4th, rev. ed. Stanley Green. LC 80-16915. 448p. 1980. 19.95 (ISBN 0-498-02344-3). A S Barnes.
World of Names: A Study in Hungarian Onomatology. Bela Kalman. LC 79-300962. 1978. 15.00x (ISBN 963-05-1399-4). Intl Pubns Serv.
World of Nations: Problems of Political Modernization. Dankwart A. Rustow. 1967. pap. 5.95 (ISBN 0-8157-7641-1). Brookings.
World of Natural Sciences & Its Phenomenology: The Human Brain & Its Universe. 2nd ed. H. Kuhlenbeck. Ed. by J. Gerlach. (Vol. 1). viii, 320p. 1981. 118.75 (ISBN 3-8055-1817-X). S Karger.
World of Night. Lururus J. Milne & Margery J. Milne. (Nature Library Ser.). (Illus.). 248p. (Orig.). 1981. pap. 5.95 (ISBN 0-06-090839-4, CN 839, CN). Har-Row.
World of O. Henry - Five One Act Plays. Jesse F. Knight. LC 77-15687. (Lion Theatrical Ser.: No. 1). 1980. pap. 3.50 (ISBN 0-930962-03-6). Lion Ent.
World of Oil. A. F. Fox. 1964. 12.25 (ISBN 0-08-010687-0); pap. 7.00 (ISBN 0-08-010686-2). Pergamon.
World of Origami. abr. ed. Isao Honda. LC 65-27101. (Illus.). 200p. 1976. pap. 11.00 (ISBN 0-87040-383-4). Japan Pubns.
World of Ottoman Art. Michael Levey. LC 76-40383. (Encore Edition). 1977. 4.95 o.p. (ISBN 0-684-16200-8, ScribT). Scribner.
World of Our Fathers. Irving Howe. 1981. pap. 3.95 (ISBN 0-553-13810-3). Bantam.
World of Physics. rev ed. R. I. Hulsizer & D. Lazarus. (gr. 11-12). 1977. text ed. 14.92 o.p. (ISBN 0-201-02967-7, Sch Div). A-W.
World of Picasso. Lael Wertenbaker. (Library of Art). (Illus.). 1967. 15.95 (ISBN 0-8094-0242-4). Time-Life.
World of Picasso. Lael Wertenbaker. LC 67-30587. (Library of Art Ser.). (Illus.). (gr. 6 up) 1967. 12.96 (ISBN 0-8094-0271-8, Pub. by Time-Life). Silver.
World of Plant Life. 2nd ed. Clarence J. Hylander. (Illus.). 1956. 19.95 (ISBN 0-02-558050-7). Macmillan.
World of Primitive Man. Paul Radin. 1971. pap. 2.45 o.p. (ISBN 0-525-47298-3). Dutton.
World of Professional Golf: Mark H. McCormack's Golf Annual 1978. Mark H. McCormack. LC 78-58848. 1978. pap. 8.95 o.p. (ISBN 0-385-14166-1); pap. 8.95 Softbound o.p. (ISBN 0-385-14179-3). Doubleday.
World of Promise. E. C. Tubb. 1980. pap. 1.75 (ISBN 0-87997-579-2, UE1579). DAW Bks.
World of Ptavvs. Larry Niven. 192p. Date not set. pap. 1.95 (ISBN 0-345-28619-7). Ballantine.
World of Ranters-Religious Radicalism in the English Revolution. A. L. Morton. 1979. pap. 6.75x (ISBN 0-85315-497-X). Humanities.
World of Rembrandt. Robert Wallace. (Library of Art). (Illus.). 1968. 15.95 (ISBN 0-8094-0244-0). Time-Life.
World of Rembrandt. Robert Wallace. LC 68-22321. (Library of Art Ser.). (Illus.). (gr. 6 up). 1968. 12.96 (ISBN 0-8094-0273-4, Pub. by Time-Life). Silver.
World of Robert Flaherty. Richard Griffith. LC 72-166104. 1972. Repr. of 1953 ed. lib. bdg. 25.00 (ISBN 0-306-70296-7). Da Capo.
World of Rodin. William H. Hale. (Library of Art). (Illus.). 1969. 15.95 (ISBN 0-8094-0254-8). Time-Life.
World of Rodin. William H. Hale. LC 70-105511. (Library of Art Ser.). (Illus.). (gr. 6 up). 1969. 12.96 (ISBN 0-8094-0283-1, Pub. by Time-Life). Silver.
World of Romantic & Modern Musical Instruments. Jeremy Montagu. LC 80-26106. (Musical Instruments Ser.). (Illus.). 136p. 1981. pap. 27.95 (ISBN 0-87951-126-5). Overlook Pr.

World of Rubens. Cicely V. Wedgewood. LC 67-27679. (Library of Art Ser.). (Illus.). (gr. 6 up). 1967. 12.96 (ISBN 0-8094-0269-6, Pub. by Time-Life). Silver.

World of Rubens. Cicely V. Wedgwood. (Library of Art). (Illus.). 1967. 15.95 (ISBN 0-8094-0240-8). Time-Life.

World of Sail & Power, No. 3. Ed. by Gerald Asaria & Erwan Quemere. (Illus.). 1980. 28.95 (ISBN 0-914814-25-7). Sail Bks.

World of Salads. Rosalie Swedlin. LC 80-18134. (Illus.). 256p. 1981. 17.95 (ISBN 0-03-053391-0); pap. 9.95 (ISBN 0-686-69291-8). HR&W.

World of Scarcities: Critical Issues in Public Policy. David Novick. LC 75-42278. 1976. 27.95 (ISBN 0-470-15002-5). Halsted Pr.

World of Serge Diaghilev. Charles Spencer. (Illus.). 174p. 1979. 14.95 o.p. (ISBN 0-670-78783-3, Studio). Viking Pr.

World of Serge Diaghilev. Charles Spencer & Philip Dyer. 1974. 9.95 o.p. (ISBN 0-236-31054-2, Pub. by Paul Elek). Merrimack Bk Serv.

World of Short Fiction. Ed. by Robert C. Albrecht. LC 69-11841. 1970. pap. text ed. 8.95 (ISBN 0-02-900350-4). Free Pr.

World of Somerset Maugham: An Anthology. Ed. by Klaus W. Jonas. LC 73-156196. 200p. 1972. Repr. of 1959 ed. lib. bdg. 18.75x (ISBN 0-8371-6147-9, JOSM). Greenwood.

World of Speed Skating. Dianne Holum. (Illus.). 320p. 1981. 17.50 (ISBN 0-89490-051-X). Enslow Pubs.

World of States: Connected Essays. J. D. Miller. 1981. price not set (ISBN 0-312-89240-3). St Martin.

World of Stone: Life, Folklore & Legends of the Aran Islands, Bk. 1. Curriculum Development Unit. text ed. 22.00x (ISBN 0-905140-15-X). Humanities.

World of the African Woman. John E. Njoku. LC 80-23832. 132p. 1980. 10.00 (ISBN 0-8108-1350-5). Scarecrow.

World of the American Elk. Joe Van Wormer. LC 77-86080. (Illus.). 1969. 8.95 (ISBN 0-397-00621-7). Lippincott.

World of the Bat. Charles E. Mohr. LC 76-7355. (Living World Ser.). (Illus.). 1976. 10.95 (ISBN 0-397-00800-7). Lippincott.

World of the Book of Mormon. Paul R. Cheesman. LC 77-18772. (Illus.). 1978. pap. text ed. 5.95 o.p. (ISBN 0-87747-649-7). Deseret Bk.

World of the Buddha: A Reader from the Three Baskets to Modern Zen. Ed. by Lucien Stryk. LC 68-11766. 1969. pap. 2.95 o.p. (ISBN 0-385-00407-9, A615, Anch). Doubleday.

World of the California Gray Whale. Tom Miller. (Illus.). 1975. pap. 4.00 (ISBN 0-914622-02-1). Baja Trail.

World of the Contemporary Counselor. C. Gilbert Wrenn. LC 72-4800. 368p. (Orig.). 1973. pap. text ed. 10.95 (ISBN 0-395-13901-5, 3-60800). HM.

World of the Family: A Comparative Study of Family Organization in Their Social & Cultural Settings. Dorothy Blitstein. 1963. text ed. 5.95 o.p. (ISBN 0-394-30072-6). Random.

World of the Florentine Renaissance Artist: Projects & Patrons, Workshop & Art Market. Martin Wackernagel. Tr. by Alison Luchs from Ger. LC 80-8583. 496p. 1981. 32.50x (ISBN 0-691-03966-6); pap. 12.50x (ISBN 0-691-10117-5). Princeton U Pr.

World of the Gull. David F. Costello. LC 74-159726. (Living World Bk. Ser.). (Illus.). 1971. 7.95 o.p. (ISBN 0-397-00730-2). Lippincott.

World of the Horse. Judith Campbell. LC 76-49701. 1977. pap. 7.95 o.p. (ISBN 0-89104-056-0). A & W Pubs.

World of the Huns: Studies in Their History & Culture. Otto J. Maenchen-Helfen. Ed. by Max Knight. LC 79-94985. 1973. 30.00x (ISBN 0-520-01596-7). U of Cal Pr.

World of the Japanese Garden. (Illus.). 416p. 1981. 37.50 (ISBN 0-8348-0029-2). Weatherhill.

World of the Japanese Garden: From Chinese Origins to Modern Landscape Art. Loraine Kuck. LC 68-26951. (Illus.). 413p. 1980. 37.50 (ISBN 0-8348-0029-2, Pub. by John Weatherhill Inc Japan). C E Tuttle.

World of the Middle Ages: A Reorientation of Medieval History. John L. LaMonte. (Illus.). 1949. 34.50x (ISBN 0-89197-473-3); pap. text ed. 19.50x (ISBN 0-89197-980-8). Irvington.

World of the New Testament. Ed. by Everett Ferguson. (Living Word New Testament Commentary, Vol. 1). 1967. 7.95 (ISBN 0-8344-0023-5). Sweet.

World of the New Testament. Sean Fryene. (New Testament Message Ser.). 9.00 (ISBN 0-89453-125-5); pap. 5.95 (ISBN 0-89453-190-5). M Glazier.

World of the Porcupine. David F. Costello. LC 66-16658. (Living World Books Ser). (Illus.). 1966. 8.95 (ISBN 0-397-00449-4); PLB 6.82 o.p. (ISBN 0-397-00934-8). Lippincott.

World of the Prairie Dog. David F. Costello. LC 70-110650. (Living World Bks Ser). (Illus.). 1970. 7.95 (ISBN 0-397-00679-9); PLB 7.82 o.p. (ISBN 0-397-00680-2, L). Lippincott.

World of the Red Fox. Leonard L. Rue, 3rd. LC 69-16165. (Living World Books Ser). 1969. 7.95 o.s.i. (ISBN 0-397-00627-6); PLB 7.82 o.s.i. (ISBN 0-397-00628-4). Lippincott.

World of the Reformation. Hans J. Hillerbrand. (Twin Brooks Ser.). 229p. 1981. pap. 6.95 (ISBN 0-8010-4248-8). Baker Bk.

World of the Ruffled Grouse. Leonard L. Rue, 3rd. Ed. by John Terres. LC 72-748. (Living World Bks). (Illus.). 291p. 1972. 8.95 (ISBN 0-397-00817-1). Lippincott.

World of the Small Commercial Fishermen: Their Lives & Their Boats. Michael Meltzer. (Illus.). 1980. pap. 4.95 (ISBN 0-486-23945-4). Dover.

World of the Tent-Makers: A Natural History of the Eastern Tent Caterpillar. V. G. Dethier. LC 80-11361. (Illus.). 160p. 1980. lib. bdg. 12.50x (ISBN 0-87023-300-9); pap. 5.95 (ISBN 0-87023-301-7). U of Mass Pr.

World of the Theatre. Robert W. Corrigan. 1979. text ed. 14.95x (ISBN 0-673-15107-7). Scott F.

World of the White-Tailed Deer. Leonard L. Rue. LC 62-11348. (Living World Book Ser). 1962. 10.95 (ISBN 0-397-00254-8). Lippincott.

World of the Wild Turkey. James C. Lewis. LC 72-2923. (Living World Bks.). (Illus.). (YA) 1973. 8.95 (ISBN 0-397-00788-4). Lippincott.

World of the Wolf. Russell J. Rutter & Douglas H. Pimlott. LC 67-16919. (Living World Books Ser). (gr. 4-9). 1968. 10.95 (ISBN 0-397-00570-9). Lippincott.

World of Titian. Jay Williams. (Library of Art). (Illus.). 1968. 15.95 (ISBN 0-8094-0245-9). Time-Life.

World of Titian. Jay Williams. LC 68-28257. (Library of Art Ser.). (Illus.). (gr. 6 up). 1968. 12.96 (ISBN 0-8094-0274-2, Pub. by Time-Life). Silver.

World of Tragedy. Ed. by John Kimmey & Ashley Brown. 1981. pap. 3.95 (ISBN 0-451-61991-9, ME1991, Ment). NAL.

World of Trees. Ed. by Staff of Ortho Books. LC 77-89692. (Illus.). 1978. pap. 4.95 Midwest-Northeast ed. (ISBN 0-917102-60-6); pap. 4.95 South ed. (ISBN 0-917102-61-4); pap. 4.95 West ed. (ISBN 0-917102-62-2). Ortho.

World of Trog. Wally Fawkes. (Illus.). 96p. 1977. bds. 8.75x (ISBN 0-8476-3128-1). Rowman.

World of Turner. Diana Hirsh. (Library of Art). (Illus.). 1969. 15.95 (ISBN 0-8094-0250-5). Time-Life.

World of Turner. Diana Hirsh. LC 73-78989. (Library of Art Ser.). (Illus.). (gr. 6 up). 1969. 12.96 (ISBN 0-8094-0279-3, Pub. by Time-Life). Silver.

World of Upstairs, Downstairs. Mollie Hardwick. LC 75-21465. 1976. 12.95 o.p. (ISBN 0-03-015571-1). HR&W.

World of Van Gogh. Robert Wallace. (Library of Art). (Illus.). 1969. 15.95 (ISBN 0-8094-0251-3). Time-Life.

World of Van Gogh. Robert Wallace. LC 70-78988. (Library of Art Ser.). (Illus.). (gr. 6 up). 1969. 12.96 (ISBN 0-8094-0280-7, Pub. by Time-Life). Silver.

World of Variations. Thomas F. McNulty & Mary O. Stevens. pap. 2.95 o.p. (ISBN 0-8076-0573-5). Braziller.

World of Velazquez. Dale Brown. (Library of Art). (Illus.). 1969. 15.95 (ISBN 0-8094-0252-1). Time-Life.

World of Velazquez. Dale Brown. LC 77-84575. (Library of Art Ser.). (Illus.). (gr. 6 up). 1969. 12.96 (ISBN 0-8094-0281-5, Pub. by Time-Life). Silver.

World of Venice. rev. ed. James Morris. LC 73-18461. (Helen & Kurt Wolff Bk). (Illus.). 1973. 8.95 (ISBN 0-15-199086-7). HarBraceJ.

World of Vermeer. Hans Koning. (Library of Art). (Illus.). 1967. 15.95 (ISBN 0-8094-0237-8). Time-Life.

World of Vermeer. Hans Koning. LC 67-15299. (Library of Art Ser.). (Illus.). (gr. 6 up). 1967. 12.96 (ISBN 0-8094-0266-1, Pub. by Time-Life). Silver.

World of Victorian Humor. Ed. by Harold Orel. LC 61-8018. (Goldentree Books in English Literature). (Illus., Orig.). 1961. pap. text ed. 8.95x (ISBN 0-89197-474-1). Irvington.

World of W. H. Auden. Ed. by Stephen Spender. (Illus.). 256p. 1975. 14.95 o.s.i. (ISBN 0-02-612940-X). Macmillan.

World of Watteau. Pierre Schneider. (Library of Art). (Illus.). 1967. 15.95 (ISBN 0-8094-0238-6). Time-Life.

World of Watteau. Pierre Schneider. LC 67-20332. (Library of Art Ser.). (Illus.). (gr. 6 up). 1967. 12.96 (ISBN 0-8094-0267-X, Pub. by Time-Life). Silver.

World of Whistler. Tom Prideaux. (Time-Life Library of Art). (Illus.). (gr. 5 up). 1970. 15.95 (ISBN 0-8094-0256-4). Time-Life.

World of Whistler. Tom Prideaux. LC 70-116437. (Library of Art Ser.). (Illus.). (gr. 6 up). 1970. 12.96 (ISBN 0-8094-0285-8, Pub. by Time-Life). Silver.

World of Willa Cather. Mildred R. Bennett. LC 61-7235. (Illus.). 1961. 13.95x (ISBN 0-8032-1151-1); pap. 3.95 (ISBN 0-8032-5013-4, BB 112, Bison). U of Nebr Pr.

World of Wine. Creighton Churchill. (Illus.). 384p. 1980. pap. 6.95 (ISBN 0-02-009460-4, Collier). Macmillan.

World of Winslow Homer. James Flexner. (Library of Art). (Illus.). 1966. 15.95 (ISBN 0-8094-0235-1). Time-Life.

World of Winslow Homer. James Flexner. LC 66-27562. (Library of Art Ser.). (Illus.). (gr. 6 up). 1966. 12.96 (ISBN 0-8094-0264-5, Pub. by Time-Life). Silver.

World of Women: Anthropological Studies of Women in the Societies of the World. Ed. by Erika Bourguignon. LC 79-11844. 384p. 1980. 24.95 (ISBN 0-03-051221-2); pap. 9.95 (ISBN 0-03-051226-3). Praeger.

World of Words. P. E. Dustoor. 1968. 10.00x (ISBN 0-210-34050-9). Asia.

World of Words: A Guide to Effective Communication. H. O. Nordberg et al. 1970. pap. 8.95 (ISBN 0-201-43007-X); tchr's guide 4.00 (ISBN 0-201-43008-8). A-W.

World of Words: A Guide to Effective Communication. H. Orville Nordberg et al. 1970. text ed. 8.95 (ISBN 0-8464-3007-X). Benjamin-Cummings.

World of Worms. Dorothy H. Patent. LC 77-17117. (Illus.). (gr. 5-9). 1978. 7.95 (ISBN 0-8234-0319-X). Holiday.

World of Yesterday. Stefan Zweig. LC 43-5821. (Illus.). xxvi, 455p. 1964. pap. 6.25x (ISBN 0-8032-5224-2, BB 181, Bison). U of Nebr Pr.

World Olympiad of Knowledge - 1984, a Novel. O. A. Battista. 1981. 9.95. Research Servs.

World on Wheels: Rolling Along from Ancient to Modern Times. Ali Mitgutsch. (Illus.). 48p. (gr. 1-6). 1975. 3.95 o.p. (ISBN 0-307-15795-4, Golden Pr); PLB 10.69 o.p. (ISBN 0-307-65795-7). Western Pub.

World One Hundred Years Ago. Michael W. Jones. 1976. 4.98 o.p. (ISBN 0-679-50699-3). McKay.

World One Hundred Years Ago. Michael W. Jones. 1980. cancelled o.p. McKay.

World Order of Baha'u'llah. 2nd rev. ed. Shoghi Effendi. LC 56-17685. 1974. 10.00 (ISBN 0-87743-031-4, 7-08-20); pap. 5.00 (ISBN 0-87743-004-7, 7-08-21). Baha'i.

World Organization. Raymond Bridgman. LC 77-147575. (Library of War & Peace; Int'l. Organization, Arbitration & Law). 38.00 (ISBN 0-8240-0341-1). Garland Pub.

World Out of Time. Larry Niven. 1976. 7.95 o.p. (ISBN 0-03-017776-6). HR&W.

World Outside: Collected Short Fiction About Women at Work. Ed. by Ann Reit. LC 77-7986. (gr. 7 up). 1977. 6.95g o.s.i. (ISBN 0-590-07484-9, Four Winds); pap. 3.95 o.s.i. (ISBN 0-685-79849-6, Four Winds). Schol Bk Serv.

World Overview of Solar Commercialization Activities, 5 vols. Incl. Overview of Energy Programs-Solar Energy Commercialization Status in Selected Countries. Systems Consultants, Inc; Vols. 1 & 2. Solar Energy Commercialization for European Countries. Payne, Inc. & Energy Systems International; Solar Energy Commercialization for Middle East Countries. Systems Consultants, Inc; Solar Energy Commercialization for African Countries. PRC Energy Analysis, Co. 260p. 1980. Set. cancelled (ISBN 0-930978-79-X); Set. pap. 39.00 (ISBN 0-930978-80-3). Solar Energy Info.

World Painting Index, 2 vols. Patricia P. Havlice. Incl. Vol. 1. Bibliography, Paintings by Unknown Artists, Painters & Their Works; Vol. 2. Titles of Works & Their Painters. LC 76-52407. 1977. 74.50 set (ISBN 0-8108-1016-6). Scarecrow.

World Peace Through World Economy. World Association Of World Federalists - Youth And Student Division - 6th Intl. Study Conference. 1968. pap. text ed. 5.75x (ISBN 0-391-02070-6). Humanities.

World Politics. James N. Rosenau et al. LC 75-22766. (Illus.). 1976. text ed. 17.95 (ISBN 0-02-927040-5). Free Pr.

World Politics & International Economics. Ed. by A. C. Fred Bergsten & Lawrence B. Krause. 1975. 18.95 (ISBN 0-8157-0916-1); pap. 6.95 (ISBN 0-8157-0915-3). Brookings.

World Politics & the Arab-Israeli Conflict. Ed. by Robert O. Freedman. (Pergamon Policy Studies). 1979. 39.00 (ISBN 0-08-023380-5). Pergamon.

World Politics Since 1945. 3rd ed. Peter Calvocoressi. 1978. pap. text ed. 11.95x (ISBN 0-582-48913-X). Longman.

World Population Crisis: Policy Implications & the Role of Law: Proceedings of the American Society of International Law Regional Meeting & the John Bassett Moore Society of International Law Symposium. Ed. by John M. Paxman. LC 80-19753. vi, 179p. 1980. Repr. of 1971 ed. lib. bdg. 22.50x (ISBN 0-313-22619-9, PAWO). Greenwood.

World Population Policies. Jyoti S. Singh. LC 78-19756. 1979. 22.95 (ISBN 0-03-044051-3). Praeger.

World Population: The Present & Futues Crisis, No. 251. 1st ed. Phyllis T. Piotrow. LC 80-69582. (Headline Ser.: No. 251). (Illus.). 80p. (Orig.). 1980. pap. 2.00 (ISBN 0-87124-064-5). Foreign Policy.

World Population: The Present & Future Crisis. Phyllis T. Piotrow. LC 80-69582. (Headline Ser.: No. 251). (Illus.). 80p. (Orig.). 1980. pap. 2.00 (ISBN 0-87124-064-5). Foreign Policy.

World Poverty & Development: A Survey of American Opinion. Paul A. Laudicina. LC 73-89873. (Monographs: No. 8). 126p. 1973. 2.50 (ISBN 0-686-28687-1). Overseas Dev Council.

World Power Foundation: Its Goals & Platform. Harold Thomas. 1980. pap. 6.95. Loompanics.

World Power Trends & U. S. Foreign Policy for the Nineteen Eighties. Ray S. Cline. 206p. 1980. lib. bdg. 20.00x (ISBN 0-89158-917-1); pap. 8.95x (ISBN 0-89158-790-X). Westview.

World Prehistory in New Perspective. 3rd ed. John Grahame Douglas Clark. LC 76-51318. (Illus.). 1977. 57.00 (ISBN 0-521-21506-4); pap. 12.95 (ISBN 0-521-29178-X). Cambridge U Pr.

World Problems in Education: A Brief Analytical Survey. (IBE: Studies & Surveys in Comparative Education Ser). 166p. 1975. pap. 9.25 (ISBN 92-3-201297-9, U730, UNESCO). Unipub.

World Protein Resources. Allen Jones. LC 74-11219. 1974. 24.95 (ISBN 0-470-44935-7). Halsted Pr.

World Radio & TV Handbook 1980. 34th ed. Jens Frost. 1980. pap. 14.95 o.p. (ISBN 0-8230-5906-5). Watson-Guptill.

World Radio TV Handbook Nineteen Eighty-One. 35th ed. Ed. by Jens M. Frost. 560p. (Orig.). 1980. pap. 16.50 (ISBN 0-8230-5907-3). Watson-Guptill.

World Railways & Rapid Transit Systems 1980-81. Goldsack. 1980. 125.00 (ISBN 0-531-03938-2). Watts.

World Railways & Rapid Transit Systems 1979-80. Goldsack. 1980. 89.50 (ISBN 0-531-03906-4). Watts.

World Regional Geography. 4th ed. Oliver K. Heintzelman & R. M. Highsmith, Jr. (Illus.). 1973. text ed. 20.95 (ISBN 0-13-969006-9). P-H.

World Religions & World Community. Robert H. Slater. LC 63-9805. (Lectures on the History of Religions Ser.: No. 6). 1963. 17.50x (ISBN 0-231-02615-3). Columbia U Pr.

World Resource Management: Key to Civilizations & Social Achievement. J. Edwin Becht & L. D. Belzung. (Illus.). 336p. 1975. text ed. 19.95 (ISBN 0-13-968107-8). P-H.

World Resources: Energy & Minerals, Vol. 1. Gunnar Alexandersson & Bjorn Kleverbring. 1978. 21.25x (ISBN 3-11-006577-0). De Gruyter.

World Resources: Engineering Solutions. 208p. 1980. 40.00x (ISBN 0-7277-0016-2, Pub. by Telford England). State Mutual Bk.

World Restored: Europe After Napoleon. Henry A. Kissinger. 8.00 (ISBN 0-8446-2384-9). Peter Smith.

World Review of Nutrition & Dietetics, Vol. 37. Ed. by G. H. Bourne. (Illus.). x, 240p. 1981. 115.00 (ISBN 3-8055-2143-X). S Karger.

World Revolution & Family Patterns. William J. Goode. LC 63-13538. 1970. pap. text ed. 8.95 (ISBN 0-02-912460-3). Free Pr.

World Revolutionary Elites: Studies in Coercive Ideological Movements. Ed. by Harold D. Lasswell & Daniel Lerner. LC 80-21600. xi, 478p. 1980. Repr. of 1965 ed. lib. bdg. 39.75x (ISBN 0-313-22572-9, LAWE). Greenwood.

World Rich in Anniversaries. rev. ed. Jean Follain. Tr. by Mary Feeney & William Matthews. (Illus.). 96p. (Fr.). 1981. text ed. 10.00 (ISBN 0-937406-01-5); deluxe ed. 50.00 (ISBN 0-937406-02-3); pap. 5.00 (ISBN 0-937406-00-7). Logbridge-Rhodes.

World Rubber Economy: Structure, Changes, & Prospects. Enzo R. Grilli et al. LC 80-554. (World Bank Occasional Papers). (Illus.). 224p. 1981. pap. text ed. 6.50x (ISBN 0-8018-2421-4). Johns Hopkins.

World Series. Julian May. LC 75-22387. (Sports Classics Ser.). (Illus.). 48p. (gr. 4-6). 1975. PLB 8.95 o.p. (ISBN 0-87191-447-6). Creative Ed.

World Series: A Complete Pictoral History. rev. ed. John Devaney & Burt Goldblatt. (Illus.). 416p. 1981. pap. 10.95 (ISBN 0-528-88044-6). Rand.

World Shipping Law, Release 2. University of Southampton. 1980. 80.00 (ISBN 0-379-10168-8). Oceana.

World Silver Coin Value Guide. Lorraine S. Durst & Sanford J. Durst. LC 80-51831. 1980. softcover 9.00 (ISBN 0-686-64441-7); lib. bdg. 12.00 (ISBN 0-915262-46-0). S J Durst.

World Since Fifteen Hundred: A Global History. 3rd ed. Leften Stavrianos. LC 74-30161. (Illus.). 576p. 1975. pap. text ed. 16.95 (ISBN 0-13-968156-6). P-H.

World Society. John W. Burton. LC 71-176252. (Illus.). 250p. 1972. 26.50 (ISBN 0-521-08425-3); pap. 7.95x (ISBN 0-521-09694-4). Cambridge U Pr.

World Soils. 2nd ed. E. M. Bridges. LC 77-90204. (Illus.). 1979. 23.95 (ISBN 0-521-21956-6); pap. 7.95x (ISBN 0-521-29339-1). Cambridge U Pr.

World Statistics in Brief. 241p. 1980. pap. 3.95 (ISBN 0-686-68981-X, UN80/17/3, UN). Unipub.

World Steel: An Economic Geography. Kenneth Warren. LC 74-24996. 1975. 19.50x (ISBN 0-8448-0651-X). Crane-Russak Co.

World Survey of Major Facilities in Controlled Fusion Research. (Nuclear Fusion). (Illus.). 356p. (Orig.). 1973. pap. 16.25 (ISBN 92-0-139073-4, IAEA). Unipub.

World Survey of Major Facilities in Controlled Fusion Research: 1976 Ed. 3rd, rev. ed. (STI-PUB,-23). (Illus.). 1977. pap. 64.25 (ISBN 92-0-139076-9, IAEA). Unipub.

World-System of Capitalism: Past & Present. Ed. by Walter L. Goldfrank. LC 78-26935. (Political Economy of the World-System Annuals: Vol. 2). 1979. 20.00x (ISBN 0-8039-1105-X); pap. 9.95x (ISBN 0-8039-1106-8). Sage.

World Systems of Traditional Resources Management. Gary A. Klee. LC 80-17711. (Scripta Ser. in Geography). 290p. 1980. 29.95 (ISBN 0-470-27008-X). Halsted Pr.

World Tables: 1980. Staff of World Bank. LC 79-3649. (World Bank Occasional Paper Ser.). (Illus.). 480p. 1980. text ed. 27.50x (ISBN 0-8018-2389-7); pap. text ed. 10.95x (ISBN 0-8018-2390-0). Johns Hopkins.

World That Could Be. Robert C. North. (Illus.). 1978. 8.95 (ISBN 0-393-05677-5); pap. 4.95 (ISBN 0-393-00882-7). Norton.

World Timbers, 3 vols. Compiled by B. J. Rendle. Incl. Vol. 1. Europe & Africa. 192p. 1969. o.p. (ISBN 0-8020-1570-0); Vol. 2. North & South America, Including Central America & the West Indies. 1969 (ISBN 0-8020-1667-7); Vol. 3. Asia, Australia & New Zealand. 1970 (ISBN 0-8020-1718-5). LC 74-398920. (Illus.). 35.00x ea. o.p. U of Toronto Pr.

World to Conquer: The Story of the First Around the World Flight. Ernest A. McKay. LC 80-23064. (Illus.). 224p. 1981. 10.95 (ISBN 0-668-05096-9, 5096). Arco.

World to Fifteen Hundred: A Global History. 2nd ed. Leften Stavrianos. (Illus.). 416p. 1975. pap. write for info. (ISBN 0-13-968198-1). P-H.

World Tobacco Directory. 26th ed. LC 53-29978. (Illus.). 1978. 60.00x o.p. (ISBN 0-901994-66-9). Intl Pubns Serv.

World Tobacco Directory 1979. 27th ed. LC 53-29978. (Illus.). 310p. 1979. 60.00x (ISBN 0-86108-049-1). Intl Pubns Serv.

World Trade & Domestic Adjustment. Tripartite report by fourteen economists from Japan, the European Community & North America. 19p. 1973. pap. 2.00 (ISBN 0-8157-9543-2). Brookings.

World Trade & Payments: An Introduction. 3rd ed. Caves & Jones. 1981. text ed. 17.95 (ISBN 0-316-13226-8). Little.

World Trade Annual Supplement, 1978, 5 vols. 110.00 ea.; Set. 550.00. Vol. 1 (ISBN 0-8027-5969-6). Vol. 2 (ISBN 0-8027-5971-8). Vol. 3 (ISBN 0-8027-5972-6). Vol. 4 (ISBN 0-8027-5973-4). Vol. 5 (ISBN 0-8027-5974-2). Walker & Co.

World Trade Annual 1972, 5 vols. Ed. by Statistical Office of the United Nations. LC 64-66238. Set. 209.00 o.s.i. (ISBN 0-8027-5914-9). Walker & Co.

World Trade Annual, 1978, 5 vols. 50.00 ea.; Set. 250.00 (ISBN 0-8027-5977-7). Vol. 1 (ISBN 0-8027-5963-7). Vol. 2 (ISBN 0-8027-5964-5). Vol. 3 (ISBN 0-8027-5965-3). Vol. 4 (ISBN 0-8027-5966-1). Vol. 5 (ISBN 0-8027-5968-8). Walker & Co.

World Trade: Constraints & Opportunities in the 80's. Ed. by Bela Balassa. (Atlantic Papers: No.36). 70p. 1979. write for info. (ISBN 0-916672-76-X). Allanheld.

World Treasury of Oral Poetry. Ed. by Ruth Finnegan. LC 77-88784. 576p. 1978. 15.00x (ISBN 0-253-36665-8). Ind U Pr.

World Treaty Index & Treaty Profiles, 6 vols. new ed. Peter H. Rohn. LC 73-83352. 3300p. 1974. text ed. 510.00 (ISBN 0-87436-132-X). ABC-Clio.

World Trucks: Berliet, No. 11. Pat Kennett. (Illus.). 88p. 1981. 19.95 (ISBN 0-85059-449-9). Aztex.

World Trucks: International, No. 12. Pat Kennett. (Illus.). 88p. 1981. pap. 19.95 (ISBN 0-85059-503-7). Aztex.

World Turned Upside Down: The Prose and Poetry of the American Revolution. Ed. by James H. Pickering. 1975. 17.50 (ISBN 0-8046-9082-0, Natl U). Kennikat.

World Uranium Geology & Resource Potential. Joint Steering Group on Uranium Resources of the OECD Nuclear Energy Agency & the International Atomic Energy Agency. LC 80-81724. (Illus.). 524p. 1980. pap. 50.00 (ISBN 0-87930-085-X). Miller Freeman.

World Vegetation. Denis R. Riley & Anthony Young. 1967. 6.95x (ISBN 0-521-06083-4). Cambridge U Pr.

World Vegetation Types. Ed. by S. R. Eyre. LC 78-147779. 1971. 20.00x (ISBN 0-231-03503-9). Columbia U Pr.

World Viewed: Reflections on the Ontology of Film. enl. ed. Stanley Cavell. (Paperback Ser.: No. 151). 1980. 12.50x (ISBN 0-674-96197-8); pap. 5.95 (ISBN 0-674-96196-X). Harvard U Pr.

World Views: A Study in Comparative History. W. Warren Wagar. LC 76-55505. 1977. pap. text ed. 9.95 o.p. (ISBN 0-03-088043-2). HR&W.

World War I in the Air: A Bibliography & Chronology. Myron J. Smith, Jr. LC 76-45461. (Illus.). 1977. 13.50 (ISBN 0-8108-0990-7). Scarecrow.

World War I, June Second, Nineteen Seventeen to October Thirteenth, Nineteen Seventeen. Ed. by Richard D. Challener. (United States Military Intelligence 1917-1927 Ser.: Vol. 1). 1978. lib. bdg. 60.50 (ISBN 0-8240-3000-1). Garland Pub.

World War II. Henri Michel. (Saxon House Bks.). 1974. 4.95 o.p. (ISBN 0-347-00001-0). Gordon-Cremonesi.

World War II Airplanes, Vol. 1. LC 77-88441. (Illus.). 1978. pap. 8.95 (ISBN 0-528-88170-1). Rand.

World War II Airplanes, Vol. 2. LC 77-88441. (Illus.). 1978. pap. 8.95 (ISBN 0-528-88171-X). Rand.

World War One, Oct. 20, 1917-Jan. 19, 1918. Ed. by Richard D. Challener. (United States Military Intelligence 1917-1927 Ser.). 1979. lib. bdg. 60.50 (ISBN 0-8240-3001-X). Garland Pub.

World War Two Almanac: Nineteen Thirty-One to Nineteen Forty-Five A Political & Military Record. new ed. Robert Goralski. (Illus.). 484p. 1981. 17.95 (ISBN 0-399-12548-5). Putnam.

World War Two at Sea: A Bibliography of Sources in English, 3 vols. Myron J. Smith, Jr. Incl. Vol. 1. European Theater. 15.00 (ISBN 0-8108-0884-6); Vol. 2. Pacific Theater. 18.00 (ISBN 0-8108-0969-9); Vol. 3. 24.00 (ISBN 0-8108-0970-2). Pt. 1: Gen. Works, Naval Hardware, & The All Hands Chronology (1941-1945) Pt. 2: Home Fronts & Special Studies. LC 75-34098. 1976. Set. 39.50 o.p. (ISBN 0-685-73560-5). Scarecrow.

World War Two German Military Collectibles. Robert McCarthy. (Illus.). 1980. pap. 6.95 (ISBN 0-89145-135-8). Collector Bks.

World War Two German Military Studies, 10 pts. in 23 vols. Ed. by Donald S. Detwiler. Incl. Pt. 1. Introduction & Guide (ISBN 0-8240-4300-6); Pt. 2. The Extinct Series (European Theatre Interrogations, 2 pts. Pt. A (ISBN 0-8240-4301-4). Pt. B (ISBN 0-8240-4302-2); Pt. 3. Command Structure, 3 pts. Pt. A (ISBN 0-8240-4303-0). Pt. B (ISBN 0-8240-4304-9). Pt. C (ISBN 0-8240-4305-7); Pt. 4. The OKW (Oberkommando der Wehrmacht) War Diary Series, 5 pts. Pt. A (ISBN 0-8240-4306-5). Pt. B (ISBN 0-8240-4307-3). Pt. C (ISBN 0-8240-4308-1). Pt. D (ISBN 0-8240-4309-X). Pt. E (ISBN 0-8240-4310-3); Pt. 5. The Western Theatre (ISBN 0-8240-4311-1); Pt. 6. The Mediterranean Theatre, 2 pts. Pt. A (ISBN 0-8240-4312-X). Pt. B (ISBN 0-8240-4313-8); Pt. 7. The Eastern Theatre, 5 pts. Pt. A (ISBN 0-8240-4314-6). Pt. B (ISBN 0-8240-4315-4). Pt. C (ISBN 0-8240-4316-2). Pt. D (ISBN 0-8240-4317-0). Pt. E (ISBN 0-8240-4318-9); Pt. 8. Diplomacy, Strategy & Military Theory, 2 pts. Pt. A (ISBN 0-8240-4319-7). Pt. B (ISBN 0-8240-4320-0); Pt. 9. German Military Government (ISBN 0-8240-4321-9); Pt. 10. Special Topics, 2 pts. Pt. A (ISBN 0-8240-4322-7). Pt. B (ISBN 0-8240-4323-5). 1979. lib. bdg. 60.50 ea., vol. Garland Pub.

World War Two Photo Album: German Destroyers & Escorts. Paul Beaver. (Illus.). 96p. 1981. pap. 5.95 (ISBN 0-89404-060-X). Aztex.

World War Two Photo Album: Panzers in the Balkans & Italy. Bruce Quarrie. (Illus.). 96p. 1981. pap. 5.95 (ISBN 0-89404-059-6). Aztex.

World War 2 Photo Album 13: German Bombers Over the Med. Bryan Philpott. 96p. 1980. 17.95 o.p. (ISBN 0-85059-393-X); pap. 11.95 o.p. (ISBN 0-85059-394-8). Aztex.

World War 2 Photo Album 14: German Capital Ships. Paul Beaver. 96p. 1980. 17.95 o.p. (ISBN 0-85059-395-6); pap. 11.95 o.p. (ISBN 0-85059-396-4). Aztex.

World We Imagine, Selected Essays. Mark Schorer. LC 68-14917. 1968. pap. 2.95 o.p. (ISBN 0-374-50712-0, N350). FS&G.

World Weather & Climate. D. Riley & L. Spolton. LC 73-75858. (Illus.). 128p. 1974. 19.50 (ISBN 0-521-20176-4); pap. 7.95x (ISBN 0-521-20175-6). Cambridge U Pr.

World Who's Who of Women. 5th ed. Ed. by Ernest Kay. (Illus.). 1167p. 1980. 65.00x (ISBN 0-900332-54-9, Pub. by Intl Biog). Biblio Dist.

World-Wide Variation in Human Growth. P. B. Eveleth & J. M. Tanner. LC 75-10042. (International Biological Programme Ser.: No. 8). (Illus.). 544p. 1977. 86.50 (ISBN 0-521-20806-8). Cambridge U Pr.

World Within a World: Baja. Ted Lewin. LC 78-7740. (Illus.). (gr. 5 up). 1979. 5.95 (ISBN 0-396-07615-7). Dodd.

World Without Sex. Ann L. Rutledge. 1981. 6.50 (ISBN 0-8062-1668-9). Carlton.

World Yearbook of Education, 1980: Professional Development of Teachers. LC 32-18413. 422p. 1980. 32.50x (ISBN 0-85038-287-4). Intl Pubns Serv.

World...Its History in Maps. rev. ed. William H. McNeill et al. (Illus.). 96p. 1980. pap. text ed. 9.10x (ISBN 0-87453-011-3, 81011). Denoyer.

Worldly Evangelicals: Who They Are--& Where They're Headed. Richard Quebedeaux. LC 77-20446. 204p. 1980. pap. 5.95 (ISBN 0-06-066728-1, RD 338, HarpR). Har-Row.

Worldmark Encyclopedia of the States. Worldmark Press Ltd. Ed. by Moshe Sachs. LC 80-8218. (Illus.). 700p. 1981. pre-july 54.95 (ISBN 0-06-014733-4, HarpT); 54.95. Har-Row.

Worldmaster Atlas. 1978. 12.95 (ISBN 0-528-83096-1); pap. 7.95 (ISBN 0-528-83094-5). Rand.

Worlds: A Novel of the Near Future. Joe Haldeman. LC 80-51774. 288p. 1981. 12.95 (ISBN 0-670-78984-4). Viking Pr.

Worlds-Antiworlds: Antimatter in Cosmology. Hannes Alfven. Tr. by Rudy Feichtner. LC 66-27947. 1966. 10.95x (ISBN 0-7167-0317-3). W H Freeman.

Worlds Apart. Owen Barfield. LC 63-17798. 1964. pap. 7.45 (ISBN 0-8195-6017-0, Pub. by Wesleyan U Pr). Columbia U Pr.

Worlds Apart. Leo P. Kelley. LC 79-51079. (Space Police Bks.). (Illus.). 64p. (gr. 4 up). 1980. PLB 7.95 (ISBN 0-516-02236-9). Childrens.

Worlds Apart: Relationships Between Families & Schools. Sara L. Lightfoot. LC 78-54506. 257p. 1981. pap. 5.95 (ISBN 0-465-09243-8). Basic.

Worlds Apart: Young People & Drug Programs. Ed. by Dennis T. Jaffe & Ted Clarke. 160p. (Orig.). 1974. pap. 1.95 o.p. (ISBN 0-394-71017-7, Vin). Random.

World's Best Fairy Tales. Ed. by The Reader's Digest. (Illus.). 1980. 16.95 (ISBN 0-89577-078-4, Pub. by Reader's Digest). Norton.

World's Best Loved Poems. Ed. by James G. Lawson. 1927. 9.95 (ISBN 0-06-065210-1, HarpR). Har-Row.

World's Best Orations, 2 Vols. Ed. by David J. Brewer. LC 75-15323. 1970. Repr. of 1901 ed. Set. 99.50 (ISBN 0-8108-0341-0). Scarecrow.

World's Best Poems. Ed. by R. L. Adams. 1981. 28.50 (ISBN 0-686-68313-7). Porter.

World's Best Poetry, Vol. I: Home & Friendship. new ed. Ed. by Bliss Carman. LC 80-84498. (Granger Anthology Ser.: Ser. I). 480p. 1981. Repr. of 1904 ed. lib. bdg. 29.95x (ISBN 0-89609-202-X). Granger Bk.

World's Chief Languages. Mario Pei. 1960. 16.50 (ISBN 0-913298-07-7). S F Vanni.

World's Darkest Days. Steven Otfinoski. Ed. by Thomas J. Mooney. (Beginning Pal Paperbacks Ser.). (Illus., Orig.). (gr. 7-12). 1977. pap. text ed. 1.25 (ISBN 0-8374-3462-9). Xerox Ed Pubns.

World's End. James Conaway. 384p. 1980. pap. 2.50. Bantam.

World's Eye. Albert M. Potts. LC 79-4009. (Illus.). 1981. price not set (ISBN 0-8131-1387-3). U Pr of Ky.

World's Fair of Eighteen Eighty-Nine. Ed. by Theodore Reff. (Modern Art in Paris 1855 to 1900). 330p. 1981. lib. bdg. 44.00 (ISBN 0-8240-4704-4). Garland Pub.

World's Fair of Eighteen Eighty-Nine: Retrospective Exhibition of Fine Arts, 1789 to 1889. Ed. by Theodore Reff. (Modern Art in Paris 1855 to 1900). (Illus.). 250p. 1981. lib. bdg. 44.00 (ISBN 0-8240-4705-2). Garland Pub.

World's Fair of Eighteen Fifty-Five: Modern Art in Paris 1855-1900. Ed. by Theodore Reff. 694p. 1981. lib. bdg. 44.00 (ISBN 0-8240-4701-X). Garland Pub.

World's Fair of Eighteen Seventy-Eight. Ed. by Theodore Reff. (Modern Art in Paris 1855 to 1900). 388p. 1981. lib. bdg. 44.00 (ISBN 0-8240-4703-6). Garland Pub.

World's Fair of Eighteen Sixty-Seven. Ed. by Theodore Reff. (Modern Art in Paris 1855 to 1900). 224p. 1981. lib. bdg. 44.00 (ISBN 0-8240-4702-8). Garland Pub.

World's Fair of Nineteen Hundred: General Catalogue. Ed. by Theodore Reff. (Modern Art in Part in Paris 1855 to 1900). 582p. 1981. lib. bdg. 44.00 (ISBN 0-8240-4706-0). Garland Pub.

World's Fair of Nineteen Hundred: Retrospective Exhibition of French Art, 1800 to 1889. Ed. by Theodore Reff. (Modern Art in Paris 1855 to 1900). (Illus.). 442p. 1981. lib. bdg. 44.00 (ISBN 0-8240-4707-9). Garland Pub.

World's Fair of Nineteen Hundred: Retrospective Exhibition of Fine Art,1889 to 1900. Ed. by Theodore Reff. (Modern Art in Paris 1855 to 1900). 581p. 1981. lib. bdg. 44.00 (ISBN 0-8240-4708-7). Garland Pub.

World's Final Hour: Evacuation or Extinction? Hal Lindsey. Orig. Title: Homo Sapiens. 1976. pap. 1.25 (ISBN 0-310-27732-9). Zondervan.

World's First Baseball Game. Burnham Holmes. LC 78-14581. (Famous Firsts Ser.). (Illus.). 1978. lib. bdg. 7.35 (ISBN 0-686-51115-8). Silver.

World's First Police Detective. Judy R. Block. LC 78-16169. (Famous Firsts Ser.). (Illus.). 1978. lib. bdg. 7.35 (ISBN 0-686-51116-6). Silver.

Worlds from Words: A Theory of Language in Fiction. James Phelan. LC 80-25844. (Chicago Originals Ser.). 256p. lib. bdg. 19.00x (ISBN 0-226-66690-5). U of Chicago Pr.

World's Great Chess Games. rev. ed. Reuben Fine. (Illus.). 1976. 14.95 o.p. (ISBN 0-679-13046-2). McKay.

World's Great Love: The Prayer of the Rosary. Fulton J. Sheen. (Classic Prayer Ser.). (Illus.). 1978. pap. 4.95 (ISBN 0-8164-2182-X). Crossroad NY.

World's Great Men of Color, Vols. 1 & 2. J. A. Rogers. LC 73-186437. (Illus.). 972p. 1972. Vol. 1. 9.95 o.p. (ISBN 0-686-66675-5, 60437); Vol. 2. 9.95 o.s.i. (ISBN 0-02-604380-7, 60437). Macmillan.

World's Great Operas. John T. Howard. LC 80-2278. 1981. Repr. of 1948 ed. 49.50 (ISBN 0-404-18848-6). AMS Pr.

World's Greatest Airplanes: The Heinkel HE 111 to the Concorde. Richard Trombley. (Superwheels & Thrill Sports Ser.). (Illus.). (gr. 4 up). 1981. PLB 6.95 (ISBN 0-8225-0501-0). Lerner Pubns.

World's Greatest Airplanes: The Wright Flyer to the Piper Cub. Richard Trombley. (Superwheels & Thrill Sports Bks.). (Illus.). (gr. 4 up). 1981. PLB 6.95 (ISBN 0-8225-0500-2). Lerner Pubns.

World's Greatest Athlete. Gerald Gardner & Dee Caruso. (gr. 7-12). 1975. pap. 1.50 (ISBN 0-590-03755-2, Schol Pap). Schol Bk Serv.

World's Greatest Blackjack Book. Lance Humble & Carl Cooper. LC 79-8930. (Illus.). 432p. 1980. 12.95 (ISBN 0-385-15370-8). Doubleday.

World's Greatest Collection of Clean Jokes. Bob Phillips. (Orig.). 1974. pap. 1.75 o.s.i. (ISBN 0-87801-018-1). Vision Hse.

World's Greatest Comics Quiz. Jerry Robinson. 192p. (Orig.). 1981. pap. 1.50 (ISBN 0-448-14292-9, Tempo). G&D.

World's Greatest Golf Jokes. Stan McDougal. 1980. 9.95 (ISBN 0-686-65057-3). Lyle Stuart.

World's Greatest Stamp Collectors. Stanley M. Bierman. LC 80-70957. (Illus.). 400p. 1981. 17.95 (ISBN 0-8119-0347-8). Fell.

World's Greatest Team: A Portrait of the Boston Celtics 1957-69. Jeff Greenfield 1976. 7.95 o.p. (ISBN 0-394-49560-8). Random.

World's Greatest Unsolved Mysteries. Ed. by Martin Ebon. (Orig.). 1981. pap. 2.25 (ISBN 0-451-09684-3, E9684, Sig). NAL.

Worlds in a Small Room. (Illus.). 1980. pap. 12.95 (ISBN 0-14-005565-7). Penguin.

World's Last Mysteries. (Illus.). 1978. 16.95 (ISBN 0-89577-044-X, Pub. by Reader's Digest). Norton.

World's Living Religions. Archie J. Bahm. (Arcturus Books Paperbacks). 384p. 1971. pap. 6.95 (ISBN 0-8093-0529-1). S Ill U Pr.

World's Living Religions. rev. ed. Robert E. Hume. LC 58-12515. 1959. pap. text ed. 5.95x (ISBN 0-684-15611-3). Scribner.

World's Most Challenging TV Quiz. Joe Walders. LC 77-11248. 1978. pap. 4.95 (ISBN 0-385-13054-6, Dolp). Doubleday.

World's Most Famous Court Trail: State of Tennessee V. John T. Scopes. John Scopes. LC 78-121106. (Civil Liberties in American History Ser). 1971. Repr. of 1925 ed. lib. bdg. 29.50 (ISBN 0-306-71975-4). Da Capo.

World's Most Famous Ghosts. Daniel Cohen. (Illus.). (gr. 4 up). 1979. pap. 1.50 (ISBN 0-671-29962-X, HI-LO). PB.

Worlds Near & Far: Nine Stories of Science Fiction & Fantasy. Ed. by Terry Carr. LC 74-10273. 224p. 1974. 7.95 o.p. (ISBN 0-525-66404-1). Elsevier-Nelson.

Worlds of Ernest Thompson Seton. Ernest T. Seton. Ed. by John G. Samson. 1976. 25.00 o.p. (ISBN 0-394-49547-0). Knopf.

Worlds of Patrick Geddes: Biologist, Town Planner, Re-Educator, Peace-Warrior. Philip Boardman. (Illus.). 1978. 40.00 (ISBN 0-7100-8548-6). Routledge & Kegan.

Worlds of Science Fiction. Ed. by Theodore W. Hipple & Robert G. Wright. (Literature Ser.). (gr. 7-12). 1979. pap. text ed. 5.88 (ISBN 0-205-06416-7, 4964160); tchrs'. ed. 2.96 (ISBN 0-685-63615-1). Allyn.

Worlds of Weird. Ed. by Leo Margulies. 1978. pap. 1.50 o.p. (ISBN 0-515-04826-7). Jove Pubns.

World's One Hundred Best Recipes. Roland Goock. Tr. by Culinary Arts Institute. LC 73-9341. (Illus.). 1973. 14.95 (ISBN 0-8326-0542-5, 1650); pap. 7.95 (ISBN 0-686-67697-1, 2650). Delair.

World's Religions. rev. ed. Charles S. Braden. (Series C). 1958. pap. 3.95 o.p. (ISBN 0-687-46374-2, Apex). Abingdon.

World's Rim: Great Mysteries of the North American Indians. Hartley B. Alexander. LC 53-7703. (Illus.). 1967. pap. 4.95 (ISBN 0-8032-5003-7, BB160, Bison). U of Nebr Pr.

World's Students in the United States: A Review & Evaluation of Research on Foreign Students. Seth Spaulding et al. LC 75-23992. (Special Studies). (Illus.). 544p. 1976. text ed. 31.95 (ISBN 0-275-56130-5). Praeger.

World's Truck Catalogue: International Listings. J. F. J. Kuipers. (Illus.). Date not set. pap. 16.95 (ISBN 0-89404-013-8). Aztex. Postponed.

World's Vanishing Birds. Cyril Littlewood. LC 72-92101. (Illus.). 64p. 1973. lib. bdg. 5.95 o.p. (ISBN 0-668-02889-0). Arco.

World's Wit & Humor: An Encyclopedia of the Classic Wit & Humor of All Nations, 15 vols. in 3 mini-print vols. Ed. by Joel C. Harris. 1973. Repr. of 1905 ed. 120.00 (ISBN 0-8108-0543-X). Scarecrow.

World's Worst Blank Book. Dana A Snow. 1976. 1.25 o.p. (ISBN 0-8431-0410-4); pap. 1.25 o.p. (ISBN 0-685-74201-6). Price Stern.

World's Worst California Jokes. Roger Price & Larry Sloan. 1980. 1.50 o.p. (ISBN 0-8431-0691-3). Price Stern.

Worldwide Adventure Travelguide, 1980. American Adventures Association. (Illus.). 1980. pap. 9.95 (ISBN 0-394-73872-1). Random.

Worldwide Inflation: Theory & Recent Experience. Ed. by Lawrence B. Krause & Walter S. Salant. LC 76-51580. 1976. 21.95 (ISBN 0-8157-5030-7); pap. 11.95 (ISBN 0-8157-5029-3). Brookings.

Worldwide Medical Interpreter: English, Vol. 1. G. Settar. 1976. pap. 12.00 (ISBN 0-87489-101-9). Med Economics.

Worldwide Medical Interpreter: Greek, Vol. 12. G. Settar. 1977. pap. 12.00 (ISBN 0-87489-112-4). Med Economics.

Worldwide Medical Interpreter: Italian, Vol. 6. G. Settar. 1977. pap. 12.00 (ISBN 0-87489-106-X). Med Economics.

Worldwide Riches Opportunites, Vol. 1. Tyler G. Hicks. 150p. 1981. pap. 25.00 (ISBN 0-914306-49-9). Intl Wealth.

Worldwide Riches Opportunities, Vol. 2. 2nd ed. Tyler G. Hicks. 150p. 1981. pap. 25.00 (ISBN 0-914306-50-2). Intl Wealth.

Worm of Consciousness & Other Essays. Nicola Chiaromonte. LC 75-31868. 120p. 1976. 10.00 o.p. (ISBN 0-15-199440-4). HarBraceJ.

Worms. Lois Darling & Louis Darling. LC 77-102408. (Illus.). 48p. (gr. 2-5). 1972. pap. 6.48 (ISBN 0-688-31773-1). Morrow.

Worms. Katherine Nespojohn. (First Bks). (Illus.). 72p. (gr. 4-6). 1972. PLB 4.47 o.p. (ISBN 0-531-00766-9). Watts.

Worms & Disease: A Manual of Medical Helminthology. Ralph Muller. (Illus.). 1975. 36.95x (ISBN 0-433-17580-X). Intl Ideas.

Worry! How to Kick the Serenity Habit in Ninety Eight Easy Steps. Robert Morley. (Illus.). 176p. 1981. 10.00 (ISBN 0-399-12596-5). Putnam.

Worship & Conflict Under Colonial Rule: A South India Case. Arjun Appadurai. (Cambridge South Asian Studies: No. 27). (Illus.). 282p. Date not set. price not set (ISBN 0-521-23122-1). Cambridge U Pr.

Worship & Hymnody. Gary R. Shiplett. (Illus.). 122p. (Orig.). 1980. pap. text ed. 5.95 (ISBN 0-916260-08-9). A Meriwether.

Worship & Politics. A. Gedraitis. 1973. pap. 2.75 o.p. (ISBN 0-686-11980-0). Wedge Pub.

Worship & Secular Man. Raimundo Panikkar. LC 72-93339. 126p. 1973. pap. 4.95x o.p. (ISBN 0-88344-788-6). Orbis Bks.

Worship in Islam. Al-Ghazzali. Ed. by Edwin E. Calverley. LC 79-2860. 242p. 1981. Repr. of 1925 ed. 21.50 (ISBN 0-8305-0032-4). Hyperion Conn.

Worship of the Church. Massey H. Shepherd, Jr. (Orig.). 1952. pap. 3.95 (ISBN 0-8164-2071-8, SP4). Crossroad NY.

Worship of the Early Church. Ferdinand Hahn. Ed. by John Reumann. Tr. by David E. Green from Ger. LC 72-87063. 144p. 1973. pap. 4.50 (ISBN 0-8006-0127-0, 1-127). Fortress.

Worship Stories. Walter L. Cook. (Object Lesson Ser.). 64p. 1980. pap. 2.95 (ISBN 0-8010-2445-5). Baker Bk.

Worship Without Walls. Carl E. Price. LC 80-51409. (Orig.). 1980. pap. 1.00x (ISBN 0-8358-0404-6). Upper Room.

Worst Person in the World. James Stevenson. LC 77-22141. (Illus.). (gr. k-3). 1978. 7.95 (ISBN 0-688-80127-7); PLB 7.63 (ISBN 0-688-84127-9). Greenwillow.

Worst TV Shows--Ever. Bart Andrews. (Illus.). 1980. pap. 6.95 (ISBN 0-525-47592-3). Dutton.

Wort Fasst Nicht Jeden. Ludwig Hohl. (Bibliothek Suhrkamp: 675). 133p. text ed. 8.30 (ISBN 3-518-01675-X, Pub. by Insel Verlag Germany). Suhrkamp.

Wortbildung Syntax & Morphologie: Festschrift Zum 60 Geburstag Von Hans Marchand Am, Oktober 1967. Ed. by Herbert E. Brekle. (Janua Linguarum, Ser. Major: No. 36). 1968. text ed. 51.75x (ISBN 90-2790-687-4). Mouton.

Worth: Father of Haute Couture. Diana De Marley. (Illus.). 220p. 1980. text ed. 29.50x (ISBN 0-8419-7400-4). Holmes & Meier.

Worth of a Smile. J. Spencer Kinard. LC 75-42298. 1976. 8.95 (ISBN 0-13-969139-1). P-H.

Worth Thinking About. Charles Gibboney. 1976. pap. 1.25 (ISBN 0-8272-4210-7). Bethany Pr.

Worthington Botts & the Steam Machine. Betty Baker. LC 80-24627. (Ready-to-Read Ser.). (Illus.). 56p. (gr. 1-4). 1981. PLB 7.95 (ISBN 0-02-708190-7). Macmillan.

Wortindex Zu Thomas Mann: Der Zauberberg. Francis Bulhof. LC 75-42984. 614p. (Sponsored by The College of Humanities, The University of Texas at Austin). 1976. 39.00 (ISBN 0-8357-0159-X, SS-00006). Univ Microfilms.

Wotan Warhead. James Follett. 224p. 1981. pap. 2.50 (ISBN 0-445-04629-5). Popular Lib.

Would-Be Writer. 3rd rev. ed. Clinton S. Burhans, Jr. LC 74-133494. 1971. text ed. 10.50 (ISBN 0-471-00058-2). Wiley.

Would You Believe? Florence Munat & Charles Munat. Ed. by Patricia McCarthy. (Pal Paperbacks Kit B Ser.). (Illus., Orig.). (gr. 7-12). 1974. pap. text ed. 1.25 (ISBN 0-8374-3505-6). Xerox Ed Pubns.

Would You Believe This Too. Deidre Sanders et al. LC 76-19815. (Illus.). (gr. 3 up). 1976. 5.95 o.p. (ISBN 0-8069-0098-9); PLB 5.89 o.p. (ISBN 0-8069-0099-7). Sterling.

Would You Believe...? Useless Information You Can't Afford to Be Without. Deidre Sanders et al. LC 74-82321. (Illus.). 128p. (gr. 7 up). 1974. 5.95 o.p. (ISBN 0-8069-0084-9); PLB 5.89 o.p. (ISBN 0-8069-0085-7). Sterling.

Would You Rather... John Burningham. LC 78-7088. (Illus.). (ps-2). 1978. 8.95 (ISBN 0-690-03917-4, TYC-J); PLB 9.79 (ISBN 0-690-03918-2). T Y Crowell.

Would You Settle for Improbable? P. J. Petersen. LC 80-69465. 160p. (gr. 5 up). 1981. 8.95 (ISBN 0-440-09601-4); PLB 8.44 (ISBN 0-440-09672-3). Delacorte.

Wound Healing & Wound Infection: Theory & Surgical Practice. Ed. by Thomas K. Hunt. 303p. 1980. 18.95x (ISBN 0-8385-9836-6). ACC.

Wound in the Heart. Allen Guttmann. LC 62-15342. 1962. 8.95 o.s.i. (ISBN 0-02-913290-8). Free Pr.

Wounded Generation: America After Vietnam. Ed. by A. D. Horne. (Washington Post Bk.). 160p. 1981. 10.95 (ISBN 0-13-969154-5); pap. 5.95 (ISBN 0-13-969147-2). P-H.

Wounded Healer: Ministry in Contemporary Society. Henri J. Nouwen. LC 72-186312. 120p. 1972. 6.95 (ISBN 0-385-02856-3). Doubleday.

Wounded Land: Book One of the Second Chronicles of Thomas Covenant. Stephen R. Donaldson. 512p. 1981. 12.95 (ISBN 0-345-28647-2); pap. 2.95 (ISBN 0-345-27831-3); 36 copy floor display. Ballantine.

Wounded Men, Broken Promises. Bob Klein. 300p. 1981. 10.95 (ISBN 0-02-563930-7). Macmillan.

Wounds of Civil War. Thomas Lodge. Ed. by J. W. Houppert. LC 68-63050. (Regents Renaissance Drama Ser). 1969. 7.95x (ISBN 0-8032-0269-5); pap. 1.65x (ISBN 0-8032-5268-4, BB 230, Bison). U of Nebr Pr.

Woven Cloth Construction. A. T. Robinson & R. Marks. 188p. 1967. 15.00 (ISBN 0-306-30662-X, Plenum Pr). Plenum Pub.

Woven Works. John Hamamura & Susan Hamamura. Ed. by Jane Vandenburgh. LC 78-17810. 1978. 14.95 (ISBN 0-87701-118-4, Prism Editions); pap. 6.95 (ISBN 0-87701-117-6, Prism Editions). Chronicle Bks.

Wovoka. Mel Boring. LC 80-24003. (Story of an American Indian Ser.). (Illus.). 64p. (gr. 5 up). 1981. PLB 6.95 (ISBN 0-87518-179-1). Dillon.

WP Book. Rita Kutie & Virginia Huffman. LC 79-18274. 1980. pap. text ed. 10.95 (ISBN 0-471-03881-4); study guide avail. (ISBN 0-471-07863-8). Wiley.

WPA & the Federal Relief Policy. Donald S. Howard. LC 72-2374. (FDR & the Era of the New Deal Ser). 888p. 1973. Repr. of 1943 ed. lib. bdg. 75.00 (ISBN 0-306-70489-7). Da Capo.

WQXR Guide to Listening Pleasure. Ed. by Howard Taubman. (Illus.). 1968. 6.95 o.s.i. (ISBN 0-02-616400-0). Macmillan.

Wrap Her in Light. Sandra Adelson. 448p. 1981. 11.95 (ISBN 0-688-03753-4). Morrow.

Wrapped in the Wind's Shawl: The Refugees of Southeast Asia. Scott C. Stone & John E. McGowan. (Illus.). 138p. (Orig.). 1980. pap. 8.95 (ISBN 0-89141-107-0). Presidio Pr.

Wrath of the Lion. Jack Higgins. 192p. 1977. pap. 1.95 (ISBN 0-449-13739-2, GM). Fawcett.

Wreath for Rivera. Ngaio Marsh. LC 75-44993. (Crime Fiction Ser). 1976. Repr. of 1949 ed. lib. bdg. 17.50 (ISBN 0-8240-2385-4). Garland Pub.

Wreath of Christmas Legends. Phyllis McGinley. (gr. 1-6). 1967. 9.95 (ISBN 0-02-765410-9). Macmillan.

Wreath of Lords & Ladies. James Fraser. LC 75-5261. (Crime Club Ser). 192p. 1975. 5.95 o.p. (ISBN 0-385-11074-X). Doubleday.

Wreath of Pale White Roses. Erika Duncan. LC 76-53373. 1977. 7.95 o.s.i. (ISBN 0-8027-0570-7); pap. 4.95 o.s.i. (ISBN 0-8027-7107-6). Walker & Co.

Wreck Diving. Dick Geyer. 192p. Date not set. pap. 6.95 (ISBN 0-695-81567-9, Assn Pr). Follett. Postponed.

Wreck of the Amoco Cadiz. David Fairhall & Philip Jordan. LC 80-17512. (Illus.). 256p. 1980. 12.95 (ISBN 0-8128-2743-0). Stein & Day.

Wreck of the Cassandra. Frederic Prokosch. 1966. 4.95 o.p. (ISBN 0-374-29324-4). FS&G.

Wreck of the Edmund Fitzgerald. Frederick Stonehouse. LC 77-93064. (Illus.). 1977. 4.95 o.p. (ISBN 0-685-87719-1). Avery Color.

Wreck of the Saginaw. Keith Robertson. (Illus.). (gr. 7 up). 1954. PLB 3.95 o.p. (ISBN 0-670-79060-5). Viking Pr.

Wrestlin Jacob: A Portrait of Religion in the Old South. Erskine Clark. LC 78-52453. 1979. 12.95 o.p. (ISBN 0-8042-1088-8); pap. 6.95 (ISBN 0-8042-1089-6). John Knox.

Wrestling. rev. ed. Rex Peery & Arnold Umbach. LC 61-12052. (Athletic Institute Ser). (Illus.). (gr. 6 up). 1967. 7.95 (ISBN 0-8069-4334-3); PLB 8.29 (ISBN 0-8069-4335-1). Sterling.

Wrestling: Coaching to Win. John K. Johnston et al. (Illus.). 1979. pap. 5.95 (ISBN 0-8015-8933-9, Hawthorn). Dutton.

Wrestling Physical Conditioning Encyclopedia. John Jesse. LC 74-5197. pap. 8.95 (ISBN 0-87095-043-6). Athletic.

Wrestling: The Making of a Champion. Bob Douglas. (Illus.). 1979. 9.95 (ISBN 0-8014-9177-0). Cornell U Pr.

Wrestling with God: An Anthology of Contemporary Religious Drama. Ed. by Norman Fedder. 1981. pap. 15.00 (ISBN 0-87602-018-X). Anchorage.

Wrestling with Luther. John R. Loeschen. LC 75-33815. 232p. 1976. 10.50 (ISBN 0-570-03256-3, 15-2164). Concordia.

Wretched of Canada: Letters to R. B. Bennett, 1930-35. Ed. by Linda M. Grayson & Michael Bliss. LC 73-163838. (Social History of Canada Ser.). 199p. 1971. pap. 5.00 (ISBN 0-8020-6127-3). U of Toronto Pr.

Wretched of the Horn: Forgotten Refugees in Black Africa. Richard Greenfield. LC 80-13204. (Illus.). 72p. (Orig.). 1981. pap. 5.95 (ISBN 0-936508-01-9). Barber Pr.

Wriggles: The Little Wishing Pig. Pauline Watson. LC 78-5855. (Illus.). (gr. k-3). 1978. 7.95 (ISBN 0-395-28828-2, Clarion). HM.

Wright: A Profile. Charles Wright & David St. John. (Profile Editions Ser.). (Illus.). 1979. pap. 4.00 o.p. (ISBN 0-931238-06-4); pap. 8.00 signed & lettered o. p. o.p. (ISBN 0-931238-07-2). Grilled Flowers Pr.

Wright Brothers. Ruth Franchere. LC 70-158689. (Biography Ser.). (Illus.). (gr. 1-5). 1972. PLB 7.89 (ISBN 0-690-90701-X, TYC-J). T Y Crowell.

Wright Brothers. Quentin Reynolds. (Landmark Ser). (Illus.). (gr. 4-6). 1950. PLB 5.99 (ISBN 0-394-90310-2, BYR). Random.

Wright Brothers. Quentin Reynolds. (gr. 4-6). 1950. 2.95 o.p. (ISBN 0-394-80310-8, BYR). Random.

Wright Brothers. Quentin Reynolds. LC 50-11766. (Landmark Bks.). (Illus.). 160p. (gr. 5-9). 1981. pap. 2.95 (ISBN 0-394-84700-8). Random.

Wright Brothers. (MacDonald Educational Ser.). (Illus., Arabic.). 3.50 (ISBN 0-686-53092-6). Intl Bk Ctr.

Wright Brothers: Heirs of Prometheus. Ed. by Richard P. Hallion. LC 78-606141. (Illus.). 146p. 1979. 19.50 (ISBN 0-87474-504-7); pap. 8.95 (ISBN 0-87474-503-9). Smithsonian.

Wright Morris: A Reader. Wright Morris. LC 77-83614. 1970. 12.95 o.s.i. (ISBN 0-06-013089-X, HarpT). Har-Row.

Wrigley's Hotel Directory, 1980. 70th ed. 272p. (Orig.). 1980. vinyl cover 19.00x (ISBN 0-8002-2698-4). Intl Pubns Serv.

Wrinkles. Lida Livingston & Constance Schrader. Date not set. pap. 2.50 (ISBN 0-345-29418-1). Ballantine.

Wrist & Hand: Clinical Orthopaedics & Related Research Ser. No. 83. Association of Bone & Joint Surgeons. Ed. by Marshall R. Urist & Anthony F. De Palma. (Illus.). 1971. 15.00 (ISBN 0-685-24744-9). Lippincott.

Wriston Speaking: A Selection of Addresses. Henry M. Wriston. LC 57-11230. 263p. 1957. 8.50 (ISBN 0-87057-048-X). Univ Pr of New England.

Write & Publish. Lucius Annese. LC 79-57036. 100p. 1980. write for info. (ISBN 0-933402-13-9); pap. 4.95 (ISBN 0-933402-14-7). Charisma Pr.

Write, Edit, & Print: Word Processing with Personal Computers. Donald H. McCunn. LC 80-67880. 1981. write for info. (ISBN 0-932538-06-1). Design Ent SF.

Write English, Bk. 1. 80p. (Orig.). 1981. pap. text ed. 4.95 (ISBN 0-88499-684-0). Inst Mod Lang.

Write English, Book 2. (Speak English Ser.). (Illus.). 64p. (Orig.). 1981. pap. write for info. (ISBN 0-88499-685-9). Inst Mod Lang.

Write for the Religion Market. John A. Moore. LC 80-25607. 128p. 1981. 9.95 (ISBN 0-88280-084-1). ETC Pubns.

Write It Right. Gail Kredenser. 1972. pap. 2.95 (ISBN 0-06-463329-2, EH 329, EH). Har-Row.

Write Right. Taya Zinkin. 128p. 1980. pap. 4.95 (ISBN 0-08-024566-8). Pergamon.

Write Right-or Left. Rosa Hagin. (gr. k-3). 1981. Set Of 6. 18.50 (ISBN 0-8027-9140-9); 4.20 ea. (ISBN 0-8027-9120-4). Walker & Co.

Write the Story of Your Life. Ruth Kanin. 1981. 12.95 (ISBN 0-8015-3871-8, Hawthorn). Dutton.

Write to Read, Level C. Florence Dann. (MCP Writing Skillbooster Ser.). (gr. 3). 1978. pap. text ed. 2.40 (ISBN 0-87895-340-X). Modern Curr.

Write to Read, Level D. Florence Dann. (MCP Writing Skillbooster Ser.). 1978. pap. text ed. 2.40 (ISBN 0-87895-410-4). Modern Curr.

Write to Read, Level E. Florence Dann. (MCP Writing Skillbooster Ser.). (gr. 5). 1978. pap. text ed. 2.40 (ISBN 0-87895-510-0). Modern Curr.

Write to Read, Level F. Florence Dann. (MCP Writing Skillbooster Ser.). (gr. 6). 1978. pap. text ed. 2.40 (ISBN 0-87895-610-7). Modern Curr.

Write True to Yourself So You Sell: 19 Lessons in Folios. Bert M. Anderson. write for info. (ISBN 0-917628-02-0). Coraco.

Write What You Mean: Practical Guidelines for Better Business Writing. (Supervisory Management Bk.). 1978. 4.95 (ISBN 0-8144-5453-4). Am Mgmt.

Writer & Public in France: From the Middle Ages to the Present Day. John Lough. 1978. text ed. 49.50x (ISBN 0-19-815749-5). Oxford U Pr.

Writer & Society: Heinrich Mann & Literary Politics in Germany, 1890-1940. David Gross. 316p. 1980. text ed. 15.00x (ISBN 0-391-00972-9). Humanities.

Writer & the Screen: On Writing for Film & Television. Wolf Rilla. 1974. pap. 4.95 (ISBN 0-688-05234-7). Morrow.

Writer As Liar. Guido Almansi. 1975. 20.00x (ISBN 0-7100-8147-2). Routledge & Kegan.

Writer Teaches Writing. Donald M. Murray. LC 68-6986. (Illus.). 1968. pap. text ed. 10.75 (ISBN 0-395-04989-X, 3-40075). HM.

Writers & Artists Yearbook 1980. 1980. pap. 12.00 o.p. (ISBN 0-87116-120-6). Writer.

Writer's & Photographer's Guide to Newspaper Markets. 2nd ed. Joan Long & Ronald Long. 175p. 1981. pap. price not set (ISBN 0-936940-01-8). Helm Pub.

Writers & Pilgrims: Medieval Pilgrimage Narratives & Their Posterity. Donald R. Howard. (Quantum Bk.). 100p. 1980. 10.95 (ISBN 0-520-03926-2). U of Cal Pr.

Writers & Politics in Modern Scandinavia. Janet Mawby. LC 78-18931. (Writers & Politics Ser.). 1979. 10.50x (ISBN 0-8419-0414-6); pap. text ed. 6.00x (ISBN 0-8419-0417-0). Holmes & Meier.

Writers & Politics in Nigeria. James Booth. LC 80-17670. (Writers & Politics Ser.). 128p. 1981. text ed. 23.75x (ISBN 0-8419-0650-5, Africana); pap. text ed. 13.95x (ISBN 0-8419-0651-3). Holmes & Meier.
Writers & Their Background: Alexander Pope. Ed. by Peter Dixon. LC 72-85534. (Writers & Their Background Ser.). xx, 324p. 1972. 15.00x (ISBN 0-8214-0113-0); pap. 6.00 (ISBN 0-8214-0114-9). Ohio U Pr.
Writers & Their Background: Geoffrey Chaucer. Ed. by Derek S. Brewer. LC 74-84295. (Writers & Their Background Ser.). xiv, 401p. 1974. 17.00x (ISBN 0-8214-0183-1); pap. 7.00x (ISBN 0-8214-0184-X). Ohio U Pr.
Writers & Their Background: John Dryden. Ed. by Earl Miner. LC 72-95818. (Writers & Their Background Ser.). xxvi, 363p. 1972. 15.00x (ISBN 0-8214-0119-X); pap. 6.95x (ISBN 0-8214-0120-3). Ohio U Pr.
Writers & Their Background: Robert Browning. Ed. by Isobel Armstrong. LC 72-96846. (Writers & Their Background Ser). xxvi, 365p. 1974. 15.00x (ISBN 0-8214-0131-9); pap. 6.00x (ISBN 0-8214-0132-7). Ohio U Pr.
Writers & Their Background: Samuel Taylor Coleridge. Ed. by R. L. Brett. LC 72-85533. (Writers & Their Background Ser.). xvii, 296p. 1975. 15.00x (ISBN 0-8214-0109-2); pap. 6.50x (ISBN 0-8214-0110-6). Ohio U Pr.
Writers at Work. Ed. by George Plimpton. LC 80-18030. (Paris Review Interviews Ser.: No. 5). (Illus.). 416p. 1981. 17.95 (ISBN 0-670-79098-2). Viking Pr.
Writers at Work, Vol. 5. Ed. by George Plimpton. (Writers at Work Ser.). 416p. 1981. pap. 8.95 (ISBN 0-14-005818-4). Penguin.
Writer's Book by Sherwood Anderson: A Critical Edition. Martha M. Curry. LC 74-22088. 1975. 19.50 (ISBN 0-8108-0737-8). Scarecrow.
Writers Choice: Twenty American Authors Introduce Their Own Best Story. Ed. by Rust Hills. LC 74-82985. 416p. 1974. pap. text ed. 7.95x (ISBN 0-582-28132-6). Longman.
Writer's Control of Tone. Edward M. White. 1970. pap. text ed. 4.95x (ISBN 0-393-09894-X, NortonC). Norton.
Writer's Craft. John Hersey. 1973. 10.95 (ISBN 0-394-31799-8). Random.
Writer's Craft: A Concise Rhetoric & Handbook. A. R. Coulthard. 416p. 1980. pap. text ed. 7.95x (ISBN 0-534-00768-6); wkbk. 3.95x (ISBN 0-534-00845-3). Wadsworth Pub.
Writer's Digest Diary, 1981. 144p. 1980. 9.95 (ISBN 0-89879-015-8). Writers Digest.
Writer's Effort: Trial & Error. Mary-Ruth Mundy. (Orig.). 1979. pap. 3.00x o.p. (ISBN 0-918342-08-2). Cambric.
Writers for Young Adults: Biographies Master Index. Adele Sarkissian. LC 79-13228. (Gale Biographical Index Ser.: Vol. 6). 1979. 36.00 (ISBN 0-8103-1083-X). Gale.
Writer's Guide. 6th ed. Wilma R. Ebbitt & David Ebbitt. 1979. pap. text ed. 8.95x (ISBN 0-673-15329-0). Scott F.
Writer's Guide & Index to English. 6th ed. Wilma R. Ebbitt & David R. Ebbitt. 1978. 12.95x (ISBN 0-673-15109-3). Scott F.
Writer's Guide to Book Publishing. Richard Balkin. 1977. 9.95 o.p. (ISBN 0-8015-8935-5); pap. 4.95 o.p. (ISBN 0-8015-8936-3). Dutton.
Writer's Guide to Book Publishing. rev. ed. Richard Balkin. 288p. 1981. 15.95 (ISBN 0-8015-8925-8, Hawthorn); pap. 8.95 (ISBN 0-8015-8926-6, Hawthorn). Dutton.
Writer's Guide to Chicago-Area Publishers & Other Freelance Markets. Jerold L. Kellman. LC 79-90014. 320p. 1979. 8.95 (ISBN 0-914090-74-7). Gabriel Hse.
Writer's Guide to Copyright. Poets & Writers, Inc. Ed. by Caroline R. Herron. LC 79-25019. (Illus.). 49p. (Orig.). 1979. pap. 4.95 (ISBN 0-913734-10-1). Poets & Writers.
Writer's Handbook. Lefcowitz. 1976. text ed. 10.50 (ISBN 0-13-969923-6); pap. text ed. 6.95 wkbk. (ISBN 0-13-969907-4); pap. text ed. 12.00 net, diagnostic test (ISBN 0-13-970012-9). P-H.
Writer's Handbook: 1980 Edition. new ed. Ed. by A. S. Burack. 1980. 16.95 (ISBN 0-87116-119-2). Writer.
Writers: Help Yourselves! Mildred I. Reid. 5.00 (ISBN 0-914062-02-6). Burkehaven Pr.
Writers: Here's How! rev ed. Mildred I. Reid. 1978. 4.00 (ISBN 0-914062-01-8). Burkehaven Pr.
Writer's Hotline Handbook. Michael Montgomery & John Stratton. (Orig.). 1981. pap. 3.95 (ISBN 0-451-61972-2, MF 1972, Mentor Bks). NAL.
Writer's Image: The Literary Portraits of Jill Krementz. Jill Krementz. LC 80-66461. (Illus.). 112p. 1980. 25.00 (ISBN 0-87923-349-4). Godine.
Writers in Exile: The Creative Use of Home in Modern Literature. Andrew Gurr. 220p. 1981. 21.00x (ISBN 0-389-20189-8). B&N.
Writers in Love. Mary K. Benet. LC 76-25560. 1977. 9.95 o.s.i. (ISBN 0-02-508900-5, 50890). Macmillan.
Writers in Residence: American Authors at Home. Glynne R. Betts. 1981. 16.95 (ISBN 0-670-79108-3, Studio). Viking Pr.
Writer's Legal Guide. Ted Crawford. LC 76-56516. 1978. 10.95 (ISBN 0-8015-8937-1, Hawthorn); pap. 5.95 (ISBN 0-8015-8938-X, Hawthorn). Dutton.
Writers: Let's Plot! rev. ed. Mildred I. Reid. 1979. 5.50 (ISBN 0-914062-03-4). Burkehaven Pr.
Writers: Make It Sell! rev. ed. Mildred I. Reid. 1976. 5.50 (ISBN 0-914062-04-2). Burkehaven Pr.
Writer's Manual. rev. ed. Roy Porter et al. 1979. 27.95 (ISBN 0-88280-087-6); pap. 17.95 (ISBN 0-88280-088-4). ETC Pubns.
Writer's Manual. Roy E. Porter et al. LC 75-43588. 1979. pap. 16.95 (ISBN 0-88280-088-4); pap. 14.95 (ISBN 0-88280-063-9). Chicago Review.
Writer's Market 1980. 50th ed. Ed. by William Brohaugh. (Illus.). 1979. 14.95 o.p. (ISBN 0-89879-000-X). Writers Digest.
Writers of the New Testament. W. H. Simcox. Date not set. 8.95 (ISBN 0-88469-139-X). BMH Bks.
Writers of the Western World. 2nd ed. Ed. by Addison Hibbard & Horst Frenz. LC 67-6008. 1967. text ed. 21.50 (ISBN 0-395-04601-7, 3-24495). HM.
Writers on the Left. Daniel Aaron. LC 61-13349. 1977. pap. 7.95 (ISBN 0-19-519970-7, GB512, GB). Oxford U Pr.
Writers Practical Handbook. Adrienne Robins. LC 79-19667. 1980. text ed. 12.95 (ISBN 0-471-03033-3); tchrs. manual avail. (ISBN 0-471-07833-6). Wiley.
Writers' Revisions: An Annotated Bibliography of Articles & Books About Writers' Revisions & Their Comments on the Creative Process. David Madden & Richard Powers. LC 80-22942. 254p. 1981. 13.50 (ISBN 0-8108-1375-0). Scarecrow.
Writer's Rhyming Dictionary. Langford Reed. 7.95 (ISBN 0-87116-044-7). Writer.
Writers: Why Stop Now? rev ed. Mildred I. Reid. 1981. 6.00 (ISBN 0-914062-05-0). Burkehaven Pr.
Writer's Work: Guide to Effective Composition. Dean Menering & Frank O'Hare. (Illus.). 1980. text ed. 12.95 (ISBN 0-13-969865-5); diagnostic test 29.95. P-H.
Writer's Work Workbook. Roseann Morgan. 248p. 1981. pap. text ed. 6.95 (ISBN 0-13-969840-X). P-H.
Writers Workbook A: Form D. G. Leggett & D. Lee. 1967. pap. text ed. 5.95 o.p. (ISBN 0-13-970087-0). P-H.
Writers Workshop Handbook of Assamese Literature, Vol. 1: A-D. P. N. Shastri & P. Lal. (Greybird Book Ser). 106p. 1975. text ed. 14.00 (ISBN 0-88253-702-4); pap. text ed. 8.00 (ISBN 0-88253-703-2). Ind-US Inc.
Writer's Workshop: Techniques in Creative Writing. Barry Maybury. 1979. 17.95 (ISBN 0-7134-1557-6, Pub. by Batsford England). David & Charles.
Writing. Richard L. Allington & Kathleen Krull. LC 80-15334. (Beginning to Learn About Ser.). (Illus.). 32p. (ps-2). 1980. PLB 9.65 (ISBN 0-8172-1321-X). Raintree Child.
Writing. Gregory Cowan & Elizabeth Cowan. LC 79-24989. 1980. text ed. 14.95 (ISBN 0-471-01559-8); tchr's manual (ISBN 0-471-07692-9); wkbk. 7.95 (ISBN 0-471-07691-0). Wiley.
Writing: A College Handbook. James A. Heffernan & John E. Lincoln. 1981. text ed. price not set (ISBN 0-393-95150-2); phamphlet free (ISBN 0-393-95163-4). Norton. Postponed.
Writing a Novel. John Braine. 224p. 1975. pap. 4.95 (ISBN 0-07-007112-8, SP). McGraw.
Writing a Novel. Dorothy Bryant. LC 78-69766. 1978. pap. 5.00 (ISBN 0-931688-02-7). Ata Bks.
Writing a Practical Guide. Joseph P. Dagher. LC 74-11784. (Illus.). 1975. pap. text ed. 10.50 (ISBN 0-395-18621-8); inst. manual 1.25 (ISBN 0-395-18803-2). HM.
Writing: A Preparation for College Composition. 2nd ed. Robert C. Slack & Beekman W. Cottrell. 1978. pap. text ed. 6.95x (ISBN 0-02-478250-5). Macmillan.
Writing About Curious Things. Joan D. Berbrich. (Orig.). (gr. 8). 1981. pap. text ed. 5.67 (ISBN 0-87720-394-6). AMSCO Sch.
Writing About Fascinating Things. Joan D. Berbrich. (Orig.). (gr. 8-10). 1980. wkbk. 5.83 (ISBN 0-87720-391-1). AMSCO Sch.
Writing About My Feelings. Charlie Daniel & Becky Daniel. (gr. 1-4). 1978. 5.95 (ISBN 0-916456-18-8, GA80). Good Apple.
Writing About People & Yourself. Joan D. Berbrich. (gr. 10-12). 1979. wkbk. 7.33 (ISBN 0-87720-382-2). AMSCO Sch.
Writing Aids Through the Grades: One Hundred Eighty-Six Developmental Writing Activities. Ruth Carlson. LC 77-108775. 1970. pap. 5.25x (ISBN 0-8077-1141-1). Tchrs Coll.
Writing Air, Written Water. Roberta Gould. 96p. (Orig.). 1980. write for info. (ISBN 0-936628-00-6). Waterside.
Writing & Difference. Jacques Derrida. Tr. by Alan Bass from Fr. LC 77-25933. 1980. pap. 6.95 (ISBN 0-226-14329-5, P865, Phoen). U of Chicago Pr.
Writing & Editing School News: A Basic Project Text in Scholastic Journalism. William Harwood. 1977. lib. bdg. 7.50 (ISBN 0-931054-04-4). Clark Pub.
Writing & Evaluating Curriculum Guide. Sharon Zenger & Weldon Zenger. LC 73-77593. 1973. pap. 3.95 o.p. (ISBN 0-8224-7506-5). Pitman Learning.
Writing & Reading in Henry James. Susanne Kappeler. LC 80-18181. 242p. 1981. 22.50x (ISBN 0-231-05198-0). Columbia U Pr.
Writing & Revising: A Workbook. J. Karl Nicholas. 250p. 1981. pap. 7.95 (ISBN 0-13-971499-5). P-H.
Writing & Selling Greeting Cards. Carl Goeller. 1980. 10.95 (ISBN 0-87116-124-9). Writer.
Writing As a Second Language. Barbara Danish. 1981. worktext 6.00 (ISBN 0-915924-10-2). Tchrs & Writers Coll.
Writing at Work: Do's, Dont's & How To's. Ernst Jacobi. 1976. 12.90 (ISBN 0-8104-5730-X); pap. 9.50 (ISBN 0-8104-5729-6). Hayden.
Writing Book. Joan G. Roloff & Robert C. Wylder. 1978. 7.95x (ISBN 0-02-477120-1). Macmillan.
Writing Business Letters & Reports. Carmella E. Mansfield & Margaret H. Bahniuk. 1981. write for info. (ISBN 0-672-97374-X); tchrs. manual avail. (ISBN 0-672-97375-8). Bobbs.
Writing by Design. Walter E. Klarner et al. LC 76-14652. (Illus.). 1977. pap. text ed. 9.50 (ISBN 0-395-24428-5); inst. manual 0.25 (ISBN 0-395-24429-3). HM.
Writing Careers. Gurney Williams, 3rd. (Career Concise Guides Ser.). (Illus.). 96p. (gr. 7 up). 1976. PLB 4.90 o.p. (ISBN 0-531-01130-5). Watts.
Writing Clear Paragraphs. Robert B. Donald et al. (Illus.). 1978. pap. text ed. 8.95 (ISBN 0-13-970350-0). P-H.
Writing Clinic. 2nd ed. Ralph E. Loewe. LC 77-17542. (Illus.). 1978. pap. text ed. 9.95 (ISBN 0-13-970434-5). P-H.
Writing Communications in Business & Industry. 2nd ed. Nelda R. Lawrence. 176p. 1974. pap. text ed. 10.95 (ISBN 0-13-970491-4). P-H.
Writing Communications in Business & Industry. 3rd ed. Nelda R. Lawrence & Elizabeth Tebeaux. (Illus.). 272p. 1981. 12.95 (ISBN 0-13-970467-1). P-H.
Writing Concepts. LaSalle Mayes et al. 1978. pap. text ed. 11.95 (ISBN 0-8403-1872-3). Kendall-Hunt.
Writing: Craft & Art. William L. Rivers. 256p. 1975. pap. text ed. 7.50 (ISBN 0-13-970202-4). P-H.
Writing Creatively. Joan D. Berbrich. (gr. 10-12). 1977. wkbk 9.08 (ISBN 0-87720-375-X). AMSCO Sch.
Writing Degree Zero. Roland Barthes. Tr. by Laver & Smith. 94p. 1977. 8.95 (ISBN 0-8090-9865-2); pap. 4.50 (ISBN 0-8090-1384-3). Hill & Wang.
Writing Effective Reports on Police Investigations: Concepts, Procedures, Samples. Robert C. Levie & Lou E. Ballard. 1978. text ed. 17.95 (ISBN 0-205-06098-6, 826098-2). Allyn.
Writing Effectively: A Practical Guide. Mary L. Kelsch & Thomas Kelsch. 192p. 1981. 10.95 (ISBN 0-13-969832-9, Spec); pap. 4.95 (ISBN 0-13-969824-8, Spec). P-H.
Writing Efficiently: A Step-by-Step Composition Course. Barbara Seale. (Illus.). 1978. pap. text ed. 8.95 (ISBN 0-13-970160-5). P-H.
Writing English As a Second Language. Jewell A. Friend. 1971. pap. 6.95x (ISBN 0-673-07536-2). Scott F.
Writing English Language Tests. J. B. Heaton. 1975. 8.75x (ISBN 0-582-55080-7). Longman.
Writing Fiction. Arturo Vivante. 1980. 10.95 (ISBN 0-87116-122-2). Writer.
Writing for a Reason. Dee Brock & C. Jeriel Howard. LC 77-12617. 1978. pap. text ed. 8.50x (ISBN 0-471-03017-1); tchrs. manual 1.00 (ISBN 0-471-04052-5). Wiley.
Writing for a Specific Purpose. Sandra McKay & Linda Rosenthal. (Illus.). 1980. pap. text ed. 7.50 (ISBN 0-13-970269-5). P-H.
Writing for Business. Mary C. Bromage. (Orig.). 1965. pap. 2.95 o.p. (ISBN 0-472-06108-9, 108, AA). U of Mich Pr.
Writing for Business. Mary C. Bromage. 176p. (Orig.). 1965. 4.95 o.p. (ISBN 0-472-09108-5). U of Mich Pr.
Writing for Cash. Beryl Sandwell & Jon Atkinson. 1975. 6.95 (ISBN 0-236-31140-9, Pub. by Paul Elek). Merrimack Bk Serv.
Writing for Decision Makers. Marya Holcombe & Judith Stein. LC 80-24900. 260p. 1980. text ed. 14.95 leaders manual (ISBN 0-534-97980-7). Lifetime Learn.
Writing for Public Relations. George A. Douglas. (Marketing & Management Ser.). 192p. 1980. pap. text ed. 8.95 (ISBN 0-675-08171-8). Merrill.
Writing for Readers. George R. Bramer & Dorothy Sedley. (Illus.). 500p. 1981. text ed. price not set (ISBN 0-675-08045-2); write for info. tchr's. ed (ISBN 0-675-08038-X); instr's. manual 3.95 (ISBN 0-686-69504-6). Merrill.
Writing for Real. Daniel Knapp & John Dennis. (Illus.). 192p. 1972. pap. text ed. 6.95 (ISBN 0-13-970525-2). P-H.
Writing for Results in Business, Government, the Sciences & the Professions. 2nd ed. David W. Ewing. LC 79-11756. 1979. 19.95 (ISBN 0-471-05036-9). Wiley.
Writing for Results: Principles & Practice. Dugan Laird. LC 77-88052. 1978. pap. text ed. 8.95 (ISBN 0-201-04114-6). A-W.
Writing for Technical & Business Magazines. Robert H. Dodds. LC 70-93486. (Human Communications Ser). 1969. 14.95 o.p. (ISBN 0-471-21725-5, Pub. by Wiley-Interscience). Wiley.
Writing for Technical & Professional Journals. John H. Mitchell. LC 67-31374. (Wiley Ser. on Human Communications). 1968. 19.95 (ISBN 0-471-61170-0, Pub. by Wiley-Interscience). Wiley.
Writing for the Fun of It: An Experience-Based Approach to Composition. Robert C. Hawley & Isabel L. Hawley. LC 73-83548. 110p. (Orig.). 1974. pap. 4.95 (ISBN 0-913636-02-9). Educ Res MA.
Writing for the Real World. Robert E. Mehaffy. 1980. pap. text ed. 9.95x (ISBN 0-673-15244-8). Scott F.
Writing for Young Children. Claudia Lewis. LC 79-6588. 168p. 1981. 10.95 (ISBN 0-385-15392-9, Anchor Pr). Doubleday.
Writing from a Legal Perspective. George D. Gopen. 250p. 1981. text ed. 11.95 (ISBN 0-8299-2123-0). West Pub.
Writing Good Sentences. rev. ed. Claude W. Faulkner. 1973. pap. text ed. 9.95x (ISBN 0-684-41242-X, ScribC). Scribner.
Writing: Growth Through Structure. Clarence A. Andrews. (gr. 10 up). 1972. pap. text ed. 5.95x (ISBN 0-02-470900-X, 47090). Macmillan.
Writing How & Why: Instructional Manual to Accompany Suki. Ed. by Matthew Lipman & Ann M. Sharp. 384p. 1980. tchrs ed. 30.00 (ISBN 0-916834-14-X). Inst Adv Philo.
Writing in Law Practice. Frank E. Cooper. 1963. text ed. 17.00 (ISBN 0-672-81021-2, Bobbs-Merrill Law). Michie.
Writing in Style. Washington Post Writers Group. 1975. pap. text ed. 8.75 (ISBN 0-395-24018-2). HM.
Writing in Subject-Matter Fields: A Bibliographic Guide, with Annotations & Writing Assignments. Eva M. Burkett. LC 76-30397. 1977. 10.00 (ISBN 0-8108-1012-3). Scarecrow.
Writing Lab. S. Weiner & R. Palmer. 1974. pap. 11.95 (ISBN 0-02-479620-4, 47962). Macmillan.
Writing Light Verse & Prose Humor. Richard Armour. 7.95 (ISBN 0-87116-064-1). Writer.
Writing Logically. Joan D. Berbrich. (gr. 11-12). 1978. wkbk 8.00 (ISBN 0-87720-332-6). AMSCO Sch.
Writing Modern English. Robert M. Gorrell & Charlton Laird. (Illus.). 288p. 1973. pap. text ed. 8.95 (ISBN 0-13-970632-1). P-H.
Writing News for Broadcast. 2nd ed. Edward Bliss, Jr. & John M. Patterson. 1978. 17.50x (ISBN 0-231-04372-4). Columbia U Pr.
Writing Now: A College Handbook. Francis Fennell. 1980. pap. text ed. 7.95 (ISBN 0-574-22050-X, 13-5050); instr's guide avail. (ISBN 0-574-22051-8, 13-5051). SRA.
Writing of History: Literary Form & Historical Understanding. Ed. by Robert H. Canary & Henry Kozicki. LC 78-4590. 1978. 19.50 (ISBN 0-299-07570-2). U of Wis Pr.
Writing of Modern Fiction. Robert Somerlott. text ed. 8.95 (ISBN 0-87116-068-4). Writer.
Writing on Your Own. George E. Sullivan & Warren Cox. Ed. by K. West & D. Johnston. (Writing Skills for Daily Living Ser.). (Illus.). 32p. (gr. 7-12). 1979. pap. text ed. 3.95x (ISBN 0-87453-099-7, 82099). Denoyer.
Writing Part Time for Fun & Money. Jack C. McLarn. LC 78-50474. 1980. pap. 4.95 (ISBN 0-913864-39-0). Enterprise Del.
Writing Performance. Donald H. Ross. LC 73-463. 240p. 1973. pap. text ed. 3.95 o.p. (ISBN 0-397-47284-6). Lippincott.
Writing Practically. Joan D. Berbrich. (Orig.). (gr. 10-12). 1976. wkbk. 7.17 (ISBN 0-87720-338-5). AMSCO Sch.
Writing Prose That Makes a Difference, & the Grammar Minimum. Oxford S. Stroud. LC 79-84651. 1979. pap. text ed. 5.00 (ISBN 0-8191-0740-9). U Pr of Amer.
Writing Psychological Reports. William T. Martin. 192p. 1972. pap. 13.50 spiral (ISBN 0-398-02352-2). C C Thomas.

Writing Room: A Resource Book for Teachers of English. Harvey S. Wiener. 352p. 1981. pap. 7.95 (ISBN 0-19-502826-0). Oxford U Pr.
Writing Room: A Resource Book for Teachers of English. Harvey S. Wiener. 352p. 1981. pap. text ed. 7.95x (ISBN 0-19-502826-0). Oxford U Pr.
Writing Schoolemaster: Brachygraphie, Orthographie, Calygraphie. Peter Bales. LC 70-26226. (English Experience Ser.: No. 194). 122p. 1969. Repr. of 1590 ed. 16.00 (ISBN 90-221-0194-0). Walter J Johnson.
Writing Scientific Papers-Reports. 8th ed. Paul W. Jones & Michael L. Keene. 365p. 1981. pap. text ed. write for info. (ISBN 0-697-03773-8). Wm C Brown.
Writing Sense: A Handbook of Composition. David R. Pichaske. LC 74-15134. 1975. pap. text ed. 5.95 (ISBN 0-02-925170-2). Free Pr.
Writing Skills. Peter W. Preksto, Jr. & Patricia S. Schaefer. (Basic Skills Library). (Illus.). (gr. 4 up). 1979. PLB 5.95 (ISBN 0-87191-716-5). Creative Ed.
Writing Skills. Virginia Underwood & Merriellyn Kett. 1977. pap. text ed. 9.50 o.p. (ISBN 0-675-08484-9); audio cassettes 125.00 o.p. (ISBN 0-686-67619-X); 2-5 sets 75.00, 6 or more sets 50.00 o.p. (ISBN 0-675-08467-9). Merrill.
Writing, Speaking & Listening. Raymond W. Hodges et al. Ed. by Barry M. Smith. LC 73-80233. (Basic Studies Program). 184p. 1973. pap. text ed. 7.65 (ISBN 0-913310-34-4). PAR Inc.
Writing Systems of the World: Alphabets, Syllabaries, Pictograms. Akira Nakanishi. LC 79-64826. (Illus.). 1981. 19.50 (ISBN 0-8048-1293-4). C E Tuttle.
Writing Teacher's Sourcebook. Ed. by Gary Tate & Edward P. Corbett. 400p. 1981. pap. text ed. 9.95x (ISBN 0-19-502878-3). Oxford U Pr.
Writing Term Papers & Reports. 4th ed. George S. Hubbell. (Orig.). 1969. pap. 2.50 (ISBN 0-06-460037-8, CO 37, COS). Har-Row.
Writing That Works. Kenneth Roman & Joel Raphaelson. LC 80-8695. 160p. 1981. 9.95 (ISBN 0-06-014843-8, HarpT). Har-Row.
Writing the Australian Crawl. William Stafford. Ed. by Donald Hall. LC 77-5711. (Poets on Poetry Ser.). pap. 5.95 (ISBN 0-472-87300-8). U of Mich Pr.
Writing the Biomedical Research Paper. Stanley M. Garn. 76p. 1970. pap. 6.95 (ISBN 0-398-00648-2). C C Thomas.
Writing the Broadway Musical. Aaron Frankel. LC 76-58925. 1977. pap. text ed. 10.00x (ISBN 0-910482-82-9). Drama Bk.
Writing the Business & Technical Report. William J. Gallagher. LC 80-19781. 120p. 1980. pap. 8.95 (ISBN 0-8436-0796-3). CBI Pub.
Writing the Creative Article. rev ed. Marjorie Holmes. 1976. 8.95 (ISBN 0-87116-100-1). Writer.
Writing the Economics Paper. Lawrence Morse. 1981. pap. text ed. 3.75 (ISBN 0-8120-2113-4). Barron.
Writing the Expository Essay. Jane Kahan & Marie K. Stone. LC 78-730063. (Illus.). 1977. pap. text ed. 99.00 (ISBN 0-89290-123-3, A322). Soc for Visual.
Writing the News: Print Journalism in the Electronic Age. Walter Fox. 1977. 8.95 (ISBN 0-8038-8081-2); pap. text ed. 4.50 (ISBN 0-8038-8082-0). Hastings.
Writing the Photoplay. J. Berg Esenwein & Arthur Leeds. 425p. 1980. Repr. of 1913 ed. lib. bdg. 35.00 (ISBN 0-8495-1350-2). Arden Lib.
Writing the Research Paper. rev. ed. Lotte Blustein & Rosemary J. Geary. (Illus.). 60p. (gr. 7-12). 1980. pap. text ed. 4.45 (ISBN 0-9605248-2-7). Blustein-Geary.
Writing the Research Paper. rev. ed. Neal F. Doubleday. 1971. pap. text ed. 5.95x (ISBN 0-669-81224-2). Heath.
Writing the Research Paper. Marilyn S. Samuels. 1978. pap. text ed. 5.67 (ISBN 0-87720-965-0). AMSCO Sch.
Writing the Research Paper: A Guide & Sourcebook. Marsha Z. Cummins & Carole Slade. LC 78-69613. (Illus.). 1978. pap. text ed. 8.75 (ISBN 0-395-27259-9); inst. manual 0.30 (ISBN 0-395-27260-2). HM.
Writing Themes About Literature. 4th ed. Edgar V. Roberts. 1977. pap. text ed. 7.95 (ISBN 0-13-970582-1). P-H.
Writing to Be Read. rev. 2nd ed. Ken Macrorie. (English Language Ser.). 288p. 1976. 11.50x (ISBN 0-8104-5980-9); pap. 9.50x (ISBN 0-8104-5979-5). Hayden.
Writing Today: A Rhetoric & Handbook. Patricia Moody. (Illus.). 512p. 1981. pap. text ed. 12.95 (ISBN 0-13-971556-8). P-H.
Writing Today: A Rhetoric Handbook. P. Moody. 1981. 10.95 (ISBN 0-13-971556-8); pap. 9.95 wkbk & key (ISBN 0-13-971572-X). P-H.
Writing with a Purpose. 6th ed. James M. McCrimmon. LC 75-24527. (Illus.). 1975. text ed. 10.95 o.p. (ISBN 0-395-19235-8). HM.
Writing with a Purpose. short, 6th ed. James M. McCrimmon. LC 76-47875. 1977. text ed. 9.95 o.p. (ISBN 0-395-25004-8); inst. guide & resource bk. 1.10 o.p. (ISBN 0-395-25012-9). HM.
Writing with a Purpose. 7th ed. James M. McCrimmon et al. LC 79-88599. 1980. text ed. 12.50 (ISBN 0-395-28253-5); instrs' manual 1.25 (ISBN 0-395-28254-3). HM.
Writing with a Purpose: Short Edition. James M. McCrimmon et al. LC 79-90088. 1979. pap. text ed. 11.50 (ISBN 0-395-28939-4). HM.
Writing with Power: Techniques for Mastering the Writing Process. Peter Elbow. 356p. 1981. 15.00 (ISBN 0-19-502912-7). Oxford U Pr.
Writing with Power: Techniques for Mastering the Writing Process. Peter Elbow. 356p. 1981. pap. 5.95 (ISBN 0-19-502913-5, GB 642, GB). Oxford U Pr.
Writing with Reason: Logic for Composition. M. C. Beardsley. (Illus.). 176p. 1976. pap. text ed. 6.95 (ISBN 0-13-970301-2). P-H.
Writing with Style: Conversations on the Art of Writing. John R. Trimble. (Illus.). 160p. 1975. pap. text ed. 6.50 (ISBN 0-13-970368-3). P-H.
Writing Without Teachers. Peter Elbow. LC 72-96608. 208p. 1975. pap. 3.95 (ISBN 0-19-501679-3, GB435, GB). Oxford U Pr.
Writing Workshop. Alan Ziegler. (Orig.). 1981. pap. 6.00 (ISBN 0-915924-11-0). Tchrs & Writers Coll.
Writingcraft: The Paragraphs & the Essays. Sheila Y. Graham. (Illus.). 192p. 1976. pap. text ed. 7.50x (ISBN 0-13-970152-4). P-H.
Writings, Bk. 4. Thucydides. Ed. by J. C. Wordsworth. (Gr). text ed. 4.95x (ISBN 0-521-06634-4). Cambridge U Pr.
Writings About Music. Steve Reich. LC 73-87481. (Nova Scotia Ser). (Illus.). 82p. 1974. 10.00x, c o.p. (ISBN 0-8147-7358-3); pap. 4.00, C (ISBN 0-8147-7357-5). NYU Pr.
Writings About Music. Steve Reich. 1974. pap. 7.00 (ISBN 0-686-67541-X, 50-26921). Eur-Am Music.
Writings & Buildings. Frank L. Wright. Ed. by Edgar Kaufmann & Ben Raeburn. (Illus.). 7.95 (ISBN 0-8180-0021-X). Horizon.
Writings & Speeches of Professor D. R. Gadgil on Co-operation. D. R. Gadgil. 1975. 8.00x o.p. (ISBN 0-88386-018-X). South Asia Bks.
Writings by & About Georg Lukacs: A Bibliography. P. Murphy. 1976. 1.00 (ISBN 0-89977-032-0). Am Inst Marxist.
Writings by Du Bois in Periodicals Edited by Others, 4 vols. Ed. by Herbert Aptheker. (Completed Published Works of W. E. B. Du Bois). 1981. Set. lib. bdg. 240.00 (ISBN 0-527-25358-8). Kraus Intl.
Writings from the Beaver Trail. Ed. by Florence Boochever & Raymond Jackson. (Illus.). 312p. (Orig.). 1979. pap. 5.50 (ISBN 0-9605090-0-3). Albany Pub Lib.
Writings from the Philokalia. E. Kadloubowsky. Tr. by G. E. Palmer. (Illus.). 1951. 18.95 (ISBN 0-571-07062-0, Pub. by Faber & Faber). Merrimack Bk Serv.
Writings in General Linguistics: Vocal Alternation & "Prinzipien der Sprachentwicklung". Ed. by Mikolaj Kruszewski. Tr. by Robert Austerlitz & Fredrich Techmer. (Amsterdam Classics in Linguistics Ser.: No. 11). 190p. 1980. text ed. 31.50x (ISBN 90-272-0972-3). Humanities.
Writings in Periodicals Edited by Du Bois: Selections from Phylon. Ed. by Herbert Aptheker. LC 80-13721. (Complete Published Works of W. E. B. Du Bois Ser.). 1980. lib. bdg. 65.00 (ISBN 0-527-25353-7). Kraus Intl.
Writings in Prose & Verse of Hezekiah Salem, Late of New England. Philip M. Freneau. LC 75-15901. (Illus.). 88p. 1975. lib. bdg. 20.00x (ISBN 0-8201-1156-2). Schol Facsimiles.
Writings of Benjamin F. Perry. Benjamin F. Perry. Ed. by Stephen Meats & Edwin T. Arnold. Incl. Vol. I. Essays, Public Letters, & Speeches. 640p. 35.00 (ISBN 0-87152-340-X); Vols. II & III. Reminiscences of Public Men. Vol. II, 576p. 35.00 ea. (ISBN 0-87152-341-8); Vol. III, 572p. 35.00 (ISBN 0-87152-342-6). LC 80-19568. (South Carolina Ser.: Bibliographical & Textual: No. 6). 1980. Repr. Set. 105.00 (ISBN 0-87152-339-6). Reprint.
Writings of Bradford. John Bradford. 1979. Set. 28.95. Banner of Truth.
Writings of Henry Barrow, 1587-1590. Leland H. Carlson. (Elizabethan Nonconformist Texts Ser.). 1962. text ed. 12.50x o.p. (ISBN 0-04-285001-0). Allen Unwin.
Writings of Henry Barrow, 1590-1591. Ed. by Leland H. Carlson. (Elizabethan Nonconformist Texts Ser.). 1962. text ed. 16.50x o.p. (ISBN 0-04-285002-9). Allen Unwin.
Writings of Hugh Swinton Legare. H. S. Legare. Ed. by Mary S. L. Bullen. LC 70-107413. (American Public Figures Ser). 1970. Repr. of 1846 ed. lib. bdg. 27.50 (ISBN 0-306-71885-5). Da Capo.
Writings of John. Gerald Dye. (Double Trouble Puzzles Ser.). (Illus.). 1977. pap. 1.25 (ISBN 0-87239-150-7, 2821). Standard Pub.
Writings of John Greenwood & Henry Barrow, 1591-1593. Ed. by Leland H. Carlson. (Elizabethan Nonconformist Texts Ser.). 1970. text ed. 17.95x o.p. (ISBN 0-04-809002-6). Allen Unwin.
Writings of John Greenwood, 1587-1590. Ed. by Leland H. Carlson. (Elizabethan Nonconformist Texts Ser.). 1962. text ed. 8.95x o.p. (ISBN 0-04-285003-7). Allen Unwin.
Writings of John Lennon: In His Own Write, a Spaniard in the Works. John Lennon. 1981. 9.95 (ISBN 0-671-43257-5). S&S.
Writings of Martin Buber. Martin Buber. Ed. by Will Herberg. (Orig.). pap. 3.95 o.p. (ISBN 0-452-00407-1, F407, Mer). NAL.
Writings of Paul Rosenfeld: An Annotated Bibliography. Charles L. Silet. LC 79-7931. 250p. 1981. lib. bdg. 35.00 (ISBN 0-8240-9532-4). Garland Pub.
Writings of President Frederick M. Smith, Vol. III: The Zionic Enterprise. Ed. by Norman D. Ruoff. 1981. pap. price not set (ISBN 0-8309-0300-3). Herald Hse.
Writings of Rafael Sabatini, 21 vols. Rafael Sabatini. 1981. Repr. of 1924 ed. Set. lib. bdg. 500.00 (ISBN 0-89987-766-4). Darby Bks.
Writings of Robert Harrison & Robert Browne. Leland H. Carlson. (Elizabethan Nonconformist Text Ser.). 1953. text ed. 6.95x o.p. (ISBN 0-04-274002-9). Allen Unwin.
Writings of Sam Houston, Eighteen Thirteen to Eighteen Thirty-Six, 8 Vols. Ed. by Amelia W. Williams & Eugene C. Barker. Set. 145.00 (ISBN 0-685-13280-3). Jenkins.
Writings of the Young Marx on Philosophy & Society. Ed. by Lloyd Easton & Kurt H. Guddat. LC 67-12896. pap. 3.50 (ISBN 0-385-07171-X, A563, Anch). Doubleday.
Writings on American History Nineteen Sixty-One, 2 vols. Compiled by James R. Masterton & Joyce E. Eberly. (Writings on American History Ser.). (Orig.). 1978. Set. lib. bdg. 55.00 (ISBN 0-527-98252-0). Kraus Intl.
Writings on the Theatre. Pierre Corneille. Ed. by H. T. Barnwell. (French Texts Ser.). 1965. pap. text ed. 12.50x (ISBN 0-631-00640-0, Pub. by Basil Blackwell). Biblio Dist.
Writings on Writing. May Sarton. Ed. by Constance Hunting. 55p. 1980. pap. 3.50 (ISBN 0-913006-20-3); pap. text ed. 3.50 (ISBN 0-913006-21-1); tchr.'s ed. 3.50 (ISBN 0-913006-22-X). Puckerbrush.
Writings to an Unfinished Accompaniment. W. S. Merwin. LC 72-92616. 128p. 1973. pap. 5.95 (ISBN 0-689-10556-8). Atheneum.
Writs of Assistance Case. M. H. Smith. 1978. 38.50x (ISBN 0-520-03349-3). U of Cal Pr.
Written Arabic: An Approach to the Basic Structures. Alfred F. Beeston. (Orig.). 1968. 10.95 (ISBN 0-521-09559-X, 559). Cambridge U Pr.
Written Communication Skills. rev. ed. Wilbert Schaal. 114p. 1980. pap. 6.60 (ISBN 0-87771-022-8). Grad School.
Written Constitutions, a Computerized Comparative Study. H. Maarseveen. 1978. 37.50 (ISBN 0-379-20361-8). Oceana.
Written English: An Introduction for Beginning Students of English As a Second Language. Robert Rainsbury. 1977. pap. 7.95 (ISBN 0-13-970673-9). P-H.
Written Expression in the Language Arts. Barbara M. Grant & Dorothy G. Hennings. LC 80-25532. (Orig.). 1981. pap. 11.95 (ISBN 0-8077-2604-4). Tchrs Coll.
Written for Children: An Outline of English-Language Children's Literature. John R. Townsend. (Illus.). 1976. pap. 6.50 (ISBN 0-87675-278-4). Horn Bk.
Written Spirit: Thematic & Rhetorical Structure in Wordsworth's the Prelude. Karl R. Johnson, Jr. (Salzburg Studies in English Literature, Romantic Reassessment: No. 72). 1978. pap. text ed. 25.00x (ISBN 0-391-01437-4). Humanities.
Wrong Man. Katrina Britt. (Harlequin Romances). 192p. 1981. pap. 1.25 (ISBN 0-373-02397-9, Pub. by Harlequin). PB.
Wrong-Way Camper & Other Stories. Jo Stanchfield. LC 72-92847. (Highway Holidays Ser). (gr. 3-6). 1973. pap. text ed. 3.54 (ISBN 0-8372-0796-7). Bowmar-Noble.
Wu Ching-Tzu. Timothy C. Wong. (World Authors Ser.: No. 495). 1978. lib. bdg. 13.50 (ISBN 0-8057-6336-8). Twayne.
Wuggie Norple Story. Daniel M. Pinkwater. LC 79-19014. (Illus.). 40p. (gr. k-3). 1980. 9.95 (ISBN 0-590-07569-1, Four Winds). Schol Bk Serv.
Wulfheim. Sax Rohmer. 1972. 5.00 (ISBN 0-685-33438-4). Bookfinger.
Wump World. Bill Peet. (gr. k-3). 1981. pap. 3.95x (ISBN 0-395-31129-2). HM.
Wunderbare Flucht Von Wilden (Captivity of Jakob Morgan). in: Columbian Almanac for 1839, Repr. Of 1839 Ed. Bd. with Low Dutch Boy Prisoner: Being an Account of the Capture of Frederick Schermerhorn When a Lad of 17 Years Old by a Party of Mohawks. Josiah Priest. Repr. of 1839 ed; True Story of the Extraordinary Feats, Adventures & Sufferings of Matthew Calkins. Josiah Priest. Repr. of 1840 ed; True Narrative of the Capture of David Ogden Among the Indians in the Time of the Revolution & of the Slavery & Sufferings He Endured. Josiah Priest. Repr. of 1840 ed; Narrative of the Extraordinary Life of John Conrad Shafford Known by Many by the Name of the Dutch Hermit. Repr. of 1840 ed; Authentic Particulars of the Death of Lieut. Thomas Boyd... in the Border War of the American Revolution Who Was Put to Death by the Indians in the Most Cruel Manner. Repr. of 1841 ed; Fort Stanwix Captive, or New England Volunteer, Being the Extraordinary Life & Adventures of Isaac Hubbell Among the Indians of Canada & the West... & the Story of His Marriage with the Indian Princess. Josiah Priest. Repr. of 1841 ed. LC 75-7079. (Indian Captivities Ser.: Vol. 56). 1977. lib. bdg. 44.00 (ISBN 0-8240-1680-7). Garland Pub.
Wunderpferdchen. Peter Jerschow. (It 490). (Orig., Ger.). 1980. pap. text ed. 6.50 (ISBN 3-458-32190-X, Pub. by Insel Verlag Germany). Suhrkamp.
Wushu - a Traditional Chinese Sport. 1978. pap. 1.50 (ISBN 0-8351-0579-2). China Bks.
Wuthering Heights. rev. ed. Emily Bronte. Ed. by William M. Sale, Jr. (Critical Editions Ser.). (Annotated). (gr. 9-12). 1972. pap. text ed. 4.95x (ISBN 0-393-09400-6, 9601). Norton.
Wuthering Heights. Emily Bronte. (gr. 9 up). 1963. 4.95g o.s.i. (ISBN 0-02-714820-3). Macmillan.
Wuthering Heights. Emily Bronte. 320p. (RL 10). 1973. pap. 1.95 (ISBN 0-451-51388-6, CJ1388, Sig Classics). NAL.
Wuthering Heights. Emily Bronte. (Literature Ser). (gr. 9-12). 1969. pap. text ed. 3.92 (ISBN 0-87720-720-8). AMSCO Sch.
Wuthering Heights. Emily Bronte. (Zodiac Press Ser.). 1978. 9.95 (ISBN 0-7011-1241-7, Pub. by Chatto Bodley Jonathan). Merrimack Bk Serv.
Wuthering Heights. Emily Bronte. Ed. by Hilda Marsden & Ion Jack. (Clarendon Edition of the Novels of the Brontes Ser.). 1976. 45.00x (ISBN 0-19-812511-9). Oxford U Pr.
Wuthering Heights. Emily Bronte. LC 78-4049. (Raintree's Illustrated Classics). (Illus.). (gr. 5-8). 1978. PLB 9.65 (ISBN 0-8393-6203-X). Raintree Child.
Wuthering Heights. Emily Bronte. pap. 1.75. Bantam.
Wuthering Heights: Student Activity Book. Marcia Sohl & Gerald Dackerman. (Now Age Illustrated Ser.). (Illus.). (gr. 4-12). 1976. wkbk. 0.95 (ISBN 0-88301-296-0). Pendulum Pr.
Wuthering Heights with Reader's Guide. Emily Bronte. (AMSCO Literature Program). (gr. 10-12). 1970. pap. text ed. 4.50 (ISBN 0-87720-809-3); with model ans. s.p. 2.90 (ISBN 0-87720-909-X). AMSCO Sch.
Wuzzles. Mike Thaler. (gr. k-3). 1976. pap. 1.25 (ISBN 0-590-10164-1, Schol Pap). Schol Bk Serv.
WW II Historical Romance. Elizabeth Aspril. Date not set. price not set. E Keys.
WW 2. Theodore A. Wilson. LC 74-11680. 1975. pap. text ed. 6.50x o.p. (ISBN 0-684-13987-1, ScribC). Scribner.
Wyatt: The Critical Heritage. Ed. by Patricia Thomson. (Critical Heritage Ser.). 196p. 1974. 24.00 (ISBN 0-7100-7907-9). Routledge & Kegan.
Wyckoff's Techniques for Stock Market Profits. Henry Hadrian. (Illus.). 150p. 1972. 65.00 (ISBN 0-913314-11-0). Am Classical Coll Pr.
Wycliffe Bible Commentary. Ed. by Everett Harrison & Charles F. Pfeiffer. 21.95 (ISBN 0-8024-9695-4). Moody.
Wycliffe Bible Encyclopedia, 2 vols. Ed. by Charles F. Pfeiffer et al. (Illus.). 1875p. 1975. 40.00 (ISBN 0-8024-9697-0). Moody.
Wycliffe Historical Geography of Bible Lands. Charles F. Pfeiffer & Howard F. Vos. 1967. 14.95 (ISBN 0-8024-9699-7). Moody.
Wycliffe in Paul's Court. W. J. Burley. LC 80-5449. (Crime Club Ser.). 192p. 1980. 8.95 (ISBN 0-385-17208-7). Doubleday.
Wyndham Lewis on Art: Collected Writings 1913-1956. Wyndham Lewis. 480p. 12.95x (ISBN 0-912158-33-6). Hennessey.
Wyndham Lewis: Paintings & Drawings. Walter Michel. LC 69-11616. (Illus.). 1970. 58.50x (ISBN 0-520-01612-2). U of Cal Pr.
Wyndward Passion. Norman Daniels. (Orig.). 1978. pap. 2.25 o.s.i. (ISBN 0-446-82669-3). Warner Bks.

Wynken, Blynken & Nod. Eugene Field. (Illus.). (gr. k-2). 1980. 6.95 (ISBN 0-8038-8046-4). Hastings.

Wynkyn De Worde & Chaucer's Canterbury Tales: A Transcription & Collation of the 1498 Edition with Caxton from the General Proloque Through the Knights Tale. William F. Hutmacher. (Costerus, New Ser.: No. 10). 1978. pap. text ed. 23.00x (ISBN 90-6203-502-7). Humanities.

Wynkyn de Worde: Father of Fleet Street. James Moran. (Illus.). pap. 10.00 (ISBN 0-913720-15-1). Sandstone.

Wyoming. 23.00 (ISBN 0-89770-126-7). Curriculum Info Ctr.

Wyoming: A Geography. Robert H. Brown. (Geographies of the United States Ser.). (Illus.). 375p. 1980. lib. bdg. 35.00 (ISBN 0-89158-560-5); text ed. 20.00 (ISBN 0-89158-560-5). Westview.

Wyoming: A Guide to Its History, Highways, & People. Federal Writers' Project of the Works Projects Administration. LC 80-23038. (Illus.). xxxviii, 490p. 1981. 24.50x (ISBN 0-8032-1958-X); pap. 9.75 (ISBN 0-8032-6854-8, BB 757, Bison). U of Nebr Pr.

Wyoming: A History. Taft A. Larson. LC 77-3592. (States & the Nation Ser.). (Illus.). 1977. 12.95 (ISBN 0-393-05626-0, Co-Pub by AASLH). Norton.

Wyoming Chronology & Factbook, Vol. 50. R. I. Vexler. 1978. 8.50 (ISBN 0-379-16189-3). Oceana.

Wyoming Industrial Minerals. 1975. 14.00. Minobras.

Wyoming Statutes, Annotated, 11 vols. with indexes & rules. 1979. write for info. (ISBN 0-87215-139-5); 1980 suppl. avail. (ISBN 0-87215-348-7). Michie.

Wyoming Sun. Edward Bryant. (Illus.). 132p. 1980. deluxe ed. 12.95; pap. 6.00. Jelm Mtn.

Wyoming Wealth: A History of Wyoming. William Bragg, Jr. Ed. by Amir Sancher. LC 76-47108. (Illus.). 1977. text ed. 14.95 (ISBN 0-89100-006-2); pap. text ed. 9.95 (ISBN 0-89100-001-1). Aviation Maint.

Wyoming Wife. Rodello Hunter. (YA) 1969. 7.95 o.p. (ISBN 0-394-45290-9). Knopf.

Wyoming's People. 2nd ed. Clarice Whittenburg & Carol Stinneford. 1978. pap. 5.75x (ISBN 0-933472-12-9). Johnson Colo.

Wyoming's People Activity Book. Rogene Boyd & Margaret Schumacher. 1978. 4.00x (ISBN 0-933472-37-4). Johnson Colo.

X

X. Beidler: Vigilante. John X. Beidler. Ed. by Helen F. Sanders & William H. Bertsche, Jr. (Western Frontier Library Ser.: Vol. 8). (Illus.). 1969. Repr. of 1957 ed. 4.95 o.p. (ISBN 0-8061-0373-6). U of Okla Pr.

X Factor. Andre Norton. 224p. 1981. pap. 2.25 (ISBN 0-449-24395-8, Crest). Fawcett.

X Marks the Spot: A Symphony in Black in Four Movements. Michael Butterworth. LC 77-92207. 1978. 7.95 o.p. (ISBN 0-385-13686-2). Doubleday.

X-Out Cigarettes. L. Vikari. 4.00 o.p. (ISBN 0-8062-1077-X). Carlton.

X-Rated Marriages. H. Page Williams. 1977. pap. 2.95 o.p. (ISBN 0-88270-242-4). Logos.

X-Ray Analysis & the Structure of Organic Molecules. Jack D. Dunitz. LC 78-15588. (George Fisher Baker Non-Resident Lectureship Ser.). 1979. 60.00x (ISBN 0-8014-1115-7). Cornell U Pr.

X-Ray & Neutron Diffraction. G. E. Bacon. 1966. text ed. 44.00 (ISBN 0-08-011999-9); pap. text ed. 19.50 (ISBN 0-08-011998-0). Pergamon.

X-Ray Astronomy. Ed. by Richard Giacconi & Giancarlo Setti. (NATO Advanced Study Institutes Series, C. Mathematical & Physical Sciences: No. 60). 400p. 1980. lib. bdg. 47.50 (ISBN 90-277-1156-9, Pub. by D. Reidel). Kluwer Boston.

X-Ray Astronomy, Including a Catalogue & Bibliography of Galactic X-Ray Sources: Proceedings of the 21st Plenary Meeting, Innsbruck, Austria, 1978. Committee on Space Research. Ed. by W. A. Baity & L. E. Peterson. (Illus.). 1979. text ed. 63.00 (ISBN 0-08-023418-6). Pergamon.

X-Ray Case Studies. Florencio A. Hipona. 1974. spiral bdg. 13.75 (ISBN 0-87488-026-2). Med Exam.

X-Ray Chart of the Human Skeleton. R. Grashey & G. S. Schwarz. 1957. 6.50 o.s.i. (ISBN 0-02-845430-8). Hafner.

X-Ray Crystallography. M. J. Buerger. LC 80-12459. 554p. 1980. Repr. of 1942 ed. lib. bdg. 32.00 (ISBN 0-89874-176-9). Krieger.

X-Ray Diagnosis for Clinical Students. 3rd ed. G. Simon. 1975. 37.50 (ISBN 0-407-00004-6). Butterworths.

X-Ray Diffraction. B. E. Warren. (Metallurgy & Materials Ser). (Illus.). 1969. 20.95 (ISBN 0-201-08524-0). A-W.

X-Ray Diffraction: In Crystals, Imperfect Crystals, & Amorphous Bodies. A. Guinier. Tr. by Paul Lorrain & Dorothee Lorrain. LC 62-13298. (Physics Ser.). (Illus.). 1963. text ed. 27.95x (ISBN 0-7167-0307-6). W H Freeman.

X-Ray Diffraction Procedures: For Polycrystalline & Amorphous Materials. 2nd ed. Harold P. Klug & Leroy E. Alexander. LC 73-21936. (Illus.). 864p. 1974. 60.00 (ISBN 0-471-49369-4, Pub. by Wiley-Interscience). Wiley.

X-Ray Diffraction Tables. Jen-Ho Fang & F. Donald Bloss. LC 66-21919. 1966. 15.00x o.p. (ISBN 0-8093-0211-X). S Ill U Pr.

X-Ray Diffraction Topography. B. K. Tanner. LC 75-45196. 1976. text ed. 32.00 (ISBN 0-08-019692-6). Pergamon.

X-Ray Diganosis Positioning Manual. Jo Carson. 1971. pap. text ed. 4.95x (ISBN 0-02-473270-2, 47327). Macmillan.

X-Ray of the Pampa. Ezequiel Martinez Estrada. Tr. by Alain Swietlicki. LC 70-165913. (Texas Pan American Ser). 415p. 1971. 17.50 (ISBN 0-292-70140-3); pap. 7.95 (ISBN 0-292-79500-9). U of Tex Pr.

X-Ray Sermons. Humphry. pap. 3.50 o.p. (ISBN 0-686-13328-5). Schmul Pub Co.

X-Ray Spectrochemical Analysis, Vol. 2. 2nd ed. L. S. Birks. (Illus.). 143p. 1969. text ed. 11.25 (ISBN 0-471-07525-6, Pub. by Wiley). Krieger.

X-Ray Technology Examination Review Book, Vol. 1. 3rd ed. Ed. by Maurice King. 186p. 1972. spiral bdg. 8.50 o.p. (ISBN 0-87488-441-1). Med Exam.

X-Ray Technology Examination Review Book, Vol. 2. 3rd ed. Ed. by O. William Crawford & Henri J. Gautot. 1973. pap. 9.50 (ISBN 0-87488-442-X). Med Exam.

X-Ray Technology Examination Review Book, Vol. 3. 2nd ed. Ed. by Richard C. Kebart et al. 1976. spiral bdg. 9.50 (ISBN 0-87488-443-8). Med Exam.

X-Raying the Pharaohs. James E. Harris & Kent R. Weeks. LC 72-1180. (Encore Edition). (Illus.). 265p. 1973. pap. 2.95 (ISBN 0-684-16899-5, SL 535, ScribT). Scribner.

X-Rays in Atomic & Nuclear Physics. N. A. Dyson. (Illus.). 256p. 1973. text ed. 26.00 o.p. (ISBN 0-582-46218-5). Longman.

X, Y & Z: A List of Those Books Examined in the Course of Compiling Science Fiction & Fantasy Literature, a Checklist, 1700 to 1974, with Contemporary Science Fiction Authors II, Which Were Judged to Fall Outside the Genre of Fantastic Literature; an Anti-Bibliography. R. Reginald. LC 80-11697. (Borgo Reference Library: Vol. 10). 160p. 1981. lib. bdg. 19.95x (ISBN 0-89370-809-7); pap. 9.95x (ISBN 0-89370-909-3). Borgo Pr.

Xavier De Maistre. Charles Lombard. (World Authors Ser.: No. 447). 1977. lib. bdg. 12.50 (ISBN 0-8057-6284-1). Twayne.

Xaviera Goes Wild. Xaviera Hollander. 368p. (Orig.). 1974. pap. 2.95 (ISBN 0-446-93657-X). Warner Bks.

Xaviera: Her Continuing Adventures by the Author of the Happy Hooker. Xaviera Hollander. (Orig.). 1973. pap. 2.95 (ISBN 0-446-93660-X). Warner Bks.

Xaviera Meets Marilyn Chambers. Xaviera Hollander & Marilyn Chambers. (Orig.). 1976. pap. 2.95 (ISBN 0-446-93979-X). Warner Bks.

Xaviera's Supersex: Her Personal Techniques for Total Lovemaking. Xaviera Hollander. 1978. pap. 2.25 o.p. (ISBN 0-451-08384-9, E8384, Sig). NAL.

Xenophobia & Immigration, 1820-1930. Thomas J. Curran. LC 74-10865. (Immigrant Heritage of American Ser). 1975. lib. bdg. 10.95 (ISBN 0-8057-3294-2). Twayne.

Xenophon's Anabasis, Bks. 1-4. Maurice W. Mather & Joseph Hewitt. (Illus.). (YA) 1976. pap. 9.95x (ISBN 0-8061-1347-2). U of Okla Pr.

Xeroradiography: Breast Calcifications. John N. Wolfe (Illus.). 184p. 1977. 29.50 (ISBN 0-398-03551-2). C C Thomas.

Xeroradiography of the Lung & Mediastinum. Ed. by G Tricomi et al. 223p. 1979. 122.00 (ISBN 0-686-63099-8, Excerpta Medica). Elsevier.

Xeroradiography: Uncalcified Breast Masses. John N. Wolfe. (Illus.). 208p. 1977. 36.75 (ISBN 0-398-03504-0). C C Thomas.

Xerxes' Invasion of Greece. Charles Hignett. 1963. 29.00x o.p. (ISBN 0-19-814247-1). Oxford U Pr.

Xhosa Ntsomi. Harold Scheub. (Oxford Library of African Literature Ser.). 1974. 45.00x (ISBN 0-19-815140-3). Oxford U Pr.

XIT Ranch of Texas & the Early Days of the Llano Estacado. J. Evetts Haley. (Western Frontier Library: No. 34). (Illus.). 1967. 8.95 (ISBN 0-8061-0728-6); pap. 3.95 (ISBN 0-8061-1428-2). U of Okla Pr.

XPD. Len Deighton. LC 80-7629. 384p. 1981. 12.95 (ISBN 0-394-51258-8). Knopf.

Xultun Tarot. 2nd ed. Peter Balin. (Illus., Orig.). 1981. 12.00 (ISBN 0-914794-33-7). Wisdom Garden.

XYZ Affair. William Stinchcombe. LC 80-544. (Contributions in American History: No. 89). (Illus.). 167p. 1980. lib. bdg. 23.95 (ISBN 0-313-22234-7, SXY/). Greenwood.

XYZ Affair, 1797-98: The Diplomacy of the Adams Administration & an Undeclared War with France. Harold C. Vaughan. LC 72-189759. (Focus Bks). (Illus.). 96p. (gr. 7 up). 1972. PLB 4.47 o.p. (ISBN 0-531-02459-8). Watts.

Y

Y Ahora Que? (Spanish Bks.). 1977. 0.25 (ISBN 0-8297-0489-2). Vida Pub.

Y Ahora, Que Hago, Senor? Chris Jones. Tr. by Susana Cabeza from Eng. 107p. (Orig., Span.). (gr. 6-9). 1978. pap. 2.50 (ISBN 0-89922-123-8). Edit Caribe.

Yacht People. Mary R. Hayes. 1979. pap. 2.25 o.p. (ISBN 0-523-40377-1). Pinnacle Bks.

Yachtmaster Offshore. John Russell. LC 77-89374. 1977. 11.95 (ISBN 0-7153-7465-6). David & Charles.

Yachts & Yachting. Vanderdecken. (Scolar Maritime Library). (Illus.). 485p. 1979. Repr. of 1873 ed. 60.00x (ISBN 0-85967-568-8, Pub. by Scolar Pr England). Biblio Dist.

Yachtsman Guide to Celestial Navigation. Stafford Campbell. (Illus.). 1979. 9.95 (ISBN 0-87165-019-3, Yachting-Zd). Ziff-Davis Pub.

Yachtsman's Doctor. R. T. Counter. 148p. 1980. 27.00 (ISBN 0-245-53425-3, Pub. by Nautical England). State Mutual Bk.

Yachtsman's Emergency Handbook. Neil Hollander & Harald Mertes. (Illus.). 320p. 1980. 14.95 (ISBN 0-87851-803-7). Hearst Bks.

Yachtsman's Legal Guide to Co-Ownership. Paula Odin & Dexter Odin. 1981. 10.00 (ISBN 0-686-69463-5). De Graff.

Yachtsman's Mate's Guide. Margie Livingston. (Yachtman's Guide Ser.). (Illus.). 128p. 1980. 8.95 (ISBN 0-87165-087-8, ZD Bks). Ziff-Davis Pub.

Yachtsman's Omnibus. Harold A. Calahan. (Illus.). 1951. 12.00 o.s.i. (ISBN 0-02-520790-3). Macmillan.

Yahweh As Prosecutor & Judge: An Investigation of the Prophetic Lawsuit (Rib Pattern) Kirsten Nielsen. (JSOT Supplement Ser.: No. 9). 104p. 1978. text ed. 25.95x (ISBN 0-905774-13-2, Pub. by JSOT Pr England); pap. text ed. 12.95x (ISBN 0-905774-08-6, Pub. by JSOT Pr England). Eisenbrauns.

Yahweh Is a Warrior. Millard C. Lind. LC 80-16038. (Christian Peace Shelf Selection Ser.). 240p. 1980. pap. 9.95x (ISBN 0-8361-1233-4). Herald Pr.

Yak, the Python, the Frog: Three Beast Poems. Hilaire Belloc. LC 74-12441. (Illus.). (ps-3). 1975. 5.95 o.s.i. (ISBN 0-8193-0785-8, Four Winds); PLB 5.41 o.s.i. (ISBN 0-8193-0786-6). Schol Bk Serv.

Yakhal' Inkomo. Mongane W. Serote. 1974. pap. 5.00 o.s.i. (ISBN 0-685-80780-0, Pub by Ravan Press). Three Continents.

Yakshi from Didarganj. P. Lal. 42p. 1973. 8.00 (ISBN 0-88253-267-7); flexible bdg. 4.00 (ISBN 0-89253-518-0). Ind-US Inc.

Yale Gertrude Stein. Gertrude Stein. LC 80-5398. 480p. 1980. text ed. 30.00x (ISBN 0-300-02574-2); pap. 6.95x (ISBN 0-300-02609-9). Yale U Pr.

Yamaha Service Repair Handbook: 80-175cc Enduro & Motocross, 1968-1978. Clymer Publications. (Illus.). 1979. pap. text ed. 9.95 (ISBN 0-89287-235-7, M410). Clymer Pubns.

Yamaha Service-Repair Handbook: 90-200cc Twins, 1966-1977. David Sales. Ed. by Eric Jorgensen. (Illus.). 1978. pap. 9.25 (ISBN 0-89287-179-2, M400). Clymer Pubns.

Yamaha Snowmobiles: Nineteen Seventy-Five to Nineteen Eighty Service, Repair & Maintenance. Mike Bishop. Ed. by Eric Jorgensen. (Illus.). 180p. (Orig.). 1980. pap. text ed. 8.95 (ISBN 0-89287-323-X, X954). Clymer Pubns.

Yamaha SR500 Singles: 1977-1979 Service-Repair-Performance. Mike Bishop. Ed. by Eric Jorgensen. (Illus.). 191p. (Orig.). 1979. pap. 9.95 (ISBN 0-89287-212-8, M407). Clymer Pubns.

Yamaha XS Seven-Fifty Triples Nineteen Seventy-Six to Nineteen Seventy-Nine Service, Repair, Performance. Ed Scott. (Illus.). 1979. pap. 9.95 (ISBN 0-89287-243-8, M40A). Clymer Pubns.

Yamaha XS 360-400 1976-1980. Chilton's Automotive Editorial Dept. (Illus.). 1980. pap. 8.95 (ISBN 0-8019-6969-7). Chilton.

Yamaha XS1100 Fours: 1978-1979 Service-Repair-Performance. Ed Scott. Ed. by Eric Jorgensen. (Illus.). 224p. (Orig.). 1980. pap. text ed. 9.95 (ISBN 0-89287-309-4, M411). Clymer Pubns.

Yamaha: XS360 & XS-400 Twins, 1976-78, Service, Repair, Maintenance. Ed. by Eric Jorgensen. (Illus.). 167p. 1978. pap. 9.95 (ISBN 0-89287-170-9, M402). Clymer Pubns.

Yamaha YZ One Hundred to Four Hundred Sixty-Five Monoshock Nineteen Seventy-Five to Nineteen Eighty: Service, Repair, Performance. Ed Scott. Ed. by Eric Jorgensen. (Illus.). 293p. (Orig.). 1980. pap. text ed. 9.95 (ISBN 0-89287-329-9, M413). Clymer Pubns.

Yamaha: 250-400cc, 2-Stroke Twins 1965-1978, Service, Repair, Performance. 3rd ed. Clymer Publications. Ed. by Eric Jorgensen. (Illus.). 1978. pap. 9.95 (ISBN 0-89287-283-7, M401). Clymer Pubns.

Yamaha: 250-500cc Enduro & Motocross, 1968-78, Service, Repair, Performance. 3rd ed. Clymer Publications. Ed. by Eric Jorgensen. (Illus.). 1978. pap. 9.95 (ISBN 0-89287-276-4, M415). Clymer Pubns.

Yamaha: 50-100cc Rotary Valve Singles, 1963-1976--Service, Repair, Maintenance. 3rd ed. Ed. by Eric Jorgensen. (Illus.). 1979. pap. 9.95 (ISBN 0-89287-220-9, M389). Clymer Pubns.

Yamaha: 650cc Twins, 1979-79, Service, Repair, Performance. Ed. by Eric Jorgensen. (Illus.). 1978. pap. 9.95 (ISBN 0-89287-233-0, M403). Clymer Pubns.

Yamsi. Dayton O. Hyde. 352p. 1974. pap. 1.95 o.p. (ISBN 0-345-24286-6). Ballantine.

Yamuna's Vedanta & Pancaratra: Integrating the Classical & the Popular. Walter G. Neevel, Jr. LC 77-4048. (Harvard Theological Review. Dissertation Ser.). 1977. pap. 9.00 (ISBN 0-89130-136-4, 020110). Scholars Pr Ca.

Yang Khi: Vases of the Sea, an Exhibition of American China Trace Porcelain. Linda Cairns-Malatt. (Illus.). 31p. (Orig.). 1979. pap. 4.00 o.s.i. (ISBN 0-89133-082-8). Preservation Pr.

Yang Wan-Li. J. D. Schmidt. LC 76-18839. (World Authors Ser: No. 413). 1976. lib. bdg. 12.50 (ISBN 0-8057-6255-8). Twayne.

Yankee. John Williams. (Orig.). 1981. pap. 2.95 (ISBN 0-440-19779-1). Dell.

Yankee Artillerymen: Through the Civil War with Eli Lilly's Indiana Battery. John W. Rowell. LC 75-5918. (Illus.). 320p. 1975. 15.50x (ISBN 0-87049-171-7). U of Tenn Pr.

Yankee Autumn in Acadiana: A Narrative of the Great Texas Overland Expedition Through Southwestern Louisiana. 2nd ed. David C. Edmonds. LC 79-67333. (Illus.). 512p. 1980. Repr. 15.95 (ISBN 0-937614-01-7). Acadiana Pr.

Yankee Church Supper Cookbook. Ed. by Clarissa Silitch. LC 80-612. 240p. 1980. pap. 9.95 (ISBN 0-686-68933-X, 3075). Yankee Bks.

Yankee Church Suppers. Ed. by Clarissa Silitch. LC 80-612. 1980. pap. 9.95 (ISBN 0-911658-14-9, 3075). Yankee Bks.

Yankee City. abr. ed. Lloyd W. Warner & V. O. Low. LC 63-7588. (Illus.). 448p. 1963. 27.50x o.p. (ISBN 0-300-01026-5). Yale U Pr.

Yankee Dan. Virgil Robinson. (Uplook Ser.). 1976. pap. 0.75 (ISBN 0-8163-0273-1, 24000-2). Pacific Pr Pub Assn.

Yankee Doodle. Edward Bangs. LC 80-17024. (Illus.). 40p. (ps-3). 1980. Repr. of 1976 ed. 9.95 (ISBN 0-590-07782-1, Four Winds). Schol Bk Serv.

Yankee Doodle. Richard Shackburg. (Illus.). (gr. 1-7). 1965. pap. 1.50 o.p. (ISBN 0-13-971879-6). P-H.

Yankee Doodle-Doo: A Collection of Songs of the Early American Stage. Grenville Vernon. LC 73-78662. 1972. Repr. of 1927 ed. 20.00 (ISBN 0-8103-3872-6). Gale.

Yankee Ghosts. Hans Holzer. LC 66-16029. 1966. 5.00 o.p. (ISBN 0-672-50856-7). Bobbs.

Yankee Lover. Virginia Nielsen. 1978. pap. 1.75 o.p. (ISBN 0-449-14020-2, GM). Fawcett.

Yankee Magazine's Guide to New England. (Illus.). 144p. 1980. pap. 1.95. Yankee Bks.

Yankee Magazine's Street Maps of Boston. 1980. pap. 4.95 (ISBN 0-911658-11-4, 3073). Yankee Bks.

Yankee on the Yangtze. Paul Quimby & Norma Youngsberg. LC 76-49387. (Nova Ser.). 1977. pap. 4.95 (ISBN 0-8127-0131-3). Southern Pub.

Yankee Pioneers: A Saga of Courage. Samuel B. Pettengill. Ed. by Laura Bohannon. (Bicentennial Historiettes). (Illus.). 86p. (gr. 7-9). 1977. pap. text ed. 0.95x (ISBN 0-915892-11-1). Regional Ctr Educ.

Yankee Quizbook. Robert Weil & James Fitzgerald. LC 80-1654. (Illus.). 144p. 1981. pap. 5.95 (ISBN 0-385-17178-1, Dolp). Doubleday.

Yankee Racehorse: U. S. Frigate Constellation. Jameson & Sternlicht. 1981. 10.00 (ISBN 0-87233-013-3). Bauhan.

Yankee Ranger. Sarah O. Jewett. Orig. Title: Tory Lover. 1975. pap. 1.50 o.p. (ISBN 0-685-57555-1, LB300DK, Leisure Bks). Nordon Pubns.

Yankee Shoes: A Light Verse Saunter Through Our Second Hundred Years. Mollee Kruger. LC 75-21446. 100p. 1975. pap. 2.50 (ISBN 0-913184-03-9). Maryben Bks.

Yankee Stranger. Elswyth Thane. (Williamsburg Ser.: No. 2). 1981. lib. bdg. 16.95 (ISBN 0-8161-3166-X, Large Print Bks). G K Hall.

Yankees in the Republic of Texas: Their Origin & Impact. Arthur C. Burnett. 1952. wrappers 7.00 (ISBN 0-685-05007-6). A Jones.

Yankel the Fool. Shan Ellentuck. LC 71-175369. 112p. (gr. 3-7). 1973. PLB 4.95 o.p. (ISBN 0-385-07524-3). Doubleday.

Yannis Manglis. Harry T. Hionides. LC 74-31099. (World Authors Ser.: Greece: No. 350). 1975. lib. bdg. 10.95 (ISBN 0-8057-2578-4). Twayne.

Yanoama Indians: A Cultural Geography. William J. Smole. (Texas Pan American Ser.). (Illus.). 478p. 1975. 15.00 (ISBN 0-292-71019-4). U of Tex Pr.

Yao Village: A Study in the Social Structure of a Malawian Tribe. J. Clyde Mitchell. (Institute of African Studies Ser). (Illus.). 238p. 1971. pap. text ed. 17.50x (ISBN 0-7190-1034-9). Humanities.

Yaqui Life: The Personal Chronicle of a Yaqui Indian. Rosalio Moises et al. LC 76-56789. Orig. Title: Tall Candle: the Personal Chronicle of a Yaqui Indian. (Illus.). 1977. 13.95x (ISBN 0-8032-0944-4); pap. 3.95 (ISBN 0-8032-5857-7, BB 637, Bison). U of Nebr Pr.

Yaqui Syntax. Jacqueline Lindenfeld. (U. C. Publ. in Linguistics: Vol. 76). 1974. pap. 12.50x (ISBN 0-520-09470-0). U of Cal Pr.

Yaquis: A Cultural History. Edward H. Spicer. LC 79-27660. 1980. 28.50x (ISBN 0-8165-0589-6); pap. 14.50x (ISBN 0-8165-0588-8). U of Ariz Pr.

Yard Buildings. Mel Marshall. LC 80-1125. (Homeowner's Bible Ser.). (Illus.). 160p. 1981. pap. 4.95 (ISBN 0-385-15400-3). Doubleday.

Yard of Tame Birds. K. Kirshina. (Illus.). 20p. 1978. pap. 1.25 (ISBN 0-8285-0003-7). Progress Pubs.

Yarn Crafts. Linda Hetzer. LC 77-29052. (Illustrated Crafts for Beginners). (Illus.). (gr. 3-7). 1978. PLB 9.95 (ISBN 0-8172-1176-4). Raintree Pubs.

Yarrow. Michael Corr. 1981. 3.00 (ISBN 0-934834-20-2). White Pine.

Yasmina's Daughter. Corinne Childs. 1981. pap. 2.50 (ISBN 0-8439-0838-6, Leisure Bks). Nordon Pubns.

Yatindramatadipika. Srinivasadasa. Tr. by Swami Adidevananda. (Sanskrit & Eng.). 2.75 o.s.i. (ISBN 0-87481-428-6). Vedanta Pr.

Yazoo: Law & Politics in the New Republic. C. Peter Magrath. LC 66-19584. (Illus.). 243p. 1966. 10.00x (ISBN 0-87057-100-1, Pub. by Brown U Pr). Univ Pr of New England.

Ye Olden Time: English Customs in the Middle Ages. Emily S. Holt. LC 72-164343. 1971. Repr. of 1884 ed. 15.00 (ISBN 0-8103-3798-3). Gale.

Yea God! The True Story of a Spiritual Leader, Freedom, Who Led His Followers from Eastern Mysticism to Christianity. Lorraine Pakkala. LC 80-11503. 250p. 1980. 11.95 (ISBN 0-89594-030-2); pap. 5.95 (ISBN 0-89594-029-9). Crossing Pr.

Yeah, but Children Need.... Karen L. Rancourt. 1978. 8.95 (ISBN 0-8467-0451-X, Pub. by Two Continents). Hippocrene Bks.

Year. Suzanne Lange. LC 78-120787. (gr. 8 up). 1970. 9.95 (ISBN 0-87599-173-4). S G Phillips.

Year & a Day. William Mayne. 112p. (gr. 4-6). 1976. PLB 6.95 o.p. (ISBN 0-525-43450-X). Dutton.

Year Around Conditioning for Army Football. Timothy Kearin. LC 80-82965. (Illus.). 128p. (Orig.). 1980. pap. text ed. 4.95 (ISBN 0-918438-60-8). Leisure Pr.

Year at the Catholic Worker. Marc Ellis. LC 78-61722. 1978. pap. 2.45 (ISBN 0-8091-2140-9). Paulist Pr.

Year Between School & University. Lea Orr. (General Ser). 60p. 1974. pap. text ed. 7.00x (ISBN 0-85633-053-1, NFER). Humanities.

Year Book. American Philosophical Society. LC 39-2034. pap. 1.50 ea. 1937-1967 (ISBN 0-87169-991-5); pap. 3.00 ea. 1968-1970; pap. 5.00 ea. 1971-1978. Am Philos.

Year Book for International Insurance - Assecuranz-Compass 1979, 2 vols. 85th ed. 1724p. 1979. Set. 275.00x (ISBN 0-8002-2233-4). Intl Pubns Serv.

Year Book of American Authors. Ida S. Taylor. 372p. 1980. lib. bdg. 30.00 (ISBN 0-89760-899-2). Telegraph Bks.

Year Book of Anesthesia, 1980. Ed. by James E. Eckenhoff et al. 400p. 1980. 27.50 (ISBN 0-8151-3040-6). Year Bk Med.

Year Book of Daily Recreation & Information. William Hone. LC 67-12947. 1967. Repr. of 1832 ed. 30.00 (ISBN 0-8103-3007-5). Gale.

Year Book of Endocrinology, 1980. Ed. by Theodore B. Schwartz & Will G. Ryan. 400p. 1980. 31.50 (ISBN 0-8151-7608-2). Year Bk Med.

Year Book of Labour Statistics,1979. 39th ed. International Labour Office, Geneva. (Illus.). 711p. 1980. 47.50 (ISBN 0-686-61301-5). Intl Labour Office.

Year Book of Medicine, 1980. David E. Rogers et al. (Illus.). 640p. 1980. 29.95 (ISBN 0-8151-7441-1). Year Bk Med.

Year Book of Social Policy in Britain, 1977. Ed. by Muriel Brown & Sally Baldwin. 1978. 36.50 (ISBN 0-7100-0066-9). Routledge & Kegan.

Year Book of Social Policy in Britain 1979. Ed. by Muriel Brown & Sally Baldwin. 272p. (Orig.). 1980. pap. 45.00 (ISBN 0-7100-0690-X). Routledge & Kegan.

Year Book of the American Bureau of Metal Statistics. annual Compiled by American Bureau of Metal Statistics Staff. 1972. 25.00 (ISBN 0-910064-05-9). Am Bur Metal.

Year Book of the American Bureau of Metal Statistics. Compiled by American Bureau of Metal Statistics Staff. LC 21-15719. 1973. 25.00 (ISBN 0-910064-06-7). Am Bur Metal.

Year Book of World Affairs, 1981. Ed. by George W. Keeton & Georg Schwarzenberger. 285p. 1981. lib. bdg. 40.00x (ISBN 0-86531-150-1). Westview.

Year from Monday: New Lectures & Writings. John Cage. LC 67-24105. 1967. 10.00 o.p. (ISBN 0-8195-3081-6, Pub. by Wesleyan U Pr); pap. 6.95 (ISBN 0-8195-6002-2). Columbia U Pr.

Year Growing Ancient. Irene H. Steiner. LC 77-16748. Date not set. cancelled (ISBN 0-312-89619-0). St Martin.

Year in Endocrinology, 1975 to 1976. Ed. by S. H. Ingbar. 327p. 1977. 29.50 (ISBN 0-306-32101-7, Plenum Pr). Plenum Pub.

Year in Russia. Maurice Baring. LC 79-2891. 296p. 1981. Repr. of 1917 ed. 23.50 (ISBN 0-8305-0060-X). Hyperion Conn.

Year in the Life of a Field. Michael Allaby. LC 80-68681. (Illus.). 192p. 1981. 22.50 (ISBN 0-7153-7889-9). David & Charles.

Year in the Life of Rosie Bernard. Barbara Brenner. (gr. 3-7). 1975. pap. 1.50 (ISBN 0-380-01630-3, 43380, Camelot). Avon.

Year in Upper Felicity. Jack Chen. (Illus.). 384p. 1973. 12.95 (ISBN 0-02-524650-X). Macmillan.

Year-Long Day: One Man's Arctic. A. E. Maxwell & Ivar Ruud. LC 75-40412. (Illus.). 1976. 8.95 o.p. (ISBN 0-397-01131-8). Lippincott.

Year of Columbus, 1492. Genevieve Foster. LC 77-85268. (Illus.). (gr. 2-6). 1969. write for info. (ISBN 0-684-12695-8, ScribJ). Scribner.

Year of Growing. Bradford. (gr. 3-5). pap. 1.25 o.p. (ISBN 0-590-05411-2, Schol Pap). Schol Bk Serv.

Year of Matthew. Eugene A. LaVerdiere. LC 80-82553. (Illus.). 200p. (Orig.). 1981. pap. 6.95 (ISBN 0-934134-06-5, Celebration Bks). Natl Cath Reporter.

Year of My Life: A Translation of Issa's Oraga Haru. rev. ed. Issa. Tr. by Nobuyuki Yuasa. LC 60-9651. (Illus.). 1973. 14.75x (ISBN 0-520-00598-8); pap. 2.45 (ISBN 0-520-02160-6, CAL35). U of Cal Pr.

Year of Small Shadow. Evelyn S. Lampman. LC 73-152694. 190p. (gr. 5-7). 1971. 5.95 o.p. (ISBN 0-15-299815-2, HJ). HarBraceJ.

Year of the Ant. George Ordish. LC 78-2260. (Illus.). 1978. 9.95 o.p. (ISBN 0-684-15523-0, ScribT). Scribner.

Year of the Apple. Michael New. LC 80-15933. (Illus.). 128p. (gr. 3-7). 1980. PLB 7.95 (ISBN 0-201-05220-2, 5220, A-W Childrens). A-W.

Year of the Bloody Sevens. William O. Steele. LC 63-16036. (Illus.). (gr. 4-6). 1963. 6.75 o.p. (ISBN 0-15-299800-4, HJ). HarBraceJ.

Year of the Capricorn. David Austin. 1981. 9.95 (ISBN 0-533-04467-7). Vantage.

Year of the Century. Dee Brown. LC 66-18538. 1975. 4.95 o.p. (ISBN 0-684-12730-X, SL338, ScribT). Scribner.

Year of the Child. Marian Engel. 192p. 1981. 9.95 (ISBN 0-312-89627-1). St Martin.

Year of the French. Thomas Flanagan. 1980. pap. 3.75 (ISBN 0-671-83301-4). PB.

Year of the Golden Ape. Colin Forbes. 320p. 1975. pap. 1.50 o.p. (ISBN 0-449-22563-1, Q2563, Crest). Fawcett.

Year of the Koala. H. D. Williamson. LC 75-12704. 1975. 8.95 o.p. (ISBN 0-684-14351-8, ScribT). Scribner.

Year of the Oath. George R. Stewart. LC 77-150422. (Civil Liberties in American History Ser). 1971. Repr. of 1950 ed. lib. bdg. 25.00 (ISBN 0-306-70103-0). Da Capo.

Year of the Robot. Wayne Chen. 150p. 1981. pap. 7.95 (ISBN 0-918398-50-9). Robotics Pr.

Year of the Unicorn. Andre Norton. 224p. 1976. pap. 1.95 (ISBN 0-441-94254-7). Ace Bks.

Year of the Waterbearer. Marguerite Dorian. 180p. 1976. 7.95 o.s.i. (ISBN 0-02-532180-3). Macmillan.

Year on Muskrat Marsh. Berniece Freschet. LC 73-19559. (Illus.). 56p. (gr. 1-4). 1974. write for info. (ISBN 0-684-13748-8, ScribJ). Scribner.

Year-Round Education. John D. McLain. LC 72-14044. 1973. 17.50x (ISBN 0-8211-1222-8); text ed. 15.75x (ISBN 0-685-36207-8). McCutchan.

Year-Round Outdoor Building Projects: An Encyclopedia of Building Techniques & Construction Plans. Richard Demske. 304p. 1980. pap. 9.95 (ISBN 0-442-21259-3). Van Nos Reinhold.

Year Santa Got Thin. Bill Bluestein & Enid Bluestein. (Illus.). 48p. (gr. k-4). 1981. 6.95 (ISBN 0-89638-045-9). CompCare.

Year the Dreams Came Back. Anita M. Feagles. (gr. 7-9). 1978. pap. 1.25 (ISBN 0-671-29875-5). Archway.

Year the Dreams Came Back. Anita MacRae. (YA) (gr. 7-9). pap. 1.25 (ISBN 0-671-29875-5). PB.

Year Two Thousand & Mental Retardation. Ed. by Stanley C. Plog. (Current Topics in Mental Health Ser.). (Illus.). 240p. 1980. 19.95 (ISBN 0-306-40252-1, Plenum Pr). Plenum Pub.

Yearbook Book. Ed. by Ian Summers. 160p. (Orig.). 1975. pap. 5.95 o.p. (ISBN 0-345-24732-9). Ballantine.

Yearbook Killer. Tom Philbin. (Orig.). 1981. pap. 1.95 (ISBN 0-449-14400-3, GM). Fawcett.

Yearbook Nineteen Eighty Mit deutschem Registerschluessel. Ed. by W. Theilheimer. (Synthetic Methods of Organic Chemistry Ser.: Vol. 34). 1980. 298.25 (ISBN 3-8055-0327-X). S Karger.

Yearbook of Adult & Continuing Education: 1980-81. 6th ed. LC 75-13805. 592p. 1980. 39.50 (ISBN 0-8379-3106-1, 031099). Marquis.

Yearbook of American & Canadian Churches, 1981. Ed. by Constant H. Jacquet, Jr. 304p. (Orig.). 1981. pap. 14.95 (ISBN 0-687-46636-9). Abingdon.

Yearbook of Astronomy, 1981. Ed. by Patrick Moore. (Illus.). 1981. 14.95 (ISBN 0-393-01415-0). Norton.

Yearbook of Fishery Statistics 1977: Catches & Landings. (Fisheries Ser.: No. 44). 1979. 24.50 (ISBN 92-5-000609-8, F1552, FAO). Unipub.

Yearbook of Industrial Statistics, 1977, 2 vols. 11th ed. United Nations. Incl. Vol. 1. General Industrial Statistics. 639p. 30.00x (ISBN 0-8002-2335-7); Vol. 2. Commodity Production Data, 1967 to 1977. 750p. 30.00x (ISBN 0-8002-2336-5). LC 76-646970. (Illus.). 1389p. 1979. write for info. Intl Pubns Serv.

Yearbook of International Communist Affairs: 1977. reference ed. Ed. by Richard F. Staar. LC 76-51879. (Publications Ser: No. 170). 1977. 30.00 (ISBN 0-8179-6701-X). Hoover Inst Pr.

Yearbook of International Trade Statistics, 1978, 2 vols. Incl. Vol. 1. Trade by Country; Vol. 2. Trade by Commodity, Commodity Matrix Tables. 1178p. 1979. Set. pap. 65.00 (UN79/17/16, UN). Unipub.

Yearbook of Nordic Statistics: Nordisk Statistisk Arsbok, 1977, Vol. 16. LC 65-1336. (Illus.). 1978. pap. 22.50x o.p. (ISBN 91-7052-342-8). Intl Pubns Serv.

Yearbook of Podiatric Medicine & Surgery 1981. Ed. by Theodore H. Clarke. (Illus.). 512p. 1980. 49.00 (ISBN 0-87993-129-9). Futura Pub.

Yearbook of Podiatry: 1978-79. Ed. by Theodore H. Clarke. (Illus.). 1979. 28.50 (ISBN 0-87993-099-3). Futura Pub.

Yearbook of School Law. Incl. 1957. Lee O. Garber. vi, 160p. pap. text ed. 4.95x (ISBN 0-8134-0455-X, 455); 1958. Lee O. Garber. viii, 180p. pap. text ed. 4.95x (ISBN 0-8134-0480-0, 480); 1959. Lee O. Garber. vi, 181p. pap. text ed. 4.95x (ISBN 0-8134-0515-7, 515); 1961. Lee O. Garber. viii, 250p. pap. text ed. 5.25x (ISBN 0-8134-0560-2, 560); 1963. Lee O. Garber. iv, 266p. pap. text ed. o.p. (ISBN 0-685-22454-6, 109); 1965. Lee O. Garber. 256p. pap. text ed. 7.95x (ISBN 0-8134-0238-7, 238); 1966. Lee O. Garber. x, 302p. pap. text ed. 7.95 (ISBN 0-8134-0858-X, 858); 1967. Lee O. Garber & E. Edmund Reutter, Jr. x, 300p. pap. text ed. o.p. (ISBN 0-685-22457-0, 909); 1968. Lee O. Garber & E. Edmund Reutter, Jr. x, 268p. pap. text ed. 7.95x (ISBN 0-8134-1022-3, 1022); 1970. Lee O. Garber & E. Edmund Reutter, Jr. x, 268p. pap. text ed. o.p. (ISBN 0-685-22459-7, 1159); 1971. Lee O. Garber & Reynolds C. Seitz. x, 228p. pap. text ed. 7.95x (ISBN 0-8134-1242-0, 1242). LC 52-2403. Interstate.

Yearbook of Special Education: 1980-81. 6th ed. LC 75-13803. 456p. 1980. 39.50 (ISBN 0-8379-3006-5, 031100). Marquis.

Yearbook of Substance Use & Abuse. Leon Brill & Charles Winick. LC 70-174271. 360p. 1980. 32.95 (ISBN 0-87705-487-8). Human Sci Pr.

Yearbook of the Association of Pacific Coast Geographers, Vol. 37, 1975. Ed. by Rodney Steiner. (Illus.). 144p. 1975. pap. 5.00 (ISBN 0-686-65495-1). Oreg St U Pr.

Yearbook of the European Convention on Human Rights. Ed. by Council of Europe. (European Convention on Human Rights: No. 22). 688p. 1980. lib. bdg. 132.00 (ISBN 90-247-2383-3, Pub. by Martinus Nijhoff). Kluwer Boston.

Yearbook of the European Convention on Human Rights, Vol. 21. Council of Europe. (Annuaire de la Convention Europeenne des droits de l'Homme, 1978). 1980. lib. bdg. 155.25 (ISBN 90-247-2215-2, Martinus Nijhoff Pubs). Kluwer Boston.

Yearbook of the European Convention on Human Rights, 1978, Vol. 21. rev. ed. Council of Europe. LC 60-1388. 844p. 1979. 195.00x (ISBN 90-247-2215-2). Intl Pubns Serv.

Yearbook of the International Law Commission Nineteen Seventy-Eight: Part One of Documents of the Thirtieth Session, Vol. 2. 289p. 1979. pap. 18.00 (UN79-5-6(PT.1), UN). Unipub.

Yearbook of the International Law Commission: Nineteen Seventy-Nine, Vol.1. 247p. 1980. pap. 17.00 (UN80-5-4, UN). Unipub.

Yearbook of the United States, Vol. 31. 1303p. 1980. pap. 50.00 (ISBN 0-686-68982-8, UN79/1/1, UN). Unipub.

Yearbook of World Affairs 1977. G. W. Keeton & G. Schwarzenberger. LC 47-29156. 1977. lib. bdg. 35.50x (ISBN 0-89158-814-0). Westview.

Yearbook of World Affairs, 1978. Ed. by George W. Keeton & Georg Schwarzenberger. LC 47-29156. 1978. lib. bdg. 37.50x (ISBN 0-89158-824-8). Westview.

Yearbook of World Affairs, 1979. Ed. by George W. Keeton & Georg Scharzenberger. 1979. lib. bdg. 37.50x (ISBN 0-89158-551-6). Westview.

Yearbook on International Communist Affairs 1979. Ed. by Richard F. Staar. LC 76-51879. (Publications Ser.: No.215). 1979. 35.00 (ISBN 0-8179-7151-3). Hoover Inst Pr.

Yearbook on International Communist Affairs, 1980. Ed. by Richard F. Staar. (Publication Ser.: No. 235). 517p. 1980. 35.00 (ISBN 0-8179-7351-6). Hoover Inst Pr.

Yearbook on International Communist Affairs: 1981. Ed. by Richard F. Staar. 1981. 35.00 (ISBN 0-8179-7501-2). Hoover Inst Pr.

Yearbook: Wisconsin Ev. Lutheran Synod, 1981. 3.75 (ISBN 0-8100-0137-3, 29-1419). Northwest Pub.

Yearbook, 1979. Facts on File Digest Staff. 1980. lib. bdg. 65.00 (ISBN 0-87196-038-9). Facts on File.

Yearbook 1981: With Reaction Titles Vol. 31 to 35 & Cumulative Index; Mit deutschem Registerschlussel. (Synthetic Methods of Organic Chemistry Ser.: Vol. 35). xx, 600p. 1981. 298.25 (ISBN 3-8055-1607-X). S Karger.

Yearbooks of the Association of Pacific Coast Geographers, Vol. 1-35. Association of Pacific Coast Geographers. Incl. Vols. 1-19. 1935 - 1957. pap. 3.00 ea.; Vol. 20-27. 1958 - 1965. pap. 3.00 ea; Vols. 28, 29, 31. 1966 - 1967, 1969. pap. 3.00 ea; Vol. 30, 1968. 6.00 (ISBN 0-686-66693-3); Vols. 32-40. 1970 - 1978. pap. 5.00 ea. LC 37-13376. Oreg St U Pr.

Yearling. Marjorie K. Rawlings. (Illus.). 1962. 20.00 (ISBN 0-684-20922-5, ScribJ); text ed. 5.56 (ISBN 0-684-51547-4, ScribC); pap. o.p. (ISBN 0-684-71878-2, SL40, ScribJ); pap. text ed. 2.84 o.p. (ISBN 0-684-51548-2, ScribC). Scribner.

Yearning for Yesterday: A Sociology of Nostalgia. Fred Davis. LC 78-19838. 1979. 12.95 (ISBN 0-02-906950-5). Free Pr.

Years Apart, Minds Away. Vivian Stephenson. (Illus.). 80p. 1979. 8.95 (ISBN 0-934444-01-3); pap. 5.95 (ISBN 0-934444-03-X). Aazunna.

Year's Best Fantasy Stories, No. 4. Ed. by Lin Carter. (Science Fiction Ser.). 1978. pap. 1.75 o.p. (ISBN 0-87997-425-7, UE1425). DAW Bks.

Year's Finest Fantasy. Ed. by Terry Carr. (YA) 1979. 9.95 o.p. (ISBN 0-399-12146-3). Berkley Pub.

Year's Finest Fantasy. Ed. by Terry Carr. 1978. pap. 1.95 o.p. (ISBN 0-425-03808-4, Medallion). Berkley Pub.

Year's Finest Fantasy. Ed. by Terry Carr. 1979. 9.95 o.p. (ISBN 0-399-12327-X). Berkley Pub.

Year's Finest Fantasy II. Ed. by Terry Carr. 1979. Repr. 9.95 o.p. (ISBN 0-425-04155-7). Berkley Pub.

Year's Letters. Algernon Charles Swinburne. Ed. by Francis J. Sypher. LC 74-15290. (Illus.). 195p. 1974. 10.00x (ISBN 0-8147-7758-9); pap. 5.00x (ISBN 0-8147-7804-6). NYU Pr.

Years of Decision: American Politics in the 1890's. R. Hal Williams. LC 78-6407. (Critical Episodes in American Politics Ser). 1978. pap. text ed. 8.95 (ISBN 0-471-94878-0). Wiley.

Years of High Purpose: From Trusteeship to Nationhood. Mason Sears. LC 80-5161. (Illus.). 205p. 1980. text ed. 15.00 (ISBN 0-8191-1052-3); pap. text ed. 8.25 (ISBN 0-8191-1053-1). U Pr of Amer.

Years of High Theory. George L. Shackle. 1967. 38.50 (ISBN 0-521-06279-9). Cambridge U Pr.

Years of Hope: Australian Art & Criticism 1959-1968. Gary Catalano. (Illus.). 224p. 1980. 33.50 (ISBN 0-19-554220-7). Oxford U Pr.

Years of Protest: A Collection of American Writings of the 1930's. Ed. by Jack Salzman & Barry Wallenstein. LC 67-13489. (Illus., Orig.). 1967. pap. 8.50 (ISBN 0-672-63614-X). Pegasus.

Years of the Locust: America, 1929-1932. Gilbert Seldes. LC 72-2384. (FDR & the Era of the New Deal Ser). vi, 355p. 1973. Repr. of 1933 ed. lib. bdg. 35.00 (ISBN 0-306-70471-4). Da Capo.

Years with Ross. James Thurber. 288p. 1975. pap. 1.95 o.p. (ISBN 0-345-24649-7). Ballantine.

Year's Work in English Studies. Incl. Vol. 43, 1962. 1964. lib. bdg. 6.50x (ISBN 0-686-51444-0); Vol. 44, 1963. 1965. lib. bdg. 6.75x (ISBN 0-686-51445-9); Vol. 45, 1964. 1966. lib. bdg. 7.50x (ISBN 0-686-51446-7); Vol. 48, 1967. 1969. lib. bdg. o.p.; Vol. 49, 1968. 1970. bds. 8.75x (ISBN 0-7195-2845-3); Vol. 50, 1969. Jubilee Volume. 1971. lib. bdg. 10.00x (ISBN 0-391-00213-9); Vol. 51, 1970. 1972. lib. bdg. 11.25x (ISBN 0-7195-2845-3); Vol. 52, 1971. 1973. lib. bdg. 11.25x (ISBN 0-686-51447-5); Vol. 53, 1972. 1974. lib. bdg. 15.00x (ISBN 0-391-00363-1); Vol. 54, 1973. 1975. lib. bdg. 15.75x (ISBN 0-391-00606-1); Vol. 55, 1975. Ed. by J. Redmond. 1974. text ed. 22.50x (ISBN 0-391-00648-7); Vol. 56, 1975. 1977. text ed. 31.25x (ISBN 0-391-00748-3). Humanities.

Year's Work in English Studies, Vol. 58, 1977. Ed. by J. Redmond et al. 639p. 1980. text ed. 39.00x (ISBN 0-391-01320-3). Humanities.

Year's Work in Modern Language Studies: 1978, Vol. 40. Ed. by Glanville Price & David A. Wells. LC 31-32540. 1198p. 1979. 80.00x (ISBN 0-900547-70-7); Vols. 1-39. write for info. Intl Pubns Serv.

Yearwood. Paul Hazel. 1981. pap. 2.50 (ISBN 0-671-41605-7). PB.

Yearwood. Paul Hazel. 1980. 10.95 (ISBN 0-316-35260-8, Pub. by Atlantic-Little Brown). Little.

Yeas & the Nays: Key Congressional Decisions 1774-1945. Albert Castel & Scott L. Gibson. 1975. 7.95 (ISBN 0-932826-15-6). New Issues MI.

Yeast Flakes Cookbook. Carlson Wade. 1973. pap. 1.25 (ISBN 0-515-02904-1). Jove Pubns.

Yeast, Mould & Plant Protoplasts. Ed. by J. R. Villanveva et al. 1974. 52.00 (ISBN 0-12-722160-3). Acad Pr.

Yeast Technology. Gerald Reed & Henry J. Peppler. (Illus.). 1973. 35.00 (ISBN 0-87055-136-1). AVI.

Yeats: A Collection of Critical Essays. Ed. by John E. Unterecker. 1963. 8.95 o.p. (ISBN 0-13-971929-6, Spec); pap. 2.45 o.p. (ISBN 0-13-971911-3, Spec). P-H.

Yeats & Nietzsche: An Exploration of Major Nietzschean Echoes in the Writings of William Butler Yeats. Otto Bohlmann. 390p. 1980. 28.50x (ISBN 0-389-20065-4). B&N.

Yeats & Patrick McCartan. John Unterecker. (Yeats Centenary Papers: No. 10). 1967. text ed. 3.75x (ISBN 0-85105-469-2, Dolmen Pr). Humanities.

Yeats As Editor. Edward O'Shea. (New Yeats Papers: Vol.12). (Illus.). 141p. 1975. pap. text ed. 6.50 (ISBN 0-85105-276-2, Dolmen Pr). Humanities.

Yeats at His Last. Stanley Sultan. (New Yeats Papers Ser.: No. 11). 48p. 1975. pap. text ed. 5.00x (ISBN 0-85105-271-1, Dolmen Pr). Humanities.

Yeats Country. Sheelah Kirby. 1977. pap. text ed. 4.00x (ISBN 0-391-00737-8, Dolmen Pr). Humanities.

Yeats Family & the Pollexfens of Sligo. William M. Murphy. (New Yeats Papers Ser.: Vol. 1). (Illus.). 88p. 1971. pap. text ed. 3.75x (ISBN 0-85105-196-0, Dolmen Pr). Humanities.

Yeats, Ireland & Facism. Elizabeth Cullingford. LC 80-12734. (Gotham Library). 256p. 1980. 25.00x (ISBN 0-8147-1380-7). NYU Pr.

Yeats on Yeats: The Last Introductions & 'Under Ben Bulben' Edward Callan. (Illus.). 96p. 1980. pap. text ed. 16.50x (ISBN 0-85105-370-X, Dolmen Pr). Humanities.

Yeats, Sligo & Ireland. A. Norman Jeffares. 1981. text ed. 23.50x (ISBN 0-86140-041-0). Humanities.

Yeats, Sligo & Ireland: Essays to Mark the 21st Yeats International Summer School. Ed. by A. Norman Jeffares. (Irish Literary Studies: No. 6). 267p. 1980. 24.75x (ISBN 0-389-20095-6). B&N.

Yeats Studies. Ed. by Robert O'Driscoll & Lorna Reynolds. Incl. Vol. 1. Yeats & the 1890's. (Illus.). 1971; Vol. 2. Theatre & the Visual Arts: a Centenary Celebration of Jack Yeats & John Synge. (Illus.). 1972. pap. 8.40x ea. (Pub. by Irish Academic Pr). Biblio Dist.

Yeats the Playwright: A Commentary on Character & Design in the Major Plays. Peter Ure. 1963. cased 16.00x (ISBN 0-7100-2351-0); pap. 6.00 (ISBN 0-7100-6550-7). Routledge & Kegan.

Yeats, the Tarot & the Golden Dawn. 2nd rev. ed. Kathleen Raine. (New Yeats Papers Ser: Vol. 2). (Illus.). 1976. pap. text ed. 7.50x (ISBN 0-85105-195-2, Dolmen Pr). Humanities.

Yeats's Last Poems Again. Curtis Bradford. (Yeats Cent. Papers: Vol. 8). 1966. pap. text ed. 1.75x (ISBN 0-85105-471-4, Dolmen Pr). Humanities.

Yeggs & the Yahbuts. Richard H. Smithies & Maura Cavanagh. (Illus.). (gr. 3-5). 1969. 3.95 (ISBN 0-394-80888-6); PLB 5.39 (ISBN 0-394-90888-0). Random.

Yeh Ming-Ch'en. J. Y. Wong. LC 75-18119. (Studies in Chinese History Literature and Institutions Ser.). (Illus.). 268p. 1976. 49.50 (ISBN 0-521-21023-2). Cambridge U Pr.

Yelllow Toad: Funny Frog Cartoons, Riddles, & Silly Stories. Mike Thaler. (gr. 3-6). 1980. pap. write for info (Bard). Avon.

Yellow Airplane. William Mayne. 1974. 6.95 o.p. (ISBN 0-525-66395-9). Elsevier-Nelson.

Yellow & Black. Robert Gibbons. (Illus.). 24p. 1980. 25.00; pap. 6.00. Four Zoas Pr.

Yellow Brick Toad: Funny Frog Cartoons, Riddles & Silly Stories. Mike Thaler. (Illus.). (gr. 3-5). 1980. pap. 1.50 (ISBN 0-671-56035-2). Archway.

Yellow Butter Purple Jelly Red Jam Black Bread. Mary Ann Hoberman. (Illus.). 64p. (ps-3). 1981. 8.95 (ISBN 0-670-79382-5). Viking Pr.

Yellow Canary Whose Eye Is So Black: Poems from Spanish-Speaking Latin America. Ed. by Cheli Duran. LC 77-6354. (Eng. & Span.). (gr. 6 up). 1977. 14.95 (ISBN 0-02-732910-0, 732910). Macmillan.

Yellow Cars of Los Angeles. Jim Walker. LC 77-71538. (Special Ser.: No. 43). 1977. 27.50 (ISBN 0-916374-25-4). Interurban.

Yellow Claw. Sax Rohmer. 1976. lib. bdg. 13.95x (ISBN 0-89968-142-5). Lightyear.

Yellow-Dog Contract. Ross Thomas. 1977. pap. 1.75 o.p. (ISBN 0-380-01828-4, 36186). Avon.

Yellow Emperor's Classic of Internal Medicine. Tr. by Ilza Veith. 1966. 17.50x (ISBN 0-520-01296-8); pap. 4.95 (ISBN 0-520-02158-4, CAL238). U of Cal Pr.

Yellow Fairy Book. Ed. by Andrew Lang. (Illus.). (gr. 4-6). pap. 4.00 (ISBN 0-486-21674-8). Dover.

Yellow House Mystery. Gertrude C. Warner. LC 53-13243. (Boxcar Children Mysteries-Pilot Bk.). (Illus.). 128p. (gr. 3-7). 6.95g (ISBN 0-8075-9365-6). A Whitman.

Yellow House on the Corner. Rita Dove. LC 80-65700. (Poetry Ser.). 1980. 9.95 (ISBN 0-915604-39-6); pap. 4.95 (ISBN 0-915604-40-X). Carnegie-Mellon.

Yellow Lola. Edward Dorn. Ed. by Tom Clark & Jeffrey Miller. LC 80-68260. Orig. Title: Japanese Neon. 132p. 1981. signed limited ed. 20.00 (ISBN 0-932274-14-5); pap. 6.00 (ISBN 0-932274-13-7). Cadmus Eds.

Yellow Peril: The Adventures of Sir John Weymouth Smythe. 1980. pap. 2.95 (ISBN 0-425-04556-0). Berkley Pub.

Yellow Rose of Texas: Her Saga & Her Song. Martha A. Turner. (Illus.). 128p. 1976. 7.45 (ISBN 0-88319-025-7). Shoal Creek Pub.

Yellowcake: The International Uranium Cartel. June Taylor & Michael Yokell. (Pergamon Policy Studies). 1980. text ed. 33.00 (ISBN 0-08-022473-3). Pergamon.

Yellowhair. Charles G. Taylor & Jason Kane. (Custeriana Monograph: No. 6). 1979. Repr. of 1977 ed. limited ed. 10.00 (ISBN 0-686-27216-1). Monroe County Lib.

Yellowstone: A Century of the Wilderness Idea. M. Sutton & A. Sutton. Ed. by Eleanor Friede. LC 72-183207. (Illus.). 224p. 1972. 8.98 o.s.i. (ISBN 0-02-615480-3). Macmillan.

Yellowstone Kelly: The Memoirs of Luther S. Kelly. Luther S. Kelly. Ed. by M. M. Quaife. LC 26-9001. (Illus.). xiv, 268p. 1973. pap. 6.50 (ISBN 0-8032-5784-8, BB 571, Bison). U of Nebr Pr.

Yellowstone National Park. Hiram M. Chittendon. LC 64-11334. (Illus.). 208p. 1964. pap. 3.95 (ISBN 0-8061-0937-8). U of Okla Pr.

Yellowstone National Park: Complete Guide & Reference Book. Cliff McAdams. (Illus.). 100p. 1981. pap. 5.95 (ISBN 0-87108-571-2). Pruett.

Yellowstone: The Story Behind the Scenery. Hugh Crandall. Ed. by Gweneth R. DenDooven. LC 76-57453. (Illus.). 1977. 7.95 (ISBN 0-916122-46-8); pap. 3.00 (ISBN 0-916122-21-2). K C Pubns.

Yemen. R. Stookey. LC 77-454. (Westview Special Studies on the Middle East). 1978. lib. bdg. 26.50x (ISBN 0-89158-300-9). Westview.

Yenne Velt: The Great Works of Jewish Fantasy & Occult, 2 vols. Ed. by Joachim Neugroschel. 736p. 1976. 25.00 (ISBN 0-88373-025-1). Stonehill Pub Co.

Yer Dailege! Kuna Women's Art. Mari L. Salvador. (Illus.). 103p. (Orig.). 1978. pap. 10.95 (ISBN 0-8263-0539-3, Pub. by Maxwell Mus Anthropology). U of NM Pr.

Yersinia Enterocolitica. Ed. by Edward J. Bottone. 240p. 1981. 69.95 (ISBN 0-8493-5545-1). CRC Pr.

Yes Is Better Than No. Byrd Bayler. 1980. pap. 1.95 (ISBN 0-686-69248-9, 50625). Avon.

Yes, Lord. Dona Hoffman. LC 74-30867. 1974. pap. 4.50 (ISBN 0-570-03195-8, 12-2596). Concordia.

Yes, My Darling Daughters: Adventures in Fathering. Ralph Schoenstein. 1976. 6.95 (ISBN 0-374-29360-0). FS&G.

Yes-No, Stop-Go: Some Patterns in Mathematic Logic. Judith L. Gersting & Kuczkowski. LC 76-46376. (Young Math Ser.). (Illus.). (gr. k-3). 1977. PLB 7.89 (ISBN 0-690-01130-X, TYC-J). T Y Crowell.

Yes Virginia, There Is Right & Wrong! Values Education Survival Kit. K. M. Gow. 248p. 1980. 15.95 (ISBN 0-471-79954-8); pap. 9.95 (ISBN 0-471-79953-X). Wiley.

Yes Yes Living in a No No World. Neil Eskelin. (Orig.). 1980. pap. 2.95 (ISBN 0-88270-417-6). Logos.

Yester Year in Clark County, Ohio, 2 vols. in one. Ed. by Mary A. Skardon. (Annual Monograph Ser.). 76p. (Repr. of 1947 & 1948 eds.). 1978. pap. 3.00. Clark County Hist Soc.

Yesterday: A Memoir of a Russian-Jewish Family. Miriam S. Zunser. Ed. by Emily W. Leider. LC 78-2150. (Illus.). 1978. 11.95 o.s.i. (ISBN 0-06-014810-1, HarpT). Har-Row.

Yesterday & Today: A Dictionary of Recent American History. Stanley Hochman. LC 79-12265. (Illus.). 407p. 1979. 21.95 (ISBN 0-07-029103-9). McGraw.

Yesterday & Today from the Kitchens of Stokely-Van Camp. (Orig.). Date not set. price not set (ISBN 0-87502-071-2). Benjamin Co.

Yesterday at the Seventh Hour. Jeanne Hale. (Orig.). 1976. pap. 1.50 o.p. (ISBN 0-88368-076-9). Whitaker Hse.

Yesterday in Ireland, 3 vols. Eyre E. Crowe. Ed. by Robert L. Wolff. (Ireland Nineteenth Century Fiction - Ser. Two: Vol. 15). 984p. 1979. Set. lib. bdg. 96.00 (ISBN 0-8240-3464-3). Garland Pub.

Yesterday, Today & Tomorrow. Ed. by Robert Rotering. (Illus.). 48p. (Orig.). 1971. pap. 4.95 o.p. (ISBN 0-88489-038-4). St Marys.

Yesterday, Today & Tomorrow: The Farmer Takes a Hand. rev. ed. Marquis W. Childs. LC 52-5629. 178p. 1980. pap. 2.25 (ISBN 0-686-28113-6). Natl Rural.

Yesterday, Today, & Tomorrow: Yesterday, Book One of a Trilogy. new ed. Leydel J. Willis. 1976. 4.95 (ISBN 0-8187-0021-1). Clodele.

Yesterdays. Harold S. Ladoo. LC 74-75919. (Anansi Fiction Ser.: No. 29). 110p. 1974. 10.95 (ISBN 0-88784-431-6, Pub. by Hse Anansi Pr Canada); pap. 4.95 (ISBN 0-88784-329-8). U of Toronto Pr.

Yesterday's Authors of Books for Children: Facts & Pictures About Authors & Illustrators of Books for Young People, 2 vols. Ed. by Anne Commire. LC 76-17501. (Yesterday's Authors of Books for Children Ser.). (Illus.). (gr. 7-12). 38.00 ea.; Vol. 1, 1977. (ISBN 0-8103-0073-7); Vol. 2 1978. (ISBN 0-8103-0090-7). Gale.

Yesterday's Child. Barbara Wood. 272p. 1981. pap. 2.50 (ISBN 0-380-50765-X, 50765). Avon.

Yesterday's Children: A Longitudinal Study of Children from Kindergarten into the Adult Years. E. Philip Kraus. 208p. 1981. Repr. of 1973 ed. lib. bdg. price not set (ISBN 0-89874-311-7). Krieger.

Yesterday's Children: A Longitudinal Study of Children from Kindergarten into the Adult Years. Philip E. Kraus. LC 72-14108. 224p. 1973. 17.95 o.p. (ISBN 0-471-50722-9, Pub. by Wiley-Interscience). Wiley.

Yesterday's House. Nancy Gardiner. (YA) 1977. 4.95 o.p. (ISBN 0-685-74269-5, Avalon). Bouregy.

Yesterday's Lily. Jeff Jones. (Illus.). 80p. 1980. pap. 8.95 (ISBN 0-8256-9552-X, Quick Fox). Music Sales.

Yesterday's Motorcycles. Paul W. Hatmon. (Superwheels & Thrill Sports Bks.). (Illus.). (YA) (gr. 4 up). 1981. PLB 6.95g (ISBN 0-8225-0429-4). Lerner Pubns.

Yesterday's News. R. B. Walker. 256p. 1980. 30.00x (ISBN -0424-00079-2, Pub. by Sydney U Pr Australia). Intl Schol Bk Serv.

Yesterday's Radicals: A Study of the Affinity Between Unitarianism & Broad Church Anglicanism in the Nineteenth Century. Dennis G. Wigmore-Beddoes. 182p. Repr. of 1971 ed. 10.00 (ISBN 0-227-67751-X). Attic Pr.

Yesterday's Scars. Carole Mortimer. (Harlequin Presents Ser.). 192p. 1980. pap. 1.50 (ISBN 0-373-10383-2, Pub. by Harlequin). PB.

Yesterday's Seasons: Memoirs of a Medical Practice in Rural Texas. Gene Schulze. LC 78-53481. 1978. 10.95 o.p. (ISBN 0-8015-0301-9). Dutton.

Yesterday's Shopping: Army & Navy Stores Catalogue 1907. (Illus.). 1472p. 1980. Repr. 63.00 (ISBN 0-7153-4692-X). David & Charles.

Yesterday's Trains. Patrick C. Dorin. (Superwheels & Thrill Sports Bks.). (Illus.). (gr. 4 up). 1981. PLB 6.95 (ISBN 0-8225-0448-0). Lerner Pubns.

Yesterday's Wings: Eighty-Two Historical Aircraft. Peter M. Bowers. pap. 7.95x o.p. (ISBN 0-911720-87-1). Aviation.

Yesterday's Woman: Domestic Realism in the English Novel. Vineta Colby. 356p. 1974. text ed. 17.00 o.p. (ISBN 0-691-06263-3). Princeton U Pr.

Yet Another Big Fat Funny Silly Book. Stoo Hample. LC 80-66202. (Illus.). 96p. (gr. 1-4). 1980. 4.95 (ISBN 0-440-09796-7); PLB 6.46 (ISBN 0-440-09797-5). Delacorte.

Yet Softly Tread the Leaves. Eliza Resford. 1981. 10.95 (ISBN 0-533-04949-0). Vantage.

Yet to Be Served: Special Issue of Exceptional Children. Ed. by M. Angele Thomas. 96p. 1979. pap. 3.75 (ISBN 0-86586-095-5). Coun Exc Child.

Yet Will I Serve Him. Hoyt E. Stone. 1976. pap. 2.25 (ISBN 0-87148-931-7). Pathway Pr.

Yetta the Trickster. Andrea Zimmerman. LC 78-6164. (Illus.). (gr. 1-4). 1978. 6.95 (ISBN 0-395-28836-3, Clarion). HM.

Yevgeniy Shvarts: Three Plays. Ed. by Avril Pyman. 288p. 1972. text ed. 14.00 (ISBN 0-08-016294-0). Pergamon.

Yevgeny Yevtushenko: Bilingual Edition. Ed. by H. Marshall. 1967. text ed. 13.75 (ISBN 0-08-012464-X). Pergamon.

Yevgeny Yevtushenko: Selected Poetry. Ed. by R. R. Milner-Gulland. 1963. 6.70 (ISBN 0-08-009808-8); pap. 5.15 (ISBN 0-08-009807-X). Pergamon.

Yevtushenko: Selected Poems. Evgeny Yevtushenko. 1962. 5.50 o.p. (ISBN 0-525-23922-7). Dutton.

Yiddish Sayings Mama Never Taught You. Tr. by Gershon Weltman & Marvin Zuckerman. LC 73-79282. (Perivale Translation Ser.: No. 2). 99p. 1976. pap. 4.95 (ISBN 0-912288-04-3). Perivale Pr.

Yiddish Stories Old & New. Ed. by Irving Howe & Eliezer Greenberg. LC 74-8116. 128p. (gr. 7 up). 1974. 6.95 (ISBN 0-8234-0246-0). Holiday.

Yiddish Word Book for English Speaking People. Samuel Rosenbaum. 199p. 1980. pap. text ed. 6.95 (ISBN 0-442-21932-6). Van Nos Reinhold.

Yield of Electronic Materials & Devices. National Materials Advisory Board. 96p. 1972. pap. 5.25 (ISBN 0-309-02108-1). Natl Acad Pr.

Yield Table for Wrap-Around Mortgage No. 707. rev. ed. 25.00 (ISBN 0-685-59991-4). Finan Pub.

Yin & Yang of Organizations. Nancy Foy. LC 80-18558. 1980. 11.95 (ISBN 0-688-03769-0). Morrow.

Yin Soon. (Sharazad Stories Ser.). (Illus., Arabic.). pap. 3.50 (ISBN 0-686-53104-3). Intl Bk Ctr.

Yo Puedo: Bilingual Leadership Program for Junior & Senior High. Uvaldo Palomares & Gerry Ball. 1980. 89.95 (ISBN 0-86584-036-9). Human Dev Train.

Yo-Yo. Diane Balson. LC 75-25723. 288p. 1976. 7.95 o.p. (ISBN 0-688-02979-5). Morrow.

Yo-Yo Kid. Rose Blue. LC 76-17623. (Values in Fiction Ser.). (Illus.). 64p. (gr. 5 up). 1976. PLB 7.75 (ISBN 0-8172-0078-9). Raintree Pubs.

Yobgorgle: Mystery Monster of Lake Ontario. rev. ed. Daniel M. Pinkwater. 160p. (gr. 3-6). 1981. pap. 1.75 (ISBN 0-553-15109-6). Bantam.

Yoga. Swami Venkatesananda. (Illus., Orig.). 1981. pap. 7.95 (ISBN 0-89407-021-5). Strawberry Hill.

Yoga - Meaning, Values & Practice. Phulgenda Sinha. 1973. pap. 2.50 (ISBN 0-88253-259-6). Ind-US Inc.

Yoga & Health. Selvarajan Yesudian & Elisabeth Haich. LC 54-6039. (Illus.). 1954. 8.95 o.p. (ISBN 0-06-007590-2, HarpT). Har-Row.

Yoga & Prayer. Michaelle. Tr. by Diane Cumming. pap. 6.50 (ISBN 0-87061-059-7). Chr Classics.

Yoga Aphorisms of Patanjali. Tr. & pref. by William Q. Judge. xxi, 74p. 1930. Repr. of 1889 ed. 3.00 (ISBN 0-938998-11-0). Theosophy.

Yoga As Philosophy & Religion. S. Dasgupta. 1978. Repr. 9.00 (ISBN 0-8426-0488-X). Orient Bk Dist.

Yoga for Athletics. Harmon Hathaway et al. 1978. 12.95 o.p. (ISBN 0-8092-7561-9); pap. 5.95 o.p. (ISBN 0-8092-7560-0). Contemp Bks.

Yoga for Beginners. Alice K. Turner. LC 73-5712. (Career Concise Guides Ser.). (gr. 5 up). 1973. PLB 4.90 o.p. (ISBN 0-531-02643-4). Watts.

Yoga for Children. Eve Diskin. LC 76-28685. (Illus.). (gr. 7-11). 1977. 8.95 o.p. (ISBN 0-668-04075-0). Arco.

Yoga for Children. Esther M. Luchs. LC 77-7268. 1977. pap. 4.95 (ISBN 0-8091-2023-2). Paulist Pr.

Yoga for Kids. Kareen Zebroff & Peter Zebroff. LC 78-52346. (Illus.). (gr. 7 up). 1978. 7.95 (ISBN 0-8069-4128-6); PLB 7.49 (ISBN 0-8069-4129-4). Sterling.

Yoga for Personal Living. Richard L. Hittleman. (Illus.). 1972. pap. 2.50 o.s.i. (ISBN 0-446-91186-0). Warner Bks.

Yoga for Physical & Mental Fitness. Sachindra K. Majumdar. LC 68-31613. (Illus.). 1968. 7.95 (ISBN 0-87396-013-0); pap. 3.95 (ISBN 0-87396-014-9). Stravon.

Yoga in Daily Life. K. S. Joshi. 163p. 1971. pap. 2.00 (ISBN 0-88253-044-5). Ind-US Inc.

Yoga in Ten Lessons. Jean M. Dechanet. LC 65-20461. (Illus.). 1966. 7.95 o.p. (ISBN 0-06-001240-4, HarpT). Har-Row.

Yoga of the Guhyasamajatantra. Alex Wayman. 1977. 24.95 (ISBN 0-89684-003-4, Pub. by Motilal Banarsidass India). Orient Bk Dist.

Yoga of Works. Sri M. Pandit. 1979. 8.00 (ISBN 0-89744-943-6). Auromere.

Yoga, Science of the Self. rev. ed. Marcia Moore & Mark Douglas. LC 67-19602. (Illus.). 1979. 10.00 (ISBN 0-912240-01-6). Arcane Pubns.

Yoga Self-Taught. Andre Van Lysebeth. LC 74-181650. (Illus.). 262p. 1972. 10.95 o.p. (ISBN 0-06-014498-X, HarpT). Har-Row.

Yoga Sutras: The Textbook of Yoga Psychology. Rammurti S. Mishra. 440p. 1973. pap. 3.50 o.p. (ISBN 0-385-08358-0, Anch). Doubleday.

Yoga System of Health. Yogi Vithaldas. 1981. pap. 3.95 (ISBN 0-686-69341-8). Cornerstone.

Yoga System of Patanjali. Tr. by J. H. Woods. (Harvard Oriental Ser.: Vol. 17). 1972. 15.00x o.p. (ISBN 0-8426-0470-7). Verry.

Yoga-System of Patanjali. James H. Woods. 1977. pap. 8.50 (ISBN 0-89684-344-0, Pub. by Motilal Banarsidass India). Orient Bk Dist.

Yoga Thing. Nancy Roberts. 1973. 8.95 (ISBN 0-8015-9024-8, Hawthorn); pap. 5.95 (ISBN 0-8015-9025-6, Hawthorn). Dutton.

Yoga: Union with the Ultimate. Archie J. Bahm. LC 60-53365. 1961. 6.50 (ISBN 0-8044-5056-0); pap. 3.95 (ISBN 0-8044-6015-9). Ungar.

Yoga: Yogic Suksma Vyayama. Dhirenda Brahmachari. (Illus.). 232p. 1975. 8.95 (ISBN 0-88253-802-0). Ind-US Inc.

Yogasutra of Patanjali. 2nd rev. ed. Bangali Baba. 1979. pap. 6.50 (ISBN 0-8426-0916-4, Pub. by Motilal Banarsidass India). Orient Bk Dist.

Yoghurt Cookbook. Pamela Westland. (Illus.). 175p. 1980. 19.95 (ISBN 0-241-89763-7, Pub. by Hamish Hamilton England). David & Charles.

Yogi & the Commissar. A. Koestler. 1967. 5.95 o.s.i. (ISBN 0-02-565850-6). Macmillan.

Yogi Bear's Animal Friends. (Play & Learn Shape Board Bks). 14p. (gr. k-3). 1981. bds. 2.95 comb bdg. (ISBN 0-89828-105-9, 6005, Ottenheimer Pubs Inc). Tuffy Bks.

Yogi of Cockroach Court. Frank Waters. LC 72-91922. 277p. 1947. pap. 5.95 (ISBN 0-8040-0613-X, SB). Swallow.

Yogi, the Commissar, & the Third-World Church. Paul D. Clasper. LC 78-183648. 96p. (Orig.). 1972. pap. 1.95 o.p. (ISBN 0-8170-0560-9). Judson.

Yogic Ways to Happiness. Swami K. Saraswati. (Illus., Orig.). 1981. pap. 5.95 (ISBN 0-89407-039-8). Strawberry Hill.

Yogurt Cookbook. Kay S. Nelson. LC 76-11508. (Cookbook Ser). (Illus.). 220p. 1976. pap. 3.00 (ISBN 0-486-23416-9). Dover.

Yogurt Cookbook. Olga Smetinoff. pap. 1.95 (ISBN 0-515-05693-6, N2417). Jove Pubns.

Yogurt Cookbook. Olga Smetinoff. LC 65-23871. 1966. pap. 4.95 (ISBN 0-8119-0402-4). Fell.

Yoke Made Easy. Alfred Doerffler. LC 75-2344. 128p. 1974. pap. 4.95 (ISBN 0-570-03027-7, 6-1155). Concordia.

Yolanda. Dominique Verseau. pap. 1.50 o.s.i. (ISBN 0-440-19452-0). Dell.

Yolanda: Slaves of Space. Dominique Verseau. 1978. pap. 1.95 o.p. (ISBN 0-8021-4018-1, GP4081). Grove.

Yolanda: The Girl from Erosphere. Dominique Verseau. 1975. pap. 1.50 o.p. (ISBN 0-685-56549-1, D9452, Dist. by Dell). Grove.

Yom Kippur & After. Galia Golan. LC 76-2278. (Soviet & East European Studies). 1977. 38.50 (ISBN 0-521-21090-9). Cambridge U Pr.

Yom Kippur War: A Case Study in Crisis Decision Making in American Foreign Policy. Ray Maghroori & Stephen M. Gorman. LC 80-5811. 98p. 1981. lib. bdg. 14.75 (ISBN 0-8191-1373-5); pap. text ed. 6.75 (ISBN 0-8191-1374-3). U Pr of Amer.

York Ballad Operas & Yorkshiremen. Ed. by Walter H. Rubsamen. (Ballad Opera Ser.). 1974. lib. bdg. 50.00 (ISBN 0-8240-0926-6). Garland Pub.

York: The Continuing City. Patrick Nuttgens. 1976. 25.00 (ISBN 0-571-09733-2, Pub. by Faber & Faber). Merrimack Bk Serv.

Yorkshire. Maurice Colbeck. 1979. 19.95 (ISBN 0-7134-3059-1, Pub. by Batsford England). David & Charles.

Yorkshire. Tudor Edwards. (Illus.). 1978. 8.95 o.p. (ISBN 0-571-11165-3, Pub. by Faber & Faber). Merrimack Bk Serv.

Yorkshire. Ian Longworth. 1967. 3.95x o.p. (ISBN 0-435-32960-X). Heinemann Ed.

Yorkshire & Humberside. rev. ed. British Tourist Authority. (Illus.). 106p. 1981. pap. write for info. (ISBN 0-86143-040-9, Pub. by Auto Assn-British Tourist Authority England). Merrimack Bk Serv.

Yorkshire & North Lincolnshire. 3rd ed. H. Tolley & K. Orrell. LC 77-87393. (Geography of the British Isles Ser.). (Illus.). 1978. limp bdg. 6.95x (ISBN 0-521-21918-3). Cambridge U Pr.

Yorkshire Cistercian Heritage: Vol. 2, Rievaulx, Jervaulx, Byland. James Hogg. (Salzburg Studien Zur Anglistik und Amerikanistik: 8). (Illus.). 1979. pap. 45.00x (ISBN 0-391-01429-3). Humanities.

Yorkshire Cistercian Heritage: Vol. 3, Fountains, Kirkstall, Meaux. James Hogg. (Salzburg Studien zur Anglistik und Amerikanistik: 8). (Illus.). 1979. pap. 45.00x (ISBN 0-391-01430-7). Humanities.

Yorkshire Cisterician Heritage: Vol. 4, Roche, Salley. James Hogg. (Salzurg Studien Zur Anglistik und Amerikanistik 8). (Illus.). 1979. pap. 45.00x (ISBN 0-391-01431-5). Humanities.

Yorkshire Cookbook. Mary H. Moore. LC 79-56056. (Illus.). 96p. 1980. 11.95 (ISBN 0-7153-7892-9). David & Charles.

Yorkshire Cookery. Joan Poulson. 1979. 24.00 (ISBN 0-7134-0142-7, Pub. by Batsford England). David & Charles.

Yorkshire Dales. Geoffrey N. Wright. 1977. 14.95 (ISBN 0-7153-7454-0). David & Charles.

Yorkshire Legends. 2nd ed. Compiled by The Dalesman. (Illus.). 71p. (Orig.). 1976. pap. 3.00 (ISBN 0-686-64123-X). Legacy Bks.

Yorkshire Relish. Elizabeth Cragoe. 1979. 17.95 (ISBN 0-241-10054-2, Pub by Hamish Hamilton). David & Charles.

Yorkshire: The Dales. Maurice Colbeck. (Illus.). 160p. 1980. 19.95 (ISBN 0-7134-2236-X, Pub. by Batsford England). David & Charles.

Yorktown Campaign & the Surrender of Cornwallis, 1781. H. P. Johnston. LC 75-146149. (Era of the American Revolution Ser). 1971. Repr. of 1881 ed. lib. bdg. 22.50 (ISBN 0-306-70142-1). Da Capo.

Yorty: Politics of a Constant Candidate. John C. Bollens & Grant B. Geyer. LC 72-95289. 250p. 1973. 6.95 (ISBN 0-913530-00-X). Palisades Pub.

Yoruba Beliefs & Sacrificial Rites. Joseph O. Awolalu. (Illus.). 1979. text ed. 28.00x (ISBN 0-582-64203-5); pap. text ed. 13.50 (ISBN 0-582-64244-2). Longman.

Yoruba Myths. Ulli Beier. LC 79-7645. (Illus.). 88p. 1980. 13.95 (ISBN 0-521-22995-2); pap. 4.50 (ISBN 0-521-22865-4). Cambridge U Pr.

Yosemite. (Guide Ser.). (Illus.). 1972. pap. 1.95 o.p. (ISBN 0-307-24028-2, Golden Pr). Western Pub.

Yosemite: The Story Behind the Scenery. rev. ed. William R. Jones. LC 80-82917. (Illus.). 1980. 7.95 (ISBN 0-916122-33-6); pap. 3.00 (ISBN 0-916122-08-5). K C Pubns.

Yosemite Waterfalls. Edgar Menning. (Illus., Orig.). 1970. pap. 1.25 o.p. (ISBN 0-913832-11-1). Mus Graphics.

Yoshitsune: A Fifteenth-Century Japanese Chronicle. Tr. by Helen C. McCullough. 1966. 18.95x (ISBN 0-8047-0270-5). Stanford U Pr.

Yossiph Shyryn. Santo Cali. Ed. by Nat Scammacca. 132p. (Ital. & Eng.). 1980. 20.00 (ISBN 0-89304-563-2); pap. 10.00 (ISBN 0-89304-564-0). Cross Cult.

You. Jack Libert. (Orig.). 1971. pap. 2.00 (ISBN 0-911732-57-8). Irego.

You. Clare Trenkle. 1966. text ed. 5.95x (ISBN 0-88323-086-0, 182); wkbk. 2.25x (ISBN 0-88323-087-9, 183). Richards Pub.

You. 320p. (Orig.). 1981. pap. 2.95 (ISBN 0-553-14478-2). Bantam.

You -- After Childbirth. Julie McKenna & Margaret Polden. (Churchill Livingstone Patient Handbook Ser.). 1980. pap. text ed. 2.25x (ISBN 0-443-02128-7). Churchill.

You Always Communicate Something. Shirley Schwarzrock & C. Gilbert Wrenn. (Coping with Ser.). (Illus.). 58p. (gr. 7-12). 1973. pap. text ed. 1.30 (ISBN 0-913476-20-X). Am Guidance.

You & Democracy. Dorothy Gordon. (Illus.). (gr. 5-9). 1951. PLB 5.95 o.p. (ISBN 0-525-43491-7). Dutton.

You & I & the World. Werner Aspenstrom. Ed. by Stanley H. Barkan. Tr. by Siv Cedering from Swedish & Eng. (Cross-Cultural Review Chapbook 5). 40p. pap. 3.50 (ISBN 0-89304-803-8). Cross Cult.

You & Me. Tessa Colina. Ed. by Jane Buerger. (Illus.). 1980. 5.95 (ISBN 0-89565-179-3, 4936). Standard Pub.

You & Me. Florence P. Heide. (Illus.). 32p. (gr. k-4). 1975. 6.95 (ISBN 0-570-03436-1, 56-1267). Concordia.

You & Me Babe. Chuck Barris. 1980. pap. write for info. (ISBN 0-671-81654-3). PB.

You & Neurosis. H. J. Eysenck. (Illus.). 224p. 1979. 14.95 (ISBN 0-8039-1287-0). Sage.

You & the Psychic Within. Joseph L. D'Albert & Richard A. Herbert. 1977. 6.00 o.p. (ISBN 0-682-48879-8). Exposition.

You & the Universe. N. J. Berrill. 224p. 1973. pap. 4.95 (ISBN 0-911336-47-8). Sci of Mind.

You & Values Education. Charles Kniker. (Educational Foundations Ser.). 1977. pap. text ed. 8.50 (ISBN 0-675-08516-0). Merrill.

You & Your Adolescent. Barry Lauton & Arthur Freese. 2244p. 1981. 9.95 (ISBN 0-684-16819-7, ScribT). Scribner.

You & Your Body. Aaron E. Klein. (gr. 3-5). 1980. pap. 1.50 (ISBN 0-671-29899-2). Archway.

You & Your Cells. Leo Schneider. LC 64-71496. (Illus.). (gr. 7-9). 1964. 5.95 o.p. (ISBN 0-15-299840-3, HJ). HarBraceJ.

You & Your Child: A Primer for Parents. K. E. Moyer. LC 74-17316. 230p. 1974. 12.95 (ISBN 0-88229-156-4). Nelson-Hall.

You & Your Eyes. 2nd rev. ed. Lawrence Lewison. 1978. 10.00 o.p. (ISBN 0-682-48926-3). Exposition.

You & Your Family. rev. ed. Illus. by Macet Al Conner & Gerry Contreras. (Bowmar-Noble Social Studies Program). Orig. Title: Man & His World. (Illus.). 152p. (gr. 1). 1979. text ed. 6.24 (ISBN 0-8372-3680-0); tchrs. ed. 9.00 (ISBN 0-8372-3681-9). Bowmar-Noble.

You & Your Feelings. Eda LeShan. 128p. (gr. 7 up). 1975. 7.95 (ISBN 0-02-757330-3). Macmillan.

You & Your Grief. Edgar N. Jackson. 1961. 3.95 (ISBN 0-8015-9036-1, Hawthorn). Dutton.

You & Your Hair. Elaine Budd. (gr. 7 up). 1978. pap. 1.25 o.p. (ISBN 0-590-03861-3, Schol Pap). Schol Bk Serv.

You & Your Husband's Mid-Life Crisis. Sally Conway. (Orig.). 1980. pap. 4.95 (ISBN 0-89191-318-1). Cook.

You & Your Job. rev. ed. Walter Lowen. 1962. pap. 0.95 o.s.i. (ISBN 0-02-080620-5, Collier). Macmillan.

You & Your Money: A Guide from God's Word. Ron Hembree. (Orig.). 1981. pap. 4.95 (ISBN 0-8010-4252-6). Baker Bk.

You & Your Poodle. Mollie Skelton. 4.95 (ISBN 0-87666-362-5, PS641). TFH Pubns.

You & Your Prostate. F. P. Twinem. (Illus.). 120p. 1980. lexotone 7.75 (ISBN 0-398-04012-5); pap. 5.95 lexotone (ISBN 0-398-04014-1). C C Thomas.

You & Your Retriever. Ralph W. Coykendall, Jr. LC 63-7707. 1963. 5.95 o.p. (ISBN 0-385-02892-X). Doubleday.

You & Your Senses. Leo Schneider. LC 56-5875. (gr. 5-9). 1960. 6.50 o.p. (ISBN 0-15-299857-8, HJ). HarBraceJ.

You & Your Superstitions. Brewton Berry. LC 78-174904. (Illus.). 249p. 1974. Repr. of 1940 ed. 20.00 (ISBN 0-8103-3985-4). Gale.

You & Your Toddler: Sharing the Developing Years. Janine Levy. (Illus.). 1981. 10.95 (ISBN 0-394-51532-3); pap. 6.95 (ISBN 0-394-74806-9). Pantheon.

You & Your Work. Byron J. Alpers & Mitchell L. Afrow. (Shoptalk - Vocational Reading Skills). (gr. 9-12). 1978. pap. text ed. 5.12 (ISBN 0-205-05825-6, 495825X). Allyn.

You & Your World. Willeta R. Bolinger. (Special Education Ser. for slow learners). (gr. 7-12,RL 2.3). 1964. pap. 3.40 (ISBN 0-8224-7650-9); tchrs' manual free (ISBN 0-8224-7651-7). Pitman Learning.

You & Yours. Kathleen Barnes & Virginia Pearce. (Illus.). 41p. (Orig.). (gr. 3-6). 1980. pap. 2.95 (ISBN 0-87747-823-6). Deseret Bk.

You Are a Money Brain. William C. Drollinger & William C. Drollinger, Sr. 1981. write for info. (ISBN 0-914244-07-8). Epic Pubns.

You Are a Money Brain. William C. Jr. Drollinger. 1981. write for info. (ISBN 0-914244-07-8). Epic Pubns.

You Are Creative! Become an Endless Producer of Good Ideas. Michael T. Brown. LC 77-84036. (Illus.). 1978. 12.95 o.p. (ISBN 0-930490-02-9). Future Shop.

You Are Extraordinary. Roger J. Williams. 1967. 6.95 o.p. (ISBN 0-394-45316-6). Random.

You Are First: The Story of Olin & Rod Stephens of Sparkman & Stephens, Inc. Francis S. Kinney. LC 78-8148. (Illus.). 1978. 17.95 (ISBN 0-396-07567-3). Dodd.

You Are My Beloved Sermon Book. Frederick Kemper & George M. Bass. 1980. pap. 6.95 (ISBN 0-570-03821-9, 12-2761). Concordia.

You Are Somebody Special. John F. Hornbrook & Allan C. Wolf. 148p. (Orig.). 1980. pap. 3.95 (ISBN 0-89841-005-3). Zoe Pubns.

You Are Somebody Special. Ed. by Charlie Shedd. 224p. 1980. pap. 2.25 (ISBN 0-553-12803-5). Bantam.

You Are the Future You Are My Hope. Pope John Paul, II. 1979. 4.95 o.s.i. (ISBN 0-8198-0632-3); pap. 3.95 (ISBN 0-8198-0633-1). Dghtrs St Paul.

You Are the Greatest: How to Get from Where You Are to Where You Want to Be. Bev Shinn & Duane Shinn. 1978. pap. 9.95 o.p. (ISBN 0-912732-52-0). Duane Shinn.

You Are the Mystery. Joan Zink & David Zink. LC 76-44601. (Illus.). 1976. 7.95 o.p. (ISBN 0-87707-178-0). CSA Pr.

You Are the Rain. R. R. Knudson. LC 73-15397. 160p. (gr. 7 up). 1974. 5.95 o.p. (ISBN 0-440-08759-7). Delacorte.

You Are the World. J. Krishnamurti. LC 73-172504. 1972. pap. 1.95 (ISBN 0-06-064871-6, RD 303, HarpR). Har-Row.

You Are What You Breathe. Robert Massy. 1980. 1.00 (ISBN 0-916438-41-4). Univ of Trees.

You Are What You Eat. Victor H. Lindlahr. LC 80-19722. 128p. 1980. Repr. of 1971 ed. lib. bdg. 9.95x (ISBN 0-89370-604-3). Borgo Pr.

You Are What You Eat: A Common-Sense Guide to the Modern American Diet. Sara Gilbert. LC 76-39806. (gr. 5 up). 1977. 8.95 (ISBN 0-02-736020-2, 73602). Macmillan.

You Are What You Think. Muriel Larsori. pap. 1.95 (ISBN 0-89728-063-6, 658463). Omega Pubns OR.

You Are What You Write. Huntington Hartford. LC 72-91262. 360p. 1973. 12.95 (ISBN 0-02-548500-8). Macmillan.

You Are Your Own Healer. Ann Wigmore. 207p. pap. 1.95. Hippocrates.

You Be the Judge from The Saturday Evening Post. LC 79-53768. (Illus.). 1979. 5.95 (ISBN 0-89387-035-8). Sat Eve Post.

You Call Me Chief: Impressions of the Life of Chief Dan George. Hilda Mortimer & Dan George. LC 78-60297. (Illus.). 192p. 1981. 11.95 (ISBN 0-385-04806-8). Doubleday.

You Can Analyze Handwriting. Robert Holder. pap. 2.00 o.p. (ISBN 0-87980-176-X). Wilshire.

You Can Be a Leader. Ben Solomon & Ethel M. Bowers. 140p. (Orig.). 1981. pap. 4.95 (ISBN 0-936626-03-8). Leadership Pr.

You Can Be a Writer: A Career & Leisure Guide. Clifford Alderman. 160p. (gr. 9-12). 1981. PLB price not set (ISBN 0-671-34047-6). Messner.

You Can Be Free. R. A. Anderson. LC 76-5074. (Harvest Ser.). 1977. pap. 3.95 (ISBN 0-8163-0292-8). Pacific Pr Pub Assn.

You Can Be the Wife of a Happy Husband. Darien B. Cooper. LC 74-77450. 156p. 1974. pap. 3.95 (ISBN 0-88207-711-2). Victor Bks.

You Can Beat the Money Squeeze. George Fooshee & Marjean Fooshee. 1980. pap. 4.95 (ISBN 0-8007-5030-6). Revell.

You Can Become the Person You Want to Be. Robert H. Schuller. 224p. 1973. 10.95 (ISBN 0-8015-9048-5, Hawthorn); pap. 3.95 (ISBN 0-8015-9049-3, Hawthorn). Dutton.

You Can Become the Person You Want to Be. Robert H. Schuller. 1976. pap. 2.50 (ISBN 0-8007-8235-6, Spire Bks). Revell.

You Can Become the Person You Want to Be. Robert H. Schuller. (Orig.). pap. 2.25 (ISBN 0-515-05970-6). Jove Pubns.

You Can Become Whole Again: A Guide to Healing for Christians in Grief. Jolanda Miller. LC 80-84652. 1981. pap. 5.00 (ISBN 0-8042-1156-6). John Knox.

You Can Buy Your Way into Heaven: But It'll Take Every Cent You Have. Joseph Felix. 1981. pap. 3.95 (ISBN 0-8407-5766-2). Nelson.

You Can Catch Fish. Bill Stokes. LC 76-12478. (Games & Activities Ser.). 48p. (gr. k-3). 1976. 9.30 (ISBN 0-8172-0627-2). Raintree Pubs.

You Can Change Your Personality--& Your Life. Kurt Haas. LC 78-11449. 1979. 11.95 (ISBN 0-88229-429-6). Nelson-Hall.

You Can Cope: Be the Person You Want to Be Through Self Help. Bernard Poduska. 1975. 12.95 (ISBN 0-13-972562-8, Spec); pap. 3.95 (ISBN 0-13-972570-9). P-H.

You Can Do It: A PR Skills Manual for Librarians. Rita Kohn & Krysta Tepper. LC 80-24217. xii, 232p. 1981. pap. 12.50 (ISBN 0-8108-1401-3). Scarecrow.

You Can Do It! How to Encourage Yourself. Lewis E. Losoncy. (Illus.). 1980. 10.95 (ISBN 0-13-976605-7, Spec); pap. 5.95 (ISBN 0-13-976597-2). P-H.

You Can Draw. Kenneth Jameson. LC 79-92494. (Start to Paint Ser.). (Illus.). 1980. pap. 3.95 (ISBN 0-8008-8755-7, Pentalic). Taplinger.

You Can Fight for Your Life. Lawrence LeShan. 1978. pap. 1.95 (ISBN 0-515-04502-0). Jove Pubns.

You Can Fly: But That Cocoon Has Got to Go. Janice Barfield. (Orig.). 1981. 7.95 (ISBN 0-310-43920-5). Zondervan.

You Can Give a Chalk Talk. W. R. Rogers. LC 80-65775. 1981. saddlewire 4.95 (ISBN 0-8054-6931-1). Broadman.

You Can Have a Family Where Everybody Wins. Earl H. Gaulke. LC 75-23574. 104p. 1975. pap. 2.50 (ISBN 0-570-03723-9, 12-2625). Concordia.

You Can Hear a Magpie Smile. Paula G. Paul. (gr. 5-8). 1980. 7.95 (ISBN 0-525-66709-1). Elsevier-Nelson.

You Can Hit the Golf Ball Farther. Evan Williams & Larry Sheehan. LC 79-50544. (Illus.). 127p. 1979. 9.95 (ISBN 0-914178-26-1, 24922); pap. 5.95 (ISBN 0-914178-29-6, 24964). Golf Digest.

You Can If You Think You Can. Norman V. Peale. 1979. pap. 2.25 (ISBN 0-8007-8381-6). Revell.

You Can Improve Your Child's School. William Rioux. 1980. 12.95 (ISBN 0-686-68754-X, 25116). S&S.

You Can Kiss This Boy Goodbye. Marvin Elkoff. 1981. 11.95 (ISBN 0-671-41145-4, Wyndham Bks). S&S.

You Can Learn to Learn. F. Christ & R. Adams. 695.00 (ISBN 0-13-976704-5). P-H.

You Can Make Horseman Clocks. Billy G. Hughes, Jr. 52p. 1980. pap. 4.00 (ISBN 0-914208-08-X). Longhorn Pr.

You Can Make It Happen: A Guide to Self-Actualization & Organizational Change. Len Sperry et al. LC 76-45156. (Illus.). 1977. pap. text ed. 8.95 (ISBN 0-201-07129-0). A-W.

You Can Make Your Life Count. Arthur Caliandro. 192p. 1981. 8.95 (ISBN 0-916392-79-1). Oak Tree Pubns.

You Can Manage Your Life: 16 Keys to Success. Don Mallough. 96p. (Orig.). 1981. pap. 3.95 (ISBN 0-8010-6114-8). Baker Bk.

You Can March for the Master. Ira North. 6.50 (ISBN 0-89225-186-7); pap. 4.00 (ISBN 0-89225-187-5). Gospel Advocate.

You Can Negotiate Anything. Herb Cohen. 1980. 12.00 (ISBN 0-8184-0305-5). Lyle Stuart.

You Can Profit from a Monetary Crisis. Harry Browne. LC 73-16686. (Illus.). 288p. 1974. 8.95 o.s.i. (ISBN 0-02-517460-6). Macmillan.

You Can Put on a Show. Lewy Olfson. LC 74-31712. (Illus.). 144p. (gr. 3 up). 1975. 6.95 o.p. (ISBN 0-8069-7020-0); PLB 6.69 o.p. (ISBN 0-8069-7021-9). Sterling.

You Can Renovate Your Own Home: A Step-by-Step Guide to Major Interior Improvements. Floyd Green & Susan E. Meyer. (Illus.). 304p. 1980. pap. 8.95 (ISBN 0-385-17006-8, Dolp). Doubleday.

You Can See the World in Forty Days. Leland T. Waggoner. LC 76-14774. (Illus.). 1978. pap. 2.45 o.p. (ISBN 0-668-04608-2, 4609). Arco.

You Can See the World in Forty Days. Leland T. Waggoner. LC 76-14774. (Illus.). 1976. 8.95 o.p. (ISBN 0-668-04040-8). Arco.

You Can Sell Your Photos. Henry Scanlon. LC 80-7854. (Illus.). 256p. 1980. 16.95 (ISBN 0-690-01902-5, HarpT); pap. 7.95 (ISBN 0-690-01903-3, HarpT). Har-Row.

You Can So Get There from Here. pap. 3.75 (ISBN 0-912552-19-0). MARC.

You Can Speak Again. Charles Nelson & Joan S. Wilentz. (Funk & W Bk.). 1976. 8.95 o.s.i. (ISBN 0-308-10257-6, TYC-T); pap. 4.95 o.s.i. (ISBN 0-308-10260-6, TYC-T). T Y Crowell.

You Can Succeed in Reading & Writing: 30 Steps in Mastering English. Murray Bromberg & Julius Liebb. (gr. 8-12). 1981. pap. text ed. 4.95 (ISBN 0-8120-2081-2). Barron.

You Can Take It with You. Max M. Rice. LC 80-68885. 160p. 1981. pap. 3.95 (ISBN 0-89636-063-6). Accent Bks.

You Can Train Your Cat. Jo Loeb & Paul Loeb. 1979. pap. 3.95 (ISBN 0-671-25147-3, Fireside). S&S.

You Can Understand the Bible. Grayson H. Ensign. (Bible Study Textbook Ser.). 1978. 13.50 (ISBN 0-89900-057-6). College Pr Pub.

You Can Win a Scholarship. rev. ed. Samuel C. Brownstein & Mitchel Weiner. LC 64-24871. (Orig.). (gr. 10-12). 1972. pap. text ed. 6.50 o.p. (ISBN 0-8120-2073-1). Barron.

You Can Win a Scholarship. Samuel C. Brownstein & Mitchel Weiner. (gr. 10-12). 1981. pap. text ed. price not set. Barron.

You Cannot Die. Ian Currie. LC 80-83590. 288p. 1981. pap. 2.50 (ISBN 0-87216-791-7). Playboy Pbks.

You Can't Do That. G. Seldes. LC 70-37287. (Civil Liberties in American History Ser). 308p. 1972. Repr. of 1938 ed. lib. bdg. 27.50 (ISBN 0-306-70201-0). Da Capo.

You Can't Do That: Beatles Bootlegs & Novelty Records, 1963-1980. Charles Reinhart. 1981. 11.95 (ISBN 0-87650-128-5). Pierian.

You Can't Hardly Get There from Here. Willie S. Ethridge. LC 65-28523. 1965. 7.95 (ISBN 0-8149-0089-5). Vanguard.

You Can't Keep a Good Woman Down: Stories by Alice Walker. Alice Walker. LC 80-8761. 180p. 1981. 10.95 (ISBN 0-15-199754-3). HarBraceJ.

You Can't Tell Me What to Do! Diane Carlson. Ed. by Richard Uhlich. (Bluejeans Paperback Ser.). (Illus., Orig.). (gr. 7-12). 1978. pap. text ed. 1.25 (ISBN 0-8374-5006-3). Xerox Ed Pubns.

You Come with Naked Hands: The Story of the San Francisco to Moscow March for Peace. Bradford Lyttle. LC 66-1279. (Illus.). 289p. 1966. 15.00 (ISBN 0-934676-08-9). Greenlf Bks.

You Dance Like an Ostrich! A Book of Similes. Sylvia R. Tester. LC 78-5833. (Using Words Ser.). (Illus.). (gr. k-3). 1978. PLB 5.50 (ISBN 0-89565-037-1). Childs World.

You Don't Have to Be in Who's Who to Know What's What. Sam Levenson. (gr. 7-12). 1980. lib. bdg. 11.95 (ISBN 0-8161-3056-6, Large Print Bks). G K Hall.

You Don't Have to Be Next. Dr. Jochen Aumiller. 1980. pap. 5.95 (ISBN 0-8065-0683-0). Lyle Stuart.

You Don't Have to Be Old When You Grow Old. Florence M. Taylor. 1979. pap. 3.95 o.p. (ISBN 0-88270-349-8). Logos.

You Don't Have to Go It Alone. Leslie B. Flynn. LC 80-66722. 160p. (Orig.). 1981. pap. 4.95 (ISBN 0-89636-058-X). Accent Bks.

You Don't Have to Slay a Dragon. John M. Stuart & Marjorie L. Stuart. LC 75-14540. (Illus.). 313p. 1976. 8.95 (ISBN 0-915730-01-4). Marburger.

You Don't Look Like Your Mother Said the Robin to the Fawn. Aileen Fisher. (Nature Ser). (gr. k-6). 1973. PLB 6.96 (ISBN 0-8372-0867-X); filmstrip & record 18.00 (ISBN 0-8372-0212-4); filmstrip & cassette 18.00 (ISBN 0-8372-0878-5). Bowmar-Noble.

You Fix It: Insulation. Carmine C. Castellano & Clifford P. Seitz. LC 74-14206. (You Fix It Ser.). (Illus.). 1975. pap. 2.95 o.p. (ISBN 0-668-03614-1). Arco.

You. Forever. T. Lobsang Rampa. pap. 2.50 (ISBN 0-685-22178-4). Weiser.

You Gentiles. Maurice Samuels. pap. 3.00x (ISBN 0-911038-08-6). Noontide.

You Go Away. Dorothy Corey. LC 75-33015. (Self Starter Bks.). (Illus.). 32p. (ps). 1975. 6.50g (ISBN 0-8075-9441-5). A Whitman.

You Got It All: A Personal Account of a White Priest in a Chicago Ghetto. Vincent M. Giese. LC 79-92505. (Illus.). 252p. 1980. pap. 5.95 (ISBN 0-87973-526-0, 526). Our Sunday Visitor.

You Have a Point There: A New & Complete Guide to Punctuation. Eric Partridge. (Orig.). 1978. pap. 7.95 (ISBN 0-7100-8753-5). Routledge & Kegan.

You Have Retinal Detachment: A Guide for Patients. Fred M. Wilson. (Illus.). 136p. 1978. 9.75 (ISBN 0-398-03700-0). C C Thomas.

You, I, & the Others. Paul Weiss. LC 79-13375. 432p. 1980. 25.95 (ISBN 0-8093-0923-8). S Ill U Pr.

You in the Seventies: Families. Inner London Education Assn. 1976. 11.95x o.p. (ISBN 0-435-46560-0). Heinemann Ed.

You in the Seventies: Individual & Society. Inner London Education Assn. 1977. 11.95x o.p. (ISBN 0-435-46561-9). Heinemann Ed.

You Know My Method: A Juxtaposition of Charles S. Peirce & Sherlock Holmes. Thomas A. Sebeok & Jean Umiker-Sebeok. LC 79-55658. (Sherlock Holmes Monograph Ser.). (Illus.). 86p. 1980. 8.95x (ISBN 0-934468-01-X). Gaslight.

You Learn by Living. Eleanor Roosevelt. LC 60-10416. 1960. 15.00 o.s.i. (ISBN 0-06-013645-6, HarpT). Har-Row.

You Live After Death. Harold Sherman. 1949. 7.95 (ISBN 0-910140-16-2). Anthony.

You Live Once. John D. MacDonald. 1978. pap. 1.75 o.p. (ISBN 0-449-14050-4, GM). Fawcett.

You Make the Difference: Leaders Guide. Girl Scouts of the U.S.A. Training Department. (Orig.). 1980. pap. text ed. 2.00 (ISBN 0-88441-330-6, 20-705). GS.

You May Quote Me. Caroll Carroll. 1980. 4.95 (ISBN 0-87786-004-1). Gold Penny.

You Me He. Sammy Tippit & Jerry Jenkins. 1978. pap. 2.50 (ISBN 0-88207-766-X). Victor Bks.

You Mean the Bible Teaches That. Charles C. Ryrie. 1974. pap. 2.50 (ISBN 0-8024-9828-0). Moody.

You Might Save Someone's Life Someday. Kenneth Klein. 324p. 1981. 11.95 (ISBN 0-316-49838-6). Little.

You, My Brother. Philip Burton. 1973. 10.95 o.p. (ISBN 0-394-48478-9). Random.

You Never Can Tell. George B. Shaw. Ed. by Daniel J. Leary. LC 79-56704. (Bernard Shaw Early Texts: Play Manuscripts in Facsimile). 1981. lib. bdg. 70.00 (ISBN 0-8240-4580-7). Garland Pub.

You Never Can Tell When You May Meet a Leopard. Goldie Down. Ed. by Tom Davis. 128p. 1980. pap. write for info. (ISBN 0-8280-0026-3). Review & Herald.

You Never Miss the Water till... The Ogallalla Story. Morton N. Bittinger & Elizabeth B. Green. 1981. 12.00 (ISBN 0-918334-33-0). WRP.

You Ought to See Herbert's House. Doris H. Lund. LC 77-185690. (gr. k-3). 1973. PLB 4.90 o.p. (ISBN 0-531-02595-0). Watts.

You Paid One Thousand Dollars for a Personal What? Thomas Dwyer & Margot Critchfield. (Orig.). 1980. pap. 11.95 (ISBN 0-07-018492-5, BYTE Bks). McGraw.

You Promised Me God. Donald Deffner. LC 12-2792. (Illus.). 1981. pap. 4.95 (ISBN 0-570-03827-8). Concordia.

You Really Don't Have To! Natural Therapy Updated. Herald Maleske. 200p. 1980. 12.95 (ISBN 0-937792-00-4). Nat Therapy.

You Shall Receive. George Otis. pap. 1.50 (ISBN 0-89728-064-4, 533250). Omega Pubns OR.

You Should Se Me in Pyjamas. Robert Giddings. 192p. 1981. 27.00 (ISBN 0-241-10534-X, Pub. by Hamish Hamilton England). David & Charles.

You Take Jesus, I'll Take God. Samuel Levine. LC 80-82731. 134p. (Orig.). 1980. 9.95 (ISBN 0-9604754-2-7); pap. 6.95 (ISBN 0-9604754-1-9). Hamoroh Pr.

You: The Complete Book of Self-Knowledge. Kay Batchelor & Kurt Brent. LC 77-93326. (Illus.). 1978. 10.95 (ISBN 0-8069-4592-3); lib. bdg. 9.89 (ISBN 0-8069-4593-1). Sterling.

You, Too, Can Be Forgiven! Myrle Morris & Gwen Medina. 1978. pap. 1.95 (ISBN 0-88368-082-3). Whitaker Hse.

You Were Meant to Be Wealthy & Can Be. Howard S. King. (Orig.). 1969. pap. 1.00 o.p. (ISBN 0-8283-1041-6). Branden.

You Were Smaller Than a Dot. Glen C. Griffin. LC 72-90685. 31p. (gr. k-6). 1980. pap. 3.95 (ISBN 0-87747-817-1). Deseret Bk.

You Will Never Be the Same. Basilea Schlink. 192p. 1972. pap. 2.95 (ISBN 0-87123-661-3, 200661). Bethany Fell.

You Wouldn't Believe It. Fern Morris. 1981. 5.75 (ISBN 0-8062-1634-4). Carlton.

You'd Better Believe It! Kenneth D. Barney. LC 75-22608. (Radiant Bk). 1976. pap. 1.95 (ISBN 0-88243-887-5, 02-0887); teacher's ed 2.50 (ISBN 0-88243-161-7, 32-0161). Gospel Pub.

You'll Hear Me Laughing. R. L. Gordon. LC 78-69534. 1979. 8.95 o.s.i. (ISBN 0-690-01791-X, TYC-T). T Y Crowell.

You'll Never Get Lost Again. Robert R. Singleton. (Illus.). 1979. 9.95 (ISBN 0-87691-294-3); pap. 6.95 (ISBN 0-87691-295-1). Winchester Pr.

You'll Never Hang Me. Lee Deighton. 160p. 1981. pap. 1.75 (ISBN 0-345-29119-0). Ballantine.

Young Admiral. James Shirley et al. Ed. by Kenneth J. Ericksen & Stephen Orgel. LC 78-66752. (Renaissance Drama Ser.). 1979. lib. bdg. 20.00 (ISBN 0-8240-9746-7). Garland Pub.

Young Adolescent. Peter Blos. LC 73-125597. 1970. 15.95 (ISBN 0-02-904310-7); pap. 3.95 (ISBN 0-02-904300-X). Free Pr.

Young Adult: Development After Adolescence. Gene Bocknek. LC 80-15148. 250p. 1980. text ed. 9.95 (ISBN 0-8185-0387-4). Brooks-Cole.

Young Adult Literature: Background & Criticisms. Ed. by Millicent Lenz & Ramona Mahood. LC 80-23489. 524p. 1980. 30.00 (ISBN 0-8389-0302-9). ALA.

Young Adult Literature in the Seventies: A Selection of Readings. Ed. by Jana Varlejs. LC 78-6562. 1978. lib. bdg. 13.50 (ISBN 0-8108-1134-0). Scarecrow.

Young Adulthood. John Scanlon. 1979. pap. 5.00 (ISBN 0-89492-005-7, Pub. by Acad Ed Dev). Interbk Inc.

Young Adventurers' Series, 6 vols. Peter L. Dixon. Incl. Deep Dive. LC 79-178208 (ISBN 0-8372-1867-5); Fast Snow. LC 70-178211 (ISBN 0-8372-1870-5); Fire Guard. LC 71-178206 (ISBN 0-8372-1869-1); Silent Flight. LC 75-178207 (ISBN 0-8372-1868-3); Test Run. LC 72-178209 (ISBN 0-8372-1866-7); Wipe Out. LC 77-178210 (ISBN 0-8372-1865-9). (gr. 3 up). 1971. 6 bks. of 1 title with tchr's guide 16.77 o.p. (ISBN 0-685-56188-7); text ed. 115.83 complete series o.p. (ISBN 0-8372-0469-0); tchr's guide 3.21, free with 10 or more books o.p. (ISBN 0-8372-0729-0); posters avail. o.p. (ISBN 0-8372-0742-8); 12.00 set o.p. (ISBN 0-686-67218-6). Bowmar-Noble.

Young Alaskans. Emerson Hough. 1976. lib. bdg. 14.25x (ISBN 0-89968-049-6). Lightyear.

Young Alaskans in the Rockies. Emerson Hough. 1976. lib. bdg. 15.25x (ISBN 0-89968-050-X). Lightyear.

Young American Series, 5 bks. Margaret W. Hudson & Ann A. Weaver. Incl. Bk. 1. In Your Family. 1973 (ISBN 0-8224-7025-X); Bk. 2. In Your Community. 1973 (ISBN 0-8224-7026-8); Bk. 3. In Your State. 1973 (ISBN 0-8224-7027-6); Bk. 4. In Your Country. 1973 (ISBN 0-8224-7028-4); Bk. 5. Know Your Rights. LC 65-158878. 1971 (ISBN 0-8224-7029-2). (Illus.). (gr. 4-12). 1973. pap. 2.00 ea.; tchrs' manual free (ISBN 0-8224-7652-5). Pitman Learning.

Young America's Cookbook. Dorothy Callahan & Alma S. Payne. LC 59-5171. (Illus.). 320p. (gr. 7-9). 1959. 6.95 (ISBN 0-684-12358-4). Scribner.

Young & Black in America. Ed. by Rae P. Alexander & Julius Lester. (Sundial Paperbks.). 1972. pap. 1.95 (ISBN 0-394-70804-0, VS4, Vin). Random.

Young & Black in America. Ed. by Rae P. Alexander & Julius Lester. (Illus.). 137p. Date not set. pap. 1.50 (ISBN 0-394-70804-0, Vin). Random.

Young & Female. Pat Ross. (Illus.). 108p. Date not set. pap. 2.95 (ISBN 0-394-70808-3, Vin). Random.

Young Apostle: A Story of Torment & Revelation. Thomas B. Eckert. LC 79-67515. 122p. 1980. 6.50 (ISBN 0-533-04471-5). Vantage.

Young Ardizzone: An Autobiographical Fragment. Edward Ardizzone. (Illus.). 1971. 7.95 o.s.i. (ISBN 0-02-503000-0). Macmillan.

Young at Any Age. Ira Von Furstenberg. (Illus.). 208p. 1981. 12.95 (ISBN 0-02-622100-4). Macmillan.

Young Bisexuals. (Illus.). pap. 5.00 (ISBN 0-910550-62-X). Centurion Pr.

Young Boys Gone. Myrtle Archer. LC 77-78983. (gr. 7 up). 1978. 7.95 o.s.i. (ISBN 0-8027-6304-9). Walker & Co.

Young Catholic Family. Andrew Greeley. (Illus.). 1980. pap. 12.95 (ISBN 0-88347-122-1). Thomas More.

Young Cherry Trees Secured Against Hares. bilingual ed. Andre Breton. LC 69-15847. Orig. Title: Jeunes Cerisiers Garantis Contre les Lievres. (Illus., Fr. & Eng.). 1969. 5.00 o.p. (ISBN 0-472-17910-1). U of Mich Pr.

Young Child As Person: Toward the Development of Healthy Conscience. Martha Snyder et al. 1980. 19.95 (ISBN 0-87705-466-5). Human Sci Pr.

Young Child: His Activities & Materials. Margaret Stant. (Illus.). 160p. 1972. pap. text ed. 9.95 (ISBN 0-13-977157-3). P-H.

Young Children & the Eucharist. Urban T. Holmes. pap. 2.95 (ISBN 0-8164-5700-X). Crossroad NY.

Young Children & Their Problems. Clyde M. Narramore. (Christian Psychology Ser). 1961. pap. 0.75 o.p. (ISBN 0-310-30222-6). Zondervan.

Young Children Thinking. Alice Yardley. 144p. 1973. 3.25 o.p. (ISBN 0-590-07331-1, Citation). Schol Bk Serv.

Young Children with Special Needs. Nancy Fallen & Jill McGovern. (Special Education Ser.). 1978. text ed. 13.95 (ISBN 0-675-08382-6). study guide 3.95 (ISBN 0-675-08383-4). Merrill.

Young Children's Thinking: Studies of Some Aspects of Piaget's Theory. Millie Almy et al. LC 66-16091. (Illus., Orig.). 1966. pap. text ed. 5.75 o.p. (ISBN 0-8077-1017-2). Tchrs Coll.

Young Christians in Russia. Michael Bourdeaux & Katharine Murray. LC 76-57846. 1977. pap. 1.95 (ISBN 0-87123-663-X, 200663). Bethany Fell.

Young Christian's Life. Richard Grunze. (gr. 7-8). 1979. 8.50 (ISBN 0-8100-0104-7, 06N0557). Northwest Pub.

Young Frankenstein. Gilbert Pearlman. (Illus.). 160p. 1974. pap. 1.50 o.p. (ISBN 0-345-24268-8). Ballantine.

Young Homemaker's Cookbook. Ann A. Weaver. (gr. 7 up). 1974. pap. 2.80 (ISBN 0-8224-7675-4); tchrs' manual free (ISBN 0-8224-7678-9). Pitman Learning.

Young Horse Management. Ann L. Hardman. 1976. 11.95 (ISBN 0-7207-0904-0, Pub. by Michael Joseph). Merrimack Bk Serv.

Young Internationalists. Ed. by Thomas A. Hiatt & Mark F. Gerzon. LC 70-188981. 224p. 1973. 12.00x (ISBN 0-8248-0218-7, Eastwest Ctr). U Pr of Hawaii.

Young Ireland. Charles G. Duffy. LC 71-127257. (Europe 1815-1945 Ser.). 796p. 1973. Repr. of 1881 ed. lib. bdg. 59.50 (ISBN 0-306-71119-2). Da Capo.

Young Israel: A History of the Modern Nation the First 20 Years. Owen S. Rachleff. (Illus.). (gr. 7 up). 1981. PLB 7.95 (ISBN 0-87460-115-0). Lion.

Young Lady of Fashion. Mary A. Gibbs. 1979. pap. 1.75 o.p. (ISBN 0-449-23843-1, Crest). Fawcett.

Young Lady's Accidence. Caleb Bingham. 1980. Repr. of 1785 ed. 30.00 (ISBN 0-8201-1360-3). Schol Facsimilies.

Young Landlords. Walter D. Meyers. 1980. pap. 1.95 (ISBN 0-686-69271-3, 52191). Avon.

Young Lions of Judah. Mike Evans & Bob Summers. 116p. 1974. pap. 1.95 o.p. (ISBN 0-88270-059-6). Logos.

Young Living. rev. ed. Nanalee Clayton. (Illus.). (gr. 7-8). 1970. text ed. 15.36 (ISBN 0-87002-011-0); tchr guide avail. (ISBN 0-685-06852-8). Bennett IL.

Young Louis Fourteenth: The Early Years of the Sun King. Burke Wilkinson. LC 70-89596. (Illus.). (gr. 7 up). 1970. 4.95g o.s.i. (ISBN 0-02-792960-4). Macmillan.

Young Man Growing up. Jessie M. Hall. 1979. 4.00 o.p. (ISBN 0-8062-1234-9). Carlton.

Young Man in American Literature: The Initiation Theme. Ed. by William Coyle. LC 68-31707. (Perspectives on American Lit. Ser). (Orig.). 1969. pap. 7.95 (ISBN 0-672-63147-4). Odyssey Pr.

Young Man in Search of Love. Isaac B. Singer. LC 77-2538. (Illus.). 1978. 12.95 (ISBN 0-385-12357-4); limited ed. o.p. 50.00 (ISBN 0-385-13492-4). Doubleday.

Young Mark Twain & the Mississippi. Harnett T. Kane. (Landmark Ser.: No. 113). (Illus.). (gr. 4-6). 1966. PLB 4.39 o.p. (ISBN 0-394-90413-3, BYR). Random.

Young Melvin & Bulger. Mark Taylor. LC 79-7118. (Illus.). 48p. (gr. 4-6). 1981. 7.95a (ISBN 0-385-15190-X); PLB (ISBN 0-385-15191-8). Doubleday.

Young Men's Gold. Daniel M. Epstein. LC 77-20739. 1978. 10.00 (ISBN 0-87951-071-4); pap. 5.95 (ISBN 0-87951-076-5). Overlook Pr.

Young Merchant & the Indian Captive, a Tale Founded on Fact, Repr. Of 1851 Ed. Henry Diffenderffer. Bd. with Revolutionary Incident, the Captivity of Capt. Jeremiah Snyder & Elias Snyder of Saugerties: In: Saugerties Telegraph, V. 5, No. 13-14, Jan. 25 & Feb. 1, 1851. Charles G. De Witt. Repr. of 1851 ed; Historical Traditions of Tennessee. the Captivity of Jane Brown & Her Family. Extract from American Whig Review, v.15, p.233-349. Repr. of 1852 ed; Scenes in Texas, Being a Recital of the Sufferings of a Lady in Her Escape from the Indians... by I. Call, Who Saw the Lady Before Her Recovery from the Affects of Her Sufferings. I. Call. Repr. of 1852 ed; Lost Child: Or the Child Claimed by Two Mothers: a Narrative of the Loss & Discovery of Casper A. Partridge Among the Menomonee Indians, with a Concise Abstract of Court Testimony, & a Review of Commissioner Buttrick's Decision. Florus B. Plimpton. Repr. of 1852 ed; Indian Battles, Murders, Sieges & Forays in the Southwest. Containing the Narratives of Gen. Hall, Col. Brown, Capt. Carr, John Davis, John Bosley, Samuel Blair, John Rains, Dr. Shelby, Thomas Everett. Repr. of 1853 ed. LC 75-7088. (Indian Captivities Ser.: Vol. 64). 1976. lib. bdg. 44.00 (ISBN 0-8240-1688-2). Garland Pub.

Young Mr. Pepys. John Hearsay. LC 73-8273. (Encore Ed.). (Illus.). 1974. 3.95 o.p. (ISBN 0-684-15948-1, ScribT). Scribner.

Young Mistley. Henry S. Merriman. Ed. by Herbert Van Thal. 1888-1966. 5.00 (ISBN 0-304-93090-3); pap. 2.95 (ISBN 0-685-09212-7). Dufour.

Young Mrs. Burton. Margaret Penn. 256p. Date not set. pap. 8.95 (ISBN 0-521-28298-5). Cambridge U Pr.

Young Mrs. Ruskin in Venice. Mary Lutyens. LC 66-28881. (Illus.). 1966. 12.50 (ISBN 0-8149-0150-6). Vanguard.

Young Mussolini & the Intellectual Origins of Fascism. A. James Gregor. 1979. 18.50x (ISBN 0-520-03799-5). U of Cal Pr.

Young Nixon: An Oral Inquiry. Ed. by Renee K. Schulte. 1978. 13.95 (ISBN 0-930046-02-1); pap. 7.95 (ISBN 0-930046-01-3). CSUF Oral Hist.

Young Offer a New Step. Wilmon H. Sheldon. 1970. 3.95 o.p. (ISBN 0-8158-0249-8). Chris Mass.

Young Only Once. Clyde M. Narramore. (gr. 8 up). pap. 2.95 (ISBN 0-310-29972-1). Zondervan.

Young People & Crime. Arthur H. Cain. LC 68-11297. (John Day Bk.). 1969. 5.95 o.s.i. (ISBN 0-381-98064-2, A93200, TYC-T). T Y Crowell.

Young People & Cultural Institutions. 87p. 1980. pap. 7.50 (ISBN 92-3-101698-9, U 1001, UNESCO). Unipub.

Young People & Drugs. Arthur H. Cain. LC 69-10816. (John Day Bk.). (YA) 1969. 4.95 o.s.i. (ISBN 0-381-98066-9, A93800, TYC-T). T Y Crowell.

Young People & Leisure. John Leigh. (International Library of Sociology & Social Reconstruction). 1971. text ed. 9.00x (ISBN 0-7100-7059-4). Humanities.

Young People & Work. Arthur H. Cain. LC 78-162597. (John Day Bk.). (YA) 1971. 4.95 o.s.i. (ISBN 0-381-98074-X, A94300, TYC-T). T Y Crowell.

Young People's Literature in Series: Fiction, Non-Fiction, & Publishers' Series, 1973-1975. Judith K. Rosenberg. LC 77-57963. 1977. lib. bdg. 17.50x (ISBN 0-87287-140-1). Libs Unl.

Young People's Science Dictionary, 2 vols. Young People's Science Encyclopedia Editors. LC 67-17925. (Illus.). (gr. 4 up). 1979. lib. bdg. 15.95 (ISBN 0-516-00274-0). Childrens.

Young Performing Horse. John Yeoman. LC 78-6304. (Illus.). 40p. (ps-3). 1978. 5.95 (ISBN 0-590-07726-0, Four Winds); PLB 5.41 (ISBN 0-8193-0971-0). Schol Bk Serv.

Young Person's Book of Catholic Words. William Jacobs. LC 80-2078. 128p. (gr. 6 up). 1981. pap. 2.75 (ISBN 0-385-17434-9, Im). Doubleday.

Young Person's Guide to Playing the Piano. 2nd ed. Sidney Harrison. (Illus.). 1973. 5.95 o.p. (ISBN 0-571-04787-4, Pub. by Faber & Faber). Merrimack Bk Serv.

Young Philosopher: A Novel, 4 vols. Charlotte Smith. (Feminist Controversy in England, 1788-1810 Ser.). 1974. Set. lib. bdg. 154.00 (ISBN 0-8240-0881-2). lib. bdg. 60.50 ea. Garland Pub.

Young Pianist: An Approach for Teachers & Students. 2nd ed. Joan Last. (Illus.). 168p. 1972. pap. 9.95x (ISBN 0-19-318420-6). Oxford U Pr.

Young Player's Guide to Cricket. Derek Randall. LC 80-66427. (Illus.). 96p. 1980. 13.50 (ISBN 0-7153-7991-7). David & Charles.

Young Player's Guide to Soccer. Jim Bebbington. LC 78-66970. 1979. 11.95 (ISBN 0-7153-7536-9). David & Charles.

Young Prophet Niebuhr: Reinhold Niebuhr's Early Search for Social Justice. Ernest F. Dibble. 1978. pap. text ed. 11.50x (ISBN 0-8191-0377-2). U Pr of Amer.

Young Readers Bible. Ed. by Henry M. Bullock & Edward C. Peterson. (Illus.). (gr. 3 up). 1978. pap. 6.95 (ISBN 0-687-46800-0). Abingdon.

Young Readers Book of Christian Symbolism. Michael Daves. (Illus.). (gr. 5 up). 1967. 10.95 (ISBN 0-687-46824-8). Abingdon.

Young Renny. Mazo De La Roche. 1976. pap. 1.50 o.p. (ISBN 0-449-22842-8, Q2842, Crest). Fawcett.

Young Rider's Companion. George Wheatley. (Adult & Young Adult Bks.). (Illus.). 120p. (gr. 4 up). 1981. PLB 14.95 (ISBN 0-8225-0767-6). Lerner Pubns.

Young Sam Johnson. James L. Clifford. (McGraw-Hill Paperbacks Ser.). (Illus.). 400p. 1981. pap. 6.95 (ISBN 0-07-011381-5). McGraw.

Young Scarron. Thomas Mozeen. (Flowering of the Novel, 1740-1775 Ser: Vol. 37). 1974. Repr. of 1752 ed. lib. bdg. 50.00 (ISBN 0-8240-1136-8). Garland Pub.

Young Scientist Book of Jets. Mark Hewish. LC 78-17507. (Young Scientist Ser.). (Illus.). (gr. 4-5). 1978. text ed. 6.95 (ISBN 0-88436-527-1). EMC.

Young Scientist Book of Spaceflight. Kenneth Gatland. (Young Scientist Ser.). (gr. 4-5). text ed. 6.95 (ISBN 0-88436-526-3). EMC.

Young Scientist Book of Stars & Planets. Christopher Maynard. LC 78-17545. (Young Scientist Ser.). (Illus.). (gr. 3-5). 1978. text ed. 6.95 (ISBN 0-88436-528-X). EMC.

Young Scientist Book of the Undersea. Christopher Pick. LC 78-17796. (Young Scientist Ser.). (Illus.). (gr. 4-5). 1978. text ed. 6.95 (ISBN 0-88436-529-8). EMC.

Young Students' Book of Child Care. 4th ed. Leonora Pitcairn. LC 76-58076. 1978. 6.50x (ISBN 0-521-21671-0). Cambridge U Pr.

Young Thomas Edison. Sterling North. (North Star Bks). (Illus.). (gr. 7-11). 1958. 2.95 o.p. (ISBN 0-395-07252-2). HM.

Young Towns of Lima. P. Lloyd. LC 79-51826. (Urbanization in Developing Countries Ser.). (Orig.). 1980. 34.50 (ISBN 0-521-22871-9); pap. 9.95 (ISBN 0-521-29688-9). Cambridge U Pr.

Young Trailers. Joseph Altsheler. 1976. lib. bdg. 15.30x (ISBN 0-89968-005-4). Lightyear.

Young Tycoons. Gloria D. Miklowitz & Madelein Yates. LC 80-8803. (Illus.). 128p. (gr. 7 up). 1981. 9.95 (ISBN 0-15-299879-9, HJ). HarBraceJ.

Young Unicorns. Madeline L'Engle. (YA) (gr. 7-12). 1980. pap. 1.75 (ISBN 0-440-99919-7, LFL). Dell.

Young United States 1783 to 1830. Edwin Tunis. LC 75-29613. (Illus.). 160p. (gr. 7 up). 1976. 12.95 (ISBN 0-690-01065-6, TYC-J). T Y Crowell.

Young Van Dyck. Alan McNairn. (Illus.). 1980. 29.95 (ISBN 0-88884-456-5, 56579-3, Pub. by Natl Mus Canada); pap. 19.95 (ISBN 0-88884-468-9, 56578-5). U of Chicago Pr.

Young Victoria. Alison Plowden. LC 80-5908. (Illus.). 208p. 1981. 12.95 (ISBN 0-8128-2766-X). Stein & Day.

Young Voices. Ed. by Charles E. Schaefer & Kathleen Mellor. (gr. 3 up). 1972. pap. 0.95 o.s.i. (ISBN 0-02-044960-7, Collier). Macmillan.

Young Voices in American Poetry-1980. Gary Wilding. LC 79-92559. 304p. (Orig.). 1980. pap. text ed. 7.95 (ISBN 0-936092-00-9, 101). Harbinger Pr.

Young Voltaire. Cleveland B. Chase. 253p. 1980. Repr. of 1926 ed. lib. bdg. 35.00 (ISBN 0-8495-0799-5). Arden Lib.

Young Voyageur: Trade & Treachery at Michilimackinac. rev. ed. Dirk Gringhuis. (Illus.). 202p. (gr. 9 up). 1969. pap. 2.50 (ISBN 0-911872-34-5). Mackinac Island.

Young Wellington in India. C. H. Philips. (Creighton Lecture in History Ser). (Illus., Orig.). 1974. pap. text ed. 2.50x (ISBN 0-485-14120-5, Athlone Pr). Humanities.

Young Wife's Tale. William Sansom. 1979. 7.95 (ISBN 0-7012-0396-X, Pub. by Chatto Bodley Jonathan). Merrimack Bk Serv.

Young Winners Flag Football. Ed. by Jerry Glashagel. (Illus.). 65p. 1980. spiral bdg. 29.95 (ISBN 0-936446-04-8). Youth Sports.

Young Winners Soccer. Ed. by Jerry Glashagel. (Illus.). 57p. 1980. spiral bdg. 29.95 (ISBN 0-936446-03-X). Youth Sports.

Young Wives Encyclopedia. Wickham Griffith. 7.95 (ISBN 0-392-08155-0, SpS). Soccer.

Young Woman's Guide to Liberation: Alternatives to a Half-Life While the Choice Is Still Yours. Karen DeCrow. LC 72-141377. 1971. pap. 7.50 (ISBN 0-672-63615-8). Pegasus.

Young Worker at College. Ethel Venables. (Society Today & Tomorrow Ser.). (Illus., Orig.). 1967. 9.95 (ISBN 0-571-08070-7, Pub. by Faber & Faber). Merrimack Bk Serv.

Young Wrestler. Thompson Clayton. LC 77-1208. (Illus.). 125p. 1977. pap. 3.95 (ISBN 0-87095-064-9). Athletic.

Young Writer at Work. Ed. by Jessie Rehder. LC 62-11938. 1962. 8.95 (ISBN 0-672-63148-2). Odyssey Pr.

Younger Goethe & the Visual Arts. W. D. Robson-Scott. (Angelica Germanica Ser.). 200p. 49.50 (ISBN 0-521-23321-6). Cambridge U Pr.

Youngest Captain. Jay Williams. LC 72-629. 48p. (gr. k-3). 1972. 5.95 o.s.i. (ISBN 0-8193-0594-4, Four Winds); PLB 5.41 o.s.i. (ISBN 0-8193-0595-2). Schol Bk Serv.

Young's Analytical Concordance to the Bible. Robert Young. 1955. 19.95 (ISBN 0-8028-8084-3); pap. 19.95 (ISBN 0-8028-8085-1). Eerdmans.

Your Adversary the Devil. J. Dwight Pentecost. 192p. 1976. pap. 4.95 (ISBN 0-310-30911-5). Zondervan.

Your Aladdin's Lamp. William H. Hornaday & Harlan Ware. 1978. pap. 7.95 (ISBN 0-911336-75-3). Sci of Mind.

Your American Government. Norman C. Thomas & Fredrick C. Stoerker. LC 79-26788. 1980. text ed. 15.95 o.p. (ISBN 0-471-03031-7); write for info tchr's ed o.p. (ISBN 0-471-06330-4); study guide o.p. (ISBN 0-471-07907-3). Wiley.

Your Ant Is a Which: Fun with Homophones. Bernice K. Hunt. LC 75-37582. (Let Me Read Ser.). (Illus.). 32p. (gr. 1-5). 1976. 4.95 o.p. (ISBN 0-15-299880-2, HJ). HarBraceJ.

Your Appointment with Success. rev. ed. Bjorn Secher. LC 75-135747. 1980. pap. 4.95 (ISBN 0-8119-0354-0). Fell.

Your Aquarium - Your Vacation - Your Relocation. G. Steven Dow. (Illus.). 64p. (Orig.). 1976. pap. 2.50 (ISBN 0-87666-456-7, M528). TFH Pubns.

Your Automatic Camera. Dennis Curtin. (Your Automatic Camera Ser.). (Illus.). 128p. (Orig.). 1980. lib. bdg. 6.95 (ISBN 0-930764-17-X). Curtin & London.

Your Automatic Camera. Dennis Curtin & Barbara London. 144p. 1980. pap. 6.95 (ISBN 0-442-25871-2). Van Nos Reinhold.

Your Automatic Camera Indoors. Barbara London & Richard Boyer. 1981. pap. 6.95 (ISBN 0-442-21956-3). Van Nos Reinhold.

Your Automatic Camera Outdoors. Barbara London & Richard Boyer. 1981. pap. 6.95 (ISBN 0-442-21955-5). Van Nos Reinhold.

Your Baby & Child: From Birth to Age Five. Penelope Leach. pap. 9.95 (ISBN 0-394-73509-9). Knopf.

Your Baby: Pregnancy, Delivery, & Infant Care. Jean P. Cohen & Roger Goirand. (Illus.). 304p. 1981. 16.95 (ISBN 0-13 978130-7, Spec); pap. 8.95 (ISBN 0-13-978122-6). P-H.

Your Biblical Garden: Plants of the Bible & How to Grow Them. Allan A. Swenson. LC 79-7703. (Illus.). 240p. 1981. 13.95 (ISBN 0-385-14898-4). Doubleday.

Your Body - Biofeedback at Its Best. Beate Jencks. LC 77-24618. (Illus.). 1978. 15.95 (ISBN 0-88229-351-6); pap. 8.95 (ISBN 0-88229-508-X). Nelson-Hall.

Your Body & How It Works. Patricia Lauber. (Gateway Ser.: No. 25). (Illus.). (gr. 3-5). 1962. 2.95 o.p. (ISBN 0-685-19707-7, BYR); PLB 5.99 (ISBN 0-394-90125-8). Random.

Your Body & How It Works. J. D. Ratcliff. 1975. 8.95 o.s.i. (ISBN 0-440-09896-3). Delacorte.

Your Body, His Temple. Alfred L. Heller. 192p. 1981. pap. 4.95 (ISBN 0-8407-5769-7). Nelson.

Your Body Works: A Guide to Health, Energy & Balance. Ed. by Gerald Kogan. LC 77-79272. (Illus.). 177p. (Orig.). 1980. pap. 10.95 (ISBN 0-930162-02-1). Transform Berkeley.

Your Book About the Way a Car Works. 2nd ed. Harry Heywood & Patrick MacNaghten. (Your Book Ser.). (Illus.). 1971. 5.95 (ISBN 0-571-04749-1, Pub. by Faber & Faber). Merrimack Bk Serv.

Your Book of Acting. Kenneth Nuttall. (Illus.). 84p. (gr. 4-9). 1972. 7.95 (ISBN 0-571-04668-1). Transatlantic.

Your Book of Animal Drawing. Cyril Cowell. (gr. 7 up). 7.50 (ISBN 0-571-05139-1). Transatlantic.

Your Book of Archaeology. Rith Whitehouse. (gr. 6 up). 1979. 6.95 (ISBN 0-571-11255-2, Pub. by Faber & Faber). Merrimack Bk Serv.

Your Book of Astronomy. 4th ed. Patrick Moore. (Illus.). (gr. 6 up). 1979. 6.95 (ISBN 0-571-04951-6, Pub. by Faber & Faber). Merrimack Bk Serv.

Your Book of Badminton. Len Wright. (gr. 4 up). 1972. 6.95 (ISBN 0-571-09890-8). Transatlantic.

Your Book of Ballet. (Illus.). 77p. (gr. 7-9). 1975. 7.95 (ISBN 0-571-10241-7). Transatlantic.

Your Book of Breadmaking. Cecilia H. Hinde. (Your Book Ser.). (Illus.). 1977. 6.95 (ISBN 0-571-10641-2, Pub. by Faber & Faber). Merrimack Bk Serv.

Your Book of Bridges. Eric De Mare. (Year Book Ser.). (Illus.). 1963. 6.95 (ISBN 0-571-05285-1, Pub. by Faber & Faber). Merrimack Bk Serv.

Your Book of Butterflies & Moths. H. B. Kettlewell. (Your Book Ser.). (Illus.). 1963. 6.95 (ISBN 0-571-05576-1, Pub. by Faber & Faber). Merrimack Bk Serv.

Your Book of Canals. P. J. Ransom. (Your Book Ser.). (Illus.). 1977. 6.95 (ISBN 0-571-10971-3, Pub. by Faber & Faber). Merrimack Bk Serv.

Your Book of Chess. Raymond Bott & Stanley Morrison. (gr. 7 up). 1968. 6.25 (ISBN 0-571-08112-6). Transatlantic.

Your Book of Contract Bridge. Terence Reese. (gr. 7 up). 1971. 5.50 (ISBN 0-571-06387-X). Transatlantic.

Your Book of Corn Dollies. Joan Rendell. (Illus.). 1976. 6.95 (ISBN 0-571-10841-5, Pub. by Faber & Faber). Merrimack Bk Serv.

Your Book of Cricket. Alan Duff & D. W. Chesterton. (Your Book Ser.). (Illus.). 1970. 6.95 (ISBN 0-571-10237-9, Pub. by Faber & Faber). Merrimack Bk Serv.

Your Book of English Country Dancing. Priscilla Lobley & Robert Lobley. (Your Book Ser.). (Illus.). (gr. 4 up). 1980. 8.95 (ISBN 0-571-11522-5, Pub. by Faber & Faber). Merrimack Bk Serv.

Your Book of Flower Arranging. Sheila MacQueen. 1972. 5.95 (ISBN 0-571-09625-5, Pub. by Faber & Faber). Merrimack Bk Serv.

Your Book of Flower Making. Priscilla Lobley. 1970. 6.95 (ISBN 0-571-09294-2, Pub. by Faber & Faber). Merrimack Bk Serv.

Your Book of Freshwater Life. John Clegg. (Illus.). (gr. 7 up). 1968. 5.95 (ISBN 0-571-08399-4). Transatlantic.

Your Book of Golf. D. C. Hudson. (Your Book Ser.). (Illus.). 1967. 6.95 (ISBN 0-571-08123-1, Pub. by Faber & Faber). Merrimack Bk Serv.

Your Book of Industrial Archaeology. Christine Vialls. (Illus.). 80p. (gr. 4-12). 1981. 9.95 (ISBN 0-571-11633-7, Pub. by Faber & Faber). Merrimack Bk Serv.

Your Book of Judo. George Glass. (Your Book Ser). (Illus.). 1978. 5.95 o.p. (ISBN 0-571-11054-1, Pub. by Faber & Faber). Merrimack Bk Serv.

Your Book of Keeping Ponies. 2nd ed. Janet Holyoake. (Your Book Ser.). (Illus.). 1968. 6.95 (ISBN 0-571-04604-5, Pub. by Faber & Faber). Merrimack Bk Serv.

Your Book of Kites. Clive Hart. (gr. 7 up). 1964. 6.50 (ISBN 0-571-04712-2). Transatlantic.

Your Book of Landscape Drawing. Edwin La Dell. (Your Book Ser.). (Illus.). 1964. 7.95 (ISBN 0-571-05888-4, Pub. by Faber & Faber). Merrimack Bk Serv.

Your Book of Men in Space. David Wilson. (Your Book Ser.). (Illus.). 1976. 6.95 (ISBN 0-571-10937-3, Pub. by Faber & Faber). Merrimack Bk Serv.

Your Book of Money. David Jones. (gr. 7 up). 1971. 6.50 (ISBN 0-571-09341-8). Transatlantic.

Your Book of Music. Imogen Holst. (Your Book Ser.). (Illus.). 1964. 4.95 o.p. (ISBN 0-571-05917-1, Pub. by Faber & Faber). Merrimack Bk Serv.

Your Book of Painting. Robert Lobley. (Your Book Ser). (Illus.). 1978. 7.95 (ISBN 0-571-10776-1, Pub. by Faber & Faber). Merrimack Bk Serv.

Your Book of Parliament. D. M. Prentice. (Your Book Ser.). (Illus.). (gr. 5 up). 1967. 7.95 (ISBN 0-571-08129-0, Pub. by Faber & Faber). Merrimack Bk Serv.

Your Book of Patience. G. F. Hervey. (Your Book Ser.). 1966. 6.95 (ISBN 0-571-06560-0, Pub. by Faber & Faber). Merrimack Bk Serv.

Your Book of Pet Keeping. Donald H. Risdon. (Illus.). (gr. 3-7). 1964. 6.75 (ISBN 0-571-05771-3). Transatlantic.

Your Book of Photography. John H. Moore. (Your Book Ser.). (Illus.). 1967. 5.95 (ISBN 0-571-08127-4, Pub. by Faber & Faber). Merrimack Bk Serv.

Your Book of Prehistoric Animals. Terry Jennings. (Illus.). 64p. (gr. 5-8). 1980. 8.95 (ISBN 0-571-11455-5, Pub. by Faber & Faber). Merrimack Bk Serv.

Your Book of Prehistoric Britain. James Dyer. (Your Book Ser.). (Illus.). (gr. 5 up). 1974. 7.95 (ISBN 0-571-09883-5, Pub. by Faber & Faber). Merrimack Bk Serv.

Your Book of Pressed & Dried Flowers. Joan Rendell. (gr. 4 up). 1979. 6.95 (ISBN 0-571-11249-8, Pub. by Faber Faber). Merrimack Bk Serv.

Your Book of Puppetry. Vicki Rutter. 1969. 5.95 (ISBN 0-571-08291-2, Pub. by Faber & Faber). Merrimack Bk Serv.

Your Book of Roman Britain. David Jones. (Your Book Ser.). (Illus.). 1978. 7.95 (ISBN 0-571-09903-3, Pub. by Faber & Faber). Merrimack Bk Serv.

Your Book of Self-Defence. Pat Butler. (Your Book Ser.). (Illus.). 1968. 5.95 o.p. (ISBN 0-571-08290-4, Pub. by Faber & Faber). Merrimack Bk Serv.

Your Book of Shell Collecting. L. W. Stratton. (Illus.). (gr. 7 up). 1968. 5.95 (ISBN 0-571-08211-4). Transatlantic.

Your Book of Soccer. Robin Trimby. (Illus.). (gr. 7 up). 1968. 6.95 (ISBN 0-571-04752-1). Transatlantic.

Your Book of Sound. D. M. Desoutter. Tr. by D. L. Jenkins. (Illus.). (gr. 7 up). 1971. 5.95 (ISBN 0-571-09530-5). Transatlantic.

Your Book of Space Travel. Denis M. Desoutter. (gr. 7 up). 6.50 (ISBN 0-571-04720-3). Transatlantic.

Your Book of Squash. R. B. Hawkey. (Your Book Ser.). (Illus.). 1966. 6.95 (ISBN 0-571-06577-5, Pub. by Faber & Faber). Merrimack Bk Serv.

Your Book of Stamps. James Watson. (Your Book Ser.). (Illus.). 1966. 3.95 o.p. (ISBN 0-571-06647-X, Pub. by Faber & Faber). Merrimack Bk Serv.

Your Book of Survival Swimming & Lifesaving. Margaret A. Jarvis. (gr. 6 up). 9.50 (ISBN 0-571-06438-8). Transatlantic.

Your Book of Swimming. 3rd ed. Margaret Jarvis. (gr. 4 up). 1979. 6.95 (ISBN 0-571-04971-0, Pub. by Faber & Faber). Merrimack Bk Serv.

Your Book of Table Tennis. Victor Barna. (gr. 7 up). 1971. 6.50 (ISBN 0-571-09345-0). Transatlantic.

Your Book of Table Tennis. Victor Barna. 1977. 6.95 (ISBN 0-571-09345-0, Pub. by Faber & Faber). Merrimack Bk Serv.

Your Book of Tall Ships. Tony Hutson. (Your Book Ser.). (Illus.). 1978. 7.95 (ISBN 0-571-10889-X, Pub. by Faber & Faber). Merrimack Bk Serv.

Your Book of Television. Norman Wymer. (Your Book Ser.). (Illus.). 1966. 4.95 o.p. (ISBN 0-571-06791-3, Pub. by Faber & Faber). Merrimack Bk Serv.

Your Book of Tennis. C. M. Jones. (gr. 4 up). 1970. 7.95 (ISBN 0-571-08767-1). Transatlantic.

Your Book of the Earth. Ray Smithers. (Your Book Ser.). (Illus.). 1966. 4.95 o.p. (ISBN 0-571-06703-4, Pub. by Faber & Faber). Merrimack Bk Serv.

Your Book of the Guitar. Graham Wade. (Your Book Ser.). (Illus.). 64p. (gr. 3-8). 1980. 8.95 (ISBN 0-571-11553-5, Pub. by Faber & Faber). Merrimack Bk Serv.

Your Book of the Weather. Kaye Larsson. (Your Book Ser.). (Illus.). 1966. 4.95 o.p. (ISBN 0-571-06610-0, Pub. by Faber & Faber). Merrimack Bk Serv.

Your Book of Traction Engines. Alan Bloom. (Your Book Ser.). (Illus.). 1975. 6.95 (ISBN 0-571-10413-4, Pub. by Faber & Faber). Merrimack Bk Serv.

Your Brain & How It Works. Herbert S. Zim. LC 78-168479. (Illus.). 64p. (gr. 3-7). 1972. PLB 6.48 (ISBN 0-688-31922-X). Morrow.

Your Brain Is Younger Than You Think: A Guide to Mental Aging. Richard M. Torack. LC 80-21239. 164p. 1981. text ed. 14.95 (ISBN 0-88229-538-1); pap. 7.95 (ISBN 0-88229-761-9). Nelson-Hall.

Your Brother's Keeper: A Guide for Families of the Mentall Ill. James R. Morrison. LC 79-27810. 352p. 1981. 20.95 (ISBN 0-88229-563-2). Nelson-Hall.

Your Business Problems Solved. Paul Jenner. LC 79-51089. 1979. 17.95 (ISBN 0-7153-7646-2). David & Charles.

Your Career As a Medical Secretary-Transcriber. S. G. Berkeley & B. E. Jackson. LC 74-34233. 1975. 12.95 (ISBN 0-471-07020-3, Pub. by Wiley Medical). Wiley.

Your Career As a Physician. Carin Quinn. LC 79-802. 1979. lib. bdg. 5.95 (ISBN 0-668-04742-9, 4742); pap. 3.50 (ISBN 0-668-04753-4, 4753). Arco.

Your Career As a Writer. Mary L. Hansen. (Arco Career Guidance Ser.). lib. bdg. 6.95 (ISBN 0-668-04500-0); pap. 3.50 (ISBN 0-668-04503-5). Arco.

Your Career: Choices, Chances, Changes. David C. Borchard et al. 368p. 1980. pap. text ed. 15.95 (ISBN 0-8403-2293-3). Kendall-Hunt.

Your Career: How to Plan It-Manage It-Change It. 2nd ed. Richard H. Buskirk. LC 80-15509. 168p. 1980. pap. 9.95 (ISBN 0-8436-0790-4). CBI Pub.

Your Career in Air Conditioning, Refrigeration & Related Engineering Careers. Donald F. Daly. LC 78-701. 1979. lib. bdg. 6.95 (ISBN 0-668-04562-0); pap. 3.50 (ISBN 0-668-04573-6). Arco.

Your Career in Art & Design. Carolyn Hawes & Margaret Johnson. LC 76-41912. 1977. pap. 3.50 (ISBN 0-668-04141-2). Arco.

Your Career in Computer-Related Occupations. William Koller. LC 78-13700. 1979. lib. bdg. 6.95 (ISBN 0-668-04610-4); pap. 3.50 (ISBN 0-668-04622-8). Arco.

Your Career in Construction. William Koller. LC 77-17396. (Arco Career Guidance Ser.). (Illus.). 1978. lib. bdg. 6.95 (ISBN 0-668-04453-5); pap. 3.50 (ISBN 0-668-04435-7). Arco.

Your Career in Federal Civil Service. Flint O. DuPre. 288p. 1981. pap. 4.95 (ISBN 0-06-463529-5, EH529, EH). Har-Row.

Your Career in Interior Design. rev ed. Robert V. Doyle. LC 75-12634. (Messner Career Bks). (Illus.). 208p. (gr. 7 up). 1975. PLB 7.79 o.p. (ISBN 0-671-32755-0). Messner.

Your Career in Journalism. rev ed. M. L. Stein. LC 77-28141. (Messner Career Ser.). (Illus.). 1978. PLB 7.79 o.p. (ISBN 0-671-32840-9). Messner.

Your Career in Music. Richard Cornell. LC 77-13361. (Arco Career Guidance Ser.). 1979. lib. bdg. 6.95 (ISBN 0-668-04459-4); pap. 3.50 (ISBN 0-668-04461-6). Arco.

Your Career in Office Occupations. Gil Klevins. LC 77-17377. (Arco Career Guidance Ser.). (Illus.). 1978. lib. bdg. 6.95 (ISBN 0-668-04449-7); pap. 3.50 (ISBN 0-668-04434-9). Arco.

Your Career in the Beauty Industry. Susan MacDonald. LC 78-17138. (Arco Career Guidance Ser.). 1979. lib. bdg. 6.95 (ISBN 0-668-04612-0); pap. 3.50 (ISBN 0-668-04623-6). Arco.

Your Career in the Fashion Industry. JoAnn Lulow. LC 78-12724. (Arco Career Guidance Ser.). 1979. lib. bdg. 6.95 (ISBN 0-668-04613-9); pap. 3.50 (ISBN 0-668-04620-1). Arco.

Your Career in the World of Work. Milton Berlye. LC 75-12236. 1975. pap. 13.00 (ISBN 0-672-21050-9). Bobbs.

Your Career in Theater, Radio, Television or Filmmaking. Michael Allosso. LC 77-14145. (Career Guidance Ser.). (YA) 1978. lib. bdg. 6.97 (ISBN 0-668-04438-1); pap. 3.50 (ISBN 0-668-04445-4). Arco.

Your Cheatin' Heart: A Biography of Hank Williams. Chet Flippo. 1981. 12.95 (ISBN 0-671-24114-1). S&S.

Your Child & His Art. V. Lowenfeld. 1954. 8.95 o.s.i. (ISBN 0-02-575900-0). Macmillan.

Your Child & Ilael Conduit Surgery: A Guidebook for Parents. Children's Hospital Medical Center, the Health Education Department, Boston, Mass. (Illus.). 120p. 1970. pap. 11.75 (ISBN 0-398-00305-X). C C Thomas.

Your Child & Religion. Johanna L. Klink. Tr. by R. A. Wilson. LC 72-1764. 256p. 1972. 6.95 (ISBN 0-8042-2239-8). John Knox.

Your Child & the Piano: How to Enrich & Share in Your Child's Musical Experience. Margaret Grant. 104p. 1980. pap. 5.95 (ISBN 0-8253-0027-4). Beaufort Bks NY.

Your Child Can Be a Model. Caroline A. Zimmerman. (Illus.). 224p. 1981. 13.95 (ISBN 0-8015-9110-4, Hawthorn). Dutton.

Your Child Can Be a Super Reader. Len Kusnetz. LC 79-84790. 128p. 1980. pap. 3.95. Liberty Pub.

Your Child Can Be a Super-Reader: A Fun & Easy Approach to Reading Improvement. Len Kusnetz. LC 79-84790. (Illus.). 132p. (Orig.). 1980. pap. 3.95 (ISBN 0-9602730-0-X, Dist. by Liberty Pub. Co). Learning Hse.

Your Child Goes to the Hospital: A Book for Parents. Harold D. Love et al. 112p. 1972. pap. 6.75 (ISBN 0-398-02346-8). C C Thomas.

Your Child? I Thought It Was My Child. Owen Spann & Nancy Spann. 1980. pap. write for info. (ISBN 0-671-83084-8). PB.

Your Child Is a Person: A Psychological Approach to Parenthood Without Guilt. Stella Chess et al. 224p. 1977. pap. 3.50 (ISBN 0-14-004439-6). Penguin.

Your Child with Asthma. Simon Godfrey. 1975. pap. text ed. 10.00x (ISBN 0-433-12300-1). Intl Ideas.

Your Children: The Victims of Public Education. Robert Allen Hill. pap. 2.95 (ISBN 0-89728-004-0). Omega Pubns OR.

Your Child's Development in the First Five Years. Ronald Illingworth. (Churchill Livingstone Patient Handbook Ser.). (Illus.). 96p. 1981. pap. text ed. 3.00 (ISBN 0-686-28941-2). Churchill.

Your Child's Ears, Nose & Throat: A Parent's Medical Guide. D. Thane Cody. LC 73-22530. (Illus.). 192p. 1975. 10.95 o.s.i. (ISBN 0-02-526540-7). Macmillan.

Your Child's Intellect: A Guide to Home-Based Preschool Education. T. H. Bell & Arden R. Thorum. LC 73-159374. (Illus.). 192p. 1972. 8.95 (ISBN 0-913420-02-6); pap. 6.95 o.p. (ISBN 0-913420-03-4). Olympus Pub Co.

Your Church Can Grow. C. Peter Wagner. LC 75-39410. (Orig.). 1976. pap. 4.95 (ISBN 0-8307-0414-0, 54-033-08). Regal.

Your Congregation's Adult Jewish Education Committee: A Manual. Harold I. Krantzler. 1978. pap. 2.50 (ISBN 0-8074-0013-0, 181730). UAHC.

Your Creative Power. Alex F. Osborn. (Lib. Rep. Ed.). 1972. 20.00x (ISBN 0-684-15314-9, ScribT). Scribner.

Your Daughters Shall Prophesy: Feminist Alternatives in Theological Education. Cornwall Collective. LC 80-14891. 155p. 1980. pap. 6.95 (ISBN 0-8298-0404-8). Pilgrim NY.

Your Days Are Numbered. 21st ed. Florence Campbell. 246p. 1980. pap. 5.50 (ISBN 0-87516-422-6). De Vorss.

Your Deaf Child: A Guide for Parents. Helmer R. Myklebust. (Amer. Lec. in Otolaryngology Ser.). (Illus.). 150p. 1979. pap. 6.75 (ISBN 0-398-03127-4). C C Thomas.

Your Deaf Child's Speech & Language. Mary Courtman-Davies. 1980. 14.95 (ISBN 0-370-30149-8, Pub. by Chatto Bodley Jonathan). Merrimack Bk Serv.

Your Dog: Companion & Helper. Milo D. Pearsall & Margaret E. Pearsall. LC 80-14115. (Illus.). 160p. 1980. 11.95 (ISBN 0-931866-07-3). Alpine Pubns.

Your Dog, His Health & Happiness: The Breeder's & Pet Owners Guide to Better Dog Care. Louis D. Vine. LC 72-88607. 446p. 1973. pap. 4.95 (ISBN 0-668-02876-9). Arco.

Your Electro-Vibratory Body: A Study of Life Force in the Human Chakras. Victor Beasley. Ed. by Christopher Hills. LC 79-5085. (Illus.). 1979. pap. 9.95 (ISBN 0-916438-27-9). Univ of Trees.

Your Environment. Saltonsall. 6.95 o.s.i. (ISBN 0-8027-0320-8). Walker & Co.

Your Erroneous Zones. Wayne W. Dyer. LC 75-35621. (Funk & W Bk.). 256p. 1976. 10.95 (ISBN 0-308-10228-2, TYC-T). T Y Crowell.

Your Erroneous Zones. Wayne W. Dyer. 1977. pap. 2.75 (ISBN 0-380-01669-9, 46243). Avon.

Your Exciting Middle Years. John C. Cooper & Rachel C. Wahlberg. LC 76-2858. 1976. pap. 3.95 o.p. (ISBN 0-87680-857-7, 98075). Word Bks.

Your Eyelids Are Growing Heavy. Barbara Paul. LC 80-2462. 192p. 1981. 9.95 (ISBN 0-385-17466-7). Doubleday.

Your Eyes. Irving Adler & Ruth Adler. LC 62-16223. (Reason Why Ser). (Illus.). (gr. 3-6). 1963. PLB 7.89 (ISBN 0-381-99947-5, A95000, JD-J). John Day.

Your Face. Jack Winder. Ed. by Alton Jordan. (I Can Read Underwater Bks). (Illus.). (gr. k-3). 1974. PLB 3.50 (ISBN 0-89868-008-5, Read Res); pap. text ed. 1.75 (ISBN 0-89868-041-7). ARO Pub.

Your Family & Its Money. Helen M. Thal. (gr. 9-12). 1973. text ed. 13.28 (ISBN 0-395-14225-3). HM.

Your Family & the Law. J. E. Horsley & J. Carlova. 1975. 9.95 (ISBN 0-87489-096-9). Med Economics.

Your Family Dog: The Complete Guide to Choosing, Caring for, Training & Showing. Maxwell Riddle. LC 78-60299. (Illus.). 528p. 1981. 16.95 (ISBN 0-385-12707-3). Doubleday.

Your Family Roots. 48p. 1977. pap. 2.95 o.p. (ISBN 0-307-11098-2, Golden Pr). Western Pub.

Your Father's Not Coming Home Anymore: Children Tell How They Survive Divorce. Michael Jackson & Jessica Jackson. Ed. by Bruce Jackson. 324p. 1981. 12.95 (ISBN 0-399-90109-4). Marek.

Your Fear of Love. Marshall Bryant Hodge. LC 67-15960. 1969. pap. 2.50 (ISBN 0-385-04372-4, C483, Dolp). Doubleday.

Your Federal Income Tax. annual ed. 1980. pap. cancelled (ISBN 0-668-00865-2). Arco.

Your Fight Has Just Begun: The Sport of Boxing. Kathlyn Gay & Ben Barnes. LC 79-28242. (Illus.). 192p. (gr. 7-12). 1980. PLB 8.29 (ISBN 0-671-33005-5). Messner.

Your Film & the Lab. Bernard Happe. (Media Manuals Ser.). Date not set. pap. 8.95 (ISBN 0-8038-8595-4). Hastings.

Your Financial Plan: A Consumer's Guide. Carole E. Scott. 1979. text ed. 19.50 scp (ISBN 0-06-045844-5, HarpC); inst. manual avail. (ISBN 0-685-63499-X). Har-Row.

Your First Airplane Trip. Pat Ross & Joel Ross. 1981. 7.95 (ISBN 0-688-41989-5). Lothrop.

Your First Airplane Trip. Pat Ross & Joel Ross. LC 80-22642. (Illus.). 40p. (gr. k-2). 1981. 7.95 (ISBN 0-688-41989-5); PLB 7.63 (ISBN 0-688-51989-X). Morrow.

Your First Book of Riding. Pierre Chambry. Date not set. price not set (ISBN 0-8120-5193-9). Barron.

Your First Car. George Fremon & Suzanne Fremon. (Illus.). 176p. (Orig.). 1981. pap. 3.95 (ISBN 0-89709-024-1). Liberty Pub.

Your First Garden. Jack Kramer. LC 73-1102. (Encore Editions). (Illus.). 128p. 1973. pap. 3.50 o.p. (ISBN 0-684-15413-7, ScribT). Scribner.

Your First Pet. Carla Stevens. LC 74-2267. (Ready-to-Read Ser). (Illus.). 128p. (gr. 1-4). 1974. 7.95g o.s.i. (ISBN 0-02-788200-4). Macmillan.

Your First Point to Point Horse. Joe Hartigan. pap. 5.25 (ISBN 0-85131-212-8, Dist. by Sporting Book Center). J A Allen.

Your Five Year Old. Louise B. Ames & Frances L. Ilg. 1981. pap. 4.95 (ISBN 0-440-59494-4, Delta). Dell.

Your Flag. Boy Scouts of America. LC 19-600. (Illus.). 64p. (gr. 6-12). 1972. pap. 1.35x (ISBN 0-8395-3188-5, 3188). BSA.

Your Food & You. Herbert S. Zim. (Illus.). (gr. 4-8). 1957. PLB 6.48 (ISBN 0-688-31568-2). Morrow.

Your Four Great Emotions. David Seabury. 1969. pap. 3.95 (ISBN 0-911336-22-2). Sci of Mind.

Your Friend, Lewanika: The Life & Times of Lubosi Lewanika Litunga of Barotseland 1842 to 1916. Gervas Clay. (Robins Ser: No. 7). (Illus.). 1968. text ed. 11.50x (ISBN 0-391-02072-2). Humanities.

Your Fringe Benefits. Vera Di Palma. 1978. 11.95 (ISBN 0-7153-7517-2). David & Charles.

Your Future & You. James Finley. (Illus.). 176p. (Orig.). (gr. 10-12). 1981. pap. 3.50 (ISBN 0-87793-223-9); tchrs. ed. 2.25 (ISBN 0-87793-224-7). Ave Maria.

Your Future As a Dental Assistant. rev. ed. Jane C. Frost. LC 70-114128. (Career Guidance Ser.). 160p. 1976. pap. 3.50 (ISBN 0-668-02238-8). Arco.

Your Future As a Dietician. American Dietetic Association Members. LC 73-114126. (Career Guidance Ser). 1971. pap. 3.50 (ISBN 0-668-02240-X). Arco.

Your Future As a Dietician. Members of the American Dietetic Assoc. (Careers in Depth Ser.). (gr. 7-12). 1976. PLB 4.98 o.p. (ISBN 0-8239-0321-4). Rosen Pr.

Your Future As a Dietitian. rev ed. Members of the American Dietetic Assoc. 140p. 1980. lib. bdg. 5.97 (ISBN 0-8239-0521-7). Rosen Pr.

Your Future As a Home Economist. Jeanne Paris. LC 77-114119. (Career Guidance Ser). 1971. pap. 3.50 (ISBN 0-668-02247-7). Arco.

Your Future As a Home Economist. Jeanne Paris. LC 72-95601. (Careers in Depth Ser). (Illus.). (gr. 7 up). 1970. PLB 5.97 o.p. (ISBN 0-8239-0191-2). Rosen Pr.

Your Future As a Physician. 2nd ed. S. William Kalb. LC 74-80997. (Career Guidance Ser.). 1974. pap. 2.95 o.p. (ISBN 0-668-02263-9). Arco.

Your Future in a Television Career. David Berlyn. (Careers in Depth). 1978. lib. bdg. 5.97 o.p. (ISBN 0-8239-0404-0). Rosen Pr.

Your Future in Accounting. Edmond Locklear, Jr. LC 73-114134. (Career Guidance Ser). 1971. pap. 3.50 (ISBN 0-668-02232-9). Arco.

Your Future in Beauty Culture. rev. ed. Lawrence Gelb. (Careers in Depth Ser.). (Illus.). 128p. 1980. lib. bdg. 5.97 (ISBN 0-8239-0201-3). Rosen Pr.

Your Future in Broadcasting. John R. Rider. LC 70-146047. (Career Guidance Ser). 125p. 1974. pap. 3.50 (ISBN 0-668-03427-0). Arco.
Your Future in Dental Assisting. Jane C. Frost. LC 75-84955. (Careers in Depth Ser). (Illus.). (gr. 7 up). 1976. PLB 5.97 o.p. (ISBN 0-8239-0175-0). Rosen Pr.
Your Future in Dentistry. Allen Vershel. LC 77-114127. (Career Guidance Ser). 1971. pap. 3.50 (ISBN 0-668-02239-6). Arco.
Your Future in Ecology. (Illus.). 1974. pap. 7.95 o.p. (ISBN 0-87618-014-4). R J Brady.
Your Future in Food Technology. rev. ed. Gale Ammerman. (Careers in Depth Ser.). 1980. lib. bdg. 5.97 (ISBN 0-8239-0314-1). Rosen Pr.
Your Future in Forestry. David H. Hanaburgh. LC 75-114121. (Career Guidance Ser). 1971. pap. 3.50 (ISBN 0-668-02245-0). Arco.
Your Future in Insurance. Armand Sommer & Daniel P. Kedzie. LC 70-114117. (Career Guidance Ser). 1971. pap. 3.50 (ISBN 0-668-02249-3). Arco.
Your Future in Interior Design. rev. ed. Michael Greer. LC 79-95600. (Illus.). (gr. 7 up). 1980. PLB 5.97 o.p. (ISBN 0-8239-0200-5). Rosen Pr.
Your Future in Interior Design. Michael Greer. (Careers in Depth Ser.). 1980. lib. bdg. 5.97 (ISBN 0-8239-0524-1). Rosen Pr.
Your Future in Library Careers. Alpha Myers & Sara Temkin. LC 75-29605. (Career Guidance Ser.). 160p. 1976. pap. 3.50 (ISBN 0-668-03913-2). Arco.
Your Future in NASA: National Aeronautic & Space Administration. Sol Levine. LC 78-114111. (Career Guidance Ser). 1971. pap. 3.50 (ISBN 0-668-02255-8). Arco.
Your Future in Nursing Careers. Alice Robinson & Mary Reres. LC 72-75218. (Illus.). 128p. 1975. pap. 3.50 (ISBN 0-668-03429-7). Arco.
Your Future in Oceanography. Norman H. Gaber. LC 76-114108. 143p. 1975. pap. 2.95 o.p. (ISBN 0-668-02258-2). Arco.
Your Future in Optometry. James R. Gregg. LC 72-114107. (Career Guidance Ser). 1971. pap. 3.50 (ISBN 0-668-02259-0). Arco.
Your Future in Photography. 2nd ed. Victor Keppler. LC 71-114104. (Career Guidance Ser.). 1974. pap. 3.50 (ISBN 0-668-02262-0). Arco.
Your Future in Pro Sports. Harry Stapler. (Careers in Depth Ser). (Illus.). 160p. (gr. 7-12). 1977. PLB 5.97 (ISBN 0-8239-0372-9). Rosen Pr.
Your Future in Publishing. Leonard Corwen. LC 72-91800. 144p. 1975. pap. 3.50 (ISBN 0-668-03428-9). Arco.
Your Future in Television Careers. Berlyn. (Careers in Depth Ser.). 1980. lib. bdg. 5.97 (ISBN 0-8239-0404-0). Rosen Pr.
Your Future in Veterinary Medicine. Wayne Riser. LC 75-29656. 160p. (YA) 1976. pap. 3.50 (ISBN 0-668-03916-7). Arco.
Your Future in Word Processing. Phyllis Peck & Gilbert Konkel. (Careers in Depth Ser.). (Illus.). 140p. (gr. 7-12). 1981. lib. bdg. 5.97 (ISBN 0-8239-0532-2). Rosen Pr.
Your Future in Your Own Business. Elmer L. Winter. LC 79-114130. 188p. 1975. pap. 3.50 (ISBN 0-668-02236-1). Arco.
Your Garden Soil. Harry Maddox. (Illus.). 223p. 1975. 14.95 (ISBN 0-7153-6661-0). David & Charles.
Your God? Leon J. Suenens. 1978. pap. 4.95 (ISBN 0-8164-2192-7). Crossroad NY.
Your God Is Too Small. John B. Phillips. 8.95 (ISBN 0-02-597410-6). Macmillan.
Your Gold & Silver. Henry Merton. (Illus.). 96p. 1981. 4.95 (ISBN 0-02-077410-9, Collier). Macmillan.
Your Government Inaction. Roger Bruns & George Vogt. 80p. 1981. pap. 3.95 (ISBN 0-312-89814-2). St Martin.
Your Greatest Power. J. Martin Kohe. 1977. 5.95 (ISBN 0-685-74305-5). Success Unltd.
Your Guide to Boating: Power or Sail. John Bohannan. (Illus., Orig.). 1965. pap. 2.50 o.p. (ISBN 0-06-463238-5, 238, EH). Har-Row.
Your Guide to Photography. 2nd ed. Helen F. Bruce. (Orig.). 1974. pap. 3.95 (ISBN 0-06-463342-X, EH 342, EH). Har-Row.
Your Guide to Physicians of King County, (Washington), 1978. King County Physicians' Task Force. 1978. pap. 5.95 (ISBN 0-685-91737-1). Madrona Pubs.
Your Guide to Voting. Robert H. Loeb. (gr. 7 up). 1977. PLB 7.90 s&l (ISBN 0-531-00391-4). Watts.
Your Handspinning. Elsie G. Davenport. (Illus.). 1964. pap. 5.50 (ISBN 0-910458-01-4). Select Bks.
Your Handweaving. Elsie G. Davenport. (Illus.). 1970. pap. 5.50 (ISBN 0-910458-03-0). Select Bks.
Your Handwriting & What It Means. William L. French. (Newcastle Self-Enrichment Ser). (Illus.). 228p. 1976. pap. 2.95 o.p. (ISBN 0-87877-036-4, G-36). Newcastle Pub.
Your Handwriting & What It Means. William L. French. LC 80-19831. 226p. 1980. Repr. of 1976 ed. lib. bdg. 9.95x (ISBN 0-89370-636-1). Borgo Pr.
Your Healing Is Within You. Canon J. Glennon. 1980. pap. 4.95 (ISBN 0-88270-457-5). Logos.
Your Health Is What You Make It: A Guide for Diet, Vitamin Supplementation, Cholesterol Control, Exercise, Mental Health, and Longevity. C. W. Whitmoyer, Sr. 1972. 10.00 o.p. (ISBN 0-682-47522-X, Banner). Exposition.
Your Health: Nutrition. Francine Klagsbrun & Samuel Klagsbrun. LC 75-87930. (gr. 4-6). PLB 3.90 o.p. (ISBN 0-531-01906-3). Watts.
Your Health Under Siege: Using Nutrition to Fight Back. Jeffrey Bland. 256p. 1981. 12.95 (ISBN 0-8289-0415-4). Greene.
Your Hearing Loss & How to Cope with It. Kenneth Lysons. 1978. 10.50 (ISBN 0-7153-7472-9). David & Charles.
Your Hearing Loss: How to Break the Sound Barrier. Marilyn M. Helleberg. LC 78-8663. 1979. 13.95 (ISBN 0-88229-341-9). Nelson-Hall.
Your Heart. James C. Thomson. Ed. by C. Leslie Thomson. 80p. 1974. pap. 3.50x (ISBN 0-8464-1058-3). Beekman Pubs.
Your Heart & How It Works. Herbert S. Zim. (Illus.). (gr. 3-7). 1959. PLB 6.48 (ISBN 0-688-31552-6). Morrow.
Your Heart: Complete Information for the Family. William Likoff et al. (Illus.). 1972. 6.95 o.s.i. (ISBN 0-397-00789-2). Lippincott.
Your Hidden Potential: A Dynamic New System for Discovering the Power Within You. Christopher Markert. LC 80-23848. 172p. 1980. Repr. of 1980 ed. lib. bdg. 14.95x (ISBN 0-89370-647-7). Borgo Pr.
Your Hidden Skills: Clues to Careers & Future Pursuits. Henry G. Pearson. (Illus.). 150p. (Orig.). 1981. pap. price not set (ISBN 0-9605368-0-9). Mowry Pr.
Your Home Computer. James White. LC 77-73316. (Illus., Orig.). 1977. pap. 10.95 (ISBN 0-918138-05-1). Dilithium Pr.
Your Homemade Greenhouse. Jack Kramer. 1980. pap. 5.95 (ISBN 0-346-12442-5). Cornerstone.
Your Host Peter Gust of the Park Lane Restaurant. Ellen Taussig. LC 79-17799. (Illus.). 1979. 14.95 (ISBN 0-89047-033-2). Herman Pub.
Your Instant Guide to Movie Making. Alan Cleave. 1977. pap. 3.75 o.p. (ISBN 0-85242-499-X, Pub. by Fountain). Morgan.
Your Introduction to Law. 2nd ed. George G. Coughlin. 1975. pap. 3.95 o.p. (ISBN 0-06-463472-8, 472, EH). Har-Row.
Your Jewish Child. Morrison D. Bial. Ed. by Daniel B. Syme. 1978. pap. 5.00 (ISBN 0-8074-0012-2, 101200). UAHC.
Your Job: Survival or Satisfaction. Jerry E. White & Mary E. White. 1976. 4.95 (ISBN 0-310-34321-6). Zondervan.
Your Job: Where to Find It---How to Get It. Leonard Corwen. LC 80-22251. 256p. 1981. lib. bdg. 11.95 (ISBN 0-668-05129-9); pap. 6.95 (ISBN 0-668-05131-0). Arco.
Your Key to Success in Law School. Theodore Silver & Howard R. Sacks. (Orig.). 1981. pap. 5.95 (ISBN 0-671-09256-1). Monarch Pr.
Your Key to the Cockpit. C. A. Stevens. (Illus.). 1980. pap. 3.00 (ISBN 0-911721-85-1, Pub. by Inflight). Aviation.
Your Keys to the Executive Suite. Richard Anderson. 32p. 1973. pap. 1.50 (ISBN 0-570-06981-5, 12-2558). Concordia.
Your Kingdom Come: Bibles Studies for the Chuch Year Based on the WCC Mission & Evangelism Theme, Melbourne 1980. (Orig.). 1980. pap. 2.25 (ISBN 0-377-00093-0). Friend Pr.
Your Left Hip Pocket. C. R. Smock. 4.95 o.p. (ISBN 0-8062-1071-0). Carlton.
Your Legal Rights As a Minor. Robert H. Loeb, Jr. & John P. Maloney. LC 73-6955. (gr. 7 up). 1974. PLB 5.88 o.p. (ISBN 0-531-02650-7). Watts.
Your Life Is What You Make It. Paul Molow. 192p. 1981. 10.00 (ISBN 0-682-49739-8). Exposition.
Your Loving Anna: Letters from the Ontario Frontier. Ed. by Louis Tivy. LC 72-86392. 1972. 10.00 o.p. (ISBN 0-8020-1927-7); pap. 3.50 o.p. (ISBN 0-8020-6166-4). U of Toronto Pr.
Your Man at the UN: People, Politics & Bueaucracy in the Making of Foreign Policy. Seymour M. Finger. LC 79-3657. 368p. 1980. 26.50x (ISBN 0-8147-2566-X). NYU Pr.
Your Marriage Can Be Great. Ed. by Thomas B. Warren. 1978. pap. 13.95 (ISBN 0-934916-44-6). Natl Christian Pr.
Your Marriage Has Possibilities. Aldyth Barber & Cyril Barber. 200p. (Orig.). 1981. pap. 4.95 (ISBN 0-89840-012-0). Heres Life.
Your Marriage Needs Three Love Affairs. John A. Lavender. LC 77-91492. 1978. pap. 2.95 o.p. (ISBN 0-916406-91-1). Accent Bks.
Your Marvelous Mind. Larry Kettelkamp. LC 80-18614. (Illus.). (gr. 5-8). 9.95 (ISBN 0-664-32670-6). Westminster.
Your Memory: How It Works & How to Improve It. Kenneth Higbee. 1977. 13.95 (ISBN 0-13-980144-8, Spec); pap. 3.95 (ISBN 0-13-980136-7). P-H.
Your Middle Years: A Doctor's Guide for Today's Woman. Wulf H. Utian. (Appleton Consumer Health Guides). 109p. 1980. 12.95 (ISBN 0-8385-9938-9); pap. 5.95 (ISBN 0-8385-9937-0). ACC.
Your Middle Years: A Doctor's Guide for Today's Woman. Utlan. 12.95 (ISBN 0-8385-9938-9). P-H.
Your Mind & Your Health. Ellen G. White. 31p. 1964. pap. 0.75 (ISBN 0-8163-0083-6, 24505-0). Pacific Pr Pub Assn.
Your Mind Can Drive You Crazy. James A. Takacs. 204p. 1980. pap. 4.95 (ISBN 0-930306-34-1). Delphi Info.
Your Money. Richard Phalon. (Illus.). 320p. 1981. 5.95 (ISBN 0-312-89823-1). St Martin.
Your Money - Going or Growing? Bernard Schneider. (Illus.). (gr. 7 up). 1978. wkbk 2.25 (ISBN 0-912486-33-3). Finney Co.
Your Money & Your Life: How to Plan Your Long Range Financial Security. Hardy. Date not set. 14.95 (ISBN 0-8144-5529-8). Am Mgmt.
Your Money Matters. Malcolm MacGregor & Stanley C. Baldwin. LC 75-56123. 1977. pap. 3.95 (ISBN 0-87123-662-1, 210662). Bethany Fell.
Your Moneyscopes. Georgia Davis. Incl. Aries (ISBN 0-346-12260-0); Taurus (ISBN 0-346-12261-9); Gemini (ISBN 0-346-12262-7); Cancer (ISBN 0-346-12263-5); Leo (ISBN 0-346-12264-3); Virgo (ISBN 0-346-12265-1); Libra (ISBN 0-346-12266-X); Scorpio (ISBN 0-346-12267-8); Sagittarius (ISBN 0-346-12268-6); Capricorn (ISBN 0-346-12269-4); Aquarius (ISBN 0-346-12270-8); Pisces (ISBN 0-346-12271-6). 1977. Set. pap. 54.00 o.p. (ISBN 0-685-75535-5); pap. 1.50 ea o.p. Cornerstone.
Your Most Enchanted Listener. Wendell Johnson. LC 55-10696. 1956. 6.95 o.s.i. (ISBN 0-06-012230-7, HarpT). Har-Row.
Your Mouth Is Your Business: The Dentists' Guide to Better Health. Hyman J. Goldberg. (Appleton Consumer Health Guides). (Illus.). 215p. 1980. 12.95 (ISBN 0-8385-9943-5); pap. 5.95 (ISBN 0-8385-9942-7). ACC.
Your Muscles & Ways to Exercise Them. Margaret Cosgrove. LC 79-22936. (Illus.). (gr. 3-6). 1980. PLB 6.95 (ISBN 0-396-07787-0). Dodd.
Your Mysterious Powers of E.S.P. pap. 1.95 (ISBN 0-451-09315-1, J9315, Sig). NAL.
Your New Life. Don Norbie. 66p. pap. 0.10. Walterick Pubs.
Your New Swiss Bank Book. rev. ed. Robert Kinsman. LC 78-74760. 1979. 17.50 (ISBN 0-87094-177-1). Dow Jones-Irwin.
Your Night to Make Dinner. LouAnn Gaeddert. (Illus.). 1977. lib. bdg. 6.90 (ISBN 0-531-01297-2). Watts.
Your Old Balls. Hale Hawkins. (Illus.). 80p. (Orig.). 1980. pap. 4.95 (ISBN 0-938194-00-3). Lively Hills.
Your Own Best Secret Place. Byrd Baylor. LC 78-21243. (Illus.). (gr. 1-4). 1979. 9.95 (ISBN 0-684-16111-7). Scribner.
Your Own Computer: (a Simple Guide to the Home Computer) (Illus.). 1980. pap. 12.95 o.p. (ISBN 0-930490-34-7). Future Shop.
Your Own Financial Aid Factory: The Guide to Locating College Money. rev. ed. Robert Leider. LC 80-11185. 184p. 1981. pap. 5.95 (ISBN 0-917760-22-0). Octameron Assocs.
Your Own Joke Book. Gertrude Crampton. (gr. 6-8). pap. 1.25 (ISBN 0-590-08125-X, Schol Pap). Schol Bk Serv.
Your Part in the Great Plan. Michael X. 1972. pap. 3.95 o.p. (ISBN 0-685-37601-X). Saucerian.
Your Paths in Ink Graphoanalysis & the Personality. Johanna L. Wyland. (Illus.). 112p. 1980. 6.95 (ISBN 0-682-49604-9). Exposition.
Your People Problems. John G. Krebs. LC 68-25949. (Harvest Ser.). 1978. pap. 3.95 (ISBN 0-686-63846-8, 24510-0). Pacific Pr Pub Assn.
Your Personal Financial I.Q. Test. Leo J. Taggart. (Essential Knowledge Library). 1979. spiral bdg. 8.00 (ISBN 0-89266-171-2). Am Classical Coll Pr.
Your Personality & the Planets. Michel Gauquelin. LC 80-5499. (Illus.). 262p. 1980. 11.95 (ISBN 0-8128-2737-6). Stein & Day.
Your Pet Bear. Bobbie Hamsa. LC 79-24938. (Far-Fetched Pets Ser.). (Illus.). 32p. (ps-3). 1980. PLB 7.95 (ISBN 0-516-03351-4). Childrens.
Your Pet Isn't Sick: (He Just Wants You to Think So) Herbert Tanzer & Nick Lyons. 1978. pap. 1.75 (ISBN 0-515-04599-3). Jove Pubns.
Your Pet Isn't Sick: He Justs Wants You to Think So. Herbert Tanzer & Nick Lyons. 1977. 6.95 o.p. (ISBN 0-525-24020-9). Dutton.
Your Pet Kangaroo. Bobbie Hamsa. LC 80-15764. (Far-Fetched Pets). (Illus.). 32p. (ps-3). 1980. PLB 7.95 (ISBN 0-516-03363-8). Childrens.
Your Pet Penguin. Bobbie Hamsa. LC 80-15588. (Far-Fetched Pets Ser.). (Illus.). 32p. (ps-3). 1980. PLB 7.95 (ISBN 0-516-03364-6). Childrens.
Your Pet's Secret Language. Jhan Robbins. 176p. 1976. pap. 2.95 (ISBN 0-446-93912-9). Warner Bks.
Your Philosophy of Education- What Is It? Arnold Griese. (Illus.). 350p. (Orig.). 1981. pap. 12.95x (ISBN 0-8302-9857-6). Goodyear.
Your Piano & Your Piano Technician. Virgil E. Smith. LC 80-82009. 1981. pap. write for info. (ISBN 0-8497-5078-4, WP71, Pub. by Kjos West). Kjos.
Your Prayers & Mine. Elizabeth Yates. (Illus.). (gr. 7-9). 1954. 3.95 o.p. (ISBN 0-395-07212-3). HM.
Your Pre-Teens Can Be Fun. Jane W. Pugel. (Uplook Ser.). 30p. 1972. pap. 0.75 (ISBN 0-8163-0084-4, 24515-9). Pacific Pr Pub Assn.
Your Pregnancy Year. Anneke Campbell. LC 77-94864. 1979. 5.95 o.p. (ISBN 0-385-14323-0, Dolp). Doubleday.
Your Private World: A Study of Intimate Gardens. Thomas Church. LC 74-99220. 1969. 9.95 o.p. (ISBN 0-87701-001-3). Chronicle Bks.
Your Problem Garden. Richard Bisgrove. 1980. 19.95 (ISBN 0-7134-1184-8, Pub. by Batsford England). David & Charles.
Your Psychic Powers & How to Develop Them. Hereward Carrington. LC 80-24076. 358p. 1980. Repr. of 1975 ed. lib. bdg. 11.95x (ISBN 0-89370-633-7). Borgo Pr.
Your Reading: A Booklist for Junior High Students. NCTE Committee on the Junior High School Book List. LC 75-21358. 448p. 1975. pap. 2.95 (ISBN 0-590-09608-7, Citation). Schol Bk Serv.
Your Remarkable Mind. Reuben Hilde. LC 76-7851. (Dimension Ser.). 1976. pap. 5.95 (ISBN 0-8163-0275-8, 24517-5). Pacific Pr Pub Assn.
Your Retirement. Herbert Askwith. 157p. 1976. pap. 1.95 o.s.i. (ISBN 0-346-12224-4). Cornerstone.
Your Right to Fly. James E. Melton. LC 80-82961. (Illus.). 217p. pap. 6.95 (ISBN 0-9604752-0-6). Global Pubns WI.
Your Right to Know: How the Free Flow of News Depends on the Journalist's Right to Protect His Sources. Charles W. Whalen. 1973. 8.95 o.p. (ISBN 0-394-48732-X). Random.
Your Rights to Privacy. Trudy Hayden & Jack Novik. (ACLU Handbook Ser.). 1980. pap. 2.50 (ISBN 0-686-69238-1, 75895). Avon.
Your Roles As a Medical Assistant. C. Hardy & N. Martin. 1974. 9.50 (ISBN 0-87489-044-6). Med Economics.
Your School's Desegregation -- How Real? A Checklist. 1971. 1.80 (ISBN 0-685-59509-9). Integrated Ed Assoc.
Your Search Key to L. C. Jovian P. Lang. (Library Learning Laboratory: No. 4). 1980. pap. 23.95 o.p.; tchr's ed. 9.95 (ISBN 0-913308-06-4); wkbk. 9.95 (ISBN 0-913308-07-2); set of nine transparencies 10.90 ea.; 94.50 set (ISBN 0-686-66113-3); library congress oversized catalog card 27.95; dewey classification-Library of congress poster 14.50. Fordham Pub.
Your Second Life. Harold L. Karpman & Sam Locke. 1977. pap. 1.75 o.s.i. (ISBN 0-515-04218-8). Jove Pubns.
Your Second Mind. Curtis A. Jones. 1979. 5.75 (ISBN 0-8062-1285-3). Carlton.
Your Secret Power: Creating Happiness, Vol. 2. D. Foster Gutridge, II. (Your Secret Power Ser.). 96p. (Orig.). 1981. pap. 5.95 (ISBN 0-938014-02-1, 1001B). Freedom Unltd.
Your Secret Power: Creating Harmony with Others, Vol. 4. D. Foster Gutridge, II. 96p. (Orig.). 1981. pap. 5.95 (ISBN 0-938014-04-8, 301D). Freedom Unltd.
Your Secret Power: Creating Love, Vol. 3. D. Foster Gutridge, II. (Your Secret Power Ser.). 96p. (Orig.). 1981. pap. 5.95 (ISBN 0-938014-03-X, 2001C). Freedom Unltd.
Your Secret Power: Creating Riches, Vol. 1. D. Foster Gutridge, II. LC 80-69710. (Your Secret Power Ser.). 80p. (Orig.). 1980. pap. 5.95 (ISBN 0-938014-01-3, 901A). Freedom Unltd.
Your Self, My Self & the Self of the Universe. Alfred B Starratt. LC 79-9971. 1979. 12.95 (ISBN 0-916144-38-0); pap. 7.95 (ISBN 0-916144-39-9). Stemmer Hse.
Your Sex Dreams. (Illus.). pap. 5.00 (ISBN 0-910550-61-1). Centurion Pr.
Your Shih Tzu. rev. ed. Will C. Mooney. LC 72-80628. (Your Dog Bk.). (Illus.). 128p. 1981. price not set (ISBN 0-87714-073-1). Denlingers.

Your Siddur. Mordecai Soloff et al. (Sacred Hebrew Ser.). (Illus.). 175p. 1981. pap. 3.50 (ISBN 0-86628-001-4). Ridgefield Pub.
Your Silent Language. Elizabeth McGough. LC 73-4253. (Illus.). 128p. (gr. 7 up). 1974. PLB 6.96 (ISBN 0-688-31820-7). Morrow.
Your Skin. Herbert S. Zim. LC 78-10878. (Illus.). (gr. 4-6). 1979. 6.95 (ISBN 0-688-22178-5); PLB 6.67 (ISBN 0-688-32178-X). Morrow.
Your Skin & How to Live in It. Jerome Z. Litt. LC 80-65323. 223p. 1980. pap. 4.95 (ISBN 0-86551-011-3). Corinthian.
Your Skin & Mine. Paul Showers. LC 65-16185. (Let's-Read-&-Find-Out Science Bk). (Illus.). (gr. k-3). 1965. PLB 7.89 (ISBN 0-690-91127-0, TYC-J); pap. 2.95 crocodile paperback ser. (ISBN 0-690-00205-X); filmstrip with record 11.95 (ISBN 0-690-91130-0); filmstrip with cassette 14.95 (ISBN 0-690-91132-7). T Y Crowell.
Your Solar Energy Home: Including Wind & Methane Applications. new ed. D. Howell. 1979. text ed. 37.00 (ISBN 0-08-022685-X); pap. text ed. 11.25 (ISBN 0-08-022686-8). Pergamon.
Your Son, Calvin Coolidge: A Selection of Letters from Calvin Coolidge to His Father. Calvin Coolidge. Ed. by Edward C. Lathem. LC 68-57427. (Illus.). 255p. 1968. text ed. 12.50x (ISBN 0-87451-058-9). U Pr of New Eng.
Your Speech Reveals Your Personality. Dominick A. Barbara. 192p. 1970. pap. 8.75 photocopy, spiral (ISBN 0-398-00089-1). C C Thomas.
Your Stable, Its Construction & Management. Toni Webber. 1976. 8.50 (ISBN 0-7207-0846-X, Pub. by Michael Joseph). Merrimack Bk Serv.
Your State: Pennsylvania. Lucille Wallower. Ed. by Patricia L. Gump. (gr. 3-4). 1963. pap. 3.50 (ISBN 0-931992-09-5). Penns Valley.
Your Stomach & Digestive Tract. Herbert S. Zim. LC 72-6734. (Illus.). 64p. (gr. 3-7). 1973. 6.00 o.p. (ISBN 0-688-21838-5); PLB 6.48 (ISBN 0-688-31838-X). Morrow.
Your Stress Personalities: A Look at Your Selves. Mary Dempcy & Rene Tihista. (Illus.). 252p. (Orig.). 1981. pap. 8.95 (ISBN 0-89141-077-5). Presidio Pr.
Your Terrarium. Mervin F. Roberts, Jr. (Orig.). pap. 3.50 (ISBN 0-87666-225-4, M511). TFH Pubns.
Your Three-Year Old. Ames & Ilg. 1980. pap. 4.95 (ISBN 0-440-59478-2, Delta). Dell.
Your Three Year Old. Louise B. Ames. 1976. 7.95 (ISBN 0-440-09883-1). Delacorte.
Your Toddler. Johnson & Johnson. 1980. 16.95 (ISBN 0-02-559550-4); pap. 10.95 (ISBN 0-02-043920-2). Macmillan.
Your Travel Agent: A Consumer's Guide. 1980. 1.95 (ISBN 0-916752-32-1). Green Hill.
Your Treasury of Inspiration. rev. ed. Compiled by Eleanor Doan. 216p. 1980. gift ed. 9.95 (ISBN 0-310-23790-4, 9525). Zondervan.
Your Trellis Garden. Kramer. Date not set. 1.49 (ISBN 0-517-31432-0). Bonanza.
Your Troubled Children. Elizabeth Skoglund. LC 74-19440. 128p. 1975. pap. 1.50 o.p. (ISBN 0-912692-50-2). Cook.
Your Two Year Old. Ames & Ilg. 1980. pap. 4.95 (ISBN 0-440-59477-4, Delta). Dell.
Your Two Year Old. Louise B. Ames. 1976. 7.95 (ISBN 0-440-09882-3). Delacorte.
Your Ups & Downs. Philip B. Knoche. (Uplook Ser.). 32p. 1970. pap. 0.75 (ISBN 0-8163-0085-2, 24535-7). Pacific Pr Pub Assn.
Your Via Dolorosa & Victory. D. Meckfennel. 4.50 o.p. (ISBN 0-8062-1126-1). Carlton.
Your Voice: Methods for Strengthening & Developing the Voice. Eugene Feuchtinger. Orig. Title: Voice Development Hints. 5.95 (ISBN 0-911012-28-1). Nelson-Hall.
Your Wedding: How to Plan & Enjoy It. Marjorie B. Woods. 1972. pap. 2.75 (ISBN 0-515-05843-2). Jove Pubns.
Your Working Life: A Guide to Getting & Holding a Job. Edwin L. Herr & Roberta Moore. LC 79-28360. Orig. Title: Career Education. (Illus.). 464p. 1980. 13.28 (ISBN 0-07-028342-7, G); tchrs. manual 3.00 (ISBN 0-07-028344-3); student wkbk. 5.00 (ISBN 0-07-028343-5). McGraw.
Your Yarn Dyeing. Elsie G. Davenport. (Illus.). 1970. pap. 5.50 (ISBN 0-910458-02-2). Select Bks.
Your Young Child & You: How to Manage Growing-up Problems in the Years from One to Five. rev. ed. Eleanor Weisberger. 1979. pap. 4.95 (ISBN 0-87690-329-4). Dutton.
Your Youth Can Be Restored. Rozella et al. 1978. 6.95 o.p. (ISBN 0-533-02792-6). Vantage.
Your 14-Day Total Shape-up Plan. Capone. (gr. 7-12). 1980. pap. 1.25 (ISBN 0-590-30913-7, Schol Pap). Schol Bk Serv.
You're a Brave Man, Charlie Brown: Selected Cartoons from "You Can Do It, Charlie Brown", Vol. II. Charles M. Schulz. (Peanuts Ser.). (Illus.). 1977. pap. 1.50 (ISBN 0-449-23878-4, Crest). Fawcett.
You're a Good Man, Charlie Brown. Clark Gesner. 1978. pap. 1.50 (ISBN 0-449-23354-5, Crest). Fawcett.
You're a Good Sport, Charlie Brown. Charles M Schulz. (gr. 1 up). 1977. pap. 1.95 (ISBN 0-590-08502-6, Schol Pap). Schol Bk Serv.
You're a Little Kid with a Big Heart. Bernard Waber. (Illus.). (gr. k-3). 1980. 8.95 (ISBN 0-395-29163-1). HM.
You're Hired! Albert Van Roden. (Illus.). 64p. 1981. pap. 2.95 (ISBN 0-89709-025-X). Liberty Pub.
You're in Charge. Cecil G. Osborne. 1976. pap. 1.25 (ISBN 0-89129-221-7). Jove Pubns.
You're in Charge. Janette Rainwater. LC 79-65000. 1979. pap. 8.50 (ISBN 0-89615-021-6). Guild of Tutors Pr.
You're in the Driver's Seat. Gerald Howland. 128p. (Orig.). 1980. pap. write for info. (ISBN 0-8289-0418-9). Greene.
You're Not Elected, Charlie Brown. Charles M. Schulz. (Illus.). 96p. (gr. 3-7). 1980. pap. 1.95 (ISBN 0-590-08820-3, Schol Pap). Schol Bk Serv.
You're Not Just a Statistic. Clark B. McCall. (Uplook Ser.). 1977. pap. 0.75 (ISBN 0-8163-0313-4, 24539-9). Pacific Pr Pub Assn.
You're Not Too Old to Have a Baby. Jane Price. 147p. 1977. 7.95 (ISBN 0-374-29606-5). FS&G.
You're Our Child: A Social-Psychological Approach to Adoption. Jerome Smith & Franklin I. Miroff. LC 80-5957. 110p. (Orig.). 1981. lib. bdg. 15.75 (ISBN 0-8191-1416-2); pap. text ed. 7.25 (ISBN 0-8191-1417-0). U Pr of Amer.
You're Richer Than You Think! Erwin W. Lutzer. 1978. pap. 2.50 (ISBN 0-88207-777-5). Victor Bks.
You're Somebody Special on a Horse. Fern G. Brown. LC 77-7506. (Pilotbooks). (Illus.). (gr. 4-8). 1977. 6.95g (ISBN 0-8075-9447-4). A Whitman.
You're Something Else, Andy Capp. Smythe. 128p. (Orig.). 1981. pap. 1.75 (ISBN 0-449-14401-1, GM). Fawcett.
You're Speaking-Who's Listening? Jeanne Ferguson & Maria B. Miller. 1980. pap. text ed. 8.95 (ISBN 0-574-22560-9, 13-5560); instr's guide avail. (ISBN 0-574-22561-7, 13-5561). SRA.
You're the Boss, Andy Capp. Smythe. (Andy Capp Cartoons Ser.). 1978. pap. 1.50 (ISBN 0-449-13631-0, GM). Fawcett.
You're the Greatest, Charlie Brown. Charles M. Schulz. LC 79-4622. (Illus.). (gr. 1 up). 1979. 3.50 (ISBN 0-394-84260-X, BYR); PLB 4.99 (ISBN 0-394-94260-4). Random.
You're the Greatest, Charlie Brown. Charles M. Schulz. (Illus.). 96p. (gr. 3-7). 1980. pap. 1.95 (ISBN 0-590-31504-8, Schol Pap). Schol Bk Serv.
You're the Only One Here Who Doesn't Look Like a Doctor: Portrait of a Woman Surgeon. Marie-Claude Wrenn. LC 77-7871. 1977. 9.95 o.p. (ISBN 0-690-01420-1, TYC-T). T Y Crowell.
You're the Scaredy-Cat. Mercer Mayer. LC 80-16859. (Illus.). 40p. (ps-3). 1980. Repr. of 1974 ed. 7.95 (ISBN 0-590-07783-X, Four Winds). Schol Bk Serv.
Yours by Choice: A Guide for Adoptive Parents. rev ed. Jane Rowe. 1971. pap. 6.00 (ISBN 0-7100-6369-5). Routledge & Kegan.
Yours Truly, King Arthur. Marc Drogin. LC 79-66643. 1981. 8.95 (ISBN 0-8008-8765-4, Pentalic). Taplinger.
Yours with Love. Mary Burchell. (Harlequin Romances Ser.). 192p. (Orig.). 1981. pap. 1.25 (ISBN 0-373-02379-0, Pub. by Harlequin). PB.
Youth & Drugs. Francis H. Wise. (Illus.). Date not set. price not set. Wise Pub.
Youth & Sex: Pleasure & Responsibility. Gordon D. Jensen. LC 72-77121. (Illus.). 1973. 11.95 (ISBN 0-911012-99-0); pap. 6.95 (ISBN 0-88229-499-7). Nelson-Hall.
Youth & Sex Today. (Illus.). pap. 5.00 (ISBN 0-910550-60-3). Centurion Pr.
Youth & Social Change. Ed. by Morton Levitt & Ben Rubenstein. LC 73-157414. 1972. 14.95x (ISBN 0-8143-1450-3). Wayne St U Pr.
Youth & the Drug Problem: A Guide for Parents & Teachers. Harold D. Love. 116p. 1971. photocopy ed. 12.00 (ISBN 0-398-01152-4). C C Thomas.
Youth, Brainwashing & the Extremist Cults. Ronald M. Enroth. 1977. 7.95 o.p. (ISBN 0-310-24270-3); pap. 4.95 (ISBN 0-310-24271-1). Zondervan.
Youth Crime & Juvenile Justice: International Perspectives. Ed. by Paul C. Friday & V. Lorne Stewart. LC 77-7820. (Praeger Special Studies). 1977. text ed. 23.95 (ISBN 0-03-022646-5). Praeger.
Youth Culture & the Universities. Bryan Wilson. 1970. 6.95 o.p. (ISBN 0-571-09233-0, Pub. by Faber & Faber). Merrimack Bk Serv.
Youth Face Today's Issues One. William J. Krutza & Philip P. DiCicco. (Contemporary Discussion Ser.). (Orig.). 1970. pap. 2.45 (ISBN 0-8010-5304-8). Baker Bk.
Youth Face Today's Issues Two. William J. Krutza & Philip P. Dicicco. (Contemporary Discussion Ser.). pap. 2.45 (ISBN 0-8010-5311-0). Baker Bk.
Youth, Heart of Darkness, Typhoon, the Secret Sharer. Joseph Conrad. (Literature Ser). (gr. 10-12). 1970. pap. text ed. 3.83 (ISBN 0-87720-748-8). AMSCO Sch.
Youth, Heart of Darkness, Typhoon, The Secret Sharer. with Reader's Guide. Joseph Conrad. (AMSCO Literature Program). (gr. 9-12). 1974. pap. text ed. 5.08 (ISBN 0-87720-819-0); tchr's ed. 3.25 (ISBN 0-87720-919-7). AMSCO Sch.
Youth Hostel Association Services. Youth Hostels Association Service. (Illus.). 512p. 1973. pap. 2.95 o.s.i. (ISBN 0-02-040900-1, Collier). Macmillan.
Youth in Agricultural Villages. Bruce L. Melvin & Elna N. Smith. LC 79-165603. (FDR & the Era of the New Deal Ser). 1971. Repr. of 1940 ed. lib. bdg. 15.00 (ISBN 0-306-70353-X). Da Capo.
Youth in Contemporary Society: Theoretical & Research Perspectives. Chris Murray. (General Ser.). 1979. pap. text ed. 17.00x (ISBN 0-85633-170-8, NFER). Humanities.
Youth in Soviet Russia. Klaus Mehnert. Tr. by Michael Davidson. LC 79-2914. 270p. 1981. Repr. of 1933 ed. 22.00 (ISBN 0-8305-0083-9). Hyperion Conn.
Youth Labor Force. Beatrice G. Reubens. LC 80-67390. (Conservation of Human Resources Ser.: No. 13). 1981. text ed. 32.50 (ISBN 0-86598-027-6). Allanheld.
Youth Ministry: A Book of Reading. Ed. by Michael Warren. LC 77-70639. 1977. pap. 2.95 (ISBN 0-8091-2018-6). Paulist Pr.
Youth Ministry: The New Team Approach. Ginny W. Holderness. LC 80-82186. (Illus.). 160p. (Orig.). 1981. pap. 9.95 (ISBN 0-8042-1410-7). John Knox.
Youth or Experience? Manning the Modern Military. Martin Binkin & Irene Kyriakopoulos. (Studies in Defense Policy). 1979. pap. 3.95 (ISBN 0-8157-0969-2). Brookings.
Youth Participation in the Development Process: A Case Study in Panama. Luis A. De Souza & Lucia Ribeiro. (International Bureau of Education Experiments & Innovations in Education Ser: No. 18). 1976. pap. 4.75 (ISBN 92-3-101308-4, U735, UNESCO). Unipub.
Youth Service & Interprofessional Studies. I. Bulman et al. 1970. 19.50 (ISBN 0-08-015736-X). Pergamon.
Youth Unemployment. Chris Murray. (General Ser.). 1979. pap. text ed. 15.00x (ISBN 0-85633-172-4, NFER). Humanities.
Youthnappers. James C. Hefley. 1977. pap. 2.25 o.p. (ISBN 0-88207-754-6). Victor Bks.
Youth's Magic Horn: Seven Stories. Jon Wahl. LC 77-29127. 1978. 6.95 o.p. (ISBN 0-525-66582-X). Elsevier-Nelson.
You've Come a Long Way, Snoopy: Selected Cartoons from "Thompson Is in Trouble", Vol. I. Charles M. Schulz. (Peanuts Ser.). (Illus.). 1979. pap. 1.50 (ISBN 0-449-24004-5, Crest). Fawcett.
You've Got a Friend, Charlie Brown: Selected Cartoons from "You'll Flip, Charlie Brown", Vol. I. Charles M. Schulz. 1979. pap. 1.50 (ISBN 0-449-23887-3, Crest). Fawcett.
Ysabel Kid. J. T. Edson. (J. T. Edson Ser.). 1978. pap. 1.50 o.p. (ISBN 0-685-54608-X, Medallion). Berkley Pub.
Ysaye. Ginsburg. Ed. by Paradise. (Illus.). 576p. 1980. text ed. 20.00 (ISBN 0-87666-620-9, Z-31). Paganiniana Pubns.
Ysengrimus. Magister Nivardus. Tr. by F. J. Sypher & Eleanor Sypher. (Illus.). 280p. 1980. 95.00x (ISBN 0-8386-3005-7). F Sypher.
Yuan Chen. Angela C. Palandri. (World Authors Ser.: No. 442). 1977. lib. bdg. 12.50 (ISBN 0-8057-6279-5). Twayne.
Yuan Porcelain & Stoneware. Margaret Medley. 1974. 48.00 (ISBN 0-571-10512-2, Pub. by Faber & Faber). Merrimack Bk Serv.
Yugoslav Coast: Atlas & Guide Book. K. Cizelj. (Illus.). 186p. 1975. pap. text ed. 13.50x (ISBN 0-89918-722-6, Y722). Vanous.
Yugoslav Economic System & Its Performance in the Nineteen Seventies. Laura D. Tyson. LC 80-24650. (Research Ser.: No. 44). x, 115p. 1980. pap. 4.50x (ISBN 0-87725-144-4). U Cal LA Indus Rel.
Yugoslav Economic System: The First Labor-Managed Economy in the Making. Branko Horvat. LC 75-46111. 1976. 20.00 o.p. (ISBN 0-87332-074-3); pap. 7.95 (ISBN 0-87332-175-8). M E Sharpe.
Yugoslav Experiment 1948-1974. Dennison Rusinow. 1978. 28.50x (ISBN 0-520-03730-8, CAMPUS 215); pap. 7.95x (ISBN 0-520-03730-8). U of Cal Pr.
Yugoslav Naive Art: Eighty Self-Taught Artists Speak About Themselves & Their Work. Nebojsa Tomasevic. (Illus.). 1976. 30.00x o.p. (ISBN 0-686-19996-0). Intl Learn Syst.
Yugoslav Search for Man: Marxist Humanism in Contemporary Yugoslavia. Oskar Gruenwald. 400p. 1981. 24.95x (ISBN 0-89789-005-1). J F Bergin.
Yugoslavia. John J. Horton. (World Bibliography Ser.: No. 1). 194p. 1978. text ed. 25.25 (ISBN 0-903450-09-7). ABC-Clio.
Yugoslavia After Tito. Andrew Borowiec. LC 77-83466. (Praeger Special Studies). 1977. 24.95 (ISBN 0-03-040916-0). Praeger.
Yugoslavia After Tito: Scenarios & Implications. Gavriel D. Ra'Anan. LC 77-4164. (Special Studies on the Soviet Union & Eastern Europe Ser.). 1978. lib. bdg. 22.00x (ISBN 0-89158-335-1). Westview.
Yugoslavian. Holloway Staff. (Harper Phrase Books for the Traveler Ser.). (Orig.). 1977. pap. text ed. 1.00 o.p. (ISBN 0-8467-0317-3, Pub. by Two Continents). Hippocrene Bks.
Yugoslavs in Louisiana. Milos M. Vujnovich. 1974. 12.50 (ISBN 0-686-61039-3). Ragusan Pr.
Yukon Gold. William D. Blankenship. LC 76-55733. 1977. 9.95 (ISBN 0-525-23945-6, Henry Robbins Bks.). Dutton.
Yukon Passage: Rafting 2,000 Miles to the Bering Sea. Keith Tryck. 288p. 1981. 15.00 (ISBN 0-8129-0926-7). Times Bks.
Yukpa Cultivation System: A Study of Shifting Cultivation in Columbia & Venezuela. Kenneth Ruddle. (Publications in Ibero-Americana Ser: Vol. 52). 1976. pap. 14.50x (ISBN 0-520-09497-2). U of Cal Pr.
Yuletide at Winterthur. (Illus.). 1980. pap. 3.50 (ISBN 0-912724-09-9). Winterthur.
Yuman & Yaqui Music. Frances Densmore. LC 72-1884. (Music Ser.). (Illus.). 272p. 1972. Repr. of 1932 ed. lib. bdg. 19.50 (ISBN 0-306-70512-5). Da Capo.
Yummers! James Marshall. LC 72-5400. (Illus.). 32p. (gr. k-3). 1973. reinforced bdg. 6.95 (ISBN 0-395-14757-3). HM.
Yusuf, Boy of Cyprus. Grace Rasp-Nuri. LC 58-5901. (Illus.). (gr. 5-9). 1958. 8.95 (ISBN 0-87599-095-9). S G Phillips.
Yvain Ou le Chevalier Au Lion. Chretien De Troyes. Ed. by Jan Nelson et al. LC 68-22800. (Medieval French Literature Ser). (Orig., Fr). 1968. pap. text ed. 5.95x (ISBN 0-89197-477-6). Irvington.
Yvar, Prince of Rus. Richard Cloke. LC 80-80543. 700p. (Orig.). 1981. pap. 6.75 (ISBN 0-917458-08-7). Kent Pubns.
Yvette. Toni Block. (Orig.). 1978. pap. 1.95 o.p. (ISBN 0-523-40211-2). Pinnacle Bks.
Yvor Winters: The Uncollected Essays & Reviews. Ed. by Francis Murphy. LC 72-91915. 320p. 1972. 12.95 (ISBN 0-8040-0604-0). Swallow.

Z

Z Eight Thousand Assembly Language Programming. Lance Leventhal et al. (Assembly Language Programming Ser.: No.5). 930p. (Orig.). 1980. pap. text ed. 19.99 (ISBN 0-931988-36-5). Osborne-McGraw.
Z-Eighty & Eighty-Eighty Assembly Language Programming. Kathe Spracklen. (Computer Programming Ser.). 192p. 1979. pap. 8.85 (ISBN 0-8104-5167-0). Hayden.
Z-Eighty Assembly Language Programming. Lance Levanthal. (Assembly Language Programming Ser.: No. 3). (Orig.). 1979. pap. text ed. 16.99 (ISBN 0-931988-21-7). Osborne-McGraw.
Z-Eighty Microprocessor Programming & Interfacing, 2 bks. Joseph C. Nichols et al. LC 79-63822. 1979. Bk. 1. pap. 11.95 (ISBN 0-672-21609-4); Bk. 2. pap. 14.95 (ISBN 0-672-21610-8, 21610); Set. pap. 24.95 (ISBN 0-672-21611-6). Sams.
Z-Eighty User's Manual. Joseph Carr. (Illus.). 352p. 1980. text ed. 17.95 (ISBN 0-8359-9517-8); pap. text ed. 10.95 (ISBN 0-8359-9516-X). Reston.
Z Warning. Dan Oran & Lonn Hoklin. 1979. 8.95 o.p. (ISBN 0-345-28096-2). Ballantine.
Zabytye Proizvedeliia. Isaak Babel. Ed. by N. Stroud. (Rus.). 1979. 15.00 (ISBN 0-88233-118-3); pap. 7.50 o.p. (ISBN 0-88233-119-1). Ardis Pubs.
Zaccheus Meets Jesus. (Tell-a-Bible Story Ser.). (Illus.). 28p. bds. 0.69 (ISBN 0-686-68647-0, 3691). Standard Pub.
Zacharie Astruc: Critic, Artist & Japoniste (1883-1907) Sharon Flescher. LC 77-94694. (Outstanding Dissertations in the Fine Arts Ser.). 1978. lib. bdg. 60.50 (ISBN 0-8240-3226-8). Garland Pub.
Zachary Goes Groundfishing. Larkin. 1980. 6.95 (ISBN 0-89272-084-0). Down East.

Zadig; or, the Book of Fate, 1749. Francois Voltaire. Ed. by Michael F. Shugrue. Incl. Amours of Zeokinizal King of the Kofiranis, 1749. Claude Crebillon. (Flowering of the Novel, 1740-1775 Ser: Vol. 25). 1974. lib. bdg. 50.00 (ISBN 0-8240-1124-4). Garland Pub.

Zagadka Tolstogo. Mark Aldanov. LC 79-91652. (Slavic Reprint Ser.: No. 7). 127p. (Rus.). 1969. pap. 3.00 (ISBN 0-87057-114-1, Pub. by Brown U Pr). Univ Pr of New England.

Zahlentheorie, 5 vols. Paul Bachmann. (Nos. 15-20). (Ger). Repr. Set. 131.00 (ISBN 0-384-02990-6). Johnson Repr.

Zahlentheorie. 4th ed. P. G. Lejeune-Dirichlet & R. Dedekind. LC 68-54716. (Ger). 1969. text ed. 29.95 (ISBN 0-8284-0213-2). Chelsea Pub.

Zaire a Week in Joseph's World. Eliot Elisofon. LC 72-81069. (Face to Face Books Ser.). (Illus.). 40p. (gr. k-2). 1973. 8.95 (ISBN 0-02-733400-7, CCPr). Macmillan.

Zaire: The Political Economy of Underdevelopment. Guy Gran. LC 79-19512. (Praeger Special Studies). 352p. 1979. 25.95 (ISBN 0-03-048916-4). Praeger.

Zalacain el Aventurero. Ed. by J. C. Babcock et al. LC 49-8551. (Graded Spanish Readers, Bk. 4). (Span). 1954. pap. text ed. 4.15 (ISBN 0-395-04127-9). HM.

Zamani: A Survey of East African History. Ed. by B. A. Ogot & J. A. Kieran. LC 68-26079. (Illus.). 1971. pap. text ed. 7.25x (ISBN 0-582-60293-9). Humanities.

Zamani Goes to Market. Muriel L. Feelings. LC 70-97032. (Illus.). (gr. 1-4). 1970. 6.95 (ISBN 0-395-28791-X, Clarion). HM.

Zambesian Past: Studies in Central African History. Eric Stokes & Richard Brown. 1966. text ed. 10.25x (ISBN 0-7190-0261-3). Humanities.

Zambia, 1890-1964: The Colonial Period. Richard Hall. (Illus.). 1977. pap. text ed. 6.50x (ISBN 0-582-64620-0). Longman.

Zambia's Foreign Policy: Studies in Diplomacy & Dependence. Douglas G. Anglin & Timothy M. Shaw. 1979. 29.50 (ISBN 0-89158-191-X). Westview.

Zanboomer. R. R. Knudson. (gr. 7-12). 1980. pap. 1.50 (ISBN 0-440-99908-1, LFL). Dell.

Zande Scheme: An Anthropological Case Study of Economic Development in Africa. Conrad C. Reining. (African Studies Ser.: No. 17). 1966. 11.95x o.s.i. (ISBN 0-8101-0205-6). Northwestern U Pr.

Zande Trickster. Ed. by Edward E. Evans-Pritchard. (Oxford Library of African Literature). 1967. 14.95x (ISBN 0-19-815123-3). Oxford U Pr.

Zane Grey. Carlton Jackson. (U. S. Authors Ser.: No. 218). 1973. lib. bdg. 10.95 (ISBN 0-8057-0338-1). Twayne.

Zane Grey's Arizona Ames: Gun Trouble in Tonto Basin. Romer Z. Grey. (Orig.). 1980. pap. 2.25 (ISBN 0-505-51479-6). Tower Bks.

Zane Grey's Arizona Ames: King of the Outlaw Horde. Romer Z. Grey. (Orig.). 1980. pap. 1.95 (ISBN 0-505-51509-1). Tower Bks.

Zane Grey's Buck Duane: King of the Range. Romer Z. Grey. (Orig.). 1980. pap. 1.95 (ISBN 0-505-51499-0). Tower Bks.

Zane Grey's Buck Duane: The Rider of Distant Trails. Romer Z. Grey. 1980. pap. 2.25 (ISBN 0-505-51469-9). Tower Bks.

Zane Grey's Laramie Nelson. Romer Z. Grey. 1980. pap. 2.25 (ISBN 0-505-51458-3). Tower Bks.

Zane Grey's Nevada Jim Lacy: Beyond the Mogollon Rim. Romer Z. Grey. (Orig.). 1980. pap. 1.95 (ISBN 0-505-51529-6). Tower Bks.

Zane Grey's Yaqui: Siege at Forlorn River. Romer Z. Grey. (Orig.). 1980. pap. 1.95 (ISBN 0-505-51519-9). Tower Bks.

Zaner-Bloser Handwriting Workbook: Cursive. Walter B. Barbe. (Illus.). 1977. 3.95 (ISBN 0-88309-098-8). Zaner-Bloser.

Zaner-Bloser Handwriting Workbook: Manuscript. Walter B. Barbe. (Illus.). 1977. 3.95 (ISBN 0-88309-097-X). Zaner-Bloser.

Zanoni: A Rosicrucian Tale. E. Bulwer-Lytton. LC 78-157505. 416p. 1971. pap. 8.95 (ISBN 0-8334-1723-1). Steinerbks.

Zany Word Search & Find Puzzles, No. 4. Bea Dow & Jack Tabatch. (Orig.). 1974. pap. 0.95 o.p. (ISBN 0-345-23893-1). Ballantine.

Zanzara. Michaela Morgan. 1978. pap. 2.25 o.p. (ISBN 0-523-40388-7, Dist. by Independent News Co.). Pinnacle Bks.

Zanzibar: Tradition & Revolution. Esmond B. Martin. 1979. 19.95 (ISBN 0-241-89937-0, Pub. by Hamish Hamilton England). David & Charles.

Zapata: A Biography. Roger Parkinson. LC 74-28202. (Illus.). 256p. (Orig.). 1980. pap. cancelled (ISBN 0-8128-6072-1). Stein & Day.

Zapata, Mexican Rebel. Ronald Syme. LC 79-128118. (Illus.). (gr. 3-7). 1971. 6.75 o.p. (ISBN 0-688-21604-8); PLB 6.96 (ISBN 0-688-31604-2). Morrow.

Zapotec Deviance: The Convergence of Folk & Modern Sociology. Henry A. Selby. LC 73-22480. 214p. 1974. 10.00x o.p. (ISBN 0-292-79800-8). U of Tex Pr.

Zarabanda. Milo Sperber. 1972. pap. text ed. 3.50 (ISBN 0-912022-32-9). EMC.

Zarco. Ignacio M. Altamirano. Ed. by Raymond L. Grismer & Miguel Ruelas. 1933. 3.95x (ISBN 0-393-09442-1, NortonC). Norton.

Zavist. Yuri Olesha. (Illus., Rus.). 1977. 15.00 o.p. (ISBN 0-88233-126-4); pap. 4.00 o.p. (ISBN 0-88233-127-2). Ardis Pubs.

ZBC of Ezra Pound. Christine Brooke-Rose. LC 75-138284. 1971. 17.50x (ISBN 0-520-01848-6); pap. 4.95x (ISBN 0-520-03041-9). U of Cal Pr.

Zealots & Rebels: A History of the Ruling Communist Party of Czechoslovakia. Zdenek L. Suda. (Publication Ser.: No. 234). 265p. (Orig.). 1980. pap. 8.95 (ISBN 0-8179-7342-7). Hoover Inst Pr.

Zeb: A Celebrated Schooner Life. Polly Burroughs. LC 72-80278. (Illus.). 1979. pap. 7.95 (ISBN 0-85699-050-7). Globe Pequot.

Zebra. Clark Howard. 1980. pap. 2.75 (ISBN 0-425-04635-4). Berkley Pub.

Zebra Finches. Cyril H. Rogers. (Illus.). 128p. 1980. 7.95 (ISBN 0-903264-19-6, 4904-9, Pub. by K & R Bks England). Arco.

Zebra Goes to School. Marjorie-Ann Watts. LC 80-2688. (Illus.). 32p. (gr. k-2). 1981. 9.95 (ISBN 0-233-97241-2). Andre Deutsch.

Zebras. Daphne M. Goodall. LC 77-608273. (Animals of the World Ser). (Illus.). (gr. 4-8). 1978. PLB 10.65 (ISBN 0-8172-1080-6). Raintree Pubs.

Zechariah. T. V. Moore. (Geneva Commentaries Ser.). 1974. 7.95 (ISBN 0-85151-078-7). Banner of Truth.

Zechariah. Merrill F. Unger. 12.95 (ISBN 0-310-33420-9). Zondervan.

Zeely. Virginia Hamilton. (gr. 5-8). 1967. 8.95 (ISBN 0-02-742470-7). Macmillan.

Zeiss Ikon Cameras: Nineteen Twenty Six-Nineteen Thirty-Nine. D. B. Tubbs. 25.00 (ISBN 0-85242-604-6, Pub. by Fountain). Morgan.

Zeit Allein Heilt Keine Wunden Psychoanalytische Erstgespraeche Mit Kindern und Eltern. Ed. by A. Eckstaedt & R. Kluwer. (Edition Taschenbuecher Wissenschaft). (Orig.). 1980. pap. text ed. 7.15 (ISBN 3-518-07908-5, Pub. by Insel Verlag Germany). Suhrkamp.

Zeitschrift Fur Historische Waffen-und Kostumkunde: Eighteen Ninety Seven to Nineteen Twenty, 10. Ed. by W. Boeheim & K. Koetschau. (Illus.). 3000p. 1973. Repr. 925.00 o.p. (ISBN 3-201-00782-X). Arma Pr.

Zelda. Nancy Milford. 1971. pap. 2.50 (ISBN 0-380-00784-3, 40014). Avon.

Zeluco: Various Views of Human Nature Taken from Life and Manners, Foreign and Domestic, 2 vols. in 1. John Moore. LC 80-2492. 1981. Repr. of 1789 ed. 89.50 (ISBN 0-404-19126-6). AMS Pr.

Zemba: Shadow No. 19. Maxwell Grant. 1977. pap. 1.25 o.p. (ISBN 0-515-04285-4). Jove Pubns.

Zen: A Way of Life. Christmas Humphries. 6.95 o.s.i. (ISBN 0-87523-154-3). Emerson.

Zen Action-Zen Person. T. P. Kasulis. LC 80-27858. 192p. 1980. 12.95 (ISBN 0-8248-0702-2). U Pr of Hawaii.

Zen & Confucius in the Art of Swordsmanship(the Tengu-Geijutsu-Ron of Chozan Shissai) Ed. by Reinhard Kammer. Tr. by Betty Fitzgerald. (Illus.). 1978. cased 16.00 (ISBN 0-7100-8737-3). Routledge & Kegan.

Zen & Creative Management. Albert Low. LC 74-33609. 288p. 1976. pap. 3.50 (ISBN 0-385-04669-3, Anch). Doubleday.

Zen & Modern Japanese Religions. Michael Pye. LC 74-155691. (Living Religions Series). (Illus.). 1973. pap. 3.50x (ISBN 0-7062-3148-1). Intl Pubns Serv.

Zen & Shinto: The Story of Japanese Philosophy. Chikao Fujisawa. LC 78-139133. 92p. Repr. of 1959 ed. lib. bdg. 13.50x (ISBN 0-8371-5749-8, FUZS). Greenwood.

Zen & the Lady. Claire M. Owens. LC 79-50288. 311p. (Orig.). 1981. pap. 6.95 (ISBN 0-88238-996-3). Great Eastern.

Zen & the Mind: A Scientific Approach to Zen Practice. Tomio Hirai. (Illus., Orig.). 1978. 9.95 (ISBN 0-87040-391-5). Japan Pubns.

Zen & the Taming of the Bull: Towards the Definition of Buddhist Thought. Walpola Rahula. 1978. text ed. 17.25x (ISBN 0-900406-69-0). Humanities.

Zen & the Ways. Trevor Leggett. (Illus.). 1978. 18.00 (ISBN 0-7100-8598-2). Routledge & Kegan.

Zen Buddhism: Selected Writings of D. T. Suzuki. D. T. Suzuki. 1956. pap. 2.50 (ISBN 0-385-09300-4, A90, Anch). Doubleday.

Zen Combat. Jay Gluck. 224p. 1976. pap. 1.75 o.p. (ISBN 0-345-25030-3). Ballantine.

Zen Comments on the Mumonkan. Zenkei Shibayama. 1975. pap. 2.25 o.p. (ISBN 0-451-61403-8, ME1403, Ment). NAL.

Zen Diary. P. Wienpahl. 6.95 o.p. (ISBN 0-685-47284-1). Weiser.

Zen Dictionary. Ed. by Ernest Wood. LC 62-12828. 1962. 4.75 o.p. (ISBN 0-8022-1925-X). Philos Lib.

Zen Environment: The Impact of Zen Meditation. Marian Mountain. 288p. 1981. 10.95 (ISBN 0-688-00350-8). Morrow.

Zen Flesh, Zen Bones. Paul Reps. LC 57-10199. (Illus.). 1957. 10.50 (ISBN 0-8048-0644-6). C E Tuttle.

Zen Flesh, Zen Bones: A Collection of Zen & Pre-Zen Writings. Ed. by Paul Reps. pap. 2.95 (ISBN 0-385-08130-8, A233, Anch). Doubleday.

Zen in the Art of Flower Arrangement: An Introduction to the Spirit of the Japanese Art of Flower Arrangement. Gustie L. Herrigel. 1974. 10.00 (ISBN 0-7100-7941-9); pap. 6.00 (ISBN 0-7100-7942-7). Routledge & Kegan.

Zen in the Art of Helping. David Brandon. 1976. 12.50 (ISBN 0-7100-8428-5). Routledge & Kegan.

Zen in the Art of Tea Ceremony. Horst Hammitzch. 104p. 1981. 7.95 (ISBN 0-312-89859-2). St Martin.

Zen Master Dogen: An Introduction with Selected Writings. Yuho Yokoi & Daizen Victoria. LC 75-33200. (Illus.). 220p. 1976. 9.75 (ISBN 0-8348-0116-7); pap. 4.75 (ISBN 0-8348-0112-4). Weatherhill.

Zen Master Hakuin: Selected Writings. Tr. by Philip B. Yampolsky from Jap. LC 75-145390. (Records of Civilization, Studies & Sources: No. 86). 1971. 17.50x (ISBN 0-231-03463-6). Columbia U Pr.

Zen Mind, Beginner's Mind. Shunryu Suzuki. Ed. by Trudy Dixon. LC 70-123326. 132p. 1970. 5.95 (ISBN 0-8348-0052-7); pap. 4.50 (ISBN 0-8348-0079-9). Weatherhill.

Zen of Running. Fred Rohe. 1975. pap. 3.95 o.p. (ISBN 0-394-73038-0). Random.

Zen Poems. 2nd ed. Nhat Hanh & Vo-Dinh. Tr. by Ted Savory from Vietnamese & Eng. (Illus.). 1976. 10.00 (ISBN 0-87775-038-6); pap. 5.00 (ISBN 0-87775-038-6). Unicorn Pr.

Zen Poems of China & Japan: The Crane's Bill. Ed. by Lucien Stryk & Takashi Ikemoto. LC 73-75168. pap. 1.95 o.p. (ISBN 0-385-04624-3, Anch). Doubleday.

Zen Poems of China & Japan: The Crane's Bill. Tr. by Lucien Stryk et al from Chinese Japanese. 208p. 1981. pap. 4.95 (ISBN 0-394-17912-9, BC). Grove.

Zen Poems of Ryokan. Tr. by Nobuyuki Yuasa from Jap. LC 80-8585. (Princeton lbrary of Asian Translations). (Illus.). 196p. 1981. 17.50x (ISBN 0-691-06466-0). Princeton U Pr.

Zen Shiatsu: How to Harmonize Yin and Yang for Better Health. Shizuto Masunaga & Wataru Ohashi. (Illus.). 176p. 1977. pap. 9.95 (ISBN 0-87040-394-X). Japan Pubns.

Zen Teaching of Huang Po: On the Transmission of the Mind. Huang Po. Tr. by John Blofeld. 1959. pap. 4.95 (ISBN 0-394-17217-5, E171, Ever). Grove.

Zen Yoga Therapy. Masahiro Oki. LC 79-1060. (Illus.). 1979. pap. 12.50 (ISBN 0-87040-459-8). Japan Pubns.

Zend-Avesta, 3 Vols. English Avesta. LC 68-30997. 1880-87. Repr. lib. bdg. 49.00x (ISBN 0-8371-3070-0, AVZE). Greenwood.

Zend-Avesta, Vols. 4, 23 & 31. Ed. by F. Max Mueller. Tr. by Legge. (Sacred Books of the East Ser.). 15.00x ea.; Vol. 4. (ISBN 0-8426-1273-4); Vol. 23. (ISBN 0-8426-1274-2); Vol. 31. (ISBN 0-8426-1275-0). Verry.

Zenia's Way. Abraham Polonsky. 1980. 9.95 (ISBN 0-690-01896-7). Lippincott & Crowell.

Zenith Color TV Service Manual, Vol. 1. Robert L. Goodman. LC 75-85325. (Schematic Servicing Manual Ser.). (Illus.). 1969. vinyl o.p. 8.95 (ISBN 0-8306-9502-8); pap. 7.95 (ISBN 0-8306-8502-2, 502). TAB Bks.

Zenobia Regina Di Palmireni. Tomaso Albinoni. Ed. by Howard M. Brown. LC 76-21018. (Italian Opera 1640-1770 Ser.: Vol. 15). 1979. lib. bdg. 75.00 (ISBN 0-8240-2614-4). Garland Pub.

Zenon von Kition: Positionen und Probleme. Andreas Graeser. 1975. 51.00x (ISBN 3-11-004673-3). De Gruyter.

Zeolite Molecular Sieves: Structure, Chemistry & Use. Donald W. Breck. LC 73-11028. 1974. 56.50 (ISBN 0-471-09985-6, Pub. by Wiley-Interscience). Wiley.

Zeolite Technology & Applications: Recent Advances. Ed. by Jeanette Scott. LC 80-19308. (Chemical Tech. Rev. 170). (Illus.). 381p. 1981. 64.00 (ISBN 0-8155-0817-4). Noyes.

Zephyr 1978-1980. Chilton's Automotive Editorial Dept. (Illus.). 1980. pap. 8.95 (ISBN 0-8019-6965-4). Chilton.

Zeppelin in Combat: A History of the German Naval Airship Division, 1912-1918. Douglas H. Robinson. LC 80-13791. (Illus.). 432p. 1980. Repr. of 1971 ed. 25.00 (ISBN 0-295-95752-2). U of Wash Pr.

Zero. C. Radhakrishnan. (Indian Writers Ser.). 110p. 1974. 6.50 (ISBN 0-88253-462-9). Ind-US Inc.

Zero-Base Budgeting: A Decision Package Manual. L. Allan Austin & Logan M. Cheek. (Illus.). 1979. 16.95 (ISBN 0-8144-5513-1). Am Mgmt.

Zero-Base Budgeting: A Practical Management Tool for Evaluating Expenses. Peter A. Pyhrr. LC 72-8358. (Systems & Controls for Financial Management Ser). 240p. 1973. 26.50 (ISBN 0-471-70234-X); pap. 12.95 (ISBN 0-471-03721-4, Pub. by Wiley-Interscience). Wiley.

Zero-Base Budgeting & Program Evaluation. Joseph S. Wholey. LC 77-4610. 1978. 15.95 (ISBN 0-669-01730-2). Lexington Bks.

Zero-Base Budgeting Comes of Age. Logan Cheek. (Illus.). 1979. pap. 8.95 (ISBN 0-8144-7516-7). Am Mgmt.

Zero-Base Budgeting Comes of Age. Logan M. Cheek. LC 77-4362. (Illus.). 1977. 23.95 (ISBN 0-8144-5442-9). Am Mgmt.

Zero Base Budgeting for Health Care Institutions. Ray Dillon. LC 79-15046. 1979. text ed. 30.00 (ISBN 0-89443-150-1). Aspen Systems.

Zero-Base Budgeting in State & Local Government: Current Experiences & Cases. Ed. by John A. Worthley & William G. Ludwin. LC 79-10162. 1979. 20.95 (ISBN 0-03-049121-5). Praeger.

Zero-Base Planning & Budgeting: A Key to Raising Productivity. L. Austin & Roy Lindberg. (Illus.). 1980. 25.00 o.p. (ISBN 0-89433-107-8). Petrocelli.

Zero Cash Success Techniques Kit. 2nd ed. Tyler G. Hicks. 876p. 1981. pap. 99.50 (ISBN 0-914306-42-1). Intl Wealth.

Zero Hour & Other Documentary Poems. Ernesto Cardenal. Ed. by Donald D. Walsh. Tr. by Paul W. Borgeson & Jonathan Cohen. LC 80-36817. 1980. 12.00 (ISBN 0-8112-0766-8); pap. 4.95 (ISBN 0-8112-0767-6, NDP502). New Directions.

Zero Is Not Nothing. Harry Sitomer & Mindel Sitomer. LC 77-11562. (Young Math Book). (gr. 1-3). 1978. PLB 7.89 (ISBN 0-690-03829-1, TYC-J). T Y Crowell.

Zero Population Growth--For Whom? Differential Fertility & Minority Group Survival. Ed. by Milton Himmelfarb & Victor Baras. LC 77-87966. (Contributions in Sociology: No. 30). (Illus.). 1978. lib. bdg. 22.50x (ISBN 0-313-20041-6, AJC/). Greenwood.

Zero Sen: Japanese Fighter. Edward T. Maloney. (Illus.). 1978. pap. 3.00 (Pub. by WW II). Aviation.

Zero-Sum Society. Lester C. Thurow. 230p. 1981. pap. 4.95 (ISBN 0-14-005807-9). Penguin.

Zero Weather. Ramon S. Morningstar. Ed. by Una Edwards. LC 80-20072. 320p. (Orig.). 1980. pap. 6.95 (ISBN 0-937770-00-0). Family Pub CA.

Zerovalent Compounds of Metals. Li Malatesta & S. Cenini. 1975. 36.50 (ISBN 0-12-466350-8). Acad Pr.

Zest for Life. Emile Zola. 1959. 13.95 (ISBN 0-236-31013-5, Pub. by Paul Elek). Merrimack Bk Serv.

Zest for Living. Gaines Dobbins. LC 76-48526. 1977. 5.95 o.p. (ISBN 0-87680-511-X, 80511). Word Bks.

Zettel. Ludwig Wittgenstein. Ed. by G. E. M. Anscombe & G. H. Von Wright. Tr. by G. E. M Anscombe. 1967. 16.75x (ISBN 0-520-01355-7); pap. 4.95x (ISBN 0-520-01635-1, CAL189). U of Cal Pr.

Zeus: A Study of Ancient Religion, 2 vols. Arthur B. Cook. Incl. Vol. 1. Zeus, God of the Bright Sky. LC 64-25839. (Illus.). 885p. Repr. of 1914 ed. 45.00x (ISBN 0-8196-0148-9); Vol. 2. Zeus, God of the Dark Sky: Thunder & Lightning, 2 pts. LC 64-25839. Repr. of 1925 ed. 90.00x set (ISBN 0-8196-0156-X); Vol. 2, Pt. 1. Text & Notes. xliii, 858p; Vol. 2, Pt. 2. Appendixes & Index. (Illus.). 539p. Biblo.

Zhukov. Otto P. Chaney, Jr. LC 74-145505. (Illus.). 1971. 19.95 o.p. (ISBN 0-8061-0951-3). U of Okla Pr.

Zigger Beans. Diane R. Massie. LC 70-117564. (Illus.). (gr. k-2). 1971. 5.95 o.s.i. (ISBN 0-8193-0416-6, Four Winds); PLB 5.41 o.s.i. (ISBN 0-8193-0417-4). Schol Bk Serv.

Ziggy & His Friends. Mike Dolan. (Illus.). 1980. 7.95g (ISBN 0-516-09203-0). Childrens.

Ziggy Christmas. Tom Wilson. 48p. (gr. 4 up). 4.95 (ISBN 0-8362-1161-8). Andrews & McMeel.

Ziggy's Class Notes. 1980. 2.95 (ISBN 0-8362-1916-3). Andrews & McMeel.

Ziggy's Door Openers. Tom Wilson. 20p. (gr. 4 up). 1980. pap. 4.95 (ISBN 0-8362-1914-7). Andrews & McMeel.

Ziggys of the World Unite. new ed. Tom Wilson. (Illus.). 96p. (Orig.). 1976. pap. 2.50 (ISBN 0-8362-0673-8). Andrews & McMeel.
Zilya's Secret Plan. Ulrich Schaffer. 1979. 3.95 o.p. (ISBN 0-8028-3514-7). Eerdmans.
Zimbabwe Controversy-a Case of Colonial Historiography. David Chanaiwa. (Foreign & Comparative Studies-Eastern African Ser.: No. 8). 142p. 1973. pap. 4.50x (ISBN 0-915984-05-9). Syracuse U Foreign Comp.
Zimbabwe Directory 1980-81: Including Botswana. 71st ed. LC 38-1460. Orig. Title: Rhodesia Directory. (Illus.). 996p. (Orig.). 1980. pap. 45.00x (ISBN 0-8002-2747-6). Intl Pubns Serv.
Zimmermann Telegram. Barbara W. Tuchman. 1966. 11.95 (ISBN 0-02-620320-0). Macmillan.
Zinc & Copper in Medicine. Z. A. Karcioglu & R. M. Sarper. (Illus.). 696p. 1980. 59.75 (ISBN 0-398-03977-1). C C Thomas.
Zinc & Its Alloys. S. W. Morgan. (Illus.). 224p. 1977. pap. 13.95x (ISBN 0-7121-0945-5, Pub. by Macdonald & Evans England). Intl Ideas.
Zinc Deficiency in Rice: A Review of Research at the International Rice Research Institute. (IRRI Research Paper Ser.: No. 9). 17p. 1977. pap. 5.00 (R049, IRRI). Unipub.
Zinc in the Environment, 2 pts. Jerome O. Nriagu. Incl. Pt. I. Ecological Cycling (ISBN 0-471-05888-2); Pt. II. Health Effects (ISBN 0-471-05889-0). LC 79-19257. (Environmental Science & Technology: a Wiley-Interscience Ser. of Texts & Monographs). 1980. 47.50 ea. (Pub. by Wiley-Interscience). Wiley.
Zion Adventure Guide. Doug Rudig. 32p. 1978. 1.95. Zion.
Zion in America. Henry L. Feingold. (Immigrant Heritage of America Ser). 1974. lib. bdg. 14.50 (ISBN 0-8057-3298-5). Twayne.
Zion South. Mark Lieberman. LC 80-66494. 1981. 12.95 (ISBN 0-87795-269-8). Arbor Hse.
Zion, the Growing Symbol. Ed. by David Premoe. 1980. pap. 5.75 (ISBN 0-8309-0301-1). Herald Hse.
Zion: The Story Behind the Scenery. rev. ed. A. J. Eardley et al. Ed. by Gweneth R. DenDooven. LC 77-157458. (Illus.). 1979. 7.95 (ISBN 0-916122-32-8); pap. 3.00 (ISBN 0-916122-07-7). K C Pubns.
Zion Trails. Reed Blake. (Illus.). 1977. pap. 1.50 o.s.i. (ISBN 0-915272-09-1). Wasatch Pubs.
Zionism in Transition. Ed. by Moshe Davis. 1980. pap. 8.00 (ISBN 0-930832-61-2). Herzl Pr.
Zionist Connection: What Price Peace? Alfred M. Lilienthal. LC 78-10556. 1978. 19.95 (ISBN 0-396-07564-9). Dodd.
Zionist Relations with Nazi Germany. Faris Glubb. 3.00. New World Press NY.
Zionist Year Book 1980. 29th ed. Ed. by Jane Moonman. LC 52-65547. (Illus.). 384p. 1980. pap. 15.00 (ISBN 0-8002-2413-2). Intl Pubns Serv.
Zip. Max Apple. 1978. 8.95 o.p. (ISBN 0-670-79692-1). Viking Pr.
Zirconium: Metallurgy of Zirconium. (Atomic Energy Review: Supplement). 1971. 21.50 (ISBN 92-0-159071-7, IAEA). Unipub.
Zirconium: Physico-Chemical Properties of Its Compounds & Alloys. LC 76-5641. (Atomic Energy Review:.No. 6). (Illus.). 1977. pap. 20.50 (ISBN 92-0-149276-6, IAEA). Unipub.
Zirka. 2nd, rev. ed. Ivan Zubenko. 171p. (Ukrainian.). 1980. pap. text ed. 6.00 (ISBN 0-686-63323-7). Slavia Lib.
Zite 'ngalera. Leonardo Vinci. Ed. by Howard M. Brown. LC 76-21072. 1979. lib. bdg. 75.00 (ISBN 0-8240-2624-1). Garland Pub.
Zoar Blue. Janet Hickman. LC 78-3828. (gr. 6 up). 1978. 8.95 (ISBN 0-02-743740-X, 74374). Macmillan.
Zodiac: A Monthly Periodical Devoted to Science, Literature & the Arts. (Illus.). 312p. 1980. Repr. of 1835 ed. 19.95x (ISBN 0-937438-00-6). Am Pine Barrens.
Zodiac Killer. Jerry Weissman. (Orig.). 1979. pap. 2.25 o.p. (ISBN 0-523-40529-4). Pinnacle Bks.
Zoe: The History of Two Lives 1845. Geraldine E. Jewsbury. Ed. by Robert L. Wolff. LC 75-1518. (Victorian Fiction Ser.). 1975. lib. bdg. 66.00 (ISBN 0-8240-1591-6). Garland Pub.
Zola Dictionary. J. G. Patterson. LC 68-27179. 1969. Repr. of 1912 ed. 18.00 (ISBN 0-8103-3173-X). Gale.
Zolotaia Nasha Zhelezka. Vasily P. Aksenov. (Rus.). 1979. 15.00 (ISBN 0-88233-479-4); pap. 5.00 (ISBN 0-88233-480-8). Ardis Pubs.
Zolotyi Homin. Pavlo Hryhorovych Tychyna. LC 68-52067. (Shkil'na Biblioteka Ser.). 1967. pap. text ed. 4.00 (ISBN 0-918884-25-X). Slavia Lib.
Zombie Maker. Steven Otfinoski. Ed. by Richard Uhlich. (Bluejeans Paperback Ser.). (Illus., Orig.). (gr. 7-12). 1978. pap. text ed. 1.25 (ISBN 0-8374-5002-0). Xerox Ed Pubns.
Zondervan Expanded Concordance. Zondervan Staff. 1968. 19.95 o.p. (ISBN 0-310-35010-7). Zondervan.
Zondervan Pastor's Annual, 1981. T. T. Crabtree. 384p. 1980. kivar 7.95 (ISBN 0-310-22641-4). Zondervan.
Zondervan's Bible Student's Library, 5 bks. Incl. Matthew Henry's Commentary; Zondervan Pictorial Bible Dictionary; Zondervan Expanded Concordance; Zondervan Topical Bible; Zondervan Pictoral Atlas. Set. 93.25 o.p. (ISBN 0-310-35298-3). Zondervan.
Zone Null. Herbert W. Franke. (Suhrkamp Taschenbuecher: Phantastische Bibliothek, Vol. 35). 208p. (Orig.). 1980. pap. text ed. 4.55 (ISBN 3-518-37085-5, Pub. by Insel Verlag Germany). Suhrkamp.
Zone of the Interior. Clancy Sigal. LC 76-4831. 288p. 1976. 8.95 o.p. (ISBN 0-690-01091-5, TYC-T). T Y Crowell.
Zone Therapy: Relieving Pain & Sickness by Nerve Pressure. Benedict Lust. (Illus.). 1980. pap. 3.95 (ISBN 0-87904-038-6). Lust.
Zoning Game: Municipal Practices & Policies. Richard F. Babcock. (Illus.). 1966. 17.50 (ISBN 0-299-04091-7); pap. 6.95 (ISBN 0-299-04094-1). U of Wis Pr.
Zoning Law & Practice, 8 vols. 4th ed. with 1979 cum. suppl. 300.00 (ISBN 0-87215-207-3); 1979 cum. suppl. 15.00 (ISBN 0-87215-325-8). Michie.
Zoning Law Anthology, Vol. Ii. Philip A. Garon. LC 78-66283. 1980. 59.95. Intl Lib.
Zoning Law Anthology, Vol. 2. Ed. by Philip A. Garon. LC 78-66283. (National Law Anthology Ser.). 1979-80. text ed. 59.95 (ISBN 0-914250-20-5). Intl Lib.
Zoo. Joan Crammond. (Illus.). 74p. (gr. 3-8). 1973. 5.95 (ISBN 0-7153-5660-7). David & Charles.
Zoo. Youldon. (ps-2). 1980. PLB cancelled (ISBN 0-531-03526-3); PLB 5.90 (ISBN 0-531-04168-9). Watts.
Zoo Animals. Donald F. Hoffmeister. Ed. by Herbert S. Zim & George S. Fichter. (Golden Guide Ser). (Illus.). (gr. k-4). 1967. PLB 9.15 (ISBN 0-307-63538-4, Golden Pr); pap. 1.95 o.p. (ISBN 0-307-24019-3). Western Pub.
Zoo Babies. William Bridges. (Illus.). (gr. k-3). 1953. PLB 6.48 o.p. (ISBN 0-688-31498-8). Morrow.
Zoo Book. Jan Pfloog. (ps-1). 1967. PLB 5.38 (ISBN 0-307-68939-5, Golden Pr). Western Pub.
Zoo City. Stephen Lewis. LC 75-35659. 32p. (gr. k-3). 1976. 8.25 (ISBN 0-688-86000-1). Greenwillow.
Zoo Doctor. William Bridges. (Illus.). (gr. 3-6). 1957. 7.95 (ISBN 0-688-21499-1). Morrow.
Zoo for All Seasons: The Smithsonian Animal World. Smithsonian Institute. (Illus.). 1979. 16.95 (ISBN 0-89577-003-2). Norton.
Zoo Friends Are at Our School Today! Mabel Watts. 1979. PLB 4.77 (ISBN 0-307-68423-7, Golden Pr). Western Pub.
Zoo Man. Herb Clement. (Illus.). (gr. 7 up). 1969. 5.95 o.s.i. (ISBN 0-02-526100-2). Macmillan.
Zoo That Never Was. R. D. Lawrence. LC 80-18956. (Illus.). 304p. 1981. 12.95 (ISBN 0-03-056811-0). HR&W.
Zoo Two Thousand: Twelve Stories of Science Fiction & Fantasy Beasts. Jane Yolen. LC 72-97773. (gr. 6 up). 1973. 7.95 (ISBN 0-395-28934-3, Clarion). HM.
Zoo Vet: Adventures of a Wild Animal Doctor. David Taylor. LC 76-56834. 1977. 8.95 o.p. (ISBN 0-397-01207-1). Lippincott.
Zoo Walkabout. Vincent Serventy. 160p. 1980. 17.95x (ISBN 0-00-216420-5, Pub. by W Collins Australia). Intl Schol Bk Serv.
Zoobook. National Zoological Park. LC 76-9653. (Illus.). 80p. 1976. 9.95 (ISBN 0-87474-846-1); pap. 4.50 (ISBN 0-87474-845-3). Smithsonian.
Zoobook. National Zoological Park, Office of Education. LC 76-9653. (Illus.). 80p. 1978. pap. 4.50 (ISBN 0-87474-845-3). Smithsonian.
Zoogeography & Diversity in Plankton. Ed. by S. Van der Spoel & A. C. Pierrot-Bults. LC 79-9494. 410p. 1979. 74.95x (ISBN 0-470-26798-4). Halsted Pr.
Zoological Mythology, 2 Vols. Angelo De Gubernatis. LC 68-58904. 1968. Repr. of 1872 ed. Set. 32.00 (ISBN 0-8103-3527-1). Gale.
Zoology. 5th ed. Alfred Elliot & Darryl E. Outka. (Illus.). 1976. 19.95 (ISBN 0-13-984021-4). P-H.
Zoology Careers. Robert E. Dunbar. (Illus.). (YA) (gr. 7 up). 1977. lib. bdg. 6.45 (ISBN 0-531-01312-X). Watts.
Zoology for Everybody, Vol. 1: A General Survey. 2nd ed. Eugen Kolisko. 1977. pap. 3.95x (ISBN 0-906492-05-X, Pub. by Kolisko Archives). St George Bk Serv.
Zoology for Everybody, Vol. 2: Birds. 2nd ed. Ed. by Eugen Kolisko. 1978. pap. 3.95x (ISBN 0-906492-08-4, Pub. by Kolisko Archives). St George Bk Serv.
Zoology for Everybody, Vol. 3: Mammals. Eugen Kolisko. (Illus.). 1979. pap. 4.50x (ISBN 0-906492-15-7, Pub. by Kolisko Archives). St George Bk Serv.
Zoology for Everybody, Vol. 4: Protozoa. Eugen Kolisko. 1980. pap. 4.25x (ISBN 0-906492-24-6, Pub. by Kolisko Archives). St George Bk Serv.
Zoology Made Simple. Dorothy F. Soule. LC 67-15392. 1967. pap. 3.50 (ISBN 0-385-08870-1, Made). Doubleday.
Zoom! Peter Townend. 208p. 1975. pap. 1.25 o.p. (ISBN 0-523-22586-5). Pinnacle Bks.
Zoom & Special Lenses. Leonard Gaunt. LC 80-41245. (Illus.). 128p. 1981. pap. 9.95 (ISBN 0-240-51069-0). Focal Pr.
Zoom Catalog. Young Viewers of Zoom. (Illus.). 1972. lib. bdg. 5.69 (ISBN 0-394-92532-7); pap. 3.50 (ISBN 0-394-82532-2). Random.
Zoophabet Needlework Book. Leslie Tillett. LC 76-45763. (Illus.). 1977. 14.95 o.p. (ISBN 0-690-01211-X, TYC-T). T Y Crowell.
Zoophabets. Tallon. (ps-3). 1980. pap. 1.95 (ISBN 0-590-30047-4, Schol Pap). Schol Bk Serv.
Zoos. John Perry. LC 70-161071. 1971. PLB 4.90 o.p. (ISBN 0-531-00754-5). Watts.
Zoos in the Making. Dorothy E. Shuttlesworth. (gr. 4-6). 1977. PLB 8.50 (ISBN 0-525-43725-8, Henry Robbins Bks.). Dutton.
Zoos Without Cages. Jane R. McCauley. LC 79-3243. 100p. 1981. 6.95 (ISBN 0-87044-335-6); PLB 8.50 (ISBN 0-87044-340-2). Natl Geog.
Zoot-Suit Murders. Thomas Sanchez. 1978. 9.95 o.p. (ISBN 0-525-24060-8, Henry Robbins). Dutton.
Zora Neale Hurston: A Literary Biography. Robert E. Hemenway. LC 77-9605. (Illus.). 1977. 15.00 (ISBN 0-252-00652-6); pap. 8.95 (ISBN 0-252-00807-3). U of Ill Pr.
Zorba. Kazantzaki. (Arabic.). pap. 7.95x (ISBN 0-686-63551-5). Intl Bk Ctr.
Zoroastrians: Their Religious Beliefs & Practices. Mary Boyce. (Library of Beliefs & Practices). 1979. 24.00 (ISBN 0-7100-0121-5). Routledge & Kegan.
Zosia & Thaddeus. 1st ed. Marion M. Coleman. LC 73-93707. 115p. 1974. pap. 4.00 (ISBN 0-910366-17-9). Alliance Coll.
Zucchini Lovers' Cookbook. rev. ed. 1979. pap. 5.25 (ISBN 0-9600982-4-0). A Gonshorowski.
Zuckerman Unbound. Philip Roth. 1981. 10.95 (ISBN 0-374-29945-5). FS&G.
Zulu-English & Zulu Dictionary. 15.00 (ISBN 0-685-77569-0, 096-8). Saphrograph.
Zulu Heart: A Novel. Shirley G. DuBois. LC 73-92801. 1973. 8.95 (ISBN 0-89388-132-5). Okpaku Communications.
Zulu Journal: Field Notes of a Naturalist in South Africa. Raymond B. Cowles. 1959. 17.50x (ISBN 0-520-00274-1); pap. 1.95 (ISBN 0-520-00276-8, CAL73). U of Cal Pr.
Zulu King Speaks: Statements Made by Cetshwayo Kampande on the History & Customs of His People. Ed. by C. deB. Webb & J. B. Wright. (Killie Campbell Africana Library Reprint: No. 3). (Illus.). 1979. text ed. 21.00x (ISBN 0-86980-153-8). Verry.
Zulu of South Africa, Cattlemen, Farmers, & Warriors. Sonia Bleeker. (Illus.). (gr. 3-6). 1970. PLB 6.67 (ISBN 0-688-31451-1). Morrow.
Zulu Tribe in Transition. D. H. Reader. 1966. text ed. 8.75x (ISBN 0-7190-0258-3). Humanities.
Zulu Warrior. Ronald Welch. LC 74-78244. (gr. 3-8). 1974. 5.95 (ISBN 0-7153-6555-X). David & Charles.
Zulu Zion & Some Swazi Zionists. Bengt Sundkler. (Oxford Studies in African Affairs Ser.). 1976. 37.50x (ISBN 0-19-822707-8). Oxford U Pr.
Zum Problem der Begabung und Intelligenz. Hans Werder. (Psychologische Praxis: Vol. 55). 190p. 1980. pap. 17.00 (ISBN 3-8055-1123-X). S Karger.
Zuni Fetishes. Frank H. Cushing. LC 66-23329. (Illus.). 1966. 7.95 (ISBN 0-916122-28-X); pap. 3.00 (ISBN 0-916122-03-4). K C Pubns.
Zur Helian Dmetrick: Das Verhaltnis Von Rhythmus und Satzewicht Im Altsachsischen. Ingeborg Hinderschiedt. (German Language & Literature Monographs: No. 8). 143p. 1980. text ed. 20.00x (ISBN 90-272-4001-9). Humanities.
Zurbaran. Jonathan Brown. LC 73-10481. (Library of Great Painters Ser.). (Illus.). 160p. 1974. 28.50 o.p. (ISBN 0-8109-0549-3). Abrams.
Zurich. G. H. Heer. 1973. bds. 7.50 (ISBN 0-911268-26-X). Rogers Bk.
Zurvan: A Zoroastrian Dilemma. Robert C. Zaehner. 1973. Repr. of 1955 ed. 19.50x (ISBN 0-8196-0280-9). Biblo.
Zwingli. G. R. Potter. LC 75-46136. (Illus.). 1977. 59.50 (ISBN 0-521-20939-0). Cambridge U Pr.
Zytologie und Mikrobiologie der Vagina. 3rd ed. J. D. Schnell. (Illus.). 92p. 1980. 35.50 (ISBN 3-8055-1428-X). S Karger.
ZZ-Two-Homotopy Theory. M. C. Crabb. (London Mathematical Lecture Note Ser.: No. 44). 100p. (Orig.). 1980. pap. 15.95 (ISBN 0-521-28051-6). Cambridge U Pr.

SUBJECT INDEX

A

AARON, HENRY, 1934-
Hahn, James & Hahn, Lynn. Henry! Henry Aaron. Schroeder, Howard, ed. (Sports Legends Ser.). (Illus.). 48p. (gr. 3-5). 1981. PLB 5.95 (ISBN 0-89686-120-1); pap. text ed. 2.95 (ISBN 0-89686-135-X). Crestwood Hse.
ABAILARD, PIERRE
see Abelard, Peter, 1079-1142
ABANDONED CHILDREN
see Child Welfare
ABANDONMENT (MARINE INSURANCE)
see Insurance, Marine
ABATTOIRS
see Slaughtering and Slaughter-Houses
ABBREVIATIONS
see also Ciphers; Code Names; Periodicals–Abbreviations of Titles; Shorthand; Signs and Symbols
also subdivision Abbreviations under subjects, e.g. Law–Abbreviations
Paxton, John, ed. Everyman's Dictionary of Abbreviations. rev. ed. 408p. 1981. 20.00x (ISBN 0-8476-6973-4). Rowman.
ABDOMEN
see also Intestines, Kidneys
Dagnini, Giorgio. Clinical Laparoscopy. (Illus.). xii, 307p. 1980. 130.00 (ISBN 88-212-0746-3, Pub. by Piccin Italy). J K Burgess.
ABDOMEN–RADIOGRAPHY
Logan & Edwards. Manual of Laparoscopy & Culdoscopy. 1981. text ed. price not set. Butterworth.
ABDOMEN–SURGERY
Maingot, Rodney. Abdominal Operations, 2 vols. 7th ed. 2802p. 1979. Set. 142.00x (ISBN 0-8385-8779-8). ACC.
Schein, Clarence J. Introduction to Abdominal Surgery: Fifty Clinical Studies. (Illus.). 416p. 1981. pap. text ed. write for info. (ISBN 0-06-142381-5, Harper Medical). Har-Row.
ABDOMINAL DELIVERY
see Cesarean Section
ABELARD, PETER, 1079-1142
Starnes, Kathleen M. Peter Abelard: His Place in History. LC 80-8298. 161p. 1981. lib. bdg. 17.50 (ISBN 0-8191-1510-X); pap. text ed. 8.75 (ISBN 0-8191-1511-8). U Pr of Amer.
ABERFAN, WALES
Thompson, G. McKecknie & Rodin, S. Colliery Spoil Tips-After Aberfan. 98p. 1980. pap. 15.00x (ISBN 0-901948-59-4, Pub. by Telford England). State Mutual Bk.
ABERRATION, CHROMATIC AND SPHERICAL
see Optical Instruments
ABILITY, EXECUTIVE
see Executive Ability
ABNORMAL CHILDREN
see Exceptional Children; Handicapped Children
ABNORMAL PSYCHOLOGY
see Psychology, Pathological
ABNORMALITIES, HUMAN
see also Dislocations; Giants; Medical Genetics; Monsters
O'Donnell, James J. & Hall, Bryan D., eds. Penetrance & Variability in Malformation Syndromes. LC 79-5115. (Alan R. Liss Ser.: Vol. 15, No. 5b). 1979. 42.00 (ISBN 0-8451-1029-2). March of Dimes.
Stehling, Linda C. & Zauder, Howard L., eds. Anesthetic Implications of Congenital Anomalies in Children. 224p. 1980. 18.50x (ISBN 0-8385-0102-8). ACC.
ABOLITION OF SLAVERY
see Abolitionists
ABOLITIONISTS
Moore, W. American Negro Slavery & Abolition. LC 73-148362. 1971. 10.00 (ISBN 0-89388-000-0); pap. 5.95. Okpaku Communications.
ABORIGINES
see Ethnology; Native Races
ABORTION
Burtchaell, James T., ed. Abortion Parley. 360p. 1980. cancelled. ACC.
Davis, John J. Abortion & the Evangelical. LC 80-82736. (The Nordland Series in Contemporary American Social Problems). 150p. (Orig.). 1980. pap. 7.95 (ISBN 0-913124-43-5). Nordland Pub.
Hodgson, Jane E. Abortion & Sterilization: Medical & Social Aspects. 1981. write for info. (ISBN 0-8089-1344-1). Grune.
Kowalczyk, J. Orthodox View on Abortion. 1979. pap. 1.50 (ISBN 0-686-27070-3). Light&Life Pub Co MN.
Mall, David & Watts, Walter F., eds. Psychological Aspects of Abortion. 1979. 15.00 (ISBN 0-89093-298-0); pap. 5.00 (ISBN 0-89093-274-3). U Pubns Amer.
Montgomery, John W. Slaughter of the Innocents. (Orig.). 1981. pap. 3.95 (ISBN 0-89107-216-0). Good News.
Schneider, Carl & Vinovskis, Maris A., eds. The Law & Politics of Abortion. LC 79-3134. 320p. 1980. 15.95x (ISBN 0-669-03386-3). Lexington Bks.
Sumner, L. W. Abortion & Moral Theory. LC 80-8578. 264p. 1981. 16.50x (ISBN 0-691-07262-0); pap. 4.95x (ISBN 0-691-02017-5). Princeton U Pr.
Zimmerman, Waldo. Condemned to Life: The Plight of the Unwanted Child. 260p. (Orig.). 1980. pap. 3.95 (ISBN 0-89260-181-7). Hwong Pub.
ABRAHAM, THE PATRIARCH
Arieti, Silvano. Abraham & the Contemporary Mind. LC 80-68187. 187p. 1981. 11.95 (ISBN 0-465-00005-3). Basic.
Matthews, A. Warren. Abraham Was Their Father. LC 81-146. vii, 266p. 1981. 19.50 (ISBN 0-86554-005-5). Mercer Univ Pr.
ABRASIVES
Farago, Francis T. Abrasive Methods Engineering, Vol. 2. LC 76-14970. (Illus.). 508p. 1980. 55.00 (ISBN 0-8311-1134-8). Indus Pr.
ABSENCE FROM SCHOOL
see School Attendance
ABSENT TREATMENT
see Mental Healing
ABSENTEE VOTING
see Voting
ABSOLUTE DIFFERENTIAL CALCULUS
see Calculus of Tensors
ABSORPTION, ATMOSPHERIC
see Solar Radiation
ABSORPTION OF GASES
see Gases–Absorption and Adsorption
ABSTINENCE
see Fasting; Temperance
ABSTRACT AUTOMATA
see Machine Theory
ABSTRACT MACHINES
see Machine Theory
ACADEMIC ACHIEVEMENT
Morris, Lynn L. & Fitz-Gibbon, Carol T. How to Measure Achievement. rev. ed. LC 78-58656. (Program Evaluation Kit Ser.: Vol. 6). (Illus.). 159p. 1978. pap. 7.50 (ISBN 0-8039-1067-3). Sage.
Morris, Lynn L., et al. Program Evaluation Kit. rev. ed. LC 78-59613. (Illus.). 1080p. 1978. pap. 49.95 (ISBN 0-8039-1073-8). Sage.
Morrris, Lynn L. & Fitz-Gibbon, Carol T. How to Present an Evaluation Report. rev. ed. LC 78-58657. (Program Evaluation Kit Ser.: Vol. 8). (Illus.). 80p. 1978. pap. 4.50 (ISBN 0-8039-1069-X). Sage.
ACADEMIC ADJUSTMENT
see Student Adjustment
ACADEMIC DEGREES
see Degrees, Academic
ACADEMIC FREEDOM
see Teaching, Freedom Of
ACADEMIES (LEARNED SOCIETIES)
see Learned Institutions and Societies; Societies
ACADEMY AWARDS (MOVING-PICTURES)
Brown, Peter. The Real Oscar. (Illus.). 256p. 1981. 15.95 (ISBN 0-87000-498-0). Arlington Hse.
Sarno, Art. Academy Awards Nineteen Eighty-One Oscar Annual. (Illus.). 1981. lib. bdg. 14.95 (ISBN 0-912076-43-7); pap. 9.95 (ISBN 0-912076-44-5). ESE Calif.
ACADIA
Reid, John G. Acadia, Maine, & New Scotland: Marginal Colonies in the Seventeenth Century. 320p. 1981. 27.50x (ISBN 0-8020-5508-7). U of Toronto Pr.
ACCELERATED READING
see Developmental Reading; Rapid Reading
ACCIDENT LAW
see also Employers' Liability; Liability for Nuclear Damages; Negligence; Workmen's Compensation
Atiyah, P. S. Accidents, Compensation & the Law. 3rd ed. (Law in Context Ser.). xxiv, 695p. 1980. 47.00x (ISBN 0-297-77754-8, Pub. by Weidenfeld & Nicolson England). Rothman.
Ison, Terence G. Accident Compensation. 240p. 1981. 37.50x (ISBN 0-7099-0249-2, Pub. by Croom Helm Ltd England). Biblio Dist.
ACCIDENTS
see also Assistance in Emergencies; Burns and Scalds; Disasters; Employers' Liability; Explosions; First Aid in Illness and Injury; Industrial Accidents; Life-Saving; Medical Emergencies; Physically Handicapped; Shipwrecks; Shock; Traumatism
also subdivision Wounds and Injuries under names of regions and organs of the body
Bernzweig, Eli P. By Accident, Not Design: The Case for Comprehensive Injury Reparations. 238p. 1980. 23.95 (ISBN 0-03-056961-3). Praeger.
ACCIDENTS–LAW AND LEGISLATION
see Accident Law
ACCIDENTS–PREVENTION
see also Industrial Safety
also subdivisions Safety Appliances or Safety Measures under subjects, e.g. Railroads–Safety Appliances, Automobiles–Safety Measures
Bell, Clinton C. Preventive Maintenance in a Corrugated Container Plant. (TAPPI Press Reports Ser.). (Illus.). 56p. 1981. pap. write for info. (ISBN 0-89852-388-5, 01-01-R088). Tappi.
Ewart, Nei. Unsafe As Houses: A Guide to Home Safety. (Illus.). 160p. 1981. 12.50 (ISBN 0-7137-1090-X, Pub. by Blandford Pr England). Sterling.
Parkinson, Virginia. Safety. (Pointers for Little Persons Ser.). (Illus.). (ps-2). 1963. PLB 5.99 (ISBN 0-8178-5062-7). Harvey.
Wolfe, Louis. Disaster Detectives. (Illus.). 160p. (gr. 8-12). 1981. PLB price not set (ISBN 0-671-34042-5). Messner.
ACCIDENTS, AIRCRAFT
see Aeronautics–Accidents
ACCIDENTS, INDUSTRIAL
see Industrial Accidents
ACCLIMATIZATION (PLANTS)
see Botany–Ecology
ACCOMMODATION (PSYCHOLOGY)
see Adjustment (Psychology)
ACCOMPANIMENT, MUSICAL
see Musical Accompaniment
ACCOUNTABILITY
see Liability (Law)
ACCOUNTING
see also Auditing; Bookkeeping; Business Mathematics; Cost Accounting; Financial Statements; Income Accounting; Managerial Accounting; Productivity Accounting; Tax Accounting
also subdivision Accounting under names of industries, professions, trades, etc., e.g. Printing–Accounting
Accounting Responses to Changing Prices: Experimentation with Four Models. 1980. pap. 14.00. Am Inst CPA.
Al Hashim, Dhia & Robertson, James W. Contemporary Issues in Accounting. LC 79-9840. (ITT Key Issue Lecture Ser.). 296p. 1979. text ed. 12.50 (ISBN 0-672-97331-6); pap. text ed. 6.95 (ISBN 0-672-97332-4). Bobbs.
APB-FASB. 13th ed. LC 79-55006. 8.00 (ISBN 0-932788-12-2). Bradley CPA.
Arnold, John, et al. Topics in Management Accounting. 256p. 1980. 33.00x (ISBN 0-86003-508-5, Pub. by Allan Pubs England); pap. 16.50x (ISBN 0-86003-609-X). State Mutual Bk.

Batty, J. Accounting for Research & Development. 237p. 1976. text ed. 23.50x (Pub. by Busn Bks England). Renouf.
Beaver, William H. Financial Reporting: An Accounting Revolution. (Contemporary Topics in Accounting Ser.). (Illus.). 240p. 1981. text ed. 12.95 (ISBN 0-13-316141-2); pap. text ed. 9.95 (ISBN 0-13-316133-1). P-H.
Benjamin, James J., et al. Financial Accounting. 3rd ed. LC 80-67311. (Illus.). 737p. 1980. pap. text ed. 18.95 (ISBN 0-931920-21-3); practice problems 4.95x; study guide 5.95x; work papers 6.95x. Dame Pubns.
--Principles of Accounting. LC 80-67313. 1100p. 1981. text ed. 18.95x (ISBN 0-931920-24-8); study guide 5.95 (ISBN 0-686-68562-8); working papers 6.95 (ISBN 0-686-68563-6); practice problem 4.95 (ISBN 0-686-68564-4). Dame Pubns.
Berger, Robert O. Practical Accounting for Lawyers. (Modern Accounting Perspectives & Practice Ser.). 450p. 1981. 25.00 (ISBN 0-471-08486-7, Pub. by Wiley-Interscience). Wiley.
Beyer, R. & Trawicki, D. J. Profitability Accounting: For Planning & Control. 2nd ed. 403p. 1972. 29.95 (ISBN 0-471-06523-4). Wiley.
Bull, R. J. Accounting in Business. 4th ed. LC 80-49870. (Illus.). 448p. 1980. text ed. 34.95 (ISBN 0-408-10669-7); pap. text ed. 19.95 (ISBN 0-408-10670-0). Butterworths.
Carsberg, Bryan. Current Issues in Accounting. Hope, Tony, ed. 304p. 1977. 34.50x (ISBN 0-86003-503-4, Pub. by Allan Pubs England); pap. 17.25x (ISBN 0-86003-603-0). State Mutual Bk.
Cashin, James A. & Lerner, Joel J. Schaum's Outline of Accounting II. 2nd ed. (Schaum's Outline Ser.). 288p. 1980. pap. 5.95 (ISBN 0-07-010252-X, SP). McGraw.
Castle, E. F. & Owens, N. P. Principles of Accounts. 5th ed. 448p. 1978. pap. text ed. 12.95x (ISBN 0-7121-1687-7, Pub. by Maconald & Evans England). Intl Ideas.
Cavert, Edward C., et al. Students Guide to Accounting, 2 vols. 512p. 1980. pap. text ed. 15.95 (ISBN 0-8403-2223-2). Kendall-Hunt.
Chukuocha, Bessie. Accounting Methods for Non-Profit Organizations. 1981. 6.95 (ISBN 0-8062-1650-6). Carlton.
Copeland, R. M., et al. Financial Accounting. LC 79-18276. 1980. 19.95 (ISBN 0-471-17173-5); working papers & study guide avail. Wiley.
Davidson, Sidney, et al. Intermediate Accounting. 2nd ed. LC 80-65795. 1088p. 1981. text ed. 24.95 (ISBN 0-03-058081-1). Dryden Pr.
Deitrick & Bizzell. Plaid for Advanced Accounting. 1981. price not set (ISBN 0-256-02398-0, 01-1435-01). Learning Syst.
Di Antonio. Plaid for CPA Review Package. 1981. price not set (ISBN 0-256-02400-6, 01-1436-01). Learning Syst.
Edwards, B. Quantitative & Accounting Methods. 192p. 1980. pap. text ed. 14.95x (ISBN 0-7121-1704-0). Intl Ideas.
Estes, R. W. Corporate Social Accounting. 166p. 1976. 18.95 (ISBN 0-471-24592-5, Pub. by Wiley-Interscience). Wiley.
Estes, Ralph W. A Dictionary of Accounting. 300p. 1981. text ed. 15.00x (ISBN 0-262-05024-2); pap. text ed. 4.95x (ISBN 0-262-55009-1). MIT Pr.
Gilbert, Robert. Business Practice Set: SAAL Manufacturing Limited Financial Operating Budget. 64p. 1981. pap. text ed. 6.95 (ISBN 0-8403-2346-8). Kendall-Hunt.
Gurry, Edward J. Quantative Methods. 6th ed. LC 78-50970. 8.00 (ISBN 0-932788-03-3). Bradley CPA.
Hay & Engstrom. Plaid for Accounting for Governmental & Nonprofit Entities. 1981. price not set (ISBN 0-256-02567-3, 01-1454-01). Learning Syst.
Horngren, C. Introduction to Financial Accounting. 1981. 21.00 (ISBN 0-13-483743-6); practice set 6.95, (ISBN 0-13-483701-0); working papers 6.95 (ISBN 0-13-483727-4); student guide 6.95 (ISBN 0-13-483750-9). P-H.
Horngren, Charles T. Introduction to Financial Accounting. 5th ed. (Ser. in Accounting). 672p. 1981. text ed. 21.95 (ISBN 0-686-69276-4). P-H.
Internal Accounting Control: Evaluation & Auditor Judgment. (Auditing Research Monograph: No. 3). 1980. pap. 9.00. Am Inst CPA.
Internal Accounting Control: Report of The Special Advisory Committee. 1979. pap. 2.75. Am Inst CPA.
Langer, Steven, ed. The Accounting-Financial Report: Industry-Government-Education-Non-Profit, Pt. II. 2nd ed. 1981. pap. 75.00 (ISBN 0-916506-61-4). Abbott Langer Assocs.
--The Accounting-Financial Report: Public Accounting Firms, Pt. I. 2nd ed. 1981. pap. 75.00 (ISBN 0-916506-60-6). Abbott Langer Assocs.
Langley. Workbook in Accounting. 3rd ed. 1981. text ed. price not set (ISBN 0-408-10680-8). Butterworth.
Leach, Ronald & Stamp, Edward. British Accounting Standards: The First Ten Years. 160p. 1980. 40.00x (ISBN 0-85941-149-4, Pub. by Woodhead-Faulkner England). State Mutual Bk.
Lowe, C. W. Project Control by Critical Pathanalysis: A Basic Guide of CPA. 258p. 1978. text ed. 30.75x (ISBN 0-220-67012-9, Pub. by Busn Bks England). Renouf.
McDermott, Russell H. Columbia Bookkeeping Systems Double Entry. (Accounting-Bookkeeping Systems Ser.). (Illus.). 130p. 1980. text ed. 49.95 (ISBN 0-9604828-3-0). Columbia Bookkeeping.
McGee, R. Accounting for Inflation: Stating a True Financial Position. 15.95 (ISBN 0-13-002337-X); pap. 7.95 (ISBN 0-13-002329-9). P-H.
McNamara, Terry S. Numeracy & Accounting. (Illus.). 370p. 1979. pap. text ed. 16.95x (ISBN 0-7121-1411-4, Pub. by Macdonald & Evans England). Intl Ideas.
Magee, C. C. Framework for Accountancy. 2nd ed. 336p. 1979. pap. text ed. 14.95x (ISBN 0-7121-0631-6, Pub. by Macdonald & Evans England). Intl Ideas.
Magee, J. O. Basic Accounting. 2nd ed. 352p. 1979. pap. text ed. 11.95x (ISBN 0-7121-0284-1, Pub. by Macdonald & Evans England). Intl Ideas.
--Company Accounts. 2nd ed. 386p. 1978. pap. 12.95x (ISBN 0-7121-0384-8, Pub. by Macdonald & Evans England). Intl Ideas.
Moroni, J. Alfred & Lahey, Francis J. An Accounting Manual for Catholic Elementary & Secondary Schools. rev. ed. 86p. 1969. 4.00. Natl Cath Educ.
Moscove, Stephen. Accounting Fundamentals: A Self-Instructional Approach. 2nd ed. 1980. pap. text ed. 10.95 (ISBN 0-8359-0061-4); wkbk. 7.95 (ISBN 0-8359-0070-3); instr's. manual avail. (ISBN 0-8359-0062-2). Reston.
Moyer, Charles R. & Kretlow, William. Contemporary Financial Management. (Illus.). 700p. 1981. text ed. 19.95 (ISBN 0-8299-0400-X). West Pub.
Municipal Accounting & Auditing: Where We Are Now, Where We Should Be Going. (COMP Papers Ser.). 170p. 1980. pap. 18.00 (ISBN 0-916450-41-4). Coun on Municipal.
National Accounting Practices in Seventy Countries, Vol. I. (Studies in Methods Ser. F.: No. 26). 226p. 1979. pap. 15.00 (ISBN 0-686-68961-5, UN79/17/19, UN). Unipub.
National Accounting Practices in Seventy Countries, Vol. II. (Studies in Methods Ser. F: No. 26). 205p. 1979. pap. 14.00 (ISBN 0-686-68962-3, UN79/17/19, UN). Unipub.
National Accounting Practices in Seventy Countries, Vol. III. (Studies in Methods Ser. F: No. 26). 203p. 1979. pap. 14.00 (ISBN 0-686-68963-1, UN79/17/19, UN). Unipub.
Needles, Belverd E., et al. Principles of Accounting. LC 80-80503. (Illus.). 1008p. 1981. text ed. 20.95 (ISBN 0-395-29527-0); study guide 6.95 (ISBN 0-395-29529-7); price not set test bank (ISBN 0-395-29538-6); practice set 1 5.95 (ISBN 0-395-29534-3); price not set achievement tests 1-14A (ISBN 0-395-29539-4); price not set achievement tests 1-14B (ISBN 0-395-29540-8); price not set achievement tests 14-28A (ISBN 0-395-29541-6); price not set achievement tests 14-28B (ISBN 0-395-29542-4). HM.
Operating a Successful Accounting Practice. 1979. pap. 7.50. Am Inst CPA.
Owler, L. W. Intermediate Accounts. 3rd ed. 400p. 1975. pap. text ed. 12.95x (ISBN 0-7121-0936-6, Pub. by Macdonald & Evans England). Intl Ideas.
Partington, A. M. Q & A Theory. LC 79-83864. 12.00 (ISBN 0-932788-08-4). Bradley CPA.
Partington, A. M. & Nieminsky, Arthur C. Practice & Theory Manual. 10th ed. 19.50 (ISBN 0-932788-11-4). Bradley CPA.
Partington, A. M. & Weinberg, Frank. Q & A Practice. LC 79-83860. 16.00 (ISBN 0-932788-06-8). Bradley CPA.
Proposals for the Improvement of Subchapter K. 1979. pap. 7.50. Am Inst CPA.
Pyle, William W. & Larson, Kermit D. Financial Accounting. 1980. 19.50x (ISBN 0-256-02259-3). Irwin.
Reports by Management: Conclusions & Recommendations of the AICPA Special Advisory Committee. 1979. pap. 1.50. Am Inst CPA.
Reynolds, et al. Elementary Accounting. 1978. 18.95 (ISBN 0-03-018021-X). Dryden Pr.
Reynolds, Issac N., et al. Elementary Accounting. 2nd ed. LC 80-65808. 1040p. 1981. pap. text ed. 19.95 (ISBN 0-03-058144-3). Dryden Pr.
Riggs, Henry E. Accounting: A Survey. 1981. text ed. 18.95 (ISBN 0-07-052851-9, C); write for info instrs.' manual (ISBN 0-07-052852-7). McGraw.
SAS. LC 79-83865. 7.00 (ISBN 0-932788-10-6). Bradley CPA.
Schrader, William J., et al. Financial Accounting: An Events Approach. 520p. 1981. text ed. 18.95x (ISBN 0-931920-29-9). Dame Pubns.
Schugart, Gary L., et al. A Survey of Accounting. LC 80-67776. 600p. 1981. text ed. 18.95x (ISBN 0-931920-25-6); study guide 5.95 (ISBN 0-686-68565-2); practice problem 4.95 (ISBN 0-686-68566-0); working papers 6.95 (ISBN 0-686-68567-9). Dame Pubns.
Sellers, James H. & Milam, Edward E. Ethics: Accounting Student Perceptions. 50p. (Orig.). 1980. pap. 4.50 (ISBN 0-938004-00-X). U MS Bus Econ.
Skousen, K. Fred, et al. Financial Accounting. 1981. text ed. write for info. (ISBN 0-87901-156-4); write or info. study guide (ISBN 0-87901-157-2); write for info. practice set, vol. 2 (ISBN 0-87901-159-9); price not set practice set, vol. 2 (ISBN 0-87901-160-2); write for info. working papers (ISBN 0-87901-158-0). Worth.
Slater, Jeffrey. Rx for Small Business Success: Accounting, Planning, & Recordkeeping Techniques for a Healthy Bottom Line. (Illus.). 256p. 1981. 18.95 (Spec); pap. 12.95 (ISBN 0-13-785006-9). P-H.
Solomon, Jerome. Financial & Accounting Handbook for the Service Industries. 560p. 1981. 29.95 (ISBN 0-8436-0854-4). CBI Pub.
Sterling, Robert R. Toward a Science of Accounting. LC 80-14502. 247p. 1980. text ed. 13.00 (ISBN 0-914348-31-0). Scholars Bk.
System of Quality Control for a CPA Firm. (Statement on Quality Control Standards Ser.: No. 1). 1979. pap. 1.35. Am Inst CPA.
Tainsh, J. A. The Key to Accounting & Costing. 119p. 1959. 11.75x (ISBN 0-85264-062-5, Pub. by Griffin England). State Mutual Bk.
Taylor, A. H. & Shearing, H. Financial & Cost Accounting for Management. 7th ed. (Illus.). 384p. 1979. pap. text ed. 15.95x (ISBN 0-7121-0633-2, Pub. by Macdonald & Evans England). Intl Ideas.
Thacker, Ronald & Ellis, Loudell. Student Guide to Management Accounting: Concepts & Applications. 336p. 1980. pap. text ed. 8.95 (ISBN 0-8359-4196-5). Reston.
Ventolo, William L., Jr. Principles of Accounting. Davidson, Sidney, ed. (Illus.). 350p. (gr. 12). 1980. text ed. 15.95 (ISBN 0-686-28726-6); pap. text ed. 11.95 (ISBN 0-686-28727-4). Performance Pub.
Wilson, J. P. Inflation, Deflation, Reflation: Managemnent & Accounting in Economic Uncertainty. 345p. 1980. text ed. 36.75x (ISBN 0-220-67015-3, Pub. by Busn Bks England). Renouf.
Young, J. M. & Buchanan, N. J. Accounting for Pensions. 160p. 1980. 39.00x (ISBN 0-85941-124-9, Pub. by Woodhead-Faulkner England). State Mutual Bk.

ACCOUNTING–DATA PROCESSING

Guidelines to Assess Computerized General Ledger & Financial Reporting Systems for Use in CPA Firms. 1980. pap. 6.50. Am Inst CPA.
Guidelines to Assess Computerized Time & Billing Systems for Use in CPA Firms. 1980. pap. 6.50. Am Inst CPA.
Jancura, Elise G. & Boos, Robert V. Establishing Controls & Auditing the Computerized Accounting System. 224p. 1980. text ed. 19.95 (ISBN 0-442-80507-1). Van Nos Reinhold.
Lindhe, Richard & Grossman, Steven D. Accounting Information Systems. 500p. 1980. text ed. 18.95x (ISBN 0-931920-23-X). Dame Pubns.
Weber, Jeffrey R. Computerized Accounts Payable System: Manual & Source Code for Microcomputers. (International Data Management Computerized Accounting System Ser.). 144p. 1981. pap. 29.95 (ISBN 0-9604892-5-8). Five Arms Corp.
--Computerized Accounts Receivable System: Manual & Source Code for Microcomputers. (International Data Management Computerized Accounting System Ser.). 144p. 1981. pap. 29.95 (ISBN 0-9604892-4-X). Five Arms Corp.
--Computerized General Ledger System: Manual & Source Code for Microcomputers. (International Data Management Computerized Accounting System Ser.). 144p. 1981. pap. 29.95 (ISBN 0-9604892-6-6). Five Arms Corp.

ACCOUNTING–EXAMINATIONS, QUESTIONS, ETC.

Here are entered collections of questions actually set in examinations. Problems for classroom use or private study are entered under Accounting–Problems, Exercises, etc.
Board of Regents of IIA. Certified Internal Auditor Examination, May 1980: Questions & Suggested Solutions, No. 7. (Illus.). 57p. 1980. pap. text ed. 3.00 (ISBN 0-89413-089-7). Inst Inter Aud.
Davidsen, et al. CPA Exam Intermediate Acct. 1980. 5.95 (ISBN 0-03-058087-0). Dryden Pr.
Davidson, Sidney, et al. C.P.A. Exam Booklet. 2nd ed. 1981. pap. text ed. 6.95 (ISBN 0-686-69576-3). Dryden Pr.

ACCOUNTING–LAW

see also Tax Accounting
Laursen, Gary A. Q & A Law. LC 79-83862. 12.00 (ISBN 0-932788-09-2). Bradley CPA.
Law Manual. 9th ed. 15.00 (ISBN 0-932788-01-7). Bradley CPA.

ACCOUNTING MACHINES

Hicks, James O., Jr. & Leininger, Wayne E. Accounting Information Systems. 500p. 1981. text ed. 15.96 (ISBN 0-8299-0384-4). West Pub.

ACCOUNTS, COLLECTING OF

see Collecting of Accounts

ACEPHALIA

see Lamellibranchiata

ACETYLENE COMPOUNDS

Tedeschi. Acetelyne Based Chemicals from Coal & Other Natural Sources. Date not set. price not set (ISBN 0-8247-1358-3). Dekker.

ACHIEVEMENT, ACADEMIC

see Academic Achievement

ACHIEVEMENT MOTIVATION

Gunneweg, Antonius H. & Schmithals, Walter. Achievement. Smith, David, tr. LC 80-26977. (Biblical Encounter Ser.). 208p. (Orig.). 1981. pap. 7.95 (ISBN 0-687-00690-2). Abingdon.
Rosenbaum, Bernard L., ed. How to Motivate Today's Workers: Motivational Models for Managers & Supervisors. (Illus.). 192p. 1981. 14.95 (ISBN 0-07-053711-9, P&RB). McGraw.

ACID BASE EQUILIBRIUM

Kildeberg, Poul. Quantitative Acid-Base Physiology. (Illus.). 142p. 1981. 15.00. Igaku-Shoin.
Lauersen, Neils H. & Hochberg, Howard. Clinical Perinatal Biochemical Monitoring. 271p. 1981. write for info. (1901-1). Williams & Wilkins.

ACIDS, FATTY

Galli, C. & Avogaro, P., eds. Polyunsaturated Fatty Acids in Nutrition: Proceedings of a Round Table in Polyunsaturated Fatty Acids in Nutrition, Milan, Italy, April 1979. (Progress in Food & Nutrition Sciences Ser.: Vol. 4, No. 5). (Illus.). 80p. 1980. pap. 26.00 (ISBN 0-08-027362-9). Pergamon.

ACOUSTIC ENGINEERING

see Acoustical Engineering

ACOUSTICAL ENGINEERING

see also Architectural Acoustics; Electro-Acoustics; Music–Acoustics and Physics; Noise; Noise Control; Telecommunication
Cogan, Robert & Escot, Pozzi. Sonic Design: Practice & Problems. (Illus.). 160p. 1981. text ed. 12.95 (ISBN 0-686-68608-X). P-H.
Temkin, Samuel. Elements of Acoustics. 544p. 1981. text ed. 23.95 (ISBN 0-471-05990-0). Wiley.
Winder, Alan A. & Loda, Charles J. Introduction to Acoustical Space Time Information Processing. (Illus.). 200p. 1980. pap. 14.95 (ISBN 0-932146-04-X). Peninsula.

ACOUSTICS

see Architectural Acoustics; Hearing; Music–Acoustics and Physics; Sound

ACQUISITION OF LANGUAGE

see Children–Language

ACQUISITIONS (LIBRARIES)

Freier, Jerold L. Acquisition Search Programs. LC 80-26356. 1981. pap. 3.95 (ISBN 0-87576-094-5). Pilot Bks.

ACRASIALES

Farr, M. L. How to Know the True Slime Molds. 200p. 1981. write for info. wire coil (ISBN 0-697-04779-2). Wm C Brown.

ACROBATS AND ACROBATISM

see also Gymnastics; Stunt Men
Coulton, Jill. Sports Acrobatics. (Illus.). 112p. 1981. 12.95 (ISBN 0-8069-9184-4, Pub. by EP Publishing England); pap. 6.95 (ISBN 0-8069-9185-2). Sterling.

ACROGENS

see Cryptogams; Mosses

ACT (PHILOSOPHY)

Davidson, Donald. Essays on Actions & Events. 320p. 1980. 29.50x (ISBN 0-19-824529-7); pap. 9.95x (ISBN 0-19-824637-4). Oxford U Pr.
Harmon, Michael M. Action Theory for Public Administration. (Longman Professional Studies in Public Administration). 256p. (Orig.). 1981. text ed. 22.50 (ISBN 0-582-28254-3); pap. text ed. 9.95 (ISBN 0-582-28255-1). Longman.

ACTING

see also Actors and Actresses; Drama; Drama in Education; Theater
Kalter, Joanmarie. Actors on Acting. LC 79-65062. (Illus.). 1981. pap. 7.95 (ISBN 0-8069-8976-9). Sterling.
Rapp, Lea B. Put Your Kid in Show Biz. LC 80-54346. (Illus.). 160p. 1981. 12.95 (ISBN 0-8069-7040-5); lib. bdg. 11.69 (ISBN 0-8069-7041-3); pap. 6.95 (ISBN 0-8069-7508-3). Sterling.
Sandler, Bernard & Posner, Steve. In Front of the Camera. 1981. 12.95 (ISBN 0-525-93176-7); pap. 7.95 (ISBN 0-525-93177-5). Dutton.
Westrom, Robert. Dialects for the Actor. 69p. (Orig.). 1978. pap. 2.95 (ISBN 0-938230-01-8). Westrom.
--Monologues for the Actor. 60p. (Orig.). 1978. pap. 2.50 (ISBN 0-938230-02-6). Westrom.
--Scenes for the Actor. 76p. (Orig.). 1979. pap. 2.95 (ISBN 0-938230-03-4). Westrom.
--Speech for the Actor. rev. ed. (Illus.). 87p. (Orig.). 1978. pap. 3.50 (ISBN 0-938230-00-X). Westrom.

ACTING–COSTUME

see Costume

ACTING–MAKE-UP

see Make-Up, Theatrical

ACTING–STUDY AND TEACHING

Malkin, Michael R. Training the Young Actor. 166p. 1981. Repr. of 1979 ed. 9.95 (ISBN 0-498-01957-8). A S Barnes.
Peachment, Brian. Educational Drama. (Illus.). 232p. 1976. pap. 13.95x (ISBN 0-7121-0552-2, Pub. by Macdonald & Evans England). Intl Ideas.
The Beverly Hills Bar Association Barristers Committee. Actor's Manual. 1981. pap. 9.95 (ISBN 0-8015-0040-0, Hawthorn). Dutton.

ACTING AS A PROFESSION

Brill, Chip & Glenn, Peter, eds. The New York Casting-Survival Guide & Datebook. 1981. 124p. 1980. pap. 10.00 (ISBN 0-87314-036-2). Peter Glenn.

ACTION SONGS

see Games with Music

ACTIVATED CARBON

see Carbon, Activated

ACTIVATION ANALYSIS

see Radioactivation Analysis

ACTIVITY PROGRAMS IN EDUCATION
see also Creative Activities and Seatwork
Count Morbida's Fang-Tastic Activity Book. (gr. 3-5). pap. 3.95 (ISBN 0-590-11813-7, Schol Pap). Schol Bk Serv.
Hendricks, Gay. The Centered Teacher: Awareness Activities for Teachers & Their Students. (Transformation Ser.). 192p. 1981. 9.95 (ISBN 0-13-122234-1, Spec); pap. 4.95 (ISBN 0-13-122226-0). P-H.
Maxim, George. The Sourcebook: Activities to Enrich Programs for Infants & Young Children. 208p. 1980. pap. text ed. 11.95x (ISBN 0-534-00854-2). Wadsworth Pub.
Morse, P. & Brand, T. Home-Style Learning: Activities for Young Children & Their Parents. 1981. pap. 5.95 (ISBN 0-13-392944-2); 10.95 (ISBN 0-13-392951-5). P-H.

ACTORS AND ACTRESSES
see also Acting; Comedians; Make-Up, Theatrical; Moving-Picture Actors and Actresses; Moving-Pictures–Biography; Theater; Theater and Society
Andersen, Christopher P. The Book of People. (Illus.). 500p. 1981. 19.95 (ISBN 0-399-12617-1, Perigee); pap. 9.95 (ISBN 0-399-50530-X). Putnam.
Cohen. Jimmy Walker-the Dyn-O-Mite Kid. (gr. 3-5). pap. 1.25 (ISBN 0-590-10268-0, Schol Pap). Schol Bk Serv.
Ekland, Britt. True Britt. (Illus.). 242p. 1981. 9.95 (ISBN 0-13-931089-4). P-H.
Fisher, Seymour & Fisher, Rhoda L. Pretend the World Is Funny & Forever: A Psychological Analysis of Comedians, Clowns, & Actors. LC 80-7777. 288p. 1981. profess. & reference 19.95 (ISBN 0-89859-073-6). L Erlbaum Assocs.
Freeman. TV '80. (gr. 7-12). 1980. pap. 1.25 (ISBN 0-590-30877-7, Schol Pap). Schol Bk Serv.
Highfill, Philip H., Jr., et al. A Biographical Dictionary of Actors, Actresses, Musicians, Dancers, Managers, & Other Stage Personnel in London, 1660-1800, 6 vols. Incl. Vol. 1. Abago to Belfille. 462p. 1973 (ISBN 0-8093-0517-8); Vol. 2. Belfort to Byzand. 494p. 1973 (ISBN 0-8093-0518-6); Vol. 3. Cabanel to Cory. 544p. 1975 (ISBN 0-8093-0692-1); Vol. 4. Coryne to Dynion. 576p. 1975 (ISBN 0-8093-0693-X); Vol. 5. Eagan to Garrett. 504p. 1978 (ISBN 0-8093-0832-0); Vol. 6. Garrick to Gyngell. 512p. 1978 (ISBN 0-8093-0833-9). LC 71-157068. (Biographical Dictionary of Actors Ser.). (Illus.). 40.00x ea. S Ill U Pr.
McCambridge, Mercedes. The Quality of Mercy: An Autobiography. 1981. 10.95 (ISBN 0-8129-0945-3). Times Bks.
Mortimer, Hilda & George, Dan. You Call Me Chief: Impressions of the Life of Chief Dan George. LC 78-60297. (Illus.). 192p. 1981. 11.95 (ISBN 0-385-04806-8). Doubleday.
Piltch, Benjamin. Popular Stars. 64p. (gr. 3-7). 1980. 3.50 (ISBN 0-934618-02-X). Skyview Pub.
Salter, Elizabeth. Helpmann: The Authorised Biography. (Illus.). 247p. 1981. text ed. 18.50x (ISBN 0-87663-349-1). Universe.
Tynan, Kenneth. Show People. 1981. pap. 2.95 (ISBN 0-425-04750-4). Berkley Pub.

ACTORS AND ACTRESSES–CORRESPONDENCE, REMINISCENCES, ETC.
Lovelace, Linda & McGrady, Mike. Ordeal. 1981. pap. 2.95 (ISBN 0-425-04749-0). Berkley Pub.
Stack, Robert & Evans, Mark. Straight Shooting. 1981. pap. 2.75 (ISBN 0-425-04757-1). Berkley Pub.
Thomas, Haywood. Apology of Actors. Bd. with A Refutation of the Apology for Actors. 20.00x (ISBN 0-8201-1198-8). Schol Facsimiles.

ACTORS AND ACTRESSES–GREAT BRITAIN
Gielgud, John. Gielgud: An Actor & His Time, a Memoir. (Illus.). 1980. 14.95 (ISBN 0-517-54179-3). Potter.

ACTORS AND ACTRESSES–UNITED STATES
Carpozi, George, Jr. That's Hollywood: Beautiful & Special People, No. 7. (Orig.). 1980. pap. 1.95 (ISBN 0-532-23281-X). Manor Bks.
--That's Hollywood: The Clossal Cowboys, No. 6. (Orig.). 1980. pap. 1.95 (ISBN 0-532-23222-4). Manor Bks.
Strasberg, Susan. Bittersweet. (Illus.). 1981. pap. 3.50 (ISBN 0-451-09760-2, E9760, Sig). NAL.

ACTRESSES
see Actors and Actresses

ACTUARIAL SCIENCE
see Insurance, Life

ACUPRESSURE
see Shiatsu

ACUPUNCTURE
Bonghan, Kim, et al. Acupuncture- the Scientific Evidence & Far-Eastern Medicine. (Illus.). pap. write for info. (ISBN 0-916508-15-3). Happiness Pr.
Lavier, J. Points of Chinese Acupuncture. Chancellor, Philip, tr. from Fr. 115p. 1974. text ed. 10.95x (ISBN 0-8464-1038-9). Beekman Pubs.
Lawson-Wood, D. & Lawson-Wood, J. Acupuncture Vitality & Revival Points. 56p. 1975. 6.00x (ISBN 0-8464-0990-9). Beekman Pubs.
--Five Elements of Acupuncture & Chinese Massage. 96p. 1976. 8.95x (ISBN 0-8464-1010-9). Beekman Pubs.
Lawson-Wood, J. & Lawson-Wood, D. Acupuncture Handbook. 141p. 1973. 6.75x (ISBN 0-8464-0989-5). Beekman Pubs.
Meeker, Charles A. Chinese Acupuncture: Do-It Yourself, a Text Book for Practitioners. 4th ed. LC 60-972. (Illus.). 210p. Date not set. 15.50 (ISBN 0-935068-07-4). Meeker Pub.
Stievater, Eric H. What Is Acuncture? How Does It Work? 48p. 1971. pap. 3.00x (ISBN 0-8464-1061-3). Beekman Pubs.
Wu Wei-P'Ing. Chinese Acupuncture. Chancellor, Philip, tr. from Fr. 184p. 1962. text ed. 10.35x (ISBN 0-8464-0999-2). Beekman Pubs.

ADAM (BIBLICAL CHARACTER)
Robinson, Stephen E. The Testament of Adam: An Examination of the Syriac & Greek Traditions. LC 80-12209. (Society of Biblical Literature Dissertation Ser.: No. 52). write for info. (ISBN 0-89130-398-7, 06-01-52); pap. write for info. (ISBN 0-89130-399-5). Scholars Pr CA.

ADAMS, HENRY, 1838-1918
Byrnes, Joseph F. The Virgin of Chartres. LC 78-75174. 128p. 1981. 17.50 (ISBN 0-8386-2369-7). Fairleigh Dickinson.
Kaplan, Harold. Power & Order: Henry Adams & the Naturalist Tradition in American Fiction. LC 80-23414. 1981. lib. bdg. price not set (ISBN 0-226-42424-3). U of Chicago Pr.

ADAMS, JOHN QUINCY, PRES. U. S., 1767-1848
Bemis, Samuel F. John Quincy Adams & the Foundations of American Foreign Policy. LC 80-23039. (Illus.). xix, 588p. 1981. Repr. of 1949 ed. lib. bdg. 49.75x (ISBN 0-313-22636-9, BEAD). Greenwood.
Bemis, Samuel Flagg. John Quincy Adams & the Union. LC 80-20402. (Illus.). xv, 546p. 1980. Repr. of 1965 ed. lib. bdg. 45.00x (ISBN 0-313-22637-7, BEJQ). Greenwood.

ADAPTATION (BIOLOGY)
see also Genetics; Man–Influence of Environment; Stress (Physiology)
Bhatia, B., et al, eds. Selected Topics in Environmental Biology. 530p. 1980. 47.50x (ISBN 0-89955-317-6, Pub. by Interprint India). Intl Schol Bk Serv.
Hainsworth, F. Reed. Animal Physiology: Adaptations in Function. (Life Sciences Ser.). (Illus.). 600p. 1981. text ed. 19.95 (ISBN 0-201-03401-8). A-W.
Kavaler, Lucy. A Matter of Degree: Heat Life & Death. LC 80-8789. 224p. 1981. 14.95 (ISBN 0-06-014854-3, HarpT). Har-Row.
Kellogg, William W. & Schware, Robert. Climate Change & Society: Consequences of Increasing Atmospheric Carbon Dioxide. (Special Study Ser.). 170p. (Orig.). 1981. lib. bdg. 15.00x (ISBN 0-86531-179-X); pap. 8.00x (ISBN 0-86531-180-3). Westview.

ADAPTATION (PSYCHOLOGY)
see Adjustment (Psychology)

ADAPTATIONS, FILM
see Film Adaptations

ADAPTIVE CONTROL SYSTEMS–MATHEMATICAL MODELS
Unbehauen, H., ed. Methods in Adaptive Control: Proceedings. (Lecture Notes in Control & Information Sciences: Vol. 24). (Illus.). 309p. 1980. pap. 21.60 (ISBN 0-387-10226-4). Springer-Verlag.

ADC
see Child Welfare

ADDING MACHINES
see Calculating-Machines

ADDISON, JOSEPH, 1672-1719
Addisoniana. 242p. 1980. Repr. of 1803 ed. lib. bdg. 75.00 (ISBN 0-8492-3207-4). R West.

ADDITION
Happy Adding. (Children's Library of Picture Bks.). (Illus.). 10p. (ps). 1979. 1.95 (ISBN 0-89346-175-X, TA61, Pub. by Froebel-Kan Japan). Heian Intl.
Lutgendorf, Philip. Addition & Subtraction. LC 79-730038. (Illus.). 1978. pap. text ed. 99.00 (ISBN 0-89290-092-X, A508-SATC). Soc for Visual.

ADDRESSES
see Lectures and Lecturing; Speeches, Addresses, etc.

ADIPOSITY
see Obesity

ADIRONDACK MOUNTAINS
Fowler, Barney. Adirondack Album, No. 1. (Illus.). 200p. (Orig.). 1981. pap. 10.25 (ISBN 0-9605556-1-7). Outdoor Assocs.
--Adirondack Album, No. 2. (Illus.). 200p. (Orig.). 1980. pap. 10.25 (ISBN 0-9605556-0-9). Outdoor Assocs.
Wadsworth, Bruce. An Adirondack Sampler, II: Backpacking Trips in the Adirondacks. (Orig.). 1981. pap. 6.95 (ISBN 0-935272-15-1). Adk Mtn Club.

ADJECTIVE LAW
see Procedure (Law)

ADJUDICATION, ADMINISTRATIVE
see Administrative Procedure

ADJUSTMENT (PSYCHOLOGY)
see also Student Adjustment
Kavaler, Lucy. A Matter of Degree: Heat Life & Death. LC 80-8789. 224p. 1981. 14.95 (ISBN 0-06-014854-3, HarpT). Har-Row.

ADJUSTMENT (STUDENTS)
see Student Adjustment

ADJUVANT ARTHRITIS
see Rheumatoid Arthritis

ADLER, FELIX, 1851-1933
Friess, Horace L. Felix Adler & Ethical Culture. (Illus.). 320p. 1981. 20.00x (ISBN 0-231-05184-0). Columbia U Pr.

ADMINISTRATION
see Administrative Law; Civil Service; Management; Political Science; State, The
also subdivision Politics and Government under names of countries, states, cities, etc.

ADMINISTRATION, AGRICULTURAL
see Agricultural Administration

ADMINISTRATION, BUSINESS
see Business

ADMINISTRATION, PUBLIC
see Public Administration

ADMINISTRATION OF CRIMINAL JUSTICE
see Criminal Justice, Administration Of

ADMINISTRATION OF JUSTICE
see Justice, Administration Of

ADMINISTRATIVE ABILITY
see Executive Ability

ADMINISTRATIVE ADJUDICATION
see Administrative Procedure

ADMINISTRATIVE AGENCIES
see also Independent Regulatory Commissions
Pitt, D. C. & Smith, B. C. Government Department: An Organizational Perspective. 166p. (Orig.). 1981. pap. 20.00 (ISBN 0-7100-0742-6). Routledge & Kegan.

ADMINISTRATIVE COMMUNICATION
see Communication in Management

ADMINISTRATIVE LAW
see also Administrative Agencies; Administrative Procedure; Civil Service; Constitutional Law; Government Liability; Independent Regulatory Commissions; Local Government; Public Administration
Dimock, Marshall E. Law & Dynamic Administration. 176p. 1980. 19.95 (ISBN 0-03-057367-X); text ed. 8.95 (ISBN 0-03-057396-3). Praeger.

ADMINISTRATIVE PROCEDURE
see also Licenses
Dimock, Marshall E. Law & Dynamic Administration. 176p. 1980. 19.95 (ISBN 0-03-057367-X); text ed. 8.95 (ISBN 0-03-057396-3). Praeger.

ADMINISTRATORS AND EXECUTORS
see Executors and Administrators

ADMIRALS
Beesly, Patrick. Very Special Admiral. (Illus.). 256p. 1981. 30.00 (ISBN 0-241-10383-5, Pub. by Hamish Hamilton England). David & Charles.
Roskill, Stephen. Admiral of the Fleet, Earl Beatty: The Last Naval Hero. LC 80-19778. 1981. 19.95 (ISBN 0-689-11119-3). Atheneum.
Smith, Charles. Lord Mountbatten: His Butler's Story. LC 80-51787. (Illus.). 224p. 1980. 12.95 (ISBN 0-8128-2751-1). Stein & Day.

ADMISSION TO COLLEGE
see Universities and Colleges–Admission

ADOLESCENCE
see also Youth
also headings beginning with the word Adolescent
Elkind, David. Children & Adolescents. 3rd ed. 272p. 1981. text ed. 15.95x (ISBN 0-19-502820-1); pap. text ed. 5.95x (ISBN 0-19-502821-X). Oxford U Pr.
Graham, Billy. Billy Graham Talks to Teenagers. (Orig.). (YA) pap. 1.25 (ISBN 0-89129-153-9). Jove Pubns.
Gross, Leonard. The Terrible Teens: A Guide for Bewildered Parents. 256p. 1981. 10.95 (ISBN 0-02-545820-5). Macmillan.
Kelly & Landers. Today's Teen. rev. ed. (gr. 7-9). 1981. text ed. 14.60 (ISBN 0-87002-323-3). Bennett IL.
Santrock, John W. Adolescence: An Introduction. 600p. 1981. pap. text ed. write for info. (ISBN 0-697-06635-5); instrs.' manual avail. (ISBN 0-697-06640-1). Wm C Brown.
Steiner, Rudolf. Waldorf Education for Adolescence. 1980. pap. 9.50x (ISBN 0-906492-37-8, Pub. by Kolisko Archives). St George Bk Serv.
Sweat, Clifford H., ed. Morals & Early Adolescent Education: From Apathy to Action. LC 80-80727. 1980. pap. text ed. 4.25 (ISBN 0-8134-2134-9, 2134). Interstate.
Tackett, Jo J. & Hunsberger, Mabel. Family-Centered Care of Children & Adolescents: Nursing Concepts in Child Health. 800p. 1981. text ed. price not set (ISBN 0-7216-8740-7). Saunders.
Towns, Payton. Educating Disturbed Adolescents: Theory & Practice. (Current Issues in Behavioral Psychology Ser.). 1981. 19.50 (ISBN 0-8089-1312-3). Grune.

ADOLESCENCE–HEALTH AND HYGIENE
see Youth–Health and Hygiene

ADOLESCENCE–PSYCHOLOGY
see Adolescent Psychology

ADOLESCENT PARENTS
Lindsay, Jeanne W. Teens Parenting: The Challenge of Babies & Toddlers. (Illus.). 320p. 1981. 14.95 (ISBN 0-930934-07-5); pap. 9.95 (ISBN 0-930934-06-7); price not set tchr's guide (ISBN 0-930934-09-1); wkbk. 2.50 (ISBN 0-930934-08-3). Morning Glory.

ADOLESCENT PSYCHOLOGY
Antonovsky, Helen F., et al. Adolescent Sexuality: A Study of Attitudes & Behavior. LC 80-8337. 176p. 1980. 18.95 (ISBN 0-669-04030-4). Lexington Bks.
Aten, Marilyn J. & McAnarney, Elizabeth R. A Behavioral Approach to the Care of Adolescents. 200p. 1981. pap. text ed. 10.50 (ISBN 0-8016-3201-3). Mosby.
Bell, Ruth, et al. Changing Bodies, Changing Lives: A Book for Teens on Sex & Relationships. (Illus.). 1981. 14.95 (ISBN 0-394-50304-X); pap. 7.95 (ISBN 0-394-73632-X). Random.
Gander & Gardiner. Child & Adolescent Development. 1981. text ed. 16.95 (ISBN 0-316-30322-4); tchrs'. manual free (ISBN 0-316-30319-4); study guide 5.95 (ISBN 0-316-30318-6). Little.
Gross, Leonard. The Terrible Teens: A Guide for Bewildered Parents. 256p. 1981. 10.95 (ISBN 0-02-545820-5). Macmillan.
Hollingworth, Leta S. The Psychology of the Adolescent. 256p. 1980. Repr. lib. bdg. 30.00 (ISBN 0-89984-294-1). Century Bookbindery.
Jones, Ray & Pritchard, Colin. Social Work with Adolescents. (Library of Social Work). 260p. 1981. 16.95 (ISBN 0-7100-0632-2); pap. write for info. (ISBN 0-7100-0633-0). Routledge & Kegan.
Rice, F. Phillip. The Adolescent: Development, Relationships, & Culture. 3rd ed. 700p. 1981. text ed. 17.95 (ISBN 0-205-07303-4, 2473038); free tchr's ed. (ISBN 0-205-07304-2). Allyn.
Streit, Fred. Research Review Nineteen Sixty-Six to Nineteen Eighty: Adolescent Problems. 71p. 1980. pap. 15.00. Essence Pubns.
Williams, Frankwood E. Adolescence Studies in Mental Hygiene. 279p. 1980. Repr. lib. bdg. 25.00 (ISBN 0-89984-511-8). Century Bookbindery.

ADOPTION
see also Foster Home Care
Aigner, Hal. Faint Trails: An Introduction to the Fundamentals of Adult Adoptee/Birth Parent Reunification Searches. 104p. (Orig.). 1980. pap. 4.95 (ISBN 0-937572-00-4). Paradigm Pr.
Lindsay, Jeanne W. Pregnant Too Soon: Adoption Is an Option. LC 79-93356. (Illus.). 208p. (gr. 8-12). 1980. write for info. Morning Glory.
Smith, Jerome & Miroff, Franklin I. You're Our Child: A Social-Psychological Approach to Adoption. LC 80-5957. 110p. (Orig.). 1981. lib. bdg. 15.75 (ISBN 0-8191-1416-2); pap. text ed. 7.25 (ISBN 0-8191-1417-0). U Pr of Amer.

ADOPTION–PERSONAL NARRATIVES
Musser, Sandra K. I Would Have Searched Forever. (Orig.). 1980. pap. 4.95 (ISBN 0-88270-487-7). Logos.

ADRENAL STEROIDS
see Steroids

ADSORPTION
see also Carbon, Activated
Application of Adsorption to Wastewater Treatment. (Illus.). 1981. text ed. 40.00 (ISBN 0-937976-03-2). Enviro Pr.
Dash, J. G. Films on Solid Surfaces. 1975. 42.50 (ISBN 0-12-203350-7). Acad Pr.

ADSORPTION OF GASES
see Gases–Absorption and Adsorption

ADULT EDUCATION
see also Non-Formal Education
Apps, Jerry W. The Adult Learner on Campus: A Guide for Instructors & Administrators. 288p. 1981. 17.95 (ISBN 0-695-81577-6, Assn Pr). Follett.
Brill, Peter L. & Hayes, John P. Taming Your Turmoil: Managing the Transitions of Adult Life. (Illus.). 256p. 1981. 15.95 (ISBN 0-13-884445-3, Spectrum); pap. 6.95 (ISBN 0-13-884437-2). P-H.
Charters, Alexander N., et al. Comparing Adult Education Worldwide. LC 80-8911. (Higher Education Ser.). 1981. text ed. price not set (ISBN 0-87589-494-1). Jossey-Bass.
Commission of Architecture of AEA. Architecture for Adult Education. 74p. 1953. 2.30. Adult Ed.
Cross, K. Patricia. Adults As Learners: Increasing Participation & Facilitating Learning. LC 80-26985. (Higher Education Series). 1981. text ed. price not set (ISBN 0-87589-491-7). Jossey-Bass.
DeCrow, Roger, ed. Adult Education Dissertation Abstracts 1963-19. League, Nehume. 1970. write for info. Adult Ed.
Haponski, William C. & McCabe, Charles. Back to School: A College Guide for Adults. Leedham, Linnea, ed. (Illus.). 256p. cancelled (ISBN 0-88421-095-2); pap. cancelled (ISBN 0-88421-172-X). Butterick Pub.
Harris, W. J. Comparative Adult Education. (Illus.). 240p. 1981. pap. text ed. 14.95 (ISBN 0-582-29510-6). Longman.
Heffernan, James M. Educational & Career Services for Adults. LC 79-3279. 1981. write for info. (ISBN 0-669-03440-1). Lexington Bks.
Helping Adults Learn: Getting off to a Good Start. 1980. video tape 195.00 (ISBN 0-87771-014-7). Grad School.
Helping Adults Learn: Getting off to a Good Start. 1980. pap. 9.00 (ISBN 0-87771-015-5). Grad School.
Helping Adults Learn: Getting off to a Good Start. 1980. Set. 200.00 (ISBN 0-87771-020-1). Grad School.
Helping Adults Learn: How & Why Adults Learn. 1980. video tape 195.00 (ISBN 0-87771-016-3). Grad School.
Helping Adults Learn: How & Why Adults Learn. 1980. 9.00 (ISBN 0-87771-017-1). Grad School.
Helping Adults Learn: How & Why Adults Learn. 1980. Set. 200.00 (ISBN 0-87771-021-X). Grad School.

Kreitlow, Burton W. Examining Controversies in Adult Education. LC 80-27058. (Higher Education Ser.). 1981. text ed. price not set (ISBN 0-87589-488-7). Jossey-Bass.

Mee, Graham. Organisation for Education. 114p. 1980. pap. text ed. 25.00 (ISBN 0-582-78300-3). Longman.

Nash, Al. Ruskin College: A Challenge to Adult & Labor Education. 1981. pap. price not set (ISBN 0-87546-084-4). NY Sch Indus Rel.

Solmen, Lewis C. & Gordon, Joanne J. The Characteristics & Needs of Adults in Postsecondary Education. 1981. 20.95 (ISBN 0-669-04361-3). Lexington Bks.

Thatcher, Rebecca. Academic Skills: A Handbook for Working Adults Returning to School. 1976. pap. 1.50 (ISBN 0-87546-248-0). NY Sch Indus Rel.

ADULT EDUCATION–INDIA

Rao, T. V. & Bhatt, Anil. Adult Education for Social Change. 1980. 15.00x (ISBN 0-8364-0648-6, Pub. by Manohar India). South Asia Bks.

ADULTERY

Lake, Tony. Affairs: How to Cope with Extra-Marital Relationships. 224p. 1981. 10.95 (ISBN 0-13-018671-6, Spec); pap. 5.95 (ISBN 0-13-018663-5). P-H.

ADULTHOOD

see also Aged; Old Age

Brill, Peter L. & Hayes, John P. Taming Your Turmoil: Managing the Transitions of Adult Life. (Illus.). 256p. 1981. 15.95 (ISBN 0-13-884445-3, Spectrum); pap. 6.95 (ISBN 0-13-884437-2). P-H.

Dacey, John. Adult Development. 1981. text ed. write for info. (ISBN 0-8302-0114-9). Goodyear.

Deffner, Donald. Celebration of Adulthood. LC 80-81839. pap. 4.50 (ISBN 0-933350-41-4). Morse Pr.

Johnson, Margaret, tr. Dezoito, Nao Ha Tempo Que Perder. (Portuguese Bks.). 1979. 1.30 (ISBN 0-8297-0656-9). Life Pubs Intl.

--Dieciocho, No Hay Tiempo Que Perder. (Spanish Bks.). (Span.). 1978. 1.65 (ISBN 0-8297-0533-3). Life Pubs Intl.

ADVENTURE AND ADVENTURERS

see also Discoveries (In Geography); Escapes; Frontier and Pioneer Life; Heroes; Sea Stories; Seafaring Life; Shipwrecks; Underwater Exploration; Voyages and Travels

Davis, John L. Treasure, People, Ships & Dreams. (Illus.). 75p. 1977. pap. 5.95 (ISBN 0-933164-20-3). U of Tex Inst Tex Culture.

Newby, Eric, ed. A Short Walk in the Hindu Kush. 1981. pap. 4.95 (ISBN 0-14-002663-0). Penguin.

Stanley, C. S. The Adventures of Carlo Pittore. (Illus.). 18p. 1979. pap. 10.00 (ISBN 0-934376-01-8). Pittore Euforico.

Street, Jack C. Travel in the Nick of Time. 1981. 4.50 (ISBN 0-8062-1707-3). Carlton.

Telford, Lawrence. From Helgoland to Hollywood. 160p. 1981. 8.00 (ISBN 0-682-49738-X). Exposition.

White, Theodore H. In Search of History. 720p. 1981. pap. cancelled (ISBN 0-446-96729-7). Warner Bks.

ADVERTISING

see also Catalogs, Commercial; Commercial Art; Marketing; Packaging; Propaganda; Public Relations; Publicity; Sales Promotion; Salesmen and Salesmanship; Television Advertising

also subdivided by topic, e.g. Advertising–Banks and Banking

Albion, Mark S. & Farris, Paul. Advertising Controversy: Evidence on the Economic Effects of Advertising. 224p. 1980. 19.95 (ISBN 0-86569-057-X). Auburn Hse.

Bellavance, Diane. Advertising & Public Relations for a Small Business. (Illus.). 80p. 1980. pap. 5.95 (ISBN 0-9605276-0-5). DBA Bks.

Broadbent, Simon. Spending Advertising Money. 3rd ed. 381p. 1979. pap. 12.25x (ISBN 0-220-67020-X, Pub. by Busn Bks England). Renouf.

Dunn. Advertising. 4th ed. 1978. 21.95 (ISBN 0-03-014341-1). Dryden Pr.

Edwards, Charles M., Jr. & Lebowitz, Carl R. Retail Advertising & Sales Promotion. (Illus.). 576p. 1981. text ed. 19.95 (ISBN 0-13-775098-6); pap. 17.95 (ISBN 0-13-775080-3). P-H.

Gibson, Arthur, et al. Truth in Advertising. 1981. Repr. of 1972 ed. soft cover 4.95x (ISBN 0-88946-912-1). E Mellen.

Gilligan, C. & Crowther, G. Advertising Management. 1976. 33.00x (ISBN 0-86003-500-X, Pub. by Allan Pubs England); pap. 16.50x (ISBN 0-86003-600-6). State Mutual Bk.

Greyser, Stephen A. Cases in Advertising & Communications Management. 2nd ed. 300p. 1981. text ed. 19.95 (ISBN 0-13-118513-6). P-H.

Nelson, Roy P. The Design of Advertising. 4th ed. 1980. text ed. 16.95x (ISBN 0-697-04348-7). Wm C Brown.

Potter, Jack & Lowell, Mark. Assessing the Effectiveness of Advertising. 281p. 1975. text ed. 24.50x (ISBN 0-220-69730-2, Pub. by Busn Bks England). Renouf.

Ries, Al & Trout, Jack. Positioning: The Battle for Your Mind. 224p. 1980. 10.95 (ISBN 0-07-065263-5, P&RB). McGraw.

Roth, Bob. International Advertising. 1981. price not set (ISBN 0-87251-058-1). Crain Bks.

Sutton, Cort. Advertising Your Way to Success: How to Create Best-Selling Advertisements in All Media. (Illus.). 208p. 1981. text ed. 18.95 (ISBN 0-686-68610-1, Spec); pap. text ed. 9.95 (ISBN 0-13-018135-8, Spec). P-H.

Thomajah, Zareh. The Thief of State Street: 30 Years of Audacious Advertising with Zareh. LC 80-82894. (Illus.). 152p. (Orig.). 1980. pap. 15.00 (ISBN 0-686-28877-7). Garabed.

Zeigler, Sherilyn & Johnson, J. Douglas. Creative Strategy & Tactics in Advertising: A Managerial Approach to Copywriting & Production. LC 80-23899. (Advertising Ser.). 360p. 1981. text ed. 19.95 (ISBN 0-88244-229-5). Grid Pub.

ADVERTISING–AGENTS

see Advertising Agencies

ADVERTISING–DIRECTORIES

Glenn, Peter, et al, eds. Madison Avenue Handbook 1981. 1981. price not set (ISBN 0-87314-011-7). Peter Glenn.

ADVERTISING–LAW

see Advertising Laws

ADVERTISING–RETAIL TRADE

see Advertising

ADVERTISING–YEARBOOKS

Crain Books Staff, ed. Advertising Yearbook. 1981. price not set (ISBN 0-87251-056-5). Crain Bks.

Infa Press & Advertisers Year Book 1979. 17th ed. 318p. 1979. 25.00x (ISBN 0-8002-2737-9). Intl Pubns Serv.

ADVERTISING, ART IN

see Commercial Art

ADVERTISING, CONSUMER

see Advertising

ADVERTISING, MAGAZINE–DIRECTORIES

see Advertising–Directories

ADVERTISING, NEWSPAPER–DIRECTORIES

see Advertising–Directories

ADVERTISING, PICTORIAL

see Posters

ADVERTISING, RETAIL

see Advertising

ADVERTISING, TELEVISION

see Television Advertising

ADVERTISING AGENCIES

Cardamone, Tom. Advertising Agency & Studio Skills. 3rd ed. 160p. 1981. 10.95 (ISBN 0-8230-0151-2). Watson-Guptill.

ADVERTISING ART

see Commercial Art

ADVERTISING BUSINESS

see Advertising Agencies

ADVERTISING LAWS

see also Competition, Unfair

Garon, Philip A. Advertising Law Anthology, Vol. LC 73-87656. 1981. 59.95 (ISBN 0-686-69402-3). Intl Lib.

Kent, Felix H. Legal & Business Problems of the Advertising Industry: 1980 Course Handbook. LC 80-80906. (Patents, Copyrights, Trademarks, & Literary Property Course Handbook Ser.). (Illus.). 465p. 1980. pap. text ed. 25.00 (ISBN 0-686-68827-9, G4-3672). PLI.

Woolley, Diana. Advertising Law Handbook. 2nd ed. 106p. 1976. text ed. 21.00x (ISBN 0-220-66306-8, Pub. by Busn Bks England). Renouf.

ADVERTISING LAYOUT AND TYPOGRAPHY

Notman, Larry. Advertising Layout Basics: Ad Kit 4. 220p. 1981. pap. 4.00x (ISBN 0-918488-09-5). Newspaper Serv.

ADVERTISING TYPOGRAPHY

see Advertising Layout and Typography

ADVOCATES

see Lawyers

AENEAS

Camps, W. A. An Introduction to Virgil's Aeneid. 174p. (Orig.). 1969. pap. 9.95x (ISBN 0-19-872024-6). Oxford U Pr.

Proutfoot, L. Dryden's Aeneid & Its Seventeenth Century Predecessors. 278p. 1980. Repr. of 1960 ed. text ed. 30.00 (ISBN 0-8495-2173-4). R West.

AERIAL LAW

see Aeronautics–Laws and Regulations

AERIAL PHOTOGRAPH READING

see Photographic Interpretation

AERIAL WARFARE

see Air Warfare

AEROBIC BACTERIA

see Bacteria, Aerobic

AERODROMES

see Airports

AERODYNAMICS

see also Aeronautics; Turbulence

Hurt, H. R., Jr. Aerodynamics for Naval Aviators. 2nd ed. (Pilot Training Ser.). (Illus.). 416p. 1975. pap. 9.95 (ISBN 0-89100-182-4, E*A-182-4). Aviation Maintenance.

AERODYNAMICS, SUBSONIC

see Aerodynamics

AEROLITES

see Meteorites

AERONAUTICAL ACCIDENTS

see Aeronautics–Accidents

AERONAUTICAL INSTRUMENTS

see also Altimeter; Flight Engineering; Guidance Systems (Flight)

Federal Aviation Administration. Instrument Flying Handbook. 3rd ed. (Pilot Training Ser.). (Illus.). 274p. 1971. pap. 6.00 (ISBN 0-89100-164-6, E*A-A*C61-27B). Aviation Maintenance.

--Instrument Rating Written Test Guide. 5th ed. (Pilot Bks.). (Illus.). 200p. 1977. pap. 3.75 (ISBN 0-89100-169-7, E*A-A*C61-8D). Aviation Maintenance.

King, John & King, Martha. Answers & Explanations to Instrument Rating Written Test Guide. (Pilot Training Ser.). (Illus.). 90p. 1978. pap. 7.95 (ISBN 0-89100-091-7, E*A-61-8A*D*G). Aviation Maintenance.

--Instrument Pilot Airplane Written Test Guide, Including Answers & Explanations. (Pilot Training Ser.). (Illus.). 290p. 1978. pap. 10.95 (ISBN 0-89100-196-4, E*A-A*C61-8D*G-1). Aviation Maintenance.

Stevens, C. A. Your Key to the Cockpit. (Illus.). 1980. pap. 3.00 (ISBN 0-911721-85-1, Pub. by Inflight). Aviation.

Williams, J. R. IFR by the Book: Techniques of Instrument Flight. (Illus.). 1980. pap. 5.95 (ISBN 0-911721-83-5, Pub. by Gen. Avn. Press). Aviation.

AERONAUTICAL SPORTS

see Airplanes–Models; Gliding and Soaring

AERONAUTICS

see also Aerodynamics; Air Lines; Air Pilots; Airplanes; Airports; Astronautics; Balloon Ascensions; Balloons; Flying Saucers; Gliding and Soaring; Helicopters; Meteorology in Aeronautics; Seaplanes

Airmart. Airmart Hardware Digest: AN, MS, & NAS. Date not set. pap. 4.95. Aviation.

Baxter, Gordon. How to Fly. 288p. 1981. 12.95 (ISBN 0-671-44801-3). Summit Bks.

Bierman, Richard B. Aviation Quarterly. (Illus.). Date not set. 12.00 (Pub. by Avn Quarterly). Aviation.

Collins, Richard. Flying Safely. rev. ed. 1981. 10.95 (ISBN 0-440-02652-0, E Friede). Delacorte.

Hitchcock, Thomas H., ed. Monogram Close-up: Mess Bf-109k. (Close-up Ser.: No. 16). Date not set. pap. 5.95 (ISBN 0-914144-16-2, Pub. by Monogram). Aviation.

--Monogram Close-up: Taifun. (Close-up Ser.: No. 5). (Illus.). Date not set. pap. 5.95 (ISBN 0-914144-05-7, Pub. by Momogram). Aviation.

Jacobs, Fred E. Takeoffs & Touchdowns: My Sixty Years of Flying. LC 80-28865. (Illus.). 304p. 1981. 12.95 (ISBN 0-498-02540-3). A S Barnes.

McAllister, Chris. Planes & Airports. (Illus.). 64p. 1981. pap. 5.95 (ISBN 0-7134-3911-4, Pub. by Batsford England). David & Charles.

Monogram Close-up: Kikka. (Close-up Ser.: No. 19). (Illus.). Date not set. pap. 5.95 (ISBN 0-914144-19-7, Pub. by Monogram). Aviation.

Feterson, Melvin N. Flight Deck Uses for HP-25: Vol. 1, Professional Assortment. 66p. 1979. spiral bdg. 10.00x (ISBN 0-938880-00-4). MNP Star.

--Flight Deck Uses for the HP-41c: Vol. 1, Manual Run Mode Edition. 59p. 1981. spiral bdg. 12.00x (ISBN 0-938880-01-2). MNP Star.

Vinson, J. R., ed. Emerging Technologies in Aerospace Structures, Design, Structural Dynamics & Materials. 326p. 1980. 40.00 (H00157). ASME.

AERONAUTICS–ACCIDENTS

see also Aeronautics–Safety Measures; Survival (After Airplane Accidents, Shipwrecks, etc.)

Lightner, Robert. Triumph Through Tragedy. 70p. (Orig.). (gr. 7 up). 1980. pap. 2.00 (ISBN 0-89323-008-1). BMA Pr.

Moorhouse, Earl. Wake up, It's a Crash: A Survivor's Account. (Illus.). 184p. 1981. 17.95 (ISBN 0-7153-8093-1). David & Charles.

AERONAUTICS–BIBLIOGRAPHY

Didelot, J., ed. Interavia ABC: World Dictionary of Aviation & Astronautics, 1980. 28th ed. 1126p. 1980. 107.50x (ISBN 0-8002-2697-6). Intl Pubns Serv.

King, Frank H. & King, Viola W. Aviation Safety Bibliography & Source Book. LC 80-21946. (Aviation Management Ser.). 80p. (Orig.). 1980. pap. write for info. (ISBN 0-89100-138-7). Aviation Maintenance.

AERONAUTICS–BIOGRAPHY

see also Air Pilots

Pryor, Sam & Burnett, John. All God's Creatures: The Autobiography of Sam Pryor. 1981. 10.00 (ISBN 0-533-04946-6). Vantage.

Stein, E. P. Flight of the Vin Fiz. 1980. cancelled (ISBN 0-8129-0839-2). Times Bks.

AERONAUTICS–EXAMINATIONS, QUESTIONS, ETC.

Astro Publishers. Military Competency Exam, with Explanations. Date not set. pap. 7.95 (Pub. by Astro). Aviation.

AERONAUTICS–FLIGHTS

see also Space Flight

Aero Staff. Airman's Information Manual, 1981. LC 70-186849. 256p. 1981. pap. write for info. (ISBN 0-8168-1360-4). Aero.

Goldstein, Avram. VFR Flight Review. (Illus.). 1979. pap. 6.50 (ISBN 0-911721-67-3, Pub. by Airguide). Aviation.

McKay, Ernest A. A World to Conquer: The Story of the First Around the World Flight. LC 80-23064. (Illus.). 224p. 1981. 10.95 (ISBN 0-668-05096-9, 5096). Arco.

Stein, E. P. Flight of the Vin Fiz. 1980. cancelled (ISBN 0-8129-0839-2). Times Bks.

AERONAUTICS–HANDBOOKS, MANUALS, ETC.

Buck, Robert N. Flying Know-How. 1975. 10.95 (ISBN 0-440-04931-8). Delacorte.

Sacchi, Louise. Ocean Flying. (McGraw-Hill Ser. in Aviation). (Illus.). 240p. 1979. 16.50 (ISBN 0-07-054405-0). McGraw.

Welch, John F., ed. Van Sickle's Modern Airmanship. 5th ed. 896p. 1980. text ed. 24.95 (ISBN 0-442-25793-7). Van Nos Reinhold.

AERONAUTICS–HISTORY

Callahan, Neal & Young, David. Fill the Heavens with Commerce: Chicago Aviation 1855 to 1926. (Illus.). 250p. 1981. 15.00 (ISBN 0-914090-99-2). Chicago Review.

Grosser, Morton. Gossamer Odyssey: The Triumph of Human-Powered Flight. (Illus.). 288p. 1981. 14.95 (ISBN 0-686-69048-6). HM.

Halpenny, Bruce B. Action Stations Two: Military Airfields of Lincolnshire & the East Midlands. (Illus.). 232p. 1981. 37.95 (ISBN 0-85059-484-7). Aztex.

Matt, Paul, et al. Historical Aviation Album, Vol. XVI. Rust, Kenn & Foxworth, Thomas, eds. (All American Ser.). (Illus.). 96p. (Orig.). 1980. pap. 10.00 (ISBN 0-911852-15-8). Hist Aviation.

O'Neil, Paul. Barnstormers & Speed Kings. Time-Life Bks. Eds., ed. (The Epic of Flight Ser.). (Illus.). 176p. 1981. 12.95 (ISBN 0-8094-3275-7). Time-Life.

Platt, Deborah L. & Wiesley, Keith. Forgotten Airplanes: Interesting History of Aviation Firsts. 176p. 1981. 10.50 (ISBN 0-934506-04-3). Westminster Comm Pubns.

Rausa, Rosario. The Blue Angels: An Illustrated History. (Illus.). 1979. 14.50 (ISBN 0-911721-82-7, Pub. by Moran). Aviation.

Sims, Edward H. Fighter Tactics & Strategy Nineteen Fourteen to Nineteen Seventy. 2nd ed. LC 80-68106. (Illus.). 266p. 1980. 12.95 (ISBN 0-8168-8795-0). Aero.

Smith, Elinor. Aviatrix. (Illus.). 32p. 1981. 12.95 (ISBN 0-15-110372-0). HarBraceJ.

Spight, Edwin & Spight, Jeanne. Eagles of the Pacific: Consairways Service During WW-II. (Illus.). 1980. 12.95 (ISBN 0-911852-88-3, Pub. by Hist Avn. Album). Aviation.

Titler, Dale. Wings of Mystery: True Stories of Aviation History. rev. ed. (Illus.). 1981. 8.95 (ISBN 0-396-07826-5). Dodd.

AERONAUTICS–JUVENILE LITERATURE

see also Airplanes–Juvenile Literature

Hooker, Linda & McCarrell, Jo, eds. Let's Go Flying: An Introduction to Aviation Coloring & Activity Book. (Illus.). 1975. wkbk 2.50 (ISBN 0-911721-88-6, Pub. by Ninety-Nines); tchr's guide avail. Aviation.

AERONAUTICS–LAWS AND REGULATIONS

Aero Staff. Federal Aviation Regulations for Pilots. LC 60-10472. 112p. 1981. pap. write for info. (ISBN 0-8168-5737-7). Aero.

Doberstein, Richard. Regulations Made Easy for Commercial Pilots. (Illus.). Date not set. pap. 4.95x (Pub. by Simplified). Aviation.

--Regulations Made Easy for Instrument Pilots. (Illus.). Date not set. pap. 4.95x (Pub. by Simplified). Aviation.

--Regulations Made Easy for Private Pilots. (Illus.). Date not set. pap. 4.95x (Pub. by Simplified). Aviation.

Reschenthaler, G. B. & Roberts, B. Perspectives on Canadian Airline Regulation. 266p. 1979. pap. text ed. 13.50x (ISBN 0-409-88604-1, Pub. by Inst Res Pub Canada). Renouf.

AERONAUTICS–MEDICAL ASPECTS

see Aviation Medicine

AERONAUTICS–PICTORIAL WORKS

Feist, Uwe. Aero Armor Series, Vol. 14. LC 80-66353. (Orig.). 1981. pap. 3.95 (ISBN 0-8168-2048-1). Aero.

Skogsberg, Bertil. Wings on the Screen. Bisset, George, tr. from Swedish. (Illus.). 192p. 1981. 25.00 (ISBN 0-498-02495-4). A S Barnes.

AERONAUTICS–POETRY

Vasko, Donna. I'd Rather Be Flying. (Illus.). 100p. 1980. spiral bdg. 6.00. Aviation.

AERONAUTICS–SAFETY MEASURES

see also Air Traffic Control

Collins, Richard. Flying Safely. rev. ed. 1981. 10.95 (ISBN 0-440-02652-0, E Friede). Delacorte.

King, Frank H. & King, Viola W. Aviation Safety Bibliography & Source Book. LC 80-21946. (Aviation Management Ser.). 80p. (Orig.). 1980. pap. write for info. (ISBN 0-89100-138-7). Aviation Maintenance.

AERONAUTICS–STUDY AND TEACHING

see also Flight Training

Crane, Dale. Technical Instruction. 140p. 1980. pap. text ed. write for info. (ISBN 0-89100-183-2). Aviation Maintenance.

AERONAUTICS–TERMINOLOGY

Balter, Deborah J. Intermediate Aeronautical Language Manual. Date not set. pap. 14.95. Aviation.

--Primary Aeronautical Language Manual. Date not set. pap. 30.95. Aviation.

AERONAUTICS–YEARBOOKS

Williams, R. E., intro. by. Aviation Europe Nineteen Eighty-One. 34th ed. (Illus.). 170p. 1980. pap. 27.50x (ISBN 0-85499-888-8). Intl Pubns Serv.

AERONAUTICS, COMMERCIAL

see also Air Lines; Air Travel; Transport Planes

Doberstein, Richard. Regulations Made Easy for Commercial Pilots. (Illus.). Date not set. pap. 4.95x (Pub. by Simplified). Aviation.

AERONAUTICS, MILITARY

see also Air Warfare; Airplanes, Military
also subdivision Aerial Operations under names of wars, e.g. World War, 1939-45–Aerial Operations

Messimer, Dwight R. No Margin for Error: The U. S. Navy's Transpacific Flight of 1925. 176p. 1981. 15.95 (ISBN 0-87021-497-7). Naval Inst Pr.

Rausa, Rosario. Gold Wings, Blue Sea: A Naval Aviator's Story. 216p. 1981. 15.95 (ISBN 0-87021-219-2). Naval Inst Pr.

AERONAUTICS, NAVAL

see Aeronautics, Military

AERONAUTICS IN AGRICULTURE

Sinclair, Donna M. The Pastor's Wife Today. LC 80-26076. (Creative Leadership Ser.). 128p. (Orig.). 1981. pap. 4.95 (ISBN 0-687-30269-2). Abingdon.

AEROPLANES

see Airplanes

AEROSOLS

Kneip, Theo J. & Lioy, Paul J., eds. Aerosols: Anthropogenic & Natural, Sources & Transport. LC 80-12891. (N.Y. Academy of Sciences Annals: Vol. 338). 618p. Date not set. 108.00x (ISBN 0-89766-064-1); pap. price not set (ISBN 0-89766-065-X). NY Acad Sci.

AEROSPACE LAW

see Aeronautics–Laws and Regulations

AESCHYLUS

Kaiser, Leo, ed. The Seven Against Thebes. Thoreau, Henry D. LC 80-2522. (Emerson Society Quarterly No. Seventeen Nineteen Fifty Nine,1-30). 1981. Repr. of 1959 ed. 14.00 (ISBN 0-404-19070-7). AMS Pr.

AESTHETICS

see Esthetics

AFFECTION

see Friendship; Love

AFFIRMATIVE ACTION PROGRAMS

see also Minorities–Employment

Pepper. Affirmative Action Plan Workbook for Federal Contractors. 2nd ed. 1979. pap. 45.00 (ISBN 0-917386-31-0). Exec Ent.

Reid, Peter. Affirmative Action Compliance Kit: Eed Dictionary. 1980. pap. 10.00 (ISBN 0-917386-35-3). Exec Ent.

--Affirmative Action Compliance Kit: Reference Guide. 1980. pap. 15.00 (ISBN 0-917386-34-5). Exec Ent.

--Affirmative Action Compliance Kit: Working Manual. 1980. pap. 75.00 (ISBN 0-917386-33-7). Exec Ent.

Simmons. California Prsonnel Managers Guide to EEO Laws. 1980. pap. 25.00 (ISBN 0-917386-40-X). Exec Ent.

Solving EEO Problems. 1980. pap. 9.95 (ISBN 0-917386-36-1). Exec Ent.

AFFLICTION

see Suffering

AFFREIGHTMENT

see Freight and Freightage

AFGHANISTAN

see also names of regions, cities, etc. in Afghanistan

Anwar, M. H. Memories of Afghanistan. 1981. 8.95 (ISBN 0-8062-1696-4). Carlton.

AFGHANISTAN–FOREIGN RELATIONS

Misra, K. P. Afghanistan in Crisis. 1981. 20.00x (ISBN 0-7069-1305-1, Pub. by Vikas India). Advent Bk.

AFGHANISTAN–HISTORY

Bosworth, C. E. The Medieval History of Iran, Afghanistan & Central Asia. 374p. 1980. 75.00x (ISBN 0-86078-000-7, Pub. by Variorum England). State Mutual Bk.

Chaffetz, David. On the Eve of Invasion: A Journey Through Afghanistan. 12.95 (ISBN 0-686-68743-4). Regnery-Gateway.

Dupree, Louis. Afghanistan: 1980 Edition. LC 76-154993. (Illus.). 784p. 1980. 35.00 (ISBN 0-691-00023-9); pap. 9.95. Princeton U Pr.

Griffiths, John C. Afganistan: Key to a Continent. 200p. 1981. 16.00 (ISBN 0-86531-080-7). Westview.

Pottinger, George. The Bubble Reputation. 256p. 1981. 15.00x (ISBN 0-7073-0286-2, Pub. by Scottish Academic Pr Scotland). Columbia U Pr.

AFGHANISTAN–POLITICS AND GOVERNMENT

Fraser-Tytler, William K., Sr. Afghanistan: A Study of Political Developments in Central and Southern Asia. 5th ed. LC 80-1931. 1981. 42.50 (ISBN 0-404-18962-8). AMS Pr.

Griffiths, John C. Afganistan: Key to a Continent. 200p. 1981. 16.00 (ISBN 0-86531-080-7). Westview.

AFL-CIO

see American Federation of Labor and Congress of Industrial Organizations

AFRICA

see also names of countries or regions of Africa, e.g. Egypt, Congo, Ghana, Sahara, etc. geographic subdivisions of Africa e.g. Africa, East; Africa, Sub-Saharan

Clement, Hal. Left of Africa. (Lost Manuscripts Ser.). 160p. 1976. 12.95. Manuscript Pr.

Higgins, Aidan. Images of Africa. 1980. pap. 3.95 (ISBN 0-7145-0775-X). Riverrun NY.

Higgins, Rosalyn. United Nations Peacekeeping, 1946-1967: Documents & Commentary, Africa, Vol. 3 Africa. 486p. 1980. 87.00x (ISBN 0-19-218321-4). Oxford U Pr.

Jarrett, H. R. Africa. 5th ed. (Illus.). 624p. (Orig.). 1979. pap. text ed. 24.00x (ISBN 0-7121-0153-5, Pub by MacDonald & Evans England). Intl Ideas.

AFRICA–ARMED FORCES

African Nationalism & Militarism & Military Ascendancy. 85p. 1979. 8.00 (ISBN 0-914970-13-5, CM 003, Conch Mag). Unipub.

AFRICA–BIBLIOGRAPHY

African Index to Continental Periodical Literature: Covering 1978, No. 3. 1980. 62.50 (Dist. by Gale Research Co.). K G Saur.

AFRICA–COLONIZATION

Jacobs, Sylvia M. The African Nexus: Black American Perspectives on the European Partitioning of Africa, 1880-1920. LC 80-660. (Contributions in Afro-American & African Studies: No. 55). (Illus.). 264p. 1981. lib. bdg. 27.50 (ISBN 0-313-22312-2, JEP/). Greenwood.

AFRICA–COMMERCE

Trado Asian-African Directory of Exporters-Importers & Manufacturers, 1980. 25th ed. LC 60-41792. 1640p. 1980. 50.00x (ISBN 0-8002-2736-0). Intl Pubns Serv.

AFRICA–DESCRIPTION AND TRAVEL

African Pastureland Ecology. (FAO Pasture & Fodder Crop Studies: No. 7). 203p. 1981. pap. 11.00 (ISBN 92-5-100873-6, F2099, FAO). Unipub.

AFRICA–ECONOMIC CONDITIONS

Ake, Claude. Revolutionary Pressures in Africa. 112p. 1978. 12.95 (Pub. by Zed Pr); pap. 6.95 (ISBN 0-905762-15-0). Lawrence Hill.

Cohen, D. & Daniel, J. The Political Economy of Africa. (Illus.). 1981. text ed. 25.00x (ISBN 0-582-64284-1); pap. text ed. 11.95x (ISBN 0-582-64285-X). Longman.

The Middle East & North Africa 1980-81. 27th ed. LC 48-3250. (Illus.). 1005p. 1980. 80.00x (ISBN 0-905118-50-2). Intl Pubns Serv.

O'Connor, A. M. Urbanization in Tropical Africa, Nineteen Sixty to Nineteen Seventy-Nine: An Annotated Bibliography. (Reference Bks.). 1981. lib. bdg. 48.00 (ISBN 0-8161-8262-0). G K Hall.

AFRICA–FOREIGN RELATIONS

Drescher, Horst. Let Us Die Fighting: Nambia Under the Germans. 1981. 18.95 (ISBN 0-905762-77-0); pap. 8.95 (ISBN 0-905762-37-1). Lawrence Hill.

AFRICA–HISTORY

Alexander, E. Curtis. Axioms & Quotations of Yosef ben-Jochannan. LC 80-70287. (Illus.). 118p. (Orig.). 1980. pap. 6.95 (ISBN 0-938818-01-5). ECA Assoc.

Cambridge History of Africa, Vols. 2-5. Incl. Vol. 2. From ca. 500 B.C. to A.D. 1050. Fage, J. D., ed. 1979. 89.50 (ISBN 0-521-21592-7); Vol. 3. Ca. 1050-1600. Oliver, R., ed. 1977. 79.50 (ISBN 0-521-20981-1); Vol. 4. Gray, R., ed. 700p. 1975. 79.50 (ISBN 0-521-20413-5); Vol. 5. Flint, J. E., ed. 700p. 1977. 79.50 (ISBN 0-521-20701-0). LC 76-2261. (Illus.). Cambridge U Pr.

Davidson, Basil, et al, eds. Behind the War in Eritrea. 150p. 1980. pap. text ed. 8.95. Barber Pr.

Easterbrook, David L. & Lohrentz, Kenneth P. African Microfilms at the E. S. Bird Library, Syracuse University: An Annotated Guide. (Foreign & Comparative Studies-African Special Publications Ser.: No.7). 72p. 1975. pap. 3.50x. Syracuse U Foreign Comp.

Gailey, Harry A., Jr. History of Africa: From Earliest Times to 1800, Vol. 1. LC 80-15898. (Illus., Orig.). 1980. pap. text ed. 9.95 (ISBN 0-89874-032-0). Krieger.

--History of Africa: From 1800 to Present, Vol. 2. rev. ed. LC 80-15898. (Orig.). 1980. pap. text ed. 12.95 (ISBN 0-89874-033-9). Krieger.

Oliver, R. & Atmore, A. Africa Since Eighteen Hundred. 3rd ed. (Illus.). 396p. Date not set. price not set (ISBN 0-521-23485-9); pap. price not set (ISBN 0-521-29975-6). Cambridge U Pr.

--African Middle Ages. (Illus.). 245p. Date not set. price not set (ISBN 0-521-23301-1); pap. price not set (ISBN 0-521-29894-6). Cambridge U Pr.

Rudman, Jack. African & Afro-American History. (College Proficiency Examination Ser.: CLEP-36). (Cloth bdg. avail. on request). pap. 9.95 (ISBN 0-8373-5436-6). Natl Learning.

Tidg, Michael & Leeming, Donald. History of Africa Eighteen-Forty to Nineteen-Fourteen, Vol. 1. (Illus.). 188p. 1981. pap. text ed. 14.24x (ISBN 0-686-69152-0, Africana). Holmes & Meier.

AFRICA–POLITICS AND GOVERNMENT

see also Pan-Africanism

Administration for Development in Africa. 61p. 1979. 8.00 (ISBN 0-914970-15-1, CM 001, Conch Mag). Unipub.

African Nationalism & Militarism & Military Ascendancy. 85p. 1979. 8.00 (ISBN 0-914970-13-5, CM 003, Conch Mag). Unipub.

Ake, Claude. Revolutionary Pressures in Africa. 112p. 1978. 12.95 (Pub. by Zed Pr); pap. 6.95 (ISBN 0-905762-15-0). Lawrence Hill.

Carter, Gwendolen M. & Morgan, E. Philip, eds. From the Frontline. (Special Project Ser.: No. 27). 252p. 1980. 26.95. Hoover Inst Pr.

Cohen, D. & Daniel, J. The Political Economy of Africa. (Illus.). 1981. text ed. 25.00x (ISBN 0-582-64284-1); pap. text ed. 11.95x (ISBN 0-582-64285-X). Longman.

Drescher, Horst. Let Us Die Fighting: Nambia Under the Germans. 1981. 18.95 (ISBN 0-905762-77-0); pap. 8.95 (ISBN 0-905762-37-1). Lawrence Hill.

Education & Politics in Tropical Africa. 301p. 1979. pap. 25.00 (ISBN 0-914970-33-X, CM 004, Conch Mag). Unipub.

Jacaz, Jane W. African Policy Crossroads. (Illus.) 68p. (Orig.). 1979. pap. text ed. 3.00 (ISBN 0-89192-315-2). Interbk Inc.

Legum, Colin. Africa Contemporary Record, Vol. 12. LC 70-7957. 1400p. 1981. text ed. 125.00x (ISBN 0-8419-0550-9, Africana). Holmes & Meier.

Marshall, H. H. From Dependence to Statehood in Commonwealth Africa: Selected Documents, World War I to Independence. LC 80-10407. 734p. 1980. lib. bdg. 50.00 (ISBN 0-379-20348-0). Oceana.

The Middle East & North Africa 1980-81. 27th ed. LC 48-3250. (Illus.). 1005p. 1980. 80.00x (ISBN 0-905118-50-2). Intl Pubns Serv.

Osei-Kwame, Peter. A New Conceptual Model for the Study of Political Integration in Africa. LC 80-5708. 307p. 1980. lib. bdg. 20.00 (ISBN 0-8191-1316-6); pap. 11.50 (ISBN 0-8191-1317-4). U Pr of Amer.

Ottaway, David & Ottaway, Marina. Afrocommunism. LC 80-24289. (New Library of African Affairs Ser.). 320p. 1981. text ed. 25.00x (ISBN 0-8419-0664-5, Africana). Holmes & Meier.

AFRICA–RELIGION

Bowman, Fred. Reorientation of African Beliefs: A Prime Necessity. 1981. 4.95 (ISBN 0-8062-1566-6). Carlton.

Van Binsbergen, Wim M. J. Religious Change in Zambia: Exploratory Studies. (Monographs from the African Studies Centre, Leiden). (Illus.). 416p. 1981. price not set (ISBN 0-7103-0000-X). Routledge & Kegan.

AFRICA–SOCIAL CONDITIONS

Newman, James L., ed. Drought, Famine & Population Movement in Africa. LC 74-25877. (Foreign & Comparative Studies-Eastern African Ser.: No. 17). 144p. 1975. pap. 4.50x (ISBN 0-915984-14-8). Syracuse U Foreign Comp.

O'Connor, A. M. Urbanization in Tropical Africa, Nineteen Sixty to Nineteen Seventy-Nine: An Annotated Bibliography. (Reference Bks.). 1981. lib. bdg. 48.00 (ISBN 0-8161-8262-0). G K Hall.

AFRICA–SOCIAL LIFE AND CUSTOMS

Kofele-Kale, Ndiva. Tribesmen & Patriots: Political Culture in a Poly-Ethnic African State. LC 80-5734. 375p. 1981. lib. bdg. 22.00 (ISBN 0-8191-1395-6); pap. text ed. 12.75 (ISBN 0-8191-1396-4). U Pr of Amer.

AFRICA, CENTRAL–HISTORY

Kalck, Pierre. Historical Dictionary of the Central African Republic. O'Toole, Thomas, tr. LC 80-21199. (African Historical Dictionaries: No. 27). 194p. 1980. 10.00 (ISBN 0-8108-1360-2). Scarecrow.

AFRICA, EAST–HISTORY

Strayer, Robert, et al. Protest Movements in Colonial East Africa-Aspects of Early African Response to European Rule. LC 73-85549. (Foreign & Comparative Studies-Eastern African Ser.: No.12). 96p. 1973. pap. 4.50x (ISBN 0-915984-09-1). Syracuse U Foreign Comp.

AFRICA, EAST–POLITICS

Strayer, Robert, et al. Protest Movements in Colonial East Africa-Aspects of Early African Response to European Rule. LC 73-85549. (Foreign & Comparative Studies-Eastern African Ser.: No.12). 96p. 1973. pap. 4.50x (ISBN 0-915984-09-1). Syracuse U Foreign Comp.

AFRICA, EAST–RELIGION

Healey, Joseph G. A Fifth Gospel: The Experience of Black Christian Values. LC 80-25033. (Illus.). 320p. (Orig.). 1981. pap. 7.95 (ISBN 0-88344-013-X). Orbis Bks.

AFRICA, NORTH–BIBLIOGRAPHY

Sources of the History of North Africa, Asia, & Oceania in Scandinavia, 2 pts. Incl. Pt. 1. Sources of the History North Africa, Asia, & Oceania in Denmark. lib. bdg. 162.00 (ISBN 3-598-21474-X); Pt. 2. Sources of the History of North Africa, Asia, & Oceania in Finland, Norway, Sweden. lib. bdg. 65.00 (ISBN 3-598-21475-8). (Guides to the Sources for the History of the Nations). 1980 (Dist. by Gale Research Co.). K G Saur.

AFRICA, NORTH–HISTORY

Sources of the History of North Africa, Asia, & Oceania in Scandinavia, 2 pts. Incl. Pt. 1. Sources of the History North Africa, Asia, & Oceania in Denmark. lib. bdg. 162.00 (ISBN 3-598-21474-X); Pt. 2. Sources of the History of North Africa, Asia, & Oceania in Finland, Norway, Sweden. lib. bdg. 65.00 (ISBN 3-598-21475-8). (Guides to the Sources for the History of the Nations). 1980 (Dist. by Gale Research Co.). K G Saur.

AFRICA, SOUTHERN–HISTORY

Bridgeman, Jon M. The Revolt of the Hereros. (Perspectives on Southern Africa Ser.). 200p. 1980. 12.50 (ISBN 0-520-04113-5). U of Cal Pr.

The Historiography of Southern Africa. (General History of Africa Studies & Documents: No. 4). 112p. 1980. pap. 8.25 (ISBN 92-3-101775-6, U1026, UNESCO). Unipub.

AFRICA, SOUTHERN–POLITICS AND GOVERNMENT

Assistance to Racist Regimes in Southern Africa: Impact on the Enjoyment of Human Rights. 41p. 1979. pap. 4.00 (ISBN 0-686-68943-7, UN79/14/3, UN). Unipub.

Carter, Gwendolen & Morgan, E. Philip, eds. From the Frontline: Speeches of Sir Seretse Khama. (Special Project Ser.: 27). 252p. 1980. 26.95. Hoover Inst Pr.

Hull, Richard W. Southern Africa: Civilizations in Turmoil. (Illus.). 240p. 1981. text ed. 17.50x (ISBN 0-8147-3410-3); pap. text ed. 9.00x (ISBN 0-8147-3411-1). NYU Pr.

AFRICA, SOUTHERN–RACE QUESTION

Assistance to Racist Regimes in Southern Africa: Impact on the Enjoyment of Human Rights. 41p. 1979. pap. 4.00 (ISBN 0-686-68943-7, UN79/14/3, UN). Unipub.

Hull, Richard W. Southern Africa: Civilizations in Turmoil. (Illus.). 240p. 1981. text ed. 17.50x (ISBN 0-8147-3410-3); pap. text ed. 9.00x (ISBN 0-8147-3411-1). NYU Pr.

AFRICA, WEST

Church, R. J. West Africa. 8th ed. (Geographies for Advanced Study Ser.). (Illus.). 560p. 1980. pap. 28.00 (ISBN 0-582-30020-7). Longman.

AFRICA, WEST–DESCRIPTION AND TRAVEL

Church, R. J. West Africa. 8th ed. (Geographies for Advanced Study Ser.). (Illus.). 560p. 1980. pap. 28.00 (ISBN 0-582-30020-7). Longman.

AFRICA, WEST–ECONOMIC CONDITIONS

Pearson, Scott R. & Stryker, J. Dirck. Rice in West Africa: Policy & Economics. LC 80-50906. (Illus.). 472p. 1981. 39.00x (ISBN 0-8047-1095-3). Stanford U Pr.

Woillet, M. J. Appropriate Technology: Scope for Co-Operation Among the Countries of the West African Economic Community. International Labour Office, Geneva, ed. ii, 104p. (Orig.). 1980. pap. 5.70 (ISBN 92-2-102359-1). Intl Labour Office.

AFRICA, WEST–HISTORY

Connah, Graham. Three Thousand Years in Africa: Man & His Environment in the Lake Chad Region of Nigeria. LC 79-41508. (New Studies in Archaeology). (Illus.). 240p. Date not set. price not set (ISBN 0-521-22848-4). Cambridge U Pr.

AFRICA, WEST–SOCIAL CONDITIONS

Zachariah, K. C. & Conde, Julian. Migration in West Africa: The Demographic Aspects. (World Bank Research Publication Ser.). (Illus.). 256p. 1980. 16.95 (ISBN 0-19-520186-8); pap. 6.95 (ISBN 0-19-520187-6). Oxford U Pr.

AFRICAN AMERICANS

see Afro-Americans

AFRICAN ART

see Art, African

AFRICAN FOLK-LORE

see Folk-Lore, African

AFRICAN LITERATURE

Grant, Alice, et al. Shindano-Swahili Essays & Other Stories. (Foreign & Comparative Studies-African Special Publications Ser.: No.6). 55p. 1971. pap. 2.50x. Syracuse U Foreign Comp.

Yarbrough, Camille. Cornrows. (Illus.). 48p. (Orig.). (gr. k-3). 1981. pap. 2.95 (ISBN 0-698-20529-4, Peppercorn). Coward.

AFRICAN LITERATURE–BIBLIOGRAPHY

Zell, Hans, ed. Reader's Guide to Contemporary African Literature. 2nd, rev ed. 300p. 1981. text ed. 20.00x (ISBN 0-686-69153-9, Africana); pap. text ed. 10.00x (ISBN 0-8419-0640-8). Holmes & Meier.

AFRICAN LITERATURE–HISTORY AND CRITICISM

Brown, Lloyd W. Women Writers in Black Africa. LC 80-1710. (Contributions in Women's Studies: No. 21). 256p. 1981. lib. bdg. 23.95 (ISBN 0-313-22540-0, BRW/). Greenwood.

Lindfors, Bernth. Mazungumzo: Interviews with East African Writers, Publishers, Editors & Scholars. LC 80-25684. (Africa Ser., Ohio University Papers in International Studies). 179p. 1981. pap. 13.00 (ISBN 0-89680-108-X). Ohio U Ctr Intl.

AFRICAN LITERATURE (ENGLISH)–HISTORY AND CRITICISM

Barthold, Bonnie J. Black Time: Fiction of Africa, the Caribbean, & the United States. LC 80-24336. (Illus.). 224p. 1981. 17.50x (ISBN 0-300-02573-4). Yale U Pr.

AFRICAN MYTHOLOGY

see Mythology, African

AFRICAN POETRY–HISTORY AND CRITICISM

Anozie, Sunday O. Structural Models & African Poetics: Towards a Pragmatic View of Literature. 220p. 1981. 37.50 (ISBN 0-7100-0467-2). Routledge & Kegan.

AFRICAN RELATIONS

see Pan-Africanism

AFRICAN SCULPTURE

see Sculpture–Africa

AFRICAN TALES

see Tales, African

AFRIKAANS FICTION

see Short Stories, Afrikaans

AFRO-AMERICAN ART
This heading used beginning January 1976. See Negro Art for earlier works.
see also Afro-American Artists
Lewis, David L. When Harlem Was in Vogue. LC 80-2704. (Illus.). 400p. 1981. 17.95 (ISBN 0-394-49572-1). Knopf.
Price, Sally & Price, Richard. Afro-American Arts of the Suriname Rain Forest. (Illus.). 240p. 1981. 37.50 (ISBN 0-520-04345-6, CAL 516); pap. 14.95 (ISBN 0-520-04412-6). U of Cal Pr.

AFRO-AMERICAN ARTISTS
This heading used beginning January 1976. See Negro Artists for earlier works.
see also Afro-American Art
N.C. Museum of Art, ed. Afro-American Artists: North Carolina USA. 1980. 8.00 (ISBN 0-88259-096-0). NCMA.

AFRO-AMERICAN AUTHORS
This heading used beginning January 1976. See Negro Authors for earlier works.
see also American Literature–Afro-American Authors
Cash, E. A. John A. Williams: The Evolution of a Black Writer. LC 73-92796. 1974. 10.00 (ISBN 0-89388-142-2). Okpaku Communications.
Payne, Ladell. Black Novelists & the Southern Literary Tradition. LC 80-21747. 144p. 1981. 11.00x (ISBN 0-8203-0536-7). U of Ga Pr.
Sylvander, Carolyn W. Jessie Redmon Fauset: Black American Writer. LC 80-51050. (Illus.). 285p. 1980. 18.50x (ISBN 0-87875-196-3). Whitston Pub.

AFRO-AMERICAN CHILDREN
This heading used beginning January 1976. See Negro Children for earlier works.
Edelman, Marian W. Portrait of Inequality: Black & White Children in America. LC 80-68585. 144p. (Orig.). 1980. pap. 5.00 (ISBN 0-938008-00-5). Childrens Defense.

AFRO-AMERICAN DIALECT
see Black English

AFRO-AMERICAN EDUCATION
see Afro-Americans–Education

AFRO-AMERICAN ENGLISH
see Black English

AFRO-AMERICAN FOLK-LORE
This heading used beginning January 1976. See Folk-Lore, Negro for earlier works.
Dundes, Alan, ed. Mother Wit from the Laughing Barrel: Readings in the Interpretation of Afro-American Folklore. LC 80-8528. 688p. 1981. lib. bdg. 38.00 (ISBN 0-8240-9456-5). Garland Pub.

AFRO-AMERICAN-JEWISH RELATIONS
see Afro-Americans–Relations with Jews

AFRO-AMERICAN JOURNALISM
see Afro-American Press

AFRO-AMERICAN LITERATURE (ENGLISH)
see American Literature–Afro-American Authors

AFRO-AMERICAN MUSIC
This heading used beginning January 1976. See Negro Music for earlier works.
see also Jazz Music; Rock Music; Spirituals (Songs)
De Larma, Dominique-Rene. Bibliography of Black Music: Reference Materials, Vol. 1. LC 80-24681. (The Greenwood Encyclopedia of Black Music). 144p. 1981. lib. bdg. 25.00 (ISBN 0-313-21340-2, DBI/01). Greenwood.

AFRO-AMERICAN MUSICIANS
This heading used beginning January 1976. See Negro Musicians for earlier works.
Berry, Lemuel, Jr. Biographical Dictionary of Black Musicians & Music Educators, Vol. II. (Illus.). 389p. (gr. 5-12). 1981. 20.00 (ISBN 0-932188-02-8). Ed Bk Pubs OK.
--Biographical Dictionary of Black Musicians & Music Educators, Vol. I. LC 78-62404. (gr. 5-12). 1978. 16.95 (ISBN 0-932188-00-1); pap. 12.95 (ISBN 0-932188-01-X). Ed Bk Pubs OK.
Handy, D. Antoinette. Black Women in American Bands & Orchestras. LC 80-19380. 394p. 1981. 17.50 (ISBN 0-8108-1346-7). Scarecrow.

AFRO-AMERICAN POETRY (ENGLISH)
see American Poetry–Afro-American Authors

AFRO-AMERICAN PRESS
This heading used beginning January 1976. See Negro Press for earlier works.
Noble, Gil. Black Is the Color of My TV Tube. (Illus.). 1981. 10.00 (ISBN 0-8184-0297-0). Lyle Stuart.
Tinney, James S. & Rector, Justine J. Issues & Trends in Afro-American Journalism. LC 80-6074. 371p. 1980. lib. bdg. 20.75 (ISBN 0-8191-1352-2); pap. text ed. 12.50 (ISBN 0-8191-1353-0). U Pr of Amer.

AFRO-AMERICAN SPIRITUALS
see Spirituals (Songs)

AFRO-AMERICAN SUFFRAGE
see Afro-Americans–Politics and Suffrage

AFRO-AMERICAN WOMEN
This heading used beginning January 1976. See Women, Negro for earlier works.
Hunez, Jean M., ed. Gifts of Power: The Writings of Rebecca Jackson, Black Visionary, Shaker Eldress. (Illus.). 370p. 1981. lib. bdg. 20.00x (ISBN 0-87023-299-1). U of Mass Pr.
Smith, Barbara. Toward a Black Feminst Criticism. (Out & Out Pamphlet Ser). pap. 1.00 (ISBN 0-918314-14-3). Out & Out.
Taylor, Ganell. A Book of Rejects. 1980. 6.95 (ISBN 0-533-04796-X). Vantage.
Walker, Alice. You Can't Keep a Good Woman Down: Stories by Alice Walker. LC 80-8761. 180p. 1981. 10.95 (ISBN 0-15-199754-3). HarBraceJ.

AFRO-AMERICANS
This heading used beginning January 1976. See Negroes for earlier works. Here are entered works on the Black people of the United States. Works on Black people outside of the United States are entered under the heading Blacks. Theoretical works discussing the Black race from an anthropological point of view are entered under the heading Black Race.
see also Freedmen; Slavery in the United States
also subdivision Afro-Americans under names of wars, e.g. World War, 1939-1945–Afro-Americans; and headings beginning with Afro-American
Asante, Molefi K. & Vandi, Abdulai S., eds. Contemporary Black Thought: Alternative Analyses in Social & Behavioral Science. LC 80-15186. (Sage Focus Editions Ser.: Vol. 26). (Illus.). 302p. 1980. 18.95 (ISBN 0-8039-1500-4). Sage.
Chapian, Marie & Sadler, Robert. Help Me Remember, Lord--Help Me Forget. (Illus.). 256p. 1981. pap. 2.95 (ISBN 0-87123-203-0, 200203). Bethany Fell.
Chicago Center for Afro-American Studies & Research, ed. Black People & the Nineteen Eighty Census: Proceedings from a Conference on the Poplation Undercount, Vol. 1. LC 80-68927. (Black People & the Nineteen Eighty Census Ser.). (Illus.). 702p. 1980. pap. 20.00 (ISBN 0-937954-01-2); pap. 15.00. Chr Ctr Afro-Am Stud.
Frye, Charles A., ed. Level Three: A Black Philosophy Reader. LC 80-5801. 217p. 1980. lib. bdg. 18.00 (ISBN 0-8191-1241-0); pap. text ed. 9.75 (ISBN 0-8191-1242-9). U Pr of Amer.
Jackson, Clyde O. Come Like the Benediction. (Illus.). 1981. 7.00 (ISBN 0-682-49723-1). Exposition.
King, Martin L., Sr. & Riley, Clayton. Daddy King. 1981. lib. bdg. 13.95 (ISBN 0-8161-3157-0, Large Print Bks). G K Hall.
Krech, Shepard, III. Praise the Bridge That Carries You Over: The Life of Joseph L. Sutton. (University Books Ser.). 1981. lib. bdg. 18.50 (ISBN 0-8161-9038-0). G K Hall.
Matney, William C., ed. Who's Who Among Black Americans, 1980-1981. 3rd ed. LC 76-643293. 1981. 49.95 (ISBN 0-915130-33-5). Who's Who Black Am.
Moikobu, Josephine. Blood & Flesh: Black American & African Identifications. LC 80-1706. (Contributions in African American Studies: No. 59). (Illus.). 224p. 1981. lib. bdg. 25.00 (ISBN 0-313-22549-4, MBF/). Greenwood.
Staples, Robert. The World of Black Singles: Changing Patterns of Male-Female Relations. LC 80-1025. (Contributions in Afro-American & African Studies: No. 57). 288p. 1981. lib. bdg. 25.00 (ISBN 0-313-22478-1, SBS/). Greenwood.
Tisdale, Joanna. Little Black Boy, I Saw Your Face. 1981. 7.95 (ISBN 0-533-04828-1). Vantage.
Towle, W. Wilder. The Oral History of James Nunn: A Unique North Carolinian. 230p. (Orig.). 1980. pap. 5.95 (ISBN 0-86629-001-X). Sunrise MO.

AFRO-AMERICANS–CHILDREN
see Afro-American Children

AFRO-AMERICANS–CIVIL RIGHTS
This heading used beginning January 1976. See Negroes–Civil Rights for earlier works.
see also Afro-Americans–Politics and Suffrage
Chafe, William H. Civilities & Civil Rights: Greensboro, North Carolina, & the Black Struggle for Freedom. (Illus.). 320p. 1981. pap. 5.95 (ISBN 0-19-502919-4, GB 644, GB). Oxford U Pr.
Keech, William R. The Impact of Negro Voting: The Role of the Vote in the Quest for Equality. LC 80-26518. (American Politics Research Series). ix, 113p. 1981. Repr. of 1968 ed. lib. bdg. 19.75x (ISBN 0-313-22774-8, KEIN). Greenwood.
Rovetch, Emily, ed. Like It Is: Arthur E. Thomas Interviews Leaders on Black America. 1981. text ed. 9.95 (ISBN 0-525-93193-7); pap. 5.95 (ISBN 0-525-93194-5); tchr's. guide 3.95 (ISBN 0-525-93195-3). Dutton.
Sitkoff, Harvard. A New Deal for Blacks: The Emergence of Civil Rights As a National Issue; the Depression Decade. 412p. 1981. pap. 6.95 (ISBN 0-19-502893-7, GB 627, OPB). Oxford U Pr.

AFRO-AMERICANS–ECONOMIC CONDITIONS
This heading used beginning January 1976. See Negroes–Economic Conditions for earlier works.
see also Afro-Americans–Employment
Hermann, Janet S. The Pursuit of a Dream. (Illus.). 288p. 1981. 17.50 (ISBN 0-19-502887-2). Oxford U Pr.
Kornweibel, Theodore, Jr., ed. In Search of the Promised Land: Essays in Black Urban History. (National University Publications, Interdisciplinary Urban Ser.). 237p. 1981. 17.50 (ISBN 0-8046-9267-X). Kennikat.

AFRO-AMERICANS–EDUCATION
This heading used beginning January 1976. See Negroes–Education for earlier works.
Fleming, John. The Lengthening Shadow of Slavery: A Historical Justification for Affirmative Action for Blacks in Higher Education. LC 76-21656. 158p. 1976. pap. 5.95 (ISBN 0-88258-074-4). Howard U Pr.
Smith, Ed. Black Students in Interracial Schools: A Guide for Students, Teachers & Schools. LC 80-81701. 134p. (Orig.). 1980. pap. 7.95 (ISBN 0-686-69010-9). Garrett Pk.
Thomas, Gail E., ed. Black Students in Higher Education: Conditions & Experiences in the 1970's. LC 80-1702. (Contributions to the Study of Education: No. 1). 424p. 1981. lib. bdg. 29.95 (ISBN 0-313-22477-3, TBS/). Greenwood.

AFRO-AMERICANS–EMPLOYMENT
This heading used beginning January 1976. See Negroes–Employment for earlier works.
Meier, August & Rudwick, Elliott. Black Detroit & the Rise of the Uaw. (Illus.). 304p. 1981. pap. 6.95 (ISBN 0-19-502895-3, GB 632, OPB). Oxford U Pr.

AFRO-AMERICANS–FOLK-LORE
see Afro-American Folk-Lore

AFRO-AMERICANS–HEALTH AND HYGIENE
Symposium at Roswell Park Memorial Institute, Buffalo, May 1980. Cancer Among Black Populations: Proceedings. Mettlin, Curtis & Murphy, Gerald P., eds. (Progress in Clinical & Biological Research Ser.: No. 53). 275p. 1981. 24.00x (ISBN 0-8451-0053-X). A R Liss.

AFRO-AMERICANS–HISTORY
This heading used beginning January 1976. See Negroes–History for earlier works.
Harding, Vincent. The Other American Revolution. Hill, Robert A., ed. LC 79-54307. (Afro-American Culture & Society Monographs: Vol. 4). 1981. pap. 8.50 (ISBN 0-934934-06-1). Ctr Afro Am St.
Hermann, Janet S. The Pursuit of a Dream. (Illus.). 288p. 1981. 17.50 (ISBN 0-19-502887-2). Oxford U Pr.
King, Anita, compiled by. Quotations in Black. LC 80-1794. (Illus.). 320p. 1981. lib. bdg. 25.00 (ISBN 0-313-22128-6, KQB/). Greenwood.
Miller, Randall M., ed. The Afro-American Slaves: Community or Chaos? 128p. (Orig.). 1981. pap. 5.50 (ISBN 0-89874-078-9). Krieger.
Rudman, Jack. African & Afro-American History. (College Proficiency Examination Ser.: CLEP-36). (Cloth bdg. avail. on request). pap. 9.95 (ISBN 0-8373-5436-6). Natl Learning.
Sealy, Adrienne V. The Color Your Way into Black History Book. (Illus.). 78p. 1980. wkbk. 4.00 (ISBN 0-9602670-6-9). Assn Family Living.
Sitkoff, Harvard. A New Deal for Blacks: The Emergence of Civil Rights As a National Issue; the Depression Decade. 412p. 1981. pap. 6.95 (ISBN 0-19-502893-7, GB 627, OPB). Oxford U Pr.
Smallwood, James M. Time of Hope, Time of Despair: Black Texans During Reconstruction. (National University Publications, Ethnic Studies). 1981. 17.50 (ISBN 0-8046-9273-4). Kennikat.
Spangler, Earl. Blacks in America. LC 71-150773. (In America Bks.). (Illus.). (gr. 5-11). 1980. PLB 5.95. Lerner Pubns.

AFRO-AMERICANS–OCCUPATIONS
see Afro-Americans–Employment

AFRO-AMERICANS–POLITICS AND SUFFRAGE
This heading used beginning January 1976. See Negroes–Politics and Suffrage for earlier works.
see also Afro-Americans–Civil Rights
Burns, William H. The Voices of Negro Protest in America. LC 80-21197. 88p. 1980. Repr. of 1963 ed. lib. bdg. 17.50x (ISBN 0-313-22219-3, BUVN). Greenwood.
Keech, William R. The Impact of Negro Voting: The Role of the Vote in the Quest for Equality. LC 80-26518. (American Politics Research Series). ix, 113p. 1981. Repr. of 1968 ed. lib. bdg. 19.75x (ISBN 0-313-22774-8, KEIN). Greenwood.
--The Impact of Negro Voting: The Role of the Vote in the Quest for Equality. LC 80-26518. (American Politics Research Ser.). ix, 113p. 1981. Repr. of 1968 ed. lib. bdg. 19.75x (ISBN 0-313-22774-8, KEIN). Greenwood.
Rovetch, Emily, ed. Like It Is: Arthur E. Thomas Interviews Leaders on Black America. 1981. text ed. 9.95 (ISBN 0-525-93193-7); pap. 5.95 (ISBN 0-525-93194-5); tchr's. guide 3.95 (ISBN 0-525-93195-3). Dutton.

AFRO-AMERICANS–PSYCHOLOGY
This heading used beginning January 1976. See Negroes–Psychology for earlier works.
Asante, Molefi K. & Vandi, Abdulai S., eds. Contemporary Black Thought: Alternative Analyses in Social & Behavioral Science. LC 80-15186. (Sage Focus Editions: Vol. 26). (Illus.). 302p. 1980. pap. 9.95 (ISBN 0-8039-1501-2). Sage.
Jacobs, Sylvia M. The African Nexus: Black American Perspectives on the European Partitioning of Africa, 1880-1920. LC 80-660. (Contributions in Afro-American & African Studies: No. 55). (Illus.). 264p. 1981. lib. bdg. 27.50 (ISBN 0-313-22312-2, JEP/). Greenwood.

AFRO-AMERICANS–RELATIONS WITH JEWS
This heading used beginning January 1976. See Negro-Jewish Relations for earlier works.
Lounds, Morris, Jr. Israel's Black Hebrews: Black Americans in Search of Identity. LC 80-5651. 231p. 1981. lib. bdg. 18.25 (ISBN 0-8191-1400-6); pap. text ed. 9.75 (ISBN 0-8191-1401-4). U Pr of Amer.

AFRO-AMERICANS–RELIGION
This heading used beginning January 1976. See Negroes–Religion for earlier works.
Whitfield, Thomas. From Night to Sunlight. LC 80-68874. 1980. pap. 4.95 (ISBN 0-8054-5291-5). Broadman.

AFRO-AMERICANS–SOCIAL CONDITIONS
This heading used beginning January 1976. See Negroes–Social Conditions for earlier works.
Kornweibel, Theodore, Jr., ed. In Search of the Promised Land: Essays in Black Urban History. (National University Publications, Interdisciplinary Urban Ser.). 237p. 1981. 17.50 (ISBN 0-8046-9267-X). Kennikat.
Swan, L. Alex. Families of Black Prisoners: Survival & Progress. (University Book Ser.). 1981. 188.95 (ISBN 0-8161-8412-7). G K Hall.
--Survival & Progress: The Afro-American Experience. LC 80-1197. (Contributions in Afro-American & African Studies: No. 58). (Illus.). 280p. 1981. lib. bdg. 25.00 (ISBN 0-313-22480-3, SSU). Greenwood.
Woods, Randall B. A Black Odyssey: John Lewis Waller & the Promise of American Life, 1878-1900. LC 80-18965. (Illus.). 272p. 1981. 20.00x (ISBN 0-7006-0207-0). Regents Pr KS.

AFRO-AMERICANS–SOCIAL LIFE AND CUSTOMS
This heading used beginning January 1976. See Negroes–Social Life and Customs for earlier works.
Asante, Molefi K. & Vandi, Abdulai S., eds. Contemporary Black Thought: Alternative Analyses in Social & Behavioral Science. LC 80-15186. (Sage Focus Editions: Vol. 26). (Illus.). 302p. 1980. pap. 9.95 (ISBN 0-8039-1501-2). Sage.

AFRO-AMERICANS–SUFFRAGE
see Afro-Americans–Politics and Suffrage

AFRO-AMERICANS–CALIFORNIA
Daniels, Douglas H. Images of Our Roots: Photographic, Oral, & Written Documents of the San Francisco Bay Area's Black Pioneers, 1850-1930. (National History Ser.). (Illus.). 1981. 22.50 (ISBN 0-89482-054-0); pap. 12.50 (ISBN 0-89482-055-9). Stevenson Pr.

AFRO-AMERICANS–MISSOURI
Kremer, et al. Missouri's Black Heritage. LC 79-54887. (Orig.). 1980. pap. text ed. 6.95x (ISBN 0-88273-115-7). Forum Pr MO.

AFRO-AMERICANS–TEXAS
Smallwood, James M. Time of Hope, Time of Despair: Black Texans During Reconstruction. (National University Publications, Ethnic Studies). 1981. 17.50 (ISBN 0-8046-9273-4). Kennikat.

AFRO-AMERICANS IN AERONAUTICS
This heading used beginning January 1976. See Negroes in Aeronautics for earlier works.
Carisella, P. J. & Ryan, James W. The Black Swallow of Death. 1972. 8.95 (Pub. by Carisella). Aviation.

AFRO-AMERICANS IN MILITARY SERVICE
see United States–Armed Forces–Afro-Americans

AFRO-AMERICANS IN THE ARMED FORCES
see United States–Armed Forces–Afro-Americans

AFTER-DINNER SPEECHES
see Public Speaking

AGAMEMNON
Smith, Peter M. On the Hymn to Zeus in Aeschylus' Agamemnon. LC 80-11327. (American Classical Studies: No. 5). 12.00x (ISBN 0-89130-387-1); pap. 7.50x (ISBN 0-89130-388-X). Scholars Pr CA.

AGARICALES
Baroni, T. J. A Revision of the Genus Rhodocybe Maire: Agaricales. (Nova Hedwigia Beiheft). (Illus.). 300p. 1981. lib. bdg. 60.00x (ISBN 3-7682-5467-4). Lubrecht & Cramer.

AGE
see Longevity; Middle Age; Old Age; Youth

AGE AND EMPLOYMENT
see also Children–Employment; Youth–Employment
Fogarty, Michael. Forty to Sixty- How We Waste the Middle Aged. 250p. 1975. pap. text ed. 8.75x (ISBN 0-7199-0904-X, Pub. by Bedford England). Renouf.

AGE AND MENTAL ABILITY
see Age and Intelligence

AGE AND INTELLIGENCE
Maas, James. Fifteen Over Seventy: Counsel from My Elders. (Illus.). 1980. pap. 3.95 (ISBN 0-915288-42-7). Shameless Hussy.

AGE OF ROCKS
see Geology, Stratigraphic

AGED
see also Aging; Architecture and the Aged; Old Age; Old Age Assistance; Retirement; Retirement Income; Social Work with the Aged
Dietrich, T. Stanton. Florida's Older Population Revisited. (Illus.). vi, 78p. (Orig.). 1978. pap. 6.00 (ISBN 0-8130-0686-4). U Presses Fla.
Kosberg, Jordan I. Abuse & Maltreatment of the Aged. 400p. Date not set. text ed. 30.00 (ISBN 0-88416-353-9). PSG Pub.
McRae, John. Elderly in the Environment: Northern Europe. (Illus.). 119p. (Orig.). 1975. pap. 7.50 (ISBN 0-8130-0687-2). U Presses Fla.
Michaels, Joe. Prime of Your Life. 288p. 1981. 17.50 (ISBN 0-87196-478-3). Facts on File.
Pampel, Fred C. Social Change & the Aged: Recent Trends in the United States. LC 79-4752. (Illus.). 240p. 1981. 22.95 (ISBN 0-669-02928-9). Lexington Bks.

Planning for the Elderly in New York City: Report of a Research Utilization Workshop. 1980. 4.00. Comm Coun Great NY.

Rhine, Shirley H. America's Aging Population: Issues Facing Business & Society, Report No. 785. (Illus.). viii, 60p. 1980. pap. 15.00 (ISBN 0-8237-0221-9). Conference Bd.

Rowlings, Cherry. Social Work with Elderly People. (Studies in the Personal Social Services: No. 3). 144p. (Orig.). 1981. text ed. 19.95x (ISBN 0-04-362036-1, 2603); pap. text ed. 7.95x (ISBN 0-04-362037-X, 2604). Allen Unwin.

AGED–CARE AND HYGIENE

see also Geriatric Nursing; Geriatrics; Nursing Homes

Bray, Jean & Wright, Sheila, eds. The Use of Technology in the Care of the Elderly & the Disabled. LC 80-17847. xii, 267p. 1980. lib. bdg. 29.95 (ISBN 0-313-22616-4, BTC/). Greenwood.

Bressler, Rubin & Conrad, Kenneth. Drug Therapy for the Elderly. (Illus.). 300p. 1981. pap. text ed. 13.95 (ISBN 0-8016-0782-5). Mosby.

Carter, Jan. Day Services for Adults Somewhere to Go. (National Institute Social Services Library: No. 40). 352p. 1981. text ed. 35.00x (ISBN 0-04-262035-X, 2620). Allen Unwin.

Davies, Bleddyn P. Variations in Services for the Aged. 164p. 1971. pap. text ed. 6.25x (ISBN 0-7135-1621-6, Pub. by Bedford England). Renouf.

Forbes, Elizabeth & Fitzsimons, Virginia. The Older Adult: A Process for Care. 300p. 1981. pap. text ed. 11.50 (ISBN 0-8016-1631-X). Mosby.

Gillies, John. A Guide to Caring for & Coping with Aging Parents. 1981. pap. 4.95 (ISBN 0-8407-5772-7). Nelson.

Gray, Muir & McKenzie, Heather. Take Care of Your Elderly Relative. 208p. 1980. 25.00x (Pub. by Beaconsfield England). State Mutual Bk.

Gregory, Peter. Telephones for the Elderly. 128p. 1973. pap. text ed. 5.00x (ISBN 0-7135-1889-8, Pub. by Bedford England). Renouf.

Hogstel, Mildred O. Nursing Care of the Older Adult. 650p. 1981. 16.95 (ISBN 0-471-06022-4, Pub. by Wiley Med). Wiley.

Kane, Robert L., et al. Geriatrics in the United States: Manpower Projections & Training Considerations. LC 80-8840. (Illus.). write for info. (ISBN 0-669-04386-9). Lexington Bks.

Kayser-Jones, Jeanie S. Old, Alone, & Neglected: Care of the Aged in Scotland & in the United States. 160p. 1981. 14.95 (ISBN 0-520-04153-4). U of Cal Pr.

Sager, Alan. Planning Home Care for the Elderly. Date not set. pns professional reference (ISBN 0-88410-725-6). Ballinger Pub.

Sargent, Jean V. An Easier Way: A Handbook for the Elderly & Handicapped. (Illus.). 216p. 1981. pap. 9.95 (ISBN 0-686-69403-1). Iowa St U Pr.

AGED–DWELLINGS

see also Old Age Homes

Goldenberg, Leon & Weese, Harry. Housing for the Elderly: New Trends in Europe. 1981. lib. bdg. 29.50 (ISBN 0-8240-7139-5). Garland Pub.

Howell, Sandra C. Designing for Aging: Patterns of Use. (Illus.). 345p. 1980. text ed. 25.00x (ISBN 0-262-08107-5). MIT Pr.

AGED–ECONOMIC CONDITIONS

see also Age and Employment; Old Age Assistance; Old Age Pensions; Retirement Income

Clark, Robert L., ed. Retirement Policy in an Aging Society. LC 79-56502. (Illus.). vii, 215p. 1980. 16.75 (ISBN 0-8223-0441-4). Duke.

Irwin, Robert. The One Hundred Thousand Dollar Decision: The Older American's Guide to Selling a Home & Choosing Retirement Housing. (Illus.). 192p. 1981. 14.95 (ISBN 0-07-032070-5, P&RB). McGraw.

Michaels, Joe. Prime of Your Life. 288p. 1981. 17.50 (ISBN 0-87196-478-3). Facts on File.

O'Rand, Angela & Vasey, Wayne, eds. Assuring the Legal Rights of Older Citizens. (Center for Gerontological Studies & Programs Ser.: Vol.27). Date not set. price not set. U Presses Fla.

AGED–EMPLOYMENT

see Age and Employment

AGED–LEGAL STATUS, LAWS, ETC.

Levin, Jack & Levin, William. Ageism: Prejudice & Discrimination Against the Elderly. 168p. 1980. pap. text ed. 7.95x (ISBN 0-534-00881-X). Wadsworth Pub.

O'Rand, Angela & Vasey, Wayne, eds. Assuring the Legal Rights of Older Citizens. (Center for Gerontological Studies & Programs Ser.: Vol.27). Date not set. price not set. U Presses Fla.

Slack, Kathleen M. Old People & London Government. 82p. 1970. pap. text ed. 5.00x (ISBN 0-7135-1620-8, Pub. by Bedford England). Renouf.

AGED–MEDICAL CARE

Barnes, Grace M., et al. Alcohol & the Elderly: A Comprehensive Bibliography. LC 80-1786. xvii, 138p. 1980. lib. bdg. 25.00 (ISBN 0-313-22132-4, BAE/). Greenwood.

Gordon, Michael. Old Enough to Feel Better: A Medical Guide for Seniors. LC 80-70351. 384p. 1981. 14.95 (ISBN 0-686-69523-2). Chilton.

Morris, Robert. Allocating Health Resources for the Aged & Disabled: Technology Versus Politics. 1981. price not set (ISBN 0-669-04329-X). Lexington Bks.

Pegals, C. Carl. Health Care & the Elderly. 300p. 1980. text ed. write for info. (ISBN 0-89443-333-4). Aspen Systems.

Wershow, Harold J. Controversial Issues in Gerontology. 1981. text ed. price not set (ISBN 0-8261-3100-X); pap. text ed. price not set (ISBN 0-8261-3101-8). Springer Pub.

AGED–NUTRITION

Albanese, Anthony A., ed. Nutrition for the Elderly. LC 80-21565. (Current Topics in Nutrition & Disease: Vol. 3). 280p. 1980. 38.00 (ISBN 0-8451-1602-9). A R Liss.

AGED–PERSONALITY

see Aged–Psychology

AGED–PSYCHIATRIC CARE

see Geriatric Psychiatry

AGED–PSYCHOLOGY

Clark, Linda. Stay Young Longer. (Orig.). pap. 1.95 (ISBN 0-515-05076-8). Jove Pubns.

Hendricks, Jan & Hendricks, Davis. Aging in Mass Society. 420p. 1981. ref. ed. 15.95 (ISBN 0-87626-017-2). Winthrop.

Poon, Leonard, ed. Aging in the Nineteen-Eighties: Psychological Issues. LC 80-18515. 1980. 19.50. Am Psychol.

Torack, Richard M. Your Brain Is Younger Than You Think: A Guide to Mental Aging. LC 80-21239. 164p. 1981. text ed. 14.95 (ISBN 0-88229-538-1); pap. 7.95 (ISBN 0-88229-761-9). Nelson-Hall.

AGED–RECREATION

Wapner, Eleanor B. Recreation for the Elderly: A Leadership Theory & Source Book. (Illus.). 192p. 1981. 16.50 (ISBN 0-89962-052-3). Todd & Honeywell.

AGED–RELIGIOUS LIFE

see also Church Work with the Aged

Laurello, Bartholomeo J. Ministering to the Aging. LC 79-90992. (Paths of Life Ser.). 90p. (Orig.). 1979. pap. 2.45 (ISBN 0-8091-2268-5). Paulist Pr.

AGED–SOCIAL CONDITIONS

Lambert, Royston. New Wine in Old Bottles? 171p. 1968. pap. text ed. 5.00x (Pub. by Bedford England). Renouf.

Ungerson, Clare. Moving Home. 99p. 1971. pap. text ed. 5.00x (Pub. by Bedford England). Renouf.

AGED–GREAT BRITAIN

Booth, Charles. The Aged Poor in England & Wales, London 1894. LC 79-56948. (The English Working Class Ser.). 1980. lib. bdg. 40.00 (ISBN 0-8240-0103-6). Garland Pub.

Gray, J. Muir & Wilcock, Gordon. Our Elders. (Illus.). 224p. 1981. text ed. 19.95x (ISBN 0-19-217698-6); pap. text ed. 10.95x (ISBN 0-19-286012-7). Oxford U Pr.

Tinker, Anthea. The Elderly in Modern Society. (Social Policy in Modern Britain Ser.). (Illus.). 320p. 1981. pap. text ed. 13.95x (ISBN 0-582-29513-0). Longman.

AGED WORKERS

see Age and Employment

AGEE, JAMES, 1909-1955

Doty, Mark A. Tell Me Who I Am: James Agee's Search for Selfhood. LC 80-22440. 176p. 1981. 15.95x (ISBN 0-8071-0758-1). La State U Pr.

AGENT (PHILOSOPHY)

see Act (Philosophy)

AGILITY

see Motor Ability

AGING

Adelman, Richard, et al, eds. Neural Regulatory Mechanisms During Aging. (Modern Aging Ser.: Vol. 1). 230p. 1980. write for info. (ISBN 0-8451-2300-9). A R Liss.

Alder, William H. & Nordin, Albert A. Immunology of Aging. 240p. 1981. 59.95 (ISBN 0-8493-5809-4). CRC Pr.

Amoss, Pamela T. & Harrell, Stevan, eds. Other Ways of Growing Old: Anthropological Perspectives. LC 79-66056. 1981. 18.50x (ISBN 0-8047-1072-4). Stanford U Pr.

Anderson, Barbara G. The Aging Game: Success, Sanity, & Sex After 60. 252p. 1981. pap. 4.95 (ISBN 0-07-001761-1). McGraw.

Botwinick, Jack. We Are Aging. 1981. text ed. cancelled (ISBN 0-8261-3380-0); pap. text ed. 11.95 (ISBN 0-8261-3381-9). Springer Pub.

Brown, Barbara A. Aging: A Christian Approach. 1980. 0.65 (ISBN 0-686-28771-1). Forward Movement.

Bumagin & Hirn. Aging Is a Family Affair. 1981. 10.95 (ISBN 0-690-01823-1). Lippincott & Crowell.

Cahill, Hope L. Old Age - a Balance Sheet. (Illus.). 102p. 1981. pap. 3.95 (ISBN 0-933174-13-6). Wide World.

Carter, Nicholas, ed. Development, Growth, & Aging. 176p. 1980. 25.00x (ISBN 0-85664-861-2, Pub. by Croom Helm England). State Mutual Bk.

Cowley, Malcolm. The View from Eighty. 1981. lib. bdg. 9.95 (ISBN 0-8161-3156-2, Large Print Bks). G K Hall.

Diller, Phyllis. The Joys of Aging & How to Avoid Them. LC 79-7863. (Illus.). 192p. 1981. 8.95 (ISBN 0-385-14555-1). Doubleday.

Duncan, Theodore G., ed. Over Fifty-Five: A Handbook on Aging. 1981. write for info. Franklin Inst Pr.

Falk, Gerhard, et al. Aging in America & Other Cultures. LC 80-83627. 135p. 1981. perfect bdg. 11.50 (ISBN 0-86548-034-6). Century Twenty One.

Flesner, David E. & Freed, Edwin D., eds. Aging & the Aged: Problems, Opportunities, Challenges. LC 80-5869. 368p. 1980. lib. bdg. 21.00 (ISBN 0-8191-1267-4); pap. text ed. 12.75 (ISBN 0-8191-1268-2). U Pr of Amer.

Foner, Anne & Schwab, Karen. Aging & Retirement. LC 80-24765. (Social Gerontology Ser.). 192p. (Orig.). 1981. pap. text ed. 8.95 (ISBN 0-8185-0444-7). Brooks-Cole.

Frankel & Richard. Be Alive As Long As You Live: The Older Person's Guide to Exercise for Joyful Living. 1981. 11.95 (ISBN 0-690-01892-4). Lippincott & Crowell.

Freese, Arthur S. The Prime of Your Life: The Book That Makes Old Age Obsolete. Orig. Title: The End of Senility. 192p. 1981. pap. 5.95 (ISBN 0-87795-316-3). Arbor Hse.

Fries, James F. & Crapo, Lawrence M. Vitality & Aging: Implications of the Rectangular Curve. 1981. text ed. price not set (ISBN 0-7167-1308-X); pap. text ed. price not set (ISBN 0-7167-1309-8). W H Freeman.

Gillies, John. A Guide to Caring for & Coping with Aging Parents. 1981. pap. 4.95 (ISBN 0-8407-5772-7). Nelson.

Hendricks, Jan & Hendricks, Davis. Aging in Mass Society. 420p. 1981. ref. ed. 15.95 (ISBN 0-87626-017-2). Winthrop.

Kart & Manard. Aging in America. 2nd ed. 1981. 10.95 (ISBN 0-88284-121-1). Alfred Pub.

Lancaster, Helen. Aging. 1980. pap. 2.50 (ISBN 0-8309-0290-2). Herald Hse.

Mandel, Evelyn. The Art of Aging. Frost, Miriam, ed. Orig. Title: The Gray Matter. (Illus.). 176p. (Orig.). 1981. 14.95 (ISBN 0-03-059063-9); pap. 8.95 (ISBN 0-03-059063-9). Winston Pr.

Martin, Kathryn. A Question of Age: The Dorm & I. 224p. 1981. price not set (ISBN 0-936988-01-0). Tompson & Rutter.

Miles, Laughton E. & Dement, William C. Sleep & Aging. (Sleep Ser.: Vol. 3, No. 2). 108p. 1981. text ed. 20.00 (ISBN 0-89004-651-4). Raven.

Murdock, Carol V. & Lawson, Kenneth. The Rainbow Generation: Over Fifty-Five & Living Forward. 176p. cancelled (ISBN 0-88421-098-7). Butterick Pub.

Partnow, Elaine. Breaking the Age Barrier. 288p. (Orig.). 1981. pap. 2.95 (ISBN 0-523-40845-5). Pinnacle Bks.

Phenice, Lillian A. Children's Perceptions of Elderly Persons. LC 80-65604. 145p. 1981. perfect bdg. 10.50 (ISBN 0-86548-054-0). Century Twenty One.

Pollak, Otto & Kelley, Nancy L. The Challenges of Aging. 224p. 1981. 9.95 (ISBN 0-88427-045-9, Dist. by Caroline Hse). North River.

Suseelan, M. A., ed. Resource Book on Aging. 112p. (Orig.). 1981. pap. 8.95 (ISBN 0-8298-0447-1). Pilgrim NY.

Verandakis, A. Hormones in Development & Aging. Date not set. text ed. price not set (ISBN 0-89335-140-7). Spectrum Pub.

Wantz, Molly S. & Gay, John E. The Aging Process: A Health Perspective. (Sociology Ser.). (Illus.). 320p. 1981. pap. text ed. 10.95 (ISBN 0-87626-008-3). Winthrop.

AGING–PSYCHOLOGICAL ASPECTS

see Aged–Psychology

AGRARIAN QUESTION

see Agriculture–Economic Aspects; Land Tenure

AGREEMENTS

see Contracts

AGRIBUSINESS

see Agriculture–Economic Aspects

AGRICULTURAL ADMINISTRATION

Osburn, Donald & Schneeberger, Kenneth. Modern Agricultural Management. 2nd ed. 370p. 1982. text ed. 16.95 (ISBN 0-8359-4550-2); instr's. manual free (ISBN 0-8359-4551-0). Reston.

AGRICULTURAL ASSOCIATIONS

see Agricultural Societies

AGRICULTURAL BANKS

see Banks and Banking

AGRICULTURAL BOTANY

see Botany, Economic

AGRICULTURAL CHEMISTRY

see also Fertilizers and Manures; Soil Chemistry; Soils

Newman. Ecological Effects of Agricultural Chemistry. 1981. text ed. price not set. Butterworth.

AGRICULTURAL CLIMATOLOGY

see Crops and Climate

AGRICULTURAL CLUBS

see Agricultural Societies

AGRICULTURAL COLONIES

Here are entered works on settlement of the land by organized groups. General works on occupation of the land are entered under the heading Land Settlement. The heading Colonization is used for works on colonial settlements.

see also Emigration and Immigration; Migration, Internal

Enyedi, Gyorgy & Volgyes, Ivan, eds. The Effect of Modern Agriculture on Rural Developement. LC 80-25232. (Pergamon Policy Studies on International Developement Comparative Rural Transformations Ser.). (Illus.). 280p. 1981. 32.50 (ISBN 0-08-027179-0). Pergamon.

AGRICULTURAL COMMODITIES

see Farm Produce

AGRICULTURAL COOPERATION

see Agriculture, Cooperative

AGRICULTURAL COOPERATION, INTERNATIONAL

see International Agricultural Cooperation

AGRICULTURAL ECONOMICS

see Agriculture–Economic Aspects

AGRICULTURAL ENGINEERING

see also Agricultural Machinery; Farm Equipment; Irrigation

Ritchie, James D. Energy Use on the Farm. Case, Virginia, ed. (Illus.). 400p. 1981. 32.50 (ISBN 0-89999-029-0). Structures Pub.

AGRICULTURAL EXHIBITIONS

see Fairs

AGRICULTURAL GEOGRAPHY

see also Geography, Economic

Courtenay, P. P. Plantation Agriculture. 2nd rev. ed. 250p. 1980. lib. bdg. 30.00x (ISBN 0-86531-090-4). Westview.

AGRICULTURAL IMPLEMENTS

see also names of particular implements

Bartlett, J. V. Handy Farm & Home Devices. (Illus.). 320p. (Orig.). 1981. pap. price not set. MIT Pr.

Tresemer, David. The Scythe Book: Mowing Hay, Cutting Weeds, & Harvesting Small Grains with Hand Tools. LC 80-70277. (Illus.). 112p. (Orig.). 1981. pap. 5.95 (ISBN 0-938670-00-X). By Hand & Foot.

AGRICULTURAL LABORERS

see also Migration, Internal; Rural-Urban Migration

Daniel, Cletus E. Bitter Harvest: A History of California Farmworkers, 1879-1941. LC 80-25664. 368p. 1981. 19.50x (ISBN 0-8014-1284-6). Cornell U Pr.

AGRICULTURAL LABORERS–HOUSING

see Housing, Rural

AGRICULTURAL LAWS AND LEGISLATION

see also Land Tenure–Law

Uchtmann, Donald L. & Looney, J. W. Agricultural Law: Principles & Cases. (Illus.). 624p. 1981. text ed. 24.95 (ISBN 0-07-065746-7). McGraw.

AGRICULTURAL MACHINERY

see also Agricultural Engineering; Agricultural Implements; Farm Equipment; Separators (Machines)

Wadley, D. A. Corporations in Recession: The Australian Agricultural Machinery Industry. (Department of Human Geography Monograph: No. 13). 109p. (Orig.). 1980. pap. 5.95 (ISBN 0-908160-26-7, 0455). Bks Australia.

AGRICULTURAL MARKETING

see Farm Produce–Marketing

AGRICULTURAL MECHANICS

see Agricultural Engineering

AGRICULTURAL PESTS

see also Aeronautics in Agriculture; Pest Control; Plant Diseases; Weeds

also subdivision Diseases and Pests under names of crops, etc., Fruit–Diseases and Pests

Pimentel, David, ed. Handbook of Pest Management in Agriculture. 1981. Vol. 1. 69.95 (ISBN 0-8493-3841-7); Vol. 2. 67.95 (ISBN 0-8493-3842-5); Vol. 3. 69.95 (ISBN 0-8493-3843-3). CRC Pr.

AGRICULTURAL PHYSICS

see also Crops and Climate

Mohsenin, Nuri N. Physical Properties of Food & Agricultural Materials: A Teachin Manual. 1981. price not set (ISBN 0-677-05630-3). Gordon.

AGRICULTURAL PRODUCTS

see Farm Produce

AGRICULTURAL PROGRAMS

see Agricultural Administration

AGRICULTURAL RESEARCH

Experiences with Three Tillage Systems on a Marine Loam Soil I: 1972-1975. (Agricultural Research Reports Ser.: No. 899). 100p. 1981. pap. 18.50 (ISBN 90-220-0741-3, PDC 219, Pudoc). Unipub.

Mukherjee, J. N. Forward with Nature: An Integrated Approach to World Problems of Technology, Energy & Agriculture. 188p. 1979. text ed. 18.00x (ISBN 0-8426-1676-4). Verry.

Research Highlights for 1978. 118p. 1979. pap. 21.50 (R 126, IRRI). Unipub.

Romberger, John A., ed. Biosystematics in Agriculture. LC 77-84408. (Beltsville Symposia in Agricultural Research Ser.: No. 2). 352p. 1978. text ed. 24.00. Allanheld.

Statistical Procedures for Agricultural Research. 294p. 1976. pap. 21.50 (R003, IRRI). Unipub.

A Summary of the Recommendations Made at the Conference on the Communication Responsibilities of the International Agricultural Research Centres. 1980p. 1980. pap. 7.50 (R031, IRRI). Unipub.

AGRICULTURAL SOCIETIES

Directory of Non-Governmental Agricultural Organizations. 6th ed. 1980. pap. 40.00 (ISBN 3-598-10147-3, Dist by Gale Research Co.). K G Saur.

AGRICULTURAL STATISTICS

see Agriculture–Statistics

AGRICULTURAL SUPPLIES

see Farm Equipment

AGRICULTURAL SURPLUSES
see Surplus Agricultural Commodities
AGRICULTURAL TOOLS
see Agricultural Implements
AGRICULTURAL WASTES
Information Sources on Bioconversion of Agricultural Wastes. (UNIDO Guide to Information Sources Ser.: No.33). 84p. 1980. pap. 4.00 (UNID-228, UN). Unipub.
Post-Harvest Prevention of Waste & Loss of Food Grains. 358p. 1974. 11.75 (APO54, APO). Unipub.
AGRICULTURAL WORKERS
see Agricultural Laborers
AGRICULTURE
see also Aeronautics in Agriculture; Aquaculture; Botany, Economic; Cattle; Crop Yields; Dairying; Domestic Animals; Farm Life; Farm Management; Farm Produce; Fertilizers and Manures; Field Crops; Food Industry and Trade; Forests and Forestry; Fruit; Fruit-Culture; Gardening; Grain; Grasses; Horticulture; International Agricultural Cooperation; Irrigation; Land Tenure; Livestock; Pastures; Reclamation of Land; Seeds; Soil Science; Soils; Trees; Vegetable Gardening; Vegetables
also headings beginning with the word Agricultural, and names of agricultural products
Agriculture: Toward Two Thousand Twentieth Session. 257p. 1981. pap. 18.50 (F2093, FAO). Unipub.
Bibliography on Socio-Economic Aspects of Asian Irrigation. 80p. 1976. pap. 6.00 (R039, IRRI). Unipub.
Blocks for Transplants. 89p. 1980. pap. 9.95x (ISBN 0-901361-37-2, Pub. by Grower Bks England). Intl Schol Bk Serv.
Brengle, Kenneth G. Principles & Practices of Dryland Farming. 1981. price not set (ISBN 0-87081-095-2). Colo Assoc.
Busch, Lawrence, ed. Science & Agricultural Development. 220p. 1981. text ed. 28.00 (ISBN 0-86598-022-5). Allanheld.
Gorenflo, Louise, et al. Farm & Rural Energy Planning Manual. (Illus.). 80p. (Orig.). 1981. pap. 5.00 (ISBN 0-937786-04-7). Inst Ecological.
Gupta, U. S. Physiological Aspects of Dryland Farming. LC 76-42138. 392p. 1977. text ed. 18.00 (ISBN 0-916672-94-8). Allanheld.
Hart, John & Orman, Larry. Endangered Harvest: The Future of Bay Area Farmland. (Orig.). 1980. pap. 3.00 (ISBN 0-9605262-0-X). PFOS.
I R R I Annual Report for Nineteen Seventy-Five. 479p. 1976. pap. 37.50 (R090, IRRI). Unipub.
I R R I Annual Report for Nineteen Seventy-Six. 418p. 1977. pap. 43.00 (R089, IRRI). Unipub.
I R R I Annual Report for Nineteen Seventy-Seven. 548p. 1978. pap. 43.00 (R088, IRRI). Unipub.
International Agricultural Machinery Workshop. Proceedings. 203p. 1978. pap. 16.00 (R036, IRRI). Unipub.
International Deep-Water Rice Workshop, 1977. Proceedings. 239p. 1977. pap. 14.50 (R028, IRRI). Unipub.
Land Evaluation for Rainfed Agriculture: Report of an Expert Consultation. (World Soil Resources Reports: No. 52). 122p. 1981. pap. 6.50 (ISBN 92-5-100994-5, F2104, FAO). Unipub.
Land Preparation & Crop Establishment for Rainfed Lowland Rice. (IRRI Research Paper Ser.: No. 22). 24p. 1979. pap. 5.00 (R062, IRRI). Unipub.
Martina, Susanna W. A Great Estate at Work. LC 79-51827. (Illus.). 308p. 1980. 54.50 (ISBN 0-521-22696-1). Cambridge U Pr.
Money in Growing. 80p. 1980. pap. 6.95x (ISBN 0-901361-39-9, Pub. by Grower Bks England). Intl Schol Bk Serv.
The Morphology & Varietal Characteristics of the Rice Plant. (Technical Bulletin Ser.: No. 4). 40p. 1965. pap. 5.00 (R022, IRRI). Unipub.
Newbury, P. A. R. A Geography of Agriculture. (Illus.). 336p. 1980. pap. text ed. 18.95x (ISBN 0-7121-0733-9). Intl Ideas.
Palz, W. & Chartier, P., eds. Energy from Biomass in Europe. (Illus.). xii, 248p. 1981. 35.00x (ISBN 0-85334-934-7). Intl Ideas.
Papavizas, George C., ed. Biological Control in Crop Production. (Beltsville Symposia in Agricultural Research Ser.: No. 5). 1981. text ed. 35.00 (ISBN 0-86598-037-3). Allanheld.
Perspectives in World Agriculture. 532p. 1981. 82.50 (ISBN 0-85198-458-4, CAB 12, CAB). Unipub.
Romberger, John A. Virology in Agriculture. LC 76-42139. (Beltsville Symposia in Agricultural Reasearch Ser.: No. 1). 320p. 1977. text ed. 23.50 (ISBN 0-916672-14-X). Allanheld.
Romberger, John A., ed. Biosystematics in Agriculture. LC 77-84408. (Beltsville Symposia in Agricultural Research Ser.: No. 2). 352p. 1978. text ed. 24.00. Allanheld.
Swedes & Turnips for the Fresh Market. 96p. 1980. pap. 9.95x (ISBN 0-901361-42-9, Pub. by Grower Bks England). Intl Schol Bk Serv.
Trained Manpower for Agricultural & Rural Development. (FAO Economic & Social Development Paper Ser.: No. 10). 132p. 1980. pap. 7.50 (ISBN 92-5-100861-2, F1963, FAO). Unipub.
Tsunoda, S., et al, eds. Brassica Crops & Wild Allies. 360p. 1980. 38.00x (ISBN 0-89955-211-0, Pub. by JSSP Japan). Intl Schol Bk Serv.
Ward, William. Reporting Agriculture Through Newspapers, Magazines, Radio, Television. 2nd ed. 402p. 1959. 15.00 (ISBN 0-8014-0441-X). Cornell U Pr.
Workshop on the Interfaces Between Agriculture, Nutrition, & Food Science, 1977. Proceedings. 143p. 1979. pap. 7.25 (R087, IRRI). Unipub.
AGRICULTURE-ADMINISTRATION
see Agricultural Administration
AGRICULTURE-DICTIONARIES, INDEXES, ETC.
Khatib, Ahmad. Chihabi's Dictionary of Agricultural & Forestry Terms: English-Arabic. 1978. 40.00x. Intl Bk Ctr.
AGRICULTURE-ECONOMIC ASPECTS
see also Farm Management; Farm Produce-Marketing; Forests and Forestry-Economic Aspects; Geography, Economic; Land Tenure; Rent
Assessment & Collection of Data on Post-Harvest Foodgrain Losses. (FAO Economic & Social Development Paper: No. 13). 71p. 1981. pap. 6.00 (ISBN 92-5-100934-1, F2072, FAO). Unipub.
Casavant & Infanger. Agricultural Economics. 1981. text ed. 17.95 (ISBN 0-8359-0184-X); instr's. manual free (ISBN 0-8359-0184-X). Reston.
FAO Trade Yearbook, 1979, Vol. 33. 357p. 1981. 30.25 (ISBN 92-5-000965-8, F2106, FAO). Unipub.
McCalla, Alix F. & Josling, Timothy E., eds. Imperfect Markets in Agricultural Trade. LC 80-67393. 182p. 1981. text ed. 28.00 (ISBN 0-916672-68-9). Allanheld.
Martin, Lee R., ed. Economics of Welfare, Rural Development, & Natural Resources in Agriculture, 1940s - 1970s. (A Survey of Agricultural Economics Literature: Vol. 3). 720p. 1981. 35.00x (ISBN 0-8166-0819-9). U of Minn Pr.
Near East Readings on Agricultural Investment Projects. (Agricultural Planning Studies: No. 20). 199p. 1980. pap. 10.75 (ISBN 92-5-100917-1, F1935, FAO). Unipub.
AGRICULTURE-ECONOMIC ASPECTS-ASIA
Anatomy of a Peasant Economy. 149p. 1978. pap. 12.50 (R040, IRRI). Unipub.
Barriers to Efficient Capital Investment in Asian Agriculture. (IRRI Research Paper Ser.: No. 24). 20p. 1979. pap. 5.00 (R064, IRRI). Unipub.
AGRICULTURE-ECONOMIC ASPECTS-CHINA
Barnett, A. Doak. China & the World Food System. LC 79-87912. (Monographs: No. 12). 128p. 1979. 5.00 (ISBN 0-686-28683-9). Overseas Dev Council.
AGRICULTURE-ECONOMIC ASPECTS-EUROPE
Prices of Agricultural Products & Selected Inputs in Europe & North America 1978-79. 88p. 1980. pap. 13.00 (ISBN 0-686-68965-8, UN80/2E7, UN). Unipub.
AGRICULTURE-ECONOMIC ASPECTS-INDIA
Mitchell, Rodger. The Analysis of Indian Agro-Ecosystems. (Environmental Science Ser.). 180p. 1980. 6.50x (ISBN 0-89955-329-X, Pub. by Interprint India). Intl Schol Bk Serv.
AGRICULTURE-ECONOMIC ASPECTS-INDONESIA
Changes in Community Institutions & Income Distribution in a West Java Village. (IRRI Research Paper Ser.: No. 50). 16p. 1981. pap. 5.00 (R131, IRRI). Unipub.
Hansen, Gary E., ed. Agricultural & Rural Development in Indonesia. (Special Studies in Social, Political, & Economic Development). 312p. 1981. lib. bdg. 20.00x (ISBN 0-86531-124-2). Westview.
AGRICULTURE-ECONOMIC ASPECTS-UNITED STATES
Prices of Agricultural Products & Selected Inputs in Europe & North America 1978-79. 88p. 1980. pap. 13.00 (ISBN 0-686-68965-8, UN80/2E7, UN). Unipub.
AGRICULTURE-HISTORY
Fitzherbert, John. Fitxharbets Booke of Husbandrie: Newlie Corrected. LC 79-84107. (English Experience Ser.: No. 926). 220p. 1979. Repr. of 1598 ed. lib. bdg. 21.00 (ISBN 90-221-0926-7). Walter J Johnson.
Rowley, R. T., ed. The Origins of Open Field Agriculture. 288p. 1981. 26.50x (ISBN 0-389-20102-2). B&N.
AGRICULTURE-LABORATORY MANUALS
Waldren, Richard P. & Ehler, Stanley W. Crop Science: Laboratory Manual. 2nd ed. 1981. write for info. (ISBN 0-8087-3717-1). Burgess.
AGRICULTURE-LAWS AND LEGISLATION
see Agricultural Laws and Legislation
AGRICULTURE-RESEARCH
see Agricultural Research
AGRICULTURE-STATISTICS
see also Crop Yields
FAO Trade Yearbook, 1979, Vol. 33. 357p. 1981. 30.25 (ISBN 92-5-000965-8, F2106, FAO). Unipub.
Higgs, Roger, et al. Agricultural Mathematics. 2nd ed. 1981. 9.25 (ISBN 0-8134-2130-6); pap. 5.95x; ans. bk. 1.00x (ISBN 0-8134-2131-4, 2131). Interstate.
Statistical Procedures for Agricultural Research. 294p. 1976. pap. 21.50 (R003, IRRI). Unipub.
AGRICULTURE-VOCATIONAL GUIDANCE
Stone, Archie A. Careers in Agribusiness & Industry. 3rd ed. LC 76-106341. (Illus.). (gr. 9-12). 12.65 (ISBN 0-8134-2073-3); text ed. 9.50x. Interstate.
AGRICULTURE-AFRICA
Gilbert, Zoe. Fruit Growing in Southern Africa. 1980. 25.00x (Pub. by Bailey & Swinton South Africa). State Mutual Bk.
An Introduction to African Pastureland Production. 192p. 1981. pap. 11.00 (ISBN 92-5-100872-8, F2075, FAO). Unipub.
Management & Utilization of Pastures, East Africa: Kenya, Tanzania, Uganda. (Pasture & Fodder Crop Studies: No. 3). 124p. 1969. pap. 7.75 (ISBN 92-5-100420-X, F1970, FAO). Unipub.
Papers Presented at the FAO-SIDA Workshop on the Use of Organic Materials As Fertilizers in Africa: Organic Recycling in Africa. 308p. 1981. pap. 16.50 (ISBN 92-5-100945-7, F2096, FAO). Unipub.
AGRICULTURE-ASIA
Agricultural Growth in Japan, Taiwan, Korea, & the Philippines. 404p. 1979. 11.00 (APO82, APO). Unipub.
An Agro-Climatic Classification for Evaluating Cropping Systems Potentials in Southeast Asian Rice Growing Regions. 10p. pap. 5.00 (R112, IRRI). Unipub.
Aliways to Rice Garden: A Case Study of the Intensification of Rice Farming in Camarines Sur, Philippines. (IRRI Research Paper Ser.: No. 36). 23p. 1979. pap. 5.00 (R076, IRRI). Unipub.
Biological Constraints to Farmers' Rice Yields in Three Philippine Provinces. (IRRI Research Paper Ser.: No. 30). 69p. 1979. pap. 5.00 (R070, IRRI). Unipub.
Brown Planthopper: Threat to Rice Production in Asia. 369p. 1979. pap. 21.50 (R038, IRRI). Unipub.
Changes in Rice Farming in Selected Areas of Asia. 377p. 1975. pap. 16.00 (R011, IRRI). Unipub.
Changes in Rice Harvesting Systems in Central Luzon & Laguna. (IRRI Research Paper Ser.: No. 31). 24p. 1979. pap. 5.00 (R071, IRRI). Unipub.
Constraints to High Yields on Asian Rice Farms: An Interim Report. 235p. 1977. pap. 11.00 (R010, IRRI). Unipub.
The Effect of the New Rice Technology on Family Labor Utilization in Laguna. (IRRI Research Paper Ser.: No. 42). 17p. 1979. pap. 5.00 (R082, IRRI). Unipub.
Farm-Level Constraints to High Yields in Asia: Nineteen Seventy-Four to Nineteen Seventy-Seven. 411p. 1979. pap. 24.50 (R013, IRRI). Unipub.
Genetic Interrelationships to Improved Rice Varieties in Asia. (IRRI Research Paper Ser.: No. 23). 34p. 1979. pap. 5.00 (R063, IRRI). Unipub.
Planning for Agricultural Area Development: The Asian Experience. 246p. 1973. 7.25 (APO53, APO). Unipub.
Rice Breeders in Asia: A Ten Country Survey of Their Backgrounds, Attitudes & Use of Genetic Materials. (IRRI Research Paper Ser.: No. 13). 18p. 1978. pap. 5.00 (R053, IRRI). Unipub.
Ward, R. Gerard & Proctor, Andrew, eds. South Pacific Agriculture: Choices & Constraints. LC 79-56229. (South Pacific Agricultural Survey 1979). 525p. 1980. text ed. 24.95 (ISBN 0-7081-1944-1, 0532). Bks Australia.
Weather & Climate Data for Philippine Rice Research. (IRRI Research Paper Ser.: No. 41). 14p. 1979. pap. 5.00 (R081, IRRI). Unipub.
AGRICULTURE-AUSTRALIA AND NEW ZEALAND
Australian Wheat Varieties, Suppl. 1. 30p. 1978. pap. 13.50 (ISBN 0-643-00325-8, CO01, CSIRO). Unipub.
Checklist of Economic Plants in Australia. 214p. 1980. pap. 9.00 (ISBN 0-643-02551-0, CO04, CSIRO). Unipub.
Hartley, W. Checklist of Economic Plants in Australia. 214p. 1980. pap. 7.50x (ISBN 0-643-02551-0, Pub. by CSIRO Australia). Intl Schol Bk Serv.
AGRICULTURE-CHINA
China: Development of Olive Production. 163p. 1981. pap. 8.75 (ISBN 92-5-100995-3, F2097, FAO). Unipub.
China: Multiple Cropping & Related Crop Production Technology. (FAO Plant Protection Paper Ser.: No. 22). 66p. 1981. pap. 6.00 (ISBN 92-5-100977-5, F2108, FAO). Unipub.
China: The Agricultural Training System. (FAO Economic & Social Development Paper Ser.: No. 11). 141p. 1980. pap. 7.50 (ISBN 92-5-100898-1, F1941, FAO). Unipub.
AGRICULTURE-CONGO
Management & the Use of Grasslands, Democratic Republic of the Congo. 152p. 1966. pap. 8.00 (F1918, FAO). Unipub.
AGRICULTURE-EUROPE-HISTORY
Donath, Ferenc. Reform & Revolution: Transformation of Hungary's Agriculture 1945-1970. Vizmathy-Susits, Gisela, tr. (Illus.). 489p. (Orig.). 1980. pap. 10.00x (ISBN 963-13-0911-8). Intl Pubns Serv.
AGRICULTURE-GREAT BRITAIN
Huggett, Frank. Farming in Great Britain. (Junior Reference Ser.). (Illus.). 64p. (gr. 7 up). 1970. 7.95 (ISBN 0-7136-1527-3). Dufour.
AGRICULTURE-INDIA
Aziz, Abdul. Organizing Agricultural Labourers in India. 1980. 7.50x (ISBN 0-8364-0651-6, Pub. by Minerva India). South Asia Bks.
Barriers to Increased Rice Production in Eastern India. (IRRI Research Search Paper Ser.: No. 25). 23p. 1979. pap. 5.00 (R065, IRRI). Unipub.
Genetic & Sociological Aspects of Rice Breeding in India. (IRRI Research Paper Ser.: No. 10). 31p. 1977. pap. 5.00 (R050, IRRI). Unipub.
Nair, P. K. Intensive Multiple Cropping with Coconuts in India: Principles, Programmes & Prospects. (Advances in Agronomy & Crop Science Ser.: Vol. 6). (Illus.). 148p. (Orig.). 1979. pap. text ed. 28.00 (ISBN 3-489-71210-2). Parey Sci Pubs.
Shingi, P. M., et al. Rural Youth: Education, Occupation & Social Outlook. 1980. 10.00x (ISBN 0-8364-0663-X, Pub. by Abhinav India). South Asia Bks.
AGRICULTURE-NEPAL
Farm Mechanization, Employment, & Income in Nepal: Traditional & Mechanized Farming in Bara District. (IRRI Research Paper Ser.: No. 38). 9p. 1979. pap. 5.00 (R078, IRRI). Unipub.
AGRICULTURE-RUSSIA
Gustafson, Thane. Reform in Soviet Politics: The Lessons of Recent Policies on Land & Water. LC 80-24286. (Illus.). 224p. Date not set. price not set (ISBN 0-521-23377-1). Cambridge U Pr.
AGRICULTURE-TANZANIA
Pitblado, J. Roger. The North Mkata Plain, Tanzania: A Study of Land Capability & Land Tenure. (Department of Geography Research Publications Ser.). 200p. 1981. pap. 8.50x (ISBN 0-8020-3378-4). U of Toronto Pr.
AGRICULTURE-TROPICS
see also Tropical Crops
On-Farm Maize Drying & Storage in the Humid Tropics. (FAO Agricultural Services Bulletin: No. 40). 69p. 1981. pap. 6.00 (ISBN 92-5-100944-9, F2077, FAO). Unipub.
AGRICULTURE-UNITED STATES
Here are entered works on agriculture in the United States as a whole, as well as specific areas of the United States.
Courtenay, P. P. Plantation Agriculture. 2nd rev. ed. 250p. 1980. lib. bdg. 30.00x (ISBN 0-86531-090-4). Westview.
Dorothea Lange: Farm Security Administration Photographs, 1935 - 1939, 2 vols. LC 80-24201. (Illus., Vol. 1 236pp.; vol. 2 176 pp.). 1980. Vol.1, 732 Photos & Maps On 9 Black & White Fiche, Captions In Text,236 Pages. 34.50 (ISBN 0-89969-000-9); Vol. 2, 622 Photos & Maps On 8 Black & White Fiche, Caption In Text, 176 Pages. 32.50 (ISBN 0-89969-001-7); Set. 67.00 (ISBN 0-89969-002-5). Text-Fiche.
AGRICULTURE-UNITED STATES-HISTORY
Saloutos, Theodore. The American Farmer & the New Deal. 312p. 1981. text ed. 17.50 (ISBN 0-8138-1760-9). Iowa St U Pr.
AGRICULTURE, COOPERATIVE
Stanton, Beryle, ed. Expanding Cooperative Horizons. (Illus.). 500p. 1980. 12.00; pap. 9.50. Am Inst Cooperation.
AGRICULTURE AND STATE-GERMANY
Abraham, David. The Collapse of the Weimar Republic: Political Economy & Crisis. LC 80-8533. 550p. 1981. 30.00x (ISBN 0-691-05322-7); pap. 12.50x (ISBN 0-691-10118-3). Princeton U Pr.
AGRICULTURE AND STATE-INDIA
Stein, Burton. Peasant State & Society in Medieval South India. (Illus.). 550p. 1980. text ed. 31.00x (ISBN 0-19-561065-2). Oxford U Pr.
AGRONOMY
see Agriculture
AGROSTOLOGY
see Grasses
AGUE
see Malaria
AHMEDABAD
Papola, T. S. Urban Informal Sector in an Urban Economy: A Study in Ahmedabad. 156p. 1981. text ed. 15.95x (ISBN 0-7069-1133-4, Pub by Vikas India). Advent Bk.
AID TO DEPENDENT CHILDREN
see Child Welfare
AID TO UNDERDEVELOPED AREAS
see Technical Assistance
AIDS TO NAVIGATION
see also Lighthouses; Nautical Charts; Radar in Navigation; Radio in Navigation
Recommendation on Basic Principles & Operational Guidance Relating to Navigational Watchkeeping. 12p. 1974. pap. 7.75 (ISBN 92-801-1032-2, IMCO 62, IMCO). Unipub.
AIR-POLLUTION
Ackerman, Bruce A. & Hassler, William T. Clean Coal - Dirty Air. (Illus.). 175p. 1981. 20.00x (ISBN 0-300-02628-5); pap. 5.95 (ISBN 0-300-02643-9). Yale U Pr.
Battan, Louis J. The Unclean Sky: A Meteorologist Looks at Air Pollution. LC 80-23434. (Selected Topics in the Atmospheric Sciences, Science Study Ser.). (Illus.). xii, 141p. 1980. Repr. of 1966 ed. lib. bdg. 19.50x (ISBN 0-313-22710-1, BAUS). Greenwood.

Clean Air Society. International Clean Air Conference, 7th, Australia. International Clean Air Conference, 1981: Proceedings. 1981. text ed. 49.95 (ISBN 0-250-40415-X). Ann Arbor Science.
Manning, William J. & Feder, William A. Biomonitoring Air Pollutants with Plants. (Illus.). x, 142p. 1981. 26.00x (ISBN 0-85334-916-9). Burgess-Intl Ideas.
Occupational Exposure to Airborne Substances Harmful to Health. 44p. 1981. pap. 6.50 (ISBN 92-2-102442-3, ILO 152, ILO). Unipub.
Smith, W. H. Air Pollution & Forests. (Springer Series on Environmental Management). (Illus.). 400p. 1981. 39.80 (ISBN 0-387-90501-4). Springer-Verlag.

AIR-POLLUTION-LAWS AND LEGISLATION

Laitos, Jan G. A Legal-Economic History of Air Pollution Controls. LC 80-67046. (Scholarly Monograph Ser.). 350p. 1980. pap. 27.50 (ISBN 0-8408-0507-1). Carrollton Pr.

AIR BASES

Halpenny, Bruce B. Action Stations Two: Military Airfields of Lincolnshire & the East Midlands. (Illus.). 232p. 1981. 37.95 (ISBN 0-85059-484-7). Aztex.

AIR-BEARING VEHICLES

see Ground-Effect Machines

AIR BRUSH ART

see Airbrush Art

AIR CARGO

see Aeronautics, Commercial

AIR CARRIERS

see Air Lines

AIR CONDITIONING

see also Refrigeration and Refrigerating Machinery; Ventilation

also specific subject with or without subdivision air-conditioning, e.g. Dwellings–Air conditioning

Gladstone, John. Air Conditioning & Mechanical Trades: Preparing for the Contractor's License Examination. LC 74-18258. (Illus.). 425p. 1980. pap. 18.95 (ISBN 0-930644-04-2). Engineers Pr.
Havrella, Raymond. Heating, Ventilating & Air Conditioning Fundamentals. LC 80-17155. (Contemporary Construction Ser.). (Illus.). 288p. (gr. 10-12). 1981. text ed. 16.95x (ISBN 0-07-027281-6, G); wkbk. avail. (ISBN 0-07-027283-2). McGraw.
Sabin, A. Ross, ed. Central Air Conditioning Service. (Illus.). 218p. (gr. 11). 1974. 20.00 (ISBN 0-938336-03-7). Whirlpool.
Schneider, Raymond K. HVAC Control Systems. 400p. 1981. text ed. 19.95 (ISBN 0-471-05180-2). Wiley.

AIR-CUSHION VEHICLES

see Ground-Effect Machines

AIR FORCE WIVES

Combs, Ann. Smith College Never Taught Me How to Salute. LC 80-8227. 216p. 1981. 9.95 (ISBN 0-690-02012-0, HarpT). Har-Row.

AIR FRAMES

see Airframes

AIR FREIGHT

see Aeronautics, Commercial

AIR GUNS

Walker, John. The Air Gun. (Illus.). 144p. 1981. 19.95 (ISBN 0-8117-0046-1). Stackpole.

AIR HOSTESSES

see Air Lines–Flight Attendants

AIR LAW

see Aeronautics–Laws and Regulations

AIR LINE HOSTESSES

see Air Lines–Flight Attendants

AIR LINES

see also Air Pilots

also names of specific air lines

Allen, Oliver E. The Airline Builders. Time-Life Books, ed. (The Epic of Flight Ser.). (Illus.). 175p. 1981. 13.95 (ISBN 0-8094-3283-8). Time Life.
Doberstein, Richard. Regulations Made Easy for Private Pilots. (Illus.). Date not set. pap. 4.95x (Pub. by Simplified). Aviation.
Quastler, I. E. Pioneer of the Third Level: A History of Air Midwest. (Illus.). 174p. 1980. pap. 7.50 (ISBN 0-9602554-1-9). Commuter Airlines.
Taneja, Nawal K. Airlines in Transition. LC 80-8735. 1981. 23.95 (ISBN 0-669-04345-1). Lexington Bks.

AIR LINES–EMPLOYEES

see also Air Pilots; Air Lines–Flight Attendants

LeRette, Jon M. Airline Job Kit. (Illus.). 82p. 1980. pap. text ed. 3.50 (ISBN 0-686-28722-3). Airline Job.

AIR LINES–FLIGHT ATTENDANTS

Barfield, Janice. You Can Fly: But That Cocoon Has Got to Go. (Orig.). 1981. 7.95 (ISBN 0-310-43920-5). Zondervan.
Rich, Elizabeth. What It's Like to Be a Flight Attendant. LC 80-6152. 192p. 1981. 12.95 (ISBN 0-8128-2785-6). Stein & Day.

AIR LINES–HOSTESSES

see Air Lines–Flight Attendants

AIR LINES–LAWS AND REGULATIONS

see Aeronautics–Laws and Regulations

AIR NAVIGATION

see Aeronautics

AIR PILOTS

Airline Transport Pilot Rating Course. (Pilot Training Ser.). (Illus.). 310p. (Orig.). 1981. price not set (ISBN 0-88487-073-1, JS304127). Jeppesen Sanderson.
Bishop, William A. Winged Warfare. (Air Combat Classics Ser.). (Illus.). 288p. 1981. 11.95 (ISBN 0-668-05162-0); pap. 5.95 (ISBN 0-668-05164-7). Arco.
Canadian Private Pilot Manual. (Pilot Training Ser.). (Illus.). 428p. 1981. pap. text ed. price not set (ISBN 0-88487-074-X, JS314131). Jeppesen Sanderson.
Decker, Erwin A. Look Pride. 1981. 7.95 (ISBN 0-8062-1642-5). Carlton.
Walker, Dale L. Only the Clouds Remain: Ted Parsons of the Lafayette Escadrille. LC 80-68357. (Illus.). 72p. 1980. pap. 6.95 (ISBN 0-937748-00-5). Alandale Pr.

AIR PILOTS–JUVENILE LITERATURE

Hayman, LeRoy. Aces, Heroes & Daredevils of the Air. 160p. (gr. 8-12). 1981. PLB price not set (ISBN 0-671-34049-2). Messner.
Pelta, Kathy. What Does an Airplane Pilot Do? LC 80-23530. (What Do They Do Ser.). (Illus.). 80p. (gr. 5 up). 1981. PLB 5.95 (ISBN 0-396-07910-5). Dodd.

AIR PISTOLS

see Air Guns

AIR PLANTS

see Epiphytes

AIR POLLUTION

see Air–Pollution

AIR PORTS

see Airports

AIR RESCUE SERVICE

see Search and Rescue Operations

AIR RIFLES

see Air Guns

AIR-SEA RESCUE

see Search and Rescue Operations

AIR STEWARDESSES

see Air Lines–Flight Attendants

AIR STEWARDS

see Air Lines–Flight Attendants

AIR STRATEGY

see Air Warfare

AIR TERMINALS

see Airports

AIR TRAFFIC CONTROL

Balter, Deborah J. Air Traffic Control Communications Manual. Date not set. pap. 14.95. Aviation.

AIR TRANSPORT

see Aeronautics, Commercial

AIR TRANSPORT MANAGEMENT

see Air Lines

AIR TRAVEL

see also Air Lines

Airguide. Airguide Traveler: Bahamas, Florida, Florida Keys, & Sea Islands. (Illus.). 1980. pap. 11.00 (ISBN 0-911721-89-4). Aviation.
Ross, Pat & Ross, Joel. Your First Airplane Trip. LC 80-22642. (Illus.). 40p. (gr. k-2). 1981. 7.95 (ISBN 0-688-41989-5); PLB 7.63 (ISBN 0-688-51989-X). Morrow.

AIR WARFARE

see also Airplanes, Military; Atomic Warfare; Chemical Warfare

also subdivision Aerial Operations under names of wars, e.g. World War, 1939-1945–Aerial Operations

Sims, Edward H. Fighter Tactics & Strategy Nineteen Fourteen to Nineteen Seventy. 2nd ed. LC 80-68106. (Illus.). 266p. 1980. 12.95 (ISBN 0-8168-8795-0). Aero.

AIRBRUSH ART

Curtis, Seng-gye T. & Hunt, Christopher. The Airbrush Book: Art, History, & Technique. 160p. 1980. 24.95 (ISBN 0-442-21213-5). Van Nos Reinhold.

AIRCRAFT, FIXED WING

see Airplanes

AIRCRAFT ACCIDENTS

see Aeronautics–Accidents

AIRCRAFT ENGINES

see Airplanes–Motors; Airplanes–Turbojet Engines

AIRCRAFT INDUSTRY

see also Airplanes; Used Aircraft

Bluestone, Barry & Jordan, Peter. Aircraft Industry Dynamics: An Analysis of Competition, Capital & Labor. 180p. 1981. 19.95 (ISBN 0-86569-053-7). Auburn Hse.

AIRCRAFT INSTRUMENTS

see Aeronautical Instruments

AIRCRAFT SAFETY MEASURES

see Aeronautics–Safety Measures

AIRCRAFT STRESS ANALYSIS

see Airframes

AIRCRAFT STRUCTURES

see Airframes

AIRDROMES

see Airports

AIRFRAMES

Aviation Maintenance Publishers. Airframe Logbook. 77p. 1975. pap. 4.95 (ISBN 0-89100-190-5, E*A-A*F*L-1). Aviation Maintenance.

AIRLINERS

see Transport Planes

AIRLINES

see Air Lines

AIRPLANE ACCIDENTS

see Aeronautics–Accidents

AIRPLANE ENGINES

see Airplanes–Motors

AIRPLANE INDUSTRY

see Aircraft Industry

AIRPLANES

see also Aircraft Industry; Bombers; Fighter Planes; Gliders (Aeronautics); Guided Missiles; Helicopters; Seaplanes; Used Aircraft

also specific makes of airplanes, e.g. Boeing bombers; Lockheed airplanes; and headings beginning with the word Airplane

Aviation Mechanincs Journal. Nineteen Eighty Aircraft & Helicopter Digest. (Illus.). 204p. 1980. text ed. 13.25 (ISBN 0-89100-184-0, E*A-184-0). Aviation Maintenance.
King, H. F. Sopwith Aircraft Nineteen Twelve to Nineteen Twenty. (Illus.). 320p. 1981. 36.00 (ISBN 0-370-30050-5, Pub. by Chatto-Bodley-Jonathan). Merrimack Bk Serv.
McAllister, Chris. Planes & Airports. (Illus.). 64p. 1981. pap. 5.95 (ISBN 0-7134-3911-4, Pub. by Batsford England). David & Charles.
Mason, Francis K. Hawker Hunter: Biography of a Thoroughbred. (Illus.). 244p. 1981. 43.95 (ISBN 0-85059-476-6). Aztex.

AIRPLANES–ACCIDENTS

see Aeronautics–Accidents

AIRPLANES–AERODYNAMICS

see Aerodynamics

AIRPLANES–COLLISIONS WITH BIRDS

see Aeronautics–Accidents

AIRPLANES–DESIGN AND CONSTRUCTION

see also Airframes

Crane, Dale. Aircraft Fabric Covering. (Aviation Maintenance Training Course Ser.). (Illus.). 54p. 1978. pap. 4.95 (ISBN 0-89100-077-1, EA-ADF). Aviation Maintenance.
Crane, Dale & Carlson, Neal. Aircraft Painting & Finishing. (Aviation Maintenance Training Course Ser.). (Illus.). 67p. 1980. pap. 5.95 (ISBN 0-89100-152-2, E*A-A*P-2). Aviation Maintenance.
Thurston, David B. Home Built Aircraft. (McGraw-Hill Series in Aviation). (Illus.). 224p. 1981. 24.95 (ISBN 0-07-064552-3, P&RB). McGraw.

AIRPLANES–ELECTRIC EQUIPMENT

see also Aeronautical Instruments

Bent, Ralph D. & McKinley, James L. Aircraft Electricity & Electronics. rev. ed. (Aviation Technology Ser.). (Illus.). 432p. 1981. pap. text ed. 16.95x (ISBN 0-07-004793-6, G). McGraw.

AIRPLANES–ELECTRONIC EQUIPMENT

Bent, Ralph D. & McKinley, James L. Aircraft Electricity & Electronics. rev. ed. (Aviation Technology Ser.). (Illus.). 432p. 1981. pap. text ed. 16.95x (ISBN 0-07-004793-6, G). McGraw.
Harris, Frank. Electronic Circuit Devices. (Avionics Technician Training Course Ser.). (Orig.). 1981. pap. write for info. (ISBN 0-89100-192-1). Aviation Maintenance.

AIRPLANES–ENGINES

see Airplanes–Motors

AIRPLANES–FREIGHT

see Aeronautics, Commercial

AIRPLANES–INSTRUMENTS

see Aeronautical Instruments

AIRPLANES–JUVENILE LITERATURE

see also Aeronautics–Juvenile Literature

Freeman, Tony. Aircraft That Work for Us. LC 80-23078. (On the Move Ser.). (Illus.). 48p. (gr. 3-6). 1981. PLB 9.25 (ISBN 0-516-03888-5). Childrens.
Gunston. Spotting Planes. (Gloustér Press Ser.). (gr. 4 up). 1980. PLB 5.90 (ISBN 0-531-03450-X, B49). Watts.
Moche, Dinah. My First Airplane Trip. (Look Look Bk). (Illus.). 24p. 1981. pap. 1.25 (ISBN 0-307-11869-X, Golden Pr). Western Pub.
Monfort, Platt. Styro-Flyers: How to Build Super Model Airplanes from Hamburger Boxes & Other Fast-Food Containers. (Illus.). 32p. (gr. 5 up). 1981. pap. 3.95 (ISBN 0-394-84715-6). Random.
Ross, Pat & Ross, Joel. Your First Airplane Trip. 1981. 7.95 (ISBN 0-688-41989-5). Lothrop.
Schleier, Curt. The Team Behind Your Airline Flight. LC 80-27174. (gr. 5-8). 1981. 9.95 (ISBN 0-664-32678-1). Westminster.
Trombley, Richard. The World's Greatest Airplanes: The Heinkel HE 111 to the Concorde. (Superwheels & Thrill Sports Ser.). (Illus.). (gr. 4 up). 1981. PLB 6.95 (ISBN 0-8225-0501-0). Lerner Pubns.
--The World's Greatest Airplanes: The Wright Flyer to the Piper Cub. (Superwheels & Thrill Sports Bks.). (Illus.). (gr. 4 up). 1981. PLB 6.95 (ISBN 0-8225-0500-2). Lerner Pubns.

AIRPLANES–MAINTENANCE AND REPAIR

see also Flight Engineering

Aviation Maintenance Publishers. Radio Logbook. 70p. 1974. pap. 3.95 (ISBN 0-89100-186-7, EA-ARL-1). Aviation Maintenance.
--Radio Logbook. 70p. 1974. text ed. 4.95 (ISBN 0-89100-195-6, EA-ARL-2). Aviation Maintenance.
Crane, Dale. A&P Mechanics General Handbook Study Guide. (Aviation Maintenance Training Course Ser.). (Illus.). 172p. 1977. pap. text ed. 6.00 (ISBN 0-89100-072-0, EA-65-9ASG). Aviation Maintenance.
--A&P Mechanics Powerplant Handbook Study Guide. (Aviation Maintenance Training Course Ser.). 161p. 1978. pap. 6.00 (ISBN 0-89100-073-9, EA-65-12ASG). Aviation Maintenance.
--Aircraft Fuel Metering Systems. (Aviation Maintenance Training Course Ser.). (Illus.). 70p. 1975. pap. 5.95 (ISBN 0-89100-057-7, EA-FMS). Aviation Maintenance.
Crane, Dale, et al. Aircraft Technical Dictionary. 2nd ed. (Aviation Maintenance Training Course Ser.). Date not set. pap. price not set (ISBN 0-89100-124-7). Aviation Maintenance.
Federal Aviation Administration. A&P Mechanics Airframe Written Examination Questions. (Aviation Maintenance Training Course Ser.). (Illus.). 113p. 1979. pap. 3.75 (ISBN 0-89100-158-1, EA-AC65-20). Aviation Maintenance.
--A&P Mechanic's Certification Guide. 4th ed. (Aviation Maintenance Training Course Ser.). 64p. 1976. pap. 2.50 (ISBN 0-89100-082-8, EA-AC65-2D). Aviation Maintenance.
--A&P Mechanics General Written Examination Questions. (Aviation Maintenance Training Course Ser.). 88p. 1979. pap. 3.75 (ISBN 0-89100-157-3, EA-AC65-20). Aviation Maintenance.
--Federal Aviation Regulations for Aviation Mechanics. 6th ed. (Aviation Maintenance Training Course Ser.). 442p. 1980. pap. 10.00 (ISBN 0-89100-177-8, E*A-F*A*R-1E). Aviation Maintenance.
Johnson, Bruce C. Basic Handtools for the Aviation Technician. (Aviation Technician Training Ser.). (Orig.). 1980. pap. write for info. (ISBN 0-89100-204-9). Aviation Maintenance.
Jones, David & Crane, Dale, eds. Aviation Maintenance Handbook & Standard Hardware Digest. 2nd ed. 1981. pap. write for info. (ISBN 0-89100-151-4). Aviation Maintenance.
Schutz, Noel W., Jr. & Derwing, Bruce L. Essentials of Aviation Technology: Aviation Mechanics. LC 80-51692. (The ALA ESP Ser.). (Illus.). xii, 180p. (Orig.). 1980. pap. text ed. 10.00 (ISBN 0-934270-10-4). Am Lang Acad.
Standard on Aircraft Maintenance. 84p. 3.75 (ISBN 0-686-68288-2). Natl Fire Prot.

AIRPLANES–MODELS

Schleicher, Robert. Building & Displaying Model Aircraft. LC 80-70385. 176p. 1981. 13.95 (ISBN 0-686-69512-7); pap. 8.95 (ISBN 0-686-69513-5). Chilton.

AIRPLANES–MOTORS

see also Flight Engineering

Aviation Maintenance Publishers. Engine Logbook. 77p. 1975. pap. 4.95 (ISBN 0-89100-187-5, E*A-E*F*L-1). Aviation Maintenance.
Smith, Herschel. Aircraft Piston Engines: From the Manly Baltzer to the Continental Tiara. (Aviation Ser.). (Illus.). 264p. 1981. 18.95 (ISBN 0-07-058472-9, P&RB). McGraw.

AIRPLANES–PILOTING

see also Flight Training

Breise, Frederic H. Fifty Years of Aviation Knowledge. 108p. 1981. 9.75 (ISBN 0-938576-00-3). F H Breise.
Canadian Private Pilot Manual. (Pilot Training Ser.). (Illus.). 428p. 1981. pap. text ed. price not set (ISBN 0-88487-074-X, JS314131). Jeppesen Sanderson.
Federal Aviation Administration. Flight Training Handbook. LC 80-70552. (Illus.). 352p. 1981. 12.95 (ISBN 0-385-17599-X). Doubleday.
Gallagher, Thomas B. Private Pilot Written Exam Course. LC 80-70132. (Illus.). 68p. (Orig.). 1981. pap. 19.95 (ISBN 0-938706-00-4). Fed Aviation.
Sacchi, Louise. Ocean Flying. (McGraw-Hill Ser. in Aviation). (Illus.). 240p. 1979. 16.50 (ISBN 0-07-054405-0). McGraw.

AIRPLANES–PILOTS

see Air Pilots

AIRPLANES–SAFETY MEASURES

see Aeronautics–Safety Measures

AIRPLANES–STRESSES

see Airframes

AIRPLANES–STRUCTURES

see Airframes

AIRPLANES–TURBOJET ENGINES

Whittle, Frank. Gas Turbine Aero-Thermodynamics: With Special Reference to Aircraft Propulsion. LC 80-41372. 240p. 1981. 30.00 (ISBN 0-08-026719-X); pap. 17.50 (ISBN 0-08-026718-1). Pergamon.

AIRPLANES, MILITARY

see also Bombers; Fighter Planes; Jet Planes, Military

King, H. F. Sopwith Aircraft Nineteen Twelve to Nineteen Twenty. (Illus.). 320p. 1981. 36.00 (ISBN 0-370-30050-5, Pub. by Chatto-Bodley-Jonathan). Merrimack Bk Serv.

AIRPLANES, PERSONAL

see Airplanes, Private

AIRPLANES, PILOTLESS

see Guided Missiles

AIRPLANES, PRIVATE

Canadian Private Pilot Manual. (Pilot Training Ser.). (Illus.). 428p. 1981. pap. text ed. price not set (ISBN 0-88487-074-X, JS314131). Jeppesen Sanderson.
Thurston, David B. Home Built Aircraft. (McGraw-Hill Series in Aviation). (Illus.). 224p. 1981. 24.95 (ISBN 0-07-064552-3, P&RB). McGraw.

AIRPLANES, USED

see Used Aircraft

AIRPLANES IN AGRICULTURE

see Aeronautics in Agriculture

AIRPORTS

see also Air Bases

Amann, Dick. Airports: Today's Small Field, Tomorrow's Neighborhood Nightmare. 1981. 45.00 (ISBN 0-917194-05-5). Prog Studies.

Cannon, Charles B. The O'Hare Story. LC 80-50072. 54p. 1981. 6.95 (ISBN 0-533-04585-1). Vantage.

Institute of Civil Engineers. Aircraft Pavement Design. 114p. 1980. 79.00x (ISBN 0-901948-04-7, Pub. by Telford England). State Mutual Bk.

--Airports for the Eighties. 220p. 1980. 80.00x (ISBN 0-901948-72-1, Pub. by Telford England). Sate Mutual Bk.

--Airports for the Future. 129p. 1980. 60.00x (ISBN 0-901948-36-5, Pub. by Telford England). State Mutual Bk.

Institute of Civil Engineers, UK. Airports--- the Challenging Future. 256p. 1980. 79.00x (ISBN 0-7277-0017-0, Pub. by Telford England). State Mutual Bk.

Senterfitt, Arnold D. Airports of Mexico & Central America. (Illus.). 1980. pap. 24.95 (Pub. by Senterfitt). Aviation.

Senter Fitt, Arnold D. Airports of Mexico & Centro America. 15th ed. (Illus.). 560p. (Orig.). 1980. pap. 24.95 (ISBN 0-937260-00-2). Senterfitt.

AKKADIAN (EAST SEMITIC) LANGUAGE

see Assyro-Babylonian Language

ALABAMA-DESCRIPTION AND TRAVEL

Couch, Robert H. Everyday Is Easter in Alabama. LC 76-21358. (Illus.). 1976. 10.00 (ISBN 0-916624-02-1). TSU Pr.

ALABAMA-HISTORY

Canfield, Rosemary, ed. Perspectives: The Alabama Heritage. LC 78-64441. 1978. 15.00 (ISBN 0-916624-27-7). TSU Pr.

Van Antwerp, Emily S. Iron Ore to Iron Lace. (Illus.). 150p. 1980. 10.00 (ISBN 0-914334-07-7). Museum Mobile.

ALABAMA-SOCIAL LIFE AND CUSTOMS

Couch, Robert H. Everyday Is Easter in Alabama. LC 76-21358. (Illus.). 1976. 10.00 (ISBN 0-916624-02-1). TSU Pr.

ALASKA

see also names of cities, regions, etc. in Alaska, e.g. Aleutian Islands

Alaska Shippers Guide. (Illus.). 208p. 1980. 19.95 (ISBN 0-88240-147-5). Alaska Northwest.

ALASKA-DESCRIPTION AND TRAVEL

Baxter, Robert. Baxter's Alaska. 1981. 9.95 (ISBN 0-913384-47-X). Rail Europe-Baxter.

Hulley, Clarence C. Alaska: Past & Present. 3rd ed. LC 80-25274. (Illus.). 477p. 1981. Repr. of 1970 ed. lib. bdg. 39.75x (ISBN 0-313-22845-0, HUAL). Greenwood.

Jochum, Helen P. Alaskan Journey. LC 80-51526. (Illus.). 153p. 1980. 10.00. Jochum.

Pearson, Roger W. & Lynch, Donald F. Alaska: A Geography. 300p. 1981. lib. bdg. 35.00x (ISBN 0-89158-903-1); text ed. 20.00x (ISBN 0-89158-903-1). Westview.

Peterson, Knut. The Lost Frontier. 1981. 10.95 (ISBN 0-87949-172-8). Ashley Bks.

Searby, Ellen. The Inside Passage Traveler: Getting Around in Southeastern Alaska. 4th ed. (Illus.). 128p. 1981. pap. 5.50 (ISBN 0-9605526-0-X). Windham Bay.

ALASKA-HISTORY

Barratt, Glen. The Russians at Port Jackson. 1980. text ed. write for info. (ISBN 0-391-02165-6); pap. text ed. write for info. (ISBN 0-391-02166-4). Humanities.

Huggins, Eli L. Kodiak & Afognak Life, 1868-1870. Pierce, Richard A., ed. (Materials for the Study of Alaska History Ser.: No. 20). (Illus.). 1981. 16.50x (ISBN 0-919642-96-9). Limestone Pr.

Hulley, Clarence C. Alaska: Past & Present. 3rd ed. LC 80-25274. (Illus.). 477p. 1981. Repr. of 1970 ed. lib. bdg. 39.75x (ISBN 0-313-22845-0, HUAL). Greenwood.

Miller, David H. The Alaska Treaty. (Materials for the Study of Alaska History Ser.: No. 18). (Illus.). 1981. 16.50x (ISBN 0-919642-94-2). Limestone Pr.

Naske, Claus M. & Rowinski, Ludwig J. Anchorage: A Pictorial History. Friedman, Donna R., ed. (Illus.). 208p. 1981. pap. price not set (ISBN 0-89865-106-9). Donning Co.

Oswalt, Wendell H. Kolmakovskiy Redoubt: The Ethnoarchaeology of a Russian Fort in Alaska. LC 80-53304. (Monumenta Archaeologica Ser.: No. 8). (Illus.). 212p. 1980. 10.50 (ISBN 0-917956-17-6). UCLA Arch.

Shelikhov, Grigorii I. Voyage to America, 1783-1786, Rus. Pierce, Richard A., ed. Ramsey, Marina, tr. (Materials for the Study of Alaska History Ser.: No. 19). (Illus.). 1981. 15.50x (ISBN 0-919642-67-5). Limestone Pr.

ALASKA-JUVENILE LITERATURE

Nault, Andy. Staying Alive in Alaska's Wild. Loftin, Tee, ed. (Illus.). 224p. (Orig.). (gr. 6-12). 1980. pap. 8.00 (ISBN 0-934812-01-2). Loftin Pubs.

ALASKA-POLITICS AND GOVERNMENT

Alaska Statutes, 11 vols. 1980. write for info. (ISBN 0-87215-143-3). Michie.

ALASKA-SOCIAL LIFE AND CUSTOMS

Huggins, Eli L. Kodiak & Afognak Life, 1868-1870. Pierce, Richard A., ed. (Materials for the Study of Alaska History Ser.: No. 20). (Illus.). 1981. 16.50x (ISBN 0-919642-96-9). Limestone Pr.

ALBANIA

Kontos, Joan F. Red Cross, Black Eagle: A Biography of Albania's American School. (East European Monographs: No. 75). 240p. 1981. text ed. 17.00x (ISBN 0-914710-69-9). East Eur Quarterly.

ALBANIA-HISTORY

Stajka, Nika. The Last Days of Freedom. 1981. 12.95 (ISBN 0-533-04637-8). Vantage.

ALBANY-HISTORY

Dumbleton, Susanne & Older, Anne. In & Around Albany: A Guide for Residents, Students & Visitors. (Illus.). 183p. (Orig.). 1980. pap. 4.50 (ISBN 0-9605460-0-6). Wash Park.

ALBEMARLE REGION, NORTH CAROLINA-HISTORY

Brown, Alexander. Juniper Waterway: A History of the Albemarle & Chesapeake Canal. LC 80-14093. 1981. price not set (ISBN 0-917376-35-8). U Pr of Va.

ALCALOIDS

see Alkaloids

ALCES

Wilder, Thornton. The Alcestiad or a Life in the Sun. 1979. pap. 2.25 (ISBN 0-380-41855-X, 41855, Bard). Avon.

ALCHEMY

see also Magic

Todd, Nancy J., ed. Journal of the New Alchemists, No. 7. (Illus.). 184p. 1981. 15.95 (ISBN 0-8289-0405-7); pap. 9.95 (ISBN 0-8289-0406-5). Greene.

Ware, James R., tr. from Chinese. Alchemy, Medicine, & Religion in the China of A. D. 320: The Nei P'ien of Ko Hung (Pao-p'u tzu) 416p. 1981. pap. price not set (ISBN 0-486-24088-6). Dover.

ALCOHOL

see also Alcoholic Beverages; Alcoholism; Distillation; Liquor Industry and Trade; Liquor Problem; Liquors; Temperance

also names of alcoholic liquors

Ladewig, D., ed. Drogen & Alkohol. (Illus.). xii, 220p. 1980. pap. 23.50 (ISBN 3-8055-1624-X). S Karger.

Seixas, Judith S. Alcohol -- What It Is, What It Does. LC 76-43344. (Read-Alone Bk.). (Illus.). 56p. (gr. 1-3). 1981. pap. 2.95 (ISBN 0-688-00462-8). Greenwillow.

Thurman, Ronald, ed. Alcohol & Aldehyde Metabolizing Systems. (Advances in Experimental Medicine & Biology Ser.). 335p. 1980. 75.00 (ISBN 0-306-40476-1, Plenum Pr). Plenum Pub.

ALCOHOL-LAW AND LEGISLATION

Sloan, I. Alcohol & Drug Abuse & the Law, Vol. 27. 1980. 5.95 (ISBN 0-379-11137-3). Oceana.

ALCOHOL-PHYSIOLOGICAL EFFECT

Clark, P. M. & Kricka, L. J. Medical Consequences of Alcohol Abuse. LC 80-41993. (Chemical Science Ser.). 282p. 1980. 97.95 (ISBN 0-470-27076-4). Halsted Pr.

ALCOHOL AND YOUTH

Svendson, Roger & Griffin, Tom. The Student Assistance Program: How It Works. 1980. pap. 3.95 (ISBN 0-89486-110-7). Hazelden.

Woodward, Nancy H. If Your Child Is Drinking... What You Can Do to Fight Alcohol Abuse at Home, at School, & in the Community. 360p. 1981. 11.95 (ISBN 0-399-12457-8). Putnam.

ALCOHOL AS FUEL

Bereny, Justin A., ed. State Government Overviews. (Alcohol Fuels Information Ser.: Vol. 4). 1981. 49.95 (ISBN 0-89934-115-2); pap. 34.95 (ISBN 0-89934-114-4). Solar Energy Info.

Davy McKee Corp. Plant Conversion Potential to Fuel Alcohol Production. 125p. 1981. pap. 24.50 (ISBN 0-89934-095-4). Solar Energy Info.

Gaither, Robert. Alcohol Fuel Book. (Illus.). 55p. (Orig.). Date not set. pap. price not set (ISBN 0-89196-084-8, Domus Bks). Quality Bks IL.

Kerley, Michael R. & Mother Earth News Staff, eds. The Mother Earth News Alcohol Fuel Handbook. 120p. (Orig.). 1980. pap. 12.95 (ISBN 0-938432-00-1). Mother Earth.

Mathewson, Stephen W. The Manual for the Home & Farm Production of Alcohol Fuel. 1980. 12.95 (ISBN 0-89815-030-2); pap. 7.95 (ISBN 0-89815-029-9). Ten Speed Pr.

Office of Technology Assessment. Energy from Biological Processes, Vol. 2. Date not set. lib. bdg. price not set (ISBN 0-89934-119-5); pap. price not set (ISBN 0-89934-120-9). Solar Energy Info.

Paul, J. K., ed. Large & Small Scale Ethyl Alcohol Manufacturing Processes from Agricultural Raw Materials. LC 80-20219. (Chemical Tech. Rev. 169, Energy Tech. Rev. 58). (Illus.). 576p. 1981. 48.00 (ISBN 0-8155-0815-8). Noyes.

Raphael Katzen Associates. Grain Motor Fuel Alcohol Technical & Economic Assessment Study. 344p. 1981. pap. 39.50 (ISBN 0-89934-063-6). Solar Energy Info.

Raphael Katzen Associates International, Inc. Farm & Cooperative Alcohol Plant Study: Technical & Economic Assessment As a Commercial Venture. 230p. 1981. pap. 20.00 (ISBN 0-89934-117-9). Solar Energy Info.

Ross, James. Fuel Alcohol: How to Make It, How to Use It. 160p. 1981. 9.95 (ISBN 0-312-30932-5); pap. 4.95 (ISBN 0-312-30933-3). St Martin.

Schnittker Assocs. Ethanol: Farm & Fuel Issues. 160p. 1981. pap. 19.50 (ISBN 0-89934-096-2). Solar Energy Info.

Solar Energy Research Institute (SERI) Guide to Commercial-Scale Ethanol Production & Financing. 305p. 1981. 34.50 (ISBN 0-89934-118-7). Solar Energy Info.

TRW - Energy Systems Planning Division. Energy Balances in the Production & End-Use of Alcohols Derived from Biomass. 125p. 1981. pap. 15.00 (ISBN 0-89934-116-0). Solar Energy Info.

U.S. National Alcohol Fuels Commission. State Initiatives on Alcohol Fuels. 102p. 1981. pap. 15.00 (ISBN 0-89934-105-5). Solar Energy Info.

U.S. National Alcohols Fuels Commission. Fuel Alcohol on the Farm. 50p. 1981. pap. 4.95 (ISBN 0-89934-097-0). Solar Energy Info.

ALCOHOL INTOXICATION

see Alcoholism

ALCOHOLIC BEVERAGE CONTROL

see Alcohol-Law and Legislation

ALCOHOLIC BEVERAGE INDUSTRY

see Brewing Industry; Distilling Industries; Wine and Wine Making

ALCOHOLIC BEVERAGES

see also Beer; Liquors; Temperance; Wine and Wine Making

Ewing, John A. Drinking: Everything You Want to Know. 130p. 1981. 10.95 (ISBN 0-8359-1474-7); pap. 6.95 (ISBN 0-8359-1473-9). Reston.

Smith, C. Carter. The Art of Mixing Drinks. (Orig.). 1981. pap. 7.95 (ISBN 0-446-97759-4). Warner Bks.

ALCOHOLICS

Coudert, Jo. The Alcoholic in Your Life. LC 70-185955. 264p. 1981. pap. 6.95 (ISBN 0-8128-6121-3). Stein & Day.

Molloy, Paul. Where Did Everybody Go? LC 79-6605. 192p. 1981. 11.95 (ISBN 0-385-04997-8). Doubleday.

Sandmaier, Marian. The Invisible Alcoholics: Women & Alcohol Abuse in America. 324p. 1981. pap. 4.95 (ISBN 0-07-054661-4). McGraw.

Twerski, Abraham J. Caution: Kindness Can Be Dangerous to the Alcholic. 1981. 10.95 (ISBN 0-13-121244-3); pap. 4.95 (ISBN 0-13-121236-2). P-H.

ALCOHOLICS-PERSONAL NARRATIVES

Al-Anon Family Group Headquarters. Al-Anon's Twelve Steps & Twelve Traditions. 140p. 5.00 (ISBN 0-910034-24-9). Al-Anon.

Carle, Cecil. Letters to Elderly Alcoholics. 1980. pap. 3.95. Hazelden.

ALCOHOLICS ANONYMOUS

Al-Anon Family Group Headquarters. Al-Anon's Twelve Steps & Twelve Traditions. 140p. 5.00 (ISBN 0-910034-24-9). Al-Anon.

Alcoholics Anonymous. 3rd, rev. ed. LC 76-4029. 575p. 1976. 5.65 (ISBN 0-916856-00-3). AAWS.

Alcoholics Anonymous Comes of Age: A Brief History of A. A. LC 57-10949. 333p. 1957. 5.75 (ISBN 0-916856-02-X). AAWS.

As Bill Sees It: Selected Writings of the A. A.'s Co-Founder. 333p. 1967. 5.00 (ISBN 0-916856-03-8). AAWS.

Twelve Steps & Twelve Traditions. LC 53-5454. 192p. 1953. 4.00 (ISBN 0-916856-01-1). AAWS.

ALCOHOLISM

see also Alcohol and Youth; Alcoholics; Liquor Industry and Trade

A., Herbie. Through Living Hell...from Alcohol & Back. 1981. 4.95 (ISBN 0-8062-1603-4). Carlton.

Barnes, Grace M., et al. Alcohol & the Elderly: A Comprehensive Bibliography. LC 80-1786. xvii, 138p. 1980. lib. bdg. 25.00 (ISBN 0-313-22132-4, BAE/). Greenwood.

Camberwell Council on Alcoholism. Women & Alcohol. LC 80-40370. 207p. 1980. 22.00 (ISBN 0-422-76960-6, 2007); pap. 10.95 (2007). Methuen Inc.

Clark, P. M. & Kricka, L. J. Medical Consequences of Alcohol Abuse. LC 80-41993. (Chemical Science Ser.). 282p. 1980. 97.95 (ISBN 0-470-27076-4). Halsted Pr.

Crumbaugh, James C., et al. Logotherapy: New Help for Problem Drinkers. LC 79-18635. 176p. 1981. 10.95 (ISBN 0-88229-421-0). Nelson-Hall.

Edwards, G. & Grant, M. Alcoholism: New Knowledge & New Responses. 368p. 1980. 35.00x (Pub. by Croom Helm England). State Mutual Bk.

Frankel, B. G. & Whitehead, P. C. Drinking & Damage: Theoretical Advances & Implications for Prevention. (Rutgers Center for Alcohol Studies Monograph: No. 14). 1981. 10.00x (ISBN 0-911290-09-5). Rutgers Ctr Alcohol.

Grant, Marcus & Gwinner, Paul. Alcoholisms in Perspectjve. 176p. 1980. 27.00x (ISBN 0-85664-790-X, Pub. by Croom Helm England). State Mutual Bk.

Lowinson, Joyce & Ruiz, Pedro. Substance Abuse. (Illus.). 900p. 1981. write for info. (5210-1). Williams & Wilkins.

Mann, Marty. Marty Mann Answers Your Questions About Drinking & Alcoholism. 128p. 1981. 8.95 (ISBN 0-03-081857-5); pap. 3.95 (ISBN 0-686-69289-6). HR&W.

--Marty Mann's New Primer on Alcoholism. 256p. 1981. 10.95 (ISBN 0-03-029595-5); pap. 5.95 (ISBN 0-686-69290-X). HR&W.

Orford, Jim & Harwin, Judith, eds. Alcohol & the Family. 200p. 1980. 25.00x (Pub. by Croom Helm England). State Mutual Bk.

Polich, J. Michael & Armor, David J. The Course of Alcoholism: Four Years After Treatment. Braiker, Harriet B., ed. (Personality Processes Ser.). 312p. 1981. 25.00 (ISBN 0-471-08682-7, Pub. by Wiley-Interscience). Wiley.

Twerski, Abraham J. Caution: Kindness Can Be Dangerous to the Alcholic. 1981. 10.95 (ISBN 0-13-121244-3); pap. 4.95 (ISBN 0-13-121236-2). P-H.

Williams, Roger J. The Prevention of Alcoholism Through Nutrition. 176p. (Orig.). 1981. pap. 2.50 (ISBN 0-553-14502-9). Bantam.

ALCOHOLISM-TREATMENT

B., Mel. Is There Life After Sobriety. 1980. pap. 4.95. Hazelden.

Barnard, Charles P. Families, Alcoholism & Therapy. (Illus.). 184p. 1981. text ed. 16.50 (ISBN 0-398-04157-1); pap. text ed. 12.75 (ISBN 0-398-04173-3). C C Thomas.

Edwards, Griffith, ed. Alcoholism Treatment in Transition. 336p. 1980. 35.00x (Pub. by Croom Helm England). State Mutual Bk.

Heath, D. W., et al, eds. Cultural Factors in Alcohol Research & Treatment. (Journal of Studies on Alcohol: Suppl. No. 9). 1981. 10.00x (ISBN 0-911290-08-7). Rutgers Ctr Alcohol.

O'Keefe, Rip. Sober Living Workbook. 1980. pap. 5.95. Hazelden.

Robinson, David. Talking Out of Alcoholism. 160p. 1980. 25.00x (ISBN 0-85664-755-1, Pub. by Croom Helm England). State Mutual Bk.

Roeck, Alan L. Twenty-Four Hours a Day. large print ed. 1980. pap. 4.95 (ISBN 0-89486-108-5). Hazelden.

Shaw, Stan, et al. Responding to Drinking Problems. 272p. 1980. 40.00x (ISBN 0-85664-525-7, Pub. by Croom Helm England). State Mutual Bk.

Steiner, Claude M. Healing Alcoholism. LC 79-2320. 208p. 1981. pap. 3.95 (ISBN 0-394-17923-4, BC). Grove.

ALCOHOLISM AND EMPLOYMENT

Hore, Brian, ed. Alcohol Problems in Employment. 200p. 1980. 35.00x (Pub. by Croom Helm England). State Mutual Bk.

Hore, Brian & Plant, Michael, eds. Alcohol Problems in Employment. 200p. 1981. 35.00x (ISBN 0-7099-1202-1, Pub. by Croom Helm LTD England). Biblio Dist.

Weiss, Richard M. Dealing with Alcoholism in the Workplace, Report No. 784. (Illus.). vii, 59p. (Orig.). 1980. pap. 15.00 (ISBN 0-8237-0220-0). Conference Bd.

Wrich, James T. The Employee Assistance Program. rev. ed. 1980. 7.95. Hazelden.

ALCORAN

see Koran

ALDEHYDES

Thurman, Ronald, ed. Alcohol & Aldehyde Metabolizing Systems. (Advances in Experimental Medicine & Biology Ser.). 335p. 1980. 75.00 (ISBN 0-306-40476-1, Plenum Pr). Plenum Pub.

ALDINGTON, RICHARD, 1892-1962

MacNiven, Ian S. & Moore, Harry T., eds. Literary Lifelines: The Richard Aldington-Larence Durrell Correspondence. 288p. 1981. 17.50 (ISBN 0-670-42817-5). Viking Pr.

ALE-HOUSES

see Hotels, Taverns, etc.

ALEXANDER THE GREAT, 356-323 B.C.

Hammond, Nicholas G. Alexander the Great: King, Commander, & Statesman. LC 80-18573. (Illus.). 358p. 1981. 24.00 (ISBN 0-8155-5058-8). Noyes.

ALFONSO 10TH, EL SABIO, KING OF CASTILE AND LEON, 1221-1284

Procter, Evelyn S. Alfonso X of Castile, Patron of Literature & Learning. LC 80-10508. (Norman Macoll Lectures: 1949). vi, 149p. 1980. Repr. of 1951 ed. lib. bdg. 19.50x (ISBN 0-313-22347-5, PRAL). Greenwood.

ALGAE

see also Kelp

also names of families of algae, e.g. Zygnemaceae

Drouet, F. Revision of the Stigonemataceae: With a Summary of the Classification of Blue-Green Algae. (Nova Hedwigia Beiheft: No. 66). (Illus.). 300p. 1981. lib. bdg. 60.00x (ISBN 3-7682-5466-6). Lubrecht & Cramer.

Johansen, H. William, ed. Coralline Algae: A First Synthesis. 272p. 1981. 74.95 (ISBN 0-8493-5261-4). CRC Pr.

ALGEBRA

see also Combinatorial Analysis; Groups, Theory Of; Mathematical Analysis; Numbers, Theory Of; Partitions (Mathematics); Probabilities; Sequences (Mathematics); Spinor Analysis

Arsove, Maynard & Leutwiler, Heinz. Algebraic Potential Theory. LC 79-24384. (Memoirs of the American Mathematical Society Ser.). 1980. 7.60 (ISBN 0-8218-2226-8). Am Math.

Cohen & Cameron. Elementary Algebra. 480p. 1981. pap. text ed. 16.95 (ISBN 0-205-07308-5, 5671728); free tchr's ed. (ISBN 0-205-07309-3). Allyn.

--Intermediate Algebra. 576p. 1980. pap. text ed. 17.80 (ISBN 0-205-07172-4, 5671728); free tchr's ed. (ISBN 0-205-07173-2). Allyn.

Cohn, P. M. Algebra, 2 vols. LC 73-2780. Vol. 1, 1974, 384p. 34.25 (ISBN 0-471-16430-5, Pub. by Wiley-Interscience); Vol. 2, 1977. 29.95 (ISBN 0-471-01823-6); Vol. 1. pap. 15.95 (ISBN 0-471-16431-3). Wiley.

Draper. Analytilic Methods in Communicative Algebra. Date not set. price not set (ISBN 0-8247-1282-X). Dekker.

Faith, C. Algebra I: Rings, Modules & Categories. (Grundlehren der Mathematischen Wissenschaften Ser.: Vol. 190). 610p. 1981. 48.00 (ISBN 0-387-05551-7). Springer-Verlag.

Hestenes, Marshall & Hill, Richard. Algebra & Trigonometry with Calculators. (Illus.). 512p. 1981. text ed. 17.95 (ISBN 0-13-021857-X). P-H.

Hungerford, T. W. Algerbra. (Graduate Texts in Mathematics: Vol. 73). 526p. 1981. 24.00 (ISBN 0-387-90518-9). Springer-Verlag.

Johnson, Richard E. Elementary Algebra. 1980. 16.95 (ISBN 0-8053-5052-7). Benjamin-Cummings.

Keedy, Mervin L. & Bittinger, Marvin L. Fundamental Algebra & Trigonometry. 2nd ed. (Mathematics-Remedial & Precalculus Ser.). (Illus.). 576p. 1981. text ed. 15.95 (ISBN 0-201-03839-0). A-W.

--Fundamental College Algebra. 2nd ed. (Mathematics-Remedial & Precalculus Ser.). 480p. 1981. text ed. 15.95 (ISBN 0-201-03847-1). A-W.

Lial, Margaret A. & Miller, Charles D. Study Guide to Accompany Intermediate Algebra. 3rd ed. 1981. pap. text ed. 5.95x (ISBN 0-673-15480-7). Scott F.

Lial, Margaret L. & Miller, Charles D. Intermediate Algebra. 3rd ed. 1981. text ed. 15.95x (ISBN 0-673-15406-8). Scott F.

McKeague, Charles P. Beginning Algebra. 1980. pap. 13.95 (ISBN 0-12-484765-X). Acad Pr.

Pacholski, L., et al, eds. Model Theory of Algebra & Arithmetics: Procedings. (Lecture Notes in Mathematics Ser.: Vol. 834). 410p. 1981. pap. 24.50 (ISBN 0-686-69431-7). Springer-Verlag.

Sellers, Gene. Elementary Algebra. LC 80-23171. 475p. (Orig.). 1981. pap. text ed. 17.95 (ISBN 0-8185-0434-X). Brooks-Cole.

Sentlowitz, Michael & Trivisone, Margaret. College Algebra. (Math - Remedial & Precalculus Ser.). 576p. 1981. text ed. 14.95 (ISBN 0-201-06626-2). A-W.

--College Algebra & Trigonometry. (Math-Remedial & Precalculus Ser.). 576p. 1981. text ed. 14.95 (ISBN 0-201-06676-9). A-W.

Siever, Norman L. Intermediate Algebra: A Clear Approach. 1981. write for info. (ISBN 0-8302-4206-6). Goodyear.

Silver, Howard A. Intermediate Algebra. 512p. 1981. text ed. 17.95 (ISBN 0-13-469411-2). P-H.

Steffensen, Arnold J. & Johnson, L. M. Algebra & Trigonometry. 1980. pap. text ed. 16.95 (ISBN 0-673-15371-1). Scott F.

--Intermediate Algebra. 1980. pap. text ed. 14.95 (ISBN 0-673-15369-X). Scott F.

Steinlage, Ralph. College Algebra & Trigonometry. 1981. text ed. write for info. (ISBN 0-8302-1640-5). Goodyear.

Wright & New. Introductory Algebra. 298p. 1981. text ed. 16.95 (ISBN 0-205-07310-7, 5673100); free tchr's ed. (ISBN 0-205-07311-5); free student's guide (ISBN 0-205-07312-3). Allyn.

ALGEBRA–EARLY WORKS TO 1800

Hughes, Barnabas E., ed. Jordanus De Nemore, De Numeris Datis: A Critical Edition & Translation. (Publications of the Center for Medieval & Renaissance Studies, UCLA). 200p. 1981. 40.00x (ISBN 0-520-04283-2). U of Cal Pr.

ALGEBRA–PROGRAMMED INSTRUCTION

Pettofrezzo, Anthony J. & Armstrong, Lee H. Intermediate Algebra: A Programmed Approach. 1981. pap. text ed. 13.95 (ISBN 0-673-15315-0). Scott F.

ALGEBRA OF LOGIC

see Logic, Symbolic and Mathematical

ALGEBRAIC CURVES

see Curves, Algebraic

ALGEBRAIC FIELDS

see Fields, Algebraic

ALGEBRAIC GEOMETRY

see Geometry, Algebraic

ALGEBRAIC NUMBERS

see Fields, Algebraic

ALGEBRAIC RINGS

see Rings (Algebra)

ALGEBRAIC TOPOLOGY

Crabb, M. C. ZZ-Two-Homotopy Theory. (London Mathematical Lecture Note Ser.: No. 44). 100p. (Orig.). 1980. pap. 15.95 (ISBN 0-521-28051-6). Cambridge U Pr.

Dold, A. Lectures on Algebraic Topology. (Grundlehren der Mathematischen Wissenschaften Ser.: Vol. 200). (Illus.). 377p. 1981. 38.00 (ISBN 0-387-10369-4). Springer-Verlag.

ALGEBRAS, LIE

see Lie Algebras

ALGEBRAS, LINEAR

see also Lie Algebras; Topology; Vector Spaces

Bratteli, O. & Robinson, D. W., eds. Operators Algebra & Quantum Statistical Mechanics, Vol. II: Equilibrium States; Models. (Texts & Monographs in Physics Ser.). 496p. 1981. 46.00 (ISBN 0-387-10381-3). Springer-Verlag.

Johnson, Lee W. & Riess, R. Dean. Introduction to Linear Algebra. LC 80-19984. (Mathematics Ser.). (Illus.). 352p. 1981. text ed. 16.95 (ISBN 0-201-03392-5). A-W.

Knoke, David & Burke, Peter J. Log-Linear Models. LC 80-17031. (Quantitative Applications in the Social Sciences Ser.: No. 20). (Illus.). 80p. 1980. pap. 3.50 (ISBN 0-8039-1492-X). Sage.

Slodowy, P. Simple Singularities & Simple Algebraic Groups. (Lecture Notes in Mathematics: Vol. 815). 175p. 1980. pap. 11.80 (ISBN 0-387-10026-1). Springer-Verlag.

Strang, W. Gilbert. Instructor's Manual for Linear Algebra & Its Applications. 2nd ed. 1980. 3.00 (ISBN 0-12-673662-6). Acad Pr.

ALGERIA–HISTORY

Heggoy, Alf A. & Crout, Robert R. Historical Dictionary of Algeria. LC 80-24126. (African Historical Dictionaries Ser.: No. 28). x, 247p. 1981. 13.50 (ISBN 0-8108-1376-9). Scarecrow.

Seymour, William H. Story of Algiers. (Illus.). 143p. 1981. pap. 6.95 (ISBN 0-911116-33-8). Pelican.

ALGOL (COMPUTER PROGRAM LANGUAGE)

Brundritt, Alan. Elementary ALGOL. (Illus.). 80p. 1976. pap. text ed. 9.95 (ISBN 0-7121-0549-2, Pub. by Macdonald & Evans Engalnd). Intl Ideas.

ALGONQUIAN LANGUAGES

Wolfart, H. Christoph & Carroll, Janet F. Meet Cree: A Guide to the Cree Language. 160p. 1981. 12.50x (ISBN 0-8032-4716-8). U of Nebr Pr.

ALGORITHMIC LANGUAGE

see ALGOL (Computer Program Language)

ALIBAMU INDIANS

see Indians of North America–Eastern States

ALIENATION (PHILOSOPHY)

Keyon, Rostam. Being & Alienation. LC 78-61109. 350p. 1981. 10.00 (ISBN 0-686-69333-7). Philos Lib.

Wallimann, Isidor. Estrangement: Marx's Conception of Human Nature & the Division of Labor. LC 80-929. (Contributions in Philosophy: No. 16). 240p. 1981. lib. bdg. 29.95 (ISBN 0-313-22096-4, WAE/). Greenwood.

ALIENATION (SOCIAL PSYCHOLOGY)

Ilie, Paul. Literature & the Inner Exile: Authoritarian Spain, 1939-1975. LC 80-18281. 208p. 1981. text ed. 14.50x (ISBN 0-8018-2424-9). Johns Hopkins.

ALIENS

see also Citizenship; Naturalization; Self-Determination, National

also Chinese in the United States; Americans in Foreign Countries, and similar headings

Mutharika, A. Peter. The Alien Under American Law. LC 80-18236. 575p. 1980. looseleaf 85.00 (ISBN 0-379-20341-3). Oceana.

ALIMENTARY CANAL

Johnson, Leonard, et al, eds. Physiology of the Gastrointestinal Tract, 2 vols. 1600p. 1981. 130.00 (ISBN 0-89004-440-6). Raven.

Keren, David F. Immunology & Immunopathology of the Gastrointestinal Tract. LC 80-11922. (Illus.). 128p. 1980. pap. text ed. 18.00 (ISBN 0-89189-076-9, 45-1-001-00). Am Soc Clinical.

Mozsik, Gy., et al, eds. Gastrointestinal Defence Mechanisms: Proceedings of a Satellite Symposium of the 28th International Congress of Physiological Sciences, Budapest, 1980. LC 80-41883. (Advances in Physiological Sciences: Vol. 29). (Illus.). 590p. 1981. 70.00 (ISBN 0-08-027350-5). Pergamon.

ALIMENTARY CANAL–SURGERY

Shackelford, Richard T. & Zuidema, George D. Surgery of the Alimentary Tract, Vol. 2. 1981. text ed. price not set (ISBN 0-7216-8084-4). Saunders.

ALIMENTATION

see Nutrition

ALKALI INDUSTRY AND TRADE

Coulter, M. O., ed. Modern Chlor-Alkali Technology. 280p. 1980. 89.95x (ISBN 0-470-27005-5). Halsted Pr.

Warren, Kenneth. Chemical Foundations: The Alkali Industry in Britain to Nineteen Twenty-Six. (Oxford Research Studies in Geography). (Illus.). 220p. 1980. text ed. 46.00x (ISBN 0-19-823231-4). Oxford U Pr.

ALKALOIDS

see also names of Alkaloids

Cordell, Goeffrey A. Introduction to Alkaloids: A Biogenetic Approach. 1056p. 1981. 50.00 (ISBN 0-471-03478-9, Pub. by Wiley-Interscience). Wiley.

Hesse, Manfred. Alkaloid Chemistry. 384p. 1981. 22.50 (ISBN 0-471-07973-1, Pub. by Wiley-Interscience). Wiley.

ALKORAN

see Koran

ALL-VOLUNTEER FORCES

see Military Service, Voluntary

ALLEGORY (ART)

see Symbolism in Art

ALLEGORY IN LITERATURE

Leonard, Frances M. Laughhter in the Court of Love: Comedy in Allegory, from Chaucer to Spencer. 192p. 1981. 18.95 (ISBN 0-937664-54-5). Pilgrim Bks OK.

ALLERGY

see also Cookery for Allergics; Pediatric Allergy

Asthma & Allergy Foundation of America & Norback, Craig T., eds. The Allergy Encyclopedia. (Orig.). 1981. pap. price not set (ISBN 0-452-25270-9, Z5270, Plume Bks). NAL.

Booth, Sterling R., Jr. Allergy Cures Your Allergist Never Mentioned. 1981. 12.95 (ISBN 0-87949-191-4). Ashley Bks.

Byron, H. & Waksman, B. H., eds. Progress in Allergy, Vol. 29. (Illus.). 250p. 1981. 90.00 (ISBN 3-8055-2434-X). S Karger.

Conrad, Marion L. Allergy Cooking. (Orig.). pap. 2.25 (ISBN 0-515-05738-X). Jove Pubns.

Crook, William G. Tracking Down Hidden Food Allergy. 2nd ed. (Illus.). 104p. (Orig.). 1980. pap. 5.95 (ISBN 0-933478-05-4). Prof Bks.

Dehejia, Harsha V. The Allergy Book. 184p. 1981. 10.95 (ISBN 0-442-21887-7). Van Nos Reinhold.

De Weck, A. L., ed. Differentiated Lymphocyte Functions & Their Ontogeny. (Progress in Allergy Ser.: Vol. 28). (Illus.). 250p. 1981. 90.00 (ISBN 3-8055-1834-X). S Karger.

Eagle, Robert. Eating & Allergy. LC 80-1860. 216p. 1981. pap. 5.95 (ISBN 0-385-17361-X, Dolp). Doubleday.

Edebo, L., ed. Endocytosis & Exocytosis in Host Defence, Vol. 17. (Monographs in Allergy). (Illus.). 240p. 1981. pap. 78.00 (ISBN 3-8055-1865-X). S Karger.

Forman, Robert. How to Control Your Allergies. 256p. (Orig.). 1979. pap. 1.95 (ISBN 0-915962-29-2). Larchmont Bks.

Giannini, Allan V. The Best Guide to Allergy. (Appleton Consumer Health Guides). 160p. 1981. 12.95 (ISBN 0-8385-0645-3); pap. 5.95 (ISBN 0-8385-0644-5). ACC.

Knight, Allan. Asthma, Hay Fever & Other Allergies. LC 80-22839. (Positive Health Guides Ser.). (Illus.). 112p. 1981. 9.95 (ISBN 0-668-04675-9); pap. 5.95 (ISBN 0-668-04681-3). Arco.

Melillo, G., et al, eds. Respiratory Allergy. 214p. 26.50. Masson Pub.

O'Connell, Edward J., et al. Self-Assessment of Current Knowledge in Pediatric Allergy. LC 79-91200. 1980. pap. 18.00 (ISBN 0-87488-238-9). Med Exam.

Smolensky, M. H. & Reinberg, A., eds. Recent Advances of the Chronobiology of Allergy & Immunology: Symposium on Chronobiology in Allergy & Immunology, Israel, 1979. LC 80-41028. (Illus.). 350p. 1980. 50.00 (ISBN 0-08-025891-3). Pergamon.

ALLEYS

see Streets

ALLIED HEALTH PERSONNEL

see also Medical Technologists; Nurses' Aides

Weston, Alan. Survey of Allied Health Professions. (Illus.). 224p. pap. text ed. 12.95 (ISBN 0-933014-63-5). College-Hill.

ALLIGATOR PEAR

see Avocado

ALLITERATION

Levy, Bernard & Szarmach, Paul, eds. The Alliterative Tradition in the Fourteenth Century. LC 80-84665. 230p. 1980. write for info. (ISBN 0-87338-255-2). Kent St U Pr.

ALLORHYTHMIA

see Arrhythmia

ALLOYS

see also Metallurgy; Pewter

also aluminum Alloys, Steel Alloys and similar headings

Morgan, S. W. Zinc & Its Alloys. (Illus.). 224p. 1977. pap. 13.95x (ISBN 0-7121-0945-5, Pub. by Macdonald & Evans England). Intl Ideas.

ALMANACS

see also Calendars; Yearbooks

Cousteau, Jacques-Yves & Cousteau Society Staff. The Cousteau Almanac of the Environment: An Inventory of Life on a Water Planet. LC 79-7862. (Illus.). 864p. 1981. pap. 12.95 (ISBN 0-385-14876-3, Dolp). Doubleday.

The Old Farmer's Almanac. (Illus.). 176p. 1980. pap. 1.00. Yankee Bks.

The Old Farmers's Almanac Gardner's Companion. (Illus.). 144p. 1980. pap. 1.50 (ISBN 0-911658-99-8). Yankee Bks.

Reader's Digest, ed. Reader's Digest Nineteen-Eighty One Almanac & Yearbook. 16th ed. (Illus.). 1981. 6.95 (ISBN 0-89577-090-3, Pub. by Reader's Digest Assoc). Norton.

Sloane, Eric. Sloan's Almanac & Weather Forecaster. 1977. pap. 3.50 (ISBN 0-8015-6877-3, Hawthorn). Dutton.

Wallace, Irving, et al. The People's Almanac Presents the Book of Lists, No. 2. 576p. 1981. pap. 2.95 (ISBN 0-553-13101-X). Bantam.

Whitaker's Almanac, 1981. 113th ed. (Illus.). 2000p. 1981. 32.00 (ISBN 0-8103-0947-5). Gale.

ALMS AND ALMS-GIVING

see Charity

ALOPECIA

see Baldness

ALPHA FETOPROTEINS

Kirkpatrick. Alpha-Getoprotein: Laboratory Procedures & Clinical Applications. 1981. write for info. Masson Pub.

ALPHABET

see also Alphabets; Initial Teaching Alphabet; Runes; Writing

also subdivision Alphabet, or Writing under groups of languages, or under particular languages, e.g. Greek Languages–Alphabet, Chinese Language–Writing

ABC. (Block Bk.). (Illus.). (ps). 1981. 2.50 (ISBN 0-686-69364-7, Golden Pr). Western Pub.

Bourke, Linda. Handmade ABC: A Manual Alphabet. LC 80-27007. (Illus.). 64p. (gr. 1-9). 1981. PLB 6.95 (ISBN 0-201-00016-4, A-W Childrens); pap. 3.95 (ISBN 0-201-00015-6). A-W.

Brown, Richard, illus. Sesame Street Do-It-Yourself Alphabet Book. (Golden Play & Learn Ser.). 14p. (ps). Date not set. pap. 2.95 (ISBN 0-307-13647-7, Golden Pr). Western Pub.

Goines, David L. A Constructed Roman Alphabet. 1981. 40.00 (ISBN 0-87923-391-5); ltd. ed. 140.00 (ISBN 0-87923-376-1). Godine.

Humez, Alexander & Humez, Nicholas. From Alpha to Omega. (Illus.). 256p. 1980. write for info. (ISBN 0-87923-386-9). Godine.

Kennedy, X. J. Did Adam Name the Vinegarron? (Illus.). 32p. 1980. 10.00 (ISBN 0-87923-389-3). Godine.

Menten, Ted. The Illuminated Alphabet. (Illus.). 1978. pap. 1.50 (ISBN 0-486-22745-6). Dover.

Stifle, J. M. ABC Book About Christmas. 1981. pap. 2.95 (ISBN 0-570-04053-1, 56-1714). Concordia.

--ABC Book About Jesus. 1981. pap. 2.95 (ISBN 0-570-04054-X, 56-1715). Concordia.

--Set of ABC Books, 2 bks. 1981. pap. 5.25 (ISBN 0-570-04055-8, 56-1716). Concordia.

Youldon, Gillian. Alphabet. (All A-Board Bks). 16p. (ps-2). 1981. 3.50 (ISBN 0-686-69397-3). Watts.

ALPHABET, INITIAL TEACHING

see Initial Teaching Alphabet

ALPHABETING

see also Files and Filing (Documents)

Lehnus, Donald J. Book Numbers: Their History, Principles, and Application. LC 80-23100. 158p. 1980. pap. 7.50 (ISBN 0-8389-0316-9). ALA.

ALPHABETS

see also Lettering

Grafton, Carol B. Bizarre & Ornamental Alphabets. (Illus.). 128p. (Orig.). 1981. pap. price not set (ISBN 0-486-24105-X). Dover.

Haden, Peter. Elementary Knowledge: A Story of the Creation of the Hebrew Alphabet. (Illus.). 68p. 1981. 22.50 (ISBN 0-87663-357-2). Universe.

Morice, Dave. A Visit from St. Alphabet. (Illus.). 20p. (Orig.). (gr. 3 up). 1980. pap. 5.00 (ISBN 0-915124-47-5). Toothpaste.

ALPINE FLORA

see also Alpine Gardens

Costin, Alec, et al. Kosciusko Alpine Flora. 408p. 1980. 35.00x (ISBN 0-643-02473-5, Pub. by CSIRO Australia). Intl Schol Bk Serv.

Kosciusko Alpine Flora. 408p. 1979. 37.50 (ISBN 0-643-02473-5, CO06, CSIRO). Unipub.

Miller, Millie. Kinnikinnick: The Mountain Flower Book. Date not set. pap. 3.95 (ISBN 0-933472-09-9). Johnson Colo.

ALPINE GARDENS

Ingwersen, Will. Alpine Garden Plants in Color. (Illus.). 168p. 1981. 12.95 (ISBN 0-7137-0968-5, Pub. by Blandford Pr England); pap. 6.95 (ISBN 0-7137-1143-4). Sterling.

ALSACE

Ellis, Geoffrey. Napoleon's Continental Blockade: The Case of Alsace. (Oxford Historical Monographs). (Illus.). 368p. 1981. 49.95 (ISBN 0-19-821881-8). Oxford U Pr.

ALTERNATIVE EDUCATION

see Non-Formal Education

ALTIMETER

Gracey, William. Measurement of Aircraft Speed & Altitude. 300p. 1980. 30.00 (ISBN 0-471-08511-1, Pub. by Wiley-Interscience). Wiley.

ALUCONIDAE

see Owls

ALUMNI

see Universities and Colleges–Alumni

AMALGAMATION OF CORPORATIONS

see Consolidation and Merger of Corporations

AMATEUR JOURNALISM

see Journalism

AMAUROSIS

see Blindness

AMAZON RIVER AND VALLEY

Goulding, Michael. The Fishes & the Forest: Explorations in Amazonian Natural History. LC 80-41201. (Illus.). 250p. 1981. 20.00x (ISBN 0-520-04131-3). U of Cal Pr.

Smith, Nigel J. Man, Fishes, & the Amazon. 176p. 1981. 20.00x (ISBN 0-231-05156-5). Columbia U Pr.

AMBULATORY CARE

see Ambulatory Medical Care

AMBULATORY MEDICAL CARE

see also Hospitals–Outpatient Services

Downie, Patricia A. & Kennedy, Pat. Lifting, Handling & Helping Patients. (Illus.). 160p. 1981. 19.95 (ISBN 0-571-11630-2, Pub. by Faber & Faber); pap. 8.95 (ISBN 0-571-11631-0). Merrimack Bk Serv.

Memo to Ambulatory Health Care Planners. 70p. (Orig.). 1976. pap. text ed. 2.00 (ISBN 0-89192-310-1). Interbk Inc.

Stratmann, William C. & Ullman, Ralph. Evaluating Hospital-Based Ambulatory Care: A Case Study. LC 77-11403. 1980. 24.95 (ISBN 0-669-02096-6). Lexington Bks.

AMERICA–BIBLIOGRAPHY

Davies, Peter, ed. The American Heritage Dictionary. Date not set. pap. 2.50 (ISBN 0-440-10207-3). Dell.

AMERICA–BIOGRAPHY

Friesen, Raymond L. From Furrows to Freeways. 1981. 6.95 (ISBN 0-533-04712-9). Vantage.

National Cyclopedia of American Biography, Vol. 59. 1980. 69.50 (ISBN 0-88371-031-5). J T White.

AMERICA–CIVILIZATION

Davies, Peter, ed. The American Heritage Dictionary. Date not set. pap. 2.50 (ISBN 0-440-10207-3). Dell.

Ford, James A. A Comparison of Formative Cultures in the Americas. (Illus.). 211p. 1969. 45.00x (ISBN 0-87474-159-9). Smithsonian.

Girgus, Sam B., ed. The American Self: Myth, Ideology, & Popular Culture. 288p. 1980. 20.00x (ISBN 0-8263-0557-1). U of NM Pr.

AMERICA–DESCRIPTION AND TRAVEL

Aerial Photo. Aerial America: From Sea to Shining Sea. Date not set. 3.95 (ISBN 0-936672-11-0). Aerial Photo.

Wagner, Eliot. My America. 1980. 13.95 (ISBN 0-671-25332-8, Kenan Pr). S&S.

AMERICA–HISTORY

Clark, Malcolm, Jr. The Eden Seekers. 320p. 1981. 15.00 (ISBN 0-686-69047-8). HM.

Maddocks, Melvin. The Atlantic Crossing. Time-Life Books, ed. (The Seafarers Ser.). (Illus.). 176p. 1981. 14.95 (ISBN 0-8094-2726-5). Time Life.

Schlereth, Thomas J. Artifacts & the American Past: Techniques for the Teaching Historian. 300p. 1981. pap. 13.95 (ISBN 0-910050-47-3). AASLH.

Scitt, Authur F. America Grows. 1981. 10.95 (ISBN 0-533-04906-7). Vantage.

AMERICA–POLITICS AND GOVERNMENT

Here are entered comprehensive works on politics and government in the western hemisphere or in three or more countries of the two Americas.

Orfila, Alejandro. The Americas in the Nineteen Eighties: An Agenda for the Decade Ahead. LC 80-5935. 166p. 1980. lib. bdg. 17.25 (ISBN 0-8191-1333-6); pap. text ed. 8.75 (ISBN 0-8191-1334-4). U Pr of Amer.

AMERICAN ABORIGINES

see Indians; Indians of North America; Indians of South America, and similar headings

AMERICAN ART

see Art, American

AMERICAN AUTHORS

see Authors, American

AMERICAN CIVIL WAR

see United States–History–Civil War, 1861-1865

AMERICAN COMPOSERS

see Composers, American

AMERICAN DRAMA (COLLECTIONS)

Barlow, Judith, ed. Plays by American Women: The Early Years. 368p. 1981. pap. 3.95 (ISBN 0-380-76620-5, 76620, Bard). Avon.

Clark, Barrett H., ed. America's Lost Plays, 21 Vols. in 11. Incl. Vols. 1 & 2. 440p. 19.50x (ISBN 0-253-30650-7); Vols. 3 & 4. 500p. 15.00x (ISBN 0-253-30651-5); Vols. 9 & 10. 568p. 15.00x (ISBN 0-253-30654-X); Vols. 11 & 12. 480p. 15.00x (ISBN 0-253-30655-8); Vols. 13 & 14. 600p. 15.00x (ISBN 0-253-30656-6); Vols. 15 & 16. 492p. 15.00x (ISBN 0-253-30657-4); Vols. 17 & 18. 704p. 15.00x (ISBN 0-253-30658-2); Vols. 19 & 20. 768p. 15.00x (ISBN 0-253-30659-0); Vol. 21. 178p. 9.95x (ISBN 0-253-30660-4). LC 63-18068. 1963-69. Ind U Pr.

Jacobus, Lee. Longman Anthology of American Drama. (Illus.). 512p. 1981. pap. text ed. 14.95 (ISBN 0-582-28242-X). Longman.

AMERICAN DRAMA–HISTORY AND CRITICISM

Loney, Glenn, ed. The House of Mirth: The Play of the Novel. LC 78-75192. 220p. 1981. 13.50 (ISBN 0-8386-2416-2). Fairleigh Dickinsonn.

Vaughn, Jack A. Early American Dramatists: From the Beginnings to 1900. LC 80-53703. (World Dramatists Ser.). (Illus.). 224p. 1981. 13.95 (ISBN 0-8044-2940-5). Ungar.

AMERICAN DRAMA–HISTORY AND CRITICISM–BIBLIOGRAPHY

Harris, Richard H., ed. Modern Drama in America & England, Nineteen Fifty-Nineteen Seventy: A Guide to Information Sources. (American Literature, English Literature & World Literatures in English Ser.: Vol. 34). 400p. 1981. 32.00 (ISBN 0-8103-1493-2). Gale.

AMERICAN DRAMA–HISTORY AND CRITICISM–20TH CENTURY

Kostelanetz, Richard, ed. Scenarios. LC 80-68155. (Illus.). 1981. pap. 16.00 (ISBN 0-686-69411-2). Assembling Pr.

AMERICAN DRAWINGS

see Drawings, American

AMERICAN ESSAYS

Youngs, T. William. American Essays, 2 vols. (Orig.). 1981. Vol. 1. pap. text ed. 8.95 ea. (ISBN 0-316-97727-6). Vol. 2 (ISBN 0-316-97729-2). training manual free (ISBN 0-316-97728-4). Little.

AMERICAN FEDERATION OF LABOR AND CONGRESS OF INDUSTRIAL ORGANIZATIONS

Levenstein, Harvey. Communism, Anticommunism, & the CIO. LC 80-787. (Contributions in American History Ser.: No. 91). 360p. 1981. lib. bdg. 29.95 (ISBN 0-313-22072-7, LEC/). Greenwood.

Martin, Katherine F. Operation Dixie: The C.I.O. Organizing Committee Papers 1946-1953-a Guide to the Microfilm Edition. 154p. 1980. pap. 25.00 (ISBN 0-667-00584-6). Microfilming Corp.

AMERICAN FICTION–BIBLIOGRAPHY

Gerhardstein, Virginia B. Dickinson's American Historical Fiction. 4th ed. LC 80-23450. 328p. 1981. 15.00 (ISBN 0-8108-1362-9). Scarecrow.

AMERICAN FICTION–HISTORY AND CRITICISM

Blackman, Murray. A Guide to Jewish Themes in American Fiction, 1940-1980. LC 80-24953. 271p. 1981. lib. bdg. 15.00 (ISBN 0-8108-1380-7). Scarecrow.

Blau, Richard M. The Body Impolitic: A Reading of Four Novels by Herman Melville. 219p. 1979. pap. text ed. 42.75x (ISBN 90-6203-571-X). Humanities.

Davis, Robert C., ed. The Fictional Father: Lacanian Readings of the Text. LC 80-26222. 240p. 1981. lib. bdg. 15.00x (ISBN 0-87023-111-1). U of Mass Pr.

Hilfer, Anthony C. The Ethics of Intensity in American Fiction. 264p. 1981. text ed. 19.95x (ISBN 0-292-72029-7). U of Tex Pr.

Kirby, David. America's Hive of Honey: Foreign Influences on American Fiction Through Henry James. LC 80-20672. 231p. 1980. 12.50 (ISBN 0-8108-1349-1). Scarecrow.

Male, Roy R., ed. Money Talks: Language & Lucre in American Fiction. LC 80-5945. 160p. 1981. 14.95 (ISBN 0-8061-1754-0). U of Okla Pr.

Pattee, Fred L., ed. Century Readings in the American Short Story. 562p. 1980. Repr. of 1927 ed. lib. bdg. 40.00 (ISBN 0-89760-708-2). Telegraph Bks.

Pilkington, William T. Critical Essays on the Western American Novel. (Reference Bks). 1980. lib. bdg. 25.00 (ISBN 0-8161-8351-1). G K Hall.

Smith, Allan G. The Analysis of Motives: Early American Psychology & Fiction. (Costerus Ser.). 189p. 1980. pap. text ed. 23.00x (ISBN 90-6203-861-1). Humanities.

Stafford, William T. Books Speaking to Books: A Contextual Approach to American Fiction. LC 80-25892. 224p. 1981. 16.50x (ISBN 0-686-69544-5). U of NC Pr.

AMERICAN FICTION–HISTORY AND CRITICISM–19TH CENTURY

Reed, Walter L. An Exemplary History of the Novel: The Quixotic Versus the Picaresque. LC 80-17908. 1981. lib. bdg. 22.00x (ISBN 0-226-70683-4). U of Chicago Pr.

Smith, Henry N. Democracy & the Novel: Popular Resistance to Classic American Writers. 214p. 1981. pap. 5.95 (ISBN 0-19-502896-1, GB 633, OPB). Oxford U Pr.

AMERICAN FICTION–HISTORY AND CRITICISM–20TH CENTURY

Blouet, Brian W. & Stitcher, Teresa L., eds. The Origins of Academic Geography in the United States. 1981. 37.50 (ISBN 0-208-01881-6, Archon). Shoe String.

AMERICAN FOLK-LORE

see Folk-Lore, American

AMERICAN INDIANS

see Indians; Indians of North America; Indians of South America, and similar headings

AMERICAN LEGENDS

see Legends, American

AMERICAN LETTERS

Beers, Henry A. Initial Studies in American Letters. 291p. 1980. Repr. of 1895 ed. lib. bdg. 30.00 (ISBN 0-89987-063-5). Darby Bks.

Forgue, Guy J., ed. Letters of H. L. Mencken. 506p. Date not set. price not set (ISBN 0-930350-17-0); pap. price not set (ISBN 0-930350-18-9). NE U Pr.

Nelson, Randy F. Almanac of American Letters. 350p. (Orig.). 1981. 16.95 (ISBN 0-86576-018-7); pap. 9.95 (ISBN 0-86576-008-X). W Kaufmann.

AMERICAN LIBRARY ASSOCIATION

Young, Arthur P. Books for Sammies: The American Library Association During World War I. (Beta Phi Mu Chapbook Ser.: No. 15). (Illus.). 175p. 1981. write for info. (ISBN 0-910230-15-3). Beta Phi Mu.

AMERICAN LITERATURE (COLLECTIONS)

Here are entered only collections from several authors. For collections of a particular period, see appropriate subdivision below, e.g. American Literature–Colonial and Revolutionary periods.

see also College Readers; Spanish-American Literature

Hogan, Edward J., et al, eds. The Aspect Anthology. (Illus.). 250p. (Orig.). 1981. pap. 3.95 (ISBN 0-939010-01-1). Zephyr.

AMERICAN LITERATURE (COLLECTIONS)–19TH CENTURY

Edel, Leon, ed. The Bodley Head Henry James, 11 vols. Incl. Vol. 1. The Europeans, Washington Square. 392p (ISBN 0-370-00616-X); Vol. 2. The Awkward Age. 430p (ISBN 0-370-00617-8); Vol. 3. The Bostonians. 448p (ISBN 0-370-00625-9); Vol. 4. The Spoils of Poynton. 208p (ISBN 0-370-00626-7); Vol. 5. The Portrait of a Lady. 626p (ISBN 0-370-00640-2); Vol. 6. What Maisie Knew. 284p (ISBN 0-370-00586-4); Vol. 7. The Wings of the Dove. 540p (ISBN 0-370-01423-5); Vol. 8. The Ambassadors. 468p (ISBN 0-370-01432-4); Vol. 9. The Golden Bowl. 604p (ISBN 0-370-01456-1); Vol. 10. The Princess Casamassima. 618p (ISBN 0-370-10237-1); Vol. 11. Daisy Miller, the Turn of the Screw. 198p (ISBN 0-370-10532-X). 1980. 12.95 ea. (Pub. by Chatto Bodley Jonathan); 130.00 set. Merrimack Bk Serv.

AMERICAN LITERATURE (COLLECTIONS)–20TH CENTURY

Bander, E. Mr. Dooley & Mr. Dunne. 150p. 1981. text ed. 12.50 (ISBN 0-87215-329-0). Michie.

Edel, Leon, ed. The Bodley Head Henry James, 11 vols. Incl. Vol. 1. The Europeans, Washington Square. 392p (ISBN 0-370-00616-X); Vol. 2. The Awkward Age. 430p (ISBN 0-370-00617-8); Vol. 3. The Bostonians. 448p (ISBN 0-370-00625-9); Vol. 4. The Spoils of Poynton. 208p (ISBN 0-370-00626-7); Vol. 5. The Portrait of a Lady. 626p (ISBN 0-370-00640-2); Vol. 6. What Maisie Knew. 284p (ISBN 0-370-00586-4); Vol. 7. The Wings of the Dove. 540p (ISBN 0-370-01423-5); Vol. 8. The Ambassadors. 468p (ISBN 0-370-01432-4); Vol. 9. The Golden Bowl. 604p (ISBN 0-370-01456-1); Vol. 10. The Princess Casamassima. 618p (ISBN 0-370-10237-1); Vol. 11. Daisy Miller, the Turn of the Screw. 198p (ISBN 0-370-10532-X). 1980. 12.95 ea. (Pub. by Chatto Bodley Jonathan); 130.00 set. Merrimack Bk Serv.

AMERICAN LITERATURE (SELECTIONS: EXTRACTS, ETC.)

Thoreau, Henry D. Walden 2vols. Sanborn, F. B., ed. LC 80-2685. 1981. Repr. of 1909 ed. 58.50 (ISBN 0-404-19080-4). AMS Pr.

AMERICAN LITERATURE–ADDRESSES, ESSAYS, LECTURES

Blackmur, R. P. Language As Gesture. LC 80-28610. (Morningside Book Ser.). 448p. 1981. pap. 8.50 (ISBN 0-231-05295-2). Columbia U Pr.

Graziano, Frank, ed. Homage to Robert Penn Warren. 80p. (Orig.). 1981. price not set (ISBN 0-937406-12-0); pap. price not set (ISBN 0-937406-11-2); price not set limited ed. (ISBN 0-937406-13-9). Logbridge-Rhodes.

Spiller, Robert E. Late Harvest: Essays & Addresses in American Literature & Culture. LC 80-543. (Contributions to American Studies: No. 49). xi, 280p. 1981. lib. bdg. 25.00 (ISBN 0-313-22023-9, SLH/). Greenwood.

AMERICAN LITERATURE–AFRO-AMERICAN AUTHORS

see also Afro-American Authors

Davidson, James J. The Vision of an Artist & Writer. 1981. 6.95 (ISBN 0-533-04806-0). Vantage.

AMERICAN LITERATURE–AFRO-AMERICAN AUTHORS–BIBLIOGRAPHY

Hall, Wendy, ed. Rare Afro-Americana: A Reconstruction of the Adger Library. (Reference Book Ser.). 1981. 25.00 (ISBN 0-8161-8175-6). G K Hall.

Research Libraries of the New York Public Library, the Schomburg Collection & the Library of Congress. Bibliographic Guide to Black Studies: 1980. (Library Catalogs-Bib. Guides Ser.). 1981. lib. bdg. 70.00 (ISBN 0-8161-6882-2). G K Hall.

AMERICAN LITERATURE–AFRO-AMERICAN AUTHORS–HISTORY AND CRITICISM

Barthold, Bonnie J. Black Time: Fiction of Africa, the Caribbean, & the United States. LC 80-24336. (Illus.). 224p. 1981. 17.50x (ISBN 0-300-02573-4). Yale U Pr.

Miller, Ronald B., ed. Black American Literature & Humanism. LC 80-5179. 122p. 1981. price not set (ISBN 0-8131-1436-5). U Pr of Ky.

AMERICAN LITERATURE–BIBLIOGRAPHY

Corse, Larry B. & Corse, Sandra B. Articles on American & British Literature: An Index to Selected Periodicals, 1950-1977. 450p. 1981. 30.00x (ISBN 0-8040-0408-0). Swallow.

AMERICAN LITERATURE–DICTIONARIES, INDEXES, ETC.

Sherwin, J. Stephen. A Word Index to Walden, Turth Textual Notes. LC 80-2517. 1981. Repr. of 1960 ed. 24.50 (ISBN 0-404-19065-0). AMS Pr.

AMERICAN LITERATURE–HISTORY AND CRITICISM

American Family Styles: Current Guide to the Literature. (Spcialized Bibliography Ser.: No. 4). 1981. 8.95 (ISBN 0-915574-11-X). Soc Sci & Soc Res.

Andrews, William L. Literary Romanticism in America. LC 80-24365. 168p. 1981. 14.95x (ISBN 0-8071-0760-3). La State U Pr.

Collisn, W. Lucas. Lucian. 180p. 1981. Repr. lib. bdg. 30.00 (ISBN 0-89987-113-5). Darby Bks.

Davis, Thomas M. & Davis, Virginia L. The Unpublished Writings of Edward Taylor, 3 vols. (American Literary Manuscripts Ser.). 1981. Set. lib. bdg. 90.00 (ISBN 0-8057-9655-X). Twayne.

Kime, Wayne. Washington Irving Miscellaneous Writings, 1803-1859. (Critical Editions Program). 1981. lib. bdg. 75.00 (ISBN 0-8057-8520-5). Twayne.

Leary, Lewis, intro. by. American Literature to Nineteen Hundred. 1981. pap. 8.95 (ISBN 0-312-02876-8). St Martin.

Luccock, Halford E. Contemporary American Literature & Religion. 300p. 1980. Repr. of 1934 ed. lib. bdg. 30.00 (ISBN 0-89984-324-7). Century Bookbindery.

MacLaine, Allan, intro. by. The Beginnings to Fifteen Fifty-Eight. 96p. 1981. pap 4.95 (ISBN 0-312-07190-6). St Martin.

Muir, Kenneth, intro. by. The Romantic Period. 140p. 1981. pap. 5.95 (ISBN 0-312-69174-2). St Martin.

Nagel, James & Astro, Richard, eds. American Literature: The New England Heritage. LC 80-8517. 250p. 1981. lib. bdg. 30.00 (ISBN 0-8240-9467-0). Garland Pub.

Raghavacharyulu, D. V. The Critical Response: Selected Essays on the American, Commonwealth,Indian & British Traditions in Literature. 1980. 13.50x (ISBN 0-8364-0632-X, Pub. by Macmillan India). South Asia Bks.

Smith, Allan G. The Analysis of Motives: Early American Psychology & Fiction. (Costerus Ser.). 189p. 1980. pap. text ed. 23.00x (ISBN 90-6203-861-1). Humanities.

Smith, Henry N. Democracy & the Novel: Popular Resistance to Classic American Writers. (A Galaxy Book: No. 633). 214p. 1981. pap. 5.95 (SBN 0-19-502896-1). Oxford U Pr.

Westbrook, Perry D. Acres of Flint: Sarah Orne Jewett & Her Contemporaries. rev. ed. LC 80-20501. 204p. 1981. 12.50 (ISBN 0-8108-1357-2). Scarecrow.

AMERICAN LITERATURE–HISTORY AND CRITICISM–19TH CENTURY

Gura, Philip F. The Wisdom of Words: Language, Theology, & Literature in the New England Renaissance. 192p. 1981. 17.50 (ISBN 0-8195-5053-1). Wesleyan U Pr.

Jenkins, Lee C. Faulkner & Black-White Relations: A Psychoanalytic Approach. LC 80-21937. 288p. 1981. 20.00x (ISBN 0-231-04744-4). Columbia U Pr.

Ziff, Larzer. Literary Democracy: The Declaration of Cultural Independence in America 1837-1861. 1981. 17.95 (ISBN 0-670-43026-9). Viking Pr.

AMERICAN LITERATURE–HISTORY AND CRITICISM–20TH CENTURY

French, Warren. Twentieth Century American Literature. 672p. 1981. pap. 12.95 (ISBN 0-312-82401-7). St Martin.

Friedman, Lenemaja, ed. Shirley Jackson. LC 74-31244. (Twayne's U. S. Authors Ser.). 182p. 1975. pap. text ed. 4.95 (ISBN 0-672-61507-X). Bobbs.

Holder, Alan. The Imagined Past. LC 78-75202. 298p. 1980. 22.50 (ISBN 0-8387-2319-5). Bucknell U Pr.

Kostelanetz, Richard, et al, eds. Tenth Assembling. LC 80-68188. (Assembling Ser.). (Illus.). 200p. 1981. pap. 4.95 (ISBN 0-686-69410-4). Assembling Pr.

Lee, Lynn. Don Marquis. (United States Authors Ser: No. 393). 1981. lib. bdg. 11.95 (ISBN 0-8057-7282-0). Twayne.

AMERICAN MUSIC

see Music, American

AMERICAN PAINTING

see Painting, American

AMERICAN PAINTINGS

see Paintings, American

AMERICAN PHILOSOPHY

see Philosophy, American

AMERICAN POETRY (COLLECTIONS)

see also Latin-American Poetry (Collections)

Bozhilov, Bozhidar. American Pages. Bozhilova, Cornelia, tr. LC 80-83427. (International Poetry: Vol. 5). 40p. 1981. 10.95 (ISBN 0-8214-0596-9); pap. 6.95 (ISBN 0-8214-0597-7). Ohio U Pr.

Cassin, Maxine, et al, eds. The Maple Leaf Rag: An Anthology of New Orleans Poetry. (Illus.). 116p. (Orig.). 1980. pap. 4.95x (ISBN 0-938498-01-0). New Orleans Poetry.

Hearn, Michael P., ed. Breakfast, Books & Dreams: A Day in Verse. LC 80-13498. (Illus.). 48p. (gr. 7-10). 1981. 9.95g (ISBN 0-7232-6189-X). Warne.

Hogan, Edward J., et al, eds. The Aspect Anthology. (Illus.). 250p. (Orig.). 1981. pap. 3.95 (ISBN 0-939010-01-1). Zephyr.

Kennedy, X. J., ed. The Tygers of Wrath: Poems of Hate, Anger, & Invective. LC 80-23212. 272p. 1981. 15.00 (ISBN 0-8203-0535-9). U of Ga Pr.

Lewis, Janet. Poems Old & New: 1918-1978. LC 80-26209. xvi, 112p. 1981. 11.00 (ISBN 0-8040-0371-8); pap. 5.95 (ISBN 0-8040-0372-6). Swallow.

AMERICAN POETRY (COLLECTIONS)–20TH CENTURY

Allen, Donald & Butterick, George F., eds. The Postmoderns: The New American Poetry Revised. rev. ed. LC 79-52054. 512p. 1981. pap. 9.95 postponed (ISBN 0-394-17458-5, Ever). Grove.

Ambrosek, Jim, et al. Third Season-Seven Poets: Poetry by Seven Eastern Oregon Poets. Gullikson, Sandra S., ed. 28p. (Orig.). 1980. pap. 3.50 (ISBN 0-9605512-0-4). Clearwater OR.

Poems by Members of the Louise Bogen Poetry Society. 1980. write for info. Crambruck.

AMERICAN POETRY–AFRO-AMERICAN AUTHORS

Ngafua, Zizwe. Nommo (the Word) (Illus.). 56p. (Orig.). 1978. pap. 4.00 (ISBN 0-917886-04-6). Shamal Bks.

AMERICAN POETRY–HISTORY AND CRITICISM

Berke, Roberta. Bounds Out of Bounds: A Compass for Recent American & British Poetry. 192p. 1981. 14.95 (ISBN 0-19-502872-4). Oxford U Pr.

Davis, Thomas M. & Davis, Virginia L., eds. Edward Taylor's Minor Poetry, Vol. 3. (American Literary Manuscripts Ser.). 1981. lib. bdg. 35.00 (ISBN 0-8057-9654-1). Twayne.

DeFord, Sara & Lott, Clarinda H. Forms of Verse, British & American. LC 77-94257. 393p. Repr. 12.95 (ISBN 0-390-26000-2). New Poets.

AMERICAN PORTRAITS

see Portraits

AMERICAN POTTERY

see Pottery, American

AMERICAN PROPAGANDA
see Propaganda, American
AMERICAN PROSE LITERATURE–HISTORY AND CRITICISM
Hellmann, John. Fables of Fact: The New Journalism As New Fiction. LC 80-23881. 175p. 1981. 11.95 (ISBN 0-252-00847-2). U of Ill Pr.
AMERICAN REPUBLICS
see America–Politics and Government
AMERICAN REVOLUTION
see United States–History–Revolution, 1775-1783
AMERICAN SCULPTURE
see Sculpture–United States
AMERICAN-SPANISH WAR, 1898
see United States–History–War of 1898
AMERICAN STATESMEN
see Statesmen–United States
AMERICAN TALES
see Tales, American
AMERICAN TELEPHONE AND TELEGRAPH COMPANY
Kleinfield, Sonny. The Biggest Company on Earth: A Profile of AT&T. LC 80-13095. 352p. 1981. 14.95 (ISBN 0-03-045326-7). HR&W.
AMERICAN THOROUGHBRED HORSE
see Thoroughbred Horse
AMERICAN WIT AND HUMOR
Aragones, Sergio. Mad As a Hatter. (Mad Ser.). (Illus., Orig.). 1981. pap. 1.75 (ISBN 0-446-94116-6). Warner Bks.
--Mad Marginals. (Mad Ser.). (Illus.). 1974. pap. 1.75 (ISBN 0-446-94284-7). Warner Bks.
Block, Herb. Herblock on All Fronts. 1981. pap. 7.95 (ISBN 0-452-25266-0, Z5266, Plume). NAL.
Boskin, Joseph. Humor & Social Change in Twentieth Century America. pap. 8.00 (ISBN 0-89073-061-X). Boston Public Lib.
Bothwell, Dick. Bum Stories. (Illus.). 60p. (Orig.). 1980. pap. 3.95x (ISBN 0-9605382-0-8). St Petersburg Times.
Carroll, Caroll. You May Quote Me. 1980. 4.95 (ISBN 0-87786-004-1). Gold Penny.
Cork, Seamus. Irish Erotic Art. 96p. 1981. 5.95 (ISBN 0-312-43601-7). St Martin.
Eads, Douglas H. The Care & Handling of the 1000 LB. Dog. (Illus.). 96p. (Orig.). 1980. pap. 4.95 (ISBN 0-89769-019-2). Pine Mntn.
Hill, L. A. Elementary Anecdotes in American English. (Anecdotes in American English Ser.). (Illus.). 72p. 1980. 2.50x (ISBN 0-19-502601-2). Oxford U Pr.
Hollander, Nicole. That Woman Must Be on Drugs. (Illus.). 128p. 1981. pap. 3.95 (ISBN 0-312-79510-6). St Martin.
Jacobs, Frank & Clarke, Bob. Mad Goes Wild. (Mad Ser.). (Illus., Orig.). 1981. pap. 1.75 (ISBN 0-446-94283-9). Warner Bks.
Jaffee, Al. Al Jaffee Fowls His Nest. 1981. pap. 1.95 (ISBN 0-451-09741-6, J9741). NAL.
--Good Lord! Not Another Book of Snappy Answers to Stupid Questions. (Mad Ser.). (Illus., Orig.). 1980. pap. 1.75 (ISBN 0-446-94450-5). Warner Bks.
Leininger, Steve. The Official Russian Joke Book. 192p. (Orig.). 1981. pap. 1.95 (ISBN 0-523-41427-7). Pinnacle Bks.
Mad Magazine Editors. Mad for Kicks. (Mad Ser.: No. 54). (Illus., Orig.). 1980. pap. 1.50 (ISBN 0-446-98461-2). Warner Bks.
Markoe, Karen & Phillips, Louis. Nutty Nock-Nocks. (Funnybones Ser.). (Illus.). 64p. (gr. 3-7). 1981. pap. 1.50 (ISBN 0-671-42249-9). Wanderer Bks.
--Sneakers. (Funnybones Ser.). (Illus.). 64p. 1981. pap. 1.50 (ISBN 0-671-42117-4). Wanderer Bks.
Meglin, Nick & Woodbridge, George. Sound of Mad. (Mad Ser.). (Illus., Orig.). 1980. pap. 1.50 (ISBN 0-446-88844-3). Warner Bks.
The Perfect Squelch: Last Laughs from the Saturday Evening Post. LC 80-67061. (Illus.). 1980. 5.95 (ISBN 0-89387-042-0). Sat Eve Post.
Porges, Peter P. How-Not-to-Do-It Book. (Mad Ser.). (Illus., Orig.). 1981. pap. 1.75 (ISBN 0-446-94190-5). Warner Bks.
Post Scripts: Humor from the Saturday Evening Post. LC 78-53039. (Illus.). 1978. 4.95 (ISBN 0-89387-022-6). Sat Eve Post.
Stokes, Jack. Monster Madness Outrageous Jokes About Weird Folks. LC 80-2068. (Illus.). 64p. (gr. 6). 1981. 8.95a (ISBN 0-385-15690-1); PLB (ISBN 0-385-15691-X). Doubleday.
AMERICAN WIT AND HUMOR–ANIMALS
Jaffee, Al. Al Jaffee Hogs the Show. (Orig.). 1981. pap. price not set (ISBN 0-451-09908-7, Sig). NAL.
Sayre, Lombard. Celestial Shaggy Dog Joke, No.2. (Illus.). 51p. (Orig.). 1980. pap. 3.95 (ISBN 0-89260-194-9). Hwong Pub.
AMERICAN WIT AND HUMOR–JUVENILE LITERATURE
Brandreth, Gyles. Total Nonsense Z to A. LC 80-54349. (Illus.). 96p. (gr. 4 up). 1981. 5.95; lib. bdg. 6.69 (ISBN 0-8069-4645-8). Sterling.
Gounaud, Karen J. A Very Nice Joke Book. 1981. 6.95 (ISBN 0-395-30445-8); pap. text ed. 2.95 (ISBN 0-395-30442-3). HM.
Rosenbloom, Joseph. Snappy Put-Downs & Funny Insults. LC 80-54348. (Illus.). 128p. (gr. 3-6). 1981. 5.95 (ISBN 0-8069-4646-6); lib. bdg. 6.69 (ISBN 0-8069-4647-4). Sterling.
AMERICAN WIT AND HUMOR–MARRIAGE AND FAMILY LIFE
Bracken, Peg. A Window Over the Sink: A Mainly Affectionate Memoir. 1981. 10.95 (ISBN 0-15-196986-8). HarBraceJ.
Hoest, Bill. I See You Burned the Cold Cuts Again. (Lockhorns No. 5). (Orig.). 1981. pap. 1.50 (ISBN 0-451-09711-4, J9711, Sig). NAL.
Phillips, Bob. A Humorous Look at Love & Marriage. LC 80-83841. 128p. 1981. pap. 2.25 (ISBN 0-89081-268-3). Harvest Hse.
Stewart, D. L. Fathers Are People Too. (Illus.). 128p. (Orig.). 1980. pap. 4.95 (ISBN 0-938492-01-2). Journal Herald.
AMERICAN WIT AND HUMOR–POLITICS, GOVERNMENT, ARMED SERVICES
Wubben, Pamela G. View from the Out House: The Joke's on the Bureaucrat. 100p. 1980. pap. 3.33 (ISBN 0-935442-04-9). One Percent.
AMERICAN WIT AND HUMOR–SOCIAL LIFE AND CUSTOMS
Boskin, Joseph. Humor & Social Change in Twentieth-Century America. pap. 8.00 (ISBN 0-89073-061-X). Boston Public Lib.
Scott, Hugh. The Best of Quincy Scott. LC 80-83078. (Illus.). 216p. 1980. pap. 7.95 (ISBN 0-87595-087-6). Oreg Hist Soc.
Sutherland, Douglas. The English Gentleman's Child. (Illus.). 1981. pap. 3.50 (ISBN 0-14-005782-X). Penguin.
AMERICAN WIT AND HUMOR–SPORTS AND GAMES
Sullivan, John, et al. The Funny Side of Football. (Illus.). 92p. (Orig.). 1980. pap. 3.95 (ISBN 0-89260-141-8). Hwong Pub.
AMERICAN WIT AND HUMOR, PICTORIAL
see also Comic Books, Strips, Etc.
Booth, George. Pussycats Need Love, Too. LC 80-17198. 128p. 1980. 8.95 (ISBN 0-396-07906-7). Dodd.
AMERICANISMS
Humphrey, Edward & Churchill, James E., eds. Americana Annual, 1981. LC 23-10041. (Illus.). 1981. write for info. (ISBN 0-7172-0212-7). Grolier Ed Corp.
AMERICANS IN FOREIGN COUNTRIES
Mehta, Gita. Karma Kola. 1981. pap. 5.95 (ISBN 0-671-25084-1, Touchstone). S&S.
AMERINDS
see Indians
AMILLENNIALISM
see Millennium
AMINO ACIDS
DeFeudis, Francis V. & Mandel, Paul, eds. Amino Acid Neurotransmitters, Vol. 29. (Advances in Biochemical Psychopharmacology). 500p. 1981. 45.00 (ISBN 0-89004-595-X). Raven.
Rattenbury, J. M. Amino Acid Analysis. 320p. 1981. 89.95 (ISBN 0-470-27141-8). Halsted Pr.
Whelton. The Aminoglycosides: Microbiology, Use & Toxicology. Date not set. price not set (ISBN 0-8247-1364-8). Dekker.
AMIS, KINGSLEY, 1922-
Gardner, Philip. Kingsley Amis. (English Authors Ser.: No. 319). 1981. lib. bdg. 11.95 (ISBN 0-8057-6809-2). Twayne.
AMISH COOKERY
see Cookery, American
AMMONIA
Strelzoff, Samuel. Technology & Manufacture of Ammonia. 220p. 1981. 22.00 (ISBN 0-471-02722-7, Pub. by Wiley-Interscience). Wiley.
AMMUNITION–LAW AND LEGISLATION
see Firearms–Laws and Regulations
AMNESIA
see also Aphasia
Cermack, Laird S. Human Memory & Amnesia. 400p. 1981. ref. ed. 24.95 (ISBN 0-89859-095-7). L Erlbaum Assocs.
AMNESTY
see also Pardon
Jenkins, David, et al. Lex Terrae. Berkowitz, David S. & Thorne, Samuel E., eds. LC 77-89226. (Classics of English Legal History in the Modern Era Ser.: Vol. 70). 313p. 1979. lib. bdg. 40.00 (ISBN 0-8240-3169-5). Garland Pub.
McKnight, Brian E. The Quality of Mercy: Amnesties & Traditional Chinese Justice. LC 80-26650. 224p. 1981. pap. 15.00x (ISBN 0-8248-0736-7). U Pr of Hawaii.
AMPHIBIANS
see also Frogs; Salamanders
Duellman, William E., et al. The South American Herpetofauna: Its Origin, Evolution, & Dispersal. (U of KS Museum of Nat. Hist. Monograph: No. 7). (Illus.). 485p. Date not set. 30.00 (ISBN 0-89338-009-1); pap. 25.00 (ISBN 0-89338-008-3). U of KS Mus Nat Hist.
Rivero, Juan A. Los Anfibios y Reptils de Puerto Rico. LC 76-11798. (Illus.). 448p. (Orig.). 1976. pap. write for info. (ISBN 0-8477-2317-8). U of PR Pr.
AMPHIMIXIS
see Reproduction
AMPHIPODA
Bousfield, E. L. Shallow-Water Gammaridean Ampphipoda of New England. LC 72-4636. (Illus.). 1973. 35.00x (ISBN 0-8014-0726-5). Comstock.
AMPLIFIERS (ELECTRONICS)
Irvine, Robert G. Operational Amplifier Characteristics & Applications. (Illus.). 416p. 1981. text ed. 24.95 (ISBN 0-13-637751-3). P-H.
AMPLIFIERS, PARAMETRIC
see Parametric Amplifiers
AMPUTEES
Cleland, Max. Strong at the Broken Places. 1980. 6.95 (ISBN 0-912376-55-4). Word Bks.
AMSTERDAM–DESCRIPTION
Arthur Frommer's Guide to Amsterdam - Holland, 1981-82. 224p. Date not set. pap. 2.95 (ISBN 0-671-41427-5). Frommer-Pasmantier.
AMUSEMENTS
see also Cards; College Sports; Conjuring; Creative Activities and Seatwork; Dancing; Entertaining; Games; Hobbies; Mathematical Recreations; Moving-Pictures; Performing Arts; Play; Puzzles; Recreation; Scientific Recreations; Sports; Theater; Toys
Barron, Cheryl C. & Scherzer, Cathy C. Great Parties for Young Children. (Illus.). 160p. 1981. 9.95 (ISBN 0-8027-0684-3); pap. 5.95 (ISBN 0-8027-7175-0). Walker & Co.
Eisenberg, Helen & Eisenberg, Larry. Fun & Fellowship Resource Book. (Game & Party Bks.). 160p. 1981. pap. 3.95 (ISBN 0-8010-3364-0). Baker Bk.
ANA
see Epigrams; Quotations
ANABOLISM
see Metabolism
ANAESTHESIA
see Anesthesia
ANAESTHETICS
see Anesthetics
ANAGRAMS
Estes, Helen E. Anagraphs: A Slew of Sight Puzzles. LC 80-54813. 1981. pap. 2.95. Walker & Co.
ANALOG COMPUTERS
Garrett, Patrick. Analog I-O Design: Acquisition, Conversion, Recovery. (Illus.). 1981. text ed. 21.95 (ISBN 0-8359-0208-0); solutions manual avail. Reston.
ANALYSIS (CHEMISTRY)
see Assaying; Chemistry, Analytic;
also and names of substances analyzed
ANALYSIS (MATHEMATICS)
see Calculus; Functions; Mathematical Analysis
ANALYSIS (PHILOSOPHY)
see also Logical Positivism; Semantics (Philosophy)
Bloom, Alfred H. Linguistic Shaping of Thought: A Study in the Impact of Language on Thinking in China & the West. 128p. 1981. prof. & reference 16.50 (ISBN 0-89859-089-2). L Erlbaum Assocs.
French, Peter, et al, eds. Foundations of Analytic Philosophy. (Midwest Studies in Philosophy: Vol. 6). 576p. 1981. 35.00 (ISBN 0-8166-1033-9); pap. 15.00 (ISBN 0-8166-1036-3). U of Minn Pr.
ANALYSIS, CHROMATOGRAPHIC
see Chromatographic Analysis
ANALYSIS, JOB
see Job Analysis
ANALYSIS, MICROSCOPIC
see Metallography; Microscope and Microscopy
ANALYSIS, SPATIAL (STATISTICS)
see Spatial Analysis (Statistics)
ANALYSIS, SPECTRUM
see Spectrum Analysis
ANALYSIS, STOCHASTIC
see Stochastic Analysis
ANALYSIS OF BLOOD
see Blood–Analysis and Chemistry
ANALYSIS OF CONTENT (COMMUNICATION)
see Content Analysis (Communication)
ANALYSIS OF FOOD
see Food–Analysis; Food Adulteration and Inspection
ANALYSIS OF SOILS
see Soils–Analysis
ANALYSIS OF TIME SERIES
see Time-Series Analysis
ANALYSIS SITUS
see Topology
ANALYTIC FUNCTIONS
Garnett, John B. Bounded Analytic Functions. (Pure & Applied Mathematics Ser.). 1981. price not set (ISBN 0-12-276150-2). Acad Pr.
ANALYTICAL CHEMISTRY
see Chemistry, Analytic
ANALYTICAL GEOMETRY
see Geometry, Analytic
ANALYTICAL PHILOSOPHY
see Analysis (Philosophy)
ANARCHISM AND ANARCHISTS
see also Libertarianism; Liberty; Socialism; Terrorism
Ritter, A. Anarchism. LC 80-40589. 196p. 1981. 27.50 (ISBN 0-521-23324-0). Cambridge U Pr.
Ward, Colin. Anarchism for Beginners. (Pantheon Documentary Comic Books). (Illus.). 1981. 8.95 (ISBN 0-394-50923-4); pap. 2.95 (ISBN 0-394-74822-0). Pantheon.
ANATOLIA
Todd, Ian. The Prehistoric of Central Anatolia I: The Neolithic Period. (Studies in Mediterranean Archaeology: Vol. LX). 177p. 1981. pap. text ed. 42.00x (ISBN 91-85058-87-4, Pub. by Astroms, Sweden). Humanities.
ANATOMY
see also Dissection; Histology; Nervous System; Physiology
also specific subjects, with or without the subdivision Anatomy
Cohn, Sidney A. & Gottlieb, Marvin. Anatomy Review. 6th ed. LC 80-20349. (Basic Science Review Bks.). 1980. pap. 8.50 (ISBN 0-87488-201-X). Med Exam.
Harrison, R. J. & Holmes, R. L., eds. Progress in Anatomy, Vol. 1. (Illus.). 250p. Date not set. price not set (ISBN 0-521-23603-7). Cambridge U Pr.
Romanes, G. J., ed. Cunningham's Textbook of Anatomy. 12th ed. (Illus.). 1080p. 1981. text ed. 39.50x (ISBN 0-19-263134-9). Oxford U Pr.
Rudman, Jack. Anatomy & Physiology. (College Proficiency Examination Ser.: CLEP-37). (Cloth bdg. avail. on request). pap. 9.95 (ISBN 0-8373-5437-4). Natl Learning.
ANATOMY–LABORATORY MANUALS
Erskine, Irene. Laboratory Guide for Anatomy & Physiology. 176p. 1980. pap. text ed. 8.95 (ISBN 0-8403-2350-6). Kendall-Hunt.
ANATOMY, COMPARATIVE
see also Morphology
also names of organs and regions of the body; also subdivision Anatomy under names of animals, e.g. Cats–Anatomy
Beaver, Bonnie V. Comparative Anatomy of Domestic Animals: A Guide. (Illus.). 209p. pap. 9.95 (ISBN 0-8138-1545-2). Iowa St U Pr.
Holmes, Bruce E. Manual of Comparative Anatomy: A Laboratory Guide & Brief Text. 416p. 1980. pap. text ed. 12.95 (ISBN 0-8403-2254-2). Kendall-Hunt.
ANATOMY, DENTAL
see Teeth
ANATOMY, HUMAN
see also Body, Human; Extremities (Anatomy)
also names of organs and regions of the body, e.g. Heart, Pelvis, Skull
Green, J. H. & Silver, P. H. An Introduction to Human Anatomy. (Illus.). 400p. 1981. pap. text ed. 16.95x (ISBN 0-19-261196-8). Oxford U Pr.
Hollinshead, W. Henry. Anatomia Humana. 1000p. 1981. pap. text ed. 26.00 (ISBN 0-06-313375-X, Pub. by by HarlA Mexico). Har-Row.
Lockhart, R. D., et al. Anatomy of the Human Body. (Illus.). 698p. 1981. pap. 35.00 (ISBN 0-571-07037-X, Pub. by Faber & Faber). Merrimack Bk Serv.
Snell, Richard S. Clinical Anatomy for Medical Students. 2nd ed. 1981. text ed. price not set. Little.
ANATOMY, HUMAN–ATLASES
Clemente, Carmine D. Anatomy - A Regional Atlas of the Human Body. 2nd ed. (Illus.). 392p. 1981. text ed. price not set (ISBN 0-8067-0322-9). Urban & S.
Zuckerman, et al. A New System of Anatomy: Being a Dissector's Guide & Atlas. 2nd ed. (Illus.). 650p. 1981. pap. text ed. 29.50x (ISBN 0-19-263136-5). Oxford U Pr.
ANATOMY, MICROSCOPIC
see Histology
ANATOMY, PATHOLOGICAL
see also Pathology
Lachman, Ernest & Faulkner, Kenneth K. Case Studies in Anatomy. 3rd ed. (Illus.). 432p. 1981. pap. text ed. 9.95x (ISBN 0-19-502813-9). Oxford U Pr.
ANATOMY, VEGETABLE
see Botany–Anatomy
ANATOMY OF PLANTS
see Botany–Anatomy
ANCESTRY
see Genealogy; Heredity
ANCIENT AND MYSTICAL ORDER ROSAE CRUCIS
see Rosicrucians
ANCIENT ART
see Art, Ancient
ANCIENT HISTORY
see History, Ancient
Baumgartel, Elise J. The Cultures of Prehistoric Egypt, 2 vols. in one. LC 80-24186. (Illus.). xxiii, 286p. 1981. Repr. of 1960 ed. lib. bdg. 63.33 (ISBN 0-313-22524-9, BAUC). Greenwoodd.
ANCIENT POTTERY
see Pottery, Ancient
ANDERSON, MARIAN, 1902-
Sims, Janet L., compiled by. Marian Anderson: An Annotated Bibliography & Discography. LC 80-1787. (Illus.). viii, 243p. 1981. lib. bdg. 29.95 (ISBN 0-313-22559-1, SIM/). Greenwood.
ANDERSON, MAXWELL, 1888-1959
Shivers, Alfred S. The Life of Maxwell Anderson. LC 80-5721. 356p. 1981. 16.95 (ISBN 0-8128-2789-9). Stein & Day.
ANDES
Bartle, Jim. Trails of the Cordillaras Blanca & Huayhuash of Peru. (Illus.). 160p. (Orig.). 1980. pap. 7.95 (ISBN 0-933982-10-0). Bradt Ent.
Benson, Elizabeth & Conklin, William. Museums of the Andes. Lafarge, Henry, ed. LC 80-8912. 1981. 16.95 (ISBN 0-88225-306-9). Newsweek.
ANDREWS, CHARLES FREER, 1871-1940
Schact, Joseph. The Origins of Muhammadan Jurisprudence. 364p. 1979. pap. text ed. 12.50x (ISBN 0-19-825357-5). Oxford U Pr.
Tinker, Hugh. The Ordeal of Love: C. F. Andrews & India. (Illus.). 356p. 1979. text ed. 17.95x. Oxford U Pr.

ANDROGENS
Laszlo, F. A., ed. Recent Results in Peptide Hormone & Androgenic Steroid Research. (Illus.). 325p. 1979. 30.00x (ISBN 963-05-2292-6). Intl Pubns Serv.

ANDROIDS
Engelberger, Joseph F. Robotics in Practice. 1981. 39.95 (ISBN 0-8144-5645-6). Am Mgmt.
Pattis, Richard E. Karel the Robot: A Gentle Introduction to the Art of Programming. 128p. 1981. pap. text ed. 8.95 (ISBN 0-471-08928-1). Wiley.

ANDROPOGON SORGHUM
see Sorghum

ANEMIA, DREPANOCYTIC
see Sickle Cell Anemia

ANESTHESIA
see also Anesthesia in Dentistry; Anesthesiology; Anesthetics; Hypnotism–Therapeutic Use; Pediatric Anesthesia
Brown, Robert C. Perchance to Dream: The Patient's Guide to Anesthesia. 96p. 1981. 10.95 (ISBN 0-686-69375-2). Nelson-Hall.
Hopkin, D. A. Hazards & Errors in Anaesthesia. (Illus.). 296p. 1981. pap. 24.80 (ISBN 0-387-10158-6). Springer-Verlag.
Katz, Jordan, et al. Anesthesia & Uncommon Diseases: Pathophysiologic & Clinical Correlations. 2nd ed. (Illus.). 600p. Date not set. text ed. price not set (ISBN 0-7216-5302-2). Saunders.
Miller, Ronald D., ed. Anesthesia. (Illus.). 1500p. 1981. lib. bdg. 65.00 (ISBN 0-443-08082-8). Churchill.
Ostlere, Gordon & Bryce-Smith, Roger. Anaesthetics for Medical Students. 9th ed. 148p. 1981. text ed. 9.75 (ISBN 0-443-01863-4). Churchill.
The Quantitative Practice of Anesthesia: Use of Closed Circuit. (Illus.). 220p. 1981. write for info. (5200-4). Williams & Wilkins.
Stoeckel, H. & Omaya, T. Endocrinology in Anaesthesia & Surgery. (Anaesthesiology & Intensive Care Medicine Ser.: Vol. 132). (Illus.). 205p. 1981. pap. 55.60 (ISBN 0-387-10211-6). Springer-Verlag.

ANESTHESIA, CONDUCTION
see Conduction Anesthesia

ANESTHESIA, SPINAL
see Spinal Anesthesia

ANESTHESIA IN CHILDHOOD
see Pediatric Anesthesia

ANESTHESIA IN DENTISTRY
Jastak, J. Theodore & Yagiela, John A. Regional Anesthesia of the Oral Cavity. 1st ed. (Illus.). 200p. 1981. text ed. 20.00 (ISBN 0-8016-2434-7). Mosby.
Spiro, Stanley R., ed. Pain & Anxiety Control in Dentistry. (Illus.). 340p. 1981. text ed. 37.50 (ISBN 0-937218-66-9, Pub. by Piccin Italy). J K Burgess.

ANESTHESIOLOGY
see also Anesthesia; Anesthetics
DeKornfeld, Thomas J. & Detmar, Michael W., eds. Anesthesiology. 5th ed. LC 61-66847. 1980. pap. 15.00. Med Exam.
Hill, D. W. Physics Applied to Anesthesia. 4th ed. LC 80-40011. (Illus.). 420p. 1980. text ed. 52.95 (ISBN 0-407-00188-3). Butterworths.

ANESTHETICS
see also Anesthesia; Ether (Anesthetic); Sedatives
Furst, Susanna & Knoll, J., eds. Opiate Receptors & the Neurochemical Correlates of Pain: Proceedings of the Third Congress of the Hungarian Pharmacological Society, Budapest, 1979. LC 80-41281. (Advances in Pharmacological Research & Practice Ser.: Vol. V). 240p. 1981. 45.00 (ISBN 0-08-026390-9). Pergamon.
Gorsky, Benjamin H. Pain: Origin & Treatment – Discussions in Patient Management. LC 80-15857. 1980. 18.00 (ISBN 0-87488-448-9); pap. 10.00 (ISBN 0-87488-447-0). Med Exam.

ANESTHETICS IN DENTISTRY
see Anesthesia in Dentistry

ANEURYSMS
Sahs, Adolph L., et al. Aneurysmal Subarachnoid Hemorrhage: Report of the Cooperative Study. (Illus.). write for info. (ISBN 0-8067-1861-7). Urban & S.

ANGELOLOGY
see Angels

ANGELS
D'Angelo, Dorie. Living with Angels. 1980. pap. 7.50 (ISBN 0-912216-22-0). Angel Pr.
Graham, Billy. Los Angeles: Agentes Secretos de Dios. Rojas, Juan, tr. from Eng. LC 76-20259. 168p. (Orig., Span.). 1976. pap. 2.75 (ISBN 0-89922-069-X). Edit Caribe.
Palmer, Tobias. An Angel in My House. 64p. 1981. pap. 1.95x (ISBN 0-912484-21-7). Joseph Nichols.
Richards, H. M., Jr. Angels: Secret Agents of God & Satan. LC 80-22223. (Flame Ser.). 64p. 1980. pap. 0.95 (ISBN 0-8127-0313-8). Southern Pub.

ANGER
El Coraje De Carol. 1980. pap. 1.30 (ISBN 0-686-69352-3). Vida Pubs.

ANGIOLOGY
see Blood-Vessels; Blood-Vessels–Diseases

ANGIOSPERMS
see also Dicotyledons
Hutchinson, J. The Genera of Flowering Plants: Angiospermae. 2 vols. 1200p. 1980. Repr. of 1964 ed. Set. lib. bdg. 129.60x (ISBN 0-686-28721-5); Vol. I. lib. bdg. 64.80x (ISBN 3-87429-177-4); Vol. 2. lib. bdg. 64.80x (ISBN 3-87429-178-2). Lubrecht & Cramer.
Mohlenbrock, Robert H. Flowering Plants: Magnolias to Pitcher Plants. LC 80-18529. (Illustrated Flora of Illinois Ser.). (Illus.). 256p. 1981. 18.95x (ISBN 0-8093-0920-3). S Ill U Pr.
Wolseley, Pat. A Field Key to the Flowering Plants of Iceland. 60p. 1980. pap. 8.95x (ISBN 0-906191-42-4, Pub. by Thule Pr England). Intl Schol Bk Serv.

ANGLE
Tudo Sobre Anjos. (Portuguese Bks.). 1979. 1.20 (ISBN 0-8297-0748-4). Life Pubs Intl.

ANGLICAN CHURCH
see Church of England

ANGLING
see Fishing

ANGLO-AMERICAN CATALOGING RULES
Aichele, Jean & Olson, Nancy B. A Manual of AACR 2 Examples for Motion Pictures & Videorecordings. McClasky, Marilyn J. & Swanson, Edward, eds. 50p. 1980. pap. 6.00 (ISBN 0-936996-11-0). Soldier Creek.
Blixrud, Julia C. A Manual of AACR 2 Examples for Serials. Snesrud, Janet E. & McClaskey, Marilyn J., eds. 50p. 1980. pap. 6.00 (ISBN 0-936996-04-8). Soldier Creek.
Clack, Doris H., ed. The Making of a Code: The Issues Underlying AACR2. LC 80-17496. 264p. 1980. pap. 15.00 (ISBN 0-8389-0309-6). ALA.
Filing Committee of the Resources & Technical Services Division American Library Association. ALA Filing Rules. LC 80-22186. 62p. 1980. pap. 3.50 (ISBN 0-8389-3255-X). ALA.
Hanley, Mary D. A Manual of AACR 2 Examples for Early Printed Books. Swanson, Edward & McClaskey, Marilyn J, eds. 1980. pap. 6.00 (ISBN 0-936996-10-2). Soldier Creek.
McClaskey, Marilyn J. & Swanson, Edward, eds. A Manual of AACR 2 Level 1 Examples. 50p. 1980. pap. 6.00 (ISBN 0-936996-03-X). Soldier Creek.
Marion, Phyllis. A Manual of AACR 2 Examples for Legal Materials. McClaskey, Marilyn J. & Swanson, Edward, eds. 50p. 1980. pap. 6.00 (ISBN 0-936996-08-0). Soldier Creek.
Moore, Barbara N. A Manual of AACR for Cartographic Materials. McClaskey, Marilyn J. & Swanson, Edward, eds. 50p. 1980. pap. 6.00 (ISBN 0-936996-07-2). Soldier Creek.
Rae, G., ed. Seminar on AACR2. 1980. pap. 17.50 (ISBN 0-85365-563-4, Pub. by Lib Assn England). Oryx Pr.
Schilling, Irene A. A Manual of AACR 2 Examples for Liturgical Works & Sacred Scripture. Swanson, Edward & McClaskey, Marilyn J., eds. 50p. 1980. pap. 6.00 (ISBN 0-936996-06-4). Soldier Creek.
Simonton, Wesley & Mannie, Phillip. A Manual of AACR 2 Examples for Musical Scores & Musical Sound Recordings. Swanson, Edward & McClasky, Marilyn J., eds. 1980. pap. 6.00 (ISBN 0-936996-05-6). Soldier Creek.
Swanson, Edward. A Manual of AACR 2 Examples for Manuscripts. 50p. 1980. pap. 6.00 (ISBN 0-936996-12-9). Soldier Creek.
Swanson, Edward & Jones, Marilyn H., eds. A Manual of AACR 2 Examples. 2nd ed. 87p. (Orig.). 1980. pap. 7.50 (ISBN 0-936996-01-3). Soldier Creek.
Swanson, Edward & McClaskey, Marilyn J., eds. A Manual of AACR 2 Advanced Examples. 50p. 1980. pap. 6.00 (ISBN 0-936996-02-1). Soldier Creek.

ANGLO-AMERICAN LAW
see Law–Great Britain; Law–United States

ANGLO-SAXON ART
see Art, Anglo-Saxon

ANGLO-SAXON CIVILIZATION
see Civilization, Anglo-Saxon

ANGLO-SAXON LITERATURE (COLLECTIONS)
Szarmach, Paul E., ed. Vercelli Homilies Nine to Twenty-Three. (Toronto Old English Ser.). 192p. 1981. 25.00x (ISBN 0-8020-5528-1). U of Toronto Pr.

ANGLO-SAXON LITERATURE–HISTORY AND CRITICISM
Bately, Janet, ed. The Old English Orosius. (Early English Text Society Ser.). (Illus.). 558p. 1981. 65.00 (ISBN 0-19-722406-7). Oxford U Pr.
Whitelock, Dorothy. From Bede to Alfred: Studies in Early Anglo-Saxon Literature & History. 368p. 1980. 75.00x (ISBN 0-86078-066-X, Pub. by Variorum England). State Mutual Bk.

ANGLO-SAXONS
Soames, Henry. The Anglo-Saxon Church: Its History, Revenues & General Character. 4th ed. LC 80-2212. 1981. Repr. of 1856 ed. 39.50 (ISBN 0-404-18786-2). AMS Pr.

ANGOLA
Bender, Gerald J. Angola Under the Portuguese: The Myth & the Reality. (Illus.). 315p. 1981. pap. 6.95x (ISBN 0-520-04274-3, CAMPUS 269). U of Cal Pr.

ANGORA RABBITS
see Rabbits

ANHYDROUS AMMONIA
see Ammonia

ANIMAL BEHAVIOR
see Animals, Habits and Behavior Of

ANIMAL COMMUNICATION
Pommery, Jean. How Human the Animals. LC 78-24613. 224p. 1981. pap. 6.95 (ISBN 0-8128-6086-1). Stein & Day.

ANIMAL DISEASES
see Veterinary Medicine

ANIMAL ECOLOGY
see also Adaptation (Biology); Animal Populations; Zoogeography
Dasmann, Raymond F. Wildlife Biology. 256p. 1981. text ed. 17.95 (ISBN 0-471-08042-X). Wiley.
Hayes, Harold. Three Levels of Time. 1981. 12.95 (ISBN 0-525-21853-X). Dutton.
Remmert, H. Arctic Animal Ecology. (Illus.). 250p. 1981. pap. 24.80 (ISBN 0-387-10169-1). Springer-Verlag.

ANIMAL ELECTRICITY
see Electrophysiology

ANIMAL FOLKLORE
see Animal Lore

ANIMAL FOOD
see also Vegetarianism;
also names of particular animal foods, e.g. Dairy products, Meat, etc.
Bickel, Hans, ed. Palatability & Flavor Use in Animal Feeds. (Advances in Animal Physiology & Animal Nutrition: Vol. 11). (Illus.). 148p. (Orig.). 1980. pap. text ed. 34.10 (ISBN 3-490-41115-3). Parey Sci Pubs.

ANIMAL HUSBANDRY
see Domestic Animals; Livestock

ANIMAL INSTINCT
see Instinct

ANIMAL INTELLIGENCE
see also Animals, Habits and Behavior of; Instinct; Learning, Psychology Of; Psychology, Comparative
Lindsay, William L. Mind in the Lower Animal in Health & Disease. (Contributions to the History of Psychology Ser.: Pts. 6 & 7, Comparative Psychology). 1980. Repr. of 1879 ed. 30.00 ea. U Pubns Amer.
Romanes, George J. Animal Intelligenge. (Contributions to the History of Psychology Ser.: No. 7, Pt. a: Orientations). 1978. 30.00 (ISBN 0-89093-156-9). U Pubns Amer.
Thorndike, E. L. Animal Intelligence: Experimental Studies. 1965. Repr. of 1911 ed. 11.95 (ISBN 0-02-853470-0). Hafner.

ANIMAL KINGDOM
see Zoology

ANIMAL LANGUAGE
see Animal Communication

ANIMAL LOCOMOTION–JUVENILE LITERATURE
Prince, J. H. How Animals Move. (Illus.). 160p. (YA) 1981. 10.95 (ISBN 0-525-66712-1). Elsevier-Nelson.

ANIMAL LORE
see also Animals, Mythical; Folk-Lore; Natural History
Schuman, Beatrice Chernuchin. Am I Greedy If I Want More? (Illus.). 179p. 1979. 9.95 (ISBN 0-8119-0329-X). Fell.

ANIMAL LUMINESCENCE
see Bioluminescence

ANIMAL MIGRATION
Baker, Robin, ed. The Mystery of Migration. LC 80-16839. (Illus.). 256p. 1981. 29.95 (ISBN 0-670-50286-3). Viking Pr.

ANIMAL NUTRITION
see also Feeds;
also subdivision Feeding and Feeds under names of animals and groups of animals, e.g. Poultry–Feeding and Feeds
Feed from Animal Wastes: State of Knowledge. (FAO Animal Production & Health Paper Ser.: No. 18). 201p. 1981. pap. 10.75 (ISBN 92-5-100946-5, F2100, FAO). Unipub.
Hardman, A. C. Equine Nutrition. (Illus.). 128p. 1981. 17.95 (ISBN 0-7207-1244-0). Merrimack Bk Serv.
Haresign, W., ed. Recent Advances in Animal Nutrition. LC 80-41606. (Studies in the Agricultural & Food Sciences). (Illus.). 256p. 1980. text ed. 38.25 (ISBN 0-408-71013-6). Butterworths.
Lassiter, J. W. & Edwards, Hardy M. Animal Nutrition. 1982. text ed. 17.95 (ISBN 0-8359-0222-6); instr's. manual free (ISBN 0-8359-0223-4). Reston.

ANIMAL OILS
see Oils and Fats

ANIMAL-ORIGIN FOOD
see Animal Food

ANIMAL PARASITES
see Parasites

ANIMAL PHOTOGRAPHY
see Photography of Animals

ANIMAL POPULATIONS
see also Fish Populations; Population Genetics
Collins, Henry H., Jr., ed. Harper & Row's Complete Field Guide to North American Wildlife: Eastern Edition. LC 80-8198. (Illus.). 810p. 1981. 17.50 (ISBN 0-690-01977-7, HarpT); flexible vinyl cover 12.95 (ISBN 0-690-01969-6). Har-Row.

ANIMAL PSYCHOLOGY
see Psychology, Comparative

ANIMAL SIGNS
see Animal Tracks

ANIMAL SYMBOLISM
see Animal Lore

ANIMAL TRACKS
Pandell, Karen & Stall, Chris. Animal Tracks of the Pacific Northwest. (Illus.). 96p. (Orig.). 1981. pap. 3.95 (ISBN 0-89886-012-1). Mountaineers.

ANIMALS
see also Animals and Civilization; Aquatic Animals; Invertebrates; Mammals; Vertebrates; Zoology
also names of kinds of animals, e.g. Bears, cats, deer, etc.
Brant, George. Introductory Animal Science. 1980. perfect binding 7.95 (ISBN 0-88252-112-8). Paladin Hse.
Chamberlain, C. C., et al. Animal Science. 1982. text ed. 17.95 (ISBN 0-8359-0224-2); instr's. manual free (ISBN 0-8359-0225-0). Reston.
Lawrence, R. D. The Zoo That Never Was. LC 80-18956. (Illus.). 304p. 1981. 12.95 (ISBN 0-03-056811-0). HR&W.
Ratcliffe, Jane. Fly High, Run Free. (Illus.). 168p. 1981. 10.95 (ISBN 0-7011-2365-6, Pub. by Chatto-Bodley-Jonathan). Merrimack Bk Serv.
The Saturday Evening Post Animal Book. LC 78-5308. (Illus.). 1978. 9.95 (ISBN 0-89387-019-6). Sat Eve Post.
Sims, R. W. Animal Identification: A Reference Guide, 2 vols. Incl. Vol. 1. Marine & Brackish Water Animals. 108p (ISBN 0-471-27765-7); Vol. 2. Land & Freshwater Animals. 108p (ISBN 0-471-27766-5). 1980. 25.00 ea. Wiley.
Stanbury, Peter & Phipps, Graeme. Australia's Animals Discovered. (Illus.). 120p. 1980. 23.40 (ISBN 0-08-024796-2). Pergamon.
Zistel, Era. Good Companions. 1981. pap. 1.75 (ISBN 0-451-09813-7, E9813, Signet Bks). NAL.

ANIMALS (IN RELIGION, FOLK-LORE, ETC.)
see Animal Lore

ANIMALS–FOOD
see Animals, Food Habits of

ANIMALS–JUVENILE LITERATURE
see also Animals, Habits and Behavior of–Juvenile Literature; Zoology–Juvenile Literature
also Juvenile works, indentified by grade key, may be found in other subdivision or in headings beginning with the word Animal
Animal Babies. (Block Bk.). (ps). 1981. 2.50 (ISBN 0-686-69365-5, Golden Pr). Western Pub.
Battaglia, Aurelius, illus. Animals Sounds. (Golden Sturdy Bk.). (Illus.). 22p. 1981. 3.50 (ISBN 0-307-12122-4, Golden Pr). Western Pub.
Bethell, Jean. Playmates. LC 80-20542. 32p. (gr. k-2). 1981. 7.95 (ISBN 0-03-053821-1). HR&W.
Bonforte, Lisa, illus. Farm Animals. LC 80-53106. (Board Bks.). (Illus.). 14p. (ps). 1981. boards 2.95 (ISBN 0-394-84767-9). Random.
Brandreth, Gyles. Amazing Facts About Animals. (Amazing Facts Books Ser.). (Illus.). 32p. (gr. 5-8). pap. 2.95 (ISBN 0-385-17017-3). Doubleday.
--Amazing Facts About Prehistoric Animals. LC 80-1085. (Amazing Facts Books Ser.). (Illus.). 32p. 1981. pap. 2.95 (ISBN 0-385-17019-X). Doubleday.
Ford, Barbara. Alligators, Raccoons, & Other Survivors: The Wildlife of the Future. LC 80-28193. (Illus.). 96p. (gr. 4-6). 1981. 8.95 (ISBN 0-688-00369-9); PLB 8.59 (ISBN 0-688-00370-2). Morrow.
Freedman, Russell. When Winter Comes. LC 80-22831. (Illus.). (gr. 1-3). 1981. PLB 7.95 (ISBN 0-525-42583-7). Dutton.
Graham, Ada & Graham, Frank. Bears in the Wild. LC 80-68732. (Audubon Reader: No. 6). (Illus.). 128p. (gr. 4-7). 1981. 8.95 (ISBN 0-440-00532-9); PLB 8.44 (ISBN 0-440-00538-8). Delacorte.
Horwitz, Eleanor & Wildlife Society Elementary Education Committee, eds. Ways of Wildlife. LC 77-2208. (Illus.). 159p. (gr. 1-6). 1977. 7.95 (ISBN 0-590-07527-6, Citation); pap. 2.95 (ISBN 0-590-09617-6). Schol Bk Serv.
McLoughlin, John C. The Tree of Animal Life: A Tale of Changing Forms & Fortunes. (Illus.). 128p. (gr. 5 up). 1981. PLB 8.95 (ISBN 0-396-07939-3). Dodd.
Night Animals. (gr. 1). Date not set. pap. cancelled (ISBN 0-590-30058-X, Schol Pap). Schol Bk Serv.
Patent, Dorothy H. Hunters & the Hunted: Surviving in the Animal World. LC 80-23559. (Illus.). 64p. (gr. 4-8). 1981. PLB 7.95 (ISBN 0-8234-0386-6). Holiday.
A Picture Book of Animal Families. (Animal Picture Bks.). (Illus.). 10p. (ps). 1979. 1.95 (ISBN 0-89346-177-6, TA05, Pub. by Froebel-Kan Japan). Heian Intl.
A Picture Book of Animals of All Lands. (Children's Library of Picture Bks.). (Illus.). 10p. (ps). 1979. 1.95 (ISBN 0-89346-171-7, TA09, Pub. by Froebel-Kan Japan). Heian Intl.
Walter, Eugene J., Jr. Why Animals Behave the Way They Do. (Illus.). 64p. (gr. 5 up). 1981. 9.95 (ISBN 0-684-16879-0). Scribner.
Williams, Garth, illus. Animal Friends Everywhere! (Golden Storytime Bks.). (Illus.). (ps). 1980. pap. 4.50 boxed set (ISBN 0-307-15514-5, Golden Pr). Western Pub.

ANIMALS, AQUATIC
see Fresh-Water Biology; Marine Fauna

ANIMALS, CRUELTY TO
see Animals, Treatment Of

ANIMALS, DISEASES OF
see Veterinary Medicine

ANIMALS, DOMESTIC
see Domestic Animals
ANIMALS, EDIBLE
see Animal Food
ANIMALS, EXPERIMENTAL
see Laboratory Animals
ANIMALS, EXTINCT
see Extinct Animals
ANIMALS, FICTITIOUS
see Animals, Mythical
ANIMALS, FOOD HABITS OF
Subcommittee on Toxicity in Animals, Board on Agricultural & Renewable Resources. Mineral Tolerance of Domestic Animals. 1980. pap. text ed. 15.50 (ISBN 0-309-03022-6). Natl Acad Pr.
ANIMALS, FOSSIL
see Paleontology
ANIMALS, GEOGRAPHICAL DISTRIBUTION OF
see Zoogeography
ANIMALS, HABITS AND BEHAVIOR OF
see also Animal Intelligence; Animal Migration; Animals, Food Habits of; Behavior Genetics; Birds–Behavior; Insect Societies; Instinct; Nature Study; Nocturnal Animals; Psychology, Comparative
also names of particular animals
Animal Welfare Institute. Animal Expressions. rev. ed. (Illus.). 54p. 1974. pap. text ed. 2.00 (ISBN 0-938414-06-2). Animal Welfare.
Barnett, S. A Modern Ethology. (Illus.). 720p. 1981. text ed. 19.95x (ISBN 0-19-502780-9). Oxford U Pr.
Dickinson, A. Contemporary Animal Learning Theory. (Problems in the Behavioral Sciences Ser.). (Illus.). 180p. 1981. 27.50 (ISBN 0-521-23469-7); pap. 9.95 (ISBN 0-521-29962-4). Cambridge U Pr.
Houpt, Katherine A. & Wolski, Thomas R. Domestic Animal Behavior for Veterinarians & Animal Scientists. text ed. 16.50 (ISBN 0-8138-1060-4). Iowa St U Pr.
Johnson, H. D. Progress in Animal Biometeorology: The Effects of Weather & Climate on Animals; Vol 1 Period 1963-1973, 2 pts. Incl. Pt. 1. Effects of Temperature on Animals: Including Effects of Humidity, Radiation & Wind. 624p. 1976. text ed. 115.00 (ISBN 90-265-0196-X); Effect of Light, High Actitude, Noise, Electric, Magnetic & Electro-Magnetic Fields, Ionization, Gravity & Air Pollutions on Animals. 322p. 1976. text ed. 57.00 (ISBN 90-265-0235-4). (Progress in Biometeorology). 1976 (Pub. by Swets Pub Serv Holland). Swets North Am.
Lawrence, R. D. The Study of Life: A Naturalist's View. (Illus.). 43p. 1980. pap. 1.50 (ISBN 0-913098-37-X). Myrin Institute.
Pommery, Jean. How Human the Animals. LC 78-24613. 224p. 1981. pap. 6.95 (ISBN 0-8128-6086-1). Stein & Day.
Shebar, Jonathan M. & Shebar, Sharon S. Animal Dads Take Over. (Illus.). 64p. (gr. 3-5). 1981. PLB 6.97 (ISBN 0-671-34003-4). Messner.
Thompson, Edward P. Passions of Animals. (Contributions to the History of Psychology Ser.: Comparative Psychology). 1980. Repr. of 1851 ed. 30.00 (ISBN 0-89093-322-7). U Pubns Amer.
Wittenberger. Animal Social Behavior. (Illus.). 748p. 1981. text ed. price not set (ISBN 0-87872-295-5). Duxbury Pr.
ANIMALS, HABITS AND BEHAVIOR OF–JUVENILE LITERATURE
see also Animals–Juvenile Literature
Black, Hallie. Animal Cooperation: A Look at Sociobiology. (Illus.). 64p. (gr. 7-9). 1981. 7.95 (ISBN 0-688-00360-5); PLB 7.63 (ISBN 0-688-00361-3). Morrow.
Chen, Tony, illus. Wild Animals. LC 80-53105. (Board Bks.). (Illus.). 14p. (ps). 1981. boards 2.95 (ISBN 0-394-84748-2). Random.
Dinneen, Betty. The Family Howl. LC 80-25385. (Illus.). 96p. (gr. 4-6). 1981. PLB 8.95 (ISBN 0-02-732150-9). Macmillan.
Fagen, Robert M. Animal Play Behavior. (Illus.). 688p. 1981. text ed. 29.95x (ISBN 0-19-502760-4); pap. text ed. 12.95x (ISBN 0-19-502761-2). Oxford U Pr.
ANIMALS, IMAGINARY
see Animals, Mythical
ANIMALS, MIGRATION OF
see Animal Migration
ANIMALS, MYTHICAL
see also Animal Lore
De Menil, Dominique, intro. by. Constant Companions: An Exhibition of Mythological Animals, Demons, & Monsters. (Illus.). 1964. pap. 6.00 (ISBN 0-914412-19-1). Inst for the Arts.
Goatsend, Slim. Thor's Goats & Other Crazy Ways to Ride Around. (Odd Books for Odd Moments Ser.). (Illus.). 72p. (Orig.). 1981. pap. 3.95 (ISBN 0-938338-07-2). Winds World Pr.
Silente, Douglas M. Half Man, Half Beast, & Other Fantastic Combinations. (Odd Books for Odd Moments Ser.). (Illus.). 72p. (Orig.). 1981. pap. 3.95 (ISBN 0-938338-02-1). Winds World Pr.
ANIMALS, NOCTURNAL
see Nocturnal Animals
ANIMALS, ORIENTATION OF
see Orientation
ANIMALS, PHOTOGRAPHY OF
see Photography of Animals
ANIMALS, POISONOUS
see Poisonous Animals
ANIMALS, PREHISTORIC
see Extinct Animals; Paleontology
ANIMALS, PROTECTION OF
see Animals, Treatment Of; Wildlife Conservation
ANIMALS, RARE
see Rare Animals
ANIMALS, RESPIRATION OF
see Respiration
ANIMALS, RESTRAINT OF
see Animals, Treatment of
ANIMALS, SEA
see Marine Fauna
ANIMALS, TREATMENT OF
Animal Welfare Institute. Humane Biology Projects. 3rd ed. (Illus.). 57p. 1977. pap. text ed. 2.00 (ISBN 0-938414-05-4). Animal Welfare.
Frey, R. G. Interests & Rights: The Case Against Animals. (Clarendon Library of Logic & Philosophy Ser.). 188p. 1980. 24.95x (ISBN 0-19-824421-5). Oxford U Pr.
Magel, Charles R. A Bibliography on Animal Rights & Related Matters. LC 80-5636. 622p. 1981. lib. bdg. 28.50 (ISBN 0-8191-1488-X). U Pr of Amer.
Walker, Ernest P. & Animal Welfare Institute, eds. First Aid & Care of Small Animals. rev. ed. (Illus.). 54p. 1980. pap. text ed. 2.00 (ISBN 0-938414-04-6). Animal Welfare.
ANIMALS AND CIVILIZATION
Magel, Charles R. A Bibliography on Animal Rights & Related Matters. LC 80-5636. 622p. 1981. lib. bdg. 28.50 (ISBN 0-8191-1488-X). U Pr of Amer.
ANIMALS AS FOOD
see Animal Food
ANIMALS IN ART
Speake, George. Anglo-Saxon Animal Art & Its Germanic Background. (Illus.). 164p. 1980. text ed. 50.00x (ISBN 0-19-813194-1). Oxford U Pr.
ANIMALS IN FOLK-LORE
see Animal Lore
ANIMALS IN RESEARCH
see Laboratory Animals
ANIMATED CARTOONS
see Moving-Picture Cartoons
ANIMATION (CINEMATOGRAPHY)
Whitaker, Harold & Halas, John. Timing for Animation. LC 80-41303. (Illus.). 144p. 1981. 25.00 (ISBN 0-240-50871-8). Focal Pr.
ANIONS
Brodsky, William A., ed. Anion & Proton Transport, Vol. 341. new ed. LC 80-15917. 610p. 1980. 107.00 (ISBN 0-89766-070-6). NY Acad Sci.
ANKLE
Bateman & Trott. The Foot & Ankle. 1980. 32.00. Thieme Stratton.
Yablon, Isadore G. Injuries to the Ankle. (Illus.). 320p. 1981. lib. bdg. 30.00 (ISBN 0-443-08095-X). Churchill.
ANNALS
see History
ANNUALS
see Almanacs; Calendars; Yearbooks
ANOMALIES, CONGENITAL
see Abnormalities, Human
ANONYMS AND PSEUDONYMS
see also Anagrams
Bates, Susannah. The Pendex: An Index of Pen Names & House Names in Fantastic, Thriller & Series Literature. LC 80-8486. 200p. 1981. lib. bdg. 22.50 (ISBN 0-8240-9501-4). Garland Pub.
Mossman, Jennifer. New Pseudonyms & Nicknames--Supplements: Supplements to Pseudonyms & Nicknames Dictionary. 1981. softbound 45.00 (ISBN 0-8103-0548-8). Gale.
Room, Adrian. Naming Names: A Consideration of Pseudonyms & Name Changes. LC 80-27801. 260p. 1981. lib. bdg. write for info. (ISBN 0-89950-025-0). McFarland & Co.
ANOREXIA NERVOSA
Palmer, R. L. Anorexia Nervosa. 160p. 1981. pap. 3.95 (ISBN 0-14-022065-8, Pelican). Penguin.
ANOREXIGENIC AGENTS
see Weight Reducing Preparations
ANOUILH, JEAN, 1910-
McIntyre, H. G. The Theatre of Jean Anoulh. 1981. 18.00x (ISBN 0-389-20182-0). B&N.
ANSELM, SAINT, ARCHBISHOP OF CANTERBURY, 1033-1109
Eadmer. The Life of St. Anselm, Archbishop of Canterbury. Southern, R. W., ed. & tr. from Latin. (Oxford Medieval Texts Ser.). 386p. 1972. 31.00x (ISBN 0-19-822225-4). Oxford U Pr.
Evans, Rosemary G. Anselm & a New Generation. 230p. 1980. 34.50x (ISBN 0-19-826651-0). Oxford U Pr.
ANSWERS TO QUESTIONS
see Questions and Answers
ANTAGONISTS ENZYME
see Enzyme Inhibitors
ANTARCTIC REGIONS
Byrd, R. E. Assault on Eternity. 352p. 1980. 9.95 (ISBN 0-87021-085-8). Naval Inst Pr.
Charney, Jonathan I., ed. The New Nationalism & the Use of Common Spaces: Issues in Marine Pollution & the Exploitation of Antarctica. 420p. 1981. text ed. 29.00 (ISBN 0-86598-012-8). Allanheld.
Gjelsvik, Tore. Results from Norwegian Antartic Research, Nineteen Seventy Four to Nineteen Seventy Seven. (Norsk Polarinstitutt Skrifter: Vol. 169). (Illus.). 117p. 1980. pap. text ed. 7.50x (ISBN 82-90307-03-9). Universitet.
Sherrard, D. G. To Antarctica with the Royal Navy. LC 79-67138. 122p. 1980. 7.95 (ISBN 0-533-04448-0). Vantage.
ANTEDILUVIAN ANIMALS
see Paleontology
ANTELOPES
see also Pronghorn Antelope
Jarman, Martha V. Impala Social Behavior: Territory, Hierarchy, Mating, & the Use of Space. (Advances in Ethology Ser.: Vol. 21). (Illus.). 96p. (Orig.). 1979. pap. text ed. 33.00 (ISBN 3-489-60936-0). Parey Sci Pubs.
ANTENNAS (ELECTRONICS)
Antenna Theory & Design. (Illus.). 608p. 1981. 38.00 (ISBN 0-13-038356-2). P-H.
Clarke, R. H. & Brown, John. Diffraction Theory & Antennas. 320p. 1980. 97.50x (ISBN 0-470-27003-9). Halsted Pr.
Jull, E. V. Aperture Antennas & Diffraction Theory. 1981. pap. price not set. Inst Electrical.
Love, A. W., ed. Electromagnetic Horn Antennas. LC 75-44649. 1976. 28.95 (ISBN 0-87942-075-8). Inst Electrical.
Stutzman, Warren L. & Thiele, Gary A. Antenna Theory & Design. 672p. 1981. text ed. 26.95 (ISBN 0-471-04458-X). Wiley.
Williams, Paul H. Antenna Theory & Design. 15.95x (ISBN 0-392-07549-0, SpS). Soccer.
ANTHOLOGIES
see also Readers
Ardizzone, Tony, ed. Intro Twelve. (Intro Ser.). 244p. 1981. pap. 6.95 (ISBN 0-936266-02-3). Assoc Writing Progs.
Blythe, Ronald, ed. Places: An Anthology of Britain. (Illus.). 270p. 1981. 19.95 (ISBN 0-19-211575-8). Oxford U Pr.
Eliot, Simon & Stern, Beverly, eds. The Age of Enlightenment: An Anthology of Eighteenth Century Texts, 2 vols. 1980. Vol. 1. 23.50x; Vol. 2. 23.50x. B&N.
Evers, Larry, ed. The South Corner of Time. 250p. 1981. 35.00x (ISBN 0-8165-0732-5); pap. 14.95 (ISBN 0-8165-0731-7). U of Ariz Pr.
Patchen, Kenneth. Still Another Pelican in the Breadbox. Morgan, Richard, ed. LC 80-82905. 96p. 1980. pap. 5.95 (ISBN 0-917530-14-4). Pig Iron Pr.
Sayre, Rose, ed. Pig Iron, Number 7: Special Woman Issue. (Literary & Art Anthology Ser.). 1980. pap. 4.95 (ISBN 0-917530-15-2). Pig Iron Pr.
Villani, Jim, ed. Literary & Art Anthology, Vol. 2. 88p. 1976. pap. 4.95 (ISBN 0-917530-02-0). Pig Iron Pr.
--Literary & Art Anthology, Vol. 3. 104p. 1977. pap. 4.95 (ISBN 0-917530-06-3). Pig Iron Pr.
--Literary & Art Anthology, Vol. 4. 104p. 1978. pap. 4.95 (ISBN 0-917530-09-8). Pig Iron Pr.
--Literary & Art Anthology, Vol. 5. 96p. 1979. pap. 4.95 (ISBN 0-917530-10-1). Pig Iron Pr.
--Literary & Art Anthology, Vol. 6. 96p. 1979. pap. 4.95 (ISBN 0-917530-11-X). Pig Iron Pr.
Villani, Jim & Sayre, Rose, eds. Pig Iron, Number 8: The New Beats. (Literary & Art Anthology Ser.). 96p. 1980. pap. 4.95 (ISBN 0-917530-16-0). Pig Iron Pr.
ANTHRACITE COAL
see Coal
ANTHRACOSIS
see Lungs–Dust Diseases
ANTHROPO-GEOGRAPHY
see also Geography, Political; Geopolitics; Human Ecology; Man–Influence of Environment; Man–Migrations
French, Brian & Squire, Stan. Human & Economic Geography. (Illus.). 216p. (Orig.). 1973. pap. text ed. 4.50x (ISBN 0-19-519769-0). Oxford U Pr.
Larkin, Robert P., et al. People, Environment & Place: An Introduction to Human Geography. (Illus.). 368p. 1981. text ed. 20.95 (ISBN 0-675-08085-1); instr's. manual 3.95 (ISBN 0-686-69496-1). Merrill.
ANTHROPOLOGY
see also Anthropo-Geography; Anthropometry; Archaeology; Civilization; Craniology; Educational Anthropology; Ethnology; Ethnopsychology; Language and Languages; Man; Medical Anthropology; Physical Anthropology; Social Change; Women
also names of races, tribes etc., and subdivision Race Question under names of countries, e.g. United States–Race Question
Bates, Daniel G. & Lees, Susan H. Contemporary Anthropology: An Anthology. 332p. 1981. pap. 8.95 (ISBN 0-394-32043-3). Knopf.
Bliss. Bliss Bibliography, Second Class H: Anthropology, Human Biology & Health Sciences. 1981. price not set (ISBN 0-408-70828-X). Butterworth.
Cordell, Linda S., ed. Tijeras Canyon: Analyses of the Past. (Illus.). 232p. 1980. 19.95 (ISBN 0-8263-0553-9, Pub. by Maxwell Mus Anthropology); pap. 9.95 (ISBN 0-8263-0565-2). U of NM Pr.
Evans-Pritchard, Edward. A History of Anthropological Thought. Singer, Andre, ed. LC 80-68955. 256p. 1981. 15.00 (ISBN 0-465-02998-1). Basic.
Majumdar, D. N. & Madan, T. N. An Introduction to Social Anthropology. x, 304p. 1981. pap. text ed. 8.95x (ISBN 0-210-33687-0). Asia.
Maquet, J., ed. On Linguistic Anthropology: Essays in Honor of Harry Hoijer, 1979. LC 80-50214. (Other Realities Ser.: Vol. 2). 140p. text ed. 12.00; pap. text ed. 9.00. Undena Pubns.
Tanner, Nancy. On Becoming Human. LC 80-21526. (Illus.). 350p. Date not set. 29.95 (ISBN 0-521-23554-5); pap. 10.95 (ISBN 0-521-28028-1). Cambridge U Pr.
Tel Ngandong Fossil Hominids: A Comparative Study of a Far Eastern Homo Erectus Group. LC 80-50035. (Publications in Anthropology: No. 78). 1980. pap. 13.50. Yale U Anthro.
ANTHROPOLOGY–ADDRESSES, ESSAYS, LECTURES
Barth, Fredrik. Features of Person & Society in Swat-Collected Essays on Pathans: Selected Essays of Frederik Barth, Vol. II. (International Library of Anthropology Ser.). 208p. 1981. 32.00 (ISBN 0-7100-0620-9). Routledge & Kegan.
--Selected Essays of Fredrik Barth: Process & Form in Social Life. (International Library of Anthropology). 1981. 35.00 (ISBN 0-7100-0720-5). Routledge & Kegan.
Harten, Lucille B., et al, eds. Anthropological Papers in Memory of Earl H. Swanson, Jr. (Special Publication of the Idaho Museum of Natural History). 200p. (Orig.). 1980. write for info. Idaho Mus Nat Hist.
Hite, Shere. The Hite Report. Date not set. pap. price not set (ISBN 0-440-13690-3). Dell.
ANTHROPOLOGY–HISTORY
Frazer, James G. The Golden Bough, 13 vols. 5380p. 1980. Repr. of 1890 ed. Set. 375.00 (ISBN 0-312-33215-7). St Martin.
Hinsley, Charles M., Jr. Savages & Scientists: The Smithsonian Institution & the Development of American Anthropology, 1846-1910. (Illus.). 225p. 1980. text ed. 15.00x (ISBN 0-87474-518-7). Smithsonian.
ANTHROPOLOGY, BIBLICAL
see Man (Theology)
ANTHROPOLOGY, CRIMINAL
see Criminal Anthropology
ANTHROPOLOGY, PHILOSOPHIC
see Philosophical Anthropology
ANTHROPOLOGY, PHILOSOPHICAL
see Philosophical Anthropology
ANTHROPOLOGY, PHYSICAL
see Physical Anthropology
ANTHROPOLOGY, THEOLOGICAL
see Man (Theology)
ANTHROPOMETRY
see also Craniology; Criminal Anthropology; Fingerprints
Crooney, John. Anthropometry for Designers. rev. ed. 144p. 1981. pap. 12.00 (ISBN 0-442-22013-8). Van Nos Reinhold.
Johanson, Donald C. & Edey, Maitland A. Lucy: The Beginnings of Human Evolution. (Illus.). 1981. 13.95 (ISBN 0-671-25036-1). S&S.
ANTHROPOSOPHY
see also Karma; Theosophy
Abels, Paul & Murphy, Michael J. Administration in the Human Sciences: A Normative Systems Approach. (P-H Ser. in Social Work). (Illus.). 256p. 1981. text ed. 16.95 (ISBN 0-686-68604-7). P-H.
Kolisko, Eugen. Human Organism in the Light of Anthropasaphy. 1980. pap. 1.95x (ISBN 0-906492-11-4, Pub. by Kolisko Archives). St George Bk Serv.
ANTI-COLONIALISM
see Colonies
ANTI-CORROSIVE PAINT
see Corrosion and Anti-Corrosives
ANTI-DISCRIMINATION LAWS
see Race Discrimination
ANTI-OBESITY DRUGS
see Weight Reducing Preparations
ANTIBIOTICS
see also Penicillin
Berdy, Janos. Heterocyclic Antibiotics. (CRC Handbook of Antibiotic Compounds: Vol. 5). 640p. 1981. 62.95 (ISBN 0-8493-3456-X). CRC Pr.
Conte, John E., Jr. & Barriere, Steven L. Manual of Antibiotics & Infectious Diseases. 4th ed. (Illus.). 275p. 1981. text ed. price not set (ISBN 0-8121-0768-3). Lea & Febiger.
Gale, E. F., et al. The Molecular Basis of Antibiotic Action. 2nd ed. 640p. 1981. 98.00 (ISBN 0-471-27915-3, Pub. by Wiley-Interscience). Wiley.
Gibbs, Ronald S. Antibiotic Therapy in Obstetrics & Gynecology. 224p. 1981. 16.50 (ISBN 0-471-06003-8, Pub. by Wiley Med). Wiley.
Korzybski, T., et al, eds. Antibiotics: Origin, Nature & Properties, 3 vols. 1979. 48.00 (ISBN 0-914826-14-X). Am Soc Microbio.
Parascandola, John, ed. The History of Antibiotics: A Symposium. (Illus.). 137p. (Orig.). 1980. pap. 5.40 (ISBN 0-931292-08-5). Am Inst Pharmacy.
Sammes, P. G. Topics in Antibiotic Chemistry, Vol. 5. LC 80-41091. 312p. 1980. 87.50 (ISBN 0-470-27050-0). Halsted Pr.

Williams, R. A. D. & Kruk, Z. L. An Introduction to the Biochemistry & Pharmacology of Antibiotics. 128p. 1980. 25.00x (ISBN 0-85664-857-4, Pub. by Croom Helm England). State Mutual Bk.

ANTIBIOTICS RESISTANCE IN MICRO-ORGANISMS
see Drug Resistance in Micro-Organisms

ANTIBODIES
see Immunoglobulins

ANTICHRIST
White, John W. The Coming World Dictator. 144p. (Orig.). 1981. pap. 2.50 (ISBN 0-87123-042-9, 200042). Bethany Fell.

ANTIGUA
Shawcross, Mike. Antigua, Guatemala: City & Area Guide. (Illus.). 74p. 1979. pap. 4.95 (ISBN 0-933982-17-8). Bradt Ent.

ANTIMILITARISM
see Militarism

ANTINEOPLASTIC AGENTS
Aszalos, Adorjan, ed. Antitumor Compounds of Natural Origin. 1981. Vol. 1. 64.95 (ISBN 0-8493-5520-6); Vol. 2. 67.95 (ISBN 0-8493-5521-4). CRC Pr.

ANTIPATHIES
see Prejudices and Antipathies

ANTIQUE COLLECTING
see Antiques

ANTIQUES
Here are entered works on old decorative or utilitarian objects having aesthetic, historic and financial value. Works on decorative art objects are entered under Art Objects.
see also Art Objects;
also particular kinds of antique objects, especially the subdivisions Catalogs, Collectors and Collecting or Exhibitions when they occur under such objects, e.g. Kitchen Utensils; Firearms–Catalogs; Glassware–Collectors and Collecting; Furniture–Exhibitions
Ash, Douglas. How to Identify English Silver Drinking Vessels. 15.00x (ISBN 0-392-07924-0, SpS). Soccer.
Barlow, Ronald S. How to Be Successful in the Antique Business. rev. ed. (Illus.). 185p. 1981. 10.95 (ISBN 0-686-69481-3, ScribT). Scribner.
Benedictus, David. The Antique Collector's Guide. LC 80-69368. 1981. 14.95 (ISBN 0-689-11146-0). Atheneum.
Boone, Gray. Gray Boone on Antiques. LC 80-84408. (Illus.). 160p. 1981. 12.95 (ISBN 0-8487-0519-X). Oxmoor Hse.
Fredgant, Don. Electrical Collectibles: Relics of the Electrical Age. (Illus.). 1981. pap. 9.95 (ISBN 0-914598-04-X). Padre Prods.
Hammond, Dorothy. Pictorial Price Guide to American Antiques. 4th ed. (Illus.). 224p. 1981. pap. 9.95 (ISBN 0-525-47660-1). Dutton.
Ingram, Terry. A Question of Polish: The Antique Market in Australia. 176p. 1980. 27.95x (ISBN 0-00-216412-4, Pub. by W Collins Australia). Intl Schol Bk Serv.
Jendrick, Barbara W., ed. Antique Advertising Paper Dolls. (Illus.). 64p. (Orig.). 1981. pap. write for info. (ISBN 0-486-24045-2). Dover.
Jenkins, Dorothy. Woman's Day Book of Antique Collectibles. (Illus.). 240p. 1981. 19.95 (ISBN 0-312-88647-0). St Martin.
Knox, Bill. A Killing in Antiques. LC 80-2967. 192p. 1981. 9.95 (ISBN 0-385-17625-2). Doubleday.
Lewis, Mel. How to Make Money from Antiques. (Illus.). 160p. 1981. 12.50 (ISBN 0-7137-1084-5, Pub. by Blandford Pr England). Sterling.
Major, Alan. Maritime Antiques. 1981. 12.95 (ISBN 0-498-02496-2). A S Barnes.
Olson, Joan & Williams, Elaine. Antique Shopping in Southern California: Comprehensive Guide to Shops in Seven Counties. (Illus.). 300p. (Orig.). 1980. pap. 8.95 (ISBN 0-9602924-0-3). Willows Pr.
Raycraft, Don. Collector's Guide to Kitchen Antiques. (Illus.). 1980. 17.95 (ISBN 0-89145-140-4). Collector Bks.
Schiffer, Herbert F. Early Pennsylvania Hardware. (Illus.). 64p. 1966. pap. 3.75 (ISBN 0-916838-42-0). Schiffer.
Start, Clarissa. We Buy Junque - We Sell Antiques. 158p. (Orig.). 1979. pap. 5.95 (ISBN 0-86629-012-5). Sunrise MO.

ANTIQUES–COLLECTORS AND COLLECTING
see Antiques

ANTIQUITIES
see also Antiques; Archaeology; Christian Antiquities; Classical Antiquities
also subdivision Antiquities under names of countries, cities, etc
Gregory, Justina, et al. Survival of Antiquity. LC 80-53219. (Studies in History Ser.: No. 48). (Illus.). 1980. pap. 10.00 (ISBN 0-87391-019-2). Smith Coll.
Noble, David. Ancient Ruins of the Southwest: An Archaeological Guide. LC 80-83016. (Illus.). 128p. 1981. pap. 8.95 (ISBN 0-87358-274-8). Northland.
Pettinato, Giovanni. The Archives of Ebla: An Empire Inscribed in Clay. LC 77-16939. (Illus.). 384p. 1981. 15.95 (ISBN 0-385-13152-6). Doubleday.

ANTIQUITIES, BIBLICAL
see Bible–Antiquities

ANTIQUITIES, CHRISTIAN
see Christian Antiquities

ANTIQUITIES, CLASSICAL
see Classical Antiquities

ANTIQUITIES, ECCLESIASTICAL
see Christian Antiquities

ANTIQUITIES, GRECIAN
see Classical Antiquities; Greece–Antiquities

ANTIQUITIES, INDUSTRIAL
see Industrial Archaeology

ANTIQUITIES, PREHISTORIC
see Man, Prehistoric

ANTIQUITIES, ROMAN
see Classical Antiquities; Rome–Antiquities

ANTISEMITISM
Glassman, Samuel. Epic of Survival: The Story of Anti-Semitism. LC 80-69018. 400p. 20.00 (ISBN 0-8197-0481-4). Bloch.
Varga, William. The Number One Nazi Jew Baiter. 1981. 9.95 (ISBN 0-8062-1623-9). Carlton.

ANTISTATIC COMPOUNDS
see Petroleum Products

ANTITANK WARFARE
see Tank Warfare

ANTITHROMBOTIC AGENTS
see Fibrinolytic Agents

ANTITOXINS
see Toxins and Antitoxins

ANTITRUST LAW
see also Corporation Law
Blair, Roger D. & Lanzillotti, Robert F., eds. The Conglomerate Corporation: An Antitrust Law & Economics Symposium. LC 80-22093. 288p. 1981. lib. bdg. 25.00 (ISBN 0-89946-051-8). Oelgeschlager.
Calkins, Richard M. Anti-Trust: Guidelines for the Business Executive. 325p. 17.50 (ISBN 0-87094-231-X). Dow Jones-Irwin.
Gellhorn, Ernest. Antitrust Law & Economics in a Nutshell. 2nd ed. (Nutshell Ser.). 426p. 1981. pap. text ed. write for info. (ISBN 0-8299-2117-6). West Pub.
Posner, Richard A. & Easterbrook, Frank H. Antitrust - Cases, Economic Notes, & Other Materials. 2nd ed. LC 80-25590. (American Casebook Ser.). (Illus.). 1980. text ed. 22.95 (ISBN 0-8299-2115-X). West Pub.
Singer, Eugene M. Antitrust Economics & Legal Analysis. LC 80-19847. (Economics Ser.). 200p. 1981. pap. 12.95 (ISBN 0-88244-227-9). Grid Pub.
Van Cise, Jerrold G. & Lifland, William T. Understanding the Antitrust Laws. 8th ed. LC 80-83813. 400p. 1980. text ed. 45.00 (ISBN 0-686-69172-5, B1-1276). PLI.

ANTLIATA
see Diptera

ANTWERP
Antwerp: An Historical Descourse, or Rather a Teragicall Historie of Antwerpe Since the Departure of King Phillip of Spaine Out of Netherland. LC 79-84083. (English Experience Ser.: No. 903). 56p. 1979. Repr. of 1586 ed. lib. bdg. 7.00 (ISBN 90-221-0903-8). Walter J Johnson.

ANXIETY
see also Fear; Obsessive-Compulsive Neuroses; Worry
Appelbaum, Steven. Stress Management for Health Care Professionals. 350p. 1980. text ed. 24.95 (ISBN 0-89443-332-6). Aspen Systems.
Klein, Donald F. & Rabkin, Judith G., eds. Anxiety: New Research & Changing Concepts. 325p. 1981. 29.50 (ISBN 0-686-69136-9). Raven.
Pease, Victor P. Anxiety into Energy. 1981. 12.95 (ISBN 0-8015-0335-3, Hawthorn). Dutton.

AORTA
Aspinall, Mary Jo. Aortic Arch Surgery. (Surgical Aspects of Cardiovasculardisease: Nursing Intervention Series). 100p. 1980. pap. 6.95 (ISBN 0-686-69603-4). ACC.

AORTIC REGURGITATION
see Heart–Diseases

AORTIC VALVE–DISEASES
Barry, Sr. Anna. Aortic Andtricuspid Valvular Disease. (Surgical Aspects of Cardiovascular Disease: Nursing Intervention Series). 100p. 1980. pap. 6.95 (ISBN 0-8385-0189-3). ACC.

APACHE INDIANS
see Indians of North America–Southwest, New

APARTHEID
see South Africa–Race Question

APARTMENT HOUSES
see also Condominium (Housing); Landlord and Tenant
Bradford, Barbara T. Luxury Designs for Apartment Living. LC 77-16899. (Illus.). 352p. 1981. 29.95 (ISBN 0-385-12769-3). Doubleday.

APES
see also Orangutans
Graham, Charles E., ed. Reproductive Biology of the Great Apes: Comparative & Biomedical Perspectives. 1981. write for info. (ISBN 0-12-295020-8). Acad Pr.

APHASIA
see also Amnesia
Aurelia, Joseph C. Aphasia Therapy Manual. 2nd ed. 1980. pap. text ed. 3.95x (ISBN 0-8134-2112-8, 2112). Interstate.
Chapey, Roberta. Language Intervention Strategies in Adult Aphasia. (Illus.). 381p. 1981. 32.00 (ISBN 0-686-69565-8, 1511-7). Williams & Wilkins.
Emerick, Lon. ALD - a New Test for Aphasia. 27.00 (ISBN 0-686-69371-X). Northern Mich.
Keith, Robert L. Graduated Language Training: For Patients with Aphasia & Children with Language Deficiencies. LC 79-91245. (Illus.). 320p. 1980. clinical test 24.95 (ISBN 0-933014-57-0). College-Hill.
Sarno, Martha T. & Hook, Olle, eds. Aphasia: Assessment & Treatment. LC 80-80488. (Illus.). 288p. 1980. 34.50 (ISBN 0-89352-086-1). Masson Pub.
Wulf, Helen H. Aphasia, My World Alone. rev. ed. 144p. 1979. 9.50x. Wayne St U Pr.

APHRODISIACS
Stark, Raymond. The Book of Aphrodisiacs. LC 80-6206. 212p. 1981. 11.95 (ISBN 0-8128-2798-8). Stein & Day.

APICULTURE
see Bee Culture

APOCALYPTIC LITERATURE
Costa, Dennis. Irenic Apocalypse: Some Uses of Apocalyptic in Dante, Petrarch & Rebelais. (Stanford French & Italian Studies: Vol. 21). 160p. 1980. pap. 20.00 (ISBN 0-915838-18-4). Anma Libri.
Hedrick, Charles W. The Apocalypse of Adam: A Literary & Source Analysis. LC 79-26013. (Society of Biblical Literature Dissertation Ser.: No. 46). Date not set. price not set (ISBN 0-89130-369-3, 060146); pap. price not set. Scholars Pr CA.
Nickelsburg, George W. Jewish Literature Between the Bible & the Mishnah: A Historical & Literary Introduction. LC 80-16176. 352p. 1981. 19.95 (ISBN 0-8006-0649-3, 1-649). Fortress.
Pietersma, Albert, et al. The Apocalypse of Elijah. LC 79-24788. 1981. price not set (ISBN 0-89130-371-5, 060219); pap. 7.50 (ISBN 0-89130-372-3). Scholars Pr CA.
Rowley, H. H. The Relevance of Apocalyptic. 3rd ed. LC 64-12221. 240p. pap. text ed. 7.95 (ISBN 0-87921-061-3). Attic Pr.

APOLOGETICS
see also Bible–Evidences, Authority, etc.; Catholic Church–Apologetic Works; Faith and Reason; Natural Theology; Religion and Science; Witness Bearing (Christianity)
also subdivision Doctrinal and Controversial works under names of particular denominations, and also subdivision Apologetic Works under religious denominations, e.g. Catholic Church–Apologetic Works
Hoover, A. J. Case for Christian Theism: An Introduction to Apologetics. 272p. 1981. pap. 6.95 (ISBN 0-8010-4251-8). Baker Bk.
Luce, Alice A., tr. Evidencias Cristianas. (Spanish Bks.). (Span.). 1978. 1.25 (ISBN 0-8297-0554-6). Life Pubs Intl.

APOLOGETICS, JEWISH
see Judaism

APOSTLES
Barclay, William. The Master's Men. (Orig.). pap. 1.50 (ISBN 0-89129-132-6). Jove Pubns.
Finegan, Jack. The Archaeology of the New Testament: The Mediterranean World of the Early Christian Apostles. (Illus.). 400p. 1981. 35.00x (ISBN 0-86531-064-5). Westview.
Livadeas, Themistocles & Charitos, Minas. The Real Truth Concerning Apostolos Makrakis. Orthodox Christian Educational Society, ed. Cummings, Denver, tr. from Hellenic. 230p. (Orig.). 1952. pap. 4.00x (ISBN 0-938366-30-0). Orthodox Chr.
Lockyer. All the Apostles of the Bible. 1972. 10.95 (ISBN 0-310-28010-9, 10052). Zondervan.

APPALACHIAN MOUNTAINS
Boone, Michele L., ed. Southern Applachian Resource Catalog, Vol. II. (Illus.). 76p. 1981. 4.00. S Appalachian Res.
Bryant, Carlene F. We're All Kin: A Cultural Study of a Mountain Neighborhood. LC 81-473. 160p. 1981. 9.50x (ISBN 0-87049-312-4). U of Tenn Pr.
Farr, Sidney S. Appalachian Women: An Annotated Bibliography. LC 80-5174. 224p. 1981. price not set (ISBN 0-8131-1431-4). U Pr of Ky.

APPARATUS, ELECTRICAL
see Electric Apparatus and Appliances

APPARATUS, MEDICAL
see Medical Instruments and Apparatus

APPARATUS, ORTHOPEDIC
see Orthopedic Apparatus

APPARATUS, SCIENTIFIC
see Scientific Apparatus and Instruments

APPARATUS, SURGICAL
see Surgical Instruments and Apparatus

APPARITIONS
see also Demonology; Ghosts; Miracles; Visions
Christian, William A., Jr. Apparitions in Late Medieval & Renaissance Spain. LC 80-8541. (Illus.). 304p. 1981. 20.00x (ISBN 0-691-05326-X). Princeton U Pr.

APPEAL
see Appellate Procedure

APPELLATE COURTS
see also Appellate Procedure
National Center for State Courts. Structural Responses to the Problems of Volume & Delay in Appellate Courts. Date not set. pap. price not set (ISBN 0-89656-048-1, R-0055). Natl Ctr St Courts.

APPELLATE PROCEDURE
see also Appellate Courts; Appellate Procedure; Briefs; Civil Procedure; Trial Practice
Moran, Michael. Standards Relating to Appeals & Collateral Review. (Juvenile Justice Standards Project Ser.). 1980. softcover 5.95 (ISBN 0-88410-815-5); casebound 12.50. Ballinger Pub.
National Center for State Courts. Structural Responses to the Problems of Volume & Delay in Appellate Courts. Date not set. pap. price not set (ISBN 0-89656-048-1, R-0055). Natl Ctr St Courts.
Purver, Jonathan & Taylor, Lawrence. Handlin Criminal Appeals, Vol. 1. LC 80-81271. 1980. 47.50. Lawyers Co-Op.

APPETIZERS
see Cookery (Appetizers)

APPLIANCES, ELECTRIC
see Electric Apparatus and Appliances

APPLICATIONS FOR POSITIONS
see also Employment Interviewing; Resumes (Employment)
Ulrich, Heinz & Conner, Robert. National Job Finding Guide. LC 79-6182. 336p. 1981. pap. 10.95 (ISBN 0-385-15782-7, Dolp). Doubleday.

APPLIED MECHANICS
see Mechanics, Applied

APPLIED PSYCHOLOGY
see Psychology, Applied

APPLIED SCIENCE
see Technology

APPOMATTOX CAMPAIGN, 1865
Cresap, Bernard. Appomatax Commander. (Illus.). 384p. 1981. 15.00 (ISBN 0-498-02432-6). A S Barnes.

APPRAISAL
see Valuation

APPRAISAL OF BOOKS
see Bibliography–Best Books; Books and Reading; Criticism; Literature–History and Criticism

APPRECIATION OF ART
see Art Appreciation

APPRECIATION OF MUSIC
see Music–Analysis, Appreciation

APPREHENSION
see Perception

APPRENTICES
see also Employees, Training of
Briggs, Vernon M., Jr. & Foltman, Felician F., eds. Apprenticeship Research: Emerging Findings & Future Trends. 1981. pap. price not set (ISBN 0-87546-085-2). NY Sch Indus Rel.

APPROXIMATION THEORY
see also Chebyshev Approximation; Numerical Analysis; Perturbation (Mathematics)
Chistensen, R. Entropy Minimax Sourcebook: General Description. 700p. 1981. text ed. 29.50 (ISBN 0-686-28918-8). Entropy Ltd.
Christensen, R., ed. Entropy Minimax Sourcebook: Applications. 800p. 1981. 59.50 (ISBN 0-686-28919-6). Entropy Ltd.
Powell, M. J. Approximation Theory & Methods. (Illus.). 300p. Date not set. price not set (ISBN 0-521-22472-1); pap. price not set (ISBN 0-521-29514-9). Cambridge U Pr.

AQUACULTURE
see also Fish-Culture
Bowden, Gerald. Coastal Aquaculture Law & Policy: A Case Study of California. (Special Studies in Agricultural Science & Policy). 300p. 1981. lib. bdg. 25.00x (ISBN 0-86531-108-0). Westview.
Chen, T. P. Aquaculture Practices in Taiwan. (Illus.). 176p. 13.75 (ISBN 0-85238-080-1, FN). Unipub.
Falkowski, Paul G., ed. Primary Productivity in the Sea: Environmental Science Research Ser. (Vol. 19). 335p. 1980. 49.50 (ISBN 0-306-40623-3). Plenum Pub.
Muir, James F. & Roberts, Ronald J., eds. Recent Advances in Aquaculture. 320p. 1980. 50.00x (Pub. by Croom Helm England). State Mutual Bk.
Report of the Ad Hoc Consultation of Aquaculture Research. (FAO Fisheries Report Ser.: No. 238). 26p. 1980. pap. 6.00 (ISBN 92-5-100949-X, F2038, FAO). Unipub.
Report of the Indo-Pacific Fishery Commision Working Party on Aquaculture & Environment. 16p. 1981. pap. 6.00 (ISBN 92-5-100962-7, F2074, FAO). Unipub.
Report on the Fourth Session of the Cooperative Programme of Research on Aquaculture of the General Fisheries Council for the Mediterranean. (FAO Fisheries Report: No. 232). 32p. 1981. pap. 6.00 (ISBN 92-5-100927-9, F2068, FAO). Unipub.

AQUARIUMS
see also Fish-Culture; Goldfish; Marine Aquariums; Tropical Fish; Water Gardens
Axelrod, Herbert R. Breeding Aquarium Fishes, Bk.6. (Illus.). 288p. 1980. 12.95 (ISBN 0-87666-536-9, H-995). TFH Pubns.

AQUATIC ANIMALS
see also Fishes; Fresh-Water Biology; Fresh-Water Fauna; Marine Fauna
Pott, Eckart. Rivers & Lakes. (Illus.). 144p. 1981. pap. 5.95 (ISBN 0-7011-2544-6, Pub. by Chatto-Bodley-Jonathan). Merrimack Bk Serv.

AQUATIC BIRDS
see Water-Birds

AQUATIC CHEMISTRY
see Water Chemistry

AQUATIC ECOLOGY
see also Fresh-Water Ecology; Marine Ecology

Buikema, Arthur L., Jr. & Hendricks, Albert C. Benzene, Xylene, & Toluene in Aquatic Systems: A Review. LC 80-67170. (Illus.). 69p. (Orig.). pap. 3.75 (ISBN 0-89364-038-7, API 847-86250). Am Petroleum.

Maki, A. W., et al, eds. Biotransformation & Fate of Chemicals in the Aquatic Environment. (Illus.). 1980. write for info. (ISBN 0-914826-28-X). Am Soc Microbio.

AQUATIC FAUNA
see Aquatic Animals

AQUATIC FLORA
see Aquatic Plants

AQUATIC PLANTS
see also Fresh-Water Flora; Marine Flora; Water Gardens

Godfrey, Robert K. & Wooten, Jean W. Aquatic & Wetland Plants of Southeastern United States: Dicotyledons. LC 80-16452. (Illus.). 864p. 1981. lib. bdg. 40.00x (ISBN 0-8203-0532-4). U of Ga Pr.

Pott, Eckart. Rivers & Lakes. (Illus.). 144p. 1981. pap. 5.95 (ISBN 0-7011-2544-6, Pub. by Chatto-Bodley-Jonathan). Merrimack Bk Serv.

AQUEOUS HUMOR

Yamaguchi. Recent Advances on the Lacrimal System. Date not set. 47.50 (ISBN 0-89352-140-X). Masson Pub.

AQUICULTURE
see Aquaculture

ARAB ARCHITECTURE
see Architecture, Islamic

ARAB ART
see Art, Islamic

ARAB CIVILIZATION
see Civilization, Arab

ARAB COUNTRIES

Amin, Samir. The Arab Nation: Nationalism & Class Struggle. 116p. 1978. 12.95 (Pub. by Zed Pr); pap. 4.95 (ISBN 0-905762-23-1). Lawrence Hill.

Lanier, Alison R. Update -- Bahrain-Qatar. (Country Orientation Ser.). 1980. pap. text ed. 25.00 (ISBN 0-933662-44-0). Intercult Network.

ARAB COUNTRIES–DESCRIPTION AND TRAVEL–GUIDE BOOKS

Lanier, Alison R. Update -- Arab Emirates. (Country Orientation Ser.). 1980. pap. text ed. 25.00 (ISBN 0-933662-42-4). Intercult Network.

ARAB COUNTRIES–FOREIGN RELATIONS

Zeine, Zeine N. Arab-Turkish Relations & the Emergence of Arab Nationalism. LC 80-25080. 156p. 1981. Repr. of 1958 ed. lib. bdg. 19.75x (ISBN 0-313-22705-5, ZEAT). Greenwood.

ARAB COUNTRIES–HISTORY

Goldston, Robert. The Sword of the Prophet. 224p. 1981. pap. 2.50 (ISBN 0-449-24393-1, Crest). Fawcett.

ARAB COUNTRIES–POLITICS AND GOVERNMENT

Ajami, Fouad. The Arab Predicament: Arab Political Thought & Practice Since 1967. 250p. Date not set. price not set (ISBN 0-521-23914-1). Cambridge U Pr.

Amin, Samir. The Arab Nation: Nationalism & Class Struggle. 116p. 1978. 12.95 (Pub. by Zed Pr); pap. 4.95 (ISBN 0-905762-23-1). Lawrence Hill.

Reid, Donald M. Lawyers & Politics in the Arab World, 1880-1960. LC 80-71053. (Studies in Middle Eastern History: No. 5). 600p. 1981. 30.00 (ISBN 0-88297-028-3). Bibliotheca.

ARAB-ISRAEL BORDER CONFLICTS, 1949-
see Israel-Arab Border Conflicts, 1949-

ARAB-ISRAEL WAR, 1973
see Israel-Arab War, 1973

ARAB-JEWISH RELATIONS
see Jewish-Arab Relations

ARAB PHILOSOPHY
see Philosophy, Arab

ARABIA

Fleming, Quentin W. A Guide to Doing Business on the Arabian Peninsula. 225p. 1981. 29.95 (ISBN 0-8144-5666-9); comb-bound 29.95 (ISBN 0-8144-7012-2). Am Mgmt.

Pirenne, Jacqueline. A la Decouverte De L'arabie. (Arabia Past & Present Ser.: Vol. 14). (Fr.). 32.50 (ISBN 0-902675-53-2). Oleander Pr.

Thomas, Bertram. Alarms and Excursions in Arabia. LC 80-1911. 1981. Repr. of 1931 ed. 36.00 (ISBN 0-404-18986-5). AMS Pr.

ARABIA–HISTORY

Sabini, John. Armies in the Sand: The Struggle for Mecca & Medina. (Illus.). 224p. 1981. 16.95 (ISBN 0-500-01246-6). Thames Hudson.

Salibi, Kamal S. History of Arabia. LC 80-11919. 1980. write for info. (ISBN 0-88206-036-8). Caravan Bks.

ARABIA–SOCIAL LIFE AND CUSTOMS

Allen, Mark. Falconry in Arabia. (Illus.). 143p. Date not set. 40.00 (ISBN 0-89182-034-5). Charles River Bks.

ARABIC LANGUAGE

Abdel-Massih, Ernest T. Introduction to Moroccan Arabic. LC 72-154239. 1977. pap. text ed. 7.00 (ISBN 0-932098-80-0). Ctr for NE & North African Stud.

Bakalla, M. The Morphological & Phonological Components of the Arabic Verb. (Meccan Arabic.). 1979. 20.00x. Intl Bk Ctr.

Du Liban, Librarie. Spoken Arabic of the Arabian Gulf. 1976. pap. 2.95x. Intl Bk Ctr.

Ghandour, Mounir. Arabic Conversation. pap. 5.00; book & cassettes 30.00. Intl Bk Ctr.

--Learn Arabic Reading & Writing I. pap. 5.00; book & cassettes 30.00. Intl Bk Ctr.

Shaikh, Shafi. A Course in Spoken Arabic. 136p. (Orig.). 1978. pap. text ed. 3.95x (ISBN 0-19-561067-9). Oxford U Pr.

Stern, A. Z. & Reif, Joseph A., eds. Useful Expressions in Arabic. (Useful Expressions). 64p. (Orig.). 1980. pap. 1.50 (ISBN 0-86628-005-7); cassette 4.50 (ISBN 0-86628-015-4). Ridgefield Pub.

Wickens, G. M. Arabic Grammar. LC 77-82523. 180p. 1980. write for info. (ISBN 0-521-21885-3); pap. 12.95 (ISBN 0-521-29301-4). Cambridge U Pr.

ARABIC LANGUAGE–DIALECTS

Härning, Kerstin E. The Analytic Genitive in the Modern Arabic Dialects. (Orientalia Gothoburgensia Ser.: No. 5). 1981. pap. text ed. 17.00 (ISBN 91-7346-087-7). Humanities.

ARABIC LANGUAGE–DICTIONARIES

Addi, Al-Sayyid. Dictionary of Persian Loan Words in the Arabic Language. 1980. 15.00x. Intl Bk Ctr.

Al-Esmani, Abed. Batal Al Abtal. pap. 5.95x. Intl Bk Ctr.

Al Quareb, Al-Mawrid & Ba'Alabaki, Munir. English-Arabic Pocket Dictionary. 1980. pap. 5.50x. Intl Bk Ctr.

Ba'Albaki, Munir. English-Arabic Dictionary: Al-Mawrid. 1981. 45.00 (ISBN 0-686-69401-5). Intl Bk Ctr.

Elias, E. A. English-Arabic; Arabic-English Dictionary. pap. 12.00x. Intl Bk Ctr.

Freytag, George W. Lexicon Arabico-Latinum. 70.00x. Intl Bk Ctr.

Manar, Al. English-Arabic Dictionary. 1971. 25.00x. Intl Bk Ctr.

Mokri, M. Al-Hadiyati 'l-Hamidiyah: Kurdish-Arabic Dictionary. 1975. 18.00x. Intl Bk Ctr.

Nasr, Mohammed. Arabic Standard Atlas. (Arabic.). pap. 10.00x. Intl Bk Ctr.

Saisse, Louis. Dictionaire Francais-Arabe. 1980. pap. 7.95x. Intl Bk Ctr.

Wortabet, John. Arabic-English Pocket Dictionary. 1980. pap. 5.50x. Intl Bk Ctr.

--English-Arabic; Arabic-English Dictionary. 1979. pap. 15.00x. Intl Bk Ctr.

--English-Arabic Pocket Dictionary. 1980. pap. 5.50x. Intl Bk Ctr.

ARABIC LITERATURE–HISTORY AND CRITICISM

Atil, Esin. Kalila Wa Dimna: Fables from a Fourteenth Century Arabic Manuscript. (Illus.). 96p. (Orig.). 1981. 17.50 (ISBN 0-87474-216-1); pap. 9.95 (ISBN 0-87474-215-3). Smithsonian.

ARABIC LITERATURE–TRANSLATIONS INTO ENGLISH

Wormhoudt, Arthur, tr. from Classical Arabic. Selections from the Quran. (Arab Translation Ser.: No. 51). 175p. 1981. pap. 6.50x (ISBN 0-916358-03-8). Wormhoudt.

ARABIC PHILOSOPHY
see Philosophy, Arab

ARABIC POETRY–TRANSLATIONS INTO ENGLISH

Wormhoudt, Arthur, tr. from Classical Arabic. Dhikra Al Tanisi. (Arab Translation Ser.: No. 53). (Illus.). 1981. pap. 6.50x (ISBN 0-916358-09-7). Wormhoudt.

Wormhoudt, Arthur, tr. Dhikra Ibn Al Hajjaj. (Arab Translation Ser.: No. 55). (Illus.). 160p. pap. 6.50x (ISBN 0-916358-04-6). Wormhoudt.

Wormhoudt, Arthur, tr. from Classical Arabic. The Diwan of Abu Tayyib Al Mutanabbi: Complete with Comments. (Arab Translation Ser.: No. 52). 200p. 1981. pap. 6.50x (ISBN 0-916358-07-0). Wormhoudt.

ARABIC TALES
see Tales, Arabic

ARABS IN PALESTINE
see Palestinian Arabs

ARANEIDA
see Spiders

ARAPAHO INDIANS
see Indians of North America–The West

ARBITRATION, INDUSTRIAL
see also Collective Bargaining; Grievance Procedures; Strikes and Lockouts

Gohmann, John W. Arbitration & Representation: Applications in Air & Rail Labor Relations. LC 80-84183. 336p. 1981. text ed. 22.50 (ISBN 0-8403-2335-2). Kendall-Hunt.

Prasow, Paul & Peters, Edward. Arbitration & Collective Bargaining. 2nd ed. 480p. 22.00x (ISBN 0-07-050674-4, C). McGraw.

Schwartz, Philip J. Coalition Bargaining. (Key Issues Ser.: No. 5). 1970. pap. 2.00 (ISBN 0-87546-241-3). NY Sch Indus Rel.

ARBITRATION, INTERNATIONAL
see also Diplomatic Negotiations in International Disputes; Disarmament

Consensus & Peace. 231p. 1981. pap. 20.75 (ISBN 92-3-101851-5, U1055, UNESCO). Unipub.

Hoeber, Francis P. How Little Is Enough? SALT & Security in the Long Run. (NSIC Strategy Paper Ser.: No. 35). 96p. 1981. pap. text ed. 5.95x (ISBN 0-8448-1383-4). Crane-Russak Co.

ARBLAY, MME. FRANCES (BURNEY) D', 1752-1840

Burney, Fanny. The Journals & Letters of Fanny Burney (Madame D'Arblay), Eighteen Twelve to Eighteen Fourteen: Vol. VII, Letters 632-834. Bloom, Edward A., et al, eds. (Illus.). 650p. 1978. 69.00x (ISBN 0-19-812468-6). Oxford U Pr.

ARBORICULTURE
see Forests and Forestry; Fruit-Culture; Nurseries (Horticulture); Tree Breeding; Trees

ARCHAEOLOGICAL SPECIMENS
see Antiquities

ARCHAEOLOGISTS

Hudson, K. Social History of Archaeology. 1980. text ed. 37.50x (ISBN 0-333-25679-4). Humanities.

Williams, Barbara. Women in Archaeology. 174p. 1981. 9.95. Walker & Co.

ARCHAEOLOGY
see also Antiquities; Architecture, Ancient; Christian Art and Symbolism; Ethnology; Funeral Rites and Ceremonies; Gems; Heraldry; Historic Sites; Indians–Antiquities; Industrial Archaeology; Man, Prehistoric; Mythology; Numismatics; Pottery; Pyramids; Stone Age; Temples
also subdivision Antiquities under names of countries, regions, cities, etc., e.g. Crete–Antiquities

Anderson, Duane C. & Semken, Holmes, eds. The Cherokee Excavations: Holocene Ecology & Human Adaptations in Northwestern Iowa. (Studies in Archaeology). 1980. 23.00 (ISBN 0-12-058260-0). Acad Pr.

Binford, Lewis R. Bones: Ancient Men & Modern Myths. LC 80-2327. (Studies in Archaeology Ser.). 1981. price not set (ISBN 0-12-100035-4). Acad Pr.

Bradford, John. Ancient Landscapes: Studies in Field Archaeology. LC 80-23204. (Illus.). xvii, 297p. 1980. Repr. of 1957 ed. lib. bdg. 49.75x (ISBN 0-313-22849-3, BRAL). Greenwood.

Clarke, David L. & Chapman, Robert. Analytical Archaeology. 2nd ed. 1981. pap. text ed. 12.50 (ISBN 0-231-04631-6). Columbia U Pr.

Cornell, James. The First Stargazers. (Illus.). 288p. 1981. 17.95 (ISBN 0-684-16799-9, ScribT). Scribner.

Gaines, Sylvia W. Data Bank Applications in Archaeology. 1980. pap. write for info. (ISBN 0-8165-0686-8). U of Ariz Pr.

Gottlieb, Carla. The Restoration of the 'Nereid Monument' at Xanthos. (Illus.). 340p. 1980. 30.00 (ISBN 0-9604420-0-6); pap. 25.00 (ISBN 0-686-28889-0). Boian Bks.

Johnson, Jane. Maroni De Chypre. (Studies in Mediterranean Archaeology Ser.: LIX). 1980. text ed. 42.00x (ISBN 91-85058-94-7). Humanities.

Jurmain, et al. Physical Anthropology & Archaeology. (Illus.). 1981. pap. text ed. 11.96 (ISBN 0-8299-0388-7). West Pub.

Kelly, Joyce. The Complete Visitor's Guide to Mesoamerican Ruins. (Illus.). 480p. 1981. 35.00 (ISBN 0-8061-1566-1). U of Okla Pr.

Mason, Ronald J. Great Lakes Archaeology. LC 80-2340. (New World Archaeological Record Ser.). 1981. price not set (ISBN 0-12-477850-X). Acad Pr.

Oswalt, Wendell H. Kolmakovskiy Redoubt: The Ethnoarchaeology of a Russian Fort in Alaska. LC 80-53304. (Monumenta Archaeologica Ser.: No. 8). (Illus.). 212p. 1980. 10.50 (ISBN 0-917956-17-6). UCLA Arch.

Prufer, Olaf. Raven Rocks: A Woodland Rockshelter in Belmont County, Ohio. Seeman, Mark F., ed. LC 80-84664. (Kent State Research Papers in Archaeology: No. 1). (Illus.). 104p. (Orig.). 1981. pap. 6.00x (ISBN 0-87338-254-4). Kent St U Pr.

Ramachandran, K. S. Archaeology of South India: Tamilnadu. 1980. 40.00x (ISBN 0-8364-0669-9, Pub. by Sundeep). South Asia Bks.

Robbins, Maurice & Irving, Mary B. The Amateur Archaeologist's Handbook. 3rd ed. LC 80-7901. (Illus.). 304p. 11.95 (ISBN 0-690-01976-9, HarpT). Har-Row.

Sorrell, Alan. Reconstructing the Past. Sorrell, Mark, ed. (Illus.). 168p. 1981. 19.50x (ISBN 0-389-20196-0). B&N.

Sullivan, George, ed. Discover Archaeology. 288p. 1981. pap. 4.95 (ISBN 0-14-046491-3). Penguin.

Weatherhill, Craig. Belerion: Ancient Sites of Land's End. 96p. 1980. 15.00x (ISBN 0-906720-01-X, Pub. by Hodge England). State Mutual Bk.

Weaver, Muriel P. The Aztecs, & Their Presecessors: Archaeology of Mesoamerica. 2nd ed. (Studies in Archaeology). 1981. write for info. (ISBN 0-12-785936-5). Acad Pr.

Whitley, David S., et al, eds. Inland Chumash Archaeological Investigations. (Monographs: Vol. XV). (Illus.). 258p. 1980. pap. 7.00 (ISBN 0-917956-18-4). UCLA Arch.

Wright, Henry T., III. An Early Town on the Deh Luran Plain: Excavations at Tepe Farukhabad. (Memoirs Ser.: No. 13). 1980. pap. write for info. (ISBN 0-932206-87-5). U Mich Mus Anthro.

ARCHAEOLOGY–ADDRESSES, ESSAYS, LECTURES

Daniel, Glyn, ed. Towards a History of Archaeology. 192p. 1981. 27.50 (ISBN 0-500-05039-2). Thames Hudson.

ARCHAEOLOGY–BIBLIOGRAPHY

Heizer, Robert F., et al. Archaeology: A Bibliographical Guide to the Basic Literature. LC 77-83376. 400p. 1980. lib. bdg. 38.00 (ISBN 0-8240-9826-9). Garland Pub.

ARCHAEOLOGY–DICTIONARIES

Champion, Sara. Dictionary of Terms & Techniques in Archeology. 1980. 15.95 (ISBN 0-87196-445-7). Facts on File.

ARCHAEOLOGY–HISTORY

Hodder, I., et al. Pattern of the Past. LC 79-8497. (Illus.). 424p. Date not set. 49.50 (ISBN 0-521-22763-1). Cambridge U Pr.

Loofs-Wissowa, H. H. E., ed. The Diffusion of Material Culture. (Asian & Pacific Archaeology Ser.: No.9). (Illus.). 393p. (Orig.). 1980. pap. 10.00x (ISBN 0-8248-0744-8). U Pr of Hawaii.

ARCHAEOLOGY–JUVENILE LITERATURE

Morrison, Velma F. Going on a Dig. LC 80-2776. (Illus.). 128p. (gr. 5 up). 1981. PLB 6.95 (ISBN 0-396-07915-6). Dodd.

ARCHAEOLOGY–METHODOLOGY

Alex, Lynn M. Exploring Iowa's Past: A Guide to Prehistoric Archaeology. LC 80-21391. (Illus.). 180p. 1980. pap. 7.95 (ISBN 0-87745-108-7). U of Iowa Pr.

Dancey, William S. Archaeology: Field Methods. (Modern Physical Anthropology Ser.). 184p. (Orig.). 1981. pap. text ed. write for info. (ISBN 0-8087-0440-0). Burgess.

Sabloff, Jeremy A., ed. Simulations in Archaeology. (School of American Research Advanced Seminar Ser.). (Illus.). 440p. 1981. 29.95x (ISBN 0-8263-0576-8). U of NM Pr.

ARCHAEOLOGY, BIBLICAL
see Bible–Antiquities

ARCHAEOLOGY, CHRISTIAN
see Christian Antiquities

ARCHAEOLOGY, CLASSICAL
see Classical Antiquities

ARCHAEOLOGY, INDUSTRIAL
see Industrial Archaeology

ARCHBISHOPS
see Bishops

ARCHERY

Foy, Tom. A Guide to Archery. (Illus.). 176p. 1981. 14.95 (ISBN 0-7207-1245-9). Merrimack Bk Serv.

Gillelan, G. Howard. The Complete Book of Bow & Arrow. rev., 3rd ed. (Illus.). 330p. 1981. pap. 9.95 (ISBN 0-8117-2118-3). Stackpole.

Glogan, Joseph. Sportsmans Book of U.S. Records. (Illus.). 96p. (Orig.). 1980. pap. text ed. 2.50 (ISBN 0-937328-00-6). NY Hunting.

ARCHERY–JUVENILE LITERATURE

Thomas, Art. Archery Is for Me. LC 81-22. (Sports for Me Bks.). (Illus.). (gr. 2-5). 1981. PLB 5.95 (ISBN 0-8225-1091-X). Lerner Pubns.

ARCHITECTS
see also Architecture As a Profession
also names of architects, Wright, Frank Lloyd

Cathcart, Richard B. Herman Sorgel. (Architecture Ser.: Bibliography A-181). 61p. pap. 6.50. Vance Biblios.

Colvin, Howard & Newman, John. Of Building: Roger North's Writings on Architects. (Illus.). 200p. 1981. 45.00 (ISBN 0-19-817325-3). Oxford U Pr.

Greenbeg, Alan & George, Michael, eds. Student's Edition of Monograph of the Work of McKim, Mead & White--1879-1915. (Illus.). 160p. 1981. 18.95 (ISBN 0-8038-6774-3); pap. 10.95 (ISBN 0-8038-6775-1). Hastings.

Hardin, Evamaria. Archimedes Russell: Upstate Architect. (Illus.). 108p. 1980. pap. 5.95 (ISBN 0-8156-0165-4). Syracuse U Pr.

Hirst, Michael. Sebastiano Del Piombo. (Studies in the History of Art & Architecture). (Illus.). 288p. 1981. 98.00 (ISBN 0-19-817308-3). Oxford U Pr.

Lemagny, J. C. & De Menil, Dominiqueintro. by. Visionary Architects: Boullee, Ledoux, Lequeu. (Illus.). 1968. pap. 8.00 (ISBN 0-914412-21-3). Inst for the Arts.

Metcalf, Pricilla. James Knowles: Victorian Editor & Architect. (Illus.). 414p. 1980. 44.00x (ISBN 0-19-812626-3). Oxford U Pr.

Simpson, Duncan. C. F. A. Voysey: An Architect of Individuality. 160p. 1981. 19.95 (ISBN 0-8230-7483-8, Whitney Lib). Watson-Guptill.

ARCHITECTURAL ACOUSTICS
see also Electro-Acoustics

Pierce, Allan D. Acoustics: An Introducton to Its Physical Principles & Applications. (Illus.). 656p. 1981. text ed. 28.95x (ISBN 0-07-049961-6, C); write for info solutions manual (ISBN 0-07-049962-4). McGraw.

ARCHITECTURAL DESIGN
see Architecture–Details; Architecture–Designs and Plans

ARCHITECTURAL DETAILS
see Architecture–Details

ARCHITECTURAL DRAWING
see also Architecture–Designs and Plans; Architecture–Details

Burden, Ernest. Entourage: A Tracing File for Architecture & Interior Design Drawing. (Illus.). 256p. 1981. 15.95 (ISBN 0-07-008930-2). McGraw.

Frishman, Bernard L. & Loshak, Lionel. Metric Architectural Drawing: A Manual for Designers & Draftsmen. 160p. 1981. 20.00 (ISBN 0-471-07724-0, Pub. by Wiley-Interscience). Wiley.

Hillary, Clarence F. Basic Architectural Drawing. (A Promotion of the Arts Library Bk.). (Illus.). 141p. 1981. 37.45 (ISBN 0-930582-98-5). Gloucester Art.
Lewis, S. Architectural Draftsman's Reference Handbook. 1981. 25.00 (ISBN 0-13-044164-3). P-H.
Weidhass, Ernest H. Architectural Drafting & Construction. 560p. 1981. text ed. 24.95; instr's hdbk. avail. Allyn.

ARCHITECTURAL ENGINEERING
see Building; Strains and Stresses; Strength of Materials; Structures, Theory Of

ARCHITECTURAL IRONWORK
Menten, Theodore. Art Nouveau Decorative Ironwork: One Hundred & Fifty Photographic Illustrations. (Illus.). 144p. 1981. pap. write for info. (ISBN 0-486-23986-1). Dover.

ARCHITECTURAL LAW AND LEGISLATION
see Building Laws

ARCHITECTURAL LIBRARIES
Vance, Mary. New Publications for Architectural Libraries, March Nineteen Eighty. (Architecture Ser.: Bibliography A-196). 64p. 1980. pap. 7.00. Vance Biblios.
--New Publications for Architecture Libraries, April Nineteen Eighty. (Architecture Ser.: Bibliography A-218). 63p. 1980. pap. 7.00. Vance Biblios.
--New Publications for Architecture Libraries, May Nineteen Eighty. (Architecture Ser.: Bibliography A-236). 55p. 1980. pap. 6.00. Vance Biblios.
--New Publications for Architecture Libraries, November Nineteen Eighty. (Architecture Ser.: Bibliography A-357). 50p. 1980. pap. 7.50. Vance Biblios.
--New Publications for Architecture Libraries, September Nineteen Eighty. (Architecture Ser.: Bibliography A-317). 55p. Date not set. pap. price not set. Vance Biblios.

ARCHITECTURAL LIGHTING
see Lighting, Architectural and Decorative

ARCHITECTURAL PERSPECTIVE
see Perspective

ARCHITECTURAL PRACTICE
see Architecture As a Profession

ARCHITECTURE
see also Building; Building Materials; Buildings; Castles; Cathedrals; Church Architecture; Concrete Construction; Environmental Engineering (Buildings); Historic Buildings; Hospitals-Design and Construction; Lighting; Lighting, Architectural and Decorative; Mosques; Moving-Picture Theaters; Naval Architecture; Palaces; Sepulchral Monuments; Strains and Stresses; Strength of Materials; Structural Engineering
also headings beginning with the word Architectural
Alexander, Christopher. The Linz Cafe. (Illus.). 96p. 1981. 19.95 (ISBN 0-19-520263-5). Oxford U Pr.
Alpern, Andrew. Handbook of Specialty Elements in Architecture. (Illus.). 448p. 1981. 32.50 (ISBN 0-07-001360-8, P&RB). McGraw.
Architectural Record Magazine. Contextual Architecture: Responding to Existing Styles. Ray, Keith, ed. (Architecture Ser.). (Illus.). 1980. 27.50 (ISBN 0-07-002332-8). McGraw.
Faulkner, Waldron. Architecture & Color. 142p. 1981. Repr. of 1972 ed. text ed. price not set. Krieger.
Friedman, Yona. Toward a Scientific Architecture. Lang, Cynthia, tr. from Fr. 208p. 1980. pap. 4.95 (ISBN 0-262-56019-4). MIT Pr.
Greene, Herb & Greene, Nanine H. Building to Last. (Illus.). 168p. 1981. 24.95. Architectural.
Greengerg, Allan M. Standards Relating to Architecture of Facilities. (Juvenile Justice Standards Project Ser.). 1980. softcover 6.95 (ISBN 0-88410-813-9); casebound 14.50. Ballinger Pub.
Hamlin, Howard M. The Five Orders of Classic Architecture. (Illus.). 148p. 1981. 69.75 (ISBN 0-930582-95-0). Gloucester Art.
Krier, Leon, et al. Rational Architecture. (Archives d'Architecture Moderne Ser.). (Illus.). 216p. (Eng. & Fr.). 1978. 37.50 (ISBN 0-8150-0931-3); pap. 29.50 (ISBN 0-8150-0921-6). Wittenborn.
Muschenheim, William. Why Architecture? 13.50 (ISBN 0-89720-033-0). Green Hill.
Owen, Robert D. Hints on Public Architecture. LC 77-17509. (Illus.). 119p. 1978. Repr. of 1849 ed. 49.50x (ISBN 0-87474-736-8). Smithsonian.
SITE. Architecture As Art. (Illus.). 112p. 1981. pap. 14.95 (ISBN 0-312-04814-9). St Martin.

ARCHITECTURE-BIBLIOGRAPHY
The Research Libraries of the New York Public Library & the Library of Congress. Bibliographic Guide to Art & Architecture: 1980. (Library Catalogs-Bib. Guides Ser.). 1981. lib. bdg. 135.00 (ISBN 0-8161-6881-4). G K Hall.
Vance Bibliographies. Index to Architecture Series Bibliography: No. a-155 to A-396, Jan. 1980 to Dec. 1980, No. A-155 To A-396, Jan. 1980 To Dec. 1980. (Architecture Ser.: Bibliography: A-397). 50p. 1981. pap. 7.50. Vance Biblios.
Vance, Mary. New Publications for Architecture Libraries: February 1980. (Architecture Ser. Bibliography a-176). 56p. 1980. pap. 6.00. Vance Biblios.

ARCHITECTURE-CLIMATIC FACTORS
see Architecture and Climate

ARCHITECTURE-CONSERVATION AND RESTORATION
see also Buildings-Repair and Reconstruction
Datel, Robin E. A Selected Annotated Bibliography of Works on Western European Building Conservation, Housing, & Inner Cities. (Architecture Ser.: Bibliography: A-396). 51p. 1980. pap. 7.50. Vance Biblios.
Flavin, Christopher. Energy & Architecture: The Solar & Conservation Potential. LC 80-54002. (Worldwatch Papers). 1980. pap. 2.00 (ISBN 0-916468-39-9). Worldwatch Inst.
Historic House Association of America. Historic Property Owner's Handbook. 2nd ed. (Illus.). 96p. (Orig.). 1981. pap. 7.95 (ISBN 0-89133-094-1). Preservation Pr.
National Trust for Historic Preservation. Conserve Neighborhoods Notebook. (Illus.). 154p. 1980. 12.95 (ISBN 0-89133-092-5). Preservation Pr.
--Preservation: Reusing America's Energy. (Illus.). 128p. (Orig.). 1981. pap. 9.95 (ISBN 0-89133-095-X). Preservation Pr.

ARCHITECTURE-DATA PROCESSING
ICS Nineteen Eighty-One: Proceedings of the International Computing Symposium on Systems Architecture. 1981. pap. text ed. price not set (ISBN 0-86103-050-8, Westbury Hse). Butterworth.
Purcell, Patrick. Computing in Design. 1981. text ed. price not set (ISBN 0-86103-045-1, Westbury Hse). Butterworth.

ARCHITECTURE-DESIGNS AND PLANS
see also Architecture, Domestic-Designs and Plans; Hospitals-Design and Construction
Abbott, Derek & Pollit, Kimball. Hill Housing: A Guide to Design & Construction. 304p. 1981. 34.50 (ISBN 0-8230-7259-2, Whitney Lib). Watson-Guptill.
Crump, Ralph W., ed. The Design Connection: Energy & Technology in Architecture. Harms, Martin J. (Preston Thomas Memorial Series in Architecture). 144p. 1981. text ed. 19.95 (ISBN 0-442-23125-3). Van Nos Reinhold.
Greenbeg, Alan & George, Michael, eds. Student's Edition of Monograph of the Work of McKim, Mead & White--1879-1915. (Illus.). 160p. 1981. 18.95 (ISBN 0-8038-6774-3); pap. 10.95 (ISBN 0-8038-6775-1). Hastings.
Hoffmann, Kurt, et al. Designing Architectural Facades: An Ideas File for Architects. (Illus.). 168p. 1975. 29.95x (ISBN 0-7114-3408-5). Intl Ideas.
Jones, J. Christopher. Design Methods: Seeds of Human Futures 1980 Edition a Review of New Topics. 440p. 1981. 22.50 (Pub. by Wiley Interscience). Wiley.
King, Jean C. & Esposito, Tony, eds. The Designer's Guide to Text Type. 320p. 1980. pap. 24.95 (ISBN 0-442-25425-3). Van Nos Reinhold.
Kinneir, Jock. Words & Buildings. 192p. 1981. 32.50 (ISBN 0-8230-7487-0, Whitney Lib). Watson-Guptill.
Maier, Manfred. Basic Principles of Design. 392p. 1981. pap. 35.00 (ISBN 0-442-21206-2). Van Nos Reinhold.
Purcell, Patrick. Computing in Design. 1981. text ed. price not set (ISBN 0-86103-045-1, Westbury Hse). Butterworth.
Salvadori, James A. Famous Architectural Illustrations from Distant Lands. (Illus.). 137p. 1981. 59.45 (ISBN 0-930582-96-9). Gloucester Art.
Underground Design. 100p. 1981. pap. 7.95 (ISBN 0-931790-20-4). Brick Hse Pub.

ARCHITECTURE-DETAILS
see also Ceilings; Doors and Doorways; Facades; Floors; Foundations; Roofs; Woodwork
Salvadori, James A. Famous Architectural Illustrations from Distant Lands. (Illus.). 137p. 1981. 59.45 (ISBN 0-930582-96-9). Gloucester Art.

ARCHITECTURE-HANDBOOKS, MANUALS, ETC.
Crump, Ralph W., ed. The Design Connection: Energy & Technology in Architecture. Harms, Martin J. (Preston Thomas Memorial Series in Architecture). 144p. 1981. text ed. 19.95 (ISBN 0-442-23125-3). Van Nos Reinhold.
Willis, Arthur J. & Willis, Christopher J. Practice & Procedure for the Quantity Surveyor. 8th ed. 239p. 1980. text ed. 30.00x (ISBN 0-246-11172-0, Pub. by Granada England); pap. text ed. 16.75x (ISBN 0-246-11242-5, Pub. by Granada England). Renouf.

ARCHITECTURE-HISTORY
Diamonstein, Barbaralee. Collaboration: Artists & Architects. 176p. (Orig.). 1981. 32.50 (Whitney Lib). Watson-Guptill.
Giedon, Sigfried. The Beginnings of Architecture: The Eternal Present, a Contribution on Constancy & Change, Vol. 2. LC 80-8733. (The A. W. Mellon Lectures in the Fine Arts, 1957, Bolligen Ser.: XXXV: 6,11). (Illus.). 604p. 1981. 42.50x (ISBN 0-691-09945-6); pap. 15.00 (ISBN 0-691-09945-6). Princeton U Pr.
Nichols, Frederick D. & Griswold, Ralph E. Thomas Jefferson, Landscape Architect. LC 77-10601. (Illus.). ix, 196p. 1981. pap. 4.95x (ISBN 0-8139-0899-X). U Pr of Va.
Whiffen, Marcus & Koeper, Frederick. American Architecture: A History, 1607-1976. 600p. 1981. text ed. 20.00 (ISBN 0-262-23105-0). MIT Pr.

ARCHITECTURE-INFLUENCE OF CLIMATE
see Architecture and Climate

ARCHITECTURE-LAW AND LEGISLATION
see Building Laws

ARCHITECTURE-PICTORIAL WORKS
Blumenson, John J. Identifying American Architecture: A Pictorial Guide to Styles & Terms, 1600-1945. rev. ed. (Illus.). 1981. 12.95 (ISBN 0-393-01428-2). Norton.
Richardson, Albert E. Monumental Classic Architecture in Great Britain & Ireland. (Illus.). 1981. 25.00 (ISBN 0-393-01451-7); pap. 10.95 (ISBN 0-393-00053-2). Norton.

ARCHITECTURE-RESTORATION
see Architecture-Conservation and Restoration

ARCHITECTURE-VOCATIONAL GUIDANCE
see Architecture As a Profession

ARCHITECTURE-ARMENIA
Strzygowski, Josef. Die Baukunst der Armenier und Europa, 2 vols. (Arbeiten des Kunsthistorischen Instituts der Universitat Wien: Nos. 9-10). (Illus.). xii, 888p. (Ger.). 1981. Repr. of 1918 ed. Set. lib. bdg. 200.00x (ISBN 0-89241-157-0). Caratzas Bros.

ARCHITECTURE-ASIA
Scott, Miriam M. & Stratton, Carol. The Art of Sukhothai. (Illus.). 200p. 1980. 35.95x (ISBN 0-19-580434-1). Oxford U Pr.

ARCHITECTURE-AUSTRALIA
Johnson, Donald L., ed. Australian Architecture, 1901 to 1951: Sources of Modernism. 240p. 1980. 35.00x (ISBN 0-424-00071-7, Pub. by Sydney U Pr Australia). Intl Schol Bk Serv.

ARCHITECTURE-EGYPT
Smith, W. Stevenson. The Art & Architecture of Ancient Egypt. rev ed. 360p. 1981. pap. 19.95 (ISBN 0-14-056114-5). Penguin.

ARCHITECTURE-EUROPE
see also Architecture, Domestic-Europe
Mainstone, Madeleine. The Seventeenth Century. LC 80-40039. (Cambridge History of Art Ser.: No. 4). (Illus.). 100p. Date not set. 19.95 (ISBN 0-521-22162-5); pap. 6.95 (ISBN 0-521-29376-6). Cambridge U Pr.

ARCHITECTURE-GREAT BRITAIN
see also Architecture, Domestic-Great Britain
Ditchfield, P. H. Vanishing Old Castles in England. (A Philosophy of History Library Book). (Illus.). 109p. 1981. 49.75 (ISBN 0-86650-003-0). Gloucester Art.
Richardson, Albert E. Monumental Classic Architecture in Great Britain & Ireland. (Illus.). 1981. 25.00 (ISBN 0-393-01451-7); pap. 10.95 (ISBN 0-393-00053-2). Norton.
Simpson, Duncan. C. F. A. Voysey: An Architect of Individuality. 160p. 1981. 19.95 (ISBN 0-8230-7483-8, Whitney Lib). Watson-Guptill.
Tallmadge, Thomas E. The Story of England's Architecture. 363p. 1980. Repr. of 1934 ed. lib. bdg. 40.00 (ISBN 0-8495-5160-9). Arden Lib.

ARCHITECTURE-GREECE
see Architecture, Greek

ARCHITECTURE-IRELAND
Murphy, John. Irish Shop Prints. (Illus.). 72p. 1981. pap. cancelled (ISBN 0-312-43623-8). St Martin.
Richardson, Albert E. Monumental Classic Architecture in Great Britain & Ireland. (Illus.). 1981. 25.00 (ISBN 0-393-01451-7); pap. 10.95 (ISBN 0-393-00053-2). Norton.

ARCHITECTURE-JAPAN
see also Architecture, Domestic-Japan
Frampton, Kenneth, ed. A New Wave of Japanese Architecture. (IAUS Exhibition Catalogues Ser.). (Illus.). 96p. 1978. pap. 12.00 (ISBN 0-932628-00-1). IAUS.

ARCHITECTURE-ROME
see Architecture, Roman

ARCHITECTURE-RUSSIA
Starr, S. Fredrick. Melnikov: Solo Architect in a Mass Society. LC 77-85566. (Illus.). 295p. 1981. pap. 9.95 (ISBN 0-691-00331-9). Princeton U Pr.

ARCHITECTURE-UNITED STATES
see also Architecture, Colonial; Architecture, Domestic-United States
Bernhardi, Robert. Building of Oakland with a Section on Piedmont. 116p. 1979. 14.95 (ISBN 0-9605472-0-7). Forest Hill.
Blumenson, John J. Identifying American Architecture: A Pictorial Guide to Styles & Terms, 1600-1945. rev. ed. (Illus.). 1981. 12.95 (ISBN 0-393-01428-2). Norton.
Gleve, Paul & Shulman, Julius. The Architecture of Los Angeles. LC 80-28988. 1981. 35.00 (ISBN 0-8310-7142-7). Howell-North.
Hunt. Encyclopedia of American Architecture. 100p. Date not set. 35.00 (ISBN 0-07-031299-0). McGraw.
Margolies, John. The End of the Road. Smith, C. Ray, ed. 96p. 1981. pap. 12.95 (ISBN 0-14-005840-0). Penguin.
Prokopoff, Stephen S. & Siegfried, Joan C. The Nineteenth-Century Architecture of Saratoga Springs. (Architecture Worth Saving in New York State Ser.). (Illus.). 104p. 1980. pap. write for info. (ISBN 0-89062-001-6). NYSCA.
Tunnard, Christopher & Pushkarev, Boris. Man-Made America: Chaos or Control. Bell, Harriet, ed. 1981. 12.95 (ISBN 0-517-54379-6, Harmony). Crown.
Vance, Mary. Historical Society Architectural Publications: Vermont, Virginia, Washington, West Virginia, Wisconsin, Wyoming. (Architecture Ser.: Bibliography A-178). 51p. 1980. pap. 5.50. Vance Biblios.

ARCHITECTURE, ANCIENT
see also Pyramids; Temples
also Architecture-Egypt; Architecture, greek and similar headings
Jett, Stephen C. & Spencer, Virginia E. Navajo Architecture: Forms, History, Distributions. 1981. text ed. 24.50x (ISBN 0-8165-0688-4); pap. text ed. 12.50x (ISBN 0-8165-0723-6). U of Ariz Pr.

ARCHITECTURE, ARAB
see Architecture, Islamic

ARCHITECTURE, BAROQUE
Lavin, Irving. Bernini & the Unity of the Visual Arts, 2 vols. (Illus.). 498p. 1980. text ed. 89.00x (ISBN 0-19-520184-1). Oxford U Fr.

ARCHITECTURE, BUDDHIST
Prip-Moller, Johannes. Chinese Buddhist Monasteries. (Illus.). 410p. 1981. 65.00 (ISBN 0-85656-034-0). Great Eastern.

ARCHITECTURE, CHURCH
see Church Architecture

ARCHITECTURE, COLONIAL
see also Architecture-United States; Architecture, Domestic-United States
Perrin, Richard W. Historic Wisconsin Buildings: A Survey in Pioneer Architecture 1835-1870. 2nd ed. (Publication in History Ser.: No. 4). (Illus.). 150p. 1981. pap. 7.95. Milwaukee Pub.

ARCHITECTURE, COMPUTER
see Computer Architecture

ARCHITECTURE, DOMESTIC
see also Apartment Houses; Bathrooms; Cottages; Country Homes; Decks (Architecture, Domestic); House Construction; Nurseries; Patios
Ball, V. K. Architecture & Interior Design: A Basic History of the Eighteenth Through Twentieth Centuries, 2 vol. set. 1980. Set. 80.00 (ISBN 0-471-08721-1, Pub. by Wiley-Interscience); Set. pap. 50.00 (ISBN 0-471-08720-3); pap. 27.50 (ISBN 0-471-08722-X). Wiley.
--Architecture & Interior Design: A Basic History of the Eighteenth Through Twentieth Centuries. 464p. 1980. pap. 27.50 (ISBN 0-471-08722-X, Pub. by Wiley-Interscience). Wiley.
Blaser, Werner. Wood Houses: Form in Rural Architecture. (Illus.). 216p. (Eng., Fr. & Ger.). 1980. text ed. 19.00 (ISBN 0-89192-300-4). Interbk Inc.
Hughes, G. T., ed. Gregynog: A History of the House. 1977. 40.00 (ISBN 0-7083-0634-9). Verry.
Karp, Ben. Ornamental Carpentry of Nineteenth-Century American Houses: One Hundred Sixty Five Photographs. rev. ed. Orig. Title: Wood Motifs in American Domestic Architecture. (Illus.). 96p. 1981. pap. price not set (ISBN 0-486-24144-0). Dover.
Weiss, Jeffrey & Gault, Lila. Small Houses. 1980. pap. 7.95 (ISBN 0-446-97346-7). Warner Bks.

ARCHITECTURE, DOMESTIC-DESIGNS AND PLANS
Abbott, Derek & Pollit, Kimball. Hill Housing: A Guide to Design & Construction. 304p. 1981. 34.50 (ISBN 0-8230-7259-2, Whitney Lib). Watson-Guptill.
Davis, Albert J. & Schubert, Robert P. Alternative Natural Energy Sources in Building Design. 2nd ed. 256p. 1981. 17.95 (ISBN 0-442-23143-1); pap. 9.95 (ISBN 0-442-22008-1). Van Nos Reinhold.
Davis, Sam. The Form of Housing. 320p. 1981. pap. text ed. 14.95 (ISBN 0-442-27218-9). Van Nos Reinhold.
Energy Efficient Building Handbook. 1981. 45.00 (ISBN 0-89336-283-2). BCC.
Homes, Today & Tomorrow. rev. ed. (gr. 9-12). 1981. text ed. 15.92 (ISBN 0-87002-326-8). Bennett Co.
Schild, Erich, et al. Structural Failure in Residential Buildings, 3 vols. Incl. Vol. 1. Flat Roofs, Roof Terraces & Balconies. 24.50x (ISBN 0-470-26305-9); Vol. 2. External Walls & Openings. 27.95x (ISBN 0-470-26789-5); Vol. 3. 154p. 29.95x (ISBN 0-470-26846-8). LC 77-28647. 1978-80. Set. 85.85x (ISBN 0-470-26898-0). Halsted Pr.

ARCHITECTURE, DOMESTIC-EUROPE
Filigree Architecture: Metal & Glass Construction. (Illus.). 216p. (Eng. Fr. & Ger.). 1980. text ed. 19.00 (ISBN 0-89192-298-9). Interbk Inc.

ARCHITECTURE, DOMESTIC-FRANCE
Chamberlain, Samuel. Domestic Architecture in Rural France. (Illus.). 64p. (Orig.). 1981. pap. 7.95 (ISBN 0-8038-1578-6). Hastings.

ARCHITECTURE, DOMESTIC-GREAT BRITAIN
O'Neill, Paul D. Lutyens: Country Houses. 168p. 1981. 19.95 (ISBN 0-8230-7361-0, Whitney Lib). Watson-Guptill.

ARCHITECTURE, DOMESTIC-IRELAND
De Breffney, Brian & Folliott, Rosemary. The Houses of Ireland: Domestic Architecture from the Medieval Castle to the Edwardian Villa. (Illus.). 240p. 1981. 19.95 (ISBN 0-500-24091-4). Thames Hudson.

ARCHITECTURE, DOMESTIC-JAPAN
Fawcett, Chris. The New Japanese House: Ritual & Anti-Ritual Patterns of Dwelling. LC 80-8224. (Illus.). 192p. 1981. 25.00 (ISBN 0-06-433010-9, HarpT). Har-Row.

Frampton, Kenneth, ed. A New Wave of Japanese Architecture. (IAUS Exhibition Catalogues Ser.). (Illus.). 96p. 1978. pap. 12.00 (ISBN 0-932628-00-1). IAUS.

ARCHITECTURE, DOMESTIC–UNITED STATES
see also Architecture–United States

Gill, Brendan. The Dream Come True: Great Houses of Los Angeles. 1980. 40.00 (ISBN 0-690-01893-2); ltd. ed 100.00 (ISBN 0-690-01961-0). Har-Row.

Handlin, David. The American Home: Architecture & Society 1815-1915. 1980. 20.00 (ISBN 0-316-34300-5); pap. text ed. 8.95 (ISBN 0-316-34299-8). Little.

Margolies, John. The End of the Road. Smith, C. Ray, ed. 96p. 1981. pap. 12.95 (ISBN 0-14-005840-0). Penguin.

Ordish, George. The Living American House: The 350-Year Story of a Home - an Ecological History. (Illus.). 1981. 11.95 (ISBN 0-686-69231-4). Morrow.

Severens, Kenneth. Southern Architecture: An Architectural & Cultural History of the South from the Colonization of America to the 20th Century. 1981. 18.95 (ISBN 0-525-20692-2). Dutton.

ARCHITECTURE, ECCLESIASTICAL
see Church Architecture

ARCHITECTURE, GOTHIC
see also Cathedrals; Church Architecture

Fitchen, John. The Construction of Gothic Cathedrals: A Study of Medieval Vault Erection. (Illus.). xxii, 344p. 1981. pap. 9.95 (ISBN 0-226-25203-5). U of Chicago Pr.

Parkhurst, Helen H. Cathedral: A Gothic Pilgrimage. 304p. 1980. Repr. of 1936 ed. lib. bdg. 40.00 (ISBN 0-8492-2174-9). R West.

ARCHITECTURE, GREEK
see also Temples
also subdivision antiquities under names of cities, e.g. Athens–Antiquities

D'Espouy, Hector. Fragments from Greek & Roman Architecture: The Classical America Edition of Hector D'Espouy's Plates. (Illus.). 1981. 19.95 (ISBN 0-393-01427-4); pap. 9.95 (ISBN 0-393-00052-4). Norton.

ARCHITECTURE, ISLAMIC
see also Mosques;
also particular buildings, e.g. Alhambra

Paccard, Andre. Traditional Islamic Craft in Moroccan Architecture, 2 vols. 1980. 495.00x (Pub. by Editions Atelier England). State Mutual Bk.

ARCHITECTURE, LIBRARY
see Library Architecture

ARCHITECTURE, MODERN–20TH CENTURY

Sorkin, Michael. Hardy Holzman Pfeiffer. 136p. 1981. 18.95 (ISBN 0-8230-7264-9, Whitney Lib). Watson-Guptill.

ARCHITECTURE, MOORISH
see Architecture, Islamic

ARCHITECTURE, MUSLIM
see Architecture, Islamic

ARCHITECTURE, NAVAL
see Naval Architecture; Ship-Building

ARCHITECTURE, ORIENTAL
see also Architecture–Japan; Architecture, Domestic–Japan; Mosques; Temples
also particular mosques, temples, etc., e.g. Jerusalem–Temple

Chanh, Amos I. The Tao of Existence. 2nd ed. LC 80-8677. (Illus.). 88p. 1981. 14.50x (ISBN 0-691-03963-1); pap. 4.95 (ISBN 0-691-00330-0). Princeton U Pr.

ARCHITECTURE, ROMAN
see also Temples

D'Espouy, Hector. Fragments from Greek & Roman Architecture: The Classical America Edition of Hector D'Espouy's Plates. (Illus.). 1981. 19.95 (ISBN 0-393-01427-4); pap. 9.95 (ISBN 0-393-00052-4). Norton.

Ragette, Friedrich. Baalbek. LC 80-19626. (Illus.). 128p. 1981. 18.00 (ISBN 0-8155-5059-6). Noyes.

ARCHITECTURE, RURAL
see Architecture, Domestic; Cottages; Country Homes

ARCHITECTURE, SARACENIC
see Architecture, Islamic

ARCHITECTURE AND CLIMATE

Lawson, T. V. Wind Effects on Buildings: Vol. 1, Design Applicatons. (Illus.). xii, 344p. 1980. 55.00x (ISBN 0-85334-887-1). Burgess-Intl Ideas.

--Wind Effects on Buildings: Volume 2--Statistics & Meteorology. (Illus.). xii, 160p. 1980. 30.00x (ISBN 0-85334-893-6). Burgess-Intl Ideas.

ARCHITECTURE AND ENERGY CONSERVATION

Shurcliff, William A. Superinsulated Houses & Double-Envelope Houses. (Illus.). 228p. 1981. 19.95 (ISBN 0-931790-19-0); pap. 12.00. Brick Hse Pub.

ARCHITECTURE AND SOCIETY

Morris, William. Architecture, Industry & Wealth: Collected Papers by William Morris. Freedberg, Sydney J.; ed. LC 77-25760. (Connoisseurship, Criticism & Art History Ser.: Vol. 13). 163p. 1979. lib. bdg. 21.00 (ISBN 0-8240-3271-3). Garland Pub.

ARCHITECTURE AND SPACE
see Space (Architecture)

ARCHITECTURE AND THE AGED

Howell, Sandra C. Designing for Aging: Patterns of Use. (Illus.). 345p. 1980. text ed. 25.00x (ISBN 0-262-08107-5). MIT Pr.

ARCHITECTURE AS A PROFESSION

Sorkin, Michael. Hardy Holzman Pfeiffer. 136p. 1981. 18.95 (ISBN 0-8230-7264-9, Whitney Lib). Watson-Guptill.

ARCHIVES
see also Libraries; Manuscripts

Cook, Michael. Archives & the Computer. LC 80-41286. 152p. 1980. text ed. 27.00 (ISBN 0-408-10734-0). Butterworths.

Directory of Business Archives in the United States & Canada. 56p. (Orig.). 1980. pap. 6.00 (ISBN 0-931828-24-4). Soc Am Archivists.

Edinburgh University Library. First Supplement to Manuscripts, Edinburgh University Library. (Library Catalogs-Supplements). lib. bdg. 115.00 (ISBN 0-8161-0319-4). G K Hall.

Levstik, Frank R., compiled by. A Directory of State Archives in the United States. 66p. (Orig.). 1980. pap. 8.00 (ISBN 0-931828-26-0). Soc Am Archivists.

ARCHIVES–GREAT BRITAIN

Gervers, Michael, ed. The Cartulary of the Order of St. John of Jerusalem (Hospitalers) in England. (Records of Social & Economic History Ser.). 618p. 1980. 169.00 (ISBN 0-19-725996-0). Oxford U Pr.

ARCHIVES–RUSSIA

Brown, John H. & Grant, Steven A. The Russian Empire & Soviet Union: A Guide to Manuscripts & Archival Materials in the United States. (Libary Catalogs Supplement). 1981. lib. bdg. 75.00 (ISBN 0-8161-1300-9). G K Hall.

ARCTIC EXPEDITIONS
see Arctic Regions

ARCTIC REGIONS
see also North Pole
also names of expeditions and names of explorers

Jones, Tristan. Ice. 1980. pap. 2.75 (ISBN 0-686-69264-0, 50757). Avon.

Seton, Ernest T. The Arctic Prairies. (Nature Library Ser.). (Illus.). 320p. 1981. pap. 5.95 (ISBN 0-06-090841-6, CN 841, CN). Har-Row.

ARGENTINE LITERATURE–HISTORY AND CRITICISM

Pastor, Beatriz. Roberto Arlt y la Rebelion Alienada. LC 80-70560. 135p. (Span.). 1980. pap. write for info. (ISBN 0-935318-05-4). Edins Hispamerica.

ARGENTINE REPUBLIC–BIOGRAPHY

Fraser, Nicholas & Navarro, Marysa. Eva Peron. (Illus.). 1981. 14.95 (ISBN 0-393-01457-6). Norton.

ARGOT
see Slang

ARGUMENTATION
see Debates and Debating; Logic; Oratory; Reasoning

ARHYTHMIA
see Arrhythmia

ARIAS
see Songs

ARID REGIONS
see also Deserts

Goodall, D. W. & Perry, R. A., eds. Arid-Land Ecosystems: Structure, Functioning & Management, Vol. 2. LC 77-84810. (International Biological Programme Ser.: No. 17). 550p. Date not set. 110.00 (ISBN 0-521-22988-X). Cambridge U Pr.

Timmerhaus, Klaus D., ed. Energy Resources Recovery in Arid Lands. (Illus.). 200p. 1981. price not set (ISBN 0-8263-0582-2); pap. price not set (ISBN 0-8263-0583-0). U of NM Pr.

ARISTOTLE

Averroes. Middle Commentary on Aristotle Topics. Butterworth, Charles E. & Ahmad Abd al-Magid Haridi, eds. (Corpvs Commentariorvm Averrois in Aristotelem). 317p. (Orig., Arabic.). 1979. pap. 10.00 (ISBN 0-936770-03-1). Am Res Ctr Egypt.

ARITHMETIC
see also Accounting; Addition; Decimal System; Division; Fractions; Metric System; Multiplication; Numeration; Percentage; Subtraction

Eliopoulos, Nicholas C. Golden Arithmetization. 403p. (Orig.). 1980. pap. text ed. 30.00x (ISBN 0-9605396-0-3). Phystiklakis & Eliopoulos.

Miller, Charles D. & Salzman, Stanley A. Arithmetic: A Text-Workbook. 1981. pap. text ed. 13.95x (ISBN 0-673-15274-X). Scott F.

Pacholski, L., et al, eds. Model Theory of Algebra & Arithmetics: Procedings. (Lecture Notes in Mathematics Ser.: Vol. 834). 410p. 1981. pap. 24.50 (ISBN 0-686-69431-7). Springer-Verlag.

Spangler, David. Arithmetic Skills in Everyday Life: A Self-Correcting Competency Assessment. 112p. 1980. pap. text ed. 2.95x (ISBN 0-534-00917-4). Wadsworth Pub.

Spangler, Richard C. Arithmetic: The Essentials. 576p. (Orig.). 1981. pap. text ed. 15.95 (ISBN 0-675-08066-5); tchr's. ed. 5.95 (ISBN 0-675-09971-4). Merrill.

Thorndike, Edward L. The Psychology of Arithmetic. 314p. 1980. Repr. of 1922 ed. lib. bdg. 30.00 (ISBN 0-89760-890-9). Telegraph Bks.

ARITHMETIC–JUVENILE LITERATURE

A Arithma Games Fractions & Mixed Numbers. (gr. 3-7). 1980. pap. 7.20 (ISBN 0-913688-49-5). Pawnee Pub.

Arithma Games-Whole Numbers. (gr. 1-4). 1980. pap. 7.20 (ISBN 0-913688-48-7). Pawnee Pub.

Quinn, Daniel & Weatherall, Donald M. Addition & Subtraction Learning Module. (ps). 1974. pap. text ed. 330.25 (ISBN 0-89290-131-4, CM-52). Soc for Visual.

ARITHMETIC, COMMERCIAL
see Business Mathematics

ARITHMETIC, MECHANICAL
see Calculating-Machines

ARIZONA–DESCRIPTION AND TRAVEL

Mazel, David. Arizona Trails. Winnett, Thomas, ed. LC 80-53682. (Wilderness Press Trail Guide Ser.). (Illus.). 192p. (Orig.). 1981. pap. 7.95 (ISBN 0-89997-003-6). Wilderness Pr.

ARIZONA–HISTORY

Love, Frank & Feitz, Leland. Brothel to Boomtown: Yuma's Lively Past. (Illus., Orig.). 1981. pap. 2.95 (ISBN 0-936564-19-9). Little London.

Weiner, Melissa. Prescott: A Pictorial History. Friedman, Donna R., ed. (Illus.). 208p. 1981. pap. write for info. (ISBN 0-89865-092-5). Donning Co.

Whitlach, John. Shoot-Out at Dawn--An Arizona Tragedy. De Mente, Boye, ed. (Illus.). 176p. (Orig.). 1980. pap. 6.95 (ISBN 0-914778-37-4). Phoenix Bks.

ARK, NOAH'S
see Noah's Ark

ARKANSAS
see also names of cities, towns, etc. in Arkansas

Bell, James W. Little Rock Handbook. (Illus.). iv, 88p. (Orig.). 1980. pap. 7.95 (ISBN 0-939130-00-9). J W Bell.

Bradley, Matt. Arkansas...Its Land & People. LC 80-81993. (Illus.). 112p. 1980. 25.00 (ISBN 0-9604642-0-4); limited gift edition 55.00 (ISBN 0-9604642-1-2). Mus Sci & Hist.

Lecompte, Janet. Pueblo, Hardscrabble, Greenhorn: The Upper Arkansas, 1832-1856. LC 77-18616. (Illus.). 354p. 1981. pap. 7.95 (ISBN 0-8061-1723-0). U of Okla Pr.

ARKANSAS–POLITICS AND GOVERNMENT

Donovan, Timothy P. & Gatewood, Willard B., Jr., eds. The Governors of Arkansas: Essays in Political Biography. 1981. text ed. 24.00x (ISBN 0-938626-00-0). U of Mo Pr.

Faubus, Orval E. Down from the Hills. (Illus.). 528p. 1980. text ed. 25.00. Faubus.

ARMADA, 1588

Walker, Bryce. The Armada. Time-Life Bks. Eds., ed. (The Seafarers Ser.). (Illus.). 176p. 1981. 14.95 (ISBN 0-8094-2697-8). Time-Life.

ARMAMENTS
see also Aeronautics, Military; Armies; Disarmament; Firearms Industry and Trade
also Armies and navies of individual countries, e.g. United States–Army; Defenses under names of countries

Abbiatico, Mario. Grandi Incisioni Su Armi D'Bagi. (Illus.). Repr. of 1976 ed. 30.00. Arma Pr.

ARMED FORCES–POLITICAL ACTIVITY

Holt, Pat M. War Powers Resolution: The Role of Congress in U. S. Armed Intervention. 1978. pap. 4.25 (ISBN 0-8447-3299-0). Am Enterprise.

ARMENIA

Lang, D. M. Armenia: Cradle of Civilisation. 3rd ed. (Illus.). 330p. 1980. 35.00 (ISBN 0-04-956009-3, 2619). Allen Unwin.

ARMENIAN ARCHITECTURE
see Architecture–Armenia

ARMENIAN ART
see Art, Armenian

ARMENIAN LANGUAGE

International Conference on Armenian Linguistics, 1st. Proceedings: Proceedings. LC 80-24203. 1980. 25.00 (ISBN 0-88206-044-9). Caravan Bks.

Koushakdjian, Mardiros & Khantrouni, Dicran. Armenian-English - English-Armenian Dictionary. 2nd, rev. ed. 1372p. 1976. 35.00 (ISBN 0-686-68934-8). Heinman.

ARMENIAN MYTHOLOGY
see Mythology, Armenian

ARMIES
see also Disarmament; Militarism; Military Art and Science; Military Service, Compulsory; Sociology, Military; Soldiers
also Armies of individual countries, e.g. Great Britain–Army

Keegan, John. World Armies. 1980. 40.00 (ISBN 0-87196-407-4). Facts on File.

ARMOR
see Arms and Armor

ARMORED MILITARY VEHICLES
see Armored Vehicles, Military

ARMORED VEHICLES, MILITARY

Armoured Fighting Vehicles of the World. 3rd ed. Date not set. price not set (ScribT). Scribner.

ARMORED VESSELS
see Warships

ARMS, COATS OF
see Heraldry

ARMS AND ARMOR
see also Firearms; Rifles

Bannermans Catalogue of Military Goods 1927. facsimile ed. LC 80-68006. (Illus.). 384p. 1981. pap. 12.95 (ISBN 0-910676-20-8). DBI.

Fadala, Sam. Black Powder Handgun. LC 81-65102. 288p. (Orig.). 1981. pap. 8.95 (ISBN 0-910676-22-4, 9266). DBI.

Feist, Uwe. Aero Armor Series, Vol. 13. 52p. 1981. pap. 3.95 (ISBN 0-8168-2046-5). Aero.

Holmes, Bill. Home Workshop Guns for Defense & Resistance: The Handgun, Vol. II. Christensen, Devon, ed. (Illus.). 144p. (Orig.). 1979. pap. 6.00 (ISBN 0-87364-154-X). Paladin Ent.

Hoyem, George A. History of the Development of Small Arms Ammunition, Vol. I: Martial Long Arms, Flintlock Through Rimfire. LC 80-67532. (Illus.). 240p. 1981. 27.50x (ISBN 0-9604982-8-1). Armory Pubns.

Johnson, Thomas M. Collecting the Edged Weapons of the Third Reich, Vol. 4. Bradach, Wilfrid, tr. LC 75-15486. (Illus.). 1981. 25.00 (ISBN 0-686-69390-6). T M Johnson.

Kemp, Anthony. Weapons & Equipment of the Marlborough Wars. (Illus.). 192p. 1981. 24.95 (ISBN 0-7137-1013-6, Pub. by Blandford Pr England). Sterling.

Lewis, Jack. Modern Gun Values. 3rd ed. (Illus.). 384p. (Orig.). 1981. pap. 9.95 (ISBN 0-910676-19-4, 5836). DBI.

Miller, Gene E. The Art of Gun Collecting. 1981. 8.95 (ISBN 0-8062-1599-2). Carlton.

Oakeshott, Ewart. European Weapons & Armour. (Illus.). 277p. 1980. 29.95 (ISBN 0-686-68855-4). Beinfeld Pub.

Scofield, Jonathan. Muskets of Seventy-Six. 1981. pap. 2.75 (ISBN 0-440-05756-6). Dell.

--Tomahawks & Long Rifles. 1981. pap. 2.75 (ISBN 0-440-09119-5). Dell.

Truby, J. David. Quiet Killers II: Silencer Update. (Illus.). 80p. (Orig.). 1979. pap. 6.00 (ISBN 0-87364-163-9). Paladin Ent.

Wilkinson. Uniforms & Weapons of the Crimean War. pap. 14.95 (ISBN 0-7134-0666-6). David & Charles.

ARMS AND ARMOR, PRIMITIVE

Scofield, Jonathan. Tomahawks & Long Rifles. 1981. pap. 2.75 (ISBN 0-440-09119-5). Dell.

ARMS CONTROL
see Disarmament

ARMSTRONG, ANNIE W., d. 1938 -

Lloyd, Eva B. Annie: Herald of Home Missions. (Orig.). 1981. pap. 1.25 (ISBN 0-8054-9502-9). Broadman.

ARMY
see Armies; Military Art and Science;
also France–Army; United States–Army, and similar headings

ARMY WAGONS
see Vehicles, Military

ARNOLD, MATTHEW, 1822-1888

Elton, Oliver. Tennyson & Matthew Arnold. 96p. 1980. Repr. of 1924 ed. lib. bdg. 12.50 (ISBN 0-8492-4411-0). R West.

Moore, Charles L. Incense & Iconoclasm. 343p. 1980. Repr. of 1915 ed. lib. bdg. 30.00 (ISBN 0-89987-573-4). Century Bookbindery.

Roe, Frederick W., intro. by. Essays & Poems of Arnold. 497p. 1980. Repr. of 1928 ed. lib. bdg. 30.00 (ISBN 0-8492-7717-5). R West.

AROMATIC COMPOUNDS

Gmehling, J., et al. Aromatic Hydrocarbons: Vol. I, Pt. 7, Vapor-Liquid Equilibrium Data Collection. Behrens, D. & Eckermann, R., eds. (Dechema Chemistry Data Ser.). 564p. 1980. text ed. 106.00x (ISBN 3-9215-6723-8, Pub. by Dechema Germany). Scholium Jntl.

Tisserand, R. B. The Art of Aromatherapy. 320p. 1977. 18.00x (ISBN 0-8464-0993-3). Beekman Pubs.

ARRHYTHMIA

Szekeres, L., ed. Pharmacology of Antiarrhythmic Agents. (Intermnational Encyclopedia of Pharmacology & Therapeutics Ser.: Section 105). (Illus.). 328p. 1980. 70.00 (ISBN 0-08-025897-2). Pergamon.

ART
see also Antiques; Archaeology; Architecture; Art Nouveau; Art Objects; Artists; Bronzes; Christian Art and Symbolism; Collage; Collectors and Collecting; Commercial Art; Composition (Art); Costume; Creation (Literary, Artistic, etc.); Cubism; Decoration and Ornament; Design, Decorative; Drawing; Engraving; Esthetics; Folk Art; Gems; Glass Painting and Staining; Graphic Arts; Illustration of Books; Impressionism (Art); Interior Decoration; Jewelry; Lithography; Mosaics; Painting; Performing Arts; Photography, Artistic; Pictures; Portraits; Posters; Post-Impressionism (Art); Pottery; Proportion (Art); Realism in Art; Sculpture; Symbolism in Art; Women in Art
also subdivision Art under special headings, e.g., jesus christ–art; also Animals in Art; Birds in Art; Nude in Art; Sea in Art, and similar headings

Branham, Richard L. & Stuhr, David D. A Language of Form: The Isometric Theory. LC 80-82996. 496p. 1980. pap. text ed. 22.95 (ISBN 0-8403-2291-7). Kendall-Hunt.

Crawford, Tad. Legal Guide for the Visual Artist. 1980. pap. 5.95 (ISBN 0-8015-4472-6, Hawthorn). Dutton.

Edelson, Mary B. Seven Cycles: Public Rituals. (Illus.). 64p. (Orig.). 1980. pap. 10.00x (ISBN 0-9604650-0-6). Edelson.

Hartley, Marsden. On Art. Scott, Gail R., ed. (Illus.). 360p. 1981. 19.95 (ISBN 0-8180-0130-5). Horizon.

Holt, Elizabeth G. The Art of All Nations, 1850-1873: A Continuation of the Triumph of Art for the Public. LC 80-1666. (Illus.). 640p. (Orig.). 1981. pap. 8.95 (ISBN 0-385-14879-8, Anch). Doubleday.
Lucie-Smith, Edward. Thinking About Art. 1980. pap. 4.95 (ISBN 0-7145-0553-6). Riverrun NY.
National Research Center of the Arts. Americans & the Arts: Highlights. (Orig.). pap. 3.00 (ISBN 0-915400-28-6). Am Council Arts.
Paradise, Lee. Readings in English: The Arts, Bk 4. (Readings in English Ser.). 112p. (gr. 9-12). 1981. pap. text ed. price not set (ISBN 0-88345-426-2, 18885). Regents Pub.
Ruskin, John. Lectures on Architecture & Painting: Delivered at Edinburgh in November 1853. Freedberg, Sydney J., ed. LC 77-25766. (Connoisseurship Criticism & Art History Ser.: Vol. 21). (Illus.). 189p. 1979. lib. bdg. 22.00 (ISBN 0-8240-3279-9). Garland Pub.
Tomkins, Calvin. Off the Wall: Robert Rauschenberg & the Art World of Our Time. 1981. pap. 5.95 (ISBN 0-14-005812-5). Penguin.
Villani, Jim, ed. Literary & Art Anthology, Vol. 2. 88p. 1976. pap. 4.95 (ISBN 0-917530-02-0). Pig Iron Pr.
--Literary & Art Anthology, Vol. 3. 104p. 1977. pap. 4.95 (ISBN 0-917530-06-3). Pig Iron Pr.
--Literary & Art Anthology, Vol. 4. 104p. 1978. pap. 4.95 (ISBN 0-917530-09-8). Pig Iron Pr.
--Literary & Art Anthology, Vol. 5. 96p. 1979. pap. 4.95 (ISBN 0-917530-10-1). Pig Iron Pr.
--Literary & Art Anthology, Vol. 6. 96p. 1979. pap. 4.95 (ISBN 0-917530-11-X). Pig Iron Pr.
Weithas, Art, ed. Twenty Years of Award Winners from the Society of Illustrators. (Illus.). 352p. 1981. 45.00 (ISBN 0-8038-7224-0, Visual Communication). Hastings.

ART–ADDRESSES, ESSAYS, LECTURES

Morris, William. Hopes & Fears for Art. Freedberg, Sydney J., ed. LC 77-19374. (Connoisseurship Criticism & Art History Ser.: Vol. 12). 217p. 1979. lib. bdg. 23.00 (ISBN 0-8240-3270-5). Garland Pub.
Ruskin, John. Lectures on Art Delivered Before the University of Oxford in Hilary Term, 1870. Freedberg, Sydney J., ed. LC 77-25767. (Connossieurship Critism & Art History: Vol. 22). 155p. 1979. lib. bdg. 14.00. Garland Pub.

ART–ANALYSIS, INTERPRETATION, APPRECIATION

see Art–Philosophy; Art–Study and Teaching; Art Criticism; Esthetics; Painting; Pictures

ART–BIBLIOGRAPHY

Korwin, Yala H. Index to Two-Dimensional Art Works, 2 vols. LC 80-25002. 1519p. 1981. 69.50 (ISBN 0-8108-1381-5). Scarecrow.
Laing, Donald A. An Annotated Bibliography of the Published Writings of Roger Fry. LC 78-68305. (Garland Reference Library of the Humanities Ser.). 200p. 1979. lib. bdg. 25.00 (ISBN 0-8240-9838-2). Garland Pub.
Muehsam, Gerd. Guide to Basic Information Sources in the Visual Arts. LC 77-17430. 289p. 1980. 27.50 (ISBN 0-87436-278-4). ABC-Clio.
The Research Libraries of the New York Public Library & the Library of Congress. Bibliographic Guide to Art & Architecture: 1980. (Library Catalogs-Bib. Guides Ser.). 1981. lib. bdg. 135.00 (ISBN 0-8161-6881-4). G K Hall.

ART–CATALOGS

see also Art–Exhibitions

Blodgett, Jean. The Coming & Going of the Shaman: Eskimo Shamanism & Art. (Illus.). 246p. 1981. pap. 17.50 (ISBN 0-88915-068-0, 08913-4, Pub. by Canadian Artic Producers Ltd). U of Chicago Pr.
Brinker, Helmut & Fischer, Eberhard. Treasures from the Rietberg Museum. LC 80-12528. (Illus.). 176p. 1980. 19.95 (ISBN 0-87848-055-2). Asia Soc.
Cathcart, Linda L. Nancy Graves: A Survey 1969 to 1980. LC 80-13227. (Illus.). 1980. pap. 15.00 (ISBN 0-914782-34-7). Buffalo Acad.
Cohn, Marjorie B. & Siegfried, Susan L. Works by J. A. D. Ingres in the Collection of the Fogg Art Museum, Vol. III. Walsh, Peter & Kaliski, Andrea, eds. (Fogg Art Museum Handbooks). (Illus.). 190p. pap. write for info. Fogg Art.
Cowan, Susan, ed. We Don't Live in Snow Houses Now. (Illus.). 194p. (Inuktitut, Eng.). 1981. pap. 11.95 (ISBN 0-920234-00-3, 08912-6, Pub. by Canadian Artic Producers Ltd). U of Chicago Pr.
Elderfield, John. New Work on Paper. (Illus.). 56p. 1980. pap. 6.95 (ISBN 0-87070-496-6). Museum Mod Art.
Korwin, Yala H. Index to Two-Dimensional Art Works, 2 vols. LC 80-25002. 1519p. 1981. 69.50 (ISBN 0-8108-1381-5). Scarecrow.
Paris, Katherine W., ed. Gloria Dell' Arte: A Renaissance Perspective. LC 79-89876. (Illus.). 88p. (Orig.). 1979. pap. 6.00 (ISBN 0-686-28885-8). Philbrook.
Rathbone, Percy C. The Forsyth Wickes Collection. LC 68-27635. (Illus.). 1968. pap. 2.50 (ISBN 0-87846-036-5, Pub. by Mus Fine Arts Boston). C E Tuttle.
Rubsamen, Gisela. The Orsini Inventories. 224p. (Orig.). 1980. pap. 44.00 (ISBN 0-89236-010-0). J P Getty Mus.
Schultz, Douglas G. & Fry, Edward F., eds. Piero Dorazio: A Retrospective. LC 79-55355. (Illus.). 1979. pap. 15.00 (ISBN 0-914782-30-4). Buffalo Acad.
Spaulding, Karen L., ed. Alfred Jensen: Paintings & Diagrams from the Years 1957-1977. LC 77-83756. (Illus.). 1978. pap. 12.00 (ISBN 0-914782-15-0, Pub. by Albright-Knox Art Gallery). C E Tuttle.

ART–COLLECTORS AND COLLECTING

see also Art As an Investment

Albin, Edgar A., et al. Selections from the Permanent Collection of the Springfield Art Museum. Landwehr, William C., ed. LC 80-53333. 100p. (Orig.). 1980. pap. text ed. 9.95 (ISBN 0-934306-03-6). Springfield.
Circle Fine Art. Circle Fine Art: Editions Catalog. LC 80-54149. (Orig.). 1980. pap. write for info. (ISBN 0-932240-01-1). Circle Fine Art.
David, Carl. Collecting & Care of Fine Art. Michelman, Herbert, ed. 160p. 1981. 10.00 (ISBN 0-517-54287-0, Michelman Books). Crown.
Handlist of the Washington University Gallery of Art Collection. (Illus.). 100p. 1981. 4.00 (ISBN 0-936316-00-4). Wash U Gallery.
Hermitage Staff. The Hermitage. 315p. 1980. 75.00 (ISBN 0-569-08426-1, Pub. by Collets Holdings England). Intl Schol Bk Serv.
Los Angeles County Museum of Art Curatorial Staff. Three Decades of Collecting: Gifts of Anna Bing Arnold. D'Andrea, Jeanne & West, Stephen, eds. (Los Angeles County Museum of Art Bulletin 1980: Vol. 26). (Illus.). 96p. (Orig.). 1981. pap. 6.00 (ISBN 0-87587-099-6). La Co Art Mus.
Nicholson, H. B. & Cordy-Collins, Alana. Pre-Columbian Art from the Land Collection. Land, L. K., ed. LC 78-78330. (Illus.). 280p. (Orig.). 1981. pap. 24.95 (ISBN 0-295-95809-X, Pub. by Calif Acad Sci). U of Wash Pr.

ART–COMPOSITION

see Composition (Art)

ART–CRITICISM

see Art Criticism

ART–DICTIONARIES, INDEXES, ETC.

Mayer, Ralph. A Dictionary of Art Terms & Techniques. LC 80-8854. (Illus.). 464p. 1981. pap. 6.95 (ISBN 0-06-463531-7, EH 531, EH). Harper-Row.

ART–DIRECTORIES

Muehsam, Gerd. Guide to Basic Information Sources in the Visual Arts: Where to Find the Facts in Every Art Field. 276p. 1980. pap. 9.95 (ISBN 0-442-21200-3). Van Nos Reinhold.
Ticho, Suzy. Directory of Artists Slide Registries. 65p. (Orig.). 1980. pap. 6.95 (ISBN 0-915400-25-1). Am Council Arts.

ART–EDUCATION

see Art–Study and Teaching

ART–EXHIBITIONS

De Menil, Dominique, intro. by. Unromantic Agony: An Exhibition. (Illus.). 1965. pap. 2.50 (ISBN 0-914412-26-4). Inst for the Arts.
Elderfield, John. New Work on Paper. (Illus.). 56p. 1980. pap. 6.95 (ISBN 0-87070-496-6). Museum Mod Art.
Moffett, Kenworth. The New Generation: A Curator's Choice. LC 80-52831. (Illus.). 96p. (Orig., Eng., Fr., & Ger.). 1980. pap. 10.00 (ISBN 0-9604746-0-9). Rhineburgh Pr.
Reff, Theodore, ed. World's Fair of Eighteen Eighty-Nine. (Modern Art in Paris 1855 to 1900). 330p. 1981. lib. bdg. 44.00 (ISBN 0-8240-4704-4). Garland Pub.
--World's Fair of Eighteen Eighty-Nine: Retrospective Exhibition of Fine Arts, 1789 to 1889. (Modern Art in Paris 1855 to 1900). (Illus.). 250p. 1981. lib. bdg. 44.00 (ISBN 0-8240-4705-2). Garland Pub.
--World's Fair of Eighteen Fifty-Five: Modern Art in Paris 1855-1900. 694p. 1981. lib. bdg. 44.00 (ISBN 0-8240-4701-X). Garland Pub.
--World's Fair of Eighteen Sixty-Seven. (Modern Art in Paris 1855 to 1900). 224p. 1981. lib. bdg. 44.00 (ISBN 0-8240-4702-8). Garland Pub.
--World's Fair of Nineteen Hundred: General Catalogue. (Modern Art in Part in Paris 1855 to 1900). 582p. 1981. lib. bdg. 44.00 (ISBN 0-8240-4706-0). Garland Pub.
--World's Fair of Nineteen Hundred: Retrospective Exhibition of French Art, 1800 to 1889. (Modern Art in Paris 1855 to 1900). (Illus.). 442p. 1981. lib. bdg. 44.00 (ISBN 0-8240-4707-9). Garland Pub.
--World's Fair of Nineteen Hundred: Retrospective Exhibition of Fine Art,1889 to 1900. (Modern Art in Paris 1855 to 1900). 581p. 1981. lib. bdg. 44.00 (ISBN 0-8240-4708-7). Garland Pub.
Sandler, Irving. Twenty Artists: Yale School of Art, 1950-1970. LC 80-54616. (Illus.). 64p. 1981. pap. write for info. (ISBN 0-89467-016-6). Yale Art Gallery.
Through the Porthole. (Illus.). 1965. pap. 2.50 (ISBN 0-914412-25-6). Inst for the Arts.

ART–GALLERIES AND MUSEUMS

see Art Museums

ART–HISTORY

Here are entered general works on art history. For works on the history of art of specific nationalities or countries see Art, Chinese; Art, French; Art, Jewish; etc., with or without the subdivision History.

Bell, John. Bell's New Pantheon, 2 vols. Feldman, Burton & Richardson, Robert D., eds. LC 78-60919. (Myth & Romanticism Ser.: Vol. 4). 809p. 1979. Set. lib. bdg. 120.00 (ISBN 0-8240-3553-4). Garland Pub.
Cast, David. The Calumny of Apelles: A Study in the Humanist Tradition. LC 80-26378. (Publication in the History of Art Ser.: No. 28). (Illus.). 320p. 1981. text ed. 32.50x (ISBN 0-300-02575-0). Yale U Pr.
Del Borgo, S. Classical Faces & Figures from the 16th to the 19th Century Fully Illustrated & Described. (Science of Man Library Bks.). (Illus.). 115p. 1981. 47.85 (ISBN 0-89901-028-8). Found Class Reprints.
Finch, Margaret. Style in Art History: An Introduction to Theories of Style & Sequence. LC 73-14705. 178p. 1974. lib. bdg. 10.00 (ISBN 0-8108-0679-7). Scarecrow.
Gombrich, E. H. The Story of Art. 13th rev. ed. LC 76-62643. (Illus.). 512p. 1981. 19.95 (ISBN 0-8014-1352-4); pap. 12.95 (ISBN 0-8014-9215-7). Cornell U Pr.
Holt, Elizabeth G., ed. A Documentary History of Art, Vol. 1. pap. 3.50 ea. (Anch); Vol. 1. pap. (ISBN 0-385-09320-9); Vol. 2. pap. (ISBN 0-385-09366-7). Doubleday.
Hughes, Robert. The Shock of the New: Art & the Century of Change. 423p. 1981. pap. text ed. 15.95 (ISBN 0-394-32800-0). Knopf.
Hutter, Heribert. Styles in Art. LC 73-88460. (Universe History of Art Ser.). (Illus.). 192p. (Orig.). 1981. pap. 6.95 (ISBN 0-87663-558-3). Universe.
Janson, H. W., et al. A Basic History of Art. 2nd ed. (Illus.). 444p. 1981. pap. text ed. 15.95 (ISBN 0-686-69326-4). P-H.
Kandinsky, Wassily. Sounds. Napier, Elizabeth R., tr. from Ger. LC 80-6211. (Illus.). 144p. 30.00 (ISBN 0-300-02510-6); pap. 11.95 (ISBN 0-300-02664-1). Yale U Pr.
Letts, Rosa M. The Renaissance. (Cambridge Introduction to the History of Art Ser.: No. 3). (Illus.). 100p. Date not set. 19.95 (ISBN 0-521-23394-1); pap. 6.95 (ISBN 0-521-29957-8). Cambridge U Pr.
Maxon, John, et al, eds. Museum Studies. (Museum Studies Ser.). (Orig.). pap. 5.00 ea.; No. 1. (ISBN 0-86559-006-0); No. 2. (ISBN 0-86559-007-9); No. 3. (ISBN 0-86559-009-5); No. 4. (ISBN 0-86559-010-9); No.5. (ISBN 0-86559-011-7); No. 6. (ISBN 0-86559-012-5); No. 7. (ISBN 0-86559-013-3). Art Inst Chi.
--Museum Studies, 1-9. (Museum Studies Ser.). (Orig.). pap. 5.00 ea; No. 8. (ISBN 0-86559-018-4); No. 9. (ISBN 0-86559-027-3). Art Inst Chi.
Nelson-Rees, Walter A. Lillie May Nicholson: 1884-1964 an Artist Rediscovered. LC 80-53867. (Illus.). 88p. 1981. 38.50 (ISBN 0-938842-00-5). WIM Oakland.
Rudman, Jack. Art History. (Undergraduate Program Field Test Ser.: UPFT-1). (Cloth bdg. avail. on request). pap. 9.95 (ISBN 0-8373-6001-3). Natl Learning.
Voelke, William. The Stavelot Triptych: Mosan Art & the Legend of the True Cross. LC 80-8970. (Illus.). 80p. 1980. pap. 3.70 (ISBN 0-87598-071-6). Pierpont Morgan.

ART–HISTORY–20TH CENTURY

see Art, Modern–20th Century

ART–MARKETING

The Arts & Tourism: A Profitable Partnership. (Orig.). 1981. pap. cacelled (ISBN 0-915400-30-8). Am Council Arts.
Crawford, Tad & Mellon, Susan. The Artist Gallery Partnership: A Practical Guide to Consignment. LC 80-28108. (Orig.). 1981. pap. 4.50 (ISBN 0-915400-26-X). Am Council Arts.
Lewis, Ralph. Making & Managing an Art & Craft Shop. LC 80-68685. (Making & Managing Ser.). (Illus.). 128p. 1981. 16.95 (ISBN 0-7153-8065-6). David & Charles.

ART–MUSEUMS

see Art Museums

ART–PHILOSOPHY

Danto, Arthur C. The Transfiguration of the Commonplace: A Philosophy of Art. 1981. text ed. 17.50x (ISBN 0-674-90345-5). Harvard U Pr.
Hildebrand, Adolf. The Problem of Form in Painting and Sculpture. Freedberg, Sydney J., ed. LC 77-19375. (Connoisseurship & Art History Ser.: Vol. 11). (Illus.). 141p. 1979. lib. bdg. 20.00 (ISBN 0-8240-3269-1). Garland Pub.

ART–RHYTHM

see Proportion (Art)

ART–STUDY AND TEACHING

Daniels, Frederick H. Mind Stimulative Correlations in Art Education. (Illus.). 110p. 1981. Repr. of 1909 ed. 37.85 (ISBN 0-89901-024-5). Found Class Reprints.
McFee, June K. & Degge, Rogena M. Art, Culture, & Environment: A Catalyst for Teaching. 416p. 1980. pap. text ed. 13.95 (ISBN 0-8403-2330-1). Kendall-Hunt.
Ocvirk, Otto G. & Bone, Robert O. Art Fundamentals: Theory & Practice. 4th ed. 225p. 1981. pap. text ed. write for info. (ISBN 0-697-03232-9). Wm C Brown.
Otis, Calvin N. A Practical Guidebook in "Spontaneous" Art. (A Promotion of the Arts Library Book). (Illus.). 123p. 1981. 29.85 (ISBN 0-930582-99-3). Gloucester Art.

ART–STUDY AND TEACHING (ELEMENTARY)

Hubbard, G. Art for Elementary Classrooms. Date not set. 14.95 (ISBN 0-13-047274-3). P-H.
Jenkins, Peggy D. Art for the Fun of It: A Guide for Teaching Young Children. (Illus.). 224p. 1980. 13.95 (Spec); pap. 6.95. P-H.

ART–SUBJECTS

see Art–Themes, Motives, Etc.

ART–TECHNIQUE

see also subdivision Technique under painting, sculpture and similar headings

Bell, I., et al. Art As You See It: Wiley Self Teaching Guide. 326p. 1979. write for info. (ISBN 0-471-03826-1). Wiley.
Otis, Calvin N. A Practical Guidebook in "Spontaneous" Art. (A Promotion of the Arts Library Book). (Illus.). 123p. 1981. 29.85 (ISBN 0-930582-99-3). Gloucester Art.
Silverthorne, Jeanne, et al. Projects: Made in Philadelphia 4. LC 80-84522. (Illus.). 1979. pap. 4.00 (ISBN 0-88454-058-8). U of Pa Contemp Art.

ART–THEFTS

see Art Thefts

ART–THEMES, MOTIVES, ETC.

Lewen, Si. A Journey. LC 80-67120. 88p. 1980. 15.00 (ISBN 0-87982-032-2). Art Alliance.

ART–THERAPEUTIC USE

see Art Therapy

ART, AFRICAN

African Art in Washington Collections. (Illus.). 60p. 1972. pap. 4.00 (ISBN 0-89192-230-X). Interbk Inc.
Masterpieces of the People's Republic of the Congo. (Illus.). 57p. (Orig.). 1980. pap. text ed. 9.95 (ISBN 0-89192-314-4). Interbk Inc.

ART, AFRO-AMERICAN

see Afro-American Art

ART, AMERICAN

see also Afro-American Art

American Paintings in the Museum of Fine Arts, Boston, 2 vols. LC 68-27634. (Illus.). 1968. Boxed Set. 40.00 (ISBN 0-87846-005-5, Pub. by Mus Fine Fine Arts Boston). C E Tuttle.
Amon Carter Museum. Future Directions for Museums of American Art. LC 80-80501. 68p. 1980. pap. 7.95 (ISBN 0-88360-033-1). Amon Carter.
Chanticleer Press. Encyclopedia of American Art. Nelson, Cy, ed. 670p. 1981. 39.95 (ISBN 0-525-93164-3). Dutton.
Cowboy Artists of America: Fifteenth Annual Exhibition Catalog 1980. LC 73-162045. (Illus.). 72p. 1980. pap. 12.95 (ISBN 0-87358-272-1); ltd. ed. 150.00 (ISBN 0-87358-273-X). Northland.
Foner, Moe. Images of Labor. (Illus.). 96p. 1981. 25.00 (ISBN 0-8298-0433-1); pap. 12.95 (ISBN 0-8298-0452-8). Pilgrim NY.
Jack Smith: Paintings & Drawings, 1949 to 1976. 96p. 1980. pap. 10.95x (ISBN 0-904461-19-X, Pub. by Geolfrith Pr England). Intl Schol Bk Serv.
McConnell, Gerald, ed. Illustrators Twenty Two: The 22nd Annual of American Illustration. (Illus.). 368p. 1981. 37.50 (ISBN 0-8038-3433-0, Visual Communication). Hastings.
McShine, Kynaston, ed. Joseph Cornell. (Illus.). 296p. 1980. 29.95 (ISBN 0-87070-271-8); pap. 13.50 (ISBN 0-87070-272-6). Museum Mod Art.
National Research Center of the Arts. Americans & the Arts. LC 80-28923. (Illus., Orig.). Date not set. pap. 10.00 (ISBN 0-915400-27-8). Am Council Arts.
Philadelphia Maritime Museum. Thomas Birch Seventeen Seventy-Nine to Eighteen Fifty-One: Paintings & Drawings. (Illus.). 64p. 1966. pap. 2.00 (ISBN 0-913346-06-3). Phila Maritime Mus.
Pippin, Horace. The Phillips Collection. LC 76-52613. (Illus.). 64p. (Orig.). 1981. pap. 10.00 (ISBN 0-295-95818-9, Pub. by Phillips). U of Wash Pr.
Rumford, Beatrix T., ed. American Folk Portraits: Paintings & Drawings from the Abbey Aldrich Rockefeller Folk Art Center. 1981. 35.00 (ISBN 0-686-69213-6). NYGS.
Schad, Tennyson & Shapiro, Ira, eds. American Showcase, Vol. 2. (Illus.). 266p. 35.00 (ISBN 0-931144-04-3); pap. 22.50 (ISBN 0-931144-03-5). Am Showcase.
--American Showcase, Vol.4. (Illus.). 40.00 (ISBN 0-931144-08-6); pap. 27.50 (ISBN 0-931144-07-8). Am Showcase.
Sporre, Dennis. Perceiving the Arts: An Introduction to the Humanities. (Illus.). 256p. 1981. text ed. 9.95 (ISBN 0-13-657031-3). P-H.

ART, AMERICAN–BIBLIOGRAPHY

The Card Catalog of the Manuscript Collections of the Archives of American Art, 10 vols. LC 80-53039. 5000p. 1981. lib. bdg. 595.00 (ISBN 0-8420-2174-4). Scholarly Res Inc.

ART, AMERICAN–HISTORY

Baum, Hank, ed. California Art Review Books. Incl. California Art Review. 272p. pap. 12.95 (ISBN 0-89087-310-0); San Francisco Art Review. 160p. pap. 9.95 (ISBN 0-89087-308-9); Los Angeles Art Review. 160p. pap. 9.95 (ISBN 0-89087-319-4). (Illus., Orig.). 1980. Celestial Arts.

Jordan, James M. & Alcorn, George T., eds. The Wildfowler's Heritage. LC 80-85152. (Illus.). 120p. 1981. 46.50 (ISBN 0-938694-03-0); deluxe ed. 125.00; deluxe ed. with remarque 175.00. Jordan & Co.

Kostelanetz, Richard. Metamorphosis in the Arts. LC 80-68968. 328p. 1981. 18.00 (ISBN 0-686-69406-6); pap. 8.00 (ISBN 0-686-69407-4). Assembling Pr.

Rose, Barbara. American Art Since Nineteen Hundred. LC 72-83563. (Illus.). 320p. 1975. text ed. 13.95x. Praeger.

Spencer, Harold. American Art: Readings from the Colonial Era to the Present. LC 80-12325. (Illus.). 1980. pap. text ed. 10.95x (ISBN 0-684-16608-9, ScribC). Scribner.

Taylor, Joshua C. The Fine Arts in America. LC 78-23643. (History of American Civilization Ser.: No. 27). xvi, 264p. 1981. pap. 7.95 (ISBN 0-226-79151-3). U of Chicago Pr.

ART, ANCIENT

see also Classical Antiquities

also Art, Greek; Art, Roman and similar headings

Loran, Eric, et al. African & Ancient Mexican Art: The Loran Collection. LC 74-84681. (Illus.). 1974. pap. 4.95 (ISBN 0-88401-004-X, Pub. by Fine Arts Mus). C E Tuttle.

ART, ANGLO-SAXON

Speake, George. Anglo-Saxon Animal Art & Its Germanic Background. (Illus.). 164p. 1980. text ed. 50.00x (ISBN 0-19-813194-1). Oxford U Pr.

ART, ARAB

see Art, Islamic

ART, ARMENIAN

Strzygowski, Josef. Die Baukunst der Armenier und Europa, 2 vols. (Arbeiten des Kunsthistorischen Instituts der Universitat Wien: Nos. 9-10). (Illus.). xii, 888p. (Ger.). 1981. Repr. of 1918 ed. Set. lib. bdg. 200.00x (ISBN 0-89241-157-0). Caratzas Bros.

ART, ASIAN

Auboyer, Jeannine, intro. by. Rarities of the Musee Guimet. LC 74-81967. (Illus.). 124p. 1975. 19.50 (ISBN 0-87848-043-9). Asia Soc.

ART, AUSTRALIAN

Catalano, Gary. The Years of Hope: Australian Art & Criticism 1959-1968. (Illus.). 224p. 1980. 33.50 (ISBN 0-19-554220-7). Oxford U Pr.

Ingram, Terrence. A Matter of Taste. 152p. 1980. 20.95x (ISBN 0-00-211444-5, Pub. by W Collins Australia). Intl Schol Bk Serv.

McCaughey, Patrick, ed. Australian Paintings of the Heidelberg School: The Jack Manton Collection. (Illus.). 160p. 1979. text ed. 65.00x (ISBN 0-19-550592-1). Oxford U Pr.

Smith, Bernard. Place, Taste, & Tradition: A Study of Australian Art Since Seventeen Eighty-Eight. 2nd ed. (Illus.). 304p. 1979. text ed. 39.50x (ISBN 0-19-550561-1). Oxford U Pr.

ART, BELGIAN

Crowe, J. A. & Cavalcaselle, G. B. The Early Flemish Painters: Notices of Their Lives & Works. Freedberg, Sydney J., ed. LC 77-18679. (Connoisseurship, Criticism, & Art History Ser.: Vol. 6). 383p. 1979. lib. bdg. 38.00 (ISBN 0-8240-3263-2). Garland Pub.

The Pierpont Morgan Library. The Stavelot Triptych, Mosan Art, & the Legend of the True Cross. (Illus.). 48p. 1980. text ed. 24.95x (ISBN 0-19-520225-2). Oxford U Pr.

ART, BRITISH

Kerslake, John. Early Georgian Portraits, 2 vols. (Illus.). 800p. Set. 160.00 (ISBN 0-312-22476-1). St. Martin.

Ruskin, John. The Art of England: Lectures Given in Oxford by John Ruskin During His Second Tenure of the Slade Professorship. Freedberg, Sydney J., ed. LC 77-25769. (Connosseurship, Criticism, & Art History Ser.: Vol. 23). 292p. 1979. lib. bdg. 21.00 (ISBN 0-8240-3281-0). Garland Pub.

ART, BRITISH–HISTORY

Armstrong, Walter. Art in Great Britain & Ireland. 332p. 1980. Repr. of 1913 ed. lib. bdg. 65.00 (ISBN 0-8492-3206-6). R West.

ART, BUDDHIST

Baskett, Mary. Footprints of the Buddha. LC 80-80133. (Illus.). 125p. (Orig.). 1980. pap. 8.95 (ISBN 0-87633-034-0). Phila Mus Art.

ART, CANADIAN

Canada: Ron Martin & Henry Saxe. (Illus.). 114p. (Orig.). 1978. pap. text ed. 5.00 (ISBN 0-89192-236-9). Interbk Inc.

Tovell, Rosemarie L. Reflections in a Quiet Pool: The Prints of David Milne. (National Gallery of Canada Ser.). (Illus.). 256p. 1981. lib. bdg. 45.00x (ISBN 0-88884-461-1, 56494-0, Pub. by Natl Mus Canada). U of Chicago Pr.

ART, CELTIC

Jope, E. M. & Jacobsthal, P. Early Celtic Art in the British Isles, 2 vols. (Illus.). 392p. 1980. text ed. 99.00x (ISBN 0-19-817318-0). Oxford U Pr.

ART, CHINESE

see also Art, Oriental

Da-Wei, Kwo. Chinese Brushwork: Its History, Aesthetics, & Techniques. (Illus.). 220p. 1981. 37.50 (ISBN 0-8390-0267-X). Alanheld & Schram.

Kwo, David, ed. Chinese Brushwork. 200p. 1981. text ed. 46.50 (ISBN 0-8390-0267-X). Allanheld.

McDougall, Bonnie S. Mao Zedong's "Talks at the Yan'an Conference on Literature & Art". A Translation of the 1943 Text with Commentary. LC 80-18443. (Michigan Papers in Chinese Studies: No. 39). 128p. 1980. pap. 5.00 (ISBN 0-89264-039-1). U of Mich Ctr Chinese.

Pope, John A., et al. The Freer Gallery of Art, Washington D. C. LC 80-82645. (Oriental Ceramics Ser.: Vol. 9). (Illus.). 180p. 1981. 65.00 (ISBN 0-87011-448-4). Kodansha.

ART, CHRISTIAN

see Christian Art and Symbolism

ART, COMMERCIAL

see Commercial Art

ART, CRETAN

Higgins, Reynold. Minoan & Mycenaean Art. rev. ed. (World of Art Ser.). (Illus.). 288p. 1981. 17.95 (ISBN 0-19-520256-2); pap. 9.95 (ISBN 0-19-520257-0). Oxford U Pr.

ART, DECORATIVE–EXHIBITIONS

Edwards, Lisa A. & Krebs, Margie M. Netsuke: The Collection of the Peabody Museum of Salem. (Illus.). 160p. 1980. 30.00 (ISBN 0-87577-059-2); pap. 17.50 (ISBN 0-87577-062-2). Peabody Mus Salem.

ART, DUTCH

Ryskamp, Charles & Vliegenthart, A. W. William & Mary & Their House. (Illus.). 266p. 1980. 59.00x (ISBN 0-19-520185-X). Oxford U Pr.

ART, EARLY CHRISTIAN

see Christian Art and Symbolism

ART, ECCLESIASTICAL

see Christian Art and Symbolism

ART, EFFECT OF

see Art Therapy

ART, EGYPTIAN

James, T. G. An Introduction to Ancient Egypt. (British Museum Bks.). 286p. 1979. 20.00 (ISBN 0-374-83343-5); pap. 8.95 (ISBN 0-374-84339-2). FS&G.

Smith, W. Stevenson. The Art & Architecture of Ancient Egypt. rev ed. 360p. 1981. pap. 19.95 (ISBN 0-14-056114-5). Penguin.

ART, ENGLISH

see Art, British

ART, ESKIMO

see Eskimos–Art

ART, EUROPEAN

Mainstone, Madeleine. The Seventeenth Century. LC 80-40039. (Cambridge History of Art Ser.: No. 4). (Illus.). 100p. Date not set. 19.95 (ISBN 0-521-22162-5); pap. 6.95 (ISBN 0-521-29376-6). Cambridge U Pr.

Reff, Theodore, ed. Exhibitions of Modern European Art. (Modern Art in Paris 1855 to 1900 Ser.). 500p. 1981. lib. bdg. 44.00 (ISBN 0-8240-4725-7). Garland Pub.

Twohig, Elizabeth S. The Megalithic Art of Western Europe. (Illus.). 432p. 1980. 89.00 (ISBN 0-19-813193-3). Oxford U Pr.

ART, FOLK

see Folk Art

ART, FRENCH

Reff, Theodore, ed. Exhibition of Character & Genre Pictures. (Modern Art in Paris 1855 to 1900 Ser.). 112p. 1981. lib. bdg. 44.00 (ISBN 0-8240-4727-3). Garland Pub.

--Exhibitions of Barbizon & Landscape Art. (Modern Art in Paris 1855 to 1900 Ser.). 449p. 1981. lib. bdg. 44.00 (ISBN 0-8240-4737-0). Garland Pub.

--Exhibitions of Classicizing Art. (Modern Art in Paris 1855 to 1900 Ser.). 395p. 1981. lib. bdg. 44.00 (ISBN 0-8240-4735-4). Garland Pub.

--Exhibitions of Draftsmen & Illustrations. (Modern Art in Paris, 1855 to 1900, Ser.). 241p. 1981. lib. bdg. 44.00 (ISBN 0-8240-4744-3). Garland Pub.

--Exhibitions of Impressionist Art, Bk. I. (Modern Art in Paris 1855 to 1900 Ser.). 356p. 1981. lib. bdg. 44.00 (ISBN 0-8240-4741-9). Garland Pub.

--Exhibitions of Impressionist Art, Bk. II. (Modern Art in Paris 1855 to 1900 Ser.). 259p. 1981. lib. bdg. 44.00 (ISBN 0-8240-4742-7). Garland Pub.

--Exhibitions of Later Realist Art. (Modern Art in Paris 1855 to 1900 Ser.). 320p. 1981. lib. bdg. 44.00 (ISBN 0-8240-4740-0). Garland Pub.

--Exhibitions of Modern Drawings. (Modern Art in Paris 1855 to 1900 Ser.). 251p. 1981. lib. bdg. 44.00 (ISBN 0-8240-4724-9). Garland Pub.

--Exhibitions of Modern Prints. (Modern Art in Paris 1855 to 1900 Ser.). 339p. 1981. lib. bdg. 44.00 (ISBN 0-8240-4726-5). Garland Pub.

--Exhibitions of Realist Art, Bk. I. (Modern Art in Paris 1855 to 1900 Ser.). 518p. 1981. lib. bdg. 44.00 (ISBN 0-8240-4738-9). Garland Pub.

--Exhibitions of Realist Art, Bk. II. (Modern Art in Paris 1855 to 1900 Ser.). 345p. 1981. lib. bdg. 44.00 (ISBN 0-8240-4739-7). Garland Pub.

--Exhibitions of Romantic Art. (Modern Art in Paris 1855 to 1900 Ser.). 340p. 1981. lib. bdg. 44.00 (ISBN 0-8240-4736-2). Garland Pub.

--Exhibitions of Sculpture. (Modern Art in Paris 1855 to 1900 Ser.). 394p. 1981. lib. bdg. 44.00 (ISBN 0-8240-4745-1). Garland Pub.

--Exhibitions of Symbolists & Nabi. (Modern Art in Paris 1855 to 1900 Ser.). 254p. 1981. lib. bdg. 44.00 (ISBN 0-8240-4743-5). Garland Pub.

--Exhibitions of the Rosicrucian Salon. (Modern Art in Paris 1855 to 1900 Ser.). 354p. 1981. lib. bdg. 44.00 (ISBN 0-8240-4730-3). Garland Pub.

--Exhibitions of the Salon Des Cent, 1894 to 1895. (Modern Art in Paris 1855 to 1900 Ser.). 175p. 1981. lib. bdg. 44.00 (ISBN 0-8240-4731-1). Garland Pub.

--Exhibitions of the Society of Printmakers. (Modern Art in Paris 1855 to 1900 Ser.). 262p. 1981. lib. bdg. 44.00 (ISBN 0-8240-4729-X). Garland Pub.

--Impressionist Group Exhibitions. (Modern Art in Paris 1855 to 1900 Ser.). 157p. 1981. lib. bdg. 44.00 (ISBN 0-8240-4723-0). Garland Pub.

--Miscellaneous Group Exhibitions. (Modern Art in Paris 1855 to 1900 Ser.). 219p. 1981. lib. bdg. 44.00 (ISBN 0-8240-4734-6). Garland Pub.

--National Fine Arts Exhibitions. (Modern Art in Paris 1855 to 1900 Ser.). 396p. 1981. lib. bdg. 44.00 (ISBN 0-8240-4733-8). Garland Pub.

--Retrospective Exhibition of Gustave Dore. (Modern Art in Paris 1855 to 1900 Ser.). 221p. 1981. lib. bdg. 44.00 (ISBN 0-8240-4746-X). Garland Pub.

--Retrospective Exhibitions of Ernest Meissonier. (Modern Art in Paris 1855 to 1900 Ser.). 353p. 1981. lib. bdg. 44.00 (ISBN 0-8240-4747-8). Garland Pub.

--Salons of the "Independants", 1884 to 1891. (Modern Art in Paris 1855 to 1900 Ser.). 253p. 1981. lib. bdg. 44.00 (ISBN 0-8240-4709-5). Garland Pub.

--Salons of the "Independants", 1892 to 1895. (Modern Art in Paris 1855 to 1900 Ser.). 320p. 1981. lib. bdg. 44.00 (ISBN 0-8240-4710-9). Garland Pub.

--Salons of the "Independants", 1896 to 1900. (Modern Art in Paris 1855 to 1900 Ser.). 280p. 1981. lib. bdg. 44.00 (ISBN 0-8240-4711-7). Garland Pub.

--Salons of the "Nationale", 1890. (Modern Art in Paris 1855 to 1900 Ser.). (Illus.). 256p. 1981. lib. bdg. 44.00 (ISBN 0-8240-4712-5). Garland Pub.

--Salons of the "Nationale", 1891. (Modern Art in Paris 1855 to 1900 Ser.). (Illus.). 302p. 1981. lib. bdg. 44.00 (ISBN 0-8240-4713-3). Garland Pub.

--Salons of the "Nationale", 1892. (Modern Art in Paris 1855 to 1900 Ser.). (Illus.). 294p. 1981. lib. bdg. 44.00 (ISBN 0-8240-4714-1). Garland Pub.

--Salons of the "Nationale", 1893. (Modern Art in Paris 1855 to 1900 Ser.). (Illus.). 275p. 1981. lib. bdg. 44.00 (ISBN 0-8240-4715-X). Garland Pub.

--Salons of the "Nationale", 1894. (Modern Art in Paris 1855 to 1900 Ser.). (Illus.). 254p. 1981. lib. bdg. 44.00 (ISBN 0-8240-4716-8). Garland Pub.

--Salons of the "Nationale", 1895. (Modern Art in Paris 1855 to 1900 Ser.). (Illus.). 288p. 1981. lib. bdg. 44.00 (ISBN 0-8240-4717-6). Garland Pub.

--Salons of the "Nationale", 1896. (Modern Art in Paris 1855 to 1900 Ser.). (Illus.). 263p. 1981. lib. bdg. 44.00 (ISBN 0-8240-4718-4). Garland Pub.

--Salons of the "Nationale", 1898. (Modern Art in Paris 1855 to 1900 Ser.). (Illus.). 259p. 1981. lib. bdg. 44.00 (ISBN 0-8240-4720-6). Garland Pub.

--Salons of the "Nationale", 1899. (Modern Art in Paris 1855 to 1900 Ser.). (Illus.). 256p. 1981. lib. bdg. 44.00 (ISBN 0-8240-4721-4). Garland Pub.

--Salons of the "Refuses". (Modern Art in Paris 1855 to 1900 Ser.). 133p. 1981. lib. bdg. 44.00 (ISBN 0-8240-4722-2). Garland Pub.

Van der Meulen, Jan & Price, Nancy W. The West Portals of Chartres Cathedral, I: The Iconology of the Creation. LC 80-5586. 1981. lib. bdg. 19.75 (ISBN 0-8191-1402-2); pap. text ed. 10.50 (ISBN 0-8191-1403-0). U Pr of Amer.

ART, GERMAN

Passavant, Johann D. Tour of a German Artist in England, 2 vols. Freedberg, Sydney J., ed. LC 77-25761. (Connoisseurship Criticism & Art History Ser.: Vol. 16). (Illus.). 658p. 1979. Set. lib. bdg. 70.00 (ISBN 0-8240-3274-8). Garland Pub.

ART, GRAPHIC

see Graphic Arts

ART, GRECO-ROMAN

This heading is used for works dealing specifically with Roman art exhibiting strong Greek influence and produced almost exclusively by greek artists, particularly in Italy until about 100 A.D.

Hofmann, Herbert. Ten Centuries That Shaped the West: Greek & Roman Art in Texas Collections. LC 71-131999. (Illus.). 1970. 18.00 (ISBN 0-914412-18-3); pap. 12.00 (ISBN 0-914412-01-9). Inst for the Arts.

ART, GREEK

see also Art, Cretan; Art, Greco-Roman; Art, Mycenaean

Cook, R. M. Greek Art. (Illus.). 222p. 1976. 12.95 (ISBN 0-374-16670-6). FS&G.

Fuseli, Henry. The Lectures of Henry Fuseli- in "Lectures on Paintings by the Royal Academicians". Freedberg, Sydney J., ed. LC 77-19376. (Connoisseurship Criticism & Art History Ser.: Vol. 10). 450p. 1979. lib. bdg. 40.00 (ISBN 0-8240-3268-3). Garland Pub.

Haynes, Denys. Greek Art & the Idea of Freedom. (Illus.). 108p. 1981. 15.95 (ISBN 0-500-23331-4). Thames Hudson.

Hofmann, Herbert. Ten Centuries That Shaped the West: Greek & Roman Art in Texas Collections. LC 71-131999. (Illus.). 1970. 18.00 (ISBN 0-914412-18-3); pap. 12.00 (ISBN 0-914412-01-9). Inst for the Arts.

Vermeule, Emily. Aspects of Death in Early Greek Art & Poetry. (Sather Classical Lectures Ser.: No. 46). 1981. pap. 7.95 (ISBN 0-520-04404-5, CAL 504). U of Cal Pr.

ART, INDIAN

see Indians of North America–Art

ART, INDIC

Gupta, S. P. The Roots of Indian Art. (Illus.). Date not set. 102.50 (ISBN 0-391-02172-9). Humanities.

ART, IRANIAN

see Art, Persian

ART, IRISH

see also Art, Celtic

Armstrong, Walter. Art in Great Britain & Ireland. 332p. 1980. Repr. of 1913 ed. lib. bdg. 65.00 (ISBN 0-8492-3206-6). R West.

ART, ISLAMIC

Atil. Esin. Renaissance of Islam: Art of the Mamluks. LC 80-607866. (Illus.). 256p. (Orig.). 1981. 47.50 (ISBN 0-87474-214-5); pap. 19.95 (ISBN 0-87474-213-7). Smithsonian.

Welch, Anthony. Shah 'Abbas & the Arts of Isfahan. LC 73-76938. (Illus.). 152p. 1973. 19.95 (ISBN 0-87848-041-2). Asia Soc.

ART, ITALIAN

Blumenthal, Arthur R. Theater Art of the Medici. LC 80-22452. (Illus.). 243p. 1981. 15.00 (ISBN 0-87451-191-7). U Pr of New Eng.

Burckhardt, Jakob. The Cicerone: An Art Guide to Painting in Italy for the Use of Travellers & Students. Freedberg, Sydney J., ed. LC 77-18677. (Connoisseurship, Criticism & Art History Ser.: Vol. 3). 305p. 1979. lib. bdg. 30.00. Garland Pub.

D'Harnoncourt, Anne & Celant, Germano. Futurism & the International Avant-Garde. LC 80-83095. (Illus.). 144p. (Orig.). 1980. pap. 10.95 (ISBN 0-87633-037-5). Phila Mus Art.

Rubsamen, Gisela. The Orsini Inventories. 224p. (Orig.). 1980. pap. 44.00 (ISBN 0-89236-010-0). J P Getty Mus.

Steer,. Alvise Vivarini: His Art & Influence. (Illus.). 200p. Date not set. price not set (ISBN 0-521-23363-1). Cambridge U Pr.

Thompson, John L. Giovanni Segantini: A Vision of His Art & of His Letters. (Illus.). 107p. 1981. 41.85 (ISBN 0-930582-94-2). Gloucester Art.

ART, JAPANESE

see also Art, Oriental

Edwards, Lisa A. & Krebs, Margie M. Netsuke: The Collection of the Peabody Museum of Salem. (Illus.). 160p. 1980. 30.00 (ISBN 0-87577-059-2); pap. 17.50 (ISBN 0-87577-062-2). Peabody Mus Salem.

Johnson, Margaret K. & Hilton, Dale K. Japanese Prints Today: Tradition with Innovation. (Illus.). 256p. (Orig.). 1980. pap. 9.95 (ISBN 0-8048-1345-0, Pub. by Shufunotomo Co Ltd Japan). C E Tuttle.

Kanzaki, Noritake. Teapots. LC 78-71255. (Form & Function Ser.: Vol. 5). (Illus.). 80p. (Orig.). 1981. pap. 8.95 (ISBN 0-87011-392-5). Kodansha.

Kudo, Kazuyoshi. Japanese Bamboo Baskets. LC 78-71255. (Form & Function Ser.: Vol. 4). (Illus.). 80p. 1981. pap. 8.95 (ISBN 0-87011-394-1). Kodansha.

Lee, Sherman E. The Genius of Japanese Design. LC 79-66246. (Illus.). 1981. 39.50 (ISBN 0-87011-395-X). Kodansha.

Polster, Edythe & Marks, Alfred H. Surimono: Prints by Elbow. (Illus.). 494p. 1980. 1500.00 (ISBN 0-8188-0120-4, Lovejoy). Paragon.

ART, JEWISH

see also Jewish Art and Symbolism

Narkiss, B., ed. The Journal of Jewish Art, Vol. 7. (Illus.). 90p. 1981. pap. 15.00 (ISBN 0-8390-0271-8). Allanheld & Schram.

ART, LATIN-AMERICAN

Barnitz, Jacqueline. Abstract Currents in Ecuadorian Art. annual (Illus.). 48p. 1977. pap. text ed. 3.00 (ISBN 0-89192-235-0). Interbk Inc.

ART, MEDIEVAL

see also Art, Romanesque

Friedman, John B. The Monstrous Races in Medieval Art & Thought. LC 80-23181. (Illus.). 272p. 1981. text ed. 20.00 (ISBN 0-674-58652-2). Harvard U Pr.

Schapiro, Meyer. Late Antique, Early Christian & Mediaeval Art: Selected Papers. Date not set. 25.00 (ISBN 0-686-68085-5). Braziller.

ART, MESOPOTAMIAN

Woolley, Charles L. The Development of Sumerian Art. LC 80-24292. (Illus.). 140p. 1981. Repr. of 1935 ed. lib. bdg. 35.00x (ISBN 0-8371-4373-X, WOSA). Greenwood.

ART, MEXICAN

Light & Color: Images from New Mexico. (Illus.). 1980. pap. 12.95 (ISBN 0-89013-134-1). Museum NM Pr.

Loran, Eric, et al. African & Ancient Mexican Art: The Loran Collection. LC 74-84681. (Illus.). 1974. pap. 4.95 (ISBN 0-88401-004-X, Pub. by Fine Arts Mus). C E Tuttle.

Scott, John F. Danzantes of Monte Alban, 2 vols. LC 79-63725. (Studies in Pre-Columbian Art & Archaeology: No. 19). (Illus.). 238p. 1978. pap. 10.00 (ISBN 0-88402-079-7, Ctr Pre-Columbian). Dumbarton Oaks.
Townsend, Richard F. State & Cosmos in the Art of Tenochtitlan. LC 79-63726. (Sutdies in Pe-Columbian Art & Archaeology: No. 20). (Illus.). 78p. 1979. pap. 5.00 (ISBN 0-88402-083-5, Ctr. Pre-Columbian). Dumbarton Oaks.

ART, MODERN

Klein, Robert. Form & Meaning: Writings on the Renaissance & Modern Art. Jay, Madeline & Wieseltier, Leon, trs. LC 80-8772. 276p. 1981. pap. 7.95 (ISBN 0-691-00328-9). Princeton U Pr.
Russell, John. The Meanings of Modern Art. LC 80-8217. (Illus.). 384p. 1981. 29.95 (ISBN 0-06-013701-0, HarpT). Har-Row.

ART, MODERN–19TH CENTURY

Sherman, Claire R. & Holcomb, Adele M., eds. Women As Interpreters of the Visual Arts, 1820-1979. LC 80-785. (Contributions in Women's Studies: No. 18). (Illus.). 512p. 1981. lib. bdg. 35.00 (ISBN 0-313-22056-5, SWS/). Greenwood.

ART, MODERN–20TH CENTURY

see also Cubism; Dadaism; Post-Impressionism (Art); Surrealism

Lambert, Rosemary. The Twentieth Century. LC 80-40456. (Cambridge Introduction to the History of Art: No. 7). (Illus.). 90p. Date not set. 19.95 (ISBN 0-521-22715-1); pap. 6.95 (ISBN 0-521-29622-6). Cambridge U Pr.
Sherman, Claire R. & Holcomb, Adele M., eds. Women As Interpreters of the Visual Arts, 1820-1979. LC 80-785. (Contributions in Women's Studies: No. 18). (Illus.). 512p. 1981. lib. bdg. 35.00 (ISBN 0-313-22056-5, SWS/). Greenwood.
Vargas, Alberto & Austin, Reid. Vargas. 1981. pap. 8.95 (ISBN 0-517-53048-1, Harmony). Crown.

ART, MODERN–20TH CENTURY–EXHIBITIONS

Arthur, John. Realism Photo-Realism. LC 80-83113. (Illus.). 123p. 1980. 25.00 (ISBN 0-86659-002-1); pap. 16.50 (ISBN 0-86659-003-X). Philbrook.
D'Harnoncourt, Anne & Celant, Germano. Futurism & the International Avant-Garde. LC 80-83095. (Illus.). 144p. (Orig.). 1980. pap. 10.95 (ISBN 0-87633-037-5). Phila Mus Art.

ART, MOORISH

see Art, Islamic

ART, MUSLIM

see Art, Islamic

ART, MYCENAEAN

Higgins, Reynold. Minoan & Mycenaean Art. rev. ed. (World of Art Ser.). (Illus.). 288p. 1981. 17.95 (ISBN 0-19-520256-2); pap. 9.95 (ISBN 0-19-520257-0). Oxford U Pr.

ART, OCCIDENTAL

see Art

ART, ORIENTAL

see also Art, Asian; Art, Chinese; Art, Japanese

Azarpay, Guitty. Sogdian Painting: The Pictorial Epic in Oriental Art. 300p. 1981. 50.00x (ISBN 0-520-03765-0). U of Cal Pr.
Tessai, Tomioka, illus. The Works of Tomioka Tessai. (Illus.). 152p. (Orig.). 1968. pap. 5.00 (ISBN 0-88397-015-5). Intl Exhibit Foun.

ART, PERSIAN

Dowlatshahi, Ali. Persian Designs & Motifs for Artists & Craftsmen. (Illus.). 1979. pap. 4.00 (ISBN 0-486-23815-6). Dover.
Welch, Anthony. Shah 'Abbas & the Arts of Isfahan. LC 73-76938. (Illus.). 152p. 1973. 19.95 (ISBN 0-87848-041-2). Asia Soc.

ART, POPULAR

see Folk Art

ART, RENAISSANCE

Fuseli, Henry. The Lectures of Henry Fuseli- in "Lectures on Paintings by the Royal Academicians". Freedberg, Sydney J., ed. LC 77-19376. (Connoisseurship Criticism & Art History Ser.: Vol. 10). 450p. 1979. lib. bdg. 40.00 (ISBN 0-8240-3268-3). Garland Pub.
Klein, Robert. Form & Meaning: Writings on the Renaissance & Modern Art. Jay, Madeline & Wieseltier, Leon, trs. LC 80-8772. 276p. 1981. pap. 7.95 (ISBN 0-691-00328-9). Princeton U Pr.
Paris, Katherine W., ed. Gloria Dell' Arte: A Renaissance Perspective. LC 79-89876. (Illus.). 88p. (Orig.). 1979. pap. 6.00 (ISBN 0-686-28885-8). Philbrook.
Wackernagel, Martin. The World of the Florentine Renaissance Artist: Projects & Patrons, Workshop & Art Market. Luchs, Alison, tr. from Ger. LC 80-8583. 496p. 1981. 32.50x (ISBN 0-691-03966-6); pap. 12.50x (ISBN 0-691-10117-5). Princeton U Pr.

ART, ROMAN

see also Art, Greco-Roman

Erhart, K. Patricia, et al. Roman Portraits: Aspects of Self & Society. (Illus.). 108p. (Orig.). 1980. pap. 7.75. J P Getty Mus.
Hiesinger, Ulrich W. & Percy, Ann, eds. A Scholar Collects: Selections from the Anthony Morris Clark Bequest. LC 80-82234. (Illus.). 171p. (Orig.). 1980. pap. 14.95 (ISBN 0-87633-036-7). Phila Mus Art.
Hofmann, Herbert. Ten Centuries That Shaped the West: Greek & Roman Art in Texas Collections. LC 71-131999. (Illus.). 1970. 18.00 (ISBN 0-914412-18-3); pap. 12.00 (ISBN 0-914412-01-9). Inst for the Arts.
Lindgren, Claire. Classical Art Forms & Celtic Mutations: Figural Art in Roman Britain. LC 80-18987. (Illus.). 244p. (Orig.). 1981. 24.00 (ISBN 0-8155-5057-X, NP). Noyes.
Paschal, Mary. The Structure of the Roman De Thebes. LC 80-66540. 96p. 1980. pap. 9.95 (ISBN 0-89729-261-8). Ediciones.

ART, ROMANESQUE

The Pierpont Morgan Library. The Stavelot Triptych, Mosan Art, & the Legend of the True Cross. (Illus.). 48p. 1980. text ed. 24.95x (ISBN 0-19-520225-2). Oxford U Pr.

ART, ROMANIAN

Cagnat, R. & Chapot, V. Manuel D'archeologie Romaine, 2 vols. (Illus., Fr.). 1981. Repr. of 1920 ed. lib. bdg. 150.00x (ISBN 0-89241-139-2). Vol. 1. 735p. Vol. 2, 574p. Caratzas Bros.

ART, RUSSIAN

Barron, Stephanie & Tuchman, Maurice, eds. The Avant-Garde in Russia: New Perspectives. (Illus.). 250p. 1980. 27.50 (ISBN 0-262-20040-6). MIT Pr.
Parker, Fan & Parker, Stephen J. Russia on Canvas: Ilya Repin. LC 79-20577. (Illus.). 196p. 1980. 27.50x (ISBN 0-271-00252-2). Pa St U Pr.

ART, SARACENIC

see Art, Islamic

ART, SCANDINAVIAN

Lindberg Press. Scandanavian Charted Designs. (Illus.). 1979. pap. 1.75 (ISBN 0-486-23787-7). Dover.

ART, SPANISH

Rowell, Margit. New Images from Spain. Flint, Lucy, tr. LC 79-92992. (Illus.). 144p. (Orig.). 1980. soft cover 8.50 (ISBN 0-89207-023-4). S R Guggenheim.

ART, TIBETAN

Copeland, Carolyn. Tankas from the Koelz Collection: Museum of Anthropology, University of Michigan. (Michigan Papers on South & Southeast Asia: No. 18). (Illus.). 100p. (Orig.). 1980. pap. 9.00x (ISBN 0-89148-018-8). Ctr S&SE Asian.

ART, TURKISH

Atil, Esin, ed. Turkish Art. LC 79-22171. (Illus.). 386p. 1981. 65.00 (ISBN 0-87474-218-8). Smithsonian.

ART AND MYTHOLOGY

Haskell, Francis & Penny, Nicholas. Taste & the Antique: The Lure of Classical Sculpture 1500-1900. LC 80-24951. (Illus.). 392p. 1981. 45.00x (ISBN 0-300-02641-2). Yale U Pr.

ART AND SCIENCE

Smith, Cyril S. A Search for Structure: Selected Essays in Science, Art & History. (Illus.). 480p. 1981. 30.00 (ISBN 0-262-19191-1). MIT Pr.

ART AND SOCIETY

see also Art and State; Folk Art

Cork, Richard. The Social Role of Art. 128p. 1980. 19.95x (ISBN 0-86092-048-8, Pub. by Douglas & McIntyre Canada). Intl Schol Bk Serv.
International Society for Education Through Art. Arts in Cultural Diversity. 292p. (Orig.). 1980. 21.95. Praeger.
National Research Center of the Arts. Americans & the Arts. LC 80-28923. (Illus., Orig.). Date not set. pap. 10.00 (ISBN 0-915400-27-8). Am Council Arts.
--Americans & the Arts: Highlights. (Orig.). pap. 3.00 (ISBN 0-915400-28-6). Am Council Arts.

ART AND STATE

Swaim, C. Richard & Mulcahy, Kevin. Public Policy & the Arts. (Special Studies in Public Policy & Public System Management). 300p. 1981. lib. bdg. 25.00x (ISBN 0-86531-115-3). Westview.

ART AND THEATER

see Theaters–Stage-Setting and Scenery

ART APPRECIATION

Feldman, Edmund B. Varieties of Visual Experience. 2nd ed. 536p. text ed. 17.95 (ISBN 0-13-940585-2). P-H.
Kung, Hans. Art & the Question of Meaning. 96p. (Ger.). 1981. 7.95 (ISBN 0-8245-0016-4). Crossroad NY.
McBride, Henry. The Flow of Art. LC 75-13774. 1975. 12.50 (ISBN 0-689-10692-0). Atheneum.

ART AS AN INVESTMENT

The Arts & Tourism: A Profitable Partnership. (Orig.). 1981. pap. cacelled (ISBN 0-915400-30-8). Am Council Arts.

ART CENTERS

Philbrook Art Center. Native American Art at Philbrook. LC 80-82374. (Orig.). 1980. pap. 8.00 (ISBN 0-86659-001-3). Philbrook.

ART COLLECTORS

see Art–Collectors and Collecting

ART CRITICISM

see also Art Appreciation

Babbit, Irving. The New Laokoon. 259p. 1980. Repr. of 1910 ed. lib. bdg. 40.00 (ISBN 0-89760-049-5). Telegraph Bks.
Berman, Avis, intro. by. Lamar Briggs: Paintings & Works on Paper. LC 80-69965. (Illus.). 108p. 1980. text ed. 260.00 (ISBN 0-938454-01-3); pap. text ed. 25.00 (ISBN 0-938454-00-5). Ai.
Clark, Kenneth. What Is a Masterpiece? (Illus.). pap. 2.95 (ISBN 0-500-27206-9). Thames Hudson.
Crowe, J. A. & Cavalcaselle, G. B. Titan, His Life & Times: With Some Account of His Family, 2 vols. Freedberg, Sydney J., ed. LC 77-19373. (Connoisseurship Criticism & Art History Ser.: Vol. 8). 1032p. 1979. lib. bdg. 80.00 (ISBN 0-8240-3265-9). Garland Pub.
Eastlake, William, ed. Portrait of an Artist with Twenty-Six Horses. (Zia Bks.). 224p. 1980. pap. 5.95 (ISBN 0-8263-0558-X). U of NM Pr.
Fuseli, Henry. The Lectures of Henry Fuseli- in "Lectures on Paintings by the Royal Academicians". Freedberg, Sydney J., ed. LC 77-19376. (Connoisseurship Criticism & Art History Ser.: Vol. 10). 450p. 1979. lib. bdg. 40.00 (ISBN 0-8240-3268-3). Garland Pub.
Hagiwara, M. P. & De Rocher, F. Theme et Variations. 592p. 1980. text ed. 16.95 (ISBN 0-471-05609-X); tchrs.' ed. avail. (ISBN 0-471-05612-X); wkbk. avail. (ISBN 0-471-05607-3); transcript avail. (ISBN 0-471-05613-8). Wiley.
Kandinsky, Wassily. Sounds. Napier, Elizabeth R., tr. from Ger. LC 80-6211. (Illus.). 144p. 30.00 (ISBN 0-300-02510-6); pap. 11.95 (ISBN 0-300-02664-1). Yale U Pr.
Krieger, Murray. Arts on the Level: The Fall of the Elite Object. LC 80-25401. (The Hodges Lectures). (Illus.). 112p. 1981. text ed. 7.50x (ISBN 0-87049-308-6). U of Tenn Pr.
Kung, Hans. Art & the Question of Meaning. 96p. (Ger.). 1981. 7.95 (ISBN 0-8245-0016-4). Crossroad NY.
Lang, Eleanor M., ed. Art of the Real World. (Masterworks of Literature Ser.). 1979. pap. 5.50x (ISBN 0-686-68076-6, M50). Coll & U Pr.
Lee, Amy F. & Lowman, Alintro. by. Watercolor, Wax & Wool: The Art of Janet Shook Lacoste. LC 80-82780. (Illus.). 88p. (Orig.). 1980. pap. 10.00 (ISBN 0-933164-81-5). U of Tex Inst Tex Culture.
Lozowick, Louis. William Gropper. (Illus.). 200p. 1981. 40.00 (ISBN 0-87982-033-0). Art Alliance.
Minneapolis Institute of Arts. Arakawa. (Illus.). 1979. 8.00. Minneapolis Inst Arts.
Quatremere de Quincy, A. C. An Essay on the Nature, the End, and the Means of Imitation in the Fine Arts. Freedberg, Sydney J., ed. LC 77-25763. (Connoisseurship, Criticism, & Art History: Vol. 18). 468p. 1979. lib. bdg. 48.00 (ISBN 0-8240-3276-4). Garland Pub.
Richardson, J. Art: The Way It Is. 1974. pap. 10.95 (ISBN 0-13-049221-3). P-H.
Ruskin, John. Lectures on Architecture & Painting: Delivered at Edinburgh in November 1853. Freedberg, Sydney J., ed. LC 77-25766. (Connoisseurship Criticism & Art History Ser.: Vol. 21). (Illus.). 189p. 1979. lib. bdg. 22.00 (ISBN 0-8240-3279-9). Garland Pub.
--Lectures on Art Delivered Before the University of Oxford in Hilary Term. 1870. Freedberg, Sydney J., ed. LC 77-25767. (Connosseurship Critism & Art History: Vol. 22). 155p. 1979. lib. bdg. 14.00. Garland Pub.
Russell, Frank D. Picasso's Guernica: The Labyrinth of Narrative and Vision. LC 79-52472. 350p. 1980. text ed. 35.00 (ISBN 0-8390-0243-2). Allanheld.
Shee, Mary-Venner. Jacques Hurtubise: Recent Works - Oeuvres Recentes. (Illus.). 64p. (Fr. & Eng.). 1981. pap. 10.00 (ISBN 0-936270-16-0). Art Mus Gall.

ART DECO

Schnessel, Michael. I Cart. West, Jane, ed. 1981. 12.95 (ISBN 0-517-54399-0). Potter.

ART EDUCATION

see Art–Study and Teaching

ART GALLERIES

see Art Museums

ART IN ADVERTISING

see Commercial Art

ART MUSEUMS

Amon Carter Museum. Future Directions for Museums of American Art. LC 80-80501. 68p. 1980. pap. 7.95 (ISBN 0-88360-033-1). Amon Carter.
Brandt, Babette. Curator's Choice: Western Edition. Aymar, Brant, ed. 1981. pap. 6.95 (ISBN 0-517-54200-5). Crown.
Faison, S. Lane, Jr. Art Museums of New England. 548p. 1981. 20.00 (ISBN 0-87923-372-9); pap. 10.00 (ISBN 0-87923-373-7). Godine.
Fromme, Babbette B. Curators' Choice: From the Collections of the Art Museums of the U. S. (Midwestern Edition) Aymar, Brandt, ed. (Illus.). 160p. 1981. pap. 6.95 (ISBN 0-517-54199-8). Crown.
--Curators' Choice: From the Collections of the Art Museums of the U. S. (Northeastern Edition) Aymar, Brandt, ed. (Illus.). 288p. 1981. pap. 8.95 (ISBN 0-517-54197-1). Crown.
--Curators' Choice: From the Collections of the Art Museums of the U. S. (Southern Edition) Aymar, Brandt, ed. (Illus.). 160p. 1981. pap. 6.95 (ISBN 0-686-69482-1). Crown.
--Curators' Choice: From the Collections of the Art Museums of the U. S. (Western Edition) (Illus.). 160p. 1981. pap. 6.95 (ISBN 0-517-54200-5). Crown.
Hills, Patricia & Tarbell, Roberta K. The Figurative Tradition & the Whitney Museum of American Art: Paintings & Sculpture from the Permanent Collection. LC 80-12650. 192p. 1980. 25.00 (ISBN 0-87413-184-7). U Delaware Pr.
Meyer, Karl E. The Art Museum: Power, Money & Ethics. (Illus.). 352p. 1981. pap. 8.95. Morrow.
Pope, John A., et al. The Freer Gallery of Art, Washington D. C. LC 80-82645. (Oriental Ceramics Ser.: Vol. 9). (Illus.). 180p. 1981. 65.00 (ISBN 0-87011-448-4). Kodansha.
Sloan, Blanche C. & Swinburne, Bruce R. Campus Art Museums & Galleries: A Profile. LC 80-23418. 64p. (Orig.). 1981. pap. price not set (ISBN 0-8093-1005-8). S Ill U Pr.

ART NOUVEAU

Lingua Press. Lingua Press Collection Two Catalogue, Vol. 2. Gaburo, Kenneth, ed. 132p. 1978. soft cover 3.95. Lingua Pr.
Reff, Theodore, ed. Exhibitions of Art Nouveau. (Modern Art in Paris Ser.). 486p. 1981. lib. bdg. 44.00 (ISBN 0-8240-4732-X). Garland Pub.
Revi, Albert C. American Art Nouveau Glass. LC 68-18778. (Illus.). 476p. 1981. Repr. 40.00 (ISBN 0-916838-40-4). Schiffer.

ART OBJECTS

Here are entered works on decorative art objects. Works on old decorative or utilitarian objects having aesthetic, historic and financial value are entered under Antiques.

see also Antiques; Miniature Objects;

also classes of art objects and names of particular objects, e.g. Bronzes, Glassware, Jewelry, Metal-work, Plate, Pottery

Crawford, Tad & Mellon, Susan. The Artist Gallery Partnership: A Practical Guide to Consignment. LC 80-28108. (Orig.). 1981. pap. 4.50 (ISBN 0-915400-26-X). Am Council Arts.
Watt, James C. Chinese Jades from Han to Ch'ing. LC 80-20115. (Illus.). 236p. 1980. 22.50 (ISBN 0-87848-057-9). Asia Soc.

ART OBJECTS–CONSERVATION AND RESTORATION

Hopkirk, Peter. Foreign Devils on the Silk Road: The Search for the Lost Cities & Treasures of Chinese Central Asia. (Illus.). 264p. 1981. lib. bdg. 27.50x (ISBN 0-87023-234-7). U of Mass Pr.

ART ROBBERIES

see Art Thefts

ART THEFTS

Hopkirk, Peter. Foreign Devils on the Silk Road: The Search for the Lost Cities & Treasures of Chinese Central Asia. (Illus.). 264p. 1981. lib. bdg. 27.50x (ISBN 0-87023-234-7). U of Mass Pr.
McLeave, Hugh. Rogues in the Gallery: The Modern Plague of Art Thefts. 1981. 14.95 (ISBN 0-87923-378-8). Godine.
Reit, Seymour V. The Day They Stole the Mona Lisa. 1981. 11.95 (ISBN 0-671-25056-6). Summit Bks.

ART THERAPY

Fleshman, Bob & Fryrear, Jerry L. The Arts in Therapy. LC 80-20334. 240p. 1981. text ed. 19.95 (ISBN 0-88229-520-9); pap. text ed. 9.95 (ISBN 0-88229-762-7). Nelson-Hall.
Spontaneous Images: Relationship Between Psyche & Soma. (Illus.). 123p. (Orig., Eng. Fr. & Ger.). 1980. pap. text ed. 16.00 (ISBN 0-89192-311-X). Interbk Inc.

ARTERIES

see also Aorta; Blood–Circulation; Blood-Vessels; Veins

Sleight, Peter, ed. Arterial Baroreceptors & Hypertension. (Illus.). 380p. 1981. text ed. 67.50x (ISBN 0-19-261259-X). Oxford U Pr.

ARTHRITIS

see also Joints–Diseases; Rheumatoid Arthritis

Adams, Ruth & Murray, Frank. All You Should Know About Arthritis. 256p. (Orig.). 1979. pap. 2.25 (ISBN 0-915962-28-4). Larchmont Bks.
Arndt, Rolf D., et al. Peripheral & Joint Arthrography. (Illus.). 188p. 1981. write for info. (0253-8). Williams & Wilkins.
Childers' Diet to Stop Arthritis: The Nightshades & Ill Health. 2nd rev. ed. 200p. 1981. pap. 9.95 (ISBN 0-938378-00-7). Horticult Pubns.
Freeman, Julian. Arthritis: The New Treatments. rev. ed. (Illus.). 1981. pap. 5.95 (ISBN 0-8092-5960-5). Contemp Bks.
G-Jo Institute. Arthritis Self-Help Program. 1980. pap. 4.50 (ISBN 0-916878-10-4). Falkynor Bks.
Hart, Frank D. Overcoming Arthritis. LC 80-22466. (Positive Health Guides Ser.). (Illus.). 112p. 1981. 9.95 (ISBN 0-668-04679-1); pap. 5.95 (ISBN 0-686-69380-9). Arco.
Occupational Therapy Dept. Christchurch Hospital. Managing with Arthritis: Aids & Advice for Coping with the Activities of Daily Living. 55p. 1980. 12.00x (ISBN 0-7233-0598-6, Pub. by Whitcoulls New Zealand). State Mutual Bk.
Robinson, Martha. Arthritis & You. 88p. 1980. 15.00x (ISBN 0-86025-847-5, Pub. by Ian Henry Pubns England). State Mutual Bk.
Wilske, Kenneth R., et al. Therapeutic Program for the Patient with Arthritis. 3rd ed. 54p. Date not set. pap. 5.00 (ISBN 0-9601944-3-6). Mason Clinic.
Ziebell, Beth. Wellness: An Arthritis Reality. LC 80-84001. 144p. 1981. pap. text ed. 6.95 (ISBN 0-8403-2329-8). Kendall-Hunt.

ARTHRITIS DEFORMAS

see Rheumatoid Arthritis

ARTHROPATHY

see Joints–Diseases

ARTHROPODA

see also Crustacea; Insects; Myriapoda

Miller, T. A. Cuticle Techniques in Arthropods. (Springer Series in Experimental Entomology). (Illus.). 410p. 1981. 59.80 (ISBN 0-387-90475-1). Springer-Verlag.

ARTHROSIS DEFORMANS

see Rheumatoid Arthritis

ARTHUR, CHESTER ALAN, PRES. U. S., 1830-1886

Doenecke, Justus D. The Presidencies of James A. Garfield & Chester A. Arthur. LC 80-18957. (The American Presidency Ser.). 232p. 1981. 15.00x (ISBN 0-7006-0208-9). Regents Pr KS.

ARTICULATION (EDUCATION)

Diedrich, William M. & Bangert, Jeff. Articulation Learning. 416p. text ed. 24.50 (ISBN 0-933014-59-7). College-Hill.

Dumont, Lora L. Consonant Articulation Drills. 2nd ed. 268p. 1980. pap. text ed. 5.95x (ISBN 0-8134-2129-2, 2129). Interstate.

ARTICULATIONS

see Joints

ARTIFICIAL BLOOD CIRCULATION

see Blood–Circulation, Artificial

ARTIFICIAL FLOWERS

Entrekin, Dee. Make Your Own Silk Flowers. LC 74-31705. (Illus.). 80p. 1981. pap. 6.95 (ISBN 0-8069-8994-7). Sterling.

ARTIFICIAL FUELS

see Synthetic Fuels

ARTIFICIAL INSEMINATION

Buffalo Reproduction & Artificail Insemination. (FAO Animal Production & Health Paper: No. 13). 370p. 1981. pap. 20.00 (ISBN 92-5-100743-8, F2086, FAO). Unipub.

Perry, Enos J. Artificial Insemination of Farm Animals. 473p. 1968. 20.00 (ISBN 0-8135-0577-1). Rutgers U Pr.

ARTIFICIAL INTELLIGENCE

see also GPS (Computer Program Language)

Barr, Avron & Feigenbaum, Edward, eds. The Handbook of Artificial Intelligence, 3 vols. 1981. 90.00 set (ISBN 0-86576-004-7); 30.00 ea. Vol. 1 (ISBN 0-86576-005-5). Vol. 2 (ISBN 0-86576-006-3). Vol. 3 (ISBN 0-86576-007-1). W Kaufmann.

Boden, Margaret. Artificial Intelligence & Natural Man. LC 76-8117. (Illus.). 537p. 1981. pap. 8.95 (ISBN 0-465-00453-9). Basic.

Feigenbaum, Edward A. Computers & Thought. LC 80-29508. 540p. 1981. Repr. of 1963 ed. lib. bdg. write for info. (ISBN 0-89874-199-8). Krieger.

Lindsay, R. K., et al. Applications of Artificial Intelligence for Organic Chemistry: The Dendral Project. (Artificial Intelligence Ser.). (Illus.). 208p. 1980. text ed. 35.00 (ISBN 0-07-037895-9, C). McGraw.

Michie, Donald. Essays on Machine Intelligence & Other Topics. 250p. 1981. write for info. (ISBN 0-677-05560-9). Gordon.

--Essays on Machine Intelligence & Other Topics. 250p. 1981. price not set (ISBN 0-677-05560-9). Gordon.

ARTIFICIAL ISLANDS

see Offshore Structures

ARTIFICIAL LAKES

see Reservoirs

ARTIFICIAL ORGANS

see also Prosthesis

Madison, Arnold. Transplanted & Artificial Body Organs. (Illus.). 192p. (gr. 7 up). 1981. 8.95 (ISBN 0-8253-0050-9). Beaufort Bks NY.

ARTIFICIAL PACEMAKER (HEART)

see Pacemaker, Artificial (Heart)

ARTIFICIAL SAMPLING

see Monte Carlo Method

ARTIFICIAL SATELLITES IN TELECOMMUNICATION

see also Radiotelephone; Television

Van Trees, H. L., ed. Satellite Communications. LC 78-65704. 1979. 42.95 (ISBN 0-87942-121-5). Inst Electrical.

ARTIFICIAL TEETH

see Prosthodontics

ARTIFICIAL THINKING

see Artificial Intelligence

ARTIFICIAL WEATHER CONTROL

see Weather Control

ARTILLERY

Foss. Artillery of the World. 3rd ed. 1981. 12.95 (ScribT). Scribner.

ARTISANS

see also Apprentices

also particular classes of artisans, e.g. Barbers; Cabinet-workers

Roosevelt, Anna C. & Smith, James, eds. The Ancestors: Native Artisans of the Americas. LC 79-89536. (Illus.). 230p. (Orig.). 1980. pap. 17.50 (ISBN 0-295-95780-8, Pub. by Mus Am Ind). U of Wash Pr.

Traisman, Barbara. Handed Down: The Artisan Tradition. LC 80-67829. 1980. pap. 12.95 (ISBN 0-916860-07-8). Bean Pub.

ARTISTIC PHOTOGRAPHY

see Photography, Artistic

ARTISTS

see also Actors and Actresses; Architects; Authors; Cartoonists; Engravers; Entertainers; Illustrators; Musicians; Painters

also names of artists, e.g. Leonardo Da Vinci

Artists Compared by Age, Sex, & Earnings in 1970 & 1976. (Report Ser.: No. 12). 56p. 1980. pap. 2.50 (ISBN 0-89062-077-6, Pub. by Ctr for Arts Info). Pub Ctr Cult Res.

Burnham, Linda F. Bob & Bob: The First Five Years. LC 80-67655. (Illus.). 100p. (Orig.). 1980. pap. 12.00 (ISBN 0-937122-00-9). Astro Artz.

Carter, Judith Q. & Carter, Richard D., eds. Herbert L. Fink: Graphic Artist. (Illus.). Date not set. price not set (ISBN 0-8093-1016-3). S Ill U Pr.

Ingle, Lydia R. Edades: Kites & Visions. (Illus.). 103p. 1980. pap. 7.50x (ISBN 0-686-28646-4). Cellar.

Schnessel, Michael. I Cart. West, Jane, ed. 1981. 12.95 (ISBN 0-517-54399-0). Potter.

ARTISTS–CORRESPONDENCE, REMINISCENCES, ETC.

Jolley, Miesje. A Crack in Time. (Illus.). 48p. (Orig.). 1980. pap. 6.00 (ISBN 0-931122-20-1). West End.

Reps, Paul. Paul Reps: Letters to a Friend (Writings & Drawings), 1939 to 1980. (Illus.). 186p. 1981. 60.00 (ISBN 0-938286-01-3); ltd. ed. 175.00 (ISBN 0-938286-00-5). Stillgate.

Roskill, Mark, ed. The Letters of Vincent Van Gogh. LC 63-13089. 1963. pap. 4.95 (ISBN 0-689-70167-5). Atheneum.

ARTISTS–DICTIONARIES

Soria, Regina. The Dictionary of Nineteenth-Century American Artists in Italy, 1760-1914. LC 74-4986. 600p. 1981. 27.50 (ISBN 0-8386-1310-1). Fairleigh Dickinson.

ARTISTS–JUVENILE LITERATURE

Lipman, Jean & Aspinwall, Margaret. Sandy Calder & His Magical Mobiles. (Illus.). (ps up). 1981. 15.00 (ISBN 0-933920-17-2); pap. 7.00 (ISBN 0-933920-18-0). Hudson Hills.

ARTISTS–CANADA

Sapp, Allen. A Cree Life: The Art of Allen Sapp. (Illus.). 1977. 24.95 (ISBN 0-295-95684-4, Pub. by Douglas & McIntyre Canada). U of Wash Pr.

ARTISTS–EUROPE

Burckhardt, Jakob. Recollections of Rubens. Freedberg, Sydney J., ed. LC 77-18674. (Connoisseurship Criticism & Art History Ser.: Vol. 4). 374p. 1979. lib. bdg. 33.00 (ISBN 0-8240-3261-6). Garland Pub.

ARTISTS–GERMANY

Causey, Andrew. Paul Nash. (Illus.). 532p. 1980. 98.00x (ISBN 0-19-817348-2). Oxford U Pr.

Mochon, Anne. Gabriele Muunter: Between Munich & Murnau. Walsh, Peter & Matthews, Paula, eds. LC 80-21810. (Illus.). 65p. 1980. pap. 9.95 (ISBN 0-916724-19-0). Fogg Art.

ARTISTS–GREAT BRITAIN

Lanyon, Andrew. A St. Ives Album. 72p. 1980. 10.00x (ISBN 0-906720-00-1, Pub. by Hodge England). State Mutual Bk.

Philip Gilbert Hamerton. 591p. 1980. Repr. of 1896 ed. lib. bdg. 50.00. Telegraph Bks.

ARTISTS–ITALY

Melvasia, Carlo C. The Life of Guido Reni. Enggass, Catherine & Enggass, Robert, trs. from Ital. LC 80-11650. (Illus.). 150p. 1981. 11.95x (ISBN 0-271-00264-6). Pa St U Pr.

ARTISTS–UNITED STATES

Cruise, Boyd. Boyd Cruise. LC 76-24712. (Illus.). 72p. 1976. 20.00x (ISBN 0-917860-01-2). Historic New Orleans.

Dawdy, Doris. Artists of the American West: A Biographical Dictionary, Vol. II. LC 72-91919. 300p. 1981. 22.95x (ISBN 0-8040-0352-1). Swallow.

George Henry Durrie (1820-63), American Winter Landscapist: Renowned Through Currier & Ives. (Illus.). 240p. 1977. 34.95 (ISBN 0-686-28866-1). M Hutson.

Kardon, Janet. Robert Zakanitch. (Illus.). 1980. pap. 10.00 (ISBN 0-88454-025-1). U of Pa Contemp Art.

Soria, Regina. The Dictionary of Nineteenth-Century American Artists in Italy, 1760-1914. LC 74-4986. 600p. 1981. 27.50 (ISBN 0-8386-1310-1). Fairleigh Dickinson.

Williams, Hobie L. The American Artists Today in Black, Vol. I. White, Mosezelle & Roberts, Bobby, II, eds. 87p. (Orig.). 1981. pap. text ed. 7.95x (ISBN 0-936026-11-1). R&M Pub Co.

--The American Artists Today in Black, Vol. II. White, Mosezelle & Roberts, Bobby, II, eds. 103p. (Orig.). Date not set. pap. text ed. 8.95 (ISBN 0-936026-12-X). R&M Pub Co.

ARTISTS, AFRO-AMERICAN

see Afro-American Artists

ARTISTS, WOMEN

see Women Artists

ARTISTS IN LITERATURE

Jeffares, Bo. The Artist in Nineteenth Century Fiction. 195p. 1979. text ed. 23.75x (ISBN 0-391-00976-1). Humanities.

ARTS, THE

see also Artists

Gingrich. Relating the Arts. write for info. (ISBN 0-87628-216-8). Ctr Appl Res.

McNiff, Shaun. The Arts & Psychotherapy. (Illus.). 280p. 19.75. C C Thomas.

The State Arts Agencies in Nineteen Seventy-Four: All Present & Accounted for. (Report Ser.: No. 8). 160p. pap. 4.50 (Pub. by Ctr Fot Arts Info). Pub Ctr Cult Res.

ARTS, THE–CRITICISM

see Art Criticism

ARTS, THE–HISTORY

see also Art Criticism

Lewis, David L. When Harlem Was in Vogue. LC 80-2704. (Illus.). 400p. 1981. 17.95 (ISBN 0-394-49572-1). Knopf.

ARTS, THE–MANAGEMENT

Benedict, Stephen, compiled by. Arts Management: An Annotated Bibliography. rev. ed. LC 80-25918. 48p. 1980. pap. 5.00 (ISBN 0-89062-046-6, Pub. by Ctr for Arts Info). Pub Ctr Cult Res.

Cultural Assistance Center. Public & Private Support for the Arts in New York City: A Review with Recommendations for Improvement in the 80's. LC 80-65497. 160p. (Orig.). 1980. pap. 6.00 (Pub. by Cultural Assist). Pub Ctr Cult Res.

Thurston, Ellen. Management Assistance for the Arts: A Survey of Programs. Benedict, Stephen, ed. LC 80-440. 54p. (Orig.). 1980. pap. 4.00 (ISBN 0-89062-046-6, Pub. by Ctr for Arts Info). Pub Ctr Cult Res.

ARTS, DECORATIVE

see Decoration and Ornament; Design, Decorative; Handicraft; Interior Decoration

also subjects referred to under these headings

ARTS, FINE

see Art; Arts, the

ARTS, GRAPHIC

see Graphic Arts

ARTS, USEFUL

see Industrial Arts; Technology

ARTS IN THE CHURCH

see Christian Art and Symbolism

ARYANS

see Indo-Europeans

ASBESTOS

Pelnar, Premysl U. Health Effects of Asbestos & of Some Other Minerals & Fibres As Reflected in the World Literature: A Compendium of References, 1906-1979. 1981. 25.00 set (ISBN 0-930376-25-0). Pathotox Pubs.

Rajhans, Gyan S. & Sullivan, John. Asbestos Sampling & Analysis. 1981. text ed. 37.50 (ISBN 0-686-69577-1). Ann Arbor Science.

ASCENSION OF CHRIST

see Jesus Christ–Ascension

ASCHAM, ROGER, 1515-1568

Dees, Jerome S. Sir Thomas Elyot & Roger Ascham: A Reference Guide. (Reference Books Ser.). 1981. 25.00 (ISBN 0-8161-8353-8). G K Hall.

ASCOMYCETES

Reynolds, R. D. Ascomycete Systematics: The Luttrellian Concept. (Springer Series in Microbiology). (Illus.). 272p. 1981. 42.80 (ISBN 0-387-90488-3). Springer-Verlag.

ASCORBIC ACID

see Vitamins

ASDIC

see Sonar

ASHE, ARTHUR

Ashe, Arthur. Off the Court. 1981. price not set (ISBN 0-453-00400-8, H400). NAL.

ASHEVILLE, NORTH CAROLINA

Harshaw, Lou. Places of Discovery I--Asheville. 1981. 10.95. Green Hill.

Tessier, Mitzi. Asheville: A Pictorial History. Fredman, Donna R., ed. (Illus.). 208p. 1981. pap. price not set (ISBN 0-89865-116-6). Donning Co.

ASIA–CIVILIZATION

Permanent International Altaistic Conference, Indiana University, 1962. Aspects of Altaic Civilization: Proceedings. Francis, David & Sinor, Denis, eds. LC 80-28299. (Uralic & Altaic Ser.: Vol. 23). ix, 263p. 1981. Repr. of 1962 ed. lib. bdg. 25.00x (ISBN 0-313-22945-7, PIAA). Greenwood.

ASIA–COMMERCE

Trado Asian-African Directory of Exporters-Importers & Manufacturers, 1980. 25th ed. LC 60-41792. 1640p. 1980. 50.00x (ISBN 0-8002-2736-0). Intl Pubns Serv.

ASIA–DESCRIPTION AND TRAVEL–GUIDEBOOKS

Waldo, Myra. Myra Waldo's Travel Guide to the Orient & Asia, 1981. (Illus.). 505p. 1981. pap. 9.95 (ISBN 0-02-098890-7, Collier). Macmillan.

ASIA–ECONOMIC CONDITIONS

Asiatic Research Center, Korea University CSIS. Northeast Asia: Prosperity & Vulnerability, Vol. I. LC 79-65209. (Significant Issues Ser.: No. 2). 79p. 1979. 5.95 (ISBN 0-89206-008-5). CSI Studies.

Hewett, Robert B., ed. Political Changes & the Economic Future of East Asia. 208p. 1981. pap. write for info. (ISBN 0-8248-0750-2). U Pr of Hawaii.

Paukert, Felix, et al. Income Distribution, Structure of Economy & Employment: A Comparative Study for Four Asian Countries. 176p. 1981. 35.00x (ISBN 0-7099-2006-7, Pub. by Croom Helm LTD England). Biblio Dist.

ASIA–FOREIGN RELATIONS

Asiatic Research Center, Korea University CSIS. Northeast Asia: Prosperity & Vulnerability, Vol. I. LC 79-65209. (Significant Issues Ser.: No. 2). 79p. 1979. 5.95 (ISBN 0-89206-008-5). CSI Studies.

ASIA–HISTORY

Jones, E. L. The European Miracle: Environments, Economies & Geopolitics in the History of Europe & Asia. 274p. Date not set. text ed. price not set (ISBN 0-521-23588-X); pap. text ed. price not set (ISBN 0-521-28055-9). Cambridge U Pr.

Stein, Aurel. Serindia, 5 vols. (Illus.). 500p. 1981. 75.00 ea. (Pub. by Motilal Banarsidass); Set. 350.00 (ISBN 0-686-69377-9); Vol. 1. (ISBN 0-89581-504-4); Vol. 2. (ISBN 0-89581-505-2); Vol. 3. (ISBN 0-89581-506-0); Vol. 4. (ISBN 0-89581-507-9); Vol. 5. (ISBN 0-89581-508-7). Lancaster-Miller.

ASIA–HISTORY–SOURCES–BIBLIOGRAPHY

Sources of the History of North Africa, Asia, & Oceania in Scandinavia, 2 pts. Incl. Pt. 1. Sources of the History North Africa, Asia, & Oceania in Denmark. lib. bdg. 162.00 (ISBN 3-598-21474-X); Pt. 2. Sources of the History of North Africa, Asia, & Oceania in Finland, Norway, Sweden. lib. bdg. 65.00 (ISBN 3-598-21475-8). (Guides to the Sources for the History of the Nations). 1980 (Dist. by Gale Research Co.). K G Saur.

ASIA–POLITICS AND GOVERNMENT

Hewett, Robert B., ed. Political Changes & the Economic Future of East Asia. 208p. 1981. pap. write for info. (ISBN 0-8248-0750-2). U Pr of Hawaii.

Northeast Asia: Prosperity & Vulnerability. 79p. 1980. pap. 7.50 (ISBN 0-89206-008-5, CSIS003, CSIS). Unipub.

ASIA–SOCIAL CONDITIONS

Bailey, Anne M., ed. The Asiatic Mode of Production: Science & Politics. (Illus.). 352p. 1981. price not set (ISBN 0-7100-0737-X) (ISBN 0-7100-0738-8). Routledge & Kegan.

Chan, Gilbert F., ed. Nationalism in East Asia: An Annotated Bibliography of Selected Works. LC 80-8490. 180p. 1981. lib. bdg. 22.00 (ISBN 0-8240-9497-2). Garland Pub.

Northeast Asia: Prosperity & Vulnerability. 79p. 1980. pap. 7.50 (ISBN 0-89206-008-5, CSIS003, CSIS). Unipub.

ASIA–STATISTICS

United Nations. Statistical Yearbook for Asia & the Pacific, 1978: Annuaire Statistique pour l'asle et le Pacifique. 11th ed. LC 76-641968. (Illus.). 536p. (Orig.). 1979. pap. 28.00x (ISBN 0-8002-1083-2). Intl Pubns Serv.

ASIA, CENTRAL–HISTORY

Bosworth, C. E. The Medieval History of Iran, Afghanistan & Central Asia. 374p. 1980. 75.00x (ISBN 0-86078-000-7, Pub. by Variorum England). State Mutual Bk.

ASIA, SOUTH–DESCRIPTION AND TRAVEL

Schiffer, Michael. Lessons of the Road. 1980. 10.95 (ISBN 0-686-68922-4, Kenan Pr). S&S.

ASIA, SOUTH–ECONOMIC CONDITIONS

Rahman, Mushtaqur & Iowa State University Research Foundation. Agrarian Egalitarianism, Land Tenures & Land Reforms in South Asia. 224p. 1980. pap. text ed. 9.95 (ISBN 0-8403-2343-3). Kendall-Hunt.

ASIA, SOUTHEASTERN–ECONOMIC CONDITIONS

Allen, Thomas W. The ASEAN Report, 2 vols. Wain, Barry, ed. Incl. Vol. 1. A Comparative Assessment of the ASEAN Countries; Vol. 2. The Evolution & Programs of ASEAN. (Illus.). 414p. 1980. Set. pap. 125.00 (ISBN 0-295-95740-9, 80-110683). U of Wash Pr.

Blauvelt, Euan & Durlacher, Jennifer, eds. Sources of Asian-Pacific Economic Information, 2 vols. LC 80-28645. 1981. Set. lib. bdg. 125.00 (ISBN 0-313-22963-5). Greenwood.

Tate, D. J. The Making of South-East Asia: Vol. 2, The Western Impact--Economic & Social Change. (Illus.). 632p. 1979. text ed. 49.50x (ISBN 0-19-580332-9). Oxford U Pr.

Viksnins, George J. Financial Deepening in the Asian Countries. 96p. (Orig.). 1980. pap. 6.50x (ISBN 0-8248-0745-6). U Pr of Hawaii.

ASIA, SOUTHEASTERN–FOREIGN RELATIONS

Purcell, Victor. The Chinese in Southeast Asia. 2nd ed. (Royal Institute of International Affairs Ser.). (Illus.). 640p. 1980. pap. 22.00x (ISBN 0-19-580463-5). Oxford U Pr.

ASIA, SOUTHEASTERN–SOCIAL CONDITIONS

Evers, Hans-Dieter, ed. The Sociology of Southeast Asia: Readings on Social Change & Development. (Illus.). 350p. 1980. 32.50 (ISBN 0-19-580408-2). Oxford U Pr.

Tate, D. J. The Making of South-East Asia: Vol. 2, The Western Impact--Economic & Social Change. (Illus.). 632p. 1979. text ed. 49.50x (ISBN 0-19-580332-9). Oxford U Pr.

ASIA MINOR–ANTIQUITIES

Todd, Ian. The Prehistoric of Central Anatolia I: The Neolithic Period. (Studies in Mediterranean Archaeology: Vol. LX). 177p. 1981. pap. text ed. 42.00x (ISBN 91-85058-87-4, Pub. by Astroms, Sweden). Humanities.

ASIAN AMERICANS

Jo Young-Hawn, ed. Political Participation of Asian-Americans- Problems and Strategies. LC 80-25074. (Occasional Papers Ser.: No. 6). (Orig.). 1980. pap. 12.00 (ISBN 0-934584-14-1). Pacific-Asian.

ASIAN ARCHITECTURE

see Architecture–Asia

ASIAN ART

see Art, Asian

ASIAN FOLK-LORE
see Folk-Lore, Asian
ASIAN PAINTINGS
see Paintings, Asian
ASIANS
see also names of individual races e.g. East Indians, Mongols.
Nandi, Proshanta & Yu, Elena, eds. Asian Americans: Identity, Adaptation & Survival. (Monograph Ser.). (Orig.). 1981. cancelled (ISBN 0-934584-13-3). Pacific-Asian.
ASSASSINATION
see also Murder; Terrorism
Brooks, Stewart M. Our Murdered Presidents: The Medical Story. (Illus.). 234p. 1966. 8.95. Fell.
Dinges, John & Landau, Saul. Assassination on Embassy Row. 432p. 1981. pap. 5.95 (ISBN 0-07-016998-5). McGraw.
Minnery, John. How to Kill, Vol. III. (Illus.). 92p. (Orig.). 1979. pap. 6.00 (ISBN 0-87364-156-6). Paladin Ent.
--How to Kill, Vol. IV. (Illus.). 92p. (Orig.). 1979. pap. 6.00 (ISBN 0-87364-162-0). Paladin Ent.
--How to Kill, Vol. V. (Illus.). 86p. 1980. pap. 5.00 (ISBN 0-87364-201-5). Paladin Ent.
ASSAULT, CRIMINAL
see Rape
ASSAYING
see also classes of metals, and names of specific metals
Muns, George F. Chemical Analysis of Ores & Minerals for Copper, Silver, Gold, & the Platinum Metals. (Illus.). 53p. (Orig.). 1980. pap. 6.50 (ISBN 0-9604924-0-2). Muns.
ASSEMBLY-LINE METHODS
see also Automation
Linhart, Robert. The Asssembly Line. Rosland, Margaret, tr. from Fr. Orig. Title: L'Etabli. 144p. (Orig.). 1981. pap. text ed. 6.95x (ISBN 0-87023-322-X). U of Mass Pr.
ASSERTIVENESS (PSYCHOLOGY)
Emmons, Michael & Richardson, David. The Assertive Christian. Frost, Miriam, ed. 156p. (Orig.). 1981. pap. 5.95 (ISBN 0-03-059057-4). Winston Pr.
Lichtenstein, Grace. Machisma: Women & Daring. LC 79-7114. 360p. 1981. 14.95 (ISBN 0-385-15109-8). Doubleday.
Sholerar, G. P. Marriage Is a Family Affair. Date not set. text ed. price not set (ISBN 0-89335-120-2). Spectrum Pub.
ASSESSMENT OF PERSONALITY
see Personality Assessment
ASSINIBOIN INDIANS
see Indians of North America–The West
ASSISTANCE IN EMERGENCIES
see also Disaster Relief; First Aid in Illness and Injury
Piliavin, Jane A., et al, eds. Emergency Intervention. 1981. price not set (ISBN 0-12-556450-3). Acad Pr.
ASSISTANCE TO UNDERDEVELOPED AREAS
see Technical Assistance
ASSOCIATION
see Social Groups
ASSOCIATION FOOTBALL
see Soccer
ASSOCIATIONS (LAW)
see Corporations, Nonprofit
ASSOCIATIONS, INSTITUTIONS, ETC.
see also Clubs; Community Life; Cooperation; Meetings; Societies
also names of specific types of associations, institutions, etc. e.g., Corporations; Public Institutions; Trade and Professional Associations; subdivision Societies under appropriate subjects
Mescon, Michael H. & Bramlette, Carl A., Jr., eds. Individual & the Future of Organizations, Vol. 9. (Franklin Foundation Lecture Ser.). 1980. pap. 3.75 (ISBN 0-88406-139-6). GA St U Busn Pub.
Scott, W. Richard. Organizations: Rationale, Natural, & Open Systems. (Ser. in Sociology). (Illus.). 320p. 1981. text ed. 16.95 (ISBN 0-13-641977-1). P-H.
Wolfers, Elsie E. & Evansen, Virginia B. Organizations, Clubs, Action Groups: How to Start Them, How to Run Them. 256p. 1981. 11.95 (ISBN 0-312-58791-0). St Martin.
Zey-Ferrell, Mary & Aiken, Michael. Complex Organizations: Critical Perspectives. pap. text ed. 11.95 (ISBN 0-673-15269-3). Scott F.
ASSOCIATIONS, INSTITUTIONS, ETC.–DIRECTORIES
Anderson, I. G., ed. Directory of European Associations: National Industrial, Trade & Professional Associations, Pt. One. 3rd ed. 500p. 1981. 125.00. Gale.
Carrol, Frieda, compiled by. The Woman's Index. LC 80-70675. 200p. 1981. 12.95 (ISBN 0-9605246-6-5); pap. 9.95. Biblio Pr Ga.
ASSOCIATIONS, INTERNATIONAL
see International Agencies
ASSURANCE (INSURANCE)
see Insurance
ASSYRO-BABYLONIAN LANGUAGE
Marcus, David. A Manual of Babylonian Jewish Aramaic. LC 80-6073. 104p. (Orig.). 1981. pap. text ed. 7.75 (ISBN 0-8191-1363-8). U Pr of Amer.
ASSYRO-BABYLONIAN LITERATURE–HISTORY AND CRITICISM
Harper, Robert F., intro. by. Assyrian & Bablyonian Literature. 462p. 1980. Repr. of 1904 ed. lib. bdg. 50.00 (ISBN 0-89984-292-5). Century Bookbindery.
ASTAIRE, FRED, 1899-
Astaire, Fred. Steps in Time. (Quality Paperbacks Ser.). (Illus.). 327p. 1981. pap. 7.95 (ISBN 0-306-80141-8). Da Capo.
ASTEROIDS
see Planets, Minor
ASTHMA
Abramson, Harold A. The Patient Speaks of Her Mother. LC 79-65234. 240p. 1980. 10.00 (ISBN 0-533-04343-3). Vantage.
Booth, Sterling R., Jr. Allergy Cures Your Allergist Never Mentioned. 1981. 12.95 (ISBN 0-87949-191-4). Ashley Bks.
Gershwin, M. Eric. Bronchial Asthma: Principles of Diagnosis & Treatment. 1981. write for info. (ISBN 0-8089-1331-X). Grune.
ASTOR, NANCY WITCHER (LANGHORNE) VISCOUNTESS
Grigg, John. Nancy Astor. (Illus.). 192p. 1981. 15.00 (ISBN 0-316-32870-7). Little.
--Nancy Astor: A Lady Unashamed. (Illus.). 192p. 1981. 15.00 (ISBN 0-316-32870-7). Little.
ASTOR FAMILY
Gates, John D. The Astor Family: A Unique Exploration of One of America's First Families. LC 79-6580. 288p. 1981. 12.95 (ISBN 0-385-14909-3). Doubleday.
ASTRAL PROJECTION
Littleton, August V. The Art & Science of Psychomancy with Concrete & Practical Applications. (Library of Scientific Psychology Bk.). (Illus.). 107p. 1981. 29.45 (ISBN 0-89920-022-2). Am Inst Psych.
ASTROBIOLOGY
see Life on Other Planets
ASTROLOGY
see also Horoscopes; Occult Sciences
Anrais, David. Man & the Zodiac. pap. 5.95 (ISBN 0-87728-014-2). Weiser.
Bemis, Pat. Astrology: An Illustrated Manual for Teachers & Students. 1978. pap. 6.00 (ISBN 0-686-68269-6). Macoy Pub.
Bennett, Judith. Sex Signs. 384p. 1981. pap. 7.95 (ISBN 0-312-71339-8). St Martin.
Best, Simon & Lollerstrom, Nick. Planting by the Moon - Nineteen Eighty-One. rev. ed. (Illus.). 128p. 1981. pap. 2.95 (ISBN 0-917086-25-2). Astro Comp Serv.
Ebestin, Reinheld. The Annual Diagram. 160p. 1980. pap. 9.95 (ISBN 0-88231-122-0). ASI Pub Inc.
Ficino, Marsilio. The Book of Life. Boer, Charles, tr. from Latin. 217p. 1980. pap. 12.50 (ISBN 0-88214-212-7). Spring Pubns.
Gale, Mort. Instant Astrology. (Illus., Orig.). 1980. pap. 6.95 (ISBN 0-446-97355-6). Warner Bks.
Greene, Liz. Looking at Astrology. LC 77-83149. (Illus.). 30p. (gr. 2-7). 1981. pap. 4.95 (ISBN 0-916360-13-X). CRCS Pubns WA.
--Star Signs for Lovers. LC 80-5890. (Illus.). 480p. 1980. 14.95 (ISBN 0-8128-2765-1). Stein & Day.
Halevi, Z'Ev Ben Shimon. Adam & the Qabalistic Tree. 1980. pap. 7.95 (ISBN 0-87728-263-3). Weiser.
Hamaker-Zondag, Karen. Interpretation: Jungian Symbolism & Astrology, Pt. 1. 192p. 1981. 7.95 (ISBN 0-87728-523-3). Weiser.
Hill, Sondra. Fun Astrology. Orig. Title: All About Astrology. (Illus.). 96p. (gr. 4-7). 1981. PLB price not set (ISBN 0-671-41629-4). Messner.
Llewellyn's Personal Guide & Astrological Almanac for 1981, 12 bks. 64p. 1980. pap. 1.50. Bantam.
March, Marion & McEvers, Joan. The Only Way to Learn Astrology: Vol. 2, Math & Aftermath. 2nd. rev. ed. (Illus.). 320p. 1981. pap. 11.95 (ISBN 0-917086-26-0). Astro Comp Serv.
Martine. The Only Astrology Book You'll Ever Need. LC 80-5403. 288p. 1981. 14.95 (ISBN 0-8128-2726-0). Stein & Day.
Millard, Margaret. Casenotes of a Medical Astrologer. 1980. pap. 7.95 (ISBN 0-87728-484-9). Weiser.
Moore, Eric V. Rhythm of the Zodiac & the Wisdom Dinner. LC 80-51680. (Illus.). 80p. (Orig.). 1980. pap. 4.00 (ISBN 0-937236-00-4, 4W). Sonrise Prods.
Morimando, Patricia. The Neptune Effect. 1979. pap. 3.95 (ISBN 0-87728-487-3). Weiser.
Nauman, Eileen. American Book of Medical Astrology. (Illus.). 368p. (Orig.). 1981. pap. 14.95 (ISBN 0-917086-28-7). Astro Comp Serv.
Nevin, Bruce E. Astrology Inside Out. (Illus.). 288p. (Orig.). 1981. pap. 9.95 (ISBN 0-914918-19-2). Para Res.
Oken, Alan. Alan Oken's Complete Astrology. 640p. 1980. pap. 9.95 (ISBN 0-553-01262-2). Bantam.
Para Research, Inc. Astrological Books in Print, 1981-82. 144p. (Orig.). 1981. pap. 4.95 (ISBN 0-686-69331-0). Para Res.
Parker, Ann E. Astrology & Alcoholism: Genetic Key to the Horoscope. 1981. pap. 7.95 (ISBN 0-87728-519-5). Weiser.
Savage, John. The Gay Astrologer. 1981. 7.95. Ashley Bks.
Schulman, Martin. The Ascendant: Your Karmic Doorway. 1981. pap. 6.95 (ISBN 0-87728-507-1). Weiser.
--The Astrology of Sexuality. 1981. pap. 7.95 (ISBN 0-87728-481-4). Weiser.
--Celestial Harmony: A Guide to Horoscope Interpretation. 1980. pap. 7.95 (ISBN 0-87728-495-4). Weiser.
Sepharial. Manual of Astrology. 263p. 1981. pap. 10.00 (ISBN 0-89540-065-0). Sun Pub.
Simmons, A. LeRoi. Ephemerides 1890-1950. 407p. 1970. text ed. 17.00 (ISBN 0-9605126-0-8). Aquarian Bk Pubs.
--Ephemeris Nineteen Fifty to Nineteen Seventy-Five. (Illus.). 375p. 1977. 14.00 (ISBN 0-9605126-1-6). Aquarian Bk Pubs.
--Twentieth Century Table of Houses. 202p. 1972. text ed. 6.00 (ISBN 0-9605126-2-4). Aquarian Bk Pubs.
Van Toen, Donna. Astrologer's Note Book. 128p. 1981. pap. 6.95 (ISBN 0-87728-521-7). Weiser.
Von Hartmann, Frank. The Techniques of Astrological Geomancy. (Illus.). 137p. 1981. 47.85 (ISBN 0-89920-019-2). Am Inst Psych.
Yott, Donald H. Conjunctions: An in Depth Delineation. 1981. pap. 6.95 (ISBN 0-87728-524-1). Weiser.
ASTROLOGY, EARLY
Johndro, L. Edward. The Stars. 1979. pap. 6.95 (ISBN 0-87728-485-7). Weiser.
ASTRONAUTICS
see also Outer Space–Exploration; Space Flight; Space Sciences; Space Ships; Space Vehicles
Bent, Ralph D. & McKinley, James L. Aircraft Electricity & Electronics. rev. ed. (Aviation Technology Ser.). (Illus.). 432p. 1981. pap. text ed. 16.95x (ISBN 0-07-004793-6, G). McGraw.
ASTRONAUTICS–BIBLIOGRAPHY
Didelot, J., ed. Interavia ABC: World Dictionary of Aviation & Astronautics, 1980. 28th ed. 1126p. 1980. 107.50x (ISBN 0-8002-2697-6). Intl Pubns Serv.
ASTRONAUTICS–JUVENILE LITERATURE
see also Space Flight–Juvenile Literature
Moche. The Star Wars Question & Answer Book About Space. (Illus.). (gr. 4). Date not set. pap. cancelled (ISBN 0-590-30065-2, Schol Pap). Schol Bk Serv.
ASTRONOMICAL PHYSICS
see Astrophysics
ASTRONOMY
see also Almanacs; Astrology; Astrophysics; Comets; Cosmogony; Earth; Life on Other Planets; Meteorites; Milky Way; Nautical Astronomy; Satellites; Solar System; Space Environment; Space Sciences; Spectrum Analysis; Stars; Sun; Transits; Zodiac
Alksne, Z. K. & Ikaunieks, Ya Y. Carbon Stars. rev. ed. Baumert, J. H., ed. (Astronomy & Astrophysics Ser.: Vol. 11). Orig. Title: Uglerodnye Zvevdy. (Illus.). 192p. pap. 24.00 (ISBN 0-912918-16-0). Pachart Pub Hse.
Andrew, Bryan H., ed. Interstellar Molecules. (International Astronomical Union Symposia: No. 87). 500p. 1980. PLB 76.50 (ISBN 90-277-1160-7, Pub. by D. Reidel); pap. 34.00 (ISBN 90-277-1161-5). Kluwer Boston.
Boehme, S, et al, eds. Astronomy & Astrophysics Abstracts, Vol. 27: Literature 1980, Pt. 1. 939p. 1981. 69.70 (ISBN 0-387-10479-8). Springer-Verlag.
Bok, Bart J. & Bok, Priscilla F. The Milky Way. 5th ed. LC 80-22544. (Harvard Books on Astronomy Ser.). (Illus.). 384p. 1981. text ed. 20.00 (ISBN 0-674-57503-2). Harvard U Pr.
Claiborne, Robert. The Summer Stargazer: Astronomy for Beginners. 1981. pap. 3.95 (ISBN 0-14-046487-5). Penguin.
Cornell, James. The First Stargazers. (Illus.). 288p. 1981. 17.95 (ISBN 0-684-16799-9, ScribT). Scribner.
Dryer, Murray & Tandberg-Hanssen, Einar, eds. Solar & Interplanetary Dynamics. (International Astronomical Union Symposia: No. 91). 570p. 1980. lib. bdg. 66.00 (ISBN 90-277-1162-3, Pub. by D. Reidel); pap. 28.95 (ISBN 90-277-1163-1). Kluwer Boston.
Finocchiaro, Maurice A. Galileo & the Art of Reasoning: Rhetorical Foundations of Logic & Scientific Method. (Philosophy of Science Studies: No. 61). 463p. 1980. lib. bdg. 42.00 (ISBN 90-277-1094-5, Pub. by D. Reidel); pap. 21.00 (ISBN 90-277-1095-3). Kluwer Boston.
Giacconi, Richard & Setti, Giancarlo, eds. X-Ray Astronomy. (NATO Advanced Study Institutes Series, C. Mathematical & Physical Sciences: No. 60). 400p. 1980. lib. bdg. 47.50 (ISBN 90-277-1156-9, Pub. by D. Reidel). Kluwer Boston.
Harwit, Martin. Cosmic Discovery: The Search, Scope, & Heritage of Astronomy. LC 80-68172. 70p. 1981. 25.00x (ISBN 0-465-01428-3). Basic.
Heiles, Carl E. Radioastronomy: Extremes of the Universe. 375p. pap. text ed. 12.00x (ISBN 0-935702-06-7). Univ Sci Bks.
Jastrow, Robert. God & the Astronomers. 1980. pap. 4.95 (ISBN 0-446-97350-5). Warner Bks.
--Red Giants & White Dwarfs. 1980. pap. 7.95 (ISBN 0-446-97349-1). Warner Bks.
Johndro, L. Edward. The Earth in the Heavens. 1979. pap. 6.95 (ISBN 0-87728-486-5). Weiser.
Mitton, Simon. Daytime Star: The Story of Our Sun. (Illus.). 192p. 1981. 14.95 (ISBN 0-684-16840-5, ScribT). Scribner.
Papon, Donald. The Lure of the Heavens: A History of Astrology. (Illus.). 320p. 1980. pap. 7.95 (ISBN 0-87728-502-0). Weiser.
Polish Academy of Science. Poetic Potentials in Information of Astronomy. 1976. pap. 1.95. Primary Pr.
Protheroe, William M., et al. Exploring the Universe. 2nd ed. (Illus.). 480p. 1981. text ed. 19.95 (ISBN 0-675-08154-8); instr's. manual 3.95 (ISBN 0-686-69491-0). Merrill.
Riban, David M. Introduction to Physical Science. (Illus.). 656p. 1981. text ed. 21.95 (ISBN 0-07-052140-9, C); instr's manual 4.95 (ISBN 0-07-052141-7). McGraw.
Vincentius, Bellovacensis. Hier Begynneth the Table of the Rubrices of This Presente Volume Namde the Myrrour of the Worlde or Thymage of the Same. Caxton, William, tr. from Fr. LC 79-84143. (English Experience Ser.: No. 960). 204p. (Eng.). 1979. Repr. of 1481 ed. lib. bdg. 30.00 (ISBN 90-221-0960-7). Walter J Johnson.
Wald, Robert M. Space, Time, & Gravity. LC 77-4038. viii, 132p. 1981. pap. 3.95 (ISBN 0-226-87031-6). U of Chicago Pr.
Wayman, Patrick A., ed. Transactions of the International Astronomical Union, Vol. XVIIB. 536p. 1980. PLB 68.50 (ISBN 90-277-1159-3). Kluwer Boston.
Wyatt, Stanley P. & Kaler, James B. Principles of Astronomy: A Short Version. 550p. 1981. text ed. 18.95 (ISBN 0-205-07315-8); instructor's manual free (ISBN 0-205-07316-6). Allyn.
ASTRONOMY–ATLASES
see Stars–Atlases
ASTRONOMY–JUVENILE LITERATURE
Edens, Cooper. Caretakers of Wonder. (Illus.). 40p. (Orig.). 1980. pap. 6.95 (ISBN 0-914676-76-8). Green Tiger.
Moche. The Star Wars Question & Answer Book About Space. (Illus.). (gr. 4). Date not set. pap. cancelled (ISBN 0-590-30065-2, Schol Pap). Schol Bk Serv.
ASTRONOMY–OBSERVERS' MANUALS
Burnham, Robert, Jr. Burnham's Celestial Handbook: An Observer's Guide to the Universe Beyond the Solar System. (Illus.). 1980. Repr. of 1978 ed. 16.50x ea. Vintage Bk Co.
Jones, Kenneth G., ed. Webb Society Deep-Sky Oberver's Handbook; Galaxies, Vol. 4. 296p. 1981. pap. 14.95 (ISBN 0-89490-050-1). Enslow Pubs.
ASTRONOMY, NAUTICAL
see Nautical Astronomy
ASTROPHYSICS
see also Spectrum Analysis
Alksne, Z. K. & Ikaunieks, Ya Y. Carbon Stars. rev. ed. Baumert, J. H., ed. (Astronomy & Astrophysics Ser.: Vol. 11). Orig. Title: Uglerodnye Zvevdy. (Illus.). 192p. pap. 24.00 (ISBN 0-912918-16-0). Pachart Pub Hse.
Boehme, S, et al, eds. Astronomy & Astrophysics Abstracts, Vol. 27: Literature 1980, Pt. 1. 939p. 1981. 69.70 (ISBN 0-387-10479-8). Springer-Verlag.
Meaburn, John. Detection & Spectronomy of Faint Light. (Astrophysics & Space Science Library: No. 56). 270p. 1980. pap. 14.95 (ISBN 90-277-1198-4, Pub. by D. Reidel). Kluwer Boston.
Sheeter, Sean. The Unified Model of the Universe: The Geometrically Unified Field Solution. (The Unified Theory of Process: Vol. 1). (Illus.). 150p. 1981. 18.98 (ISBN 0-9605378-0-5); pap. 9.50 (ISBN 0-9605378-1-3). Process Pr.
Texas Symposium on Relativistic Astrophysics, 9th. Proceedings. Perry, Judith J., et al, eds. LC 80-11614. (N.Y. Academy of Sciences Annals: Vol. 336). 599p. 1980. 105.00x (ISBN 0-89766-045-5). NY Acad Sci.
Zondag-Hamaker, Karen. Astro-Psychology. 1980. pap. 7.95 (ISBN 0-87728-465-2). Weiser.
ASYLUM, RIGHT OF
see also Extradition
Grahl-Madsen, Atle. Territorial Asylum. LC 80-10498. (Monograph in the Uppsala University Swedish Institute of International Law). 231p. 1980. lib. bdg. 28.00 (ISBN 0-379-20706-0). Oceana.
ASYLUMS
see also Old Age Homes; Poor; Psychiatric Hospitals
Rothman. Conscience & Convenience: The Asylum & Its Alternatives in Progressive America. (Orig.). 1980. pap. text ed. 8.95 (ISBN 0-316-75775-6). Little.
ATARACTIC DRUGS
see Tranquilizing Drugs
ATATURK, KAMAL, PRES. TURKEY, d. 1938
Walker, Barbara K., et al. To Set Them Free: The Early Years of Mustafa Kemal Ataturk. LC 80-21127. (Illus.). 96p. 1981. 14.95 (ISBN 0-936988-00-2); pap. 9.95 (ISBN 0-936988-02-9). Tompson & Rutter.
ATHEISM
see also Theism
Ellis, Albert. The Case Against Religion: A Psychotherapist's View. 1976. pap. 3.00. Am Atheist.

Harris, T. L. Unholy Pilgrimage: A Visit to Russia to Find What Twenty Years of Official Atheism Had Done for the Russian People. 195p. Repr. of 1937 ed. text ed. 2.95. Attic Pr.
Ingersoll, Robert G. Atheist Truth Vs. Religion's Ghosts. 1980. pap. 3.29. Am Atheist.
--A Few Reasons for Doubting the Inspiration of the Bible. 1976. pap. 3.00. Am Atheist.
Johnson, B. C. The Atheist Debater's Handbook: The/Skeptics Bookshelf. 100p. 1981. 15.95 (ISBN 0-87975-152-5); pap. 9.95 (ISBN 0-87975-154-1). Prometheus Bks.
McCabe, Joseph. The Logic & Virtue of Atheism. 1980. pap. 3.29. Am Atheist.
Murray, Jon G. Essays of an Atheist Activist. 1980. pap. 3.29. Am Atheist.
O'Hair, Madalyn M. The American Atheist Radio Series of Ingersoll the Magnificent. 1977. pap. 3.00. Am Atheist.
--An Atheist Primer. 1980. pap. 3.00. Am Atheist.
--Women & Atheism: The Ultimate Liberation. 1979. pap. 3.00. Am Atheist.

ATHEISM AND CHRISTIANITY
see Christianity and Atheism

ATHENS–DESCRIPTION
Blue Guide - Athens. 1981. pap. 19.95 (ISBN 0-528-84623-X). Rand.
Taylor, William. Athenian Odyssey. 4.95 (ISBN 0-89353-025-5). Green Hill.

ATHENS–HISTORY
Cargill, Jack. The Second Athenian League: Empire or Free Alliance. 325p. 1981. 17.50x (ISBN 0-520-04069-4). U of Cal Pr.

ATHENS, GEORGIA–HISTORY
Reap, James. Athens: A Pictorial History. Friedman, Donna R., ed. (Illus.). 208p. 1981. pap. price not set (ISBN 0-89865-110-7). Donning Co.

ATHLETES
Black, William T. Mormon Athletes. (Illus.). 6.95 (ISBN 0-87747-842-2). Deseret Bk.

ATHLETES–BIOGRAPHY
Fife, Eric S. Against the Clock: The Story of Ray Buker, Sr., Olympic Runner & Missionary Statesman. (Illus.). 224p. (Orig.). 1981. pap. 5.95 (ISBN 0-310-24351-3). Zondervan.

ATHLETES, WOMEN
Jones, Betty M. Wonder Women of Sports. LC 80-20232. (Step-up Book Ser.: No. 33). (Illus.). 72p. (gr. 2-5). 1981. PLB 4.99 (ISBN 0-394-94475-5); pap. 3.95 boards (ISBN 0-394-84475-0). Random.

ATHLETIC GOODS
see Sporting Goods

ATHLETIC MEDICINE
see Sports Medicine

ATHLETICS
see also Boxing; College Sports; Fencing; Gymnastics; Olympic Games; Physical Education and Training; Skating; Sports; Swimming; Track-Athletics; Walking; Weight Lifting
also names of specific sports names of schools, colleges, etc.
Green, Barry & Green, Alan. The Directory of Athletic Scholarships: Where They Are & How to Get Them. 312p. 1981. 14.95 (ISBN 0-399-12620-1, Perigee); pap. 6.95 (ISBN 0-399-50533-4). Putnam.
Klafs, Carl E. & Arnheim, Daniel D. Modern Principles of Athletic Training. 5th ed. (Illus.). 580p. 1981. text ed. 21.95 (ISBN 0-8016-2682-X). Mosby.
Reilly, Thomas, ed. Sports Fitness & Sports Injuries. (Illus.). 304p. 1981. 45.00 (ISBN 0-571-11628-0, Pub. by Faber & Faber); pap. 28.00 (ISBN 0-571-11629-9). Merrimack Bk Serv.

ATHLETICS–APPARATUS AND EQUIPMENT
see also Sporting Goods
DeVore, Steven, et al. Sybervision: Muscle Memory Programming for Any Sport. (Illus.). 250p. 1981. 12.95 (ISBN 0-914090-98-4). Chicago Review.

ATHLETICS–MEDICAL ASPECTS
see Sports Medicine

ATLANTA
Brambilla, Robert. Learning from Atlanta. (Learningfrom the U. S. A. Ser.). 150p. (Orig.). 1981. pap. text ed. 6.95 (ISBN 0-87855-835-7). Transaction Bks.

ATLANTIC ALLIANCE
see North Atlantic Treaty Organization

ATLANTIC OCEAN
Mitchell-Thome, Raoul C. Geology of the South Atlantic Islands. (Beitraege zur regionalen Geologie der Erde: Vol. 10). (Illus.). 366p. 1970. lib. bdg. 90.05x (ISBN 3-443-11010-X, Pub by Gebrueder Borntraeger Germany). Lubrecht & Cramer.
Rona, Peter A. The Central North Atlantic Ocean Basin & Continental Margins: Geology, Geophysics, Geochemistry, & Resources, Including the Trans-Atlantic Geotraverse (TAG) (Illus.). 99p. 1980. pap. 45.00 (ISBN 0-08-026259-7). Pergamon.

ATLANTIC STATES
Pennypacker, Arabelle, ed. Reading for Young People: The Middle Atlantic. LC 80-16021. 162p. 1980. pap. 8.00 (ISBN 0-8389-0295-2). ALA.

ATLANTIS
Donnelly, Ignatius. Atlantis: Antediluvidan World. LC 80-8340. (Harper's Library of Spiritual Wisdom). (Illus.). 512p. 1981. pap. 6.95 (ISBN 0-06-061960-0, HarpR). Har-Row.

ATLASES
see also Bible–Geography
also subdivision Maps under names of countries, cities, etc., e.g. United States–Maps; London–Maps; also subdivision Atlases under subjects, e.g. Anatomy, Human–Atlases
American Youth Hostels. The American Bicycle Atlas. 1981. pap. 5.95 (ISBN 0-525-93172-4). Dutton.
Rand McNally. Pocket Atlas. LC 80-83201. (Illus.). 160p. 1980. pap. 4.95 (ISBN 0-528-83097-X). Rand.

ATLASES–BIBLIOGRAPHY
Research Libraries of the New York Public Library & the Library of Congress. Bibliographic Guide to Maps & Atlases: 1980. (Library Catalogs-Bib. Guides Ser.). 1981. lib. bdg. 95.00 (ISBN 0-8161-6890-3). G K Hall.

ATLASES, AMERICAN
see Atlases

ATLASES, ASTRONOMICAL
see Stars–Atlases

ATLASES, HISTORICAL
see Geography, Historical–Maps

ATMOSPHERE
see also Meteorology
also headings beginning with the word Atmospheric
Anthes, Richard, et al. The Atmosphere. 3rd ed. (Illus.). 384p. 1981. text ed. 17.95 (ISBN 0-675-08043-6); instr's. manual 3.95 (ISBN 0-686-69485-6). Merrill.
Cole, Alan. Introduction to the Atmosphere Lab Manual. 1980. loose leaf shrink wrapped 4.75 (ISBN 0-88252-110-1). Paladin Hse.
Kato, S. & Roper, R. G. Electric Current & Atmospheric Motion. (Advances in Earth & Planetary Sciences Ser.: No. 7). 294p. 1980. 24.50x (ISBN 0-89955-314-1, Pub. by JSSP Japan). Intl Schol Bk Serv.
Murcray, David G., ed. Handbook of High Resolution Infrared Spectra of Gases of Atmospheric Interest. 304p. 1981. 49.95 (ISBN 0-8493-2950-7). CRC Pr.
Schaefer, Vincent J. & Day, John A. A Field Guide to the Atmosphere. (Illus.). 384p. 1981. 13.95 (ISBN 0-395-24080-8). HM.

ATMOSPHERE, UPPER
Kato, Susumo, ed. Dynamics of the Upper Atmosphere. (Developments in Earth & Planetary Sciences Ser.: No. 1). 233p. 1980. PLB 29.95 (ISBN 90-277-1132-1, Pub. by D. Reidel). Kluwer Boston.

ATMOSPHERIC ABSORPTION OF SOLAR RADIATION
see Solar Radiation

ATMOSPHERIC NUCLEATION
Kellogg, William W. & Schware, Robert. Climate Change & Society: Consequences of Increasing Atmospheric Carbon Dioxide. (Special Study Ser.). 170p. (Orig.). 1981. lib. bdg. 15.00x (ISBN 0-86531-179-X); pap. 8.00x (ISBN 0-86531-180-3). Westview.

ATMOSPHERIC RADIOACTIVITY
see also Atomic Energy and Meteorology
Atomospheric Dispersion in Nuclear Power Plant Siting. (Safety Ser.: No. 50-SG-S3). 1981. pap. 14.75 (ISBN 92-0-623180-4, ISP 549, IAEA). Unipub.

ATOM BOMB
see Atomic Bomb

ATOMIC BOMB
see also Atomic Energy; Atomic Power; Hydrogen Bomb
Japan Broadcasting Corporation, ed. Unforgettable Fire: Pictures Drawn by Atomic Bomb Survivors. (Illus.). 1981. 15.95 (ISBN 0-394-51585-4); pap. 7.95 (ISBN 0-394-74823-9). Pantheon.

ATOMIC BOMB (INTERNATIONAL LAW)
see Atomic Weapons (International Law)

ATOMIC BOMB AND DISARMAMENT
see Atomic Weapons and Disarmament

ATOMIC DAMAGES, LIABILITY FOR
see Liability for Nuclear Damages

ATOMIC ENERGY
see also Atomic Bomb; Atomic Power; Atomic Power Industry; Masers; Nuclear Engineering; Nuclear Fission; Nuclear Reactors
INIS: Authority List for Journal Titles. (INIS-11(Rev.9)). 228p. 1981. pap. 14.00 (ISBN 0-686-69441-4, IN11R9, IAEA). Unipub.
Stewart, Hugh B. Transitional Energy Policy 1980-2030: Alternative Nuclear Technologies. (Pergamon Policy Studies on Science & Technology). 266p. 1981. 30.00 (ISBN 0-08-027183-9); pap. 12.50 (ISBN 0-08-027182-0). Pergamon.

ATOMIC ENERGY–INTERNATIONAL CONTROL
see Atomic Power–International Control

ATOMIC ENERGY–LAW AND LEGISLATION
see Atomic Power–Law and Legislation

ATOMIC ENERGY–MORAL AND RELIGIOUS ASPECTS
Hessel, Dieter T., ed. Energy Ethics: A Christian Response. (Orig.). 1979. pap. 4.25 (ISBN 0-377-00094-9). Friend Pr.

ATOMIC ENERGY–POPULAR WORKS
Calder, Nigel. Nuclear Nightmares. 1981. pap. 3.95 (ISBN 0-14-005867-2). Penguin.

ATOMIC ENERGY AND METEOROLOGY
see also Air–Pollution
Atomospheric Dispersion in Nuclear Power Plant Siting. (Safety Ser.: No. 50-SG-S3). 1981. pap. 14.75 (ISBN 92-0-623180-4, ISP 549, IAEA). Unipub.

ATOMIC ENERGY INDUSTRIES–SAFETY REGULATIONS
see Atomic Power–Law and Legislation

ATOMIC FUEL
see Nuclear Fuels

ATOMIC MEDICINE
see Nuclear Medicine

ATOMIC NUCLEI
see Nuclear Physics

ATOMIC PILES
see Nuclear Reactors

ATOMIC POWER
see also Atomic Bomb; Atomic Energy; Atomic Power Plants
Bupp, Irvin C. & Derian, Jean-Claude. The Failed Promise of Nuclear Power: The Story of Light Water. LC 77-20419. (Illus.). 241p. 1981. pap. 5.95 (ISBN 0-465-02273-1). Basic.
Doern, G. Bruce. Canadian Nuclear Policies. 1980. pap. text ed. 14.95x (ISBN 0-920380-25-5, Pub. by Inst Res Pub Canada). Renouf.
Freedman, Lawrence. Britain & Nuclear Weapons. 1981. text ed. 27.50x (ISBN 0-333-30494-2). Humanities.
Grossman, Karl. Cover Up: What You Are Not Supposed to Know About Nuclear Power. 1980. 11.95 (ISBN 0-531-07405-6, Permanent Pr). Watts.
McCormick, Norman J. Reliability & Risk Analysis: Methods & Nuclear Power Applications. 1981. write for info. (ISBN 0-12-482360-2). Acad Pr.
Weiss, Ann E. The Nuclear Question. LC 80-8806. (Illus.). 192p. (gr. 7 up). 1981. 10.95 (ISBN 0-15-257596-0, HJ). HarBraceJ.

ATOMIC POWER–HISTORY
Bickel, Lennard. The Deadly Element: The Story of Uranium. LC 78-66243. (Illus.). 320p. 1980. pap. 7.95 (ISBN 0-8128-6089-6). Stein & Day.
Browne, Corinne & Munroe, Robert. The Dragon's Tail: America's Continuing Nuclear Experiment. (Illus.). 288p. 1981. 10.95 (ISBN 0-688-03691-0). Morrow.

ATOMIC POWER–INTERNATIONAL CONTROL
Harris, Stuart & Oshima, Keichi, eds. Australia & Japan: Nuclear Energy Issues in the Pacific. (Australia-Japan Economic Relations Research Project Monograph: No. 3). (Illus.). 245p. 1980. pap. text ed. 9.95 (ISBN 0-9596197-2-0). Bks Australia.
Lovins, Amory B. & Lovins, L. H. Energy- War: Breaking the Nuclear Links. LC 80-8713. 228p. 1981. pap. 4.95 (ISBN 0-06-090852-1, CN 852, CN). Har-Row.

ATOMIC POWER–LAW AND LEGISLATION
see also Liability for Nuclear Damages; Radioactive Substances–Safety Regulations
Chicken, J. C. Nuclear Power Hazard Control Policy. LC 80-40992. (Illus.). 300p. 1981. 35.00 (ISBN 0-08-023254-X); pap. 17.50 (ISBN 0-08-023255-8). Pergamon.
Commissioning Procedures for Nuclear Plants. (Safety Ser.: No. 50-SG-04). pap. 9.00 (ISBN 0-686-69439-2, ISP 574, IAEA). Unipub.
Factors Relevant to the Decommissioning of Land-Based Nuclear Reactor Plants. (Safety Ser.: No. 52). 28p. 1981. pap. 4.75 (ISBN 0-686-69440-6, ISP 541, IAEA). Unipub.
Muntzing, L. Manning, ed. Nuclear Power & Its Regulation in the United States. (Illus.). 125p. 1980. pap. 30.00 (ISBN 0-08-027139-1). Pergamon.
Protection System & Related Features in Nuclear Power Plants. (Safety Ser.: No. 50-SG-D3). 55p. 1981. pap. 7.00 (ISBN 0-686-69442-2, ISP 551, IAEA). Unipub.

ATOMIC POWER ENGINEERING
see Nuclear Engineering

ATOMIC POWER INDUSTRY
Manpower Requirements & Developement for Nuclear Power Programmes. 628p. 1980. pap. 78.50 (ISBN 92-0-050080-3, ISP523, IAEA). Unipub.

ATOMIC POWER PLANTS
American Society of Civil Engineers, compiled by. Structural Analysis & Design of Nuclear Plant Facilities. LC 80-65828. (ASCE Manual & Report on Engineering Practice Ser.: No. 58). 576p. 1980. text ed. 140.00 (ISBN 0-87262-238-X). Am Soc Civil Eng.
Division 1 - Nuclear Power Plant Components: General Requirements. (Boiler & Pressure Vessel Code Ser.: Sec. 3). 1980. 55.00 (P0003R); pap. 80.00 loose-leaf (V0003R). ASME.
Freeman, Leslie J. Nuclear Witnesses: Insiders Speak Out. (Illus.). 1981. 14.95 (ISBN 0-393-01456-8). Norton.
Hickey, Albert E., ed. Simulation & Training Technology for Nuclear Power Plant Safety. 350p. 1981. pap. 40.00 (ISBN 0-89785-975-8). AIR Systems.
In-Service Inspection for Nuclear Power Plants. (Saftey Ser.: No. 50-Sg-02). 47p. 1980. pap. 7.25 (ISBN 92-0-123180-6, IAEA). Unipub.
Inspection & Enforcement by the Regulatory Body for Nuclear Power Plants. (Safety Ser.: No. 50-Sg-G4). 43p. 1980. pap. 7.00 (ISBN 0-686-68220-3, ISP557, IAEA). Unipub.
Nuclear Power & Safety. 1980. 50.00x (Pub. by Norwegian Info Norway). State Mutual Bk.
Operating Experience with Nuclear Power Stations in Member States: Performance Analysis Report 1978. 27p. 1980. pap. 5.50 (ISBN 92-0-659080-4, ISP570, IAEA). Unipub.
Protection Against Internally Generated Missles & Their Secondary Effects in Nuclear Power Plants. (Safety Ser.: No. 50-SG-D4). 43p. 1980. pap. 6.50 (ISBN 92-0-123880-0, ISP 552, IAEA). Unipub.
Sills, David L., et al, eds. Accident at Three Mile Island: The Human Dimensions. 200p. (Orig.). 1981. lib. bdg. 20.00x (ISBN 0-86531-165-X); pap. text ed. 12.00x (ISBN 0-86531-187-0). Westview.

ATOMIC SPECTRA
Bruce, W. R. & Johns, H. E. The Spectra of X Rays Scattered in Low Atomic Number Materials. 1980. 10.00x (Pub. by Brit Inst Radiology). State Mutual Bk.

ATOMIC WARFARE
see also Air Warfare; Atomic Bomb; Atomic Weapons; Hydrogen Bomb
Barnaby, Frank. Prospects for Peace. (Illus.). 105p. 1980. 21.50 (ISBN 0-08-027399-8); pap. 11.50 (ISBN 0-08-027398-X). Pergamon.
Boynton, John. Nuclear War: Can You Survive? (Illus.). 64p. pap. 4.95. Astroart Ent.

ATOMIC WARFARE AND SOCIETY
see War and Society

ATOMIC WEAPONS
see also Atomic Bomb; Atomic Weapons and Disarmament; Ballistic Missiles; Hydrogen Bomb
Bertram, Christoph, ed. Strategic Deterrence in a Changing Environment. LC 80-67841. (Adelphi Library: Vol. 6). 200p. 1981. text ed. 29.50 (ISBN 0-916672-75-1). Allanheld.
Lovins, Amory B. & Lovins, L. Hunter. Energy & War: Breaking the Nuclear Link. 180p. 1980. 10.00 (ISBN 0-913890-44-8). Friends Earth.
Mandelbaum, Michael. The Nuclear Revolution: International Politics Before & After Hiroshima. LC 80-24194. 256p. Date not set. price not set (ISBN 0-521-23819-6); pap. price not set (ISBN 0-521-28239-X). Cambridge U Pr.
Strauss, Erwin S. Basement Nukes: The Consequences of Cheap Weapons of Mass Destruction. 1980. pap. 6.95. Loompanics.

ATOMIC WEAPONS (INTERNATIONAL LAW)
Shaker, Mohamed I. The Nuclear Non-Proliferation Treaty: Origin & Implementation 1959 to 1979, 3 vols. LC 80-17359. 1980. lib. bdg. 40.00 ea. (ISBN 0-379-20470-3). Vol. 1 (ISBN 0-379-20470-3). Vol. 2 (ISBN 0-379-20471-1). Vol. 3 (ISBN 0-379-20472-X). Oceana.

ATOMIC WEAPONS AND DISARMAMENT
Barton, John H. The Politics of Peace: An Evaluation of Arms Control. LC 79-67776. 296p. 1981. text ed. 18.50x (ISBN 0-8047-1081-3). Stanford U Pr.
Burt, Richard, ed. Arms Control & Defense Postures in the Nineteen-Eighties. (Special Studies in National Security & Defense Policy Ser.). 220p. 1981. lib. bdg. 24.00x (ISBN 0-86531-162-5). Westview.
George, J. Socialism for the Dead. LC 79-67320. 354p. 1980. 12.95 (ISBN 0-533-04454-5). Vantage.
Labrie, Roger, ed. SALT Handbook: Key Documents & Issues, 1972-1979. 1979. pap. 12.25 (ISBN 0-8447-3316-4). Am Enterprise.
Shaker. Nuclear Non-Proliferation Treaty, Vols. 1-3. 1980. 40.00 ea. Oceana.

ATOMISM
Gangopadhyaya, Mrinalkanti. Indian Atomosm: History & Sources. 384p. 1980. pap. text ed. write for info. (ISBN 0-391-02177-X). Humanities.

ATOMS
see also Electrons; Magnetic Resonance; Neutrons; Nuclear Physics; Protons
Bolton, W. Atoms and Quanta, Book 7. LC 80-41395. (Study Topics in Physics Ser.). 96p. 1980. pap. text ed. write for info. (ISBN 0-408-10658-1). Butterworths.
CIAMDA Eighty: An Index to the Literature on Atomic & Molecular Collision Data Relevant to Fusion Research. 498p. 1980. pap. 31.25 (ISBN 92-0-039080-3, ISP550, IAEA). Unipub.
Weissbluth, Mitchel. Atoms & Molecules: Student Edition. 1980. lib ed 24.50 (ISBN 0-12-744452-1). Acad Pr.

ATOMS–SPECTRA
see Atomic Spectra

ATOMS, NUCLEI OF
see Nuclear Physics

ATONEMENT–BIBLICAL TEACHING
Smeaton, George. Doctrine of the Atonement According to the Apostles. Date not set. 17.95 (ISBN 0-88469-136-5). BMH Bks.

ATONEMENT–HISTORY OF DOCTRINE
Hengel, Martin. The Atonememt: The Origins of the Doctrine in the New Testament. Bowden, John, tr. from Ger. LC 80-2384. 128p. 1981. pap. 6.95 (ISBN 0-8006-1446-1, 1-1446). Fortress.

ATTACK AND DEFENSE (MILITARY SCIENCE)
see also Deterrence (Strategy)
Bray, Frank T. & Moodie, Michael. Defense Technology & the Atlantic Alliance: Competition or Collaboration? LC 77-80297. (Foreign Policy Report Ser.). 5.00 (ISBN 0-89549-000-5). Inst Foreign Policy Anal.

The Directory of Defense Electronic Products & Services: U. S. Suppliers, 1981. rev. 7th ed. 228p. pap. write for info. (ISBN 0-931634-06-7). Info Clearing House.
Goure, Leon, et al. The Emerging Strategic Environment: Implications for Ballistic Missile Defense. LC 79-53108. 75p. 1979. 6.50. Inst Foreign Policy Anal.
Hanks, Robert J. The Unnoticed Challenge: Soviet Maritime Strategy & the Global Choke Points. LC 80-83751. (Special Report Ser.). 68p. 1980. 6.50 (ISBN 0-89549-025-0). Inst Foreign Policy Anal.
Record, Jeffrey. Force Reductions in Europe: Starting Over. LC 80-83753. (Special Report Ser.). 92p. 1980. 6.50 (ISBN 0-89549-027-7). Inst Foreign Policy Anal.

ATTENDANCE, CHURCH
see Church Attendance

ATTENDANCE, SCHOOL
see School Attendance

ATTITUDE (PSYCHOLOGY)
see also Conformity; Empathy; Frustration; Job Satisfaction
Kardos, Lajos, ed. Attitudes, Interaction & Personality. Dajka, B., et al, trs. (Illus.). 149p. 1980. 10.50x (ISBN 963-05-2088-5). Intl Pubns Serv.
Mehrabian, Albert. Silent Messages: Implicit Communication of Emotions & Attitudes. 2nd ed. 208p. 1980. pap. text ed. 8.95x (ISBN 0-534-00910-7). Wadsworth Pub.
Wegener, Bernd, ed. Social Attitudes & Psychophysical Measurement: 432p. 1981. professional reference text 24.95 (ISBN 0-89859-083-3). L Erlbaum Assocs.

ATTITUDE AND POSTURE OF MAN
see Man–Attitude and Movement

ATTORNEYS
see Lawyers

ATTRIBUTES OF GOD
see God–Attributes

ATTRITION
see Penance

ATYPICAL CHILDREN
see Exceptional Children

AUCTIONS
see also Sales
Auctions of Nineteen Seventy-Nine. Date not set. pap. 10.00 (ISBN 0-936032-03-0). Thoroughbred Own & Breed.
Engelmeier, Philip A. Auctioneering. Paulaha, Richard & Engelmeier, Darlette, eds. Orig. Title: Be a Journeyman Auctioneer. (Illus.). 70p. (Orig.). 1980. pap. 10.00. Engelmeier.
Leab, Daniel J. & Leab, Katharine K. The Auction Companion. LC 80-8208. 224p. 1981. 12.95 (ISBN 0-06-012556-X, HarpT); pap. 5.95 (ISBN 0-06-090850-5, CN 850). Har-Row.
Webster, Jonathan & Webster, Harriet. The Underground Marketplace. LC 80-54401. (Illus.). 208p. 1981. text ed. 12.50x (ISBN 0-87663-348-3); pap. 6.95 (ISBN 0-87663-555-9). Universe.

AUDEN, WYSTAN HUGH, 1907-1973
Griffin, Howard. Conversations with W. H. Auden. LC 80-24381. 128p. 1981. 12.95 (ISBN 0-912516-55-0); pap. 4.95 (ISBN 0-912516-56-9). Grey Fox.
Mendelson, Edward. Early Auden. 1981. 16.95 (ISBN 0-670-28712-1). Viking Pr.
Mitchell, Donald. Britten & Auden in the Thirties: The Year 1936. LC 80-25980. (Illus.). 174p. 1981. 15.00 (ISBN 0-295-95814-6). U of Wash Pr.

AUDI (AUTOMOBILE)
see Automobiles, Foreign–Types–Audi

AUDIENCES
see Television Audiences

AUDIENCES, TELEVISION
see Television Audiences

AUDIO EQUIPMENT
see Sound–Apparatus

AUDIO TAPES
see Phonotapes

AUDIO-VISUAL AIDS
see Audio-Visual Materials

AUDIO-VISUAL EDUCATION
see also Audio-Visual Materials; Visual Education also subdivision Audio-Visual Aids, or Study and Teaching under subjects, e.g. Music–Audio-Visual aids
Lebaron, John. Making Television: A Video Guide for Teachers. (Orig.). 1981. pap. 12.50 (ISBN 0-8077-2636-2). Tchrs Coll.

AUDIO-VISUAL EQUIPMENT
Here are entered general works on projects, screens, sound equipment, pointers, tables, exhibit boards, etc. see also names of particular equipment, e.g. Moving picture projects, Record changers
Schroeder, Don & Lare, Gary. Audiovisual Equipment & Materials: A Basic Repair & Maintenance Manual. LC 79-384. 172p. 1979. pap. text ed. 10.00 (ISBN 0-8108-1206-1). Scarecrow.

AUDIO-VISUAL LIBRARY SERVICE
Photograph A-V Program Directory. LC 80-83469. (Illus.). 224p. 1980. 24.50 (ISBN 0-936524-00-6). PMI Inc.

AUDIO-VISUAL MATERIALS
see also Filmstrips; Moving-Pictures; Phonorecords also subdivision Audio-visual aids, or study and teaching under subjects, e.g. Music
Edgerton, Mills F., Jr., ed. Sight & Sound: The Sensible & Sensitive Use of Audio-Visual Aids. 1969. pap. 7.95x (ISBN 0-915432-69-2). NE Conf Teach.
Educational Film Locator: Of the Consortium of University Film Centers & R. R. Bowker. 2nd ed. 2500p. 1980. 50.00 (ISBN 0-8352-1295-5). Bowker.
Swain, Dwight. Scripting for Video & Audiovisual Media. 1981. 22.95 (ISBN 0-240-51075-5). Focal Pr.
Weber, O., ed. Audiovisual Market Place A Multimedia Guide 1981: A Multimedia Guide. 11th ed. LC 69-18201. 1981. pap. 32.50 (ISBN 0-8352-1333-1). Bowker.

AUDIO-VISUAL MATERIALS CENTERS
see Instructional Materials Centers

AUDIOLOGY
see also Deafness
Bess, Fred H. & McConnell, Freeman E. Audiology, Education & the Hearing Impaired Child. (Illus.). 225p. 1981. pap. text ed. 15.95 (ISBN 0-8016-0671-3). Mosby.
Chermak, Gail D. Handbook of Audiological Rehabilitation. (Illus.). 480p. 1981. 43.75 (ISBN 0-398-04170-9). C C Thomas.
Rudman, Jack. Speech Pathology & Audiology. (Undergraduate Program Field Test Ser.: UPFT-25). (Cloth bdg. avail. on request). pap. 9.95 (ISBN 0-8373-6025-0). Natl Learning.
Smith, Carol. Auditory Discrimination Practice Exercises. 1981. pap. 3.95 (ISBN 0-8134-2168-3, 2168). Interstate.

AUDIOMETER
see Audiometry

AUDIOMETRY
Aten, James. The Denver Auditory Phoneme Sequencing Test. LC 79-651. (Illus.). 310p. 1979. clinical test 59.95 (ISBN 0-933014-51-1). College-Hill.

AUDIT, MANAGEMENT
see Management Audit

AUDITING
see also Accounting; Financial Statements; Tax Auditing; also subdivision Accounting under names of industries, trades, etc.
Audit Committee. 1978. pap. 1.50. Am Inst CPA.
Auditing Manual. 9th ed. 15.00 (ISBN 0-932788-00-9). Bradley CPA.
Brink, V. Z., et al. Modern Internal Auditing: An Operational Approach. 3rd ed. 795p. 1973. 34.50 (ISBN 0-471-06524-2). Wiley.
Computer Assisted Audit Techniques. (Audit & Accounting Guide Ser.). 1979. pap. 5.00. Am Inst CPA.
Cornick, Delroy L. Auditing in the Electronic Environment: Theory, Practice & Literature. LC 80-81813. 300p. 1980. 19.75 (ISBN 0-912338-23-7); microfiche 14.75. Lomond.
Edds, John A. Management Auditing: Concepts & Practice. 432p. 1980. text ed. 20.95 (ISBN 0-8403-2209-7). Kendall-Hunt.
Howard, Leslie R. Auditing. 6th ed. 320p. (Orig.). 1978. pap. text ed. 11.95x (ISBN 0-7121-0169-1, Pub. by Macdonald & Evans England). Intl Ideas.
Hubbard, Thomas D., et al. Readings & Cases in Auditing. rev. ed. LC 79-52071. 550p. (Orig.). 1980. pap. text ed. 10.95x (ISBN 0-931920-22-1). Dame Pubns.
International Auditing Guidelines. 1980. pap. 2.75. Am Inst CPA.
Loebbecke, James K. & Arens, Alvin A. Applications of Statistical Sampling to Auditing. (Illus.). 400p. 1981. 23.95 (ISBN 0-13-039156-5). P-H.
Marlin, John T. Compliance with Revenue Sharing Auditing Requirements: The New York State Case. (Government Auditing Ser.). 67p. 1980. pap. 7.50 (ISBN 0-916450-31-7). Coun on Municipal.
Meigs. et al. Plaid for Auditing. rev. ed. 1981. write for info. (ISBN 0-256-02399-9, 01-1172-02). Learning Syst.
Q & A Auditing. LC 79-83863. 16.00 (ISBN 0-932788-07-6). Bradley CPA.
Report on Special Committee on Audit Committee. 1978. pap. 1.50. Am Inst CPA.
Roush, John H., Jr. Management Audits of Subordinate Claims Offices of National Insurance Companies. LC 74-31546. 197p. 17.00. J H Roush.
Rousmaniere, Peter F. The Federal Challenge: S.1236. (Government Auditing Ser.). 52p. 1979. pap. 6.00 (ISBN 0-916450-30-9). Coun on Municipal.
Rousmaniere, Peter F., et al, eds. Local Government Auditing: A Manual for Public Officials. Olenick, Arnold & Pirnicory, Vincent. 90p. 1979. pap. 14.95 (ISBN 0-916450-27-9). Coun on Municipal.
Smith, Kussel & DePaula. Internal Control & Audit. 24.50x (ISBN 0-392-07955-0, SpS). Soccer.
Solomon, Morton B., et al. Main Hurdman & Cranston Guide to Preparing Financial Reports, 1981. 272p. 1981. 75.00 (ISBN 0-471-09104-9, Pub. by Wiley-Interscience). Wiley.
Staples Frederick. Auditing Manual. 181p. 1980. pap. 9.50. Counting Hse.
Washbrook, H. The Board & Management Audit. 262p. 1978. text ed. 30.75x (ISBN 0-220-66334-3, Pub. by Busn Bks England). Renouf.

AUDITING–LAW
see Accounting–Law

AUDITING, TAX
see Tax Auditing

AUDUBON, JOHN JAMES, 1785-1851
Audubon, Maria R. Audubon & His Journal, 2 vols. Aaron, Daniel, ed. (American Men & Women of Letters Audubon & His Journals Ser.). (Illus.). 1100p. 1981. pap. 14.95 (ISBN 0-87754-174-4). Chelsea Hse.
Clement, Roland C. The Living World of Audubon. (Illus.). 1980. 9.95 (ISBN 0-686-68770-1, Fireside). S&S.

AUGUSTINE, SAINT, ABP. OF CANTERBURY, d. 604
Bathory, Peter D. Political Theory As Public Confession. 307p. 1981. 24.95 (ISBN 0-87855-405-X); text ed. 24.95 (ISBN 0-686-68058-8). Transaction Bks.

AURELIUS ANTONINUS, MARCUS, EMPEROR OF ROME, 121-180
Haynie, Charles R. Caesar's Prophet. Date not set. 8.95 (ISBN 0-533-04844-3). Vantage.

AUROBINDO, SRI, 1872-1950
Chaudhuri, Haridas. Integral Philosophy of Sri Aurobindo. Spiegelberg, Frederic, ed. 350p. 1980. 6.00 (ISBN 0-89744-992-4, Pub. by Cultural Integration). Auromere.
--Sri Aurobindo: Prophet of Life Divine. 270p. (Orig.). 1973. pap. 3.50 (ISBN 0-89744-994-0, Pub. by Cultural Integration). Auromere.

AUSTEN, JANE, 1775-1817
Cecil, David. Poets & Story-Tellers. 201p. 1980. Repr. of 1968 ed. lib. bdg. 30.00 (ISBN 0-8495-0852-5). Arden Lib.
Stanley, Hiram M. Essays on Literary Art: Tennyson, Wordsworth, Jane Austen, Thoreau. 164p. 1980. Repr. of 1897 ed. lib. bdg. 25.00 (ISBN 0-8414-8035-4). Folcroft.
Wilson, Mona. Jane Austin & Some Contemporaries. 304p. 1980. Repr. of 1938 ed. lib. bdg. 20.00 (ISBN 0-8492-2973-1). R West.

AUSTIN (AUTOMOBILE)
see Automobiles, Foreign–Types–Austin

AUSTRALIA–BIBLIOGRAPHY
National Library of Australia. Australian National Bibliography, 1976. 16th ed. LC 63-33739. 1464p. 1977. 67.50x (ISBN 0-8002-1048-4). Intl Pubns Serv.

AUSTRALIA–BIOGRAPHY
Dalziel, Allan. Evatt the Enigma: Controverial Australian. 9.95x (ISBN 0-392-07809-0, SpS). Soccer.
Down, Goldie. You Never Can Tell When You May Meet a Leopard. Davis, Tom, ed. 128p. 1980. pap. write for info. (ISBN 0-8280-0026-3). Review & Herald.
Duffield, Robert. Rogue Bull. 320p. 1980. 20.95x (ISBN 0-00-216423-X, Pub. by W Collins Australia); pap. 8.95x (ISBN 0-00-634515-8). Intl Schol Bk Serv.
King, Hazel. Elizabeth Macarthur & Her World. 240p. 1980. 27.50x (ISBN 0-424-00080-6, Pub. by Sydney U Pr Australia). Intl Schol Bk Serv.
Radi, Heather, et al. Biographical Register of the New South Wales Parliament 1901-70. (Australian Parliaments, Biographical Notes: No. 6). 302p. 1979. text ed. 37.95 (ISBN 0-7081-1756-2, 0575, Pub. by ANUP Australia); pap. text ed. 18.95 (ISBN 0-7081-1757-0, 0574). Bks Australia.
Sumner, L. E., ed. Business Who's Who of Australia, 1980. 14th ed. LC 64-56752. 805p. 1980. write for info (ISBN 0-8002-2741-7). Intl Pubns Serv.
Walter, James. The Leader: A Political Biography of Gough Whitlam. (Illus.). 295p. 1981. text ed. 18.00x (ISBN 0-7022-1557-0). U of Queensland Pr.

AUSTRALIA–CIVILIZATION
Smith, Bernard. Place, Taste, & Tradition: A Study of Australian Art Since Seventeen Eighty-Eight. 2nd ed. (Illus.). 304p. 1979. text ed. 39.50x (ISBN 0-19-550561-1). Oxford U Pr.

AUSTRALIA–COLONIZATION
Glover, Rhoda, et al. Plantagenet "Rich & Beautiful...". A History of the Shire of Plantagenet, Western Australia. 429p. 1980. 21.00x (ISBN 0-85564-175-4, Pub. by U of West Australia Pr Australia). Intl Schol Bk Serv.
Journals of Several Expeditions Made in Western Australia. 262p. 1980. 19.95x (ISBN 0-85564-185-1, Pub. by U of West Australia Pr Australia). Intl Schol Bk Serv.
Willey, Keith. When the Sky Fell Down. 231p. 1980. 13.95x (ISBN 0-00-216434-5, Pub. by W Collins Australia). Intl Schol Bk Serv.

AUSTRALIA–COMMERCE
Firkens, Peter, ed. A History of Commerce & Industry in Western Australia. 223p. 1980. 17.95x (ISBN 0-85564-150-9, Pub. by U of West Australia Pr Australia). Intl Schol Bk Serv.

AUSTRALIA–CONSTITUTIONAL HISTORY
McMinn, Winston G. A Constitutional History of Australia. 228p. 1979. text ed. 29.95x (ISBN 0-19-550562-X). Oxford U Pr.

AUSTRALIA–DESCRIPTION AND TRAVEL
Collings, Lawrence & Ruhen, Olaf. On & Around Sydney Harbour. 128p. 1980. 13.95x (ISBN 0-00-216407-8, Pub. by W Collins Australia). Intl Schol Bk Serv.
Dorward, Douglas. Wild Australia. (Illus.). 128p. 1980. 20.95x (ISBN 0-00-211446-1, Pub. by W Collins Australia). Intl Schol Bk Serv.
Serventy, Vincent. Zoo Walkabout. 160p. 1980. 17.95x (ISBN 0-00-216420-5, Pub. by W Collins Australia). Intl Schol Bk Serv.
White, John & Morison, Margaret P. Western Towns & Buildings. 364p. 1980. 22.50x (ISBN 0-85564-156-8, Pub. by U of West Australia). Intl Schol Bk Serv.

AUSTRALIA–DESCRIPTION AND TRAVEL–GUIDEBOOKS
Bone, Robert W. Maverick Guide to Australia. rev. ed. (The Maverick Guide Ser.). (Illus.). 324p. (Orig.). 1981. pap. 9.95 (ISBN 0-88289-278-9). Pelican.
Mortlock, A. J. & Hueneke, K. Beyond the Cotter. LC 79-53837. (Canberra Companions Ser.). (Illus.). 66p. (Orig.). 1980. pap. 3.95 (ISBN 0-7081-1581-0, 0541). Bks Australia.
Yeomans, John. The Twenty Best Sights of Sydney. 128p. 1980. pap. 4.95x (ISBN 0-686-68862-7, Pub. by W Collins Australia). Intl Schol Bk Serv.

AUSTRALIA–DISCOVERY AND EXPLORATION
Glover, Rhoda, et al. Plantagenet "Rich & Beautiful...". A History of the Shire of Plantagenet, Western Australia. 429p. 1980. 21.00x (ISBN 0-85564-175-4, Pub. by U of West Australia Pr Australia). Intl Schol Bk Serv.
Journals of Several Expeditions Made in Western Australia. 262p. 1980. 19.95x (ISBN 0-85564-185-1, Pub. by U of West Australia Pr Australia). Intl Schol Bk Serv.
Webster, E. M. Whirlwinds in the Plain: Ludwig Leichardt - Friends, Foes & History. 484p. 1980. 40.00x (ISBN 0-522-84181-3, Pub. by Melbourne U Pr Australia). Intl Schol Bk Serv.

AUSTRALIA–ECONOMIC CONDITIONS
Crawford, John & Okita, Saburo, eds. Australia & Japan: Issues in the Economic Relationship. (Australia-Japan Economic Relations Research Project Monograph: No. 2). (Illus.). 140p. 1980. pap. text ed. 5.95 (ISBN 0-9596197-1-2). Bks Australia.
Denger, Louis A. A Few Pieces of Australia, 1979. 1981. 8.95 (ISBN 0-533-04458-8). Vantage.
Rowan, David. Australian Monetary Policy. (Illus.). 313p. 1981. text ed. 22.50x (ISBN 0-86861-360-6, 2318); pap. text ed. 13.95x (ISBN 0-86861-368-1, 2319). Allen Unwin.
Theophanpous, Andrew. Australian Democracy in Crisis: A New Theoretical Introduction to Australian Politics. 224p. 1980. 27.00 (ISBN 0-19-554200-2). Oxford U Pr.

AUSTRALIA–EMIGRATION AND IMMIGRATION
Sherington, Geoffrey. Australia's Immigrants. (Australian Experience Ser.). 216p. 1981. text ed. 16.95x (ISBN 0-86861-010-0, 2511); pap. text ed. 9.95x (ISBN 0-86861-018-6, 2512). Allen Unwin.

AUSTRALIA–FOREIGN RELATIONS
Babbage, Ross. Rethinking Australia's Defence. (Illus.). 312p. 1981. text ed. 30.25x (ISBN 0-7022-1486-8). U of Queensland Pr.
Bell, Coral, ed. Agenda for the Eighties. LC 80-65340. 256p. 1980. pap. text ed. 18.95 (ISBN 0-7081-1086-X, 0469, Pub. by ANUP Australia). Bks Australia.
Cuddy, Dennis L. Contemporary Australian-American Relations. LC 80-65615. 155p. 1981. perfect bdg. 12.95 (ISBN 0-86548-027-3). Century Twenty One.

AUSTRALIA–HISTORY
Breeden, Stanley & Breeden, Kay. Australia's North. (A Natural History of Australia Ser.: No. 3). 208p. 1980. 34.95x (ISBN 0-00-211441-0, Pub. by W Collins Australia). Intl Schol Bk Serv.
Hudson, W. J., ed. Australia & the League of Nations. 224p. 1980. 20.00x (ISBN 0-424-00084-9, Pub. by Sydney U Pr Australia). Intl Schol Bk Serv.
Lea-Scarlett, Errol. Roots & Branches: Ancestry for Australians. 256p. 1980. pap. 6.95x (ISBN 0-00-216415-9, Pub. by W Collins Australia). Intl Schol Bk Serv.
Serville, Paul De. Port Philip Gentlemen. (Illus.). 256p. 1980. 49.00x (ISBN 0-19-554212-6). Oxford U Pr.
Souter, Gavin. Lion & Kangaroo. 344p. 1980. 8.95x (ISBN 0-00-634512-3, Pub. by W Collins Australia). Intl Schol Bk Serv.

AUSTRALIA–IMPRINTS
Austrailian Books in Print. 1980. 39.50 (ISBN 0-8352-1316-1). Bowker.

AUSTRALIA–INDUSTRIES
Firkens, Peter, ed. A History of Commerce & Industry in Western Australia. 223p. 1980. 17.95x (ISBN 0-85564-150-9, Pub. by U of West Australia Pr Australia). Intl Schol Bk Serv.

AUSTRALIA–NATIVE RACES
Bell, Diane & Ditton, Pam. Law. (Illus.). 147p. 1980. pap. text ed. 9.95 (ISBN 0-908160-77-1). Bks Australia.
Kolig, Erich. Silent Revolution: The Effects of Westernization on Aboriginal Religion. (Illus.). 240p. 1981. text ed. 18.50x (ISBN 0-89727-020-7). Inst Study Hum.
Lemos, M. De. Aboriginal Students in Victoria. (ACER Research Monograph: No. 3). 1979. pap. 18.00 (ISBN 0-85563-193-7). Verry.

Sansom, Basil. The Camp at Wallaby Cross: Aboriginal Fringe Dwellers in Darwin. 280p. 1980. text ed. 17.00x (ISBN 0-391-01696-2, Pub. by Australian Inst Australia); pap. text ed. 9.75x (ISBN 0-391-01697-0). Humanities.

Shapiro, Warren. Miwuyt Marriage: The Cultural Anthropology of Affinity in Northeast Arnhem Land. (Illus.). 240p. 1981. text ed. 18.50x (ISBN 0-89727-021-5). Inst Study Hum.

AUSTRALIA–POLITICS AND GOVERNMENT

Babbage, Ross. Rethinking Australia's Defence. (Illus.). 312p. 1981. text ed. 30.25x (ISBN 0-7022-1486-8). U of Queensland Pr.

Hughes, Colin A. The Government of Queensland. (Governments of the Australian States & Territories Ser.). (Illus.). 322p. 1981. text ed. 36.25x (ISBN 0-7022-1515-5); pap. text ed. 19.25x (ISBN 0-7022-1516-3). U of Queensland Pr.

Kahn, Herman & Pepper, Thomas. Will She Be Right? The Future of Australia. (Illus.). 199p. 1981. text ed. 18.75 (ISBN 0-7022-1568-6); pap. 7.25 (ISBN 0-7022-1569-4). U of Queensland Pr.

McMinn, Winston G. A Constitutional History of Australia. 228p. 1979. text ed. 29.95x (ISBN 0-19-550562-X). Oxford U Pr.

Penniman, Howard R., ed. Australian National Elections of 1977. 1980. pap. 8.25 (ISBN 0-8447-3357-1). Am Enterprise.

Sharkansky, Ira. Wither the State? Politics & Public Enterprise in Three Countries. 9.95 (ISBN 0-934540-01-2); pap. 7.95 (ISBN 0-934540-00-4). Chatham Hse Pubs.

Stilwell, Frank J. Economic Crisis, Cities & Regions: An Analysis of Current Urban & Regional Problems in Australia. 192p. 1980. 14.50 (ISBN 0-08-024810-1); pap. 8.95 (ISBN 0-08-024809-8). Pergamon.

Theophanpous, Andrew. Australian Democracy in Crisis: A New Theoretical Introduction to Australian Politics. 224p. 1980. 27.00 (ISBN 0-19-554200-2). Oxford U Pr.

AUSTRALIA–POPULATION

Lonsdale, Richard E. & Holmes, John H., eds. Settlement Systems in Sparsely Populated Regions: The United States & Australia. LC 80-27278. (Pergamon Policy Studies on Urban Affairs; Comparative Rural Transformation Ser.). (Illus.). 360p. 1981. 40.00 (ISBN 0-08-023111-X). Pergamon.

Stenhouse, N. S. Busselton Norms. 1980. pap. 8.50x (ISBN 0-85564-164-9, Pub. by U of West Australia Pr Australia). Intl Schol Bk Serv.

AUSTRALIA–RELIGION

Broome, Richard. Treasure in Earthen Vessels: Protestant Christianity in New South Wales Society 1900-1914. 216p. 1981. text ed. 36.25x (ISBN 0-7022-1525-2). U of Queensland Pr.

Kolig, Erich. Silent Revolution: The Effects of Westernization on Aboriginal Religion. (Illus.). 240p. 1981. text ed. 18.50x (ISBN 0-89727-020-7). Inst Study Hum.

AUSTRALIA–SOCIAL CONDITIONS

Burnley, I. H., et al, eds. Mobility & Community Change in Australia. (Studies in Society & Culture). (Illus.). 286p. 1981. text ed. 30.25x (ISBN 0-7022-1446-9). U of Queensland Pr.

AUSTRALIA–SOCIAL LIFE AND CUSTOMS

Denger, Louis A. A Few Pieces of Australia, 1979. 1981. 8.95 (ISBN 0-533-04458-8). Vantage.

Mackenzie, Toni. A Small Place in the Country. 240p. 1980. pap. 6.95 (ISBN 0-00-216408-6, Pub. by W Collins Australia). Intl Schol Bk Serv.

Troy, P. N., ed. A Just Society? Essays on Equity in Australia. 192p. 1981. text ed. 22.50x (ISBN 0-86861-234-0, 2655). Allen Unwin.

AUSTRALIAN ABORIGINES–GOVERNMENT RELATIONS

see Australia–Native Races

AUSTRALIAN ABORIGINES–LANGUAGES

see Australian Languages

AUSTRALIAN ARCHITECTURE

see Architecture–Australia

AUSTRALIAN ART

see Art, Australian

AUSTRALIAN AUTHORS

see Authors, Australian

AUSTRALIAN LANGUAGES

Austin, P. A Grammar of Diyari, South Australia. (Cambridge Studies in Linguistics Monographs: No. 32). (Illus.). 230p. Date not set. price not set (ISBN 0-521-22849-2). Cambridge U Pr.

Dixon, R. M. & Blake, B. J., eds. Handbook of Australian Languages, Vol. 1. (Handbook of Australian Languages Ser.). 390p. (Orig.). 1980. pap. text ed. 23.95 (ISBN 0-7081-1201-3, 0435). Bks-Australia.

AUSTRALIAN LITERATURE–BIBLIOGRAPHY

Lock, Fred & Lawson, Alan. Australian Literature: A Reference Guide. 2nd ed. (Australian Bibliographies Ser.). 134p. 1980. pap. text ed. 10.95x (ISBN 0-19-554214-2). Oxford U Pr.

AUSTRALIAN LOVEBIRD

see Budgerigars

AUSTRALIAN NATIONAL CHARACTERISTICS

see National Characteristics, Australian

AUSTRALIAN PAINTERS

see Painters–Australia

AUSTRALIAN POETRY (COLLECTIONS)

Shoate, Alec & Main, Barbara Y., eds. Summerland. 242p. 1980. 16.95x (ISBN 0-85564-166-5, Pub. by U of West Australia Pr Australia). Intl Schol Bk Serv.

AUSTRIA–DESCRIPTION AND TRAVEL–GUIDEBOOKS

Zellers, Margaret. Austria...the Inn Way. 162p. 1981. 4.95 (ISBN 0-937334-01-4). Berkshire Traveller.

AUSTRIA–ECONOMIC CONDITIONS

Hankel, Wilhelm. Prosperity Amidst Crisis: Austria's Economic Policy & the Energy Crunch. Steinberg, Jean, tr. 234p. 1980. lib. bdg. 20.00x (ISBN 0-86531-101-3). Westview.

AUSTRIA–HISTORY

see also Hungary–History

Gulick, Charles A. Austria from Habsburg to Hitler, 2 vols. Incl. Vol. I. Labor's Workshop of Democracy; Vol. II. Fascism's Subversion of Democracy. (California Library Reprint Ser.: No. 109). 1936p. 1981. Repr. of 1948 ed. Set. 85.00x (ISBN 0-520-04211-5). U of Cal Pr.

Pauley, Bruce. Hitler & the Forgotten Nazis. LC 80-17006. 360p. 1981. 19.00x (ISBN 0-8078-1456-3). U of NC Pr.

Seton-Watson, Hugh & Seton-Watson, Christopher. The Making of a New Europe: R. W. Seton-Watson & the Last Years of Austria-Hungary. 528p. 1981. 50.00 (ISBN 0-295-95792-1). U of Wash Pr.

AUSTRIAN LITERATURE–HISTORY AND CRITICISM

Sharp, Francis M. The Poet's Madness: A Reading of George Trakl. (Illus.). 264p. 1981. 17.50x (ISBN 0-8014-1297-8). Cornell U Pr.

AUSTRIAN MUSIC

see Music, Austrian

AUTHORITARIANISM

see also National Socialism

Spitz, David. Patterns of Anti-Democratic Thought: An Analysis & Criticism, with Special Reference to the American Political Mind in Recent Times. LC 80-22640. 347p. 1981. Repr. of 1965 ed. lib. bdg. 27.50x (ISBN 0-313-22392-0, SPPD). Greenwood.

AUTHORITY (RELIGION)

see also Bible–Evidences, Authority, Etc.; Church–Authority; Liberty of Speech in the Church; Popes–Infallibility; Tradition (Theology)

Autoridade Espirituale. 1980. pap. 1.85 (ISBN 0-686-69356-6). Vida Pubs.

Nee, Watchman, tr. Autoridad Espiritual. (Spanish Bks.). (Span.). 1978. 1.75 (ISBN 0-8297-0805-7). Life Pubs Intl.

--L' Autorite Spirituelle. (French Bks.). (Fr.). 1979. 1.75 (ISBN 0-686-28817-3). Life Pubs Intl.

AUTHORS

see also Anonyms and Pseudonyms; Women Authors also particular classes of writers, e.g. Dramatists, Historians, Poets; also names of authors, e.g. Shakespeare, William

Author's Names 1981. 1981. 125.00 (ISBN 0-8352-1095-2). Bowker.

Beckett, Samuel, et al. New Writing & Writers Thirteen. 1980. pap. 6.00 (ISBN 0-7145-3541-9). Riverrun NY.

Boll, Heinrich, et al. New Writing & Writers Fifteen. 1980. pap. 6.00 (ISBN 0-7145-3561-3). Riverrun NY.

Bond, et al. New Writing & Writers, No. 14. text ed. 13.00x. Humanities.

Bowler, Christine, et al. New Writers Eight. 1980. pap. 6.00 (ISBN 0-7145-0015-1). Riverrun NY.

Burns, Alan, et al. New Writers One. 1980. pap. 6.00 (ISBN 0-7145-0397-5). Riverrun NY.

Burns, Carol, et al. New Writers Six. 1980. pap. 6.00 (ISBN 0-7145-0407-6). Riverrun NY.

Burroughs, William, et al. New Writing & Writers Sixteen. 1980. pap. 6.00 (ISBN 0-7145-3638-5). Riverrun NY.

Castelain, Daniel, et al. New Writers Five. 1980. pap. 6.00 (ISBN 0-7145-0405-X). Riverrun NY.

Commire, Anne, ed. Something About the Author, Vol. 21. LC 72-27107. 300p. 1980. 38.00 (ISBN 0-8103-0093-1). Gale.

--Something About the Author, Vol. 22. LC 72-27107. (Illus.). 375p. 1981. 38.00 (ISBN 0-8103-0085-0). Gale.

Derleth, August W. Three Literary Men. 56p. 1980. Repr. of 1963 ed. lib. bdg. 15.00 (ISBN 0-8482-0645-2). Norwood Edns.

Engelbarts, Rudolf. Librarian Authors. LC 80-28035. 123p. 1981. lib. bdg. write for info. (ISBN 0-89950-007-2). McFarland & Co.

Evory, Ann. Contemporary Authors. (New Revision Ser.: Vol. 2). 500p. 1981. 58.00 (ISBN 0-8103-1931-4). Gale.

Evory, Ann, ed. Contemporary Authors. (New Revisions Ser.: No. 3). 500p. 1981. 58.00 (ISBN 0-8103-1932-2). Gale.

Galloway, David, et al. New Writers Twelve. 1980. pap. 6.00 (ISBN 0-7145-3545-1). Riverrun NY.

International Portrait Gallery: Vol. 12, Children's Authors & Illustrators Supplement. (Illus.). 64p. 1981. 35.00 (ISBN 0-686-69448-1, IPG-12). Gale.

International Portrait Gallery: Vol. 9, Writers for Young Adults Supplement. (Illus.). 64p. 1981. 35.00 (ISBN 0-686-69445-7, IPG-9). Gale.

Lebel, J. J. & Marowitz, Charles. New Writers Four. 1980. pap. 6.00 (ISBN 0-7145-0403-3). Riverrun NY.

Locher, Frances C., ed. Contemporary Authors: A Bio-Bibliographical Guide to Current Writers in Fiction, General Non-Fiction, Poetry, Journalism, Drama, Motion Pictures, Television & Other Fields, Vol. 101. LC 62-52046. 900p. 1981. 58.00 (ISBN 0-8103-1901-2). Gale.

Madsen, Svend A., et al. New Writers Eleven. 1980. pap. 6.00 (ISBN 0-7145-0814-4). Riverrun NY.

Morris, Tina, et al. New Writers Seven. 1980. pap. 6.00 (ISBN 0-7145-0013-5). Riverrun NY.

Rasp, Renate, et al. New Writers Nine. 1980. pap. 6.00 (ISBN 0-7145-0017-8). Riverrun NY.

Reilly, John M., ed. Twentieth Century Crime & Mystery Writers. (Twentieth Century Writers Ser.). 1600p. 1980. 50.00x (ISBN 0-312-82417-3). St Martin.

Salas, Floyd, et al. New Writers Ten. 1980. pap. 6.00 (ISBN 0-7145-0752-0). Riverrun NY.

Taylor, Anne R. Male Novelists & Their Female Voices: Literary Masquerades. LC 80-50841. 238p. 1981. 15.00x (ISBN 0-87875-195-5). Whitston Pub.

Trocchi, Alexander, et al. New Writers Three. 1980. pap. 6.00 (ISBN 0-7145-0401-7). Riverrun NY.

Varady, Tibor, et al. New Writing & Writers Eighteen. 1980. pap. 6.00 (ISBN 0-7145-3815-9). Riverrun NY.

Vestdijk, Simon, et al. New Writers Two. 1980. pap. 6.00 (ISBN 0-7145-0399-1). Riverrun NY.

Vinson, James & Kirkpatrick, Daniel, eds. Great Novelists & Prose Writers. (Great Writers of the English Language Ser.). 1400p. 1979. 45.00x (ISBN 0-312-34624-7). St Martin.

AUTHORS–CORRESPONDENCE, REMINISCENCES, ETC.

Buchwald, Ann & Buchwald, Art. Seems Like Yesterday. 1981. pap. 2.75 (ISBN 0-425-04833-0). Berkley Pub.

Burney, Fanny. The Journals & Letters of Fanny Burney (Madame D'Arblay), Eighteen Twelve to Eighteen Fourteen: Vol. VII, Letters 632-834. Bloom, Edward A., et al, eds. (Illus.). 650p. 1978. 69.00x (ISBN 0-19-812468-6). Oxford U Pr.

Ellis, Henry, illus. Original Letters of Eminent Literary Men of the 16th, 17th, & 18th Centuries. 460p. 1980. Repr. lib. bdg. 85.00 (ISBN 0-89984-199-6). Century Bookbindery.

Jordan, Rudolf. The Autobiography of Rudolf Jordan. LC 80-70948. (Illus.). 227p. 1981. 10.95 (ISBN 0-8119-0415-6). Fell.

Orel, Harold, ed. Thomas Hardy's Personal Writings. 295p. 1981. text ed. 10.00x (ISBN 0-333-05493-8, Pub. by Macmillan, England). Humanities.

Sagan, Francoise. Nightbird. (Clarkson N. Potter Bks.). (Illus.). 1980. 9.95 (ISBN 0-517-54224-2). Crown.

AUTHORS, AFRO-AMERICAN

see Afro-American Authors

AUTHORS, AMERICAN

Anderson, Richard. Robert Coover. (United States Authors Ser.: No. 300). 1981. lib. bdg. 11.95 (ISBN 0-8057-7330-4). Twayne.

Bucco, Martin. Rene Wellek. (United States Authors Ser.: No. 410). 1981. lib. bdg. 12.95 (ISBN 0-8057-7339-8). Twayne.

Davis, Cheri. W. S. Merwin. (United States Authors Ser.: No. 360). 1981. lib. bdg. 11.95 (ISBN 0-8057-7301-0). Twayne.

Eckley, Grace. Finley Peter Dunne. (United States Authors Ser.: No. 402). 1981. lib. bdg. 11.95 (ISBN 0-8057-7295-2). Twayne.

Hamilton, Nigel. The Brothers Mann. LC 78-15114. 431p. pap. 9.95 (ISBN 0-300-02668-4). Yale U Pr.

Jeffries, Richard. The Story of My Heart: My Autobiography. 144p. 1980. pap. 3.95 (ISBN 0-7043-3257-4, Pub. by Quartet England). Horizon.

Kazin, Alfred. Bright Book of Life: American Novelists & Storytellers from Hemingway to Mailer. LC 80-24576. 334p. 1980. pap. text ed. 6.95 (ISBN 0-268-00664-4). U of Notre Dame Pr.

Kesterson, David B. Bill Nye. (United States Authors Ser: No. 403). 1981. lib. bdg. 11.95 (ISBN 0-8057-7332-0). Twayne.

Kipler, James, ed. American Novelists Since World War II: Second Series. (Dictionary of Literary Biography Ser.: Vol. 6). (Illus.). 300p. 1980. 54.00 (ISBN 0-8103-0908-4). Gale.

Lee, Lynn. Don Marquis. (United States Authors Ser: No. 393). 1981. lib. bdg. 11.95 (ISBN 0-8057-7282-0). Twayne.

Long, Terry L. Granville Hicks. (United States Authors Ser.: No. 387). 1981. lib. bdg. 11.95 (ISBN 0-8057-7319-3). Twayne.

Martine, James J., ed. American Novelists Nineteen Ten to Nineteen Forty-Five, 2 vols. (Dictionary of Literary Biography Ser.). (Illus.). 800p. 1981. Set. 108.00 (ISBN 0-8103-0931-9). Gale.

Moore, Harry T. Contemporary American Novelists. LC 64-20254. (Crosscurrents-Modern Critiques Ser.). 1966. pap. 7.95 (ISBN 0-8093-0195-4). S Ill U Pr.

Morris, Wright. Will's Boy: A Memoir. LC 80-8708. 192p. 1981. 11.95 (ISBN 0-06-014856-X, HarpT). Har-Row.

Pannick, Gerald. Richard Palmer Blackmur. (United States Authors Ser.: No. 409). 1981. lib. bdg. 12.95 (ISBN 0-8057-7338-X). Twayne.

Perry, Lilla S. My Friend Carl Sandburg: The Biography of a Friendship. Perry, E. Caswell, ed. LC 80-21908. 234p. 1981. 12.00 (ISBN 0-8108-1367-X). Scarecrow.

Rolfe, Lionel. Literary L. A. (Illus.). 96p. (Orig.). 1981. pap. 5.95 (ISBN 0-87701-177-X). Chronicle Bks.

The Selected Papers of E. S. Pearson. 327p. 1966. 25.00x (ISBN 0-85264-705-0, Pub. by Griffin England). State Mutual Bk.

Shi, David. Matthew Josephson, Bourgeois Bohemiam. LC 80-24493. (Illus.). 328p. 1981. 19.95 (ISBN 0-300-02563-7). Yale U Pr.

Taylor, Ida S. The Year Book of American Authors. 372p. 1980. lib. bdg. 30.00 (ISBN 0-89760-899-2). Telegraph Bks.

Welch, Lew. I Remain: The Letters of Lew Welch with the Correspondence of His Friends, Volume 2. Allen, Donald, ed. LC 79-21574. 208p. 1980. 12.00 (ISBN 0-912516-41-0); pap. 5.95 (ISBN 0-912516-42-9). Grey Fox.

White, Helen. Jesse Hill Ford: An Annotated Checklist of His Published Works & of His Papers. (Mississippi Valley Collection Bulletin, No. 7). (Illus.). 55p. 1974. pap. 5.95x (ISBN 0-87870-083-8). Memphis St Univ.

AUTHORS, AMERICAN–BIBLIOGRAPHY

Silet, Charles L. The Writings of Paul Rosenfeld: An Annotated Bibliography. LC 79-7931. 250p. 1981. lib. bdg. 35.00 (ISBN 0-8240-9532-4). Garland Pub.

AUTHORS, AUSTRALIAN

Irvin, Eric. Gentleman George - King of Melodrama. (Illus.). 234p. 1981. text ed. 18.00x (ISBN 0-7022-1536-8). U of Queensland Pr.

James, Clive. Unreliable Memoirs. LC 80-24245. 176p. 1981. 10.00 (ISBN 0-394-51263-4). Knopf.

AUTHORS, CANADIAN

Cameron, Elspeth. Hugh MacLennan: A Writers Life. 424p. 1981. 25.00 (ISBN 0-8020-5556-7). U of Toronto Pr.

Leeker, Robert, ed. The Annotated Bibliography of Canada's Major Authors: Margaret Atwood, Leonard Cohen, Archibald Lampman, E. J. Pratt, & Al Purdy, Vol.iI. (Reference Book Ser.). 1981. 26.00 (ISBN 0-8161-8552-2). G K Hall.

AUTHORS, ENGLISH

Atkins, John. Six Novelists Look at Society. 1980. 11.95 (ISBN 0-7145-3535-4). Riverrun NY.

Darton, Harvey F. From Surtees to Sassoon, Some Eng. Contrasts. (1938-1928) 222p. 1980. Repr. lib. bdg. 25.00 (ISBN 0-8492-4219-3). R West.

Dawson, William J. & Dawson, Coningsby W. The Great English Letter-Writers, 2 vols. 1980. Set. lib. bdg. 50.00 (ISBN 0-8492-4218-5). R West.

Greene, Graham. Ways of Escape. Date not set. 12.95 (ISBN 0-671-41219-1). S&S.

Hinchliffe, Arnold P. Harold Pinter. rev. ed. (English Authors Ser.: No. 51). 1981. lib. bdg. 9.95 (ISBN 0-8057-6784-3). Twayne.

Hooton, Joy H. A. D. Hope. (Australian Bibliographies Ser.). 286p. 1979. text ed. 12.95x (ISBN 0-19-550523-9). Oxford U Pr.

Kilpatrick, Sarah. Fanny Burney. LC 80-5891. (Illus.). 256p. 1981. 14.95 (ISBN 0-8128-2761-9). Stein & Day.

Philip Gilbert Hamerton. 591p. 1980. Repr. of 1896 ed. lib. bdg. 50.00. Telegraph Bks.

Salwak, Dale. John Wain. (English Authors Ser.: No. 316). 1981. lib. bdg. 11.95 (ISBN 0-8057-6806-8). Twayne.

Scott-Kilvert, Ian, ed. British Writers, Vol. IV. LC 78-23483. 1981. lib. bdg. 55.00 (ISBN 0-684-16635-6). Scribner.

--British Writers, Vol. V. LC 78-23483. 1981. lib. bdg. 55.00 (ISBN 0-684-16636-4). Scribner.

--British Writers, Vol. III. LC 78-23483. 1980. lib. bdg. 55.00 (ISBN 0-684-16408-6). Scribner.

Scott-Kilvert, Ian & British Council, eds. British Writers, Vol. II. LC 78-23483. (British Council Pamphlet Ser.). 1979. lib. bdg. 55.00 (ISBN 0-684-16407-8). Scribner.

Williams, I. Emyr Humphreys. (Writers of Wales). 1980. pap. 9.00 (ISBN 0-7083-0750-7). Verry.

AUTHORS, FRENCH

Boissier, Gaston. Great French Writers: Madame De Sevigne. 154p. 1980. Repr. of 1887 ed. lib. bdg. 25.00 (ISBN 0-8495-0476-7). Arden Lib.

Bree, Germaine. Women Writers in France: Variations on a Theme. 104p. 1973. 7.00 (ISBN 0-8135-0771-5). Rutgers U Pr.

Slater, Maya. Humour in the Works of Proust. (Oxford Modern Languages & Literature Monographs). 200p. 1979. text ed. 22.00x (ISBN 0-19-815534-4). Oxford U Pr.

Verlaine, Paul. Confessions of a Poet. Wolf, Ruth S. & Richardson, Joanna, trs. from Fr. 192p. 1981. Repr. of 1950 ed. lib. bdg. 30.00 (ISBN 0-89987-876-8). Darby Bks.

AUTHORS, GERMAN

Bachem, Michael. Heimito Von Doderer. (World Authors Ser.: No. 595). 1981. lib. bdg. 14.95 (ISBN 0-8057-6437-2). Twayne.

AUTHORS, IRISH

Banim, John & Banim, Michael. The Life of John Banim, the Irish Novelist. Wolff, Robert L., ed. (Ireland, Nineteenth Century Fiction - Ser. Two: Vol. 25). 350p. 1979. lib. bdg. 32.00 (ISBN 0-8240-3474-0). Garland Pub.

Carleton, William. The Life of William Carleton. Wolff, Robert L., ed. (Ireland Nineteenth Century Fiction - Ser. Two: Vol. 44). 728p. 1979. lib. bdg. 32.00 (ISBN 0-8240-3493-7). Garland Pub.
Smith, Elizabeth. The Irish Journals of Elizabeth Smith Eighteen Forty to Eighteen Fifty. Thomson, David & McGusty, Moyra, eds. (Illus.). 352p. 1980. 29.00x (ISBN 0-19-822471-0). Oxford U Pr.
Wolff, Robert L. William Carleton, Irish Peasant Novelist: A Preface to His Fiction. LC 79-4399. 200p. 1980. lib. bdg. 18.00 (ISBN 0-8240-3527-5). Garland Pub.

AUTHORS, ITALIAN
Abba, Giuseppe C. The Diary of One of Garibaldi's Thousand. Vincent, E. R., tr. from Ital. LC 80-24181. (Oxford Library of Italian Classics). (Illus.). xxi, 166p. 1981. Repr. of 1962 ed. lib. bdg. 18.75x (ISBN 0-313-22446-3, ABDO). Greenwood.
Sabatini, Rafael. The Writings of Rafael Sabatini, 21 vols. 1981. Repr. of 1924 ed. Set. lib. bdg. 500.00 (ISBN 0-89987-766-4). Darby Bks.

AUTHORS, JEWISH
Waldman, Bess. The Book of Tziril: A Family Chronicle. 270p. 1981. pap. 6.00x (ISBN 0-916288-09-9). Micah Pubns.

AUTHORS, RUSSIAN
Payne, R. The Apocalypse of Our Time & Other Writings by Vasily Razanov. 1977. text ed. 10.95 (ISBN 0-03-028911-4, HoltC). HR&W.

AUTHORS, SCOTTISH
Wilson, A. N. The Laird of Abbotsford: A View of Sir Walter Scott. 214p. 1980. text ed. 24.95x (ISBN 0-19-211756-4). Oxford U Pr.

AUTHORS, SPANISH
Alberti, Rafael. The Lost Grove: The Autobiography of a Spanish Poet in Exile. Berns, Gabriel, ed. (Illus.). 331p. 1981. pap. 5.95 (CAL 464). U of Cal Pr.
Gonzalez, Justo. Historia de un Amor. (Illus.). 168p. (Orig., Span.). 1979. pap. 3.50 (ISBN 0-89922-151-3). Edit Caribe.
Johnson, Roberta. Carmen Laforet. (World Authors Ser: No. 601). 1981. lib. bdg. 14.50 (ISBN 0-8057-6443-7). Twayne.

AUTHORS, WOMEN
see Women Authors

AUTHORS AND PRINTERS
see Authorship–Handbooks, Manuals, etc.

AUTHORSHIP
Here are entered guides to authorship in general. Guides in individual fields are entered under appropriate terms if in common usage, e.g. Playwriting, Technical Writing, Television Authorship; otherwise under the name of the genre or subject with subdivision Authorship, e.g. Poetry–Authorship. The subdivision Authorship is also used under names of individual authors or works in cases of dubious or disputed authorship, e.g. Shakespeare, William, 1564-1616–Authorship.
see also Authors; Autobiography; Biography (As a Literary Form); Characters and Characteristics in Literature; Copyright; Creative Writing; Editing; Fiction–Authorship; Fiction–Technique; Historiography; Journalism; Literature; Moving-Picture Authorship; Report Writing; Rhetoric; Short Story; Versification; Women Authors
Alderman, Clifford. You Can Be a Writer: A Career & Leisure Guide. 160p. (gr. 9-12). 1981. PLB price not set (ISBN 0-671-34047-6). Messner.
Betts, Glynne R. Writers in Residence: American Authors at Home. 1981. 16.95 (ISBN 0-670-79108-3, Studio). Viking Pr.
Brande, Dorothea. Becoming a Writer. LC 80-53146. 256p. 1981. pap. 5.95 (ISBN 0-87477-164-1). J P Tarcher.
Elbow, Peter. Writing with Power: Techniques for Mastering the Writing Process. 356p. 1981. 15.00 (ISBN 0-19-502912-7). Oxford U Pr.
--Writing with Power: Techniques for Mastering the Writing Process. 356p. 1981. pap. 5.95 (ISBN 0-19-502913-5, GB 642, GB). Oxford U Pr.
Gopen, George D. Writing from a Legal Perspective. 250p. 1981. text ed. 11.95 (ISBN 0-8299-2123-0). West Pub.
Grant, Barbara M. & Hennings, Dorothy G. Written Expression in the Language Arts. LC 80-25532. (Orig.). 1981. pap. 11.95 (ISBN 0-8077-2604-4). Tchrs Coll.
Gurr, Andrew. Writers in Exile: The Creative Use of Home in Modern Literature. 220p. 1981. 21.00x (ISBN 0-389-20189-8). B&N.
Hellyer, Clement D. Making Money with Words. (Illus.). 256p. 1981. 10.95 (ISBN 0-13-547414-0, Spec); pap. 5.95 (ISBN 0-13-547406-X). P-H.
Highsmith, Patricia, ed. Plotting & Writing Suspense Fiction. 1981. 10.95 (ISBN 0-87116-125-7). Writer.
Male, Roy R., ed. Money Talks: Language & Lucre in American Fiction. LC 80-5945. 160p. 1981. 14.95 (ISBN 0-8061-1754-0). U of Okla Pr.
Plimpton, George, ed. Writers at Work. LC 80-18030. (The Paris Review Interviews Ser.: No. 5). (Illus.). 416p. 1981. 17.95 (ISBN 0-670-79098-2). Viking Pr.
Polking, Kirk, ed. Jobs for Writers. LC 80-16070. 256p. 1980. 10.95 (ISBN 0-89879-019-0). Writers Digest.
Sarton, May. Writings on Writing. Hunting, Constance, ed. 55p. 1980. pap. 3.50 (ISBN 0-913006-20-3); pap. text ed. 3.50 (ISBN 0-913006-21-1); tchr.'s ed. 3.50 (ISBN 0-913006-22-X). Puckerbrush.
Schrammn, Wilbur L. The Story Workshop. 458p. 1980. Repr. of 1938 ed. lib. bdg. 20.00 (ISBN 0-89984-423-5). Century Bookbindery.
Shaw, Dave & Eisman, Greg. Beyond Ideas into Information: A Writing Workbook. 192p. 1980. pap. text ed. 6.95 (ISBN 0-8403-2218-6). Kendall-Hunt.
Smith, Agnes. Speaking As a Writer. Ross-Robertson, David, tr. LC 78-65831. (Illus.). 76p. (Orig.). 1979. 7.75 (ISBN 0-9602342-0-9); pap. 5.95 (ISBN 0-9602342-1-7). Westwind Pr.
Vardaman, G. T. & Vardaman, P. B. Successful Writing: A Short Course for Professionals. 1977. 39.95 (ISBN 0-471-02428-7). Wiley.

AUTHORSHIP–HANDBOOKS, MANUALS, ETC.
see also Medical Writing; Technical Writing
Adleman, Robert. How to Write Anything. LC 80-81879. 1981. pap. 6.95 (ISBN 0-933350-37-6). Morse Pr.
Boggess, Louise. How to Write Fillers & Short Features That Sell. 2nd ed. LC 80-8682. 256p. 1981. 10.95 (ISBN 0-06-010492-9, HarpT). Har-Row.
Cox, Sidney. Indirections for Those Who Want to Write. 1981. pap. 8.95 (ISBN 0-87923-389-3). Godine.
Doubtfire, Dianne. The Craft of Novel Writing. 1981. pap. 5.95 (ISBN 0-8052-8087-1, Pub. by Allison & Busby England). Schocken.
Highsmith, Patricia. Plotting & Writing Suspense Fiction. rev. ed. 1981. 10.95 (ISBN 0-87116-125-7). Writer.
Holley, Frederick S., ed. Los Angeles Times Stylebook: A Manual for Writers, Editors, Journalists & Students. 1981. pap. 6.95 (ISBN 0-452-00552-3, F552, Mer). NAL.
Mathieu, Aron. The Book Market: How to Write, Publish & Market Your Book. LC 80-71059. 512p. 1981. 14.95 (ISBN 0-939014-00-9). Andover Pr.
Montgomery, Michael & Stratton, John. The Writer's Hotline Handbook. (Orig.). 1981. pap. 3.95 (ISBN 0-451-61972-2, MF 1972, Mentor Bks). NAL.
Moore, John A. Write for the Religion Market. LC 80-25607. 128p. 1981. 9.95 (ISBN 0-88280-084-1). ETC Pubns.
Quennell, Peter. The Sign of the Fish. (Illus.). 255p. 1980. Repr. of 1960 ed. lib. bdg. 30.00 (ISBN 0-8492-2209-5). R West.
Romero, Donald G. A Handbook on Professional Magazine Article Writing. 1975. 3.95 (ISBN 0-87543-127-5). Lucas.
Swain, Dwight V. Techniques of the Selling Writer. LC 73-7419. 330p. 1981. pap. 7.50 (ISBN 0-8061-1191-7). U of Okla Pr.
Wilbur, L. Perry. Build a Second Income Writing Articles. 224p. 1981. pap. text ed. 7.95 (ISBN 0-471-08426-3). Wiley.

AUTISM
see also Fantasy
Gillium, James E. Autism: Diagnosis, Instruction, Management, & Research. write for info. (ISBN 0-398-04072-9). C C Thomas.
Morgan, Sam B. The Unreachable Child: An Introduction to Early Childhood Autism. 208p. 1981. text ed. 15.95 (ISBN 0-87870-202-4); pap. text ed. 7.95 (ISBN 0-87870-201-6). Memphis St Univ.
Readings in Autism. rev. ed. (Special Education Ser.). (Illus.). 224p. pap. text ed. write for info. Spec Learn Corp.
Tinbergen, E. A. & Tinbergen, N. Early Childhood Autism: An Ethological Approach. (Advances in Ethology Ser.: Vol. 10). (Illus.). 53p. (Orig.). 1972. pap. text ed. 14.00 (ISBN 3-489-78036-1). Parey Sci Pubs.

AUTOBIOGRAPHIES
Benziger, Barbara F. The Prison of My Mind. LC 80-54811. 184p. 1981. pap. 5.95 (ISBN 0-8027-7172-6). Walker & Co.
Browne, Corinne. Casualty: A Memoir of Love & War. 1981. 12.95 (ISBN 0-393-01422-3). Norton.
Jensen, Marilyn. Phillis Wheatley, Negro Slave of John Wheatley. pap. 9.95. Lion.
Shields, Mary L. Sea Run. LC 80-52406. 352p. 1981. 11.95 (ISBN 0-87223-665-X). Seaview Bks.

AUTOBIOGRAPHY
see also Biography (As a Literary Form)
O'Hara, Daniel T. Tragic Knowledge: Yeat's Autobiography & Hermeneutics. LC 80-26825. 224p. 1981. 20.00x (ISBN 0-231-05204-9). Columbia U Pr.
Pilling, John. Autobiography & Imagination: Studies in Self-Scrutiny. 200p. 1981. price not set (ISBN 0-7100-0730-2). Rqutledge & Kegan.
Western, Leone N. The Gold Key to Writing Your Life History. LC 80-83026. (Illus.). 124p. 1981. pap. 7.95 (ISBN 0-918146-20-8). Peninsula WA.
Winslow, Donald J. Life-Writing: A Glossary of Terms in Biography, Autobiography, & Related Forms. (Biography Monographs Ser.). 64p. (Orig.). pap. 4.50x (ISBN 0-8248-0748-0). U Pr of Hawaii.

AUTOBIOGRAPHY–TECHNIQUE
see Autobiography

AUTOCODES
see Programming Languages (Electronic Computers)

AUTOGENOUS WELDING
see Welding

AUTOGRAPHS–CATALOGS
see Autographs–Collections

AUTOGRAPHS–COLLECTIONS
Collecting Autographs. 96p. (gr. 4-7). 1981. price not set (ISBN 0-671-34025-5). Messner.

AUTOMATA
see also Machine Theory
Knoedel, W. & Schneider, H. J., eds. Parallel Processes & Related Automata. (Computing Supplementum Ser.: No. 3). 203p. 1981. pap. 59.00 (ISBN 0-387-81606-2). Springer-Verlag.

AUTOMATED BATTLEFIELD
see Electronics in Military Engineering

AUTOMATIC COMPUTERS
see Computers

AUTOMATIC CONTROL
see also Automation; Cybernetics; Feedback Control Systems; Guidance Systems (Flight); Process Control
Bryson, A. E. & Ho, Y. C. Applied Optimal Control: Optimization, Estimation, & Control. rev. ed. LC 75-16114. (Illus.). 481p. 1981. pap. 15.95 (ISBN 0-89116-228-3). Hemisphere Pub.
Laskiewicz, H. J. & Zaremba, M., eds. Pneumatic & Hydraulic Components & Instruments in Automatic Control: Proceedings of the IFAC Symposium, Warsaw, Poland, 20-23 May 1980. (IFAC Proceedings Ser.). (Illus.). 308p. 1981. 75.00 (ISBN 0-08-027317-3). Pergamon.
Leondes, C. T., ed. Control of Dynamic Systems: Advances in Theory & Application, Vols. 9, 10, 13 & 15. Incl. Vol. 9. 44.00 (ISBN 0-12-012709-1); Vol. 10. 44.00 (ISBN 0-12-012710-5); Vol. 13. 1977. 39.00 (ISBN 0-12-012713-X); Vol. 15. 1979. 22.50 (ISBN 0-12-012715-6). 1973. Acad Pr.
Letherman, K. M. Automatic Controls for Heating & Airconditioning: Principles & Applications. (International Series on Heating, Ventilation & Refrigeration: Vol. 15). (Illus.). 220p. 1981. 30.00 (ISBN 0-08-023222-1). Pergamon.

AUTOMATIC COUNTING DEVICES
see Digital Counters

AUTOMATIC DATA PROCESSING
see Electronic Data Processing

AUTOMATIC DATA PROCESSORS
see Computers

AUTOMATIC DATA STORAGE
see Information Storage and Retrieval Systems

AUTOMATIC DIGITAL COMPUTERS
see Electronic Digital Computers

AUTOMATIC DRAFTING
see Computer Graphics

AUTOMATIC FACTORIES
see Automation

AUTOMATIC INDEXING
Richmond, Phyllis A. Introduction to PRECIS for North American Usage. 340p. 1981. lib. bdg. 25.00x (ISBN 0-87287-240-8). Libs Unl.

AUTOMATIC MACHINE-TOOLS
see Machine-Tools

AUTOMATIC PRODUCTION
see Automation

AUTOMATIC PROGRAMMING LANGUAGES
see Programming Languages (Electronic Computers)

AUTOMATIC SPEECH RECOGNITION
Fu, K. S., ed. Digital Pattern Recognition. 2nd ed. (Communication & Cybernetics: Vol. 10). (Illus.). 234p. 1980. pap. 29.80 (ISBN 0-387-10207-8). Springer-Verlag.

AUTOMATIC TRANSMISSIONS, AUTOMOBILE
see Automobiles–Transmission Devices

AUTOMATION
see also Assembly-Line Methods; Automatic Control; Feedback Control Systems; Man-Machine Systems; Systems Engineering
Bolz, Roger W., ed. How to Automate Your Plant Successfully. LC 80-67334. (Illus.). 184p. (Orig.). 1980. pap. 28.50 (ISBN 0-930220-03-X). Conquest.
Rapid Methods & Automation in Microbiology & Immunology: A Bibliography. 250p. 24.00 (ISBN 0-904147-07-X). Info Retrieval.

AUTOMATION–SOCIAL ASPECTS
Faunce, William. Problems of an Industrial Society. 2nd ed. Munson, Eric M., ed. 256p. 1981. pap. text ed. 8.95 (ISBN 0-07-020105-6, C). McGraw.

AUTOMOBILE BODIES
see Automobiles–Bodies

AUTOMOBILE BUYING
see Automobile Purchasing

AUTOMOBILE DRIVERS' LICENSES
see Automobile Drivers' Tests

AUTOMOBILE DRIVERS' TESTS
Drivers License Guide Co. Drivers License Guide Nineteen Eighty-One. (Illus.). 96p. 1981. pap. 9.45. Drivers License.
--U. S. Identification Manual. rev. ed. (Illus.). 700p. 1981. text ed. 90.00. Drivers License.

AUTOMOBILE DRIVING
Abodaher, David J. So You're Ready to Drive a Car. (Illus.). 128p. (gr. 7 up). 1981. PLB price not set. Messner.
Mbodaher, David J. So You're Ready to Drive a Car. (Illus.). 128p. (gr. 8 up). 1981. write for info. (ISBN 0-671-32891-3). Messner.

AUTOMOBILE DRIVING–SAFETY MEASURES
see Traffic Safety

AUTOMOBILE FUEL SYSTEMS
see Automobiles–Fuel Systems

AUTOMOBILE INDUSTRY AND TRADE
see also Automobiles–Prices; Used Car Trade
Conde, John A. The Cars That Hudson Built. (Illus.). 224p. 1980. 19.95 (ISBN 0-9605048-0-X). Arnold-Porter Pub.
Hartley, John R. Management of Vehicle Production. (Illus.). 216p. 1980. text ed. 32.00 (ISBN 0-408-00396-0). Butterworths.

AUTOMOBILE INSURANCE
see Insurance, Automobile

AUTOMOBILE MAINTENANCE
see Automobiles–Maintenance and Repair

AUTOMOBILE OPERATION
see Automobile Driving

AUTOMOBILE PRICES
see Automobiles–Prices

AUTOMOBILE PURCHASING
Autos, 1981: Ratings, Specifications & Best Buys. rev. ed. 96p. (Orig.). Date not set. pap. 2.50 (ISBN 0-89552-071-0). DMR Pubns.
Douglas, Herman. Are You Paying Too Much for Your Car? Sweitzer, Peggy, ed. 1979. write for info. Web Pub Hse.
Edmonston, Phil. The Used Car Guide. (Illus.). 254p. 1981. pap. 8.95 (ISBN 0-8253-0051-7). Beaufort Bks NY.
Green, Michael L., ed. Car Facts, 1981. rev. ed. (Buyer's Guide Ser.). 96p. (Orig.). Date not set. pap. 2.50 (ISBN 0-89552-069-9). DMR Pubns.
--Economy Cars, 1981. rev. ed. (Buyer's Guide Ser.). 96p. (Orig.). Date not set. pap. 2.50 (ISBN 0-89552-073-7). DMR Pubns.
Ross, James. How to Buy a Car. 160p. 1981. pap. 3.95 (ISBN 0-312-39546-9); prepack 39.50 (ISBN 0-312-39547-7). St Martin.

AUTOMOBILE RACING
see also Automobiles, Racing; Drag Racing; Karting
Barber, DeNonie. Their Last Lap at Indy: A Book of Tributes. (Illus.). 1980. 8.95 (ISBN 0-916620-49-2). Portals Pr.
Chapin, Kim. Fast As White Lightning: The Story of Stock Car Racing. (Illus.). 1981. 11.95. Dial.
Hamilton, Maurice. Autocourse, Nineteen Eighty to Nineteen Eighty-One, No. 29. (Illus.). 240p. 1981. 39.95 (ISBN 0-905138-12-0, Pub. by Hazelton England). Motorbooks Intl.
Lerner, Mark. Careers in Auto Racing. LC 80-12047. (Illus.). (gr. 2-5). 1980. PLB 4.95 (ISBN 0-8225-0343-3). Lerner Pubns.

AUTOMOBILE RACING–JUVENILE LITERATURE
Abodaher, David J. Great Moments in Sports Car Racing. (Illus.). 96p. (gr. 4-6). 1981. PLB 7.29 (ISBN 0-686-69302-7). Messner.
Lerner, Mark. Quarter-Midget Racing Is for Me. LC 81-41. (Sports for Me Bks.). (Illus.). (gr. 2-5). 1981. PLB 5.95 (ISBN 0-8225-1125-8). Lerner Pubns.
Scalzo, Joe. Speedway. 192p. 1981. pap. 1.95 (ISBN 0-448-17200-3, Tempo). G&D.
Wilkinson, Sylvia. Can-Am. (World of Racing Ser.). (Illus.). 48p. (gr. 4 up). 1981. PLB 9.25 (ISBN 0-516-04710-8). Childrens.
--Endurance Cars. (World of Racing Ser.). (Illus.). 48p. (gr. 4 up). 1981. PLB 9.25 (ISBN 0-516-04712-4). Childrens.
--Stock Cars. (World of Racing Ser.). (Illus.). 48p. (gr. 4 up). 1981. PLB 9.25 (ISBN 0-516-04715-9). Childrens.
--Super Vee. (World of Racing Ser.). (Illus.). 48p. (gr. 4 up). 1981. PLB 9.25 (ISBN 0-516-04714-0). Childrens.

AUTOMOBILE RADIOS
see Automobiles–Radio Equipment

AUTOMOBILE REPAIR
see Automobiles–Maintenance and Repair

AUTOMOBILE TOURING
see also Travel
Reader's Digest. Drive America. (Illus.). 1981. 22.95 (ISBN 0-89577-085-7, Pub. by Reader's Digest). Norton.

AUTOMOBILE TRANSMISSION
see Automobiles–Transmission Devices

AUTOMOBILE TRUCKS
see Motor-Trucks

AUTOMOBILES
see also Motorcycles; Motor-Trucks
also names of automobiles under Automobiles–Types; Automobiles, Foreign–Types, e.g. Automobiles–Types–Ford; Automobiles, Foreign–Types–Volkswagen; also headings beginning with the word automobile
Burness, Tad. American Car Spotter's Guide: 1966-1980. (Illus.). 432p. (Orig.). 1981. pap. 16.95 (ISBN 0-87938-102-7). Motorbooks Intl.
Harding, Anthony, ed. Motorist's Miscellany. 17.50x (ISBN 0-392-05932-0, SpS). Soccer.
The Saturday Evening Post Automobile Book. LC 78-9002. (Illus.). 1977. 12.95 (ISBN 0-89387-012-9). Sat Eve Post.

AUTOMOBILES–AIR-CONDITIONING
Samuels, Clifford L. Automotive Air Conditioning. (Illus.). 288p. 1981. pap. text ed. 13.95 (ISBN 0-13-054205-9). P-H.

AUTOMOBILES–BODIES
Chilton's Editorial Dept., ed. Chilton's Mechanics' Handbook: Automobile Sheet Metal Repair, Vol. III. (Illus.). 300p. 1981. pap. 14.95 (ISBN 0-686-69516-X). Chilton.

Schmidt, Robert P. Autobody Repair & Refinishing. 350p. 1981. text ed. 18.95 (ISBN 0-8359-0247-1); instr's. manual free (ISBN 0-8359-0248-X). Reston.

Storer, Jay, ed. Basic Bodywork & Painting. 5th, rev. ed. LC 73-79967. (Illus.). 192p. (Orig.). 1981. pap. 4.95 (ISBN 0-8227-5057-0). Petersen Pub.

AUTOMOBILES-COLLECTORS AND COLLECTING

see also Automobiles-History

Davies, Robert A. The Story of the Black Beauty. 1981. 10.00 (ISBN 0-8062-1712-X). Carlton.

Hornung, Clarence. Antique Automobiles. (Illus.). 1978. pap. 1.75 (ISBN 0-486-22742-1). Dover.

Wise, David B. Automobile Archaeology. (Illus.). 160p. 1981. 35.95 (ISBN 0-85059-455-3). Aztex.

AUTOMOBILES-DICTIONARIES

Toboldt, William K. & Johnson, Larry. Automotive Encyclopedia. rev. ed. (Illus.). 792p. 1981. text ed. 16.00 (ISBN 0-87006-314-6). Goodheart.

AUTOMOBILES-DIESEL MOTORS

see Automobiles-Motors

AUTOMOBILES-DRIVING

see Automobile Driving

AUTOMOBILES-ELECTRIC EQUIPMENT

Weathers, Thomas & Hunter, Claud. Fundamentals of Electricity & Automotive Electrical Systems. (Illus.). 256p. 1981. text ed. 16.95 (ISBN 0-13-337030-5). P-H.

AUTOMOBILES-ENGINES

see Automobiles-Motors

AUTOMOBILES-FUEL SYSTEMS

see also Carburetors

Ireland, Glen E. Automotive Fuel, Ignition, & Emission Control Systems. 1980. pap. 10.95 (ISBN 0-534-00866-6, Breton Pubs). Wadsworth Pub.

Mother Earth News Staff. How to Convert Your Vehicle to Propane. Hoffman, Robert, ed. 50p. (Orig.). 1981. pap. 7.50 (ISBN 0-938432-01-X). Mother Earth.

Urich, Mike. Forty-One Fifty Holley Carburetor Handbook. (Orig.). 1980. pap. 3.95 (ISBN 0-89586-047-3). H P Bks.

--Twenty-Three Hundred Holley Carburetor Handbook. (Orig.). 1981. pap. 3.95 (ISBN 0-89586-048-1). H P Bks.

AUTOMOBILES-GEARING

see Automobiles-Transmission Devices

AUTOMOBILES-HANDBOOKS, MANUALS, ETC.

see also subdivision-Types-specific type, e.g. Automobiles-Types-Ford, etc.

Danielson. Transmission Systems for Technicians, No. 2. 1981. text ed. price not set (ISBN 0-408-00562-9). Butterworth.

General Motors X Cars Tune-up & Repair. (Orig.). (gr. 9-12). 1981. pap. 6.95 (ISBN 0-8227-5058-9). Petersen Pub.

AUTOMOBILES-HISTORY

see also Automobiles-Collectors and Collecting

Wise, David B. Automobile Archaeology. (Illus.). 160p. 1981. 35.95 (ISBN 0-85059-455-3). Aztex.

AUTOMOBILES-IGNITION

Ireland, Glen E. Automotive Fuel, Ignition, & Emission Control Systems. 1980. pap. 10.95 (ISBN 0-534-00866-6, Breton Pubs). Wadsworth Pub.

AUTOMOBILES-INSURANCE

see Insurance, Automobile

AUTOMOBILES-JUVENILE LITERATURE

Knudson, Richard L. Fabulous Cars of the 1920s & 1930s. LC 80-343. (Superwheels & Thrill Sports Bks.). (Illus.). (gr. 4 up). 1981. PLB 6.95 (ISBN 0-8225-0504-5). Lerner Pubns.

Ray, John. Cars. (Junior Reference Ser.). (Illus.). 96p. (gr. 7 up). 7.96 (ISBN 0-7136-1322-X). Dufour.

Rich, Mark. Custom Cars & Trucks. (On the Move Ser.). (Illus.). 48p. (gr. 3-6). 1981. PLB 9.25 (ISBN 0-516-03886-9). Childrens.

AUTOMOBILES-MAINTENANCE AND REPAIR

Advice About Buying a Car, Car Maintenance, Car Repair. (Home Adviser Ser.). 80p. (Orig.). 1981. pap. 1.95 (ISBN 0-8326-2405-5, 7053). Delair.

Chilton's Easy Car Care. 2nd ed. Orig. Title: La Cautela Facil Del Automovil Chilton. (Illus.). 384p. (Spanish.). pap. 9.95. Chilton.

Chilton's Editorial Dept., ed. Chilton's Import Car Repair Manual. LC 78-20243. (Illus.). 1536p. 1981. 19.95 (ISBN 0-8019-7029-6). Chilton.

--Chilton's Mechanics' Handbook: Automobile Sheet Metal Repair, Vol. III. (Illus.). 300p. 1981. pap. 14.95 (ISBN 0-686-69516-X). Chilton.

Fendell, Bob. How to Make Your Car Last a Lifetime. LC 80-19759. (Illus.). 216p. 1981. 12.95 (ISBN 0-03-053661-8); pap. 6.95 (ISBN 0-03-053656-1). HR&W.

Fifty-Two Hundred Holley Carburetor Handbook. (Orig.). 1981. pap. 3.95 (ISBN 0-89586-050-3). H P Bks.

General Motors X Cars Tune-up & Repair. (Orig.). (gr. 9-12). 1981. pap. 6.95 (ISBN 0-8227-5058-9). Petersen Pub.

Robert Bentley, Inc. Volkswagen Rabbit Diesel Service Manual 1977-1981, Including Pickup Truck. rev. ed. (Illus.). 480p. (Orig.). 1981. pap. 18.50 (ISBN 0-8376-0104-5). Bentley.

--Volkswagen Rabbit-Scirocco Service Manual 1980-1981, Gasoline Models, Including Pickup Truck. rev. ed. (Illus.). 600p. (Orig.). 1981. pap. 18.50 (ISBN 0-8376-0099-5). Bentley.

Schmidt, Robert P. Autobody Repair & Refinishing. 350p. 1981. text ed. 18.95 (ISBN 0-8359-0247-1); instr's. manual free (ISBN 0-8359-0248-X). Reston.

Storer, Jay, ed. Basic Bodywork & Painting. 5th, rev. ed. LC 73-79967. (Illus.). 192p. (Orig.). 1981. pap. 4.95 (ISBN 0-8227-5057-0). Petersen Pub.

Young, Paul. Datsun Tune-up for Everybody. (Illus.). 1980. pap. 7.95 (ISBN 0-89815-026-4). Ten Speed Pr.

--Honda Tune-up for Everybody. (Illus.). 144p. (Orig.). 1981. pap. 7.95 (ISBN 0-89815-031-0). Ten Speed Pr.

AUTOMOBILES-MODELS

Wieland, James & Force, Edward. Corgi Toys: The Ones with Windows. (Illus.). 1981. 8.95 (ISBN 0-87938-123-X). Motorbooks Intl.

AUTOMOBILES-MOTORS

see also Automobiles, Racing-Motors

Barlow, Roger. The Diesel Car Book. LC 80-8913. (Illus.). 288p. (Orig.). 1981. pap. 7.95 (ISBN 0-394-17895-5, Ever). Grove.

Crouse, William H. & Anglin, Donald L. Workbook for Automotive Engines. 6th ed. (Automotive Technology Ser.). (Illus.). 96p. 1981. pap. 6.95 (ISBN 0-07-014826-0, G). McGraw.

Day, Richard. Automotive Engine Tuning. 1981. pap. text ed. 14.95 (ISBN 0-8359-0270-6). Reston.

How to Rebuild Small-Block Mopar. (Orig.). 1981. pap. 7.95 (ISBN 0-89586-091-0). H P Bks.

Mackerle, J. Air-Cooled Automotive Engines. 518p. 1972. 59.00x (ISBN 0-85264-205-9, Pub. by Griffin England). State Mutual Bk.

AUTOMOBILES-PAINTING

Storer, Jay, ed. Basic Bodywork & Painting. 5th, rev. ed. LC 73-79967. (Illus.). 192p. (Orig.). 1981. pap. 4.95 (ISBN 0-8227-5057-0). Petersen Pub.

AUTOMOBILES-PRICES

Badnow, William R., ed. Edmund's Nineteen Eighty-One Foreign Car Prices. (Edmund's Car Price Guides Ser.). (Orig.). 1981. pap. 2.50 (ISBN 0-440-02207-X, Pub. by Edmund). Dell.

--Edmund's Nineteen Eighty-One New Car Prices. (Orig.). 1981. pap. 2.50 (ISBN 0-440-02236-3, Pub. by Edmund). Dell.

--Edmund's Nineteen Eighty-One Used Car Prices. (Edmund's Car Price Guides Ser.). (Orig.). 1981. pap. 2.50 (ISBN 0-440-02209-6, Pub. by Edmund). Dell.

--Edmund's Used Car Prices. (Orig.). Date not set. pap. price not set (ISBN 0-440-02952-X, Pub by Edmund). Dell.

Consumer Guide -- Complete Guide to Used Cars, 1981. 1981. pap. 3.50 (ISBN 0-451-09785-8, E9785, Sig). NAL.

Consumer Guide, ed. Consumer Guide: Nineteen Eighty-One Cars. 1981. pap. 3.50 (ISBN 0-451-09625-8, Sig). NAL.

Green, Michael L., ed. New & Used Foreign Car Prices. rev. ed. (Buyer's Guide Ser.). 96p. (Orig.). Date not set. pap. 2.50 (ISBN 0-89552-067-2). DMR Pubns.

--New Car Prices Buyer's Guide, 1981. rev. ed. (Buyer's Guide Ser.). 128p. (Orig.). Date not set. pap. 2.50 (ISBN 0-89552-068-0). DMR Pubns.

--New Truck & Van Prices, 1981. rev. ed. (Buyer's Guide Ser.). 96p. (Orig.). Date not set. pap. 2.50 (ISBN 0-89552-070-2). DMR Pubns.

--Used Car Prices. rev. ed. (Buyer's Guide Ser.). 96p. (Orig.). Date not set. pap. 2.50 (ISBN 0-89552-065-6). DMR Pubns.

--Used Truck & Van Prices. rev. ed. (Buyer's Guide Ser.). 96p. (Orig.). Date not set. pap. 2.25 (ISBN 0-89552-066-4). DMR Pubns.

Jones, Brian N. Car Values: 1981 Edition. 4th ed. (Illus.). 272p. (Orig.). 1981. pap. 12.95 (ISBN 0-528-88138-8). Rand.

AUTOMOBILES-PURCHASING

see Automobile Purchasing

AUTOMOBILES-RADIO EQUIPMENT

Salm, Walter G. Auto Audio: How to Select & Install Stereo Equipment. 144p. 1980. pap. 7.70 (ISBN 0-8104-0759-0). Hayden.

AUTOMOBILES-REPAIRING

see Automobiles-Maintenance and Repair

AUTOMOBILES-SERVICING

see Automobiles-Maintenance and Repair

AUTOMOBILES-SPRINGS AND SUSPENSION

Campbell, Colin. New Directions in Suspension Design: Making the Fast Car Faster. LC 80-24348. (Illus.). 224p. 1981. 18.50 (ISBN 0-8376-0150-9). Bentley.

AUTOMOBILES-TOURING

see Automobile Touring

AUTOMOBILES-TRANSMISSION DEVICES

Brycha, M. Automatic Transmissions. 2nd ed. 1981. 16.95 (ISBN 0-13-054577-5). P-H.

Danielson. Transmission Systems for Technicians, No. 2. 1981. text ed. price not set (ISBN 0-408-00562-9). Butterworth.

Husselbee, William. Automatic Transmission Service: A Text-Workbook. (Orig.). 1981. pap. 9.95 (ISBN 0-8359-0266-8). Reston.

Sessions, Ron. Hydra-Matic Transmissions. (Orig.). 1981. pap. 9.95 (ISBN 0-89586-051-1). H P Bks.

Tucker, Howard. Automatic Transmissions Workbook on Service & Repair. LC 80-67593. (Automotive Technology Ser.). (Illus.). 64p. (Orig.). 1981. pap. text ed. 6.00 (ISBN 0-8273-1894-4). Delmar.

AUTOMOBILES-TYPES-BUICK

Dunham, Terry B., et al. Buick: The Complete History. Doerflinger, William, ed. (Automobile Quarterly Library Ser.). 444p. 1981. 59.95 (ISBN 0-525-07230-6). Dutton.

AUTOMOBILES-TYPES-CAMARO

Miller, Ray. Camaro! Chevy's Classy Chassis. (Illus.). 320p. 1981. write for info. (ISBN 0-913056-10-3). Evergreen Pr.

AUTOMOBILES-TYPES-CHALLENGER

Colt & Challenger Nineteen Seventy-One to Eighty. LC 80-70346. (Illus.). 242p. 1980. pap. 8.95. Chilton.

AUTOMOBILES-TYPES-CHEVROLET

see also Automobiles-Types-Nova

Chevrolet Nineteen Sixty-Eight to Seventy-Nine. (Illus.). 268p. (Spanish.). 1979. pap. 8.95. Chilton.

Colt & Challenger Nineteen Seventy-One to Eighty. LC 80-70346. (Illus.). 242p. 1980. pap. 8.95. Chilton.

AUTOMOBILES-TYPES-CHRYSLER

How to Rebuild Small-Block Mopar. (Orig.). 1981. pap. 7.95 (ISBN 0-89586-091-0). H P Bks.

AUTOMOBILES-TYPES-DODGE

see also Automobiles-Types-Challenger

Champ-Arrow-Sapporo 1978-81. LC 80-70347. (Illus.). 208p. 1980. pap. 8.95. Chilton.

AUTOMOBILES-TYPES-FORD

see also Automobiles-Types-Pinto; Automobiles, Foreign-Types-Zephyr

Ford Nineteen Sixty-Eight to Seventy-Nine. (Illus.). 304p. (Spanish.). 1980. pap. 8.95. Chilton.

Moline, Mary. The Best of Ford. (Illus.). 1973. 10.00 (ISBN 0-913444-01-4, Pub. by Rumbleseat Press). Motorbooks Intl.

--Model A Miseries & Cures. (Illus.). 1972. pap. 6.00 (ISBN 0-913444-00-6, Pub. by Rumbleseat Press). Motorbooks Intl.

Sorensen, Lorin. The Ford Road. (Illus.). 1978. 19.95 (ISBN 0-87938-078-0, Pub. by Silverado Pubns Co). Motorbooks Intl.

AUTOMOBILES-TYPES-LINCOLN

Bonsall, Thomas E. The Linclon Motorcar: Sixty Years of Excellence. 325p. 1981. 32.95 (ISBN 0-934780-05-6). Bookman Dan.

--The Lincoln Motorcar: Sixty Years of Excellence. (Illus.). 1981. 32.95 (ISBN 0-934780-05-6). Bookman Dan.

AUTOMOBILES-TYPES-MERCURY

Pinto & Bobcat Ninteen Eighty-One to Eighty. LC 80-70340. (Illus.). 280p. 1980. pap. 8.95. Chilton.

AUTOMOBILES-TYPES-NOVA

Ahlstrand, Alan. Chevy Nova Nineteen Seventy-One to Nineteen Seventy-Nine: Shop Manual. Jorgensen, Eric, ed. (Illus.). 362p. (Orig.). 1980. pap. text ed. 10.95 (ISBN 0-89287-317-5, A133). Clymer Pubns.

AUTOMOBILES-TYPES-PINTO

Pinto & Bobcat Ninteen Eighty-One to Eighty. LC 80-70340. (Illus.). 280p. 1980. pap. 8.95. Chilton.

AUTOMOBILES-TYPES-PLYMOUTH

Arrow & D-Fifty Pick-Ups 1979-81. LC 80-70343. (Illus.). 192p. pap. 8.95. Chilton.

Champ-Arrow-Sapporo 1978-81. LC 80-70347. (Illus.). 208p. 1980. pap. 8.95. Chilton.

AUTOMOBILES, DIESEL

see Automobiles-Motors

AUTOMOBILES, FOREIGN

Chilton's Automotive Editorial Dept. Fairmont Zephyr 1978-1980. (Illus.). 1980. pap. 8.95 (ISBN 0-8019-6965-4). Chilton.

AUTOMOBILES, FOREIGN-MAINTENANCE AND REPAIR

see Automobiles-Maintenance and Repair

AUTOMOBILES, FOREIGN-TYPES-AUDI

Audi Four Thousand-Five Thousand 1977-81. LC 80-70341. (Illus.). 208p. 1980. pap. 8.95. Chilton.

AUTOMOBILES, FOREIGN-TYPES-AUSTIN

Wyatt, R. J. The Austin. LC 80-68896. (Illus.). 256p. 1981. 38.00 (ISBN 0-7153-7948-8). David & Charles.

AUTOMOBILES, FOREIGN-TYPES-DATSUN

Ahlstrand, Alan. Datsun 810: 1977-1980 Shop Manual. Jorgensen, Eric, ed. (Illus.). 296p. 1980. pap. 10.95 (ISBN 0-89287-334-5). Clymer Pubns.

Datsun Nineteen Seventy-Three to Eighty. (Illus.). 288p. 1979. pap. 8.95. Chilton.

How to Modify Your Datsun- Four & Six Cylinder. (Orig.). 1981. pap. 9.95 (ISBN 0-89586-092-9). H P Bks.

Young, Paul. Datsun Tune-up for Everybody. (Illus.). 1980. pap. 7.95 (ISBN 0-89815-026-4). Ten Speed Pr.

AUTOMOBILES, FOREIGN-TYPES-FERRARI

Clarke, R. M., ed. Ferrari Cars Nineteen Sixty-Nine to Nineteen Seventy-Three. (Brooklands Bks.). (Illus., Orig.). 1980. pap. 11.95. Motorbooks Intl.

AUTOMOBILES, FOREIGN-TYPES-FIAT

Fiat Nineteen Sixty-Nine to Eighty-One. LC 80-70348. (Illus.). 262p. 1980. pap. 8.95. Chilton.

AUTOMOBILES, FOREIGN-TYPES-HONDA

Young, Paul. Honda Tune-up for Everybody. (Illus.). 144p. (Orig.). 1981. pap. 7.95 (ISBN 0-89815-031-0). Ten Speed Pr.

AUTOMOBILES, FOREIGN-TYPES-JAGUAR

Lord Montague. Jaguar. 2nd rev. ed. LC 80-27039. (Illus.). 240p. 1981. 19.95 (ISBN 0-498-02547-0). A S Barnes.

AUTOMOBILES, FOREIGN-TYPES-LOTUS

Clarke, R. M., ed. Lotus Elan Nineteen Sixty-Two to Nineteen Seventy-Three. (Brooklands Bks.). (Illus.). 100p. (Orig.). 1980. pap. 11.95. Motorbooks Intl.

AUTOMOBILES, FOREIGN-TYPES-MAZDA

Mazda RX-7 Nineteen Seventy-Eight to Eighty-One. LC 80-70342. (Illus.). 208p. 1980. pap. 8.95. Chilton.

AUTOMOBILES, FOREIGN-TYPES-PANTERA

Clarke, R. M., ed. Pantera & Mangusta Nineteen Sixty-Nine to Nineteen Seventy-Four. (Illus.). 70p. (Orig.). 1980. pap. 8.95 (ISBN 0-907073-00-X). Motorbooks Intl.

AUTOMOBILES, FOREIGN-TYPES-PORSCHE

Clarke, R. M. Porsche Nine Fourteen: Nineteen Sixty-Nine to Nineteen Seventy-Five. (Brooklands Bks.). (Illus.). 100p. (Orig.). 1980. 11.95 (ISBN 0-906589-84-3). Motorbooks Intl.

Frere, Paul. Porsche Nine Eleven Story. 2nd ed. (Illus.). 200p. 1981. 37.95 (ISBN 0-85059-482-0). Aztex.

--Porsche Racing Cars of the Seventies. LC 80-23773. (Illus.). 256p. 1981. 16.95 (ISBN 0-668-05113-2, 5113). Arco.

AUTOMOBILES, FOREIGN-TYPES-RABBIT

Sloniger, Jerry. The VW Story. (Illus.). 216p. 1981. 37.95 (ISBN 0-85059-441-3). Aztex.

AUTOMOBILES, FOREIGN-TYPES-TOYOTA

Toyota Celica & Supra 1971-81. LC 80-70267. (Illus.). 224p. pap. 8.95. Chilton.

Toyota Corolla-Carina-Tercel 1970-81. LC 80-70345. (Illus.). 224p. 1980. pap. 8.95. Chilton.

Toyota Pick-Ups Nineteen Seventy to Eighty-One. LC 80-70344. (Illus.). 224p. 1980. pap. 8.95. Chilton.

AUTOMOBILES, FOREIGN-TYPES-VOLKSWAGEN

see also Automobiles, Foreign-Types-Rabbit

Robert Bentley, Inc. Volkswagen Rabbit Diesel Service Manual 1977-1981, Including Pickup Truck. rev. ed. (Illus.). 480p. (Orig.). 1981. pap. 18.50 (ISBN 0-8376-0104-5). Bentley.

--Volkswagen Rabbit-Scirocco Service Manual 1980-1981, Gasoline Models, Including Pickup Truck. rev. ed. (Illus.). 600p. (Orig.). 1981. pap. 18.50 (ISBN 0-8376-0099-5). Bentley.

Sloniger, Jerry. The VW Story. (Illus.). 216p. 1981. 37.95 (ISBN 0-85059-441-3). Aztex.

Volkswagen Nineteen Seventy to Seventy-Nine. (Illus.). 288p. (Spanish.). 1980. pap. 8.95. Chilton.

VW Ninteen Seventy to Nineteen Eighty-One. LC 80-70339. (Illus.). 288p. 1980. pap. 8.95. Chilton.

AUTOMOBILES, FOREIGN-TYPES-VOLVO

Volvo Nineteen Seventy to Eighty-One. (Illus.). 288p. 1980. pap. 8.95. Chilton.

AUTOMOBILES, FOREIGN-TYPES-ZEPHYR

Chilton's Automotive Editorial Dept. Fairmont Zephyr 1978-1980. (Illus.). 1980. pap. 8.95 (ISBN 0-8019-6965-4). Chilton.

AUTOMOBILES, RACING

Hungness, Carl, et al. USAC Sprint History: Twenty-Five Years of United States Sprint Car Racing. Mahoney, John & Cadou, Jep, eds. (Illus.). 208p. 1981. pap. 14.95 (ISBN 0-915088-26-6). C. Hungness.

AUTOMOBILES, RACING-MOTORS

Hot Rod Magazine Editors, ed. Bolt-on Performance. (Hot Rod Shop Ser.). (Illus.). 1981. pap. 8.95 (ISBN 0-8227-6013-4). Petersen Pub.

AUTOMORPHIC FORMS

Gerritzen, L. & Van Der Put, M. Schottky Groups & Mumford Curves. (Lecture Notes in Mathematics: Vol. 817). 317p. 1980. pap. 19.50 (ISBN 0-387-10229-9). Springer-Verlag.

AUTOMOTIVE FUEL SYSTEMS

see Automobiles-Fuel Systems

AUTOMOTIVE TRANSPORTATION

see Transportation, Automotive

AUTOMOTIVE VEHICLES

see Motor Vehicles

AUTONOMIC NERVOUS SYSTEM

see Nervous System, Autonomic

AUTONOMY

see also Self-Determination, National

Deci, Edward L. The Psychology of Self-Determination. LC 80-8373. 1980. 19.95 (ISBN 0-669-04045-2). Lexington Bks.

Marshall, H. H. From Dependence to Statehood, Vol. 1. 1980. 50.00 (ISBN 0-379-20348-0). Oceana.

Shapiro, David. Autonomy & Rigid Character. LC 80-68953. 167p. 1981. 12.95x (ISBN 0-465-00567-5). Basic.

AUTOSUGGESTION

see Hypnotism

AUTUMN

Allington, Richard L. & Krull, Kathleen. Autumn. LC 80-25190. (Beginning to Learn About Ser.). (Illus.). 32p. (ps-2). 1981. PLB 9.65 (ISBN 0-8172-1343-0). Raintree Child.

AVIATION

see Aeronautics

AVIATION ACCIDENTS

see Aeronautics-Accidents

AVIATION INDUSTRY

see Air Lines; Aircraft Industry

AVIATION LAW

see Aeronautics-Laws and Regulations

AVIATION MEDICINE
Engle, Eloise & Lott, Arnold. Man in Flight: Biomedical Achievements in Aerospace. LC 79-63780. (A Supplement to the American Astronautical Society History Ser.). (Illus.). 414p. 1979. 20.00x (ISBN 0-915268-24-8). Univelt Inc.
Goeltz, Judith. Jet Stress: What It Is & How to Cope with It. Donsbach, Kurt W., ed. LC 79-89366. 350p. 1980. 9.95 (ISBN 0-86664-000-2). Inst Pubs.
AVIATION REGULATIONS
see Aeronautics–Laws and Regulations
AVIATORS
see Air Pilots
AVITAMINOSIS
Coburn, Stephen P. The Chemistry & Metabolism of the Vitamin B6 Antagonist, 4' Deoxypyridoxine. 224p. 1981. 69.95 (ISBN 0-8493-5783-7). CRC Pr.
AVOCADO
Some Avocado Varieties for Australia. 35p. 1978. pap. 5.00 (ISBN 0-643-02276-7, CO10, CSIRO). Unipub.
AVOCATIONS
see Hobbies
AWARDS
see Rewards (Prizes, etc.)
AXES
Schreier, Konrad F., Jr. Marbles, Knives & Axes. LC 78-15942. 70p. 1978. pap. 4.50 (ISBN 0-917714-19-9). Beinfeld Pub.
AXIOLOGY
see Values
AYURVEDIC MEDICINE
see Medicine, Hindu
AZORIN
see Martinez Ruiz, Jose, 1873-
AZTALAN, WISCONSIN
Orozco, E. C. Republican Protestantism in Aztlan. 261p. 1980. 22.00 (ISBN 0-686-28883-1); pap. 11.00 (ISBN 0-686-28884-X). Petereins Pr.
AZTECS
Stevenson, Robert. Music in Aztec & Inca Territory. (California Library Reprint Ser.: No. 64). 1977. Repr. of 1968 ed. 38.50x (ISBN 0-520-03169-5). UCDLA.
Weaver, Muriel P. The Aztecs, & Their Presecessors: Archaeology of Mesoamerica. 2nd ed. (Studies in Archaeology). 1981. write for info. (ISBN 0-12-785936-5). Acad Pr.
AZTECS–JUVENILE LITERATURE
Lewis, Brenda R. Growing up in Aztec Times. (Growing up Ser.). (Illus.). 72p. (gr. 7-9). 1981. 15.95 (ISBN 0-7134-2734-5, Pub. by Batsford England). David & Charles.

B

BABEL, ISAAC, 1894-1941
Mendelson, Danuta. Metaphor in the Works of Isaac Babel. 1981. 17.50 (ISBN 0-88233-702-5). Ardis Pubs.
BABIES
see Infants
BABY FOODS
see Infants–Nutrition
BABY SITTERS
Saunders, Rubie. Baby-Sitting: A Concise Guide. (YA) (gr. 7-9). 1979. pap. 1.50 (ISBN 0-671-56012-3). PB.
Sherman. The Babysitter's Guide. (Illus.). (gr. 7-12). 1980. pap. 1.25 (ISBN 0-590-31342-8, Schol Pap). Schol Bk Serv.
BABYLONIAN LANGUAGE
see Assyro-Babylonian Language
BABYSITTERS
see Baby Sitters
BACH, JOHANN CHRISTIAN, 1735-1782
Mellers, Wilfrid. Bach & the Dance of God. 1981. 39.95 (ISBN 0-19-520232-5). Oxford U Pr.
BACH, JOHANN SEBASTIAN, 1685-1750
Daw, Stephen. The Music of Johann Sebastion Bach. LC 78-68624. (Illus.). 240p. 1981. 19.50 (ISBN 0-8386-1682-8). Fairleigh Dickinson.
BACHELORS
Keefer, Anna. For Women Only. 112p. 1980. pap. 5.95 (ISBN 0-89305-037-7). Anna Pub.
BACK PACKING
see Backpacking
BACKACHE
Grahame, R. & Anderson, J. A. Low Back Pain, Vol. 2. (Annual Research Reviews). 83p. 1981. 14.00 (ISBN 0-88831-095-1). Eden Med Res.
Kurland, Howard. Back Pains. (Illus.). 1981. 12.95 (ISBN 0-671-41379-1). S&S.
The Low-Back Patient & Therapeutic Exercise Handouts 1979. Date not set. Set Of 25. 25.00. Masson Pub.
BACKBONE
see Spine
BACKGAMMON
Becker, Bruce. Backgammon for Blood. 1974. 8.95 (ISBN 0-87690-123-2). Dutton.
BACKPACKING
Bridge, Raymond. America's Backing Guide. rev. ed. 448p. 1981. 14.95 (ISBN 0-684-16872-3, ScribT). Scribner.
Elliott, Cheri. Backpacker's Digest. 3rd ed. (Illus.). 1981. pap. 8.95 (ISBN 0-910676-21-6, 6536). DBI.
Robinson, Don. Backpacking. (Illus.). 112p. 1981. 12.95 (ISBN 0-8069-9180-1, Pub. by EP Publishing England); pap. 6.95 (ISBN 0-8069-9182-8). Sterling.
Wadsworth, Bruce. An Adirondack Sampler, II: Backpacking Trips in the Adirondacks. (Orig.). 1981. pap. 6.95 (ISBN 0-935272-15-1). Adk Mtn Club.
Wood, Robert S. Pleasure Packing for the Eighties. 2nd rev. ed. (Illus.). 256p. 1981. pap. 6.95 (ISBN 0-89815-035-3). Ten Speed Pr.
BACKWARD AREAS
see Underdeveloped Areas
BACKWARD CHILDREN
see Mentally Handicapped Children
BACON, FRANCIS, VISCOUNT ST. ALBANS, 1561-1626
Ince, Richard. England's High Chancellor: Francis Bacon-a Romance. 324p. 1980. Repr. of 1935 ed. lib. bdg. 35.00 (ISBN 0-89984-297-6). Century Bookbindery.
BACON, FRANCIS, 1909-
Quinton, Anthony. Bacon. (Past Masters Ser.). 1981. 7.95 (ISBN 0-8090-2790-9); pap. 2.95 (ISBN 0-8090-1414-9). Hill & Wang.
Sylvester, David. Interviews with Francis Bacon. rev., enl. ed. (Illus.). 176p. 1981. pap. 9.95 (ISBN 0-500-27196-8). Thames Hudson.
BACTERIA
see also Viruses
also names of specific bacteria, e.g. staphyloccoccus
McLaren, Anne. Germ Cells & Soma: A New Look at Old Problem. LC 80-54221. (Silliman Lectures: No. 5). (Illus.). 128p. 1981. 15.00 (ISBN 0-300-02694-3). Yale U Pr.
Seeley, Harry W., Jr. & VanDemark, Paul J. Microbes in Action: A Laboratory Manual of Microbiology. 3rd ed. (Illus.). 1981. write for info. (ISBN 0-7167-1259-8); instrs'. manual avail. W H Freeman.
--Selected Exercises from Microbes in Action: A Laboratory Manual of Microbiology. 3rd ed. (Illus.). 1981. price not set (ISBN 0-7167-1260-1). W H Freeman.
BACTERIA, AEROBIC
Stafford, D. A., et al, eds. Anaerobic Digestion. (Illus.). xii, 528p. 1980. 95.00x (ISBN 0-85334-904-5). Burgess-Intl Ideas.
BACTERIAL RESISTANCE TO ANTIBIOTICS
see Drug Resistance in Micro-Organisms
BACTERIOLOGY
see also Bacteria; Biological Products; Germ Theory of Disease; Immunity; Medicine, Preventive; Sewage–Purification; Sewage Disposal
also subdivision Bacteriology under particular subjects, e.g. Milk–Bacteriology
Holt, John G. Supplement to the Index Bergeyana. 387p. 1981. write for info. (4106-1). Williams & Wilkins.
BACTERIOLOGY–LABORATORY MANUALS
Gerhardt, Philipp, ed. Manual of Methods for General Bacteriology. (Illus.). 1981. pap. 25.00 (ISBN 0-914826-29-8); flexible bdg. 21.00 (ISBN 0-914826-30-1). Am Soc Microbio.
BADGES OF HONOR
see Medals
BADMINTON (GAME)
Grice, Tony. Badminton. 2nd ed. (Illus.). 71p. 1980. pap. text ed. 3.95x (ISBN 0-89641-053-6). American Pr.
BAGDAD
Alexander, Constance. Baghdad in Bygone Days: From the Journals and Correspondence of Claudius Rich, Traveler, Artist, Linguist, Antiquary, and British Resident of Baghdad, 1808-1821. LC 80-1939. 1981. Repr. of 1928 ed. 41.50 (ISBN 0-404-18951-2). AMS Pr.
BAHA'I FAITH
see Bahaism
BAHAISM
Christensen, Deborah. God & Me. (Sunflower Bks. for Young Children: Bk. 3). (Illus., Orig.). (ps-2). 1980. pap. 2.00 (ISBN 0-87743-143-4, 7-53-03). Baha'i.
--My Baha'i Book. (Sunflower Bks. for Young Children: Bk. 1). (Illus., Orig.). (ps-2). 1980. pap. 2.00 (ISBN 0-87743-141-8, 7-53-01). Baha'i.
--My Favorite Prayers & Passages. (Sunflower Bks. for Young Children: Bk. 2). (Illus., Orig.). (ps-2). 1980. pap. 2.00 (ISBN 0-87743-142-6, 7-53-02). Baha'i.
--Our Baha'i Holy Places. (Sunflower Bks. for Young Children: Bk. 4). (Illus., Orig.). (ps-2). 1980. pap. 2.00 (ISBN 0-87743-144-2, 7-03-04). Baha'i.
Mahmoudi, Jalil. A Concordance to the Hidden Words of Baha'u'llah. (Orig.). 1980. pap. 5.00 (ISBN 0-87743-148-5, 7-68-52). Baha'i.
Wittman, Debbie D. The Birth of the Baha'i Faith. (Illus., Orig.). (gr. 5-9). 1980. pap. 1.00 (ISBN 0-87743-146-9, 7-52-55). Baha'i.
BAHAMAS
Dupuch, S. P., ed. Bahamas Handbook & Businessman's Annual, 1980 to 1981. 18th ed. (Illus.). 478p. (Orig.). 1980. pap. 15.00x (ISBN 0-8002-2694-1). Intl Pubns Serv.
Pye, Michael. The King Over the Water. (Illus.). 288p. 1981. 12.95 (ISBN 0-03-057551-6). HR&W.
BAHAMAS–DESCRIPTION AND TRAVEL
Airguide. Airguide Traveler: Bahamas, Florida, Florida Keys, & Sea Islands. (Illus.). 1980. pap. 11.00 (ISBN 0-911721-89-4). Aviation.
Wilensky, Julius M. Cruising Guide to the Abacos & the Northern Bahamas. rev. 2nd ed. Weber, Carol, ed. LC 80-50792. (Illus.). 220p. 1980. pap. 17.25 (ISBN 0-918752-03-5). Wescott Cove.
BAIL–GREAT BRITAIN
Coke, Edward & Highmore, Anthony, Jr. A Little Treatise on Baile & Maineprize. Berkowitz, David S. & Thorne, Samuel E., eds. LC 77-86576. (Classics of English Legal History in the Modern Era Ser.: Vol. 13). 352p. 1979. lib. bdg. 40.00 (ISBN 0-8240-3062-1). Garland Pub.
BAILMENTS
see also Auctions
Jones, Sir William. An Essay on the Law of Bailments. Berkowitz, David S., ed. Thorne, Samuel E. LC 77-86562. (Classics of English Legal History in the Modern Era Ser.: Vol. 14). 132p. 1979. lib. bdg. 40.00 (ISBN 0-8240-3063-X). Garland Pub.
BAIT
see also Fishing Lures
Bennett, D. W. Secrets of Baitfishing. Campbell, M., ed. (North East Fishing Ser.). (Illus.). 128p. 1981. pap. 4.95 (ISBN 0-88839-087-4). Hancock Hse.
BAJA CALIFORNIA
Honter, Jim. Offbeat Baja. 156p. 1977. pap. 5.95 (ISBN 0-87701-093-5). Chronicle Bks.
BAKING
see also Bread; Cookies; Pastry
Pack-Miller, Lisa, et al. Easy Natural Breads Even a Kid Can Bake. Frompovich, Catherine J., ed. (Illus.). 14p. (gr. 3 up). 1980. pap. 1.50 (ISBN 0-935322-07-8). C J Frompovich.
Time-Life Bks. Eds., ed. Pies & Pastries. (The Good Cook Ser.). (Illus.). 176p. 1981. 12.95 (ISBN 0-8094-2895-4). Time-Life.
Wolter, Annette & Teubner, Christian. On Tasting Best of Baking. (Orig.). 1980. 14.95 (ISBN 0-89586-041-4); pap. 9.95 (ISBN 0-89586-071-6). H P Bks.
BALAENOPTERA
see Whales
BALANCE (ART)
see Proportion (Art)
BALANCE OF NATURE
see Ecology
BALANCE SHEETS
see Financial Statements
BALANCING (GYMNASTICS)
see Acrobats and Acrobatism
BALDNESS
Margo. Growing New Hair! How to Keep What You Have & Fill in Where It's Thin, by Margo, for Men Only. LC 80-66699. (Illus.). 112p. 1980. 7.95 (ISBN 0-394-51417-3). Autumn Pr.
BALDWIN, STANLEY BALDWIN, 1ST EARL, 1867-1947
Stannage, Tom. Baldwin Thwarts the Opposition: The British General Election of 1935. 320p. 1980. 50.00x (ISBN 0-7099-0341-3, Pub. by Croom Helm Ltd England). Biblio Dist.
BALFOUR, ARTHUR JAMES BALFOUR, 1ST EARL OF, 1848-1930
St. James, Ian. Balfour Conspiracy. LC 80-69378. 1981. 10.95 (ISBN 0-689-11140-1). Atheneum.
BALKAN PENINSULA–HISTORY
Djordjevic, Dmitrije & Fischer-Galati, Stephen. The Balkan Revolutionary Tradition. LC 80-24039. 272p. 1981. 17.50x (ISBN 0-231-05098-4). Columbia U Pr.
Krekic, Barisa. Dubrovnik, Italy & the Balkans in the Late Middle Ages. 332p. 1980. 75.00x (ISBN 0-86078-070-8, Pub. by Variorum England). State Mutual Bk.
BALKAN QUESTION
see Eastern Question (Balkan)
BALL ROOM DANCING
see Ballroom Dancing
BALLADS
Farmer, John S. Merry Songs & Ballads: Musa Pedestris, 6 vols. Set. 61.50x (ISBN 0-8154-0066-7). Cooper Sq.
Ord, John. The Bothy Songs & Ballads of Aberdeen. Banff & Moray, Angus & the Mearns. 493p. 1980. Repr. of 1930 ed. lib. bdg. 25.00 (ISBN 0-8492-7307-2). R West.
Wright, Thomas. Songs & Ballads, with Other Short Poems, Chiefly of the Reign of Philip & Mary. 214p. 1980. Repr. of 1860 ed. lib. bdg. 45.00 (ISBN 0-8495-5827-1). Arden Lib.
BALLADS, AMERICAN
Fuson, Henry H. Ballads of the Kentucky Highlands. 219p. 1980. Repr. of 1931 ed. text ed. 25.00 (ISBN 0-8492-4706-3). R West.
BALLADS, ENGLISH
see also Folk-Songs, English
Palmer, Roy, ed. Everyman's Book of British Ballads. (Illus.). 256p. 1981. 22.50x (ISBN 0-460-04452-4, Pub. by J. M. Dent England). Biblio Dist.
BALLET
Here are entered works on the ballet. Ballet scores are entered under the heading Ballets.
Barnes, Clive. Inside the American Ballet Theatre. 1977. pap. 9.95 (Hawthorn). Dutton.
Glasstone, Richard. Better Ballet. LC 78-55577. (Better Sport Ser.). (Illus.). 95p. 1977. 8.50x (ISBN 0-7182-1453-6). Intl Pubns Serv.
Haggin, B. H. Discovering Balanchine. (Illus.). 196p. 1981. 19.95 (ISBN 0-8180-0404-5). Horizon.
Montadori Editors, ed. The Simon & Schuster Book of the Ballet. (Illus.). 1980. 24.95 (ISBN 0-671-25099-X). S&S.
Montague, Sarah. Pas De Deux: Great Partnerships in Dance. LC 80-54502. (Illus.). 112p. 1981. text ed. 12.50x (ISBN 0-87663-346-7); pap. 7.95x (ISBN 0-87663-553-2). Universe.
Zorina, Vera. Dancer's Choice: The Ballet in Music & Pictures. Date not set. 27.00 (ISBN 0-03-057982-1, HarpT). Har-Row.
BALLET–HISTORY
Martens, Frederick H. The Book of the Opera & the Ballet & the History of the Opera. LC 80-2289. 1981. Repr. of 1925 ed. 22.50 (ISBN 0-404-18857-5). AMS Pr.
BALLET–JUVENILE LITERATURE
Gross. If You Were a Ballet Dancer. (gr. 3). 1979. pap. 1.50 (ISBN 0-590-05746-4, Schol Pap). Schol Bk Serv.
Sorine, D. At Every Turn! It's Ballet. LC 80-19232. (Illus.). 49p. (ps-3). 1981. 8.95 (ISBN 0-394-84473-4); pap. 1.95 (ISBN 0-394-94473-9). Knopf.
BALLET DANCERS
see Dancers
BALLET DANCING
Glasstone, Richard. Better Ballet. LC 78-55577. (Better Sport Ser.). (Illus.). 95p. 1977. 8.50x (ISBN 0-7182-1453-6). Intl Pubns Serv.
Paskevska, Anna. Both Sides of the Mirror: The Science & Art of Ballet. LC 79-51362. (Illus.). 200p. 1981. 22.50 (ISBN 0-87127-112-5). Dance Horiz.
BALLETS
Beaumont, Cyril W. Michel Fokine & His Ballets. LC 80-69956. (Illus.). 1981. pap. 8.95 (ISBN 0-87127-120-6). Dance Horiz.
BALLISTIC MISSILES
Goure, Leon, et al. The Emerging Strategic Environment: Implications for Ballistic Missile Defense. LC 79-53108. 75p. 1979. 6.50. Inst Foreign Policy Anal.
BALLOON ASCENSIONS
Coombs, Charles. Hot-Air Ballooning. LC 80-26704. (Illus.). 128p. (gr. 4-6). 1981. 7.95 (ISBN 0-688-00364-8); PLB 7.63 (ISBN 0-688-00365-6). Morrow.
Time-Life Books Editors & Jackson, Donald D. The Aeronauts. (The Epic of Flight Ser.). (Illus.). 176p. 1980. 12.95 (ISBN 0-8094-3268-4). Time-Life.
BALLOONS
see also Aeronautics; Balloon Ascensions
Time-Life Books Editors & Botting, Douglas. The Giant Airships. (The Epic of Flight). (Illus.). 176p. 1981. 12.95 (ISBN 0-8094-3270-6). Time-Life.
BALLROOM DANCING
Moore, Alex. The Revised Techniques of Ballroom Dancing. 9th ed. 108p. 1980. pap. text ed. 12.50x (ISBN 0-392-07521-0, LTB). Soccer.
Simic, Charles. Classic Ballroom Dances. LC 80-14470. 1980. 8.95 (ISBN 0-8076-0973-0); pap. 4.95 (ISBN 0-8076-0974-9). Braziller.
BALOCHI LANGUAGE
see Baluchi Language
BALSA WOOD–JUVENILE LITERATURE
Haney, Lynn. I Am a Dancer. (Illus.). 64p. (gr. 10 up). 1981. 8.95 (ISBN 0-399-20724-4); pap. 4.95 (ISBN 0-399-20792-9). Putnam.
BALTIMORE
McGrain, John W. Good Old Company Towns. (Baltimore County Heritage Publication Ser.). (Illus.). 1981. pap. price not set (ISBN 0-937076-01-5). Baltimore Co Pub Lib.
Stevens, Elisabeth. Elisabeth Stevens Nineteen Eighty-One Guide to Baltimore's Inner Harbor. (Illus.). 64p. 1981. pap. 2.50 (ISBN 0-916144-86-0). Stemmer Hse.
BALTO-SLAVIC LANGUAGES
see Slavic Languages
BALUCHI LANGUAGE
Barker, M. A. Spoken Baluchi, 2 bks. Incl. Bk. I. 526p. cancelled (ISBN 0-87950-425-0); cancelled (ISBN 0-87950-427-7); cancelled (ISBN 0-87950-428-5); Bk. II. 667p. 1980. cancelled (ISBN 0-87950-426-9); cancelled Bks. I & II (ISBN 0-87950-429-3). (Spoken Language Ser.). 1980. Spoken Lang Serv.
BAMBOO
Bamboo Research in Asia. 228p. 1981. pap. 15.00 (ISBN 0-88936-267-X, I*O*R*C 159, IDRC). Unipub.
BANACH SPACES
see also Hilbert Space
Banas & Goebel. Measures of Noncompactness in Banach Spaces. 112p. 1980. 59.75 (ISBN 0-8247-6981-3). Dekker.
BANANA
Report of the Seventh Session of the Intergovernmental Group on Bananas. 17p. 1981. pap. 6.00 (ISBN 92-5-100950-3, F2091, FAO). Unipub.
BAND MUSIC
see also Orchestral Music
Band Music Guide. 17.50. Instrumental Co.
Fennell, Frederick. Basic Band Repertory: British Band Classics from the Conductor's Point of View. 1980. pap. 6.00. Instrumental Co.
BANDITS
see Brigands and Robbers
BANDMASTERS
see Conductors (Music)

BANDS (MUSIC)
see also Wind Instruments
Fennell, Frederick. Basic Band Repertory: British Band Classics from the Conductor's Point of View. 1980. pap. 6.00. Instrumental Co.
BANGLADESH–ECONOMIC CONDITIONS
Faaland, Just, ed. Aid & Influence: The Case of Bangladesh. LC 80-13481. 1980. 25.00 (ISBN 0-312-01492-9). St Martin.
BANG'S DISEASE
see Brucellosis in Cattle
BANK LOANS
see Loans
BANK ROBBERIES
see Brigands and Robbers
BANKERS
Canfield, Cass. Outrageous Fortunes: The Story of the Medici, the Rothschilds, & J. Pierpont Morgan. (Illus.). 1981. 10.95 (ISBN 0-15-170513-5). HarBraceJ.
BANKING
see Banks and Banking
BANKING LAW
see also Negotiable Instruments
also topics in the field of banking, e.g. Trust Companies
Garon, Philip A. Banking Law Anthology, Vol.1. 1981. 59.95. Intl Lib.
Karam, N. H., tr. Banking Laws of Kuwait. 275p. 1979. 22.00x (ISBN 0-86010-139-8, Pub.by Graham & Trotman England). State Mutual Bk.
BANKRUPTCY
see also Corporate Reorganizations
King, Lawrence, et al. Municipal Bankruptcy Law & Its Implications. (COMP Papers: No. P-6). 81p. (Orig.). 1980. pap. 12.00 (ISBN 0-916450-39-2). Coun on Municipal.
Kosel, Janice. Bankruptcy: Do It Yourself in California. 1980. 12.00 (ISBN 0-917316-29-0). Nolo Pr.
Newton, Grant W. Bankruptcy & Insolvency Accounting. 2nd ed. 500p. 1981. 29.95 (ISBN 0-471-07992-8). Ronald Pr.
Nicholas, Ted. How to Get Out of Debt. (Illus.). 146p. 1980. 14.95 (ISBN 0-913864-60-9). Enterprise Del.
Rogers, Harry E. How to Do a Bankruptcy. 2nd ed. 7.95. Green Hill.
Wagner, Michael P. Minnesota Legal Forms: Bankruptcy. Mason Publishing Staff, ed. 150p. 1981. ring binder 15.00 (ISBN 0-917126-92-0). Mason Pub.
Weintraub, Benjamin. What Every Credit Executive Should Know About Chapter Eleven of the Bankruptcy Code. LC 80-82081. 133p. 1980. pap. 9.50 (ISBN 0-934914-32-X). NACM.
BANKS AND BANKING
see also Bankers; Credit; Foreign Exchange; Interest and Usury; Liquidity (Economics); Money; Negotiable Instruments
Bank Frauds: Their Detection & Prevention. 2nd ed. 276p. 1965. 19.95 (ISBN 0-471-06574-9). Wiley.
Bequai, August. The Cashless Society: EFTS at the Crossroads. LC 80-21517. 350p. 1981. 19.95 (ISBN 0-471-05654-5, Pub. by Wiley-Interscience). Wiley.
Campbell, Colin & Campbell, Rosemary. Money & Banking. 4th ed. LC 80-65792. 608p. 1981. text ed. 18.95 (ISBN 0-03-058076-5). Dryden Pr.
Cox, Edwin B., et al. The Bank Director's Handbook. (Illus.). 200p. 1981. 19.95 (ISBN 0-86569-056-1). Auburn Hse.
Frankel, S. Herbert. Money & Banking. 1980. pap. 4.25 (ISBN 0-8447-3398-9). Am Enterprise.
Keyserling, Leon H. & Conference of Economic Staff. Money, Credit, & Interest Rates: Their Gross Mismanagement by the Federal Reserve System. (Illus.). 1980. 3.00. Conf Econ Prog.
Moore, William G. The Use of the Magnetic Ink Character Reader. 1979. pap. text ed. 1.99 (ISBN 0-934488-00-2). Williams Ent.
Richardson, Linda. Banking & Sales: A Consultative Guide to Cross Selling Financial Products & Services. 165p. 1981. 19.95 (ISBN 0-471-09010-7, Pub. by Wiley-Interscience). Wiley.
Sametz, Arnold, ed. Securities Activities of Commercial Banks. LC 80-8339. 1981. write for info. (ISBN 0-669-04031-2). Lexington Bks.
Skousen, Mark. The Insider's Banking & Credit Almanac. 14.95 (ISBN 0-932496-01-6). Green Hill.
BANKS AND BANKING–DATA PROCESSING
Veith, Richard H. Multinational Computer Nets: The Case of International Banking. 160p. 1981. 18.95x (ISBN 0-669-04092-4). Lexington Bks.
BANKS AND BANKING–DICTIONARIES
Perry, F. E. A Dictionary of Banking. 304p. 1979. text ed. 19.95x (ISBN 0-7121-0428-3, Pub. by Macdonald & Evans England). Intl Ideas.
BANKS AND BANKING–DIRECTORIES
Hicks, Tyler G. Go Where the Money Is: Mideast & North African Banks & Financial Institutions. 2nd ed. 150p. 1981. pap. 15.00 (ISBN 0-914306-56-1). Intl Wealth.
BANKS AND BANKING–HISTORY
Greenberg, Dolores. A Study of Morton, Bliss & Company. LC 78-66830. 288p. 1980. 22.50 (ISBN 0-87413-148-0). U Delaware Pr.
BANKS AND BANKING–LAWS AND LEGISLATION
see Banking Law
BANKS AND BANKING–AFRICA
Hicks, Tyler G. Go Where the Money Is: Mideast & North African Banks & Financial Institutions. 2nd ed. 150p. 1981. pap. 15.00 (ISBN 0-914306-56-1). Intl Wealth.
BANKS AND BANKING–CANADA
Ebel, Jurgen. Banking in Canada. Blythe, L. N., ed. 80p. (Orig.). 1978. pap. text ed. 10.95x (ISBN 0-7121-0259-0, Pub. by Macdonald & Evans England). Intl Ideas.
BANKS AND BANKING–INDIA
Hasan, Khaja S. Banking in India. Blythe, L. N., ed. 112p. (Orig.). 1979. pap. text ed. 10.95x (ISBN 0-7121-0260-4, Pub. by Macdonald & Evans England). Intl Ideas.
BANKS AND BANKING–SWITZERLAND
Ziegler, Jean. Switzerland Exposed. (Allison & Busby Motive Ser.). 180p. 1981. pap. 7.95 (ISBN 0-8052-8077-4, Pub. by Allison & Busby England). Schocken.
BANKS AND BANKING, INDUSTRIAL
see Loans, Personal
BANKS AND BANKING, INTERNATIONAL
Kammert, James L. International Commercial Banking Management. 336p. 1981. 19.95 (ISBN 0-8144-5680-4). Am Mgmt.
McKitterick, Nathaniel & Middleton, Jenkins B. The Bankers of the Rich & the Bankers of the Poor: The Role of Export Credit in Development Finance. LC 72-76253. (Monographs: No. 6). 70p. 1972. 2.00 (ISBN 0-686-28689-8). Overseas Dev Council.
Sydell, Alfred E. The Approaching Collapse of the International Banking System. (Illus.). 127p. 1981. 67.85 (ISBN 0-930008-75-8). Inst Econ Pol.
Veith, Richard H. Multinational Computer Nets: The Case of International Banking. 160p. 1981. 18.95x (ISBN 0-669-04092-4). Lexington Bks.
Ziegler, Jean. Switzerland Exposed. (Allison & Busby Motive Ser.). 180p. 1981. pap. 7.95 (ISBN 0-8052-8077-4, Pub. by Allison & Busby England). Schocken.
BANNOCK INDIANS
see Indians of North America–Northwest, Pacific
BANQUETS
see Dinners and Dining
BAPTISM
Byrum, R. R. Holy Spirit Baptism & the Second Cleansing. 108p. pap. 60.75; pap. 2.00 3 copies. Faith Pub Hse.
Cantelon, Willard, tr. Le Bapteme Dans le Saint-Sprit. (French Bks.). (Fr.). 1979. 0.95 (ISBN 0-8297-0929-0). Life Pubs Intl.
Davis, Susan. A Way to Remember. Davis, Tom, ed. 32p. (ps up). 1980. pap. write for info. (ISBN 0-8280-0023-9). Review & Herald.
Riggle, H. M. Christian Baptism, Feet Washing & the Lord's Supper. 264p. 3.50. Faith Pub Hse.
Warns, Johannes. Baptism. Date not set. 11.50 (ISBN 0-86524-063-9). Klock & Klock.
BAPTISM–BIBLICAL TEACHING
Todd, Richard E., ed. Baptism. (Grace Bible Ser.). (Illus.). 16p. (Orig.). (gr. 1-6). 1980. pap. 0.50 (ISBN 0-9605324-0-4). R E Todd.
BAPTISTS
Hastings, C. B. Introducing Southern Baptists. 176p. (Orig.). 1981. pap. 6.95 (ISBN 0-8091-2364-9). Paulist Pr.
Howe, Claude L., Jr. Glimpses of Baptist Heritage. 1981. pap. 5.75 (ISBN 0-8054-6559-6). Broadman.
Russell, Lester F. Black Baptist Secondary Schools in Virginia, 1887-1957: A Study in Black History. LC 80-22414. 218p. 1981. 12.50 (ISBN 0-8108-1373-4). Scarecrow.
BAPTISTS–CLERGY
McSwain, Larry L. & Treadwell, William C., Jr. Conflict Ministry in the Church. 1981. pap. 6.95 (ISBN 0-8054-2540-3). Broadman.
BAPTISTS–GOVERNMENT
Dale, Robert D. To Dream Again. 1981. pap. 4.95 (ISBN 0-8054-2541-1). Broadman.
BAPTISTS–HISTORY
Duncan, R. S. A History of the Baptists in Missouri. Date not set. Repr. of 1882 ed. price not set. Church History.
Jackson, J. H. A Story of Christian Activism: History of the National Baptist Convention U. S. A., Inc. LC 80-17408. (Illus.). 790p. 1980. 19.95 (ISBN 0-935990-01-1). Townsend Pr.
Miles, Delos. Church Growth - a Mighty River. 1981. pap. 5.95 (ISBN 0-8054-6227-9). Broadman.
Yance, Norman A. Religion Southern Style: Southern Baptists & Society in Historical Pspective. LC 78-61185. (Special Studies Ser.: No. 4). 1978. 3.95 (ISBN 0-932180-03-5). Assn Baptist Profs.
BAR
see Lawyers
BAR ASSOCIATIONS
Maine Bar Directory, 1981. 1981. price not set (ISBN 0-89442-022-4). Tower Pub Co.
BARBARY CORSAIRS
see Pirates
BARBECUE COOKERY
see Cookery, Barbecue
BARBERS
Rockwell, Anne & Rockwell, Harlow. My Barber. LC 80-29467. (Ready-to-Read Ser.). (Illus.). 24p. (ps-2). 1981. PLB 7.95 (ISBN 0-02-777630-1). Macmillan.
BARGAINING
see Collective Bargaining; Negotiation
BARGELLO
see Canvas Embroidery
BARLEY
Australian Barleys. 64p. 1979. pap. 13.50 (ISBN 0-643-00344-4, CO02, CSIRO). Unipub.
Fitzsimmons, R. W. & Wrigley, C. W. Australian Barleys. 86p. 1980. 9.95x (ISBN 0-643-00344-4, Pub. by CSIRO Australia). Intl Schol Bk Serv.
BARMAIDS
see Bartenders
BARNUM, PHINEAS TAYLOR, 1810-1891
Harris, Neil. Humbug: The Art of P. T. Barnum. LC 80-26944. xiv, 338p. 1981. pap. 8.95 (ISBN 0-226-31752-8). U of Chicago Pr.
BAROQUE ARCHITECTURE
see Architecture, Baroque
BAROQUE LITERATURE–HISTORY AND CRITICISM
Erdman, David V., et al, eds. The Romantic Movement: A Selective & Critical Bibliography for Nineteen Seventy-Nine. LC 80-8494. 350p. 1980. lib. bdg. 35.00 (ISBN 0-8240-9512-X). Garland Pub.
BAROQUE MUSIC
see Music, Baroque
BAROQUE SCULPTURE
see Sculpture, Baroque
BARRACUDAS
Jacobs, Francine. Barracuda: Tiger of the Sea. (Illus.). 48p. (gr. 1-4). 1981. 8.95 (ISBN 0-8027-6413-4); lib. bdg. 9.85 (ISBN 0-8027-6414-2). Walker & Co.
BARREN FIG TREE (PARABLE)
see Jesus Christ–Parables
BARRISTERS
see Lawyers
BARS (DRINKING ESTABLISHMENTS)
see Hotels, Taverns, Etc.
BARTENDERS
Van Kleek, Peter E. Beverage Management & Bartending. 144p. 1981. pap. text ed. 7.95 (ISBN 0-8436-2209-1). CBI Pub.
BARTER
Corden, W. M. Inflation, Exchange Rates, & the World Economy: Lectures on International Monetary Economics. (Business & Society Studies). 1980. pap. write for info. (ISBN 0-226-11584-4). U of Chicago Pr.
BARTH, KARL, 1886-1968
Barth, Karl. Karl Barth Letters: 1961 to 1968. Bromiley, Geoffrey W., tr. LC 80-29140. 288p. 1981. 14.95 (ISBN 0-8028-3536-8). Eerdmans.
Casalis, George. Portrait of Karl Barth. Brown, Robert M., tr. LC 80-25829. viii, 135p. 1981. Repr. of 1963 ed. lib. bdg. 17.50x (ISBN 0-313-22775-6, CAKB). Greenwood.
Sykes, S. W. Karl Barth: Studies of His Theological Method. 214p. 1979. text ed. 29.00x (ISBN 0-19-826649-9). Oxford U Pr.
BARTHIANISM
see Dialectical Theology
BARUCH, BERNARD MANNES, 1870-1965
Schwarz, Jordan A. The Speculator: Bernard M. Baruch in Washington, 1917-1965. LC 80-17386. (Illus.). 688p. 1981. 27.50 (ISBN 0-8078-1396-6). U of NC Pr.
BARYSHNIKOV, MIKHAIL
Smakov, Gennady. Baryshnikov: From Russia to the West. (Illus.). 1981. 17.50 (ISBN 0-374-10908-7). FS&G.
BASEBALL
see also Pitching (Baseball); Softball; World Series (Baseball)
Bouton, Jim. Ball Four, Plus Ball Five. rev. ed. LC 80-6165. 432p. 1981. 12.95 (ISBN 0-8128-2771-6). Stein & Day.
Davenport, John W. Baseball's Pennant Races: A Graphic View. 1981. 19.95 (ISBN 0-934794-02-2); pap. 12.95 (ISBN 0-934794-03-0). First Impressions.
Forker, Dom. The Ultimate Baseball Quiz Book. (Orig.). 1981. pap. 1.95 (ISBN 0-451-09679-7, J9679, Sig). NAL.
Hollander, Zander, ed. The Complete Handbook of Baseball - 1981 Edition. (Orig.). 1981. pap. 2.95 (ISBN 0-451-09682-7, Sig). NAL.
Kelly, Robert. Baseball Trivia Puzzler, No. 1. (Orig.). 1981. pap. 1.95 (ISBN 0-440-00393-8). Dell.
Lally, Richard. A Bartender's Guide to Baseball. 304p. (Orig.). 1981. pap. 2.50 (ISBN 0-446-91736-2). Warner Bks.
Liss, Howard. The Pocket Book of Baseball. 1981. pap. 2.75 (ISBN 0-671-41862-9). PB.
McBride, Joseph. High & Inside: The Complete Guide to Baseball Slang. 288p. (Orig.). 1981. pap. 2.50 (ISBN 0-446-91939-X). Warner Bks.
Marshall, Bob. Diary of a Yankee-Hater. 256p. (Orig.). 1981. pap. 7.95 (ISBN 0-531-09945-8). Watts.
Mazer, Bill & Fischler, Stan. The Amazing Bill Mazer's Baseball Trivia. 224p. (Orig.). 1981. pap. 2.50 (ISBN 0-446-91784-2). Warner Bks.
Sugar, Burt R. The Baseball Trivia Book. LC 75-44566. Orig. Title: Who Was Harry Steinfeldt? & Other Baseball Trivia Questions. 176p. 1981. pap. 1.95 (ISBN 0-87216-824-7). Playboy Pbks.
Sullivan, George. Baseball Rules Illustrated. 96p. (Orig.). 1981. pap. 3.95 (ISBN 0-346-12524-3). Cornerstone.
Uecker, Bob & Herskowitz, Mickey. The Catcher in the Wry. 320p. 1981. 10.95 (ISBN 0-399-12586-8). Putnam.
Walton, Ed. The Rookies. LC 80-5892. 288p. 1981. 14.95 (ISBN 0-8128-2778-3). Stein & Day.
BASEBALL–BIOGRAPHY
see also names of baseball players, e.g. Ruth, George Herman
Charboneau, Joe, et al. Super Joe: The Life & Legend of Joe Charboneau. LC 80-6169. 256p. 1981. 12.95 (ISBN 0-8128-2806-2). Stein & Day.
Honig, Donald & Ritter, Lawrence S. One Hundred Greatest Baseball Players of All Time. Thomas, Pamela, ed. 288p. 1981. 15.95 (ISBN 0-517-54300-1). Crown.
Marazzi, Rich & Fiorito, Len. Aaron to Zuverink: A Nostalgic Look at the Baseball Players of the Fifties. LC 80-5893. 352p. 1981. 14.95 (ISBN 0-8128-2775-9). Stein & Day.
Martin, Billy. Number One. 1981. pap. 3.25 (ISBN 0-440-16229-7). Dell.
BASEBALL–HISTORY
Allen, Maury. Baseball's One Hundred: A Personal Ranking of the Best Players in Baseball History. (Illus.). 352p. 1981. 14.95 (ISBN 0-89104-208-3); pap. 6.95 (ISBN 0-89104-200-8). A & W Pubs.
Dickey, Glenn. The History of National League Baseball: Since 1876. LC 80-6261. 336p. 1981. 13.95 (ISBN 0-8128-2818-6); pap. 9.95 (ISBN 0-8128-6101-9). Stein & Day.
Fleming, G. H. The Unforgettable Season. LC 80-18299. (Illus.). 336p. 1981. 16.95 (ISBN 0-03-056221-X). HR&W.
Honig, Donald. Brooklyn Dodgers. (Illus.). 192p. 1981. 16.95 (ISBN 0-312-10600-9). St Martin.
Honig, Donald & Ritter, Lawrence S. One Hundred Greatest Baseball Players of All Time. Thomas, Pamela, ed. 288p. 1981. 15.95 (ISBN 0-517-54300-1). Crown.
Kubik, Richard S. Baseball Transition Nineteen Fifty to Nineteen Seventy-Nine. (Illus.). 124p. 1981. 10.00 (ISBN 0-682-49676-6). Exposition.
Marazzi, Rich. The Stein & Day Baseball Date Book, 1981. (Illus.). 128p. 1980. 6.95 (ISBN 0-8128-2770-8). Stein & Day.
Onigman, Marc. This Date in Braves History. LC 80-6158. (This Date Ser.). 288p. 1981. pap. 9.95 (ISBN 0-8128-6106-X). Stein & Day.
Reichler, Joseph L. The Great All-Time Baseball Record Book: A Unique Sourcebook of Facts, Feats & Figures. (Illus.). 608p. 1981. 19.95 (ISBN 0-02-603100-0). Macmillan.
Rosenthal, Harold. The Ten Best Years of Baseball: An Informal History of the Fifties. 184p. 1981. pap. 5.95 (ISBN 0-442-27063-1). Van Nos Reinhold.
BASEBALL–JUVENILE LITERATURE
Batting Secrets of the Major Leaguers. (Illus.). 112p. 1981. write for info. (ISBN 0-671-41315-5). Messner.
Buck, Ray. Dave Parker: The Cobra Swirl. LC 80-39987. (Sports Stars Ser.). (Illus.). 48p. (gr. 2-8). 1981. PLB 7.35 (ISBN 0-516-04310-2). Childrens.
Burchard, Marshall. Sports Hero: Ron Guidry. (Sports Hero Ser.). (Illus.). 96p. (gr. 7-10). 1981. PLB 6.99 (ISBN 0-399-61178-9). Putnam.
Burchard, S. H. Sports Star: Tommy John. LC 80-8794. (Sports Star Ser.). (Illus.). 64p. (gr. 4-6). 1981. 6.95 (ISBN 0-15-278038-6, HJ). HarBraceJ.
Remmers, Mary. Ducks on the Pond: A Little League Lexicon. (Illus.). (gr. 1-6). 1981. pap. price not set (ISBN 0-88319-056-7). Shoal Creek Pub.
Sullivan, George. Better Baseball for Boys. rev. ed. LC 80-22022. (Better Sports Ser.). (Illus.). 64p. (gr. 5 up). 1981. PLB 6.95 (ISBN 0-396-07912-1). Dodd.
Weber. All-Pro Baseball Stars 1980. (gr. 7-12). 1980. pap. 1.25 (ISBN 0-590-31537-4, Schol Pap). Schol Bk Serv.
BASEBALL CLUBS
see also names of individual clubs, e.g. New York Baseball Club (American League)
Markham, Jesse W. & Teplitz, Paul V. Baseball Economics & Public Policy. LC 79-6032. 1981. write for info. (ISBN 0-669-03607-2). Lexington Bks.
BASEDOW'S DISEASE
see Graves' Disease
BASES, MILITARY
see Military Bases
BASIC (COMPUTER PROGRAM LANGUAGE)
Brady & Richardson. Plaid for Basic Programming Language. rev. ed. 1981. write for info. (ISBN 0-256-02124-4, 14-1037-02). Learning Syst.
Davis, William S. BASIC: Getting Started. 69p. 1981. pap. text ed. 5.95 (ISBN 0-201-03258-9). A-W.
Didday, Richard & Page, Rex. Using BASIC. 450p. 1980. pap. text ed. 10.36 (ISBN 0-8299-0357-7). West Pub.
Finkel, L. & Brown, J. Data Files in Basic. (Wiley Self Teaching Guide Ser.). 320p. 1981. write for info. (ISBN 0-471-08333-X). Wiley.
--Data Files in BASIC. (Wiley Self-Teaching Guides). 320p. 1981. write for info. (ISBN 0-471-08333-X). Wiley.
Finkel, Leroy & Brown, Jerald R. Data File Programming in Basic. (Self-Teaching Guide Ser.). 320p. 1981. pap. text ed. 9.95 (ISBN 0-471-08333-X). Wiley.

Guido, Raymond. Calculating with Basic. (Da Capo Quality Paperbacks Ser.). (Illus.). 80p. 1981. pap. text ed. 8.95 (ISBN 0-306-80144-2). Da Capo.
Inman, Don. More TRS-80 Basic. (Self-Teaching Guide Ser.). 300p. 1981. pap. text ed. 8.95 (ISBN 0-471-08010-1). Wiley.
Parker, A. J. VS Basic for Business: For the IBM 360-370. 1982. pap. text ed. 12.95 (ISBN 0-8359-8439-7). Reston.
Parker, Alan & Stewart, John. Apple Basic for Business: For the Apple II. 1981. text ed. 16.95 (ISBN 0-8359-0228-5); pap. text ed. 11.95 (ISBN 0-8359-0226-9); instrs'. manual avail. (ISBN 0-8359-0229-3). Reston.
Peckham, Herbert C. BASIC: A Hands-on Method. 2nd ed. (Illus.). 320p. 1980. pap. text ed. 12.95 (ISBN 0-07-049160-7). McGraw.
Poirot, James L. Microcomputer Systems & Applied BASIC. (Illus.). 150p. (Orig.). (gr. 6-12). 1980. pap. 8.95 (ISBN 0-88408-136-2). Sterling Swift.
Poirot, James L. & Retzlaff, Don A. Microcomputer Workbook: Apple II Ed. 2nd ed. 137p. (gr. 11-12). 1981. pap. text ed. 5.95 (ISBN 0-88408-139-7). Sterling Swift.
Sawatzky, Jasper J. & Chen, Shu-Jen. Programming in Basic-Plus. LC 80-27869. 336p. 1981. pap. 13.95 (ISBN 0-471-07729-1). Wiley.
Thompson, Robert G. BASIC: A First Course. (Data Processing Ser.). (Illus.). 352p. 1981. text ed. 13.95 (ISBN 0-675-08057-6); tchr's. manual avail. Merrill.
Trombetta, Michael. Basic for Business Students. LC 80-15605. 320p. 1981. pap. text ed. 9.95 (ISBN 0-201-07611-X). A-W.

BASIL, SAINT, 329-379
Basilius. The Ascetic Works of Saint Basil. Clarke, W. K., tr. & intro. by. LC 80-2352. 1981. Repr. of 1925 ed. 47.50 (ISBN 0-404-18902-4). AMS Pr.
St. Basil the Great on the Holy Spirit. Anderson, David, tr. from Greek. LC 80-25502. 1980. pap. 3.95 (ISBN 0-913836-74-5). St Vladimirs.

BASKET-BALL
see Basketball

BASKET MAKING
Adovasio, James M. Basketry Technology: A Guide to Identification & Analysis. (Manuals on Archeology Ser.: No. 1). (Illus.). x, 182p. 1977. 18.00x (ISBN 0-202-33035-4). Taraxacum.
Rossbach, Ed. The New Basketry. 128p. 1980. pap. 7.95 (ISBN 0-442-23996-3). Van Nos Reinhold.

BASKETBALL
Basketball--Hockey Trivia Puzzle, No. 1. 1981. pap. 1.95 (ISBN 0-440-00738-0). Dell.
Devaney, John. The Pocket Book of Pro Basketball 1980. 1980. pap. 2.75 (ISBN 0-671-41863-7). PB.
Hallander, Zander, ed. Complete Handbook of Pro Basketball-1981. pap. 2.75 (ISBN 0-451-09471-9, 9471, Sig). NAL.
Isaacs, Neil D. & Motta, Dick. Sports Illustrated Basketball. rev. ed. LC 80-7896. (Illus.). 160p. 1981. 8.95 (ISBN 0-690-01990-4, HarpT); pap. 5.95 (ISBN 0-690-01992-0). Har-Row.
--Sports Illustrated Basketball. rev. ed. LC 80-7896. (Illus.). 160p. 1981. pap. 5.95 (ISBN 0-690-01992-0, CN 865, CN). Har-Row.
Rudman, Daniel, ed. Take It to the Hoop. (Illus.). 300p. (Orig.). 1980. 25.00; pap. 8.95 (ISBN 0-913028-76-2). North Atlantic.

BASKETBALL-JUVENILE LITERATURE
All-Pro Basketball Stars 1980. (gr. 7-12). 1980. pap. 1.25 (ISBN 0-590-31238-3, Schol Pap). Schol Bk Serv.
Levin, Rich. Magic Johnson: Court Magician. LC 80-25814. (Sports Stars Ser.). (Illus.). 48p. (gr. 2-8). 1981. PLB 7.35 (ISBN 0-516-04313-7). Childrens.
Rosenthal, Bert. Larry Bird: Cool Man on the Court. LC 80-27094. (Sport Stars Ser.). (Illus.). 48p. (gr. 2-8). 1981. PLB 7.35 (ISBN 0-516-04312-9). Childrens.

BASKETS
Teleki, Gloria A. Baskets of Rural America. (Illus.). 1975. pap. 7.50 (ISBN 0-525-47409-9). Dutton.

BASS, ELECTRIC
see Guitar

BASS DRUM
see Drum

BASS FISHING
see also specific varieties of bass, e.g. Striped Bass
Hannon, Douglas & Carter, Horace. Hannon's Field Guide for Bass Fishing. LC 80-68668. (Illus.). 208p. (Orig.). 1981. pap. 5.95 (ISBN 0-937866-01-6). D Hannon.

BAT
see Bats

BATES LABORATORY ASPIRATOR
see Separators (Machines)

BATH, ENGLAND-HISTORY
Neale, R. S. Bath Sixteen Eighty to Eighteen Fifty: A Social History. (Illus.). 400p. 1981. price not set (ISBN 0-7100-0639-X). Routledge & Kegan.

BATHROOMS
Weiss, Jeffrey. Great Bathrooms. 96p. 1981. pap. 9.95 (ISBN 0-312-34486-4). St Martin.

BATIK
Donahue, Leo O. Encyclopedia of Batik Designs. LC 80-67121. 520p. 1981. 60.00 (ISBN 0-87982-035-7). Art Alliance.

BATRACHIA
see Amphibians

BATS
Laycock, George. Bats in the Night. LC 80-25834. (Illus.). 64p. (gr. 1-5). 1981. 9.95 (ISBN 0-590-07653-1, Four Winds). Schol Bk Serv.

BATTLES
see also Naval Battles
also names of battles, e.g. Gettysburg, Battle of; subdivision Campaigns or Campaigns and Battles under names of wars, e.g. European War, 1914-1918 campaigns; United States-History-Civil war, 1861-1865-Campaigns and Battles
Bruce, George. Harbottle's Dictionary of Battles. 3rd rev. ed. 304p. 1981. 14.95 (ISBN 0-442-22336-6); pap. 7.95 (ISBN 0-442-22335-8). Van Nos Reinhold.
Terraine, John. The Road to Passchendaele: The Flanders Offensive of 1917: a Study in Inevitability. (Illus.). xxiv, 365p. 1977. 27.50. Shoe String.
Whiting, Charles. Death of a Division. LC 80-5717. (Illus.). 176p. 1981. 11.95 (ISBN 0-8128-2760-0). Stein & Day.

BATTLESHIPS
see Warships

BAUDELAIRE, CHARLES PIERRE, 1821-1867
Baudelaire, Charles. The Painter of Modern Life & Other Essays. Freedberg, Sydney J., ed. LC 77-18671. (Connoisseurship Criticism & Art History Ser.: Vol. 1). 224p. 1979. lib. bdg. 27.00 (ISBN 0-8240-3257-8). Garland Pub.
Concordance to Baudelaire's les Fleurs Du Mal. 417p. 1965. 22.75 (ISBN 0-8173-9602-0). U of Ala Pr.

BAY OF PIGS INVASION
see Cuba-History-Invasion, 1961

BAYEUX TAPESTRY
see Tapestry

BEACH BIRDS
see Shore Birds

BEACHES
Kopper, Philip. The Wild Edge: Life & Lore of the Great Atlantic Beaches. 288p. 1981. pap. 6.95 (ISBN 0-14-046497-2). Penguin.

BEACONSFIELD, BENJAMIN DISRAELI, 1ST EARL OF, 1804-1881
Baily, F. E. The Perfect Age. 187p. 1981. Repr. of 1946 ed. lib. bdg. 30.00 (ISBN 0-89987-064-3). Darby Bks.
Disraeli, Benjamin. The Complete Letters of Benjamin Disraeli, 1815 to 1834. Matthews, John, et al, eds. 640p. 1981. 45.00x (ISBN 0-8020-5523-0). U of Toronto Pr.

BEARDSLEY, AUBREY VINCENT, 1872-1898
Beardsley, Aubrey V. Last Letters of Aubrey Beardsley. 158p. 1980. Repr. of 1904 ed. lib. bdg. 20.00 (ISBN 0-8482-4200-9). Norwood Edns.

BEARINGS, GAS-LUBRICATED
see Gas-Lubricated Bearings

BEARS-JUVENILE LITERATURE
Goudey, Alice E. Here Come the Bears. LC 54-5924. (Illus.). 96p. (gr. 1-5). 1954. 5.95 (ISBN 0-684-13365-2, ScribJ). Scribner.

BEASTS
see Domestic Animals; Zoology

BEATITUDES
Crosby, Michael H. The Spirituality of the Beatitudes: Matthew's Challenge for First World Christians. 256p. (Orig.). 1981. pap. 7.95 (ISBN 0-88344-465-8). Orbis Bks.
Staton, Julia & Staton, Knofel. Check Your Character (Instructor) LC 80-199950. 132p. (Orig.). 1980. pap. 2.50 (ISBN 0-87239-421-2, 39992). Standard Pub.
Staton, Knofel. Check Your Character (Student) 116p. (Orig.). 1980. pap. 2.25 (ISBN 0-87239-422-0, 39993). Standard Pub.

BEATLES
ESE California. John Lennon. (Front Page News Book Ser.). 1981. lib. bdg. 12.95 (ISBN 0-912076-46-1); pap. 5.95 (ISBN 0-912076-45-3). ESE Calif.
Lennon, John. The Writings of John Lennon: In His Own Write, a Spaniard in the Works. 1981. 9.95 (ISBN 0-671-43257-5). S&S.

BEAUTIFUL, THE
see Art-Philosophy; Esthetics

BEAUTY
see Art-Philosophy; Beauty, Personal; Esthetics

BEAUTY, PERSONAL
see also Beauty Culture; Charm; Clothing and Dress; Cosmetics; Costume; Hair; Hairdressing; Hand; Perfumes; Skin; Teeth
Arpel, Adrien. How to Look Ten Years Younger. 1981. pap. 8.95 (ISBN 0-446-97823-X). Warner Bks.
Avon Products. Looking Good, Feeling Beautiful. 14.95 (ISBN 0-671-25224-0). S&S.
Gold, Sharon. The Woman's Day Book of Beauty, Health & Fitness Hints. LC 80-12022. (Illus.). 166p. 1980. pap. 5.95 (ISBN 0-688-08611-X, Quill). Morrow.
Gross, Joy. The Thirty-Day to a Born-Again Body. 1981. pap. 2.75 (ISBN 0-425-04733-4). Berkley Pub.
Hannon, Sharron. Working Woman's Beauty Book. LC 78-19959. 220p. 1981. pap. 7.95. Stein & Day.
Liddell, Louise A. Clothes & Your Appearance. rev. ed. LC 80-25167. (Illus.). 352p. 1980. 13.20 (ISBN 0-87006-311-1). Good Heart.
McCullough, Prudence. The Do-It-Yourself Super Spa Home Weekend. (Illus., Orig.). 1981. pap. 6.95 (ISBN 0-8092-7083-8). Contemp Bks.
Meredith, Bronwen. The Vogue Body & Beauty Book. (Illus.). 360p. 1981. pap. 6.95 (ISBN 0-89104-199-0). A & W Pubs.
The Natural Way to Beauty. 3.98. Mayflower Bks.
Parkhill, Joe. Health, Beauty & Happiness. spiral 5.95 (ISBN 0-88427-014-9). Green Hill.
Ross, Judith & Acton, Susan. Beauty Makeover Guide. LC 78-19956. 190p. 1981. pap. 6.95 (ISBN 0-8128-6113-2). Stein & Day.
Rubinstein, Helena. Food for Beauty. rev. ed. 256p. 1977. pap. 1.95 (ISBN 0-915962-19-5). Larchmont Bks.
Saffon, M. J. The Fifteen Minute-a-Day Natural Face Lift. 112p. 1981. pap. 3.95 (ISBN 0-446-97788-8). Warner Bks.
Shelmire, Bedford. The Doctor's Overnight Beauty Program. (Illus.). 192p. 1981. 12.95 (ISBN 0-312-21489-8). St Martin.
Stein, Frances P. & Udell, Rochelle. Hot Tips: One Thousand Real Life Fashion & Beauty Tricks. (Illus.). 224p. 1981. 12.95 (ISBN 0-399-12580-9). Putnam.
Tiegs, Cheryl. The Way to Natural Beauty. (Illus.). 1980. 12.95 (ISBN 0-686-68753-1, 24894). S&S.
Walden, Barbara & Lindner, Vicki. Easy Glamour. (Illus.). 224p. 1981. 9.95 (ISBN 0-688-00416-4). Morrow.
Yeager, Trisha. The California Beauty Book: A Total Guide to Bringing Out Your Natural Beauty. (Illus.). 240p. 1981. pap. 9.95 (ISBN 0-936602-11-2). Harbor Pub CA.
York, Alexandra. Lose Ten Years in Ten Days. (Illus.). 192p. 1981. 10.95 (ISBN 0-02-633270-1). Macmillan.

BEAUTY CULTURE
see also Beauty, Personal; Cosmetics; Hairdressing
Ahern, Jerry J. Textbook of Cosmetology. 330p. 1980. pap. text ed. 7.00 (ISBN 0-8299-0309-7); study guide 4.50 (ISBN 0-8299-0319-4); answers to study guide avail. (ISBN 0-8299-0354-2); state board review questions 0.75 (ISBN 0-8299-0375-5); answers to state board review questions avail. (ISBN 0-8299-0379-8). West Pub.
Colletti, Anthony B. La Cosmetologia, la Guia Keystone Para Aprender el Arte De Embellecer. rev. ed. (Span.). 1981. text ed. 16.78 (ISBN 0-912126-61-2, 1260-00); pap. text ed. 12.15 (ISBN 0-912126-62-0, 1261-00). Keystone Pubns.
--Cosmetology Instructor's Guide, No. 1. (Keystone Publications' Audio-Visual Program Ser.). 88p. 1976. 7.10 (ISBN 0-912126-16-7). Keystone Pubns.
--Cosmetology Instructor's Guide, No. 2. (Keystone Publications' Audio-Visual Program Ser.). 80p. 1976. 7.10311 (ISBN 0-912126-17-5). Keystone Pubns.
--Cosmetology Instructor's Guide, No. 3. (Keystone's Publications' Audio-Visual Program Ser.). 136p. 1976. 7.10 (ISBN 0-912126-18-3). Keystone Pubns.
--Cosmetology Instructor's Guide, No. 4. (Keystone Publications' Audio-Visual Program Ser.). 112p. 7.10 (ISBN 0-912126-19-1). Keystone Pubns.
--Cosmetology Review Book. 1981. pap. text ed. 5.00 (ISBN 0-912126-56-6, 1267-00). Keystone Pubns.
--Cosmetology: The Keystone Guide to Beauty Culture. rev. ed. 1981. text ed. 10.00 (ISBN 0-912126-59-0, 1248-00); pap. text ed. 7.14 (ISBN 0-912126-60-4, 1249-00). Keystone Pubns.
Gelb, Lawrence. Your Future in Beauty Culture. rev. ed. (Careers in Depth Ser.). (Illus.). 128p. 1980. lib. bdg. 5.97 (ISBN 0-8239-0201-3). Rosen Pr.

BEAUVOIR, SIMONE DE, 1908-
Ascher, Carol. Simone De Beauvoir: A Life of Freedom. LC 80-70361. 256p. 1981. 13.95 (ISBN 0-8070-3240-9). Beacon Pr.

BEBOP MUSIC
see Jazz Music

BECKETT, SAMUEL BARCLAY, 1906-
Albright, Daniel. Representation & the Imagination: Beckett, Kafka, Nabokov, & Schoenberg. LC 80-26975. (Chicago Originals Ser.). 256p. 1981. lib. bdg. 20.00x (ISBN 0-226-01252-2). U of Chicago Pr.
Toppen. From Caxton to Beckett. 1979. text ed. 42.75x (ISBN 90-6203-581-7). Humanities.

BED-WETTING
see Enuresis
Meadow. Help for Bedwetting. Date not set. pap. text ed. 2.75 (ISBN 0-443-02236-4). Churchill.

BEDDING (HORTICULTURE)
see Gardening

BEDOUINS
Lancaster, William. The Rwala Bedouin Today. (Changing Cultures Ser.). (Illus.). 192p. Date not set. price not set (ISBN 0-521-23877-3); pap. price not set (ISBN 0-521-28275-6). Cambridge U Pr.

BEDS AND BEDSTEADS
Boeschen, John. Successful Bed Book. Case, Virginia A., ed. (Successful Ser.). (Illus.). 200p. 1981. 18.95 (ISBN 0-89999-030-4); pap. 8.95 (ISBN 0-89999-031-2). Structures Pub.

BEDUINS
see Bedouins

BEE CULTURE
see also Honey
Cannon, Hal, compiled by. The Grand Beehive. (Illus.). 88p. (Orig.). 1980. pap. 9.50 (ISBN 0-87480-190-7). U of Utah Pr.
Hopper, Ted. Guide to Bees & Honey. (Illus.). 260p. 1981. 12.50 (ISBN 0-7137-0782-8, Pub. by Blandford Pr England). Sterling.
Lonik, Larry J. The Healthy Taste of Honey: Bee People's Recipes, Anecdotes & Lore. Campbell, Jean, ed. (Orig.). 1981. deluxe ed. write for info. (ISBN 0-89865-020-8). Donning Co.
Moffett, Joseph O. Some Beekeepers & Associates, Pt. I. (Illus.). 140p. lib. bdg. 19.90; pap. 9.90 (ISBN 0-686-28741-X). Moffett.
Morse, Roger A. Bees & Beekeeping. LC 74-14082. (Illus.). 320p. 1975. 17.50x (ISBN 0-8014-0920-9). Comstock.
Sechrist, Edward L. Amateur Beekeeping. LC 55-11865. (Illus.). 148p. 1981. pap. 4.95 (ISBN 0-8159-5001-2). Devin.

BEEKEEPING
see Bee Culture

BEER
see also Malt
Canaday, Downs. The Beer Drinker's Guide to Early Retirement. (Illus.). 96p. 1981. pap. 5.95 (ISBN 0-931896-03-7). Cove View.
Dersch, Lou. Beer, Bubbles & Bucks. 225p. 1981. 9.95 (ISBN 0-86629-008-7). Sunrise MO.
Robertson, James. Great American Beer Book. 1980. pap. 2.95 (ISBN 0-446-93073-3). Warner Bks.
Shanken, Marvin R. The Impact American Beer Market Review & Forecast: Nineteen-Eighty-One Edition. 2nd ed. (Illus.). 60p. 1981. pap. price not set (ISBN 0-918076-15-3). Tasco.
Whitehouse, Albert. Home Brewing: An Illustrated Guide. LC 80-68689. (Illus.). 1981. 12.95 (ISBN 0-7153-7985-2). David & Charles.

BEETHOVEN, LUDWIG VAN, 1770-1827
Deane, Forbes, et al. Fidelio: Beethoven. Hammond, Tom & Blumer, Rodney, trs. 1981. pap. 4.95 (ISBN 0-7145-3823-X). Riverrun NY.
Greene, David B. Temporal Processes in Beethoven's Music. 1981. price not set (ISBN 0-677-05600-1). Gordon.
Hopkins, Antony. The Nine Symphonies of Beethoven. LC 80-27053. (Illus.). 296p. 1981. 20.00 (ISBN 0-295-95823-5). U of Wash Pr.
Lam, Basil. Beethoven String Quartets, 2 vols. Incl. Vol. 1. (BBC Music Guides Ser.: No. 32). 64p. pap. (ISBN 0-295-95423-X); Vol. 2. (BBC Music Guides Ser.: No. 33). 64p. pap. (ISBN 0-295-95424-8). LC 75-5008. (Illus.). 1975. pap. 1.95 ea. U of Wash Pr.

BEHAVIOR
see Conduct of Life; Etiquette

BEHAVIOR (PSYCHOLOGY)
see Animals, Habits and Behavior Of; Human Behavior

BEHAVIOR, COMPARATIVE
see Psychology, Comparative

BEHAVIOR GENETIC ANALYSIS
see Behavior Genetics

BEHAVIOR GENETICS
Eglash, Albert, ed. Psychogenesis of Coronary Heart Disease: A Syllabus for Medical Researchers. (Bibliographies in Psychosomatic Medicine Ser.: No. 1, Myocardial Infraction). (Illus.). 110p. (Orig.). 1980. lib. bdg. 20.00 (ISBN 0-935320-20-2). Quest Pr.
Ehrman, Lee & Parsons, Peter. Behavior Genetics & Evolution. (Illus.). 448p. 1981. text ed. 22.95 (ISBN 0-07-019276-6, C). McGraw.
Giannini, A. James. Psychitric, Psychologenic, & Somatopsychic Disorders Handbook. 1978. pap. 14.50 (ISBN 0-87488-596-5). Med Exam.

BEHAVIOR IN ORGANIZATIONS
see Organizational Behavior

BEHAVIOR MODIFICATION
see also Behavior Therapy
Bijou, Sidney W. & Ruiz, Roberto. Contribution of Behavior Modification to Education. 352p. 1980. text ed. 24.95 (ISBN 0-89859-024-8). L Erlbaum Assocs.
Lazarus, Arnold A. The Practice of Multimodal Therapy. (Illus.). 256p. 1981. 18.95 (ISBN 0-07-036813-9, P&R&B). McGraw.
Malott, Richard. Contingency Management in Education & Other Equally Exciting Places. 2nd ed. (Illus.). 260p. 1972. pap. text ed. 10.00 (ISBN 0-914474-08-1); instr's. quiz manual avail. F Fournies.
Malott, Richard, et al. Behavior Analysis & Behavior Modification: An Introduction. LC 78-380. (Illus.). 442p. (Orig.). 1978. pap. 11.00 (ISBN 0-914474-20-0); tests avail. F Fournies.
Stuart, Richard B., ed. Violent Behavior: Social Learning Approaches to Prediction, Management & Treatment. 400p. 1981. 20.00 (ISBN 0-87630-262-2). Brunner-Mazel.
Watson, David L. & Tharp, Roland G. Self Directed Behavior: Self-Modification for Personal Adjustment. 3rd ed. LC 80-24411. 300p. 1981. text ed. 10.95 (ISBN 0-8185-0443-9). Brooks-Cole.

BEHAVIOR OF CHILDREN
see Children-Management; Etiquette for Children and Youth

BEHAVIOR PROBLEMS (CHILDREN)
see Problem Children

BEHAVIOR THERAPY
Ader, Robert, ed. Psychoneuroimmunology. LC 80-265. (Behavioral Medicine Ser.). 1981. price not set (ISBN 0-12-043780-5). Acad Pr.

Algozzine, Bob, et al. Sourcebook of Research & Practice in Behavioral Disorders. 375p. 1981. text ed. price not set (ISBN 0-89443-345-8). Aspen Systems.

Caine, Tom, et al. Personal Styles in Neurosis: Implications for Small Group Psychotherapy & Behavior Therapy. (International Library of Group Psychotherapy & Group Process). 224p. write for info. (ISBN 0-7100-0617-9). Routledge & Kegan.

Commons, Michael & Nevin, John A., eds. Discriminative Properties of Reinforcement Schedules. (The Quantitative Analysis of Behavior Ser.). 1981. price not set professional reference (ISBN 0-88410-377-3). Ballinger Pub.

Daitzman, Reid J. Clinical Behavior: Therapy & Behavior Modification, Vol. 2. LC 79-14455. 304p. 1980. lib. bdg. 32.50 (ISBN 0-8240-7217-0). Garland Pub.

Hersen, Michel & Bellack, Alan, eds. Behavioral Assessment: A Practical Handbook. 2nd ed. (Pergamon General Psychology Ser.: No. 98). (Illus.). 500p. 1981. 42.50 (ISBN 0-08-025956-1); pap. 19.50 (ISBN 0-08-025955-3). Pergamon.

Imber, Steve, ed. Readings in Emotional & Behavioral Disorders. rev. ed. (Special Education Ser.). (Illus.). 224p. pap. text ed. 9.95 (ISBN 0-89568-294-X). Spec Learn Corp.

Kaszniak, Alfred W. An Introduction to the Biological Bases of Behavior for the Health Professions. (Behavioral Sciences for Health Care Professionals Ser.). 128p. (Orig.). 1981. lib. bdg. 15.00x (ISBN 0-86531-010-6); pap. text ed. 6.00x (ISBN 0-86531-011-4). Westview.

Lazarus, Arnold A. The Practice of Multimodal Therapy. (Illus.). 256p. 1981. 18.95 (ISBN 0-07-036813-9, P&R&B). McGraw.

O'Banion, Dan R. An Ecological & Nutritional Approach to Behavioral Medicine. (Illus.). 248p. 1981. price not set (ISBN 0-398-04457-0). C C Thomas.

Rachman, S., ed. Advances in Behaviour Research & Therapy, Vol. 2. (Illus.). 186p. 1980. 84.00 (ISBN 0-08-027110-3). Pergamon.

Sgro, Joseph A., ed. Virginia Tech Symposium on Applied Behavioral Science, Vol. I. LC 80-8614. 1981. 28.95 (ISBN 0-669-04332-X). Lexington Bks.

Strub, Richard L. & Black, F. William. Organic Brain Syndromes: An Introduction to Neurobehavioral Disorders. (Illus.). 500p. 1981. text ed. 25.00 (ISBN 0-8036-8209-3, 8209-3). Davis Co.

Walker, C. Eugene, et al. Clinical Procedures for Behavior Therapy. (Illus.). 464p. 1981. text ed. 18.95 (ISBN 0-13-137794-9). P-H.

Weiss, Stephen M., et al, eds. Perspectives on Behavioral Medicine 1980, Vol. I. (Serial Publication). 1981. price not set (ISBN 0-12-532101-5). Acad Pr.

BEHAVIORAL GENETICS

see Behavior Genetics

BEHAVIORAL PHARMACOLOGY

see Psychopharmacology

BEHAVIORISM (PSYCHOLOGY)

Cozby, Paul C. Methods in Behavioral Research. 2nd ed. (Illus.). 300p. 1981. pap. text ed. price not set (ISBN 0-87484-521-1). Mayfield Pub.

Gordon, Laura B. Behavioral Intervention in Health Care. (Behavioral Sciences for Health Care Professionals Ser.). 128p. 1981. lib. bdg. 15.00x (ISBN 0-86531-018-1); pap. text ed. 6.00x (ISBN 0-86531-019-X). Westview.

Hardin, Veralee & Busch, Robert L. Manual for Behavior Rating Scale. 1975. saddle stitched 19.75. Lucas.

BEIRUT, LEBANON

Tabbara, Lina M. Survival in Beirut. (Illus.). 186p. 1977. cased 16.00; pap. 7.00. Three Continents.

BEL CANTO

Coffin, Berton. Coffin's Overtones of Bel Canto: Phonetic Basis of Artistic Singing with One Hundred Chromatic Vowel-Chart Exercises. LC 80-21958. 254p. 1980. text ed. 20.00 (ISBN 0-8108-1370-X); Accompanying Chart. 7.50; Set. 27.50. Scarecrow.

Corte, Andrea D., ed. Canto E Bel Canto P.F. Tosi: Opinioni De Cantori Antchi E Moderni Seventeen Twenty Three. LC 80-2268. 1981. Repr. of 1933 ed. 31.50 (ISBN 0-404-18823-0). AMS Pr.

BELGIAN ART

see Art, Belgian

BELGIAN LITERATURE (FLEMISH)

see Flemish Literature

BELGIUM–DESCRIPTION AND TRAVEL

Lanier, Alison R. Update -- Belgium. (Country Orientation Ser.). 1980. pap. text ed. 25.00 (ISBN 0-933662-28-9). Intercult Network.

BELGIUM–DESCRIPTION AND TRAVEL–GUIDEBOOKS

Bristow, Philip. Through the Belgian Canals. 160p. 1980. 9.00x (ISBN 0-245-50975-5, Pub. by Nautical England). State Mutual Bk.

BELGIUM–JUVENILE LITERATURE

Goldstein, Frances. Children's Treasure Hunt Travel to Belgium & France. LC 80-85012. (Children's Treasure Hunt Travel Guide Ser.). (Illus.). 230p. (Orig.). (gr. k-12). 1981. pap. 4.95 (ISBN 0-933334-02-8). Paper Tiger Pap.

BELIEF AND DOUBT

Here are entered works treating the subject from the philosophical standpoint. Works on religious belief are entered under the heading Faith.

see also Faith; Truth

Comportamento Do Crente. (Portuguese Bks.). 1979. write for info. (ISBN 0-8297-0650-X). Life Pubs Intl.

Connolly, John R. Dimensions of Belief & Unbelief. LC 80-67241. 373p. 1981. lib. bdg. 21.75 (ISBN 0-8191-1389-1); pap. text ed. 12.75 (ISBN 0-8191-1390-5). U Pr of Amer.

Koffarnus, Richard. Why Believe? LC 80-53673. 96p. (Orig.). 1981. pap. 2.25 (ISBN 0-87239-425-5, 40090). Standard Pub.

Williams, Morris, tr. Le Comportement Du Croyant. (French Bks.). (Fr.). 1979. write for info. (ISBN 0-8297-0833-2). Life Pubs Intl.

BELLE-ALLIANCE, BATTLE OF, 1815

see Waterloo, Battle Of, 1815

BELLES-LETTRES

see Literature

BELLY DANCE

Aradoon, Zarifa. Belly Dance Costume Book. rev. ed. Bain, David, ed. LC 77-88919. (Illus.). 1981. pap. 15.00 (ISBN 0-930486-04-8). Dream Place.

BELOUTCHI LANGUAGE

see Baluchi Language

BELT CONVEYORS

see Conveying Machinery

BEMIS'S HEIGHTS, BATTLE OF, 1777

see Saratoga Campaign, 1777

BENEDICTINES

Fry, Timothy, et al, eds. The Rule of Saint Benedict RB 1980: In Latin and English with Notes. 650p. 1981. 21.95 (ISBN 0-8146-1211-3); pap. 16.95 (ISBN 0-8146-1220-2). Liturgical Pr.

Lunn, David. The English Benedictines, Fifteen Forty to Sixteen Eighty-Eight: Reformation to Revolution. (Illus.). 282p. 1980. 24.95x. B&N.

Oury, Guy-Marie. St. Benedict: Blessed by God. Otto, John A., tr. from Fr. LC 80-13253. Orig. Title: Ce que croyait Benoit. (Orig.). 1980. pap. text ed. 4.50 (ISBN 0-8146-1181-8). Liturgical Pr.

Turner & Rogers. The Benedictines in Britain. Date not set. 12.95 (ISBN 0-8076-0992-7). Braziller.

BENEDICTUS, SAINT, ABBOT OF MONTE CASSINO, 480-550

Oury, Guy-Marie. St. Benedict: Blessed by God. Otto, John A., tr. from Fr. LC 80-13253. Orig. Title: Ce que croyait Benoit. (Orig.). 1980. pap. text ed. 4.50 (ISBN 0-8146-1181-8). Liturgical Pr.

BENEFIT SOCIETIES

see Friendly Societies

BENEVOLENT INSTITUTIONS

see Asylums; Hospitals

BENGAL–SOCIAL CONDITIONS

Ray, Ratnalakha. Change in Bengal Agrarian Society, Seventeen Sixty to Eighteen Fifty. 1980. 20.00x (ISBN 0-8364-0646-X, Pub. by Manohar India). South Asia Bks.

BENI MARIN DYNASTY

Cigar, Norman, ed. Muhammad Al-Qadiris Nashr Al Mathani: The Chronicles. (Fontes Historiae Africanae Ser.). (Illus.). 400p. 1980. 89.00 (ISBN 0-19-725994-4). Oxford U Pr.

BENNETT, ARNOLD, 1867-1931

Darton, Harvey. Arnold Bennett. 127p. 1980. Repr. lib. bdg. 17.50 (ISBN 0-89760-131-9). Telegraph Bks.

Hepburn, James. Arnold Bennett: The Critical Heritage. (The Critical Heritage Ser.). 576p. 1981. pap. 48.50 (ISBN 0-7100-0512-1). Routledge & Kegan.

BENTON, THOMAS HART, 1889-1975

Burroughs, Polly. Thomas Hart Benton: A Portrait. LC 77-16903. (Illus.). 208p. 1981. 29.95 (ISBN 0-385-12342-6). Doubleday.

BENTONITE

Folk, R. L., et al. Field Excursion, Central Texas: Tertiary Bentonites of Central Texas. 53p. 1973. Repr. of 1961 ed. 1.25 (GB 3). Bur Econ Geology.

BENZENE

Buikema, Arthur L., Jr. & Hendricks, Albert C. Benzene, Xylene, & Toluene in Aquatic Systems: A Review. LC 80-67170. (Illus.). 69p. (Orig.). pap. 3.75 (ISBN 0-89364-038-7, API 847-86250). Am Petroleum.

BEOWULF–BIBLIOGRAPHY

Short, Douglas D. Beowulf Scholarship: An Annotated Bibliography. LC 79-7924. 353p. 1980. lib. bdg. 38.00 (ISBN 0-8240-9530-8). Garland Pub.

BERING LAND BRIDGE

Hadleigh-West, Frederick. The Archaeology of Beringia. (Illus.). 320p. 1981. 30.00x (ISBN 0-231-05172-7). Columbia U Pr.

BERNARD DE CLAIRVAUX, SAINT, 1091?-1153

Elder, E. Rozanne & Sommerfeldt, John R., eds. The Chimaera of His Age: Studies in Medieval Cistercian History V. (Cistercian Studies Ser.: No. 63). 146p. 1980. pap. 8.95 (ISBN 0-87907-863-4). Cistercian Pubns.

BERNINI, GIOVANNI LORENZO, 1598-1680

Lavin, Irving. Bernini & the Unity of the Visual Arts, 2 vols. (Illus.). 498p. 1980. text ed. 89.00x (ISBN 0-19-520184-1). Oxford U Pr.

BERRIES

Fulwiler, Kyle D. The Berry Cookbook. 120p. 1981. pap. 5.95 (ISBN 0-914718-59-2). Pacific Search.

Hendrickson, Robert. The Berry Book: The Illustrated Home Gardener's Guide to Growing & Using Over 50 Kinds & 300 Varieties of Berries from Strawberries, Blueberries & Raspberries to Currants, Dewberries, & Gooseberries. LC 78-22326. (Illus.). 192p. 1981. 9.95 (ISBN 0-385-13589-0). Doubleday.

Nuts, Berries & Grapes. (Country Home Ser.). 96p. 2.95 (ISBN 0-88453-009-4). Berkshire Traveller.

BERRIGAN, DANIEL

Deedy, Jack. Apologies, Good Friends... An Interim Biography of Daniel Berrigan, S. J. 152p. 1981. pap. 6.95 (ISBN 0-8190-0641-6). Fides Claretian.

BERRY, CHUCK, 1926-

Dewitt, Howard A. Chuck Berry: Rock'n'roll Music. (Illus.). 120p. (Orig.). 1981. 12.95 (ISBN 0-938840-01-0); pap. 5.95 (ISBN 0-938840-00-2). Horizon Bks CA.

BERTALANFFY, LUDWIG VON, 1901-1972

Von Bertalanffy, Ludwig. A Systems View of Man: Collected Essays by Ludwig Von Bertalanffy. LaViolette, Paul, ed. 190p. 1981. lib. bdg. 16.00 (ISBN 0-86531-084-X); pap. 7.95 (ISBN 0-86531-094-7). Westview.

BEST BOOKS

see Bibliography–Best Books

BEST SELLERS

see also Bibliography–Best Books

Bocca, Geoffrey. Best-Seller: A Nostalgic Celebration of the Less Than Great Books You Have Always Been Afraid to Admit You Loved. 1981. 12.95 (Wyndham Bks). S&S.

Sutherland, John. Best Sellers: Popular Fiction of the 1970s. 272p. 1981. 18.95 (ISBN 0-7100-0750-7). Routledge & Kegan.

BETA FUNCTIONS

see Functions, Beta

BETCHERRYGAH

see Budgerigars

BETHUNE, MARY JANE (MCCLEOD), 1875-1955

Carruth, Ella K. She Wanted to Read: The Story of Mary Bethune. (Illus.). (gr. 3-5). 1969. pap. 1.25 (ISBN 0-671-29861-5). PB.

BETON

see Concrete

BETTING

see Gambling

BEVERAGES

see also Alcoholic Beverages

also names of beverages, e.g. Cocoa, Coffee, Tea

Adams, Ruth & Murray, Frank. All You Should Know About Beverages for Your Health & Well Being. 286p. 1976. pap. 1.75 (ISBN 0-915962-17-9). Larchmont Bks.

Paterson, Wilma. A Country Cup: Old & New Recipes for Drinks of All Kinds Made from Wild Plants & Herbs. (Illus.). 88p. (Orig.). 1981. 11.95 (ISBN 0-7207-1234-3). Merrimack Bk Serv.

Smith, C. Carter. The Art of Mixing Drinks. (Orig.). 1981. pap. 7.95 (ISBN 0-446-97759-4). Warner Bks.

Van Kleek, Peter E. Beverage Management & Bartending. 144p. 1981. pap. text ed. 7.95 (ISBN 0-8436-2209-1). CBI Pub.

Woodroof, J. G. & Phillips, G. Frank. Beverages: Carbonated & Noncarbonated. rev. ed. (Illus.). 1981. lib. bdg. 45.00 (ISBN 0-87055-381-X). AVI.

BHAGAVADGITA

Feurstein, G. Bhagavad Gita: A Critical Rendering. 1981. text ed. write for info. (ISBN 0-391-02191-5). Humanities.

Ghandhi, Mohandas K. The Teaching of the Gita. Hingorani, Anand T., ed. 103p. (Orig.). 1981. pap. 2.00 (ISBN 0-934676-26-7). Greenlf Bks.

BHAGAVATAS

Gill, Harjeet S. A Phulkari from Bhatinda. 1980. 17.50x (ISBN 0-89955-322-2, Pub. by Interprint India). Intl Schol Bk Serv.

Gopal, Madan. Tulasi Das. 120p. 1980. 6.95x (ISBN 0-89955-320-6, Pub. by Interprint India). Intl Schol Bk Serv.

The Song Celestial: Shrimad Bhagavad Gita. 151p. 1980. 6.50x (ISBN 0-89955-328-1, Pub. by Interprint India). Intl Schol Bk Serv.

BHAGVATAS

see Bhagavatas

BHAGVATS

see Bhagavatas

BHUTTO, ZULFIQUAR ALI, 1928-

Bhutto, Z. My Execution. 1980. 10.00x (ISBN 0-8364-0650-8, Pub. by Muswati India). South Asia Bks.

BIBLE–ANIMALS

see Bible–Natural History

BIBLE–ANTHROPOLOGY

see Man (Theology)

BIBLE–ANTIQUITIES

see also Christian Antiquities

also subdivision Antiquities under names of Biblical countries and cities

Baez-Camargo, Gonzalo. Comentario Arqueologica de la Biblia. 339p. (Orig., Span.). 1979. pap. 7.25 (ISBN 0-89922-148-3). Edit Caribe.

Chavez, Moises. Enfoque Arqueologico del Mundo de la Biblia. LC 76-25325. 138p. (Orig., Span.). pap. 3.25 (ISBN 0-89922-076-2). Edit Caribe.

Finegan, Jack. The Archaeology of the New Testament: The Mediterranean World of the Early Christian Apostles. (Illus.). 400p. 1981. 35.00x (ISBN 0-86531-064-5). Westview.

Lance, H. Darrell. The Old Testament & the Archaeologist. Tucker, Gene M., ed. LC 80-2387. (Guides to Biblical Scholarship: Old Testament Ser.). 112p. (Orig.). 1981. pap. 4.50 (ISBN 0-8006-0467-9, 1-467). Fortress.

Perkins, Ann L. The Comparative Archeology of Early Mesopotamia. LC 49-10748. (Studies in Ancient Oriental Civilization: No. 25). (Illus.). xx, 201p. (Orig.). 1977. pap. text ed. 14.00x (ISBN 0-226-62396-3). Oriental Inst.

Thompson, J. A. The Bible & Archaeology. wnd, rev. ed. 512p. 1981. 13.95 (ISBN 0-8028-3545-7). Eerdmans.

BIBLE–ARCHAEOLOGY

see Bible–Antiquities

BIBLE–ATLASES

see Bible–Geography–Maps

BIBLE–BIOGRAPHY

see also Apostles; Prophets; Women In the Bible

also names of individuals mentioned in the Bible, e.g. Moses; Mary, Virgin

Barron, Sr. Mary C. Unveiled Faces: Men & Women of the Bible. (Illus.). 120p. 1981. pap. 4.50 (ISBN 0-8146-1212-1). Liturgical Pr.

Coggins, Richard. Who's Who in the Bible: From Historic Sources. (Illus.). 232p. 1981. 16.50x (ISBN 0-686-69582-8). B&N.

Crouch, Brodie. Study of Minor Prophets. pap. 2.50 (ISBN 0-89315-291-9). Lambert Bk.

Dugan, LeRoy. Old Testament Heroes, No. 1. 80p. (Orig.). (ps-4). 1981. pap. 1.49 oversized, saddle stitched (ISBN 0-87123-705-9, 220705). Bethany Fell.

Ivins, Dan. God's People in Transition. Date not set. 5.95 (ISBN 0-8054-6932-X). Broadman.

Turner, J. J. Study of Bible Leaders. pap. 2.50 (ISBN 0-89315-290-0). Lambert Bk.

BIBLE–BIOGRAPHY–O. T.

Nickelsburg, George W. Jewish Literature Between the Bible & the Mishnah: A Historical & Literary Introduction. LC 80-16176. 352p. 1981. 19.95 (ISBN 0-8006-0649-3, 1-649). Fortress.

Scruggs, Rachel I. Come, Follow Me. 1981. 7.95 (ISBN 0-533-04769-2). Vantage.

BIBLE–BIRDS

see Bible–Natural History

BIBLE–BOTANY

see Bible–Natural History

BIBLE–CANON

Reid, John K. The Authority of Scripture: A Study of the Reformation & Post-Reformation Understanding of the Bible. LC 79-8716. 286p. 1981. Repr. of 1962 ed. lib. bdg. 25.00x (ISBN 0-313-22191-X, REAS). Greenwood.

BIBLE–CATECHISMS, QUESTION-BOOKS, ETC.

see also Bible Games and Puzzles

Makrakis, Apostolos. Divine & Sacred Catechism. Orthodox Christian Educational Society, ed. 224p. 1946. 4.00x (ISBN 0-938366-15-7). Orthodox Chr.

Redemptorist Pastoral Publication. The Illustrated Catechism. 112p. (Orig.). 1981. pap. 3.95 (ISBN 0-89243-135-0). Liguori Pubns.

BIBLE–CHARACTERS

see Bible–Biography

BIBLE–CODICES

see Bible–Manuscripts

BIBLE–COMMENTARIES

Here are entered only commentaries on the whole Bible. Commentaries on the New Testament, and portions of the New Testament, precede commentaries on the Old Testament, and portions of the Old testament.

Berry, R. L. Steps Heavenward. 123p. pap. 1.00. Faith Pub Hse.

Biblia a Su Alcance, 8 bks. Incl. Bk. 1. Genesis a Nehemias. write for info. (ISBN 0-8297-0736-0); Bk. 2. Job a Jeremias. 3.25 (ISBN 0-8297-0737-9); Bk. 3. Lamentaciones a Malaquias. 3.25 (ISBN 0-8297-0738-7); Bk. 4. Mateo a 11 Corintios. 3.25 (ISBN 0-8297-0739-5); Bk. 5. Galatas-Romanos-Filipenses-Colosenses. 3.25 (ISBN 0-686-28838-6); Bk. 6. Filomeno 1-11 Timothy-Tito-Hebreos. 3.25 (ISBN 0-8297-0741-7); Bk. 7. Santiago 1-11 Pedro-Judas 1-11-11 John. 3.25 (ISBN 0-8297-0742-5); Bk. 8. Apocalipsis. 2.25 (ISBN 0-8297-0743-3). 1977. Life Pubs Intl.

Crouch, Owen. What the Bible Says About the Bible. (What the Bible Says Ser.). 400p. 1981. 13.50 (ISBN 0-89900-082-7). College Pr Pub.

Ellicott, Charles J. Ellicott's Four Volume Bible Commentary (Unabridged) 4580p. 1981. Repr. 119.95 (ISBN 0-310-43878-0). Zondervan.

Gunneweg, Antonius H. & Schmithals, Walter. Achievement. Smith, David, tr. LC 80-26977. (Biblical Encounter Ser.). 208p. (Orig.). 1981. pap. 7.95 (ISBN 0-687-00690-2). Abingdon.

Harper, W. R. Amos & Hosea. LC 5-7893. (International Critical Commentary Ser.). 608p. Repr. of 1905 ed. text ed. 20.00x (ISBN 0-567-05018-1). Attic Pr.

Ironside, H. A. The Best of H. A. Ironside. (Best Ser.). 296p. (Orig.). 1981. pap. 4.95 (ISBN 0-8010-5033-2). Baker Bk.

Lange, John P. Lange's Commentary on the Holy Scriptures, 12 vols. 1980. Repr. Set. 219.00 (ISBN 0-310-27198-3). Zondervan.

Lockyer, Herbert. Light to Live by (Wedding Edition) 384p. 1981. 7.95 (ISBN 0-310-28260-8). Zondervan.

Lubich, Chiara. Words to Live By. Moran, Hugh, ed. Dauphinais, Raymond, tr. from Fr. & Ital. LC 80-82419. Orig. Title: Paroles Pour Vivre. 160p. (Orig.). 1980. pap. 4.50 (ISBN 0-911782-08-7). New City.

O'Donovan, Daniel, tr. Bernard of Clairvaux, Treatises III: On Grace & Free Choice, in Praise of the New Knighthood. (Cistercian Studies Ser.: No. 3). 1977. 10.95 (ISBN 0-87907-119-2); pap. 4.95 (ISBN 0-87907-719-0). Cistercian Pubns.

Penelope, Sr., tr. William of St. Thierry: On Contemplating God, Prayer, Meditations. (Cistercian Fathers Ser.: No. 3). 1970. pap. 4.00 (ISBN 0-87907-903-7). Cistercian Pubns.

Randolph, Boris. Bible Verses in Verse. LC 80-67992. 144p. 1980. pap. 3.95 (ISBN 0-87516-424-2). De Vorss.

Riedel, Eunice, et al. The Book of the Bible. 560p. 1981. pap. 3.95 (ISBN 0-553-14649-1). Bantam.

Sabourin, Leopold. The Bible & Christ: The Unity of the Two Testaments. LC 80-14892. 208p. (Orig.). 1980. pap. 6.95 (ISBN 0-8189-0405-4). Alba.

Smith, F. G. What the Bible Teaches. 576p. Repr. of 1914 ed. 5.50. Faith Pub Hse.

Spurgeon, Charles H. Guide to Commentaries. Date not set. 0.30 (ISBN 0-686-28947-1). Banner of Truth.

Turretin, Francis. The Doctrine of Scripture: Locus 2 of Institutio Theologiae Elencticae. Beardslee, John W., III, ed. 200p. (Orig.). 1981. 12.95 (ISBN 0-8010-8858-5); pap. 7.95 (ISBN 0-8010-8857-7). Baker Bk.

Vincent, Thomas. The Shorter Catechism Explained from Scripture. (Puritan Paperbacks). 282p. (Orig.). 1980. pap. 3.95 (ISBN 0-85151-314-X). Banner of Truth.

Wells, Paul R. James Barr & the Bible: Critique of a New Liberalism. 1980. pap. 12.00 (ISBN 0-87552-546-6). Presby & Reformed.

Whyte, A. Commentary on the Shorter Catechism. (Handbook for Bible Classes Ser.). 213p. pap. text ed. 8.95 (ISBN 0-567-28144-2). Attic Pr.

BIBLE-COMMENTARIES-N. T.

Here are entered only Commentaries on the New Testament as a whole.

Bratcher, R. G., ed. Marginal Notes for the New Testament. 1980. softcover 2.30 (ISBN 0-8267-0026-8, 08558). United Bible.

Cullmann, Oscar. The Christology of the New Testament. rev. ed. Guthrie, Shirley C. & Hall, Charles A., trs. LC 59-10178. pap. 11.95. Westminster.

Fitzmyer, J. A. To Advance the Gospel: New Testament Essays. 320p. 1981. 19.50 (ISBN 0-8245-0008-3). Crossroad NY.

Forestell, J. T. Targumic Traditions & the New Testament. LC 79-19293. (Society of Biblical Literature Aramaic Studies: No. 4). pap. 12.00 (06 13 04). Scholars Pr CA.

Hollinson, Harry. Background to the New Testament. 4.00x (ISBN 0-392-07650-0, SpS). Soccer.

Malina, Bruce J. The New Testament World: Insights from Cultural Anthropology. (Illus.). 224p. 1981. pap. 8.95 (ISBN 0-8042-0423-3). John Knox.

Pritchard, John P. A Literary Approach to the New Testament. LC 72-1793. (Illus.). 355p. 1981. pap. 7.95 (ISBN 0-8061-1710-9). U of Okla Pr.

Pruitt, Fred. The New Testament Church & Its Symbols. 131p. 1.00. Faith Pub Hse.

Religious Education Staff. Insights: Spirit Masters for Reading the New Testament. (To Live Is Christ Ser.). 1978. 12.95 (ISBN 0-697-01674-8). Wm C Brown.

Reuchlin, Abelard. The True Authorship of the New Testament. 1979. pap. 2.00. Vector Assocs.

Schell, William G. The Ordinances of the New Testament. 67p. pap. 0.50. Faith Pub Hse.

Simcox, W. H. Writers of the New Testament. Date not set. 8.95 (ISBN 0-88469-139-X). BMH Bks.

Trapp, John. A Commentary on the New Testament. 864p. 1981. Repr. of 1865 ed. 19.95 (ISBN 0-8010-8855-0). Baker Bk.

BIBLE-COMMENTARIES-N. T. ACTS

Alexander, J. A. Acts of the Apostles, 2 vols. in 1. (Banner of Truth Geneva Series Commentaries). 1980. 19.95 (ISBN 0-85151-309-3). Banner of Truth.

Horton, Stanley M. The Book of Acts: A Radiant Commentary on the New Testament. LC 80-65892. 304p. 1981. 10.95 (ISBN 0-88243-317-2, 02-0317). Gospel Pub.

Lindsay, T. M. Acts, Vol. 2, Chapts. 13-28. (Handbooks for Bible Classes). 165p. 1950. text ed. 3.50 (ISBN 0-567-08117-6). Attic Pr.

BIBLE-COMMENTARIES-N. T. CATHOLIC EPISTLES

Here are entered commentaries on the Catholic Epistles as a whole, as well as on one or more of the following Epistles: James, John, Jude, Peter.

Bigg, Charles. Saint Peter & Saint Jude, 2 vols. LC 2-12311. (International Critical Commentary Ser.). 376p. Repr. of 1978 ed. Vol. 1, 534p. 20.00x (ISBN 0-567-05036-X); Vol. 2, 580p. 22.00x (ISBN 0-567-05012-2). Attic Pr.

Brooke, A. E. The Johannine Epistles. LC 13-170. (International Critical Commentary Ser.). 336p. 1912. text ed. 17.50x (ISBN 0-567-05037-8). Attic Pr.

Brown, John. First Peter, 2 vols. 1980. 29.95 (ISBN 0-85151-204-6); Vol. 1, 577 Pp. (ISBN 0-85151-205-4); Vol. 2, 640 Pp. (ISBN 0-85151-206-2). Banner of Truth.

--Parting Counsels: Exposition of II Peter 1. (Banner of Truth Geneva Series Commentaries). 1980. 11.50 (ISBN 0-85151-301-8). Banner of Truth.

Criswell, W. A. Expository Sermons on the Epistles of Peter. 216p. (Orig.). 1980. pap. 4.95 (ISBN 0-310-22811-5). Zondervan.

Hastings, James. The Great Texts of the Bible: James-Jude. 439p. Repr. of 1912 ed. 5.00x (ISBN 0-567-06719-X). Attic Pr.

Kelly, J. N. A Commentary of the Pastoral Epistles. (Thornapple Commentaries Ser.). 272p. 1981. pap. 6.95 (ISBN 0-8010-5428-1). Baker Bk.

Moffatt, James. James, Hebrews. LC 24-21703. (International Critical Commentary Ser.). 336p. Repr. of 1924 ed. text ed. 17.50 (ISBN 0-567-05034-3). Attic Pr.

Ropes, J. H. Saint James. LC 16-6543. (International Critical Commentary Ser.). 336p. Repr. of 1916 ed. 17.50x (ISBN 0-567-05035-1). Attic Pr.

Selwyn, Edward G. The First Epistle of St. Peter. 2nd ed. (Thornapple Commentaries Ser.). 517p. 1981. pap. 10.95 (ISBN 0-8010-8199-8). Baker Bk.

BIBLE-COMMENTARIES-N. T. COLOSSIANS

Abbott, T. K. Ephesians & Colossians. LC 40-15742. (International Critical Commentary Ser.). 392p. Repr. of 1979 ed. 21.00x (ISBN 0-567-05030-0). Attic Pr.

Moule, H. C. G. Colossian & Philemon Studies. Date not set. 10.50 (ISBN 0-86524-052-3). Klock & Klock.

Trevethan, Thomas. Our Joyful Confidence: The Lordship of Jesus in Colossians. 220p. (Orig.). 1981. pap. 5.95 (ISBN 0-87784-749-5). Inter Varsity.

Vaughan, Curtis. Colossians & Philemon: A Study Guide Commentary. (Study Guide Commentary Ser.). 144p. (Orig.). 1981. pap. 3.50 (ISBN 0-310-33583-3). Zondervan.

Wilson, Geoffrey B. Colossians & Philemon. (Wilson'a New Testament Commentaries). 111p. (Orig.). 1980. pap. 3.95 (ISBN 0-85151-313-1). Banner of Truth.

BIBLE-COMMENTARIES-N. T. CORINTHIANS

Plummer, Alfred. Corinthians II. LC 16-915. (International Critical Commentary Ser.). 462p. Repr. of 1916 ed. text ed. 23.00x (ISBN 0-567-05028-9). Attic Pr.

Robertson, A. & Plummer, A. Corinthians I. (International Critical Commentary Ser.). 496p. Repr. of 1978 ed. write for info. (ISBN 0-567-05027-0). Attic Pr.

Wilson, Geoffrey. First Corinthians. 1978. pap. 3.95. Banner of Truth.

--Second Corinthians. 1979. pap. 3.95 (ISBN 0-85151-295-X). Banner of Truth.

BIBLE-COMMENTARIES-N. T. EPHESIANS

Abbott, T. K. Ephesians & Colossians. LC 40-15742. (International Critical Commentary Ser.). 392p. Repr. of 1979 ed. 21.00x (ISBN 0-567-05030-0). Attic Pr.

Criswell, W. A. Ephesians: An Exposition. 308p. 1981. pap. 6.95 (ISBN 0-310-22781-X). Zondervan.

Lloyd-Jones, D. Martyn. Christian Unity: An Exposition of Ephesians 4: 1-16. 280p. 1981. 9.95 (ISBN 0-8010-5607-1). Baker Bk.

Wilson, Geoffrey. Ephesians. 1978. pap. 2.95 (ISBN 0-85151-263-1). Banner of Truth.

BIBLE-COMMENTARIES-N. T. EPISTLES OF JOHN

see Bible-Commentaries-N. T. Catholic Epistles

BIBLE-COMMENTARIES-N. T. EPISTLES OF PAUL

Coniaris, A. M. Treasures from Paul's Letters, Vol. I. 1978. pap. 5.95 (ISBN 0-937032-05-0). Light & Life Pub Co MN.

--Treasures from Paul's Letters, Vol. II. 1979. pap. 5.95 (ISBN 0-937032-06-9). Light & Life Pub Co MN.

Epistles of Paul: Hebrews. (Banner of Truth Geneva Series Commentaries). 1978. 21.95. Banner of Truth.

Leggett, Gary. Letters to Timothy. LC 80-82830. (Radiant Life Ser.). 128p. 1981. 1.95 (ISBN 0-88243-877-8, 02-0877). Gospel Pub.

Lightfoot, J. B. Notes on the Epistles of St. Paul. Date not set. 12.95 (ISBN 0-88469-137-3). BMH Bks.

Stanley, Arthur P. Epistles of Paul to the Corinthians. Date not set. 20.95 (ISBN 0-86524-051-5). Klock & Klock.

BIBLE-COMMENTARIES-N. T. GALATIANS

Burton, E. D. Galatians. LC 20-21079. (International Critical Commentary Ser.). 632p. 1920. text ed. 23.00x (ISBN 0-567-05029-7). Attic Pr.

Stagg, Frank. Galatians & Romans. (Knox Pereaching Guides Ser.). 160p. (Orig.). 1980. pap. 4.50 (ISBN 0-8042-3238-5). John Knox.

Wilson, Geoffrey. Galatians. 1979. pap. 3.50 (ISBN 0-85151-294-1). Banner of Truth.

BIBLE-COMMENTARIES-N. T. GOSPELS

Here are entered commentaries on the Gospels as a whole, as well as on the Individual Gospels, Matthew, Mark, Luke, John.

Alexander, Joseph A. Mark. (Thornapple Commentaries Ser.). 1980. pap. 8.95 (ISBN 0-8010-0150-1). Baker Bk.

--Matthew. (Thornapple Commentaries Ser.). 1980. pap. 8.95 (ISBN 0-8010-0146-3). Baker Bk.

Aquinas, Thomas. Commentary on the Gospel of St. John, 2 pts. Weisheipl, James A., ed. Larcher, Fabian R., tr. from Lat. LC 66-19306. (Aquinas Scripture Ser.: Vol. 4, Pt. 1). (Illus.). 512p. 1980. 35.00x (ISBN 0-87343-031-X). Magi Bks.

Belo, Fernando. A Materialist Reading of the Gospel of Mark. O'Connell, Matthew, tr. LC 80-24756. 384p. (Orig.). 1981. pap. 12.95 (ISBN 0-88344-323-6). Orbis Bks.

Bernard, J. H. Saint John, 2 vols. LC 29-17737. (International Critical Commentary Ser.). Repr. of 1928 ed. Vol. 1, 480p. 22.00x (ISBN 0-567-05024-6); Vol. 2, 456p. 22.00x (ISBN 0-567-05025-4). Attic Pr.

Byrum, R. R. Shadows of Good Things, or the Gospel in Type. (Illus.). 144p. pap. 1.50. Faith Pub Hse.

Chantry, Walter. Today's Gospel. 1980. pap. 2.45. Banner of Truth.

Chantry, Walter J. God's Righteous Kingdom. 151p. (Orig.). 1980. pap. 3.50 (ISBN 0-85151-310-7). Banner of Truth.

Clark, Gordon H. First John: A Commentary. 1980. pap. 4.75 (ISBN 0-87552-166-5). Presby & Reformed.

Cooper, Al. Examining the Gospels. 1981. 4.75 (ISBN 0-8062-1601-8). Carlton.

Crissey, Clair. Layman's Bible Book Commentary: Matthew, Vol. 15. 1981. 4.75 (ISBN 0-8054-1185-2). Broadman.

Danker, Frederick W. Jesus & the New Age According to Saint Luke. LC 72-83650. 255p. 1980. pap. 12.00 (ISBN 0-915644-21-5). Clayton Pub Hse.

Garvie, A. E. The Joy of Finding: An Exposition of Luke 15: 11-32. (Short Course Ser.). 146p. 1914. text ed. 2.95 (ISBN 0-567-08313-6). Attic Pr.

Godet, F. Commentary on the Gospel of Saint Luke, 2 vols. 5th ed. 920p. 1976. pap. text ed. 27.50x (ISBN 0-567-27446-2). Attic Pr.

Gould, E. P. Saint Mark. LC 25-17683. (International Critical Commentary Ser.). 376p. 1896. text ed. 20.00x (ISBN 0-567-05022-X). Attic Pr.

Hengstenberg, E. W. Commentary on the Gospel of John, 2 vols. Date not set. Set. 34.95 (ISBN 0-86524-047-7). Klock & Klock.

Hinnebusch, Paul. St. Matthew's Earthquake: Judgement & Discipleship in the Gospel of Matthew. 154p. (Orig.). 1980. pap. 3.95 (ISBN 0-89283-093-X). Servant.

Hoefler, Richard C. A Sign in the Straw. 128p. (Orig.). 1980. pap. text ed. 6.25 (ISBN 0-89536-465-4). CSS Pub.

Hurtado, Larry. Text-Critical Methodology & the Pre-Caesarean Text. 112p. (Orig.). 1981. pap. 13.00 (ISBN 0-8028-1872-2). Eerdmans.

Kelly, William. The Gospel of Luke. Date not set. 16.95 (ISBN 0-86524-046-9). Klock & Klock.

Kingsbury, Jack D. Jesus Christ in Matthew, Mark, & Luke. Krodel, Gerhard, ed. LC 80-69755. (Proclamation Commentaries Ser.: The New Testament Witnesses for Preaching). 144p. (Orig.). 1981. pap. 4.25 (ISBN 0-8006-0596-9, 1-596). Fortress.

Lorber, Jokob. The Dream of Zorel. Ozols, Violet, tr. from Ger. 124p. Date not set. pap. 5.00 (ISBN 0-934616-17-5). Valkyrie Pr.

Marcion Of Sinope. The Gospel of the Lord. Hill, James H., tr. LC 78-63171. (Heresies II Ser.). 80p. 1980. Repr. of 1891 ed. 13.50 (ISBN 0-404-16186-3). AMS Pr.

Mays, James L., ed. Interpreting the Gospels. LC 80-8057. 320p. 1981. pap. 13.50 (ISBN 0-8006-1439-9, 1-1439). Fortress.

Montague, George T. Mark: Good News for Hard Times: A Popular Commentary on the the Earliest Gospel. 200p. (Orig.). 1981. pap. 5.95 (ISBN 0-89283-096-4). Servant.

Obach, Robert E. & Kirk, Albert. A Commentary on the Gospel of John. 288p. 1981. pap. 6.95 (ISBN 0-8091-2346-0). Paulist Pr.

Painter, John. Reading John's Gospel Today. LC 79-25332. (Biblical Foundations Ser.). Orig. Title: John: Witness & Theologian. 170p. 1980. pap. 5.95 (ISBN 0-8042-0522-1). John Knox.

Philaretos, Sotirios D. The Decalogue & the Gospel. Orthodox Christian Educational Society, ed. Cummings, D., tr. from Hellenic. 62p. (Orig.). Date not set. pap. 1.50x (ISBN 0-938366-43-2). Orthodox Chr.

Plummer, Alfred. St. Luke. 5th ed. (International Critical Commentary Ser.). 688p. Repr. of 1901 ed. text ed. 23.00x (ISBN 0-567-05023-8). Attic Pr.

Reith, G. St. John: Chapters 1-8, Vol. I. (Handbooks for Bible Classes Ser.). 197p. Repr. of 1889 ed. text ed. 7.50 (ISBN 0-567-08114-1). Attic Pr.

--St. John: Chapters 8-21, Vol. II. (Handbooks for Bible Classes). 178p. Repr. of 1889 ed. text ed. 7.50 (ISBN 0-567-08115-X). Attic Pr.

Savoy, Gene. The Lost Gospel of Jesus, Authorized Version: The Hidden Teachings of Christ. LC 78-71277. (The Sacred Teachings of Light Ser.: Codex VIII). (Illus.). xiii, 85p. 1978. text ed. 39.50 (ISBN 0-936202-02-5). Intl Comm Christ.

Swihart, Stephen D. Logos International Bible Commentary, Vo. 1. 1981. write for info. (ISBN 0-88270-500-8). Logos.

Van Doren, W. H. Gospel of John, 2 vols. in 1. rev. ed. LC 80-8080. (Kregal Bible Study Classics Ser.). 1100p. 1981. Repr. of 1878 ed. text ed. 22.95 (ISBN 0-8254-3953-1). Kregel.

Woods, Guy N. John. 1981. 8.95 (ISBN 0-89225-207-3). Gospel Advocate.

BIBLE-COMMENTARIES-N. T. HEBREWS

Ford, Charles W. Learning from Hebrews. LC 80-67467. (Radiant Life Ser.). 128p. (Orig.). 1981. 1.95 (ISBN 0-88243-915-4, 02-0915); teacher's ed 2.50 (ISBN 0-88243-188-9, 32-0188). Gospel Pub.

Gerber, Aaron. Abraham: The First Hebrew. 180p. 1981. 12.50 (ISBN 0-89962-208-9). Todd & Honeywell.

Hastings, James. The Great Texts of the Bible: Thessalonians-Hebrews. 495p. Repr. of 1914 ed. text ed. 5.00x (ISBN 0-567-06718-1). Attic Pr.

Hudson, James T. The Epistle to the Hebrews: Its Meaning & Message. 78p. Repr. of 1937 ed. 3.50 (ISBN 0-567-02144-0). Attic Pr.

Jewett, Robert. Letter to Pilgrims. 244p. (Orig.). 1981 pap. 7.95 (ISBN 0-8298-0425-0). Pilgrim NY.

Moffatt, James. James, Hebrews. LC 24-21703. (International Critical Commentary Ser.). 336p. Repr. of 1924 ed. text ed. 17.50 (ISBN 0-567-05034-3). Attic Pr.

Way, Arthur S. Letters of Paul, Hebrews & Psalms. 468p. 1981. text ed. 12.95 (ISBN 0-8254-4016-5). Kregel.

Wilson, Geoffrey. Hebrews. 1976. pap. 3.95 (ISBN 0-85151-099-X). Banner of Truth.

BIBLE-COMMENTARIES-N. T. JAMES

see Bible-Commentaries-N. T. Catholic Epistles

BIBLE-COMMENTARIES-N. T. JOHN

see Bible-Commentaries-N. T. Gospels

BIBLE-COMMENTARIES-N. T. JUDE

see Bible-Commentaries-N. T. Catholic Epistles

BIBLE-COMMENTARIES-N. T. LUKE

see Bible-Commentaries-N. T. Gospels

BIBLE-COMMENTARIES-N. T. MARK

see Bible-Commentaries-N. T. Gospels

BIBLE-COMMENTARIES-N. T. MATTHEW

see Bible-Commentaries-N. T. Gospels

Raymond, John. Twenty-Six Lessons on Matthew, Vol. II. (Bible Student Study Guide Ser.). 180p. 1981. pap. 2.95 (ISBN 0-89900-171-8). College Pr Pub.

BIBLE-COMMENTARIES-N. T. PASTORAL EPISTLES

Here are entered commentaries on the Pastoral epistles as a whole as well as those on Titus or Timothy.

Fairbairn, Patrick. The Pastoral Epistles. Date not set. 14.95 (ISBN 0-86524-053-1). Klock & Klock.

Lock, W. Pastoral Epistles. (International Critical Commentary Ser.). 212p. 1924. text ed. 17.50x (ISBN 0-567-05033-5). Attic Pr.

BIBLE-COMMENTARIES-N. T. PETER

see Bible-Commentaries-N. T. Catholic Epistles

BIBLE-COMMENTARIES-N. T. PHILEMON

Moule, H. C. G. Colossian & Philemon Studies. Date not set. 10.50 (ISBN 0-86524-052-3). Klock & Klock.

Vaughan, Curtis. Colossians & Philemon: A Study Guide Commentary. (Study Guide Commentary Ser.). 144p. (Orig.). 1981. pap. 3.50 (ISBN 0-310-33583-3). Zondervan.

Vincent, M. R. Philippians & Philemon. LC 4-1629. (International Critical Commentary Ser.). 248p. Repr. of 1904 ed. text ed. 17.50x (ISBN 0-567-05031-9). Attic Pr.

Wilson, Geoffrey B. Colossians & Philemon. (Wilson'a New Testament Commentaries). 111p. (Orig.). 1980. pap. 3.95 (ISBN 0-85151-313-1). Banner of Truth.

BIBLE-COMMENTARIES-N. T. PHILIPPIANS

Eddleman, H. Leo. Commentary on Philippians. 176p. (Orig.). 1981. pap. 4.75 (ISBN 0-682-49700-2). Exposition.

Vincent, M. R. Philippians & Philemon. LC 4-1629. (International Critical Commentary Ser.). 248p. Repr. of 1904 ed. text ed. 17.50x (ISBN 0-567-05031-9). Attic Pr.

Vos, Howard F. Philippians: A Study Commentary. (Study Guide Commentary Ser.). 96p. (Orig.). 1980. pap. 2.95 (ISBN 0-310-33863-8). Zondervan.

BIBLE-COMMENTARIES-N. T. REVELATION

Beasley-Murray, G. R. Revelation. Black, Matthew, ed. (New Century Bible Commentary Ser.). 352p. (Orig.). 1981. pap. 7.95 (ISBN 0-8028-1885-4). Eerdmans.

Charles, R. H. Revelation, Vol. I. LC 21-5413. (International Critical Commentary Ser.). 568p. 1920. text ed. 22.00x (ISBN 0-567-05038-6). Attic Pr.

--Revelation, Vol. II. LC 21-5413. (International Critical Commentary Ser.). 506p. 1920. text ed. 22.00x (ISBN 0-567-05039-4). Attic Pr.

Eller, Vernard. War & Peace from Genesis to Revelation. 232p. 1981. pap. 8.95 (ISBN 0-8361-1947-9). Herald Pr.

Fiorenza, Elizabeth S. Invitation to the Book of Revelation: A Commentary on the Apocalypse with Complete Text from the Jerusalem Bible. LC 79-6744. 224p. 1981. pap. 3.95 (ISBN 0-385-14800-3, Im). Doubleday.

Hastings, James. The Great Texts of the Bible: Revelation. 432p. Repr. of 1915 ed. 5.00x (ISBN 0-567-06720-3). Attic Pr.

Ladd, George E. El Apocalipsis de Juan: Un Comentario. Canclini, Arnoldo, tr. from Eng. LC 78-50625. 269p. (Orig., Span.). 1978. pap. 5.50 (ISBN 0-89922-111-4). Edit Caribe.

Morris, Leon. Creo en la Revelacion. Blanch, Miguel, tr. from Eng. (Serie Creo). 223p. (Orig., Span.). 1979. pap. 3.95 (ISBN 0-89922-140-8). Edit Caribe.

BIBLE–COMMENTARIES–N. T. ROMANS

Cranfield, C. E. Romans, Vol.i. (International Critical Commentary Ser.). 480p. Repr. of 1980 ed. text ed. 24.00x (ISBN 0-567-05040-8). Attic Pr.

--Romans, Vol. Ii. (International Critical Commentary Ser.). 448p. Repr. of 1979 ed. text ed. 28.50x (ISBN 0-567-05041-6). Attic Pr.

Hastings, James. The Great Texts of the Bible: Romans 8-16. 479p. Repr. of 1911 ed. text ed. 5.00x (ISBN 0-567-06714-9). Attic Pr.

Hunt, Gladys. Romans: Made Righteous by Faith. (Fisherman Bible Studyguide Ser.). 94p. (Orig.). 1981. saddle stitch 2.25 (ISBN 0-87788-733-0). Shaw Pubs.

Sanday, W. & Headlam, A. C. Romans. 5th ed. (International Critical Commentary Ser.). 568p. Repr. of 1977 ed. 23.00x (ISBN 0-567-05026-2). Attic Pr.

Smith, Sherwood. Thirteen Lessons on Romans, Vol. II. LC 81-65030. (Bible Student Study Guides Ser.). 180p. 1981. pap. 2.95 (ISBN 0-89900-170-X). College Pr Pub.

Stagg, Frank. Galatians & Romans. (Knox Pereaching Guides Ser.). 160p. (Orig.). 1980. pap. 4.50 (ISBN 0-8042-3238-5). John Knox.

Watson, Thomas. A Divine Cordial. (Summit Ser.). 96p. 1981. pap. 2.45 (ISBN 0-8010-9646-4). Baker Bk.

BIBLE–COMMENTARIES–N. T. THESSALONIANS

Frame, J. E. Thessalonians. LC 12-23430. (International Critical Commentary Ser.). 336p. Repr. of 1912 ed. 17.50x (ISBN 0-567-05032-7). Attic Pr.

Hastings, James. The Great Texts of the Bible: Thessalonians-Hebrews. 495p. Repr. of 1914 ed. text ed. 5.00x (ISBN 0-567-06718-1). Attic Pr.

Saunders, Ernest W. I Thessalonians, II Thessalonians, Philippians, Philemen. Hayes, John H., ed. (Preaching Guides Ser.). (Orig.). 1981. pap. 4.50 (ISBN 0-8042-3241-5). John Knox.

Wilson, Geoffrey. First & Second Thessalonians. 1975. pap. 2.45 (ISBN 0-85151-227-5). Banner of Truth.

BIBLE–COMMENTARIES–N. T. TIMOTHY

see Bible–Commentaries–N. T. Pastoral Epistles

BIBLE–COMMENTARIES–N. T. TITUS

see Bible–Commentaries–N. T. Pastoral Epistles

BIBLE–COMMENTARIES–O. T.

Here are entered only Commentaries on the Old Testament as a whole.

Alexander, David. Fotovision del Antiguo Testamento. Vega, Pedro, tr. from Eng. (Illus.). 157p. (Span.). 1976. 8.50 (ISBN 0-89922-062-2). Edit Caribe.

Bratcher, R. G., ed. Marginal Notes for the Old Testament. 1980. softcover 2.50 (ISBN 0-8267-0025-X, 08557). United Bible.

Delitzsch, Franz. Old Testament History of Redemption. Date not set. pap. 6.95 (ISBN 0-88469-141-1). BMH Bks.

Francisco, C. T. Introduccion Al Antiguo Testamento. Lacue, Juan J., tr. Orig. Title: Introducing the Old Testament. 350p. (Span.). 1980. pap. 4.25 (ISBN 0-311-04010-1). Casa Bautista.

Harrelson, Walter J. From Fertility Cult to Worship. LC 66-14929. (Scholars Press Reprint Ser.: No. 4). pap. 9.00x (ISBN 0-89130-379-0, 00 07 04). Scholars Pr CA.

MacDonald, William. Old Testament Digest: Gen-Deut, Vol. 1. 1981. pap. 7.50 (ISBN 0-937396-59-1). Walterick Pubs.

Martens, Elmer A. God's Design: Focusing an Old Testament Theology. 368p. 1981. 12.95 (ISBN 0-8010-6115-6). Baker Bk.

Morgan, Donn F. Wisdom in the Old Testament Tradition. LC 80-84653. 17.50 (ISBN 0-8042-0188-9); pap. 8.95 (ISBN 0-8042-0189-7). John Knox.

Napier, Davie. Song of the Vineyard: A Guide Through the Old Testament. rev. ed. LC 78-14672. 360p. 1981. pap. 11.95 (ISBN 0-8006-1352-X, 1-1352). Fortress.

Patrick, Dale. The Rendering of God in the Old Testament, No. 10. Brueggemann, Walter & Donahue, John R., eds. LC 80-2389. (Overtures to Biblical Theology Ser.). 176p. (Orig.). 1981. pap. 8.95 (ISBN 0-8006-1533-6, 1-1533). Fortress.

Payne, J. Barton. New Perspectives on the Old Testament. Date not set. 14.95 (ISBN 0-88469-134-9). BMH Bks.

BIBLE–COMMENTARIES–O. T. AMOS

see Bible–Commentaries–O. T. Minor Prophets

BIBLE–COMMENTARIES–O. T. CHRONICLES

see Bible–Commentaries–O. T. Historical Books

BIBLE–COMMENTARIES–O. T. DANIEL

see Bible–Commentaries–O. T. Prophets

BIBLE–COMMENTARIES–O. T. DEUTERONOMY

see Bible–Commentaries–O. T. Pentateuch

BIBLE–COMMENTARIES–O. T. ECCLESIASTES

see Bible–Commentaries–O. T. Poetical Books

BIBLE–COMMENTARIES–O. T. ESTHER

see Bible–Commentaries–O. T. Historical Books

BIBLE–COMMENTARIES–O. T. EXODUS

see Bible–Commentaries–O. T. Pentateuch

BIBLE–COMMENTARIES–O. T. EZEKIEL

see Bible–Commentaries–O. T. Prophets

BIBLE–COMMENTARIES–O. T. EZRA

see Bible–Commentaries–O. T. Historical Books

BIBLE–COMMENTARIES–O. T. GENESIS

see Bible–Commentaries–O. T. Pentateuch

BIBLE–COMMENTARIES–O. T. HABAKKUK

see Bible–Commentaries–O. T. Minor Prophets

BIBLE–COMMENTARIES–O. T. HAGGAI

see Bible–Commentaries–O. T. Minor Prophets

BIBLE–COMMENTARIES–O. T. HISTORICAL BOOKS

Adeney, Walter D. The Books of Ezra & Nehemiah. Date not set. 11.50 (ISBN 0-86524-050-7). Klock & Klock.

Batten, L. W. Ezra & Nehemiah. LC 13-12806. (International Critical Commentary Ser.). 400p. Repr. of 1913 ed. 20.00x (ISBN 0-567-05008-4). Attic Pr.

Curtis, E. L. & Madsen, A. A. Chronicles, I & II. LC 10-14958. (International Critical Commentary Ser.). 560p. Repr. of 1910 ed. text ed. 23.00x (ISBN 0-567-05007-6). Attic Pr.

Farrar, F. W. The First Book of Kings. Date not set. 16.75 (ISBN 0-86524-035-3). Klock & Klock.

--The Second Book of Kings. Date not set. 16.75 (ISBN 0-86524-036-1). Klock & Klock.

Montgomery, J. A. & Gehman, H. S. Kings I & II. LC 52-8522. (International Critical Commentary Ser.). 624p. Repr. of 1951 ed. 23.00x (ISBN 0-567-05006-8). Attic Pr.

Moore, G. F. Judges. LC 25-19368. (International Critical Commentary Ser.). 528p. 1895. text ed. 23.00x (ISBN 0-567-05004-1). Attic Pr.

Paton, L. B. Esther. LC 8-30156. (International Critical Commentary Ser.). 360p. Repr. of 1908 ed. text ed. 20.00x (ISBN 0-567-05009-2). Attic Pr.

Raleigh, Alexander. The Book of Esther. Date not set. 9.00 (ISBN 0-86524-037-X). Klock & Klock.

Smith, H. P. First & Second Samuel. LC 99-1607. (International Critical Commentary Ser.). 462p. 1899. text ed. 20.00x (ISBN 0-567-05005-X). Attic Pr.

Soggin, J. Alberto. Judges: A Commentary. Bowden, John, tr. from Ital. (Old Testament Library). 1981. text ed. price not set (ISBN 0-664-21368-5). Westminster.

Woudstra, Marten H. The Book of Joshua. LC 80-23413. (New International Commentary on the Old Testament). 400p. 1981. 16.95 (ISBN 0-8028-2356-4). Eerdmans.

BIBLE–COMMENTARIES–O. T. HOSEA

see Bible–Commentaries–O. T. Minor Prophets

BIBLE–COMMENTARIES–O. T. ISAIAH

see Bible–Commentaries–O. T. Prophets

BIBLE–COMMENTARIES–O. T. JEREMIAH

see Bible–Commentaries–O. T. Prophets

BIBLE–COMMENTARIES–O. T. JOB

see Bible–Commentaries–O. T. Poetical Books

BIBLE–COMMENTARIES–O. T. JOEL

see Bible–Commentaries–O. T. Minor Prophets

BIBLE–COMMENTARIES–O. T. JONAH

see Bible–Commentaries–O. T. Minor Prophets

BIBLE–COMMENTARIES–O. T. JOSHUA

see Bible–Commentaries–O. T. Historical Books

BIBLE–COMMENTARIES–O. T. JUDGES

see Bible–Commentaries–O. T. Historical Books

BIBLE–COMMENTARIES–O. T. KINGS

see Bible–Commentaries–O. T. Historical Books

BIBLE–COMMENTARIES–O. T. LAMENTATIONS

see Bible–Commentaries–O. T. Prophets

BIBLE–COMMENTARIES–O. T. LEVITICUS

see Bible–Commentaries–O. T. Pentateuch

BIBLE–COMMENTARIES–O. T. MALACHI

see Bible–Commentaries–O. T. Minor Prophets

BIBLE–COMMENTARIES–O. T. MICAH

see Bible–Commentaries–O. T. Minor Prophets

BIBLE–COMMENTARIES–O. T. MINOR PROPHETS

Crouch, Brodie. Study of Minor Prophets. pap. 2.50 (ISBN 0-89315-291-9). Lambert Bk.

De Waard, J. & Smalley, W. A. Translators Handbook on the Book of Amos. (Helps for Translators Ser.). 1979. softcover 2.50 (ISBN 0-8267-0128-0, 08577). United Bible.

Inman, V. Kerry. Prophets of Doom in an Age of Optimism. (Orig.). 1981. pap. 4.95 (ISBN 0-934688-02-8). Great Comm Pubns.

Martin, Hugh. Jonah. (Banner of Truth Geneva Series Commentaries). 1978. 10.95 (ISBN 0-85151-115-5). Banner of Truth.

Mitchell, H. G., et al. Haggai, Zechariah, Malachi, & Jonah. LC 12-22008. (International Critical Commentary Ser.). 544p. Repr. of 1912 ed. 23.00x (ISBN 0-567-05020-3). Attic Pr.

Moore, T. V. Haggi, Malachi, & Zechariah. (Banner of Truth Geneva Series Commentaries). 1979. 10.95 (ISBN 0-85151-288-7). Banner of Truth.

Smith, J. M., et al. Micah, Zephaniah, Nahum, Habakkuk, Obadiah & Joel. (International Critical Commentary Ser.). 560p. 1911. text ed. 23.00x (ISBN 0-567-05019-X). Attic Pr.

Watts, John D. W. Obadiah. Date not set. pap. 4.95 (ISBN 0-88469-138-1). BMH Bks.

BIBLE–COMMENTARIES–O. T. NAHUM

see Bible–Commentaries–O. T. Minor Prophets

BIBLE–COMMENTARIES–O. T. NEHEMIAH

see Bible–Commentaries–O. T. Historical Books.

BIBLE–COMMENTARIES–O. T. NUMBERS

see Bible–Commentaries–O. T. Pentateuch

BIBLE–COMMENTARIES–O. T. OBADIAH

see Bible–Commentaries–O. T. Minor Prophets

BIBLE–COMMENTARIES–O. T. PENTATEUCH

Asimov, Isaac & Baron, Carole. In the Beginning. 1981. 10.95 (ISBN 0-517-54336-2). Crown.

Bonar, Andrew. Leviticus. (Banner of Truth Geneva Series Commentaries). 1978. 14.95 (ISBN 0-85151-086-8). Banner of Truth.

Dods, M. Genesis. (Handbooks for Bible Classes Ser.). 224p. Repr. of 1956 ed. 3.50 (ISBN 0-567-08101-X). Attic Pr.

Driver, S. R. Deuteronomy. 3rd ed. LC 2-25926. (International Critical Commentary Ser.). 556p. 20.00x (ISBN 0-567-05003-3). Attic Pr.

Gray, G. Buchanan. Numbers. LC 3-31887. (International Critical Commentary Ser.). 544p. 1930. text ed. 23.00x (ISBN 0-567-05002-5). Attic Pr.

Hastings, James. The Great Texts of the Bible: Genesis-Numbers. 458p. Repr. of 1911 ed. text ed. 5.00x (ISBN 0-567-06701-7). Attic Pr.

Hoff, Pablo, tr. El Pentateuco. (Spanish Bks.). 1979. 2.95 (ISBN 0-8297-0876-6). Life Pubs Intl.

Kelley, William T. Genesis-Exodus: An Access Guide. 128p. (Orig.). 1981. pap. 4.95 (ISBN 0-8215-5927-3). Sadlier.

Mayes, A. D. Deuteronomy. Clements, Ronald E., ed. (New Century Bible Commentary Ser.). (Orig.). 1981. pap. 8.95 (ISBN 0-8028-1882-X). Eerdmans.

--Deuteronomy. (New Century Bible Ser.). 352p. Repr. of 1979 ed. 19.50x (ISBN 0-551-00804-0). Attic Pr.

Origins of Faith & Life: Genesis A. (New Horizons Bible Study Ser.). 1981. pap. 1.75 leader's guide (ISBN 0-89367-052-9); pap. 2.25 study guide (ISBN 0-89367-053-7). Light & Life.

Skinner, John. Genesis. (International Critical Commentary Ser.). 640p. 1930. text ed. 23.00x (ISBN 0-567-05001-7). Attic Pr.

BIBLE–COMMENTARIES–O. T. POETICAL BOOKS

Barton, G. A. Ecclesiastes. LC 8-15777. (International Critical Commentary Ser.). 236p. Repr. of 1908 ed. 17.50x (ISBN 0-567-05014-9). Attic Pr.

Briggs, C. A. & Briggs, E. G. Psalms. LC 6-26084. (International Critical Commentary). 22.00x (ISBN 0-567-05011-4). Attic Pr.

Brown, John. The Sufferings & the Glories of the Messiah. (Giant Summit Bks.). 352p. 1981. pap. 5.95 (ISBN 0-8010-0792-5). Baker Bk.

Campbell, Murdoch. From Grace to Glory: Meditations of the Psalms. 1979. pap. 3.95 (ISBN 0-85151-028-0). Banner of Truth.

Driver, S. R. & Gray, G. Buchanan. Job. LC 21-15647. (International Critical Commentary Ser.). 816p. Repr. of 1921 ed. 23.00x (ISBN 0-567-05010-6). Attic Pr.

Hastings, James. The Great Texts of the Bible: Job-Psalm 23. 518p. Repr. of 1913 ed. text ed. 5.00x (ISBN 0-567-06703-3). Attic Pr.

Hembree, Ron. The Shepherd Psalm. (Direction Bks). 64p. 1981. pap. text ed. 1.75 (ISBN 0-8010-4249-6). Baker Bk.

Keller, Phillip. La Vida En el Redil. Vargas, Carlos A., tr. from Eng. LC 76-14500. 141p. (Orig., Span.). 1976. pap. 2.50 (ISBN 0-89922-073-8). Edit Caribe.

McNeil, Brian. Christ in the Psalms. 90p. 1980. pap. 2.95 (ISBN 0-8091-2341-X). Paulist Pr.

Makrakis, Apostolos. Commentary on the Psalms of David. Orthodox Christian Educational Society, ed. Cummings, Denver, tr. from Hellenic. 990p. 1950. 10.00x (ISBN 0-938366-19-X). Orthodox Chr.

The Psalms, 3 vols. Date not set. 43.50 set (ISBN 0-86524-038-8). Klock & Klock.

Sidders, Max. S. O. S. An Exposition of the Song of Solomon. 1981. 5.95 (ISBN 0-533-04640-8). Vantage.

Spurgeon, Charles H. Great Verses from the Psalms. 278p. 1981. pap. 6.95 (ISBN 0-310-32901-9). Zondervan.

Toy, C. H. Proverbs. LC 99-5903. (International Critical Commentary Ser.). 592p. Repr. of 1899 ed. text ed. 23.00x. Attic Pr.

Walsh, Kilian, tr. Bernard of Clairvaux on the Song of Songs, Vol. I. (Cistercian Fathers Er.: No. 4). pap. 4.00 (ISBN 0-87907-104-4). Cistercian Pubns.

Wardlaw, Ralph. Book of Proverbs. Date not set. 27.50 (ISBN 0-86524-042-6). Klock & Klock.

Way, Arthur S. Letters of Paul, Hebrews & Psalms. 468p. 1981. text ed. 12.95 (ISBN 0-8254-4016-5). Kregel.

Westermann, Claus. The Structure of the Book of Job: A Form-Critical Analysis. Muenchow, Charles A., tr. from Ger. LC 80-2379. 160p. 1981. 14.95 (ISBN 0-8006-0651-5, 1-651). Fortress.

William of St. Thierry: Exposition on the Song of Songs. (Cistercian Fathers Ser.: No. 6). 1970. 7.95 (ISBN 0-7165-1006-5). Cistercian Pubns.

Young, Edwin H. The Lord Is... LC 80-68750. 1981. pap. 3.25 (ISBN 0-8054-1526-2). Broadman.

BIBLE–COMMENTARIES–O. T. PROPHETS

see also Bible–Commentaries–O. T. Minor Prophets

Brown, John. The Sufferings & the Glories of the Messiah. (Giant Summit Bks.). 352p. 1981. pap. 5.95 (ISBN 0-8010-0792-5). Baker Bk.

Cooke, G. A. Ezekiel. LC 38-12281. (International Critical Commentary Ser.). 608p. Repr. of 1936 ed. text ed. 23.00x (ISBN 0-567-05016-5). Attic Pr.

Dasbach, Fernando L. Blight or Bloom. 198p. 1981. 12.50. Regenbogen-Verlag.

Gray, G. Buchanan. Isaiah: Chapters 1-39. (International Critical Commentary Ser.). 576p. 1912. text ed. 23.00x (ISBN 0-567-05015-7). Attic Pr.

Huey, F. B., Jr. Jeremiah: A Study Guide Commentary. (Study Guide Commentary Ser.). 144p. (Orig.). 1981. pap. 3.95 (ISBN 0-310-36063-3). Zondervan.

Montgomery, A. Daniel. LC 27-14200. (International Critical Commentary Ser.). 520p. Repr. of 1927 ed. 23.00x (ISBN 0-567-05017-3). Attic Pr.

Smith, F. G. Prophetic Lectures on Daniel & Revelations. 260p. pap. 3.50. Faith Pub Hse.

Tatford, Frederick. Daniel & His Prophecy. Date not set. 8.25 (ISBN 0-86524-045-0). Klock & Klock.

Whybray, R. N. Isaiah Forty to Sixty-Six. Clements, Ronald E., ed. (New Century Bible Commentary). 320p. (Orig.). 1981. pap. 7.95 (ISBN 0-8028-1884-6). Eerdmans.

BIBLE–COMMENTARIES–O. T. PROVERBS

see Bible–Commentaries–O. T. Poetical Books

BIBLE–COMMENTARIES–O. T. PSALMS

see Bible–Commentaries–O. T. Poetical Books

BIBLE–COMMENTARIES–O. T. RUTH

see Bible–Commentaries–O. T. Historical Books

BIBLE–COMMENTARIES–O. T. SAMUEL

see Bible–Commentaries–O. T. Historical Books

BIBLE–COMMENTARIES–O. T. SONG OF SOLOMON

see Bible–Commentaries–O. T. Poetical Books

BIBLE–COMMENTARIES–O. T. ZECHARIAH

see Bible–Commentaries–O. T. Minor Prophets

BIBLE–COMMENTARIES–O. T. ZEPHANIAH

see Bible–Commentaries–O. T. Minor Prophets

BIBLE–CONCORDANCES

Concordancia De la Biblia. (Spanish Bks.). (Span.). 1980. 1.25 (ISBN 0-8297-0775-1). Life Pubs Intl.

Goodrick, Edward W. & Kohlenberger, John P. The NIV Complete Concordance. 1056p. 1981. 19.95 (ISBN 0-310-43650-8). Zondervan.

Moulton, W. F., et al. A Concordance to the Greek Testament: According to the Texts of Westcott & Hort, Tischendorf & the English Revisers. 5th ed. 1120p. 1978. text ed. 45.00x (ISBN 0-567-01021-X). Attic Pr.

Parker, George. Lexico-Concordancia Del Nuevo Testamento En Griego y Espanol. Orig. Title: Lexicon-Concordance of the New Testament in Greek & Spanish. 1000p. (Span.). Date not set. pap. price not set (ISBN 0-311-42066-4). Casa Bautista.

Vigram, George V. The Englishman's Greek Concordance of the New Testament. rev. ed. 1980. pap. 23.95 (ISBN 0-8054-1388-X). Broadman.

BIBLE–COVENANTS

see Covenants (Theology)

BIBLE–CRITICISM, HIGHER

see Bible–Criticism, Interpretation, etc.; Bible–Introductions

BIBLE–CRITICISM, INTERPRETATION, ETC.

Here are entered works on the Bible as a whole. Works on the New Testament as a whole and on portions of the New Testament precede works on the Old Testament.

see also Sex in the Bible

Allen, Horace T., Jr. A Handbook for the Lectionary. 1980. softcover 9.95 (ISBN 0-664-24347-9). Westminster.

Barnes, W. Emery. Gospel Criticism & Form Criticism. 83p. 1936. pap. text ed. 3.50 (ISBN 0-567-02020-7). Attic Pr.

Dawes, Walter A. The Ghost of Old Capernaum. (Illus.). 358p. (Orig.). 1980. pap. text ed. 24.95 (ISBN 0-686-28901-3). New Capernaum.

--Impact: The Religion of the Twenty-First Century. (Illus.). 79p. (Orig.). 1980. pap. text ed. 8.95 (ISBN 0-938792-05-9). New Capernaum.

Ellinger, K. Biblia Hebraica Stuttgartensia. 1977. 19.25 (ISBN 3-438-05218-0, 60555). United Bible.

Gaffin, Richard B., Jr., ed. Redemptive History & Biblical Interpretation: The Shorter Writings of Geerhardus Vos. 1980. 17.50 (ISBN 0-87552-270-X). Presby & Reformed.

Henley, Marshall. Positive Salvation. Date not set. 6.95 (ISBN 0-533-04861-3). Vantage.

Henrichsen, Walter A. Entendamos. Cook, David A., tr. from Eng. 112p. (Orig., Span.). 1979. pap. 2.75 (ISBN 0-89922-131-9). Edit Caribe.

Inch, Morris A. & Bullock, C. Hassell, eds. The Literature & Meaning of Scripture. 360p. 1981. 14.95 (ISBN 0-8010-5032-4). Baker Bk.

Jensen, Irving L. Jensen's Bible Study Charts. 128p. 1981. pap. 19.95 (ISBN 0-8024-4296-X). Moody.

Lampkin, G. V. God's Word As It Was in the Beginning. 1981. 6.95 (ISBN 0-533-04646-7). Vantage.

March, W. Eugene, ed. Texts & Testaments: Critical Essays on the Bible & Early Church Fathers. 321p. 1980. 15.00 (ISBN 0-911536-80-9). Trinity U Pr.

Mini-Guide to the Contents of the Books of the Bible. pap. 0.50. Reiner.

Morris, Leon. Testaments of Love: A Study of Love in the Bible. (Orig.). 1981. pap. price not set (ISBN 0-8028-1874-9). Eerdmans.

Vos, Geerhardus. Redemptive History & Biblical Interpretation. Gaffin, Richard B., Jr., ed. 584p. 1981. 17.50 (ISBN 0-8010-9286-8). Baker Bk.

Walsh, Chad. A Rich Feast: Encountering the Bible from Genesis to Revelation. LC 80-8356. 192p. 1981. 9.95 (ISBN 0-06-069249-9, HarpR, HarpR). Har-Row.

BIBLE–CRITICISM, INTERPRETATION, ETC.–N. T.

Barclay, William. The New Testament: A New Translation. 576p. (Orig.). 1980. pap. 2.95x (ISBN 0-664-24358-4). Westminster.

Eusebius. The Proof of the Gospel, 2 vols. in one. Ferrar, W. J., ed. (Twin Brooks Ser.). 568p. 1981. pap. 12.95 (ISBN 0-8010-3366-7). Baker Bk.

Lohse, Eduard. The Formation of the New Testament. Boring, M. Eugene, tr. LC 80-27032. 256p. (Orig.). 1981. pap. 8.95 (ISBN 0-687-13294-0). Abingdon.

McCray, Walter A. Who Says? A Black Perspective on the Authority of New Testament Exegesis Highlighting the Foundation for Its Interpretations & Applications. Bentley, William H., ed. 75p. (Orig.). 1981. pap. 3.00 (ISBN 0-933176-35-X). Black Light Fellow.

Makrakis, Apostolos. Interpretation of the Entire New Testament (Revelation Not Included, 2 vols. Orthodox Christian Educational Society, ed. Alexander, Albert G., tr. from Hellenic. 2052p. (Vol. 1, 1127 pp.;vol. 2, 925 pp.). 1949. Set. 20.00x (ISBN 0-938366-08-4). Orthodox Chr.

Yamauchi, Edwin. Harper's World of the New Testament. LC 80-8606. (Illus.). 144p. (Orig.). 1981. pap. 9.95 (ISBN 0-06-069708-3, HarpR). Har-Row.

Yeager, Randolph O., ed. The Renaissance New Testament, Vol. 7. 1981. 19.95 (ISBN 0-88289-457-9). Pelican.

BIBLE–CRITICISM, INTERPRETATION, ETC.–N. T. ACTS

Guthrie, Donald. The Apostles. 432p. 1981. pap. 10.95 (ISBN 0-310-25421-3). Zondervan.

Timmer, John. Acts, a Study Guide. (Revelation Ser. for Adults). 1981. pap. text ed. 1.45 (ISBN 0-933140-20-7). Bd of Pubns CRC.

BIBLE–CRITICISM, INTERPRETATION, ETC.–N. T. COLOSSIANS

see Bible–Criticism, Interpretation, etc.–N. T. Epistles

BIBLE–CRITICISM, INTERPRETATION, ETC.–N. T. CORINTHIANS

see Bible–Criticism, Interpretation, Etc.–N. T. Epistles

BIBLE–CRITICISM, INTERPRETATION, ETC.–N. T. EPHESIANS

see Bible–Criticism, Interpretation, Etc.–N. T. Epistles

BIBLE–CRITICISM, INTERPRETATION, ETC.–N. T. EPISTLES

Here are entered books on the Epistles as a whole, or on one or more of the following, Colossians, Corinthians, Ephesians, Galatians, Hebrews, James, Epistles of John, Jude, Peter, Philemon, Romans, Thessalonians, Timothy, Titus.

Arichea, D. C. & Nida, E. A. Translators Handbook on the First Letter from Peter. (Helps for Translators Ser.). 1980. softcover 2.35 (ISBN 0-8267-0152-3, 08624). United Bible.

Hayes, John, ed. First & Second Corinthians. write for info (ISBN 0-8042-3239-3). John Knox.

Hogg, C. F. & Vine, W. E. Epistles of Paul the Apostle to the Thessalonians. 5.95 (ISBN 0-89315-040-1). Lambert Bk.

Karris, Robert. Romans: An Access Guide. 128p. (Orig.). 1981. pap. 4.95 (ISBN 0-8215-5926-5). Sadlier.

Laws, Sophie. The Epistle of James. LC 80-8349. (Harper's New Testament Commentaries Ser.). 288p. 1981. 14.95 (ISBN 0-06-064918-6, HarpR). Har-Row.

Lull, David J. The Spirit in Galatia: Paul's Interpretation of Pneuma As Divine Power. LC 79-26094. (Society of Biblical Literature Dissertation: No. 49). 13.50x (ISBN 0-89130-367-7, 06-01-49); pap. 9.00x (ISBN 0-89130-368-5). Scholars Pr CA.

MacDonald, William. Letter to Titus. 54p. pap. 1.50. Walterick Pubs.

Martin, Ralph. Reconciliation: A Study of Paul's Theology. Toon, Peter, ed. LC 80-16340. (New Foundations Theological Library). 272p. 1981. 18.50 (ISBN 0-8042-3709-3); pap. 11.95 (ISBN 0-8042-3729-8). John Knox.

Nystrom, Carolyn. A Woman's Workshop on Romans-Leader's Manual. 112p. (Orig.). 1981. pap. 1.95 (ISBN 0-310-41911-5). Zondervan.

--A Woman's Workshop on Romans-Student's Manual. 144p. (Orig.). 1981. pap. 2.95 (ISBN 0-310-41921-2). Zondervan.

Wiersbe, Warren. Be Complete. 160p. 1981. pap. 3.50 (ISBN 0-88207-257-9). Victor Bks.

BIBLE–CRITICISM, INTERPRETATION, ETC.–N. T. EPISTLES OF JOHN

see Bible–Criticism, Interpretation, Etc.–N. T. Epistles

BIBLE–CRITICISM, INTERPRETATION, ETC.–N. T. GALATIANS

see Bible–Criticism, Interpretation, Etc.–N. T. Epistles

BIBLE–CRITICISM, INTERPRETATION, ETC.–N. T. GOSPELS

Here are entered works on the gospels as a whole, or on one or more of the gospels: John, Luke, Mark, Matthew.

Bailey, Robert Q. The Servant Story (Mark) Study Guide. (New Horizons Bible Study Ser.). 64p. 1980. pap. 2.25 (ISBN 0-89367-049-9). Light & Life.

Clark, Elizabeth. John the Beloved: An Essene Understanding of the Book of Revelations. 1981. 6.95 (ISBN 0-533-04781-1). Vantage.

Craddock, Fred B. The Gospels. LC 80-26270. 160p. (Orig.). 1981. pap. 6.95 (ISBN 0-687-15655-6). Abingdon.

DeLamotte, Roy C. The Alien Christ. LC 80-5902. 276p. 1980. lib. bdg. 18.75 (ISBN 0-8191-1304-2); pap. text ed. 10.50 (ISBN 0-8191-1305-0). U Pr of Amer.

Dewey, Joanna. Markan Public Debate: Literary Technique, Concentric Structure & Theology in Mark 2: 1-3: 6. LC 79-17443. (Society of Biblical Literature Ser.: No. 48). 12.00x (ISBN 0-89130-337-5); pap. 7.50x (ISBN 0-89130-338-3). Scholars Pr CA.

Harrington, Daniel J. The Gospel According to Mark: An Access Guide. 128p. (Orig.). 1981. pap. 4.95 (ISBN 0-8215-9835-X). Sadlier.

Hebart, Friedemann. One in the Gospel. 1981. pap. 4.25 (ISBN 0-570-03830-8, 12-2796). Concordia.

Heidenreich, Alfred. Healings in the Gospels. 1980. pap. 7.25 (ISBN 0-903540-36-3, Pub. Floris Books). St George Bk Serv.

Higgins, A. J. The Son of Man in the Teaching of Jesus. LC 79-42824. (Society for New Testament Studies Monographs: No. 40). 186p. Date not set. 24.50 (ISBN 0-521-22363-6). Cambridge U Pr.

Hurtado, Larry. Text-Critical Methodology & the Pre-Caesarean Text. 112p. (Orig.). 1981. pap. 13.00 (ISBN 0-8028-1872-2). Eerdmans.

Killinger, John. A Devotional Guide to John. 144p. 1981. 7.95 (ISBN 0-8499-0256-8). Word Bks.

Makrakis, Apostolos. The Interpretation of the Gospel Law. Orthodox Christian Educational Society, ed. Cummings, Denver, tr. from Hellenic. 317p. 1955. 6.00x (ISBN 0-938366-10-6). Orthodox Chr.

Maloney, Elliott C. Semitic Interference in Marcan Syntax. LC 80-13016. (Society of Biblical Literature Dissertation Ser.: No. 51). 15.00x (06 01 51); pap. 10.50x (ISBN 0-89130-406-1). Scholars Pr CA.

Martin, Ralph. Reconciliation: A Study of Paul's Theology. Toon, Peter, ed. LC 80-16340. (New Foundations Theological Library). 272p. 1981. 18.50 (ISBN 0-8042-3709-3); pap. 11.95 (ISBN 0-8042-3729-8). John Knox.

Newman, B. M. & Nida, E. A. Translators Handbook on the Gospel of John. (Helps for Translators Ser.). 1980. softcover 4.85 (ISBN 0-8267-0137-X, 08620). United Bible.

Patton, Carl S. Sources of the Synoptic Gospels. 263p. 1980. Repr. of 1915 ed. lib. bdg. 50.00 (ISBN 0-89984-385-9). Century Bookbindery.

Robinson, James M. The Problem of History in Mark. LC 57-857. (Scholars Press Reprint Ser.). pap. 6.00 (ISBN 0-89130-334-0, 000703). Scholars Pr CA.

BIBLE–CRITICISM, INTERPRETATION, ETC.–N. T. HEBREWS

see Bible–Criticism, Interpretation, Etc.–N. T. Epistles

BIBLE–CRITICISM, INTERPRETATION, ETC.–N. T. JAMES

see Bible–Criticism, Interpretation, Etc.–N. T. Epistles

BIBLE–CRITICISM, INTERPRETATION, ETC.–N. T. JOHN

see Bible–Criticism, Interpretation, etc.–N. T. Gospels

BIBLE–CRITICISM, INTERPRETATION, ETC.–N. T. JUDE

see Bible–Criticism, Interpretation, Etc.–N. T. Epistles

BIBLE–CRITICISM, INTERPRETATION, ETC.–N. T. LUKE

see Bible–Criticism, Interpretation, Etc.–N. T. Gospels

BIBLE–CRITICISM, INTERPRETATION, ETC.–N. T. MARK

see Bible–Criticism, Interpretation, Etc.–N. T. Gospels

BIBLE–CRITICISM, INTERPRETATION, ETC.–N. T. MATTHEW

see Bible–Criticism, Interpretation, Etc.–N. T. Gospels

BIBLE–CRITICISM, INTERPRETATION, ETC.–N. T. PETER

see Bible–Criticism, Interpretation, Etc.–N. T. Epistles

BIBLE–CRITICISM, INTERPRETATION, ETC.–N. T. PHILEMON

see Bible–Criticism, Interpretation, Etc.–N. T. Epistles

BIBLE–CRITICISM, INTERPRETATION, ETC.–N. T. REVELATION

Bock, Emil. The Apocalypse. 1980. pap. 12.50 (ISBN 0-903540-42-8, Pub. by Floris Books). St George Bk Serv.

Heading, John. From Now to Eternity (Revelation) 1981. pap. 3.95 (ISBN 0-937396-15-X). Walterick Pubs.

Makrakis, Apostolos. Interpretation of the Book of Revelation. Orthodox Christian Educational Society, ed. Alexander, A. G., tr. from Hellenic. 564p. 1972. 8.00x (ISBN 0-938366-12-2). Orthodox Chr.

Smith, F. G. The Revelation Explained. 464p. 5.50. Faith Pub Hse.

BIBLE–CRITICISM, INTERPRETATION, ETC.–N. T. ROMANS

see Bible–Criticism, Interpretation, Etc.–N. T. Epistles

BIBLE–CRITICISM, INTERPRETATION, ETC.–N. T. THESSALONIANS

see Bible–Criticism, Interpretation, Etc.–N. T. Epistles

BIBLE–CRITICISM, INTERPRETATION, ETC.–N. T. TIMOTHY

see Bible–Criticism, Interpretation, Etc.–N. T. Epistles

BIBLE–CRITICISM, INTERPRETATION, ETC.–N. T. TITUS

see Bible–Criticism, Interpretation, Etc.–N. T. Epistles

BIBLE–CRITICISM, INTERPRETATION, ETC.–O. T

Alter, Robert. The Art of Biblical Narrative. LC 80-68958. 208p. 1981. 13.95 (ISBN 0-465-04420-4). Basic.

Crenshaw, James L. Old Testament Wisdom: An Introduction. LC 80-82183. 262p. 1981. 16.50 (ISBN 0-8042-0143-9); pap. 9.95 (ISBN 0-8042-0142-0). John Knox.

BIBLE–CRITICISM, INTERPRETATION, ETC.–O. T. AMOS

see Bible–Criticism, Interpretation, Etc.–O. T. Minor Prophets

BIBLE–CRITICISM, INTERPRETATION, ETC.–O. T. CHRONICLES

see Bible–Criticism, Interpretation, Etc.–O. T. Historical Books

BIBLE–CRITICISM, INTERPRETATION, ETC.–O. T. DANIEL

see Bible–Criticism, Interpretation, Etc.–O. T. Prophets

BIBLE–CRITICISM, INTERPRETATION, ETC.–O. T. DEUTERONOMY

see Bible–Criticism, Interpretation, Etc.–O. T. Pentateuch

BIBLE–CRITICISM, INTERPRETATION, ETC.–O. T. ECCLESIASTES

see Bible–Criticism, Interpretation, etc.–O. T. Poetical Books

BIBLE–CRITICISM, INTERPRETATION, ETC.–O. T. ESTHER

see Bible–Criticism, Interpretation, Etc.–O. T. Historical Books

BIBLE–CRITICISM, INTERPRETATION, ETC.–O. T. EXODUS

see Bible–Criticism, Interpretation, Etc.–O. T. Pentateuch

BIBLE–CRITICISM, INTERPRETATION, ETC.–O. T. EZEKIEL

see Bible–Criticism, Interpretation, Etc.–O. T. Prophets

BIBLE–CRITICISM, INTERPRETATION, ETC.–O. T. EZRA

see Bible–Criticism, Interpretation, Etc.–O. T. Historical Books

BIBLE–CRITICISM, INTERPRETATION, ETC.–O. T. GENESIS

see Bible–Criticism, Interpretation, Etc.–O. T. Pentateuch

BIBLE–CRITICISM, INTERPRETATION, ETC.–O. T. HABAKKUK

see Bible–Criticism, Interpretation, Etc.–O. T. Minor Prophets

BIBLE–CRITICISM, INTERPRETATION, ETC.–O. T. HAGGAI

see Bible–Criticism, Interpretation, Etc.–O. T. Minor Prophets

BIBLE–CRITICISM, INTERPRETATION, ETC.–O. T. HISTORICAL BOOKS

Here are entered works on the historical Books as a whole, as well as on one or more of the following: Chronicles, Esther, Ezra, Joshua, Judges, Kings, Nehemiah, Ruth, Samuel.

Bodine, Walter R. The Greek Text of Judges: Recensional Developments. LC 80-12578. (Harvard Semitic Monographs: No. 23). 15.00x (ISBN 0-89130-400-2). Scholars Pr CA.

Campbell, Donald K. No Time for Neutrality. 144p. 1981. pap. 3.95 (ISBN 0-88207-337-0). Victor Bks.

BIBLE–CRITICISM, INTERPRETATION, ETC.–O. T. HOSEA

see Bible–Criticism, Interpretation, Etc.–O. T. Minor Prophets

BIBLE–CRITICISM, INTERPRETATION, ETC.–O. T. ISAIAH

see Bible–Criticism, Interpretation, Etc.–O. T. Prophets

BIBLE–CRITICISM, INTERPRETATION, ETC.–O. T. JEREMIAH

see Bible–Criticism, Interpretation, Etc.–O. T. Prophets

BIBLE–CRITICISM, INTERPRETATION, ETC.–O. T. JOB

see Bible–Criticism, Interpretation, Etc.–O. T. Poetical Books

BIBLE–CRITICISM, INTERPRETATION, ETC.–O. T. JOEL

see Bible–Criticism, Interpretation, Etc.–O. T. Minor Prophets

BIBLE–CRITICISM, INTERPRETATION, ETC.–O. T. JONAH

see Bible–Criticism, Interpretation, Etc.–O. T. Minor Prophets

BIBLE–CRITICISM, INTERPRETATION, ETC.–O. T. JOSHUA

see Bible–Criticism, Interpretation, Etc.–O. T. Historical Books

BIBLE–CRITICISM, INTERPRETATION, ETC.–O. T. JUDGES

see Bible–Criticism, Interpretation, Etc.–O. T. Historical Books

BIBLE–CRITICISM, INTERPRETATION, ETC.–O. T. KINGS

see Bible–Criticism, Interpretation, Etc.–O. T. Historical Books

BIBLE–CRITICISM, INTERPRETATION, ETC.–O. T. LAMENTATIONS

see Bible–Criticism, Interpretation, Etc.–O. T. Prophets

BIBLE–CRITICISM, INTERPRETATION, ETC.–O. T. LEVITICUS

see Bible–Criticism, Interpretation, Etc.–O. T. Pentateuch

BIBLE–CRITICISM, INTERPRETATION, ETC.–O. T. MALACHI

see Bible–Criticism, Interpretation, Etc.–O. T. Minor Prophets

BIBLE–CRITICISM, INTERPRETATION, ETC.–O. T. MICAH

see Bible–Criticism, Interpretation, Etc.–O. T. Minor Prophets

BIBLE–CRITICISM, INTERPRETATION, ETC.–O. T. MINOR PROPHETS

Here are entered works on the 12 minor prophets as a whole, as well as books on one or more of the minor prophets.

see also Bible–Criticism, Interpretation, Etc.–O. T. Prophets

Twombly, Gerald H. Major Themes from the Minor Prophets. (Adult Study Guide). 144p. (Orig.). 1981. pap. 3.95 (ISBN 0-88469-132-2). BMH Bks.

BIBLE–CRITICISM, INTERPRETATION, ETC.–O. T. NAHUM

see Bible–Criticism, Interpretation, Etc.–O. T. Minor Prophets

BIBLE–CRITICISM, INTERPRETATION, ETC.–O. T. NEHEMIAH

see Bible–Criticism, Interpretation, Etc.–O. T. Historical Books

BIBLE–CRITICISM, INTERPRETATION, ETC.–O. T. NUMBERS

see Bible–Criticism, Interpretation, Etc.–O. T. Pentateuch

BIBLE–CRITICISM, INTERPRETATION, ETC.–O. T. OBADIAH

see Bible–Criticism, Interpretation, Etc.–O. T. Minor Prophets

BIBLE–CRITICISM, INTERPRETATION, ETC.–O. T. PENTATEUCH

Here are entered works on the pentateuch as a whole, as well as books on one or more of the following: Deuteronomy, Exodus, Genesis, Leviticus, Numbers.

Gribbin, John. Genesis: The Origins of Man & the Universe. 1981. 13.95 (ISBN 0-440-02832-9). Delacorte.

Halevi, Z'ev. Kabbalah & Exodus. LC 80-50743. (Illus.). 234p. 1980. pap. 7.95 (ISBN 0-394-73950-7). Shambhala Pubns.

BIBLE–CRITICISM, INTERPRETATION, ETC.–O. T. POETICAL BOOKS

Here are entered works on the poetical books as a whole, as well as books on one or more of the following: Job, Ecclesiastes, Psalms, Proverbs, Song of Solomon; For works on Lamentations see Bible–Criticism, Interpretation, Etc–O. T. Prophets.

Chandler, Lotus H. The Book of Proverbs in Rhyme from the Holy Bible. LC 79-56329. 1981. 6.95 (ISBN 0-533-04528-2). Vantage.

Habel, Norman C. Job. Hayes, John, ed. LC 80-82193. (Knox Preaching Guides). 96p. (Orig.). 1981. pap. 4.50 (ISBN 0-8042-3216-4). John Knox.

MacDonald, William. Enjoying the Psalms, 2 vols. 1981. pap. 4.95 ea. Vol. 1 (ISBN 0-937396-34-6). Vol. 2 (ISBN 0-937396-35-4). Walterick Pubs.

Westermann, Claus. Praise & Lament in the Psalms. rev. enl. ed. Crim, Keith & Soulen, Richard, trs. from German. 1981 (ISBN 0-8042-1791-2). pap. 9.50 (ISBN 0-8042-1792-0). John Knox.

BIBLE–CRITICISM, INTERPRETATION, ETC.–O. T. PROPHETS

Here are entered works on the prophets as a whole as well as those on one or more of the following: Isaiah, Daniel, Lamentations, Ezekiel, Jeremiah.

Croatto, J. Severino. Exodus: A Hermeneutics of Freedom. 112p. (Orig.). 1981. pap. 4.95 (ISBN 0-88344-111-X). Orbis Bks.

Macintosh, A. A. Isaiah XXI: A Palimpsest. LC 79-41375. 160p. 1980. 29.50 (ISBN 0-521-22943-X). Cambridge U Pr.

BIBLE–CRITICISM, INTERPRETATION, ETC.–O. T. PROVERBS

see Bible–Criticism, Interpretation, Etc.–O. T. Poetical Books

BIBLE–CRITICISM, INTERPRETATION, ETC.–O. T. PSALMS

see Bible–Criticism, Interpretation, Etc.–O. T. Poetical Books

BIBLE–CRITICISM, INTERPRETATION, ETC.–O. T. RUTH

see Bible–Criticism, Interpretation, Etc.–O. T. Historical Books

BIBLE–CRITICISM, INTERPRETATION, ETC.–O. T. SAMUEL
see Bible–Criticism, Interpretation, Etc.–O. T. Historical Books

BIBLE–CRITICISM, INTERPRETATION, ETC.–O. T. SONG OF SOLOMON
see Bible–Criticism, Interpretation, Etc.–O. T. Poetical Books

BIBLE–CRITICISM, INTERPRETATION, ETC.–O. T. WISDOM LITERATURE
Murphy, Roland E. Wisdom Literature: Ruth, Esther, Job, Proverbs, Ecclesiastes, Canticles. (The Forms of the Old Testament Literature Ser.). (Orig.). 1981. pap. write for info. (ISBN 0-8028-1877-3). Eerdmans.

BIBLE–CRITICISM, INTERPRETATION, ETC.–O. T. ZECHARIAH
see Bible–Criticism, Interpretation, Etc.–O. T. Minor Prophets

BIBLE–CRITICISM, INTERPRETATION, ETC. O. T. ZEPHANIAH
see Bible–Criticism, Interpretation, Etc.–O. T. Minor Prophets

BIBLE–CRITICISM, INTERPRETATION, ETC.–THEORY, METHODS, ETC.
see Bible–Hermeneutics

BIBLE–CRITICISM, TEXTUAL–N. T.
Bratcher, R. G., ed. Old Testament Quotations in the New Testament. rev. ed. 1980. Repr. of 1967 ed. softcover 1.25 (ISBN 0-8267-0000-4, 08503). United Bible.
--Section Headings for the New Testament. 1961. pap. 0.85 (ISBN 0-8267-0001-2, 08505). United Bible.
Hurtado, Larry. Text-Critical Methodology & the Pre-Caesarean Text. 112p. (Orig.). 1981. pap. 13.00 (ISBN 0-8028-1872-2). Eerdmans.

BIBLE–CURIOSA
see Bible–Miscellanea

BIBLE–DEVOTIONAL LITERATURE
see Bible–Meditations

BIBLE–DICTIONARIES
Beers, V. Gilbert. The Children's Illustrated Bible Dictionary. 1981. pap. 6.95 (ISBN 0-8407-5755-7). Nelson.
De Foulkes, E. Tamez & De Foulkes, I. W. Diccionario Conciso Griego-Espanol Del Nuevo Testamento. 1978. vinyl 3.50 (ISBN 3-438-06005-1, 56530). United Bible.
Greenfield, William. The Greek-English Lexicon to the New Testament. 216p. 1981. pap. 5.95 (ISBN 0-310-20351-1). Zondervan.
Nelson, Wilton M., ed. Diccionario Ilustrado de la Biblia. (Illus.). 735p. (Span.). 1974. 24.95 (ISBN 0-89922-033-9); pap. 15.95 (ISBN 0-89922-099-1). Edit Caribe.
Osbourn, William, Jr. A Hebrew & English Lexicon to the Old Testament. 287p. 1981. pap. 5.95 (ISBN 0-310-20361-9). Zondervan.
Smith, Barbara. The Westminster Concise Bible Dictionary. LC 80-25771. 1981. pap. 5.95 (ISBN 0-664-24363-0). Westminster.
Tenney, Merill E., tr. Diccionario Biblico. (Spanish Bks.). (Span.). 1979. 3.50 (ISBN 0-8297-0540-6); pap. 2.50 (ISBN 0-686-28811-4). Life Pubs Intl.
Thayer, J. H., ed. Greek-English Lexicon of the New Testament: Being Grimm's Wilke's Clavis Novi Testamenti, Transl. Revised & Enlarged. 4th ed. 746p. Repr. of 1901 ed. text ed. 25.00x (ISBN 0-567-01015-5). Attic Pr.

BIBLE–DRAMA
see Mysteries and Miracle-Plays

BIBLE–EVIDENCES, AUTHORITY, ETC.
see also Miracles
Pearlman, Myer, tr. Conhecendo As Doutrinas Da Biblia. (Portugese Bks.). (Port.). 1979. 2.95 (ISBN 0-8297-0647-X). Life Pubs Intl.
Ryrie, Charles. We Believe in Biblical Innerancy. 61p. 1981. pap. 0.35 (ISBN 0-937396-53-2). Walterick Pubs.

BIBLE–EXAMINATIONS, QUESTION-BOOKS, ETC.
see Bible–Catechisms, Question-Books, etc.

BIBLE–EXEGESIS
see Bible–Commentaries; Bible–Hermeneutics

BIBLE–FESTIVALS
see Fasts and Feasts

BIBLE–FOLK-LORE
see Folk-Lore, Jewish

BIBLE–GARDENS
see Bible–Natural History

BIBLE–GEOGRAPHY
Cohn, Robert L. The Shape of Sacred Space: Four Biblical Studies. Cherry, Conrad, ed. LC 80-11086. (Studies in Religion: No. 23). 12.00x (ISBN 0-89130-383-9, 01 00 23); pap. 7.50x (ISBN 0-89130-384-7). Scholars Pr CA.
De Money, Netta D., tr. Geografia Historica Do Mundo Biblico. (Portuguese Bks.). 1979. 2.25 (ISBN 0-8297-0723-9). Life Pubs Intl.
De Money, Netta K., tr. Geografia Historica Del Mundo Biblico. (Spanish Bks.). (Span.). 1979. 2.95 (ISBN 0-8297-0558-9). Life Pubs Intl.

BIBLE–GEOGRAPHY–MAPS
Cleeve, Richard. The Student Map Manual: Historical Geography of the Bible Landa. Monson, J., et al, eds. 168p. 1980. 34.95 (ISBN 0-310-42980-3). Zondervan.

BIBLE–GLOSSARIES, VOCABULARIES, ETC.
see Bible–Dictionaries

BIBLE–HANDBOOKS, MANUALS, ETC.
Alexander, David & Alexander, Pat, eds. Eerdmans' Concise Bible Handbook. LC 80-20131. (Illus.). 384p. (Orig.). 1981. pap. 9.95 (ISBN 0-8028-1875-7). Eerdmans.
Alexander, Pat, ed. Eerdmans' Concise Bible Encyclopedia. LC 80-19885. (Illus.). 256p. (Orig.). 1981. pap. 8.95 (ISBN 0-8028-1876-5). Eerdmans.

BIBLE–HERMENEUTICS
Here are entered works on the principles of Biblical Criticism. Critical works on the Bible are entered under Bible–Criticism, Interpretation, Etc.
Chavez, Moises. Hermeneutica: El Arte de la Parafrasis Libre. 132p. (Orig., Span.). 1978. pap. 3.50 (ISBN 0-89922-142-4). Edit Caribe.
Lund, A. & Luce, A., trs. Hermeneutica E Introduccion Biblica. (Spanish Bks.). (Span.). 1978. 1.90 (ISBN 0-8297-0564-3). Life Pubs Intl.

BIBLE–HIGHER CRITICISM
see Bible–Criticism, Interpretation, etc.; Bible–Introductions

BIBLE–HISTORY
This head is used for work on the History of Bible texts or versions. For works on historical events see Bible–History of Biblical Events, or Bible–History of Contemporary Events.
Blaikie, W. G. & Matthews, C. D. A Manual of Bible History. rev. ed. 432p. 1940. 13.95 (ISBN 0-471-07008-4). Wiley.
De Money, Netta D., tr. Geografia Historica Do Mundo Biblico. (Portugese Bks.). 1979. 2.25 (ISBN 0-8297-0723-9). Life Pubs Intl.
De Money, Netta K., tr. Geografia Historica Del Mundo Biblico. (Spanish Bks.). (Span.). 1979. 2.95 (ISBN 0-8297-0558-9). Life Pubs Intl.
Franzmann, Werner H. Bible History Commentary: Old Testament. LC 80-53145. (Illus.). 616p. 1981. 15.95 (ISBN 0-938272-04-7). Wis Ev Luth.
Keller, Werner. The Bible As History. 2nd, rev. ed. Rehork, Joachim, ed. Neil, William & Rasmussen, B. H., trs. from Ger. LC 80-22218. Orig. Title: Und Die Bibel Hat Docht Recht. (Illus.). 448p. 1981. 16.95 (ISBN 0-688-03724-0). Morrow.

BIBLE–HISTORY OF BIBLICAL EVENTS
see also Palestine–History
Hill, Andrew E., compiled by. Baker's Handbook of Bible Lists. 288p. (Orig.). 1981. pap. 6.95 (ISBN 0-8010-4242-9). Baker Bk.

BIBLE–HISTORY OF BIBLICAL EVENTS–JUVENILE LITERATURE
see Bible Stories

BIBLE–HISTORY OF BIBLICAL EVENTS–N. T.
Levitt, Zola & McCall, Tom. Once Through the New Testament. LC 80-69306. 160p. 1981. pap. 5.95 (ISBN 0-915684-78-0). Christian Herald.

BIBLE–HISTORY OF BIBLICAL EVENTS–SOURCES
see Bible–Evidences, Authority, etc.

BIBLE–HISTORY OF CONTEMPORARY EVENTS, ETC.
see also Palestine–History
Thompson, J. A. The Bible & Archaeology. wnd, rev. ed. 512p. 1981. 13.95 (ISBN 0-8028-3545-7). Eerdmans.

BIBLE–HOMILETICAL USE
Allen, Horace T., Jr. A Handbook for the Lectionary. 1980. softcover 9.95 (ISBN 0-664-24347-9). Westminster.
Criswell, W. A. Expository Sermons on the Epistles of Peter. 216p. (Orig.). 1980. pap. 4.95 (ISBN 0-310-22811-5). Zondervan.
Fuller, Reginald H. The Use of the Bible in Preaching. LC 80-2377. 80p. (Orig.). 1981. pap. 3.50 (ISBN 0-8006-1447-X, 1-1447). Fortress.
Stagg, Frank. Galatians & Romans. (Knox Pereaching Guides Ser.). 160p. (Orig.). 1980. pap. 4.50 (ISBN 0-8042-3238-5). John Knox.

BIBLE–ILLUSTRATIONS
see Bible–Pictures, Illustrations, etc.

BIBLE–INFLUENCE
Von Dobschutz, E. The Influence of the Bible on Civilization. 200p. Repr. of 1914 ed. text ed. 2.95 (ISBN 0-567-02093-2). Attic Pr.
Warshaw, Thayer S. A Compact Guide to Bible Based Beliefs. LC 80-19820. 49p. (Orig.). 1981. pap. 1.50 (ISBN 0-687-09254-X). Abingdon.

BIBLE–INTERPRETATION
see Bible–Commentaries; Bible–Criticism, Interpretation, etc.; Bible–Hermeneutics

BIBLE–INTRODUCTIONS
Asimov, Isaac. Asimov's Guide to the Bible, Vol. 1. LC 68-23566. 12.50 (ISBN 0-385-07399-2). Doubleday.
Hughes, Gerald & Travis, Stephen. Harper's Introduction to the Bible. LC 80-8607. (Illus.). 144p. (Orig.). 1981. pap. 9.95 (ISBN 0-06-064078-2). Har-Row.

BIBLE–INTRODUCTIONS–N. T.
Here are entered Introductions to the New Testament as a whole, or to any part except the Gospels, which are listed separately below.
Foulkes, Richard. Panorama del Nuevo Testamento. LC 75-15161. 112p. (Orig., Span.). 1975. pap. 2.50 (ISBN 0-89922-048-7). Edit Caribe.
Moffatt, James. An Introduction to the Literature of the New Testament. 3rd ed. (International Theological Library). 704p. Repr. of 1918 ed. 13.95x (ISBN 0-567-07213-4). Attic Pr.

BIBLE–INTRODUCTIONS–N. T. GOSPELS
Foulkes, Richard. Panorama del Nuevo Testamento. LC 75-15161. 112p. (Orig., Span.). 1975. pap. 2.50 (ISBN 0-89922-048-7). Edit Caribe.

BIBLE–INTRODUCTIONS–O. T.
Here are listed Introductions to the Old Testament as a whole, or to any part except Apocryphal writings, which are listed separately under Bible–Introductions–Apocrypha and Apocryphal Books.
Driver, S. R. An Introduction to the Literature of the Old Testament. 9th ed. (International Theological Library). 640p. Repr. of 1913 ed. 13.95x (ISBN 0-567-07205-3). Attic Pr.

BIBLE–JUVENILE LITERATURE
see also Bible Stories
Amstutz, Beverly. Benjamin & the Bible Donkies. (Illus.). 1981. pap. 2.50 (ISBN 0-937836-03-6). Precious Res.
Beers, V. Gilbert. The Children's Illustrated Bible Dictionary. 1981. pap. 6.95 (ISBN 0-8407-5755-7). Nelson.
Boehlke, Neal A. Man Who Met Jesus at Bethesda. (Arch Bk.). (gr. k-4). 1981. pap. 0.79 (ISBN 0-570-06143-1, 59-1260). Concordia.
Booth, Julianne. Books of the New Testament. (Arch Book Supplement Ser.). 1981. pap. 0.79 (ISBN 0-570-06150-4, 59-1305). Concordia.
--Books of the Old Testament. (Arch Book Supplement Ser.). 1981. pap. 0.79 (ISBN 0-570-06151-2, 59-1306). Concordia.
Burrage, Barbara. Bible Quizzerama Puzzle Book. 48p. (Orig.). (gr. 6 up). 1981. pap. 1.25 (ISBN 0-87239-446-8, 2836). Standard Pub.
Coleman, William. Far Out Facts About the Bible. (gr. 4-9). 1980. pap. 2.50 (ISBN 0-89191-336-X). Cook.
Dean, Bessie. Paul's Letters. (Story Books to Color). (Illus.). 72p. (Orig.). (gr. k-5). 1980. pap. 3.95 (ISBN 0-88290-170-2). Horizon Utah.
Grogg, Evelyn. Bible Lessons for Little People: Revised with Learning Centers. rev. ed. Eberle, Sarah, rev. by. LC 80-53878. 144p. 1981. pap. 6.95 (ISBN 0-87239-430-1, 3368). Standard Pub.
Johnson, Irene. Life & Letters of Paul. (Find-a-Word Puzzles Ser.). 48p. (Orig.). (gr. 6 up). 1981. pap. 1.25 (ISBN 0-87239-448-4, 2838). Standard Pub.
Keller, W. Phillip. A Child's Look at the Twenty-Third Psalm. LC 80-976. (Illus.). 96p. 1981. 7.95 (ISBN 0-385-15456-9, Galilee). Doubleday.
Marquardt, Merv. Song for Joseph. (Arch Bks.: No. 18). (gr. k-4). 1981. pap. 0.79 (ISBN 0-570-06146-6, 59-1263). Concordia.
Meu Livro De Jesus. (Portugese Bks.). (Port.). 1979. 3.00 (ISBN 0-8297-0758-1). Life Pubs Intl.
Mi Libro De Relatos Biblicos. (Spanish Bks.). 1977. 3.50 (ISBN 0-8297-0755-7). Life Pubs Intl.
Miles, A. Marie. Bible: Chain of Truth. 168p. pap. 1.25. Faith Pub Hse.
Moncure, Jane. Kindness. (What Does the Bible Say? Ser.). (Illus.). 32p. 4.95 (ISBN 0-89565-167-X, 4929). Standard Pub.
Ninety-Two Puzzlers from Old & New Testaments. 48p. (Orig.). (gr. 6 up). 1981. pap. 1.25 (ISBN 0-87239-450-6, 2841). Standard Pub.
Nystrom, Carolyn. Lord, I Want to Have a Quiet Time. LC 80-69305. 224p. (gr. 7-12). 1981. pap. 5.95 (ISBN 0-915684-77-2). Christian Herald.
Schoolland, Marian M. Leading Little Ones to God: A Child's Book of Bible Teaching. rev., 2nd ed. (Illus.). 96p. 1981. 9.95 (ISBN 0-8028-4035-3). Eerdmans.
World Book Childcraft International, Inc. Best-Loved Bible Stories: Old Testament & New Testament, 2 vols. LC 79-55309. (Illus.). 90p. (gr. 4-8). 1980. write for info. (ISBN 0-7166-2059-6). World Bk-Childcraft.

BIBLE–LANGUAGE, STYLE
see also Bible–Parables; Greek Language, Biblical; Hebrew Language
Moulton, J. H., et al. A Grammar of the New Testament Greek: Style, Vol. 4. LC 7-13420. 1976. text ed. 15.00x (ISBN 0-567-01018-X). Attic Pr.
Simcox, W. H. Language of the New Testament. Date not set. 8.95 (ISBN 0-88469-140-3). BMH Bks.
Turner, Nigel. Grammatical Insights into the New Testament. LC 66-71386. 208p. Repr. of 1965 ed. text ed. 15.95x (ISBN 0-567-01017-1). Attic Pr.

BIBLE–LAW
see Jewish Law

BIBLE–LITERARY CRITICISM
see Bible–Criticism, Interpretation, etc.; Bible–Introductions

BIBLE–MANUSCRIPTS
see also Dead Sea Scrolls
Finegan, Jack. Encountering New Testament Manuscripts. pap. 7.95 (ISBN 0-8028-1836-6). Eerdmans.

BIBLE–MAPS
see Bible–Geography–Maps

BIBLE–MEDITATIONS
McAlpine, Campbell. Alone with God: A Manual of Biblical Meditation. 1981. pap. 3.95 (ISBN 0-87123-000-3, 210000). Bethany Fell.

BIBLE–MIRACLES
see Jesus Christ–Miracles; Miracles

BIBLE–MISCELLANEA
Biddle, Maureen. Fifty Craft Projects with Bible Verses & Patterns. LC 80-53872. (Illus.). 64p. (Orig.). 1981. pap. 3.50 (ISBN 0-87239-428-X, 2148). Standard Pub.

BIBLE–NATURAL HISTORY
Swenson, Allan A. Your Biblical Garden: Plants of the Bible & How to Grow Them. LC 79-7703. (Illus.). 240p. 1981. 13.95 (ISBN 0-385-14898-4). Doubleday.

BIBLE–OUTLINES, SYLLABI, ETC.
see Bible–Study

BIBLE–PARABLES
see also Jesus Christ–Parables
Chekijian, Vartan S. The Strange Dreams. 109p. 1980. 5.95 (ISBN 0-533-03227-X). Vantage.
Hubbard, David A. Pictures of the New Kingdom. 110p. (Orig.). 1981. pap. 2.95 (ISBN 0-87784-471-2). Inter-Varsity.
Miller, John W. Step by Step Through the Parables. 192p. (Orig.). 1981. pap. 6.95 (ISBN 0-8091-2379-7). Paulist Pr.
Morgan, G. Campbell. The Parable of the Father's Heart. (Morgan Library). 96p. 1981. pap. 2.95 (ISBN 0-8010-6118-0). Baker Bk.
Schindler, Regine. The Lost Sheep. LC 80-68546. Orig. Title: Das Verlorene Shaf. 32p. (gr. k-3). 1981. Repr. 5.95 (ISBN 0-687-22780-1). Abingdon.

BIBLE–PHILOLOGY
see Greek Language, Biblical; Hebrew Language

BIBLE–PICTURES, ILLUSTRATIONS, ETC.
see also subdivisions Art under names of Bible characters and Biblical subjects, e.g. Jesus Christ–Art
Holy Bible: Norman Rockwell Commemorative Edition. (Illus.). 1979. 39.95 (ISBN 0-89387-037-4). Sat Eve Post.

BIBLE–POETRY
see Hebrew Poetry

BIBLE–PRAYERS
see also Jesus Christ–Prayers; Lord's Prayer; Prayer–Biblical Teaching
Geissler, Eugene S., ed. Bible Prayerbook. LC 80-71052. 528p. (Orig.). 1981. pap. 4.95 (ISBN 0-87793-218-2). Ave Maria.
Pink, A. W. Effectual Fervent Prayer. White, Donald R., ed. 176p. 1981. 8.95 (ISBN 0-8010-7059-7). Baker Bk.

BIBLE–PRINTING
see Bible–History

BIBLE–PROPHECIES
see also Apocalyptic Literature; Prophets
Brubaker, Ray. What in the World Is Happening? 1981. pap. 3.95 (ISBN 0-8407-5767-0). Nelson.
Lindsey, Hal & Carlson, C. C. The Late Great Planet Earth. 176p. 1980. pap. 2.50. Zondervan.
Lockyer. All the Promises of the Bible. 1962. 10.95 (ISBN 0-310-28130-X, 10074). Zondervan.
Longley, Arthur. Earth Will Be Invaded from Outer Space. (Orig.). 1981. pap. 4.95 (ISBN 0-88270-505-9). Logos.
McCune, James A. America, the True Church & the End of the Age: Where the United States Fits in Biblical Prophecy. (Illus.). 227p. (Orig.). 1980. pap. 5.95 (ISBN 0-9604732-0-3). Yorkshire Pub.
Popoff, Peter & Tanner, Don. Forecasts for Nineteen-Eighty Two. LC 80-69975. (Illus.). 50p. 1980. pap. 1.00 (ISBN 0-938544-00-4). Faith Messenger.
Shorrosh, Anis A. Jesus, Prophecy & the Middle East. 1981. pap. 3.95 (ISBN 0-8407-5764-6). Nelson.

BIBLE–READERS
see Readers–Bible

BIBLE–READING
Fish, Sidney M. Weekly Torah Reader: Book of Genesis. rev. ed. 1977. pap. 3.45x (ISBN 0-8197-0036-3). Bloch.
No Volvera a Mi Vacia. LC 76-55490. 365p. (Orig., Span.). 1976. pap. 2.95 (ISBN 0-89922-080-0). Edit Caribe.
Not by Bread Alone: Bible Readings for the Weekdays of Lent. (Illus.). 112p. 1972. pap. 1.95 (ISBN 0-87793-087-2). Ave Maria.

BIBLE–SCIENCE
see Bible and Science

BIBLE–SERMONS
Here are entered works containing sermons which are successively based on at least one whole book of the Bible, virtually forming a commentary in sermon form.
Smith, Robert A. Sermons from the Bible. 1981. pap. 3.00 (ISBN 0-912128-21-6). Pubns Living.

BIBLE–STORIES
see Bible Stories

BIBLE–STUDY
see also Bible Stories
Abecedario Biblico. (Spanish Bks.). 1978. 1.30 (ISBN 0-8297-0494-9). Life Pubs Intl.
Ackland, Dojnald F. Broadman Comments, July-September, 1981. 1981. pap. 2.15 (ISBN 0-8054-1463-0). Broadman.
Ackland, Donald F. Broadman Comments: April-June, 1981. (Orig.). 1981. pap. 2.15 (ISBN 0-8054-1462-2). Broadman.

Adult Vacation Bible School. Incl. pap. 1.95 saddlewire, adult member (ISBN 0-8054-3821-1); pap. 2.10 saddlewire, adult teacher (ISBN 0-8054-3822-X); Ages 4-5. pap. 0.70 saddlewire, pupil (ISBN 0-8054-3813-0); pap. 1.75 saddlewire, teacher (ISBN 0-8054-3814-9); Ages 6-8. (gr. 1-3). pap. 0.70 saddlewire, pupil (ISBN 0-8054-3815-7); pap. 1.75 saddlewire, teacher (ISBN 0-8054-3816-5); Ages 9-11. pap. 0.70 saddlewire, pupil (ISBN 0-8054-3817-3); pap. 1.75 saddlewire, teacher (ISBN 0-8054-3818-1); Planbook, 1981. pap. 0.80 saddlewire (ISBN 0-8054-3811-4); Youth. (gr. 7-12). pap. 0.85 saddlewire, pupil (ISBN 0-8054-3819-X); pap. 2.05 saddlewire, teacher (ISBN 0-8054-3820-3). 1980. Broadman.

Alexander, David. Manual Biblico Llustrado. Vega, Pedro, et al, trs. from Eng. (Illus.). 680p. (Span.). 1976. 26.95 (ISBN 0-89922-077-0). Edit Caribe.

Barr, James. The Scope & Authority of the Bible. LC 80-21394. 1981. pap. 7.95 (ISBN 0-664-24361-4). Westminster.

Barton, Donald W. Journey into the Word. 130p. (Orig.). 1981. pap. 3.50 (ISBN 0-938736-00-0). Life Enrich.

Bennett, Alan D. Unlocking the Beauty of the Bible: A Study Guide. 5.00. UAHC.

Bennett, Georgaan. What the Bible Says About Goodness. LC 80-69626. (What the Bible Says Ser.). 350p. 1981. 13.50 (ISBN 0-89900-080-0). College Pr Pub.

Blaiklock, E. M. Blaiklock's Handbook to the Bible. 1981. pap. 5.95 (ISBN 0-8007-5055-1). Revell.

Boadt, Lawrence, et al, eds. Biblical Studies: Meeting Ground of Jews & Christians. LC 80-82812. (Stimulus Bk). 220p. (Orig.). 1981. pap. 7.95 (ISBN 0-8091-2344-4). Paulist Pr.

Breneman, Mervin, ed. Biblia con Notas. 1696p. (Span.). 1981. 14.95 (ISBN 0-89922-164-5); imitation leather 18.95 (ISBN 0-686-69098-2). Edit Caribe.

Brown, David. Meet the Bible. 1980. 1.25 (ISBN 0-686-28784-3). Forward Movement.

Cartlidge, David R. & Dungan, David L. Documents for the Study of the Gospels. LC 79-21341. 300p. (Orig.). 1980. 14.95 (1-640); pap. 8.95 (ISBN 08006-1640-5, 1-1640). Fortress.

The Catholic Bible Study Course, 6 vols. 1980. Set. pap. text ed. 125.00 (ISBN 0-8434-0766-2, Consortium); 6 wkbks. incl. McGrath.

The Catholic Bible Study Course, 12 vols. Incl. Vol. 1. Pentateuch. Bryce, Glendon E. 250p (ISBN 0-8434-0745-X); Vol. 2. A Guide Through Pentateuch (ISBN 0-8434-0746-8); Vol. 3. Historical Literature. Miller, Charles, ed. 250p (ISBN 0-8434-0747-6); Vol. 4. A Guide Through Historical Literature (ISBN 0-8434-0748-4); Vol. 5. Wisdom Literature. Lillie, Betty J. 250p (ISBN 0-8434-0749-2); Vol. 6. A Guide Through Wisdom Literature (ISBN 0-8434-0750-6); Vol. 7. Prophetic Literature. Branick, Vincent. 250p (ISBN 0-8434-0751-4); Vol. 8. A Guide Through Prophetic Literature (ISBN 0-8434-0752-2); Vol. 9. Mark-Matthew-Luke. Sargent, Robert, ed. 250p (ISBN 0-8434-0754-9); Vol. 10. A Guide Through Mark-Matthew-Luke (ISBN 0-8434-0754-9); Vol. 11. John & Epistles. Grassi, Joseph, ed. 250p (ISBN 0-8434-0755-7); Vol. 12. A Guide Through John & Epistles (ISBN 0-8434-0756-5). Date not set. Set. 125.00 (ISBN 0-686-68786-8); Vols. 1 & 2. 25.00; Vols. 3 & 4. 25.00; Vols. 5 & 6. 25.00; Vols. 7 & 8. 25.00; Vols. 9 & 10. 25.00; Vols. 11 & 12. 25.00. McGrath.

Clark, Gordon H. First & Second Peter. 1980. pap. 4.95. Presby & Reformed.

Cohn, Robert L. The Shape of Sacred Space: Four Biblical Studies. Cherry, Conrad, ed. LC 80-11086. (Studies in Religion: No. 23). 12.00x (ISBN 0-89130-383-9, 01 00 23); pap. 7.50x (ISBN 0-89130-384-7). Scholars Pr CA.

Curso Biblico Elemental, 3 vols. Incl. Vol. 1. Nueva Vida En Cristo - Nuestra Biblia. Walker, Luisa J. 1.95 (ISBN 0-8297-0526-0); tchr's guide 1.50 (ISBN 0-686-28834-3); Vol. 2. Poder Divino-Preguntas y Respuestas-Administradores Fieles. Grams, M. David, et al. 1.95 (ISBN 0-686-28835-1); tchr's guide 2.00 (ISBN 0-686-28836-X); Vol. 3. Iglesia En Marcha-Nuestros Cantos-Nuestra Salud. Hodges, Melvin, et al. 1.95 (ISBN 0-8297-0530-9); tchr's guide 2.00 (ISBN 0-686-28837-8). 1977. Set. 5.20 (ISBN 0-686-28832-7); Set. tchr's guide 5.00 (ISBN 0-686-28833-5). Life Pubs Intl.

De La Fuente, Tomas. Auxiliares Basicos Para el Estudio Biblico. (Illus.). 424p. (Span.). 1980. pap. 4.80 (ISBN 0-311-42067-2). Casa Bautista.

Earle, Ralph. Peloubet's Notes 1981-82. 408p. (Orig.). 1981. pap. 4.95 (ISBN 0-8010-3363-2). Baker Bk.

Fairweather, W. From Exile to Advent. 5th ed. (Handbooks for Bible Classes Ser.). 210p. pap. text ed. 3.50 (ISBN 0-567-28128-0). Attic Pr.

Fromer, Margaret & Nystrom, Carolyn. James: Roadmap for Down-to-Earth Christians (Student & Teacher) (Young Fisherman Bible Studyguide). (Illus.). 80p. 1981. tchr.'s ed. 4.95 (ISBN 0-87788-420-X, 420-X); wkbk. 3.95 (ISBN 0-87788-419-6, 419-X). Shaw Pubs.

Gerstner, John. Bible Inerrancy Primer. Date not set. pap. 1.95 (ISBN 0-88469-144-6). BMH Bks.

Gonzalez, Justo & Gonzalez, Catherine. In Accord-Let Us Worship. (Orig.). 1981. pap. 3.95 (ISBN 0-377-00111-2). Friend Pr.

Havlik, John. How to Enjoy Reading the Bible. 1981. 7.95 (ISBN 0-8054-1137-2). Broadman.

Jeske, Richard L. Understanding & Teaching the Bible. Rast, Harold W., ed. LC 80-69756. (A Lead Book). 128p. (Orig.). 1981. pap. 3.25 (ISBN 0-8006-1601-4, 1-1601). Fortress.

Keyes, Nelson B. El Fascinante Mundo De la Biblia. Orig. Title: Story of the Bible World. (Illus.). 216p. (Span.). 1980. 15.95 (ISBN 0-311-03664-3, Edit Mundo); pap. 11.95 (ISBN 0-311-03665-1, Edit Mundo). Casa Bautista.

Kuiper, R. B. The Bible Tells Us So: Twelve Short Chapters on Major Themes of the Bible. 1978. pap. 2.95 (ISBN 0-85151-001-9). Banner of Truth.

Kunz, Marilyn & Schell, Catherine. Efesios y Filemon. Orozco, Julio, tr. from Eng. LC 77-83811. (Encuentros Biblicos Ser.). 55p. (Orig., Span.). 1977. pap. 1.25 (ISBN 0-89922-095-9). Edit Caribe.

--El Evangelio Segun San Lucas. Roberts, Grace S., tr. from Eng. LC 75-42950. (Encuentros Biblicos). 64p. (Orig., Span.). pap. 1.25 (ISBN 0-89922-063-0). Edit Caribe.

--Se Encontraron Con Jesus. Velez, Jose R., tr. from Eng. LC 76-1299. (Encuentros Biblicos). 55p. (Orig., Span.). 1976. pap. 1.25 (ISBN 0-89922-065-7). Edit Caribe.

--Uno Corintios: Llamado a la Madurez. Velez, Jose R., tr. from Eng. LC 76-1298. (Encuentros Biblicos). 77p. (Orig., Span.). 1976. pap. 1.25 (ISBN 0-89922-064-9). Edit Caribe.

McClain, Alva J. Bible Truths. 1981. pap. 1.00 (ISBN 0-88469-013-X). BMH Bks.

MacDonald, William. Let Me Introduce You to the Bible. 1981. pap. 1.95 (ISBN 0-937396-22-2). Walterick Pubs.

Makrakis, Apostolos. The Bible & the World & Triluminal Science. Orthodox Christian Educational Society, ed. Cummings, Denver, tr. from Hellenic. 531p. 1950. 6.00x (ISBN 0-938366-18-1). Orthodox Chr.

Manley, G. T. Nuevo Auxiliar Biblica. Flores, Jose, tr. from Eng. 572p. (Span.). 1958. pap. 8.50 (ISBN 0-89922-001-0). Edit Caribe.

Mears, Henrietta C. What the Bible Is All About. 698p. 1980. pap. 7.95 (ISBN 0-89066-024-7). World Wide Pubs.

Palau, Luis. Con Quien Me Casare? LC 76-42154. 127p. (Orig., Span.). 1975. pap. 2.25 (ISBN 0-89922-050-9). Edit Caribe.

Peace, Richard. Aprendamos a Amar a Dios. Roberts, Grace S., tr. from Eng. LC 75-29951. (Orig., Span.). 1975. pap. 1.50 (ISBN 0-89922-056-8). Edit Caribe.

--Aprendamos a Amar a Otros. Roberts, Grace S., tr. from Eng. LC 75-29980. 71p. (Orig., Span.). 1975. pap. 1.50 (ISBN 0-89922-057-6). Edit Caribe.

--Aprendamos a Amarnos a Nosotros Mismos. Roberts, Grace S., tr. from Eng. LC 75-29987. 69p. (Orig., Span.). 1975. pap. 1.50 (ISBN 0-89922-058-4). Edit Caribe.

Pearlman, Myer, tr. A Traves De la Biblia. (Spanish Bks.). 1977. 4.25 (ISBN 0-8297-0501-5); pap. 3.25 (ISBN 0-686-28805-X). Life Pubs Intl.

--Atraves Da Biblia. (Portugese Bks.). (Port.). 1979. 3.95 (ISBN 0-8297-0641-0). Life Pubs Intl.

Perry, Mac. The Bible: Why Trust It? (Orig.). 1981. pap. 4.95 (ISBN 0-88270-493-1). Logos.

Perschke, Louis M. Helps & Hints at Bible Study. 176p. 1981. 8.50 (ISBN 0-682-49733-9). Exposition.

Piet, John H. A Path Through the Bible. 1981. pap. 8.95 (ISBN 0-664-24369-X). Westminster.

Prince, Derek. Three Messages for Israel: Jewish Edition. 64p. (Orig.). 1977. pap. 1.50 (ISBN 0-934920-21-4). Derek Prince.

Robinson, James H. & Darline, R. One Hundred Bible Quiz Activities for Church School Classes. 1981. pap. 3.95 (ISBN 0-570-03829-4, 12-2794). Concordia.

Salem, Luis. Hogares de la Biblia. 107p. (Orig., Span.). pap. 1.95 (ISBN 0-89922-079-7). Edit Caribe.

Santa Biblia Dios Habla Hoy. 1504p. 1980. write for info. (Edit Mundo). Casa Bautista.

Schutz, Albert L. Exodus--Exodus: The Cabalistic Bible. Lowenkopf, Anne N., ed. (Orig.). Date not set. 15.50 (ISBN 0-686-69116-4); pap. 8.95 (ISBN 0-936596-04-X). Quantal.

Selbie, W. B. Belief & Life: Studies in the Thought of the Fourth Gospel. (Short Course Ser.). 151p. 1916. text ed. 2.95 (ISBN 0-567-08314-4). Attic Pr.

Smith, Thomas A. Discovering Discipleship: A Resource for Home Bible Studies. (Illus.). 64p. (Orig.) 1981. pap. 2.75 (ISBN 0-87239-438-7, 88570). Standard Pub.

Stout, John L. What the Bible Does Not Say. LC 80-84340. (Illus.). 208p. 1981. 10.95 (ISBN 0-8187-0042-4). Harlo Pr.

Tickle, John. Discovering the Bible, Bk. 2. 96p. (Orig.) 1980. pap. 3.95 (ISBN 0-89243-133-4). Liguori Pubns.

--Un Estudio de la Biblia. Diaz, Olimpia, Sr., tr. from Eng. 96p. 1980. pap. 1.95 (ISBN 0-89243-131-8). Liguori Pubns.

Torrey, R. A., tr. Ce Que la Bible Enseigne. (French Bks.). (Fr.). 1979. 6.00 (ISBN 0-686-28818-1). Life Pubs Intl.

Viertel, Weldon. La Biblia Y Su Interpretation. Orig. Title: The Bible & Its Interpretation. 208p. Date not set. pap. write for info. (ISBN 0-311-03670-8). Casa Bautista.

Wadsworth, Michael, ed. Ways of Reading the Bible. 225p. 1981. 27.50x (ISBN 0-389-20162-6). B&N.

Weiner, Robert T. & Ellen, Rose, Jr. Bible Studies on the Overcoming Life II. 134p. 1976. 3.95 (ISBN 0-686-68912-7). Maranatha Hse.

Weiner, Robert T. & Weiner, Rose E. Bible Studies on the Overcoming Life. 110p. 1976. 3.95 (ISBN 0-686-68913-5). Maranatha Hse.

Weiner, Rose E. & Weiner, Robert T., Jr. Bible Studies for the Preparation of the Bride. 195p. 1980. 4.95 (ISBN 0-686-68911-9). Maranatha Hse.

Your Kingdom Come: Bibles Studies for the Chuch Year Based on the WCC Mission & Evangelism Theme, Melbourne 1980. (Orig.). 1980. pap. 2.25 (ISBN 0-377-00093-0). Friend Pr.

BIBLE–STUDY–OUTLINES, SYLLABI, ETC.

Ackland, Donald F., et al. Broadman Comments, Nineteen Eighty-One-Eighty-Two. 1981. pap. 4.75 (ISBN 0-8054-1465-7). Broadman.

Bailey, Keith M. Leader's Guide for Opening the Old Testament. 50p. (Orig.). 1980. pap. 1.25 (ISBN 0-87509-283-7). Chr Pubns.

Campbell, Frank R. God's Message in Troubled Times. 1981. pap. 3.95 (ISBN 0-8054-2239-0). Broadman.

BIBLE–STUDY–N. T.

Besson, Pablo, tr. from Greek. Nuevo Testamento De Nuestro Senor Jesucristo. 576p. (Span.). 1980. pap. write for info. (ISBN 0-311-48710-6, Edit Mundo). Casa Bautista.

Carr, A. W. Angels & Principalities. (Society for the New Testament Studies Monographs: No. 42). 240p. Date not set. price not set (ISBN 0-521-23429-8). Cambridge U Pr.

Chavez, Moises. Hebreo Biblico Texto Programado: Tomo 1. (Span.). Date not set. pap. price not set (ISBN 0-311-42068-0, Edit Mundo). Casa Bautista.

Harvey, A. E. New English Bible Companion to the New Testament. 1979. 59.50 (ISBN 0-521-07705-2); pap. 19.50 (ISBN 0-521-50539-9). Cambridge U Pr.

Hebreo Biblico Ejercicios Programados: Tomo 2. 192p. (Span.). Date not set. pap. price not set (ISBN 0-311-42069-9, Edit Mundo). Casa Bautista.

Jensen, Irving L. Jensen's Survey of the New Testament. 608p. 1981. text ed. 14.95 (ISBN 0-8024-4308-7). Moody.

LaVerdiere, Eugene. The New Testament in the Life of the Church. LC 80-67403. 192p. (Orig.). 1980. pap. 4.95 (ISBN 0-87793-213-1). Ave Maria.

Rochais, G. Les Recits de Resurrection des Morts dans le Nouveau Testament. LC 79-41615. (Society for New Testament Studies Monographs). 240p. (Fr.). Date not set. price not set (ISBN 0-521-22381-4). Cambridge U Pr.

Viertel, Weldon E. El Evangelio y Epistolas De Juan: Texto Programado. 304p. (Span.). 1981. pap. write for info. (ISBN 0-311-04347-X). Casa Bautista.

--Los Hechos De los Apostoles: Texto Programado. 208p. (Span.). 1981. pap. write for info. (ISBN 0-311-04348-8). Casa Bautista.

BIBLE–STUDY–O. T.

Cowles, H. Robert. Opening the Old Testament. LC 80-65149. (Illus.). 158p. (Orig.). Date not set. pap. 4.50 (ISBN 0-87509-279-9). Chr Pubns.

Hodson, Geoffrey. The Hidden Wisdom in the Holy Bible, Vol. 4. LC 67-8724. 375p. (Orig.). 1981. pap. 5.95 (ISBN 0-8356-0548-5, Quest). Theos Pub Hse.

Roberts, Douglas, tr. Ao Adao, Com Amor. (Portugese Bks.). (Port.). 1979. 1.55 (ISBN 0-8297-0857-X). Life Pubs Intl.

Sperry, Sidney B. The Spirit of the Old Testament. LC 70-119330. (Classics in Mormon Literature Ser.). 246p. 1980. Repr. 5.95 (ISBN 0-87747-832-5). Deseret Bk.

Wood, Fred M. Fire in My Bones. 2nd ed. 1981. pap. 3.50 (ISBN 0-8054-1219-0). Broadman.

BIBLE–SYMBOLISM

see Symbolism in the Bible

BIBLE–TEACHINGS

see Bible–Theology

BIBLE–THEOLOGY

see also names of specific doctrines, with or without the subdivision Biblical Teaching

Chafer, Lewis S. Systematic Theology, 8 vols. 2700p. 1981. Repr. 89.95 (ISBN 0-310-22378-4). Zondervan.

Nelson, P. C., tr. Doctrinas Biblicas. (Spanish Bks.). (Span.). 1979. pap. 1.75 (ISBN 0-8297-0539-2). Life Pubs Intl.

--Doutrinas Biblicas. (Portuguese Bks.). 1979. 1.25 (ISBN 0-8297-0658-5). Life Pubs Intl.

BIBLE–THEOLOGY–N. T.

Goppelt, Leonard. Theology of the New Testament: Jesus & the Gospels, Vol I. Alsup, John E., tr. LC 80-28947. 316p. 1981. 15.95 (ISBN 0-8028-2384-X). Eerdmans.

Guthrie, Donald. New Testament Theology. 1056p. 1981. text ed. 24.95 (ISBN 0-87784-965-X). Inter-Varsity.

Stevens, G. B. The Theology of the New Testament. 2nd ed. (International Theological Library). 636p. Repr. of 1918 ed. text ed. 13.95x (ISBN 0-567-07215-0). Attic Pr.

BIBLE–THEOLOGY–O. T.

Davidson, A. B. The Theology of the Old Testament. (International Theological Library Ser.). 567p. Repr. of 1904 ed. text ed. 13.95x (ISBN 0-567-27206-0). Attic Pr.

BIBLE–TRANSLATIONS

see Bible–Versions

BIBLE–VERSIONS

Here are entered works on Versions of the Bible in any language except English. For English Version see subdivision Versions, English.

Arichea, D. C. & Nida, E. A. Translators Handbook on the First Letter from Peter. (Helps for Translators Ser.). 1980. softcover 2.35 (ISBN 0-8267-0152-3, 08624). United Bible.

Fernandez, Enrique F. Las Biblias Castellanas del Exilio. LC 76-5154. (Illus.). 190p. (Span.). 1976. pap. 3.50 (ISBN 0-89922-067-3). Edit Caribe.

Friberg, Timothy & Friberg, Barbara, eds. Analytical Greek New Testament. 1000p. 1981. 16.95 (ISBN 0-8010-3496-5). Baker Bk.

Lee, S., ed. Syriac Bible, Peshitta Version. 9.40 (ISBN 0-564-03212-3, 82566). United Bible.

Newman, B. M. & Nida, E. A. Translators Handbook on the Gospel of John. (Helps for Translators Ser.). 1980. softcover 4.85 (ISBN 0-8267-0137-X, 08620). United Bible.

Stokes, Mack B. The Bible in the Wesleyan Heritage. LC 80-23636. 96p. (Orig.). 1981. pap. 3.95 (ISBN 0-687-03100-1). Abingdon.

Yeager, Randolph O., ed. The Renaissance New Testament, Vol. 7. 1981. 19.95 (ISBN 0-88289-457-9). Pelican.

BIBLE–VERSIONS, ENGLISH

Lewis, Jack P. The English Bible: From KJV to NIV. 400p. 1981. 15.95 (ISBN 0-8010-5599-7). Baker Bk.

BIBLE–WOMEN

see Women in the Bible

BIBLE–ZOOLOGY

see Bible–Natural History

BIBLE AND SCIENCE

see also Creation

Reid, James. Dios, el Atomo, y el Universo. Orozco, Julio, tr. from Eng. LC 76-55491. 240p. (Orig., Span.). 1977. pap. 3.50 (ISBN 0-89922-083-5). Edit Caribe.

BIBLE GAMES AND PUZZLES

see also Bible–Catechisms, Question-Books, etc.

Botrom, Alice C. Bible Word Puzzles. (Illus.). 30p. (Orig.). 1980. pap. 1.50 (ISBN 0-89323-005-7). BMA Pr.

Crain, Steve. Bible Fun Book, No. 7. 32p. (Orig.). (gr. k-4). 1981. oversized saddle stitched .89 (ISBN 0-87123-766-0, 220766). Bethany Fell.

Doan, Eleanor. Bible Word Search Puzzles, No. 2. (Fun-to-Learn Ser.). 96p. (Orig.). 1980. pap. 1.75 (ISBN 0-310-23812-9). Zondervan.

Hendricks, William & Noord, Glenn Van. Bible Word Chain Puzzles. (Quiz & Puzzle Bks.). 96p. (Orig.). 1981. pap. 2.95 (ISBN 0-8010-4238-0). Baker Bk.

Marks, Thomas J. Bible Study Puzzle Book. (gr. 9 up). 1981. pap. 2.50 saddlewire (ISBN 0-8054-9106-6). Broadman.

Reynolds, Erma. Bible Places Quiz Book. (Quiz & Puzzle Books Ser.). 112p. (Orig.). 1981. pap. 2.45 (ISBN 0-8010-7703-6). Baker Bk.

BIBLE IN THE SCHOOLS

see Religion in the Public Schools

BIBLE PUZZLES

see Bible Games and Puzzles

BIBLE STORIES

Beers, V. G. Out of the Treasure Chest. (Muffin Family Ser.). (Illus.). 96p. (ps-6). 1981. 8.95 (ISBN 0-8024-6099-2). Moody.

Brem, M. M. La Historia de Maria. (Libros Arco Ser.). (Illus.). 32p. (Orig., Span.). (gr. 1-3). 1979. pap. 0.95 (ISBN 0-89922-145-9). Edit Caribe.

Crockett, Maline C. Stories to See & Share. 80p. 1980. pap. 2.95 (ISBN 0-87747-828-7). Deseret Bk.

Hirsh, Marilyn, illus. The Tower of Babel. LC 80-21196. (Illus.). 32p. (ps-2). 1981. PLB 6.95 (ISBN 0-8234-0380-7). Holiday.

Lo Que Nos Dice la Biblia. 1980. pap. 6.95 (ISBN 0-686-69351-5). Vida Pubs.

Martin, Charles E., illus. The Story of Jonah. (Look Look Bks). (Illus.). 24p. (ps). 1981. pap. 1.25 (ISBN 0-307-11863-0, Golden Pr). Western Pub.

Patten, Donald W. The Biblical Flood & the Ice Epoch. 1966. 9.00; pap. 7.50. Pacific Mer.

Peale, Norman V. Bible Stories. pap. 2.25 (ISBN 0-89129-049-4). Jove Pubns.

Schoolland, Marian M. Leading Little Ones to God: A Child's Book of Bible Teaching. rev., 2nd ed. (Illus.). 96p. 1981. 9.95 (ISBN 0-8028-4035-3). Eerdmans.

Wilkerson, David. Promesas de Jesus. Orig. Title: Jesus Person Pocket Promise Book. 95p. (Span.). 1974. pap. 1.95 (ISBN 0-89922-027-4). Edit Caribe.

BIBLE STORIES–N. T.

see also Jesus Christ–Biography–Juvenile Literature

Robertson, Jenny. Paul the Traveler. (Ladybird Bible Ser.). (Illus.). 32p. (ps-4). 1980. Repr. 1.95 (ISBN 0-310-42890-4). Zondervan.

Stoddard, Sandol. Five Who Found the Kingdom: New Testament Stories. LC 80-1663. (Illus.). 128p. (gr. 7). 1981. 8.95a (ISBN 0-385-17169-2); PLB (ISBN 0-385-17170-6). Doubleday.

BIBLE STORIES–O. T.

Napier, B. Davie. Come Sweet Death. rev. ed. 64p. 1981. pap. 4.95 (ISBN 0-8298-0422-6). Pilgrim NY.

BIBLE TRANSLATING

see Bible–Versions

BIBLICAL ANTHROPOLOGY

see Man (Theology)

BIBLICAL ARCHAEOLOGY

see Bible–Antiquities

BIBLICAL CHARACTERS

see Bible–Biography

BIBLICAL GREEK

see Greek Language, Biblical

BIBLICAL LAW

see Jewish Law

BIBLICAL RESEARCH

see Bible–Criticism, Interpretation, etc.

BIBLIOGRAPHICAL EXHIBITIONS

Annual '79: Bologna Book Fair. 8.00. Boston Public Lib.

Character of the Year Project: A Catalog. (Bologna Children's Book Fair). pap. 10.00. Boston Public Lib.

Taylor, Earl R., compiled by. A Checklist of the Robert A Feer Collection of World Fairs of North America. pap. 3.00. Boston Public Lib.

BIBLIOGRAPHY

see also Anonyms and Pseudonyms; Archives; Book Collecting; Bookbinding; Books; Books and Reading; Cataloging; Classification–Books; Information Storage and Retrieval Systems; Libraries; Library Science; Manuscripts; Periodicals–Indexes; Printing; Reference Books

also names of literature, e.g. American Literature; also names of persons, places and subjects, with or without the subdivision bibliography

American Book Publishing Record 1876-1949. 1980. 1975.00 (ISBN 0-8352-1245-9). Bowker.

Bowers, Fredson, ed. Studies in Bibliography, Vol. 34. LC 49-3353. 1981. 20.00x (ISBN 0-8139-0898-1). U Pr of Va.

Performing Arts 1876-1981. 1981. 150.00 (ISBN 0-8352-1372-2). Bowker.

BIBLIOGRAPHY–BEST BOOKS

see also Reference Books–Bibliography

Raphael, Frederic, et al. List of Books. 1981. 10.95 (ISBN 0-517-54017-7, Harmony). Crown.

Sutherland, John. Best Sellers: Popular Fiction of the 1970s. 272p. 1981. 18.95 (ISBN 0-7100-0750-7). Routledge & Kegan.

BIBLIOGRAPHY–EXHIBITIONS

see Bibliographical Exhibitions

BIBLIOGRAPHY–HISTORY

Sources of the History of North Africa, Asia, & Oceania in Scandinavia, 2 pts. Incl. Pt. 1. Sources of the History of North Africa, Asia, & Oceania in Denmark. lib. bdg. 162.00 (ISBN 3-598-21474-X); Pt. 2. Sources of the History of North Africa, Asia, & Oceania in Finland, Norway, Sweden. lib. bdg. 65.00 (ISBN 3-598-21475-8). (Guides to the Sources for the History of the Nations). 1980 (Dist. by Gale Research Co.). K G Saur.

BIBLIOGRAPHY–PAPERBACK EDITIONS

Paperbound Books in Print 1981: Fall, 1981, 2 vols. 4000p. 1981. Set. 43.00 (ISBN 0-8352-1331-5). Bowker.

Paperbound Books in Print 1981: Spring & Fall, 1981 (Full Coverage, 4 vols. 8000p. 1981. Set. 75.00 (ISBN 0-8352-1329-3). Bowker.

Paperbound Books in Print 1981: Spring, 1981, 2 vols. 4000p. 1981. Set. 43.00 (ISBN 0-8352-1330-7). Bowker.

BIBLIOGRAPHY–RARE BOOKS

see also Manuscripts

Hall, Katherine R. E. B. White: A Bibliographic Catalogue of Printed Materials in the Department of Rare Books, Cornell University Library. (Garland Reference Library of the Humanities Ser.). 550p. 1979. lib. bdg. 40.00 (ISBN 0-8240-9549-9). Garland Pub.

BIBLIOGRAPHY–REFERENCE BOOKS

see Reference Books

Walsh, Michael J., et al. Religious Bibliographies in Serial Literature: A Guide. LC 81-312. 224p. 1981. lib. bdg. 35.00 (ISBN 0-313-22987-2, WRB/). Greenwood.

BIBLIOGRAPHY, CRITICAL

see Bibliography–Best Books; Books and Reading; Criticism; Literature–History and Criticism; also subdivision History and Criticism under names of literatures, e.g. American Literatures–History and Criticism

BIBLIOTHERAPY

see also Therapeutics

Stephens, Jacquelyn W. A Practical Guide in the Use & Implementation of Bibliotherapy. 64p. 1981. PLB 6.95 (ISBN 0-89962-045-0). Todd & Honeywell.

BICAMERALISM

see Legislative Bodies

BICYCLES AND TRICYCLES

see also Cycling; Mopeds; Motorcycles

Alderson, Frederick. Bicycles. (Junior Reference Ser.). (Illus.). 64p. (gr. 7 up). 1974. 7.95 (ISBN 0-7136-1464-1). Dufour.

American Society of Civil Engineers, compiled by. Bicycle Transportation: A Civil Engineer's Notebook. LC 80-70171. 189p. pap. text ed. 15.50 (ISBN 0-87262-260-6). Am Soc Civil Eng.

Armstrong, Diana. Bicycle Camping. (Illus., Orig.). 1981. pap. 8.95. Dial.

Cuthbertson, Tom. Better Bikes: A Manual for an Alternative Mode of Transportation. LC 80-5101. (Illus.). 1980. 7.95 (ISBN 0-89815-025-6); pap. 4.95 (ISBN 0-89815-024-8). Ten Speed Pr.

--The Bike Bag Book. (Illus.). 128p. (Orig.). 1981. pap. 2.95 (ISBN 0-89815-039-6). Ten Speed Pr.

Marino, John, et al. John Marino's Bicycling Book. (Illus.). 320p. 1981. 12.95 (ISBN 0-87477-131-5). J P Tarcher.

Marshall, Jeff. The Bicycle Rider's Bible. LC 79-6868. (Outdoor Bible Ser.). (Illus.). 176p. 1981. pap. 4.50 (ISBN 0-385-15134-9). Doubleday.

Olney, Ross R. Riding High: Bicycling for Young People. LC 80-28566. (Illus.). 192p. (gr. 5 up). 1981. 8.95 (ISBN 0-688-41979-8); PLB 8.59 (ISBN 0-688-51979-2). Morrow.

Teresi, Dick & Colligan, Doug. The Cyclist's Manual. LC 76-1344. (Illus.). 1981. 14.95 (ISBN 0-8069-5562-7); lib. bdg. 13.29 (ISBN 0-8069-5563-5). Sterling.

BIGFOOT

see Sasquatch

BILIARY CALCULI

see Calculi, Biliary

BILINGUALISM

see also Education, Bilingual

Palomares, Uvaldo & Ball, Gerry. Yo Puedo: Bilingual Leadership Program for Junior & Senior High. 1980. 89.95 (ISBN 0-86584-036-9). Human Dev Train.

Turner, Paul, ed. Bilingualism in the Southwest. 2nd, rev. ed. 1982. pap. text ed. write for info. (ISBN 0-8165-0729-5). U of Ariz Pr.

BILL OF RIGHTS (U. S.)

see United States–Constitution

BILLS AND NOTES

see Negotiable Instruments

BILLS OF CREDIT

see Negotiable Instruments

BILLS OF FARE

see Menus

BILLY THE KID

Adams, Ramon F. A Fitting Death for Billy the Kid. LC 60-5112. (Illus.). 310p. 1981. 14.95 (ISBN 0-8061-0458-9). U of Okla Pr.

BILUCHI LANGUAGE

see Baluchi Language

BINARY STARS

see Stars, Double

BINDING OF BOOKS

see Bookbinding

BINGHAM, GEORGE CALEB, 1811-1899

Grand, Evalyne S. The Fifty Dollar Gift. 178p. 1979. 11.95 (ISBN 0-86629-017-6). Sunrise MO.

BIOCHEMICAL ENGINEERING

Trudinger, P. A. Biogeochemistry of Ancient & Modern Environments. 723p. 1981. 52.00 (ISBN 0-387-10303-1). Springer-Verlag.

BIOCHEMICAL EVOLUTION

see Chemical Evolution

BIOCHEMISTRY

see Biological Chemistry

BIOCHEMISTRY, QUANTUM

see Quantum Biochemistry

BIOCLIMATOLOGY

see also Crops and Climate

Eighth International Biometeorological Congress 9-15 September 1979. Biometeorology Seven: Proceedings, Supplement to Volume 24, of the International Journal of Biometeorology, Pts. 1 & 2. Zemel, Z. & Hyslop, N., eds. 1981. pap. text ed. 78.95 (ISBN 90-265-0354-7). Swets North Am.

--Biometeorology Seven: Proceedings, Supplement to Volume 24 of the International Journal of Biometeorology, Pt. 2. Zemel, Z. & Hyslop, N., eds. 1981. pap. text ed. 44.75 (ISBN 90-265-0350-4). Swets North Am.

Johnson, H. D. Progress in Animal Biometeorology: The Effects of Weather & Climate on Animals; Vol 1 Period 1963-1973, 2 pts. Incl. Pt. 1. Effects of Temperature on Animals: Including Effects of Humidity, Radiation & Wind. 624p. 1976. text ed. 115.00 (ISBN 90-265-0196-X); Effect of Light, High Actitude, Noise, Electric, Magnetic & Electro-Magnetic Fields, Ionization, Gravity & Air Pollutions on Animals. 322p. 1976. text ed. 57.00 (ISBN 90-265-0235-4). (Progress in Biometeorology). 1976 (Pub. by Swets Pub Serv Holland). Swets North Am.

Tromp, Solco W. Progress in Human Biometeorology: The Effect of Weather & Climate on Man & His Living Environment, Period 1963 to 1970-75, Vol. 1. Incl. Pt. 1. The Micro & Macroenvironments in the Atmosphere & Their Effects on Basic Physiological Mechanisms of Man. 726p. 1974. pap. text ed. 144.00 (ISBN 90-265-0167-6); Pt. 2. Pathological Biometeorology. 444p. 1977. pap. text ed. 86.50 (ISBN 90-265-0245-1); Pt. 3. Biometeorological Aspects of Plants, Trees & Animals in Human Life. 158p. 1972. pap. text ed. 31.50 (ISBN 90-265-0156-0). (Progress in Biometeorology Ser., Pub. by Swets Pub Serv Holland). Swets North Am.

Zemel, Z. & Hyslop, N. St. G., eds. Biometeorology: Proceedings of the Eighth International Biometeorological Congress 9-15 September 1979.Supplement to Volume 24 of the International Journal of Biometeorology, No.7, Pt.1. vi, 150p. 1980. pap. text ed. 44.75 (ISBN 90-265-0349-0). Swets North Am.

BIOCOMPATIBLE MATERIALS

see Biomedical Materials

BIODYNAMIC GARDENING

see Organic Gardening

BIOELECTRICITY

see Electrophysiology

BIOENERGETICS

see also Energy Metabolism

Sanadi, D. Rao, ed. Current Topics in Bioenergetics, Vol. XI. (Serial Publications). 1981. write for info. (ISBN 0-12-152511-2). Acad Pr.

BIOENGINEERING

see also Agricultural Engineering; Bionics; Biosynthesis; Biotelemetry; Human Engineering; Sanitary Engineering

House, David. The Biogas Handbook. LC 80-8998. Orig. Title: The Compleat Biogas Handbook. (Illus.). 224p. 1981. pap. 10.95 (ISBN 0-915238-47-0). Peace Pr.

Welkowitz, Walter, ed. Bioengineering: Proceedings of the Ninth Northeast Conference, March, 1981, Rutgers University, Piscataway, New Jersey. (Illus.). 432p. 1981. pap. 60.00 (ISBN 0-08-027207-X). Pergamon.

BIOFEEDBACK TRAINING

Danskin, David G. & Crow, Mark A. Biofeedback: An Introduction & Guide. 150p. (Orig.). 1981. pap. text ed. price not set (ISBN 0-87484-530-0). Mayfield Pub.

Heisel, Dorelle. Biofeedback Strategies for Interpersonal Relationships. 1981. write for info. Gordon.

Hume, Wilfrid I. Biofeedback, Vol. 1. Horrobin, D. F., ed. (Biofeedback Research Review Ser.). 126p. 1980. Repr. of 1977 ed. 9.95 (ISBN 0-87705-965-9). Human Sci Pr.

BIOGEOGRAPHY

see Geographical Distribution of Animals and Plants

BIOGRAPHY

see also Autobiographies; Bibliography; Christian Biography; Genealogy; Heraldry; Portraits

also names of individuals, e.g. Burns, Robert; Einstein, Albert; or classes of persons, e.g. Actors, Authors; and subdivision Biography under particular subjects and under names of countries, cities, etc., e.g. Great Britain–Biography; women–Biography

Aurandt, Paul. More of Paul Harvey's the Best of the Story. 208p. 1981. pap. 2.50 (ISBN 0-553-14594-0). Bantam.

Burroughs, William S. The Last Words of Dutch Schultz. LC 80-54557. (Illus.). 128p. 1981. pap. 4.95 (ISBN 0-394-17852-1). Seaver Bks.

Cecil, David, ed. Modern Biography. 229p. 1980. Repr. of 1938 ed. lib. bdg. 15.00 (ISBN 0-8492-3971-0). R West.

DeMarco, Guy. Third from the Sun. 64p. 1981. 10.00 (ISBN 0-682-49670-7). Exposition.

Dowling, William C. Language & Logos in Boswell's Life of Johnson. LC 80-8545. (Essays in Literature Ser.). 232p. 1981. 15.00x (ISBN 0-691-06455-5). Princeton U Pr.

Greenwood, John D. Namesakes of the Eighties. 1980. 22.00. Freshwater.

The International Who's Who 1980-1981. 44th ed. LC 35-10257. 1409p. 1980. 90.00x (ISBN 0-905118-48-0). Intl Pubns Serv.

Langness, L. L. & Frank, Gelya F. Lives: An Anthropological Approach to Biography. Edgerton, R. N., ed. (Chandler & Sharp Publications in Anthropology Ser.). 224p. (Orig.). 1981. pap. 5.95 (ISBN 0-88316-542-2). Chandler & Sharp.

Shawcross, J. P. The Daily Biographer. 388p. 1980. Repr. of 1915 ed. lib. bdg. 50.00 (ISBN 0-8492-8118-0). R West.

Sherman, Lucille. Lady on the Run. LC 80-83999. 1981. pap. 4.95 (ISBN 0-89081-278-0). Harvest Hse.

Tennyson, Charles. Life's All a Fragment: Tennyson. 264p. 1980. Repr. of 1953 ed. lib. bdg. 30.00 (ISBN 0-89760-881-X). Telegraph Bks.

Unger, Leonard, ed. American Writers: A Collection of Literary Biographies, 6 vols. LC 73-1759. 1979. Set. lib. bdg. 275.00 (ISBN 0-684-16104-4). Scribner.

BIOGRAPHY–BIBLIOGRAPHY

Rex, Percy F. The Prolific Pencil. Burrows, Fredrika A. & Sullwold, Stephen W., eds. LC 80-51482. (Illus.). 312p. 1980. 15.00 (ISBN 0-88492-037-2). W S Sullwold.

Who's Who 1981-82. 133rd ed. 2700p. 1981. 99.50x (ISBN 0-686-69393-0). St Martin.

BIOGRAPHY–HISTORY AND CRITICISM

see Biography (As a Literary Form)

BIOGRAPHY–20TH CENTURY

Wintle, Justin. Makers of Modern Culture. 704p. 1981. 34.95 (ISBN 0-87196-493-7). Facts on File.

BIOGRAPHY (AS A LITERARY FORM)

see also Autobiography

Winslow, Donald J. Life-Writing: A Glossary of Terms in Biography, Autobiography, & Related Forms. (Biography Monographs Ser.). 64p. (Orig.). pap. 4.50x (ISBN 0-8248-0748-0). U Pr of Hawaii.

BIOLOGICAL ANTHROPOLOGY

see Physical Anthropology

BIOLOGICAL CHEMISTRY

see also Acid Base Equilibrium; Biochemical Engineering; Bioenergetics; Biosynthesis; Blood–Analysis and Chemistry; Chemical Genetics; Chromatographic Analysis; Enzymes; Metabolism; Molecular Biology; Quantum Biochemistry

Adrian, R. H. Reviews of Physiology, Biochemistry, & Pharmacology, Vol. 88. (Illus.). 280p. 1981. 52.00 (ISBN 0-387-10408-9). Springer-Verlag.

Adrian, R. H., ed. Reviews of Physiology, Biochemistry & Pharmacology, Vol. 89. (Illus.). 260p. 1981. 54.30 (ISBN 0-387-10495-X). Springer-Verlag.

Brewster, Marge A. & Naito, Herbert K., eds. Nutritional Elements & Clinical Biochemistry. 450p. 1980. 45.00 (ISBN 0-306-40569-5, Plenum Pr). Plenum Pub.

Bryce, Charles, ed. Biochemical Education. 208p. 1981. 33.00x (ISBN 0-7099-0600-5, Pub. by Croom Helm LTD England). Biblio Dist.

Buechel, T., et al, eds. Biological Chemistry of Organelle Formation: Proceedings. (Colloquium Mosbach Ser.: Vol. 31). (Illus.). 290p. 1981. 44.00 (ISBN 0-387-10458-5). Springer-Verlag.

Campbell, Paul N. & Greville, G. D., eds. Essays in Biochemistry, Vols. 1-5 & 8-15. Incl. Vol. 1. 1965 (ISBN 0-12-158101-2); Vol. 2. 1966 (ISBN 0-12-158102-0); Vol. 3. 1967 (ISBN 0-12-158103-9); Vol. 4. 1968 (ISBN 0-12-158104-7); Vol. 5. 1970 (ISBN 0-12-158105-5); Vol. 8. 1972 (ISBN 0-12-158108-X); Vol. 9. 1974 (ISBN 0-12-158109-8); Vol. 10. 1974 (ISBN 0-12-158110-1); Vol. 11. 1976 (ISBN 0-12-158111-X); Vol. 12. 1977 (ISBN 0-12-158112-8); Vol. 13. 1978 (ISBN 0-12-158113-6); Vol. 14. 1978 (ISBN 0-12-158114-4); Vol. 15. 1979 (ISBN 0-12-158115-2). (Illus.). pap. 13.00 ea. Acad Pr.

Chapeville, F. & Haenni, A. O., eds. Chemical Recognition in Biology. (Molecular Biology, Biochemistry & Biophysics: Vol. 32). (Illus.). 430p. 1980. 57.80 (ISBN 0-387-10205-1). Springer-Verlag.

Davies, P. L. Biochemistry: Level Three. (Illus.). 224p. (Orig.). 1980. pap. text ed. 19.95x (ISBN 0-7121-0276-0). Intl Ideas.

Dugas, H. & Penney, C. Bioorganic Chemistry: A Chemical Approach to Enzyme Action. (Springer Advanced Texts in Chemistry Ser.). (Illus.). 416p. 1981. 29.80 (ISBN 0-387-90491-3). Springer-Verlag.

Glick, David M. Biochemistry Review. LC 80-19927. (Basic Science Review Bks.). 1980. pap. 8.50. Med Exam.

Goldberg, David M. Clinical Biochemistry Review, Vol. 2. 416p. 1981. 24.00 (ISBN 0-471-08297-X, Pub. by Wiley Med). Wiley.

Harrison, P. M. & Hoare, R. J. Metals in Biochemistry. LC 79-41813. 80p. 1980. pap. 5.95 (ISBN 0-412-13160-9, 6361). Methuen Inc.

Porter, John W. & Spurgeon, Sandra L. Biosynthesis of Isoprenoid Compounds. 350p. 1981. 35.00 (ISBN 0-471-04807-0, Pub. by Wiley-Interscience). Wiley.

Powell, Eric F. Biochemistry Up to Date. 66p. 1963. pap. 5.00x (ISBN 0-8464-0995-X). Beekman Pubs.

Russell, N. J., et al. Blood Biochemistry. 128p. 1980. 24.00x (Pub. by Croom Helm England). State Mutual Bk.

Semenza, G. Of Oxygen, Energy & Nutrients, Vol. 1, Pt. 1. (Evolving Life Sciences Ser: First-Hand Accounts of Scientific Ideas & Events). 440p. 1981. 90.00 (ISBN 0-471-27923-4, Pub. by Wiley-Interscience). Wiley.

Van Tamelen, E. E., ed. Bioorganic Chemistry, 2 vols. Incl. Vol. 1. Enzyme Action. 1977. 49.75 (ISBN 0-12-714301-7); Vol. 2. 1978. 52.50, by subscription 83.00 (ISBN 0-12-714302-5). Acad Pr.

BIOLOGICAL CHEMISTRY–LABORATORY MANUALS

Strong, F. M. & Koch, H. Gilbert. Biochemistry Laboratory Manual. 3rd ed. 260p. 1981. write for info. wire coil (ISBN 0-697-04705-9). Wm C Brown.

BIOLOGICAL CHEMISTRY–PROBLEMS, EXERCISES, ETC.

Dawes, E. A. Quantitative Problems in Biochemistry. 6th ed. (Illus.). 340p. 1981. text ed. 32.00 (ISBN 0-582-44402-0). Longman.

Wood, W. B. Biochemistry: A Problems Approach. 2nd ed. 1981. 12.95; solutions manual 3.95. Benjamin-Cummings.

BIOLOGICAL CLOCKS

see Biological Rhythms

BIOLOGICAL CONTROL SYSTEMS

see also Biofeedback Training; Homeostasis

Leondes, C. T., ed. Control of Dynamic Systems: Advances in Theory & Application, Vols. 9, 10, 13 & 15. Incl. Vol. 9. 44.00 (ISBN 0-12-012709-1); Vol. 10. 44.00 (ISBN 0-12-012710-5); Vol. 13. 1977. 39.00 (ISBN 0-12-012713-X); Vol. 15. 1979. 22.50 (ISBN 0-12-012715-6). 1973. Acad Pr.

Toates, F. M. Control Theory in Biology & Experimental Psychology. 1980. text ed. 21.00x (ISBN 0-09-119660-4, Hutchinson U Lib). Humanities.

BIOLOGICAL ELECTRONICS

see Electronics in Biology

BIOLOGICAL ENGINEERING

see Bioengineering

BIOLOGICAL FORM
see Morphology
BIOLOGICAL MECHANICS
see Biomechanics
BIOLOGICAL PHYSICS
see also Biological Control Systems; Biomechanics; Biomedical Engineering; Bionics; Cells; Electronics in Biology; Homeostasis; Medical Physics; Molecular Biology; Radiobiology; Rheology (Biology)
Blumenfeld, L. A. Problems of Biological Physics. (Springer Series in Synergetics: Vol. 7). (Illus.). 300p. 1981. 36.00 (ISBN 0-387-10401-1). Springer-Verlag.
Guelph. Biophysics Handbook II. 208p. 1980. pap. text ed. 8.95 (ISBN 0-8403-2281-X). Kendall-Hunt.
Noble, D. & Blundell, T. L., eds. Progress in Biophysics & Molecular Biology, Vol. 35. (Illus.). 206p. 1981. 62.50 (ISBN 0-08-027122-7). Pergamon.
University of Guelph. Biophysics Handbook I. 208p. 1980. pap. text ed. 8.95 (ISBN 0-8403-2280-1). Kendall-Hunt.
BIOLOGICAL PRODUCTS
Vincent, J. F. & Currey, J. D., eds. The Mechanical Properties of Biological Materials. LC 80-40111. (Society of Experimental Biology Symposia Ser.: No. 34). (Illus.). 400p. 1981. 69.50 (ISBN 0-521-23478-6). Cambridge U Pr.
BIOLOGICAL RHEOLOGY
see Rheology (Biology)
BIOLOGICAL RHYTHMS
Scheving, Lawrence E. & Halberg, Franz. Chronobiology: Principles & Applications to Shifts in Schedules. (NATO Advanced Study Institute: Behavioral Social Sciences, No. 3). 597p. 1980. 65.00x (ISBN 90-286-0940-7). Sijthoff & Noordhoff.
BIOLOGICAL STRUCTURE
see Morphology
BIOLOGICAL TELEMETRY
see Biotelemetry
BIOLOGY
see also Adaptation (Biology); Anatomy; Bioclimatology; Bioengineering; Biomathematics; Biometry; Botany; Cells; Cytology; Developmental Biology; Electronics in Biology; Embryology; Evolution; Fresh-Water Biology; Genetics; Heredity; Human Biology; Hybridization; Life (Biology); Marine Biology; Medical Microbiology; Metabolism; Microbiology; Microscope and Microscopy; Morphogenesis; Natural History; Parasites; Parasitology; Photobiology; Phylogeny; Physiology; Psychobiology; Radiobiology; Reproduction; Sex (Biology); Symbiosis; Zoology
Adams, David. Essentials of Oral Biology. (Dental Ser.). (Illus.). 152p. 1981. text ed. 12.50 (ISBN 0-443-02095-7). Churchill.
Black. Materials in the Biological Environment. 320p. 1981. 32.50 (ISBN 0-8247-1267-6). Dekker.
Cheremisinoff, Paul N. Bioconversion Sourcebook: (Abstracts) 1981. text ed. 29.95 (ISBN 0-250-40424-9). Ann Arbor Science.
Cold Spring Harbor Symposia on Quantitative Biology: Movable Genetic Elements, Vol. XLV. (Cold Spring Harbor Symposia on Quantitative Biology Ser.). 1981. price not set (ISBN 0-87969-044-5). Cold Spring Harbor.
Committee on Research Priorities in Tropical Biology. Research Priorities in Tropical Biology. xii, 116p. 1980. pap. text ed. 8.25 (ISBN 0-309-03043-9). Natl Acad Pr.
Curtis, Helena & Barnes, N. Sue. Invitation to Biology. 3rd ed. 1981. text ed. write for info. (ISBN 0-87901-131-9); write for info. study guide (ISBN 0-87901-139-4). Worth.
Halvorson, Harlyn O. & Van Holde, Kensal E., eds. The Origins of Life & Evolution. LC 80-21901. (MBL Lectures in Biology: Vol. 1). 136p. 1980. 16.00 (ISBN 0-8451-2200-2). A R Liss.
Jaeger, W., ed. Biological Growth & Spread: Proceedings. (Lecture Notes in Biomathematics: Vol. 38). 511p. 1981. pap. 34.00 (ISBN 0-387-10257-4). Springer-Verlag.
Mani, M. S. & Giddings, L. E. Ecology of Highlands. (Monographiae Biologicae: No. 40). (Illus.). 236p. 1980. lib. bdg. 58.00 (ISBN 90-6193-093-6, Pub. by Dr. W. Junk). Kluwer Boston.
Maniatis, T., et al, eds. Molecular Cloning Lab Manual. Sambrook, J. (Orig.). 1981. pap. text ed. 24.00 (ISBN 0-87969-136-0). Cold Spring Harbor.
Mercer, E. H. The Foundations of Biological Theory. 290p. 1981. 30.00 (ISBN 0-471-08797-1, Pub. by Wiley Interscience). Wiley.
Nelson, Gareth & Platnick, Norman I. Systematics & Biogeography: Cladistics & Vicariance. LC 80-20828. (Illus.). 592p. 1981. text ed. 35.00x (ISBN 0-231-04574-3). Columbia U Pr.
OAS General Secretariat Department of Scientific & Technological Affairs. A Vida Da Celula. (Serie De Biologia: No. 5). (Illus.). 117p. (Orig.). Repr. of 1968 ed. 2.00 (ISBN 0-8270-1141-5). OAS.
Prescott, David & Turner, James, eds. Methods in Cell Biology: Three-Dimensional Ultrastructure in Biology, Vol. 22. 1981. write for info. (ISBN 0-12-564122-2). Acad Pr.
Rudman, Jack. Biology. (Undergraduate Program Field Test Ser.: UPFT-2). (Cloth bdg. avail. on request) (ISBN 0-8373-6002-1). pap. 9.95 (ISBN 0-686-68259-9). Natl Learning.
Scott, George P. & McMillin, J. M. Dissipative Structures & Spatiotemporal Organization Studies in Biomedical Research. (Illus.). 271p. 1980. pap. text ed. 9.95. Iowa St U Pr.
Skulachev, V. P., ed. Soviet Scientific Review: Biology Review, Vol. 2, Section D. 1981. write for info. (ISBN 3-7186-0058-7). Harwood Academic.
BIOLOGY–ADDRESSES, ESSAYS, LECTURES
Biology Coloquium, 29th, Oregon State Univ. Biochemical Coevolution: Proceedings. Chambers, Kenton L., ed. LC 52-19235. 128p. 1970. text ed. 6.00 (ISBN 0-87071-168-7). Oreg St U Pr.
Halvorson, Harlyn O. & Van Holde, Kensal E., eds. The Origins of Life & Evolution. LC 80-21901. (MBL Lectures in Biology: Vol. 1). 136p. 1980. 16.00 (ISBN 0-8451-2200-2). A R Liss.
Huxley, Julian. Essays of a Biologist. 304p. 1980. Repr. of 1929 ed. lib. bdg. 25.00 (ISBN 0-8495-2274-9). Arden Lib.
BIOLOGY–COLLECTED WORKS
Skulachev, V. P., ed. Soviet Scientific Reviews: Biology Reviews, Vol. 2, Section D. 1981. write for info. (ISBN 3-7186-0058-7). Harwood Academic.
BIOLOGY–DATA PROCESSING
Lewis, R., ed. Computers in Life Sciences. 128p. 1980. 25.00x (Pub. by Croom Helm England). State Mutual Bk.
BIOLOGY–DICTIONARIES
Daintith, John, ed. The Facts on File Dictionary of Biology. 288p. 1981. 14.95 (ISBN 0-87196-510-0). Facts on File.
Gray, Peter. Encyclopedia of the Biological Sciences. LC 80-28590. 1056p. 1981. Repr. lib. bdg. price not set (ISBN 0-89874-326-5). Krieger.
Roe, Keith E. & Frederick, Richard G. Dictionary of Theoretical Concepts in Biology. LC 80-19889. 312p. 1981. 17.50 (ISBN 0-8108-1353-X). Scarecrow.
BIOLOGY–ECOLOGY
see Ecology
BIOLOGY–LABORATORY MANUALS
Gerrath, Jean, et al. A Plant Biology Lab Manual for a One Semester Course Form & Function. 144p. 1980. pap. text ed. 6.95 (ISBN 0-8403-2272-0). Kendall-Hunt.
Griffith, Jack S., et al. Biology One Hundred & Twenty: Laboratory Manual for Man & His Environment. 128p. 1980. pap. text ed. 7.95 (ISBN 0-8403-2228-3). Kendall-Hunt.
Hartman, Margaret & Russell, Mercer P. Laboratory Manual for Biology of Animals. 1980. coil binding 7.50 (ISBN 0-88252-108-X). Paladin Hse.
Jope, Charlene A. Cellular & Molecular Laboratory Manual. 64p. 1981. pap. text ed. 5.95 (ISBN 0-8403-2353-0). Kendall-Hunt.
Knox, Carol & Rowsey, Katheryn. Problems in Biology. (Illus.). 90p. (Orig.). (gr. 10-11). 1980. lab manual 2.95 (ISBN 0-88334-132-8). Ind Sch Pr.
Schultz, Janet L. Biology & Man Laboratory Guide. 80p. 1980. pap. text ed. 5.95 (ISBN 0-8403-2351-4). Kendall-Hunt.
Scott, Leroy & Weih, Starr. Biology Laboratory Manual. 1980. coil binding 8.95 (ISBN 0-88252-106-3). Paladin Hse.
Wall, Wendell. Laboratory Manual for Introductory Biology. coil binding 10.95 (ISBN 0-88252-101-2). Paladin Hse.
BIOLOGY–MATHEMATICAL MODELS
Burton. Modeling of Differential Equations in Biology. 296p. 1980. 35.00 (ISBN 0-8247-1075-4). Dekker.
Burton, T. A., ed. Mathematical Biology-a Conference on Theoretical Aspects of Molecular Science: Proceedings of a Conference Held at Southern Illinois University at Carbondale, May 27-28, 1980. (Illus.). 241p. 1981. 30.00 (ISBN 0-08-026348-8). Pergamon.
BIOLOGY–PERIODICITY
see Biological Rhythms
BIOLOGY–STATISTICAL MODELS
see Biometry
BIOLOGY, ELECTRONICS IN
see Electronics in Biology
BIOLOGY, MOLECULAR
see Molecular Biology
BIOLUMINESCENCE
Deluca, Marlene & McElroy, William, eds. Bioluminescience & Chemiluminescence: Basic Chemistry & Analytical Applications. 1981. price not set (ISBN 0-12-208820-4). Acad Pr.
BIOMASS ENERGY
see also Refuse As Fuel
Office of Technology Assessment, U.S. Congress. Energy from Biological Processes. 200p. 1981. lib. bdg. 20.00x (ISBN 0-86531-171-4). Westview.
BIOMATERIALS
see Biomedical Materials
BIOMATHEMATICS
see also Biology–Mathematical Models; Biometry
Ohta, T. Evolution & Variation of Multigene Families. (Lecture Notes in Biomathematics: Vol. 37). 131p. 1980. pap. 9.80 (ISBN 0-387-09998-0). Springer-Verlag.
BIOMECHANICS
see also Human Engineering
Engle, Eloise & Lott, Arnold. Man in Flight: Biomedical Achievements in Aerospace. LC 79-63780. (A Supplement to the American Astronautical Society History Ser.). (Illus.). 414p. 1979. 20.00x (ISBN 0-915268-24-8). Univelt Inc.
Fung, Y. C. Biomechanics: Mechanical Properties of Living Tissues. (Illus.). 400p. 1980. 29.80 (ISBN 0-387-90472-7). Springer-Verlag.
Ghista, D. N., et al, eds. Perspective in Biomechanics, Vol. I. (Perspectives in Biomechanics Ser.). 902p. 1981. 205.00 (ISBN 3-7186-0006-4). Harwood Academic.
Simonian, Charles. Fundamentals of Sports Biomechanics. (Illus.). 224p. 1981. text ed. 13.95 (ISBN 0-13-344499-6). P-H.
BIOMEDICAL ENGINEERING
see also Biomedical Materials; Electronics in Biology; Medical Instruments and Apparatus
Francois, D. Advances in Fracture Research: Proceedings of the 5th International Conference on Fracture, 1981, Cannes, France. LC 80-41879. (International Series on the Strength & Fracture of Materials & Structures). 3000p. 1981. 450.00 (ISBN 0-08-025428-4); pap. 375.00 (ISBN 0-08-024776-8). Pergamon.
Tischler, Morris. Experiments in General & Biomedical Instrumentation. Haas, Mark, ed. (Illus.). 176p. 1980. pap. text ed. 8.95x (ISBN 0-07-064781-X, G). McGraw.
Traister, Robert. Principles of Biomedical Instrumentation & Monitoring. 300p. 1981. text ed. 24.95 (ISBN 0-8359-5611-3). Reston.
BIOMEDICAL MATERIALS
Szycher, Michael & Robinson, William J., eds. Synthetic Biomedical Polymers: Concepts & Applications. LC 80-52137. (Illus.). 235p. 1980. 39.00 (ISBN 0-87762-290-6). Technomic.
BIOMETEROLOGY
see Bioclimatology
BIOMETRY
see also Biomathematics; Mathematical Statistics
Hubert, J. J. & Carter. Biostatistics: 1064 Answers. 64p. 1980. pap. text ed. 3.95 saddle stitched (ISBN 0-8403-2288-7). Kendall-Hunt.
--Biostatistics: 1064 Questions. LC 80-82899. 160p. 1980. pap. text ed. 6.95 (ISBN 0-8403-2287-9). Kendall-Hunt.
Sokal, Robert R. & Rohlf, F. James. Biometry: The Principles & Practices of Statistics in Biological Research. 2nd ed. LC 81-4. 1981. text ed. price not set (ISBN 0-7167-1254-7). W H Freeman.
BIOMETRY–TABLES, ETC.
Pearson, E. S. & Hartley, H. O., eds. Biometrika Tables for Statisticians, Vol. 1. 270p. 1976. 25.00x (ISBN 0-85264-700-X, Pub. by Griffin England). State Mutual Bk.
--Biometrika Tables for Statisticians, Vol. 2. 1976. 30.00x (ISBN 0-85264-701-8, Pub. by Griffin England). State Mutual Bk.
Rimm, Alfred A., et al. Basic Biostatistics in Medicine & Epidemiology. 352p. 1980. pap. text ed. 16.50x (ISBN 0-8385-0528-7). ACC.
BIONICS
see also Artificial Intelligence; Optical Data Processing
DECHEMA, Deutsche Gesellschaft Fuer Chemisches Apparatewesen E. V., ed. Biotechnology: Proceedings of the First European Congress on Biotechnology. (Dechema Monographs: Vol. 82). 304p. 1979. pap. text ed. 37.50 (ISBN 3-527-10765-7). Verlag Chemie.
Rothman, Harry, et al, eds. Biotechnology: A Review & Annotated Bibliography. 1980. 25.00 (ISBN 0-08-027177-4). Pergamon.
Wiseman, A. Topics in Enzyme & Fermentation Biotechnology, Vol. 5. 300p. 1980. 95.00 (ISBN 0-470-27089-6). Halsted Pr.
Wunderluch, Klaus & Gloede, Wolfgang. Nature As Constructor. Varecha, Vladimir, tr. from Ger. LC 80-18311. (Illus.). 196p. 1981. 19.95 (ISBN 0-668-05102-7, 5102). Arco.
BIONOMICS
see Ecology
BIOPHYSICS
see Biological Physics
BIOPSYCHOLOGY
see Psychobiology
BIORHYTHMS
see Biological Rhythms
BIOSCIENCES
see Life Sciences
BIOSTATISTICS
see Biometry
BIOSYNTHESIS
see also Protein Biosynthesis
Corcoran, J. W., ed. Biosynthesis. (Antibiotics Ser.: Vol. 4). (Illus.). 500p. 1981. 97.00 (ISBN 0-387-10186-1). Springer-Verlag.
Manitto, P. Biosynthesis of Natural Products Polyketides Terpenoids Steroids & Phnylpropano Ds. 550p. 1981. 117.95 (ISBN 0-470-27100-0). Halsted Pr.
BIOTECHNOLOGY
see Bionics; Human Engineering
BIOTELEMETRY
Kimmich, H. P., ed. Wildlife Biotelemetry. (Journal: Biotelemetry & Patient Monitoring: Vol. 7, No. 3-4). (Illus.). 116p. 1980. pap. write for info. (ISBN 3-8055-2093-X). S Karger.
BIOTIC COMMUNITIES
Nitecki, Matthew H. Biotic Crises in Ecological & Evolutionary Time. LC 80-70597. 1981. 25.00 (ISBN 0-12-519640-7). Acad Pr.
BIRD-HOUSES
Kesselman, Judi R. & Peterson, Franklynn. I Can Use Tools. (Illus.). 32p. (gr. 1-4). 1981. 5.95 (ISBN 0-525-66725-3). Elsevier-Nelson.
BIRD WATCHING
Alden, Peter & Gooders, John. Finding Birds Around the World. (Illus.). 704p. 1980. 16.95 (ISBN 0-395-29114-3). HM.
Bowers, Mary B., ed. Stories About Birds & Bird Watchers: From Bird Watcher's Digest. LC 80-7925. (Illus.). 192p. 1981. 12.95 (ISBN 0-689-11093-6). Atheneum.
Rivera Cianchini, Osvaldo & Mojica Sandoz, Luis. Pajaros Notables De Puerto Rico: Guia Para Observadores De Aves. (Illus.). v, 101p. 1980. write for info. (ISBN 0-8477-2324-0); pap. write for info. (ISBN 0-8477-2325-9). U of PR Pr.
BIRDS
see also Cage-Birds; Ornithology; Water-Birds also names of particular birds, e.g. Robins
Bowers, Mary B., ed. Stories About Birds & Bird Watchers: From Bird Watcher's Digest. LC 80-7925. (Illus.). 192p. 1981. 12.95 (ISBN 0-689-11093-6). Atheneum.
Epple, August & Stetson, Milton. Avian Endocrinology. 1980. lib ed. 34.00 (ISBN 0-12-240250-2). Acad Pr.
Goodwin, Derek. Birds of Man's World. LC 77-74922. (Illus.). 190p. 1978. 12.50 (ISBN 0-8014-1167-X). Comstock.
Holland, John. Bird Spotting. (Illus.). 292p. 1981. pap. 6.95 (ISBN 0-7137-1148-5, Pub. by Blandford Pr England). Sterling.
Terres, John K. Songbirds in Your Garden. 3rd st ed. Conrad, Jeff, ed. (Illus.). 228p. 1980. pap. 6.95 (ISBN 0-8015-6945-1, Hawthorn). Dutton.
Vriends, Matthew M. Encyclopedia of Softbilled Birds. (Illus.). 221p. 1980. 12.95 (ISBN 0-87666-891-0, H-1026). TFH Pubns.
BIRDS–BEHAVIOR
Kress, Stephen W. Audubon Society Handbook for Birders. (Illus.). 320p. 1981. 14.95 (ISBN 0-684-16336-5, ScribT). Scribner.
Tanabe, Y., et al, eds. Biological Rhythms in Birds: Neural & Endocrine Aspects. 373p. 1980. 49.60 (ISBN 0-387-10311-2). Springer-Verlag.
BIRDS–COLLISIONS WITH AIRPLANES
see Aeronautics–Accidents
BIRDS–ECONOMIC ASPECTS
see Birds, Injurious and Beneficial
BIRDS–EMBRYOLOGY
see Embryology–Birds
BIRDS–JUVENILE LITERATURE
Ames, Felicia. The Bird You Care for. Date not set. pap. 1.75 (ISBN 0-451-07527-7, E7527, Sig). NAL.
Haley, Neale. Birds for Pets & Pleasure. LC 80-68740. (Illus.). 224p. (gr. 8). 1981. PLB 8.44 (ISBN 0-440-00476-4); pap. 4.95 (ISBN 0-440-00475-6). Delacorte.
Hess, Lilo. Bird Companions. (Illus.). 32p. (gr. 4-7). 1981. 9.95 (ISBN 0-684-16874-X). Scribner.
Jacobs, Francine. Bermuda Petrel: The Bird That Would Not Die. LC 80-20466. (Illus.). 40p. (gr. k-3). 1981. 7.95 (ISBN 0-688-00240-4); PLB 7.63 (ISBN 0-688-00244-7). Morrow.
Little, Brown Editiors, ed. Birds: West Coast Edition. (Explorer's Notebooks). (Illus.). 32p. (Orig.). (gr. 5 up). 1981. pap. 1.95 (ISBN 0-316-52776-9). Little.
Little, Brown Editors, ed. Birds: East Coast Edition. (Explorer's Notebooks). (Illus.). 32p. (Orig.). (gr. 5 up). 1981. pap. 1.95 (ISBN 0-316-52775-0). Little.
Radlauer, Ruth & Radlauer, Ed. Bird Mania. LC 80-21833. (Mania Bks). (Illus.). 32p. (gr. k-4). 1981. PLB 7.95g (ISBN 0-516-07782-1, Elk Grove Bks). Childrens.
Wheeler, Ruth L. Story of Birds of North America. LC 65-14630. (Story of Science Ser.). (Illus.). (gr. 5-10). 1965. PLB 7.29 (ISBN 0-8178-3542-3). Harvey.
BIRDS–LEGENDS AND STORIES
Gustafson, Anita. Burrowing Birds. LC 80-29058. (Illus.). 64p. (gr. 4-6). 1981. 7.95 (ISBN 0-688-41977-1); PLB 7.63 (ISBN 0-688-51977-6). Morrow.
BIRDS–PICTORIAL WORKS
Rice, Don. Birds: A Picture Source Book. 160p. 1980. pap. 8.95 (ISBN 0-442-20395-0). Van Nos Reinhold.
BIRDS–ALASKA
Armstrong, Robert H. & Alaska Magazine Editors. Guide to the Birds of Alaska. 320p. 1980. pap. 15.95 (ISBN 0-88240-143-2). Alaska Northwest.
BIRDS–ASIA
Ali, Salim & Ripley, Dillon. Compact Edition of the Handbook of the Birds of India & Pakistan, Together with Those of Bangladesh, Nepal, Bhutan & Sri Lanka. (Illus.). 816p. 1980. 96.95 (ISBN 0-19-561245-0). Oxford U Pr.
Ripley, S. Dillon. A Naturalist's Adventure in Nepal: Search for the Spiny Babbler. (Illus.). 301p. 1981. Repr. of 1953 ed. 12.50 (ISBN 0-87474-810-0). Smithsonian.
BIRDS–INDIA
Ali, Salim & Ripley, Dillon. Compact Edition of the Handbook of the Birds of India & Pakistan, Together with Those of Bangladesh, Nepal, Bhutan & Sri Lanka. (Illus.). 816p. 1980. 96.95 (ISBN 0-19-561245-0). Oxford U Pr.

BIRDS–LATIN-AMERICA
Lill, A. Lek Behavior in the Golden-Headed Manakin, Pipra erythrocephala in Trinidad (West Indies) (Advances in Ethology Ser.: Vol. 18). (Illus.). 84p. (Orig.). 1976. pap. text ed. 34.00 (ISBN 3-489-72536-0). Parey Sci Pubs.
BIRDS–NEW ZEALAND
Marshall, Janet, et al. Common Birds in New Zealand, 2 vols. (Mobil New Zealand Nature Ser.). (Illus.). 1973. Vol. 1. pap. 7.50 (ISBN 0-589-00730-0, Pub. by Reed Bks Australia); Vol. 2. pap. 7.50 (ISBN 0-589-00759-9). C E Tuttle.
--Uncommon Birds in New Zealand. (Mobil New Zealand Nature Ser.). (Illus.). 96p. 1975. pap. 7.50 (ISBN 0-589-00941-9, Pub. by Reed Bks Australia). C E Tuttle.
BIRDS–PUERTO RICO
Feliciano-Mendoza, Ester & Rodriquez-Baez, Felix. Ala y Trino: Pajaros De Puerto Rico Libro De Ninos Para Colorear. LC 79-24763. (Orig., Span.). 1980. pap. write for info. (ISBN 0-8477-3600-8). U of PR Pr.
Rivera Cianchini, Osvaldo & Mojica Sandoz, Luis. Pajaros Notables De Puerto Rico: Guia Para Observadores De Aves. (Illus.). v, 101p. 1980. write for info. (ISBN 0-8477-2324-0); pap. write for info. (ISBN 0-8477-2325-9). U of PR Pr.
BIRDS–UNITED STATES
see also Birds–Alaska
Sutton, George M. Fifty Common Birds of Oklahoma & the Southern Great Plains. LC 77-24336. (Illus.). 113p. 1981. pap. 6.95 (ISBN 0-8061-1704-4). U of Okla Pr.
BIRDS, AQUATIC
see Water-Birds
BIRDS, INJURIOUS AND BENEFICIAL
see also Birds of Prey
Weber, Walter. Health Hazards from Pigeons, Starlings & English Sparrows. LC 79-55324. Date not set. 13.00 (ISBN 0-913702-10-2). Thomson Pub Ca.
BIRDS, RARE
see Rare Birds
BIRDS AS PETS
see Cage-Birds
BIRDS OF PREY
see also Owls
Weick, Friedhelm & Brown, Leslie. Birds of Prey of the World: A Coloured Guide to Identification of All the Diurnal Species Order Falconiformes. (Illus.). 159p. (Orig.). 1980. 48.00 (ISBN 3-490-08518-3). Parey Sci Pubs.
Wildlife Education, Ltd. Birds of Prey. (Zoobooks). (Illus.). 20p. (Orig.). 1980. pap. 1.00 (ISBN 0-937934-01-1). Wildlife Educ.
BIRTH (IN RELIGION, FOLK-LORE, ETC.)
The New Technologies of Birth & Death: Medical, Legal & Moral Dimensions. LC 80-83425. xvi, 196p. (Orig.). 1980. pap. 8.95 (ISBN 0-935372-07-5). Pope John Ctr.
BIRTH CONTROL
see also Abortion; Contraception; Intrauterine Contraceptives
Baker, Lynn S. The Fertility Fallacy: Sexuality in the Post Pill Age. LC 80-50715. 224p. 1981. 11.95 (ISBN 0-03-057656-3). HR&W.
Banerjee, Sumanta. Family Planning Communication: A Critique of the Indian Programme. (Illus.). 218p. 1980. text ed. 10.50x (ISBN 0-391-02169-9). Humanities.
Echoes from the Past. LC 79-90484. (Illus.). 128p. 1979. 25.00 (ISBN 0-934586-03-9). Plan Parent.
Factors Affecting the Use & Non-Use of Contraception Findings from a Comparative Analysis of Selected KAP Surveys. (Population Studies: No. 69). 109p. 1979. pap. 9.00 (ISBN 0-686-68956-9, UN79/13/6, UN). Unipub.
Lieberman, E. J. & Peck, Ellen. Sex & Birth Control: A Guide for the Young. rev. ed. LC 79-7094. (Illus.). 304p. 1981. 10.95 (ISBN 0-690-01837-1, HarpT). Har-Row.
Nortman, Dorothy & Hofstatter, Ellen. Population & Family Planning Programs. 10th ed. LC 80-52443. (Illus.). 96p. (Orig.). 1980. pap. 4.50 (ISBN 0-87834-041-6). Population Coun.
Okpaku, S. Family Planning & Preventive Psychiatry. 1981. 20.00 (ISBN 0-89388-003-5). Okpaku Communications.
Planned Parenthood Federation of America, Inc. Echoes from the Past. (Illus.). 128p. 1979. 25.00 (ISBN 0-934586-03-9). Plan Parent.
Polgar, Steven, ed. Culture & Population: A Collection of Current Studies. LC 80-20070. (Carolina Population Center, Monograph: 9). vi, 195p. 1980. Repr. of 1971 ed. lib. bdg. 19.75x (ISBN 0-313-22620-2, POCP). Greenwood.
Sala, Andre & Duxler, Margot. Expectations: A Completely Unexpected Guide to Planned & Unplanned Parenthood. (Illus.). 100p. 1981. pap. 2.95 (ISBN 0-399-50516-4, Perigee). Putnam.
Social Welfare & Family Planning: Concepts, Strategies & Methods Report of a U. N. Project, 1971-1978. 107p. 1979. pap. 8.00 (ISBN 0-686-68972-0, UN79/4/6, UN). Unipub.
Tucker, Tarvez. Birth Control. 1981. pap. 2.50 (ISBN 0-440-00566-3). Dell.
BIRTH CONTROL–RELIGIOUS ASPECTS
Davis, John J. Abortion & the Evangelical. LC 80-82736. (The Nordland Series in Contemporary American Social Problems). 150p. (Orig.). 1980. pap. 7.95 (ISBN 0-913124-43-5). Nordland Pub.
Roetzer, Josef. Family Planning the Natural Way. Date not set. pap. 6.95 (ISBN 0-8007-1185-8). Revell.
Trobisch, Ingrid & Roetzer, Elisabeth. An Experience of Love: Understanding Natural Family Planning. Date not set. 6.95 (ISBN 0-8007-1184-X). Revell.
BIRTH CONTROL–ASIA
Krannich, Ronald L. & Krannich, Caryl R. The Politics of Family Planning Policy: Thailand--a Case of Successful Implementation. (Monograph: No. 19). 115p. 1980. pap. 9.00x (Pub. by Northern Ill Univ Ctr S E Asian Stud); pap. text ed. 9.00. Cellar.
BIRTH CONTROL–INDIA
Khan, M. E. & Prasad, C. V. Fertility Control in India. 1980. 14.00x (ISBN 0-8364-0628-1, Pub. by Manohar India). South Asia Bks.
BIRTH DEFECTS
see Abnormalities, Human
BIRTH-RATE
see Population
BISCUITS, ENGLISH
see Cookies
BISHOPS
see also Church Polity; Popes–Primacy
Cabestrero, Teofilo. Mystic of Liberation: A Portrait of Bishop Pedro Casaldaliga of Brazil. Walsh, Donald D., tr. LC 80-25402. (Illus.). 176p. (Orig.). 1981. pap. 7.95 (ISBN 0-88344-324-4). Orbis Bks.
Erdozain, Placido. Archbishop Romero: Martyr of Salvador. McFadden, John & Warner, Ruth, trs. (Illus.). 128p. (Orig.). 1981. pap. 4.95 (ISBN 0-88344-019-9). Orbis Bks.
BISMARCK, OTTO, FURST VON, 1815-1898
Stieber, Wilhelm J. The Chancellor's Spy: The Revelations of the Chief of Bismarck's Secret Service. Van Heurck, Jan, tr. from German. LC 79-52090. Orig. Title: Spion Des Kanzlers. 272p. 1981. 12.50 (ISBN 0-394-50869-6). Grove.
BIVALVES
see Lamellibranchiata
BLACK AFRICANS
see Blacks
BLACK AMERICANS
see Afro-Americans
BLACK ART (WITCHCRAFT)
see Witchcraft
BLACK CARIB INDIANS
see Indians of Central America
BLACK ENGLISH
Fasold, Ralph. Tense Marking in Black English: A Linguistic and Social Analysis. (Urban Language Ser.). 1972. pap. text ed. 8.00 (ISBN 0-87281-031-3). Ctr Appl Ling.
BLACK JACK (GAME)
see Blackjack (Game)
BLACK LITERATURE (AFRICAN)
see African Literature
BLACK LITERATURE (AMERICAN)
see American Literature–Afro-American Authors
BLACK MARKET
Ray, S. K. Economics of the Black Market. (Replica Edition Ser.). 250p. 1981. lib. bdg. 20.00x (ISBN 0-86531-149-8). Westview.
BLACK MASS
see Satanism
BLACK MONKS
see Benedictines
BLACK POETRY (AMERICAN)
see American Poetry–Afro-American Authors
BLACK RACE
Here are entered theoretical works discussing the Black race from an anthropological point of view. Works on Black people outside of the United States are entered under the heading Blacks. Works on the Black people of the United States are entered under the heading Afro-Americans.
see also Blacks
Lawrence, Cherrie M. & Anzaldua, Gloria, eds. This Bridge Called My Back: Writings by Radical Women of Color. (Orig.). 1981. pap. price not set (ISBN 0-930436-10-5). Persephone.
BLACK SEA
Report of the Technical Consultation on the Assessment & Management of the Black Sea Turbot (GFCM) Working Party on Resource Evaluation & Fishery Statistics. 23p. 1980. pap. 7.50 (ISBN 92-5-100879-5, F1964, FAO). Unipub.
BLACK-TAILED DEER
see Mule Deer
BLACKBIRDS
Britton, Anne. Blackie: The Biography of Blackbird. 6.95 (ISBN 0-392-07664-0, SpS). Soccer.
BLACKFEET INDIANS
see Indians of North America–Northwest, Pacific
BLACKJACK (GAME)
Patterson, Jerry L. Blackjack's Winning Formula. 91p. 1980. write for info. (ISBN 0-9605112-0-2). Casino Gaming.
BLACKS
This heading used beginning January 1976. See Negroes for earlier materials. Here are entered works on Black people outside of the United States. Works on the Black people of the United States are entered under the heading Afro-Americans. Theoretical works discussing the Black race from an anthropological point of view are entered under the heading Black Race.
see also Afro-Americans
also headings beginning with Black
Asante, Molefi K. & Vandi, Abdulai S., eds. Contemporary Black Thought: Alternative Analyses in Social & Behavioral Science. LC 80-15186. (Sage Focus Editions Ser.: Vol. 26). (Illus.). 302p. 1980. 18.95 (ISBN 0-8039-1500-4). Sage.
Frye, Charles A., ed. Level Three: A Black Philosophy Reader. LC 80-5801. 217p. 1980. lib. bdg. 18.00 (ISBN 0-8191-1241-0); pap. text ed. 9.75 (ISBN 0-8191-1242-9). U Pr of Amer.
BLACKS–CIVIL RIGHTS
This heading used beginning January 1976. See Negroes–Civil Rights for earlier works.
see also Blacks–Politics and Government
Haywood, Harry. Negro Liberation. 1978. pap. 3.95 (ISBN 0-930720-50-4). Liberator Pr.
BLACKS–ECONOMIC CONDITIONS
This heading used beginning January 1976. See Negroes–Economic Conditions for earlier works.
Trower-Subira, George. Black Folks' Guide to Making Big Money in America. 184p. 1980. 11.00 (ISBN 0-9605304-0-1). VSBE.
BLACKS–POLITICS AND GOVERNMENT
This heading used beginning January 1976. See Negroes–Politics and Suffrage for earlier works.
Karnig, Albert & Welch, Susan. Black Representation & Urban Policy. LC 80-16714. 1981. 20.00x (ISBN 0-226-42534-7). U of Chicago Pr.
BLACKS–RELIGION
This heading used beginning January 1976. See Negroes–Religion for earlier works.
Erskine, Noel L. Decolonizing Theology: A Caribbean Perspective. LC 80-21784. 160p. (Orig.). 1981. pap. 6.95 (ISBN 0-88344-087-3). Orbis Bks.
BLACKS–SUFFRAGE
see Blacks–Politics and Government
BLACKS–JAMAICA
Heuman, Gad J. Between Black & White: Race, Politics, & the Free Coloreds in Jamaica, 1792-1865. LC 80-661. (Contributions in Comparative Colonial Studies: No. 5). (Illus.). 240p. 1981. lib. bdg. 35.00 (ISBN 0-313-20984-7, HBW/). Greenwood.
BLACKS–UNITED STATES
see Afro-Americans
BLACKSMITHING
see also Welding
McRaven, Charles. Country Blacksmithing. LC 80-7876. (Illus.). 208p. 1981. 14.95 (ISBN 0-06-014870-5, HarpT). Har-Row.
--Country Blacksmithing. LC 80-7876. (Illus.). 208p. 1981. pap. 9.95 (ISBN 0-06-090870-X, CN870, CN). Har-Row.
BLADDER
see also Prostate Gland–Diseases
Connolly, John G., ed. Carcinoma of the Bladder. (Progress in Cancer Research & Therapy Ser.). 275p. 1981. 27.00 (ISBN 0-89004-536-4). Raven.
Oliver, R. T., et al, eds. Bladder Cancer: Principles of Combination Therapy. (Illus.). 272p. 1981. text ed. 69.00 (ISBN 0-407-00187-5). Butterworth.
BLAKE, WILLIAM, 1757-1827
Butlin, Martin. The Paintings & Drawings of William Blake. LC 80-6221. (Paul Mellon Centre for Studies in British Art). (Illus.). 1408p. 1981. 250.00x (ISBN 0-300-02550-5). Yale U Pr.
Gilchrist, Alexander. Life of William Blake: With Selections from His Poems & Other Writings, 2 vols. enl. ed. (Illus.). 993p. 1969. Set. 35.00. Phaeton.
Leader, Zachery. Reading Blake's Poems. (Illus.). 256p. 1981. 27.50 (ISBN 0-7100-0635-7). Routledge & Kegan.
BLANC, JEAN JOSEPH CHARLES LOUIS, 1811-1882
Loubere, Leo A. Louis Blanc: His Life & His Contribution to the Rise of French Jacobin-Socialism. LC 80-23424. (Northwestern University Studies in History: No. 1). xii, 256p. 1980. Repr. of 1961 ed. lib. bdg. 27.50x (ISBN 0-313-22690-3, LOBL). Greenwood.
BLAVATSKY, HELENE PETROVNA (HAHN-HAHN), 1831-1891
Blavatsky, Helena P. H. P. Blavatsky Collected Writings, Vol. XII. De Zirkoff, Boris, ed. LC 80-53953. (Illus.). 849p. 1981. cloth 18.95 (ISBN 0-8356-0228-1). Theos Pub Hse.
BLAZONRY
see Heraldry
BLESSINGS, TABLE
see Grace at Meals
BLIGH, WILLIAM, 1754-1817
Mackaness, George, ed. A Book of the Bounty' William Bligh & Others. Kennedy, Gavin. (Everyman's Reference Library). 1981. 14.50x (ISBN 0-460-00950-8, Pub. by J. M. Dent England). Biblio Dist.
BLIND–EDUCATION
National Accreditation Council. Section D-9, Low Vision Services. (Self-Study & Evaluation Guide). 1981. 1.50. NACASBVH.
BLIND–REHABILITATION
Crawford, Fred L. Career Planning for the Blind: A Manual for Students & Teachers. 189p. 1966. 3.95 (ISBN 0-374-11905-8). FS&G.
Read, Ralph. When the Cook Can't Look: A Cooking Handbook for the Blind & Visually Impaired. 144p. 1981. 9.95 (ISBN 0-8264-0034-5). Continuum.
BLINDNESS
Scott, Robert A. The Making of Blind Men. 160p. 1981. pap. 4.95 (ISBN 0-87855-687-7). Transaction Bks.
BLIXEN, KAREN, 1885-1962
Dinesen, Isak. Letters from Africa, 1914 to 1931. Lasson, Frans, ed. Born, Anne, tr. LC 80-25856. 1981. 25.00 (ISBN 0-226-15309-6). U of Chicago Pr.
BLOCK ANESTHESIA
see Conduction Anesthesia
BLOOD
see also Serum Protein
Ellerbe, Suellyn. Fluid & Blood Component Therapy in the Critically Ill. (Contemporary Issues in Critical Care Nursing). (Illus.). 224p. 1981. lib. bdg. 20.00 (ISBN 0-443-08129-8). Churchill.
EMBO Workshop, Weizmann Institute of Science, Rehovot, Israel, 1980, et al. Platelets: Cellular Response Mechanisms & Their Biological Significance: Proceedings. 340p. 1980. 52.50 (ISBN 0-471-27896-3, Pub. by Wiley-Interscience). Wiley.
BLOOD–ANALYSIS AND CHEMISTRY
see also Blood Sugar
Love, G. D., et al, eds. Clinical Aspects of Blood Viscosity & Ceell Deformability. (Illus.). 250p. 1981. 41.30 (ISBN 0-387-10299-X). Springer-Verlag.
Russell, N. J., et al. Blood Biochemistry. 128p. 1980. 24.00x (Pub. by Croom Helm England). State Mutual Bk.
BLOOD–CIRCULATION
see also Aorta; Arteries; Blood Flow; Blood Pressure; Blood-Vessels; Cardiovascular System; Heart; Microcirculation; Peripheral Circulation; Veins
De Sousa, Maria. Lymphocyte Circulation: Experimental & Clinical Aspects. 316p. 1981. 57.00 (ISBN 0-471-27854-8, Pub. by Wiley-Interscience). Wiley.
Granger, Neil & Bulkley, Gregory B. Measurement of Blood Flow: Applications to the Splanchnic Circulation. (Illus.). 496p. 1981. write for info. (3730-7). Williams & Wilkins.
Rainer, Lick F. Atlas a Color De Oirugia. 600p. 1981. pap. text ed. write for info. (ISBN 0-06-315030-1, Pub. by HarlA Mexico). Har-Row.
Tardos,., et al, eds. Pharmacological Control of Heart & Circulation: Proceedings of the Third Congress of the Hungarian Pharmacological Society, Budapest, 1979. LC 80-41281. (Advances in Pharmacological Research & Practice Ser.: Vol. I). 445p. 1981. 84.00 (ISBN 0-08-026386-0). Pergamon.
Wolf, Stewart, et al, eds. Structure & Function of the Circulation, Vol. 1. 825p. 1980. 75.00 (ISBN 0-306-40278-5). Plenum Pub.
BLOOD–CIRCULATION, ARTIFICIAL
Ionescu. Techniques in Extracorporeal Circulation. 2nd ed. 1981. text ed. price not set (ISBN 0-407-00173-5). Butterworth.
BLOOD–COAGULATION
see also Fibrinolysis; Hemophilia
Lijnen, H. R., et al, eds. Synthetic Substrates in Clinical Blood Coagulation Assays. (Developments in Hematology Ser.: No. 1). 142p. 1981. PLB 23.50 (ISBN 90-247-2409-0, Pub. Bymartinus Nijhoff). Kluwer Boston.
Protides of the Biological Fluids, Colloquium 28: Proceedings of the 28th Colloquium on Protides of the Biological Fluids, Brussels, 5-8 May 1980. LC 58-5908. (Illus.). 600p. 1980. 120.00 (ISBN 0-08-026370-4). Pergamon.
BLOOD–CORPUSCLES AND PLATELETS
see Blood Cells
BLOOD–DISEASES
see also Hemophilia; Hyperlipemia
Lusher. Acquired Bleeding Disorders in Children: Abnormalities of Hemostasis. (Monographs in Pediatric Hematology-Oncology: Vol. 3). 1981. price not set (ISBN 0-89352-127-2). Masson Pub.
BLOOD–FLOW
see Blood Flow
BLOOD–GAS CONTENT
see Blood Gases
BLOOD–PRESSURE
see Blood Pressure
BLOOD–TRANSFUSION
Kasprisin, Duke O. & Kasprisin, Christina A. Introduction to Transfusion Therapy: A Programmed Text. LC 80-17972. 1980. pap. 10.50 (ISBN 0-87488-822-0). Med Exam.
Kretschmer, V. Leukozytenseparation und Transfusion. (Beitraege Zu Infusionstherapie und Klinische Ernaehrung Ser.: Vol. 6). (Illus.). viii, 200p. 1981. 18.00 (ISBN 3-8055-1946-X). S Karger.
Petz & Swisher. Clinical Practice of Blood Transfusion. Date not set. text ed. price not set (ISBN 0-443-08067-4). Churchill.

Petz, Lawrence D. & Swisher, Scott N., eds. Clinical Practice of Blood Transfusion. (Illus.). 640p. 1981. lib. bdg. 55.00 (ISBN 0-443-08067-4). Churchill.

BLOOD, GASES IN
see Blood Gases

BLOOD CELLS
see also Erythrocytes

Hollan, S. R., et al. Genetics, Structure & Function of Blood Cells: Proceedings of the 28th International Congress of Physiological Sciences, Budapest, 1980. LC 80-41876. (Advances in Physiological Sciences: Vol. 6). (Illus.). 310p. 1981. 40.00 (ISBN 0-08-026818-8). Pergamon.

Love, G. D., et al, eds. Clinical Aspects of Blood Viscosity & Ceell Deformability. (Illus.). 250p. 1981. 41.30 (ISBN 0-387-10299-X). Springer-Verlag.

BLOOD CHEMISTRY
see Blood–Analysis and Chemistry

BLOOD CORPUSCLES
see Blood Cells

BLOOD FLOW

Chmiel, Horst & Walitza, Eckehard. Rheology of Blood & Synovial Fluids. 184p. 1981. 42.00 (ISBN 0-471-27858-0, Pub. by Wiley-Interscience). Wiley.

Oka, S. Cardiovascular Hemorheology. (Illus.). 200p. Date not set. price not set (ISBN 0-521-23650-9). Cambridge U Pr.

BLOOD GASES

Huch, Albert, et al, eds. Continous Transcutaneous Blood Gas Monitorin. LC 79-2586. (Alan R. Liss Ser.: Vol. 15, No. 4). 1979. 68.00 (ISBN 0-8451-1027-6). March of Dimes.

Lauersen, Neils H. & Hochberg, Howard. Clinical Perinatal Biochemical Monitoring. 271p. 1981. write for info. (1901-1). Williams & Wilkins.

BLOOD GLUCOSE
see Blood Sugar

BLOOD PRESSURE
see also Blood–Circulation; Hypotension

Coleman, Thomas G. Blood Pressure Control, Vol. 1. 248p. 1980. 32.50 (ISBN 0-88831-088-9). Eden Med Res.

Hutchinson, James C. Hypertension: A Practitioner's Guide to Therapy. 1975. spiral bdg. 13.00 (ISBN 0-87488-709-7). Med Exam.

Rosenvold, Lloyd. Drop Your Blood Pressure. 176p. (Orig.). 1980. pap. 2.50 (ISBN 0-515-05721-5). Jove Pubns.

Soffer, Richard L. Biochemical Regulation of Blood Pressure. 425p. 1981. 35.00 (ISBN 0-471-05600-6, Pub. by Wiley-Interscience). Wiley.

BLOOD PRESSURE, HIGH
see Hypertension

BLOOD PRESSURE, LOW
see Hypotension

BLOOD SUGAR
see also Hypoglycemia

Adams, Ruth & Murray, Frank. Is Blood Sugar Making You a Nutritional Cripple? rev. ed. 174p. (Orig.). 1975. pap. 1.75 (ISBN 0-915962-11-X). Larchmont Bks.

Bernstein, Richard K. Diabetes: The Glucograph Method for Normalizing Blood Sugar. Behrman, Marion, ed. (Illus.). 320p. 1981. 14.95 (ISBN 0-517-54155-6). Crown.

BLOOD TRANSFUSION
see Blood–Transfusion

BLOOD-VESSELS
see also Arteries; Blood–Circulation; Veins
also names of organs and regions of the body, with or without the subdivision Blood Vessels

Abramson, David I. & Casey, M. Beth. Self-Assessment of Current Knowledge in Peripheral Vascular Disorders. 1980. pap. 18.00 (ISBN 0-87488-291-5). Med Exam.

BLOOD-VESSELS–DISEASES
see also Aneurysms

New York Heart Association. Nomenclature & Criteria for Diagnosis of Diseases of the Heart & Great Vessels. 8th ed. LC 78-71219. 349p. 1979. text ed. 14.95 (ISBN 0-316-60536-0); pap. text ed. 11.95 (ISBN 0-316-60537-9). Little.

BLOOD-VESSELS–GRAFTS
see Vascular Grafts

BLOODHOUNDS
see Dogs–Breeds–Bloodhounds

BLOWOUTS, OILWELL
see Oil Well Blowouts

BLUE COLLAR WORKERS
see Labor and Laboring Classes

BLUE LAWS
see Sunday Legislation

BLUE-PRINTS

Brown, Walter C. Blueprint Reading for Construction. LC 79-23958. 1980. pap. text ed. 13.92 spiral. Goodheart.

--Blueprint Reading for Construction. LC 79-23958. (Illus.). 338p. (Orig.). 1980. pap. text ed. 13.92 (ISBN 0-87006-286-7). Good Heart.

McDonnell, Leo & Ball, John. Blueprint Reading & Sketching for Carpenters: Residential. 3rd ed. LC 80-66027. (Blueprint Reading Ser.). (Illus.). 160p. 1981. pap. text ed. 9.80 (ISBN 0-8273-1354-3); price not set instr's guide (ISBN 0-8273-1355-1). Delmar.

Taylor, David. Elementary Blueprint Reading for Machinists. LC 80-65572. (Blueprint Reading Ser.). 160p. 1981. pap. text ed. 4.60 (ISBN 0-8273-1895-2); instr's. guide 1.50 (ISBN 0-8273-1892-8). Delmar.

BLUE SKY LAWS
see Securities

BLUEFISH

Bennett, D. W. Secrets of Blue Fishing. Campbell, M., ed. (North East Fishing Ser.). (Illus.). 50p. (Orig.). 1981. pap. 3.95 (ISBN 0-88839-086-6). Hancock Hse.

BLUEPRINTS
see Blue-Prints

BLUES (SONGS, ETC.)
see also Spirituals (Songs)

Charters, Samuel. Roots of the Blues: An African Search. 160p. 1981. 15.00 (ISBN 0-7145-2705-X). Merrimack Bk Serv.

Germain, Edward, ed. Blues Anthology. 1981. 15.00x (ISBN 0-916156-50-8); pap. 6.50x (ISBN 0-916156-49-4). Cherry Valley.

Green Note Music Publications Staff. Improvising Blues Guitar, Vol. 2. (Guitar Transcription Ser.). 1980. pap. 7.25 (ISBN 0-912910-11-9). Green Note Music.

Palmer, Robert. Deep Blues. LC 80-52000. (Illus.). 1981. 13.95 (ISBN 0-670-49511-5). Viking Pr.

BLUNDERS
see Errors, Popular

BOARD GAMES
see also specific games, e.g. Chess

Provenzo, Asterie B. & Provenzo, Eugene F. Play It Again: Historic Board Games You Can Make & Play. (Illus.). 288p. 1981. 17.95 (ISBN 0-13-683367-5, Spec); pap. 8.95 (ISBN 0-13-683359-4, Spec). P-H.

BOARDING-HOUSES
see Hotels, Taverns, etc.

BOARDS OF DIRECTORS
see Directors of Corporations

BOARDS OF SUPERVISION (CORPORATION LAW)
see Directors of Corporations

BOAT-BUILDING
see also Fiberglass Boats; Ship-Building

Bailey, Frank. Small Boat Design for Beginners. (Illus.). 88p. (Orig.). 1980. pap. 8.25 (ISBN 0-589-50203-4, Pub. by Reed Bks Australia). C E Tuttle.

Gannaway, Dave. Small Boat Building. 1980. 6.00x (ISBN 0-245-52656-0, Pub. by Nautical England). State Mutual Bk.

Greeve, Alec. Build Your Boat with Me. 14.95x (ISBN 0-392-07731-0, SpS). Soccer.

Sims, E. H. Boatbuilding in Alluminum Alloy. 124p. 1980. 18.00x (ISBN 0-245-53128-9, Pub. by Nautical England). State Mutual Bk.

BOAT HANDLING
see Boats and Boating

Meisel, Tony. A Manual of Singlehanded Sailing. LC 80-22856. (Illus.). 224p. 1981. lib. bdg. 12.95 (ISBN 0-668-04998-7, 4998). Arco.

BOAT MODELS
see Ship Models

BOAT RACING
see Yacht Racing

BOATS, SUBMARINE
see Submarines

BOATS AND BOATING
see also Boat-Building; Canoes and Canoeing; Fiberglass Boats; Fishing Boats; Life-Boats; Motor-Boats; Sailing; Ships; Steamboats and Steamboat Lines; Submarines; Yachts and Yachting

Block, Richard A., ed. Motorboat Operator License Preparation Course. rev. ed. (Illus.). 269p. 1980. pap. text ed. 18.00 (ISBN 0-934114-29-3). Marine Educ.

--Understanding T-Boat Regulations. (Illus.). 143p. 1979. pap. text ed. 12.00 (ISBN 0-934114-22-6). Marine Educ.

Brewer, Edward S. & Betts, Jim. Understanding Boat Design. 3rd ed. LC 70-147872. (Illus.). 1980. pap. 7.95 (ISBN 0-87742-015-7). Intl Marine.

BUC's Older Boat Price Guide 1980. 38.00 (ISBN 0-911778-83-7). Buc Intl.

Damour, Jacques. One Hundred & One Tips & Hints for Your Boat. Howard-Williams, Jeremy, tr. from Fr. (Illus.). 1981. 13.95 (ISBN 0-393-03262-0). Norton.

Engineering Applications, No. 1: Installation & Maintenance of Engines in Fishing Vessels. (FAO Fisheries Technical Paper Ser.: No. 196). 136p. 1980. pap. 7.25 (ISBN 92-5-100862-0, F1948, FAO). Unipub.

Gannaway, Dave. Buying a Secondhand Boat. 104p. 1980. 15.00x (ISBN 0-245-53446-6, Pub. by Nautical England). State Mutual Bk.

Glasspool, John. Boats of the Longshoremen. 136p. 1980. 18.00x (ISBN 0-245-53111-4, Pub. by Nautical England). State Mutual Bk.

Jarman, Colin. Buying a Boat. LC 80-68904. (Illus.). 160p. 1981. 19.95 (ISBN 0-7153-7960-7). David & Charles.

Jones, Charles. Boat Maintenance: Ideas & Practice. 192p. 1980. 12.00x (ISBN 0-245-52347-2, Pub. by Nautical England). State Mutual Bk.

Markow, Herbert L. Small Boat Law: Nineteen Seventy-Nine to Nineteen Eighty Supplement. 1981. pap. write for info. (ISBN 0-934108-02-1). H L Markow.

Martin, Fred W. Nineteen Hundred & One Album of Designs for Boats, Launches & Yachts. rev. ed. LC 80-69290. (Illus.). 80p. 1980. pap. 5.00. Altair Pub Co.

Noel, John V. The Boating Dictionary: Sail & Power. 304p. 1981. text ed. 16.95 (ISBN 0-442-26048-2). Van Nos Reinhold.

Painter, A. A. Consumer Protection for Boat Users. 104p. 1980. 12.00x (ISBN 0-245-53450-4, Pub. by Nautical England). State Mutual Bk.

Toghill, Jeff. Boat Owner's Fitting-Out Manual. 224p. 22.95 (ISBN 0-442-26199-3). Van Nos Reinhold.

Ware, Michael. Narrow Boats at Work. 144p. 1980. 23.85x (ISBN 0-86190-006-5, Pub. by Allan Pubs England). State Mutual Bk.

Watney, John. Boat Electrics. LC 80-68680. (Illus.). 160p. 1981. 24.50 (ISBN 0-7153-7957-7). David & Charles.

Whittier, Bob. Most Common Boat Maintenance Problems. (Illus.). 256p. 1981. lib. bdg. 12.95 (ISBN 0-668-04877-8, 4877). Arco.

BOATS AND BOATING–JUVENILE LITERATURE

Scott, Geoffrey. Egyptian Boats. LC 80-27676. (A Carolrhoda on My Own Bk). (Illus.). 48p. (gr. k-3). 1981. PLB 5.95 (ISBN 0-87614-138-6). Carolrhoda Bks.

Zeck, Gerry & Zeck, Pam. Sternwheel Paddleboats. (Illus.). 32p. (gr. k-3). Date not set. PLB 5.95 (ISBN 0-87614-143-2). Carolrhoda Bks.

BODY, HUMAN
see also Anatomy, Human; Mind and Body

Fisher, John. Body Magic. LC 78-6387. (Illus.). 158p. 1980. pap. 6.95 (ISBN 0-8128-6088-8). Stein & Day.

Scott, Russell. The Body As Property. 1981. 14.95 (ISBN 0-670-17743-1). Viking Pr.

BODY AND MIND
see Mind and Body

BODY AND SOUL (PHILOSOPHY)
see Mind and Body

BODY AND SOUL (THEOLOGY)
see Man (Theology)

BODY MECHANICS
see Posture

BODY SURFING
see Surfing

BOEHM FLUTE
see Flute

BOGART, HUMPHREY, 1899-1957

Samuels, M. Screen Greats: Bogart. 1980. pap. 2.95 (ISBN 0-931064-31-7). O'Quinn Studio.

BOHEMIAN HYMNS (LANGUAGE, NEWSPAPERS, ETC.)
see Czech Language

BOILER-SCALE
see Steam-Boilers

BOILER WATER
see Feed-Water

BOILERS
see also Feed-Water; Fuel; Heating; Pressure Vessels; Steam-Boilers

Armstrong, H. C. & Lewis, C. V. Practical Boiler Firing. 4th ed. 387p. 1954. 10.95x (ISBN 0-85264-065-X, Pub. by Griffin England). State Mutual Bk.

Code Cases Book: Boilers & Pressure Vessels. (Boiler & Pressure Vessel Code Ser.). 1980. pap. 100.00 loose-leaf (V00120). ASME.

Code Cases Book: Boilers & Pressure Vessels. (Boilers & Pressure Vessel Code Ser.). 1980. pap. 100.00 loose-leaf (V00120). ASME.

Code Cases Book: Nuclear Components. (Boilers & Pressure Vessel Code Ser.). 1980. pap. 140.00 loose-leaf (V0012N). ASME.

Code Cases Book: Nuclear Components. (Boiler & Pressure Vessel Code Ser.). 1980. loose leaf 140.00 (V0012). ASME.

Companies Holding Boiler & Pressure Vessel Certificates of Authorization for Use of Code Symbol Stamps: 1980 Edition, Three Issues. 1978. 675.00 (EX0052). ASME.

Companies Holding Boiler & Pressure Vessel Certificates of Authorization for Use of Code Symbol Stamps: 1980 Edition-Three Issues, No. EX0052. 1980. 75.00. ASME.

Division 1: Appendices. (Boiler & Pressure Vessel Code Ser.: Sec. 3). 1980. 100.00 (P0003A); pap. 125.00 loose-leaf (V0003A). ASME.

Division 1: Subsection NB-Class 1 Components. (Boiler & Pressure Vessel Code Ser.: Sec. 3). 1980. 70.00 (P0003B); pap. 100.00 loose-leaf (V0003B). ASME.

Division 1: Subsection NC-Class 2 Components. (Boiler & Pressure Vessel Code Ser.: Sec. 3). 1980. 70.00 (P0003C); pap. 100.00 loose-leaf (V0003C). ASME.

Division 1: Subsection ND-Class 3 Components. (Boiler & Pressure Vessel Code Ser.: Sec. 3). 1980. 70.00 (P0003D); pap. 100.00 loose-leaf (V0003D). ASME.

Division 1: Subsection NE Class MC Components. (Boiler & Pressure Vessel Code Ser.: Sec. 3). 1980. bound edition 70.00 (P0003E); pap. 100.00 loose-leaf (P0003E). ASME.

Division 1: Subsection NF-Component Supports. (Boiler & Pressure Vessel Code Ser.: Sec. 3). 1980. 55.00 (P0003F); pap. 65.00 loose-leaf (V0003F). ASME.

Division 1: Subsection NG-Core Support Structures. (Boiler & Pressure Vessel Code Ser.: Sec. 3). 1980. 55.00 (P0003G); pap. 65.00 loose-leaf (V0003G). ASME.

Heating Boilers. (Boilers & Pressure Vessel Code Ser.: Sec. 4). 1980. 65.00 (P00040); pap. 85.00 loose-leaf (V00040). ASME.

Interpretations of the ASME Boiler & Pressure Vessel Code. 1980. annual subscription 30.00 (E0098); special 3-yr. subscription 70.00. ASME.

Martin, A. E., ed. Emission Control Technology for Industrial Boilers. LC 80-26046. (Pollution Tech. Rev. 74 Ser.: Energy Tech. Rev. 62). (Illus.). 405p. 1981. 48.00 (ISBN 0-8155-0833-6). Noyes.

Material Specifications: Ferrous Materials, 3 pts, Pt. A. (Boiler & Pressure Vessel Code Ser.: Sec II). 1980. 125.00 (P0002A); loose-leaf 172.00 (V0002A). ASME.

Material Specifications: Welding Rods, Electrodes & Filler Metals. (Boiler & Pressure Vessel Code Ser.: Sec II). 1980. 55.00 (P0002C); pap. 70.00 loose-leaf (V0002C). ASME.

BOILING
see Ebullition

BOLIVIA

Pecher, R. & Schmiermann, W. The Southern Cordillera Real. (Illus.). 57p. (Orig.). 1977. pap. 7.95 (ISBN 0-686-69199-7). Bradt Ent.

BOLSHEVISM
see Communism

BOMBERS
see also Lancaster (Bombers)

Clark, Ronald W. The Role of the Bomber. (Illus.). 1980. 14.95 (ISBN 0-690-01720-0). Quality Bks IL.

Gunston, Bill. The Illustrated Guide to Bombers of World War II. LC 80-67628. (Illustrated Military Guides). (Illus.). 4094p. 1981. 7.95 (ISBN 0-668-05094-2, 5094). Arco.

Lewis, Peter. The British Bomber Since 1914. LC 67-15743. 1967. 9.95 (ISBN 0-370-00121-4). Aero.

Philpott, Bryan. German Bombers Over Russia: World War Two Photo Album. (Illus.). 96p. 1981. pap. 5.95 (ISBN 0-89404-050-2). Aztex.

--German Bombers Over the Med: World War Two Photo Album. (Illus.). 96p. 1981. pap. 5.95 (ISBN 0-89404-037-5). Aztex.

Slow to Take Offense: Bombers, Cruise Missles & Prudent Deterrence. 136p. 1980. pap. 15.00 (ISBN 0-89206-015-8, CSIS017, CSIS). Unipub.

BONAPARTE, NAPOLEON
see Napoleon 1st, Emperor of the French, 1769-1821

BONDING (TECHNOLOGY)
see Sealing (Technology)

BONDS
see also Municipal Bonds; Stocks

Holt, Robert L. Bonds: How to Double Your Money Quickly & Safely. LC 80-66576. 1980. 10.00x (ISBN 0-930926-03-X). Calif Health.

BONDS–TAXATION
see Taxation of Bonds, Securities, etc.

BONDS, CHEMICAL
see Chemical Bonds

BONDS, MUNICIPAL
see Municipal Bonds

BONE MARROW
see Marrow

BONES–ABNORMALITIES AND DEFORMITIES

Schajowicz, F. Tumors & Tumor Like Lesions of Bone & Joints. (Illus.). 650p. 65.00 (ISBN 0-387-90492-1). Springer-Verlag.

BONES–DISEASES
see also Bones–Radiography; Exostosis; Necrosis; X-Rays

Edeiken, Jack. Roentgen Diagnosis of Diseases of the Bone. (Golden's Diagnostic Radiology Ser.: Section No. 6). (Illus.). 1752p. 1981. price not set (2744-1). Williams & Wilkins.

Rimoin, David L., ed. International Nomenclature of Constitutional Diseases of Bone Wih Bibliography. LC 79-54820. (March of Dimes Birth Defects Foundation Ser.: Vol. 15, No. 10). 1979. write for info. March of Dimes.

Rywlin, Arkadi M. Histopathology of the Bone Marrow. LC 75-41570. (Series in Laboratory Medicine). 229p. 1976. text ed. 22.50 (ISBN 0-316-76369-1). Little.

BONES–RADIOGRAPHY

Griffiths, Harry. Basic Bone Radiology. 182p. 1980. text ed. 15.50x (ISBN 0-8385-0535-X). ACC.

BONHEUR, ROSA, 1822-1889

Ashton, Dore & Hare, Denise B. Rosa Bonheur: A Life & a Legend. LC 80-36749. (Illus.). 192p. 1981. 20.00 (ISBN 0-670-60813-0). Viking Pr.

BONHOEFFER, DIETRICH, 1906-1945

Klassen, A. J. A Bonhoeffer Legacy: Essays in Understanding. 186p. (Orig.). 1981. pap. 13.95 (ISBN 0-8028-1744-0). Eerdmans.

Marty, Martin E., ed. The Place of Bonhoeffer: Problems & Possibilities in His Thought. LC 79-8718. 224p. 1981. Repr. of 1962 ed. lib. bdg. 22.50x (ISBN 0-313-20812-3, MAPL). Greenwood.

BONNEY, WILLIAM H., 1859-1881
see Billy the Kid

BONS MOTS
see Wit and Humor

BOOK COLLECTING
Johnson, Barbara L. Book Scouting: How to Turn Your Love for Books in Print. (Illus.). 192p. 1981. 10.95 (Spec); pap. 4.95. P-H.
Taylor, Robert H. Certain Small Works. LC 79-3891. (Illus.). 164p. 1980. 12.00 (ISBN 0-87811-023-2). Princeton Lib.
BOOK COLLECTING–BIBLIOGRAPHY
McCrimmon, Barbara. GK One: The Publication of the General Catalogue of Printed Books in British Museum, 1881-1900. 1980. write for info. (ISBN 0-208-01874-3, Linnet). Shoe String.
BOOK ILLUSTRATION
see Illustration of Books
BOOK INDUSTRIES AND TRADE
see also Bookbinding; Booksellers and Bookselling; Imprints (In Books); Paper Making and Trade; Printing; Publishers and Publishing
Bowker Annual of Library & Book Trade Information 1981. 26th ed. LC 55-12434. (Illus.). 600p. 1981. 32.50 (ISBN 0-8352-1343-9). Bowker.
Huenefeld, John & Wiley, Virginia. Planning & Control Guides & Forms for Small Book Publishers. LC 80-21051. 72p. 1980. 44.00 (ISBN 0-931932-01-7). Huenefeld Co.
Lengenfelder, Helga, ed. International Bibliography of the Book Trade & Librarianship 1976-79. (Handbook of International Documentation & Information Ser.: Vol. 2). 800p. 1981. 95.00 (ISBN 3-598-20504-X, Dist. by Gale Research). K G Saur.
BOOK INDUSTRIES AND TRADE–EXHIBITION
see Bibliographical Exhibitions
BOOK LISTS
see Bibliography–Best Books
BOOK NUMBERS
see Alphabeting
BOOK ORNAMENTATION
Brenni, Vito J., compiled by. Book Illustration & Decoration: A Guide to Research. LC 80-1701. (Art Reference Collection Ser.: No. 1). viii, 191p. 1980. lib. bdg. 27.50 (ISBN 0-313-22340-8, BBI/). Greenwood.
BOOK PRICES
see Books–Prices
BOOK RARITIES
see Bibliography–Rare Books
BOOK REPAIRING
see Books–Conservation and Restoration
BOOK REVIEWING
Here are entered works on the technique of writing reviews. Collections of reviews are entered under the heading Books–Reviews.
Oppenheimer, Evelyn. Oral Book Reviewing to Stimulate Reading: A Practical Guide in Technique for Lecture & Broadcast. LC 80-20006. 168p. 1980. 10.00 (ISBN 0-8108-1352-1). Scarecrow.
Steiner, Dale R., ed. Historical Journals: A Handbook for Writers & Reviewers. 1981. price not set (ISBN 0-87436-312-8). ABC-Clio.
BOOK REVIEWS
see Books–Reviews
BOOK SALES
see Books–Prices; Booksellers and Bookselling
BOOK TRADE
see Book Industries and Trade; Booksellers and Bookselling; Publishers and Publishing
BOOKBINDING
see also Book Ornamentation
Diehl, Edith. Bookbinding: Its Background & Technique. (Illus.). 748p. 1980. pap. 12.00 (ISBN 0-486-24020-7). Dover.
Riberholt, K. & Drastrup, A. Bookbinding at Home: The Basics of Bookbinding Simply Explained in Words & Diagrams. (Illus.). 96p. (Orig.). 1981. pap. 5.95 (ISBN 0-8069-9270-0). Sterling.
BOOKBINDING–EXHIBITIONS
see Bibliographical Exhibitions
BOOKKEEPING
see also Accounting; Auditing; Business Mathematics; Calculating-Machines; Cash Registers; Cost Accounting; Financial Statements
also subdivision Accounting under specific industries, professions, trades, etc.
Magee, J. O. Basic Bookkeeping. 256p. (Orig.). 1979. pap. text ed. 10.00x (ISBN 0-7121-0274-4, Pub. by Macdonald & Evans England). Intl Ideas.
Quint, B. G. Clear & Simple Guide to Bookkeeping. (Clear & Simple Guides Ser.). (Illus.). 96p. (Orig.). 1981. pap. 4.95 (ISBN 0-671-42108-5). Monarch Pr.
BOOKS
see also Bibliography; Cataloging; Classification–Books; Copyright; Illustration of Books; Imprints (In Books); Libraries; Literature; Manuscripts; Printing; Publishers and Publishing
also headings beginning with the word Book
American Book Publishing Record Annual Cumulative 1980. 1260p. 1981. text ed. 59.00 (ISBN 0-8352-1245-9). Bowker.
British Museum - Library. General Catalogue of Printed Books: Compact Edition. Basic Catalogue (to 1955, 27 vols. compact ed. 1967. Set. 750.00 (ISBN 0-918414-04-0). Readex Bks.
British Museum - Library. General Catalogue of Printed Books: Compact Edition. Second Supplement (1966-1970, 3 vols. compact ed. 1974. Set. 120.00 (ISBN 0-918414-06-7). Readex Bks.
British Museum - Library. General Catalogue of Printed Books: Compact Edition. Third Supplement (1971-1975, 2 vols. compact ed. 1980. Set. 150.00 (ISBN 0-918414-07-5). Readex Bks.
Rawlings, Gertrude B. The Story of Books. 160p. 1980. Repr. of 1901 ed. lib. bdg. 25.00 (ISBN 0-89984-431-6). Century Bookbindery.
Taylor, Robert H. Certain Small Works. LC 79-3891. (Illus.). 164p. 1980. 12.00 (ISBN 0-87811-023-2). Princeton Lib.
BOOKS–APPRAISAL
see Bibliography–Best Books; Books and Reading; Criticism; Literature–History and Criticism
BOOKS–BEST SELLERS
see Best Sellers
BOOKS–COLLECTORS AND COLLECTING
see Book Collecting
BOOKS–CONSERVATION AND RESTORATION
Averkamp, Marcella. Preserving Paper & Photographic Materials: A Handbook for Curators & Librarians. LC 80-26028. (Illus.). 88p. (Orig.). 1981. pap. 7.95x (ISBN 0-87020-203-0). State Hist Soc Wis.
BOOKS–EXHIBITIONS
see Bibliographical Exhibitions
Annual '79: Bologna Book Fair. 8.00. Boston Public Lib.
Character of the Year Project: A Catalog. (Bologna Children's Book Fair). pap. 10.00. Boston Public Lib.
Taylor, Earl R., compiled by. A Checklist of the Robert A Feer Collection of World Fairs of North America. pap. 3.00. Boston Public Lib.
BOOKS–FORMAT
Morrison, C. L., ed. Pithy Sayings from FORMAT Interviews, Vol. II. 1980. pap. 2.50 (ISBN 0-932508-07-3). Seven Oaks.
BOOKS–PRESERVATION
see Books–Conservation and Restoration
BOOKS–PRICES
Leab, Katharine K. & Leab, Daniel J., eds. American Book Prices Current: 1980, Vol. 86. 1200p. 1981. 79.75 (ISBN 0-914022-10-5); prepub. 62.30 (ISBN 0-686-68816-3). Bancroft Parkman.
Leab, Katherine & Leab, Daniel, eds. American Book Prices Current, Vol. 86. 1981. 79.75 (ISBN 0-914022-11-3). Am Book Prices.
McGrath, Daniel F., ed. Bookman's Price Index: A Guide to the Values of Rare & Other Out-of-Print Books. LC 64-8723. (Bookman's Price Index Ser.: Vol. 21). 900p. 1981. 78.00 (ISBN 0-8103-0621-2). Gale.
BOOKS–REPAIRING
see Books–Conservation and Restoration
BOOKS–RESTORATION
see Books–Conservation and Restoration
BOOKS–REVIEWS
Here are entered collections of reviews; Works on the technique of writing reviews are entered under the heading Book Reviewing.
see also Book Reviewing
Books of the Times: The New York Times Daily Book Reviews, 1980. (Illus.). 648p. 1981. 20.00 (ISBN 0-405-14021-5). Arno.
Eddy, Donald D. Samuel Johnson - Book Reviewer in the Literary Magazine: Or Universal Review 1756-1758. LC 78-53000. 170p. 1979. lib. bdg. 17.00 (ISBN 0-8240-3425-2). Garland Pub.
Tarbert, Gary C., ed. Book Review Index: Annual Cumulation Covering 1980. LC 65-9908. (Book Review Index Ser.). 1981. 78.00 (ISBN 0-8103-0571-2). Gale.
BOOKS–REVIEWS–BIBLIOGRAPHY
Jacques Cattell Press, ed. Library Journal Book Review 1980. LC 68-59515. 760p. 32.50 (ISBN 0-8352-1344-7). Bowker.
BOOKS, FILMED
see Film Adaptations
BOOKS, ILLUSTRATED
see Illustration of Books
BOOKS, LARGE TYPE
see Large Type Books
BOOKS, RARE
see Bibliography–Rare Books
BOOKS, REFERENCE
see Reference Books
BOOKS AND READING
see also Best Sellers; Bibliography–Best Books; Books–Reviews; Classification–Books; Libraries; Literature; Readability (Literary Style); Reference Books
Smith, Agnes. Speaking As a Writer. Ross-Robertson, David, tr. LC 78-65831. (Illus.). 76p. (Orig.). 1979. 7.75 (ISBN 0-9602342-0-9); pap. 5.95 (ISBN 0-9602342-1-7). Westwind Pr.
What Shall I Read? 2d ed. 1978. 12.95x (ISBN 0-85365-560-X, Pub. by Lib Assn England). Oryx Pr.
BOOKS AND READING FOR CHILDREN
see also Children'S Literature (Collections); also subdivisions under Children's Literature
Children's Books International III: Proceedings. 1978. 7.50. Boston Public Lib.
Children's Books International IV: Proceedings. 1979. 7.50. Boston Public Lib.
Made to Measure: Children's Books in Developing Countries. 129p. 1981. pap. 8.25 (ISBN 92-3-101783-7, U1047, UNESCO). Unipub.
BOOKS FOR CHILDREN
see Children'S Literature (Collections); also subdivisions under Children's Literature
BOOKS FOR THE DEAF
see Deaf, Books for the
BOOKS OF KNOWLEDGE
see Encyclopedias and Dictionaries
BOOKSELLERS AND BOOKSELLING
see also Books–Prices; Catalogs, Booksellers'; Copyright; Publishers and Publishing
Annual '79: Bologna Book Fair. 8.00. Boston Public Lib.
Character of the Year Project: A Catalog. (Bologna Children's Book Fair). pap. 10.00. Boston Public Lib.
Heath, Wendy Y., ed. Book Auction Records: Vol. 76, Aug. 1978-July 1979. LC 5-18641. 518p. 1980. 162.50x (ISBN 0-7129-1012-3). Intl Pubns Serv.
Taylor, Earl R., compiled by. A Checklist of the Robert A Feer Collection of World Fairs of North America. pap. 3.00. Boston Public Lib.
White, Ken. Bookstore Planning & Design. (Illus.). 192p. 1982. 34.50 (ISBN 0-07-069851-1). McGraw.
BOOKSELLERS AND BOOKSELLING–DIRECTORIES
Directory of Publishing & Bookselling in Brazil. 179p. 1980. 50.00x (ISBN 0-901618-22-5, Pub. by Brit Coun England). State Mutual Bk.
Staff of American Book Collector. Directory of Specialized American Bookdealers 1981-1982. 256p. 1981. lib. bdg. 19.95 (ISBN 0-668-05203-1). Arco.
BOOKSELLERS' CATALOGS
see Catalogs, Booksellers'
BOOTH, JOHN WILKES, 1838-1865
Townsend, George A. The Life, Crime, & Capture of John Wilkes Booth. LC 80-129018. (Illus.). 65p. pap. text ed. 10.00 (ISBN 0-686-28746-0). J L Barbour.
BOOTS AND SHOES–REPAIRING
Thomas, Bill & Stebel, Sid. Shoe Leather Treatment... LC 79-56300. (Illus.). 1979. 11.95 (ISBN 0-312-90861-X). J P Tarcher.
BORDEN, LIZZIE ANDREW, 1860-1927
Porter, Edwin & Libris, Edouard, eds. The Fall River Tragedy: With an Essay on the True Borden Murderer by Edouard Libris. rev. ed. 350p. 1981. lib. bdg. 15.00; pap. 10.00. Forty Whacks.
BORDER LIFE
see Frontier and Pioneer Life
BORGES, JORGE LUIS, 1899-
Bell-Villada, Gene H. Borges & His Fiction: A Guide to His Mind & Art. LC 80-17426. 352p. 1981. 19.00x (ISBN 0-8078-1458-X); pap. 10.00x (ISBN 0-8078-4075-0). U of NC Pr.
BORING
Here are entered works relating to the operation of cutting holes in earth or rock. Material dealing with workshop operations in metal, wood, etc. is entered under Drilling and Boring.
see also Wells
Institute of Civil Engineers, UK. Safety in Wells & Boreholes. 1980. pap. 12.00x (ISBN 0-901948-57-8, Pub. by Telford England). State Mutual Bk.
BORMANN, MARTIN, 1900-1945
Manning, Paul. Martin Bormann: Nazi in Exile. (Illus.). 320p. 1981. 14.95 (ISBN 0-686-69395-7). Lyle Stuart.
BORON
Mellor. Mellor's Comprehensive Treatise on Inorganic & Theoretical Chemistry: Pt. 5 Boron. (Illus.). 825p. 1980. lib. bdg. 170.00 (ISBN 0-582-46277-0). Longman.
BORSTAL SYSTEM
see Juvenile Detention Homes
BOSS RULE
see Corruption (In Politics)
BOSTON–DESCRIPTION
Hogarth, Paul. Paul Hogarth's Walking Tour of Old Boston. (Illus.). 1978. pap. 7.95 (ISBN 0-87690-295-6). Dutton.
Yankee Magazine's Street Maps of Boston. 1980. pap. 4.95 (ISBN 0-911658-11-4, 3073). Yankee Bks.
BOSTON BASEBALL CLUB (AMERICAN LEAGUE)
Lindberg, Rick. Stuck on the Sox. 192p. (Orig.). 1978. pap. 1.95 (ISBN 0-930528-02-6). Sassafras Pr.
BOSTON PUBLIC LIBRARY
Upon the Objects to Be Attained by the Establishment of a Public Library: Report of the Trustees of the Public Library of the City of Boston. 1852. Repr. 3.50. Boston Public Lib.
Wadlin, Horace G. The Boston Public Library of the City of Boston: A History. (Published by the Trustees of the Boston Public Library). 1911. 35.00. Boston Public Lib.
Whitehill, Walter M. Boston Public Library: A Centennial History. (Published by Harvard University). 1956. 4.75. Boston Public Lib.
BOSTON SYMPHONY ORCHESTRA
Dickson, Harry E. Arthur Fiedler & the Boston Pops. 276p. 1981. 12.95 (ISBN 0-686-69044-3). HM.
BOSTON TEA PARTY, 1773
Fowler, William & Coyle, E. Wallace. The American Revolution: Changing Perspectives. 2nd ed. LC 79-88424. (Illus.). 231p. 1981. pap. text ed. 9.95x (ISBN 0-930350-21-9). NE U Pr.
Labaree, Benjamin W. The Boston Tea Party. 2nd ed. (Illus.). 347p. 1981. Repr. of 1966 ed. price not set (ISBN 0-930350-16-2). NE U Pr.
BOSWELL, JAMES, 1740-1795
Dowling, William C. Language & Logos in Boswell's Life of Johnson. LC 80-8545. (Essays in Literature Ser.). 232p. 1981. 15.00x (ISBN 0-691-06455-5). Princeton U Pr.
Ingram, Allan. Boswell's Creative Gloom: A Study of Imagery & Melancholy in the Writings of James Boswell. 1981. 28.50x (ISBN 0-389-20157-X). B&N.
BOTANICAL CHEMISTRY
see also Plant Hormones
Stumpf, P. K. & Hatch, M. D., eds. The Biochemistry of Plants: A Comprehensive Treatise, Photosynthesis, Vol. 8. 1981. write for info. Acad Pr.
BOTANICAL GEOGRAPHY
see Phytogeography
BOTANICAL RESEARCH
Douglass, A. E. Climatic Cycle & Tree Growth, 3 vols. in one. (Vols. 1 & 2, A Study of the Annual Rings of Trees in Relation to Climate & Solar Activity; Vol. 3, A Study of Cycles). 1971. 75.00 (ISBN 3-7682-0720-X). Lubrecht & Cramer.
Nair, P. K., ed. Glimpses in Plant Research. 300p. 1980. 35.00x (Pub. by Croom Helm England). State Mutual Bk.
BOTANY
see also Alpine Flora; Aquatic Plants; Botanical Research; Climbing Plants; Fertilization of Plants; Flowers; Fresh-Water Biology; Fresh-Water Flora; Fruit; Growth (Plants); House Plants; Marine Flora; Microscope and Microscopy; Natural History; Paleobotany; Phytogeography; Plants; Seeds; Shrubs; Trees; Tropical Plants; Vegetables; Weeds; Wild Flowers; Woody Plants
also divisions, classes, etc. of the vegetable kingdom, e.g. Cryptograms, Fungi; also headings beginning with the word plant; and names of plants
Batra, Lekh R., ed. Insect Fungus Symbiosis: Nutrition, Mutualism & Commensalism. LC 78-20640. 288p. 1979. text ed. 27.50 (ISBN 0-470-26671-6). Allanheld.
Blake, S. F. Geographical Guide to Floras of the World. (Landmark Reprints in Plant Science). 1961. text ed. 40.00 (ISBN 0-86598-006-3). Allanheld.
Ellenberg, H., ed. Progress in Botany, Vol. 42. 430p. 1981. 56.00 (ISBN 0-387-10430-5). Springer-Verlag.
Ewan, J. Introduction to the Reprint of Pursh's Flora Americae Septentrionalis. 118p. 1980. pap. text ed. 18.00 (ISBN 3-7682-1272-6). Lubrecht & Cramer.
Haslam, S. M. & Wolseley, P. A. River Vegetation: Its Identification, Assessment & Management; a Field Guide to the Macrophytic Vegetation of British Watercourses. 96p. Date not set. text ed. price not set (ISBN 0-521-23186-8); pap. text ed. price not set (ISBN 0-521-23187-6). Cambridge U Pr.
Kramer, Jack. Picture Encyclopedia of Small Plants. LC 78-1089. 192p. 1981. pap. 8.95 (ISBN 0-8128-6083-7). Stein & Day.
Mukherji, S. M. Pericyclic Reactions: A Mechanistic Study. 1980. 16.00x (ISBN 0-8364-0637-0, Pub. by Macmillan India). South Asia Bks.
Raven, Peter H., et al. Biology of Plants. 3rd ed. 1981. text ed. write for info. (ISBN 0-87901-132-7); write for info. lab manual (ISBN 0-87901-142-4); prep guide avail. (ISBN 0-87901-143-2). Worth.
Romberger, J. A. Meristems, Growth & Development in Woody Plants. (Landmark Reprints in Plant Science Ser.). 1963. text ed. 15.00 (ISBN 0-86598-005-5). Allanheld.
Schumann, Donna N. Living with Plants: A Guide to the Practical Application of Botany. (Illus.). 328p. (Orig.). 1980. pap. 14.20 (ISBN 0-916422-20-8). Mad River.
Skellern, Claire & Rogers, Paul. Basic Botany. (Illus.). 208p. (Orig.). 1977. pap. text ed. 9.95x (ISBN 0-7121-0255-8, Pub. by Macdonald & Evans England). Intl Ideas.
Smith, J. P. & Sawyer, J. O. Keep to the Vascular Plants of Northwest California. 1981. pap. price not set. Mad River.
--Keys to the Vascular Plants of Northwest California. rev. ed. 160p. 1980. pap. text ed. write for info (ISBN 0-916422-23-2). Mad River.
Smith, J. P., Jr. A Key to the Genera of Grasses of the Conterminous United States. 1981. pap. price not set. Mad River.
Ting, Irwin P. Plant Psysiology. LC 80-16448. (Illus.). 635p. 1981. text ed. 19.95 (ISBN 0-201-07406-0). A-W.
Watling, Roy. How to Identify Mushrooms to Genus V. Using Cultural & Developmental Features. 1981. pap. price not set. Mad River.
BOTANY–ANATOMY
see also Botany–Morphology
Leaver, C. J., ed. Genome Organization & Expression in Plants. (NATO Advanced Study Institutes Ser., Series A, Life Sciences: Vol. 29). 600p. 1980. 59.50 (ISBN 0-306-40340-4). Plenum Pub.
BOTANY–CLASSIFICATION
see also Plants–Identification
Kapoor, V. C. Taxonomic Approach to Insects. 500p. 1980. 25.00x (Pub. by Croom Helm England). State Mutual Bk.
Plant Taxonomic Literature in Australian Libraries. 520p. 1978. pap. 31.50 (ISBN 0-643-00286-3, CO15, CSIRO). Unipub.

BOTANY–ECOLOGY
see also Epiphytes; Forest Ecology; Phytogeography; Plant Communities; Symbiosis
Osmond, C. B., et al. Physiological Processes in Plant Ecology: Towards a Synthesis with Atriplex. (Ecololgical Studies: Vol. 36). (Illus.). 500p. 1980. 49.80 (ISBN 0-387-10060-1). Springer-Verlag.
Report of the Government Consultation on the International Plant Protection Convention. 50p. 1977. pap. 6.00 (ISBN 92-5-100355-6, F1983, FAO). Unipub.
BOTANY–GEOGRAPHICAL DISTRIBUTION
see Phytogeography
BOTANY–HISTOLOGY
see Botany–Anatomy
BOTANY–MAPPING
see Vegetation Mapping
BOTANY–MORPHOLOGY
see also Botany–Anatomy
Li, Sui-Fong. Studies on the Tolerance to Elevated Temperatures in Pleurotus Ostreatus (Jacq. Ex Fr.) Kummer: A Contribution to Taxonomy & the Genetics of the Fruiting Process. (Bibliotheca Mycologica: No. 76). (Illus.). 88p. 1981. pap. text ed. 15.00x (ISBN 3-7682-1276-9). Lubrecht & Cramer.
BOTANY–PATHOLOGY
see Plant Diseases
BOTANY–PHYSIOLOGY
see Plant Physiology
BOTANY–PHYTOGRAPHY
see Botany
BOTANY–RESEARCH
see Botanical Research
BOTANY–STRUCTURE
see Botany–Anatomy
BOTANY–TAXONOMY
see Botany–Classification
BOTANY–AFRICA
Barkuizen, B. The Succulents of Southern Africa. 1980. 60.00x (Pub. by Bailey & Swinton South Africa). State Mutual Bk.
BOTANY–AUSTRALIA
Groves, R. H., ed. Australian Vegetation. LC 80-40421. (Illus.). 350p. Date not set. price not set (ISBN 0-521-23436-0); pap. price not set (ISBN 0-521-29950-0). Cambridge U Pr.
Lands of the Alligator Rivers Area, Northern Territory. (Land Research Ser.: No. 38). 171p. 1976. pap. 13.50 (ISBN 0-643-00208-1, CO19, CSIRO). Unipub.
Levitt, Dulcie. Plants & People: Aboriginal Uses of Plants on Groote Eylandt. (Australian Institute of Aborigianl Studies). 1981. text ed. price not set (ISBN 0-391-02195-8); pap. text ed. write for info. Humanities.
BOTANY–CANADA
Taylor, Ronald J. & Leviton, Alan E., eds. Mosses of North America. 170p. (Orig.). 1980. 11.95 (ISBN 0-934394-02-4). AAASPD.
BOTANY–GREAT BRITAIN
Clapham, A. R., et al. Excursion Flora of the British Isles. 3rd ed. LC 79-51679. 600p. Date not set. 29.95 (ISBN 0-521-23290-2). Cambridge U Pr.
Walters, S. M. Shaping of Cambridge Botany. (Illus.). 128p. Date not set. price not set (ISBN 0-521-23795-5). Cambridge U Pr.
Webb, D. A. An Irish Flora. (Illus.). 14.95. Dufour.
BOTANY–LATIN AMERICA
Leon, H. & Alain, Hermano. Flora de Cuba, 2 vols. (Illus.). 2317p. (Span., Lat.). 1979. Repr. of 1946 ed. lib. bdg. 280.80 five parts bound in 2 vols. (ISBN 3-87429-077-8). Lubrecht & Cramer.
BOTANY–NORWAY
Ronning, Olaf & Bjaerevoll, Olav. Flowers of Svalbard. (Illus.). 56p. 1981. pap. 14.00x (ISBN 82-00-05398-9). Universitet.
BOTANY–UNITED STATES
Ewan, Joseph, ed. A Short History of Botany in the United States. 1969. 8.95 (ISBN 0-02-844360-8). Hafner.
Godfrey, Robert K. & Wooten, Jean W. Aquatic & Wetland Plants of Southeastern United States: Dicotyledons. LC 80-16452. (Illus.). 864p. 1981. lib. bdg. 40.00x (ISBN 0-8203-0532-4). U of Ga Pr.
Martin, W. C. & Hutchins, C. R. A Flora of New Mexico, 2 vols. (Illus.). 3000p. 1980. lib. bdg. 160.00x (ISBN 3-7682-1263-7, Pub. by Cramer Germany). Lubrecht & Cramer.
Smth, Clifton F. A Flora of the Santa Barbara Region, California. LC 76-9164. 331p. 1976. pap. text ed. 12.50 (ISBN 0-936494-00-X). Santa Barbara Mus Nat Hist.
BOTANY, AGRICULTURAL
see Botany, Economic
BOTANY, ECONOMIC
see also Forest Products; Grain; Grasses; Plants, Edible; Weeds
Gill, N. T. & Vear, K. C. Agricultural Botany 1: Dicotyledonous Crops. 3rd ed. (Illus.). 268p. 1980. 45.00x (ISBN 0-7156-1250-6, Pub. by Duckworth England). Biblio Dist.
--Agricultural Botany 2: Monocotyledonous Crops. 3rd ed. Barnard, A. D., rev. by. (Illus.). 259p. 1980. 45.00x (ISBN 0-7156-1251-4, Pub by Duckworth England). Biblio Dist.
BOTANY, FOSSIL
see Paleobotany
BOTANY, MEDICAL
see also Herbs; Materia Medica, Vegetable; Medicine, Medieval; Plants–Assimilation
Barlow, Max G. Medicinal Botany II: From the Shepard's Purse. 1981. 25.95x (ISBN 0-9602812-1-5). Spice West.
Ceres. Herbs for First-Aid & Minor Ailments. LC 80-53453. (Everybodys Home Herbal Ser.). (Illus.). 64p. 1981. pap. 1.95 (ISBN 0-394-74925-1). Shambhala Pubns.
Heinerman, John. The Treatment of Cancer with Herbs. 1980. 12.95 (ISBN 0-89557-047-5). Bi World Indus.
The Old Herb Doctor. 1981. Repr. lib. bdg. 13.95 (ISBN 0-89370-652-3). Borgo Pr.
Powell, Eric F. Tranquilization with Harmless Herbs. 1980. 3.00x (ISBN 0-8464-1054-0). Beekman Pubs.
Speight, Phyllis. Arnica the Wonder Herb. 1977. text ed. 3.00x (ISBN 0-686-68090-1). Beekman Pubs.
Wren, R. C. Potter's New Cyclopaedia of Botanical Drugs & Preparations. 1980. text ed. 23.95x (ISBN 0-8464-1039-7). Beekman Pubs.
BOTANY, STRUCTURAL
see Botany–Anatomy
BOTANY, SYSTEMATIC
see Botany–Classification
BOTANY OF THE BIBLE
see Bible–Natural History
BOTSWANA
Carter, Gwendolen & Morgan, E. Philip, eds. From the Frontline: Speeches of Sir Seretse Khama. (Special Project Ser.: 27). 252p. 1980. 26.95. Hoover Inst Pr.
Colclough, Christopher & McCarthy, Stephen. The Politocal Economy of Botswana: A Study of Growth & Distribution. (Illus.). 308p. 1980. 37.50 (ISBN 0-19-877136-3). Oxford U Pr.
BOTTLES
Hastin, Bud. Bud Hastin's Avon Bottle Encyclopedia. 8th ed. (Illus.). 530p. 1981. 18.95. Avons Res.
Western Collector: Handbook & Price Guide to Avon Bottles, 1977-78. 320p. 14.95. Avons Res.
Western Collector: Handbook & Price Guide to Avon Bottles, 1975-76. 224p. 12.95. Avons Res.
BOTTOM DEPOSITS (OCEANOGRAPHY)
see Marine Sediments; Sedimentation and Deposition
BOUCICAULT, DION, 1820-1890
Fawkes, Richard. Dion Boucicault: A Biography. 274p. 1980. 21.95 (ISBN 0-7043-2221-8, Pub. by Quartet England). Horizon.
BOULEE, ETIENNE LOUIS, 1728-1799
Lemagny, J. C. & De Menil, Dominiqueintro. by. Visionary Architects: Boullee, Ledoux, Lequeu. (Illus.). 1968. pap. 8.00 (ISBN 0-914412-21-3). Inst for the Arts.
BOUNTY (SHIP)
Mackaness, George, ed. A Book of the Bounty' William Bligh & Others. Kennedy, Gavin. (Everyman's Reference Library). 1981. 14.50x (ISBN 0-460-00950-8, Pub. by J. M. Dent England). Biblio Dist.
BOURBON WHISKEY
see Whiskey
BOURNE, RANDOLPH, 1886-1918
Vitelli, James R. Randolph Bourne. (United States Authors Ser.: No. 408). 1981. lib. bdg. 12.95 (ISBN 0-8057-7337-1). Twayne.
BOUTIQUES
see Stores, Retail
BOUVIER D'FLANDRES (DOG)
see Dogs–Breeds–Bouvier D'Flandres
BOVINE BRUCELLOSIS
see Brucellosis in Cattle
BOWLING
Allen, George & Ritger, Dick. The Complete Guide to Bowling Strikes: The Encyclopedia of Strikes. LC 80-53200. (Illus.). 240p. 1981. 14.95 (ISBN 0-933554-02-8); pap. 9.95 (ISBN 0-933554-03-6). Ritger Sports.
Annarino, A. Bowling: Individualized Instructional Program. 1973. pap. 4.25 (ISBN 0-13-080440-1). P-H.
Liss, Howard. Bowling Talk. (gr. 4-6). 1974. pap. 0.75 (ISBN 0-671-29619-1). PB.
Taylor, Dawson. Mastering Bowling. (Mastering Ser.). (Illus.). 1981. 12.95 (ISBN 0-8092-7049-8); pap. 6.95 (ISBN 0-8092-7047-1). Contemp Bks.
Weiskopf, Herm & Pezzano, Chuck. Sports Illustrated: Bowling. LC 80-7887. (Illus.). 160p. 1981. pap. 5.95 (ISBN 0-690-02006-6, CN 866, CN). Har-Row.
BOXING
see also T'ai chi Ch'uan
Fraser, Raymond. Fighting Fisherman: The Life of Yvon Durelle. LC 80-703. (Illus.). 288p. 1981. 11.95 (ISBN 0-385-15863-7). Doubleday.
Okpaku, Joseph. Superfight No. II: The Story Behind the Fights Between Muhammad Ali & Joe Frazier. LC 74-74429. 1974. 6.95 (ISBN 0-89388-165-1). Okpaku Communlications.
Thomas, Art. Boxing Is for Me. LC 80-20086. (Sports for Me Bks.). (Illus.). (gr. 2-5). 1981. PLB 5.95 (ISBN 0-8225-1133-9). Lerner Pubns.
BOY SCOUTS
Albright, Gretchen E. Survival Sanctuary: A Scouts Guide to Preparedness. LC 80-54281. (Illus.). 146p. (Orig.). 1980. pap. 4.95 (ISBN 0-938064-00-2). Secure Futures.
Boy Scouts, of America. Den Chief Handbook. LC 79-55446. (Illus.). 128p. (gr. 6-12). 1980. flexible bdg. 1.75x. BSA.
BOYS–EMPLOYMENT
see Children–Employment; Youth–Employment
BRACHYGRAPHY
see Abbreviations; Shorthand
BRACKISH WATER BIOLOGY
see Marine Biology; Marine Fauna; Marine Flora
BRADY, MATTHEW B., 1823-1896
Harrison, et al. Matthew Brady. (Illus.). 35p. (gr. 1-9). 1981. 2.95 (ISBN 0-86575-190-0). Dormac.
BRAHMAN MYTHOLOGY
see Mythology, Hindu
BRAHMS, JOHANNES, 1833-1897
Matthews, Denis. Brahms Piano Music. LC 75-27955. (BBC Music Guides: No. 37). (Illus.). 64p. (Orig.). 1978. pap. 2.95 (ISBN 0-295-95480-9). U of Wash Pr.
BRAIDISM
see Hypnotism
BRAIN
see also Cerebellum; Cerebral Cortex; Dreams; Hypothalamus; Memory; Mind and Body; Nervous System; Pituitary Body; Psychology; Sleep; Telencephalon; Thalamus
Donhoffer, Sz. Homeothermia of the Brain. (Illus.). 140p. (Orig.). 1980. pap. 13.50x (ISBN 963-05-2405-8). Intl Pubns Serv.
Giles, Floyd H., et al. Developing Human Brain: Growth & Epidemiologic Neuropathology. Date not set. write for info. (ISBN 0-88416-254-0). PSG Pub.
Gluhbegovic, Nedzad & Williams, Terence H. The Human Brain. (Illus.). 176p. 1980. text ed. 27.50 (ISBN 0-06-140945-6, Harper Medical). Har-Row.
Katsuki, Yasuji & Sato, Masayasu. Brain Mechanisms of Sensation. 320p. 1981. 28.50 (ISBN 0-471-08148-5, Pub. by Wiley Med). Wiley.
Kuhlenbeck, H. The World of Natural Sciences & Its Phenomenology: The Human Brain & Its Universe. 2nd ed. Gerlach, J., ed. (Vol. 1). viii, 320p. 1981. 118.75 (ISBN 3-8055-1817-X). S Karger.
Kuhlenbeck, H. & Gerlach, J. The Brain & Its Mind. 2nd ed. (The Human Brain & Its Universe: Vol. 2). (Illus.). x, 398p. 1981. 118.75 (ISBN 3-8055-2403-X). S Karger.
Monro, Alexander. Three Treatises: On the Brain, the Eye, & the Ear. Bd. with Croonian Lectures on Cerebrqal Localization. Ferrier, D. (Contributions to the History of Psychology Ser., Vol. VII, Pt. E: Psysiological Psychology). 1980. Repr. of 1797 ed. 30.00 (ISBN 0-89093-326-X). U Pubns Amer.
Montemurro, Donald G. & Bruni, J. Edward. The Human Brain in Dissection. 1981. text ed. price not set (ISBN 0-7216-6438-5). Saunders.
Noble, Daniel. Brain & Its Physiology. (Contributions to the History of Pcychology E, V, Physiological Psychology Ser.). 1980. Repr. of 1846 ed. 30.00 (ISBN 0-89093-324-3). U Pubns Amer.
Siesjo, B. K. Brain Energy Metabolism. 607p. 1978. 79.50 (ISBN 0-471-99515-0). Wiley.
Smith, Carlton G. Serial Discussions of the Human Brain. (Illus.). 100p. 1981. text ed. price not set (ISBN 0-8067-1811-0). Urban & S.
Tasker, Ronald R., et al. The Thalmus & the Midbrain of Man: A Physiological Atlas Using Electrical Stimulatiob. (American Lecture Neurosurgery Ser.). (Illus.). 464p. write for info. (ISBN 0-398-04475-9). C C Thomas.
Young, J. Z. Programs of the Brain. (Illus.). 334p. 1981. pap. 6.95 (ISBN 0-19-286019-4, GB 641, GB). Oxford U Pr.
BRAIN–DISEASES
see also Amnesia; Aphasia; Brain Damage; Cerebral Edema; Cerebral Palsy; Cerebrovascular Disease; Electroencephalography; Encephalitis; Leucodystrophy; Nervous System–Diseases; Psychology, Pathological; Thrombosis
McDowell, Fletcher H., ed. Current Concepts in Cerebravascular Disease. (Progress in Cardiovascular Disease Ser.). 1980. write for info. (ISBN 0-8089-1353-0). Grune.
Safar, Peter & Grenvik, Ake. Brain Failure & Resuscitation. (Clinics in Critical Care Medicine). (Illus.). 256p. 1981. lib. bdg. 22.50 (ISBN 0-443-08143-3). Churchill.
Wackenheim, A., et al. Cheirolumbar Dysostosis. (Illus.). 102p. 1981. pap. 34.30 (ISBN 0-387-10371-6). Springer-Verlag.
BRAIN–LOCALIZATION OF FUNCTIONS
Ferrier, David. Functions of the Brain. (Contributions to the History of Psychology E, III, Physiological Psychology Ser.). 1978. Repr. of 1886 ed. 30.00 (ISBN 0-89093-176-3). U Pubns Amer.
Gall, Franz J. On the Functions of the Brain & Each of Its Parts. Lewis, W., tr. from Ger. (Contributions to the History of Psychology Ser.). 1980. Repr. of 1835 ed. 30.00 ea. U Pubns Amer.
Jacobs, Barry L. & Gelperin, Alan, eds. Serotonin Transmission & Behavior. 430p. 1981. text ed. 45.00x (ISBN 0-686-69226-8). MIT Pr.
Pfaff, D. W. Estrogens & Brain Function: Neural Analysis of a Hormone-Controlled Mammalian Reproductive Behavior. (Illus.). 272p. 1980. 24.90 (ISBN 0-387-90487-5). Springer-Verlag.
Pompeiano, O. & Ajmone-Marsan, C., eds. Brain Mechanisms & Perceptual Awareness. (IBRO Ser.: No. 8). 1981. text ed. price not set (ISBN 0-89004-603-4). Raven.
Springer, Sally P. & Deutsch, Georg. Left Brain, Right Brain. LC 80-25453. (Psychology Ser.). (Illus.). 1981. text ed. 11.95x (ISBN 0-7167-1269-5); pap. text ed. 6.95x (ISBN 0-7167-1270-9). W H Freeman.
BRAIN–RESEARCH
McDowell, Fletcher H., ed. Current Concepts in Cerebravascular Disease. (Progress in Cardiovascular Disease Ser.). 1980. write for info. (ISBN 0-8089-1353-0). Grune.
BRAIN–SURGERY
see also Stereoencephalotomy
Riechert, T. Stereotactic Brain Operations: Methods, Clinical Aspects, Indications. (Illus.). 387p. 1980. 120.00 (ISBN 3-456-80457-1, Pub. by Hans Huber). J K Burgess.
BRAIN DAMAGE
Richter, Derek, ed. Addiction & Brain Damage. 320p. 1980. 45.00x (Pub. by Croom Helm England). State Mutual Bk.
BRAIN DEATH
New Jersey Supreme Court. In the Matter of Karen Quinlan, Vol. 1: The Complete Legal Briefs, Court Proceedings, & Decision in the Superior Court of New Jersey. 575p. 1975. 29.50 (ISBN 0-89093-100-3). U Pubns Amer.
New Jersey Supreme Court, et al. In the Matter of Karen Quinlan: Volume 2, The Complete Briefs, Oral Agruments, & Opinion in the New Jersey Supreme Court. 1976. 22.50 (ISBN 0-89093-114-3). U Pubns Amer.
Stickel, D. L. The Brain Death Criterion of Human Death. (Illus.). 73p. 1981. 19.00 (ISBN 0-08-025814-X). Pergamon.
BRAIN DRAIN
Kao, Charles H. Brain Drain. 178p. 1980. 10.50x (ISBN 0-89955-157-2, Pub. by Mei Ya Pub Taiwan); pap. 5.95x (ISBN 0-89955-188-2). Intl Schol Bk Serv.
BRAIN EDEMA
see Cerebral Edema
BRAIN FUNCTION LOCALIZATION
see Brain–Localization of Functions
BRANCH LIBRARIES
see Libraries–Branches, Delivery Stations, Etc.
BRAND MANAGEMENT
see Product Management
BRAND NAMES
see Trade-Marks
BRANDEIS, LOUIS DEMBITZ, 1856-1941
Urofsky, Melvin. Louis B. Brandeis & the Progressive Tradition. 208p. 1981. 11.95 (ISBN 0-316-88787-0). Little.
Urofsky, Melvin I. Lows D. Brandeis & the Progressive Tradition. (Library of American Biography). 1980. pap. text ed. 4.95 (ISBN 0-316-88788-9). Little.
BRANDS (COMMERCE)
see Trade-Marks
BRANDY
Ramos, Adam & Ramos, Joseph. California Brandy: The Wine Drinker's Spirit. (Illus.). 1981. 12.95 (ISBN 0-914598-66-X). Padre Prods.
BRASS BAND MUSIC
see Band Music
BRASS BANDS
see Bands (Music)
BRASS INSTRUMENTS
see Wind Instruments
BRAUN, ALBERT, 1889-
Emerson, Dorothy. Among the Mescalero Apaches: The Story of Father Albert Braun, O. F. M. LC 73-76302. 1980. pap. 8.50 (ISBN 0-8165-0714-7). U of Ariz Pr.
BRAVERY
see Courage
BRAZIL–DESCRIPTION AND TRAVEL
Lanier, Alison R. Update -- Brazil. (Country Orientation Ser.). 1980. pap. text ed. 25.00 (ISBN 0-933662-36-X). Intercult Network.
BRAZIL–ECONOMIC CONDITIONS
Anuario Estatistico Do Brazil. 40th ed. LC 73-642043. (Illus.). 853p. (Portuguese.). 1980. pap. 85.00x (ISBN 0-8002-2696-8). Intl Pubns Serv.
Tyler, William G. The Brazilian Industrial Economy. LC 79-5440. 1981. price not set (ISBN 0-669-03448-7). Lexington Bks.
BRAZIL–ECONOMIC POLICY
Tyler, William G. Advanced Developing Countries As Export Competitors in Third World Markets: The Brazilian Experience, Vol. II. LC 80-67710. (Significant Issues Ser.: No. 9). 88p. 1980. 5.95 (ISBN 0-89206-022-0). CSI Studies.
BRAZIL–FOREIGN RELATIONS
Selcher, Wayne A., ed. Brazil in the International System. (Special Studies on Latin America & the Caribbean). 300p. 1981. lib. bdg. 26.50x (ISBN 0-89158-907-4). Westview.
BRAZIL–HISTORY
Conniff, Michael L. Urban Politics in Brazil: The Rise of Populism, 1925-1945. LC 80-54060. (Pitt Latin American Ser.). (Illus.). 280p. 1981. 19.95x (ISBN 0-8229-3438-8). U of Pittsburgh Pr.
BRAZIL–POLITICS AND GOVERNMENT
Daland, Robert T. Exploring Brazilian Bureaucracy: Performance & Pathology. LC 80-67246. 455p. 1981. lib. bdg. 24.24 (ISBN 0-8191-1468-5); pap. text ed. 15.75 (ISBN 0-8191-1469-3). U Pr of Amer.

Selcher, Wayne A., ed. Brazil in the International System. (Special Studies on Latin America & the Caribbean). 300p. 1981. lib. bdg. 26.50x (ISBN 0-89158-907-4). Westview.

BRAZIL–SOCIAL CONDITIONS

Anuario Estatistico Do Brazil. 40th ed. LC 73-642043. (Illus.). 853p. (Portuguese.). 1980. pap. 85.00x (ISBN 0-8002-2696-8). Intl Pubns Serv.

Flory, Thomas. Judge & Jury in Imperial Brazil, 1808-1871: Social Control & Political Stability in the New State. 288p. 1981. text ed. 25.00x (ISBN 0-292-74015-8). U of Tex Pr.

BREAD

see also Baking

Pack-Miller, Lisa, et al. Easy Natural Breads Even a Kid Can Bake. Frompovich, Catherine J., ed. (Illus.). 14p. (gr. 3 up). 1980. pap. 1.50 (ISBN 0-935322-07-8). C J Frompovich.

Roberts, Ada L. The New Book of Favorite Breads from Rose Lane Farm. 2nd, rev. ed. (Illus.). 192p. 1981. pap. 3.00 (ISBN 0-486-24091-6). Dover.

Time-Life Books. Breads. (The Good Cook Ser.). (Illus.). 176p. 1981. 12.95 (ISBN 0-8094-2900-4). Time Life.

BREADSTUFFS

see Grain; Wheat

BREAKAGE, SHRINKAGE, ETC. (COMMERCE)

Barnes, Robert M. Technical Commodity Yearbook, 1981. 128p. 1980. text ed. 37.50 (ISBN 0-686-69348-5). Van Nos Reinhold.

BREAKERS

see Ocean Waves

BREAKFASTS

St. John Thomas, David. The Breakfast Book. LC 80-69350. (Illus.). 96p. 1981. 11.95x (ISBN 0-7153-8094-X). David & Charles.

BREAST–CANCER

Cshl Banbury Center Report 8 - Hormones & Breast Cancer, et al. Proceedings. Siiteri, Pentti K. & Welsch, Clifford W., eds. (Banbury Report Ser.: Vol. 8). 1981. 60.00 (ISBN 0-87969-207-3). Cold Spring Harbor.

Lewison, Edward F. & Montague, Albert C. Diagnosis & Treatment of Breast Cancer: International Clinical Congress. (Illus.). 268p. 1981. write for info. (4954-2). Williams & Wilkins.

McGrath, Charles M., et al, eds. Cell Biology of Breast Cancer. LC 80-13804. 1981. 33.00 (ISBN 0-12-483940-1). Acad Pr.

Milan, Albert R. Breast Self-Examination. LC 79-56529. (Illus.). 128p. 1980. pap. 3.50 (ISBN 0-89480-124-4). Liberty Pub.

Shapero, Lucy & Goodman, Anthony A. Never Say Die: A Doctor & Patient Talk About Breast Cancer. (Appleton Consumer Health Guides). 170p. 1980. 10.95 (ISBN 0-8385-6718-5). ACC.

Smithers, D. W., et al. Cancer of the Breast. 1980. 10.00x (Pub. by Brit Inst Radiology England). State Mutual Bk.

BREAST–DISEASES

Bulbrook, R. D. & Taylor, D. Jane, eds. Commentaries on Research in Breast Disease, Vol. 2. 175p. 1981. price not set (ISBN 0-8451-1901-X). A R Liss.

BREAST FEEDING

Feinberg, Richard, et al. Tempest in a Tea House: American Attitudes Toward Breast-Feeding. 50p. (Orig.). 1980. pap. 2.95 (ISBN 0-933522-06-1). Kent Popular.

Worthington, Bonnie & Taylor, Lynda. Nutrition During Pregnancy & Breast Feeding. (Illus.). 1980. pap. 2.50. Budlong.

BREATH AND BREATHING (IN RELIGION, FOLK-LORE, ETC.)

see also Yoga, Hatha

Iyengar, B. K. Light on Pranayama: The Yogic Art of Breathing. 320p. 1981. 12.95 (ISBN 0-8245-0048-2). Crossroad NY.

BREATHING

see Respiration

BREVIARIES

see Liturgies

BREWING INDUSTRY

see also Beer

Breweries & Malsters in Europe, 1980. 69th ed. LC 46-33153. Orig. Title: Brauereien und Malzereien in Europa 1980. 610p. (Orig., Eng, Fr. & Ger.). 1980. 92.50x (ISBN 3-8203-0034-1). Intl Pubns Serv.

Dersch, Lou. Beer, Bubbles & Bucks. 225p. 1981. 9.95 (ISBN 0-86629-008-7). Sunrise MO.

BRIC-A-BRAC

see Art Objects

BRICKLAYING

see also Masonry

Initial Skills in Bricklaying: A Practical Guide. LC 80-41756. (Illus.). 100p. 1981. 18.00 (ISBN 0-08-025424-1); pap. 10.00 (ISBN 0-08-025423-3). Pergamon.

BRIDAL CUSTOMS

see Marriage Customs and Rites

BRIDGE (GAME)

see Contract Bridge

BRIDGE CONSTRUCTION

see Bridges; Masonry; Strains and Stresses

BRIDGE WHIST

see also Contract Bridge

Mollo, Victor. Bridge in the Fourth Dimension. 1974. 11.95 (ISBN 0-571-10634-X, Pub. by Faber & Faber). Merrimack Bk Serv.

BRIDGES

see also Trusses

also names of individual bridges

De Mare, Eric. Your Book of Bridges. (Year Book Ser.). (Illus.). 1963. 6.95 (ISBN 0-571-05285-1, Pub. by Faber & Faber). Merrimack Bk Serv.

Guide for Bridge Maintenance Management. 1980. 3.00. AASHTO.

Institute of Civil Engineers, UK. Mechanization for Road & Bridge Construction. 54p. 1980. 55.00x (ISBN 0-901948-58-6, Pub. by Telford England). State Mutual Bk.

Interim Specifications - Bridges. 1980. 4.00. AASHTO.

Interim Specifications for Bridges. 1979. 4.00. AASHTO.

Lee, Trevor R. & Wood, L. J. Adjustment in the Urban System: The Tasman Bridge Collapse & Its Effects on Metropolitan Hobart. 85p. 1980. pap. 13.50 (ISBN 0-08-026810-2). Pergamon.

Manual for Maintenance Inspection of Bridges. 1978. 2.50. AASHTO.

Thomas Telford Ltd. Editorial Staff. Informal Meeting, Steel Box Girder Bridges. 118p. 1980. pap. 25.00x (Pub. by Telford England). State Mutual Bk.

Thomas Telford Ltd, Editorial Staff. Steel Box Girder Bridges. 324p. 1980. 60.00x (Pub. by Telford England). State Mutual Bk.

White, et al. Bridge Maintenance: Inspection & Evaluation. 272p. 1981. 32.75 (ISBN 0-8247-1086-X). Dekker.

BRIDGES–JUVENILE LITERATURE

MacGregor, Anne & MacGregor, Scott. Bridges. LC 80-23305. (Illus.). 56p. (gr. 4 up). 1981. PLB 9.55 (ISBN 0-688-51997-0); pap. 5.95 (ISBN 0-688-41997-6). Morrow.

BRIDGES, COVERED

see Covered Bridges

BRIDLE PATHS

see Trails

BRIEFHAND

see Shorthand

BRIEFS

Harvard Law School Board of Student Advisers. Introduction to Advocacy: Brief Writing & Oral Argument in Moot Court Competition. 3rd ed. 100p. 1980. text ed. write for info. (ISBN 0-88277-019-5). Foundation Pr.

BRIGANDS AND ROBBERS

see also Outlaws; Robbery; Rogues and Vagabonds; Thieves; Thugs

Edge, L. L. Run the Cat Roads: A True Story of Bank Robbers in the Thirties. LC 80-25930. 1981. 12.50 (ISBN 0-934878-01-3). Dembner Bks.

O'Neal, Bill. Henry Brown: The Outlaw-Marshall. (Illus.). 165p. 12.95; leatherbound collector's edition 75.00. Creative Pubns.

Tattersall, Peter D. Conviction. LC 80-82368. (Illus.). 374p. 1980. 12.95 (ISBN 0-8119-0407-5, Pegasus Rex). Fell.

Vanderwood, Paul J. Disorder & Progress: Bandits, Police, & Mexican Development. LC 80-22345. (Illus.). xx, 269p. 1981. 19.95x (ISBN 0-8032-4651-X, Bison); pap. 7.95 (ISBN 0-8032-9600-2, BB 767). U of Nebr Pr.

BRIGHT CHILDREN

see Gifted Children

BRITISH ARCHITECTURE

see Architecture–Great Britain

BRITISH COMMONWEALTH OF NATIONS

see Commonwealth of Nations

BRITISH DRAWINGS

see Drawings, British

BRITISH FOLK-LORE

see Folk-Lore, British

BRITISH IN AFRICA

Grant, Nellie. Nellie's Story. Huxley, Elspeth, ed. 352p. 1981. Repr. 12.95 (ISBN 0-688-00475-X). Morrow.

Hurd, David. Home to My Island. (Illus.). 192p. 1981. 9.50 (ISBN 0-682-49727-4). Exposition.

Tidrick, Kathryn. Heart-Beguiling Araby. (Illus.). 256p. Date not set. price not set (ISBN 0-521-23483-2). Cambridge U Pr.

BRITISH IN EUROPE

Harrison, G. B., ed. Anthony Munday: The English Romayne Lyfe. 105p. 1980. Repr. of 1925 ed. lib. bdg. 22.50 (ISBN 0-89760-543-8). Telegraph Bks.

BRITISH IN FOREIGN COUNTRIES

Butcher, John G. The British in Malaya, Eighteen Eighty to Nineteen Forty-One: The Social History of a European Community in Colonial South-East Asia. (Illus.). 314p. 1979. 34.95x (ISBN 0-19-580419-8). Oxford U Pr.

BRITISH LITERATURE

see English Literature (Collections); Irish Literature (Collections); Scottish Literature (Collections); and subdivisions under these headings, e.g. English Literature–History and Criticism

BRITISH MUSIC

see Music, British

BRITISH PAINTINGS

see Paintings, British

BRITISH POETRY

see English Poetry (Collections); Irish Poetry (Collections); Irish Poetry (English) (Collections); Scottish Poetry (Collections); Welsh Poetry (Collections); and subdivisions under these headings, e.g. English Poetry–History and Criticism

BRITISH PORCELAIN

see Porcelain

BRITISH PORTRAITS

see Portraits

BRITISH SCIENCE

see Science, British

BRITISH TALES

see Tales, British

BRITISH WIT AND HUMOR

see English Wit and Humor

BRITTEN, BENJAMIN, 1913-1976

Kennedy, Michael. Britten. (The Master Musicians Ser.). (Illus.). 364p. 1981. 22.50x (ISBN 0-460-03175-9, Pub. by J. M. Dent England). Biblio Dist.

Mitchell, Donald. Britten & Auden in the Thirties: The Year 1936. LC 80-25980. (Illus.). 174p. 1981. 15.00 (ISBN 0-295-95814-6). U of Wash Pr.

BROADCASTING

see also Radio Broadcasting; Television Broadcasting

International Broadcasting Convention. (IEE Conference Publications Ser.: No. 191). 354p. (Orig.). 1980. soft cover 59.50 (ISBN 0-85296-222-3). Inst Elect Eng.

Windlesham. Broadcasting in a Free Society. (Mainstream Ser.). 172p. 1980. 19.50x (ISBN 0-631-11371-1, Pub. by Basil Blackwell). Biblio Dist.

BROMELIACIAE

Benzing, David H. Biology of the Bromeliads. 300p. (Orig.). 1980. pap. write for info (ISBN 0-916422-21-6). Mad River.

BRONCHITIS

Booth, Sterling R., Jr. Allergy Cures Your Allergist Never Mentioned. 1981. 12.95 (ISBN 0-87949-191-4). Ashley Bks.

BRONCHOCELE

see Goiter

BRONTE, CHARLOTTE, 1816-1855

Byron, May C. A Day with Charlotte Bronte. 50p. 1980. Repr. lib. bdg. 8.50 (ISBN 0-8495-0462-7). Arden Lib.

BRONTE FAMILY

The Bronte Sisters. 1200p. Date not set. 9.98 (ISBN 0-7064-1348-2). Mayflower Bks.

Buono, Dello & Joseph, Carmen. Rare Early Essays on the Brontes. 218p. 1980. lib. bdg. 17.50 (ISBN 0-8482-0646-0). Norwood Edns.

Cannon, John. The Road to Haworth. (Illus.). 176p. 1981. 10.95 (ISBN 0-670-60079-2). Viking Pr.

BRONZES

Bode, Wilhelm. The Italian Bronze Statuettes of the Renaissance. Draper, James D., ed. Gretor, William, tr. LC 80-82165. (Illus.). 1980. 295.00 (ISBN 0-937370-00-2). MAS De Reinis.

BROOKLYN

Bedell, Harry. Brooklyn: Where Else. 1981. 8.50 (ISBN 0-8062-1621-2). Carlton.

Landesman, Alter F. A History of New Lots, Brooklyn to Eighteen Eighty-Seven. LC 76-30367. 1977. 12.50 (ISBN 0-8046-9172-X). Kennikat.

BROTHELS

see Prostitution

BROWN, CHARLES BROCKDEN, 1771-1810

Rosenthal, Bernard. Critical Essays on Charles Brockden Brown. (Critical Essays on American Literature). 1981. lib. bdg. 25.00 (ISBN 0-8161-8255-8). Twayne.

BROWNE, CHARLES FARRAR, 1834-1867

Seitz, Don C. Artemus Ward: Charles Farrar Browne. 338p. 1980. Repr. of 1919 ed. lib. bdg. 40.00 (ISBN 0-89760-824-0). Telegraph Bks.

BROWNING, ROBERT, 1812-1889

Altick, Richard D. Robert Browning: The Ring & the Book. LC 80-53977. 707p. 1981. text ed. 30.00x (ISBN 0-300-02677-3); pap. 7.95. Yale U Pr.

Pettigrew, John, ed. Robert Browning, the Poems, Vol. I. LC 80-53976. 1218p. 1981. text ed. 35.00x (ISBN 0-300-02675-7); pap. 12.95 (ISBN 0-300-02683-8). Yale U Pr.

--Robert Browning, the Poems, Vol. II. LC 80-53976. 1156p. 1981. text ed. 35.00x (ISBN 0-300-02676-5); pap. 12.95 (ISBN 0-300-02684-6). Yale U Pr.

Russell, Frances T. One Word More on Browning. 157p. 1980. Repr. of 1927 ed. text ed. 28.00 (ISBN 0-8492-7709-4). R West.

BROWNING, ROBERT, 1812-1889–CRITICISM AND INTERPRETATION

Alexander, William J. An Introduction to the Poetry of Robert Browning. 210p. 1980. Repr. of 1889 ed. lib. bdg. 22.50 (ISBN 0-89987-006-6). Darby Bks.

BRUCELLOSIS IN CATTLE

Straub, O. C. Bovine Hematology. (Illus.). 64p. (Orig.). 1981. pap. text ed. 18.00. Parey Sci Pub.

BRUNCHES

see Breakfasts

BRUNEL, ISAMBARD KINGDOM, 1806-1859

Pugsley, Alfred, ed. The Works of Isambard Kingdom Brunel - an Engineering Appreciation. 232p. 1980. 40.00x (ISBN 0-7277-0030-8, Pub. by Telford England). State Mutual Bk.

BRUNELLESCHI, FILIPPO, 1377-1446

Saalman, Howard. Filippo Brunelleschi: The Cupola of Santa Maria Del Fiore. (Studies in Architecture). (Illus.). 391p. 1980. 140.00 (ISBN 0-8390-0268-8). Allanheld & Schram.

BRYCE CANYON NATIONAL PARK

Yandell, M. D. National Parkways, Zion & Bryce Canyon National Parks. (Illus.). 64p. 1972. 2.95. Zion.

BUBER, MARTIN, 1878-1965

Cohn, Margot & Buber, Rafael, eds. Martin Buber: A Bibliography of His Writings, 1897-1978. 164p. 1980. 35.00 (ISBN 3-598-10146-5, Dist by Gale Research Co.). K G Saur.

Susser, Bernard. Existence & Utopia: The Social & Political Thought of Martin Buber. LC 78-75188. 260p. 1981. 15.00 (ISBN 0-8386-2292-5). Fairleigh Dickinson.

Vermes, Pamela. Buber on God & the Perfect Man. Neusner, J., et al, eds. LC 80-23406. (Brown Judaic Studies). 1981. 15.00 (ISBN 0-89130-426-6); pap. 10.50 (ISBN 0-89130-427-4). Scholars Pr CA.

BUBONIC PLAGUE

see Plague

BUBONIDAE

see Owls

BUCCANEERS

see also Brigands and Robbers; Pirates; Sea Stories

Golden Book of Buccaneers. (gr. 3-7). Date not set. 6.95 (ISBN 0-307-16811-5, Golden Pr). Western Pub.

BUCKINGHAM PALACE

John de St. Jorre. The Guards. 1981. 25.00 (ISBN 0-517-54376-1). Crown.

BUDDHISM

see also Lamaism; Meditation (Buddhism); Zen Buddhism

also headings beginning with the word Buddhist

Aronson, Harvey B. Love & Sympathy in Theravada Buddhism. 1980. 11.00x (ISBN 0-8364-0627-3, Pub. by Motilal Banarsidass). South Asia Bks.

Beyer, Stephen. The Buddhist Experience: Sources & Interpretations. 1974. pap. text ed. 7.95x (ISBN 0-8221-0127-0). Dickenson.

Bhikkhu, Suratano. In the Conquest of True Freedom. LC 78-63079. 100p. 1980. 5.95 (ISBN 0-533-03965-7). Vantage.

Bloom, Alfred. Tannisho: A Resource for Modern Living. LC 80-39523. 112p. (Orig.). 1981. pap. 4.95 (ISBN 0-938474-00-6). Buddhist Study.

David-Neel, Alexandra. Buddhism. pap. 2.75 (ISBN 0-380-46185-4, 46185, Discus). Avon.

Kaviratna, Harishchandra. Dhammapada, Wisdom of the Buddha. 1980. 8.50 (ISBN 0-911500-39-1); softcover 5.00 (ISBN 0-911500-40-5). Theos U Pr.

Moses, Larry W. The Political Role of Mongol Buddhism. (Indiana University Uralic & Altaic Ser.: Vol. 133). x, 299p. 1977. 14.95 (ISBN 0-933070-01-2). Ind U Res Inst.

Narain, A. K. Studies in History of Buddhism: Papers Presented at the International Conference on the History of Buddhism at the University of Wisconsin, Madison August 19-21,1976. 421p. 1980. text ed. 40.50 (ISBN 0-391-02212-1). Humanities.

SGam po pa. The Jewel Ornament of Liberation. Guenther, Herbert V., tr. from Tibetan. LC 72-146507. (The Clear Light Ser.). 349p. 1981. pap. 9.95 (ISBN 0-87773-717-7). Great Eastern.

The Teaching of Buddha. 307p. 1977. Repr. of 1966 ed. 6.00 (ISBN 0-89346-167-9, Bukkyo Denka Kyokai Japan). Heian Intl.

The Teaching of Buddha: Pocket Edition. 244p. 1970. Repr. of 1966 ed. 5.00 (ISBN 0-89346-168-7, Bukkyo Dendo Kyokai Japan). Heian Intl.

BUDDHISM–HISTORY

Paul, Diana. The Buddhist Feminine Ideal: Queen Srimala & the Tathagatagarbha American Academy of Religion. LC 79-12031. (Dissertation Ser.: No. 30). 12.00x (ISBN 0-89130-284-0); pap. 7.50x (ISBN 0-89130-303-0). Scholars Pr CA.

BUDDHISM–CHINA

Prip-Moller, Johannes. Chinese Buddhist Monasteries. (Illus.). 410p. 1981. 65.00 (ISBN 0-85656-034-0). Great Eastern.

BUDDHISM–INDIA

Bhattacharyya, Benoytosh. An Introduction to Buddhist Esoterism. 1980. Repr. of 1931 ed. 19.00x (ISBN 0-686-69019-2, Pub. by Motilal Banarsidas). South Asia Bks.

Chattopadhyaya, Debiprasad, ed. Taranath's History of Buddhism in India. Lama Chimpa, Alaka Chattopadhyaya & Chattopadhyaya, Alalca, trs. from Tibetan. 500p. 1980. Repr. of 1608 ed. text ed. write for info. (ISBN 0-391-02176-1). Humanities.

BUDDHISM–JAPAN

Nanjio, Bunyiu, tr. from Japanese. Short History of the Twelve Buddhist Sects. (Studies in Japanese History & Civilization). 1979. Repr. of 1886 ed. 19.75 (ISBN 0-89093-252-2). U Pubns Amer.

BUDDHISM–TIBET

Trungpa, Chogyam. Born in Tibet. LC 76-53358. (The Clear Light Ser.). (Illus.). 1981. pap. 8.95 (ISBN 0-87773-718-5). Great Eastern.

BUDDHIST ARCHITECTURE

see Architecture, Buddhist

BUDDHIST ART

see Art, Buddhist

BUDDHIST DOCTRINES

Guenther, Herbert V. Treasures on the Tibetan Middle Way. LC 75-40260. 166p. 1981. pap. 5.95 (ISBN 0-87773-002-4). Great Eastern.

Luk, Charles, tr. from Chinese. The Vimalakirti Nirdesa Sutra. LC 71-189851. 175p. 1981. pap. 5.95 (ISBN 0-87773-072-5). Great Eastern.

Rinpoche, Namgyal. The Path of Victory: Discourses on the Paramita. Gelong, Karma S., ed. LC 80-84669. (Illus.). 75p. (Orig.). 1980. pap. 5.00 (ISBN 0-9602722-1-6). Open Path.

BUDDHIST LITERATURE

Amore, Roy C. & Shinn, Larry D. Lustful Maidens & Ascetic Kings: Buddhist & Hindu Stories of Life. (Illus.). 150p. 1981. 14.95 (ISBN 0-19-502838-4); pap. 5.95 (ISBN 0-19-502839-2). Oxford U Pr.

Guenther, Herbert V. Philosophy & Psychology in the Abhidharma. LC 75-40259. 282p. 1981. pap. 6.95 (ISBN 0-87773-081-4). Great Eastern.

Wei Wu-Wei. Posthumous Pieces. 245p. 1981. pap. 5.00 (ISBN 0-85656-027-8). Great Eastern.

--The Tenth Man. 246p. 1981. pap. 6.00 (ISBN 0-85656-013-8). Great Eastern.

BUDDHIST THEOLOGY

see Buddhist Doctrines

BUDGERIGARS

Leyland, Eric. Budgerigars for Pleasure & Profit. 6.50x (SpS). Soccer.

BUDGET

see also Program Budgeting

Sweeny, H. W. & Rachlin, Robert. Handbook of Budgeting: Systems & Controls for Financial Management. 700p. 1981. 34.50 (ISBN 0-471-05621-9). Ronald Pr.

BUDGET IN BUSINESS

Alexander Hamilton Institute, Inc. Manual De Practicas Orcamentaries Modernas. Jenks, James M., ed. (Illus.). 84p. (Orig., Portuguese.). 1978. pap. 58.25x (ISBN 0-86604-002-1, TX-15-336). Hamilton Inst.

--Manual De Practicia Presupuestaria Moderna. Jenks, James M., ed. (Illus.). 90p. (Orig., Span.). 1976. pap. 52.75x (ISBN 0-86604-001-3, A783161). Hamilton Inst.

--Le Manuel De Pratiques Budgetaires Modernes. Jenks, Jjames M., ed. (Illus.). 87p. (Orig., Fr.). 1978. pap. 49.50 (ISBN 0-86604-003-X, TX-30-652). Hamilton Inst.

BUDGETS, HOUSEHOLD

see Home Economics–Accounting

BUDGETS, TIME

see Time Allocation

BUFFALOES

Buffalo Reproduction & Artificail Insemination. (FAO Animal Production & Health Paper: No. 13). 370p. 1981. pap. 20.00 (ISBN 92-5-100743-8, F2086, FAO). Unipub.

BUICK AUTOMOBILE

see Automobiles–Types–Buick

BUILDER'S PLANT

see Construction Equipment

BUILDING

see also Architecture; Bricklaying; Carpentry; Ceilings; Concrete Construction; Construction Equipment; Construction Industry; Doors and Doorways; Environmental Engineering (Buildings); Floors; Foundations; House Construction; Masonry; Materials; Roofs; Trusses; Underground Construction; Walls

Billington, N. S. & Roberts, B. M. Building Services Engineering: A Review of Its Development. (International Series on Building Environmental Engineering: Vol. 1). 500p. 1981. 80.00 (ISBN 0-08-026741-6); pap. 24.00 (ISBN 0-08-026742-4). Pergamon.

Building to Last. (Illus.). 168p. 1981. 24.95 (ISBN 0-8038-0028-2). Hastings.

Greene, Herb & Greene, Nanine H. Building to Last. (Illus.). 168p. 1981. 24.95. Architectural.

Inwood, Robert & Bruyere, Christian. In Harmony with Nature. LC 80-54351. (Illus.). 224p. 1981. pap. 7.95 (ISBN 0-8069-7504-0). Sterling.

Ove Arup Partnership. Building Design for Energy Economics. 160p. 1981. 38.00 (ISBN 0-86095-850-7). Longman.

Technology Assessment & Utilization Committee. A National Strategy for Improving Productivity in Building & Construction. LC 80-81951. xii, 209p. 1980. pap. text ed. 8.25 (ISBN 0-309-03080-3). Natl Acad Pr.

Timber Research & Development Association. Structural Recommendations for Timber Frame Housing. (Illus.). 1981. 38.00 (ISBN 0-86095-890-6). Longman.

BUILDING–ACCOUNTING

see Construction Industry–Accounting

BUILDING–AMATEURS' MANUALS

see also Building–Handbooks, Manuals, etc.

Demske, Richard. Year-Round Outdoor Building Projects: An Encyclopedia of Building Techniques & Construction Plans. 304p. 1980. pap. 9.95 (ISBN 0-442-21259-3). Van Nos Reinhold.

BUILDING–CONTRACTS AND SPECIFICATIONS

Crooney, John. Anthropometry for Designers. rev. ed. 144p. 1981. pap. 12.00 (ISBN 0-442-22013-8). Van Nos Reinhold.

Metric Conversion in the Construction Industries: Planning, Coordination & Timing. 62p. 1980. 15.00. Am Natl.

Pierce, Jotham D., Jr. Construction Contracts in the Eighties. LC 80-80760. (Real Estate Law & Practice Course Handbook Ser.). 896p. 1980. pap. text ed. 25.00 (ISBN 0-686-68821-X, N4-4348). PLI.

Rosen, Harold J. Construction Specifications Writing Principles & Procedures. 2nd ed. 240p. 1981. 24.95 (ISBN 0-471-08328-3, Pub. by Wiley-Interscience). Wiley.

Saunt. Revision Notes on Building Measurement. 1981. text ed. price not set. Butterworth.

Timber Research & Development Association. Structural Recommendations for Timber Frame Housing. (Illus.). 1981. 38.00 (ISBN 0-86095-890-6). Longman.

Wallach, Paul & Hepler, Don. Reading Construction Drawings: Trade Edition. (Illus.). 320p. 1980. 18.95 (ISBN 0-07-067940-1, P&RB). McGraw.

BUILDING–COSTS

see Building–Estimates

BUILDING–DETAILS

Wallach, Paul & Hepler, Don. Reading Construction Drawings: Trade Edition. (Illus.). 320p. 1980. 18.95 (ISBN 0-07-067940-1, P&RB). McGraw.

Weidhass, Ernest H. Architectural Drafting & Construction. 560p. 1981. text ed. 24.95; instr's hdbk. avail. Allyn.

BUILDING–ESTIMATES

Building Cost File, compiled by. The Berger Building Cost File 1981: General Construction Trades with Comparative Building Systems & Costs, 4 editions, Vol. 1. Incl. Eastern Edition (ISBN 0-442-21240-2); Western Edition (ISBN 0-442-21238-0); Central Edition (ISBN 0-442-21237-2); Southern Edition (ISBN 0-442-21236-4). 210p. 1980. pap. text ed. 34.95 ea. Van Nos Reinhold.

--The Berger Building Cost File 1981: Mechanical & Electrical Trades with Comparative Building Systems Costs, 4 editions, Vol. II. Incl. Eastern Edition (ISBN 0-442-21235-6); Western Edition (ISBN 0-442-21234-8); Central Edition (ISBN 0-442-21232-1); Southern Edition (ISBN 0-442-21231-3). 105p. 1980. pap. text ed. 24.95 ea. Van Nos Reinhold.

Crystal-Smith. Estimating for Building & Civil Engineering Works. 7th ed. 1981. text ed. write for info. (ISBN 0-408-00515-7). Butterworth.

Dodge Construction Systems Costs, 1981. 262p. 1981. 43.80 (ISBN 0-07-017327-3). McGraw.

Dodge Cost Information Systems Division. Dodge Guide to Public Works & Heavy Construction Costs, 1981. 232p. 1981. 31.80 (ISBN 0-07-017326-5). McGraw.

--Dodge Manual for Building Construction Pricing & Scheduling, 1981. 292p. 1981. 29.80 (ISBN 0-07-017328-1). McGraw.

Engelsman, Coert. Engelsman's General Construction Cost File 1981. 409p. 1980. pap. text ed. 29.95 (ISBN 0-442-12222-5). Van Nos Reinhold.

--Residential Cost Manual 1981: New Construction, Remodeling, & Valuation. 347p. 1980. pap. text ed. 29.95 (ISBN 0-442-12224-1). Van Nos Reinhold.

Godfrey, Robert S. Mechanical & Electrical Cost Data, 1981. 4th ed. LC 79-643328. 400p. 1981. pap. 29.50 (ISBN 0-911950-31-1). Means.

BUILDING–HANDBOOKS, MANUALS, ETC.

see also Building–Amateurs' Manuals

Ambrose, James. Simplified Design of Building Foundations. 384p. 1981. 20.00 (ISBN 0-471-06267-7, Pub. by Wiley-Interscience). Wiley.

Hall. Building Service & Equipment Four: Checkbook. 1981. text ed. price not set (ISBN 0-408-00613-7). Butterworth.

Hodgkinson, Allan. A J Handbook of Building Structure. 2nd ed. (Illus.). 428p. (Orig.). 1980. pap. 37.50x (ISBN 0-85139-273-3). Intl Pubns Serv.

Pritchard. Building Science & Materials Two: Checkbook. 1981. text ed. price not set. Butterworth.

BUILDING–JUVENILE LITERATURE

Van Ryzin, Lani. A Patch of Earth. (Illus.). 64p. (gr. 3-5). 1981. PLB 6.97 (ISBN 0-686-69298-5). Messner.

BUILDING–LAWS AND LEGISLATION

see Building Laws

BUILDING–MATERIALS

see Building Materials

BUILDING–PRICE BOOKS

see Building–Estimates

BUILDING–SPECIFICATIONS

see Building–Contracts and Specifications

BUILDING–SUPERINTENDENCE

Calvert. Introduction to Building Management. 4th ed. 1981. text ed. price not set (ISBN 0-408-00520-3); pap. price not set. Butterworth.

BUILDING, CONCRETE

see Concrete Construction

BUILDING, EARTHQUAKE-PROOF

see Earthquakes and Building

BUILDING, HOUSE

see House Construction

BUILDING, UNDERGROUND

see Underground Construction

BUILDING BLOCK DESIGN

see Unit Construction

BUILDING CODES

see Building Laws

BUILDING DYNAMICS

see Structural Dynamics

BUILDING FAILURES

see also Buildings–Protection

Davis, I., ed. Disasters & the Small Dwelling. 220p. 1981. 30.00 (ISBN 0-08-024753-9). Pergamon.

BUILDING INDUSTRY

see Construction Industry

BUILDING LAWS

see also Building–Contracts and Specifications; Zoning Law

Brown, Diana M. Building Codes & Residential Construction: An Annotated Bibliography. (Architecture Ser.: Bibliography A-334). 60p. 1980. pap. 6.50. Vance Biblios.

BUILDING MATERIALS

see also Asbestos; Cement; Ceramics; Concrete; Insulating Materials; Plastics; Reinforced Concrete; Steel, Structural; Strength of Materials; Structural Engineering; Tiles; Timber; Wood

Bhatnager, V. M. Building Materials. 300p. 1981. 40.00x (ISBN 0-86095-866-3). Longman.

Dagostino, Frank. Materials of Construction. 1981. text ed. 18.95 (ISBN 0-8359-4286-4). Reston.

Hall. Building Service & Equipment Four: Checkbook. 1981. text ed. price not set (ISBN 0-408-00613-7). Butterworth.

Herubin, Charles & Marotta, Theodore. Basic Construction Materials. 2nd ed. 1981. text ed. 17.50 (ISBN 0-8359-0362-1); solutions manual avail. (ISBN 0-8359-0363-X). Reston.

Maguire, Byron W. Construction Materials. 375p. 1981. text ed. 19.95 (ISBN 0-8359-0935-2). Reston.

Pritchard. Building Science & Materials Two: Checkbook. 1981. text ed. price not set. Butterworth.

BUILDING MATERIALS–SPECIFICATIONS

see Building–Contracts and Specifications

BUILDING REPAIR

see Buildings–Repair and Reconstruction; Dwellings–Maintenance and Repair

BUILDING SUPERINTENDENCE

see Building–Superintendence

BUILDING TRADES–ACCOUNTING

see Construction Industry–Accounting

BUILDINGS

see also Architecture; Building; Historic Buildings also names of particular types of building and construction e.g. Dwellings; School-houses; Concrete Construction

Neufert, E. Architect's Data: The Handbook of Building Types, 2nd (International) English Edition. 420p. 1980. 69.95x (ISBN 0-470-26947-2). Halsted Pr.

BUILDINGS–ACOUSTICS

see Architectural Acoustics

BUILDINGS–DETAILS

see Architecture–Details; Building–Details

BUILDINGS–ENVIRONMENTAL ENGINEERING

see Environmental Engineering (Buildings)

BUILDINGS–MATERIALS

see Building Materials

BUILDINGS–PROTECTION

see also Buildings–Repair and Reconstruction

McGavin, Gary L. Earthquake Protection of Essential Building Equipment: Design, Engineering, Installation. 496p. 1981. 25.00 (ISBN 0-471-06270-7, Pub. by Wiley-Interscience). Wiley.

Mills, Edward D., ed. Building Maintenance & Preservation: A Guide for Design & Management. (Illus.). 192p. 1980. pap. text ed. 39.95 (ISBN 0-408-00470-3). Butterworths.

BUILDINGS–REPAIR AND RECONSTRUCTION

see also Architecture–Conservation and Restoration; Dwellings–Maintenance and Repair; Dwellings–Remodeling

Hutchins, Nigel. Restoring Old Houses. 240p. 1980. 29.95 (ISBN 0-442-29625-8). Van Nos Reinhold.

Mills, Edward D., ed. Building Maintenance & Preservation: A Guide for Design & Management. (Illus.). 192p. 1980. pap. text ed. 39.95 (ISBN 0-408-00470-3). Butterworths.

Old-House Journal Staff, ed. The Old-House Journal 1981 Catalog: A Buyer's Guide. (Illus.). 142p. (Orig.). 1981. pap. 9.95 (ISBN 0-87951-125-7). Overlook Pr.

Vance, Mary. Remodeling: A Bibliography of Periodical Articles. (Architecture Ser.: Bibliography A-295). 68p. 1980. pap. 7.50. Vance Biblios.

BUILDINGS, LIBRARY

see Library Architecture

BUILDINGS, PREFABRICATED

Consumer Guide Editors. The Complete Book of Prefabs, Kits & Manufactured Houses. 160p. 1981. pap. 7.95 (ISBN 0-449-90051-7, Columbine). Fawcett.

BUILDINGS, RECONSTRUCTION OF

see Buildings–Repair and Reconstruction

BUILDINGS, RESTORATION OF

see Architecture–Conservation and Restoration

BULGARIA–HISTORY

Moser, Charles. Dimitrov of Bulgaria. 14.95. Green Hill.

Runciman, Steven. A History of the First Bulgarian Empire. LC 80-2369. 1981. Repr. of 1930 ed. 48.50 (ISBN 0-404-18916-4). AMS Pr.

Slavov, Atanas. The Thaw in Bulgarian Literature. (East European Monographs: No. 84). 200p. 1981. 15.00x (ISBN 0-914710-78-8). East Eur Quarterly.

BULGARIAN QUESTION

see Eastern Question (Balkan)

BULK SOLIDS HANDLING

Loeffler, F. J. & Proctor, C. R., eds. Units & Bulk Materials Handling. 289p. 1980. 60.00 (H00163). ASME.

BULLETIN BOARDS

Harden, B. M. & Williams, D. L. Bulletin Boards Made the Easy Way. (Illus.). 64p. 1981. 5.00 (ISBN 0-682-49731-2). Exposition.

BULLION

see Precious Metals

BULLOCK, SETH, 1849-1919

Kellar, Kenneth C. Seth Bullock: Frontier Marshall. LC 72-92726. 191p. 1972. 4.95 (ISBN 0-87970-126-9). North Plains.

BULLS AND BEARS

see Stock-Exchange

BUNYAN, JOHN, 1628-1688

Talon, Henri A. John Bunyan, The Man & His Works. 340p. 1980. Repr. of 1951 ed. lib. bdg. 35.00 (ISBN 0-89987-810-5). Darby Bks.

BUNYAN, PAUL–SONGS AND MUSIC

Callarman, Frederick A. Paulevala: Land of Hurrahs. 88p. (Orig.). 1981. pap. 1.98 (ISBN 0-930092-01-5). Callarman Hse.

BUONARROTI, MICHELANGELO

see Michelangelo (Buonarroti, Michelangelo), 1475-1564

BUREAUCRACY

see also Civil Service

Bruns, Roger & Vogt, George. Your Government Inaction. 80p. 1981. pap. 3.95 (ISBN 0-312-89814-2). St Martin.

Cooper, John L. The Anti-Gravity Force. LC 80-83402. 160p. 1981. pap. text ed. 9.95 (ISBN 0-8403-2300-X). Kendall-Hunt.

Dynamics of Public Bureaucracy: An Introduction to Public Management. 2nd ed. (Illus.). 480p. 1981. pap. text ed. 16.95 (ISBN 0-87626-199-3). Winthrop.

Kramer, Fred A. Perspectives on Public Bureaucracy. 3rd ed. (Illus.). 236p. 1981. pap. text ed. 7.95 (ISBN 0-87626-659-6). Winthrop.

BURIAL

see also Funeral Rites and Ceremonies; Sepulchral Monuments

Zelevansky, Paul. The Case for the Burial of Ancestors, Bk. 1. 1981. 25.00 (ISBN 0-9605610-3-X); pap. 15.00 (ISBN 0-9605610-2-1). Zartscorp.

BURIAL LAWS

Bernard, H. Y. Law of Death & Disposal of the Dead. 2nd ed. 1979. 5.95 (ISBN 0-379-11000-8). Oceana.

BURIAL STATISTICS

see Mortality

BURIED CITIES

see Cities and Towns, Ruined, Extinct, etc.

BURIED TREASURE

see Treasure-Trove

BURKE, EDMUND, 1729-1797

Bryant, Donald C. Edmund Burke & His Literary Friends. 323p. 1980. Repr. of 1939 ed. lib. bdg. 35.00 (ISBN 0-8482-0133-7). Norwood Edns.

Young, George M. Today & Yesterday: Tennyson, Burke, Thackeray, Shakespeare. 312p. 1980. lib. bdg. 15.00 (ISBN 0-8482-3125-2). Norwood Edns.

BURMA–HISTORY

Johnson, Mary O. Burma Diary Nineteen Thirty-Eight to Nineteen Forty-Two. 1981. 5.75 (ISBN 0-8062-1697-2). Carlton.

BURNE-JONES, EDWARD COLEY, SIR, 1833-1898

Burne-Jones, Edward. The Pre-Raphaelite Drawings of Edward Burne-Jones. (Dover Art Library). (Illus.). 48p. (Orig.). 1981. pap. price not set (ISBN 0-486-24113-0). Dover.

Ruskin, John. The Art of England: Lectures Given in Oxford by John Ruskin During His Second Tenure of the Slade Professorship. Freedberg, Sydney J., ed. LC 77-25769. (Connossseurship, Criticism, & Art History Ser.: Vol. 23). 292p. 1979. lib. bdg. 21.00 (ISBN 0-8240-3281-0). Garland Pub.

BURNEY, FANNY

see Arblay, Mme. Frances (Burney) D', 1752-1840

BURNS, ROBERT, 1759-1796

Findlay, Jessie Patrick. Footprints of Robert Burns. 174p. 1980. Repr. of 1923 ed. lib. bdg. 22.50 (ISBN 0-8492-4725-X). R West.

BURNS AND SCALDS

Feller, I. International Bibliography on Burns, 1981 Supplement. 1981. pap. 12.00 (ISBN 0-917478-12-6). Natl Inst Burn.

National Institute for Burn Medicine. NIBM: A Decade of Progress in Burn Medicine. LC 80-82419. (Illus.). pap. write for info. Natl Inst Burn.

Rickham, P. P. & Hecker, W. C. Management of the Burned Child. (Progress in Pediatric Surgery Ser.: Vol. 14). 1981. write for info. (ISBN 0-8067-1514-6). Urban & S.

BURROUGHS, EDGAR RICE, 1875-1950

Holtsmark, Erling B. Tarzan & Tradition: Classical Myth in Popular Literature. LC 80-1023. (Contributions to the Study of Popular Culture: No. 1). (Illus.). 216p. 1981. lib. bdg. 22.50 (ISBN 0-313-22530-3, HOT/). Greenwood.

BURROUGHS, WILLIAM S., 1914-

Bockris, Victor. With William Burroughs. 288p. 1981. 14.95 (ISBN 0-394-51809-8); pap. 7.95 (ISBN 0-394-17828-9). Seaver Bks.

BURYING GROUNDS

see Burial; Cemeteries

BUSHWHACKERS

see Guerrillas

BUSINESS

see also Accounting; Advertising; Applications for Positions; Bookkeeping; Budget in Business; Business Enterprises; Business Mathematics; Businessmen; Catalogs, Commercial; Commerce; Commercial Law; Competition; Controllership; Corporations; Credit; Department Stores; Entrepreneur; Executives; Financial Statements; Industrial Management; Mail-Order Business; Marketing; Markets; Office Management; Profit; Purchasing; Real Estate Business; Salesmen and Salesmanship; Shipment of Goods; Small Business; Success; Trade-Marks; Warehouses; Wealth; Women in Business

Anderson, R. G. Business Systems. (Illus.). 240p. (Orig.). 1977. pap. 9.95x (ISBN 0-7121-0254-X, Pub. by Macdonald & Evans England). Intl Ideas.

--Case Studies in Systems Design. (Illus.). 208p. (Orig.). 1980. pap. text ed. 10.00x (ISBN 0-7121-0387-2). Intl Ideas.

Association for University Business & Economic Research-AUBER. AUBER Membership Directory 1980. (Orig.). 1980. pap. 10.00. Bureau Busn Res U Wis.

Boone, Louis E. & Kurtz, David L. Contemporary Business. 2nd ed. 1979. 18.95 (ISBN 0-03-043646-X). Dryden Pr.

Bruyn, S. T. The Social Economy: People Transforming Modern Business. 392p. 1977. 29.95 (ISBN 0-471-01985-2). Wiley.

Evans, Paul & Bartolome, Fernando. Must Success Cost So Much? The Human Toll of Corporate Life. LC 81-68964. 256p. 1981. 13.95 (ISBN 0-465-04746-7). Basic.

Fleming, Quentin W. A Guide to Doing Business on the Arabian Peninsula. 225p. 1981. 29.95 (ISBN 0-8144-5666-9); comb-bound 29.95 (ISBN 0-8144-7012-2). Am Mgmt.

Hall, L. Secretarial & Administrative Practice. 3rd ed. (Illus.). 304p. 1978. pap. 10.95 (ISBN 0-7121-1958-2, Pub. by Macdonald & Evans England). Intl Ideas.

Handern, Geoff. Business Organisation & Management. 1978. 22.50x (ISBN 0-86003-023-7, Pub. by Allan Pubs England); pap. 11.25x (ISBN 0-86003-124-1). State Mutual Bk.

Hegar, Kathryn W. It's Everybody's Business: Study Guide & Readings for "Introduction to Business, Third Ed.". 3rd ed. (Illus.). 400p. 1981. 8.95 (ISBN 0-13-506659-X). P-H.

Hodgetts, Richard M. Introduction to Business. 2nd ed. LC 80-21284. (Business Ser.). (Illus.). 600p. 1981. text ed. 15.95 (ISBN 0-201-03894-3). A-W.

--Introduction to Business. 2nd ed. LC 76-12797. 1981. text ed. write for info. (ISBN 0-201-02897-2); write for info. resource guide; write for info. study guide (ISBN 0-201-03896-X). A-W.

Hofer, Charles W., et al. A Casebook in Business Policy & Planning. 150p. Date not set. price not set instr's. manual (ISBN 0-8299-0614-2). West Pub.

Initiative Fur Morgen: Strategien in Wettbewerb der 80er Jahre. 247p. (Orig., Ger.). 1980. pap. text ed. 22.50 (ISBN 3-7184-1002-8). Interbk Inc.

International Business & Management Institute. Little Known Business Secrets & Shortcuts for Entrepreneurs & Managers. (Illus.). 110p. (Orig.). pap. 25.00 (ISBN 0-935402-03-9). Intl Comm Serv.

Klug, John R. Basic Book of Business. 350p. 1980. Repr. of 1977 ed. 50.00 (ISBN 0-932648-16-9). Boardroom.

--The Book of Business Answers. 1981. 50.00 (ISBN 0-932648-16-9). Boardroom.

McCutcheon, J. R. Business One Twenty One. 224p. 1981. pap. 9.95 lab manual (ISBN 0-8403-2368-9). Kendall-Hunt.

McKenzie, Richard B. Restrictions on Business Mobility: Political Rhetoric & Economic Reality. 1979. pap. 4.25 (ISBN 0-8447-3338-5). Am Enterprise.

McPhatter, William. The Business Beat: Its Impact & Its Problems. LC 80-16599. (ITT Key Issue Lecture Ser.). 168p. pap. text ed. 4.95. Bobbs.

Mandell, Steven L., et al. Introduction to Business: Concepts & Applications. (Illus.). 580p. 1981. pap. text ed. 15.95 (ISBN 0-8299-0393-3). West Pub.

--Introduction to Business Concepts & Applications: Test Bank. 1980. write for info. (ISBN 0-8299-0527-8). West Pub.

Mangham, Ian & Bate, Paul. Exploring Participation. 320p. 1981. 38.50 (ISBN 0-471-27921-8, Pub. by Wiley-Interscience). Wiley.

Naidich, Arnold. Protect Your Company from A-Z. 1976. 49.95. Busn Res Pubns.

Payne, Jack. The Complete New Encyclopedia of Little-Known, Highly Profitable Business Opportunities. rev. ed. LC 74-75380. 256p. 1980. Repr. of 1971 ed. 10.95 (ISBN 0-8119-0345-1). Fell.

Pluta, Joseph, ed. Economic & Business Issues of the Nineteen Eighties. LC 80-68658. 235p. (Orig.). 1980. pap. 7.00 (ISBN 0-87755-242-8). U of Tex Busn Res.

Poe, Roy, et al. Getting Involved with Business. (Illus.). 576p. (gr. 9-10). 1980. text ed. 12.16 (ISBN 0-07-050335-4, G); learning activity kit I 4.60 (ISBN 0-07-050336-2). McGraw.

Porter, Michael E. Competitive Strategy: Techniques for Analyzing Industries & Competitors. (Illus.). 1980. 15.95 (ISBN 0-02-925360-8). Macmillan.

Die Rationalisierungsfalle. 123p. (Orig., Ger.). 1979. pap. text ed. 20.00 (ISBN 0-89192-297-0). Interbk Inc.

Rivers, William E. Business Reports: Samples from the "Real World". (Illus.). 272p. 1981. pap. 9.95 (ISBN 0-13-107656-6). P-H.

Rudman, Jack. Business. (Undergraduate Program Field Test Ser.: UPFT-3). (Cloth bdg. avail. on request). pap. 9.95 (ISBN 0-8373-6003-X). Natl Learning.

Shaw, W. C. & Day, C. J. The Businessman's Complete Checklist. 1978. text ed. 24.50x (ISBN 0-220-66359-9, Pub. by Busn Bks England). Renouf.

Tetreault, Wilfred F. Buying & Selling Business Opportunities: A Sales Transaction Handbook. LC 80-18771. 208p. 1981. text ed. 19.95 (ISBN 0-201-07711-6). A-W.

Thomas, R. E. Business Policy. 256p. 1977. 36.00x (ISBN 0-86003-502-6, Pub. by Allan Pubs England); pap. 18.00x (ISBN 0-86003-602-2). State Mutual Bk.

--The Government of Business. 224p. 1976. 30.00x (ISBN 0-86003-501-8, Pub. by Allan Pubs England); pap. 15.00x (ISBN 0-86003-601-4). State Mutual Bk.

Wallace, Melvin. Partners in Business. 200p. 1981. 14.95 (ISBN 0-913864-66-8); pap. 7.95 (ISBN 0-913864-67-6). Enterprise Del.

BUSINESS–BIBLIOGRAPHY

Dalton's Directory: Business & Industry. 18th ed. 500p. Date not set. 57.00x. Dalton.

Directory of Business Archives in the United States & Canada. 56p. (Orig.). 1980. pap. 6.00 (ISBN 0-931828-24-4). Soc Am Archivists.

Research Libraries of the New York Public Library & the Library of Congress. Bibliographic Guide to Business & Economics: 1980. (Library Catalogs-Bib. Guides). 1981. lib. bdg. 225.00 (ISBN 0-8161-6883-0). G K Hall.

BUSINESS–DATA PROCESSING

Brandon, Dick H. & Segelstein, Sidney. Business Computers: How to Select Hardware, Software, Services. LC 80-26751. 302p. 1981. write for info. (ISBN 0-932648-18-5). Boardroom.

Brown, Gary D. Beyond Cobol: Survival in Business Applications Programming. 225p. 1981. 17.50 (ISBN 0-471-09030-1, Pub. by Wiley-Interscience). Wiley.

Clifton, H. D. Systems Analysis for Business Data Processing. 3rd ed. 242p. 1978. text ed. 30.75x (ISBN 0-220-66369-6, Pub. by Busn Bks England). Renouf.

Davis, William S. Computers & Business Information Processing. LC 80-10946. 448p. 1981. pap. text ed. 14.95 (ISBN 0-201-03161-2). A-W.

Honess, Brian C. Structured Business Problem Solving with Fortran. 300p. 1981. text ed. 13.95 (ISBN 0-205-07332-8); free (ISBN 0-205-07328-X). Allyn.

Lucas, Harold. Computers in Management & Business Studies. 2nd ed. (Illus., Orig.). 1979. pap. text ed. 19.95x (ISBN 0-7121-0390-2, Pub. by Macdonald & Evans England). Intl Ideas.

Mackle, M. Computers in Business. 2nd ed. 80p. 1970. text ed. 3.40 (ISBN 0-7715-0724-0). Forkner.

Morris, Ralph. Computer Basics for Managers. 241p. 1980. text ed. 23.50x (ISBN 0-09-141570-5, Pub. by Busn Bks England). Renouf.

Russel, Robert A. The Electronic Briefcase: The Office of the Future. 52p. 1978. pap. text ed. 3.00x (ISBN 0-920380-05-0, Pub. by Inst Res Pub Canada). Renouf.

Sardinias, Joseph L., Jr. Computing Today: An Introduction to Business Data Processing. 512p. 1981. text ed. 17.95 (ISBN 0-686-69273-X); pap. 5.95 student guide (ISBN 0-13-165100-5). P-H.

Watson, Hugh J. Computer Simulation in Business. 400p. 1981. text ed. 16.95 (ISBN 0-471-03638-2). Wiley.

BUSINESS–DICTIONARIES

Giordano, Albert G. Concise Dictionary of Business Terminology. 464p. 1981. text ed. 14.95 (ISBN 0-13-166553-7, Spec); pap. text ed. 5.95 (ISBN 0-13-166546-4). P-H.

Henni, Mustapha. Dictionaire Des Termes Economiques et Commerciaux: Francais-Arabe. 20.00x. Intl Bk Ctr.

Sachs, Rudolf. British American Business Terms. 144p. (Orig.). 1975. pap. text ed. 10.00x (ISBN 0-7121-0242-6, Pub. by Macdonald & Evans England). Intl Ideas.

BUSINESS–EXAMINATIONS, QUESTIONS, ETC.

Bobrow, Jerry & Covino, William A. GMAT (Graduate Management Admissions Test) Date not set. pap. text ed. cancelled. Cliffs.

BUSINESS–HANDBOOKS, MANUALS, ETC.

Blagrove, Luanna C. Business Problems & Solutions for Proprietors & Partnerships. 160p. 1981. 24.95; pap. 19.95 (ISBN 0-9604466-9-9). Blagrove Pubns.

--How to Have an Ideal Business Client in Four Months. (Illus.). 67p. (Orig.). 1981. pap. 9.95 (ISBN 0-9604466-6-4). Blagrove Pubns.

--Introduction to Proprietor & Partnership Businesses. 160p. 1981. 24.95; pap. 19.95. Blagrove Pubns.

--The Professional's Business Guide for Proprietor & Partnerships. rev. ed. (Illus.). 185p. 1981. 29.95 (ISBN 0-9604466-5-6). Blagrove Pubns.

Fiederer, S. M. Easy Money. LC 80-54016. 1981. pap. 14.95 (ISBN 0-938584-00-6, 123058). United Pub NY.

Fox, Harrison W., Jr. & Schnitzer, Martin. Doing Business in Washington: How to Win Friends & Influence Governemnt. LC 80-2313. (Illus.). 1981. 14.95 (ISBN 0-02-910460-2). Free Pr.

Klein, Bertram. How to Make Money Listing Business Opportunities. 1981. 9.95 (ISBN 0-533-04710-2). Vantage.

Milbrath, Mona A. Credentials: A Guide to Business Designations. LC 80-66740. 221p. (Orig.). 1980. pap. 9.95 (ISBN 0-936324-01-5). Blue River.

BUSINESS–INFORMATION SERVICES

Beardsley, Rick, ed. The Videolog in Business. 1980-81 ed. (Videolog Ser.). 300p. 1981. pap. 39.50 (ISBN 0-88432-070-7). J Norton Pubs.

BUSINESS–SOCIAL ASPECTS

see Industry–Social Aspects

BUSINESS–STUDY AND TEACHING

see Business Education

BUSINESS–TAXATION

see Business Tax

BUSINESS, CHOICE OF

see Vocational Guidance

BUSINESS ADMINISTRATION

see Business

BUSINESS AND GOVERNMENT

see Industry and State

BUSINESS AND POLITICS

McKenzie, Richard B. Restrictions on Business Mobility: Political Rhetoric & Economic Reality. 1979. pap. 4.25 (ISBN 0-8447-3338-5). Am Enterprise.

BUSINESS AND SOCIAL PROBLEMS

see Industry–Social Aspects

BUSINESS ARITHMETIC

see Business Mathematics

BUSINESS BUDGETING

see Budget in Business

BUSINESS COMMUNICATION

see Communication in Management

BUSINESS CONSULTANTS

Bidgood, Reginald. Future Markets for Consultancy: Professional Business Development Abroad. (Illus.). 160p. 1980. 21.00x (ISBN 0-7198-2830-9). Intl Ideas.

Dean, Sandra L. Success As a Consultant: The Complete Guide. 225p. 1981. 14.95 (ISBN 0-913864-61-7). Enterprise Del.

Shenson, Howard L. How to Strategically Negotiate the Consulting Contract. 107p. 1980. pap. text ed. 24.00 (ISBN 0-930686-10-1). Bermont Bks.

The Successful Consultant's Guide to Fee Setting. 167p. 1980. text ed. 34.00 (ISBN 0-930686-11-X). Bermont Bks.

BUSINESS CORPORATIONS

see Corporations

BUSINESS CORRESPONDENCE

see Commercial Correspondence

BUSINESS CYCLES

see also Business Forecasting; Economic Forecasting; Economic Stabilization

Barro, Robert J. Money, Expectations & Business Cycles: Essays in Macroeconomics. (Economic Theory, Econometrics & Mathematical Economic Ser.). 1981. write for info. (ISBN 0-12-079550-7). Acad Pr.

Strigel, W. Business Cycle Analysis: Papers Presented at the Fourteenth CIRET Conference Proceedings - Lisbon 1979. 456p. 1980. text ed. 50.00x (ISBN 0-566-00368-6, Pub. by Gower Pub. Co England). Renouf.

BUSINESS ECONOMICS

see Managerial Economics

BUSINESS EDUCATION

see also Accounting; Bookkeeping; Commercial Law; Penmanship; Shorthand; Typewriting

Chaffee, John, Jr. Business-School Partnerships: A Plus for Kids. 1980. pap. 11.95 (ISBN 0-87545-018-0). Natl Sch PR.

Leeds, C. S., et al. Management & Business Studies. 2nd ed. 448p. 1978. pap. text ed. 16.95x (ISBN 0-7121-1298-7, Pub. by Macdonald & Evans England). Intl Ideas.

Macdonald, Eleanor & Little, Julia. The Successful Secretary. (Illus.). 176p. 1980. pap. 9.95x (ISBN 0-7121-1976-0). Intl Ideas.

Musselman, Vernon L. & Hughes, Eugene H. Study Guide & Applied Readings to Introduction to Modern Business: Issues & Environment. 8th ed. 272p. 1981. pap. text ed. 7.95 (ISBN 0-13-488080-3). P-H.

BUSINESS ENGLISH

see English Language–Business English

BUSINESS ENTERPRISES

Here are entered works on business concerns as legal entities.

see also Business Tax; Government Business Enterprises; International Business Enterprises; Investments, Foreign

Baty, Gordon. Entrepreneurship in the Eighties. 1981. text ed. 17.95 (ISBN 0-8359-1745-2); pap. text ed. 12.95 (ISBN 0-8359-1744-4). Reston.

Baumback, C. Baumback's Guide to Entrepreneurship. 1981. 13.95 (ISBN 0-13-066761-7). P-H.

Hodgetts. Business Enterprise. 1977. 11.95 (ISBN 0-7216-4709-X). Dryden Pr.

Miklowitz, Gloria D. & Yates, Madelein. The Young Tycoons. LC 80-8803. (Illus.). 128p. (gr. 7 up). 1981. 9.95 (ISBN 0-15-299879-9, HJ). HarBraceJ.

Steindl, Josef. Random Processes & the Growth of Firms. 1965. 22.00 (ISBN 0-02-852950-2). Hafner.

Suzman, Cedric L., et al. Southeast Export: Profiles, Typology & the Role of Technology in Selected U. S. Firms. (Research Monograph: No. 90). 1981. spiral bdg. 15.00 (ISBN 0-88406-146-9). GA St U Busn Pub.

BUSINESS ENTERPRISES–FINANCE

Ramey, Emmett & Wong, Alex. The Loan Package. 180p. 1981. 3 ring binder 29.95 (ISBN 0-916378-12-8). Oasis Pr.

BUSINESS ENTERPRISES–ASIA

Asian Business Directory 1978. (Illus.). 2655p. 1980. 100.00 (ISBN 0-8002-2732-8). Intl Pubns Serv.

BUSINESS ETHICS

see also Competition; Success

Behrman, Jack N. Discourses on Ethics & Business. LC 80-23626. 192p. 1981. lib. bdg. 20.00 (ISBN 0-89946-064-X). Oelgeschlager.

Westin, Alan F., ed. Whistle-Blowing! Loyalty & Dissent in the Corporation. LC 80-15800. 192p. 1980. 12.50 (ISBN 0-07-069483-4, P&RB). McGraw.

BUSINESS EXECUTIVES

see Executives

BUSINESS FAILURES

see Bankruptcy

BUSINESS FORECASTING

Barro, Robert J. Money, Expectations & Business Cycles: Essays in Macroeconomics. (Economic Theory, Econometrics & Mathematical Economic Ser.). 1981. write for info. (ISBN 0-12-079550-7). Acad Pr.

Pluta, Joseph E., ed. Economic & Business: Issues of the 1980's. 1980. 7.00. U of Tex Busn Res.

UCLA Business Forecast for the Nation & California. 1981. 40.00 (ISBN 0-686-69435-X). UCLA Busn Forecasting.

BUSINESS GAMES

see Management Games

BUSINESS INSURANCE

see Insurance, Business

BUSINESS LAW

see also Commercial Law; Forms (Law)

Babb, Hugh W. & Martin, Charles. Business Law. 3rd ed. 400p. (Orig.). 1981. pap. 4.95 (ISBN 0-06-460198-6, COS 198, COS). Har-Row.

Business Law: Alternate Editions. 1978. 21.95 (ISBN 0-03-045481-6). Dryden Pr.

Clarkson, Kenneth W., et al. Alternate Test Items to Accompany West's Business Law: Text & Cases. 169p. Date not set. price not set (ISBN 0-8299-0508-1). West Pub.

--West's Business Law: Alternate UCC Comprehensive Edition. 750p. 1981. text ed. 13.95 (ISBN 0-8299-0366-6). West Pub.

--West's Business Law: Alternate UCC Comprehensive Edition. write for info. alt. test items (ISBN 0-8299-0526-X). West Pub.

Donnell, John D., et al. Law for Business. 18.95x (ISBN 0-256-02316-6). Irwin.

Hadden, Tom. Company Law & Capitalism. 2nd ed. (Law in Context Ser.). 1977. 25.00x (ISBN 0-297-77334-8, Pub. by Weidenfeld & Nicolson England). Rothman.

Harron, Thomas. Business Law. 992p. 1981. text ed. 21.95 (ISBN 0-686-69609-3). Allyn.

Howell, et al. Business Law. 1978. 20.95 (ISBN 0-03-016711-6). Dryden Pr.

Howell, Rate A., et al. Business Law: Text & Cases. 2nd ed. LC 80-65801. 1104p. 1981. text ed. 21.95 (ISBN 0-03-058111-7). Dryden Pr.

Kaufman, S. L. Investors Legal Guide. 2nd ed. 1979. 5.95 (ISBN 0-379-11126-8). Oceana.

Mitchell, Ewan. The Director's Lawyer & the Company Secretary's Legal Guide. 4th ed. 645p. 1978. text ed. 43.00x (ISBN 0-220-66346-7, Pub. by Busn Bks England). Renouf.

Oliver, R. A. & Lewis, D. G. The Content of Sixth-Form General Studies. 144p. 1974. 12.00x (ISBN 0-7190-0586-8, Pub. by Manchester U Pr England). State Mutual Bk.

Sengupta, Surajit. Business Law in India. 894p. (Orig.). 1979. pap. text ed. 9.95x (ISBN 0-19-560658-2). Oxford U Pr.

Simmonds, K. Multinational Corporations Law, Vols. 1-2. 1979. Set. 75.00 (ISBN 0-379-20373-1). Oceana.

--Multinational Corporations Law, Release 3. 1980. 50.00. Oceana.

BUSINESS LETTERS

see Commercial Correspondence

BUSINESS LITERATURE SEARCHING

see Information Storage and Retrieval Systems–Business

BUSINESS MACHINES

see Calculating-Machines; Electronic Office Machines

BUSINESS MATHEMATICS

Business Mathematics. 2nd ed. (Illus.). 400p. 1979. pap. 11.95x (ISBN 0-7121-0282-5, Pub. by Macdonald & Evans England). Intl Ideas.

Clar, Lawrence M, et al. Business Mathematics. Latham, Calvin, ed. 1980. text ed. 15.95x (ISBN 0-686-65089-1). Macmillan.

Felton, James. Business Mathematics: A Better Course. 640p. 1981. pap. 15.95 (ISBN 0-205-07323-9, 1073230); tchr's ed. free (ISBN 0-205-07324-7, 1073249). Allyn.

Funk, Jerry. Sportset: A Math Practice Set. 100p. pap. text ed. 5.95 (ISBN 0-686-69610-7); free. Allyn.

Giordano, Al. Business Mathematics - Electronic Calculation. (Illus.). 304p. 1981. text ed. 17.95 (ISBN 0-13-105163-6); pap. text ed. 13.95 (ISBN 0-13-105155-5). P-H.

Golden, Edward J. The Art & Science of Real Estate Investment Analysis. 300p. 1980. pap. text ed. 15.00 (ISBN 0-9604532-0-2). Adv Prof Seminars.

Groebner, David & Shannon, Patrick. Business Statistics: A Decision-Making Approach. (Illus.). 800p. 1981. text ed. 20.95 (ISBN 0-675-08083-5); tchr's. manual avail.; lab manual avail. (ISBN 0-675-08084-3); test bank avail. Merrill.

King, Horace M. A Clear Introduction to Business Mathematics. 2nd ed. 580p. pap. text ed. 15.95x (ISBN 0-89863-035-5). Star Pub CA.

Nickerson, Charles A. & Nickerson, Ingeborg A. Business Mathematics: A Consumer Approach. (Illus.). 256p. 1981. pap. text ed. 13.95 (ISBN 0-675-08071-1); tchr's. manual avail. Merrill.

Wallace & Pitz. Mathematics for Business with Machine Applications. 448p. 1977. text ed. 17.27 (ISBN 0-7715-0901-4); tchr's. manual with text solutions 11.93 (ISBN 0-7715-0902-2); tchr's. ed., wkbk. 1 9.27 (ISBN 0-7715-0904-9); tchr's. ed., wkbk. 2 9.93 (ISBN 0-7715-0906-5); wkbk. 1, units 1-9 4.60 (ISBN 0-7715-0903-0); wkbk. 2, units 10-22 5.27 (ISBN 0-7715-0905-7). Forkner.

Williams, Walter E. & Reed, James H. Fundamentals of Business Mathematics. 2nd ed. 580p. 1981. text ed. write for info. (ISBN 0-697-08049-8); wkbk avail. (ISBN 0-697-08056-0); instrs' manual avail. (ISBN 0-697-08057-9). Wm C Brown.

BUSINESS MATHEMATICS–PROGRAMMED INSTRUCTION

Soracco, Lionel J., Jr. Math House Proficiency Review Tapes: Applications Involving Money, Unit D. (YA) (gr. 7 up). 1980. manual & cassettes 159.95 (ISBN 0-917792-06-8). Math Hse.

BUSINESS MEN

see Businessmen

BUSINESS MERGERS

see Consolidation and Merger of Corporations

BUSINESS PSYCHOLOGY

see Psychology, Industrial

BUSINESS-REPLY MAIL

see Postal Service

BUSINESS REPORT WRITING

Alred, Gerald J., et al. Business & Technical Writing: An Annotated Bibliography of Books, 1880-1980. LC 80-29211. 249p. 1981. 12.50 (ISBN 0-8108-1397-1). Scarecrow.

Dawe & Dornan. One-to-One: Resources for Conference-Centered Writing. (Orig.). 1981. pap. text ed. 7.95 (ISBN 0-316-17722-9); tchrs'. manual free (ISBN 0-316-17723-7). Little.

Hemphill, Charles. Business Communications with Writing Improvement Exercises. 256p. 1981. pap. text ed. 11.95 (ISBN 0-13-093880-7). P-H.

Hillman, Howard. The Art of Writing Business Reports & Proposals. (Illus.). 256p. 1981. 12.50 (ISBN 0-8149-0850-0). Vanguard.

BUSINESS RESEARCH

see Economic Research

BUSINESS SPANISH

see Spanish Language–Business Spanish

BUSINESS STABILIZATION

see Economic Stabilization

BUSINESS TAX

see also Licenses

Hoffman. Federal Taxation: Corporations, Partnerships, Estates & Trusts. 420p. 1979. write for info. (ISBN 0-8299-0491-3); solutions manual avail. West Pub.

Kahn, Douglas A. Basic Corporate Taxation. 3rd ed. LC 80-27245. 531p. 1980. pap. text ed. 18.95 (ISBN 0-8299-2114-1). West Pub.

Taxation of the Formation & Combination of Business Enterprises. (Statement of Tax Policy Ser.: No. 5). 1980. pap. 6.50. Am Inst CPA.

BUSINESSMEN

Case, Everett N. & Case, Josephine Y. Owen D. Young & American Enterprise: A Biography. 1981. 25.00 (ISBN 0-87923-360-5). Godine.

Shook, Robert L. The Entrepreneurs. LC 79-2735. (Illus.). 192p. 1981. pap. 3.95 (ISBN 0-06-464043-4, B*N 4043). Har-Row.

Tandon, Prakash. Return to the Punjab. 300p. 1981. 18.50x (ISBN 0-520-01759-5). U of Cal Pr.

BUSINESSWOMEN

see Women in Business

BUSING OF SCHOOL CHILDREN

see School Children–Transportation

BUSY WORK

see Creative Activities and Seatwork

BUTCHERING

see Slaughtering and Slaughter-Houses

BUTTERFLIES

Christensen, James R. Field Guide to the Butterflies of the Pacific Northwest. LC 80-52967. (GEM Bks. - Natural History). (Illus.). 200p. (Orig.). 1981. pap. 12.95 (ISBN 0-89301-074-X). U Pr of Idaho.

DeTreville, Susan & DeTreville, Stan. Butterflies & Moths. (Illus.). 32p. (Orig.). 1981. pap. 3.50 (ISBN 0-89844-026-2). Troubador Pr.

Dornfield, Ernst. Butterflies of Oregon. 275p. 1980. 25.00 (ISBN 0-917304-58-6, Pub. by Timber Pr). Intl Schol Bk Serv.

Ferris, Clifford D. & Brown, F. Martin, eds. Butterflies of the Rocky Mountain States. LC 80-22274. (Illus.). 500p. 1981. 35.00 (ISBN 0-8061-1552-1); pap. 15.95 (ISBN 0-8061-1733-8). U of Okla Pr.

Treat, Asher E. Mites of Moths & Butterflies. LC 75-7147. (Illus.). 368p. 1975. 45.00x (ISBN 0-8014-0878-4). Comstock.

BUYERS' GUIDES

see Consumer Education

also subdivision directories under particular lines of business industry

BUYING

see Purchasing

BUYING, AUTOMOBILE

see Automobile Purchasing

BUYING, INDUSTRIAL

see Industrial Procurement

BYRON, GEORGE GORDON NOEL BYRON, 6TH BARON, 1788-1824

Gamba, Pietro. A Narrative of Lord Byron's Last Journey to Greece. 314p. 1980. Repr. of 1945 ed. lib. bdg. 45.00 (ISBN 0-8495-2046-0). Arden Lib.

Hearn, R. B. Byron Criticism Since Nineteen Fifty-Two. (Romantic Reassessment: No. 83: 2). 1980. pap. text ed. 25.00x (ISBN 0-391-02188-5). Humanities.

McGann, Jerome J., ed. Lord Byron: The Complete Poetical Works, Vol. I. 516p. 1980. 98.00x (ISBN 0-19-811890-2); pap. 59.00 (ISBN 0-19-812763-4). Oxford U Pr.

Marchand, Leslie A. Prefaces to Byron. 131p. 1980. Repr. of 1979 ed. lib. bdg. 30.00 (ISBN 0-8414-5876-6). Folcroft.

Rainwater, Frank. Lord Byron: A Study of the Development of His Philosophy, with Special Emphasis Upon the Dramas. 50p. 1980. Repr. of 1949 ed. lib. bdg. 8.50 (ISBN 0-8492-7731-0). R West.

Trueblood, Paul G. Byron & Europe: The Interplay of Poetry & Politics. 1980. write for info. (ISBN 0-391-02164-8). Humanities.

BYSSINOSIS

see Lungs–Dust Diseases

BYZANTINE EMPIRE–CIVILIZATION

Anastos, Milton V. Studies in Byzantine Intellectual History. 432p. 1980. 78.00x (ISBN 0-86078-031-7, Pub. by Variorum England). State Mutual Bk.

Browning, Robert. Studies on Byzantine History, Literature & Education. 390p. 1980. 60.00x (ISBN 0-86078-003-1, Pub. by Variorum England). State Mutual Bk.

BYZANTINE EMPIRE–HISTORY

Alexander, Paul J. Religious & Political History & Thought in the Byzantine Empire. 360p. 1980. 60.00x (ISBN 0-86078-016-3, Pub. by Variorum England). State Mutual Bk.

Anastos, Milton V. Studies in Byzantine Intellectual History. 432p. 1980. 78.00x (ISBN 0-86078-031-7, Pub. by Variorum England). State Mutual Bk.

Browning, Robert. Studies on Byzantine History, Literature & Education. 390p. 1980. 60.00x (ISBN 0-86078-003-1, Pub. by Variorum England). State Mutual Bk.

Jenkins, Romilly J. Studies on Byzantine History of the 9th & 10th Centuries. 386p. 1980. 50.00x (ISBN 0-902089-07-2, Pub. by Variorum England). State Mutual Bk.

McCarren, Vincent P. Michigan Papyri XIV. (American Studies in Papyrology: No. 22). 15.00x (ISBN 0-89130-295-6). Scholars Pr CA.

Meyendorff, John. Byzantium & the Rise of Russia. LC 80-40110. 340p. Date not set. 69.50 (ISBN 0-521-23183-3). Cambridge U Pr.

BYZANTINE EMPIRE–POLITICS AND GOVERNMENT

Alexander, Paul J. Religious & Political History & Thought in the Byzantine Empire. 360p. 1980. 60.00x (ISBN 0-86078-016-3, Pub. by Variorum England). State Mutual Bk.

C

CABALA

see also Occult Sciences; Symbolism of Numbers

Halevi, Z'ev. Kabbalah & Exodus. LC 80-50743. (Illus.). 234p. 1980. pap. 7.95 (ISBN 0-394-73950-7). Shambhala Pubns.

Rowlands, Henry. Mona Antiqua Restaurata. Feldman, Burton & Richardson, Robert D., eds. LC 78-60894. (Myth & Romanticism Ser.: Vol. 21). 399p. 1979. lib. bdg. 60.00 (ISBN 0-8240-3570-4). Garland Pub.

Schutz, Albert. Call Adonoi: Manual of Practical Cabalah & Gestalt Mysticism. 114p. 1980. pap. 8.95. Ross-Erikson.

CABBALA

see Cabala

CABINET OFFICERS

see also Prime Ministers

Vexler, R. I. Vice Presidents & Cabinet Members: Biographies Arranged Chronologically by Administration, Vols. 1-2. 1975. 35.00 ea. Vol. 1 (ISBN 0-379-12089-5). Vol. 2 (ISBN 0-379-12090-9). Oceana.

CABINET-WORK

see also Furniture Making; Home Workshops; Woodwork

Burch, Monte. The Home Cabinetmaker: Building Fine Furniture, Built-Ins, Millwork. LC 79-4747. (Popular Science Bk.). (Illus.). Date not set. 19.95 (ISBN 0-06-010349-3, HarpT). Har-Row.

Jones, Peter. Start-to-Finish Cabinetmaking. 1980. pap. 7.95 (ISBN 0-8359-7062-0). Reston.

Lewis, Gaspar J. Cabinetmaking, Pattermaking, & Millwork. 448p. 1981. 18.95 (ISBN 0-442-24785-0). Van Nos Reinhold.

CABINS

see Log Cabins

CABLE TELEVISION

see Community Antenna Television

CABLES, ELECTRIC

see Electric Cables

CACTUS

Bechtel, Helmut. Cactus Identifier. LC 76-51168. (Illus.). 256p. 1981. pap. 6.95 (ISBN 0-8069-8960-2). Sterling.

Watson, Robert. Night-Blooming Cactus. LC 80-65999. 1980. 10.00 (ISBN 0-689-11090-1); pap. 5.95. Atheneum.

CADASTRAL SURVEYS

see Real Property

CAESAREAN SECTION

see Cesarean Section

CAESARS

see Roman Emperors

CAFES

see Hotels, Taverns, etc.; Restaurants, Lunchrooms, etc.

CAFETERIAS, ETC.

see Restaurants, Lunchrooms, etc.

CAGE-BIRDS

see also names of cage-birds, e.g. Canaries

Lint, Kenton C. & Lint, Alice M. Diets for Birds in Captivity. (Illus.). 192p. 1981. 50.00 (ISBN 0-7137-1087-X, Pub. by Blandford Pr England). Sterling.

CAGNEY, JAMES, 1899-

Cagney, James. Cagney by Cagney. 1981. pap. 2.75 (ISBN 0-671-41757-6). PB.

CAKE DECORATING

Spencer, Louise. Cake Decorating Ideas & Designs. LC 80-54334. (Illus.). 1981. 14.95 (ISBN 0-8069-0214-0); lib. bdg. 13.29 (ISBN 0-8069-0215-9); pap. 9.95 (ISBN 0-8069-7502-4). Sterling.

CALAMITIES

see Disasters

CALCIUM METABOLISM

Parsons, John A., ed. Endocrinology of Calcium Metabolism. (Comprehensive Endocrinology Ser.). 375p. 1981. 36.00 (ISBN 0-89004-344-2). Raven.

CALCULATING-MACHINES

Here are entered works on calculators, as well as all mechanical computers of pre-1945 vintage. Works on modern electronic computers first developed after 1945 are entered under Computers.

see also Accounting Machines; Computers; Cybernetics; Digital Counters; Programmable Calculators

Hestenes, Marshall & Hill, Richard. Algebra & Trigonometry with Calculators. (Illus.). 512p. 1981. text ed. 17.95 (ISBN 0-13-021857-X). P-H.

Meck, H. R. Scientific Analysis for Programmable Calculators. (Illus.). 160p. 1981. 13.95 (ISBN 0-13-796417-X, Spec); pap. 6.95 (ISBN 0-13-796409-9). P-H.

Moschytz, G. S. Active Filter Design Handbook: For Use with Programmable Pocket Calculators & Minicomputers. 296p. 1981. 49.95 (ISBN 0-471-27850-5, Pub. by Wiley-Interscience). Wiley.

Peterson, Melvin N. Flight Deck Uses for HP-25: Vol. 1, Professional Assortment. 66p. 1979. spiral bdg. 10.00x (ISBN 0-938880-00-4). MNP Star.

--Flight Deck Uses for the HP-41c: Vol. 1, Manual Run Mode Edition. 59p. 1981. spiral bdg. 12.00x (ISBN 0-938880-01-2). MNP Star.

CALCULATING-MACHINES, ELECTRONIC

see Computers

CALCULATORS

see Calculating-Machines

CALCULATORS, PROGRAMMABLE

see Programmable Calculators

CALCULI, BILIARY

Caprini, Joseph A., et al. Gallstones. (Discussions in Surgical Management Ser.). 1979. pap. 10.50 (ISBN 0-87488-953-7). Med Exam.

Wolpers, C. Gallensteine Im Roentgenbild. (Illus.). 66p. 1980. soft cover 20.50 (ISBN 3-8055-2031-X). S Karger.

CALCULUS

see also Differential Equations; Functions; Mathematical Analysis; Nonlinear Theories; Surfaces

Arya, Jagdish C. & Lardner, Robin W. Applied Calculus for Business & Economics. (Illus.). 528p. 1981. text ed. 18.95 (ISBN 0-13-039255-3). P-H.

Dixon, Charles. Advanced Calculus. 192p. 1981. 36.00 (ISBN 0-471-27913-7, Pub. by Wiley-Interscience); pap. 17.95 (ISBN 0-471-27914-5). Wiley.

Gillet, Philip. Calculus & Analytic Geometry. 928p. 1981. text ed. 28.95 (ISBN 0-669-00641-6); instr's. guide avail. (ISBN 0-669-02702-2); solutions guide vol. 1 6.95 (ISBN 0-669-00642-4); solutions guide vol. 2 6.95 (ISBN 0-669-03212-3); solutions guides vol. 3 6.95 (ISBN 0-669-03213-1). Heath.

Goldstein, L. Calculus & It's Applications. 1980. 21.95 (ISBN 0-13-111963-X). P-H.

Grabiner, Judith. The Origins of Cauchy's Rigorous Calculus. 368p. 1981. text ed. 27.50x (ISBN 0-262-07079-0). MIT Pr.

Gulati, Bodh R. A Short Course in Calculus. LC 79-67409. 560p. 1981. text ed. 17.95 (ISBN 0-03-047466-3). Dryden Pr.

Marsden, Jerrold & Weinstein, Alan. Calculus Unlimited. 1980. pap. text ed. 6.95 (ISBN 0-8053-6932-5). Benjamin-Cummings.

Mikusinski, Jan. Operational Calculus, Vol. 1. 2nd ed. (International Series in Pure & Applied Mathematics: Vol. 109). (Illus.). 320p. 1981. 27.00 (ISBN 0-08-025071-8). Pergamon.

Rosenstein, Joseph G. Linear Orderings. LC 80-2341. (Pure & Applied Mathematics Ser.). 1981. write for info. (ISBN 0-12-597680-1). Acad Pr.

Sikorski, R. Advanced Calculus: Functions of Several Variables. 1969. 15.95 (ISBN 0-02-852280-X). Hafner.

Simmons, George F. Precalculus Primer. (Illus.). 176p. (Orig.). Date not set. pap. 7.95 (ISBN 0-86576-009-8). W Kaufmann.

CALCULUS–PROBLEMS, EXERCISES, ETC.

Downing, Douglas. Calculus by Discovery. 224p. (gr. 10-12). 1981. pap. text ed. 4.50 (ISBN 0-8120-2380-3). Barron.

CALCULUS, ABSOLUTE DIFFERENTIAL

see Calculus of Tensors

CALCULUS, DIFFERENTIAL

Bear, H. S. Introduction to Differential Equations. (Illus.). 490p. 1981. pap. text ed. 19.50 (ISBN 0-9605502-0-8). Manoa Pr.

CALCULUS OF DIFFERENCES

see Difference Equations

CALCULUS OF SPINORS

see Spinor Analysis

CALCULUS OF TENSORS

see also Spinor Analysis

Bishop, Richard & Goldberg, Samuel. Tensor Analysis on Manifolds. (Illus.). 1980. pap. 6.00 (ISBN 0-486-64039-6). Dover.

CALCULUS OF VARIATIONS

see also Functional Analysis

Goldstine, H. H. A History of the Calculus of Vatriations from the Seventeenth Through the Nineteenth Century. (Studies in the History of Mathematics & Physical Sciences Ser.: Vol. 5). (Illus.). 410p. 1981. 48.00 (ISBN 0-387-90521-9). Springer-Verlag.

CALDWELL, ERSKINE (PRESTON), 1903-

MacDonald, Scott. Critical Essays on Erskine Caldwell. (Critical Essays on American Literature). 1981. lib. bdg. 25.00 (ISBN 0-8161-8299-X). Twayne.

CALDWELL, TAYLOR, PSEUD.

Stearn, Jess. In Search of Taylor Caldwell. LC 80-6150. 224p. 1981. 12.95 (ISBN 0-8128-2791-0). Stein & Day.

CALENDAR–REFORM

see Calendar Reform

CALENDAR, ECCLESIASTICAL

see Church Calendar

CALENDAR REFORM

Makris, Kallistos. The God-Inspired Orthodox Julian Calendar VS. the False Gregorian Papal Calendar. Vlesmas, Jerry, tr. from Hellenic. 118p. (Orig.). 1971. pap. 2.00x (ISBN 0-938366-36-X). Orthodox Chr.

CALENDARS

see also Almanacs; Devotional Calendars

Keane, Jerryl. Book of Calendars. 700p. 1981. lib. bdg. 22.50 (ISBN 0-87196-467-8). Facts on File.

Makris, Kallistos. The God-Inspired Orthodox Julian Calendar VS. the False Gregorian Papal Calendar. Vlesmas, Jerry, tr. from Hellenic. 118p. (Orig.). 1971. pap. 2.00x (ISBN 0-938366-36-X). Orthodox Chr.

CALIFORNIA

see also names of cities, regions, etc. in California, e.g. San Francisco; Death Valley

Gold, Herbert. A Walk on the West Side: California on the Brink. LC 80-70216. 208p. 1981. 10.95 (ISBN 0-87795-305-8); pap. 4.95 (ISBN 0-87795-322-8). Arbor Hse.

CALIFORNIA–ANTIQUITIES

Finnerty, W. Patrick, et al. Community Structure & Trade at Isthmus Cove: A Salvage Excavation on Catalina Island (Calif.) (Pacific Coast Archaeological Society Occasional Papers: No. 1). 81p. 1981. pap. 2.95. Acoma Bks.

CALIFORNIA–BIOGRAPHY

Jackson, H. C. The Good 'uns: A Memoir of H.C. "Bud Jackson. (Illus.). 280p. 1980. 17.95 (ISBN 0-914330-38-1). Pioneer Pub Co.

Sisk, B. F. A Congressional Record: The Memoir of Bernie Sisk. Dickman, A. I., ed. LC 80-84208. (Illus.). 280p. 1980. 20.00 (ISBN 0-914330-36-5). Panorama West.

CALIFORNIA–DESCRIPTION AND TRAVEL

Bailey, Bernadine. Picture Book of California. rev ed. (gr. 3-5). 1981. 5.50g. A Whitman.

Grossberg, Milton. Family Bike Rides. (Illus.). 128p. (Orig.). 1981. pap. 5.95 (ISBN 0-87701-148-6). Chronicle Bks.

Ilian, Martin. Bay Area Sports & Recreation Directory. 224p. (Orig.). 1981. pap. 7.95 (ISBN 0-87701-164-8). Chronicle Bks.

Jackson, Ruth A. Combing the Coast: San Francisco to Santa Cruz. (Illus.). 116p. (Orig.). 1981. pap. 4.95 (ISBN 0-87701-140-0). Chronicle Bks.

Moffat, Gwen. Hard Road West: Alone on the California Trail. 1981. 12.95 (ISBN 0-670-36145-3). Viking Pr.

Newey, Bob. East Bay Trails. 4th, rev. ed. LC 80-69075. (Illus.). 144p. 1981. pap. 4.95 (ISBN 0-9605186-0-6). Footloose Pr.

CALIFORNIA–DESCRIPTION AND TRAVEL–GUIDEBOOKS

Arrigoni, Patricia. Making the Most of Marin. (Illus., Orig.). 1981. pap. 7.95 (ISBN 0-89141-108-9). Presidio Pr.

Crain, Jim. Historic Country Inns of California. LC 77-727. 170p. 1980. pap. 5.95 (ISBN 0-87701-208-3). Chronicle Bks.

Hart, Herbert M. Tour Guide to Old Forts of Oregon, Idaho, Washington, California, Vol. 3. (Illus.). 65p. (Orig.). 1981. pap. 3.95 (ISBN 0-87108-582-8). Pruett.

McKinney, John. A Day Hiker's Guide to Southern California. 160p. (Orig.). 1981. pap. 8.85 (ISBN 0-88496-163-X). Capra Pr.

CALIFORNIA–GOLD DISCOVERIES

Chamberlain, Newell D. The Call of Gold. (Illus.). 185p. 1981. pap. 5.95 (ISBN 0-934136-12-2). Western Tanager.

Umbeck, John R. A Theory of Property Rights-with Special Applications to the California Gold Rush. (Illus.). 160p. 1981. text ed. 9.50 (ISBN 0-8138-1675-0). Iowa St U Pr.

CALIFORNIA–HISTORY

DeWitt, Howard A. Readings in California Civilization: Interpretative Issues. LC 80-83492. 240p. 1981. pap. text ed. 12.95 (ISBN 0-8403-2311-5). Kendall-Hunt.

Hutchings, James M. Seeking the Elephant, Eighteen Forty-Nine: James Mason Hutchings' Journal of His Overland Trek to California. Sargent, Shirley, ed. LC 80-67777. (American Trail Ser.: No. XII). (Illus.). 210p. 1981. 30.00 (ISBN 0-87062-136-X). A H Clark.

Quinn, Arthur. Broken Shore: The Marin Peninsula, a Perspective on California History. (Illus.). 288p. 1981. 14.95 (ISBN 0-87905-085-3). Peregrine Smith.

Read, Ethel M. Lo, the Poor Indian: A Saga of the Suisun Indians of California. LC 80-82306. 580p. (Orig.). 1980. 18.00 (ISBN 0-914330-34-9); pap. 10.00 (ISBN 0-914330-37-3). Panorama West.

Rintoul, William. Oildorado: Boom Times on the West Side. LC 78-50141. (Illus.). 240p. 1980. pap. 7.95 (ISBN 0-934136-07-6, Valley Calif). Western Tanager.

Starr, Kevin. Americans & the California Dream, 1850-1915. (Illus.). 512p. 1981. pap. 11.50 (ISBN 0-87905-083-7). Peregrine Smith.

Summers, June N. Good Morning, Tecate. (Illus.). 62p. (Orig.). 1972. pap. text ed. 4.00 (ISBN 0-686-28871-8). J N Summers.

CALIFORNIA–HISTORY, LOCAL

Fresno City & County Historical Society. Fresno California Illustrated. LC 80-68522. (Illus.). 192p. 1980. Repr. 13.95 (ISBN 0-914330-35-7). Pioneer Pub Co.

Hicks, John & Hicks, Regina. Cannery Row. (A Pictorial History: No. 1). (Illus.). 48p. 1972. pap. 2.95 (ISBN 0-914606-01-8). Creative Bks.

Parks, Annette W. Qhawala-li: Water Coming Down Place; "A History of Gualalal, Mendocino County, California. LC 80-82462. (Illus.). 150p. 1981. 24.95 (ISBN 0-9605550-0-5); pap. 12.95 (ISBN 0-9605550-1-3). FreshCut.

Pierce, Marjorie. East of the Gabilans. LC 76-56566. 190p. 1981. 17.95 (ISBN 0-934136-14-9); pap. 9.95 (ISBN 0-934136-11-4). Western Tanager.

Sioli, P., ed. History of el Dorado County, California. facsimile ed. 272p. Repr. of 1883 ed. quarto 35.00. Holmes.

CALIFORNIA–SOCIAL CONDITIONS

Tunstall, Jeremy & Walker, David. Media Made in California: Hollywood, Politics, & the News. (Illus.). 224p. 1981. 15.95 (ISBN 0-19-502922-4). Oxford U Pr.

CALIFORNIA, LOWER

see Baja California

CALISTHENICS

see Callisthenics

CALLAS, MARIA, 1923-1977

Stassinopoulos, Arianna. Maria Callas: The Woman Behind the Legend. 1981. 13.95 (ISBN 0-671-25583-5). S&S.

CALLIGRAPHERS

Peladeau, Marius B. Stephen R. Deane: Early Maine Folk Calligrapher. (Illus.). 128p. 1981. 22.50 (ISBN 0-931474-15-9). TBW Bks.

CALLIGRAPHY

Baker, Arthur. New Calligraphic Ornaments & Flourishes. (Pictorial Archive Ser.). (Orig.). 1981. pap. price not set (ISBN 0-486-24095-9). Dover.

Homelsky, Geri & Kaufman, Herb. Calligraphy in the Copperplate Style. (Illus.). 50p. (Orig.). 1981. pap. 1.75 (ISBN 0-486-24037-1). Dover.

Jessen, Peter. Masterpieces of Calligraphy: Two Hundred & Sixty-One Examples, 1500-1800. (Illus.). 1981. pap. price not set (ISBN 0-486-24100-9). Dover.

Lehman, Charles. Italic Handwriting & Calligraphy for the Beginner: A Craft Manual. (Illus.). 160p. (Orig.). 1981. pap. 3.95 (ISBN 0-8008-4290-1, 80-53415, Pentalic). Taplinger.

Leptich, Anne & Evans, Jacque. Calligrapher's Reference Book. pap. 6.00 (ISBN 0-87980-386-X). Wilshire.

--Calligraphy for Fun & Profit. pap. 6.00 (ISBN 0-87980-385-1). Wilshire.

Maguire, Kitty. Heart to Hand: A Calligraphy Manual. (Illus.). 68p. 1980. text ed. 25.00 limited ed of 50 (ISBN 0-9604818-0-X); pap. 12.00 (ISBN 0-9604818-1-8). Anemone Edns.

Stevens, John. Sacred Calligraphy of the East. LC 80-53446. (Illus.). 176p. (Orig.). 1981. pap. 9.95 (ISBN 0-394-74832-8). Shambhala Pubn.

Sullivan, Michael. The Three Perfections: Chinese Painting, Poetry & Calligraphy. LC 80-18189. (Illus.). 64p. 10.00 (ISBN 0-8076-0996-X); pap. 4.95 (ISBN 0-8076-0997-8). Braziller.

CALLING

see Vocation

CALLISTHENICS

see also Gymnastics; Physical Education and Training

Kirby, Colleen & Roberts, Laura. Putting You in Creative Aerobic Dance: The Fun & Fitness of a Lifetime Sport Through Movement to Music. Fritze, David, ed. LC 80-84937. (Illus.). 150p. (Orig.). 1981. pap. write for info. Korakas-Roberts-Kirby.

Wassersug, Joseph D. Jarm-How to Jog with Your Arms to Live Longer. 1981. 11.95 (ISBN 0-87949-197-3). Ashley Bks.

CALUMNY

see Libel and Slander

CALVIN, JEAN, 1509-1564

Calvin, John. Calvin's Letters. pap. 4.95 (ISBN 0-686-28946-3). Banner of Truth.

Van Halsema, Thea B. This Was John Calvin. (Christian Biography Ser.). 184p. 1981. pap. 3.95 (ISBN 0-8010-9283-3). Baker Bk.

CALVINISM

see also Covenants (Theology); New England Theology; Predestination

Calvin, John. Letters of John Calvin. 261p. 1980. pap. 4.95 (ISBN 0-85151-323-9). Banner of Truth.

Conforti, Joseph. Samuel Hopkins & the New Divinity Movement: Calvinism, the Congregational Ministry, & Reform in New England Between the Great Awakenings. 240p. (Orig.). 1981. pap. 12.95 (ISBN 0-8028-1871-4). Eerdmans.

Martin, Albert N. Practical Implications of Calvinism. 1979. pap. 0.75 (ISBN 0-85151-296-8). Banner of Truth.

Ross, Bob L. Killing Effects of Calvinism. 1980. pap. 1.25. Pilgrim Pubns.

Seaton, Jack. The Five Points of Calvinism. 1979. pap. 0.95. Banner of Truth.

CAMBISTRY

see Foreign Exchange; Weights and Measures

CAMBODIA

Sobel. Cambodia: Holocaust in Asia. 200p. 1981. lib. bdg. 17.50 (ISBN 0-87196-209-8). Facts on File.

CAMBODIA–POLITICS AND GOVERNMENT

Samphan, Khieu. Cambodia's Economy & Industrial Development, Data Paper No. 113. Summers, Laura, tr. 129p. 1979. 6.00 (ISBN 0-87727-111-9). Cornell SE Asia.

Shawcross, William. Sideshow. rev. ed. 1981. price not set (ISBN 0-671-25414-6, Touchstone). S&S.

CAMBRIAN PERIOD

see Geology, Stratigraphic–Cambrian

CAMBRIDGE, ENGLAND–HISTORY

Taylor, A., et al. Early Cambridgestive. (Cambridge Town, Gown & Country Ser.: Vol. 28). 192p. 1977. 20.00 (ISBN 0-900891-08-4). Oleander Pr.

CAMBRIDGE UNIVERSITY–HISTORY

Garland, Martha M. Cambridge Before Darwin. LC 80-40327. 224p. 1980. 34.50 (ISBN 0-521-23319-4). Cambridge U Pr.

Taylor, A., et al. Early Cambridgestive. (Cambridge Town, Gown & Country Ser.: Vol. 28). 192p. 1977. 20.00 (ISBN 0-900891-08-4). Oleander Pr.

CAMELS

Gauthier-Pilters, Hilde & Dagg, Anne I. The Camel: Its Evolution, Ecology, Behavior, & Relationship to Man. LC 80-23822. 1981. lib. bdg. 26.00x (ISBN 0-226-28453-0). U of Chicago Pr.

CAMERA LENSES

see Lenses, Photographic

CAMERAS

see also Moving-Picture Cameras

Focal Editorial Staff, ed. Cameras: The Facts, a Collector's Guide, 1957-1964. LC 80-41969. (Illus.). 528p. 1981. 45.00 (ISBN 0-240-51062-3). Focal Pr.

London, Barbara & Boyer, Richard. Your Automatic Camera Indoors. 1981. pap. 6.95 (ISBN 0-442-21956-3). Van Nos Reinhold.

--Your Automatic Camera Outdoors. 1981. pap. 6.95 (ISBN 0-442-21955-5). Van Nos Reinhold.

McKeown, James M. & McKeown, Joan C. Price Guide to Antique & Classic Still Cameras 1981-1982. LC 81-65028. (Illus.). 176p. 1981. pap. 12.95 (ISBN 0-931838-01-0). Centennial Photo Serv.

CAMERAS–TYPES–POLAROID LAND

Olshaker, Mark. The Instant Image: Edwin Land & the Polaroid Experience. LC 77-15965. (Illus.). 292p. 1980. pap. 8.95 (ISBN 0-8128-6093-4). Stein & Day.

CAMORRA

see Mafia

CAMP COOKERY

see Cookery, Outdoor

CAMP COUNSELORS

Stutts, Evelyn C. All That You Need to Know About Camp Counseling. (Illus.). 1981. 4.95 (ISBN 0-8062-1708-1). Carlton.

CAMP MAINTENANCE

see Camp Sites, Facilities, etc.

CAMP MANAGEMENT

see Camps

CAMP SITES, FACILITIES, ETC.

VanMeer, Mary. See America Free. VanMeer, Leo, ed. LC 80-53384. (Illus.). 725p. (Orig.). 1981. pap. 6.95 (ISBN 0-937826-00-6). VanMeer Pubns.

Wheeler's RV Resort & Campground Guide: Nineteen Eighty-One. (Illus.). 1981. pap. 6.95 (ISBN 0-670-75955-4). Viking Pr.

CAMPAIGNS, PRESIDENTIAL

see Presidents–United States–Election

CAMPANELLA, TOMMASO, 1568-1639

Grillo, Francesco. Tommaso Campanella in America: A Supplement to the Critical Bibliography. 48p. 1957. 5.00x (ISBN 0-913298-49-2). S F Vanni.

CAMPBELLITES

see Disciples of Christ

CAMPERS AND COACHES, TRUCK

see also Vans

Wolters, Richard A. Living on Wheels: The Secrets of a Safe, Happy, & Comfortable Living in a Motor Home. 1973. 8.95 (ISBN 0-87690-100-3). Dutton.

CAMPING

see also Backpacking; Camp Sites, Facilities, etc.; Camps; Cookery, Outdoor; Outdoor Life; Survival (After Airplane Accidents, Shipwrecks, etc.)

Armstrong, Diana. Bicycle Camping. (Illus., Orig.). 1981. pap. 8.95. Dial.

Drabik, Harry. The Spirit of Canoe Camping. (Illus.). 126p. 1981. pap. 5.95 (ISBN 0-931714-11-7). Nodin Pr.

Farmer, Charles & Farmer, Kathleen. Family Book of Camping Lists. (Illus.). 224p. (Orig.). 1981. pap. 6.95 (ISBN 0-8117-2136-1). Stackpole.

Hauser, Verne. River Camping: Touring by Canoe, Raft, Dory, & Kayak. (A Soltice Press Bk.). (Illus.). 1981. pap. 9.95 (ISBN 0-8037-7256-4). Dial.

Jacobson, Clifford. Wilderness Canpeina & Campina. (Illus.). 1977. 13.95 (ISBN 0-87690-228-X); pap. 6.95 (ISBN 0-87690-229-8). Dutton.

McManus, Patrick. They Shoot Canoes, Don't They? 228p. 1981. 10.95 (ISBN 0-03-058646-1). HR&W.

Neimark, Paul. Camping & Ecology. (Wilderness World Ser.). (Illus.). 64p. (gr. 3 up). 1981. PLB 9.25 (ISBN 0-516-02451-5). Childrens.

Thomas, Dian. Roughing It Easy, Two. (Illus.). 224p. (Orig.). 1978. pap. 2.75 (ISBN 0-446-95843-3). Warner Bks.

Vigil, Alberta G. The Complete Camper's Cookbook: Nearly 200 Easy Recipes for Family Outdoor Cooking. (Illus.). 104p. (Orig.). 1981. pap. 5.95 (ISBN 0-932906-09-5). Pan-Am Publishing Co.

CAMPING–OUTFITS, SUPPLIES, ETC.

Platten, David. Making Camping & Outdoor Gear. LC 80-68902. (Illus.). 160p. 1981. 16.95 (ISBN 0-7153-8023-0). David & Charles.

CAMPING–EUROPE

Automobile Assication. AA Camping & Caravanning in Europe. rev. ed. (Illus.). 416p. 1981. pap. write for info. (Pub. by Auto Assn-British Tourist Authority England). Merrimack Bk Serv.

CAMPING–GREAT BRITAIN

Automobile Association. AA Camping & Caravanning in Britain. rev. ed. (Illus.). 256p. 1981. pap. write for info. (ISBN 0-86145-041-8, Pub. by Auto Assn-British Tourist Authority England). Merrimack Bk Serv.

CAMPS

see also Camp Sites, Facilities, etc.; Camping

Van Krevelen, Alice. Summer Camp: A Guidebook for Parents. LC 80-26726. (Illus.). 168p. 1981. 11.95 (ISBN 0-88229-296-X). Nelson-Hall.

CAMPS–COUNSELORS

see Camp Counselors

CAMPUS CULTURES

see Educational Anthropology

CAMUS, ALBERT, 1913-1960

Gay-Crosier, Raymond. Albert Camus Nineteen Eighty. LC 80-22240. 330p. (Orig., Fr.). 1981. pap. 16.00 (ISBN 0-8130-0691-0). U Presses Fla.

Rizzuto, Anthony. Camus' Imperial Vision. 1981. price not set (ISBN 0-8093-1002-3). S Ill U Pr.

CANAANITE MYTHOLOGY

see Mythology, Canaanite

CANADA–ARMED FORCES

Summers, Jack L. & Chartrand, Rene. Military Uniforms in Canada. (Illus.). 220p. 1981. 35.00 (ISBN 0-660-10346-X, 56434-7, Pub. by Natl Mus Canada). U of Chicago Pr.

CANADA–ARMY

Summers, Jack L. & Chartrand, Rene. Military Uniforms in Canada. (Illus.). 220p. 1981. 35.00 (ISBN 0-660-10346-X, 56434-7, Pub. by Natl Mus Canada). U of Chicago Pr.

CANADA–BIOGRAPHY

Barnett, Herbert E. & Fraser, Hugh, eds. Who's Who in Canada 1980-81. 70th ed. (Illus.). 1496p. 1980. 75.00x (ISBN 0-8002-2744-1). Intl Pubns Serv.

Jones, Andrew & Rutman, Leonard. In the Children's Aid: J. J. Kelso & Child Welfare in Ontario. 256p. 1981. 17.50 (ISBN 0-8020-5491-9). U of Toronto Pr.

Salverson, Laura G. Confessions of an Immigrant's Daughter. (Social History of Canada Ser.). 400p. 1981. 30.00x (ISBN 0-8020-2424-6); pap. 15.00 (ISBN 0-8020-6434-5). U of Toronto Pr.

Who's Who in the East. 18th ed. 944p. 1981. 62.50 (ISBN 0-8379-0618-0). Marquis.

CANADA–COMMERCE

Fraser's Canadian Trade Directory, 1980, 3 vols. 69th ed. LC 39-5763. 1980. Set. 95.00x (ISBN 0-8002-2707-7). Intl Pubns Serv.

Hay, K. A. Friends or Acquaintances? Canada & Japan's Other Trading Partners in the Early 1980's. 52p. 1978. pap. text ed. 3.00x (ISBN 0-920380-15-8, Pub. by Inst Res Pub Canada). Renouf.

Walker, David F. Canadian Industrial Space-Economy. 261p. 1980. 27.95 (ISBN 0-470-27061-6). Halsted Pr.

CANADA–DESCRIPTION AND TRAVEL

Baxter, Robert. Baxter's Western Canada. 1981. 9.95 (ISBN 0-913384-41-0). Rail-Europe-Baxter.

Canada Handbook. 343p. 1980. pap. 11.75 (ISBN 0-660-10203-X, SSC145, SSC). Unipub.

CANADA–DESCRIPTION AND TRAVEL–GUIDEBOOKS

Hall, Gerry. Offbeat Canada. (Orig.). 1981. pap. 2.50 (ISBN 0-451-09842-0, E9842, Sig). NAL.

Thompson, John. Country Bed & Breakfast Places in Canada. rev ed. 1981. pap. 7.95 (ISBN 0-88879-045-7). Berkshire Traveller.

CANADA–ECONOMIC CONDITIONS

Bird, Richard M. The Growth of Public Employment in Canada. 190p. 1979. pap. text ed. 12.95x (ISBN 0-920380-17-4, Pub. by Inst Res Pub Canada). Renouf.

Bucovetsky, Meyer W. Studies in Public Employment & Compensation in Canada. 177p. 1979. pap. text ed. 14.95x (ISBN 0-409-88601-7, Pub. by Inst Res Pub Canada). Renouf.

Cundiff, W. E. & Reid, Mado. Issues in Canadian-U. S. Transborder Computer Data Flows. 89p. 1979. pap. text ed. 6.50x (ISBN 0-920380-12-3, Pub. by Inst Res Pub Canada). Renouf.

Doern, G. Bruce & Maslove, Allan M. Public Evaluation of Government Spending. 192p. 1979. pap. text ed. 10.95x (ISBN 0-920380-19-0, Pub. by Inst Res Pub Canada). Renouf.

Foot, David K. Public Employment & Compensation in Canada: Myths & Realities. 188p. 1978. pap. text ed. 10.95x (ISBN 0-409-88600-9, Pub. by Inst Res Pub Canada). Renouf.

--Public Employment in Canada: Statistical Series. 217p. 1979. pap. text ed. 15.00x (ISBN 0-409-88603-3, Pub. by Inst Res Pub Canada). Renouf.

Hudson, Michael. Canada in the New Monetary Order: Borrow? Devalue? Restructure! 117p. 1978. pap. text ed. 6.95x (ISBN 0-920380-06-9, Pub. by Inst Res Pub Canada). Renouf.

Marmorek, Jan. Over a Barrell: A Guide to the Canadian Energy Crisis. LC 80-1068. 224p. 1981. 12.95 (ISBN 0-385-17192-7); pap. 6.95 (ISBN 0-385-17195-1). Doubleday.

Maslove, A. & Swimmer, G. Wage Controls in Canada, 1975-78. 182p. 1980. pap. text ed. 11.95x (ISBN 0-920380-50-6, Pub. by Inst Res Pub Canada). Renouf.

Protheroe, David R. Imports & Politics. 170p. 1980. pap. text ed. 8.95x (ISBN 0-920380-45-X, Pub. by Inst Res Pub Canada). Renouf.

Rowley, J. W. & Stanbury, W. T. Competition Policy in Canada: Stage II, Bill C-13. 311p. 1978. pap. text ed. 12.95x (ISBN 0-920380-02-6, Pub. by Inst Res Pub Canada). Renouf.

Stanbury, W. T. Studies on Regulation in Canada. 249p. 1978. pap. text ed. 9.95x (ISBN 0-920380-04-2, Pub. by Inst Res Pub Canada). Renouf.

Thompson, Fred & Stanbury, W. T. The Political Economy of Interest Groups in the Legislative Process in Canada. 53p. 1979. pap. text ed. 3.00x (ISBN 0-920380-27-1, Pub. by Inst Res Pub Canada). Renouf.

Tsurumi, Y. Sogoshosha: Engines of Export-Based Growth. 91p. 1980. pap. text ed. 8.95x (ISBN 0-920380-58-1, Pub. by Inst Res Pub Canada). Renouf.

Walker, David F. Canadian Industrial Space-Economy. 261p. 1980. 27.95 (ISBN 0-470-27061-6). Halsted Pr.

CANADA–FOREIGN ECONOMIC RELATIONS

Institute for Research on Public Policy, Canada & Brookings. Conferences on Canadian-U. S. Economic Relations. 94p. 1978. pap. text ed. 3.00x (ISBN 0-920380-09-3, Pub. by Inst Res Pub Canada). Renouf.

CANADA–FOREIGN RELATIONS

Stacey, C. P. Canada & the Age of Conflict: A History of Canadian External Policies, Vol. II; 1921-48--the Mackenzie King Era. 480p. 1981. 30.00x (ISBN 0-8020-2397-5); pap. 12.50 (ISBN 0-8020-6420-5). U of Toronto Pr.

CANADA–HISTORY

Bothwell, Robert, et al. Canada Since Nineteen Forty-Five: Power, Politics, & Provincialism. 496p. 1981. 19.95 (ISBN 0-8020-2417-3). U of Toronto Pr.

Creighton, Donald. Story of Canada. 1971. pap. 3.95 (ISBN 0-571-09070-2, Pub. by Faber & Faber). Merrimack Bk Serv.

Stacey, C. P. Canada & the Age of Conflict: A History of Canadian External Policies, Vol. II; 1921-48--the Mackenzie King Era. 480p. 1981. 30.00x (ISBN 0-8020-2397-5); pap. 12.50 (ISBN 0-8020-6420-5). U of Toronto Pr.

CANADA–POLITICS AND GOVERNMENT

Armstrong, Christopher. The Politics of Federalism: Ontario's Relations with the Federal Government 1867-1942. (Ontario Historical Studies). 316p. 1981. 20.00 (ISBN 0-8020-3374-1). U of Toronto Pr.

Bishop, Olga B. Canadian Official Publications. (Guides to Official Publications Ser.: Vol. 9). 308p. 1981. 40.00 (ISBN 0-08-024697-4). Pergamon.

Bothwell, Robert, et al. Canada Since Nineteen Forty-Five: Power, Politics, & Provincialism. 496p. 1981. 19.95 (ISBN 0-8020-2417-3). U of Toronto Pr.

Bourinot, John G. Parliamentary Procedure & Practice in the Dominion of Canada. 785p. 1980. Repr. 70.00x (ISBN 0-7165-2021-4, Pub. by Irish Academic Pr). Biblio Dist.

Doern, G. Bruce. Canadian Nuclear Policies. 1980. pap. text ed. 14.95x (ISBN 0-920380-25-5, Pub. by Inst Res Pub Canada). Renouf.

--Government Intervention in the Canadian Nuclear Industry. 1980. pap. text ed. 8.95x (ISBN 0-920380-46-8, Pub. by Inst Res Pub Canada). Renouf.

Feldman, Elliot J. & Nevitte, Neil. The Future of North America: Canada, the United States, & Quebec Nationalism. 378p. 1979. pap. text ed. 9.50x (ISBN 0-87674-045-X, Pub. by Inst Res Pub Canada). Renouf.

French, Richard & Beliveau, Andre. The R. C. M. P. & the Management of National Security. 77p. 1979. pap. text ed. 6.95x (ISBN 0-920380-18-2, Pub. by Inst Res Pub Canada). Renouf.

Hartle, Douglas G. Public Policy Decision Making & Regulation. 218p. 1979. pap. text ed. 12.95x (ISBN 0-920380-20-4, Pub. by Inst Res Pub Canada). Renouf.

Hartley, Karen. Energy R & D Decision Making for Canada. 108p. 1979. pap. text ed. 3.00x (ISBN 0-920380-40-9, Pub. by Inst Res Pub Canada). Renouf.

Millar, Perry S. & Baar, Carl. Judicial Administration in Canada. (Institute of Public Administration of Canada, Ipac Ser.). (Illus.). 550p. 1981. 35.95x (ISBN 0-7735-0367-6); pap. 18.95x (ISBN 0-7735-0368-4). McGill-Queens U Pr.

Organization of the Government of Canada. 635p. 1981. pap. 37.00 (ISBN 0-660-10496-2, SSC 149, SSC). Unipub.

Protheroe, David R. Imports & Politics. 170p. 1980. pap. text ed. 8.95x (ISBN 0-920380-45-X, Pub. by Inst Res Pub Canada). Renouf.

Savoie, Donald J. Federal-Provincial Collaboration: The Canada-New Brunswick General Development Agreement. (Institute of Public Administration of Canada (IPAC) Ser.). 220p. 1981. 25.00x (ISBN 0-7735-0373-0); pap. 11.95x (ISBN 0-7735-0374-9). McGill-Queens U Pr.

Shere, Waris. Miracles of Survival: Canada & French Canada. 160p. 1981. 7.50 (ISBN 0-682-49730-4). Exposition.

Smith, David E. The Regional Decline of a National Party: Liberals on the Prairies. (Canadian Government Ser.). 184p. 1981. 14.00x (ISBN 0-8020-2421-1); pap. 6.50 (ISBN 0-8020-6430-2). U of Toronto Pr.

Thompson, Fred & Stanbury, W. T. The Political Economy of Interest Groups in the Legislative Process in Canada. 53p. 1979. pap. text ed. 3.00x (ISBN 0-920380-27-1, Pub. by Inst Res Pub Canada). Renouf.

CANADA–POPULATION

Stone, Leroy O. Canadian Population Trends & Public Policy Through the 1980's. 1977. pap. text ed. 4.00x (ISBN 0-7735-0288-2, Pub. by Inst Res Pub Canada). Renouf.

CANADA–SOCIAL CONDITIONS

Breton, Raymond. The Canadian Condition: A Guide to Research in Public Policy. 65p. 1977. pap. text ed. 2.95x (ISBN 0-920380-00-X, Pub. by Inst Res Pub Canada). Renouf.

Stone, Leroy O. & MacLean, Michael J. Future Income Prospects for Canada's Senior Citizens. 104p. 1979. pap. text ed. 7.95x (ISBN 0-920380-13-1, Pub. by Inst Res Pub Canada). Renouf.

CANADA–SOCIAL LIFE AND CUSTOMS

Mouton, Claude. The Montreal Canadians. 256p. 1981. 19.95 (ISBN 0-442-29634-7). Van Nos Reinhold.

CANADA–STATISTICS

Hobrook, Jay M. Shipton Quebec Canada Eighteen Twenty Five Census. LC 76-364055. 1976. pap. 7.50 (ISBN 0-931248-07-8). Holbrook Res.

Holbrook, Jay M. Ascott Quebec Canada Eighteen Twenty Five Census. LC 80-117991. 1976. pap. 7.50 (ISBN 0-931248-06-X). Holbrook Res.

CANADIAN AUTHORS

see Authors, Canadian

CANADIAN LITERATURE–BIBLIOGRAPHY

Leeker, Robert, ed. The Annotated Bibliography of Canada's Major Authors: Margaret Atwood, Leonard Cohen, Archibald Lampman, E. J. Pratt, & Al Purdy, Vol.iI. (Reference Book Ser.). 1981. 26.00 (ISBN 0-8161-8552-2). G K Hall.

CANADIAN LITERATURE–HISTORY AND CRITICISM

Woodcock, George. The World of Canadian Writing: Critiques & Recollections. LC 80-15497. 312p. 1981. pap. price not set (ISBN 0-295-95808-1). U of Wash Pr.

CANADIAN MUSIC

see Music, Canadian

CANADIAN SONGS

see Songs, Canadian

CANALS

Hadfield, Charles. British Canals: An Illustrated History. 4th ed. (Canals of the British Isles Ser.). (Illus.). 8.95. David & Charles.

--The Canal Age. LC 80-69343. (Illus.). 240p. 1981. 22.50 (ISBN 0-7153-8079-6). David & Charles.

Ware, Michael. Narrow Boats at Work. 144p. 1980. 23.85x (ISBN 0-86190-006-5, Pub. by Allan Pubs England). State Mutual Bk.

CANAPES

see Cookery (Appetizers)

CANARY ISLANDS

Mercer, John. The Canary Islanders: Their Prehistory Conquest & Survival. (Illus.). 285p. 1980. 32.50x (ISBN 0-389-20213-4). B&N.

CANARY PARROT

see Budgerigars

CANBERRA, AUSTRALIA

Johnson, Donald. Canberra & Walter Burley Griffin: A Bibliography of Eighteen Seventy-Six to Nineteen Seventy-Six & a Guide to Published Sources. (Illus.). 128p. (Orig.). 1980. pap. 6.50x (ISBN 0-19-554203-7). Oxford U Pr.

CANCER

see also Antineoplastic Agents; Carcinogenesis; Kaposi's Sarcoma

also subdivision Cancer or Diseases under name of organs or regions of the body

Cameron, Ewan & Pauling, Linus. Cancer & Vitamin C. 1981. pap. 5.95 (ISBN 0-446-97735-7). Warner Bks.

Cancer Treatment: Why So Many Failures? What You Can Do About It. 1980. write for info (ISBN 0-9601644-1-3). GE-PS Cancer.

Connolly, John G., ed. Carcinoma of the Bladder. (Progress in Cancer Research & Therapy Ser.). 275p. 1981. 27.00 (ISBN 0-89004-536-4). Raven.

Critser, James R., Jr. Cancer: Diagnosis & Therapy. (Ser. 10CDT - 80). 1981. 60.00 (ISBN 0-914428-77-2). Lexington Data.

Crooke, Stanley T. & Prestayko, Archie W. Cancer & Chemotherapy: Introduction to Clinical Oncology, Vol. 2. LC 79-8536. 1981. write for info. (ISBN 0-12-197802-8). Acad Pr.

Dietz, J. Herbert. Rehabilitation Oncology. 224p. 1981. 24.50 (ISBN 0-471-08414-X, Pub. by Wiley Med). Wiley.

Donavan, Marilee. Cancer Care: A Guide for Patient Education. 288p. 1981. pap. 11.50 (ISBN 0-8385-1028-0). ACC.

Hodgson, Thomas A. Social & Economic Implications of Cancer in the United States. Cox, Klaudia, ed. (Ser. 3, No. 20). 50p. 1980. pap. text ed. 1.50 (ISBN 0-8406-0203-0). Natl Ctr Health Stats.

Levine. Cancer in the Young. 1981. write for info. Masson Pub.

Lewison, Edward F. & Montague, Albert C. Diagnosis & Treatment of Breast Cancer: International Clinical Congress. (Illus.). 268p. 1981. write for info. (4954-2). Williams & Wilkins.

Maher, Tom & Schwartz, Malcolm. Doctor Discusses Cancer. (Illus.). 1981. pap. 2.50 (ISBN 0-686-69338-8). Budlong.

Moss, Ralph W. The Cancer Syndrome. LC 79-2300. 320p. 1981. pap. 7.95 (ISBN 0-394-17896-3, BC). Grove.

Newell, Guy R. & Ellison, Neil M., eds. Cancer & Nutrition: Etiology & Treatment. 475p. 1981. 45.00 (ISBN 0-89004-631-X). Raven.

Oliver, R. T., et al, eds. Bladder Cancer: Principles of Combination Therapy. (Illus.). 272p. 1981. text ed. 69.00 (ISBN 0-407-00187-5). Butterworth.

Simmons, Harold E. The Psychogenic Biochemical Aspects of Cancer. 1979. pap. 9.95 (ISBN 0-87312-010-8). Gen Welfare.

Stening, Malcolm. Cancer & Related Lesions of the Vulva. (Illus.). 184p. 1980. text ed. 45.00 (ISBN 0-909337-22-5). ADIS Pr.

Symposium at Roswell Park Memorial Institute, Buffalo, May 1980. Cancer Among Black Populations: Proceedings. Mettlin, Curtis & Murphy, Gerald P., eds. (Progress in Clinical & Biological Research Ser.: No. 53). 275p. 1981. 24.00x (ISBN 0-8451-0053-X). A R Liss.

Symposium in Honor of the Jackson Laboratory's Fiftieth Anniversary, Bar Harbor, Maine, July 1979. Mammalian Genetics & Cancer: Proceedings. Russell, Elizabeth S., ed. 1981. 42.00x (ISBN 0-8451-0045-9). A R Liss.

The G-Jo Institute. Pathways from Cancer: A Directory. 1980. pap. 3.00 (ISBN 0-916878-08-2). Falkynor Bks.

Welvaart, K., et al, eds. Colorectal Cancer. (Boerhaave Series for Postgraduate Medical Education: No. 18). (Illus.). 290p. 1981. PLB 58.00 (ISBN 90-6021-465-X, Pub. by Leiden U Pr). Kluwer Boston.

CANCER–CHEMOTHERAPY

Al-Rashid, Rashid A. Pediatric Cancer Chemotherapy. (Medical Outline Ser.). 1979. 26.00 (ISBN 0-87488-685-6); pap. 17.00 (ISBN 0-87488-663-5). Med Exam.

Carter. Chemotherapy of Cancer. 2nd ed. 400p. 1981. 15.75 (ISBN 0-471-08045-4, Pub. by Wiley Medical). Wiley.

Crooke, S. T. & Prestayko, A. W., eds. Cancer & Chemotherapy: Antineoplastic Agents, Vol. 3. 1981. write for info. (ISBN 0-12-197803-6). Acad Pr.

Greenspan, Ezra. Clinical Interpretation & Practice of Cancer Chemotherapy. 1981. text ed. price not set (ISBN 0-89004-566-6). Raven.

Mihich, Enrico. New Leads in Cancer Chemotherapeutics. 1981. lib. bdg. 27.50 (ISBN 0-8161-2148-6, Hall Medical). G K Hall.

Pilapil, F. & Studva, K., eds. Programmed Instruction: Understanding Cancer & Chemotherapy. 80p. 1979. pap. 6.50 (ISBN 0-89352-081-0). Masson Pub.

Sartorelli, A. C., et al, eds. Molecular Actions & Targets for Cancer Chemotherapeutic Agents. (Bristol-Myers Cancer Symposia Ser.). 1981. 45.00 (ISBN 0-12-619280-4). Acad Pr.

Scoy-Mosher, M. V. Chemotherapy: A Manual for Patients & Their Families. Date not set. Set Of 100. pap. 40.00. Masson Pub.

Skipper, Howard E. Cancer Chemotherapy, Vol. 10: Some Thoughts Regarding the Modes of Action of Drugs on Cells & on Application of Available Pharmacokinetic Data (Anticancer Drugs) LC 78-24299. (Illus.). 132p. (Orig.). 1980. pap. 14.25 (ISBN 0-8357-0557-9, SS-00140, Pub. by Southern Res Inst). Univ Microfilms.

CANCER–DIAGNOSIS

Critser, James R., Jr. Cancer: Diagnosis & Therapy. (Ser. 10CDT - 80). 1981. 60.00 (ISBN 0-914428-77-2). Lexington Data.

Delellis. Diagnostic Immunohistochemistry of Tumor Markers. 1981. write for info. Masson Pub.

Sherbet, G. V., ed. Phenomenon of Control of Growth in Neoplastic & Differentiative Systems. (Illus.). xii, 184p. 1981. 58.75 (ISBN 3-8055-2305-X). S Karger.

Van Nagell, John R., Jr. & Barber, Hugh R., eds. Modern Concepts of Gynecological Oncology. 350p. 1981. text ed. 30.00 (ISBN 0-88416-268-0). PSG Pub.

Wolf, P., ed. Tumor Associated Markers: The Importance of Identification in Clinical Medicine. LC 79-87540. (Illus.). 208p. 1979. 25.50 (ISBN 0-89352-065-9). Masson Pub.

CANCER–PERSONAL NARRATIVES

see Cancer Patients–Personal Narratives

CANCER–PREVENTION

Heyden, Siegfried & Pittillo, Elen S. Sensible Talk About Cancer: A Physician's Program for Prevention. 128p. (Orig.). 1981. pap. 3.95 (ISBN 0-8326-2247-8, 7440). Delair.

Murphy, Gerald D., ed. Cancer: Signals & Safeguards. (Illus.). 364p. 1981. text ed. 27.50 (ISBN 0-88416-229-X). PSG Pub.

Newbold, H. L. Vitamin C Against Cancer. LC 79-5301. (Illus.). 384p. 1981. pap. 7.95 (ISBN 0-8128-6098-5). Stein & Day.

Shaw, Charles R., ed. Prevention of Occupational Cancer. 256p. 1981. 72.95 (ISBN 0-8493-5625-3). CRC Pr.

CANCER–PSYCHOLOGICAL ASPECTS

Koocher, Gerald P. & O'Malley, John E. The Damocles Syndrome: Psychosocial Consequences of Surviving Childhood Cancer. 1981. 15.95 (ISBN 0-07-035340-9). McGraw.

CANCER–RADIOTHERAPY

George. Modern Interstitial & Intracavitary Radiation Cancer Management, Vol. 6. (Cancer Management Ser.). 1981. write for info. Masson Pub.

CANCER–RESEARCH

see Cancer Research

CANCER CELLS

McKinnell, R. G., ed. Differentiation & Neoplasia. (Results & Problems in Cell Differentiation: Vol. 11). (Illus.). 350p. 1980. 76.20 (ISBN 0-387-10177-2). Springer-Verlag.

Skipper, Howard E. Cancer Chemotherapy, Vol. 10: Some Thoughts Regarding the Modes of Action of Drugs on Cells & on Application of Available Pharmacokinetic Data (Anticancer Drugs) LC 78-24299. (Illus.). 132p. (Orig.). 1980. pap. 14.25 (ISBN 0-8357-0557-9, SS-00140, Pub. by Southern Res Inst). Univ Microfilms.

Takahashi, Masayoshi. Color Atlas of Cancer Cytology. 2nd ed. LC 80-85297. (Illus.). 550p. 1981. 125.00 (ISBN 0-89640-050-6). Igaku-Shoin.

CANCER NURSING

Wang, Rosemary Y. & Kelley, Ann M. Self-Assessment of Current Knowledge in Oncology Nursing. 1979. spiral bdg. 10.50 (ISBN 0-87488-236-2). Med Exam.

CANCER PATIENTS–PERSONAL NARRATIVES

Graham, Jory. In the Company of Others. LC 78-22252. 288p. 1981. 10.95 (ISBN 0-15-144642-3). HarBraceJ.

Greenfield, Natalee. First Do No Harm. 176p. 1981. pap. 1.95 (ISBN 0-448-17227-5, Tempo). G&D.

Keatinge, Margaret C. Fighting Back: A Manual for Survival with Cancer. LC 79-67759. 146p. 1980. 8.95 (ISBN 0-533-04480-4). Vantage.

Lawson, Jill, tr. Gueri Du Cancer. (French Bks.). (Fr.). 1979. 1.85 (ISBN 0-686-28820-3). Life Pubs Intl.

--Sanado De Cancer. (Spanish Bks.). 1979. 1.40 (ISBN 0-8297-0532-5). Life Pubs Intl.

CANCER RESEARCH

Burchenal, Joseph & Oettgen, Herbert. Cancer: Achievements, Challenges, & Prospects for the 1980's, Vol. 1. 1981. write for info. (ISBN 0-8089-1351-4). Grune.

Burchenal, Joseph, ed. Cancer: Achievements, Challenges, & Prospects for the 1980's, Vol. 2. Oettgen, Herbert. 1981. write for info. Grune.

Goodfield, June. An Imagined World: A Story of Scientific Discovery. LC 79-1664. (Illus.). 288p. 1981. 12.95 (ISBN 0-06-011641-2, HarpT). Har-Row.

Hoogstraten, Barth, ed. Cancer Research: Impact of the Cooperative Groups. LC 80-82668. 480p. 1980. 44.50 (ISBN 0-89352-092-6). Masson Pub.

Moss, Ralph W. The Cancer Syndrome. LC 79-2300. 320p. 1981. pap. 7.95 (ISBN 0-394-17896-3, BC). Grove.

Weinhouse, Sidney & Klein, George, eds. Advances in Cancer Research, Vol. 34. (Serial Publication Ser.). 1981. write for info. (ISBN 0-12-006634-3). Acad Pr.

CANDLEMAKING

Guy, Gary V. Easy to Make Candles. (Illus.). 1980. pap. 2.00 (ISBN 0-486-23881-4). Dover.

CANIDAE

Nowak, Ronald M. North American Quarternary Canis. Wiley, E. O., ed. (U of KS Museum of Nat. Hist. Monograph: No. 6). (Illus.). 154p. 1979. pap. 10.00 (ISBN 0-89338-007-5). U of KS Mus Nat Hist.

CANNING AND PRESERVING

Hersom, A. C. & Hulland, E. D. Canned Foods. 1981. text ed. 35.00 (ISBN 0-8206-0288-4). Chem Pub.

Seranne, Ann. The Home Canning & Preserving Book. 1975. pap. 4.95 (ISBN 0-06-463424-8, EH). Har-Row.

Sunset Editors. Canning, Freezing & Drying. 2nd ed. LC 80-53480. (Illus.). 128p. 1981. pap. 4.95 (ISBN 0-376-02213-2, Sunset Books). Sunset-Lane.

Turgeon, Charlotte. The Saturday Evening Post Small-Batch Canning & Freezing Cookbook. LC 78-53040. (Illus.). 1978. 8.95 (ISBN 0-89387-020-X); pap. 4.95 (ISBN 0-89387-020-X). Sat Eve Post.

U. S. Dept. of Agriculture. Home Canning of Fruits & Vegetables. (Illus.). 31p. Repr. pap. 2.50. Shorey.

CANOES AND CANOEING

Angier, Bradford & Taylor, Zack. Introduction to Canoeing. (Illus.). 192p. (Orig.). 1981. pap. 8.95 (ISBN 0-8117-2010-1). Stackpole.

Aquadro, Charles, et al. Canoeing the Brandywine: A Naturalist's Guide. 1980. 2.25x. Brandywine Conserv.

Canoe Trails of Northern Wisconsin. (Illus.). 64p. (Orig.). 1981. pap. 6.95 (ISBN 0-915024-25-X). Tamarack Edns.

Deschner, Whit. Does the Wet Suit You? The Confessions of a Kayak Bum. LC 80-70510. (Illus.). 96p. 1981. pap. 6.45 (ISBN 0-9605388-0-1). Tern Pr.

Dowd, John. Sea Kayaking: A Manual for Long-Distance Touring. (Illus.). 300p. 1981. 10.00 (ISBN 0-295-95807-3). U of Wash Pr.

Drabik, Harry. The Spirit of Canoe Camping. (Illus.). 126p. 1981. pap. 5.95 (ISBN 0-931714-11-7). Nodin Pr.

Gilpatrick, Gil. Building a Strip Canoe: Easy Step-by-Step Instructions & Patterns for 5 Canoe Models. (Illus.). 96p. (Orig.). 1979. pap. 8.95 (ISBN 0-89933-000-2). DeLorme Pub.

--The Canoe Guide's Handbook: Planning a Trip for 2 to 20 People. (Illus., Orig.). 1981. pap. price not set (ISBN 0-89933-011-8). DeLorme Pub.

--The Canoe Guide's Handbook: Planning a Trip for 2 to 20 People. (Illus., Orig.). 1981. pap. 7.95 (ISBN 0-89933-011-8). DeLorme Pub.

Harrison, Dave. Sports Illustrated Canoeing. LC 80-8687. (Illus.). 192p. 1981. 8.95 (ISBN 0-06-014853-5, HarpT); pap. 5.95 (ISBN 0-06-090874-2, CN874, HarpT). Har-Row.

Harrison, David & Harrison, Judy. Canoe Tripping with Kids. (Illus.). 144p. (Orig.). 1981. pap. 9.95 (ISBN 0-8289-0426-X). Greene.

Hauser, Verne. River Camping: Touring by Canoe, Raft, Dory, & Kayak. (A Soltice Press Bk.). (Illus.). 1981. pap. 9.95 (ISBN 0-8037-7256-4). Dial.

Jacobson, Clifford. Wilderness Canpeina & Campina. (Illus.). 1977. 13.95 (ISBN 0-87690-228-X); pap. 6.95 (ISBN 0-87690-229-8). Dutton.

Mason, Bill. Path of the Paddle: An Illustrated Guide to the Art of Canoeing. 192p. 1980. 24.95 (ISBN 0-442-29630-4). Van Nos Reinhold.

Urban, John & Williams, Walley. AMC White Water Handbook for Canoe & Kayak. (Illus.). 200p. 1981. pap. 4.95 (ISBN 0-910146-28-4). Appalach Mtn.

CANON LAW

see also Ecclesiastical Courts; Ecclesiastical Law

also special legal headings with Canon Law added in parentheses, e.g. Marriage (Canon Law)
Kuttner, Stephan. Medieval Councils, Decretals & Collections of Canon Law: Selected Essays. 338p. 1980. 75.00x (ISBN 0-86078-071-6, Pub. by Variorum England). State Mutual Bk.

CANONS, FUGUES, ETC.
see also Glees, Catches, Rounds, etc.
Agapius, et al. The Rudder. Orthodox Christian Educational Society & Makrakis, Apostolos, eds. Cummings, Denver, tr. from Hellenic. Orig. Title: Pedalion. 1097p. 1957. 15.00x (ISBN 0-938366-00-9). Orthodox Chr.

CANS
see Containers

CANTEENS (RECREATION CENTERS)
see Recreation Centers

CANVAS EMBROIDERY
Witt, Susan. Susan Witt's Classics for Needlepoint. LC 80-84410. (Illus.). 160p. 1981. 17.95 (ISBN 0-8487-0525-4). Oxmoor Hse.

CANVAS EMBROIDERY-PATTERNS
Nicoletti, Sally. Japanese Motifs for Needlepoint. LC 80-22650. (Illus.). 136p. 1981. 14.95 (ISBN 0-688-00163-7). Morrow.
Zimikes, Martha R. Iron-on Transfers from a Treasury of Needlework Designs: Ready-to-Use Patterns for Needlepoint & Embroidery. 96p. 1981. pap. 9.95 (ISBN 0-442-23119-9). Van Nos Reinhold.

CANVAS WORK (NEEDLEPOINT)
see Canvas Embroidery

CANYONS
Cordell, Linda S., ed. Tijeras Canyon: Analyses of the Past. (Illus.). 232p. 1980. 19.95 (ISBN 0-8263-0553-9, Pub. by Maxwell Mus Anthropology); pap. 9.95 (ISBN 0-8263-0565-2). U of NM Pr.

CAOUTCHOUC
see Rubber

CAPE COD
Sargent, Bill. Shallow Waters: A Year of Cape Cod's Pleasant Bay. (Illus.). 144p. 1981. 17.95 (ISBN 0-395-29481-9). HM.
Taber, Gladys. Still Cove Journal. Colby, Constance T., intro. by. LC 80-8220. (Illus.). 192p. 1981. 10.95 (ISBN 0-06-014227-8, HarpT). Har-Row.

CAPE COD-DESCRIPTION AND TRAVEL
Finch, Robert. Common Ground: A Naturalist's Cape Cod. (Illus.). 1981. 12.50 (ISBN 0-87923-383-4); ltd. ed. 40.00 (ISBN 0-87923-384-2). Godine.

CAPE COD-HISTORY
Kaye, Glen. Cape Cod: The Story Behind the Scenery. DenDooven, Gweneth R., ed. LC 80-81370. (Illus.). 1981. 7.95 (ISBN 0-916122-74-3); pap. 3.00 (ISBN 0-916122-73-5). K C Pubns.

CAPE OF GOOD HOPE-HISTORY
Scholtz, P. L., et al. Race Relations at the Cape of Good Hope, Sixteen Fifty-Two to Seventeen Ninety-Five: A Bibliography. (Reference Bks.). 1981. lib. bdg. 27.50 (ISBN 0-8161-8500-X). G K Hall.

CAPE TOWN
Western, John. Outcast Capetown. (Illus.). 352p. 1981. 20.00 (ISBN 0-8166-1025-8). U of Minn Pr.

CAPITAL
see also Banks and Banking; Capitalism; Liquidity (Economics); Interest and Usury; Investments; Monopolies; Profit; Saving and Investment; Wealth
Fetter, Frank A. Capital, Interest, & Rent: Essays in the Theory of Distribution. Rothbard, Murray N., ed. & intro. by. 1977. write for info. NYU Pr.
Lachmann, Ludwig M. Capital, Expectations, & the Market Process: Essays on the Theory of the Market Economy. Grinder, Walter E., ed. & intro. by. 1977. write for info. NYU Pr.

CAPITAL-TAXATION
see Capital Levy

CAPITAL AND LABOR
see Industrial Relations

CAPITAL EXPORTS
see Foreign Exchange; Investments, Foreign

CAPITAL FORMATION
see Saving and Investment

CAPITAL IMPORTS
see Foreign Exchange; Investments, Foreign

CAPITAL INVESTMENTS
see also Art as an Investment
Betancourt, Roger & Clague, Christopher. Capacity Utilization: A Theoretical & Empirical Analysis. LC 80-22410. (Illus.). 320p. Date not set. price not set (ISBN 0-521-23583-9). Cambridge U Pr.
Hull, J. C. The Evaluation of Risk in Business Investment. LC 80-40136. (Illus.). 192p. 1980. 27.00 (ISBN 0-08-024075-5); pap. 15.00 (ISBN 0-08-024074-7). Pergamon.

CAPITAL LEVY
see also Property Tax
Analysis of Capital Cost Recovery. (Statement of Tax Policy Ser.: No. 7). 1980. pap. 3.50. Am Inst CPA.

CAPITAL OUTPUT RATES
see Cost Effectiveness

CAPITAL PUNISHMENT
Jackson, Bruce & Christian, Diane. Death Row. LC 79-53752. (Illus.). 312p. 1981. pap. 6.95 (ISBN 0-8070-3203-4). Beacon Pr.

CAPITALISM
see also Capital; Christianity and Economics; Entrepreneur; Technocracy
Campbell, Mike. Capitalism in the UK: A Marxist Perspective. 216p. 1981. 28.00x (ISBN 0-7099-0089-9, Pub. by Croom Helm LTD England). Biblio Dist.
Corrigan, Philip. Capitalism, State Formation & Marx Theory. 258p. 1980. 9.95 (ISBN 0-7043-3311-2, Pub. by Quartet England). Horizon.
Hadden, Tom. Company Law & Capitalism. 2nd ed. (Law in Context Ser.). 1977. 25.00x (ISBN 0-297-77334-8, Pub. by Weidenfeld & Nicolson). Rothman.
--Company Law & Capitalism. 2nd ed. (Law in Context Ser.). 1977. 25.00x (ISBN 0-297-77334-8, Pub. by Weidenfeld & Nicolson England). Rothman.
Hallam, Arthur F. Christian Capitalism. 182p. (Orig.). 1981. pap. 14.95 (ISBN 0-938770-00-4). Capitalist Pr OH.
Hilferding, Rudolf. Finance Capital: A Study of the Latest Phase of Capitalist Development. Bottomore, Tom, tr. from Ger. 500p. 1981. 60.00 (ISBN 0-7100-0618-7). Routledge & Kegan.
Katsaros, Thomas & Teluk, John. Capitalism: A Cooperative Venture. LC 80-8163. 161p. 1981. lib. bdg. 17.50 (ISBN 0-8191-1484-7); pap. text ed. 8.50 (ISBN 0-8191-1485-5). U Pr of Amer.
Lefebvre, Henri. The Survival of Capitalism. (Allison & Busby Motive Ser.). 140p. 1981. pap. 7.95 (ISBN 0-8052-8076-6, Pub. by Allison & Busby England). Schocken.
Lefever, Ernest, ed. Will Capitalism Survive? A Challenge by Paul Johnson with Twelve Responses. 79p. 1979. pap. 3.00 (ISBN 0-89633-026-5). Ethics & Public Policy.
Lekachman, Robert. Capitalism for Beginners. Van Loon, Bron, tr. (Pantheon Documentary Comic Books). 1981. 8.95 (ISBN 0-394-51027-5); pap. 2.95 (ISBN 0-394-73863-2). Pantheon.
Novak, Michael. American Vision: Essay on the Future of Democratic Capitalism. 1978. pap. 4.25 (ISBN 0-8447-3324-5). Am Enterprise.
Novak, Michael, ed. Capitalism &Socialism: A Theological Inquiry. 1979. 12.25 (ISBN 0-8447-2153-0); pap. 6.25 (ISBN 0-8447-2154-9). Am Enterprise.
--Denigration of Capitalism. 1979. pap. 4.25 (ISBN 0-8447-3364-4). Am Enterprise.
Schweickart, David. Capitalism or Worker Control: An Ethical & Economic Appraisal. 266p. 1980. 22.95 (ISBN 0-03-056724-6). Praeger.
Sethi, S. Prakash & Swanson, Carl L. Private Enterprise & Public Purpose. (Management & Administration Ser.). 480p. 1981. pap. text ed. 12.95 (ISBN 0-471-07697-X). Wiley.
Smith, Joan. Social Issues & Problems: The Contradictions of Capitalism. (Sociology Ser.). 416p. 1981. pap. text ed. 11.95 (ISBN 0-87626-813-0). Winthrop.
Warren, Bill. Imperialism: Pioneer of Capitalism. 296p. 1981. 19.50x (ISBN 0-8052-7089-2, Pub. by NLB England); pap. 8.50 (ISBN 0-8052-7088-4). Schocken.

CAPITALIZATION (FINANCE)
see Corporations-Finance; Securities; Valuation

CAPTAINS OF SHIPS
see Shipmasters

CARBINES
see Rifles

CARBOHYDRATE METABOLISM
see also Phosphorylation
Candy, David S. Biological Functions of Carbohydrates. LC 80-18668. (Tertiary Level Biology Ser.). 197p. 1980. 34.95 (ISBN 0-470-27038-1). Halsted Pr.
Cobelli, E. & Bergman, R. N. Carbohydrate Metabolism: Quantitative Physiology & Mathematical Modelling. 432p. 1981. 77.00 (ISBN 0-471-27912-9, Pub. by Wiley Interscience). Wiley.

CARBOHYDRATES
see also Low Carbohydrate Diet
also names of compounds belonging to this group, e.g. Cellulose, Dextrose
Carbohydrates in Human Nutrition. (Food & Nutrition Paper Ser.: No. 15). 82p. 1980. pap. 6.00 (ISBN 92-5-100903-1, F2040, FAO). Unipub.
Devon, T. K. & Scott, A. I. Handbook of Naturally Occurring Compounds, 2 vols. Incl. Vol. 1. Acetogenins, Shikimates & Carbohydrates. 1975. 51.50 (ISBN 0-12-213601-2); Vol. 2. Terpenes. 1972. 42.00 (ISBN 0-12-213602-0). Acad Pr.
Netzer, Corinne T. Brand Name Carbohydrate Gram Counter. (Orig.). 1981. pap. 2.75 (ISBN 0-440-10658-3). Dell.
Tipson, R. Stuart & Horton, Derek, eds. Advances in Carbohydrate Chemistry & Biochemistry, Vol. 39. (Serial Publication Ser.). write for info. Acad Pr.

CARBOHYDRATES IN THE BODY
see also Carbohydrate Metabolism
Candy, David S. Biological Functions of Carbohydrates. LC 80-18668. (Tertiary Level Biology Ser.). 197p. 1980. 34.95 (ISBN 0-470-27038-1). Halsted Pr.

CARBON
see also Coal; Diamonds
Perrich, Jerry R., ed. Congressional Staff Directory, Ltd. 272p. 1981. 69.95 (ISBN 0-8493-5693-8). CRC Pr.

CARBON, ACTIVATED
Rice, Rip G. Biological Activated Carbon for Drinking Water. 1981. text ed. 69.90 2 vol. set (ISBN 0-250-40429-X); text ed. 39.95 vol. 1 (ISBN 0-250-40427-3); text ed. 39.95 vol. 2 (ISBN 0-250-40428-1). Ann Arbor Science.

CARBON COMPOUNDS
Mori, K., et al. Synthetic Chemistry of Insect Phermones & Juvenile Hormones. (Recent Developments in the Chemistry of Natural Carbon Compounds: Vol. 9). (Illus.). 420p. 1979. 40.00x (ISBN 963-05-1632-2). Intl Pubns Serv.

CARBON DIOXIDE
Kellogg, William W. & Schware, Robert. Climate Change & Society: Consequences of Increasing Atmospheric Carbon Dioxide. (Special Study Ser.). 170p. (Orig.). 1981. lib. bdg. 15.00x (ISBN 0-86531-179-X); pap. 8.00x (ISBN 0-86531-180-3). Westview.

CARBON MONOXIDE
Ford, Peter, ed. Catalytic Activation of Carbon Monoxide. (ACS Symposium Ser.: No. 152). 1981. price not set (ISBN 0-8412-0620-1). Am Chemical.

CARBONATED BEVERAGES
see Beverages

CARBONIC ACID
see Carbon Dioxide

CARBONIC OXIDE
see Carbon Monoxide

CARBONIFEROUS PERIOD
see Geology, Stratigraphic-Carboniferous

CARBURETORS
Brown's Book of Carburetors. 154p. 1980. 9.95. Madison Pub.
Dennis, Brad & Rutan, Al. Vaporizing Carburetors: One Hundred Miles per Gallon--the Real Facts. (Illus.). 150p. (Orig.). 1981. pap. 14.95 (ISBN 0-936222-06-9). Rutan Pub.
Fifty-Two Hundred Holley Carburetor Handbook. (Orig.). 1981. pap. 3.95 (ISBN 0-89586-050-3). H P Bks.
Urich, Mike. Forty-One Fifty Holley Carburetor Handbook. (Orig.). 1980. pap. 3.95 (ISBN 0-89586-047-3). H P Bks.
--Twenty-Three Hundred Holley Carburetor Handbook. (Orig.). 1981. pap. 3.95 (ISBN 0-89586-048-1). H P Bks.

CARCINOGENESIS
Borek, Carmia & Williams, Gary M., eds. Differentiation & Carcinogenesis in Liver Cell Cultures. new ed. LC 80-20918. (Vol. 349). 429p. 1980. 83.00 (ISBN 0-89766-087-0). NY Acad Sci.
McKinnell, R. G., ed. Differentiation & Neoplasia. (Results & Problems in Cell Differentiation: Vol. 11). (Illus.). 350p. 1980. 76.20 (ISBN 0-387-10177-2). Springer-Verlag.
Mayneord, W. V. & Clark, R. H. Carcinogenesis & Radiation Risk: A Biomathematical Reconnaissance. 1980. 35.00x (Pub. by Brit Inst Radiology England). State Mutual Bk.
Pullman, Bernard, et al, eds. Carcinogenesis: Fundamental Mechanisms & Environmental Effects. (Jerusalem Symposium: No. 13). 560p. PLB 63.00 (ISBN 90-277-1171-2, Pub. by D. Reidel). Kluwer Boston.

CARCINOMA
see Cancer; Tumors

CARD GAMES
see Cards

CARD SYSTEM IN BUSINESS
see Files and Filing (Documents)

CARD TRICKS
Hugard, Jean & Braue, Frederick. Royal Road to Card Magic. 1949. 9.50 (ISBN 0-571-11399-0, Pub. by Faber & Faber). Merrimack Bk Serv.

CARDIAC DISEASES
see Heart-Diseases

CARDIAC FUNCTION TESTS
see Heart Function Tests

CARDIAC PACING
see Pacemaker, Artificial (Heart)

CARDIAC PATIENTS
see Cardiacs

CARDIAC RESUSCITATION
Advice About First Aid, High Blood Pressure, Heart Attack. (Home Adviser Ser.). 80p. (Orig.). 1981. pap. 1.95 (ISBN 0-8326-2404-7, 7054). Delair.

CARDIACS
see also Coronary Care Units
Amundsen, Lou. Cardiac Rehabilitation. (Clinics in Physical Therapy Ser.). (Illus.). 224p. 1981. lib. bdg. 18.00 (ISBN 0-443-08147-6). Churchill.
Appels, A. & Falger, P., eds. The Role of Psychosocial Factors in the Pathogenesis of Coronary Heart Disease, 1980. (Journal: Psychotherapy & Psychosomatics: Vol. 34, No. 2-3). (Illus.). iv, 160p. 1981. pap. price not set (ISBN 3-8055-2286-X). S Karger.
Cohen, Lawrence S., et al. Physical Conditioning & Cardiovascular Rehabilitation. 344p. 1981. 25.00 (ISBN 0-471-08713-0, Pub. by Wiley-Med). Wiley.
Cohn & Madrid. Coming Back: A Guide to Recovering from Heart Attack & Living Confidently. 10.95 (ISBN 0-201-04562-1). A-W.
Gardocki, Gloria J. & Pokras, Robert. Utilization of Short-Stay Hospitals by Persons with Heart Disease & Malignant Neoplasms. Shipp, Audrey, ed. (Ser. Thirteen: No. 52). 50p. 1981. pap. 1.75 (ISBN 0-8406-0214-6). Natl Ctr Health Stats.
Huszar, Robert S. Emergency Cardiac Care. 2nd ed. (Illus.). 350p. 1981. pap. text ed. 14.95 (ISBN 0-87619-863-9). R J Brady.
Seymour, Roger J. Heart Attack Survival Manual. 144p. 1981. 11.95 (ISBN 0-13-385740-9, Spec); pap. 5.95 (ISBN 0-13-385732-8). P-H.

CARDINAL VIRTUES
see Virtue and Virtues

CARDINALS
Zekowski, Arlene & Berne, Stanley. Cardinals & Saints. LC 58-11713. 1958. 75.00 (ISBN 0-913844-10-1). Am Canadian.

CARDIOGRAPHY
Nanda, Navin. Two Dimensional Echocardiography. 1981. write for info. (ISBN 0-87993-134-5). Futura Pub.

CARDIOLOGY
see also Heart-Diseases; Pediatric Cardiology
Abbasi, Abdul S. Echocardiographic Interpretation. (Illus.). 448p. 1981. text ed. price not set (ISBN 0-398-04153-9). C C Thomas.
Berman, Danieal S. & Mason, Dean T. Clinical Nuclear Cardiology. (Clinical Cardiology Monographs Ser.). 1981. write for info. (ISBN 0-8089-1356-5). Grune.
Chiu, Ray C. Myocardial Protection in Regional & Global Ischemia, Vol. 1. (Annual Research Reviews). 177p. 1981. 26.00 (ISBN 0-88831-097-8). Eden Med Res.
Donoso, Ephraim, ed. Advances & Controversies in Cardiology. (Current Cardiovascular Topics: Vol. VI). (Illus.). 350p. 1981. text ed. 35.00 (ISBN 0-86577-024-7). Thieme-Stratton.
Gillette, Paul C., et al, eds. Pediatric Cardiac Dysrhythmias. (Clinical Cardiology Monographs). 1981. price not set (ISBN 0-8089-1332-8). Grune.
Goldberger, Emanuel. A Textbook of Clinical Cardiology. (Illus.). 934p. 1981. text ed. 35.00 (ISBN 0-8016-1864-9). Mosby.
Hamer, John & Rowlands, Derek J. Recent Advances in Cardiology, Vol. 8. (Recent Advances Ser.). (Illus.). 360p. 1980. lib. bdg. 50.00 (ISBN 0-443-01995-9). Churchill.
Moller, James H. & Neal, William A. Heart Disease in Infancy. 522p. 1980. 36.50x (ISBN 0-8385-3671-9). ACC.
Reddy, P. S., et al, eds. Pericardial Disease. 1981. text ed. price not set (ISBN 0-89004-586-0). Raven.
Roberts, William C., et al. Cardiology: 81. (Illus.). 400p. 1981. text ed. 35.00 (ISBN 0-914316-22-2). Yorke Med.
Rowlands & Humern, eds. Recent Advances in Cardiology, No. 8. (R-A in Cardiology Ser.). (Illus.). 1981. text ed. price not set. Churchill.
Seal, Anna L. Cardiogenic Shock. (Myocardial Infarction Ser.). 100p. 1980. pap. 6.95x (ISBN 0-8385-1056-6). ACC.
Stocker, F. & Weber, J. W., eds. Neuere Aspekte Kinderkardiologie. (Paediatrische Fortbildungskurse Fuer Die Praxis: Vol. 51). (Illus.). vi, 130p. 1980. pap. 41.50 (ISBN 3-8055-0926-X). S Karger.
Vogel, J. H., ed. Current Concepts in Clinical Cardiology. (Advances in Cardiology Ser.: Vol. 27). (Illus.). viii, 360p. 1980. 118.75 (ISBN 3-8055-0098-X). S Karger.

CARDIOVASCULAR AGENTS
see also Vasodilators
Tardos,., et al, eds. Pharmacological Control of Heart & Circulation: Proceedings of the Third Congress of the Hungarian Pharmacological Society, Budapest, 1979. LC 80-41281. (Advances in Pharmacological Research & Practice Ser.: Vol. I). 445p. 1981. 84.00 (ISBN 0-08-026386-0). Pergamon.

CARDIOVASCULAR DISEASE NURSING
see also Coronary Care Units
Karch, Amy M. Cardiac Care: A Guide for Patient Education. (The Patient Education Series). 1981. pap. 11.50 (ISBN 0-8385-1041-8). ACC.

CARDIOVASCULAR DRUGS
see Cardiovascular Agents

CARDIOVASCULAR SYSTEM
see also Blood-Circulation; Blood-Vessels; Heart
Abramson, David I. & Casey, M. Beth. Self-Assessment of Current Knowledge in Peripheral Vascular Disorders. 1980. pap. 18.00 (ISBN 0-87488-291-5). Med Exam.
Berne, Robert M. & Levy, Matthew N. Cardiovascular Physiolgy. 4th ed. (Illus.). 304p. 1981. pap. text ed. 16.50 (ISBN 0-8016-0655-1). Mosby.
Critser, James R., Jr. Clinical Assays. (Ser. 10CA 80). 1981. 80.00 (ISBN 0-914428-78-0). Lexington Data.
Cupps, Thomas R. & Fauci, Anthony S. The Vasculitides. 1981. pap. price not set. Saunders.
Haimovici, Henry. Vascular Emergencies. 1981. 34.50 (ISBN 0-686-69607-7). ACC.
Heller, Lois J. & Mohrman, David E. Cardiovascular Physiology. Mixter, Richard W., ed. (Illus.). 176p. 1980. pap. text ed. 9.95 (ISBN 0-07-027973-X). McGraw.
Honig, Carl R. Modern Cardiovascular Physiology. 1981. text ed. write for info. (ISBN 0-316-37214-5); pap. text ed. write for info (ISBN 0-316-37215-3). Little.

Kovach, A. G. B., et al, eds. Cardiovascular Physiology, Microcirculation & Capillary Exchange: Proceedings of the 28th International Congress of Physiological Sciences, Budapest, 1980. LC 80-41873. (Advances in Physiological Sciences: Vol. 7). (Illus.). 400p. 1981. 50.00 (ISBN 0-08-026819-6). Pergamon.

--Cardiovascular Physiology, Heart, Peripheral Circulation & Methodology: Proceedings of the 28th International Congress of Physiological Sciences, Budapest, Hungary, 1980. LC 80-41875. (Advances in Physiological Sciences). (Illus.). 400p. 1981. 50.00 (ISBN 0-08-026820-X). Pergamon.

--Cardiovascular Physiology-Neural Control Mechanisms: Proceesings of the 28th International Congress of Physiological Sciences, Budapest, 1980. LC 80-41927. (Advances in Physiological Sciences: Vol. 9). (Illus.). 400p. 1981. 50.00 (ISBN 0-08-026821-8). Pergamon.

Rosenquist, Glenn C. & Bergsma, Daniel, eds. Morphogenesis & Malinformation of the Cardiovascular System. LC 78-14527. (Alan R. Liss Ser.: Vol. 14, No. 7). 1978. 46.00 (ISBN 0-8451-1023-3). March of Dimes.

Wells, Sara J., et al. Manual of Cardiovascular Assessment. 1981. pap. text ed. 14.95 (ISBN 0-8359-4233-3). Reston.

CARDIOVASCULAR SYSTEM–DISEASES

see also Cardiovascular Disease Nursing

also specific diseases, e.g. Varix

Advances in Diagnosis & Therapy, Muenchen, November 1980. Congress on Microcirculation & Ischemic Vascular Diseases. Messmer, K. & Fagrell, B., eds. (Illus.). 240p. 1981. pap. 24.00 (ISBN 3-8055-2417-X). S Karger.

Davies, M. J. Pathology of Cardiac Valves. LC 80-40487. (Butterworths Postgraduate Pathology Ser.). 192p. 1980. text ed. 52.95 (ISBN 0-407-00179-4). Butterworths.

Mehta, Jawahar & Mehta, Paulette, eds. Platelets & Prostaglandins in Cardiovascular Disease. 300p. 1981. write for info. (ISBN 0-87993-089-6). Futura Pub.

CARDIOVASCULAR SYSTEM–SURGERY

James, Edwin C., et al. Thoracic and Cardiovascular Surgery Continuing Education Review. 1980. pap. 16.00 (ISBN 0-87488-439-X). Med Exam.

Strandness, D. E. & Thiele, Brian L. Selected Topics in Venous Disorders: Pathophysiology & Treatment. LC 80-69527. (Illus.). 1981. 29.50 (ISBN 0-87993-154-X). Futura Pub.

CARDS

see also Card Tricks

also names of card games, e.g. Cribbage, Contract Bridge

Bumppo, Natty. The Columbus Book of Euchre. (Illus.). 64p. 1981. pap. price not set (ISBN 0-9604894-2-8). Borf Bks.

CARDS, GREETING

see Greeting Cards

CARE OF SOULS

see Pastoral Counseling; Pastoral Theology

CAREER EDUCATION

see Vocational Education

CAREER WOMEN

see Women–Employment

CAREERS

see Professions; Vocational Guidance

CARGO AIRCRAFT

see Transport Planes

CARGO HANDLING

Code of Safe Practice for Bulk Cargoes. (Illus.). 137p. 1977. 15.25 (IMCO). Unipub.

Code of Safe Practice for Ships Carrying Timber Deck Cargoes. 31p. 1974. 7.00 (IMCO). Unipub.

IMCO-ILO Guidelinesfor Training in the Packing of Cargo in Freight Containers. (Illus.). 21p. 1978. 7.00 (IMCO). Unipub.

Institute of Civil Engineers, UK. Transport of Hazardous Materials. 160p. 1980. 39.00x (ISBN 0-7277-0058-8, Pub. by Telford England). State Mutual Bk.

International Maritime Dangerous Goods Code: Annex 1: Packing Recommendations, Glossary of Packagings, Illustrations of Packagings, 1977 Edition. (Illus.). 196p. 1977. 16.50 (IMCO). Unipub.

International Maritime Dangerous Goods Code Amendments 16-78. 1978. 38.50 (IMCO). Unipub.

International Maritime Dangerous Goods Code: Amendments 14-76 & 15-77, 4 vols. 800p. 1978. 55.00 (IMCO). Unipub.

International Maritime Dangerous Goods Code: Brochure. (Illus.). 4p. 1975. 4.25 (IMCO). Unipub.

Kemp, J. F. & Young, P. Notes on Cargo Work. 4th ed. (Kemp & Young Ser.). (Illus., Orig.). 1981. pap. text ed. 9.50x (ISBN 0-540-07332-6). Sheridan.

Keyes, Lucille S. Regulatory Reform in Air Cargo Transportation. 1980. pap. 4.25 (ISBN 0-8447-3371-7). Am Enterprise.

Recommendation Concerning Fire Safety Requirements for Cargo Ships. 25p. 1976. 7.00 (IMCO). Unipub.

Recommendations on the Safe Use of Pesticides in Ships. 14p. 1973. 5.50 (IMCO). Unipub.

CARGO PLANES

see Transport Planes

CARGO SHIPS

see also Tankers

Clark, Merrian E. Ford's Freighter Travel Guide: Published Semi-Annually, March & September. 57th ed. D'Ascenzo, Juliann & Wilson, Bonnie, eds. LC 54-3845. (Illus.). 140p. pap. 4.95 (ISBN 0-916486-57-5). Fords Travel.

CARIBBEAN AREA

Macpherson, John. Caribbean Lands. 4th ed. (Illus.). 192p. 1980. pap. text ed. 6.95x (ISBN 0-582-76565-X). Longman.

CARIBBEAN AREA–DESCRIPTION AND TRAVEL–GUIDE-BOOKS

Street, Donald M., Jr. Street's Cruising Guide to the Eastern Caribbean, Vol. 1. 1981. pap. 27.95 spiral bdg. (ISBN 0-393-03250-7). Norton.

Zellers, Margaret. Caribbean...the Inn Way. rev. ed. 240p. 1980. 4.95 (ISBN 0-937334-00-6). Berkshire Traveller.

CARIBBEAN AREA–ECONOMIC CONDITIONS

Delson, Roberta M. Readings in Caribbean History & Economics: An Introduction to the Region. 300p. 1981. write for info. (ISBN 0-677-05280-4). Gordon.

CARIBBEAN AREA–HISTORY

Claypole, William & Robottom, John. Caribbean Story: Foundations, Bk. 1. (Longman Caribbean Ser.). (Illus.). 198p. (Orig.). 1981. pap. text ed. 9.95 (ISBN 0-582-76534-X). Longman.

Delson, Roberta M. Readings in Caribbean History & Economics: An Introduction to the Region. 300p. 1981. write for info. (ISBN 0-677-05280-4). Gordon.

CARIBBEAN AREA–POPULATION

Cook, Sherburne F. & Borah, Woodrow. Essays in Population History, 3 vols. Incl. Vols. 1 & 2. Mexico & the Caribbean. 1971. 27.50x ea. Vol. 1 (ISBN 0-520-01764-1). Vol. 2 (ISBN 0-520-02272-6); Vol. 3. Mexico & California. 1979. 25.00x (ISBN 0-520-03560-7). U of Cal Pr.

CARIBBEAN AREA–SOCIAL CONDITIONS

Erskine, Noel L. Decolonizing Theology: A Caribbean Perspective. LC 80-21784. 160p. (Orig.). 1981. pap. 6.95 (ISBN 0-88344-087-3). Orbis Bks.

Wooding, Charles J. Evolving Culture: A Cross-Cultural Study of Surinam, West Africa & the Caribbean. LC 80-5612. 343p. 1981. lib. bdg. 21.75 (ISBN 0-8191-1377-8); pap. text ed. 12.00 (ISBN 0-8191-1378-6). U Pr of Amer.

CARIBBEAN COOKERY

see Cookery, Caribbean

CARIBBEAN LITERATURE–HISTORY AND CRITICISM

Barthold, Bonnie J. Black Time: Fiction of Africa, the Caribbean, & the United States. LC 80-24336. (Illus.). 224p. 1981. 17.50x (ISBN 0-300-02573-4). Yale U Pr.

CARICATURES AND CARTOONS

see also Cartoonists; Comic Books, Strips, Etc.; Moving-Picture Cartoons; Wit and Humor, Pictorial also American Wit and Humor, Pictorial; English Wit and Humor, Pictorial; and similar headings

Booth, George, et al, eds. Animals, Animals, Animals. LC 79-1653. (Illus.). 256p. 1981. pap. 8.95 (ISBN 0-06-090853-X, C*N 853, CN). Har-Row.

Cates, Ann. Guilt Trips. (Illus.). 100p. (Orig.). 1980. pap. 2.95 (ISBN 0-937768-00-6). Expressions TX.

Lenburg, Jeff. The Complete Encyclopedia of Animated Cartoon Series. (Illus.). 192p. 1981. 24.95 (ISBN 0-87000-495-6). Arlington Hse.

Peyton, Mike. Hurrican Zoe & Other Sailing. 96p. 1980. 9.00x (ISBN 0-245-53132-7, Pub. by Nautical England). State Mutual Bk.

Robinson, Jerry. World's Greatest Comics Quiz. 192p. (Orig.). 1981. pap. 1.50 (ISBN 0-448-14292-9, Tempo). G&D.

Schulz, Charles. Sing for Your Supper, Snoopy. 128p. 1981. pap. 1.75 (ISBN 0-449-24403-2, Crest). Fawcett.

Schulz, Charles M. Things I Learned After It As Too Late: (& Other Minor Truths) (Illus.). 1981. pap. 4.95 (ISBN 0-686-69128-8). HR&W.

Smythe. You're Something Else, Andy Capp. 128p. (Orig.). 1981. pap. 1.75 (ISBN 0-449-14401-1, GM). Fawcett.

Trudeau, G. B. He's Never Heard of You, Either. (Doonesbury Ser.). (Illus., Orig.). 1981. pap. 4.95 (ISBN 0-03-049196-7). HR&W.

CARICATURISTS

see Cartoonists

CARLYLE, JANE BAILLIE (WELSH) 1801-1866

Sanders, Charles R. & Fielding, Kenneth J., eds. The Collected Letters of Thomas & Jane Welsh Carlyle, Vols. 8-9. LC 71-101132. (Illus., Consolidated Index in Vol. 9). 1981. Vol. 8, 1835-1836. 30.00 (ISBN 0-8223-0433-3); Vol. 9, 1836-1837. 30.00 (ISBN 0-8223-0434-1); Set. 59.75 (ISBN 0-686-69104-0). Duke.

CARLYLE, THOMAS, 1795-1881

Sanders, Charles R. & Fielding, Kenneth J., eds. The Collected Letters of Thomas & Jane Welsh Carlyle, Vols. 8-9. LC 71-101132. (Illus., Consolidated Index in Vol. 9). 1981. Vol. 8, 1835-1836. 30.00 (ISBN 0-8223-0433-3); Vol. 9, 1836-1837. 30.00 (ISBN 0-8223-0434-1); Set. 59.75 (ISBN 0-686-69104-0). Duke.

CARMAN, WILLIAM BLISS, 1861-1929

Gundy, H. Pearson, ed. Letters of Bliss Carman. (Illus.). 500p. 1981. 55.00 (ISBN 0-7735-0364-1). McGill-Queens U Pr.

CARNIVAL

see Masks

CAROLS

Himnos De Gloria y Triunfo. (Spanish Bks.). 1977. 3.75 (ISBN 0-8297-0567-8). Life Pubs Intl.

Tillman, June, et al, eds. The Galliard Book of Carols. (Illus.). 248p. 1980. 30.00x (ISBN 0-389-20146-4). B&N.

CAROTINOIDS

Bauerfeind, Jack C., ed. Carotenoid As Colorants & Vitamin A Precursors: Technological & Nutritional Applications. LC 79-8850. (Food Science & Technology Ser.). 1981. write for info. (ISBN 0-12-082850-2). Acad Pr.

CARPENTERS

Krenov, James. James Krenov Worker in Wood. (Illus.). 128p. 1981. 24.95 (ISBN 0-442-26336-8). Van Nos Reinhold.

CARPENTRY

see also Cabinet-Work; Doors and Doorways; Floors; Roofs; Walls; Woodwork; Woodworking Machinery

Baker, Glenn E. & Miller, Rex. Carpentry Fundamentals. (Contemporary Construction Ser.). (Illus.). 512p. (gr. 10-12). 1981. 16.95 (ISBN 0-07-003361-7, G); tchrs. manual & key 1.50 (ISBN 0-07-003363-3); write for info wkbk. (ISBN 0-07-003362-5). McGraw.

Feirer & Hutchings. Carpentry Construction & Building. rev. ed. 1981. text ed. 24.60 (ISBN 0-87002-327-6). Bennett IL.

Feirer, John & Hutchings, Gilbert R. Carpentry & Building Constructions. rev. ed. (Illus.). 1981. 37.50 (ISBN 0-684-16981-9, ScribT). Scribner.

Leggatt, Alex. Carpentry for the Home. (Illus.). 144p. 1981. 22.50 (ISBN 0-7134-1886-9, Pub. by Batsford England). David & Charles.

Marshall, Mel. How to Choose & Use Lumber, Plywood, Panelboards, & Laminates. LC 79-4710. 1980. pap. 4.95 (ISBN 0-06-090724-X, CN 724, CN). Har-Row.

Oumet, Ronald P. Eighty Woodcraft Projects. 320p. 1980. 17.95 (ISBN 0-8246-0260-9). Jonathan David.

CARPETBAG RULE

see Reconstruction

CARPETS

see also Rugs; Weaving

Carpet Annual 1980: Year Book & Directory of the World's Carpet Industries & Trade. 45th ed. 372p. 1979. 42.50x (ISBN 0-8002-2745-X). Intl Pubns Serv.

CARRIAGES AND CARTS

see also Vehicles

Lockwood, Stan. Kaleidoscope of Char-a-Bancs & Coaches. (Illus.). 1980. 20.00x (ISBN 0-906116-02-3). Intl Pubns Serv.

Smith, D. J. Collecting & Restoring Horse-Drawn Vehicles. (Illus.). 192p. 1981. 39.95 (ISBN 0-85059-429-4). Aztex.

--Collecting & Restoring Horse-Drawn Vehicles. 120p. 1981. 39.95 (ISBN 0-85059-429-4). Aztex.

CARRIER PIGEONS

see Pigeons

CARROLL, LEWIS

see Dodgson, Charles Lutwidge, 1832-1898

CARS (AUTOMOBILES)

see Automobiles

CARTER, JIMMY, PRES. U. S., 1924-

Seminar on Energy Policy: The Carter Proposals. 1979. pap. 3.25 (ISBN 0-8447-3355-5). Am Enterprise.

CARTER FAMILY

Cash, June C. Among My Klediments. 160p. 1981. pap. 4.95 (ISBN 0-310-38171-1). Zondervan.

CARTIER, GEORGE ETIENNE, SIR, 1814-1873

Young, Brian. George-Etienne Cartier: Montreal Bourgeois. (Illus.). 200p. 1981. 23.95x (ISBN 0-7735-0370-6); pap. 10.95x (ISBN 0-7735-0371-4). McGill-Queens U Pr.

CARTOGRAPHY

see also Nautical Charts; Vegetation Mapping

Appel, Carl L. Provenzalische Lautlehre: Mit Einer Karte. LC 80-2165. (Provenzalische Chrestomathie Ser.). 1981. Repr. of 1918 ed. 30.00 (ISBN 0-404-19027-8). AMS Pr.

Freeman, Herbert & Pieroni, Goffredo G., eds. Map Data Processing. 1980. 26.00 (ISBN 0-12-267180-5). Acad Pr.

CARTOGRAPHY–HISTORY

Wilford, John N. The Mapmakers. LC 80-2716. (Illus.). 448p. 1981. 20.00 (ISBN 0-394-46194-0). Knopf.

CARTOONISTS

Adams, John P. & Marschall, Richard. Milton Caniff, Rembrandt of the Comic Strip. rev. ed. LC 80-70395. (Illus.). 64p. 1981. pap. 6.95x (ISBN 0-918348-04-8). Flying Buttress.

CARTOONS

see Caricatures and Cartoons

CARTRIDGES

Suydam, Charles R. U. S. Cartridges & Their Handguns. (Illus.). 333p. 1976. 15.95 (ISBN 0-917714-04-0); pap. 9.95 (ISBN 0-917714-07-5). Beinfeld Pub.

CARTS

see Carriages and Carts

CARTULARIES

see Archives

CARY, JOYCE, 1888-1957

Cook, Cornelia. Joyce Cary: Liberal Principles. (Barnes & Noble Critical Studies). 240p. 1981. 28.50x (ISBN 0-389-20201-0). B&N.

CASANOVA DE SEINGALT, GIACOMO GIROLAMO, 1725-1798

Dobree, Bonamy. Three Eighteenth Century Figures: Sarah Churchill, John Wesley, Giacomo Casanova. LC 80-19398. xi, 248p. 1981. Repr. of 1962 ed. lib. bdg. 25.00x (ISBN 0-313-22682-2, DOTF). Greenwood.

CASE WORK, SOCIAL

see Social Case Work

CASH, JOHNNY

Cash, June C. Among My Klediments. 160p. 1981. pap. 4.95 (ISBN 0-310-38171-1). Zondervan.

Smith, John L. Another Song to Sing: An Illustrated Discography of Johnny Cash. (Illus.). 1981. pap. 5.95 (ISBN 0-915608-06-5). Country Music Found.

CASH REGISTERS

Klimo, Kate, ed. My Cash Register Book. (Playboards Ser.). (Illus.). 12p. (ps-k). Date not set. boards 2.95 (ISBN 0-671-42527-7, Little Simon). S&S.

Odiorne, George S. The Change Resisters: How They Prevent Progress & What Managers Can Do About Them. (Illus.). 304p. 1981. 16.95 (ISBN 0-13-127902-5, Spec); pap. 7.95 (ISBN 0-13-127894-0). P-H.

CASSATT, MARY, 1845-1926

Getlein, Frank. Mary Cassatt: Paintings & Prints. LC 80-66523. (Illus.). 160p. 1980. 22.50 (ISBN 0-89659-181-6); pap. 14.95 (ISBN 0-89659-155-7). Abbeville Pr.

CASSAVA

Cassava Cultural Practices. 152p. 1980. pap. 10.00 (ISBN 0-88936-245-9, IDRC151, IDRC). Unipub.

CASSIRER, ERNST, 1874-1945

Cassirer, Ernst. Symbol, Myth & Culture: Essays & Lectures of Ernst Cassirer 1935-45. Verne, Donald P., ed. LC 78-9887. 368p. 1981. pap. 9.95x (ISBN 0-300-02666-8). Yale U Pr.

CASTAWAYS

see Survival (After Airplane Accidents, Shipwrecks, etc.)

CASTE–INDIA

Sarma, Jyotimoyee. Caste Dynamics Among the Bengali Hindus. 1980. 11.50x (ISBN 0-8364-0633-8, Pub. by Mukhopadhyay India). South Asia Bks.

CASTILE–HISTORY

Marquez-Sterling, Manuel. Fernan Gonzalez, First Count of Castile: The Man & the Legend. LC 80-15095. (Romance Monographs: No. 40). (Illus.). 160p. 1980. write for info. Romance.

CASTILIAN LANGUAGE

see Spanish Language

CASTING

see Founding; Plaster Casts; Plastics–Molding

CASTING (FISHING)

see Spin Fishing

CASTLES

see also Palaces;

also names of castles, e.g. Windsor Castle

Ditchfield, P. H. Vanishing Old Castles in England. (A Philosophy of History Library Book). (Illus.). 109p. 1981. 49.75 (ISBN 0-86650-003-0). Gloucester Art.

Fry, Plantagenet S. The David & Charles Book of Castles. LC 80-69352. (Illus.). 496p. 1981. 33.00 (ISBN 0-7153-7976-3). David & Charles.

CASTRO, FIDEL, 1927-

Halperin, Maurice. The Taming of Fidel Castro. 1981. 16.95 (ISBN 0-520-04184-4). U of Cal Pr.

CASUALTY INSURANCE

see Insurance, Casualty

CAT

see Cats

CAT, DOMESTIC

see Cats

CATABOLISM

see Metabolism

CATALOGING

see also Anglo-American Cataloging Rules; Bibliography; Classification–Books; Imprints (In Books); Library Science

Downing, Mildred H. Introduction to Cataloging & Classification. 5th ed. LC 80-20299. (Illus.). 240p. 1981. lib. bdg. 14.95x (ISBN 0-89950-017-X). McFarland & Co.

Formats Used in the Library Multimedia Union Catalog. LC 79-4055. 59p. 1979. 6.00 (ISBN 0-913578-19-3). Inglewood Ca.

INIS: Authority List for Corporate Entries & Report Number Prefixes. 472p. 1980. pap. 29.75 (ISBN 92-0-178280-2, IN6-R13, IAEA). Unipub.

INIS: Descriptive Cataloguing Rules. 72p. 1980. pap. 5.50 (ISBN 92-0-178180-6, IAEA). Unipub.

Slocum, Robert B. Sample Cataloguing Forms: Illustrations of Solutions to Problems of Description (with Particular Reference to Chapters 1-13 of the Anglo-American Cataloging Rules, Second Edition) 3rd ed. LC 80-21507. (Illus.). 121p. 1980. 11.00 (ISBN 0-8108-1364-5). Scarecrow.

CATALOGING OF AUDIO-VISUAL MATERIALS

see Cataloging of Non-Book Materials

CATALOGING OF NON-BOOK MATERIALS

see also cataloging of individual types of materials, e.g. Cataloging of Maps

Laertacher, David V. A Nonbook Cataloguing Sampler. 100p. 1975. pap. 5.00 (ISBN 0-912556-04-8). Hi Willow.

CATALOGS

see Library Catalogs;

also subdivision Catalogs under specific subjects, e.g. Engravings–Catalogs; Manuscripts–Catalogs
CATALOGS, BOOKSELLERS'
Leab, Katherine & Leab, Daniel, eds. American Book Prices Current, Vol. 86. 1981. 79.75 (ISBN 0-914022-11-3). Am Book Prices.
CATALOGS, COMMERCIAL
Pinkerton, Steve & Pinkerton, Betsy. The Great Book of Catalogs. 8.95 (ISBN 0-9602882-0-1). Green Hill.
CATALOGS, FILM
see Moving-Pictures–Catalogs
CATALOGS, LIBRARY
see Library Catalogs
CATALOGS, PUBLISHERS'
British Publishers' Catalog Annual: 1980. 1980. catalog collection 275.00 (ISBN 0-930466-33-0). Meckler Bks.
European Publishers' Catalog Annual: 1980. 80000p. 1980. catalog collection 410.00 (ISBN 0-930466-32-2). Meckler Bks.
German Books in Print, Nineteen Eighty to Eighty-One: Authors-Titles-Keywords, 4 vols. 10th ed. Set. 250.00 (ISBN 3-7657-0862-3, Dist by Gale Research Co.). K G Saur.
German Books in Print, Nineteen Eighty to Eighty-One: ISBN Register. 637p. 1980. 95.00 (ISBN 3-7657-0986-7, Dist. by Gale Research Co.). K G Saur.
German Books in Print, Nineteen Eighty to Eighty-One: Subject Guide, 3 vols. 3rd ed. 1980. Set. 240.00 (Dist. by Gale Research Co.). K G Saur.
Lingua Press. Lingua Press Collection Three Catalogue, Vol. 3. Gaburo, Kenneth, ed. (Illus.). 150p. 1981. softcover 8.50. Lingua Pr.
CATALOGS, STAR
see Stars–Catalogs
CATALOGS, SUBJECT
see also Automatic Indexing; Subject Headings
Subject Guide to Books in Print 1980-81, 2 vols. 5700p. 1980. Set. 79.50 (ISBN 0-8352-1308-0). Bowker.
Subject Guide to Large Print Book Catalog. LC 76-30595. 110p. 1976. 5.00 (ISBN 0-913578-15-0). Inglewood Ca.
CATALOGS, UNION
Formats Used in the Library Multimedia Union Catalog. LC 79-4055. 59p. 1979. 6.00 (ISBN 0-913578-19-3). Inglewood Ca.
Hoffman, Herbert H. WORKMAC: A Bibliographic Format for Works in Analytic On-Line Library Union Catalogs. 1980. pap. 5.00x (ISBN 0-89537-016-6). Headway Pubns.
CATALONIA
Lewis, Archibald R. The Development of Southern French & Catalan Society Seven Eighteen to Ten Fifty. LC 80-2019. 1981. Repr. of 1965 ed. 47.50 (ISBN 0-404-18575-4). AMS Pr.
CATALYSIS
see also Fluidization
Frankenburg, W. G., et al. Advances in Catalysis & Related Subjects, Vol. 29. Date not set. 45.00 (ISBN 0-12-007829-5). Acad Pr.
CATALYSTS
Business Communication Co. Catalysis, C-023: New Directions. 1981. 800.00 (ISBN 0-89336-271-9). BCC.
DECHEMA, Deutsche Gesellschaft Fuer Chemisches Apparatewesen E. V., ed. Characterization of Immobilized Biocatalysts. (DECHEMA Monographs: Vol. 84). 400p. (Orig.). 1979. pap. text ed. 46.00 (ISBN 3-527-10767-3). Verlag Chemie.
Schuit, G. G. & Prins, R., eds. Chemistry & Chemical Engineering of Catalytic Processes. (NATO-Advanced Study Institute Ser.). 660p. 1980. 75.00x (ISBN 9-0286-0730-7). Sijthoff & Noordhoff.
Thomas, J. M. & Lambert, R. M. Characterization of Catalysts. 1980. write for info. (ISBN 0-471-27874-2, Pub. by Wiley-Interscience). Wiley.
CATAPHORESIS
see Electrophoresis
CATARACT
Morgan, Joe W. Cataracts & Their Treatment. 144p. 1981. 6.95 (ISBN 0-8059-2775-1). Dorrance.
CATARRH
see Cold (Disease)
CATASTROPHES
see Disasters
CATAWBA INDIANS
see Indians of North America–Eastern States
CATCHES
see Glees, Catches, Rounds, etc.
CATECHETICAL ILLUSTRATIONS
see Homiletical Illustrations
CATECHETICS
see also Catechisms; Christian Education; Confirmation–Instruction and Study
also subdivision Catechisms and Creeds under names of Christian denominations, e.g. Catholic Church–Catechisms and Creeds
Hill, Brennan & Newland, Mary R., eds. Theologians & Catechists in Dialogue: The Albany Forum. 64p. (Orig.). 1977. pap. 2.25 (ISBN 0-697-01671-4). Wm C Brown.
Sork, David, et al. Growing & Sharing: The Catechist Formation Book. 128p. (Orig.). 1981. pap. 6.95 (ISBN 0-8091-2365-7). Paulist Pr.
CATECHETICS–CATHOLIC CHURCH
Focus on American Catechetics: A Commentary on the General Catechetical Directory. 101p. 1972. 2.95. Natl Cath Educ.
Kelley, Francis D., pref. by. Media & Catechetics Today: Towards the Year 2000. 3.00. Natl Cath Educ.
CATECHISMS
see also Bible–Catechisms, Question-Books, etc.; Catechetics; Creeds
also subdivision Catechisms and Creeds under names of religions, religious denominations, etc., e.g. Catholic Church–Catechisms and Creeds
Westminster Assembly. Shorter Catechism with Scripture Proofs. Date not set. 0.75 (ISBN 0-686-28948-X). Banner of Truth.
CATECHOLAMINES
Kunos, George. Adrenoceptors & Catecholamine Action. (Neurotransmitter Receptors Ser.: Vol. 1). 300p. 1981. 29.50 (ISBN 0-471-05725-8, Pub. by Wiley-Interscience). Wiley.
CATEGORIES (PHILOSOPHY)
Esposito, Joseph L. Evolutionary Metaphysics: The Development of Peirce's Theory of Catagories. LC 80-15736. (Illus.). x, 152p. 1980. 15.00x (ISBN 0-8214-0551-9). Ohio U Pr.
CATERERS AND CATERING
see also Breakfasts; Desserts; Dinners and Dining; Menus
Glew, G., ed. Advances in Catering Technology. (Illus.). xii, 450p. 1980. 99.00x (ISBN 0-85334-844-8). Burgess-Intl Ideas.
CATERINA DA SIENA, SAINT, 1347-1380
see Catherine of Siena, Saint, 1347-1380
CATFISHES
Lee, Jasper S. Commercial Catfish Farming. 2nd ed. (Illus.). 1981. 10.00 (ISBN 0-8134-2156-X, 2156). Interstate.
CATHEDRALS
see also Architecture, Gothic;
also subdivision Churches under names of cities, e.g. New York (City)–Churches
British Tourist Authority. Discovering Cathedrals. (Illus.). 80p. 1981. pap. write for info. (ISBN 0-85263-472-2, Pub. by Auto Assn-British Tourist Authority England). Merrimack Bk Serv.
Franzwa, Gregory M. The Old Cathedral. 2nd ed. LC 80-15885. (Illus.). 1980. 14.95 (ISBN 0-935284-18-4). Patrice Pr.
Parkhurst, Helen H. Cathedral: A Gothic Pilgrimage. 304p. 1980. Repr. of 1936 ed. lib. bdg. 40.00 (ISBN 0-8492-2174-9). R West.
Rodin, Auguste. Cathedrals of France. rev. ed. Geissbuhler, Elisabeth C., tr. from Fr. (Illus.). 278p. 20.00x (ISBN 0-933806-07-8). Black Swan CT.
CATHER, WILLA SIBERT, 1873-1947
Gerber, Phillip L., ed. Willa Cather. LC 75-2287. (Twayne's U. S. Authors Ser.). 187p. 1975. pap. text ed. 4.95 (ISBN 0-672-61508-8). Bobbs.
Rapin, Rene. Willa Cather. 115p. 1980. Repr. of 1930 ed. lib. bdg. 12.50 (ISBN 0-8492-7730-2). R West.
CATHERINE OF SIENA, SAINT, 1347-1380
Curtayne, Alice. St. Catherine of Siena. LC 80-53745. 1980. pap. write for info. (ISBN 0-89555-162-4). Tan Bks Pubs.
CATHERINE 2ND, EMPRESS OF RUSSIA, 1729-1796
De Madariaga, Isabel. Russia in the Age of Catherine the Great. LC 80-21993. (Illus.). 728p. 1981. 40.00x (ISBN 0-300-02515-7). Yale U Pr.
CATHODE RAY OSCILLOSCOPE
Here are entered works on the test instrument in which the variations in an electrical quantity appear temporarily as a visible waveform on the screen of a cathode ray tube. Works on the instrument combining a cathode ray oscilloscope and a camera to produce a permanent record of a waveform are entered under Cathode ray oscillograph.
Middleton, Robert G. Know Your Oscilloscope. 4th ed. LC 80-52230. 1980. pap. 8.95. Sams.
--One Hundred & One Ways to Use Your Oscilloscope. 3rd ed. 1980. pap. 6.95 (ISBN 0-672-21794-5). Sams.
--Troubleshooting with the Oscilloscope. 4th ed. LC 80-51719. 1980. 9.95 (ISBN 0-672-21738-4). Sams.
CATHODE RAY TUBES
Kane, Gerry. The CRT Controller Handbook. 250p. (Orig.). 1980. pap. 6.99 (ISBN 0-931988-45-4). Osborne-McGraw.
CATHOLIC CHURCH
see also Canon Law; Fasts and Feasts; Inquisition
Hellwig, Monika K. Unnderstanding Catholicism. 192p. (Orig.). 1981. pap. 3.50 (ISBN 0-8091-2384-3). Paulist Pr.
Likoudis, James & Whitehead, K. D. The Pope, the Council, & the Mass. 1981. 14.95 (ISBN 0-8158-0400-8). Chris Mass.
CATHOLIC CHURCH–APOLOGETIC WORKS
Benko, Stephen. Los Evangelicos, los Catolicos y la Virgen Maria. Olmedo, Alfonso, tr. from Eng. Orig. Title: Protestants, Catholics & Mary. Date not set. pap. price not set (ISBN 0-311-05041-7). Casa Bautista.
CATHOLIC CHURCH–BIBLIOGRAPHY
Mathieson, Moria B. The Complete Guide to Careers in the Catholic Church for Religious & Laity. 200p. (Orig.). 1980. pap. text ed. 15.00 (ISBN 0-8434-0759-X, Consortium). McGrath.
CATHOLIC CHURCH–BIOGRAPHY
Wilhelmsen, Frederick. Citizens of Rome: Reflections from the Life of a Roman Catholic. 12.95 (ISBN 0-89385-010-1); pap. 4.95 (ISBN 0-89385-005-5). Green Hill.
CATHOLIC CHURCH–CLERGY
see also Bishops; Cardinals; Priests; Retreats; Theological Seminaries, Catholic
Watson, Thomas E. The Roman Catholic Hierarchy. (Studies in Populism). 1980. lib. bdg. 69.95 (ISBN 0-686-68883-X). Revisionist Pr.
CATHOLIC CHURCH–DOCTRINAL AND CONTROVERSIAL WORKS
Gratsch, Edward, et al. Principles of Catholic Theology: A Synthesis of Dogma & Morals. LC 80-26272. 401p. (Orig.). 1981. pap. 10.95 (ISBN 0-8189-0407-0). Alba.
Overberg, Kenneth R. An Inconsistent Ethic? Teachings of the American Catholic Bishops. LC 80-512. 220p. 1980. lib. bdg. 17.75 (ISBN 0-8191-1318-2); pap. text ed. 9.75 (ISBN 0-8191-1319-0). U Pr of Amer.
CATHOLIC CHURCH–HISTORY
see also Schism–Eastern and Western Church
also names of specific councils of the Catholic Church
Capetti, Giselda, ed. Cronistoria, 5 vols. 400p. (Orig.). 1980. Set. pap. write for info. (ISBN 0-89944-043-6); Vol. 1. pap. (ISBN 0-89944-044-4); Vol. 2. pap. (ISBN 0-89944-045-2); Vol. 3. pap. (ISBN 0-89944-046-0); Vol. 4. pap. (ISBN 0-89944-047-9); Vol. 5. pap. (ISBN 0-89944-048-7). D Bosco Pubns.
Murphy, Francis X. This Church, These Times: The Roman Catholic Church Since Vatican II. (Illus.). 128p. 1981. cancelled (ISBN 0-695-81446-X, Assn Pr). Follett.
CATHOLIC CHURCH–LITURGY AND RITUAL
Bain, Georgia, ed. Understanding the Sunday Readings: July, August, September 1980. (Understanding the Sunday Readings Ser.). 173p. 1980. 8.95 (ISBN 0-8434-0741-7, Consortium). McGrath.
Official Catholic Teachings, Update 1977. LC 80-82422. (Official Catholic Teachings Ser.). 350p. 1980. text ed. 35.00 (ISBN 0-8434-0742-5, Consortium). McGrath.
Official Catholic Teachings, Update 1978. LC 80-82423. (Official Catholic Teachings Ser.). 400p. 1980. text ed. 35.00 (ISBN 0-8434-0743-3, Consortium). McGrath.
Official Catholic Teachings, Update 1979. LC 80-82424. (Official Catholic Teachings Ser.). 400p. 1980. text ed. 35.00 (ISBN 0-8434-0744-1, Consortium). McGrath.
Ryrie, Charles C. What You Should Know About the Rapture. (What You Know Ser.). 128p. 1981. pap. 2.95 (ISBN 0-8024-9416-1). Moody.
Understanding the Sunday Readings: October, November, December 1980. (Understanding the Sunday Readings Ser.). Date not set. 8.95 (ISBN 0-8434-0758-1, Consortium). McGrath.
CATHOLIC CHURCH–MARRIAGE
see Marriage–Catholic Church
CATHOLIC CHURCH–MODERNISM
see Modernism–Catholic Church
CATHOLIC CHURCH–SACRAMENTS
see Sacraments–Catholic Church
CATHOLIC CHURCH IN AFRICA
Healey, Joseph G. A Fifth Gospel: The Experience of Black Christian Values. LC 80-25033. (Illus.). 320p. (Orig.). 1981. pap. 7.95 (ISBN 0-88344-013-X). Orbis Bks.
CATHOLIC CHURCH IN AUSTRALIA
Wiltgen, R. M. The Founding of the Roman Catholic Church in Oceania 1825-1850. LC 78-74665. (Illus.). 610p. 1980. text ed. 36.95 (ISBN 0-7081-0835-0, 0572). Bks Australia.
CATHOLIC CHURCH IN ITALY
Harrison, G. B., ed. Anthony Munday: The English Romayne Lyfe. 105p. 1980. Repr. of 1925 ed. lib. bdg. 22.50 (ISBN 0-89760-543-8). Telegraph Bks.
CATHOLIC CHURCH IN THE NETHERLANDS
Bakvis, Herman. Catholic Power in the Netherlands. (Illus.). 550p. 1981. 35.95x (ISBN 0-7735-0367-6); pap. 18.95x (ISBN 0-7735-0368-4). McGill-Queens U Pr.
CATHOLIC CHURCH IN THE UNITED STATES–EDUCATION
Catechists Never Stop Learning. 97p. 1972. 2.00. Natl Cath Educ.
Creating an Early Learning Center in an Unused Building. 55p. 1972. 2.00. Natl Cath Educ.
Developing the Competencies of the Religion Teacher. 162p. 1974. 3.00. Natl Cath Educ.
Differentiated Patterns of Education in Catholic Elementary Schools. 74p. 1973. 2.95. Natl Cath Educ.
Diocese of Cleveland & Torrence, Rosemary. Mending Our Nets. 160p. (Orig.). 1980. pap. 7.95 (ISBN 0-697-01757-5). Wm C Brown.
Directory-Department of Chief Administrators of Catholic Education. 62p. 3.00. Natl Cath Educ.
Directory of Catholic Residential Schools. 1978. 2.00. Natl Cath Educ.
Doctoral Dissertations on Catholic Education 1968-1975. 67p. 1975. 3.00. Natl Cath Educ.
Guidelines for Selected Personnel Practices in Catholic Schools II. 58p. 1977. 3.75. Natl Cath Educ.
Harper, Mary-Angela. Ascent to Excellence in Catholic Education: A Guide to Effective Decision-Making. 7.95. Natl Cath Educ.
Kelley, Francis D., pref. by. The Vocation & Spirituality of the DRE: An NPCD Publication. 3.50. Natl Cath Educ.
Murdick, Olin J. & Meyers, Jack F., eds. Boards of Education-a Primer. 78p. 1972. 2.00. Natl Cath Educ.
The National Conference on Catholic School Finance III. 84p. 1977. 3.00. Natl Cath Educ.
The National Conference on Catholic School Finance II. 71p. 1975. 3.00. Natl Cath Educ.
The National Conference on Catholic School Finance I. 75p. 1974. 3.00. Natl Cath Educ.
NCEA-GANLEY's Catholic Schools in America. 322p. 30.00. Natl Cath Educ.
The Parish School Boards: Voice of the Community. 67p. 1973. 3.00. Natl Cath Educ.
Planning for Catholic Education. 62p. 1971. 2.00. Natl Cath Educ.
A Report on United States Catholic Schools, 1972-73. 98p. 1973. 2.00. Natl Cath Educ.
A Report on United States Catholic Schools 1971-72. 67p. 1972. 2.00. Natl Cath Educ.
A Report on United States Catholic Schools, 1970-71. 54p. 1971. 2.00. Natl Cath Educ.
A Statistical Report on Catholic Elementary & Secondary Schools for the Years 1967-68 to 1969-70. 104p. 1970. 3.00. Natl Cath Educ.
Unionism in Catholic Schools. 70p. 1976. 4.00. Natl Cath Educ.
U.S. Catholic Schools 1973-74. 92p. 1974. 2.00. Natl Cath Educ.
CATHOLIC LITERATURE–HISTORY AND CRITICISM
Tarr, Sr. Mary. Catholicism in Gothic Fiction. Bleiler, E. F., ed. LC 78-60815. (The Fiction of Popular Culture Ser.: Vol. 16). 148p. 1979. lib. bdg. 15.00 (ISBN 0-8240-9652-5). Garland Pub.
CATHOLIC THEOLOGICAL SEMINARIES
see Theological Seminaries, Catholic
CATHOLICISM
see Catholicity
CATHOLICITY
see also Ecumenical Movement
The Catholic Bible Study Course, 12 vols. Incl. Vol. 1. Pentateuch. Bryce, Glendon E. 250p (ISBN 0-8434-0745-X); Vol. 2. A Guide Through Pentateuch (ISBN 0-8434-0746-8); Vol. 3. Historical Literature. Miller, Charles, ed. 250p (ISBN 0-8434-0747-6); Vol. 4. A Guide Through Historical Literature (ISBN 0-8434-0748-4); Vol. 5. Wisdom Literature. Lillie, Betty J. 250p (ISBN 0-8434-0749-2); Vol. 6. A Guide Through Wisdom Literature (ISBN 0-8434-0750-6); Vol. 7. Prophetic Literature. Branick, Vincent. 250p (ISBN 0-8434-0751-4); Vol. 8. A Guide Through Prophetic Literature (ISBN 0-8434-0752-2); Vol. 9. Mark-Matthew-Luke. Sargent, Robert, ed. 250p (ISBN 0-8434-0754-9); Vol. 10. A Guide Through Mark-Matthew-Luke (ISBN 0-8434-0754-9); Vol. 11. John & Epistles. Grassi, Joseph, ed. 250p (ISBN 0-8434-0755-7); Vol. 12. A Guide Through John & Epistles (ISBN 0-8434-0756-5). Date not set. Set. 125.00 (ISBN 0-686-68786-8); Vols. 1 & 2. 25.00; Vols. 3 & 4. 25.00; Vols. 5 & 6. 25.00; Vols. 7 & 8. 25.00; Vols. 9 & 10. 25.00; Vols. 11 & 12. 25.00. McGrath.
Chilson, Richard. Creed for a Young Catholic. LC 80-2073. 128p. 1981. pap. 2.75 (ISBN 0-385-17436-5, Im). Doubleday.
Empie, Paul C. Lutherans & Catholics in Dialogue: Personal Notes for a Study. LC 80-69754. (Orig.). 1981. pap. 3.95 (ISBN 0-8006-1449-6, 1-1449). Fortress.
Hill, Brennan & Newland, Mary R., eds. Why Be a Catholic? 108p. (Orig.). 1979. pap. 2.00 (ISBN 0-697-01713-3). Wm C Brown.
Jacobs, William. A Young Person's Book of Catholic Words. LC 80-2078. 128p. (gr. 6 up). 1981. pap. 2.75 (ISBN 0-385-17434-9, Im). Doubleday.
Lambert, O. C. Catholicism Against Itself, Vol. 1. 7.50 (ISBN 0-89315-005-3). Lambert Bk.
--Catholicism Against Itself, Vol. 2. 7.50 (ISBN 0-89315-006-1). Lambert Bk.
CATHOLICS
Davis, Charles. Why I Left the Roman Catholic Church. 1976. pap. 3.00. Am Atheist.
Simms, Carolynne. Letters from a Roman Catholic. 1976. pap. 3.00. Am Atheist.
Taylor, Bill. A Tale of Two Cities: The Mormons-Catholics. 1981. pap. 4.00 (ISBN 0-933046-02-2). Little Red Hen.
CATHOLICS IN THE UNITED STATES
Shanabruch, Charles. Chicago's Catholics: An Evolution of an American Identity. LC 80-53071. (Studies in American Catholicism: Vol. 4). 288p. 1981. text ed. 18.95 (ISBN 0-268-01840-5). U of Notre Dame Pr.
CATIONS
Penczek, S., et al. Cationic Ring-Opening Polymerization of Heterocyclic Monomers. (Advances in Polymer Science Ser.: Vol. 37). (Illus.). 156p. 1981. 46.00 (ISBN 0-387-10209-4). Springer-Verlag.
CATS
Buchan, Vivian. Cat Sun Signs. LC 79-65117. (Illus.). 156p. 1981. pap. 5.95 (ISBN 0-8128-6097-7). Stein & Day.

Frazier, Anitra & Eckroate, Norma. The Natural Cat: A Holistic Guide for Finnicky Owners. (Illus.). 208p. 1981. 11.95 (ISBN 0-936602-12-0); pap. 7.95 (ISBN 0-936602-13-9). Harbor Pub CA.

Green, Martin. The Home Pet Vet Guide for Cats. pap. cancelled (ISBN 0-686-68438-9, 43406). Avon.

Lennon, Lynn, photos by. Categorically Speaking. (Illus.). 128p. (Orig.). 1981. pap. 6.95 (ISBN 0-670-20685-7, Studio). Viking Pr.

Payne, Christina & Cutts, Paddy. Pedigree Cats & Kittens: How to Choose & Care for Them. (Illus.). 64p. 1981. pap. 5.95 (ISBN 0-7134-3915-7, Pub. by Batsford England). David & Charles.

Randolph, Elizabeth. How to Be Your Cat's Best Friend. (Illus.). 224p. 1981. 11.95 (ISBN 0-316-73376-8). Little.

Wilbourn, Carole C. The Inner Cat: A New Approach to Cat Behavior. LC 77-20189. (Illus.). 204p. 1980. pap. 4.95 (ISBN 0-8128-6081-0). Stein & Day.

CATS–DISEASES

Sheppard, K. The Treatment of Cats by Homoeopathy. 62p. 1960. 3.50x (ISBN 0-8464-1055-9). Beekman Pubs.

CATS–JUVENILE LITERATURE

see also Cats–Legends and Stories; Cats–Pictures, Illustrations, Etc.

Sanders, Ruth M. A Book of Cats & Creatures. LC 80-70012. (gr. 2-6). 1981. PLB 8.95 (ISBN 0-525-26773-5). Dutton.

Shea, George. Big Cats. LC 80-23227. (Creatures Wild & Free). (gr. 1-6). 1981. text ed. 5.95 (ISBN 0-88436-774-6). EMC.

Zaum, Marjorie. All About Cats As Pets. (Illus.). 64p. (gr. 3-5). 1981. PLB 6.97 (ISBN 0-686-69306-X). Messner.

Zokeisha. Kittens. (Puppet Story Board Bks.). (Illus.). 12p. (ps-k). Date not set. boards 2.95 (ISBN 0-686-69451-1, Little Simon). S&S.

CATS–LEGENDS AND STORIES

Teacher, Lawrence, ed. Cat Notebook: Being an Illlustrated Book with Quotes. (Illus.). 96p. (Orig.). 1981. lib. bdg. 12.90 (ISBN 0-89471-131-8); pap. 4.95 (ISBN 0-89471-133-4). Running Pr.

CATS–PICTURES, ILLUSTRATIONS, ETC.

Kliban, B. The Cat Calender Book. LC 80-54618. 144p. 1981. 17.50 (ISBN 0-89480-155-4). Workman Pub.

Suares, Jean C., ed. Photographed Cat. LC 80-665. (Illus.). 128p. 1980. pap. 8.95 (ISBN 0-385-17080-7, Dolp). Doubleday.

CATTLE

see also Cattle Breeding; Cattle Trade; Cows
also names of specific breeds, e.g. Aberdeen-Angus Cattle

Albers, Michael D. The Terror. (Orig.). 1980. pap. 2.25 (ISBN 0-532-23311-5). Manor Bks.

Cattle, Economics & Development. 253p. 1981. 62.50 (ISBN 0-85198-452-5, CAB 14, CAB). Unipub.

Cattle, Sheep, & Hogs. (Country Home Ser.). 96p. 2.95 (ISBN 0-88453-005-1). Berkshire Traveller.

Cleveland, Hugh. Cattle Pricing Guide. 3rd rev. ed. (Illus.). 1980. pap. 7.95 (ISBN 0-89145-137-4). Collector Bks.

Summers, Ian & Kagan, Dan. Cattle Mutilations. 288p. (Orig.). 1981. pap. 2.95. Bantam.

CATTLE–DISEASES

see also Brucellosis in Cattle

Kahrs, Robert F. Viral Diseases of Cattle. (Illus.). 224p. 1981. text ed. 15.00 (ISBN 0-8138-0860-X). Iowa St U Pr.

Rosenberger, Gustav. Clinical Examination of Cattle. (Illus.). 469p. 1980. 95.00 (ISBN 0-7216-7705-3). Saunders.

CATTLE BREEDING

see also Dairying

Dobie, J. Frank. Cow People. (Illus.). 317p. 1981. pap. 6.95 (ISBN 0-292-71060-7). U of Tex Pr.

Herman, Harry A. Improving Cattle by the Millions: NAAB & the Development & Worldwide Application of Artificial Insemination. LC 80-25899. 352p. 1981. text ed. 30.00x (ISBN 0-8262-0320-5). U of Mo Pr.

CATTLE TRADE

see also Cowboys; Ranch Life

May, Cheryl. Cattle Management. 350p. 1981. text ed. 16.95 (ISBN 0-8359-0721-X); instr's. manual free. Reston.

CATV

see Community Antenna Television

CAUSALITY

see Causation

CAUSATION

Miller, John W. The Paradox of Cause & Other Essays. 192p. 1981. pap. 5.95 (ISBN 0-393-00032-X). Norton.

CAUSE AND EFFECT

see Causation

CAVES

see also Speleology
also names of caves, e.g. Lascaux Cave

Mitchell, Robert W. & Reddell, James R., eds. Studies on the Cavernicole Fauna of Mexico & Adjacent Regions. (Association for Mexican Cave Studies: Bulletin 5). 201p. 1973. 13.00. Speleo Pr.

Reddell, James R. A Preliminary Bibliography of Mexican Cave Biology with a Checklist of Published Records. (Association for Mexican Cave Studies: Bulletin 3). 184p. 1971. 10.00. Speleo Pr.

Reddell, James R., ed. Studies on the Caves & Cave Fauna of the Yucatan Peninsula. (Association for Mexican Cave Studies: Bulletin 6). 296p. 1977. 13.00. Speleo Pr.

Reddell, James R. & Mitchell, Robert W., eds. Studies on the Cavernicole Fauna of Mexico. (Association for Mexican Cave Studies: Bulletin 4). 239p. 1971. 13.00. Speleo Pr.

CAVINO, GIOVANNI DAL, 1500-1570

Lawrence, Richard H. The Paduans, Medals by Giovanni Cavino. (Illus.). pap. 5.00 (ISBN 0-916710-74-2). Obol Intl.

CAXTON, WILLIAM, 1422-1491

Toppen. From Caxton to Beckett. 1979. text ed. 42.75x (ISBN 90-6203-581-7). Humanities.

CAYAKS

see Canoes and Canoeing

CAYCE, EDGAR, 1877-1945

ARE Study Group No. 1. Suche Nach Gott, Bk I. Kronberger, Helge F., tr. from Eng. 135p. (Ger.). 1978. pap. 10.00 (ISBN 0-87604-131-4). ARE Pr.

CB RADIO

see Citizens Band Radio

CBR WARFARE

see Atomic Warfare; Chemical Warfare

CEILINGS

Greener. The Everything Book of Floors, Walls, & Ceilings. (Illus.). 250p. 1980. 14.95 (ISBN 0-8359-1803-3); pap. 7.95 (ISBN 0-8359-1802-5). Reston.

CELESTIAL NAVIGATION

see Nautical Astronomy

CELIBACY

Constantelos, D. J. Marriage, Sexuality & Celibacy: A Greek Orthodox Perspective. 1975. pap. 3.95 (ISBN 0-937032-15-8). Light&Life Pub Co MN.

CELL BIOLOGY

see Cytology

CELL CULTURE

Cameron, Ivan L. & Pool, Thomas B., eds. The Transformed Cell. (Cell Biology Ser.). 1981. price not set (ISBN 0-12-157160-2). Acad Pr.

Chaleff, R. S. Genetics of Higher Plants: Applications of Cell Culture. (Development & Cell Biology Monographs: No. 9). 208p. Date not set. price not set (ISBN 0-521-22731-3). Cambridge U Pr.

Maramorosh, Karl, ed. Advances in Cell Culture, Vol. I. (Serial Publication Ser.). 1981. write for info. (ISBN 0-12-007901-1). Acad Pr.

--Advances in Cell Culture, Vol. 2. (Serial Publication). 1981. price not set (ISBN 0-12-007902-X). Acad Pr.

CELL DIFFERENTIATION

Borek, Carmia & Williams, Gary M., eds. Differentiation & Carcinogenesis in Liver Cell Cultures. new ed. LC 80-20918. (Vol. 349). 429p. 1980. 83.00 (ISBN 0-89766-087-0). NY Acad Sci.

McKinnell, R. G., ed. Differentiation & Neoplasia. (Results & Problems in Cell Differentiation: Vol. 11). (Illus.). 350p. 1980. 76.20 (ISBN 0-387-10177-2). Springer-Verlag.

CELL MOTILITY

see Cells–Motility

CELL NUCLEI

Busch, Harris, ed. The Cell Nucleus: Nuclear Particles, Vol. 8. 1981. write for info. (ISBN 0-12-147608-1). Acad Pr.

CELL WALLS

see Plasma Membranes

CELLS

see also Blood Cells; Cancer Cells; Contractility (Biology); Cytology; Embryology; Epithelium; Histology; Membranes (Biology); Pathology, Cellular; Plasma Membranes; Protozoa; Ultrastructure (Biology)

Blecher, Melvin & Barr, Robert S. Receptors & Human Disease. (Illus.). 350p. 1981. write for info. (0609-6). Williams & Wilkins.

Golub, Edward S. The Cellular Basis of the Immune Response. rev. & 2nd ed. LC 80-28080. (Illus.). 325p. 1981. pap. text ed. price not set (ISBN 0-87893-212-7). Sinauer Assoc.

Horecker, Bernard & Estabrook, Ronald, eds. Current Topics in Cellular Regulation: Biological Cycles, Vol. 18. (Serial Publication Ser.). 1981. write for info. (ISBN 0-12-152818-9); lib ed. (ISBN 0-12-152892-8); microfiche ed. (ISBN 0-12-152893-6). Acad Pr.

Jackson, David. Cell System of Production. 170p. 1978. text ed. 23.50x (ISBN 0-220-66345-9, Pub. by Busn Bks England). Renouf.

Jasmin, G., ed. Cell Markers. (Methods & Achievements in Experimental Pathology: Vol. 10). (Illus.). vi, 294p. 1981. 90.00 (ISBN 3-8055-1736-X). S Karger.

Margulis, Lynn. Symbiosis in Cell Evolution: Life & Its Environment on the Early Earth. LC 80-26695. (Illus.). 1981. text ed. 27.95x (ISBN 0-7167-1255-5); pap. text ed. 13.95x (ISBN 0-7167-1256-3). W H Freeman.

Pannese, E. The Satellite Cells of the Sensory Canglia. (Advances in Antomy, Embryology & Cell Biology Ser.: Vol. 65). (Illus.). 98p. 1981. pap. 33.00 (ISBN 0-387-10219-1). Springer-Verlag.

Pollack, Robert, ed. Readings in Mammalian Cell Culture. 2nd ed. 1981. pap. text ed. 26.00 (ISBN 0-686-69552-6). Cold Spring Harbor.

Salanki, J., et al, eds. Physiology of Non-Excitable Cells: Proceedings of the 28th International Congress of Physiological Sciences, Budapest, 1980. LC 80-41874. (Advannces in Physiological Sciences: Vol. 3). (Illus.). 350p. 1981. 40.00 (ISBN 0-08-026815-3). Pergamon.

CELLS–MOTILITY

Cameron, Ivan L. & Pool, Thomas B., eds. The Transformed Cell. (Cell Biology Ser.). 1981. price not set (ISBN 0-12-157160-2). Acad Pr.

CELLULAR BIOLOGY

see Cytology

CELLULAR PATHOLOGY

see Pathology, Cellular

CELLULOSE

see also Polysaccharides

Bikales, N. M. & Segal, L. Cellulose & Cellulose Derivatives, Vol. 5, Pts. 4 & 5. 1411p. 1971. Set. 130.00 (ISBN 0-471-39038-0). Wiley.

CELTIC ART

see Art, Celtic

CELTS

see also Druids and Druidism

Lindgren, Claire. Classical Art Forms & Celtic Mutations: Figural Art in Roman Britain. LC 80-18987. (Illus.). 244p. (Orig.). 1981. 24.00 (ISBN 0-8155-5057-X, NP). Noyes.

CEMENT

see also Concrete; Pavements

Cedric Willson Symposium on Expansive Cement. 1980. 30.60 (SP-64). ACI.

Gutcho, M. H., ed. Cement & Mortar Technology & Additives: Developments Since 1977. LC 80-19343. (Chemical Tech. Rev. 173). 540p. (Orig.). 1981. 54.00 (ISBN 0-8155-0822-0). Noyes.

CEMETERIES

see also Burial Laws

Rezatto, Helen. Mount Moriah: Kill a Man, Start a Cemetery. LC 80-81127. (Illus.). 256p. 1980. 7.95 (ISBN 0-87970-150-1). North Plains.

CENA, ULTIMA

see Lord's Supper

CENDRARS, BLAISE, 1887-1961

Cendrars, Blaise. The Astonished Man. LC 80-9056. 260p. 1981. 12.95 (ISBN 0-8128-2814-3). Stein & Day.

--Planus. LC 80-9057. 220p. 1981. 12.95 (ISBN 0-8128-2816-X). Stein & Day.

CENOZOIC PERIOD

see Geology, Stratigraphic–Cenozoic

CENSORSHIP OF THE PRESS

see Liberty of the Press

CENSUS

see also subdivision Census under names of countries, cities, etc. e.g. United States–Census

Chicago Center for Afro-American Studies & Research, ed. Black People & the Nineteen Eighty Census: Proceedings from a Conference on the Poplation Undercount, Vol. 1. LC 80-68927. (Black People & the Nineteen Eighty Census Ser.). (Illus.). 702p. 1980. pap. 20.00 (ISBN 0-937954-01-2); pap. 15.00. Chr Ctr Afro-Am Stud.

Hobrook, Jay M. Shipton Quebec Canada Eighteen Twenty Five Census. LC 76-364055. 1976. pap. 7.50 (ISBN 0-931248-07-8). Holbrook Res.

Holbrook, Jay M. Ascott Quebec Canada Eighteen Twenty Five Census. LC 80-117991. 1976. pap. 7.50 (ISBN 0-931248-06-X). Holbrook Res.

CENTIPEDES

Lewis, J. G. The Biology of Centipedes. (Illus.). 350p. Date not set. price not set (ISBN 0-521-23413-1). Cambridge U Pr.

CENTRAL EUROPE

see Europe, Central

CENTRAL NERVOUS SYSTEM

see also Brain; Spinal Cord

Association for Research in Nervous Mental Disease. The Circulation of the Brain & Spinal Cord, Vol. 18. 1966. 27.50 (ISBN 0-02-842900-1). Hafner.

Myrianthopoulos, Ntinos C. & Bergsma, Daniel, eds. Recent Advances in the Developmental Biology of Central Nervous System Malformations. LC 79-4947. (Alan R. Liss Ser.: Vol. 15, No. 3). 1979. 16.00 (ISBN 0-8451-1026-8). March of Dimes.

Palmer, Gene C., ed. Neuropharmacology of Central Nervous System & Behavioral Disorders. LC 80-1107. 1981. 59.00 (ISBN 0-12-544760-4). Acad Pr.

Szentagothai, J., et al. Regulatory Functions of the Cns - Sybsystems: Proceedings of the 28th International Congress of Physiological Sciences, Budapest, 1980. LC 80-41884. (Advances in Physiological Sciences: Vol. 2). (Illus.). 293p. 1981. 35.00 (ISBN 0-08-027371-8). Pergamon.

--Regulatory Functions of the CNS- Motion & Organization Principles: Proceedings of the 28th International Congress of Physiological Sciences, Budapest, 1980. LC 80-41885. (Advances in Physiological Sciences: Vol. 1). (Illus.). 300p. 1981. 35.00 (ISBN 0-08-026814-5). Pergamon.

CENTRAL NERVOUS SYSTEM–DISEASES

see also Brain–Diseases

Buckley, Joseph P. & Ferrario, Carlos, eds. Central Nervous System Mechanisms in Hypertension. 425p. 1981. 39.95 (ISBN 0-89004-545-3). Raven.

CENTRIFUGAL FORCE

see also Gravitation

Centrifugation: A Practical Approach. 224p. 16.00 (ISBN 0-904147-10-X); pap. 9.00 (ISBN 0-904147-11-8). Info Retrieval.

Weissberger, Arnold & Hsu, Hsien-Wen. Separations by Centrifugal Phenomena. (Techniques of Chemistry Ser.: Vol. 16). 400p. 49.50 (ISBN 0-471-05564-6, Pub. by Wiley-Interscience). Wiley.

CENTRIFUGAL PUMPS

Karasik. Centrifugal Pump Clinic. 488p. 1981. 39.50 (ISBN 0-8247-1016-9). Dekker.

Standard for the Installation of Centrifugal Fire Pumps. 134p. 5.00 (ISBN 0-686-68287-4). Natl Fire Prot.

Yedidiah, S. Centrifugal Pump Problems. 232p. 1980. 35.00 (ISBN 0-87814-131-6). Pennwell Pub.

CERAMICS

Here are entered general works on the technology of fired earth products, or clay products intended for industrial and technical use. Works on earthenware, chinaware, and art objects are entered under Pottery or Pottery Craft.; Particular objects and types are entered under their specific names, e.g. Bricks; clay; pipe; Refractory Materials; Tiles; Vases.

Peak, Carl E. The Decorative Touch: How to Decorate, Glaze, & Fire Your Pots. (Creative Handicrafts Ser.). (Illus.). 160p. 1981. 17.95 (ISBN 0-13-198085-8, Spec); pap. 8.95 (ISBN 0-13-198077-7). P-H.

CERAMICS (ART)

see Pottery

CERAMICS, DENTAL

see Dentistry–Ceramics

CEREAL PRODUCTS

Jenkyn, J. F. & Plumb, R. T. Strategies for the Control of Cereal Disease: Organized by the British Plant Pathologist, Vol. 2. 250p. 1981. 47.50 (ISBN 0-470-27049-7). Halsted Pr.

CEREALS

see Grain

CEREBELLUM

Brodal, A. & Kawamura, K. The Olivocerebellar Projection: A Review. (Advances in Anatomy, Embryology & Cell Biology Ser.: Vol. 64). (Illus.). 144p. 1981. pap. 46.10 (ISBN 0-387-10305-8). Springer-Verlag.

CEREBRAL CORTEX

Braak, H. Architectonics of the Human Telencephalic Cortex. (Studies of Brain Functions: Vol. 4). (Illus.). 147p. 1981. 27.50 (ISBN 0-387-10312-0). Springer-Verlag.

Luria, Aleksandr R. Higher Cortical Functions in Man. rev. & expanded ed. 655p. 1980. 27.50 (ISBN 0-306-10966-2, Consultants Bureau). Plenum Pub.

Schmitt, F. O., et al, eds. The Cerebral Cortex: Proceedings of a Neurosciences Research Program Colloquium. (Illus.). 576p. 1981. text ed. 50.00x (ISBN 0-262-19189-X). MIT Pr.

CEREBRAL DEATH

see Brain Death

CEREBRAL EDEMA

De Vlieger, M. Brain Edema. 185p. 1981. 27.50 (ISBN 0-471-04477-6, Pub. by Wiley-Med). Wiley.

CEREBRAL ISCHEMIA

Carney, Andrew L. & Anderson, Evelyn M., eds. Diagnosis & Treatment of Brain Ischemia, Vol. 30. (Advances in Neurology). 450p. 1981. 43.00 (ISBN 0-89004-529-1). Raven.

Cowley, R. Adams & Trump, Benjamin F. Pathophysiology of Shock, Anoxia & Ischemia. 600p. 1981. write for info. (2149-4). Williams & Wilkins.

Peerless, S. & McCormick, C. W., eds. Microsurgery for Cerebral Ischemia. (Illus.). 362p. 1981. 89.80 (ISBN 0-387-90495-6). Springer-Verlag.

CEREBRAL LOCALIZATION

see Brain–Localization of Functions

CEREBRAL PALSY

Bobath, Karel. A Neurophysical Basis for the Treatment of Cerebral Palsy. (Clinics in Developmental Medicine Ser.: No. 75). 106p. 1980. 19.50. Lippincott.

CEREBROVASCULAR DISEASE

see also Cerebral Ischemia; Stroke Patients

Hess, Lucille & Bahr, Robert. What Every Family Should Know About Strokes. (Appleton Consumer Health Guides). 128p. 1981. 12.95 (ISBN 0-8385-9717-3); pap. 5.95 (ISBN 0-8385-9716-5). ACC.

CEREBRUM

see Brain

CEREMONIAL PURITY

see Purity, Ritual

CEREMONIES

see Etiquette; Rites and Ceremonies

CEROPLASTIC

see Wax Modeling

CERTIFICATION OF TEACHERS

see Teachers–Certification

CERVANTES SAAVEDRA, MIGUEL DE, 1547-1616–BIBLIOGRAPHY

Drake, Dana B. Cervantes' Novelas Ejemplares: A Selective, Annotated Bibliography. 2nd,rev. ed. LC 80-8492. 250p. 1981. lib. bdg. 35.00 (ISBN 0-8240-9473-5). Garland Pub.

CESAREAN SECTION

Meyer, Linda D. The Cesarean (R) Evolution: A Handbook for Parents & Professionals. rev., 2nd ed. (Illus.). 150p. 1981. pap. 5.95 (ISBN 0-9603516-1-2). C Franklin Pr.

Mitchell, Kathleen & Nason, Marty. Cesarean Birth: A Couple's Guide for Decision & Preparation. 208p. 1981. pap. 7.95 (ISBN 0-936602-17-1). Harbor Pub CA.

CESSIO BONORUM
see Bankruptcy
CESSNA (AIRPLANES)
National Flightshops. All Those Cessna 150's: Owners Manuals 1959-1977. Date not set. pap. 12.95 (Pub. by National Flightshops). Aviation.
CESTODA
Arai, Hisao, ed. Biology of the Tapeworm Hymenolepis Diminuta. 1980. 45.00 (ISBN 0-12-058980-X). Acad Pr.
Upadhyay, H. P. Monograpgh of Ceratocystis & Ceratocystiopsis. (Illus.). 288p. 1981. 27.50x (ISBN 0-8203-0539-1). U of Ga Pr.
CEVENNES MOUNTAINS
Stevenson, Robert L. Travels with a Donkey in the Cevennes. 1980. 12.95 (ISBN 0-906223-17-2). Dufour.
CHAETOPODA
see also Oligochaeta
Ashworth, J. H. Catalogue of the Chaetopoda in the British Museum (Natural History) A. Polychaeta. (Illus.). xii, 175p. 1912. 15.00x (ISBN 0-565-00102-7, Pub. by British Mus Nat Hist England). Sabbot-Natural Hist Bks.
CHAIN REACTION PILES
see Nuclear Reactors
CHALCOGENIDES
Dhar, D. N. The Chemistry of Chalcones & Related Compounds. 300p. 1981. 29.50 (ISBN 0-471-08007-1, Pub. by Wiley-Interscience). Wiley.
CHALICOSIS
see Lungs–Dust Diseases
CHAMBER MUSIC
Schubert, Franz. Complete Chamber Music for Strings. pap. 8.95 (ISBN 0-486-21463-X). Dover.
CHAMBERLAIN, WILTON NORMAN, 1936-
Hahn, James & Hahn, Lynn. Wilt! Wilton Chamberlain. Schroeder, Howard, ed. (Sports Legends Ser.). (Illus.). 48p. (Orig.). (gr. 3-5). 1981. PLB 5.95 (ISBN 0-89686-124-4); pap. text ed. 2.95 (ISBN 0-89686-139-2). Crestwood Hse.
CHAMPIGNONS
see Mushrooms
CHAMPLAIN, LAKE
Hill, Ralph N. Lake Champlain: Key to Liberty. 296p. 1978. 14.95 (ISBN 0-936896-01-9). VT Life Mag.
CHANCE
see also Games of Chance (Mathematics); Probabilities
Eigen, Manfred & Winkler, Ruthild. Laws of the Game: How the Principles of Nature Govern Chance. LC 79-3494. (Illus.). 384p. 1981. 17.95 (ISBN 0-394-41806-9). Knopf.
Peirce, Charles S. Chance, Love & Logic. 317p. 1980. Repr. of 1923 ed. lib. bdg. 50.00 (ISBN 0-89984-386-7). Century Bookbindery.
CHANCERY
see Equity; Equity Pleading and Procedure
CHANGE
Samuel, Herbert L. Grooves of Change: A Book of Memoirs. LC 80-1913. 1981. Repr. of 1946 ed. 39.50 (ISBN 0-404-18985-7). AMS Pr.
CHANGE, EDUCATIONAL
see Educational Innovations
CHANGE, SOCIAL
see Social Change
CHANGE OF LIFE IN WOMEN
see Menopause
CHANNEL ISLANDS
Blue Guide - Channel Islands. 24.95 (ISBN 0-528-84620-5); pap. 15.95 (ISBN 0-528-84619-1). Rand.
CHANNELS (HYDRAULIC ENGINEERING)
see also Canals; Harbors; Lakes; Reservoirs; Rivers
Stelczer, K. Theory & Practice of Bed-Load Transport. 1981. 22.00 (ISBN 0-918334-38-1). WRP.
CHANSONS DE GESTE
Cook, Robert F. Chanson D'Antioche, Chanson De Geste: Le Cycle de la Croisade Estil Epique? (Purdue University Monographs in Romance Languages: No. 2). 115p. 1980. text ed. 17.25x (ISBN 90-272-1712-2, Athlone Pr). Humanities.
CHANTS (PLAIN, GREGORIAN, ETC.)–INSTRUCTION AND STUDY
Rayburn, John. Gregorian Chant: A History of Controversy Concerning Its Rhythm. LC 80-27616. xiv, 90p. 1981. Repr. of 1964 ed. lib. bdg. 19.75x (ISBN 0-313-22811-6, RAGR). Greenwood.
CHANUKAH
see Hanukkah (Feast of Lights)
CHAP-BOOKS
see also Comic Books, Strips, etc.
McDaniel, Wilma E. Tollbridge. 32p. 1980. 3.00 (ISBN 0-936556-01-3). Contact Two.
CHAP-BOOKS–BIBLIOGRAPHY
Mendel, Roberta, ed. The Pin Prick Press Annual Index of Serial & Chapbook Publications, 1980. (Orig.). 1981. pap. 3.00 (ISBN 0-936424-07-9, 007). Pin Prick.
CHAPELS
Wroth, William. The Chapel of Our Lady of Talpa. 1979. pap. 7.50. Taylor Museum.
CHAPLIN, CHARLES SPENCER, 1889-1977
Sacranie, Raj. Charlie Chaplin. (Profiles Ser.). (Illus.). 64p. (gr. 3-6). 1981. 7.95 (ISBN 0-241-10481-5, Pub. by Hamish Hamilton England). David & Charles.
CHARACTER
see also Conduct of Life; Temperament; Virtue and Virtues
Bain, Alexander. On the Study of Character, Including an Estimate of Phrenology. (Contributions to the History of Psychology Ser.: Orientations). 1980. Repr. of 1861 ed. 30.00 (ISBN 0-89093-316-2). U Pubns Amer.
CHARACTER EDUCATION
see Moral Education
CHARACTER SKETCHES–HISTORY AND CRITICISM
see Characters and Characteristics in Literature
CHARACTERS AND CHARACTERISTICS IN LITERATURE
see also Jews in Literature; Shakespeare, William, 1564-1616–Characters; Women in Literature
Fitzgerald, Percy H. The History of Pickwick. 1980. Repr. of 1891 ed. lib. bdg. 45.00 (ISBN 0-8492-4631-8). R West.
CHARISMATA
see Gifts, Spiritual
CHARISMATIC MOVEMENT
see Pentecostalism
CHARITABLE INSTITUTIONS
see Asylums
CHARITABLE USES, TRUSTS AND FOUNDATIONS
Foundation Center. Corporate Foundation Profiles. LC 80-69622. 512p. (Orig.). 1980. pap. 50.00 (ISBN 0-87954-038-9). Foundation Ctr.
CHARITIES–HISTORY
Young, Frances M. Thankfulness Unites: The History of the United Thank Offering. 1979. 1.75 (ISBN 0-686-28795-9). Forward Movement.
CHARITY
see also Love (Theology)
Merchant, Jane. The Greatest of These. (Orig.). pap. 1.25 (ISBN 0-89129-175-X). Jove Pubns.
CHARITY LAWS AND LEGISLATION
see also Charitable Uses, Trusts and Foundations
Report of the Goodman Committee. Charity Law & Voluntary Organisations. 150p. 1976. pap. text ed. 5.00x (ISBN 0-7199-0910-4, Pub. by Bedford England). Renouf.
CHARLATANS
see Impostors and Imposture; Quacks and Quackery
CHARLEMAGNE, 742-814
Rice, Edward. The Age of Charlemagne. 112p. 1963. 2.95 (ISBN 0-374-29492-5). FS&G.
CHARLES 1ST, KING OF GREAT BRITAIN, 1600-1649
Abbott, Jacob. Makers of History, Charles I. 285p. 1980. Repr. of 1903 ed. lib. bdg. 20.00 (ISBN 0-89984-002-7). Century Bookbindery.
CHARLESTON, SOUTH CAROLINA–HISTORY
Jackson, Melvin H. Privateers in Charleston, 1793 to 1796. (Illus.). 160p. 1969. 17.50x (ISBN 0-87474-158-0). Smithsonian.
CHARM
Davis, Katrina. Charm Course for College Coeds. (Illus.). 80p. (Orig.). 1981. pap. 9.95 (ISBN 0-937242-05-5). Scandia Pubs.
CHARTRES, FRANCE
James, John. The Contractors of Chartres. (Illus.). 232p. 1980. 60.00 (ISBN 0-7099-0180-1, Pub. by Croom Held Ltd England). Biblio Dist.
CHARTS, NAUTICAL
see Nautical Charts
CHASE, SAMUEL, 1741-1811
Haw, James, et al. Stormy Patriot: The Life of Samuel Chase. LC 80-83807. (Illus.). 305p. 1980. 14.95 (ISBN 0-938420-00-3). Md Hist.
CHASIDISM
see Hasidism
CHASSIS MOUNTED COACHES
see Campers and Coaches, Truck
CHATEAUX
see Castles
CHATTELS
see Personal Property
CHATTERTON, THOMAS, 1752-1770
Nevill, John C. Thomas Chatterton. 261p. 1980. Repr. of 1948 ed. lib. bdg. 30.00 (ISBN 0-8495-4020-8). Arden Lib.
CHAUCER, GEOFFREY, d. 1400
Edmunds, Edward W. Chaucer & His Poetry. 218p. 1980. Repr. of 1920 ed. lib. bdg. 8.00 (ISBN 0-8495-1349-9). Arden Lib.
Goddard, Harold C. Chaucer's Legend of Good Women. 107p. 1980. Repr. of 1908 ed. lib. bdg. 20.00 (ISBN 0-8495-1959-4). Arden Lib.
Pace, George B. & David, Alfred, eds. The Minor Poems, Pt. 1. LC 80-5943. (Works of Geoffrey Chaucer Ser., Variorum Ed.: Vol. V). 200p. 1981. 25.00 (ISBN 0-8061-1629-3). U of Okla Pr.
Rye, Walter. Chaucer: A Norfolk Man. 104p. 1980. Repr. of 1915 ed. lib. bdg. 20.00 (ISBN 0-8495-4636-2). Arden Lib.
Tyrwhitt, Thomas. An Essay on the Language & Versification of Chaucer. 76p. 1980. Repr. of 1775 ed. text ed. 15.00 (ISBN 0-8492-8409-0). R West.
CHAUCER, GEOFFREY, d. 1400–STUDY (FOR OUTLINES, STUDY GUIDES, ETC.)
Tyrwhitt, Thomas. An Introductory Discourse to the Canterbury Tales. 52p. 1980. Repr. of 1778 ed. lib. bdg. 15.00 (ISBN 0-8495-5161-7). Arden Lib.
CHEBYSHEV APPROXIMATION
Chistensen, R. Entropy Minimax Sourcebook: General Description. 700p. 1981. text ed. 29.50 (ISBN 0-686-28918-8). Entropy Ltd.
Christensen, R., ed. Entropy Minimax Sourcebook: Applications. 800p. 1981. 59.50 (ISBN 0-686-28919-6). Entropy Ltd.
CHEER LEADERS
see Cheers and Cheerleading
CHEERS AND CHEERLEADING
Hawkins, Jim W. Cheerleading Is for Me. (Sports for Me Bks.). (Illus.). (gr. 2-5). 1981. PLB 5.95 (ISBN 0-8225-1127-4). Lerner Pubns.
CHEESE
see also Cookery (Dairy Products)
Ensrud, Barbara. The Pocket Guide to Cheese. 144p. 1981. pap. 4.95 (ISBN 0-399-50518-0, Perigee). Putnam.
CHEETAHS
Frame, George & Frame, Lory. Swift & Enduring: Cheetahs & Wild Dogs of the Serengeti. 1981. 15.95 (ISBN 0-525-93060-4). Dutton.
--Swift & Enduring: Cheetahs & Wilddogs of the Serengeti. (Illus.). 256p. 1980. 15.95 (ISBN 0-525-93060-4). Dutton.
CHEEVER, JOHN
Bosha, Francis J. John Cheever: A Reference Guide. (Reference Books Ser.). 1981. 20.00 (ISBN 0-8161-8447-X). G K Hall.
CHEIROPTERA
see Bats
CHEKHOV, ANTON PAVLOVICH, 1860-1904
Emeljanow, Victor, ed. Chekhov: The Critical Heritage. (The Critical Heritage Ser.). 496p. 1981. 50.00 (ISBN 0-7100-0374-9). Routledge & Kegan.
CHEMICAL ANALYSIS
see Chemistry, Analytic
CHEMICAL BONDS
Chisholm, Malcolm, ed. Reactivity of Metal-Metal Bonds. (ACS Symposium Ser.: No. 155). 1981. price not set (ISBN 0-8412-0624-4). Am Chemical.
CHEMICAL COMPOSITION OF THE EARTH
see Geochemistry
CHEMICAL ELEMENTS
see also Trace Elements; Valence (Theoretical Chemistry)
also names of elements
Friend, J. N. Man & the Chemical Elements. 354p. 1961. 19.50x (ISBN 0-85264-053-6, Pub. by Griffin England). State Mutual Bk.
Lavender, J. P., ed. Clinical & Experimental Applications of Krypton81m. 1980. 75.00x (Pub. by Brit Inst Radiology England). State Mutual Bk.
CHEMICAL ENGINEERING
see also Fluidization; Mechanical Engineering; Metallurgy
Chang, Huan-Yang & Over, Ira Earl. Selected Numerical Methods & Computer Programs for Chemical Engineers. 235p. (Orig.). 1981. pap. text ed. 11.95 (ISBN 0-88408-131-1). Sterling Swift.
European Federation of Chemical Engineering, European Symposium, Amsterdam, Holland, June 3-5, 1980. Particle Technology Nineteen Eighty: Proceedings, Vols. A & B. Schonert, K., et al, eds. (E FCE Publication Ser.: No. 7). 1232p. 1980. text ed. 79.00x (ISBN 3-921567-27-0, Pub. by Dechema Germany). Scholium Intl.
Finlayson, Bruce A. Nonlinear Analysis in Chemical Engineering. (M-H Chemical Engineering Ser.). (Illus.). 384p. 1980. text ed. 44.50 (ISBN 0-07-020915-4). McGraw.
Moore. Principles of Chemical Metallurgy. 1981. text ed. price not set (ISBN 0-408-00567-X); pap. text ed. price not set (ISBN 0-408-00430-4). Butterworth.
Schuit, G. G. & Prins, R., eds. Chemistry & Chemical Engineering of Catalytic Processes. (NATO-Advanced Study Institute Ser.). 660p. 1980. 75.00x (ISBN 9-0286-0730-7). Sijthoff & Noordhoff.
Teja, A. S. Chemical Engineering & the Environments. LC 80-26427. 115p. 1981. 27.95 (ISBN 0-470-27106-X). Halsted Pr.
--Chemical Engineering & the Environment. (Critical Reports on Applied Chemistry). 115p. 1981. 27.95 (ISBN 0-470-27106-X). Halsted Pr.
CHEMICAL EQUILIBRIUM
Denbigh, K. G. The Principles of Chemical Equilibrium. (Illus.). 506p. Date not set. 59.50 (ISBN 0-521-23682-7); pap. 19.95 (ISBN 0-521-28150-4). Cambridge U Pr.
CHEMICAL EVOLUTION
Biology Coloquium, 29th, Oregon State Univ. Biochemical Coevolution: Proceedings. Chambers, Kenton L., ed. LC 52-19235. 128p. 1970. text ed. 6.00 (ISBN 0-87071-168-7). Oreg St U Pr.
Gutfreund, H. Biochemical Evolution. 320p. Date not set. text ed. price not set (ISBN 0-521-23549-9); pap. text ed. price not set (ISBN 0-521-28025-7). Cambridge U Pr.
CHEMICAL GENETICS
see also Molecular Biology
Applied Genetics: A Booming Industry C-032. 1981. 950.00 (ISBN 0-89336-285-9). BCC.
CHEMICAL GEOLOGY
see Geochemistry; Mineralogy, Determinative; Rocks–Analysis
CHEMICAL INDUSTRIES
Here are entered works on industries based largely on chemical processes. Material dealing with the manufacture of chemicals as such is entered under Chemicals–Manufacture and Industry.
Annual Bulletin of Trade in Chemical Products, Vol. 5. 285p. 1980. pap. 19.00 (UN79-2E29, UN). Unipub.
European Federation of Chemical Engineering, 2nd Intl. Conference on Phase Equilibria & Fluid Properties in the Chemical Industry, Berlin, 1980. Phase Equilibria & Fluid Properties in the Chemical Industry: Proceedings, Pts. 1 & 2. (EFCE Publication Ser.: No. 11). 1012p. 1980. text ed. 82.50x (ISBN 3-921567-35-1, Pub. by Dechema Germany). Scholium Intl.
Evans, L. S. Chemical & Process Plant: A Guide to the Selection of Engineering Materials. 2nd ed. LC 80-20355. 190p. 1981. 34.95 (ISBN 0-470-27064-0). Halsted Pr.
CHEMICAL INDUSTRIES–GERMANY
Wunder, Dietrich, intro. by. Directory of the West German Chemical Industry-Firmenhandbuch Chemische Industrie, 1979 to 1981, 2 vols. 10th ed. 512p. 1979. 115.00x (ISBN 3-430-12758-0). Intl Pubns Serv.
CHEMICAL INDUSTRIES–GREAT BRITAIN
Warren, Kenneth. Chemical Foundations: The Alkali Industry in Britain to Nineteen Twenty-Six. (Oxford Research Studies in Geography). (Illus.). 220p. 1980. text ed. 46.00x (ISBN 0-19-823231-4). Oxford U Pr.
CHEMICAL KINETICS
see Chemical Reaction, Rate of
CHEMICAL PROCESS CONTROL
Whitaker, Norman. Process Instrumentation Primer. 128p. 1980. 27.50 (ISBN 0-87814-128-6). Pennwell Pub.
CHEMICAL REACTION, RATE OF
Wojciechowski, Bohdan W. Chemical Kinetics for Chemical Engineers. 2nd ed. (Illus.). 333p. 1981. pap. text ed. 11.95 (ISBN 0-88408-130-3). Sterling Swift.
CHEMICAL REACTIONS
see also Chemical Reactors; Friedel-Crafts Reaction; Phosphorylation
Christoph, S. G. Collision Theory & Statistical Theory of Chemical Reactions. (Lectures Notes in Chemistry: Vol. 18). (Illus.). 322p. 1980. pap. 27.70 (ISBN 0-387-10012-1). Springer-Verlag.
Daudel, Raymond, et al, eds. Quantum Theory of Chemical Reactions: Solvent Effect, Reaction Mechanisms, Photochemical Processes, Vol. 11. 340p. 1980. PLB 42.00 (ISBN 90-277-1182-8). Kluwer Boston.
Fiechter, A., ed. Reactors & Reactions. (Advances in Biochemical Engineering Ser.: Vol. 19). (Illus.). 250p. 1981. 57.90 (ISBN 0-387-10464-X). Springer-Verlag.
Villermaux, J. & Trambouze, P., eds. Chemical Reaction Engineering: Sixth International Symposium on Chemical Reaction Engineering--Plenary Lectures, Vol. 2. LC 79-41749. (Illus.). 259p. 1980. pap. 40.00 (ISBN 0-08-026234-1). Pergamon.
CHEMICAL REACTORS
Fiechter, A., ed. Reactors & Reactions. (Advances in Biochemical Engineering Ser.: Vol. 19). (Illus.). 250p. 1981. 57.90 (ISBN 0-387-10464-X). Springer-Verlag.
CHEMICAL REAGENTS
see Chemical Tests and Reagents
CHEMICAL STRUCTURE
see also Chemical Bonds; Molecular Structure; Valence (Theoretical Chemistry)
Moskowitz, H. R. & Warren, Craig, eds. Odor Quality & Chemical Structure. (ACS Symposium Ser.: No. 148). 1981. price not set (ISBN 0-8412-0607-4). Am Chemical.
CHEMICAL SYMBOLS
see Abbreviations
CHEMICAL TESTS AND REAGENTS
Fieser, Mary, et al. Reagents for Organic Synthesis, Vol. 9. (Reagents for Organic Synthesis Ser.). 688p. 1981. 35.00 (ISBN 0-471-05631-6, Pub. by Wiley-Interscience). Wiley.
Pizey, J. S. Synthetic Reagents Vol. 4: Mercuric Acetate Periodic Acid & Periodates Sulfuryl Chloride. 200p. 1981. 110.00 (ISBN 0-470-27133-7). Halsted Pr.
CHEMICAL WARFARE
Brown, Frederic J. Chemical Warfare: A Study in Restraints. LC 80-27993. xix, 355p. 1981. Repr. of 1968 ed. lib. bdg. 31.75x (ISBN 0-313-22823-X, BRCHW). Greenwood.
CHEMICALS
see also groups of chemicals, e.g. Acids, Explosives, and individual chemical substances, e.g. Carbolic Acid
Chem Sources USA. 22nd ed. 1981. 120.00 (ISBN 0-937020-00-1). Directories Pub.
Walker, Colin. Environmental Pollution by Chemicals. 1980. pap. text ed. 7.75x (ISBN 0-09-123891-9, Hutchinson U Lib). Humanities.
CHEMICALS–LAW AND LEGISLATION
Legal Data Profiles for Selected Chemicals. (IRPTC Ser.: No. 2). 280p. 1981. pap. 28.00 (ISBN 0-686-69542-9, UNEP 40, UNEP). Unipub.
CHEMICALS–MANUFACTURE AND INDUSTRY
see also Chemical Industries; Electrochemistry, Industrial

also specific chemical industries

European Federation of Chemical Engineering, 2nd Intl. Conference on Phase Equilibria & Fluid Properties in the Chemical Industry, Berlin, 1980. Phase Equilibria & Fluid Properties in the Chemical Industry: Proceedings, Pts. 1 & 2. (EFCE Publication Ser.: No. 11). 1012p. 1980. text ed. 82.50x (ISBN 3-921567-35-1, Pub. by Dechema Germany). Scholium Intl.

CHEMILUMINESCENCE

Deluca, Marlene & McElroy, William, eds. Bioluminescence & Chemiluminescence: Basic Chemistry & Analytical Applications. 1981. price not set (ISBN 0-12-208820-4). Acad Pr.

CHEMISTRY

see also Agricultural Chemistry; Alchemy; Assaying; Biological Chemistry; Botanical Chemistry; Catalysis; Color; Combustion; Crystallography; Electrochemistry; Explosives; Gases–Liquefaction; Geochemistry; Pharmacy; Photochemistry; Poisons; Spectrum Analysis; Water Chemistry

also headings beginning with the word Chemical

Banerjea, D. Coordination Chemistry: Twentieth International Conference on Coordination Chemistry, Calcutta, India, 10-14 Dec. 1979. LC 80-41163. 286p. 1980. 75.00 (ISBN 0-08-023942-0). Pergamon.

Boschke, F. L., ed. Van der Waals Systems. (Topics in Current Chemistry: Vol. 93). (Illus.). 140p. 1980. 40.20 (ISBN 0-387-10058-X). Springer-Verlag.

Brown, Theodore L. & LeMay, H. E. Chemistry, The Central Science: Solutions to Exercises. 272p. 1980. 6.96 (ISBN 0-13-128538-6). P-H.

Brown, Theodore L. & LeMay, H. Eugene. Chemistry: The Central Science. 2nd ed. 832p. 1981. text ed. 22.95 (ISBN 0-13-128504-1). P-H.

Buttle, J. W., et al. Chemistry: A Unified Approach. 1981. text ed. price not set (ISBN 0-408-70938-3). Butterworth.

Chang, Raymond. Chemistry. Incl. Losey, Eugene. wkbk. 6.95 (ISBN 0-394-32447-1); Goldwhite, Harold & Spielman, John. solutions to problem sets 4.95 (ISBN 0-394-32519-2). 815p. 1981. text ed. 23.95 (ISBN 0-394-31224-4). Random.

Chemistry. (Undergraduate Program Field Test Ser.: UPFT-4). (Cloth bdg. avail. on request). pap. 9.95 (ISBN 0-8373-6004-8). Natl Learning.

Chemistry of Art. 1980. 3.00 (ISBN 0-910362-13-0). Chem Educ.

Dack, M. R. Techniques of Chemistry: Vol. 8, Pt. 1, Solutions & Solubilities. 475p. 1975. 48.50 (ISBN 0-471-93266-3). Wiley.

Devon, T. K. & Scott, A. I. Handbook of Naturally Occurring Compounds, 2 vols. Incl. Vol. 1. Acetogenins, Shikimates & Carbohydrates. 1975. 51.50 (ISBN 0-12-213601-2); Vol. 2. Terpenes. 1972. 42.00 (ISBN 0-12-213602-0). Acad Pr.

Geffner, Saul L. & Kass, Gerard A. Contemporary Chemistry. (Orig.). (gr. 10-12). 1981. pap. text ed. price not set (ISBN 0-87720-100-5). AMSCO Sch.

Herron, Dudley. Understanding Chemistry. Incl. Kean, Elizabeth. wkbk. 6.95 (ISBN 0-394-32423-4); Copes, Jane. lab manual 6.95 (ISBN 0-394-32437-4). 515p. 1981. text ed. 16.95 (ISBN 0-394-32087-5). Random.

Izatt, Reed M. & Christensen, James J. Progess in Macrocyclic Chemistry, Vol. 2. (Progress in Macrocyclic Chemistry Ser.). 384p. 1981. 35.00 (ISBN 0-471-05178-0, Pub. by Wiley-Interscience). Wiley.

King, Edward L. Chemistry. 1100p. 1981. text ed. 23.95 (ISBN 0-394-32761-6). Random.

Kirk & Othmer. Encyclopedia of Chemical Technology, 12 vols. 3rd ed. Incl. Vol. 1. A-Alkanolamines. 967p (ISBN 0-471-02037-0); Vol. 2. Alkoxides, Metals & Antibiotics (Peptides) 1036p (ISBN 0-471-02038-9); Vol. 3. Antibiotics (Phenazines) 958p (ISBN 0-471-02039-7); Vol. 4. Blood, Coagulants & Anticoagulants to Cardiovascular Agents. 930p (ISBN 0-471-02040-0); Vol. 5. Castor Oil to Chlorosulfuric Acid. 880p (ISBN 0-471-02041-9); Vol. 6. Chocolate & Cocoa to Copper. 869p (ISBN 0-471-02042-7); Vol. 7. Copper Alloys to Distillations (ISBN 0-471-02043-5); Vol. 8. Diuretics to Emulsions (ISBN 0-471-02044-3); Vol. 9. Enamels: Porcelain or Vitreous to Ferrites. 902p (ISBN 0-471-02062-1); Vol. 10. Ferroelectrics to Fluorine Compounds. 962p (ISBN 0-471-02063-X); Vol. 11. Fluorine Compounds to Gold & Gold Compounds (ISBN 0-471-02064-8); Vol. 12. Gravity Concentration to Hidroxy Carboxylic Acids (ISBN 0-471-02065-6). 1978-80. 145.00 ea. (Pub. by Wiley-Interscience). Wiley.

Miller, G. Tyler, Jr. Chemistry: A Basic Introduction. 2nd ed. 560p. 1980. text ed. 18.95x (ISBN 0-534-00878-X). Wadsworth Pub.

Riban, David M. Introduction to Physical Science. (Illus.). 656p. 1981. text ed. 21.95 (ISBN 0-07-052140-9, C); instr's manual 4.95 (ISBN 0-07-052141-7). McGraw.

Rossiter, B. W. Techniques of Chemistry: Vol. 9, Chemical Experimentation Under Extreme Conditions. 369p. 1980. 28.50 (ISBN 0-471-93269-8). Wiley.

Scott, Arthur F., ed. Survey of Progress in Chemistry, 8 vols. Incl. Vol. 1. 1963. 40.50 (ISBN 0-12-610501-4); Vol. 2. 1965. 40.50 (ISBN 0-12-610502-2); Vol. 3. 1966. 40.50 (ISBN 0-686-62064-X); Vol. 4. 1968. 40.50 (ISBN 0-12-610504-9); Vol. 5. 1969. 40.50 (ISBN 0-12-610505-7); Vol. 6. 1974. 51.50 (ISBN 0-12-610506-5); Vol. 7. 1976. 40.00 (ISBN 0-12-610507-3); lib. ed 50.50 (ISBN 0-12-610574-X); microfiche 29.00 (ISBN 0-12-610575-8); Vol. 8. 1978. 43.00 (ISBN 0-12-610508-1); lib. ed. 55.50 (ISBN 0-12-610576-6); microfiche 31.50 (ISBN 0-12-610577-4); Vol. 9. 1980. 35.00 (ISBN 0-12-610509-X); lib. bdg. 45.50 (ISBN 0-12-610578-2); microfiche 24.50 (ISBN 0-12-610579-0). Acad Pr.

Scott, George P. & McMillin, J. M. Dissipative Structures & Spatiotemporal Organization Studies in Biomedical Research. (Illus.). 271p. 1980. pap. text ed. 9.95. Iowa St U Pr.

Summerlin, Lee R. Chemistry for the Life Sciences. Incl. P. S. Associates. wkbk. 6.95 (ISBN 0-394-32457-9); Hendrickson, William & Healy, Juanita. lab manual 6.95 (ISBN 0-394-32520-6). 631p. 1981. text ed. 19.95 (ISBN 0-394-32215-0). Random.

Tonnis, John & Rausch, Gerald. Chemical Investigations for the Nonscientist. 1980. coil binding 6.95 (ISBN 0-88252-109-8). Paladin Hse.

Vol'Pin, M., ed. Soviet Scientific Reviews 011section B: Chemistry Reviews, Vol.2. (Soviet Scientific Reviews). 480p. 1980. 90.00 (ISBN 3-7186-0018-8). Harwood Academic.

Vol'Pin, M. E., ed. Soviet Scientific Review: Chemistry Review, Vol. 3, Section B. 1981. write for info. (ISBN 3-7186-0057-9). Harwood Academic.

--Soviet Scientific Reviews: Chemistry Reviews, Vol. 3, Section B. 1981. price not set (ISBN 3-7186-0057-9). Harwood Academic.

Weissberger, A. & Perry, E. S. Techniques of Chemistry: Vol. 13 Laboratory Engineering & Manipulations. 3rd ed. 531p. 1979. 47.50 (ISBN 0-471-03275-1). Wiley.

Weissberger, A., ed. Techniques of Chemistry. Incl. Vol. 1. Physical Methods of Chemistry, 5 pts. Rossiter, B. 1971-72; Pt. 1A. Components of Scientific Instruments. 40.50 (ISBN 0-471-92724-4); Pt. 2A. Electrochemical Methods. 68.00 (ISBN 0-471-92727-9); Pt. 3A. o.p. (ISBN 0-471-92729-5); Pt. 1B. Automatic Recording & Control, Computers in Chemical Research. 36.50 (ISBN 0-471-92725-2); Pt. 2B. o.p. (ISBN 0-471-92728-7); Pt. 3B. Spectroscopy & Spectometry in Infrared, Visible & Ultraviolet. 62.50 (ISBN 0-471-92731-7); Pt. 3C. Polarimetry. 47.95 (ISBN 0-471-92732-5); Pt. 3D. X-Ray, Nuclear, Molecular Beam & Radioactivity Methods. 62.95 (ISBN 0-471-92733-3); Pt. 4. Determination of Mass, Transport & Electrical-Magnetic Properties. 54.50; Pt. 5. o.p. (ISBN 0-471-92734-1); Pt. 6. Supplement & Cumulative Index. LC 75-29544. 256p. 1976. 31.50 (ISBN 0-471-92899-2); Vol. 2. Organic Solvents: Physical Properties & Methods of Purification. 3rd ed. Riddick, John A. & Bunger, William B. LC 72-114919. 1971. Pt. 1. 60.50 (ISBN 0-471-92726-0); Vol. 3. Photochromism. Brown, G. H. LC 45-8533. 1971. 93.00 (ISBN 0-471-92894-1); Vol. 4. Elucidation of Organic Structures by Physical & Chemical Methods, 3 pts. Bentley, K. W. & Kirby, G. W. 1972-73. Pt. 1. 57.00 (ISBN 0-471-92896-8); Pt. 2. 58.00 (ISBN 0-471-92897-6); Pt. 3. o.p. (ISBN 0-471-92898-4); Vol. 5. Techniques of Electroorganic Synthesis, 2 pts. Weingerb, N. L., ed. Pt. 1. 84.50; Pt. 2. 75.00 (ISBN 0-471-93272-8); Vol. 6. Investigation of Rates & Mechanisms of Reactions, 2 pts. 3rd ed. Lewis, E. S., ed. LC 73-8850. 1974. Pt. 1. 77.00 (ISBN 0-471-93095-4); Pt. 2. 52.50 (ISBN 0-471-93127-6); Vol. 7. Membranes in Separations. Hwang, S. T. & Kammermeyer, K. LC 74-2218. 1975. 60.50 (ISBN 0-471-93268-X); Vol. 10. Applications of Biochemical Systems in Organic Chemistry, 2 pts. Jone, Bryan J., et al, eds. 1976. Pt. 1. 45.00 (ISBN 0-471-93267-1); Pt. 2. 50.00 (ISBN 0-471-93270-1). Pub. by Wiley-Interscience). Wiley.

Williams, Arthur L., et al. Introduction to Chemistry. 3rd ed. (Chemistry Ser.). (Illus.). 896p. 1981. text ed. 21.95 (ISBN 0-201-08726-X). A-W.

CHEMISTRY–ADDRESSES, ESSAYS, LECTURES

Scott, Arthur F., ed. Survey of Progress in Chemistry, 8 vols. Incl. Vol. 1. 1963. 40.50 (ISBN 0-12-610501-4); Vol. 2. 1965. 40.50 (ISBN 0-12-610502-2); Vol. 3. 1966. 40.50 (ISBN 0-686-62064-X); Vol. 4. 1968. 40.50 (ISBN 0-12-610504-9); Vol. 5. 1969. 40.50 (ISBN 0-12-610505-7); Vol. 6. 1974. 51.50 (ISBN 0-12-610506-5); Vol. 7. 1976. 40.00 (ISBN 0-12-610507-3); lib. ed 50.50 (ISBN 0-12-610574-X); microfiche 29.00 (ISBN 0-12-610575-8); Vol. 8. 1978. 43.00 (ISBN 0-12-610508-1); lib. ed. 55.50 (ISBN 0-12-610576-6); microfiche 31.50 (ISBN 0-12-610577-4); Vol. 9. 1980. 35.00 (ISBN 0-12-610509-X); lib. bdg. 45.50 (ISBN 0-12-610578-2); microfiche 24.50 (ISBN 0-12-610579-0). Acad Pr.

Varmuza, K. Pattern Recognition in Chemistry. (Lecture Notes in Chemistry Ser.: Vol. 21). (Illus.). 217p. 1981. pap. 21.00 (ISBN 0-387-10273-6). Springer-Verlag.

CHEMISTRY–COLLECTED WORKS

Vol'Pin, M. E., ed. Soviet Scientific Reviews: Chemistry Reviews, Vol. 3, Section B. 1981. price not set (ISBN 3-7186-0057-9). Harwood Academic.

CHEMISTRY–DATA PROCESSING

Lykos, Peter. Personal Computers in Chemistry. 250p. 1980. 25.00 (ISBN 0-471-08508-1, Pub. by Wiley-Interscience). Wiley.

CHEMISTRY–DICTIONARIES

Barcelo, J. R. Spanish-English - English-Spanish Chemical Vocabulary. vii, 111p. (Orig.). 1980. pap. 7.50 (ISBN 84-205-0696-6). Heinman.

Bennett, H. Encyclopedia of Chemical Trademarks & Synonyms, Vol. 1 A-E. 1981. 55.00 (ISBN 0-8206-0286-8). Chem Pub.

Daintith, John, ed. The Facts on File Dictionary of Chemistry. 224p. 1981. 14.95 (ISBN 0-87196-513-5). Facts on File.

CHEMISTRY–LABORATORY MANUALS

see also Chemistry, Inorganic–Laboratory Manuals; Glass Blowing and Working

Armstrong, Roger W. Laboratory Manual for Chemistry: A Lige Science Approach. 1980. pap. write for info. (ISBN 0-02-303920-5). Macmillan.

Eastham, R. C. Interpretation Klinisch-Chemischer Laborresultate. 2nd ed. Peheim, E., tr. Colombo, J. P., ed. xii, 248p. 1981. pap. 17.00 (ISBN 3-8055-1879-X). S Karger.

Ifft, James B. & Roberts, Julian L., Jr. Frantz - Malm's Chemistry in the Laboratory. (Illus.). 1981. 8.95x (ISBN 0-7167-1238-5); tchrs. manual avail.; individual exercises 0.50 ea. W H Freeman.

Kemp, Kenneth C. Laboratory Experiments to Chemistry: The Central Science. 2nd ed. 378p. 1981. wkbk. 10.95 (ISBN 0-13-128520-3). P-H.

Scottish Schools Science Equipment Research Centre, ed. Hazardous Chemicals: A Manual for Schools & Colleges. 1979. pap. 12.95xlab. manual (ISBN 0-05-003204-6). Longman.

CHEMISTRY–MATHEMATICS

Gabbay, S. M. Elementary Mathematics for Basic Chemistry & Physics. 128p. (Orig.). 1980. pap. 9.95 (ISBN 0-9604722-0-7). Basic Science Prep Ctr.

CHEMISTRY–PROBLEMS, EXERCISES, ETC.

LeLorenzo, Ronald. Problem Solving in General Chemistry. 496p. 1980. pap. text ed. 10.95 (ISBN 0-669-02924-6). Heath.

CHEMISTRY–TERMINOLOGY

Bennett, H. Encyclopedia of Chemical Trademarks & Synonyms, Vol. 1 A-E. 1981. 55.00 (ISBN 0-8206-0286-8). Chem Pub.

CHEMISTRY, AGRICULTURAL

see Agricultural Chemistry

CHEMISTRY, ANALYTIC

see also Chromatographic Analysis; Electrolysis; Mineralogy, Determinative; Radioactivation Analysis; Spectrophotometry

also subdivision analysis under special subjects, e.g. Gases–Analysis; Rocks–Analysis

Boschke, F. L., ed. Analytical Problems. (Topics in Current Chemistry Ser.: Vol. 95). (Illus.). 210p. 1981. 56.70 (ISBN 0-387-10402-X). Springer-Verlag.

Hieftje, Gary, et al, eds. Lasers in Chemical Analysis. LC 80-84082. (Contemporary Instrumentation & Analysis). (Illus.). 352p. 1981. price not set (ISBN 0-89603-027-X). Humana.

Kateman, G. & Pijpers, F. W. Quality Control in Analytical Chemistry. (Chemical Analysis Ser.). 320p. 1981. 28.50 (ISBN 0-471-46020-6, Pub. by Wiley-Interscience). Wiley.

Kolthoff, I. M. & Elving, P. J. Treatise on Analytical Chemistry, 3 pts. Incl. Pt. 1, Vols. 10-12. Theory & Practice of Analytical Chemistry. Vol. 10, 1972, 595p. 46.50 (ISBN 0-470-49966-4); Vol. 11, 1975. 60.00 (ISBN 0-471-49967-6); Vol. 12, 1976. 32.50 (ISBN 0-471-49968-4); Pt. 2, Vols. 4, 10, 12 & 14-15. Analytical Chemistry of the Elements & of Inorganic & Organic Compounds. Vol. 4, 1966, 452p. 39.50 (ISBN 0-470-49986-9); Vol. 10, 1978. 50.00 (ISBN 0-471-49998-6); Vol. 12, 1976. 27.25 (ISBN 0-470-50002-6); Vol. 14, 1971. 44.95 (ISBN 0-471-50005-4); Vol. 15, 1976. 50.00 (ISBN 0-471-50009-7); Pt. 3, Vols. 3-4. Analytical Chemistry in Industry. 60.00 (ISBN 0-471-50012-7); 60.00 (ISBN 0-471-02765-0). LC 59-12439 (Pub. by Wiley-Interscience). Wiley.

Schenk, et al. Introduction to Analytical Chemistry. 2nd ed. 540p. 1981. text ed. 21.95 (ISBN 0-205-07236-4, 6872360); student's manual. Allyn.

CHEMISTRY, ANALYTIC–QUALITATIVE

see also Spectrum Analysis

Franks, Relix. Polywater: The History of an Artifact. 100p. 1981. 17.50x (ISBN 0-262-06073-6). MIT Pr.

CHEMISTRY, ANALYTIC–QUANTITATIVE

Klecka, William R. Discriminant Analysis. LC 80-50927. (Quantitative Applications in the Social Sciences Ser.: No. 19). (Illus.). 71p. 1980. pap. 3.50 (ISBN 0-8039-1491-1). Sage.

Kumar, Vinay. Experimental Techniques in Quantitative Chemical Analysis. LC 80-69043. 183p. (Orig.). 1981. pap. text ed. 10.00 (ISBN 0-8191-1509-6). U Pr of Amer.

CHEMISTRY, BIOLOGICAL

see Biological Chemistry

CHEMISTRY, BOTANICAL

see Botanical Chemistry

CHEMISTRY, CLINICAL

Glickson. Biomycin: Chemistry & Clinical Applications. Date not set. price not set (ISBN 0-8247-1289-7). Dekker.

Hood, W. A-Z of Clinical Chemistry. LC 80-23908. 386p. 1980. 19.95 (ISBN 0-470-27029-2). Halsted Pr.

Lijnen, H. R., et al, eds. Synthetic Substrates in Clinical Blood Coagulation Assays. (Developments in Hematology Ser.: No. 1). 142p. 1981. PLB 23.50 (ISBN 90-247-2409-0, Pub. Bymartinus Nijhoff). Kluwer Boston.

Price, Christopher P. & Spencer, Kevin, eds. Centrifugal Analysers in Clinical Chemistry. 520p. 1980. 59.95 (ISBN 0-03-058854-5). Praeger.

Richterich, R. Clinical Chemistry: Theory, Practice & Interpretation. Colombo, J. P., ed. 672p. 1981. price not set (ISBN 0-471-27809-2, Pub. by Wiley-Interscience). Wiley.

Robinson, R. Clinical Chemistry & Automation: A Study in Laboratory Proficiency. 188p. 1971. 21.95x (ISBN 0-85264-204-0, Pub. by Griffin England). State Mutual Bk.

CHEMISTRY, INDUSTRIAL

see Chemical Engineering

CHEMISTRY, INORGANIC

see also Earths, Rare; Metals

also names and classes of inorganic compounds

Anderson, Rubin. Adsorption of Inorganics at Solid Liquid Interfaces. 1981. text ed. 39.95 (ISBN 0-250-40226-2, Dist. by Butterworths). Ann Arbor Science.

Burns, D. T. & Townshend, A. Inorganic Reaction Chemistry: Reactions of the Elements, Vol. 2. Carter, A. H., ed. (Ser. in Analytical Chemistry). 410p. 1981. 97.50 (ISBN 0-470-27105-1). Halsted Pr.

Emeleus, H. J. & Sharpe, A. G., eds. Advances in Inorganic Chemistry & Radiochemistry, Vol. 24. (Serial Publication Ser.). 1981. write for info. (ISBN 0-12-023624-9). Acad Pr.

Martell, Arthur E. Inorganic Chemistry in Biology & Medicine. LC 80-23248. (ACS Symposium Ser.: No. 140). 1980. 39.50 (ISBN 0-8412-0588-4). Am Chemical.

Mellor. Mellor's Comprehensive Treatise on Inorganic & Theoretical Chemistry: Pt. 5 Boron. (Illus.). 825p. 1980. lib. bdg. 170.00 (ISBN 0-582-46277-0). Longman.

CHEMISTRY, INORGANIC–LABORATORY MANUALS

Nathan, Larry C. Laboratory Project in Modern Coordination Chemistry. LC 80-25233. 93p. (Orig.). 1981. pap. text ed. 8.95 (ISBN 0-8185-0433-1). Brooks-Cole.

CHEMISTRY, MEDICAL AND PHARMACEUTICAL

see also Chemistry, Clinical; Drugs; Materia Medica; Pharmacy; Poisons

De las Heras, F. G. & Vega, S. Medicinal Chemistry Advances: Proceedings of the Seventh International Symposium on Medicinal Chemistry, Torremolinos, 2-5 September 1980. (Illus.). 500p. 1981. 80.00 (ISBN 0-08-025297-4); pap. 25.00 (ISBN 0-08-026198-1). Pergamon.

Lavender, J. P., ed. Clinical & Experimental Applications of Krypton81m. 1980. 75.00x (Pub. by Brit Inst Radiology England). State Mutual Bk.

Quantitative Aspects of Chemical Pharmacology. 256p. 1980. 80.00x (ISBN 0-85664-892-2, Pub. by Croom Helm England). State Mutual Bk.

Shargel, Leon & Yu, Andrew B. Applied Biopharmaceutics & Pharmacokinetics. 288p. 1980. pap. text ed. 18.50x (ISBN 0-8385-0206-7). ACC.

CHEMISTRY, NUCLEAR

see Nuclear Chemistry

CHEMISTRY, ORGANIC

see also Carbon Compounds; Condensation Products (Chemistry); Surface Active Agents

also names of classes of organic compounds, e.g. Alkaloids; Carbohydrates; Proteins; also names of individual organic substances, e.g. Benzene

Bailey. Organic Chemistry: A Brief Survey of Concepts & Applications. 2nd ed. 500p. 1981. text ed. 19.95 (ISBN 0-205-07233-X, 6872336); free tchr's ed. (ISBN 0-205-07234-8); free student's guide (ISBN 0-205-07235-6). Allyn.

Basic Organic Chemistry: Arabic Translation, Pt. 1. 256p. 1978. 6.95 (ISBN 0-471-04526-8). Wiley.

Bentley, K. W. & Kirby, G. W. Techniques of Chemistry: Vol. 4, 2 Pts. Elucidation of Organic Structures by Physical & Chemical Methods. 2nd ed. 1250p. 1972. Pt. 1. 57.00 (ISBN 0-471-92896-8); Pt. 2. 58.00 (ISBN 0-471-92897-6). Wiley.

Butler, A. R. & Perkins, J. M., eds. Organic Reaction Mechanism. Incl. Vol. 9. 1973. 96.95 (ISBN 0-471-12690-X); Vol. 10. 1974. 119.95 (ISBN 0-471-12693-4); Reprint A. 7.50 (ISBN 0-471-01531-8); Reprint B. 8.95 (ISBN 0-471-01532-6); Vol. 11. 1975. 115.95 (ISBN 0-471-01864-3); Vol. 12. 1976. 125.50 (ISBN 0-471-99523-1). LC 66-23143. 1975-1978 (Pub. by Wiley-Interscience). Wiley.

The Eighth Symposium on Nucleic Acids Chemistry: Proceedings. (Nucleic Acids Symposium Ser.: No. 8). 198p. 1980. 20.00 (ISBN 0-904147-28-2). Info Retrieval.

Fernandez, Jack E. Organic Chemistry: An Introduction. (Illus.). 528p. 1981. text ed. 19.95 (ISBN 0-686-68299-8). P-H.

Freidlina, R. Kh., ed. Organic Sulfer Chemistry: Ninth International Symposium on Organic Sulfur Chemistry, Riga, USSR, 9-14 June 1980. (IUPAC Symposium Ser.). (Illus.). 270p. 1981. 81.00 (ISBN 0-08-026180-9). Pergamon.

Holiday & Hunt. Intermediate Chemistry: Organic Chemistry. 1981. text ed. price not set (ISBN 0-408-70915-4). Butterworth.

International Symposium in Chemical Synthesis of Nucleic Acids, Egestorf, West Germany, May 1980. Nucleic Acid Synthesis: Applications to Molecular Biology & Genetic Engineering. (Nucleic Acids Symposium Ser.: No. 7). 396p. 1980. 40.00 (ISBN 0-904147-26-6). Info Retrieval.

Izatt, Reed M. & Christensen, James J. Progress in Macrocyclic Chemistry, Vol. 2. 300p. 1981. 35.00 (ISBN 0-471-05178-0, Pub. by Wiley-Interscience). Wiley.

Jones, J. B., et al. Techniques of Chemistry: Vol. 10 Applications of Biochemical Systems in Organic Chemistry, 2 pts. 522p. 1976. Pt. 1. 50.00 (ISBN 0-471-93267-1); Pt. 2, 575pp. 55.00 (ISBN 0-471-93270-1); Set. 80.95 (ISBN 0-471-02279-9). Wiley.

Lednicer, Daniel & Mitscher, Lester A. Organic Chemistry of Drug Synthesis, 2 vols. LC 76-28387. Vol. 1, 1977. 28.50 (ISBN 0-471-52141-8, Pub. by Wiley-Interscience); Vol. 2, 1980. 28.00 (ISBN 0-471-04392-3). Wiley.

Rabjohn, N. Organic Syntheses Collective Volumes, Vol. 4. 1036p. 1963. 39.00 (ISBN 0-471-70470-9, 2-203). Wiley.

Schrader, B. & Meier, W., eds. Raman-IR Atlas of Organic Compounds. 1974-1976. Set. 467.70. Vol. 1,345p (ISBN 3-527-25539-7). Vol. 2,386p (ISBN 3-527-25541-9). Vol. 3,507p (ISBN 3-527-25542-7). Verlag Chemie.

Silverstein, Robert M. & Bassler, G. Clayton. Spectrometric Indentification of Organic Compounds. 4th ed. Morrill, Terence C., ed. 704p. 1981. text ed. 20.95 (ISBN 0-471-02990-4). Wiley.

Van Tamelen, E. E., ed. Bioorganic Chemistry, 2 vols. Incl. Vol. 1. Enzyme Action. 1977. 49.75 (ISBN 0-12-714301-7); Vol. 2. 1978. 52.50, by subscription 83.00 (ISBN 0-12-714302-5). Acad Pr.

Weissberger, A. Technique of Organic Chemistry. Incl. Vol. 2. Catalytic, Photochemical & Electrolytic Reactions. 2nd ed. 1956. 42.00 (ISBN 0-470-92862-X); Vol. 3, Pt. 2. Laboratory Engineering. 1957. 36.95 (ISBN 0-470-92928-6). (All other vols. in set o.p., Pub. by Wiley-Interscience). Wiley.

Zubrick, James W. Work in the Hood: The First Entertaining Organic Chemistry Laboratory Guide. LC 80-69113. (Illus.). 120p. (Orig.). 1980. pap. 4.50 (ISBN 0-937926-00-0). Scienspot.

CHEMISTRY, ORGANIC–SYNTHESIS

see also Biosynthesis; Plastics; Polymers and Polymerization; Synthetic Products

Trost, Barry M. & Hutchinson, C. R., eds. Organic Synthesis - Today & Tomorrow: Third IUPAC Symposium on Organic Synthesis, Madison, Wisconsin, U.S.A., 15-20 June 1980. (IUAC Symposium Ser.). (Illus.). 360p. 1981. 96.00 (ISBN 0-08-025268-0). Pergamon.

Wade, L. G., Jr. & O'Donnell, Martin J., eds. Annual Reports in Organic Synthesis, 1979, Vol. 10. 1980. 23.50 (ISBN 0-12-040810-4). Acad Pr.

CHEMISTRY, PATHOLOGICAL

see Chemistry, Medical and Pharmaceutical

CHEMISTRY, PHARMACEUTICAL

see Chemistry, Medical and Pharmaceutical

CHEMISTRY, PHYSICAL AND THEORETICAL

see also Adsorption; Atoms; Catalysis; Chemical Bonds; Chemical Equilibrium; Chemical Reaction, Rate of; Chemical Structure; Colloids; Coordination Compounds; Crystallography; Electrochemistry; Electrolysis; Electrolytes; Gases–Liquefaction; Mass Transfer; Nuclear Chemistry; Nuclear Physics; Photochemistry; Polymers and Polymerization; Quantum Chemistry; Quantum Theory; Radiochemistry; Solid State Chemistry; Surface Chemistry; Thermodynamics; Valence (Theoretical Chemistry)

Buckingham. International Review in Physical Chemistry. 1981. text ed. price not set (ISBN 0-408-12271-4). Butterworth.

Christensen, James J. & Hansen, Lee D. Handbook of Proton Ionization Heats. 286p. Repr. of 1976 ed. lib. bdg. write for info. (ISBN 0-89874-344-3). Krieger.

Dolphin, David, ed. The Porphyrins. Incl. Vol. 1, Pt. A. 59.00 (ISBN 0-12-220101-9); Physical Chemistry. Vol. 3, Pt. A. 71.00 (ISBN 0-12-220103-5); Vol. 4, Pt. B. 50.00 (ISBN 0-12-220104-3); Vol. 5, Pt. C. 57.50 (ISBN 0-12-220105-1). LC 77-14197. 1978-79. Acad Pr.

Henderson, Douglas, ed. Theoretical Chemistry: Theory of Scattering-Papers in Honor of Henry Eyring, Vol. 6a. (Serial Publication). 1981. write for info. (ISBN 0-12-681906-8). Acad Pr.

--Theoretical Chemistry: Theory of Scattering: Papers in Honor of Henry Eyring, Vol. 6B. (Serial Publications). 1981. price not set (ISBN 0-12-681907-6). Acad Pr.

Isaacs, Neil S. Liquid Phase High Pressure Chemistry. 384p. 1981. 100.00 (ISBN 0-471-27849-1, Pub. by Wiley-Interscience). Wiley.

Izatt, Reed M. & Christensen, James J. Progress in Macrocyclic Chemistry, Vol. 2. 300p. 1981. 35.00 (ISBN 0-471-05178-0, Pub. by Wiley-Interscience). Wiley.

Laurent, J. P., ed. Coordination Chemistry-Twenty One: Twenty First International Conference on Coodination Chemistry, Toulouse, France 7-11 July 1980. (IUPAC Symposium Ser.). 200p. 1981. 54.00 (ISBN 0-08-025300-8). Pergamon.

Mellor. Mellor's Comprehensive Treatise on Inorganic & Theoretical Chemistry: Pt. 5 Boron. (Illus.). 825p. 1980. lib. bdg. 170.00 (ISBN 0-582-46277-0). Longman.

CHEMISTRY, QUANTUM

see Quantum Chemistry

CHEMISTRY, SOIL

see Soil Chemistry

CHEMISTRY, SOLID STATE

see Solid State Chemistry

CHEMISTRY, SURFACE

see Surface Chemistry

CHEMISTRY, SYNTHETIC

see Chemistry, Organic–Synthesis

CHEMISTRY, TECHNICAL–FORMULAE, RECEIPTS, PRESCRIPTIONS

Bennett, H., ed. Chemical Formulary, 22 vols. Incl. Vol. 1, 1933 (ISBN 0-8206-0259-0). Vol. 2, 1935 (ISBN 0-8206-0260-4). Vol. 3, 1936 (ISBN 0-8206-0261-2). Vol. 4, 1939 (ISBN 0-8206-0262-0). Vol. 5, 1941 (ISBN 0-8206-0263-9). Vol. 6, 1943 (ISBN 0-8206-0264-7). Vol. 7, 1945 (ISBN 0-8206-0265-5); Vol. 8, 1948 (ISBN 0-8206-0266-3). Vol. 9, 1950 (ISBN 0-8206-0267-1). Vol. 10, 1957 (ISBN 0-8206-0268-X). Vol. 11, 1961 (ISBN 0-8206-0269-8). Vol. 12, 1965 (ISBN 0-8206-0270-1). Vol. 13, 1967 (ISBN 0-8206-0271-X). Vol. 14, 1968 (ISBN 0-8206-0272-8); Vol. 15, 1970 (ISBN 0-8206-0273-6). Vol. 16, 1971 (ISBN 0-8206-0274-4). Vol. 17, 1973 (ISBN 0-8206-0275-2). Vol. 18, 1975 (ISBN 0-8206-0276-0). Vol. 19, 1976 (ISBN 0-8206-0277-9). Vol. 20, 1977 (ISBN 0-8206-0278-7). Vol. 21, 1979 (ISBN 0-8206-0279-5). Vol. 22, 1979 (ISBN 0-8206-0280-9). 22.50 ea. Chem Pub.

CHEMISTRY, THEORETICAL

see Chemistry, Physical and Theoretical

CHEMISTRY IN WARFARE

see Chemical Warfare

CHEMISTRY OF FOOD

see Food–Analysis; Food–Composition

CHEMORECEPTORS

European Chemoreception Research Organisation, Symposium, Netherlands, 1979. Preference Behaviour & Chemoreception: Proceedings. (ECRO Minisymposium Ser.). 350p. 1979. 26.00 (ISBN 0-904147-12-6). Info Retrieval.

European Chemoreception Research Organisation, 2nd Interdisciplinary Symposium, Switzerland, 1975. Structure-Activity Relationships in Chemoreception: Proceedings. 197p. 20.00 (ISBN 0-904147-03-7). Info Retrieval.

CHEMOTHERAPY

see also Antibiotics; Psychopharmacology

also subdivision Chemotherapy under diseases, e.g. Cancer–Chemotheraphy

Becker, Teresa M. Cancer Chemotherapy: A Manual for Nurses. (Little, Brown Spiral Training Manual Ser.). 1981. pap. text ed. price not set. Little.

Bernstein, Jerold G. Handbook of Drug Therapy in Psychiatry. 1981. write for info. (ISBN 0-88416-323-7). PSG Pub.

Bressler, Rubin & Conrad, Kenneth. Drug Therapy for the Elderly. (Illus.). 300p. 1981. pap. text ed. 13.95 (ISBN 0-8016-0782-5). Mosby.

Carter. Chemotherapy of Cancer. 2nd ed. 400p. 1981. 15.75 (ISBN 0-471-08045-4, Pub. by Wiley Medical). Wiley.

Crooke, Stanley T. & Prestayko, Archie W. Cancer & Chemotherapy: Introduction to Clinical Oncology, Vol. 2. LC 79-8536. 1981. write for info. (ISBN 0-12-197802-8). Acad Pr.

International Congress of Chemotherapy, 11th & Interscience Conference on Antimicrobial Agents & Chemotherapy, 19th. Current Chemotherapy & Infectious Disease: Proceedings, 2 vols. Nelson, John D. & Grassi, Carlo, eds. (Illus.). 1980. Set. 75.00 (ISBN 0-914826-22-0). Am Soc Microbio.

Mathe, G. & Muggia, F. M., eds. Cancer Chemo- & Immunopharmacology, Part I: Chemopharmacology. (Recent Results in Cancer Research Ser.: Vol. 74). (Illus.). 315p. 1981. 66.00 (ISBN 0-387-10162-4). Springer-Verlag.

--Cancer Chemo- & Immunopharmacology, Part II: Immunopharmacology, Relations, & General Problems. (Recent Results in Cancer Research Ser.: Vol. 75). (Illus.). 260p. 1981. 52.00 (ISBN 0-387-10163-2). Springer-Verlag.

Pagliaro, Louis A., et al, eds. Problems in Pediatric Drug Therapy. LC 78-50204. 313p. 1979. text ed. 19.50 (ISBN 0-914768-29-8, 16). Drug Intl Pubns.

Pilapil, F. & Studva, K., eds. Programmed Instruction: Understanding Cancer & Chemotherapy. 80p. 1979. pap. 6.50 (ISBN 0-89352-081-0). Masson Pub.

Romankiewicz, John A., et al. Handbook of Essential Drug Therapy for Critical Care Nurses. LC 79-90429. 211p. 1980. pap. text ed. 12.50 spiral bound (ISBN 0-914768-35-2). Drug Intl Pubns.

Schoenfeld, H., ed. Antiparasitic Chemotherapy. (Antibiotics & Chemotherapy. Ser.: Vol. 30). (Illus.). 200p. 1981. 72.00 (ISBN 3-8055-2160-X). S Karger.

--Pharmacokinetics 1981. (Antibiotics & Chemotherapy Ser.: Vol. 31). (Illus.). 200p. 1981. 72.00 (ISBN 3-8055-2448-X). S Karger.

Scoy-Mosher, M. V. Chemotherapy: A Manual for Patients & Their Families. Date not set. Set Of 100. pap. 40.00. Masson Pub.

CHERAW INDIANS

see Indians of North America–Eastern States

CHEREMISSIAN LANGUAGE

Sebeok, Thomas A. Cheremis Literary Reader: With Glossary. (Indiana University Uralic & Altaic Ser.: Vol. 132). 120p. 1978. 17.00 (ISBN 2-8017-0096-7). Ind U Res Inst.

CHEROKEE INDIANS

see Indians of North America–Eastern States

CHERUBIM

see Angels

CHESAPEAKE AND OHIO CANAL

Brown, Alexander. Juniper Waterway: A History of the Albemarle & Chesapeake Canal. LC 80-14093. 1981. price not set (ISBN 0-917376-35-8). U Pr of Va.

CHESAPEAKE BAY

Hamer, Red. Four Seasons of the Chesapeake Bay: Fall-Winter, Vol. II. Hamer, Barbara H., ed. (Illus.). 128p. 1981. 27.50 (ISBN 0-9605400-2-4). Four Seas Bk.

--Four Seasons of the Chesapeake Bay: Spring-Summer, Vol. 1. Hamer, Barbara H., ed. (Illus.). 128p. 1980. 27.50 (ISBN 0-9605400-0-8). Four Seas Bk.

Smith, Daniel B. Inside the Great House: Planter Family Life in Eighteenth-Century Chesapeake Society. LC 80-14557. (Illus.). 368p. 1980. 17.50x (ISBN 0-8014-1313-3). Cornell U Pr.

CHESAPEAKE BAY RETRIEVER

see Dogs–Breeds–Chesapeake Bay Retriever

CHESS

Harding, T. D. Queen's Gambit Declined: Semi-Slav. (Illus.). 176p. 1981. pap. 18.50 (ISBN 0-7134-2448-6, Pub. by Batsford England). David & Charles.

Keene & Edwards. Chess Players Bedside Book. 14.95 (Pub. by Batsford England); pap. 10.95. David & Charles.

Kotov, Alexander. Train Like a Grandmaster. (Clubplayer's Library Ser.). (Illus.). 112p. 1981. pap. 11.95 (ISBN 0-7134-3609-3, Pub. by Batsford England). David & Charles.

Levy, D. N. Sacrifices in the Sicilian. (Batsford Chess Ser.). 196p. 1981. 19.95 (ISBN 0-7134-2596-2, Pub. by Batsford England); pap. 10.95 (ISBN 0-7134-2597-0). David & Charles.

--Sicilian Dragon: Classical & Levenfish Variations. 96p. 1981. pap. 11.95 (ISBN 0-7134-2744-2, Pub. by Batsford England). David & Charles.

Lifshitz, A. Test Your Chess IQ, 2 bks. Neat, K. P., ed. Incl. Bk. 1. 128p. 15.70 (ISBN 0-08-023120-9); pap. 8.90 (ISBN 0-08-024118-2); Bk. 2. 224p. 20.00 (ISBN 0-08-026881-1); pap. 13.40 (ISBN 0-08-026880-3). LC 80-41072. (Pergamon Russian Chess Ser.). (Illus.). 1981. Pergamon.

McCormick, Gene H. & Soltis, Andy. Bird's Defense to the Ruy Lopez. LC 80-28210. (Illus.). 220p. 1981. lib. bdg. write for info. McFarland & Co.

O'Connell, F. J. Batsford Fide Chess Yearbook, 1975-1976. 159p. 1976. 16.95 (ISBN 0-7134-1223-2). David & Charles.

Osborn, Leslie A. King of the Hill. Date not set. 7.95 (ISBN 0-533-04592-4). Vantage.

Pachman, Ludek. Complete Chess Strategy: Play on the Wings, Vol. 3. 176p. 1981. 3.95 (ISBN 0-346-12517-0). Cornerstone.

Povah, Nigel. Chess Training. 176p. 1981. 19.95 (ISBN 0-571-11604-3, Pub. by Faber & Faber); pap. 8.95 (ISBN 0-571-11608-6). Merrimack Bk Serv.

CHESS–BIOGRAPHY

Botvinnik, M. M. Mikhail Botvinnik: Soviet Chess Patriarch. LC 80-40437. (Pergamon Russian Chess Ser.). (Illus.). 230p. 1981. pap. 19.00 (ISBN 0-08-024120-4). Pergamon.

Denker, Arnold S. My Best Games of Chess 1929-75. Orig. Title: If You Must Play Chess. 190p. 1981. pap. price not set (ISBN 0-486-24035-5). Dover.

CHESS–COLLECTIONS OF GAMES

see also Chess–Tournaments

Botvinnik, M. M. Selected Games: 1967-1970. LC 80-40181. (Pergamon Russian Chess Ser.). (Illus.). 318p. 1981. 29.00 (ISBN 0-08-024124-7); pap. 13.95 (ISBN 0-08-024123-9). Pergamon.

Thomas, Hilary. Complete Games of Mikhail Tal, 1936-59. LC 80-69576. 192p. 1981. 15.00 (ISBN 0-668-05187-6, 5187). Arco.

Wicker, Kevin. Two Hundred Brilliancies. LC 80-54188. (Illus.). 144p. 1981. 15.00 (ISBN 0-668-05214-7, 5214). Arco.

CHESS–END GAMES

Levenfish & Smuslov. Rook Endings. pap. 10.95 (ISBN 0-7134-0449-3, Pub. by Batsford England). David & Charles.

CHESS–OPENINGS

Cafferty. Chess Openings for You. 16.95 (ISBN 0-7134-1976-8, Pub. by Batsford England); pap. 10.95 (ISBN 0-7134-1977-6). David & Charles.

Chandler, Murray. Sicilian 2c3. (Algebraic Chess Openings Ser.). (Illus.). 96p. 1981. pap. 11.50 (ISBN 0-7134-1933-4, Pub. by Batsford England). David & Charles.

Edwards, Raymond. Basic Chess Openings. rev. ed. (Routledge Chess Handbooks Ser.: No. 4). (Illus., Orig.). 1981. pap. price not set (ISBN 0-7100-0853-8). Routledge & Kegan.

Flesch, Janos. The Morra Gambit. (Algebraic Chess Openings Ser.). (Illus.). 176p. 1981. pap. 14.50 (ISBN 0-7134-2188-6, Pub. by Batsford England). David & Charles.

Keene, Raymond & Talbot, Shaun. French Defence: Tarrasch Variation. (Algebraic Chess Openings Ser.). (Illus.). 112p. 1981. pap. 11.95 (ISBN 0-7134-1898-2, Pub. by Batsford England). David & Charles.

Watson, John L. English: Franco, Slav & Flank Defence. (Contemporary Chess Openings Ser.). (Illus.). 112p. 1981. 19.50 (ISBN 0-7134-2690-X, Pub. by Batsford England). David & Charles.

CHESS–TOURNAMENTS

Edmondson, E. B. Chess Scandals: The Nineteen Seventy-Eight World Championship Match. (Pergamon Chess Ser.). (Illus.). 260p. 1981. 24.00 (ISBN 0-08-024145-X); pap. 14.40 (ISBN 0-08-024144-1). Pergamon.

Hartston, W. R. & Reuben, S. London Nineteen Eighty: Phillips & Drew Kings Chess Tournament. (Pergamon Chess Ser.). (Illus.). 230p. 1981. 21.60 (ISBN 0-08-024141-7); pap. 21.60 (ISBN 0-08-024140-9). Pergamon.

Nimzovich, Aron. Selected Games from the Carlsbad International Chess Tournament 1929. Marfia, Jim, tr. from Rus. 143p. (Orig.). 1981. pap. price not set (ISBN 0-486-24115-7). Dover.

CHESS GAMES

see Chess–Collections of Games

CHESS OPENINGS

see Chess–Openings

CHEST–DISEASES–DIAGNOSIS

Borrie, John. Management of Thoracic Emergencies. 3rd ed. (Illus.). 500p. 1979. 39.50x (ISBN 0-8385-6124-1). ACC.

Emerson, Peter, ed. Thoracic Medicine. 1981. text ed. price not set (ISBN 0-407-00210-3). Butterworth.

Glinz, W. Chest Trauma: Diagnosis & Management. (Illus.). 310p. 1981. 58.00 (ISBN 0-387-10409-7). Springer-Verlag.

Haft, Jacob I., ed. Differential Diagnosis of Chest Pain & Other Cardiac Symptoms. LC 80-68061. (Advances in the Management of Clinical Heart Disease Monograph: Vol. 4). (Illus.). 230p. 1980. 26.50 (ISBN 0-87993-150-7). Futura Pub.

CHEST–SURGERY

Coordinating Committee for Continuing Education in Thoracic Surgery. Self-Education-Self Assessment in Thoracic Surgery. 208p. 1980. pap. text ed. 100.00 (ISBN 0-8403-2331-X). Kendall-Hunt.

James, Edwin C., et al. Thoracic and Cardiovascular Surgery Continuing Education Review. 1980. pap. 16.00 (ISBN 0-87488-439-X). Med Exam.

Kaiser, Gerard A., et al. Thoracic Surgery Case Studies. 1979. pap. 15.75 (ISBN 0-87488-056-4). Med Exam.

CHESTER COUNTY, PENNSYLVANIA–BIOGRAPHY

Hamer, Red. The Four Seasons of Chester County. (Illus.). 96p. 1979. 24.95 (ISBN 0-9605400-0-8). Four Seas Bk.

CHETAHS

see Cheetahs

CHEVROLET AUTOMOBILE

see Automobiles–Types–Chevrolet

CHEYENNE INDIANS

see Indians of North America–The West

CHICAGO–DESCRIPTION

Caro, Ruth, et al. The Lake Is Always East. 128p. 1981. spiral bdg. 2.95 (ISBN 0-695-81566-0). Follett.

Heimovics, Rachel B. Chicago Jewish Source Book. 336p. 1981. pap. 6.95 (ISBN 0-695-81568-7). Follett.

Klimovitch, Don, et al. The Chicago Book. (Illus., Orig.). 1981. pap. 5.95 (ISBN 0-8092-5893-5). Contemp Bks.

Krantz, Les. Portrait of Chicago. Pfeiffer, Douglas, ed. (Portrait of America Ser.). (Illus.). 80p. (Orig.). 1981. pap. text ed. 5.95 (ISBN 0-912856-70-X). Graphic Arts Ctr.

Robert Lang Adams & Associates, ed. The Chicago Job Bank: A Comprehensive Guide to Major Employers Throughout Greater Chicago. (Job Bank Ser.). 300p. (Orig.). 1981. pap. 9.95 (ISBN 0-937860-05-0). Adams Inc MA.

CHICAGO–HISTORY

Davis, Perry. Chicago: Creating New Traditions. LC 76-45167. (Illus.). 1976. 12.50 (ISBN 0-913820-03-2); pap. 7.95 (ISBN 0-913820-05-9). Chicago Hist.

Jones, Peter D. & Holli, Melvin G., eds. Ethnic Chicago. 336p. (Orig.). 1981. pap. 12.95 (ISBN 0-8028-1821-8). Eerdmans.

CHICAGO BASEBALL CLUB (NATIONAL LEAGUE, CUBS)

Gold, Eddie. Eddie Gold's White Sox & Cubs Trivia Book. 144p. 1981. pap. 3.95 (ISBN 0-695-81574-1). Follett.

Schwab, Rick. Stuck on the Cubs. 192p. (Orig.). 1977. pap. 1.95 (ISBN 0-930528-01-8). Sassafras Pr.

CHICAGO BASEBALL CLUB (AMERICAN LEAGUE)

Gold, Eddie. Eddie Gold's White Sox & Cubs Trivia Book. 144p. 1981. pap. 3.95 (ISBN 0-695-81574-1). Follett.

CHICANOS

see Mexican Americans

CHICKASAW INDIANS

see Indians of North America–Eastern States

CHICKENS
see Poultry
CHIEF JUSTICES
see Judges
CHILD ABUSE

Burt, Robert A. & Wald, Michael. Standards Relating to Abuse & Neglect. (Juvenile Justice Standards Project Ser.). Date not set. softcover 7.95 (ISBN 0-88410-830-9); casebound 16.50 (ISBN 0-88410-242-4). Ballinger Pub.

Evans, Alan L. Personality Characteristics & Disciplinary Attitudes of Child-Abusing Mothers. LC 80-69240. 145p. 1981. perfect bdg. 11.95 (ISBN 0-86548-033-8). Century Twenty One.

Finkelhor, David. Sexually Victimized Children. LC 79-7104. 1981. pap. text ed. 7.95 (ISBN 0-02-910400-9). Free Pr.

Harkness, Don, ed. Humanistic Issues in Child Abuse. 100p. (Orig.). 1981. pap. 3.50 (ISBN 0-934996-13-X). Am Stud Pr.

Kadushin, Alfred & Martin, Judith A. Child Abuse: An Interactional Event. (Illus.). 360p. 1981. 25.00x (ISBN 0-231-04774-6). Columbia U Pr.

Mrazek, Patricia B. & Kempe, C. H. Sexually Abused Children & Their Families. 300p. 1981. 72.01 (ISBN 0-08-026796-3). Pergamon.

Polansky, Norman A., et al. Damaged Parents: An Anatomy of Child Neglect. LC 80-22793. (Illus.). 288p. 1981. 15.00 (ISBN 0-226-67221-2). U of Chicago Pr.

Sexual Abuse of Children: Implications from the Sexual Trauma Treatment Program of Connecticut-Special Report of Two Research Utilization Workshops. 1979. 3.00. Comm Coun Great NY.

Starr, R. H., ed. Child Abuse Predictions: Policy Implications. 1981. pns professional reference (ISBN 0-88410-378-1). Ballinger Pub.

CHILD AND MOTHER
see Mother and Child
CHILD AND PARENT
see Parent and Child
CHILD BEHAVIOR
see Child Psychology; Children–Management; Etiquette for Children and Youth
CHILD BIRTH
see Childbirth
CHILD CARE CENTERS
see Day Care Centers
CHILD CUSTODY
see Custody of Children
CHILD DEVELOPMENT
see also Child Psychology; Children–Growth

Asher, Steven & Gottman, John, eds. The Development of Children's Friendships. LC 80-25920. (Illus.). 336p. Date not set. price not set (ISBN 0-521-23103-5); pap. price not set (ISBN 0-521-29806-7). Cambridge U Pr.

Book Review Committee. Family Life & Child Development: Selective Bibliography Cumulative Through 1979. (Jewish Board of Family & Children Services). 1979. pap. 3.00 (ISBN 0-87183-187-2). Jewish Bd Family.

Carter, Nicholas, ed. Development, Growth, & Aging. 176p. 1980. 25.00x (ISBN 0-85664-861-2, Pub. by Croom Helm England). State Mutual Bk.

Gander & Gardiner. Child & Adolescent Development. 1981. text ed. 16.95 (ISBN 0-316-30322-4); tchrs'. manual free (ISBN 0-316-30319-4); study guide 5.95 (ISBN 0-316-30318-6). Little.

Gappa, Sylvia & Glenn, Deirdre. Room to Grow. LC 80-81681. (Learning Handbooks Ser.). 1981. pap. 5.95 (ISBN 0-8224-5875-6). Pitman Learning.

Jones, Barbara S. Movement Themes: Topics for Early Childhood Learning Through Creative Movement. LC 80-65608. 115p. 1981. perfect bdg. 8.50 (ISBN 0-86548-042-7). Century Twenty One.

Kannenberg, Gary D. From Birth to Twelve: How to Be a Successful Parent to Infants & Children. LC 80-69331. 125p. 1981. 7.95 (ISBN 0-86548-043-5). Century Twenty One.

Leach, Penelope. Your Baby & Child: From Birth to Age Five. pap. 9.95 (ISBN 0-394-73509-9). Knopf.

Powell, Marcene L. Assessment & Management of Developmental Changes & Problems in Children. (Illus.). 350p. 1981. pap. 12.95 (ISBN 0-8016-1520-8). Mosby.

Rosenzweig, Mark R. & Brown, T. A., eds. Intelligence & Affectivity: Their Relationship During Child Development. Brown, T. A. & Kaegi, C. E., trs. (Illus.). 1981. 8.00 (ISBN 0-8243-2901-5). Annual Reviews.

Sahler, Olle J. The Child from Three to Eighteen. (Illus.). 260p. 1981. softcover 12.50 (ISBN 0-8016-4290-6). Mosby.

Tate-O'Brien, Judith. Welcome: Christian Parenting. 68p. (Orig.). 1980. pap. 4.00 (ISBN 0-936098-15-5); instrs.' guide 3.00 (ISBN 0-686-68853-8). Natl Marriage.

Tudor, Mary J. Child Development. 544p. 1981. text ed. 22.95 (ISBN 0-07-065412-3, HP). McGraw.

Verny, Thomas & Kelly, John. The Secret Life of the Unborn Child. 256p. 1981. 12.95 (ISBN 0-671-25312-3). Summit Bks.

Warrell, Susan E. Helping Young Children Grow: A Humanistic Approach to Parenting & Teaching. 240p. 1980. 12.95 (Spec); pap. 5.95. P-H.

White, Earl. Nourishing Self Esteem: A Parent Handbook for Nurturing Love. (Illus.). 95p. (Orig.). 1981. pap. text ed. 5.00 (ISBN 0-686-69561-5). Whitenwife Pubns.

CHILD DISCIPLINE
see Discipline of Children
CHILD HEALTH
see Child Welfare; Children–Care and Hygiene
CHILD LABOR
see Children–Employment; Youth–Employment
CHILD NEGLECT
see Child Abuse
CHILD PLACING
see Adoption; Foster Home Care
CHILD PSYCHOLOGY
see also Cognition (Child Psychology); Educational Psychology; Infant Psychology; Learning, Psychology of

Berger, Brigitte & Callahan, Sidney, eds. Child Care & Mediating Structures. 1979. 9.25 (ISBN 0-8447-2162-X); pap. 4.25. Am Enterprise.

Bursynski, P. R., ed. To Be a Child: A Book of Photographic Essays on the Psychological Rights of the Child. 65p. 1979. 10.00 (ISBN 0-917668-03-0). Intl Schl Psych.

Cooper, John O. Measuring Behavior. 2nd ed. (Special Education Ser.). (Illus.). 224p. 1981. pap. text ed. 7.95 (ISBN 0-675-08078-9). Merrill.

Drescher, John M. Siete Necesidades Basicas Del Nino. 160p. (Span.). 1981. pap. write for info. (ISBN 0-311-46085-2). Casa Bautista.

Field, Tiffany, ed. Culture & Early Interactions. 300p. 1981. ref. ed. 19.95 (ISBN 0-89859-097-3). L Erlbaum Assocs.

Gabel, Stewart, ed. Behavioral Problems of Childhood. 1981. price not set (ISBN 0-8089-1336-0). Grune.

Gillmore, John & Gillmore, Eunice. Give Your Child a Future: How to Develop a Productive Personality. 1981. pap. 6.95 (ISBN 0-89803-038-2). Caroline Hse.

Hetherington-Parke. Contemporary Readings in Child Psychology. 2nd ed. Nave, Patricia S., ed. 448p. 1981. pap. text ed. 11.97 (ISBN 0-07-028426-1, C). McGraw.

Ilg, Frances L., et al. Child Behavior. rev. ed. LC 80-8371. (Illus.). 1981. 14.95 (ISBN 0-06-014829-2, HarpT). Har-Row.

Kauffman, James M. Characteristics of Children's Behavior Disorders. 2nd ed. (Special Education Ser.). (Illus.). 352p. 1981. pap. text ed. 17.95 (ISBN 0-675-08055-X); write for info. instrs'. manual. Merrill.

Nagera, Humberto. Developmental Understanding of the Child. LC 80-69668. 378p. 1981. 30.00 (ISBN 0-87668-432-0). Aronson.

Nash, Eric, ed. Behavioral Assessment Childhood Disorders. Terdal, Leif. (Behavioral Assessment Ser.). 750p. 1981. 27.50 (ISBN 0-89862-141-0). Guilford Pr.

Pinard, Adrien. The Conservation of Conservation: The Child's Acquisition of a Fundamental Concept. Feider, Helga, tr. LC 80-26339. (Chicago Originals Ser.). 200p. 1981. lib. bdg. 14.00x (ISBN 0-226-66834-7). U of Chicago Pr.

Sarnoff, Charles. Latency. LC 75-42548. 400p. 1981. Repr. of 1976 ed. 25.00 (ISBN 0-686-69588-7). Aronson.

Smith, P. K. & Connolly, K. J. The Ecology of Preschool Behaviour. LC 79-42647. (Illus.). 400p. Date not set. 49.50 (ISBN 0-521-22331-8). Cambridge U Pr.

Solomon, Ben & Bowers, Ethel M. You Can Be a Leader. 140p. (Orig.). 1981. pap. 4.95 (ISBN 0-936626-03-8). Leadership Pr.

Sully, James. Studies in Childhood. (Contributions to the History of Psycholgy Ser.: Psychometrics & Educational Psychology). 1978. Repr. of 1978 ed. 30.00 (ISBN 0-89093-162-3). U Pubns Amer.

Taylor, A. R. The Study of the Child. 215p. 1980. Repr. of 1910 ed. lib. bdg. 35.00. Telegraph Bks.

Toback, Charles. Pediatrician's Psychological Handbook. LC 79-92916. 1980. pap. 10.50 (ISBN 0-87488-687-2). Med Exam.

Vance, R. & Hall, Marilyn C. How to Select Reinforcers. 1980. pap. 3.25 (ISBN 0-89079-052-3). H & H Ent.

Van Houten, Ron. How to Use Reprimands. 1980. pap. 3.25 (ISBN 0-89079-051-5). H & H Ent.

Yando, Regina & Seitz, Victoria. Intellectual & Personality Characteristics of Children: Social-Class & Ethnic-Group Differences. 136p. 1979. profess./reference text 12.95 (ISBN 0-89859-001-9). Erlbaum Assocs.

CHILD PSYCHOTHERAPY

Hoffman, Leon. The Evaluation & Care of Severely Disturbed Children & Their Families. 1981. text ed. write for info. (ISBN 0-89335-129-6). Spectrum Pub.

Reisman, John M. Principles of Psychotherapy with Children. LC 80-29581. 354p. 1981. Repr. of 1973 ed. lib. bdg. price not set (ISBN 0-89874-317-6). Krieger.

CHILD PSYCHOTHERAPY–RESIDENTIAL TREATMENT

Hoffman, Leon. The Evaluation & Care of Severely Disturbed Children & Their Families. 1981. text ed. write for info. (ISBN 0-89335-129-6). Spectrum Pub.

CHILD REARING
see Children–Management
CHILD STUDY
see Child Development; Child Psychology
CHILD WELFARE
see also Child Abuse; Children–Law; Day Care Centers; Foster Home Care; Juvenile Delinquency

Bursynski, P. R., ed. To Be a Child: A Book of Photographic Essays on the Psychological Rights of the Child. 65p. 1979. 10.00 (ISBN 0-917668-03-0). Intl Schl Psych.

CWLA Directory of Member Agencies & Associates Listing. LC 78-646558. (Orig.). 1981. pap. text ed. 10.00 (ISBN 0-87868-201-5). Child Welfare.

Gratch, Alan S. Board Members Are Child Advocates. (Orig.). 1980. pap. text ed. 4.95 (ISBN 0-87868-198-1). Child Welfare.

Lemmon, John, ed. Family Law & Child Welfare: Selected Current Trends in Legal Social Work Practice. (Law & Social Work Quarterly Ser.: Vol. 1, No. 1). 112p. 1981. text ed. 12.95 (ISBN 0-917724-64-X). Haworth Pr.

Salary Study 1981. 1981. pap. text ed. 5.75 (ISBN 0-87868-203-1). Child Welfare.

The Worker Burnout Phenomenon: Implications of Current Research for the Child Protective System. 1978. 1.00. Comm Coun Great NY.

CHILD WELFARE–LAW AND LEGISLATION
see Children–Law
CHILD WELFARE–GREAT BRITAIN

Holman, Bob. Kids at the Door: A Preventative Project on a Council Estate. (Practical of Social Work Ser.: No. 8). 208p. 1981. 25.00x (ISBN 0-631-12586-8, Pub. by Basil Blackwell England); pap. 12.50x (ISBN 0-631-12587-6). Biblio Dist.

O'Neill, Tom. A Place Called Hope: Caring for Children in Distress. (Practice of Social Work Ser.: No. 7). 128p. 1981. 22.50x (ISBN 0-631-12963-4, Pub. by Basil Blackwell England); pap. 8.95x (ISBN 0-631-12654-6). Biblio Dist.

Packman, Jean. The Child's Generation: Child Care Policy in Britain. 2nd ed. (Aspects of Social Policy Ser.). 200p. 1981. pap. 12.50x (ISBN 0-631-12664-3, Pub. by Basil Blackwell England). Biblio Dist.

CHILDBIRTH
see also Labor (Obstetrics)

Anderson, Barbara & Shapiro, Pamela. Emergency Childbirth Handbook. 1979. pap. 7.40 (ISBN 0-8273-1761-1). Delmar.

Berezin, Nancy. The Gentle Birth Book: A Practical Guide to Leboyer Family-Centered Delivery. 1981. pap. 2.95 (ISBN 0-671-41990-0). PB.

Bradley, Robert A. Husband Coached Childbirth. 3rd ed. LC 80-8683. (Illus.). 256p. 1981. 9.95 (ISBN 0-06-014850-0, HarpT). Har-Row.

Cohen, Jean P. & Goirand, Roger. Your Baby: Pregnancy, Delivery, & Infant Care. (Illus.). 304p. 1981. 16.95 (ISBN 0-13-978130-7, Spec); pap. 8.95 (ISBN 0-13-978122-6). P-H.

Dalton, Katharina. Depression After Childbirth: How to Recognize & Treat Postnatal Illness. (Illus.). 192p. 1981. 13.95 (ISBN 0-19-217701-X); pap. 6.95 (ISBN 0-19-286008-9). Oxford U Pr.

Ewy, Donna & Ewy, Rodger. The Cycle of Life. (Illus.). 384p. 1981. 17.95 (ISBN 0-525-93181-3). Dutton.

Fielding, Kathy. The Total Experiance of Having Your Baby at Home. 2.95 (ISBN 0-912216-23-9). Green Hill.

Hodson, Geoffrey. The Miracle of Birth. rev. ed. LC 80-53950. (Illus.). 100p. 1981. pap. 3.95 (ISBN 0-8356-0545-0). Theos Pub Hse.

Horos, Carol. Prepared Childbirth. Date not set. pap. 2.25 (ISBN 0-440-07087-2). Dell.

Kieffer, Joyce L. To Have, To Hold. 2nd ed. (Illus.). 80p. 1981. pap. 4.95 (ISBN 0-933794-02-9). Train Res Assoc.

Milburn, Joyce & Smith, Lynette. The Natural Childbirth Book. 224p. (Orig.). 1981. pap. 5.95 (ISBN 0-87123-399-1, 210339). Bethany Fell.

Perkins, Elizabeth R. Education for Childbirth & Parenthood. 180p. 1980. bds. 27.50x (ISBN 0-7099-0273-5, Pub. by Croom Helm Ltd England). Biblio Dist.

CHILDBIRTH–PSYCHOLOGY

Feher, Elizabeth. The Psychology of Birth: Roots of Human Personality. 224p. 1981. 12.95 (ISBN 0-8264-0039-6). Continuum.

CHILDHOOD
see Children
CHILDREN
see also Church Work with Children; Day Care Centers; Education of Children; Etiquette for Children and Youth; Exceptional Children; Heredity; Infants; Kindergarten; Play; Prenatal Influences; Stepchildren; Television and Children; Youth

Duboscq, Genevieve. My Longest Night. Woodward, Richard S., tr. from Fr. LC 80-23169. (Illus.). 288p. 1981. 12.95 (ISBN 0-394-51590-0). Seaver Bks.

Elkind, David. Children & Adolescents. 3rd ed. 272p. 1981. text ed. 15.95x (ISBN 0-19-502820-1); pap. text ed. 5.95x (ISBN 0-19-502821-X). Oxford U Pr.

CHILDREN–AMUSEMENTS
see Amusements
CHILDREN–BOOKS AND READING
see Books and Reading for Children
CHILDREN–CARE AND HYGIENE
see also Baby Sitters; Children–Diseases; Children–Nutrition; Health Education; Infants–Care and Hygiene; Nurses and Nursing; Pediatric Nursing; Physical Education for Children; School Children–Food; School Health; School Nursing

Adler, Jack. Fundamentals of Group Child Care: A Textbook & Instructional Guide for Child Care Workers. 1981. price not set reference (ISBN 0-88410-198-3). Ballinger Pub.

All About Raising Children, Nineteen Eighty-One. 1980. 10.95 (ISBN 0-911094-07-5). Pacific Santa Barbara.

Ames, Louise B. & Ilg, Frances L. Your Five Year Old. 1981. pap. 4.95 (ISBN 0-440-59494-4, Delta). Dell.

Berger, Brigitte & Callahan, Sidney, eds. Child Care & Mediating Structures. 1979. 9.25 (ISBN 0-8447-2162-X); pap. 4.25. Am Enterprise.

Blackstone, Tessa. Education & Day Care for Young Children in Need: The American Experience. 72p. 1973. pap. text ed. 1.90x (ISBN 0-7199-0875-2, Pub. by Bedford,England). Renouf.

Clark, Oliver. Never Catch Colds Again. 64p. 1979. pap. 6.95x (ISBN 0-8464-1035-4). Beekman Pubs.

Davies, Bleddyn. Variatons in Childrens Services Among Urban Authorities. 159p. 1972. pap. text ed. 6.25x (ISBN 0-7135-1676-3, Pub. by Bedford England). Renouf.

De Mille, Richard. Put Your Mother on the Ceiling: Children's Imagination Games. LC 67-23698. 192p. (gr. 1 up). 1981. Repr. of 1967 ed. 9.95 (ISBN 0-915520-39-7). Ross-Erikson.

Griffith, H. Winter, et al. Information & Instructions for Pediatric Patients. LC 80-51712. 320p. 1980. 35.00 (ISBN 0-938372-00-9). Winter Pub Co.

Heagarty, Margaret C., et al. Child Health: Basics for Primary Care. 454p. 1980. pap. text ed. 16.95 (ISBN 0-8385-1111-2). ACC.

Huggins, Hal A. Why Raise Ugly Kids? How You Can Fulfill Your Child's Health & Happiness Potential. (Illus.). 256p. 1981. 12.95 (ISBN 0-87000-507-3). Arlington Hse.

Jelliffe, D. B. & Jelliffe, E. F., eds. Advances in International Maternal & Child Health, Vol. 1. 250p. 1981. text ed. 45.00x (ISBN 0-19-261281-6). Oxford U Pr.

King, Michael. Childhood, Welfare & Justice. 160p. 1981. pap. 16.95 (ISBN 0-7134-3713-8, Pub. by Batsford England). David & Charles.

Krueger, Caryl W. Six Weeks to Better Parenting: The Complete Guide for Creative Raising of Children 2-12. 348p. 1981. pap. 8.95 (ISBN 0-938632-05-1). Belleridge.

Levy, Janine. You & Your Toddler: Sharing the Developing Years. (Illus.). 1981. 10.95 (ISBN 0-394-51532-3); pap. 6.95 (ISBN 0-394-74806-9). Pantheon.

Mante, Daisy R. & Mathisen, Bonnie W. Growing Better Brighter Children. 160p. (Orig.). Date not set. pap. price not set (ISBN 0-931310-02-4). Jifunza Educ.

Mitchell, Rose G. & Mackenzie, James, eds. Child Health in the Community. 2nd ed. (Illus.). 352p. 1980. text ed. 37.50 (ISBN 0-443-02195-3). Churchill.

Olness, Karen. Parenting Happy Healthy Children. 1981. 9.95 (ISBN 0-9602790-4-0). The Garden.

--Raising Happy Healthy Children. 1981. pap. 3.95 (ISBN 0-9602790-5-9). The Garden.

Pillitteri, Adele. Child Health Nursing: Care of the Growing Family. 2nd ed. 1981. text ed. write for info (ISBN 0-316-70793-7). Little.

Prensky, Arthur L. & Palkes, Helen. Care of the Neurologically Handicapped Child. (Illus.). 350p. 1981. text ed. 18.95x (ISBN 0-19-502917-8). Oxford U Pr.

Schaffer, H. R. Child Care & the Family. 88p. 1968. pap. text ed. 5.00x (ISBN 0-7135-1511-2, Pub. by Bedford England). Renouf.

Sherbon, Florence B. The Child: His Origin, Development & Care. 707p. 1980. Repr. of 1934 ed. lib. bdg. 50.00 (ISBN 0-89984-422-7). Century Bookbindery.

Smith, David H. & Hokelman, Robert A. Controversies in Child Health & Pediatrics. (Illus.). 480p. 1981. text ed. 29.95 (ISBN 0-07-058510-5, HP). McGraw.

Tackett, Jo J. & Hunsberger, Mabel. Family-Centered Care of Children & Adolescents: Nursing Concepts in Child Health. 800p. 1981. text ed. price not set (ISBN 0-7216-8740-7). Saunders.

Thomson, Jessie. Natural & Healthy Childhood. 120p. 1976. pap. 6.00x (ISBN 0-8464-1034-6). Beekman Pubs.

Weinfeld, Nanci R. Helpful Hints & Tricks for New Moms & Dads. LC 80-53669. (Illus.). 96p. (Orig.). 1981. pap. 3.95 (ISBN 0-528-88041-1). Rand.

Wigmore, Ann. Healthy Children: Nature's Way. 120p. pap. 1.95. Hippocrates.

CHILDREN–CHARITIES
see Child Welfare
CHILDREN–CUSTODY
see Custody of Children
CHILDREN–DISCIPLINE
see Discipline of Children
CHILDREN–DISEASES
see also Infants–Diseases; Pediatric Allergy; Pediatric Nursing
also names of diseases, e.g. Chicken Pox, Whooping Cough

Clark, Oliver. Never Catch Colds Again. 64p. 1979. pap. 6.95x (ISBN 0-8464-1035-4). Beekman Pubs.

Levine. Cancer in the Young. 1981. write for info. Masson Pub.

Lusher. Acquired Bleeding Disorders in Children: Abnormalities of Hemostasis. (Monographs in Pediatric Hematology-Oncology: Vol. 3). 1981. price not set (ISBN 0-89352-127-2). Masson Pub.

Thomson, Jessie. Natural & Healthy Childhood. 120p. 1976. pap. 6.00x (ISBN 0-8464-1034-6). Beekman Pubs.

Walker & Smith. Practical Approach to Gastroenterology & Procedures in Childhood. (Postgraduate Pediatric Ser.). 1981. text ed. price not set. Butterworth.

CHILDREN–DISEASES–DIAGNOSIS

see also Pediatric Radiology

Kalokerinos, Archie. Every Second Child. LC 80-84435. 138p. 1981. pap. 2.95 (ISBN 0-87983-250-9). Keats.

CHILDREN–DISEASES–PSYCHOSOMATIC ASPECTS

see Pediatrics–Psychosomatic Aspects

CHILDREN–EDUCATION

see Education of Children

CHILDREN–EMPLOYMENT

see also Apprentices; Labor Supply; Youth–Employment

Tann, Jennifer. Children at Work. (History in Focus Ser.). (Illus.). 72p. (gr. 6 up). 1981. 14.95 (ISBN 0-7134-3553-4, Pub. by Batsford England). David & Charles.

CHILDREN–ETIQUETTE

see Etiquette for Children and Youth

CHILDREN–FOOD

see Children–Nutrition

CHILDREN–GROWTH

Gappa, Sylvia & Glenn, Deirdre. Room to Grow. LC 80-81681. (Learning Handbooks Ser.). 1981. pap. 5.95 (ISBN 0-8224-5875-6). Pitman Learning.

Leach, Penelope. Your Baby & Child: From Birth to Age Five. pap. 9.95 (ISBN 0-394-73509-9). Knopf.

Riggs, Maida L. Jump to Joy: Helping Children Grow Through Active Play. (Illus.). 176p. 1980. 12.95 (Spec); pap. 6.95. P-H.

Young, Harben B., et al. Height & Weight of Children in Relation to Socioeconomic Status: Tunisia & the United States. Shipp, Audrey, ed. 50p. Date not set. pap. text ed. 1.75 (ISBN 0-8406-0206-5). Natl Ctr Health Stats.

CHILDREN–HEALTH

see Children–Care and Hygiene

CHILDREN–HYGIENE

see Children–Care and Hygiene

CHILDREN–JUVENILE LITERATURE

see also names of geographic areas, countries, etc. for books about the children of those areas

Oxenbury, Helen. Family. (Baby Board Bks.). (Illus.). 12p. (ps-k). Date not set. boards 3.50 (ISBN 0-671-42110-7, Little Simon). S&S.

CHILDREN–LANGUAGE

Hakes, D. T. The Development of Metalinguistic Abilities in Children. (Springer Series in Language & Communication: Vol. 9). (Illus.). 119p. 1980. 22.50 (ISBN 0-387-10295-7). Springer-Verlag.

Murry, Thomas & Murry, John, eds. Infant Communication: Cry & Early Speech. (Illus.). 342p. 1980. text ed. 28.95 (ISBN 0-933014-62-7). College-Hill.

Pinnell, Gay S., ed. Discovering Language with Children. LC 80-24795. 132p. (Orig.). 1980. pap. 5.50 (ISBN 0-8141-1210-2, 12102). NCTE.

Reynell, Joan. Language Developement & Assessment. (Studies in Developmental Pediatrics Ser.: Vol. 1). 178p. 1980. text ed. 16.50 (ISBN 0-88416-377-6). PSG Pub.

Stibbs, Andrew. Assessing Children's Language: Guidelines for Teachers. 1980. pap. text ed. 4.25x (ISBN 0-7062-3853-2, Pub. by Ward Lock Educational England). Hayden.

Tavakolian, Susan, ed. Language Acquisition & Linguistic Theory. (Illus.). 336p. 1981. text ed. 19.95x (ISBN 0-262-20039-2). MIT Pr.

Teller, Virginia & White, Sheila J., eds. Studies in Child Language & Multilingualism. LC 80-16810. 187p. 1980. 28.00x (ISBN 0-89766-078-1). NY Acad Sci.

CHILDREN–LAW

see also Adoption; Children–Employment; Custody of Children; Guardian and Ward; Juvenile Courts; Juvenile Delinquency; Parent and Child (Law); Stepchildren

Feld, Barry & Levy, Robert J. Standards Relating to Rights of Minors. (Juvenile Justice Standards Project Ser.). 1980. softcover 7.95 (ISBN 0-88410-810-4); casebound 16.50 (ISBN 0-88410-243-2). Ballinger Pub.

Flicker, Barbara. Standards for Juvenile Justice: A Summary & Analysis. (Juvenile Justice Standards Project Ser.). 1981. softcover 7.95 (ISBN 0-88410-758-2); casebound 16.50 (ISBN 0-88410-831-7). Ballinger Pub.

Lemmon, John, ed. Family Law & Child Welfare: Selected Current Trends in Legal Social Work Practice. (Law & Social Work Quarterly Ser.: Vol. 1, No. 1). 112p. 1981. text ed. 12.95 (ISBN 0-917724-64-X). Haworth Pr.

Prescott, Peter S. The Child Savers. LC 80-2705. 320p. 1981. 12.95 (ISBN 0-394-50235-3). Knopf.

Tann, Jennifer. Children at Work. (History in Focus Ser.). (Illus.). 72p. (gr. 6 up). 1981. 14.95 (ISBN 0-7134-3553-4, Pub. by Batsford England). David & Charles.

CHILDREN–MANAGEMENT

see also Baby Sitters; Child Abuse; Discipline of Children; Moral Education; Parent and Child; Problem Children

Brooks, Jane B. The Process of Parenting. (Illus.). 460p. (Orig.). 1981. write for info (ISBN 0-87484-474-6). Mayfield Pub.

Byers, J. W. Parent & Child. 60p. pap. 0.50. Faith Pub Hse.

Campbell, Jean M. Reaching Out with Love: Encounters with Troubled Youth. 144p. (Orig.). 1981. pap. 2.95 (ISBN 0-87239-453-0, 3652). Standard Pub.

Crary, Elizabeth. Without Spanking or Spoiling: A Practical Approach to Toddler & Preschool Guidance. LC 79-18253. (Illus.). 104p. (Orig.). 1979. pap. 6.95 (ISBN 0-9602862-0-9); write for info leaders' guide (ISBN 0-9602862-1-7). Parenting Pr.

Dardig, Jill C. & Heward, William L. Sign Here: A Contracting Book for Children & Their Parents. 2nd ed. LC 76-18757. (Illus.). 166p. 1981. pap. 10.00 (ISBN 0-917472-04-7); leader's manual 3.00 (ISBN 0-914474-27-8). F Fournies.

Davis, Ken & Taylor, Tom. Kids & Cash. 320p. 1981. pap. 2.95 (ISBN 0-553-14152-X). Bantam.

Dillow, Linda & Arp, Claudia. Sanity in the Summertime. 224p. 1981. 8.95 (ISBN 0-8407-5237-7); pap. 4.95 (ISBN 0-8407-5754-9). Nelson.

Dodson, Fitzhugh & Ruben, Paula. How to Grandparent. LC 80-7849. 304p. 1981. 12.95 (ISBN 0-690-01874-6, HarpT). Har-Row.

Engelmann, Seigfried & Engelmann, Therese. Give Your Child a Superior Mind. 320p. 1981. 5.95 (ISBN 0-346-12532-4). Cornerstone.

Fay, Jennifer & Adams, Caren. What Do I Say? Protecting Your Child from Sexual Assault. (Illus.). 96p. (Orig.). 1981. pap. 3.95 (ISBN 0-915166-24-0). Impact Pubs Cal.

Friedland, Ronnie & Kort, Carol, eds. The Mother's Book. 384p. 1981. 14.95 (ISBN 0-686-69055-9). HM.

Illingworth, Ronald. Your Child's Development in the First Five Years. (Churchill Livingstone Patient Handbook Ser.). (Illus.). 96p. 1981. pap. text ed. 3.00 (ISBN 0-686-28941-2). Churchill.

Johnston, Madeline. Channels Worth Watching. Van Dolson, Bobbie J., ed. 64p. 1981. pap. write for info. (ISBN 0-8280-0030-1). Review & Herald.

Krueger, Caryl W. Six Weeks to Better Parenting: The Complete Guide for Creative Raising of Children 2-12. 348p. 1981. pap. 8.95 (ISBN 0-938632-05-1). Belleridge.

Levy, Janine. You & Your Toddler: Sharing the Developing Years. (Illus.). 1981. 10.95 (ISBN 0-394-51532-3); pap. 6.95 (ISBN 0-394-74806-9). Pantheon.

Moore, Raymond & Moore, Dorothy. Home Grown Kids. 1981. 9.95 (ISBN 0-8499-0270-3). Word Bks.

Phillips, Mike. Blueprint for Raising a Child. 1978. pap. 3.95 (ISBN 0-88270-280-7). Logos.

Schwartz, Bernard & Pugh, James M. How to Get Your Children to Be Good Students-How to Get Your Students to Be Good Children. LC 80-27826. 150p. 1981. 8.95 (ISBN 0-13-409862-5). P-H.

Servey, Richad W. Elementary Social Studies: A Skills Emphasis. 600p. 1981. text ed. 17.95 (ISBN 0-205-07213-5, 2372134). Allyn.

Spellmann, Charles M. & Williams, Rachel. Pitching in: How to Teach Your Children to Work Around the House. (Illus.). 1981. pap. 4.95 (ISBN 0-915190-31-1). Jalmar Pr.

Stevens, Laura J. & Stoner, Rosemary B. How to Improve Your Child's Behavior Through Diet. 1981. pap. 3.50 (ISBN 0-451-09812-9, E9812, Signet Bks). NAL.

Teele, James E. Mastering Stress in Child Rearing: Parental Coping Versus Spontaneous Remission. LC 79-48006. 1981. price not set (ISBN 0-669-03622-6). Lexington Bks.

Weinfeld, Nanci R. Helpful Hints & Tricks for New Moms & Dads. LC 80-53669. (Illus.). 96p. (Orig.). 1981. pap. 3.95 (ISBN 0-528-88041-1). Rand.

Wellington, Paul A., ed. Parenting Alone. 1980. pap. 2.50 (ISBN 0-8309-0297-X). Herald Hse.

Wolfe, David, et al. The Child Management Program for Abusive Parents. (Illus.). 192p. (Orig.). 1981. pap. write for info. (ISBN 0-89305-035-0). Anna Pub.

CHILDREN–MANAGEMENT–PERSONAL NARRATIVES

Felker, Evelyn. Raising Other People's Kids: Successful Child-Rearing in the Restructured Family. 160p. (Orig.). 1981. pap. 4.95 (ISBN 0-8028-1868-4). Eerdmans.

CHILDREN–MANAGEMENT–PROGRAMMED INSTRUCTION

Norwak, Mary. Self-Sufficiency for Children. (Illus.). 96p. (gr. 8 up). 1981. 10.95 (ISBN 0-7207-1095-2). Merrimack Bk Serv.

CHILDREN–MEDICAL CARE

see Pediatrics

CHILDREN–NUTRITION

see also Infants–Nutrition; School Children–Food

Bond, Jenny T., et al, eds. Infant & Child Feeding. (Nutrition Foundation Ser.). 1981. write for info. (ISBN 0-12-113350-8). Acad Pr.

Pipes, Peggy L. Nutrition in Infancy & Childhood. 2nd ed. (Illus.). 288p. 1981. pap. text ed. 11.95 (ISBN 0-8016-3941-7). Mosby.

Richert, Barbara. Getting Your Kids to Eat Right. 192p. (Orig.). 1981. pap. 5.95 (ISBN 0-346-12519-7). Cornerstone.

Wilkinson, J. F. Don't Raise Your Child to Be a Fat Adult. 1981. Repr. pap. 2.50 (ISBN 0-451-09902-8, E9902, Sig). NAL.

CHILDREN–POETRY

Ross, H. K., ed. Great Story Poems - Collection. (Illus.). 160p. 1981. PLB 6.95. Lion.

CHILDREN–PRAYER-BOOKS AND DEVOTIONS

see also Grace at Meals

Crane, Ila H. My First Prayer Book. LC 79-91677. 32p. (gr. k up). 1981. 5.95 (ISBN 0-89896-100-9). Larksdale.

Roberts, Don. Prayers for the Young Child. 1981. pap. 5.95 (ISBN 0-570-04051-5, 56-1717). Concordia.

CHILDREN–PROTECTION

see Child Welfare

CHILDREN–PSYCHOLOGY

see Child Psychology

CHILDREN–RECREATION

see Amusements; Creative Activities and Seatwork; Games

CHILDREN–SPEECH

see Children–Language

CHILDREN–SURGERY

see also Orthopedia; Pediatric Orthopedia

Lilly, John R., et al. Pediatric Surgery Case Studies. 1978. spiral bdg. 19.50 (ISBN 0-87488-069-6). Med Exam.

Raffensperger, John G., ed. Swenson's Pediatric Surgery. 4th ed. 960p. 1980. 78.50x (ISBN 0-8385-8756-9). ACC.

CHILDREN–TRAINING

see Children–Management

CHILDREN–TRANSPORTATION

see School Children–Transportation

CHILDREN–VOCABULARY

see Children–Language

CHILDREN, ABNORMAL AND BACKWARDS

see Exceptional Children; Handicapped Children; Mentally Handicapped Children

CHILDREN, ADOPTED

see Adoption

CHILDREN, AFRO-AMERICAN

see Afro-American Children

CHILDREN, APHASIC

see Aphasia

CHILDREN, BOOKS AND READING FOR

see Books and Reading for Children

CHILDREN, CUSTODY OF

see Custody of Children

CHILDREN, DEAF

see also Deaf–Means of Communication

Griffin, Betty F. Family to Family. 78p. 1980. pap. text ed. 5.75 (ISBN 0-88200-140-X, 16008). Alexander Graham.

CHILDREN, DEAF–EDUCATION

see Deaf–Education

CHILDREN, EXCEPTIONAL

see Exceptional Children

CHILDREN, RETARDED

see Mentally Handicapped Children

Ross, Bette M. Our Special Child: A Guide to Successful Parenting of Handicapped Children. LC 80-54815. 192p. 1981. 12.95 (ISBN 0-8027-0678-9). Walker & Co.

CHILDREN AND DEATH

Furman, Erna. A Child's Parent Dies: Studies in Childhood Bereavement. LC 73-86894. 352p. 1981. pap. 7.95x (ISBN 0-300-02645-5). Yale U Pr.

Hammond, Janice M. When My Mommy Died: A Child's View of Death. (Illus.). 27p. (Orig.). (ps-5). 1980. pap. 3.95 (ISBN 0-9604690-0-1). Cranbrook Pub.

Kubler-Ross, Elisabeth. Coping with Death & Dying. (Illus.). 192p. 1980. 9.95 (ISBN 0-686-69030-3). Macmillan.

CHILDREN AND TELEVISION

see Television and Children

CHILDREN AS ARTISTS

see also Folk Art

Mattel, E. & Mayan, B. Meaning in Children's Art. 1981. 15.95 (ISBN 0-13-567115-9); pap. 12.95 (ISBN 0-13-567107-8). P-H.

CHILDREN IN AUSTRALIA

Brown, Ray, ed. Children Australia. 320p. 1981. text ed. 22.50x (ISBN 0-86861-186-7, 2567); pap. text ed. 12.50x (ISBN 0-86861-194-8, 2568). Allen Unwin.

CHILDREN IN GREAT BRITAIN

Allen, Eleanor. Victorian Children. (Junior Reference Ser.). (Illus.). 64p. (gr. 7 up). 7.95 (ISBN 0-7136-1324-6). Dufour.

Bedford, Jessie. English Children in the Olden Time. 336p. 1980. Repr. of 1907 ed. lib. bdg. 30.00 (ISBN 0-8492-3777-7). R West.

King, Michael. Childhood, Welfare & Justice. 160p. 1981. pap. 16.95 (ISBN 0-7134-3713-8, Pub. by Batsford England). David & Charles.

CHILDREN'S ALMANACS

see Almanacs

CHILDREN'S BOOKS

see Children's Literature (Collections)

also subdivisions under Children's Literature

CHILDREN'S COURTS

see Juvenile Courts

CHILDREN'S DISEASES

see Children–Diseases

CHILDREN'S DRAMA

see Children'S Plays

CHILDREN'S ETIQUETTE

see Etiquette for Children and Youth

CHILDREN'S HYMNS

Beautiful Ways Songs. pap. 0.30. Faith Pub Hse.

CHILDREN'S LIBRARIES

see School Libraries

CHILDREN'S LITERATURE (COLLECTIONS)

see also Books and Reading for Children; Children's Plays; Children's Poetry; Children's Stories; Fairy Tales; Picture-Books for Children; Readers

also subdivision Juvenile Literature under particular subjects, e.g. Astronomy–Juvenile Literature

Egoff, Sheila A., ed. One Ocean Touching: Papers from the First Pacific Rim Conference on Children's Literature. LC 78-31308. 260p. 1979. lib. bdg. 13.00 (ISBN 0-8108-1199-5). Scarecrow.

Twain, Mark. Tom Sawyer. LC 80-22095. (Raintree Short Classics). (Illus.). 48p. (gr. 4-8). 1981. PLB 9.95 (ISBN 0-8172-1665-0). Raintree Pubs.

CHILDREN'S LITERATURE–BIBLIOGRAPHY

see also School Libraries

Baldwin Library of Childrens Literature, Universityof Florida, Gainesville. Index to Children's Literature in English Before 1900: Catalog of the Baldwin Library of the University of Florida at Gainesville. (Library Catalogs Supplements). 1981. lib. bdg. 325.00 (ISBN 0-686-69555-0). G K Hall.

Children's Books in Print 1980-1981. 935p. 1980. 35.00 (ISBN 0-8352-1311-0). Bowker.

Davis, Enid. A Comprehensive Guide to Children's Literature with a Jewish Theme. LC 80-54139. 256p. 1981. 18.95x (ISBN 0-8052-3760-7). Schocken.

Dreyer, Sharon S. The Bookfinder: A Guide to Children's Literature About the Needs & Problems of Youth Aged 2 to 15, 2 vols. 1981. Set. text ed. 69.50 (ISBN 0-913476-44-7); Vol. 1. text ed. 32.00 (ISBN 0-686-69405-8); Vol. 2. text ed. 37.50 (ISBN 0-913476-46-3). Am Guidance.

Library of Congress Classification Adapted for Children's Materials. 3rd ed. LC 76-48893. 131p. 1976. 5.00 (ISBN 0-913578-14-2). Inglewood Ca.

Subject Guide to Children's Books in Print 1980-1981. 1980. 35.00 (ISBN 0-8352-1312-9). Bowker.

Subject Guide to Children's Books in Print 1980-1981. 540p. 1980. 35.00 (ISBN 0-8352-1312-9). Bowker.

Tarbert, Gary C., ed. Children's Book Review Index: Nineteen-Eighty Annual. LC 75-27408. (Children's Book Review Index Ser.). 350p. 1981. 46.00 (ISBN 0-8103-0631-X). Gale.

CHILDREN'S LITERATURE–HISTORY AND CRITICISM

Association for the Library Service to Children. The Arbuthnot Lectures Nineteen-Seventy to Nineteen Seventy-Nine. LC 79-26095. 214p. 1980. 12.50 (ISBN 0-8389-3240-1). ALA.

Butler, Francelia, et al, eds. Children's Literature: Annual of the Modern Language Association Division on Children's Literature Association, Vol. 9. LC 79-711. (Illus.). 272p. 1981. text ed. 27.50x (ISBN 0-300-02623-4); pap. 8.95 (ISBN 0-300-02642-0). Yale U Pr.

Egoff, Sheila, et al, eds. Only Connect: Readings on Children's Literature. 2nd ed. (Illus.). 482p. 1980. pap. 8.95 (ISBN 0-19-540309-6). Oxford U Pr.

Inglis, F. The Promise of Happiness. LC 80-49986. 250p. Date not set. 39.50 (ISBN 0-521-23142-6). Cambridge U Pr.

Riehl, Jospeh E. Charles Lamb's Children's Literature. (Romantic Reassessment Ser.: No. 94). 1980. pap. text ed. 25.00x (ISBN 0-391-02189-3). Humanities.

Scott, Dorothea H. Chinese Popular Literature & the Child. LC 80-10412. 192p. 1980. 15.00 (ISBN 0-8389-0289-8). ALA.

Smith, Elva S. & Hodges, Margaret. The History of Children's Literature: A Syllabus with Selected Bibliographies. LC 79-28323. 312p. 1980. 40.00 (ISBN 0-8389-0286-3). ALA.

CHILDREN'S PLAYS

Arneson, Donald. Doing Something Nice, Inc. & Other Short Plays for Kids. (Illus.). 72p. (Orig.). (gr. 3-6). 1978. write for info. (ISBN 0-934778-00-0); pap. write for info. Bookmaker.

Bedard, Roger L. Dramatic Literature for Children: A Century in Review. Date not set. text ed. price not set (ISBN 0-87602-019-8); pap. text ed. price not set (ISBN 0-87602-020-1). Anchorage.

Davis, Jed H. & Evans, Mary J. Theatre, Children & Youth. 1981. text ed. 19.95 (ISBN 0-87602-016-3); pap. 16.25 (ISBN 0-87602-017-1). Anchorage.

Slade, P. Child Drama. 1979. pap. 25.00 (ISBN 0-340-20968-2). Verry.

CHILDREN'S PLAYS–PRESENTATION, ETC.

Cornelison, Gayle, ed. Directory of Children's Theatre in the United States. 1980. pap. 9.00; ATA members 7.00. Am Theatre Assoc.

CHILDREN'S POETRY

see also Nursery Rhymes

Ainsworth, Catherine H. Jump Rope Verses Around the United States. (Folklore Bks.). 24p. 1980. 2.00 (ISBN 0-933190-01-8). Clyde Pr.

Atwood, Ann. Fly with the Wind, Flow with the Water. (Illus.). 32p. (gr. 1-5). 1979. 9.95 (ISBN 0-684-16103-6). Scribner.

Auden, W. H. Collected Shorter Poems: 1927 to 1957. 352p. Date not set. pap. 3.95 (ISBN 0-394-72015-6, V-2015, Vin). Random.

Bennett, Jill, compiled by. Roger Was a Razor Fish & Other Poems. LC 80-17166. (Illus.). 48p. (gr. 2-6). 1981. 7.95 (ISBN 0-688-41986-0). Morrow.

Creed, Lisa, ed. The House Within Me: An Anthology of Poems by Children from Little River School. 64p. (Orig.). (ps). 1981. pap. 4.00 (ISBN 0-932112-10-2). Carolina Wren.

Cummings, E. E. & Firmage, George J., eds. Hist Whist & Other Poems for Children. (Illus.). 1981. 9.95 (ISBN 0-87140-640-3). Liveright.

Dacey, Philip. The Boy Under the Bed. LC 80-8858. (Johns Hopkins Poetry & Fiction). 1981. text ed. 10.95x (ISBN 0-8018-2601-2); pap. text ed. 5.95x (ISBN 0-8018-2602-0). Johns Hopkins.

Gernhardt, Robert. One More Makes Four. Taylor, Elizabeth W., tr. (Illus.). 32p. (gr. k up). 1981. 9.95 (ISBN 0-224-01577-X, Pub. by Chatto-Bodley-Jonathan). Merrimack Bk Serv.

Hagerup, Inger & Tate, Joan. Helter Skelter. (Illus.). 32p. (gr. k-8). 1981. 7.95 (ISBN 0-7207-1198-3). Merrimack Bk Serv.

London Bridge Is Falling Down. LC 67-17695. (Illus.). (gr. k-3). 1967. pap. 1.49 (ISBN 0-385-08025-5, Zephyr). Doubleday.

Moore, Vardine. Mice Are Rather Nice. LC 80-23121. 112p. (gr. 3-7). 1981. PLB 7.95 (ISBN 0-689-30819-1). Atheneum.

Powell, Charles. The Poets in the Nursery. 79p. Repr. of 1920 ed. lib. bdg. 25.00 (ISBN 0-8492-4221-5). R West.

Stevenson, Robert L. A Child's Garden of Verses. (Children's Library of Picture Bks.). (Illus.). 10p. (ps). 1979. 1.95 (ISBN 0-89346-178-4, TA60, Pub. by Froebel-Kan Japan). Heian Intl.

CHILDREN'S PRAYERS

see Children–Prayer-Books and Devotions

CHILDREN'S SERMONS

Coniaris, A. M. Eighty Talks for Orthodox Young People. 1975. pap. 3.50 (ISBN 0-937032-16-6). Light&Life Pub Co MN.

CHILDREN'S STORIES

see also Adventure and Adventurers; Christmas Stories; Detective and Mystery Stories–Juvenile Literature; Fairy Tales; Missionary Stories; Science Fiction (Collections); Sea Stories; Short Stories; Western Stories

also subdivision Legends and Stories under names of animals, e.g. Dogs–Legends and Stories

Benet, Stephen V. Devil & Daniel Webster & Other Stories. (Illus.). (YA) (gr. 7-9). 1967. pap. 1.50 (ISBN 0-671-29943-3). PB.

Ellis, Joyce K., compiled by. Saved by a Broken Pole & Other Stories. 75p. (Orig.). (gr. 2-6). 1980. pap. 1.75 (ISBN 0-89323-007-3). BMA Pr.

Ireson, Barbara, ed. Tales Out of Time. 224p. (gr. 10 up). 1981. 8.95 (ISBN 0-399-20786-4). Philomel.

CHILDREN'S THEATER

see Children's Plays–Presentation, etc.

CHILDREN'S WIT AND HUMOR

see Wit and Humor, Juvenile

CHILE–DESCRIPTION AND TRAVEL

Villagran, M. C. Vegetationsgeschichtliche und Pflanzensoziologische Untersuchungen Im Vicente Perez Nationalpark: Chile. (Dissertationes Botanicae: No. 54). (Illus.). 166p. (Ger.). 1981. pap. text ed. 25.00x (ISBN 3-7682-1265-3). Lubrecht & Cramer.

CHILE–ECONOMIC CONDITIONS

Greenberg, James B. Santiago's Sword: Chatino Peasant Religion & Economics. 250p. 1981. 16.95x (ISBN 0-520-04135-6). U of Cal Pr.

CHILI CON CARNE

Bridges, Bill. The Great American Chili Book. LC 78-5384. 224p. 1981. 12.95 (ISBN 0-89256-074-6); pap. 6.95 (ISBN 0-89256-130-0). Rawson Wade.

Neely, Martina & Neely, William. The International Chili Society Official Chili Cookbook. (Illus.). 224p. 1981. 10.95 (ISBN 0-312-41988-0). St Martin.

CHILIASM

see Millennium

CHILLS AND FEVER

see Malaria

CHILOPODA

see Centipedes

CHIN

Yang Ywing-Ming. Shaolin Chin Na. LC 80-53546. (Illus.). 144p. (Orig.). 1980. pap. 6.95 (ISBN 0-86568-012-4). Unique Pubns.

CHINA

Bedeski, Robert E. State Building in Modern China. (China Research Monographs: No. 18). 200p. 1981. pap. 8.00 (ISBN 0-912966-28-9). IEAS Ctr Chinese Stud.

Huang Jiemin. China. 83p. Date not set. 50.00 (ISBN 0-07-056830-8). McGraw.

Massimino, Sal T. How to Sell to the People's Republic of China. LC 80-18997. (Illus.). 176p. 1980. 16.95 (ISBN 0-444-00454-8, Thomond Pr). Elsevier.

Scherer, John L., ed. China Facts & Figures Annual (CHIFFA, Vol. 3, 1981. 37.00 (ISBN 0-87569-036-X). Academic Intl.

CHINA–ARMED FORCES

Nelsen, Harvey W. The Chinese Military System: An Organizational Study of the Chinese People's Liberation Army. (Special Studies on China & East Asia). (Illus.). 266p. (Orig.). 1981. lib. bdg. 25.00x (ISBN 0-86531-069-6); pap. text ed. 15.00x (ISBN 0-86531-192-7). Westview.

CHINA–BIOGRAPHY

Bartke, Wolfgang. Who's Who in the People's Republic of China. (Illus.). 750p. 1981. 100.00 (ISBN 0-87332-183-9). M E Sharpe.

Chang, Yu-Chuan. Wang Shou-Jen As a Statesman. (Studies in Chinese History & Civilization). 517p. 1977. Repr. of 1940 ed. 21.00 (ISBN 0-89093-094-5). U Pubns Amer.

De Rachwiltz, I. & Wang, M. Index to Biographical Material in Chin & Yuan Literary Works - Third Series. LC 78-52594. (Faculty of Asian Studies Oriental Monograph: No. 20). 341p. 1980. pap. text ed. 19.95 (ISBN 0-7081-0179-8, 0556). Bks Australia.

Douglas, Robert K. Li-Hung-Chang. (Studies in Chinese History & Civilization). 1977. Repr. of 1895 ed. 19.75 (ISBN 0-89093-110-0). U Pubns Amer.

Lui, Adam Yuen-Chung. The Hanlin Academy: Training Ground for the Ambitious, 1644-1850. (Illus.). 1980. write for info. (ISBN 0-208-01833-6, Archon). Shoe String.

Wei, Cho-Min. The Political Principles of Mencius. (Studies in Chinese Government & Law). 99p. 1977. Repr. of 1916 ed. 11.50 (ISBN 0-89093-063-5). U Pubns Amer.

Wellington, V. K. V. K. Wellington Koo's Foreign Policy: Some Selected Documents. King, Wuncz, ed. (Studies in Chinese History & Civilization). 141p. 1977. Repr. of 1931 ed. 16.00 (ISBN 0-89093-071-6). U Pubns Amer.

CHINA–CIVILIZATION

Bodde, Derk. Essays on Chinese Civilization. Le Blanc, Charles & Borei, Dorothy, eds. LC 80-8586. (Princeton Ser. of Collected Essays). 504p. 1981. 25.00x (ISBN 0-691-03129-0); pap. 8.95x (ISBN 0-691-00024-7). Princeton U Pr.

Djung, Lu-Dzai. History of Democratic Education in Modern China. (Studies in Chinese History & Civilization). 258p. 1977. Repr. of 1934 ed. 19.00 (ISBN 0-89093-080-5). U Pubns Amer.

Douglas, Robert K. Li-Hung-Chang. (Studies in Chinese History & Civilization). 1977. Repr. of 1895 ed. 19.75 (ISBN 0-89093-110-0). U Pubns Amer.

Grantham, Alexandra E. Manchu Monarch: An Interpretation of Chia Ch'ing. (Studies in Chinese History & Civilization). 1977. Repr. of 1934 ed. 19.00 (ISBN 0-89093-076-7). U Pubns Amer.

Hsu, Shu-Hsi. Essays on the Manchurian Problem. (Studies in Chinese History & Civilization). 349p. 1977. 22.00 (ISBN 0-89093-093-7). U Pubns Amer.

Kent, Percy H. Passing of the Manchus. (Studies in Chinese History & Civilization). 1977. 24.00 (ISBN 0-89093-089-9). U Pubns Amer.

Pratt, Helen G. China & Her Unfinished Revolution. (Studies in Chinese History & Civilization). 173p. 1977. Repr. of 1937 ed. 16.00 (ISBN 0-89093-091-0). U Pubns Amer.

Smith, Arthur H. Chinese Characteristics. 342p. 1980. Repr. of 1894 ed. lib. bdg. 40.00 (ISBN 0-89760-849-6). Telegraph Bks.

T'Ang, Leang-Li. New Social Order in China. (Studies in Chinese History & Civilization). 1977. Repr. of 1936 ed. 22.00 (ISBN 0-89093-090-2). U Pubns Amer.

T'Ang, Leang-Ti. China in Revolt: How a Civilization Became a Nation. (Studies in Chinese History & Civilization). 176p. 1977. Repr. of 1927 ed. 18.00 (ISBN 0-89093-070-8). U Pubns Amer.

Tawney, R. H., tr. from Chinese. Agrarian China: Selected Source Materials from Chinese Authors. (Studies in Chinese History & Civilization). 257p. 1977. Repr. of 1938 ed. 18.75 (ISBN 0-89093-084-8). U Pubns Amer.

Wong, Theodore R. Chronological Tables of the Chinese Dynasties. Lyman, E. R., ed. (Studies in Chinese History & Civilization). 103p. 1977. Repr. of 1902 ed. 12.00 (ISBN 0-89093-092-9). U Pubns Amer.

CHINA–COMMERCE

Azif, Herbert B. China Trade: A Guide to Doing Business with the People's Republic of China. LC 80-84105. (Illus.). 200p. (Orig.). Date not set. pap. price not set (ISBN 0-9605190-0-9). Intraworld Trade.

Perkins, Dwight, ed. Rural Small-Scale Industry in the People's Republic of China. 1981. pap. 7.95 (ISBN 0-520-04401-0, CAL 499). U of Cal Pr.

Perry, Phillip M. China Business Directory. LC 80-52703. (Illus.). 352p. 1980. 55.00 (ISBN 0-87762-286-8). Technomic.

CHINA–DESCRIPTION AND TRAVEL

Arthur Frommer's Guide to China, 1981-82. 464p. Date not set. pap. 8.95 (ISBN 0-671-43030-0). Frommer-Pasmantier.

China Travel & Tour Service. The Official Guidebook of China: 1980-1981 Edition. pap. 9.95 (ISBN 0-86519-000-3). Green Hill.

Herdan, Innes. Introduction to China. 1979. pap. 3.95 (ISBN 0-8351-0643-8). China Bks.

Huang Shou-Fu & T'An Chung-Yo. Mount Omei Illustrated Guide. Phelps, Dryden L., tr. from Chinese. (Illus.). 472p. 1981. pap. 15.00 (ISBN 0-85656-113-4). Great Eastern.

Miller, Arthur & Morath, Inge. Chinese Encounters. (Illus.). 256p. 1981. pap. 9.95 (ISBN 0-14-005781-1). Penguin.

CHINA–DESCRIPTION AND TRAVEL–1949-

Fifteen Cities in China. 1980. pap. 4.95 (ISBN 0-8351-0736-1). China Bks.

Lee, Robert. China Journal: Glimpses of a Nation in Transition. (Illus., Orig.). 1980. 9.25 (ISBN 0-934788-00-6); pap. 5.25 (ISBN 0-686-28891-2). E-W Pub Co.

Townsend, James R. & Bush, Richard C., eds. The People's Republic of China: A Basic Handbook. 2nd, rev. ed. (Illus., Orig.). 1980. pap. text ed. 4.50 (ISBN 0-936876-13-1). Learn Res Intl Stud.

CHINA–ECONOMIC CONDITIONS

Lamb, Jefferson D. The Development of the Agrarian Movement & Agrarian Legislation in China. LC 78-74319. (Modern Chinese Economy Ser.: Vol. 12). 254p. 1980. lib. bdg. 33.00 (ISBN 0-8240-4261-1). Garland Pub.

CHINA–ECONOMIC CONDITIONS–1949-

Jones, John F., ed. Building China: Studies in Integrated Development. 158p. 1981. 14.95 (ISBN 0-295-95821-9, Pub. by Chinese Univ Hong Kong). U of Wash Pr.

Time Periodicals Ltd., ed. Straits Times Dictionary of Singapore. 948p. 1980. 58.50x (ISBN 0-8002-2750-6). Intl Pubns Serv.

CHINA–FOREIGN RELATIONS

Chang, Yu-Chuan. Wang Shou-Jen As a Statesman. (Studies in Chinese History & Civilization). 517p. 1977. Repr. of 1940 ed. 21.00 (ISBN 0-89093-094-5). U Pubns Amer.

Downen, Robert. The Taiwan Pawn in the China Game: Congress to the Rescue, Vol. I. LC 79-88334. (Significant Issues Ser.: No. 1). 80p. 1979. 5.95 (ISBN 0-89206-007-7). CSI Studies.

Ewing, Thomas E. Between the Hammer & the Anvil? Chinese & Russian Policies in Outer Mongolia, 1911-1921. (Indiana University Uralic & Altaic Ser.: Vol. 138). 300p. 1980. 20.00 (ISBN 0-933070-06-3). Ind U Res Inst.

Gilbert, Rodney V. The Unequal Treaties: China & the Foreigner. (Studies in Chinese History & Civilization). 248p. 1977. Repr. of 1929 ed. 19.50 (ISBN 0-89093-075-9). U Pubns Amer.

Marshall, George C. Marshall's Mission to China: The Report & Appended Documents. 1976. Set. 60.00 (ISBN 0-89093-115-1). U Pubns Amer.

Tai, En-Sai. Treaty Ports in China: A Study in Diplomacy. (Studies in Chinese History & Civilization). 202p. 1977. 17.50 (ISBN 0-89093-083-X). U Pubns Amer.

Tomimas, Shutaro. The Open-Door Policy & the Territorial Integretiy of China. (Studies in Chinese History & Civilization). 1977. 17.00 (ISBN 0-89093-095-3). U Pubns Amer.

Wellington, V. K. V. K. Wellington Koo's Foreign Policy: Some Selected Documents. King, Wuncz, ed. (Studies in Chinese History & Civilization). 141p. 1977. Repr. of 1931 ed. 16.00 (ISBN 0-89093-071-6). U Pubns Amer.

CHINA–FOREIGN RELATIONS–1949-

Armstrong, J. D. Revolutionary Diplomacy: Chinese Foreign Policy & the United Front Doctrine. 259p. 1981. 21.00x (ISBN 0-520-03251-9, CAMPUS 268); pap. 5.95x (ISBN 0-520-04273-5). U of Cal Pr.

Papp, Daniel S. Vietnam: The View from Moscow, Peking, Washington. LC 80-20117. (Illus.). 263p. 1981. lib. bdg. 17.95x (ISBN 0-89950-010-2). McFarland & Co.

CHINA–FOREIGN RELATIONS–RUSSIA

Stoessinger, John G. Nations in Darkness: China, Russia, & America. 3rd ed. 263p. 1981. pap. text ed. 6.95 (ISBN 0-394-32657-1). Random.

Stuart, Douglas T. & Tow, William T., eds. China, the Soviet Union & the West: Strategic & Political Dimensions for the Nineteen Eighties. (Special Studies in International Relations). 320p. (Orig.). 1981. lib. bdg. 27.50x (ISBN 0-86531-091-2); pap. text ed. 12.50x (ISBN 0-86531-168-4). Westview.

Ular, Alexander. Russo-Chinese Empire. (Studies in Chinese History & Civilization). 334p. 1977. Repr. of 1904 ed. 24.00 (ISBN 0-89093-086-4). U Pubns Amer.

CHINA–FOREIGN RELATIONS–UNITED STATES

Stoessinger, John G. Nations in Darkness: China, Russia, & America. 3rd ed. 263p. 1981. pap. text ed. 6.95 (ISBN 0-394-32657-1). Random.

Stueck, William W., Jr. The Road to Confrontation: American Policy Toward China & Korea, 1947 - 1950. LC 80-11818. (Illus.). 337p. 1981. 22.00x (ISBN 0-8078-1445-8); pap. 10.00x (ISBN 0-8078-4080-7). U of NC Pr.

CHINA–HISTORY

Here are entered general works on Chinese history. Smaller periods are listed chronologically at the end of the History subject headings.

China-the Sick Dragon. LC 78-65281. 1979. write for info. Sundowner Serv.

Ching-Shan. Diary of His Excellency Ching-Shan: Being a Chinese Account of the Boxer Trouble. Duyvendak, Jan J., tr. from Chinese. (Studies in Chinese History & Civilization). 134p. 1977. Repr. of 1924 ed. 14.50 (ISBN 0-89093-074-0). U Pubns Amer.

Dennerline, Jerry. The Chia-Ting Loyalists: Confucian Leadership & Social Change in Seventeenth-Century China. LC 80-21417. (Historical Publications Miscellany Ser.: No. 126). (Illus.). 416p. 1981. text ed. 35.00 (ISBN 0-300-02548-3). Yale U Pr.

Douglas, Robert K. Li-Hung-Chang. (Studies in Chinese History & Civilization). 1977. Repr. of 1895 ed. 19.75 (ISBN 0-89093-110-0). U Pubns Amer.

Grantham, Alexandra E. Manchu Monarch: An Interpretation of Chia Ch'ing. (Studies in Chinese History & Civilization). 1977. Repr. of 1934 ed. 19.00 (ISBN 0-89093-076-7). U Pubns Amer.

Hsia, Ching-Lin. Studies in Chinese Diplomatic History. 226p. 1977. Repr. of 1925 ed. 17.00 (ISBN 0-89093-088-0). U Pubns Amer.

Hsu, Shu-Hsi. Essays on the Manchurian Problem. (Studies in Chinese History & Civilization). 349p. 1977. 22.00 (ISBN 0-89093-093-7). U Pubns Amer.

Huang, Ray. Fifteen-Eighty-Seven, a Year of No Significance: The Mingdynasty in Decline. LC 80-5392. (Illus.). 396p. 1981. 19.95x (ISBN 0-300-02518-1). Yale U Pr.

Keightley, David, et al, eds. Early China, No. 5. 131p. 1980. pap. 7.00 (ISBN 0-912966-26-2). IEAS Ctr Chinese Stud.

Kent, Percy H. Passing of the Manchus. (Studies in Chinese History & Civilization). 1977. 24.00 (ISBN 0-89093-089-9). U Pubns Amer.

Morton. China: Its History & Culture. 1981. 10.95 (ISBN 0-690-01863-0). Lippincott & Crowell.

Pratt, Helen G. China & Her Unfinished Revolution. (Studies in Chinese History & Civilization). 173p. 1977. Repr. of 1937 ed. 16.00 (ISBN 0-89093-091-0). U Pubns Amer.

Spence, Jonathan & Wills, John E., Jr. From Ming to Ch'ing: Conquest, Region, & Continuity in Seventeenth-Century China. LC 78-15560. (Illus.). 437p. 1981. pap. 8.95x (ISBN 0-300-02672-2). Yale U Pr.

T'Ang, Leang-Li. Inner History of the Chinese Revolution. (Studies in Chinese Government & Law). 391p. 1977. Repr. of 1930 ed. 23.50 (ISBN 0-89093-066-X). U Pubns Amer.

--New Social Order in China. (Studies in Chinese History & Civilization). 1977. Repr. of 1936 ed. 22.00 (ISBN 0-89093-090-2). U Pubns Amer.

T'Ang, Leang-Ti. China in Revolt: How a Civilization Became a Nation. (Studies in Chinese History & Civilization). 176p. 1977. Repr. of 1927 ed. 18.00 (ISBN 0-89093-070-8). U Pubns Amer.

Tawney, R. H., tr. from Chinese. Agrarian China: Selected Source Materials from Chinese Authors. (Studies in Chinese History & Civilization). 257p. 1977. Repr. of 1938 ed. 18.75 (ISBN 0-89093-084-8). U Pubns Amer.

Ular, Alexander. Russo-Chinese Empire. (Studies in Chinese History & Civilization). 334p. 1977. Repr. of 1904 ed. 24.00 (ISBN 0-89093-086-4). U Pubns Amer.

Wakeman, Fredric, Jr., ed. Ming & Qing: Historical Studies in the People's Republic of China. (China Research Monographs: No. 17). 1981. pap. 8.00 (ISBN 0-912966-27-0). IEAS Ctr Chinese Stud.

Wong, Theodore R. Chronological Tables of the Chinese Dynasties. Lyman, E. R., ed. (Studies in Chinese History & Civilization). 103p. 1977. Repr. of 1902 ed. 12.00 (ISBN 0-89093-092-9). U Pubns Amer.

Wright, Arthur F., ed. Perspctives on the T'ang. Twitchett. LC 72-91310. 542p. 1981. pap. 10.95x (ISBN 0-300-02674-9). Yale U Pr.

Wu, Kuo-Cheng. Ancient Chinese Political Theories. (Studies in Chinese Government & Law). 340p. 1977. Repr. of 1928 ed. 24.00 (ISBN 0-89093-068-6). U Pubns Amer.

CHINA–HISTORY–EARLY TO 1643

De Rachwiltz, I. & Wang, M. Index to Biographical Material in Chin & Yuan Literary Works - Third Series. LC 78-52594. (Faculty of Asian Studies Oriental Monograph: No. 20). 341p. 1980. pap. text ed. 19.95 (ISBN 0-7081-0179-8, 0556). Bks Australia.

Huang, Ray. Fifteen-Eighty-Seven, a Year of No Significance: The Mingdynasty in Decline. LC 80-5392. (Illus.). 396p. 1981. 19.95x (ISBN 0-300-02518-1). Yale U Pr.

Langlois, John D., Jr., ed. China Under Mongol Rule. LC 80-8559. (Illus.). 532p. 1981. 30.00x (ISBN 0-691-03127-4); pap. 12.50x (ISBN 0-691-10110-8). Princeton U Pr.

Pokotilov, Dmitri & Loewenthal, Rudolf. History of the Eastern Mongols During the Ming Dynasty from 1368 to 1631. (Studies in Chinese History & Civilization). 148p. 1977. Repr. of 1947 ed. 17.00 (ISBN 0-89093-087-2). U Pubns Amer.

CHINA–HISTORY–1643-1856

Tulisen. Narrative of the Chinese Embassy to the Khan of the Tourgouth Tartars, 1712-1715. Staunton, George L., tr. from Chinese. (Studies in Chinese History & Civilization). 330p. Date not set. Repr. of 1821 ed. 24.00 (ISBN 0-89093-073-2). U Pubns Amer.

CHINA–HISTORY–19TH CENTURY

see also Taiping Rebellion, 1850-1864; Nien Rebellion, 1853-1868

Godley, Michael R. The Mandarin-Capitalists from Nanyang: Overseas Chinese Enterprise in the Modernisation of China 1893-1911. (Cambridge Studies in Chinese History, Literature & Institutions Ser.). (Illus.). 288p. Date not set. price not set (ISBN 0-521-23626-6). Cambridge U Pr.

Perry, Elizabeth J. Chinese Perspectives on the Nien Rebellion. 150p. 1981. 18.50 (ISBN 0-87332-191-X). M E Sharpe.

CHINA–HISTORY–1900-

Lane, Peter. China in the Twentieth Century. 16.95 (ISBN 0-7134-0973-8, Pub. by Batsford England). David & Charles.

Mehra, Parshotam. The North-East Frontier: A Documentary Study of the Internecine Rivalry Between India, Tibet & China, Vol. 1, 1906-14. 270p. 1979. text ed. 9.95x (ISBN 0-19-561158-6). Oxford U Pr.

Scalapino, Robert A. & Yu, George T. The Chinese Anarchist Movement. LC 80-23499. (University of California Institute of International Studies, Center for Chinese Studies, Research Ser.). vi, 81p. 1980. Repr. of 1961 ed. lib. bdg. 19.75x (ISBN 0-313-22586-9, SCCM). Greenwood.

Thornton, Richard C. China: A Political History. 500p. (Orig.). 1981. lib. bdg. 27.50x (ISBN 0-86531-197-8); pap. text ed. 12.00x (ISBN 0-86531-198-6). Westview.

CHINA–HISTORY–1937-1949

Rea, Kenneth W. & Brewer, John C., eds. The Forgotten Ambassador: The Reports of John Leighton Stuart, 1946-1949. (Replica Edition Ser.). 350p. 1981. lib. bdg. 25.00x (ISBN 0-86531-157-9). Westview.

CHINA–HISTORY–1949-

Armstrong, J. D. Revolutionary Diplomacy: Chinese Foreign Policy & the United Front Doctrine. 259p. 1981. 21.00x (ISBN 0-520-03251-9, CAMPUS 268); pap. 5.95x (ISBN 0-520-04273-5). U of Cal Pr.

Harding, Harry. Organizing China: The Problem of Bureaucracy, 1949-1976. LC 79-67772. 280p. 1981. text ed. 25.00x (ISBN 0-8047-1080-5). Stanford U Pr.

Jones, John F., ed. Building China: Studies in Integrated Development. 158p. 1981. 14.95 (ISBN 0-295-95821-9, Pub. by Chinese Univ Hong Kong). U of Wash Pr.

Townsend, James R. & Bush, Richard C., eds. The People's Republic of China: A Basic Handbook. 2nd, rev. ed. (Illus., Orig.). 1980. pap. text ed. 4.50 (ISBN 0-936876-13-1). Learn Res Intl Stud.

CHINA–HISTORY–1949-–PICTORIAL WORKS

Riboud, Marc. Visions of China: Photographs by Marc Riboud, 1957-1980. (Illus.). 1981. 30.00 (ISBN 0-394-51535-8); pap. 14.95 (ISBN 0-394-74840-9). Pantheon.

CHINA–INTELLECTUAL LIFE–1949-

Loescher, Gil & Loescher, Ann D. China: Pushing Toward the Year 2000. LC 80-8802. (Illus.). 160p. (gr. 7 up). 1981. 10.95 (ISBN 0-15-217506-7, HJ). HarBraceJ.

CHINA–KINGS AND RULERS

MacKinnon, Stephen R. Power & Politics in Late Imperial China: Yuan Shi-kai in Beijing & Tianjin, 1901-1908. (Center for Chinese Studies Ser.). (Illus.). 400p. 1981. 18.50x (ISBN 0-520-04025-2). U of Cal Pr.

CHINA–OFFICIALS AND EMPLOYEES

Radiopress-Tokyo, ed. China Directory-1971. 9th ed. 657p. 1980. 85.00x (ISBN 0-8002-2752-2). Intl Pubns Serv.

Wang Fan-Hsi. Chinese Revolutionary, Memoirs 1919-49. Benton, Gregor, tr. 256p. 1980. 45.00 (ISBN 0-19-211746-7). Oxford U Pr.

CHINA–POLITICS AND GOVERNMENT

Bau, Mingchien J. Modern Democracy in China: Studies in Chinese Government & Law. 467p. 1977. Repr. of 1923 ed. 25.00 (ISBN 0-89093-060-0). U Pubns Amer.

Chang, Yu-Kon, et al, trs. from Chinese. Civil Code of the Republic of China. Hsia, Ching-Lin. (Studies in Chinese Government & Law). 400p. 1977. Repr. of 1930 ed. 26.50 (ISBN 0-89093-055-4). U Pubns Amer.

Cheng, F. T., tr. from Chinese. The Chinese Supreme Court Decisions: Relating to General Principles of Civil Law, Obligations & Commercial Law. 229p. 1979. Repr. of 1923 ed. 22.50 (ISBN 0-89093-065-1). U Pubns Amer.

Constitution & Supplementary Laws & Documents of the Republic of China. (Studies in Chinese Government & Law). 198p. 1977. Repr. of 1924 ed. 21.00 (ISBN 0-89093-059-7). U Pubns Amer.

Hu, Sheng. Imperialism & Chinese Politics. (Studies in Chinese Government & Law). 308p. 1977. Repr. of 1955 ed. 19.50 (ISBN 0-89093-054-6). U Pubns Amer.

Kwang, Eu-Yang. Political Reconstruction of China. (Studies in Chinese Government & Law). 190p. 1977. Repr. of 1922 ed. 18.50 (ISBN 0-89093-058-9). U Pubns Amer.

Lanier, Alison R. Update: Peoples Republic of China. Pusch, Margaret D., ed. (Country Orientation Ser.). 150p. (Orig.). 1980. pap. 25.00 (ISBN 0-933662-44-0). Intercult Pr.

Lynn, Jermyn Chi-Mung. Political Parties in China. (Studies in Chinese Government & Law). 255p. 1977. Repr. of 1930 ed. 19.50 (ISBN 0-89093-069-4). U Pubns Amer.

Politics in China. 2nd ed. (Comparative Politics Ser.). 1980. pap. text ed. 7.95 (ISBN 0-316-85131-0). Little.

Republic of China. Laws, Ordinances, Regulations, & Rules Relating to the Judicial Administration of the Republic of China. (Studies in Chinese Government & Law). 364p. 1977. Repr. of 1923 ed. 24.00 (ISBN 0-89093-062-7). U Pubns Amer.

Riasanovsky, V. A. Chinese Civil Law. (Studies in Chinese Government & Law). 1977. Repr. of 1938 ed. 22.50 (ISBN 0-89093-061-9). U Pubns Amer.

T'Ang, Leang-Li. Inner History of the Chinese Revolution. (Studies in Chinese Government & Law). 391p. 1977. Repr. of 1930 ed. 23.50 (ISBN 0-89093-066-X). U Pubns Amer.

Thornton, Richard C. China: A Political History. 500p. (Orig.). 1981. lib. bdg. 27.50x (ISBN 0-86531-197-8); pap. text ed. 12.00x (ISBN 0-86531-198-6). Westview.

Tyau, Min-Chi'En T. China's New Constitution & International Problems. (Studies in Chinese Government & Law). 286p. 1977. Repr. of 1918 ed. 19.50 (ISBN 0-89093-064-3). U Pubns Amer.

Wang, Joseph E., ed. Selected Legal Documents of the People's Republic of China. LC 76-5167. (Studies in Chinese Government & Law). 564p. 1979. 32.50 (ISBN 0-89093-067-8). U Pubns Amer.

--Selected Legal Documents of the People's Republic of China: Volume II. LC 76-5167. (Studies in Chinese Government & Law). 564p. 1979. 32.50 (ISBN 0-89093-241-7). U Pubns Amer.

Wei, Cho-Min. The Political Principles of Mencius. (Studies in Chinese Government & Law). 99p. 1977. Repr. of 1916 ed. 11.50 (ISBN 0-89093-063-5). U Pubns Amer.

Wu, Kuo-Cheng. Ancient Chinese Political Theories. (Studies in Chinese Government & Law). 340p. 1977. Repr. of 1928 ed. 24.00 (ISBN 0-89093-068-6). U Pubns Amer.

CHINA–POLITICS AND GOVERNMENT–1949-

Bloodworth, Dennis & Ching Ping. Heirs Apparent: What Happens When Mao Dies? 272p. 1973. 7.95 (ISBN 0-374-16898-9). FS&G.

Harding, Harry. Organizing China: The Problem of Bureaucracy, 1949-1976. LC 79-67772. 280p. 1981. text ed. 25.00x (ISBN 0-8047-1080-5). Stanford U Pr.

Leys, Simon. Broken Images. (Allison & Busby's Motive Ser.). 160p. 1981. pap. 8.95 (ISBN 0-8052-8069-3, Pub. by Allison & Busby England). Schocken.

--The Chairwoman's New Clothes: Mao & the Cultural Revolution. (Allison & Busby Motive Ser.). 270p. 1981. pap. 8.95 (ISBN 0-8052-8080-4, Pub. by Allison & Busby England). Schocken.

The Taiwan Pawn in the China Game. 80p. 1979. pap. 7.50 (ISBN 0-89206-007-7, CSIS002, CSIS). Unipub.

CHINA–RELATIONS (GENERAL) WITH FOREIGN COUNTRIES–1949-

Hsiung, James C. & Kim, Samuel S., eds. China in the Global Community. 288p. 1980. 27.95 (ISBN 0-03-057009-3). Praeger.

CHINA–RELIGION

Maspero, Henri. Taoism & Chinese Religion. Kierman, Frank A., tr. from Fr. LC 80-13444. Orig. Title: Le Taoisme et les religions Chinoises. 656p. 1981. lib. bdg. 32.50x (ISBN 0-87023-308-4). U of Mass Pr.

Ware, James R., tr. from Chinese. Alchemy, Medicine, & Religion in the China of A. D. 320: The Nei P'ien of Ko Hung (Pao-p'u tzu) 416p. 1981. pap. price not set (ISBN 0-486-24088-6). Dover.

CHINA–SOCIAL CONDITIONS

Menpes, Mortimer. China. 139p. 1980. Repr. of 1909 ed. lib. bdg. 35.00 (ISBN 0-89987-562-9). Darby Bks.

Myrdal, Jan. Report from a Chinese Village. (Illus.). 1981. pap. 6.95 (ISBN 0-394-74802-6). Pantheon.

Sun Yun Chiang, Cecilia & Carr, Allan. Mandarin Way. rev. & expanded ed. Silva, Sharon, ed. LC 80-66580. (Illus.). 288p. 1980. 11.95 (ISBN 0-89395-062-9); pap. 7.95 (ISBN 0-89395-059-9). Cal Living Bks.

CHINA–SOCIAL CONDITIONS–1949-

Croll, Elisabeth. The Politics of Marriage in Contemporary China. LC 80-40586. (Contemporary China Institute Publications Ser.). (Illus.). 224p. Date not set. 36.00 (ISBN 0-521-23345-3). Cambridge U Pr.

Jones, John F., ed. Building China: Studies in Integrated Development. 158p. 1981. 14.95 (ISBN 0-295-95821-9, Pub. by Chinese Univ Hong Kong). U of Wash Pr.

CHINA–SOCIAL LIFE AND CUSTOMS

Blair, Patricia, ed. Development in the People's Republic of China: A Selected Bibliography. LC 76-53149. (Occasional Papers: No. 8). 94p. 1976. 2.50 (ISBN 0-686-28696-0). Overseas Dev Council.

Blake, C. Fred. Ethnic Groups & Social Change in a Chinese Market Town. (Asian Studies at Hawaii: No. 27). 192p. (Orig.). 1981. pap. 10.50x (ISBN 0-8248-0720-0). U Pr of Hawaii.

Comrade Editor: Letters to the People's Daily. 1980. pap. 4.95 (ISBN 0-8351-0734-5). China Bks.

Croll, Elisabeth. The Politics of Marriage in Contemporary China. LC 80-40586. (Contemporary China Institute Publications Ser.). (Illus.). 224p. Date not set. 36.00 (ISBN 0-521-23345-3). Cambridge U Pr.

Fei, Hsiao-Tung. Peasant Life in China: A Field Study of Country Life in the Yangtze Valley. (Studies in Chinese History & Civilization). (Illus.). 296p. 1977. Repr. of 1939 ed. 21.00 (ISBN 0-89093-081-3). U Pubns Amer.

Fraser, John. The Chinese: Portrait of a People. LC 80-26314. (Illus.). 463p. 1980. 14.95 (ISBN 0-671-44873-0). Summit Bks.

Lanier, Alison R. Update: Peoples Republic of China. Pusch, Margaret D., ed. (Country Orientation Ser.). 150p. (Orig.). 1980. pap. 25.00 (ISBN 0-933662-44-0). Intercult Pr.

MacDonald, Malcolm. Inside China. (Illus.). 208p. 1981. 19.95 (ISBN 0-316-54188-5). Little.

McKnight, Brian E. The Quality of Mercy: Amnesties & Traditional Chinese Justice. LC 80-26650. 224p. 1981. pap. 15.00x (ISBN 0-8248-0736-7). U Pr of Hawaii.

T'Ang, Leang-Li. New Social Order in China. (Studies in Chinese History & Civilization). 1977. Repr. of 1936 ed. 22.00 (ISBN 0-89093-090-2). U Pubns Amer.

Tun Li-Ch'En. Annual Customs & Festivals in Peking. Bodde, Derk, tr. from Chinese. (Illus.). 175p. 1981. 10.00 (ISBN 0-85656-029-4). Great Eastern.

CHINA (PORCELAIN)

see Porcelain

CHINAWARE

see Porcelain; Pottery

CHINESE ART

see Art, Chinese

CHINESE FICTION

Lau, Joseph, et al, eds. Modern Chinese Stories & Novellas, Nineteen Nineteen to Nienteen Forty-Nine. LC 80-27572. (Modern Asian Literature Ser.). 608p. (Eng.). 1981. 35.00x (ISBN 0-231-04202-7); pap. 15.00x (ISBN 0-231-04203-5). Columbia U Pr.

CHINESE FICTION–HISTORY AND CRITICISM

Hegel, Robert E. The Novel in Seventeenth-Century China. (Illus.). 320p. 1981. 20.00x (ISBN 0-231-04928-5). Columbia U Pr.

CHINESE FOLK-LORE

see Folk-Lore, Chinese

CHINESE IN FOREIGN COUNTRIES

Purcell, Victor. The Chinese in Southeast Asia. 2nd ed. (Royal Institute of International Affairs Ser.). (Illus.). 640p. 1980. pap. 22.00x (ISBN 0-19-580463-5). Oxford U Pr.

CHINESE IN THE UNITED STATES

Kingston, Maxine H. China Men. 288p. 1981. pap. 3.50 (ISBN 0-345-29482-3). Ballantine.

McCunn, Ruthanne L. An Illustrated History of the Chinese in America. LC 79-50114. (Illus.). 136p. 1979. 11.95 (ISBN 0-932538-01-0); pap. 6.95 (ISBN 0-932538-02-9). Design Ent SF.

Nee, Victor G. & Nee, Brett De B. Lontime Californ' A Documentary Study of an American Chinatown. (Pantheon Village Ser.). 1981. pap. 6.95 (ISBN 0-394-73846-2). Pantheon.

CHINESE LANGUAGE

Choi, Juliet. Teacher's Manual for Beginning Chinese for Intermediate Schools. xxii, 331p. 1980. tchrs' ed. 29.00x (ISBN 0-89644-641-7). Chinese Materials.

Choi, Juliet & Defrancis, John. Beginning Chinese for Intermediate Schools, 2 vols. viii, 145p. (Orig.). 1980. Set. pap. text ed. 15.45 (ISBN 0-89644-639-5). Chinese Materials.

--Character Workbook for Beginning Chinese for Intermediate Schools, 2 vols. viii, 115p. (Orig.). (gr. 7-12). 1980. Set. pap. text ed. 15.45x (ISBN 0-89644-640-9). Chinese Materials.

Eddy, Peter, et al. Chinese Language Study in American Higher Education: State of the Art. (Language in Education Ser.: No. 30). 1980. pap. text ed. 7.95 (ISBN 0-87281-129-8). Ctr Appl Ling.

Jordan, David. Guide to the Romanization of Chinese. 78p. 1980. 3.95 (ISBN 0-89955-156-4, Pub. by Mei Ya Pub Taiwan). Intl Schol Bk Serv.

CHINESE LANGUAGE–CONVERSATION AND PHRASE BOOKS

Eddy, Peter, et al. Chinese Language Study in American Higher Education: State of the Art. (Language in Education Ser.: No. 30). 1980. pap. text ed. 7.95 (ISBN 0-87281-129-8). Ctr Appl Ling.

Peking University Faculty. Modern Chinese: A Second Course. rev. ed. 500p. 1981. pap. price not set (ISBN 0-486-24155-6). Dover.

Sivam, Avraham J. & Ikeda, Yutaka. Useful Expressions in Chinese. (Useful Expressions Ser.). 64p. (Orig.). 1981. pap. 1.50 (ISBN 0-86628-023-5). Ridgefield Pub.

CHINESE LANGUAGE–DICTIONARIES

English-Chinese & Chinese-English Dictionary. 1977. 7.95 (ISBN 0-8351-0725-6). China Bks.

Goodrich, Chauncey. A Pocket Dictionary: Chinese-English, & Pekingese Syllabary. 341p. 1981. pap. 2.50 (ISBN 0-85656-131-2). Great Eastern.

Kimball, Richard L. China Beginner's Traveler's Dictionary. 1980. pap. 6.95 (ISBN 0-8351-0732-9). China Bks.

Lee, Bennett & Barme, Geremie. China Traveler's Phrasebook. 1980. pap. 5.95 (ISBN 0-8351-0729-9). China Bks.

Makkai, Adam. A Dictionary of American Idioms in Chinese. Gates & Boatner. eds. 396p. 1981. pap. 10.95 (ISBN 0-8120-2386-2). Barron.

Montanaro, John S. Chinese-English Phrase Book for Travellers. 200p. 1981. pap. text ed. 4.95 (ISBN 0-471-08298-8). Wiley.

A Pocket English-Chinese Dictionary. 1980. pap. 4.95 (ISBN 0-8351-0727-2). China Bks.

CHINESE LANGUAGE–READERS

Elementary Chinese Readers, 4 vols. Incl. Vol. 1 (ISBN 0-8351-0778-7); Vol. 2 (ISBN 0-8351-0779-5); Vol. 3 (ISBN 0-8351-0780-9); Vol. 4 (ISBN 0-8351-0781-7). 1980. pap. 4.95 ea. China Bks.

CHINESE LANGUAGE–WRITING

Dian Wen K. Chinn. Practical Chinese Letter Writing. xii, 124p. (Orig.). 1980. pap. text ed. 9.50x (ISBN 0-89644-642-5). Chinese Materials.

CHINESE LITERATURE (COLLECTIONS)

Lu Xun: Selected Works, 4 vols. 1980. Set. 24.95 (ISBN 0-8351-0747-7). China Bks.

Nieh, Hualing. Literature of the Hundred Flowers, 2 vols. LC 80-36748. 1981. Vol. 1, 288p. 27.50 (ISBN 0-231-05074-7); Vol. 2, 560p. 42.50 (ISBN 0-231-05076-3). Columbia U Pr.

CHINESE LITERATURE–HISTORY AND CRITICISM

Deeney, John J., ed. Chinese-Western Comparative Literature & Strategy. 220p. 1981. 17.50 (ISBN 0-295-95810-3, Pub. by Chinese Univ Hong Kong). U of Wash Pr.

De Rachwiltz, I. & Wang, M. Index to Biographical Material in Chin & Yuan Literary Works - Third Series. LC 78-52594. (Faculty of Asian Studies Oriental Monograph: No. 20). 341p. 1980. pap. text ed. 19.95 (ISBN 0-7081-0179-8, 0556). Bks Australia.

Scott, Dorothea H. Chinese Popular Literature & the Child. LC 80-10412. 192p. 1980. 15.00 (ISBN 0-8389-0289-8). ALA.

CHINESE MEDICINE

see Medicine, Chinese

CHINESE PAINTING

see Painting, Chinese

CHINESE PAINTINGS

see Paintings, Chinese

CHINESE POETRY

Sullivan, Michael. The Three Perfections: Chinese Painting, Poetry & Calligraphy. LC 80-18189. (Illus.). 64p. 10.00 (ISBN 0-8076-0996-X); pap. 4.95 (ISBN 0-8076-0997-8). Braziller.

CHINESE POETRY–HISTORY AND CRITICISM

Soong, Stephen C., ed. Song Without Music: Chinese Tz'u Poetry. (Renditions Ser). (Illus.). 286p. 1981. 20.00 (ISBN 0-295-95811-1, Pub. by Chinese Univ Hong Kong). U of Wash Pr.

Stryk, Lucien, et al, trs. from Chinese Japanese. Zen Poems of China & Japan: The Crane's Bill. 208p. 1981. pap. 4.95 (ISBN 0-394-17912-9, BC). Grove.

CHINESE POETRY–TRANSLATIONS INTO ENGLISH

Lattimore, David, tr. The Harmony of the World: Chinese Poems. rev. & enl. ed. (Illus.). 1980. pap. 4.50 (ISBN 0-914278-31-2). Cooper Beech.

CHINESE PORCELAIN

see Porcelain, Chinese

CHINESE POTTERY

see Pottery, Chinese

CHINESE PRISONERS

see Prisoners, Chinese

McKnight, Brian E. The Quality of Mercy: Amnesties & Traditional Chinese Justice. LC 80-26650. 224p. 1981. pap. 15.00x (ISBN 0-8248-0736-7). U Pr of Hawaii.

CHINESE QUESTION

see China–History; Eastern Question (Far East)

CHINESE TALES

see Tales, Chinese

CHINOOK INDIANS

see Indians of North America–Northwest, Pacific

CHIPPEWA INDIANS

see Indians of North America–Northwest, Old

CHIROGRAPHY

see Penmanship; Writing

CHIROPODY

see Podiatry

CHIROPRACTIC

see also Naturopathy

DeGiacomo, F. P. Chiropractic Analysis Through Palpation. McDonnell, James, ed. (Illus.). 192p. 1980. 12.00 (ISBN 0-938470-00-0). NY Chiro Coll.

Haldeman, Scott, ed. Modern Developments in the Principles & Practice of Chiropractic. 480p. 1980. 28.50x (ISBN 0-8385-6350-3). ACC.

Schafer, R. C., ed. Chiropractic Physical & Spinal Diagnosis. (Illus.). 578p. 1980. text ed. 30.00 (ISBN 0-936948-00-0). Am Chiro Acad.

Wilk, Chester A. Everything You Should Know About Chiropractic. LC 80-53014. 1980. write for info. Wilk Pub.

CHIROPTERA

see Bats

CHIROTHERAPY

see Massage

CHITTAHS

see Cheetahs

CHLOROPLASTS

Electrical Events Associated with Primary Photosynthetic Reactions in Chloroplast Membranes. (Agricultural Research Reports Ser.: No. 905). 86p. 1981. pap. 16.75 (ISBN 90-220-0756-1, PDC 218, Pudoc). Unipub.

CHOCOLATE

see also Cookery (Chocolate)

Lawrence, Paul A. In Praise of Chocolate. (Illus.). 60p. (Orig.). 1981. pap. 6.95 (ISBN 0-938034-03-0). PAL Pr.

CHOCTAW INDIANS

see Indians of North America–Eastern States

CHOICE OF BOOKS

see Bibliography–Best Books; Books and Reading

CHOICE OF COLLEGE

see College, Choice of

CHOICE OF PROFESSION

see Vocational Guidance

CHOIR BOOKS

see Service Books (Music)

CHOLELITHIASIS

see Calculi, Biliary

CHOLESTEROL

Gruberg, Edward & Raymond, Stephen. Beyond Cholesterol. 208p. 1981. 9.95 (ISBN 0-312-07779-3). St Martin.

Hausman, Patricia. Jack Sprat's Legacy: The Science & Politics of Fat & Cholesterol. 320p. 1981. 12.95 (ISBN 0-399-90111-6). Marek.

CHOMSKY, NOAM

Allen, J. P. & Van Buren, Paul, eds. Chomsky: Selected Readings. 166p. 1981. pap. 6.95 (ISBN 0-19-437046-1). Oxford U Pr.

Lawrence, Irene. Linguistics & Theology: The Significance of Noam Chomsky for Theological Construction. LC 80-24210. (ATLA Monograph: No. 16). 214p. 1980. 12.50 (ISBN 0-8108-1347-5). Scarecrow.

CHOPIN, FRYDERYK FRANCISZEK, 1810-1849

Weinstock, Herbert. Chopin: The Man & His Music. (Music Ser.). (Illus.). xiv, 336p. 1981. Repr. of 1949 ed. lib. bdg. 27.50 (ISBN 0-306-76081-9). Da Capo.

CHOPIN, KATE O'FLAHERTY, 1851-1904

Seyerstead, Per. Kate Chopin: A Critical Biography. LC 77-88740. (Southern Literary Ser.). 256p. 1980. pap. 5.95 (ISBN 0-8071-0678-X). La State U Pr.

CHORAL MUSIC

Here are entered works on choral music. Collections of choral compositions are entered under Choruses.

Young, Percy M. The Choral Tradition. rev. ed. 400p. 1981. pap. 8.95 (ISBN 0-393-00058-3). Norton.

CHORAL MUSIC–BIBLIOGRAPHY

Tortolano, William. Original Music for Men's Voices: A Selected Bibliography. 2nd ed. LC 80-25917. 206p. 1981. 12.50 (ISBN 0-8108-1386-6). Scarecrow.

CHORDATA

see also Vertebrates

McNeill, Alexander R. The Chordates. (Illus.). 500p. Date not set. text ed. price not set (ISBN 0-521-23658-4); pap. text ed. price not set (ISBN 0-521-28141-5). Cambridge U Pr.

CHOSES

see Personal Property

CHRESTOMATHIES

see Readers

CHRETIEN DE TROYES, 12TH CENTURY

Topsfield, L. T. Chretien de Troyes. 300p. Date not set. 49.50 (ISBN 0-521-23361-5). Cambridge U Pr.

CHRIST

see Jesus Christ

CHRISTENING

see Baptism

CHRISTIAN ANTIQUITIES

see also Architecture, Gothic; Christian Art and Symbolism; Church Architecture; Fasts and Feasts; Sepulchral Monuments

Fuellenbach, John. Ecclesiastical Office & the Primacy of Rome: An Evaluation of Recent Theological Discussion of 1 Clement. (Studies in Christian Antiquity: Vol. 20). 278p. 25.00x (ISBN 0-8132-0551-4, Pub. by Cath U of America Pr). Intl Schol Bk Serv.

Leclercq, H. Manuel D'archeologie Chretienne: Depuis les origines jusqu'au VIII siecle, 2 vols. (Illus., Fr.). 1981. Repr. of 1907 ed. lib. bdg. 160.00x (ISBN 0-89241-148-1). Vol. 1, 592p. Vol. 2, 682p. Caratzas Bros.

CHRISTIAN ARCHAEOLOGY

see Christian Antiquities

CHRISTIAN ART AND SYMBOLISM

see also Bible–Pictures, Illustrations, etc.; Cathedrals; Christian Antiquities; Church Architecture; Crib in Christian Art and Tradition; Emblems; Icons; Jewish Art and Symbolism; Mosaics; Symbolism in the Bible; Symbolism of Numbers

also subdivision Art under various subjects, e.g. Jesus Christ–Art

De Fleury, C. Rohault. La Sainte Vierge: Etudes Archeologiques et Iconographiques, 2 vols. (Illus., Fr.). 1981. Repr. of 1878 ed. Set. 325.00x (ISBN 0-89241-154-6). Caratzas Bros.

Fleury, C. Rohault. La Messe: Etudes Archeologiques sur ses Monuments, 8 vols. (Illus.). 1722p. (Fr.). 1981. Repr. of 1889 ed. lib. bdg. 600.00x (ISBN 0-89241-153-8). Caratzas Bros.

Leclercq, H. Manuel D'archeologie Chretienne: Depuis les origines jusqu'au VIII siecle, 2 vols. (Illus., Fr.). 1981. Repr. of 1907 ed. lib. bdg. 160.00x (ISBN 0-89241-148-1). Vol. 1, 592p. Vol. 2, 682p. Caratzas Bros.

MacCormack, Sabine. Art & Ceremony in Late Antiquity. (The Transformation of the Classical Heritage Ser.). (Illus.). 450p. 1981. 35.00x (ISBN 0-520-03779-0). U of Cal Pr.

Saleske, Theodore E. Easter. (Living Values Ser.). (Illus.). 64p. (Orig.). 1980. pap. 3.95 (ISBN 0-89107-206-3). Good News.

Schapiro, Meyer. Late Antique, Early Christian & Mediaeval Art: Selected Papers. Date not set. 25.00 (ISBN 0-686-68085-5). Braziller.

CHRISTIAN BIOGRAPHY

see also Apostles; Bishops; Cardinals; Clergy; Fathers of the Church; Missionaries; Monasticism and Religious Orders; Saints; Theologians

Bandel, Betty. Sing the Lord's Song in a Strange Land: The Life of Justin Morgan. LC 78-73309. 264p. 1981. 24.50 (ISBN 0-8386-2411-1). Fairleigh Dickinson.

Barfield, Janice. You Can Fly: But That Cocoon Has Got to Go. (Orig.). 1981. 7.95 (ISBN 0-310-43920-5). Zondervan.

Beckwith, Elizabeth. If I Take the Wings of the Morning. 1979. 2.00 (ISBN 0-686-28780-0). Forward Movement.

Berio, Paquita. Ahora Brillan las Estrellas. 134p. (Orig., Span.). 1981. pap. 2.50 (ISBN 0-89922-201-3). Edit Caribe.

Bolshakoff, Sergius. Russian Mystics. (Cistercian Studies: No. 26). Orig. Title: I Mistici Russi. 303p. 1981. pap. 6.95 (ISBN 0-87907-926-6). Cistercian Pubns.

Byers, A. L. Birth of a Reformation: Life & Labours of D. S. Warner. (Illus.). 496p. Repr. 5.50. Faith Pub Hse.

Byrum, Isabel. The Poorhouse Waif & His Divine Teacher. 223p. pap. 2.00. Faith Pub Hse.

Hale, Mabel. The Hero of Hill House. 224p. pap. 2.00. Faith Pub Hse.

Jackson, S. Trevena. Fanny Crosby's Story. (Christian Biography Ser.). 198p. 1981. pap. 2.95 (ISBN 0-8010-5127-4). Baker Bk.

Johnson, Cecelia D. Her Life for His Friends: A Biography of Terry McHugh. LC 80-25996. 1980. pap. 7.95 (ISBN 0-8190-0640-8). Fides Claretian.

Lawrence, Carl. Majken. 192p. 1981. pap. 4.95 (ISBN 0-8407-5762-X). Nelson.

Memoirs of George E. Harmon. (Illus.). 56p. 0.60; 2 copies 1.00. Faith Pub Hse.

Naylor, C. W. The Redemption of Howard Gray. 72p. pap. 0.50. Faith Pub Hse.

Orr, C. E. The Hidden Life. 112p. pap. 0.75. Faith Pub Hse.

Owen, Robert & Howard, David M. Victor el Victorioso. Orellana, Eugenio, tr. from Eng. 152p. (Orig., Span.). 1981. pap. 2.95 (ISBN 0-89922-206-4). Edit Caribe.

Popoff, Peter. A New Fire Is Blazing. Tanner, Don, ed. LC 80-67993. (Illus.). 194p. (Orig.). 1980. pap. 4.95 (ISBN 0-938544-02-0). Faith Messenger.

Poulos, Nellie. Life's Story & Healings. 160p. pap. 1.50. Faith Pub Hse.

Prewitt, Cheryl & Slattery, Kathryn S. The Cheryl Prewitt Story. LC 80-2896. (Illus.). 216p. 1981. 11.95 (ISBN 0-385-17021-1, Galilee). Doubleday.

Rinker, Rosalind. Dentro del Circulo. Cochrane, James R., tr. from Eng. 110p. (Orig., Span.). 1976. pap. 2.25 (ISBN 0-89922-075-4). Edit Caribe.

Ryle, J. C. Christian Leaders of the Eighteenth Century: Includes Whitefield, Wesley, Grimshaw, Romaine, Rowlands, Berridge, Venn, Walker, Harvey, Toplady, & Fletcher. 1978. pap. 5.45 (ISBN 0-85151-268-2). Banner of Truth.

Squire, Aelred. Aelred of Rievaulx: A Study. (Cistercian Studies Ser.: No. 50). 192p. 1981. price not set (ISBN 0-87907-950-9); pap. price not set. Cistercian Pubns.

Staubach, Roger & Luksa, Frank. Roger Staubach: Time Enough to Win. 256p. 1980. 9.95 (ISBN 0-8499-0274-6). Word Bks.

Stover, Ruby E. Life's Golden Gleanings. 94p. pap. 1.00. Faith Pub Hse.

Susag, S. O. Personal Experiences of S. O. Susag. 191p. pap. 1.75. Faith Pub Hse.

Taylor, Hudson & Thompson, Phyllis. God's Adventurer. (Illus.). 1978. pap. 2.25 (ISBN 0-85363-094-1). OMF Bks.

Williams, Efie M. Just Mary. 96p. pap. 0.75. Faith Pub Hse.

Young, Fay. The Awakening. 64p. 1981. 5.00 (ISBN 0-682-49701-0). Exposition.

CHRISTIAN BIOGRAPHY–JUVENILE LITERATURE

Wilson, William. With Their Whole Strength. LC 80-2084. 128p. (gr. 6 up). 1981. pap. 2.75 (ISBN 0-385-17435-7, Im). Doubleday.

CHRISTIAN BRETHREN

Getz, Gene A. Encouraging One Another. 1981. pap. 3.95 (ISBN 0-88207-256-0). Victor Bks.

CHRISTIAN COMMUNICATION

see Communication (Theology)

CHRISTIAN DEVOTIONAL CALENDARS

see Devotional Calendars

CHRISTIAN DEVOTIONAL LITERATURE

see Devotional Literature

CHRISTIAN DOCTRINE

see Theology, Doctrinal

CHRISTIAN DOCTRINE (CATHOLIC CHURCH)

see Catechetics–Catholic Church

CHRISTIAN EDUCATION

Here are entered works dealing with instruction in the Christian religion in schools and private life; Works on the relation of the church to education in general, and works on the history of the part that the church has taken in secular education are entered under Church and education.

see also Bible–Study; Catechetics; Catechisms; Christian Leadership; Church and Education; Church Schools; Theology–Study and Teaching

Ashton, Leila. Checks from God. (My Church Teaches Ser.). 32p. (ps-1). 1981. pap. 1.50 (ISBN 0-8127-0314-6). Southern Pub.

Baynes, Richard W. God's OK -- You're OK? Perspective on Christian Worship. LC 79-67440. 96p. (Orig.). 1981. pap. 1.95 (ISBN 0-87239-382-8, 40088). Standard Pub.

Boyer, Orlando, tr. Esforca-Te Para Ganhar Almas. (Portugese Bks.). (Port.). 1979. 1.60 (ISBN 0-8297-0662-3). Life Pubs Intl.

Graendorf, Werner, ed. Introduction to Biblical Christian Education. 1981. text ed. 11.95 (ISBN 0-8024-4128-9). Moody.

Griggs, Patricia R. Using Storytelling in Christian Education. LC 80-26468. 64p. (Orig.). 1981. pap. 4.95 (ISBN 0-687-43117-4). Abingdon.

Hart, Thomas N. The Art of Christian Listening. 128p. (Orig.). 1981. pap. 4.95 (ISBN 0-8091-2345-2). Paulist Pr.

Henrichsen, Walter A. How to Disciple Your Children. 120p. 1981. pap. 3.95 (ISBN 0-88207-260-9). Victor Bks.

Hurst, D. V., tr. E Ele Concedeu Uns Para Mestres. (Portugese Bks.). 1979. 2.35 (ISBN 0-8297-0838-3). Life Pubs Intl.

Powers, Bruce P., ed. Christian Education Handbook. 1981. pap. 7.95 (ISBN 0-8054-3229-9). Broadman.

Sell, Charles M. Family Ministry: Family Life Through the Church. 272p. 11.95 (ISBN 0-310-42580-8). Zondervan.

Truman, Ruth. How to Be a Liberated Christian. LC 80-27302. 160p. 1981. 7.95 (ISBN 0-687-17710-3). Abingdon.

Wagner, C. Peter & Dayton, Edward R. Unreached Peoples, Eighty-One. (Orig.). 1981. pap. 8.95 (ISBN 0-89191-331-9). Cook.

Walker, Arthur L., Jr. Educating for Christian Missions. (Orig.). 1981. pap. 5.95 (ISBN 0-8054-6934-6). Broadman.

CHRISTIAN ETHICS

see also Christian Life; Christianity and Economics; Commandments, Ten; Love (Theology); Pastoral Medicine; Pastoral Psychology; Perfection; Virtue and Virtues

also subdivision Moral and Religious Aspects under specific subjects, e.g. Amusements–Moral and Religious Aspects

Barth, Karl. The Christian Life. Bromiley, Geoffrey W., ed. LC 80-39942. 328p. 1981. 14.95 (ISBN 0-8028-3523-6). Eerdmans.

Boice, James M. The Sermon on the Mount. 328p. (Orig.). 1981. pap. 7.95 (ISBN 0-310-21511-0). Zondervan.

Geisler, Norman. La Etica Christiana del Amor. Canclini, Arnoldo, tr. from Eng. LC 77-15813. 126p. (Orig., Span.). 1977. pap. 2.50 (ISBN 0-89922-103-3). Edit Caribe.

Geisler, Norman L. Options in Contemporary Christian Ethics. 128p. (Orig.). 1981. pap. 4.95 (ISBN 0-8010-3757-3). Baker Bk.

Hauerwas, Stanley. A Community of Character: Toward a Constructive Christian Social Ethic. LC 80-53072. 320p. 1981. text ed. 20.00 (ISBN 0-268-00733-0). U of Notre Dame Pr.

McCormick, Richard A. Notes on Moral Theology. LC 80-5682. 902p. 1981. lib. bdg. 24.50 (ISBN 0-8191-1439-1); pap. text ed. 15.00 (ISBN 0-8191-1440-5). U Pr of Amer.

Thieliche, Helmut. Theological Ethics, 3 vols. Incl. Foundations. Vol. I. pap. 10.95 (ISBN 0-8028-1791-2); Politics. Vol. II. pap. 10.95 (ISBN 0-8028-1792-0); Vol. III. Sex. pap. 6.95 (ISBN 0-8028-1794-7). LC 78-31858. Set. 29.50 (ISBN 0-8028-1795-5). Eerdmans.

CHRISTIAN ETHICS–ORTHODOX EASTERN AUTHORS

Harakas, Stanley S. For the Health of Body & Soul. 48p. (Orig.). 1980. pap. 1.95 (ISBN 0-916586-42-1). Hellenic Coll Pr.

CHRISTIAN EVIDENCES

see Apologetics

CHRISTIAN GIVING

see Stewardship, Christian

CHRISTIAN HYMNS

see Hymns

CHRISTIAN LEADERSHIP

Cornwall, Judson. Profiles of a Leader. (Orig.). 1981. pap. 4.95 (ISBN 0-88270-503-2). Logos.

Eims, Leroy. Disciples in Action. 324p. 1981. pap. 5.95 (ISBN 0-88207-343-5). Victor Bks.

Grollenberg, Lucas, et al. Minister? Pastor? Prophet? Grassroots Leadership in the Churches. 112p. (Dutch.). 1981. 9.95 (ISBN 0-8245-0017-2). Crossroad NY.

CHRISTIAN LIFE

see also Character; Christian Education; Christian Ethics; Conduct of Life; Devotional Exercises; Faith; Family–Religious Life; Monastic and Religious Life; Perfection; Prayer; Revivals; Sanctification; Spiritual Life; Stewardship, Christian

also subdivision Religious Life under classes of persons and institutions, e.g. Children–Religious Life

Adams, Jay E. Shepherding God's Flock. one vol. ed. 1979. pap. 8.95 (ISBN 0-87552-058-8). Presby & Reformed.

Adams, Walter E. Crisis at the Twenty-Third Hour. 175p. 1981. pap. 4.50 (ISBN 0-937408-03-4). Gospel Pubns FL.

Amate Siquiera un Poco. LC 78-57808. 182p. (Orig., Span.). 1978. pap. 3.95 (ISBN 0-89922-120-3). Edit Caribe.

Ardente No Espiritu. (Portuguese Bks.). 1979. write for info. (ISBN 0-8297-0787-5). Vida Pub.

Baker, Caleb. Two Roads & Two Destinies. 59p. pap. 0.25; chart 0.50. Walterick Pubs.

Barth, Karl. The Christian Life. Bromiley, Geoffrey W., ed. LC 80-39942. 328p. 1981. 14.95 (ISBN 0-8028-3523-6). Eerdmans.

Bascio, Patrick. Building a Just Society. LC 80-27238. 176p. (Orig.). 1981. pap. text ed. 5.95 (ISBN 0-88344-205-1). Orbis Bks.

Beardsley, Lou. How to Be a Better Mother-in-Law. 176p. (Orig.). 1981. pap. 4.95 (ISBN 0-89081-281-0). Harvest Hse.

Beasley, Manley & Robinson, Ras. Laws for Liberated Living. 212p. 1980. pap. 4.95 (ISBN 0-937778-01-X); 3.00 (ISBN 0-937778-02-8). Fulness Hse.

Benson, Bob. In Quest of the Shared Life. 168p. 1981. pap. 4.95 (ISBN 0-914850-55-5). Impact Tenn.

Berrigan, Daniel. Ten Commandments for the Long Jaul. (Journeys in Faith Ser.). 128p. 1981. 7.95 (ISBN 0-687-41240-4). Abingdon.

Blackman, Clifford L. Our Foolish Ways. 1981. 5.75 (ISBN 0-8062-1718-9). Carlton.

Blanton, Alma E. God & Mrs. Adam. (Illus.). 152p. (Orig.). 1978. pap. 4.95 (ISBN 0-938134-00-0, G-1). Loving Pubs.

Bly, Stephen. Radical Discipleship. 128p. (Orig.). 1981. pap. 3.95 (ISBN 0-8024-8219-8). Moody.

Bogart, Lois S. Life Can Be Beautiful. 1981. 4.95 (ISBN 0-8062-1589-5). Carlton.

Bonar, Horatius. When God's Children Suffer. LC 80-84441. (Shepherd Classics Ser.). 144p. 1981. pap. 5.95 (ISBN 0-87983-245-2). Keats.

Bonilla, Plutarco. Los Milagros Tambien Son Parabolas. LC 78-59240. 166p. (Orig., Span.). 1978. pap. 3.50 (ISBN 0-89922-114-9). Edit Caribe.

Boom, Corrie T. Tramp for the Lord. (Orig.). pap. 2.25 (ISBN 0-515-05828-9). Jove Pubns.

Bristol, Lee H., Jr. Renewal from Within. 1978. 1.00 (ISBN 0-686-28790-8). Forward Movement.

Bro, Bernard. The Little Way. pap. 5.95 (ISBN 0-87061-052-X). Chr Classics.

Brown, Delwin. To Set at Liberty: Christian Faith & Human Freedom. LC 80-21783. 144p. (Orig.). 1981. pap. 6.95 (ISBN 0-88344-501-8). Orbis Bks.

Brown, Robert M. Making Peace in the Global Village. LC 80-27213. (Orig.). 1981. pap. 5.95 (ISBN 0-664-24343-6). Westminster.

Bruchez, Dardo. Mensaje a la Conciencia. 128p. (Orig., Span.). 1979. pap. 2.50 (ISBN 0-89922-143-2). Edit Caribe.

Burroughs, Jeremiah. The Rare Jewel of Christian Contentment. 1979. pap. 3.95 (ISBN 0-85151-091-4). Banner of Truth.

Burton, Wilma. Sidewalk Psalms... & Some from Country Lanes. LC 79-92015. 119p. 1980. 6.95 (ISBN 0-89107-165-2). Good News.

Cameron, Miriam. Hello, I'm God & I'm Here to Help You. (Orig.). 1980. pap. 1.95 (ISBN 0-446-90063-X). Warner Bks.

Carson, Mary F. & Duba, Arlo D. Alabad a Dios. Gonzalez, Justo L., tr. from Eng. 86p. (Orig., Span.). 1979. pap. 2.50 (ISBN 0-89922-155-6). Edit Caribe.

Carter, James E. Christ & the Crowds. 1981. 3.25 (ISBN 0-8054-5181-1). Broadman.

Catherwood, Frederick. First Things First. 128p. 1981. pap. 5.95 (ISBN 0-87784-472-0). Inter Varsity.

Chalker, Kenneth W. Dare to Defy: Challenging Sterotypes & Looking at Relationships in a Christian Context. LC 80-54478. 144p. 1981. pap. 4.50x (ISBN 0-8358-0418-6). Upper Room.

Chambers, Oswald. Daily Thoughts for Disciples. 251p. 1976. 6.95. Chr Lit.

--Still Higher for His Highest. 192p. 1970. 5.95. Chr Lit.

Charles, J. Norman & Charles, Sharon. Heaven on Earth, Family Style. (Orig.). 1980. pap. 4.95 (ISBN 0-88270-495-8). Logos.

Cho, Paul Y. Solving Life's Problems. (Orig.). 1980. pap. 4.95 (ISBN 0-88270-450-8). Logos.

Christoff, Nicholas B. Saturday Night, Sunday Morning: Singles of the Church. LC 77-7841. 160p. 1980. pap. 4.95 (ISBN 0-06-061381-5, RD 341, HarpR). Har-Row.

Churches Alive Inc. Growth Group Member's Notebook. (Illus.). 105p. (Orig.). 1980. pap. text ed. 5.00 (ISBN 0-934396-11-6). Churches Alive.

Colson, Charles. Naci de Nuevo. Ward, Rhode, tr. from Eng. LC 77-81645. 419p. (Orig., Span.). 1977. pap. 3.95 (ISBN 0-89922-087-8). Edit Caribe.

Coniaris, A. M. Making God Real in the Orthodox Christian Home. 1977. pap. 4.95 (ISBN 0-937032-07-7). Light & Life Pub Co MN.

Conley, Herbert N. Living & Dying Gracefully. LC 79-65569. 70p. 1979. 4.95 (ISBN 0-8091-0298-6). Paulist Pr.

Cook, James. Grace Upon Grace. 6.95. Eerdmans.

Cooper, John C. The Joy of the Plain Life. 200p. 1981. pap. 4.95 (ISBN 0-914850-62-8, 14015P). Impact Tenn.

Costas, Orlando. Compromiso y Mision. 159p. (Orig., Span.). 1979. pap. 3.50 (ISBN 0-89922-165-3). Edit Caribe.

Crowther, Duane S. Thus Saith the Lord. LC 80-83862. 300p. 1981. 7.95 (ISBN 0-88290-168-0, 1061). Horizon Utah.

Curtin, Rosalie, et al. R.C.I.A. A Practical Approach to Christian Initiation. 136p. (Orig.). 1981. pap. 6.95. Wm C Brown.

Donfried, Karl P. The Dynamic Word: New Testament Insights for Contemporary Christians. LC 80-8905. 244p. 1981. 12.95 (ISBN 0-06-061945-7). Har-Row.

Dooley, Anne M. A Quest for Religious Maturity: The Obsessive-Compulsive Personality--Implications for Pastoral Counseling. LC 80-67255. 124p. (Orig.). 1981. lib. bdg. 16.00 (ISBN 0-8191-1442-1); pap. text ed. 7.50 (ISBN 0-8191-1443-X). U Pr of Amer.

Dunning, James B. New Wine: New Wineskins. 128p. (Orig.). 1981. pap. 6.80 (ISBN 0-8215-9807-4). Sadlier.

Eims, LeRoy. Disciples in Action. (Orig.). 1981. pap. price not set (ISBN 0-89109-477-6). NavPress.

Elliot, Elisabeth. The Mark of a Man. 1981. 7.95 (ISBN 0-8007-1178-5). Revell.

Elsdon, Ronald. Bent World. 200p. (Orig.). 1981. pap. 5.95 (ISBN 0-87784-834-3). Inter-Varsity.

Emmons, Michael & Richardson, David. The Assertive Christian. Frost, Miriam, ed. 156p. (Orig.). 1981. pap. 5.95 (ISBN 0-03-059057-4). Winston Pr.

Evans, Colleen T. Love Is an Everyday Thing. (Orig.). pap. 1.50 (ISBN 0-89129-243-8). Jove Pubns.

Ewens, James M. Pass It on. (Orig.). pap. 1.50 (ISBN 0-89129-051-6). Jove Pubns.

Farnsworth, Kirk E. & Lawhead, Wendell H. Life Planning. 96p. (Orig.). 1981. pap. 6.95 (ISBN 0-87784-840-8). Inter-Varsity.

Feinberg, Charles L. Daniel: The Man & His Visions. LC 80-70117. 212p. 1981. 8.95 (ISBN 0-915684-86-1). Christian Herald.

Ferguson, Sinclair B. Taking the Christian Life Seriously: Biblical Teaching on Christian Maturity. Orig. Title: Add to Your Life. 192p. 1981. pap. 5.95 (ISBN 0-310-43891-8). Zondervan.

Foster, Richard J. Freedom of Simplicity. LC 80-8351. 192p. 1981. 9.95 (ISBN 0-06-062832-4, HarpR). Har-Row.

Fowler, James W. Stages of Faith: The Psychology of Human Development & the Quest for Meaning. LC 80-7757. 224p. 1981. 10.95 (ISBN 0-06-062840-5, HarpR). Har-Row.

Frost, Robert, tr. Vida Desbordante. (Spanish Bks.). (Span.). 1978. 1.95 (ISBN 0-8297-0606-2). Vida Pub.

--Vida Transbordante. (Portugese Bks.). (Port.). 1979. write for info. (ISBN 0-8297-0919-3). Vida Pub.

Gagliostro, Vincenza. Am I OK - If I Feel the Way I Do? LC 80-2077. 128p. 1981. pap. 2.75 (ISBN 0-385-17437-3, Im). Doubleday.

Galilea, Segundo. Following Jesus. Phillips, Helen, tr. 128p. (Orig.). 1981. pap. 4.95 (ISBN 0-88344-136-5). Orbis Bks.

Getz, Gene A. Encouraging One Another. 1981. pap. 3.95 (ISBN 0-88207-256-0). Victor Bks.

Gibson, Jean. Intermediate Christian Training. 1981. pap. 6.50 (ISBN 0-937396-60-5). Walterick Pubs.

Goodyear, Imogene, ed. The Beauty of Wholeness: Program Resource for Women 1981. 1980. pap. 4.00 (ISBN 0-8309-0294-5). Herald Hse.

Gordon, Arthur. Touch of Wonder. (Orig.). pap. 1.75 (ISBN 0-515-04811-9). Jove Pubns.

Gorun, Joel R. Focus on Growth in the Church: School Ed. (To Live Is Christ Ser.). 1980. teacher's manual 3.85 (ISBN 0-697-01722-2). Wm C Brown.

Gossett, Don. How to Conquer Fear. Orig. Title: How You Can Rise Above Fear. 160p. 1981. pap. 2.95 (ISBN 0-88368-092-0). Whitaker Hse.

Graham, Billy. Billy Graham Talks to Teenagers. (Orig.). (YA) pap. 1.25 (ISBN 0-89129-153-9). Jove Pubns.

--Nacer a Una Nueva Vida. Ward, Rhode, tr. from Eng. LC 78-52622. 191p. (Orig., Span.). 1978. pap. 3.50 (ISBN 0-89922-110-6). Edit Caribe.

Hall, Douglas J. Lighten Our Darkness: Toward an Indigenous Theology of the Cross. LC 75-38963. pap. 9.95 (ISBN 0-664-24359-2). Westminster.

Hansen, Harold I. America's Witness for Christ. LC 80-84565. 350p. 1981. 8.95 (ISBN 0-88290-174-5). Horizon Utah.

Harakas, S. Living the Liturgy. 1974. pap. 3.50 (ISBN 0-937032-17-4). Light&Life Pub Co MN.

Haring, Bernard. Free & Faithful in Christ: Light to the World, Vol. 3. 500p. 1981. 19.50 (ISBN 0-8245-0009-1). Crossroad NY.

--Free & Faithful in Christ: The Truth Will Set You Free, Vol. 2. 560p. 1979. 17.50 (ISBN 0-8164-0205-1). Crossroad NY.

Harlan, Jeff. The Rapture. 1980. pap. 2.95. Maranatha Hse.

Harris, Charles. What's Ahead? (Radiant Life Ser.). 128p. (Orig.). 1981. pap. price not set. Gospel Pub.

Hawthorne, Minnie. Here We Go Again Lord. 1981. 4.50 (ISBN 0-8062-1659-X). Carlton.

Helldorfer, Martin. The Work Trap. LC 80-53205. (Illus.). 140p. 1981. pap. 4.95 (ISBN 0-88489-127-5). St Mary's.

Hendricks, Howard & Hendricks, Jeanne. Footprints: Walking Through the Passages of Life. LC 80-25868. (Illus.). 96p. 1981. pap. 8.95 (ISBN 0-930014-55-3). Multnomah.

Henry, Matthew. The Secret of Communion with God. LC 79-93431. (Shepperd Classics Ser.). 144p. 1981. pap. 5.95 (ISBN 0-87983-245-2). Keats.

Herring, Clyde L. When God & I Talk. (gr. 7-12). 1981. pap. 3.50 (ISBN 0-8054-5334-2). Broadman.

Hession, Roy. Not I but Christ. 1980. pap. 2.95. Chr Lit.

Higgs, Ralph, tr. El Espiritu Mismo. (Spanish Bks.). 1979. 1.90 (ISBN 0-8297-0551-1). Life Pubs Intl.

Hoeksema, Herman. When I Survey. LC 76-57122. 1977. 9.95 (ISBN 0-8254-2817-3). Kregel.

Hoeksma, Homer C. Voice of Our Fathers. LC 80-8082. 1980. 18.95 (ISBN 0-8254-2841-6). Kregel.

Hover, Margot K. & Breidenbach, Monica E. Chrisitan Family Almanac. 128p. (Orig.). 1980. pap. 9.95 (ISBN 0-697-01740-0). Wm C Brown.

Huffman, John A., Jr. Wholly Living. 132p. 1981. pap. 3.95 (ISBN 0-89693-005-X). Victor Bks.

Hunter, Emily. Como Ser Encantadora (Para Alumna) Mendoza De Mann, Wilma & Mariotti, F. A., trs. Orig. Title: Christian Charm Notebook. (Illus.). 56p. (Span.). Date not set. pap. price not set (ISBN 0-311-46054-2). Casa Bautista.

Jackson, Dave. Dial Nine One Nine. 160p. 1981. pap. text ed. 5.95 (ISBN 0-8361-1952-5). Herald Pr.

Jackson, Hulen. Sunshine Through the Shadows. 4.95 (ISBN 0-89315-283-8). Lambert Bk.

Jameson, Kenneth P. & Wilber, Charles K., eds. Religious Values & Development. (Illus.). 154p. 1981. 34.50 (ISBN 0-08-026107-8). Pergamon.

Jegen, Mary E. & Wilbur, Charles K., eds. Growth with Equity: Strategies for Meeting Human Needs. LC 78-70818. 242p. (Orig.). 1979. pap. 4.95. Paulist Pr.

John Paul, Pope, II. Faith According to St. John of the Cross. Aumann, Jordan, tr. LC 80-82265. Orig. Title: Doctrina de Fide apud S. Joannem a Cruce. 376p. (Orig.). 1981. price not set (ISBN 0-89870-010-8); pap. price not set (ISBN 0-89870-005-1). Ignatius Pr.

Joiner, William L. Wanting, Becoming, Believing. 152p. 1981. pap. 5.95 (ISBN 0-8170-0884-5). Judson.

Jones, Chris. Y Ahora, Que Hago, Senor? Cabeza, Susana, tr. from Eng. 107p. (Orig., Span.). (gr. 6-9). 1978. pap. 2.50 (ISBN 0-89922-123-8). Edit Caribe.

Jones, Jerry, compiled by. First Person, Singular. 175p. 1981. pap. 4.95 (14018P). Impact Tenn.

Judd, Mary T. Love & Lifestyles. LC 80-54285. (Illus.). 200p. (Orig.). (gr. 12). 1981. pap. text ed. 5.25 (ISBN 0-88489-132-1). St Mary's.

Kaiser, Richard. Overing Discouragement. LC 79-84746. 128p. 1981. pap. 2.50 (ISBN 0-89081-269-1). Harvest Hse.

Karo, Nancy & Mickelson, Alvera. La Aventura de Morir. Flores, Jose, tr. from Eng. LC 77-15812. 197p. (Orig., Span.). 1977. pap. 3.50 (ISBN 0-89922-098-3). Edit Caribe.

Kasper, Walter. Introduction to Christian Faith. Smith, David, tr. from Ger. 224p. 1981. pap. 4.95 (ISBN 0-8091-2324-X). Paulist Pr.

Keller, W. Phillip. Walking with God. 1980. 7.95 (ISBN 0-8007-1140-8). Revell.

Kempis, Thomas A. Of the Imitation of Christ. 256p. 1981. pap. 2.50 (ISBN 0-88368-094-7). Whitaker Hse.

Kibildis, Ralph. Turning Road. 112p. 1981. 1.95 (ISBN 0-914544-34-9). Living Flame Pr.

Kirk, Margaret. God Was a Stranger. 1980. pap. 2.75 (ISBN 0-85363-130-1). OMF Bks.

Klug, Ronald. Following Christ. 1981. pap. 3.50 (ISBN 0-570-03826-X, 12-2791). Concordia.

Kraft, Charles H. Communicating the Gospel God's Way. LC 80-53945. 60p. 1980. pap. 2.95x (ISBN 0-87808-742-7). William Carey Lib.

Larkin, Francis. Understanding the Heart. rev. ed. LC 80-81066. 127p. 1980. pap. write for info. (ISBN 0-89870-007-8). Ignatius Pr.

Leach, Virgil. Attitudes I. Date not set. pap. 2.95 (ISBN 0-89137-803-0). Quality Pubns.

--Attitudes II. 1981. pap. 2.95 (ISBN 0-89137-804-9). Quality Pubns.

Legere, J. Roy. Commissioned by the Lord Himself. 168p. 1980. 7.95 (ISBN 0-935488-00-6); pap. 3.95 (ISBN 0-935488-01-4). Apostolic Formation.

Leon, Jorge A. Cada Muchacho Necesita un Modelo Vivo. 96p. (Span.). 1981. pap. write for info. (ISBN 0-311-46087-9). Casa Bautista.

--Psicologia Pastoral de la Iglesia. LC 77-43121. 192p. (Orig., Span.). 1978. pap. 4.95 (ISBN 0-89922-113-0). Edit Caribe.

Levine, Samuel. You Take Jesus, I'll Take God. LC 80-82731. 134p. (Orig.). 1980. 9.95 (ISBN 0-9604754-2-7); pap. 6.95 (ISBN 0-9604754-1-9). Hamoroh Pr.

Lewis, C. S. El Problema del Dolor. Vilela, Ernesto S., tr. from Eng. LC 77-16715. 156p. (Orig., Span.). 1977. pap. 2.95 (ISBN 0-89922-097-5). Edit Caribe.

Lockerbie, D. Bruce. Timeless Moment. LC 80-65332. 126p. 1980. pap. 3.95 (ISBN 0-89107-181-4, Cornerstone Bks). Good News.

Lockerbie, Jeanette. Forgive, Forget & Be Free. LC 80-69304. 148p. 1981. 7.95 (ISBN 0-915684-76-4). Christian Herald.

Loder, James E. The Transforming Moment: Understanding Convictional Experiences. LC 80-8354. 256p. 1981. 12.95 (ISBN 0-06-065276-4, HarpR). Har-Row.

Lutz, Lorry. Born to Loose, Bound to Win. LC 80-83877. 192p. (Orig.). 1981. pap. 5.95 (ISBN 0-89081-274-8). Harvest Hse.

Macaulay, Susan S. Something Beautiful from God. LC 80-67388. 1980. 11.95 (ISBN 0-89107-189-X, Cornerstone Bks); pap. 6.95 (ISBN 0-89107-186-5). Good News.

McCarty, Michele. Believing. 160p. 1980. pap. text ed. 4.25 (ISBN 0-697-01753-2); tchr's manual 5.00. Wm C Brown.

--Relating. 128p. (Orig.). (gr. 11-12). 1979. pap. text ed. 4.00 (ISBN 0-697-01710-9); tchr's manual 5.00 (ISBN 0-697-01711-7). Wm C Brown.

McCasland, David C. Open to Change. 144p. 1981. pap. 3.95 (ISBN 0-88207-258-7). Victor Bks.

MacMillan, John A. Encounter with Darkness. 116p. pap. 1.95 (ISBN 0-87509-287-X). Chr Pubns.

Makrakis, Apostolos. Concerning Our Duties to God. Orthodox Christian Educational Society, ed. 170p. 1958. pap. text ed. 2.00x (ISBN 0-938366-13-0). Orthodox Chr.

Malinski, Mieczyslaw. Our Daily Bread. 142p. 1979. 7.95 (ISBN 0-8164-0439-9). Crossroad NY.

Marie Eugene. I Am a Daughter of the Church. M Verda Clare, tr. 1981. pap. cancelled (ISBN 0-87061-050-3). Chr Classics.

Martino, Mario. God, Why Me? 1981. 4.95 (ISBN 0-8062-1703-0). Carlton.

Maston, T. B. Consejos a la Juventud. Duffer, H. F., Jr., tr. Orig. Title: Advice to Youth. 60p. (Span.). 1980. pap. 1.00 (ISBN 0-311-46005-4). Casa Bautista.

Merrill, Vic. Can You Hear Me, God? 96p. 1981. 6.00 (ISBN 0-682-49740-1). Exposition.

Merton, Thomas. Introductions East & West. (Illus.). 175p. 1981. 19.95 (ISBN 0-87775-139-0); pap. 9.95 (ISBN 0-87775-140-4). Unicorn Pr.

Miller, Donald E. The Case for Liberal Christianity. LC 80-8355. 160p. 1980. 9.95 (ISBN 0-06-065753-7). Har-Row.

Molow, Paul. Your Life Is What You Make It. 192p. 1981. 10.00 (ISBN 0-682-49739-8). Exposition.

Moran, Hugh, ed. Words to Live by: Chiara Lubich & Christians from All Over the World. Dauphinais, Raymond & Moran, Hugh, trs. from Fr. & Ital. LC 80-82419. 1980. pap. 4.50 (ISBN 0-911782-08-7). New City.

Morison, Frank. Quien Movio la Piedra? Ward, Rhode, tr. from Eng. LC 77-11752. 206p. (Orig., Span.). 1977. pap. 3.95 (ISBN 0-89922-100-9). Edit Caribe.

Murray, Andrew. Absolute Surrender. 128p. 1981. pap. 2.50 (ISBN 0-88368-093-9). Whitaker Hse.

--Like Christ. 240p. 1981. pap. 2.50 (ISBN 0-88368-099-8). Whitaker Hse.

Nee, Watchman. Normal Christian Life Study Guide. Foster, ed. 1978. pap. 1.25. Chr Lit.

Niklas, Gerald R. The Making of a Pastoral Person. 159p. (Orig.). 1981. pap. 5.95 (ISBN 0-8189-0409-7). Alba.

Norbie, Don. Your New Life. 66p. pap. 0.10. Walterick Pubs.

Notaro, Thom. Van Til & the Use of Evidence. 1980. pap. 3.75 (ISBN 0-87552-353-6). Presby & Reformed.

Ogilvie, Lloyd J. Radiance of the Inner Splendor. LC 80-51524. 144p. 1980. pap. text ed. 4.95x (ISBN 0-8358-0405-4). Upper Room.

Oliver, Lucille. Cry for the World. 1981. pap. price not set (ISBN 0-8309-0307-0). Herald Hse.

Orr, C. E. Helps to Holy Living. 64p. pap. 0.40; pap. 1.00 3 copies. Faith Pub Hse.

--How to Live a Holy Life. 112p. 0.75; pap. 2.00 3 copies. Faith Pub Hse.

Palau, Luis. Exito. Sipowicz, Edwin, tr. from Eng. LC 78-57804. 144p. (Orig., Span.). 1978. pap. 3.50 (ISBN 0-89922-115-7). Edit Caribe.

Parrick, Jerry. A Twentieth Century Miracle. (Orig.). 1981. pap. 4.95 (ISBN 0-88270-488-5). Logos.

Pate, Don. He Shall Be Like a Tree. (Horizon Ser.). 128p. 1981. pap. price not set (ISBN 0-8127-0315-4). Southern Pub.

Patterson, Katherine. Partners in Pluralism: A Study Guide. (Orig.). 1981. pap. 2.95 (ISBN 0-377-00111-2). Friend Pr.

Peale, Norman V. Norman Vincent Peale's Treasury of Joy & Enthusiasm. 1981. 9.95 (ISBN 0-8007-1180-7). Revell.

Pentecost, Dwight. Designed to Be Like Him. 1981. pap. 5.95 (ISBN 0-8024-2132-6). Moody.

Phillips, Keith. The Making of a Disciple. 1981. 7.95 (ISBN 0-8007-1181-5). Revell.

Polland, Madeleine A. All Their Kingdoms. 1981. 11.95 (ISBN 0-440-00019-X). Delacorte.

Powers, Susan. The Inspirational Series, 12 bks. (Illus.). 1980. 2.95 ea. Mayflower Bks.

Prather, Hugh. A Book of Games: A Course in Spiritual Play. LC 80-2840. (Illus.). 176p. 1981. pap. 5.95 (ISBN 0-385-14779-1, Dolp). Doubleday.

Premoe, David, ed. Zion, the Growing Symbol. 1980. pap. 5.75 (ISBN 0-8309-0301-1). Herald Hse.

Price, Eugenia. Just As I Am. (Orig.). 1976. pap. 1.75 (ISBN 0-89129-187-3). Jove Pubns.

--Learning to Live. (Orig.). pap. 1.95 (ISBN 0-89129-193-8). Jove Pubns.

Prime, Derek. Created to Praise. 128p. (Orig.). 1981. pap. 2.95 (ISBN 0-87784-825-4). Inter-Varsity.

Rapoport, Nessa. Preparing for Sabbath. LC 80-21539. 304p. 1981. 10.95 (ISBN 0-688-00294-3). Morrow.

Read, D. H. I Am Persuaded. (Scholar As Preacher Ser.). 190p. Repr. of 1961 ed. text ed. 7.75 (ISBN 0-567-04430-0). Attic Pr.

Reiss, Walter. Thank God for My Breakdown. 1980. 4.95 (ISBN 0-8100-0114-4). Northwest Pub.

Roberts, Dana. Understanding Watchman Nee. (Orig.). 1981. pap. 4.95 (ISBN 0-88270-489-3). Logos.

Roberts, Dennis. Well... Excuse Me. LC 80-84233. 64p. (Orig.). 1981. pap. 1.25 (ISBN 0-89081-265-9). Harvest Hse.

Robinson, Ras, ed. The Finest of Fulness. 192p. 1979. pap. 3.95 (ISBN 0-937778-00-1). Fulness Hse.

Rose, Tom & Metcalf, Robert. The Coming Victory. (The Coronation Ser.: No. 5). 206p. (Orig.). 1980. pap. 6.95x (ISBN 0-686-28757-6). Chr Stud Ctr.

Rosenthal, Joan. The Lord Is My Strength. (Orig.). pap. 1.25 (ISBN 0-89129-086-9). Jove Pubns.

Roseveare, Helen. Living Faith. (Orig.). 1981. pap. 3.95 (ISBN 0-8024-4941-7). Moody.

Salem, Luis. El Dios de Nuestros Libertadores. LC 77-165. (Illus.). 172p. (Orig., Span.). 1977. pap. 2.75 (ISBN 0-89922-093-2). Edit Caribe.

Sanford, John A. The Man Who Wrestled with God. 144p. 1981. pap. 6.95 (ISBN 0-8091-2367-3). Paulist Pr.

Sargent, Rodney. Christian in the Making. (Orig.). 1981. pap. price not set. NavPress.

Savage, Hughley. How to Find True Peace & Hapiness-Plus Inherit Eternal Life. (Orig.). 1980. pap. 2.00 (ISBN 0-9605150-0-3). Savage.

Schall, James V. Christianity & Life. LC 79-89759. 130p. (Orig.). 1981. pap. write for info. (ISBN 0-89870-004-3). Ignatius Pr.

Schmitt, Dotty. The Delight of Being His Daughter. 1981. pap. 4.95 (ISBN 0-88270-509-1). Logos.

Schuller, Robert A., ed. Robert Schuller's Life Changers. 1981. 7.95 (ISBN 0-8007-1182-3). Revell.

Scrogin, Michael. When God Intrudes. 112p. 1981. pap. 4.95 (ISBN 0-8170-0903-5). Judson.

Seerveld, C. Rainbows for the Fallen World. 1980. 14.95x (ISBN 0-919071-00-7); pap. 9.95x (ISBN 0-919071-01-5). Radix Bks.

Sergio, Lisa. Jesus & Woman: An Exciting Discovery of What He Offered Her. LC 75-4365. 139p. 1980. pap. 4.95 (ISBN 0-914440-44-6). EPM Pubns.

Sertillanges, A. D. The Intellectual Life. pap. 5.95 (ISBN 0-87061-053-8). Chr Classics.

Shearer, Helen. Invest in You. 1981. 5.75 (ISBN 0-8062-1600-X). Carlton.

Shedd, Charlie W. Letters to Philip. (Orig.). pap. 1.95 (ISBN 0-515-05827-0). Jove Pubns.

Shields, Steven L. No Greater Sacrifice. LC 80-83864. 250p. 1980. 6.95 (ISBN 0-88290-166-4, 1059). Horizon Utah.

Sill, Sterling W. Lessons from Great Lives. LC 80-84567. 300p. 1981. 7.95 (ISBN 0-88290-172-9, 2049). Horizon Utah.

--The Upward Reach. LC 80-83863. 350p. 1980. 8.50 (ISBN 0-88290-167-2, 1060). Horizon Utah.

Simpson, Albert B. The Christ Life. LC 80-69301. 96p. pap. 1.75 (ISBN 0-87509-291-8). Chr Pubns.

Simpson, F. Dale. Seven Steps Along the Way. 1981. pap. write for info. (ISBN 0-89137-527-9). Quality Pubns.

Slover, Luella, ed. Life After Youth. 1981. pap. write for info. (ISBN 0-8309-0303-8). Herald Hse.

Smith, B. J. & Ingley, James M. The Last of the Generations. 1981. 8.95 (ISBN 0-533-04609-2). Vantage.

Smith, Charles. What If I Don't Go Overseas. 1981. pap. 0.50 (ISBN 0-87784-182-9). Inter-Varsity.

Smith, Louis A. & Barndt, Joseph R. Beyond Brokeness. (Orig.). 1980. pap. 2.95 (ISBN 0-377-00100-7). Friend Pr.

Smith, Robert A. Seeking & Finding. 1974. 1.75 (ISBN 0-912128-08-9). Pubns Living.

Sommerfeldt, John R., ed. Abba: Guides to Wholeness & Holiness East & West. (Cistercian Studies Ser.: No. 38). 1981. price not set (ISBN 0-87907-838-3). Cistercian Pubns.

Spray, Pauline E. Coping with Tension. (Direction Bks). 136p. 1981. pap. 2.95 (ISBN 0-8010-8189-0). Baker Bk.

Stedman, Ray C. Authentic Christianity. (Orig.). pap. 1.75 (ISBN 0-89129-249-7). Jove Pubns.

Stern, Chaim, ed. Gates of Forgiveness: Selichot. 1980. pap. 2.00 ea. Eng. Ed (ISBN 0-916694-57-7). Hebrew Ed (ISBN 0-916694-74-7). Central Conf.

Stewart, Don. Miracle Happiness. (Orig.). 1981. pap. 2.95 (ISBN 0-88270-483-4). Logos.

Stoffel, Ernest L. The Dragon Bound: Revelation Speaks to Our Times. 120p. (Orig.). 1981. pap. 4.50 (ISBN 0-8042-0227-3). John Knox.

The Stream on the Other Side of the Mind. 300p. 1981. 30.00 (ISBN 0-913028-82-7); pap. 8.95 (ISBN 0-686-69476-7). North Atlantic.

Stringfellow, Bill. All in the Name of the Lord. 176p. 1981. pap. 2.95 (ISBN 0-939286-00-9). Concerned Pubns.

Swindoll, Charles R. Make up Your Mind. (Illus.). 100p. 1981. pap. 8.95 (ISBN 0-930014-61-8). Multnomah.

Tait, Vera D. Take Command. LC 80-53217. 144p. 1981. 3.95 (ISBN 0-87159-150-2). Unity Bks.

Tapscott, Betty. Out of the Valley. 128p. 1981. pap. 3.95 (ISBN 0-8407-5761-1). Nelson.

Tate-O'Brien, Judith. Love in Deed. rev. ed. (Illus.). 68p. 1980. pap. 2.95 (ISBN 0-936098-07-4). Natl Marriage.

Tchividjian, Gigi. A Woman's Quest for Serenity. 1981. 7.95 (ISBN 0-8007-1183-1). Revell.

Ten Boom, Corrie, tr. Andarilha Para O Senhor. (Portugese Bks.). (Port.). 1979. 1.50 (ISBN 0-8297-0638-0). Life Pubs Intl.

--Mision Ineludible. (Spanish Bks.). (Span.). 1978. 1.95 (ISBN 0-8297-0586-4). Life Pubs Intl.

Thomas a Kempis. The Imitation of Christ. Blaiklock, E. M., tr. 228p. 1981. pap. 4.95 (ISBN 0-8407-5760-3). Nelson.

Toon, Peter. God's Kingdom for Today. LC 80-65331. (Christian Faith for Today Ser.). 128p. 1980. pap. 3.95 (ISBN 0-89107-188-1, Cornerstone Bks). Good News.

Torrey, R. A. How to Bring Men to Christ. 128p. 1981. pap. 2.50 (ISBN 0-88368-098-X). Whitaker Hse.

Toye, Charles. Prayers & Meditations for Healing. LC 80-82813. 96p. (Orig.). 1981. pap. 3.95 (ISBN 0-8091-2342-8). Paulist Pr.

Tozer, Aiden W. Renewed Day by Day. LC 80-69301. 380p. pap. 6.95 (ISBN 0-87509-292-6). Chr Pubns.

True Bounds of Christian Freedom. 1978. pap. 3.95 (ISBN 0-85151-083-3). Banner of Truth.

Valenti, Tony & Yonan, Grazia P. The Tony Valenti Story. 160p. (Orig.). 1981. write for info. (ISBN 0-88243-752-6, 02-0752). Gospel Pub.

Van Zant, William. Seven Epistles of Love. 1981. 5.95 (ISBN 0-8062-1719-7). Carlton.

Vicker, Denise. God Let Me Out of This Marriage. Boneck, John, ed. LC 80-83459. 160p. 1981. pap. 3.50 (ISBN 0-89221-080-X). New Leaf.

Vincent, Harold. Sonship Training. 64p. (Orig.). 1980. pap. 1.50 (ISBN 0-89841-009-6). Zoe Pubns.

Wagner, Maurice. La Sensacion de Ser Alguien. Cook, David A., tr. from Eng. LC 77-16714. 300p. (Orig., Span.). 1977. pap. 4.95 (ISBN 0-89922-104-1). Edit Caribe.

Walker, Winifred. Valley of Vision: Discovering God Around the World. 64p. (Orig.). 1981. pap. write for info. Upper Room.

Warren, Max. Creo en la Gran Comision. Sipowicz, Edwin, tr. from Eng. LC 78-54272. (Serie Creo). 205p. (Orig., Span.). 1978. pap. 3.95 (ISBN 0-89922-112-2). Edit Caribe.

Watkins, Janet. Savoring the Sabbath. LC 80-83865. 80p. (Orig.). 1980. pap. 4.95 (ISBN 0-88290-165-6, 1058). Horizon Utah.

Watson. I Believe in the Church. pap. 4.95. Eerdmans.

Watt, Gordon. The Meaning of the Cross. 1970. pap. 1.25. Chr Lit.

Weaver, Richard. In Praise of Jesus. 1981. 4.95 (ISBN 0-8062-1711-1). Carlton.

Wellington, Paul A., ed. Planning to Stay Together. 1980. pap. 4.00 (ISBN 0-8309-0308-9). Herald Hse.

Wenger, J. C. The Family Faith. (No. 10). 72p. 1981. pap. 0.95 (ISBN 0-686-69151-2). Herald Pr.

White, Ellen G. Steps to Jesus. 128p. 1980. 3.95 (ISBN 0-8127-0316-2); pap. 1.95 (ISBN 0-8127-0318-9). Southern Pub.

Wilkerson, David. Beyond the Cross & the Switchblade. (Orig.). pap. 1.75 (ISBN 0-89129-151-2). Jove Pubns.

Wilkinks, Ronald J. The Emerging Church. (To Live Is Christ Ser.). 1981. pap. 4.10 (ISBN 0-697-01760-5). Wm C Brown.

Wilson, Leland. Silver City. 96p. (Orig.). 1980. pap. 3.95 (ISBN 0-87178-790-3). Brethren.

Winn, Albert C. A Sense of Mission: Guidance from the Gospel of John. 1981. pap. price not set (ISBN 0-664-24365-7). Westminster.

Young, Douglas. A Strange Judgment. Hunting, Constance, ed. (Orig.). 1981. pap. 4.95 (ISBN 0-913006-23-8). Puckerbrush.

Zehr, Paul M. God Dwells with His People. 216p. 1981. pap. 7.95 (ISBN 0-8361-1939-8). Herald Pr.

CHRISTIAN LIFE–BIOGRAPHY

see Christian Biography

CHRISTIAN LITERATURE, EARLY–HISTORY AND CRITICISM

Augustine, St. St. Augustine: The Greatness of the Soul, Vol. 9. Quasten, J. & Plumpe, J., eds. Colleran, Joseph M., tr. (Ancient Christian Writers Ser.: No. 9). 255p. 1950. 11.95 (ISBN 0-8091-0060-6). Paulist Pr.

CHRISTIAN MINISTRY

see Clergy–Office

CHRISTIAN PERFECTION

see Perfection

CHRISTIAN PRIESTHOOD

see Priesthood

CHRISTIAN REFORMED CHURCH

Brink, William P. & DeRidder, Richard R. Manual of Christian Reformed Church Government: 1980 Edition. rev. ed. LC 80-24129. 1980. pap. text ed. 4.45 (ISBN 0-933140-19-3). Bd of Pubns CRC.

CHRISTIAN SCIENCE

see also Faith-Cure; Mental Healing

Kimball, Edward A. Lectures & Articles on Christian Science. (Illus.). 1976. 10.00 (ISBN 0-911588-01-9). N S Wait.

CHRISTIAN SOCIOLOGY

see Sociology, Christian

CHRISTIAN STEWARDSHIP

see Stewardship, Christian

CHRISTIAN SYMBOLISM

see Christian Art and Symbolism

CHRISTIAN THEOLOGIANS

see Theologians

CHRISTIAN UNION

see also Ecumenical Movement

Tully, Mary Jo & Hirstein, Sandra J. Focus on Believing. (Light of Faith Ser.). (Orig.). (gr. 3 up). 1981. pap. text ed. 3.00 (ISBN 0-697-01767-2); tchr's ed. 7.60 (ISBN 0-697-01768-0). Wm C Brown.

--Focus on Belonging. (Light of Faith Ser.). (Orig.). (gr. 2 up). 1981. pap. text ed. 2.65 (ISBN 0-697-01765-6); tchrs' ed. 7.60 (ISBN 0-697-01766-4). Wm C Brown.

--Focus on Celebrating. (Light of Faith Ser.). (Orig.). (gr. 5 up). 1981. pap. text ed. 3.00 (ISBN 0-697-01771-0); tchrs' ed. 7.60. Wm C Brown.

--Focus on Living. (Light of Faith Ser.). (Orig.). (gr. 4 up). 1981. pap. text ed. 3.00 (ISBN 0-697-01769-9); tchrs' ed. 7.60 (ISBN 0-697-01770-2). Wm C Brown.

--Focus on Relating. (Light of Faith Ser.). (Orig.). (gr. 6). 1981. pap. text ed. 3.00 (ISBN 0-697-01773-7); tchrs' ed. 7.60 (ISBN 0-697-01774-5). Wm C Brown.

CHRISTIAN UNION–CATHOLIC CHURCH

Bakker, Jim. Survival: Unity to Live. Boneck, John & Dudley, Cliff, eds. LC 80-84504. 150p. 1980. 7.95 (ISBN 0-89221-081-8). New Leaf.

CHRISTIANITY

see also Catholicity; Church; Ecumenical Movement; God; Homosexuality and Christianity; Jesus Christ; Miracles; Missions; Protestantism; Reformation; Sociology, Christian; Theism; Theology; Women in Christianity

also headings beginning with the word Christian and Church; and names of Christian churches and sects, e.g. Catholic Church, Lutheran Church, Huguenots

Bain, John A. The Foundations of Christian Faith. 112p. Repr. of 1936 ed. 2.95 (ISBN 0-567-02015-0). Attic Pr.

Coe, Ben. Christian Churches at the Crossroads. 1980. pap. write for info. (ISBN 0-87808-178-X). William Carey Lib.

Daniels, Marilyn. The Dance in Christianity. (Illus.). 112p. (Orig.). 1981. pap. 4.95 (ISBN 0-8091-2381-9). Paulist Pr.

Groff, John W. The Mystic Journey. 1980. 1.45 (ISBN 0-686-28785-1). Forward Movement.

Guinan, Michael D. Gospel Poverty: Witness to the Risen Christ. 96p. (Orig.). 1981. pap. 3.95 (ISBN 0-8091-2377-0). Paulist Pr.

Hanson, Anthony & Hanson, Richard. Reasonable Belief: An Outline of the Christian Faith. 300p. 1981. 24.95 (ISBN 0-19-213235-0). Oxford U Pr.

Harkness, Georgia. Understanding the Christian Faith. (Festival Ser.). 192p. 1981. pap. 1.95 (ISBN 0-687-42955-2). Abingdon.

Harvey, Van A. The Historian & the Believer: The Morality of Historical Knowledge & Christian Belief. 1981. pap. price not set (ISBN 0-664-24367-3). Westminster.

Holl, Karl. The Distinctive Elements in Christianity. Hope, Norman V., tr. LC 38-24885. 79p. pap. text ed. 3.50. Attic Pr.

Johnson, Sherman E. Belonging: An Introduction to the Christian Church. 1978. 1.65 (ISBN 0-686-28773-8). Forward Movement.

Kennedy, James W. Anglican Partners. 1978. 2.00 (ISBN 0-686-28772-X). Forward Movement.

Lewis, C. S. Christianismo...y Nada Mas. Orozco, Julio, tr. from Eng. LC 77-85609. 216p. (Orig., Span.). 1977. pap. 3.50 (ISBN 0-89922-096-7). Edit Caribe.

McKinney, W. A., ed. Creation, Christ & Culture: Studies in Honor of T. F. Torrance. 336p. Repr. of 1976 ed. text ed. 17.95x (ISBN 0-567-01019-8). Attic Pr.

Mather, Cotton. Great Works of Christ in America, 2 vols. 1979. Set. 37.95; Vol. 1. (ISBN 0-85151-280-1); Vol. 2. (ISBN 0-85151-280-1). Banner of Truth.

The Reasonableness of Christianity. 311p. Repr. of 1927 ed. text ed. 4.95. Attic Pr.

Reisinger, Ernest C. The Carnal Christian: What Should We Think of the Carnal Christian? 75p. Date not set. 0.75. Banner of Truth.

Ryken, Leland, ed. The Christian Imagination: Essays on Literature & the Arts. 344p. (Orig.). 1981. pap. 9.95 (ISBN 0-8010-7702-8). Baker Bk.

Simcox, Carroll E. Learning to Believe: A Meditation on the Christian Creed. LC 80-2372. 112p. 1981. pap. 5.95 (ISBN 0-8006-1497-6, 1-1497). Fortress.

Torrance, Thomas F., ed. Belief in Science & in Christian Life. 160p. 1981. pap. 11.00x (ISBN 0-905312-11-2, Pub. by Sottish Academic Pr Scotland). Columbia U Pr.

Wood, Charles M. The Formation of Christian Understanding: An Essay in Theological Hermeneutics. (Orig.). 1981. pap. price not set (ISBN 0-664-24373-8). Westminster.

Woods, H. G. At the Temple Church. (Scholar As Preacher Ser.). 252p. Repr. of 1911 ed. 7.75 (ISBN 0-567-04406-8). Attic Pr.

CHRISTIANITY–APOLOGETIC WORKS

see Apologetics

CHRISTIANITY–BIBLIOGRAPHY

Address Book of Some Assemblies of Christians (Current) 1981. pap. 3.95 (ISBN 0-937396-03-6). Walterick Pubs.

CHRISTIANITY–BIOGRAPHY

see Christian Biography

CHRISTIANITY–COMMUNICATION

see Communication (Theology)

CHRISTIANITY–CONTROVERSIAL LITERATURE

see also Atheism; Free Thought; Secularism

Khomiakov, Aleksiei S. L' Eglise Latine et le Protestantisme, Au Point De Vue De l'Eglise d'Orient. LC 80-2362. 1981. Repr. of 1872 ed. 49.00 (ISBN 0-404-18908-3). AMS Pr.

CHRISTIANITY–ESSENCE, GENIUS, NATURE

Wilken, Robert L. The Myth of Christian Beginnings. LC 80-11884. 218p. 1980. pap. text ed. 4.95 (ISBN 0-268-01348-9). U of Notre Dame Pr.

CHRISTIANITY–EVIDENCES

see Apologetics

CHRISTIANITY–HISTORY

see Church History

CHRISTIANITY–ORIGIN

see also Church–Foundation

Jackson, John G. Pagan Origins of the Christ Myth. 1980. pap. 3.00. Am Atheist.

CHRISTIANITY–PHILOSOPHY

see also Transcendence of God

Clark, Gordon H. A Christian View of Men & Things. (Twin Brooks Ser.). 325p. 1981. pap. 8.95 (ISBN 0-8010-2466-8). Baker Bk.

Conner, T. Doctrina Cristiana. Robleto, Adolfo, tr. Orig. Title: Christian Doctrine. 408p. (Span.). Date not set. pap. price not set (ISBN 0-311-09012-5). Casa Bautista.

Makrakis, Apostolos. The Foundation of Philosophy--a Refutation of Skepticism, the True Jesus Christ, the Science of God & Man; the God of the Christians. Orthodox Christian Educational Society, ed. Lekatsos, Anthony & Cummings, Denver, trs. from Fr. 103p. 1955. 6.00x (ISBN 0-938366-07-6). Orthodox Chr.

--The Orthodox Approach to Philosophy. Orthodox Christian Educational Society, ed. Cummings, Denver, tr. from Hellenic. (The Logos & Holy Spirit in the Unity of Christian Thought Ser.: Vol. 1). 82p. 1977. pap. 2.50x (ISBN 0-938366-06-8). Orthodox Chr.

--The Paramount Doctrines of Orthodoxy--the Tricompositeness of Man, Apology of A. Makrakis & the Trial of A. Makrakis. Orthodox Christian Educational Society, ed. Cummings, Denver, tr. from Hellenic. 380p. 1954. 10.00x (ISBN 0-938366-17-3). Orthodox Chr.

--Philosophy: An Orthodox Christian Understanding. Orthodox Christian Educational Society, ed. Cummings, Denver, tr. from Hellenic. (The Logos & Holy Spirit in the Unity of Christian Thought Ser.: Vol. 5). 279p. 1977. pap. 3.50x (ISBN 0-938366-02-5). Orthodox Chr.

--The Political Philosophy of the Orthodox Church. Orthodox Christian Educational Society, ed. Cummings, Denver, tr. from Hellenic. Orig. Title: The Orthodox Definition of Political Science. 163p. (Orig.). 1965. pap. 2.00x (ISBN 0-938366-11-4). Orthodox Chr.

CHRISTIANITY–POLITY

see Church Polity

CHRISTIANITY–PSYCHOLOGY

Makrakis, Apostolos. Psychology: An Orthodox Christian Perspective. Orthodox Christian Educational Society, ed. Cummings, Denver, tr. from Hellenic. (The Logos & Holy Spirit in the Unity of Christian Thought Ser.: Vol. 2). 151p. 1977. pap. 3.50x (ISBN 0-938366-05-X). Orthodox Chr.

CHRISTIANITY–RENEWAL

see Church Renewal

CHRISTIANITY–UNION BETWEEN CHURCHES

see Christian Union

CHRISTIANITY–20TH CENTURY

Marchant, James. The Reunion of Christendom: A Survey of Present Position. 329p. 1980. Repr. of 1929 ed. lib. bdg. 30.00 (ISBN 0-8495-3771-1). Arden Lib.

Metz, Johann B. The Emergent Church: The Future of Christianity in a Post-Bourgeois World. 160p. (Ger.). 1981. 10.95 (ISBN 0-8245-0036-9). Crossroad NY.

Osborn, E. F. The Beginning of Christian Philosophy. LC 79-8911. 256p. Date not set. price not set; pap. price not set (ISBN 0-521-29855-5). Cambridge U Pr.

CHRISTIANITY AND ATHEISM

Bloch, E. Atheism in Christianity. 12.50 (ISBN 0-8164-9102-X). Continuum.

CHRISTIANITY AND ECONOMICS

see also Sociology, Christian; Stewardship, Christian

Hallam, Arthur F. Christian Capitalism. 182p. (Orig.). 1981. pap. 14.95 (ISBN 0-938770-00-4). Capitalist Pr OH.

CHRISTIANITY AND LAW

see Religion and Law

CHRISTIANITY AND LITERATURE

Lawrence, Irene. Linguistics & Theology: The Significance of Noam Chomsky for Theological Construction. LC 80-24210. (ATLA Monograph: No. 16). 214p. 1980. 12.50 (ISBN 0-8108-1347-5). Scarecrow.

CHRISTIANITY AND OTHER RELIGIONS

see also Paganism

Copeland, E. L. El Cristianismo y Otras Religiones. Mora, Abdias A., tr. Orig. Title: Christianity & World Religious. (Illus.). 192p. (Span.). Date not set. pap. price not set (ISBN 0-311-05760-8, Edit Mundo). Casa Bautista.

Hick, John & Hebblethwaite, Brian, eds. Christianity & Other Religions: Selected Readings. LC 80-2383. 256p. 1981. pap. 6.95 (ISBN 0-8006-1444-5, 1-1444). Fortress.

Schultz, Joseph P. Judaism & the Gentile Faiths: Comparative Studies in Religion. LC 75-5250. 405p. 1981. 19.50 (ISBN 0-8386-1707-7). Fairleigh Dickinson.

CHRISTIANITY AND OTHER RELIGIONS–GREEK

Capel, Evelyn. Making of Christianity & the Greek Spirit. 1980. pap. 10.75 (ISBN 0-903540-41-X, Pub. by Floris Books). St George Bk Serv.

CHRISTIANITY AND OTHER RELIGIONS–JUDAISM

Jocz, Jakob. The Jewish People & Jesus Christ After Auschwitz. 172p. (Orig.). 1981. pap. 6.95 (ISBN 0-8010-5123-1). Baker Bk.

Lapide, Pinchas & Moltmann, Jurgen. Jewish Monotheism & Christian Trinitarian Doctrine. Swidler, Leonard, tr. from Ger. LC 80-8058. 96p. 1981. pap. 4.50 (ISBN 0-8006-1405-4, 1-1405). Fortress.

Sanders, E. P., et al, eds. Jewish & Christian Self-Definition, Vol. 2: Aspects of Judaism in the Greco-Roman Period. LC 80-2391. 450p. 1981. 17.95 (ISBN 0-8006-0660-4, 1-660). Fortress.

CHRISTIANITY AND PHILOSOPHY

see Philosophy and Religion

CHRISTIANITY AND POLITICS

Eliopoulos, Nicholas. Oneness of Politics & Religion. 126p. (Orig.). 1970. pap. 3.00x (ISBN 0-9605396-1-1). Phystiklakis & Eliopoulos.

CHRISTIANITY AND SCIENCE

see Religion and Science

CHRISTIANITY AND THE WORLD

see Church and the World

CHRISTIANITY AND WAR

see War and Religion

CHRISTIANITY IN (AFRICA, ASIA, ETC.)

see Christians in (Africa, Asia, etc.)

CHRISTIANS, JEWISH

see Jewish Christians

CHRISTIANS IN AFRICA

Healey, Joseph G. A Fifth Gospel: The Experience of Black Christian Values. LC 80-25033. (Illus.). 320p. (Orig.). 1981. pap. 7.95 (ISBN 0-88344-013-X). Orbis Bks.

CHRISTIANS IN JAPAN

Paske-Smith, Montague, ed. Japanese Traditions of Christianity: Being Some Old Translations from the Japanese, with British Consular Reports of the Persecutions of 1868-1872. (Studies in Japanese History & Civilization). 1979. Repr. of 1930 ed. 17.50 (ISBN 0-89093-257-3). U Pubns Amer.

Phillips, James M. From the Rising of the Sun: Christians & Society in Contemporary Japan. LC 80-24609. (Illus.). 352p. (Orig.). 1981. pap. 14.95 (ISBN 0-88344-145-4). Orbis Bks.

CHRISTIANS IN RUSSIA

Sawatsky, Walter. Soviet Evangelicals Since World War II. LC 81-94121. (Illus.). 560p. 1981. 19.95 (ISBN 0-8361-1238-5); pap. 14.95 (ISBN 0-8361-1239-3). Herald Pr.

CHRISTIANS IN THE NEAR EAST

Lotfi, Nasser. Iranian Christian. 160p. 1980. 8.95 (ISBN 0-8499-0275-4). Word Bks.

CHRISTMAS

see also Jesus Christ–Nativity

Bell, Irving. Christmas in Old New England. 54p. (gr. 3-8). 1981. 8.95 (ISBN 0-917780-02-7). April Hill.

Beyer, Douglas. Basic Beliefs of Christmas. 64p. 1981. pap. 3.50 (ISBN 0-8170-0896-9). Judson.

Cooke, Gillian. A Celebration of Christmas. 1980. 16.95 (ISBN 0-686-68353-6). Putnam.

Rosenthal, Barbara & Rosenthal, Nadia. Christmas: New Ideas for an Old-Fashioned Celebration. 1980. 12.95 (ISBN 0-517-53695-1). Potter.

Sparks, Judith, ed. Christman Programs for the Church, No. 14. 64p. (Orig.). 1981. pap. 2.75 (ISBN 0-87239-437-9, 8614). Standard Pub.

CHRISTMAS–DRAMA

see Christmas Plays

CHRISTMAS–JUVENILE LITERATURE

Eastman, Moira & Poussard, Wendy. The Christmas Book. LC 80-68368. (Illus.). 40p. 1980. 5.95 (ISBN 0-87793-214-X). Ave Maria.

Stifle, J. M. ABC Book About Christmas. 1981. pap. 2.95 (ISBN 0-570-04053-1, 56-1714). Concordia.

World Book-Childcraft International, Inc. Christmas in France. LC 80-50994. (Around the World Christmas Program Ser.). (Illus.). 80p. (ps-9). 1980. write for info. (ISBN 0-7166-3106-7). World Bk-Childcraft.

Ziegler, Sandra. Our Christmas Handbook. (Illus.). 112p. pap. 5.95 (ISBN 0-89565-180-7, 3041). Standard Pub.

CHRISTMAS BOOKS

see Christmas; Christmas Plays; Christmas Stories

CHRISTMAS CAROLS

see Carols

CHRISTMAS COOKERY

Fox, Betsy. Visions of Sugar Plums. 1980. 6.95 (ISBN 0-935746-00-5). Green Hill.

Poole, Shona C. The Christmas Cookbook. LC 79-63631. 259p. 1981. pap. 5.95 (ISBN 0-689-70606-5, 267). Atheneum.

Voth, Norma J. Festive Cakes of Christmas. 80p. 1981. pap. 2.95 (ISBN 0-8361-1956-8). Herald Pr.

CHRISTMAS PLAYS

see also Crib in Christian Art and Tradition

Berry, Linda. Christmas Plays for Older Children. (gr. 5-7). 1981. saddle wire 1.65 (ISBN 0-8054-9733-1). Broadman.

Payne, Darwin R. A Christmas Carol. LC 80-18827. 128p. 1981. pap. price not set (ISBN 0-8093-0999-8). S Ill U Pr.

CHRISTMAS STORIES

Jones, Swiftwater. Jake Claus, Santa's Brother. LC 79-56509. 1980. 5.95 (ISBN 0-533-04534-7). Vantage.

The Saturday Evening Post Christmas Book. 3rd ed. LC 76-24034. (Illus.). 1978. 11.95 (ISBN 0-89387-001-3). Sat Eve Post.

The Saturday Evening Post Christmas Stories. LC 80-67058. (Illus.). 1980. 11.95 (ISBN 0-89387-046-3). Sat Eve Post.

Sheppard, Donna C. Williamsburg Christmas. LC 80-7487. (Illus.). 84p. (Orig.). 1980. 9.95 (ISBN 0-87935-053-9); pap. 4.95 (ISBN 0-87935-054-7). Williamsburg.

CHRISTOLOGY

see Jesus Christ

CHROMATICS

see Color

CHROMATOGRAPHIC ANALYSIS

see also Gas Chromatography; Liquid Chromatography; Thin Layer Chromatography

Provder, Theodore, ed. Size Exclusion Chromatography (GPC) LC 80-22015. (ACS Symposium Ser.: No. 138). 1980. 30.75 (ISBN 0-8412-0586-8). Am Chemical.

CHROMATOGRAPHY, THIN LAYER

see Thin Layer Chromatography

CHROMIUM

Saner, Gunay, ed. Chromium in Nutrition & Disease. LC 80-81854. (Current Topics in Nutrition & Disease: Vol. 2). 146p. 1980. 16.00 (ISBN 0-8451-1601-0). A R Liss.

CHROMOSOME NUMBERS

Robinson, Arthur, et al, eds. Sex Chromosome Aneuploidy: Prospective Studies on Children. LC 78-13921. (Alan R. Liss Ser.: Vol. 15, No. 1). 1979. 32.00 (ISBN 0-8451-1024-1). March of Dimes.

CHROMOSOMES

see also Chromosome Numbers; Genetics; Human Chromosomes; Sex Chromosomes

M. D. Anderson Symposia on Fundamental Cancer Research, 33rd. Genes, Chromosomes, & Neoplasia. Arrighi, Frances E., et al, eds. 550p. 1981. 49.50 (ISBN 0-89004-532-1). Raven.

Therman, E. Human Chromosomes. (Illus.). 235p. 1981. 19.80 (ISBN 0-387-90509-X). Springer-Verlag.

CHRONOGRAMS

see Anagrams

CHRONOPHOTOGRAPHY

see Cinematography

CHRYSANTHEMUMS

Nutritional Disorders in Chrysanthemums. 42p. 1980. pap. 22.75 (ISBN 90-220-0718-9, Pudoc). Unipub.

CHRYSLER CORPORATION

Stuart, Reginald. Bailout: America's Billion Dollar Gamble on the "New" Chrysler Corporation. LC 80-70279. (Illus.). 210p. (Orig.). 1981. pap. write for info. (ISBN 0-89708-050-5). And Bks.

CHURCH

see also Christian Union; Christianity; Church Work; Ecumenical Movement; Jesus Christ–Mystical Body; Mission of the Church

Milash, Nikodim. Das Kirchenrecht der Morgenlandischen Kirche. 2nd ed. LC 80-2360. 1981. Repr. of 1905 ed. 83.00 (ISBN 0-404-18910-5). AMS Pr.

Surrey, Peter J. The Small Town Church. (Creative Leadership Ser.). 128p. (Orig.). 1981. pap. 4.95 (ISBN 0-687-38720-5). Abingdon.

Wilson, Robert L. Shaping the Congregation. LC 80-22228. (Into Our Third Century Ser.). 144p. (Orig.). 1981. pap. 3.95 (ISBN 0-687-38334-X). Abingdon.

CHURCH–ADDRESSES, ESSAYS, LECTURES

McGavran, Donald, frwd. by. Christian Churches at the Crossroads. 160p. (Orig.). 1980. pap. write for info. (ISBN 0-87808-178-X). William Carey Lib.

CHURCH–AUTHORITY

see also Liberty of Speech in the Church

Cleveland, E. E. The Gates Shall Not. (Horizon Ser.). 96p. 1980. pap. write for info. (ISBN 0-8127-0325-1). Southern Pub.

CHURCH–FOUNDATION

see also Christianity–Origin; Popes–Primacy

Hurlbut, Lyman, tr. Historia Da Igraja. (Portuguese Bks.). 1979. write for info. (ISBN 0-8297-0667-4). Life Pubs Intl.

Turner, J. J. Church According to the Bible. pap. 1.95 (ISBN 0-89315-016-9). Lambert Bk.

CHURCH–HISTORY OF DOCTRINES

Cleveland, E. E. The Gates Shall Not. (Horizon Ser.). 96p. 1980. pap. write for info. (ISBN 0-8127-0325-1). Southern Pub.

Hodges, Melvin, tr. Edificare My Iglesia. (Spanish Bks.). 1979. 1.50 (ISBN 0-8297-0544-9); wkbk. 0.80 (ISBN 0-8297-0545-7). Life Pubs Intl.

Pearlman, Myer, tr. Teologia Biblica y Sistematica. (Spanish Bks.). 1978. 4.25 (ISBN 0-8297-0603-8); pap. 3.25 (ISBN 0-8297-0602-X). Life Pubs Intl.

CHURCH–MISSION

see Mission of the Church

CHURCH–REFORM

see Church Renewal

CHURCH ADMINISTRATION

see Church Management

CHURCH AND EDUCATION

see also Church Schools; Religion in the Public Schools; Teaching, Freedom Of; Theology–Study and Teaching

also names of particular religious denominations with the subdivision Education, e.g. Catholic Church–Education

McMillan, Richard C., ed. Education, Religion, & the Supreme Court. LC 78-74196. (Special Studies Ser.: No. 6). 1979. 4.95 (ISBN 0-932180-05-1). Assn Baptist Profs.

Makrakis, Apostolos. The Two Contrariant Schools, Concerning the Establishment of a Christian University. Orthodox Christian Educational Society, ed. Cummings, Denver, tr. from Hellenic. 87p. (Orig.). 1949. pap. 2.00x (ISBN 0-938366-27-0). Orthodox Chr.

Wilkes, Peter, ed. Christianity Challenges the University. 108p. 1981. pap. 3.95 (ISBN 0-87784-474-7). Inter Varsity.

CHURCH AND HOMOSEXUALITY

see Homosexuality and Christianity

CHURCH AND SLAVERY

see Slavery and the Church

CHURCH AND SOCIAL PROBLEMS

see also Slavery and the Church; Sociology, Christian

De Santa Ana, Julio. Towards a Church of the Poor. LC 80-25667. (Orig.). 1981. pap. 8.95 (ISBN 0-88344-502-6). Orbis Bks.

Grocott, Allan M. Convicts, Clergymen & Churches. 356p. 1980. 27.50x (ISBN 0-424-00072-5, Pub. by Sydney U Pr Australia). Intl Schol Bk Serv.

Scrogin, Michael. When God Intrudes. 112p. 1981. pap. 4.95 (ISBN 0-8170-0903-5). Judson.

Searle, Mark, ed. Liturgy & Social Justice. 1980. pap. write for info (ISBN 0-8146-1209-1). Liturgical Pr.

CHURCH AND SOCIETY

see Church and the World

CHURCH AND STATE

see also Asylum, Right Of; Christianity and Politics; Church and Education; Church Polity; Ecclesiastical Law; Government, Resistance To; Religion and State; Religion in the Public Schools; Taxation, Exemption From

McDonagh, Edna. Church & Politics: From Theology to a Case History of Zimbabwe. LC 80-53070. 200p. 1980. text ed. 12.95 (ISBN 0-268-00734-9); pap. text ed. 5.95 (ISBN 0-268-00736-5). U of Notre Dame Pr.

Manning, Leonard F. The Law of Church-State Relations in a Nutshell. LC 80-22991. (Nutshell Ser.). 314p. 1980. pap. text ed. 6.95 (ISBN 0-8299-2113-3). West Pub.

Mechling, Jay, ed. Church State & Public Policy. 1979. 10.25 (ISBN 0-8447-2159-X); pap. 5.25 (ISBN 0-8447-2160-3). Am Enterprise.

Nuttall, Clayton L. The Conflict: The Separation of the Church & State. LC 80-21267. 144p. 1980. pap. 4.95 (ISBN 0-87227-076-9, RBP5088). Reg Baptist.

Weber, Paul J. & Gilbert, Dennis A. Private Churches & Public Money: Church-Government Fiscal Relations. LC 80-1793. (Contributions to the Study of Religion: No. 1). (Illus.). 256p. 1981. lib. bdg. 27.95 (ISBN 0-313-22484-6, WCM/). Greenwood.

CHURCH AND STATE–CHURCH OF ENGLAND

see Church and State in Great Britain

CHURCH AND STATE–HISTORY

Greenslade, Stanley L. Church & State from Constantine to Theodosius. LC 79-8712. 93p. 1981. Repr. of 1954 ed. lib. bdg. 19.50x (ISBN 0-313-20793-3, GRCS). Greenwood.

CHURCH AND STATE IN GREAT BRITAIN

Here are entered works dealing not only with church and state in England, Scotland and Ireland, or in any two of them, but also works dealing with England alone.

Boehmer, Heinrich. Kirche und Staat in England und in Normandie Im XI. und XII. Jahrhundert: Eine Historische Studie. LC 80-2234. 1981. Repr. of 1899 ed. 57.50 (ISBN 0-404-18755-2). AMS Pr.

Tillman, Helene. Die Papstlichen Legaten in England Bis Zur Beendigung der Legation Gualas, 1218. LC 80-2208. 1981. Repr. of 1926 ed. 27.50 (ISBN 0-404-18795-1). AMS Pr.

CHURCH AND STATE IN ITALY

Cipolla, Carlo M. Faith, Reason, & the Plague in Seventeenth-Century Tuscany. 128p. 1981. pap. 3.95 (ISBN 0-393-00045-1). Norton.

CHURCH AND STATE IN THE UNITED STATES

Spykman, Gordon, et al. Society, State, & Schools: A Case for Structural & Confessional Pluralism. 224p. (Orig.). 1981. pap. 11.95 (ISBN 0-8028-1880-3). Eerdmans.

CHURCH AND THE WORLD

Here are entered works on the position and responsibilities of the Christian church in secular society.

see also Christianity and Economics; Christianity and Politics; Church and Social Problems; Kingdom of God; Sociology, Christian

Baumgartel, Elise J. The Cultures of Prehistoric Egypt. LC 80-24186. (Illus.). 268p. 1981. Repr. of 1955 ed. lib. bdg. 60.00x (ISBN 0-313-22524-9, BACU). Greenwood.

Marty, Martin E. The Public Church. 192p. 1981. 10.95 (ISBN 0-8245-0019-9). Crossroad NY.

CHURCH AND WAR

see War and Religion

CHURCH ANTIQUITIES

see Christian Antiquities

CHURCH ARCHITECTURE

see also Architecture, Gothic; Cathedrals; Chapels

Fitchen, John. The Construction of Gothic Cathedrals: A Study of Medieval Vault Erection. (Illus.). xxii, 344p. 1981. pap. 9.95 (ISBN 0-226-25203-5). U of Chicago Pr.

Hodges, Melvin, tr. Um Guia Para Fundacao De Igrejas. (Portuguese Bks.). 1979. 1.10 (ISBN 0-686-28807-6). Vida Pub.

Vosko, Richard S. Through the Eye of a Rose Window: A Perspective on the Environment for Worship. 1981. pap. text ed. 8.95 (ISBN 0-89390-028-1). Resource Pubns.

CHURCH ARCHITECTURE–DESIGNS AND PLANS

Hodges, Melvin, tr. Como Fundar Iglesias. (Spanish Bks.). (Span.). 1978. 1.50 (ISBN 0-8297-0560-0). Life Pubs Intl.

CHURCH ARCHITECTURE–GREAT BRITAIN

Child, Mark. English Church Architecture. (Illus.). 120p. 1981. 19.95 (ISBN 0-7134-2776-0, Pub. by Batsford England). David & Charles.

CHURCH ATTENDANCE

see also Public Worship

Lawson, LeRoy. The Family of God: The Meaning of Church Membership. LC 80-53497. 64p. (Orig.). 1981. pap. 1.50 (ISBN 0-87239-432-8, 39970). Standard Pub.

CHURCH BIOGRAPHY

see Christian Biography

CHURCH BUILDINGS

see Church Architecture

CHURCH CALENDAR

see also Fasts and Feasts

Makris, Kallistos. The God-Inspired Orthodox Julian Calendar VS. the False Gregorian Papal Calendar. Vlesmas, Jerry, tr. from Hellenic. 118p. (Orig.). 1971. pap. 2.00x (ISBN 0-938366-36-X). Orthodox Chr.

CHURCH COURTS

see Ecclesiastical Courts

CHURCH DISCIPLINE

see also Celibacy; Ecclesiastical Courts; Inquisition; Marriage, Mixed; Penance

also subdivision Discipline under names of religions, religious denominations, etc., e.g. Catholic Church–Discipline

Dobson, James, tr. Atrevete a Disciplinar. (Spanish Bks.). (Span.). 1978. 1.90 (ISBN 0-8297-0499-X). Life Pubs Intl.

--Ouse Disciplinar. (Portuguese Bks.). 1979. 1.45 (ISBN 0-8297-0768-9). Life Pubs Intl.

CHURCH FATHERS

see Fathers of the Church

CHURCH FESTIVALS

see Fasts and Feasts

CHURCH FINANCE

see also Stewardship, Christian; Taxation, Exemption From; Tithes

also subdivision Finance under Church denominations and under special topics, e.g. Church of England–Finance

Horton, Claude A. Money Counts: A Handbook on Local Church Finance. 88p. 1980. pap. 4.95 (ISBN 0-89367-051-0). Light & Life.

McLeod, Thomas E. The Work of the Church Treasurer. 80p. 1981. pap. 6.95 (ISBN 0-8170-0908-6). Judson.

CHURCH-GOING

see Church Attendance

CHURCH GOVERNMENT

see Church Polity

CHURCH HISTORY

This heading is subdivided first according to subject matter, e.g. Church History–Philosophy, and second, chronologically, according to the period of history covered.

see also Church and State; Creeds; Fathers of the Church; Inquisition; Miracles; Missions; Monasticism and Religious Orders; Papacy; Persecution; Protestantism; Reformation; Religious Thought; Revivals; Sects

also subdivision Church History under names of countries; names of denominations, sects, churches, councils, etc.; headings beginning with the word Christian

Baker, R. A. Compendio De la Historia Cristiana. Almanza, Francisco G., tr. Orig. Title: A Summary of Christian History. 372p. (Span.). Date not set. pap. price not set (ISBN 0-311-15032-2). Casa Bautista.

Gonzalez, Justo L. La Era de las Tinieblas. (Y Hasta Lo Ultimo De la Tierra: una Historia Ilustrada Del Christianismo Ser.: Tomo III). (Illus.). 199p. (Orig., Span.). 1978. pap. 4.50 (ISBN 0-89922-128-9). Edit Caribe.

--La Era de los Altos Ideales. (Y Hasta Lo Ultimo De la Tierra: una Historia Ilustrada Del Christianismo Ser.: Tomo IV). (Illus.). 197p. (Orig., Span.). 1979. pap. 4.50 (ISBN 0-89922-135-1). Edit Caribe.

--La Era de los Conquistadores. (Y Hasta Lo Ultimo de la Tierra: una Historia Ilustrada del Cristianismo: Tomo VII). (Illus.). 218p. (Span.). 1981. pap. 4.50 (ISBN 0-89922-162-9). Edit Caribe.

--La Era de los Gigantes. (Y Hasta Lo Ultimo De la Tierra: una Historia Ilustrada Del Christianismo Ser.: Tomo II). (Illus.). 184p. (Orig., Span.). 1978. pap. 4.50 (ISBN 0-89922-117-3). Edit Caribe.

--La Era de los Martires. (Y Hasta Lo Ultimo De la Tierra: una Historia Ilustrada Del Christianismo Ser.: Tomo I). (Illus.). 189p. (Orig., Span.). 1978. pap. 4.50 (ISBN 0-89922-109-2). Edit Caribe.

--La Era de los Reformadores. (Y Hasta Lo Ultimo De la Tierra: una Historia Ilustrada Del Christianismo Ser.: Tomo VI). (Illus.). 219p. (Orig., Span.). 1980. pap. 4.50 (ISBN 0-89922-154-8). Edit Caribe.

--La Era de los Suenos Frustrados. (Y Hasta Lo Ultimo De la Tierra: una Historia Ilustrada Del Christianismo Ser.: Tomo V). (Illus.). 182p. (Orig., Span.). 1979. pap. 4.50 (ISBN 0-89922-139-4). Edit Caribe.

--Luces Bajo el Almud. LC 77-11753. 76p. (Orig., Span.). 1977. pap. 1.95 (ISBN 0-89922-102-5). Edit Caribe.

Hood, John C. Icelandic Church Saga. LC 79-8720. (Illus.). xii, 241p. 1981. Repr. of 1946 ed. lib. bdg. 27.50x (ISBN 0-313-22194-4, HOIC). Greenwood.

Hurlbut, Lyman & Flower, J. R. History of the Christian Church. 1979. 3.35 (ISBN 0-8297-0575-9); pap. 2.35 (ISBN 0-8297-0574-0). Life Pubs Intl.

Izbicki, Thomas M. Protector of the Faith: Cardinal Johannes De Turrecremata & the Defense of the Institutional Church. 1981. price not set (ISBN 0-8132-0558-1). Cath U Pr.

Ketcherside, Carl. Which Church. pap. 0.50. Reiner.

McGiffert, A. C. A History of Christianity in the Apostolic Age. (International Theologica Library). 692p. Repr. of 1897 ed. text ed. 13.95x (ISBN 0-567-07207-X). Attic Pr.

Moore, G. F. History of Religions: Judaism, Christianity, Mohammedanism, Vol. II. (International Theological Library). 568p. 1920. text ed. 13.95x (ISBN 0-567-07203-7). Attic Pr.

Nuttall, G. Christian Pacifism in History. pap. 1.25 (ISBN 0-8164-9235-2). Continuum.

Pruitt, Fred. Past, Present & Future of the Church. 72p. 0.60. Faith Pub Hse.

Riggle, H. M. The Christian Church: Its Rise & Progress. 488p. 5.00. Faith Pub Hse.

Roberts, Frank. To All Generations, a Study of Church History. 276p. (Orig.). 1981. pap. text ed. price not set (ISBN 0-933140-17-7); price not set tchr's manual (ISBN 0-933140-18-5). Bd of Pubns CRC.

Tewinkel, Joseph M. Built Upon the Cornerstone. LC 80-65148. 178p. (Orig.). 1981. pap. 3.95 (ISBN 0-87509-280-2); pap. 1.50 leaders guide (ISBN 0-686-69527-5). Chr Pubns.

Treadgold, Donald W. A History of Christianity. LC 78-78118. 277p. (Orig.). 1979. 22.50 (ISBN 0-913124-35-4); pap. 7.95 (ISBN 0-913124-35-4). Nordland Pub.

Tvedtnes, John. The Church of the Old Testament. rev. ed. LC 80-18595. 111p. 1980. 5.95 (ISBN 0-87747-827-9). Deseret Bk.

Wilken, Robert L. The Myth of Christian Beginnings. LC 80-11884. 218p. 1980. pap. text ed. 4.95 (ISBN 0-268-01348-9). U of Notre Dame Pr.

CHURCH HISTORY–PRIMITIVE AND EARLY CHURCH, ca. 30-600

see also Apostles; Fathers of the Church; Jewish Christians

Greenslade, Stanley L. Church & State from Constantine to Theodosius. LC 79-8712. 93p. 1981. Repr. of 1954 ed. lib. bdg. 19.50x (ISBN 0-313-20793-3, GRCS). Greenwood.

Guthrie, Donald. The Apostles. 432p. 1981. pap. 10.95 (ISBN 0-310-25421-3). Zondervan.

Lawson, LeRoy. The New Testament Church Then & Now. (Orig.). 1981. pap. 3.95 (ISBN 0-87239-443-3, 88585). Standard Pub.

Maier, Paul. The Flames of Rome. LC 80-2561. (Illus.). 384p. 1981. 12.95 (ISBN 0-385-17091-2, Galilee). Doubleday.

March, W. Eugene, ed. Texts & Testaments: Critical Essays on the Bible & Early Church Fathers. 321p. 1980. 15.00 (ISBN 0-911536-80-9). Trinity U Pr.

Matsagouras, E. The Early Church Fathers As Educators. 1977. pap. 3.95 (ISBN 0-937032-10-7). Light & Life Pub Co MN.

Norbie, D. R. Early Church. 1981. pap. 10.00 (ISBN 0-937396-13-3). Walterick Pubs.

Schell, William G. Biblical Trace of the Church. 173p. pap. 1.50. Faith Pub Hse.

CHURCH HISTORY–MIDDLE AGES, 600-1500

see also Crusades; Inquisition; Mysticism–Middle Ages, 600-1500; Papacy

Alexander, Paul J. Religious & Political History & Thought in the Byzantine Empire. 360p. 1980. 60.00x (ISBN 0-86078-016-3, Pub. by Variorum England). State Mutual Bk.

Cheney, Mary G. Roger, Bishop of Worcestor Eleven Sixty Four to Eleven Seventy Nine: An English Bishop of the Age of Becket. (Oxford Historical Monographs). (Illus.). 320p. 1980. 49.50 (ISBN 0-19-821879-6). Oxford U Pr.

Chibnall, Marjorie, ed. The Ecclesiastical History of Orderic Vitalis, Vol. 1. (Oxford Medieval Texts Ser.). (Illus.). 416p. 1980. 79.00 (ISBN 0-19-822243-2). Oxford U Pr.

Evans, Rosemary G. Anselm & a New Generation. 230p. 1980. 34.50x (ISBN 0-19-826651-0). Oxford U Pr.

Hamilton, Bernard. The Latin Church in the Crusader States: The Secular Church. 402p. 1980. 40.00x (ISBN 0-86078-072-4, Pub. by Variorum England). State Mutual Bk.

Ullman, Walter. The Church & the Law in the Earlier Middle Ages. 406p. 1980. 60.00x (ISBN 0-902089-79-X, Pub. by Variorum England). State Mutual Bk.

Ullmann, Walter. The Papacy & Political Ideas in the Middle Ages. 408p. 1980. 60.00x (ISBN 0-902089-87-0, Pub. by Variorum England). State Mutual Bk.

Williams, John. The Holy Table, Name & Thing, More Patiently, Properly, & Literally Used Under the New Treatment, Than That of an Altar. LC 79-84146. (English Experience Ser.: No.962). 244p. 1979. Repr. of 1637 ed. lib. bdg. 22.00 (ISBN 90-221-0962-3). Walter J Johnson.

CHURCH HISTORY–REFORMATION, 1517-1648

see Reformation

CHURCH HISTORY–MODERN PERIOD, 1500-

see also Missions–History; Protestantism–History; Reformation; Sects

Thompson, Bard. Renaissance & Reformation. (Texts & Studies in Religion, Vol. 11). (Orig.). 1981. soft cover 24.95x (ISBN 0-88946-915-6). E Mellen.

CHURCH LAW

see Ecclesiastical Law

CHURCH LEADERSHIP

see Christian Leadership

CHURCH LIBRARIES

see Libraries, Church

CHURCH MANAGEMENT

see also Church Finance

Colson, Howard P. & Rigdon, Raymond M. Understanding Your Church's Curriculum. rev. ed. LC 80-67351. 1981. pap. 4.95. Broadman.

Derrick, Christopher. Church Authority & Intellectual Freedom. LC 81-80129. 95p. (Orig.). 1981. pap. price not set (ISBN 0-89870-011-6). Ignatius Pr.

Harms, William C. Who Are We & Where Are We Going: A Parish Planning Guide. 96p. (Orig.). 1981. pap. 9.00 (ISBN 0-8215-9806-6). Sadlier.

Hodges, Melvin, tr. Crecimiento De la Iglesia. (Spanish Bks.). (Span.). 1979. 1.50 (ISBN 0-8297-0905-3). Life Pubs Intl.

Horton, Claude A. Money Counts: A Handbook on Local Church Finance. 88p. 1980. pap. 4.95 (ISBN 0-89367-051-0). Light & Life.

McLeod, Thomas E. The Work of the Church Treasurer. 80p. 1981. pap. 6.95 (ISBN 0-8170-0908-6). Judson.

Maves, Paul B. Older Volunteers in Church & Community. 96p. 1981. pap. 6.95 (ISBN 0-8170-0889-6). Judson.

Rusbuldt, Richard E., et al. Medidas Principales En la Planificacion De la Iglesia Local: Key Steps in Local Church Planning. Rodriguez, Oscar E., tr. from Eng. 134p. (Span.). 1981. pap. 5.95 (ISBN 0-8170-0933-7). Judson.

CHURCH MEMBERSHIP

see also Baptism; Church Discipline; Lord's Supper

Lewis, Douglass. Resolving Church Conflicts: A Case Study Approach for Local Congregations. LC 80-8347. 192p. (Orig.). 1981. pap. 6.95 (ISBN 0-06-065244-6, HarpR). Har-Row.

CHURCH MUSIC

see also Carols; Choral Music; Hymns; Liturgies; Organ Music

Bennett, Marian, ed. Songs for Preschool Children. LC 80-25091. 96p. 1981. pap. 5.95 (ISBN 0-87239-429-8, 5754). Standard Pub.

Boyd, Jack. Leading the Lord's Singing. 1981. pap. write for info. (ISBN 0-89137-603-8). Quality Pubns.

Fellowes, Edmund H. English Cathedral Music. 5th, rev. ed. Westrup, J. A., ed. LC 80-24400. (Illus.). xi, 283p. 1981. Repr. of 1973 ed. lib. bdg. 27.50x (ISBN 0-313-22643-1, FEEC). Greenwood.

Grahams, Betty L., tr. Ministrando Con Musica. (Portugese Bks.). (Port.). 1979. write for info. (ISBN 0-8297-0732-8). Life Pubs Intl.

Grams, Betty J., tr. Ministrando Con Musica. (Spanish Bks.). 1978. 2.50 (ISBN 0-8297-0584-8). Life Pubs Intl.

Hannum, Harold E. Let the People Sing. Davis, Tom, ed. 112p. 1981. pap. write for info. (ISBN 0-8280-0029-8). Review & Herald.

Lawrence, Joy & Ferguson, John. A Musician's Guide to Church Music. 280p. 1981. 16.95 (ISBN 0-8298-0424-2). Pilgrim NY.

CHURCH MUSIC–CHORUSES AND CHOIR BOOKS

see Service Books (Music)

CHURCH MUSIC–SERVICE BOOKS

see Service Books (Music)

CHURCH OF CHRIST OF LATTER-DAY SAINTS

see Church of Jesus Christ of Latter-Day Saints; Mormons and Mormonism

CHURCH OF ENGLAND

see also Church and State in Great Britain

Edwards, David L. What Anglican (Episcopalians) Believe. 1975. 1.00 (ISBN 0-686-28799-1). Forward Movement.

Hodges, George. Short History of the Episcopal Church. 1967. 1.10 (ISBN 0-686-28793-2). Forward Movement.

CHURCH OF ENGLAND–DOCTRINAL AND CONTROVERSIAL WORKS

Calderwood, David. A Solution of Doctor Resolutus, His Resolutions for Kneeling. LC 79-84093. (English Experience Ser.: No. 913). 60p. 1979. Repr. of 1619 ed. lib. bdg. 8.00 (ISBN 90-221-0913-5). Walter J Johnson.

Staniloae, Dumitru. Theology & the Church. Barry, Robert, tr. from Romanian. LC 80-19313. 240p. 1980. pap. 6.95 (ISBN 0-913836-69-9). St Vladimirs.

CHURCH OF ENGLAND–HISTORY

Barrow, Andrew. The Flesh Is Weak: An Intimate History of the Church of England. (Illus.). 254p. 1981. 29.95 (ISBN 0-241-10234-0, Pub. by Hamish Hamilton England). David & Charles.

O'Day, Rosemary & Heal, Felicity. Princes & Paupers in the English Church. 1981. 27.50x (ISBN 0-389-20200-2). B&N.

Watson, Edward W. The Church of England. LC 80-22643. (Home University Library of Modern Knowledge: No. 90). 192p. 1981. Repr. of 1961 ed. lib. bdg. 25.00x (ISBN 0-313-22683-0, WAEN). Greenwood.

CHURCH OF JESUS CHRIST OF LATTER-DAY SAINTS

Burton, Malcom K. Disorders in the Kingdom. 1981. 11.95 (ISBN 0-533-04751-X). Vantage.

CHURCH POLITY

see also Cardinals; Church and State; Church Discipline; Church Finance; Church Membership; Clergy; Ecclesiastical Law

also subdivision Government under church denominations, e.g. Church of England–Government

Lewis, Douglass. Resolving Church Conflicts: A Case Study Approach for Local Congregations. LC 80-8347. 192p. (Orig.). 1981. pap. 6.95 (ISBN 0-06-065244-6, HarpR). Har-Row.

CHURCH REFORM

see Church Renewal

CHURCH RENEWAL

see also Mission of the Church

Avis, Paul D. The Church in the Theology of the Reformers. Toon, Peter & Martin, Ralph, eds. LC 80-16186. (New Foundations Theological Library). 256p. 1981. 18.50 (ISBN 0-8042-3708-5); pap. 11.95 (ISBN 0-8042-3728-X). John Knox.

Hesselgrave, David & Hesselgrave, Ronald. What in the World Has Gotten into the Church? 128p. 1981. pap. 3.95 (ISBN 0-8024-9386-6). Moody.

Miller, Paul M. Leading the Family of God. 216p. 1981. pap. 7.95 (ISBN 0-8361-1950-9). Herald Pr.

Richards, Lawrence O. A New Face for the Church. 288p. (Orig.). 1981. pap. 6.95 (ISBN 0-310-31901-3). Zondervan.

CHURCH SCHOOLS

Blazier, Kenneth D. Una Escuela Biblica 002a: A Growing Church School. De Olivieri, Evelyn R., tr. from Eng. 64p. (Span.). 1981. pap. 3.25 (ISBN 0-8170-0928-0). Judson.

CHURCH UNITY

see Christian Union

CHURCH USHERS

Enlow, David R. Church Usher: Servant of God. LC 80-66769. 64p. (Orig.). 1980. pap. 1.95 (ISBN 0-87509-284-5). Chr Pubns.

CHURCH WORK

see also Christian Leadership; Church and Social Problems; Church Management; Church Ushers; Christian Leadership; City Missions; Evangelistic Work; Pastoral Counseling; Pastoral Psychology; Revivals; Sunday-Schools; Women in Church Work

Billups, Ann. Perspectives: Discussion Starters on Attitudes & Values for Church Groups. 224p. 1981. pap. 11.95 (ISBN 0-8170-0905-1). Judson.

Boys, Mary C., ed. Ministry & Education in Conversation. LC 80-53204. 160p. (Orig.). 1981. pap. 6.95 (ISBN 0-88489-126-7). St Mary's.

Campbell, Thomas C. & Reierson, Gary B. The Gift of Adminstration. LC 80-24594. 1981. soft cover 6.95 (ISBN 0-664-24357-6). Westminster.

Hater, Robert J. The Ministry Explosion. 96p. (Orig.). 1979. pap. 3.25 (ISBN 0-697-01709-5). Wm C Brown.

Rusbuldt, Richard E. Basic Leader Skills: Handbook for Church Leaders. 64p. 1981. pap. 4.95 (ISBN 0-8170-0920-5). Judson.

Schillebeeckx, Edward. Ministry. 160p. (Dutch.). 1981. 12.95 (ISBN 0-8245-0030-X). Crossroad NY.

Shelp, Earl E. & Sunderlan, Ronald, eds. A Biblical Basis for Ministry. Achtmeier, Paul J., et al. (Orig.). 1981. pap. price not set (ISBN 0-664-24371-1). Westminster.

Spurgeon, C. H. All Round Ministry. 1978. pap. 5.45 (ISBN 0-85151-277-1). Banner of Truth.

Trevino, Alejandro. El Predicador: Platicas a Mis Estudiantes. 155p. 1980. pap. 2.30 (ISBN 0-311-42016-8). Casa Bautista.

CHURCH WORK WITH ADULTS

see Church Work

CHURCH WORK WITH CHILDREN

I Believe in God. 52p. 1975. 3.00. Natl Cath Educ.

CHURCH WORK WITH CRIMINALS

Pederson, Duane. How to Establish a Jail & Prison Ministry. 132p. 1981. pap. 3.95 (ISBN 0-8407-5675-5). Nelson.

CHURCH WORK WITH THE AGED

Kerr, Horace L. How to Minister to Senior Adults in Your Church. 1980. 4.95 (ISBN 0-8054-3222-1). Broadman.

CHURCHES–LIBRARIES

see Libraries, Church

CHURCHES–MANAGEMENT

see Church Management

CHURCHES–CANADA

Jacquet, Constant H., Jr., ed. Yearbook of American & Canadian Churches, 1981. 304p. (Orig.). 1981. pap. 14.95 (ISBN 0-687-46636-9). Abingdon.

CHURCHES–GERMANY

Matheson, Peter. The Third Reich & the Christian Churches. LC 80-26767. 112p. (Orig.). 1981. pap. 5.95 (ISBN 0-8028-1873-0). Eerdmans.

CHURCHES–UNITED STATES

Jacquet, Constant H., Jr., ed. Yearbook of American & Canadian Churches, 1981. 304p. (Orig.). 1981. pap. 14.95 (ISBN 0-687-46636-9). Abingdon.

Schumacher, Claire W. This Is Our St. Rose Church in Proctor Minnesota. (Illus.). 100p. 1976. pap. 3.00 (ISBN 0-917378-02-4). Schumacher Pubns.

CHURCHILL, CHARLES, 1731-1764

Dobree, Bonamy. Three Eighteenth Century Figures: Sarah Churchill, John Wesley, Giacomo Casanova. LC 80-19398. xi, 248p. 1981. Repr. of 1962 ed. lib. bdg. 25.00x (ISBN 0-313-22682-2, DOTF). Greenwood.

Vines, Sherard. Georgian Satirists: Edward Young, Christopher Smart, Charles Churchill. 217p. 1980. Repr. of 1934 ed. lib. bdg. 25.00 (ISBN 0-8495-5528-0). Arden Lib.

CHURCHILL, WINSTON LEONARD SPENCER, SIR, 1874-1965

Colville, John. Winston Churchill & His Inner Circle. 1981. 13.95 (ISBN 0-671-42583-8, Wyndham Bks). S&S.

Lewin, Ronald. Churchill As Warlord. LC 72-96544. (Illus.). 308p. 1981. pap. 6.95 (ISBN 0-8128-6099-3). Stein & Day.

Pitt, Barrie. Churchill & His Generals. 224p. 1981. pap. 2.50 (ISBN 0-553-14610-6). Bantam.

CHURCHYARDS

see Cemeteries

CIA

see United States–Central Intelligence Agency

CIGARETTE HABIT

see Smoking

CINEMA

see Moving-Pictures

CINEMATOGRAPHY

see also Moving-Picture Cameras

Manwell, Roger. Art & Animation: The Story of the Halas & Batchelor Animation Studio. (Illus.). 128p. 1980. 26.50 (ISBN 0-8038-0494-6, Visual Communications). Hastings.

CINESIOLOGY

see Kinesiology

CIO

see American Federation of Labor and Congress of Industrial Organizations

CIPHERS

see also Abbreviations; Code Names; Cryptography; Writing

Gleason, Norma. Cryptograms & Spygrams. 128p. (Orig.). 1981. pap. price not set. Dover.

CIRCUITS, ELECTRIC

see Electric Circuits

CIRCUITS, INTEGRATED

see Integrated Circuits

CIRCULATION OF THE BLOOD

see Blood–Circulation

CIRCULATORY SYSTEM

see Cardiovascular System

CIRCUS–JUVENILE LITERATURE

White, Paul. Fairs & Circuses. (Junior Reference Ser.). (Illus.). 64p. (gr. 7 up). 1972. 7.95 (ISBN 0-7136-1323-8). Dufour.

CISTERCIANS–HISTORY

Elder, E. Rozanne, ed. Cistercians in the Late Middle Ages. (Cistercian Studies: No. 64). (Illus., Orig.). 1980. pap. 8.95 (ISBN 0-87907-865-0). Cistercian Pubns.

Elder, E. Rozanne, et al, eds. Cistercians in the Late Middle Ages: Studies in Medievel Cistercian History VI. (Cistercian Studies: No. VI). 161p. (Orig.). 1981. pap. 8.97 (ISBN 0-87907-864-2). Cistercian Pubns.

Lillich, Meredith, et al, eds. Studies in Cistercian Art & Architecture I. (Cistercian Studies: No. 66). (Illus., Orig.). 1981. pap. price not set (ISBN 0-87907-866-9). Cistercian Pubns.

CITIES AND TOWNS

see also Community; Education, Urban; Markets; Parks; Sociology, Urban; Streets; Urbanization; Villages

also headings beginning with the word City, Municipal and Urban; names of individual cities and towns

Bryfogle, R. Charles. City in Print: An Urban Studies Bibliography, Supplement Three. 1979. pap. 15.00 (ISBN 0-918010-01-2). Dawson & Co.

Darden, Joe T., ed. The Ghetto: Readings with Interpretations. (National University Publications, Interdisciplinary Urban Ser.). 1981. 19.50 (ISBN 0-8046-9277-7); pap. 9.95 (ISBN 0-8046-9279-3). Kennikat.

Drucker, Mark, ed. Urban Decision Making...a Guide to Information Sources. LC 80-19252. (Urban Studies Information Guide Ser. Part of the Gale Information Guide Library: Vol. 13). 200p. 1981. 30.00 (ISBN 0-8103-1481-9). Gale.

Lynch, Kevin. A Theory of Good City Form. (Illus.). 526p. 1981. text ed. 25.00x (ISBN 0-262-12085-2). MIT Pr.

Mumford, Lewis. The Culture of Cities. LC 80-23130. (Illus.). xviii, 586p. 1981. Repr. of 1970 ed. lib. bdg. 45.00x (ISBN 0-313-22746-2, MUCC). Greenwood.

CITIES AND TOWNS–HISTORY

Botero, Giovanni. A Treatise, Concerning the Causes of the Magnificence & Greatness of Cities. LC 79-84090. (English Experience Ser.: No. 910). 128p. (Eng.). 1979. Repr. of 1606 ed. lib. bdg. 13.00 (ISBN 90-221-0910-0). Walter J Johnson.

Buenker, John, et al, eds. Urban History...a Guide to Information Sources. LC 80-19643. (American Government & History Ser.,Part of the Gale Information Guide Library: Vol. 9). 400p. 1981. 30.00 (ISBN 0-8103-1479-7). Gale.

Jones, Emrys. Towns & Cities. LC 80-24687. (Illus.). viii, 152p. 1981. Repr. of 1966 ed. lib. bdg. 19.50x (ISBN 0-313-22724-1, JOTC). Greenwood.

CITIES AND TOWNS–JUVENILE LITERATURE

Rosario, Idalia. Idalia's Project ABC-Proyecto ABC. LC 80-21013. (Illus.). 32p. (ps-2). 1981. 6.95 (ISBN 0-03-044141-2). HR&W.

CITIES AND TOWNS–MOVEMENT TO

see Rural-Urban Migration

CITIES AND TOWNS–PLANNING

see City Planning

CITIES AND TOWNS–SURVEYING

see Surveying

CITIES AND TOWNS–AFRICA

Peil, Margaret. Cities & Suburbs: Urban Life in West Africa. LC 80-26440. (New Library of African Affairs). 330p. 1981. text ed. 24.00x (ISBN 0-8419-0685-8). Holmes & Meier.

CITIES AND TOWNS–CANADA

Armstrong, Frederick H., et al. Bibliography of Canadian Urban History: Part V: Western Canada. (Public Adminstration Ser.: Bibliography P-541). 72p. 1980. pap. 7.50. Vance Biblios.

CITIES AND TOWNS–EGYPT

Margoliouth, David S. Cairo, Jerusalem, & Damascus, Three Chief Cities of the Egyptian Sultans. LC 80-1918. (Illus.). 1981. Repr. of 1907 ed. 54.50 (ISBN 0-404-18980-6). AMS Pr.

CITIES AND TOWNS–EUROPE

Burtenshaw, D. The City in West Europe. 320p. 1981. 47.50 (ISBN 0-471-27929-3, Pub. by Wiley-Interscience). Wiley.

Schmal, Henk, ed. Patterns of European Urbanisation Since 1500. 400p. 1981. 31.00x (ISBN 0-7099-0365-0, Pub. by Croom Helm LTD England). Biblio Dist.

CITIES AND TOWNS–GREAT BRITAIN

Lanyon, Andrew. A St. Ives Album. 72p. 1980. 10.00x (ISBN 0-906720-00-1, Pub. by Hodge England). State Mutual Bk.

Lawless, P. Britain's Inner Cities. 1981. text ed. 25.85 (ISBN 0-06-318184-3, Pub. by Har-Row Ltd England); pap. text ed. 13.10 (ISBN 0-06-318185-1). Har-Row.

CITIES AND TOWNS–JAPAN

Ponsonby-Fane, Richard A. Imperial Cities: The Capitals of Japan from the Oldest Times Until 1229. (Studies in Japanese History & Civilization). 1979. 21.50 (ISBN 0-89093-251-4). U Pubns Amer.

CITIES AND TOWNS–MEXICO

Saville, Marshall H. Bibliographic Notes on Xochioalco, Mexico. (INM Ser.: Vol. 11, No.6). 1928. pap. 1.00 (ISBN 0-934490-28-7). Mus Am Ind.

CITIES AND TOWNS–NEAR EAST

Blake, G. H. & Lawless, R. I., eds. The Changing Middle Eastern City. (Illus.). 273p. 1980. 28.50x. B&N.

The Islamic City: Selected Papers from the Colloquium Held at the Middle East Centre. 210p. 1980. pap. 13.50 (ISBN 92-3-101665-2, U1033, UNESCO). Unipub.

CITIES AND TOWNS–RUSSIA

Priselkov, Mikhail D. Khanskie Iarlyki Russkim Metropolitam. LC 80-2364. 1981. Repr. of 1916 ed. 25.50 (ISBN 0-686-69404-X). AMS Pr.

CITIES AND TOWNS–UNITED STATES

Baldwin, Carl R. Echoes of Their Voices. 400p. 1978. 10.95 (ISBN 0-86629-003-6). Sunrise MO.

Fazio, Michael W. & Prenshaw, Peggy W., eds. Order & Image in the American Small Town. LC 80-24300. (Southern Quarterly Ser.). 1981. price not set (ISBN 0-87805-130-9). U Pr of Miss.

Hepburn, Mary A., et al. City Government in Georgia. LC 79-24128. 150p. (Orig.). (gr. 8-12). 1980. pap. 7.50 (ISBN 0-89854-052-6). U of GA Inst Govt.

Johnson, Charles O. & Jackson, Charles W. City Behind a Fence: Oak Ridge, Tennessee, 1942-1946. LC 80-15897. (Illus.). 272p. 1981. 18.50 (ISBN 0-87049-303-5); pap. 9.50 (ISBN 0-87049-309-4). U of Tenn Pr.

Lang, Michael. Gentrification & the Resegregation of American Cities. 1981. price not set professional reference (ISBN 0-88410-697-7). Ballinger Pub.

Mumford, Lewis. The Highway & the City. LC 80-22641. viii, 246p. 1981. Repr. of 1953 ed. lib. bdg. 25.00x (ISBN 0-313-22747-0, MUHC). Greenwood.

Murphy, Patricia & Taylor-Gordon, Elaine. The Business-Woman's Guide to Thirty American Cities. 400p. 1981. 19.95 (ISBN 0-312-92072-5); pap. 9.95 (ISBN 0-312-92073-3). St Martin.

Palm, Risa. The Geography of American Cities. (Illus.). 384p. 1981. text ed. 18.95x (ISBN 0-19-502785-X). Oxford U Pr.

CITIES AND TOWNS, MOVEMENT TO

see Urbanization

CITIES AND TOWNS, RUINED, EXTINCT, ETC.

Paher, Stanley W. Southwestern Arizona Ghost Tours. (Illus.). 2.95 (ISBN 0-913814-32-6). Nevada Pubns.

Urbanek, Mae. Ghost Trails of Wyoming. (Illus.). 236p. 1978. 16.95; pap. 8.95. Urbanek.

CITIZENS BAND RADIO

see also Models and Modelmaking–Radio Control Systems

Murray, Joan. A CB Picture Dictionary. LC 80-1725. (Illus.). 64p. (gr. 5 up). 8.95a (ISBN 0-385-14782-1); PLB (ISBN 0-385-14783-X). Doubleday.

Smelser, Newt. Beginner's CB & Two-Way Radio Repairing. LC 80-23818. (Illus.). 232p. 1981. text ed. 29.95 (ISBN 0-88229-573-X); pap. text ed. 14.95 (ISBN 0-88229-763-5). Nelson-Hall.

CITIZENS RADIO SERVICE

see Citizens Band Radio

CITIZENSHIP

see also Aliens; Civics; Naturalization; Political Rights; Self-Determination, National

Sherwin-White, A. N. The Roman Citizenship. 2nd ed. 496p. 1980. pap. 24.95x (ISBN 0-19-814847-X). Oxford U Pr.

Van Dyne, Frederick. Citizenship of the United States. xxvii, 385p. 1980. Repr. of 1904 ed. lib. bdg. 28.50x (ISBN 0-8377-1229-7). Rothman.

Wise, John S. A Treatise on American Citizenship. (Studies in Constitutional Law). viii, 340p. 1981. Repr. of 1906 ed. lib. bdg. 30.00x (ISBN 0-8377-1306-4). Rothman.

CITRUS FRUIT INDUSTRY

Citrus Fruit. (International Standardisation of Fruit & Vegetables Ser.). 103p. (Orig.). 1980. pap. 17.50 (ISBN 9-2640-2112-4). OECD.

CITRUS FRUITS

see also Citrus Fruit Industry

Nagy, Steven & Attaway, John, eds. Citrus Nutrition & Quality. LC 80-22562. (ACS Symposium Ser.: No. 143). 1980. 36.25 (ISBN 0-8412-0595-7). Am Chemical.

Ray, Richard & Walheim, Lance. Citrus. (Gardening Ser.). (Orig.). 1980. pap. 7.95 (ISBN 0-89586-076-7). H P Bks.

CITY GOVERNMENT

see Municipal Government

CITY MISSIONS

Pelham, Joseph, et al. To Hear & to Heed. 1978. 1.50 (ISBN 0-686-28797-5). Forward Movement.

CITY PLANNING

see also Community Development; Housing; Industries, Location of; Parks; Regional Planning; Social Surveys; Space (Architecture); Suburbs; Urban Renewal

Basile, Ralph J., et al. Downtown Development Handbook. LC 80-50928. (Community Builder Handbook Ser.). (Illus.). 278p. 1980. 34.00 (ISBN 0-87420-591-3, D12). Urban Land.

Black, J. Thomas, et al. UDAG Partnerships: Nine Case Studies. (Illus.). 108p. 1980. pap. 10.00 (ISBN 0-87420-594-8, U12). Urban Land.

Branch, Melville C. Comparative Urban Desigh-Rare Engravings: 1830-1843. 108p. 49.50 (ISBN 0-686-69145-8, Co Pub by U of Cal Pr). Arno.

--Continuous City Planning: Integrating Municipal & City Planning. 192p. 1980. 21.95 (ISBN 0-471-08943-5, Pub. by Wiley-Interscience). Wiley.

Broady, Maurice. Planning for People. 119p. 1968. pap. text ed. 4.00x (ISBN 0-7199-0765-9, Pub. by Bedford England). Renouf.

Cook, Charles C., intro. by. Land Valuation Methods: Urban Land. (Lincoln Institute Monograph: No. 80-1). (Illus.). 200p. 1980. pap. text ed. 10.00. Lincoln Inst Land.

Ferris, John. Participation in Urban Planning. 95p. 1972. pap. text ed. 6.25x (ISBN 0-7135-1714-X, Pub. by Bedford England). Renouf.

Hopkins, George D., Jr. Urban Ecology Through the Adaptive Use of Existing Buildings: A Selected Bibliography, Revising A-22 of Oct. 1978. (Architecture Ser.: Bibliography a-281). 78p. 1980. pap. 8.50. Vance Biblios.

Mumford, Lewis. The Culture of Cities. LC 80-23130. (Illus.). xviii, 586p. 1981. Repr. of 1970 ed. lib. bdg. 45.00x (ISBN 0-313-22746-2, MUCC). Greenwood.

Palen. City Scenes: Problems & Prospects. 2nd ed. 1981. pap. text ed. 9.95 (ISBN 0-316-68871-1). Little.

Portugali, Juval. Distribution, Allocation, Social Structure & Spatial Form: Elements of Planning Theory. (Progress in Planning: Vol. 14, Part 3). (Illus.). 83p. 1980. pap. 13.50 (ISBN 0-08-026808-0). Pergamon.

Ravetz, Alison. Remaking Cities. 375p. 1980. 37.50x (ISBN 0-85664-293-2, Pub. by Croom Helm Ltd England). Biblio Dist.

Scott, A. J. The Urban Land Nexus & the State. 256p. 1980. 24.00 (ISBN 0-85086-079-2, 6390). Methuen Inc.

Szanton, Peter. Not Well Advised. LC 80-69174. 175p. 1981. text ed. 11.95x (ISBN 0-87154-874-7). Russell Sage.

Todaro, Michael P. & Stilkind, Jerry. City Bias & Rural Neglect: The Dilemma of Urban Development. LC 80-26071. (Public Issues Papers). (Illus.). xiv, 93p. (Orig.). 1981. pap. text ed. 2.50 (ISBN 0-87834-042-4). Population Coun.

CITY PLANNING–BIBLIOGRAPHY

Branch, Melville C. & Mazza, Eliane G. Selected Annotated Bibliography on New Town Planning & Development. (Architecture Ser.: Bibliography a-216). 133p. 1980. pap. 14.00. Vance Biblios.

Vance, Mary. City Planning: A Selected List of Books, 1970-1978. (Architecture Ser.: Bibliography A-224). 99p. 1980. pap. 10.50. Vance Biblios.

CITY PLANNING–LAW AND LEGISLATION

see City Planning and Redevelopment Law

CITY PLANNING–PUBLIC OPINION

Schill, Michael H. Neighborhood Reinvestment & Displacement: A Working Paper. LC 80-85160. 64p. 1981. pap. 2.50x (ISBN 0-938882-01-5). PURRC.

CITY PLANNING–AUSTRALIA

Archer, R. W. Land Pooling by Local Government for Planned Urban Development in Perth. (Lincoln Institute Monograph: No. 80-4). (Illus.). 69p. 1980. pap. 5.00 (Australian Institute of Urban Studies). Lincoln Inst Land.

Stilwell, Frank J. Economic Crisis, Cities & Regions: An Analysis of Current Urban & Regional Problems in Australia. 192p. 1980. 14.50 (ISBN 0-08-024810-1); pap. 8.95 (ISBN 0-08-024809-8). Pergamon.

CITY PLANNING–CHINA

Ma, Laurence J. & Hanten, Edward W., eds. Urban Development in Modern China. (Special Studies on China & East Asia). 250p. 1981. lib. bdg. 20.00x (ISBN 0-86531-120-X). Westview.

CITY PLANNING–EUROPE

Mumford, Lewis. The Highway & the City. LC 80-22641. viii, 246p. 1981. Repr. of 1953 ed. lib. bdg. 25.00x (ISBN 0-313-22747-0, MUHC). Greenwood.

CITY PLANNING–GREAT BRITAIN

Cartwright, Richard M. Design of Urban Space: A GLC Manual. 208p. 1981. 44.95 (ISBN 0-470-27066-7). Halsted Pr.

Cooke, Philip. Dependent Development in United Kingdom Regions with Particular Reference to Wales. (Progress on Planning Ser.: Vol. 15, Part 1). 90p. 1980. pap. 13.50 (ISBN 0-08-026809-9). Pergamon.

Daniels, P. W. Office Location & the Journey to Work: A Comparative Study of Five Urban Centers. 175p. 1980. text ed. 30.00x (ISBN 0-566-00352-X, Pub. by Gower Pub Co England). Renouf.

CITY PLANNING–INDIA

Hall, Derek R. A Spatial Analysis of Urban Community Development Policy in India. (Geography & Public Policy Research Studies Ser.). 192p. 1981. 33.75 (ISBN 0-471-27862-9, Pub. by Wiley-Interscience). Wiley.

Prakash, S. Financing of Planned Development in India. 1968. 7.50 (ISBN 0-8426-1682-9). Verry.

CITY PLANNING–LATIN AMERICA

Butterworth, Douglas & Chance, John K. Latin American Urbanization. LC 80-18486. (Urbanization in Developing Countries Ser.). (Illus.). 320p. 1981. text ed. 29.95 (ISBN 0-521-23713-0); pap. text ed. 8.95 (ISBN 0-521-28175-X). Cambridge U Pr.

CITY PLANNING–RUSSIA

Pallot, Judith & Shaw, Denis. Planning in the Soviet Union. LC 80-24723. 320p. 1981. lib. bdg. 25.00x (ISBN 0-8203-0550-2). U of Ga Pr.

CITY PLANNING–UNITED STATES

Bryce, Herrington J., ed. Cities & Firms. LC 80-8367. (The Urban Roundtable Ser.). 272p. 1980. 18.95x (ISBN 0-669-04042-8). Lexington Bks.

Hillert, Margaret. City Fun. (Just Beginning-to-Read Ser.). 32p. 1980. PLB 4.39 (ISBN 0-695-41457-7); pap. 1.50 (ISBN 0-695-31457-2). Follett.

Lang, Michael. Gentrification & the Resegregation of American Cities. 1981. price not set professional reference (ISBN 0-88410-697-7). Ballinger Pub.

Mowry, George E. & Brownell, Blaine E. The Urban Nation: Nineteen Twenty to Nineteen Eighty. Donald, David H., ed. 1981. 12.50 (ISBN 0-8090-9541-6); pap. 5.95 (ISBN 0-8090-0148-9). Hill & Wang.

Mumford, Lewis. The Highway & the City. LC 80-22641. viii, 246p. 1981. Repr. of 1953 ed. lib. bdg. 25.00x (ISBN 0-313-22747-0, MUHC). Greenwood.

National Archives of the United States Office of Education. Washington: Design for the Federal City. 1981. pap. 9.95 (ISBN 0-87491-417-5). Acropolis.

Palley, Marian L. & Palley, Howard A. Urban America & Public Policies. 2nd ed. 336p. 1981. pap. text ed. 8.95 (ISBN 0-669-04004-5). Heath.

Ramati, Racquel & Urban Design Group of the Department of City Planning, New York. How to Save Your Own Street. LC 78-14709. (Illus.). 176p. 1981. pap. 19.95 (ISBN 0-385-14814-3, Dolp). Doubleday.

Willis, F. Roy. Western Civilization: An Urban Perspective, 2 vols. 3rd ed. (Vol. 1, 688 pp.:vol. 2, 560 pp.). 1981. Vol. 1. pap. text ed. 12.95 (ISBN 0-669-03364-2); Vol. 2. pap. text ed. 12.95 (ISBN 0-669-03365-0); instructor's guide (ISBN 0-669-03366-9). Heath.

CITY PLANNING AND REDEVELOPMENT LAW

see also Regional Planning; Zoning Law

Nathan, Richard P. & Webman, Jerry A., eds. The Urban Development Action Grant Program: Papers & Conference Proceedings on Its First Two Years of Operation. LC 80-84901. (Illus.). 124p. 1980. pap. 5.00 (ISBN 0-938882-00-7). PURRC.

Schnidman, Frank & Silveman, Jane A., eds. Management & Control of Growth: Updating the Law. LC 80-50920. (Management & Control of Growth Ser.: Vol. V). 352p. 1980. pap. text ed. 19.50 (ISBN 0-87420-592-1, M12). Urban Land.

CITY SCHOOLS

see Education, Urban

CITY SURVEYING

see Surveying

CITY TRANSIT

see Local Transit

CITY UNIVERSITY OF NEW YORK

Lavin, David E., et al. Right Versus Privilege: The Open Admissions Experiment at the City University of New York. LC 80-69571. (Illus.). 1981. 24.95 (ISBN 0-02-918080-5). Free Pr.

CIVIC PLANNING

see City Planning

CIVIC RIGHTS

see Political Rights

CIVICS

Here are entered general works and works about the United States in particular. For works dealing with specific states see names of individual states, with or without the subdivision Politics and Government.

see also Citizenship; Civil Rights; Political Ethics; Political Rights

Roberts, Susan A., et al. Civics for New Mexicans. LC 80-52284. 375p. 1980. 25.00 (ISBN 0-8263-0547-4). U of NM Pr.

CIVIL AERONAUTICS

see Aeronautics, Commercial

CIVIL AVIATION

see Aeronautics, Commercial

CIVIL DISOBEDIENCE

see Government, Resistance to

CIVIL DISORDERS

see Riots

CIVIL ENGINEERING

see also Bridges; Canals; Dams; Docks; Excavation; Foundations; Hydraulic Engineering; Irrigation; Marine Engineering; Masonry; Mechanical Engineering; Piling (Civil Engineering); Public Works; Railroad Engineering; Reclamation of Land; Rivers; Roads; Sanitary Engineering; Steel, Structural; Streets; Strength of Materials; Structural Dynamics; Surveying; Tunnels and Tunneling; Walls; Water-Supply Engineering

also subdivision Public Works under names of countries, cities, etc. e.g. United States–Public Works

The Aesthetic Aspects of Civil Engineering Design. 120p. 1980. pap. 25.00x (ISBN 0-901948-13-6, Pub. by Telford England). State Mutual Bk.

American Society of Civil Engineers, compiled by. Guide for Field Testing of Bridges. LC 80-69154. 72p. 1980. pap. text ed. 12.00 (ISBN 0-87262-255-X). Am Soc Civil Eng.

--Selected Papers by Alfred M. Freudenthal. 816p. 1981. pap. text ed. 54.00 (ISBN 0-87262-263-0). Am Soc Civil Eng.

Chen, W. F. & Ting, E. C., eds. Fracture in Concrete. LC 80-69656. 110p. 1980. pap. text ed. 12.00 (ISBN 0-87262-259-2). Am Soc Civil Eng.

Christian, John. Management, Machines & Methods in Civil Engineering. 375p. 1981. 34.95 (ISBN 0-471-06334-7, Pub. by Wiley-Interscience). Wiley.

Civil Engineering Procedure. 3rd ed. 112p. 1980. 25.00x (ISBN 0-7277-0113-4, Pub. by Telford England). State Mutual Bk.

De Vore, R. William & Graves, Donald H., eds. Symposium on Surface Mining Hydrology, Sedimentology, & Reclamation 1980: Proceedings. (Illus., Orig.). 1980. pap. 33.50 (ISBN 0-89779-044-8, UKYBU123); microfiche 5.50 (ISBN 0-89779-045-6). OES Pubns.

Edge, Billy L., ed. Coastal Zone '80, 3 vols. LC 80-69152. 2470p. 1980. pap. text ed. 110.00 (ISBN 0-87262-258-4). Am Soc Civil Eng.

Fuller, Frank. Deep Foundations. LC 80-69155. 540p. 1981. pap. text ed. 25.00 (ISBN 0-87262-256-8). Am Soc Civil Eng.

Hart, Gary. Dynamic Response of Structures. LC 80-70135. 992p. 1981. pap. text ed. 65.00 (ISBN 0-87262-261-4). Am Soc Civil Eng.

Haswell & Silva. Civil Engineering Contracts. 1981. text ed. price not set (ISBN 0-408-00526-2). Butterworth.

Lindeburg, Michael R. Surveying Law for the California Civil Professional Engineering Exam. (Engineering Review Manual Ser.). (Illus.). 154p. 1981. pap. 9.50 (ISBN 0-932276-26-1). Prof Engine.

O'Neill, Michael W. & Dobry, Ricardo, eds. Dynamic Response of Pile Foundations: Analytical Aspects. LC 80-69151. 112p. 1980. pap. text ed. 12.00 (ISBN 0-87262-257-6). Am Soc Civil Eng.

Scott, John S. Dictionary of Civil Engineering. 3rd ed. LC 80-24419. 308p. 1980. 19.95 (ISBN 0-470-27087-X). Halsted Pr.

Snethen, Donald. Expansive Soils, 2 vols. LC 66-140. 900p. 1981. pap. text ed. 46.00 (ISBN 0-87262-245-2). Am Soc Civil Eng.

Stopher, Peter R., et al, eds. New Horizons in Travel-Behavior Research. LC 78-24830. 1981. price not set (ISBN 0-669-02850-9). Lexington Bks.

CIVIL ENGINEERING–BIBLIOGRAPHY

Institute of Civil Engineers. ICE Yearbook 1980. 848p. 1980. pap. 69.00 (ISBN 0-7277-0081-2, Pub. by Telford England). State Mutual Bk.

CIVIL ENGINEERING–DATA PROCESSING

Surface Modelling by Computer. 112p. 1980. 28.00x (ISBN 0-7277-0029-4, Pub. by Telford England). State Mutual Bk.

CIVIL ENGINEERING–ESTIMATES AND COSTS

see Engineering–Estimates and Costs

CIVIL ENGINEERING–MANAGEMENT

see Engineering–Management

CIVIL ENGINEERS

Institute of Civil Engineers. ICE Yearbook 1980. 848p. 1980. pap. 69.00 (ISBN 0-7277-0081-2, Pub. by Telford England). State Mutual Bk.

CIVIL GOVERNMENT

see Political Science

CIVIL LAW

see also Liability (Law); Roman Law

Domat, Jean. The Civil Law in Its Natural Order, 2 vols. Cushing, Luther S., ed. Strahan, William, tr. from Fr. 1763p. 1981. Repr. of 1850 ed. Set. lib. bdg. 97.50x (ISBN 0-8377-0511-8). Rothman.

Howe, William W. Studies in the Civil Law, & Its Relations to the Law of England & America. xv, 340p. 1980. Repr. of 1896 ed. lib. bdg. 27.50x (ISBN 0-8377-0631-9). Rothman.

CIVIL LAW–ROME

see Roman Law

CIVIL LAW (JEWISH LAW)

see Jewish Law

CIVIL LAW (ROMAN LAW)

see Roman Law

CIVIL LIBERTY

see Liberty

CIVIL-MILITARY RELATIONS

see Militarism

CIVIL PROCEDURE

see also Appellate Procedure; Equity Pleading and Procedure; Instructions to Juries; Judgments; Jury; Probate Law and Practice; Trial Practice

Landers, Jonathan M. & Martin, James A. Basic Civil Procedure: Cases & Materials. 1196p. 1981. price not set. Little.

CIVIL PROCEDURE–FRANCE

New Code of Civil Procedure in France, Bk. 1. 1978. 32.50 (ISBN 0-379-20266-2). Oceana.

CIVIL RIGHTS

see also Liberty; Liberty of Speech; Liberty of the Press; Petition, Right of; Political Rights; Race Discrimination; Teaching, Freedom of

Brownlie, Ian, ed. Basic Documents of Human Rights. 2nd ed. 450p. 1981. 67.50 (ISBN 0-19-876124-4); pap. 24.95 (ISBN 0-19-876125-2). Oxford U Pr.

Cohen, Roy. Stand up for Your Rights. 14.95 (ISBN 0-671-25341-7). S&S.

Council of Europe, ed. Yearbook of the European Convention on Human Rights. (European Convention on Human Rights: No. 22). 688p. 1980. lib. bdg. 132.00 (ISBN 90-247-2383-3, Pub. by Martinus Nijhoff). Kluwer Boston.

Cummings, Richard. Proposition Fourteen: A Secessionist Remedy. LC 80-8917. 128p. 1981. pap. 5.95 postponed (ISBN 0-394-17890-4, Ever). Grove.

Gunther, Gerald. Cases & Materials on Individual Rights in Constitutional Law. 3rd, abr. ed. LC 80-70238. (University Casebook Ser.). 1337p. 1980. text ed. write for info. (ISBN 0-88277-021-7). Foundation Pr.

Lefever, Ernest W., ed. Morality & Foreign Policy: A Symposium on President Carter's Stance. 82p. 1977. pap. 3.00 (ISBN 0-89633-005-2). Ethics & Public Policy.

OAS General Secretariat Inter-American Commission of Human Rights. Manual De Normas Wicentes En Materia De Derechos Humanos. (Human Rights Ser.). 153p. 1980. text ed. 6.00 (ISBN 0-8270-1153-9). OAS.

Schuster, Edward J. Human Rights Today: Evolution or Revolution? LC 80-84737. 1981. 12.00 (ISBN 0-686-68868-6). Philos Lib.

Tardu, M. Human Rights: The International Petition System, Release 1. 1980. 35.00 (ISBN 0-379-20252-2). Oceana.

United Nations. The International Bill of Human Rights. 132p. 1981. 7.95 (ISBN 0-934558-06-X); pap. 2.95 (ISBN 0-934558-07-8). Entwhistle Bks.

Williamson, Henry H., Jr. To Be Self-Evident. 280p. 1980. 8.95 (ISBN 0-533-04016-7). Vantage.

Wirsing, Robert G., ed. Protection of Ethnic Minorities: Comparative Perspectives. LC 80-25618. (Pergamon Policy Studies on International Politices Ser.). 350p. 1981. 39.50 (ISBN 0-08-025556-6). Pergamon.

CIVIL RIGHTS–STUDY AND TEACHING

The Teaching of Human Rights. 258p. 1980. pap. 13.25 (ISBN 92-3-101781-0, U1036, UNESCO). Unipub.

CIVIL RIGHTS–HAITI

OAS General Secretariat Inter-American Commision of Human Rights. Informe Sobre la Situacion De los Derechos Humanos En Haiti. (Human Rights Ser.). 77p. 1980. text ed. 5.00 (ISBN 0-8270-1095-8). OAS.

OAS General Secretariat Inter-American Commission of Human Rights, ed. Rapport Sur la Situation Des Droits De L'homme En Haiti. (Human Rights Ser.). 76p. 1980. 5.00 (ISBN 0-8270-1098-2). OAS.

OAS General Secretariat Inter-American Commission of Human Rights. Report on the Situation of Human Rights in Haiti. (Human Rights Ser.). 81p. 1980. lib. bdg. 5.00 (ISBN 0-8270-1096-6). OAS.

CIVIL RIGHTS–ISLAMIC COUNTRIES

Butler, William J. & Levasseur, Georges. Human Rights & the Legal System in Iran. 80p. (Orig.). 1976. pap. text ed. 2.50 (ISBN 0-89192-084-6). Interbk Inc.

CIVIL RIGHTS–LATIN AMERICA

OAS General Secretariat. Manual De Normas Vigentes En Materia De Direitos Humanos: Actualizado Em Julho De 1980. (Human Rights Ser.). 149p. (Port.). 1980. pap. text ed. 4.00 (ISBN 0-8270-1203-9). OAS.

OAS General Secretariat Inter-American Commission of Human Rights. Report on the Situation of Human Rights in Argentina. (Human Rights Ser.). 266p. (Orig.). 1980. 12.00 (ISBN 0-8270-1099-0). OAS.

Sukedo, Iris D. The Sociology of Racial Intergration in Guyana. 224p. 1981. 9.50 (ISBN 0-682-49686-3). Exposition.

CIVIL RIGHTS–UNITED STATES

see also Afro-Americans–Civil Rights; United States–Constitution

Allen Bakke Vs. Regents of the University of California, 6 vols. 1978. 44.00 ea. Oceana.

Chafe, William H. Civilities & Civil Rights: Greensboro, North Carolina, & the Black Struggle for Freedom. (Illus.). 320p. 1981. pap. 5.95 (ISBN 0-19-502919-4, GB 644, GB). Oxford U Pr.

Ewing, David. Freedom Inside the Organization: Bringing Civil Liberties to the Workplace. 1977. 10.00 (ISBN 0-87690-249-2). Dutton.

Hamlin, David. The Nazi-Skokie Conflict: A Civil Liberties Battle. LC 80-68165. 192p. 1981. 12.95 (ISBN 0-8070-3230-1). Beacon Pr.

Lamont, Corliss. Freedom Is As Freedom Does: Civil Liberties in America. 330p. (Orig.). 1981. pap. 5.95 (ISBN 0-8180-0350-2). Horizon.

Lamont, Corliss, ed. Freedom of Choice Affirmed. 214p. (Orig.). 1981. pap. 4.95 (ISBN 0-8180-1329-X). Horizon.

Lockhart, William B., et al. Cases & Materials on Constitutional Rights & Liberties. 5th ed. LC 80-54541. (American Casebook Ser.). 1298p. 1980. text ed. 21.95 (ISBN 0-8299-2135-4). West Pub.

Mann, Stanley C. One Against the Storm. (Illus.). 221p. (Orig.). pap. write for info. (ISBN 0-938662-00-7). Quest Utah.

Nineteen-Eighty Case Supplement, Civil Rights: Leading Cases. Date not set. 8.95 (ISBN 0-316-08819-6). Little.

Viorst, Milton. Fire in the Streets. 1981. 8.95 (ISBN 0-671-42814-4, Touchstone). S&S.

CIVIL RIGHTS–UNITED STATES–SONGS AND MUSIC–HISTORY AND CRITICISM

OAS General Secretariat. Manual De Normas Vigentes En Materia De Direitos Humanos: Actualizado Em Julho De 1980. (Human Rights Ser.). 149p. (Port.). 1980. pap. text ed. 4.00 (ISBN 0-8270-1203-9). OAS.

CIVIL RIGHTS (INTERNATIONAL LAW)

Falk, Richard A. Human Rights & State Sovereignty. 180p. 1981. text ed. 24.00x (ISBN 0-8419-0619-X); pap. text ed. 9.75x (ISBN 0-8419-0620-3). Holmes & Meier.

International Association for Philosophy of Law & Social Philosophy. Equality & Freedom, Vols. 1-3. 1977. Set. 35.00 (ISBN 0-379-00657-X). Oceana.

Lillich, Richard B., ed. U. S. Ratification of the Human Rights Treaties: With or Without Reservations? (Procedural Aspects of International Law Ser.). 1980. write for info. (ISBN 0-8139-0881-7). U Pr of Va.

Morgenthau, Hans J. Human Rights & Foreign Policy. LC 79-53084. (First Distinguished CRIA Lecture on Morality & Foreign Policy Ser.). 1979. pap. 4.00 (ISBN 0-87641-216-9). Coun Rel & Intl.

United Nations. The International Bill of Human Rights. 132p. 1981. 7.95 (ISBN 0-934558-06-X); pap. 2.95 (ISBN 0-934558-07-8). Entwhistle Bks.

CIVIL RIGHTS WORKERS

Mays, Benjamin E. Lord, the People Have Driven Me on. 1981. 7.95 (ISBN 0-533-04503-7). Vantage.

CIVIL SERVICE

see also Administrative Law; Bureaucracy; Collective Bargaining–Government Employees; Municipal Officials and Employees; Strikes and Lockouts–Civil Service

also subdivision Officials and Employees–Appointments, Qualifications, Tenure, etc. under the names of countries, cities, etc. e.g. United States–Officials and Employees–Appointments, Qualifications, Tenure, etc.

McGill, Dan M. Financing the Civil Service Retirement System. 1979. 11.00x (ISBN 0-256-02250-X). Irwin.

Murphy, Thomas P., et al. Contemporary Public Administration: A Study in Emerging Realities. LC 80-83377. 517p. 1981. text ed. 14.95 (ISBN 0-87581-269-4). Peacock Pubs.

Young, Joseph & Young, Lucille, eds. Nineteen Eighty-One Federal Employees' Almanac. 156p. (Orig.). 1981. pap. 2.75 (ISBN 0-910582-01-7). Fed Employees.

CIVIL SERVICE–EXAMINATIONS

see Civil Service Examinations

CIVIL SERVICE–POSITIONS

see Civil Service Positions

CIVIL SERVICE–VOCATIONAL GUIDANCE

see Civil Service Positions

CIVIL SERVICE–CHINA–HISTORY

Miyazaki, Ichisada. China's Examination Hell: The Civil Service Examinations of Imperial China. Schirokauer, Conrad, tr. from Chinese. LC 80-54223. 142p. 1981. pap. 4.95 (ISBN 0-300-02639-0). Yale U Pr.

CIVIL SERVICE–GREAT BRITAIN

Kelley, Mike. White-Collar Proletariat: The Industrial Behaviour of British Civil Servants. 208p. (Orig.). 1980. pap. 21.75 (ISBN 0-7100-0623-3). Routledge & Kegan.

Paz, D. G. The Politics of Working-Class Education in Britain, 1830-1850. 199p. 1981. lib. bdg. 30.00x (ISBN 0-87023-326-2). U of Mass Pr.

CIVIL SERVICE–UNITED STATES

Brown, E. M. The Helicopter in Civil Operations. 208p. 1981. 17.95 (ISBN 0-442-24528-9). Van Nos Reinhold.

R. B. Uleck Associates. Federal Career Guide. (Illus., Orig.). 1979. pap. 5.95 (ISBN 0-937562-03-3). Uleck Assoc.

CIVIL SERVICE, INTERNATIONAL

see International Officials and Employees

CIVIL SERVICE EXAMINATIONS

Here are entered general works and works on United States civil service examinations. Examinations for specific cities in the United States or for countries other than the United States are entered under the appropriate subdivisions.

Riemer, Edwin & Leibling, Louis. Barron's How to Prepare for Civil Service Examinations: Clerks, Stenographers, Typists. 4th ed. (Barron's Educational Ser.). 405p. 1981. pap. text ed. 5.95 (ISBN 0-8120-2033-2). Barron.

Wiener, Solomon. The High School Graduate Guide for Scoring High on Civil Service Tests. 160p. (Orig.). (gr. 12). 1981. pap. 4.95 (ISBN 0-671-42776-8). Monarch Pr.

--How to Take Simple Tests for Civil Service Jobs & Score Higher. 160p. (Orig.). 1981. pap. 4.95 (ISBN 0-671-42777-6). Monarch Pr.

CIVIL SERVICE PENSIONS

see also subdivisions Pensions and Salaries, Pensions, etc. under names of industries, professions, etc. e.g. Teachers–Salaries, Pensions, etc.

McGill, Dan M. Financing the Civil Service Retirement System. 1979. 11.00x (ISBN 0-256-02250-X). Irwin.

Patterson, Archibald L. The Administration of Public Employee Retirement Systems: Georgia & the Nation. 100p. (Orig.). 1981. pap. price not set (ISBN 0-89854-073-9). U of GA Inst Govt.

CIVIL SERVICE POSITIONS

DuPre, Flint O. Your Career in Federal Civil Service. 288p. 1981. pap. 4.95 (ISBN 0-06-463529-5, EH529, EH). Har-Row.

Editorial Board. Civil Service Handbook. 7th ed. 128p. (Orig.). 1981. pap. 4.00 (ISBN 0-668-05166-3, 5166). Arco.

CIVIL WAR

Eckstein, Harry, ed. Internal War: Problems & Approaches. LC 80-23162. x, 339p. 1980. Repr. of 1964 ed. lib. bdg. 27.50x (ISBN 0-313-22451-X, ECIW). Greenwood.

CIVIL WAR–GREAT BRITAIN

see Great Britain–History–Puritan Revolution, 1642-1660

CIVIL WAR–UNITED STATES

see United States–History–Civil War, 1861-1865

CIVILIZATION

Includes works treating of culture or civilization in general. Literature dealing with the culture of peoples and races ordinarily classed as civilized and not confined to one country are entered under the headings Civilization, Greek; Civilization, Germanic; Civilization, Homeric; etc.; Works on the civilization of a single country are entered under the name of the country with the subdivision Civilization, e.g. United States–Civilization; Works treating of the culture of uncivilized tribes are entered under the name of the tribe.

see also Animals and Civilization; Anthropology; Archaeology; Art; Culture; Education; Ethics; Ethnology; Humanism; Inventions; Learning and Scholarship; Migrations of Nations; Progress; Religions; Renaissance; Social Evolution; Social Problems; Social Sciences; Society, Primitive; Technology and Civilization

Holliday, Robin. The Science of Human Progress. 112p. 1981. 21.00 (ISBN 0-19-854711-0). Oxford U Pr.

Williamson, Samuel. Origins of a Tragedy. (Problems in Civilization Ser.). (Orig.). 1981. pap. text ed. 3.95x (ISBN 0-88273-409-1). Forum Pr MO.

CIVILIZATION–ADDRESSES, ESSAYS, LECTURES

Kilpatrick, William H. Education for a Changing Civilization: Three Lectures Delivered on the Luther Laflin Kellogg Foundation at Rutgers University 1926. 143p. 1980. Repr. of 1926 ed. lib. bdg. 15.00 (ISBN 0-89760-426-1). Telegraph Bks.

CIVILIZATION–PHILOSOPHY

see also Philosophical Anthropology

Parker, Frank A. Whither Civilization? 1981. 10.00 (ISBN 0-533-04882-6). Vantage.

Schweitzer, Albert. The Philosophy of Civilization. Campion, C. T., tr. from Ger. LC 80-27122. xvii, 347p. 1981. pap. 6.00 (ISBN 0-8130-0694-5). U Presses Fla.

CIVILIZATION, AMERICAN

see America–Civilization; United States–Civilization

CIVILIZATION, ANCIENT

Cazeau, Charles J. & Scott, Stuart D., Jr. Exploring the Unknown: Great Mysteries Reexamined. (Da Capo Quality Paperbacks Ser.). (Illus.). 1981. pap. 8.95 (ISBN 0-306-80139-6). Da Capo.

Cotterell, Arthur, ed. Encyclopedia of Ancient Civilizations. Renfrew, Colin. 320p. 1980. 29.95 (ISBN 0-8317-2790-X). Mayflower Bks.

CIVILIZATION, ANGLO-SAXON

Clemoes, P. Anglo-Saxon England, Vol. 9. LC 78-190423. (Anglo-Saxon England Ser.). (Illus.). 330p. Date not set. 56.00 (ISBN 0-521-23449-2). Cambridge U Pr.

CIVILIZATION, ARAB

see also Civilization, Islamic

Permanent International Altaistic Conference, 18th Meeting, Bloomington, June 29-July 5, 1975. Aspects of Altaic Civilization II: Proceedings. Draghi, Paul A. & Clark, Larry V., eds. (Indiana University Uralic & Altaic Ser.: Vol. 134). 212p. 1978. 34.00 (ISBN 0-933070-02-0). Ind U Res Inst.

CIVILIZATION, GREEK

see also Hellenism

Finley, M. I., ed. The Legacy of Greece: A New Appraisal. (Illus.). 480p. 1981. 16.95 (ISBN 0-19-821915-6). Oxford U Pr.

CIVILIZATION, HISPANIC

see also Spain–Civilization

Handelsman, Michael H. & Heslin, William H., Jr. La Cultura Hispanica: Dentro y Fuera de los Estados Unidos. 128p. 1981. pap. text ed. 7.95 (ISBN 0-394-32653-9). Random.

Martin, D. La Vida Espanola. 3rd ed. (Span.). 1970. pap. 8.50 (ISBN 0-13-522458-6). P-H.

CIVILIZATION, INDO-EUROPEAN

see Indo-Europeans

CIVILIZATION, IRANIAN

Abbot, John. The Iranians: How They Live & Work. 168p. 1978. text ed. 8.95 (ISBN 0-03-042496-8, HoltC). HR&W.

CIVILIZATION, ISLAMIC

see also Civilization, Arab

Rodinson, Maxime. The Arabs. Goldhammer, Arthur, tr. LC 80-25916. (Illus.). 140p. 1981. lib. bdg. price not set (ISBN 0-226-72355-0); pap. price not set (ISBN 0-226-72356-9). U of Chicago Pr.

CIVILIZATION, JEWISH

see Jews–Civilization

CIVILIZATION, MEDIEVAL

see also Art, Medieval; Feudalism; Middle Ages; Monasticism and Religious Orders; Renaissance

Benson, Larry D & Leyerle, John, eds. Chivalric Literature: Essays on Relations Between Literature and Life in the Later Middle Ages. LC 80-17514. (Studies in Medieval Culture: XIV). (Illus.). 176p. (Orig.). 1980. pap. 10.80 (ISBN 0-918720-09-5). Medieval Inst.

Clogan, P. M., ed. Medievalia et Humanistica, Vols. 1-3 & 6-9. Incl. Vol. 1. LC 75-32451. 251p. 1976 (ISBN 0-521-21032-1); Vol. 2. Medieval & Renaissance Studies in Review. LC 75-32452. 223p (ISBN 0-521-21033-X); Vol. 3. Social Dimension in Medieval & Renaissance Studies. LC 75-32453. 328p (ISBN 0-521-21034-8); Vol. 6. LC 75-16872. 1979 (ISBN 0-521-20999-4); Vol. 7. Studies in Medieval & Renaissance Culture: Medieval Poetics. LC 76-12914. 1977 (ISBN 0-521-21331-2); Vol. 8. Studies in Medieval & Renaissance Culture Transformation & Continuity. LC 75-32451. 1978 (ISBN 0-521-21783-0); Vol. 9. LC 75-32451. 1979 (ISBN 0-521-22446-2). 36.00 ea. Cambridge U Pr.

Grabois, Ayreh. The Illustrated Encyclopedia of Medeival Civilization. (Illus.). 752p. 1980. 25.00 (ISBN 0-7064-0856-X). Mayflower Bks.

Hamilton, Bernard. Medieval Inquisition: Foundations of Medieval History. LC 80-27997. 110p. (Orig.). 1981. pap. text ed. 13.00x (ISBN 0-8419-0695-5). Holmes & Meier.

Sommerfeldt, John R. & Elder, E. Rozanne, eds. Studies in Medieval Culture, Vols. 6 & 7. combined ed. 1976. write for info. Medieval Inst.

Sommerfeldt, John R. & Elder, Rozanne E., eds. Studies in Medieval Culture, Vols. 8 & 9. combined ed. 1976. write for info. Medieval Inst.

Sommerfeldt, John R. & Seiler, Thomas H., eds. Studies in Medieval Culture, Vol. 1. 1977. write for info. Medieval Inst.

--Studies in Medieval Culture, Vol. 10. 1977. write for info. Medieval Inst.

--Studies in Medieval Culture, Vol. 12. 1978. write for info. Medieval Inst.

Tierney, Brian & Linehan, Peter, eds. Authority & Power. 274p. 1981. 59.50. Cambridge U Pr.

CIVILIZATION, MODERN–1950-

Benoit, Emile. Progress & Survival: An Essay on the Future of Mankind. Gohn, Jack B., ed. 144p. 1980. 17.95 (ISBN 0-03-056911-7). Praeger.

CIVILIZATION, MUSLIM

see Civilization, Islamic

CIVILIZATION, OCCIDENTAL

Angell, J. William & Helm, Robert M. Meaning & Value in Western Thought: A History of Ideas in Western Culture. LC 80-67174. (The Ancient Foundations Ser.: Vol. I). 434p. 1981. lib. bdg. 22.75 (ISBN 0-8191-1368-9); pap. text ed. 13.95 (ISBN 0-8191-1369-7). U Pr of Amer.

Cheilik, Michael. Western Civilization Vol. II, Since 1715. LC 80-66627. (Cliffs Rapid Review Ser.). 112p. (Orig.). (gr. 10-12). 1980. pap. text ed. 3.95 (ISBN 0-8220-1742-3). Cliffs.

Christopher, John B., et al. Civilization in the West, Pt. II. 4th ed. (Illus.). 512p. 1981. pap. text ed. 13.95 (ISBN 0-13-134932-5). P-H.

Gray, William G. An Outlook on Our Inner Western Way. 1980. pap. 6.95 (ISBN 0-87728-493-8). Weiser.

Parker, Frank A. Whither Civilization? 1981. 10.00 (ISBN 0-533-04882-6). Vantage.

Rudofsky, Bernard. Now I Lay Me Down to Eat: Notes & Footnotes on the Lost Art of Living. LC 80-714. (Illus.). 196p. 1980. pap. 10.95 (ISBN 0-385-15716-9, Anch). Doubleday.

Willis, F. Roy. Western Civilization: An Urban Perspective, 2 vols. 3rd ed. (Vol. 1, 688 pp.:vol. 2, 560 pp.). 1981. Vol. 1. pap. text ed. 12.95 (ISBN 0-669-03364-2); Vol. 2. pap. text ed. 12.95 (ISBN 0-669-03365-0); instructor's guide (ISBN 0-669-03366-9). Heath.

CIVILIZATION, OCCIDENTAL–HISTORY

Mork, Gordon R. Modern Western Civilization: A Concise History. LC 80-6198. 253p. (Orig.). 1981. lib. bdg. 19.25 (ISBN 0-8191-1434-0); pap. text ed. 10.00 (ISBN 0-8191-1435-9). U Pr of Amer.

CIVILIZATION, PRIMITIVE

see Society, Primitive

CIVILIZATION, SPANISH

see Civilization, Hispanic; Spain–Civilization

CIVILIZATION, WESTERN

see Civilization, Occidental

CIVILIZATION AND MACHINERY

see Technology and Civilization

CIVILIZATION AND SCIENCE

see Science and Civilization

CIVILIZATION AND TECHNOLOGY

see Technology and Civilization

CLANS AND CLAN SYSTEM

see also Kinship; Society, Primitive

also names of clans

Weiss, Al. Ninja: Clan of Death. (Orig.). 1981. pap. 2.50 (ISBN 0-671-43046-7). PB.

CLARES, POOR

see Poor Clares

CLARINET

Richmond, Stanley. Clarinet & Sax0 Phone Experience. 1980. 25.00x (Pub.by Darton-Longman-Todd England). State Mutual Bk.

CLARISSES
see Poor Clares
CLARK, GEORGE ROGERS, 1752-1818
Pease, Theodore C. & Pease, Marguerite J. George Rogers Clark & the Revolution in Illinois, Seventeen Sixty-Three to Seventeen Eighty-Seven. 1929. 3.00 (ISBN 0-912226-12-9). Ill St Hist So.
CLASS CONFLICT
see Social Conflict
CLASS DISTINCTION
see Social Classes
CLASS STRUGGLE
see Social Conflict
CLASSES, SOCIAL
see Social Classes
CLASSICAL ANTIQUITIES
see also Archaeology; Art, Greek; Art, Roman; Gems; Musical Instruments; Mythology, Classical; Pottery, Ancient; Pottery, Greek
also subdivision Antiquities under names of countries, e.g. Greece–Antiquities
Anderson, William S. & Puhvel, Jaan, eds. California Studies in Classical Antiquity, Vol. 12. LC 68-26906. (Illus.). 400p. 1981. 15.00x (ISBN 0-520-04055-4). U of Cal Pr.
CLASSICAL ARCHAEOLOGY
see Classical Antiquities
CLASSICAL DANCING
see Modern Dance
CLASSICAL FIELD THEORY
see Field Theory (Physics)
CLASSICAL LITERATURE–BIBLIOGRAPHY
American School of Classical Studies at Athens. Catalogue of the Gennadius Library: American School of Classical Studies at Athens. (Library Catalogs: Supplement 2). 1981. lib. bdg. 160.00 (ISBN 0-8161-0011-X). G K Hall.
CLASSICAL MYTHOLOGY
see Mythology, Classical
CLASSIFICATION
see also Information Storage and Retrieval Systems
also subdivision Classification under names of special subjects, e.g. Botany–Classification
Downing, Mildred H. Introduction to Cataloging & Classification. 5th ed. LC 80-20299. (Illus.). 240p. 1981. lib. bdg. 14.95x (ISBN 0-89950-017-X). McFarland & Co.
Schwartz, Barry. Vertical Classification: A Study in Structuralism & the Sociology of Knowledge. LC 80-24207. (Chicago Original Paperback Ser.). 232p. 1981. lib. bdg. 17.00x (ISBN 0-226-74208-3). U of Chicago Pr.
CLASSIFICATION–BOOKS
see also Classification, Library of Congress
Winans, Robert B. A Descriptive Checklist of Book Catalogues Separately Printed America. 1981. 35.00 (ISBN 0-912296-47-X, Dist. by U Pr of Va). Am Antiquarian.
CLASSIFICATION–BOOKS–BIBLIOGRAPHY
University of Cambridge. Classification Scheme & List of Subject Headings for the Squire Library of the Library of Cambridge. 1974. 20.00 (ISBN 0-379-20060-0). Oceana.
CLASSIFICATION–BOTANY
see Botany–Classification
CLASSIFICATION–PLANTS
see Botany–Classification
CLASSIFICATION, LIBRARY OF CONGRESS
Library of Congress Classification Adapted for Children's Materials. 3rd ed. LC 76-48893. 131p. 1976. 5.00 (ISBN 0-913578-14-2). Inglewood Ca.
CLASSROOM MANAGEMENT
Nier, Charles J. Dynamics of Classroom Structure. LC 80-69330. 140p. 1981. perfect bdg. 11.50 (ISBN 0-86548-052-4). Century Twenty One.
Phillips, Betty W., ed. Management of Behavior in the Classroom: A Handbook of Psychological Strategies. LC 79-66965. 232p. 1980. pap. text ed. 9.80x (ISBN 0-87424-162-6). Western Psych.
Raffini, James P. Discipline: Negotiating Conflicts with Today's Kids. 192p. 1980. 10.95 (Spec); pap. 3.95. P-H.
CLAUDIUS, EMPEROR OF ROME, B.C.10-A.D.54
Momigliano, Arnaldo. Claudius, the Emperor & His Achievement. rev. ed. Hogarth, W. D., tr. from Ital. LC 80-26158. xv, 143p. 1981. Repr. of 1961 ed. lib. bdg. 17.50x (ISBN 0-313-20813-1, MOCE). Greenwood.
CLAY, CASSIUS MARCELLUS, 1942-
Edwards, A. & Wohl, G. The Picture Life of Muhammad Ali. 1977. pap. 1.75 (ISBN 0-380-01904-3, 51623, Camelot). Avon.
CLAY, HENRY, 1777-1852
Curry, W. H. Sun Rising on the West: The Saga of Henry Clay & Elizabeth Smith. 1979. write for info. Crosby County.
CLAY
see also Ceramics; Modeling; Particles
Thomas Telford Editorial Staff, Ltd., ed. Clay Fills. 330p. 1980. 90.00x (ISBN 0-7277-0069-3, Pub. by Telford England). State Mutual Bk.
CLAY MODELING
see Modeling
CLEAN AND UNCLEAN
see Purity, Ritual
CLEANLINESS, RITUAL
see Purity, Ritual
CLEFT LIP
see Harelip
CLEFT PALATE
Edwards, et al. Advances in the Management of Cleft Palate. (Illus.). 1981. text ed. 30.00 (ISBN 0-443-01601-1). Churchill.
Melnick, Michael & Bixler, David, eds. Etiology of Cleft Lip & Cleft Palate. (Progress in Clinical & Biological Research: Vol. 46). 566p. 1980. 40.00 (ISBN 0-8451-0046-7). A R Liss.
CLEMENS, SAMUEL LANGHORNE, 1835-1910
Emberson, Frances G. Mark Twain's Vocabulary. 53p. 1980. Repr. of 1935 ed. lib. bdg. 12.50 (ISBN 0-89987-206-9). Darby Bks.
CLEMENS, SAMUEL LANGHORNE, 1835-1910–JUVENILE LITERATURE
Frevert, Patricia D. Mark Twain, an American Voice. Redpath, Ann, ed. (People to Remember Ser.). (Illus.). 32p. (gr. 5-9). 1981. PLB 5.95 (ISBN 0-87191-802-1). Creative Ed.
CLERGY
see also Bishops; Celibacy; Elders (Church Officers); Monasticism and Religious Orders; Pastoral Theology; Priests; Theologians; Women Clergy
also subdivision Clergy under church denominations, e.g. Church of England–Clergy
Ditchfield, P. H. The Old-Time Parson. 342p. 1980. Repr. of 1908 ed. lib. bdg. 35.00 (ISBN 0-89760-130-0). Telegraph Bks.
Gold, Don. The Priest. LC 80-22752. 320p. 1981. 13.95 (ISBN 0-03-053981-1). Hr&W.
Grollenberg, Lucas, et al. Minister? Pastor? Prophet? Grassroots Leadership in the Churches. 112p. (Dutch.). 1981. 9.95 (ISBN 0-8245-0017-2). Crossroad NY.
Harvey, H. El Pastor. Trevifio, Alejandro, tr. Orig. Title: The Pastor. 232p. (Span.). 1980. pap. 2.60 (ISBN 0-311-42025-7). Casa Bautista.
Laity, Edward. Priesthood, Old & New. 1980. 1.95 (ISBN 0-86544-012-3). Salvation Army.
Lindsay, Gordon. John Alexander Dowie: A Life of Tragedies & Triumphs. 1980. 4.95 (ISBN 0-89985-985-2). Christ Nations.
Mother Martha. Papa Nicholas Planas. Holy Transfiguration Monastery, ed. & tr. from Greek. (Orig.). 1981. pap. price not set (ISBN 0-913026-18-2). St Nectarios.
Nall, T. Otto. Builder of Bridges. LC 80-50241. 222p. 1980. text ed. 6.95x (ISBN 0-8358-0400-3). Upper Room.
Ramsden, William E. Ministries Through Non-Parish Institutions. LC 80-22294. (Into Our Third Century Ser.). 96p. (Orig.). 1981. pap. 3.95 (ISBN 0-687-27037-5). Abingdon.
Riggs, Ralph M., tr. O Guia Do Pastor. (Portugese Bks.). (Port.). 1979. 3.25 (ISBN 0-8297-0665-8); pap. 2.25 (ISBN 0-686-28815-7). Life Pubs Intl.
Robinson, Joseph A. Gilbert Crispin, Abbot of Westminster: A Study of the Abby Under Norman Rule. LC 80-2211. 1981. Repr. of 1911 ed. 32.50 (ISBN 0-404-18785-4). AMS Pr.
Scataglini, Alberto, et al, trs. Brujula Para el Ministro. (Spanish Bks.). 1979. 3.75 (ISBN 0-8297-0877-4). Life Pubs Intl.
Ziegler, Edward K. Tapestry of Grace. 158p. (Orig.). 1980. pap. 5.95 (ISBN 0-87178-834-9). Brethren.
CLERGY–CORRESPONDENCE, REMINISCENCES, ETC.
see also subdivision Clergy–Correspondence, Reminiscences, etc. under particular denominations, e.g. Catholic Church–Clergy–Correspondence, Reminiscences, etc.
Biebel, David. Jonathan: You Left Too Soon. 192p. 1981. 8.95 (ISBN 0-8407-5235-0). Nelson.
Krumm, John W. Why Choose the Episcopal Church? 1974. 1.35 (ISBN 0-686-28800-9). Forward Movement.
Lowman, J. Warren. Up from the Depths. 183p. 1926. pap. 3.00 (ISBN 0-917714-28-8). Beinfeld Pub.
McDuffie, Jack. Walk Out with Me. 1979. 1.80 (ISBN 0-686-28798-3). Forward Movement.
Paul, Cecil R. Passages of a Pastor. 128p. 1981. 6.95 (ISBN 0-310-43070-4, 11160). Zondervan.
Pruitt, Fred & Pruitt, Lawrence. God's Gracious Dealings. (Illus.). 496p. 5.00. Faith Pub Hse.
CLERGY–MAJOR ORDERS
see Bishops; Clergy
CLERGY–OFFICE
Brister, C. W., et al. Beginning Your Ministry. LC 80-25763. 160p. (Orig.). 1981. pap. 6.95 (ISBN 0-687-02780-2). Abingdon.
McElvaney, William K. The People of God in Ministry. LC 80-26077. 176p. (Orig.). 1981. pap. 6.95 (ISBN 0-687-30660-4). Abingdon.
CLERGY–RELIGIOUS LIFE
see also Retreats; Spiritual Direction
Manual Del Ministro. (Spanish Bks.). 1979. 2.50 (ISBN 0-8297-0581-3). Life Pubs Intl.
Manual Do Ministro. (Portugese Bks.). (Port.). 1979. 2.85 (ISBN 0-8297-0672-0). Life Pubs Intl.
CLERGY, TRAINING OF
see also Theology–Study and Teaching
Charry, Dana. Mental Health Skills for Clergy. 160p. 1981. 10.95 (ISBN 0-8170-0886-1). Judson.
CLERGYMEN'S WIVES
Benjamin, Carol. The Rib Section. (Orig.). 1981. pap. 4.95 (ISBN 0-88270-498-2). Logos.
Sinclair, Donna M. The Pastor's Wife Today. LC 80-26076. (Creative Leadership Ser.). 128p. (Orig.). 1981. pap. 4.95 (ISBN 0-687-30269-2). Abingdon.
CLERICAL CELIBACY
see Celibacy
CLERICAL MEDICINE
see Pastoral Medicine
CLERICAL PSYCHOLOGY
see Pastoral Psychology
CLEVELAND
Jedick, Peter. Cleveland: Where the East Coast Meets the Midwest. (Illus.). 105p. (Orig.). 1980. pap. 11.95 (ISBN 0-9605508-1-X). Jedick Ent.
CLEVELAND–HISTORY
Jedick, Peter. Cleveland: Where the East Coast Meets the Midwest. (Illus.). 105p. (Orig.). 1980. pap. 11.95 (ISBN 0-9605508-1-X). Jedick Ent.
CLIMATE
see Climatology
CLIMATE, INFLUENCE OF
see Architecture and Climate; Man–Influence of Environment
CLIMATE AND ARCHITECTURE
see Architecture and Climate
CLIMATOLOGY
see also Architecture and Climate; Bioclimatology; Meteorology; Rain and Rainfall; Weather
also names of countries, cities, etc. with or without the subdivision Climate
Bach, Wilfrid, et al, eds. Interactions of Energy & Climate. 568p. 1980. lib. bdg. 58.00 (ISBN 90-277-1179-8, Pub. by D. Reidel); pap. 26.50 (ISBN 90-277-1177-1). Kluwer Boston.
Griffiths, John F. & Driscoll, Dennis M. Survey of Climatology. 352p. 1981. text ed. 19.95 (ISBN 0-675-09994-3); instr's. manual 3.95 (ISBN 0-686-69500-3). Merrill.
Landsberg, Helmut. The Urban Climate. (International Geophysics Ser.). 1981. write for info. (ISBN 0-12-435960-4). Acad Pr.
Skinner, Brian J., ed. Climates Past & Present. (The Earth & Its Inhabitants: Selected Readings from American Scientist Ser.). (Illus.). 200p. (Orig.). 1981. pap. 9.95 (ISBN 0-913232-91-2). W Kaufmann.
CLIMATOLOGY, AGRICULTURAL
see Crops and Climate
CLIMBING PLANTS
Galet, Pierre. A Practical Ampelography: Grapevine Indentification. Morton, Lucie, tr. LC 78-59631. (Illus.). 192p. 1979. 28.50x (ISBN 0-8014-1240-4). Comstock.
Stokes, Donald. The Natural History of Wild Shrubs & Vines. LC 80-8219. (Illus.). 256p. 1981. 12.95 (ISBN 0-06-014163-8, HarpT). Har-Row.
CLINICAL CHEMISTRY
see Chemistry, Clinical
CLINICAL ENDOCRINOLOGY
see also Pediatric Endocrinology
Beardwell, C. Clinical Endocrinology: Pituitary, Vol. 1. (Butterworths International Medical Reviews Ser.). 1981. text ed. price not set (ISBN 0-407-02272-4). Butterworth.
Bloodworth, J. M., Jr. Endocrine Pathology: General & Surgical. 2nd ed. (Illus.). 950p. 1981. write for info. (0854-4). Williams & Wilkins.
Thomson, John A. Introduction to Clinical Endocrinology. 2nd ed. (Churchill Livingstone Medical Text Ser.). (Illus.). 220p. 1981. text ed. 10.75 (ISBN 0-443-02307-7). Churchill.
CLINICAL ENGINEERING
see Biomedical Engineering
CLINICAL ENZYMOLOGY
Burlina, A. & Galzigna, L., eds. Clinical Enzymology Symposia, Vol. 2. (Illus.). 646p. 1980. text ed. 49.50 (ISBN 88-212-0772-2, Pub. by Piccin Italy). J K Burgess.
Colowick, S. P., et al, eds. Methos in Enzymology: Lipids, Pt. D, Vol. 72. (Serial Publications). 1981. price not set (ISBN 0-12-181972-8). Acad Pr.
Foster, R. L. The Nature of Enzymology. 384p. 1980. 79.00x (ISBN 0-85664-434-X, Pub. by Croom Helm England). State Mutual Bk.
Meister, Alton, ed. Advances in Enzymology & Related Areas of Molecular Biology. Vol. 45, 1977. 36.50 (ISBN 0-471-02726-X, Pub. by Wiley-Interscience); Vol. 46, 1978. 41.50 (ISBN 0-471-02993-9); Vol. 47, 1978. 42.50 (ISBN 0-471-04116-5); Vol. 51, 1980, 225p. 29.50 (ISBN 0-471-05653-7). Wiley.
Nord, F. F. Advances in Enzymology. Incl. Vol. 14. 1953. 28.50 (ISBN 0-470-64647-0); Vol. 15. 1954. 31.50 (ISBN 0-470-64680-2); Vol. 23. 1961. 34.00 (ISBN 0-470-64944-5); Vol. 25. 1963. 34.00 (ISBN 0-470-64948-8). LC 41-9213 (Pub. by Wiley-Interscience). Wiley.
CLINICAL LABORATORY TECHNICIANS
see Medical Technologists
CLINICAL MEDICINE
see Medicine, Clinical
CLINICAL PARASITOLOGY
see Medical Parasitology
CLINICAL PSYCHOLOGY
Choca, James. Manual for Clinical Psychology Practicums. LC 80-18731. 172p. 1980. 15.00 (ISBN 0-87630-258-4); pap. 9.95 (ISBN 0-87630-240-1). Brunner-Mazel.
Corsini, Raymond. Handbook of Innovative Psychotherapies. 1100p. 1981. 40.00 (ISBN 0-471-06229-4, Pub. by Wiley-Interscience). Wiley.
CLINICAL PSYCHOLOGY–STUDY AND TEACHING
Lenburg, Carrie. The Clinical Performance Examination. 384p. 1979. 14.75 (ISBN 0-8385-1168-6). ACC.
CLINICAL RADIOLOGY
see Radiology, Medical
CLINICAL RECORDS
see Medical Records
CLITELLATA
see Oligochaeta
CLOCK AND WATCH MAKERS
Clutten, Cecil, ed. Britten's Old Clocks & Watches & Their Makers. 8th ed. (Illus.). 1973. 50.00 (ISBN 0-525-93140-6). Dutton.
CLOCK AND WATCH MAKING
see also Clocks and Watches
Chapalay & Mottier, ed. Swiss Watchmaking Year-Book, 1980-1981. 83rd ed. LC 46-34872. Orig. Title: Quid Horloger: Annuaire De L'Horlogerie Suisse. 602p. (Orig.). 1980. pap. write for info. (ISBN 0-8002-2751-4). Intl Pubns Serv.
Good, Richard. Watches in Color. (Illus.). 218p. 1981. pap. 6.95 (Pub. by Blandford Pr England). Sterling.
CLOCKS AND WATCHES
see also Clock and Watch Making; Time Measurements
Clutten, Cecil, ed. Britten's Old Clocks & Watches & Their Makers. 8th ed. (Illus.). 1973. 50.00 (ISBN 0-525-93140-6). Dutton.
Daniels, George & Markarian, Ohannes. Watches & Clocks in the Sir David Salomons Collection. (Illus.). 320p. 1981. 80.00x (ISBN 0-85667-074-X, Pub. by Sotheby Parke Bernet England). Biblio Dist.
The Hamburg-American Clock Company. 176p. 1980. soft cover 10.20 (ISBN 0-933396-10-4). Antique Clocks.
Husher, R. W. & Welch, W. W. A Study of Simon Willard's Clocks. LC 80-65021. (Illus.). 292p. 1980. 35.00x (ISBN 0-9603944-0-0). Husher & Welch.
Loomes, Brian. White Dial Clocks: The Complete Guide. (Illus.). 192p. 1981. price not set (ISBN 0-7153-8073-7). David & Charles.
Schorsch, Anita. The Warner Collector' Guide to American Clocks: 0the/Collectors' Guide to American Clocks. (Orig.). 1981. pap. 9.95 (ISBN 0-446-97633-4). Warner Bks.
Shugart, Cooksey. The Complete Guide to American Pocket Watches 1981: Pocket Watches from 1809-1950. Schrieber, Peter, ed. 1981. pap. 8.95 (ISBN 0-517-54378-8, Harmony). Crown.
CLOCKS AND WATCHES–JUVENILE LITERATURE
Imbo, M. Mi Querido Reloj. Mann, Philip, ed. Kreps, Georgian, tr. from Eng. (Shape Board Lay Book). Orig. Title: The Happy Clock Book. (Illus.). 14p. (Span.). (ps-3). 1981. bds. 3.50 plastic comb bdg (ISBN 0-89828-204-7, 5008SP). Tuffy Bks.
Klimo, Kate, ed. My Clock Book. (Playboards Ser.). (Illus.). 12p. (ps-k). Date not set. boards 2.95 (ISBN 0-671-42528-5, Little Simon). S&S.
CLOISTERS
see Monasteries
CLONING
see also Plant Propagation
Salman, Sydney E., ed. Cloning of Human Tumor Stem Cells. LC 80-19600. (Progress in Clinical & Biological Research: Vol. 48). 366p. 1980. 44.00 (ISBN 0-8451-0048-3). A R Liss.
CLOSE CORPORATIONS
Painter, William E. Corporate & Tax Aspects of Closely Held Corporations. 670p. 1981. write for info (ISBN 0-316-68868-1). Little.
CLOSED CORPORATIONS
see Close Corporations
CLOTH
see Textile Fabrics
CLOTHIERS
see Clothing Trade
CLOTHING
see Clothing and Dress; Costume
CLOTHING AND DRESS
Here are entered works dealing with clothing as a covering for the body and works on the art of dress. Descriptive and historical works on the costumes of particular countries, nations, or periods are entered under Costume.
see also Costume; Dressmaking; Fashion; Hats; Models, Fashion
Audette, Vicki. Dress for Less: One Thousand & One for Saving Money on Clothes. Grooms, Kathe, ed. (A Consumer-Aid Bk.). (Illus.). 160p. 1981. pap. 3.95 (ISBN 0-915658-33-X). Meadowbrook Pr.
Hearon, Shelby. Painted Dresses. LC 80-69644. 1981. 11.95 (ISBN 0-689-11155-X). Atheneum.
Humphreys, John. The Sportsman Head to Toe. (Illus.). 96p. (Orig.). 1980. pap. 8.50 (ISBN 0-85242-733-6). Intl Pubns Serv.
Jackson, Carole. Color Me Beautiful. 216p. 1981. pap. 8.95 (ISBN 0-345-29015-1). Ballantine.
Liddell, Louise A. Clothes & Your Appearance. rev. ed. LC 80-25167. (Illus.). 352p. 1981. text ed. 13.20 (ISBN 0-87006-311-1). Goodheart.
--Clothes & Your Appearance. rev. ed. LC 80-25167. (Illus.). 352p. 1980. 13.20 (ISBN 0-87006-311-1). Good Heart.
Rex, Chris. Comfort Clothes. LC 80-69534. (Illus.). 80p. (Orig.). pap. 7.95 (ISBN 0-89087-312-7). Celestial Arts.

--Comfort Clothes: How to Make & Wear West African Style Garments. LC 80-69534. (Illus.). 80p. 1981. 7.95 (ISBN 0-89087-312-7). Celestial Arts.

Schrader, Constance. Nine to Five: The Complete Looks, Clothes & Personality Handbook for the Working Woman. (Illus.). 200p. 1981. 13.95 (ISBN 0-13-622555-1); pap. 6.95 (ISBN 0-13-622563-2). P-H.

Stuvel, Pieke. A Touch of Style: Sewing Simple, Inventive Clothes. 96p. 1981. pap. 4.95 (ISBN 0-14-046482-4). Penguin.

Wallach, Janet. Working Wardrobe: An Easy, Affordable Approach to Successful Dressing. 1981. 14.95 (ISBN 0-87491-072-2). Acropolis.

CLOTHING AND DRESS–CLEANING

see Laundry

CLOTHING AND DRESS–JUVENILE LITERATURE

Charlton, Leigh & Swanberg, Annette. Glad Rags II. (Illus.). 168p. (Orig.). 1981. pap. 7.95 (ISBN 0-87701-178-8). Chronicle Bks.

Oxenbury, Helen. Dressing. (Baby Board Bks.). (Illus.). 12p. (ps-k). Date not set. boards 3.50 (ISBN 0-671-42113-1, Little Simon). S&S.

CLOTHING TRADE

International Labour Office. Contract Labour in the Clothing Industry: Second Tripartite Technical Meeting for the Clothing Industry, Geneva, 1980, Report II. ii, 75p. (Orig.). 1980. pap. 7.15 (ISBN 92-2-102432-6). Intl Labour Office.

--The Employment Effects on the Clothing Industry of Changes in International Trade: Second Tripartite Technical Meeting for the Clothing Industry, Geneve, 1980, Report III. ii, 49p. (Orig.). 1980. pap. 7.15 (ISBN 92-2-102433-4). Intl Labour Office.

--General Report: Second Tripartite Technical Meeting for the Clothing Industry, Geneva, 1980. v, 154p. (Orig.). 1980. pap. 11.40 (ISBN 92-2-102431-8). Intl Labour Office.

Solinger, Jacob. The Apparel Manufacturing Handbook. 800p. 1981. text ed. 60.00 (ISBN 0-442-21904-0). Van Nos Reinhold.

CLOUD MODIFICATION

see Weather Control

CLOWNS

see also Comedians

Radlauer, Ed & Radlauer, Ruth. Clown Mania. LC 80-21826. (Mania Bks). (Illus.). 32p. (gr. k-4). 1981. PLB 7.95g (ISBN 0-516-07783-X, Elk Grove Bks). Childrens.

Sanders, Toby. How to Be a Compleat Clown. LC 78-7520. (Illus.). 288p. 1980. pap. 7.95 (ISBN 0-8128-6090-X). Stein & Day.

Stolzenberg, Mark. Clown: For Circus & Stage. LC 80-54337. (Illus.). 1981. 12.95 (ISBN 0-8069-7034-0); lib. bdg. 11.69 (ISBN 0-8069-7035-9). Sterling.

CLUBS

see also Societies; Women–Societies and Clubs

also names of individual clubs

Thorndike, Edward. The Human Nature Club. 231p. 1980. Repr. of 1900 ed. lib. bdg. 25.00 (ISBN 0-8492-8410-4). R West.

Wolfers, Elsie E. & Evansen, Virginia B. Organizations, Clubs, Action Groups: How to Start Them, How to Run Them. 256p. 1981. 11.95 (ISBN 0-312-58791-0). St Martin.

CLYDE COMPANY

Brown, Philip L., ed. Clyde Company Papers. Incl. Vol. 2. 1836-40. 1952. 8.00x (ISBN 0-19-711411-3); Vol. 5. 1851-53. 1963. 11.25x (ISBN 0-19-711594-2); Vol. 6. 1854-58. 1968. 12.00x (ISBN 0-19-711627-2); Vol. 6. 1854-58. 1968. 12.00x (ISBN 0-19-711627-2). Oxford U Pr.

COACHES

see Carriages and Carts

COACHES, TRUCK

see Campers and Coaches, Truck

COAL

see also Coal Mines and Mining

Ackerman, Bruce A. & Hassler, William T. Clean Coal Dirty Air. (Illus.). 175p. 1981. 20.00x (ISBN 0-300-02628-5); pap. 5.95 (ISBN 0-300-02643-9). Yale U Pr.

Bloch, Carolyn C. Coal Information Sources & Data Bases. LC 80-22344. 128p. 1981. 24.00 (ISBN 0-8155-0830-1). Noyes.

Braunstein & Copenhaver. Environmental, Health & Control Aspects of Coal Conversion: An Information Overview, 2 vols. 1338p. 1981. Set. text ed. 90.00 (ISBN 0-250-40445-1). Ann Arbor Science.

Business Communications Co. Future for Coal As a Fuel & Chemical, E-004. 1980. 825.00 (ISBN 0-89336-273-5). BCC.

Coal Burning with Clean Emissions: F.G.D.(Flue Gas Desulfurization. 1981. price not set. Inform.

Coal Cleaning: Rediscovered for the Eighties. 1981. price not set. Inform.

Evans, T. J. Bituminous Coal in Texas. (Illus.). 65p. 1974. 2.00 (HB 4). Bur Econ Geology.

Falbe, Jurgen. Chemical Feedstocks from Coal. 730p. 1981. 50.00 (ISBN 0-471-05291-4, Pub. by Wiley-Interscience). Wiley.

Meyers. Coal Handbook. Date not set. price not set (ISBN 0-8247-1270-6). Dekker.

Morrison, James W. The Complete Coalburning Stove & Furnace Guide. (Illus.). 288p. 1981. 11.95 (ISBN 0-668-05097-7, 5097-7). Arco.

The National Coal Policy Project. 83p. 1979. pap. 10.00 (ISBN 0-686-68797-3, CSIS016, CSIS). Unipub.

Nelson, Robert V. Coal: The New Energy Source. Ide, Arthur F., ed. LC 79-9940. (E Equals M C Squared Ser.). (Illus.). 70p. (Orig.). 1981. 12.00 (ISBN 0-86663-804-0); pap. 7.50 (ISBN 0-86663-805-9). Ide Hse.

Sullivan, Richard F., ed. Upgrading Coal Liquids. (ACS Symposium Ser.: No. 156). 1981. price not set (ISBN 0-8412-0629-5). Am Chemical.

COAL–COMBUSTION

see Combustion

COAL–JUVENILE LITERATURE

Davey, John. Mining Coal. (Junior Reference Ser.). (Illus.). 64p. 7.95 (ISBN 0-7136-1596-6). Dufour.

COAL LANDS

see Coal

COAL MINERS–GREAT BRITAIN

Brown, Harold. Most Splendid Men. (Illus.). 192p. 1981. 12.50 (ISBN 0-7137-1107-8, Pub. by Blandford Pr England). Sterling.

Thompson, G. McKecknie & Rodin, S. Colliery Spoil Tips-After Aberfan. 98p. 1980. pap. 15.00x (ISBN 0-901948-59-4, Pub. by Telford England). State Mutual Bk.

COAL MINES AND MINING

Casper, Barry M. & Wellstone, Paul D. Powerline: The First Battle of America's Energy War. 336p. 1981. lib. bdg. 18.50x (ISBN 0-87023-320-3); pap. 7.95 (ISBN 0-87023-321-1). U of Mass Pr.

Electric Power Research Institute. The Kaiparowits Coal Project & the Environment. 1980. text ed. 14.95 (ISBN 0-250-40399-4). Ann Arbor Science.

Spearman, James E. United States Metallurgical Coal Industry. 209p. 1980. 12.50 (ISBN 0-937058-00-9). West Va U Lib.

Strip-Mineable Coals Guidebook. LC 80-81269. 1980. 103.00. Minobras.

Technology & Labour in Japanese Coal Mining. 65p. 1980. pap. 5.00 (ISBN 92-808-0082-5, TUNU090, UNU). Unipub.

Zimmerman, Martin B. The U. S. Coal Industry: The Economics of Policy Change. 256p. 1982. text ed. 27.50. MIT Pr.

COAL MINES AND MINING–JUVENILE LITERATURE

see Coal–Juvenile Literature

COAL MINES AND MINING–SAFETY REGULATIONS

Reeder, R. T., ed. Fifth Institute on Coal Mine Health & Safety: Proceedings. (Fifth Proceedings Ser.). (Illus.). 380p. (Orig.). 1980. pap. text ed. 12.00 (ISBN 0-918062-41-1). Colo Sch Mines.

COAL OIL

see Petroleum

COAST-PILOT GUIDES

see Pilot Guides

COASTAL ECOLOGY

see Seashore Ecology

COASTAL ZONE MANAGEMENT

see also Marine Pollution

Barnes, R. S. Coastal Lagoons. LC 80-40041. (Cambridge Studies in Modern Biology: No. 1). (Illus.). 130p. 1980. 29.50 (ISBN 0-521-23422-0); pap. 11.95 (ISBN 0-521-29945-4). Cambridge U Pr.

Center for Ocean Management Studies, ed. Comparative Marine Policy. 336p. 1980. 26.95 (ISBN 0-03-058307-1). Praeger.

Proceedings of the Jakarta Workshop on Coastal Resources Managements. 106p. 1980. pap. 15.00 (ISBN 0-686-68813-9, TUNU100, UNU). Unipub.

COASTS

see also Coastal Zone Management; Ocean Waves

Ringold, Paul L. & Clark, John. The Coastal Almanac: For 1980--the Year of the Coast. LC 80-22501. (Geology Ser.). (Illus.). 1980. 19.95x (ISBN 0-7167-1285-7); pap. 9.95x (ISBN 0-7167-1286-5). W H Freeman.

COASTWISE NAVIGATION

Oldale, Adrienne & Oldale, Peter. Navigating Britain's Coastline: Portland to Dover. LC 80-68901. (Illus.). 88p. 1981. 18.50 (ISBN 0-7153-7960-7). David & Charles.

Toghill, Jeff. Coastal Navigation for Beginners. 1980. pap. 7.95x (ISBN 0-8464-1001-X). Beekman Pubs.

COATINGS, PROTECTIVE

see Protective Coatings

COATS OF ARMS

see Heraldry

COBOL (COMPUTER PROGRAM LANGUAGE)

Brown, Gary D. Beyond Cobol: Survival in Business Applications Programming. 225p. 1981. 17.50 (ISBN 0-471-09030-1, Pub. by Wiley-Interscience). Wiley.

Chappell, James D. Cobol Demand Processing Manual. 80p. 1981. pap. text ed. 6.95 (ISBN 0-8403-2376-X). Kendall-Hunt.

Grauer, R. Cobol: A Vehicle for Information Systems. 1981. 18.95 (ISBN 0-13-139709-5). P-H.

Grauer, Robert T. A Cobol Book of Practice & Reference. (P-H Software Ser.). (Illus.). 352p. 1981. pap. text ed. 15.95 (ISBN 0-13-139717-6). P-H.

Grauer, Robert T. & Crawford, Marshal A. Structured COBOL: A Pragmatic Approach. (Illus.). 544p. 1981. pap. text ed. 19.95 (ISBN 0-13-854455-7). P-H.

Philippakis, Andreas S. & Kazmier, Leonard J. Structured COBOL. 2nd ed. Stewart, Charles E., ed. (Illus.). 448p. 1981. pap. text ed. 13.95 (ISBN 0-07-049801-6); instrs'. manual 5.95 (ISBN 0-07-049802-4). McGraw.

Popkin, Gary S. Introductory Structured COBOL Programming. 496p. 1981. text ed. 18.95 (ISBN 0-442-26771-1). Van Nos Reinhold.

Schecter, David & Yukoff, George. The Structured COBOL Report Writer. 1981. text ed. 17.95 (ISBN 0-8359-7097-3). Reston.

Welburn, Tyler. Structured COBOL: Fundamentals & Style. (Illus.). 640p. (Orig.). 1981. pap. text ed. price not set (ISBN 0-87484-543-2). Mayfield Pub.

COCAINE

Lee, David. Cocaine Handbook. 192p. 1981. price not set. And-or Pr.

COCHITI INDIANS

see Indians of North America–Southwest, New

COCKATEELS

Kates, Steve. Encyclopedia of Cockatoos. (Illus.). 221p. 1980. 20.00 (ISBN 0-87666-896-1, H-1023). TFH Pubns.

Rogers, Cyril H. Cockatiels. (Illus.). 80p. 1981. 3.95 (ISBN 0-903264-26-9, 5212-0, Pub. by K & R Bks England). Arco.

Sturman, Julie & Schults, Dorothy. Breeding Cockatiels. (Illus.). 93p. 1980. 2.95 (ISBN 0-87666-889-9, KW-099). TFH Pubns.

COCONUT

Nair, P. K. Intensive Multiple Cropping with Coconuts in India: Principles, Programmes & Prospects. (Advances in Agronomy & Crop Science Ser.: Vol. 6). (Illus.). 148p. (Orig.). 1979. pap. text ed. 28.00 (ISBN 3-489-71210-2). Parey Sci Pubs.

CODE NAMES

see also Ciphers

Gardner, Martin. Codes, Ciphers & Secret Writing. (gr. 5-7). 1979. pap. 1.25 (ISBN 0-671-29954-9). PB.

CODICILS

see Wills

COEFFICIENT OF EXPANSION

see Gases

COELENTERATA

The Coelomycetes. 694p. 1981. 115.00 (ISBN 0-85198-446-0, CAB 7, CAB). Unipub.

COEXISTENCE

see United States–Foreign Relations–Russia; World Politics–1945-

COFFEE

Davids, Kenneth & Duniec, M. L. Coffee: A Revised Guide to Buying, Brewing & Enjoying. rev. ed. (Illus.). 192p. 1981. pap. 6.95 (ISBN 0-89286-186-X). One Hurd One Prods.

Stewart, Hilary. Wild Teas, Coffees, & Cordials. (Illus.). 128p. 1981. 7.95 (ISBN 0-295-95804-9). U of Wash Pr.

COFFEE TRADE

Priovolos, Theophilos. Coffee & the Ivory Coast: An Econometric Study. LC 80-8630. (The Wharton Econometric Studies). (Illus.). 240p. 1981. 24.95 (ISBN 0-669-04331-1). Lexington Bks.

COGNAC

see Brandy

COGNITION

see also Knowledge, Theory Of; Perception

Anderson, John R., ed. Cognitive Skills & Their Acquisition. (Carnegie Symposia on Cognition). 384p. 1981. ref. 24.95 (ISBN 0-89859-093-0). L Erlbaum Assocs.

Bickhard, Mark H. Cognition, Convention, & Communication. 210p. 1980. 24.95 (ISBN 0-03-056098-5). Praeger.

Bresnan, Joan, ed. The Mental Representation of Grammatical Relations. (Cognitive Theory & Mental Representation Ser.: Vol. 1). 700p. 1981. text ed. 35.00x (ISBN 0-262-02158-7). MIT Pr.

Estes, W. K., ed. Handbook of Learning & Cognitive Processes, 6 vols. Incl. Vol. 1. Introduction to Concepts & Issues. LC 75-20113. 303p. 1975. o.p. (ISBN 0-470-24585-9); Vol. 2. Conditioning & Behavior Therapy. LC 75-20113. 350p. 1975. 18.50 (ISBN 0-470-24586-7); Vol. 3. Approaches to Human Learning & Motivation. LC 76-15010. 1976. 18.50 (ISBN 0-470-15121-8); Vol. 4. Attention & Memory. LC 76-26002. 1976. o.p. (ISBN 0-470-98908-4); Vol. 5. Human Information Processing. LC 78-3847. 1978. 26.50 (ISBN 0-470-26310-5); Vol. 6. Linguistic Functions in Cognitive Theory. 1978. 18.00 (ISBN 0-470-26311-3). Halsted Pr.

Flowers, John H., ed. Nebraska Symposium on Motivation, 1980: Human Cognition. LC 53-11655. (Nebraska Symposium on Motivation: Vol. 28). 264p. 1981. 16.50x (ISBN 0-8032-0620-8); pap. 9.95x (ISBN 0-8032-0621-6). U of Nebr Pr.

Fodor, Jerry A. Representations: Philosophical Essays on the Foundations of Cognitive Science. LC 81-24313. (Illus.). 384p. 1981. text ed. 20.00 (ISBN 0-89706-011-3). Bradford Bks.

Hamilton, David L., ed. Cognitive Processes in Stereotyping & Intergroup Behavior. 384p. 1981. prof. - refer. 24.95 (ISBN 0-89859-081-7). L Erlbaum Assocs.

Harvey, John L., ed. Cognition, Social Behavior, & the Environment. 600p. 1981. ref. 29.95 (ISBN 0-89859-082-5). L Erlbaum Assocs.

Haugeland, John C. Mind Design: Philosophy, Psychology, Artifical Intelligence. LC 81-24275. Orig. Title: Mind Design. (Illus.). 368p. 1981. text ed. 21.50 (ISBN 0-89706-004-0); pap. text ed. 10.00 (ISBN 0-89706-005-9). Bradford Bks.

Kettelkamp, Larry. Your Marvelous Mind. LC 80-18614. (Illus.). (gr. 5-8). 9.95 (ISBN 0-664-32670-6). Westminster.

Mayer, Richard E. The Promise of Cognitive Psychology. LC 80-39997. (Psychology Ser.). (Illus.). 1981. text ed. 10.95x (ISBN 0-7167-1275-X); pap. text ed. 5.95x (ISBN 0-7167-1276-8). W H Freeman.

Pirozzolo, Francis J. & Wittrock, Merlin C. Neuropsychological & Cognitive Processes in Reading. (Perspectives in Neurolinguistics & Psycholinguistics Ser.). 1981. price not set (ISBN 0-12-557360-X). Acad Pr.

Shapiro, Edna K. & Weber, Evelyn, eds. Cognitive & Affective Growth: Developmental Interaction. 240p. 1981. ref. 19.95 (ISBN 0-89859-092-2). L Erlbaum Assocs.

Stone, Gerald L. A Cognitive-Behavioral Approach Psychology: Implications for Practice, Research, & Training. LC 80-21344. 256p. 1980. 21.95 (ISBN 0-03-055926-X). Praeger.

Weimer, Walter B. & Palermo, David, eds. Cognition & the Symbolic Processes, Vol. 2. 426p. 1981. professional ref. text 24.95 (ISBN 0-89859-066-3). L Erlbaum Assocs.

COGNITION (CHILD PSYCHOLOGY)

Biber, Barbara, et al. Promoting Cognitive Growth: A Developmental-Interaction Point of View. 2nd ed. LC 72-154558. (Illus.). 64p. 1977. pap. text ed. write for info. (126). Natl Assn Child Ed.

COIFFURE

see Hairdressing

COIN COLLECTING

see Numismatics–Collectors and Collecting

COINAGE

see also Gold; Mints; Money; Quantity Theory of Money; Silver Question

Baldwin, A. The Coinages of Lapsakos. (Illus.). 111p. 1980. 30.00 (ISBN 0-916710-70-X). Obol Intl.

MacDonald, George. The Evolution of Coinage. viii, 148p. 1980. 20.00 (ISBN 0-916710-73-4). Obol Intl.

COINING, ILLICIT

see Counterfeits and Counterfeiting

COINS

Here are entered lists of coins, specimens, etc. Works about coins are entered under the heading numismatics.

see also Tokens

also names of coins

Hultsch, F. Die Polemaischen Munz-und Rechnugswerte. 66p. (Ger.). 15.00 (ISBN 0-916710-81-5). Obol Intl.

Leighton, Philip. Coins & Tokens. (Junior Reference Ser.). (Illus.). 64p. (gr. 7 up). 1972. 7.95 (ISBN 0-7136-1238-X). Dufour.

Thompson, Richard. World Coins & Their Values. 224p. (gr. 8 up). Date not set. 3.95 (ISBN 0-307-24408-3, Golden Pr). Western Pub.

COINS–COLLECTORS AND COLLECTING

see Numismatics–Collectors and Collecting

COINS, AMERICAN

Badnow, William R., ed. Edmund's United States Coin Prices. (Orig.). 1981. pap. 2.50 (ISBN 0-440-01794-7, Pub. by Edmund). Dell.

Beginners Coin Collecting Kit: For U. S. Coins. (gr. 4 up). 1980. 5.95 (ISBN 0-307-09394-8). Western Pubs OH.

Bowse, Robert A., ed. United States Coin Prices, 1980 to 1981. (Illus.). 304p. (Orig.). 1980. pap. 3.95 (ISBN 0-937458-04-X). Harris & Co.

COINS, ANCIENT

A Catalogue of the Coins of Dalmatia et Albania (1410-1797) (Illus.). 1980. pap. 5.00 (ISBN 0-916710-67-X). Obol Intl.

Heiss, Aloiss. Description Generale Des Monnaies Des Rois Wisigoths d'Espagne. (Illus.). iv, 185p. (Fr.). 1980. Repr. 30.00 (ISBN 0-916710-64-5). Obol Intl.

Imhoof-Blumer, F. Mallos, Megarsos, Antioche du Pyramos. 37p. (Fr.). 1979. pap. 5.00 (ISBN 0-916710-58-0). Obol Intl.

COINS, BRITISH

Galster, Georg. Sylloge of Coins of the British Isles-National Museum, Copenhagen, Royal Collection of Coins & Metals: Anglo-Saxon Coins, Aethelred II, Vol. 2. 1966. 25.75x (ISBN 0-19-725896-4). Oxford U Pr.

Smart, Veronica, ed. Sylloge of Coins of the British Isles, Vol. 28. 164p. 1981. 74.00 (ISBN 0-19-726002-0). Oxford U Pr.

COINS, CHINESE

Coole, Arthur B. The Earliest Round Coins of China. (Encyclopedia of Chinese Coins Ser.: Vol. 7). 325p. Date not set. lib. bdg. 35.00 (ISBN 0-88000-122-4). Quarterman.

COINS, CYPRIAN

Lambros, Paul. Unpublished Coins of the Medieval Kingdom of Cyprus. Toumazou, Michael, tr. from Gr. (Illus.). 170p. (Eng., Fr., Gr.). 20.00 (ISBN 0-916710-76-9). Obol Intl.

COINS, ENGLISH

see Coins, British

COINS, GREEK
Bompois, H. F. Examen Chronologique des Monnais Frappes par la Communaute des Macedoniens Avant, Pendant et Apes la Conquete Romaine. (Illus.). 102p. (Fr.). 20.00 (ISBN 0-916710-77-7). Obol Intl.
Jameson, R. Monnaies Grecques Antiques et Romaines. 1007p. (Fr.). 1980. Repr. 295.00 (ISBN 0-916710-65-3). Obol Intl.
Kambanis, M. L. Notes Sur le Classement Chronologique Des Monnaies D'athenes (Series Avec Noms De Magistrats) (Illus., Fr.). pap. 5.00 (ISBN 0-916710-78-5). Obol Intl.
Milne, J. G. Greek & Roman Coins & the Study of History. (Illus.). 128p. 1980. 30.00. Obol Intl.
Ravel, O. E. Numismatique Grecque Falsifications Moyens Pour les Reconnaitre. 105p. (Fr.). 1980. Repr. of 1946 ed. 20.00 (ISBN 0-916710-71-8). Obol Intl.
Seltman, Charles. Masterpieces of Greek Coinage. (Illus.). 128p. 1980. 20.00 (ISBN 0-916710-72-6). Obol Intl.

COINS, MEDIEVAL
Lambros, Paul. Unpublished Coins of the Medieval Kingdom of Cyprus. Toumazou, Michael, tr. from Gr. (Illus.). 170p. (Eng., Fr., Gr.). 20.00 (ISBN 0-916710-76-9). Obol Intl.

COINS, MEXICAN
Grove, Frank W. The Coins of Mexico. 1981. lib. bdg. 60.00 (ISBN 0-88000-123-2). Quarterman.

COINS, ROMAN
Jameson, R. Monnaies Grecques Antiques et Romaines. 1007p. (Fr.). 1980. Repr. 295.00 (ISBN 0-916710-65-3). Obol Intl.
Mattingly, H. Aes & Pecunia Records of Roman Currency Down to 269 B. C. Date not set. pap. 3.00 (ISBN 0-916710-51-3). Obol Intl.
Milne, J. G. Greek & Roman Coins & the Study of History. (Illus.). 128p. 1980. 30.00. Obol Intl.
Newell, Edward F. The Pre-Imperial Coinage of Roman Antioch. 45p. 1980. pap. 5.00 (ISBN 0-916710-66-1). Obol Intl.

COLD–PHYSIOLOGICAL EFFECT
Killian, H. Cold & Frost Injuries: Rewarming Damages. (Disaster Medicine: Vol. 3). (Illus.). 260p. 1981. pap. 49.60 (ISBN 0-387-08991-8). Springer-Verlag.

COLD (DISEASE)
Clark, Oliver. Never Catch Colds Again. 64p. 1979. pap. 6.95x (ISBN 0-8464-1035-4). Beekman Pubs.

COLD COOKERY
see Cookery (Cold Dishes)

COLD STRESS (BIOLOGY)
see Cold–Physiological Effect

COLD WAR
see World Politics–1945-

COLERIDGE, SAMUEL TAYLOR, 1772-1834
Garnett, Richard. Coleridge. 111p. 1980. Repr. of 1904 ed. lib. bdg. 12.50 (ISBN 0-89987-307-3). Darby Bks.
Marks, Emerson R. Coleridge on the Language of Verse. (Princeton Essays in Literature). 116p. 1981. 9.50x (ISBN 0-691-06458-X). Princeton U Pr.

COLERIDGE, SAMUEL TAYLOR, 1772-1834–BIBLIOGRAPHY
Haney, John L. A Bibliography of Samuel Taylor Coleridge. 144p. 1980. Repr. of 1903 ed. lib. bdg. 20.00 (ISBN 0-8495-2299-4). Arden Lib.
Milton, Mary Lee. The Poetry of Samual Traylor Coleridge: An Annotated Bibliography of Criticism, 1935 to 1970. LC 80-83650. 250p. 1981. lib. bdg. 30.00 (ISBN 0-8240-9451-4). Garland Pub.

COLERIDGE-TAYLOR, SAMUEL, 1875-1912
Roper, Derek. Wordsworth & Coleridge - Lyrical Ballads 1805. 2nd ed. 432p. 1976. pap. 12.95 (ISBN 0-7121-0140-3, Pub. by Macdonald & Evans England). Intl Ideas.

COLITIS
Goulston, S. J. & McGovern, V. J. The Basic Facts About Colitis. (Illus.). 144p. 1981. 25.00 (ISBN 0-08-026862-5); pap. 11.20 (ISBN 0-08-026861-7). Pergamon.

COLLABORATIONISTS
see Treason

COLLAGE
see also Fabric Pictures
Romano, Clare & Ross, John. The Complete Collagraph: The Art & Technique of Printmaking from Collage Plates. (Illus.). 1980. 29.95 (ISBN 0-02-926770-6). Macmillan.

COLLAGEN DISEASES
see also Arthritis; Rheumatoid Arthritis
Cousins, Norman. Anatomy of an Illness As Perceived by the Patient. 176p. 1981. pap. 4.95 (ISBN 0-553-01293-2). Bantam.

COLLAPSE OF BUILDINGS
see Building Failures

COLLECTING
see Collectors and Collecting

COLLECTING OF ACCOUNTS
Felix, Ervin J. Banknote Collector's Guide & Companion. DeLenc, Marcus F., ed. (Illus.). 144p. (Orig.). pap. 1.50 (ISBN 0-937458-03-1). Harris & Co.
Whalen, Harold B. & Nickerson, Robert L. Getting Paid: Practical Credit Collection Techniques for Business & Industry. LC 80-82730. (Illus.). 135p. (Orig.). 1980. pap. 10.00 (ISBN 0-937788-00-7). Kalum Pr.

COLLECTION LETTERS
see Collecting of Accounts

COLLECTIVE BARGAINING
see also Arbitration, Industrial; Strikes and Lockouts; Trade-Unions
Herman, E. Edward. Collective Bargaining & Labor Relations. (Illus.). 576p. 1981. text ed. 19.95 (ISBN 0-13-140558-6). P-H.
Lieberman, Myron. Public-Sector Bargaining: A Policy of Reappraisal. LC 80-8426. 1980. 19.95 (ISBN 0-669-04110-6). Lexington Bks.
Neal, Richard G. & Felts, Frances I. Bargaining Tactics: A Reference Manual for Public Sector Labor Negotiations. LC 80-83023. 275p. 1981. 30.00 (ISBN 0-686-28742-8); pap. 25.00 (ISBN 0-686-28743-6). Neal Assoc.
O'Reilly, Robert C. & O'Reilly, Marjorie I. Librarians & Labor Relations: Employment Under Union Contracts. LC 80-1049. (Contributions in Librarianship & Information Science Ser.: No. 35). 208p. 1981. lib. bdg. 25.00 (ISBN 0-313-22485-4, OLL/). Greenwood.
Prasow, Paul & Peters, Edward. Arbitration & Collective Bargaining. 2nd ed. 480p. 22.00x (ISBN 0-07-050674-4, C). McGraw.
Stokes, Arch. The Collective Bargaining Handbook for Hotels, Restaurants & Institutions. (The Stokes Employee Relations Ser.). 352p. 1981. spiral bdg. 39.95 (ISBN 0-8436-2149-4). CBI Pub.

COLLECTIVE BARGAINING–CIVIL SERVICE
see Collective Bargaining–Government Employees

COLLECTIVE BARGAINING–EDUCATION
Thomson, A. W. J. Introduction to Collective Bargining in Higher Education. (Key Issues Ser.: No. 16). 1974. pap. 2.00 (ISBN 0-87546-250-2). NY Sch Indus Rel.

COLLECTIVE BARGAINING–ENGINEERS
Howie, Will. Trade Unions & the Professional Engineer. 80p. 1980. 15.00x (ISBN 0-7277-0044-8, Pub. by Telford England). State Mutual Bk.

COLLECTIVE BARGAINING–GOVERNMENT EMPLOYEES
Salerno, Charles. Police at the Bargaining Table. 1981. write for info (ISBN 0-398-04462-7). C C Thomas.

COLLECTIVE PSYCHOTHERAPY
see Group Psychotherapy

COLLECTIVE SECURITY
see Security, International

COLLECTIVE SETTLEMENTS–ISRAEL
Leviatan, Uri, ed. Work & Organization in Kibbutz Industry. Rosner, Menachem, tr. 204p. 1980. lib. bdg. 20.00 (ISBN 0-8482-1640-7). Norwood Edns.

COLLECTORS AND COLLECTING
see also Antiques; Book Collecting; Hobbies
also names of objects collected, e.g. Postage-Stamps–Collectors and Collecting
Connolly, Robert D. The New Collector's Directory for the 1980's. rev. 2nd ed. (Illus.). 168p. 1980. pap. 5.95 (ISBN 0-914598-38-4). Padre Prods.
DiNoto, Andrea. Collector's Guide to U.S. Auctions & Flea Markets. 320p. (Orig.). 1981. pap. 7.95 (ISBN 0-14-046481-6). Penguin.
Herzog, David A. Collecting Today for Tomorrow. LC 79-18557. (Illus.). 192p. 1981. pap. 4.95 (ISBN 0-668-04883-2, 4883). Arco.
Kirsch, Francine. Collecting Chromos. LC 80-26616. (Illus.). 288p. 1981. 25.00 (ISBN 0-498-02517-9). A S Barnes.
Klamkin, Marian & Klamkin, Charles. Collectibles: A Compendium. LC 77-37677. (Illus.). 288p. 1981. pap. 10.95 (ISBN 0-385-12176-8, Dolp). Doubleday.
Wiliams, Guy. Instructions to Young Collectors. 9.75x (ISBN 0-392-07941-0, SpS). Soccer.

COLLECTORS AND COLLECTING–DIRECTORIES
Beitman, Hartford. Directory of Antique Radio Collectors & Suppliers. 5th ed. (Orig.). 1980. pap. 3.00x (ISBN 0-938630-00-8); notebook 4.00x (ISBN 0-938630-01-6). Antique Radio.
Rogers, Carole. How to Collect: A Complete Guide. 1981. 12.95 (ISBN 0-525-93190-2); pap. 6.95 (ISBN 0-525-47671-7). Dutton.

COLLEGE, CHOICE OF
Brawner, Julie R., et al. From the Kudzu to the Ivy: How to Find Your College: a Southerner's Guide to Northeastern Colleges. 256p. (Orig.). (YA) (gr. 11-12). 1980. pap. 5.95. Kudzu-Ivy.

COLLEGE ADMISSION
see Universities and Colleges–Admission

COLLEGE ATHLETICS
see Athletics; College Sports; Track-Athletics

COLLEGE CHEERS
see Cheers and Cheerleading

COLLEGE COSTS
Peterson's Guides Editors, compiled by. After Scholarships, What: Sixteen Ways to Reduce Your College Costs. 400p. 1981. pap. 8.00 (ISBN 0-87866-129-8). Petersons Guid.

COLLEGE DEGREES
see Degrees, Academic

COLLEGE ENTRANCE REQUIREMENTS
see Universities and Colleges–Admission

COLLEGE FACULTY
see Universities and Colleges–Faculty

COLLEGE GRADUATES
Moravisin, Sylvester. Why Our Universities Are Turning Out Ordinary Barbarians. (American Culture Library). (Illus.). 105p. 1981. 47.85 (ISBN 0-89266-299-9). Am Classical Coll Pr.

COLLEGE LIBRARIES
see Libraries, University and College

COLLEGE LIFE
see College Students

COLLEGE PRESIDENTS
see Universities and Colleges–Administration

COLLEGE RADIO STATIONS
see Radio Stations

COLLEGE READERS
Here are entered selections of reading material in the English language, literary as well as non-literary, compiled for teaching rhetoric, comprehension and related topics on the college level; General literary selections are entered under appropriate literature headings, e. g. American Literature.
Kolzow, Lee & Lehman, Jane. College Reading: Strategies for Success. (Illus.). 352p. 1981. pap. text ed. 8.95 (ISBN 0-13-150052-X). P-H.
Stubbs, Marcia & Barnet, Sylvan. The Little Brown Reader. 2nd ed. 1980. pap. text ed. 8.95 (ISBN 0-316-82002-4); instr's manual free (ISBN 0-316-82003-2). Little.

COLLEGE SPORTS
see also Baseball; Basketball; Football; Intramural Sports; Soccer; Sports; Track-Athletics
also names of colleges, universities, etc., with or without the subdivision Athletics
Florence, Mal. Trojan Heritage: A Pictorial History of USC Football. LC 80-84556. (Illus.). 184p. 1980. 16.95 (ISBN 0-938694-01-4). JCP Corp VA.

COLLEGE STUDENT ORIENTATION
Brechner, Irv. The College Survival Kit. 96p. 1980. pap. 2.95. Bantam.
Carnes, Ralph & Carnes, Valerie. The Essential College Survival Handbook: An Insider's Guide to Making College Work for You. 224p. 1981. 12.95 (ISBN 0-87223-684-6); pap. 6.95 (ISBN 0-87223-694-3). Playboy.
Case, Harry L. Commencement Address: A Talk to University Freshmen & Other Heretical Essays. Date not set. 7.95 (ISBN 0-533-04579-7). Vantage.
Haponski, William C. & McCabe, Charles. Back to School: A College Guide for Adults. Leedham, Linnea, ed. (Illus.). 256p. cancelled (ISBN 0-88421-095-2); pap. cancelled (ISBN 0-88421-172-X). Butterick Pub.
Rich, Dale. How You Can Get Straight A's in College by Beating the System. 123p. (Orig.). 1981. 9.95 (ISBN 0-89896-099-1). Larksdale.
Shanahan, William F. The Parent Student College Planning Guide. LC 80-24467. 224p. (Orig.). 1981. pap. 6.95 (ISBN 0-668-04996-0, 4996). Arco.

COLLEGE STUDENTS
Council on Learning's National Task Force. What College Students Know About Their World. LC 80-69768. 56p. (Orig.). 1980. pap. 5.95 (ISBN 0-915390-30-2). Change Mag.
Educational Testing Service & Council on Learning. What College Students Know. LC 80-69767. 200p. (Orig.). 1980. pap. 10.95 (ISBN 0-915390-31-0). Change Mag.
Strang, William A. & Feldman, Howard. Non-Resident Students & the U. W. Madison Summer Session: An Evaluation of Demand & an Estimate of Local Economic Impact. (Wisconsin Economy Studies: No. 17). (Orig.). 1979. pap. 2.50. Bureau Busn Res U Wis.

COLLEGE STUDENTS–ORIENTATION
see College Student Orientation

COLLEGES
see Universities and Colleges

COLLINS, MICHAEL, 1890-1922
O'Broin, Leon. Michael Collins. (Gill's Irish Lives Ser.). 156p. 1980. 20.00 (ISBN 0-7171-1076-1, Pub. by Gill & Macmillan Ireland); pap. 6.50 (ISBN 0-7171-0968-2). Irish Bk Ctr.

COLLINS, WILKIE, 1824-1889
Andrews, R. V. Wilkie Collins, a Critical Survey of His Prose Fiction with a Bibliography. Bleiler, E. F., ed. LC 78-60801. (The Fiction of Popular Culture Ser.: Vol. 1). 367p. 1979. lib. bdg. 35.00 (ISBN 0-8240-9667-3). Garland Pub.

COLLISIONS, AIRCRAFT
see Aeronautics–Accidents

COLLOGEN
see Collagen Diseases

COLLOIDS
see also Particles; Rheology
Gel Electrophoresis: A Practical Approach. 1980. write for info. Info Retrieval.
Kerker, Milton, ed. Colloid & Interface Science, Vols. 2-5. Incl. Vol. 2. Aerosols, Emulsions & Surfactants. 35.00 (ISBN 0-12-404502-2); Vol. 3. Adsorption, Catalysis, Solid Surfaces, Wetting, Surface Tension & Water. 37.50 (ISBN 0-12-404503-0); Vol. 4. Hydrosols & Rheology. 36.50 (ISBN 0-12-404504-9); Vol. 5. Biocolloids, Polymers, Monolayers, Membranes & General Papers. 36.50 (ISBN 0-12-404505-7). 1976. Set. 122.00. Acad Pr.
Shaw, D. J. Introduction to Colloid & Surface Chemistry. 3rd ed. LC 80-49871. 256p. 1980. text ed. 14.95 (ISBN 0-408-71049-7). Butterworths.

COLLOQUIAL ENGLISH
see English Language–Conversation and Phrase Books; English Language–Spoken English
Cassell. Cassell's Colloquials, 4 bks. Incl. French. 160p. pap. 3.95 (ISBN 0-02-079420-7); German. 176p. pap. 3.95 (ISBN 0-02-079410-X); Spanish. 256p. pap. 4.95 (ISBN 0-02-079430-4); Italian. 192p. pap. 3.95 (ISBN 0-02-079440-1). 1981. Macmillan.

COLOMBIA–ECONOMIC CONDITIONS
OAS General Secretariat. Short-Term Economic Reports: Colombia, Vol. 1. 2nd ed. (Short Term Economic Reports Ser.). 77p. 1980. pap. text ed. 5.00 (ISBN 0-8270-1261-6). OAS.

COLOMBO, CRISTOFORO
see Columbus, Christopher (Cristoforo Colombo), 1446-1506

COLON (ANATOMY)–DISEASES
Rossini, F. P., ed. Slide Atlas of Coloscopy. Ferrari, A. (Illus.). 58p. 1980. Repr. of 1979 ed. text ed. 110.00x (ISBN 88-212-0791-9, Pub. by Piccin Italy). J K Burgess.

COLONIAL AFFAIRS
see Colonies

COLONIAL ARCHITECTURE
see Architecture, Colonial

COLONIALISM
see Colonies; Imperialism

COLONIES
see also Agricultural Colonies; Colonies in America; Colonization; Emigration and Immigration; Land Settlement
also subdivision Colonies under names of countries, e.g. France–Colonies
Sociological Theories: Race & Colonialism. 499p. 1981. pap. 34.00 (ISBN 92-310-1635-0, U1050, UNESCO). Unipub.

COLONIES IN AMERICA
Reid, John G. Acadia, Maine, & New Scotland: Marginal Colonies in the Seventeenth Century. 320p. 1981. 27.50x (ISBN 0-8020-5508-7). U of Toronto Pr.
Risjord, Norman K. Representative Americans: The Colonists, Vol. I. (Representative Americans Ser.). 272p. 1980. pap. text ed. 6.95 (ISBN 0-669-02831-2). Heath.

COLONITIS
see Colitis

COLONIZATION
see also Agricultural Colonies; Colonies; Emigration and Immigration; Migration, Internal
Weinstein, Warren & Grotpeter, John J. Pattern of African Decolonialization-a New Interpretation. LC 73-83839. (Foreign & Comoarative Studies-Eastern African Ser.: No. 10). 123p. 1973. pap. 4.50x (ISBN 0-915984-07-5). Syracuse U Foreign Comp.

COLOR
see also Colors; Dyes and Dyeing
Babbitt, Edwin D. Principles of Light & Color. (Illus.). 578p. Date not set. 20.00 (ISBN 0-89540-060-X). Sun Pub.
Blake, Wendon. The Color Book. (Illus.). 256p. 25.00 (ISBN 0-8230-0694-8). Watson-Guptill.
Ellinger, Richard G. Color Structure & Design. 144p. 1980. pap. 9.95 (ISBN 0-442-23941-6). Van Nos Reinhold.
Faiss, Fritz. Concerning the Way of Color. 12.50. Green Hut.
Le Blon, J. C. Coloritto. 98p. 1980. 12.50 (ISBN 0-442-24723-0). Van Nos Reinhold.
Light & Color: Images from New Mexico. (Illus.). 1980. pap. 12.95 (ISBN 0-89013-134-1). Museum NM Pr.
Parramon, J. M. Color. (Orig.). Date not set. pap. 4.95 (ISBN 0-89586-075-9). H P Bks.
Verity, Enid. Color Observed. 184p. 1980. 18.95 (ISBN 0-442-21906-7). Van Nos Reinhold.

COLOR–JUVENILE LITERATURE
Shape & Colors, No. 1. (Shapes & Colors Ser.). 1980. 1.95 (ISBN 0-8431-0165-2). Price Stern.
Shapes & Colors, No. 3. (Shapes & Colors Ser.). 1980. 1.95 (ISBN 0-8431-0167-9). Price Stern.
Shapes & Colors, No. 4. (Shapes & Colors Ser.). 1980. 1.95 (ISBN 0-8431-0168-7). Price Stern.

COLOR–PHYSIOLOGICAL EFFECT
Ott, John N. The Dynamics of Color & Light: How They Affect Human Health & Behavior. (Illus.). 256p. 1981. 10.00 (ISBN 0-8159-5314-3). Devin.

COLOR–PSYCHOLOGICAL ASPECTS
Kargere, Audrey. Color & Personality. pap. 3.95 (ISBN 0-686-69317-5). Weiser.

COLOR PHOTOGRAPHY–PRINTING PROCESSES
Gassan, Arnold. The Color Print Book: A Survey of Contemporary Photographic Printmaking Methods for the Creative Photographer. (The Extended Photo Media Ser.: No. 3). (Illus., Orig.). 1980. pap. 9.95 (ISBN 0-87992-023-8). Light Impressions.

COLOR PRINTS (PHOTOGRAPHY)
see Color Photography–Printing Processes

COLORADO–DESCRIPTION AND TRAVEL
Baldwin, Charles. Colorado Gem & Mineral Collecting Localities. pap. 4.95 (ISBN 0-933472-08-0). Johnson Colo.
Crouter, George. Colorado's Highest: The Magestic Fourteeners. (Illus.). 144p. 16.50 (ISBN 0-913582-22-0). Sundance.

Fetter, Richard L., et al. Front Range Restaurants: The One Hundred Best. 1980. pap. 7.95 (ISBN 0-933472-46-3). Johnson Colo.
Gunnufson, Kent, photos by. Tracking the Snow-Shoe Itinerant. LC 80-54041. (Illus.). 128p. 1981. text ed. 18.95 (ISBN 0-9605366-0-4); pap. text ed. 11.95 (ISBN 0-9605366-1-2). Snowstorm.
Miller, Millie. Kinnikinnick: The Mountain Flower Book. Date not set. pap. 3.95 (ISBN 0-933472-09-9). Johnson Colo.

COLORADO–HISTORY
Clark, Nancy. Littleton: A Pictorial History. Friedman, Donna R., ed. (Illus.). 208p. 1981. pap. price not set (ISBN 0-89865-112-3). Donning Co.
Mangan, Terry W. Colorado on Glass: First 50 Years of Glass-Plate Photography in Colorado. (Illus.). 416p. 47.00 (ISBN 0-913582-13-1). Sundance.
Turk, Gayle. Trial & Triumph. (Illus.). 60p. (Orig.). 1978. pap. 2.50 (ISBN 0-936564-11-3). Little London.

COLORADO RIVER AND VALLEY
Fradkin, Philip L. A River, No More: The Colorado River & the West. LC 80-2713. (Illus.). 384p. 1981. 15.95 (ISBN 0-394-41579-5). Knopf.

COLORADO SPRINGS
Sprague, Marshall. Newport in the Rockies: The Life & Good Times of Colorado Spring. rev. ed. LC 80-52995. 1981. 15.95 (ISBN 0-8040-0412-9, SB); pap. 9.95 (ISBN 0-8040-0413-7). Swallow.

COLORED PEOPLE (U. S.)
see Afro-Americans

COLORED REFUGEES
see Slavery in the United States–Fugitive Slaves

COLORS
see also Color
Hefter. The Strawberry Book of Colors. 120p. Date not set. 4.50 (ISBN 0-07-027826-1). McGraw.
Thomas, Anne W. Colors from the Earth. 132p. 1980. 13.95 (ISBN 0-442-25786-4). Van Nos Reinhold.

COLPOSCOPE
see Colposcopy

COLPOSCOPY
Mestwerdt. Atlas of Colposcopy. Meier, A., ed. 1981. text ed. price not set (ISBN 0-7216-6268-4). Saunders.

COLT, SAMUEL, 1814-1892
Barnard, Henry & Butler, J. D. Armsmear. (Illus.). 399p. 1976. 16.95 (ISBN 0-686-68856-2). Beinfeld Pub.

COLT REVOLVER
Garton, George. Colt's SAA: Post War Models. 166p. 17.95 (ISBN 0-917714-23-7). Beinfeld Pub.
Wilson, Robert L. The Book of Colt Engraving. 2nd ed. (Illus.). 560p. 1980. 50.00 (ISBN 0-917714-30-X). Beinfeld Pub.

COLUMBAE
see Pigeons

COLUMBIA RIVER AND VALLEY
Nelson, Sharlene & LeMieux, Joan. Cruising the Columbia & Snake Rivers: Eleven Cruises in the Inland Waterway. 192p. 1981. pap. 8.95 (ISBN 0-914718-57-6). Pacific Search.
Sharp, William F. Slavery on the Spanish Frontier: The Colombian Choco, 1680-1810. LC 76-18767. (Illus.). 253p. 1981. pap. 6.95 (ISBN 0-8061-1759-1). U of Okla Pr.

COLUMBIDAE
see Pigeons

COLUMBUS, CHRISTOPHER (CRISTOFORO COLOMBO), 1446-1506
Brother Nectario M. Juan Colon Alias Christopher Columbus. Josephson, Emanuel M., ed. LC 72-166573. (Blacked-Out History Ser.). 1971. pap. 5.00 (Pub. by Chedney). Alpine Ent.
Nagro, C. F. Christopher Columbus: Man of Destiny & Vision. 1981. 9.50 (ISBN 0-533-04809-5). Vantage.

COLUMBUS, CHRISTOPHER (CRISTOFORO COLOMBO), 1446-1506-BIBLIOGRAPHY
Tornoe. Columbus in the Arctic. 1965. text ed. 5.50x. Humanities.

COLUMBUS, OHIO
Rucker, Marion E. & LaPidus, Anne. Ohio Magazine's Offical Guide to Columbus & Central Ohio. rev. ed. LC 80-53248. (Illus.). 272p. (Orig.). 1980. pap. 5.95 (ISBN 0-938040-00-6). Ohio Mag.

COLUMNISTS
see Journalists

COMANCHE INDIANS
see Indians of North America–The West

COMBAT VEHICLES
see Armored Vehicles, Military

COMBINATIONS IN RESTRAINT OF TRADE
see Monopolies; Restraint of Trade

COMBINATIONS OF LABOR
see Strikes and Lockouts

COMBINATORIAL ANALYSIS
see also Graph Theory
Breen. Convexity & Related Combinatorial Geometry. Date not set. price not set (ISBN 0-8247-1278-1). Dekker.
Stillwell, J. Classical Topology & Combinatorial Group Theory. (Graduate Texts in Mathematics Ser.: Vol. 72). (Illus.). 301p. 1980. 32.00 (ISBN 0-387-90516-2). Springer-Verlag.

COMBUSTION
see also Chemical Warfare; Fuel; Heat
Chigier, N. A., ed. Progress in Energy & Combustion Science, Vol. 6, Pt. 2. 102p. 1980. pap. 24.50 (ISBN 0-08-026059-4). Pergamon.
Remenyi, Karoly. Combustion Stability. Darabant, E., tr. (Illus.). 175p. 1980. 20.00x (ISBN 963-05-2023-0). Intl Pubns Serv.

COMECON
Vienna Institute for Comparative Economic Studies, ed. COMECON Foreign Trade Data Nineteen Eighty. LC 80-28569. (Illus.). 509p. 1981. lib. bdg. 40.00 (ISBN 0-313-22988-0, VIC/). Greenwood.

COMEDIANS
see also Clowns
Fisher, Seymour & Fisher, Rhoda L. Pretend the World Is Funny & Forever: A Psychological Analysis of Comedians, Clowns, & Actors. LC 80-7777. 288p. 1981. profess. & reference 19.95 (ISBN 0-89859-073-6). L Erlbaum Assocs.

COMEDY
Leonard, Frances M. Laughhter in the Court of Love: Comedy in Allegory, from Chaucer to Spencer. 192p. 1981. 18.95 (ISBN 0-937664-54-5). Pilgrim Bks OK.
Quevedo y Villegas, Francisco G. de. The Comical Works of Don Francisco de Quevedo. 2nd ed. Stevens, John, tr. LC 80-2494. 1981. Repr. of 1709 ed. 69.50 (ISBN 0-404-19128-2). AMS Pr.

COMETS
Periodic comets are entered under the name of the discoverer, e.g. Halley's Comet.
Berger, Melvin. Comets, Meteors & Asteroids. (Illus.). 64p. (gr. 10 up). 1981. PLB 6.99 (ISBN 0-399-61148-7). Putnam.
Calder, Nigel. The Comet Is Coming. 176p. 1981. 12.95 (ISBN 0-670-23216-5). Viking Pr.

COMFORT, STANDARD OF
see Cost and Standard of Living

COMIC BOOKS, STRIPS, ETC.
see also Chap-Books; Newspapers–Sections, Columns, etc.
Linke, Frances. Space Patrol III. Linke, Ray, ed. (Illus.). 205p. 1980. 25.00 (ISBN 0-933276-07-9). Nin-Ra Ent.
Marschall, Rick. Rembrandt of the Comic Strip. 1981. 6.95 (ISBN 0-918348-04-8). Green Hill.

COMIC LITERATURE
see Comedy

COMIC OPERA
see Opera

COMIC STRIPS
see Comic Books, Strips, etc.

COMMANDMENTS, TEN
Watson, Thomas. The Ten Commandments. 1976. 9.95 (ISBN 0-85151-146-5). Banner of Truth.

COMMENSALISM
see Symbiosis

COMMENTARIES, BIBLICAL
see Bible–Commentaries

COMMENTATORS
see Journalists

COMMERCE
see also Barter; Black Market; Business; Business Mathematics; Businessmen; Competition, International; Customs Unions; Export Marketing; Export Sales; Foreign Exchange; Freight and Freightage; Geography, Economic; Harbors; Inland Water Transportation; Insurance, Marine; International Business Enterprises; Interstate Commerce; Investments, Foreign; Maritime Law; Markets; Money; Monopolies; Neutrality; Purchasing; Restraint of Trade; Retail Trade; Shipment of Goods; Shipping; Sterling Area; Trade-Marks; Transportation; Warehouses
also subdivision Commerce under names of countries, cities, etc.; names of articles of commerce, e.g. Cotton, Leather, Lumber; headings beginning with the word Commercial
Allen, R. C. Professional Trading System. 1981. 20.00 (ISBN 0-910228-10-8). Best Bks.
Baldwin & Richardson. International Trade & Finance. 2nd ed. 1981. pap. text ed. 8.95 (ISBN 0-316-07922-7). Little.
Bhagwati, Jagdish, ed. International Trade: Selected Readings. 456p. 1981. text ed. 25.00x (ISBN 0-262-02160-9); pap. text ed. 9.95x (ISBN 0-262-52060-5). MIT Pr.
Bradley, Bill, ed. Days of Commerce. (Special Ser.: No.X-8). 1981. pap. write for info. (ISBN 0-916374-45-9). Interurban.
Carlson, Jack & Graham, Hugh. The Economic Importance of Exports to the United States, Vol. Ii. LC 80-66694. (Significant Issues Ser.: No. 6). 128p. 1980. 5.95 (ISBN 0-89206-019-0). CSI Studies.
Caves & Jones. World Trade & Payments: An Introduction. 3rd ed. 1981. text ed. 17.95 (ISBN 0-316-13226-8). Little.
De Saint Phalle, Thibaut. U. S. Productivity & Competitiveness in International Trade, Vol. II. LC 80-68434. (Significant Issues Ser.: No. 12). 115p. 1980. 5.95 (ISBN 0-89206-028-X). CSI Studies.
DeVos, Ton. U. S. Multinationals & Worker Participation in Management: The American Experience in the European Community. LC 80-23597. 1981. lib. bdg. 29.95 (ISBN 0-89930-004-9, DUM/, Quorum Bks). Greenwood.
Enet, Daniel. Exporting for Small & Medium Sized Firms. 150p. 1977. text ed. 22.00x (ISBN 0-220-66329-7, Pub. by Busn Bks England). Renouf.
Flammang, Robert. U S Programs That Impede U. S. Export Competitiveness: The Regulatory Environment, Vol. II. LC 80-80933. (Significant Issues Ser.: No. 3). 45p. 1980. 5.95 (ISBN 0-89206-017-4). CSI Studies.
Hartland-Thunberg, Penelope. The Political & Strategic Importance of Exports, Vol. I. LC 79-2785. (Significant Issues Ser.: No. 3). 35p. 1979. 4.00 (ISBN 0-89206-009-3). CSI Studies.
Ingham, Barbara. Tropical Exports & Economic Development. Date not set. 22.50 (ISBN 0-312-81918-8). St Martin.
International Trade 1979-80. 192p. 1981. pap. 18.00 (G144, GATT). Unipub.
Kettell, Brian. The Finance of International Trade. LC 80-28878. (Illus.). xviii, 175p. 1981. lib. bdg. 40.00 (ISBN 0-89930-011-1, KFI/, Quorum Bks). Greenwood.
Krueger, Anne O., et al. Trade & Employment in Developing Countries, Vol. 1: Individual Studies. LC 80-15826. (National Bureau of Economic Research Ser.). (Illus.). 1981. lib. bdg. 39.00x (ISBN 0-226-45492-4). U of Chicago Pr.
McGuire, E. Patrick, ed. Consumer Protection: Implications for the International Trade, Report No. 789. (Illus.). vii, 63p. (Orig.). 1980. pap. 15.00 (ISBN 0-8237-0225-1). Conference Bd.
Mikesell, Raymond F. & Farah, Mark G. U. S. Export Competitiveness in Manufactures in Third World Countries, Vol. II. LC 80-67711. (Significant Issues Ser.: No. 9). 144p. 1980. 5.95 (ISBN 0-89206-026-3). CSI Studies.
Nineteen Seventy-Eight Yearbook of International Trade Statistics, 2 vols. 1178p. 1979. Set. pap. 65.00 (UN79-17-16, UN). Unipub.
Office of Technology Assessment Congress of the United States, ed. Technology & East West Trade. LC 80-26121. 312p. 1981. text ed. 25.00 (ISBN 0-86598-041-1). Allanheld.
Operations & Effects of the Generalized System of Preferences. 146p. 1979. pap. 11.00 (ISBN 0-686-68964-X, UN79/2D2., UN). Unipub.
The Political & Strategic Importance of Exports. (Significant Issues Ser.: Vol. I, No. 3). 35p. 1979. pap. 5.00 (ISBN 0-89206-009-3, CSIS004, CSIS). Unipub.
Rubin, Seymour J. & Graham, Thomas R., eds. Environment & Trade: The Relation of International Trade & Environmental Policy. 380p. 1981. text ed. 28.50 (ISBN 0-86598-032-2). Allanheld.
Swift, Eric. Managing Your Export Office. 150p. 1977. text ed. 22.00x (ISBN 0-220-66310-6, Pub. by Busn Bks England). Renouf.
Technology & East West Trade: Office of Technology Assessment, Congress of the U. S. LC 80-26121. 312p. 1981. text ed. 25.00 (ISBN 0-86598-041-1). Allanheld.
Whiting, D. P. International Trade & Payments. (Illus.). 160p. 1978. pap. 11.95x (ISBN 0-7121-0952-8). Intl Ideas.
Winters, L. Alan. An Econometric Model of the Export Sector. (Cambridge Studies in Applied Econometrics). 192p. Date not set. price not set (ISBN 0-521-23720-3). Cambridge U Pr.
World Trade Annual Supplement, 1978, 5 vols. 110.00 ea.; Set. 550.00. Vol. 1 (ISBN 0-8027-5969-6). Vol. 2 (ISBN 0-8027-5971-8). Vol. 3 (ISBN 0-8027-5972-6). Vol. 4 (ISBN 0-8027-5973-4). Vol. 5 (ISBN 0-8027-5974-2). Walker & Co.
World Trade Annual, 1978, 5 vols. 50.00 ea.; Set. 250.00 (ISBN 0-8027-5977-7). Vol. 1 (ISBN 0-8027-5963-7). Vol. 2 (ISBN 0-8027-5964-5). Vol. 3 (ISBN 0-8027-5965-3). Vol. 4 (ISBN 0-8027-5966-1). Vol. 5 (ISBN 0-8027-5968-8). Walker & Co.
Wyatt, David H. Essential of International Trade. LC 79-88237. (The ALA ESP Ser.). (Illus.). v, 205p. (Orig.). 1979. pap. text ed. 10.00 (ISBN 0-934270-07-4). Am Lang Acad.
Zauberman, Alfred. Topics in Trade Coordination in Planned Economics. 108p. 1980. text ed. 32.50x (ISBN 0-8419-5085-7). Holmes & Meier.

COMMERCE–DIRECTORIES
Hicks, Tyler G. Worldwide Riches Opportunites, Vol. 1. 150p. 1981. pap. 25.00 (ISBN 0-914306-49-9). Intl Wealth.
--Worldwide Riches Opportunities, Vol. 2. 2rd ed. 150p. 1981. pap. 25.00 (ISBN 0-914306-50-2). Intl Wealth.
Zils, Michael, ed. World Guide to Trade Associations. 2nd ed. (Handbook of International Documentation & Information Ser.: Vol. 12). 845p. 1980. 180.00 (ISBN 3-598-20513-9, Dist by Gale Research Co.). K G Saur.

COMMERCE–HISTORY
Ashton, Eliyahu. Studies on the Levantine Trade in the Middle Ages. 372p. 1980. 60.00x (ISBN 0-86078-020-1, Pub. by Variorum England). State Mutual Bk.
D'Arms, John H. Commerce & Social Standing in Ancient Rome. LC 80-25956. (Illus.). 224p. 1981. text ed. 20.00 (ISBN 0-674-14475-9). Harvard U Pr.
Miller, Russell. The East Indiamen. Time-Life Books, ed. (The Seafarers Ser.). (Illus.). 176p. 1981. 14.95 (ISBN 0-8094-2689-7). Time-Life.

COMMERCE–STATISTICS
see Commercial Statistics

COMMERCE CLAUSE (U. S. CONSTITUTION)
see Interstate Commerce

COMMERCIAL AERONAUTICS
see Aeronautics, Commercial

COMMERCIAL ARITHMETIC
see Business Mathematics

COMMERCIAL ART
Billig, O. & Burton-Bradley, B. G. The Painted Message. 1978. 19.50 (ISBN 0-470-99126-7). Wiley.
Cardamone, Tom. Advertising Agency & Studio Skills. 3rd ed. 160p. 1981. 10.95 (ISBN 0-8230-0151-2). Watson-Guptill.
Muller-Brockmann, Josef. A History of Visual Communication. 2nd ed. (Illus.). 334p. 1981. pap. 29.50 (ISBN 0-8038-3059-9, Visual Communication). Hastings.

COMMERCIAL AVIATION
see Aeronautics, Commercial

COMMERCIAL CATALOGS
see Catalogs, Commercial

COMMERCIAL CORNERS
see Monopolies; Stock-Exchange

COMMERCIAL CORRESPONDENCE
see also English Language–Business English; Form Letters
Gartside, I. Model Business Letters. 2nd ed. 416p. 1974. pap. 13.95x (Pub. by Macdonald & Evans England). Intl Ideas.
Hemphill, Charles. Business Communications with Writing Improvement Exercises. 256p. 1981. pap. text ed. 11.95 (ISBN 0-13-093880-7). P-H.
Michell, Ewan. The Businessman's Guide to Letter-Writing & to the Law on Letters. 2nd ed. 222p. 1979. text ed. 23.50x (ISBN 0-220-66326-2, Pub. by Busn Bks England). Renouf.
Mitchell, Ewan. The Director's & Company Secretary's Handbook of Draft Legal Letters. 2nd ed. 596p. 1979. text ed. 43.00x (ISBN 0-220-67001-3, Pub. by Busn Bks England). Renouf.
Poynter, Dan. Business Letters for Publishers: Creative Correspondence Outlines. 82p. 1981. 14.95 (ISBN 0-915516-28-4); magnetic recorded disc 29.95 (ISBN 0-915516-29-2). Para Pub.

COMMERCIAL CREDIT
see Credit

COMMERCIAL DESIGN
see Commercial Art

COMMERCIAL EDUCATION
see Business Education

COMMERCIAL ETHICS
see Business Ethics

COMMERCIAL FISHING
see Fisheries

COMMERCIAL GEOGRAPHY
Staff of World Bank. World Tables: 1980. LC 79-3649. (World Bank Occasional Paper Ser.). (Illus.). 480p. 1980. text ed. 27.50x (ISBN 0-8018-2389-7); pap. text ed. 10.95x (ISBN 0-8018-2390-0). Johns Hopkins.

COMMERCIAL LAW
Here are entered general works and works on commercial law in the United States. For commercial law of other countries, see subdivisions below.
see also Accounting–Law; Antitrust Law; Auctions; Bailments; Banking Law; Bankruptcy; Business; Business Enterprises; Business Law; Collecting of Accounts; Competition, Unfair; Contracts; Corporation Law; Debt; Food Law and Legislation; Foreign Exchange; Foreign Trade Regulation; Forms (Law); Insurance Law; Landlord and Tenant; Leases; Licenses; Maritime Law; Negotiable Instruments; Partnership; Personal Property; Real Property; Restraint of Trade; Sales; Security (Law); Trade-Marks; Trade Regulation; Trusts and Trustees; Warehouses
Clark, Barkley, ed. Warranties in the Sale of Goods 1980: Course Handbook, 2 vols. LC 78-643376. (Nineteen Eighty to Nineteen Eighty-One Commercial Law & Practice Course Handbook Ser.). 1131p. 1980. pap. text ed. 25.00 (ISBN 0-686-69173-3, A6-3091). PLI.
Cooke, Frederick H. The Law of Trade & Labor Combinations As Applicable to Boycotts, Strikes, Trade Conspiracies, Monopolies, Pools, Trusts, & Kindred Topics. xxv, 214p. 1981. Repr. of 1898 ed. lib. bdg. 24.00x (ISBN 0-8377-0430-8). Rothman.
Credit Manual of Commercial Laws, 1981 Ed. 1980. 32.00 (ISBN 0-934914-37-0). NACM.
Illustrations of Accounting for Joint Ventures. (Financial Report Survey Ser.: No. 21). 1980. pap. 8.00. Am Inst CPA.
OAS General Secretariat International Trade & Export Development Program. Sistema Generalizado De Preferencial De Estados Unidos: Cobertura Y Procedimientos Administrativos Vignetes En 1980. (International Trade Ser.). 58p. pap. text ed. 5.00 (ISBN 0-8270-1125-3). OAS.
Thompson, George C. & Brady, Gerald P. Shortened CPA Law Review. (Business Ser.). 560p. 1980. text ed. 17.95x (ISBN 0-686-69155-5). Kent Pub Co.

COMMERCIAL PAPER
see Negotiable Instruments

COMMERCIAL POLICY
see also Commercial Treaties; Commodity Control; Competition, Unfair; Customs Unions; Foreign Trade Regulation; Free Ports and Zones

also subdivision Commerce or Commercial Policy under names of countries

Hazari, Bharat, et al. Non-Traded & Intermediate Goods & the Pure Theory of International Trade. 1981. 29.95 (ISBN 0-312-57728-1). St Martin.

Helleiner, Gerald K. Intra - Firm Trade & the Developing Countries. 1981. 25.00 (ISBN 0-312-42538-4). St Martin.

Trade Liberalization & the National Interest. (Significant Issues Ser.: Vol. II, No. 2). 52p. 1980. pap. 7.50 (ISBN 0-89206-016-6, CSIS010, CSIS). Unipub.

U. S. Programs That Impede U. S. Export Competitiveness: The Regulatory Environment. (Significant Issues Ser.: Vol. II, No. 3). 45p. 1980. pap. 7.50 (ISBN 0-89206-017-4, CSIS011, CSIS). Unipub.

COMMERCIAL PRODUCTS

see also Commodity Control; Commodity Exchanges; Forest Products; Geography, Economic; Marine Resources; New Products; Synthetic Products
also names of individual products

Consumers Index to Product Evaluations & Information Sources, 1980 Annual. 1981. 59.50 (ISBN 0-87650-130-7). Pierian.

COMMERCIAL PRODUCTS-BREAKAGE, SHRINKAGE, ETC.

see Breakage, Shrinkage, etc. (Commerce)

COMMERCIAL SCHOOLS

see Business Education

COMMERCIAL STATISTICS

see also subdivision Commerce under names of countries, cities, etc. e.g. France-Commerce

Yearbook of International Trade Statistics, 1978, 2 vols. Incl. Vol. 1. Trade by Country; Vol. 2. Trade by Commodity, Commodity Matrix Tables. 1178p. 1979. Set. pap. 65.00 (UN79/17/16, UN). Unipub.

COMMERCIAL TREATIES

Baldwin, Robert E. Multilateral Trade Negotiations: Toward Greater Liberalization? 1979. pap. 3.75 (ISBN 0-8447-1082-2). Am Enterprise.

Erb, Guy F. Negotiations on Two Fronts: Manufactures & Commodities. LC 78-57199. (Development Papers: No. 25). 80p. 1978. pap. 1.50 (ISBN 0-686-28674-X). Overseas Dev Council.

COMMERCIALS, TELEVISION

see Television Advertising

Gradus, Ben. Directing the Television Commercial. (Communication Arts Books). 228p. 1981. 16.95x (ISBN 0-8038-1575-1, Communications Arts); pap. 9.95x (ISBN 0-8038-1577-8). Hastings.

COMMISSIONS, INDEPENDENT REGULATORY

see Independent Regulatory Commissions

COMMISSIONS OF INQUIRY

see Governmental Investigations

COMMISSIONS OF THE FEDERAL GOVERNMENT

see Independent Regulatory Commissions

COMMITMENT

Leavenworth, Carol. Love & Commitment: You Don't Have to Settle for Less. (Illus.). 192p. 1981. 10.95t (ISBN 0-13-540971-3, Spec); pap. 5.95b (ISBN 0-13-540963-2). P-H.

COMMODITIES

see Commercial Products

COMMODITY CONTROL

Behrman, Jere R. International Commodity Agreements: An Evaluation of the UNCTAD Integrated Commodity Programme. LC 77-90146. (Monographs: No. 9). 112p. 1977. 5.00 (ISBN 0-686-28686-3). Overseas Dev Council.

Erb, Guy F. Negotiations on Two Fronts: Manufactures & Commodities. LC 78-57199. (Development Papers: No. 25). 80p. 1978. pap. 1.50 (ISBN 0-686-28674-X). Overseas Dev Council.

COMMODITY EXCHANGES

see also Commercial Products; Marketing; Markets

Angell, George. Computer Proven Commodity Spreads. 1981. write for info. Windsor.

Chamberlain, G. H. Trading in Options. 144p. 1980. 30.00x (ISBN 0-85941-168-0, Pub. by Woodhead-Faulkner England). State Mutual Bk.

Gemmill, G. T. ICCH Commodities Yearbook 1980-81. 304p. 1980. 75.00x (ISBN 0-85941-071-4, Pub. by Woodhead-Faulkner England). State Mutual Bk.

Koch, Harvey. Fastest Way to Get Rich: Trading in Financial Futures. LC 80-6155. 224p. 1981. 12.95 (ISBN 0-8128-2782-1). Stein & Day.

Rose, Leon & Rose, Joy, eds. Commodity Money Management Yearbook, 1980. (Illus.). 1981. 39.50 (ISBN 0-936624-01-9). LJR Inc.

Sarnoff, Paul. Trading in Financial Futures. 144p. 1980. 30.00x (ISBN 0-85941-133-8, Pub. by Woodhead-Faulkner England). State Mutual Bk.

Watling, T. & Morley, J. Successful Commodity Futures Trading. 2nd ed. 244p. 1974. text ed. 29.50x (ISBN 0-220-66340-8, Pub. by Busn Bks England). Renouf.

Yarry, Mark R. The Fastest Game in Town: Commodities. 192p. 1981. 9.95 (ISBN 0-13-307884-1). P-H.

COMMON BUSINESS ORIENTED LANGUAGE

see COBOL (Computer Program Language)

COMMON LAW-GREAT BRITAIN

Bacon, Francis & Francis, Richard. Examples of a Treatise on Universal Justice or the Fountains of Equity, by Aphorisms. Berkowitz, David S. & Thorne, Samuel E., eds. LC 77-86639. (Classics of English Legal History in the Modern Era Ser.: Vol. 33). 125p. 1979. lib. bdg. 40.00 (ISBN 0-8240-3082-6). Garland Pub.

Berkowitz, David S. & Thorne, Samuel E., eds. Baron & Feme. LC 77-86664. (Classics of English Legal History in the Modern Era Ser.: Vol. 43). 445p. 1979. lib. bdg. 40.00 (ISBN 0-8240-3092-3). Garland Pub.

COMMON MARKET COUNTRIES

see European Economic Community

COMMON SCHOOLS

see Public Schools

COMMONS (SOCIAL ORDER)

see Labor and Laboring Classes

COMMONWEALTH, THE

see State, The

COMMONWEALTH OF NATIONS

Smith, T. E. Commonwealth Migration: Flows & Policies. 1980. text ed. 40.00x (ISBN 0-333-27898-4). Humanities.

COMMUNE DE PARIS, 1871

see Paris-History-Commune, 1871

COMMUNICABLE DISEASES

see also Bacteriology; Epidemics; Epidemiology; Germ Theory of Disease; Immunity; Medicine, Preventive; Virus Diseases; Zoonoses
also names of communicable diseases, e.g. Chicken-Pox, Malarial Fever

Christie, A. B. Infectious Diseases: Epidemiology & Clinical Practice. 3rd ed. (Illus.). 1981. text ed. 95.00 (ISBN 0-443-02263-1). Churchill.

Conte, John E., Jr. & Barriere, Steven L. Manual of Antibiotics & Infectious Diseases. 4th ed. (Illus.). 275p. 1981. text ed. price not set (ISBN 0-8121-0768-3). Lea & Febiger.

Gibbs, Ronald S. Antibiotic Therapy in Obstetrics & Gynecology. 224p. 1981. 16.50 (ISBN 0-471-06003-8, Pub. by Wiley Med). Wiley.

Holloway, William J., ed. Infectious Disease Reviews, Vol VI. LC 78-50693. (Illus.). 192p. 1981. monograph 23.75 (ISBN 0-87993-151-5). Futura Pub.

International Congress of Chemotherapy, 11th & Interscience Conference on Antimicrobial Agents & Chemotherapy, 19th. Current Chemotherapy & Infectious Disease: Proceedings, 2 vols. Nelson, John D. & Grassi, Carlo, eds. (Illus.). 1980. Set. 75.00 (ISBN 0-914826-22-0). Am Soc Microbio.

Moss, Gordon E. Illness, Immunity & Social Interaction. 298p. 1981. Repr. of 1973 ed. text ed. price not set (ISBN 0-89874-266-8). Krieger.

Noble, Robert C. Sexually Transmitted Diseases. LC 78-71163. (Discussions in Patient Management Ser.). 1979. pap. 9.50 (ISBN 0-87488-881-6). Med Exam.

Remington, Jack S. & Swartz, Morton N. Current Clinical Topics in Infectious Diseases, No. 2. (Illus.). 304p. 1981. text ed. 30.00 (ISBN 0-07-051851-3, HP). McGraw.

Simmons, Richard. Surgical Infectious Disease. 1981. 65.00 (ISBN 0-8385-8729-1). ACC.

COMMUNICABLE DISEASES-LAW AND LEGISLATION

see Public Health Laws

COMMUNICATION

Here are entered works on human communication, including both the primary techniques of language, pictures, etc., and the secondary techniques which facilitate the process, such as the press and radio.
see also Communications Research; Content Analysis (Communication); Cybernetics; Information Science; Information Theory; Intercultural Communication; Language and Languages; Mass Media; Oral Communication; Persuasion (Psychology); Semantics (Philosophy); Visual Aids

American Psychological Association. Language & Communication: Student Booklet. (Human Behavior Curriculum Peoject Ser.). 64p. (Orig.). (gr. 9-12). 1981. pap. text ed. 3.95 (ISBN 0-8077-2625-7). Tchrs Coll.

--Language & Communication: Teachers Handbook & Duplication Masters. (Human Behavir Curriculum Project Ser.). 48p. (Orig.). (gr. 9-12). 1981. pap. 9.95 (ISBN 0-8077-2626-5). Tchrs Coll.

Ansberger, Carolyn & Green, Mary J. Here's How to Handle "L". 1980. 50.00 (ISBN 0-88450-709-2, 30598-B). Communication Bks.

Aptoelectronics: Growth G-062. 1981. 850.00 (ISBN 0-89336-286-7). BCC.

Ausberger, Carloyn & Green, Mary J. Here's How to Handle "S". 1979. 50.00 (ISBN 0-88450-708-4, 3057-B). Communications Skill.

Ausberger, Carolyn & Green, Mary J. Here's How to Handle "R". 1975. 50.00 (ISBN 0-88450-707-6, 2023-B). Communication Skill.

Berko, Roy M. & Wolvin, Andrew D. Communicating: A Social & Career Focus. 2nd ed. (Illus.). 432p. 1981. pap. text ed. 10.50 (ISBN 0-395-29170-4). HM.

Bickhard, Mark H. Cognition, Convention, & Communication. 210p. 1980. 24.95 (ISBN 0-03-056098-5). Praeger.

Bryant, Al. Keep in Touch. 1981. 8.95. Word Bks.

Cravis, Howard. Communications Network Analysis. LC 75-39314. 1981. price not set (ISBN 0-669-00443-X). Lexington Bks.

DeFleur, Melvin L. & Dennis, Everette E. Understanding Mass Communication. LC 80-82762. (Illus.). 528p. 1981. pap. text ed. 11.95 (ISBN 0-395-29722-2); price not set instr's. manual (ISBN 0-395-29723-0). HM.

DeVito, Joseph A. Communication: Concepts & Processes. 3rd ed. (Illus.). 320p. 1981. pap. text ed. 10.95 (ISBN 0-13-153411-4). P-H.

DuVall, J. Barry, et al. Getting the Message. LC 79-57016. (Technology Ser.). 384p. 1981. text ed. 15.50 (ISBN 0-87192-123-5, 000-6); tchr's guide 18.60 (ISBN 0-87192-125-1, 00-6A); activity manual 5.95 (ISBN 0-87192-124-3, 00-6B). Davis Mass.

Emmert, Philip & Donaghy, William. Human Communication: Elements & Contexts. LC 80-17595. (Speech Ser.). (Illus.). 46p. 1981. text ed. 12.95 (ISBN 0-201-03597-9). A-W.

Esau, Helmut, et al. Language & Communication. 1980. pap. 8.75. Hornbeam Pr.

Ferguson, Stewart & Ferguson, Sherry D. Interrcom: Readings in Organizational Communication. 432p. 1980. 12.95x (ISBN 0-8104-5127-1). Hayden.

Forsdale, Louis. Perspectives on Communication. LC 80-16616. (Speech Ser.). (Illus.). 400p. 1981. text ed. 12.95 (ISBN 0-201-04571-0). A-W.

Gustason, G. & Zaevolkow, E., eds. Using Signing Exact English in Total Communication. LC 80-84549. 62p. 1980. 4.50 (ISBN 0-916708-04-7). Modern Signs.

Hills, Philip, ed. The Future of the Printed Word. LC 80-1716. 172p. 1980. lib. bdg. 25.00 (ISBN 0-313-22693-8, HIP/). Greenwood.

Holmes, Jack K. Coherent Communication with Applications to Pseudo-Noise Spread Spectrum Synchronization. 850p. 1981. 50.00 (ISBN 0-471-03301-4, Pub. by Wiley-Interscience). Wiley.

Intergovernmental Conference on Communication Policies in Asia & Oceania: Final Report. 87p. 1980. pap. 7.50 (ISBN 0-686-68811-2, U1022, UNESCO). Unipub.

International Technical Communication Conference, 27th, Minneapolis, May 14-17, 1980. Technical Communication--the Bridge of Understanding: Proceedings. Society for Technical Communication, ed. 1058p. 1980. pap. text ed. 35.00x (ISBN 0-914548-32-8). Univelt Inc.

Janowitz, Morris & Hirsch, Paul, eds. Reader in Public Opinion & Mass Communication. 3rd ed. LC 80-2444. 448p. 1981. pap. text ed. 10.95 (ISBN 0-02-916020-0). Free Pr.

Johannesen, Richard L. Ethics in Human Communication. LC 74-24780. 176p. pap. text ed. 5.95x (ISBN 0-917974-58-1). Waveland Pr.

Kates, Linda & Schein, Jerome. A Complete Guide to Communication with Deaf Blind Persons. (Illus.). 108p. 1981. pap. text ed. 3.95 (ISBN 0-913072-40-0). Natl Assn Deaf.

Krippendorff, Klaus. Content Analysis: An Introduction to Its Methodology. LC 80-19166. (CommText Ser.: Vol. 5). (Illus.). 191p. 1980. 15.00 (ISBN 0-8039-1497-0); pap. 7.95 (ISBN 0-8039-1498-9). Sage.

Larson, Charles U. Communication: Everyday Encounters. 240p. pap. text ed. 10.95 (ISBN 0-917974-60-3). Waveland Pr.

Lehman, Maxwell, ed. Communication Technologies & Information Flow. (PPS on Science & Technology Ser.). (Illus.). 175p. 1981. 20.00 (ISBN 0-08-027169-3); pap. 12.50 (ISBN 0-08-027528-1). Pergamon.

Lewis, Norman. Word Power Made Easy. pap. 2.95 (ISBN 0-671-42416-5). PB.

Lindell, Anne. Intensive English for Communication: Book Two. (Illus.). 294p. 1980. pap. text ed. 6.95x (ISBN 0-472-08572-7). U of Mich Pr.

McCabe & Bender. Speaking Is a Practical Matter. 4th ed. 384p. 1981. pap. text ed. 12.95 (ISBN 0-205-07230-5, 4872304); free tchr's ed. (ISBN 0-205-07231-3). Allyn.

Many Voices, One World. 312p. 1980. pap. 13.50 (ISBN 92-3-101802-7, U1034, UNESCO). Unipub.

Melody, William H., et al. Culture, Communication, & Dependency: The Tradition of H. A. Innis. 288p. 1980. text ed. write for info. (ISBN 0-89391-065-1). Ablex Pub.

Michaels, Claire F. & Carello, Claudia A. Direct Perception. (Illus.). 224p. 1981. text ed. 18.00 (ISBN 0-13-214791-2). P-H.

Middleton, Karen P. & Jussawalla, Meheroo. The Economics of Communication: A Selected Bibliography with Asbstracts. LC 80-50505. (Pergamon Policy Studies on Internatioanl Development). 250p. 1981. 25.00 (ISBN 0-08-026325-9). Pergamon.

--The Economics of Comnunication: A Selected Bibliography with Abstracts Published in Cooperation with the Eeast-West Center, Hawaii. LC 80-20505. (Pergamon Policy Studies on International Development). 1981. 25.000 (ISBN 0-08-026325-9). Pergamon.

OECD. Information Computer Communications Policy (ICCP) 4. 233p. (Orig.). 1980. pap. 14.50 (ISBN 92-64-12035-1, 93-80-01-1). OECD.

Ribeiro, Manoel A., tr. Conversas Intimas. (Portugese Bks.). (Port.). 1979. 1.00 (ISBN 0-8297-0651-8). Life Pubs Intl.

Sherif, Muzafer & Hovland, Carl I. Social Judgment: Assimilation & Contrast Effects in Communication & Attitude Change. LC 80-21767. (Yale Studies in Attitude & Communication: Vol. 4). xii, 218p. 1981. Repr. of 1961 ed. lib. bdg. 25.00x (ISBN 0-313-22438-2, SHSO). Greenwood.

Smythe, Dallas W. Dependency Road: Communications, Capitalism, Consciousness & Canada. 300p. 1981. text ed. price not set (ISBN 0-89391-067-8). Ablex Pub.

Stevenson, Dwight W., et al, eds. Courses, Components, & Exercises in Technical Communication. 1981. pap. price not set (ISBN 0-8141-0877-6). NCTE.

Theobald, Robert. Beyond Despair: Directions for America's Third Century. rev. ed. 208p. 1981. 11.95 (ISBN 0-932020-04-6); pap. 7.95 (ISBN 0-932020-05-4). Seven Locks Pr.

Twyford, John. Graphic Communication. (Illus.). 120p. (gr. 9-12). 1981. pap. 17.50 (ISBN 0-7134-3388-4, Pub. by Batsford England). David & Charles.

Verderber, Rudolph F. Communicate. 3rd ed. 384p. 1980. pap. text ed. 10.95x (ISBN 0-534-00885-2). Wadsworth Pub.

Vervalin, Charlie, ed. Communication Guidelines for Technical Professionals. 220p. (Orig.). 1981. pap. 15.95 (ISBN 0-87201-127-5). Gulf Pub.

Wicklein, John. The New Communications & Freedom. 1981. 14.95 (ISBN 0-670-50658-3). Viking Pr.

Zannes, Estelle. Communication: The Widening Circle. LC 80-15150. (Speech Ser.). 324p. 1981. pap. text ed. 10.95 (ISBN 0-201-08997-1). A-W.

COMMUNICATION (THEOLOGY)

see also Evangelistic Work

Buckingham, Jamie. The Last Word. 1978. pap. 3.95 (ISBN 0-88270-404-4). Logos.

Lawless, Agnes & Goodboy, Eadie. The Word. (Aglow Bible Study Bk.: No. E-4). (Illus.). 64p. (Orig.). 1980. pap. 1.95 (ISBN 0-930756-59-2, 4220-E4). Women's Aglow.

Main, John. Word into Silence. 96p. 1981. pap. 3.95 (ISBN 0-8091-2369-X). Paulist Pr.

Skudlarek, William. The Word in Worship. LC 80-25525. (Abingdon Preacher's Library). 128p. (Orig.). 1981. pap. 4.95 (ISBN 0-687-46131-6). Abingdon.

COMMUNICATION-BIBLIOGRAPHY

Stofferahn, Curtis W. & Korsching, Peter F. Communication, Diffusion & Adoption of Innovations: A Bibliographical Update. (Public Administration Ser.: Bibliography P-433). 50p. 1980. pap. 5.50. Vance Biblios.

COMMUNICATION-CONTENT ANALYSIS

see Content Analysis (Communication)

COMMUNICATION-RESEARCH

see Communications Research

Bustanoby, Andre & Bustanoby, Fay. Just Talk to Me. 192p. (Orig.). 1981. pap. text ed. 5.95 (ISBN 0-310-22181-1). Zondervan.

COMMUNICATION-AFRICA

Communication Policies in Kenya. 94p. 1980. pap. 7.50 (ISBN 92-3-101774-8, U1032, UNESCO). Unipub.

Communication Policies in Zaire. 59p. 1980. pap. 5.25 (ISBN 92-3-101602-4, U1018, UNESCO). Unipub.

COMMUNICATION, BUSINESS

see Communication in Management

COMMUNICATION, INTERCULTURAL

see Intercultural Communication

COMMUNICATION AMONG ANIMALS

see Animal Communication

COMMUNICATION IN EDUCATION

see also Education; Education Libraries

Prentice, Lloyd. Words, Pictures, Media: Communication in Educational Politics. 91p. 1976. pap. text ed. 4.00 (ISBN 0-917754-01-8). Inst Responsive.

COMMUNICATION IN INDUSTRY

see Communication in Management

COMMUNICATION IN MANAGEMENT

see also Business Report Writing

Adams, James R. Media Planning. 2nd ed. 232p. 1977. pap. 12.25x (ISBN 0-220-66337-8, Pub. by Busn Bks England). Renouf.

Anastasi, Thomas E., Jr. The Manager's Desk Guide to Communication. 300p. 1981. 15.95 (ISBN 0-8436-0855-2). CBI Pub.

Aronoff, Craig, et al. Getting Your Message Across: A Practical Guide to Business Communication. (Illus.). 500p. 1981. text ed. 13.95 (ISBN 0-8299-0362-3). West Pub.

Chappell, R. T. & Read, W. L. Business Communications. 4th ed. 232p. (Orig.). 1979. pap. text ed. 13.95x (ISBN 0-7121-0272-8, Pub. by Macdonald & Evans England). Intl Ideas.

Fallon, William K., ed. Effective Communication on the Job. 3rd ed. 273p. 1981. 15.95 (ISBN 0-8144-5698-7). Am Mgmt.

Feinberg. Applied Business Communications. 1981. 15.95 (ISBN 0-88284-125-4). Alfred Pub.

Fisher, Dalmar. Communication in Organizations. (Illus.). 480p. 1981. text ed. 16.95 (ISBN 0-8299-0374-7). West Pub.

Gartside, I. Model Business Letters. 2nd ed. 416p. 1974. pap. 13.95x (Pub. by Macdonald & Evans England). Intl Ideas.

Gartside, L. Modern Business Correspondence. 3rd ed. (Illus.). 480p. 1976. pap. 14.95x (ISBN 0-7121-1392-4, Pub. by Macdonald & Evans England). Intl Ideas.
Goodworth, Clive T. Effective Speaking & Presentation for the Company Executive. 204p. 1980. text ed. 12.25x (Pub. by Busn Bks England). Renouf.
Greyser, Stephen A. Cases in Advertising & Communications Management. 2nd ed. 300p. 1981. text ed. 19.95 (ISBN 0-13-118513-6). P-H.
Himstreet & Baty. Plaid for Business Communications. rev. ed. 1981. price not set (ISBN 0-256-02720-X, 12-1175-02). Learning Syst.
Holtz, Herman R. & Schmidt, Terry D. The Winning Proposal: How to Write It. (Business Communication Ser.). (Illus.). 384p. 1981. text ed. 18.95x (ISBN 0-07-029649-9). McGraw.
Huseman, Richard B., et al. Business Communication. LC 80-65802. 448p. 1981. text ed. 16.95 (ISBN 0-03-050946-7). Dryden Pr.
--Readings in Business Communication. 1981. pap. text ed. 8.95 (ISBN 0-03-058206-7). Dryden Pr.
International Association of Business Communicators. Inside Organizational Communication. (Longman Public Communication Ser.). 384p. (Orig.). 1981. text ed. 22.50 (ISBN 0-582-28235-7); pap. text ed. 12.50 (ISBN 0-582-28234-9). Longman.
Koehler, Jerry W. & Sisco, John I. Public Communication in Business & the Professions. 300p. 1981. text ed. 11.36 (ISBN 0-8299-0417-4). West Pub.
Marlow, Eugene. Managing the Corporate Media Center. (The Video Bookshelf Ser.). (Illus.). 175p. 1981. text ed. 19.95 (ISBN 0-914236-68-7). Knowledge Indus.
Penrose, John M. Applications in Business Communication. 1981. pap. text ed. 7.95 (ISBN 0-03-058202-4). Dryden Pr.
Quible, Zane K., et al. Introduction to Business Communication. (Illus.). 496p. 1981. text ed. 16.95 (ISBN 0-13-479055-3). P-H.
Ragan Report Editors. Organizational Communication: Questions & Answers. 124p. (Orig.). 1980. pap. 10.00 (ISBN 0-931368-04-9). Ragan Comm.
Roman, Kenneth & Raphaelson, Joel. Writing That Works. LC 80-8695. 160p. 1981. 9.95 (ISBN 0-06-014843-8, HarpT). Har-Row.
Walter, Gordon A. The Handbook of Experiential Learning & Change. 600p. 1981. 29.95 (ISBN 0-471-08355-0, Pub. by Wiley-Interscience). Wiley.

COMMUNICATION IN MANAGEMENT–BIBLIOGRAPHY
Jacobi, Ernst. Work at Writing: A Workbook to Accompany Writing at Work. 112p. 1980. pap. text ed. 5.50x (ISBN 0-8104-6117-X). Hayden.

COMMUNICATION IN MEDICINE
see also Health Education; Medical Libraries; Medical Writing; Medicine–Information Services
Ashworth, Pat M. Care to Communicate. (RCN Research Monographs). 184p. (Orig.). 1980. pap. 10.00 (ISBN 0-443-02412-X). Churchill.
Edwards, Barba J. & Brilhart, John K. Communications in Nursing Practice. (Illus.). 240p. 1981. pap. text ed. 9.95 (ISBN 0-8016-0786-8). Mosby.
Metzger, Norman & Munn, Harry. Communication in Health Care. 150p. 1981. text ed. price not set (ISBN 0-89443-356-3). Aspen Systems.
Reeder, Robert C. The Sourcebook of Medical Communications. (Illus.). 325p. 1981. text ed. 29.00 (ISBN 0-8016-4177-2). Mosby.

COMMUNICATION IN THE SOCIAL SCIENCES
DeLo, James S. & Green, William A. Multicultural Transactions: A Workbook Focusing on Communication Between Groups. LC 80-69328. 125p. 1981. perfect bdg. 11.50 (ISBN 0-86548-030-3). Century Twenty One.
Pearce, W. Barnett & Cronen, Vernon E. Communication, Action & Meaning: The Creation of Social Realities. 308p. 1980. 29.95 (ISBN 0-03-057611-3). Praeger.

COMMUNICATION OF TECHNICAL INFORMATION
see also Technical Libraries; Technical Writing
Danielson. Radio Systems for Technicians, No. 2. 1981. text ed. price not set (ISBN 0-408-00561-0). Butterworth.
Fear, David E. Technical Communication. 2nd ed. 1981. pap. text ed. 9.95x (ISBN 0-673-15401-7). Scott F.
International Technical Communication Conference, 27th, Minneapolis, May 14-17, 1980. Technical Communication--the Bridge of Understanding: Proceedings. Society for Technical Communication, ed. 1058p. 1980. pap. text ed. 35.00x (ISBN 0-914548-32-8). Univelt Inc.
Puzman, Josef & Porizek, Radoslav. Communication Control in Computer Networks. (Wiley Series in Computing). 300p. 1981. 36.00 (ISBN 0-471-27894-7, Pub. by Wiley Interscience). Wiley.
Turner, Barry T. Effective Technical Writing & Speaking. 2nd ed. 220p. 1978. text ed. 22.00x (ISBN 0-220-66344-0, Pub. by Busn Bks England). Renouf.

COMMUNICATION SATELLITES
see Artificial Satellites in Telecommunication

COMMUNICATION SKILLS (ELEMENTARY EDUCATION)
see English Language–Study and Teaching (Elementary)

COMMUNICATION THEORY
see Information Theory

COMMUNICATIONS RELAY SYSTEMS
see Artificial Satellites in Telecommunication

COMMUNICATIONS RESEARCH
see also Content Analysis (Communication)
Cragan, John F. & Shields, Donald C. Applied Communication Research: A Dramatistic Approach. 432p. 1981. text ed. 17.95x (ISBN 0-917974-53-0). Waveland Pr.
Stempel, Guido H., III & Westley, Bruce H. Research Methods in Mass Communication. (Illus.). 480p. 1981. text ed. 19.95 (ISBN 0-13-774240-1). P-H.
Tucker, Raymond, et al. Research in Speech Communication. (Ser. in Speech Communication). (Illus.). 352p. 1981. text ed. 18.95 (ISBN 0-13-774273-8). P-H.

COMMUNICATIVE DISORDERS
Schubert, E. D. Hearing: Its Function & Dysfunction. (Disorders of Human Communications: Vol. 1). (Illus.). 200p. 1980. 29.50 (ISBN 0-387-81579-1). Springer-Verlag.
Weiss, Curtis E. & Lillywhite, Harold S. Communicative Disorders: Prevention & Early Intervention. 2nd ed. (Illus.). 398p. 1981. pap. text ed. 12.50 (ISBN 0-8016-5389-4). Mosby.

COMMUNION
see Lord's Supper

COMMUNION SERMONS
Meeter, John. He Took Bread & Broke It. 1981. 6.95 (ISBN 0-533-04729-3). Vantage.

COMMUNISM
Here are entered general works. For works on communism in specific countries, see subdivisions below.
see also Communists; Marxian Economics; Nationalism and Socialism; Socialism; Women and Socialism
Alexander, Robert J. The Right Opposition: The Lovestoneites & the International Communist Opposition of the 1930's. LC 80-1705. (Contributions in Political Science: No. 54). 312p. 1981. lib. bdg. 32.50 (ISBN 0-313-22070-0, AOP/). Greenwood.
Corrigan, Philip. Capitalism, State Formation & Marx Theory. 258p. 1980. 9.95 (ISBN 0-7043-3311-2, Pub. by Quartet England). Horizon.
Hirszowicz, Maria, ed. The Bureaucratic Leviathan: A Study in the Sociology of Communism. 224p. 1980. text ed. 27.50x (ISBN 0-8147-3406-5). NYU Pr.
Hudson, C. Wayne. The Marxist Philosophy of Ernest Bloch. Date not set. price not set (ISBN 0-312-51860-9). St Martin.
Karl Marx-Frederick Engels: Collected Works, Vol. 16. (Illus.). 8.50 (ISBN 0-7178-0516-6). Intl Pub Co.
LaRouche, Lyndon H., Jr. What Every Conservative Should Know About Communism. LC 80-20325. (Illus.). 149p. (Orig.). 1980. pap. 3.95 (ISBN 0-933488-06-8). New Benjamin.
Merleau-Ponty, Maurice. Humanism & Terror: An Essay on the Communist Problem. O'Neill, John, tr. from Fr. LC 80-21672. xlvii, 189p. 1980. Repr. of 1969 ed. lib. bdg. 25.00x (ISBN 0-313-22748-9, MEHU). Greenwood.
Wawrzkowicz, Peter. In the Shadow of Hammer & Sickle. Date not set. 6.95 (ISBN 0-8062-1657-3). Carlton.

COMMUNISM–HISTORY
Alexander, Robert J. The Right Opposition: The Lovestoneities & the International Communist Opposition of the 1930's. LC 80-1711. (Contributions in Political Science Ser.: No. 54). 320p. 1981. lib. bdg. 32.50 (AOP/). Greenwood.

COMMUNISM–AFRICA
Ottaway, David & Ottaway, Marina. Afrocommunism. LC 80-24289. (New Library of African Affairs Ser.). 320p. 1981. text ed. 25.00x (ISBN 0-8419-0664-5, Africana). Holmes & Meier.

COMMUNISM–EUROPE
Boggs, Carl. The Impasse of European Communism. 1981. lib. bdg. 20.00x (ISBN 0-89158-784-5). Westview.
Schwab, George, ed. Eurocommunism: The Ideological & Political-Theoretical Foundations. LC 80-26864. (Contributions in Political Science: No. 60). 352p. 1981. lib. bdg. 25.00 (ISBN 0-313-22908-2). Greenwood.
—Eurocommunism: The Ideological & Political-Theoretical Foundations. (Contributions in Political Science: No. 60). (Illus.). 352p. 1981. lib. bdg. 25.00 (ISBN 0-313-22908-2, SEU/). Greenwood.

COMMUNISM–GREAT BRITAIN
Wallerstein, Immanual, ed. On the European Workers' Movements and Eurocommunism. 100p. 1980. pap. 5.001311. Synthesis Pubns.

COMMUNISM–HUNGARY
Volgyes, Ivan. Hungary: A Profile. (Nations of Contemporary Eastern Europe). (Illus.). 128p. 1981. lib. bdg. 16.50x (ISBN 0-89158-929-5). Westview.

COMMUNISM–INDIA
Fonseca, A. J., ed. The Marxian Dilemma: Transformation of Values to Prices. 1980. 10.00x (ISBN 0-8364-0654-0, Pub. by Manohar India). South Asia Bks.

COMMUNISM–INDONESIA
Tichelman, Fritjov. The Social Evolution of Indonesia: The Asiatic Mode of Production & Its Legacy. (Studies in Social History: No. 5). 314p. 1980. lib. bdg. 44.75 (ISBN 90-247-2389-2, Pub. by Martinus Nijhoff). Kluwer Boston.

COMMUNISM–JAPAN
Itoh, Makoto. Value & Crisis: Essays on Marxian Economics in Japan. LC 80-8084. 192p. 1980. 13.50 (ISBN 0-85345-556-2); pap. 7.00 (ISBN 0-85345-557-0). Monthly Rev.

COMMUNISM–RUSSIA
Berdyaev, Nicolas. The Origin of Russian Communism. 239p. 1980. Repr. of 1937 ed. lib. bdg. 30.00 (ISBN 0-89760-047-9). Telegraph Bks.

COMMUNISM–UNITED STATES
Bales, James. Communism Killed Kennedy but Did America Learn? 3.95 (ISBN 0-89315-015-0). Lambert Bk.
Revolutionary Continuity: Marxist Leadership in the U. S., 1848-1917. 1981. 20.00 (ISBN 0-913460-85-0); pap. 5.45 (ISBN 0-913460-84-2). Monad Pr.

COMMUNISM AND SOCIETY
Burger, et al. Marxism, Science & the Movement of History. (Philosophical Currents Ser.: No. 27). 1981. pap. text ed. 34.25x. Humanities.
Gilbert, Alan. Marx's Politics: Communists & Citizens. 320p. 1981. 19.00 (ISBN 0-8135-0903-3). Rutgers U Pr.

COMMUNIST COUNTRIES–POLITICS AND GOVERNMENT
Staar, Richard F., ed. Yearbook on International Communist Affairs: 1981. 1981. 35.00 (ISBN 0-8179-7501-2). Hoover Inst Pr.

COMMUNIST PARTY OF FRANCE
Lange, Peter & Vannicelli, Maurizio, eds. The Communist Parties of Italy France & Spain: Postwar Change & Continuity, a Casebook. (Casebook Series on European Politics & Society: No. 1). 392p. 1981. text ed. 42.00x (ISBN 0-04-329033-7, 2644-5); pap. text ed. 18.50 (ISBN 0-686-69601-8). Allen Unwin.

COMMUNIST PARTY OF ITALY
Lange, Peter & Vannicelli, Maurizio, eds. The Communist Parties of Italy France & Spain: Postwar Change & Continuity, a Casebook. (Casebook Series on European Politics & Society: No. 1). 392p. 1981. text ed. 42.00x (ISBN 0-04-329033-7, 2644-5); pap. text ed. 18.50 (ISBN 0-686-69601-8). Allen Unwin.

COMMUNIST PARTY OF THE UNITED STATES OF AMERICA
Hall, Gus. Basics: For Peace, Democracy & Social Progress. 348p. (Orig.). 1980. 14.00 (ISBN 0-7178-0580-8); pap. 4.50 (ISBN 0-7178-0578-6). Intl Pub Co.

COMMUNISTS
Wolfe, Bertram D. Strange Communists I Have Known. LC 65-14401. 232p. 1981. pap. 7.95 (ISBN 0-8128-6120-5). Stein & Day.

COMMUNITY
see also Community Life; Community Organizations
McDowell, Charles P. Community Relations & Criminal Justice. 500p. Date not set. text ed. price not set (ISBN 0-87084-558-6). Anderson Pub Co.

COMMUNITY AND LIBRARIES
see Libraries and Community

COMMUNITY AND SCHOOL
Here are entered works on ways in which the community at large, as distinct from government, may aid the school program.
Burges, Bill. Facts for a Change: Citizen Action Research for a Better Schools. 125p. (Orig.). 1976. pap. text ed. 5.00 (ISBN 0-917754-03-4). Inst Responsive.
Davies, Don, ed. Schools Where Parents Make a Difference. 163p. (Orig.). 1976. pap. text ed. 3.95 (ISBN 0-917754-00-X). Inst Responsive.
Davies, Don & Zerchykov, Ross, eds. Citizen Participation in Education: Annotated Bibliography. 386p. (Orig.). 1978. pap. text ed. 15.00 (ISBN 0-917754-05-0). Inst Responsive.
Davies, Don, et al. Federal & State Impact on Citizen Participation in the Schools. 147p. (Orig.). 1978. pap. text ed. 5.00 (ISBN 0-917754-02-4). Inst Responsive.
Hamer, Irving, et al, eds. Opening the Door: Citizen Roles in Educational Collective Bargaining. 194p. (Orig.). 1979. pap. 4.50 (ISBN 0-917754-11-5). Inst Responsive.
Huguenin, Kathleen, et al. Narrowing the Gap Between Intent & Practice: A Report to Policy-Makers on Community Organizations & School Decisionmaking. 118p. (Orig.). 1979. pap. 5.00 (ISBN 0-917754-13-1). Inst Responsive.
Wachtel, Betsy & Powers, Brian. Rising Above Decline. Seymour, Nancy, ed. 198p. (Orig.). 1979. pap. 4.50 (ISBN 0-917754-14-X). Inst Responsive.

COMMUNITY ANTENNA TELEVISION
Hollowell, Mary L. The Cable-Broadband Communications Book, 1980-1981, Vol. 2. (Video Bookshelf Ser.). 300p. 1980. text ed. 29.95x (ISBN 0-914236-79-2). Knowledge Indus.

COMMUNITY COLLEGES
The Community, Technical, & Junior College in the United States. 96p. 1978. 3.50 (IIE). Unipub.
Cosand, Joseph P. Perspective: Community Colleges in the Nineteen Eighties. (ERIC Monographs Ser.). 60p. (Orig.). pap. 5.00 (ISBN 0-87117-049-3). Am Assn Comm Jr Coll.

COMMUNITY COUNCILS
see Community Organizations

COMMUNITY DEVELOPMENT
see also City Planning; Factories–Location; Technical Assistance
Baine, Sean. Community Action & Local Government. 96p. 1975. pap. text ed. 8.75x (ISBN 0-7135-1842-1, Pub. by Bedford England). Renouf.
Bossong, Ken & Simpson, Jan. Appropriate Community Technologies Sourcebook. (Illus.). 180p. (Orig.). 1981. pap. text ed. 7.50 (ISBN 0-89988-055-X). Citizens Energy.
Broady, Maurice. Tomorrow's Community- the Development of Neighborhood Organisations. 86p. 1979. pap. text ed. 7.40x (ISBN 0-7199-0966-X, Pub. by Bedford England). Renouf.
Corbett, Michael N. A Better Place to Live: New Designs for Tomorrow's Communities. Stoner, Carol, ed. (Illus.). 256p. (Orig.). 1981. pap. 14.95 (ISBN 0-87857-348-8). Rodale Pr Inc.
Durand-Drouhin, Jean-Louis & Szwengrub, Lili-Marie, eds. Rural Community Studies in Europe: Trends, Selected & Annotated Bibliographies, Analyses, Vol. I. LC 80-41523. (Publications of the Vienna Centre Ser.). (Illus.). 342p. 1981. 70.50 (ISBN 0-08-021384-7). Pergamon.
Hunter, Guy, et al, eds. Policy & Practice in Rural Development. LC 76-15078. 526p. text ed. 19.50 (ISBN 0-86598-002-0). Allanheld.
Largo, Gerald A. Community & Liturgy: An Historical Overview. LC 80-1434. 151p. 1980. lib. bdg. 16.25 (ISBN 0-8191-1302-6); pap. text ed. 7.75 (ISBN 0-8191-1303-4). U Pr of Amer.
Newman, Oscar. Community of Interest. (Illus.). 368p. 1981. pap. 8.95 (ISBN 0-385-11124-X, Anch). Doubleday.
Penland & Williams. Community Psychology & Coordination. Date not set. price not set (ISBN 0-8247-6144-8). Dekker.
Ramati, Racquel & Urban Design Group of the Department of City Planning, New York. How to Save Your Own Street. LC 78-14709. (Illus.). 176p. 1981. pap. 19.95 (ISBN 0-385-14814-3, Dolp). Doubleday.
Sackman, Harold & Boehm, Barry W., eds. Planning Community Information Utilities. LC 72-83727. (Illus.). viii, 501p. 1972. 15.00 (ISBN 0-88283-000-7). AFIPS Pr.
Trained Manpower for Agricultural & Rural Development. (FAO Economic & Social Development Paper Ser.: No. 10). 132p. 1980. pap. 7.50 (ISBN 92-5-100861-2, F1963, FAO). Unipub.
Wadhva, Charan D. Rural Banks for Rural Development. 1980. 16.00x (ISBN 0-8364-0642-7, Pub. by Macmillan India). South Asia Bks.

COMMUNITY HEALTH
see Public Health

COMMUNITY HEALTH SERVICES
Blomquist, Kathleen B., et al. Community Health Nursing Continuing Education Review. 1979. pap. 9.50 (ISBN 0-87488-401-2). Med Exam.
Bruce, Nigel. Teamwork for Preventive Care, Vol. I. (Social Policy Research Monographs). 264p. 1980. 55.00 (ISBN 0-471-27883-1, Pub. by Wiley-Interscience). Wiley.
Freeman, Ruth B. & Heinrich, Janet. Community Health Nursing Practice. 2nd ed. (Illus.). 500p. 1981. text ed. price not set (ISBN 0-7216-3877-5). Saunders.

COMMUNITY JUNIOR COLLEGES
see Community Colleges

COMMUNITY LEADERSHIP
Thomson, J. S., ed. Community Leaders & Noteworthy Americans. 10th ed. 609p. 1980. 44.95x (ISBN 0-934544-02-6, Pub. by Intl Biog). Biblio Dist.

COMMUNITY LIFE
see also Community and School; Community Development; Community Leadership; Community Organizations; Libraries and Community
Library Association-the Working Party on Community Information, ed. Community Information: What Libraries Can Do. 1980. pap. 9.25x (ISBN 0-85365-872-2, Pub. by Lib Assn England). Oryx Pr.

COMMUNITY MENTAL HEALTH SERVICES
Butterworth, C. A. & Skidmore, D. Caring for the Mentally Ill in the Community. 160p. 1980. 27.00x (Pub by Croom Helm England). State Mutual Bk.
Penland & Williams. Community Psychology & Coordination. Date not set. price not set (ISBN 0-8247-6144-8). Dekker.

COMMUNITY ORGANIZATIONS
see also Community Power; Urban Renewal
Bullock, Paul, ed. Directory of Community Services Organizations in Greater Los Angeles. 255p. 1980. 6.50 (ISBN 0-89215-106-4). U Cal LA Indus Rel.
Dowden, C. James. Community Associations: A Guide for Public Officials. LC 79-57077. (Community Association Ser.). (Illus.). 88p. 1980. pap. text ed. 13.50 (ISBN 0-87420-590-5, C18). Urban Land.

Gittell, Marilyn, et al. Limits to Citizen Participation: The Decline of Community Organizations. LC 80-15950. (Sage Library of Social Research: Vol. 109). (Illus.). 280p. 1980. 18.00 (ISBN 0-8039-1478-4); pap. 8.95 (ISBN 0-8039-1479-2). Sage.
Hillary, George. A Research Odyssey: Developing & Testing a Community Theory. 158p. 1981. 15.95 (ISBN 0-87855-400-9); text ed. 15.95 (ISBN 0-686-68061-8). Transaction Bks.
Okagaki, Alan & Benson, Jim. County Energy Plan Guidebook. 2nd ed. (Illus.). 200p. (Orig.). 1979. pap. text ed. 10.00x (ISBN 0-937786-01-2). Inst Ecologica.
Peebles, Marvin L. Directory of Management Resources for Community Based Organizations: Third Annual. 100p. 1981. spiral bdg. 12.00 (ISBN 0-939020-03-3). MLP Ent.
Wesley, Roland. So You Think You Want to Be in the Helping Profession As a Community Organizer. LC 80-65603. 135p. 1981. perfect bdg. 11.50 (ISBN 0-86548-059-1). Century Twenty One.

COMMUNITY POWER
Barber, Daniel M. Citizen Participation in American Communities: Strategies for Success. LC 80-83336. 144p. 1980. pap. 8.95 (ISBN 0-8403-2299-2). Kendall-Hunt.

COMMUNITY SONG-BOOKS
see Songs

COMMUNITY SURVEYS
see Social Surveys

COMOPODA
see Lamellibranchiata

COMPANIES
see Corporations; Partnership

COMPANIES, INSURANCE
see Insurance Companies

COMPANY INSURANCE
see Insurance, Business

COMPANY LAW
see Corporation Law

COMPARATIVE ANATOMY
see Anatomy, Comparative

COMPARATIVE BEHAVIOR
see Psychology, Comparative

COMPARATIVE ECONOMICS
Bhattacharyya, M. N. Comparison of Box-Jenkins & Bonn Monetary Prediction Performance. (Lecture Notes in Economics & Mathematical Systems: Vol. 178). (Illus.). 146p. 1980. pap. 15.00 (ISBN 0-387-10011-3). Springer-Verlag.

COMPARATIVE EDUCATION
see also Intercultural Education
Holmes, Brian. Comparative Education: Some Considerations of Method. (Unwin Education Bks.). (Illus.). 1981. text ed. 22.50 (ISBN 0-04-370101-9, 2624/5); pap. text ed. 9.50 (ISBN 0-04-370102-7). Allen Unwin.
Regional Disparities in Educational Development: A Controversial Issue. 257p. 1981. pap. 18.75 (ISBN 92-803-1085-2, U1048, UNESCO). Unipub.
Regional Disparities in Educational Development: Diagnosis & Policies for Reduction. 409p. 1981. pap. 18.75 (ISBN 92-803-1086-0, U1049, UNESCO). Unipub.

COMPARATIVE GOVERNMENT
see also subdivision Politics and Government under names of countries, cities, etc.
Wirsing, Robert G., ed. Protection of Ethnic Minorities: Comparative Perspectives. LC 80-25618. (Pergamon Policy Studies on International Politices Ser.). 350p. 1981. 39.50 (ISBN 0-08-025556-6). Pergamon.

COMPARATIVE GOVERNMENT–OUTLINES, SYLLABI, ETC.
Chilcote, Ronald H. Theories of Comparative Politics: The Search for a Paradigm. 492p. (Orig.). 1981. lib. bdg. 30.00x (ISBN 0-89158-970-8); pap. 15.00x (ISBN 0-89158-971-6). Westview.

COMPARATIVE GRAMMAR
see Grammar, Comparative and General

COMPARATIVE LAW
Here are entered works on the comparison of various systems of law as a method of legal study and research. Comparative studies of individual legal topics or branches of the law are entered under the respective headings applying to these subjects.
see also Law–History and Criticism
Campbell, D. L. Comparative Law Yearbook, Vol. III. 294p. 1980. 47.50x (ISBN 90-286-0340-9). Sijthoff & Noordhoff.
Cross, Rupert. The Precedent in English Law. 3rd ed. 252p. 1977. pap. 11.95x (ISBN 0-19-876073-6). Oxford U Pr.
Seed Legislation. (Legislative Study: No. 16). 122p. 1981. pap. 6.75 (ISBN 92-5-100832-9, F2083, FAO). Unipub.

COMPARATIVE LITERATURE
see Literature, Comparative

COMPARATIVE MORPHOLOGY
see Anatomy, Comparative; Morphology

COMPARATIVE PHYSIOLOGY
see Physiology, Comparative

COMPARATIVE POLITICS
see Comparative Government

COMPARATIVE PSYCHOLOGY
see Psychology, Comparative

COMPARATIVE RELIGION
see Christianity and Other Religions; Religions

COMPASSION (ETHICS)
see Sympathy

COMPENSATION
see Pensions; Wages

COMPETENT AUTHORITY
see also Administrative Procedure; Jurisdiction
Roesch, Ronald & Golding, Stephen L. Competency to Stand Trial. LC 80-12456. 251p. 1981. 19.95 (ISBN 0-252-00825-1). U of Ill Pr.

COMPETITION
see also Government Competition; Monopolies; Supply and Demand
Zweigert, Konrad & Kropholler, Jan. Law of Copyright, Competition & Industrial Property. Kolle, Gert & Hallstein, Hans P., eds. (Sources of International Uniform Law Ser.: Vol. III-A First Supplement). 1340p. 1980. 175.00x (ISBN 9-0286-0099-X). Sijthoff & Noordhoff.

COMPETITION, GOVERNMENT
see Government Competition

COMPETITION, INTERNATIONAL
see also Commercial Treaties; International Cooperation
Gee, Sherman. Technology Transfer, Innovation, & International Competitiveness. 240p. 1980. 21.00 (ISBN 0-471-08468-9, Pub. by Wiley-Interscience). Wiley.

COMPETITION, UNFAIR
see also Advertising Laws; Patents; Price Policy; Restraint of Trade; Trade-Marks
U. S. Federal Trade Commission. Memorandum on Unfair Competition at the Common Law. 305p. 1980. Repr. of 1916 ed. lib. bdg. 28.50x (ISBN 0-8377-1228-9). Rothman.

COMPETITIONS
see Rewards (Prizes, etc.)

COMPETITIVE EXAMINATIONS
see Civil Service Examinations

COMPLEXION
see Beauty, Personal; Cosmetics

COMPONENTS CONSTRUCTION
see Buildings, Prefabricated

COMPOSERS
Clinkscale, Edward, ed. Les Oeuvres Completes d'antoine de Fevin. (Gesamtausgaben - Collected Works Ser.: Vol. XI, No. 1). xvi, 134p. (Eng. & Ger.). 1980. lib. bdg. 55.00 (ISBN 0-912024-68-2). Inst Mediaeval.

COMPOSERS–CORRESPONDENCE, REMINISCENCES, ETC.
see Musicians–Correspondence, Reminiscences, etc.

COMPOSERS–DICTIONARIES
see Music–Bio-Bibliography

COMPOSERS, AMERICAN
Bandel, Betty. Sing the Lord's Song in a Strange Land: The Life of Justin Morgan. LC 78-73309. 280p. 1981. 17.50 (ISBN 0-8386-2411-1). Fairleigh Dickinson.

COMPOSERS, AMERICAN–BIBLIOGRAPHY
OAS General Secretariat Technical Unit of Performing Arts. Compositores De America, No. 8. rev. ed. (Composers of the Americas Ser.). (Illus.). 157p. (Eng. -Span.). 1980. Repr. of 1962 ed. 7.00 (ISBN 0-8270-1085-0). OAS.

COMPOSERS, BRITISH
Bent, Margaret. Dunstaple. (Studies of Composers: No. 17). 96p. 1981. pap. 14.95 (ISBN 0-19-315225-8). Oxford U Pr.

COMPOSITE MATERIALS
Bunsell, A. R., et al, eds. Advances in Composite Materials: Proceedings of the Third International Conference on Composite Materials, Paris, France, 26-29 August, 1980. LC 80-40997. 2000p. 1980. 200.00 (ISBN 0-08-026717-3). Pergamon.
Tsai, Stephen W. & Hahn, H. Thomas. Introduction to Composite Materials. LC 80-51965. 475p. 1980. 35.00 (ISBN 0-87762-288-4). Technomic.

COMPOSITES, FIBROUS
see Fibrous Composites

COMPOSITION (ART)
see also Painting; Proportion (Art)
Parramon, J. M. Composition. (Orig.). 1981. pap. 4.95 (ISBN 0-89586-084-8). H P Bks.

COMPOSITION (MUSIC)
see also Musical Accompaniment
Engel, Lehman. The Musical Theater Workshop. (Sound Seminars Ser.). bk., tapes, listening guide 350.00x (ISBN 0-88432-065-0, 11500). J Norton Pubs.
Leinsdorf, Erich. The Composer's Advocate: A Radical Orthodoxy for Musicians. LC 80-17614. (Illus.). 232p. 1981. 14.95 (ISBN 0-300-02427-4). Yale U Pr.

COMPOSITION (PHOTOGRAPHY)
Bruck, Axel. Practical Composition. LC 80-40759. (Practical Photography Ser.). (Illus.). 164p. 1981. 19.95 (ISBN 0-240-51060-7). Focal Pr.

COMPOSITION (PRINTING)
see Type-Setting

COMPOSITION (RHETORIC)
see Letter-Writing; Rhetoric;
also subdivision Composition and Exercises under names of languages

COMPOUNDS, UNSATURATED
Devon, T. K. & Scott, A. I. Handbook of Naturally Occurring Compounds, 2 vols. Incl. Vol. 1. Acetogenins, Shikimates & Carbohydrates. 1975. 51.50 (ISBN 0-12-213601-2); Vol. 2. Terpenes. 1972. 42.00 (ISBN 0-12-213602-0). Acad Pr.

COMPREHENSIVE HEALTH CARE DELIVERY ORGANIZATIONS
see Health Maintenance Organizations

COMPRESSED GAS
see Gases, Compressed

COMPTROLLERSHIP
see Controllership

COMPULSION (PSYCHOLOGY)
see Obsessive-Compulsive Neuroses

COMPULSORY MILITARY SERVICE
see Military Service, Compulsory

COMPULSORY SCHOOL ATTENDANCE
see Educational Law and Legislation; School Attendance

COMPUTABILITY THEORY
see Recursive Functions

COMPUTABLE FUNCTIONS
see Recursive Functions

COMPUTATIONAL LINGUISTICS
see Linguistics–Data Processing; Programming Languages (Electronic Computers)

COMPUTER ARCHITECTURE
see also Computer Engineering
Reynolds, R. A. Computer Methods for Architects. (Illus.). 160p. 1980. text ed. 39.95 (ISBN 0-408-00476-2). Butterworths.

COMPUTER-ASSISTED INSTRUCTION
Bork, Alfred. Learning with Computers. (Illus.). 250p. 1981. 24.00 (ISBN 0-932376-11-8). Digital Pr.
O'Neil, Harold F., ed. Computer-Based Instruction: A State-of-the-Art Assessment. (Educational Technology Ser.). 1981. price not set (ISBN 0-12-526760-6). Acad Pr.

COMPUTER CIRCUITS
see Computers–Circuits

COMPUTER CONTROL
see Automation

COMPUTER DEBUGGING
see Debugging (Electronic Computers)

COMPUTER DEPARTMENT SECURITY MEASURES
see Electronic Data Processing Departments–Security Measures

COMPUTER DRAWING
Clark, David R. Computers for Image-Making. (Audio-Visual Media for Education & Research Ser.: Vol. 2). (Illus.). 166p. 1980. 29.00 (ISBN 0-08-024058-5); pap. 14.50 (ISBN 0-08-024059-3). Pergamon.

COMPUTER ENGINEERING
see also Computer Architecture
Configuring Distributed Computer Systems. 1981. pap. 5.00 (ISBN 0-918734-28-2). Reymont.
Osaki, S. & Nishio, T. Reliability Evaluation of Some Fault-Tolerant Computer Architectures. (Lecture Notes in Computer Science Ser.: Vol. 97). 129p. 1981. pap. 9.80 (ISBN 0-387-10274-4). Springer-Verlag.
Siewiorek, Daniel & Swarz, Robert. The Design & Evaluation of Reliable Computing Structures. 520p. Date not set. 35.00 (ISBN 0-932376-13-4). Digital Pr.
Siewiorek, Daniel, et al. Principles of Computer Structures. (Computer Science Ser.). (Illus.). 768p. 1981. text ed. 29.95 (ISBN 0-07-057302-6, C). McGraw.
Tomek, Ivan. Introduction to Computer Organization Workbook. (Illus., Orig.). 1981. pap. text ed. price not set (ISBN 0-914894-70-6). Computer Sci.
Utley, B. G. IBM System-38: Technical Developments. (IBM Systems Design & Development Ser.). (Illus.). 109p. 1980. pap. 5.50 (ISBN 0-933186-03-7, G-580-0237-1). IBM Armonk.

COMPUTER GRAPHICS
Cosentino, John, ed. Computer Graphics Marketplace. 1981. pap. 22.50 (ISBN 0-912700-91-2). Oryx Pr.
Foundyller, Charles M. Turnkey CAD-CAM Computer Graphics: A Survey & Buyers' Guide for Manufacturers, 3 pts, Pts. 1,2, & 3. (Illus.). 476p. 1980. Set. spiral with laminated covers 199.00x (ISBN 0-938484-04-4). Daratech.
--Turnkey CAD-CAM Computer Graphics: A Survey & Buyers' Guide for Manufacturers, Pts. 1 & 2. Incl. Pt. 1. 254p. 84.00x (ISBN 0-938484-01-X); Pt. 2. 120p. 69.00x (ISBN 0-938484-02-8). (Illus.). 374p. 1980. Set. spiral with laminated covers 153.00x (ISBN 0-938484-00-1). Daratech.
--Turnkey CAD-CAM Computer Graphics: A Survey & Buyers' Guide for Manufacturers, Pt. 3. (Illus.). 102p. 1980. spiral with laminated covers 46.00x (ISBN 0-938484-03-6). Daratech.
Pavlidis, Theo. Computer Graphics & Pictorial Information Processing. (Illus.). 1981. text ed. price not set (ISBN 0-914894-65-X). Computer Sci.

COMPUTER LANGUAGES
see Programming Languages (Electronic Computers)

COMPUTER MATHEMATICS
see Numerical Analysis

COMPUTER MEMORY SYSTEMS
see Computer Storage Devices

COMPUTER MUSIC
Brun, Herbert & Gaburo, Kenneth. Collaboration One. 24p. 1976. soft cover saddle-stitched 15.00. Lingua Pr.

COMPUTER PROGRAM LANGUAGES
see Programming Languages (Electronic Computers)

COMPUTER PROGRAMMING
see Programming (Electronic Computers)

COMPUTER PROGRAMMING MANAGEMENT
Dunn, Robert & Ullman, Richard. Quality Assurance for Computer Software. (Illus.). 1981. 19.50 (ISBN 0-07-018312-0, P&R&B). McGraw.
Lorin, Harold & Deitel, Harvey. Operating Systems. LC 80-10625. (Computer Science: Systems Programming (IBM) Ser.). (Illus.). 480p. 1981. text ed. 18.95 (ISBN 0-201-14464-6). A-W.
McClure, Carma. Managing Software Development & Maintenance. 224p. 1981. text ed. 16.95 (ISBN 0-442-22569-5). Van Nos Reinhold.
Metzger, Philip. Managing a Programming Project. 2nd ed. (Illus.). 288p. 1981. text ed. 21.50 (ISBN 0-13-550772-3). P-H.

COMPUTER PROGRAMS
Beebe, William, intro. by. Autofact West Proceedings, Vol. 1. LC 80-53423. (Illus.). 939p. 1980. pap. 55.00 (ISBN 0-87263-065-X). SME.
Berg, H. K. & Giloi, W. K., eds. The Use of Formal Specification of Software & Firmware. (Informatik-Fachberichte Ser.: Vol. 36). 388p. 1981. pap. 27.50 (ISBN 0-387-10442-9). Springer-Verlag.
Burnham, Don, intro. by. Manufacturing Productivity Solutions II. LC 80-54415. (Illus.). 161p. 1980. pap. text ed. 20.00 (ISBN 0-87263-106-0). SME.
Bywater, R. Hardware-Software Design of Digital Systems. 1981. 28.00 (ISBN 0-13-383950-8). P-H.
Dunn, Robert & Ullman, Richard. Quality Assurance for Computer Software. (Illus.). 1981. 19.50 (ISBN 0-07-018312-0, P&R&B). McGraw.
Gilder, Jules H. Basic Computer Programs in Science & Engineering. 256p. 1980. pap. 9.95 (ISBN 0-8104-0761-2). Hayden.
Glass, Robert L. & Noiseux, Ronald A. Software Maintenance Guidebook. (Illus.). 208p. 1981. text ed. 21.95 (ISBN 0-13-821728-9). P-H.
McCarty, Frank, intro. by. Autofact West Proceedings, Vol. 2. LC 80-53423. (Illus.). 842p. 1980. pap. 55.00 (ISBN 0-87263-066-8). SME.
Martin, James. Computer Networks & Distributed Processing: Software, Techniques, & Architecture. (Illus.). 544p. 1981. text ed. 32.50 (ISBN 0-13-165258-3). P-H.
Muchnick, Steven S. & Jones, Neil D. Program Flow Analysis: Theory & Application. (Software Ser.). (Illus.). 448p. 1981. 21.50 (ISBN 0-13-729681-9). P-H.
Norback, Craig T. The Computer Invasion. 304p. 1981. text ed. 18.95 (ISBN 0-442-26121-7). Van Nos Reinhold.
People's Computer Company. Dr. Dobb's Journal of Computer Calesthenics & Orthodontia: Running Light Without Overbyte, 3 vols. 1980. pap. 18.95 ea.; Vol. 1. pap. (ISBN 0-8104-5475-0); Vol. 2. pap. (ISBN 0-8104-5484-X); Vol. 3. pap. (ISBN 0-8104-5490-4). Hayden.
Sagan, Hans & Meyer, Carl D., Jr. Ten Easy Pieces: Creative Programming for Fun & Profit. 192p. 1980. pap. 7.95 (ISBN 0-8104-5160-3). Hayden.
Sandford, D. M. Using Sophisticated Models in Resolution Theorem Proving. (Lecture Notes in Computer Science Ser.: Vol. 90). (Illus.). 239p. 1981. pap. 14.00 (ISBN 0-387-10231-0). Springer Verlag.
Sternberg, Charles. Basic Computer Programs for the Home. 336p. 1979. pap. 9.95 (ISBN 0-8104-5154-9). Hayden.
Taraman, Khalil S., ed. CAD-CAM, Meeting Today's Productivity Challenge. LC 80-69006. (Manufacturing Update Ser.). (Illus.). 281p. 1980. 29.00 (ISBN 0-87263-063-3). SME.

COMPUTER SECURITY MEASURES
see Electronic Data Processing Departments–Security Measures

COMPUTER SIMULATION, DIGITAL
see Digital Computer Simulation

COMPUTER SOFTWARE
see Computer Programs; Programming (Electronic Computers); Programming Languages (Electronic Computers);
also similar headings

COMPUTER STORAGE DEVICES
Jung, Walter G. IC Array Cookbook. 208p. 1980. pap. 8.85 (ISBN 0-8104-0762-0). Hayden.
Miller, Stephen W., ed. Memory & Storage Technolgy, Vol II. (The Information Technology Ser.). (Illus.). 182p. 1977. pap. 20.00 (ISBN 0-88283-015-5). AFIPS Pr.
Sauer, Charles & Chandy, Mani K. Contemporary Systems Performance Modeling. (Illus.). 384p. 1981. text ed. 18.95 (ISBN 0-13-165175-7). P-H.
Schank, Roger C. & Riesbeck, Christopher K. Inside Computer Understanding: Five Programs Plus Miniatures. LC 80-18314. (Artificial Intelligence Ser.). 368p. 1981. profess. & reference 24.95 (ISBN 0-89859-071-X). L Erlbaum Assocs.

COMPUTERS
Here are entered works on modern electronic computers first developed after 1945. Works on calculators, as well as all mechanical computers of pre-1945 vintage, are entered under Calculating-Machines.
see also Electronic Data Processing; Electronic Digital Computers; Information Storage and Retrieval Systems; Minicomputers
also headings beginning with the word Computer
Bernstein, Jeremy. The Analytical Engine: Computers-Past, Present, & Future. rev. ed. 128p. 1981. 8.95; pap. 4.95. Morrow.

Bibel, W. & Kowalski, R., eds. Fifth Conference on Automated Deduction, les Arcs Proceedings. (Lecture Notes in Computer Science: Vol. 87). (Illus.). 385p. 1980. pap. 22.00 (ISBN 0-387-10009-1). Springer-Verlag.

Bursky, Dave. The S-One Hundred Bus Handbook. 280p. 1980. pap. 14.50 (ISBN 0-8104-0897-X). Hayden.

Encarnacao, J. Computer Aided Design Modelling, Systems Engineering, CAD Systems. (Lecture Notes in Computer Science Ser.: Vol. 89). 459p. 1981. pap. 27.00 (ISBN 0-387-10242-6). Springer-Verlag.

Fuori, William M. Introduction to the Computer: The Tool of Business. 3rd ed. (Illus.). 720p. 1981. text ed. 17.95 (ISBN 0-13-480343-4); pap. 5.95 study guide (ISBN 0-13-480368-X). P-H.

Goldstine, Herman H. The Computer from Pascal to Von Neumann. LC 70-173755. (Illus.). 400p. 1980. 22.50x (ISBN 0-691-08104-2); pap. 6.95 (ISBN 0-691-02367-0). Princeton U Pr.

Hsiao, T. C., ed. Computer Dissertations: Second Supplement, 1979-1980. LC 78-59418. 300p. 1981. 25.00 (ISBN 0-686-28922-6). Sci & Tech Pr.

Inman, Don, et al. Introduction to TI BASIC. 300p. (gr. 10-12). 1980. pap. 10.95 (ISBN 0-8104-5185-9). Hayden.

National Computer Conference, 1977. AFIPS Proceedings, Vol. 46. Korfhage, Robert R., ed. LC 55-44701. (Illus.). xiv, 1026p. 1977. 60.00 (ISBN 0-88283-007-4). AFIPS Pr.

National Computer Conference, 1978. AFIPS Proceedings, Vol. 47. Ghosh, Sakti P. & Liu, Leonard Y., eds. LC 55-44701. (Illus.). xxxiv, 1300p. 1978. 60.00 (ISBN 0-88283-006-6). AFIPS Pr.

National Computer Conference, 1979. AFIPS Proceedings, Vol. 48. Merwin, Richard E., ed. LC 55-44701. (Illus.). xi, 1114p. 1979. 60.00 (ISBN 0-88283-005-8). AFIPS Pr.

National Computer Conference, 1980. AFIPS Proceedings, Vol. 49. Medley, Donald B., ed. LC 80-66206. (Illus.). 1980. 60.00 (ISBN 0-88283-003-1). AFIPS Pr.

Nijholt, A. Context-Free Grammars: Covers, Normal Forms, & Parsing. (Lecture Notes in Computer Science Ser.: Vol. 93). 253p. 1981. pap. 16.80 (ISBN 0-387-10245-0). Springer-Verlag.

Stern, Nancy. History of Computing: From ENIAC to UNIVAC. (Illus.). 280p. 1981. 21.00 (ISBN 0-932376-14-2). Digital Pr.

Willis, Jerry & Miller, Merl. Computers for Everybody. 140p. 1981. pap. 4.95 (ISBN 0-918398-49-5). Dilithium Pr.

COMPUTERS–APPRAISAL

see Computers–Valuation

COMPUTERS–CIRCUITS

Jung, Walter G. IC Array Cookbook. 208p. 1980. pap. 8.85 (ISBN 0-8104-0762-0). Hayden.

COMPUTERS–DEBUGGING

see Debugging (Electronic Computers)

COMPUTERS–DESIGN AND CONSTRUCTION

see Computer Engineering

COMPUTERS–DICTIONARIES

Kelly-Bootle, Stan. The Devil's DP Dictionary. (Illus.). 160p. 1981. 5.95 (ISBN 0-07-034022-6, P&RB). McGraw.

COMPUTERS–DIRECTORIES

Hsiao, T. C., ed. Computer Faculty Directory (U. S. Edition) 350p. 1981. 35.00 (ISBN 0-686-28923-4). Sci & Tech Pr.

COMPUTERS–HANDBOOKS, MANUALS, ETC.

Atkin, J. K. Computer Science. 2nd ed. (Illus.). 224p. (Orig.). 1980. pap. 12.95x (ISBN 0-7121-0396-1). Intl Ideas.

Huffman & Bruce. How to Debug Your Personal Computer. 175p. 1980. pap. 7.95 (ISBN 0-8359-2924-8). Reston.

Jensen, C. W. & Fisher, Eugene. The I E E E Four Eighty-Eight Interface Parts Handbook. 280p. (Orig.). 1980. pap. 6.99 (ISBN 0-931988-50-0). Osborne-McGraw.

Kane, Gerry. The CRT Controller Handbook. 250p. (Orig.). 1980. pap. 6.99 (ISBN 0-931988-45-4). Osborne-McGraw.

Leventhal, Lance, et al. Z Eight Thousand Assembly Language Programming. (Assembly Language Programming Ser.: No.5). 930p. (Orig.). 1980. pap. text ed. 19.99 (ISBN 0-931988-36-5). Osborne-McGraw.

Ling, Robert F. & Roberts, Harry V. Users Manual for IDA. (Data Analysis Ser.). 300p. 1980. pap. text ed. 12.50 (ISBN 0-07-037905-X, C). McGraw.

Osborne, Adam. PET-CBM Personal Computer Guide. 2nd ed. 530p. 1980. pap. 15.00 (ISBN 0-931988-55-1). Osborne-McGraw.

Winger, Martin. Electronic Calculator Handbook for Pilots. (Illus.). Date not set. spiral bdg. 3.95 (ISBN 0-911721-77-0, Pub. by Winger). Aviation.

COMPUTERS–JUVENILE LITERATURE

Bitter, Gary. Exploring with Computers. (Illus.). (gr. 4-7). 1981. PLB price not set (ISBN 0-671-34034-4). Messner.

COMPUTERS–LAW AND LEGISLATION

Brooks, Daniel T., ed. Computer Law: Purchasing, Leasing, & Licensing Hardware, Software & Services. LC 80-82741. (Nineteen Eighty to Nineteen Eighty-One Commercial Law & Practice Course Handbook Ser.). 382p. 1981. pap. 25.00 (ISBN 0-686-69165-2, A4-3089). PLI.

Gemignami, Michael. Law & the Computer: A Guide for Computer Professionals. 320p. 1981. 18.95 (ISBN 0-8436-1604-0). CBI Pub.

Gilchrist, Bruce & Wessel, Milton R. Government Regulation of the Computer Industry. LC 72-83726. ix, 247p. 1972. 12.50 (ISBN 0-88283-028-7). AFIPS Pr.

Leininger, Joseph E. & Gilchrist, Bruce, eds. Computers, Society & Law: The Role of Legal Education. LC 73-93427. (Illus.). 264p. 1973. pap. 6.00 (ISBN 0-88283-001-5). AFIPS Pr.

Winkler, Stanley & Wewer, William, eds. Computers, Law & Public Policy. LC 80-69245. (Executive Information Ser.). 400p. Date not set. price not set (ISBN 0-88283-030-9). AFIPS Pr.

COMPUTERS–MEMORY SYSTEMS

see Computer Storage Devices

Bursky, Dave. Memory Systems Design & Applications. 240p. pap. 11.95 (ISBN 0-8104-0980-1). Hayden.

COMPUTERS–PROGRAMMING

see Programming (Electronic Computers)

COMPUTERS–STORAGE DEVICES

see Computer Storage Devices

COMPUTERS–TIME-SHARING SYSTEMS

Bull, G. M. Dartmouth Time-Sharing System. LC 80-41327. (Computers & Their Applications Ser.). 240p. 1980. 65.00 (ISBN 0-470-27082-9). Halsted Pr.

COMPUTERS–VALUATION

Hord, R. Michael. The Illiac IV: The First Super Computer. (Illus.). 1981. text ed. price not set (ISBN 0-914894-71-4). Computer Sci.

COMPUTERS–VOCATIONAL GUIDANCE

Hsiao, T. C., tr. Directory of Computer Education & Research. 1100p. 1981. 120.00. Sci & Tech Pr.

COMPUTERS, ELECTRONIC

see Computers; Electronic Digital Computers

COMPUTERS AND CIVILIZATION

Ackoff, Russell. The Second Industrial Revolution. 1978. 0.75 (ISBN 0-686-28791-6). Forward Movement.

Logsdon, Tom. Computers & Social Controversy. (Illus.). 123p. 1980. pap. text ed. write for info. wkbk (ISBN 0-914894-68-4). Computer Sci.

Sanders, Donald H. Computers in Society. 3rd ed. 536p. 1981. text ed. 16.95 (ISBN 0-07-054672-X, C); instructor's manual 4.95 (ISBN 0-07-054673-8); study guide 7.95 (ISBN 0-07-054674-6); test bank 5.95 (ISBN 0-07-054675-4). McGraw.

Shackel, B., ed. Man-Computer Interaction: Human Factors of Computers & People. (NATO Advanced Study Institute Ser.: Applied Sciences, No. 44). 550p. 1980. 60.00x (ISBN 90-286-0910-5). Sijthoff & Noordhoff.

COMPUTING MACHINES

see Calculating-Machines

COMPUTING MACHINES (COMPUTERS)

see Computers

COMSTOCK LODE, NEVADA

Lord, Eliot. Comstock Miners & Mining. (Illus.). 578p. Repr. of 1959 ed. 20.00 (ISBN 0-8310-7008-0). A S Barnes.

--Comstock Miners & Mining. (Illus.). 578p. 1981. Repr. of 1959 ed. 20.00 (ISBN 0-8310-7008-0). Howell-North.

CONCENTRATION CAMPS

see also Political Prisoners;

also names of individual concentration camps, e.g. Oswiecim (Concentration Camp)

Feig, Konnilyn G. Hitler's Death Camps. (Illus.). 400p. 1981. 29.50x (ISBN 0-8419-0675-0); pap. 12.50x (ISBN 0-8419-0676-9). Holmes & Meier.

Heger, Heinz. The Men with the Pink Triangle. Fernbach, David, tr. LC 80-69205. (Illus.). 120p. (Orig.). 1980. pap. 4.95 (ISBN 0-932870-06-6). Carrier Pigeon.

Lewen, Si. A Journey. LC 80-67120. 88p. 1980. 15.00 (ISBN 0-87982-032-2). Art Alliance.

Mueller, Filip. Eyewitness Auschwitz. LC 78-66257. (Illus.). 192p. 1981. pap. 6.95 (ISBN 0-8128-6084-5). Stein & Day.

CONCEPTION

see also Contraception

Hafez, E. S. Human Reproduction: Conception & Contraception. 2nd ed. (Illus.). 932p. 1980. text ed. 47.50 (ISBN 0-06-141066-7, Harper Medical). Har-Row.

CONCEPTION–PREVENTION

see Contraception

CONCEPTION OF GEOMETRY

see Geometry Concept

CONCEPTUALISM

see also Realism

Hewitt. Conceptual Physics: A New Introduction to Your Environment. 4th ed. 1981. text ed. 16.95 (ISBN 0-316-35969-6); tchrs'. manual free (ISBN 0-316-35971-8); test bank avail. Little.

Vacca, Richard T. Content Area Reading. 1981. text ed. 14.95 (ISBN 0-316-89488-5). Little.

CONCERT HALLS

see Music-Halls

CONCHIFERA

see Lamellibranchiata

CONCHOLOGY

see Mollusks; Shells

CONCORD RIVER–DESCRIPTION AND TRAVEL

Karabatsos, James. A Word-Index to a Week on the Concord & Merrimack Rivers. LC 80-2510. 1981. Repr. of 1971 ed. 18.50 (ISBN 0-404-19058-8). AMS Pr.

CONCORDANCES

see also Bible–Concordances

also subdivision Concordances under names of authors, e.g. Shakespeare, William–Concordances

Cruden, Alexander. Cruden's Unabridged Concordance. 14.95 (ISBN 0-8010-2316-5). Baker Bk.

CONCRETE

see also Cement; Pavements; Prestressed Concrete; Reinforced Concrete

ACI Manual of Concrete Practice, 5 pts. Incl. Pt. 1. 29.92; Pt. 2. 29.95; Pt. 3. 29.95; Pt. 4. 29.95; Pt. 5. 29.95. 1980. ACI.

Institute of Civil Engineers, UK. Concrete Afloat. 208p. 1980. 55.00x (ISBN 0-7277-0048-0, Pub. by Telford England). State Mutual Bk.

Thomas Telford Ltd. Editorial Staff. Non-Destructive Testing of Concrete & Timber. 126p. 1980. 80.00x (ISBN 0-901948-27-6, Pub. by Telford England). State Mutual Bk.

Wynne, George. Reinforced Concrete. 1981. text ed. 19.95 (ISBN 0-8359-6638-0); instrs'. manual avail. (ISBN 0-8359-6639-9). Reston.

CONCRETE, PRESTRESSED

see Prestressed Concrete

CONCRETE, REINFORCED

see Reinforced Concrete

CONCRETE BUILDING

see Concrete Construction

CONCRETE CONSTRUCTION

see also Prestressed Concrete; Prestressed Concrete Construction; Reinforced Concrete; Reinforced Concrete Construction

ACI Detailing Manual. 1980. 44.95 (SP-66). ACI.

Anchor, R. D. Design of Liquid-Retaining Concrete Structures. 176p. 1981. 49.95 (ISBN 0-470-27123-X). Halsted Pr.

Billington, David P. Thin-Shell Concrete Structures. 2nd ed. (Illus.). 432p. 1981. 24.50. McGraw.

Concrete Design: U. S. & European Practices. 1979. 29.50 (SP-59); 22.75. ACI.

Dalzell, J. Ralph. Simplified Concrete Masonry Planning & Building. 2nd, rev. ed. Merritt, Frederick S., rev. by. LC 81-385. 398p. 1981. Repr. of 1972 ed. lib. bdg. price not set (ISBN 0-89874-278-1). Krieger.

Douglas McHenry International Symposium on Concrete & Concrete Structures. 1978. 28.95 (SP-55). ACI.

Ferguson, Phil M. Reinforced Concrete Fundamentals: SI Version. 4th ed. 736p. 1981. text ed. 28.95 (ISBN 0-471-05897-1). Wiley.

Guide to the Use of Waterproofing, Dampproofing, Protective & Decorative Barrier Systems for Concrete. 1979. 17.15 (515.1R-79); 12.30. ACI.

International Symposium on Polymers in Concrete. Proceedings. 1978. 22.25 (SP-58); 17.50. ACI.

Performance of Concrete in Marine Environment. 1980. 32.95 (SP-65). ACI.

Refractory Concrete. 1978. 22.25 (SP-57); 17.25. ACI.

Ropke, John C. Concrete: Problems, Causes, & Cures. (Illus.). 192p. 1981. 21.50 (ISBN 0-07-053609-0). McGraw.

Scharff, Robert. Successful & Masonry. Case, Virginia A., ed. (Successful Ser.). 144p. 1981. 18.95 (ISBN 0-89999-023-1); pap. 8.95 (ISBN 0-89999-024-X). Structures Pub.

Superplasticizers in Concrete. 1979. 30.95 (SP-62); member 24.50. ACI.

Thomas Telford Ltd. Editorial Staff. Prestressed Concrete Pressure Vessels. 762p. 1980. 79.00x (ISBN 0-901948-45-4, Pub. by Telford England). State Mutual England.

--Ultimate Load Design of Concrete Structures. 104p. 1980. 25.00 (Pub. by Telford England). State Mutual Bk.

Vibrations of Concrete Structures. 1979. 22.25 (SP-60); 17.75. ACI.

CONDEMNATION OF LAND

see Eminent Domain

CONDENSATION PRODUCTS (CHEMISTRY)

see also Plastics; Polymers and Polymerization

Fain, B. Theory of Rate Processesin Condensed Media. (Lecture Notes in Chemistry Ser.: Vol. 20). (Illus.). 166p. 1981. 17.50 (ISBN 0-387-10249-3). Springer Verlag.

CONDOLENCE, ETIQUETTE OF

see Etiquette

CONDOMINIUM (CIVIL LAW)

see Condominium (Housing)

CONDOMINIUM (HOUSING)

Bullock, Paul. How to Profit from Condominium Conversions. 1981. 17.95 (ISBN 0-913864-64-1). Enterprise Del.

Dinkelspiel, John R. & Selesnick, Herbert. Condominiums: The Effects of Conversion on a Community. 160p. 1981. 19.95 (ISBN 0-86569-059-6). Auburn Hse.

Heatter, Justin W. Buying a Condominium. 1981. 10.95 (ISBN 0-938602-01-2); pap. 6.95 (ISBN 0-938602-00-4). Green Hill.

Jackson, F. Scott & Lippman, William J., eds. Condominium & Cooperative Conversions 1980: Course Handbook. LC 80-81527. (Nineteen Seventy-Nine to Nineteen Eighty Real Estate Law & Practice Course Handbook Ser.). 549p. 1981. pap. 25.00 (ISBN 0-686-69166-0, N4-4352). PLI.

Natelson, Robert G. Condos. (Orig.). 1981. price not set. Cornerstone.

--How to Buy & Sell a Condominium. 160p. (Orig.). 1981. pap. 4.95 (ISBN 0-346-12537-5). Cornerstone.

CONDOMINIUM (REAL PROPERTY)

see Condominium (Housing)

CONDUCT OF LIFE

see also Anger; Business Ethics; Character; Charity; Charm; Christian Life; Courage; Culture; Ethics; Etiquette; Family Life Education; Friendship; Interpersonal Relations; Justice; Love; Loyalty; Obedience; Self-Control; Self-Culture; Self-Respect; Spiritual Life; Success; Sympathy; Temperance; Virtue and Virtues; Worry

also subdivision Conduct of Life under names of classes of persons, e.g. Youth–Conduct of Life

Adler, Mortimer J. Six Great Ideas. 256p. 1981. 12.95 (ISBN 0-02-500560-X). Macmillan.

Bender, David L. Constructing a Life Philosophy: Opposing Viewpoints. (Opposing Viewpoints Ser.). 144p. (gr. 12). 1980. lib. bdg. 8.95 (ISBN 0-89908-329-3); pap. text ed. 3.95 (ISBN 0-89908-304-8). Greenhaven.

Bernstein, Joanna. Loss & How to Cope with It. 160p. (gr. 6 up). 1981. pap. 3.95 (ISBN 0-395-30012-6, Clarion). HM.

Betteridge, Clair B. Primer for Change. 1981. 8.95 (ISBN 0-8062-1717-0). Carlton.

Caliandro, Arthur. You Can Make Your Life Count. 192p. 1981. 8.95 (ISBN 0-916392-79-1). Oak Tree Pubns.

Cargas, Harry J. & Radley, Roger J. Keeping a Spiritual Journal. LC 80-2072. 128p. (gr. 6 up). 1981. pap. 2.75 (ISBN 0-385-17439-X, Im). Doubleday.

Causly, Henry. Remedies for Positive Living. 1981. 4.75 (ISBN 0-8062-1690-5). Carlton.

Clemens, David A. Living, Vol. 3. LC 79-55503. (Steps to Maturity Ser.). 1980. tchrs' manual 14.95 (ISBN 0-86508-006-2); students' manual 12.50 (ISBN 0-86508-005-4). BCM Inc.

Culture, Behavior, & Personality. 2nd ed. 320p. 1981. 22.95x (ISBN 0-686-69599-2); pap. text ed. 11.95x (ISBN 0-686-69600-X). Aldine Pub.

Davis, Carolyn. Making Every Moment Count. (Illus.). 1980. 7.95 (ISBN 0-87707-225-6). CSA Pr.

Deffner, Donald. Two Lives to Live. LC 80-81840. 1981. pap. 4.50 (ISBN 0-933350-40-6). Morse Pr.

Edwards, John F. How to Quit the Rat Race-Successfully. 1981. 9.95 (ISBN 0-937590-00-2); pap. 5.95 (ISBN 0-937590-01-0). Green Hill.

Erskine, Jim & Moran, Goerge. Hug a Teddy: And One Hundred & Seventy-One Other Ways to Keep Safe & Secure. 1980. 5.95 (ISBN 0-517-54215-3, 542153); 10 copy prepack 59.50 (ISBN 0-517-54239-0). Potter.

Firestone, Robert & Catlett, Joyce. The Truth. 320p. 1981. 12.95 (ISBN 0-02-538380-9). Macmillan.

Fitzgerald, Ernest A. God Writes Straight with Crooked Lines. LC 80-65997. 144p. 1981. 7.95 (ISBN 0-689-11073-1). Atheneum.

Gandhi, Mohandas K. To the Perplexed. Hingorani, Anand T., ed. 229p. 1981. 6.00 (ISBN 0-934676-27-5). Greenlf Bks.

Gilbert, Sara. Trouble at Home. 192p. (gr. 7 up). 1981. 7.95 (ISBN 0-688-41995-X); PLB 7.63 (ISBN 0-688-51995-4). Morrow.

Girard, Joe. How to Sell Yourself. 352p. 1981. pap. 5.95 (ISBN 0-446-97336-X). Warner Bks.

Graham, Billy. Billy Graham Talks to Teenagers. (Orig.). (YA) pap. 1.25 (ISBN 0-89129-153-9). Jove Pubns.

Greiff, Barrie S. & Munter, Preston K. Tradeoffs: Executive, Family, & Organizational Life. 1981. pap. 3.50 (ISBN 0-451-61960-9, ME1960, Ment). NAL.

Hadfield, J. A. Psychology & Morals. 245p. 1980. Repr. of 1926 ed. lib. bdg. 30.00 (ISBN 0-8492-5282-2). R West.

Hendricks, C. & Leavenworth, C. Living: The Adult Centering Book. 1978. 8.95 (ISBN 0-13-538512-1); pap. 3.95 (ISBN 0-13-538504-0). P-H.

Hosen, Ron. Who Would You Like to Be. 200p. (Orig.). 1980. pap. 4.95 (ISBN 0-89260-195-7). Hwong Pub.

Hugman, Bruce. Act Natural. 95p. 1977. text ed. 9.90x (ISBN 0-7199-0933-3, Pub. by Bedford England). Renouf.

Hutschnecker, Arnold A. Hope: The Dynamics of Self-Fulfillment. 320p. 1981. 11.95 (ISBN 0-399-12589-2). Putnam.

Jorgensen, Roy. Energy Philosophy: A System of Self-Mastery & Increased Personal Energy. LC 80-83506. (Illus.). 260p. (Orig.). 1980. pap. 7.95 (ISBN 0-938226-01-0). Pacific Edns.

Key, Wilson B. The Clam Plate Orgy & Other Subliminal Techniques for Manipulating Your Behavior. (Illus.). 1981. pap. 2.95 (ISBN 0-686-69108-3, E9723, Sig). NAL.

Krutza, William J. So Now You're a Graduate. 88p. 1981. 4.95 (ISBN 0-8010-5433-8). Baker Bk.

Leichtman, Robert R. & Japikse, Carl. The Art of Living, Vol. 2. (Illus.). 249p. (Orig.). 1980. pap. 5.00 (ISBN 0-89804-033-7). Ariel Pr.

Lindskoog, Kathryn. A Partir del Eden. Orozco, Julio, tr. from Eng. LC 77-73843. 144p. (Orig., Span.). 1977. pap. 2.50 (ISBN 0-89922-092-4). Edit Caribe.

Macaba. The Road Back. 2nd ed. 200p. (Orig.). 1979. pap. 9.75 (ISBN 0-911038-89-2). Noontide.

MacDonald, William. Chasing the Wind. 1981. pap. 1.95 (ISBN 0-937396-07-9). Walterick Pubs.

Moncure, Jane B. Kindness. rev. ed. LC 80-39535. (What Is It? Ser.). (Illus.). 32p. (gr. k-3). 1981. PLB 5.50 (ISBN 0-89565-204-8). Childs World.

Morley, Robert. Worry! How to Kick the Serenity Habit in Ninety Eight Easy Steps. (Illus.). 176p. 1981. 10.00 (ISBN 0-399-12596-5). Putnam.

Moskowitz, Robert. How to Organize Your Work & Your Life. LC 80-1815. (Illus.). 312p. 1981. 12.95 (ISBN 0-385-17011-4). Doubleday.

--How to Organize Your Work & Your Life. LC 80-1815. (Illus.). 312p. 1981. pap. 6.95 (ISBN 0-385-17011-4, Dolp). Doubleday.

Narramore, Clyde & Narramore, Ruth. Como Dominar la Tension Nerviosa. Ward, Rhode, tr. from Eng. 216p. (Orig., Span.). 1978. pap. 3.95 (ISBN 0-89922-129-7). Edit Caribe.

National Federation of Community Assoc. Creative Living. 76p. 1974. pap. text ed. 3.75x (ISBN 0-7199-0896-5, Pub. by Bedford England). Renouf.

Price, Eugenia. Learning to Live. (Orig.). pap. 1.95 (ISBN 0-89129-193-8). Jove Pubns.

Reel, Joseph P. Use Both Brains. LC 80-82602. (Illus.). 104p. (Orig.). 1980. pap. 14.95 (ISBN 0-938024-00-0). Human Dev Pr.

Rosenthal, Joan. The Lord Is My Strength. (Orig.). pap. 1.25 (ISBN 0-89129-086-9). Jove Pubns.

Rutstrum, Calvin. A Columnist Looks at Life. 133p. (Orig.). 1981. pap. 5.95 (ISBN 0-931714-10-9). Nodin Pr.

Schutz, Susan P., ed. One Day at a Time: Making the Most Out of Life. (Illus., Orig.). 1981. pap. 4.95 (ISBN 0-88396-131-8). Blue Mtn Pr CO.

Schweitzer, Albert. A Treasury of Albert Schweitzer. LC 65-20328. 352p. 1965. 6.00 (ISBN 0-8022-1518-1). Philos Lib.

Shedd, Charlie W. Letters to Philip. (Orig.). pap. 1.95 (ISBN 0-515-05827-0). Jove Pubns.

Wahlroos, Sven. Excuses: How to Spot Them, Deal with Them, & Stop Using Them. (Illus.). 1981. 11.95 (ISBN 0-02-623300-2). Macmillan.

Wakin, E. E. How to Turn Down into up. (gr. 9). 1980. pap. 1.25 (ISBN 0-590-31263-4, Schol Pap). Schol Bk Serv.

Wydro, Kenneth. Think on Your Feet: The Art of Thinking & Speaking Under Pressure. 192p. 1981. text ed. 11.95 (ISBN 0-13-917815-5, Spec); pap. text ed. 4.95 (ISBN 0-13-917807-4, Spec). P-H.

CONDUCT OF LIFE–QUOTATIONS, MAXIMS, ETC.

Carroll, Carroll. Carroll's First Book of Proverbs or Life Is a Fortune Cookie. (Illus.). 96p. 1981. pap. 4.95 (ISBN 0-87786-004-1). Gold Penny.

CONDUCTION ANESTHESIA

Cosmi, Ermelando V. Obstetric Anesthesia & Perinatology. 500p. 1981. 33.50 (ISBN 0-8385-7196-4). ACC.

CONDUCTIVITY OF ELECTROLYTES

see Electrolytes

CONDUCTORS (MUSIC)

Dickson, Harry E. Arthur Fiedler & the Boston Pops. 276p. 1981. 12.95 (ISBN 0-686-69044-3). HM.

Lewis, Lawrence. Guido Cantelli: Portrait of a Maestro. LC 80-29385. (Illus.). 176p. 1981. 11.95 (ISBN 0-498-02493-8). A S Barnes.

Remick, Dorothy C. Stephen S. Townsend. (Illus.). 160p. 1981. 12.50 (ISBN 0-89962-050-7). Todd & Honeywell.

CONDUCTORS, RAILROAD

see Railroad Conductors

CONFEDERATE STATES OF AMERICA–REGIMENTAL HISTORIES

see United States–History–Civil War, 1861-1865–Regimental Histories

CONFERENCES

see Congresses and Conventions; Meetings

CONFESSIONS OF FAITH

see Creeds

CONFIRMATION–INSTRUCTION AND STUDY

Reichert, Richard. Born in the Spirit of Jesus. 84p. (Orig.). 1980. pap. text ed. 2.75 (ISBN 0-697-01725-7); tchr's manual 3.50 (ISBN 0-697-01726-5); spirit masters 10.95 (ISBN 0-697-01727-3). Wm C Brown.

CONFISCATIONS

see also subdivision Finance, Commerce, Confiscations, etc. under names of certain wars, e.g. United States–History–Civil War, 1861-1865–finance, Commerce, Confiscations, etc.

Friedman, Samy. Expropriation in International Law. rev. ed. Jackson, Ivor C., tr. from Fr. LC 80-26295. (The Library of World Affairs: No. 20). 236p. 1981. Repr. of 1953 ed. lib. bdg. 29.75x (ISBN 0-313-20840-9, FREI). Greenwood.

CONFLICT OF LAWS

see also Aliens; Public Policy (Law)

International Institute for the Unification of Private Law. Digest of Legal Activities of International & Other Institutions, Release 1. 4th ed. 1980. 85.00 (ISBN 0-379-00545-X). Oceana.

CONFORMITY

see also Deviant Behavior; Dissenters; Persuasion (Psychology); Social Values

Morris, Terence. Deviance & Control. 1980. pap. text ed. 9.25x (ISBN 0-09-126871-0, Hutchinson U Lib). Humanities.

CONGENITAL ABNORMALITIES

see Abnormalities, Human

CONGENITAL DISEASES

see Medical Genetics

CONGREGATIONAL CHURCHES

Smith, Donald P. Congregations Alive. (Orig.). pap. write for info. (ISBN 0-664-24370-3). Westminster.

CONGRESS OF INDUSTRIAL ORGANIZATIONS

see American Federation of Labor and Congress of Industrial Organizations

CONGRESSES AND CONVENTIONS

see also International Organization; Treaties; also names of particular congresses

Review - Nineteen Seventy Nine Session of the Congress: Nineteen Seventy-Nine Session of the Congress. 1980. pap. 3.75 (ISBN 0-8447-0228-5). Am Enterprise.

Review: Nineteen Seventy-Eight Session of the Congress. 1979. pap. 3.75 (ISBN 0-8447-0215-3). Am Enterprise.

Review: Nineteen Seventy-Six Session of the Congress. 1977. pap. 2.00 (ISBN 0-8447-0183-1). Am Enterprise.

Union List of Conference Proceedings in Libraries of the Federal Republic of Germany Including Berlin (West, 2 vols. 907p. 1978. Set. 375.00 (ISBN 3-7940-3004-4, Dist by Gale Research Co). K G Saur.

CONGRESSIONAL INVESTIGATIONS

see Governmental Investigations

Greene, Robert W. The Sting Man. (Illus.). 256p. 1981. 12.95 (ISBN 0-525-20985-9). Dutton.

CONGRESSMEN

see Legislators

CONIFERAE

Bailey, L. H. The Cultivated Conifers in North America: Comprising the Pine Family & the Taxads. (Landmark Reprints in Plant Science). 1933. text ed. 27.00 (ISBN 0-86598-007-1). Allanheld.

CONJURING

Here are entered works on modern (parlor) magic, legerdemain, prestidigitation, etc. Works dealing with occult science (supernatural arts) are entered under the heading Magic.

see also Card Tricks; Magic; Medicine-Man; Tricks

Townsend, Charles B. Merlin's Catalog of Magic. (Puzzler Ser.). 128p. (Orig.). (gr. 9 up). 1981. pap. 4.95 (ISBN 0-8437-2099-9). Hammond Inc.

CONJURING–JUVENILE LITERATURE

Fulves, Karl. The Children's Magic Kit: Sixteen Easy-to-Do Tricks Complete with Cardboard Cutouts. (Illus.). 32p. (Orig.). (gr. 3-6). Date not set. pap. price not set (ISBN 0-486-24019-3). Dover.

Reed, Graham. Magic for Every Occasion. (Illus.). 128p. (gr. 5 up). 1981. 9.95 (ISBN 0-525-66733-4). Elsevier-Nelson.

CONNECTICUT–DESCRIPTION AND TRAVEL

Lewis, Thomas R. Near the Tidal River: Readings in the Historical Geography of Central Connecticut. LC 80-6181. 156p. 1981. lib. bdg. 17.50 (ISBN 0-8191-1464-2); pap. text ed. 8.00 (ISBN 0-8191-1465-0). U Pr of Amer.

CONNECTICUT–HISTORY

Decker, Robert O. The Whaling City, a History of New London. LC 74-30794. (Illus.). 413p. 1976. 15.00 (ISBN 0-87106-053-1). New London County.

Galonska, Michael. Connecticut Supplement. 2nd ed. 196p. 1980. pap. 7.95 (ISBN 0-695-81499-0). Follett.

CONNECTICUT–SOCIAL CONDITIONS

Hall, Trish. The New Connecticut Yankees. (Illus.). (gr. 9-12). 1981. 7.95 (ISBN 0-938348-07-8); pap. 2.95 (ISBN 0-938348-08-6); limited edition 12.95 (ISBN 0-938348-06-X). Cottage Indus.

CONRAD, JOSEPH, 1857-1924

Anon. Joseph Conrad, a Pen Portrait. 24p. 1980. Repr. of 1913 ed. lib. bdg. 10.00 (ISBN 0-8482-1309-2). Norwood Edns.

Bender, Todd K. & Parins, James W. A Concordance to Conrad's Nigger of the Narcissus. LC 79-8417. 150p. 1981. lib. bdg. 35.00 (ISBN 0-8240-9519-7). Garland Pub.

Conrad, John. Joseph Conrad-Times Remembered. LC 79-41596. (Illus.). 212p. Date not set. price not set (ISBN 0-521-22805-0). Cambridge U Pr.

Tennant, Roger. Joseph Conrad. LC 80-69393. 1981. 12.95 (ISBN 0-689-11152-5). Atheneum.

Watt, Ian. Conrad in the Nineteenth Century. 1981. pap. 7.95 (ISBN 0-520-04405-3, CAL 507). U of Cal Pr.

CONRAD, JOSEPH, 1857-1924–BIBLIOGRAPHY

Bender, Todd K. Concordances to Conrad's Victory. LC 79-8416. 150p. 1980. lib. bdg. 35.00 (ISBN 0-8240-9520-0). Garland Pub.

CONSCIENCE

see also Free Will and Determinism

Carlson, Edgar M. The Church & the Public Conscience. LC 79-8710. xii, 104p. 1981. Repr. of 1956 ed. lib. bdg. 17.50x (ISBN 0-313-22195-2, CACH). Greenwood.

CONSCIENTIOUS OBJECTORS

see also Pacifism

Mitchell, Hobart. We Would Not Kill. 1980. write for info (ISBN 0-913408-63-8). Friends United.

CONSCIOUSNESS

see also Belief and Doubt; Knowledge, Theory of; Personality; Self

Jahn, R. G. The Role of Consciousness in the Physical World. (AAAS Selected Symposium: No. 57). 136p. 1981. lib. bdg. 15.00x (ISBN 0-89158-955-4). Westview.

Ong, Walter J. Fighting for Life: Contest, Sexuality, & Consciousness. LC 80-66968. (Illus.). 240p. 1981. 14.95 (ISBN 0-8014-1342-7). Cornell U Pr.

Pearce, Joseph C. The Bond of Power. 1981. 10.95 (ISBN 0-525-06950-X). Dutton.

Valle, Ronald S. & Eckartsberg, Rolf Von, eds. The Metaphors of Consciousness. 500p. 1981. 25.00 (ISBN 0-306-40520-2, Plenum Pr). Plenum Pub.

CONSCIOUSNESS, MULTIPLE

see Personality, Disorders of

CONSCIOUSNESS EXPANDING DRUGS

see Hallucinogenic Drugs

CONSCRIPT LABOR

see Contract Labor

CONSCRIPTION, MILITARY

see Military Service, Compulsory

CONSERVATION EDUCATION

see Conservation of Natural Resources–Study and Teaching

CONSERVATION OF ART OBJECTS

see Art Objects–Conservation and Restoration

CONSERVATION OF BOOKS

see Books–Conservation and Restoration

CONSERVATION OF BUILDINGS

see Architecture–Conservation and Restoration

CONSERVATION OF ENERGY RESOURCES

see Energy Conservation

CONSERVATION OF FORESTS

see Forest Conservation

CONSERVATION OF NATURAL RESOURCES

see also Energy Conservation; Forest Conservation; Human Ecology; Nature Conservation; Reclamation of Land; Recycling (Waste, etc.); Soil Conservation; Wildlife Conservation

Allen, Robert. How to Save the World: Strategy for World Conservation. (Illus.). 144p. 1981. pap. 4.95 (ISBN 0-8226-0366-7). Littlefield.

Blacksell, Mark & Gilg, Andrew. The Countryside: Planning & Change. (Resource Management Ser.: No. 2). (Illus.). 288p. (Orig.). 1981. text ed. 35.00x (ISBN 0-04-711008-2, 2599); pap. text ed. 17.50x (ISBN 0-04-711009-0, 2560). Allen Unwin.

Brookins, Douglas G. Earth Resources, Energy & the Environment. (Illus.). 160p. (Orig.). 1981. pap. text ed. 6.95 (ISBN 0-675-08113-0). Merrill.

Bryant, Jeannette, ed. Conservation Directory. 301p. 1981. 6.00 (ISBN 0-912186-39-9). Natl Wildlife.

Conservation & Development in Northern Thailand. 114p. 1980. pap. 15.00 (ISBN 92-808-0077-9, TUNU083, UNU). Unipub.

Cousteau, Jacques-Yves. A Bill of Roghts for Future Generations. (Illus.). 33p. (Orig.). 1980. pap. 1.50 (ISBN 0-913098-31-0). Myrin Institute.

Ford, Phyllis M. Principles & Practices of Outdoor-Environment Education. LC 80-23200. 350p. 1981. text ed. 15.95 (ISBN 0-471-04768-6). Wiley.

Frick, G. William, ed. Environmental Glossary. LC 80-67274. 225p. 19.50 (ISBN 0-86587-080-2). Gov Insts.

Gabor, D., et al. Beyond the Age of Waste: A Report to the Club of Rome. 2nd ed. LC 80-41614. (Illus.). 265p. 1981. lib. bdg. 42.00 (ISBN 0-08-027303-3); pap. 19.00 (ISBN 0-08-027304-1). Pergamon.

The Guide for Citizen Action. (Illus.). 1980. pap. 3.98 (ISBN 0-930698-12-6). Natl Audubon.

Hyde, William F. Timber Supply, Land Allocation, & Economic Efficiency. LC 80-8021. (Illus.). 248p. 1980. text ed. 19.00x (ISBN 0-8018-2489-3). Johns Hopkins.

The IUCN Plant Red Data Book. 540p. 1978. pap. 20.00 (ISBN 2-88032-202-2, IUCN84, IUCN). Unipub.

Kain, Roger. Planning for Conservation: An International Perspective. 1980. 30.00 (ISBN 0-312-61400-4). St Martin.

Leistritz, F. Larry & Murdock, Steven H. The Socioeconomic Impact of Resource Development: Methods for Assessment. (Social Impact Assessment Ser.: No. 6). 250p. 1981. lib. bdg. 22.50x (ISBN 0-89158-978-3). Westview.

Libecap, Gary. Locking up the Range: Federal Land Controls & Grazing. (Pacific Institute for Public Policy Research Ser.). 1981. price not set professional reference (ISBN 0-88410-382-X). Ballinger Pub.

McLeod, G. C. Georges Bank: Past, Present, & Future. (Special Studies on Natural Resources & Energy Management). 225p. 1981. lib. bdg. 22.00x (ISBN 0-86531-199-4). Westview.

McNall, Preston E. & Kircher, Harry B., eds. Our Natural Resources. 5th ed. LC 80-83584. (Illus.). (gr. 7-12). 1981. text ed. 10.95x (ISBN 0-8134-2166-7, 2166). Interstate.

Oregon State University Biology Colloquium, 40th. Forests: Fresh Perspectives from Ecosystems Analysis. Proceedings. Waring, Richard H., ed. LC 80-14883. (Illus.). 210p. 1980. pap. 12.00 (ISBN 0-87071-179-2). Oreg St U Pr.

Papageorgiou, Nikolaos. Population Energy Relationships of the Agrimi (Capra Aegagrus Cretica) on Theodorou Island, Greece. (Illus.). 56p. (Orig.). pap. text ed. 14.10 (ISBN 3-490-21518-4). Parey Sci Pubs.

Perception of Desertification. 134p. 1981. pap. 22.75 (ISBN 92-808-0190-2, TUNU 104, UNU). Unipub.

Population Environment Relations in Tropical Islands: The Case of Eastern Fiji. (MAB Technical Notes Ser.: No. 13). 233p. 1981. pap. 18.00 (ISBN 92-3-101821-3, U1054, UNESCO). Unipub.

Price, Larry W. Mountains & the Man: A Study of Process & Environment. (Illus.). 496p. 1981. 22.50 (ISBN 0-520-03263-2). U of Cal Pr.

Reichley, A. James. Conservatives in an Age of Change: The Nixon & Ford Administrations. 500p. 1981. 26.95 (ISBN 0-8157-7380-3); pap. 11.95 (ISBN 0-8157-7379-X). Brookings.

Robert Clark, Gillean. Resource Recovery Planning & Management. 1981. text ed. 24.00 (ISBN 0-250-40298-X). Ann Arbor Science.

Skinner, Brian J., ed. Use & Misuse of Earth's Surface. (The Earth & Its Inhabitants: Selected Readings from American Scientist Ser.). (Illus.). 200p. (Orig.). 1981. pap. 9.95 (ISBN 0-913232-95-5). W Kaufmann.

Skurzynski, Gloria. Safeguarding the Land. LC 80-8805. (Illus.). 192p. (gr. 7-12). 1981. pap. 3.95 (ISBN 0-15-269957-0, VoyB). HarBraceJ.

Smith, Frank E. Conservation in the United States, 5 vols. 1971. Set. 150.00x (ISBN 0-442-37775-4). Van Nos Reinhold.

Spofford, Walter O., Jr., et al, eds. Energy Development in the Southwest: Problems of Water, Fish & Wildlife in the Upper Colorado River Basin. LC 80-8020. (Resources for the Future Research Ser.: Paper R-18). 1980. Set Of 2 Vols. pap. text ed. 25.00x (ISBN 0-8018-2495-8). Johns Hopkins.

Trends in Environmental Policy & Law. (IUCN Environmental Policy & Law Paper Ser.: No. 15). 404p. 1981. pap. 30.75 (ISBN 2-88032-085-2, IUCN94, IUCN). Unipub.

Vogt, Frederick, ed. Energy Conservation & Use of Renewable Energies in the Bio-Industries: Proceedings of the International Seminar on Energy Conservation & the Use of Solar & Other Renewable Energies in Agriculture, Horticulture & Fishculture, 15-19 September, 1980, Polytechnic of Central London. LC 80-49739. (Illus.). 580p. 1981. 100.00 (ISBN 0-08-026866-8). Pergamon.

Working Group Meeting on Energy Planning & Committee on Natural Resources. Proceedings, Fifth Session. (Energy Resources Development Ser: No. 20). 151p. 1980. pap. 12.00 (UN79-2F11, UN). Unipub.

World Resources: Engineering Solutions. 208p. 1980. 40.00x (ISBN 0-7277-0016-2, Pub. by Telford England). State Mutual Bk.

Young, Oran R. Natural Resources & the State: The Political Economy of Resource Management. 1981. 16.50 (ISBN 0-520-04285-9). U of Cal Pr.

CONSERVATION OF NATURAL RESOURCES–STUDY AND TEACHING

Environmental Education in the Light of the Tbilisi Conference. (Education on the Move Ser.: No. 3). 100p. 1980. pap. 7.00 (ISBN 92-3-101787-X, U1035, UNESCO). Unipub.

Franklin Institute. ENGUIDE: A Guide to Bibliographic Data for Users of Environmental Information. 100p. 1980. pap. text ed. 14.95. Franklin Inst Pr.

Intergovernmental Conference on Environmental Education: Final Report. 101p. 1980. pap. 7.50 (ISBN 0-686-68812-0, U1021, UNESCO). Unipub.

An Overview Environmental Training. (UNEP Report Ser.: No. 9). 150p. 1980. pap. 14.00 (UNEP037, UNEP). Unipub.

CONSERVATION OF NATURE

see Nature Conservation

CONSERVATION OF PETROLEUM

see Petroleum Conservation

CONSERVATION OF POWER RESOURCES

see Energy Conservation

CONSERVATION OF RESOURCES

see Conservation of Natural Resources

CONSERVATION OF THE SOIL

see Soil Conservation

CONSERVATION OF WATER

see Water-Conservation

CONSERVATION OF WILDLIFE

see Wildlife Conservation

CONSERVATISM

see also Authoritarianism

Rossiter, Clinton L. Conservatism in America: The Thankless Persuasion. 2nd, rev. ed. LC 80-27937. xii, 306p. 1981. Repr. of 1962 ed. lib. bdg. 27.50x (ISBN 0-313-22720-9, ROCN). Greenwood.

Stark, Gary D. Entrepreneurs of Ideology: Neoconservative Publishers in Germany, 1890-1933. LC 80-14906. 384p. 1981. 26.50x (ISBN 0-8078-1452-0). U of NC Pr.

CONSERVATORIES

see Greenhouses

CONSOLATION

see also Joy and Sorrow

Cruz, Nicky & Harris, Madalene. Lonely, but Never Alone. 192p. (Orig.). 1981. pap. 5.95 (ISBN 0-310-43361-4). Zondervan.

CONSOLIDATION AND MERGER OF CORPORATIONS
see also Corporate Reorganizations
Clapp, Andrew D. Merger Yearbook Nineteen Eighty. 1981. 68.00 (ISBN 0-939008-03-3). Cambridge Corp.
Fraser, Ronald. Consolidations; A Simplified Approach. LC 80-83431. 128p. 1981. pap. text ed. 9.15 (ISBN 0-8403-2303-4). Kendall-Hunt.
Samuels, J. M. Readings on Mergers & Takeovers. 1972. 39.95 (ISBN 0-236-17619-6, Pub. by Paul Elek). Merrimack Bk Serv.
CONSPIRACY
Hazell, Robert. Conspiracy & Civil Liberties. 128p. 1974. pap. text ed. 6.25x (ISBN 0-7135-1909-6, Pub. by Bedford England). Renouf.
CONSTANTINE, DONATION OF
see Donation of Constantine
CONSTIPATION
Fuller, Richard R. Constipation Control: An Exercise Program to Achieve Regularity. 64p. 1981. 5.00 (ISBN 0-682-49690-1). Exposition.
CONSTITUTIONAL HISTORY
see also Democracy; Political Science
also subdivision Constitutional History under names of countries, states, etc. e.g. Great Britian–Constitutional History
McWhinney, Edward. Constitution-Making. 240p. 1981. 20.00x (ISBN 0-8020-5553-2). U of Toronto Pr.
CONSTITUTIONAL LAW
see also Administrative Law; Citizenship; Civil Rights; Democracy; Eminent Domain; Executive Power; Federal Government; Government Liability; Legislation; Legislative Bodies; Martial Law; Political Rights; Sovereignty
also subdivision Constitutional Law under names of countries, e.g. United States–Constitutional Law
Constitution & Supplementary Laws & Documents of the Republic of China. (Studies in Chinese Government & Law). 198p. 1977. Repr. of 1924 ed. 21.00 (ISBN 0-89093-059-7). U Pubns Amer.
Constitutional Interpretation, Cases-Essays-Materials. 2nd ed. LC 79-14772. 1490p. 1979. text ed. 19.95 (ISBN 0-8299-2052-8). West Pub.
Genovese, Michael A. The Supreme Court, the Constitution, & Presidential Power. LC 80-5695. 345p. 1980. lib. bdg. 20.50 (ISBN 0-8191-1322-0); pap. text ed. 11.75 (ISBN 0-8191-1323-9). U Pr of Amer.
Gunther, Gerald. Cases & Materials on Individual Rights in Constitutional Law. 3rd, abr. ed. LC 80-70238. (University Casebook Ser.). 1337p. 1980. text ed. write for info. (ISBN 0-88277-021-7). Foundation Pr.
Ito, Hirobumi. Commentaries on the Constitution of the Empire of Japan. (Studies in Japanese Law & Government). 310p. 1979. Repr. of 1906 ed. 25.00 (ISBN 0-89093-212-3). U Pubns Amer.
Klotter, John C. & Kanovitz, Jacqueline R. Constitutional Law. 4th ed. (Justice Administration Legal Ser.). 900p. Date not set. price not set (ISBN 0-87084-492-X). Anderson Pub Co.
Pierce, Franklin. Federal Usurpation. xx, 437p. 1980. Repr. of 1908 ed. lib. bdg. 35.00x (ISBN 0-8377-1007-3). Rothman.
Rotunda, Ronald D. Modern Constitutional Law: Cases & Notes. (American Casebook Ser.). 1058p. 1981. text ed. price not set (ISBN 0-8299-2136-2). West Pub.
Sedgwick, Theodore. A Treatise on the Rules Which Govern the Interpretation & Construction of Statutory & Constitutional Law. 2nd ed. Pomeroy, John N., ed. xlviii, 692p. 1981. Repr. of 1874 ed. lib. bdg. 49.50x (ISBN 0-8377-1115-0). Rothman.
Wise, John S. A Treatise on American Citizenship. (Studies in Constitutional Law). viii, 340p. 1981. Repr. of 1906 ed. lib. bdg. 30.00x (ISBN 0-8377-1306-4). Rothman.
CONSTITUTIONAL LAW–HISTORY
see Constitutional History
CONSTITUTIONAL LIMITATIONS
see Constitutional Law
CONSTITUTIONS
see also Constitutional History; Constitutional Law
also subdivision Constitutional Law under names of countries, states, etc.
Maarseveen, H. Written Constitutions, a Computerized Comparative Study. 1978. 37.50 (ISBN 0-379-20361-8). Oceana.
McWhinney, Edward. Constitution-Making. 240p. 1981. 20.00x (ISBN 0-8020-5553-2). U of Toronto Pr.
CONSTRUCTION
see Architecture; Building; Engineering
CONSTRUCTION, CONCRETE
see Concrete Construction
CONSTRUCTION, HOUSE
see House Construction
CONSTRUCTION BLOCK PRINCIPLE
see Unit Construction
CONSTRUCTION EQUIPMENT
see also Pumping Machinery
Watkins, Fincham. Construction Science & Materials for Technicians 2. 1981. text ed. price not set (ISBN 0-408-00483-6). Butterworth.
CONSTRUCTION INDUSTRY
Here are entered works dealing comprehensively with the construction business, including finance, planning, management, and skills.
see also Building
Chudley. Construction Technology One: Checkbook. 1981. text ed. price not set (ISBN 0-408-00602-1, Westbury Hse). Butterworth.
Engelsman, Coert. Nineteen Hundred Eighty-One Heavy Construction Cost File: Unit Prices. 256p. 1980. pap. text ed. 24.50 (ISBN 0-442-12223-3). Van Nos Reinhold.
Hazards in Construction. 1980. 60.00x (Pub. by Telford England). State Mutual Bk.
Metric Conversion in the Construction Industries: Planning, Coordination & Timing. 62p. 1980. 15.00. Am Natl.
Technology Assessment & Utilization Committee. A National Strategy for Improving Productivity in Building & Construction. LC 80-81951. xii, 209p. 1980. pap. text ed. 8.25 (ISBN 0-309-03080-3). Natl Acad Pr.
Thomas Telford Ltd. Editorial Staff. Safety on Construction Sites. 122p. 1980. 75.00x (Pub. by Telford England). State Mutual Bk.
CONSTRUCTION INDUSTRY–ACCOUNTING
Building Cost File, compiled by. The Berger Building Cost File 1981: General Construction Trades with Comparative Building Systems & Costs, 4 editions, Vol. 1. Incl. Eastern Edition (ISBN 0-442-21240-2); Western Edition (ISBN 0-442-21238-0); Central Edition (ISBN 0-442-21237-2); Southern Edition (ISBN 0-442-21236-4). 210p. 1980. pap. text ed. 34.95 ea. Van Nos Reinhold.
--The Berger Building Cost File 1981: Mechanical & Electrical Trades with Comparative Building Systems Costs, 4 editions, Vol. II. Incl. Eastern Edition (ISBN 0-442-21235-6); Western Edition (ISBN 0-442-21234-8); Central Edition (ISBN 0-442-21232-1); Southern Edition (ISBN 0-442-21231-3). 105p. 1980. pap. text ed. 24.95 ea. Van Nos Reinhold.
Engelsman, Coert. Engelsman's General Construction Cost File 1981. 409p. 1980. pap. text ed. 29.95 (ISBN 0-442-12222-5). Van Nos Reinhold.
CONSTRUCTION INDUSTRY–CONTRACTS AND SPECIFICATIONS
see Building–Contracts and Specifications
CONSTRUCTION INDUSTRY–ESTIMATES
see Building–Estimates
CONSTRUCTION INDUSTRY–MANAGEMENT
see also Building–Superintendence
Volpe, S. P. Construction Management Practices. 181p. 1972. 18.50 (ISBN 0-471-91010-4). Wiley.
CONSTRUCTION MACHINERY
see Construction Equipment
CONSTRUCTION OF ROADS
see Road Construction
CONSTRUCTIVE MATHEMATICS
see also Logic, Symbolic and Mathematical
Slisenko, A. O., ed. Studies in Constructive Mathematics & Mathematical Logic, Pt. 3. LC 69-12507. (Seminars in Mathematics Ser.: Vol. 16). 1971. 25.00 (ISBN 0-306-18816-3, Consultants). Plenum Pub.
CONSULTANTS, BUSINESS
see Business Consultants
CONSULTANTS, EDUCATIONAL
see Educational Consultants
CONSUMER ADVERTISING
see Advertising
CONSUMER BEHAVIOR
see Consumers
CONSUMER EDUCATION
Here are entered works on the selection and most efficient use of consumer goods and services, as well as works on means and methods of educating the consumer.
see also Consumers; Consumption (Economics); Home Economics
also specific consumer problems, e.g. Food adulturation and Inspection; Installment Plan; Labels
Best, Arthur. When Consumers Complain. LC 80-21789. 256p. 1981. 16.95 (ISBN 0-231-05124-7). Columbia U Pr.
Brazil, Diane. South Bay Bargain Guide. (Illus.). 96p. (Orig.). 1981. pap. 4.95 (ISBN 0-87701-142-7). Chronicle Bks.
Cockerell, H. A. & Dickinson, G. M. Motor Insurance & the Consumer. 192p. 1980. 30.00x (ISBN 0-85941-146-X, Pub. by Woodhead-Faulkner England). State Mutual Bk.
Consumer Guide, ed. Consumer Guide: Nineteen Eighty-One Buying Guide. 1981. pap. 3.50 (ISBN 0-451-09623-1, E9623, Sig). NAL.
Consumers Index to Product Evaluations & Information Sources: 1979 Annual. 1980. 59.50 (ISBN 0-87650-126-9). Pierian.
Consumer's Union. Consumer's Union Guide to Consumer Service. 1981. write for info. Little.
Farrell, H. Clyde & Kens, Paul. Buying, Renting & Borrowing in Texas: The Rules of the Game. LC 80-52895. (Illus.). 278p. 1980. 10.95 (ISBN 0-937606-00-6); pap. 6.95 (ISBN 0-937606-01-4). Tex Consumer.
Flesch, Yolande. Free Things for Homeowners. 96p. (Orig.). 1981. pap. 4.95 (ISBN 0-346-12533-2). Cornerstone.
Forkner, Jerry & Schatz, Gail. Consumer Education Learning Activities. 64p. (Orig.). 1981. pap. 10.95 (ISBN 0-89994-252-0). Soc Sci Ed.
Fulkerson, Katherine. The Merchandise Buyers' Game. 1981. pap. text ed. 2.95 (ISBN 0-933836-13-9). Simtek.
Horowitz, David. Fight Back: & Don't Get Ripped off. LC 78-19498. 304p. 1981. pap. 2.95 (ISBN 0-06-250392-8, P 5001, PL). Har-Row.
Hulme, Francis. Directory of Buyers. 2nd ed. 1981. pap. 7.95x (ISBN 0-936588-01-2). Buyer's Directory.
Leasure, Jan. Jan's Consumer Savings. (Illus.). 175p. 1981. pap. write for info. (ISBN 0-930256-08-5). Almar.
Leipsic, Reggie. Save Money Buying Meat, Poultry, & Fish. (Illus.). 200p. (Orig.). 1981. pap. 6.95 (ISBN 0-89141-113-5). Presidio Pr.
Miller, Roger L. Economic Issues for Consumers. 3rd ed. (Illus.). 600p. 1980. text ed. 19.95 (ISBN 0-8299-0396-8). West Pub.
Moldafsky, Annie. The Good Buy Book -- South. 228p. (Orig.). 1981. pap. 4.95 (ISBN 0-528-88046-2). Rand.
Norback, Peter & Norback, Craig. The Consumer's Energy Handbook. 272p. 1981. 19.95 (ISBN 0-442-26066-0); pap. 14.95 (ISBN 0-442-26067-9). Van Nos Reinhold.
Rosenbloom, Joseph. Consumer Complaint Guide. 8th ed. LC 73-182375. 1981. 12.50 (ISBN 0-02-469590-4). Macmillan.
Ross, James. How to Buy a Car. 160p. 1981. pap. 3.95 (ISBN 0-312-39546-9); prepack 39.50 (ISBN 0-312-39547-7). St Martin.
Simpson, Colleen E. & Hirshman, S. Stalking the Seattle Bargain: A Complete Bargain Hunter's Catalogue & Consumer Education Guide. (Illus.). 160p. (Orig.). 1980. pap. 3.95 (ISBN 0-938406-00-0). Simpson-Hirshman.
Sloane, Martin. The Nineteen Eighty-One Guide to Coupons & Refunds. 2nd rev. ed. (Orig.). 1981. pap. 2.95 (ISBN 0-553-14617-3). Bantam.
Webster, Jonathan & Webster, Harriet. The Underground Marketplace. LC 80-54401. (Illus.). 208p. 1981. text ed. 12.50x (ISBN 0-87663-348-3); pap. 6.95 (ISBN 0-87663-555-9). Universe.
Widing, Thomas L. Budget Shopper's Guide to the Delaware Valley. rev. ed. LC 80-84929. 160p. (Orig.). 1981. pap. 3.95 (ISBN 0-917908-03-1). Hamilton Hse.
Wolgemuth, Kathleen D. Hawaii's Super Shopper. LC 80-83398. 128p. (Orig.). 1980. pap. 3.50 (ISBN 0-9604798-0-5). Island Writers.
Wood, Merle. The Davis Family: A Personal Recordkeeping Practice Set. 2nd ed. (Illus.). (gr. 10-12). 1981. 6.28 (ISBN 0-07-071623-4, G). McGraw.
CONSUMER LOANS
see Loans, Personal
CONSUMER ORGANIZATIONS
see Cooperative Societies
CONSUMER PRICE INDEX
see Cost and Standard of Living
CONSUMER PRODUCTS
see Commercial Products
CONSUMER PROTECTION
see also Consumer Education; Drugs–Adulteration and Analysis; Food Adulteration and Inspection; Food Law and Legislation
Cohen, Roy. Stand up for Your Rights. 14.95 (ISBN 0-671-25341-7). S&S.
Debating Consumer Protection Policy 1980-81: High School Debate Analysis. 1980. pap. 3.75 (ISBN 0-8447-1831-9). Am Enterprise.
Epstin, David G. & Nickles, Steve H. Consumer Law in a Nutshell. 2nd ed. (Nutshell Ser.). 400p. 1981. pap. text ed. 6.95 (ISBN 0-8299-2130-3). West Pub.
Kane, T. Gregory. Consumers & the Regulators. 123p. 1980. pap. text ed. 10.95x (ISBN 0-920380-60-3, Pub. by Inst Res Pub Canada). Renouf.
McGuire, E. Patrick, ed. Consumer Protection: Implications for the International Trade, Report No. 789. (Illus.). vii, 63p. (Orig.). 1980. pap. 15.00 (ISBN 0-8237-0225-1). Conference Bd.
CONSUMERS
Here are entered works on consumer behavior. Consumers' guides are entered under Consumer Education; works on the economic theory of consumption under Consumption (economics).
see also Consumer Education; Consumer Protection; Consumption (Economics); Cooperation
Blackwell, et al. Contemporary Cases Consumer Behavior. 1977. 10.95. Dryden Pr.
Block & Roering. Essentials of Cons. Behavior. 1979. 19.95 (ISBN 0-03-041961-1). Dryden Pr.
Cohen, Dorothy. Consumer Behavior. 504p. 1981. pap. text ed. 19.95 (ISBN 0-394-31160-4). Random.
Deaton, Angus. Essays in the Theory & Measurement of Consumer Behavior. 300p. Date not set. price not set (ISBN 0-521-22565-5). Cambridge U Pr.
Engel, et al. Consumer Behavior. 3rd ed. 1978. 20.95 (ISBN 0-03-089673-8). Dryden Pr.
Kassarjian, Harold & Robertson, Thomas. Perspectives in Consumer Behavior. 1981. pap. text ed. 10.95x (ISBN 0-673-15394-0). Scott F.
Wasserman, Paul & Morgan, Jean, eds. Consumer Sourcebook, 2 vols. 3rd ed. 1800p. 1981. Set. 78.00 (ISBN 0-8103-0383-3). Gale.
Williams, Terrell G. Consumer Behavior: Concepts & Strategies. 600p. pap. text ed. 14.36 (ISBN 0-8299-0420-4). West Pub.
CONSUMPTION
see Tuberculosis
CONSUMPTION (ECONOMICS)
Works designed to inform and educate the consumer are entered under the heading Consumer Education. Works on consumer behavior are entered under the heading Consumers.
see also Consumer Education; Marketing; Supply and Demand
The Big Rock Candy Mountain: A Paradigm of the Values of the Mass Consumption Society. 20p. 1981. pap. 10.00 (ISBN 92-808-0154-6, TUNU 106, UNU). Unipub.
CONTACT LENSES
Critser, James R., Jr. Prosthetics & Contact Lens: Series 10PC - 79. 1981. refer. - ring bdg. 60.00 (ISBN 0-686-69159-8). Lexington Data.
Stone, Janet & Musset, Anthony. Contact Lens Design Tables. 1981. text ed. price not set. Butterworth.
CONTACT PRINTS
see Blue-Prints
CONTACT VERNACULARS
see Languages, Mixed
CONTAGIOUS ABORTION
see Brucellosis in Cattle
CONTAGIOUS DISEASES
see Communicable Diseases
CONTAINER INDUSTRY
Bell, Clinton C. Preventive Maintenance in a Corrugated Container Plant. (TAPPI Press Reports Ser.). (Illus.). 56p. 1981. pap. write for info. (ISBN 0-89852-388-5, 01-01-R088). Tappi.
CONTAINERS
see also Baskets; Packaging; Sealing (Technology)
International Convention for Safe Containers. 23p. 1977. 7.00 (IMCO). Unipub.
CONTAINERS, PRESSURIZED
see Pressure Vessels
CONTAMINATED FOOD
see Food Contamination
CONTAMINATION OF ENVIRONMENT
see Pollution
CONTEMPLATION
see also Meditation
Keating, Thomas. The Heart of the World: An Introduction to Contemplative Christianity. 96p. 1981. 8.95 (ISBN 0-8245-0014-8). Crossroad NY.
CONTEMPORARY ART
see Art, Modern–20th Century
CONTEMPORARY SCULPTURE
see Sculpture, Modern–20th Century
CONTEMPT OF CONGRESS
see Contempt of Legislative Bodies
CONTEMPT OF COURT
Sullivan, Harold W. Contempts by Publication: The Law of Trial by Newspaper. xiv, 230p. 1980. Repr. of 1941 ed. lib. bdg. 24.00x (ISBN 0-8377-1114-2). Rothman.
CONTEMPT OF LEGISLATIVE BODIES
Rapalje, Stewart. A Treatise on Contempt Including Civil & Criminal Contempts of Judicial Tribunals, Justices of the Peace, Legislative Bodies, Municipal Boards, Committees, Notaries, Commissioners, Referees & Other Officers Exercising Judicial & Quasi-judicial Functions: With Practice & Forms. xliv, 273p. 1981. Repr. of 1890 ed. lib. bdg. 32.50x (ISBN 0-8377-1030-8). Rothman.
CONTENT ANALYSIS (COMMUNICATION)
Stavroulakis, P., ed. Interference Analysis of Communication. LC 80-18464. 1980. 34.95 (ISBN 0-87942-135-5). Inst Electrical.
CONTESTS
see Rewards (Prizes, etc.)
CONTINENTAL SHELF
Marine Board, Assembly of Engineering, National Research Council. Outer Continental Shelf Frontier Technology. LC 80-82152. 1980. pap. text ed. 8.50 (ISBN 0-309-03084-6). Natl Acad Pr.
CONTINUED FRACTIONS
see Fractions, Continued
CONTINUING EDUCATION CENTERS
Hendrickson, Gayle A. Promoting Continuing Education Programs. 80p. (Orig.). 1980. pap. 10.50 (ISBN 0-89964-169-5). CASE.
Ilsley, Paul & Niemi, John A. Recruiting & Training Volunteers. (Adult Education Association Professional Development Ser.). (Illus.). 176p. 1980. text ed. 12.95x (ISBN 0-07-000556-7, C). McGraw.
Sanford, R. Nevitt & Comstock, Craig. Learning After College. new ed. 277p. (Orig.). 1980. 14.50 (ISBN 0-917430-04-2); pap. 9.95 (ISBN 0-917430-03-4). Montaigne.
Study of the Quality of Continuing Legal Education in the United States. 29.00; 2 copies 16.24 ea.; 3 or more copies 11.60 ea. ALI-ABA.
CONTINUUM MECHANICS
see also Field Theory (Physics); Fluid Mechanics; Magnetohydrodynamics; Sound
Billington, E. W. & Tate, A. The Physics of Deformation & Flow. (Illus.). 720p. 1981. text ed. 59.00 (ISBN 0-07-005285-9, C). McGraw.
Gurtin, Morton E. An Introduction to Continuum Mechanics. (Mathematics in Science & Engineering Ser.). 1981. write for info. (ISBN 0-12-309750-9). Acad Pr.

CONTINUUM PHYSICS
see Field Theory (Physics)
CONTORTION
see Acrobats and Acrobatism
CONTRACEPTION
see also Birth Control
Baker, Lynn S. The Fertility Fallacy: Sexuality in the Post-Pill Age. LC 80-50715. 224p. 1981. 11.95 (ISBN 0-7216-1492-2). Saunders.
Hafez, E. S. Human Reproduction: Conception & Contraception. 2nd ed. (Illus.). 932p. 1980. text ed. 47.50 (ISBN 0-06-141066-7, Harper Medical). Har-Row.
Jackson, M., et al. Vaginal Contraception. 1980. lib. bdg. 29.95 (ISBN 0-8161-2211-3, Medical Publications). G K Hall.
Zatuchni, Gerald, et al. Vaginal Contraception: New Developments. (PARFR Series on Fertility Regulation). (Illus.). 384p. 1980. text ed. 17.50 (ISBN 0-06-142901-5, Harper Medical). Har-Row.
CONTRACEPTIVES, ORAL
see Oral Contraceptives
CONTRACT BRIDGE
Amsbury. Bridge: Bidding Naturally. 1979. 17.95 (ISBN 0-7134-1619-X, Pub. by Batsford England). David & Charles.
Flint, Jeremy & Greenwood, David. Instructions for the Defence. (Illus.). 125p. 1981. 12.50 (ISBN 0-370-30032-7, Pub. by Chatto-Bodley-Jonathan). Merrimack Bk Serv.
Goren, Charles H. Goren's Bridge Complete. LC 80-2247. 736p. 1981. 14.95 (ISBN 0-385-17441-1). Doubleday.
Jannerston, Eric. The Only Chance. Kelsey, H. W., tr. (Illus.). 176p. 1981. 12.95 (ISBN 0-370-30266-4, Pub. by Chatto-Bodley-Jonathan). Merrimack Bk Serv.
Kelsey, H. W. Advanced Play at Bridge. 192p. 1981. pap. 6.95 (ISBN 0-571-11677-9, Pub. by Faber & Faber). Merrimack Bk Serv.
Mollo, Victor. Bridge in the Fourth Dimension: Further Adventures of the Hideous Hog. 192p. 1981. pap. 6.95 (ISBN 0-571-11675-2, Pub. by Faber & Faber). Merrimack Bd Serv.
Reese, Terence & Dormer, Albert. The Bridge Player's Alphabetical Handbook. 224p. 1981. 19.95 (ISBN 0-571-11599-3, Pub. by Faber & Faber). Merrimack Bk Serv.
Rubens, Jeff. The Secrets of Winning Bridge. 241p. 1981. pap. 4.00 (ISBN 0-486-24076-2). Dover.
Seabrook. Bridge: From Average to Expert. 1979. 17.95 (ISBN 0-7134-1623-8, Pub. by Batsford England). David & Charles.
Sheinwold, Pat. Successful Bridge Partnerships. 208p. 1981. 4.95 (ISBN 0-686-69323-X). Cornerstone.
Sowter. Bridge: Improve Your Defence. 1979. 17.95 (ISBN 0-7134-1621-1, Pub. by Batsford England). David & Charles.
CONTRACT BRIDGE–DUPLICATE PLAY
Sands, Norma. Standard American Bridge Updated. pap. 4.95 (ISBN 0-686-28759-2). Rocky Mtn Bks.
CONTRACT LABOR
see also Chinese in Foreign Countries; Indentured Servants
International Labour Office. Contract Labour in the Clothing Industry: Second Tripartite Technical Meeting for the Clothing Industry, Geneva, 1980, Report II. ii, 75p. (Orig.). 1980. pap. 7.15 (ISBN 92-2-102432-6). Intl Labour Office.
CONTRACTILITY (BIOLOGY)
Grinnell, Alan D., et al, eds. The Regulation of Muscle Contraction: Excitation-Contraction Coupling. (UCLA Forum in Medical Sciences: Vol. 22). 1981. price not set (ISBN 0-12-303780-8). Acad Pr.
CONTRACTING PARTIES TO THE GENERAL AGREEMENT ON TARIFFS AND TRADE
Basic Instruments & Selected Documents: Protocols, Decisions, Reports, 1978 to 1979 & Thirty-Fifth Session. 26th supl. ed. 393p. 1981. pap. 25.00 (G141, GATT). Unipub.
Trade Relations Under Flexible Exchange Rates. (Studies in International Trade: No. 8). 80p. 1981. pap. 8.00 (G143, GATT). Unipub.
CONTRACTIONS
see Abbreviations; Ciphers
CONTRACTORS OPERATIONS–ACCOUNTING
see Construction Industry–Accounting
CONTRACTS
see also Bailments; Leases; Liability (Law); Negotiable Instruments; Partnership; Sales
also subdivision Contracts and Specifications under particular subjects, e.g. Building–Contracts and Specifications
Chitty, Joseph, Jr. A Practical Treatise on the Law of Contracts. Berkowitz, David S. & Thorne, Samuel E., eds. LC 77-86636. (Classics of English Legal History in the Modern Era Ser.: Vol. 25). 807p. 1979. lib. bdg. 40.00 (ISBN 0-8240-3074-5). Garland Pub.
Farnsworth, E. Allan & Young, William F. Cases & Materials on Contracts. 3rd ed. LC 80-15040. (University Casebook Ser.). 1203p. write for info. (ISBN 0-88277-009-8). Foundation Pr.
Howell, John C. The Complete Guide to Business Contracts. 160p. 1980. pap. 5.95 (Spec). P-H.
Levasseur, Alain A. Precis in Conventional Obligations. 300p. 1980. text ed. 18.00 (ISBN 0-87215-334-7). Michie.
Sammet, George, Jr. & Kelley, Clifton G. Subcontract Management Handbook. 370p. 1981. 24.95 (ISBN 0-8144-5639-1). Am Mgmt.
CONTRACTS–CASES
Farnsworth, E. Allan & Young, William F. Cases & Materials on Contracts. 3rd ed. LC 80-15040. (University Casebook Ser.). 1203p. write for info. (ISBN 0-88277-009-8). Foundation Pr.
CONTRACTUAL LIMITATIONS
see Contracts
CONTRITION
see Penance
CONTROL (PSYCHOLOGY)
Cudlipp, Hugh. The Prerogative of the Harlot: Press Barons & Power. (Illus.). 304p. 1981. 13.50 (ISBN 0-370-30238-9, Pub. by Chatto-Bodley-Jonathan). Merrimack Bk Serv.
Steiner, Claude. The Other Side of Power. LC 80-8921. 192p. 1981. 16.50 (ISBN 0-394-51950-7, Ever); pap. 6.95 (ISBN 0-394-17926-9). Grove.
CONTROL, INVENTORY
see Inventory Control
CONTROL, PRODUCTION
see Production Control
CONTROL BIOPHYSICS
see Biological Control Systems
CONTROL ENGINEERING
see Automatic Control
CONTROL EQUIPMENT
see Automatic Control
CONTROL OF INDUSTRIAL PROCESSES
see Process Control
CONTROL OF PESTS
see Pest Control
CONTROL SYSTEMS, BIOLOGICAL
see Biological Control Systems
CONTROL THEORY
see also Automatic Control; Biological Control Systems
Bryson, A. E. & Ho, Y. C. Applied Optimal Control: Optimization, Estimation, & Control. rev. ed. LC 75-16114. (Illus.). 481p. 1981. pap. 15.95 (ISBN 0-89116-228-3). Hemisphere Pub.
Hermann, Robert. Cartanian Geometry, Nonlinear Waves, & Control Theory, Pt. B. Ackerman, Michael, tr. (Interdisciplinary Mathematics Ser.: Vol. 21). 585p. 1980. text ed. 60.00x (ISBN 0-915692-29-5, QA649.H46). Math Sci Pr.
Leondes, C. T., ed. Control of Dynamic Systems: Advances in Theory & Application, Vols. 9, 10, 13 & 15. Incl. Vol. 9. 44.00 (ISBN 0-12-012709-1); Vol. 10. 44.00 (ISBN 0-12-012710-5); Vol. 13. 1977. 39.00 (ISBN 0-12-012713-X); Vol. 15. 1979. 22.50 (ISBN 0-12-012715-6). 1973. Acad Pr.
MacFarlane, A. G., ed. Frequency: Response Methods in Control Systems. LC 79-90572. 1979. 39.95 (ISBN 0-87942-125-8). Inst Electrical.
Strejc, Vladimir. State Space Theory of Discrete Linear Control. 1981. price not set (ISBN 0-471-27594-8, Pub. by Wiley-Interscience). Wiley.
Toates, F. M. Control Theory in Biology & Experimental Psychology. 1980. text ed. 21.00x (ISBN 0-09-119660-4, Hutchinson U Lib). Humanities.
CONTROLLED READING
see Developmental Reading
CONTROLLED RELEASE PREPARATIONS
see Delayed-Action Preparations
CONTROLLERSHIP
see also Accounting; Auditing; Budget in Business
Willson, James D. & Campbell, John B. Controllership: The Work of the Managerial Accountant. 3rd ed. 800p. Date not set. write for info. (ISBN 0-471-05711-8). Wiley.
CONURBATIONS
see Metropolitan Areas
CONVALESCENCE
see also Nursing Homes
Burstein. The Get Well Hotel. 113p. Date not set. lib. bdg. 4.95 (ISBN 0-07-009244-3). McGraw.
Schaller, Agnes P. & Kinney, Analee. Seasonal Parties for Convalescents. 1981. write for info (ISBN 0-398-04452-X). C C Thomas.
CONVENTIONS
see Treaties
CONVENTIONS (CONGRESSES)
see Congresses and Conventions
CONVENTIONS, POLITICAL
see Political Conventions
CONVERSION OF WASTE PRODUCTS
see Recycling (Waste, etc.)
CONVERT MAKING
see Evangelistic Work
CONVERTERS, ELECTRIC
see Electric Current Converters
CONVEYING MACHINERY
see also Bulk Solids Handling; Hydraulic Conveying
Smith, D. K. Package Conveyors: Design & Estimating. 136p. 1972. 25.00x (ISBN 0-85264-213-X, Pub. by Griffin England). State Mutual Bk.
CONVICTION
see Belief and Doubt; Truth
CONVICTS
see Prisoners
CONVULSION THERAPY
see Shock Therapy
COOK, STANLEY ARTHUR, 1873-1949
Hunt, William R. To Stand at the Pole: The Dr. Cook-Admiral Peary North Pole Controversy. LC 80-6156. 272p. 1981. 14.95 (ISBN 0-8128-2773-2). Stein & Day.
COOK-BOOKS
see Cookery
COOKE, WILLIAM FOTHERGILL, SIR, 1806-1879
Betty Crocker's Cookbook. 816p. 1980. pap. 2.95. Bantam.
COOKERY
see also Baking; Bread; Breakfasts; Canning and Preserving; Caterers and Catering; Christmas Cookery; Coffee; Desserts; Diet; Dinners and Dining; Electric Cookery; Flavoring Essences; Food; Food Processor Cookery; Frying; Menus; Pancakes, Waffles, Etc.; Pastry; Quantity Cookery; Salads; Sandwiches; Soups; Stews; Vegetarian Cookery
Advice About Household Appliances, Cooking, Entertaining. (Home Adviser Ser.). 80p. (Orig.). 1981. pap. 1.95 (ISBN 0-8326-2403-9, 7052). Delair.
Allen, Gayle & Allen, Robert F. Three Worlds Cookbook. LC 75-19542. (Illus.). 239p. 1975. pap. 7.95 (ISBN 0-87983-096-4). Keats.
Andrea, Bob. Akron-Canton Epicure. (Epicure Ser.). 1981. pap. 4.95 (ISBN 0-89716-080-0). Peanut Butter.
The Any Oven Cookbook. (Orig.). pap. 5.95 (ISBN 0-87502-083-6). Benjamin Co.
Armour & Company Kitchens. The Quick-Easy Armour Cookbook. (Orig.). 5.95 (ISBN 0-87502-082-8). Benjamin Co.
Bauman, Wes. Country Kitchen Cookbook. 8.95 (ISBN 0-8423-0448-7). Tyndale.
Better Homes & Gardens. Better Homes & Gardens New Cookbook. 832p. 1981. pap. 3.95 (ISBN 0-553-14866-4). Bantam.
Better Homes & Gardens Books Editors, ed. Easy Bazaar Crafts. (Illus.). 96p. 1981. 4.95 (ISBN 0-696-00665-0). Meredith Corp.
--Good Food & Fitness. (Illus.). 96p. 1981. 4.95 (ISBN 0-696-00635-9). Meredith Corp.
--Short-Cut Recipes. (Illus.). 96p. 1981. 4.95 (ISBN 0-696-00655-3). Meredith Corp.
Better Homes & Gardens Editors, ed. Casual Entertaining Cook Book. (Illus.). 96p. 1981. 4.95 (ISBN 0-696-00490-9). Meredith Corp.
Bjorn, Thyra F. The Home Has a Heart. (Orig.). pap. 1.75 (ISBN 0-89129-033-8). Jove Pubns.
Blinn, Lynn. Decisions: What to Eat. (Home Economics Ser.). (Illus.). 300p. (Orig.). 1981. pap. text ed. price not set (ISBN 0-8273-1853-7); price not set instr's guide (ISBN 0-8273-1854-5). Delmar.
Bloch, Barbara. If It Doesn't Pan Out: How to Cope with Cooking Disasters. LC 80-26508. 1981. 8.95 (ISBN 0-934878-02-1). Dembner Bks.
Bradley, Richard. The Country Housewife & Lady's Director. 500p. 1980. Repr. of 1736 ed. 37.50x (ISBN 0-907325-01-7, Pub. by Prospect England). U Pr of Va.
Brenner, Eleanor P. Gourmet Cooking Without Salt. LC 79-6856. (Illus.). 416p. 1981. 15.95 (ISBN 0-385-14821-6). Doubleday.
Cadwallader, Sharon. Whole Earth Cooking for the Eighties. (Illus.). 128p. 1981. 9.95 (ISBN 0-312-87050-7); pap. 5.95 (ISBN 0-312-87051-5). St Martin.
Carlson, Estelle. The I'm Too Busy Cook Book: Recipes for Busy People Who Love to Cook. (Illus.). 59p. (Orig.). 1981. pap. write for info. Pot of Gold.
Caviani, Mabel, et al. Simplified Quantity Ethnic Recipies. (Ahrens Ser.). 272p. 1980. 15.95 (ISBN 0-8104-9474-4). Hayden.
Claiborne, Craig. Craig Claiborne's Favorites, Vol. 3. 1981. pap. 2.95 (ISBN 0-446-93808-4). Warner Bks.
Clark, Nancy. The Athlete's Kitchen: A Nutrition Guide & Cookbook. (Illus.). 276p. 1981. pap. 9.95 (ISBN 0-8436-2212-1). CBI Pub.
Collings, Michael & Collings, Judith. Whole Wheat Harvest-Recipes for Unground Wheat. pap. 2.95 (ISBN 0-89036-143-6). Hawkes Pub Inc.
Crandall, Dorothy & Ambuter, Jeanne. Mrs. Filbert's His & Her Cookbook. 7.95 (ISBN 0-916752-13-5). Green Hill.
D. C. Comics. DC Super Heroes Super Healthy Cookbook. (Illus., Orig.). 1981. 8.95 (ISBN 0-446-51227-3). Warner Bks.
The Ekco Economy Cookbook. 7.95 (ISBN 0-916752-25-9). Green Hill.
Elena, Tony S., Jr. Good Food. LC 80-65651. 128p. (Orig.). 1981. pap. 6.95 (ISBN 0-89087-265-1). Celestial Arts.
Eliason, Karine, et al. More Make-A-Mix Cookery. (Orig.). 1980. pap. 5.95 (ISBN 0-89586-055-4). H P Bks.
Elliot, Sharon A. Dinner Can Be a Picnic All Year Round. LC 80-70050. 1981. pap. 5.95 (ISBN 0-9601398-4-2). Fresh Pr.
Elmont, Nancy. The Four Seasons Cookbook. LC 80-70101. (Illus.). 144p. 1981. 8.95 (ISBN 0-916752-47-X). Dorison Hse.
--The Four Seasons Cookbook. 1981. 11.95 (ISBN 0-916752-47-X). Green Hill.
Emery, William. Culinary Design & Decoration. 135p. 1980. 26.95 (ISBN 0-8436-2187-7). CBI Pub.
Erickson, Charlotte. The Freezer Cookbook. (Illus.). 1981. pap. 8.95 (ISBN 0-8092-5888-9). Contemp Bks.
--Shortcut Cooking. rev. ed. (Illus.). 1981. pap. 6.95 (ISBN 0-8092-5887-0). Contemp Bks.
Ericson, Georgia. Aunt Hack's Rock House Kitchen: A Cookbook with a Story. 1977. write for info. Crosby County.
Farm Journal Food Editors. Farm Journal's Everyday Favorite Recipes. 128p. (Orig.). 1980. pap. 3.50x (ISBN 0-89795-011-9). Farm Journal.
Fellowship Church, Baton Rouge, La, Members. Quickies for Singles. McKee, Gwen, ed. (Illus.). 80p. 1980. pap. 4.95 (ISBN 0-937552-03-8). Quail Ridge.
Franey, Pierre. The New York Times Sixty Minute Gourmet. 352p. 1981. pap. 6.95 (ISBN 0-686-69133-4, Columbine). Fawcett.
Gallo, Patrick J. Old Bread, New Wine: A Portrait of the Italiann-Americans. LC 80-20401. 360p. 1981. 16.95 (ISBN 0-88229-146-7). Nelson-Hall.
Gans, Irvin. The Gourmet Doggie Bag Cookbook. Date not set. 6.95 (ISBN 0-533-04764-1). Vantage.
Grosser, Arthur E. The Cookbook Decoder: or, Culinary Alchemy Explained. 192p. 1981. 9.95 (ISBN 0-8253-0033-9). Beaufort Bks NY.
Hartbarger, Janie C. & Hartbarger, Neil J. Eating for the Eighties. LC 80-53187. 256p. 1981. 12.95 (ISBN 0-03-059077-9); pap. 6.95 (ISBN 0-03-059076-0). HR&W.
Haven, Diana. Menus for Romance. (Candlelight Romance Cookbook Ser.). (Orig.). pap. 1.50 (ISBN 0-440-16169-X). Dell.
Hayden, Naura. Hip, High Protein, Low-Cal Easy Does It Cookbook. 1981. pap. price not set (ISBN 0-671-42390-8). PB.
Herbert, Charlotte H. Charlotte Hughes Herbert's Cookery for Special Occasions. (Illus.). 1980. pap. 7.85 (ISBN 0-9604928-0-1). Sullivan Prod.
Holiday Magazine Award Cookbook. LC 76-41562. (Illus.). 1976. 12.50 (ISBN 0-89387-002-1). Sat Eve Post.
Hunt-Wesson Kitchens. The Cooking Lite Feeling Right Cookbook. 1980. 2.99 (ISBN 0-671-41778-9, Fireside). S&S.
Hunter, Catherine A. The Square Meal Cookbook. 206p. (Orig.). 1980. pap. write for info. Ref Guides.
The Index. in gift box 9.95 (ISBN 0-932398-03-0). Good Food Bks.
Jester, Pat. Easy Suppers. (Orig.). 1980. pap. 5.95 (ISBN 0-89586-064-3). H P Bks.
Jones, Jeanne. Diet for a Happy Heart: A Low-Cholesterol, Low-Saturated Fat, Low Calorie Cookbook. rev. ed. (Illus.). 192p. 1981. pap. 6.95 (ISBN 0-89286-183-5). One Hurd One Prods.
Junior League of New Orleans Inc. Jambalaya. (Illus.). 256p. (Orig.). 1980. pap. 7.95 (ISBN 0-9604774-0-3). Jr League New Orleans.
Kaplan, Lisa. The Good Sign Cookbook. LC 80-67482. (Illus.). 80p. 1980. pap. 3.50 (ISBN 0-937730-00-9). Good Sign.
Kirschner, Heidi. Fireless Cookery. 144p. 1981. pap. 5.95 (ISBN 0-914842-58-7). Madrona Pubs.
Lamborn, George D., ed. Entirely Entertaining. 212p. (Orig.). 1979. pap. 5.95. Jr League Montclair-Newark.
Leavitt, Sophie. All New Sophie Lavitt's Penny Pincher's Cookbook. 512p. 1980. pap. 2.95 (ISBN 0-553-13329-2). Bantam.
Leiderman, David & Liederman, Susan V. David's Cookies Cookie Cookbook. (Illus.). 128p. 1981. 8.95 (ISBN 0-89480-151-1); pap. 4.95 (ISBN 0-89480-149-X). Workman Pub.
Leonard, Jon N. & Taylor, Elaine A. The Live Longer Now Cookbook. 384p. 1981. pap. 2.50 (ISBN 0-441-48521-9). Charter Bks.
Longacre, Doris J. More with with Cookbook. 336p. 1981. pap. 3.95 (ISBN 0-553-13930-4). Bantam.
McCartney, Wilma M. Ring the Doorbell with Your Elbow: A Cookbook of "Portables". rev. ed. LC 80-84349. (Illus.). 136p. 1981. pap. 6.95 (ISBN 0-933050-07-0). New Eng Pr VT.
Macpherson, Ruth. Be a Guest at Your Own Party. (Illus., Orig.). 1981. pap. 6.95 (ISBN 0-8437-3377-2). Hammond Inc.
McWilliams, Margaret. Illustrated Guide to Food Preparation. 4th rev. ed. 1981. pns (ISBN 0-8087-3409-1). Burgess.
Marks, Celia. Come into My Kitchen. 1969. spiral bd. 7.95. Plum Nelly.
Martinez, Pam. Sugarless Cooking. 5.95 (ISBN 0-934230-05-6). Green Hill.
Maud, Marjory V. Divide & Conquer or Life Among the Left Overs. (Illus.). 1981. 9.95 (ISBN 0-938562-00-2). Single Impressinons.
Maynard, Dave. Dave Maynard's Tried & True All-Night Radio Secret Family Recipe Cookbook. (Illus.). 256p. pap. 6.95 (ISBN 0-201-05008-0). A-W.
The Mennonite Cookbook. LC 80-28579. (Illus.). 294p. 1981. spiral bdg. 9.95 (ISBN 0-8253-0041-X). Beaufort Bks NY.
Mini Meals in Minutes. 7.95 (ISBN 0-916752-09-7). Green Hill.
Murphy, Margaret D. The Farberware Convection Turbo Oven Cookbook. 1981. 8.95 (ISBN 0-916752-44-5). Green Hill.

Nelson, Kay S. Complete International Breakfast - Brunch Cookbook. LC 80-5714. 296p. 1981. 14.95 (ISBN 0-8128-2786-4). Stein & Day.

Nemet, Roslyn. Cook to Your Heart's Content. 1981. pap. 1.75 (ISBN 0-8439-0870-X, Leisure Bks). Nordon Pubns.

Offutt, Nelson T. More Than a Cookbook. LC 79-93281. 1981. pap. 5.95 (ISBN 0-89709-019-5). Liberty Pub.

Older, Julia & Sherman, Steve. Soup & Bread: One Hundred Recipes for Bowl & Board. 2nd ed. 128p. 1981. pap. 8.95 (ISBN 0-8289-0338-7). Greene.

Pierot, Suzanne W. Suzanne's Cooking Secrets. (Illus.). 1981. 12.95 (ISBN 0-393-01458-4); pap. 5.95 (ISBN 0-393-00055-9). Norton.

Ramsey, Gerald. Morning, Noon & Night Cookbook. 2nd ed. LC 63-16652. 272p. 8.95 (ISBN 0-87074-178-0). SMU Press.

Reynolds, Bruford S. Money Saving Recipes Through Sprouting & Gardening. pap. 4.95 (ISBN 0-89036-134-7). Hawkes Pub Inc.

Riccio, Dolores & Bingham, Joan. The Complete All-in-the-Oven Cookbook: The Cookbook for Saving Time & Energy. LC 80-5712. 300p. 1981. 12.95 (ISBN 0-8128-2699-X). Stein & Day.

Rotz, Anna O. Heritage Hill Farm Cookbook. 96p. 1980. 6.00 (ISBN 0-9605108-0-X). Rotz.

Schur, Sylvia, ed. Recipes for Busy People. (Orig.). 1980. pap. 2.50 (ISBN 0-446-91542-4). Warner Bks.

Shank, et al. Guide to Modern Meals. O'Neill, Martha, ed. (Illus.). 640p. (gr. 10-12). 1980. 17.28 (ISBN 0-07-056416-7, W); tchrs. resource guide avail. (ISBN 0-07-047514-8). McGraw.

Stanaford, Penny. Create-A-Cookbook: Guide to Easy Meal Planning. (Illus.). 68p. 1980. 10.95 (ISBN 0-9604850-0-7). Postscript.

Standish, Marjorie. Cooking Down East. 12th ed. (Illus.). 260p. 1980. 8.95 (ISBN 0-930096-14-2). G Gannett.

Stout, Rex & Viking Press Eds. The Nero Wolfe Cookbook. 224p. 1981. pap. 3.95 (ISBN 0-14-005754-4). Penguin.

Straubing, H. The Nymphomaniac's Cookbook. (Illus.). 144p. 1980. 4.95 (ISBN 0-87786-003-3); pap. 2.97 (ISBN 0-686-69011-7). Gold Penny.

The Sunbeam Frypan Cookbook. 1981. 8.95 (ISBN 0-916752-43-7). Green Hill.

Thackeray, Helen, compiled by. Lion House Recipes. LC 80-19719. (Illus.). 122p. 1980. 8.95 (ISBN 0-87747-831-7). Deseret Bk.

Tracy, Marian. Real Food: Simple, Sensuous & Splendid. pap. 5.95 (ISBN 0-14-046468-9). Penguin.

Truax, Carol. All About Steam Cooking. LC 79-6878. (Illus.). 272p. 1981. 12.95 (ISBN 0-385-15548-4). Doubleday.

Turgeon, Charlotte. The Saturday Evening Post Small-Batch Canning & Freezing Cookbook. LC 78-53040. (Illus.). 1978. 8.95 (ISBN 0-89387-020-X); pap. 4.95 (ISBN 0-89387-020-X). Sat Eve Post.

Turgeon, Charlotte & Turgeon, Charles. The Saturday Evening Post Time to Entertain Cookbook. LC 78-73386. 1978. 9.95 (ISBN 0-89387-025-0). Sat Eve Post.

Uvezian, Sonia. Complete International Sandwich Cookbook. LC 80-5715. 288p. 1981. 14.95 (ISBN 0-8128-2787-2). Stein & Day.

Voth, Norma J. Festive Cakes of Christmas. 80p. 1981. pap. 2.95 (ISBN 0-8361-1956-8). Herald Pr.

Ward, Patricia A. Farm Journal's Speedy Skillet Meals. (Illus.). 232p. 1980. 8.95 (ISBN 0-89795-009-7). Farm Journal.

Weight Watchers International. Weight Watchers Holiday & Party Cookbook. 1980. 12.95 (ISBN 0-453-01005-9, TE-5). NAL.

Wenham, Lynette. The Cook & Carry Book. (Illus.). 160p. (Orig.). 1980. pap. 8.95 (ISBN 0-589-01275-4, Pub. by Reed Bks Australia). C E Tuttle.

Wilde, Mary P. The Best of Ethnic Home Style Cooking. LC 80-50406. 240p. 1981. 10.95 (ISBN 0-87477-138-2). J P Tarcher.

Wishbone, Lipton Kitchens. Not for Salads Only from Wishbone. (Orig.). Date not set. price not set (ISBN 0-87502-081-X). Benjamin Co.

Wold, Tina & Frost, John. Men & Women Use... Menus. LC 80-68806. 120p. (Orig.). 1980. pap. 5.95 (ISBN 0-9604802-0-X). Frost Art.

Wright, Carol. The Holiday Cook: Recipes & Shopping Away from Home. LC 80-68682. (Illus.). 160p. 1981. 14.50 (ISBN 0-7153-8017-6). David & Charles.

Wubben, Pamela G. Wood Stove Cookery. 50p. 1981. pap. 3.75 (ISBN 0-935442-05-7). One Percent.

Yesterday & Today from the Kitchens of Stokely-Van Camp. (Orig.). Date not set. price not set (ISBN 0-87502-071-2). Benjamin Co.

Zahn, Carl F., compiled by. The Fine Arts Cookbook, Two. (Illus.). 195p. 1981. 14.95 (ISBN 0-8436-2211-3). CBI Pub.

Zumwalt, Betty. Ketchup Pickles Sauces: 19th Century Food in Glass. (Illus.). 480p. 1980. 25.00x (ISBN 0-686-28760-6). M West Pubs.

COOKERY–JUVENILE LITERATURE

Baker, Margaret. Food & Cooking. (Junior Reference Ser.). (Illus.). 64p. (gr. 7 up). 7.95 (ISBN 0-7136-1465-X). Dufour.

Haines, Gail K. Baking in a Box, Cooking on a Can. LC 80-26678. (Illus.). 128p. (gr. 4-6). 1981. PLB 6.67 (ISBN 0-688-00376-1); pap. 4.95 (ISBN 0-688-00373-7). Morrow.

Sanders. The Arrow Book of Good "N" Easy Cooking. (gr. 3-5). 1980. pap. 1.25 (ISBN 0-590-30066-0, Schol Pap). Schol Bk Serv.

The Saturday Evening Post I Can Cook Children's Cookbook. LC 80-67055. (Illus., Orig.). (gr. 1 up). 1980. 7.95 (ISBN 0-89387-049-8). Sat Eve Post.

Stori, Mouse. I'll Eat Anything If I Can Make It Myself. (Illus.). 176p. spiral bdg. 7.95. Chicago Review.

Veitch, B. & Harms, T. A Child's Cookbook. (ps-4). 1981. 8.95 (ISBN 0-201-09430-4, 09426, Sch Div); tchr's guide free; recipe step book 15.00 (ISBN 0-686-69466-X). A-W.

COOKERY–REDUCING RECIPES

Claiborne, Craig. Craig Claiborne's Gourmet Diet. 1981. pap. 2.95 (ISBN 0-345-29579-X). Ballantine.

Hunter, Frances. Skinnie Minnie Recipe Book. 1976. pap. 2.95 (ISBN 0-917726-06-5). Hunter Bks.

COOKERY–VOCATIONAL GUIDANCE

Culinary Institute of America. The Professional Chef. 5th ed. Folsom, LeRoj, ed. 608p. Date not set. text ed. 29.95 (ISBN 0-8436-2201-6). CBI Pub.

Foodservice Editors of CBI. The Professional Host. LC 80-15609. (Illus.). 496p. 1980. 24.95 (ISBN 0-8436-2154-0). CBI Pub.

COOKERY (APPETIZERS)

Edwinn, Gloria. Just for Starters. LC 80-51771. 272p. 1981. 14.95 (ISBN 0-670-41093-4). Viking Pr.

Orcutt, Georgia. Soups, Chowders & Stews. Taylor, Sandra, ed. (Flair of New England Ser.). 1981. pap. 8.95 (ISBN 0-911658-17-3, 3078). Yankee Bks.

Walker, Michael. The Cocktail Book. (Orig.). 1980. pap. 4.95 (ISBN 0-89586-069-4). H P Bks.

COOKERY (BEAN CURD)

Andersen, Jeul. The Tofu Primer: A Beginner's Book of Bean Cake Cookery. (Illus.). 50p. (Orig.). 1981. pap. 2.95 (ISBN 0-916870-33-2). Creative Arts Bk.

Landgrebe, Gary. Tofu at Center Stage. LC 80-69560. (Illus.). 112p. (Orig.). 1981. pap. 5.95 (ISBN 0-9601398-3-4). Fresh Pr.

COOKERY (BEEF)

Neely, Martina & Neely, William. The International Chili Society Official Chili Cookbook. (Illus.). 224p. 1981. 10.95 (ISBN 0-312-41988-0). St Martin.

COOKERY (BUTTERMILK)

see Cookery (Dairy Products)

COOKERY (CEREALS)

McMichael, Betty & McDonald, Karen M. Cooking with Love & Cereal. LC 80-69312. 224p. 1981. spiral bdg. 9.95 (ISBN 0-915684-80-2). Christian Herald.

COOKERY (CHEESE)

see Cookery (Dairy Products)

COOKERY (CHICKEN)

Hollander, Mary K. Chicken Favorites. Herbert, Susan H., ed. (Illus.). 64p. (Orig.). 1981. pap. 2.50 (ISBN 0-915942-18-6). Owlswood Prods.

Kay, Sophie & Consumer Guide Editors. The Chicken Cookbook. 160p. (Orig.). 1981. pap. 6.95 (ISBN 0-449-90049-5, Columbine). Fawcett.

COOKERY (CHOCOLATE)

Lawrence, Paul A. In Praise of Chocolate. (Illus.). 60p. (Orig.). 1981. pap. 6.95 (ISBN 0-938034-03-0). PAL Pr.

COOKERY (COLD DISHES)

Hecht, Helen. Cold Cuisine. LC 80-69374. 1981. 11.95 (ISBN 0-689-11130-4). Atheneum.

COOKERY (DAIRY PRODUCTS)

Editors of Time-Life Books. Eggs & Cheese. (The Good Cook Ser.). (Illus.). 176p. 1981. 12.95 (ISBN 0-8094-2887-3). Time-Life.

Monroe, Elvira. Say Cheesecake - & Smile. 220p. 1981. pap. 5.95 (ISBN 0-933174-11-X). Wide World.

The Shopwell Dairy Lovers' Cookbook. 6.95 (ISBN 0-916752-10-0). Green Hill.

COOKERY (DRIED FOODS)

Raigan, E. F. The Saturday Evening Post Dried Foods Cookbook. LC 80-67060. (Illus.). 1980. pap. 5.95 (ISBN 0-89387-041-2). Sat Eve Post.

The Saturday Evening Post Family Cookbook: Collectors Edition. LC 74-18928. (Illus.). 1979. pap. 5.95 (ISBN 0-89387-030-7). Sat Eve Post.

COOKERY (EGGS)

Editors of Time-Life Books. Eggs & Cheese. (The Good Cook Ser.). (Illus.). 176p. 1981. 12.95 (ISBN 0-8094-2887-3). Time-Life.

COOKERY (FISH)

see Cookery (Sea Food)

COOKERY (FLOWERS)

Buchner, Greet. Cooking with Flowers. (Illus.). 8.95 (ISBN 0-7225-0236-2). Dufour.

COOKERY (FROZEN FOODS)

Murphy, Margaret D. Freezer Cookery. 7.95 (ISBN 0-916752-02-X). Green Hill.

COOKERY (FRUCTOSE)

Byrd, Anita. Cooking with Fructose. LC 80-25086. 128p. 1981. 8.95 (ISBN 0-668-05138-8); pap. 4.95 (ISBN 0-668-05142-6). Arco.

COOKERY (FRUIT)

Celebrity Kitchen & United Fresh Fruit & Vegetable Association. The Fresh Fruit & Vegetable Book: A Complete Guide to Enjoying Fresh Fruits & Vegetables. LC 80-8390. (Illus.). 320p. 1981. pap. 3.95 (ISBN 0-06-463527-9, EH 527). Har-Row.

Fulwiler, Kyle D. The Berry Cookbook. 120p. 1981. pap. 5.95 (ISBN 0-914718-59-2). Pacific Search.

COOKERY (GAME)

Cone, Joan. Fish & Game Cooking. 1981. pap. 7.95 (ISBN 0-914440-45-4). EPM Pubns.

Marsh, Judy & Dyer, Carole, eds. The Maine Way -- a Collection of Maine Fish & Game Recipes: A Collection of Marine Fish & Game Recipes. (Illus.). 96p. (Orig.). 1978. pap. 3.95 (ISBN 0-686-69324-8). DeLorme Pub.

Sagstetter, Brad. The Venison Handbook. LC 80-84354. (Illus., Orig.). 1981. 5.95 (ISBN 0-89896-075-4). Larksdale.

COOKERY (GROUND BEEF)

see Cookery (Beef)

COOKERY (HAMBURGER)

see Cookery (Beef)

COOKERY (HERBS AND SPICES)

Gordon, Lesley. A Country Herbal. (Illus.). 208p. 1980. 19.95 (ISBN 0-8317-4446-4). Mayflower Bks.

Heffern, Richard. The Herb Buyers Guide. (Orig.). pap. 1.50 (ISBN 0-515-04635-3). Jove Pubns.

Muenscher, Minnie W. Minnie Muenscher's Herb Cookbook. LC 77-90908. (Illus.). 224p. 1978. 11.50 (ISBN 0-8014-1166-1). Comstock.

Schlerman, Gene. Schlerman in the Kitchen. 240p. 1980. 12.95 (ISBN 0-914842-56-0). Madrona Pubs.

COOKERY (HONEY)

Parkhill, Joe M. Here's to You Honey: The Book That Takes Where the World of Honey Leaves off, Vol. 2. 160p. 1980. spiral bdg 6.95. Country Bazaar.

--Honey-God's Gift-for Health & Beauty: Cooking & Canning with Honey, Food Value Versus Sugar. 158p. 1980. spiral bdg 6.95 (ISBN 0-936744-03-0). Country Bazaar.

COOKERY (MACARONI)

Nathan, Joan. The Larosa International Pasta Cookbook. 7.95 (ISBN 0-916752-25-9). Green Hill.

Time-Life Books Editors. Pasta. (The Good Cook Ser.). (Illus.). 176p. 1981. 12.95 (ISBN 0-8094-2891-1). Time-Life.

White, Merry. Pasta & Noodles. 288p. 1981. pap. 5.95 (ISBN 0-14-046504-9). Penguin.

COOKERY (MEAT)

see also Chili Con Carne; Cookery, Barbecue; Cookery (Game)

Meat Meals in Minutes. write for info. (ISBN 0-87502-085-2). Benjamin Co.

Murphy, Margaret D. Meat Makes the Meal. 7.95 (ISBN 0-916752-11-9). Green Hill.

Sagstetter, Brad. The Venison Handbook. LC 80-84354. (Illus., Orig.). 1981. 5.95 (ISBN 0-89896-075-4). Larksdale.

COOKERY (MILK)

see Cookery (Dairy Products)

COOKERY (NATURAL FOODS)

Better Homes & Gardens Books Editors, ed. Meatless Main Dishes. (Illus.). 96p. 1981. 4.95 (ISBN 0-696-00645-6). Meredith Corp.

Black, Maggie & Howard, Pat. Eating Naturally: Recipes for Food with Fibre. 148p. 1981. 21.00 (ISBN 0-571-11602-7, Pub. by Faber & Faber); pap. 9.50 (ISBN 0-571-11603-5). Merrimack Bk Serv.

Blauer, Stephen. Rejuvenation: Dr. Ann Wigmore's Complete Diet & Health Program. 197p. pap. 4.95. Hippocrates.

Bricklin, Mark & Claessens, Charon. Natural Healing Cookbook: Over Four Hundred Fifty Delicious Ways to Get Better & Stay Healthy. (Illus.). 416p. 1981. 16.95 (ISBN 0-87857-338-0). Rodale Pr Inc.

Bumgarner, Marlene A. Organic Cooking for (Not-So-Organic) Mothers. Olson, Sue, ed. LC 80-23089. (Illus.). 160p. (Orig.). pap. 5.50 (ISBN 0-938006-01-0); spiral bdg. 4.95 (ISBN 0-938006-00-2). Chesbro.

Dalsass, Diana. Cashews & Lentils, Apples & Oats. (Illus.). 1981. 14.95 (ISBN 0-8092-5935-4); pap. 7.95 (ISBN 0-8092-5934-6). Contemp Bks.

Edwards, William, et al. The Renaissance Cookbook, Vol. 1. (Illus.). 184p. 1980. 5.95 (ISBN 0-938054-01-5); pap. 3.25 (ISBN 0-938054-00-7). Tri-B Pubns.

Parsons, Mothey. Almonds to Zoybeans: A Natural Foods Cookbook. (Illus.). 192p. 1973. pap. 1.50. Larchmont Bks.

Pickard, Mary A. Feasting Naturally: From Your Own Recipes. LC 80-68229. 1980. spiral bdg. 7.95 (ISBN 0-934474-18-4). Cookbook Pubs.

SerVaas, Cory, et al. The Saturday Evening Post Fiber & Bran Better Health Cookbook. LC 77-7804. (Illus.). 1977. 12.95 (ISBN 0-89387-008-0). Sat Eve Post.

--The Saturday Evening Post Fiber & Bran Better Health Cookbook. LC 80-67052. (Illus.). 1977. pap. 6.50 (ISBN 0-89387-048-X). Sat Eve Post.

Shurtleff, William & Aoyagi, Akiko. The Book of Miso. 768p. 1981. pap. 3.50 (ISBN 0-345-29107-7). Ballantine.

Szilard, Paula & Woo, Juliana J. The Electric Vegetarian: Natural Cooking the Food Processor Way. 1981. 12.95. Johnson VA.

Wigmore, Ann. Healthy Children: Nature's Way. 120p. pap. 1.95. Hippocrates.

--Recipes for Life. Kimball, Betsy, ed. (Illus.). 181p. pap. text ed. 7.95. Hippocrates.

--Spiritual Diet. (Health Digest Ser.: No. 152). 64p. pap. 1.50. Hippocrates.

Wunderlich, Elinor. Easy Whole-Food Recipes. LC 80-81655. (Orig.). 1980. pap. 3.95 (ISBN 0-910812-26-8). Johnny Reads.

COOKERY (NOODLES)

see Cookery (Macaroni)

COOKERY (POULTRY)

see also Cookery (Chicken)

Foley, Joseph & Foley, Joan. The Chesapeake Bay Fish & Fowl Cookbook: A Treasury of Old & New Recipes from Maryland's Eastern Shore. (Illus.). 192p. 1981. 13.95 (ISBN 0-02-539560-2). Macmillan.

COOKERY (SEA FOOD)

Beard, James. James Beard's Fish Cookery. 1967. pap. 2.75 (ISBN 0-446-95680-5). Warner Bks.

Cone, Joan. Fish & Game Cooking. 1981. pap. 7.95 (ISBN 0-914440-45-4). EPM Pubns.

D'Ermo, Dominique. Dominique's Famous Fish, Game & Meat Recipes. 1981. 12.95 (ISBN 0-87491-083-8); pap. 6.95 (ISBN 0-87491-080-3); ltd. edition hidebound 50.00 (ISBN 0-87491-082-X). Acropolis.

Foley, Joseph & Foley, Joan. The Chesapeake Bay Fish & Fowl Cookbook: A Treasury of Old & New Recipes from Maryland's Eastern Shore. (Illus.). 192p. 1981. 13.95 (ISBN 0-02-539560-2). Macmillan.

Hardigree, Peggy A. The Freefood Seafood Book. 224p. (Orig.). 1981. pap. 8.95 (ISBN 0-8117-2068-3). Stackpole.

Hovey, Eddy. Shark Gourmet Seafood of the Future. Sharp, George, ed. LC 80-52109. (Illus.). 111p. pap. 6.95 (ISBN 0-937496-00-6). Sea Harvest.

Marsh, Judy & Dyer, Carole, eds. The Maine Way -- a Collection of Marine Fish & Game Recipes: A Collection of Marine Fish & Game Recipes. (Illus.). 96p. (Orig.). 1978. pap. 3.95 (ISBN 0-686-69324-8). DeLorme Pub.

Rubin, Cynthia & Rubin, Jerome. The Oster Every Day a Gourmet Cookbook. 7.95 (ISBN 0-916752-29-1). Green Hill.

Schmidt, R. Marilyn. The Simply Seafood Cookbook of East Coast Fish. (Illus.). 150p. (Orig.). 1980. pap. 7.95 (ISBN 0-937996-00-9). Barnegat.

--The Simply Seafood Cookbook of East Coast Shellfish. (Illus.). 150p. (Orig.). 1980. pap. 7.95 (ISBN 0-937996-01-7). Barnegat.

Sunset Editors. Seafood Cook Book. 5th ed. LC 80-53482. (Illus.). 128p. 1981. pap. 4.95 (ISBN 0-376-02586-7, Sunset Books). Sunset-Lane.

COOKERY (SMOKED FOODS)

Kramer, Matt. Smoke Cooking. pap. 3.95 (ISBN 0-8015-6896-X, Hawthorn). Dutton.

COOKERY (SOUR CREAM AND MILK)

see Cookery (Dairy Products)

COOKERY (SPAGHETTI)

see Cookery (Macaroni)

COOKERY (VEGETABLES)

Beaven, Betsey, et al, eds. The Political Palate: A Feminist Vegetarian Cookbook. (Illus.). 352p. (Orig.). 1980. pap. 8.95 (ISBN 0-9605210-0-3, Dist. by Crossing Press). Sanguinaria.

Binding, G. J. Vegetables & Herbs with a Difference. 64p. 1972. pap. 3.00x (ISBN 0-8464-1059-1). Beekman Pubs.

Celebrity Kitchen & United Fresh Fruit & Vegetable Association. The Fresh Fruit & Vegetable Book: A Complete Guide to Enjoying Fresh Fruits & Vegetables. LC 80-8390. (Illus.). 320p. 1981. pap. 3.95 (ISBN 0-06-463527-9, EH 527). Har-Row.

Cornog, Mary, ed. Growing & Cooking Potatoes. LC 80-52993. 1981. pap. 7.95 (ISBN 0-911658-15-7, 3076). Yankee Bks.

Grigson, Jane. Jane Grigson's Vegetable Book. 1981. pap. 6.95 (ISBN 0-14-046352-6). Penguin.

Kerr, Don & Kerr, Vivian. Kerr's Country Kitchen. (Illus.). 164p. 1981. pap. 6.95 (ISBN 0-933614-08-X). Peregrine Pr.

Singh, Manju S. The Spice Box: A Vegetarian Indian Cookbook. (Illus.). 224p. 1981. 12.95 (ISBN 0-89594-052-3); pap. 6.95 (ISBN 0-89594-053-1). Crossing Pr.

Sunset Editors. Vegetarian Cooking. LC 80-53483. (Illus.). 96p. (Orig.). 1981. pap. 3.95 (ISBN 0-376-02910-2, Sunset Books). Sunset-Lane.

Szilard, Paula & Woo, Juliana J. The Electric Vegetarian: Natural Cooking the Food Processor Way. 1981. 12.95. Johnson VA.

Tenison, Marika H. Cooking with Vegetables. (Illus.). 284p. 1981. 16.95 (ISBN 0-224-01597-4, Pub. by Chatto-Bodley-Jonathan). Merrimack Bk Serv.

Turgeon, Charlotte. Of Cabbages & Kings Cookbook. LC 77-85390. (Illus.). 1977. 8.95 (ISBN 0-89387-014-5). Sat Eve Post.

Wubben, Pamela G. The Rhubarb Cookbook. LC 79-66754. (Illus.). 65p. 1979. 4.95 (ISBN 0-935442-00-6). One Percent.

COOKERY (VERMICELLI)

see Cookery (Macaroni)

COOKERY (WILD FOODS)

D'Ermo, Dominique. Dominique's Famous Fish, Game & Meat Recipes. 1981. 12.95 (ISBN 0-87491-083-8); pap. 6.95 (ISBN 0-87491-080-3); ltd. edition hidebound 50.00 (ISBN 0-87491-082-X). Acropolis.

COOKERY, AMERICAN

see also Cookery, Creole

Ayala, Mitzi. The Farmers' Cookbook: A Collection of Favorite Recipes, Economical Meal Planning Methods & Other Tips & Pointers for America's Farm Kitchens. (Illus.). 240p. 1981. 12.50 (ISBN 0-686-69457-0). Harbor Pub CA.

Berolzheimer, Ruth, ed. Culinary Arts Institute Encyclopedic Cookbook. 1980. 8.95 (ISBN 0-671-41408-9, Fireside). S&S.

Blackburn, Lois J. Florida Food Fare: & Food for Thought. (Illus.). 120p. (Orig.). 1980. pap. 5.00 (ISBN 0-938910-00-0). Pecalhen.

Burrows, Marion. Keep It Simple. 256p. 1981. 10.95 (ISBN 0-688-00450-4). Morrow.

Callahan, Dorothy & Payne, Alma S. Young America's Cookbook. LC 59-5171. (Illus.). 320p. (gr. 7-9). 1959. 6.95 (ISBN 0-684-12358-4). Scribner.

Callaway, Cason J., Jr. & Flowers, Charles M., eds. A Southern Collection. (Illus.). 318p. (Orig.). 1979. pap. 8.50. Jr League Columbus.

Carlson, Verne. The Cowboy Cookbook. LC 80-68342. (Illus.). 186p. 1981. 10.95 (ISBN 0-937844-00-4); pap. 6.95 (ISBN 0-937844-01-2). Caverne Pub.

Clark, Emery, illus. Recipes & Reminiscences of New Orleans. (Illus.). 237p. (Orig.). 1971. pap. 6.95 (ISBN 0-9604718-0-4). Old Ursuline.

Combes, Angela, ed. The Vermont Symphony Cookbook. (Illus.). 128p. 1981. pap. cancelled (ISBN 0-8397-8571-2). Eriksson.

Cookbook Committee, 1979, ed. Indianapolis Collects & Cooks. (Illus.). 208p. 1980. pap. text ed. 11.75 (ISBN 0-936260-00-9). Ind Mus Art.

Crabtree, Catherine G. A'la Aspen: Restaurant Recipes. rev. ed. pap. 6.50 (ISBN 0-937070-05-X). Crabtree.

--A'la Vail: Restaurant Recipes. LC 80-67564. pap. 6.50 (ISBN 0-937070-03-3). Crabtree.

D. C. Comics. D C Super Heroes Super Healthy Cookbook. (Illus., Orig.). 1981. pap. 8.95 (ISBN 0-446-51227-3). Warner Bks.

Dillow, Louise B. & Carver, Deenie B. Mrs. Blackwell's Heart-of-Texas Cookbook. (Illus.). 130p. 1980. pap. 6.95 (ISBN 0-931722-06-3). Corona Pub.

Eberly, Carole. More Michigan Cooking... & Other Things, Vol. 2. (Illus.). 112p. (Orig.). 1981. pap. 4.95 (ISBN 0-932296-07-6). Eberly Pr.

Foley, Joseph & Foley, Joan. The Chesapeake Bay Fish & Fowl Cookbook: A Treasury of Old & New Recipes from Maryland's Eastern Shore. (Illus.). 192p. 1981. 13.95 (ISBN 0-02-539560-2). Macmillan.

Geoghegan, Sheilah. Dining Out & Dining in: Memorable Menus & Recipes from Washington's Finest Restaurants. 128p. 1981. 10.00 (ISBN 0-914440-47-0). EPM Pubns.

Groff, Betty & Wilson, Jose. Betty Groff's Country Goodness Cookbook. LC 80-1093. (Illus.). 336p. 1981. 17.95 (ISBN 0-385-12120-2). Doubleday.

Hachten, Harva. The Flavor of Wisconsin: An Informal History of Food & Eating in the Badger State. LC 80-26172. (Illus.). 300p. 1981. 12.95 (ISBN 0-87020-204-9). State Hist Soc Wis.

Hayes, Irene. What's Cooking in Kentucky, 2 vols. Date not set. spiral bdg. 6.95x ea. Vol. 1, 204pp (ISBN 0-938402-02-1). Vol. 2, 196pp (ISBN 0-938402-03-X). Hayes Bk Co.

Hess, Karen, ed. Martha Washington's Book of Cookery. LC 80-18257. 464p. 1981. 19.95 (ISBN 0-231-04930-7). Columbia U Pr.

Jenkins, Ruth, et al. Four Great Southern Cooks. LC 80-68989. (Illus.). 200p. (Orig.). 1980. pap. 7.95 (ISBN 0-938072-00-5). DuBose Pub.

Judd, Rue & Worley, Ann. It's a Long Way to Guacamole: The Tex-Mex Cookbook. (Illus.). 106p. (Orig.). 1978. pap. 6.00 (ISBN 0-9604842-0-5). J&W Tex-Mex.

Junior League of Rochester, Inc. Applehood & Motherpie. Kessler, Tracy K., ed. 330p. 1981. 12.95 (ISBN 0-9605612-0-X). Jr League Rochester.

Miller, Mark E., ed. Amish Cooking. 320p. 1981. Repr. 14.95 (ISBN 0-8361-1958-4). Herald Pr.

Nebraska Centennial Cookbook. (Illus.). 1966. pap. 6.95 (ISBN 0-8220-1620-6). Centennial.

Northcountry Cookbook: Compilation of Northcountry Recipes. 1980. 7.95 (ISBN 0-932212-17-4). Avery Color.

Patent, Greg. More Big Sky Cooking. (Big Sky Cooking Ser.: No. 2). (Illus.). 151p. (Orig.). 1980. pap. 9.50. Eagle Comm.

Ragan, W. Gordon. Georgia Cookbook. 2nd ed. LC 78-70630. (Illus.). 1980. 9.95 (ISBN 0-916620-50-6). Portals Pr.

Research Staff of Inst. of Texan Cultures. The Melting Pot: Ethnic Cuisine in Texas. (Illus.). 230p. 1977. 10.95 (ISBN 0-933164-18-1). U of Tex Inst Tex Culture.

Robinson, Delmer. Appalachian Hill Country Cook Book. LC 80-83183. (Illus.). 156p. 1980. 9.95 (ISBN 0-934750-04-1). Jalamap.

Rothenbuehler, Mary L., ed. Family Secrets: Recipes from Grandma Fowler's Kitchen. (Illus., Orig.). 1981. pap. 2.25 (ISBN 0-939010-00-3). Zephyr.

Seighman, Ruth. A Taste of Quality: Favorite Recipes from the Merillat Kitchens of America. 1980. write for info. (ISBN 0-937304-01-8). Impressions.

Serrane, Ann, ed. The Southern Junior League Cookbook. 640p. 1981. pap. 7.95 (ISBN 0-345-29518-8). Ballantine.

Silitch, Clarissa, ed. Yankee Church Supper Cookbook. LC 80-612. 240p. 1980. pap. 9.95 (ISBN 0-686-68933-X, 3075). Yankee Bks.

Stamm, Sara B. Favorite New England Recipes. (Illus.). 304p. 1972. pap. 9.75 (ISBN 0-911658-87-4). Yankee Bks.

Standish, Marjorie. Keep Cooking the Maine Way. 5th ed. (Illus.). 260p. 1980. 8.95 (ISBN 0-930096-15-0). G Gannett.

Swendson, Patsy & Swendson, Ole. A Couple of Cooks. (Illus.). 1980. 5.95. Corona Pub.

Weist, Lois A. What's Cooking in Towne & Country USA, Vol. I. (Special Collectors' Keepsake Ser.). (Illus.). 240p. 1979. 14.99 (ISBN 0-938166-00-X). Weist Pub OH.

--What's Cooking in Towne & Country USA, Vol. II. (Special Collectors' Keepsake Ser.). (Illus.). 250p. 1979. 14.99 (ISBN 0-938166-01-8). Weist Pub OH.

COOKERY, AMISH

see Cookery, American

COOKERY, BARBECUE

see also Cookery, Outdoor

Waldo, Myra. The Great International Barbeque Book. 216p. 1981. pap. 4.95 (ISBN 0-07-067778-6). McGraw.

COOKERY, BURMESE

Khaing, Mi Mi. Cook & Entertain the Burmese Way. 12.95 (ISBN 0-89720-017-9). Green Hill.

COOKERY, CAMP

see Cookery, Outdoor

COOKERY, CARIBBEAN

Schulman, Estella F. Now Listen Good: A Collection of Authentic West Indian Recipes. 6.95 (ISBN 0-88427-037-8). Green Hill.

COOKERY, CHINESE

The Cooking of China. Date not set. price not set. Time-Life.

Fessler, Stella L. Chinese Seafood Cooking. 1981. pap. price not set (ISBN 0-452-25265-2, Z5265, Plume). NAL.

Huang, Dorothy. Dorothy Huang's Chinese Cooking. Harju, Lorry B., ed. 200p. 1980. 12.95. Pinewood.

Lo, Kenneth. Chinese Regional Cooking. 1981. pap. 4.95 (ISBN 0-394-73870-5). Pantheon.

Ma, Nancy C. Mrs. Ma's Favorite Chinese Recipes. LC 68-13739. (Illus.). 145p. 1980. pap. 7.95 (ISBN 0-87011-427-1). Kodansha.

Myers, Barbara. The Chinese Restaurant Cookbook. LC 80-6229. 348p. 1981. 14.95 (ISBN 0-8128-2803-8). Stein & Day.

Tsujita, Mariko & Ikeda, Kyoko. Chinese Cooking for Everyone. (Illus.). 96p. 1980. 4.50 (ISBN 0-86628-003-0). Ridgefield Pub.

COOKERY, COLD

see Cookery (Cold Dishes)

COOKERY, CREOLE

Clark, Emery, illus. Recipes & Reminiscences of New Orleans. (Illus.). 237p. (Orig.). 1971. pap. 6.95 (ISBN 0-9604718-0-4). Old Ursuline.

COOKERY, EUROPEAN

Tyrack, Mildred & Van Eperen, Jeannine, eds. Five Generations of Obesity: A Compilation of Family Recipes Making Getting Fat Look Easy. (Illus.). 116p. (Orig.). 1981. pap. 4.95 (ISBN 0-937268-03-8). Alpha Printing.

COOKERY, FRENCH

Ancelet, Danielle. Cuisine of France. (Illus.). 184p. 1981. 15.95 (ISBN 0-312-17834-4). St Martin.

Benoist, Elizabeth. The Dish Ran Away with the Spoon. 212p. 1980. pap. 5.95 (ISBN 0-86629-007-9). Sunrise MO.

Brown, Michael. Food & Wine of Southwest France. (Illus.). 216p. 1981. 35.00 (ISBN 0-7134-1847-8, Pub. by Batsford England). David & Charles.

Darling, Renny. The Joy of Eating French Food: Great French Dishes Made Easy. 1980. pap. 8.95 (ISBN 0-930440-05-6). Royal Calif.

David, Elizabeth. French Provincial Cooking. rev. ed. LC 80-8369. (Illus.). 520p. 1981. 16.95 (ISBN 0-06-014827-6, HarpT). Har-Row.

Olney, Richard. The French Menu Cookbook. LC 80-24423. (Illus.). 446p. Date not set. pap. 8.95 (ISBN 0-689-70607-3, 268). Atheneum.

Spurlock, Rae. Modern French Cooking. LC 79-23751. 208p. 1981. 16.95 (ISBN 0-88229-480-6). Nelson-Hall.

Virion, Charles. Charles Virion's French Country Cookbook. Backman, Beth, ed. (Illus.). 416p. 1980. pap. 7.95 (ISBN 0-8015-1198-4, Hawthorn). Dutton.

Willan, Anne. LaVarenne's Basic French Cookery. (Orig.). 1980. 12.95 (ISBN 0-89586-086-4); pap. 7.95 (ISBN 0-89586-056-2). H P Bks.

--LaVarenne's Basic French Cookery. 1980. 12.95 (ISBN 0-89586-086-4). H P Bks.

--Paris Kitchen: An Introduction to the La Varenne Cooking School. LC 80-27346. (Illus.). 288p. 1981. price not set (ISBN 0-688-00411-3). Morrow.

COOKERY, HEBREW

see Cookery, Jewish

COOKERY, HUNGARIAN

Karoly, Gundel. Hungarian Cookery-Book: One Hundred Forty Hungarian Specialities. 10th rev. ed. (Illus.). 103p. 1980. 7.50x (ISBN 963-13-0949-5). Intl Pubns Serv.

COOKERY, INDIC

Ady, Doris M. Curries from the Sultan's Kitchen. rev. ed. (Illus.). 126p. 1980. pap. 8.25 (ISBN 0-589-50188-7, Pub. by Reed Books Australia). C E Tuttle.

COOKERY, INDONESIAN

Copeland, Marks & Soeharjo, Mintari. The Indonesian Kitchen. LC 80-69385. 1981. write for info. (ISBN 0-689-11142-8). Atheneum.

Owen, Sri. Indonesian Food & Cooking. rev. ed. (Illus.). 256p. 1980. pap. 10.95x (ISBN 0-907325-00-9, Pub. by Prospectengland). U Pr of Va.

Samuel-Hool, Leonie. To All My Grandchildren: Lessons in Indonesian Cooking. Hool, Sherman, ed. LC 80-84766. (Illus.). 120p. 1981. 12.95 (ISBN 0-936016-50-7); pap. 7.95 (ISBN 0-936016-75-2). Liplop.

COOKERY, ITALIAN

Love, Louise. Complete Book of Pizza. 2nd ed. (Illus.). 1981. pap. write for info. Sassafras Pr.

McNair, James K. Adventures in Italian Cooking. Ortho Books Editorial Staff, ed. LC 80-66345. (Illus.). 96p. (Orig.). 1981. pap. 4.95 (ISBN 0-917102-89-4, Ortho Bks). Chevron Chem.

Polvay, Marina. Cucina Magra, Cucina Sana: Slim & Healthy Italian Cooking. (Illus.). 192p. 1981. 13.95 (ISBN 0-13-195081-9, Spec); pap. 6.95 (ISBN 0-13-195073-8). P-H.

COOKERY, JAPANESE

Omura, Yoshiaki, et al. The Tofu-Miso High Efficiency Diet. 208p. 1981. 10.95 (ISBN 0-668-05178-7); pap. 6.95 (ISBN 0-668-05180-9). Arco.

COOKERY, JEWISH

Bellin, Mildred G. The Jewish Cookbook. 1980. write for info. (ISBN 0-8197-0058-4). Bloch.

Frucht, Phyllis, et al, eds. The Best of Jewish Cooking. 1981. pap. 9.95 (ISBN 0-686-69080-X). Dial.

Jackson, Judy. The Home Book of Jewish Cookery. 176p. 1981. 24.00 (ISBN 0-571-11697-3, Pub. by Faber & Faber); pap. 9.95 (ISBN 0-571-11737-6). Merrimack Bk Serv.

Shosteck, Patti. A Lexicon of Jewish Cooking. rev. ed. 1981. pap. 6.95 (ISBN 0-8092-5995-8). Contemp Bks.

COOKERY, MEXICAN

Judd, Rue & Worley, Ann. It's a Long Way to Guacamole: The Tex-Mex Cookbook. (Illus.). 106p. (Orig.). 1978. pap. 6.00 (ISBN 0-9604842-0-5). J&W Tex-Mex.

COOKERY, MICROWAVE

see Microwave Cookery

COOKERY, ORIENTAL

Wright, Jeni. The Encyclopedia of Asian Cooking. (Illus.). 224p. 1980. 20.00 (ISBN 0-7064-0990-6); pap. 9.95 (ISBN 0-7064-1354-7). Mayflower Bks.

COOKERY, OUTDOOR

see also Cookery, Barbecue

Barker, Harriett. The One-Burner Gourmet. rev. ed. (Illus.). 1981. pap. 7.95 (ISBN 0-8092-5883-8). Contemp Bks.

Morton, Nancy A. Picnics with Pizzazz. (Orig.). 1981. pap. 5.95 (ISBN 0-8092-5922-2). Contemp Bks.

Vigil, Alberta G. The Complete Camper's Cookbook: Nearly 200 Easy Recipes for Family Outdoor Cooking. (Illus.). 104p. (Orig.). 1981. pap. 5.95 (ISBN 0-932906-09-5). Pan-Am Publishing Co.

--The Complete Campers Cookbook: Nearly 200 Easy Recipes for Family Outdoor Cooking. LC 80-83880. (Illus.). 104p. 1981. pap. 5.95 (ISBN 0-932906-09-5). Pan-Am Publishing Co.

Woodruff, Leroy L. Cooking the Dutch Oven Way. (Illus.). 144p. 1980. pap. 4.95 (ISBN 0-934802-01-7). Ind Camp Supply.

COOKERY, PENNSYLVANIA GERMAN

see Cookery, American

COOKERY, QUANTITY

see Quantity Cookery

COOKERY, SOUTHERN

see Cookery, American

COOKERY, THAI

Brennan, Jennifer. The Original Thai Cookbook. (Illus.). 276p. 1981. 12.95 (ISBN 0-399-90110-8) Marek.

COOKERY, VEGETARIAN

see Vegetarian Cookery

COOKERY FOR ALLERGICS

Conrad, Marion L. Allergy Cooking. (Orig.). pap. 2.25 (ISBN 0-515-05738-X). Jove Pubns.

COOKERY FOR DIABETICS

Jones, Jeanne. More Calculated Cooking: Practical Recipies for Diabetics & Dieters. 192p. (Orig.). 1981. 10.95 (ISBN 0-89286-185-1); pap. 6.95 (ISBN 0-89286-184-3). One Hurd One Prods.

Salmon, Margaret B. Diabetic Diet Exchange Lists for Low Sodium Diets. (Illus.). 1979. pap. 1.50 (ISBN 0-918662-06-0). Techkits.

--Dieta Siabetica Para Buena Salud. (Illus.). 1979. pap. 1.50 (ISBN 0-918662-06-0). Techkits.

COOKERY FOR INSTITUTIONS, ETC.

see Quantity Cookery

COOKERY FOR LARGE NUMBERS

see Quantity Cookery

COOKERY FOR THE PHYSICALLY HANDICAPPED

see also Physically Handicapped–Rehabilitation

Read, Ralph. When the Cook Can't Look: A Cooking Handbook for the Blind & Visually Impaired. 144p. 1981. 9.95 (ISBN 0-8264-0034-5). Continuum.

COOKERY FOR THE SICK

see also Cookery for Allergics; Cookery for Diabetics; Diet in Disease; Low-Fat Diet; Salt-Free Diet; Sugar-Free Diet

Finsand, Mary J. Caring & Cooking for the Hyperactive Child. LC 80-54335. 192p. 1981. 12.95 (ISBN 0-8069-5560-0); lib. bdg. 11.69 (ISBN 0-8069-5561-9); pap. 6.95 (ISBN 0-8069-8980-7). Sterling.

Forsythe, Elizabeth. The Low-Fat Gourmet. 156p. 1981. 14.95 (ISBN 0-7207-1226-2). Merrimack Bk Serv.

COOKIES

Leiderman, David & Liederman, Susan V. David's Cookies Cookie Cookbook. (Illus.). 128p. 1981. 8.95 (ISBN 0-89480-151-1); pap. 4.95 (ISBN 0-89480-149-X). Workman Pub.

Thaler, Mike. Complete Cookie Book. 1980. pap. 1.95 (ISBN 0-380-76133-5, 76133, Camelot). Avon.

COOKING UTENSILS

see Kitchen Utensils

COOLEY'S ANEMIA

see Thalassemia

COOLIDGE, CALVIN, PRES. U. S., 1872-1933

Ferrell, Robert H., et al. The Talkative President: The off-the-Record Press Conferences of Calvin Coolidge. Friedel, Frank, ed. LC 78-66526. (The History of the United States Ser.: Vol. 6). 287p. 1979. lib. bdg. 23.00 (ISBN 0-8240-9706-8). Garland Pub.

COOLIE LABOR

see Chinese in Foreign Countries

COOLING APPLIANCES

see Refrigeration and Refrigerating Machinery

COOPERATION

Here are entered works on the theory and history of cooperation and the cooperative movement.

see also Agriculture, Cooperative; Cooperative Societies; International Cooperation; Profit-Sharing; Trade-Unions

Regan, Donald. Utilitarianism & Cooperation. 296p. 1980. text ed. 37.50x (ISBN 0-19-824609-9); pap. 15.95x. Oxford U Pr.

COOPERATION, INTERNATIONAL

see International Cooperation

COOPERATIVE AGRICULTURE

see Agriculture, Cooperative

COOPERATIVE ASSOCIATIONS

see Cooperative Societies

COOPERATIVE DISTRIBUTION

see Cooperation; Cooperative Societies

COOPERATIVE PRODUCTION

see Cooperation; Cooperative Societies

COOPERATIVE SOCIETIES

Here are entered works dealing specifically with the nature and organization of cooperative enterprises and the laws governing them. Works on the theory and history of cooperation and the cooperative movement are entered under the heading Cooperation.

see also Agriculture, Cooperative

Bartolke-Bergmann. Integrated Cooperatives in the Industrial Society. 1980. text ed. 22.50x (ISBN 90-232-1772-1). Humanities.

Roy, Ewell P. Cooperatives: Development, Principles & Management. 4th ed. 1981. 11.95 (ISBN 0-8134-2143-8, 2143); pap. text ed. 8.95x. Interstate.

Wright, David H. Co-Operatives & Community. 118p. 1979. pap. text ed. 8.75x (ISBN 0-7199-0952-X, Pub. by Bedford England). Renouf.

COOPERATIVE STORES

see Cooperative Societies

COORDINATES

Laurent, J. P., ed. Coordination Chemistry-Twenty One: Twenty First International Conference on Coodination Chemistry, Toulouse, France 7-11 July 1980. (IUPAC Symposium Ser.). 200p. 1981. 54.00 (ISBN 0-08-025300-8). Pergamon.

COORDINATION COMPOUNDS

see also Ligand Field Theory

Berezin, B. D. Coordination Compounds of Porphyrins & Phthalocyanine. 256p. 1981. 52.00 (ISBN 0-471-27857-2, Pub. by Wiley-Interscience). Wiley.

COPPER ENGRAVING

see Engraving

COPPER IN THE BODY

Spiro, Thomas G. Copper Proteins. (Metal Ions in Biology Ser.: Vol. 3). 356p. 1981. 37.50 (ISBN 0-471-04400-8, Pub. by Wiley Interscience). Wiley.

COPPER MINES AND MINING

Schlitt, W. J., ed. Leaching & Recovering Copper from As-Mined Materials. LC 79-57347. (Illus.). 124p. 1980. pap. 15.00x (ISBN 0-89520-272-7). Soc Mining Eng.

Whiteley, Robert J. Geophysical Case Study of the Woodlawn Orebody, New South Wales Australia. LC 79-42637. (Illus.). xviii, 592p. 1980. 80.00 (ISBN 0-08-023996-X). Pergamon.

COPY-BOOKS

see Writing

COPYRIGHT

see also Patent Laws and Legislation; Trade-Marks

Copyright Law Survey. 206p. 1980. binder 34.50 (ISBN 92-805-0011-2, WIPO62, WIPO). Unipub.

Organization of American States. Copyright Protection in the Americas. 1979. looseleaf 150.00 (ISBN 0-379-20675-7). Oceana.

--Copyright Protection in the Americas, Release 1, Vol. 2. 1980. 75.00 (ISBN 0-379-20675-7). Oceana.

Silfen, Martin E. Counseling Clients in the Entertainment Industry 1980. 2 vols. LC 80-80021. (Patents, Copyrights, Trademarks, & Literary Property Course Handbook Ser.). 1433p. 1980. pap. text ed. 25.00 (ISBN 0-686-68822-8, G6-3666). PLI.

Strong, William S. A Layman's Guide to Copyright. 192p. 1981. text ed. 12.50 (ISBN 0-262-19194-6). MIT Pr.

Wincor, R. Copyright, Patents & Trademarks. 1980. 5.95 (ISBN 0-379-11138-1). Oceana.

WIPO Glossary of the Terms of the Law of Copyright & Neighboring Rights. 281p. 1980. pap. 39.50 (ISBN 92-805-0016-3, WIPO63, WIPO). Unipub.

Zweigert, Konrad & Kropholler, Jan. Law of Copyright, Competition & Industrial Property. Kolle, Gert & Hallstein, Hans P., eds. (Sources of International Uniform Law Ser.: Vol. III-A First Supplement). 1340p. 1980. 175.00x (ISBN 9-0286-0099-X). Sijthoff & Noordhoff.

COPYRIGHT–UNITED STATES

Miller, Jerome K. U. S. Copyright Documents: An Annotated Collection for Use by Educators & Librarians. LC 80-24768. 360p. 1980. lib. bdg. 25.00x (ISBN 0-87287-239-4). Libs Unl.

Organization of American States. Copyright Protection in the Americas. 1979. looseleaf 150.00 (ISBN 0-379-20675-7). Oceana.

--Copyright Protection in the Americas, Release 1, Vol. 2. 1980. 75.00 (ISBN 0-379-20675-7). Oceana.

CORE CURRICULUM

see Education–Curricula

CORN

Guidelines for Integrated Control of Maize Pests. (FAO Plant Production & Protection Paper Ser.: No. 18). 98p. 1980. pap. 6.00 (ISBN 92-5-100875-2, F1942, FAO). Unipub.

On-Farm Maize Drying & Storage in the Humid Tropics. (FAO Agricultural Services Bulletin: No. 40). 69p. 1981. pap. 6.00 (ISBN 92-5-100944-9, F2077, FAO). Unipub.

Shurtleff, M. C. Compendium of Corn Diseases. 2nd ed. (Compendium Ser.: No. 1). (Illus.). 124p. 1980. 11.00 (ISBN 0-89054-029-2). Am Phytopathol Soc.

Smil, Vaclav & Nachman, Paul. Energy Analysis & Agriculture: An Application to U.S. Corn Production. (Special Studies in Agricultural Science & Policy). 175p. 1981. lib. bdg. 22.00x (ISBN 0-86531-167-6). Westview.

CORNERS, COMMERCIAL

see Monopolies; Stock-Exchange

CORONA, SOLAR

see Sun

CORONADO, FRANCISCO VAZQUEZ DE

see Vazquez De Coronado, Francisco, 1510-1549

CORONARY ARTERIES–DISEASES

see Coronary Heart Disease

CORONARY ARTERIOSCLEROSIS

see Coronary Heart Disease

CORONARY CARE UNITS

Cohn & Madrid. Coming Back: A Guide to Recovering from Heart Attack & Living Confidently. 10.95 (ISBN 0-201-04562-1). A-W.

CORONARY HEART DISEASE

see also Heart–Infarction

Barnett, H. J., et al, eds. Acetylsalicylic Acid: New Uses for an Old Drug. 1981. text ed. price not set (ISBN 0-89004-647-6). Raven.

Carlson, Lars A. & Pernow, Bengt, eds. Metabolic Risk Factors in Ischemic Cardiovascular Disease. 1981. text ed. price not set (ISBN 0-89004-614-X). Raven.

Gensini, Goffredo G., ed. Coronary Arteriography. 2nd ed. 1981. write for info. (ISBN 0-87993-130-2). Futura Pub.

CORONARY THROMBOSIS

see Coronary Heart Disease

CORPORATE FINANCE

see Corporations–Finance

CORPORATE INSURANCE

see Insurance, Business

CORPORATE MERGERS

see Consolidation and Merger of Corporations

CORPORATE PLANNING

Baysinger, Barry D., et al. Barriers to Corporate Growth. LC 80-8603. 1981. price not set (ISBN 0-669-04323-0). Lexington Bks.

Mueller, Robert K. The Incompleat Board: The Unfolding of Corporate Governance. LC 80-8639. 1981. 29.95 (ISBN 0-669-04339-7). Lexington Bks.

CORPORATE REORGANIZATIONS

see also Bankruptcy; Consolidation and Merger of Corporations

Bibeault, Donald. Corporate Turnaround: How Managers Turn Losers into Winners. 416p. 1981. 22.95 (ISBN 0-07-005190-9). McGraw.

CORPORATION DIRECTORS

see Directors of Corporations

CORPORATION EXECUTIVES

see Executives

CORPORATION FINANCE

see Corporations–Finance

CORPORATION INCOME TAX

see Corporations–Taxation

CORPORATION LAW

Here are entered general works, and works on the United States For works on other countries, see local subdivisions below.

see also Bonds; Close Corporations; Consolidation and Merger of Corporations; Corporate Reorganizations; Corporations, Nonprofit; Directors of Corporations; Public Utilities; Securities; Stocks

Cary, William & Eisenberg, Melvin A. Cases & Materials on Corporations. 5th ed. LC 80-18042. (University Casebook Ser.). 1829p. pap. 2.50 (ISBN 0-88277-012-8). Foundation Pr.

Cary, William L. & Eisenberg, Melvin A. Cases & Materials on Corporations. abr. 5th ed. LC 80-68866. (University Casebook Ser.). 1085p. 1980. text ed. 21.50 (ISBN 0-88277-017-9). Foundation Pr.

Eppler, Klaus & Gilroy, Thomas, eds. Representing Publicly Traded Corporations, 1980, 2 vols. LC 80-83000. (Nineteen-Eighty to Nineteen Eighty-One Corporate Law & Practice Course Handbook Ser.). 1925p. 1980. pap. text ed. 40.00 (ISBN 0-686-69171-7, B6-6555). PLI.

Hadden, Tom. Company Law & Capitalism. 2nd ed. (Law in Context Ser.). 1977. 25.00x (ISBN 0-297-77334-8, Pub. by Weidenfeld & Nicolson). Rothman.

Howell, John C. Corporate Executive's Legal Handbook. 144p. 1980. pap. 5.95 (Spec). P-H.

Manning, Bayless. A Concise Textbook on Legal Capital. 2nd ed. (University Textbook Ser.). 180p. 1981. pap. text ed. write for info. (ISBN 0-88277-020-9). Foundation Pr.

Mautz, R. K., et al. Internal Control in U. S. Corporations: The State of the Art. LC 80-66623. 1980. 6.50 (ISBN 0-910586-33-0). Finan Exec.

Professional Report Editors & Kirk, John. Incorporating Your Business. (Illus.). 1981. 15.00 (ISBN 0-8092-5903-6). Contemp Bks.

Reese, Reuben A. The True Doctrine of Ultra Vires in the Law of Corporations, Being a Concise Presentation of the Doctrine in Its Application to the Powers & Liabilities of Private & Municipal Corporations. lxxi, 338p. 1981. Repr. of 1897 ed. lib. bdg. 30.00x (ISBN 0-8377-1031-6). Rothman.

CORPORATION TAX

see Corporations–Taxation

CORPORATIONS

Here are entered works on business associations organized as legal persons. For works dealing with United States corporations see the subdivision United States which follows.

see also Bonds; Close Corporations; Corporate Planning; Corporate Reorganizations; Cooperative Societies; Corporation Law; Directors of Corporations; International Business Enterprises; Public Utilities; Securities; Stocks

Bradley, James W. & Korn, Donald H. Acquisition & Corporate Development: A Contemporary Perspective for the Manager. LC 79-7719. (An Arthur D. Little Bk.). (Illus.). 1981. price not set (ISBN 0-669-03170-4). Lexington Bks.

Bradshaw, Thornton & Vogel, David. Corporations & Their Critics. 1980. 14.95 (ISBN 0-07-007075-X). McGraw.

Howell, John C. Form Your Own Corporation. 128p. 1980. pap. 5.95 (Spec). P-H.

Millstein, Ira M. & Katsh, Salem M. The Limits of Corporate Power: Existing Constraints on the Exercise of Corporate Discretion. LC 80-69280. (Studies of the Modern Corporation). (Illus.). 1981. 15.95 (ISBN 0-02-921490-4). Free Pr.

Seth, S. Up Against the Corporate Wall: Modern Corporations & Social Issues of the 80's. 4th ed. 1981. pap. 11.95 (ISBN 0-13-938308-5); 14.95 (ISBN 0-13-938316-6). P-H.

CORPORATIONS–BIBLIOGRAPHY

Miletich, John J. Corporate Power, Leadership, & Success: A Selective Bibliography to 1977. (Public Administration Ser.: Bibliography P-518). 49p. 1980. pap. 5.50. Vance Biblios.

CORPORATIONS–CONSOLIDATION

see Consolidation and Merger of Corporations

CORPORATIONS–FINANCE

see also Corporate Reorganizations; Corporations–Taxation

Bierman, H. Decision Making & Planning for the Corporate Treasurer. 195p. 1977. 27.95 (ISBN 0-471-07238-9). Wiley.

Troy, Kathryn. Managing Corporate Contributions, Report No. 792. (Illus.). vii, 95p. (Orig.). 1980. pap. 30.00 (ISBN 0-8237-0228-6). Conference Bd.

Van Arsdell, P. M. Corporation Finance: Policy, Planning, Administration. 1739p. 1968. 39.95. Wiley.

CORPORATIONS–LAWS AND LEGISLATION

see Corporation Law

CORPORATIONS–MERGER

see Consolidation and Merger of Corporations

CORPORATIONS–REORGANIZATION

see Corporate Reorganizations

CORPORATIONS–TAXATION

Sobeloff, Jonathan & Weidenbruch, Peter P. Federal Income Taxation of Corporations & Stockholders in a Nutshell. 2nd ed. (Nutshell Ser.). 351p. 1981. pap. 6.95 (ISBN 0-8299-2122-2). West Pub.

CORPORATIONS–CANADA

Gorecki, P. K. & Stanbury, W. T. Perspectives on the Royal Commission on Corporate Concentration. 308p. 1979. pap. text ed. 15.95x (ISBN 0-409-88606-8, Pub. by Inst Res Pub Canada). Renouf.

CORPORATIONS–LATIN AMERICA

Wiarda, Howard J. Corporatism & National Development in Latin America. (Replica Edition Ser.). 325p. 1981. lib. bdg. 27.00x (ISBN 0-86531-031-9). Westview.

CORPORATIONS–UNITED STATES

Herman, Edward S. Corporate Control, Corporate Power. LC 80-29447. (Illus.). 336p. 1981. 17.95 (ISBN 0-521-23996-6). Cambridge U Pr.

CORPORATIONS–UNITED STATES–FINANCE

Diener, Royce. How to Finance Your Growing Business. 416p. 1981. pap. 8.95 (ISBN 0-13-406546-8, Spec). P-H.

CORPORATIONS–UNITED STATES–TAXATION

Seixas, John R. Tax Havens & Offshore Companies. (Illus.). 159p. (Orig.). 1979. pap. 9.95 (ISBN 0-937456-00-4). Dragon Co.

Sobeloff, Jonathan & Weidenbruch, Peter P. Federal Income Taxation of Corporations & Stockholders in a Nutshell. 2nd ed. (Nutshell Ser.). 351p. 1981. pap. 6.95 (ISBN 0-8299-2122-2). West Pub.

CORPORATIONS, BUSINESS

see Corporations

CORPORATIONS, MEMBERSHIP

see Corporations, Nonprofit

CORPORATIONS, NONPROFIT

Accounting Principles & Reporting Practices for Certain Nonprofit Oragnizations. 1979. pap. 4.00 (SOP 78-10). Am Inst CPA.

Barocci, Thomas A. Non-Profit Hospitals: Their Structure, Human Resources, & Economic Importance. LC 80-22075. (Illus.). 224p. 1980. 19.95 (ISBN 0-86569-054-5). Auburn Hse.

Hunter, Richard J., Jr. Not-for-Profit Business: Readings, Legal Documents & Commentary. 273p. 1980. pap. text ed. 12.95 (ISBN 0-89651-509-5). Icarus.

Maddalena, Lucille A. A Communications Manual for Nonprofit Organizations. 286p. 1981. 17.95 (ISBN 0-8144-5606-5). Am Mgmt.

Rados, David L. Marketing for Non-Profit Organizations. LC 80-25948. (Illus.). 512p. 1981. 24.95 (ISBN 0-86569-055-3). Auburn Hse.

CORPULENCE

see Obesity

CORPUSCLES, BLOOD

see Blood Cells

CORPUSCULAR THEORY OF MATTER

see Electrons

CORRECTIONAL SERVICES

see Corrections

CORRECTIONS

see also Pardon; Probation; Punishment

Allen, Francis A. The Decline of the Rehabilitative Ideal: Penal Policy & Social Purpose. LC 80-25098. (Storrs Lectures). 160p. 1981. 15.00x (ISBN 0-300-02565-3). Yale U Pr.

Krantz, Sheldon. Cases & Materials on the Law of Corrections & Prisoners' Rights. 2nd ed. (American Casebook Ser.). 786p. 1981. text ed. 22.95 (ISBN 0-8299-2127-3). West Pub.

McDowell, Charles P. Community Relations & Criminal Justice. 500p. Date not set. text ed. price not set (ISBN 0-87084-558-6). Anderson Pub Co.

O'Brien, Edward L. & Fisher, Margaret E. Practical Law for Correctional Personnel: A Resource Manual & a Training Curriculum (by the National Street Law Institute) Austern, David T., ed. (Illus.). 205p. 1980. pap. text ed. write for info. (ISBN 0-8299-1034-4). West Pub.

Roberg, Roy R. & Webb, Vincent J. Critical Issues in Corrections: Problems, Trends, & Prospects. 300p. 1981. pap. text ed. 10.95 (ISBN 0-8299-0405-0). West Pub.

Rutherford, Andrew & Cohen, Fred. Standards Relating to Corrections Administration. (Juvenile Justice Standards Project Ser.). 1980. softcover 7.95 (ISBN 0-88410-821-X); casebound 16.50 (ISBN 0-88410-750-7). Ballinger Pub.

Truitt, John O. & Brewer, Donald D. Dynamics of Corrections Administration. (Illus.). 125p. 1981. pap. text ed. price not set (ISBN 0-87084-854-2). Anderson Pub Co.

CORRELATION OF FORCES

see Force and Energy

CORRESPONDENCE

see Commercial Correspondence; Letter-Writing; Letters

CORRESPONDENT BANKS

see Banks and Banking

CORRESPONDENTS, FOREIGN

see Journalists

CORROSION AND ANTI-CORROSIVES

see also Paint; Protective Coatings

Dechema: the West German National Scientific Society. Seawater Corrosion Data. (Chemical Engineering Book Ser.). 160p. 1981. 57.50 (ISBN 0-07-016207-7). McGraw.

Thomas Telford Editorial Staff, Ltd. Corrosion in Civil Engineering. 172p. 1980. 40.00x (ISBN 0-7277-0079-0, Pub. by Telford England). State Mutual Bk.

West, J. M. Basic Corrosion & Oxidation. 247p. 1981. 69.95 (ISBN 0-470-27080-2). Halsted Pr.

CORRUPTION (IN POLITICS)

see also Lobbying

Esalen, Wilner W. Too Small to Die. LC 79-57586. 114p. 1981. 7.95 (ISBN 0-533-04575-4). Vantage.

CORSAIRS

see Pirates

CORTEX, CEREBRAL

see Cerebral Cortex

COSMETICS

see also Beauty, Personal; Beauty Culture; Perfumes

Corson. Fashions in Makeup. 1980. text ed. 78.00. Humanities.

Elder, Robert L., ed. Cosmetic Ingredient: Their Safety Assessment. (Illus.). 1980. pap. text ed. 19.00 (ISBN 0-930376-19-6). Pathotox Pubs.

Mono, Madeleine. Making Eyes with Madeleine Mono. LC 80-7892. (Illus.). 128p. 1981. 10.95 (ISBN 0-690-01945-9, HarpT). Har-Row.

Place, Stan & Budd, Elaine. Stan Place's Guide to Make-Up: How to Look Like Yourself Only Better. (Illus.). 192p. 1981. 17.95 (ISBN 0-385-15537-9). Doubleday.

COSMETOLOGY

see Beauty Culture

COSMOGONY

see also Creation

Chaisson, Eric. Cosmic Dawn: The Origins of Matter & Life. (Illus.). 320p. 1981. 14.95 (ISBN 0-316-13590-9, Pub. by Atlantic Monthly Pr). Little.

Smith, William F. The Shaping of the Earth. (Illus.). 128p. 1981. 7.00 (ISBN 0-682-49715-0). Exposition.

Van Woerden, Hugo, et al, eds. Oort & the Universe. 210p. 1980. PLB 29.00 (ISBN 0-686-28847-5, Pub. by D. Reidel); pap. 12.95 (ISBN 90-277-1209-3). Kluwer Boston.

COSMOGONY, BIBLICAL

see Creation

COSMOLOGY

see also Astronomy; Creation; Earth; Life on Other Planets; Philosophy; Space Sciences; Theosophy

Chaisson, Eric. Cosmic Dawn: The Origins of Matter & Life. (Illus.). 320p. 1981. 14.95 (ISBN 0-316-13590-9, Pub. by Atlantic Monthly Pr). Little.

Davies, Paul. Other Worlds. 1981. 11.95 (ISBN 0-671-42227-8). S&S.

Goldsmith, Donald. The Evolving Universe. 1981. 18.95 (ISBN 0-8053-3327-4). Benjamin-Cummings.

Harrison, Edward R. Cosmology: The Science of the Universe. LC 80-18703. (Illus.). 480p. Date not set. price not set (ISBN 0-521-22981-2). Cambridge U Pr.

Heidmann, J. Relativistic Cosmology: An Introduction. (Illus.). 168p. 1980. pap. 24.80 (ISBN 0-387-10138-1). Springer-Verlag.

Smith, William F. The Shaping of the Earth. (Illus.). 128p. 1981. 7.00 (ISBN 0-682-49715-0). Exposition.

Stafford, Harry C. Culture & Cosmology: Essays on the Birth of World View. LC 80-5642. 371p. 1981. lib. bdg. 21.25 (ISBN 0-8191-1371-9); pap. text ed. 12.50 (ISBN 0-8191-1372-7). U Pr of Amer.

Van Woerden, Hugo, et al, eds. Oort & the Universe. 210p. 1980. PLB 29.00 (ISBN 0-686-28847-5, Pub. by D. Reidel); pap. 12.95 (ISBN 90-277-1209-3). Kluwer Boston.

COSMOLOGY, BIBLICAL

see Creation

COST ACCOUNTING

see also Managerial Accounting

Morse, Wayne J. Cost Accounting: Processing, Evaluating, & Using Cost Data. (Illus.). 752p. 1981. text ed. 18.95 (ISBN 0-201-04677-6). A-W.

Owler, L. W. & Brown, J. L. Wheldon Costing Simplified. 5th ed. (Illus.). 336p. 1978. pap. text ed. 11.95x (ISBN 0-7121-2309-1, Pub. by Macdonald & Evans England). Intl Ideas.

--Wheldon's Cost Accounting & Costing Methods. 14th ed. (Illus.). 784p. 1978. text ed. 21.00x (ISBN 0-7121-2334-2, Pub. by Macdonald & Evans England). Intl Ideas.

Tagliaferri, Louis E. Creative Cost Improvement for Managers. (Self-Teaching Guide Ser.). 208p. 1981. pap. text ed. 8.95 (ISBN 0-471-08708-4). Wiley.

Tainsh, J. A. The Key to Accounting & Costing. 119p. 1959. 11.75x (ISBN 0-85264-062-5, Pub. by Griffin England). State Mutual Bk.

Taylor, A. H. & Shearing, H. Financial & Cost Accounting for Management. 7th ed. (Illus.). 384p. 1979. pap. text ed. 15.95x (ISBN 0-7121-0633-2, Pub. by Macdonald & Evans England). Intl Ideas.

Wald, J. Bigg's Cost Accounts. (Illus.). 400p. (Orig.). 1978. pap. text ed. 15.95x (ISBN 0-7121-0263-9, Pub. by Macdonald & Evans England). Intl Ideas.

COST AND STANDARD OF LIVING

see also Food Prices; Home Economics–Accounting; Rent; Saving and Thrift; Wages

Annual Price Survey of Family Living Costs in the Greater New York Area, 1979: Family Budget Costs. 1980. write for info. Comm Coun Great NY.

McLachlan, Christopher A. Inflation-Wise: How to Do Almost Everything for Less. 1981. pap. 4.95 (ISBN 0-380-76836-4). Avon.

Spiegel, Janet. Stretching the Food Dollar: Practical Solutions to the Challenges of the 80's. (Urban Life Ser.). (Illus.). 96p. (Orig.). 1981. pap. 4.95 (ISBN 0-87701-172-9). Chronicle Bks.

COST BENEFIT ANALYSIS

see Cost Effectiveness

COST CONTROL
see also Cost Accounting
Shah, Pravin. Cost Control & Information Systems: A Complete Guide to Effective Design & Implementation. (Illus.). 608p. 1981. 24.95 (ISBN 0-07-056369-1, P&RB). McGraw.
COST EFFECTIVENESS
Hospital Financial Management Association. Cost Effectiveness Notebook: Nineteen Eighty Update. 1980. write for info. (ISBN 0-930228-14-6). Hospital Finan.
Pearce, David & Nash, Christopher. Social Appraisal of Projects: A Text in Cost-Benefit Analysis. 400p. 1981. 22.95 (ISBN 0-470-27137-X). Halsted Pr.
Qayum, Abdul. Social Cost-Benefit Analysis. 250p. 1979. pap. 9.95 (ISBN 0-913244-16-3). Hapi Pr.
COST OF LIVING
see Cost and Standard of Living
COST OF MEDICAL CARE
see Medical Care, Cost of
COST REDUCTION
see Cost Control
COSTUME
see also Arms and Armor; Clothing and Dress; Cosmetics; Dressmaking; Fans; Fashion; Jewelry; Make-Up, Theatrical; Millinery
also individual articles of apparel, e.g. Hosiery; Gloves
Bruun-Rasmussen, Ole & Petersen, Grete. Make-up, Costumes & Masks for the Stage. LC 76-19803. (Illus.). 96p. (gr. 4-12). 1981. pap. 6.95 (ISBN 0-8069-8992-0). Sterling.
Emery, Joy S. Stage Costume Techniques. (Ser. in Theatre & Drama). (Illus.). 368p. 1981. 18.95 (ISBN 0-13-840330-9). P-H.
Erte. Erte's Costumes & Sets for "Der Rosenkavalier" in Full Color. (Illus.). 48p. 1980. pap. 6.95 (ISBN 0-486-23998-5). Dover.
COSTUME–HISTORY
Cumming, Valerie. Exploring Costume History. (Illus.). 72p. 1981. 17.95 (ISBN 0-7134-1829-X, Pub. by Batsford England). Doubleday.
Lubin, Leonard. The Elegant Beast. LC 80-52645. (Illus.). 48p. 1981. pap. 10.95 (ISBN 0-670-29097-1, Studio). Viking Pr.
COSTUME–EUROPE
Yarwood, Doreen. Costume of the Western World. 192p. 1980. 17.50x. St Martin.
COSTUME–GREAT BRITAIN
McClintock, H. F. Handbook on the Traditional Old Irish Dress. (Illus.). 8.95. Dufour.
COSTUME–UNITED STATES
Yarwood, Doreen. Costume of the Western World. 192p. 1980. 17.50x. St Martin.
COSTUME, ANCIENT
see Costume–History
COSTUME, MEDIEVAL
see Costume–History
COSTUME, MILITARY
see Uniforms, Military
COSTUME, THEATRICAL
see Costume
COSTUME DESIGNERS–BIOGRAPHY
De Marley, Diana. Worth: Father of Haute Couture. (Illus.). 220p. 1980. text ed. 29.50x (ISBN 0-8419-7400-4). Holmes & Meier.
COTENANCY
see Condominium (Housing)
COTTAGES
see also Architecture, Domestic; Country Homes
Downing, Andrew J. Victorian Cottage Residences. Harney, George E., ed. (Illus.). 352p. 1981. pap. price not set (ISBN 0-486-24078-9). Dover.
COTTON
see also Fibers
Lord, E. Manual of Cotton Spinning: The Characteristics of Raw Cotton, Vol. 2, Pt. 1. 333p. 1971. 45.00x (ISBN 0-686-63772-0). State Mutual Bk.
COTTON COMBING
Lord, E. Manual of Cotton Spinning: The Characteristics of Raw Cotton, Vol. 2, Pt. 1. 333p. 1971. 45.00x (ISBN 0-686-63772-0). State Mutual Bk.
COTTON MANUFACTURE
see also Cotton Combing
Mazzaoui, Maureen F. The Italian Cotton Industry in the Later Middle Ages: Eleven Hundred to Sixteen Hundred. LC 80-41023. (Illus.). 272p. Date not set. price not set (ISBN 0-521-23095-0). Cambridge U Pr.
Transformation & Development of Technology in the Japanese Cotton Industry. 86p. 1980. pap. 5.00 (ISBN 92-808-0091-4, TUNU093, UNU). Unipub.
COUNSELING
see also Genetic Counseling; Marriage Counseling; Pastoral Counseling; Personnel Service in Education; Social Case Work; Vocational Guidance
Blocher, D. H. Developmental Counseling. 2nd ed. 320p. 1974. 17.50 (ISBN 0-471-06894-2). Wiley.
Borck, Leslie E. & Fawcett, Stephen B. Learning Counseling & Problem-Solving Skills. 350p. (Orig.). 1981. text ed. 26.00 (ISBN 0-917724-30-5); pap. text ed. 13.95 (ISBN 0-917724-35-6). Haworth Pr.
Brechner, Irv. The College Survival Kit. 96p. 1980. pap. 2.95. Bantam.
Eddy, John, et al. Counseling Methods: Developing Counselors. LC 80-6315. 285p. 1981. lib. bdg. 19.25 (ISBN 0-8191-1474-X); pap. text ed. 10.25 (ISBN 0-8191-1475-8). U Pr of Amer.
--Counseling Theories: Developing Counselors. LC 80-6316. 138p. 1981. lib. bdg. 16.50 (ISBN 0-8191-1476-6); pap. text ed. 7.50 (ISBN 0-8191-1477-4). U Pr of Amer.
Galloway, David. Teaching & Counselling. 192p. 1981. pap. 13.50 (ISBN 0-582-48987-3). Longman.
Kennedy, Eugene. Crisis Counseling: The Essential Guide for Non-Professional Counselors. 208p. 1981. 12.95 (ISBN 0-8264-0038-8). Continuum.
Pedersen, Paul B., et al, eds. Counseling Across Cultures. rev. & expanded ed. 368p. (Orig.). 1981. pap. 10.00x (ISBN 0-8248-0725-1). U Pr of Hawaii.
Watts, A. G. Counselling at Work. 92p. 1977. text ed. 7.40x (ISBN 0-7199-0925-2, Pub. by Bedford England); pap. text ed. 4.40x (ISBN 0-7199-0924-4, Pub. by Bedford England). Renouf.
COUNSELING, PASTORAL
see Pastoral Counseling
COUNSELING, RABBINICAL
see Pastoral Counseling (Judaism)
COUNSELORS, CAMP
see Camp Counselors
COUNTERESPIONAGE
see Intelligence Service
COUNTERFEITS AND COUNTERFEITING
Hill, G. F. Becker the Counterfeiter. 111p. 1979. 20.00 (ISBN 0-916710-52-1). Obol Intl.
Internaional Numismatic Symposium, Warsaw & Budapest, 1976. Proceedings. Niro-Sey, K. & Gedai, I., eds. (Illus.). 221p. 1980. 27.50x (ISBN 963-05-2055-9). Intl Pubns Serv.
Ravel, O. E. Numismatique Grecque Falsifications Moyens Pour les Reconnaitre. 105p. (Fr.). 1980. Repr. of 1946 ed. 20.00 (ISBN 0-916710-71-8). Obol Intl.
COUNTERINTELLIGENCE
see Intelligence Service
COUNTERS, DIGITAL
see Digital Counters
COUNTING
see Numeration
COUNTING DEVICES, DIGITAL
see Digital Counters
COUNTING-OUT RHYMES
Crowther, Robert. The Most Amazing Hide & Seek Counting Book. (Illus.). 14p. 1981. 8.95 (ISBN 0-670-48997-2). Viking Pr.
Lewin, Betsy. Cat Count. LC 80-25849. (Illus.). 32p. (ps-2). 1981. PLB 5.95 (ISBN 0-396-07928-8). Dodd.
COUNTRY AND WESTERN MUSIC
see Country Music
COUNTRY HOMES
Franklin, Jill. The Gentleman's Country House & Its Plan 1835-1914. (Illus.). 272p. 1981. 40.00 (ISBN 0-7100-0622-5). Routledge & Kegan.
O'Neill, Paul D. Lutyens: Country Houses. 168p. 1981. 19.95 (ISBN 0-8230-7361-0, Whitney Lib). Watson-Guptill.
Planning a Country Place. (Country Home Ser.). 96p. 2.95 (ISBN 0-88453-003-5). Berkshire Traveller.
COUNTRY LIFE
see also Agricultural Societies; Farm Life; Outdoor Life; Rural Conditions; Sociology, Rural
Bailey, Liberty H. The Holy Earth. LC 80-27854. (Illus.). 124p. 1980. pap. 4.95 (ISBN 0-9605314-6-7). NY St Coll Ag.
Czestochowski, Joseph S. John Stewart Curry & Grant Wood: A Portrait of Rural America. 240p. 1981. text ed. 26.00x (ISBN 0-8262-0336-1). U of Mo Pr.
Hartley, Dorothy. Lost Country Life. (Illus.). 1981. pap. 6.95 (ISBN 0-394-74838-7). Pantheon.
Kyle, Louisa V. Country Woman's Scrapbook. Dunn, Joseph, ed. LC 80-84557. (Illus.). 120p. 1980. 10.95 (ISBN 0-938694-02-2). JCP Corp VA.
COUNTRY LIFE–CHINA
Fei, Hsiao-Tung. Peasant Life in China: A Field Study of Country Life in the Yangtze Valley. (Studies in Chinese History & Civilization). (Illus.). 296p. 1977. Repr. of 1939 ed. 21.00 (ISBN 0-89093-081-3). U Pubns Amer.
COUNTRY LIFE–GREAT BRITAIN
Horn, Pamela. The Rural World: Social Change in the English Counryside 1780-1850. 1981. 25.00 (ISBN 0-312-69606-X). St Martin.
COUNTRY MUSIC
see also Country Musicians
Cobin, Everettt J. Storm Over Nashville: A Case Against "Modern" Country Music. 202p. (Orig.). 1980. pap. text ed. 9.95 (ISBN 0-932534-01-5). Ashlar Pr.
COUNTRY MUSICIANS
Hefley, James. How Sweet the Sound. 1981. pap. 2.95 (ISBN 0-8423-1449-0). Tyndale.
Paris, Mike & Comber, Chris. Jimmie the Kid: The Life of Jimmie Rodgers. (Da Capo Quality Paperbacks Ser.). (Illus.). 211p. 1981. pap. 6.95 (ISBN 0-306-80133-7). Da Capo.
COUNTY GOVERNMENT
Kalinich, David P. & Postill, Frederick J. Principles of County Jail Administration Management. 1981. write for info (ISBN 0-398-04140-7). C C Thomas.
COUP D'ETAT OF 1851
see France–History–Second Republic, 1848-1852
COUPLES PSYCHOTHERAPY
see Family Psychotherapy
COUPS D'ETAT
Rosenblum, Mort. Coups & Earthquakes: Reporting the World to America. LC 79-1680. 240p. 1981. pap. 4.95 (ISBN 0-06-090856-4, CN 856, CN). Har-Row.
COURAGE
see also Fear; Heroes
Moncure, Jane B. Courage. rev. ed. LC 80-39515. (What Is It? Ser.). (Illus.). 32p. (gr. k-3). 1981. PLB 5.50 (ISBN 0-89565-202-1). Childs World.
Schuller, Robert H. Discover Courage to Face Your Future. (Orig.). 1978. pap. 1.25 (ISBN 0-89081-156-3). Harvest Hse.
COURSES OF STUDY
see Education–Curricula
COURT, CONTEMPT OF
see Contempt of Court
COURT ADMINISTRATION
Cohen, Fred. Standards Relating to Dispositional Procedures. (Juvenile Justice Standards Project Ser.). 1980. softcover 5.95 (ISBN 0-88410-808-2); casebound 16.50 (ISBN 0-88410-233-5). Ballinger Pub.
Freed, Daniel J. & Terrell, Timothy P. Standards Relating to Interim Status: The Release, Control & Detention of Accused Juvenile Offenders Between Arrest & Disposition. (Juvenile Justice Standards Project Ser.). 1980. softcover 7.95 (ISBN 0-88410-812-0); casebound 16.50 (ISBN 0-88410-244-0). Ballinger Pub.
Rubin, Ted. Standards Relating to Court Organization & Administration. (Juvenile Justice Standards Project Ser.). 1980. softcover 7.95; casebound 16.50 (ISBN 0-88410-231-9). Ballinger Pub.
Shapiro, Martin. Courts: A Comparative & Political Analysis. LC 80-18263. 1981. lib. bdg. 20.00x (ISBN 0-226-75042-6). U of Chicago Pr.
Singer, Linda R. Standards Relating to Dispositions. (Junvenile Justice Standards Project Ser.). 1980. softcover 7.95 (ISBN 0-88410-816-3); casebound 16.50 (ISBN 0-88410-229-7). Ballinger Pub.
Whitebread, Charles. Standards Relating to Transfer Between Courts. (Juvenile Justice Standards Project Ser.). 1980. softcover 5.95 (ISBN 0-88410-818-X); casebound 12.50 (ISBN 0-88410-230-0). Ballinger Pub.
COURT MANAGEMENT
see Court Administration
COURT OFFICIALS AND EMPLOYEES
see Courts–Officials and Employees
COURT REPORTING
see Newspaper Court Reporting
COURT REPORTING (BY NEWSPAPER)
see Newspaper Court Reporting
COURT REPORTS
see Law Reports, Digests, etc.
COURTING
see Courtship
COURTLY LOVE
see also Love; Troubadours; Trouveres
Schmidgall, Gary. Shakespeare & the Courtly Aesthetic. (Illus.). 344p. 1981. 22.50x (ISBN 0-520-04130-5). U. of Cal Pr.
COURTS
Here are entered works on courts in general and in the United states; For works on courts in foreign countries see appropriate subdivision, e.g. Courts–Great Britain.
see also Appellate Courts; Appellate Procedure; Civil Procedure; Contempt of Court; Criminal Procedure; Ecclesiastical Courts; Judges; Judgments; Jurisdiction; Jury; Justice, Administration Of; Juvenile Courts; Psychology, Forensic
Flory, Thomas. Judge & Jury in Imperial Brazil, 1808-1871: Social Control & Political Stability in the New State. 288p. 1981. text ed. 25.00x (ISBN 0-292-74015-8). U of Tex Pr.
Genovese, Michael A. The Supreme Court, the Constitution, & Presidential Power. LC 80-5695 345p. 1980. lib. bdg. 20.50 (ISBN 0-8191-1322-0); pap. text ed. 11.75 (ISBN 0-8191-1323-9). U Pr of Amer.
Hindus, Michael S., et al. The Files of the Massachusetts Superior Court, 1859-1959: An Analysis & a Plan for Action. (Reference Publications Ser.). 1980. lib. bdg. 50.00 (ISBN 0-8161-9037-2). G K Hall.
Law Enforcement Assistance Administration. Public Image of Courts, Nineteen Seventy-Seven: General Public Data. LC 79-91248. 1980. 16.00 (ISBN 0-89138-962-8). ICPSR.
Nelson, William E. Dispute & Conflict Resolution in Plymouth County, Massachusetts, 1725 - 1825. LC 80-17403. (Studies in Legal History). 240p. 1980. 19.50x (ISBN 0-8078-1454-7). U of NC Pr.
Phillips, Charles D. Sentencing Councils in the Federal Courts: An Evaluation. LC 79-3784. 128p. 1980. 19.95x (ISBN 0-669-03514-9). Lexington Bks.
Racz, Attila. Courts & Tribunals: A Comparative Study. Zehery, Miklos, tr. 246p. 1980. 25.00x (ISBN 963-05-1799-X). Intl Pubns Serv.
COURTS–ADMINISTRATION
see Court Administration
COURTS–OFFICIALS AND EMPLOYEES
see also Judges
Crockett, George W., et al, eds. National Roster of Black Judicial Officers, 1980. 120p. (Orig.). 1980. pap. 2.95 (8562). Am Judicature.
COURTS, ECCLESIASTICAL
see Ecclesiastical Courts
COURTSHIP
see also Dating (Social Customs); Love; Marriage
Fielding, William J. Strange Customs of Courtship & Marriage. 315p. 1980. Repr. of 1942 ed. lib. bdg. 25.00 (ISBN 0-89987-259-X). Darby Bks.
COVENANTS (THEOLOGY)
see also Dispensationalism; Grace (Theology); Salvation
Acceptanc: Establishing the Covenant, Vol. 8. 250p. Date not set. 11.95. Maznaim.
Booker, Richard. The Miracle of the Scarlet Thread. (Orig.). (YA) 1981. pap. 4.95 (ISBN 0-88270-499-0). Logos.
Morris, Danny. Discovery Our Family Covenant. 1981. pap. 2.25x (ISBN 0-8358-0419-4). Upper Room.
Smith, Mont. What the Bible Says About the Covenant. (What the Bible Says Ser.). 400p. 1981. 13.50 (ISBN 0-89900-083-5). College Pr Pub.
COVERED BRIDGES
Allen, Richard S. Covered Bridges of the Northeast. (Illus.). 128p. 1981. pap. 9.95 (ISBN 0-8289-0439-1). Greene.
Sangster, Tom & Sangster, Dess L. Alabama's Covered Bridges. LC 80-68408. (Illus.). 100p. (Orig.). 1980. pap. 20.00 (ISBN 0-938252-00-3); includes 13 lithographs 29.50, 1st 500 numbered & signed by artist Tom Sangster (ISBN 0-686-69146-6). Coffeetable.
COW
see Cows
COWBOY SLANG
Dary, David. Cowboy Culture. LC 80-2699. (Illus.). 1981. 17.95 (ISBN 0-394-42605-3). Knopf.
COWBOYS
see also Ranch Life; Rodeos
Berger, Bruce. Gordon Snidow Portrays the Cowboy Heritage Hangin'on. LC 80-83021. (Illus.). 128p. 1980. 40.00 (ISBN 0-87358-266-7); pap. 18.50 (ISBN 0-87358-265-9); ltd. ed. avail. (ISBN 0-87358-267-5). Northland.
Carpozi, George, Jr. That's Hollywood: The Clossal Cowboys, No. 6. (Orig.). 1980. pap. 1.95 (ISBN 0-532-23222-4). Manor Bks.
Dary, David. Cowboy Culture. LC 80-2699. (Illus.). 1981. 17.95 (ISBN 0-394-42605-3). Knopf.
Hume, Sandy. Western Man: Photographs from the National Western Stock Show. 1980. 18.95 (ISBN 0-933472-48-X); pap. 12.95 (ISBN 0-933472-49-8). Johnson Colo.
Polk, Frank. F-F-Frank Polk: An Uncommonly Frank Autobiography. LC 78-51848. 136p. pap. 9.50 (ISBN 0-87358-276-4). Northland.
COWPER, WILLIAM, 1731-1800
King, James & Ryskamp, Charles, eds. The Letters & Prose Writings of William Cowper, Volume II: Letters 1782-1786. (Illus.). 586p. 1981. 98.00 (ISBN 0-19-812607-7). Oxford U Pr.
Nicholson, Norman. William Cowper. 167p. 1980. Repr. of 1951 ed. text ed. 25.00 (ISBN 0-8492-1973-6). R West.
COWS
see also Cattle; Dairying;
also particular breeds of cattle
Grohman, Joan S. Keeping a Family Cow. (Illus.). 192p. 1981. 9.95 (ISBN 0-684-16867-7, ScribT). Scribner.
COZZENS, JAMES GOULD, 1903-
Bruccoli, Matthew J. James Gould Cozzens: A Descriptive Bibliography. LC 80-53553. (Pittsburgh Ser in Bibliography). (Illus.). 256p. 1981. 32.95x (ISBN 0-8229-3435-3). U of Pittsburgh Pr.
CRAFTS (HANDICRAFTS)
see Handicraft
CRAFTSMEN
see Artisans
CRAMMING
see Study, Method of
CRANE, HART, 1899-1932
Trachtenberg, Alan. Hart Crane: A Collection of Critical Essays. (Twentieth Century Views Ser.). 224p. 1981. 13.95 (ISBN 0-13-383935-4, Spec); pap. 5.95 (ISBN 0-13-383927-3). P-H.
CRANE, STEPHEN, 1871-1900
Nagel, James. Stephen Crane & Literary Impressionism. LC 80-16051. 200p. 1980. 16.50x (ISBN 0-271-00267-0). Pa St U Pr.
CRANES, DERRICKS, ETC.
Dickie, D. E. & Short, Douglas. Crane Handbook. 1981. text ed. price not set (ISBN 0-408-00445-2, Newnes-Butterworth). Butterworths.
CRANIOLOGY
Here are entered works dealing with skulls from an anthropological, archaeological, or ethnological point of view. Strictly anatomical and pathological literature is entered under Skull. Treatises on methods of measuring the skull are entered under Craniometry.
see also Brain; Jaws; Man, Prehistoric; Skull–Abnormities and Deformities
Cranial Manipulation Roots. 177p. pap. 9.00 (ISBN 0-917628-03-9). Coraco.
Craniopathy: (Cranial Adjusting) 93 Technics in 10 Folios. 1975. 92.00 (ISBN 0-917628-01-2). Coraco.
CRANIUM
see Craniology; Skull

CRATER MOUND, ARIZONA
Abrahams, Harold J. Heroic Efforts at Meteor Crater, Arizona: Selected Correspondence Between Daniel Moreau Barringer & Elihu Thomson. LC 78-75170. 480p. 1981. 20.00 (ISBN 0-8386-2399-9). Fairleigh Dickinson.
CRAWFORD, FRANCIS MARION, 1854-1909
Moran, John C. An F. Marion Crawford Companion. LC 80-1707. (Illus.). 608p. 1981. lib. bdg. 45.00 (ISBN 0-313-20926-X, MCC/). Greenwood.
CRAYFISH
see Crustacea
CREATION
see also Cosmology; Earth; Evolution; Geology; God; Man
Fagan, Brian M. In the Beginning. 4th ed. 1981. text ed. 16.95 (ISBN 0-686-68258-0). Little.
McKay, Donald M. Science, Chance & Providence. (Riddell Memorial Lectures Ser.). (Illus.). 78p. 1978. text ed. 13.95x. Oxford U Pr.
Tarneja, Sukh R. Nature, Spirituality & Science. 240p. 1980. text ed. 27.50x (ISBN 0-7069-1203-9, Pub by Vikas India). Advent Bk.
CREATION (LITERARY, ARTISTIC, ETC.)
see also Creative Ability; Creative Thinking (Education); Creative Writing; Inspiration; Planning
Doczi, Gyorgy. The Power of Limits: Proportional Harmony in Art, Architecture, Nature, & Man. LC 77-90883. (Illus.). 224p. 1981. 19.95 (ISBN 0-394-51352-5); pap. 9.95 (ISBN 0-394-73580-3). Shambhala Pubns.
Endogenous Intellectual Creativity: Reflections on Some ETIC & EMIC Paradigms. 22p. 1980. pap. 5.00 (ISBN 92-808-0118-X, TUNU098, UNU). Unipub.
The First Asian Symposium on Intellectual Creativity in Endogenous Culture. 74p. 1980. pap. 6.75 (ISBN 92-808-0189-9, TUNU081, UNU). Unipub.
Gruber, Howard E. Darwin on Man: A Psychological Study of Scientific Creativity. 2nd ed. LC 80-28453. 1981. lib. bdg. price not set (ISBN 0-226-31008-6); pap. price not set (ISBN 0-226-31007-8). U of Chicago Pr.
Ryrie, Charles. We Believe in Creation. 62p. 1981. pap. 0.35 (ISBN 0-937396-54-0). Walterick Pubs.
Seeley, J. High Contrast: Creative Imagemaking for Photographers, Designers & Graphic Artists. 1980. 24.95 (ISBN 0-442-23888-6). Van Nos Reinhold.
CREATIVE ABILITY
see also Creation (Literary, Artistic, etc.); Creative Thinking (Education)
LeBoeuf. Imagineering: How to Think & Act Creatively. 88p. Date not set. 9.95 (ISBN 0-07-036952-6). McGraw.
Pearce, Joseph C. The Bond of Power. 1981. 10.95 (ISBN 0-525-06950-X). Dutton.
Raudsepp, Eugene. How Creative Are You? 196p. 1981. pap. 4.95 (ISBN 0-686-69593-3, Perigee). Putnam.
Willings, David. The Creatively Gifted: Recognising & Developing the Creative Personality. 184p. 30.00x (ISBN 0-85941-120-6, Pub. by Woodhead-Faulkner England). State Mutual Bk.
CREATIVE ACTIVITIES AND SEATWORK
see also Activity Programs in Education; Paper Work
Howard, Nina. Do Your Own Thing. (Illus.). 96p. (ps-6). 1980. 9.90 (ISBN 0-917206-12-6). Children Learn Ctr.
Katz, Marjorie P. Fingerprint Owls & Other Fantasies. LC 72-85648. 64p. 1981. pap. cancelled (ISBN 0-87131-341-3). M Evans.
Michener, Dorothy & Muschlitz, Beverly. Day in Day Out. LC 80-82304. (Illus.). 160p. 1980. pap. text ed. 8.95 (ISBN 0-913916-71-4). Incentive Pubns.
Sussman, Ellen. Smiling Sentences: Sight Word Activities to Cut & Paste. (Spirit Duplicating Masters Ser.). (Illus.). 24p. (gr. 2-3). 1980. 4.95 (ISBN 0-933606-08-7). Monkey Sisters.
--Sunny Sentences: Sight Word Activities to Cut & Paste. (Spirit Duplicating Masters Ser.). (Illus.). 24p. (gr. 1-2). 1980. 4.95 (ISBN 0-933606-07-9). Monkey Sisters.
CREATIVE THINKING (EDUCATION)
see also Creative Ability
Rawlinson, J. Geoffrey. Creative Thinking & Brainstorming. LC 80-22724. 144p. 1981. 14.95 (ISBN 0-470-27091-8). Halsted Pr.
CREATIVE WRITING
Cook, Albert S. Adapt the Living. LC 80-17828. 85p. 1981. 8.95 (ISBN 0-8040-0350-5); pap. 4.50 (ISBN 0-8040-0359-9). Swallow.
Madden, David & Powers, Richard. Writers' Revisions: An Annotated Bibliography of Articles & Books About Writers' Revisions & Their Comments on the Creative Process. LC 80-22942. 254p. 1981. 13.50 (ISBN 0-8108-1375-0). Scarecrow.
Wasson, John M. Subject & Structure: An Anthology for Writers. 7th ed. 1981. pap. text ed. 7.95 (ISBN 0-316-92423-7); tchrs'. manual free (ISBN 0-316-92424-5). Little.
CREATIVITY
see Creation (Literary, Artistic, etc.); Creative Ability; Creative Thinking (Education)
CRECHES (DAY NURSERIES)
see Day Care Centers
CREDIT
see also Banks and Banking; Collecting of Accounts; Credit Management; Debt; Liquidity (Economics); Loans
Credit Manual of Commercial Laws, 1981 Ed. 1980. 32.00 (ISBN 0-934914-37-0). NACM.
Skousen, Mark. The Insider's Banking & Credit Almanac. 14.95 (ISBN 0-932496-01-6). Green Hill.
Yeager, Leland B. Proposals for Government Credit Allocation. 1977. pap. 2.75 (ISBN 0-8447-3281-8). Am Enterprise.
CREDIT ADMINISTRATION
see Credit Management
CREDIT CARDS
Galanoy, Terry. Charge It: Inside the Credit Card Conspiracy. 264p. 1981. 11.95 (ISBN 0-399-12555-8). Putnam.
CREDIT MANAGEMENT
see also Collecting of Accounts
Barzman, Sol. Everyday Credit Checking: A Practical Guide. rev. ed. LC 80-82080. 289p. 1980. 13.95 (ISBN 0-934914-36-2). NACM.
Bass, R. M. Credit Management: How to Manage Credit Effectively. 352p. 1979. pap. 14.75x (ISBN 0-220-67029-3, Pub. by Busn Bks England). Renouf.
CREEDS
see also Catechisms
also subdivision Catechisms and Creeds under names of religions, religious denominations, etc. e.g. Catholic Church–Catechisms and Creeds
Hodge, A. A. Confession of Faith. 1978. 12.95 (ISBN 0-85151-275-5). Banner of Truth.
CREEDS–HISTORY AND CRITICISM
Kelly, J. N. Early Christian Creeds. 3rd ed. 446p. 1979. text ed. 25.00x (ISBN 0-582-48931-8). Longman.
CREEK INDIANS
see Indians of North America–Eastern States
CREELEY, ROBERT, 1926-
Olson, Charles & Creeley, Robert. Charles Olson & Robert Creeley: The Complete Correspondence, Vol. 3. Butterick, George F., ed. (Illus.). 200p. (Orig.). 1981. 20.00 (ISBN 0-87685-483-8); deluxe ed. 30.00 (ISBN 0-87685-484-6); pap. 7.50 (ISBN 0-87685-482-X). Black Sparrow.
CREOLE DIALECTS
Hancock, I. F. Readings in Creole Studies. (Story-Scientia Linguistics Ser.: No. 2). 1980. text ed. 62.25x (ISBN 90-6439-163-7). Humanities.
CREOLES
Valdman, Albert & Highfield, Arnold, eds. Theoretical Orientations in Creole Studies. LC 80-26273. 1980. lib ed 29.50 (ISBN 0-12-710160-8). Acad Pr.
CREPES (COOKERY)
see Pancakes, Waffles, Etc.
CRESTS
see Heraldry
CRETAN ART
see Art, Cretan
CREWEL WORK
see Embroidery
CRIB IN CHRISTIAN ART AND TRADITION
Swarzenski, Hanns. An Eighteenth Century Creche. LC 66-25450. (Illus.). 1966. pap. 2.00 (ISBN 0-87846-142-6, Pub. by Mus Fine Arts Boston). C E Tuttle.
CRIME AND CRIMINALS
Here are entered general works. For books dealing with crime and criminals in specific areas see the appropriate geographic subdivision, e.g. Crime and Criminals–United States.
see also Anarchism and Anarchists; Assassination; Brigands and Robbers; Crime and the Press; Crime Prevention; Drug Abuse and Crime; Female Offenders; Impostors and Imposture; Organized Crime; White Collar Crimes
also headings beginning with the word Criminal
Allen, Harry E., et al. Crime & Punishment: An Introduction to Criminology. LC 80-69715. (Illus.). 464p. 1981. text ed. 14.95 (ISBN 0-02-900460-8). Free Pr.
Barlow. Introduction to Criminology. 2nd ed. 1981. text ed. 16.95 (ISBN 0-316-08115-9); tchrs'. manual free (ISBN 0-316-08116-7). Little.
Blumberg, Abraham S. Current Perspectives on Criminal Behavior. 2nd ed. 442p. 1981. pap. text ed. 10.95 (ISBN 0-394-32156-1). Knopf.
Bucknill, John C. Unsoundness of Mind in Relation to Criminal Acts. Bd. with Care of the Insane & Their Legal Control; Factors of the Unsound Mind. Guy, W. A. (Contributions to the History of Psychology Ser., Vol. IV Pt. F: Insanity & Jurisprudence). 1980. Repr. of 1854 ed. 30.00 (ISBN 0-89093-329-4). U Pubns Amer.
Carpozi, George, Jr. Great Crimes of the Century: Murderers Leave Clues, No. 8. (Orig.). 1980. pap. 1.95 (ISBN 0-532-23130-9). Manor Bks.
--Great Crimes of the Century: The Savage Killers, No. 7. (Orig.). 1980. pap. 1.95 (ISBN 0-532-23129-5). Manor Bks.
--Great Crimes of the Century: The Senseless Slayers, No. 5. (Orig.). 1979. pap. 1.95 (ISBN 0-532-23165-1). Manor Bks.
--Great Crimes of the Century: The Weird Murderers, No. 6. (Orig.). 1979. pap. 1.95 (ISBN 0-532-23113-9). Manor Bks.
Carroll. White Collar Crime. 1981. text ed. 18.95. Butterworth.
Chase, Bob. Diggs. 1981. 10.00 (ISBN 0-533-04670-X). Vantage.
Clinard, Marshall B. & Yeager, Peter C. Corporate Crime. 1980. 16.95 (ISBN 0-02-905710-8). Macmillan.
Conrad, John P. Justice & Consequences. LC 78-348. (The Dangerous Offender Project Ser.). 1981. price not set (ISBN 0-669-02190-3). Lexington Bks.
Fox, James A., ed. Frontiers in Quantitative Criminology. (Quantitative Studies in Social Relations). 1981. price not set (ISBN 0-12-263950-2). Acad Pr.
Gibbons, Don C. Changing the Lawbreaker. 1981. pap. text ed. 8.95 (ISBN 0-86598-017-9). Allanheld.
Greenberg, David F., ed. Crime & Class: Essays in Marxist Criminology. 350p. (Orig.). 1981. write for info (ISBN 0-87484-505-X). Mayfield Pub.
Grocott, Allan M. Convicts, Clergymen & Churches. 356p. 1980. 27.50x (ISBN 0-424-00072-5, Pub. by Sydney U Pr Australia). Intl Schol Bk Serv.
Hays. Getting Away with Murder: The Law & Bishop Legrand. 1981. 14.95 (ISBN 0-690-01941-6). Lippincott & Crowell.
Hirshi, Travis & Gottfredson, Michael, eds. Understanding Crime: Current Theory & Research. LC 80-19376. (Sage Research Progress Ser. in Criminology: Vol. 18). (Illus.). 144p. 1980. 12.95 (ISBN 0-8039-1517-9); pap. 6.50 (ISBN 0-8039-1518-7). Sage.
Hylton, John. Reintegrating the Offender: Assessing the Impact of Community Corrections. LC 80-5730. 334p. 1981. lib. bdg. 20.75 (ISBN 0-8191-1387-5); pap. text ed. 11.75 (ISBN 0-8191-1388-3). U Pr of Amer.
Kranes, David. Criminals. 256p. (Orig.). pap. 2.50 (ISBN 0-441-12174-8). Charter Bks.
Lowney & Winslow. Deviant Reality: Alternative World Views. 2nd ed. 420p. 1980. pap. text ed. 10.95 (ISBN 0-205-07243-7, 8172439). Allyn.
Lowry, Timothy S. Rock Springs: Sodom & Gomorrah in America. LC 80-29293. (Illus.). 224p. 1981. 11.95 (ISBN 0-8253-0044-4). Beaufort Bks NY.
Madison, Arnold. Vandalism: The Not-So-Senseless Crime. 160p. (gr. 6 up). 1981. pap. 3.95 (ISBN 0-395-30009-6, Clarion). HM.
Morris, Norval & Tonry, Michael. Crime & Justice: An Annual Review of Research. (Vol. II). 480p. 1981. pap. 7.95 (ISBN 0-226-53959-8). U of Chicago Pr.
Nash, Jay R. Look for the Woman. De Kay, George C., ed. (Illus.). 320p. 1981. 14.95 (ISBN 0-87131-336-7). M Evans.
Nash, Jay R., ed. Almanac of World Crime. LC 79-6871. (Illus.). 432p. 1981. 19.95 (ISBN 0-385-15003-2). Doubleday.
Price, Barbara R. & Baunach, Phyllis J., eds. Criminal Justice Research: New Models & Findings. LC 80-20145. (Illus.). 143p. 1980. 12.95 (ISBN 0-8039-1509-8); pap. 6.50 (ISBN 0-8039-1510-1). Sage.
Sagarin, Edward, ed. Taboos in Criminology. LC 80-18175. (Sage Research Progress Ser. in Criminology: Vol. 15). 152p. 1980. 12.95 (ISBN 0-8039-1513-6); pap. 6.50 (ISBN 0-8039-1514-4). Sage.
Shelley, Louise I. Crime & Modernization: The Impact of Industrialization & Urbanization on Crime. LC 80-24044. (Science & International Affairs Ser.). 216p. 1981. 22.50x (ISBN 0-8093-0983-1). S Ill U Pr.
Shoham, S. Giora, ed. Israel Studies in Criminology, Vol. V. 228p. 1980. 20.00x (ISBN 965-20-0026-4, Pub. by Turtledove Pr Israel). Intl Schol Bk Serv.
Tobias, Ronald. They Shoot to Kill: A Psycho-Survey of Criminal Sniping. 240p. (Orig.). 1981. 14.95 (ISBN 0-87364-207-4). Paladin Ent.
CRIME AND CRIMINALS–ADDRESSES, ESSAYS, LECTURES
Inciardi, James A. & Faupel, Charles E., eds. History & Crime: Implications for Criminal Justice Policy. LC 80-19532. (Focus Editions Ser.: Vol. 27). (Illus.). 288p. 1980. 18.95 (ISBN 0-8039-1410-5); pap. 9.95 (ISBN 0-8039-1411-3). Sage.
Shelley, Louise I., ed. Readings in Comparative Criminology. LC 80-19533. (Science & International Affairs). 312p. 1981. 25.00x (ISBN 0-8093-0938-6). S Ill U Pr.
CRIME AND CRIMINALS–BIOGRAPHY
Schwarz, Ted. The Hillside Strangler: A Murderer's Mind. LC 80-2435. 264p. 1981. 12.95 (ISBN 0-385-17337-7). Doubleday.
Tattersall, Peter D. Conviction. LC 80-82368. (Illus.). 374p. 1980. 12.95 (ISBN 0-8119-0407-5, Pegasus Rex). Fell.
CRIME AND CRIMINALS–STATISTICAL METHODS
see Criminal Statistics
CRIME AND CRIMINALS–STATISTICS
see Criminal Statistics
CRIME AND CRIMINALS–LATIN AMERICA
Brana-Shute, Rosemary & Brana-Shute, Gary, eds. Crime & Punishment in the Caribbean. LC 80-21078. (Illus.). x, 146p. 1980. pap. 6.00 (ISBN 0-8130-0685-6). U Presses Fla.
CRIME AND CRIMINALS–UNITED STATES
Carter, Timothy J., et al, eds. Rural Crime: Integrating Research & Prevention. 1981. text ed. 25.00 (ISBN 0-86598-023-3). Allanheld.
Chanan, Michael, ed. Santiago Alvarez. (BFI Dossier Ser.: No. 2). 71p. (Orig.). 1980. pap. 7.50 (ISBN 0-918432-35-9). NY Zoetrope.
Christensen, R., et al. Futuristic Community Development: East Central Florida Crime Impact 1974-1984. xxii, 390p. Date not set. pap. 15.00 (ISBN 0-686-28750-9, 04-80-04). Entropy Ltd.
Feiden, Doug. The Ten Million Dollar Getaway: The Inside Story of the Lufthansa Heist. (Orig.). pap. 2.50 (ISBN 0-515-05452-6). Jove Pubns.
Felony Arrests: Their Prosecution & Disposition in New York City's Courts. (Vera Studies in Criminal Justice (Professional Studies)). (Illus.). 192p. (Orig.). 1981. 17.50 (ISBN 0-582-28195-4); pap. 6.95 (ISBN 0-582-28187-3). Longman.
Fisher, Gene. The Fear of Crime: In Public Housing. 1981. 8.50 (ISBN 0-8062-1573-9). Carlton.
Glassman, Craig. Off the Wall. (Illus.). 277p. 1980. 12.95 (ISBN 0-8119-0410-5, Pegasus Rex). Fell.
Muller, Fred. America's Coming Nightmare Inflation, Economic Collapse & Crime Revolution. 120p. 1980. 10.00 (ISBN 0-686-68648-9). State Ptg.
Nelli, Humbert S. The Business of Crime: Italians & Syndicate Crime in the United States. LC 80-27196. xiv, 314p. 1981. pap. 6.95 (ISBN 0-226-57132-7). U of Chicago Pr.
Rashke, Richard. The Killing of Karen Silkwood. 1981. 12.95 (ISBN 0-395-30233-1). HM.
Schwarz, Ted. The Hillside Strangler: A Murderer's Mind. LC 80-2435. 264p. 1981. 12.95 (ISBN 0-385-17337-7). Doubleday.
Triplett, Frank. The History of the Great American Crimes. (American Culture Library Bks.). (Illus.). 127p. 1981. 69.75 (ISBN 0-89901-031-8). Found Class Reprints.
Wilkerson, Michael & Wilkerson, Dick. Someone Cry for the Children: The Unsolved Girl Scout Murders of Oklahoma & the Case of Gene Leroy Hart. 256p. 1981. 10.95 (ISBN 0-8037-8283-7). Dial.
CRIME AND CRIMINALS, SEXUAL
see Sex Crimes
CRIME AND DRUG ABUSE
see Drug Abuse and Crime
CRIME AND THE PRESS
see also Contempt of Court; Newspaper Court Reporting
Sullivan, Harold W. Contempts by Publication: The Law of Trial by Newspaper. xiv, 230p. 1980. Repr. of 1941 ed. lib. bdg. 24.00x (ISBN 0-8377-1114-2). Rothman.
CRIME DETECTION
see Criminal Investigation
CRIME PREVENTION
see also Criminal Psychology
Fennelly. Handbook of Loss Prevention & Crime Prevention. 1981. text ed. price not set. Butterworth.
O'Block, Robert L. Security & Crime Prevention. c ed. (Illus.). 378p. 1981. pap. text ed. 13.95 (ISBN 0-8016-3738-4). Mosby.
Ratledge, Marcus W. Don't Become the Victim. 120p. 1981. pap. 6.00 (ISBN 0-87364-211-2). Paladin Ent.
Strauss, Sheryl, ed. Security Problems in a Modern Society. (Illus.). 314p. 1980. text ed. 9.95 (ISBN 0-409-95079-3). Butterworths.
CRIME STATISTICS
see Criminal Statistics
CRIME STORIES (COLLECTIONS)
see Detective and Mystery Stories (Collections)
CRIME SYNDICATES
see Organized Crime
CRIMEAN WAR, 1853-1856
see also Eastern Question (Balkan)
Wilkinson. Uniforms & Weapons of the Crimean War. pap. 14.95 (ISBN 0-7134-0666-6). David & Charles.
CRIMES AND MISDEMEANORS
see Criminal Law
CRIMINAL ANTHROPOLOGY
see also Crime Prevention; Criminal Psychology
Sagarin, Edward, ed. Taboos in Criminology. LC 80-18175. (Sage Research Progress Ser. in Criminology: Vol. 15). 152p. 1980. 12.95 (ISBN 0-8039-1513-6); pap. 6.50 (ISBN 0-8039-1514-4). Sage.
CRIMINAL ANTHROPOMETRY
see Anthropometry; Criminal Anthropology
CRIMINAL COURTS–STATISTICS
see Criminal Statistics
CRIMINAL DEFENSES
see Defense (Criminal Procedure)
CRIMINAL EVIDENCE
see Evidence, Criminal
CRIMINAL INVESTIGATION
see also Detectives; Evidence, Criminal; Fingerprints; Legal Documents; Medical Jurisprudence; Wire-Tapping
Background GmBH. Without a Trace. Partisan Press Staff, ed. (Illus.). 128p. (Orig.). 1980. pap. 4.95 (ISBN 0-935150-00-5). Partisan Pr.
Bennett, Wayne W. & Hess, Karen M. Criminal Investigation. (Criminal Justice Ser.). 450p. 1980. text ed. 15.95 (ISBN 0-8299-0342-9). West Pub.
Grau, Joseph J. Criminal & Civil Investigation Handbook. (Illus.). 1088p. 1982. 39.50 (ISBN 0-07-024130-9). McGraw.
Sennewald, Charles A. The Process of Investigation: Concepts & Strategies for the Security Professional. 255p. 1981. text ed. 21.95 (ISBN 0-409-95018-1). Butterworths.

CRIMINAL JUSTICE, ADMINISTRATION OF
see also Amnesty; Crime and Criminals; Criminal Investigation; Criminal Law; Criminal Procedure; Impeachments; Juvenile Courts; Juvenile Delinquency; Law Enforcement; Pardon; Police; Prisons; Probation; Punishment
Alper, Benedict S. & Nichols, Lawrence T. Beyond the Courtroom: Community Justice & Programs in Conflict Resolution. LC 78-20376. write for info. (ISBN 0-669-02724-3). Lexington Bks.
Bender, David L., ed. Criminal Justice: Opposing Viewpoints. (Opposing Viewpoints Ser.). (gr. 12). 1981. lib. bdg. 8.95 (ISBN 0-89908-332-3); pap. text ed. 3.95 (ISBN 0-89908-307-2). Greenhaven.
Bottomley, A. Keith. Prison Before Trial. 117p. 1970. pap. text ed. 5.00x (ISBN 0-7135-1816-2, Pub. by Bedford England). Renouf.
Cohen, Henry. Brutal Justice: The Ordeal of an American City. 248p. 1980. lib. bdg. 10.00x (ISBN 0-89444-027-6). John Jay Pr.
Cohen, Henry, ed. Criminal Justice History: An International Annual, 1980, Vol. I. (Criminal Justice History Ser.). (Illus.). 294p. 1980. lib. bdg. 20.00x (ISBN 0-686-28890-4). Crime & Justice Hist.
Cohn, Alvin W. & Ward, Benjamin, eds. Improving Management in Criminal Justice. LC 80-18331. (Sage Research Progress Ser. in Criminology: Vol. 17). (Illus.). 159p. 1980. 12.95 (ISBN 0-8039-1515-2); pap. 6.50 (ISBN 0-8039-1516-0). Sage.
Conrad, John P. Justice & Consequences. LC 78-348. (The Dangerous Offender Project Ser.). 1981. price not set (ISBN 0-669-02190-3). Lexington Bks.
Dow, Paul E. Discretionary Justice. 1981. price not set reference (ISBN 0-88410-835-X). Ballinger Pub.
Flekenes, George T. Michigan Criminal Justice Law Manual. (Criminal Justice Ser.). 300p. 1981. pap. text ed. 18.95 (ISBN 0-8299-0369-0). West Pub.
Foster, C. A., et al. Introduction to the Administration of Justice. 2nd ed. LC 78-13498. 347p. 1979. 17.50 (ISBN 0-471-04079-7). Wiley.
Frankel, Marvin E. Partisan Justice. 1981. pap. 4.95 (ISBN 0-8090-1395-9). Hill & Wang.
Herman, Melvin. Administrative Justice & Supplementary Benefits. 68p. 1972. pap. text ed. 5.00x (ISBN 0-7135-1711-5, Pub. by Bedford England). Renouf.
Keeble, Ursula. Aids & Adaptations. 320p. 1979. pap. text ed. 14.90x (ISBN 0-7199-0963-5, Pub. by Bedford England). Renouf.
Klein, Malcolm W & Teilmann, Katherine S., eds. Handbook of Criminal Justice Evaluation. LC 80-16909. (Illus.). 693p. 1980. 39.95 (ISBN 0-8039-1052-5). Sage.
Krehel, Peter. Spiritual Fingerprint. 1981. 10.95 (ISBN 0-8062-1675-1). Carlton.
McDowell, Charles P. Community Relations & Criminal Justice. 500p. Date not set. text ed. price not set (ISBN 0-87084-558-6). Anderson Pub Co.
Misner, Gordon E. & Crim, D. Criminal Justice Studies: Their Trans-Disciplinary Nature. (Illus.). 350p. 1981. pap. text ed. 14.95 (ISBN 0-8016-3457-1). Mosby.
Pearson, Richard, et al. Criminal Justice Education: The End of the Beginning. 220p. (Orig.). 1980. pap. 5.50x (ISBN 0-89444-030-6). John Jay Pr.
Robinson, Henry, et al. Certain Considerations in Order to a More Speedy, Cheap, and Equal Distribution of Justice Throughout the Nation. Berkowitz, David S. & Thorne, Samuel E., eds. LC 77-86668. (Classics of English Legal History in the Modern Era Ser.: Vol. 49). 317p. 1979. lib. bdg. 40.00 (ISBN 0-8240-3098-2). Garland Pub.
Senna, Joseph J. & Siegel, Larry J. Introduction to Criminal Justice. 2nd ed. (Criminal Justice Ser.). (Illus.). 550p. 1981. text ed. 16.95 (ISBN 0-8299-0409-3). West Pub.
Wright, Kevin N., ed. Crime & Criminal Justice in a Declining Economy. LC 80-26623. 128p. 1981. lib. bdg. 20.00 (ISBN 0-89946-046-1). Oelgeschlager.

CRIMINAL JUSTICE, ADMINISTRATION OF–STATISTICS
see Criminal Statistics

CRIMINAL LAW
see also Abortion; Adultery; Capital Punishment; Competition, Unfair; Conspiracy; Contempt of Court; Counterfeits and Counterfeiting; Criminal Justice, Administration of; Criminal Procedure; Embezzlement; Fraud; Gambling; Infanticide; International Offenses; Libel and Slander; Lotteries; Murder; Obscenity (Law); Pardon; Poisoning; Probation; Punishment; Rape; Riots; Robbery; Sex Crimes; Suicide; Tax Evasion; Treason
Culbertson, Robert G. & Tezak, Mark R. Order Under Law-Readings in Criminal Justice. 272p. 1981. pap. text ed. 6.95x (ISBN 0-917974-52-2). Waveland Pr.
Ferguson. Readings on Concepts of Criminal Law. (Criminal Justice Ser.). 1975. pap. text ed. 12.95 (ISBN 0-8299-0619-3). West Pub.
Greenawalt, R. Kent & Low, Peter W., eds. Model Penal Code & Commentaries, 3 vols, Pt. II. 1427p. 105.00 set (ISBN 0-686-69005-2); postage & handling 9.00 (ISBN 0-686-69006-0). Am Law Inst.
Michael, Jerome & Adler, Mortimer J. Crime, Law & Social Science. (Social Science Classics Ser.). 440p. 1982. 19.95 (ISBN 0-87855-362-2); text ed. 19.95 (ISBN 0-686-68056-1); pap. 7.95 (ISBN 0-87855-786-5); pap. text ed. 7.95 (ISBN 0-686-68057-X). Transaction Bks.
Sigler, Jay A. Understanding Criminal Law. 1981. text ed. 16.95 (ISBN 0-316-79054-0); training manual free (ISBN 0-316-79055-9). Little.

CRIMINAL LAW–PLEADING AND PROCEDURE
see Criminal Procedure

CRIMINAL LAW–STATISTICS
see Criminal Statistics

CRIMINAL LAW–CHINA
McKnight, Brian E. The Quality of Mercy: Amnesties & Traditional Chinese Justice. LC 80-26650. 224p. 1981. pap. 15.00x (ISBN 0-8248-0736-7). U Pr of Hawaii.
Meijer, Marinus J. Introduction to Modern Criminal Law in China. (Studies in Chinese Government & Law). 1977. Repr. of 1950 ed. 20.00 (ISBN 0-89093-057-0). U Pubns Amer.

CRIMINAL LAW–GREAT BRITAIN
Smith, Roger. Trial by Medicine: The Insanity Defense in Victorian England. 280p. 1981. 33.00x (ISBN 0-85224-407-X, Pub.by Edinburgh U Pr Scotland). Columbia U Pr.

CRIMINAL LAW–LATIN AMERICA
Brana-Shute, Rosemary & Brana-Shute, Gary, eds. Crime & Punishment in the Caribbean. LC 80-21078. (Illus.). x, 146p. 1980. pap. 6.00 (ISBN 0-8130-0685-6). U Presses Fla.

CRIMINAL LAW, INTERNATIONAL
see International Offenses

CRIMINAL PROCEDURE
see also Appellate Procedure; Criminal Law; Defense (Criminal Procedure); Evidence, Criminal; Extradition; Instructions to Juries; Judgments; Jury; Probation; Psychology, Forensic; Sentences (Criminal Procedure); Torture; Trial Practice
Israel, Jerold H. & LaFave, Wayne R. Criminal Procedure in a Nutshell: Constitutional Limitations. 3rd ed. LC 80-23164. (Nutshell Ser.). 438p. 1980. pap. text ed. 6.95 (ISBN 0-8299-2107-9). West Pub.
Jones, David A. The Law of Criminal Procedure: An Analysis & Critique. 600p. 1981. text ed. 17.95 (ISBN 0-316-47283-2); tchrs'. manual free (ISBN 0-316-47284-0). Little.
Kamisar, Yale, et al. Basic Criminal Procedure, Cases, Comments & Questions. 5th ed. LC 52-52950. (American Casebook Ser.). 920p. 1980. pap. text ed. 13.95 (ISBN 0-8299-2109-5). West Pub.
McGehee, Lucius P. Due Process of Law Under the Federal Constitution. (Studies in Constitutional Law). x, 452p. 1981. Repr. of 1906 ed. lib. bdg. 37.50x (ISBN 0-8377-0837-0). Rothman.
Sedgwick, Jeffery L. Deterring Criminals: Policy Making & the American Political Tradition. 1980. pap. 4.25 (ISBN 0-8447-3385-7). Am Enterprise.
Weston, Paul B. & Wells, Kenneth M. The Administration of Justice. 4th ed. (Illus.). 240p. 1981. text ed. 14.95 (ISBN 0-686-69272-1). P-H.

CRIMINAL PROCEDURE–CASES
Moenssens, Andre A., et al. Cases & Comments on Criminal Procedure. (Contemporary Legal Education Ser.). 900p. 1979. text ed. 21.00 (ISBN 0-672-83683-1). Bobbs.

CRIMINAL PROCEDURE–STATISTICS
see Criminal Statistics

CRIMINAL PSYCHOLOGY
see also Forensic Psychiatry; Psychology, Forensic; Psychology, Pathological; Sex Crimes
Bucknill, John C. Unsoundness of Mind in Relation to Criminal Acts. Bd. with Care of the Insane & Their Legal Control; Factors of the Unsound Mind. Guy, W. A. (Contributions to the History of Psychology Ser., Vol. IV Pt. F: Insanity & Jurisprudence). 1980. Repr. of 1854 ed. 30.00 (ISBN 0-89093-329-4). U Pubns Amer.
Lewis, Dorothy O., ed. Psychobiological Vulnerabilities to Delinquency. 1981. text ed. write for info. (ISBN 0-89335-136-9). Spectrum Pub.
Michael, Jerome & Adler, Mortimer J. Crime, Law & Social Science. (Social Science Classics Ser.). 440p. 1982. 19.95 (ISBN 0-87855-362-2); text ed. 19.95 (ISBN 0-686-68056-1); pap. 7.95 (ISBN 0-87855-786-5); pap. text ed. 7.95 (ISBN 0-686-68057-X). Transaction Bks.
Monahan, John, ed. Who Is the Client? The Ethics of Psychological Intervention in the Criminal Justice System. LC 80-14101. 1980. 7.50 (ISBN 0-912704-14-4). Am Psychol.

CRIMINAL STATISTICS
Felony Arrests: Their Prosecution & Disposition in New York City's Courts. (Vera Studies in Criminal Justice (Professional Studies)). (Illus.). 192p. (Orig.). 1981. 17.50 (ISBN 0-582-28195-4); pap. 6.95 (ISBN 0-582-28187-3). Longman.
Law Enforcement. National Crime Surveys: National Sample, 1973-1978. LC 78-71979. 1979. 10.00 (ISBN 0-89138-991-1). ICPSR.

CRIMINALS
see Crime and Criminals

CRIMINOLOGY
see Crime and Criminals

CRIPPLES
see Physically Handicapped

CRISIS INTERVENTION (PSYCHIATRY)
Burgess, Ann W. & Baldwin, Bruce. Crisis Intervention Theory & Practice: A Clinical Guide. (Illus.). 288p. 1981. text ed. 14.95 (ISBN 0-13-193466-X); pap. text ed. 11.95 (ISBN 0-686-69274-8). P-H.
France, Joseph B. Crisis Therapy. LC 80-83967. 1980. pap. text ed. 8.75x (ISBN 0-918970-28-8). Intl Gen Semantics.
Greenstone, James L. & Leviton, Sharon. Hotline: The Crisis Intervention Directory. 350p. 1981. lib. bdg. 45.00 (ISBN 0-87196-373-6). Facts on File.
Hafen, Brent Q. & Karren, Keith J. Prehospital Emergency Care & Crisis Intervention. 570p. 1981. pap. 13.95x (ISBN 0-89582-057-9); wkbk. 5.95x (ISBN 0-89582-058-7); text & wkbk. 17.00x. Morton Pub.

CRISIS THEOLOGY
see Dialectical Theology

CRITICAL CARE UNITS
see Intensive Care Units

CRITICAL MATERIALS
see Strategic Materials

CRITICISM
Here are entered works on the principles of criticism in general and of literary criticism in particular. Criticism in a specific field is entered under the appropriate heading, e.g. Art Criticism; English Literature–History and Criticism; English Poetry–History and Criticism; Literature–History and Criticism; Music–History and Criticism. Criticism of the work of an individual is entered under the name of the individual.
see also Bible–Criticism, Interpretation, etc.; Book Reviewing; Books–Reviews; Esthetics; Hermeneutics; Literature–History and Criticism; Moving-Picture Criticism; Style, Literary;
also Criticism in specific fields e.g. Art Criticism; English Literature–History and Criticism; also names of individuals, with or without the subdivision Criticism and Interpretation
Beardsley, Monroe C. Aesthetics: Problems in the Philosophy of Criticism. 2nd ed. (Illus.). 688p. 1981. 25.00 (ISBN 0-915145-09-X); pap. text ed. 14.50 (ISBN 0-915145-08-1). Hackett Pub.
Belsey, Catherine. Critical Practice. 176p. 1980. 17.00 (ISBN 0-416-72940-1, 2022); pap. 7.95 (ISBN 0-416-72950-9, 2021). Methuen Inc.
Bouhours, Dominique. Art of Criticism. Repr. of 1705 ed. write for info. Schol Facsimil.
Browne, M. Neil & Keely, Stuart M. Asking the Right Questions. 224p. 1981. pap. text ed. 6.95 (ISBN 0-13-049395-3). P-H.
Earnest, Ernest. A Forward to Literature. 332p. 1980. Repr. of 1945 ed. lib. bdg. 25.00 (ISBN 0-89987-205-0). Century Bookbindery.
Gunton, Sharon, ed. Contemporary Literary Criticism: Excerpts from Criticism of the Works of Today's Novelists, Poets, Playwrights, & Other Creative Writers. LC 76-38938. (Contemporary Literary Criticism Ser.: Vol. 17). 600p. 1981. 58.00 (ISBN 0-8103-0107-5). Gale.
--Contemporary Literary Criticism: Vol. 18, Excerpts from Criticism of the Works of Today's Novelists, Poets, Playwrights & Other Creative Writers. LC 76-38938. (Contemporary Literary Criticism Ser.: Vol. 17). 600p. 1981. 58.00 (ISBN 0-8103-0123-7). Gale.
Leavis, F. R. Towards Standards of Criticism. 200p. 1981. pap. 7.25x (ISBN 0-85315-388-4, Pub. by Lawrence & Wishart Ltd England). Humanities.
Wellek, Rene. Four Critics: Croce, Valery, Lukacs, & Ingarden. LC 80-54429. (The Walker-Ames Lecture Ser.). 104p. 1981. 8.95 (ISBN 0-295-95800-6). U of Wash Pr.
--A History of Modern Criticism: 1750-1950: Volume 1 - the Later Eighteenth Century. 358p. Date not set. pap. price not set (ISBN 0-521-28295-0). Cambridge U Pr.
--A History of Modern Criticism: 1750-1950: Volume 2 - the Romantic Age. 460p. Date not set. pap. price not set (ISBN 0-521-28296-9). Cambridge U Pr.

CRITICISM–ADDRESSES, ESSAYS, LECTURES
Bowman, James C. Contemporary American Criticism. 330p. 1980. Repr. of 1926 ed. lib. bdg. 35.00 (ISBN 0-8495-0457-0). Arden Lib.
Smith, Agnes. Speaking As a Writer. Ross-Robertson, David, tr. LC 78-65831. (Illus.). 76p. (Orig.). 1979. 7.75 (ISBN 0-9602342-0-9); pap. 5.95 (ISBN 0-9602342-1-7). Westwind Pr.

CRITICISM (PHILOSOPHY)
Eagleton, Terry. Walter Benjamin: Or Toward a Revolutionary Criticism. 224p. 1981. 19.50 (ISBN 0-8052-7100-7, Pub. by NLB England); pap. 8.50 (ISBN 0-8052-7099-X). Schocken.

CROCHETING
see also Lace and Lace Making
American School of Needlework. The Great Afghan Book. Thomas, Mary, ed. (Illus.). 160p. 1981. 16.95 (ISBN 0-8069-5444-2, Columbia Hse). Sterling.
Drysdale, Rosemary. Miniature Crocheting & Knitting for Dollhouses. (Illus.). 50p. 1981. pap. 2.00 (ISBN 0-486-23964-0). Dover.
Kettelle, F. W. Filet Crochet. 1978. pap. 1.50 (ISBN 0-486-23745-1). Dover.
Lep, Antoinette. Traditional Quilt Block Patterns for Crocheting. 48p. (Orig.). 1981. pap. write for info. (ISBN 0-486-23967-5). Dover.
Ough, Anne R. New Directions in Crochet. LC 80-52646. (Illus.). 248p. 1981. 17.95 (ISBN 0-670-40008-4, Studio). Viking Pr.
Staff of Workbasket Magazine. Aunt Ellen's Crochet Handbook: A Treasury of Techniques & Projects. LC 80-85484. (Illus., Orig.). 1981. pap. 2.95 (ISBN 0-86675-325-7, 3257). Mod Handicraft.
Weiss, Rita. Crocheting Afgans. (Illus.). 1979. pap. 1.50 (ISBN 0-486-23883-0). Dover.
--Crocheting Edgings. (Illus.). 48p. 1980. pap. 1.75 (ISBN 0-486-24031-2). Dover.
--Floral Doilies for Crocheting. (Illus.). 1979. pap. 1.75 (ISBN 0-486-23789-3). Dover.

CROCKER, CHARLES, 1822-1888
Hunt, Harrison J. North to the Horizon. Thompson, Ruth H., ed. LC 80-69081. (Illus.). 135p. 1981. 11.95 (ISBN 0-89272-080-8). Down East.

CROCKERY
see Pottery

CROCKERY COOKERY, ELECTRIC
see Electric Cookery, Slow

CROP REPORTS
see Agriculture–Statistics

CROP STATISTICS
see Agriculture–Statistics

CROP YIELDS
see also Agriculture–Statistics; Crops and Climate
International Bibliography on Cropping Systems Nineteen Seventy-Three to Nineteen Seventy-Four. 300p. 1976. pap. 36.00 (IRRI). Unipub.
Risk & Uncertainty As Factors in Crop Improvement Research. (IRRI Research Paper Ser.: No. 15). 19p. 1978. pap. 5.00 (R055, IRRI). Unipub.

CROPS
see Agriculture; Field Crops; Plants, Cultivated

CROPS AND CLIMATE
see also Crop Yields; Meteorology, Agricultural
Raper, C. David & Kramer, Paul J. Crop Reactions to Water & Temperature Stresses in Humid, Temperate Climates. (Special Studies in Agricultural Science & Policy). 425p. 1981. lib. bdg. 30.00x (ISBN 0-686-69585-2). Westview.
Slater, Lloyd E. & Levin, Susan K., eds. Climate's Impact on Food Supplies. (Selected Symposium Ser.: No. 62). 250p. 1981. lib. bdg. 20.00x (ISBN 0-86531-166-8). Westview.
Symposium on Climate & Rice. Proceedings. 565p. 1976. pap. 37.50 (R025, IRRI). Unipub.
Tropical Climate & Its Influence on Rice. (IRRI Research Paper Ser.: No. 20). 25p. 1979. pap. 5.00 (R060, IRRI). Unipub.
Weather & Climate Data for Philippine Rice Research. (IRRI Research Paper Ser.: No. 41). 14p. 1979. pap. 5.00 (R081, IRRI). Unipub.

CROSBY, BING
Shepherd, Donald & Slatzer, Robert. Bing Crosby. (Illus.). 320p. 1981. 13.95 (ISBN 0-312-07866-8). St Martin.

CROSS-COUNTRY RUNNING
see Running

CROSS-EXAMINATION
see also Evidence (Law)
Bailey, F. Lee & Rothblatt, Henry. Cross-Examination in Criminal Trials, Vol. 1. LC 78-18628. 1978. 47.50. Lawyers Co-Op.

CROSS-STITCH
see also Samplers
Hauschild, Jana. Danish Cross-Stitched Zodiac Samplers: Charted Designs for the Astrological Year. (Illus.). 1980. pap. 2.25 daddlewire (ISBN 0-486-24032-0). Dover.
Jessen, Ellen. Peruvian Designs for Cross-Stitch. 64p. 1980. pap. 6.95 (ISBN 0-442-21926-1). Van Nos Reinhold.

CROSS-WORD PUZZLES
see Crossword Puzzles

CROSSWORD PUZZLES
Gillespie, Robert. Tempo Daily Crosswords, No. 4. 128p. (gr. 4 up). 1981. pap. 1.50 (ISBN 0-448-05727-1, Tempo). G&D.
Hart, Harold H., compiled by. The Mammoth Book of Crossword Puzzles. 512p. 1981. pap. 8.95 (ISBN 0-89104-204-0). A & W Pubs.
Kurzban, Stan, et al. The Compleat Cruciverbalist: How to Solve & Compose Crossword Puzzles for Fun & Profit. 156p. 1980. 9.95 (ISBN 0-442-25738-4). Van Nos Reinhold.
Preston, Charles. Dow Jones Crosswords for the Serious, Bk. 3. 60p. 1981. pap. 3.50 (ISBN 0-87094-238-7). Dow Jones-Irwin.
Rafferty, Kathleen. Dell Crossword Dictionary. 1981. pap. 2.95 (ISBN 0-440-16314-5). Dell.
Rafferty, Kathleen, ed. The Big Dell Book of Crosswords & Pencil Puzzles. (Orig.). 1981. pap. 6.95 (ISBN 0-440-50970-X, Dell Trade Pbks). Dell.
Sunners, William. How to Make & Sell Original Crosswords & Other Puzzles. LC 80-52333. (Illus.). 256p. 1981. 12.95 (ISBN 0-8069-4632-6); lib. bdg. 11.69 (ISBN 0-8069-4633-4). Sterling.
Toye, Randall & Gaffney, Judith H. The Agatha Christie Crossword Puzzle Book. 132p. (Orig.). 1981. pap. 6.95 (ISBN 0-686-69122-9). HR&W.

CROTALUS
see Rattlesnakes

CROW INDIANS
see Indians of North America–The West

CROWDS
see also Riots

Penrose, L. S. On the Objective Study of Crowd Behavior. 78p. 1981. Repr. of 1952 ed. text ed. price not set. Krieger.

CROWS

Goodwin, Derek. Crows of the World. LC 76-20194. (Illus.). 352p. 1976. 32.50x (ISBN 0-8014-1057-6). Comstock.

CRUCIFIXION OF CHRIST

see Jesus Christ-Crucifixion

CRUDE OIL

see Petroleum

CRUELTY TO CHILDREN

see Child Abuse

CRUSADES

Here are entered works on the crusades in general. Specific crusades are listed chronologically at the end of this entry.

Prawer, Joshua. Crusader Institutions. (Illus.). 536p. 1980. 89.00x (ISBN 0-19-822536-9). Oxford U Pr.

CRUSADES-FOURTH, 1202-1204

Godfrey, John. Twelve Hundred & Four - the Unholy Crusade. (Illus.). 256p. 1980. 28.50 (ISBN 0-19-215834-1). Oxford U Pr.

CRUSADES-LATER, 13TH, 14TH, AND 15TH CENTURIES

Hamilton, Bernard. The Latin Church in the Crusader States: The Secular Church. 402p. 1980. 40.00x (ISBN 0-86078-072-4, Pub. by Variorum England). State Mutual Bk.

CRUSTACEA

see also Amphipoda; Lobsters

Morris, S. F. Catalogue of Type & Figured Fossil Crustacea (Exc. Ostracoda), Chelicerata & Myriapoda in the British Museum (Natural History) (Illus.). 56p. 1980. pap. 13.00x (ISBN 0-565-00828-5). Sabbot-Natural Hist Bks.

CRYOGENICS

see Low Temperature Engineering; Low Temperatures; Refrigeration and Refrigerating Machinery

Toscano, W. M., et al. Cryogenic Processes & Equipment in Energy Systems. 193p. 1980. 40.00 (H00164). ASME.

CRYPTANALYSIS

see Cryptography

CRYPTESTHESIA

see Extrasensory Perception

CRYPTOGAMS

see also Algae; Fungi; Lichens; Mosses

Esser, Karl. Cryptograms: Cyanobacteria, Algae, Fungi, Lichens, Textbook & Practical Guide. Hackston, Michael G. & Webster, John, trs. LC 80-41070. 624p. Date not set. text ed. price not set (ISBN 0-521-23621-5); pap. text ed. price not set (ISBN 0-521-28080-X). Cambridge U Pr.

CRYPTOGRAPHY

see also Ciphers

Gleason, Norma. Cryptograms & Spygrams. 128p. (Orig.). 1981. pap. price not set. Dover.

CRYSTAL OPTICS

Bloss, Donald F. The Spindle Stage: Principles & Practice. LC 80-21488. (Illus.). 416p. Date not set. price not set (ISBN 0-521-23292-9). Cambridge U Pr.

Personick, Stewart D. Optical Fiber Transmission Systems. (Applications of Communications Theory Ser.). 210p. 1981. 25.00 (ISBN 0-306-40580-6, Plenum Pr). Plenum Pub.

CRYSTALLINE SEMICONDUCTORS

see Semiconductors

CRYSTALLOGRAPHY

see also Crystal Optics; Crystals; Geology; Mineralogy also names of minerals

Vainshtain, B. K. Modern Crystallography I. (Springer Series in Solid-State Sciences: Vol. 15). (Illus.). 420p. 1981. 54.50 (ISBN 0-387-10052-0). Springer-Verlag.

Whittaker, E. J. Crystallography: An Introduction for Earth Science (and Other Solid State) Students. LC 80-41188. (Illus.). 240p. 1981. 33.00 (ISBN 0-686-69443-0); pap. 19.50 (ISBN 0-08-023804-1). Pergamon.

CRYSTALS

see also Domain Structure; Semiconductors also names of particular types of crystals

Freyhardt, H. C., ed. Organic Crystals, Germanates, Semiconductors. (Crystals, Growth, Properties & Applications: Vol. 4). (Illus.). 250p. 1980. 55.50 (ISBN 0-387-10298-1). Springer-Verlag.

OAS General Secretariat. Aplicacoes Da Teoria De Grupos Na Espectroscopia De Raman E Do Infravermelho. (Fisica Monografia: No. 14). 102p. 1980. pap. text ed. 2.00 (ISBN 0-8270-1126-1). OAS.

Silinish, E. A. Organic Molecular Crystals: Their Electronic States. (Springer Series in Solid State Sciences: Vol. 16). (Illus.). 410p. 1980. 54.50 (ISBN 0-387-10053-9). Springer-Verlag.

Stoiber, Richard E. & Morse, Stearns A. Microscopic Identification of Crystals. 286p. 1981. Repr. of 1972 ed. lib. bdg. 16.50 (ISBN 0-89874-276-5). Krieger.

CRYSTALS-OPTICAL PROPERTIES

see Crystal Optics

CRYSTALS, LIQUID

see Liquid Crystals

CUB SCOUTS

see Boy Scouts

CUBA-ECONOMIC CONDITIONS

Mesa-Lago, Carmelo. The Economy of Socialist Cuba: A Two-Decade Appraisal. 296p. 1981. price not set (ISBN 0-8263-0578-4); pap. price not set (ISBN 0-8263-0585-7). U of NM Pr.

CUBA-HISTORY-INVASION, 1961

Randall, Margaret. Women in Cuba--Twenty Years Later. (Illus.). 182p. 1981. 15.95 (ISBN 0-918266-15-7); pap. 6.95 (ISBN 0-918266-14-9). Smyrna.

Taylor, Maxwell, et al. Operations Zapata: The "Ultrasensitive" Report & Testimony of the Board of Inquiry on the Bay of Pigs. 1980. 24.00 (ISBN 0-89093-185-2); pap. 8.00 (ISBN 0-89093-186-0). U Pubns Amer.

CUBA-POLITICS AND GOVERNMENT

Fidel Castro on Internationalism, Nineteen Seventy-Five to Nineteen Eighty. 1981. 30.00 (ISBN 0-87348-610-2); pap. 7.95 (ISBN 0-87348-610-2). Path Pr NY.

Horowitz, Irving L. Cuban Communism. 550p. 1981. pap. 9.95 (ISBN 0-87855-838-1). Transaction Bks.

Navarro, Antonio. Tocayo: The True Story of a Resistance Leader in Castro's Cuba. 288p. 1981. 14.95 (ISBN 0-87000-508-1). Arlington Hse.

CUBA-SOCIAL CONDITIONS

Randall, Margaret. Women in Cuba--Twenty Years Later. (Illus.). 182p. 1981. 15.95 (ISBN 0-918266-15-7); pap. 6.95 (ISBN 0-918266-14-9). Smyrna.

CUBAN INVASION, 1961

see Cuba-History-Invasion, 1961

CUBAN LITERATURE-HISTORY AND CRITICISM

Fernandez-Vazquez, Antonio. La Novelistica Cubana De la Revolucion. LC 79-52159. (Coleccion Polymita Ser.). 157p. (Span.). 1980. pap. 9.95 (ISBN 0-89729-228-6). Ediciones.

CUBISM

see also Post-Impressionism (Art)

Daix, Pierre & Rosselet, Joan. Picasso, a Catalogue Raisonne of the Paintings & Related Works. LC 78-71109. (Illus.). 1979. 125.00 (ISBN 0-8212-0672-9, 706981). NYGS.

CULDOSCOPY

Logan & Edwards. Manual of Laparoscopy & Culdoscopy. 1981. text ed. price not set. Butterworth.

CULTIVATED PLANTS

see Plants, Cultivated

CULTS

Here are entered works on groups or movements whose system of religious beliefs or practices differs significantly from the major world religions and which are often gathered around a specific diety or person. Works on the major world religions are entered under Religions. Works on religious groups whose adherents recognize special teachings or practices which fall within the normative bounds of the major world religions are entered under Sects.

see also Sects

Bradlee, Ben, Jr. & Van Atta, Dale. Prophet of Blood: The Story of the "Mormon Manson". (Illus.). 384p. 1981. 12.95 (ISBN 0-399-12371-7). Putnam.

Burstein, A. Religion, Cults & the Law. 1980. 5.95 (ISBN 0-379-11133-0). Oceana.

Hunt, Dave. A Study Guide for the Cult Explosion. 128p. (Orig.). 1981. pap. 2.95 (ISBN 0-89081-280-2). Harvest Hse.

McCoy, Duke. How to Organize & Manage Your Own Religious Cult. 1980. pap. 6.95. Loompanics.

Shupe, Anson D., Jr. & Bromley, David G. The New Vigilantes: Deprogrammers, Anti-Cultists & the New Religions. LC 80-23276. (Sage Library of Social Research: Vol. 113). 272p. 1980. 18.00 (ISBN 0-8039-1542-X); pap. 8.95 (ISBN 0-8039-1543-8). Sage.

CULTURAL ANTHROPOLOGY

see Ethnology

CULTURAL CHANGE

see Social Change

CULTURAL EVOLUTION

see Social Change; Social Evolution

CULTURAL EXCHANGE PROGRAMS

see Cultural Relations

CULTURAL RELATIONS

Cultural Co-operation: Studies & Experiences in the Cultural Content of Education. (Joint Study: No. 9). 100p. 1980. pap. 7.50 (ISBN 0-686-68809-0, U1023, UNESCO). Unipub.

CULTURALLY DEPRIVED

see Socially Handicapped

CULTURE

see also Civilization; Education; Educational Anthropology; Humanism; Intercultural Communication; Learning and Scholarship; Self-Culture; Social Evolution; United States-Popular Culture

Binion, Rudolph. Soundings. 275p. 1981. 18.95 (ISBN 0-914434-16-0); pap. 8.95 (ISBN 0-914434-17-9). Psychohistory Pr.

Culture, Behavior, & Personality. 2nd ed. 320p. 1981. 22.95x (ISBN 0-686-69599-2); pap. text ed. 11.95x (ISBN 0-686-69600-X). Aldine Pub.

Goodenough, Ward. Culture, Language & Society. 1981. 9.95; pap. 5.95. Benjamin-Cummings.

McFee, June K. & Degge, Rogena M. Art, Culture, & Environment: A Catalyst for Teaching. 416p. 1980. pap. text ed. 13.95 (ISBN 0-8403-2330-1). Kendall-Hunt.

Ong, Walter J. The Presence of the Word: Some Prolegomena for Cultural & Religious History. xvi, 360p. 1981. pap. 8.95x (ISBN 0-8166-1043-6). U of Minn Pr.

Peters, Nancy J., et al, eds. Free Spirits. 1981. pap. price not set (ISBN 0-87286-128-7). City Lights.

Rossi, Ino, ed. The Logic of Culture: Advances in Structural Theory & Methods. 320p. 1981. text ed. 24.95x (ISBN 0-89789-015-9). J F Bergin.

Stafford, Harry C. Culture & Cosmology: Essays on the Birth of World View. LC 80-5642. 371p. 1981. lib. bdg. 21.25 (ISBN 0-8191-1371-9); pap. text ed. 12.50 (ISBN 0-8191-1372-7). U Pr of Amer.

Suarez-Torrez, David. Contrastes Culturales. 336p. 1981. text ed. 11.95 case (ISBN 0-669-02662-X). Heath.

Wagner, Roy W. The Invention of Culture. rev., exp. ed. 1981. lib. bdg. 21.00x (ISBN 0-226-86933-4); pap. 5.95 (ISBN 0-226-86934-2). U of Chicago Pr.

Williams, Raymond. Problems in Materialism & Culture: Selected Essays. 288p. 1981. 19.50x (ISBN 0-8052-7093-0, Pub. by NLB England); pap. 8.75 (ISBN 0-8052-7092-2). Schocken.

Wittgenstein, Ludwig. Culture & Value. Von Wright, G. H., ed. Winch, Peter, tr. LC 80-15234. 1980. 20.00x (ISBN 0-226-90432-6). U of Chicago Pr.

CULTURE, EVOLUTION OF

see Social Evolution

CULTURE AND EDUCATION

see Educational Anthropology

CULTURE OF CELLS

see Cell Culture

CULTURES (BIOLOGY)

see also Cell Culture

Yonisuke, Ikeda. JFCC Catalogue of Cultures. 3rd ed. 320p. 1980. 35.00x (ISBN 0-89955-221-8, Pub. by JSSP Japan). Intl Schol Bk Serv.

CULTUS, DISPARITY OF

see Marriage, Mixed

CUPS AND SAUCERS

see Porcelain; Pottery

CURE OF SOULS

see Pastoral Counseling; Pastoral Theology

CURIOSITIES AND WONDERS

A general and miscellaneous form heading, not to be confused with Curiosa which stands for literary and bibliographical curiosities.

Alder, Vera S. From the Mundane to the Magnificent. 1980. pap. 5.95 (ISBN 0-87728-504-7). Weiser.

Aylward, Jim. Things No One Ever Tells You. 144p. (Orig.). 1981. pap. 1.95 (ISBN 0-446-90707-3). Warner Bks.

Barron, Neil. Anatomy of Wonder. 2nd ed. 450p. 1981. 22.50 (ISBN 0-8352-1339-0). Bowker.

Cazeau, Charles J. & Scott, Stuart D., Jr. Exploring the Unknown: Great Mysteries Reexamined. (Da Capo Quality Paperbacks Ser.). (Illus.). 1981. pap. 8.95 (ISBN 0-306-80139-6). Da Capo.

McWhirter, Norris, ed. Guinness Book of World Records. 19th ed. 672p. 1981. pap. 3.50 (ISBN 0-553-14500-2). Bantam.

McWhirter, Ross & McWhirter, Norris. Guinness Book of Young Recordbreakers. rev. ed. LC 76-1161. (Guinness Illustrated Collection of World Records for Young Readers). (Illus.). 96p. (gr. 3 up). 1981. 5.95 (ISBN 0-8069-0216-7); PLB 6.69 (ISBN 0-8069-0217-5). Sterling.

Phillips, Louis. Freaky Facts. Schneider, Meg, ed. (Funnybones Ser.). 64p. 1981. pap. 1.50 (ISBN 0-671-42247-2). S&S.

Worthington, George. In Search of World Records. LC 80-82032. (gr. 10-12). 1980. 12.95 (ISBN 0-938282-01-8); pap. 9.95 (ISBN 0-938282-02-6). Hang Gliding.

CURRENCY

see Money

CURRENTS, ELECTRIC

see Electric Currents

CURRICULA (COURSES OF STUDY)

see Education-Curricula

CURRICULUM DEVELOPMENT

see Curriculum Planning

CURRICULUM PLANNING

Bank, Adrianne, et al. A Practical Guide to Program Planning: A Teaching Models Approach. (Orig.). 1981. pap. 14.95 (ISBN 0-8077-2641-9). Tchrs Coll.

Beauchamp, George A. Curriculum Theory. 4th ed. LC 80-84104. 225p. 1981. pap. text ed. 8.50 (ISBN 0-87581-270-8). Peacock Pubs.

Caribbean Co-Operation for Curriculum Develoment & Reform in Teacher Training. (Experiments & Innovations in Education Ser.: No. 39). 46p. 1980. pap. 3.50 (U 1041, UNESCO). Unipub.

Curriculum: U. S. Capacities, Developing Countries' Needs. 244p. 1979. 14.00 (IIE). Unipub.

Davis, Ed. Teachers As Curriculum Evaluators. (Classroom & Curriculum in Australia Ser.: No. 4). 180p. 1981. text ed. 21.00x (ISBN 0-86861-090-9, 2517); pap. text ed. 9.95x (ISBN 0-86861-098-4, 2518). Allen Unwin.

Gail, Meredith D. Handbook for Evaluating & Selecting Curriculum Materials. 190p. 1981. pap. text ed. 9.95 (ISBN 0-205-07301-8, 2373017). Allyn.

Kelly, A. V. Curriculum Context. 1980. 18.50 (IntlDept). Har-Row.

Kissock, Craig. Curriculum Planning for Social Studies & Teaching Cultural Approach. 125p. 1981. 28.00 (ISBN 0-471-27868-8, Pub. by Wiley Interscience). Wiley.

Lawn, Martin. Rethinking Curriculum Studies: A Radical Approach. 224p. 1981. 27.95 (ISBN 0-470-27097-7). Halsted Pr.

McNeil, John D. Curriculum: A Comprehensive Approach. 2nd ed. 1981. text ed. 14.95 (ISBN 0-316-56308-0). Little.

CURRY COUNTY, OREGON

Jones, Edith W. Excerpts from the Curry County Echoes, Vol. II. (Illus.). 110p. (Orig.). 1981. pap. 47.00 (ISBN 0-932368-08-5). Curry County.

CURTAIN WALLS

see Walls

CURVED SURFACES

see Surfaces

CURVES, ALGEBRAIC

see also Geometry, Algebraic

Campillo, A. Algebroid Curves in Positive Characteristic. (Lecture Notes in Mathematics Ser.: Vol. 813). 168p. 1980. pap. text ed. 11.80 (ISBN 0-387-10022-9). Springer-Verlag.

Gerritzen, L. & Van Der Put, M. Schottky Groups & Mumford Curves. (Lecture Notes in Mathematics: Vol. 817). 317p. 1980. pap. 19.50 (ISBN 0-387-10229-9). Springer-Verlag.

Griffiths, Phillip A. An Introduction to the Theory of Special Divisors on Algebraic Curves. LC 80-16415. (Conference Board of Mathematical Sciences Ser.). 1980. 5.60 (ISBN 0-8218-1694-2). Am Math.

Orzech. Plane Algerbraic Curves. 224p. 1981. 29.75 (ISBN 0-8247-1159-9). Dekker.

CUSTER, GEORGE ARMSTRONG, 1839-1876

Hammer, Kenneth M. The Glory March. (Custeriana Monograph Ser.: No. 7). 1980. pap. 2.50. Monroe County Lib.

Marquis, Thomas B. Keep the Last Bullet for Yourself: The True Story of Custer's Last Stand. Irvine, Keith & Faherty, Robert, eds. LC 75-39093. (Illus.). 1980. pap. 5.95 (ISBN 0-917256-14-X). Ref Pubns.

Masters, Joseph G. Shadows Fall Across the Little Horn: Custer's Last Stand. 62p. 1951. 20.00. South Pass Pr.

Van De Water, Frederic F. Glory Hunter: A Life of General Custer. LC 63-20840. (Illus.). 1964. Repr. of 1934 ed. 15.00. Argosy.

CUSTODY OF CHILDREN

Gap Committee on the Family. Divorce, Child Custody & the Family, Vol. 10. LC 80-25935. (Publications Ser.: No. 106). 1980. pap. 12.95 (ISBN 0-910958-10-6, 106, Mental Health Materials Center). Adv Psychiatry.

CUSTOMS UNIONS

El-Agra, A. M. & Jones, A. J. Theory of Customs Unions. 1981. 25.00 (ISBN 0-312-79737-0). St Martin.

CUTANEOUS DISEASES

see Skin-Diseases

CUTIS

see Skin

CUTTING FLUIDS

see Metal-Working Lubricants

CUTTING OF GEMS

see Gem Cutting

CYANIDES

Doudoroff, Peter. A Critical Review of Recent Literature on Toxicity of Cyanides to Fish. LC 80-68588. 71p. (Orig.). 1980. pap. 3.60 (ISBN 0-89364-039-5, API 847-87000). Am Petroleum.

CYBERNETICS

see also Biological Control Systems; Bionics; Computers; Information Theory; Information Theory in Psychology; System Analysis; Systems Engineering

Trappl, Robert, et al, eds. Progress in Cybernetics & Systems Research, 5 vols. Incl. Vol. 1. General Systems, Engineering Systems, Biocybernetics & Neural Systems. 24.50 (ISBN 0-470-88475-4); Vol. 2. Socio-Economic Systems, Cognition & Learning, Systems Education, Organization & Management. 24.50 (ISBN 0-470-88476-2); Vol. 3. General Systems Methodology, Fuzzy Mathematics & Fuzzy Systems, Biocybernetics & Theoretical Neurobiology. 40.00 (ISBN 0-470-26371-7); Vol. 4. Cybernetics of Cognition & Learning, Structure & Dynamics of Socioeconomic Systems, Health Care Systems, Engineering Systems Methodology. 40.00 (ISBN 0-470-99380-4); Vol. 5. Organization & Management, Organic Problem-Solving in Management System Approach in Urban & Regional Planning, Computer Performance, Control & Evaluation of Computer Linguistics. 50.00 (ISBN 0-470-26553-1). LC 75-6641. 1975-79. Halsted Pr.

CYCLES (BICYCLES)

see Bicycles and Tricycles

CYCLES IN BIOLOGY

see Biological Rhythms

CYCLING

see also Bicycles and Tricycles; Motorcycles; Motorcycling

Allen, John S. The Complete Book of Bicycle Commuting. (Illus.). 320p. 1980. 12.95 (ISBN 0-87857-342-9); pap. 9.95 (ISBN 0-87857-344-5). Rodale Pr Inc.

Editors of Bicycling. Best Bicycle Tours, Vol. 2. Fones, Kathy, ed. (Bicycling Magazine Book Ser.). (Illus.). 96p. (Orig.). 1981. pap. 2.95 (ISBN 0-87857-324-0). Rodale Pr Inc.

Faria, I. E. & Cavanagh, P. R. The Psychology & Biomechanics of Cycling. 179p. 1978. 14.95 (ISBN 0-471-25490-8). Wiley.

Lieb, Thom. Everybody's Book of Bicycle Riding. McCullagh, Chuck, ed. (Illus.). 336p. 1981. 12.95 (ISBN 0-87857-322-4); pap. 9.95 (ISBN 0-87857-323-2). Rodale Pr Inc.

MacFarlan, Allan A. Boy's Book of Biking. (Illus.). 1970. pap. 1.25 (ISBN 0-671-29739-2). PB.

Madden, Virginia M. Across America on the Yellow Brick Road. (Illus.). 1980. pap. 8.95 (ISBN 0-937760-00-5). Crow Canyon.

Miller, Christian. Daisy, Daisy: A Journey Across America on a Bicycle. LC 80-2946. 192p. 1981. 11.95 (ISBN 0-385-17475-6). Doubleday.

Neumann, Phyllis L. Sonoma County Bike Trails. (Illus.). 112p. (Orig.). pap. 3.95 (ISBN 0-686-28739-8). Sonoma County.

Sloane, Eugene A. The All New Complete Book of Bicycling. (Illus.). 1981. 19.95 (ISBN 0-671-24967-3). S&S.

Teresi, Dick & Colligan, Doug. The Cyclist's Manual. LC 76-1344. (Illus.). 1981. 14.95 (ISBN 0-8069-5562-7); lib. bdg. 13.29 (ISBN 0-8069-5563-5). Sterling.

CYCLOIDS, MIXED (CHEMISTRY)
see Heterocyclic Compounds

CYCLONES (MACHINES)
see Separators (Machines)

CYCLOPEDIAS
see Encyclopedias and Dictionaries

CYMRIC LANGUAGE
see Welsh Language

CYPRUS–DESCRIPTION AND TRAVEL

Blue Guide - Cyprus. 1980. pap. 22.95 (ISBN 0-528-84617-5). Rand.

Maier, Franz G. Cyprus. 1968. 11.95 (ISBN 0-236-17602-1, Pub. by Paul Elek). Merrimack Bk Serv.

CYPRUS–HISTORY

Polyviou, Polyvios G. Cyprus: Conflict & Negotiation 1960-1980. 246p. 1981. text ed. 40.00x (ISBN 0-8419-0683-1). Holmes & Meier.

CYPRUS–POLITICS AND GOVERNMENT

Polyviou, Polyvios G. Cyprus: Conflict & Negotiation 1960-1980. 246p. 1981. text ed. 40.00x (ISBN 0-8419-0683-1). Holmes & Meier.

CYSTOSCOPY
see Bladder

CYSTOSTOMY
see Bladder

CYSTS
see also Tumors

Harnisch, Herbert. Clinical Aspects & Treatment of Cysts of the Jaws. (Illus.). 237p. 1974. 38.00. Quint Pub Co.

CYTOGENETICS

Atchley, W. R. & Woodruff, David S. Evolution & Speciation: Essays in Honor of M.J.D. White. (Illus.). 496p. Date not set. price not set (ISBN 0-521-23823-4). Cambridge U Pr.

Blackman, R. L., et al. Insect Cytogenetics. (Royal Entomological Society of London Symposium Ser.). 272p. 1981. 69.95 (ISBN 0-470-27126-4). Halsted Pr.

Cytogenetics in Animal Reproduction. (Illus.). 96p. 1981. 45.00 (ISBN 0-85198-444-4, CAB 8, CAB). Unipub.

Goldstein, L. & Prescott, David, eds. Cell Biology: A Comprehensive Treatise, 2 vols. Incl. Vol. 1. 1978. 47.00 (ISBN 0-12-289501-0); by subscription 40.50 (ISBN 0-686-61588-3); Vol. 2. The Structure & Replication of Genetic Material. 1979. 47.00, by subscription 40.50 (ISBN 0-12-289502-9). LC 78-10457. Acad Pr.

CYTOGENETICS–DICTIONARIES

Bergsma, Daniel, ed. An International System for Human Cytogenetic Namenclature. LC 78-61295. (S. Karger Ser.: Vol. 14, No. 8). 1978. 10.00. March of Dimes.

CYTOLOGY
see also Cell Differentiation; Cells; Cytogenetics

Boeck, P., et al. Peroxisomes & Related Particles in Animal Tissues. (Cell Biology Monographs: Vol. 7). (Illus.). 250p. 1980. 79.00 (ISBN 0-387-81582-1). Springer-Verlag.

Bourne, G. H. & Danielli, J. F. International Review of Cytology, Vol. 69. (Serial Publications Ser.). 1981. 38.00 (ISBN 0-12-364469-0). Acad Pr.

Bourne, G. H. & Danielli, J. F., eds. International Review of Cytology, Vol. 71. 1981. write for info. (ISBN 0-12-364471-2). Acad Pr.

Bourne, G. H. & Muggleton-Harris, Audrey L., eds. International Review of Cytology: Supplement 12. (Serial Publication). 1981. price not set (ISBN 0-12-364373-2). Acad Pr.

Bourne, Geoffrey & Danielli, James, eds. International Review of Cytology, Vol. 72. (Serial Publication). 1981. price not set (ISBN 0-12-364472-0). Acad Pr.

Bourne, Geoffrey H. & Danielli, James F., eds. International Review of Cytology, Vol. 70. (Serial Publication). 1981. price not set (ISBN 0-12-364470-4). Acad Pr.

Daems, W. T., et al, eds. Cell Biological Aspects of Disease: The Plasma Membrane & Lysosomes. (Boerhaave Series for Postgraduate Medical Education: No. 19). 330p. 1981. PLB 68.50 (ISBN 90-6021-466-8, Pub. by Leiden U Pr). Kluwer Boston.

Fawcett, Don. The Cell. 2nd ed. (Illus.). 928p. 1981. text ed. write for info. (ISBN 0-7216-3584-9). Saunders.

Goldstein, L. & Prescott, David, eds. Cell Biology: A Comprehensive Treatise, 2 vols. Incl. Vol. 1. 1978. 47.00 (ISBN 0-12-289501-0); by subscription 40.50 (ISBN 0-686-61588-3); Vol. 2. The Structure & Replication of Genetic Material. 1979. 47.00, by subscription 40.50 (ISBN 0-12-289502-9). LC 78-10457. Acad Pr.

Hendy, Bruce. Membrane Physiology & Cell Excitation. 160p. 1980. 30.00x (Pub. by Croom Helm England). State Mutual Bk.

Jope, Charlene A. Cellular & Molecular Laboratory Manual. 64p. 1981. pap. text ed. 5.95 (ISBN 0-8403-2353-0). Kendall-Hunt.

Kline, Tilde S. Handbook of Fine Needle Aspiration Biopsy Cytology. (Illus.). 210p. 1981. text ed. 27.50 (ISBN 0-8016-2701-X). Mosby.

Koss, Leopold G. & Coleman, Dulcie V. Advances in Clinical Cytology. LC 80-49874. 380p. 1980. text ed. 66.95 (ISBN 0-407-00174-3). Butterworths.

Leopoldo & De Meis. The Sarcoplasmic Reticulum: With Special Reference to Transport & Energy Transduction. (Transport in the Life Sciences Ser.). 150p. 1981. 25.00 (ISBN 0-471-05025-3, Pub. by Wiley-Interscience). Wiley.

Schwartz, Lagar M. & Azar, Miguel M., eds. Advanced Cell Biology. 1168p. 1981. text ed. 39.50 (ISBN 0-442-27471-8). Van Nos Reinhold.

Schweiger, H. G., ed. International Cell Biology 1980 - 1981. (Illus.). 1180p. 1981. 68.00 (ISBN 0-387-10475-5). Springer-Verlag.

Steer, M. W. Understanding Cell Structure. (Illus.). 120p. Date not set. price not set (ISBN 0-521-23745-9); pap. text ed. price not set (ISBN 0-521-28198-9). Cambridge U Pr.

Takahashi, Masayoshi. Color Atlas of Cancer Cytology. 2nd ed. LC 80-85297. (Illus.). 550p. 1981. 125.00 (ISBN 0-89640-050-6). Igaku-Shoin.

Vasiliev, J. M. & Gelfand, I. M. Neoplastic & Normal Cells in Culture. LC 80-40075. (Development & Cell Biology: No. 8). (Illus.). 300p. Date not set. price not set (ISBN 0-521-23149-3). Cambridge U Pr.

CYTOPATHOLOGY
see Pathology, Cellular

CYTOTOXIC DRUGS
see Antineoplastic Agents

CZARTORYSKI, ADAM JERZY, KSIAZE, 1770-1861

Kukiel, Marian. Czartoryski & European Unity: 1770-1861. LC 80-22899. (Poland's Millenium Ser. of the Kosciuszko Foundation). (Illus.). xvii, 354p. 1981. Repr. of 1955 ed. lib. bdg. 35.00x (ISBN 0-313-22511-7, KUCZ). Greenwood.

CZECH LANGUAGE

Gardiner, Duncan B. Intonation & Music: The Semantics of Czech Prosody. LC 79-67358. (Physsardt Series in Prague Linguistics: No. 2). (Illus.). 1980. pap. 10.00 (ISBN 0-916062-04-X). Physsardt.

Kolafova, V. & Slaba, D. Czech-English-Czech Dictionary. (For Travel Ser.). 394p. 1979. text ed. write for info. (ISBN 0-89918-302-6). Vanous.

CZECHOSLOVAKIA–HISTORY

Krystufek, Zdenek. The Soviet Regime in Czechoslovakia. (East European Monographs: No. 81). 320p. 1981. text ed. 21.00x (ISBN 0-914710-75-3). East Eur Quarterly.

Levy, Alan. Many Heroes. 2nd ed. LC 80-65002. 384p. 1980. Repr. of 1972 ed. 12.50 (ISBN 0-933256-12-4, Pub. by Second Chance Pr). Watts.

Seton-Weston, R. W. A History of the Czechs & Slovaks. 413p. 1980. Repr. of 1943 ed. lib. bdg. 50.00 (ISBN 0-8492-2974-X). R West.

CZECHOSLOVAKIA–POLITICS AND GOVERNMENT

Taborsky, Edward. President Edvard Benes, Between East & West: 1938-1948. LC 80-83829. (Publication Ser.: No. 246). (Illus.). 280p. 1981. 19.95 (ISBN 0-8179-7461-X). Hoover Inst Pr.

D

DACTYLOGRAPHY
see Fingerprints

DACTYLOLOGY
see Deaf–Means of Communication

DADAISM

Tzara, Tristan. Seven Dada Manifestos. Wright, Barbara, tr. 1979. 8.95 (ISBN 0-7145-3557-5); pap. 4.95. Riverrun NY.

DAHLIAS

Hammett, Keith. The World of Dahlias. (Illus.). 144p. 1980. 17.50 (ISBN 0-589-01265-7, Pub. by Reed Bks Australia). C E Tuttle.

DAILY READINGS (SPIRITUAL EXERCISES)
see Devotional Calendars

DAIRIES
see Dairying

DAIRY INDUSTRY
see Dairying

DAIRY PRODUCTS
see also Dairying;
also names of specific dairy products, e.g. milk, cheese, etc.

Hostage, Jacqueline. Living...Without Milk. 3rd ed. LC 78-72504. (Illus.). 128p. (Orig.). 1981. text ed. 7.95 (ISBN 0-932620-06-X); pap. 3.95 (ISBN 0-932620-05-1). Betterway Pubns.

DAIRYING
see also Cheese; Cows; Dairy Products

Cullity, Maurice. The History of Dairying in Western Australia. 488p. 1980. 35.00x (ISBN 0-85564-177-0, Pub. by U of West Australia Pr Australia). Intl Schol Bk Serv.

Lowe, F. R. Milking Machines: A Comprehensive Guide for Farmers, Herdsmen & Students. (Illus.). 200p. 1981. 30.00 (ISBN 0-08-024381-9); pap. 15.00 (ISBN 0-08-024382-7). Pergamon.

DAKOTA INDIANS
see Indians of North America–The West

DAMASCUS

Londonderry, Robert S. A Journey to Damascus, Through Egypt, Nubia, Arabia Petroea, Palestine & Syria. LC 80-1925. 1981. Repr. of 1947 ed. 69.50 (ISBN 0-404-18976-8). AMS Pr.

DAMPING (MECHANICS)
see also Shock (Mechanics)

Torvik, P. J., ed. Damping Applications for Vibration Control. (AMD: Vol. 38). 160p. 1980. 24.00 (G00171). ASME.

DAMS
see also Flood Dams and Reservoirs
also particular dams, e.g. Grand Coulee Dam

Environmental Effects of Dams & Impoundments in Canada: Experience & Procepts. (Bulletin: No. 205). 1981. pap. 4.75 (ISBN 0-660-10485-7, SSC 147, SSC). Unipub.

Thomas Telford Editorial Staff, Ltd. Arch Dams: A Review of British Research & Development. 168p. 1980. 60.00x (ISBN 0-901948-14-4, Pub. by Telford England). State Mutual Bk.

DANCE THERAPY

Lyon, Barbara. Dance Toward Wholeness: Moving Methods to Heal Individuals & Groups. Adams, Doug, ed. (Illus.). 112p. 1981. pap. text ed. 5.95 (ISBN 0-686-28737-1). Sharing Co.

DANCERS

Montague, Sarah. Pas De Deux: Great Partnerships in Dance. LC 80-54502. (Illus.). 112p. 1981. text ed. 12.50x (ISBN 0-87663-346-7); pap. 7.95x (ISBN 0-87663-553-2). Universe.

Salter, Elizabeth. Helpmann: The Authorised Biography. (Illus.). 247p. 1981. text ed. 18.50x (ISBN 0-87663-349-1). Universe.

Solrac, Odelot. Tortola Valencia & Her Times. 1981. 11.95 (ISBN 0-533-04563-0). Vantage.

DANCING
see also Ballet; Ballroom Dancing; Dancers; Modern Dance; Tap Dancing
also names of dances

Haselbach, Barbara. Improvisation, Dance, & Movement. Murray, Margaret, tr. from Ger. Orig. Title: Improvisation, Tanz, Bewegung. 1980. Repr. of 1976 ed. pap. 19.00 (ISBN 0-918812-15-1). Magnamusic.

Hayden, Melissa. Dancer to Dancer: Advice for Today's Dancer. LC 80-940. (Illus.). 192p. 1981. 19.95 (ISBN 0-385-15582-4, Anchor Pr). Doubleday.

--Dancer to Dancer: Advice for Today's Dancer. LC 80-940. (Illus.). 192p. 1981. 19.95 (ISBN 0-385-15550-6, Anch). Doubleday.

Hays, Joan F. Modern Dance: A Biochemical Approach to Teaching. (Illus.). 312p. 1981. pap. text ed. 13.95 (ISBN 0-8016-2179-8). Mosby.

Mouzaki, Rozanna. Greek Dances for Americans. Dallas-Damis, Athena, tr. LC 77-25604. (Illus.). 192p. 1981. pap. 9.95 (ISBN 0-385-14041-X). Doubleday.

The Nature of Dance As a Creative Art Activity. 1980. 12.50x (ISBN 0-912536-11-X). Mettler Studios.

Richard, Glasstone. Dancing As a Career for Men. LC 80-54339. (Illus.). 120p. (gr. 10 up). 1981. 8.95 (ISBN 0-8069-4640-7); lib. bdg. 9.29 (ISBN 0-8069-4641-5). Sterling.

DANCING–HISTORY

Clarke, Mary, et al. A History of Dance. 1981. 35.00 (ISBN 0-517-54282-X). Crown.

Morgan, Barbara. Martha Graham: Sixteen Dances in Photographs. rev. ed. LC 80-81766. (Illus.). 168p. 1980. Repr. of 1941 ed. 35.00 (ISBN 0-87100-176-4). Morgan.

Sorell, Walter. Dance in Its Time. LC 80-913. (Illus.). 480p. 1981. 19.95 (ISBN 0-385-13418-5). Doubleday.

DANCING–JUVENILE LITERATURE

McCarter, Albert D. & Reed, Glenn. I'm Dancing! (Illus.). 32p. (gr. k-3). 1981. 9.95 (ISBN 0-686-69284-5). Scribner.

Pollack. The Disco Handbook. (gr. 7-12). 1980. pap. 1.50 (ISBN 0-590-30003-2, Schol Pap). Schol Bk Serv.

Sorine, D. Imagine That! It's Modern Dance. LC 80-19232. (Illus.). 48p. (ps-3). 1981. PLB 4.99 (ISBN 0-394-84474-2); PLB 8.95 (ISBN 0-394-94474-7). Knopf.

DANCING–LIBRARIES AND MUSEUMS
see Music Libraries

DANCING–STUDY AND TEACHING

Hayes, Elizabeth R. Dance Composition & Production. LC 80-69958. (Illus.). 210p. 1981. pap. 8.95 (ISBN 0-87127-121-4). Dance Horiz.

Wydro, Luigi & Wydro, Kenneth. The Luigi Jazz Dance Technique. LC 80-1091. (Illus.). 192p. Date not set. pap. 12.95 (ISBN 0-385-15588-3, Dolph). Doubleday.

DANCING–THERAPEUTIC USE
see Dance Therapy

DANCING–LATIN AMERICA

Laird, Walter. Technique of Latin Dancing. rev. ed. (Illus.). 180p. 1980. pap. text ed. 19.50 (ISBN 0-392-07535-0, LTB). Soccer.

DANCING–UNITED STATES

Livingston, Peter, et al. The Complete Book of Country Swing & Western Dance. LC 80-70555. 1981. pap. 9.95 (ISBN 0-385-17601-5, Dolp). Doubleday.

Siegel, Marcia B. The Shapes of Change. 400p. 1981. pap. 3.95 (ISBN 0-380-53892-X, 53892, Discus). Avon.

Terry, Walter. The Dance in America. (Dance Ser.). (Illus.). xiv, 274p. 1981. Repr. of 1971 ed. lib. bdg. 25.00 (ISBN 0-306-76059-2). Da Capo.

DANCING, BALLET
see Ballet Dancing

DANES IN FOREIGN COUNTRIES

Hale, Frederick. Danes in Wisconsin. LC 80-26088. (Illus., Orig.). 1981. pap. 2.00 (ISBN 0-87020-205-7). State Hist Soc Wis.

DANIEL, THE PROPHET–JUVENILE LITERATURE

Daniel & the Lions. (Tell-a-Bible Story Ser.). (Illus.). 28p. bds. 0.69 (ISBN 0-686-68640-3, 3684). Standard Pub.

DANTE ALIGHIERI, 1265-1321

Boyde, P. Dante: Philomythes & Philosopher. LC 80-40551. (Illus.). 520p. Date not set. 55.00 (ISBN 0-521-23598-7). Cambridge U Pr.

Butler, Arthur J. Dante His Times & His Work. 201p. 1980. Repr. of 1895 ed. lib. bdg. 30.00 (ISBN 0-8495-0475-9). Arden Lib.

Fowlie, Wallace. A Reading of Dante's Inferno. LC 80-19025. 248p. 1981. lib. bdg. 18.00 (ISBN 0-226-25887-4); pap. 6.50 (ISBN 0-226-25888-2). U of Chicago Pr.

Grayson, Cecil. The World of Dante: Essays on Dante & His Times. (Illus.). 204p. 1980. text ed. 36.00x. Oxford U Pr.

Nolan, David, ed. Dante Soundings. 1981. 22.50x (ISBN 0-8476-3633-X). Rowman.

DARK AGES
see Middle Ages

DARK ROOMS
see Photography–Studios and Dark Rooms

DARKROOM TECHNIQUE IN PHOTOGRAPHY
see Photography–Processing

DARROW, CLARENCE SEWARD, 1857-1938

Hunsberger, Willard D. Clarence Darrow: A Bibliography. LC 80-26317. viii, 215p. 1981. 12.50 (ISBN 0-8108-1384-X). Scarecrow.

DARWIN, CHARLES ROBERT, 1809-1882

Angell, J. R., et al. Darwinism. Bd. with Natural Inheritance. Galton, Francis. (Contributions to the History of Psychology Ser., Vol. IV, Pt. D: Comparative Psychology). 1978. 30.00 (ISBN 0-89093-173-9). U Pubns Amer.

Gruber, Howard E. Darwin on Man: A Psychological Study of Scientific Creativity. 2nd ed. LC 80-28453. 1981. lib. bdg. price not set (ISBN 0-226-31008-6); pap. price not set (ISBN 0-226-31007-8). U of Chicago Pr.

Kelly, Alfred. The Descent of Darwin: The Popularization of Darwinism in Germany, 1860-1914. LC 80-19445. 200p. 1981. 18.50x (ISBN 0-8078-1460-1). U of NC Pr.

DARWINISM
see Evolution

DATA BASE MANAGEMENT

Barber, Derek, ed. Data Networks: Development & Uses. 690p. 1980. pap. text ed. 160.00x (ISBN 0-903796-59-7, Pub. by Online Conferences England). Renouf.

Bernard, Joseph, et al. HALO: A Data Base Management System. 1981. pap. 12.95 (ISBN 0-8359-2720-2). Reston.

Date, C. J. Introduction to Database Systems. 3rd ed. LC 80-17603. (IBM Systems Programming Ser.). (Illus.). 704p. 1981. text ed. 20.95 (ISBN 0-201-14471-9). A-W.

The Development of Integrated Data Bases for Social, Economic & Demographic Statistics. (Studies in Methods Ser. F: No. 27). 62p. 1979. pap. 6.00 (ISBN 0-686-68950-X, UN79/17/14, UN). Unipub.

Federal Communications Commission Planning Conference November 8 & 9, 1976 & Hopewell, Lynn. Computers & Communications: Proceedings. (Illus.). 197p. 1976. pap. 10.00 (ISBN 0-88283-022-8). AFIPS Pr.

Fernandez, Eduardo B., et al. Database Security & Integrity. LC 80-15153. (IBM Systems Programming Ser.). (Illus.). 288p. 1981. text ed. 18.95 (ISBN 0-201-14467-0). A-W.

Gaydasch, Alex. Principles of Electronic Data Processing Management. 300p. 1982. text ed. 18.95 (ISBN 0-8359-5604-0); instr's. manual free (ISBN 0-8359-5605-9). Reston.
Korfhage, Robert R., ed. Computer Networks & Communication. (The Information Technology Ser.: Vol. IV). 150p. 1977. pap. 20.00 (ISBN 0-88283-017-1). AFIPS Pr.
Martin, J. End User's Guide to Data Base. 1981. 21.50 (ISBN 0-13-277129-2). P-H.
Olle, T. W. The CODASYL Approach to Data Base Management. 287p. 1978. 26.95 (ISBN 0-471-99579-7, 1-320). Wiley.
Perkinson, Richard C. Handbook of Data Analysis & Data Base Design. 175p. 1981. pap. 29.50 (ISBN 0-89435-045-5). QED Info Sci.
Planning the Purchase & Use of Data Base Management Systems. 1981. pap. 5.00 (ISBN 0-918734-29-0). Reymont.
Puzman, Josef & Porizek, Radoslav. Communication Control in Computer Networks. (Wiley Series in Computing). 300p. 1981. 36.00 (ISBN 0-471-27894-7, Pub. by Wiley Interscience). Wiley.
Rubin, Martin L. Handbook of Data Processing Management, 6 vols. 1971. Set. 175.00 (ISBN 0-442-80343-5). Van Nos Reinhold.
Tsichritzis, Dennis & Klug, Anthony, eds. The ANSI-X3-SPARC DBMS Framework Report of the Study Group on Database Management Systems. (Illus.). xii, 19p. 1978. saddle-stitch 7.00 (ISBN 0-88283-013-9). AFIPS Pr.
Vetter, M. & Maddison, R. Data Base Design Methodology. 1980. 28.00 (ISBN 0-13-196535-2). P-H.

DATA DISPLAY SYSTEMS
see Information Display Systems

DATA PROCESSING
see Electronic Data Processing; Information Storage and Retrieval Systems
FAO-UNEP Workshop on the Aquatic Sciences & Fisheries Information System (ASFIS) (FAO Fisheries Report Ser.: No. 243). 49p. 1981. pap. 6.00 (ISBN 92-5-000991-7, F2109, FAO). Unipub.

DATA SMOOTHING FILTERS
see Digital Filters (Mathematics)

DATA TRANSMISSION SYSTEMS
see also Library Information Networks
Barber, Derek, ed. Data Networks: Development & Uses. 690p. 1980. pap. text ed. 160.00x (ISBN 0-903796-59-7, Pub. by Online Conferences England). Renouf.
Tugal, Dogan & Tugal, Osman. Data Transmission: Analysis; Design; Applications. (Illus.). 384p. 1982. 19.50 (ISBN 0-07-065427-1). McGraw.

DATE ETIQUETTE
see Dating (Social Customs)

DATES, BOOKS OF
see Calendars

DATING (SOCIAL CUSTOMS)
Eisner. Dating & Hanging Out. (gr. 7-12). Date not set. pap. cancelled (ISBN 0-590-30031-8, Schol Pap). Schol Bk Serv.
Shaw, Mara L. How to Meet Men...and Be Successful with Them. 1981. 9.95 (ISBN 0-9605602-0-3). Shaw Inc.
Trabucco, Peter D. Panning for Gold in a Single's Bar. (Illus.). 96p. (Orig.). 1980. pap. 6.95 (ISBN 0-9605106-0-5). PT Marketing.
Weber, Eric. How to Pick up Girls. 1981. 4.95 (ISBN 0-914094-00-9). Green Hill.

DATSUN (AUTOMOBILE)
see Automobiles, Foreign–Types–Datsun

DAVID, KING OF ISRAEL
Blaikie, William G. David, King of Israel. Date not set. 14.50 (ISBN 0-86524-054-X). Klock & Klock.
Castleman, Robbie. David: Man After God's Own Heart, 2 vols. (Fisherman Bible Studyguide Ser.). 72p. 1981. saddle stitched 2.25 ea. Vol. 1 (ISBN 0-87788-164-2). Vol. 2 (ISBN 0-87788-165-0). Shaw Pubs.
Petersen, Mark E. Three Kings of Israel. LC 80-36697. 179p. 1980. 6.95 (ISBN 0-87747-829-5). Deseret Bk.
Pink, Arthur W. The Life of David, 2 vols. in one. (Giant Summit Ser.). 768p. 1981. pap. 10.95 (ISBN 0-8010-7061-9). Baker Bk.

DAVID, KING OF ISRAEL–JUVENILE LITERATURE
David & Goliath. (Tell-a-Bible Story Ser.). (Illus.). 28p. bds. 0.69 (ISBN 0-686-68639-X, 3683). Standard Pub.

DAVID, JACQUES-LOUIS, 1748-1825
Brookner, Anita. Jacques-Louis David. LC 79-3386. (Icon Editions). (Illus.). 1981. 35.00 (ISBN 0-06-430507-4, HarpT). Har-Row.

DA VINCI, LEONARDO
see Leonardo Da Vinci, 1452-1519

DAVIS, THOMAS OSBORNE, 1814-1845
Yeats, William B. Tribute to Thomas Davis. 55p. 1980. Repr. of 1947 ed. lib. bdg. 8.50 (ISBN 0-8492-3121-3). R West.

DAY CAMPS
see Camps

DAY CARE CENTERS
see also Nursery Schools
Anholt, Uni V. In Search of Heffalumps. (Illus.). 88p. (Orig.). pap. 5.95 (ISBN 0-9601996-0-8). Beeberry Bks.
Endsley, Richard & Bradbard, Marilyn. Quality Day Care: A Handbook of Choices for Parents & Caregivers. (Illus.). 256p. 1981. 13.95 (Spectrum); pap. 5.95. P-H.
Kamerman, Sheila B. & Kahn, Alfred J. Child Care, Family Benefits & Working Parents. (Illus.). 352p. 1981. text ed. 25.00x (ISBN 0-231-05170-0). Columbia U Pr.

DAY DREAMS
see Fantasy

DAY NURSERIES
see Day Care Centers

DDT (INSECTICIDE)
Dunlap, Thomas R. DDT: Scientists, Citizens, & Public Policy. LC 80-8546. 304p. 1981. 18.50x (ISBN 0-691-04680-8). Princeton U Pr.

DEAD SEA SCROLLS
Nickelsburg, George W. Jewish Literature Between the Bible & the Mishnah: A Historical & Literary Introduction. LC 80-16176. 352p. 1981. 19.95 (ISBN 0-8006-0649-3, 1-649). Fortress.

DEAF
see also Children, Deaf
Collier, Charles. Essay on the Principles of Education, Physiologically Considered. Bd. with Art of Instructing the Infant Deaf & Dumb. (Contributions to the History of Psychology, Vol. V, Pt. B: Psychometrics & Educational Psychology). 1980. Repr. of 1856 ed. 30.00 (ISBN 0-89093-319-7). U Pubns Amer.
Gannon, Jack. Deaf Heritage: A Narrative History of Deaf America. 1981. text ed. 19.00x (ISBN 0-913072-38-9); pap. text ed. 12.00x (ISBN 0-913072-39-7). Natl Assn Deaf.
Richards, Judith. How Does It Feel to Be Deaf? (Illus.). (gr. 4-7). Date not set. PLB price not set (ISBN 0-671-34030-1). Messner.

DEAF–EDUCATION
see also Deaf–Means of Communication; Teachers of the Deaf
Arrowsmith, John P. Art of Instructing the Infant Deaf & Dumb: Including De L'Epee's Method of Educating Mutes. (Contributions to the History of Psychology B, Psychometrics & Educational Psychology Ser.). 1980. Repr. of 1819 ed. 30.00 (ISBN 0-89093-319-7). U Pubns Amer.
Naiman, Doris. Education for Severely Handicapped Hearing Impaired Students. 84p. 1981. pap. text ed. 6.95x (ISBN 0-913072-34-6). Natl Assn Deaf.
O'Neill, John J. & Oyer, Herbert J. Visual Communication for the Hard of Hearing: History, Research & Methods. 2nd ed. (Illus.). 224p. 1981. text ed. 14.95 (ISBN 0-13-942466-0). P-H.
Osguthorpe, Russel T. Manager's Guide to the Tutor-Notetaker. 122p. 1980. pap. text ed. 6.00 (ISBN 0-88200-129-9, N6796). Alexander Graham.
--Tutor-Notetaker. 98p. (Orig.). 1980. pap. text ed. 6.00 (ISBN 0-88200-131-0, N6680). Alexander Graham.
Subtelny, Joanne D., ed. Speech Assessment & Speech Improvement for the Hearing Impaired. 420p. 1980. pap. text ed. 19.95 (ISBN 0-88200-138-8, A0138). Alexander Graham.
Van Eijndhoven, J., ed. Religious Education of the Deaf. (Modern Approaches to the Diagnosis & Instruction of Multi-Handicapped Children Ser.: Vol. 11). 168p. 1973. text ed. 20.25 (ISBN 90-237-4111-0, Pub. by Swets Pub. Ser Holland). Swets North Am.

DEAF–MEANS OF COMMUNICATION
Baker, Charlotte & Battison, Robbin. Sign Language & the Deaf Community: Essays in Honor of William Stokoe. (Illus.). 267p. 1981. text ed. 12.00 (ISBN 0-913072-37-0); pap. text ed. 8.00 (ISBN 0-913072-36-2). Natl Assn Deaf.
Hoemann, Harry W. & Lucafo, Rosemarie. I Want to Talk: A Child Model of American Sign Language. 189p. 1981. pap. text ed. 7.95x (ISBN 0-913072-41-9). Natl Assn Deaf.
Kates, Linda & Schein, Jerome. A Complete Guide to Communication with Deaf Blind Persons. (Illus.). 108p. 1981. pap. text ed. 3.95 (ISBN 0-913072-40-0). Natl Assn Deaf.

DEAF, BOOKS FOR THE
Bornstein, Harry. Count & Color. (Signed English Ser.). 18p. 1973. pap. 1.85 (ISBN 0-913580-20-1). Gallaudet Coll.
--The Pet Shop. (Signed English Ser.). 16p. pap. 1.85 (ISBN 0-913580-54-6). Gallaudet Coll.

DEAF MUTES
see Deaf

DEAFNESS
Here are entered works on the lack of sense of hearing, including the lack combined with the inability to speak, i.e. deaf-mutism. Works on the inability to speak whether from any functional or physical case other than deafness are entered under Mutism.
see also Ear; Hearing; Hearing Aids
Fellendorf, George W., ed. Supplement to Bibliography on Deafness: 1977 to 1979. 1980. pap. text ed. 4.95 (ISBN 0-88200-139-6, L9435). Alexander Graham.
Gregory, Peter. Deafness & Public Responsibility. 56p. 1964. pap. text ed. 3.75x (Pub. by Bedford England). Renouf.
Jacobs, Leo M. A Deaf Adult Speaks Out. 2nd, rev. ed. xiv, 192p. 1981. 7.95 (ISBN 0-913580-63-5); pap. 5.95 (ISBN 0-913580-71-6). Gallaudet Coll.
Levin, L. Stefan & Knight, Connie, eds. Genetic & Environmental Hearing Loss: Syndromic & Nonsyndromic. (Birth Defects: Oringinal Article Ser.: Vol. XVI, No. 7). 100p. 1980. write for info. (ISBN 0-8451-1040-3). A R Liss.
Star, Robin R. We Can, Vol. 1. 88p. (gr. 4 up). 1980. PLB 5.00 (ISBN 0-88200-135-3, C2670). Alexander Graham.
--We Can, Vol. 2. 98p. (gr. 4 up). 1980. PLB 5.00 (ISBN 0-88200-136-1, C2786). Alexander Graham.
Stein, Laszlo K., et al. Deafness & Mental Health. 1981. write for info. (ISBN 0-8089-1347-6). Grune.

DEAFNESS IN CHILDREN
see Children, Deaf

DEATH
see also Children and Death; Future Life; Heaven; Hell; Martyrdom; Mortality
Bender, David L., ed. Death & Dying: Opposing Viewpoints. (Opposing Viewpoints Ser.). (gr. 12). 1980. lib. bdg. 8.95 (ISBN 0-89908-331-5); pap. text ed. 3.95 (ISBN 0-89908-306-4). Greenhaven.
Bernard, H. Y. Law of Death & Disposal of the Dead. 2nd ed. 1979. 5.95 (ISBN 0-379-11000-8). Oceana.
Bichat, Xavier. Physiological Researches on Life & Death. Gold, F., tr. from Fr. Bd. with Outlines of Phrenology; Phrenology Examined. (Contributions to the History of Psychology, Vol. II, Pt. E: Physiological Psychology). 1978. Repr. of 1827 ed. 30.00 (ISBN 0-89093-175-5). U Pubns Amer.
Duda, Deborah. Dying at Home with Dignity. (Illus., Orig.). 1981. pap. 7.00 (ISBN 0-686-69339-6). John Muir.
Goodman, Lisl M. Death & the Creative Life. 1981. text ed. price not set (ISBN 0-8261-3500-5). Springer Pub.
Horan, Dennis J. & Mall, David, eds. Death, Dying, & Euthanasia. 1977. 24.00 (ISBN 0-89093-139-9); pap. 10.00 (ISBN 0-89093-140-2). U Pubns Amer.
Sivaram, M. Death & Nachiketas. 192p. 1981. text ed. 15.00x (ISBN 0-7069-1284-5, Pub by Vikas India). Advent Bk.
Wilcox & Sutton. Understanding Death & Dying. 2nd ed. 1981. 10.95 (ISBN 0-88284-122-X). Alfred Pub.

DEATH–JUVENILE LITERATURE
Krementz, Jill. How It Feels When a Parent Dies. LC 80-8808. (Illus.). 128p. 1981. 9.95 (ISBN 0-394-51911-6). Knopf.

DEATH–MEDITATIONS
Hein, Marvin. Like a Shock of Wheat. LC 80-22224. 192p. 1981. pap. 7.95 (ISBN 0-8361-1938-X). Herald Pr.

DEATH–PSYCHOLOGY
see also Children and Death
Furman, Erna. A Child's Parent Dies: Studies in Childhood Bereavement. LC 73-86894. 352p. 1981. pap. 7.95x (ISBN 0-300-02645-5). Yale U Pr.
Grollman, Earl A., ed. What Helped Me: When My Loved One Died. LC 80-68166. 160p. 1981. 9.95 (ISBN 0-8070-3228-X). Beacon Pr.
Marshall, George. Facing Death & Grief. 250p. 1981. 15.95 (ISBN 0-87975-140-1). Prometheus Bks.
Peachey, Mark. Facing Terminal Illness. 72p. 1981. pap. 2.25 (ISBN 0-8361-1948-7). Herald Pr.

DEATH–RELIGIOUS AND MORAL ASPECTS
Brennan, Hill. The Near Death Experience: A Christian Approach. 64p. (Orig.). 1981. pap. 3.50 (ISBN 0-697-01758-3). Wm C Brown.
Kaiser, Otto & Lohse, Eduard. Death & Life. Steely, John E., tr. LC 80-21265. (Biblical Encounter Ser.). 176p. 1981. pap. 6.95 (ISBN 0-687-10332-0). Abingdon.
The New Technologies of Birth & Death: Medical, Legal & Moral Dimensions. LC 80-83425. xvi, 196p. (Orig.). 1980. pap. 8.95 (ISBN 0-935372-07-5). Pope John Ctr.

DEATH, MERCY
see Euthanasia

DEATH AND CHILDREN
see Children and Death

DEATH DUTIES
see Inheritance and Transfer Tax

DEATH IN LITERATURE
Vermeule, Emily. Aspects of Death in Early Greek Art & Poetry. (Sather Classical Lectures Ser.: No. 46). 1981. pap. 7.95 (ISBN 0-520-04404-5, CAL 504). U of Cal Pr.

DEATH PENALTY
see Capital Punishment

DEATH RATE
see Mortality

DEATH VALLEY
Gebhardt, Chuck. Inside Death Valley. rev. 3rd ed. LC 80-83123. (Illus.). 166p. 1980. pap. 5.95 (ISBN 0-9601410-1-4). C Gebhardt.

DEATHBED WORDS
see Last Words

DEBATES AND DEBATING
see also Discussion; Oratory; Parliamentary Practice
Ranney, Austin, ed. Past & Future of Presidential Debates. 1979. pap. 7.25 (ISBN 0-8447-3330-X). Am Enterprise.
Rusher, William A. How to Win Arguments. LC 79-6874. 264p. 1981. 10.95 (ISBN 0-385-15255-8). Doubleday.

DEBENTURES
see Bonds

DEBT
see also Bankruptcy; Collecting of Accounts; Credit
David, Ann. How to Get Out of Debt & Stay Out of Debt. 160p. 1980. 5.95 (ISBN 0-346-12480-8). Cornerstone.

DEBUGGING (ELECTRONIC COMPUTERS)
see also Computer Programming Management
Ghani, Noordin & Farrell, Edward. Microprocessor System Debugging. (Computer Engineering Ser.). 160p. 1981. 28.00 (ISBN 0-471-27860-2, Pub. by Wiley-Interscience). Wiley.
Huffman & Bruce. How to Debug Your Personal Computer. 175p. 1980. pap. 7.95 (ISBN 0-8359-2924-8). Reston.

DEBUSSY, CLAUDE, 1862-1918
Thompson, Oscar. Debussy Man & Artist. 395p. 1980. Repr. of 1940 ed. lib. bdg. 30.00 (ISBN 0-89984-474-X). Century Bookbindery.

DECALOGUE
see Commandments, Ten

DECEIT
see Fraud

DECENNALIA
see Roman Emperors

DECIMAL SYSTEM
Fineberg, Marjorie & Shaw, John. Decimals. LC 79-730043. (Illus.). 1978. pap. text ed. 99.00 (ISBN 0-89290-095-4, A511-SATC). Soc for Visual.
Learning Achievement Corp. Decimals, Percent & Money: Measurement & Transportation. Zak, Therese A., ed. (MATCH Ser.). (Illus.). 144p. 1981. text ed. 5.28 (ISBN 0-07-037114-8, G). McGraw.
Learning Achievement Corporation. Fractions & Food: Fractions, Decimals & Electronic Communications. Zak, Therese A., ed. (MATCH Ser.). (Illus.). 144p. Date not set. text ed. 5.28 (ISBN 0-07-037113-X, G). McGraw.

DECIMAL SYSTEM–PROGRAMMED INSTRUCTION
Soracco, Lionel J., Jr. Math House Proficiency Review Tapes: Operations with Decimals & Percent, Unit B. (YA) (gr. 7 up). 1980. manual & cassettes 159.95 (ISBN 0-917792-04-1). Math Hse.

DECISION (PSYCHOLOGY)
see Decision-Making

DECISION-MAKING
see also Management Games
Alexander Hamilton Institute, Inc. Como los Ejecutivos Toman Decisiones. Jenks, James M., ed. (Illus.). 79p. (Orig., Span.). 1976. pap. 43.75 (ISBN 0-86604-006-4). Hamilton Inst.
--How Executives Make Decisions. Jenks, James M., ed. (Illus.). 79p. (Orig.). 1976. pap. 48.25 (ISBN 0-86604-005-6, A783159). Hamilton Inst.
Fick, G. & Sprague, R. H., Jr., eds. Decision Support Systems--Issues & Challenges: Proceedings of an International Task Foce Meeting, June 23-25, 1980. (IIASA Proceedings: Vol. 11). (Illus.). 190p. 1980. pap. 29.50 (ISBN 0-08-027321-1). Pergamon.
Hammond, Kenneth R., et al. Human Judgement & Decision Making: Theories, Methods & Procedures. 272p. 1980. 25.95 (ISBN 0-03-057567-2). Praeger.
Heller, Frank A. Competence & Power in Managerial Decision-Making. Wilpert, Bernhard, ed. 256p. 1981. 34.50 (ISBN 0-471-27837-8, Pub. by Wiley-Interscience). Wiley.
Hon, David C. Trade-Offs: For the Person Who Can't Have Everything. (Illus.). 150p. 1981. text ed. 14.95 (ISBN 0-89384-048-3). Learning Concepts.
Howell, William C. & Fleishman, Edwin A., eds. Information Processing & Decision Making. (Human Performance & Productivity Ser.: Vol. 2). 1981. professional ref. text 19.95 (ISBN 0-89859-090-6). L Erlbaum Assocs.
McCarty, Michele. Deciding. (Orig.). (gr. 11-12). 1981. pap. text ed. 4.25 (ISBN 0-697-01778-8); tchrs' manual 5.00 (ISBN 0-697-01779-6). Wm C Brown.
Nelkin, Dorothy. Controversy: Politics of Technical Decisions. LC 78-21339. (Focus Editions Ser.: Vol. 8). 256p. 1979. 18.95 (ISBN 0-8039-1209-9); pap. 9.95 (ISBN 0-8039-1210-2). Sage.
Radford, K. J. Modern Managerial Decision Making. 1981. text ed. 17.95 (ISBN 0-8359-4571-5); instr's. manual avail. (ISBN 0-8359-4229-5). Reston.
Taffler, Richard. Answers: Decision-Making Techniques for Managers. rev. ed. (Illus.). 256p. 1981. 13.95 (ISBN 0-13-037861-5, Spectrum); pap. text ed. 6.95 (ISBN 0-13-037853-4). P-H.
Trueman, Richard E. Quantitative Methods for Decision Making in Business. 3rd ed. LC 80-65810. 384p. 1981. text ed. 19.95 (ISBN 0-03-051356-1). Dryden Pr.
Zeleny, Milan. Multiple Criteria Decision Making. 1981. write for info instrs.' manual (ISBN 0-07-072795-3, C); price not set instr's manual (ISBN 0-07-072796-1). McGraw.

DECISION-MAKING–MATHEMATICAL MODELS
Hensher, David A. Applied Discrete-Choice Modelling. Johnson, Lester W., ed. LC 80-23517. 468p. 1980. 29.95 (ISBN 0-470-27078-0). Halsted Pr.

DECISION-MAKING, JUDICIAL
see Judicial Process

DECISION-MAKING IN SCHOOL MANAGEMENT
Tanner, C. Kenneth & Williams, Earl J. Educational Planning & Decision Making: A View Through the Organizational Process. LC 80-8631. 1981. write for info. (ISBN 0-669-04330-3). Lexington Bks.
DECISION PROCESSES
see Decision-Making
DECKS (ARCHITECTURE, DOMESTIC)
Hamilton, Geoff. Design & Build a Patio or Terrace. 4.50. David & Charles.
DECLAMATION
see Public Speaking
DECLARATION OF INDEPENDENCE
see United States–Declaration of Independence
DECORATION, INTERIOR
see Interior Decoration
DECORATION AND ORNAMENT
see also Alphabets; Antiques; Art Objects; Bronzes; Carpets; Decoupage; Design; Design, Decorative; Embroidery; Flower Arrangement; Folk Art; Furniture; Gems; Glass Painting and Staining; Illustration of Books; Interior Decoration; Jewelry; Lettering; Metal-Work; Mosaics; Painting; Pottery; Sculpture; Stencil Work; Table Setting and Decoration; Tapestry; Textile Design; Wood-Carving
Roda, Janet. No-Sew Decorating. (Orig.). 1981. pap. 9.95 (ISBN 0-440-56207-4, Delta). Dell.
DECORATION AND ORNAMENT–ART DECO
see Art Deco
DECORATIVE ARTS
see Decoration and Ornament; Design, Decorative; Interior Decoration
also the specific subjects referred to under these headings
DECORATIVE DESIGN
see Design, Decorative
DECORATIVE LIGHTING
see Lighting, Architectural and Decorative
DECOUPAGE
Kirsch, Francine. Collecting Chromos. LC 80-26616. (Illus.). 288p. 1981. 25.00 (ISBN 0-498-02517-9). A S Barnes.
DECOYS (HUNTING)
Shourds, Harry V. & Hillman, Anthony. Carving Duck Decoys, with Full-Size Patterns for Hollow Contruction. (Illus.). 64p. (Orig.). 1981. pap. price not set (ISBN 0-486-24083-5). Dover.
DEDICATION, FEAST OF
see Hanukkah (Feast of Lights)
DEDUCTION (LOGIC)
see Logic
DEDUCTIVE LOGIC
see Logic
DEEP-SEA DEPOSITS
see Marine Sediments; Sedimentation and Deposition
DEEP-SEA EXPLORATION
see Marine Biology; Marine Fauna; Marine Flora
DEER
see also Antelopes; Elk; White-Tailed Deer
Dasmann, William. Deer Range: Management & Improvement. 2nd ed. LC 80-28280. Orig. Title: If Deer Are to Survive. (Illus.). 175p. 1981. lib. bdg. write for info (ISBN 0-89950-027-7). McFarland & Co.
Herbert, Harry J. The Population Dynamics of the Waterbuck, Kobus ellipsiprymnus (Ogilby, 1833), in the Sabi-Sand Wildtuin. (Mammalia Depicta Ser.). (Illus.). 68p. (Orig.). 1972. pap. text ed. 20.00. Parey Sci Pubs.
Jungius, Harmut. The Biology & Behavior of the Reedbuck (Redunca arundium Boddaert 1785) in the Kruger National Park. (Illus.). 106p. (Orig.). 1971. pap. text ed. 20.00 (ISBN 3-490-02818-X). Parey Sci Pubs.
DEER HUNTING
Sell, Francis E. Art of Successful Deer Hunting. 1980. pap. 5.95 (ISBN 0-932558-13-5). Willow Creek.
Smith, Richard P. Deer Hunting. rev. ed. (Illus.). 256p. 1981. pap. 9.95 (ISBN 0-8117-2132-9). Stackpole.
DEFALCATION
see Embezzlement
DEFAMATION
see Libel and Slander
DEFECTIVE SPEECH
see Speech, Disorders Of
DEFECTS, BIRTH
see Abnormalities, Human
DEFENSE (CRIMINAL PROCEDURE)
see also Trial Practice
Garbus, Martin. Ready for the Defense. 320p. 1971. write for info. FS&G.
DEFENSE (LAW)
see Defense (Criminal Procedure)
DEFENSE (MILITARY SCIENCE)
see Attack and Defense (Military Science)
DEFENSE, PERCEPTUAL
see Perception
DEFENSES, CRIMINAL
see Defense (Criminal Procedure)
DEFORMATIONS (MECHANICS)
see also Continuum Mechanics; Fracture Mechanics; Plasticity; Rheology; Strains and Stresses
Billington, E. W. & Tate, A. The Physics of Deformation & Flow. (Illus.). 720p. 1981. text ed. 59.00 (ISBN 0-07-005285-9, C). McGraw.
DEFORMATIONS, CONTINUOUS
see Homotopy Theory
DEFORMITIES
see Abnormalities, Human
DEGREES, ACADEMIC
Martindale, Don. Ideals & Realities of Academic Advising. (Intercontinental Series in Sociology: No. 3). 207p. 1980. lib. bdg. 14.95 (ISBN 0-933142-02-1). Intercont Press.
Peterson's Guides Editors, ed. Who Offers Part-Time Degree Programs? A National Survey of Postsecondary Institutions Offering Daytime, Evening, Weekend, Summer & External Degree Programs-1981 Edition. 250p. 1981. pap. 6.00 (ISBN 0-87866-121-2). Petersons Guid.
DEHYDRATION OF FOOD
see Food–Drying
DEHYDROFROZEN FOOD
see Food, Frozen
DEITIES
see Gods
DEJECTION
see Depression, Mental
DE KOONING, WILLEM, 1904-
Hess, Thomas B. & Feldman, Morton. Six Painters: Mondrian, DeKooning, Guston, Kline, Pollock, Rothko. LC 67-30452. (Illus.). 1968. pap. 3.00 (ISBN 0-914412-22-1). Inst for the Arts.
DELACROIX, EUGENE, 1798-1863
Johnson, Lee, ed. The Painting of Eugene Delacroix: A Critical Catalogue, Vols. 1 & 2: 1816-1831. (Illus.). 556p. 1981. Set. 195.00 (ISBN 0-19-817314-8). Oxford U Pr.
DELAUNAY, SONIA
Buck, Robert T., et al, eds. Sonia Delaunay: A Retrospective. LC 79-57450. (Illus.). 236p. 1980. pap. 27.50 (ISBN 0-914782-32-0). Buffalo Acad.
Kotik, Charlotta, ed. With Paper, About Paper. LC 80-69318. (Illus.). 1980. pap. 7.50 (ISBN 0-914782-35-5). Buffalo Acad.
DELAWARE
see also names of cities, counties, etc. in Delaware
Fagan, Michael. Beautiful Delaware. Shangle, Robert D., ed. LC 80-21494. (Illus.). 72p. 1980. 14.95 (ISBN 0-89802-207-X); pap. 7.95 (ISBN 0-89802-208-8). Beautiful Am.
DELAWARE–HISTORY
Munroe, John A. Federalist Delaware: 1775-1815. 286p. 1980. Repr. of 1954 ed. 16.50 (ISBN 0-374-96024-0). Octagon.
DELAWARE INDIANS
see Indians of North America–Eastern States
DELAYED-ACTION PREPARATIONS
Johnson, J. C., ed. Sustained Release Medications. LC 80-23455. (Chemical Technology Review: No. 177). (Illus.). 412p. 1981. 54.00 (ISBN 0-8155-0826-3). Noyes.
Shargel, Leon & Yu, Andrew B. Applied Biopharmaceutics & Pharmacokinetics. 288p. 1980. pap. text ed. 18.50x (ISBN 0-8385-0206-7). ACC.
DELINQUENCY, JUVENILE
see Juvenile Delinquency
DELINQUENT WOMEN
see Female Offenders
DELIVERY, ABDOMINAL
see Cesarean Section
DELIVERY (OBSTETRICS)
see Labor (Obstetrics)
DELPHINIDAE
see Dolphins
DELUSIONAL INSANITY
see Paranoia
DELUSIONS
see Errors, Popular; Impostors and Imposture; Superstition; Witchcraft
DEMAND AND SUPPLY
see Supply and Demand
DEMENTIA PRAECOX
see Schizophrenia
DEMILUNES OF HEIDENHAIN
see Salivary Glands
DEMINERALIZATION OF SALINE WATERS
see Saline Waters–Demineralization
DEMOCRACY
see also Equality; Federal Government; Liberty; Socialism
Agar, Herbert. The Perils of Democracy. LC 66-11684. (Background Ser.). 95p. 1965. 6.25 (ISBN 0-8023-1001-X). Dufour.
Cooper, James F. The American Democrat. LC 80-83794. 280p. 1981. 9.00 (ISBN 0-913966-91-6); pap. 4.00 (ISBN 0-913966-92-4). Liberty Fund.
Cummings, Richard. Proposition Fourteen: A Secessionist Remedy. LC 80-8917. 128p. 1981. pap. 5.95 postponed (ISBN 0-394-17890-4, Ever). Grove.
Julien, Claude. The Suicide of the Democracies. 1980. 13.95 (ISBN 0-7145-1061-0). Riverrun NY.
Lecky, William E. Democracy & Liberty. LC 80-82371. 1981. Set. 18.00 (ISBN 0-913966-80-0); Vol. I, 520p. (ISBN 0-913966-82-7); Vol. II 528p. (ISBN 0-913966-83-5); Set. pap. 6.00 (ISBN 0-913966-81-9). Vol. I (ISBN 0-913966-84-3). Vol. II. (ISBN 0-913966-85-1). Liberty Fund.
Lipset, Seymour M. Political Man: The Social Bases of Politics. LC 80-8867. 584p. 1981. pap. text ed. 7.50x (ISBN 0-8018-2522-9). Johns Hopkins.
Novak, Michael. American Vision: Essay on the Future of Democratic Capitalism. 1978. pap. 4.25 (ISBN 0-8447-3324-5). Am Enterprise.
Novak, Michael, ed. Democracy & Mediating Structures: A Theological Inquiry. 1980. 13.25 (ISBN 0-8447-2175-1); pap. 7.25 (ISBN 0-8447-2176-X). Am Enterprise.
Spitz, David. Patterns of Anti-Democratic Thought: An Analysis & Criticism, with Special Reference to the American Political Mind in Recent Times. LC 80-22640. 347p. 1981. Repr. of 1965 ed. lib. bdg. 27.50x (ISBN 0-313-22392-0, SPPD). Greenwood.
Stankiewicz, W. J. Approaches to Democracy: Philosophy of Government at the Close of the Twentieth Century. 1981. 25.00 (ISBN 0-312-04668-5). St Martin.
Watson, Richard A. & Fitzgerald, Michael R. Promise & Performance of American Democracy: National Editon. 4th ed. 570p. 1981. text ed. 14.95 (ISBN 0-471-08380-1). Wiley.
--Promise & Performance of American Democracy: State Edition. 4th ed. 650p. 1981. text ed. 16.95 (ISBN 0-471-08381-X). Wiley.
DEMOCRACY–ADDRESSES, ESSAYS, LECTURES
Humayun, Kabir. Science, Democracy, and Islam: And Other Essays. LC 80-2195. 1981. Repr. of 1955 ed. 20.00 (ISBN 0-404-18967-9). AMS Pr.
DEMOCRATIC PARTY, NATIONAL CONVENTION, CHICAGO, 1968
Langle, James I. Representation & Presidential Primaries: The Democratic Party in the Post-Reform Era. LC 80-1791. (Contributions in Political Science Ser.: No. 57). (Illus.). 192p. 1981. lib. bdg. 25.00 (ISBN 0-313-22482-X, LEP/). Greenwood.
DEMOCRATIC PARTY, NATIONAL CONVENTION, LOS ANGELES, 1960
Langle, James I. Representation & Presidential Primaries: The Democratic Party in the Post-Reform Era. LC 80-1791. (Contributions in Political Science Ser.: No. 57). (Illus.). 192p. 1981. lib. bdg. 25.00 (ISBN 0-313-22482-X, LEP/). Greenwood.
DEMOGRAPHY
see also Fertility, Human; Geopolitics; Mortality; Population
also subdivision Population under names of countries
Brandon, Belinda B., ed. The Effect of the Demographics of Individual Households on Their Telephone Useage. 432p. 1980. write for info. (ISBN 0-88410-695-0). Ballinger Pub.
Cavalli-Sforza, L. L. & Feldman, M. W. Cultural Transmission & Evolution: A Quantitative Approach. May, Robert M., ed. LC 80-8539. (Monographs in Population Biology: No. 16). (Illus.). 368p. 1981. 20.00x (ISBN 0-691-08280-4); pap. 8.95x (ISBN 0-691-08283-9). Princeton U Pr.
Smith, T. E. Commonwealth Migration: Flows & Policies. 1980. text ed. 40.00x (ISBN 0-333-27898-4). Humanities.
United Nations Demographic Yearbook 1978. 463p. 1980. pap. 36.00 (ISBN 0-686-68978-X, UN79/13/1, UN). Unipub.
World Statistics in Brief. 241p. 1980. pap. 3.95 (ISBN 0-686-68981-X, UN80/17/3, UN). Unipub.
DEMONIAC POSSESSION
see also Satanism
Irvine, Doreen. Freed from Witchcraft. 192p. 1981. pap. 3.95 (ISBN 0-8407-5771-9). Nelson.
DEMONOLOGY
see also Apparitions; Devil; Magic; Occult Sciences; Satanism; Superstition; Witchcraft
De Menil, Dominique, intro. by. Constant Companions: An Exhibition of Mythological Animals, Demons, & Monsters. (Illus.). 1964. pap. 6.00 (ISBN 0-914412-19-1). Inst for the Arts.
DEMOUNTABLE BUILDINGS
see Buildings, Prefabricated
DENDROLOGY
see Trees
DENMARK–HISTORY
Davidson, Hilda E., ed. Saxo Grammaticus: History of the Danes, Vol. II. Fisher, Peter, tr. (Illus.). 209p. 1980. 35.00x (ISBN 0-8476-6938-6). Rowman.
DENMARK–SOCIAL CONDITIONS
Dominant Ways of Life in Denmark--Alternative Ways of Life in Denmark. 77p. 1980. pap. 5.00 (ISBN 92-808-0140-6, TUNU095, UNU). Unipub.
DENOMINATIONAL SCHOOLS
see Church Schools
DENOMINATIONS, RELIGIOUS
see Religions; Sects;
also particiular denominations and sects
DENTAL ANATOMY
see Teeth
DENTAL ANESTHESIA
see Anesthesia in Dentistry
DENTAL ASSISTANTS
Anderson, Pauline C. The Dental Assistant. 3rd ed. 372p. 1981. text ed. 14.95 (ISBN 0-442-21873-7). Nos Van Reinhold.
Dental Assisting Manuals. Incl. No. I. Professionalism, Legal Considerations, & Office Management. Earl, Ethel M. (Illus.). 110p. 1980. pap. text ed. 6.00x (ISBN 0-8078-1375-3); No. II. Basic Sciences. Burkes, E. Jeff, Jr. & Wood, Matthew T. (Illus.). 120p. 1980. pap. text ed. 7.00x (ISBN 0-8078-1376-1); No. III. Preclinical Sciences. Wood, Matthew T. & Burkes, E. Jeff, Jr. (Illus.). 130p. 1980. pap. text ed. 7.00x (ISBN 0-8078-1377-X); No. IV. Communication, Psychology, Nutrition, & Preventive Dentistry. George, Mary C., et al. (Illus.). 160p. 1980. pap. text ed. 8.00x (ISBN 0-8078-1378-8); No. V. Dental Radiology. Matteson, Stephen R., et al. (Illus.). 130p. 1980. pap. text ed. 8.00x (ISBN 0-8078-1379-6); No. VI. Dental Materials & Technical Application. Leinfelder, Karl E., et al. (Illus.). 150p. 1980. pap. text ed. 10.00x (ISBN 0-8078-1380-X); No. VII. Clinical Sciences. Strickland, William D. & Wilder, Aldridge D., Jr. (Illus.). 140p. 1980. pap. text ed. 10.00x (ISBN 0-8078-1381-8); No. VIII. Clinical Chairside Assisting. Strickland, William D. & Wilder, Aldridge D., Jr. (Illus.). 160p. 1980. pap. text ed. 10.00x (ISBN 0-8078-1382-6). U of NC Pr.
Douglas, Mary A. Secretarial Dental Assistant. 304p. 1981. text ed. 14.95 (ISBN 0-442-21860-5). Van Nos Reinhold.
Rudman, Jack. National Dental Assistant Boards (NDAB) (Admission Test Ser.: AT-87). (Cloth bdg. avail. on request). 17.95 (ISBN 0-8373-5087-5). Natl Learning.
DENTAL CARE
Schissel, Marvin. Dentistry & Its Victims. 336p. 1981. 11.95 (ISBN 0-312-19391-2). St Martin.
DENTAL CERAMICS
see Dentistry–Ceramics
DENTAL HYGIENE
Here are entered works on dental hygiene as practiced by dental hygienists. Works on dental hygiene for the layman are entered under Teeth–Care and Hygiene.
Barsh, Laurence I. Dental Planning for the Adult Patient. (Illus.). 376p. 1981. text ed. price not set (ISBN 0-7216-1533-3). Saunders.
DENTAL MATERIA MEDICA
see Materia Medica, Dental
DENTAL MEDICINE
see Teeth–Diseases
DENTAL PATHOLOGY
see Teeth–Diseases
DENTAL PROSTHESIS
see Prosthodontics
DENTAL RADIOGRAPHY
see Teeth–Radiography
DENTAL RADIOLOGY
see Teeth–Radiography
DENTAL SURGERY
see Dentistry; Dentistry, Operative
DENTAL WRITING
see Medical Writing
DENTISTRY
see also Anesthesia in Dentistry; Diagnosis, Radioscopic; Endodontics; Hypnotism–Therapeutic Use; Occlusion (Dentistry); Prosthodontics; Teeth
Anderson, Pauline C. The Dental Assistant. 3rd ed. 372p. 1981. text ed. 14.95 (ISBN 0-442-21873-7). Nos Van Reinhold.
Beeching, Brian. Interpreting Dental Radiographs. (Illus.). 142p. 1981. PLB 33.55 (ISBN 0-906141-20-6, Pub. by Update Books Ltd). Kluwer Boston.
Celenza, Frank V. Occlusal Morphology. 110p. 1980. pap. 18.00 (ISBN 0-931386-33-0). Quint Pub Co.
Celenza, Frank V. & Nasedkin, John N. Occlusion, the State of the Art. (Illus.). 165p. 1978. 32.00 (ISBN 0-931386-00-4). Quint Pub Co.
Dental Assisting Manuals. Incl. No. I. Professionalism, Legal Considerations, & Office Management. Earl, Ethel M. (Illus.). 110p. 1980. pap. text ed. 6.00x (ISBN 0-8078-1375-3); No. II. Basic Sciences. Burkes, E. Jeff, Jr. & Wood, Matthew T. (Illus.). 120p. 1980. pap. text ed. 7.00x (ISBN 0-8078-1376-1); No. III. Preclinical Sciences. Wood, Matthew T. & Burkes, E. Jeff, Jr. (Illus.). 130p. 1980. pap. text ed. 7.00x (ISBN 0-8078-1377-X); No. IV. Communication, Psychology, Nutrition, & Preventive Dentistry. George, Mary C., et al. (Illus.). 160p. 1980. pap. text ed. 8.00x (ISBN 0-8078-1378-8); No. V. Dental Radiology. Matteson, Stephen R., et al. (Illus.). 130p. 1980. pap. text ed. 8.00x (ISBN 0-8078-1379-6); No. VI. Dental Materials & Technical Application. Leinfelder, Karl E., et al. (Illus.). 150p. 1980. pap. text ed. 10.00x (ISBN 0-8078-1380-X); No. VII. Clinical Sciences. Strickland, William D. & Wilder, Aldridge D., Jr. (Illus.). 140p. 1980. pap. text ed. 10.00x (ISBN 0-8078-1381-8); No. VIII. Clinical Chairside Assisting. Strickland, William D. & Wilder, Aldridge D., Jr. (Illus.). 160p. 1980. pap. text ed. 10.00x (ISBN 0-8078-1382-6). U of NC Pr.
Dentist's Desk Reference: Materials, Instruments & Equipment. (Illus.). 1981. 13.95 (ISBN 0-686-69611-5). Am Dental.
Dyce, James M. Stress & Decision Making in the Dental Practice. (Illus.). 165p. 1973. 24.00. Quint Pub Co.
Faschlicht, Samuel. Tooth Mutilations & Dentistry in Pre-Columbian Mexico. (Illus.). 152p. 1976. 46.00. Quint Pub Co.
Freedman, Kenneth. Management of the Geriatric Dental Patient. (Illus.). 148p. 1980. 42.00 (ISBN 0-931386-05-5). Quint Pub Co.

Fusayama, Takao. Two Layers of Carious Dentin & New Conservative Restoration. 190p. 1981. 42.00. Quint Pub Co.
Gaerny, Arnold. Removable Closure of the Interdental Space. (Illus.). 196p. 1972. 52.50. Quint Pub Co.
Grundler, Horst. The Study of Tooth Shapes: A Systematic Procedure. (Illus.). 104p. 1976. 24.00 (ISBN 3-87652-561-6). Quint Pub Co.
Imagines Demostrandae: Dentists Guide. (Illus.). 76p. 1978. 120.00 (ISBN 3-87652-031-2). Quint Pub Co.
Jong, Anthony. Dental Public Health & Community Dentistry. (Illus.). 300p. Date not set. pap. text ed. 12.95 (ISBN 0-8016-2575-0). Mosby.
Menaker, Lewis. Biological Basis of Dental Caries: An Oral Biology Textbook. (Illus.). 532p. 1980. 45.00 (ISBN 0-06-141726-2, Harper Medical). Har-Row.
Muhlemann, Hans R. Introduction to Oral Preventive Medicine. (Illus.). 253p. 1976. 22.00. Quint Pub Co.
Paul, J. Ellis. Manual of Four-Handed Dentistry. (Illus.). 155p. 1980. 42.00 (ISBN 0-931386-09-8). Quint Pub Co.
Salinas, Carlos F. & Jorgenson, Ronald J., eds. Dentistry in the Interdisciplinary Treatment of Genetic Diseases. (Birth Defects: Original Article Ser.: Vol. XVI, No. 5). 216p. 1980. 26.00 (ISBN 0-8451-1039-X). A R Liss.
Simonsen, Richard J. Clinical Applications of the Acid Etch Technique. (Illus.). 123p. 1978. 42.00 (ISBN 0-931386-01-2). Quint Pub Co.
Stahl, S. Sigmund, et al. What Dentists Do: A Patient's Guide to Modern Dentistry. (Appleton Consumer Health Guides). (Illus.). 226p. 1980. 12.95 (ISBN 0-8385-9712-2); pap. 5.95 (ISBN 0-8385-9711-4). ACC.
Vrijhoef, M., et al. Dental Amalgam. (Illus.). 114p. 1980. 46.00 (ISBN 0-931386-16-0). Quint Pub Co.
Warner, Richard & Segal, Herman. Ethical Issues of Imformed Consent in Dentistry. 112p. 1980. pap. 12.00 (ISBN 0-931386-33-0). Quint Pub Co.
Wells, Jack E., et al, eds. Review of Basic Sciences & Clinical Dentistry, 2 vols. Incl. Vol. 1. Basic Science. 262p. text ed. 27.50 (ISBN 0-06-142657-1); Vol. 2. Clinical Dentistry. 466p. text ed. 42.50 (ISBN 0-06-142658-X). (Illus.). 1400p. 1980. text ed. write for info. (Harper Medical). Har-Row.
White. Clinical Oral Periatrics. 148p. 1981. 68.00 (ISBN 0-931386-32-2). Quint Pub Co.

DENTISTRY–CERAMICS
Kuwata, Mashiro. Theory & Practice of Ceramo Metal Restorations. (Illus.). 150p. 1980. 58.00 (ISBN 0-931386-15-2). Quint Pub Co.
McLean, John. The Science & Art Dental Ceramics, Vol. 1. (Illus.). 334p. 1979. 42.00 (ISBN 0-931386-04-7). Quint Pub Co.
--The Science & Art of Dental Ceramics, Vol. II. (Illus.). 496p. 1978. 120.00 (ISBN 0-931386-11-X). Quint Pub Co.

DENTISTRY–HISTORY
Hoffman-Axthelm, Walter A. History of Dentistry. (Illus.). 400p. 1981. 46.00. Quint Pub Co.

DENTISTRY–PRACTICE
Griffin, A. J. How to Avoid People Problems & Increase Lab Productivity. 112p. 1980. pap. 12.00 (ISBN 0-931386-17-9). Quint Pub Co.
Kimmel, K. & Walker, R. O. Practising Dentistry. (Illus.). 258p. 1972. 46.00. Quint Pub Co.
Schijatscky, Milan. Life-Threatening Emergencies in the Dental Practice. (Illus.). 163p. 1975. 24.50. Quint Pub Co.
Schon, Fritz. Teamwork in the Dental Practice. (Illus.). 88p. 1971. 27.50. Quint Pub Co.

DENTISTRY–PSYCHOLOGICAL ASPECTS
Spiro, Stanley R., ed. Pain & Anxiety Control in Dentistry. (Illus.). 340p. 1981. text ed. 37.50 (ISBN 0-937218-66-9, Pub. by Piccin Italy). J K Burgess.

DENTISTRY–STUDY AND TEACHING
Shugar, Gershon J., et al. How to Get into Medical & Dental School. rev. ed. LC 80-23397. 160p. 1981. lib. bdg. 8.00 (ISBN 0-668-05105-1); pap. 6.00 (ISBN 0-668-05112-4). Arco.

DENTISTRY, OPERATIVE
Here are entered works on that field of dentistry concerned with restoring diseased or defective teeth to a state of normal function, health and aesthetics.
Baum, Lloyd, et al. Textbook of Operative Dentistry. (Illus.). 450p. 1981. text ed. price not set (ISBN 0-7216-1601-1). Saunders.

DENTISTRY, PROSTHETIC
see Prosthodontics

DENTISTRY, PSYCHOSOMATIC
see Dentistry–Psychological Aspects

DENTISTRY, RESTORATIVE
see Dentistry, Operative

DENTURES
see Prosthodontics

DENVER–DESCRIPTION
Kane, Kay & Gold, Louise. Discover Denver: A Pennywise Survival Handbook. (Illus.). 184p. (Orig.). 1980. pap. 5.95 (ISBN 0-9604430-0-2). Gold-Kane Ent.

DENVER–HISTORY
Jones, William. Denver: A Pictorial History. (Illus., Orig.). Date not set. pap. 10.95 (ISBN 0-87108-575-5). Pruett.
Turk, Gayle. Trial & Triumph. (Illus.). 60p. (Orig.). 1978. pap. 2.50 (ISBN 0-936564-11-3). Little London.

DEONTOLOGY
see Ethics

DEOXYRIBONUCLEIC ACID
Alberts, Bruce & Fox, C. Fred, eds. Mechanistic Studies of DNA Replication & Genetic Recombination. (ICN-UCLA Symposia on Molecular & Cellular Biology Ser.: Vol. XIX). 1980. 48.00 (ISBN 0-12-048850-7). Acad Pr.
Freidberg & Hanawalt. DNA Repair, Pt. 1A. 312p. 1981. 29.75 (ISBN 0-8247-6848-5). Dekker.
Gueriguian, J. L., et al, eds. Insulins, Growth Hormone, & Recombinant DNA Technology. 250p. 1981. 25.00 (ISBN 0-89004-544-5). Raven.
Watson, James D. & Tooze, John, eds. Recombinant DNA: A Scrapbook Edited by James D. Watson & John Tooze. (Illus.). 1981. text ed. price not set (ISBN 0-7167-1292-X). W H Freeman.

DEPARTMENT STORES
Hendrickson, Robert. The Grand Emporiums: The Illustrated History of America's Great Department Stores. LC 78-7555. (Illus.). 616p. 1980. pap. 9.95 (ISBN 0-8128-6092-6). Stein & Day.

DEPENDENCIES
see Colonies

DEPENDENTS OF MILITARY PERSONNEL
see Air Force Wives

DEPOSITION AND SEDIMENTATION
see Sedimentation and Deposition

DEPOSITS, DEEP-SEA
see Marine Sediments; Sedimentation and Deposition

DEPRESSANTS
see Sedatives

DEPRESSION, MENTAL
see also Manic-Depressive Psychoses
Emery, Gary. Defeating Depression. 12.95 (ISBN 0-671-24866-9). S&S.
Johnson, James E. Freedom from Depression. (Orig.). 1981. pap. 2.95 (ISBN 0-88270-494-X). Logos.
Littauer, Florence. Blow Away the Black Clouds. LC 80-85334. 1981. pap. 3.95 (ISBN 0-89081-285-3). Harvest Hse.
Nordvedt, Matilda, tr. Por el Tunel De la Depresion. (Spanish Bks.). (Span.). 1979. 1.60 (ISBN 0-8297-0796-4). Life Pubs Intl.
Norvedt, Matilda, tr. Derrotando O Desespero E Depressao. (Portuguese Bks.). 1979. 1.25 (ISBN 0-8297-0828-6). Life Pubs Intl.
Ross, Harvey. Fighting Depression. 221p. (Orig.). 1975. pap. 1.95. Larchmont Bks.
Sturgeon, Wina. Depression. 256p. 1981. pap. 5.95 (ISBN 0-346-12514-6). Cornerstone.

DEPRESSIONS–1929
Brunner, Karl, ed. The Great Depression Revisited. (Rochester Studies in Economics & Policy Issues: Vol. 2). 368p. 1980. lib. bdg. 20.00 (ISBN 0-89838-051-0, Pub by Martinus Nijhoff). Kluwer Boston.
Coode, Thomas H. & Bauman, John F. People, Poverty, & Politics: Pennsylvanians During the Great Depression. LC 78-75198. 280p. 1981. 24.50 (ISBN 0-8387-2320-9). Bucknell U Pr.
Day, Richard B. Crisis & the "Crash". Soviet Studies of the West(1917-1939) 320p. 1981. 22.50 (Pub. by NLB England). Schocken.
Galbraith, John K. The Great Crash of Nineteen Twenty-Nine. 1980. pap. 2.75 (ISBN 0-686-69255-1, 50799, Discus). Avon.
Lowitt, Richard & Beasley, Maurine, eds. One Third of a Nation: Lorena Hickok Reports on the Great Depression. (Illus.). 450p. 1981. 18.95 (ISBN 0-252-00849-9). U of Ill Pr.

DEPRESSIVE PSYCHOSES
see Depression, Mental

DEPRIVATION, MATERNAL
see Maternal Deprivation

DERMATITIS
see Skin–Diseases

DERMATOGLYPHICS
see also Fingerprints
Wertelecki, Wladimir & Plato, Chris C., eds. Dermatoglyphics Fifty Years Later. LC 79-2595. (Alan R. Liss Ser.: Vol. 15, No. 6). 1979. 76.00 (ISBN 0-8451-1031-4). March of Dimes.

DERMATOLOGY
see also Pediatric Dermatology; Skin–Diseases
Ackerman, A. Bernard, et al. Differential Diagnosis in Dermatopathology. (Illus.). 200p. 1981. text ed. 86.00 (ISBN 0-8121-0800-0). Lea & Febiger.
Korting. Practical Dermatology of the Genital Region. 1981. text ed. price not set (ISBN 0-7216-5498-3). Saunders.
Lynch, Peter J. Dermatology for the House Officer: Problem Oriented Approach. 225p. 1981. write for info. softcover (5250-0). Williams & Wilkins.
Pinkus, Herman. A Guide to Dermatohistopathology. 3rd ed. 672p. 1981. 40.00 (ISBN 0-8385-3151-2). ACC.
Roenigk, Henry H., Jr. Office Dermatology. (Illus.). 340p. 1981. write for info. (7316-8). Williams & Wilkins.
Rosen, Theodore & Martin, Sandy. Atlas of Black Dermatology. 1981. text ed. price not set (ISBN 0-316-75709-8). Little.
Schuppli, R., ed. Schweizerische Gesellschaft Fuer Dermatologie und Venerologie, 61. Jahresversammlung, Lausanne, Oktober 1979. (Illus.). viii, 68p. 1981. pap. 6.75 (ISBN 3-8055-2353-X). S Karger.

DERRICKS
see Cranes, Derricks, etc.

DERVISHES
Shah, Amina. The Tale of Four Dervishes & Other Sufi Tales. LC 80-8895. 288p. (Orig.). 1981. pap. 5.95 (ISBN 0-06-067256-0). Har-Row.

DESALINIZATION OF WATER
see Saline Waters–Demineralization

DESCARTES, RENE, 1596-1650
Gaukroger, Stephen, ed. Descartes: Philosophy, Mathematics & Physics. (Harvester Readings in the History of Science & Philosophy Ser.: No. 1). 329p. 1980. 30.00x (ISBN 0-389-20084-0). B&N.

DESCENT
see Genealogy; Heredity

DESEGREGATION
Baez, Tony, et al. Desegregation & Hispanic Students: A Community Perspective. LC 80-80311. 84p. (Orig.). 1980. pap. 3.50 (ISBN 0-89763-023-8). Natl Clearinghse Bilingual Ed.

DESEGREGATION IN EDUCATION
see School Integration

DESERTS
see also names of deserts e.g.; Kalahari Desert, Sahara Desert; also headings beginning with the word Desert
Benson, Lyman & Darrow, Robert A. Trees & Shrubs of the Southwestern Deserts. rev. ed. 1981. text ed. 49.50x (ISBN 0-8165-0591-8). U of Ariz Pr.
Davey, Keith. Australian Desert Life. 6.50x (ISBN 0-392-07552-0, SpS). Soccer.
Helms, Christopher L. & DenDooven, Gweneth R., eds. The Sonoran Desert. LC 80-82918. (Illus.). 1980. 8.95 (ISBN 0-916122-72-7); pap. 3.75 (ISBN 0-916122-71-9). K C Pubns.
Lopez, Barry H. Desert Notes: Reflections in the Eye of the Raven. 96p. pap. 2.25 (ISBN 0-380-53819-9, 53819, Bard). Avon.
McGinnies, William G. Discovering the Desert: The Legacy of the Carnegie Desert Botanical Laboratory. 1981. text ed. 21.95x (ISBN 0-8165-0719-8); pap. text ed. 9.50x (ISBN 0-8165-0728-7). U of Ariz Pr.
Social & Environmental Aspects of Desertification. 40p. 1980. pap. 6.75 (ISBN 0-686-68814-7, TUNU085, UNU). Unipub.

DESERTS–JUVENILE LITERATURE
Baylor, Byrd. The Desert Is Theirs. (Illus.). 32p. (gr. 1-5). pap. 2.95 (ISBN 0-689-70481-X, A-108, Aladdin). Atheneum.
Watson, Jane W. Deserts of the World: Future Threat or Promise? (Illus.). 136p. (gr. 10-12). 1981. 12.95 (ISBN 0-399-20785-6). Philomel.

DESIGN
see also Pattern-Making; Printing–Layout and Typography; Textile Design
Corpron, Carlotta & Sandweiss, Martha A. Carlotta Corpron: Designer with Light. 64p. 1980. 14.95 (ISBN 0-292-71064-X); pap. 9.95 (ISBN 0-292-71065-8). U of Tex Pr.
Design for the Eighties. (Illus.). 1981. text ed. 40.00 (ISBN 0-937976-05-9). Enviro Pr.
Design: Science-Method. 1980. pap. text ed. 46.80. Butterworths.
Ferebee, Ann. A History of Design from the Victorian Era to the Present. 128p. 1980. pap. 7.95 (ISBN 0-442-23115-6). Van Nos Reinhold.
Huchingson, Dale. New Horizons for Human Factors in Design. (Illus.). 512p. Date not set. text ed. 22.95 (ISBN 0-07-030815-2, C). McGraw.
Industrial Design Magazine. Designer's Choice: The Best Products, Graphics & Environments of 1980. Finley, George, ed. 120p. 1980. pap. 7.95 (ISBN 0-07-031710-0, P&RB). McGraw.
Learning Achievement Corporation. Geometry & Design & Maintenance: Ratio, Proportion, Reading Graphs & Data. Zak, Therese A., ed. (MATCH Ser.). (Illus.). 128p. 1981. text ed. 5.28 (ISBN 0-07-037115-6, G). McGraw.
Locke, John. Isometric Perspective Designs & How to Create Them. (Illus.). 64p. (Orig.). 1981. pap. price not set (ISBN 0-486-24123-8). Dover.
Maier, Manfred. Basic Principles of Design. 392p. 1981. pap. 35.00 (ISBN 0-442-21206-2). Van Nos Reinhold.
Schafer, R. Murray. The Tuning of the World: Toward a Theory of Soundscape Design. 1980. write for info.; pap. text ed. 11.50x (ISBN 0-8122-1109-X). U of Pa Pr.

DESIGN–JUVENILE LITERATURE
Ames, Lee. Graff-a-Doodle Do. (Illus.). 96p. 1981. pap. 3.95 (ISBN 0-686-69181-4). G&D.
Heller, Ruth. Designs. (Creative Coloring Activity Pandabacks). (Illus.). 32p. 1981. pap. 1.25 (ISBN 0-448-49621-6). G&D.
--More Designs. (Creative Coloring Activity Pandabacks). (Illus.). 32p. 1981. pap. 1.25 (ISBN 0-448-49622-4). G&D.

DESIGN, ARCHITECTURAL
see Architecture–Designs and Plans; Architecture–Details

DESIGN, DECORATIVE
see also Decoration and Ornament; Decoupage; Drawing; Folk Art; Lettering; Tapestry; Textile Design
Benedictus, Edouard. Benedictus' Art Deco Designs in Color. (Illus.). 1980. pap. 6.00 (ISBN 0-486-23971-3). Dover.
Dye, Daniel S. The New Book of Chinese Lattice Designs. (Pictorial Archive Ser.). (Illus.). 128p. (Orig.). 1981. pap. price not set (ISBN 0-486-24128-9). Dover.
Harvey, Virginia I. Color & Design in Macrame. (Illus.). 104p. 1980. pap. 9.95 (ISBN 0-914842-55-2). Madrona Pubs.
Lee, Sherman E. The Genius of Japanese Design. LC 79-66246. (Illus.). 1981. 39.50 (ISBN 0-87011-395-X). Kodansha.
Nicoletti, Sally. Japanese Motifs for Needlepoint. LC 80-22650. (Illus.). 136p. 1981. 14.95 (ISBN 0-688-00163-7). Morrow.
Verneuil, M. P. & Grafton, Carol B. One Hundred & Five Art Nouveau Designs in Full Color. (Pictorial Archive Ser.). (Illus.). 48p. (Orig.). 1981. pap. price not set (ISBN 0-486-24112-2). Dover.

DESIGN, DECORATIVE–PLANT FORMS
Gaber, Susan. A Treasury of Flower Designs for Artists, Embroiderers & Craftsmen: 100 Garden Favorites. (Illus.). 80p. (Orig.). 1981. pap. price not set (ISBN 0-486-24096-7). Dover.
Sibbett, Ed. Ready-to-Use Floral Designs. (Illus.). 64p. pap. 2.50 (ISBN 0-486-23976-4). Dover.

DESIGN, ENGINEERING
see Engineering Design

DESIGN, INDUSTRIAL
see also Engineering Design; Environmental Engineering; Human Engineering; Mechanical Drawing; Unit Construction
Design for the Eighties. (Illus.). 1981. text ed. 40.00 (ISBN 0-937976-05-9). Enviro Pr.
Haddon, Randolph J. The Basic Guidebook for Industrial Designers. (Illus.). 129p. 1981. 47.45 (ISBN 0-930582-92-6). Gloucester Art.

DESIGN OF EXPERIMENTS
see Experimental Design

DESIGN PERCEPTION
see Pattern Perception

DESIGNED GENETIC CHANGE
see Genetic Engineering

DESIGNS, FLORAL
see Design, Decorative–Plant Forms

DESOXYRIBONUCLEIC ACID
see Deoxyribonucleic Acid

DESSERTS
see also Puddings
The C&H Complete Dessert Cookbook. Date not set. price not set (ISBN 0-87502-087-9). Benjamin Co.

DESTINY
see Fate and Fatalism

DESTITUTION
see Poverty

DESTROYERS (WARSHIPS)
see Warships

DESTRUCTION OF PROPERTY
see Vandalism

DESTRUCTION OF THE JEWS (1939-1945)
see Holocaust, Jewish (1939-1945)

DETAILS, ARCHITECTURAL
see Architecture–Details

DETECTIVE AND MYSTERY STORIES (COLLECTIONS)
see also Horror Tales
Asimov, Isaac, et al. Miniature Mysteries: One Hundred Malicious Little Mystery Stories. 256p. 1981. 12.95 (ISBN 0-8008-5251-6). Taplinger.
Gardner, Erle S. Ellery Queen Presents. Bd. with Erle Stanley Gardner; The Amazing Adventures of Lester Leith. 192p. 1981. 9.95. Davis Pubns.
Hitchcock, Alfred. Stories to Be Read with the Door Locked. 1981. pap. 2.25 (ISBN 0-440-10138-7). Dell.
Mystery & Suspense from the Saturday Evening Post. LC 76-41561. 1976. 5.95 (ISBN 0-89387-005-6). Sat Eve Post.
Queen, Ellery, ed. Ellery Queen's Crime Cruise Round the World. 288p. 1981. 9.95 (ISBN 0-8037-2189-7). Davis Pubns.
--Ellery Queen's Doors to Mystery. 288p. 1981. 9.95 (ISBN 0-8037-2194-3). Davis Pubns.

DETECTIVE AND MYSTERY STORIES–BIBLIOGRAPHY
Hoch, Edward D. Best Detective Stories of the Year: Thirty-Fifth Annual Collection. 224p. 1981. 10.95 (ISBN 0-525-06440-0). Dutton.
Reilly, John M., ed. Twentieth Century Crime & Mystery Writers. (Twentieth Century Writers Ser.). 1600p. 1980. 50.00x (ISBN 0-312-82417-3). St Martin.

DETECTIVE AND MYSTERY STORIES–HISTORY AND CRITICISM
Charney, Hanna. The Detective Novel of Manners: Hedonism, Morality, & the Life of Reason. LC 79-17634. 160p. 1981. 16.50 (ISBN 0-8386-3004-9). Fairleigh Dickinson.
Haining, Peter. Mystery! An Illustrated History of Crime & Detective Fiction. LC 80-6170. 1981. 15.95 (ISBN 0-8128-2805-4). Stein & Day.
Johnson, Timothy W., et al. Crime Fiction Criticism: An Annotated Bibliography. LC 80-8497. 450p. 1981. lib. bdg. 40.00 (ISBN 0-8240-9490-5). Garland Pub.
Skene Melvin, David & Skene Melvin, Ann. Crime, Detective, Espionage, Mystery, & Thriller Fiction & Film: A Comprehensive Bibliography of Critical Writing Through 1979. LC 80-1194. 384p. 1980. lib. bdg. 29.95 (ISBN 0-313-22062-X, MCD/). Greenwood.

DETECTIVE AND MYSTERY STORIES–JUVENILE LITERATURE
Brenner, Barbara. Mystery of the Plumed Serpent. LC 80-17316. (Capers Ser.). (Illus.). 128p. (gr. 3-6). 1981. PLB 4.99 (ISBN 0-394-94531-X); pap. 1.95 (ISBN 0-394-84531-5). Knopf.
DETECTIVE AND MYSTERY STORIES–TECHNIQUE
Highsmith, Patricia. Plotting & Writing Suspense Fiction. rev. ed. 1981. 10.95 (ISBN 0-87116-125-7). Writer.
DETECTIVES
see also Criminal Investigation; Police; Secret Service
Sennewald, Charles A. The Process of Investigation: Concepts & Strategies for the Security Professional. 255p. 1981. text ed. 21.95 (ISBN 0-409-95018-1). Butterworths.
DETENTE
Brownfeld, Allan C. The Price of Detente. 180p. 1981. 10.00 (ISBN 0-8159-6517-6). Devin.
Crampton, Richard. The Hollow Detente: Anglo-German Relations in the Balkans, 1911-1914. (Illus.). 250p. 1980. text ed. 18.75x (ISBN 0-391-02159-1). Humanities.
Frei, Daniel, ed. Definitions & Measurement of Detente: East & West Perspectives. LC 80-27960. 256p. 1981. lib. bdg. 22.50 (ISBN 0-89946-080-1). Oelgeschlager.
Imai, Ryukichi & Barton, John, eds. Arms Control II: A New Approach to International Security. LC 80-22700. 352p. 1981. lib. bdg. 25.00 (ISBN 0-89946-069-0). Oelgeschlager.
DETENTION CAMPS
see Concentration Camps
DETENTION HOMES, JUVENILE
see Juvenile Detention Homes
DETERMINATIVE MINERALOGY
see Mineralogy, Determinative
DETERMINISM AND INDETERMINISM
see Free Will and Determinism
DETERRENCE (STRATEGY)
Bertram, Christoph, ed. Strategic Deterrence in a Changing Environment. LC 80-67841. (Adelphi Library: Vol. 6). 200p. 1981. text ed. 29.50 (ISBN 0-916672-75-1). Allanheld.
DETROIT–HISTORY
Ferry, W. Hawkins. Building of Detroit: A History. rev. ed. (Illus.). 1980. 40.00 (ISBN 0-8143-1665-4). Wayne St U Pr.
DETROIT BASEBALL CLUB
Hawkins, John C. This Date in Detroit Tigers History. LC 80-5435. (This Date Ser.). 288p. 1981. pap. 9.95 (ISBN 0-8128-6067-5). Stein & Day.
DEVELOPMENT (BIOLOGY)
see Developmental Biology
DEVELOPMENT, CHILD
see Child Development
DEVELOPMENTAL ABNORMALITIES
see Abnormalities, Human
DEVELOPMENTAL BIOLOGY
see also Aging; Child Development; Embryology; Growth; Psychobiology
Deutsch, Henri & Bustow, Sheldon M. Developmental Disabilities: A Training Guide. (American Health Care Association Ser.). 192p. 1981. 15.95 (ISBN 0-8436-0851-X). CBI Pub.
Karp, Gerald & Berrill, N. J. Development. 2nd ed. (Illus.). 640p. 1981. text ed. 21.95 (ISBN 0-07-033340-8, C). McGraw.
DEVELOPMENTAL DYSLEXIA
see Reading Disability
DEVELOPMENTAL PSYCHOLOGY
Here are entered works on the psychological development of the individual from infancy to old age. Works on the evolutionary psychology of man in terms of origin and development, whether in the individual or in the species, are entered under Genetic Psychology.
see also Child Psychology
Brehm, Sharon S., et al, eds. Developmental Social Psychology: Theory & Research. (Illus.). 352p. 1981. text ed. 19.95x (ISBN 0-19-502840-6); pap. text ed. 11.95x (ISBN 0-19-502841-4). Oxford U Pr.
Clifford, Margaret M. & Grandgenett, Myrna. Activities & Readings in Learning & Development. LC 80-84892. (Illus.). 256p. 1981. pap. text ed. price not set (ISBN 0-395-29924-1). HM.
Dworetzky, John. Developmental Psychology. (Illus.). 550p. 1981. pap. text ed. 12.76 (ISBN 0-8299-0368-2). West Pub.
La Barba, Richard. Foundations of Developmental Psychology. LC 80-615. 1980. lib ed 18.95 (ISBN 0-12-432350-2); write for info. (ISBN 0-12-432355-3). Acad Pr.
Lamb, Michael E. & Brown, Ann L., eds. Advances in Developmental Psychology. Vol. 1. (Advances in Developmental Psychology Ser.). 400p. 1981. prof. ref. 24.95 (ISBN 0-89859-094-9). L Erlbaum Assocs.
Pollack, Margaret. Adaptive Development. (Studies in Developmental Pediatrics Ser: Vol. 3). 240p. 1981. text ed. 17.50 (ISBN 0-88416-380-6). PSG Pub.
Simons, Richard C. & Pardes, Herbert. Understanding Human Behavior in Health & Illness. 2nd ed. (Illus.). 760p. 1981. write for info. (7740-6). Williams & Wilkins.
DEVELOPMENTAL READING
see also Rapid Reading
Kennedy, Edward C. Methods in Teaching Developmental Reading. 2nd ed. LC 80-52445. 368p. 1981. pap. text ed. 9.95 (ISBN 0-87581-258-9). Peacock Pubs.
DEVIANT BEHAVIOR
see also Crime and Criminals; Conformity
Douglas & Waksler. Deviance. 1981. text ed. 16.95 (ISBN 0-316-19111-6); tchrs'. manual free (ISBN 0-316-19112-4). Little.
--The Sociology of Deviance: An Introduction. 512p. 1981. text ed. 16.95 (ISBN 0-316-19111-6); tchr's ed free (ISBN 0-316-19112-4). Little.
Lowney & Winslow. Deviant Reality: Alternative World Views. 2nd ed. 420p. 1980. pap. text ed. 10.95 (ISBN 0-205-07243-7, 8172439). Allyn.
Morris, Terence. Deviance & Control. 1980. pap. text ed. 9.25x (ISBN 0-09-126871-0, Hutchinson U Lib). Humanities.
DEVIATION, SEXUAL
see Sexual Deviation
DEVIL
see also Demonology; Satanism
Adams, Walter E. The Devil Is a Mean Man. 140p. (Orig.). 1981. pap. 3.95 (ISBN 0-937408-01-8). Gospel Pubns Fl.
Cruz, Nicky, tr. Sata Anda Solto. (Portugese Bks.). (Port.). 1979. 1.30 (ISBN 0-8297-0686-0). Life Pubs Intl.
--Satana Anda Suelto. (Spanish Bks.). (Span.). 1978. 1.90 (ISBN 0-8297-0595-3). Life Pubs Intl.
DEVIL-WORSHIP
see Satanism
DEVOTIONAL CALENDARS
Devotion for Every Day, 1981-1982: Fourteenth Annual. 384p. (Orig.). 1981. pap. 2.95 (ISBN 0-87239-433-6, 3082). Standard Pub.
Lang, J. David, ed. Devotion for Every Day, 1981-1982: Third Annual. 384p. (Orig.). 1981. pap. 5.50 large type ed. (ISBN 0-87239-434-4, 4082). Standard Pub.
Zeigler, Mildred. Onward & Upward. 60p. 1981. pap. 4.00 (ISBN 0-86629-027-3). Sunrise MO.
DEVOTIONAL EXERCISES
see also Church Music; Devotional Calendars; Hymns; Liturgies; Lord's Prayer; Lord's Supper; Meditations; Prayer
also subdivision Prayer-books and devotions under particular denominations; children's prayers; women–prayerbooks and devotions, etc.
Fair, Harold L. Class Devotions: For Use with the 1981-82 International Lessons. 1981. pap. 3.95 (ISBN 0-687-08621-3). Abingdon.
Tozer, A. W. Renewed Day by Day: Three Hundred & Sixty Five Daily Devotions. 1981. 12.95 (ISBN 0-8010-8861-5). Baker Bk.
DEVOTIONAL LITERATURE
see also Religious Literature;
also subdivision Devotional Literature under specific subjects, e.g. Jesus christ–devotional Literature
Autton, Norman. In Times of Sickness. 1978. 1.40 (ISBN 0-686-28781-9). Forward Movement.
Balaguer, Josemaria E. de. The Way. 228p. 1979. pap. 2.95 (ISBN 0-933932-35-9). Scepter Pubs.
Bawa Muhaiyaddeen, M. R. A Book of God's Love. Marcus, Sharon & Marcus, Karin, eds. Macan-Markar, Ajwad, et al, trs. from Tamil. (Illus.). 126p. 1981. 7.95 (ISBN 0-914390-19-8). Fellowship Pr.
Blalock, Jack E., Jr. It's All There If You Want It: And Here Is the Map. LC 80-69519. 250p. (Orig.). 1980. 12.95 (ISBN 0-9605156-1-5); pap. 10.95 (ISBN 0-9605156-1-5). Better Am Corp.
Boom, Corrie T. A Prisoner & Yet. (Orig.). pap. 1.95 (ISBN 0-515-05334-1). Jove Pubns.
Chinmoy, Sri. O My Pilot Beloved. 54p. (Orig.). 1980. pap. 2.00 (ISBN 0-88497-502-9). Aum Pubns.
Cook, Lyndon W. & Cannon, Donald Q. A New Light Breaks Forth. pap. 7.95 (ISBN 0-89036-148-7). Hawkes Pub Inc.
Coughlin, Kevin. Finding God in Everyday Life. 80p. (Orig.). 1981. pap. 3.95 (ISBN 0-8091-2351-7). Paulist Pr.
D'Arcy, Paula. Song for Sarah. 128p. 1981. pap. 2.50 (ISBN 0-553-14728-5). Bantam.
Editors of Ideals. The Book of Comfort & Joy. LC 80-1192. 96p. 1981. 9.95 (ISBN 0-385-17289-3, Galilee). Doubleday.
Estrada, Jose R. Dias Sin Gloria. 64p. (Span.). 1980. pap. 1.45 (ISBN 0-311-08213-0, Edit Mundo). Casa Bautista.
Evans, Colleen T. Give Us This Day Our Daily Bread: Asking for & Sharing Life's Necessities. LC 78-20070. 168p. 1981. 9.95 (ISBN 0-385-14091-6, Galilee). Doubleday.
Fettig, Art. Mentor: Secrets Ot the Ages. (Illus.). 112p. 1981. 9.95 (ISBN 0-8119-0333-8). Fell.
Fields, Mary E. Foundations in Truth. LC 80-67931. 275p. 1980. 10.00 (ISBN 0-87516-423-4). De Vorss.
Finegold, Julius J. & Thetford, William N., eds. Choose Once Again. LC 76-20363. (Illus.). 112p. 1981. 8.95 (ISBN 0-89087-285-6). Celestial Arts.
Gillies, Marilyn. Tracings. LC 80-67934. 84p. 1981. pap. 4.95 (ISBN 0-9605170-0-6). Earth-Song.
Helman, Patricia K. At Home in the World. 120p. (Orig.). 1980. pap. 4.95 (ISBN 0-87178-065-8). Brethren.
Holmes, Marjorie. Lord, Let Me Love. 288p. 1981. pap. 2.75 (ISBN 0-553-14915-6). Bantam.
Hooker, Thomas. The Poor Doubting Christian Drawn to Christ. (Summit Bks). 168p. 1981. pap. 2.95 (ISBN 0-8010-4246-1). Baker Bk.
Kaufman, Barry N. A Miracle to Believe in. LC 80-942. 320p. 1981. 12.95 (ISBN 0-385-14991-3). Doubleday.
Law, William. William Law on Christian Perfection. 144p. 1981. pap. 2.95 (ISBN 0-87123-117-4, 210117). Bethany Fell.
Lee, Laurel. Signs of Spring. 128p. 1981. pap. 2.25 (ISBN 0-553-14342-5). Bantam.
Lerin, Alfredo, compiled by. Quinientas Ilustraciones. 324p. (Span.). 1980. pap. 4.95 (ISBN 0-311-42037-0). Casa Bautista.
Lynn, Claire. Wjere Living Waters Flow. (Illus.). 99p. (Orig.). 1979. pap. 2.00 (ISBN 0-89323-002-2). BMA Pr.
Lynn, Claire, compiled by. Build on the Rock. (Illus.). 52p. (Orig.). (ps-7). 1979. pap. 2.50 (ISBN 0-89323-000-6). BMA Pr.
Medeiros, Huberto C. Thy Kingdom Come. 1980. write for info. (ISBN 0-8198-7307-1); pap. write for info. (ISBN 0-8198-7308-X). Dghtrs St Paul.
Murray, Andrew. Thy Will Be Done. (Summit Bks). 200p. 1981. pap. 3.45 (ISBN 0-8010-6109-1). Baker Bk.
--Waiting on God. 160p. 1981. pap. 2.50 (ISBN 0-88368-101-3). Whitaker Hse.
Newman, Daisy. A Procession of Friends. 1980. pap. 10.95 (ISBN 0-913408-59-X). Friends United.
Quiros, T. E. Por Sendas Biblicas. 162p. (Span.). Date not set. pap. price not set (ISBN 0-311-08753-1). Casa Bautista.
Richardson, Agnes. Jesus Calls Us His Sheep. (Illus.). 1981. 4.95 (ISBN 0-8062-1636-0). Carlton.
Rogers, W. R. You Can Give a Chalk Talk. LC 80-65775. 1981. saddlewire 4.95 (ISBN 0-8054-6931-1). Broadman.
Sheen, Fulton J. God Love You. LC 80-23085. 224p. 1981. pap. 4.50 (ISBN 0-385-17486-1, Im). Doubleday.
Spurgeon, Charles H. Daily Help. (Summit Ser.). 296p. 1981. pap. 3.95 (ISBN 0-8010-8195-5). Baker Bk.
Swindoll, Charles. Hand Me Another Brick. 176p. 1981. pap. 2.25 (ISBN 0-553-14524-X). Bantam.
Taylor, Charles L. Gleanings. 1979. 2.00 (ISBN 0-686-28779-7). Forward Movement.
Wilkerson, David. Racing Toward Judgement. (Orig.). pap. 1.50 (ISBN 0-89129-035-4). Jove Pubns.
Zickgraf, Cordula. I Am Learning to Live Because You Must Die: A Hospital Diary. Scheidt, David L., tr. from Ger. LC 80-2371. 144p. 1981. pap. 6.95 (ISBN 0-8006-1434-8, 1-1434). Fortress.
DEVOTIONAL LITERATURE (SELECTIONS: EXTRACTS, ETC.)
Blackburn, Joyce. A Book of Praises. 128p. (Orig.). (YA) 1980. pap. 3.95 (ISBN 0-310-42061-X). Zondervan.
Bolding, Amy. Easy Devotions to Give. (Paperback Program Ser.). 96p. (Orig.). 1981. pap. 2.95 (ISBN 0-8010-0794-1). Baker Bk.
Bryant, Al, ed. Climbing the Heights. 384p. 1981. pap. 4.95 (ISBN 0-310-22061-0). Zondervan.
Byrum, Isabel. The Pilot's Voice. (Illus.). 146p. pap. 1.50. Faith Pub Hse.
Chrysostomos, Archimandrite. The Ancient Fathers of the Church: Translated Narratives from the Evertinos on Passions & Perfection in Christ. (Illus.). 118p. 1980. 7.95 (ISBN 0-916586-77-4); pap. 4.95. Hellenic Coll Pr.
Coleman, William L. Singing Penguins & Puffed-up Toads. 128p. (ps-4). 1981. pap. 3.95 (ISBN 0-87123-554-4, 210554). Bethany Fell.
DePree, Gladis & DePree, Gordon. A Time to Grow. 112p. (Orig.). 1981. pap. 3.95 (ISBN 0-310-23681-9). Zondervan.
Eck, Margaret. Lest We Forget. 72p. pap. 0.75; pap. 2.00 3 copies. Faith Pub Hse.
Guideposts Treasury of Inspirational Classics. 1981. pap. 2.95 (ISBN 0-553-14271-2). Bantam.
Hale, Mabel. Stories of Home Folks. 160p. pap. 1.50. Faith Pub Hse.
Murray, Andrew. Believer's Daily Renewal. 144p. 1981. pap. 2.95 (ISBN 0-87123-147-6, 210147). Bethany Fell.
Orr, C. E. Food for Lambs. 168p. pap. 1.50. Faith Pub Hse.
--Heavenly Life for Earthly Living. 60p. 0.40; 3 copies. Faith Pub Hse.
--Odors from Golden Vials. 78p. pap. 0.60. Faith Pub Hse.
Riggle, H. M. The Kingdom of God & the One Thousand Years Reign. 160p. pap. 1.50. Faith Pub Hse.
Shaw, Jean. Second Cup of Coffee. 192p. (Orig.). 1981. pap. 2.95 (ISBN 0-310-43542-0). Zondervan.
Spurgeon, Charles H. Spurgeon's Morning & Evening. 736p. 1980. Repr. 10.95 (ISBN 0-310-32940-X). Zondervan.
Teasley, D. O. Rays of Hope. 95p. pap. 0.75. Faith Pub Hse.
Tengbom, Mildred. Does Anyone Care How I Feel? 128p. (gr. 4 up). 1981. pap. 3.95 (ISBN 0-87123-142-5, 210142). Bethany Fell.
Williams, Effie. The Man of His Counsel. 112p. pap. 1.00. Faith Pub Hse.
DEVOTIONAL THEOLOGY
see Devotional Exercises; Devotional Literature; Meditations; Prayers;
also subdivision Prayer-Books and Devotions under names of Christian denominations, religious orders, classes of persons, etc.
DEVOTIONAL YEARBOOKS
see Devotional Calendars
DEVOTIONS
see Devotional Exercises
DEWEY, JOHN, 1859-1952
Dewey, John. The Later Works of John Dewey, Nineteen Twenty-Five to Nineteen Fifty-Three: Volume 1, Nineteen Twenty-Five. Boydston, Jo Ann, et al, eds. 1981. price not set (ISBN 0-8093-0986-6). S Ill U Pr.
Lamont, Corliss, ed. Dialogue on John Dewey. 155p. (Orig.). 1981. pap. 4.95 (ISBN 0-8180-1328-1). Horizon.
DEXTERITY
see Motor Ability
DHYANA (MEDITATION)
see Meditation (Buddhism)
DHYANA (SECT)
see Zen Buddhism
DIABETES
see also Insulin
Ahuja, M. M. Epidemology of Diabetes in Developing Countries. 124p. 1980. pap. 5.95x (ISBN 0-89955-316-8, Pub. by Interprint India). Intl Schol Bk Serv.
Bernstein, Richard K. Diabetes: The Glucograph Method for Normalizing Blood Sugar. Behrman, Marion, ed. (Illus.). 320p. 1981. 14.95 (ISBN 0-517-54155-6). Crown.
Craig, Oman & Apley, John. Childhood Diabetes. 2nd ed. (Postgraduate Pediatric Ser.). 1981. text ed. price not set (ISBN 0-407-00209-X). Butterworth.
Farquhar, James W. The Diabetic Child. (Patient Handbook Ser.). (Illus.). 96p. 1981. pap. 2.95 (ISBN 0-443-02193-7). Churchill.
Kivelowitz, Terri. Diabetes: A Guide to Self-Management for Patients & Their Families. (Illus.). 224p. 1981. 12.95 (ISBN 0-13-208637-9, Spec); pap. 5.95 (ISBN 0-13-208629-8). P-H.
Podolsky, Stephen, ed. Clinical Diabetes: Modern Management. 608p. 1980. 30.00x (ISBN 0-8385-1123-6). ACC.
Skyler, Jay S. & Cahill, George F., eds. Diabetes Mellitus. (Illus.). 400p. 1981. text ed. write for info. (ISBN 0-914316-23-0). Yorke Med.
Steiner, George & Lawrence, Patricia A. Educating Diabetic Patients. 1981. text ed. price not set (ISBN 0-8261-2760-6); pap. text ed. price not set (ISBN 0-8261-2761-4). Springer Pub.
Van Son, Allene. Diabetes: A Guide for Patient Education. 288p. 1981. pap. 9.50 (ISBN 0-8385-1596-7). ACC.
DIABETIC DIET
see Cookery for Diabetics
Steiner, George & Lawrence, Patricia A. Educating Diabetic Patients. 1981. text ed. price not set (ISBN 0-8261-2760-6); pap. text ed. price not set (ISBN 0-8261-2761-4). Springer Pub.
DIAGNOSIS
see also Children–Diseases–Diagnosis; Diagnosis, Radioscopic; Endoscope and Endoscopy; Medicine, Clinical; Microscopy, Medical; Pain; Pathology; Physical Diagnosis; Radiesthesia; Veterinary Medicine–Diagnosis
also subdivisions Diseases–Diagnosis or Diseases under names of organs and regions of the body, e.g. Lungs–diseases–diagnosis; also subdivisions Diagnosis under particular diseases, e.g. Tuberculosis–Diagnosis
Ali, Majid, et al. Visa Qualifying Examination Review, Vol. 1: Basic Sciences. LC 78-61617. 1978. pap. 11.75 (ISBN 0-87488-124-2). Med Exam.
Baker, Michael A. Visa Qualifying Examination Review, Vol. 2: Clinical Sciences. LC 78-61618. 1978. pap. 11.75 (ISBN 0-87488-125-0). Med Exam.
Dagnini, Giorgio. Clinical Laparoscopy. (Illus.). xii, 307p. 1980. 130.00 (ISBN 88-212-0746-3, Pub. by Piccin Italy). J K Burgess.
Hersh, Leroy, ed. New Developments in Clinical Instrumentation. 192p. 1981. 49.95 (ISBN 0-8493-5305-X). CRC Pr.
Holbrook, John H. Physical Diagnosis Review. LC 79-88046. 1979. pap. 8.50 (ISBN 0-87488-135-8). Med Exam.
Intermed Communications, ed. Diagnostics. (Nurse's Reference Library). (Illus.). 1200p. 1981. text ed. 19.95 (ISBN 0-916730-29-8). Intermed Comm.
Krupp, Marcus A. & Chatton, Milton J., eds. Current Medical Diagnosis & Treatment. rev. ed. LC 74-641062. (Illus.). 1100p. 1981. lexotone cover 21.00 (ISBN 0-87041-251-5). Lange.
Lee, Bok Y. Handbook of Noninvasive Diagnostic Techniques. 352p. 1981. pap. 15.00 (ISBN 0-8385-3620-4). ACC.
Seedor, Marie M. Aids to Nursing Diagnosis. 3rd ed. (Nursing Education Monograph: No. 6). 1980. pap. 8.95 (ISBN 0-397-54120-1, Pub. by Columbia U Pr). Lippincott.
Swartz, Mark H., ed. An Introduction to Physical Diagnosis. Date not set. text ed. price not set (ISBN 0-89004-562-3). Raven.
DIAGNOSIS, RADIOSCOPIC
see also Pediatric Radiology; X-Rays

also subdivision names of organs with or without the subdivision Radiography

Edeiken, Jack. Roentgen Diagnosis of Diseases of the Bone. (Golden's Diagnostic Radiology Ser.: Section No. 6). (Illus.). 1752p. 1981. price not set (2744-1). Williams & Wilkins.

Harris, John H., Jr. & Harris, William H. The Radiology of Emergency Medicine. 2nd ed. (Illus.). 550p. 1981. write for info. (3883-4). Williams & Wilkins.

Juhl, John H. Paul & Juhl's Essentials of Roentgen Interpretation. 4th ed. (Illus.). 1184p. 1981. text ed. price not set (ISBN 0-06-142143-X, Harper Medical). Har-Row.

DIAGNOSIS, ULTRASONIC

see also Ultrasonics in Medicine

Athey, Patricia A. & Hadlock, Frank P. Ultrasound in Obstetrics & Gynecology. (Illus.). 400p. 1981. text ed. 45.00 (ISBN 0-8016-0374-9). Mosby.

Thompson, H. E. & Bernstine, R. L. Diagnostic Ultrasound in Clinical Obstetrics & Gynecology. 192p. 1978. 34.95 (ISBN 0-471-86080-8, 1-322). Wiley.

DIAGNOSIS, VETERINARY

see Veterinary Medicine–Diagnosis

DIAGNOSTIC PSYCHOLOGICAL TESTING

see Clinical Psychology

DIAGNOSTIC ULTRASONICS

see Diagnosis, Ultrasonic

DIAGRAMS, STATISTICAL

see Statistics–Charts, Tables, etc.; Statistics–Graphic Methods

DIALECTIC (LOGIC)

see Logic

DIALECTIC (RELIGION)

see Dialectical Theology

DIALECTIC LOGIC

see Logic

DIALECTICAL THEOLOGY

Crisis, Cambios y Conflictos. 1980. pap. 1.40 (ISBN 0-686-69360-4). Vida Pubs.

DIALECTS

see Creole Dialects; Grammar, Comparative and General; Languages, Mixed

also subdivisions Dialects; Idioms, Corrections, Errors; Provincialisms under names of languages

DIAMOND DRILLING

see Boring

DIAMONDS

see also Gems

Green, Timothy S. The World of Diamonds. LC 80-26196. (Illus.). 1981. price not set (ISBN 0-688-03731-3). Morrow.

DIAPHRAGMS (MECHANICAL DEVICES)

DiGiovanni. Flat & Corrugated Diapharm Design Handbook. Date not set. price not set. Dekker.

Institute of Civil Engineers. A Review of Diaphragm Walls. 158p. 1980. 35.00x (ISBN 0-7277-0045-6, Pub. by Telford England). State Mutual Bk.

DIARIES–BIBLIOGRAPHY

Barrett, William T., II, ed. The Overland Journal of Amos Piatt Josselyn. 129p. 1978. octavo 10.00. Holmes.

DIATOMACEAE

Wujek, E. D. & Rupp, R. F. Diatoms of the Tittabawassee River, Michigan. (Bibliotheca Phycologica: No. 50). (Illus.). 160p. 1981. pap. text ed. 25.00x (ISBN 3-7682-1271-8, Pub. by Cramer Germany). Lubrecht & Cramer.

DIAZ, PORFIRIO, PRES. MEXICO, 1830-1915

Gil, Carlos A., ed. Age of Porfirio Diaz: Selected Readings. LC 76-57535. (Illus.). 191p. 5.95 (ISBN 0-8263-0284-X). U of NM Pr.

DICKENS, CHARLES, 1812-1870

Dello Buono, Carmen J. Rare Early Essays on Charles Dickens. 207p. 1980. lib. bdg. 22.50 (ISBN 0-8482-0647-9). Norwood Edns.

Fitzgerald, Percy H. The History of Pickwick. 1980. Repr. of 1891 ed. lib. bdg. 45.00 (ISBN 0-8492-4631-8). R West.

Fyfe, Thomas A. Who's Who in Dickens. 352p. Repr. of 1913 ed. lib. bdg. 30.00 (ISBN 0-8495-1713-3). Arden Lib.

Horton, Susan R. The Reader in the Dickens World. LC 80-53031. 215p. 1981. 29.95 (ISBN 0-8229-1140-X). U of Pittsburgh Pr.

Jones, Charles H. A Short Life of Charles Dickens with Selections from His Letters. 260p. 1980. Repr. of 1900 ed. lib. bdg. 30.00 (ISBN 0-8414-5406-X). Folcroft.

Lambert, Mark. Dickens & the Suspended Quotation. LC 80-22072. 208p. 1981. 16.50 (ISBN 0-300-02555-6). Yale U Pr.

Neale, Charles M. An Index to Pickwick. 75p. 1980. Repr. of 1897 ed. lib. bdg. 12.50 (ISBN 0-89987-603-X). Darby Bks.

Newman, S. J. Dickens at Play. 1981. 14.95 (ISBN 0-312-19980-5). St Martin.

DICKENS, CHARLES, 1812-1870–BIBLIOGRAPHY

Podeschi, John B. Dickens & Dickensiana: A Catalogue of the Richard Gimbel Collection in the Yale University Library. LC 79-66938. 594p. 1981. text ed. 65.00x (ISBN 0-300-03506-3). Yale U Pr.

Wright, Thomas. The Life of Charles Dickens. 392p. 1980. Repr. of 1935 ed. lib. bdg. 45.00 (ISBN 0-8492-2999-5). R West.

DICKINSON, EMILY NORCROSS, 1830-1886

Ferlazzo, Paul J., ed. Emily Dickinson. (Twayne's U. S. Authors Ser.). 168p. 1976. pap. text ed. 4.95 (ISBN 0-672-61511-8). Bobbs.

Frisbiewhicher, George. This Was a Poet: A Critical Biography of Emily Dickinson. 337p. 1980. 17.50 (ISBN 0-208-01900-6, Archon); pap. 9.50 tchr.'s ed. (ISBN 0-208-01901-4). Shoe String.

Porter, David. Dickinson: The Modern Idiom. LC 80-24322. 336p. 1981. text ed. 20.00 (ISBN 0-674-20444-1). Harvard U Pr.

DICOTYLEDONS

Godfrey, Robert K. & Wooten, Jean W. Aquatic & Wetland Plants of Southeastern United States: Dicotyledons. LC 80-16452. (Illus.). 864p. 1981. lib. bdg. 40.00x (ISBN 0-8203-0532-4). U of Ga Pr.

DICTATION (OFFICE PRACTICE)

see also Shorthand

Gonzalez, Jean. Complete Guide to Effective Dictation. 1980. pap. text ed. 12.95 (ISBN 0-534-00811-9). Kent Pub Co.

Schrag, Adele F. How to Dictate. LC 80-26747. (Illus.). 96p. 1981. pap. text ed. 3.60 (ISBN 0-07-055601-6). McGraw.

Uris, Auren. The Dictation Book. rev. ed. 113p. pap. text ed. 8.95 (ISBN 0-935220-05-4). Intl Word Process.

DICTATORS

Miller, Arthur S. Democratic Dictatorship: The Emergent Constitution of Control. LC 80-25424. (Contributions in American Studies: No. 54). 312p. 1981. lib. bdg. 29.95 (ISBN 0-313-22836-1, MDD/). Greenwood.

DICTIONARIES

see Encyclopedias and Dictionaries;

also particular languages or subjects with or without the subdivision dictionaries

DIDACTICS

see Teaching

DIDEROT, DENIS, 1713-1784

Schwartz, Leon. Diderot & the Jews. LC 78-73304. 220p. 1981. 14.50 (ISBN 0-8386-2377-8). Fairleigh Dickinson.

DIE CASTING

Schubert, Paul B., ed. Die Methods: Design, Frabrication, Maintainance & Application, Bk. 1. LC 66-19984. (Illus.). 464p. 1966. 18.00 (ISBN 0-8311-1013-9). Indus Pr.

DIESEL ENGINE

see Diesel Motor

DIESEL LOCOMOTIVE ENGINES

see Diesel Locomotives

DIESEL LOCOMOTIVES

New England Diesels. 28.95. Chatham Pub CA.

DIESEL MOTOR

see also Automobiles–Motors; Marine Diesel Motors

Barlow, Roger. The Diesel Car Book. LC 80-8913. (Illus.). 288p. (Orig.). 1981. pap. 7.95 (ISBN 0-394-17895-5, Ever). Grove.

Weathers, Tom & Hunter, Claud. Diesel Engines for Automobiles & Small Trucks. 300p. 1981. text ed. 16.95 (ISBN 0-8359-1288-4); instr's. manual free (ISBN 0-8359-1289-2). Reston.

DIET

see also Animal Food; Beverages; Cookery; Cookery–Reducing Recipes; Food; Food, Raw; Food Habits; Low Carbohydrate Diet; Low-Fat Diet; Menus; Nutrition; Reducing Diets; School Children–Food; Vegetarianism

Adcock, Larry. How to Weigh Less for the Rest of Your Life. 1980. pap. 2.25 (ISBN 0-446-92084-3). Warner Bks.

Alter, Robert M. The No-Nibbling Book: One Hundred Twenty-Eight Things to Do at the Refrigerator Door So You Won't Open It. 144p. 1981. 9.95 (ISBN 0-399-12581-7). Putnam.

Edelstein, Barbara. The Woman Doctor's Diet for Teenage Girls. 288p. 1981. pap. 2.50 (ISBN 0-345-28879-3). Ballantine.

--The Woman Doctor's Diet for Women. 199p. 1981. pap. 2.50 (ISBN 0-345-29488-2). Ballantine.

Ernst, K. F. The Complete Calorie Counter for Dining Out. (Orig.). 1981. pap. 2.95 (ISBN 0-515-05500-X). Jove Pubns.

--The Complete Carbohydrate Counter for Dining Out. 1981. pap. 2.95 (ISBN 0-515-05698-7). Jove Pubns.

Franz, William & Franz, Barbara. To Eat or Not to Eat: A Young People's Guide to Dietary Goals for the United States. (Illus.). 160p. (gr. 9-12). 1981. PLB price not set (ISBN 0-671-42563-3). Messner.

Jones, Jeanne. Diet for a Happy Heart: A Low-Cholesterol, Low-Saturated Fat, Low Calorie Cookbook. rev. ed. (Illus.). 192p. 1981. pap. 6.95 (ISBN 0-89286-183-5). One Hurd One Prods.

Karow, Juliette. The Necessary Diet. (Orig.). 1981. pap. 5.95 (ISBN 0-89865-085-2). Donning Co.

Kaufman, William I. The Diet Diary. (Watch Your Diet Ser.). (Orig.). 1981. pap. 1.75 (ISBN 0-515-05915-3). Jove Pubns.

Macleod, W. & Macleod, G. M.I.N.D. Over Weight: How to Stay Slim the Rest of Your Life. 1981. pap. 7.95 (ISBN 0-13-583385-X). P-H.

Mason, Sally W. The New Holistic Way to Lose Weight & Rejuvenate. rev. ed. (Illus.). 228p. 1980. Repr. of 1979 ed. 9.95 (ISBN 0-8119-0348-6). Fell.

Parriott, Sara. Calories Don't Count When... LC 79-84900. (Illus.). 96p. 1979. pap. 2.95 (ISBN 0-87477-105-6). J P Tarcher.

Rush, David, et al, eds. Diet in Pregnancy: A Randomized Controlled Trail of Nutritional Supplements. LC 79-3846. (Alan R. Liss Ser.: Vol. 16, No. 3). 1980. 26.00 (ISBN 0-8451-1037-3). March of Dimes.

Vincent, L. M. Competing with the Sylph: Dancers & the Pursuit of the Ideal Body Form. 143p. 1980. pap. 5.95 (ISBN 0-8362-2407-8). Andrews & McMeel.

Whitley, Craig. Recipes for Runners: A Complete Nutrition Guide for Runners. (Illus.). 272p. 1981. cancelled (ISBN 0-913276-34-0). Stone Wall Pr.

Wigmore, Ann. You Are Your Own Healer. 207p. pap. 1.95. Hippocrates.

Williams, Sue R. Nutrition & Diet Therapy. 4th ed. (Illus.). 875p. 1981. text ed. 19.95 (ISBN 0-8016-5554-4). Mosby.

DIET, LOW SUGAR

see Sugar-Free Diet

DIET IN DISEASE

see also Cookery–Reducing Recipes; Cookery for Diabetics; Cookery for the Sick; High-Fiber Diet; Low-Fat Diet; Salt-Free Diet; Sugar-Free Diet

Childers' Diet to Stop Arthritis: The Nightshades & Ill Health. 2nd rev. ed. 200p. 1981. pap. 9.95 (ISBN 0-938378-00-7). Horticult Pubns.

Davis, Ben. Rapid Healing Foods. LC 79-22770. 1980. 10.95 (ISBN 0-13-753137-0, Parker). P-H.

Howe, Phyllis. Basic Nutrition in Health & Disease: Including Selection & Care of Food. 7th ed. 450p. 1981. pap. text ed. price not set (ISBN 0-7216-4796-0). Saunders.

DIET THERAPY

see Diet in Disease

DIETARY FIBER

see High-Fiber Diet

DIETETICS

see Diet; Diet in Disease; Nutrition

DIETING

see Reducing

DIETING FOR WEIGHT LOSS

see Reducing Diets

DIFFERENCE (PSYCHOLOGY)

Ellis, Robert S. The Psychology of Individual Differences. 533p. 1980. Repr. of 1930 ed. lib. bdg. 45.00 (ISBN 0-89760-204-8). Telegraph Bks.

DIFFERENCE EQUATIONS

Miranker, Willard L. Numerical Methods for Stiff Equations & Singular Perturbation Problems. (Mathematics & Its Applications Ser.: No. 5). 216p. 1980. lib. bdg. 29.95 (ISBN 90-277-1107-0, Pub. by D. Reidel). Kluwer Boston.

DIFFERENTIAL ANALYZERS, ELECTRONIC

see Electronic Differential Analyzers

DIFFERENTIAL CALCULUS

see Calculus, Differential

DIFFERENTIAL EQUATIONS

see also Differential Operators; Electronic Differential Analyzers; Existence Theorems; Functions; Potential, Theory of; Surfaces

Bateman, Harry. Differential Equations. LC 66-23754. 1967. 11.95 (ISBN 0-8284-0190-X). Chelsea Pub.

Bear, H. S. Introduction to Differential Equations. (Illus.). 490p. 1981. pap. text ed. 19.50 (ISBN 0-9605502-0-8). Manoa Pr.

Bucy, R. S., et al. Stochastic Differential Equations. McKean, H. P. & Keller, J. B., eds. LC 72-13266. (SIAM-AMS Proceedings). 1973. 22.00 (ISBN 0-8218-1325-0). Am Math.

Burghes, D. N. & Borrie, Y. M. Modelling with Differential Equations. (Mathematics & Its Applications Ser.). 160p. 1981. 29.95 (ISBN 0-470-27101-9). Halsted Pr.

Burton. Modeling of Differential Equations in Biology. 296p. 1980. 35.00 (ISBN 0-8247-1075-4). Dekker.

Derrick, William R. & Grossman, Stanley I. Elementary Differential Equations with Applications. 2nd ed. (Mathematics Ser.). (Illus.). 576p. 1981. text ed. price not set (ISBN 0-201-03162-0). A-W.

--Elementary Differential Equations with Applications: A Short Course. 2nd ed. (Mathenatics Ser.). (Illus.). 384p. 1981. text ed. 18.95 (ISBN 0-201-03164-7). A-W.

Everett, W. N., ed. Ordinary & Partial Differential Equations. (Lecture Notes in Mathematics Ser.: Vol. 827). (Illus.). 271p. 1981. pap. 16.80 (ISBN 0-387-10252-3). Springer-Verlag.

Johnstone, I. A Probabilistic Study of Linear Elliptic-Parabolic Equations of Second Order. (Notes on Pure Mathematics Ser.: No. 12). 217p. (Orig.). 1980. pap. text ed. 14.95 (ISBN 0-908160-32-1, 0564). Bks Australia.

Leighton, Walter. First Course in Ordinary Differential Equations. 5th ed. 304p. 1980. text ed. 21.95x (ISBN 0-534-00837-2). Wadsworth Pub.

Martini, R., ed. Geometrical Approaches to Differential Equations: Proceedings. (Lecture Notes in Mathematics: Vol. 810). (Illus.). 339p. 1980. pap. 19.50 (ISBN 0-387-10018-0). Springer-Verlag.

Muller-Pfeiffer, Erich. Spectralk Theory of Ordinary Differential Equations. LC 80-42097. (Mathematics & Its Application Ser.). 260p. 1981. 51.95 (ISBN 0-470-27103-5). Halsted Pr.

Nikol'ski, S. M., ed. Theory & Applications of Differentiable Functions of Several Variables, Vol. 4. LC 68-1677. (Proceedings of the Steklov Institute). 1974. 43.60 (ISBN 0-8218-3017-1, STEKLO-117). Am Math.

Reid, William T. Sturmian Theory for Ordinary Differential Equations. (Applied Mathematical Sciences: Vol. 31). 559p. 1981. pap. 26.80 (ISBN 0-387-90542-1). Springer-Verlag.

Sperline, Meredith E. Ordinary Differential Equations: Solutions & Applications. LC 80-6101. 584p. 1981. pap. text ed. 17.95 (ISBN 0-8191-1358-1). U Pr of Amer.

Stech, et al. Integral & Functional Differential Equations. Date not set. price not set (ISBN 0-8247-1354-0). Dekker.

DIFFERENTIAL EQUATIONS, NONLINEAR

Fucik, Svatopluk. Solvability of Nonlinear Equations & Boundry Value Problems. (Mathematics & Its Applications Ser.: No. 4). 400p. 1980. lib. bdg. 29.95 (ISBN 90-277-1077-5, Pub. by D. Reidel). Kluwer Boston.

Kakshmikantham, V. Nonlinear Differential Equations in Abstract Spaces. (I.S. Nonlinear Mathematics Series; Theory, Methods and Applications: Vol. 2). 272p. 1981. 45.00 (ISBN 0-08-025038-6). Pergamon.

DIFFERENTIAL EQUATIONS, PARTIAL

Everett, W. N., ed. Ordinary & Partial Differential Equations. (Lecture Notes in Mathematics Ser.: Vol. 827). (Illus.). 271p. 1981. pap. 16.80 (ISBN 0-387-10252-3). Springer-Verlag.

Varadhan, S. R. S. Diffusion Problems & Partial Differential Equations. (Tate Institute Lectures on Mathematics Ser.). 315p. 1981. pap. 10.70 (ISBN 0-387-08773-7). Springer-Verlag.

Vemuri, V. & Karplus, Walter. Digital Computer Treatment of Partial Differential Equations. (Illus.). 480p. 1981. text ed. 26.50 (ISBN 0-13-212407-6). P-H.

Vichenevetsky, Robert. Computer Methods for Partial Differential Equations: Elliptical Equations & the Finite Element Method, Vol. 1. (Illus.). 400p. 1981. text ed. 28.00 (ISBN 0-686-69327-2). P-H.

DIFFERENTIAL GEOMETRY

see Geometry, Differential

DIFFERENTIAL OPERATORS

see also Differential Equations

Browder, F., ed. Nonlinear Functional Analysis, Pts. 1 & 2. LC 74-3414. (Proceedings of Symposia in Pure Mathematics Ser.). 1968. Set. 44.80. Am Math.

Taylor, Michael E. Pseudodifferential Operators. LC 80-8580. (Princeton Mathematical Ser.: No. 34). 468p. 1981. 30.00x (ISBN 0-691-08282-0). Princeton U Pr.

DIFFERENTIAL THERMAL ANALYSIS

see Thermal Analysis

DIFFERENTIATION OF CELLS

see Cell Differentiation

DIFFRACTION HOLOGRAPHY

see also subdivision diffraction under subjects, e.g. X-rays–Diffraction

French, Alfred D. & Gardner, Kenncorwin H., eds. Fiber Diffraction Methods. LC 80-21566. (ACS Symposium Ser.: No. 141). 1980. 34.50 (ISBN 0-8412-0589-2). Am Chemical.

Jull, E. V. Aperture Antennas & Diffraction Theory. 1981. pap. price not set. Inst Electrical.

DIFFUSE COLLAGEN DISEASES

see Collagen Diseases

DIGESTIVE ORGANS–DISEASES

Korelitz, Burton I., ed. Inflammatory Bowel Diseases. 332p. 1981. text ed. 27.50 (ISBN 0-88416-310-5). PSG Pub.

Rotter, Jerome I., et al, eds. The Genetics & Heterogeneity of Common Gastrointestinal Disorders. 1980. 35.00 (ISBN 0-12-598760-9). Acad Pr.

Rotterdam, Heidrun Z. & Sommers, Sheldon C. Biopsy Diagnosis of the Digestive Tract. (Biopsy Interpretation Ser.). 1981. text ed. price not set (ISBN 0-89004-541-0). Raven.

DIGESTS OF CASES (LAW)

see Law Reports, Digests, Etc.

DIGITAL COMPUTER CIRCUITS

see Electronic Digital Computers–Circuits

DIGITAL COMPUTER SIMULATION

see also Artificial Intelligence

Schmidt, B. GPSS Fortran. (Computing Ser.). 544p. 1981. write for info. (ISBN 0-471-27881-5, Pub. by Wiley-Interscience). Wiley.

Watson, Hugh J. Computer Simulation in Business. 400p. 1981. text ed. 16.95 (ISBN 0-471-03638-2). Wiley.

DIGITAL COMPUTERS, ELECTRONIC

see Electronic Digital Computers

DIGITAL COUNTERS

Oberman, R. M. Counting & Counters. 192p. 1981. 29.95 (ISBN 0-470-27118-3). Halsted Pr.

DIGITAL DIFFERENTIAL ANALYZERS, ELECTRONIC

see Electronic Differential Analyzers

DIGITAL ELECTRONICS

Digital Signal Processing Committee, ed. Programs for Digital Signal Processing. LC 79-89028. 1979. 35.95; tape version 50.00. Inst Electrical.

Holdsworth. Digital Logic Design. 1981. text ed. price not set (ISBN 0-408-00404-5); pap. text ed. price not set (ISBN 0-408-00566-1). Butterworth.

Leach, Donald P. Experiments in Digital Principles. 2nd ed. (Illus.). 176p. 1980. 14.95x (ISBN 0-07-036916-X, G). McGraw.

Lenk, John D. Handbook of Digital Electronics. (Illus.). 384p. 1981. text ed. 21.95 (ISBN 0-13-377184-9). P-H.

Taub, Herbert. Digital Circuits & Microprocessors. (Electrical Engineering Ser.). (Illus.). 608p. 1981. text ed. 26.95x (ISBN 0-07-062945-5, C); solutions manual 12.95 (ISBN 0-07-062946-3). McGraw.

Young, George. Digital Electronics: A Hands-on Learning Approach. (gr. 12). 1980. pap. 8.95 (ISBN 0-8104-5668-0). Hayden.

DIGITAL FILTERS (MATHEMATICS)

Huang, T. S., ed. Two-Dimensional Digital Signal Processing I: Linear Filters. (Topids in Applied Physics Ser.: Vol. 42). (Illus.). 1981. 46.60 (ISBN 0-686-69432-5). Springer-Verlag.

--Two-Dimensional Digital Signal Processing II: Transforms & Median Filters. (Topics in Applied Physics Ser.: Vol. 43). (Illus.). 260p. 1981. 46.60 (ISBN 0-686-69433-3). Springer-Verlag.

Taylor. Digital Filter Design Handbook. Date not set. price not set (ISBN 0-8247-1357-5). Dekker.

DIGITAL SIMULATION

see Digital Computer Simulation

DILTHEY, WILHELM, 1833-1911

Bulhof, Ilse N. Wilhelm Dilthey: A Hermeneutic Approach to the Study of History & Culture. (Martinus Nijhoff Philosophy Library: No. 2). 225p. 1980. lib. bdg. 37.00 (ISBN 90-247-2360-4, Pub. by Martinus Nijhoff). Kluwer Boston.

Ermarth, Michael. Wilhelm Dilthey: The Critique of Historical Reason. write for info. (ISBN 0-226-21743-4). U of Chicago Pr.

DIMAGGIO, JOSEPH PAUL, 1914-

DeGregorio, George. Joe DiMaggio: An Informal Biography. LC 80-6159. 272p. 1981. 12.95 (ISBN 0-8128-2777-5). Stein & Day.

DIMENSIONAL ANALYSIS

see also Engineering Mathematics

McKay & Patera. McKay & Patera Tables of Dimensions. 336p. Date not set. 39.75 (ISBN 0-8247-1227-7). Dekker.

DINESEN, ISAK, PSEUD.

see Blixen, Karen, 1885-1962

DINING

see Dinners and Dining

DINING ESTABLISHMENTS

see Restaurants, Lunchrooms, Etc.

DINNERS AND DINING

see also Cookery; Desserts; Drinking Customs; Food; Menus

Taylor, Derek. How to Sell Banquets. rev. ed. 224p. 1981. 16.95 (ISBN 0-8436-2198-2). CBI Pub.

DINOSAURIA

Gilbert, John. Dinosaurs Discovered. LC 80-82756. (Illus.). 96p. 1981. 8.95 (ISBN 0-88332-252-8). Larousse.

DINOSAURIA–JUVENILE LITERATURE

Hoff, Syd. Amy's Dinosaur. LC 80-14082. (Illus.). 48p. (ps-2). 1980. pap. 3.95 (ISBN 0-671-41338-4, Pub. by Windmill). S&S.

Sattler, Helen R. Dinosaurs of North America. (Illus.). 160p. (gr. 2 up). 1981. 10.95 (ISBN 0-688-51952-0). Morrow.

DIOCESAN SCHOOLS

see Church Schools

DIOPTRICS

see Refraction

DIPLOMACY

see also Diplomatic Negotiations in International Disputes; Diplomats; Treaties

also subdivision Foreign Relations under names of countries, e.g. United States–Foreign Relations

Plischke, Elmer, ed. Modern Diplomacy: The Art &The Artisans. 1979. pap. 9.25 (ISBN 0-8447-3350-4). Am Enterprise.

DIPLOMATIC NEGOTIATIONS IN INTERNATIONAL DISPUTES

Fischer. A Collection of International Concessions & Related Instruments, Vols. 9-10. 1980. 45.00 ea. Vol. 9 (ISBN 0-379-10084-3). Vol. 10 (ISBN 0-379-10085-1). Oceana.

International Center for Settlement of Investment Disputes. Investment Laws of the World, Binder 10. 1979. 75.00 (ISBN 0-379-00650-2). Oceana.

Posses, F. The Art of International Negotiation. 195p. 1978. text ed. 23.50x (ISBN 0-220-66315-7, Pub. by Busn Bks England). Renouf.

DIPLOMATIC PROTESTS

see Diplomacy

DIPLOMATS

Asbell, Bernard. The Senate Nobody Knows. LC 80-8928. 480p. 1981. pap. text ed. 6.95x (ISBN 0-8018-2620-9). Johns Hopkins.

Devine, Michael J. John W. Foster: Politics & Diplomacy in the Imperial Era-1873-1917. LC 80-17387. (Illus.). 200p. 1981. 14.95x (ISBN 0-8214-0437-7). Ohio U Pr.

DIPLOMATS' WIVES

Helms, Cynthia. An Ambassador's Wife in Iran. LC 80-25090. (Illus.). 284p. 1981. 9.95 (ISBN 0-396-07881-8). Dodd.

DIPSOMANIA

see Alcoholism

DIPTERA

see also Flies

also particular kinds of flies, gnats, etc. e.g. Mosquitoes

Theodor, Oskar. Diptera: Asilidae Insecta II, Vol. 2. (Fauna Palaestina). (Illus.). 458p. 1981. text ed. 30.00x (ISBN 0-87474-910-7). Smithsonian.

--An Illustrated Catalogue of the Rothschild Collection of Nycteribiidae (Diptera) in the British Museum (Natural History) (Illus.). viii, 506p. 1967. 66.50x (ISBN 0-565-00655-X, Pub. by British Mus Nat Hist England). Sabbot-Natural Hist Bks.

DIRECT PRIMARIES

see Primaries

DIRECT TAXATION

see Income Tax; Taxation

DIRECTION, SENSE OF

see Orientation

DIRECTION, SPIRITUAL

see Spiritual Direction

DIRECTORS, MOVING-PICTURE

see Moving-Picture Producers and Directors

DIRECTORS OF CORPORATIONS

Batty, J. The Board & the Presentation of Financial Information to Management. 340p. 1978. text ed. 36.75x (ISBN 0-220-66352-1, Pub. by Busn Bks England). Renouf.

Betts, Peter W. The Board & Administrative Management: Management for the Board. 192p. 1977. text ed. 23.50x (ISBN 0-220-66338-6, Pub. by Busn Bks England). Renouf.

Frean, David. The Board & Management Development. 188p. 1980. text ed. 30.75x (ISBN 0-220-66304-1, Pub. by Busn Bks England). Renouf.

Galley, J. N. The Board & Computer Management. 185p. 1978. text ed. 23.50x (ISBN 0-220-67000-5, Pub. by Busn Bks England). Renouf.

Washbrook, H. The Board & Management Audit. 262p. 1978. text ed. 30.75x (ISBN 0-220-66334-3, Pub. by Busn Bks England). Renouf.

DISABILITY, READING

see Reading Disability

DISABILITY EVALUATION

see also Industrial Accidents

Ferry, Ted S. Modern Accident Investigation & Analysis: An Executive Guide to Accident Investigation. 350p. 1981. 30.00 (ISBN 0-471-07776-3). Page-Ficklin.

DISABILITY INSURANCE

see Insurance, Disability

DISABLED

see Handicapped

DISARMAMENT

see also Arbitration, International; Atomic Weapons and Disarmament; Militarism; Peace; Sea-Power; Security, International

Barton, John H. The Politics of Peace: An Evaluation of Arms Control. LC 79-67776. 296p. 1981. text ed. 18.50x (ISBN 0-8047-1081-3). Stanford U Pr.

Bertram, Christoph, ed. Arms Control & Military Force. LC 80-67836. (Adelphi Library: Vol. 3). 272p. 1981. text ed. 32.50 (ISBN 0-916672-70-0). Allanheld.

Haavelsrud, M. Disarmament Education. 1981. text ed. write for info. (ISBN 0-86103-043-5, Westbury Hse). Butterworth.

Hoeber, Francis P. How Little Is Enough? SALT & Security in the Long Run. (NSIC Strategy Paper Ser.: No. 35). 96p. 1981. pap. text ed. 5.95x (ISBN 0-8448-1383-4). Crane-Russak Co.

Hoover, Robert A. Arms Control: The Interwar Naval Limitation Agreements. (Monograph Series in World Affairs). 124p. (Orig.). 1980. pap. 4.00 (ISBN 0-87940-062-5). U of Denver Intl.

Labrie, Roger, ed. SALT Handbook: Key Documents & Issues, 1972-1979. 1979. pap. 12.25 (ISBN 0-8447-3316-4). Am Enterprise.

Laszlo, Ervin & Keys, Donald, eds. Disarmament: The Human Factor: Pproceedings of a Colloquium on the Societal Context for Disarmament. 200p. 1981. 25.00 (ISBN 0-08-024703-2). Pergamon.

Record, Jeffrey. Force Reductions in Europe: Starting Over. LC 80-83753. (Special Report Ser.). 92p. 1980. 6.50 (ISBN 0-89549-027-7). Inst Foreign Policy Anal.

Statement of the Honorable Henry A. Kissinger with Respect to the Treaty on Strategic Arms Limitation Before the Committee on Foreign Relations of the U. S. Senate, July 31, 1979. (Significant Issues Ser.: Vol. I, No. 4). 35p. 1979. pap. 5.00 (ISBN 0-686-68798-1, CSIS005, CSIS). Unipub.

The United Nations Disarmament Yearbook: 1978, Vol. 3. 535p. 1979. 30.00 (ISBN 0-686-68979-8, UN79/9/2, UN). Unipub.

DISARMAMENT AND ATOMIC WEAPONS

see Atomic Weapons and Disarmament

DISASTER RELIEF

see also Emergency Medical Services

Foster, H. D. Disaster Planning: The Preservation of Life & Property. (Springer Series on Environmental Management). (Illus.). 275p. 1981. 29.80 (ISBN 0-387-90498-0). Springer-Verlag.

Stoffer, R. & Lavalla, Rick. Emergency Prepardedness Education: An Overview. 74p. pap. 3.00 (ISBN 0-913724-23-8). Survival Ed Assoc.

DISASTERS

see also Accidents; Building Failures; Natural Disasters; Shipwrecks

Davis, I., ed. Disasters & the Small Dwelling. 220p. 1981. 30.00 (ISBN 0-08-024753-9). Pergamon.

Gleser, Goldine C., et al. Buffalo Creek Revisted: Prolonged Psychological Effects of a Disaster. (Personality & Psychopathology Ser.). 1981. price not set (ISBN 0-12-286260-0). Acad Pr.

Goodman, Jeffrey. We Are the Earthquake Generation. 1980. pap. 2.75 (ISBN 0-425-04991-4). Berkley Pub.

Popoff, Peter. Calamities, Catastrophies, & Chaos. Tanner, Don, ed. LC 80-69974. (Illus.). 108p. 1980. pap. 2.50 (ISBN 0-938544-01-2). Faith Messenger.

Whittow, John. Disasters: The Anatomy of Environmental Hazards. LC 79-5236. (Illus.). 405p. 1981. pap. 9.95 (ISBN 0-8203-0542-1). U of Ga Pr.

DISCIPLES, TWELVE

see Apostles

DISCIPLES OF CHRIST

Moloney, F. J. Disciples & Prophets. 240p. 1981. 9.95 (ISBN 0-8245-0049-0). Crossroad NY.

DISCIPLES OF CHRIST–HISTORY

Updegraff, John C. The Christian Church (Disciples of Christ) in Florida: Its History & Development. 384p. 1981. write for info. (ISBN 0-89305-034-2). Anna Pub.

DISCIPLES OF CHRIST–LITURGY AND RITUAL

McWhirter, David. Millenial Harbinger - Index. LC 81-65031. (Millenial Harbinger Ser.). 864p. 1981. 19.95 (ISBN 0-89900-228-5). College Pr Pub.

DISCIPLESHIP

see Christian Life

DISCIPLINE, ECCLESIASTICAL

see Church Discipline

DISCIPLINE OF CHILDREN

Dreikurs, Rudolph. Discipline Without Tears. 1974. pap. 3.95 (ISBN 0-8015-2132-7, Hawthorn). Dutton.

Raffini, James P. Discipline: Negotiating Conflicts with Today's Kids. 192p. 1980. 10.95 (Spec); pap. 3.95. P-H.

DISCOURSES

see Lectures and Lecturing; Speeches, Addresses, etc.

DISCOVERERS

see Discoveries (In Geography)

DISCOVERIES (IN GEOGRAPHY)

see also Antarctic Regions; Arctic Regions; Geography–History; Voyages and Travels

also subdivision Discovery and Exploration under names of countries, etc.

Hanbury-Tenison, Robin. Mulu: The Rain Forest. (Illus.). 176p. 1980. 22.50x (ISBN 0-297-77768-8, Pub. by Weidenfeld & Nicolson England). Biblio Dist.

Hilder, Brett. The Voyage of Torres: The Discovery of the Southern Coastline of New Guinea & Torres Strait by Captain Luis Baez De Torres in 1606. (Illus.). 194p. 1981. 21.75x (ISBN 0-7022-1275-X). U of Queensland Pr.

DISCOVERIES (IN SCIENCE)

see Industrial Arts; Inventions; Patents; Science

DISCRIMINATION

Here are entered general works on social discrimination based on race, religion, sex, social minority status, or other factors.

see also Civil Rights; Discrimination in Education; Discrimination in Employment; Minorities; Race Discrimination; Sex Discrimination

Levin, Jack & Levin, William. Ageism: Prejudice & Discrimination Against the Elderly. 168p. 1980. pap. text ed. 7.95x (ISBN 0-534-00881-X). Wadsworth Pub.

DISCRIMINATION, RACE

see Race Discrimination

DISCRIMINATION, SEXUAL

see Sex Discrimination

DISCRIMINATION AGAINST WOMEN

see Sex Discrimination

DISCRIMINATION IN EDUCATION

see also Segregation in Education

Quay, Richard H. In Pursuit of Equality of Educational Opportunity: A Selective Bibliography & Guide to the Research Literature. LC 76-52691. 200p. 1978. lib. bdg. 23.00 (ISBN 0-8240-9872-2). Garland Pub.

Spender, Dale, ed. Men's Studies Modified: The Impact of Feminism on the Academic Disciplines. (Athene Ser.: Vol. 1). 350p. 1981. 40.00 (ISBN 0-08-026770-X); pap. 18.90 (ISBN 0-08-026117-5). Pergamon.

DISCRIMINATION IN EMPLOYMENT

see also Age and Employment;

also subdivision Employment under names of social or racial groups, e.g. Afro-Americans–Employment; Women–Employment; etc

Livernash, E. Robert, ed. Comparable Worth: Issues & Alternatives. LC 80-67644. 260p. 1980. 21.00 (ISBN 0-937856-01-0). Equal Employ.

Shaeffer, Ruth G. Nondiscrimination in Employment-& Beyond, Report No. 782. vi, 108p. (Orig.). 1980. pap. 30.00 (ISBN 0-8237-0218-9). Conference Bd.

Shedd, Joe. White Workers & Black Trainees: An Outline of Some of the Issues Raised by Special Training Programs for the Disadvantaged. (Key Issues Ser.: No. 13). 1973. pap. 2.00. NY Sch Indus Rel.

Stasz, Clarice. The American Nightmare: The Success Ideal & Work Discrimination. LC 80-6191. 192p. 1981. 14.95 (ISBN 0-8052-3765-8). Schocken.

Taylor, Lynda K. A Fairer Slice of the Cake: The Task Ahead. 228p. 1976. text ed. 21.00x (ISBN 0-220-66284-3, Pub. by Busn Bks England). Renouf.

DISCRIMINATION IN EMPLOYMENT–LAW AND LEGISLATION

Modjeska, Lee. Handling Employment Discrimination Cases, Vol. 1. LC 78-70830. 1980. 47.50. Lawyers Co-Op.

Player, Mack A. Federal Law of Employment Discrimination in a Nutshell. rev. ed. LC 80-22475. (Nutshell Ser.). 357p. 1980. pap. text ed. 6.95 (ISBN 0-8299-2111-7). West Pub.

Sullivan, Charles A., et al. Federal Statutory Law of Employment Discrimination. 1000p. 1980. text ed. 45.00 (ISBN 0-672-83697-1). Bobbs.

DISCS

see Phonorecords

DISCUSSION

see also Debates and Debating; Meetings; Negotiation

Baird, John E., Jr. & Weinberg, Sanford B. Group Communication: Essence of Synergy. 270p. 1981. pap. text ed. write for info. (ISBN 0-697-04181-6); resourse manual avail. (ISBN 0-697-04187-5). Wm C Brown.

DISEASE (PATHOLOGY)

see Pathology

DISEASE, DIET IN

see Diet in Disease

DISEASE GERMS

see Germ Theory of Disease

DISEASE OUTBREAKS

see Epidemics

DISEASE RESISTANCE OF PLANTS

see Plants–Disease and Pest Resistance

DISEASES–CAUSES AND THEORIES OF CAUSATION

see also Accidents; Communicable Diseases; Germ Theory of Disease; Heredity; Infection; Traumatism

Blecher, Melvin & Barr, Robert S. Receptors & Human Disease. (Illus.). 350p. 1981. write for info. (0609-6). Williams & Wilkins.

Branwood. Diagnosis & Interpretations of Changing Patterns in Multiple Disease States. 1981. price not set (ISBN 0-89352-025-X). Masson Pub.

Caplan, Arthur L., et al. Concepts of Health & Disease: Interdisciplinary Perspectives. 608p. 1981. pap. text ed. write for info. (ISBN 0-201-00973-0). A-W.

Clegg, E. J. & Garlick, J. P., eds. Disease & Urbanization. (Symposia of the Society for the Study of Human Biology: Vol. 20). 1980. text ed. 22.25x (ISBN 0-85066-190-0). Humanities.

Koenig. Illnesses of Our Time. 1980. pap. 3.25x (ISBN 0-906492-36-X, Pub. by Kolisko Archives). St George Bk Serv.

Morgagni, John B. The Seats & Causes of Disease Investigated by Anatomy, 3 vols. Alexander, Benjamin, tr. LC 60-13365. (History of Medicine Ser.). 1980. Repr. of 1960 ed. Set. monograph 85.00 (ISBN 0-87993-148-5). Futura Pub.

DISEASES–OUTBREAKS

see Epidemics

DISEASES–PREVENTION

see Medicine, Preventive

DISEASES, COMMUNICABLE

see Communicable Diseases

DISEASES, INCURABLE

see Incurable Diseases

DISEASES, MENTAL

see Mental Illness; Psychology, Pathological; Psychoses

DISEASES, OCCUPATIONAL

see Occupational Diseases

DISEASES OF ANIMALS

see Veterinary Medicine

DISEASES OF CHILDREN

see Children–Diseases; Infants–Diseases

DISEASES OF OCCUPATIONS

see Occupational Diseases

DISEASES OF PLANTS

see Plant Diseases

DISEASES OF THE BLOOD, DISEASES OF THE BRAIN, DISEASES OF THE HEART

see subdivision Diseases under specific subjects, e.g. Blood–Diseases; Brain–Diseases

DISK RECORDING

see Phonorecords; Sound–Recording and Reproducing

DISLOCATIONS

see also organs and parts of the body, with or without the subdivision Dislocation

Connolly, John F., ed. DePalma's the Management of Fractures & Dislocations: An Atlas, 2 vols. 3rd ed. (Illus.). 2000p. Date not set. Set. text ed. price not set (ISBN 0-7216-2666-1); Vol. 1. price not set (ISBN 0-7216-2702-1); Vol. 2. price not set (ISBN 0-7216-2703-X). Saunders.

DISORDERS OF NUTRITION

see Nutrition Disorders

DISORDERS OF PERSONALITY

see Personality, Disorders Of

DISORDERS OF SPEECH

see Speech, Disorders Of

DISPARITY OF CULTUS

see Marriage, Mixed

DISPENSATIONALISM

Periodos Biblicos. (Spanish Bks.). 1977. 1.50 (ISBN 0-8297-0590-2). Life Pubs Intl.

DISPERSOIDS
see Colloids
DISPLAY SYSTEMS, INFORMATION
see Information Display Systems
DISPOSAL OF REFUSE
see Refuse and Refuse Disposal
DISRAELI, BENJAMIN
see Beaconsfield, Benjamin Disraeli, 1st Earl of, 1804-1881
DISRAELI, ISAAC, 1766-1848
Butler, David. Disraeli: Portrait of a Romantic. (Orig.). 1980. pap. 2.75 (ISBN 0-446-85776-9). Warner Bks.
DISSECTION
see also Zoology–Laboratory Manuals
Crafts, R. C. & Binhammer, R. T. A Guide to Regional Dissection: Study of the Human Body. 4th ed. LC 79-14417. 324p. 13.50 (ISBN 0-471-05154-3). Wiley.
DISSENTERS
Smith, Don P. Shadows of Chaos. rev. ed. 1981. pap. 5.00 (ISBN 0-937514-09-8). World Merch Import.
Zanjani, Sally S. The Unspiked Rail: Memoir of a Nevada Rebel. LC 80-39920. (Lancehead Ser.). (Illus.). xv, 357p. 1981. price not set (ISBN 0-87417-064-8). U of Nev Pr.
DISSERTATIONS, ACADEMIC–BIBLIOGRAPHY
Brown, Pia T., compiled by. O. S. U. Theses & Dissertations, Nineteen Seventy-One to Nineteen Seventy-Seven. (Bibliographic Ser.: No. 17). 128p. 1980. pap. 4.00 (ISBN 0-87071-137-7). Oreg St U Pr.
Sims, Michael. United States Doctoral Dissertations in Third World Studies, 1869-1978. 436p. 1980. 60.00. African Studies Assn.
DISSOCIATION OF PERSONALITY
see Personality, Disorders Of
DISTILLATION
see also Alcohol; Brandy; Liquors
Fundamentals of Multicomponent Distillation. (Chemical Engineering Ser.). (Illus.). 624p. 1981. text ed. 39.95 (ISBN 0-07-029567-0, C). McGraw.
DISTILLING INDUSTRIES
see also Liquor Industry and Trade
Shanken, Marvin R. The Impact American Distilled Spirits Market Review & Forecast: Nineteen-Eighty-One Edition. 6th ed. (Illus.). 60p. 1981. pap. price not set (ISBN 0-918076-14-5). Tasco.
DISTRIBUTION, COOPERATIVE
see Cooperation; Cooperative Societies
DISTRIBUTION OF INCOME
see Income
DISTRIBUTION OF WEALTH
see Wealth
DISTRICT NURSES
see Nurses and Nursing
DIVES AND LAZARUS (PARABLE)
see Jesus Christ–Parables
DIVINE HEALING
see Christian Science; Faith-Cure; Miracles
DIVINE IMMANENCE
see Immanence of God
DIVINE TRANSCENDENCE
see Transcendence of God
DIVING
see also Swimming
Fulton, John A. & Gordon, Steven M. Diving West. rev. ed. (Updated Every 2 to 4 Years Ser.). (Illus.). 96p. (Orig.). 1980. pap. 4.95 (ISBN 0-938206-01-X). ChartGuide.
Geyer, Dick. Wreck Diving. 192p. Date not set. pap. 6.95 (ISBN 0-695-81567-9, Assn Pr). Follett.
DIVING, SUBMARINE
see also Manned Undersea Research Stations; Scuba Diving; Underwater Exploration
Vallintine, Reginald. Divers & Diving. (Illus.). 176p. 1981. 12.95 (ISBN 0-7137-0855-7, Pub. by Blandford Pr England); pap. 6.95 (ISBN 0-7137-1128-0). Sterling.
DIVINING-ROD
see also Radiesthesia
Steffy, Robert E. The Dowser's Primer. 60p. 1980. pap. 4.50 (ISBN 0-935648-04-6). Halldin Pub.
DIVINITY OF CHRIST
see Jesus Christ–Divinity
DIVISION
Hunt, R. Multiplication & Division. LC 78-730962. 1978. pap. text ed. 99.00 (ISBN 0-89290-093-8, A509-SATC). Soc for Visual.
DIVISION OF LABOR
see also Machinery in Industry
Wallimann, Isidor. Estrangement: Marx's Conception of Human Nature & the Division of Labor. LC 80-929. (Contributions in Philosophy: No. 16). 240p. 1981. lib. bdg. 29.95 (ISBN 0-313-22096-4, WAE/). Greenwood.
DIVISION OF POWERS
see Federal Government
DIVORCE
see also Divorcees; Custody of Children; Remarriage
Adam, J. & N. Divorce: How & When to Let Go. 9.95 (ISBN 0-13-216416-7); pap. 4.95 (ISBN 0-13-216408-6). P-H.
Adams, Jay E. Marriage, Divorce & Remarriage. 120p. 1981. pap. 3.50 (ISBN 0-8010-0168-4). Baker Bk.
--Marriage, Divorce & Remarriage. 1980. pap. 3.50 (ISBN 0-87552-068-5). Presby & Reformed.
Bergler, Edmund. Divorce Won't Help. 1978. 12.95 (ISBN 0-87140-635-7); pap. 3.95 (ISBN 0-87140-124-X). Liveright.
Collins, Jackie. The World Is Full of Divorced Women. 416p. (Orig.). 1981. pap. 2.95 (ISBN 0-446-83183-2). Warner Bks.
Fayerweather Street School. The Kids' Book of Divorce. Rofes, Eric, ed. 112p. 1981. 7.95 (ISBN 0-86616-003-5). Lewis Pub Co.
Gap Committee on the Family. Divorce, Child Custody & the Family, Vol. 10. LC 80-25935. (Publications Ser.: No. 106). 1980. pap. 12.95 (ISBN 0-910958-10-6, 106, Mental Health Materials Center). Adv Psychiatry.
Gershenson, Milton G. & Birzon, Paul I., eds. New York Matrimonial Practice Under Equitable Distribution: Course Handbook. LC 80-83148. 364p. 1980. pap. 25.00 (ISBN 0-686-69170-9, F4-3706). PLI.
Gilstrap, Frank. How to Do Your Own Texas Divorce for Under Forty Dollars. 80p. (Orig.). 1980. pap. 7.95 (ISBN 0-938356-00-3). How-to Pr.
Greteman, Jim. Coping with Divorce. (Illus.). 80p. 1981. spiralbound 3.95 (ISBN 0-87793-226-3). Ave Maria.
Hart, Nicky. When Marriage Ends: A Study in Status Passage. 277p. 1976. pap. 11.95 (ISBN 0-422-74690-8, 6371). Methuen Inc.
Haynes, John M. Divorce Mediation: A/Practical Guide for Therapists & Counselors. LC 80-25065. 1981. text ed. 17.95 (ISBN 0-8261-2590-5); pap. text ed. price not set (ISBN 0-8261-2591-3). Springer Pub.
Irving, Howard I. Divorce Mediation. LC 80-54399. 216p. 1981. 11.95 (ISBN 0-87663-351-3). Universe.
Jackson, Michael & Jackson, Jessica. Your Father's Not Coming Home Anymore: Children Tell How They Survive Divorce. Jackson, Bruce, ed. 324p. 1981. 12.95 (ISBN 0-399-90109-4). Marek.
Kahn, Lawrence E. When Couples Part: How the Legal System Can Work for You. 192p. 1981. 10.95 (ISBN 0-531-09944-X). Watts.
Lawyers & Judges Publishing Staff. About Divorce: Eighty-Two Questions & Answers. rev. ed. 1978. pap. 0.95 (ISBN 0-88450-052-7, 6110-B). Lawyers & Judges.
McCrory, Margaret. The Nineteen-Seventy's Divorce Revolution. pap. 3.95. Green Hill.
Mitnick, Harold. How to Handle Your Divorce Step by Step. LC 80-80875. 177p. 1981. 21.95; pap. 14.95 (ISBN 0-936550-00-7). Lone Oak.
Morgenbesser, Mel & Nehls, Nadine. Joint Custody: An Alternative for Divorcing Families. LC 80-22182. (Illus.). 176p. 1981. 13.95 (ISBN 0-88229-620-5). Nelson-Hall.
Morrison, R. H. Divorce Dirty Tricks. 265p. 1980. 9.95 (ISBN 0-937484-03-2). Pegasus Rex NJ.
--Divorce Dirty Tricks. 248p. 1980. 9.95 (ISBN 0-8119-0408-3, Pegasus Rex). Fell.
Phillips, Roderick. Family Breakdown in Late Eighteenth Century France: Divorces in Rouen 1792-1803. (Illus.). 288p. 1980. 55.00 (ISBN 0-19-822572-5). Oxford U Pr.
Plateris, Alexander A. & Shipp, Audrey. Duration of Marriage to Divorce United States. (Ser. 21: No. 38). 50p. 1981. pap. text ed. 1.75 (ISBN 0-8406-0217-0). Natl Ctr Health Stats.
Tatar, Elayne S. Divorce-Texas Style. Date not set. price not set (ISBN 0-89896-060-6). Larksdale.
Weed, James A. National Estimates of Marriage Dissolution & Suvivorship. Cox, Klaudia, ed. (Ser. 3, No. 19). 50p. 1980. pap. text ed. 1.75 (ISBN 0-8406-0196-4). Natl Ctr Health Stats.
Wheeler, Michael, ed. Divided Children. 223p. 1981. pap. 4.95 (ISBN 0-14-005777-3). Penguin.
Wilkinson, Martin. Children & Divorce. (Practice of Social Work Ser.: No. 6). 288p. 1981. 25.00x (ISBN 0-631-12514-0, Pub. by Basil Blackwell England); pap. 12.50x (ISBN 0-631-12524-8). Biblio Dist.
DIVORCE–JUVENILE LITERATURE
Norvedt, Matilda. Daddy Isn't Coming Home. (Pathfinder Ser.). 96p. (Orig.). (gr. 3-6). 1981. pap. 2.95 (ISBN 0-310-43941-8). Zondervan.
Sinberg, Janet. Divorce Is a Grown up Problem. 1978. pap. 2.95 (ISBN 0-380-01901-9, 37333). Avon.
DIVORCE (CANON LAW)
Charles, R. H. Divorce & the Roman Doctrine of Nullity. 100p. 1927. text ed. 2.95 (ISBN 0-567-22067-2). Attic Pr.
DIVORCEES
see also Single-Parent Family
Willison, Marilyn M. Diary of a Divorced Mother. 192p. 1981. pap. 2.50 (ISBN 0-553-14501-0). Bantam.
Young, James J. Growing Through Divorce. LC 79-90993. (Paths of Life Ser.). 60p. (Orig.). 1979. pap. 2.45 (ISBN 0-8091-2267-7). Paulist Pr.
DIZZINESS
see Vertigo
DNA
see Deoxyribonucleic Acid
DO-IT-YOURSELF WORK
see specific fields of activity for do-it-yourself manuals in such fields, e.g. House Painting; Interior Decoration
DOCKS
see also Harbors
Cornick, H. F. Dock & Harbour Engineering: The Design of Docks, Vol. 1. 338p. 80.00x (ISBN 0-85264-037-4, Pub. by Griffin England). State Mutual Bk.
Dock & Harbour Engineering: The Design of Harbours, Vol. 2. 352p. 1969. 80.00x (ISBN 0-85264-041-2, Pub. by Griffin England). State Mutual Bk.
DOCTOR-PATIENT RELATIONSHIP
see Physician and Patient
DOCTORS
see Physicians
DOCTORS' DEGREES
see Degrees, Academic
DOCTRINAL ANTHROPOLOGY
see Man (Theology)
DOCTRINAL THEOLOGY
see Theology, Doctrinal
DOCTRINE, CHRISTIAN (CATHOLIC CHURCH)
see Catechetics–Catholic Church
DOCTRINES
see Dogma; Theology, Doctrinal
DOCUMENTARY FILMS
see Moving-Pictures, Documentary
DOCUMENTARY PHOTOGRAPHY
see Photography, Documentary
DOCUMENTS, CONSERVATION OF
see Archives
DOCUMENTS, IDENTIFICATION OF
see Legal Documents
DODGSON, CHARLES LUTWIDGE, 1832-1898
Carroll, Lewis, pseud. Lewis Carroll & the Kitchins. Cohen, Morton N., tr. LC 79-92406. (Carroll Studies: No. 4). (Illus.). 80p. (Orig.). pap. 15.00 (ISBN 0-930326-04-0). Lewis Carroll Soc.
Guiliano, Edward. Lewis Carroll: An Annotated International Bibliography, 1960-1977. LC 80-13975. 1981. 15.00x (ISBN 0-8139-0862-0). U Pr of Va.
DOG
see Dogs
DOG BREEDING
Seranne, Anne. The Joy of Breeding Your Own Show Dog. LC 80-16081. (Illus.). 272p. 1980. 11.95 (ISBN 0-87605-413-0). Howell Bk.
DOG GUIDES
see Guide Dogs
DOG-SHOWS
Tietjen, Sari B. The Dog Judge's Handbook. LC 80-36820. (Illus.). 224p. 1980. 10.95 (ISBN 0-87605-512-9). Howell Bk.
DOGMA
see also Theology, Doctrinal
Dallmayr, Fred A. Beyond Dogma & Despair: Toward a Critical Phenomenology of Politics. LC 80-53179. 256p. 1981. text ed. 19.95 (ISBN 0-268-00661-X). U of Notre Dame Pr.
DOGMATIC THEOLOGY
see Theology, Doctrinal
DOGS
Here are entered works on dogs in general. For works on specific breeds of dogs see subdivision breeds, further subdivided by specific names, e.g. Dogs–Breeds–Dalmatians.
see also Dog Breeding; Dog-Shows; Guide Dogs; Hunting Dogs
Damroth, Marion. Country Dogs & City Cousins(the Care & Loving of All Puppies) LC 80-81371. (Illus.). 125p. Date not set. price not set (ISBN 0-937118-01-X). Home Frosted.
Fairchild, William. Astrology for Dogs (& Owners) (Illus.). 95p. 1981. 8.95 (ISBN 0-241-10380-0, Pub. by Hamish Hamilton England). David & Charles.
Green, Martin. The Home Pet Vet Guide for Dogs. pap. cancelled (ISBN 0-686-68439-7, 43414). Avon.
DOGS–BREEDING
see Dog Breeding
DOGS–BREEDS–BLOODHOUNDS
Lowe, Brian. Hunting the Clean Boot: The Working Bloodhound. (Illus.). 240p. 1981. 22.50 (ISBN 0-7137-0950-2). Sterling.
DOGS–BREEDS–BOUVIER D'FLANDRES
McLean, Claire. The Bouvier Des Flandres. 19.95 (ISBN 0-87714-077-4). Green Hill.
DOGS–BREEDS–CHESAPEAKE BAY RETRIEVER
Cherry, Eloise H. The Complete Chesapeake Bay Retriever. LC 80-25037. (Illus.). 288p. 1981. 14.95 (ISBN 0-87605-074-7). Howell Bk.
--Complete Chesapeake Bay Retriever. LC 80-25037. 1981. write for info. (ISBN 0-87605-074-7). Howell Bk.
--The Complete Chesapeake Bay Retriever. LC 80-25037. (Illus.). 288p. 1981. 14.95 (ISBN 0-87605-074-7). Howell Bk.
DOGS–BREEDS–ENGLISH SHEEP DOGS
Woods, Sylvia & Owen, Ray. Old English Sheepdogs. (Illus.). 224p. 1981. 22.00 (ISBN 0-571-11620-5, Pub. by Faber & Faber). Merrimack Bk Serv.
DOGS–BREEDS–GREYHOUNDS
Clarke, H. Edwards. The Greyhound. rev., 7th ed. 222p. 1980. text ed. 24.95x (ISBN 0-09-141410-5, SpS). Soccer.
DOGS–BREEDS–SOFTCOATED WHEATEN TERRIER
Holmes, Maureen. The Wheaten Years: The History of Ireland's Soft Coated Wheaten Terrier. LC 77-88422. 14.95. B P Reynolds.
DOGS–DISEASES
Herriott, James. Illustrated Textbook of Dog Diseases. (Illus.). 284p. 1980. 7.95 (ISBN 0-87666-733-7, PS-770). TFH Pubns.
Sheppard, K. The Treatment of Dogs by Homoeopathy. 1980. 4.00 (ISBN 0-8464-1056-7). Beekman Pubs.
DOGS–EXHIBITIONS
see Dog-Shows
DOGS–JUVENILE LITERATURE
Rockwell, Jane. Dogs & Puppies. (Illus.). (gr. 4-6). 1979. pap. 1.50 (ISBN 0-671-56038-7). PB.
Selsam, Millicent & Hunt, Joyce. A First Look at Dogs. Springer, Harriett, tr. (A First Look at Ser.). 32p. (gr. 1-4). 1981. 7.95 (ISBN 0-8027-6409-6); lib. bdg. 8.85 (ISBN 0-8027-6421-5). Walker & Co.
DOGS–TRAINING
Benjamin, Carol L. Dog Problems. LC 80-1082. 192p. 1981. 10.95 (ISBN 0-385-15710-X). Doubleday.
Dog Training. Date not set. price not set. TFH Pubns.
Mr. Lucky's Trick Dog Training Book. 4.95 (ISBN 0-87714-086-3). Green Hill.
Woodhouse, Barbara. Dog Training My Way. LC 72-82833. (Illus.). 128p. 1981. pap. 5.95 (ISBN 0-8128-6082-9). Stein & Day.
DOGS–TRAINING–JUVENILE LITERATURE
Lowe, Brian. Hunting the Clean Boot: The Working Bloodhound. (Illus.). 240p. 1981. 22.50 (ISBN 0-7137-0950-2). Sterling.
DOGS IN LITERATURE
Donovan, John A. Dogs in Shakespeare. 9.95 (ISBN 0-87714-074-X). Green Hill.
DOLL MAKING
see Dollmaking
DOLLMAKING
Greenhouse, Jean. Making Miniature Toys & Dolls. 1980. 19.95 (ISBN 0-7134-3271-3). David & Charles.
DOLLS
see also Dollmaking
Angione, Genevieve. All Bisque & Half Bisque Dolls. LC 76-77265. (Illus.). 357p. 1981. Repr. 25.00 (ISBN 0-916838-39-0). Schiffer.
Antique Dolls Go to a Paper Doll Wedding. 8p. (gr. 8-12). 1978. pap. 3.50 (ISBN 0-914510-09-6). Evergreen.
Frame, Linda J. Folk & Forign Costume Dolls. (Illus.). 1980. pap. 9.95 (ISBN 0-89145-143-9). Collector Bks.
Nason, Janet. Dolls of the Nineteen Thirties Paper Dolls. 8p. (gr. 8-12). 1978. pap. 3.50 (ISBN 0-914510-08-8). Evergreen.
Price Guide for Composition Dolls. 3rd ed. 1981. 6.50 (ISBN 0-686-69470-8). R Shoemaker.
Price Guide for Madame Alexander Dolls. 3rd ed. 1981. 7.50 (ISBN 0-686-69471-6). R Shoemaker.
Robison, Joleen & Sellers, Kay. Advertising Dolls. (Illus.). 1980. pap. 9.95 (ISBN 0-89145-134-X). Collector Bks.
Rosamond, Peggy J. Antique French Doll Coloring Books. 8p. (gr. 8-12). pap. 3.50 (ISBN 0-914510-06-1). Evergreen.
--Antique French Doll Paper Dolls. 8p. (gr. 8-12). 1976. pap. 3.50. Evergreen.
Smith, Patricia. China & Parian Dolls. (Illus.). 1980. pap. 9.95 (ISBN 0-89145-144-7). Collector Bks.
--German Dolls II. (Illus.). 1980. pap. 9.95 (ISBN 0-89145-151-X). Collector Bks.
--Price Guide to Madame Alexander Dolls, No. 7. (Illus.). 1981. 3.95 (ISBN 0-89145-167-6). Collector Bks.
Swanberg, Nancie. Great Ballet Paper Dolls. (Illus.). 32p. (Orig.). 1981. pap. 3.50 (ISBN 0-89844-027-0). Troubador Pr.
DOLPHINS
Carter, Samuel, III. Happy Dolphins. (Illus.). (YA) (gr. 7-9). 1972. pap. 1.25 (ISBN 0-671-29726-0). PB.
Morris. Dolphin. (Illus.). (gr. 2-3). Date not set. pap. cancelled (ISBN 0-590-30026-1, Schol Pap). Schol Bk Serv.
DOMAIN, EMINENT
see Eminent Domain
DOMAIN CONFIGURATION
see Domain Structure
DOMAIN STRUCTURE
Odel, T. H. Ferromagnetodynamics: The Dynamics of Magnetic Bubbles Domains & Domain Walls. 232p. 1981. 54.95 (ISBN 0-470-27084-5). Halsted Pr.
DOMESTIC ANIMALS
see also Animals, Treatment of; Cats; Cattle; Cows; Dogs; Goats; Horses; Livestock; Pets; Sheep; Swine
Berry, W. T., Jr., et al. Basic Animal Science. (Illus.). 187p. Repr. wire coil lab. manual 6.95 (ISBN 0-89641-052-8). American Pr.
Craig, James V. Domestic Animal Behavior: Causes & Implications for Animal Care & Management. (Illus.). 400p. 1981. text ed. 19.95 (ISBN 0-13-218339-0). P-H.
Jochle, Wolfgang & Lamond, Ross. Control of Reproductive Functions in Domestic Animals. (Current Topics in Veterinary Medicine & Animal Science Ser.: No. 7). (Illus.). 1981. PLB 39.50 (ISBN 90-247-2400-7, Pub. by Martinus Nijhoff). Kluwer Boston.
DOMESTIC ANIMALS–DISEASES
see Veterinary Medicine
DOMESTIC ANIMALS–JUVENILE LITERATURE
A Picture Book of Farmyard Friends. (Children's Library of Picture Bks.). (Illus.). 10p. (ps). 1979. 1.95 (ISBN 0-89346-172-5, TA12, Froebel-Kan Japan). Heian Intl.

DOMESTIC APPLIANCES
see Household Appliances
DOMESTIC ARCHITECTURE
see Architecture, Domestic
DOMESTIC ECONOMY
see Home Economics
DOMESTIC RELATIONS
see also Children–Law; Family; Guardian and Ward; Husband and Wife; Parent and Child (Law)
Cothren, Paige. Let None Deal Treacherously. 224p. (Orig.). 1981. pap. 4.95 (ISBN 0-937778-03-6). Fulness Hse.
David, Miriam E. The State, the Family, & Education. (Radical Social Policy Ser.). 304p. (Orig.). 1980. pap. 17.50 (ISBN 0-7100-0601-2). Routledge & Kegan.
Green, Samuel & Long, John V. Modern Family Law, 3 vols. 1800p. Date not set. Set. 180.00 (ISBN 0-07-024275-5). McGraw.
Hill, Myron G., Jr., et al. Smith's Review of Family Law. 2nd ed. (Smith's Review Ser.). 140p. 1981. pap. text ed. 10.95 (ISBN 0-8299-0515-4). West Pub.
Schafly, Phyllis. Power Ideas for a Happy Family. (Orig.). pap. 1.75 (ISBN 0-515-05104-7). Jove Pubns.
Zanzucchi, Anne M. Family Portrait, from a Mother's Diary. Szczesniak, Lenny, tr. from It. LC 81-80031. Orig. Title: Giorno per Giorno. 100p. 1981. pap. 2.95 (ISBN 0-911782-19-2). New City.
DOMESTIC SCIENCE
see Home Economics
DOMESTICATION
see Domestic Animals; Plants, Cultivated
DOMESTICS
see Servants
DOMINICAN REPUBLIC–POLITICS AND GOVERNMENT
Atkins, G. Pope. Arms & Politics in the Dominican Republic. (Special Studies on Latin America & the Caribbean). 158p. 1981. lib. bdg. 20.00x (ISBN 0-86531-112-9). Westview.
DOMINION OF THE SEA
see Maritime Law; Sea-Power
DOMINIONS, BRITISH
see Commonwealth of Nations
DONATION OF CONSTANTINE
Constantine I. A Treatise of the Donation of Gyfts & Endowment of Possessyons Gyven & Graunted Unto Sylvester Pope of Rome by Constantyne Emperour of Rome. Marshall, William, tr. LC 79-84096. (English Experience Ser.: No. 916). 152p. (Eng.). 1979. Repr. of 1534 ed. lib. bdg. 24.00 (ISBN 90-221-0916-X). Walter J Johnson.
DONATIONS
see Charitable Uses, Trusts and Foundations
DONNE, JOHN, 1573-1631
Carey, John. John Donne: Life, Mind & Art. 336p. 1981. 19.95 (ISBN 0-19-520242-2). Oxford U Pr.
Slights, Camille W. The Casuistical Tradition in Shakespeare, Donne, Herbert, & Milton. LC 80-8576. 352p. 1981. 26.50x (ISBN 0-691-06463-6). Princeton U Pr.
DONNER PARTY
Limburg, Peter R. Deceived: The Story of the Donner Party. (Illus.). 256p. (gr. 7 up). Date not set. PLB 7.95 (ISBN 0-396-07942-3). Dodd.
DOOLITTLE, JAMES HAROLD, 1896-
Glines, Carroll V. Jimmy Doolittle: Master of the Calculated Risk. 208p. 1980. pap. 4.95 (ISBN 0-442-23102-4). Van Nos Reinhold.
DOOMSDAY BOOK
Galbraith, Vivian H. The Making of Domesday Book. LC 80-2224. 1981. Repr. of 1961 ed. 36.50 (ISBN 0-404-18761-7). AMS Pr.
DOORS AND DOORWAYS
Hoffmann, Gretl. Doors: Excellence in International Design. (Illus.). 144p. 1977. 35.00x (ISBN 0-8230-7135-9). Intl Ideas.
DOSIMETRY
see Drugs–Dosage; Radiation–Dosage; Radiation Dosimetry
DOSTOEVSKII, FEDOR MIKHAILOVICH, 1821-1881
Morson, Gary S. The Boundaries of Genre: Dostoevsky's "Diary of a Writer" & the Traditions of Literary Utopia. 272p. 1981. text ed. 25.00x (ISBN 0-292-70732-0). U of Tex Pr.
Passage, Charles. Character Names in Dostoevsky's Fiction. 1981. 16.00 (ISBN 0-88233-616-9). Ardis Pubs.
DOUBLE CONSCIOUSNESS
see Personality, Disorders Of
DOUBLE EMPLOYMENT
see Supplementary Employment
DOUBLE ENTRY BOOKKEEPING
see Bookkeeping
DOUBLE STARS
see Stars, Double
DOUBT
see Belief and Doubt
DOUGLAS, WILLIAM ORVILLE, 1898-
Douglas, William O. The Court Years: Nineteen Thirty-Nine to Nineteen Seventy-Five. (Illus.). 434p. 16.95 (ISBN 0-394-49240-4). Random.
DOVES
see Pigeons
DOWSING
see Divining-Rod
DRAFT, MILITARY
see Military Service, Compulsory
DRAFTING, MECHANICAL
see Mechanical Drawing
DRAFTING-ROOM PRACTICE
see Drawing-Room Practice
DRAG RACING
Olney, Ross R. Modern Drag Racing Superstars. LC 80-25908. (High Interest-Low Vocabulary Ser.). (Illus.). 112p. (gr. 4). 1981. PLB 5.95 (ISBN 0-396-07925-3). Dodd.
DRAGON FLIES
Pinhey, E. C. A Survey of the Dragonflies (Order Odonata) of Eastern Africa. (Illus.). vii, 214p. 1961. 18.50x (ISBN 0-565-00216-3, Pub. by Brit Mus Nat Hist England). Sabbot-Natural Hist Bks.
DRAMA
Here are entered works dealing with the subject of the drama in general. Works on the history and criticism of the drama are entered under Drama–History and Criticism. Collections of drama are entered under Drama–Collections, Collections of drama of specific nationalities are entered as English Drama, French Drama, etc.
see also Acting; Ballet; Characters and Characteristics in Literature; Children's Plays; Christmas Plays; Comedy; Dramatic Criticism; Dramatists; Melodrama; Monologue; Mysteries and Miracle-Plays; Opera; Psychodrama; Puppets and Puppet-Plays; Television Plays; Theater; Tragedy
also drama of specific nationalities, e.g. English Drama, French Drama; subdivision Drama under special subjects and names of persons, e.g. Indians of North America–Drama; Lincoln, Abraham, Pres., United States–drama
Brownstein, Oscar L. & Daubert, Darlene M. Analytical Sourcebook of Concepts in Dramatic Theory. LC 80-1200. 584p. 1981. lib. bdg. 45.00 (ISBN 0-313-21309-7, BRN/). Greenwood.
Rudman, Jack. Drama & Theatre. (Undergraduate Program Field Test Ser.: UPFT-5). (Cloth bdg. avail. on request). pap. 9.95 (ISBN 0-8373-6005-6). Natl Learning.
DRAMA–ADDRESSES, ESSAYS, LECTURES
Lagerkvist, Par & Buckman, Thomas R. Modern Theatre: Seven Plays & an Essay. LC 64-11582. 1966. 14.95x (ISBN 0-8032-0098-6). U of Nebr Pr.
DRAMA–BIBLIOGRAPHY
Mikhail, E. H. An Annotated Bibliography of Modern Anglo-Irish Drama. LC 80-51874. 306p. 1981. 20.00x (ISBN 0-87875-201-3). Whitston Pub.
DRAMA–BIOGRAPHY
see Dramatists
DRAMA–COLLECTIONS
Montes-Huidobro, Matias. Ojos Para No Ver. LC 79-52160. (Coleccion Teatro Ser.). (Illus.). 59p. (Span.). 1980. pap. 5.95 (ISBN 0-89729-229-4). Ediciones.
Nuttall, Jeff. Performance Art Scripts, Vol. II. 1981. 13.95 (ISBN 0-7145-3789-6); pap. 6.95 (ISBN 0-7145-3712-8). Riverrun NY.
Pinget, Robert. Plays, Vol. II. 1980. pap. 4.95 (ISBN 0-7145-0036-4). Riverrun NY.
Richards, Stanley, ed. Best Mystery & Suspense Plays of the Modern Theatre. 1979. pap. 7.95 (ISBN 0-380-46466-7). Avon.
Sanchez-Boudy, Jose. La Rebelion De los Negros. LC 79-56654. (Coleccion Teatro Ser.). 78p. (Orig., Span.). Date not set. pap. 5.95 (ISBN 0-89729-247-2). Ediciones.
Seven Expressionist Plays. 1980. pap. 6.95 (ISBN 0-7145-0521-8). Riverrun NY.
DRAMA–COLLECTIONS–20TH CENTURY
Fedder, Norman, ed. Wrestling with God: An Anthology of Contemporary Religious Drama. 1981. pap. 15.00 (ISBN 0-87602-018-X). Anchorage.
Guernsey, Otis L., Jr., ed. The Best Plays of 1979-1980. (The Burns Mantle Yearbook of the Theatre Ser.). (Illus.). 550p. 1981. 20.00 (ISBN 0-396-07907-5). Dodd.
Lagerkvist, Par & Buckman, Thomas R. Modern Theatre: Seven Plays & an Essay. LC 64-11582. 1966. 14.95x (ISBN 0-8032-0098-6). U of Nebr Pr.
Malpede, Karen & Chaikin, Joseph. Three Works by the Open Theater. LC 74-13837. (Illus.). 1975. 12.50 (ISBN 0-910482-54-3). Drama Bk.
Miller, Arthur. Arthur Miller's Collected Plays, Vol. II. LC 80-52008. 704p. 1981. 17.95 (ISBN 0-670-13598-4). Viking Pr.
Ostrow, Eileen J., ed. Center Stage: An Anthology of 21 Contemporary Black American Plays. LC 80-53143. (Illus.). 352p. (Orig.). 1981. pap. price not set. Sea Urchin.
DRAMA–HISTORY AND CRITICISM
see also Theater–United States
also similar headings
Barnet, et al. Types of Drama. 3rd ed. Date not set. pap. text ed. 11.95 (ISBN 0-316-08208-2). Little.
Foss, George R. What the Author Meant. 196p. 1980. Repr. of 1932 ed. lib. bdg. 25.00 (ISBN 0-89984-204-6). Century Bookbindery.
Olauson, Judith. The American Woman Playwright: A View of Criticism & Characterization. LC 80-51605. 190p. 1981. 12.50x (ISBN 0-87875-198-X). Whitston Pub.
Orr, John. Tragic Drama & Modern Society: Studies in the Social & Literary Theroy of Drama from 1870 to the Present. LC 80-18156. Date not set. price not set (ISBN 0-312-81354-6). St Martin.
Redmond, J. Drama, Dance & Music. (Themes in Drama Ser.: No. 3). (Illus.). 260p. Date not set. 36.00 (ISBN 0-521-22180-3). Cambridge U Pr.
Scouten, Arthur, intro. by. Restoration & Eighteenth Century Drama. 160p. 1981. pap. 5.95 (ISBN 0-312-67787-1). St Martin.
Traversi, Derek, intro. by. Renaissance Drama. 128p. 1981. pap. 5.95 (ISBN 0-312-67160-1). St Martin.
DRAMA–HISTORY AND CRITICISM–20TH CENTURY
Innes, Chritoper. Holy Theatre: Ritual & the Avant Garde. (Illus.). 280p. Date not set. price not set (ISBN 0-521-22542-6). Cambridge U Pr.
Styan, J. L. Modern Drama in Theory & Practice, 3 vols. Incl. Vol. 1. Realism & Naturalism. Cloth (ISBN 0-521-22737-2); Vol. 2. Symbolism, Surrealism & the Absurd. Cloth (ISBN 0-521-22738-0); Vol. 3. Expressionism & Epic Theatre. Cloth (ISBN 0-521-22739-9). LC 79-15947. (Illus.). 250p. Date not set. 75.00 set; 29.50 ea. Cambridge U Pr.
DRAMA–PRODUCTION AND DIRECTION
see Theater–Production and Direction
DRAMA–SELECTIONS
see Drama–Collections
DRAMA–STORIES, PLOTS, ETC.
Louis, Louise. Honeybee Cousin. (Illus.). 88p. (gr. 4-11). 1979. PLB 5.99. Pen-Art.
DRAMA–STUDY AND TEACHING
see also Drama in Education
England, A. Scripted Drama. 260p. Date not set. price not set (ISBN 0-521-23235-X). Cambridge U Pr.
Griffith, Peter. The School Play: A Complete Handbook. (Illus.). 168p. 1981. 14.95 (ISBN 0-7134-3541-0, Pub. by Batsford England). David & Charles.
DRAMA, MODERN
see Drama; Drama–Collections–20th Century
DRAMA IN EDUCATION
see also Acting; Theater
McCaslin, Nellie. Children & Drama. 2nd ed. 320p. 1981. text ed. 9.95 (ISBN 0-686-28848-3). Longman.
DRAMATIC CRITICISM
Here are entered works on criticism of the drama as presented on the stage.
see also Moving-Picture Criticism
Miller, Tice L. Bohemians & Critics: American Theatre Criticism in the Nineteenth Century. LC 80-24430. x, 190p. 1981. 12.00 (ISBN 0-8108-1377-7). Scarecrow.
Phillips, Henry. The Theatre & Its Critics in Seventeenth-Century France. (Modern Language & Literature Monographs). 272p. 1980. 36.00 (ISBN 0-19-815535-2). Oxford U Pr.
DRAMATIC EDUCATION
see Acting–Study and Teaching
DRAMATIC MONOLOGUE
see Monologue
DRAMATIC MUSIC
see Music in Theaters; Musical Revue, Comedy, Etc.; Opera
DRAMATISTS
Cotton, Nancy. Women Playwrights in England: 1363-1750. LC 78-73155. 256p. 1980. 15.00 (ISBN 0-8387-2381-0). Bucknell U Pr.
Craig, Edward G. Index to the Story of My Days. 320p. Date not set. price not set (ISBN 0-521-23609-6); pap. price not set (ISBN 0-521-28070-2). Cambridge U Pr.
Daoust, Yvette. Roger Planchon: Director & Playwright. (Illus.). 200p. Date not set. 44.95 (ISBN 0-521-23414-X). Cambridge U Pr.
Lazarus, A. L. & Jones, Victor H. Beyond Graustark: George Barr McCutcheon - Playwright Discovered. (National University Publications, Literary Criticism Ser.). 1981. 15.00 (ISBN 0-8046-9280-7). Kennikat.
Vinson, James & Kirkpatrick, Daniel, eds. Great Dramatists. (Great Writers of the English Language Ser.). 700p. 1979. 45.00 (ISBN 0-312-34570-4). St Martin.
DRAMSHOPS
see Hotels, Taverns, etc.; Liquor Industry and Trade
DRAW-POKER
see Poker
DRAWING
see also Architectural Drawing; Design, Decorative; Drawings; Figure Drawing; Graphic Methods; Illustration of Books; Mechanical Drawing; Painting; Perspective; Proportion (Art)
also Birds in Art; Dogs–Pictures, Illustrations, Etc., and similar headings
Savitt, Sam. Draw Horses with Sam Savitt. LC 80-21812. (Illus.). 96p. 1981. 14.95 (ISBN 0-670-28259-6, Studio). Viking Pr.
DRAWING–INSTRUCTION
see also Airbrush Art; Commercial Art; Computer Drawing
also special subjects of instruction, e.g. Figure Drawing; Flower Painting and Illustration; Birds Art; and similar headings; also subdivision Pictures, Illustrations, etc. under names of animals, e.g. Cats–Pictures, Illustrations, etc.
Blake, Vernon. The Way to Sketch: With Special Reference to Water Color. (Illus.). 144p. (Unabridged replication of 2nd ed.). 1981. pap. price not set (ISBN 0-486-24119-X). Dover.
Filson, Henry J. Senior Hi Artist. (Draw-Sketch Practice Ser.). (Illus.). 44p. 1978. plastic bdg. 3.75 (ISBN 0-918554-02-0). Old Violin.
--Sketch & Draw Today. (Draw-Sketch Practice Ser.). (Illus.). 122p. 1976. plastic bdg. 12.00 (ISBN 0-918554-00-4). Old Violin.
Hoff, Syd. Syd Hoff's How to Draw Dinosaurs. (Illus.). 64p. (gr. 3 up). 1981. pap. 3.95 (ISBN 0-671-42553-6). Windmill Bks.
Lohan, Frank J. Pen & Ink Themes. (Illus.). 1981. 12.95 (ISBN 0-8092-7016-1); pap. 5.95 (ISBN 0-8092-7015-3). Contemp Bks.
Martinez-Juarez, Alberto. The Drawing. 1981. 5.95 (ISBN 0-8062-1590-9). Carlton.
Parramon, J. M. Drawing. (Orig.). 1980. pap. 4.95 (ISBN 0-89586-072-4). H P Bks.
Zappalorti, Robert. Drawing Sharp Focus Still Lifes. 192p. 1981. 18.95 (ISBN 0-8230-1435-5). Watson-Guptill.
DRAWING–INSTRUCTION–JUVENILE LITERATURE
Ames, Lee J. Draw Fifty Dogs. LC 79-6853. (Illus.). 64p. (gr. 4-6). 1981. 6.95a (ISBN 0-385-15686-3); PLB (ISBN 0-385-15687-1). Doubleday.
Filson, Henry J. Little Hands with First Drawing Practice. (Draw-Sketch Practice Ser.). (Illus.). 28p. (gr. 5 up). 1978. bdg. 2.75plastic (ISBN 0-918554-01-2). Old Violin.
Tallarico, Tony. I Can Draw Cars, Trucks, & Other Wheels. Scheider, Meg, ed. (I Can Draw Ser.). 80p. (Orig.). (gr. 3-7). 1981. pap. 2.75 (ISBN 0-671-42535-8). Wanderer Bks.
DRAWING, ARCHITECTURAL
see Architectural Drawing
DRAWING-ROOM PRACTICE
Amiss, John M. & Jones, Franklin D. The Use of Handbook Tables & Formulas. 21st ed. Ryffel, Henry H., ed. LC 75-10949. (Illus.). 224p. 8.00 (ISBN 0-8311-1131-3). Indus Pr.
DRAWINGS
see also Graffiti; Lithographs
Burroughs, Ben. Sketches. LC 56-11909. 160p. 1980. pap. 8.50 (ISBN 0-8303-0048-1). Fleet.
Chi Chen. Chen Chi Watercolors, Drawings, Sketches: Deluxe Edition. (Illus.). 108p. 1980. leather bound 100.00 (ISBN 0-9604652-1-9). Chen Chi Studio.
Roe, Halper. Tears of the Prophets. LC 75-33530. (Illus.). 1975. 15.00 (ISBN 0-916326-01-2). Bloch.
DRAWINGS–CATALOGS
Latham, Robert. Catalogue of the Pepys Library at Magdalene College, Cambridge, Vol. 3: Pt. 1 - Prints & Drawings (General) Aspitall, A., ed. 160p. 1981. 135.00x (ISBN 0-8476-3637-2). Rowman.
Ludlow, Norman H., Jr. Clip Book Number Eleven: Communicate the Action. (Illus.). 64p. (Orig.). 1980. pap. 13.95 (ISBN 0-916706-22-2). N H Ludlow.
DRAWINGS–EXHIBITIONS
Geeenberg, Reesa. The Drawings of Alfred Pellan. (National Gallery of Canada Ser.). (Illus.). 192p. 1981. pap. 15.95 (ISBN 0-88884-458-1, 56319-7, Pub. by Natl Mus Canada). U of Chicago Pr.
Jacques, Michael. Images of Age. LC 80-69225. (Illus.). 146p. 1980. 30.00 (ISBN 0-89011-550-8). Abt Assoc.
Smith, Philip C. More Marine & Drawings in the Peabody Museum. (Illus.). 19?p. 1979. 35.00 (ISBN 0-87577-064-9); boxed numbered 50.00 (ISBN 0-686-68319-6). Peabody Mus Salem.
DRAWINGS, AMERICAN
Andrews, Benny. Between the Lines. LC 78-60633. (Illus.). 111p. 1978. 19.95 (ISBN 0-918618-13-4); lib. bdg. 9.95 (ISBN 0-918618-12-6). Pella Pub.
Baro, Gene. Robert Gordy: Paintings & Drawings. (Illus.). 1981. pap. price not set (ISBN 0-89494-011-2). New Orleans Mus Art.
DRAWINGS, BRITISH
Hammond, Charlie. Charlie Hammond's Sketch-Book. (Illus.). 84p. 1980. 19.95 (ISBN 0-19-212974-0). Oxford U Pr.
DRAWINGS, EUROPEAN
Here are entered works on European artists as a whole, as well as those on artists of specific European countries.
Denison, Cara D. & Mules, Helen B. European Drawings, 1375-1825. (Fine Art Ser.). (Illus.). 316p. (Orig.). 1981. pap. price not set. Dover.
DRAWINGS, FRENCH
Oberhuber, Konrad & Jacoby, Beverly S., eds. French Drawings from a Private Collection: Louis XIII to Louis XVI. LC 80-65383. 182p. 1980. pap. 7.50 (ISBN 0-916724-42-5). Fogg Art.
Reff, Theodore, ed. Exhibitions of Modern Drawings. (Modern Art in Paris 1855 to 1900 Ser.). 251p. 1981. lib. bdg. 44.00 (ISBN 0-8240-4724-9). Garland Pub.
DREADNOUGHTS
see Warships
DREAMS
see also Fantasy; Psychoanalysis; Sleep
Faraday, Ann. Dream Power. 1981. pap. 2.50 (ISBN 0-425-04863-2). Berkley Pub.
Lillie, Sally L. Judging the Dreamer. 52p. 1980. pap. 4.50x (ISBN 0-938564-00-5). P a Abbott.
Lowe, Elizabeth. Coping with Recurring Dreams & Nightmares. 1980. 1.50 (ISBN 0-686-28864-5). Dreams Unltd.
--Dreams & Spiritual Experiences. 1980. 1.50 (ISBN 0-686-28863-7). Dreams Unltd.

--How to Understand Dreams. 1979. 1.50 (ISBN 0-686-28862-9). Dreams Unltd.
McLeod, Stuart R. Dreams: A Portrait of the Psyche. LC 80-65607. 170p. 1981. perfect bdg. 14.95 (ISBN 0-86548-046-X). Century Twenty One.
Nicoll, Maurice. Dream Psychology. 1979. pap. 4.95 (ISBN 0-87728-475-X). Weiser.
Torda, C. Memory & Dreams: A Modern Physics Approach. (Illus.). 453p. 1980. 24.95. Walters.
Wippler, Migene. Dreams and What They Mean. pap. 2.25. Merit Pubns.
Yancy, Wallace. The Dream Dictionary. 1981. 6.95 (ISBN 0-8062-1685-9). Carlton.

DREDGING
Institute of Civil Engineers, UK. Dredging. 124p. 1980. 70.00x (ISBN 0-901948-40-3, Pub. by Telford England). State Mutual Bk.

DREISER, THEODORE, 1871-1945
Pizer, Donald. Critical Essays on Theodore Dreiser. (Critical Essays on American Literature). 1981. lib. bdg. 25.00 (ISBN 0-8161-8257-4). Twayne.

DREPANOCYTIC ANEMIA
see Sickle Cell Anemia

DRESS
see Clothing and Dress

DRESSAGE
see Horsemanship

DRESSMAKING
see also Needlework; Sewing
Cotten, Emmi. Clothes Make Magic. 2nd, rev. ed. Rateaver, Bargyla & Rateaver, Gylver, eds. LC 79-55932. (Conservation Gardening & Farming Ser. C: The Home). (Illus.). 223p. (gr. 9-10). 1980. pap. 10.00 (ISBN 0-915966-00-X). Rateavers.
Martensson, Kerstin. Kwik-Sew Method for Easy Sewing. (Illus.). pap. 6.95 (ISBN 0-913212-09-1). Kwik Sew.

DRILLING AND BORING
Here are entered works relating to the drilling and boring of holes in metal, wood, other materials, as carried on in workshops, etc., for building and constructive purposes.
Gingery, David J. The Drill Press. LC 80-66142. (Build Your Own Metal Working Shop from Scrap Ser.: Bk. 5). (Illus.). 72p. (Orig.). 1981. pap. 6.95 (ISBN 0-9604330-4-X). D J Gingery.

DRILLING AND BORING MACHINERY
Gingery, David J. The Dividing Head & Deluxe Accessories. LC 80-66142. (Build Your Own Metal Working Shop from Scrap: Bk. 6). (Illus.). 112p. (Orig.). 1981. pap. 7.95 (ISBN 0-9604330-5-8). D J Gingery.

DRINK QUESTION
see Liquor Problem

DRINKING AND YOUTH
see Alcohol and Youth

DRINKING CUSTOMS
Edmunds, Lowell. The Silver Bullet: The Martini in American Civilization. LC 80-1196. (Contributions in American Studies: No. 52). (Illus.). 160p. 1981. lib. bdg. 19.95 (ISBN 0-313-22225-8, ESB/). Greenwood.

DRINKING WATER
Rice, Rip G. Biological Activated Carbon for Drinking Water. 1981. text ed. 69.90 2 vol. set (ISBN 0-250-40429-X); text ed. 39.95 vol. 1 (ISBN 0-250-40427-3); text ed. 39.95 vol. 2 (ISBN 0-250-40428-1). Ann Arbor Science.

DRINKS
see Beverages; Liquors

DRIVERS' TESTS, AUTOMOBILE
see Automobile Drivers' Tests

DRIVING, AUTOMOBILE
see Automobile Driving

DRIVING TESTS, AUTOMOBILE
see Automobile Drivers' Tests

DROMEDARIES
see Camels

DROUGHTS
see also Rain and Rainfall
Institute of Civil Engineers, UK. Operational Aspects of the Drought of 1975-76. 142p. 1980. pap. 50.00x (ISBN 0-7277-0059-6, Pub. by Telford England). State Mutual Bk.

DRUG ABUSE
see also Alcoholism; Hallucinogenic Drugs; Marihuana; Narcotic Habit
Andrews, Theodora. A Bibliography of Drug Abuse: A Supplement, 1977 to 1980. 200p. 1981. lib. bdg. price not set (ISBN 0-87287-252-1). Libs Unl.
Bauman, Carl E. Predicting Adolescent Drug Use: Utility Structure & Marijuana. 192p. 1980. 22.95 (ISBN 0-03-050636-0). Praeger.
Crenshaw, Mary A. The End of the Rainbow. 224p. 1981. 12.95 (ISBN 0-02-528810-5). Macmillan.
Drug Abuse Bibliography for 1977. 730p. 1980. 42.50x (ISBN 0-87875-176-9). Whitston Pub.
Fort, Joel. The Addicted Society. LC 80-8918. 256p. 1981. pap. 3.95 (ISBN 0-394-17889-0, B454, BC). Grove.
Harris, Teresa. God! Please Stop Drugs. Date not set. 5.95 (ISBN 0-533-04435-9). Vantage.
Hoben, Brent. Drug & Alcohol Emergencies. 1980. pap. 4.95. Hazelden.
Lennard, Henry L. The Valium Papers. LC 80-84546. 150p. (Orig.). 1981. pap. 9.95 (ISBN 0-935824-02-2). Gondolier.
Lowinson, Joyce & Ruiz, Pedro. Substance Abuse. (Illus.). 900p. 1981. write for info. (5210-1). Williams & Wilkins.
Meftah, Michael. Smoking & Chemical Abuse. 1981. 5.75 (ISBN 0-8062-1616-6). Carlton.
Nahas, Gabriel G. & Frick, Henry C., II, eds. Drug Abuse in the Modern World: a Perspective for the Eighties: Proceedings of a Symposium Held at the College of Physicians & Surgeons of Columbia University, New York, N.Y. (Illus.). 320p. 40.00 (ISBN 0-08-026300-3). Pergamon.
Richter, Derek, ed. Addiction & Brain Damage. 320p. 1980. 45.00x (Pub. by Croom Helm England). State Mutual Bk.
Wikler, Abraham. Opioid Dependence--Mechanisms & Treatment. 300p. 1980. 27.50 (ISBN 0-306-40591-1, Plenum Pr). Plenum Pub.

DRUG ABUSE–CASE STUDIES
Peele, Stanton. The Addiction Experience. 1980. pap. 1.50. Hazelden.

DRUG ABUSE AND CRIME
see also Drugs–Laws and Legislation
Moore, Jim. Flip Line. 300p. (Orig.). 1981. pap. 2.95. Tuppence.

DRUG ADDICTION
see Drug Abuse; Narcotic Habit

DRUG ADULTERATION
see Drugs–Adulteration and Analysis

DRUG HABIT
see Drug Abuse; Narcotic Habit

DRUG INDUSTRY
see Drug Trade

DRUG METABOLISM
Bridges, J. W. & Chasseaud, L. F., eds. Progress in Drug Metabolism, Vols. 1-4. Incl. Vol. 1. 1977. 46.00 (ISBN 0-471-10370-5); Vol. 2. 1977. 48.50 (ISBN 0-471-99442-1); Vol. 3. LC 75-19446. 1979. 52.95 (ISBN 0-471-99711-0); Vol. 4. LC 79-42723. 304p. 1980. 72.00 (ISBN 0-471-27702-9). Pub. by Wiley-Interscience). Wiley.
International Conference on Drug Absorption, Edinburgh, 1979. Proceedings. Nimmo, W. S. & Prescott, L. F., eds. 355p. 1980. text ed. 45.00 (ISBN 0-909337-30-6). ADIS Pr.
Tuchmann-Depleiss, M. Drug Effects on the Fetus. (Illus.). 267p. 1975. text ed. 21.50 (ISBN 0-9599827-4-4). ADIS Pr.
Weizman Institute of Science, Rehovot, Israel, Feb. 1980 & Littauer, U. Z. Drug Receptors in the Central Nervous System - Based on a Workshop Sponsored by the European Molecular Biology Organization: Proceedings. 350p. 1980. 43.00 (ISBN 0-471-27893-9, Pub. by Wiley-Interscience). Wiley.

DRUG RESEARCH
see Pharmaceutical Research

DRUG RESISTANCE IN MICRO-ORGANISMS
see also Micro-Organisms; Pharmacology
Mitsuhashi, S., et al, eds. Antibiotic Resistance: Proceedings. (Illus.). 410p. 1981. 55.50 (ISBN 0-387-10322-8). Springer-Verlag.

DRUG THERAPY
see Chemotherapy

DRUG TRADE
Adriani, John. Drugs, the Drug Industry & Prices. LC 70-176187. 192p. 1981. 10.50 (ISBN 0-87527-196-0). Green.
Behrman, Jack N. Tropical Diseases: Responses of Pharmaceutical Companies. 1980. pap. 4.25 (ISBN 0-8447-3393-8). Am Enterprise.
Blum, et al, eds. Pharmaceuticals & Health Policy: An International Perspective on Provision & Control. 387p. 1981. text ed. 38.00x (ISBN 0-8419-0682-3). Holmes & Meier.
Helms, Robert, ed. International Supply of Medicines: Implications of U. S. Regulatory Reform. 1980. 14.25 (ISBN 0-8447-2190-5); pap. 6.25 (ISBN 0-8447-2191-3). Am Enterprise.
Kalman. Drug Assay. 2nd ed. 1981. price not set. Masson Pub.

DRUG TRADE–LAW AND LEGISLATION
see Drugs–Laws and Legislation; Pharmacy–Laws and Legislation

DRUGS
see also Botany, Medical; Drug Metabolism; Materia Medica; Medicine–Formulae, Receipts, Prescriptions; Pharmacology; Pharmacy; Poisons
also names of particular drugs and groups of drugs, e.g. Narcotics, Stimulants
Advice About Drugs, Food, Fitness. (Home Adviser Ser.). 80p. (Orig.). 1981. pap. 1.95 (ISBN 0-8326-2408-X, 7050). Delair.
Coley, Chris & Wolfe, Sidney. Four Hundred Drugs That Don't Work. 6.95. Green Hill.
Domino, E. F., ed. PCP Phencyclidine: Historical & Current Perspectives. LC 80-81498. (Illus.). 300p. 1980. 30.00x (ISBN 0-916182-03-7). NPP Bks.
Enna, Salvatore J., et al, eds. Antidepressants: Neurochemical, Behavioral, & Clinical Perspectives. 275p. 1981. 27.00 (ISBN 0-89004-534-8). Raven.
Gannon, Frank. Drugs, What They Are- How They Look- What They Do. LC 70-148361. 1971. 8.95 (ISBN 0-89388-005-1). Okpaku Communications.
Kalman. Drug Assay. 2nd ed. 1981. price not set. Masson Pub.
Ladewig, D., ed. Drogen & Alkohol. (Illus.). xii, 220p. 1980. pap. 23.50 (ISBN 3-8055-1624-X). S Karger.
McGgrady, Pat. The Persecuted Drug: The Story of DMSO. 312p. (Orig.). 1981. pap. 2.50 (ISBN 0-441-15101-9). Charter Bks.
Modell, Walter, ed. Drugs in Current Use & New Drugs 1981. 1981. pap. text ed. 8.95 (ISBN 0-8261-0159-3). Springer Pub.
O'Flaherty, Ellen. Toxicants & Drugs: Kinetics & Synamics. 320p. 1981. 27.50 (ISBN 0-471-06047-X, Pub. by Wiley-Interscience). Wiley.
Rote Liste, 1980. (Illus., Ger.). 1980. 35.00x (ISBN 3-87193-055-5). Intl Pubns Serv.
Siest, G., ed. Drug Effects on Laboratory Test Results. (Developments in Clinical Biochemistry: No. 2). (Illus.). 338p. 1981. PLB 49.50 (ISBN 0-686-28843-2, Pub. by Martinus Nijhoff). Kluwer Boston.
Silverman, Milton, et al. Pills & the Public Purse. 300p. 1981. 14.95 (ISBN 0-520-04381-2). U of Cal Pr.
Sunshine, Irving, ed. CRC Handbook of Spectrophotometric Data of Drugs. 432p. 1981. 62.95 (ISBN 0-8493-3571-X). CRC Pr.
Tognoni, Gianni, et al, eds. Frontiers in Therapeutic Drug Monitoring. (Monographs of the Mario Negri Institute for Pharmacological Research). 200p. 1980. text ed. 21.50 (ISBN 0-89004-508-9). Raven.

DRUGS–ADULTERATION AND ANALYSIS
Baer, Daniel M. & Dito, William R., eds. Interpretation of Therapeutic Drug Levels. (Illus.). 400p. 1981. text ed. 35.00 (ISBN 0-89189-080-7, 45-9-009-00). Am Soc Clinical.
Darvas, F. & Knoll, J., eds. Chemical Structure - Biological Activity Relationships, Quantitative Approaches: Proceedings of the Third Congress of the Hungarian Pharmacological Society, Budapest, 1979. LC 80-41281. (Advances in Pharmacological Research & Practice Ser.: Vol. III). 355p. 1981. 67.00 (ISBN 0-08-026388-7). Pergamon.
Nursing Drug Handbook 81. 1000p. 1981. text ed. 15.95 (ISBN 0-916730-33-6). Intermed Comm.
Professional Guide to Drugs. (Illus.). 1150p. 1981. text ed. 17.95 (ISBN 0-916730-34-4). Intermed Comm.
Urquhart, John, ed. Controlled Release Pharmaceuticals. LC 80-70561. 160p. 1981. pap. 27.00 (ISBN 0-917330-34-X). Am Pharm Assn.

DRUGS–DICTIONARIES
Gonzales, Gertrude D. & Lewis, Arthur J., eds. Modern Drug Encyclopedia & Therapeutic Index, No. 16. 16th ed. LC 34-12823. 1100p. 1981. text ed. 40.00 (ISBN 0-914316-21-4). Yorke Med.
Physicians' Desk Reference for Nonprescription Drugs. 12.25 (ISBN 0-87489-957-5). Med Economics.

DRUGS–DOSAGE
Norville, Mary F. Drug Dosage & Solutions Workbook. (Illus.). 128p. (Orig.). 1981. pap. text ed. 9.95 (ISBN 0-87619-920-1). R J Brady.
Nursing Drug Handbook 81. 1000p. 1981. text ed. 15.95 (ISBN 0-916730-33-6). Intermed Comm.
Professional Guide to Drugs. (Illus.). 1150p. 1981. text ed. 17.95 (ISBN 0-916730-34-4). Intermed Comm.

DRUGS–LAWS AND LEGISLATION
Merrill, Richard A. & Hutt, Peter B. Food & Drug Law, Cases & Materials. LC 80-23167. (University Casebook Ser.). 959p. 1980. text ed. write for info. (ISBN 0-88277-016-0). Foundation Pr.
Morris, Louis, et al, eds. Product Labeling. LC 80-22728. (Banbury Report Ser.: Report 6). 325p. 1980. 45.00x (ISBN 0-87969-205-7). Cold Spring Harbor.
Sloan, I. Alcohol & Drug Abuse & the Law, Vol. 27. 1980. 5.95 (ISBN 0-379-11137-3). Oceana.
Walker, William O., III. Drug Control in the Americas. (Illus.). 328p. 1981. price not set (ISBN 0-8263-0579-2). U of NM Pr.

DRUGS–RESEARCH
see Pharmaceutical Research

DRUGS, ANTINEOPLASTIC
see Antineoplastic Agents

DRUGS, CARDIOVASCULAR
see Cardiovascular Agents

DRUGS, CYTOTOXIC
see Antineoplastic Agents

DRUGS, DERMATOLOGIC
see Dermatology

DRUGS AND YOUTH
Bauman, Carl E. Predicting Adolescent Drug Use: Utility Structure & Marijuana. 192p. 1980. 22.95 (ISBN 0-03-050636-0). Praeger.
Griffin, LaDean. Escape the Drug Scene. pap. 3.95 (ISBN 0-89036-141-X). Hawkes Pub Inc.
Linkletter, Art & Gallup, George, Jr. My Child on Drugs? Youth & the Drug Culture. (Orig.). 1981. pap. 3.50 (ISBN 0-87239-456-5, 5015). Standard Pub.
Tessler, Diane J. Drugs, Kids & Schools: Practical Strategies for Educators & Other Concerned Adults. LC 80-17294. 1980. pap. 8.95 (ISBN 0-8302-2224-3). Goodyear.
Wise, Francis H. Youth & Drugs. (Illus.). Date not set. price not set. Wise Pub.

DRUGS BY MOUTH
see Oral Medication

DRUIDS AND DRUIDISM
Rowlands, Henry. Mona Antiqua Restaurata. Feldman, Burton & Richardson, Robert D., eds. LC 78-60894. (Myth & Romanticism Ser.: Vol. 21). 399p. 1979. lib. bdg. 60.00 (ISBN 0-8240-3570-4). Garland Pub.

DRUM
Moon, John C. An Instructor for the Drum. (Musick of the Fifes & the Drum: Vol. Iv). (Illus.). 56p. (Orig.). 1981. pap. 3.95 (ISBN 0-87935-059-8); record 5.95 (ISBN 0-686-69569-0); Set. pap. 8.95 (ISBN 0-87935-060-1). Williamsburg.

DRUMMOND, WILLIAM, 1585-1649
Masson, David. Drummond on Hawthornden: The Story of His Life & Writings. 490p. 1980. Repr. of 1873 ed. lib. bdg. 50.00 (ISBN 0-8492-6834-6). R West.

DRUNKARDS
see Alcoholics

DRUNKENNESS
see Alcoholics; Alcoholism; Liquor Problem; Temperance

DRYDEN, JOHN, 1631-1700
Proutfoot, L. Dryden's Aeneid & Its Seventeenth Century Predecessors. 278p. 1980. Repr. of 1960 ed. text ed. 30.00 (ISBN 0-8495-2173-4). R West.

DUAL EMPLOYMENT
see Supplementary Employment

DUBLIN
Haliday, Charles. The Scandinavian Kingdom of Dublin. 300p. 1980. Repr. of 1884 ed. 15.00 (ISBN 0-7165-0052-3, Pub. by Irish Academic Pr Ireland). Biblio Dist.
Wright, G. N. An Historical Guide to the City of Dublin. 2nd ed. 260p. 1981. Repr. of 1825 ed. 20.00x (ISBN 0-906127-21-1, Pub. by Irish Academic Pr Ireland). Biblio Dist.

DU BOIS, WILLIAM EDWARD BURGHARDT, 1868-1963
DuBois, Shirley G. His Day Is Marching on: Memoirs of W. E. B. DuBois. LC 71-14693. 1971. 10.00 (ISBN 0-89388-156-2); pap. 5.95 (ISBN 0-89388-157-0). Okpaku Communications.

DUBROVNIK, YUGOSLAVIA
Krekic, Barisa. Dubrovnik, Italy & the Balkans in the Late Middle Ages. 332p. 1980. 75.00x (ISBN 0-86078-070-8, Pub. by Variorum England). State Mutual Bk.

DUCK SHOOTING
see also Decoys (Hunting)
Jordan, James M. & Alcorn, George T., eds. The Wildfowler's Heritage. LC 80-85152. (Illus.). 120p. 1981. 46.50 (ISBN 0-938694-03-0); deluxe ed. 125.00; deluxe ed. with remarque 175.00. Jordan & Co.

DUCTLESS GLANDS
see Endocrine Glands

DUDLEY, ROBERT, EARL OF LEICESTER, 1533-1588
Wilson, Derek. Sweet Robin: A Biography of Robert Dudley, Earl of Leicester, 1533-1588. (Illus.). 304p. 1981. 54.00 (ISBN 0-241-10149-2, Pub. by Hamish Hamilton England). David & Charles.

DUMB (DEAF MUTES)
see Deaf

DUMBNESS
see Mutism

DUNCAN, ISADORA 1878-1927
Desti, Mary. The Untold Story: The Life of Isadora Duncan 1921-1927. (Dance Ser.). (Illus.). 281p. 1981. Repr. of 1929 ed. lib. bdg. 25.00 (ISBN 0-306-76044-4). Da Capo.
Schneider, Ilya I. Isadora Duncan: The Russian Years. Magarshack, David, tr. from Rus. (Da Capo Qauality Paperbacks Ser.). (Illus.). 221p. 1981. pap. 6.95 (ISBN 0-306-80142-6). Da Capo.

DUNGEONS
see Prisons

DUNSTABLE, JOHN, 1370?-1453
Bent, Margaret. Dunstaple. (Studies of Composers: No. 17). 96p. 1981. pap. 14.95 (ISBN 0-19-315225-8). Oxford U Pr.

DUPLICATE CONTRACT BRIDGE
see Contract Bridge–Duplicate Play

DURHAM, ENGLAND (COUNTY)
see also Durham, New Hampshire
Thorold, Henry. County Durham: A Shell Guide. (Illus.). 192p. 1981. 14.95 (ISBN 0-571-11640-X, Pub. by Faber & Faber). Merrimack Bk Serv.

DURRELL, LAWRENCE, 1912-
MacNiven, Ian S. & Moore, Harry T., eds. Literary Lifelines: The Richard Aldington-Larence Durrell Correspondence. 288p. 1981. 17.50 (ISBN 0-670-42817-5). Viking Pr.

DURUM WHEAT
see Wheat

DUST DISEASES
see Lungs–Dust Diseases

DUTCH ART
see Art, Dutch

DUTCH LANGUAGE
Bellin. Classical Dutch. 19.95 (ISBN 0-7134-3211-X, Pub. by Batsford England). David & Charles.
Stern, A. Z. & Reif, Joseph A., eds. Useful Expressions in Dutch. (Useful Expressions). 64p. 1980. pap. 1.50 (ISBN 0-86628-004-9). Ridgefield Pub.

DUTCH LITERATURE–HISTORY AND CRITICISM
Krahn, Cornelius. Dutch Anabaptism. 320p. 1981. pap. 18.00 (ISBN 0-8361-1243-1). Herald Pr.

DUTCH LITERATURE–TRANSLATIONS INTO ENGLISH
De Wit, Joost & Barkan, Stanley H., eds. Fifty Dutch & Flemish Novelists. 220p. 25.00 (ISBN 0-89304-031-2); pap. 15.00 (ISBN 0-89304-032-0). Cross Cult.

DUTCH PAINTING
see Painting, Dutch
DUTIES
see Taxation
DUTIES OF MEMBERS OF CONGRESS
see United States–Congress–Powers and Duties
DVORAK, ANTONIN, 1841-1904
Layton, Robert. Dvorak Symphonies & Concertos. LC 77-82650. (BBC Music Guides: No. 38). (Illus.). 64p. (Orig.). 1978. pap. 2.95 (ISBN 0-295-95505-8). U of Wash Pr.
DWARF FRUIT TREES
Tukey, Harold B. Dwarfed Fruit Trees. LC 77-12289. (Illus.). 576p. 1978. 32.50x (ISBN 0-8014-1126-2). Comstock.
DWARF TREES
see Dwarf Fruit Trees
DWELLINGS
see also Apartment Houses; Architecture, Domestic; Bathrooms; Country Homes; House Construction; Kitchens; Log Cabins; Patios
Keller, Suzanne, ed. Building for Women. LC 80-8783. 1981. price not set (ISBN 0-669-04368-0). Lexington Bks.
Shapiro, Barry & Boericke, Arthur. Handmade Homes: The Natural Way to Build Houses. (Illus.). Date not set. 17.95 (ISBN 0-440-03340-3). Delacorte.
Werning, David & Werning, Mary K. The Mistake Proof Earth Shelter Handbook. (Illus.). 160p. 1981. price not set (ISBN 0-89196-087-2, Domus Bks); pap. price not set. Quality Bks IL.
DWELLINGS–ENERGY CONSERVATION
Clayton, Michael. Cutting the Cost of Energy: A Practical Guide for the Householder. LC 80-67579. (Illus.). 160p. 1981. 16.95 (ISBN 0-7153-7927-5). David & Charles.
Coffed, Frank. The Self-Sufficient House. LC 80-13434. (Illus.). 1981. 16.95 (ISBN 0-03-053611-1); pap. 8.95 (ISBN 0-686-69126-1). HR&W.
Henkin, William A. Energy-Saving Projects for the Home. Ortho Books Editorial Staff, ed. LC 80-66348. (Illus.). 112p. (Orig.). 1981. pap. 5.95 (ISBN 0-917102-86-X, Ortho Bks). Chevron Chem.
Lindahl, Judy. Energy Saving Decorating. new ed. (Illus.). 128p. (Orig.). 1981. pap. 4.95 (ISBN 0-9603032-3-5). Lindahl.
Mecca, Stephen J. & Robertshaw, Joseph E. Home Energy Management: Principles & Practices. (Illus.). 160p. 1981. 12.00 (ISBN 0-89433-146-9). Petrocelli.
Palz, W & Steemers, Tc, eds. Solar Houses in Europe: How They Have Worked. LC 80-49715. (Illus.). 320p. 1981. 40.00 (ISBN 0-08-026743-2); pap. 20.00 (ISBN 0-08-026744-0). Pergamon.
DWELLINGS–HEATING AND VENTILATION
see Heating
DWELLINGS–JUVENILE LITERATURE
Unstead, R. J. Houses. (Junior Reference Ser.). (Illus.). 96p. (gr. 7 up). 7.95 (ISBN 0-7136-1301-7). Dufour.
Youldon, Gillian. Homes. (All A-Board Bks). (Illus.). 16p. (ps-2). 1981. 3.50 (ISBN 0-531-02539-X). Watts.
DWELLINGS–MAINTENANCE AND REPAIR
see also Buildings–Repair and Reconstruction
Advice About Tools & Home Repair. (Home Adviser Ser.). 80p. (Orig.). 1981. pap. 1.95 (ISBN 0-8326-2406-3, 7055). Delair.
Bingham, John. The Handbook for Apartment Living. LC 80-70350. 288p. (gr. 11-12). 1981. 13.95 (ISBN 0-686-69519-4); pap. 8.95 (ISBN 0-686-69520-8). Chilton.
Brann, Donald R. How to Build Outdoor Projects. 210p. 1981. pap. 5.95 (ISBN 0-87733-807-8). Easi-Bild.
Flynn, Joyce. About the House. 6.95 (ISBN 0-916752-08-9). Green Hill.
Gundrey, Elizabeth. Simple Home Repairs. (Orig.). 1980. pap. 6.95x (ISBN 0-8464-1050-8). Beekman Pubs.
Harris, M. The Muckraker's Manual: How to Do Your Own Investigative Reporting. 1980. pap. 7.95. Loompanics.
Hildebrand, Ron. Projects for the Home. Ortho Books Editorial Staff, ed. LC 80-66343. (Illus.). 96p. (Orig.). 1981. pap. 4.95 (ISBN 0-917102-85-1, Ortho Bks). Chevron Chem.
Miller, Michael C. The Guide to Home Renovation: For Those Without the Time or Inclination to Do It Themselves. LC 80-70390. (Illus.). 136p. (Orig.). 1981. pap. 7.95 (ISBN 0-686-69518-6). Chilton.
Old-House Journal Staff, ed. The Old-House Journal 1981 Catalog: A Buyer's Guide. (Illus.). 142p. (Orig.). 1981. pap. 9.95 (ISBN 0-87951-125-7). Overlook Pr.
Richardson, Barry. Remedial Treatment of Buildings. (The Construction Press Ser.). (Illus.). 236p. 1981. 42.00 (ISBN 0-904406-74-1). Longman.
Ritchie, James. Successful Homeowner's Tools. (Successful Ser.). 192p. 1980. 14.95 (ISBN 0-912336-85-4); pap. 7.95 (ISBN 0-912336-86-2). Structures Pub.
Rusk, Katherine. Renovating the Victorian House: A Guide for Aficionados of Old Houses. (Illus.). 250p. (Orig.). 1981. pap. 8.95 (ISBN 0-89286-187-8). One Hurd One Prods.
Sunset Editors. Roofing & Siding. LC 80-53487. (Illus.). 112p. (Orig.). 1981. pap. 4.95 (ISBN 0-376-01490-3, Sunset Bks). Sunset-Lane.
Time-Life Books Editors. Special Purpose Rooms. (Home Repair & Improvement Ser.). (Illus.). 128p. 1981. 10.95 (ISBN 0-8094-3458-X). Time-Life.
DWELLINGS–REMODELING
see also Buildings–Repair and Reconstruction
Bracken, John & Stone, Linda. Restoring the Victorian House. (Illus.). 192p. 1981. pap. 8.95 (ISBN 0-87701-222-9). Chronicle Bks.
Burch, Monte. Masonry & Concrete. Horowitz, Shirley & Kummings, Gail, eds. (Illus.). 144p. (Orig.). 1981. pap. 6.95 (ISBN 0-932944-30-2). Creative Homeowner.
Corbett, Michael N. A Better Place to Live: New Designs for Tomorrow's Communities. Stoner, Carol, ed. (Illus.). 256p. (Orig.). 1981. pap. 14.95 (ISBN 0-87857-348-8). Rodale Pr Inc.
Godfrey, Robert S. Repair & Remodeling Cost Data, 1981. 2nd ed. 325p. 1981. pap. 32.00 (ISBN 0-911950-34-6). Means.
Hague, William. Remodel, Don't Move: Make Your Home Fit Your Lifestyle. LC 80-498. (Illus.). 256p. 1981. 14.95 (ISBN 0-385-15910-2). Doubleday.
Hildebrand, Ron. Projects for the Home. Ortho Books Editorial Staff, ed. LC 80-66343. (Illus.). 96p. (Orig.). 1981. pap. 4.95 (ISBN 0-917102-85-1, Ortho Bks). Chevron Chem.
Hutchins, Nigel. Restoring Old Houses. 240p. 1980. 29.95 (ISBN 0-442-29625-8). Van Nos Reinhold.
Marshall, Mel. Yard Buildings. LC 80-1125. (Homeowner's Bible Ser.). (Illus.). 160p. 1981. pap. 4.95 (ISBN 0-385-15400-3). Doubleday.
Myers, Stanley & Figiel, Richard. Creative Home Remodeling. (Illus.). 240p. 1981. text ed. 16.95 (ISBN 0-13-189613-X, Spec); pap. text ed. 7.95 (ISBN 0-13-189605-9, Spec). P-H.
DYEING
see Dyes and Dyeing
DYES AND DYEING
see also Batik
Rice, Miriam C. How to Use Mushrooms for Color. rev. ed. (Illus.). 145p. 1980. pap. 7.95 (ISBN 0-916422-19-4). Mad River.
Venkataraman, Krishnasami, ed. The Chemistry of Synthethic Dyes, 8 vols. Incl. Vol. 1. 1952. 62.50 (ISBN 0-12-717001-4); Vol. 2. 1952. 62.50 (ISBN 0-12-717001-4); Vol. 3. 1970. 62.50 (ISBN 0-12-717003-0); Vol. 4. 1971. 62.50 (ISBN 0-12-717004-9); Vol. 5. 1972. 68.00 (ISBN 0-12-717005-7); Vol. 6. 1973. 62.50 (ISBN 0-12-717006-5); Vol. 7. 1974. 62.50 (ISBN 0-12-717007-3); Vol. 8. 1978. 62.50 (ISBN 0-12-717008-1). (Organic & Biological Chemistry Ser.). Set. 412.00 (ISBN 0-12-717002-2). Acad Pr.
DYING WORDS
see Last Words
DYNAMIC DISPLAY SYSTEMS
see Information Display Systems
DYNAMICS
see also Aerodynamics; Control Theory; Force and Energy; Hydrodynamics; Mechanics; Perturbation (Mathematics); Physics; Plasma Dynamics; Quantum Theory; Rotational Motion; Statics; Thermodynamics
Blaquiere, A., et al, eds. Dynamical Systems & Microphysics. (CISM - International Centre for Mechanical Sciences Courses & Lectures: Vol. 261). (Illus.). ix, 412p. 1980. pap. 39.00 (ISBN 0-387-81533-3). Springer-Verlag.
The Design of Counting Systems for Dynamic Studies & Uptake Measurements. 1980. 10.00 (Pub. by Brit Inst Radiology England). State Mutual Bk.
Gumowski, I. & Mira, C. Recurrence & Discrete Dynamic Systems. (Lecture Notes in Mathematics: Vol. 809). (Illus.). 272p. 1980. pap. 16.80 (ISBN 0-387-10017-2). Springer-Verlag.
McClamroch, N. H. State Models of Dynamic Systems. (Illus.). 248p. 1980. 17.80 (ISBN 0-387-90490-5). Springer-Verlag.
Nitecki, Z. & Robinson, C., eds. Global Theory of Dynamical Systems: Proceedings. (Lecture Notes in Mathematics Ser.: Vol. 819). 499p. 1981. pap. 29.50 (ISBN 0-387-10236-1). Springer-Verlag.
DYNAMICS, STRUCTURAL
see Structural Dynamics
DYSLEXIA
see also Reading Disability
Levinson, H. N. A Solution to the Riddle Dyslexia. (Illus.). 398p. 1981. 24.80 (ISBN 0-387-90515-4). Springer-Verlag.
Pavlidis, George & Miles, Timothy R. Dyslexia Research & Its Applications to Education. 264p. 1981. 29.75 (ISBN 0-471-27841-6, Pub. by Wiley Interscience). Wiley.
DYSLEXIA, DEVELOPMENTAL
see Reading Disability

E

EAR
see also Hearing
External Ear Malformations: Epidemiology, Genetics & Natural History. LC 79-2501. (Alan R. Liss Ser.: Vol. 15, No. 9). 1979. 18.00 (ISBN 0-8451-1034-9). March of Dimes.
Gorlin, Robert J., ed. Morphogenesis & Malformation of the Ear. LC 80-18892. (Birth Defects: Original Article Ser.: Vol XVI, No. 4). 367p. 1980. 44.00 (ISBN 0-8451-1038-1). A R Liss.
--Morphogenesis & Malformation of the Ear. LC 80-18892. (Alan R. Liss: Vol. 16,No. 4). 1980. 44.00 (ISBN 0-8451-1038-1). March of Dimes.
Monro, Alexander. Three Treatises: On the Brain, the Eye, & the Ear. Bd. with Croonian Lectures on Cerebrqal Localization. Ferrier, D. (Contributions to the History of Psychology Ser., Vol. VII, Pt. E: Psysiological Psychology). 1980. Repr. of 1797 ed. 30.00 (ISBN 0-89093-326-X). U Pubns Amer.
Silverstein, Alvin & Silverstein, Virginia. The Story of Your Ear. (Illus.). 64p. (gr. 5-9). 1981. PLB 6.99 (ISBN 0-698-30704-6). Coward.
EARLE, AUGUSTUS
Hackforth-Jones, Jocelyn. Augustus Earle: Travel Artist: Paintings & Drawings in the Rex Nan Kivell Collection National Library of Australia. 157p. 1980. 50.00x (ISBN 0-85967-631-5, Pub. by Scolar Pr England). Biblio Dist.
EARLY MAN
see Fossil Man
EARLY PRINTED BOOKS
see Bibliography–Rare Books
EARTH
see also Antarctic Regions; Arctic Regions; Atmosphere; Climatology; Cosmogony; Cosmology; Creation; Earthquakes; Geography; Geology; Geophysics; Glacial Epoch; Meteorology; Ocean; Oceanography; Physical Geography
Bendick. The Big Strawberry Book of the Earth: Our Ever-Changing Planet. 110p. Date not set. 6.95 (ISBN 0-07-004514-3). McGraw.
Fiennes, R. N. Ecology & Earth History. 250p. 1980. 40.00x (Pub. by Croom Helm England). State Mutual Bk.
Ozima, Minoru. The Earth: Its Birth & Growth. Wakabayashi, J. F., tr. (Illus.). 180p. Date not set. price not set (ISBN 0-521-23500-6); pap. price not set (ISBN 0-521-28005-2). Cambridge U Pr.
Smith, William F. The Shaping of the Earth. (Illus.). 128p. 1981. 7.00 (ISBN 0-682-49715-0). Exposition.
Thompson, William I. Passages About Earth: An Exploration of the New Planetary Culture. LC 73-14298. 192p. 1981. pap. 3.95 (ISBN 0-06-090835-1, CN 835, CN). Har-Row.
EARTH–CHEMICAL COMPOSITION
see Geochemistry
EARTH–CRUST
see also Plate Tectonics
Mineralogical Society Geochemistry Group, November 1 & 2, 1978. The Evidence of Chemical Heterogeneity in the Earth's Mantle. Bailey, D. K., et al, eds. (Illus.). 357p. 1980. text ed. 100.00x (ISBN 0-85403-144-8, Pub. by Royal Soc London). Scholium Intl.
EARTH–MAPS
see World Maps
EARTH, EFFECT OF MAN ON
see Man–Influence on Nature
EARTH SCIENCE
see Earth; Geology; Physical Geography
EARTH SCIENCES
see also Atmosphere; Climatology; Geochemistry; Geography; Geology; Geophysics; Hydrology; Meteorology; Oceanography
Brandreth, Gyles. Amazing Facts About Our Earth. LC 80-1087. (Amazing Facts Books Ser.). (Illus.). 32p. (gr. 5-8). 1981. pap. 2.95 (ISBN 0-385-17016-5). Doubleday.
EARTHENWARE
see Pottery
EARTHQUAKES
see also Seismology
Ben-Chieh Liu, et al. Earthquake Risk & Damage Functions: Applications to New Madrid. (Special Studies in Earth Sciences). 300p. 1981. lib. bdg. 24.50x (ISBN 0-86531-144-7). Westview.
Conference Sponsored by ASCE Construction Division, May 1980, San Francisco, CA. Social & Economic Impact of Earthquakes on Utility Lifelines: Proceedings. Isenberg, J., ed. LC 80-69153. 250p. pap. text ed. 21.00 (ISBN 0-87262-254-1). Am Soc Civil Eng.
Eiby, G. A. Earthquakes. 209p. 1980. 14.95 (ISBN 0-442-25191-2). Van Nos Reinhold.
Instrumentation for Ground Vibration & Earthquakes. 176p. 1980. pap. 65.00x (ISBN 0-7277-0052-9, Pub. by Telford England). State Mutual Bk.
Mack, Gerstle. Nineteen Hundred Six: Surviving the Great Earthquake & Fire. 96p. (Orig.). pap. 5.95 (ISBN 0-87701-176-1). Chronicle Bks.
Obermeyer, William G., Jr. & Jue-Obermeyer, Pauline M. Earthquake: Are You Prepared? LC 80-50463. (Illus.). 68p. (Orig.). 1980. pap. 2.95 (ISBN 0-936706-01-5). CERA.
Rikitake, Tsuneji, ed. Current Research in Earthquake Prediction, Vol. 1. (Developments in Earth & Planetary Sciences Ser.: No. 2). 400p. 1981. PLB 37.00 (ISBN 0-686-28846-7, Pub. by D. Reidel). Kluwer Boston.
Ritchie, David. The Ring of Fire. LC 80-69391. (Illus.). 296p. 1981. 12.95 (ISBN 0-689-11150-9). Atheneum.
Shibata, H. & Ariman, T., eds. Recent Advances in Lifeline Earthquake Engineering in Japan. (PVP: No. 43). 158p. 1980. 24.00 (H00170). ASME.
EARTHQUAKES–JUVENILE LITERATURE
Kimball, Virginia. Earthquake Ready. LC 80-8997. (Illus.). 128p. (Orig.). (gr. 6 up). 1981. pap. 5.95 (ISBN 0-915238-46-2). Peace Pr.
EARTHQUAKES AND BUILDING
Earthquake Problems Related to the Siting of Critical Facilities, Committee on Seismology. Earthquake Research for the Safer Siting of Critical Facilities. LC 80-82030. 1980. pap. text ed. 5.50 (ISBN 0-309-03082-X). Natl Acad Pr.
McGavin, Gary L. Earthquake Protection of Essential Building Equipment: Design, Engineering, Installation. 496p. 1981. 25.00 (ISBN 0-471-06270-7, Pub. by Wiley-Interscience). Wiley.
EARTHS, RARE
see also kinds of rare earths, e.g. Cerium
Subbarao, E. C. & Wallace, W. E., eds. Science & Technology of Rare Earth Materials. 1980. 29.00 (ISBN 0-12-675640-6). Acad Pr.
EARTHWORMS
Hess, Lilo. The Amazing Earthworm. (Illus.). 48p. (gr. 2-7). 1979. 7.95 (ISBN 0-684-16079-X). Scribner.
EAST–DESCRIPTION AND TRAVEL
Waldo, Myra. Myra Waldo's Travel Guide to the Orient & Asia, 1981. (Illus.). 505p. 1981. pap. 9.95 (ISBN 0-02-098890-7, Collier). Macmillan.
EAST–HISTORY
Le Monde Oriental De 395 a 1081. LC 80-2356. 1981. Repr. of 1936 ed. 72.50 (ISBN 0-404-18906-7). AMS Pr.
EAST GERMANY
see Germany, East
EAST INDIA COMPANY (ENGLISH)
Miller, Russell. The East Indiamen. Time-Life Books, ed. (The Seafarers Ser.). (Illus.). 176p. 1981. 14.95 (ISBN 0-8094-2689-7). Time-Life.
EAST INDIAN LITERATURE
see Indic Literature
EAST INDIAN PHILOSOPHY
see Philosophy, Indic
EAST INDIES
Special Index One: Annual Lists & General Index of the Parliamentary Papers Relating to the East Indies 1801-1907. (Bibliography on Parliamentary Papers Ser.). 248p. Repr. of 1909 ed. 61.00x (Pub. by Irish Academic Pr Ireland). Biblio Dist.
EASTER
see also Jesus Christ–Resurrection
Vaughan, Jenny. The Easter Book. LC 80-83362. (Illus.). 48p. (gr. 1-6). 1981. 4.95 (ISBN 0-448-11541-7); lib. bdg. 10.15 (ISBN 0-448-13492-6). G&D.
EASTER–SERMONS
Vawter, Bruce & Carl, William J., III. Easter. LC 79-7377. (Proclamation 2: Aids for Interpreting the Lessons of the Church Year, Ser. A). 64p. (Orig.). 1981. pap. 6.95 (ISBN 0-8006-4095-0, 1-4095). Fortress.
EASTER CAROLS
see Carols
EASTER EGGS
Milhous, Katherine. The Egg Tree. (Illus.). 32p. (gr. k-3). pap. 2.95 (ISBN 0-689-70492-5, A-119, Aladdin). Atheneum.
EASTER ISLAND
McCall, Grant. Rapanui: Tradition & Survival on Easter Island. LC 80-54833. 176p. 1981. text ed. 16.95x (ISBN 0-8248-0746-4). U Pr of Hawaii.
EASTERN CHURCHES
see also Orthodox Eastern Church
Lopez, Robert S. Byzantium & the World Around It: Economic & Institutional Relations. 318p. 1980. 50.00x (ISBN 0-86078-030-9, Pub. by Variorum England). State Mutual Bk.
Nicol, Donald M. Byzantium: Its Ecclesiastical History & Relations with the Western World. 336p. 1980. 60.00x (ISBN 0-902089-35-8, Pub. by Variorum England). State Mutual Bk.
EASTERN CHURCHES–LITURGY AND RITUAL
Weitzmann, Kurt. Byzantine Liturgical Psalters & Gospels. 322p. 1980. 200.00x (ISBN 0-86078-064-3, Pub. by Variorum England). State Mutual Bk.
EASTERN GERMANY
see Germany, East
EASTERN ORTHODOX CHURCH
see Orthodox Eastern Church
EASTERN QUESTION (BALKAN)
see also Balkan Peninsula–History; Crimean War, 1853-1856
Djordjevic, Dmitrije & Fischer-Galati, Stephen. The Balkan Revolutionary Tradition. LC 80-24039. 272p. 1981. 17.50x (ISBN 0-231-05098-4). Columbia U Pr.
EASTERN QUESTION (FAR EAST)
Tomimas, Shutaro. The Open-Door Policy & the Territorial Integretiy of China. (Studies in Chinese History & Civilization). 1977. 17.00 (ISBN 0-89093-095-3). U Pubns Amer.
EASTERN SCHISM
see Schism–Eastern and Western Church
EASTERN STATES–DESCRIPTION AND TRAVEL–GUIDEBOOKS
Whitman, John. The Best Free Attractions in the East. Grooms, Kathe, ed. (The Best Free Attractions Ser.). (Illus., Orig.). 1981. pap. 3.95 (ISBN 0-915658-35-6). Meadowbrook Pr.
EATING
see Dinners and Dining
EBONITE
see Rubber

EBULLITION

Collier, J. G. Convective Boiling & Condensation. 2nd ed. (Illus.). 460p. 1981. text ed. 59.50 (ISBN 0-07-011798-5). McGraw.

ECCLESIASTICAL ANTIQUITIES

see Christian Antiquities

ECCLESIASTICAL ARCHITECTURE

see Church Architecture

ECCLESIASTICAL ART

see Christian Art and Symbolism

ECCLESIASTICAL BIOGRAPHY

see Christian Biography

ECCLESIASTICAL CALENDAR

see Church Calendar

ECCLESIASTICAL COURTS

see also Church Discipline

Phillimore, Robert. The Principal Ecclesiastical Judgments Delivered in the Court of Arches 1867 to 1875. xiii, 420p. 1981. Repr. of 1876 ed. lib. bdg. 35.00x (ISBN 0-8377-2504-6). Rothman.

ECCLESIASTICAL DISCIPLINE

see Church Discipline

ECCLESIASTICAL FASTS AND FEASTS

see Fasts and Feasts

ECCLESIASTICAL HISTORY

see Church History

ECCLESIASTICAL INSTITUTIONS

see Religious and Ecclesiastical Institutions

ECCLESIASTICAL LAW

see also Asylum, Right Of; Canon Law; Ecclesiastical Courts; Privileges and Immunities; Sunday Legislation; Tithes

also subdivision Government under denominations, e.g. Church of England–Government

Ullman, Walter. The Church & the Law in the Earlier Middle Ages. 406p. 1980. 60.00x (ISBN 0-902089-79-X, Pub. by Variorum England). State Mutual Bk.

ECCLESIASTICAL OFFICE

see Clergy–Office

ECCLESIASTICAL POLITY

see Church Polity

ECCLESIASTICAL RITES AND CEREMONIES

see Liturgies; Rites and Ceremonies; Sacraments

ECCLESIASTICAL THEOLOGY

see Church

ECCLESIASTICAL TRIBUNALS

see Ecclesiastical Courts

ECHINOIDEA

see Sea-Urchins

ECHO RANGING

see Sonar

ECOLOGY

see also Animal Ecology; Animal Populations; Aquatic Ecology; Bioclimatology; Botany–Ecology; Conservation of Natural Resources; Forest Ecology; Fresh-Water Ecology; Geographical Distribution of Animals and Plants; Grassland Ecology; Human Ecology; Marine Ecology

Berrill, Michael & Berrill, Deborah. A Sierra Club Naturalist's Guide to the North Atlantic Coast. (Sierra Club Naturalist's Guides). (Illus.). 512p. (Orig.). 1981. 24.95 (ISBN 0-87156-242-1); pap. 10.95 (ISBN 0-87156-243-X). Sierra.

Blacksell, Mark & Gilg, Andrew. The Countryside: Planning & Change. (Resource Management Ser.: No. 2). (Illus.). 288p. (Orig.). 1981. text ed. 35.00x (ISBN 0-04-711008-2, 2599); pap. text ed. 17.50x (ISBN 0-04-711009-0, 2560). Allen Unwin.

Cousteau, Jacques-Yves. The Cousteau Almanac of the Environment: An Inventory of Life on a Water Planet. 864p. 1981. 24.95 (ISBN 0-385-14875-5). Doubleday.

Directory of Wetlands of International Importance in the Western Paleartic. 506p. 1981. pap. 27.50 (IUCN 87, IUCN). Unipub.

Earthday X Colloquium, University of Denver, April 21-24, 1980. Ecological Consciousness: Essays from the Earthday X Colloquium. Schultz, Robert C. & Hughes, J. Donald, eds. LC 80-6084. 510p. 1981. lib. bdg. 26.50 (ISBN 0-8191-1496-0); pap. text ed. 16.75 (ISBN 0-8191-1497-9). U Pr of Amer.

The Ecological Effects of Biological & Chemical Control of Undisirable Plants & Animals. 118p. 1961. pap. 7.50 (ISBN 0-686-68189-4, IUCN85, IUCN). Unipub.

Fiennes, R. N. Ecology & Earth History. 250p. 1980. 40.00x (Pub. by Croom Helm England). State Mutual Bk.

Grace, J., et al. Plants & Their Atmospheric Enviroment. (British Ecological Society Symposia Ser.). 428p. 1981. 89.95 (ISBN 0-470-27125-6). Halsted Pr.

Ito, Y. Comparative Ecology. 2nd ed. Kikkawa, J., tr. LC 79-41581. (Illus.). 350p. Date not set. text ed. 54.00 (ISBN 0-521-22977-4); pap. text ed. 19.95 (ISBN 0-521-29845-8). Cambridge U Pr.

Newman. Ecological Effects of Agricultural Chemistry. 1981. text ed. price not set. Butterworth.

On Coexistence: A Casual Approach to Diversity & Stability in Grassland Vegetation. (Agricultural Research Reports Ser.: No. 902). 164p. 1981. pap. 25.75 (ISBN 90-220-0747-2, PDC 217, Pudoc). Unipub.

Pilat, J. F. Ecological Politics: The Rise of the Green Movement. LC 80-52547. (The Washington Papers: No. 77). 96p. 1980. pap. 3.50 (ISBN 0-8039-1535-7). Sage.

A Review-Coastal Ecosystems, Nineteen Eighty. (UNEP Report Ser.: No. 4). 65p. 1980. pap. 7.50 (UNEP 033, UNEP). Unipub.

A Review-Island Ecosystems. (UNEP Report Ser.: No. 3). 34p. 1980. pap. 6.00 (UNEP 032, UNEP). Unipub.

A Review-Mountain Ecosystems, Nineteen Eighty. (UNEP Report Ser.: No. 2). 38p. 1980. pap. 6.00 (UNEP 031, UNEP). Unipub.

A Summary of UNEP Activities: Technical Assistance, 1980. (UNEP Report Ser.: No. 8). 115p. 1980. pap. 11.00 (UNEP 036, UNEP). Unipub.

Wolf, Joyce. An Ecology Alphabet. (Illus.). (gr. 3-6). 1981. PLB price not set (ISBN 0-671-42692-3). Messner.

ECOLOGY, HUMAN

see Human Ecology

Hayes, Harold. Three Levels of Time. 1981. 12.95 (ISBN 0-525-21853-X). Dutton.

ECONOMETRICS

see also Economics, Mathematical; Statistics

Abbott, Carl. Boosters & Businessmen: Popular Economic Thought & Urban Growth in the Antebellum Middle West. LC 80-1795. (Contributions in American Studies: No. 53). (Illus.). 1981. lib. bdg. 27.50 (ISBN 0-313-22562-1, ABB/). Greenwood.

Allard, R. J. An Approach to Econometrics. 240p. 1974. 27.00x (ISBN 0-86003-003-2, Pub. by Allan Pubs England); pap. 13.50x (ISBN 0-86003-102-0). State Mutual Bk.

Cassidy, Henry J. Using Econometrics: A Beginner's Guide. 1981. text ed. 18.95 (ISBN 0-8359-8135-5); instr's. manual free (ISBN 0-8359-8136-3). Reston.

Chow, Gregory C. Econometric Analysis by Control Methods. (Wiley Series in Probability & Mathematical Statistics). 325p. 1981. 31.95 (ISBN 0-471-08706-8, Pub. by Wiley-Interscience). Wiley.

Kendrick, David. Stochastic Control of Economic Models. (Economic Handbook Ser.). (Illus.). 288p. 1981. text ed. 39.50 (ISBN 0-07-033962-7, C). McGraw.

Lucas, Robert E., Jr. & Sargent, Thomas J., eds. Rational Expectations & Econometric Practice. 672p. 1981. 35.00x (ISBN 0-8166-0916-0); pap. 14.95x (ISBN 0-8166-0917-9). U of Minn Pr.

Spirey, W. Allen & Wrobleski, William J. Econometric Model Performance in Forecasting & Policy Assessment. 1979. pap. 4.25 (ISBN 0-8447-3327-X). Am Enterprise.

Stewart, Jon. Understanding Econometrics. 1980. text ed. 18.25x (ISBN 0-09-126230-5, Hutchinson U Pr); pap. text ed. 10.25x (ISBN 0-09-126231-3). Humanities.

Stewart, Mark B. & Kenneth, Wallis F. Introductory Econometrics. 2nd ed. 352p. 1981. 24.95 (ISBN 0-470-27132-9). Halsted Pr.

Wolters, J. Stochastic Dynamic Properties of Linear Econometric Models. (Lecture Notes in Economics & Mathematical Systems: Vol. 182). (Illus.). 154p. 1981. pap. 15.00 (ISBN 0-387-10240-X). Springer Verlag.

ECONOMIC ASSISTANCE, AMERICAN

Sommer, John G. Beyond Charity: U. S. Voluntary Aid for a Changing Third World. LC 77-89276. 192p. 1977. pap. 3.95 (ISBN 0-686-28706-1). Overseas Dev Council.

ECONOMIC BOTANY

see Botany, Economic

ECONOMIC CONDITIONS

see Economic History

ECONOMIC CYCLES

see Business Cycles

ECONOMIC DEVELOPMENT

Here are entered general works on the theory and policy of economic development. Works restricted to a particular area are entered under the name of the area.

see also Industrialization; Saving and Investment; Underdeveloped Areas

Cole, J. P. The Development Gap: A Spatial Analysis of World Poverty & Inequality. 416p. 1981. write for info. (ISBN 0-471-27796-7, Pub. by Wiley-Interscience). Wiley.

D'A. Shaw, Robert. Rethinking Economic Development. (Development Papers: No. 8). 58p. 1972. pap. 1.00 (ISBN 0-686-28680-4). Overseas Dev Council.

Fourth Franklin Conference. Innovation & the American Economy. 140p. 1980. pap. text ed. 8.95 (ISBN 0-89168-033-0). Franklin Inst Pr.

Greenwood, Michael. Migration & Economic Growth in the United States: National, Regional & Metropolitan Perspectives. (Studies in Urban Economics). 1981. price not set (ISBN 0-12-300650-3). Acad Pr.

Ingham, Barbara. Tropical Exports & Economic Development. Date not set. 22.50 (ISBN 0-312-81918-8). St Martin.

Laudicina, Paul A. World Poverty & Development: A Survey of American Opinion. LC 73-89873. (Monographs: No. 8). 126p. 1973. 2.50 (ISBN 0-686-28687-1). Overseas Dev Council.

Roemer, Stern. Cases in Economic Development Projects: Policies & Statistics. 1981. text ed. price not set (ISBN 0-408-10730-8); pap. text ed. price not set (ISBN 0-408-10729-4). Butterworth.

ECONOMIC DEVELOPMENT–MATHEMATICAL MODELS

Ohkawa, Kazushi & Key, Bernard. Asian Socioeconomical Development: A National Accounts Approach. 326p. 1980. text ed. 27.50. U Pr of Hawaii.

Ohkawa, Kazushi & Key, Bernard, eds. Asian Socioeconomic Development: A National Accounts Approach. 326p. 1980. text ed. 27.50x (ISBN 0-8248-0743-X). U Pr of Hawaii.

ECONOMIC DEVELOPMENT–SOCIAL ASPECTS

Wolfgang, Marvin E. & Lambert, Richard D., eds. Social Effects of Inflation. (The Annals of the American Academy of Political & Social Science: No. 456). 250p. 1981. 7.50 (ISBN 0-87761-264-1); pap. 6.00 (ISBN 0-87761-265-X). Am Acad Pol Soc Sci.

ECONOMIC FORECASTING

see also Business Forecasting; Economic Indicators

Pluta, Joseph E., ed. Economic & Business: Issues of the 1980's. 1980. 7.00. U of Tex Busn Res.

Servan-Schreiber, Jean-Jacques. The World Challenge. 1981. 14.95 (ISBN 0-671-42524-2). S&S.

Smart, C. F. & Stanbury, W. T. Studies on Crisis Management. 195p. 1978. pap. text ed. 9.95x (ISBN 0-920380-03-4, Pub. by Inst Res Pub Canada). Renouf.

ECONOMIC FORECASTING–MATHEMATICAL MODELS

Spirey, W. Allen & Wrobleski, William J. Econometric Model Performance in Forecasting & Policy Assessment. 1979. pap. 4.25 (ISBN 0-8447-3327-X). Am Enterprise.

ECONOMIC GEOGRAPHY

see Geography, Economic

ECONOMIC GROWTH

see Economic Development

ECONOMIC HISTORY

see also subdivision Economic conditions under names of countries, regions, cities, etc. Also Automation–Economic aspects

Main Economic Indicators, Historical Statistics 1960 to 1979. (Illus.). 637p. (Orig., Fr. & Eng.). 1980. pap. text ed. 27.50x (ISBN 92-64-02110-8). OECD.

ECONOMIC INDICATORS

Main Economic Indicators, Historical Statistics 1960 to 1979. (Illus.). 637p. (Orig., Fr. & Eng.). 1980. pap. text ed. 27.50x (ISBN 92-64-02110-8). OECD.

ECONOMIC INTEGRATION, INTERNATIONAL

see International Economic Integration

ECONOMIC ORNITHOLOGY

see Birds, Injurious and Beneficial

ECONOMIC POISONS

see Pesticides

ECONOMIC POLICY

see also Commercial Policy; Comparative Economics; Economic Development; Economic Stabilization; Full Employment Policies; Government Ownership; Government Spending Policy; Industrial Laws and Legislation; Industrialization; Industry and State; Inflation (Finance); International Economic Relations; Labor Supply; Manpower Policy; Monetary Policy; Social Policy; Subsidies; Technical Assistance; Unemployed; Wage-Price Policy; Welfare Economics also subdivisions Commercial Policy and Economic Policy under names of countries

Aliber, Robert Z., ed. The Political Economy of Monetary Reform. LC 76-26692. 320p. 1977. text ed. 21.00 (ISBN 0-86598-001-2). Allanheld.

Atkinson, A. B., ed. Wealth, Income, & Inequality. 2nd ed. (Illus.). 450p. 1981. 42.00x (ISBN 0-19-877143-6); pap. 21.00x (ISBN 0-19-877144-4). Oxford U Pr.

Bartlett, Bruce R. A Walk on the Supply Side: Economic Policies for the Eighties & Beyond. 256p. 1981. 14.95 (ISBN 0-87000-505-7). Arlington Hse.

Benoit, Emile. Progress & Survival: An Essay on the the Future of Mankind. Gohn, Jack B., ed. 144p. 1980. 17.95 (ISBN 0-03-056911-7). Praeger.

Culyer, A. J. The Political Economy of Social Policy. 1980. 27.50 (ISBN 0-312-62242-2). St Martin.

Grant, R. M. & Shaw, G. K. Current Issues in Economic Policy. 320p. 28.50x (ISBN 0-86003-029-6, Pub. by Allan Pubs England); pap. 14.25x (ISBN 0-86003-128-4). State Mutual Bk.

Keeley, Michael C. Labor Supply & Public Policy: A Critical Review. (Studies in Labor Economics Ser.). 1981. price not set (ISBN 0-12-403920-0). Acad Pr.

United Nations. World Economic Survey, 1979-80. LC 48-1401. 116p. (Orig.). 1980. pap. 10.00x (ISBN 0-8002-1108-1). Intl Pubns Serv.

Weiss, Leonard. Economics & Society. 2nd ed. 576p. 1981. text ed. 18.95 (ISBN 0-471-03160-7). Wiley.

World Statistics in Brief. 241p. 1980. pap. 3.95 (ISBN 0-686-68981-X, UN80/17/3, UN). Unipub.

ECONOMIC RELATIONS, FOREIGN

see International Economic Relations

ECONOMIC RESEARCH

see also Economic Surveys

Association for University Business & Economic Research-AUBER. Readings in Business & Economic Research Management: Execution & Enterprise, Vol. 1. 1980. pap. 7.50 (ISBN 0-86603-000-X). Bureau Busn Res U Wis.

Smith, Charles B. A Guide to Business Research: Developing, Conducting & Writing Research Projects. LC 79-22991. 200p. 1981. text ed. 16.95 (ISBN 0-88229-546-2); pap. text ed. 8.95 (ISBN 0-88229-750-3). Nelson-Hall.

ECONOMIC STABILIZATION

Cline, William R. & Weintraub, Sidney. Economic Stabilization in Developing Countries. LC 80-70079. 514p. 1981. 26.95 (ISBN 0-8157-1466-1); pap. 11.95 (ISBN 0-8157-1465-3). Brookings.

ECONOMIC STATISTICS

see Economic History (for collections of statistics), Statistics (for works on the theory and methodology of economic statistics)

ECONOMIC SURVEYS

World Economic Survey: Niniteen Seventy-Nine to Nineteen Eighty. 116p. 1980. pap. 10.00 (UN80-2C2, UN). Unipub.

ECONOMIC THEORY

see Economics

ECONOMIC UNION

see International Economic Integration

ECONOMICS

see also Banks and Banking; Barter; Business; Capital; Capitalism; Christianity and Economics; Commerce; Comparative Economics; Competition; Consumption (Economics); Cooperation; Cost and Standard of Living; Credit; Debt; Demography; Division of Labor; Econometrics; Economic Development; Economic Forecasting; Economic History; Economic Policy; Economists; Employment (Economic Theory); Entrepreneur; Finance; Finance, Public; Government Ownership; Income; Individualism; Industry; Institutional Economics; Interest and Usury; Labor and Laboring Classes; Labor Economics; Land Use; Macroeconomics; Managerial Economics; Marxian Economics; Microeconomics; Money; Monopolies; Population; Profit; Property; Rent; Risk; Saving and Investment; Saving and Thrift; Socialism; Statistics; Supply and Demand; Taxation; Transportation; Value; Wages; Wealth; Welfare Economics

Agrawal, A. N. & Lal, Kundan. Economic Planning. 2nd rev. ed. 400p. 1980. text ed. 18.95 (ISBN 0-7069-1256-X, Pub. by Vikas India). Advent Bk.

Andrews, Linda. Philosophy of Economics. (Foundations of Philosophy Ser.). (Illus.). 200p. 1981. pap. text ed. 7.95 (ISBN 0-13-663336-6). P-H.

Bagby, Wesley M. Contemporary American Economic & Political Problems. LC 80-22510. 296p. 1981. text ed. 19.95 (ISBN 0-88229-328-1); pap. text ed. 9.95 (ISBN 0-88229-765-1). Nelson-Hall.

Bhooshan, B. S., ed. Towards Alternative Settlement Strategies: The Role of Small & Intermediate Centers in Development Process. x, 404p. 1980. text ed. 25.00x (ISBN 0-86590-005-1). Apt Bks.

Bingham, Robert C. Economic Concepts: A Programmed Approach. 6th ed. (Illus.). 384p. 1981. pap. text ed. 7.95 (ISBN 0-07-044936-8, C). McGraw.

Brinkman, Richard L. Cultural Economics. LC 78-62056. 450p. 1981. pap. text ed. 15.95 (ISBN 0-913244-15-5). Hapi Pr.

Brotchie, J. F., et al. TOPAZ - General Planning Technique & Its Applications at the Regional, Urban, & Facility Planning Levels. (Lecture Notes in Economics & Mathematical Systems: Vol. 180). (Illus.). 356p. 1980. pap. 29.00 (ISBN 0-387-10020-2). Springer-Verlag.

Buchanan, James M. & Thirlby, G. F., eds. L.S.E Essays on Cost. (The Institute for Humane Studies Ser. in Economic Theory). 1981. text ed. 20.00x (ISBN 0-8147-1034-4); pap. text ed. 7.00x (ISBN 0-8147-1035-2). NYU Pr.

Chisholm, Roger & McCarty, Marilu. Principles of Economics. 2nd ed. 1981. text ed. 18.95x (ISBN 0-673-15492-0). Scott F.

Clawson, Elmer. Our Economy: How It Works. 1980. 12.64 (ISBN 0-201-01057-7, Sch Div); tchr's. ed. 8.24. A-W.

Close, Frank A., et al. Study Guide to Accompany Principles of Economics. 2nd ed. 1981. pap. text ed. 6.95x (ISBN 0-673-15494-7). Scott F.

Coghlan, Richard. Money Credit & the Economy. (Illus.). 192p. 1981. text ed. 35.00x (ISBN 0-04-332079-1, 2649). Allen Unwin.

Crowson, P. C. & Richards, B. A. Economics for Managers. (Illus.). 248p. 1978. pap. 16.95x (ISBN 0-7131-3397-X). Intl Ideas.

The Current Development of the World Economy. 74p. 1980. pap. 5.00 (ISBN 92-808-0150-3, TUNU096, UNU). Unipub.

De Jong, Frits J., et al, eds. Quadrilingual Economics Dictionary. 1981. lib. bdg. 48.00 (ISBN 90-247-2243-8, Pub. by Martinus Nijhoff). Kluwer Boston.

Elliott, Ralph N. An Elementary Introduction into the Elliott's Wave Theory. (The New Stock Market Reference Library). (Illus.). 91p. 1981. 27.55 (ISBN 0-918968-92-5). Inst Econ Fina.

Fellner, William, ed. Contemporary Economic Problems, 1980. 1980. pap. 8.25 (ISBN 0-8447-3386-5). Am Enterprise.

Fellner, William J., ed. Contemporary Economic Problems, 1979. 1979. pap. 9.25 (ISBN 0-8447-1334-1). Am Enterprise.

Fels, et al. Casebook of Economic, Microeconomic Problems & Policies: Practice in Thinking. 4th ed. 112p. 1978. 5.95 (ISBN 0-8299-0479-4); staff notes avail. West Pub.

Frey, Bruno S. Modern Political Economy, Paper. 166p. 1980. pap. text ed. 13.95 (ISBN 0-470-26999-5). Halsted Pr.

Friedman, Milton & Friedman, Rose. Free to Choose: A Personal Statement. 352p. 1981. pap. 2.95 (ISBN 0-380-52548-8, 52548). Avon.

Galbraith, John K. Economics & the Public Purpose. 1980. pap. 2.95 (ISBN 0-451-61864-5, ME1864, Ment). NAL.

Gaskin, Maxwell, ed. The Political Economy of Tolerable Survival. 224p. 1981. 30.00x (ISBN 0-7099-0266-2, Pub. by Croom Helm Ltd England). Biblio Dist.

Giffen, Robert. Economic Inquiries & Studies, 2 vols. (The Development of Industrial Society Ser.). 916p. 1981. Repr. 65.00x (ISBN 0-7165-1758-2, Pub. by Irish Academic Pr). Biblio Dist.

Ginsburg, Helen, ed. Poverty, Economics, & Society. LC 80-6115. 361p. 1981. lib. bdg. 21.50 (ISBN 0-8191-1385-9); pap. text ed. 11.95 (ISBN 0-8191-1386-7). U Pr of Amer.

Grant, Lorenzo G. The Weight of the Historical Inevitabilities at the End of the 20th Century & the Future of Humanity. (Illus.). 141p. 1981. 41.75 (ISBN 0-930008-76-6). Inst Econ Finan.

Hanson, J. L. An Introduction to Applied Economics. 3rd ed. (Illus.). 512p. 1980. pap. text ed. 17.50x (ISBN 0-7121-0963-3). Intl Ideas.

--An Outline of Monetary Theory. 4th ed. 160p. 1980. pap. text ed. 9.95x (ISBN 0-7121-1533-1). Intl Ideas.

--A Textbook of Economics. 7th ed. (Illus.). 640p. 1977. pap. text ed. 15.95x (ISBN 0-7121-2020-3, Pub. by Macdonald & Evans England). Intl Ideas.

Hazlitt, Henry. Economics in One Lesson. 218p. 1981. pap. 4.95 (ISBN 0-87000-517-0). Arlington Hse.

Henderson, Hazel. Politics of the Solar Age: The Alternative to Economics. LC 80-1723. (Illus.). 312p. 1981. pap. 5.95 (ISBN 0-385-17150-1, Anchor Pr); pap. 5.95 (ISBN 0-385-17151-X). Doubleday.

Jones, Aubrey, ed. Economics & Equality. 176p. 1976. 27.00x (ISBN 0-86003-010-5, Pub. by Allan Pubs England). State Mutual Bk.

Karl Marx-Frederick Engels: Collected Works, Vol. 14. 1980. 8.50 (ISBN 0-7178-0514-X). Intl Pub Co.

Keyserling, Leon H. Liberal & Conservative National Economic Policies & Their Consequences, 1919-79. (Illus.). 1979. 3.00. Conf Econ Prog.

Lachmann, Ludwig M. Capital, Expectations, & the Market Process: Essays on the Theory of the Market Economy. Grinder, Walter E., ed. & intro. by. 1977. write for info. NYU Pr.

LaRouche, Lyndon H., Jr. Basic Economics for Conservative Democrats. LC 80-5684. (Illus.). 172p. (Orig.). 1980. pap. 3.95 (ISBN 0-933488-04-1). New Benjamin.

LaRouche, Lyndon H., Jr. & Goldman, David. The Ugly Truth About Milton Friedman. LC 80-20623. (Illus.). 350p. (Orig.). 1980. pap. 3.95 (ISBN 0-933488-09-2). New Benjamin.

Leipziger, Danny M., ed. The Basic Human Needs Approach to Development: Some Policy Issues. LC 80-19938. 256p. 1981. lib. bdg. 20.00 (ISBN 0-89946-021-6). Oelgeschlager.

Levi, Maurice. Economics Deciphered: A Layman's Guide. LC 80-68173. 192p. 1981. 11.95 (ISBN 0-465-01794-0). Basic.

Livingstone, Ian, ed. Development Economics & Policy Readings. (Illus.). 368p. (Orig.). 1981. text ed. 38.95x (ISBN 0-04-382025-5, 2581); pap. text ed. 15.00x (ISBN 0-04-382026-3, 2582). Allen Unwin.

McArthur, Alfred G. & Loveridge, John W. Economic Theory & Organization. (Illus.). 400p. 1980. pap. 16.95x. Intl Ideas.

Marx, K. & Engels, F. Mega, Vol. 1, Pt.10. 1390p. 60.00 (Pub. by Dietz Germany). Imported Pubns.

--Mega, Vol. 1, Pt. 22. 1790p. 60.00 (Pub. by Dietz Germany). Imported Pubns.

--Mega, Vol. 2, Pt. 1.1. 464p. 60.00 (Pub. by Dietz Germany). Imported Pubns.

--Mega, Vol. 2,pt. 3.1. 499p. 60.00 (Pub. by Dietz Germany). Imported Pubns.

--Mega, Vol. 2,pt. 3.2. 800p. 60.00 (Pub. by Dietz Germany). Imported Pubns.

--Mega, Vol. 2,pt. 3.3. 930p. 60.00 (Pub. by Dietz Germany). Imported Pubns.

--Mega, Vol. 2,pt. 3.4. 479p. 60.00 (Pub. by Dietz Germany). Imported Pubns.

--Mega, Vol. 3,pt. 1. 479p. 60.00 (Pub. by Dietz Germany). Imported Pubns.

--Mega, Vol. 4,pt. 1. 1047p. 60.00 (Pub. by Dietz Germany). Imported Pubns.

Mayer, Martin. The Fate of the Dollar. 1981. Repr. pap. 3.50 (ISBN 0-451-09612-6, E9612, Sig). NAL.

Menger, Carl. Principles of Economics. Dingwall, James & Hoselitz, Bert F., trs. (The Institute for Humane Studies Ser. in Economic Theory). 328p. 1981. text ed. 20.00x (ISBN 0-8147-5380-9); pap. text ed. 7.00x (ISBN 0-8147-5381-7). NYU Pr.

Mises, Ludwig Von. The Ulitmate Foundation of Economic Science: An Essay on Method. 1978. wrtie for info. NYU Pr.

Morgan, E. V. First Approach to Economics. pap. 26.00x (ISBN 0-392-07843-0, SpS). Soccer.

Odagiri, Hiroyuki. The Theory of Growth in a Corporate Economy: Management Prefernce, Research & Development & Economic Growth. LC 80-23494. (Illus.). 256p. Date not set. price not set (ISBN 0-521-23132-9). Cambridge U Pr.

Odum, Howard T. & Odum, Elisabeth C. Energy Basis for Man & Nature. 2nd ed. (Illus.). 352p. 1981. text ed. 19.50 (ISBN 0-07-047511-3, C); pap. text ed. 12.95 (ISBN 0-07-047510-5, C); instrs'. manual avail. McGraw.

Pasinetti, L. Structural Change & Economic Growth. (Illus.). 337p. Date not set. price not set (ISBN 0-521-23607-X). Cambridge U Pr.

Pluta, Joseph, ed. Economic & Business Issues of the Nineteen Eighties. LC 80-68658. 235p. (Orig.). 1980. pap. 7.00 (ISBN 0-87755-242-8). U of Tex Busn Res.

Remington, Alexander M. Anatomy of the Economic Forces Which Decide the Life & Death of Our Modern Societies. (Illus.). 148p. 1981. 49.75 (ISBN 0-918968-91-7). Inst Econ Finan.

Ritter, Lawrence S. & Silber, William L. Money. 4th, rev. ed. 336p. 1981. 12.95x (ISBN 0-465-04718-1); pap. 6.95x (ISBN 0-465-04720-3). Basic.

Rothbard, Murray N. Man, Economy, & State: A Treatise on Economic Principles. 1978. write for info. NYU Pr.

--Power & Market: Government & the Economy. 1977. write for info. NYU Pr.

Rothwell, Roy & Zegveld, Walter. Technological Innovation & Public Policy. LC 81-493. (Contributions in Economics & Economic History Ser.: No. 42). 400p. 1981. lib. bdg. 35.00 (ISBN 0-313-22989-9, RTE/). Greenwood.

Roy, Ewell P., et al. Economics: Applications to Agriculture & Agribusiness. 3rd ed. x, 455p. 1981. 17.00 (ISBN 0-8134-2113-6, 2113); text ed. 12.75x. Interstate.

Rudman, Jack. Economics. (Undergraduate Program Field Test Ser.: UPFT-6). (Cloth bdg. avail. on request). pap. 9.95 (ISBN 0-8373-6006-4). Natl Learning.

Sapsford, David. Labour Market Economics. (Illus.). 240p. 1981. text ed. 30.00x (ISBN 0-04-331082-6, 2621/2); pap. text ed. 14.95x3210-04-331083-4 (ISBN 0-04-331083-4). Allen Unwin.

Schotter, Andrew. The Economic Theory of Social Institutions. (Illus.). 240p. Date not set. 29.50 (ISBN 0-521-23044-6). Cambridge U Pr.

Schulz, T. Paul. Population Economics. LC 80-36830. (Perspectives in Economics Ser.). 224p. 1981. pap. text ed. price not set (ISBN 0-201-08371-X). A-W.

Shaw, George B. The Intelligent Woman's Guide to Socialism, Capitalism, Sovietism, & Fascism. 1981. pap. 3.95 (ISBN 0-14-040034-6). Penguin.

Simon, Herbert. Sciences of the Artificial. 2nd, rev. ed. 192p. 1981. text ed. 15.00 (ISBN 0-262-19193-8); pap. 4.95 (ISBN 0-262-69073-X). MIT Pr.

Sirkin, Gerald, ed. Lexeconics: The Interaction of Law & Economics. (Social Dimensions of Economics, CCNY Ser.: Vol. 2). 272p. 1981. lib. bdg. 17.50 (ISBN 0-89838-053-7, Pub. by Martinus Nijhoff). Kluwer Boston.

Smith, Adam, pseud. Paper Money. 288p. 1981. 13.95 (ISBN 0-671-44825-0). Summit Bks.

Usher, Dan. The Economic Prerequisite to Democracy. 224p. 1981. 17.50x (ISBN 0-231-05280-4). Columbia U Pr.

Von Mises, Ludwig. Epistemological Problems of Economics. (The Institue for Humane Studies Ser. in Economic Theory). 264p. 1981. 20.00x (ISBN 0-8147-8757-6); pap. 7.00x (ISBN 0-8147-8758-4). NYU Pr.

Watson, Thomas E. Handbook of Politics & Economics. (Studies in Populism). 1980. lib. bdg. 75.00 (ISBN 0-686-68879-1). Revisionist Pr.

ECONOMICS–ADDRESSES, ESSAYS, AND LECTURES

Copeland, Morris A. Essays in Socioeconomic Evolution. 1981. 10.00 (ISBN 0-533-04328-X). Vantage.

Drucker, Peter F. Toward the Next Economics & Other Essays. LC 80-8370. 256p. 1981. 11.95 (ISBN 0-06-014828-4, HarpT). Har-Row.

Long, Frank, ed. Economic Planning Studies. (International Studies in Economics & Econometrics: No. 8). 198p. 1980. pap. 11.95 (ISBN 90-277-1194-1, Pub. by D. Reidel). Kluwer Boston.

Marschak, Jacob. Economic Information, Decision, & Prediction, 3 vols. (Theory & Decision Library: No. 7). 1980. Vol. I, 389 Pp. pap. 14.95 (ISBN 90-277-1195-X, Pub. by D. Reidel); Vol. II, 362 Pp. pap. 14.95 (ISBN 90-277-1196-8); Vol. III, 399 Pp. pap. 14.95 (ISBN 90-277-1197-6). Kluwer Boston.

Robinson, Joan. What Are the Questions? & Other Essays: Further Contributions to Economics. 214p. 1981. 17.50x (ISBN 0-87332-199-5); pap. 8.95x (ISBN 0-87332-200-2). M E Sharpe.

Weizsaecker, C. C. Barriers to Entry: A Theoretical Treatment. (Lecture Notes in Economics & Mathematical Systems Ser.: Vol. 185). (Illus.). 220p. 1981. pap. 19.00 (ISBN 0-387-10272-8). Springer-Verlag.

ECONOMICS–BIBLIOGRAPHY

Research Libraries of the New York Public Library & the Library of Congress. Bibliographic Guide to Business & Economics: 1980. (Library Catalogs-Bib. Guides). 1981. lib. bdg. 225.00 (ISBN 0-8161-6883-0). G K Hall.

ECONOMICS–DICTIONARIES

Henni, Mustapha. Dictionaire Des Termes Economiques et Commerciaux: Francais-Arabe. 20.00x. Intl Bk Ctr.

ECONOMICS–HISTORY

Flumiani, Carlo M. The Economic Philosophy of History & Basic Patterns in the Growth & Decline of Nations. (Illus.). 117p. 1981. 59.85 (ISBN 0-930008-77-4). Inst Econ Finan.

Grant, Lorenzo G. The Weight of the Historical Inevitabilities at the End of the 20th Century & the Future of Humanity. (Illus.). 141p. 1981. 41.75 (ISBN 0-930008-76-6). Inst Econ Finan.

Malynes, Gerard De. Consuetudo, Vel Lex Mercatoria, or the Ancient Law-Merchant. LC 79-84121. (English Experience Ser.: No. 940). 524p. 1979. Repr. of 1622 ed. lib. bdg. 78.00 (ISBN 90-221-0940-2). Walter J Johnson.

Matyas, Antal. History of Modern Non-Marxian Economics. Veges, Istvan, tr. (Illus.). 598p. 1980. 50.00x (ISBN 963-05-1894-5). Intl Pubns Ser.

Seddon, Edmund. Modern Economic History. (Illus.). 384p. 1979. pap. text ed. 11.95x (ISBN 0-7121-1286-3, Pub. by Macdonald & Evans England). Intl Ideas.

ECONOMICS–INFORMATION SERVICES

Gould, Jay M. Input-Output Databases. 1978. lib. bdg. 22.50 (ISBN 0-8240-7058-5). Garland Pub.

ECONOMICS–MATHEMATICAL MODELS

Kendrick, David. Stochastic Control of Economic Models. (Economic Handbook Ser.). (Illus.). 288p. 1981. text ed. 39.50 (ISBN 0-07-033962-7, C). McGraw.

ECONOMICS–METHODOLOGY

see also Economics, Mathematical

Bradley, Iver F. & South, John B. Introductory Statistics for Business Economics. LC 80-65789. 640p. 1981. text ed. 18.95 (ISBN 0-03-053026-1). Dryden Pr.

ECONOMICS–RESEARCH

see Economic Research

ECONOMICS–STUDY AND TEACHING

Burns. Great Ideas for Teaching Economics. 846p. 1981. pap. write for info. (ISBN 0-8302-2304-5). Goodyear.

Holley, B. & Skelton, V. Economics Education Fourteen to Sixteen. 250p. 1981. pap. text ed. 15.25x (ISBN 0-85633-215-1, NFER). Humanities.

Toch, Henry. Economics for Professional Studies. (Illus.). 240p. 1977. pap. 12.95 (ISBN 0-7121-0568-9, Pub. by Macdonald & Evans England). Intl Ideas.

ECONOMICS, COMPARATIVE

see Comparative Economics

ECONOMICS, INTERNATIONAL

see also International Economic Relations

Corden, W. M. Inflation, Exchange Rates, & the World Economy: Lectures on International Monetary Economics. (Business & Society Studies). 1980. pap. write for info. (ISBN 0-226-11584-4). U of Chicago Pr.

Hieronymi, Otto, ed. The New Economic Nationalism. 300p. 1980. 29.95 (ISBN 0-03-056676-2). Praeger.

Kenan, Peter B. Essays in International Economics. (Princeton Series of Collected Essays). 432p. 1980. 22.50 (ISBN 0-691-04225-X); pap. 5.95 (ISBN 0-691-00364-5). Princeton U Pr.

Laffer & Miles. International Economics: In an Integrated World. 416p. 1981. pap. write for info. (ISBN 0-8302-4028-4). Goodyear.

Mundell, Robert A. & Swoboda, Alexander K., eds. Monetary Problems of the International Economy. pap. write for info. (ISBN 0-226-55066-4). U of Chicago Pr.

ECONOMICS, MATHEMATICAL

see also Economics–Mathematical Models

Bradley, Iver F. & South, John B. Introductory Statistics for Business Economics. LC 80-65789. 640p. 1981. text ed. 18.95 (ISBN 0-03-053026-1). Dryden Pr.

Stewart, Jon. Understanding Econometrics. 1980. text ed. 18.25x (ISBN 0-09-126230-5, Hutchinson U Pr); pap. text ed. 10.25x (ISBN 0-09-126231-3). Humanities.

ECONOMICS, MEDICAL

see Medical Economics

ECONOMICS AND CHRISTIANITY

see Christianity and Economics

ECONOMISTS

LaRouche, Lyndon H., Jr. & Goldman, David. The Ugly Truth About Milton Friedman. LC 80-20623. (Illus.). 350p. (Orig.). 1980. pap. 3.95 (ISBN 0-933488-09-2). New Benjamin.

ECONOMY

see Saving and Thrift

ECUADOR

Cueva, Agustin. The Process of Political Domination in Ecuador. Salti, Danielle, tr. from Span. 190p. 1981. 14.95 (ISBN 0-87855-338-X). Transaction Bks.

Martin, Paul. Island of Immunity: Health Secrets from the Andes. (Illus.). 176p. 1981. 10.00 (ISBN 0-8159-5828-5). Devin.

ECUMENICAL MOVEMENT

see also Christian Union

For All God's People: Ecumenical Prayer Cycle. 240p. (Orig.). 1981. pap. cancelled (ISBN 0-88344-012-1). Orbis Bks.

International Ecumenical Bibliography: 1973-1975, Vols. 12-14. LC 68-132921. Orig. Title: Internationale Oekumenische Bibliographie. 672p. 1980. 80.00x (ISBN 0-8002-2756-5). Intl Pubn Serv.

World Council of Churches. Classified Catalog of the Ecumenical Movement: First Supplement. (Library Catalogs-Supplements Ser.). 1981. lib. bdg. 95.00 (ISBN 0-686-69558-5). G K Hall.

ECUMENICAL MOVEMENT–CATHOLIC CHURCH

see Christian Union–Catholic Church

EDEMA

see Cerebral Edema

EDIBLE FUNGI

see Mushrooms, Edible

EDIBLE MUSHROOMS

see Mushrooms, Edible

EDIBLE OILS AND FATS

see Oils and Fats, Edible

EDIBLE PLANTS

see Plants, Edible

EDISON, THOMAS ALVA, 1847-1931

Johnson, Ann D. The Value of Creativity: The Story of Thomas Edison. (Valuetales Ser.). (Illus.). 64p. (gr. k-6). 1981. 6.95 (ISBN 0-916392-72-4). Oak Tree Pubns.

Wachhorst, Wyn. Thomas Alva Edison: The Biography of a Myth. 288p. 1981. 15.00 (ISBN 0-262-23108-5). MIT Pr.

EDISON EFFECT

see Thermionic Emission

EDITING

see also Authorship–Handbooks, Manuals, Etc.; Moving-Pictures–Editing

Beach, Mark. Editing Your Own Newsletter. 76p. 1980. pap. 6.95x (ISBN 0-9602664-2-9, Pub. by Coast to Coast Bks). Intl Schol Bk Serv.

EDITORIALS

Spencer, M. Lyle. Editorial Writing, Ethics, Policy Practice. 362p. 1980. Repr. of 1924 ed. lib. bdg. 30.00 (ISBN 0-89984-419-7). Century Bookbindery.

EDITORS (JOURNALISM)

see Journalists

EDUCATION

see also Adult Education; Books and Reading; Business Education; Christian Education; Church and Education; Communication in Education; Culture; Drama in Education; Education and State; Education of Children; Education of Women; Educators; Foreign Study; Home and School; International Education; Learning, Psychology of; Learning and Scholarship; Libraries; Library Education; Moral Education; Moving-Pictures in Education; Nature Study; Physical Education and Training; Private Schools; Professional Education; Public Schools; Religious Education; Religious Education of Young People; Role Playing; Scholarships; Schools; Self-Culture; Socialization; Students; Study, Method of; Teachers; Teaching; Technical Education; Television in Education; Universities and Colleges; Vocational Education; Youth

also subdivision Study and Teaching under special subjects; subdivision Education under names of denominations, sects, etc., e.g. Catholic Church–Education, and under special classes of people and social groups, e.g. Deaf–Education; and headings beginning with the word Educational

Berman & Shevitz. The Basics & Beyond. 1981. pap. text ed. write for info. (ISBN 0-8302-0992-1). Goodyear.

Bever, Thomas G., ed. Dips in Learning. 300p. 1981. prof. - refer. 19.95 (ISBN 0-89859-096-5). L Erlbaum Assocs.

Blackham, H. J. Education for Personal Autonomy. 211p. 1978. pap. text ed. 7.40x (ISBN 0-7199-0936-8, Pub. by Bedford England). Renouf.

Campbell, Clyde. Toward Perfection in Learning. LC 68-59444. 142p. 1969. 5.50. Pendell Pub.

Chamberlin, J. Gordon. The Educating Act: A Phenomenological View. LC 80-6076. 202p. 1981. lib. bdg. 17.75 (ISBN 0-8191-1449-9); pap. text ed. 8.75 (ISBN 0-8191-1450-2). U Pr of Amer.

Chapman, J. C., et al. Principles of Education. Cubberley, Ellwood P., ed. 645p. 1980. Repr. of 1924 ed. lib. bdg. 25.00 (ISBN 0-8495-0851-7). Arden Lib.

Christensen, James E., ed. Perspectives on Education As Educology. LC 80-6078. 396p. 1981. lib. bdg. 25.50 (ISBN 0-686-69075-3); pap. text ed. 14.75 (ISBN 0-8191-1394-8). U Pr of Amer.

Council on Learning's National Task Force. Education for a Global Century: Issues & Some Solutions. LC 80-69769. 112p. (Orig.). Date not set. pap. 7.95 (ISBN 0-915390-29-9). Change Mag.

Crosby, Nina. Tomorrow's Decisions Today: The Corporation. 51p. (Orig.). 1979. pap. text ed. 4.95 (ISBN 0-914634-72-0, 7910). DOK Pubs.

Cyster, R., et al. Parental Involvement in Primary Schools. 210p. 1981. pap. text ed. 19.25x (ISBN 0-85633-211-9, NFER). Humanities.

Davies, Don & Zerchykov, Ross, eds. Citizen Participation in Education: Annotated Bibliography. 386p. (Orig.). 1978. pap. text ed. 15.00 (ISBN 0-917754-05-0). Inst Responsive.

Drazan, Joseph G. The Unknown Eric: A Selection of Documents for the General Library. LC 80-25975. 239p. 1981. lib. bdg. 12.50 (ISBN 0-8108-1402-1). Scarecrow.

Draze, Dianne. Patchwork (Activities in Flexible Thinking) (Illus., Orig.). 1980. pap. text ed. 7.00 (ISBN 0-931724-13-9); tchr's ed. avail. Dandy Lion.

First Things First: Quality Education & the Way to Achieve It. 3.50 (ISBN 0-686-28653-7). Quality Educ.

Herbart, J. F. Science of Education. Bd. with Education of Man. (Contributions to the History of Psychology Ser.). 1978. Repr. of 1902 ed. 30.00 (ISBN 0-89093-161-5). U Pubns Amer.

Ignas, Edward & Corsini, Raymond J., eds. Comparative Educational Systems. LC 80-52449. 450p. 1981. text ed. 12.50 (ISBN 0-87581-260-0). Peacock Pubs.

Jacks, Maurice Leonard. The Education of Good Men. LC 80-19910. 192p. 1980. Repr. of 1955 ed. lib. bdg. 19.50x (ISBN 0-313-22800-0, JAEG). Greenwood.

Jeter, Jan, ed. Approaches to Individualized Education. LC 80-67363. 83p. (Orig.). 1980. pap. 4.75 (ISBN 0-87120-101-1, 611-80204). Assn Supervision.

OAS General Secretariat, Dept. of Educational Affairs. Glosario de Technologia Educativa. (Illus.). 83p. (Span.). 1978. pap. text ed. 3.00 (ISBN 0-8270-1060-5). OAS.

OECD. School & Community, Vol. II. (Illus.). 129p. 1980. pap. 8.00x (ISBN 92-64-12082-3, 96-80-01-1). OECD.

Partington, Geoffrey. The Idea of an Historical Education. 257p. 1981. pap. text ed. 20.75x (ISBN 0-85633-202-X, NFER). Humanities.

Prescott, Daniel A. Emotion & the Educative Process: A Report of the Committee on the Relation of Emotion to the Educative Process. 323p. 1980. Repr. of 1938 ed. lib. bdg. 25.00 (ISBN 0-89760-707-4). Telegraph Bks.

Rosner, Jerome. Perceptual Skills Curriculum, 4 programs. Incl. Introductory Guide. LC 73-83888. 96p. tchr's ed. 7.50 (ISBN 0-8027-8025-3); Prog. 1. Visual-Motor Skills. 327p. pap. text ed. 24.90 (ISBN 0-8027-8026-1); Prog. 2. Auditory Motor Skills. 304p. pap. text ed. 15.95 (ISBN 0-8027-8027-X); Prog. 3. General Motor Skills. 144p. pap. text ed. 7.95 (ISBN 0-8027-8028-8); Prog. 4. Introducing Letters & Numerals, Pts. 1 & 2. 562p. pap. text ed. 46.90 (ISBN 0-8027-8029-6). 1973. Walker Educ.

Rowan, Patricia. What Sort of Life? 138p. 1981. pap. text ed. 15.25x (ISBN 0-85633-200-3, NFER). Humanities.

Rudman, Jack. Education. (Undergraduate Program Field Test Ser.: UPFT-7). (Cloth bdg. avail. on request). pap. 9.95 (ISBN 0-8373-6007-2). Natl Learning.

--Undergraduate Program Field Test Series. (Cloth bdg. avail. on request). pap. 9.95 ea. (ISBN 0-8373-6000-5). Natl Learning.

Rutter, M., et al, eds. Education, Health & Behavior. 390p. 1981. Repr. of 1970 ed. text ed. price not set (ISBN 0-89874-268-4). Krieger.

Satterly, David. Assessment in Schools. (Theory & Practice in Education Ser.: Vol. 1). 320p. 1981. 40.00x (ISBN 0-631-11151-4, Pub. by Basil Blackwell England); pap. 19.95x (ISBN 0-631-12564-7). Biblio Dist.

Taba, Hilda. The Dynamics of Education: A Methodology of Progressive Educational Thought. 278p. 1980. Repr. of 1932 ed. lib. bdg. 35.00 (ISBN 0-89760-880-1). Telegraph Bks.

Thayer, Louis, ed. Fifty Strategies for Experimental Learning: Book Two. 260p. (Orig.). 1981. pap. write for info. (ISBN 0-88390-164-1). Univ Assocs.

Thomas, J. R. The Self in Education. 114p. 1981. pap. text ed. 18.00x (ISBN 0-85633-212-7, NFER). Humanities.

Thomas, John W. Making Changes: A Guide to Future Oriented Education. (Education Futures: No. 6). (Illus.). (gr. 6-12). 1981. pap. text ed. 8.95 (ISBN 0-88280-081-7); tchrs' ed. 19.95 (ISBN 0-88280-082-5). ETC Pubns.

Turney, C., et al. Isolated Schools. 152p. 1980. pap. 8.50x (ISBN 0-424-00068-7, Pub. by Sydney U Pr Australia). Intl Schol Bk Serv.

Walker, Ronald & Institute for Responsive Action Staff. Education for All People: A Grassroots Primer. 155p. (Orig.). 1979. pap. text ed. 6.00 (ISBN 0-917754-09-3). Inst Responsive.

Webster, Geral S. How to Bring up a Child to Become a Financial Leader. (A Human Development Library Bk.). (Illus.). 113p. 1981. 31.75 (ISBN 0-89266-294-8). Am Classical Coll Pr.

Yardumian, Charles. The Problem of Cheating in Schools: Its Psychological Meaning & the Future of the American Society. (American Culture Library Bk.). (Illus.). 107p. 1981. 29.95 (ISBN 0-89266-293-X). Am Classical Coll Pr.

EDUCATION–ADDRESSES, ESSAYS, LECTURES

Kilpatrick, William H. Education for a Changing Civilization: Three Lectures Delivered on the Luther Laflin Kellogg Foundation at Rutgers University 1926. 143p. 1980. Repr. of 1926 ed. lib. bdg. 15.00 (ISBN 0-89760-426-1). Telegraph Bks.

EDUCATION–AIMS AND OBJECTIVES

see also Educational Accountability; Educational Equalization; Educational Planning; Educational Sociology

Benjamin, Robert. Making Schools Work: A Reporter's Journey Through Some of America's Most Remarkable Schools. 208p. 1981. 12.95 (ISBN 0-8264-0040-X). Continuum.

Bisconti, Ann S. & Kessler, Jean G. Other Stepping Stones: A Study of Learning Experiences That Contribute to Effective Performance in Early & Long-Run Jobs. pap. 8.95 (ISBN 0-913936-15-4). Coll Placement.

Bloom, Benjamin S. & Madaus, George F. Evaluation to Improve Learning. (Illus.). 352p. (Orig.). 1981. pap. text ed. 13.95 (ISBN 0-07-006109-2). McGraw.

Born, Warren C., ed. Goals Clarification: Curriculum, Teaching, Evaluation. 1975. pap. 7.95x. NE Conf Teach.

Buss, William G. & Goldstein, Stephen R. Standards Relating to Schools & Education. (Juvenile Justice Standards Project Ser.). Date not set. softcover 7.95 (ISBN 0-88410-841-4). Ballinger Pub.

Clegg, Alec. About Our Schools. (Illus.). 160p. 1981. 24.50x (ISBN 0-631-12881-6, Pub. by Basil Blackwell); pap. 9.95 (ISBN 0-631-12832-8). Biblio Dist.

Clift, J. C. & Imrie, B. W. Assessing Students Appraising Teaching. 160p. 1981. 24.95 (ISBN 0-470-27098-5). Halsted Pr.

Edwards, Harry T. Higher Education & the Unholy Crusade Against Governmental Regulation. LC 80-26334. 62p. (Orig.). 1980. pap. text ed. 5.95x (ISBN 0-934222-04-5). Inst Ed Management.

Gow, Lesley & McPherson, Andrew. Tell Them from Me. 137p. 1980. 30.65 (ISBN 0-08-025738-0); pap. 13.45 (ISBN 0-08-025739-9). Pergamon.

Kozol, Jonathan. On Being a Teacher. 208p. 1981. 12.95 (ISBN 0-8264-0035-3). Continuum.

O'Neill, William. Educational Ideologies. (Orig.). 1981. pap. text ed. 17.95x (ISBN 0-8302-2305-3). Goodyear.

Robb, George P. & Williamson, Ann P. An Introduction to Individual Appraisal. (Illus.). 360p. write for info. (ISBN 0-398-04473-2); pap. write for info. (ISBN 0-398-04474-0). C C Thomas.

Simon, Brian, ed. Education of the Eighties: A Central Issue. Taylor, William. 256p. 1981. 45.00 (ISBN 0-7134-3679-4, Pub. by Batsford England); pap. 14.95 (ISBN 0-7134-3680-8). David & Charles.

Stanton, Jim & Zerchykov, Ross. Overcoming Barriers to School Effectiveness. 153p. (Orig.). 1979. pap. 6.50 (ISBN 0-917754-10-7). Inst Responsive.

Tucker, N. The Child & the Book. 275p. Date not set. 29.95 (ISBN 0-521-23251-1). Cambridge U Pr.

Zalatimo, Suleiman & Sleeman, Phillip. A Systems Approach to Learning Environents. 1975. pap. 12.40 (ISBN 0-913178-68-3). Redgrave Pub Co.

EDUCATION–BIBLIOGRAPHY

Berry, Dorothea M. A Bibliographic Guide to Educational Research. 2nd ed. LC 80-20191. 224p. 1980. 11.00 (ISBN 0-8108-1351-3). Scarecrow.

Education Index. Incl. Vols. 9-19, 1953-69; Vols. 20-29, 1969-79; Vol. 30, 1980. 60.00 ea. Wilson.

El-Hi Textbooks in Print 1981. 800p. 1981. 38.00 (ISBN 0-8352-1357-9). Bowker.

Guide to State Education Agencies. 48p. (Orig.). 1980. pap. 3.50 (ISBN 0-89763-027-0). Natl Clearinghse Bilingual Ed.

Quay, Richard H. In Pursuit of Equality of Educational Opportunity: A Selective Bibliography & Guide to the Research Literature. LC 76-52691. 200p. 1978. lib. bdg. 23.00 (ISBN 0-8240-9872-2). Garland Pub.

Sandhu, Harpreet & Bukkila, Laura. Guide to Publishers & Distributors Serving Minority Languages. rev. ed. 176p. 1980. pap. 4.50 (ISBN 0-89763-051-3). Natl Clearinghse Bilingual Ed.

The Research Libraries of the New York Public Library & Columbia University, Teachers College Library. Bibliographic Guide to Education: 1980. (Library Catalog-Bib.Guides Ser.). 1981. lib. bdg. 85.00 (ISBN 0-8161-6880-6). G K Hall.

EDUCATION–COSTS

Here are entered works on institutional costs in the field of education.

Costs at U. S. Educational Institutions. 156p. 1979. 20.00 (IIE). Unipub.

EDUCATION–CURRICULA

Works on the curriculum of a particular denomination, sect, or order are entered under name of denominations, etc., with subdivision Education.

see also Articulation (Education)

also subdivision Curricula under various subdivisions of Education, e.g. Education, Secondary–Curricula; also heading Universities and colleges; also subdivision Study and Teaching under special subjects

Change Magazine Editors. Educating for the World View. LC 80-68195. 80p. 1980. pap. 3.00 (ISBN 0-915390-26-4). Change Mag.

Giroux, Henry A., et al, eds. Curriculum & Instruction: Alternatives in Education. LC 80-84142. 1981. price not set (ISBN 0-8211-0615-5); text ed. price not set. McCutchan.

Gordon, Peter. Study of Curriculum. 192p. 1981. 27.00 (ISBN 0-686-69077-X, Pub. by Batsford England); pap. 13.50 (ISBN 0-7134-2092-8). David & Charles.

Kirby, Alice M., ed. Curriculum: Content & Change. 128p. (Orig.). 1980. pap. 4.95 (ISBN 0-88200-141-8, C2883). Alexander Graham.

Lawn, Martin. Rethinking Curriculum Studies. 224p. 27.95 (ISBN 0-470-27097-7). Halsted Pr.

--Rethinking Curriculum Studies: A Radical Approach. 224p. 1981. 27.95 (ISBN 0-470-27097-7). Halsted Pr.

Mason, Ralph E. & Haines, Peter G. Cooperative Occupational Education & Work Experience in the Curriculum. 3rd ed. (Illus.). 1981. text ed. 11.75x (ISBN 0-8134-2150-0, 2150). Interstate.

Wilcox, B. & Eustace, P. J. Tooling up for Curriculum Review. 101p. 1981. pap. text ed. 23.50x (ISBN 0-85633-210-0, NFER). Humanities.

EDUCATION–DATA PROCESSING

see also Computer-Assisted Instruction

Patton, Peter C. & Holoien, Renee A., eds. Computing in the Humanities. LC 79-3185. 1981. price not set (ISBN 0-669-03397-9). Lexington Bks.

Rushby, N. J. Introduction to Educational Computing. 224p. 1980. 30.00x (Pub. by Croom Helm England). State Mutual Bk.

Sterling Swift Publishing Co. Educational Software Directory: Apple II Edition. 104p. 1981. pap. 11.95 (ISBN 0-88408-141-9); Educational 9.95. Sterling Swift.

EDUCATION–DICTIONARIES

Gieber, Robert L. An English-French Glossary of Educational Terminology. LC 80-5652. 212p. 1980. lib. bdg. 18.00 (ISBN 0-8191-1344-1); pap. text ed. 9.25 (ISBN 0-8191-1345-X). U Pr of Amer.

EDUCATION–DIRECTORIES

The Place of Information in Educational Development. 135p. 1981. pap. 9.25 (ISBN 92-3-101822-1, U1059, UNESCO). Unipub.

The World of Learning 1980-81. 2000p. 1981. 125.00 (ISBN 0-905118-52-9, EUR 25, Europa). Unipub.

EDUCATION–EARLY WORKS TO 1800

Battersby, W. J. De La Salle: A Pioneer of Modern Education. 236p. 1981. Repr. of 1949 ed. lib. bdg. 40.00 (ISBN 0-89987-065-1). Darby Bks.

EDUCATION–EXAMINATIONS, QUESTIONS, ETC.

Bobrow, Jerry & Covino, William A. ACT (American College Testing) Date not set. pap. text ed. cancelled. Cliffs.

Covino, William A., et al. GRE (Graduate Record Examination) Date not set. pap. text ed. cancelled. Cliffs.

Gochnour, Elizabeth. Gochnour Idiom Screening Test (GIST) 1977. pap. text ed. 3.95x (ISBN 0-8134-2049-0, 1970). Interstate.

Robinson, Jacqueline & Robinson, Dennis M. High School Entrance Examinations. LC 80-22278. 512p. 1981. lib. bdg. 9.00 (ISBN 0-668-05149-3); pap. 6.50 (ISBN 0-668-05155-8). Arco.

EDUCATION–EXPERIMENTAL METHODS

see also Activity Programs in Education; Educational Innovations

Abt, Wendy P., et al. Reforming Schools: Problems in Program Implementation & Evaluation. LC 80-23339. (Contemporary Evaluation Research Ser.: Vol. 4). (Illus.). 200p. 1981. 20.00 (ISBN 0-8039-1459-8); pap. 9.95 (ISBN 0-8039-1460-1). Sage.

Chacksfield, E. M., et al. Music & Language with Young Children. 192p. 1981. pap. 6.50x (Pub. by Basil Blackwell England). Biblio Dist.

EDUCATION–FINANCE

see also College Costs; Education–Costs; Educational Equalization

American Education Finance Association. Perspectives in State School Support Programs. Date not set. price not set prof. reference (ISBN 0-88410-197-5). Ballinger Pub.

Lake, Sara, ed. Declining Enrollments, Declining Resources. (Special Interest Resource Guides in Education Ser.). (Orig.). 1981. pap. text ed. 9.50x (ISBN 0-912700-86-6). Oryx Pr.

Moroni, J. Alfred & Lahey, Francis J. An Accounting Manual for Catholic Elementary & Secondary Schools. rev. ed. 86p. 1969. 4.00. Natl Cath Educ.

EDUCATION–HISTORY

Here are entered general works on the history of education. For works on history of specific areas see the geographical subdivisions which follow.

see also Comparative Education

Fraley, Angela E. Schooling & Innovation: The Rhetoric & the Reality. 288p. 1981. text ed. write for info. (ISBN 0-9605520-0-6). Gibson Pubs.

Froebel, Frederich. Educations of Man. Hailmann, W. N., tr. from German. (Contributions to the History of Psychology B, I: Psychometrics Ser.). 1978. Repr. of 1887 ed. write for info. (ISBN 0-89093-161-5). U Pubns Amer.

Perkinson, Henry J., ed. Two Hundred Years of American Educational Thought. LC 75-43907. (Educational Policy, Planning, & Theory Ser.). 1980. pap. 9.95x (ISBN 0-582-28198-9). Longman.

Willis, Earl T. Education & First Principles: A Historical Perspective. LC 80-16408. ix, 132p. 1980. 12.74 (ISBN 0-8130-0646-5). U Presses Fla.

EDUCATION–INTEGRATION

see School Integration

EDUCATION–JUVENILE LITERATURE

Forte, Imogene. Think About It: Middle Grades. LC 80-84619. (Think About It Ser.). (Illus.). 96p. (gr. 4-6). 1981. pap. text ed. 5.95 (ISBN 0-913916-98-6, IP 98-6). Incentive Pubn.

--Think About It: Primary. LC 80-84619. (Think About It Ser.). (Illus.). 88p. (gr. 1-3). 1981. pap. text ed. 5.95 (ISBN 0-913916-97-8, IP 97-8). Incentive Pubn.

L'Engle, Madeleine. The Anti-Muffins. (The Education of the Public & the Public School Ser.). (Illus.). 48p. (gr. 3-6). 1981. 7.95 (ISBN 0-8298-0415-3). Pilgrim NY.

Muntean, Michaela. I Like School. (Sesame Street Early Bird Bks). (Illus.). 32p. (ps). 1981. 3.50 (ISBN 0-307-11602-6, Golden Pr). Western Pub.

Relf, Patricia. Show & Tell. (Sesame Street Early Bird Bks). (Illus.). 32p. (ps). 1981. 3.50 (ISBN 0-307-11606-9, Golden Pr). Western Pub.

Trager. School Survival Guide. (gr. 7-12). Date not set. pap. cancelled (ISBN 0-590-30915-3, Schol Pap). Schol Bk Serv.

EDUCATION–LAWS AND LEGISLATION

see Educational Law and Legislation

EDUCATION–PERSONNEL SERVICE

see Personnel Service in Education

EDUCATION–PHILOSOPHY

see also Educational Anthropology

Derrick, Christopher. Escape from Scepticism: Liberal Education As If Truth Mattered. 2.45 (ISBN 0-89385-002-0). Green Hill.

Fraley, Angela E. Schooling & Innovation: The Rhetoric & the Reality. 288p. 1981. text ed. write for info. (ISBN 0-9605520-0-6). Gibson Pubs.

Griese, Arnold. Your Philosophy of Education- What Is It? (Illus.). 350p. (Orig.). 1981. pap. 12.95x (ISBN 0-8302-9857-6). Goodyear.

O'Hear, Anthony. Education, Society & Human Nature: An Introduction to the Philosophy of Education. 192p. 1981. price not set (ISBN 0-7100-0747-7); pap. price not set (ISBN 0-7100-0748-5). Routledge & Kegan.

Okafor, Festus C., ed. Philosophy of Education & Third World Perspective. LC 80-50732. 346p. (Orig.). 1981. 15.00x (ISBN 0-931494-06-0); pap. 10.00x (ISBN 0-931494-07-9). Brunswick Pub.

Ozmon, Howard & Craver, Samuel. Philosophical Foundations of Education. 2nd ed. (General Education Ser.). 320p. Date not set. text ed. 14.95 (ISBN 0-675-08049-5). Merrill.

Perkinson, Henry J., ed. Two Hundred Years of American Educational Thought. LC 75-43907. (Educational Policy, Planning, & Theory Ser.). 1980. pap. 9.95x (ISBN 0-582-28198-9). Longman.

Soltis, Jonas, ed. Philosophy & Education. LC 80-83743. (National Society for the Study of Education 80th Yearbooks: Pt. I). 288p. 1981. lib. bdg. price not set. U of Chicago Pr.

EDUCATION–PSYCHOLOGY

see Educational Psychology

EDUCATION–RESEARCH

see Educational Research

EDUCATION–SEGREGATION

see Segregation in Education

EDUCATION–STATISTICAL METHODS

see Educational Statistics

EDUCATION–UNDERDEVELOPED AREAS

Curriculum: U. S. Capacities, Developing Countries' Needs. 244p. 1979. 14.00 (IIE). Unipub.

EDUCATION–YEAR-BOOKS

International Yearbook of Education, Vol. XXXII, 1980. 242p. 1980. pap. 12.25 (ISBN 92-3-101634-2, U1039, UNESCO). Unipub.

World of Learning 1980-81, 2 vols. 31st ed. LC 47-30172. 2000p. 1981. 130.00 (Pub. by Europa England). Gale.

World Yearbook of Education, 1980: Professional Development of Teachers. LC 32-18413. 422p. 1980. 32.50x (ISBN 0-85038-287-4). Intl Pubns Serv.

EDUCATION–AFRICA

Hall, Susan J. Africa in U. S. Schools, K-12: A Survey. 39p. (Orig.). 1978. pap. text ed. 4.00 (ISBN 0-89192-292-X). Interbk Inc.

Heyneman, Stephen P. Conflict Over What Is to Be Learned in Schools: A History of Curriculum Politics in Africa. (Foreign & Comparative Studies-Eastern African Ser.: No. 2). 113p. 1971. pap. 4.50x (ISBN 0-915984-01-6). Syracuse U Foreign Comp.

EDUCATION–ASIA

Education in Asia & Oceania: Reviews, Reports, & Notes. (UNESCO Regional Office for Education in Asia & Oceania: Vol.17). 99p. 1980. pap. 9.00 (UB88, UNESCO Reginal Office). Unipub.

Richards, P. & Leonor, M. Education & Income Distribution in Asia. 208p. 1981. 35.50x (ISBN 0-7099-2201-9, Pub. by Croom Helm Ltd England). Biblio Dist.

Technical & Vocational Education in Asia & Oceania. (Bulletin of the UNESCO Regional Office for the Education in Asia & Oceania: Vol.21). 316p. 1980. pap. 8.00 (UB 87, UNESCO Regional Office). Unipub.

EDUCATION–AUSTRALIA

Denger, Louis A. A Few Pieces of Australia, 1979. 1981. 8.95 (ISBN 0-533-04458-8). Vantage.

D'Urso, S. & Smith, R. A., eds. Changes, Issues & Prospects in Australian Education. 2nd ed. (Illus.). 333p. 1981. pap. text ed. 19.95x (ISBN 0-7022-1582-1). U of Queensland Pr.

Neal, W. D., ed. Education in Western Australia. 324p. 1980. 22.50x (ISBN 0-85564-147-9, Pub. by U of West Australia Pr Australia). Intl Schol Bk Serv.

Rosier, M. J. Changes in Secondary School Mathematics in Australia, 1964-1978. (ACER Research Monographs: No. 8). 1980. pap. 20.00 (ISBN 0-85563-208-9). Verry.

EDUCATION–BRAZIL
Directory of English Studies in Brazil. 185p. 1980. 50.00x (ISBN 0-901618-21-7, Pub. by Brit Coun England). State Mutual Bk.
EDUCATION–CANADA
Goulson, Cary F. A Source Book of Royal Commissions & Other Major Governmental Inquiries in Canadian Education 1787-1978. 248p. 1981. 20.00x (ISBN 0-8020-2408-4). U of Toronto Pr.
EDUCATION–CHINA
Djung, Lu-Dzai. History of Democratic Education in Modern China. (Studies in Chinese History & Civilization). 258p. 1977. Repr. of 1934 ed. 19.00 (ISBN 0-89093-080-5). U Pubns Amer.
EDUCATION–CHINA–1949-
White, Gordon. Party & Professionals: The Political Role of Teachers in Contemporary China. 350p. 1981. 25.00 (ISBN 0-87332-188-X). M E Sharpe.
EDUCATION–EUROPE
Handbook on International Study for U. S. Nationals: Study in Europe, Vol. 1. 307p. 1976. 10.00 (IIE). Unipub.
Handbook on International Study for U. S. Nationals: Study in the American Republics Area, Vol. 2. 230p. 1976. 12.00 (IIE). Unipub.
Kay, Joseph. The Social Condition & Education of the People in England & Europe, 2 vols. (The Development of Industrial Society Ser.). 1156p. 1980. Repr. 50.00x (ISBN 0-7165-1565-2, Pub. by Irish Academic Pr). Biblio Dist.
Teaching Abroad. 87p. 1976. 6.00 (IIE). Unipub.
EDUCATION–GREAT BRITAIN
Fenwick, Keith & McBride, Peter. The Government of Education: The Politics & Administration of Education in Britain. 256p. 1981. 20.00x (ISBN 0-85520-255-6, Pub. by Martin Robertson England); pap. 9.95x (ISBN 0-85520-254-8). Biblio Dist.
Halsey, Albert H. & Heath, Anthony F. Origins & Destinations: Family, Class & Education in Modern Britain. (Illus.). 250p. 1980. text ed. 29.50x (ISBN 0-19-827224-3); pap. 12.95x (ISBN 0-19-827249-9). Oxford U Pr.
Lyons, Charles H., et al. Education for What? British Policy Versus Local Initiative. (Foreign & Comparative Studies-Eastern African Ser.: No. 13). 100p. 1973. pap. 4.50x (ISBN 0-915984-10-5). Syracuse U Foreign Comp.
Paz, D. G. The Politics of Working-Class Education in Britain, 1830-1850. 199p. 1981. lib. bdg. 30.00x (ISBN 0-87023-326-2). U of Mass Pr.
EDUCATION–GREAT BRITAIN–HISTORY
Kay, Joseph. The Social Condition & Education of the People in England & Europe, 2 vols. (The Development of Industrial Society Ser.). 1156p. 1980. Repr. 50.00x (ISBN 0-7165-1565-2, Pub. by Irish Academic Pr). Biblio Dist.
Mangan, J. A. Athleticism in the Victorian & Edwardian Public School. (Illus.). 336p. Date not set. price not set (ISBN 0-521-23388-7). Cambridge U Pr.
EDUCATION–INDIA
Outdoor Primary Education in Bangladesh. (Experiments & Innovations in Education Ser.: No. 40). 60p. 1980. pap. 4.00 (ISBN 92-3-101816-7, U1042, UNESCO). Unipub.
Prakash, Shri. Educational System of India. 1980. 9.50 (ISBN 0-391-02182-6). Humanities.
Rao, T. V. & Bhatt, Anil. Adult Education for Social Change. 1980. 15.00x (ISBN 0-8364-0648-6, Pub. by Manohar India). South Asia Bks.
Shah, O. P. Education in India Today. 1980. 15.00x (ISBN 0-8364-0634-6, Pub. by Mukhopadhyay India). South Asia Bks.
Shingi, P. M., et al. Rural Youth: Education, Occupation & Social Outlook. 1980. 10.00x (ISBN 0-8364-0663-X, Pub. by Abhinav India). South Asia Bks.
EDUCATION–IRAN
Parker, Francis & Parker, Betty J. American Dissertations on Foreign Education: Iran & Iraq, Vol. XII. 425p. 1980. 28.50x (ISBN 0-87875-151-3). Whitston Pub.
EDUCATION–IRAQ
Parker, Francis & Parker, Betty J. American Dissertations on Foreign Education: Iran & Iraq, Vol. XII. 425p. 1980. 28.50x (ISBN 0-87875-151-3). Whitston Pub.
EDUCATION–ISLANDS OF THE PACIFIC
Education in Asia & Oceania: Reviews, Reports, & Notes. (UNESCO Regional Office for Education in Asia & Oceania: Vol.17). 99p. 1980. pap. 9.00 (UB88, UNESCO Reginal Office). Unipub.
Technical & Vocational Education in Asia & Oceania. (Bulletin of the UNESCO Regional Office for the Education in Asia & Oceania: Vol.21). 316p. 1980. pap. 8.00 (UB 87, UNESCO Regional Office). Unipub.
EDUCATION–ISRAEL
Parker, Francis & Parker, Betty J. American Dissertations on Foreign Education: Israel, Vol. XIII. 464p. 1980. 32.00x (ISBN 0-87875-152-1). Whitston Pub.
EDUCATION–JAPAN
Bowman, Mary J. Educational Choice Second Labor Markets in Japan. LC 80-25557. 320p. 1981. lib. bdg. 19.00x (ISBN 0-226-06923-0). U of Chicago Pr.
EDUCATION–LATIN AMERICA
Lauerhass, Ludwig & A Raujo-Haugse, Vera L. De. Education in Latin America: A Bibliography. (Reference Books Ser.). lib. bdg. 55.00 (ISBN 0-8161-8516-6). G K Hall.
EDUCATION–PERU
Barndt, Deborah. Education & Social Change: A Photographic Study of Peru. 1980. pap. text ed. 19.95 (ISBN 0-8403-2283-6). Kendall-Hunt.
EDUCATION–UNITED STATES
see also Afro-Americans–Education
Cohen, Sol, compiled by. Education in the United States: A Documentary History, 5 vols. LC 73-3099. 1974. Set. lib. bdg. 200.00 (ISBN 0-313-20141-2). Greenwood.
Davies, Don, ed. Communities & Their Schools. (Study of the Schooling in the United States Ser.). 352p. 1981. 16.95 (ISBN 0-07-015503-8, P&RB). McGraw.
Lightfoot, Sara L. Worlds Apart: Relationships Between Families & Schools. LC 78-54506. 257p. 1981. pap. 5.95 (ISBN 0-465-09243-8). Basic.
Lockerbie, D. Bruce. Who Educates Your Child? 216p. (Orig.). 1981. pap. 5.95 (ISBN 0-310-44001-7). Zondervan.
Nisbet, John, et al. Towards Community Education: An Evaluation of Community Schools. 144p. 1980. 20.25 (ISBN 0-08-025735-6). Pergamon.
Ravitch, Diane & Goodenow, Ronald, eds. Educating an Urban People: The New York Experience. 1981. text ed. 22.50 (ISBN 0-8077-2600-1). Tchrs Coll.
Rotter, Joseph C., et al. Significant Influence People: A Sip of Discipline & Encouragement. LC 80-69233. 110p. 1981. perfect bdg. 8.95 (ISBN 0-86548-055-9). Century Twenty One.
Spiller, Robert E. Late Harvest: Essays & Addresses in American Literature & Culture. LC 80-543. (Contributions to American Studies: No. 49). xi, 280p. 1981. lib. bdg. 25.00 (ISBN 0-313-22023-9, SLH/). Greenwood.
EDUCATION–UNITED STATES–FINANCE
Edwards, Harry T. Higher Education & the Unholy Crusade Against Governmental Regulation. LC 80-26334. 62p. (Orig.). 1980. pap. text ed. 5.95x (ISBN 0-934222-04-5). Inst Ed Management.
EDUCATION–UNITED STATES–HISTORY
Gibson, Betty S. Pride of the Golden Bear. 560p. 1981. text ed. 23.75 (ISBN 0-8403-2397-2). Kendall-Hunt.
Nasaw, David. Schooled to Order: A Social History of Public Schooling in the United States. 316p. 1981. pap. 5.95 (ISBN 0-19-502892-9, GB 626, OPB). Oxford U Pr.
Smith, Ed. Black Students in Interracial Schools: A Guide for Students, Teachers & Schools. LC 80-81701. 134p. (Orig.). 1980. pap. 7.95 (ISBN 0-686-69010-9). Garrett Pk.
Smith, Philip L. Sources of Progressive Thought in American Education. LC 80-8290. 217p. 1980. lib. bdg. 18.75 (ISBN 0-8191-1300-X); pap. text ed. 9.75 (ISBN 0-8191-1301-8). U Pr of Amer.
Walch, Timothy & Sedlak, Michael W., eds. American Educational History: A Guide to Informational History. LC 80-19646. (American Government & History Information Guide Ser.: Vol. 10). 350p. 1981. 30.00 (ISBN 0-8103-1478-9). Gale.
EDUCATION, ART
see Art–Study and Teaching
EDUCATION, BILINGUAL
Bergin, Victoria. Special Education Needs in Bilingual Programs. 64p. (Orig.). 1980. pap. 3.00 (ISBN 0-89763-026-2). Natl Clearinghse Bilingual Ed.
Bibliography of Resources in Bilingual Education: Curricular Materials. 322p. (Orig.). 1980. pap. 4.00 (ISBN 0-89763-016-5). Natl Clearinghse Bilingual Ed.
Brisk, Maria E., et al. Working with the Bilingual Community. LC 79-84372. 90p. (Orig.). 1979. pap. 4.50 (ISBN 0-89763-013-0). Natl Clearinghse Bilingual Ed.
Cohen, Andrew D. Describing Bilingual Education Classrooms: The Role of the Teacher in Evaluation. LC 80-80307. 64p. (Orig.). 1980. pap. 3.00 (ISBN 0-89763-050-5). Natl Clearinghse Bilingual.
Fishman, Joshua A. & Keller, Gary D., eds. Bilingual Education for Hispanic Students in the United States. (Orig.). 1981. pap. 17.95 (ISBN 0-8077-2603-6). Tchrs Coll.
Greenberg, Jean, et al. Guide to Current Research. (Resources in Bilingual Education Ser.). (Orig.). 1981. pap. write for info. (ISBN 0-89763-052-1). Natl Clearinghse Bilingual Ed.
Guide to Title Seven ESEA: Bilingual Education Programs 1979 to 1980. LC 80-80697. 126p. 1980. pap. 2.50 (ISBN 0-89763-024-6). Natl Clearinghse Bilingual Ed.
Leibowitz, Arnold H. Bilingual Education Act: A Legislative Analysis. LC 80-80121. 70p. (Orig.). 1980. pap. 4.20 (ISBN 0-89763-022-X). Natl Clearinghse Bilingual Ed.
National Association for Bilingual Education. Proceedings of the Eighth Annual International Bilingual Bicultural Education Conference. (Orig.). 1981. pap. write for info. (ISBN 0-89763-054-8). Natl Clearinghse Bilingual Ed.
Reilly, Marta T., et al. Guide to Resource Organizations. (Resources in Bilingual Education Ser.). (Orig.). 1981. pap. write for info. (ISBN 0-89763-053-X). Natl Clearinghse Bilingual Ed.
San Juan Cafferty, Pastora & Rivera-Martinez, Carmen. The Politics of Language: The Dilemma of Bilingual Education for Puerto Ricans. (Replica Edition Ser.). 200p. 1981. lib. bdg. 20.00x (ISBN 0-86531-170-6). Westview.
Schneider, Susan G., et al. Outstanding Dissertations in Bilingual Education. LC 8-80120. 127p. 1980. pap. 4.85 (ISBN 0-89763-020-3). Natl Clearinghse Bilingual Ed.
Trueba, Henry T., et al, eds. Culture & the Bilingual Classroom: Studies in Classroom Ethnography. (Bilingual Multicultural Education Ser.). 288p. (Orig.). 1981. pap. text ed. 15.95 (ISBN 0-88377-182-9). Newbury Hse.
EDUCATION, BUSINESS
see Business Education
EDUCATION, CHARACTER
see Moral Education
EDUCATION, CHRISTIAN
see Religious Education
EDUCATION, COMPARATIVE
see Comparative Education
EDUCATION, ELEMENTARY
see also Creative Activities and Seatwork; Education of Children;
also subdivision Study and Teaching (Elementary) under special subjects, e.g. Science–Study and Teaching (Elementary)
Brierley, John. Children's Well-Being. 171p. 1981. pap. text ed. 18.75x (ISBN 0-85633-218-6, NFER). Humanities.
Cherry, Clare. Think of Something Quiet. LC 80-82981. (Early Childhood Library). 1981. pap. 5.95 (ISBN 0-8224-6949-9). Pitman Learning.
Daniels, Patricia, ed. Let's Discover Series, 16 vols. Incl. Vol. 1. Warm-blooded Animlas. LC 80-22951; Vol. 2. Prehistoric World. LC 80-22949; Vol. 3. People & Customs. LC 80-22960; Vol. 4. Cold-blooded Animals. LC 80-24150; Vol. 5. The Earth. LC 80-22952; Vol. 6. The Sea. LC 80-22953; Vol. 7. People of Long Ago. LC 80-22955; Vol. 8. What People Do. LC 80-22965; Vol. 9. You & Your Body. LC 80-22970; Vol. 10. Sport & Entertainment. LC 80-22975; Vol. 11. The World of Machines. LC 80-22980; Vol. 12. Land Travel. LC 80-22954; Vol. 13. Ships & Boats. LC 80-22959; Vol. 14. Flying. LC 80-22964; Vol. 15. Outer Space. LC 80-22974; Vol. 16. Index. LC 80-22978. (Illus.). (gr. k-3). 1981. Set, 80 Pages Ea. PLB 239.79 (ISBN 0-8172-1782-7). Raintree Pubs.
Eyre, Linda & Eyre, Richard. Teaching Children Joy. (Illus.). 194p. 1980. 6.95 (ISBN 0-87747-816-3). Deseret Bk.
Gregory. Go Ahead Series, Gr. 1. Incl. Bk. 1. Tom's Little Feet. pap. text ed. (ISBN 0-8009-0819-8); pkg. of 10 copies 9.28 (ISBN 0-8009-0917-8); Bk. 2. Big Egg. pap. text ed. (ISBN 0-8009-0822-8); Bk. 3. Red Kite. pap. text ed. (ISBN 0-8009-0824-4); pkg. of 10 copies 9.28 (ISBN 0-8009-0921-6); Bk. 4. Grandma the Kitten. pap. text ed. (ISBN 0-8009-0826-0); pkg. of 10 copies 9.28 (ISBN 0-8009-0923-2); Bk. 5. Dog Who Wanted a Boy. pap. text ed. (ISBN 0-8009-0828-7); pap. text ed. 9.28 pkg. of 10 copies (ISBN 0-8009-0925-9). 1969. pap. text ed. 1.04 ea.; tchr's. ed. for Go Ahead Ser, Gr. 1-3 9.28 (ISBN 0-8009-0919-4). McCormick-Mathers.
--Go Ahead Series, Gr. 2. Incl. Bk. 1. Bill & I. (ISBN 0-8009-0830-9); pkg. of 10 (ISBN 0-8009-0927-5); Bk. 2. Blue Weed. pap. text ed. (ISBN 0-8009-0832-5); pkg. of 10 (ISBN 0-8009-0929-1); Bk. 3. House on Wheels. pap. text ed. (ISBN 0-8009-0834-1); pkg. of 10 (ISBN 0-8009-0931-3); Bk. 4. New Shoes. pap. text ed. (ISBN 0-8009-0836-8); pkg. of 10 (ISBN 0-8009-0934-8); Bk. 5. Balloon Book. pap. text ed. (ISBN 0-8009-0838-4); pkg. of 10 (ISBN 0-8009-0936-4); Bk. 6. An Umbrella for May. (ISBN 0-8009-0840-6); pap. text ed. kpkg. of 10 (ISBN 0-8009-0938-0); Bk. 7. Boat. pap. text ed. (ISBN 0-8009-0842-2); pkg. of 10 (ISBN 0-8009-0940-2). 1969-70. pap. text ed. 1.04 ea.; pkgs. of 10 of same title 9.28 ea.; tchr's. ed. for Go Ahead 8ser, Gr. 1-3 9.25 (ISBN 0-8009-0919-4). McCormick-Mathers.
--Go Ahead Series, Gr. 3. Incl. Bk. 2. Little Clown. pap. text ed. (ISBN 0-8009-0844-9); pkg. of 10 (ISBN 0-8009-0942-9); Bk. 2310#10#.00. Yellow Horse. pap. text ed. (ISBN 0-8009-0846-5); pkg. of 10 (ISBN 0-8009-0944-5); Bk. 3. Sue's Tree. pap. text ed. (ISBN 0-8009-0850-3); pkg. of 10 (ISBN 0-8009-0946-1); Bk. 4. Mr. Long's Long Feet. pap. text ed. (ISBN 0-8009-0853-8); pkg. of 10 (ISBN 0-8009-0948-8); Bk. 5. Nine on Team. pap. text ed. (ISBN 0-8009-0855-4); pkg. of 10 (ISBN 0-8009-0951-8); Bk. 6. Happy the Merry-Go-Round. pap. text ed. (ISBN 0-8009-0857-0); pkg. of 10 (ISBN 0-8009-0953-4). pap. text ed. 1.16 ea.; pkgs. of 10 of same title 10.60 ea.; tchr's. ed. for Go Ahead Ser, Gr. 1-3 9.28 (ISBN 0-8009-0919-4). McCormick-Mathers.
Piechowiak, Ann & Cook, Myra. Complete Guide to the Elementary Learning Center. 252p. pap. 8.95 (ISBN 0-13-160309-4, Reward). P-H.
Ryan, Bernard, Jr. How to Help Your Child Start School: A Practical Guide for Parents & Teachers of Four to Six Year Olds. 166p. 1981. pap. 4.95 (ISBN 0-399-50539-3, Perigee). Putnam.
EDUCATION, ETHICAL
see Moral Education; Religious Education
EDUCATION, HIGHER
see also Degrees, Academic; Federal Aid to Higher Education; Higher Education and State; Junior Colleges; Professional Education; Technical Education; Universities and Colleges; Universities and Colleges–Graduate Work
also subdivision Study and Teaching (Higher) under special subjects, e.g. English Language–Study and Teaching (Higher)
Brickman, William W. Two Millenia of International Relations in Higher Education. 263p. 1980. Repr. of 1976 ed. lib. bdg. 25.00 (ISBN 0-8414-1660-5). Folcroft.
Cosand, Joseph P. Perspective: Community Colleges in the Nineteen Eighties. (ERIC Monographs Ser.). 60p. (Orig.). pap. 5.00 (ISBN 0-87117-049-3). Am Assn Comm Jr Coll.
Haburton, Eleanor. Study Skills for College. (Illus.). 176p. 1981. pap. text ed. 6.95 (ISBN 0-87626-860-2). Winthrop.
Hecquet, Ignace, et al. Recent Student Flows in Higher Education. 189p. (Orig.). 1976. pap. text ed. 5.00 (ISBN 0-89192-313-6). Interbk Inc.
Helmantoler, Michael C., ed. Mass Media College Catalog. rev. ed. 132p. 1980. pap. 15.00 (ISBN 0-87117-048-5). Am Assn Comm Jr Coll.
Hoy, John C., ed. Higher Education & the New England Economy in the Nineteen-Eighties. 160p. 1981. 10.00x (ISBN 0-87451-197-6). U Pr of New Eng.
Kerr, Clark, et al. Twelve Systems of Higher Education: Six Decisive Issues. 214p. (Orig.). 1978. pap. text ed. 8.00 (ISBN 0-89192-211-3). Interbk Inc.
Kowalski, Casimir J. & Cangemi, Joseph P. Higher Education in the United States & Latin America. 128p. (Orig.). 1981. 8.50 (ISBN 0-8022-2385-0). Philos Lib.
Matterson, Alan. Polytechnics & Colleges. (Illus.). 320p. 1981. text ed. 34.00 (ISBN 0-582-49095-2). Longman.
Methods & Techniques in Post-Secondary Education. (Educational Studies & Documents Ser.: No. 31). 138p. 1980. pap. 7.00 (ISBN 92-3-101575-3, U1045, UNESCO). Unipub.
Owen, David. High School. 252p. 1981. 12.95 (ISBN 0-670-37149-1). Viking Pr.
Robbins, Lord. Higher Education Revisited. 230p. 1980. text ed. 34.00x (ISBN 0-8419-5082-2). Holmes & Meier.
Smartt, Steven S. Fact Book on Higher Education in the South: Nineteen Seventy-Nine & Nineteen Eighty. rev. ed. 1980. pap. 3.50. S Regional Ed.
Thomas, Gail E., ed. Black Students in Higher Education: Conditions & Experiences in the 1970's. LC 80-1702. (Contributions to the Study of Education: No. 1). 424p. 1981. lib. bdg. 29.95 (ISBN 0-313-22477-3, TBS/). Greenwood.
Tuckman, Howard P. & Whalen, Edward L., eds. Subsidies to Higher Education: The Issues. 320p. 1980. 27.95 (ISBN 0-03-055791-7). Praeger.
EDUCATION, HIGHER–AIMS AND OBJECTIVES
Kay, Anthony & Rumble, Greville, eds. Distance Teaching. 350p. 1981. 37.50x (ISBN 0-89397-099-9). Nichols Pub.
Moravisin, Sylvester. Why Our Universities Are Turning Out Ordinary Barbarians. (American Culture Library). (Illus.). 105p. 1981. 47.85 (ISBN 0-89266-299-9). Am Classical Coll Pr.
St. Denis, Albert, ed. Success Oriented Supervision. rev. ed. 1980. 44.15 (ISBN 0-87771-019-8). Grad School.
Teichler, Erich, et al. Higher Education & the Needs of Society. (NFER Ser.). 141p. 1980. pap. text ed. 11.00x (ISBN 0-85633-209-7, NFER). Humanities.
EDUCATION, HIGHER–CURRICULA
Kay, Anthony & Rumble, Greville, eds. Distance Teaching. 350p. 1981. 37.50x (ISBN 0-89397-099-9). Nichols Pub.
EDUCATION, HIGHER–1965-
Pierce, Lucia & Pierce, Lucia. International Training. 1981. pap. 7.95x (ISBN 0-915432-81-1). NE Conf Teach Foreign.
EDUCATION, HIGHER–ASIA
Narita, Katsuya. Systems of Higher Education: Japan. (Design & Management of Systems of Higher Education Ser.). 154p. (Orig.). 1978. pap. text ed. 5.50 (ISBN 0-89192-202-4). Interbk Inc.
EDUCATION, HIGHER–EUROPE
Higher Education Reform: Implications for Foreign Students. 172p. 1978. 12.00 (IIE). Unipub.
Peisert, Hansgert. Systems of Higher Education: Federal Republic of Germany. (Design & Management of Systems of Higher Education Ser.). 240p. (Orig.). 1978. pap. text ed. 8.00 (ISBN 0-89192-206-7). Interbk Inc.
EDUCATION, HIGHER–GREAT BRITAIN
Careers Research & Advisory Centre, ed. Graduate Studies: The Guide to Postgraduate Study in the UK, 1980 to 1981. 7th ed. 1191p. 1980. 135.00x (ISBN 0-86021-342-0). Intl Pubns Serv.

EDUCATION, HIGHER–LATIN AMERICA

Kowalski, Casimir J. & Cangemi, Joseph P. Higher Education in the United States & Latin America. 128p. (Orig.). 1981. 8.50 (ISBN 0-8022-2385-0). Philos Lib.

EDUCATION, INDUSTRIAL

see Technical Education

EDUCATION, INTERCULTURAL

see Intercultural Education

EDUCATION, INTERNATIONAL

see International Education

EDUCATION, JEWISH

see Jews–Education

EDUCATION, MORAL

see Moral Education

EDUCATION, MUSICAL

see Music–Instruction and Study

EDUCATION, OUTDOOR

see Outdoor Education

EDUCATION, PHYSICAL

see Physical Education and Training

EDUCATION, PRESCHOOL

see also Education of Children; Kindergarten; Nursery Schools; Religious Education of Pre-School Children

Barbe, Walter B. Resource Book for the Kindergarten Teacher. (Illus.). 1980. 34.95 (ISBN 0-88309-103-8). Zaner-Bloser.

Barbe, Walter B., et al. Basic Skills in Kindergarten: Foundations for Formal Learning. 1980. 10.00 (ISBN 0-88309-104-6). Zaner-Bloser.

Clift, Phillip, et al. The Aims, Role & Deployment of Staff in the Nursery. (Report of the National Foundation for Educational Research in England & Wales). 224p. 1980. pap. text ed. 18.75x (ISBN 0-85633-197-X). Humanities.

Connell, Donna. Teach Your Preschooler to Write. (Illus.). 132p. (Orig.). 1980. pap. 7.95 (ISBN 0-9604192-0-9). Can Do Bks.

Eliason, Claudia & Jenkins, Loa T. A Practical Guide to Early Childhood Curriculum. 2nd ed. (Illus.). 330p. 1981. pap. text ed. 12.95 (ISBN 0-8016-1511-9). Mosby.

Hymes, James L. Teaching the Child Under Six. 3rd ed. (Illus.). 224p. Date not set. pap. text ed. 7.95 (ISBN 0-675-08063-0). Merrill.

Johnson, Janeen A. Games to Improve Perceptual Skills of Pre-Schoolers: Ideas for Parents & Teachers. 1978. pap. text ed. 0.25 (ISBN 0-8134-2049-0, 2049); for 25 copies 4.38; for 100 copies 14.75. Interstate.

Lucas, Virginia H., et al. Kindergarten Program. (Illus.). 1980. pupil bk. 2.97 (ISBN 0-88309-101-1); tchr's guide 4.97 (ISBN 0-88309-102-X). Zaner-Bloser.

Lundsteen, Sara & Bernstein-Tarrow, Norma. Guiding Young Children's Learning. (Illus.). 528p. 1981. text ed. 16.95 (ISBN 0-07-039105-X, C); instrs'. manual avail. (ISBN 0-07-039106-8). McGraw.

Osbon, D. Keith. Early Childhood Education in Historical Perspective. rev. ed. 1980. 11.95 (ISBN 0-918772-08-7); pap. 5.95 (ISBN 0-918772-07-9). Ed Assocs.

EDUCATION, PRIMARY

see also Creative Activities and Seatwork; Education of Children

Chacksfield, E. M., et al. Music & Language with Young Children. 192p. 1981. pap. 6.50x (Pub. by Basil Blackwell England). Biblio Dist.

Jones, Roy. Primary School Management. 160p. 1980. 14.95 (ISBN 0-7153-7843-0). David & Charles.

Kirbya, N. Personal Values in Primary Education. 1981. text ed. 18.35 (ISBN 0-06-318130-4, Pub. by Har-Row Ltd England); pap. 9.25 (ISBN 0-06-318131-2). Har-Row.

Osbon, D. Keith. Early Childhood Education in Historical Perspective. rev. ed. 1980. 11.95 (ISBN 0-918772-08-7); pap. 5.95 (ISBN 0-918772-07-9). Ed Assocs.

EDUCATION, PROFESSIONAL

see Professional Education

EDUCATION, RELIGIOUS

see Religious Education

EDUCATION, RURAL

Education in a Rural Environment. (Education & Rural Development Ser.: No. 2). 63p. 1980. pap. 7.00 (ISBN 92-3-101764-0, U1046, UNESCO). Unipub.

Sher, Jonathan P., ed. Rural Education in Urbanized Nations: Issues & Innovations. (Special Studies in Education). 425p. 1981. lib. bdg. 27.50x (ISBN 0-89158-964-3). Westview.

EDUCATION, SCIENTIFIC

see Science–Study and Teaching

EDUCATION, SECONDARY

see also Private Schools; Public Schools
also subdivision Study and Teaching (Secondary) under special subjects, e.g. Science–Study and Teaching (Secondary)

Beechick, Ruth. Teaching Juniors. LC 80-68886. (Teacher Training Ser.). 192p. (Orig.). 1981. pap. 3.95 (ISBN 0-89636-062-8). Accent Bks.

Briault, Eric & Smith, Frances. Falling Rolls in Secondary Schools, Pt. 2. 403p. 1980. pap. text ed. 27.50x (ISBN 0-85633-208-9, NFER). Humanities.

Henson, Kenneth T. Secondary Teaching Methods. 384p. 1980. text ed. 14.95 (ISBN 0-669-03316-2). Heath.

Jackson, et al, eds. Student Activities in Secondary Schools: A Bibliography. Battiste. 92p. 1980. pap. 4.00 (ISBN 0-88210-109-9). Natl Assn Principals.

James, Phillip H. The Reorganization of Secondary Education. 145p. 1980. pap. text ed. 19.25x (ISBN 0-85633-214-3, NFER). Humanities.

Loew, H. Assessing Study Abroad Programs for Secondary School Students. (Language in Education Ser.: No. 29). 1980. pap. text ed. 2.95 (ISBN 0-87281-128-X). Ctr Appl Ling.

Russell, Lester F. Black Baptist Secondary Schools in Virginia, 1887-1957: A Study in Black History. LC 80-22414. 218p. 1981. 12.50 (ISBN 0-8108-1373-4). Scarecrow.

Steiner, Rudolf. Waldorf Education for Adolescence. 1980. pap. 9.50x (ISBN 0-906492-37-8, Pub. by Kolisko Archives). St George Bk Serv.

Study Abroad XXIII 1981-82, 1982-83. 1011p. 1981. pap. 12.95 (ISBN 92-3-001840-6, U1061, UNESCO). Unipub.

Sweat, Clifford H., ed. Morals & Early Adolescent Education: From Apathy to Action. LC 80-80727. 1980. pap. text ed. 4.25 (ISBN 0-8134-2134-9, 2134). Interstate.

Walter, Ralph. Unmet Needs in Secondary Education. 144p. 1981. 5.00 (ISBN 0-8059-2773-5). Dorrance.

Williams, L. A. Secondary Schools for American Youth. 529p. 1980. Repr. of 1944 ed. lib. bdg. 25.00 (ISBN 0-89984-524-X). Century Bookbindery.

EDUCATION, SECONDARY–AIMS AND OBJECTIVES

Briault, Eric & Smith, Frances. Falling Rolls in Secondary Schools, Pt. 1. 1980. pap. text ed. 16.00x (ISBN 0-85633-207-0, NFER). Humanities.

EDUCATION, TECHNICAL

see Technical Education

EDUCATION, THEOLOGICAL

see Religious Education; Theology–Study and Teaching

EDUCATION, URBAN

Mayberry, Claude, Jr., ed. Urban Education: The City As a Living Curriculum. LC 80-67288. (Orig.). 1980. pap. text ed. 6.50 (ISBN 0-87120-100-3, 611-80206). Assn Supervision.

Parks, Arnold G. Urban Education: An Annotated Bibliography. LC 80-69234. 135p. 1981. perfect bdg 9.50 (ISBN 0-86548-053-2). Century Twenty One.

EDUCATION, VISUAL

see Visual Education

EDUCATION, VOCATIONAL

see Vocational Education

EDUCATION AND ANTHROPOLOGY

see Educational Anthropology

EDUCATION AND CHURCH

see Church and Education

EDUCATION AND RELIGION

see Church and Education

EDUCATION AND SOCIOLOGY

see Educational Sociology

EDUCATION AND STATE

see also Art and State; Community and School; Higher Education and State; Scholarships

David, Miriam E. The State, the Family, & Education. (Radical Social Policy Ser.). 304p. (Orig.). 1980. pap. 17.50 (ISBN 0-7100-0601-2). Routledge & Kegan.

Davies, Don, et al. Federal & State Impact on Citizen Participation in the Schools. 147p. (Orig.). 1978. pap. text ed. 5.00 (ISBN 0-917754-04-2). Inst Responsive.

Reitman. Education, Society & Change. 496p. 1981. pap. text ed. 13.50 (ISBN 0-205-07254-2, 2373541); free tchr's ed. (ISBN 0-205-07255-0, 237255X). Allyn.

EDUCATION AS A PROFESSION

Choosing College Major in Education. 10.95 (ISBN 0-679-50957-7); pap. 5.95 (ISBN 0-679-50958-5). McKay.

Jones, Marilyn. Exploring Careers in Special Education. (Careers in Depth Ser.). (Illus.). 128p. 1981. lib. bdg. 5.97 (ISBN 0-8239-0539-X). Rosen Pr.

EDUCATION FOR LIBRARIANSHIP

see Library Education

EDUCATION LIBRARIES

Cline, Hugh F. & Sinnott, Loraine T. Building Library Collections: Policies & Practices in Academic Libraries. LC 80-8602. (Illus.). 192p. 1981. 15.95x (ISBN 0-669-04321-4). Lexington Bks.

EDUCATION OF ADULTS

see Adult Education

EDUCATION OF CHILDREN

see also Education, Elementary; Education, Preschool; Education, Primary; Physical Education for Children; School Social Work; Schools

Blackstone, Tessa. Education & Day Care for Young Children in Need: The American Experience. 72p. 1973. pap. text ed. 1.90x (ISBN 0-7199-0875-2, Pub. by Bedford England). Renouf.

Engelmann, Seigfried & Engelmann, Therese. Give Your Child a Superior Mind. 320p. 1981. 5.95 (ISBN 0-346-12532-4). Cornerstone.

Jacobs, Wilma J. Any Love Notes Today? LC 76-48409. 143p. (Orig.). 1976. pap. 4.95 (ISBN 0-89146-002-0). Learn Pathways.

Kraus, E. Philip. Yesterday's Children: A Longitudinal Study of Children from Kindergarten into the Adult Years. 208p. 1981. Repr. of 1973 ed. lib. bdg. price not set (ISBN 0-89874-311-7). Krieger.

Lundsteen, Sara & Bernstein-Tarrow, Norma. Guiding Young Children's Learning. (Illus.). 528p. 1981. text ed. 16.95 (ISBN 0-07-039105-X, C); instrs'. manual avail. (ISBN 0-07-039106-8). McGraw.

Towns, Payton. Educating Disturbed Adolescents: Theory & Practice. (Current Issues in Behavioral Psychology Ser.). 1981. 19.50 (ISBN 0-8089-1312-3). Grune.

EDUCATION OF GIRLS

see Education of Women

EDUCATION OF THE BLIND

see Blind–Education

EDUCATION OF THE DEAF

see Deaf–Education

EDUCATION OF WOMEN

Kersey, Shirley N. Classics in the Education of Girls & Women. LC 80-20711. 335p. 1981. 17.50 (ISBN 0-8108-1354-8). Scarecrow.

Misenheimer, Helen E. Rousseau on the Education of Women. LC 80-5857. 109p. 1981. lib. bdg. 15.75 (ISBN 0-8191-1404-9); pap. text ed. 7.50 (ISBN 0-8191-1405-7). U Pr of Amer.

The School Education of Girls. 180p. 1981. pap. 10.50 (ISBN 92-3-101782-9, U1058, UNESCO). Unipub.

EDUCATIONAL ACCOUNTABILITY

Benjamin, Robert. Making Schools Work: A Reporter's Journey Through Some of America's Most Remarkable Schools. 208p. 1981. 12.95 (ISBN 0-8264-0040-X). Continuum.

EDUCATIONAL ADMINISTRATION

see School Management and Organization; Universities and Colleges–Administration

EDUCATIONAL AIMS AND OBJECTIVES

see Education–Aims and Objectives; Education, Higher–Aims and Objectives

EDUCATIONAL ANTHROPOLOGY

Cultural Co-operation: Studies & Experiences in the Cultural Content of Education. (Joint Study: No. 9). 100p. 1980. pap. 7.50 (ISBN 0-686-68809-0, U1023, UNESCO). Unipub.

EDUCATIONAL CHANGE

see Educational Innovations

EDUCATIONAL CONSULTANTS

Conoley, Jane C., ed. Consultation in Schools: Theory, Research Procedures. LC 80-2329. (Educational Technology Ser.). 1981. price not set (ISBN 0-12-186020-5). Acad Pr.

EDUCATIONAL DISCRIMINATION

see Discrimination in Education

Weinberg, Meyer, compiled by. The Education of Poor & Minority Children: A World Bibliography, 2 vols. LC 80-29441. 1981. lib. bdg. 95.00 (ISBN 0-313-21996-6, WEC/). Greenwood.

EDUCATIONAL EQUALIZATION

Banks. Multiethnic Eduction: Theory & Practice. 300p. 1981. text ed. 17.50 (ISBN 0-205-07300-X, 2373009); pap. text ed. 10.50 (ISBN 0-205-07293-3, 2372932). Allyn.

Tomlinson, Sally. Educational Subnormality. (International Library of Sociology Ser.). 300p. 1981. price not set (ISBN 0-7100-0697-7). Routledge & Kegan.

Weinberg, Meyer, compiled by. The Education of Poor & Minority Children: A World Bibliography, 2 vols. LC 80-29441. 1981. lib. bdg. 95.00 (ISBN 0-313-21996-6, WEC/). Greenwood.

EDUCATIONAL EXCHANGES

see also Students, Interchange Of; Teachers, Interchange Of

Cohen, Gail A., ed. The Learning Traveler: Vacation Study Abroad, Vol. 2. rev. ed. 186p. 1981. pap. text ed. 8.00 (ISBN 0-87206-107-8). Inst Intl Educ.

Higher Education Reform: Implications for Foreign Students. 172p. 1978. 12.00 (IIE). Unipub.

International Educational Exchange: A Bibliography. 156p. 1970. 6.00 (IIE). Unipub.

EDUCATIONAL FACILITIES

see School Facilities

EDUCATIONAL GAMES

Harrison, James D. Community & Environmental Simulations: Annotated Guide to Over 200 Games for College & Community Education. (Public Administration Ser.: Bibliographies: P-675). 138p. 1981. 15.00. Vance Biblios.

Johnson, Janeen A. Games to Improve Perceptual Skills of Pre-Schoolers: Ideas for Parents & Teachers. 1978. pap. text ed. 0.25 (ISBN 0-8134-2049-0, 2049); for 25 copies 4.38; for 100 copies 14.75. Interstate.

Lucas, Katherine & Lucas, Louse. Who Owns the Unicorn. (Illus., Orig.). (gr. 4-12). 1980. pap. text ed. 3.95 (ISBN 0-914634-69-0, 7918). DOK Pubs.

Munini, Diane J. Developmental Arts...Hands-on Enrichment Activities for Young Children. 2nd rev. ed. LC 80-70128. 68p. 1980. pap. 6.50 (ISBN 0-9605372-0-1). Developmental Arts.

Sparling, Joseph & Lewis, Isabelle. Learning Games for the First Three Years. 320p. 1981. pap. 2.95 (ISBN 0-425-04752-0). Berkley Pub.

--Learninggames for the First Three Years. 1981. pap. 2.95 (ISBN 0-425-04752-0). Berkley Pub.

Sternlict, Manny & Hurwitz, Abraham. Games Children Play: Instructive & Creative Play Activities for the Mentally Retarded & Developmentally Disabled Child. 128p. 1980. 12.95 (ISBN 0-442-25857-7). Van Nos Reinhold.

Wieckert, Jeanne E. & Bell, Irene W. Classroom Skills Through Games for the Middle School, Vol. 2. (Illus.). 250p. 1981. lib. bdg. 17.50x (ISBN 0-87287-236-X). Libs Unl.

EDUCATIONAL GUIDANCE

see Personnel Service in Education

EDUCATIONAL INNOVATIONS

see also Education–Experimental Methods; Educational Technology; Non-Formal Education

Barnett, Regina R. Let Out the Sunshine. 144p. (Orig.). 1981. pap. text ed. 12.00 (ISBN 0-697-01762-1). Wm C Brown.

Carelli, M. Dino, ed. A New Look at the Relation Between School Education and Work: Second All-European Conference for Directors of Educational Research Institutions, Madrid 11-13 Sept. 79. (International Studies in Education Ser.: No. 37). vi, 164p. 1980. pap. text ed. 16.00 (ISBN 90-265-0355-5). Swets North Am.

Morgan, Lorraine L., et al. Beyond the Open Classroom: Toward Informal Education. LC 80-69235. 140p. 1981. perfect bdg. 9.50 (ISBN 0-86548-050-8). Century Twenty One.

EDUCATIONAL LAW AND LEGISLATION

see also School Management and Organization; Segregation in Education; Teachers–Legal Status, Laws, etc.

Savage, David. Education Laws Nineteen Seventy-Eight: A Guide to New Directions in Federal Aid. 120p. 1979. pap. 11.95 (ISBN 0-87545-015-6). Natl Sch PR.

Spiva, Ulysses V. Legal Outlook: A Message to College & University People. LC 80-69232. 115p. 1981. perfect bdg. 9.95 (ISBN 0-86548-057-5). Century Twenty One.

Vander Horck, Karl J. A Dutch Uncle's Guidebook to School Law. 194p. (Orig.). 1980. pap. 6.95 (ISBN 0-87839-035-9). North Star.

EDUCATIONAL LAW AND LEGISLATION–CASES

Edwards, Harry T. Higher Education & the Unholy Crusade Against Governmental Regulation. LC 80-26334. 62p. (Orig.). 1980. pap. text ed. 5.95x (ISBN 0-934222-04-5). Inst Ed Management.

EDUCATIONAL LIBRARIES

see Education Libraries

EDUCATIONAL MEASUREMENTS

see Educational Tests and Measurements

EDUCATIONAL PLANNING

see also Educational Innovations; School Management and Organization

Information: An Essential Factor in Educational Planning & Policy. 303p. 1981. pap. 18.75 (ISBN 92-3-101668-7, U1056, UNESCO). Unipub.

EDUCATIONAL POLICY

see Education and State

EDUCATIONAL PSYCHOLOGY

see also Achievement Motivation; Child Psychology; Imagination; Learning, Psychology Of; Listening; Memory; Perception; Psychology, Applied; Thought and Thinking

Baatz, Charles A. & Baatz, Olga K., eds. The Psychological Foundations of Education: A Guide to Information Sources. (Education Information Guide Ser.: Vol. 10). 350p. 1981. 30.00 (ISBN 0-8103-1467-3). Gale.

Bijou, Sidney W. & Ruiz, Roberto. Contribution of Behavior Modification to Education. 352p. 1980. text ed. 24.95 (ISBN 0-89859-024-8). L Erlbaum Assocs.

Carroll, James L., ed. Contemporary School Psychology: Readings from Psychology in the Schools. 2nd ed. 1981. pap. text ed. 12.95x (ISBN 0-88422-014-1). Clinical Psych.

--Contemporary School Psychology: Readings from Psychology in the Schools. 2nd ed. 1981. pap. 12.50x (ISBN 0-88422-014-1). Clinical Psych.

Clarizio, Harvey, et al. Contemporary Issues in Educational Psychology. 4th ed. 1981. pap. text ed. 9.95 (ISBN 0-205-07331-X). Allyn.

Clifford, Margaret M. Practicing Educational Psychology. (Illus.). 752p. 1981. pap. text ed. write for info. (ISBN 0-395-29921-7); write for info. set test bank (ISBN 0-395-29925-X); write for info. instr's manual (ISBN 0-395-29923-3). HM.

Collier, Charles. Essay on the Principles of Education, Physiologically Considered. Bd. with Art of Instructing the Infant Deaf & Dumb. (Contributions to the History of Psychology, Vol. V, Pt. B: Psychometrics & Educational Psychology). 1980. Repr. of 1856 ed. 30.00 (ISBN 0-89093-319-7). U Pubns Amer.

Curtis, Bernard & Mays, Wolfe, eds. Phenomenology & Education: Self-Consciousness & Its Development. 150p. 1978. pap. 9.95 (ISBN 0-416-70960-5, 6368). Methuen Inc.

Entwistle, Noel. Styles of Learning & Teaching: An Integrated Outline of Educational Psychology for Students, Teachers, & Lecturers. 1981. price not set (ISBN 0-471-27901-3, Pub. by Wiley-Interscience). Wiley.

Farley, Frank & Gordon, Neal J., eds. Education & Psychology: The State of the Union. LC 80-82902. 300p. 1981. write for info (ISBN 0-8211-0506-X); text ed. write for info. McCutchan.

Hine, James R. Will We Meet Each Other's Needs? 1979. pap. text ed. 7.50 (ISBN 0-8134-2052-0, 2052). Interstate.

Kratochwill, Thomas R. Advances in School Psychology, Vol. 1. (Advances in School Psychology Ser.). 368p. 1981. profess. & reference 24.95 (ISBN 0-89859-076-0). L Erlbaum Assocs.
Owen, et al. Educational Psychology: An Introduction. 2nd ed. 1981. pap. text ed. 15.95 (ISBN 0-316-67729-9); tchrs'. manual free (ISBN 0-316-67730-2). Little.
Pedagogical Seminary: (Selections) Hall, G. Stanley, ed. (Contributions to the History of Psychology Ser.: Psychometric & Educational Psychology). 1980. 30.00 (ISBN 0-89093-320-0). U Pubns Amer.
Rhine, W. Ray, ed. Making Schools More Effective: New Directions from Follow Through. (Educational Psychology Ser.). 1981. price not set (ISBN 0-12-587060-4). Acad Pr.
Roweton, William E. My Reflections on Educational Psychology, Science & American Schools. LC 80-8262. 124p. 1980. lib. bdg. 15.75 (ISBN 0-8191-1329-8); pap. text ed. 7.50 (ISBN 0-8191-1330-1). U Pr of Amer.
Siann, Gerda & Ugwuegbu, Denis. Educational Psychology in a Changing World. (Illus.). 256p. (Orig.). 1980. text ed. 22.50x (ISBN 0-04-370099-3, 2587); pap. text ed. 11.50x (ISBN 0-04-370100-0, 2588). Allen Unwin.
Sprinthall, Richard & Sprinthall, Normal. Educational Psychology: A Developmental Approach. 3rd ed. LC 80-15223. (Illus.). 624p. 1981. pap. text ed. 14.95 (ISBN 0-201-06872-9). A-W.
Stones, E. Psychopedagogy: Psychological Theory & the Practice of Teaching. 490p. 1979. 21.95 (ISBN 0-416-71330-0, 2525); pap. 13.95 (ISBN 0-416-71340-8, 6420). Methuen Inc.

EDUCATIONAL RESEARCH
Berry, Dorothea M. A Bibliographic Guide to Educational Research. 2nd ed. LC 80-20191. 224p. 1980. 11.00 (ISBN 0-8108-1351-3). Scarecrow.
Borg, Walter R. Applying Educational Research: A Practical Guide for Teachers. 368p. (Orig.). 1981. text ed. 14.50 (ISBN 0-582-28145-8). Longman.
Burges, Bill. Facts for a Change: Citizen Action Research for a Better Schools. 125p. (Orig.). 1976. pap. text ed. 5.00 (ISBN 0-917754-03-4). Inst Responsive.
Carelli, M. Dino, ed. A New Look at the Relation Between School Education and Work: Second All-European Conference for Directors of Educational Research Institutions, Madrid 11-13 Sept. 79. (International Studies in Education Ser.: No. 37). vi, 164p. 1980. pap. text ed. 16.00 (ISBN 90-265-0355-5). Swets North Am.
Gay, L. R. Educational Research. 2nd ed. (Illus.). 464p. 1981. write for info student guide (ISBN 0-675-08021-5); price not set student guide (ISBN 0-675-08020-7); instr's. manual 3.95 (ISBN 0-686-69490-2). Merrill.

EDUCATIONAL SOCIOLOGY
see also Education–Aims and Objectives; Socially Handicapped Children–Education
Rodehaver, Myles W., et al. The Sociology of the School. LC 80-26021. x, 262p. 1981. Repr. of 1957 ed. lib. bdg. 27.50x (ISBN 0-313-22897-3, ROSSC). Greenwood.

EDUCATIONAL STATISTICS
UNESCO Statistical Yearbook 1980. 1280p. 1981. pap. 104.00 (ISBN 92-3-001835-X, U1062, UNESCO). Unipub.

EDUCATIONAL SURVEYS
Here are entered works on the technique of conducting school surveys, evaluating school efficiency, etc. Specific surveys are entered under the name of the school or subject surveyed.
Guba, Egon G. & Lincoln, Yvonna S. Effective Evaluation: Improving the Usefulness of Evaluation Results Through Responsive & Naturalistic Approaches. LC 80-8909. (Social & Behavioral Science Ser.). 1981. text ed. price not set (ISBN 0-87589-493-3). Jossey-Bass.
Improving Assessment of Schoolchildren: A Guide to Evaluating Cognitive, Emotional & Physical Problems. LC 80-26130. (Social & Behavioral Science Ser.). 1981. text ed. write for info. (ISBN 0-87589-488-7). Jossey-Bass.

EDUCATIONAL TECHNOLOGY
see also Audio-Visual Education; Computer-Assisted Instruction; Teaching–Aids and Devices
Association for Educational & Training Technology. Aspects of Educational Technology: Educational Technology to the Year 2000, Vol. 14. Evans, Leo & Winterburn, Roy, eds. 450p. 1980. 37.50x (ISBN 0-85038-383-8). Nichols Pub.
O'Neil, Harold F., Jr., ed. Issues in Instructional Systems Development. 224p. 1979. 17.50 (ISBN 0-12-526640-5). Acad Pr.
Poirot, James L. Computers & Education. (Illus.). 96p. (Orig.). 1980. pap. 6.95 (ISBN 0-88408-137-0). Sterling Swift.
Roid, Gale & Haladyna, Tom. A Technology for Test-Item Writing. 1981. price not set. Acad Pr.

EDUCATIONAL TELEVISION
see Television in Education

EDUCATIONAL TESTS AND MEASUREMENTS
see also Grading and Marking (Students)
also names of specific tests, or subdivision Examinations, Questions, Etc. under subjects
Guidelines for Selecting Basic & Life Skills Tests. 1980. pap. 4.25 (ISBN 0-89354-830-8). Northwest Regional.
Hills, John R. Measurement & Evaluation. 2nd ed. (Illus.). 480p. 1981. pap. text ed. 14.95 (ISBN 0-675-08044-4); instr's. manual 3.95 (ISBN 0-686-69495-3). Merrill.
Lazarus, Mitchel. Goodbye to Excellence: A Critical Look at Minimum Competency Testing. (NAESP Studies in Education & Public Policy). 192p. (Orig.). 1981. lib. bdg. 16.00x (ISBN 0-89158-771-3); pap. text ed. 6.50x (ISBN 0-89158-897-3). Westview.
Lewy, Arieh & Nevo, David. Evaluation Roles. 500p. 1981. price not set (ISBN 0-677-16290-1). Gordon.
Northwest Regional Educational Laboratory. Competency-Based Education: Beyond Minimum Competency Testing. Nickes, Ruth, ed. Date not set. pap. price not set (ISBN 0-8077-2606-0). Tchrs Coll.

EDUCATIONAL WORKSHOPS
see Teachers' Workshops

EDUCATORS
see also Teachers
Peters, R. S. Essays on Educators. (Unwin Education Bks). 160p. 1981. text ed. 19.95x (ISBN 0-04-370103-5, 2626-7); pap. text ed. 7.95x (ISBN 0-04-370104-3). Allen Unwin.
Sokolosky, Barbara A., ed. American Association of University Women Archives 1881-1976. 115p. 1980. pap. write for info. (ISBN 0-667-00651-6). Microfilming Corp.

EDUCATORS–UNITED STATES
Holtzclaw, Robert F. William Henry Holtzclaw: Scholar in Ebony. LC 76-29278. (Illus.). 252p. 1977. 8.92 (ISBN 0-913228-19-2). Keeble Pr.

EDWARD, THE CONFESSOR, KING OF ENGLAND, SAINT, d. 1066
Oleson, Trygovi J. The Witenagemot in the Reign of Edward the Confessor: A Study in the Constitutional History of Eleventh-Century England. LC 80-2217. 1981. Repr. of 1955 ed. 29.50 (ISBN 0-404-18769-2). AMS Pr.

EDWARD 8TH, KING OF GREAT BRITAIN, 1894-1972
Bryan, James & Murphy, Charles. The Windsor Story. 1981. pap. 3.95 (ISBN 0-440-19346-X). Dell.

EELS
Forrest, David M. Eel Capture, Culture, Processing & Marketing. (Illus.). 206p. 20.25 (ISBN 0-85238-070-4, FN). Unipub.
Usui, Atsushi. Eel Culture. (Illus.). 190p. 19.50 (FN). Unipub.

EELWORMS
see Nematoda

EFFECT AND CAUSE
see Causation

EFFICIENCY, PERSONAL
see Success

EFFICIENCY ENGINEERS
see Business Consultants

EFFICIENCY RATING
see Employees, Rating Of

EFFIGIES, SEPULCHRAL
see Sepulchral Monuments

EGG (BIOLOGY)
see Embryology

EGGS
see also Cookery (Eggs)
Horsting, Al G. The Complete Book on Hatching Egg Care & Sanitation. 1981. write for info. Franklin Inst Pr.

EGGS, EASTER
see Easter Eggs

EGO (PSYCHOLOGY)
Walsh, Roger & Vaughn, Frances. Beyond Ego. 272p. 1981. pap. 6.95 (ISBN 0-87477-175-7). J P Tarcher.
Watkins, John G. & Watkins, Helen H. Ego-States & Hidden Observers & the Women in Black & the Lady in White. (Sound Seminars Ser.). 1980. transcript & tapes 29.50x (ISBN 0-88432-066-9, 29400-29401). J Norton Pubs.

EGYPT–ANTIQUITIES
Cohen, I. Bernard. The Birth of a New Physics. LC 78-25792. (Illus.). 200p. 1981. Repr. of 1960 ed. lib. bdg. 19.75x (ISBN 0-313-20773-9, COBN). Greenwood.
Hayes, William C. Scepter of Egypt: A Background for the Study of Egyptian Antiquities in the Metropolitan Museum of Art. Incl. Vol. 1. From the Earliest Times to the End of the Middle Kingdom. 25.00 (ISBN 0-87099-072-1); pap. 18.50 (ISBN 0-686-60651-5); Vol. 2. The Hyksos Period & the New Kingdom (1675-1080 B.C.) 16.95 o.p. (ISBN 0-87099-074-8); pap. 18.50 (ISBN 0-87099-191-4). LC 52-7286. (Illus.). 1959. Metro Mus Art.
Holz, R. K., et al. Mendes I. Hall, E. S. & Bothmer, B. V., eds. (Illus.). 83p. 45.00 (ISBN 0-936770-02-3). Am Res Ctr Egypt.
Stewart, H. M. Egyptian Stelae, Relief & Printings from the Petrie Collection. (Modern Egyptology Ser.). 100p. 40.00x (ISBN 0-85668-171-7, Pub. by Aris & Phillips England). Intl Schol Bk Serv.

EGYPT–CIVILIZATION
Cohen, I. Bernard. The Birth of a New Physics. LC 78-25792. (Illus.). 200p. 1981. Repr. of 1960 ed. lib. bdg. 19.75x (ISBN 0-313-20773-9, COBN). Greenwood.
Leca, Ange-Pierre. The Egyptian Way of Death: Mummies & the Cult of the Immortal. LC 78-68326. (Illus.). 312p. 1981. 12.95 (ISBN 0-385-14609-4). Doubleday.
Smith, W. Stevenson. The Art & Architecture of Ancient Egypt. rev ed. 360p. 1981. pap. 19.95 (ISBN 0-14-056114-5). Penguin.

EGYPT–DESCRIPTION AND TRAVEL
Burgoyne. Light of Egypt, 2 vol. (Illus.). 1980. pap. 15.00 (ISBN 0-89540-064-2). Sun Pub.
Lanier, Alison R. Update -- Egypt. (Country Orientation Ser.). 1980. pap. text ed. 25.00 (ISBN 0-933662-32-7). Intercult Network.

EGYPT–ECONOMIC CONDITIONS
Ikram, Khalid. Egypt: Economic Management in a Period of Transition. LC 80-552. (World Bank Country Economic Report). (Illus.). 464p. 1981. text ed. 32.50x (ISBN 0-8018-2418-4); pap. text ed. 10.50x (ISBN 0-8018-2419-2). Johns Hopkins.
Tignor, Robert L. & Abdel-Khalek, Goudal, eds. Political Economy of Income Distribution in Egypt. LC 80-26932. (The Political Economy of Income Distribution in Developing Countries Ser.). 500p. 1981. text ed. 45.00x (ISBN 0-8419-0633-5). Holmes & Meier.

EGYPT–HISTORY
see also Mamelukes
Budge, Ernest A. Short History of the Egyptian People. 280p. 1980. lib. bdg. 30.00 (ISBN 0-8482-0148-5). Norwood Edns.
Frith, Francis. Egypt & the Holy Land in Historic Photographs: Seventy-Seven Views. Van Haaften, Julia, ed. 112p. 1981. pap. 7.00 (ISBN 0-486-24048-7). Dover.

EGYPT–HISTORY–TO 640
Cohen, I. Bernard. The Birth of a New Physics. LC 78-25792. (Illus.). 200p. 1981. Repr. of 1960 ed. lib. bdg. 19.75x (ISBN 0-313-20773-9, COBN). Greenwood.
Drew-Bear, Marie. Le Nome Hermopolite. LC 78-13005. (American Studies in Papyrology: No. 21). 45.00x (ISBN 0-89130-258-1, 310021). Scholars Pr CA.

EGYPT–JUVENILE LITERATURE
Payne, Elizabeth. The Pharaohs of Ancient Egypt. LC 80-21392. (Landmark Bks.). (Illus.). 192p. (gr. 5-9). 1981. pap. 2.95 (ISBN 0-394-84699-0). Random.

EGYPT–POLITICS AND GOVERNMENT
Abdel-Fadil, M. The Political Economy of Nasserism. LC 80-49995. (Cambridge Department of Applied Economics, Occasional Papers: No. 52). (Illus.). 140p. 1980. 24.95 (ISBN 0-521-22313-X); pap. 13.95 (ISBN 0-521-29446-0). Cambridge U Pr.
Bell, Charles Frederic M. Khedives and Pashas: Sketches of Contemporary Egyptian Rulers and Statesmen. by One Who Knows Them Well. LC 80-2196. 1981. Repr. of 1884 ed. 30.00 (ISBN 0-404-18954-7). AMS Pr.
Kedourie, Elie & Haim, Sylvia G., eds. Modern Egypt: Studies in Politics & Society. 136p. 1980. 25.00 (ISBN 0-7146-3168-X, F Cass Co). Biblio Dist.
Kosman, William Y. Sadat's Realistic Peace Initiative. Date not set. 8.95 (ISBN 0-533-04614-9). Vantage.
Tignor, Robert L. & Abdel-Khalek, Goudal, eds. Political Economy of Income Distribution in Egypt. LC 80-26932. (The Political Economy of Income Distribution in Developing Countries Ser.). 500p. 1981. text ed. 45.00x (ISBN 0-8419-0633-5). Holmes & Meier.

EGYPT–RELIGION
Anan Isho, compiled by. The Wit & Wisdom of the Christian Fathers of Egypt: The Syrian Version of the Apophthegmata Patrum. Wallis Budge, Ernest A., tr. LC 80-2354. 1981. Repr. of 1934 ed. 53.50 (ISBN 0-404-18900-8). AMS Pr.

EGYPT–SOCIAL CONDITIONS
Kedourie, Elie & Haim, Sylvia G., eds. Modern Egypt: Studies in Politics & Society. 136p. 1980. 25.00 (ISBN 0-7146-3168-X, F Cass Co). Biblio Dist.

EGYPT–SOCIAL LIFE AND CUSTOMS
James, T. G. An Introduction to Ancient Egypt. (British Museum Bks.). 286p. 1979. 20.00 (ISBN 0-374-83343-5); pap. 8.95 (ISBN 0-374-84339-2). FS&G.

EGYPTIAN ARCHITECTURE
see Architecture–Egypt

EGYPTIAN ART
see Art, Egyptian

EIDETIC IMAGERY
Fauver, William & Birch, Robert L. Memory Dynamics: A Complete Memory System. 1981. 49.95; spiral binding 39.95. Knowledge Bank.

EIKONS
see Icons

EINSTEIN, ALBERT, 1879-1955
Dukas, Helen & Hoffman, Banesh. Albert Einstein, the Human Side: New Glimpses from His Archives. LC 78-70289. 168p. 1981. pap. 3.95 (ISBN 0-691-02368-9). Princeton U Pr.
Grunfeld, Frederic V. Prophets Without Honor: A Background to Freud, Kafka, Einstein & Their World. 1980. 5.95x (ISBN 0-07-025087-1). McGraw.
Roberts, Alan W. Einstein As I Knew Him. 7.95 (ISBN 0-89523-001-1). Green Hill.

EISENHOWER, DWIGHT DAVID, PRES. U. S., 1890-1969
Branyan, Robert L. The Eisenhower Administration, Nineteen Fifty-Three to Nineteen Sixty-One: A Documentary History, 2 vols. LC 71-164935. 1971. Set. lib. bdg. 85.00 (ISBN 0-313-20126-9). Greenwood.
Divine, Robert A. Eisenhower & the Cold War. (Illus.). 160p. 1981. 14.95 (ISBN 0-19-502823-6). Oxford U Pr.
--Eisenhower & the Cold War. 160p. 1981. pap. 3.95 (ISBN 0-19-502824-4, 621, GB). Oxford U Pr.
Egleton, Clive. The Eisenhower Deception. LC 80-69372. 1981. 10.95 (ISBN 0-689-11127-4). Atheneum.
Ewald, William B., Jr. Eisenhower the President: Crucial Days, 1951-1960. LC 80-22929. 420p. 1981. 12.95 (ISBN 0-13-246868-9). P-H.

EISENSTAEDT, ALFRED
Honnef, Klaus, et al. Eisenstaedt: Germany. (Illus.). 112p. (Orig.). 1981. pap. 12.50 (ISBN 0-87474-530-6). Smithsonian.

EL DORADO
Sioli, P., ed. History of el Dorado County, California. facsimile ed. 272p. Repr. of 1883 ed. quarto 35.00. Holmes.

ELASTIC SOLIDS
see also Deformations (Mechanics); Strains and Stresses; Vibration
Wempner, Gerald. Mechanics of Solids with Application to Thin Bodies. (Mechanics of Elastics & Viscoelastic Solids). 620p. 1980. 35.00x (ISBN 90-286-0880-X). Sijthoff & Noordhoff.

ELASTIC TISSUE
Robert, A. M. & Robert, L., eds. Biology & Pathology of Elastic Tissues. (Frontiers of Matrix Biology Ser.: Vol. 8). (Illus.). viii, 232p. 1980. 74.25 (ISBN 3-8055-3078-1). S Karger.

ELASTICITY
see also Continuum Mechanics; Plasticity; Shells; Strains and Stresses; Strength of Materials
Gladwell, G. M. Contact Problems in the Classical Theory of Elasticity. (Mechanics of Elastic & Viscoelastic Solids Ser.). 716p. 1980. 60.00x (ISBN 9-0286-0440-5); pap. 35.00x (ISBN 9-0286-0760-9). Sijthoff & Noordhoff.
Wempner, Gerald. Mechanics of Solids with Application to Thin Bodies. (Mechanics of Elastics & Viscoelastic Solids). 620p. 1980. 35.00x (ISBN 90-286-0880-X). Sijthoff & Noordhoff.

ELDERS (CHURCH OFFICERS)
Taylor, Robert, Jr. Elder & His Work. 6.95 (ISBN 0-89315-041-X); pap. 6.95 (ISBN 0-89315-042-8). Lambert Bk.

ELECTIONS
see also Nominations for Office; Presidents–United States–Election; Primaries; Voters, Registration Of; Voting; Women–Suffrage
also subdivision Election or Elections under subjects, e.g. Presidents–United States–election; Great Britain–Parliament–Elections
Mirchandani, G. G. State Assembly Elections. 240p. 1980. text ed. 22.50x (ISBN 0-7069-1288-8, Pub. by Vikas India). Advent Bk.
Reitman, A. The Election Process. 2nd ed. 1980. 5.95. Oceana.
Simpson, Dick. Winning Elections: A Handbook in Participatory Politics. rev. & enl. ed. (Illus.). 240p. 1981. 13.95x (ISBN 0-8040-0365-3); text ed. 7.95x (ISBN 0-8040-0366-1). Swallow.

ELECTIONS–JAPAN
Passm, Herbert, ed. Season of Voting: Japanese Elections of 1976 & 1977. 1979. pap. 6.25 (ISBN 0-8447-3343-1). Am Enterprise.

ELECTIONS–NEW ZEALAND
Penniman, Howard R., ed. New Zealand at the Polls: The General Election of 1978. 1980. pap. 7.95 (ISBN 0-8447-3376-8). Am Enterprise.

ELECTIONS–UNITED STATES
see also Afro-Americans–Politics and Suffrage; Presidents–United States–Election; United States–Congress–Elections
Gray, Lee L. How We Chose A President. 5th ed. 1980. 8.95 (ISBN 0-312-39411-X). St Martin.
Hirschfield, Robert S. Selection-Election. 1980. 264p. 1981. text ed. price not set. Aldine Pub.
Pomper, Gerald M. The Election of 1980: Reports & Interpretations. 224p. (Orig.). 1980. 12.95 (ISBN 0-934540-10-1); pap. text ed. 7.95 (ISBN 0-934540-09-8). Chatham Hse Pubs.
Ranney, Austin, ed. Past & Future of Presidential Debates. 1979. pap. 7.25 (ISBN 0-8447-3330-X). Am Enterprise.
--Presidential Nominating Process: Can It Be Improved? 1980. pap. 3.25 (ISBN 0-8447-3397-0). Am Enterprise.
Silva, Ruth C. Rum, Religion, & Votes: Nineteen Twenty-Eight Re-Examined. LC 80-24997. ix, 76p. 1981. Repr. of 1962 ed. lib. bdg. 22.50x (ISBN 0-313-22768-3, SIRR). Greenwood.
--Rum, Religion, & Votes: Nineteen Twenty-Eight Re-Examined. LC 80-24997. 85p. 1981. Repr. of 1962 ed. lib. bdg. 22.50 (ISBN 0-313-22768-3, SIRR). Greenwood.

ELECTIONS, PRIMARY
see Primaries

ELECTORAL COLLEGE
see Presidents–United States–Election

ELECTRIC ACCOUNTING MACHINES
see Accounting Machines

ELECTRIC APPARATUS AND APPLIANCES
see also Household Appliances
Brewster, Albert H., Jr. How to Convert Gasoline Lawn Mowers for Cordless Electric Mowing. 3rd ed. LC 76-48500. (Illus.). 1981. pap. 10.00x (ISBN 0-918166-03-9). Amonics.
Brittan, John. Electronics for Appliances. Sabin, A. Ross, ed. (Illus.). 172p. (gr. 11). 1979. 20.00 (ISBN 0-938336-09-6). Whirlpool.
Fredgant, Don. Electrical Collectibles: Relics of the Electrical Age. (Illus.). 1981. pap. 9.95 (ISBN 0-914598-04-X). Padre Prods.
Keefe, William F. Successful Home Appliances: The 1980's Energy & Money Saving Guide. Case, Virginia, ed. (Successful Ser.). (Illus.). 1981. 18.95 (ISBN 0-89999-019-3); pap. 8.95 (ISBN 0-89999-020-7). Structures Pub.
Pacheko, Jose, tr. from Eng. Electricidad Basica Para Apparatas Caseros. (Illus.). 140p. (Span.). 1975. 20.00 (ISBN 0-938336-10-X). Whirlpool.
Sabin, A. Ross, ed. Automatic Dishwasher, Disposer, Trash Masher Compactor. (Illus.). 168p. (gr. 11). 1978. 20.00 (ISBN 0-938336-07-X). Whirlpool.
--Automatic Dryers. (Illus.). 160p. (gr. 11). 20.00 (ISBN 0-938336-05-3). Whirlpool.
--Automatic Washers. (Illus.). 200p. (gr. 11). 1975. 20.00 (ISBN 0-938336-04-5). Whirlpool.
--Basic Electricity for Appliances. (Illus.). 255p. (gr. 11). 1973. 20.00 (ISBN 0-938336-00-2). Whirlpool.
--Commercial Ice Makers. (Illus.). 273p. (gr. 11). 1980. 20.00 (ISBN 0-938336-08-8). Whirlpool.
--Range Service (Gas, Electric, Microwave) (Illus.). 253p. (gr. 11). 1979. 20.00 (ISBN 0-938336-06-1). Whirlpool.

ELECTRIC APPARATUS AND APPLIANCES–MAINTENANCE AND REPAIR
Hahn, James & Hahn, Lynn. Aim for a Job in Appliance Repair. (Aim High Ser.). 128p. 1981. lib. bdg. 5.97 (ISBN 0-8239-0541-1). Rosen Pr.

ELECTRIC BASS
see Guitar

ELECTRIC CABLES
see also Electric Wiring
Knox. Power Cable Handbook. 1981. text ed. price not set. Butterworths.

ELECTRIC CIRCUITS
see also Electric Networks; Electronic Circuits
Aatre, V. K. Network Theory & Filter Design. 432p. 1981. 18.95 (ISBN 0-470-26934-0). Halsted Pr.
Floyd, Thomas L. Principles of Electric Circuits. (Illus.). 768p. 1981. text ed. 19.95 (ISBN 0-675-08081-9); tchr's. ed. 3.95 (ISBN 0-686-69499-6). Merrill.
Yorke, R. Electric Circuit Theory. LC 80-41323. (Applied Electricity & Electronics Ser.). (Illus.). 272p. 1981. 30.00 (ISBN 0-08-026133-7); pap. 15.00 (ISBN 0-08-026132-9). Pergamon.

ELECTRIC COMMUNICATION
see Telecommunication

ELECTRIC CONVERTERS
see Electric Current Converters

ELECTRIC COOKERY
see also Microwave Cookery
Consumer Guide Editors & Ojakangas, Beatrice A. The Convection Oven Cookbook. (Illus.). 1980. pap. 6.95 (ISBN 0-449-90042-8, Columbine). Fawcett.
Reingold, Carmel B. Convection Oven Cookbook. 1980. 13.95 (ISBN 0-690-01980-7, HarpT); pap. 7.95 (ISBN 0-690-01982-3, HarpT). Har-Row.

ELECTRIC COOKERY, SLOW
Lomask, Martha. Low, Slow, Delicious: Recipes for Casseroles & Electric Slow-Cooking Pots. (Illus.). 160p. 1981. 19.95 (ISBN 0-571-11384-2, Pub. by Faber & Faber). Merrimack Bk Serv.

ELECTRIC CROCKERY COOKERY
see Electric Cookery, Slow

ELECTRIC CURRENT CONVERTERS
Wood, Peter. Switching Power Converters. 464p. 1981. text ed. 26.50 (ISBN 0-442-24333-2). Van Nos Reinhold.

ELECTRIC CURRENTS
see also Electric Transformers
Kato, S. & Roper, R. G. Electric Current & Atmospheric Motion. (Advances in Earth & Planetary Sciences Ser.: No. 7). 294p. 1980. 24.50x (ISBN 0-89955-314-1, Pub. by JSSP Japan). Intl Schol Bk Serv.

ELECTRIC ENGINEERING
see also Electric Apparatus and Appliances; Electric Machinery; Electric Power Distribution; Electric Power Systems; Electro-Acoustics; Electromechanical Devices; Radio; Telephone
Carlson, A. Bruce & Gisser, David G. Electrical Engineering: Concepts & Applications. LC 80-21519. (Electrical Engineering Ser.). 640p. 1981. text ed. price not set (ISBN 0-201-03940-0). A-W.
D'Azzo, John & Houpis, Constantine. Linear Control System Analysis & Design. 2nd ed. (Electrical Engineering Ser.). (Illus.). 864p. 1981. text ed. write for info (ISBN 0-07-016183-6, C); write for info solutions manual (ISBN 0-07-016184-4). McGraw.
Fink, Donald G. & Christiansen, Donald. Electronics Engineer's Handbook. 2nd ed. 2496p. Date not set. 46.50 (ISBN 0-07-020981-2). McGraw.
Gandhi, Om P. Microwave Engineering & Applications. (Illus.). 543p. 1981. 60.00 (ISBN 0-08-025589-2); pap. 24.50 (ISBN 0-08-025588-4). Pergamon.
Gas Discharges & Their Applications. (IEE Conference Publication Ser.: No. 189). (Illus.). 560p. (Orig.). 1980. soft cover 79.00. Inst Elect Eng.
Gregory, B. A. An Introduction to Electric Instrumentation & Measurement. LC 80-22869. 435p. 1981. pap. 29.95 (ISBN 0-470-27092-6). Halsted Pr.
Hamilton, R. Electrical Principles for Technicians. (Electrical & Telecommunications Technicians Ser.). (Illus.). 200p. 1980. 37.50 (ISBN 0-19-859360-0). Oxford U Pr.
Jowett, C. E. Application of Engineering in Microelectronic Industries. 184p. 1975. text ed. 22.00x (ISBN 0-220-66278-9, Pub. by Busn Bks England). Renouf.

ELECTRIC ENGINEERING–APPARATUS AND APPLIANCES
see Electric Apparatus and Appliances

ELECTRIC ENGINEERING–DICTIONARIES
Jackson, K. G. & Feinberg, R. Dictionary of Electrical Engineering. 2nd ed. 1981. text ed. price not set (ISBN 0-408-00450-9, Newnes-Butterworth). Butterworth.

ELECTRIC ENGINEERING–LAWS AND LEGISLATION
Flach, George W. Changes in the 1981 National Electrical Code. 144p. 1981. pap. 6.95 (ISBN 0-13-127852-5). P-H.
Garland, J. D. National Electrical Code Reference Book, 1981. 3rd ed. (Illus.). 640p. 1981. 21.95 (ISBN 0-13-609321-3). P-H.
Harmon, T. & Allen, C. Guide to the National Electral Code R. 1981. 21.95 (ISBN 0-13-370478-5). P-H.

ELECTRIC ENGINEERING–VOCATIONAL GUIDANCE
see Engineering–Vocational Guidance

ELECTRIC EQUIPMENT OF AUTOMOBILES
see Automobiles–Electric Equipment

ELECTRIC HOUSEHOLD APPLIANCES
see Household Appliances

ELECTRIC MACHINERY
see also Electric Current Converters; Electric Motors; Electric Transformers
Hindmarsh, J. Electrical Machines & Their Applications. LC 79-20595. (Illus.). 800p. (Arabic.). 1981. pap. 20.00 (ISBN 0-08-026158-2). Pergamon.
McPherson, George. An Introduction to Electrical Machines & Transformers. 544p. 1981. text ed. 22.95 (ISBN 0-471-05586-7); tchrs.' ed. avail. (ISBN 0-471-07954-5). Wiley.
Metzger, D. Electric Components, Instruments & Troubleshooting. 1981. 28.95 (ISBN 0-13-250266-6). P-H.
Nasar, Syed A. Schaum's Outline of Electric Machines & Electromechanics. (Schaum's Outline Ser.). (Illus.). 208p. 1981. pap. 6.95 (ISBN 0-07-045886-3, SP). McGraw.

ELECTRIC MECHANICAL DEVICES
see Electromechanical Devices

ELECTRIC MOTORS
see also Electric Transformers
Bottle, E. K. Fractional Horse-Power Electric Motors: A Guide to Types & Applications. 209p. 1948. 10.95x (ISBN 0-85264-051-X, Pub. by Griffin England). State Mutual Bk.

ELECTRIC NETWORKS
Aatre, V. K. Network Theory & Filter Design. 432p. 1981. 18.95 (ISBN 0-470-26934-0). Halsted Pr.
Balabanian, Norman & Bickert, Theodore. Linear Network Theory: Analysis, Properties, Design & Synthesis. 450p. 1981. text ed. 32.95 (ISBN 0-916460-10-X). Matrix Pubns.
Sonde, B. S. Introduction to System Design Using Integrated Circuits. 261p. 1981. 24.95 (ISBN 0-470-27110-8). Halsted Pr.

ELECTRIC POTENTIAL
see Electric Currents; Potential, Theory Of

ELECTRIC POWER DISTRIBUTION
see also Electric Networks; Electric Wiring
Brown. Transfer Station Techniques Manual. 1981. text ed. 39.95 (ISBN 0-250-40426-5). Ann Arbor Science.

ELECTRIC POWER SYSTEMS
Here are entered works on the complex assemblage of equipment and circuits for generating, transmitting, transforming, and distributing electric energy.
see also Electric Power Distribution
Horowitz, S. H. Protective Relaying for Power Systems. 560p. 1980. 39.95 (ISBN 0-471-08968-0, Pub. by Wiley-Interscience); pap. 26.00 (ISBN 0-471-08967-2). Wiley.
United Nations Economic Commission for Europe. Combined Production of Electric Power & Heat: Proceedings of a Seminar Organized by the Committee on Electric Power of the United Nations Economic Commission for Europe, Hamburg, FR Germany, 6-9 November 1978. LC 80-755. (Illus.). 150p. 32.00 (ISBN 0-08-025677-5). Pergamon.

ELECTRIC PRECIPITATION
see Electrostatic Precipitation

ELECTRIC RAILROADS
see also Street-Railroads
Henry Huntington & the Pacific Electric. pap. 10.00. Chatham Pub CA.

ELECTRIC RAILROADS–CARS
Albert, Richard C. Trolleys from the Mines: Street Railways of Centre, Clearfield, Indiana & Jefferson Counties, Pennsylvania. (Illus.). 100p. (Orig.). 1980. pap. 9.00 (ISBN 0-911940-32-4). Cox.
Cummings, O. R. Street Cars of Boston, Vol.6: Birneys, Type 5, Semiconvertibles, Parlor, Private, & Mail Cars. (Illus.). 84p. 1980. pap. 9.00 (ISBN 0-911940-34-0). Cox.

ELECTRIC SIGNAL THEORY
see Signal Theory (Telecommunication)

ELECTRIC STREET-RAILROADS
see Street-Railroads

ELECTRIC TESTING
Gill, Paul. Electrical Equipment Testing & Maintenance Handbook. 350p. 1981. text ed. 16.95 (ISBN 0-8359-1625-1). Reston.

ELECTRIC TRANSFORMERS
McPherson, George. An Introduction to Electrical Machines & Transformers. 544p. 1981. text ed. 22.95 (ISBN 0-471-05586-7); tchrs.' ed. avail. (ISBN 0-471-07954-5). Wiley.

ELECTRIC WIRING
see also Electric Cables
Colvin, Thomas. Electrical Wiring: Residential, Utility Bldgs, & Service Areas. 10.95 (ISBN 0-89606-030-6). Green Hill.
Graf, R. & Whalen, G. Home Wiring. 1981. 14.95 (ISBN 0-13-392977-9). P-H.
Mix, Floyd M. Housewiring Simplified. LC 80-21122. (Illus.). 176p. 1981. text ed. 8.00 (ISBN 0-87006-309-X). Goodheart.
Mullin, Ray C. Electrical Wiring Residential: Based on 1981 National Electrial Code. 7th ed. 288p. 1981. 14.95. Van Nos Reinhold.
Mullin, Ray C. & Smith, Robert L. Electrical Wiring - Commercial. 4th rev. ed. LC 80-65467. (Electrical Trades Ser.). (Illus.). 208p. 1981. pap. text ed. 10.00 (ISBN 0-8273-1953-3); price not set instr's. guide (ISBN 0-8273-1954-1). Delmar.
Richter, H. P. & Schwan, W. C., eds. Wiring Simplified. 33rd ed. LC 33-7980. 160p. 1981. 3.50 (ISBN 0-9603294-1-2). Park Pub.
Watkins, A. J. Electrical Installation Calculations, Vol. 1. 3rd ed. 100p. 1980. 13.00x (ISBN 0-7131-3422-4, Pub. by Arnold Pubs England). State Mutual Bk.
--Electrical Installation Calculations: SJ Units, Vol. 2. 2nd ed. 106p. 1980. 13.00x (Pub. by Arnold Pubs England). State Mutual Bk.
--Electrical Installation Calculations: S1 Units, Vol. 3. 154p. 1980. 13.00x (ISBN 0-7131-3224-8, Pub. by Arnold Pubs England). State Mutual Bk.

ELECTRIC WIRING–DIAGRAMS
Watkins, A. J. Electrical Installation Calculations, Vol. 1. 3rd ed. 100p. 1980. 13.00x (ISBN 0-7131-3422-4, Pub. by Arnold Pubs England). State Mutual Bk.
--Electrical Installation Calculations: SJ Units, Vol. 2. 2nd ed. 106p. 1980. 13.00x (Pub. by Arnold Pubs England). State Mutual Bk.
--Electrical Installation Calculations: S1 Units, Vol. 3. 154p. 1980. 13.00x (ISBN 0-7131-3224-8, Pub. by Arnold Pubs England). State Mutual Bk.

ELECTRICAL ENGINEERING
see Electric Engineering

ELECTRICALLY EXPLODED WIRES
see Exploding Wire Phenomena

ELECTRICITY
see also Electrons; Magnetism; Telephone; X-Rays also headings beginning with Electric and Electro
Bird, May. Electrical Principles Three Checkbook. text ed. write for info. (ISBN 0-408-00636-6); pap. text ed. write for info. (ISBN 0-408-00601-3). Butterworth.
--Electrical Principles Two Checkbook. 1981. text ed. price not set (ISBN 0-408-00635-8); pap. text ed. price not set (ISBN 0-408-00600-5). Butterworth.
Chapple, M. A-Level Physics: Electricity & Semiconducters, Vol.3. 2nd ed. (Illus.). 288p. (Orig.). 1980. pap. text ed. 11.95x (ISBN 0-7121-0158-6). Intl Ideas.
D'Arcangelo, B. F., et al. Mathematics for Plumbers & Pipefitters. 3rd rev. ed. (Applied Mathematics Ser.). (Illus.). 210p. 1981. pap. text ed. price not set (ISBN 0-8273-1291-1); price not set instr's. guide. Delmar.
DeGuilmo, Joseph M. Electricity-Electronics: Principles & Applications. LC 79-54909. (Electronics Technology Ser.). (Illus.). 672p. (Orig.). 1981. pap. 19.60 (ISBN 0-8273-1686-0); price not set instr's. guide (ISBN 0-8273-1687-9). Delmar.
Gerrish, H. & Dugger, W., Jr. Exploring Electricity & Electronics: Basic Fundamentals. rev. ed. LC 80-20830. (Illus.). 208p. 1981. text ed. 9.96 (ISBN 0-87006-308-1). Goodheart.
McKenzie, Bruce A. & Zachariah, Gerald. Understanding & Using Electricity. 2nd ed. 1981. text ed. 1.95x. Interstate.
Patrick, Dale & Dugger, William E., Jr. Electricity & Electronics Laboratory Manual. rev. ed. (Illus.). 372p. (gr. 7 up). 1980. 4.96. Goodheart.
Rexford, Kenneth. Electrical Control for Machines. LC 80-70918. (Electrical Maintenance Ser.). (Illus.). 332p. 1981. pap. text ed. 9.80 (ISBN 0-8273-1983-5); write for info. instr's guide (ISBN 0-8273-1984-3). Delmar.
Sprott, Julien C. Introduction to Modern Electronics. 512p. 1981. text ed. 22.95 (ISBN 0-471-05840-8). Wiley.
Weathers, Thomas & Hunter, Claud. Fundamentals of Electricity & Automotive Electrical Systems. (Illus.). 256p. 1981. text ed. 16.95 (ISBN 0-13-337030-5). P-H.
Wildi, Theodore. Electrical Power Technology. 704p. 1981. write for info. solns. manual (ISBN 0-471-07764-X); price not set solns. manual (ISBN 0-471-09239-8). Wiley.

ELECTRICITY–APPARATUS AND APPLIANCES
see Electric Apparatus and Appliances

ELECTRICITY–DISTRIBUTION
see Electric Power Distribution

ELECTRICITY–JUVENILE LITERATURE
Math, Irwin. Wires & Watts: Understanding & Using Electricity. (Illus.). 96p. (gr. 7 up). 1981. 8.95 (ISBN 0-686-69287-X). Scribner.

ELECTRICITY–LAWS AND LEGISLATION
see Electric Engineering–Laws and Legislation

ELECTRICITY, ANIMAL
see Electrophysiology

ELECTRICITY ON SHIPS
Watson. Marine Electrical Practice. 5th ed. 1981. text ed. price not set (ISBN 0-408-00498-3). Butterworth.

ELECTRO-ACOUSTICS
see also Magnetic Recorders and Recording; Phonograph
Merhaut, Josef. Theory of Electroacoustics. (Illus.). 336p. 1981. 44.95 (ISBN 0-07-041478-5, C). McGraw.

ELECTROBIOLOGY
see Electrophysiology

ELECTROCARDIOGRAPHY
Blake, Thomas M. The Practice of Electrocardiography. LC 80-13084. 1980. 18.95 (ISBN 0-87488-903-0); pap. 12.00 (ISBN 0-87488-997-9). Med Exam.
Chung, Edward K. Electrocardiography: Practical Applications with Vectorial Principles. 2nd ed. (Illus.). 693p. 1980. text ed. 42.50 (ISBN 0-06-140642-2, Harper Medical). Har-Row.
Goldberger, Ary L. & Goldberger, Emanuel. Clinical Electrocardiography: A Simplified Approach. 2nd ed. LC 80-27024. (Illus.). 278p. 1981. text ed. 14.95 (ISBN 0-8016-1865-7). Mosby.
Kernicki, Jeanette & Weiler, Kathi. Electocardiography for Nurses: Physiological Correlates Electrical Disturbances of the Heart. 304p. 1981. 17.95 (ISBN 0-471-05752-5, Pub. by Wiley Med). Wiley.
Lemmerz, A. H. & Schmidt, R. R. Auswertung und Deutung Des EKG. 12th ed. (Illus.). xii, 260p. 1981. pap. 29.50 (ISBN 3-8055-1932-X). S Karger.

ELECTROCHEMISTRY
see also Electrolysis
Burgess. Elementary Electrochemistry. 3rd ed. 1981. text ed. price not set (ISBN 0-408-70931-6). Butterworth.
Gerischer, Heinz. Advances in Electrochemistry & Electrochemical Engineering, Vol. 12. Tobias, Charles W., ed. 40404p. 1981. write for info. (ISBN 0-471-87530-9, Pub. by Wiley-Interscience). Wiley.
Hertz, H. G. Electrochemistry: A Reformaulation of the Basic Principles. (Lecture Notes in Chemistry: Vol. 17). (Illus.). 254p. 1980. pap. 24.80 (ISBN 0-387-10008-3). Springer-Verlag.

ELECTROCHEMISTRY, INDUSTRIAL
see also Electrostatic Precipitation
Trescott, Martha M. The Rise of the American Electrochemicals Industry, 1880-1910: Studies in the American Technological Environment. LC 80-23469. (Contributions in Economics & Economic History Ser.: No. 38). (Illus.). 424p. 1981. lib. bdg. 45.00 (ISBN 0-313-20766-6, TRI/). Greenwood.

ELECTRODES
Luebbers, D. W., ed. Progress in Enzyme & Ion-Selective Electrodes. (Illus.). 240p. 1981. pap. 34.30 (ISBN 0-387-10499-2). Springer-Verlag.
Material Specifications: Welding Rods, Electrodes & Filler Metals, 3 pts, Pt. C. (Boiler & Pressure Vessel Code Ser.: Sec. II). 1980. loose leaf 70.00 (P0002C); pap. 70.00 l00se leaf (V0002C). ASME.

ELECTROENCEPHALOGRAPHY
Cooper, R. & Osselton, J. W. EEG Technology. 3rd ed. Shaw, J. C., ed. (Illus.). 304p. 1980. text ed. 29.95 (ISBN 0-407-16002-7). Butterworths.
Kiloh, L. G., et al. Clinical Electroencephalography. 4th ed. 1981. text ed. price not set (ISBN 0-407-00160-3). Butterworth.
Nunez, Paul L. Electric Fields of the B. (Illus.). 500p. 1981. text ed. 35.00x (ISBN 0-19-502796-5). Oxford U Pr.

ELECTROLYSIS
see also Electrolytes; Ions
Shapiro, Julius. Electrolysis, Key to a Beautiful Body. LC 80-24691. (Illus.). 246p. 1981. 8.95 (ISBN 0-396-07903-2). Dodd.

ELECTROLYTE SOLUTIONS
Inman, Douglas & Lovering, David G., eds. Ionic Liquids. 445p. 1981. 49.50 (ISBN 0-306-40412-5, Plenum Pr). Plenum Pub.
Schwoyer, William E., ed. Polyelectrolytes for Water & Wastewater Treatment. 304p. 1981. 74.95 (ISBN 0-8493-5439-0). CRC Pr.

ELECTROLYTES
see also Electrolyte Solutions

Nozik, Art J., ed. Photoeffects at Semiconductor-Electrolyte Interfaces. LC 80-27773. (Symposium Ser.: No. 146). 1981. 39.00 (ISBN 0-8412-0604-X). Am Chemical.

ELECTROMAGNETIC INTERACTIONS

Hobbs, B. A., ed. A Special Issue Surveying Electromagnetic Induction in the Earth & Moon. 185p. pap. 23.50 (ISBN 90-277-9041-8, Pub. by D. Reidel). Kluwer Boston.

Schmucker, U., ed. Electromagnetics Induction in the Earth & Moon. (Advances in Earth & Planetary Sciences Ser.: No. 9). 200p. 1980. lib. bdg. 26.50 (ISBN 90-277-1131-3, Pub. by D. Reidel). Kluwer Boston.

Stavroulakis, Peter. Interference Analysis of Communication Systems. 472p. 1980. 38.00 (ISBN 0-471-08674-6, Pub. by Wiley-Interscience); pap. 25.75 (ISBN 0-471-08673-8). Wiley.

ELECTROMAGNETIC MEASUREMENTS

Verma, Rajni K. Master Tables for Electromagnetic Depth Sounding Interpretation. (IFI Data Base Library Ser.). 480p. 1980. 75.00 (ISBN 0-306-65188-2, IFI). Plenum Pub.

ELECTROMAGNETIC THEORY

see also Electromagnetic Waves; Electrons; Field Theory (Physics); Light

Petit, R. Electromagnetic Theory of Gratings. (Topics in Current Physics Ser.: Vol. 22). (Illus.). 284p. 1981. 38.35 (ISBN 0-387-10193-4). Springer-Verlag.

Skitok, J. & Marshall, R. Electromagnetic Concepts & Applications. 1981. 28.00 (ISBN 0-13-248963-5). P-H.

ELECTROMAGNETIC WAVES

Hudson, J. E. Adaptive Arrays. (IEE Electromagnetic Waves Ser.). 1981. price not set (Pub. by Peregrinus England). Inst Electrical.

Wait, James R. Wave Propagation Theory. LC 80-23286. 400p. 1981. 40.01 (ISBN 0-08-026345-3); pap. 20.01 (ISBN 0-08-026344-5). Pergamon.

ELECTROMAGNETICS

see Electromagnetism

ELECTROMAGNETISM

see also Magnetic Materials; Magnetohydrodynamics; Masers

Copson, David A. Informational Bioelectromagnetics. 650p. 1981. text ed. 24.95 (ISBN 0-916460-09-6). Matrix Pubns.

ELECTROMECHANICAL DEVICES

see also Electric Machinery

Melcher, James R. Continuum Electromechanics. (Illus.). 700p. 1981. text ed. 37.50x (ISBN 0-262-13165-X). MIT Pr.

Nasar, Syed A. Schaum's Outline of Electric Machines & Electromechanics. (Schaum's Outline Ser.). (Illus.). 208p. 1981. pap. 6.95 (ISBN 0-07-045886-3, SP). McGraw.

ELECTRON CIRCUITS–DESIGN

see Electronic Circuit Design

ELECTRON EMISSION

see Electrons–Emission

ELECTRON MICROSCOPE

Becker, R. P. & Johari, O. Scanning Electron Microscopy 1980, No. II. LC 72-626068. (Illus.). xiv, 658p. 50.00 (ISBN 0-931288-12-6). Scanning Electron.

Daumeister, W., ed. Electron Microscopy at Molecular Dimensions. (Proceedings in Life Sciences). (Illus.). 300p. 1980. 57.90 (ISBN 0-387-10131-4). Springer-Verlag.

Electron Microscopy in Human Medicine, Vol. 7: Digestive System. (Electron Microscopy in Human Medicine Ser.). 250p. 1980. 58.00 (ISBN 0-07-032507-3, HP). McGraw.

Griffith, Jack D. Electron Microscopy in Biology, Vol.1. (Electron Microscopy in Biology Ser.). 325p. 1981. 32.50 (ISBN 0-471-05525-5, Pub. by Wiley-Interscience). Wiley.

Hall, Cecil E. Introduction to Electron Microscopy. 2nd ed. LC 80-39788. 410p. 1981. Repr. of 1966 ed. lib. bdg. price not set (ISBN 0-89874-302-8). Krieger.

Johari, Om. Scanning Electron Microscopy 1980, Pt. I. LC 72-626068. (Illus.). xvi, 608p. 1980. 50.00 (ISBN 0-931288-11-8). Scanning Electron.

Johari, Om & Becker, R. P., eds. Scanning Electron Microscopy 1980, No. III. LC 72-62608. (Illus.). xx, 670p. 50.00 (ISBN 0-931288-13-4). Scanning Electron.

Spence, J. C. Experimental High-Resolution Electron Microscopy. (Monographs on the Physics & Chemistry of Materials). (Illus.). 384p. 1981. 74.00 (ISBN 0-19-851365-8). Oxford U Pr.

Weakley, Brenda. A Beginner's Handbook of Biological Transmission Electron Microscopy. (Illus.). 272p. (Orig.). 1981. pap. 16.50 (ISBN 0-443-02091-4). Churchill.

Wischnitzer, Saul. Introduction to Electron Microscopy. 3rd ed. LC 80-15266. 320p. 1980. 19.75 (ISBN 0-08-026298-8). Pergamon.

ELECTRON PARAMAGNETIC RESONANCE

Gordy, W. Techniques of Chemistry: Vol. 15 Theory & Application of Electron Spin Resonance. 625p. 1980. 39.95 (ISBN 0-471-93162-4). Wiley.

Molin, Y. N., et al. Spin Exchange: Principles & Applications in Chemistry & Biology. (Springer Series in Chemical Physics: Vol. 8). (Illus.). 242p. 1980. 39.00 (ISBN 0-387-10095-4). Springer-Verlag.

Poole, C. P. Electron Spin Resonance: A Comprehensive Treatise on Experimental Technique. 922p. 1967. 50.00 (ISBN 0-470-69386-X). Wiley.

ELECTRON PROBES

see Probes (Electronic Instruments)

ELECTRON RESONANCE

see Electron Paramagnetic Resonance

ELECTRON SPECTROSCOPY

Bonnelle, C. & Mande, C., eds. Advances in X-Ray Spectroscopy: A Reference Text in Honour of Professor Y Cauchois. (Illus.). 400p. 1981. 60.00 (ISBN 0-08-025266-4). Pergamon.

ELECTRON SPIN RESONANCE

see Electron Paramagnetic Resonance

ELECTRONIC APPARATUS AND APPLIANCES

see also Airplanes–Electronic Equipment; Antennas (Electronics); Computers; Electronic Office Machines; Electronic Toys; Industrial Electronics; Microwave Devices; Miniature Electronic Equipment; Probes (Electronic Instruments)

Morgan, Alfred. The Boy's Second Book of Radio & Electronics. LC 57-6078. (Illus.). 288p. (gr. 7-9). 1977. 6.95 (ISBN 0-684-13154-4). Scribner.

ELECTRONIC BATTLEFIELD

see Electronics in Military Engineering

ELECTRONIC BRAINS

see Artificial Intelligence; Computers

ELECTRONIC CALCULATING-MACHINES

see Computers

ELECTRONIC CIRCUIT DESIGN

Comer, David J. Electronic Design with Integrated Circuits. LC 80-23365. (Electrical Engineering Ser.). (Illus.). 416p. 1981. text ed. 24.95 (ISBN 0-201-03931-1). A-W.

O'Malley, John. Schaum's Outline of Basic Circuit Analysis. (Schaum's Outline Ser.). 400p. 1981. pap. 6.95 (ISBN 0-07-047820-1). McGraw.

ELECTRONIC CIRCUITS

see also Computers–Circuits; Electronic Digital Computers–Circuits; Integrated Circuits; Semiconductors

Chua, L. & Lin, P. Computer-Aided Analysis of Electronic Circuits: Algorathms & Computational Techniques. 1975. 32.95 (ISBN 0-13-165415-2). P-H.

Harris, Frank. Electronic Circuit Devices. (Avionics Technician Training Course Ser.). (Orig.). 1981. pap. write for info. (ISBN 0-89100-192-1). Aviation Maintenance.

O'Malley, John. Schaum's Outline of Basic Circuit Analysis. (Schaum's Outline Ser.). 400p. 1981. pap. 6.95 (ISBN 0-07-047820-1). McGraw.

Su, Kendall L. A Collection of Solved Problems in Circuits, Electronics, & Signal Analysis, Vol. 1. 96p. 1980. pap. text ed. 5.50 (ISBN 0-8403-2262-3). Kendall-Hunt.

Weber, Samuel, ed. Electronic Circuits Notebook: Proven Designs for Systems Applications. LC 80-29479. (Electronic Magazine Bks.). (Illus.). 344p. (Orig.). 1981. professional 14.95 (ISBN 0-07-606720-3, R-026). McGraw.

ELECTRONIC COMPUTER–DEBUGGING

see Debugging (Electronic Computers)

ELECTRONIC COMPUTER–PROGRAMMING

see Programming (Electronic Computers)

ELECTRONIC COMPUTERS

see Computers

ELECTRONIC DATA PROCESSING

see also Artificial Intelligence; Data Transmission Systems; Debugging (Electronic Computers); Data Base Management; Office Practice; Optical Data Processing; Programming (Electronic Computers); Programming Languages (Electronic Computers); Real-Time Data Processing

also subdivision Data Processing under subjects, e.g. Business–Data Processing

Anderson, R. G. Data Processing & Management Information Systems. 3rd ed. (Illus.). 480p. 1980. pap. text ed. 15.95x (ISBN 0-7121-0417-8). Intl Ideas.

Bjorner, D., ed. Abstract Software Specifications. (Lecture Notes in Computer Sciences: Vol. 86). 567p. 1980. pap. 31.00 (ISBN 0-387-10007-5). Springer-Verlag.

Burkhard, R. E. & Derigs, U. Assignment & Matching Problems: Solution Methods with FORTRAN-Programs. (Lecture Notes in Economics & Mathematical Systems Ser.: Vol. 184). 148p. 1981. pap. 15.00 (ISBN 0-387-10267-1). Springer-Verlag.

Condon, Robert. Data Processing with Applications. abr. ed. 1981. pap. text ed. 12.95 (ISBN 0-8359-1259-0); instr's. manual free (ISBN 0-8359-1260-4). Reston.

Cundiff, W. E. & Reid, Mado. Issues in Canadian-U. S. Transborder Computer Data Flows. 89p. 1979. pap. text ed. 6.50x (ISBN 0-920380-12-3, Pub. by Inst Res Pub Canada). Renouf.

Dixon, W. J. & Brown, M. B., eds. BMDP 1981. (Orig.). 1981. pap. 20.00x (ISBN 0-520-04408-8). U of Cal Pr.

Exton, William, Jr. Cost-Effective Error Reduction in Data Processing. 275p. 1981. 20.95 (ISBN 0-471-04682-5, Pub. by Wiley-Interscience). Wiley.

Fernandez, Judi N. Using CPM: A Self Teaching Guide. Ashley, Ruth, ed. (Self-Teaching Guide Ser.). 240p. 1981. pap. text ed. 8.95 (ISBN 0-471-08011-X). Wiley.

Gaydasch, Alex. Principles of Electronic Data Processing Management. 300p. 1982. text ed. 18.95 (ISBN 0-8359-5604-0); instr's. manual free (ISBN 0-8359-5605-9). Reston.

Kroenke, David M. Business Computer Systems: An Introduction. (Illus.). 576p. 1980. 15.95x (ISBN 0-938188-00-3). Mitchell Pub.

Ling, Robert F. & Roberts, Harry V. Users Manual for IDA. (Data Analysis Ser.). 300p. 1980. pap. text ed. 12.50 (ISBN 0-07-037905-X, C). McGraw.

Mandell, Steven L. Principles of Data Processing. 2nd ed. (West Series in Data Processing & Information Systems). (Illus.). 165p. 1981. pap. text ed. write for info. (ISBN 0-8299-0392-5). West Pub.

Martin, James. Design & Strategy for Distributed Data Processing. (Illus.). 672p. 1981. text ed. 37.50 (ISBN 0-13-201657-5). P-H.

Miller, Alan R. Eighty-Eighty - ZEighty Assembly Language: Techniques for Improved Programming. 224p. 1980. pap. text ed. 8.95 (ISBN 0-471-08124-8). Wiley.

Mittman, Benjamin & Borman, Lorraine. Personalized Data Base Systems. 326p. 1981. Repr. of 1975 ed. lib. bdg. price not set (ISBN 0-89874-298-6). Krieger.

Moore, William G. The Adjunct to Understanding Data Processing: The Course on Modern Data Processing & Accounting Procedures. 1979. pap. text ed. 2.99 (ISBN 0-934488-01-0). Williams Ent.

Morris, Carl & Rolph, John. Introduction to Data Analysis & Statistical Inference. (Illus.). 416p. 1981. pap. text ed. 13.95. P-H.

Nyborg, Philip S. & McCarter, Pender M., eds. Information Processing in the United States: A Quantitative Summary. (Illus.). vii, 55p. 1977. saddle-stitch 6.00 (ISBN 0-686-68785-X). AFIPS Pr.

Parker, Donn B. Ethical Conflicts in Computer Science & Technology. vi, 201p. 1979. 20.00 (ISBN 0-88283-009-0); wkbk 15.00 (ISBN 0-88283-010-4). AFIPS Pr.

Perkinson, Richard C. Handbook of Data Analysis & Data Base Design. 175p. 1981. pap. 29.50 (ISBN 0-89435-045-5). QED Info Sci.

Reitman, Julian. Computer Simulation Applications. 438p. 1981. Repr. lib. bdg. price not set (ISBN 0-89874-310-9). Krieger.

Report of the AFIPS Panel on Transborder Data Flow. Proceedings. Turn, Rein, ed. LC 79-93002. (Transborder Data Flow: Concerns in Privacy Protection & Free Flow of Information: Vol. 1). (Illus.). xviii, 186p. 1979. pap. 15.00 (ISBN 0-88283-004-X). AFIPS Pr.

Roberts, Harry V. Conversational Statistics. (Data Analysis Series). 256p. 1974. pap. text ed. 15.95 (ISBN 0-07-053135-8, C). McGraw.

Sackman, Harold & Nie, Norman, eds. The Information Utility & Social Choice. LC 78-129364. (Illus.). 310p. 1970. 9.00 (ISBN 0-88283-019-8). AFIPS Pr.

Sanders, Donald H. Computers in Society. 3rd ed. 536p. 1981. text ed. 16.95 (ISBN 0-07-054672-X, C); instructor's manual 4.95 (ISBN 0-07-054673-8); study guide 7.95 (ISBN 0-07-054674-6); test bank 5.95 (ISBN 0-07-054675-4). McGraw.

Skelcher, Derek. Word Processing Equipment Survey. 222p. (Orig.). 1980. pap. 125.00x (ISBN 0-903796-56-2, Pub. by Online Conferences England). Renouf.

Smith, Billy E. Managing the Information Systems Audit: A Case Study-Policies, Procedures, & Guidelines. (Illus.). 65p. 1980. pap. text ed. 22.50 (ISBN 0-89413-086-2); avail. wkbk. (ISBN 0-89413-087-0). Inst Inter Aud.

Smith, J. E. Integrated Injection Logic. 424p. 1980. 34.00 (ISBN 0-471-08675-4, Pub. by Wiley-Interscience); pap. 22.00 (ISBN 0-471-08676-2). Wiley.

Stephens, Graham. Data Communications. 1981. text ed. price not set (ISBN 0-86103-046-X, Westbury Hse). Butterworth.

Tanenbaum, Andrew S. Computer Networks: Toward Distributed Processing Systems. (Illus.). 544p. 1981. text ed. 28.00 (ISBN 0-13-165183-8). P-H.

Tugal, Dogan & Tugal, Osman. Data Transmission: Analysis; Design; Applications. (Illus.). 384p. 1982. 19.50 (ISBN 0-07-065427-1). McGraw.

Turn, Rein & Roth, Alexander D., eds. Supporting Documents: Transborder Data Flows: Concerns in Privacy Protection & Free Flow of Information, Vol. II. 300p. 1979. pap. 25.00 (ISBN 0-88283-024-4). AFIPS Pr.

ELECTRONIC DATA PROCESSING–AUDITING

Cornick, Delroy L. Auditing in the Electronic Environment: Theory, Practice & Literature. LC 80-81813. 300p. 1980. 19.75 (ISBN 0-912338-23-7); microfiche 14.75. Lomond.

Sardinas, Joseph & Burch, John G. EDP Auditing: A Primer. 200p. 1981. pap. text ed. 10.95 (ISBN 0-471-12305-6). Wiley.

ELECTRONIC DATA PROCESSING–DICTIONARIES

Kelly-Bootle, Stan. The Devil's DP Dictionary. (Illus.). 160p. 1981. 5.95 (ISBN 0-07-034022-6, P&RB). McGraw.

Ross, Ronald G. Data Dictionaries & Data Administration: Concepts & Practices for Data Resource Management. 549p. 1981. 25.95 (ISBN 0-8144-5596-4). Am Mgmt.

ELECTRONIC DATA PROCESSING–STUDY AND TEACHING

Concepts in Business Data Processing: A Student Guide. pap. 7.95 (ISBN 0-13-166413-1); pap. 7.95 issues (ISBN 0-13-093906-4). P-H.

Davis, William S. Computers & Business Information Processing. LC 80-10946. 448p. 1981. pap. text ed. 14.95 (ISBN 0-201-03161-2). A-W.

ELECTRONIC DATA PROCESSING–VOCATIONAL GUIDANCE

Berger, Raymond M. Computer Programmer Job Analysis Reference Text. (Illus.). 195p. 1974. pap. 10.00 (ISBN 0-88283-021-X). AFIPS Pr.

ELECTRONIC DATA PROCESSING DEPARTMENTS–MANAGEMENT

Keen, Jeffrey S. Managing Systems Development. (Information Processing). 320p. 1981. 27.50 (ISBN 0-471-27839-4, Pub. by Wiley-Interscience). Wiley.

Perkinson, Richard C. Handbook of Data Analysis & Data Base Design. 175p. 1981. pap. 29.50 (ISBN 0-89435-045-5). QED Info Sci.

Ross, Ronald G. Data Dictionaries & Data Administration: Concepts & Practices for Data Resource Management. 549p. 1981. 25.95 (ISBN 0-8144-5596-4). Am Mgmt.

Shneiderman, Ben, ed. Database Management Systems. LC 76-41070. (Information Technology Ser.: Vol. I). (Illus.). 137p. 1976. pap. 15.00 (ISBN 0-88283-014-7). AFIPS Pr.

ELECTRONIC DATA PROCESSING DEPARTMENTS–SECURITY MEASURES

Browne, Peter S. Securtiy: Checklist for Computer Center Self-Audits. LC 79-56012. (Illus.). 189p. 1979. pap. 35.00 (ISBN 0-88283-024-4). AFIPS Pr.

Dinardo, C. T., ed. Computers & Security, Vol. III. (The Information Technology Ser.). (Illus.). 247p. 1977. pap. 20.00 (ISBN 0-88283-016-3). AFIPS Pr.

Krauss, Leonard I. SAFE: Security Audit & Field Evaluation for Computer Facilities & Information Systems. 308p. 1981. 29.95 (ISBN 0-8144-5526-3). Am Mgmt.

Parker, Donn. Computer Security Management. 304p. 1981. text ed. 21.95 (ISBN 0-8359-0905-0). Reston.

Perry, William E. Management Guide to Computer Security & Control. (Business Data Processing: a Wiley Ser.). 275p. 1981. 20.95 (ISBN 0-471-05235-3, Pub. by Wiley-Interscience). Wiley.

ELECTRONIC DATA PROCESSING IN PROGRAMMED INSTRUCTION

see Computer-Assisted Instruction

ELECTRONIC DIFFERENTIAL ANALYZERS

Vemuri, V. & Karplus, Walter. Digital Computer Treatment of Partial Differential Equations. (Illus.). 480p. 1981. text ed. 26.50 (ISBN 0-13-212407-6). P-H.

Vichenevetsky, Robert. Computer Methods for Partial Differential Equations: Elliptical Equations & the Finite Element Method, Vol. 1. (Illus.). 400p. 1981. text ed. 28.00 (ISBN 0-686-69327-2). P-H.

ELECTRONIC DIGITAL COMPUTERS

see also Computer-Assisted Instruction; Computer Graphics; Digital Computer Simulation; Minicomputers; Sequential Machine Theory

AFIPS Taxonomy Committee & Ashenhurst, Robert L. Taxonomy of Computer Science & Engineering. LC 79-57474. ix, 462p. 1980. 35.00 (ISBN 0-88283-008-2). AFIPS Pr.

Dunning, Kenneth A. Getting Started in General Purpose Simulation System. LC 80-28281. 117p. (Orig.). 1981. pap. 5.95x (ISBN 0-910554-34-X). Eng Pr.

Hall, Douglas V. & Hall, Marybelle B. Experiments in Microprocessors & Digital Systems. (Illus.). 176p. 1981. 7.95x (ISBN 0-07-025576-8, G). McGraw.

Hogan, Thom. CP-M User's Guide. 350p. (Orig.). 1981. pap. 12.99 (ISBN 0-931988-44-6). Osborne-McGraw.

Isermann, R. & Kaltenecker, H. Digital Computer Applications to Process Control: Proceedings of the Sixth IFAC-IFIP Conference, Dusseldorf, Federal Republic of Germany, 14-17 October 1980. LC 80-41343. (IFAC Proceedings). 550p. 1981. 100.00 (ISBN 0-08-026749-1). Pergamon.

Kroenke, David M. Business Computer Systems: An Introduction. (Illus.). 576p. 1980. 15.95x (ISBN 0-938188-00-3). Mitchell Pub.

Lucas, Jay P. & Adams, Russell E., eds. Personal Computing: Proceedings. (Illus.). viii, 439p. 1979. pap. 12.00 (ISBN 0-88283-020-1). AFIPS Pr.

Lukoff, Herman. From Dits to Bits...a Personal History of the Electronic Computer. LC 79-90567. 200p. 1979. 14.95 (ISBN 0-89661-002-0). Robotics Pr.

Maryanski, Fred J. Digital Computer Simulation. 336p. 1980. 15.95 (ISBN 0-8104-5118-2). Hayden.

Mehlmann, Marilyn. When People Use Computers: An Approach to Developing an Interface. (Ser. in Software). (Illus.). 160p. 1981. text ed. 15.00 (ISBN 0-13-956219-2). P-H.

Olesky, J. & Rutkowski, G. Microprocessors & Digital Computer Technology. 1981. 22.95 (ISBN 0-13-581116-3). P-H.

Press, Larry & Whittaker, Lou, eds. Personal Computing Digest. (Illus.). vi, 211p. 1980. pap. 12.00 (ISBN 0-88283-012-0). AFIPS Pr.

Rutkowski, George B. & Olesky, Jerome E. Microprocessor & Digital Computer Technology. (Illus.). 416p. 1981. text ed. 22.95 (ISBN 0-13-581116-3). P-H.
Subramanyam, B. R., ed. Computer Applications in Large Scale Power Systems: Proceedings of the Symposium, New Delhi, India, 16-19 August 1979, 3 vols. (Illus.). 1100p. 1980. 205.00 (ISBN 0-08-024450-5). Pergamon.
Tomek, Ivan. Introduction to Computer Organization. (Illus.). 200p. 1981. text ed. 21.95 (ISBN 0-914894-08-0). Computer Sci.
Warren, Carl & Miller, Merl. From the Counter to the Bottom Line. LC 79-52263. 225p. 1979. pap. 13.95 (ISBN 0-918398-11-8). Dilithium Pr.
Wicklein, John. Electronic Nightmare: The New Communications & Freedom. LC 80-54199. 320p. 1981. 15.95 (ISBN 0-670-50658-3). Viking Pr.
Willis, Jerry. Peanut Butter & Jelly Guide to Computers. LC 78-70238. 225p. 1978. pap. 8.95 (ISBN 0-918398-13-4). Dilithium Pr.

ELECTRONIC DIGITAL COMPUTERS–CIRCUITS

Bennetts, R. G. Introduction to Digital Board Testing. (Computer Systems Engineering Ser.). 1981. text ed. price not set (ISBN 0-8448-1385-0). Crane-Russak Co.

ELECTRONIC DIGITAL COMPUTERS–DESIGN AND CONSTRUCTION

Bywater, R. Hardware-Software Design of Digital Systems. 1981. 28.00 (ISBN 0-13-383950-8). P-H.
Garside, R. G. The Architecture of Digital Computers. (Oxford Applied Mathematics & Computing Science Ser.). (Illus.). 376p. 1980. text ed. 74.00x (ISBN 0-19-859627-8); pap. text ed. 34.50x (ISBN 0-19-859638-3). Oxford U Pr.

ELECTRONIC DIGITAL COMPUTERS–JUVENILE LITERATURE

D'Ignazio, Fred. Super Games & Projects to Do with Your Home Computer. LC 79-6860. (Illus.). 144p. (gr. 6). 1981. 9.95a (ISBN 0-385-15313-9); PLB (ISBN 0-385-15314-7). Doubleday.

ELECTRONIC DIGITAL COMPUTERS–MEMORY SYSTEMS

see Computer Storage Devices

ELECTRONIC DIGITAL COMPUTERS–PROGRAMMING

see also Computer Programs; Data Base Management also names of specific computers, with or without the subdivision programming

Freeman, Herbert & Lewis, P. M., II, eds. Software Engineering. 1980. 21.00 (ISBN 0-12-267160-0). Acad Pr.
Halpern, M. I., ed. Annual Review in Automatic Programming. (Illus.). 222p. 1980. 55.00 (ISBN 0-08-020242-X). Pergamon.
Riddle, W. E. & Fairley, R. E. Software Development Tools. (Illus.). 280p. 1980. pap. 19.80 (ISBN 0-387-10326-0). Springer-Verlag.
Stevens, Wayne P. Using Structured Design: How to Make Programs Simple, Changeable, Flexible & Reusable. 232p. 1981. 21.95 (ISBN 0-471-08198-1, Pub. by Wiley-Interscience). Wiley.
Weber, J. R. How to Use Your Apple II Computer. LC 80-70465. (IDM's How to Use Your Microcomputer Ser.). 250p. (gr. 10-12). 1981. 19.95 (ISBN 0-938862-02-2); pap. 14.95 (ISBN 0-938862-03-0). Five Arms Corp.
--How to Use Your TRS-80 Model II Computer. LC 80-70467. (IDM's How to Use Your Microcomputer Ser.). 250p. (gr. 10-12). 1981. 19.95 (ISBN 0-938862-00-6); pap. 14.95 (ISBN 0-938862-01-4). Five Arms Corp.

ELECTRONIC EQUIPMENT, MINIATURE

see Miniature Electronic Equipment

ELECTRONIC GAMES

see Electronic Toys

ELECTRONIC MUSIC

see also Computer Music

Griffiths, Paul. A Guide to Electronic Music. 128p. pap. 6.95 (ISBN 0-500-27203-4). Thames Hudson.
Strange, Allen. Electronic Music: Systems, Techniques & Controls. 2nd ed. 1981. pap. text ed. 7.95x (ISBN 0-697-03602-2). Wm C Brown.
Willman. Electronic Music for Young People. write for info. (ISBN 0-87628-210-9). Ctr Appl Res.

ELECTRONIC OFFICE MACHINES

see also Computers; Office Practice

Future Office Systems Market, 2 vols. 493p. 1980. Set. 1000.00 (ISBN 0-686-28894-7, A778). Frost & Sullivan.

ELECTRONIC ORGAN

Norman, Herbert & Norman, H. John. The Organ Today. (Illus.). 224p. 1981. 25.00 (ISBN 0-7153-8053-2). David & Charles.

ELECTRONIC PROBES

see Probes (Electronic Instruments)

ELECTRONIC TOYS

Blumenthal, Howard J. Complete Guide to Electronic Games. 1981. pap. price not set (ISBN 0-452-25268-7, Z5268, Plume). NAL.
Consumer Guide Editors, ed. Complete Book of Video Games. 1977. pap. 1.95. Warner Bks.

ELECTRONIC WARFARE

see Electronics in Military Engineering

ELECTRONIC WORK FUNCTION

see Electrons–Emission

ELECTRONICS

see also Cybernetics; Electronic Apparatus and Appliances; Electronic Circuits; Electronics in Biology; Electronics in Military Engineering; High-Fidelity Sound Systems; Industrial Electronics; Microelectronics; Microwaves; Miniature Electronic Equipment; Semiconductors

Beards, Peter. Electronics: Level II. (Illus.). 192p. 1980. pap. text ed. 12.95x (ISBN 0-7121-0581-6). Intl Ideas.
Bolton, W. Electronic Systems, Bk. 8. LC 80-41394. (Study Topics in Physics Ser.). 96p. 1980. pap. text ed. write for info. (ISBN 0-408-10659-X). Butterworths.
DeGuilmo, Joseph M. Electricity-Electronics: Principles & Applications. LC 79-54909. (Electronics Technology Ser.). (Illus.). 672p. (Orig.). 1981. pap. 19.60 (ISBN 0-8273-1686-0); price not set instr's. guide (ISBN 0-8273-1687-9). Delmar.
Electronics Magazine Editors. An Age of Innovation: The World of Electronics, 1930-2000. LC 80-14816. (Illus.). 274p. 1980. text ed. 18.50 (ISBN 0-07-606688-6, R-013). McGraw.
Gerrish, H. & Dugger, W., Jr. Exploring Electricity & Electronics: Basic Fundamentals. rev. ed. LC 80-20830. (Illus.). 208p. 1981. text ed. 9.96 (ISBN 0-87006-308-1). Goodheart.
Grossman, Morris. For-Hhundred Ideas for Ddesign, Vol.4. 376p. 1980. 13.95 (ISBN 0-8104-0950-X). Hayden.
Hardy, James. Communications Electronics. 1981. text ed. 18.95 (ISBN 0-8359-0892-5); instr's. manual free (ISBN 0-8359-0893-3). Reston.
Knight, S. A. Electronics for Technicians Three. (Newnes-Butterworth Technical Ser.). (Illus.). 192p. 1980. pap. text ed. 15.95 (ISBN 0-408-00458-4). Butterworths.
Kyriacou, Demetrios. Basics of Electrooranic Synthesis. 230p. 1980. 24.50 (ISBN 0-471-07975-8, Pub. by Wiley-Interscience). Wiley.
McWane, John W. Introduction to Electronics & Instrumentation. 1981. text ed. 19.95 (ISBN 0-534-00938-7, Breton Pubs). Wadsworth Pub.
Marton, C. & Harmuth, H. F., eds. Advances in Electronics & Electron Physics, Supplement 14: Nonsinusoidal Waves for Radar & Radio Communication. (Serial Publication Ser.). 1981. write for info. (ISBN 0-12-014575-8). Acad Pr.
Marton, L. & Marton, Claire, eds. Advances in Electronic & Electron Physics, Vol. 55. (Serial Publication). 1981. 47.50 (ISBN 0-12-014655-X); lib. bdg. 62.00 (ISBN 0-12-014710-6); microfiche ed. 33.50 (ISBN 0-12-014711-4). Acad Pr.
Sprott, Julien C. Introduction to Modern Electronics. 512p. 1981. text ed. 22.95 (ISBN 0-471-05840-8). Wiley.

ELECTRONICS–APPARATUS AND APPLIANCES

see Electronic Apparatus and Appliances

ELECTRONICS–DICTIONARIES

Amos, S. W. Dictionary of Electronics. 1981. text ed. price not set (ISBN 0-408-00331-6, Newnes-Butterworth). Butterworth.
Oppermann, Alfred, ed. Dictionary of Electronics: English-German. 692p. 1980. 120.00 (ISBN 3-598-10312-3, Dist. by Gale Research Co.). K G Saur.

ELECTRONICS–HANDBOOKS, MANUALS, ETC.

Fredericksen, Thomas M. Intuitive IC Electronics: A Sophisticated Primer for Engineers & Technicians. (Illus.). 208p. 1981. 18.50 (ISBN 0-07-021923-0, P&RB). McGraw.

ELECTRONICS–LABORATORY MANUALS

Patrick, Dale & Dugger, William E., Jr. Electricity & Electronics Laboratory Manual. rev. ed. (Illus.). 372p. (gr. 7 up). 1980. 4.96. Goodheart.
Wells, Andy J. Audio Servicing: Text/Lab Manual. 1st ed. (Illus.). 144p. 9.95 (ISBN 0-07-069247-5). McGraw.

ELECTRONICS IN BIOLOGY

Office of Technology Assessment. Energy from Biological Processes. 205p. 1981. lib. bdg. 34.50 (ISBN 0-89934-090-3); pap. 22.50 (ISBN 0-89934-107-1). Solar Energy Info.

ELECTRONICS IN INDUSTRY

see Industrial Electronics

ELECTRONICS IN MILITARY ENGINEERING

The Directory of Defense Electronic Products & Services: U. S. Suppliers, 1981. rev. 7th ed. 228p. pap. write for info. (ISBN 0-931634-06-7). Info Clearing House.

ELECTRONS

see also Electromagnetic Theory; Electron Paramagnetic Resonance; Electronics; Ions; Neutrons; Photoelectricity; Plasma (Ionized Gases); Protons; Spin-Lattice Relaxation

Marton, L. & Marton, Claire, eds. Advances in Electronic & Electron Physics, Vol. 55. (Serial Publication). 1981. 47.50 (ISBN 0-12-014655-X); lib. bdg. 62.00 (ISBN 0-12-014710-6); microfiche ed. 33.50 (ISBN 0-12-014711-4). Acad Pr.

ELECTRONS–EMISSION

see also Electron Spectroscopy; Photoelectricity; Thermionic Emission

Zuppinger, A., et al, eds. High Energy Electrons in Radiation Therapy. (Illus.). 130p. 1980. pap. 28.40 (ISBN 0-387-10188-8). Springer-Verlag.

ELECTROPHONIC MUSIC

see Electronic Music

ELECTROPHORESIS

Gel Electrophoresis: A Practical Approach. 1980. write for info. Info Retrieval.

ELECTROPHYSIOLOGY

see also Electroencephalography; Muscle; Nerves

Cronin. Mathematics of Cell Electrophysiology. 144p. 1981. 19.75 (ISBN 0-8247-1157-2). Dekker.
Electrical Events Associated with Primary Photosynthetic Reactions in Chloroplast Membranes. (Agricultural Research Reports Ser.: No. 905). 86p. 1981. pap. 16.75 (ISBN 90-220-0756-1, PDC 218, Pudoc). Unipub.
Proceedings of a Workshop, Palo Alto, California, July 1979, et al. Conduction Velocity Distributions: A Population Approach to Electrophysiology of Nerve. Dorfman, Leslie J. & Cummins, Kenneth L., eds. (Progress in Clinical & Biological Research Ser.: No. 52). 338p. 1981. 30.00x (ISBN 0-8451-0052-1). A R Liss.
Schoffeniels, E. & Neumann, E., eds. Molecular Aspects of Bioelectricity: Proceedings of the Symposium in Honour of David Nachmansohn, Liege, May 19-20, 1980. (Illus.). 360p. 1980. 72.00 (ISBN 0-08-026371-2). Pergamon.

ELECTROSTATIC PRECIPITATION

Katz, Jacob. The Art of Electrostatic Precipitation. (Illus.). 350p. 1980. text ed. 45.00x (ISBN 0-9603986-1-9). Scholium Intl.

ELEMENTARY EDUCATION

see Education, Elementary

ELEMENTARY PARTICLES (PHYSICS)

see Particles (Nuclear Physics)

ELEMENTS, CHEMICAL

see Chemical Elements

ELEPHANTS

Freeman, Dan. Elephants: The Vanishing Giants. (Illus.). 192p. 1981. 20.00 (ISBN 0-399-12567-1). Putnam.

ELEPHANTS–JUVENILE LITERATURE

Overbeck, Cynthia. Elephants. (Lerner Natural Science Bks.). (Illus.). (gr. 4-9). 1981. PLB 7.95 (ISBN 0-8225-1452-4). Lerner Pubns.
Wildlife Education, Ltd. Elephants. (Zoobooks). (Illus.). 20p. (Orig.). 1980. pap. 1.00 (ISBN 0-937934-00-3). Wildlife Educ.

ELEVATED TEMPERATURES

see High Temperatures

ELIADE, MIRCEA, 1907-

Eliade, Mircea. Autobiography: Volume I, Journey East, Journey West 1907-1937. LC 80-8357. 352p. 1981. 17.50 (ISBN 0-06-065227-6, HarpR). Har-Row.

ELIOT, GEORGE, PSEUD., I.E. MARIAN EVANS, AFTERWARDS CROSS, 1819-1880

Baker, William. Some George Eliot Notebooks: An Edition of the Carl H. Pforzheimer Library's George Eliot Ecolgrph Notebooks Mss 707, 708, 709, 710, Vol.iII-711. (Romantic Reassessment Ser.: No.46). 267p. 1980. pap. text ed. 25.00 (ISBN 0-391-01309-2). Humanities.
Buono, Dello & Joseph, Carmen. Rare Early Essays on George Eliot. 211p. 1980. lib. bdg. 25.00 (ISBN 0-8482-3660-2). R West.
Deakin, Mary H. The Early Life of George Eliot. 188p. 1980. Repr. of 1913 ed. lib. bdg. 30.00 (ISBN 0-8495-1121-6). Arden Lib.
Dello Buono, Carmen J. Rare Early Essays on George Eliot. 202p. 1980. lib. bdg. 25.00 (ISBN 0-8482-3661-0). Norwood Edns.
Wiesenfarth, Joseph. George Eliot: A Writer's Notebook, 1854-1879, Collected Writings. LC 80-23271. Date not set. write for info. (ISBN 0-8139-0887-6). U Pr of Va.

ELIOT, GEORGE, PSEUD., I.E. MARIAN EVANS, AFTERWARDS CROSS, 1819-1880–BIBLIOGRAPHY

Muir, Percival N. A Bibliography of the First Editions of Books by George Eliot (Mary Ann Evans) (1819-1880) 52p. 1980. Repr. of 1927 ed. lib. bdg. 10.00 (ISBN 0-8492-6833-8). R West.

ELIOT, THOMAS STEARNS, 1888-1965

Lobb, Edward. T. S. Eliot & the Romantic Critical Tradition. 208p. 1981. 20.00 (ISBN 0-7100-0636-5). Routledge & Kegan.
Rajnath. T. S. Eliot's Theory of Poetry. 1980. text ed. 12.50x (ISBN 0-391-01755-1). Humanities.

ELIZABETH, QUEEN OF ENGLAND, 1533-1603

Abbott, Jacob. History of Elizabeth, Queen of England. 252p. 1980. Repr. lib. bdg. 20.00 (ISBN 0-8492-3226-0). R West.
Smith, Lacey B. Elizabeth I. LC 79-54031. (Problems in Civilization Ser.). (Orig.). 1980. pap. text ed. 3.95x (ISBN 0-88273-407-5). Forum Pr MO.

ELIZABETH, QUEEN OF ENGLAND, 1533-1603–DRAMA

Boas, Frederick S. Queen Elizabeth in Drama & Related Studies. 212p. 1980. Repr. lib. bdg. 25.00 (ISBN 0-8492-3588-X). R West.

ELK

Krakel, Dean, II. Season of the Elk. LC 75-42982. (Illus.). 128p. 1980. 20.00 (ISBN 0-913504-28-9); pap. 12.95 (ISBN 0-913504-29-7). Lowell Pr.

ELLINGTON, DUKE, 1899-1974

Dance, Stanley. The World of Duke Ellington. (Da Capo Quality Paperbacks Ser.). xii, 311p. pap. 7.95 (ISBN 0-306-80136-1). Da Capo.
Ellington, Mercer & Dance, Stanley. Duke Ellington in Person. 236p. pap. 5.95 (ISBN 0-306-80104-3). Da Capo.

ELMORAN

see Masai

ELOCUTION

see also Acting; Debates and Debating; Lectures and Lecturing; Oratory; Preaching; Public Speaking; Readers; Voice

Philip, D. Frank. Manual of Elocution for the Ministry. 122p. Repr. of 1948 ed. text ed. 3.50 (ISBN 0-567-02207-2). Attic Pr.

ELVES

see Fairies

ELYOT, THOMAS, SIR, 1490-1546

Dees, Jerome S. Sir Thomas Elyot & Roger Ascham: A Reference Guide. (Reference Books Ser.). 1981. 25.00 (ISBN 0-8161-8353-8). G K Hall.

EMANCIPATION OF SLAVES

see Slavery–Emancipation

EMANCIPATION OF WOMEN

see Women's Rights

EMBEZZLEMENT

McCullough, William W. Sticky Fingers: A Close Look at Embezzlement---America's Fastest Growing Crime. 259p. 1981. 10.95 (ISBN 0-8144-5688-X). Am Mgmt.

EMBLEMS

see also Christian Art and Symbolism; Heraldry; Seals (Numismatics); Symbolism

Stiling, Marjorie. Famous Brand Names, Emblems and Trademarks. LC 80-69353. (Illus.). 64p. 1981. 8.95 (ISBN 0-7153-8098-2). David & Charles.

EMBROIDERY

see also Canvas Embroidery; Fabric Pictures; Needlework; Samplers; Smocking

Gross, Nancy D. & Fontana, Frank. Shishi Embroidery: Traditional Mirrorwork of India, Pakistan & Afghanistan. (Illus.). 80p. (Orig.). Date not set. pap. price not set (ISBN 0-486-24043-6). Dover.
Haraszty, Eszter. The Embroiderer's Portfolio of Flower Designs. (Illus.). 1981. 22.95 (ISBN 0-87140-643-8). Liveright.
Klimova, Nina T. Folk Embroidery of the USSR. 152p. 1981. 19.95 (ISBN 0-442-24464-9). Van Nos Reinhold.
Messent, Jan. Embroidery & Nature. (Illus.). 168p. 1980. 22.75 (ISBN 0-8231-4258-2). Branford.
Ness, Pamela M. Assissi Embroidery. (Illus.). 1978. pap. 1.75 (ISBN 0-486-23743-5). Dover.
Ondori Staff. A Treasury of Embroidery Samples. LC 80-84416. (Illus.). 96p. 1981. pap. 5.95 (ISBN 0-87040-496-2). Japan Pubns.

EMBROIDERY, INDIAN

see Indians of North America–Art

EMBRYOLOGY

see also Cells; Developmental Biology; Fetus; Genetics; Morphogenesis; Reproduction

Carlson, Bruce M. Patten's Foundations of Embryology. 4th, rev. ed. (Organismal Biology Ser.). (Illus.). 608p. 1981. text ed. 21.95 (ISBN 0-07-009875-1, C). McGraw.
Langman, Jan. Medical Embryology. 4th ed. 328p. 1981. write for info. (4858-9). Williams & Wilkins.
Roe, Shirley A. Matter, Life & Generation: Eighteenth Century Embryology & the Haller-Wolff Debate. LC 80-19611. (Illus.). 216p. Date not set. price not set (ISBN 0-521-23540-5). Cambridge U Pr.
Sandler. Amniotic Fluid & Its Clinical Significance. Date not set. price not set (ISBN 0-8247-1346-X). Dekker.

EMBRYOLOGY–BIRDS

Rager, G. The Development of Retinotectal Projection in the Chicken. (Advances in Anatomy, Embryology & Cell Biology: Vol. 63). (Illus.). 92p. 1980. pap. 30.70 (ISBN 0-387-10121-7). Springer-Verlag.

EMBRYOLOGY–FISHES

Selected Bibliography on Pelagic Fish Egg & Larva Surveys. (FAO Fisheries Circular: No. 706). 97p. 1980. pap. 6.00 (ISBN 0-686-68187-8, F2023, FAO). Unipub.

EMBRYOLOGY–INSECTS

Hinton, H. E. Biology of Insect Eggs, 3 vols. LC 77-30390. (Illus.). 1500p. 1980. Set. 350.00 (ISBN 0-08-021539-4). Pergamon.

EMERGENCIES

see Accidents; First Aid in Illness and Injury; Medical Emergencies

EMERGENCIES, ASSISTANCE IN

see Assistance in Emergencies

EMERGENCY MEDICAL SERVICES

Brennan, William T. & Crowe, James W. Guide to Problems & Practices in First Aid & Emergency Care. 4th ed. 192p. 1981. wire coil 7.95x (ISBN 0-697-07390-4). Wm C Brown.
Chayet, Neil L. Legal Implications of Emergency Care. 1981. pap. 12.50 (ISBN 0-686-69605-0). ACC.
Eckert, Charles. Emergency-Room Care. 4th ed. 1981. text ed. price not set; pap. text ed. price not set. Little.
Hafen, Brent Q. & Karren, Keith J. Prehospital Emergency Care & Crisis Intervention. 570p. 1981. pap. 13.95x (ISBN 0-89582-057-9); wkbk. 5.95x (ISBN 0-89582-058-7); text & wkbk. 17.00x. Morton Pub.
Huszar, Robert S. Emergency Cardiac Care. 2nd ed. (Illus.). 350p. 1981. pap. text ed. 14.95 (ISBN 0-87619-863-9). R J Brady.

McRae, James T. Emergency Medicine Case Studies. LC 79-88721. 1979. pap. 15.50 (ISBN 0-87488-002-5). Med Exam.
McSwain, Norman, Jr. & Skelton, Mary B. Surgical Procedures in Emergency Medicine. 300p. 1982. text ed. 29.95 (ISBN 0-8359-7394-8). Reston.
Mannon, James M. Emergency Encounters: A Study of an Urban Ambulance Service. (National University Publications, Sociology of Medicine Ser.). 1981. 15.00 (ISBN 0-8046-9281-5). Kennikat.
Meislin, Harvey W. & Dresnick, Stephen J. Skills & Procedures of Emergency & General Medicine. 250p. 1982. text ed. 29.95 (ISBN 0-8359-7009-4). Reston.
Springer, Llewellyn W. Emergency Treatment of Accute Respiratory Disease. 3rd ed. (Illus.). 180p. 1981. pap. text ed. 11.95 (ISBN 0-87619-862-0). R J Brady.
Sternbach, George, ed. The Organization & Administration of Emergency Medical Care. LC 78-74611. 117p. 1979. 9.50 (ISBN 0-87762-269-8). Technomic.
Wasserberger, Jonathan & Eubanks, David. Paramedic Procedures. 2nd ed. (Illus.). 284p. 1981. pap. text ed. 12.95 (ISBN 0-8016-5353-3). Mosby.

EMERGENCY NURSING

McRae, James T. Emergency Medicine Case Studies. LC 79-88721. 1979. pap. 15.50 (ISBN 0-87488-002-5). Med Exam.

EMERGENCY POWERS

see Executive Power

EMERGENCY RELIEF

see Disaster Relief

EMERSON, RALPH WALDO, 1803-1882

Berry, Edmund G. Emerson's Plutarch. LC 80-2525. 1981. Repr. of 1961 ed. 37.00 (ISBN 0-404-19250-5). AMS Pr.
Bishop, Jonathan. Emerson on the Soul. LC 80-2527. 1981. Repr. of 1964 ed. 29.50 (ISBN 0-404-19251-3). AMS Pr.
Brooks, Van Wyck. The Life of Emerson. LC 80-2528. 1981. Repr. of 1932 ed. 37.00 (ISBN 0-404-19252-1). AMS Pr.
Cameron, Kenneth W. Emerson the Essayist: An Outline of His Philosophical Development Through 1836. 2 vols. LC 80-2529. 1981. Repr. of 1945 ed. Set. 92.00 (ISBN 0-404-19280-7). Vol. 1 (ISBN 0-404-19281-5). Vol. 2 (ISBN 0-404-19282-3). AMS Pr.
Cheyfitz, Eric. The Trans-Parent: Sexual Politics in the Lanuage of Emerson. LC 80-25750. 224p. 1981. text ed. 13.50 (ISBN 0-8018-2450-8). Johns Hopkins.
Dillaway, Newton. Prophet of America: Emerson & the Problems of Today. LC 80-2530. 1981. Repr. of 1936 ed. 44.50 (ISBN 0-404-19254-8). AMS Pr.
The Emerson Centenary. LC 80-2531. (AMS Anthology Ser.). 1981. 49.50 (ISBN 0-404-19256-4). AMS Pr.
Emerson: The Nineteenth Century. LC 80-2541. (AMS Anthology Ser.). 1981. 57.50 (ISBN 0-404-19257-2). AMS Pr.
Emerson: The Twentieth Century. LC 80-2547. 1981. 57.50 (ISBN 0-404-19273-4). AMS Pr.
Firkins, Oscar W. Ralph Waldo Emerson. LC 80-2532. 1981. Repr. of 1915 ed. 44.50 (ISBN 0-404-19258-0). AMS Pr.
Gay, Robert M. Emerson: A Study of the Poet As Seer. LC 80-2533. 1981. Repr. of 1928 ed. 32.75 (ISBN 0-404-19259-9). AMS Pr.
Goren, Leyla. Elements of Brahmanism in the Transcendentalism of Emerson. LC 80-2534. 1981. Repr. of 1959 ed. 18.50 (ISBN 0-404-19260-2). AMS Pr.
Harding, Walter R. Emerson's Library. LC 80-2535. 1981. Repr. of 1967 ed. 37.50 (ISBN 0-404-19261-0). AMS Pr.
Harrison, John S. The Teachers of Emerson. LC 80-2536. 1981. Repr. of 1910 ed. 37.00 (ISBN 0-404-19263-7). AMS Pr.
Holmes, Oliver W. Ralph Waldo Emerson. LC 80-23687. (American Men & Women of Letters Ser.). 330p. 1981. pap. 5.95 (ISBN 0-87754-157-4). Chelsea Hse.
Hopkins, Vivian C. Spires of Forms: A Study of Emerson's Aesthetic Theory. LC 80-2537. 1981. Repr. of 1951 ed. 33.50 (ISBN 0-404-19263-7). AMS Pr.
Hubbard, Stanley. Nietzche und Emerson. LC 80-2538. 1981. Repr. of 1958 ed. 25.50 (ISBN 0-404-19264-5). AMS Pr.
Malloy, Charles. The Poems of Emerson: Selected Criticism from the Coming Age & the Arena, 1899-1905. LC 80-2539. 1981. 32.50 (ISBN 0-404-19265-3). AMS Pr.
Nicoloff, Philip L. Emerson on Race & History: An Examination of English Traits. LC 80-2540. 1981. Repr. of 1961 ed. 33.50 (ISBN 0-404-19266-1). AMS Pr.
Paul, Sherman. Emerson's Angle of Vision: Man & Nature in American Experience. LC 80-2542. 1981. Repr. of 1952 ed. 33.50 (ISBN 0-404-19267-X). AMS Pr.
Perry, Bliss, ed. The Heart of Emerson's Journals. 357p. 1980. Repr. of 1926 ed. lib. bdg. 30.00 (ISBN 0-89987-670-6). Darby Bks.
Porte, Joel. Emerson & Thoreau: Transcendentalists in Conflict. LC 80-2512. 1981. Repr. of 1966 ed. 29.50 (ISBN 0-404-19060-X). AMS Pr.
Ramakrishna, Rao V. Emerson, His Muse & Message. 312p. 1980. lib. bdg. 35.00 (ISBN 0-8482-5869-X). Norwood Edns.
Rao, Adapa R. Emerson & Social Reform. 132p. 1981. text ed. 10.25 (ISBN 0-391-02199-0). Humanities.
Reminiscences of Emerson: An AMS Anthology. LC 80-2543. 1981. 57.50 (ISBN 0-404-19268-8). AMS Pr.
Russell, Phillips. Emerson, the Wisest American. LC 80-2544. 1981. Repr. of 1929 ed. 37.00 (ISBN 0-404-19269-6). AMS Pr.
Scudder, Townshend. The Lonely Wayfaring Man: Emerson & Some Englishmen. LC 80-2545. 1981. Repr. of 1936 ed. 32.50 (ISBN 0-404-19270-X). AMS Pr.
Simon, Julius. Ralph Waldo Emerson in Deutschland: 1851-1932. LC 80-2546. (Ger.). 1981. Repr. of 1936 ed. 25.50 (ISBN 0-404-19271-8). AMS Pr.
Wahr, Frederick B. Emerson & Goethe. 197p. 1980. Repr. of 1915 ed. lib. bdg. 25.00 (ISBN 0-8492-2979-0). R West.
Wynkoop, William M. Three Children of the Universe: Emerson's Views of Shakespeare, Bacon, & Milton. LC 80-2548. 1981. Repr. of 1966 ed. 25.50 (ISBN 0-404-19272-6). AMS Pr.
Zink, Harriet R. Emerson's Use of the Bible. 75p. 1980. Repr. of 1935 ed. lib. bdg. 15.00 (ISBN 0-8495-6206-6). Arden Lib.

EMERSON, RALPH WALDO, 1803-1882–BIBLIOGRAPHY

Bryer, J. R. & Rees, R. A., eds. Emerson Bibliographies. LC 80-2526. (AMS Anthology Ser.). 1981. 34.50 (ISBN 0-404-19255-6). AMS Pr.

EMIGRATION AND IMMIGRATION

see also Agricultural Colonies; Aliens; Anthropo-Geography; Colonization; Man–Migrations; Migration, Internal; Naturalization; Refugees
also subdivision Emigration and Immigration under names of countries; and names of special nationalities, e.g. Americans in Foreign Countries, British in Asia

Austin, Aleine. Matthew Lyon: "New Man" of the Democratic Revolution, 1749-1822. LC 80-281. (Illus.). 208p. 1980. 16.50x (ISBN 0-271-00262-X). Pa St U Pr.
Jones, Catherine. Immigration & Social Policy in Britain. 275p. 1977. pap. 9.95 (ISBN 0-422-74680-0, 6363). Methuen Inc.
National Lawyers Guild. Immigration & Defense. 2nd ed. LC 79-9735. 1979. 60.00 (ISBN 0-87632-109-0). Boardman.

EMIGRATION AND IMMIGRATION LAW

Chaplin, Stewart. Suspension of the Power of Alienation, & Postponement of Vesting, Under the Laws of New York, Mich Igan, Minnesota & Wisconsin. xxxix, 370p. 1981. Repr. of 1891 ed. lib. bdg. 30.00x (ISBN 0-8377-0428-6). Rothman.
Williams, Rod. How to Immigrate Without a Lawyer. 200p. 1980. pap. 19.95 (ISBN 0-89260-198-1). Hwong Pub.

EMIN PASHA RELIEF EXPEDITION, 1887-1889

Walters, Alphonse J. Stanleys Emin Pasha Expedition. LC 80-1910. (Illus.). 1981. Repr. of 1890 ed. 43.00 (ISBN 0-404-18988-1). AMS Pr.

EMINENT DOMAIN

see also Government Liability

Friedman, Samy. Expropriation in International Law. rev. ed. Jackson, Ivor C., tr. from Fr. LC 80-26295. (The Library of World Affairs: No. 20). 236p. 1981. Repr. of 1953 ed. lib. bdg. 29.75x (ISBN 0-313-20840-9, FREI). Greenwood.

EMISSION, THERMIONIC

see Thermionic Emission

EMISSION OF ELECTRONS

see Electrons–Emission

EMOTIONAL HEALTH

see Mental Health

EMOTIONAL MATURITY

Clemens, David A. Living, Vol. 3. LC 79-55503. (Steps to Maturity Ser.). 1980. tchrs' manual 14.95 (ISBN 0-86508-006-2); students' manual 12.50 (ISBN 0-86508-005-4). BCM Inc.
Derenski, Arlene & Landsburg, Sally. Older Women - Younger Men. 272p. 1981. 11.95 (ISBN 0-316-51366-0). Little.

EMOTIONAL STRESS

see Stress (Psychology)

EMOTIONALLY DISTURBED CHILDREN

see Mentally Ill Children; Problem Children

EMOTIONS

see also Anger; Anxiety; Attitude (Psychology); Belief and Doubt; Control (Psychology); Emotional Maturity; Empathy; Fear; Frustration; Grief; Joy and Sorrow; Love; Pain; Prejudices and Antipathies; Rigidity (Psychology); Sympathy; Temperament; Transference (Psychology); Worry

Ainsworth, Stanley. Positive Emotional Power: How to Manage Your Feelings. (Illus.). 256p. 1981. 12.95 (ISBN 0-13-687616-1); pap. 6.95 (ISBN 0-686-69330-2). P-H.
Bain, Alexander. Emotions & the Will. (Contributions to the History of Psychology Ser.: No. 5, Pt. a: Orientations). 1978. Repr. of 1859 ed. 30.00 (ISBN 0-89093-154-2). U Pubns Amer.
Lutzer, Erwin. Managing Your Emotions. LC 80-69311. 128p. 1981. 7.95 (ISBN 0-915684-81-0). Christian Herald.
Mehrabian, Albert. Silent Messages: Implicit Communication of Emotions & Attitudes. 2nd ed. 208p. 1980. pap. text ed. 8.95x (ISBN 0-534-00910-7). Wadsworth Pub.
Prescott, Daniel A. Emotion & the Educative Process: A Report of the Committee on the Relation of Emotion to the Educative Process. 323p. 1980. Repr. of 1938 ed. lib. bdg. 25.00 (ISBN 0-89760-707-4). Telegraph Bks.
Seamands, David A. Healing of Our Damaged Emotions. 1981. pap. 3.95 (ISBN 0-88207-228-5). Victor Bks.
Unger, Carl. Trails of Thinking, Feeling & Willing. 1980. pap. 3.00 (ISBN 0-916786-47-1). St George Bk Serv.

EMPATHY

Moncure, Jane B. Caring. rev. ed. LC 80-27506. (What Is It? Ser.). (Illus.). (gr. k-3). 1981. PLB 5.50 (ISBN 0-89565-201-3). Childs World.

EMPEDOCLES, fl. 490-430 B.C.

Wright, M. R., ed. Empedocles - the Extant Fragments. LC 80-17923. 416p. 1981. text ed. 45.00 (ISBN 0-300-02475-4). Yale U Pr.

EMPLOYEE BENEFITS

see Non-Wage Payments

EMPLOYEE-EMPLOYER RELATIONS

see Industrial Relations

EMPLOYEE OWNERSHIP

Abrahamsson, Bengt & Brostrom, Anders. The Rights of Labor. LC 80-16233. 301p. 25.00 (ISBN 0-8039-1477-6). Sage.

EMPLOYEES, RATING OF

see also Performance Standards

Watling, Tom. Plan for Promotion: Advancement & the Manager. 237p. 1977. text ed. 19.75x (ISBN 0-220-66327-0, Pub. by Busn Bks England). Renouf.

EMPLOYEES, RECRUITING OF

see Recruiting of Employees

EMPLOYEES, SUPERVISION OF

see Supervision of Employees

EMPLOYEES, TRAINING OF

Here are entered works on the training of employees on the job. Works on retraining persons with obsolete vocational skills are entered under Occupational Retraining. Works on vocational instruction within the standard educational system are entered under Vocational Education. Works on the vocationally oriented process of endowing people with a skill after either completion or termination of their formal education are entered under Occupational Training.
see also Apprentices; Executives, Training Of; Technical Education

Aboud, Grace. Hiring & Training the Disadvantaged for Public Employment. (Key Issues Ser.: No. 11). 1973. pap. 2.00 (ISBN 0-87546-202-2). NY Sch Indus Rel.
Gardner, James E. Training Interventions in Job Skill Development. LC 80-23810. (Illus.). 224p. 1981. text ed. 12.95 (ISBN 0-201-03097-7). A-W.

EMPLOYEES, TRANSFER OF

Here are entered works on the transfer of employees from one department or position to another within the same company, within the same geographical location.

Gruenfeld, Elaine F. Promoton: Practices, Policies, & Affirmative Action. (Key Issues Ser.: No. 17). 1975. pap. 3.00 (ISBN 0-87546-222-7). NY Sch Indus Rel.

EMPLOYEES' REPRESENTATION IN MANAGEMENT–GERMANY

Thimm, Alfred L. The False Promise of Codetermination. LC 80-8422. 288p. 1980. 27.95x (ISBN 0-669-04108-4). Lexington Bks.

EMPLOYER-EMPLOYEE RELATIONS

see Industrial Relations

EMPLOYERS' LIABILITY

see also Industrial Accidents; Occupational Diseases; Workmen's Compensation

Janner, Greville. Janner's Product Liability. 405p. 1979. text ed. 36.75x (ISBN 0-220-67008-0, Pub. by Busn Bks England). Renouf.

EMPLOYMENT (ECONOMIC THEORY)

see also Job Vacancies; Manpower Policy

Creedy. The Economics of Unemployment in Britain. 1981. text ed. price not set (ISBN 0-408-10703-0). Butterworth.
Malinvaud, Edmond & Fitouss, Jean-Paul, eds. Unemployment in Western Countries. LC 79-29710. 560p. 1980. 40.00 (ISBN 0-312-83268-0). St Martin.
Pepitone-Rockwell, Fran, ed. Dual Career Couples. LC 80-15747. (Sage Focus Editions Ser.: Vol. 24). (Illus.). 294p. 1980. 18.95 (ISBN 0-8039-1436-9); pap. 9.95x (ISBN 0-8039-1437-7). Sage.
Ridker, Ronald. Employment in South Asia: Problems, Prospects & Prescriptions. (Occasional Papers: No. 1). 74p. 1971. 1.00 (ISBN 0-686-28697-9). Overseas Dev Council.

EMPLOYMENT, SUPPLEMENTARY

see Supplementary Employment

EMPLOYMENT AND AGE

see Age and Employment

EMPLOYMENT AND ALCOHOLISM

see Alcoholism and Employment

EMPLOYMENT DISCRIMINATION

see Discrimination in Employment

EMPLOYMENT INTERVIEWING

Coghill, Mary A. Lie Detector in Employment. (Key Issues Ser.: No. 2). 1973. pap. 2.00 (ISBN 0-87546-208-1). NY Sch Indus Rel.
Fraser, John M. Employment Interviewing. 5th ed. (Illus.). 224p. 1978. pap. 13.95 (ISBN 0-7121-0570-0, Pub. by Macdonald & Evans England). Intl Ideas.
Goodworth, C. T. Effective Interviewing for Employment Selection. 138p. 1979. text ed. 22.00x (ISBN 0-220-67005-6, Pub. by Busn Bks England). Renouf.
McQuaig, Jack, et al. How to Interview & Hire Productive People. LC 80-70952. 204p. 1981. 9.95 (ISBN 0-8119-0332-X). Fell.

EMPLOYMENT MANAGEMENT

see Personnel Management

EMPLOYMENT OF CHILDREN

see Children–Employment

EMPLOYMENT OF WOMEN

see Women–Employment

EMPLOYMENT OF YOUTH

see Youth–Employment

EMPLOYMENT TESTS

Manese, Wilfredo R. Employment Testing, Validation & the Law: A Primer. 213p. 1979. 55.00 (ISBN 0-9604586-0-3). EGM Ent.
Rosen, Doris B. Employment Testing & Minority Groups. (Key Issues Ser.: No. 6). 1970. pap. 2.00 (ISBN 0-87546-239-1). NY Sch Indus Rel.
Wiener, Solomon. The College Graduate Guide for Scoring High on Employment Tests. 160p. (Orig.). 1981. pap. 4.95 (ISBN 0-686-69227-6). Monarch Pr.

EMULSIONS

Influence of Fat Crystals in the Oil Phase of Stability of Oil-in-Water Emulsions. (Agricultural Research Report: No. 901). 1981. pap. 18.75 (ISBN 0-686-69540-2, PDC 216, Pudoc). Unipub.

ENAMEL PAINTS

see Paint

ENCEPHALITIS

Monath, Thomas P., ed. St Louis Encephalitis. LC 79-53721. (Illus.). 700p. 1980. text ed. 20.00x (ISBN 0-87553-090-7). Am Pub Health.

ENCEPHALOGRAPHY

see Electroencephalography

ENCULTURATION

see Socialization

ENCYCLOPEDIAS AND DICTIONARIES

Encyclopedias and dictionaries of a particular subject are entered under the subject with subdivisions Dictionaries, Dictionaries, Juvenile or, in the case of countries, cities, etc. or ethnic groups, dictionaries and encyclopedias e.g. Botany–Dictionaries; Catholic Church–Dictionaries Juvenile.
see also Handbooks, Vade-Mecums, etc.; Questions and Answers
also particular subjects with or without the subdivision Dictionaries

Algemene Winkler Prins Encyclopedie, 14 vols. (Dutch.). 1975-1977. 725.00 set. Pergamon.
Allgemeine Enzyclopaedie der Wissenschaften und Kuste (Ersch-Gruber, 167 vols. (Ger.). 1969. Set. write for info. Pergamon.
Beebe, Brooke M. & Rosenblatt, Ruth Y. The Dictionary. LC 77-730283. (Illus.). (gr. 3-5). 1977. pap. text ed. 64.00 (ISBN 0-89290-121-7, A151-SAR). Soc for Visual.
Cayne, Bernard S., ed. Encyclopedia Americana, 30 vols. LC 80-84517. (Illus.). 1981. write for info. (ISBN 0-7172-0112-0). Grolier Ed Corp.
Diccionario Enciclopedico Espasa, 12 vols. (Span.). 1978. Set. 165.00. Pergamon.
Diccionario Enciclopedico Illustrado Sopena, 5 vols. (Span.). 1978. Set. 425.00. Pergamon.
Enciclopedia Hoepli, 14 vols. (Ital.). 1976. Set. 550.00. Pergamon.
Enciclopedia Powszechna, 4 vols. (Pol.). 1973-1976. Set. 180.00. Pergamon.
Gascoigne. World List Annual 1979. (World List Ser.). 1980. text ed. 29.95 (ISBN 0-408-70858-1). Butterworths.
Gran Enciclopedia Rialp, 24 vols. (Span.). 1971-1876. Set. 1425.00. Pergamon.
Grand Enciclopedia Universale Curcio, 20 vols. (Ital.). 1976-1977. Set. 980.00. Pergamon.
Howard, Vernon. The Esoteric Encyclopedia of Eternal Knowledge. LC 80-6203. 256p. 1981. 9.95 (ISBN 0-8128-2797-X); pap. 6.95 (ISBN 0-8128-6117-5). Stein & Day.
Humphrey, Edward, ed. Encyclopedia International, 20 vols. LC 80-84815. (Illus.). 1981. write for info. (ISBN 0-7172-0712-9). Grolier Ed Corp.
Kane, Joseph N., ed. Famous First Facts. 4th ed. 1981. write for info. Wilson.
Kister, Kenneth F. Encyclopedia Buying Guide. 3rd ed. LC 76-645701. 388p. 1981. 22.50 (ISBN 0-8352-1353-6). Bowker.
Kordo, Herbert, ed. New Book of Popular Science, 6 vols. LC 80-83090. (Illus.). 1981. write for info. (ISBN 0-7172-1211-4). Grolier Ed Corp.
Larousse de la Langue Francaise, 2 vols. (Fr.). 1977. 98.50 set. Pergamon.
Shapiro, William E., ed. New Book of Knowledge, 21 vols. LC 80-82958. (Illus.). 1981. write for info. (ISBN 0-7172-0512-6). Grolier Ed Corp.
Shapiro, William E. & Mamberg, Fern, eds. New Book of Knowledge Annual, 1981. LC 79-26807. (Illus.). 1981. write for info. (ISBN 0-7172-0612-2). Grolier Ed Corp.
Sween, Roger, ed. Encyclopedia Buyers' Guide. vi, 74p. 1981. pap. 4.50 (ISBN 0-914054-51-1). Index Co.
Wallace, Irving, et al. The Book of Lists Two. 1981. pap. 3.50 (ISBN 0-553-13101-X). Bantam.

END OF THE WORLD

see also Antichrist

Berlitz, Charles. Doomsday Nineteen Ninety-Nine A.D. LC 80-1084. (Illus.). 240p. 1981. 11.95 (ISBN 0-385-15982-X). Doubleday.
Graham, Billy. Till Armageddon. 1981. 8.95 (ISBN 0-8499-0195-2). Word Bks.
Walwoord, John F. & Walwoord, John E., trs. Armagedom. (Portuguese Bks.). 1979. 1.40 (ISBN 0-8297-0639-9). Life Pubs Intl.
--Armagedon. (Spanish Bks.). (Span.). 1979. 1.90 (ISBN 0-8297-0495-7). Life Pubs Intl.

ENDANGERED SPECIES
see Rare Animals

ENDLESS PUNISHMENT
see Hell

ENDOCRINE GLANDS
see also Hormones; Hypothalamus; Pineal Body; Pituitary Body; Thyroid Gland
Bloodworth, J. M., Jr. Endocrine Pathology: General & Surgical. 2nd ed. (Illus.). 950p. 1981. write for info. (0854-4). Williams & Wilkins.
Stoeckel, H. & Omaya, T. Endocrinology in Anaesthesia & Surgery. (Anaesthesiology & Intensive Care Medicine Ser.: Vol. 132). (Illus.). 205p. 1981. pap. 55.60 (ISBN 0-387-10211-6). Springer-Verlag.

EDOCRINE GLANDS-RADIOGRAPHY
Ashkar, F. S., ed. Thyroid & Endocrine System Investigations with Radionuclides & Radioassays. (Illus.). 544p. 1979. 40.50 (ISBN 0-89352-070-5). Masson Pub.

ENDOCRINE GYNECOLOGY
Barwin, B. Norman, et al. Self-Assessment of Current Knowledge in Infertility & Gynecologic Endocrinology. 1979. spiral bdg. 14.50 (ISBN 0-87488-231-1). Med Exam.

ENDOCRINOLOGY
see also Clinical Endocrinology; Endocrine Glands; Endocrine Gynecology; Hormones; Hormones, Sex; Neuroendocrinology; Ovaries; Pediatric Endocrinology; Pineal Body; Pituitary Body; Testicle; Thyroid Gland
Briggs, Michael & Corbin, Alan, eds. Progress in Hormone Biochemistry & Pharmacholog, Vol. 1. (Endocrinology Ser.). (Illus.). 300p. 1980. 34.95 (ISBN 0-88831-076-5). Eden Med Res.
Chopra, I. J. Triiodothyronines in Health & Disease. (Monographs in Endocrinology: Vol. 18). (Illus.). 160p. 1981. 46.00 (ISBN 0-387-10400-3). Springer-Verlag.
Edebo, L., ed. Endocytosis & Exocytosis in Host Defence, Vol. 17. (Monographs in Allergy). (Illus.). 240p. 1981. pap. 78.00 (ISBN 3-8055-1865-X). S Karger.
Epple, August & Stetson, Milton. Avian Endocrinology. 1980. lib ed 34.00 (ISBN 0-12-240250-2). Acad Pr.
Frajese, G., et al, eds. Oligozoospermia. 1981. text ed. price not set (ISBN 0-89004-589-5). Raven.
Gold, Jay J. & Josimovich, John B. Gynecological Endocrinology. 3rd ed. (Illus.). 918p. 1980. pap. 62.50 (ISBN 0-06-140954-5, Harper Medical). Har-Row.
Goldworthy, Graham J. Endocrinology. LC 80-18704. 184p. 1981. 34.95 (ISBN 0-470-27034-9). Halsted Pr.
Pethes, G., et al, eds. Recent Advances of Avian Endocrinology: Proceedings of a Satellite Symposium of the 28th International Congress of Physiological Sciences, Budapest, Hungary, 1980. LC 80-42007. (Advances in Physiological Sciences: Vol. 33). (Illus.). 450p. 1981. 50.00 (ISBN 0-08-027355-6). Pergamon.
Stark, E., et al, eds. Endocrinology, Neuroendocrinology, Neuropeptides- Part 1: Proceedings of the 28th International Congress of Physiological Sciences, Budapest, 1980. LC 80-42047. (Advances in Physiological Sciences: Vol. 13). (Illus.). 350p. 1981. 40.00 (ISBN 0-08-026827-7). Pergamon.
--Endocrinology, Neuroendocrinology, Neuropeptides-Part II: Proceedings of the 28th International Congress of Physiological Sciences, Budapest, 1980. LC 80-42046. (Advances in Physiological Sciences Ser.: Vol. 14). (Illus.). 350p. 1981. 40.00 (ISBN 0-08-026871-4). Pergamon.
Thomas, John A. Textbook of Endocrine Pharmacology. Date not set. price not set (ISBN 0-8067-1901-X). Urban & S.

ENDODONTICS
Pyner, David. Simplefied Painless Endodontics for the General Dentist: An Alternative to N 2. (Illus.). 171p. 1980. 48.00 (ISBN 0-931386-12-8). Quint Pub Co.
Shoji, Yoshiro. Systematic Endodontics. (Illus.). 126p. 1977. 22.00. Quint Pub Co.

ENDOGENOUS RHYTHMS
see Biological Rhythms

ENDOMETRIUM
Robertson, W. B. The Endometrium. (Postgraduate Pathology Ser.). 1981. text ed. 52.95 (ISBN 0-407-00171-9). Butterworth.

ENDOSCOPE AND ENDOSCOPY
Sugawa, Choichi & Schuman, Bernard M. Primer of Gastrointestinal Fiberoptic Endoscopy. 1981. text ed. write for info (ISBN 0-316-82150-0). Little.

ENDOWED CHARITIES
see Charitable Uses, Trusts and Foundations

ENDURANCE, PHYSICAL
see Physical Fitness

ENEMY ALIENS
see Aliens

ENERGY
see Force and Energy; Power Resources

ENERGY, BIOMASS
see Biomass Energy

ENERGY AND STATE
see Energy Policy

ENERGY CONSERVATION
Here are entered general works on the conservation of all forms of energy. Works on the conservation of a specific form of energy are entered under that form, e.g. Petroleum Conservation. Works on the conservation of energy as a physical concept are entered under Force and Energy.
see also Architecture and Energy Conservation; Energy Policy; Petroleum Conservation; Recycling (Waste, etc.)
Aird, Catherine. The Religious Body. 176p. 1980. pap. 1.95 (ISBN 0-553-13951-7). Bantam.
Annual Bulletin of General Energy Statistics for Europe, Nineteen Seventy-Eight, Vol. XI. 157p. 1980. pap. 12.00 (UN80/2E8, UN). Unipub.
Bergman, M., ed. Subsurface Space--Environment Protection, Low Cost Storage, Energy Savings: Proceedings of the International Symposium, Stockholm, Sweden, June 23-27, 1980, 3 vols. (Illus.). 1500p. 1980. 250.00 (ISBN 0-08-026136-1). Pergamon.
California Energy Commission. California Renewable Energy Information Series, 6 vols. Incl. Vol. 1. Exploring New Energy Sources for California: The 1980-81 Report of the Legislature. 106p. pap. 17.95 (ISBN 0-89934-085-7); Vol. 2. Comparative Evaluation of Nontraditional Energy Sources. 122p. pap. 17.95 (ISBN 0-89934-086-5); Vol. 3. Wind Energy Overview: Wind-Elastic Power, Wind Energy Program Progress Report & Wind Resource Assessment. 104p. pap. 17.95 (ISBN 0-89934-087-3); Vol. 4. Impact of Large Wind Energy Systems in California. 200p. pap. 19.95 (ISBN 0-89934-088-1); Vol. 5. Solar & Wind Programs, Final Environmental Impact Reports. 195p. pap. 24.50 (ISBN 0-89934-110-1); Vol. 6. Program Plan for the Maximum Implementation of Solar Energy Through 1990. pap. 24.50 (ISBN 0-89934-109-8). 1981. pap. Solar Energy Info.
Chigier, N. A., ed. Progress in Energy & Combustion Science, Vol. 6, Pt. 2. 102p. 1980. pap. 24.50 (ISBN 0-08-026059-4). Pergamon.
Conaway, James. World's End. 384p. 1980. pap. 2.50. Bantam.
Cunningham, Chet. Two Hundred & Twenty-Two Ways to Save Gas: And Get the Best Possible Mileage. LC 80-26423. (Illus.). 96p. 1981. pap. 3.95 (ISBN 0-13-935213-9). P-H.
Cussler, Clive. Raise the Titanic! 384p. 1980. pap. 2.75 (ISBN 0-553-13880-4). Bantam.
Darmstadter, Joel, et al. How Industrial Societies Use Energy: A Comparative Analysis. LC 77-83780. (Illus.). 300p. 1978. text ed. 18.50x (ISBN 0-8018-2041-3). Johns Hopkins.
Diamond, Stuart. No-Cost Low Cost Energy Tips: Fifty-Two Ways to Save One Thousand Dollars a Year in Energy Cost Without Sacrifice. 112p. 1980. pap. 1.95 (ISBN 0-553-14239-9). Bantam.
Dunkerley, Joy. Trends in Energy Use in Industrial Countries. LC 80-8022. (Resources for the Future Research Ser.: Paper R-19). (Illus., Orig.). 1980. pap. text ed. 8.00x (ISBN 0-8018-2487-7). Johns Hopkins.
The Economic Commission for Europe & Energy Conservation. 76p. 1980. pap. 7.00 (UN80-2E4, UN). Unipub.
The Economy of Energy Conservation in Educational Facilities. 82p. (Orig.). 1973. pap. text ed. 4.00. Interbk Inc.
Energy & Agriculture. 302p. 1981. pap. 18.00 (ISBN 0-643-02654-1, CSIRO 56, CSIRO). Unipub.
The Energy Conservation Idea Handbook. 171p. (Orig.). 1980. pap. 12.00 (ISBN 0-89492-047-2). Acad Educ Dev.
Gardner, Robert. Save That Energy. (Illus.). 192p. (gr. 8-12). 1981. PLB price not set (ISBN 0-671-34066-2). Messner.
Garton, George S. How to Really Save Money & Energy in Cooling Your Home. pap. 9.95 (ISBN 0-931624-00-2). Green Hill.
Gordon, Richard. World Energy Problems: An Economic Analysis. (Illus.). 320p. 1981. text ed. 30.00x (ISBN 0-262-07080-4). MIT Pr.
Helcke, G. The Energy Saving Guide: Tables for Assessing the Profitability of Energy Saving Measures with Explanatory Notes and Worked Examples. Published for the Commission of the European Communities. LC 80-41528. 230p. 1981. 45.00 (ISBN 0-08-026738-6); pap. 15.50 (ISBN 0-08-026739-4). Pergamon.
Krockover, Gerald & Devito, Alfred. Activities Handbook for Energy Education. (Illus.). 192p. (Orig.). 1981. pap. 10.95 (ISBN 0-8302-2717-2). Goodyear.
Mahon, Harold P., et al. Efficient Energy Management. (Illus.). 496p. 1981. 24.95 (ISBN 0-13-791434-2). P-H.
National Trust for Historic Preservation. Preservation: Reusing America's Energy. (Illus.). 128p. (Orig.). 1981. pap. 9.95 (ISBN 0-89133-095-X). Preservation Pr.
Nelson, Robert V. & Nelson, Rosalie K. E Equals M C Squared: Energy - Management, Conservation & Communication, 17 vols. Ide, Arthur F., ed. (Illus., Orig.). 1981. write for info. (ISBN 0-86663-800-8); pap. write for info. (ISBN 0-86663-801-6). Ide Hse.
Norback, Peter & Norback, Craig. The Consumer's Energy Handbook. 272p. 1981. 19.95 (ISBN 0-442-26066-0); pap. 14.95 (ISBN 0-442-26067-9). Van Nos Reinhold.
Payne, Gordon. Energy Managers' Handbook. 2nd ed. 1980. text ed. 25.00 (ISBN 0-86103-032-X); pap. text ed. 19.50 (ISBN 0-86103-033-8). Butterworths.
Skinner, Brian J., ed. Earth's Energy & Mineral Resources. (The Earth & Its Inhabitants: Selected Readings from American Scientist Ser.). (Illus.). 200p. 1980. pap. 8.95 (ISBN 0-913232-90-4). W Kaufmann.
Sobel, Lester A., ed. Energy Crisis: Nineteen Seventy-Seven to Nineteen Seventy-Nine, Vol. 4. 1980. lib. bdg. 17.50 (ISBN 0-87196-284-5). Facts on File.
Sunset Editors. Energy-Saving Projects. LC 80-53485. (Illus.). 96p. (Orig.). 1981. pap. 3.95 (ISBN 0-376-01230-7, Sunset Bks.). Sunset-Lane.
Veit, Lawrence A. Economic Adjustment to an Energy-Short World. (Atlantic Papers Ser.: No. 38). 78p. 1980. write for info. 0.00 (ISBN 0-916672-78-6). Allanheld.

ENERGY CONSERVATION, MICROBIAL
see Biomass Energy

ENERGY METABOLISM
Mount, Laurence E. Energy Metabolism. LC 80-40265. (Studies in the Agricultural & Food Sciences). (Illus.). 416p. 1980. text ed. 79.95 (ISBN 0-408-10641-7). Butterworths.

ENERGY POLICY
see also Energy Conservation
Berg, Mark R., et al. Jobs & Energy in Michigan: The Next Twenty Years. LC 80-24884. (Illus.). 262p. 1981. 17.95 (ISBN 0-87944-264-6); pap. 11.95 (ISBN 0-87944-263-8). U of Mich Soc Res.
Choucri, Nazli. International Energy Policy: Petroleum, Prices, Power & Payments. (Illus.). 352p. 1981. text ed. 35.00x (ISBN 0-262-03075-6). MIT Pr.
Council on Energy Resources. National Energy Policy: A Continuing Assessment. (Illus.). 395p. 1978. 4.00. Bur Econ Geology.
DeSouza, Glenn R. Energy Policy & Forecasting: Economic, Financial, & Technological Dimensions. LC 79-9671. (Arthur D. Little Bk.). 1980. write for info. (ISBN 0-669-03614-5). Lexington Bks.
Jaques Cattell Press, ed. Energy Research Programs. 450p. 1981. 75.00 (ISBN 0-8352-1352-8). Bowker.
Ladman, Jerry R., et al, eds. U.S.-Mexican Energy Relationships: Realities & Prospects. LC 80-8878. 1981. price not set (ISBN 0-669-04398-2). Lexington Bks.
Nemetz, Peter N. Energy Policy: The Global Challenge. 1979. pap. text ed. 20.50x (ISBN 0-920380-30-1, Pub. by Inst Res Pub Canada). Renouf.
Okagaki, Alan & Benson, Jim. County Energy Plan Guidebook. 2nd ed. (Illus.). 200p. (Orig.). 1979. pap. text ed. 10.00x (ISBN 0-937786-01-2). Inst Ecologica.
Pachauri. International Energy Policy. 600p. 1980. 35.00 (ISBN 0-471-08984-2, Wiley-Interscience). Wiley.
Pluta, Joseph E., ed. The Energy Picture: Problems & Prospects. LC 80-68659. 185p. 1980. pap. 6.00. U of Tex Busn Res.
Prast, William G. Securing U. S. Energy Supplies: The Private Sector As an Instrument of Public Policy. LC 79-2978. 1981. 15.95x (ISBN 0-669-03305-7). Lexington Bks.
Pronin, Monica, ed. Energy Index Nineteen Eighty. LC 73-89098. 600p. 1981. 135.00 (ISBN 0-89947-010-6). Environ Info.
Seminar on Energy Policy: The Carter Proposals. 1979. pap. 3.25 (ISBN 0-8447-3355-5). Am Enterprise.
Servan-Schreiber, Jean-Jacques. The World Challenge. 1981. 14.95 (ISBN 0-671-42524-2). S&S.
Stewart, Hugh B. Transitional Energy Policy 1980-2030: Alternative Nuclear Technologies. (Pergamon Policy Studies on Science & Technology). 266p. 1981. 30.00 (ISBN 0-08-027183-9); pap. 12.50 (ISBN 0-08-027182-0). Pergamon.
Stobaugh, Robert & Yergin, Daniel, eds. Energy Future: The Report of the Energy Project at the Harvard Business School. 1980. pap. 2.95 (ISBN 0-345-29349-5). Ballantine.
Working Group Meeting on Energy Planning & Committee on Natural Resources. Proceedings, Fifth Session. (Energy Resources Development Ser: No. 20). 151p. 1980. pap. 12.00 (UN79-2F11, UN). Unipub.

ENERGY RECOVERY FROM WASTE
see Refuse As Fuel

ENERGY RESOURCES
see Power Resources

ENFORCEMENT OF LAW
see Law Enforcement

ENGELS, FRIEDRICH, 1820-1895
Hazelkorn, Ellen. Marx & Engels: On Ireland - an Annotated Checklist. (Bibliographical Ser.: No. 15). 1981. 2.00 (ISBN 0-89977-031-2). Am Inst Marxist.
Karl Marx-Frederick Engels: Collected Works, Vol. 16. (Illus.). 8.50 (ISBN 0-7178-0516-6). Intl Pub Co.

ENGINEERING
see also Agricultural Engineering; Architecture; Bioengineering; Biomedical Engineering; Boring; Bridges; Building Materials; Canals; Chemical Engineering; Civil Engineering; Dams; Docks; Electric Engineering; Engineers; Engines; Environmental Engineering; Harbors; Hydraulic Engineering; Irrigation; Low Temperature Engineering; Marine Engineering; Masonry; Mechanical Drawing; Mechanical Engineering; Mechanics; Mensuration; Nuclear Engineering; Ocean Engineering; Plant Engineering; Railroad Engineering; Reclamation of Land; Reliability (Engineering); Reservoirs; Rivers; Roads; Sanitary Engineering; Statics; Steam-Engines; Strength of Materials; Structural Engineering; Subways; Surveying; Systems Engineering; Tunnels and Tunneling; Ventilation; Walls; Water-Supply Engineering
Berkofsky, Louis, et al, eds. Settling the Desert. 272p. 1981. write for info. (ISBN 0-677-16280-4). Gordon.
Coates, Donald R., ed. Geomorphology & Engineering. (Binghamton Symposia in Geomorphology: International Ser.: No. 7). (Illus.). 384p. 1980. text ed. 30.00x (ISBN 0-04-551040-7, 2584). Allen Unwin.
The Engineer in the Community. 172p. 1980. 45.00x (Pub. by Telford England). State Mutual Bk.
Engineering & Technology Degrees, 1980, 3 pts. Incl. Pt. 1. By Schools. 25.00; Pt. 2. By Minorities. 75.00; Pt. 3. By Curriculum. 25.00. 1981. Set. 100.00 (201-80). AAES.
Engineering & Technology Enrollments, 1979, 2 pts. Incl. Pt. 1. Engineering Enrollments. 45.00; Pt. 2. Technology Enrollments. 45.00. 1980. Set. 75.00. AAES.
Engineering Societies in the Life of a Country. 174p. 1980. 24.00x (ISBN 0-901948-02-0, Pub. by Telford England). State Mutual Bk.
The Environment in Engineering Education. (Studies in Engineering Education: No. 9). 110p. 1980. pap. 9.25 (ISBN 92-3-101793-4, U1028, UNESCO). Unipub.
Fisk, Edward R. Construction Engineer's Form Book. 256p. 1981. text ed. 40.00 (ISBN 0-471-06307-X). Wiley.
Gas Discharges & Their Applications. (IEE Conference Publication Ser.: No. 189). (Illus.). 560p. (Orig.). 1980. soft cover 79.00. Inst Elect Eng.
Goals for Engineering Profession. Date not set. 3.50 (515). AAES.
Helander, Martin. Human Factors-Ergonomics for Building & Construction. (Construction Management & Engineering Ser.). 400p. 1981. 35.00 (ISBN 0-471-05075-X, Pub. by Wiley-Interscience). Wiley.
Heriam, J. L. Engineering Mechanics, 2 vols. Incl. Vol. 1. Statics: SI Version. text ed. 18.95 (ISBN 0-471-05558-1); Arabic ed. (ISBN 0-471-06312-6); Vol. 2. Dynamics: SI Version. text ed. 17.95 (ISBN 0-471-05559-X); Arabic ed. (ISBN 0-471-06311-8). LC 79-11173. 1980. Wiley.
--Engineering Mechanics, 2 vols. Incl. Vol. 1. Statics. text ed. 18.95x (ISBN 0-471-59460-1); Vol. 2. Dynamics. text ed. 19.95x (ISBN 0-471-59461-X). LC 77-24716. 1978. Wiley.
Heriman, J. L. ARA Engineering Mechanics, 2 vols. Incl. Vol. 1. SI Statics (ISBN 0-471-06312-6); Vol. 2. SI Dynamics (ISBN 0-471-06311-8). 1980. 18.95 ea. Wiley.
Hobbs, F. D. & Doling, J. F. Planning for Engineers & Surveyors. LC 80-41553. (Illus.). 230p. 1980. 30.00 (ISBN 0-08-025459-4); pap. 15.00 (ISBN 0-08-025458-6). Pergamon.
Iowa State University Research Foundation. Fundamentals of Engineering Review. LC 80-83440. 208p. 1980. pap. text ed. 14.95 (ISBN 0-8403-2305-0). Kendall-Hunt.
McDonagh, et al. Engineering Science for Technicians, Vol. 2. (Illus.). 1978. pap. 11.00x (ISBN 0-7131-3398-8). Intl Ideas.
Mathewson, Christopher C. Engineering Geology. (Illus.). 416p. 1981. text ed. 24.95 (ISBN 0-675-08032-0). Merrill.
Measuring & Forecasting Engineering Personnel Requirements. Date not set. 50.00 (126-79). AAES.
Nunney. Engineering Technology One. 1981. text ed. price not set (ISBN 0-408-00511-4). Butterworth.
Pau. Failure Diagnoses & Performance Monitoring. Date not set. price not set (ISBN 0-8247-1018-5). Dekker.
Pawlicki, T. How to Build a Flying Saucer: And Other Proposals in Specultive Engineering. 1980. pap. 6.95 (ISBN 0-13-402461-3). P-H.
The Placement of Engineering & Technology Graduates. Date not set. 25.00 (210-80). AAES.
Rudman, Jack. Engineering. (Undergraduate Program Field Test Ser.: UPFT-8). (Cloth bdg. avail. on request). pap. 9.95 (ISBN 0-8373-6008-0). Natl Learning.

Salaries of Engineers in Education - 1980. Date not set. 15.00 (307-80). AAES.
Savage. Basic Engineering Craft Activities. 1980. pap. text ed. write for info. (ISBN 0-408-00568-8). Butterworths.
Simonton, Dave. Directory of Engineering Document Sources. 2nd ed. 436p. 1974. perfect bnd. 39.95x (ISBN 0-912702-06-0). Global Eng.
Survey of Employee Benefits of Engineers - 1977. Date not set. 20.00 (510-77). AAES.

ENGINEERING–AUTHORSHIP
see Technical Writing

ENGINEERING–CONTRACTS AND SPECIFICATIONS
Burchess, D. Specifications & Quantities. 2nd ed. (Illus.). 136p. 1980. pap. text ed. 12.95x (ISBN 0-7114-5640-2). Intl Ideas.
Shoup, T., et al. Introduction to Engineering Design with Design Projects. 1981. pap. 15.95 (ISBN 0-13-482364-8); pap. 8.95 wkbk. (ISBN 0-13-716274-X). P-H.

ENGINEERING–DATA PROCESSING
see also Structures, Theory of–Data Processing
Graham, J. A., ed. Use of Computers in Managing Material Property Data. (MPC: No. 14). 64p. 1980. 18.00 (G00192). ASME.
Ryder, A. & Malcolmson, E. The Engineers' Computer Handbook. 336p. 1980. 95.00x (ISBN 0-7277-0078-2, Pub. by Telford England). State Mutual Bk.

ENGINEERING–DESIGN
see Engineering Design

ENGINEERING–ESTIMATES AND COSTS
see also Cost Effectiveness
Crystal-Smith. Estimating for Building & Civil Engineering Works. 7th ed. 1981. text ed. write for info. (ISBN 0-408-00515-7). Butterworth.
An Introduction to Engineering Economics. 192p. 1980. 21.00x (Pub. by Telford England). State Mutual Bk.
Management of Large Capital Projects. 246p. 1980. 60.00x (ISBN 0-7277-0066-9, Pub. by Telford England). State Mutual Bk.
The Middle East: Life & Work for the Civil Engineer. 85p. 1980. 29.00x (ISBN 0-7277-0064-2, Pub. by Telford England). State Mutual Bk.

ENGINEERING–GRAPHIC METHODS
see Engineering Graphics

ENGINEERING–HANDBOOKS, MANUALS, ETC.
Management of Large Capital Projects. 246p. 1980. 60.00x (ISBN 0-7277-0066-9, Pub. by Telford England). State Mutual Bk.
Manual of Applied Geology for Engineers. 414p. 1980. pap. 75.00x (ISBN 0-7277-0038-3, Pub. by Telford England). State Mutual Bk.
Parmley, Robert O. Field Engineer's Manual. 608p. 1981. 19.50 (ISBN 0-07-048513-5, P&RB). McGraw.
Roland, Hall C. The Armchair Engineer. 120p. (Orig.). 1981. pap. 4.95 (ISBN 0-918398-51-7). Dilithium Pr.
Yuen, Aubrey. Geometric & Positional Tolerancing Reference & Work Book. 2nd ed. 90p. 1973. perfect bnd 7.95x (ISBN 0-912702-07-9). Global Eng.

ENGINEERING–HISTORY
Baynes, Ken & Pugh, Francis. The Art of the Engineer. LC 80-29190. (Illus.). 240p. 1981. 60.00 (ISBN 0-87951-128-1). Overlook Pr.
Turner, Roland & Goulden, Steven L., eds. Greag Engineers: From Antiquity Through the Industrial Revolution, Vol. I. (Illus.). 630p. 1981. 65.00x (ISBN 0-312-34574-7). St Martin.

ENGINEERING–MANAGEMENT
Amos, John M. & Sarchet, Bernard R. Management for Engineers. (P-H Ser. in Industrial Systems Engineering). (Illus.). 384p. 1981. text ed. 18.95 (ISBN 0-686-68606-3). P-H.
Christian, John. Management, Machines & Methods in Civil Engineering. 375p. 1981. 34.95 (ISBN 0-471-06334-7, Pub. by Wiley-Interscience). Wiley.

ENGINEERING–MATERIALS
see Materials

ENGINEERING–PROBLEMS, EXERCISES, ETC.
Ferziger, J. H. Numerical Methods for Engineering Applications. 400p. 1981. 36.00 (ISBN 0-471-06336-3, Pub. by Wiley-Interscience). Wiley.
Irvine. Engineering Technology Problem Solving. Date not set. price not set (ISBN 0-8247-1169-6). Dekker.
Yuen, Aubrey. Geometric & Positional Tolerancing Reference & Work Book. 2nd ed. 90p. 1973. perfect bnd 7.95x (ISBN 0-912702-07-9). Global Eng.

ENGINEERING–STATISTICS
Volk, William. Engineering Statistics with a Programmable Calculator. Davidson, Robert L., ed. (Illus.). 320p. 1981. text ed. 17.50 (ISBN 0-07-067552-X, P&RB). McGraw.

ENGINEERING–VOCATIONAL GUIDANCE
Guidelines to Professional Employment for Engineers & Scientists. Date not set. 1.00 (511-78). AAES.
Reyes-Guerra, David R. & Fischer, Alan M. Peterson's Guide to Undergraduate Engineering Study. (Orig.). 1981. pap. 14.00 (ISBN 0-87866-163-8). Petersons Guides.

ENGINEERING, AGRICULTURAL
see Agricultural Engineering

ENGINEERING, ARCHITECTURAL
see Building; Strains and Stresses; Strength of Materials; Structures, Theory of

ENGINEERING, BIOMEDICAL
see Biomedical Engineering

ENGINEERING, CHEMICAL
see Chemical Engineering

ENGINEERING, CIVIL
see Civil Engineering

ENGINEERING, CLINICAL
see Biomedical Engineering

ENGINEERING, ELECTRICAL
see Electric Engineering

ENGINEERING, GENETIC
see Genetic Engineering

ENGINEERING, HYDRAULIC
see Hydraulic Engineering

ENGINEERING, INDUSTRIAL
see Industrial Engineering

ENGINEERING, MARINE
see Marine Engineering

ENGINEERING, MECHANICAL
see Mechanical Engineering; Mechanics, Applied

ENGINEERING, MEDICAL
see Biomedical Engineering

ENGINEERING, RAILROAD
see Railroad Engineering

ENGINEERING, SANITARY
see Sanitary Engineering

ENGINEERING, STRUCTURAL
see Structural Engineering

ENGINEERING, TRAFFIC
see Traffic Engineering

ENGINEERING, WATER-SUPPLY
see Water-Supply Engineering

ENGINEERING ANALYSIS
see Engineering Mathematics

ENGINEERING CYBERNETICS
see Automation

ENGINEERING DESIGN
see also Materials; Structural Design; Systems Engineering;
also subdivisions Design and Design and Construction under special subjects, e.g. Machinery–Design; Automobiles–Design and Construction
The Aesthetic Aspects of Civil Engineering Design. 120p. 1980. pap. 25.00x (ISBN 0-901948-13-6, Pub. by Telford England). State Mutual Bk.
Design for the Eighties. (Illus.). 1981. text ed. 40.00 (ISBN 0-937976-05-9). Enviro Pr.
Institute of Civil Engineers, UK. Thames Barrier Design. 202p. 1980. 50.00x (ISBN 0-7277-0057-X, Pub. by Telford England). State Mutual Bk.
Problems in Engineering Drawing for Design & Communications. 8th ed. pap. 8.95 ea. Vol. 1 (ISBN 0-13-716373-8). Vol. 2 (ISBN 0-13-716381-9). P-H.

ENGINEERING DRAWING
see Mechanical Drawing

ENGINEERING GRAPHICS
see also Computer Graphics;
also subdivision Graphic Methods under specific subjects
Kundis, Lawrence E. Point, Line, Plane & Solid: A Basic Text Workbook for Engineering Graphics. 2nd ed. 368p. 1980. pap. text ed. 16.95 (ISBN 0-8403-2310-7). Kendall-Hunt.

ENGINEERING GRAPHICS–DATA PROCESSING
see Computer Graphics

ENGINEERING LITERATURE SEARCHING
see Information Storage and Retrieval Systems–Engineering

ENGINEERING MATERIALS
see Materials

ENGINEERING MATHEMATICS
see also Dimensional Analysis; Mechanics, Applied; Structures, Theory of
Bajpai, A. C., et al. Specialist Techniques in Engineering Mathematics. 416p. 1980. 57.25 (ISBN 0-471-27907-2, Pub. by Wiley-Interscience); pap. 26.00 (ISBN 0-471-27908-0). Wiley.
Ferziger, J. H. Numerical Methods for Engineering Applications. 400p. 1981. 36.00 (ISBN 0-471-06336-3, Pub. by Wiley-Interscience). Wiley.
Kaplan, Wilfred. Advanced Mathematics for Engineers. LC 80-19492. (Mathematics Ser.). (Illus.). 960p. 1981. text ed. 22.95 (ISBN 0-201-03773-4). A-W.

ENGINEERS
see also Civil Engineers; Engineering–Vocational Guidance; Inventors; Mechanical Engineers; Technologists
Carvill. Famous Names in Engineering. 1981. text ed. price not set (ISBN 0-408-00536-X). Butterworth.
The Engineer in the Community. 172p. 1980. 45.00x (Pub. by Telford England). State Mutual Bk.
Engineering Societies in the Life of a Country. 174p. 1980. 24.00x (ISBN 0-901948-02-0, Pub. by Telford England). State Mutual Bk.

ENGINEERS–COLLECTIVE BARGAINING
see Collective Bargaining–Engineers

ENGINES
see also Fire-Engines; Fuel; Locomotives; Marine Engines; Pumping Machinery; Steam-Boilers; Steam-Engines
Chilton's Editorial Dept., ed. Chilton's Mechanics' Handbook: Engine Rebuilding, Engine Repair, Engine Theory, Vol. II. (Illus.). 300p. (Orig.). 1981. pap. text ed. 14.95 (ISBN 0-686-69515-1). Chilton.
Engineering Applications, No. 1: Installation & Maintenance of Engines in Fishing Vessels. (FAO Fisheries Technical Paper Ser.: No. 196). 136p. 1980. pap. 7.25 (ISBN 92-5-100862-0, F1948, FAO). Unipub.
Smith, Ross. Propane Conversion of Engines. rev. ed. (Applied Technology Ser.). (Illus.). 76p. 1980. pap. 8.45 (ISBN 0-938260-01-4). Smith & Assoc.
--Propane Conversion of Engines. rev. ed. (Applied Technology Ser.). (Illus.). 76p. 1980. pap. 9.15. Ashford.
Turner, J. Howard. Care & Operation of Small Engines, 2 vols. 4th ed. Vol. 1. 7.95 (ISBN 0-914452-23-1); Vol. 2. 9.95 (ISBN 0-914452-24-X). Green Hill.
--Maintenance & Repair of Small Engines. 9.95 (ISBN 0-914452-45-2). Green Hill.

ENGLAND
see also Great Britain;
also specific countries, cities and geographic areas in England
Clemoes, Peter A., ed. Anglo-Saxon England, 8 vols. Incl. Vol. 1. 320p. 1972. 47.50 (ISBN 0-521-08557-8); Vol. 2. 300p. 1973. 47.50 (ISBN 0-521-20218-3); Vol. 3. 320p. 1974. 47.50 (ISBN 0-521-20574-3); Vol. 4. 270p. 1975. 47.50 (ISBN 0-521-20868-8); Vol. 5. 1976. 47.50 (ISBN 0-521-21270-7); Vol. 6. 1977. 47.50 (ISBN 0-521-21701-6); Vol. 7. 1979. 47.50 (ISBN 0-521-22164-1); Vol. 8. 1980. 57.50 (ISBN 0-521-22788-7). LC 78-19043. (Illus.). Cambridge U Pr.

ENGLAND–ANTIQUITIES
Wilson, David M. The Archaeology of Anglo-Saxon England. (Illus.). 532p. Date not set. pap. price not set (ISBN 0-521-28390-6). Cambridge U Pr.

ENGLAND–CIVILIZATION
see Great Britain–Civilization

ENGLAND–DESCRIPTION AND TRAVEL
see also Great Britain–Description and Travel
Capek, Karel. Letters from England. Selver, Paul, tr. 192p. 1980. Repr. of 1926 ed. lib. bdg. 25.00 (ISBN 0-8495-0952-1). Arden Lib.
Norden, John. England: An Intended Guyde, for English Travailers. LC 79-84125. (English Experience Ser.: No. 944). 84p. 1979. Repr. of 1625 ed. lib. bdg. 14.00 (ISBN 90-221-0944-5). Walter J Johnson.

ENGLAND–DESCRIPTION AND TRAVEL–GUIDEBOOKS
Crookston, Peter, ed. Village England. 1980. 16.95 (ISBN 0-686-68275-0). Methuen Inc.

ENGLAND–GENEALOGY
see Great Britain–Genealogy

ENGLAND–HISTORY
see Great Britain–History

ENGLAND–SOCIAL CONDITIONS
see Great Britain–Social Conditions

ENGLAND–SOCIAL LIFE AND CUSTOMS
see also Great Britain–Social Life and Customs
Byrne, Muriel S., ed. The Lisle Letters, 6 vols. LC 80-12019. 1981. Set. 250.00x (ISBN 0-226-08801-4). U of Chicago Pr.
Cooper, Jilly. Class. LC 80-2718. (Illus.). 288p. 1981. 12.95 (ISBN 0-394-51414-9). Knopf.
Halsey, Albert H. & Heath, Anthony F. Origins & Destinations: Family, Class & Education in Modern Britain. (Illus.). 250p. 1980. text ed. 29.50x (ISBN 0-19-827224-3); pap. 12.95x (ISBN 0-19-827249-9). Oxford U Pr.
Ovchinnikov, V. V. Britain Observed: A Russian's View. LC 80-40657. 224p. 1981. 22.50 (ISBN 0-08-023603-0); pap. 8.50 (ISBN 0-08-023608-1). Pergamon.
Thompson, Denys. Change & Tradition in Rural England: An Anthology of Writings on Country Life. LC 79-41613. 288p. 1981. 27.50 (ISBN 0-521-22546-9). Cambridge U Pr.
Urwick, E. J., ed. Study of Boy Life in Our Cities: London, 1904. LC 79-56942. (The English Working Class Ser.). 1980. lib. bdg. 28.00 (ISBN 0-8240-0125-7). Garland Pub.

ENGLAND, CHURCH OF
see Church of England

ENGLISH ARCHITECTURE
see Architecture–Great Britain

ENGLISH ART
see Art, British

ENGLISH AS A FOREIGN LANGUAGE
see English Language–Study and Teaching–Foreign Students

ENGLISH CHANNEL
Coles, K. A. Channel Harbours & Anchorages. 5th ed. 198p. 1980. 24.00 (ISBN 0-245-53086-X, Pub. by Nautical England). State Mutual Bk.

ENGLISH COMPOSERS
see Composers, British

ENGLISH DRAMA–HISTORY AND CRITICISM
Espeland, Pamela. The Story of Pygmalion. LC 80-15792. (Myths for Modern Children Ser.). (Illus.). 32p. (gr. 1-4). 1981. PLB 6.95 (ISBN 0-87614-127-0). Carolrhoda Bks.
Ewbank, Inga-Stina. Essays & Studies Nineteen Eighty, Vol.33. (Essays & Studies). 158p. 1980. pap. text ed. 22.00x (ISBN 0-391-01766-7). Humanities.
Jeffrey, Rosalind. Chess in the Mirror: A Study of Theatrical Cubism in Francis Warner's Requiem & Its Maquettes. 1981. text ed. 13.00 (ISBN 0-85455-020-8). Humanities.
Salgado, Gamini. English Drama: A Critical Introduction. 1981. write for info. (ISBN 0-312-25429-6). St Martin.

ENGLISH DRAMA–HISTORY AND CRITICISM–BIBLIOGRAPHY
Harris, Richard H., ed. Modern Drama in America & England, Nineteen Fifty-Nineteen Seventy: A Guide to Information Sources. (American Literature, English Literature & World Literatures in English Ser.: Vol. 34). 400p. 1981. 32.00 (ISBN 0-8103-1493-2). Gale.

ENGLISH DRAMA–HISTORY AND CRITICISM–TO 1500
Ingram, Reginald W., ed. Coventry. (Records of Early English Drama Ser.). 700p. 1981. 47.50x (ISBN 0-8020-5542-7). U of Toronto Pr.

ENGLISH DRAMA–HISTORY AND CRITICISM–EARLY MODERN AND ELIZABETHAN, 1500-1600
Helterman, Jeffrey. Symbolic Action in the Plays of the Wakefield Master. LC 80-18273. (South Atlantic Modern Language Association Award Study). 216p. 1981. lib. bdg. 17.50x (ISBN 0-8203-0534-0). U of Ga Pr.
Yearsley, Percival M. Doctors in Elizabethan Drama. 128p. 1980. Repr. of 1933 ed. lib. bdg. 20.00 (ISBN 0-8495-6101-9). Arden Lib.
Young, Stephen B. & Orgel, Stephen, eds. Match at Midnight (1633) LC 79-54324. (Renaissance Drama Second Ser.). 270p. 1980. lib. bdg. 30.00 (ISBN 0-8240-4481-9). Garland Pub.

ENGLISH DRAMA–HISTORY AND CRITICISM–RESTORATION, 1660-1700
Brown, Laura. English Dramatic Form, Sixteen-Sixty to Seveenteen-Sixty: An Essay in Generic History. LC 80-25702. 264p. 1981. 19.50x (ISBN 0-300-02585-8). Yale U Pr.
Gossett, Suzanne, ed. Hierarchomachia, or the Antibishop. LC 78-75201. 300p. 1981. 14.50 (ISBN 0-8387-2151-6). Bucknell U Pr.

ENGLISH DRAMA–HISTORY AND CRITICISM–18TH CENTURY
Stone, George W., Jr., ed. The Stage & the Page: London's "Whole Show" in the Eighteenth Century Theatre. 1981. 14.95x (ISBN 0-520-04201-8). U of Cal Pr.

ENGLISH DRAMA–HISTORY AND CRITICISM–20TH CENTURY
Dean, Joan F. Tom Stoppard: Comedy As Moral Matrix. LC 80-26400. 128p. 1981. text ed. 9.00x (ISBN 0-8262-0332-9). U of Mo Pr.
Drakakis, John. British Radio Drama. 300p. Date not set. 47.50 (ISBN 0-521-22183-8); pap. 15.95 (ISBN 0-521-29383-9). Cambridge U Pr.

ENGLISH DRAMA–IRISH AUTHORS
see Irish Drama (English)

ENGLISH DRAMA–OUTLINES, SYLLABI, ETC.
see English Literature–Outlines, Syllabi, etc.

ENGLISH ESSAYS
Here are entered only collections of essays by several authors.
Gissing, George. The Town Traveller. 247p. 1980. Repr. of 1927 ed. lib. bdg. 25.00 (ISBN 0-89984-231-3). Century Bookbindery.
Hannay, James. Essays from "The Quarterly Review". 390p. 1980. Repr. of 1861 ed. lib. bdg. 45.00 (ISBN 0-89984-282-8). Century Bookbindery.
Lobban, J. H., intro. by. English Essays. 257p. 1980. Repr. lib. bdg. 30.00 (ISBN 0-89987-507-6). Century Bookbindery.
Muggerbridge, Malcolm. The Thirties, Nineteen Thirty to Nineteen Forty. 327p. 1980. Repr. of 1940 ed. lib. bdg. 30.00 (ISBN 0-89987-574-2). Darby Bks.
Williams, W. E., ed. A Book of English Essays. 1981. pap. 3.95 (ISBN 0-14-043153-5). Penguin.

ENGLISH FICTION–HISTORY AND CRITICISM
Asthana, Rama K. Henry James: A Study in the Aesthetics of the Novel. 130p. 1980. Repr. of 1936 ed. text ed. 11.25 (ISBN 0-391-02180-X). Humanities.
Davis, Robert C., ed. The Fictional Father: Lacanian Readings of the Text. LC 80-26222. 240p. 1981. lib. bdg. 15.00x (ISBN 0-87023-111-1). U of Mass Pr.
Day, Kenneth F. Eden Phillpots on Dartmoor. (Illus.). 248p. 1981. 19.95 (ISBN 0-7153-8118-0). David & Charles.
Weygandt, Cornelius. A Century of the English Novel. 1980. Repr. of 1925 ed. write for info. (ISBN 0-89760-916-6). Telegraph Bks.

ENGLISH FICTION–HISTORY AND CRITICISM–19TH CENTURY
Lascelles, Mary. The Story-Teller Retrieves the Past: Historical Fiction & Fictitious History in the Art of Scott, Stevenson, Kipling, & Some Others. 116p. 1980. 29.50x (ISBN 0-19-812802-9). Oxford U Pr.
Levine, George. The Realistic Imagination: English Fiction from Frankenstein to Lady Chatterley. LC 80-17444. 1981. lib. bdg. 25.00x (ISBN 0-226-47550-6). U of Chicago Pr.
Reed, Walter L. An Exemplary History of the Novel: The Quixotic Versus the Picaresque. LC 80-17908. 1981. lib. bdg. 22.00x (ISBN 0-226-70683-4). U of Chicago Pr.

ENGLISH FICTION–OUTLINES, SYLLABI, ETC.
see English Literature–Outlines, Syllabi, etc.

ENGLISH FOLK-LORE
see Folk-Lore, English

ENGLISH FOLK SONGS
see Folk-Songs, English

ENGLISH IN AFRICA
see British in Africa

ENGLISH IN FOREIGN COUNTRIES
see British in Foreign Countries

ENGLISH LANGUAGE
see also COBOL (Computer Program Language)

Dixson, Robert J. Modern American English: Teacher's Manual 3. (Modern American English Ser.). (Illus.). 187p. 1978. pap. text ed. 4.95 (ISBN 0-88345-322-3). Regents Pub.

Flachmann, Kim. Focus: A College English Handbook. (Illus.). 448p. 1981. pap. text ed. 6.95 (ISBN 0-395-29728-1); instrs' manual 0.75. HM.

Pierce, Joe E. How English Really Works. 235p. pap. 12.95 (ISBN 0-913244-18-X). Hapi Pr.

Vines, Lois. Guide to Language Camps in the United States. (Language in Education Ser.: No. 26). 1980. pap. text ed. 3.95 (ISBN 0-87281-114-X). Ctr Appl Ling.

ENGLISH LANGUAGE–MIDDLE ENGLISH, 1100-1500

Edwards, A. S. & Pearsall, Derek, eds. Middle English Prose: Essays on Bibliographical Problems. LC 80-8595. 150p. 1981. lib. bdg. 25.00 (ISBN 0-8240-9453-0). Garland Pub.

Hartung, Albert E. & Severs, Burke, eds. Manual of Writings in Middle English, 1050-1500, 6 vols. Incl. Vol. 1. 338p. 1967. 17.50 (ISBN 0-208-00893-4); pap. 10.50; Vol. 2. 329p. 1970. 17.50 (ISBN 0-208-00894-2); Vol. 3. 960p. 1972. 17.50 (ISBN 0-208-01220-6); Vol. 4. 1313p. 1973. 17.50 (ISBN 0-208-01342-3); Vol. 5. 440p. 1976. 25.00 (ISBN 0-208-01459-4); Vol. 6. 500p. 1980. 25.00 (ISBN 0-208-01715-1). Shoe String.

Sweet, Henry. The Oldest English Text. 668p. 1980. Repr. of 1885 ed. lib. bdg. 85.00 (ISBN 0-8482-6221-2). Norwood Edns.

ENGLISH LANGUAGE–ABBREVIATIONS
see Abbreviations

ENGLISH LANGUAGE–AMERICANISMS
see Americanisms

ENGLISH LANGUAGE–ANALYSIS AND PARSING
see English Language–Grammar

ENGLISH LANGUAGE–ANTONYMS
see English Language–Synonyms and Antonyms

ENGLISH LANGUAGE–BUSINESS ENGLISH

De Capno, A. Clear & Simple Guide to Business Spelling. (Clear & Simple Guides Ser.). 96p. (Orig.). 1981. pap. 4.95 (ISBN 0-686-68915-1). Monarch Pr.

Lawrence, Nelda R. & Tebeaux, Elizabeth. Writing Communications in Business & Industry. 3rd ed. (Illus.). 272p. 1981. 12.95 (ISBN 0-13-970467-1). P-H.

Paxson, William. The Business Writing Handbook. 288p. (Orig.). 1981. pap. 3.95 (ISBN 0-553-14344-1). Bantam.

Pryse, B. Elizabeth. Successful Communication in Business. 272p. 1981. pap. 10.95x (ISBN 0-631-11601-X, Pub. by Basil Blackwell). Biblio Dist.

Smith, Leial R. English for Careers Business Professionals & Technical. 2nd ed. 528p. 1981. pap. text ed. 13.95 (ISBN 0-471-08991-5). Wiley.

Visco, Louis J. The Manager As an Editor: Reviewing Memos, Letters & Reports. 172p. 1981. pap. 8.95 (ISBN 0-8436-0852-8). CBI Pub.

Warner, Joan. Business English Handbook. 1981. text ed. 14.95 (ISBN 0-8359-0574-8). Reston.

ENGLISH LANGUAGE–COMPOSITION AND EXERCISES
Here are entered works of an elementary character containing exercises in, and treatises on English composition. More advanced works on English composition are entered under the headings English Language–Rhetoric and English Language–Style.
see also English Language–Grammar; English Language–Rhetoric; English Language–Style; English Language–Text-Books for Foreigners

Arnaudet, Martin L. & Barrett, Mary E. Paragraph Development: A Guide for Students of English As a Second Language. (ESL Ser.). (Illus.). 160p. 1981. pap. text ed. 7.95 (ISBN 0-13-648618-5). P-H.

Basic Skills Word List. 1980. pap. 14.95 (ISBN 0-932166-02-4). Instruct Object.

Bell. I Learn to Write: 1978 Ed, 9 bks. Incl. Bk. A. (gr. k). pap. text ed. 2.92 (ISBN 0-8009-0255-6); tchr's. ed. 4.40 (ISBN 0-8009-0257-2); Bks. B-I. (gr. 1-8). pap. text ed. 2.44 ea. Bk. B (ISBN 0-8009-0259-9). Bk. C (ISBN 0-8009-0263-7). Bk. D (ISBN 0-8009-0269-6). Bk. E (ISBN 0-8009-0274-2). Bk. F (ISBN 0-8009-0278-5). Bk. G (ISBN 0-8009-0282-3). Bk. H (ISBN 0-8009-0288-2). Bk. I (ISBN 0-8009-0292-0); Bks. B-I, Tchr's. Eds. pap. 3.88 ea. Bk. B (ISBN 0-8009-0261-0). Bk. C (ISBN 0-8009-0265-3). Bk. D (ISBN 0-8009-0272-6). Bk. E (ISBN 0-8009-0276-9). Bk. F (ISBN 0-8009-0280-7). Bk. G (ISBN 0-8009-0286-6). Bk. H (ISBN 0-8009-0290-4). Bk. I (ISBN 0-8009-0294-7); Bks. C-G, Texas Edition. (gr. 2-6). Bk. C, Transition. pap. text ed. 2.00 (ISBN 0-8009-0250-5); Bks. D-G. pap. text ed. 2.20 ea. Bk. D (ISBN 0-8009-0240-8). Bk. E (ISBN 0-8009-0242-4). Bk. F (ISBN 0-8009-0244-0). Bk. G (ISBN 0-8009-0246-7). tchr's. ed. for Bk. C 3.88 (ISBN 0-8009-0252-1); Helping the Left-Handed Child. pap. 0.44 (ISBN 0-8009-0305-6); How Parents Help Pre-School Children Write. pap. 0.64 (ISBN 0-8009-0302-1); Learn Manuscript Writing - Student Bk. pap. 2.32 (ISBN 0-8009-0300-5); Transition - When? pap. 0.044 (ISBN 0-8009-0307-2). (gr. k-8). ABC reference & desk cards, charts, practice paper, pencils & pens avail.; 1968 & 1973 eds. of texts & tchr's. bks. also avail. Write for further info. McCormick-Mathers.

Blanton, Linda L. Intermediate Composition Practice, Bk I. (Illus., Orig.). (gr. 7-12). 1981. pap. text ed. 5.95 (ISBN 0-88377-194-2). Newbury Hse.

Bossone, Richard M. & Ashe, Amy E. English Proficiency: Developing Your Reading & Writing Power, Bk. 1. 320p. (gr. 7-9). 1980. 10.32 (ISBN 0-07-006589-6, W); tchrs. manual 6.00 (ISBN 0-07-006590-X). McGraw.

Burleigh, Robert & Gray, Mary Jane. Basic Writing Skills. LC 77-730072. (Illus.). (gr. 6-8). 1976. pap. text ed. 225.00 (ISBN 0-89290-115-2, CM-39). Soc for Visual.

Canavan, P. Joseph. The Effective Writer's Companion. 1981. pap. text ed. 8.95x (ISBN 0-673-15449-1). Scott F.

Chapman, John. Welcome to English: Let's Begin. new ed. (Welcome to English Ser.). (Illus.). 48p. 1980. pap. 2.50 (ISBN 0-88345-379-7); tchr's manual 1.95 (ISBN 0-88345-448-3). Regents Pub.

Connell, Donna. Teach Your Preschooler to Write. (Illus.). 132p. (Orig.). 1980. pap. 7.95 (ISBN 0-9604192-0-9). Can Do Bks.

Croteau, Leo H. Generative Rhetoric, a Teaching Guide for English Composition. 300p. 1980. tchrs.' ed. 25.00 (ISBN 0-9602582-0-5). Neechee Assoc.

Danish, Barbara. Writing As a Second Language. 1981. worktext 6.00 (ISBN 0-915924-10-2). Tchrs & Writers Coll.

Davis, Barbara, et al. The Evaluation of Composition Instruction. LC 80-68774. 160p. (Orig.). 1981. pap. 6.95x (ISBN 0-918528-11-9). Edgepress.

Direct Measures of Writing Skills: Issues & Applications. 1980. pap. 3.75 (ISBN 0-89354-829-4). Northwest Regional.

Elsbree, Langdon, et al. The Heath Handbook of Composition. 10th ed. 448p. 1981. text ed. 8.95 (ISBN 0-669-03352-9); pap. text ed. 7.95 (ISBN 0-669-03353-7); instr's guide with tests avail. (ISBN 0-669-03356-1); wkbk. 4.95 (ISBN 0-669-03456-8). Heath.

Haley-James, Shirley, ed. Perspectives on Writing in Grades 1-8. 1981. pap. price not set (ISBN 0-8141-3519-6). NCTE.

Heffernan, James A. & Lincoln, John E. Writing: A College Handbook. 1981. text ed. price not set (ISBN 0-393-95150-2); phamphlet free (ISBN 0-393-95163-4). Norton.

Hirsch, E. D., Jr. The Philosophy of Composition. LC 77-4944. xiv, 200p. 1981. pap. 4.95 (ISBN 0-226-34243-3). U of Chicago Pr.

Horlock, Carole. Initial Consonants. (Illus.). 44p. (gr. 1-3). 1980. pap. 5.95 (ISBN 0-933358-60-1). Enrich.

Hudson & Weaver. Reading, Writing & Speaking: Here & Now. (Illus.). 1980. pap. 2.95x (ISBN 0-88323-160-3, 248). Richards Pub.

Judy, Stephen N. & Judy, Susan J. An Introduction to the Teaching of Writing. 225p. 1981. pap. text ed. 10.95 (ISBN 0-471-06222-7). Wiley.

Kelsch, Mary L. & Kelsch, Thomas. Writing Effectively: A Practical Guide. 192p. 1981. 10.95 (ISBN 0-13-969832-9, Spec); pap. 4.95 (ISBN 0-13-969824-8, Spec). P-H.

Klink, William. Sentence Writing. LC 80-5805. (Illus.). 141p. (Orig.). 1981. pap. text ed. 7.50 (ISBN 0-8191-1430-8). U Pr of Amer.

Konek, Carol, et al. The Source Book. 192p. (Orig.). 1981. pap. text ed. 7.95 (ISBN 0-582-28201-2); tchrs'. manual free (ISBN 0-582-28252-7). Longman.

Kroitor, Harry. The Five Hundred Word Theme Workbook. (Illus.). 224p. 1981. pap. 6.95 (ISBN 0-13-321612-8). P-H.

Lorch, Sue. Basic Writing: A Practical Approach. 300p. 1981. pap. text ed. 8.95. Winthrop.

Lynch, Robert E. & Swanzey, Thomas B. The Example of Science: An Anthology for College Composition. 320p. 1981. pap. text ed. 9.95 (ISBN 0-686-69275-6). P-H.

Measuring the Skills of Composition. 1981. pap. 11.95 (ISBN 0-932166-04-0). Instruct Object.

Mills, Helen. Commanding Paragraphs. 2nd ed. 1981. pap. text ed. 9.95x (ISBN 0-673-15442-4). Scott F.

Moody, Patricia. Writing Today: A Rhetoric & Handbook. (Illus.). 512p. 1981. pap. text ed. 12.95 (ISBN 0-13-971556-8). P-H.

Morgan, Roseann. The Writer's Work Workbook. 248p. 1981. pap. text ed. 6.95 (ISBN 0-13-969840-X). P-H.

New Voyages in English 7. 464p. 1979. 5.95 (ISBN 0-8294-0288-8); tchr's ed. 5.95. Loyola.

New Voyages in English 8. 5.95 (ISBN 0-8294-0286-1); tchr's ed. 5.95 (ISBN 0-8294-0287-X). Loyola.

Nicholas, J. Karl. Writing & Revising: A Workbook. 250p. 1981. pap. 7.95 (ISBN 0-13-971499-5). P-H.

An Orthographic Way of Writing English Prosody. 1976. pap. 1.95. Primary Pr.

Pack, Alice C. & Henrichsen, Lynn. Sentence Combination: Writing & Combining Standard English Sentences, Bk. II. 128p. (Orig.). 1981. pap. text ed. 5.95 (ISBN 0-88377-174-8). Newbury Hse.

Phelps-Terasaki, Diana & Phelps, Trisha. Disorders of Written Language: Methods & Programming for Redemiation. 350p. 1981. text ed. price not set (ISBN 0-89443-360-1). Aspen Systems.

Price, Jonathan. Thirty Days to More Powerful Writing. 192p. (Orig.). 1981. pap. 5.95 (ISBN 0-449-90047-9, Columbine). Fawcett.

Rafter, Rosalie & Alaia, Cheri. RCT Writing: A Workbook. 225p. (gr. 9-12). 1981. pap. 5.75 (ISBN 0-937820-10-5). Westsea Pub.

Schaal, Wilbert. Written Communication Skills. rev. ed. 114p. 1980. pap. 6.60 (ISBN 0-87771-022-8). Grad School.

Schor, Sandra & Fishman, Judith. The Random House Guide to Writing. 2nd ed. 464p. 1981. pap. text ed. 10.95 (ISBN 0-394-32608-3). Random.

Schuster, Edgar H. Sentence Mastery B: Pupil's Edition. (Sentence Mastery Ser.). (Illus.). 160p. (gr. 8). 1980. 3.96 (ISBN 0-07-055622-9, W). McGraw.

Sedley, Dorothy. College Writer's Workbook. 240p. 1981. pap. text ed. 7.95 (ISBN 0-675-08022-3); instr's. manual 3.95 (ISBN 0-686-69486-4). Merrill.

Smith, N. A. New Enlightenment. 1980. pap. 6.95 (ISBN 0-7145-3604-0). Riverrun NY.

Strong, William. Sentence Combing & Paragraph Building. (Illus.). 320p. 1981. pap. text ed. 8.95 (ISBN 0-394-31264-3). Random.

Teaching the Skills of Composition. 1980. pap. 11.95 (ISBN 0-932166-03-2). Instruct Object.

Vail, Priscilla. One Thousand One Games for Better Writing: Writing Easily, Clearly & Enthusiastically. LC 80-54818. (Illus.). 288p. 1981. 16.95 (ISBN 0-8027-0682-7). Walker & Co.

Weathers, Winston. An Alternative Style: Options in Compostition. 144p. 1980. text ed. 6.19x (ISBN 0-686-69598-4). Hayden.

Wendell, Barrett. English Composition. 316p. 1980. Repr. of 1903 ed. lib. bdg. 30.00 (ISBN 0-8495-5654-6). Arden Lib.

Wiener, Harvey S. The Writing Room: A Resource Book for Teachers of English. 352p. 1981. pap. 7.95 (ISBN 0-19-502826-0). Oxford U Pr.

Yehl, Joan K. & Bandlow, Richard F. P. O. W. E. R. The Reading - Writing Connection. (Illus.). 320p. 1981. pap. text ed. 8.95 (ISBN 0-675-08064-9); instr's. manual 3.95 (ISBN 0-686-69497-X). Merrill.

Ziegler, Alan. The Writing Workshop. (Orig.). 1981. pap. 6.00 (ISBN 0-915924-11-0). Tchrs & Writers Coll.

ENGLISH LANGUAGE–COMPOSITION AND EXERCISES–PROGRAMMED INSTRUCTION
see English Language–Programmed Instruction

ENGLISH LANGUAGE–CONVERSATION AND PHRASE BOOKS

Coe, Graham. Colloquial English. (Illus.). 192p. (Orig.). 1981. pap. 9.50 (ISBN 0-7100-0740-X). Routledge & Kegan.

Dobson, Julia M. & Hawkins, Gerald S. Conversation in English: Professional Careers. (Illus.). 108p. (gr. 9-12). 1978. pap. text ed. 3.96 (ISBN 0-278-46440-8). Litton Educ Pub.

Dobson, Julia M. & Sedwick, Frank. Conversation in English: Points of Departure. 2nd ed. (Illus.). 112p. 1981. pap. text ed. 3.80 (ISBN 0-278-46430-0). Litton Educ Pub.

Fitzpatrick, Anthony. English for International Conferences: A Language Course for Those Working in the Field of Science, Economics, Politics & Administration. (MFLP Ser.). 64p. 1980. pap. 60.00 includes 4 cassettes (ISBN 0-08-027225-8). Pergamon.

Montanare, John S. Chinese-English Phrase Book for Travellers. 200p. 1981. pap. text ed. 4.95 (ISBN 0-471-08298-8). Wiley.

ENGLISH LANGUAGE–DIAGRAMING
see English Language–Grammar

ENGLISH LANGUAGE–DIALECTS
see also Americanisms

Adams, Ramon F. Western Words: A Dictionary of the American West. LC 68-31369. 355p. 1981. pap. 9.95 (ISBN 0-8061-1173-9). U of Okla Pr.

Collis, Harry. Colloquial English. 96p. 1981. pap. text ed. write for info. (ISBN 0-88345-428-9). Regents Pub.

Gimson, A. C. An Introduction to the Pronunciation of English. 3rd ed. 352p. 1980. 19.00x (Pub. by Arnold Pubs England). State Mutual Bk.

Haycraft, Brita & Lee, W. R. It Depends on How You Say It: Dialogues in Everyday Social English. LC 80-41174. (Illus.). 128p. 1981. 12.00 (ISBN 0-08-025315-6); pap. 4.95 (ISBN 0-08-025314-8). Pergamon.

Schur, Norman W., ed. English English. 2nd ed. 300p. 1980. 28.00 (ISBN 0-8103-1096-1). Verbatim.

Wright, Peter. Cockney Dialect. 192p. 1981. 22.50 (ISBN 0-7134-2242-4, Pub. by Batsford England). David & Charles.

ENGLISH LANGUAGE–DICTIONARIES
see also English Language–Dictionaries, Juvenile; also subdivisions Etymology; Glossaries, Vocabularies, etc.; Idioms, Corrections, Errors; Rime; Synonyms and Antonyms; Terms and Phrases under English Language

Goldstein, Sam. The Birdicide of Cock Robin, & Other Murderous Words Ending in Cide. (Illus.). 68p. (Orig.). 1981. pap. 3.95 (ISBN 0-938338-04-8). Winds World Pr.

Kirkpatrick, E. M., ed. Chambers Universal Learners' Dictionary. 928p. 1980. 25.00x (ISBN 0-550-10632-4, Pub. by W & R Chambers Scotland). State Mutual Bk.

Macedonian-English, English-Macedonian Dictionary, 2 vols. 1978. Set. 20.00. Macedonian-English 476pp. English-Macedonian 422pp. Heinman.

New Webster's English Dictionary. (Handy Reference Bks.). (Orig.). 1981. pap. 3.50 (ISBN 0-8326-0056-3, 6480). Delair.

The New Webster's Quick Reference Dictionary. 1981. pap. 1.95 (ISBN 0-8326-0051-2, 6604). Delair.

New Webster's Thesaurus. (Handy Reference Bks.). (Orig.). 1981. pap. 3.50 (ISBN 0-8326-0055-5, 6482). Delair.

Oxford English Dictionary: Compact Edition, 2 vols. compact ed. 16569p. 1971. 75.00 (ISBN 0-918414-08-3). Readex Bks.

Schafer, Jurgen. Documentation in the O. E. D. Shakespeare & Nashe As Test Cases. (Illus.). 186p. 1980. text ed. 29.50x (ISBN 0-19-811938-0). Oxford U Pr.

Stein, Jess, ed. The Random House Dictionary. (Orig.). 1981. pap. 2.25 (ISBN 0-345-29096-8). Ballantine.

Wetterau, Bruce. The Last Crossword Dictionary. (Orig.). 1981. pap. 3.50 (ISBN 0-451-09910-9, E9910). NAL.

Zettler, Howard G., ed. Ologies & Isms: A Thematic Dictionary. 2nd ed. 300p. 1981. 28.00 (ISBN 0-8103-1055-4). Gale.

ENGLISH LANGUAGE–DICTIONARIES–ARABIC

Al Quareb, Al-Mawrid & Ba'Alabaki, Munir. English-Arabic Pocket Dictionary. 1980. pap. 5.50x. Intl Bk Ctr.

Ba'Albaki, Munir. English-Arabic Dictionary: Al-Mawrid. 1981. 45.00 (ISBN 0-686-69401-5). Intl Bk Ctr.

Elias, E. A. English-Arabic; Arabic-English Dictionary. pap. 12.00x. Intl Bk Ctr.

Manar, Al. English-Arabic Dictionary. 1971. 25.00x. Intl Bk Ctr.

Wahba, Magdi. Dictionary of Literary & Linguistic Terms: Arabic-Arabic. 25.00x. Intl Bk Ctr.

Wortabet, John. Arabic-English Pocket Dictionary. 1980. pap. 5.50x. Intl Bk Ctr.

--English-Arabic; Arabic-English Dictionary. 1979. pap. 15.00x. Intl Bk Ctr.

--English-Arabic Pocket Dictionary. 1980. pap. 5.50x. Intl Bk Ctr.

ENGLISH LANGUAGE–DICTIONARIES–ARMENIAN

Koushakdjian, Mardiros & Khantrouni, Dicran. Armenian-English - English-Armenian Dictionary. 2nd, rev. ed. 1372p. 1976. 35.00 (ISBN 0-686-68934-8). Heinman.

ENGLISH LANGUAGE–DICTIONARIES–CHINESE

English-Chinese & Chinese-English Dictionary. 1977. 7.95 (ISBN 0-8351-0725-6). China Bks.

Goodrich, Chauncey. A Pocket Dictionary: Chinese-English, & Pekingese Syllabary. 341p. 1981. pap. 2.50 (ISBN 0-85656-131-2). Great Eastern.

Makkai, Adam. A Dictionary of American Idioms in Chinese. Gates & Boatner, eds. 396p. 1981. pap. 10.95 (ISBN 0-8120-2386-2). Barron.

Montanaro, John S. Chinese-English Phrase Book for Travellers. 200p. 1981. pap. text ed. 4.95 (ISBN 0-471-08298-8). Wiley.

A Pocket English-Chinese Dictionary. 1980. pap. 4.95 (ISBN 0-8351-0727-2). China Bks.

ENGLISH LANGUAGE–DICTIONARIES–CZECH

Jouklova, Z. Technical Dictionary: English, Czech, English. 510p. (Czech.). 1970. 12.00x (ISBN 0-89918-301-8). Vanous.

Kolafova, V. & Slaba, D. Czech-English-Czech Dictionary. (For Travel Ser.). 394p. 1979. text ed. write for info. (ISBN 0-89918-302-6). Vanous.

ENGLISH LANGUAGE–DICTIONARIES–FRENCH

Cruikshank, Eleanor P. French-English Instant Vocabulary Francais-Anglais. 88p. 1980. pap. 4.00 (ISBN 0-9605284-0-7). Cruikshank.

Gieber, Robert L. An English-French Glossary of Educational Terminology. LC 80-5652. 212p. 1980. lib. bdg. 18.00 (ISBN 0-8191-1344-1); pap. text ed. 9.25 (ISBN 0-8191-1345-X). U Pr of Amer.

ENGLISH LANGUAGE–DICTIONARIES–GERMAN

Pheby, John. The Oxford-Duden Pictorial German-English Dictionary. The Dudenredaktion & German Section of Oxford Pr Dictionary Department, eds. (Illus.). 776p. 1980. text ed. 24.95x (ISBN 0-19-864135-4). Oxford U Pr.

Traupman, John C., ed. The Bantam New College German & English Dictionary. 768p. (Orig.). (gr. 7-12). 1981. pap. 2.50 (ISBN 0-553-14155-4). Bantam.

ENGLISH LANGUAGE–DICTIONARIES–GREEK

Greenfield, William. The Greek-English Lexicon to the New Testament. 216p. 1981. pap. 5.95 (ISBN 0-310-20351-1). Zondervan.

ENGLISH LANGUAGE–DICTIONARIES–HEBREW

Osbourn, William, Jr. A Hebrew & English Lexicon to the Old Testament. 287p. 1981. pap. 5.95 (ISBN 0-310-20361-9). Zondervan.

ENGLISH LANGUAGE–DICTIONARIES–HINDI

Pathak, R. C., ed. Hindi-English - English-Hindi Illustrated Dictionary, 2 vols. (Illus.). 1978. Set. 25.00 (ISBN 0-686-68936-4). Vol. 1, Hindi-Eng., 1512pp. Vol. 2. Eng.-Hindi, 1432pp. Heinman.

ENGLISH LANGUAGE–DICTIONARIES–HUNGARIAN

Orszagh, Laszlo. Hungarian-English - English-Hungarian Dictionary, 2 vols. 11th, rev. ed. 1977. Set. 15.00 (ISBN 0-686-68937-2). Vol. 1, Hung.-Eng., 464pp (ISBN 963-05-1255-6). Vol. 2, Eng.-Hung., 608pp (ISBN 963-05-1256-4). Heinman.

ENGLISH LANGUAGE–DICTIONARIES–ICELANDIC AND OLD NORSE

Sigurdsson, Angrimur & Bogason, Sigurdur O. Icelandic-English - English-Icelandic Dictionary, 2 vols. 3rd ed. 1980. Set. 130.00 (ISBN 0-686-68938-0). Vol. 1, Icelandic-Eng., 942pp. Vol. 2, Eng.-Icelandic, 862pp. Heinman.

ENGLISH LANGUAGE–DICTIONARIES–ITALIAN

Denti, Renzo. Dizionario Tecnico Italiano-Inglese--Inglese-Italiano. 9th rev. ed. 1811p. 1979. 44.00x (ISBN 88-203-1052-X). S F Vanni.

Lucchesi, Mario. Dizionario Medico Ragionato Inglese-Italiano: Termini, Abbreviazioni, Sigle, Eponimi e Sinonimi Medici, Medico-Biologici e Delle Specializzazionni Mediche. 1490p. 1978. 98.00x (ISBN 0-913298-52-2). S F Vanni.

Motta, Giuseppe. Dizionario Commerciale Inglese-Italiano--Italiano-Inglese: Economia, Legge, Finanza, Banca, Etc. 1051p. 1978. 40.00x (ISBN 0-913298-50-6). S F Vanni.

ENGLISH LANGUAGE–DICTIONARIES–JAPANESE

Kawamoto, Shigeo, et al, eds. The Kodansha Japanese-English Dictionary. Shimizu, Hamoru & Harita, Shigehisa, trs. 1250p. 1980. flexible soft-binding 19.95 (ISBN 0-87011-421-2). Kodansha.

ENGLISH LANGUAGE–DICTIONARIES–MAORI

Biggs, Bruce, ed. The Complete English-Maori Dictionary. 250p. 1981. 34.00 (ISBN 0-19-647989-4). Oxford U Pr.

ENGLISH LANGUAGE–DICTIONARIES–RUSSIAN

Kuznetsov, B., ed. Russian-English Polytechnical Dictionary. LC 80-41193. 900p. 1981. 100.00 (ISBN 0-08-023609-X). Pergamon.

ENGLISH LANGUAGE–DICTIONARIES–SPANISH

Barcelo, J. R. Spanish-English - English-Spanish Chemical Vocabulary. vii, 111p. (Orig.). 1980. pap. 7.50 (ISBN 84-205-0696-6). Heinman.

Mills, Dorothy H. & Martinez, Jorge C. Dictionary for the Health Professional: English-Spanish-Spanish-English. LC 79-90820. (Illus.). 250p. 1981. pap. 21.20 (ISBN 0-935356-03-7). Mills Pub Co.

New Webster's Quick Reference English-Spanish Dictionary. (Quick Reference Ser.). (Orig.). 1981. pap. 1.95 (ISBN 0-8326-0054-7, 6607). Delair.

ENGLISH LANGUAGE–DICTIONARIES–SWAHILI

Lipton, Gladys & Munoz, Olivia. Diccionario Del Ingles Americano. (Illus.). 368p. (gr. 10-12). 1981. pap. 2.95 (ISBN 0-8120-2319-6). Barron.

ENGLISH LANGUAGE–DICTIONARIES–TAGALOG

Guzman, Maria O. Tagalog-English - English-Tagalog Dictionary. rev. ed. xxxix, 678p. 1977. pap. 12.50 (ISBN 0-686-68939-9). Heinman.

ENGLISH LANGUAGE–DICTIONARIES–TURKISH

Goodenough, Ward H. & Sugita, Hiroshi. Trukese-English Dictionary. LC 79-54277. (Memoir Ser.: Vol. 141). 1980. 10.00 (ISBN 0-87169-141-8). Am Philos.

ENGLISH LANGUAGE–DICTIONARIES, JUVENILE

Madrigal, Margarita. Open Door to Spanish, Bk. 2. (Open Door to Spanish Ser.). 200p. (gr. 5-12). 1981. pap. text ed. 3.75 (ISBN 0-88345-427-0, 18470). Regents Pub.

ENGLISH LANGUAGE–ERRORS

see English Language–Idioms, Corrections, Errors

ENGLISH LANGUAGE–ETYMOLOGY

McDonald, Irene B. Language: All About It. 112p. (Orig.). (gr. 10-12). 1980. pap. text ed. 3.25x (ISBN 0-88334-140-9). Ind Sch Pr.

Maleska, Eugene. A Pleasure in Words. 1981. 15.95 (ISBN 0-671-24881-2). S&S.

--Take My Words. 1981. 14.95 (ISBN 0-671-24881-2). S&S.

ENGLISH LANGUAGE–ETYMOLOGY–JUVENILE LITERATURE

Lewis, Norman. Instant Word Power. (Orig.). 1981. pap. text ed. price not set (ISBN 0-87720-963-4). AMSCO Sch.

ENGLISH LANGUAGE–EXERCISES

see English Language–Composition and Exercises

ENGLISH LANGUAGE–EXPOSITION

see Exposition (Rhetoric)

ENGLISH LANGUAGE–GRAMMAR

see also English Language–Text-Books for Foreigners

Azur, Betty S. Understanding & Using English Grammar. (Illus.). 416p. 1981. pap. text ed. 10.95 (ISBN 0-13-936492-7, Spec). P-H.

Bordman, Marcia Beth, et al. Practical English Structure. (Practical English Structure Ser: ol. 1). (Illus.). 224p. 1981. text ed. 6.95 (ISBN 0-913580-65-1). Gallaudet Coll.

Burnham, Philip & Lederer, Richard. Basic Verbal Skills. 2nd ed. 243p. (gr. 9-12). 1980. pap. text ed. 4.95x (ISBN 0-88334-134-4). Ind Sch Pr.

--Workbook for Basic Verbal Skills. 2nd ed. 74p. (gr. 9-12). 1980. 2.50 (ISBN 0-88334-130-1). Ind Sch Pr.

Clark, Sarah. From Grammar to Paragraphs. 306p. 1981. pap. text ed. 8.95 (ISBN 0-394-32560-5). Random.

Cook, John L., et al. A New Way to Proficiency in English. 336p. 1980. pap. 9.95x (ISBN 0-631-12652-X, Pub. by Basil Blackwell). Biblio Dist.

DeCarrico, Jeanette S. Anaphoric Options of Indefinite Noun Phrases in English. (Linguistics Research Monograph Ser.: Vol. 3). 1981. text ed. 32.00 (ISBN 0-932998-03-8). Noit Amrofer.

Fox, Edward J. & Moore, Malcolm T. Junior Words, Phrases, Clauses: Exercises in Elementary Grammar. 89p. (Orig.). (gr. 4-6). 1980. pap. 3.25x (ISBN 0-88334-127-1). Ind Sch Pr.

--Words, Phrases, Clauses: Exercises in English Grammar. 3rd ed. 120p. (gr. 6-12). 1980. pap. text ed. 3.50 (ISBN 0-88334-128-X). Ind Sch Pr.

Greene, Samuel S. First Lessons in Grammar. Repr. of 1848 ed. write for info. (ISBN 0-8201-1349-2). Schol Facsimil.

Lutgendorf, Philip & James, Shirley M. The Parts of Speech. LC 77-730079. (Illus.). (gr. 7-9). 1976. pap. text ed. 95.00 (ISBN 0-89290-118-7, A134-SAR). Soc for Visual.

Mooney, Frank V. & Thomas, Cleveland A. Basic English Usage: The Parts of Speech. (Illus.). (gr. 7-12). 1962. pap. text ed. 37.80 (ISBN 0-89290-116-0, A133-SA). Soc for Visual.

New Voyages in English One. 168p. 1981. pap. 2.50 (ISBN 0-8294-0361-2); tchrs'. ed. 2.50 (ISBN 0-8294-0362-0). Loyola.

New Voyages in English Two. 168p. 1981. pap. 2.50 (ISBN 0-8294-0363-9); tchrs'. ed. 2.50 (ISBN 0-686-69394-9). Loyola.

Shepherd, James F. RSVP: The Houghton Mifflin Reading, Study, & Vocabulary Program. (Illus.). 352p. 1981. pap. text ed. 8.50 (ISBN 0-395-29342-1); write for info. instr's manual (ISBN 0-395-29343-X). HM.

Thomson, A. J. & Martinet, A. V. A Practical English Grammar. 3rd ed. 384p. 1980. pap. 7.95 (ISBN 0-19-431336-0). Oxford U Pr.

--A Practical English Grammar: Exercise One. 176p. 1980. 5.50x (ISBN 0-19-431337-9). Oxford U Pr.

--A Practical English Grammar: Exercises Two. 205p. 1980. 5.50x (ISBN 0-19-431338-7). Oxford U Pr.

Waterston, Elizabeth. Brush up Your Basics: Clear Thinking, Clear Writing. 112p. 1981. pap. text ed. 5.95 (ISBN 0-8403-2387-5). Kendall-Hunt.

Zorach, Cecile. English Grammar for Students of German. LC 80-82773. 1980. pap. 4.50 (ISBN 0-934034-02-8). Olivia & Hill.

ENGLISH LANGUAGE–GRAMMAR–PROGRAMMED INSTRUCTION

see English Language–Programmed Instruction

ENGLISH LANGUAGE–GRAMMAR, 1950-

Wiener, Harvey S. The Writing Room: A Resource Book for Teachers of English. 352p. 1981. pap. text ed. 7.95x (ISBN 0-19-502826-0). Oxford U Pr.

ENGLISH LANGUAGE–IDIOMS, CORRECTIONS, ERRORS

Makkai, Adam. A Dictionary of American Idioms in Chinese. Gates & Boatner, eds. 396p. 1981. pap. 10.95 (ISBN 0-8120-2386-2). Barron.

ENGLISH LANGUAGE–METRICS AND RHYTHMICS

see English Language–Rhythm; English Language–Style

ENGLISH LANGUAGE–ORTHOGRAPHY AND SPELLING

Ainsworth-Land, Vaune & Fletcher, Norma. Casting a Spell. (Illus., Orig.). 1980. pap. text ed. 7.95 (ISBN 0-914634-65-8, 7909). DOK Pubs.

Bremer. Skills in Spelling: 1973 Ed, Bks. A-H. Incl. Bk. A. (gr. 1). pap. text ed. 3.44 (ISBN 0-8009-0551-2); tchr's ed. 5.04 (ISBN 0-8009-0555-5); 1967 ed. of text & tchr's. ed. also avail. Write for further info.; Bk. B. (gr. 2). text ed. 6.88 (ISBN 0-8009-0649-7); pap. text ed. 3.44 (ISBN 0-8009-0564-4); tchr's. ed. for hardcover text 5.04 (ISBN 0-8009-0651-9); tchr's. ed. for pap. text 4.56 (ISBN 0-8009-0568-7); 1967-68 eds. of texts & tchr's ed. also avail. Write for further info.; Bk. C. (gr. 3). text ed. 6.88 (ISBN 0-8009-0653-5); pap. text ed. 3.44 (ISBN 0-8009-0576-8); tchr's. ed. for hardcover text 6.04 (ISBN 0-8009-0655-1); tchr's. ed. for pap. text 4.56 (ISBN 0-8009-0580-6); 1964 & 1967-68 eds. of texts & tchr's. ed. avail. Write for further info.; Bk. D. (gr. 4). text ed. 6.88 (ISBN 0-8009-0657-8); pap. text ed. 3.44 (ISBN 0-8009-0588-1); tchr's. ed. for hardcover text 5.04 (ISBN 0-8009-0659-4); tchr's. ed. for pap. text 4.56 (ISBN 0-8009-0593-8); 1964 & 1967-68 eds. of texts & tchr's. eds. also avail. Write for further info.; Bk. E. (gr. 5). text ed. 6.88 (ISBN 0-8009-0661-6); pap. text ed. 3.44 (ISBN 0-8009-0601-2); tchr's. ed. for hardcover text 5.04 (ISBN 0-8009-0663-2); tchr's. ed. for pap. text 4.56 (ISBN 0-8009-0605-5); 1967-68 eds. of texts & tchr's. eds. also avail. Write for further info.; Bk. F. (gr. 6). text ed. 6.88 (ISBN 0-8009-0665-9); pap. text ed. 3.44 (ISBN 0-8009-0614-4); tchr's. ed. for hardcover text 5.04 (ISBN 0-8009-0667-5); tchr's. ed. for pap. text 4.56 (ISBN 0-8009-0618-7); 1967-68 eds. also avail. Write for further info.; Bk. G. (gr. 7). text ed. 6.88 (ISBN 0-8009-0669-1); pap. text ed. 3.44 (ISBN 0-8009-0626-8); tchr's. ed. for hardcover text 5.04 (ISBN 0-8009-0671-3); tchr's. ed. for pap. text 4.56 (ISBN 0-8009-0630-6); 1964 & 1967-68 eds. also avail. Write for further info.; Bk. H. (gr. 8). text ed. 6.88 (ISBN 0-8009-0674-8); pap. text ed. 3.44 (ISBN 0-8009-0638-1); tchr's. ed. for hardcover text 5.04 (ISBN 0-8009-0676-4); tchr's. ed. for pap. text 4.56 (ISBN 0-8009-0643-8); 1964 & 1967-68 eds. also avail. Write for further info.. (gr. 1-8). McCormick-Mathers.

Crosby & Emery. Building College Spelling Skills. 192p. (Orig.). 1981. pap. text ed. 7.95 (ISBN 0-316-16186-1); tchrs'. manual free (ISBN 0-316-16188-8). Little.

Gregorvich, Barbara & Manoni, Mary H. Learning to Spell Correctly. LC 78-730054. (Illus.). 1978. pap. text ed. 99.00 (ISBN 0-89290-127-6, 331-SATC). Soc for Visual.

Hurtekant, Barbara. How to Teach Your Child to Spell: A Guide for Parents. LC 80-24308. 1980. pap. 7.95 (ISBN 0-937838-40-3); tchr's ed. 7.95 (ISBN 0-937838-41-1). Open Roads.

Kirkpatrick, E. M. & Schwartz, C. M. Chambers Spell Well. 256p. 1980. 10.00x (ISBN 0-550-11821-7, Pub. by W & R Chambers Scotland). State Mutual Bk.

Lewis, Norman. Instant Word Power. (Orig.). 1981. pap. text ed. price not set (ISBN 0-87720-963-4). AMSCO Sch.

New Webster's Quick Reference Speller. (Quick Reference Ser.). (Orig.). 1981. pap. 1.95 (ISBN 0-8326-0053-9, 6606). Delair.

New Webster's Speller. (Handy Reference Bks.). (Orig.). 1981. pap. 3.50 (ISBN 0-8326-0042-3, 6481). Delair.

Raygor, A. & Scnmelzer, R. Word Attack & Spelling: An Audio Tutorial. 1981. 250.00 (ISBN 0-13-963215-8); student wkbk. 7.95 (ISBN 0-13-963223-9). P-H.

Sanderlin, David. Spelling for the Aviation Technician. 75p. (Orig.). 1980. write for info. (ISBN 0-89100-180-8). Aviation Maintenance.

Smalley, W. A., et al. Orthography Studies. 1964. 3.00 (ISBN 0-8267-0027-6, 08508). United Bible.

Spelling Program: Diagnostic & Prescriptive, 30 bks. (gr. 2 up). 1981. Set. 73.95 (ISBN 0-686-69580-1); pap. 2.25 test booklet (ISBN 0-686-69581-X). B Loft.

Wallace, Mary L. Spelling. Raygor, Alton, ed. (Communication Skills Ser.). 288p. 1981. pap. text ed. 7.95 (ISBN 0-07-067901-0, C). McGraw.

Williams, Ralph M. Phonetic Spelling for College Students. LC 80-24084. 180p. 1980. Repr. of 1960 ed. lib. bdg. 27.50x (ISBN 0-313-22650-4, WIPS). Greenwood.

ENGLISH LANGUAGE–ORTHOGRAPHY AND SPELLING–PROGRAMMED INSTRUCTION

Baggett, Richard C. A Programmed Approach to Good Spelling! 160p. 1981. pap. text ed. 6.95 (ISBN 0-13-729764-5). P-H.

ENGLISH LANGUAGE–PARSING

see English Language–Grammar

ENGLISH LANGUAGE–PHONOLOGY

Here are entered works on the history of sounds or letters and the laws which govern their changes.

Anttila, Elizabeth K. English Oral Production. 1980. pap. write for info. (ISBN 0-8477-3333-5). U of PR Pr.

Brook, G. L. English Sound Changes. 175p. 6.00x (ISBN 0-7190-0111-0, Pub.by Manchester U Pr England). State Mutual Bk.

Gimson, A. C. An Introduction to the Pronunciation of English. 3rd ed. 352p. 1980. 19.00x (Pub. by Arnold Pubs England). State Mutual Bk.

Robson, Ernest. Phonetic Music. 1981. 19.00. Primary Pr.

ENGLISH LANGUAGE–PHRASES AND TERMS

see English Language–Terms and Phrases

ENGLISH LANGUAGE–PRIMERS

see Readers

ENGLISH LANGUAGE–PROGRAMMED INSTRUCTION

Brengelman, Fred. Shaping Sentences & Paragraphs: A Systematic Approach to Sentence & Paragraph Construction. 128p. 1980. pap. 6.95 (ISBN 0-8403-2292-5). Kendall-Hunt.

Ljung, Magnus. Reflections on the English Progressive. (Gothenberg Studies in English: 46). 166p. 1981. pap. text ed. 19.75x (ISBN 91-7346-080-X, Pub. by Acta Univertatis, Sweden). Humanities.

Thomson, A. J. & Martinet, A. V. A Practical English Grammar: Exercise One. 176p. 1980. 5.50x (ISBN 0-19-431337-9). Oxford U Pr.

--A Practical English Grammar: Exercises Two. 205p. 1980. 5.50x (ISBN 0-19-431338-7). Oxford U Pr.

Widdowson, H. G., ed. Reading & Thinking in English: Discourse in Action. (Reading & Thinking in English Ser.). (Illus.). 128p. 1980. pap. 5.95 (ISBN 0-19-451357-2); 10.95 (ISBN 0-19-451358-0). Oxford U Pr.

ENGLISH LANGUAGE–PRONUNCIATION

Here are entered works on the pronunciation of words (as distinct from that of particular sounds or letters) especially with reference to best usage.

Cercignani, Fausto. Shakespeare's Works & Elizabethan Pronunciation. 448p. 1981. 74.00 (ISBN 0-19-811937-2). Oxford U Pr.

An Orthographic Way of Writing English Prosody. 1976. pap. 1.95. Primary Pr.

ENGLISH LANGUAGE–READERS

see Readers

ENGLISH LANGUAGE–REVERSE DICTIONARIES

see English Language–Synonyms and Antonyms

ENGLISH LANGUAGE–RHETORIC

see also English Language–Composition and Exercises; English Language–Style; Exposition (Rhetoric)

Buckley, Edmund H. & Solkov, Arnold. A Conceptual Approach to College Writing. 2nd ed. 112p. 1980. pap. text ed. 6.95 (ISBN 0-8403-2308-5). Kendall-Hunt.

Corbett, Edward P. The Little English Handbook: Choices & Conventions. 3rd ed. 300p. 1981. pap. text ed. 5.95 (ISBN 0-471-07856-5). Wiley.

Croteau, Leo H. Generative Rhetoric, a Teaching Guide for English Composition. 300p. 1980. tchrs.' ed. 25.00 (ISBN 0-9602582-0-5). Neechee Assoc.

Holcombe, Marya & Stein, Judith. Writing for Decision Makers. LC 80-24900. 260p. 1980. text ed. 14.95 leaders manual (ISBN 0-534-97980-7). Lifetime Learn.

McMahan, Elizabeth. A Crash Course in Composition. 3rd ed. 272p. 1980. pap. text ed. 8.95 (ISBN 0-07-045458-2, C); instructor's manual 4.95 (ISBN 0-07-045459-0). McGraw.

Ruggiero. Art of Writing. 1981. 11.95 (ISBN 0-88284-118-1); manuel free (ISBN 0-88284-129-7). Alfred Pub.

Tate, Gary & Corbett, Edward P., eds. The Writing Teacher's Sourcebook. 400p. 1981. pap. text ed. 9.95x (ISBN 0-19-502878-3). Oxford U Pr.

Wiener, Harvey S. The Writing Room: A Resource Book for Teachers of English. 352p. 1981. pap. text ed. 7.95x (ISBN 0-19-502826-0). Oxford U Pr.

ENGLISH LANGUAGE–RHYTHM

Wilson, Katherine M. The Real Rhythm in English Poetry. 171p. 1980. Repr. of 1929 ed. lib. bdg. 25.00 (ISBN 0-89987-860-1). Darby Bks.

ENGLISH LANGUAGE–SELF-INSTRUCTION

see also English Language–Programmed Instruction

Claire, Elizabeth. A Foreign Student's Guide to Dangerous English. (Illus.). 92p. (Orig.). 1980. pap. 4.95 (ISBN 0-937630-00-4). Eardley Pubns.

ENGLISH LANGUAGE–SENTENCES

Lutgendorf, Philip & Gray, Mary Jane. Sentence Structure. LC 77-730353. (Illus.). (gr. 7-9). 1977. pap. text ed. 95.00 (ISBN 0-89290-119-5, A144). Soc for Visual.

Mooney, Frank V. & Thomas, Cleveland A. Basic English Usage: The Sentence. (Illus.). (gr. 7-12). 1964. pap. text ed. 49.50 (ISBN 0-89290-117-9, A133SB). Soc for Visual.

ENGLISH LANGUAGE–SENTENCES–PROGRAMMED INSTRUCTION

Brengelman, Fred. Shaping Sentences & Paragraphs: A Systematic Approach to Sentence & Paragraph Construction. 128p. 1980. pap. 6.95 (ISBN 0-8403-2292-5). Kendall-Hunt.

ENGLISH LANGUAGE–SPELLING

see English Language–Orthography and Spelling

ENGLISH LANGUAGE–SPOKEN ENGLISH

Dixon, Robert. El Ingles En Accion: See It& Say It in English. pap. 1.75 (ISBN 0-451-08060-2, E8060, Sig). NAL.

ENGLISH LANGUAGE–STUDY AND TEACHING

British European Centre, Paris. Explorations: The English Language Course of the British European Centre. (Pergamon Institute of English Courses Ser.). 160p. 1981. pap. 5.95 (ISBN 0-08-025358-X). Pergamon.

Editors of NCTE Committee & Stanford, Gene, eds. Classroom Practices in Teaching English, 1980-1981: Dealing with Differences. (Classroom Practices in Teaching English Ser.). 144p. 1980. 5.00 (ISBN 0-8141-0690-0, 06900). NCTE.
Spann, Sylvia & Culp, Mary B., eds. Thematic Units in Teaching English & the Humanities. 2nd ed. (Orig.). (gr. 6-12). 1980. pap. text ed. 6.00 (ISBN 0-8141-5376-3). NCTE.
Wiener, Harvey S. The Writing Room: A Resource Book for Teachers of English. 352p. 1981. pap. 7.95 (ISBN 0-19-502826-0). Oxford U Pr.

ENGLISH LANGUAGE–STUDY AND TEACHING–FOREIGN STUDENTS

Cooper, Stephen. Graduate Theses & Dissertations in ESL: 1978-79. (Language in Education Ser.: No. 27). 1980. pap. text ed. 2.95 (ISBN 0-87281-127-1). Ctr Appl Ling.
--Graduate Theses Dissertations in E S L: Nineteen Seventy-Six to Nineteen Seventy-Seven. (Language in Education Ser.: No. 3). 1978. pap. text ed. 2.95 (ISBN 0-87281-079-8). Ctr Appl Ling.
Cooper, T., et al. Sentence Combining in Second Language Construction. (Language in Education Ser.: No. 31). 1980. pap. text ed. 7.95 (ISBN 0-87281-130-1). Ctr Appl Ling.
Duff, Alan. The Third Language: Recurrent Problems of Translation into English. LC 80-41116. (Language Teaching Methodology Ser.). 160p. 1981. 23.65 (ISBN 0-08-027248-7); pap. 11.95 (ISBN 0-08-025334-2). Pergamon.
English Language & Orientation Programs in the United States. 130p. 1980. 5.00 (IIE). Unipub.
Erazmus, Edward T. & Cargas, Harry J. English As a Second Language: A Reader. 3rd ed. 1980. pap. text ed. 9.95 (ISBN 0-697-03958-7). Wm C Brown.
Ferreira, Linda. Notion by Notion. 96p. (Orig.). 1981. pap. text ed. 3.95 (ISBN 0-88377-199-3). Newbury Hse.
Gruber, Edward C. Test of English As a Foreign Language (TOEFL) rev. ed. (Exam Preparation Ser.). 528p. (gr. 12). 1981. pap. text ed. 6.95 (ISBN 0-671-18987-5). Monarch Pr.
Lado, Robert. Lado English Series, Bk. 6. (Illus.). 202p. (gr. 7-12). 1980. pap. text ed. 3.75 (ISBN 0-88345-333-9); wkbk 2.25 (ISBN 0-88345-339-8). Regents Pub.
McDonough, Steven H. Psychology in Foreign Language Teaching. (Illus.). 176p. 1981. text ed. 25.00x (ISBN 0-04-418002-0, 2628-9); pap. text ed. 8.95x (ISBN 0-04-418003-9). Allen Unwin.
Teaching a Second Language: A Guide for the Student Teacher. (Language in Education Ser.: No. 28). 1980. pap. text ed. 4.95 (ISBN 0-87281-127-1). Ctr Appl Ling.

ENGLISH LANGUAGE–STUDY AND TEACHING (ELEMENTARY)

Butterworth, John H., 3rd. Tripper, the Sound Hound Book One: The Round Sounds. (Illus.). 1981. 4.50 (ISBN 0-533-04390-5). Vantage.
Dacey, John. Where the World Is, Teaching Basic Skills Outdoors. (Illus.). 192p. (Orig.). 1981. pap. 10.95 (ISBN 0-8302-9605-0). Goodyear.
Fletcher, Cynthia H. My Jesus Pocketbook of ABC's. (Illus.). 32p. (Orig.). (ps). pap. 0.49 (ISBN 0-937420-01-8). Stirrup Assoc.
Lind, Carolyn P., pseud. One Hundred Four Ideas for Improving Your Young Child's Language Skills. (Illus.). 80p. (Orig.). 1980. pap. 10.00 (ISBN 0-9604940-0-6). Lindell Pubs.

ENGLISH LANGUAGE–STUDY AND TEACHING (SECONDARY)

Carter, Candy & Rashkis, Zora, eds. Ideas for Teaching English in the Junior High & Middle School. LC 80-25921. 320p. 1980. 15.00 (ISBN 0-8141-2253-1). NCTE.
Glatthorn, Allan A. A Guide for an English Curriculum for the Eighties. 1980. pap. 6.50 (ISBN 0-8141-1922-0). NCTE.

ENGLISH LANGUAGE–STYLE

Shopen, T. & Willaims, J., eds. Styles & Variables in English. (English Ser.). (Illus.). 14.95 (ISBN 0-87626-866-1). Winthrop.

ENGLISH LANGUAGE–SYNONYMS AND ANTONYMS

New Webster's Quick Reference Thesaurus. (Quick Reference Ser.). (Orig.). 1981. pap. 1.95 (ISBN 0-8326-0052-0, 6605). Delair.
Townley, Helen M. & Gee, Ralph C. Thesaurus-Making: Grow Your Own Word-Stock. (Grafton Ser.). 208p. 1981. lib. bdg. 25.00x (ISBN 0-86531-107-2). Westview.

ENGLISH LANGUAGE–SYNTAX

DeCarrico, Jeanette S. Anaphoric Options of Indefinite Noun Phrases in English. (Linguistics Research Monograph Ser.: Vol. 3). 1981. text ed. 32.00 (ISBN 0-932998-03-8). Noit Amrofer.

ENGLISH LANGUAGE–TERMS AND PHRASES

LaRoche, Nancy & Urdang, Laurence, eds. Picturesque Expressions: A Thematic Dictionary. LC 80-22705. 300p. 1980. 35.00 (ISBN 0-8103-1122-4). Gale.
Mellado De Hunter, Elena. Anglicimos Profesionales De Puerto Rico. LC 80-17935. (Coleccion Mente y Palabra). 241p. (Span.). 1980. 6.25 (ISBN 0-8477-0578-1); pap. 5.00 (ISBN 0-8477-0579-X). U of PR Pr.

ENGLISH LANGUAGE–TEXT-BOOKS FOR FOREIGNERS

see also English Language–Self-Instruction

Annand, William S. & Wise, Sheldon. The ALA TOEFL Course. 2nd ed. (Orig.). 1980. Set Includes Tchrs.' Handbk, Classwork Bk, Homework Bk. pap. text ed. write for info. (ISBN 0-934270-00-7). Antiquary Pr.
Bolitho, Red & Tomlinson, Brian. Discover English. (Illus.). 168p. (Orig.). 1980. pap. text ed. 9.95x (ISBN 0-04-371076-X, 2586). Allen Unwin.
Close, R. A. English As a Foreign Language. 3rd ed. 224p. (Orig.). 1981. pap. text ed. 10.95x (ISBN 0-04-425025-8, 2638). Allen Unwin.
Conversational English in Ten Days. 1981. pap. 14.95 including tape (ISBN 0-686-69460-0). Plymouth Pr.
Dobson, Julia M. & Hawkins, Gerald S. Conversation in English: Professional Careers. (Illus.). 108p. (gr. 9-12). 1978. pap. text ed. 3.96 (ISBN 0-278-46440-8). Litton Educ Pub.
Fingado, Gail, et al. The English Connection: A Text for Speakers of Englisn As a Second Language. (English Ser.). 416p. 1981. text ed. 12.95 (ISBN 0-87626-236-1). Winthrop.
First Steps in Reading & Writing: Books One & Two. (Gateway to English Program Ser.). (Illus., Orig.). (gr. 7-12). 1981. pap. text ed. 4.50 ea. Vol. 1 (ISBN 0-88377-186-1). Vol. 2 (ISBN 0-88377-195-0). Newbury Hse.
Flint, Austin. Insights: A Contemporary Reader. 192p. (Orig.). 1981. pap. text ed. 5.95 (ISBN 0-88377-185-3). Newbury Hse.
Hileman, Josephine & Colman, Bruce. Coming to America. (Newbury House Readers Ser.: Stage 3 - Intermediate). 48p. (Orig.). (gr. 7-12). 1981. pap. text ed. 1.95 (ISBN 0-88377-196-9). Newbury Hse.
McPartland, Pamela. Take It Easy: American Indians & Two Word Verbs for Students of English As a Foreign Language. (ESL Ser.). 176p. 1981. pap. text ed. 6.95 (ISBN 0-13-882902-0). P-H.
Malkemes, Fred & Pires, Deborah S. Looking at English: An ESL Text-Workbook for Beginners, Bk. 1. (English As a Second Language Ser.). (Illus.). 256p. 1981. pap. text ed. 7.95 (ISBN 0-13-540401-0). P-H.
Malkenes, Fred & Pires, Deborah S. Looking at English: An ESL Text-Workbook for Beginners, Bk. 2. (Illus.). 288p. 1981. pap. text ed. 8.95 (ISBN 0-13-540427-4). P-H.
Monte, Provindencia C., ed. Learning Modules for the Basic Course in English, Vol. 1. LC 79-22332. 304p. 1980. pap. 8.00 (ISBN 0-8477-3324-6). U of PR Pr.
Mouthany, J. R. English Without Teacher & Dictionary: English-Arabic. 7.95x. Intl Bk Ctr.
Rackmill, Ruth. Let's Have Fun with English. LC 80-68407. 120p. 1981. perfect bdg. 6.95 (ISBN 0-86548-061-3). Century Twenty One.
Sayasithsena, Souksomboun, tr. Delta's Effective English As a Second Language for the 21st Century Laotian Supplement. 104p. (Orig.). 1980. pap. 4.95 (ISBN 0-937354-02-3). Delta Systems.
Widdowson, H. G., ed. Reading & Thinking in English: Discourse in Action. (Reading & Thinking in English Ser.). (Illus.). 128p. 1980. pap. 5.95 (ISBN 0-19-451357-2); 10.95 (ISBN 0-19-451358-0). Oxford U Pr.
Wishon, George E. & Burks, Julia M. Let's Write English. rev. ed. 430p. (gr. 9-12). 1980. pap. text ed. 5.20 (ISBN 0-278-47520-5); tchrs. ed. 1.20 (ISBN 0-278-47522-1). Litton Educ Pub.
Woodford, Protase E. & Kernan, Doris. Bridges to English, Bk. 1. Rebisz, J., ed. LC 80-21012. (Illus.). 144p. 1980. pap. text ed. 5.64 (ISBN 0-07-034481-7, W); write for info. tchrs. ed. (ISBN 0-07-034482-5); wkbk. 3.52 (ISBN 0-07-034483-3); cassettes avail. (ISBN 0-07-034484-1); cue cards avail. (ISBN 0-07-034485-X); tests avail. (ISBN 0-07-034486-8). McGraw.
Yorkey, Richard C., et al. English for International Communication: InterCom, Bk. 1. (Illus.). 200p. 1981. pap. text ed. price not set (ISBN 0-278-49201-0); price not set tchr's. ed. (ISBN 0-278-49216-9); price not set wkbk (ISBN 0-278-49230-4); price not set audio prog. (ISBN 0-278-49245-2). Litton Educ Pub.

ENGLISH LANGUAGE–TEXT-BOOKS FOR FOREIGNERS–CHINESE

Montanare, John S. Chinese-English Phrase Book for Travellers. 200p. 1981. pap. text ed. 4.95 (ISBN 0-471-08298-8). Wiley.
Yen, Isabella Y. English for Speakers of Mandarin Chinese. (English As a Foreign Language Ser.). 356p. 1981. text & cassettes 85.00x (ISBN 0-87950-603-2); cassettes 80.00 (ISBN 0-686-69430-9). text ed. 10.00x (ISBN 0-87950-301-7). Spoken Lang Serv.

ENGLISH LANGUAGE–TEXT-BOOKS FOR FOREIGNERS–SPANISH

Mellado De Hunter, Elena. Anglicimos Profesionales De Puerto Rico. LC 80-17935. (Coleccion Mente y Palabra). 241p. (Span.). 1980. 6.25 (ISBN 0-8477-0578-1); pap. 5.00 (ISBN 0-8477-0579-X). U of PR Pr.
Savaiano, Eugene & Winget, Lynn W. Two Thousand & One Modismos Espanoles e Ingleses. (Barron's Educational Ser.). 336p. 1981. pap. 3.95 (ISBN 0-8120-2314-5). Barron.

ENGLISH LANGUAGE–TEXT-BOOKS FOR FOREIGNERS–VIETNAMESE

Gage, William W. English for Speakers of Vietnamese. (English As a Foreign Language Ser.). 366p. 1981. text & 9 cassettes 85.00 (ISBN 0-87950-617-2); cassettes separate 80.00 (ISBN 0-87950-616-4). Spoken Lang Serv.

ENGLISH LANGUAGE–USAGE

Burnham, Philip & Lederer, Richard. Basic Verbal Skills. 2nd ed. 243p. (gr. 9-12). 1980. pap. text ed. 4.95x (ISBN 0-88334-134-4). Ind Sch Pr.
--Workbook for Basic Verbal Skills. 2nd ed. 74p. (gr. 9-12). 1980. 2.50 (ISBN 0-88334-130-1). Ind Sch Pr.
Cook, John L., et al. A New Way to Proficiency in English. 336p. 1980. pap. 9.95x (ISBN 0-631-12652-X, Pub. by Basil Blackwell). Biblio Dist.
Howard, Philip. Words Fail Me. 1981. 13.95 (ISBN 0-19-520237-6). Oxford U Pr.
Lamberts, J. J. A Short Introduction to English Usage. 400p. 1981. Repr. lib. bdg. write for info. (ISBN 0-89874-328-1). Krieger.
Mooney, Frank V. & Thomas, Cleveland A. Basic English Usage: The Parts of Speech. (Illus.). (gr. 7-12). 1962. pap. text ed. 37.80 (ISBN 0-89290-116-0, A133-SA). Soc for Visual.

ENGLISH LANGUAGE–VOCABULARY

see Vocabulary

ENGLISH LANGUAGE–VOWELS

Horlock, Carole. Initial Vowels. (Illus.). 24p. (gr. 1-3). 1980. pap. 3.95 (ISBN 0-933358-61-X). Enrich.

ENGLISH LETTERS

Dawson, William J. & Dawson, Coningsby W. The Great English Letter-Writers, 2 vols. 1980. Set. lib. bdg. 50.00 (ISBN 0-8492-4218-5). R West.
Duckitt, M. & Wragg, H. Selected English Letters: Fifteenth to Nineteenth Centuries. 599p. 1981. Repr. of 1941 ed. lib. bdg. 20.00 (ISBN 0-89987-158-5). Darby Bks.
Dunton, John. Teague Land or a Journey Among the Wilde Irish. 80p. 1981. Repr. 10.00x (ISBN 0-906127-25-4, Pub. by Irish Academic Pr Ireland). Biblio Dist.
King, James & Ryskamp, Charles, eds. The Letters & Prose Writings of William Cowper, Volume II: Letters 1782-1786. (Illus.). 586p. 1981. 98.00 (ISBN 0-19-812607-7). Oxford U Pr.
MacKenzie, M., ed. The Letters of Sidney & Beatrice Webb. Incl. Vol. 1.; Vol. 2. (ISBN 0-685-85982-7); Vol. 3.. LC 77-1665. 1978. 69.95 ea.; Set. 185.00 (ISBN 0-521-22015-7). Cambridge U Pr.
Selected English Letters: Fifteen to Nineteen Centuries. anthology ed. 460p. 1980. Repr. of 1913 ed. lib. bdg. 12.50 (ISBN 0-8495-1060-0). Arden Lib.
Strauss, Richard & Von Hofmannsthal, Hugo. The Correspondence Between Richard Strauss & Hugo Von Hofmannsthal. Hammelmann, Hanns & Osers, Ewald, trs. LC 80-40072. 576p. 1981. 67.50 (ISBN 0-521-23476-X); pap. 17.95 (ISBN 0-521-29911-X). Cambridge U Pr.
Wilmot, John. The Letters of John Wilmot, Earl of Rochester. Treglown, Jeremy, ed. LC 80-20592. 1980. lib. bdg. 26.00x (ISBN 0-226-81181-6). U of Chicago Pr.

ENGLISH LETTERS–HISTORY AND CRITICISM

Duckitt, M. & Wragg, H. Selected English Letters: Fifteenth to Nineteenth Centuries. 599p. 1981. Repr. of 1941 ed. lib. bdg. 20.00 (ISBN 0-89987-158-5). Darby Bks.

ENGLISH LITERATURE (COLLECTIONS)–TO 1100

see Anglo-Saxon Literature (Collections)

ENGLISH LITERATURE (COLLECTIONS)–MIDDLE ENGLISH (1100-1500)

Edwards, A. S. & Pearsall, Derek, eds. Middle English Prose: Essays on Bibliographical Problems. LC 80-8595. 150p. 1981. lib. bdg. 25.00 (ISBN 0-8240-9453-0). Garland Pub.

ENGLISH LITERATURE (COLLECTIONS)–EARLY MODERN, 1500-1700

Jonson, Ben. Work of Ben Jonson. Herford, C. H., et al, eds. Incl. Vol. 1. 42.00x (ISBN 0-19-811352-8); Vol. 2. 42.00x (ISBN 0-19-811353-6); Vol. 5. 46.50x (ISBN 0-19-811356-0); Vol. 7. 49.00x (ISBN 0-19-811358-7); Vol. 8. 49.00x (ISBN 0-19-811359-5); Vol. 10. 49.00x (ISBN 0-19-811361-7); Vol. 11. 49.00x (ISBN 0-19-811362-5). 1925-52. Oxford U Pr.

ENGLISH LITERATURE (COLLECTIONS)–TO 1700

Carey, John. English Renaissance Studies: Presented to Dame Helen Gardner in Honour of Her Seventieth Birthday. (Illus.). 312p. 1980. 44.00x (ISBN 0-19-812093-1). Oxford U Pr.

ENGLISH LITERATURE (COLLECTIONS)–18TH CENTURY

Bellringer, A. W. & Jones, C. B., eds. The Romantic Age in Prose. (Costerus Ser.: Vol. XXIX). 159p. 1981. pap. text ed. 28.50x (Pub. by Radopi, Holland). Humanities.

ENGLISH LITERATURE–BIBLIOGRAPHY

Corse, Larry B. & Corse, Sandra B. Articles on American & British Literature: An Index to Selected Periodicals, 1950-1977. 450p. 1981. 30.00x (ISBN 0-8040-0408-0). Swallow.
Hull, Suzanne W. Chaste, Silent & Obedient: English Books for Women, 1475-1640. (Illus.). 1980. write for info. (ISBN 0-87328-115-2). Huntington Lib.

ENGLISH LITERATURE–HISTORY AND CRITICISM

Aldington, Richard. A Book of Characters from Theophrastus Joseph Hall, Sir Thomas Overbury, Nicolas Breton, John Earle, Thomas Fuller, & Other English Authors; Jean De la Bruyere, Vauvenargues, & Other French Authors. 559p. 1980. Repr. of 1924 ed. lib. bdg. 50.00 (ISBN 0-8482-0049-7). Norwood Edns.
Daiches, David & Flower, John. Literary Landscape of the British Isles: A Narrative Atlas. 288p. 1981. pap. 7.95 (ISBN 0-14-005735-8). Penguin.
Haynes, E S. Early Victorian & Other Papers. 78p. 1980. Repr. lib. bdg. 25.00 (ISBN 0-89984-287-9). Century Bookbindery.
Ironic Historian: The Narrator of Books 3 & 4 of the Faerie Queene. (Elizabethan Studies: No. 98). 1980. pap. text ed. 25.00x (ISBN 0-391-02186-9). Humanities.
MacLaine, Allan, intro. by. The Beginnings to Fifteen Fifty-Eight. 96p. 1981. pap. 4.95 (ISBN 0-312-07190-6). St Martin.
Moody, W. V. & Lovett, R. M. A History of English Literature. 591p. 1980. Repr. lib. bdg. 30.00 (ISBN 0-89760-547-0). Telegraph Bks.
Muir, Kenneth, intro. by. The Romantic Period. 140p. 1981. pap. 5.95 (ISBN 0-312-69174-2). St Martin.
Murphy, James J. Renaissance Rhetoric: A Short Title Catalogue. LC 80-8501. 400p. 1981. lib. bdg. 50.00 (ISBN 0-8240-9487-5). Garland Pub.
Panitz, Esther L. The Alien in Their Midst: Images of the Jews in English Literature. LC 78-75183. 150p. 1981. 10.50 (ISBN 0-8386-2318-2). Fairleigh Dickinson.
Raghavacharyulu, D. V. The Critical Response: Selected Essays on the American, Commonwealth,Indian & British Traditions in Literature. 1980. 13.50x (ISBN 0-8364-0632-X, Pub. by Macmillan India). South Asia Bks.
Redmond, J., et al, eds. Year's Work in English Studies, Vol. 58, 1977. 639p. 1980. text ed. 39.00x (ISBN 0-391-01320-3). Humanities.
Reed, Henry. Lectures on English Literature from Chaucer to Tennyson. 411p. 1980. Repr. of 1876 ed. lib. bdg. 40.00 (ISBN 0-89984-430-8). Century Bookbindery.
Tolkien, J. R. The Old English Exodus. Turville-Petre, Joan, ed. 128p. 1981. 24.00 (ISBN 0-19-811177-0). Oxford U Pr.
Waller, G. F. Mary Sidney, Countess of Pembroke: A Critical Study of Her Writings & Literary Milieu. (Elizabethan Studies: No. 87). 1980. pap. text ed. 25.00x (ISBN 0-391-02161-3). Humanities.

ENGLISH LITERATURE–HISTORY AND CRITICISM–ADDRESSES, ESSAYS AND LECTURES

Buono, Dello & Joseph, Carmen. Rare Early Essays on the Brontes. 218p. 1980. lib. bdg. 17.50 (ISBN 0-8482-0646-0). Norwood Edns.
Wylie, Laura J. Studies in the Revolution of English Criticism. 212p. 1980. Repr. of 1903 ed. text ed. 25.00 (ISBN 0-8492-2997-9). R West.

ENGLISH LITERATURE–HISTORY AND CRITICISM–MIDDLE ENGLISH (1100-1500)

Darrah, John. The Real Camelot: Paganism & the Arthurian Romances. 160p. 1981. 13.95 (ISBN 0-500-01250-4). Thames Hudson.

ENGLISH LITERATURE–HISTORY AND CRITICISM–EARLY MODERN, 1500-1700

Huntley, Frank L. Essays in Persuasion: On Seventeenth-Century English Literature. LC 80-14477. 1981. 14.00x (ISBN 0-226-36088-1). U of Chicago Pr.

ENGLISH LITERATURE–HISTORY AND CRITICISM–19TH CENTURY

Baily, F. E. The Perfect Age. 187p. 1981. Repr. of 1946 ed. lib. bdg. 30.00 (ISBN 0-89987-064-3). Darby Bks.
David, Deirdre. Fictions of Resolution in Three Victorian Novels. LC 80-16262. 304p. 1981. text ed. 20.00x (ISBN 0-231-04980-3). Columbia U Pr.
Hogg, James, ed. Romantic Reassessmeent: Studies in Nineteenth Century Literature. (Salzberg Studies in English Literature: 87-2). 144p. 1981. pap. text ed. 25.00x (ISBN 0-391-02245-8, Pub. by Salzburg, Austria). Humanities.
Landow, George P. Victorian Types, Victorian Shadows: Biblical Typology in Victorian Literature, Art & Thought. 256p. 1980. 24.95 (ISBN 0-7100-0598-9). Routledge & Kegan.
Walker, Hugh. The Age of Tennyson. 309p. 1980. Repr. of 1932 ed. lib. bdg. 25.00 (ISBN 0-89760-914-X). Telegraph Bks.

ENGLISH LITERATURE–HISTORY AND CRITICISM–20TH CENTURY

Fonstad, Karen W. The Atlas of the Middle-Earth. 224p. 1981. 14.95 (ISBN 0-686-69045-1). HM.
Hobsbaum, Phillip. A Reader's Guide to D. H. Lawrence. 160p. 1981. 17.95 (ISBN 0-500-14023-5); pap. 9.95 (ISBN 0-500-15017-6). Thames Hudson.
Swinnerton, Frank. Background with Chorus. 236p. 1980. Repr. of 1956 ed. lib. bdg. 30.00 (ISBN 0-8492-8124-5). R West.

ENGLISH LITERATURE–INDIC AUTHORS

Ramakrishna, D., ed. Indian-English Prose: An Anthology. 1981. text ed. write for info. (ISBN 0-391-02190-7). Humanities.

ENGLISH LITERATURE–IRISH AUTHORS

see Irish Literature (English)

ENGLISH LITERATURE–OUTLINES, SYLLABI, ETC.
Bender, Todd K. & Parins, James W. A Concordance to Conrad's Nigger of the Narcissus. LC 79-8417. 150p. 1981. lib. bdg. 35.00 (ISBN 0-8240-9519-7). Garland Pub.
ENGLISH LITERATURE–STYLE
see English Language–Style
ENGLISH MUSIC
see Music, English
ENGLISH PAINTINGS
see Paintings, British
ENGLISH PHILOSOPHERS
see Philosophers–Great Britain
ENGLISH POETRY (COLLECTIONS)
see also American Poetry (Collections); Irish Poetry (English) (Collections); Poetry
Chase, Nan E., ed. Bountiful: A Poetry Digest. (First Annual Ser.). (Illus.). 53p. pap. 4.25 (ISBN 0-938512-00-5). Brigadoon.
Hoagland, Kathleen, ed. One Thousand Years of Irish Poetry. 832p. 1981. 12.95 (ISBN 0-517-34295-2). Devin.
Kennedy, X. J., ed. The Tygers of Wrath: Poems of Hate, Anger, & Invective. LC 80-23212. 272p. 1981. 15.00 (ISBN 0-8203-0535-9). U of Ga Pr.
Tomlinson, Charles, ed. The Oxford Book of Verse in English Translation. 750p. 1980. 37.50 (ISBN 0-19-214103-1). Oxford U Pr.
ENGLISH POETRY–BIBLIOGRAPHY
Brogan, T. V., ed. English Versification: 1570-1980: a Reference Guide with a Global Appendix. LC 80-8861. 832p. 1981. text ed. 47.50x (ISBN 0-8018-2541-5). Johns Hopkins.
ENGLISH POETRY–HISTORY AND CRITICISM
Allen, Don C., ed. Four Poets on Poetry. LC 80-20856. (Percy Graeme Turnbull Memorial Lectures on Poetry, 1958). 111p. 1980. Repr. of 1959 ed. lib. bdg. 19.50x (ISBN 0-313-22405-6, ALFP). Greenwood.
Baum, Joan M. The Theatrical, Composition of the Major English Romantic Poets. (Salzburg Studies in Poetic Drama: No. 57). 1980. pap. text ed. 25.00x (ISBN 0-391-02187-7). Humanities.
Berke, Roberta. Bounds Out of Bounds: A Compass for Recent American & British Poetry. 192p. 1981. 14.95 (ISBN 0-19-502872-4). Oxford U Pr.
De Almeida, Hermione. Byron & Joyce Through Homer: Don Juan & Ulysses. 256p. 1981. 20.00x (ISBN 0-231-05092-5). Columbia U Pr.
DeFord, Sara & Lott, Clarinda H. Forms of Verse, British & American. LC 77-94257. 393p. Repr. 12.95 (ISBN 0-390-26000-2). New Poets.
Edgecombe, Rodney. Sweetness Readie Penn'd Imagery, Syntax & Metric in the Poetry of George Herbert. (Elizabethan Studies). 1980. pap. text ed. 25.00x (ISBN 0-391-02185-0). Humanities.
Fraser, G. S. A Short History of English Poetry. 250p. 1981. 23.50x (ISBN 0-389-20174-X); pap. 9.95x (ISBN 0-389-20175-8). B&N.
Harland, Marion. Literary Hearthstones: William Cowper. 237p. 1980. Repr. of 1899 ed. lib. bdg. 30.00 (ISBN 0-89984-286-0). Century Bookbindery.
ENGLISH POETRY–HISTORY AND CRITICISM–MIDDLE ENGLISH (1100-1500)
Levy, Bernard & Szarmach, Paul, eds. The Alliterative Tradition in the Fourteenth Century. LC 80-84665. 230p. 1980. write for info. (ISBN 0-87338-255-2). Kent St U Pr.
ENGLISH POETRY–HISTORY AND CRITICISM–EARLY MODERN, 1500-1700
Jorgens, Elise B. The Well Tun'd Word: Musical Interpretations of English Poetry, 1597-1651. (Illus.). 320p. 1981. 25.00x (ISBN 0-8166-1029-0). U of Minn Pr.
Miles, Josephine. The Primary Language of Poetry in the 1640's. LC 78-11614. (Univ. of California Publications in English: Vol. 19, No. 1). (Illus.). 160p. 1979. Repr. of 1948 ed. lib. bdg. 16.50x (ISBN 0-313-20661-9, MIPP). Greenwood.
ENGLISH POETRY–HISTORY AND CRITICISM–19TH CENTURY
Hair, Donald S. Domestic & Heroic in Tennyson's Poetry. 272p. 1981. 25.00x (ISBN 0-8020-5530-3). U of Toronto Pr.
ENGLISH POETRY–OUTLINES, SYLLABI, ETC.
see English Literature–Outlines, Syllabi, etc.
ENGLISH POETRY–TRANSLATIONS FROM FOREIGN LITERATURE
Tomlinson, Charles, ed. The Oxford Book of Verse in English Translation. 750p. 1980. 37.50 (ISBN 0-19-214103-1). Oxford U Pr.
ENGLISH POETRY–TRANSLATIONS FROM JAPANESE
Sato, Hiroaki & Watson, Burton, eds. From the Country of Eight Islands: An Anthology of Japanese Poetry. 480p. 1981. 17.50 (ISBN 0-295-95798-0). U of Wash Pr.
ENGLISH PORCELAIN
see Porcelain
ENGLISH PROSE LITERATURE (COLLECTIONS)
Edwards, A. S. & Pearsall, Derek, eds. Middle English Prose: Essays on Bibliographical Problems. LC 80-8595. 150p. 1981. lib. bdg. 25.00 (ISBN 0-8240-9453-0). Garland Pub.
ENGLISH SCHOOL CERTIFICATE EXAMINATION
see High School Equivalency Examination

ENGLISH WIT AND HUMOR
Bell, Alan. Sydney Smith. (Illus.). 240p. 1980. 29.95 (ISBN 0-19-812050-8). Oxford U Pr.
ENGLISH WIT AND HUMOR, PICTORIAL
Searle, Ronald. The Situation Is Hopeless. LC 80-15868. (Illus.). 64p. 1981. 12.95 (ISBN 0-670-64731-4, Studio). Viking Pr.
ENGRAVERS
Bleile, C. Roger. American Engravers. (Illus.). 191p. 1980. 29.95 (ISBN 0-917714-29-6). Beinfeld Pub.
ENGRAVING
see also Etching; Gems
Norman, Barbara. Glass Engraving. LC 80-18031. (Illus.). 208p. 1981. 25.00 (ISBN 0-668-05081-0, 5081). Arco.
ENGRAVING–HISTORY
Ottley, William Y. An Inquiry into the Origin & Early History of Engraving Upon Copper & Wood, 2 vols. Freedberg, Sydney J., ed. LC 77-25757. (Connoisseurship Criticism & Art History Ser.: Vol. 14). 835p. 1979. Set. lib. bdg. 80.00 (ISBN 0-8240-3272-1). Garland Pub.
ENGRAVINGS–EXHIBITIONS
De Bry, Theodor. Conquistadores, Aztecs & Incas: A Facasimile of 16th Century Engravings. (Illus.). 108p. 1981. 60.00 (ISBN 0-8390-0257-2). Allanheld & Schram.
ENHARMONIC ORGAN
see Organ
ENIGMAS
see Curiosities and Wonders
ENLIGHTENMENT
Engell, James. The Creative Imagination: Enlightenment to Romanticism. 1981. write for info. Harvard U Pr.
ENTEROPATHY
see Intestines–Diseases
ENTERPRISES
see Business Enterprises; Entrepreneur
ENTERTAINERS
see also Actors and Actresses; Clowns; Comedians; Dancers; Musicians
Donahue, Phil, et al. Donahue: My Own Story. 288p. 1981. pap. 2.95 (ISBN 0-449-24358-3, Crest). Fawcett.
Doonican, Val. The Special Years: An Autobiography. (Illus.). 192p. 1981. 17.95 (ISBN 0-241-10499-8, Pub. by Hamish Hamilton England). David & Charles.
Fortunato, P. When We Were Young: An Album of Stars. 1980. 8.95 (ISBN 0-13-956482-9); pap. 2.50 (ISBN 0-13-956474-8). P-H.
ENTERTAINING
see also Amusements; Dinners and Dining; Etiquette; Games
Advice About Household Appliances, Cooking, Entertaining. (Home Adviser Ser.). 80p. (Orig.). 1981. pap. 1.95 (ISBN 0-8326-2403-9, 7052). Delair.
Jones, Terri & Jones, Evelyn J. Green Felt & Funny-Money: A Complete Guide to Throwing a Home Casino Party. Piper, Sue, ed. (Illus.). 1980. pap. text ed. 6.95 (ISBN 0-686-28734-7). Univ Marketing.
Olney, Judith. Entertainments. (Illus.). 196p. 1981. 19.95 (ISBN 0-8120-5410-5). Barron.
Post, Elizabeth & Staffieri, Anthony. The Complete Book of Entertaining. LC 80-7879. (Illus.). 384p. 1981. 14.95 (ISBN 0-690-01970-X, HarpT). Har-Row.
Post, Emily. The Emily Post Institute Book of Home Entertaining. 1981. 12.95 (ISBN 0-690-01970-X). Lippincott & Crowell.
Sheinhold, Patricia F. The Jolly Time Party Book. 6.95 (ISBN 0-916752-21-6). Green Hill.
Willan, Ann. Entertaining: Complete Menus for All Occasions. (Illus.). 216p. 1981. 22.50 (ISBN 0-7134-3408-2, Pub. by Batsford England). David & Charles.
ENTHUSIASM
Wilkins, Alfred T., Jr. & Dunn, Joseph. The Real Race. LC 80-85152. (Illus.). 210p. 1981. 10.95 (ISBN 0-938694-04-9). Jordan & Co.
ENTOMOLOGY
Shenfelt, R. D. Hymenopterorum Catalogus. (Hymenopterorum Catalogus Ser.: No. 16). 573p. 1980. pap. 137.00 (ISBN 0-686-28664-2, Pub. by Dr. W. Junk). Kluwer Boston.
ENTOMOLOGY–JUVENILE LITERATURE
see Insects–Juvenile Literature
ENTRANCE EXAMINATIONS
see Universities and Colleges–Examinations
ENTREPRENEUR
see also Business Enterprises; Capitalism; Profit
Gladson, Deek. The Miser's Manual: A Guide to Frofitable Self-Employment. 1981. pap. 4.00 (ISBN 0-686-69465-1); plastic bdg. 6.00 (ISBN 0-89316-626-X). Exanimo Pr.
Kingstone, Brett M. The Student Entrepreneur's Guide. 192p. (Orig.). 1981. pap. 4.95 (ISBN 0-89815-045-0). Ten Speed Pr.
Nicholas, Ted. The Ted Nicholas Small Business Course. 500p. (Orig.). 1981. pap. 14.95 (ISBN 0-913864-65-X). Enterprise Del.
Schieffermann, Vance A. The Art of Successful Entrepreneurship & How to Get It. (Illus.). 1981. 49.95 (ISBN 0-918968-82-8). Inst Econ Pol.

Shook, Robert L. The Entrepreneurs: Twelve Who Took Risks & Succeeded. LC 79-2735. (Illus.). 192p. 1981. pap. 3.95 (ISBN 0-06-464043-4, BN 4043, EH). Har-Row.
ENTROPY
Christensen, R. Entropy Minimax Sourcebook: Computer Implementation. x, 254p. 1980. 37.50. Entropy Ltd.
--Entropy Minimax Sourcebook: Philosophical Origins. x, 218p. 1980. 32.50. Entropy Ltd.
ENURESIS
Azrin, Nathan H. & Besalel, Victoria A. A Parent's Guide to Bedwetting Control: A Step by Step Method. 1981. pap. price not set (ISBN 0-671-82774-X). PB.
Belman, A. Barry & Kaplan, George W. Urologic Problems in Pediatrics. (Major Problems in Clinical Pediatrics Ser.: Vol. 22). (Illus.). 200p. 1981. text ed. price not set (ISBN 0-7216-1678-X). Saunders.
ENVIRONMENT
see Adaptation (Biology); Ecology; Human Ecology; Anthropo-Geography; Man–Influence of Environment; Man–Influence on Nature
ENVIRONMENT, HUMAN
see Human Ecology
ENVIRONMENT AND STATE
see Environmental Policy
ENVIRONMENTAL, SPACE
see Space Environment
ENVIRONMENTAL CONTROL
see Environmental Engineering; Environmental Law; Environmental Policy
ENVIRONMENTAL EDUCATION
see Conservation of Natural Resources–Study and Teaching
ENVIRONMENTAL ENGINEERING
see also Environmental Health; Environmental Policy; Environmental Protection; Environmental Testing; Human Engineering; Lighting; Noise Control; Pollution; Sanitary Engineering
Billington, N. S. & Roberts, B. M. Building Services Engineering: A Review of Its Development. (International Series on Building Environmental Engineering: Vol. 1). 500p. 1981. 80.00 (ISBN 0-08-026741-6); pap. 24.00 (ISBN 0-08-026742-4). Pergamon.
Butlin, J. A., ed. The Economics of Environmental & Natural Resources Policy. 200p. 1981. lib. bdg. 27.50x (ISBN 0-86531-190-0); pap. text ed. 14.00x (ISBN 0-86531-196-X). Westview.
Cloudesley-Thompson, J. D. Terrestrial Environments. 262p. 1980. 29.00x (ISBN 0-85664-001-8, Pub. by Croom Helm England). State Mutual Bk.
Cousteau, Jacques-Yves. The Cousteau Almanac of the Environment: An Inventory of Life on a Water Planet. 864p. 1981. 24.95 (ISBN 0-385-14875-5). Doubleday.
Directory of Institutions & Individuals Active in Environmentally Sound & Appropriate Technologies. (UNEP Reference Ser.: Vol. 1). 152p. 1979. pap. 20.00 (ISBN 0-08-025658-9, PERG20, UNEP). Unipub.
Fatigue Eighty-One. 1981. text ed. price not set (ISBN 0-86103-042-7, Westbury Hse). Butterworth.
Institute of Civil Engineers, UK. Highways & the Environment. 1980. pap. 15.00x (ISBN 0-7277-0065-0, Pub. by Telford England). State Mutual Bk.
OECD. Siting Procedures for Major Energy Facilities: Some National Cases. (Illus.). 142p. (Orig.). 1980. pap. text ed. 8.00x (ISBN 92-64-11986-8). OECD.
O'Riordan, Timothy & Sewell, W. R. Project Appraisal & Policy Review. (Studies in Environmental Management & Resource Development). 320p. 1981. 35.75 (ISBN 0-471-27853-X, Pub. by Wiley-Interscience). Wiley.
Perry, Allen H. Environmental Hazards in the British Isles. (Illus.). 192p. (Orig.). 1981. text ed. 27.50 (ISBN 0-04-910069-6, 2601); pap. text ed. 14.95 (ISBN 0-04-910070-X, 2602). Allen Unwin.
Pfafflin, James & Ziegler, Edward, eds. Advances in Environmental Science & Engineering, Vol. 4. 240p. 1981. write for info. (ISBN 0-677-16250-2). Gordon.
Pronin, Monica, ed. Environment Index Nineteen Eighty. LC 73-189498. 800p. 1981. 135.00 (ISBN 0-89947-011-4). Environ Info.
Shaw, A. M., ed. International Dictionary of Consulting & Environmental Engineers. 2nd rev. ed. 1981. 10.00. Intl Research Serv.
Siebert, Horst. Economics of the Environment. LC 80-7442. 1981. price not set (ISBN 0-669-03693-5). Lexington Bks.
ENVIRONMENTAL ENGINEERING (BUILDINGS)
see also Architectural Acoustics; Ventilation
Aho, Arnold J. Materials, Energies & Environmental Design. 1981. lib. bdg. 28.50 (ISBN 0-8240-7178-6). Garland Pub.
Hopkins, George D., Jr. Urban Ecology Through the Adaptive Use of Existing Buildings: A Selected Bibliography, Revising A-22 of Oct. 1978. (Architecture Ser.: Bibliography a-281). 78p. 1980. pap. 8.50. Vance Biblios.
ENVIRONMENTAL HEALTH
see also Environmental Engineering; Man–Influence of Environment; Pollution; Public Health

Calabrese, Edward J. Nutrition & Environmental Health: The Influence of Nutritional Status on Pollutant Toxicity & Carcinogenicity, 2 vols. Incl. Vol. 1. The Vitamins. 60.00 (ISBN 0-471-04833-X); Vol. 2. Minerals & Macronutrients. 544p. 35.00 (ISBN 0-471-08207-4). LC 79-21089. (Environmental Science & Technology Ser.). 1980 (Pub. by Wiley-Interscience). Wiley.
ENVIRONMENTAL HEALTH ENGINEERING
see Sanitary Engineering
ENVIRONMENTAL LAW
see also Air–Pollution–Laws and Legislation; Natural Resources–Law and Legislation
British Institute of International & Comparative Law. Selected Documents on International Environmental Law. 1977. 15.00 (ISBN 0-379-00348-1). Oceana.
Environmental Statutes: 1981 Edition. 663p. 1981. pap. 16.96 (ISBN 0-86587-089-6). Gov Insts.
Findley, Roger W. & Farber, Daniel A. Environmental Law: Cases & Materials. (American Casebook Ser.). 639p. 1981. text ed. 19.95. West Pub.
Manual on Environmental Legislation. 116p. 1981. pap. 13.00 (UNEP46, UNEP). Unipub.
Nordic Countries Legislation on the Environment with Special Emphasis on Conservation: A Survey. (Environmental Policy & Law Paper: No. 14). 44p. 1980. pap. 10.75 (IUCN 83, IUCN). Unipub.
Trends in Environmental Policy & Law. (IUCN Environmental Policy & Law Paper Ser.: No. 15). 404p. 1981. pap. 30.75 (ISBN 2-88032-085-2, IUCN94, IUCN). Unipub.
ENVIRONMENTAL MANAGEMENT
see Environmental Engineering; Environmental Policy
ENVIRONMENTAL POLICY
see also Environmental Law
Barney, Gerald O., ed. The Global Two Thousand Report to the President of the U. S.--Entering the 21st Century: The Summary Report--Special Edition with Environment Projections & the Government's Global Model, Vol. 1. (Pergamon Policy Studies Ser.). 200p. 1980. 30.00 (ISBN 0-08-024617-6); pap. 9.50 (ISBN 0-08-024616-8). Pergamon.
Bergman, M., ed. Subsurface Space--Environment Protection, Low Cost Storage, Energy Savings: Proceedings of the International Symposium, Stockholm, Sweden, June 23-27, 1980, 3 vols. (Illus.). 1500p. 1980. 250.00 (ISBN 0-08-026136-1). Pergamon.
Environmental Studies Board. Long-Range Environmental Outlook. x, 198p. 1980. pap. text ed. 10.50 (ISBN 0-309-03038-2). Natl Acad Pr.
Fullenbach. European Environmental Policy East & West. 1981. text ed. price not set (ISBN 0-408-10689-1). Butterworth.
Gilpin, Alan. Environmental Policy in Australia. (Australian Environment Ser.: No. 8). (Illus.). 380p. 1981. text ed. 36.25x (ISBN 0-7022-1366-7); pap. text ed. 21.75x (ISBN 0-7022-1367-5). U of Queensland Pr.
Limbrey, Susan & Evans, J. G., eds. The Effect of Man on the Landscape: The Lowland Zone. 160p. 1980. pap. 29.95x (ISBN 0-900312-60-2, Pub. by Council Brit Arch England). Intl Schol Bk Serv.
Liroff, Richard A. & Davis, G. Gordon. Conflict in the North Country: A Study of the Implementation of Regional Land Use Controls by the Adirondack Park Agency. 1981. price not set (ISBN 0-88410-643-8). Ballinger Pub.
Mann, Dean, ed. Environmental Policy. (Orig.). 1980. pap. 5.00 (ISBN 0-918592-43-7). Policy Studies.
Odum, Howard T. & Odum, Elisabeth C. Energy Basis for Man & Nature. 2nd ed. (Illus.). 352p. 1981. text ed. 19.50 (ISBN 0-07-047511-3, C); pap. text ed. 12.95 (ISBN 0-07-047510-5, C); instrs'. manual avail. McGraw.
Trends in Environmental Policy & Law. (IUCN Environmental Policy & Law Paper Ser.: No. 15). 404p. 1981. pap. 30.75 (ISBN 2-88032-085-2, IUCN94, IUCN). Unipub.
United Nations Environment Programme Annual Review, 1978. 86p. 1981. pap. 10.00 (ISBN 92-807-1013-3, UNEP45, UNEP). Unipub.
ENVIRONMENTAL POLLUTION
see Pollution
ENVIRONMENTAL PROTECTION
see also Conservation of Natural Resources; Environmental Engineering; Environmental Law; Environmental Policy
Bernard, Harold. The Greenhouse Effect. LC 80-8710. 256p. 1981. pap. 4.95 (ISBN 0-06-090855-6, C*N 855, CN). Har-Row.
Duffus, John H. Environmental Toxicology. (An Environmental Science Ser.). 132p. 1981. 15.95 (ISBN 0-470-27051-9). Halsted Pr.
Kay, David A., et al. Environmental Protection: The International Dimension. 320p. 1981. text ed. 28.50 (ISBN 0-86598-034-9). Allanheld.
Lobell, John. The Little Green Book: A Guide to Self-Reliant Living in the '80s. LC 80-53445. (Illus.). 224p. (Orig.). 1981. pap. 5.95 (ISBN 0-394-74924-3). Shambhala Pubn.
Mandelker, Daniel R. Environment & Equity: A Regulatory Challenge. (Regulation of American Business & Industry (RABI) Ser.). 240p. 1981. 24.95 (ISBN 0-07-039864-X, P&RB). McGraw.
Medawar, Jean. Lifeclass. (Illus.). 80p. (gr. 3-6). 1981. 13.50 (ISBN 0-686-69427-9, Pub. by Hamish Hamilton England). David & Charles.

Rajagopal, R., ed. Environmental Mediation & Conflict Management: A Selection of Papers Presented at the 5th Annual Conference of the NAEP, Washington Dc, April 21-23 1980. 120p. 1981. pap. 10.00 (ISBN 0-08-026261-9). Pergamon.

A Summary of UNEP Activities: Technical Assistance, 1980. (UNEP Report Ser.: No. 8). 115p. 1980. pap. 11.00 (UNEP 036, UNEP). Unipub.

ENVIRONMENTAL STUDIES

see Conservation of Natural Resources–Study and Teaching

ENVIRONMENTAL TESTING

Hsu, T. C., ed. Cytogenetic Testing of Environmental Mutagens. LC 79-88262. 430p. 1981. text ed. 35.00 (ISBN 0-916672-56-5). Allanheld.

ENZYME INHIBITORS

Brodbeck, V. Enzyme Inhibitors. 270p. (Orig.). Date not set. pap. price not set. Verlag Chemie.

ENZYMES

see also Clinical Enzymology; Enzyme Inhibitors; Fibrinolysis; Fibrinolytic Agents; Malt

also names of enzymes, e.g. Diastase, Pepsin

Biochemical Societies of France, Great Britain, Italy, & the Netherlands. Joint Meeting, Venice, 1976. Phosphorylated Proteins & Related Enzymes: Proceedings. 121p. 8.00. Info Retrieval.

Desnick, Robert J., ed. Enzyme Therapy in Genetic Diseases: Part 2. LC 79-48026. (Alan R. Liss Ser.: Vol. 16, No. 1). 1980. 64.00. March of Dimes.

Dugas, H. & Penney, C. Bioorganic Chemistry: A Chemical Approach to Enzyme Action. (Springer Advanced Texts in Chemistry Ser.). (Illus.). 416p. 1981. 29.80 (ISBN 0-387-90491-3). Springer-Verlag.

Luebbers, D. W., ed. Progress in Enzyme & Ion-Selective Electrodes. (Illus.). 240p. 1981. pap. 34.30 (ISBN 0-387-10499-2). Springer-Verlag.

Methods in Enzymology, Vols. 47-62. Incl. Vol. 47. Enzyme Structure, Pt. E. Hirs, C. H. & Timasheff, S. N., eds. 1977. 59.50 (ISBN 0-12-181947-7); Vol. 48. Enzyme Structures, Pt. F. Hirs, C. H., ed. 1978. 57.00 (ISBN 0-12-181948-5); Vol. 49. Enzyme Structure, Pt. G. Hirs, C. H. & Timasheff, S. N., eds. 1978. 57.00 (ISBN 0-12-181949-3); Vol. 50. Complex Carbohydrates, Pt. C. Colowick, Sidney P. & Kaplan, Nathan O., eds. 1978. 51.00 (ISBN 0-12-181950-7); Vol. 51. Purine & Pyrimidine Nucleotide Metabolism. Colowick, Sidney P., et al, eds. 1978. 47.50 (ISBN 0-12-181951-5); Vol. 52. Biomembranes, Pt. C, Biological Oxidations; Microsomal Electron Transport & Cytochrome P-450 Systems. Colowick, Sidney P. & Kaplan, Nathan O., eds. 1978. 48.00 (ISBN 0-12-181952-3); Vol. 53. Pt. D Biological Oxidations; Mitochondrial & Microbial Systems. Fleischer, Sidney & Packer, Lester, eds. 1978. 48.00 (ISBN 0-12-181953-1); Vol. 54. Pt. E Biological Oxidations; Specialized Techniques. Fleischer, Sidney & Packer, Lester, eds. 1978. 47.00 (ISBN 0-12-181954-X); Vol. 55. Pt. F, Bioenergetics Oxidative Phosphorylation. Colowick, Sidney P. & Fleischer, Sidney, eds. 1979. 58.00 (ISBN 0-12-181955-8); Vol. 56. Biomembranes, Pt. G; Bioenergetics, Biogenesis of Mitochondria, Organization & Transport. Colowick, Sidney P., et al, eds. 1979. 52.00 (ISBN 0-686-62056-9); Vol. 57. Bioluminescence & Chemiluminescence. Deluca, Marlene, ed. 1978. 48.00 (ISBN 0-12-181957-4); Vol. 58. Cell Culture. Colowick, Sidney & Jacoby, William, eds. 1979. 50.00 (ISBN 0-12-181958-2); Vol. 59. Nucleic Acids & Proteins Synthesis, Pt. G, Moldave. Colowick, Sidney, ed. 1979. 52.50 (ISBN 0-12-181959-0); Vol. 60. Pt. H, Moldave. Colowick, Sidney, ed. 1979. 52.50 (ISBN 0-12-181960-4); Vol. 61. Enzyme Structure, Pt. H. Colowick, Sidney & Hirs, C. H., eds. 1979. 48.00 (ISBN 0-12-181961-2); Vol. 62. Vitamins & Coenzymes, Pt. D. Colowick, Sidney, et al, eds. 1979. 50.00 (ISBN 0-12-181962-0). Acad Pr.

Mora, Jaime & Palacios, Rafael, eds. Glutamine: Metabolism, Enzymology & Regulation. 1980. 28.00 (ISBN 0-12-506040-8). Acad Pr.

Schwimmer, Sigmund. Source Book of Food Enzymology. (Illus.). 1981. lib. bdg. 79.50 (ISBN 0-87055-369-0). AVI.

ENZYMOLOGY, CLINICAL

see Clinical Enzymology

EOLITHIC PERIOD

see Stone Age

EPIC POETRY–HISTORY AND CRITICISM

Rosenberg, D. N. Oaten Reeds & Trumpets: Pastoral & Epic in Virgil, Spenser, & Milton. LC 80-17974. 288p. 1981. 22.50 (ISBN 0-8387-5002-8). Bucknell U Pr.

EPICTETUS

Oldfather, W. A. A Bibliography of Epictetus. 177p. 1952. octavo 7.00. Holmes.

EPIDEMICS

see also Communicable Diseases;

also names of communicable diseases, e.g. Yellow Fever

Cliff, A. D., et al. Spatial Diffusion: An Historical Geography of Epidemics in an Island Community. (Cambridge Geographical Studies: No. 14). (Illus.). 244p. Date not set. price not set (ISBN 0-521-22840-9). Cambridge U Pr.

Goldblum, N., et al, eds. Rift Valley Fever. (Contributions to Epidemiology & Biostatistics Ser.: Vol. 3). (Illus.). 200p. 1981. pap. 60.00 (ISBN 3-8055-1770-X). S Karger.

EPIDEMIOLOGY

see also Epidemics

Bruce, W. Robert, et al, eds. Banbury Report 7-the Carcinogen & Mutagen Formation in the Gastrointestinal Tract. (Banbury Report Ser.). (Illus.). 1981. 60.00x (ISBN 0-87969-206-5). Cold Spring Harbor.

Comparative Epidemiology: A Tool for Better Disease Management. 122p. 1981. pap. 33.25 (ISBN 90-220-0721-9, PDC 212, Pudoc). Unipub.

Frauenthal, J. C. Mathematical Modeling in Epidemiology. (Universitexts Ser.). 118p. 1980. pap. 16.80 (ISBN 0-387-10328-7). Springer-Verlag.

Litlienfeld, Abraham M. Times, Places & Persons: Aspects of the History of Epidemiology. LC 80-8090. (The Henry F. Sigerist Supplements to the Bulletin of the History of Medicine, New Ser.: No. 4). 160p. 1980. pap. text ed. 9.00x (ISBN 0-8018-2425-7). Johns Hopkins.

Meteorological Factors Affecting the Epidemology of the Cotton Leaf Worm & the Pink Boolworm. (Technical Note Ser.: No. 167). 46p. 1980. pap. 10.00 (ISBN 92-63-10532-4, W473, WMO). Unipub.

Mortimer, James A. & Schuman, Leonard M., eds. The Epidemiology of Dementia. (Illus.). 200p. 1981. text ed. 18.95x (ISBN 0-19-502906-2). Oxford U Pr.

Morton, N. E. Outline of Genetic Epidemiology. (Illus.). x, 250p. 1981. pap. 25.75 (ISBN 3-8055-2269-X). S Karger.

Sartwell, Philip E. & Nathanson, Neal, eds. Epidemiologic Reviews: 1980, Vol. 2. LC 79-7564. (Epidemiologic Reviews Ser.). (Illus.). 240p. 1980. text ed. 13.50x (ISBN 0-8018-2404-4). Johns Hopkins.

Tartakow, I. Jackson & Vorperian, John H. Foodborne & Waterborne Diseases: Their Epidemiological Character. (Illus.). 1981. pap. 19.00 (ISBN 0-87055-368-2). AVI.

EPIDERMIS

see Skin

EPIGRAMS

see also Quotations

Cunningham, J. V. Collected Poems and Epigrams. LC 71-132578. 142p. 1971. pap. 8.95 (ISBN 0-8040-0517-6). Swallow.

Howell, Peter. A Commentary on Book One of the Epigrams of Martial. 369p. 1980. text ed. 65.00x (Athlone Pr). Humanities.

Mendel, Roberta. Epigrams to Live & Die by. (Sketchbook Ser.). (Illus., Orig.). 1981. pap. 4.00 (ISBN 0-936424-08-7, 008). Pin Prick.

Page, D. L., ed. Further Greek Epigrams. LC 79-42646. (Illus.). 700p. Date not set. price not set (ISBN 0-521-22903-0). Cambridge U Pr.

EPILEPSY

Janz, D., et al, eds. Epilepsy, Pregnancy, & Child. 1981. text ed. price not set (ISBN 0-89004-654-9). Raven.

Penry, J. Kiffin & Dam, Mogens, eds. Advances in Epileptology Research. (Twelfth Eplilepsy International Symposium, Copenhagen, Denmark). 1981. text ed. price not set (ISBN 0-89004-611-5). Raven.

EPIPHYTES

Biological Nitrogen Fixation by Epiphytic Microoganisms in Rice Fields. (IRRI Research Paper Ser.: No. 47). 14p. 1981. pap. 5.00 (ISBN 0-686-69532-1, R 117, IRRI). Unipub.

EPISCOPAL CHURCH

see Church of England; Protestant Episcopal Church in the U. S. A.

EPISTEMOLOGY

see Knowledge, Theory Of

EPITHELIUM

see also Mucous Membrane

Macknight, Anthony D. & Leader, John P., eds. Epithelial Ion & Water Transport. 380p. 1981. 35.00 (ISBN 0-89004-537-2). Raven.

EPIZOA

see Parasites

EQUAL EMPLOYMENT OPPORTUNITY

see Discrimination in Employment

EQUAL OPPORTUNITY IN EMPLOYMENT

see Discrimination in Employment

EQUALITY

see also Democracy; Individualism; Liberty; Social Classes; Socialism

Atkinson, A. B., ed. Wealth, Income, & Inequality. 2nd ed. (Illus.). 450p. 1981. 42.00x (ISBN 0-19-877143-6); pap. 21.00x (ISBN 0-19-877144-4). Oxford U Pr.

Berreman, Gerald D. Social Inequality: Comparative & Developmental Approaches. (Studies in Anthropology). 1981. price not set (ISBN 0-12-093160-5). Acad Pr.

Carens, Joseph H. Equality, Moral Incentives, & the Market. LC 80-36774. (Illus.). 1981. lib. bdg. 19.00x (ISBN 0-226-09269-0). U of Chicago Pr.

Collins, Margaret S., et al, eds. Science & the Question of Human Equality. (AAAS Selected Symposium: No. 58). 180p. 1981. lib. bdg. 16.00x (ISBN 0-89158-952-X). Westview.

Green, Philip. The Pursuit of Inequality. 1981. 14.95 (ISBN 0-394-50676-6). Pantheon.

Haksar, Vinit. Equality, Liberty & Perfectionism. (Clarendon Library of Logic & Philosophy Ser.). 310p. 1979. text ed. 24.95x (ISBN 0-19-824418-5). Oxford U Pr.

Redenius, Charles. The American Ideal of Equality & Constitutional Change: From Jefferson's Declaration to the Burger Court. (National University Publications, Political Science Ser.). 1981. 17.50 (ISBN 0-8046-9282-3). Kennikat.

Reich, Michael. Racial Inequality: A Political-Economic Analysis. LC 80-8573. 320p. 1981. 20.00x (ISBN 0-691-04227-6); pap. 6.95 (ISBN 0-691-00365-3). Princeton U Pr.

Reied, Morton H., ed. Systems of Equality & Inequality in Human Society. 240p. 1981. 20.95 (ISBN 0-89789-012-4). J F Bergin.

Ryan, William. Equality. 1981. 15.95 (ISBN 0-394-50493-3). Pantheon.

EQUATIONS, DIFFERENCE

see Difference Equations

EQUATIONS, DIFFERENTIAL

see Differential Equations

EQUATIONS, INTEGRAL

see Integral Equations

EQUESTRIANISM

see Horsemanship

EQUILIBRIUM

see also Statics

Garrido, L., ed. Systems Far from Equilibrium: Sitges Conference. (Lecture Notes in Physics Ser.: Vol. 132). 403p. 1981. pap. 27.70 (ISBN 0-387-10251-5). Springer Verlag.

EQUILIBRIUM, CHEMICAL

see Chemical Equilibrium

EQUILIBRIUM, THERMAL

see Heat; Thermodynamics

EQUIPMENT, POLLUTION CONTROL

see Pollution Control Equipment

EQUITATION

see Horsemanship

EQUITY

see also Equity Pleading and Procedure; Trusts and Trustees

Allen Bakke Vs. Regents of the University of California, 6 vols. 1978. 44.00 ea. Oceana.

Fonblanque, John. A Treatise of Equity. Ballow, Henry, et al, eds. LC 77-86649. (Classics of English Legal History in the Modern Era Ser.: Vol. 34). 775p. 1979. lib. bdg. 40.00 (ISBN 0-8240-3083-4). Garland Pub.

Troy, P. N., ed. Equity in the City. 192p. 1981. text ed. 22.50x (ISBN 0-86861-250-2, 2647). Allen Unwin.

EQUITY PLEADING AND PROCEDURE

Crownover, Arthur, Jr. Gibson's Suits in Chancery, 2 vols. 5th ed. 1100p. 1955. text ed. 50.00 (ISBN 0-87215-083-6). Michie.

EQUIVALENCY EXAMINATION, HIGH SCHOOL

see High School Equivalency Examination

ERASMUS, DESIDERIUS, d. 1536

Boyle, Marjorie O. Christening Pagan Mysteries: Erasmus in Pursuit of Wisdom. (Erasmus Studies). 168p. 1981. 15.00x (ISBN 0-8020-5525-7). U of Toronto Pr.

ERGONOMETRICS

see Work Measurement

ERGONOMICS

see Human Engineering

ERIE CANAL

Spier, Peter. Erie Canal. LC 70-157625. (gr. 1-3). 1970. pap. 1.95 (ISBN 0-385-05234-0, Zephyr). Doubleday.

ERLANG TRAFFIC FORMULA

see Queuing Theory

ERNST, MAX, 1891-

Hofmann, Werner, et al. Max Ernst: Inside the Sight. LC 77-125283. (Illus.). 1973. pap. 6.00 (ISBN 0-914412-06-X). Inst for the Arts.

EROSION

see also Geomorphology; Glaciers; Sedimentation and Deposition

DeBoodt, M. & Gabriels, D. Assessment of Erosion. 400p. 1981. 67.50 (ISBN 0-471-27899-8, Pub. by Wiley-Interscience). Wiley.

EROSION CONTROL

see Soil Conservation

EROTICA

see also Obscenity (Law); Pornography; Sex in Moving-Pictures

Lorde, Audre. Uses of the Erotic: The Erotic As Power. (Out & Out Pamphlet Ser.). pap. 1.00 (ISBN 0-918314-09-7). Out & Out.

ERRORS, POPULAR

see also Superstition

Burnam, Tom. More Misinformation. 1981. pap. 2.50 (ISBN 0-345-29251-0). Ballantine.

Robbins, R. H., ed. Sir Thomas Browne's Pseudodoxia Epidemica. (Oxford English Texts Ser.). (Illus.). 1000p. 1980. 129.00 (ISBN 0-19-812706-5). Oxford U Pr.

ERSE

see Gaelic Language

ERUDITION

see Learning and Scholarship

ERUPTIVE ROCKS

see Rocks, Igneous

ERYTHROCYTES

Instrumentation Laboratory Spring Symposium, Boston, Ma, April 1980. Erythrocyte Pathobiology: Proceedings. Wallach, Donald F., ed. (Progress in Clinical & Biological Research Ser.: No. 54). 250p. 1981. price not set (ISBN 0-8451-0054-8). A R Liss.

ESCAPES

Rivers, Gayle & Hudson, James. The Contract Rescue. LC 80-1850. (Illus.). 240p. 1981. 11.95 (ISBN 0-385-17200-1). Doubleday.

ESCHATOLOGY

see also Antichrist; Apocalyptic Literature; Death; Dispensationalism; End of the World; Future Life; Heaven; Hell; Immortality; Kingdom of God; Millennium; Resurrection; Second Advent; Time (Theology)

Hendren, Bob. Life Without End. LC 80-54164. (Journey Bks.). 144p. (Orig.). 1981. pap. 2.35 (ISBN 0-8344-0118-5). Sweet.

White, H. Roy. The Meaning & Significance of Christian Hope. 1981. 5.95 (ISBN 0-533-04536-3). Vantage.

ESKIMO ART

see Eskimos–Art

ESKIMOS

Brumble, H. David, III. An Annotated Bibliography of American Indian & Eskimo Autobiographies. LC 80-23449. 190p. 1981. 10.95x (ISBN 0-8032-1175-9). U of Nebr Pr.

ESKIMOS–ART

Smith, James G. Arctic Art: Eskimo Ivory. 127p. soft cover 19.95x (ISBN 0-934490-37-6). Mus Am Ind.

ESKIMOS–CANADA

Cowan, Susan, ed. We Don't Live in Snow Houses Now. (Illus.). 194p. (Inuktitut, Eng.). 1981. pap. 11.95 (ISBN 0-920234-00-3, 08912-6, Pub. by Canadian Artic Producers Ltd). U of Chicago Pr.

ESP

see Extrasensory Perception; Psychical Research

ESPIONAGE

see also Spies

Foote, Alexander. Handbook for Spies. 12.50x (ISBN 0-392-07888-0, SpS). Soccer.

Mosley, Leonard. Druid. LC 80-69367. 1981. 12.95 (ISBN 0-689-11106-1). Atheneum.

ESPIONAGE, BRITISH

see also Great Britain–Special Operations Executive

Masterman, J. C. The Double Cross System. 4.95 (ISBN 0-686-28851-3). Academy Chi Ltd.

ESPIONAGE, GERMAN

Stieber, Wilhelm J. The Chancellor's Spy: The Revelations of the Chief of Bismarck's Secret Service. Van Heurck, Jan, tr. from German. LC 79-52090. Orig. Title: Spion Des Kanzlers. 272p. 1981. 12.50 (ISBN 0-394-50869-6). Grove.

ESPIONAGE, RUSSIAN

CIA. Rote Kapelle: The CIA's History of Soviet Intelligence & Espionage Networks in Western Europe, 1936-1945. Kesaris, Paul, ed. 1979. 29.50 (ISBN 0-89093-203-4). U Pubns Amer.

ESPIONAGE STORIES

see Spy Stories

ESSAY

Here are entered works on the essay as a literary form. collections of essays are entered under the heading Essays.

Lopez Gonzalez, Julio. El Ensayo y Su Ensenanza: Dos Ejemplos Puertorriquenos. LC 80-17712. (Coleccion Mente y Palabra). 146p. 1980. 6.25 (ISBN 0-8477-0568-4); pap. 5.00 (ISBN 0-8477-0569-2). U of PR Pr.

ESSAYS

see also English Essays; French Essays; and similar headings; and subdivision Addresses, Essays, Lectures under specific subjects

Allen, Grant. Physiological Aesthetics. 283p. 1980. Repr. of 1877 ed. lib. bdg. 35.00 (ISBN 0-8495-0064-8). Arden Lib.

Barthes, Roland. Barthes Reader. Sontag, Susan, ed. 1981. 17.95 (ISBN 0-8090-2815-8); pap. 8.95 (ISBN 0-8090-1394-0). Hill & Wang.

Beckwith, B. P. Radical Essays. 1981. 6.00 (ISBN 0-686-69571-2). Beckwith.

British Academy, 1979. Proceedings, Vol. LXV. (Illus.). 500p. 1981. 175.00 (ISBN 0-19-725998-7). Oxford U Pr.

Gerould, Katharine F. Vain Obliations. 324p. 1980. Repr. of 1915 ed. lib. bdg. 25.00 (ISBN 0-89987-306-5). Century Bookbindery.

Godwin, William. Essays. 293p. 1980. Repr. of 1873 ed. lib. bdg. 35.00 (ISBN 0-8492-4974-0). R West.

Goodman, Ellen. Close to Home. 1980. pap. 2.50 (ISBN 0-449-24351-6, Crest). Fawcett.

Heron, David W., ed. A Unifying Influence: Essays of Raynard Coe Swank. LC 80-28595. 237p. 1981. 13.50 (ISBN 0-8108-1407-2). Scarecrow.

James, C. L. R. The Future in the Present: Selected Writings of C. L. R. James. LC 77-73129. 228p. 1980. pap. 6.95 (ISBN 0-88208-125-X). Lawrence Hill.

Jordan, June. Civil Wars. LC 80-68164. 192p. 1981. 12.95 (ISBN 0-8070-3232-8). Beacon Pr.

McKitterick, D., ed. Stanley Morison: Selected Essays, 2 vols. LC 78-54718. (Illus.). 250p. Date not set. Set. 275.00 (ISBN 0-521-22338-5). Vol. 1 (ISBN 0-521-22456-X). Vol. 2 (ISBN 0-521-22457-8). Cambridge U Pr.

Maculay, Lord. Literary Essays: Contributed by the Edinburgh Review. 706p. 1980. Repr. of 1923 ed. lib. bdg. 30.00 (ISBN 0-89760-544-6). Telegraph Bks.

Mazzini, Joseph. The Duties of Man & Other Essays. 327p. 1980. lib. bdg. 15.00 (ISBN 0-89760-546-2). Telegraph Bks.

Morowitz, Harold J. The Wine of Life & Other Essays on Societies, Energy & Living Things. 240p. 1981. pap. 2.95 (ISBN 0-553-14353-0). Bantam.

Morris, Leavitt F. An Editor at Large. 160p. 1981. 12.50 (ISBN 0-682-49705-3). Exposition.

Neruda, Pablo. Passions & Impressions. Peden, Margaret S., tr. from Span. 1981. 17.95 (ISBN 0-374-22994-5). FS&G.

Spingarn, Joel E., ed. Critical Essays of the Seventeenth Century, 3 vols. Incl. Vol. 1. 364p. 12.50x (ISBN 0-253-31551-4); Vol. 2. 368p. 12.50x (ISBN 0-253-31552-2); Vol. 3. 384p. 12.50x (ISBN 0-253-31553-0). LC 57-10727. 1957. Set. 32.50x (ISBN 0-253-31554-9). Ind U Pr.

Taylor, Ann M. Short Model Essays. (Orig.). 1981. pap. text ed. 6.95 (ISBN 0-316-83358-4); tchrs'. manual free (ISBN 0-316-83359-2). Little.

Young, G. M. Last Essays: Scott, Newman, Push Kiv, Hardy. 288p. 1980. Repr. of 1950 ed. lib. bdg. 20.00 (ISBN 0-8495-6149-3). Arden Lib.

ESTATE PLANNING

see also Estates (Law); Inheritance and Transfer Tax; Insurance; Investments; Tax Planning; Taxation; Trusts and Trustees

Brosterman, Robert. The Complete Estate Planning Guide. rev. ed. 1981. pap. 2.95 (ISBN 0-451-61962-5, ME1692, Ment). NAL.

Casner, A. James. Estate Planning, Vols. 1-6. 1980. text ed. 250.00 (ISBN 0-316-13148-2). Vol. 1. Vol. 2 (ISBN 0-316-13149-0). Vol. 3 (ISBN 0-316-13150-4). Vol. 4 (ISBN 0-316-13151-2). Vol. 5 (ISBN 0-316-13152-0). Vol. 6 (ISBN 0-316-13153-9). Little.

Drollinger, William C. & Drollinger, William C. Jr. Tax Shelters & Tax-Free Income for Everyone, Vol II. 4th ed. 1981. write for info. (ISBN 0-914244-06-X). Epic Pubns.

Holzman, Robert S. Encyclopedia of Estate Planning. LC 80-19441. 312p. 1980. 50.00 (ISBN 0-932648-15-0). Boardroom.

Howell, John C. Estate Planning for the Small Business Owner. 176p. 1980. pap. 5.95 (Spec). P-H.

Leimberg, Stepan R., et al. The Tools & Techniques of Estate Planning. 3rd ed. 376p. 1980. pap. 20.00 (ISBN 0-87218-406-4). Natl Underwriter.

Schain, George M. Estates, Gifts & Fiducuaries: Planning & Taxation. 3rd ed. Gold, Jeffrey S., ed. 444p. 1980. 29.95 (ISBN 0-07-055120-0, P&RB); wkbk. & 10 cassettes 195.00 (ISBN 0-07-079056-6). McGraw.

Whitman, Robert. Simplified Guide to Estate Planning & Administration. 192p. 1981. pap. 6.95 (ISBN 0-671-09136-0). Monarch Pr.

ESTATE PLANNING–UNITED STATES

Clay, William C. The Dow-Jones Irwin Guide to Estate Planning. 3rd ed. 176p. 1981. pap. 2.50 (ISBN 0-553-14913-X). Bantam.

ESTATES (LAW)

see also Estate Planning; Future Interests

Ferguson, M. Carr, et al. Federal Income Taxation of Estates & Beneficiaries. 749p. (Orig.). 1970. text ed. 40.00 (ISBN 0-316-27889-0); text ed. 12.50 1979 supplement (ISBN 0-316-27899-8). 1980 supplement (ISBN 0-316-27900-5). Little.

Michaelson, Arthur M. Income Taxation of Estates & Trusts. 11th ed. LC 80-83758. 220p. 1980. text ed. 35.00 (ISBN 0-686-69169-5, J1-1434). PLI.

ESTHER, FEAST OF

see Purim (Feast of Esther)

ESTHETICS

see also Art; Art–Philosophy; Color; Criticism; Cubism; Dadaism; Form (Esthetics); Impressionism (Art); Literature–Esthetics; Music–Philosophy and Esthetics; Painting; Poetry; Post-Impressionism (Art); Realism in Art; Realism in Literature; Rhythm; Romanticism; Sculpture; Surrealism; Values

Beardsley, Monroe C. Aesthetics: Problems in the Philosophy of Criticism. 2nd ed. (Illus.). 688p. 1981. 25.00 (ISBN 0-915145-09-X); pap. text ed. 14.50 (ISBN 0-915145-08-1). Hackett Pub.

Eagleton, Terry. Walter Benjamin: Or Toward a Revolutionary Criticism. 224p. 1981. 19.50 (ISBN 0-8052-7100-7, Pub. by NLB England); pap. 8.50 (ISBN 0-8052-7099-X). Schocken.

Falk, Eugene H. The Poetics of Roman Ingarden. LC 79-29655. 272p. 1980. 20.00x (ISBN 0-8078-1436-9); pap. 11.00x (ISBN 0-8078-4068-8). U of NC Pr.

Hogarth, William. The Artistic & Psychological Analysis of Beauty. (Illus.). 127p. 1981. 31.45 (ISBN 0-930582-90-X). Gloucester Art.

Inman, Billie A. Walter Pater's Reading: A Bibliography of His Library Borrowings & Literary References, 1858 to 1873. LC 78-68284. 390p. 1981. lib. bdg. 40.00 (ISBN 0-8240-9790-4). Garland Pub.

Kirchman, Milton. Mannerism & Imagination: A Reexamination of Sixteenth Century Italian Aesthetic. (Elizabethan Studies: No. 88). 1980. pap. text ed. 25.00x (ISBN 0-391-02162-1). Humanities.

Landorf, Joyce, tr. La Belleza Radiante. (Spanish Bks.). (Span.). 1978. 1.90 (ISBN 0-8297-0807-3). Life Pubs Intl.

Reid, Louis A. A Study in Aesthetics. 415p. 1980. Repr. of 1931 ed. lib. bdg. 45.00 (ISBN 0-8495-4635-4). Arden Lib.

Silk, M. S. & Stern, J. P. Nietzsche on Tragedy. LC 80-40433. 500p. Date not set. price not set (ISBN 0-521-23262-7). Cambridge U Pr.

ESTIMATES

see subdivision Estimates and Estimates and Costs under technical subjects, e.g. Building–Estimates; Engineering–Estimates and Costs

ESTIMATION OF DISABILITY

see Disability Evaluation

ESTRANGEMENT (PHILOSOPHY)

see Alienation (Philosophy)

ESTRANGEMENT (SOCIAL PSYCHOLOGY)

see Alienation (Social Psychology)

ESTROGEN

Pfaff, D. W. Estrogens & Brain Function: Neural Analysis of a Hormone-Controlled Mammalian Reproductive Behavior. (Illus.). 272p. 1980. 24.90 (ISBN 0-387-90487-5). Springer-Verlag.

Simmons, Harold. The Side Effects of Estrogen Drug Therapy: Contraception & Menopause. 1979. pap. 4.95 (ISBN 0-87312-007-8). Gen Welfare.

ETCHING

see also Engraving; Metals–Finishing

Nord, Barry & Nord, Elaine. Glass Etching-Pattern Book I: Fruit, Flowers, & Birds. (Illus.). 50p. (Orig.). 1980. pap. 3.95 (ISBN 0-935656-02-2, 101C). Chrome Yellow.

--Glass Etching-Pattern Book II: Wildlife, Alphabets, Geometrics. (Illus.). 50p. (Orig.). 1980. pap. 3.95 (ISBN 0-935656-03-0, 101D). Chrome Yellow.

ETERNAL LIFE

see Future Life

ETERNAL PUNISHMENT

see Hell

ETERNITY

Here are entered works of the philosophical concept of eternity, Eschatological works are entered under the heading Future Life.

see also Future Life; Time (Theology)

Van Dorn, Charles H. Six Things Everyone Should Know. 201p. 1980. 7.95 (ISBN 0-533-03707-7). Vantage.

ETHANOL

see Alcohol

ETHER (ANESTHETIC)

Patai, S. Supplement E Chemistry of Ethers Crown Ethers Hydroxyl Group & Their Sulphur Analogs. 1192p. 1980. Set. write for info. (ISBN 0-471-27618-9, Pub. by Wiley-Interscience). Pt. 1 (ISBN 0-471-27771-1). Pt. 2 (ISBN 0-471-27772-X). Wiley.

ETHERS

Cantor, G. N. & Hodge, M. J. Conceptions of Ether: Studies in the History of Ether Theories 1740 to 1900. LC 80-21174. (Illus.). 350p. Date not set. price not set (ISBN 0-521-22430-6). Cambridge U Pr.

ETHICAL EDUCATION

see Moral Education; Religious Education

Barry, James, ed. Ethics on a Catholic University Campus: Symposium. 1980. pap. 5.95 (ISBN 0-8294-0369-8). Loyola.

ETHICAL THEOLOGY

see Christian Ethics

ETHICS

see also Anger; Animals, Treatment of; Business Ethics; Character; Charity; Christian Ethics; Christian Life; Conduct of Life; Conscience; Courage; Crime and Criminals; Divorce; Etiquette; Free Will and Determinism; Friendship; Gambling; Good and Evil; Happiness; Joy and Sorrow; Judgment (Ethics); Justice; Legal Ethics; Love; Loyalty; Medical Ethics; Moral Education; Nursing Ethics; Obedience; Peace; Political Ethics; Professional Ethics; Religious Ethics; Responsibility; Science and Ethics; Secularism; Self-Realization; Self-Respect; Sexual Ethics; Social Problems; Spiritual Life; Spirituality; Success; Suicide; Sympathy; Temperance; Temptation; Utilitarianism; Values; Virtue and Virtues; Vocation; War; Will also subdivision Moral and Religious Aspects under specific subjects, e.g. Atomic Warfare–Moral and Religious Aspects

Callahan, Daniel & Bok, Sissela, eds. Ethics Teaching in Higher Education. (Hastings Center Monograph Ser.). 275p. 1980. 19.50 (ISBN 0-306-40522-9). Plenum Pub.

Foot, Philippa. Virtues & Vices & Other Essays in Moral Philosophy. 1981. pap. 5.95 (ISBN 0-520-04396-0, CAL 494). U of Cal Pr.

Gonsalves, Milton. Fagothey's Right & Reason: Ethics in Theory & Practice. 7th ed. 630p. 1981. text ed. 19.95 (ISBN 0-8016-1541-0). Mosby.

Grisez, Germain & Shaw, Russell. Beyond the New Morality: The Responsibilities of Freedom. rev. ed. LC 80-18293. 240p. 1980. text ed. 10.95 (ISBN 0-268-00663-6); pap. 4.95 (ISBN 0-268-00665-2). U of Notre Damepr.

Howie, John. Perspectives for Moral Decisions. LC 80-6102. 192p. 1981. lib. bdg. 17.50 (ISBN 0-8191-1375-1); pap. text ed. 9.00 (ISBN 0-8191-1376-X). U Pr of Amer.

Johannesen, Richard L. Ethics in Human Communication. LC 74-24780. 176p. pap. text ed. 5.95x (ISBN 0-917974-58-1). Waveland Pr.

Kant, Immanuel. Grounding for the Metaphysics of Morals. Ellington, James W., tr. from Ger. (HPC Philosophical Classics Ser.). 125p. 1981. lib. bdg. 12.50 (ISBN 0-915145-01-4); pap. text ed. 2.75 (ISBN 0-915145-00-6). Hackett Pub.

Sellers, James H. & Milam, Edward E. Ethics: Accounting Student Perceptions. 50p. (Orig.). 1980. pap. 4.50 (ISBN 0-938004-00-X). U MS Bus Econ.

Swabey, W. C. Ethical Theory from Hobbes to Kant. LC 60-53161. 1961. 4.75 (ISBN 0-8022-1680-3). Philos Lib.

ETHICS–ADDRESSES, ESSAYS, LECTURES

Pimsleur. Opinions, Committees on Professional Ethics, Release 1. 1980. 150.00 (ISBN 0-379-20670-6). Oceana.

ETHICS–HISTORY

Fiering, Norman. Moral Philosophy at Seventeenh-Century Harvard: A Discipline in Transition. LC 80-18282. 368p. 1981. 24.00x (ISBN 0-8078-1459-8). U of NC Pr.

Hersh, Richard H., et al. Promoting Moral Growth: From Piaget to Kohlberg. LC 78-19945. 256p. 1979. pap. text ed. write for info. Longman.

ETHICS, CHRISTIAN

see Christian Ethics

ETHICS, COMMERCIAL

see Business Ethics

ETHICS, JEWISH

see also Jewish Way of Life

Vorspan, Albert. Great Jewish Debates & Dilemmas: Perspectives on Moral Issues in Conflict in the 80's. LC 80-21057. 240p. (gr. 10-12). 1980. pap. text ed. 5.95 (ISBN 0-8074-0049-1). UAHC.

ETHICS, LEGAL

see Legal Ethics

ETHICS, MEDICAL

see Medical Ethics

ETHICS, MODERN–20TH CENTURY

Hoffman, Stanley. Duties Beyond Borders: On the Limits & Possibilities of Ethical International Politics. 288p. 1981. 18.00 (ISBN 0-8156-0167-0); pap. 9.95 (ISBN 0-8156-0168-9). Syracuse U Pr.

ETHICS, POLITICAL

see Political Ethics

ETHICS, PRACTICAL

see Conduct of Life; Ethics

ETHICS, RELIGIOUS

see Religious Ethics

ETHICS, SEXUAL

see Sexual Ethics

ETHICS AND RELIGION

see Religion and Ethics

ETHICS AND SCIENCE

see Science and Ethics

ETHIOPIA–FOREIGN RELATIONS

Bates, Darrell. The Abyssinian Difficulty: The Emperor Theodorus & the Magdala Campaign, 1867-68. (Illus.). 256p. 27.50x (ISBN 0-19-211747-5). Oxford U Pr.

ETHIOPIA–HISTORY

Bates, Darrell. The Abyssinian Difficulty: The Emperor Theodorus & the Magdala Campaign, 1867-68. (Illus.). 256p. 27.50x (ISBN 0-19-211747-5). Oxford U Pr.

ETHNIC GROUPS

Here are entered theoretical works on groups of people who are bound together by common ties of ancestry and culture. Works on the subjective sense of belonging to an individual ethnic group are entered under Ethnicity. Works on all or several of the ethnic groups located in a particular region or country are entered under Ethnology with appropriate local subdivisions, e.g. ethnology–Indonesia. Works on individual ethnic groups are entered under the name of the group, e.g. Italian Americans.

see also Ethnicity; Minorities; Race Relations

McCormick, Regina. Ethnic Heritage Studies Program Catalog: 1974-1979. (Illus.). 152p. (Orig.). 1980. pap. 9.95 (ISBN 0-89994-247-4). Soc Sci Ed.

Sowell, Thomas. Ethnic America: A History. (Illus.). 336p. 1981. 16.95 (ISBN 0-465-02074-7). Basic.

ETHNIC IDENTITY

see Ethnicity

ETHNIC PSYCHOLOGY

see Ethnopsychology

ETHNICITY

Here are entered works on the subjective sense of belonging to an individual ethnic group. Works on groups of people who are bond together by common ties of ancestry and culture are entered under Ethnic groups.

Bates, Robert H. Ethnicity in Contemporary Africa. LC 73-86994. (Foreign & Comparative Studies-Eastern African Ser.: No. 14). 59p. 1973. pap. 3.50x (ISBN 0-915984-11-3). Syracuse U Foreign Comp.

Hoffman, Stanley. Duties Beyond Borders: On the Limits & Possibilities of Ethical International Politics. 288p. 1981. 18.00 (ISBN 0-8156-0167-0); pap. 9.95 (ISBN 0-8156-0168-9). Syracuse U Pr.

Morrison, Minion K. Ethnicity & Political Integration: Ashanti, Ghana. (Foreign & Comparative Studies Program African Ser.: No. XXXVI). 1981. pap. text ed. price not set (ISBN 0-915984-59-8). Syracuse U Foreign Comp.

Stack, John F., Jr., ed. Ethnic Identities in a Transnational World. LC 80-1199. (Contributions in Political Science Ser.: No. 52). 264p. 1981. lib. bdg. 27.50 (ISBN 0-313-21088-8, SEI/). Greenwood.

Van der Merwe, Hendrik & Schrire, Robert A., eds. Race & Ethnicity: South African & International Perspectives. 240p. 1981. pap. 12.95x (ISBN 0-8476-3651-8). Rowman.

ETHNOGRAPHY

see Ethnology

ETHNOLOGY

see also Anthropo-Geography; Anthropometry; Archaeology; Civilization; Costume; Ethnic Groups; Ethnicity; Ethnopsychology; Folk-Lore; Head-Hunters; Kinship; Language and Languages; Man–Migrations; Man, Prehistoric; Native Races; Race Relations; Religion, Primitive; Society, Primitive; Socialization also individual ethnic groups and peoples, e.g. Indo-Europeans; Caucasian Race; Bantus

Alland, Alexander. To Be Human: An Introduction to Cultural Anthropology. 401p. 1981. text ed. 13.95 (ISBN 0-471-06213-8). Wiley.

Conformity & Conflict: Readings in Cultural Anthropology. 4th ed. 397p. 1980. pap. text ed. 7.95 (ISBN 0-316-80735-4); free instructors manual (ISBN 0-316-80749-4). Little.

Goodenough, Ward H. Description & Comparison in Cultural Anthropology. LC 80-67925. (Lewis Henry Morgan Lectures). 192p. 1981. 22.50 (ISBN 0-521-23740-8); pap. 6.95 (ISBN 0-521-28196-2). Cambridge U Pr.

Gunda, Bela. Ethnographica Carpatho-Balcanica. (Illus.). 427p. (Eng, Fr. & Ger.). 1979. 45.00x (ISBN 963-05-1747-7). Intl Pubns Serv.

Haley, Frances, ed. Ethnic Studies Sampler: The Best of the Title IX Project Materials. (Orig.). 1981. pap. write for info. (ISBN 0-89994-251-2). Soc Sci Ed.

Keyes, Charles F., ed. Ethnic Change. LC 80-54426. (Publications on Ethnicity & Nationality of the School of International Studies: No. 2). 306p. 1981. 20.00 (ISBN 0-295-95812-X). U of Wash Pr.

ETHNOLOGY–BIBLIOGRAPHY

Ethnic Chronologies Series, 31 vols. 1979. Set. 275.00 (ISBN 0-379-00494-1). Oceana.

ETHNOLOGY–DICTIONARIES

Murdock, George P. Atlas of World Cultures. LC 80-53030. (Illus.). 152p. 1981. 9.95x (ISBN 0-8229-3432-9). U of Pittsburgh Pr.

ETHNOLOGY–HISTORY

Frazer, James G. The Golden Bough, 13 vols. 5380p. 1980. Repr. of 1890 ed. Set. 375.00 (ISBN 0-312-33215-7). St Martin.

ETHNOLOGY–AFRICA

Wooding, Charles J. Evolving Culture: A Cross-Cultural Study of Surinam, West Africa & the Caribbean. LC 80-5612. 343p. 1981. lib. bdg. 21.75 (ISBN 0-8191-1377-8); pap. text ed. 12.00 (ISBN 0-8191-1378-6). U Pr of Amer.

ETHNOLOGY–AMERICA

Hill, W. W. Ethnography of Santa Clara Pueblo. Lange, Charles H., ed. (Illus.). 550p. 1981. 35.00x (ISBN 0-8263-0555-5). U of NM Pr.

ETHNOLOGY–ANGOLA

Esterman, Carlos. Ethnography of Southwestern Angola: The Hero People, Vol. 3. LC 75-8794. (Illus.). 1981. text ed. 39.50x (ISBN 0-8419-0206-2, Africana). Holmes & Meier.

ETHNOLOGY–AUSTRALIA

Falkenberg, Johannes & Falkenberg, Aslaug. The Affinal Relationship System of the Australian Aborigines in the Port Keats District. 224p. 1981. pap. 23.00x. Universitet.

ETHNOLOGY–GREAT BRITAIN

Strathern, Marilyn. Kinship at the Core: An Anthropology of Elmdon, a Village in North-West Essex. LC 80-40550. (Illus.). 336p. Date not set. price not set (ISBN 0-521-23360-7). Cambridge U Pr.

ETHNOLOGY–INDIA

Trautmann, Thomas R. Dravidian Kinship. LC 80-24214. (Cambridge Studies in Social Anthropology: No. 36). (Illus.). 704p. Date not set. price not set (ISBN 0-521-23703-3). Cambridge U Pr.

ETHNOLOGY–SOUTH AMERICA

O'Leary, Timothy J. Etnographic Bibliography of South America. LC 63-20695. (Bibliography Ser). 1980. pap. 27.50 (ISBN 0-87536-224-9). HRAFP.

ETHNOLOGY–UNITED STATES

see also Afro-Americans; Asian Americans; Italian Americans

Bailyn, Bernard, et al. The Great Republic: A History of the American People. 2nd ed. 1008p. 1981. text ed. 19.95 (ISBN 0-669-02753-7); pap. text ed. 12.95 vol. 1 (ISBN 0-669-02754-5); pap. text ed. 12.95 vol. 2 (ISBN 0-669-02755-3); instr's guide avail. (ISBN 0-669-02757-X); student guide 5.95 (ISBN 0-669-02756-1). Heath.

Jones, Peter D. & Holli, Melvin G., eds. Ethnic Chicago. 336p. (Orig.). 1981. pap. 12.95 (ISBN 0-8028-1821-8). Eerdmans.

Rose, Peter I. They & We: Racial & Ethnic Relations in the United States. 252p. 1981. pap. text ed. 7.95 (ISBN 0-394-32402-1). Random.

Ward, Charles A., et al, eds. Studies on Ethnicity: The East European Experience in America. (East European Monographs: No. 73). 256p. 1980. 17.50x (ISBN 0-914710-67-2). East Eur Quarterly.

ETHNOPSYCHOLOGY
see also Psychology, Applied; Race Awareness; Social Psychology
Hofstede, Geert. Culture's Consequences: International Differences in Work-Related Values. LC 80-16327. (Sage Ser. on Cross-Cultural Research & Methodology: Vol. 5). (Illus.). 475p. 1980. 29.95 (ISBN 0-8039-1444-X). Sage.
ETHOLOGY
see Character; Ethics; Human Behavior
ETHOLOGY (ZOOLOGY)
see Animals, Habits and Behavior of
ETHOLOGY, COMPARATIVE
see Psychology, Comparative
ETHYL ALCOHOL
see Alcohol
ETIOLOGY
see Diseases–Causes and Theories of Causation
ETIQUETTE
see also Air Force Wives; Charm; Dating (Social Customs); Dinners and Dining; Entertaining; Etiquette for Children and Youth; Letter-Writing
also subdivision; social life and custom under names of countries
Davis, Katrina. Charm Course for College Coeds. (Illus.). 80p. (Orig.). 1981. pap. 9.95 (ISBN 0-937242-05-5). Scandia Pubs.
Stewart, Marjabelle Y. Marjabelle Stewart's Book of Modern Table Manners. (Illus.). 192p. 1981. 14.95 (ISBN 0-312-51525-1); pap. 7.95 (ISBN 0-312-51526-X). St Martin.
Vanderbilt, Amy. The Amy Vanderbilt Complete Book of Etiquette: A Guide to Contemporary Living. Balderige, Letitia, rev. by. 272p. 1981. pap. 3.50 (ISBN 0-553-14582-7). Bantam.
ETIQUETTE–JUVENILE LITERATURE
see Etiquette for Children and Youth
ETIQUETTE FOR CHILDREN AND YOUTH
Allison, Alida. The Children's Manners Book. (Illus.). 32p. (Orig.). 1981. pap. 3.95 (ISBN 0-8431-0437-6). Price Stern.
ETYMOLOGY
see Language and Languages–Etymology;
also subdivisions Etymology and Semantics under particular languages or groups of languages
EUCALYPTUS
Boland, D. J., et al. Eucalyptus Seed. (Illus.). 191p. 1980. 25.00x (ISBN 0-643-02586-3, Pub. by Timber Pr.). Intl Schol Bk Serv.
Botanists of the Eucalypts. 160p. 1978. pap. 13.50 (ISBN 0-643-00271-5, CO07, CSIRO). Unipub.
EUCHARIST
see Lord's Supper
EURIPIDES, d. 406 B.C.–CRITICISM, TEXTUAL
Kovacs, David. The Andromache Oof Euripides: An Interpretation. LC 80-11220. write for info. (ISBN 0-89130-389-8); lib. bdg. 10.00x (ISBN 0-89130-390-1). Scholars Pr CA.
EUROPE
see also European Economic Community
also names of countries, cities and geographic areas in Europe
Boyer, Carl, 3rd. Ancestral Lines Revised. 1981. 40.00 (ISBN 0-936124-05-9). C Boyer.
Fischer-Galati, Stephen, ed. Eastern Europe in the Nineteen Eighties. 384p. (Orig.). 1981. lib. bdg. 25.00x (ISBN 0-89158-198-7); pap. 11.50x (ISBN 0-686-69586-0). Westview.
Robertson, A. H., ed. European Yearbook-Annuaire Europeen, Vol. XXVI. 696p. (Fr., Eng.). 1980. lib. bdg. 110.00 (ISBN 90-247-2298-5, Pub. by Marinus Nijhoff). Kluwer Boston.
EUROPE–ANTIQUITIES
Heggie, Douglas C. Megalithic Science: Ancient Mathematics & Science in Northwest Europe. (Illus.). 256p. 1981. 27.50 (ISBN 0-500-05036-8). Thames Hudson.
EUROPE–BIOGRAPHY
Wood, David & Wood, Alan, eds. The Times Guide to the European Parliament. (Illus.). 360p. 1980. 45.00x (ISBN 0-930466-30-6). Meckler Bks.
EUROPE–CIVILIZATION
Finley, M. I., ed. The Legacy of Greece: A New Appraisal. (Illus.). 480p. 1981. 16.95 (ISBN 0-19-821915-6). Oxford U Pr.
EUROPE–CIVILIZATION–HISTORY
Trueblood, Paul G. Byron & Europe: The Interplay of Poetry & Politics. 1980. write for info. (ISBN 0-391-02164-8). Humanities.
EUROPE–DESCRIPTION AND TRAVEL–GUIDEBOOKS
see also Restaurants, Lunchrooms, etc.–Europe
Automobile Assication. AA Camping & Caravanning in Europe. rev. ed. (Illus.). 416p. 1981. pap. write for info. (Pub. by Auto Assn-British Tourist Authority England). Merrimack Bk Serv.
Automobile Association. AA Motoring in Europe. rev. ed. (Illus.). 416p. 1981. pap. write for info. (Pub. by Auto Assn-British Tourist Authority England). Merrimack Bk Serv.
--AA Touring Map of Western Europe. (Illus.). Date not set. pap. price not set (ISBN 0-86145-001-9). Merrimack Bk Serv.
Lo Bello, Nino. European Detours: A Trave Guide to Unsual Sights. (Illus.). 176p. 1981. 8.95 (ISBN 0-8437-3375-6). Hammond Inc.
McGahey, Stan. Playboys Guide to Good Times: Europe. LC 80-84372. 256p. (Orig.). 1981. pap. 2.95 (ISBN 0-87216-819-0). Playboy Pbks.
Oakes, George W. & Chapman, Alexandra. Turn Right at the Fountain. 4th, rev. ed. LC 80-17568. (Illus.). 352p. 1981. 14.95 (ISBN 0-03-047171-0); pap. 7.95 (ISBN 0-686-69129-6). HR&W.
Paddington Press. Europe Business Travel Guide. 480p. 1981. 19.95 (ISBN 0-87196-338-8); pap. 11.95 (ISBN 0-87196-344-2). Facts on File.
Rubenstein, Hilary. Europe's Wonderful Little Hotels & Inns. (Illus.). 512p. 1981. 12.95 (ISBN 0-312-92188-8); pap. 8.95 (ISBN 0-312-92189-6). St Martin.
Waldo, Myra. Myra Waldo's Travel Guide to Northern Europe, 1981. (Illus.). 730p. 1981. pap. 9.95 (ISBN 0-02-098910-5, Collier). Macmillan.
--Myra Waldo's Travel Guide to Southern Europe, 1981. (Illus.). 770p. 1981. pap. 9.95 (ISBN 0-02-098930-X, Collier). Macmillan.
Yeadon, David. Backroads of Southern Europe. LC 80-8222. (Illus.). 256p. 1981. 15.00 (ISBN 0-06-014779-2, CN 838, HarpT); pap. 6.95 (ISBN 0-06-090838-6). Har-Row.
Youth Hostels Association. Standard Youth Hosteler's Guide to Europe. rev. ed. (Illus.). 498p. 1981. 6.95 (ISBN 0-02-098950-4, Collier). Macmillan.
EUROPE–DIRECTORIES
Boehm, Klaus & Morris, Brian. Who Decides What in Europe. 256p. 1981. lib. bdg. 27.50 (ISBN 0-87196-388-4). Facts on File.
EUROPE–ECONOMIC CONDITIONS
Berger, Suzanne, ed. Organizing Interests in Western Europe: Pluralism, Corporatism & the Transformation of Politics. LC 80-16378. (Cambridge Studies in Modern Political Economies). (Illus.). 464p. Date not set. price not set (ISBN 0-521-23174-4). Cambridge U Pr.
Economic Survey of Europe in Nineteen Seventy-Seven: The European Economy in Nineteen Seventy-Eight, Pt.1. 166p. 1980. pap. 12.00 (UN79-2E1, UN). Unipub.
Leigh, L. H. Economic Crime in Europe. Date not set. write for info. (ISBN 0-312-22788-4). St Martin.
Lomax, D. F. & Gutmann, P. T. The Euromarkets & International Financial Policies. 275p. 1980. 29.95x (ISBN 0-470-26923-5). Halsted Pr.
NATO. Economic Reforms in Eastern Europe & Prospects for the 1980s. (NATO Colloquim, 16-18 April 1980, Brussels, Belgium). (Illus.). 325p. 1980. 60.00 (ISBN 0-08-026801-3). Pergamon.
EUROPE–ECONOMIC INTEGRATION
Kruse, Douglas C. Monetary Integration in Western Europe. LC 80-40980. (European Studies Ser.). (Illus.). 256p. 1980. text ed. 42.95 (ISBN 0-408-10666-2). Butterworths.
Pollard, Sidney. Integration of the European Economy Since 1815. (Studies on Contemporary Europe: No. 4). 96p. 1981. text ed. 15.95x (ISBN 0-04-336069-6, 2615-6); pap. text ed. 6.95x (ISBN 0-04-336070-X). Allen Unwin.
EUROPE–FOREIGN ECONOMIC CONDITIONS
Andren, Nils & Birnbaum, Karl E. Belgrade & Beyond: The CSCE Process in Perspective. (East West Perspectives: No. 5). 27.50x (ISBN 90-286-0250-X). Sijthoff & Noordhoff.
Buckley, Peter J. & Roberts, Brian R. European Direct Investment in the U.S.A. Before World War I. 1981. 25.00 (ISBN 0-312-26940-4). St Martin.
EUROPE–HISTORIOGRAPHY
Cohen, William. European Empire Building. LC 79-57459. (Problems in Civilization Ser.). (Orig.). 1980. pap. text ed. 3.95x (ISBN 0-88273-410-5). Forum Pr MO.
EUROPE–HISTORY
Here are entered general works on European history. For works covering shorter periods of time see chronological subdivisions below.
Binion, Rudolph. Soundings. 275p. 1981. 18.95 (ISBN 0-914434-16-0); pap. 8.95 (ISBN 0-914434-17-9). Psychohistory Pr.
Bowle, John. A History of Europe. xii, 626p. 1981. lib. bdg. write for info. (06856-0, Pub. by Secker & Warburg). U of Chicago Pr.
Burke, P., ed. The New Cambridge Modern History, Vol. XIII. LC 57-14935. (The New Cambridge Modern History Ser.). 384p. 1980. pap. 13.95 (ISBN 0-521-28017-6). Cambridge U Pr.
Deak, Istvan. Everyman in Europe: Essays in Social History, Vol. 1. 224p. 1981. pap. text ed. 9.95 (ISBN 0-13-293621-6). P-H.
Francis, Carol B. Europe Dimensions: A Study-Activity Guide. (Orig.). 1981. pap. 3.95 (ISBN 0-377-00108-2). Friend Pr.
Godfrey, James. Revolutionary Justice: A Study of the Organization, Personnel & Procedure of the Paris Tribunal 1793-1795. (Perspectives in Europen History Ser.: No. 42). vi, 166p. 1981. Repr. of 1951 ed. lib. bdg. 15.00x (ISBN 0-87991-640-0). Porcupine Pr.
Jones, E. L. The European Miracle: Environments, Economies & Geopolitics in the History of Europe & Asia. 274p. Date not set. text ed. price not set (ISBN 0-521-23588-X); pap. text ed. price not set (ISBN 0-521-28055-9). Cambridge U Pr.
Jones, R. Ben. The Making of Contemporary Europe. 225p. 1981. text ed. 38.50x (ISBN 0-8419-0668-8); pap. text ed. 19.50x (ISBN 0-8419-0669-6). Holmes & Meier.
Kelly, D. R. The Beginning of Ideology. 358p. Date not set. price not set (ISBN 0-521-23504-9). Cambridge U Pr.
Shennan, J. H. The Origins of the Modern European State, Fourteen Fifty to Seventeen Twenty-Five. 1980. text ed. 14.50x (ISBN 0-09-119030-4, Hutchinson U Pr); pap. text ed. 9.25x (ISBN 0-09-119031-2). Humanities.
Steves, Rick. Europe - Through the Back Door. 2nd ed. 112p. 1981. pap. 5.95 (ISBN 0-686-28770-3). Steves Wide World.
EUROPE–HISTORY–BIBLIOGRAPHY
International Biographical Dictionary of Central Emigres, 1933-1945. (Politics, Economics, & Public Life Ser.: Vol. I). 875p. 1980. 210.00 (ISBN 3-598-10088-4, Dist by Gale Research). K G Saur.
EUROPE–HISTORY–476-1492
see also Middle Ages–History
Duby, Georges. The Age of the Cathedrals: Art & Society, 980-1420. Levieux, Eleanor & Thompson, Barbara, trs. LC 80-22769. (Illus.). 1981. price not set (ISBN 0-226-16769-0). U of Chicago Pr.
Folz, Robert. The Concept of Empire in Western Europe from the Fifth to the Fourteenth Century. Ogilvie, Sheila A., tr. from French. LC 80-18796. xv, 250p. 1980. Repr. of 1969 ed. lib. bdg. 27.50x (ISBN 0-313-22453-6, FOCO). Greenwood.
A History of Europe from Thirteen Seventy-Eight to Fourteen Ninety-Four. 3rd ed. LC 80-23759. (Methuen's History of Medieval & Modern Europe: IV). (Illus.). xiii, 545p. 1980. Repr. of 1949 ed. lib. bdg. 45.00x (ISBN 0-8371-8091-0, WAHEU). Greenwood.
Hlawitscka, Eduard. Franken, Alemannen, Bayern und Burgunder in Oberitalien, 774-962. LC 80-2025. 1981. Repr. of 1960 ed. 38.50 (ISBN 0-404-18569-X). AMS Pr.
Holmes, Urban T., Jr. Daily Living in the Twelfth Century: Based on the Observations of Alexander Neckam in London & Paris. LC 80-19991. (Illus.). ix, 337p. 1980. Repr. of 1973 ed. lib. bdg. 29.50x (ISBN 0-313-22796-9, HODL). Greenwood.
Rice, Edward. The Age of Charlemagne. 112p. 1963. 2.95 (ISBN 0-374-29492-5). FS&G.
Rose, J. H. The Revolutionary & Napoleonic Era. 387p. 1980. Repr. of 1894 ed. lib. bdg. 40.00 (ISBN 0-89760-737-6). Telegraph Bks.
Sanders, Ivor J. Feudal Military Service in England: A Study of the Constitutional & Military Powers of the Barones in Medieval England. LC 80-23778. (Oxford Historical Ser., British Ser.). xv, 173p. 1980. Repr. of 1956 ed. lib. bdg. 19.25x (ISBN 0-313-22725-X, SAFM). Greenwood.
Tout, Thomas F. The Empire & the Papacy, Nine Eighteen to Twelve Seventy-Three. 8th ed. LC 80-18865. (Periods of European History: Period II). (Illus.). vii, 526p. 1980. Repr. of 1965 ed. lib. bdg. 35.00x (ISBN 0-313-22372-6, TOEP). Greenwood.
University of Wisconsin, Division of Humanities. Twelfth-Century Europe & the Foundations of Modern Society. Clagett, Marshall, et al, eds. LC 80-21872. (Illus.). xvi, 219p. 1980. Repr. of 1966 ed. lib. bdg. 29.75x (ISBN 0-313-22798-5, WITC). Greenwood.
EUROPE–HISTORY–1492-1648
Mark, Peter A. Africans in European Eyes-the Portrayal of Black Africans in Fourteenth & Fifteenth Century Europe. LC 74-25878. (Foreign & Comparative Studies-Eastern African Ser.: No. 16). 98p. 1975. pap. 4.50x (ISBN 0-915984-13-X). Syracuse U Foreign Comp.
EUROPE–HISTORY–17TH CENTURY
Gutmann, Myron P. War & Rural Life in the Early Modern Low Countries. 322p. 1980. text ed. 34.25 (ISBN 90-232-1740-3). Humanities.
EUROPE–HISTORY–18TH CENTURY
Gutmann, Myron P. War & Rural Life in the Early Modern Low Countries. 322p. 1980. text ed. 34.25 (ISBN 90-232-1740-3). Humanities.
EUROPE–HISTORY–1789-1815
Leeds, C. A. European History Seventeen Eighty-Nine to Nineteen Fourteen. 448p. 1979. pap. 13.95x (ISBN 0-7121-0575-1, Pub. by Macdonald & Evans England). Intl Ideas.
EUROPE–HISTORY–19TH CENTURY
Santi, Paul & Hill, Richard, eds. The Europeans in the Sudan Eighteen Thirty Four to Eighteen Seventy Eight. (Illus.). 352p. 1980. 45.00 (ISBN 0-19-822718-3). Oxford U Pr.
EUROPE–HISTORY–1815-1871
Leeds, C. A. European History Seventeen Eighty-Nine to Nineteen Fourteen. 448p. 1979. pap. 13.95x (ISBN 0-7121-0575-1, Pub. by Macdonald & Evans England). Intl Ideas.
EUROPE–HISTORY–1871-1918
Leeds, C. A. European History Seventeen Eighty-Nine to Nineteen Fourteen. 448p. 1979. pap. 13.95x (ISBN 0-7121-0575-1, Pub. by Macdonald & Evans England). Intl Ideas.
Mayer, Arno. The Persistence of the Old Regime: Europe to the Great War. 1981. 16.95 (ISBN 0-394-51141-7). Pantheon.
EUROPE–HISTORY–20TH CENTURY
Radice, Lisanne. Prelude to Appeasement: East European Central Diplomacy in the Early 1930's. (East European Quarterly Ser.: No. 80). 256p. 1981. text ed. 17.50x (ISBN 0-914710-74-5). East Eur Quarterly.
EUROPE–HISTORY–1945-
Thackrah, J. R. Europe Since the Second World War. 288p. 1979. pap. 9.95x (Pub. by Macdonald & Evans England). Intl Ideas.
EUROPE–INTELLECTUAL LIFE
Stromberg, R. European Intellectual History Since Seventeen Eighty-Nine. 3nd ed. 1981. pap. 4.95 (ISBN 0-13-291955-9). P-H.
EUROPE–POLITICS AND GOVERNMENT
Butler, David & Marquand, David. European Elections & British Politics. 208p. 1981. text ed. 25.00 (ISBN 0-582-29528-9); pap. text ed. 11.95 (ISBN 0-582-29529-7). Longman.
Flinn, Michael W. The European Demographic System: 1500 to 1820. LC 80-19574. (Studies in Comparative History: No. 11). 220p. 1981. text ed. 15.00 (ISBN 0-8018-2426-5). Johns Hopkins.
Hachey, Thomas E. & Weber, Ralph E. European Ideologies Since Seventeen Eighty-Nine: Rebels, Radicals & Political Ferment. 200p. (Orig.). 1981. pap. text ed. 5.50 (ISBN 0-89874-082-7). Krieger.
Jacob, Margaret C. The Radical Enlightenment: Pantheists, Fremasons & Republicans. (Early Modern Europe Today Ser.). (Illus.). 352p. 1981. text ed. 29.50x (ISBN 0-04-901029-8, 2595). Allen Unwin.
Oakeshott, Michael. The Social & Political Doctrines of Contemporary Europe. 241p. 1980. Repr. of 1947 ed. lib. bdg. 35.00 (ISBN 0-89987-625-0). Darby Bks.
Pridham, Geoffrey & Pridham, Pippa. Transnational Party Co-Operation & European Integration. 304p. 1981. text ed. 34.00x (ISBN 0-04-329032-9, 2591). Allen Unwin.
Shennan, J. H. The Origins of the Modern European State, Fourteen Fifty to Seventeen Twenty-Five. 1980. text ed. 14.50x (ISBN 0-09-119030-4, Hutchinson U Pr); pap. text ed. 9.25x (ISBN 0-09-119031-2). Humanities.
Smith, Gordon. Politics in Western Europe. 3rd ed. LC 80-81211. 344p. 1980. 24.75 (ISBN 0-8419-0627-0); pap. 9.75 (ISBN 0-8419-0628-9). Holmes & Meier.
Smith, Gordon B., et al, eds. Soviet & East European Law & the Scientific-Technical Revolution. (Pergamon Policy Studies on International Politics). (Illus.). 330p. 1981. 34.00 (ISBN 0-08-027195-2). Pergamon.
Stamm, Theo. Political Parties in Europe. 1981. 42.50 (ISBN 0-930466-28-4). Meckler Bks.
EUROPE–POLITICS AND GOVERNMENT–1789-1900
Trueblood, Paul G. Byron & Europe: The Interplay of Poetry & Politics. 1980. write for info. (ISBN 0-391-02164-8). Humanities.
EUROPE–POLITICS AND GOVERNMENT–20TH CENTURY
Berger, Suzanne, ed. Organizing Interests in Western Europe: Pluralism, Corporatism & the Transformation of Politics. LC 80-16378. (Cambridge Studies in Modern Political Economies). (Illus.). 464p. Date not set. price not set (ISBN 0-521-23174-4). Cambridge U Pr.
Fitzgerald, Walter. The New Europe: An Introduction to Its Political Geography. LC 80-24065. (Illus.). xiii, 298p. 1980. Repr. of 1946 ed. lib. bdg. 29.75x (ISBN 0-313-21006-3, FINE). Greenwood.
EUROPE–RELIGION
Francis, Carol B. Europe Dimensions: A Study-Activity Guide. (Orig.). 1981. pap. 3.95 (ISBN 0-377-00108-2). Friend Pr.
Tout, Thomas F. The Empire & the Papacy, Nine Eighteen to Twelve Seventy-Three. 8th ed. LC 80-18865. (Periods of European History: Period II). (Illus.). vii, 526p. 1980. Repr. of 1965 ed. lib. bdg. 35.00x (ISBN 0-313-22372-6, TOEP). Greenwood.
Will, James E. Must Walls Divide? The Creative Witness of the Churches in Europe. (Orig.). 1981. pap. 3.75 (ISBN 0-377-00106-6). Friend Pr.
EUROPE–SOCIAL CONDITIONS
Deak, Istvan. Everyman in Europe: Essays in Social History, Vol. 1. 224p. 1981. pap. text ed. 9.95 (ISBN 0-13-293621-6). P-H.
Hachey, Thomas E. & Weber, Ralph E. European Ideologies Since Seventeen Eighty-Nine: Rebels, Radicals & Political Ferment. 200p. (Orig.). 1981. pap. text ed. 5.50 (ISBN 0-89874-082-7). Krieger.
Jacob, Margaret C. The Radical Enlightenment: Pantheists, Fremasons & Republicans. (Early Modern Europe Today Ser.). (Illus.). 352p. 1981. text ed. 29.50x (ISBN 0-04-901029-8, 2595). Allen Unwin.
Kay, Joseph. The Social Condition & Education of the People in England & Europe, 2 vols. (The Development of Industrial Society Ser.). 1156p. 1980. Repr. 50.00x (ISBN 0-7165-1565-2, Pub. by Irish Academic Pr). Biblio Dist.
Oakeshott, Michael. The Social & Political Doctrines of Contemporary Europe. 241p. 1980. Repr. of 1947 ed. lib. bdg. 35.00 (ISBN 0-89987-625-0). Darby Bks.
EUROPE–STATISTICS
Europa Yearbook Nineteen Eighty-One, 2 vols. 22nd ed. (Illus.). 3600p. 1981. 150.00. Gale.
EUROPE, CENTRAL
Here are entered works on the area included in the basins of the Danube, Elbe, and rhine rivers.
Wells, P. S. Culture Contact & Culture Change. LC 80-40212. (New Studies in Archaeology). (Illus.). 195p. 1981. 24.95 (ISBN 0-521-22808-5). Cambridge U Pr.

EUROPE, CENTRAL-HISTORY
International Biographical Dictionary of Central Emigres, 1933-1945. (Politics, Economics, & Public Life Ser.: Vol. I). 875p. 1980. 210.00 (ISBN 3-598-10088-4, Dist by Gale Research). K G Saur.
EUROPE, EASTERN-BIBLIOGRAPHY
New York Public Library, Research Libraries & Library of Congress. Bibliographic Guide to Soviet & East European Studies, 1980. (Library Catalogs - Bibliographic Guides Ser.). 1981. lib. bdg. 195.00 (ISBN 0-8161-6894-6). G K Hall.
Terry, Garth M. East European Languages & Literatures: A Subject & Name Index to Articles in English-Language Journals, 1900-1977. 275p. 1978. 47.50. ABC-Clio.
EUROPE, EASTERN-POLITICS AND GOVERNMENT
Bahro, Rudolph. The Alternative in Eastern Europe. 464p. 1981. 19.50 (ISBN 0-8052-7056-6, Pub. by NLB England); pap. 9.50 (ISBN 0-8052-7098-1). Schocken.
Singer, Daniel. The Road to Gdansk: Eastern Europe on the Move. LC 80-39914. 288p. 1981. 15.00 (ISBN 0-85345-567-8). Monthly Rev.
EUROPE, EASTERN-SOCIAL LIFE AND CUSTOMS
Sanders, Irwin, et al. East European Presantries: Social Reflections-an Annotated Bibliography of Periodical Articles, Vol.2. (Reference Books Ser.). 1981. 16.00 (ISBN 0-8161-8488-7). G K Hall.
Singer, Daniel. The Road to Gdansk: Eastern Europe on the Move. LC 80-39914. 288p. 1981. 15.00 (ISBN 0-85345-567-8). Monthly Rev.
EUROPEAN ARCHITECTURE
see Architecture-Europe
EUROPEAN ART
see Art, European
EUROPEAN COMMON MARKET (1955-)
see Europe-Economic Integration; European Economic Community
EUROPEAN DRAWINGS
see Drawings, European
EUROPEAN ECONOMIC COMMUNITY
Action by the European Community Through Its Financial Instruments-Documentation. 316p. 1980. pap. 25.00 (ISBN 2-8029-0023-4, ED11, Edns Delta). Unipub.
Campbell, A. Common Market Law, Vol. 3. 2nd ed. 1973. 65.00 (ISBN 0-379-16063-3). Oceana.
The Economic Commission for Europe & Energy Conservation. 76p. 1980. pap. 7.00 (UN80-2E4, UN). Unipub.
El-Agraa, A. M. The Economics of the European Community. 1980. 37.50 (ISBN 0-312-23285-3). St Martin.
Minshall, G. N. The New Europe, an Economic Geography of the EEC. 2nd ed. LC 78-6581. 288p. 1981. pap. text ed. 17.50x (ISBN 0-8419-6221-9). Holmes & Meier.
Parker, Geoffrey. Logic of Unity. 3rd ed. (Illus.). 224p. 1981. pap. text ed. 14.95 (ISBN 0-582-30031-2). Longman.
Principal Companies of the European Economic Community 1980-81. 1980. 127.00 (ISBN 0-531-03942-0); pap. 111.00 (ISBN 0-531-03950-1). Watts.
Seers, Dudley, et al, eds. Integration & Unequal Development. (Studies in the Integration of Western Europe). 1981. write for info. (ISBN 0-312-41890-6). St Martin.
Usher, John. European Community Law & National Law. (Studies on Contemporary Europe: No. 3). 96p. (Orig.). 1981. text ed. 15.95x (ISBN 0-04-341017-0, 2593); pap. text ed. 6.95x (ISBN 0-04-341018-9, 2594). Allen Unwin.
EUROPEAN LITERATURE
see Literature
EUROPEAN PAINTING
see Painting, European
EUROPEAN PARLIAMENT
Palmer, Michael. The European Paraliament: What It Is - What It Does - How It Works. 128p. 1981. 14.50 (ISBN 0-08-024536-6); pap. 7.20 (ISBN 0-08-024535-8). Pergamon.
Wood, David & Wood, Alan, eds. The Times Guide to the European Parliament. (Illus.). 360p. 1980. 45.00x (ISBN 0-930466-30-6). Meckler Bks.
EUROPEAN PORCELAIN
see Porcelain
EUROPEAN WAR, 1914-1918
Hardach, Gerd. The First World War, Nineteen Fourteen to Nineteen Eighteen. (History of the World Economy in the Twentieth Century Ser.: Vol. 2). 1981. pap. 6.95 (ISBN 0-520-04397-9, CAL 495). U of Cal Pr.
Hillgruber, Andreas. Germany & the Two World Wars. Kirby, William C., tr. LC 80-27036. 144p. 1981. text ed. 14.50 (ISBN 0-674-35321-8). Harvard U Pr.
Marston, Frank S. The Peace Conference of Nineteen Nineteen: Organization & Procedure. LC 80-28997. xi, 276p. 1981. Repr. of 1944 ed. lib. bdg. 25.00x (ISBN 0-313-22910-4, MAPEC). Greenwood.
Stokesbury, James L. A Short History of World War I. LC 80-22206. (Illus.). 352p. 1981. 13.95 (ISBN 0-688-00128-9). Morrow.
--A Short History of World War I. LC 80-22207. (Illus.). 352p. 1981. pap. 7.95 (ISBN 0-688-00129-7, Quill). Morrow.
Terraine, John. To Win a War: Nineteen Eighteen, The Year of Victory. LC 79-7119. (Illus.). 288p. 1981. 14.95 (ISBN 0-385-15316-3). Doubleday.
EUROPEAN WAR, 1914-1918-AERIAL OPERATIONS
Flammer, Philip M. Vivid Air: The Lafayette Escadrille. LC 80-22059. (Illus.). 288p. 1981. 17.50 (ISBN 0-8203-0537-5). U of Ga Pr.
EUROPEAN WAR, 1914-1918-AMERICAN PROPAGANDA
see Propaganda, American
EUROPEAN WAR, 1914-1918-BIBLIOGRAPHY
Phillips, Jill M. The Darkling Plain: A Bibliography of Books About World War I. (Bibliographies for Librarians Ser.). 1980. lib. bdg. 69.95 (ISBN 0-8490-3207-5). Gordon Pr.
EUROPEAN WAR, 1914-1918-BIOGRAPHY
Brittain, Vera. Testament of Youth. 1980. 13.95 (ISBN 0-686-68866-X). Seaview Bks.
--Testament of Youth. 1980. 13.95 (ISBN 0-686-68995-X); pap. 7.45 (ISBN 0-686-68996-8). Wideview Bks.
Udet, Ernst. Ace of the Iron Cross. Ulanoff, Stanley M., ed. Riehn, Richard K., tr. from Ger. LC 80-26156. (Air Combat Classics). (Illus.). 256p. 1981. 9.95 (ISBN 0-668-05161-2); pap. 5.95 (ISBN 0-668-05163-9). Arco.
EUROPEAN WAR, 1914-1918-PEACE
Marks, Sally. Innocent Abroad: Belgium at the Paris Peace Conference of 1919. LC 80-13698. (Illus.). 456p. 1980. 26.00x (ISBN 0-8078-1451-2). U of NC Pr.
EUROPEAN WAR, 1914-1918-PERSONAL NARRATIVES
Maginnis, John J. Profile of a Citizen Soldier. (Illus.). 254p. 1981. 9.95 (ISBN 0-89962-046-9). Todd & Honeywell.
Nagel, Fritz. Fritz: The World War I Memoirs of a German Lieutenant. Baumgartner, Richard A., ed. (Illus.). 160p. (Orig.). 1980. pap. 6.95 (ISBN 0-9604770-0-4). Der Angriff.
EUROPEAN WAR, 1939-1945
see World War, 1939-1945
EUROPEANS IN AFRICA
Santi, Paul & Hill, Richard, eds. The Europeans in the Sudan Eighteen Thirty Four to Eighteen Seventy Eight. (Illus.). 352p. 1980. 45.00 (ISBN 0-19-822718-3). Oxford U Pr.
EUSEBIUS PAMPHILI, BISHOP OF CAESAREA
Grant, Robert M. Eusebius As Church Historian. 192p. 1980. 29.95 (ISBN 0-19-826441-0). Oxford U Pr.
EUTHANASIA
God, Phyllis. God. Date not set. 7.95 (ISBN 0-533-04754-4). Vantage.
Grisez, Germain & Boyle, Joseph M., Jr. Life & Death with Liberty & Justice: A Contribution to the Euthanasia Debate. LC 78-31249. 544p. 1980. pap. text ed. 9.95 (ISBN 0-268-01263-6). U of Notre Dame Pr.
Horan, Dennis J. & Mall, David, eds. Death, Dying, & Euthanasia. 1977. 24.00 (ISBN 0-89093-139-9); pap. 10.00 (ISBN 0-89093-140-2). U Pubns Amer.
Wallace, Samuel E. & Eser, Albin, eds. Suicide & Euthanasia: The Rights of Personhood. LC 80-28799. 176p. 1981. 12.50x (ISBN 0-87049-299-3). U of Tenn Pr.
EVALUATION, JOB
see Job Evaluation
EVALUATION OF LITERATURE
see Bibliography-Best Books; Books and Reading; Criticism; Literature-History and Criticism
EVALUATION OF SCHOOLS
see Educational Surveys
EVANGELICAL RELIGION
see Evangelicalism
EVANGELICALISM
Apperlman, Hyman. Sermons on Evangelism. (Pocket Pulpit Library). 96p. 1981. pap. 1.95 (ISBN 0-8010-0068-8). Baker Bk.
Farrior, Louise H. Una Dedicacion Valiente. Gonzalez, Justo L., tr. from Eng. 123p. (Orig., Span.). 1979. pap. 2.25 (ISBN 0-89922-134-3). Edit Caribe.
Gasco, Hugo. Despierta, Continente Mio. LC 78-50624. 159p. (Orig., Span.). 1978. pap. 3.50 (ISBN 0-89922-108-4). Edit Caribe.
Jay, Elisabeth. The Religion of the Heart: Anglican Evangelicalism & the Nineteenth-Century Novel. 1979. write for info. (ISBN 0-19-812092-3). Oxford U Pr.
Kuiper, R. B. God Centred Evangelism. 1978. pap. 3.95 (ISBN 0-85151-110-4). Banner of Truth.
Miller, C. J. Evangelism & Your Church. 1980. pap. 2.95 (ISBN 0-87552-290-4). Presby & Reformed.
Murray, Iain. El Obstaculo Al Evangelismo. (Span.). Date not set. pap. 0.60 (ISBN 0-686-28950-1). Banner of Truth.
Samuel, D. N. The Evangelical Succession. 144p. pap. 7.95 (ISBN 0-227-67834-6). Attic Pr.
Schaeffer, Franky. Addicted to Mediocrity. (Illus.). 128p. 1981. pap. 4.95 (ISBN 0-89107-214-4). Good News.
Smith, Bailey E. Real Evangelistic Preaching. 1981. 6.95 (ISBN 0-8054-6229-5). Broadman.
Stephens, Ken. Discipleship Evangelism. LC 81-80258. 1981. pap. 6.95 (ISBN 0-89081-283-7). Harvest Hse.
Watson, David. Creo en la Evangelizacion. Schwieters, Elsa S., tr. from Eng. (Serie Creo). 235p. (Orig., Span.). 1979. pap. 3.95 (ISBN 0-89922-133-5). Edit Caribe.
EVANGELISTIC WORK
see also Communication (Theology); Missions; Revivals
Anderson, Gerald H. & Stransky, Thomas F., eds. Mission Trends No. Five: Faith Meets Faith. (Mission Trends Ser.). 320p. (Orig.). 1981. pap. 3.95 (ISBN 0-8028-1821-8). Eerdmans.
Hughes, Richard & Serig, Joseph A., eds. Evangelism: The Ministry of the Church. 1981. pap. 12.00 (ISBN 0-8309-0304-6). Herald Hse.
Lesick, Lawrence T. The Lane Rebels: Evangelicalism & Antislavery in Antebellum America. LC 80-24123. (Studies in Evangelicalism: No. 2). 287p. 1980. 15.00 (ISBN 0-8108-1372-6). Scarecrow.
Ogilvie, Lloyd J. How to Know God's Will. LC 80-84824. 1981. pap. 4.95 (ISBN 0-89081-282-9). Harvest Hse.
Olford, Stephen. Lord, Open the Heavens! A Heartcry for Revival. LC 80-52053. 144p. 1980. pap. 3.95x (ISBN 0-87788-335-1). Shaw Pubs.
Pearlman, Myer, tr. Evangelismo Personal. (Spanish Bks.). 1978. 1.25 (ISBN 0-8297-0552-X). Life Pubs Intl.
Reapsome, James, et al, eds. Evangelical Missions Quarterly, Vols. 13-15. LC 71-186301. 803p. 1980. Repr. 19.95 (ISBN 0-87808-709-5). William Carey Lib.
Sumner, Robert L. After the Revival--What? 1980. pap. 3.95 (ISBN 0-87398-026-3). Bibl Evang Pr.
EVANGELISTS
Green, John L. Pioneer Evangelists of the Church of God in the Pacific Northwest. 164p. pap. 2.00. Faith Pub Hse.
Pratt, Josiah, ed. Thought of the Evangelical Leaders: John Newton, Thomas Scott, Charles Simeon, Etc. 1978. 15.95 (ISBN 0-85151-270-4). Banner of Truth.
EVAPORATION OF FOOD
see Food-Drying
EVASION, FISCAL
see Tax Evasion
EVE (BIBLICAL CHARACTER)
De Vinck, Catherine. A Book of Eve. 1979. text ed. 6.00 (ISBN 0-911726-40-3); stero record incl. Alleluia Pr.
EVELYN, JOHN, 1620-1706
Bowle, John. John Evelyn & His Cracked World. (Illus.). 256p. 1981. price not set (ISBN 0-7100-0721-3). Routledge & Kegan.
Hiscock, W. G. John Evelyn & His Family Circle. 256p. 1980. Repr. of 1955 ed. lib. bdg. 35.00 (ISBN 0-8495-2374-5). Arden Lib.
EVERLASTING PUNISHMENT
see Hell
EVIDENCE (LAW)
see also Cross-Examination; Evidence, Criminal; Medical Jurisprudence; Psychology, Forensic; Wire-Tapping
Bentham, Jeremy. A Treatise on Judicial Evidence, Extracted from the Manuscripts of Jeremy Bentham. Dumont, M., ed. xvi, 366p. 1981. Repr. of 1825 ed. lib. bdg. 35.00x (ISBN 0-8377-0318-2). Rothman.
Best, William M. & Stephen, James F. A Treatise on the Principles of Evidence & Practice As to Proofs in the Court of Common Law. Berkowitz, David S. & Thorne, Samuel E., eds. LC 77-86653. (Classics of English Legal History in the Modern Era Ser.: Vol.37). 594p. 1979. lib. bdg. 40.00 (ISBN 0-8240-3086-9). Garland Pub.
Broun, Kenneth S. & Meisenholder, Robert. Problems in Evidence. 2nd ed. (American Casebook Ser.). 1981. pap. text ed. 6.95 (ISBN 0-8299-2125-7). West Pub.
Lawyers & Judges Publishing Staff. About Your Deposition: Ninety-Five Questions & Answers. rev. ed. 1979. pap. 0.95 (ISBN 0-88450-051-9, 6109-B). Lawyers & Judges.
Louisell, David W. & Kaplan, John. Cases & Materials on Evidence. 4th ed. (University Casebook Ser.). 899p. 1981. write for info. (ISBN 0-88277-018-7). Foundation Pr.
McCormick, Charles T., et al. Cases & Materials on Evidence. 5th ed. LC 80-22463. 1083p. 1980. text ed. write for info. (ISBN 0-8299-2112-5). West Pub.
Rothstein, Paul F. Evidence in a Nutshell, State & Federal Rules. 2nd ed. (Nutshell Ser.). 401p. 1981. pap. text ed. 6.95 (ISBN 0-8299-2131-1). West Pub.
EVIDENCE, CRIMINAL
see also Torture; Wire-Tapping
Klotter, John C. Criminal Evidence. 3rd rev. ed. LC 79-55201. (Criminal Justice Studies). 500p. 1980. text ed. 18.95 (ISBN 0-87084-500-4). Anderson Pub Co.
Rothstein, Paul F. Evidence in a Nutshell, State & Federal Rules. 2nd ed. (Nutshell Ser.). 401p. 1981. pap. text ed. 6.95 (ISBN 0-8299-2131-1). West Pub.
EVIDENCES, CHRISTIAN
see Apologetics
EVIDENCES OF CHRISTIANITY
see Apologetics
EVIDENCES OF THE BIBLE
see Bible-Evidences, Authority, etc.
EVIL
see Good and Evil
EVIL SPIRITS
see Demonology
EVOLUTION
see also Adaptation (Biology); Anatomy, Comparative; Biology; Creation; Embryology; Genetics; Heredity; Holism; Human Evolution; Man-Influence of Environment; Natural Selection; Phylogeny
Alfassa, Mirra & Enginger, Bernard. Mother's Agenda, Vol. 2, 1961. Orig. Title: L'agenda De Mere. 500p. (Orig.). 1981. pap. 8.95 (ISBN 0-938710-01-X). Inst Evolutionary.
Darwin, Charles. The Collected Papers of Charles Darwin, 2 vol. set. Barrett, Paul H., ed. 886p. pap. 13.50. U of Chicago Pr.
Dillon, Lawrence S. Ultrastructure,Macromolecules, & Evolution. 750p. 1981. 69.50 (ISBN 0-306-40528-8, Plenum Pr). Plenum Pub.
Erickson, Lonni R. The Teaching of Evolution in Public Schools: A Comparison of Evolution & Special Creation. (Illus.). 40p. (Orig.). 1980. pap. 3.95 (ISBN 0-937242-03-9). Scandia Pubs.
Frankel, O. H. & Soule, M. E. Conservation & Evolution. LC 80-40528. (Illus.). 300p. Date not set. 49.50 (ISBN 0-521-23275-9); pap. 17.95 (ISBN 0-521-29889-X). Cambridge U Pr.
Haeckel, Ernst. Last Words on Evolution. McCabe, Joseph, tr. from Ger. Bd. with Contributions to the Study of the Behavior of Lower Organisms. Jennings, H. S; An Essay. Spencer, Herbert. (Contributions to the History of Psychology Ser.: No. 3, Pt. D). 1978. Repr. of 1906 ed. 30.00 (ISBN 0-89093-172-0). U Pubns Amer.
Halvorson, Harlyn O. & Van Holde, Kensal E., eds. The Origins of Life & Evolution. LC 80-21901. (MBL Lectures in Biology: Vol. 1). 136p. 1980. 16.00 (ISBN 0-8451-2200-2). A R Liss.
Hanson, Earl D. Understanding Evolution. (Illus.). 560p. 1981. text ed. 19.95x (ISBN 0-19-502784-1). Oxford U Pr.
Hayes, Harold. Three Levels of Time. 1981. 12.95 (ISBN 0-525-21853-X). Dutton.
Hill, Harold, tr. Homme Ou Singe, Mr. Darwin? (French Bks.). (Fr.). 1979. 1.75 (ISBN 0-8297-0840-5). Life Pubs Intl.
--Las Monerias De Darwin. (Spanish Bks.). (Span.). 1977. 1.60 (ISBN 0-8297-0771-9). Life Pubs Intl.
Jantsch, Erich, ed. The Evolutionary Vision: Toward a Unifying Paradigm of Physical, Biological, & Sociocultural Evolution. (AAAS Selected Symposium: No. 6). 200p. 1981. lib. bdg. 17.50x (ISBN 0-86531-140-4). Westview.
Skinner, Brian J., ed. Paleontology & Paleoenvironments. (The Earth & Its Inhabitants: Selected Readings from American Scientist Ser.). (Illus.). 250p. (Orig.). 1981. pap. 8.95 (ISBN 0-913232-93-9). W Kaufmann.
Volpe, Peter E. Understanding Evolution. 4th ed. 240p. 1981. pap. text ed. write for info. (ISBN 0-697-04646-X). Wm C Brown.
Wilson, Colin. Starseekers. LC 80-1273. 256p. 1981. 15.95 (ISBN 0-385-17253-2). Doubleday.
EVOLUTION-ADDRESSES, ESSAYS, LECTURES
Atchley, W. R. & Woodruff, David S. Evolution & Speciation: Essays in Honor of M.J.D. White. (Illus.). 496p. Date not set. price not set (ISBN 0-521-23823-4). Cambridge U Pr.
Medawar, Peter B. The Uniqueness of the Individual. 192p. 1981. pap. write for info. (ISBN 0-486-24042-8). Dover.
EWP
see Exploding Wire Phenomena
EX-NUNS
Ellis, Elizabeth A. The Least of My Sisters. LC 79-66928. 229p. 8.95 (ISBN 0-533-04426-X). Vantage.
EX-SERVICE MEN
see Veterans
EXAMINATION OF THE BLOOD
see Blood-Analysis and Chemistry
EXAMINATION OF WITNESSES
see Cross-Examination
EXAMINATIONS, MEDICAL
see Diagnosis
EXAMINATIONS, PREPARATION FOR
see Study, Method Of
EXCAVATION
see also Tunnels and Tunneling
Ground Engineering. 132p. 1980. 75.00x (ISBN 0-901948-09-8, Pub. by Telford England). State Mutual Bk.
Roberts, A. Applied Geotechnology: A Text for Students & Engineers on Rock Excavation & Related Topics. (Illus.). 416p. 1981. 50.00 (ISBN 0-08-024015-1); pap. 25.00 (ISBN 0-08-024014-3). Pergamon.
EXCEPTIONAL CHILDREN
see also Gifted Children; Handicapped Children
Lewis, Michael & Rosenblum, Leonard, eds. The Uncommon Child. (Genesis of Behavior Ser.: Vol. 3). 335p. 1981. 25.00 (ISBN 0-306-40499-0, Plenum Pr). Plenum Pub.
Mandell, Colleen J. & Fiscus, Edward D. Understanding Exceptional Children. (Illus.). 550p. 1981. text ed. 12.76 (ISBN 0-8299-0394-1). West Pub.
Perino, Sheila C. & Perino, Joseph. Parenting Exceptional Children: A Manual. 208p. 1981. 19.95 (ISBN 0-8352-1354-4). Bowker.

Porter Sargent Staff, ed. The Directory for Exceptional Children. 9th ed. LC 54-4975. (Special Education Ser.). (Illus.). 1384p. 1981. 30.00 (ISBN 0-87558-097-1). Porter Sargent.

EXCEPTIONAL CHILDREN–EDUCATION

Battle, James. Canadian Self-Esteem Inventories for Children & Adults. 1981. pap. 45.50 for complete battery (ISBN 0-686-69429-5). Spec Child.

Blake, Kathryn. Educating Exceptional Pupils: An Introduction to Contemporary Practices. LC 80-15222. (Illus.). 528p. 1981. text ed. 15.95 (ISBN 0-201-00083-0). A-W.

Cutler, Barbara C. Unraveling the Special Education Maze: An Action Guide for Parents. LC 80-54006. 260p. (Orig.). 1981. pap. text ed. 7.95 (ISBN 0-87822-224-3, 2243). Res Press.

Ducanis, Alex J. & Golin, Anne K. The Interdisciplinary Team: A Handbook for the Education of Exceptional Children. 200p. 1981. text ed. price not set. Aspen Systems.

Gallagher, James J. Study Guide for Educating Exceptional Children. 3rd ed. (Illus.). 208p. 1980. pap. text ed. write for info. (ISBN 0-395-28690-5). HM.

Gillet, Pamela. Career Edition for Exceptional Children & Youth: Career Edition for Excepional Children & Youth. LC 80-84931. 340p. 1981. text ed. 18.95 (ISBN 0-913420-90-5). Olympus Pub Co.

Jones, Marilyn. Exploring Careers in Special Education. (Careers in Depth Ser.). (Illus.). 128p. 1981. lib. bdg. 5.97 (ISBN 0-8239-0539-X). Rosen Pr.

Michaelis, Carol T. Home & School Partnerships in Exceptional Education. 375p. 1980. text ed. 27.95 (ISBN 0-89443-330-X). Aspen Systems.

EXCESS PROFITS TAX

Seidman, J. Seidman's Legislative History of Excess Profit Tax Laws: 1917-1946. 1959. 15.00. P-H.

EXCHANGE (BARTER)

see Barter

EXCHANGE, FOREIGN

see Foreign Exchange

EXCHANGE OF PRISONERS OF WAR

see Prisoners of War

EXCHANGES, COMMODITY

see Commodity Exchanges

EXCHANGES, EDUCATIONAL

see Educational Exchanges

EXCHANGES, PRODUCE

see Commodity Exchanges

EXCHANGES, STOCK

see Stock-Exchange

EXECUTIVE ABILITY

see also Leadership; Management; Personnel Management; Planning

Goodworth, Clive T. Effective Speaking & Presentation for the Company Executive. 204p. 1980. text ed. 12.25x (Pub. by Busn Bks England). Renouf.

EXECUTIVE AGENCIES

see Administrative Agencies

EXECUTIVE INVESTIGATIONS

see Governmental Investigations

EXECUTIVE POWER

see also Pardon; Prerogative, Royal; Presidents–United States; Prime Ministers

also subdivision; officials and employees–appointments, qualifications, etc. under names of countries

Genovese, Michael A. The Supreme Court, the Constitution, & Presidential Power. LC 80-5695. 345p. 1980. lib. bdg. 20.50 (ISBN 0-8191-1322-0); pap. text ed. 11.75 (ISBN 0-8191-1323-9). U Pr of Amer.

Lines, James. The Role of the Chief Executive. 172p. 1978. text ed. 24.50x (ISBN 0-220-66355-6, Pub. by Busn Bks England). Renouf.

Meltsner, Arnold J., ed. Towards Presidential Governance. 300p. (Orig.). 1981. pap. write for info. (ISBN 0-917616-40-5). Inst Contemporary.

Reber, Jan & Shaw, Paul. Executive Protection Manual. 1976. 39.95 (ISBN 0-916070-02-6); soft cover 29.95. MTI Tele.

EXECUTIVES

see also Executive Ability; Government Executives; Personnel Management; Women Executives

Kozmetsky, Ronya & Kozmetsky, George. Making It Together: A Survival Manual for the Executive Family. LC 80-69284. 1981. 12.95 (ISBN 0-02-917910-6). Free Pr.

Louis, Arthur. The Tycoons. 1981. 11.95 (ISBN 0-671-24974-6). S&S.

Pond, Samuel A. & Bricker, George W., eds. Bricker's International Directory: University Executive Development Programs. 12th ed. LC 73-110249. 600p. 1980. 85.00x (ISBN 0-9604804-0-4). S A Pond.

Pryor, Sam & Burnett, John. All God's Creatures: The Autobiography of Sam Pryor. 1981. 10.00 (ISBN 0-533-04946-6). Vantage.

Siu, Ralph G. Transcending the Power Game: The Way to Executive Serenity. LC 79-25299. 1980. 14.95 (ISBN 0-471-06001-1, Pub. by Wiley-Interscience). Wiley.

Sumner, L. E., ed. Business Who's Who of Australia, 1980. 14th ed. LC 64-56752. 805p. 1980. write for info (ISBN 0-8002-2741-7). Intl Pubns Serv.

EXECUTIVES–HEALTH PROGRAMS

Alexander Hamilton Institute, Inc. El Ejecutivo Bajo Stress. Jenks, James M., ed. (Illus.). 72p. (Orig., Span.). 1976. pap. 44.75x (ISBN 0-86604-008-0, A783158). Hamilton Inst.

--Executivo Sob Tensao. Jenks, James M., ed. (Illus.). 71p. (Orig., Portuguese.). 1978. pap. 50.75x (ISBN 0-86604-009-9). Hamilton Inst.

Alexander Institute, Inc. The Exectutive Under Stress. Jenks, Jamess M., ed. (Illus.). 71p. (Orig.). 1976. pap. 49.25x (ISBN 0-86604-007-2, A783157). Hamilton Inst.

Melhuish, A. Executive Health. 190p. 1978. text ed. 24.50x (ISBN 0-220-66351-3, Pub. by Busn Bks England). Renouf.

Times Bks. & British Medical Association. The Book of Executive Health: A Guide for Men & Women Executives Who Want to Live Longer. (Illus.). 224p. 1981. 12.95 (ISBN 0-13-080010-4, Spec); pap. 5.95 (ISBN 0-13-080002-3). P-H.

EXECUTIVES–RECRUITING

Jaques Cattell Press, ed. Association of Executive Recruiting Consultants. 2nd ed. 300p. 1981. 38.50 (ISBN 0-8352-1355-2). Bowker.

EXECUTIVES–GREAT BRITAIN

Fidler, John. The British Business Elite: Its Attitudes to Class, Status & Power. 384p. 1981. price not set (ISBN 0-7100-0770-1). Routledge & Kegan.

EXECUTIVES, TRAINING OF

Jones, Andrew N. & Cooper, Cary L. Combating Managerial Obsolescence. LC 80-16307. 192p. 1980. lib. bdg. 19.95 (ISBN 0-86003-509-3, JCO/). Greenwood.

EXECUTIVES, TRAINING OF–DIRECTORIES

Pond, Samuel A. & Bricker, George W., eds. Bricker's International Directory of University Executive Development Programs: 1981. 12th ed. LC 73-110249. 1980. 85.00 (ISBN 0-9604804-0-4). Bricker's Intl.

EXECUTORS AND ADMINISTRATORS

see also Probate Law and Practice; Trusts and Trustees

Fearne, Charles. An Essay on the Learning of Contingent Remainders & Executory Devises, 2 vols. 10th ed. Butler, Charles & Smith, Josiah W., eds. 1980. Repr. of 1844 ed. Set. PLB 95.00x (ISBN 0-8377-0539-8). Rothman.

EXEMPTION FROM MILITARY SERVICE

see Military Service, Compulsory

EXEMPTION FROM TAXATION

see Taxation, Exemption From

EXERCISE

see also Callisthenics; Exercise Therapy; Gymnastics; Physical Education and Training; Physical Fitness; Yoga, Hatha

also particular types of exercise, e.g. Fencing, Rowing, Running

Beaulieu, John E. Stretching for All Sports. (Illus.). 214p. 7.95 (ISBN 0-87095-079-7). Athletic.

Carnes, Ralph & Carnes, Valerie. Bodysculpture. (Illus.). 192p. 1981. pap. 5.95 (ISBN 0-312-08735-7). St Martin.

Cox, Beverly & Benois, George. Cellulite: Defeat It Through Diet & Exercise. (Illus.). 192p. 1981. 12.50 (ISBN 0-8149-0845-4); pap. 9.95 (ISBN 0-8149-0846-2). Vanguard.

Diagram Group. The Complete Encyclopedia of Exercises. 336p. 1981. pap. 9.95 (ISBN 0-442-23148-2). Van Nos Reinhold.

Fienup-Riordan, Ann. Shape Up with Baby: Exercise Games for the New Parent & Child. LC 80-82128. (Illus., Orig.). 1980. pap. 5.95 (ISBN 0-937604-04-6). Pennypress.

Gaines, Charles & Butler, George. Staying Hard. (Orig.). 1980. pap. 8.95 (ISBN 0-671-41265-5, Kenan Pr). S&S.

Gilmore, C. P. Exercising for Fitness. Time-Life Books, ed. (Health Ser.). (Illus.). 176p. 1981. 12.95 (ISBN 0-8094-3754-6). Time Life.

Hockert, Valerie. The Whole Body Tone-up Book. LC 80-53499. (Orig.). 1980. pap. 5.95 (ISBN 0-935698-01-9). Tasa Pub Co.

Jones, Jeanne & Kientzler, Kharma. Fitness First-a-Fourteen-Day Diet & Exercise Program. LC 80-11320. (Illus.). 154p. (Orig.). 1980. pap. 6.95 (ISBN 0-89286-162-2). One Hund One Prods.

Jones, Lucile. Hop, Skip, & Jump. Van Dolson, Bobbie J., ed. 32p. 1981. pap. price not set (ISBN 0-8280-0038-7). Review & Herald.

Kaye, Anna & Mathan, Don C. Reflexology for Good Health. pap. 3.00 (ISBN 0-87980-383-5). Wilshire.

Marchetti, Albert. Dr. Marchetti's Walking Book. LC 78-66258. 142p. 1981. pap. 6.95 (ISBN 0-8128-6114-0). Stein & Day.

Mason, Sally W. The New Holistic Way to Lose Weight & Rejuvenate. rev. ed. (Illus.). 228p. 1980. Repr. of 1979 ed. 9.95 (ISBN 0-8119-0348-6). Fell.

Smithdeal, Judy. Quick & Easy Exercises for Figure Beauty. pap. 2.00 (ISBN 0-87980-381-9). Wilshire.

Thomas, Gregory S., et al. Exercise & Health: The Evidence & the Implications. LC 80-23376. 128p. 1981. lib. bdg. 17.50 (ISBN 0-89946-048-8). Oelgeschlager.

Walker, Morton. Rebounding Aerobics. Angelo, Frank, ed. LC 80-83600. (Illus.). 240p. (Orig.). 1980. pap. 6.95 (ISBN 0-938302-19-1). NIRH.

Wallis, Celestina, et al. Anuska's Complete Body Makeover Book. (Illus.). 224p. 1981. 11.95 (ISBN 0-399-12579-5). Putnam.

EXERCISE–PHYSIOLOGICAL EFFECT

Di Prampero, P. E. & Poortsmans, J., eds. Physiological Chemistry of Exercise & Training. (Medicine & Sport Ser.: Vol. 13). (Illus.). xii, 200p. 1981. 76.75 (ISBN 3-8055-2028-X). S Karger.

EXERCISE, DEVOTIONAL

see Devotional Exercises

EXERCISE THERAPY

Carter, Albert E. Rebound to Better Health: Includes Trampolining. 59p. 1977. pap. 2.95 (ISBN 0-938302-10-8). NIRH.

Cohen, Lawrence S., et al. Physical Conditioning & Cardiovascular Rehabilitation. 344p. 1981. 25.00 (ISBN 0-471-08713-0, Pub. by Wiley-Med). Wiley.

Dellon, A. Lee. Evaluation of Sensibility & Reeducation of Sensation of the Hand. (Illus.). 140p. 1981. write for info. (2427-2). Williams & Wilkins.

Fuller, Richard R. Constipation Control: An Exercise Program to Achieve Regularity. 64p. 1981. 5.00 (ISBN 0-682-49690-1). Exposition.

The Low-Back Patient & Therapeutic Exercise Handouts 1979. Date not set. Set Of 25. 25.00. Masson Pub.

Maleske, Herald. You Really Don't Have To! Natural Therapy Updated. 200p. 1980. 12.95 (ISBN 0-937792-00-4). Nat Therapy.

Sullivan, Patricia, et al. Manual of Therapeutic Exercise. 1981. text ed. 15.95 (ISBN 0-8359-4245-7). Reston.

EXERCISES, DEVOTIONAL

see Devotional Exercises

EXHIBITIONS

see also Fairs

also particular exhibitions, e.g. Chicago–World's Columbian Exposition, 1893; exhibitions under special subjects, e.g. Paintings–Exhibitions

Abbott, Carl. The Great Extravaganza: Portland & the Lewis & Clark Expedition. LC 80-83179. (Illus.). 104p. 1981. pap. 5.95 (ISBN 0-87595-088-4). Oreg Hist Soc.

Harrison, Helen A., ed. Dawn of a New Day: The New York World's Fair, 1939-1940. (Illus.). 128p. 1980. 24.95x (ISBN 0-8147-3407-3); pap. 12.95x (ISBN 0-8147-3408-1). NYU Pr.

Reff, Theodore, ed. World's Fair of Eighteen Eighty-Nine. (Modern Art in Paris 1855 to 1900). 330p. 1981. lib. bdg. 44.00 (ISBN 0-8240-4704-4). Garland Pub.

--World's Fair of Eighteen Eighty-Nine: Retrospective Exhibition of Fine Arts, 1789 to 1889. (Modern Art in Paris 1855 to 1900). (Illus.). 250p. 1981. lib. bdg. 44.00 (ISBN 0-8240-4705-2). Garland Pub.

--World's Fair of Eighteen Fifty-Five: Modern Art in Paris 1855-1900. 694p. 1981. lib. bdg. 44.00 (ISBN 0-8240-4701-X). Garland Pub.

--World's Fair of Eighteen Sixty-Seven. (Modern Art in Paris 1855 to 1900). 224p. 1981. lib. bdg. 44.00 (ISBN 0-8240-4702-8). Garland Pub.

--World's Fair of Nineteen Hundred: General Catalogue. (Modern Art in Part in Paris 1855 to 1900). 582p. 1981. lib. bdg. 44.00 (ISBN 0-8240-4706-0). Garland Pub.

--World's Fair of Nineteen Hundred: Retrospective Exhibition of French Art, 1800 to 1889. (Modern Art in Paris 1855 to 1900). (Illus.). 442p. 1981. lib. bdg. 44.00 (ISBN 0-8240-4707-9). Garland Pub.

--World's Fair of Nineteen Hundred: Retrospective Exhibition of Fine Art,1889 to 1900. (Modern Art in Paris 1855 to 1900). 581p. 1981. lib. bdg. 44.00 (ISBN 0-8240-4708-7). Garland Pub.

EXHIBITS

see Exhibitions

EXISTENCE THEOREMS

I Only Work Here. 15.00; pap. 7.95. Primary Pr.

Nicholas, J. W. Psience: A General Theory of Existence. LC 77-11135. pap. 3.95 (ISBN 0-915520-09-5). Ross-Erikson.

EXISTENTIALISM

Kenyon, Roger A. Existential Structures: An Analytic Enquiry. LC 76-4222. 1976. 6.00 (ISBN 0-8022-2181-5). Philos Lib.

EXOBIOLOGY

see Life on Other Planets

EXOPHTHALMIC GOITER

see Graves' Disease

EXOSTOSIS

Edebo, L., ed. Endocytosis & Exocytosis in Host Defence, Vol. 17. (Monographs in Allergy). (Illus.). 240p. 1981. pap. 78.00 (ISBN 3-8055-1865-X). S Karger.

EXPANSION (U. S. POLITICS)

see Imperialism

EXPANSION OF GASES

see Gases

EXPEDITIONS, ANTARCTIC

see Antarctic Regions;

also names of expeditions, and names of explorers

EXPEDITIONS, ARCTIC

see Arctic Regions;

also names of expeditions, and names of explorers

EXPENDITURES, PUBLIC

see also Budget; Government Spending Policy

Anton, Thomas J., et al. Moving Money: An Empirical Analysis of Federal Expenditure Patterns. LC 80-21700. 272p. 1980. text ed. 20.00 (ISBN 0-89946-066-6). Oelgeschlager.

Consultant's Library Editors. The Successful Consultant's Guide to Winning Government Contracts. 122p. pap. write for info. leatherette (ISBN 0-930686-12-8). Bermont Bks.

Johnston, Ronald J. Governments & the Geography of Federal Spending in the U.S.A. 208p. 1981. write for info. (ISBN 0-471-27865-3, Pub. by Wiley-Interscience). Wiley.

Morris, Vera. Distributional Effects of Public Expenditure. 176p. 1980. 21.50x (ISBN 0-86003-030-X, Pub. by Allan Pubs England); pap. 10.50x (ISBN 0-86003-129-2). State Mutual Bk.

Schick, Allen. Congress & Money: Budgeting, Spending & Taxing. LC 80-53322. 600p. 1980. 27.50 (ISBN 0-87766-278-9). Urban Inst.

EXPERIMENTAL ANIMALS

see Laboratory Animals

EXPERIMENTAL DESIGN

Gardner, David M. & Belk, Russell W. A Basic Bibliography on Experimental Design in Marketing. LC 80-19563. (Bibliography Ser.: No. 37). 59p. 1980. pap. 6.00 (ISBN 0-87757-142-2). Am Mktg.

EXPERIMENTAL MEDICINE

see Medicine, Experimental

EXPERIMENTAL METHODS IN EDUCATION

see Education–Experimental Methods

EXPERIMENTAL PATHOLOGY

see Pathology, Experimental

EXPERIMENTAL PSYCHIATRY

see Psychiatric Research

EXPERIMENTAL PSYCHOLOGY

see Psychology, Experimental

EXPERIMENTAL SURGERY

see Surgery, Experimental

EXPERIMENTAL ZOOLOGY

see Zoology, Experimental

EXPERIMENTATION ON MAN, MEDICAL

see Human Experimentation in Medicine

EXPLODING WIRE PHENOMENA

Chace, W. G. & Moore, H. K., eds. Exploding Wires, 4 vols. Incl. Vol. 1. 373p. 1959. 32.50 (ISBN 0-306-37521-4); Vol. 2. 321p. 1962. 32.50 (ISBN 0-306-37522-2); Vol. 3. 410p. 1964. 37.50 (ISBN 0-306-37523-0); Vol. 4. 348p. 1968. 39.50 (ISBN 0-306-37524-9). LC 59-14822 (Plenum Pr). Plenum Pub.

EXPLORATION, SUBMARINE

see Underwater Exploration

EXPLORATION OF SPACE

see Outer Space–Exploration

EXPLORATION OF THE DEEP SEA

see Marine Biology; Marine Fauna; Marine Flora

EXPLOSIONS

Bartknecht, W. Explosions: Course, Prevention, Protection. Burg, H. & Almond, T., trs. from Ger. (Illus.). 251p. 1981. 74.40 (ISBN 0-387-10216-7). Springer-Verlag.

EXPLOSIVES

Berman, I. & Schroeder, J. W., eds. Explosive Welding, Forming, Plugging, & Compaction. (PVP: No. 44). 119p. 1980. 20.00 (H00171). ASME.

Yinon, Jehuda & Zitrin, Shmuel. The Analysis of Explosives. (Pergamon Ser. in Analytic Chemistry: Vol. 3). (Illus.). 300p. 1981. 60.00 (ISBN 0-08-023846-7); pap. 25.00 (ISBN 0-08-023845-9). Pergamon.

EXPORT AND IMPORT CONTROLS

see Foreign Trade Regulation

EXPORT MARKETING

The Impact of U. S. Foreign Direct Investment on U. S. Export Competitiveness in Third World Markets. (Significant Issues Ser.: Vol. II, No. 1). 25p. 1980. pap. 5.00 (ISBN 0-89206-014-X, CSIS009, CSIS). Unipub.

EXPORT SALES

The Economic Importance of Exports of the United States. (Significant Issues Ser.: Vol. II, No. 5). 119p. 1980. pap. 10.00 (ISBN 0-89206-019-0, CSIS013, CSIS). Unipub.

EXPORTS

see Commerce

EXPOSITION (RHETORIC)

Kahan, Jane & Stone, Marie K. Writing the Expository Essay. LC 78-730063. (Illus.). 1977. pap. text ed. 99.00 (ISBN 0-89290-123-3, A322). Soc for Visual.

EXPOSITIONS

see Exhibitions

EXPRESSIONISM

see also Dadaism; Surrealism

Bronner, Stephen & Kellner, Douglas, eds. Passion & Rebellion: The Expressionist Movement & Its Heritage. 400p. 1981. lib. bdg. price not set (ISBN 0-89789-016-7); pap. text ed. price not set (ISBN 0-89789-017-5). J F Bergin.

EXPROPRIATION

see Eminent Domain

EXPULSION

see United States–Emigration and Immigration

EXTEMPORIZATION (MUSIC)

see Improvisation (Music)

EXTERMINATION

see Pest Control

also names of specific pests, with or without the subdivision extermination

EXTERMINATION, JEWISH (1939-1945)

see Holocaust, Jewish (1939-1945)

EXTINCT ANIMALS

see also Paleontology; Rare Animals

Zallinger, Peter. Prehistoric Animals. (Pictureback Ser.). (Illus.). 32p. (ps-3). 1981. PLB 4.99 (ISBN 0-394-93737-6); pap. 1.25 (ISBN 0-394-83737-1). Random.

EXTINCT CITIES
see Cities and Towns, Ruined, Extinct, etc.

EXTRACORPOREAL CIRCULATION
see Blood–Circulation, Artificial

EXTRADITION
see also Asylum, Right Of

Grahl-Madsen, Atle. Territorial Asylum. LC 80-10498. (Monograph in the Uppsala University Swedish Institute of International Law). 231p. 1980. lib. bdg. 28.00 (ISBN 0-379-20706-0). Oceana.

Van den Wijngaert, Christine. The Political Offence Exception to Extradition. 260p. 1980. lib. bdg. 53.00 (ISBN 90-268-1185-3, Pub. by Kluwer Law & Taxation). Kluwer Boston.

EXTRAGALACTIC NEBULAE
see Galaxies

EXTRASENSORY PERCEPTION
see also Psychical Research

Frazier, Kendrick, ed. Borderlands Beyond Science: Skeptical Inquiries into the Paranormal. LC 80-84403. (Critiques of the Paranormal Ser.). 400p. 1981. 19.95 (ISBN 0-87975-147-9); pap. 9.95 (ISBN 0-87975-148-7). Prometheus Bks.

EXTRATERRESTRIAL ENVIRONMENT
see Space Environment

EXTRATERRESTRIAL LIFE
see Life on Other Planets

EXTREMITIES (ANATOMY)
see also Hand; Leg

Moberg. The Upper Limb on Tetraplegia. 1979. 18.00. Thieme Stratton.

EXTRINSIC EVIDENCE
see Evidence (Law)

EYE
see also Aqueous Humor; Fundus Oculi; Lacrimal Organs; Vision

Hall, Dorothy. Iridology: How the Eyes Reveal Your Health & Personality. LC 80-84439. (Illus.). 256p. (Orig.). 1981. pap. 8.95 (ISBN 0-87983-241-X). Keats.

Monro, Alexander. Three Treatises: On the Brain, the Eye, & the Ear. Bd. with Croonian Lectures on Cerebrqal Localization. Ferrier, D. (Contributions to the History of Psychology Ser., Vol. VII, Pt. E: Psysiological Psychology). 1980. Repr. of 1797 ed. 30.00 (ISBN 0-89093-326-X). U Pubns Amer.

EYE–CARE AND HYGIENE

Bates, W. H. Better Eyesight Without Glasses. 208p. (Orig.). 1981. pap. 2.95 (ISBN 0-03-058012-9). HR&W.

Revien, Leon & Gabor, Mark. Dr. Revien's Eye Exercise Program for Athletes: How to Direct Your Eyes to Win in 15 Minutes a Day. LC 80-54623. (Illus.). 192p. 1981. pap. 4.95 (ISBN 0-89480-152-X). Workman Pub.

EYE–JUVENILE LITERATURE

Amstutz, Beverly. The Fly Has Lots of Eyes. (Illus.). 1981. pap. 2.50 (ISBN 0-937836-04-4). Precious Res.

Rahn, Joan E. Eyes & Seeing. LC 80-23988. (Illus.). 128p. (gr. 5-9). 1981. PLB 8.95 (ISBN 0-689-30828-0). Atheneum.

EYE–MOVEMENTS

Fisher, Dennis F., et al, eds. Eye Movements: Cognition & Visual Perception. (Eye Movements Ser.). 368p. 1981. ref. 19.95 (ISBN 0-89859-084-1). L Erlbaum Assocs.

EYE–SURGERY

McCord, Clinton D., Jr. Oculoplastic Surgery. 300p. 1981. 29.00 (ISBN 0-89004-633-6). Raven.

Shafer, Donald M. Manual on Retinal Detachment. 150p. 1981. write for info. (1550-8). Williams & Wilkins.

EYE–WOUNDS AND INJURIES

Menna, F., ed. Therapeutic Effects in Ocular Lesions Obtained by Systemic & Topical Administration of an Activator of the Oxygen Metabolism. (Journal: Ophthalmologica: Vol. 180, Suppl. 1). (Illus.). vi, 92p. 1980. 19.75 (ISBN 3-8055-1686-X). S Karger.

EYE-GLASSES
see also Contact Lenses

Corson, Richard. Fashions in Eyeglasses: From the 14th Century to the Present Day. rev. ed. (Illus.). 1980. Repr. of 1967 ed. text ed. 70.00x (ISBN 0-7206-3282-X). Humanities.

EYE IN LITERATURE

Donaldson-Evans, Lancelot K. Love's Fatal Glance: A Study of Eye Imagery in the Poets of the Ecole lyonnaise. LC 80-10415. (Romance Monographs: No. 39). 155p. 1980. 14.50 (ISBN 84-499-3694-2). Romance.

EYEGROUNDS
see Fundus Oculi

F

FABRIC PICTURES

Fiberarts Magazine, ed. The Fiberarts Design Book. (Illus.). 176p. 1980. 24.95 (ISBN 0-8038-2394-0, Visual Communications); pap. 15.95 (ISBN 0-8038-2395-9). Hastings.

Rodmell, Ken. How to Use Type. 120p. 1981. pap. 7.95 (ISBN 0-442-29801-3). Van Nos Reinhold.

FABRICS
see Textile Fabrics

FABRICS, NONWOVEN
see Nonwoven Fabrics

FACADES
see also Architecture–Details

Hoffmann, Kurt, et al. Designing Architectural Facades: An Ideas File for Architects. (Illus.). 168p. 1975. 29.95x (ISBN 0-7114-3408-5). Intl Ideas.

FACE–ABNORMITIES AND DEFORMITIES

Melnick, Michael & Jorgenson, Ronald, eds. Developmental Aspects of Craniofacial Dysmorphology. LC 79-2487. (Alan R. Liss Ser.: Vol. 15, No. 8). 1979. 16.00 (ISBN 0-8451-1033-0). March of Dimes.

FACE–SURGERY

Pirruccello, Frank W. Plastic & Reconstructive Surgery of the Face: Cosmetic Surgery. (Illus.). 200p. 1981. write for info. (6891-1). Williams & Wilkins.

FACETIAE
see Wit and Humor;
see American Wit and Humor, English Wit and Humor, and similar headings subdivided by subject, e.g. American Wit and Humor–Sports

FACTORIES–LOCATION
see also Industries, Location of

Rowe, James E. Industrial Plant Location. (Public Administation Ser.: Bibliography P-575). 52p. 1980. pap. 5.50. Vance Biblios.

FACTORIES–MAINTENANCE AND REPAIR
see Plant Maintenance

FACTORIES–MANAGEMENT
see Factory Management

FACTORIES–NOISE
see Industrial Noise

FACTORY AND TRADE WASTE
see also Agricultural Wastes; Petroleum Waste; Pollution; Refuse and Refuse Disposal

Brown, Michael. Laying Waste: The Poisoning of America by Toxic Chemicals. 1981. pap. 3.50. WSP.

Connon, James. A Clear View - Guide to Industrial Pollution Control. LC 75-15321. 1975. pap. 4.00. Inform.

Curi, K. Treatment & Disposal of Liquid & Solid Industrial Wastes: Proceedings of the Third Turkish-German Environmental Engineering Symposium, Istanbul, July 1979. LC 80-40993. (Illus.). 515p. 1980. 75.00 (ISBN 0-08-023999-4). Pergamon.

Managing Industrial & Agricultural Wastes: Some Experiences. 137p. 1980. pap. 13.25 (ISBN 92-833-1460-3, APO 89, APO). Unipub.

Purdue University Industrial Waste Conference, 35th. Proceedings. Bell, John M., ed. 1981. text ed. 59.95 (ISBN 0-250-40363-3). Ann Arbor Science.

FACTORY MANAGEMENT
see also Assembly-Line Methods; Industrial Engineering; Office Management; Personnel Management; Plant Engineering; Production Control; Production Engineering; Quality Control

Guide to Operation "F". 95p. 1973. 5.00 (APO23, APO). Unipub.

Lockyer, K. G. Factory Management. 24.50x (ISBN 0-392-07793-0, SpS). Soccer.

Saunders, N. F. Factory Organization & Management. 24.50x (ISBN 0-392-07812-0, SpS). Soccer.

FACTORY NOISE
see Industrial Noise

FACTORY WASTE
see Factory and Trade Waste

FACULTY (EDUCATION)
see Educators; Teachers; Universities and Colleges–Faculty

FAIENCE
see Pottery

FAILURE (PSYCHOLOGY)

Raudsepp, Eugene. Success & Failure. (Best Thoughts Ser.). (Illus.). 80p. (Orig.). 1981. pap. 2.50 (ISBN 0-8431-0390-6). Price Stern.

FAILURE OF METALS
see Metals–Fracture

FAILURE OF SOLIDS
see Fracture Mechanics

FAILURE TO ASSIST IN EMERGENCIES
see Assistance in Emergencies

FAIR EMPLOYMENT PRACTICE
see Discrimination in Employment

FAIR TRADE
see Competition, Unfair

FAIRBANKS, ALASKA

Naske, Claus M. & Rowinski, Ludwig J. Fairbanks: A Pictorial History. Friedman, Donna R., ed. (Illus.). 208p. 1981. pap. price not set (ISBN 0-89865-108-5). Donning Co.

FAIRIES

O'Brien, John. Elves, Gnomes & Other Little People: A Coloring Book. (Illus.). 48p. 1980. pap. 2.00 (ISBN 0-486-24049-5). Dover.

FAIRS
see also Exhibitions; Markets

Better Homes & Gardens Books Editors, ed. Easy Bazaar Crafts. (Illus.). 96p. 1981. 4.95 (ISBN 0-696-00665-0). Meredith Corp.

Gale, Janice & Gale, Stephen. Guide to Fairs, Festivals & Fun Events. (Illus.). 190p. 1981. pap. 6.95 (ISBN 0-937928-00-3). Sightseer.

Sunrise Publishing Company Editors, ed. The Greatest of Expositions: St. Louis World's Fair, 1904. rev. ed. 1981. pap. 8.95 (ISBN 0-86629-029-X). Sunrise MO.

White, Paul. Fairs & Circuses. (Junior Reference Ser.). (Illus.). 64p. (gr. 7 up). 1972. 7.95 (ISBN 0-7136-1323-8). Dufour.

FAIRY TALES
see also Folk-Lore; Legends; Tales

Alice in Wonderland. (Illustrated Junior Library). (Illus.). 304p. 1981. pap. 4.95 (ISBN 0-448-11004-0). G&D.

Andersen's Fairy Tales. (Illustrated Junior Library). (Illus.). 352p. 1981. pap. 4.95 (ISBN 0-448-11022-9). G&D.

Brothers Grimm. Cinderella. LC 80-15394. (Illus.). 32p. (gr. k-3). 1981. 7.95 (ISBN 0-688-80299-0); PLB 7.63 (ISBN 0-688-84299-2). Greenwillow.

Diamond, Donna, adapted by. & illus. The Bremen Town Musicians: A Grimms' Fairytale. LC 80-36838. (Illus.). 32p. (gr. k-2). 1981. 8.95 (ISBN 0-440-00826-3); PLB 8.44 (ISBN 0-440-00827-1). Delacorte.

Garcia, David. Fairy Tales of Puerto Rico. (Children's Bks: No. 166). (Illus.). 50p. (gr. 1-5). 1981. 6.95 (ISBN 0-934642-02-8). Puerto Rico Almanacs.

Grimm's Fairy Tales. (Illustrated Junior Library). (Illus.). 384p. 1981. pap. 4.95 (ISBN 0-448-11009-1). G&D.

Heidi. (Illustrated Junior Library). (Illus.). 336p. 1981. pap. 4.95 (ISBN 0-448-11012-1). G&D.

Izawa, T. & Hijkata, S., illus. Hansel & Gretel. (Puppet Storybooks). (Illus.). 18p. (gr. k-2). 1981. 3.50 (ISBN 0-448-09754-0). G&D.

--Snow White & the Seven Dwarfs. (Puppet Storybooks). (Illus.). 18p. (gr. k-2). 1981. 3.50 (ISBN 0-448-09757-5). G&D.

Lang, Andrew. Favorite Andrew Dang Fairy Tale Books in Many Colors: Red, Green & Blue Fairy Tale Books. (Illus.). 1979. pap. 14.95 boxed set (ISBN 0-486-23407-X). Dover.

McKinley, Robin. The Door in the Hedge. LC 80-21903. 224p. (gr. 7 up). 1981. 8.95 (ISBN 0-688-00312-5). Greenwillow.

Rockwell, Anne. Up a Tall Tree. LC 79-7695. (Reading-on-My-Own Bks.). (Illus.). 64p. (gr. 2). 1981. 4.95a (ISBN 0-385-15556-5); PLB (ISBN 0-385-15557-3). Doubleday.

Ross, Tony. Jack & the Beanstalk. LC 80-67493. (Illus.). 32p. (gr. k-2). 1981. 8.95 (ISBN 0-440-04168-6); PLB 8.44 (ISBN 0-440-04174-0). Delacorte.

Spock, Marjorie. Fairy Worlds & Workers: A Natural History of the Middle Kingdom. 1980. pap. 5.95 (ISBN 0-916786-46-3). St George Bk Serv.

Story of the Ugly Duckling. (Children's Library of Picture Bks.). (Illus.). 10p. 1971. 1.95 (ISBN 0-89346-126-1, TA35, Pub. by Froebel-Kan Japan). Heian Intl.

Wizard of Oz. (Illustrated Junior Library). (Illus.). 224p. 1981. pap. 4.95 (ISBN 0-448-11026-1). G&D.

FAIRY TALES–CLASSIFICATION
see also Literature, Comparative–Themes, Motives

Waelti-Walters, Jennifer. Fairy Tales & the Female Imagination. 225p. 1981. price not set (ISBN 0-920792-07-3). Eden Women.

FAIRY TALES–HISTORY AND CRITICISM

Duffy, Maureen. The Erotic World of Faery. 1980. pap. 3.50 (ISBN 0-686-69241-1, 48108, Discus). Avon.

FAIRY TALES–THEMES, MOTIVES
see Fairy Tales–Classification

FAITH
see also Atheism; Faith and Reason; Hope; Salvation; Sanctification; Truth

Armstrong, Anne, tr. Viendo Lo Invisible. (Spanish Bks.). (Span.). 1979. 1.90 (ISBN 0-8297-0670-4). Vida Pub.

Bloesch, Donald G. Faith & Its Counterfeits. 108p. (Orig.). 1981. pap. 3.95 (ISBN 0-87784-822-X). Inter Varsity.

Brown, Willis M. How I Got Faith. 199p. 2.00. Faith Pub Hse.

Cook, Micheal L. The Jesus of Faith: A Study in Christology. 192p. (Orig.). pap. 6.95 (ISBN 0-8091-2349-5). Paulist Pr.

Corrigan, John T. Archives: The Light of Faith. (Catholic Library Association Studies in Librarianship: No. 4). 1980. 4.00 (ISBN 0-87507-008-6). Cath Lib Assn.

Eareckson, Joni & Musser, Joe. Joni. (Illus.). 256p. 1980. pap. 2.95 (ISBN 0-310-23982-6). Zondervan.

Ferries, George. The Growth of Christian Faith. 385p. Repr. of 1905 ed. 3.50 (ISBN 0-567-02106-8). Attic Pr.

Flesseman-Van Leer, E. A Faith for Today. Steely, John E., tr. LC 79-56514. (Special Studies Ser.: No. 7). 1980. 6.95 (ISBN 0-932180-06-X). Assn Baptist Profs.

Happold, F. C. Religious Faith & Twentieth Century Man. 192p. 1981. 6.95 (ISBN 0-8245-0046-6). Crossroad NY.

Hermission, Hans-Jurgen & Lohse, Eduard. Faith. Stott, Douglas, tr. LC 80-22542. (Biblical Encounter Ser.). 176p. 1981. pap. 6.95 (ISBN 0-687-12520-0). Abingdon.

Hickman, Martha W. The Growing Season. LC 80-68983. 128p. (Orig.). 1980. pap. write for info. (ISBN 0-8358-0411-9). Upper Room.

Johnson, Luke T. Sharing Possessions: Mandate & Symbol of Faith, No. 9. Brueggemann, Walter & Donahue, John R., eds. LC 80-2390. (Overtures to Biblical Theology Ser.). 176p. (Orig.). 1981. pap. 8.95 (ISBN 0-8006-1534-4, 1-1534). Fortress.

Kelly, Douglas, et al. The Westminster Confession of Faith: A New Edition. 102p. 1980. pap. 5.95 (ISBN 0-87921-060-5). Attic Pr.

McDonald, H. D. Salvation. (Foundations for Faith). 4.95 (ISBN 0-89107-225-X). Good News.

McPherson, J. The Westminster Confession of Faith. (Handbooks for Bible Classes). 175p. pap. text ed. 8.95 (ISBN 0-567-28143-4). Attic Pr.

Melanchthon, Philipp. The Justification of Man by Faith Only. Lesse, Nicholas, tr. LC 79-84123. (English Experience Ser.: No. 942). 204p. 1979. Repr. of 1548 ed. lib. bdg. 15.00 (ISBN 90-221-0942-9). Walter J Johnson.

Newton, John. Out of the Depths. (Shepherd Illustrated Classics). (Illus.). 144p. 1981. pap. 5.95 (ISBN 0-87983-243-6). Keats.

Romaine, William. The Life of Faith. (Summit Bks.). 178p. 1981. pap. 1.95 (ISBN 0-8010-7704-4). Baker Bk.

Roy, Paul S. The Faith Experience: Communal Spirituality for Justice. 240p. (Orig.). 1981. pap. 8.95 (ISBN 0-8091-2380-0). Paulist Pr.

Sobosan, Jeffrey. The Ascent to God. 1981. 9.95 (ISBN 0-88347-128-0). Thomas More.

Williams, Paul L., ed. Christian Faith in a Neo-Pagan Society: Proceedings of the Fellowship of Catholic Scholara. LC 81-80229. 128p. (Orig.). 1981. pap. 5.95 (ISBN 0-937374-02-4); pap. text ed. 4.50 (ISBN 0-937374-03-2). NE Bks.

FAITH, CONFESSIONS OF
see Creeds

FAITH AND REASON
see also Philosophy and Religion; Religion and Science

Gewirth, Alan. Reason & Morality. 416p. 1981. pap. 9.95x (ISBN 0-226-28876-5). U of Chicago Pr.

FAITH-CURE
see also Christian Science; Mental Healing; Miracles

Bartow, Donald W. The Adventures of Healing: How to Use New Testament Practices & Receive New Testament Results. rev. ed. 371p. 1981. pap. 5.95 (ISBN 0-938736-02-7). Life Enrich.

Divine Physical Healing, Past & Present. 272p. pap. 2.50. Faith Pub Hse.

MacNutt, Francis. The Prayer That Heals. LC 80-69770. 120p. (Orig.). 1981. pap. 2.95 (ISBN 0-87793-219-0). Ave Maria.

FAITH HEALING
see Faith-Cure

FALCONRY

Allen, Mark. Falconry in Arabia. (Illus.). 143p. Date not set. 40.00 (ISBN 0-89182-034-5). Charles River Bks.

Glasier. Falconry & Hawking. 53.00 (ISBN 0-7134-0232-6). David & Charles.

FALL
see Autumn

FAMILIES OF MILITARY PERSONNEL
see Air Force Wives

FAMILY
see also Children; Clans and Clan System; Divorce; Domestic Relations; Family Life Education; Family Life Surveys; Fathers; Foster Home Care; Grandparents; Heredity, Human; Home; Kinship; Marriage; Mothers; Parent and Child; Single-Parent Family; Twins; Widows

Ball, Gerry. Circle of Warmth: Family Program. 1980. 34.95 (ISBN 0-86584-040-7). Human Dev Train.

--Grounds for Growth: Comprehensive Theory Manual. 1980. 14.95 (ISBN 0-86584-009-1). Human Dev Train.

Cook, et al. Family Mediation Workbook. Polk, Donice, ed. 90p. (Orig.). 1980. pap. 10.00. D Polk.

Corwin, Sheila. Marriage & the Family & Child-Rearing Practices. Zak, Therese A., ed. (Lifeworks Ser.). (Illus.). 160p. 1981. text ed. 4.56 (ISBN 0-07-013198-8). McGraw.

Coward, Raymond T. & Smith, William M., eds. The Family in Rural Society. (Special Studies in Contemporary Social Issues). 280p. 1981. lib. bdg. 25.00x (ISBN 0-86531-121-8). Westview.

Cox, Frank D. Human Intimacy: Marriage, the Family & Its Meaning. 2nd ed. (Illus.). 475p. 1981. text ed. 13.56 (ISBN 0-8299-0367-4). West Pub.

Dempsey, John J. The Family & Public Policy: The Issue of the 1980s. (Illus.). 120p. 1981. text ed. price not set (ISBN 0-933716-15-X). P H Brookes.

Gap Committee on the Family. Divorce, Child Custody & the Family, Vol. 10. LC 80-25935. (Publications Ser.: No. 106). 1980. pap. 12.95 (ISBN 0-910958-10-6, 106, Mental Health Materials Center). Adv Psychiatry.

Hiesberger, Jean M., ed. Healing Family Hurts. LC 79-90991. (Paths of Life Ser.). 124p. (Orig.). 1979. pap. 2.45 (ISBN 0-8091-2266-9). Paulist Pr.

Hirsch, Julia. Family Photographs: Content, Meaning & Effect. LC 80-25591. (Illus.). 160p. 1981. 12.95 (ISBN 0-19-502889-9). Oxford U Pr.

Howe, Florence & Rothermich, John A., eds. Household & Kin: Families in Flux. (Women's Lives - Women's Work Ser.). 208p. (Orig.). Date not set. pap. text ed. 4.71 (ISBN 0-07-020427-6). Webster-McGraw.

Kinton, Jack. American Family Styles. 1981. pap. 2.95 (ISBN 0-915574-22-5). Soc Sci & So.

Laucks, Eulah C. The Meaning of Children: Attitudes & Opinions of a Selected Group of U.S. University Graduates. (Special Studies in Contemporary Social Issues). 225p. 1981. lib. bdg. 20.00x (ISBN 0-89158-881-7). Westview.

Masnick, George & Bane, Mary Jo. The Nation's Families: 1960-1990. LC 80-20531. (Illus.). 200p. (Orig.). 1980. 17.95 (ISBN 0-86569-050-2); pap. 10.00 (ISBN 0-86569-051-0). Auburn Hse.

Oppenheim. Living Today. (gr. 9-12). 1981. text ed. price not set (ISBN 0-87002-343-8). Bennett Co.

Schafly, Phyllis. Power Ideas for a Happy Family. (Orig.). pap. 1.75 (ISBN 0-515-05104-7). Jove Pubns.

Shapiro, David S. & Shapiro, Elaine S. The Search for Love & Achievement: Marriage & the Family in a Changing World. 2nd ed. 1980. pap. text ed. 10.95x (ISBN 0-917974-48-4). Waveland Pr.

Steiner, Gilbert Y. The Futility of Family Policy. 250p. 1981. 15.95 (ISBN 0-8157-8124-5); pap. 5.95 (ISBN 0-8157-8123-7). Brookings.

Tufte, Virginia & Myerhoff, Barbara. Changing Images of the Family: Multidisciplinary Perspectives. LC 79-537. (Illus.). 413p. 1981. pap. 6.95 (ISBN 0-300-02671-4). Yale U Pr.

Wright, H. Norman. How to Be a Better-Than-Average In-Law. 1981. pap. 3.95 (ISBN 0-88207-342-7). Victor Bks.

Zanzucchi, Anne M. Family Portrait, from a Mother's Diary. Szczesniak, Lenny, tr. from It. LC 81-80031. Orig. Title: Giorno per Giorno. 100p. 1981. pap. 2.95 (ISBN 0-911782-19-2). New City.

FAMILY–HISTORY

Howard, Ronald L. A Social History of American Family Sociology, 1865-1940. Mogey, John H. & Van Leeuwen, Louis Th., eds. LC 80-1790. (Contributions in Family Studies Ser.: No. 4). 168p. 1981. lib. bdg. 22.50 (ISBN 0-313-22767-5, MOA/). Greenwood.

Phillips, Roderick. Family Breakdown in Late Eighteenth Century France: Divorces in Rouen 1792-1803. (Illus.). 288p. 1980. 55.00 (ISBN 0-19-822572-5). Oxford U Pr.

Quitt, Martin & Fox, Vivian. Loving, Parenting, & Dying: The Family Cycle in England & America, Past & Present. 200p. 1980. 27.00 (ISBN 0-914434-14-4); pap. 10.95 (ISBN 0-914434-15-2). Psychohistory Pr.

Swerdlow, Amy, et al. Household & Kin: Families in Flux. (Women's Lives - Women's Work Ser.). (Illus.). 192p. (Orig.). (gr. 11-12). 1981. 14.95 (ISBN 0-912670-91-6); pap. 5.95 (ISBN 0-912670-68-1). Feminist Pr.

Thwing, Charles F. & Thwing, Carrie F. The Family: An Historical & Social Study. 258p. 1980. Repr. of 1913 ed. lib. bdg. 40.00 (ISBN 0-8495-5157-9). Arden Lib.

FAMILY–JUVENILE LITERATURE

Lessin, Roy. Families Are God's Idea. (God's Idea Books Ser.). (Illus.). 32p. (ps-4). 1981. pap. 1.25 (ISBN 0-87123-177-8, 210177). Bethany Fell.

--Kids Are God's Idea. (God's Idea Books Ser.). (Illus.). 32p. (ps-4). 1981. pap. 1.25 (ISBN 0-87123-178-6, 210178). Bethany Fell.

FAMILY–LAW

see Domestic Relations

FAMILY–PRAYER-BOOKS AND DEVOTIONS

Henshaw, Paul & Weemshall, H. Family Worship. 84p. 1981. pap. 2.25x (ISBN 0-8358-0421-6). Upper Room.

Jurries, Ginger & Mulder, Karen. Fun Ideas for Family Devotions (with Activity Pages) (Illus.). 176p. (Orig.). 1981. pap. 5.95 (ISBN 0-87239-415-8, 2968). Standard Pub.

Seifert, Lois. Our Family Night in: Workbook of Convant Living. 200p. (Orig.). pap. 3.95x (ISBN 0-8358-0420-8). Upper Room.

FAMILY–RELIGIOUS LIFE

Meier, Paul & Meier, Richard. Family Foundations. 96p. (Orig.). 1981. 8.95 (ISBN 0-8010-6117-2); pap. 4.95 (ISBN 0-8010-6122-9). Baker Bk.

Sell, Charles M. Family Ministry: Family Life Through the Church. 272p. 11.95 (ISBN 0-310-42580-8). Zondervan.

Stephens, John F. Spirit Filled Family, No. 11. 48p. (Orig.). 1980. pap. 1.50 (ISBN 0-89841-008-8). Zoe Pubns.

Sweeting, George. Special Sermons on the Family. (Special Sermon Ser.). 144p. 1981. pap. 2.95 (ISBN 0-8024-8208-2). Moody.

Webb, Barbara O. Families Sharing God. 48p. 1981. pap. 3.50 (ISBN 0-8170-0900-0). Judson.

FAMILY–CHINA

Wilkinson, Hiran P. Family in Classical China. (Studies in Chinese History & Civilization). 239p. 1977. Repr. of 1926 ed. 19.50 (ISBN 0-89093-085-6). U Pubns Amer.

FAMILY–FRANCE

Phillips, Roderick. Family Breakdown in Late Eighteenth Century France: Divorces in Rouen 1792-1803. (Illus.). 288p. 1980. 55.00 (ISBN 0-19-822572-5). Oxford U Pr.

FAMILY–GREAT BRITAIN

Greve, John. London's Homeless. 76p. 1964. pap. text ed. 3.75x (Pub. by Bedford England). Renouf.

Land, Hilarly. Large Families in London. 154p. 1969. pap. text ed. 6.25x (ISBN 0-7135-1577-5, Pub. by Bedford England). Renouf.

FAMILY BUDGETS

see Home Economics–Accounting

FAMILY CASE WORK

see Family Social Work

FAMILY COURTS

see Juvenile Courts

FAMILY GROUP THERAPY

see Family Psychotherapy

FAMILY HISTORIES

see subdivision genealogy under countries, e.g., United States–Genealogy; and individual families, e.g. Lee Family

FAMILY LAW

see Domestic Relations

FAMILY LIFE EDUCATION

see also Counseling; Finance, Personal; Home Economics; Interpersonal Relations; Marriage Counseling; Sex Instruction

Acus, Leah K. Quarreling Kids: Stop the Fighting & Develop Loving Relationship Within the Family. (Illus.). 192p. 1981. 10.95 (ISBN 0-13-748012-1, Spec); pap. 5.95 (ISBN 0-13-748004-0). P-H.

Campbell, Philip. Future Family. LC 80-84365. 1981. pap. 4.95 (ISBN 0-933350-39-2). Morse Pr.

Entwisle, Doris B. & Doering, Susan G. The First Birth: A Family Turning Point. LC 80-22741. (Illus.). 304p. 1981. text ed. 25.00x (ISBN 0-8018-2408-7). Johns Hopkins.

Family Factbook. 2nd ed. 670p. 1981. price not set (ISBN 0-8379-4602-6). Marquis.

Family in Transition: Rethinking Marriage, Sexuality, Child Rearing & Family Organization. 3rd ed. 579p. 1980. pap. text ed. 9.95 (ISBN 0-316-79722-7); free test bank by Harrentsian (ISBN 0-316-79704-9). Little.

Farrell, Kathy & Sweeney, Mary. What Can We Do Today, Mommy. (Illus.). 127p. (Orig.). 1980. 6.95 (ISBN 0-9604118-0-1). Growing Together.

Getty, Kathleen & Humphries, Winifred. Understanding the Family. 608p. 1981. pap. 12.95 (ISBN 0-8385-9265-1). ACC.

Hutter, Mark. The Family & Social Change: Comparative Perspectives. 500p. 1981. text ed. 16.95 (ISBN 0-471-08394-1). Wiley.

Meister, Robert. Fathers: Daughters, Sons, Fathers Reveal Their Deepest Feelings. 224p. 1981. 12.95 (ISBN 0-399-90107-8). Marek.

Myers, Betsy. How to Protect Your Home & Family. 110p. 1981. pap. cancelled (ISBN 0-686-68067-7). Cornerstone.

National Information Center for Special Education Materials (NICSEM) NICSEM Mini-Index to Special Education Materials: Family Life & Sex Education. LC 80-82540. 1980. pap. 16.00 (ISBN 0-89320-043-3). Univ SC Natl Info.

Scanzoni, John & Szinovacz, Maximiliane. Family Decision-Making: Sex Roles & Change Over the Life Cycle. LC 80-18243. (Sage Library of Social Research: Vol. 111). (Illus.). 312p. 1980. 18.00 (ISBN 0-8039-1533-0); pap. 8.95 (ISBN 0-8039-1534-9). Sage.

Stoop, Dave. A Parent's Cry for Help. rev. ed. LC 78-62916. 144p. 1981. pap. 2.50 (ISBN 0-89081-270-5). Harvest Hse.

Thodes, Sonya & Wilson, Josleen. Surviving Family Life: The Seven Crises of Living Together. 300p. 1981. 11.95 (ISBN 0-399-12507-8). Putnam.

Trojan, Judith. American Family Life Films. LC 80-14748. 508p. 1981. 25.00 (ISBN 0-8108-1313-0). Scarecrow.

Understanding Us: Family Development 1. 8.95 (ISBN 0-917340-10-8). Interpersonal Comm.

Wright, Norman. An Answer to in-Law Relationships. (Orig.). pap. 1.25 (ISBN 0-89081-076-1). Harvest Hse.

--An Answer to Parent-Teen Relationships. (Orig.). pap. 1.25 (ISBN 0-89081-075-3). Harvest Hse.

--An Answer to Submission & Decision Making. pap. 1.25 (ISBN 0-89081-078-8). Harvest Hse.

FAMILY LIFE SURVEYS

American Family Styles: Current Guide to the Literature. (Spcialized Bibliography Ser.: No. 4). 1981. 8.95 (ISBN 0-915574-11-X). Soc Sci & Soc Res.

Nye, F. Ivan & Berardo, Felix M., eds. Emerging Conceptual Frameworks in Family Analyses. (Special Studies on the Family). 356p. 1981. 13.95 (ISBN 0-03-057043-3). Praeger.

FAMILY MEDICINE

Geyman, John P. Archives of Family Practice, 1981. 448p. 1981. 36.00 (ISBN 0-8385-0325-X). ACC.

Geyman, John P., ed. Archives of Family Practice 1980. 416p. 1980. 34.50x (ISBN 0-8385-0324-1). ACC.

--Profile of the Residency-Trained Family Physician in the United States 1970-1979. 72p. 1980. pap. 7.00x (ISBN 0-8385-7961-2). ACC.

McWhinney, Ian R. An Introduction to Family Medicine. (Illus.). 224p. 1981. text ed. 16.95x (ISBN 0-19-502807-4); pap. text ed. 9.95 (ISBN 0-19-502808-2). Oxford U Pr.

Parents Magazine Enterprises. Parents' Magazine's Mother's Encyclopedia & Everyday Guide to Family Health. Rossman, Isidore, ed. 1981. pap. 9.95 (Delta). Dell.

Pieroni, Robert E. Family Practice Review, Vol. 2. LC 79-91973. 1980. pap. 14.50 (ISBN 0-87488-181-1). Med Exam.

Rosen, Gerald M., et al, eds. Behavioral Science in Family Practice. 300p. 1980. 19.50x (ISBN 0-8385-0638-0). ACC.

Yen, Ernest Y. Review & Assessment in Family Practice. 288p. 1980. pap. 12.95x (ISBN 0-8385-2539-3). ACC.

FAMILY PLANNING

see Birth Control

FAMILY PRACTICE (MEDICINE)

see Family Medicine

FAMILY PSYCHOTHERAPY

Erickson, Gerald D. & Hogan, Terrence P. Family Therapy: An Introduction to Theory & Technique. 2nd ed. 448p. (Orig.). 1980. pap. text ed. 12.95 (ISBN 0-8185-0437-4). Brooks-Cole.

Freeman, David S. Techniques of Family Therapy. LC 80-69669. 350p. 1981. 25.00 (ISBN 0-87668-431-2). Aronson.

Green, Robert J. & Framo, James L., eds. Family Therapy: The Major Approaches. 620p. 1981. text ed. 30.00 (ISBN 0-8236-1885-4). Intl Univs Pr.

Hansen, James C. & Rosenthal, David. Strategies & Techniques in Family Therapy. (Illus.). 480p. 1981. 28.50 (ISBN 0-398-04435-X); pap. 19.75 (ISBN 0-398-04154-7). C C Thomas.

Hiesberger, Jean M., ed. Healing Family Hurts. LC 79-90991. (Paths of Life Ser.). 124p. (Orig.). 1979. pap. 2.45 (ISBN 0-8091-2266-9). Paulist Pr.

Hoffman, Lynn. Foundations of Family Therapy. LC 80-68956. 416p. 1981. 25.00x (ISBN 0-465-02498-X). Basic.

Howells, John G. Advances in Family Psychiatry, Vol. 2. LC 101. 1980. text ed. 29.95 (ISBN 0-8236-0101-3). Intl Univs Pr.

Kempler, Walter. Experiential Psychotherapy Within Families. 320p. 1981. 20.00 (ISBN 0-87630-267-3). Brunner-Mazel.

Lieberman, Stuart. Transgenerational Family Therapy. 240p. 1980. 39.00x (ISBN 0-85664-776-4, Pub. by Croom Helm England). State Mutual Bk.

Madanes, Cloe. Strategic Family Therapy. LC 80-26286. (Social & Behavioral Science Ser.). 1981. text ed. 14.95 (ISBN 0-87589-487-9). Jossey-Bass.

Okpaku, S. Family Planning & Preventive Psychiatry. 1981. 20.00 (ISBN 0-89388-003-5). Okpaku Communications.

Wile, B. Couples Therapy: A Nontraditional Approach. 240p. 1981. 22.50 (ISBN 0-471-07811-5, Pub. by Wiley Interscience). Wiley.

FAMILY SOCIAL WORK

see also Family Life Education; Marriage Counseling

Geismar, Ludwig L. Family & Community Functioning: A Manual of Measurement for Social-Work Practice & Policy. 2nd, rev. ed. LC 80-17785. 317p. 1980. 15.00 (ISBN 0-8108-1332-7); pap. 9.75 (ISBN 0-8108-1341-6). Scarecrow.

Howard, Ronald L., et al. A Social History of American Family Sociology, 1865-1940. Mogey, John H. & Van Leeuwen, Louis T., eds. LC 80-1790. (Contributions in Family Studies: No. 4). 168p. 1981. lib. bdg. 22.50 (ISBN 0-313-22767-5, MOA/). Greenwood.

Karpf, Maurice J. The Scientific Basis of Social Work. 424p. 1981. Repr. of 1931 ed. lib. bdg. 35.00 (ISBN 0-8495-3049-0). Arden Lib.

Rich, William. Smaller Families Through Social & Economic Progress. LC 72-97989. (Monographs: No. 7). 74p. 1973. 2.00 (ISBN 0-686-28688-X). Overseas Dev Council.

FAMILY THERAPY

see Family Psychotherapy

FAMILY WORSHIP

see Family–Prayer-Books and Devotions; Family–Religious Life

FAMINES

Newman, James L., ed. Drought, Famine & Population Movement in Africa. LC 74-25877. (Foreign & Comparative Studies-Eastern African Ser.: No. 17). 144p. 1975. pap. 4.50x (ISBN 0-915984-14-8). Syracuse U Foreign Comp.

FANCY DRESS

see Costume

FANS

Mayor, Susan. Collecting Fans. (The Christies International Collectors Ser.). (Illus.). 128p. 1980. 14.95 (ISBN 0-8317-3199-0). Mayflower Bks.

FANTASY

Featherman, Buzz. The Fun & Fantasy Book. LC 80-54612. (Illus.). 144p. (Orig.). 1981. pap. text ed. 6.95 (ISBN 0-932238-04-1). Word Shop.

--The Fun & Fantasy Book. new ed. (Illus.). 1980. 6.95 (ISBN 0-932238-03-3). Word Shop.

Ferman, Edward L. & Greenberg, Martin H., eds. Fantasy & Science Fiction, April Nineteen Sixty-Five. (Alternatives Ser.). 160p. Date not set. price not set (ISBN 0-8093-1007-4). S Ill U Pr.

Fisher, Paul. Mont Cant Gold. LC 80-23851. 264p. (gr. 5-9). 1981. PLB 10.95 (ISBN 0-689-30808-6, Argo). Atheneum.

FAR EASTERN QUESTION

see Eastern Question (Far East)

FARE, BILLS OF

see Menus

FARM ANIMALS

see Domestic Animals

FARM CROPS

see Field Crops

FARM EQUIPMENT

see also Agricultural Engineering; Agricultural Implements; Agricultural Machinery

Jenkins, J. Geraint. The English Farm Wagon: Origins & Structure. (Illus.). 264p. 1981. 22.50 (ISBN 0-7153-8119-9). David & Charles.

FARM IMPLEMENTS

see Agricultural Implements

FARM LABORERS

see Agricultural Laborers

FARM LIFE

see also Country Life; Rural Conditions; Sociology, Rural

Sifford, Darrell. A Love of the Land. (Illus.). 288p. 1980. 11.95 (ISBN 0-89795-010-0). Farm Journal.

Thomas, Sherry. We Didn't Have Much but We Sure Had Plenty: Stories of Rural Women. LC 80-956. (Illus.). 208p. 1981. pap. 7.95 (ISBN 0-385-14951-4, Anch). Doubleday.

FARM LIFE CLUBS

see Agricultural Societies

FARM MACHINERY

see Agricultural Machinery

FARM MANAGEMENT

Boy Scouts of America. Farm & Ranch Management. (Illus.). 32p. (gr. 6-12). 1980. pap. 0.70x (3348). BSA.

Buckett, M. An Introduction to Farm Organisation & Mamagement. (Illus.). 280p. 1981. 50.00 (ISBN 0-08-024433-5); pap. 21.00 (ISBN 0-08-024432-7). Pergamon.

Farm Level Water Management in Selected Asian Countries. 159p. 1980. pap. 13.25 (ISBN 92-833-1461-1, APO 88, APO). Unipub.

Farm Planning in the Early Stages of Development. (Agricultural Services Bulletin: No. 1). 106p. 1968. pap. 6.00 (F1971, FAO). Unipub.

Forster, D. Lynn & Erven, Bernard L. Foundations for Managing the Farm Business. LC 80-20832. (Agricultural Economics Ser.). 320p. 1981. text ed. 20.95 (ISBN 0-88244-230-9). Grid Pub.

FARM MECHANICS

see Agricultural Engineering

FARM PRODUCE

see also Field Crops; Food Industry and Trade; Surplus Agricultural Commodities

Boone, L. V., et al, eds. Producing Farm Crops. 3rd ed. 1981. 14.60 (ISBN 0-8134-2151-9); text ed. 10.95x. Interstate.

FARM PRODUCE–MARKETING

Here are entered works on the marketing of farm produce from the point of view of the farmer.

see also Field Crops; Food Industry and Trade; Surplus Agricultural Commodities

also subdivision Marketing under specific commodities, e.g. Eggs–Marketing

Assessment & Collection of Data on Post-Harvest Foodgrain Losses. (FAO Economic & Social Development Paper: No. 13). 71p. 1981. pap. 6.00 (ISBN 92-5-100934-1, F2072, FAO). Unipub.

Farm Sales & Pick Your Own. 91p. 1980. pap. 9.95 (ISBN 0-901361-28-3, Pub. by Grower Bks England). Intl Schol Bk Serv.

Finney, Essex E., Jr., ed. Handbook of Transportation & Marketing in Agriculture: Volume 1: Food Commodities. 317p. 1981. 59.95 (ISBN 0-8493-3851-4). CRC Pr.

FARM PRODUCE–TRANSPORTATION

Finney, Essex E., Jr., ed. Handbook of Transportation & Marketing in Agriculture: Volume 1: Food Commodities. 317p. 1981. 59.95 (ISBN 0-8493-3851-4). CRC Pr.

FARM SHOPS

see Agricultural Machinery

FARM SUPPLIES

see Farm Equipment

FARM SURPLUSES

see Surplus Agricultural Commodities

FARM TOOLS

see Agricultural Implements

FARMERS' COOPERATIVES

see Agriculture, Cooperative

FARMERS' ORGANIZATIONS

see Agricultural Societies

FARMING

see Agriculture

FAROE

Leikur & Torshavn. Islands & People. 150p. 1980. 27.50 (ISBN 0-906191-22-X, Pub. by Thule Pr England). Intl Schol Bk Serv.

FARRIERY

see Horses; Veterinary Medicine; Veterinary Surgery

FASHION

see also Clothing and Dress; Costume; Dressmaking

Jackson, Carole. Color Me Beautiful. 216p. 1981. pap. 8.95 (ISBN 0-345-29015-1). Ballantine.

Jarnow, Jeannette A. Inside the Fashion Business: Text & Readings. 3rd ed. 450p. 1981. text ed. 20.95 (ISBN 0-471-06038-0). Wiley.

Troxell, Mary D. & Stone, Elaine. Fashion Merchandising. 3rd ed. LC 80-25077. (Gregg McGraw-Hill Marketing Ser.). (Illus.). 480p. 16.50 (ISBN 0-07-065280-5). McGraw.

FASHION–HISTORY

Carter. The Changing World of Fashion: 1900 to the Present. Date not set. price not set (ISBN 0-517-31110-0). Bonanza.

Newton, Stella M. Fashion in the Age of the Black Prince: A Study of the Years 1340-1365. (Illus.). 151p. 1980. 37.50x (ISBN 0-8476-6939-4). Rowman.

FASHION MODELS

see Models, Fashion

FAST DAYS

see Fasts and Feasts

FAST-RESPONSE DATA PROCESSING
see Real-Time Data Processing
FASTER READING
see Rapid Reading
FASTING
see also Fasts and Feasts
Ryan, Thomas. Fasting Rediscovered: A Guide to Health & Wholeness for Your Body-Spirit. LC 80-81581. 176p. (Orig.). 1981. pap. 5.95 (ISBN 0-8091-2323-1). Paulist Pr.
FASTS AND FEASTS
Here are entered works on religious fasts and feasts in general and on Christian fasts and feasts.
see also Christmas; Easter; Festivals; Lent; Pentecost Festival
Falwell, Jerry. Fasting. 1981. pap. 2.25 (ISBN 0-8423-0849-0). Tyndale.
Nieting, Lorenz. Lesser Festivals 4: Saints' Days & Special Occasions. Achtemeier, Elizabeth, et al, eds. LC 79-7377. (Proclamation Two Ser.: Aids for Interpreting the Lessons of the Church Year). 64p. (Orig.). 1981. pap. 2.50 (ISBN 0-8006-1396-1, 1-1396). Fortress.
Reid, Richard & Crum, Milton, Jr. Lesser Festivals 3: Saints' Days & Special Occasions. Achtemeier, Elizabeth, et al, eds. LC 79-7377. (Proclamation 2: Aids for Interpreting the Lessons of the Church Year). 64p. (Orig.). 1981. pap. 2.50 (ISBN 0-8006-1395-3, 1-1395). Fortress.
Zimmerman, Martha. How to Celebrate the Feasts. (Illus.). 160p. (Orig.). 1981. pap. 4.95 (ISBN 0-87123-228-6, 210228). Bethany Fell.
FASTS AND FEASTS–JUDAISM
see also names of individual fasts and feast, e.g. sukkoth
Kanter, Shamai. Rabban Gamaliel II: The Legal Traditions. LC 80-12229. (Brown Judaic Studies: No. 8). 15.00x (ISBN 0-89130-403-7, 14 00 08); pap. 10.50x (ISBN 0-89130-404-5). Scholars Pr CA.
FAT
Here is entered material on fat in its relation to the animal organism. Works on the technological aspects of fats in general are entered under the heading Oils and Fats.
see also Low-Fat Diet
Cox, Beverly & Benois, George. Cellulite: Defeat It Through Diet & Exercise. (Illus.). 192p. 1981. 12.50 (ISBN 0-8149-0845-4); pap. 9.95 (ISBN 0-8149-0846-2). Vanguard.
Hausman, Patricia. Jack Sprat's Legacy: The Science & Politics of Fat & Cholesterol. 320p. 1981. 12.95 (ISBN 0-399-90111-6). Marek.
FATE AND FATALISM
see also Free Will and Determinism; Predestination
Turner, Bryan S. For Weber: Essays in the Sociology of Fate. 360p. 1981. price not set (ISBN 0-7100-0780-9). Routledge & Kegan.
FATHER AND CHILD
Lockerbie, D. Bruce. Fatherlove: Learning to Give the Best You've Got. LC 80-711. 240p. 1981. 10.95 (ISBN 0-385-15865-3, Galilee). Doubleday.
FATHERS
see also Adolescent Parents; Grandparents; Stepfathers
Colman, Arthur & Colman, Libby. Earth Father-Sky Father: The Changing Concept of Fathering. (Illus.). 224p. 1981. 12.95t (ISBN 0-13-223032-1, Spec); pap. 5.95b (ISBN 0-13-223024-0). P-H.
Lessin, Roy. Dads Are God's Idea. (God's Idea Books Ser.). (Illus.). 32p. (ps-4). 1981. pap. 1.25 (ISBN 0-87123-176-X, 210176). Bethany Fell.
FATHERS OF THE CHURCH
Here are entered works on the life and thought of the Fathers of the Church, a term that embraces the leaders of the early church to the time of Gregory the Great in the West and John of Damascus in the east. Works on their writing are entered under the heading Christian Literature, Early.
see also Persecution
Matsagouras, E. The Early Church Fathers As Educators. 1977. pap. 3.95 (ISBN 0-937032-10-7). Light & Life Pub Co MN.
Plott, John C. Global History of Philosophy: The Patristic-Sutra Period, Vol. 3. 1980. 27.00 (ISBN 0-8426-1680-2). Verry.
FATIGUE, MENTAL
Schuller, Robert H. Discover How to Turn Activity into Energy. (Orig.). 1978. pap. 1.25 (ISBN 0-89081-135-0). Harvest Hse.
FATIGUE OF MATERIALS
see Materials–Fatigue
FATIMA, PORTUGAL (SHRINE)
Johnston, Francis. Fatima. (The Great Sign). 1980. Repr. of 1979 ed. write for info. Tan Bks Pubs.
FATNESS
see Obesity
FATS
see Fat; Oils and Fats
FATTY ACIDS
see Acids, Fatty
FAULKNER, WILLIAM, 1897-1962
Minter, David. William Faulkner: His Life & Work. LC 80-13089. 325p. 1980. text ed. 16.95x (ISBN 0-8018-2347-1). Johns Hopkins.
Oberhelman, Harley D. The Presence of Faulkner in the Writings of Garcia Marquez. (Graduate Studies, Texas Tech Univ.: No. 22). (Illus.). 1980. pap. 7.00 (ISBN 0-89672-080-2). Tex Tech Pr.
Turner, Dixie M. A Jungian Psychoanalytic Interpretation of William Faulkner's "As I Lay Dying". LC 80-5582. 107p. 1981. lib. bdg. 16.50 (ISBN 0-8191-1451-0); pap. text ed. 7.50 (ISBN 0-8191-1452-9). U Pr of Amer.
FAULKNER, WILLIAM, 1897-1962–DICTIONARIES, INDEXES, ETC.
Bonner, Thomas, Jr. & Falcon, Guillermo N. William Faulkner, the William B. Wisdom Collection: A Descriptive Catalog. LC 79-26556. (Illus.). 1980. pap. 13.00 (ISBN 0-9603212-2-5). Tulane Univ.
Polk, Noel & Privratsky, Kenneth L. The Sound & the Fury: A Concordance to the Novel. LC 80-12310. (The Faulkner Concordances Ser.: No. 5). 412p. 1980. Set. 62.00 (ISBN 0-8357-0513-7, IS-00108, Pub. by Faulkner Concordance). A-L (ISBN 0-8357-0558-7). M-Z (ISBN 0-8357-0559-5). Univ Microfilms.
FAUNA
see Animals; Fresh-Water Biology; Zoology
FAUNA, PREHISTORIC
see Paleontology
FAUST
Kelly, James W. The Faust Legend in Music. LC 74-75893. (Detroit Reprints in Music). 1976. 10.00 (ISBN 0-911772-81-2). Info Coord.
FBI
see United States–Federal Bureau of Investigation
FEAR
see also Anxiety; Courage; Phobias
Angell, James W. Learning to Manage Our Fears. 128p. 1981. 6.95 (ISBN 0-687-21329-0). Abingdon.
Buckley, Michael. Why Are You Afraid. pap. 5.95 (ISBN 0-87061-060-0). Chr Classics.
Gossett, Don. How to Conquer Fear. Orig. Title: How You Can Rise Above Fear. 160p. 1981. pap. 2.95 (ISBN 0-88368-092-0). Whitaker Hse.
Saliba, David R. A Psychology of Fear: The Nightmare Formula of Edgar Allan Poe. LC 80-8267. 277p. 1980. lib. bdg. 18.50 (ISBN 0-8191-1269-0); pap. text ed. 10.25 (ISBN 0-8191-1270-4). U Pr of Amer.
Tuan, Yi-Fu. Landscapes of Fear. LC 79-1890. 272p. 1981. pap. 8.95 (ISBN 0-8166-1021-5). U of Minn Pr.
FEAST OF DEDICATION
see Hanukkah (Feast of Lights)
FEAST OF ESTHER
see Purim (Feast of Esther)
FEAST OF LIGHTS
see Hanukkah (Feast of Lights)
FEAST OF THE MACCABEES
see Hanukkah (Feast of Lights)
FEASTS
see Fasts and Feasts
FECUNDITY
see Fertility
FEDERAL AID TO HIGHER EDUCATION
Tuckman, Howard P. & Whalen, Edward L., eds. Subsidies to Higher Education: The Issues. 320p. 1980. 27.95 (ISBN 0-03-055791-7). Praeger.
FEDERAL BUREAU OF INVESTIGATION
see United States–Federal Bureau of Investigation
FEDERAL CORPORATION TAX
see Corporations–Taxation
FEDERAL GOVERNMENT
see also Democracy; Grants-In-Aid; Intergovernmental Fiscal Relations; State Governments
also subdivision Constitution and subdivision Politics and Government under names of federal states, e.g. United States–Constitution; France–Politics and Government
Boogman, J. C. & Van Der Plaat, G. N., eds. Federalism: History & Current Significance of a Form of Government. (Illus.). 307p. 1980. pap. 16.90 (ISBN 90-247-9003-4, Pub by Martinus Nijhoff). Kluwer Boston.
Di Marzo, Luigi. Component Units of Federal States & International Agreement. LC 80-83265. 272p. 1980. 45.00x (ISBN 90-286-0330-1). Sijthoff & Noordhoff.
Schultz, Richard J. Federalism & the Regulatory Process. 91p. 1979. pap. text ed. 1.50x (ISBN 0-686-68857-0, Pub. by Inst Res Pub Canada). Renouf.
Szanton, Peter, ed. Federal Reorganization. 1981. pap. 12.95x (ISBN 0-934540-11-X). Chatham Hse Pubs.
FEDERAL PARTY
Fairfield, Roy P., ed. The Federalist Papers. 2nd ed. LC 80-8862. 368p. 1981. pap. text ed. 5.95x (ISBN 0-8018-2607-1). Johns Hopkins.
FEDERAL REVENUE SHARING
see Intergovernmental Fiscal Relations
FEDERAL-STATE FISCAL RELATIONS
see Intergovernmental Fiscal Relations
FEDERAL-STATE RELATIONS
see Federal Government
FEDERAL THEOLOGY
see Covenants (Theology)
FEDERALISM
see Federal Government
FEDERALISTS (U. S.)
see Federal Party
FEDERATION, INTERNATIONAL
see International Organization
FEE SYSTEM (TAXATION)
see Taxation
FEEBLE MINDED
see Mental Deficiency; Mentally Handicapped
FEED
see Feeds
FEED-WATER
Pincus, Leo I. Practical Boiler Water Treatment: Including Air-Conditioning Systems. 284p. 1981. Repr. lib. bdg. price not set (ISBN 0-89874-255-2). Krieger.
FEEDBACK CONTROL SYSTEMS
see also Biological Control Systems
Mees, A. I. Dynamics of Feedback Systems. LC 80-40501. 212p. 1981. 35.75 (ISBN 0-471-27822-X, Pub. by Wiley-Interscience). Wiley.
FEEDING
see Animal Nutrition
FEEDING BEHAVIOR
see Animals, Food Habits of
FEEDS
see also Animal Nutrition
also subdivision Feeding and Feeds under names of animals and groups of animals, e.g. Poultry–Feeding and Feeds
Feed from Animal Wastes: State of Knowledge. (FAO Animal Production & Health Paper Ser.: No. 18). 201p. 1981. pap. 10.75 (ISBN 92-5-100946-5, F2100, FAO). Unipub.
Perry, T. W., ed. Feed Formulations. 3rd ed. 1981. 12.35 (ISBN 0-8134-2174-8); text ed. 9.25x. Interstate.
FEELING
see Perception; Touch
FEELINGS
see Emotions
FEET
see Foot
FEIGL, HERBERT
Cohen, Robert S., ed. Herbert Feigl: Inquiries & Provocations, Selected Writings. 1929 to 1974. (Vienna Circle Collection: No. 14). 450p. 1980. lib. bdg. 50.00 (ISBN 90-277-1101-1, Pub. by D. Reidel); pap. 23.50 (ISBN 90-277-1102-X). Kluwer Boston.
FELLOWSHIPS
see Scholarships
FELONY
see Criminal Law
FEMALE
see Women
FEMALE OFFENDERS
see also Reformatories for Women
Freedman, Estelle B. Their Sister's Keepers: Women's Prison Reform in America, 1830-1930. LC 80-24918. (Women & Culture Ser.). 256p. 1981. text ed. 18.50 (ISBN 0-472-10008-4). U of Mich Pr.
Giallombardo, Rose. The Social World of Imprisoned Girls. 314p. 1981. Repr. text ed. price not set (ISBN 0-89874-285-4). Krieger.
Lombroso, Cesare. Basic Characteristics Typical of Women Criminals. (The Library of Scientific Psychology). (Illus.). 1981. 74.95 (ISBN 0-89901-032-6). Found Class Reprints.
Sturgeon, S. & Rans, L. The Woman Offender: A Bibliographic Sourcebook. vi, 63p. 1975. pap. 5.00 (ISBN 0-686-28749-5). Entropy Ltd.
FEMALE SEX HORMONE
see Hormones, Sex
FEMALE STERILIZATION
see Sterilization of Women
FEMALE STUDIES
see Women'S Studies
FEMININITY (PSYCHOLOGY)
see also Sex (Psychology)
Terman, Lewis M. & Miles, Catherine C. Sex & Personality. 600p. 1980. Repr. of 1936 ed. lib. bdg. 50.00 (ISBN 0-89987-811-3). Darby Bks.
FEMINISM
see also Sex Discrimination; Women–History; Women–Legal Status, Laws, etc.; Women's Rights; Women–Social Conditions
Barrett, Michele. Women's Oppression Today: Problems in Marxist Feminst Analysis. 280p. 1981. 19.50x (ISBN 0-8052-7091-4, Pub. by NLB England); pap. 8.50 (ISBN 0-8052-7090-6). Schocken.
Follis, Anne B. I'm Not a Women's Libber, but... 128p. 1981. 7.95 (ISBN 0-687-18687-0). Abingdon.
Friedan, Betty. The Second Stage. 320p. 1981. 12.95 (ISBN 0-671-41034-2). Summit Bks.
Joseph, Gloria & Lewis, Jill. Common Differences. LC 79-6885. 240p. 1981. pap. 7.95 (ISBN 0-385-14271-4, Anch). Doubleday.
Lawrence, Cherrie M. & Anzaldua, Gloria, eds. This Bridge Called My Back: Writings by Radical Women of Color. (Orig.). 1981. pap. price not set (ISBN 0-930436-10-5). Persephone.
Miller, Sally M., ed. Flawed Liberation: Socialism & Feminism. LC 80-1050. (Contributions to Women's Studies Ser.: No. 19). 240p. 1981. lib. bdg. 27.50 (ISBN 0-313-21401-8, MFL/). Greenwood.
Reeves, Joyce A. Motherless Victim. 1981. 5.95 (ISBN 0-8062-1576-3). Carlton.
Richards, Janet R. The Sceptical Feminist: A Philosophical Enquiry. 320p. 1980. 32.00 (ISBN 0-7100-0673-X). Routledge & Kegan.
Roberts, Helen, ed. Doing Feminist Research. 224p. (Orig.). 1981. pap. price not set (ISBN 0-7100-0772-8). Routledge & Kegam.
Smith, Barbara. Toward a Black Feminst Criticism. (Out & Out Pamphlet Ser). pap. 1.00 (ISBN 0-918314-14-3). Out & Out.
Tingley, Elizabeth & Tingley, Donald F., eds. Women & Feminism: A Guide to Information Sources. (American Government & History Information Guide Ser.: Vol. 12). 325p. 1981. 30.00 (ISBN 0-8103-1492-4). Gale.
FEMINIST STUDIES
see Women'S Studies
FEMUR
McArdle, J. Functional Morphology of the Hip & Thigh of the Lorisiformes. (Contributions to Primatology Ser.: Vol. 17). (Illus.). 148p. 1981. pap. 19.25 (ISBN 3-8055-1767-X). S Karger.
FENCES
see also Hedges
Russell, James E. Walks, Walls & Fences. Horowitz, Shirley M. & Auer, Marilyn M., eds. (Illus., Orig.). 1981. pap. 6.95 (ISBN 0-932944-36-1). Creative Homeowner.
FENCING
Garret, Maxwell R. & Poulson, Mary H. Foil Fencing: Skills, Safety, Operations, & Responsibilities for the 1980s. LC 80-18426. (Illus.). 160p. 1981. text ed. 9.75x (ISBN 0-271-00273-5). Pa St U Pr.
FERMENTS
see Enzymes
FERRARI (AUTOMOBILE)
see Automobiles, Foreign–Types–Ferrari
FERROCEMENT
see Reinforced Concrete
FERROMAGNETIC DOMAIN
see Domain Structure
FERROMAGNETISM
see also Domain Structure
Odel, T. H. Ferromagnetodynamics: The Dynamics of Magnetic Bubbles Domains & Domain Walls. 232p. 1981. 54.95 (ISBN 0-470-27084-5). Halsted Pr.
FERTILITY
Bollack, C. G. & Clavert, A., eds. Epididymis & Fertility: Biology & Pathology. (Progress in Reproductive Biology Ser.: Vol. 8). (Illus.). viii, 192p. 1981. 58.75 (ISBN 3-8055-2157-X). S Karger.
Chowdhury, R. H. Social Aspects of Fertility. 200p. 1980. text ed. 22.50x (ISBN 0-7069-1211-X, Pub by Vikas India). Advent Bk.
Cunningham, G. R., et al, eds. Regulation of Male Fertility. (Clinics in Andrology Ser.: No. 5). (Illus.). 245p. 1981. PLB 68.50 (ISBN 90-247-2373-6, Pub. by Martinus Nijhoff). Kluwer Boston.
International Planned Parenthood Federation. Handbook of Infertility. Kleinman, Ronald L. & Senayake, Pramilla, eds. (Illus.). 58p. (Orig.). 1979. pap. 6.50x (ISBN 0-86089-034-1). Intl Pubns Serv.
Potts, Malcolm & Selman, Peter. Society & Fertility. (Illus.). 384p. 1979. 27.50x (ISBN 0-7121-1960-4, Pub. by Macdonald & Evans England). Intl Ideas.
Robertson, W. B. The Endometrium. (Postgraduate Pathology Ser.). 1981. text ed. 52.95 (ISBN 0-407-00171-9). Butterworth.
FERTILITY, HUMAN
see also subdivision Population under names of countries
Chamie, Joseph. Religion & Fertility: Arab Christian-Muslim Differentials. LC 80-19787. (ASA Rose Monograph Ser.). (Illus.). 176p. Date not set. price not set (ISBN 0-521-23677-0); pap. price not set (ISBN 0-521-28147-4). Cambridge U Pr.
Zatuchni, Gerald I., et al. Research Frontiers in Fertility Regulation. (Illus.). 416p. 1981. text ed. write for info. (ISBN 0-06-142902-3, Harper Medical). Har-Row.
FERTILIZATION OF PLANTS
Physiochemical Properties of Submerged Soils in Relationship to Fertility. (IRRI Research Paper Ser.: No. 5). 32p. 1977. pap. 5.00 (R045, IRRI). Unipub.
FERTILIZERS AND MANURES
see also Agricultural Chemistry; Nitrogen Fertilizers; Nitrates; Soil Fertility
Papers Presented at the FAO-SIDA Workshop on the Use of Organic Materials As Fertilizers in Africa: Organic Recycling in Africa. 308p. 1981. pap. 16.50 (ISBN 92-5-100945-7, F2096, FAO). Unipub.
FESTIVAL OF HANUKKAH
see Hanukkah (Feast of Lights)
FESTIVALS
see also Fasts and Feasts; Music Festivals
also names of particular festivals, e.g. Christmas; Hanukkah (Feast of Lights)
Gale, Janice & Gale, Stephen. Guide to Fairs, Festivals & Fun Events. (Illus.). 190p. 1981. pap. 6.95 (ISBN 0-937928-00-3). Sightseer.
Huxford, Sharon & Huxford, Bob. Collector's Encyclopedia of Fiesta. 4th rev. ed. (Illus.). 1981. pap. 8.95 (ISBN 0-89145-168-4). Collector Bks.
Truck, Fred, ed. The Des Moines Festival of the Avant-Garde Invites You to a Show Without Really Being There. (Orig.). pap. text ed. 7.50 (ISBN 0-938236-02-4). Cookie Pr.
Tun Li-Ch'En. Annual Customs & Festivals in Peking. Bodde, Derk, tr. from Chinese. (Illus.). 175p. 1981. 10.00 (ISBN 0-85656-029-4). Great Eastern.
FESTIVALS–JEWS
see Fasts and Feasts–Judaism

FESTSCHRIFTEN–BIBLIOGRAPHY

Reinberg, Gerald, et al, eds. A Festschrift for Maurice Goldhaber. new ed. LC 80-20599. (Transaction Ser.: Vol. 40). 293p. 1980. 25.00 (ISBN 0-89766-086-2). NY Acad Sci.

FETICIDE

see Abortion

FETUS

see also Obstetrics

Lauersen, Neils H. & Hochberg, Howard. Clinical Perinatal Biochemical Monitoring. 271p. 1981. write for info. (1901-1). Williams & Wilkins.

FETUS–ABNORMALITIES AND DEFORMITIES

Athey, Patricia A. & Hadlock, Frank P. Ultrasound in Obstetrics & Gynecology. (Illus.). 400p. 1981. text ed. 45.00 (ISBN 0-8016-0374-9). Mosby.

Golbus, Mitchell S. & Hall, Bryan D., eds. Diagnosti Approaches to Malformed Fetus, Abortus, Stillborn & Deceased Newborn. LC 79-2369. (Alan R. Liss Ser.: Vol. 15, No. 5a). 1979. 22.00 (ISBN 0-8451-1028-4). March of Dimes.

FETUS–DISEASES

Milunsky, Aubrey, et al, eds. Advances in Perinatal Medicine, Vol. 1. 450p. 1981. 35.00 (ISBN 0-306-40482-6, Plenum Pr). Plenum Pub.

FETUS, DEATH OF

see also Abortion

Golbus, Mitchell S. & Hall, Bryan D., eds. Diagnosti Approaches to Malformed Fetus, Abortus, Stillborn & Deceased Newborn. LC 79-2369. (Alan R. Liss Ser.: Vol. 15, No. 5a). 1979. 22.00 (ISBN 0-8451-1028-4). March of Dimes.

FEUDAL CASTLES

see Castles

FEUDALISM

see also Clans and Clan System; Land Tenure; Middle Ages

Bellette, Emile. La Succession Aux Fiefs Dans les Coutumes Flamandes. LC 80-1997. 1981. Repr. of 1926 ed. 23.50 (ISBN 0-404-18553-3). AMS Pr.

Cahen, Claude. La Regime Feodal De l'Italie Normande. LC 80-1995. 1981. Repr. of 1923 ed. 22.00 (ISBN 0-404-18555-X). AMS Pr.

Calmette, Joseph L. La Societe Feodale. LC 80-1994. 1981. Repr. of 1923 ed. 26.50 (ISBN 0-404-18556-8). AMS Pr.

English, Barbara. The Lord of Holderness, Ten Eighty-Six to Twelve Sixty: A Study in Feudal Society. (Illus.). 288p. 1979. 49.50x (ISBN 0-19-713437-8). Oxford U Pr.

Mor, Carlo G. L' Eta Feudale, 2 vols. LC 80-2016. 1981. Repr. of 1952 ed. Set. 110.00 (ISBN 0-404-18609-2). AMS Pr.

Perrin, Charles E. La Societe Feodale Allemande et Ses Institutions Du Xe Au XIIe Siecle. LC 80-2013. 1981. Repr. of 1956 ed. 34.50 (ISBN 0-404-18583-5). AMS Pr.

Sanchez-Albornoz y Menduina, Claudio. En Torno a los Origenes del Feudalismo, 3 vols. LC 80-2004. 1981. Repr. of 1942 ed. Set. 110.00 (ISBN 0-404-18590-8). Vol. 1 (ISBN 0-404-18591-6). Vol. 2 (ISBN 0-404-18592-4). Vol. 3 (ISBN 0-404-18593-2). AMS Pr.

Thompson, James W. Feudal Germany. LC 80-2001. 1981. Repr. of 1928 ed. 67.50 (ISBN 0-404-18601-7). AMS Pr.

FEUDALISM–FRANCE

Lagoulle, Henri. Essai Sur la Conception Juridique De la Propriete Fonciere Dans le Tres Anciendroit Normand: Premiere Partie, la Conception Feodale. LC 80-2020. 1981. Repr. of 1902 ed. 47.50 (ISBN 0-404-18574-6). AMS Pr.

Petit-Dutaillis, Charles E. The Feudal Monarchy in France & England from the Tenth to the Thirteenth Century. LC 80-2011. 1981. Repr. of 1936 ed. 44.50 (ISBN 0-404-18585-1). AMS Pr.

FEUDALISM–GREAT BRITAIN

Petit-Dutaillis, Charles E. The Feudal Monarchy in France & England from the Tenth to the Thirteenth Century. LC 80-2011. 1981. Repr. of 1936 ed. 44.50 (ISBN 0-404-18585-1). AMS Pr.

FIAT (AUTOMOBILE)

see Automobiles, Foreign–Types–Fiat

FIAT MONEY

see Paper Money

FIBER IN THE DIET

see High-Fiber Diet

FIBER OPTICS

Centro Studi e Laboratori Telecomumicazioni. Optical Fibre Communication. (Illus.). 928p. 1980. 39.50 (ISBN 0-07-014882-1, P&RB). McGraw.

Hewlett-Packard. Optoelectronics-Fiber-Optics Applications Manual. 2nd ed. (Illus.). 448p. 1981. 27.50 (ISBN 0-07-028606-X, P&RB). McGraw.

Hill, D. A. Fibre Optics. 176p. 1977. text ed. 29.50x (ISBN 0-220-66333-5, Pub. by Busn Bks England). Renouf.

Kao, C. K. Optical Fiber Technology II. 304p. 1980. 24.00 (ISBN 0-471-09169-3, Pub. by Wiley-Interscience); pap. 15.75 (ISBN 0-471-09171-5). Wiley.

Sharma, A. B., et al. Optical Fiber Systems & Their Components. (Springer Ser. in Optical Sciences: Vol. 24). (Illus.). 250p. 1981. 38.35 (ISBN 0-387-10437-2). Springer-Verlag.

Weik, Martin H. Fiber Optics & Lightwave Communications Standard Dictionary. 320p. 1980. text ed. 18.50 (ISBN 0-442-25658-2). Van Nos Reinhold.

FIBER PLANTS

see Fibers

FIBER SCULPTURE

see Tapestry

FIBERGLASS BOATS

Jones, Charles. Glass Fibre Yachts: Improvement & Repair. 128p. 1980. 12.00x (Pub. by Nautical England). State Mutual Bk.

FIBERS

see also Cotton; Fibrous Composites; Paper

French, Alfred D. & Gardner, Kenncorwin H., eds. Fiber Diffraction Methods. LC 80-21566. (ACS Symposium Ser.: No. 141). 1980. 34.50 (ISBN 0-8412-0589-2). Am Chemical.

Hearle, J. W., ed. Mechanics of Flexible Fiber Assemblies. (NATO-Advanced Study Institute Ser.). 700p. 1980. 72.50x (ISBN 9-0286-0720-X). Sijthoff & Noordhoff.

Report of the Fifteenth Session of the Intergovernmental Group on Hard Fibres to the Committee on Commodity Problems. 1980. pap. 6.00 (ISBN 92-5-100905-8, F1951, FAO). Unipub.

FIBRINOLYSIS

Protides of the Biological Fluids, Colloquium 28: Proceedings of the 28th Colloquium on Protides of the Biological Fluids, Brussels, 5-8 May 1980. LC 58-5908. (Illus.). 600p. 1980. 120.00 (ISBN 0-08-026370-4). Pergamon.

FIBRINOLYTIC AGENTS

Forster, Werner, et al. Prostaglandins & Thromboxins: Proceedings of the Third International Symposium on Prostaglandins & Thromboxanes in the Cardiovascular System, Hale-Salle, GDR, 5-7 May 1980. LC 80-41802. (Illus.). 500p. 1981. 80.00 (ISBN 0-08-027369-6). Pergamon.

FIBROUS COMPOSITES

Lenoe, Edward M., et al, eds. Fibrous Composites in Structural Design. 900p. 1980. 85.00 (ISBN 0-306-40354-4). Plenum Pub.

FICINO, MARSILIO, 1433-1499

Ficino, Marsilio. The Letters of Marsilio Ficino, Vol. 3, Bk. 4. 160p. 1980. 39.00x (ISBN 0-85683-045-3, Pub. by Shepheard-Walwyn England). State Mutual Bk.

FICTION

see also Children's Stories; Detective and Mystery Stories (Collections); Fairy Tales; Fishing Stories; Folk-Lore; Historical Fiction; Horror Tales; Hunting Stories; Legends; Nature Stories; Romanticism; Science Fiction (Collections); Sea Stories; Short Stories; Spy Stories; Tales; Western Stories also American Fiction, English Fiction, French Fiction, and similar headings; and subdivision Fiction under historical events and characters, etc. e.g. Gettysburg, Battle of, 1863–Fiction; Napolean 1st, Emperor of the French, 1769-1821–Fiction; World War, 1939-1945–Fiction

Beaty, Jerome, ed. The Norton Introduction to Fiction. 2nd ed. 640p. 1981. pap. text ed. 8.95x (ISBN 0-393-95156-1); classroom guide avail. (ISBN 0-393-95159-6). Norton.

FICTION (COLLECTIONS)

Schmidt, Stanley, ed. Analog's Golden Anniversary Anthology. 384p. 1980. 10.95 (ISBN 0-8037-0217-5). Davis Pubns.

Scholes, Robert, ed. Elements of Fiction: An Anthology. 984p. 1981. pap. text ed. 9.95x (ISBN 0-19-502881-3). Oxford U Pr.

FICTION–AUTHORSHIP

Macnichol, Kenneth. Twelve Lectures on the Technique of Fiction Writing. 385p. 1980. lib. bdg. 40.00 (ISBN 0-89760-545-4). Telegraph Bks.

FICTION–HISTORY AND CRITICISM

Cockshut, A. O., intro. by. The Novel to Nineteen Hundred. 320p. 1981. pap. 7.95 (ISBN 0-312-57965-9). St Martin.

Conger, Syndy M. & Welsch, Janice R., eds. Narrative Strategies: Original Essays in Film & Prose Fiction. (Essays in Literature Ser.: Bk. 4). 140p. (Orig.). 1981. pap. 8.00x (ISBN 0-934312-03-6). Western Ill Univ.

Federman, Raymond, ed. Surfiction: Fiction Now & Tomorrow. rev. ed. 1981. pap. 7.95. Swallow.

Gilman, Stephen. Galdos & the Art of the European Novel, Eighteen Sixty-Seven to Eighteen Eighty-Seven. LC 80-8550. 416p. 1981. 27.50x (ISBN 0-691-06456-3). Princeton U Pr.

Kunar, Raj. The New Concept of the Novel. 49p. 1980. Repr. of 1959 ed. lib. bdg. 6.00 (ISBN 0-8482-1446-3). Norwood Edns.

McCleary, George F. On Detective Fiction & Other Things. 161p. 1980. Repr. of 1960 ed. lib. bdg. 20.00 (0-8492-6600-9). R West.

Miller, D. A. Narrative & Its Discontents: Problems of Closure in the Traditional Novel. LC 80-8565. 320p. 1981. 20.00x (ISBN 0-691-06459-8). Princeton U Pr.

Phelan, James. Worlds from Words: A Theory of Language in Fiction. LC 80-25844. (Chicago Originals Ser.). 256p. lib. bdg. 19.00x (ISBN 0-226-66650-7). U of Chicago Pr.

Reed, Walter L. An Exemplary History of the Novel: The Quixotic Versus the Picaresque. LC 80-17908. 1981. lib. bdg. 22.00x (ISBN 0-226-70683-4). U of Chicago Pr.

Skene Melvin, David & Skene Melvin, Ann. Crime, Detective, Espionage, Mystery, & Thriller Fiction & Film: A Comprehensive Bibliography of Critical Writing Through 1979. LC 80-1194. 384p. 1980. lib. bdg. 29.95 (ISBN 0-313-22062-X, MCD/). Greenwood.

FICTION–HISTORY AND CRITICISM–20TH CENTURY

Devlin, Laura K. Looking Inward: Studies in James Joyce, E.M. Forster, & the Twentieth Century Novel. 1980. lib. bdg. 59.95 (ISBN 0-87700-269-X). Revisionist Pr.

Schulz, Max F. Black Humor Fiction of the Sixties: A Pluralistic Definition of Man & His World. LC 72-85538. 156p. 1980. pap. 5.95x (ISBN 0-8214-0574-8). Ohio U Pr.

FICTION–TECHNIQUE

see also Detective and Mystery Stories–Technique

Brophy, Jere, et al. Student Characteristics & Teaching. (Professional Ser.). 224p. 1981. text ed. 22.50 (ISBN 0-582-28152-0). Longman.

Burns, Alan & Sugnet, Charles. The Imagination on Trial: Conversations with the British & American Novelists. 192p. 1981. 16.95x (ISBN 0-8052-8084-7); pap. 7.95 (ISBN 0-8052-8083-9). Schocken.

Doubtfire, Dianne. The Craft of Novel Writing. 1981. pap. 5.95 (ISBN 0-8052-8087-1, Pub. by Allison & Busby England). Schocken.

Hellmann, John. Fables of Fact: The New Journalism As New Fiction. LC 80-23881. 175p. 1981. 11.95 (ISBN 0-252-00847-2). U of Ill Pr.

Highsmith, Patricia. Plotting & Writing Suspense Fiction. rev. ed. 1981. 10.95 (ISBN 0-87116-125-7). Writer.

McCarthy, Mary. Ideas & the Novel. 7.95 (ISBN 0-15-143682-7). HarBraceJ.

FICTION, HISTORICAL

see Historical Fiction

FICTITIOUS ANIMALS

see Animals, Mythical

FICTITIOUS NAMES

see Anonyms and Pseudonyms

FIDUCIA

see Trusts and Trustees

FIEFS

see Feudalism; Land Tenure

FIELD ATHLETICS

see Track-Athletics

FIELD CROPS

see also Grain; Horticulture; Tropical Crops also names of specific crops, e.g. Cotton, Hay

Checklist of Economic Plants in Australia. 214p. 1980. pap. 9.00 (ISBN 0-643-02551-0, CO04, CSIRO). Unipub.

China: Multiple Cropping & Related Crop Production Technology. (FAO Plant Protection Paper Ser.: No. 22). 66p. 1981. pap. 6.00 (ISBN 92-5-100977-5, F2108, FAO). Unipub.

Crops on a Few Acres. (Country Home Ser.). 96p. 2.95 (ISBN 0-88453-010-8). Berkshire Traveller.

FIELD SPORTS

see Hunting; Sports

FIELD THEORY (PHYSICS)

see also Continuum Mechanics; Electromagnetic Theory; Gravitation; Quantum Field Theory

Bolton, W. Fields, Bk. 5. LC 80-41166. (Study Topics in Physics Ser.). 96p. 1980. pap. text ed. write for info. (ISBN 0-408-10656-5). Butterworths.

Lee, T. D. Field Theory & Particle Analysis. (Contemporary Concepts in Physics Ser.). 1981. 35.00 (ISBN 0-686-69595-X); pap. 14.00 (ISBN 0-686-69596-8). Harwood Academic.

Urban, P., ed. Field Theory & Strong Interactions: Proceedings. (Acta Physica Austriaca Supplementum Ser.: No. 22). (Illus.). 815p. 1981. 98.00 (ISBN 0-387-81615-1). Springer-Verlag.

FIELD THEORY, QUANTIZED

see Quantum Field Theory

FIELDING, HENRY, 1707-1754

Kalpakgian, Mitchell. The Marvellous in Fielding's Novels. LC 80-1411. 243p. 1981. lib. bdg. 18.75 (ISBN 0-8191-1505-3); pap. text ed. 9.75 (ISBN 0-8191-1506-1). U Pr of Amer.

McCrea, Brian. Henry Fielding & the Politics of Mid-Eighteenth-Century England. LC 80-14711. (South Atlantic Modern Language Association Award Study, 1979). 328p. 1981. 20.00x (ISBN 0-8203-0531-6). U of Ga Pr.

FIELDS, ALGEBRAIC

see also Numbers, Theory of; Rings (Algebra)

Gerritzen, L. & Van Der Put, M. Schottky Groups & Mumford Curves. (Lecture Notes in Mathematics: Vol. 817). 317p. 1980. pap. 19.50 (ISBN 0-387-10229-9). Springer-Verlag.

Hsu, D. F. Cyclic Neofields & Combinatorial Designs. (Lecture Notes in Mathematics Ser.: Vol. 824). (Illus.). 230p. 1981. pap. 14.00 (ISBN 0-387-10243-4). Springer-Verlag.

FIGHTER PLANES

Gunston, Bill. The Illustrated Guide to German, Italian & Japanese Fighters of World War II. LC 80-67627. (Illustrated Military Guides). (Illus.). 160p. 1981. 7.95 (ISBN 0-668-05093-4, 5093). Arco.

Maloney, Edward T. Zero Sen: Japanese Fighter. (Illus.). 1978. pap. 3.00 (Pub. by WW II). Aviation.

Philpott, Bryan. German Fighters Over England: World War Two Photo Album. (Illus.). 96p. 1981. softcover 5.95 (ISBN 0-89404-056-1). Aztex.

Rhodes, Arnold. The Republic F-84: From "Lead Sled" to "Super Hawg". (Illus.). 128p. 1981. pap. 9.95 (ISBN 0-89404-054-5). Aztex.

FIGHTING

see Battles; Boxing; Karate; Military Art and Science; Naval Art and Science; War

FIGHTING, HAND-TO-HAND

see Hand-To-Hand Fighting

FIGURATION

see Figurative Art

FIGURATIVE ART

Hills, Patricia & Tarbell, Roberta K. The Figurative Tradition & the Whitney Museum of American Art: Paintings & Sculpture from the Permanent Collection. LC 80-12650. 192p. 1980. 25.00 (ISBN 0-87413-184-7). U Delaware Pr.

FIGURE DRAWING

Carter, Stanley N. Practical Instruction in Figure Drawing. (A Promotion of the Arts Library Book). (Illus.). 103p. 1981. 27.45 (ISBN 0-86650-002-2). Gloucester Art.

Goldstein, Nathan. Figure Drawing: The Structure, Anatomy, & Expressive Design of Human Form. (Illus.). 330p. 1981. text ed. 20.95 (ISBN 0-13-314518-2); pap. text ed. 17.95 (ISBN 0-13-314435-6). P-H.

FIGURE PAINTING

see also Genre Painting

Kinstler, Everett R. Painting Faces, Figures & Landscapes. 144p. 1981. 22.50 (ISBN 0-8230-3625-1). Watson-Guptill.

FIGURE SKATING

see Skating

FIGURINES

see Bronzes; Dolls; Jade

FIJI ISLANDS

Population Environment Relations in Tropical Islands: The Case of Eastern Fiji. (MAB Technical Notes Ser.: No. 13). 233p. 1981. pap. 18.00 (ISBN 92-3-101821-3, U1054, UNESCO). Unipub.

FILAMENT REINFORCED COMPOSITES

see Fibrous Composites

FILES AND FILING (DOCUMENTS)

see also Alphabeting

Stewart, Jeffrey R., Jr., et al. Filing Systems & Records Management. 3rd ed. LC 80-21605. (Illus.). 240p. 1981. text ed. 10.95 (ISBN 0-07-061471-7, G); instructor's manual & key avail. (ISBN 0-07-061473-3); practice materials avail. (ISBN 0-07-061472-5). McGraw.

FILIBUSTERS (WEST INDIAN BUCCANEERS)

see Buccaneers

FILING SYSTEMS

see Files and Filing (Documents)

FILIPINO FOLK-LORE

see Folk-Lore, Filipino

FILIPINOS IN HAWAII

Teodoro, Luis V., ed. Out of This Struggle: The Filipinos in Hawaii. (Illus.). 168p. 1981. 12.95 (ISBN 0-8248-0747-2). U Pr of Hawaii.

FILLMORE, MILLARD, PRES. U. S., 1800-1874

Grayson, Benson L. The Unknown President: The Administration of President Millard Fillmore. LC 80-5962. 179p. 1981. lib. bdg. 17.75 (ISBN 0-8191-1456-1); pap. text ed. 8.75 (ISBN 0-8191-1457-X). U Pr of Amer.

FILLS (EARTHWORK)

American Society of Civil Engineers, compiled by. Sanitary Landfill, Manual 39. (ASCE Manual & Report on Engineering Practice Ser.: No. 39). 92p. looseleaf binder 27.50 (ISBN 0-87262-215-0). Am Soc Civil Eng.

FILM ACTORS

see Moving-Picture Actors and Actresses

FILM ADAPTATIONS

Laurence, Frank M. Hemingway & the Movies. LC 79-1437. 336p. 1980. 20.00 (ISBN 0-87805-115-5). U Pr of Miss.

FILM AUTHORSHIP

see Moving-Picture Authorship

FILM CATALOGS

see Moving-Pictures–Catalogs

FILM EDITING (CINEMATOGRAPHY)

see Moving-Pictures–Editing

FILM MUSIC

see Moving-Picture Music

FILM STARS

see Moving-Picture Actors and Actresses

FILM STRIPS

see Filmstrips

FILMS

see Filmstrips; Microfilms; Moving-Pictures

FILMS, THIN

see Thin Films

FILMS FROM BOOKS

see Film Adaptations

FILMSTRIPS

Carroll, Walter J., ed. Olympic's Film Finder: Nineteen Eighty-One Business Edition. 1981. 24.00x (ISBN 0-88367-600-1). Olympic Media.

FILTERS, DIGITAL (MATHEMATICS)

see Digital Filters (Mathematics)

FILTERS AND FILTRATION

see also Separators (Machines)

Ghausi, M. & Laker, K. Modern Filter Design: Active RC & Switched Capacitor. 1980. 34.95 (ISBN 0-13-594663-8). P-H.

Sarner. Plastic-Packed Trickling Filters. new ed. 1980. text ed. 12.50 (ISBN 0-250-40371-4, Butterworths). Ann Arbor Science.

FINAL CAUSE
see Causation
FINANCE
see also Bankruptcy; Banks and Banking; Bonds; Budget in Business; Business Mathematics; Capital; Church Finance; Commerce; Controllership; Credit; Finance, Personal; Finance, Public; Foreign Exchange; Income; Inflation (Finance); Insurance; Interest and Usury; International Finance; Investments; Liquidity (Economics); Loans; Money; Profit; Saving and Investment; Securities; Stock-Exchange; Wealth also subdivision Finance under special subjects, e.g. Corporations–Finance; Railroads–Finance

Archer, S. H., et al. Financial Management: An Introduction. 724p. 1979. 23.50 (ISBN 0-471-02987-4); study guide 9.50 (ISBN 0-471-02988-2). Wiley.
Aydon, Cyril. How to Finance Your Company. 206p. 1976. text ed. 19.50x (ISBN 0-220-66309-2, Pub. by Busn Bks England). Renouf.
Bogen, J. I. & Shipman, S. S. Financial Handbook. 4th ed. 1208p. 1968. 40.95 (ISBN 0-471-06556-0). Wiley.
Clugston, Donald. All That Money & No Cash. 128p. 1981. 7.50 (ISBN 0-682-49678-2). Exposition.
Dickmeyer, Nathan & Hughes, K. Scott. Financial Self-Assessment: A Workbook for Colleges. 72p. 1980. pap. text ed. 15.00 (ISBN 0-915164-11-6). Natl Assn Coll.
Ford, John K. A Framework for Financial Analysis. 176p. 1981. pap. text ed. 9.95 (ISBN 0-13-330241-5). P-H.
Goff, Walter S. Finance for Managers. 296p. 1980. pap. text ed. 14.95x (ISBN 0-7121-0636-7). Intl Ideas.
Guide for a Review of a Financial Forecast. 1980. pap. 6.00. Am Inst CPA.
Hartley, W. C. Cash: Planning, Forecasting & Control. 210p. 1976. text ed. 24.50x (ISBN 0-220-66288-6, Pub. by Busn Bks England). Renouf.
How to Survive the Money Crash. 9.95 (ISBN 0-89081-174-1). Harvest Hse.
Kidwell, David S. & Peterson, Richard L. Financial Institutions & Markets. LC 80-65804. 640p. 1981. text ed. 18.95 (ISBN 0-03-046066-2). Dryden Pr.
Kim, Suk H. & Guithues, Henry J. Capital Expenditure Analysis. LC 80-6070. 338p. 1981. 20.00 (ISBN 0-8191-1462-6); pap. 11.25. U Pr of Amer.
Mathewson, Kent & Neenan, William B., eds. Financing the Metropolis. 352p. 1980. 29.95 (ISBN 0-03-056886-2). Praeger.
Miller, Jama. Theory of Finance. 1972. 21.95 (ISBN 0-03-086732-0). Dryden Pr.
Modern Dev. Fin. Mngt. 1976. pap. 16.95 (ISBN 0-275-89360-X). Dryden Pr.
OECD. Published Offical Sources of Financial Statistics. (Illus.). 132p. (Orig.). 1980. pap. 11.00x (ISBN 92-64-02095-0). OECD.
Pratt, Stanley E. Guide to Venture Capital Sources. 5th ed. 1981. 49.50 (ISBN 0-914470-12-4). Capital Pub Corp.
Pring, Martin J. How to Forecast Interest Rates: A Guide to Profits for Consumers, Managers & Investors. 192p. 1981. 14.95 (ISBN 0-07-050865-8, P&RB). McGraw.
Prodham, B. The Board & Financial Management. 175p. 1979. text ed. 24.50 (ISBN 0-220-66354-8, Pub. by Business Books England). Renouf.
Randle, Paul A. & Swensen, Philip R. Financial Planning for the Executive. (Finance Ser.). (Illus.). 300p. 1981. text ed. 15.95. Lifetime Learn.
Rockley, L. E. Finance for the Non-Accountant. 3rd ed. 337p. 1979. pap. 12.25x (ISBN 0-220-67022-6, Pub. by Busn Bks England). Renouf.
--Finance for the Purchasing Executive. 191p. 1978. text ed. 24.50x (ISBN 0-220-66362-9, Pub. by Busn Bks England). Renouf.
Simmons, James G. How to Obtain Financing & Make Your Best Deal with Any Bank, Finance or Leasing Company. (Illus.). 380p. (Orig.). 1980. pap. 19.95 (ISBN 0-937700-00-2). Cambrian.
Simons, Leon. The Basic Arts of Financial Management. 2nd ed. 249p. 1978. text ed. 25.75x (ISBN 0-220-66370-X, Pub. by Busn Bks England). Renouf.
Skousen, K. Fred, et al. Financial Accounting. 1981. text ed. write for info. (ISBN 0-87901-156-4); write or info. study guide (ISBN 0-87901-157-2); write for info. practice set, vol. 2 (ISBN 0-87901-159-9); price not set practice set, vol. 2 (ISBN 0-87901-160-2); write for info. working papers (ISBN 0-87901-158-0). Worth.
Solomon, Morton B., et al. Main Hurdman & Cranston Guide to Preparing Financial Reports, 1981. 272p. 1981. 75.00 (ISBN 0-471-09104-9, Pub. by Wiley-Interscience). Wiley.
Wilson, J. P. Inflation, Deflation, Reflation: Managmennt & Accounting in Economic Uncertainty. 345p. 1980. text ed. 36.75x (ISBN 0-220-67015-3, Pub. by Busn Bks England). Renouf.
Wood, E. G. Costing Matters for Managers. 199p. 1974. text ed. 24.50x (Pub. by Busn Bks England). Renouf.

FINANCE–MATHEMATICAL MODELS
Thore, Sten. Programming the Network of Financial Intermediation. 224p. 1983. pap. text ed. 14.00x (ISBN 82-00-05379-2). Universitet.

FINANCE–AFRICA
Okigbo, P. N. Nigeria's Financial System. (Illus.). 320p. 1981. text ed. 25.00x (ISBN 0-582-59733-1). Longman.

FINANCE, CHURCH
see Church Finance
FINANCE, INTERNATIONAL
see International Finance
FINANCE, MUNICIPAL
see Municipal Finance
FINANCE, PERSONAL
see also Estate Planning; Home Economics–Accounting; Insurance; Investments; Saving and Thrift

Advice About Insurance, Credit, Budgeting. (Home Adviser Ser.). 80p. (Orig.). 1981. pap. 1.95 (ISBN 0-8326-2407-1, 7051). Delair.
Anderson, Jim. How to Live Rent Free in the 1980's: It's Not Too Late! 1980. write for info. (ISBN 0-932574-04-1). Brun Pr.
Baker, C. R. & Hayes, R. S. Lease Financing: A Practical Guide. 256p. 1981. 17.95 (ISBN 0-471-06040-2, Pub. by Wiley Interscience). Wiley.
Barngrover, Charles L., et al. Personal Finance. 2nd ed. LC 80-18010. (Finance Ser.). 520p. 1981. text ed. 19.95 (ISBN 0-88244-216-3). Grid Pub.
Carrol, Frieda. How to Get Something for Almost Nothing & More. LC 78-59909. 52p. (Orig.). 1981. pap. text ed. 5.00 (ISBN 0-9605246-0-6). Biblio Pr GA.
--Prescriptions for Survival. LC 78-72312. 148p. 1981. pap. text ed. 14.95 (ISBN 0-9605246-1-4). Biblio Pr GA.
Cohen. Plaid for Personal Finance. 3rd ed. 1981. write for info. (ISBN 0-256-02126-0, 06-0117-03). Learning Syst.
Del Bueno, Dorothy. Money: A Financial Guide for Nurses. (Illus.). 208p. 1981. text ed. 12.50 (ISBN 0-86542-007-6). Blackwell Sci.
Felix, Joseph. You Can Buy Your Way into Heaven: But It'll Take Every Cent You Have. 1981. pap. 3.95 (ISBN 0-8407-5766-2). Nelson.
Gitman. Personal Finance. 1978. 18.95 (ISBN 0-03-020821-1). Dryden Pr.
Gitman, Lawrence J. Personal Finance. 2nd ed. LC 80-65798. 672p. 1981. text ed. 18.95 (ISBN 0-03-058094-3). Dryden Pr.
Hardy. Your Money & Your Life: How to Plan Your Long Range Financial Security. Date not set. 14.95 (ISBN 0-8144-5529-8). Am Mgmt.
Hembree, Ron. You & Your Money: A Guide from God's Word. (Orig.). 1981. pap. 4.95 (ISBN 0-8010-4252-6). Baker Bk.
Hover, Craig R. Beyond the Valley of the Dollar. (Illus.). 224p. Date not set. 10.95 (ISBN 0-89913-004-6). Entity Pub Co.
Johnstad, Jack & Johnstad, Lois. Attaining Financial Peace of Mind: A Practical Guide for the Thinking Person. LC 80-67104. (Illus.). 320p. 1980. pap. 8.95 (ISBN 0-937346-00-4). Bright Spirit.
Kaufman, Daniel. How to Get Out of Debt. 208p. (Orig.). 1981. pap. 2.50 (ISBN 0-523-41197-9). Pinnacle Bks.
Lang, Larry. Strategy for Personal Finance. 2nd ed. 1981. text ed. 17.95 (ISBN 0-07-036281-5, C); instructor's manual 4.95 (ISBN 0-07-036283-1); wkbk. 5.95 (ISBN 0-07-036282-3). McGraw.
Lassen, Richard. Currency Management. 168p. 1980. 40.00x (ISBN 0-85941-154-0, Pub. by Woodhead-Faulkner England). State Mutual Bk.
Mackevich, Gene. The Woman's Money Book. 224p. 1981. pap. 2.95 (ISBN 0-553-14711-0). Bantam.
Meyer, Martin J. Don't Bank on It. 240p. pap. 2.50 (ISBN 0-671-41606-5). PB.
Minkow, Rosalie. Money Management for Women. LC 80-84373. 256p. (Orig.). 1981. pap. 2.50 (ISBN 0-87216-816-6). Playboy Pbks.
Mumford, Amy R. It Only Hurts Between Paydays. 2nd ed. 160p. 1981. pap. 2.25 (ISBN 0-89636-067-9). Accent Bks.
Phalon, Richard. Your Money. (Illus.). 320p. 1981. 5.95 (ISBN 0-312-89823-1). St Martin.
Purgraski, Carolyn B., et al. Sorting Out Money Values & Student Packet of Ready-to-Be-Duplicated Worksheets. rev. ed. (Sorting Life Out Ser.). 292p. 1981. tchr's. ed. 25.00 (ISBN 0-930004-02-7); student packet, 68p. free. C E M Comp.
Rathbone, David. How to Keep the Money You Owe: One Hundred One (Legal(Ways to Confound Your Creditors. (Illus.). 70p. (Orig.). 1981. pap. 10.00. Phoenix Laguna.
Rogers, Mary & Joyce, Nancy. Women & Money. 1979. pap. 2.25 (ISBN 0-686-68425-7, 46003). Avon.
Warner, Ralph & Honigsberg, Peter. California Debtor's Handbook. 3rd ed. 1979. pap. 5.95 (ISBN 0-917316-14-2). Nolo Pr.
Weiss, Martin D. The Great Money Panic: A Guide for Survival & Action. (Illus.). 256p. 1981. 15.95 (ISBN 0-87000-502-2). Arlington Hse.
Wolf, Harold. Personal Finance. 6th ed. 700p. 1981. 19.95 (ISBN 0-205-07298-4, 1072986); tchr's ed. free (ISBN 0-205-07299-2, 1072994). Allyn.

FINANCE, PUBLIC
see also Bonds; Budget; Expenditures, Public; Government Spending Policy; Grants-In-Aid; Intergovernmental Fiscal Relations; Loans; Money; Municipal Finance; Paper Money; Taxation; Taxation, State also subdivision Finance under special subjects, e.g. Education–Finance; World War, 1939-1945–Finance

Coe, Charles K. Maximizing Revenue: Minimizing Expenditure. 76p. (Orig.). 1981. pap. 7.50 (ISBN 0-89854-070-4). U of GA Inst Govt.
Wheaton, William C., ed. Interregional Movements & Regional Growth. (Papers on Public Economics Ser.: Vol. 2). 253p. (Orig.). 1980. pap. 7.50 (ISBN 0-87766-257-6, 26600). Urban Inst.

FINANCE, PUBLIC–UNITED STATES
see also Taxation, State
Coghland, Richard & Sykes, Carolyn. Managing the Money Supply. 224p. 1980. 21.00x (ISBN 0-85941-164-8, Pub. by Woodhead-Faulkner England). State Mutual Bk.

FINANCIAL ACCOUNTING
see Accounting
FINANCIAL INSTITUTIONS
see also Banks and Banking; Insurance Companies
Seitz, Neil & Yeager, Frederick. Financial Institution Management. 450p. 1982. text ed. 18.95 (ISBN 0-8359-2022-4); instr's. manual free (ISBN 0-8359-2023-2). Reston.

FINANCIAL NEWS
see Newspapers–Sections, Columns, etc.
FINANCIAL STATEMENTS
see also subdivision Accounting under special subjects, e.g. Agriculture–Accounting

Compilation & Review of Financial Statements. (Statements on Standards for Accounting & Review Services Ser.: No. 1). 1978. pap. 1.50. Am Inst CPA.
Illustrations of Auditors' Reports on Comparitve Financial Statements. (Financial Report Survey Ser.: No. 18). 1979. pap. 9.50. Am Inst CPA.
Langer, Steven, ed. The Accounting-Financial Report: Industry-Government-Education-Non-Profit, Pt. II. 2nd ed. 1981. pap. 75.00 (ISBN 0-916506-61-4). Abbott Langer Assocs.
--The Accounting-Financial Report: Public Accounting Firms, Pt. I. 2nd ed. 1981. pap. 75.00 (ISBN 0-916506-60-6). Abbott Langer Assocs.
--Available Pay Survey Reports: An Annotated Bibliography, Pts. 2 & 3. 2nd ed. 1980. Pt. 1. pap. 39.50 (ISBN 0-916506-45-2); Pt. 2. pap. 19.50 (ISBN 0-916506-46-0). Abbott Langer Assocs.
Management Reports on Financial Statements. (Financial Report Survey Ser.: No. 19). 1980. pap. 9.00. Am Inst CPA.
Reporting on Comparative Financial Statements. (Statements on Standards for Accounting & Review Services Ser.: No. 2). 1979. pap. 1.50. Am Inst CPA.
Stockwell, Herbert G. How to Read a Financial Statement: Adapted Especially to Needs of Credit Men, Bankers & Investors. 443p. 1980. Repr. of 1925 ed. lib. bdg. 30.00 (ISBN 0-8495-5049-1). Arden Lib.

FINCH, PETER
Harrris, Leonard. The Hamptons. 1981. 13.95 (ISBN 0-671-61000-7, Wyndham Bks). S&S.

FINCHES
Roberts, Mervin F. Breeding Zebra Finches. (Illus.). 96p. 1980. 2.95 (ISBN 0-87666-883-X, KW-056). TFH Pubns.

FINDING LISTS
see Library Catalogs
FINE ARTS
see Art; Arts, the
FINGER ALPHABET
see Deaf–Means of Communication
FINGER-PRESSURE THERAPY
see Shiatsu
FINGERPRINTS
Katz, Marjorie P. Fingerprint Owls & Other Fantasies. Katz, Herbert M., ed. LC 72-85648. (Illus.). 54p. 1981. pap. 3.95 (ISBN 0-87131-341-3). M Evans.
Wertelecki, Wladimir & Plato, Chris C., eds. Dermatoglyphics Fifty Years Later. LC 79-2595. (Alan R. Liss Ser.: Vol. 15, No. 6). 1979. 76.00 (ISBN 0-8451-1031-4). March of Dimes.

FINISHES AND FINISHING
see also Metals–Finishing; Paint; Wood Finishing
Gillies, M. T., ed. Solventless & High Solids Industrial Finishes: Recent Developments. LC 80-21553. (Chemical Technology Review: No. 179). (Illus.). 342p. 1981. 48.00 (ISBN 0-8155-0828-X). Noyes.

FINISHING, FURNITURE
see Furniture Finishing
FINITE ARITHMETIC
see Modular Arithmetic
FINITE AUTOMATA
see Sequential Machine Theory
FINITE DIFFERENCES
see Difference Equations
FINITE ELEMENT METHOD
Becker, Eric B., et al. Finite Elements: An Introduction, Vol. I. (Illus.). 256p. 1981. 24.95 (ISBN 0-13-317057-8). P-H.
Mercier, B. Lectures on Topics in Finite Element Solution of Elliptic Problems. (Tata Institute Lectures on Mathematics). (Illus.). 191p. 1980. pap. 8.00 (ISBN 0-387-09543-8). Springer-Verlag.

FINITE GROUPS
Gashutz, W. Lectures on Subgroups of Sylow Type in Finite Soluble Groups. Kuhn, U., tr. (Notes on Pure Mathematics Ser.: No. 11). 100p. (Orig.). 1980. pap. text ed. 7.95 (ISBN 0-908160-22-4, 0571). Bks Australia.
Jones, Vaughan. Actions of Finite Groups on the Hyperfinite Type II (to the First Power) Factor. LC 80-22560. (Memoirs Ser.: No. 237). 4.40 (ISBN 0-8218-2237-3, MEMO-237). Am Math.
Reiner, Irving & Curtis, Charles W. Representation Theory of Finite Groups & Orders. (Pure & Applied Mathematics: Texts, Monographs & Tracts). 900p. 1981. 60.00 (ISBN 0-471-18994-4, Pub. by Wiley-Interscience). Wiley.
Tsuzuku, T. Finite Groups & Finite Geometrics. (Cambridge Tracts in Mathematics Ser.: No. 78). (Illus.). 250p. Date not set. price not set (ISBN 0-521-22242-7). Cambridge U Pr.

FINLAND
Central Statistical Office of Finland. Statistical Yearbook of Finland, 1978. 75th ed. Laakso, Elia, ed. LC 59-42150. (Illus.). 577p. (Eng, Finnish, Swed.). 1980. vinyl bnd. 38.00x (ISBN 0-8002-2731-X). Intl Pubns Serv.

FINLAND–FOREIGN RELATIONS
Paasivirt, Juhani. Finland & Europe: The Period of Autonomy & the International Crises, 1808-1914. Kirby, D. G., ed. Upton, Anthony F., tr. from Finnish. (The Nordic Ser.: Vol. 7). 300p. 1981. 29.50x (ISBN 0-8166-1046-0). U of Minn Pr.

FINLAND–HISTORY
see also Russo-Finnish War, 1939-1940
Erfurth, Waldemar. Last Finnish War. 1979. 22.00 (ISBN 0-89093-205-0). U Pubns Amer.

FINLAND–POLITICS AND GOVERNMENT
Paasivirt, Juhani. Finland & Europe: The Period of Autonomy & the International Crises, 1808-1914. Kirby, D. G., ed. Upton, Anthony F., tr. from Finnish. (The Nordic Ser.: Vol. 7). 300p. 1981. 29.50x (ISBN 0-8166-1046-0). U of Minn Pr.

FINLAND–SOCIAL LIFE AND CUSTOMS
Irwin, John L. The Finns & the Lapps: How They Live & Work. 171p. 1973. text ed. 8.95 (ISBN 0-03-030206-4, HoltC). HR&W.
Rajanen, Aini. Of Finnish Ways. LC 80-28932. (Heritage Books). (Illus.). 232p. 1981. 8.95 (ISBN 0-87518-214-3). Dillon.

FINNO-HUNGARIAN LANGUAGES
see Finno-Ugrian Languages
FINNO-RUSSIAN WAR, 1939-1940
see Russo-Finnish War, 1939-1940
FINNO-UGRIAN LANGUAGES
see also Cheremissian Language
Sinor, Denis, ed. Studies in Finno-Ugric Linguistics: In Honor of Alo Raun. (Indiana University Uralic & Altaic Ser.: Vol. 131). 440p. 1977. 70.00 (ISBN 0-933070-00-4). Ind U Res Inst.

FINNS IN THE UNITED STATES
Hannula, Reino N. Blueberry God: The Education of a Finnish-American. LC 80-54183. 1981. 12.00 (ISBN 0-9605044-0-0). Quality Hill.

FIRE-DEPARTMENT PUMPERS
see Fire-Engines
FIRE-DEPARTMENTS–JUVENILE LITERATURE
Loeper, John. By Hook & Ladder. LC 80-36738. (Illus.). 96p. (gr. 4-6). 1981. PLB 7.95 (ISBN 0-689-30816-7). Atheneum.

FIRE-ENGINES
Fire Engines. (Golden Sturdy Shape Bks.). (Illus.). 14p. (ps). 1981. 2.95 (ISBN 0-307-12263-8, Golden Pr). Western Pub.

FIRE EXTINCTION
see also Fire Fighters; Fire-Engines
IFSTA Committee. Fire Service Rescue Practices. 5th ed. Carlson, Gene, ed. (IFSTA Ser.: No. 108). 1981. pap. 7.00 (ISBN 0-87939-044-1). Intl Fire Serv.
Mann, Philip. Bomba de Incendios. Kreps, Georgian, tr. from Eng. (Shape Board Play Book). Orig. Title: Fire Engines. (Illus., Span.). (ps-3). 1981. bds. 3.50 plastic comb bdg (ISBN 0-89828-202-0, 5006SP). Tuffy Bks.

FIRE FIGHTERS
Earnest, Ernest. The Volunteer Fire Company. LC 78-8785. (Illus.). 224p. 1980. pap. 6.95 (ISBN 0-8128-6094-2). Stein & Day.
Hamilton, Richard & Barnard, Charles N. Twenty Thousand Alarms. LC 74-33553. 256p. 1981. pap. 2.50 (ISBN 0-87216-810-7). Playboy Pbks.
ISTA Committee. Fire Service Instructor Training. 4th ed. Carlson, Gene, ed. (Illus.). 1981. pap. text ed. 7.00 (ISBN 0-87939-045-X, IFSTA 302). Intl Fire Serv.
McGannon, Robert E. Firefighter, F. D. 7th ed. LC 80-25047. 256p. (Orig.). 1981. pap. 8.00 (ISBN 0-668-05170-1, 5170). Arco.
Wallington, Neil. Firemen at War: The Work of London's Firefighters in the Second World War. LC 80-68692. (Illus.). 160p. 1981. 19.95 (ISBN 0-7153-7964-X). David & Charles.

FIRE FIGHTING
see Fire Extinction
FIRE PREVENTION
see also Fire Extinction; Fire Fighters; Fireproofing also subdivision Fires and Fire Prevention under various classes of institutions and buildings, e.g. Schools–Fires and Fire Prevention
Bhatnagar, ViJay M., ed. Fire Retardants: Proceeding of the First European Conference on Flammability & Fire Retardants. LC 78-66105. 1979. pap. 35.00 (ISBN 0-87762-264-7). Technomic.

Commerce & Community Affairs Dept. Fire Protection Administration for Small Communities & Fire Protection Districts. LC 79-93086. (Illus.). 1980. pap. text ed. 15.00 (ISBN 0-87939-037-9). Intl Fire Serv.
Earnest, Ernest. The Volunteer Fire Company. LC 78-8785. (Illus.). 224p. 1980. pap. 6.95 (ISBN 0-8128-6094-2). Stein & Day.
Marchant. Design for Fire Safety. 1981. text ed. price not set (ISBN 0-408-00487-8). Butterworth.
Vervalin, Charles H., ed. Fire Protection Manual for Hydrocarbon Processing Plants, Vol. 2. (Illus.). 300p. 1981. text ed. 49.95 (ISBN 0-87201-288-3). Gulf Pub.

FIRE PROOFING
see Fireproofing

FIRE PUMPS
see Fire-Engines

FIRE RESISTANT POLYMERS
Critser, James R., Jr. Flame Retardants for Plastics, Rubber, Textiles & Paper: Series No. 2-7980, July 1979 - June 1980. 136p. 1981. refer. - ring bdg. 110.00 (ISBN 0-914428-73-X). Lexington Data.

FIREARMS
see also Air Guns; Rifles; Shooting; Shot-Guns
also names of specific kinds of firearms, e.g. Colt Revolver; Machine Guns; Mauser Rifle; Winchester Rifle
Muller, Heinrich. Guns, Pistols, & Revolvers. LC 80-52998. (Illus.). 240p. 1981. 29.95 (ISBN 0-312-35392-8). St Martin.
Sellers, Frank. Sharp's Firearms. LC 77-71186. 358p. 1978. 34.95 (ISBN 0-917714-12-1). Beinfeld Pub.

FIREARMS-COLLECTORS AND COLLECTING
Madaus, H. Michael. The Warner Collector's Guide to American Long Arms. (Orig.). 1981. pap. 9.95 (ISBN 0-446-97628-8). Warner Bks.
Pocket Guide to Guns. (Illus.). 1980. pap. 1.95 (ISBN 0-89145-154-4). Collector Bks.

FIREARMS-HISTORY
Bianchi, John. Blue Steel & Gunleather. Mason, James D., ed. (Illus.). 213p. 1978. 9.95 (ISBN 0-917714-15-6). Beinfeld Pub.
Cooper, Jeff. Fireworks: A Gunsite Anthology. LC 80-83992. 1981. 19.95 (ISBN 0-916172-07-4). Janus Pr.
Hamilton, T. M., ed. Indian Trade Guns. 10.95 (ISBN 0-913150-43-6). Pioneer Pr.
Oakeshott, Ewart. European Weapons & Armour. (Illus.). 277p. 1980. 29.95 (ISBN 0-686-68855-4). Beinfeld Pub.

FIREARMS-IDENTIFICATION
Hill, Richard T. & Anthony, William E. Confederate Longarms & Pistols: A Pictorial Study. Hill, Olivia R., ed. (Illus.). 304p. 1978. 29.95 (ISBN 0-87833-309-6); lib. bdg. 26.95 (ISBN 0-686-28758-4). Confed Arms.
Madaus, H. Michael. The Warner Collector's Guide to American Long Arms. (Orig.). 1981. pap. 9.95 (ISBN 0-446-97628-8). Warner Bks.
Suydam, Charles R. U. S. Cartridges & Their Handguns. (Illus.). 333p. 1976. 15.95 (ISBN 0-917714-04-0); pap. 9.95 (ISBN 0-917714-07-5). Beinfeld Pub.

FIREARMS-LAWS AND REGULATIONS
Cook, Philip J. & Lambert, Richard D., eds. Gun Control. (The Annals of the American Academy of Political & Social Science Ser.: No. 455). 250p. 1981. 7.50x (ISBN 0-87761-262-5); pap. 6.00x (ISBN 0-87761-263-3). Am Acad Pol Soc Sci.
Kates, Dan B. Restricting Handguns: The Liberal Sceptics Speak Out. 9.95 (ISBN 0-88427-033-5). Green Hill.

FIREARMS CONTROL
see Firearms-Laws and Regulations

FIREARMS INDUSTRY AND TRADE
see also Gunsmithing
Bleile, C. Roger. American Engravers. (Illus.). 191p. 1980. 29.95 (ISBN 0-917714-29-6). Beinfeld Pub.

FIREFIGHTERS
see Fire Fighters

FIREMEN
see Fire Fighters

FIREPROOFING
see also Fire Resistant Polymers
Bhatnagar, ViJay M., ed. Fire Retardants: Proceeding of the First European Conference on Flammability & Fire Retardants. LC 78-66105. 1979. pap. 35.00 (ISBN 0-87762-264-7). Technomic.
Marchant. Design for Fire Safety. 1981. text ed. price not set (ISBN 0-408-00487-8). Butterworth.

FIRES IN SHIPS
see Ships-Fires and Fire Prevention

FIREWOOD
see Wood As Fuel

FIRMS
see Business Enterprises

FIRST AID FOR ANIMALS
Walker, Ernest P. & Animal Welfare Institute, eds. First Aid & Care of Small Animals. rev. ed. (Illus.). 54p. 1980. pap. text ed. 2.00 (ISBN 0-938414-04-6). Animal Welfare.

FIRST AID IN ILLNESS AND INJURY
see also Accidents; Burns and Scalds; Emergency Medical Services; Medical Emergencies
Advice About First Aid, High Blood Pressure, Heart Attack. (Home Adviser Ser.). 80p. (Orig.). 1981. pap. 1.95 (ISBN 0-8326-2404-7, 7054). Delair.
The American Medical Association's Handbook of First Aid & Emergency Care. (Illus.). 1980. pap. 5.95 (ISBN 0-394-73668-0). Random.
Barber, Janet & Dillman, Peter. Emergency Patient Care for the EMT: A Guide for the EMT. 1981. 15.95 (ISBN 0-8359-1671-5). Reston.
Boy Scouts of America. First Aid. (Illus.). 56p. (gr. 6-12). 1981. pap. 0.70x. BSA.
Brennan, William T. & Crowe, James W. Guide to Problems & Practices in First Aid & Emergency Care. 4th ed. 192p. 1981. wire coil 7.95x (ISBN 0-697-07390-4). Wm C Brown.
Hartunian, Paul. Lifesavers: A Guide to Free First Aid, Health & Safety Information. 50p. (Orig.). 1981. pap. 3.95. Tri-Med.
Madda, Frank C., ed. Outdoor Emergency Medicine. (Illus.). 277p. (Orig.). 1981. pap. 3.95 (ISBN 0-938278-00-2). BioServ Corp.
Medical First Aid Guide for Use in Accidents Involving Dangerous Goods. (Illus.). 147p. 1973. 16.50 (IMCO). Unipub.
Renouf, Jane & Hulse, Stewart. First Aid for Hill Walkers & Climbers. (Illus.). 169p. 1978. pap. 5.95 (ISBN 0-14-046293-7). Bradt Ent.
Scott, R. W. Handy Medical Guide for Seafarers: Fishermen, Trawlermen & Yachtsmen. (Illus.). 96p. 7.50 (ISBN 0-85238-007-0, FN). Unipub.
Survival First Aid: Practical Guide to Life's Presercation in Wars & Cataclysms for Self & Others. Skills &Preparedness. LC 80-84992. (Illus.). 1981. 10.00 (ISBN 0-916508-14-5); pap. 8.00 (ISBN 0-686-69456-2). Happiness Pr.

FISCAL EVASION
see Tax Evasion

FISCAL RELATIONS, INTERGOVERNMENTAL
see Intergovernmental Fiscal Relations

FISH
see Fishes

FISH AS FOOD
see also Cookery (Sea Food)
Kreuzer, Rudolf, ed. Freezing & Irradiation of Fish. (Illus.). 548p. 41.25 (ISBN 0-85238-008-9, FN). Unipub.
Mutkoski, Stephen A. & Schurer, Marcia L. Meat & Fish Management for Food Service. 1981. text ed. 17.95 (ISBN 0-534-00907-7, Breton Pubs). Wadsworth Pub.
O'Farrell, R. C. Seafood Fishing for Amateur & Professional. (Illus.). 196p. 10.00 (ISBN 0-85238-097-6, FN). Unipub.
Papers Presented at the FAO-SIDA Workshop on the Use of Organic Materials As Fertilizers in Africa: Organic Recycling in Africa. 308p. 1981. pap. 16.50 (ISBN 92-5-100945-7, F2096, FAO). Unipub.
Report of the EIFAC, IUNS & ICES Working Group on the Standardization of Methodology in Fish Nutrition Research. (EIFAC Technical Paper Ser.: No. 36). 24p. 1980. pap. 6.75 (ISBN 92-5-100918-X, F2048, FAO). Unipub.

FISH BY-PRODUCTS
see Fishery Products

FISH-CULTURE
see also Aquariums
Axelrod, Herbert R. Breeding Aquarium Fishes, Bk.6. (Illus.). 288p. 1980. 12.95 (ISBN 0-87666-536-9, H-995). TFH Pubns.
Hepher, Dalfour & Pruginin, Yoel. Commercial Fish Farming: With Special Reference to Fish Culture in Israel. 250p. 1981. 25.00 (ISBN 0-686-69368-X, Pub. by Wiley-Interscience). Wiley.
Huet, Marcel. Textbook of Fish Culture: Breeding & Cultivation of Fish. (Illus.). 454p. 41.25 (ISBN 0-85238-020-8, FN). Unipub.
McNeil, William J. & Himsworth, Daniel C., eds. Salmonid Ecosystems of the North Pacific. LC 80-17800. (Illus.). 348p. pap. 15.00 (ISBN 0-87071-335-3); pap. text ed. 15.00 (ISBN 0-686-68208-4). Oreg St U Pr.
Report on the Fourth Session of the Cooperative Programme of Research on Aquaculture of the General Fisheries Council for the Mediterranean. (FAO Fisheries Report: No. 232). 32p. 1981. pap. 6.00 (ISBN 92-5-100927-9, F2068, FAO). Unipub.

FISH FARMING
see Fish-Culture

FISH HATCHERIES
see Fish-Culture

FISH LAW
see Fishery Law and Legislation

FISH POPULATIONS
Nikolskii, G. V. Theory of Fish Population Dynamics As the Biological Background for Rational Exploitation & Management of Fishery Resources. Jones, R., ed. Bradley, J. E., tr. from Rus. (Illus.). 323p. 1980. Repr. of 1969 ed. lib. bdg. 43.25x (ISBN 3-87429-171-5). Lubrecht & Cramer.
A Review of the World Resources of Mesopelagic Fish. (FAO Fish Tech Paper: No. 193). 151p. 1981. pap. 8.50 (ISBN 92-5-100924-4, F2074, FAO). Unipub.
Stokes, F. Joseph. Handguide to the Coral Reef Fishes of the Caribbean. LC 79-27224. (Illus.). 160p. 1980. 9.95 (ISBN 0-690-01919-X). Lippincott & Crowell.

FISH TRADE
see also Fishery Products
Mead, John T. Marine Refrigeration & Fish Preservation. rev. ed. LC 80-25359. (Illus.). 1980. 25.00 (ISBN 0-912524-19-7). Busn News.
Nowak, W. S. The Marketing of Shellfish. (Illus.). 280p. 15.25 (ISBN 0-85238-010-0, FN). Unipub.
OECD. Financial Support to the Fishing Industry. (Illus.). 161p. (Orig.). 1980. pap. 6.50x (ISBN 92-64-12087-4, 53-80-01-1). OECD.

FISH WASTE
see Fishery Products

FISHERIES
see also Fish Trade; Fishes; Fishing Boats; Trawls and Trawling
Clepper, Henry, ed. Marine Recreational Fisheries, Vol. 5. LC 76-22389. 1980. 15.00. Sport Fishing.
Comparitive Studies on Fresh-Water Fisheries. (FAO Fisheries Technical Paper: No. 198). 54p. 1981. pap. 6.00 (ISBN 92-5-100952-X, FAO). Unipub.
FAO Species Catalogue, Vol. 1: Shrimps & Prawns of the World; an Annotated Catalogue of Species of Interest to Fisheries. (FAO Fisheries Synopsis Ser.: No. 125, Vol. 1). 287p. 1980. pap. 15.50 (ISBN 92-5-100896-5, F1939, FAO). Unipub.
General Fisheries Council for the Mediterranean. Report of the First Session of the Working Party on Acoustic Methods for Fish Detection & Abundance Estimation of the General Fisheries Council for the Mediterranean. (FAO Fisheries Report: No. 231). 27p. 1980. pap. 6.00 (ISBN 92-5-100928-7, F2039, FAO). Unipub.
Hart, Paul & Pitcher, Tony. Fisheries Ecology. 224p. 1980. 35.00x (ISBN 0-85664-894-9, Pub. by Croom Helm England). State Mutual Bk.
Hela, Ilmo & Laevastu, Taivo. Fisheries Oceanography. (Illus.). 254p. 22.00 (ISBN 0-85238-009-7, FN). Unipub.
Lackey, Robert T. Fisheries Management. LC 80-20028. 422p. 1980. 34.95 (ISBN 0-470-27056-X). Halsted Pr.
Manual of Fisheries Science, Pt. 2: Methods of Resource Investigation & Their Application. (FAO Fisheries Technical Paper Ser.: No. 115, Rev. 1). 224p. Date not set. pap. 14.50 (ISBN 92-5-100842-6, F854, FAO). Unipub.
Manual of Methods for Fish Stock Assessment, Pt. II: Tables of Yield Functions. rev. ed. (FAO Fisheries Technical Paper Ser.: No. 38, Rev. 1). 1980. pap. 6.00 (ISBN 92-5-000840-6, F848, FAO). Unipub.
OECD. Financial Support to the Fishing Industry. (Illus.). 161p. (Orig.). 1980. pap. 6.50x (ISBN 92-64-12087-4, 53-80-01-1). OECD.
--Review of Fisheries in OECD Member Countries Nineteen Seventy-Nine. (Illus.). 253p. (Orig.). 1980. pap. 12.00 (ISBN 92-64-12103-X). OECD.
Report of the ACMRR Working Party on the Scientific Basis of Determining Management Measures. (FAO Fisheries Report Ser.: No. 236). 149p. 1980. pap. 10.50 (ISBN 92-5-100938-4, F2051, FAO). Unipub.
Report of the Fifteenth FAO Regional Conference for Asia & the Pacific. 97p. 1981. pap. 6.00 (ISBN 92-5-100963-5, F2084, FAO). Unipub.
Report of the Sixth Session of the Fishery Committee for the Eastern Central Atlantic (CECAF) (FAO Fisheries Report: No. 229). 70p. 1980. pap. 6.00 (ISBN 92-5-100900-7, F1952, FAO). Unipub.
Report of the Sixth Session of the Indian Ocean Fishery Commission. (FAO Fisheries Report: No. 234). 35p. 1981. pap. 6.00 (ISBN 92-5-100930-9, F2088, FAO). Unipub.
Report of the Thirs Session of the Committee on Resource Managment of the General Fisheries Council for the Mediterranean. (FAO Fisheries Report: No. 240). 20p. 1981. pap. 6.00 (ISBN 92-5-100966-X, F2087, FAO). Unipub.
Trilingual Dictionary of Fisheries Technological Terms-Curing. (FAO Fisheries Ser.: No. 12). 91p. 1980. pap. 10.25 (ISBN 0-686-68188-6, F483, FAO). Unipub.

FISHERIES-BIBLIOGRAPHY
World List of Aquatic Sciences & Fisheries Serial Titles. (FAO Fisheries Technical Paper: No. 147). 128p. 1980. pap. 7.00 (ISBN 92-5-100904-X, F1946, FAO). Unipub.
World List of Aquatic Sciences & Fisheries Serial Titles. (FAO Fisheries Technical Paper: No. 148). 128p. 1980. pap. 6.00 (ISBN 92-5-000882-1, F1947, FAO). Unipub.

FISHERIES-LAW
see Fishery Law and Legislation

FISHERIES-STATISTICS
Report of the Technical Consultation on the Assessment & Management of the Black Sea Turbot (GFCM) Working Party on Resource Evaluation & Fishery Statistics. 23p. 1980. pap. 7.50 (ISBN 92-5-100879-5, F1964, FAO). Unipub.

FISHERIES-AFRICA
Papers Presented at the FAO-SIDA Workshop on the Use of Organic Materials As Fertilizers in Africa: Organic Recycling in Africa. 308p. 1981. pap. 16.50 (ISBN 92-5-100945-7, F2096, FAO). Unipub.

FISHERIES-AUSTRALIA
Pownall, Peter. Fisheries of Australia. (Illus.). 160p. 1979. 20.50 (ISBN 0-85238-101-8, FN). Unipub.

FISHERIES-INDIA
Indian Ocean Fishery Commission. Report of the Sixth Joint Meeting of the Indian Ocean Fishery Commission, Committee on Management of Indian Ocean Tuna. 18p. 1980. pap. 6.00 (ISBN 92-5-100939-2, F2045, FAO). Unipub.
Papers Presented at the Indo-Pacific Fisheries Commission Workshop on Fish Silage Production & Its Use. (FAO Fisheries Report: No. 230). 1980. pap. 6.00 (ISBN 92-5-100921-X, F1940, FAO). Unipub.

FISHERIES-NORWAY
S. E. Haugan Consulting. Fish Versus Oil. 1980. 50.00x (Pub. by Norwegian Info Norway). State Mutual Bk.
Underal, Arild. The Politics of International Fisheries Management. 234p. 1981. pap. 20.00x. Universitet.

FISHERMEN
Seufert, Francis A. Wheels of Fortune. Vaughan, Thomas, ed. LC 80-81719. (Illus.). 304p. 1981. 19.95 (ISBN 0-87595-083-3); pap. 12.95 (ISBN 0-87595-069-8). Oreg Hist Soc.

FISHERY LAW AND LEGISLATION
see also Sealing
McLeod, G. C. Georges Bank: Past, Present, & Future. (Special Studies on Natural Resources & Energy Management). 225p. 1981. lib. bdg. 22.00x (ISBN 0-86531-199-4). Westview.

FISHERY METHODS
see Fisheries

FISHERY PRODUCTS
see also Canning and Preserving
Papers Presented at the Indo-Pacific Fisheries Commission Workshop on Fish Silage Production & Its Use. (FAO Fisheries Report: No. 230). 1980. pap. 6.00 (ISBN 92-5-100921-X, F1940, FAO). Unipub.
Scheuer, Paul J., ed. Marine Natural Products: Chemical & Biological Perspectives, Vol. 4. 1981. price not set (ISBN 0-12-624004-3). Acad Pr.

FISHES
see also Aquariums; Fish As Food; Fish-Culture; Fisheries; Fishing; Tropical Fish;
also names of classes, orders, etc. of fishes, e.g. Bass, salmon
Advances in Fish Science & Technology. 512p. 1980. pap. 95.00 (ISBN 0-85238-108-5, FN 87, FN). Unipub.
Anderson, Lee. Economic Analysis of Fisheries Management Plans. 300p. 1981. text ed. 49.95 (ISBN 0-250-40389-7). Ann Arbor Science.
Casier, Edgar. Faune Ichthyologique Du London Clay: Text & Atlas. (Illus.). xiv, 496p. 1966. 87.50x (ISBN 0-565-00654-1, Pub. by British Mus Nat Hist England). Sabbot-Natural Hist Bks.
Gordon, Bernard L. Secret Lives of Fishes. rev. ed. (Illus.). 306p. 1980. pap. text ed. 7.95 (ISBN 0-910258-12-0). Book & Tackle.
McNeil, William J. & Himsworth, Daniel C., eds. Salmonid Ecosystems of the North Pacific. LC 80-17800. (Illus.). 348p. pap. 15.00 (ISBN 0-87071-335-3); pap. text ed. 15.00 (ISBN 0-686-68208-4). Oreg St U Pr.
The New Alchemy Backyard Fish Farm Book. 100p. 1981. pap. 4.95 (ISBN 0-931790-21-2). Brick Hse Pub.
Oren, O. H., ed. Aquaculture of Grey Mullets. LC 79-53405. (International Biological Programme: No. 26). (Illus.). 450p. Date not set. price not set (ISBN 0-521-22926-X). Cambridge U Pr.

FISHES-COLLECTION AND PRESERVATION
Midgalski, Edward C. How to Make Fish Mounts & Other Fish Trophies. 2nd ed. 288p. 1981. 15.95 (ISBN 0-471-07990-1, Pub. by Wiley-Interscience). Wiley.
Phillips, Archie & Phillips, Bubba. How to Mount Fish. (Illus.). 144p. 1981. 19.95 (ISBN 0-8117-0787-3). Stackpole.

FISHES-DISEASES
Doudoroff, Peter. A Critical Review of Recent Literature on Toxicity of Cyanides to Fish. LC 80-68588. 71p. (Orig.). 1980. pap. 3.60 (ISBN 0-89364-039-5, API 847-87000). Am Petroleum.
Roberts, Ronald J. & Shepherd, C. Jonathan. Handbook of Trout & Salmon Diseases. (Illus.). 172p. 21.25 (ISBN 0-85238-066-6, FN). Unipub.

FISHES-EMBRYOLOGY
see Embryology-Fishes

FISHES-FOOD
Fish Feed Technology: Lectures Presented at the FAO - UNDP Training Course in Fish Feed Technology. (Agriculture Development Coordination Programme Ser.), 400p. 1980. pap. 21.50 (ISBN 92-5-100901-5, F1944, FAO). Unipub.

FISHES-JUVENILE LITERATURE
Noel, Spike. Fish & the Sea. (Junior Reference Ser.). (Illus.). 64p. (gr. 7 up). 1972. 7.95 (ISBN 0-7136-1239-8). Dufour.

FISHES-PHYSIOLOGY
Ali, M. A., ed. Environmental Physiology of Fishes. (NATO Advanced Study Institutes Ser, A-Life Sciences: Vol. 35). 685p. 1981. 69.50 (ISBN 0-306-40574-1, Plenum Pr). Plenum Pub.
Silva, Tony & Kotlar, Barbara. Discus. (Illus.). 98p. 1980. 2.95 (ISBN 0-87666-535-0, KW-097). TFH Pubns.

FISHES-AFRICA
Voss, J. Color Patterns of African Cichlids. Orig. Title: Les Livrees Ou Patrons De Coloration Chezles Poissons Chichlides Africains. (Illus.). 128p. 1980. 7.95 (ISBN 0-87666-503-2, PS-755). TFH Pubns.

FISHES–ATLANTIC COAST
Hildebrand, Samuel F. & Schroeder, William C. The Fishes of the Chesapeake Bay. LC 72-5565. (Illus.). 388p. 1972. Repr. of 1928 ed. 8.00x. Smithsonian.
FISHES–AUSTRALIA
Thomson, J. M. A Field Guide to the Common Sea & Estuary Fishes of Ono-Tropical Australia. 144p. 1980. 17.95x (ISBN 0-00-219271-3, Pub. by W Collins Ausftralia). Intl Schol Bk Serv.
FISHES–CANADA
Shrimps of the Pacific Coast of Canada. 280p. 1981. 32.50 (ISBN 0-660-10177-7, SSC 148, SSC). Unipub.
FISHES–GREAT BRITAIN
Varley, Margaret. British Freshwater Fishes: Factors Affecting Their Distribution. (Illus.). 148p. 15.00 (ISBN 0-85238-107-7, FN). Unipub.
FISHES–LATIN AMERICA
Smith, Nigel J. Man, Fishes, & the Amazon. 176p. 1981. 20.00x (ISBN 0-231-05156-5). Columbia U Pr.
FISHES–NEW ZEALAND
McDowall, R. M. Freshwater Fish in New Zealand. (Mobil New Zealand Nature Ser.). (Illus.). 80p. (Orig.). 1980. pap. 6.95 (ISBN 0-589-01327-0, Pub. by Reed Bks Australia). C E Tuttle.
FISHES–PACIFIC OCEAN
Walford, Lionel A. Marine Fishes of the Pacific Coast from Alaska to the Equator. LC 74-80976. 205p. 1975. Repr. of 1937 ed. 15.00x (ISBN 0-87474-153-X). Smithsonian.
FISHES–UNITED STATES
Naiman, Robert J. & Solt, David L. Fishes in North American Deserts. 360p. 1981. 35.00 (ISBN 0-471-08523-5, Pub. by Wiley-Interscience). Wiley.
FISHES, TROPICAL
see Tropical Fish
FISHING
see also Bait; Bass Fishing; Fishery Law and Legislation; Fly Fishing; Salmon Fishing; Spin Fishing; Trout Fishing
Becker, A. C., Jr. The Complete Book of Fishing. LC 76-18477. (Illus.). 217p. 1981. Repr. of 1977 ed. 20.00 (ISBN 0-498-01973-X). A S Barnes.
Berners, Juliana. A Treatise on Fishing with a Hook. 9.95. Green Hill.
Brandt, Andres von. Fish Catching Methods of the World. 2nd ed. (Illus.). 256p. 19.50 (ISBN 0-85238-026-7, FN). Unipub.
Deindorfer, Robert G. Positive Fishing. LC 79-67600. 224p. 1981. 10.95 (ISBN 0-87223-660-9). Seaview Bks.
Foster, Muriel. Days on Sea, Loch & River. (Illus.). 124p. 1981. 4.95 (ISBN 0-7181-1788-3). Merrimack Bk Serv.
Garrison, Chuck. Offshore Fishing: In Southern California & Baja. (Illus., Orig.). 1980. pap. 4.95 (ISBN 0-87701-166-4). Chronicle Bks.
Haig-Brown, Roderick. Bright Waters, Bright Fish. (Illus.). 160p. 1980. 19.95 (ISBN 0-917304-59-4, Timber Pr). Intl Schol Bk.
--Bright Waters, Bright Fish. 1980. ltd. ed. 75.00 (ISBN 0-918400-05-8, Champoeg Pr). Intl Schol Bk.
Hayden, Mike. Pier Fishing on San Francisco Bay. (Illus.). 116p. (Orig.). 1981. pap. 5.95 (ISBN 0-87701-138-9). Chronicle Bks.
Hodson, Alfred. The Fishing Cadet's Handbook. (Illus.). 108p. 7.50 (ISBN 0-85238-011-9, FN). Unipub.
Iversen, Edwin S. Farming the Edge of the Sea. 2nd ed. (Illus.). 440p. 37.50 (ISBN 0-85238-079-8, FN). Unipub.
Judd, Stan. Inshore Fishing: Its Skills, Risks, Rewards. (Illus.). 144p. 10.00 (ISBN 0-85238-096-8, FN). Unipub.
Ketting, Kees & Peeters, Henk. Two Hundred Fishing Tips: Zander. (Illus.). 88p. (Orig.). 1980. pap. 5.00 (ISBN 0-85242-615-1). Intl Pubns Serv.
Lee, Jasper S. Commercial Catfish Farming. 2nd ed. (Illus.). 1981. 10.00 (ISBN 0-8134-2156-X, 2156). Interstate.
McNally, Tom. Pocket Fishing Guide. 1981. pap. 1.95 (ISBN 0-528-84548-9). Rand.
Milne, P. H. Fish & Shellfish Farming in Coastal Waters. (Illus.). 208p. 24.75 (ISBN 0-85238-022-4, FN). Unipub.
Mitchell, John. On the Line. 9.50x (ISBN 0-392-06594-0, SpS). Soccer.
O'Farrell, R. C. Seafood Fishing for Amateur & Professional. (Illus.). 196p. 10.00 (ISBN 0-85238-097-6, FN). Unipub.
Pratt, Mary M. Better Angling with Simple Science. (Illus.). 144p. 9.50 (ISBN 0-85238-069-0, FN). Unipub.
Regulation of Fishing Effort. (FAO Fisheries Technical Paper: No. 197). 82p. 1981. pap. 6.00 (ISBN 92-5-100947-3, F2067, FAO). Unipub.
Sainsbury, John C. Commercial Fishing Methods: An Introduction to Vessels & Gear. (Illus.). 120p. 13.75 (ISBN 0-85238-076-3, FN). Unipub.
Stewart, Hilary. Indian Fishing: Early Methods on the Northwest Coast. LC 77-950. (Illus.). 136p. 1981. pap. 15.00 (ISBN 0-295-95803-0). U of Wash Pr.
Tedone, David. Complete Shellfisherman's Guide. (Illus.). 200p. 1981. pap. 7.95 (ISBN 0-933614-09-8). Peregrine Pr.
Vanderweide, Harry. The Book of Maine Fishing Maps. (Illus.). 96p. (Orig.). 1980. pap. 6.95 (ISBN 0-89933-007-X). DeLorme Pub.
FISHING–ANECDOTES, FACETIAE, ETC.
see Fishing Stories
FISHING–BIBLIOGRAPHY
Glogan, Joseph. Sportsmans Book of U.S. Records. (Illus.). 96p. (Orig.). 1980. pap. text ed. 2.50 (ISBN 0-937328-00-6). NY Hunting.
FISHING–DICTIONARIES
Fisherman's Handbook. (Illus.). 319p. 1980. 37.00 (ISBN 0-85238-106-9, FN85, FN). Unipub.
FISHING–IMPLEMENTS AND APPLIANCES
see also Fishing Tackle
EIFAC Fishing Gear Intercalibration Experiments. 92p. 1980. pap. 7.50 (ISBN 92-5-100864-7, F1954, FAO). Unipub.
Garner, John. Modern Inshore Fishing Gear. 2nd ed. 13.75 (FN). Unipub.
Nedelec, C., ed. FAO Catalogue of Small Scale Fishing Gear. (Illus.). 192p. 24.25 (ISBN 0-85238-077-1, FN). Unipub.
Sainsbury, John C. Commercial Fishing Methods: An Introduction to Vessels & Gear. (Illus.). 120p. 13.75 (ISBN 0-85238-076-3, FN). Unipub.
Wilson, Gloria. More Scottish Fishing Craft & Their Work: Their Work in Great Lining, Small Lining, Seining, Pair Trawling, Drifting, Potting & Trawling. (Illus.). 170p. 8.75 (ISBN 0-85238-048-8, FN). Unipub.
FISHING–JUVENILE LITERATURE
Neimark, Paul. Fishing. (Wilderness World Ser.). (Illus.). 64p. (gr. 3 up). 1981. PLB 9.25 (ISBN 0-516-02452-3). Childrens.
FISHING–GREAT BRITAIN
Wilson, Gloria. More Scottish Fishing Craft & Their Work: Their Work in Great Lining, Small Lining, Seining, Pair Trawling, Drifting, Potting & Trawling. (Illus.). 170p. 8.75 (ISBN 0-85238-048-8, FN). Unipub.
FISHING–NORTH AMERICA
Stearns, Mary Lee. Haida Culture in Custody: The Masset Band. LC 80-50862. (Illus.). 315p. 1980. 24.50 (ISBN 0-295-95763-8). U of Wash Pr.
FISHING–UNITED STATES
Bennett, D. W. Secrets of Striped Bass Fishing. (N. E. Fishing Ser.). (Illus.). 70p. (Orig.). 1981. pap. 6.95 (ISBN 0-88839-103-X). Hancock Hse.
Konizeski, Dick. The Montanans' Fishing Guide: West of the Continental Divide, Vol. I. rev. ed. Fbursk, Dale A., ed. (Illus.). 325p. 1980. pap. 7.95 (ISBN 0-87842-139-4). Mountain Pr.
FISHING BOATS
Pair Trawling with Small Boats. (FAO Training Ser.: No. 1). 77p. 1981. pap. 6.75 (ISBN 92-5-100627-X, F2095, FAO). Unipub.
FISHING LURES
Bennett, D. W. Secrets of Baitfishing. Campbell, M., ed. (North East Fishing Ser.). (Illus.). 128p. 1981. pap. 4.95 (ISBN 0-88839-087-4). Hancock Hse.
FISHING REGULATIONS
see Fishery Law and Legislation
FISHING STORIES
see also American Wit and Humor–Sports and Games
McManus, Patrick. They Shoot Canoes, Don't They? 228p. 1981. 10.95 (ISBN 0-03-058646-1). HR&W.
FISHING TACKLE
Barnard, Philip. The Tackle Box Fishing Guide. LC 78-69685. (Illus.). 128p. 1981. 7.95 (ISBN 0-498-02254-4). A S Barnes.
Kimball, Art & Kimball, Scott. Collecting Old Fishing Tackle. LC 80-122941. (Illus.). 1980. 30.00 (ISBN 0-9604906-0-4); pap. 19.00 (ISBN 0-9604906-1-2). Aardvark Pubs.
FISSION, NUCLEAR
see Nuclear Fission
FITTING (ENGINEERING)
see Machine-Shop Practice
FITZGERALD, FRANCIS SCOTT KEY, 1896-1940
Bruccoli, Matthew J. Some Kind of Epic Grandeur: The Life of F. Scott Fitzgerald. LC 80-8740. (Illus.). 384p. 1981. 17.50 (ISBN 0-15-183242-0). HarBraceJ.
Eble, Kenneth. F. Scott Fitzgerald. LC 77-429. (Twayne's U. S. Authors Ser.). 187p. 1977. pap. text ed. 4.95 (ISBN 0-672-61503-7). Bobbs.
Fitzgerald, F. Scott. Afternoon of an Author. (Hudson River Edition Ser.). 1981. write for info. (ISBN 0-684-16469-8, ScribT). Scribner.
--The Letters of F. Scott Fitzgerald. (Hudson River Edition Ser.). 1981. write for info. (ISBN 0-684-16476-0, ScribT). Scribner.
FITZGERALD, FRANCIS SCOTT KEY, 1896-1940–BIBLIOGRAPHY
Fitzgerald, F. Scott. Great Gatsby. (Hudson River Edition Ser.). 1981. write for info. (ISBN 0-684-16498-1, ScribT). Scribner.
FITZPATRICK, THOMAS, 1799?-1854
Hafen, Leroy R. Broken Hand: The Life of Thomas Fitzpatrick, Mountain Man, Guide & Indian Agent. LC 80-23451. (Illus.). xiv, 359p. 1981. pap. 6.50 (ISBN 0-8032-7208-1, BB 753, Bison). U of Nebr Pr.
FIVE YEAR PLAN (RUSSIA)
see Russia–Economic Policy
FIXED COSTS
see Overhead Costs
FIXED IDEAS
see Hysteria; Obsessive-Compulsive Neuroses
FIXED WING AIRCRAFT
see Airplanes
FLAGS–UNITED STATES
Blotnick, Elihu & Robinson, Barbara. Free-for-All: The Reds, the Whites & the Blues. (Illus.). 64p. (Orig.). 1981. pap. 6.95 (ISBN 0-915090-02-3). Calif Street.
FLAME RETARDANT POLYMERS
see Fire Resistant Polymers
FLASH-LIGHT PHOTOGRAPHY
see Photography, Flash-Light
FLASKS
see Bottles
FLAT RACING
see Horse-Racing
FLATFISHES
Rae, B. Bennet. The Lemon Sole. (Illus.). 108p. 7.00 (ISBN 0-85238-013-5). Unipub.
FLAVORING ESSENCES
Heath, Henry B. Source Book of Flavors. (Illus.). 1981. lib. bdg. 79.50 (ISBN 0-87055-369-0). AVI.
FLEMISH LANGUAGE
see Dutch Language
FLEMISH LITERATURE
De Wit, Joost & Barkan, Stanley H., eds. Fifty Dutch & Flemish Novelists. 220p. 25.00 (ISBN 0-89304-031-2); pap. 15.00 (ISBN 0-89304-032-0). Cross Cult.
FLEMISH PAINTINGS
see Paintings, Flemish
FLESH FOODS
see Animal Food
FLIES
Theodor, Oskar. Diptera: Asilidae Insecta II, Vol. 2. (Fauna Palaestina). (Illus.). 458p. 1981. text ed. 30.00x (ISBN 0-87474-910-7). Smithsonian.
FLIGHT–MEDICAL ASPECTS
see Aviation Medicine
FLIGHT, UNPOWERED
see Gliding and Soaring
FLIGHT ATTENDANTS
see Air Lines–Flight Attendants
FLIGHT ENGINEERING
Aviation Maintenance Publishers. Airframe Logbook. 77p. 1975. pap. 4.95 (ISBN 0-89100-190-5, E*A-A*F*L-1). Aviation Maintenance.
FLIGHT TRAINING
see also Airplanes–Piloting
Crane, Dale. So You Think You Know...? Quiz Book. (Aviation Training Ser.). (Illus.). 297p. 1980. pap. 6.95 (ISBN 0-89100-071-2, E*A-Q*B). Aviation Maintenance.
Federal Aviation Administration. Flight Training Handbook. 2nd ed. (Pilot Training Ser.). (Illus.). 325p. 1980. pap. 7.40 (ISBN 0-89100-165-4, EA-AC61-21A). Aviation Maintenance.
--Flight Training Handbook. LC 80-70552. (Illus.). 352p. 1981. 12.95 (ISBN 0-385-17599-X). Doubleday.
Taylor, S. E. & Parmar, H. A. Ground Studies for Pilots. Incl. Vol. I. Radio Aids. 3rd ed. 200p. 1979. text ed. 26.50x (ISBN 0-246-11169-0); Vol. II. Plotting & Flight Planning. 130p. 1976. text ed. 19.95x (ISBN 0-246-11176-3); Vol. III. Navigation General. 232p. 1979. text ed. 26.50x (ISBN 0-246-11177-1). Pub. by Granada England). Renouf.
Vasko, Donna M. I'd Rather Be Flying. 100p. (Orig.). 1980. pap. 5.95 (ISBN 0-9604308-0-6). Calligraphy Donna.
FLOOD CONTROL
see also Flood Dams and Reservoirs
Institute of Civil Engineers, UK. Reservoir Flood Standards. 1980. pap. 20.00x (ISBN 0-7277-0023-5, Pub. by Telford England). State Mutual Bk.
FLOOD DAMS AND RESERVOIRS
Institute of Civil Engineers, UK. Reservoir Flood Standards. 1980. pap. 20.00x (ISBN 0-7277-0023-5, Pub. by Telford England). State Mutual Bk.
FLOOD PROTECTION
see Flood Control
FLOODS
see also Flood Control; Reclamation of Land; Rivers; also subdivision floods under names of rivers, cities, etc.
Institute of Civil Engineers, UK. Flood Studies Conference. 106p. 1980. 75.00x (ISBN 0-7277-0014-6, Pub. by Telford England). State Mutual Bk.
--Floods & Reservoir Safety: An Engineering Guide. 1980. pap. 25.00x (ISBN 0-7277-0033-2, By Telford England). State Mutual Bk.
FLOORS
Greener. The Everything Book of Floors, Walls, & Ceilings. (Illus.). 250p. 1980. 14.95 (ISBN 0-8359-1803-3); pap. 7.95 (ISBN 0-8359-1802-5). Reston.
FLORA
see Botany; Plants
FLORAL DECORATION
see Flower Arrangement
FLORAL DESIGN
see Design, Decorative–Plant Forms
FLORENCE–HISTORY
Holmes, Timothy. Vile Florentines. 196p. 1981. 10.95 (ISBN 0-312-84677-0). St Martin.
Porter, Bernard H. I Ricordi Di Firenze. 60p. 1981. lib. bdg. 28.50 (ISBN 0-686-68872-4). Porter.
FLORIDA–DESCRIPTION AND TRAVEL
Baxter, Robert. Baxter's Florida. 1981. 9.95 (ISBN 0-913384-34-8). Rail-Europe-Baxter.
Bowe, Richard J. Pictorial History of Florida. 3rd ed. 1970. 10.00 (ISBN 0-913122-14-9). Mickler Hse.
How to Live in Florida on Ten Thousand Dollars a Year, 1981-82. 224p. Date not set. pap. 7.95 (ISBN 0-671-41397-X). Frommer-Pasmantier.
FLORIDA–DESCRIPTION AND TRAVEL–GUIDEBOOKS
Airguide. Airguide Traveler: Bahamas, Florida, Florida Keys, & Sea Islands. (Illus.). 1980. pap. 11.00 (ISBN 0-911721-89-4). Aviation.
Grove, Judi. A Vacationer's Guide to Orlando. (Illus.). 150p. (Orig.). 1981. pap. 4.95x (ISBN 0-914788-39-6). East Woods.
Hargrove, Jim & Cooper, Harry. Five Hundred Things to Do in Florida for Free. 140p. Date not set. pap. 3.95 (ISBN 0-695-81564-4). Follett.
FLORIDA–ECONOMIC CONDITIONS
Thompson, Ralph B., ed. Florida Statistical Abstract, 1980. (Illus.). 695p. 1980. 20.00x (ISBN 0-8130-0677-5); pap. 11.50 (ISBN 0-8130-0678-3). U Presses Fla.
FLORIDA–HISTORY
Bowe, Richard J. Pictorial History of Florida. 3rd ed. 1970. 10.00 (ISBN 0-913122-14-9). Mickler Hse.
Tenney, Frank F., Jr. The Enchanting Experience: Naples - Marco Island. Woolfolk, Doug, ed. (Illus.). 112p. 1981. 10.00 (ISBN 0-86518-016-4). Moran Pub Corp.
FLORIDA–POLITICS AND GOVERNMENT
Dauer, Manning J., ed. Florida's Politics & Government. LC 80-20723. (Orig.). 1980. pap. 10.00x (ISBN 0-8130-0671-6). U Presses Fla.
Thompson, Ralph B., ed. Florida Statistical Abstract, 1980. (Illus.). 695p. 1980. 20.00x (ISBN 0-8130-0677-5); pap. 11.50 (ISBN 0-8130-0678-3). U Presses Fla.
FLORIDA–SOCIAL LIFE AND CUSTOMS
Thompson, Ralph B., ed. Florida Statistical Abstract, 1980. (Illus.). 695p. 1980. 20.00x (ISBN 0-8130-0677-5); pap. 11.50 (ISBN 0-8130-0678-3). U Presses Fla.
FLORIDA KEYS
Airguide. Airguide Traveler: Bahamas, Florida, Florida Keys, & Sea Islands. (Illus.). 1980. pap. 11.00 (ISBN 0-911721-89-4). Aviation.
FLORISTS
Mitchell, H. Retail Floral Shop Management. 1982. text ed. 16.95 (ISBN 0-8359-6676-3); instr's. manual free (ISBN 0-8359-6677-1). Reston.
FLOTATION
Ranney, M. W., ed. Flotation Agents & Processes: Technology & Applications. LC 80-19191. (Chemical Tech. Rev. 172). (Illus.). 372p. 1981. 48.00 (ISBN 0-8155-0821-2). Noyes.
FLOUNDERS
see Flatfishes
FLOW, MULTIPHASE
see Multiphase Flow
FLOW, TWO-PHASE
see Two-Phase Flow
FLOW OF WATER
see Hydraulics
FLOWER ARRANGEMENT
Adams, Mary. Natural Flower Arranging. (Illus.). 120p. 1981. 19.95 (ISBN 0-7134-2677-2, Pub. by Batsford England). David & Charles.
Cutler, Katherine. Flower Arranging for All Occasions. rev. ed. LC 80-2850. (Illus.). 256p. 1981. 12.95 (ISBN 0-385-18508-1). Doubleday.
Flower Arranging: A Manual. 1972. 5.50 (ISBN 0-87543-106-2). Lucas.
Guertner, Beryl. Australian Book of Flower Arrangements. (Illus.). 12.50x (ISBN 0-392-06790-0, ABC). Soccer.
McDaniel, G. Floral Design & Arrangement. 250p. 1981. text ed. 16.95 (ISBN 0-8359-2072-0); instr's. manual free (ISBN 0-8359-2073-9). Reston.
Tozer, Zibby. The Art of Flower Arranging. (Orig.). 1981. pap. 7.95 (ISBN 0-446-97760-8). Warner Bks.
FLOWER DRAWING
see Flower Painting and Illustration
FLOWER GARDENING
Crooks, Michael. Growing Flowers. (Practical Gardening Ser.). (Illus.). 112p. (Orig.). 1979. pap. 10.50 (ISBN 0-589-01241-X, Pub. by Reed Bks Australia). C E Tuttle.
Watts, Leslie. Flower & Vegetable Plant Breeding. (Orig.). 1980. pap. 22.50 (ISBN 0-901361-35-6, Pub. by Grower Bks England). Intl Schol Bk Serv.
FLOWER PAINTING AND ILLUSTRATION
see also Flowers in Art
Ryskamp, Charles, pref. by. Flowers in Books & Drawings, Nine Forty to Eighteen Forty. LC 80-83208. (Illus.). 84p. 1980. pap. 6.95 (ISBN 0-87598-072-4). Pierpont Morgan.
FLOWER PRINTS
see Flowers in Art
FLOWERING PLANTS
see Angiosperms
FLOWERS
see also Botany; Cookery (Flowers); Fertilization of Plants; Flower Arrangement; Flower Gardening; Plants; Wild Flowers
also names of flowers, e.g. Carnations, Roses, Violets
Anderson, Frank J. Cultivated Flowers. (Abbeville Library of Art Ser.). (Illus.). 112p. (Orig.). 1981. pap. 4.95 (ISBN 0-89659-182-4). Abbeville Pr.

Fish, Margery. Cottage Garden Flowers. 1980. pap. 7.95 (ISBN 0-571-11462-8, Pub. by Faber& Faber). Merrimack Bk Serv.

Hutcheson, Gladys. The Flower Book. 96p. 1980. 19.75x (ISBN 0-7050-0071-0, Pub. by Skilton & Shaw England). State Mutual Bk.

FLOWERS–ARRANGEMENT

see Flower Arrangement

FLOWERS–JUVENILE LITERATURE

Little, Brown Editors, ed. Flowers: East Coast Edition. (Explorer's Notebooks). (Illus.). 32p. (Orig.). (gr. 5 up). 1981. pap. 1.95 (ISBN 0-316-52773-4). Little.

--Flowers: West Coast Edition. (Explorer's Notebooks). (Illus.). 32p. (Orig.). (gr. 5 up). 1981. pap. 1.95 (ISBN 0-316-52774-2). Little.

Overbeck, Cynthia. Sunflowers. (Lerner Natural Science Bks.). (Illus.). (gr. 4-10). 1981. PLB 7.95 (ISBN 0-8225-1457-5). Lerner Pubns.

FLOWERS–MARKETING

see also Florists

Mitchell, H. Retail Floral Shop Management. 1982. text ed. 16.95 (ISBN 0-8359-6676-3); instr's. manual free (ISBN 0-8359-6677-1). Reston.

FLOWERS–PICTORIAL WORKS

Sanders, Rosanne. The Remembering Garden. (Clarkson N. Potter Bks.). (Illus.). 1980. 17.95 (ISBN 0-517-54169-6). Crown.

FLOWERS, ARTIFICIAL

see Artificial Flowers

FLOWERS, PAINTING OF

see Flower Painting and Illustration

FLOWERS, PROTECTION OF

see Plants, Protection Of

FLOWERS, WILD

see Wild Flowers

FLOWERS IN ART

see also Design, Decorative–Plant Forms; Flower Painting and Illustration;

also names of specific flowers in art, e.g. Roses in Art

Ryskamp, Charles, pref. by. Flowers in Books & Drawings, Nine Forty to Eighteen Forty. LC 80-83208. (Illus.). 84p. 1980. pap. 6.95 (ISBN 0-87598-072-4). Pierpont Morgan.

FLUID BED PROCESSES

see Fluidization

FLUID DYNAMICS

see also Aerodynamics; Fluid Film Bearings; Fluidization; Gas Dynamics; Hydrodynamics; Magnetohydrodynamics; Mass Transfer; Multiphase Flow; Wakes (Fluid Dynamics)

Collier, J. G. Convective Boiling & Condensation. 2nd ed. (Illus.). 460p. 1981. text ed. 59.50 (ISBN 0-07-011798-5). McGraw.

Cranfield Fluidics Conference, 1st. Proceedings. 1965. 24.00. BHRA Fluid.

Cranfield Fluidics Conference, 6th. Proceedings. 1974. 45.00. BHRA Fluid.

Cranfield Fluidics Conference, 7th. Proceedings. 1977. 58.00 (ISBN 0-900983-50-7). BHRA Fluid.

Drzewiecki, T. M. & Franke, M. E., eds. Twentieth Anniversary of Fluidics Symposium. 232p. 1980. 30.00 (G00177). ASME.

Fluidics Quarterly, Vol. 11. (Illus.). 1979. 115.00 (ISBN 0-88232-052-1). Delbridge Pub Co.

FLUID FILM BEARINGS

see also Gas-Lubricated Bearings

Gross, William & Matsch, Lee A. Fluid Film Lubrication. Vohr, John H. & Wildman, Manfred, eds. LC 80-36889. 773p. 1980. 35.00 (ISBN 0-471-08357-7, Pub. by Wiley-Interscience). Wiley.

FLUID MECHANICS

see also Diaphragms (Mechanical Devices); Fluid Dynamics; Fluids; Hydraulic Engineering; Hydraulics; Hydrodynamics

Childress, Stephen. Mechanics of Swimming & Flying. LC 80-23364. (Cambridge Studies in Mathematical Biology: No. 2). (Illus.). 170p. Date not set. price not set (ISBN 0-521-23613-4); pap. price not set (ISBN 0-521-28071-0). Cambridge U Pr.

Plint, M. A. & Boswirth, L. Fluid Mechanics: A Laboratory Course. 186p. 1978. 30.00x (ISBN 0-85264-245-8, Pub. by Griffin England). State Mutual Bk.

Ruzicka, Jaromir & Hansen, Elo H. Flow Injection Analysis. 250p. 1981. 32.50 (ISBN 0-471-08192-2, Pub. by Wiley-Interscience). Wiley.

Schreier, Stefan. Compressible Flow. 768p. 1981. 40.00 (ISBN 0-471-05691-X, Pub. by Wiley-Interscience). Wiley.

FLUID POWER TECHNOLOGY

see also Hydraulic Machinery; Pneumatic Machinery

Stephens, H. S. & Radband, D. Papers Presented at the Sixth Fluid Power Symposium. (Orig.). 1981. pap. 78.00 library ed. (ISBN 0-686-69307-8). BHRA Fluid.

Stephens, H. S. & Jarvis, B., eds. Papers Presented at the Fifth International Symposium on Jet Cutting. (Illus.). 438p. (Orig.). 1980. pap. 99.00x (ISBN 0-906085-41-1). BHRA Fluid.

FLUID THERAPY

Ellerbe, Suellyn. Fluid & Blood Component Therapy in the Critically Ill. (Contemporary Issues in Critical Care Nursing). (Illus.). 224p. 1981. lib. bdg. 20.00 (ISBN 0-443-08129-8). Churchill.

FLUIDIZATION

Yates, J. G. Fluidized Bed Reactors. 1981. text ed. price not set. Butterworth.

FLUIDIZED SYSTEMS

see Fluidization

FLUIDS

see also Fluid Dynamics; Fluid Mechanics; Gases; Hydraulic Engineering

European Federation of Chemical Engineering, 2nd Intl. Conference on Phase Equilibria & Fluid Properties in the Chemical Industry, Berlin, 1980. Phase Equilibria & Fluid Properties in the Chemical Industry: Proceedings, Pts. 1 & 2. (EFCE Publication Ser.: No. 11). 1012p. 1980. text ed. 82.50x (ISBN 3-921567-35-1, Pub. by Dechema Germany). Scholium Intl.

Fluidics Quarterly: The Journal of Fluid Control, Vol. 13. (Illus.). 1981. 124.00 (ISBN 0-88232-062-9). Delbridge Pub Co.

FLUIDS–THERAPEUTIC USE

see Fluid Therapy

FLUORIDES

Chambers, Richard D. Fluorine in Organic Chemistry. 410p. 1981. Repr. of 1973 ed. lib. bdg. price not set (ISBN 0-89874-345-1). Krieger.

FLUORINE

see also Organofluorine Compounds

Chambers, Richard D. Fluorine in Organic Chemistry. 410p. 1981. Repr. of 1973 ed. lib. bdg. price not set (ISBN 0-89874-345-1). Krieger.

FLUTE

Duetti Facili per Flauti in Do: Twenty Nine Duets for Recorder & Flute. pap. 1.95 (ISBN 0-916786-45-5). St George Bk Serv.

Mather, Roger. The Art of Playing the Flute: Breath Control. LC 80-52140. (A Series of Workbooks: Vol. 1). (Illus.). 88p. (Orig.). 1980. pap. 6.95 (ISBN 0-9604640-0-X). Romney Pr.

FLUXIONS

see Calculus

FLY

see Flies

FLY FISHING

Malo, John. Fly Fishing for Panfish: A Beginner's Guide. LC 80-26788. (Illus.). 150p. 1981. 8.95 (ISBN 0-87518-208-9). Dillon.

FLYING BOATS

see Seaplanes

FLYING CLASSES

see Flight Training

FLYING SAUCERS

Berlitz, Charles & Moore, William L. The Roswell Incident. 1980. 10.00 (ISBN 0-686-69014-1). G&D.

Coundakis, Anthony L. Mannerism on Space Communication. 256p. 1981. 12.50 (ISBN 0-682-49734-7). Exposition.

Fuller, Curtis. Proceedings of the First International UFO Congress. 1980. pap. 2.75 (ISBN 0-446-95159-5). Warner Bks.

Hopkin, Budd. Invisible Epidemic: A Documented Study of the UFO Abduction Experience. 256p. 1981. 12.95 (ISBN 0-399-90102-7). Marek.

Messier, Charles. The Messier Catalogue. Niles, P. H., ed. LC 80-70586. 52p. (Orig.). 1981. pap. 1.50 (ISBN 0-9602738-2-4). Auriga.

Pawlicki, T. How to Build a Flying Saucer: And Other Proposals in Specultive Engineering. 1980. pap. 6.95 (ISBN 0-13-402461-3). P-H.

Rutledge, Harley D. Project Identification: The First Scientific Field Study of UFO Phenomena. (Illus.). 1981. 12.95 (ISBN 0-13-730713-6); pap. 7.95 (ISBN 0-13-730705-5). P-H.

Sheaffer, Robert. The UFO Verdict: Examining the Evidence. LC 80-84406. (Critiques of the Paranormal Ser.). 275p. 1981. 15.95 (ISBN 0-87975-146-0). Prometheus Bks.

Story, Ronald D. UFO's & the Limits of Science. LC 80-25543. (Illus.). 224p. 1981. 10.95 (ISBN 0-688-00144-0). Morrow.

Stubbs. U. F. O. Unidentified Flying Object. 7.95 (ISBN 0-233-97197-1). Andre Deutsch.

Vesco, Renato. Intercept but Don't Shoot. 336p. 1981. pap. 2.50 (ISBN 0-553-13205-9). Bantam.

FLYING SAUCERS (GAME)

see Frisbee (Game)

FLYNN, ERROL

Flynn, Errol. My Wicked, Wicked Ways. 1981. pap. 2.75. Berkley Pub.

Higham, Charles. Errol Flynn: The Untold Story. 1981. pap. 3.50 (ISBN 0-440-12307-0). Dell.

FOAMED MATERIALS

U.S. Foamed Plastics Markets & Directory. LC 63-59134. 100p. 1979. pap. 25.00 (ISBN 0-87762-277-9). Technomic.

FODDER

see Feeds

FOETUS

see Fetus

FOLK ART

see also Children As Artists

Bishop, Robert. Treasures of American Folk Art. 12.50 (ISBN 0-8109-2218-5). Abrams.

Vaughan, Betty A. Folk Art Painting: A Bit of the Past & Present. (Illus.). 52p. (Orig.). 1981. pap. 7.95 (ISBN 0-9605172-0-0). BETOM Pubns.

FOLK ART–AFRICA

Finnegan, Ruth H. Limba Stories & Story-Telling. LC 80-25904. (Oxford Library of African Literature). xii, 352p. 1981. Repr. of 1967 ed. lib. bdg. 28.75x (ISBN 0-313-22723-3, FILS). Greenwood.

FOLK ART–EUROPE

Vaughan, Betty A. Folk Art Painting: A Bit of the Past & Present. (Illus.). 52p. (Orig.). 1981. pap. 7.95 (ISBN 0-9605172-0-0). BETOM Pubns.

FOLK ART–HUNGARY

Kolar, Walter W., ed. The Folk Arts of Hungary. LC 80-54019. (Illus.). 190p. (Orig.). 1980. pap. 10.00 (ISBN 0-936922-01-X). Tamburitza.

FOLK ART–POLAND

Pokropek, Marian. Guide to Folk Art & Folklore in Poland. Paszkiewicz, Magdalena M., tr. from Polish. (Illus.). 307p. 1980. 20.00x (ISBN 83-213-3014-2). Intl Pubns Serv.

FOLK COSTUME

see Costume

FOLK LITERATURE

see also Chap-Books; Fairy Tales; Legends; Nursery Rhymes; Tales

Ranelagh, E. L. The Past We Share: The Near Eastern Ancestry of Western Folk Literature. (Illus.). 288p. 1980. 21.95 (ISBN 0-7043-2234-X, Pub. by Quartet England). Horizon.

FOLK LITERATURE–THEMES, MOTIVES

see also Literature, Comparative–Themes, Motives

Newall, Venetia J., ed. Folklore Studies in the Twentieth Century: Proceedings of the Centenary Conference of the Folklore Society. 1981. 85.00x (ISBN 0-8476-3638-0). Rowman.

FOLK-LORE

see also Animal Lore; Chap-Books; Counting-Out Rhymes; Devil; Divining-Rod; Fairies; Fairy Tales; Ghosts; Legends; Marriage Customs and Rites; Myth; Mythology; Nursery Rhymes; Oral Tradition; Plant Lore; Superstition; Tales; Valentines; Witchcraft

Boatright, Mody C. Folklore of the Oil Industry. LC 63-21186. 228p. 1980. Repr. of 1963 ed. 6.95 (ISBN 0-87074-007-5). SMU Press.

Crossley-Holland, Kevin, ed. The Faber Book of Northern Folk-Tales. (Illus.). 157p. (gr. 3-12). 1981. 11.95 (ISBN 0-571-11519-5, Pub. by Faber & Faber). Merrimack Bk Serv.

Fontenrose, Joseph. The Delphic Oracle: Its Responses & Operations. 1981. pap. 10.95 (ISBN 0-520-04359-6, CAL 490). U of Cal Pr.

Laubach, David C. Introduction to Folklore. 192p. (gr. 10-12). 1980. pap. 6.25 (ISBN 0-8104-6039-4). Hayden.

Phelps, Ethel J. The Maid of the North & Other Folk Tales Heroines. LC 80-21500. (Illus.). 192p. (gr. 2-6). 1981. 10.95 (ISBN 0-03-056893-5). HR&W.

Rodway, Avril. Fairies. (The Leprechaun Library). (Illus.). 64p. 1981. 3.95 (ISBN 0-399-12610-4). Putnam.

Sonntag, Linda. Frogs. (The Leprechaun Library). (Illus.). 64p. 1981. 3.95 (ISBN 0-399-12611-2). Putnam.

Sutton-Smith, Brian. Folkstories of Children. LC 80-5010. (American Folklore Society Ser.). 1980. 19.95x (ISBN 0-686-61087-3). U of Pa Pr.

Thompson, Stith. Motif-Index of Folk-Literature, 6 Vols. rev. ed. Incl. Vol. 1. 560p. 32.50x (ISBN 0-253-33881-6); Vol. 2. 520p. 32.50x (ISBN 0-253-33882-4); Vol. 3. 520p. 32.50x (ISBN 0-253-33883-2); Vol. 4. 500p. 32.50x (ISBN 0-253-33884-0); Vol. 5. 568p. 32.50x (ISBN 0-253-33885-9); Vol. 6. 896p. 45.00x (ISBN 0-253-33886-7). LC 55-8055. 1955-58. Set. 160.00x (ISBN 0-253-33887-5). Ind U Pr.

FOLK-LORE–BIBLIOGRAPHY

Simmons, Merle E., ed. Folklore Bibliography for Nineteen Seventy-Six. (Indiana University Folklore Institute Monograph Ser.: Vol. 33). 256p. 1981. text ed. 17.50 (ISBN 0-89727-023-1). Inst Study Hum.

FOLK-LORE–JUVENILE LITERATURE

Foley, Tom, illus. Sakshi Gopal: A Witness for the Wedding. (Illus.). 16p. (gr. 1-4). 1981. pap. 2.95 (ISBN 0-89647-010-5). Bala Bks.

Hillert, Margaret. Little Red Riding Hood. (Just Beginning-to-Read Ser.). (Illus.). 32p. (gr. 1-6). 1981. PLB 4.39 (ISBN 0-695-41543-3); pap. 1.50 (ISBN 0-695-31543-9). Follett.

--Tom Thumb. (Just Beginning-to-Read Ser.). (Illus.). 32p. (gr. 1-6). 1981. PLB 4.39 (ISBN 0-695-41542-5); pap. 1.50 (ISBN 0-695-31542-0). Follett.

Izawa, T. & Hijkata, S., illus. Jack & the Beanstalk. (Puppet Storybooks). (Illus.). 18p. (gr. k-2). 1981. 3.50 (ISBN 0-448-09758-3). G&D.

FOLK-LORE, AFRICAN

Bassey, Linus A., ed. African Wise Sayings. 1980. pap. write for info. African Policy.

Egejuru, Phanuel. Origin & Survival of African Folktales in the New World. Date not set. 8.95 (ISBN 0-933184-23-9); pap. 4.95 (ISBN 0-933184-24-7). Flame Intl.

Garcia-Cortez, Julio. Pataki: Leyendas Y Misterios De los Orishas Africanos. LC 79-54684. (Coleccion Ebano Y Canela Ser.). (Illus.). 250p. (Span.). 1980. pap. 14.95 (ISBN 0-89729-236-7). Ediciones.

Keidel, Eudene. African Fables, Bk. 2. (Illus.). 112p. 1981. pap. 3.25 (ISBN 0-8361-1945-2). Herald Pr.

Pitcher, Diana. Tokoloshi: African Folk Tales Retold. LC 80-69843. (Illus.). 64p. (gr. 3 up). 1981. Repr. 9.95 (ISBN 0-89742-049-7). Dawne-Leigh.

FOLK-LORE, AFRO-AMERICAN

see Afro-American Folk-Lore

FOLK-LORE, AMERICAN

Ainsworth, Catherine H. Polish-American Folktales. LC 77-80771. (Folklore Bks.). x, 102p. 1980. 5.00 (ISBN 0-933190-04-2). Clyde Pr.

Bauman, Richard & Abrahams, Roger D., eds. And Other Neighborly Names: Social Process & Cultural Image in Texas Folklore. (Illus.). 333p. 1981. text ed. 25.00x (ISBN 0-292-70352-X). U of Tex Pr.

Boatwright, Mody C., et al, eds. Madstones & Twisters. LC 58-9269. (Texas Folklore Society Publication Ser.: No. 28). 180p. 1980. Repr. of 1958 ed. 5.95 (ISBN 0-87074-017-2). SMU Press.

Dobie, J. Frank, et al, eds. In the Shadow of History. (Texas Folklore Society Publication Ser.: No. 25). 192p. 1980. Repr. of 1939 ed. 6.95 (ISBN 0-87074-173-X). SMU Press.

Dorson, Richard M. American Folklore & the Historian. pap. write for info. (ISBN 0-226-15869-1). U of Chicago Pr.

Hendricks, George D. Roosters, Rhymes, & Railroad Tracks. 200p. 1980. pap. 6.95 (ISBN 0-87074-177-2). SMU Press.

Kalin, Berkeley & Robinson, Clayton, eds. Myths & Realities: Conflicting Values in America. (Mississippi Valley Collection Bulletin, No. 5). 78p. 1972. pap. 5.95x (ISBN 0-87870-081-1). Memphis St Univ.

Roberts, Leonard. I Bought Me a Dog. (Illus.). 1976. pap. 1.25. Pikeville Coll.

Scott, Beth & Norman, Michael. Haunted Wisconsin. LC 80-22151. (Illus.). 256p. (Orig.). 1980. pap. 9.95 (ISBN 0-88361-082-5). Stanton & Lee.

Wofford, Vera D. Hale County, Facts & Folklore. 18.00 (ISBN 0-686-68989-5). Pioneer Bk Tx.

FOLK-LORE, ASIAN

Coburn, Jewell R. Encircled Kingdom: Legends & Folktales of Laos. LC 79-53838. (Illus.). 100p. 1979. 8.95 (ISBN 0-918060-03-6). Burn-Hart.

Van Duong, Quyen & Coburn, Jewell R. Beyond the EAST Wind: Legends & Folktales of Vietnam. LC 76-50345. (Illus.). 100p. 1976. 8.95 (ISBN 0-918060-01-X). Burn-Hart.

FOLK-LORE, BRITISH

Briggs, Katherine M. British Folktales. (Fairy Tale & Folklore Library). 1980. pap. 5.95 (ISBN 0-394-73993-0). Pantheon.

FOLK-LORE, CHINESE

Frog Rider: Folk Tales from China. 1980. pap. 1.95 (ISBN 0-8351-0764-7). China Bks.

FOLK-LORE, ENGLISH

Nicholson, John. Folk-Lore of East Yorkshire. 168p. 1980. Repr. of 1972 ed. lib. bdg. 20.00 (ISBN 0-8492-1984-1). R West.

FOLK-LORE, FILIPINO

Fuentes, Milma M. & Edito T. De La Cruz, trs. A Treasury of Mandaya & Mansaka Folk Literature. (Illus.). 130p. (Mandaya, Mansaka.). 1980. pap. 8.25x (ISBN 0-686-28808-4). Cellar.

FOLK-LORE, INDIAN

Here are entered works on the folk-lore of the American Indians; Collections of Indan tales, legends, or myths are entered under Indians of North America–Legends; Indians of South America–Legends; etc.

Coffer, William E. Where Is the Eagle? 288p. 1981. 16.95 (ISBN 0-442-26163-2). Van Nos Reinhold.

Myles, Colette G., ed. The Butterflies Carried Him Home & Other Indian Tales. (Illus.). 65p. 1981. 5.00 (ISBN 0-686-28917-X). Artmans Pr.

--The Butterflies Carried Him Home: And Other Indian Tales. LC 80-70506. (Illus.). 65p. (Orig.). 1981. pap. 4.95 (ISBN 0-9605468-1-2). Artmans Pr.

FOLK-LORE, ITALIAN

Salomone-Marino, Salvatore. Customs & Habits of the Sicilian Peasants. Norris, Rosalie N., ed. & tr. from It. LC 80-65583. (Illus.). 256p. 1981. 19.50 (ISBN 0-8386-3010-3). Fairleigh Dickinson.

Spalding, Henry, ed. Joys of Italian Humor & Folklore. LC 80-13750. 360p. 1980. 16.95 (ISBN 0-8246-0255-2). Jonathan David.

FOLK-LORE, JAPANESE

Fischer, Sally. The Tale of the Shining Princess. Keene, Donald, tr. LC 80-1943. (Illus.). 72p. 1981. 10.95 (ISBN 0-670-63971-0). Viking Pr.

FOLK-LORE, JEWISH

Braude, William G. & Kapstein, Israel J., trs. from Heb. Tanna Debe Eliyyahu. 660p. 1980. 27.50 (ISBN 0-8276-0174-3). Jewish Pubn.

FOLK-LORE, KOREAN

Zong, In Sob, compiled by. & tr. Folk Tales from Korea. 176p. 1979. write for info. (ISBN 0-930878-15-9). Hollym Intl.

FOLK-LORE, MEDICAL

see Folk Medicine

FOLK-LORE, MEXICAN

Bullock, J. Benbow. Vaya Con Dios. (Illus.). 150p. 1981. pap. 6.95 (ISBN 0-937024-02-3). Gourmet Guides.

Dobie, J. Frank, ed. Puro Mexicano. LC 35-1517. (Texas Folklore Society Publication Ser.: No. 12). 272p. 1980. Repr. of 1935 ed. 7.95 (ISBN 0-87074-041-5). SMU Press.

FOLK-LORE, PALESTINE

Hanauer, James E. Folklore of the Holy Land. 280p. 1980. Repr. of 1935 ed. lib. bdg. 30.00 (ISBN 0-8492-5272-5). R West.

FOLK-LORE, POLISH

Ainsworth, Catherine H. Polish-American Folktales. LC 77-80771. (Folklore Bks.). x, 102p. 1980. 5.00 (ISBN 0-933190-04-2). Clyde Pr.

Pokropek, Marian. Guide to Folk Art & Folklore in Poland. Paszkiewicz, Magdalena M., tr. from Polish. (Illus.). 307p. 1980. 20.00x (ISBN 83-213-3014-2). Intl Pubns Serv.

FOLK-LORE, PUERTO RICAN

Garcia, David. Fairy Tales of Puerto Rico. (Children's Bks: No. 166). (Illus.). 50p. (gr. 1-5). 1981. 6.95 (ISBN 0-934642-02-8). Puerto Rico Almanacs.

FOLK-LORE OF ANIMALS

see Animal Lore

FOLK-LORE OF BIRTH

see Birth (In Religion, Folk-Lore, etc.)

FOLK LORE OF NUMBERS

see Counting-Out Rhymes

FOLK-LORE OF PLANTS

see Plant Lore

FOLK-LORE OF WOMEN

see Women (In Religion, Folklore, etc.)

FOLK MEDICINE

Gerrick, David J. & Dietsche, Doreen. Old Time Cures - Farmers Folklore. 104p. (Orig.). 1980. pap. 3.95 (ISBN 0-686-68571-7). Dayton Labs.

Meyer, George G., et al. Folk Medicine & Herbal Healing. write for info. (ISBN 0-398-04470-8). C C Thomas.

FOLK-PSYCHOLOGY

see Ethnopsychology

FOLK-SONGS, ENGLISH

see also Ballads, English

Barrett, William A. English Folk Songs Collected, Arranged & Provided with Symphonies & Accompaniments for the Pianoforte. 95p. 1980. Repr. of 1891 ed. lib. bdg. 15.00 (ISBN 0-8492-3758-0). R West.

FOLK-SONGS, JAPANESE

Isaku, Patia R. Mountain Storm, Pine Breeze: Folk Song in Japan. 1981. text ed. 12.95x (ISBN 0-8165-0564-0); pap. 6.50 (ISBN 0-8165-0722-8). U of Ariz Pr.

FOLK-SONGS, YORUBAN

Ismaili, Rashidah, et al. Womanrise (Anthology) Rivera, Louis R., ed. (Illus.). 128p. (Orig.). 1978. pap. 4.25 (ISBN 0-917886-05-4). Shamal Bks.

FOLK-TALES

see Folk Literature; Folk-Lore; Legends; Tales

FONDA, JANE

Erlanger, Ellen. Jane Fonda. (The Achievers Ser.). (Illus.). (gr. 4-9). 1981. PLB 5.95 (ISBN 0-8225-0485-5). Lerner Pubns.

FONTANEL

see Skull

FOOD

see also Animal Food; Animals, Food Habits of; Beverages; Cookery; Diet; Farm Produce; Fish as Food; Flavoring Essences; Food, Natural; Fruit; Grain; Markets; Meat; Nutrition; Nuts; Vegetables; Vegetarianism

also headings beginning with the word Food; also particular foods and beverages, e.g. Bread, Milk; also subdivision Food under subjects, e.g. Fishes–Food; Indians of North America–Food

Adams, Rex. Miracle Medical Foods. 304p. (Orig.). 1981. pap. 2.50 (ISBN 0-446-91940-3). Warner Bks.

--Miracle Medicine Foods. LC 77-6245. 1977. pap. 3.95 (ISBN 0-13-585463-6, Reward). P-H.

Advice About Drugs, Food, Fitness. (Home Adviser Ser.). 80p. (Orig.). 1981. pap. 1.95 (ISBN 0-8326-2408-X, 7050). Delair.

Brown, Jo G. The Good Food Compendium. LC 78-22306. (Illus.). 336p. 1981. pap. 10.95 (ISBN 0-385-13523-8, Dolp). Doubleday.

Dennis, P. O., et al, eds. Food Control in Action. (Illus.). xii, 280p. 1980. 45.00x (ISBN 0-85334-894-4). Burgess-Intl Ideas.

Fetterman, Elsie. Buying Food. (Consumer Casebook Ser.). (Illus.). 80p. (gr. 10-12). 1981. pap. text ed. 5.00 (ISBN 0-87005-268-3). Fairchild.

Klinger, Judith L. The Food Inflation Fighters Handbook. (Illus.). 1980. pap. 5.95 (ISBN 0-449-90030-4, Columbine). Fawcett.

Lang, George. Lang's Compendium of Culinary Nonsense & Trivia. (Illus.). 1980. 10.00 (ISBN 0-517-54148-3). Potter.

Time-Life Editors. Foods of the World. 1980. 14.95 (ISBN 0-686-68054-5). Time-Life.

United States Department of Agriculture. The World Food Situation: Problems & Prospects to 1985, Vol. 2. 1976. 37.50 (ISBN 0-379-00573-5). Oceana.

World Food Programme: Report of the Eighth Session of the UN - FAO Committee on Food Aid Policies & Programmes. 55p. 1980. pap. 7.50 (ISBN 92-5-100895-7, F1967, FAO). Unipub.

Wright, Carol. The Holiday Cook: Recipes & Shopping Away from Home. LC 80-68682. (Illus.). 160p. 1981. 14.50 (ISBN 0-7153-8017-6). David & Charles.

FOOD–ANALYSIS

see also Food–Composition

Charalambous, George, ed. Analysis & Control of Less-Desirable Flavors in Foods & Beverages. 1980. 24.50 (ISBN 0-12-169065-2). Acad Pr.

Crook, William G. Tracking Down Hidden Food Allergy. 2nd ed. (Illus.). 104p. (Orig.). 1980. pap. 5.95 (ISBN 0-933478-05-4). Prof Bks.

Ericksson, C. Maillard Reactions in Food: Proceedings of the International Symposium, Uddevalla, Sweden, September 1979. (Progress in Food & Nutrition Science Ser.: Vol. 5). (Illus.). 500p. 1981. 156.00 (ISBN 0-08-025496-9). Pergamon.

FAO Evaluation of Malthion Residues in Food. 28p. 1980. pap. 6.00 (F1977, FAO). Unipub.

FAO-WHO Evaluation of Chlordane Residues in Food. 68p. 1973. pap. 6.00 (F1974, FAO). Unipub.

FAO-WHO Evaluation of Diazinon Residues in Food. 61p. 1973. pap. 6.00 (F1975, FAO). Unipub.

FAO-WHO Evaluation of Dichlorvos Residues in Food. 82p. 1973. pap. 6.00 (F1979, FAO). Unipub.

FAO-WHO Evaluation of Dieldrin Residues in Food. 99p. 1973. pap. 6.00 (F1978, FAO). Unipub.

FAO-WHO Evaluation of Endosulfan Residues in Food. 33p. 1973. pap. 6.00 (F1982, FAO). Unipub.

FAO-WHO Evaluation of Ethion Residues in Food. 42p. 1973. pap. 6.00 (F1973, FAO). Unipub.

FAO-WHO Evaluation of Parathion Residues in Food. 20p. 1973. pap. 6.00 (F1976, FAO). Unipub.

FAO-WHO Evaluation of Phosphamidon Residues in Food. 25p. 1973. pap. 6.00 (F1981, FAO). Unipub.

FAO-WHO Evaluation of Residues of Fentin Compounds in Food. 51p. 1973. pap. 6.00 (F1980, FAO). Unipub.

King, R. D., ed. Developments in Food Analysis Techniques-2. (Illus.). ix, 268p. 1981. 46.00x (ISBN 0-85334-921-5). Burgess-Intl Ideas.

Manuals of Food Quality Control: Microbiological Analysis. (FAO Food & Nutrition Paper: No. 14-4). 119p. 1981. pap. 7.75 (ISBN 92-5-100849-3, F2070, FAO). Unipub.

Pesticide Residues in Food-1979 Evaluations. 568p. 1981. pap. 30.25 (ISBN 92-5-100958-9, F2089, FAO). Unipub.

Report of the Thirteenth Session Codex Alimentarius Commission. 103p. 1981. pap. 6.00 (ISBN 92-5-100912-0, F2071, FAO). Unipub.

Schwartz, George. Food Power. 204p. 1981. pap. 4.95 (ISBN 0-07-055674-1). McGraw.

FOOD–COMPOSITION

see also Food–Analysis

Adams, Rex. Miracle Medical Foods. 304p. (Orig.). 1981. pap. 2.50 (ISBN 0-446-91940-3). Warner Bks.

Charalambous, George, ed. Analysis & Control of Less-Desirable Flavors in Foods & Beverages. 1980. 24.50 (ISBN 0-12-169065-2). Acad Pr.

Ericksson, C. Maillard Reactions in Food: Proceedings of the International Symposium, Uddevalla, Sweden, September 1979. (Progress in Food & Nutrition Science Ser.: Vol. 5). (Illus.). 500p. 1981. 156.00 (ISBN 0-08-025496-9). Pergamon.

Hawthorn, John. Foundations of Food Science. (Illus.). 1981. text ed. price not set (ISBN 0-7167-1295-4); pap. text ed. price not set (ISBN 0-7167-1296-2). W H Freeman.

Manuals of Food Quality Control, 3 vols. Incl. Vol. 1. Food Control Laboratory. 75p. pap. 7.50 (ISBN 92-5-100839-6, F1960); Vol. 2. Additives, Contaminants, Techniques. 317p. pap. 20.75 (ISBN 92-5-100867-1, F1961); Vol. 3. Commodities. 420p. pap. 26.75 (ISBN 92-5-100844-2, F1962). (FAO Food & Nutrition Papers: No. 14). 1980 (FAO). Unipub.

Manuals of Food Quality Control: Microbiological Analysis. (FAO Food & Nutrition Paper: No. 14-4). 119p. 1981. pap. 7.75 (ISBN 92-5-100849-3, F2070, FAO). Unipub.

Rockland, Louis B. & Stewart, George F., eds. Water Activity: Influences on Food Quality: Proceedings of Second International Symposium on Properties of Water Affecting Food Quality. LC 79-26632. 1980. 60.00 (ISBN 0-12-591350-8). Acad Pr.

Schwimmer, Sigmund. Source Book of Food Enzymology. (Illus.). 1981. lib. bdg. 79.50 (ISBN 0-87055-369-0). AVI.

FOOD–CONTAMINATION

see Food Contamination

FOOD–DRYING

Wubben, Pamela G. Drying Foods Naturally: A Handbook for Preserving Foods & Using Them Later. 80p. 1980. pap. 4.50 (ISBN 0-935442-01-4). One Percent.

--The Food Dryer Handbook. 55p. 1980. pap. 3.50 (ISBN 0-935442-02-2). One Percent.

FOOD–FREEZING

see Food, Frozen

FOOD–HISTORY

Heiser, Charles B., Jr. Seed to Civilization: The Story of Food. 2nd ed. LC 80-18208. (Illus.). 1981. text ed. 19.95x (ISBN 0-7167-1264-4); pap. text ed. 9.95x (ISBN 0-7167-1265-2). W H Freeman.

Ritchie, Carson I. Food in Civilization: How History Has Been Affected by Human Tastes. 192p. 1981. 8.95 (ISBN 0-8253-0037-1). Beaufort Bks NY.

FOOD–INSPECTION

see Food Adulteration and Inspection

FOOD–JUVENILE LITERATURE

Simon, Seymour. About the Food You Eat. Date not set. price not set. McGraw.

FOOD–LAW AND LEGISLATION

see Food Law and Legislation

FOOD–PACKAGING

Hersom, A. C. & Hulland, E. D. Canned Foods. 1981. text ed. 35.00 (ISBN 0-8206-0288-4). Chem Pub.

Palling, S. J., ed. Developments in Food Packaging - One. (Illus.). xv, 192p. 1980. 45.00x (ISBN 0-85334-917-7). Burgess-Intl Ideas.

FOOD–PRESERVATION

see also Canning and Preserving; Fishery Products; Food–Drying; Food, Frozen

Glanfield, P., compiled by. Applied Cook-Freezing. (Illus.). xii, 203p. 1980. 35.00x (ISBN 0-85334-888-X). Burgess-Intl Ideas.

Kerr, Don & Kerr, Vivian. Kerr's Country Kitchen. (Illus.). 164p. 1981. pap. 6.95 (ISBN 0-933614-08-X). Peregrine Pr.

Tilbury, R. H., ed. Developments in Food Preservatives, No. 1. x, 168p. 1981. 34.00x (ISBN 0-85334-918-5). Intl Ideas.

Turgeon, Charlotte. The Saturday Evening Post Small-Batch Canning & Freezing Cookbook. LC 78-53040. (Illus.). 1978. 8.95 (ISBN 0-89387-020-X); pap. 4.95 (ISBN 0-89387-020-X). Sat Eve Post.

Yepsen, Roger B., Jr., ed. Home Food Systems: Rodale's Catalog of Methods & Tools for Producing, Processing & Preserving Naturally Good Foods. (Illus.). 512p. 1981. 18.95 (ISBN 0-87857-325-9); pap. 15.95 (ISBN 0-87857-320-8). Rodale Pr Inc.

FOOD–PRICES

see Food Prices

FOOD, CHEMISTRY OF

see Food–Analysis; Food–Composition

FOOD, COST OF

see Cost and Standard of Living

FOOD, FROZEN

see also Cookery (Frozen Foods)

U. S. Dept. of Agriculture. Home Freezing of Fruits & Vegetables. (Illus.). 48p. pap. 2.50 (ISBN 0-8466-6056-3). Shorey.

FOOD, HEALTH

see Food, Natural

FOOD, NATURAL

see also Cookery (Natural Foods)

Adams, Ruth. Eating in Eden. 196p. (Orig.). 1976. pap. 1.75 (ISBN 0-915962-16-0). Larchmont Bks.

Adams, Ruth & Murray, Frank. All You Should Know About Health Foods. 352p. pap. 2.50 (ISBN 0-915962-01-2). Larchmont Bks.

--The Good Seeds, the Rich Grains, the Hardy Nuts for a Healthier, Happier Life. rev. ed. 303p. 1973. pap. 1.75 (ISBN 0-915962-07-1). Larchmont Bks.

Blauer, Stephen. Rejuvenation: Dr. Ann Wigmore's Complete Diet & Health Program. 197p. pap. 4.95. Hippocrates.

Wigmore, Ann. Be Your Own Doctor: Let Living Food Be Your Medicine. 176p. pap. text ed. 1.95. Hippocrates.

--How to Grow Living Foods in Seven Days. pap. text ed. write for info. Hippocrates.

--Recipes for Life. Kimball, Betsy, ed. (Illus.). 181p. pap. text ed. 7.95. Hippocrates.

--Spiritual Diet. (Health Digest Ser.: No. 152). 64p. pap. 1.50. Hippocrates.

--Spiritual-Physical Survival Through Sprouting. (Health Digest Ser.: No. 153). 63p. pap. 1.50. Hippocrates.

FOOD, ORGANICALLY GROWN

see Food, Natural

FOOD, PURE

see Food Adulteration and Inspection; Food Law and Legislation

FOOD, RAW

see also Vegetarianism

Baker, Elizabeth & Baker, Elton. The Uncook Book: Raw Food Adventures to a New Health High. (Illus.). 198p. 1981. pap. 5.95 (ISBN 0-937766-05-4). Drelwood Pubns.

FOOD, SMOKED

see Cookery (Smoked Foods)

FOOD, WILD

see also Cookery (Wild Foods)

Stewart, Hilary. Wild Teas, Coffees, & Cordials. (Illus.). 128p. 1981. 7.95 (ISBN 0-295-95804-9). U of Wash Pr.

FOOD ADULTERATION AND INSPECTION

see also Food Contamination; Meat Inspection

Roberts, Howard R. Food Safety. 448p. 1981. 39.50 (ISBN 0-471-06458-0, Pub. by Wiley-Interscience). Wiley.

FOOD AID PROGRAMS

see Food Relief

FOOD ALLERGY

see Allergy

FOOD ANIMALS

see Animal Food

FOOD CHEMISTRY

see Food–Analysis; Food–Composition

FOOD CONSUMPTION

Changes in Food Habits in Relation to Increase of Productivity. 370p. 1973. 13.75 (APO14, APO). Unipub.

FOOD CONTAMINATION

Pesticide Residues in Food 1979. (FAO Plant Production & Protection Paper Ser.: No. 20). 97p. 1980. pap. 6.00 (ISBN 92-5-100922-8, F1936, FAO). Unipub.

Pesticide Residues in Food-1979 Evaluations. 568p. 1981. pap. 30.25 (ISBN 92-5-100958-9, F2089, FAO). Unipub.

Pim, Linda. The Invisible Additives: Environmental Contamination of Food. 195p. 1981. 9.95 (ISBN 0-385-17001-7); pap. 6.95 (ISBN 0-385-17002-5). Doubleday.

Reilly, Conor. Metal Contamination of Food. xvi, 231p. 1980. 42.50x (ISBN 0-85334-905-3). Burgess-Intl Ideas.

Roberts, Howard R. Food Safety. 448p. 1981. 39.50 (ISBN 0-471-06458-0, Pub. by Wiley-Interscience). Wiley.

FOOD CONTROL

see Food Supply

FOOD CUSTOMS

see Food Habits

FOOD FOR INVALIDS

see Cookery for the Sick

FOOD FOR SCHOOL CHILDREN

see School Children–Food

FOOD HABITS

see also Diet; Nutrition

Simoons, Frederick J. Eat Not This Flesh: Food Avoidances in the Old World. LC 80-22232. (Illus.). xiii, 241p. 1981. Repr. of 1967 ed. lib. bdg. 29.75x (ISBN 0-313-22772-1, SIEN). Greenwood.

FOOD HABITS OF ANIMALS

see Animals, Food Habits of

FOOD HANDLING

Guthrie, Rufus K. Food Sanitation. 2nd ed. (Illus.). 1980. lib. bdg. 21.50 (ISBN 0-87055-361-5). AVI.

FOOD INDUSTRY AND TRADE

see also Farm Produce; Food Prices; Food Supply also individual processed food and processing industries, e.g. Cheese and Dairying; Meat Industry and Trade

Ayres, John C. & Kirschman, John C., eds. Impact of Toxiology on Food Processing. (Institute of Food Technologists Basic Symposia Ser.). (Illus.). 1981. lib. bdg. price not set (ISBN 0-87055-388-7). AVI.

Doyle, Edwin S. & Mittler, Abe, eds. Control of Critical Points in Food Processing: A Systems Approach. (Illus.). 270p. 1977. text ed. 25.00 (ISBN 0-937774-04-9). Food Processors.

FAO Production Yearbook, Vol. 33. 309p. 1980. pap. 25.25 (ISBN 92-5-000936-4, F2050, FAO). Unipub.

Fox, Brian A. & Cameron, Allan G. Food Science: A Chemical Approach. 3rd ed. 1977. 10.50x (ISBN 0-8448-0938-1). Crane-Russak Co.

Harper, Judson M. Extrusion of Foods. 1981. Vol. 1. 59.95 (ISBN 0-8493-5203-7); Vol. 2. 46.95 (ISBN 0-8493-5204-5). CRC Pr.

Heldman, D. R. & Singh, R. P. Food Process Engineering. (Illus.). 1981. pap. text ed. 24.00 (ISBN 0-686-69097-4). AVI.

Lilley. Information Sources in Agriculture & Food Science. (Butterworths Guides to Information Sources Ser.). 1981. text ed. price not set (ISBN 0-408-10612-3). Butterworth.

Linko, P., et al, eds. Food Process Engineering: Vol. 1 Food Processing Systems. (Illus.). xii, 981p. 1980. 210.00x (ISBN 0-85334-896-0). Burgess-Intl Ideas.

--Food Process Engineering: Volume 2--Enzyme Engineering in Food Processing. (Illus.). vii, 328p. 1980. 75.00x (ISBN 0-85334-897-9). Burgess-Intl Ideas.

Muller, H. G. & Tobin, G. Nutrition & Food Processing. 240p. 1980. 35.00x (ISBN 0-85664-540-0, Pub. by Croom Helm England). State Mutual Bk.

Strang, William A. Restaurant & Food Store Surveys, 1979: Evaluating the Potential for a Small Business Information System in Wisconsin. (Wisconsin Economy Studies: No. 18). (Orig.). 1979. pap. 5.00 (ISBN 0-86603-007-7). Bureau Busn Res U Wis.

Workshop on the Interfaces Between Agriculture, Nutrition, & Food Science, 1977. Proceedings. 143p. 1979. pap. 7.25 (R087, IRRI). Unipub.

FOOD INDUSTRY AND TRADE–LAW AND LEGISLATION

see Food Law and Legislation

FOOD INSPECTION

see Food Adulteration and Inspection

FOOD LAW AND LEGISLATION

see also subdivision Law and legislation under individual foods

Manuals of Food Quality Control, 3 vols. Incl. Vol. 1. Food Control Laboratory. 75p. pap. 7.50 (ISBN 92-5-100839-6, F1960); Vol. 2. Additives, Contaminants, Techniques. 317p. pap. 20.75 (ISBN 92-5-100867-1, F1961); Vol. 3. Commodities. 420p. pap. 26.75 (ISBN 92-5-100844-2, F1962). (FAO Food & Nutrition Papers: No. 14). 1980 (FAO). Unipub.

Merrill, Richard A. & Hutt, Peter B. Food & Drug Law, Cases & Materials. LC 80-23167. (University Casebook Ser.). 959p. 1980. text ed. write for info. (ISBN 0-88277-016-0). Foundation Pr.

Schultz, Harold W. Food Law Handbook. (Illus.). 1981. lib. bdg. 79.50 (ISBN 0-87055-372-0). AVI.

FOOD OF ANIMALS

see Animals, Food Habits of

FOOD PLANTS

see Plants, Edible

FOOD PRESERVATION

see Food–Preservation

FOOD PRICES

Food Price Policies & Nutrition in Latin America. (Food & Nutrition Bulletin Ser.: Suppl. 3). 170p. 1980. pap. 15.00 (ISBN 92-808-0128-7, TUNU087, UNU). Unipub.

Samtur, Susan J. & Tuleja, Tad. Cashing in at the Checkout. 1980. pap. 1.95 (ISBN 0-446-90585-2). Warner Bks.

FOOD PROCESSING

see Food Industry and Trade

FOOD PROCESSOR COOKERY

Gethers, Judith. The Fabulous Food Processor. 384p. (Orig.). 1981. pap. 7.95 (ISBN 0-345-29586-2). Ballantine.

Mandel, Abby. Abby Mandel's Cuisinart Classroom. McElheny, Ruth, ed. (Illus.). 288p. (Orig.). 1980. pap. 12.50 (ISBN 0-936662-03-4). Cuisinart Cooking.

Reingold, Carmel B. Cuisinart Food Processor Cookbook. 1981. pap. price not set (Delta). Dell.

Szilard, Paula & Woo, Juliana J. The Electric Vegetarian: Natural Cooking the Food Processor Way. 1981. 12.95. Johnson VA.

--Electric Vegetarian: Natural Cooking the Food Processor Way. 1980. pap. 10.95 (ISBN 0-933472-50-1). Johnson Colo.

FOOD RELIEF

Cadet, Melissa L. Food Aid & Policy for Economic Development: An Annotated Bibliography & Directory. (Illus.). 187p. (Orig.). 1981. 24.95 (ISBN 0-938398-00-8); pap. 16.95. Trans Tech Mgmt.

Manual on Management of Group Feeding Programmes. (FAO Food & Nutrition Paper Ser.). 124p. 1980. pap. 7.00 (ISBN 92-5-100931-7, F2041, FAO). Unipub.

United States Department of Agriculture. The World Food Situation: Problems & Prospects to 1985, Vol. 2. 1976. 37.50 (ISBN 0-379-00573-5). Oceana.

FOOD SANITATION

see Food Handling

FOOD SERVICE

Here are entered works on quantity preparation and service of food for outside the home. Works dealing solely with quantity food preparation are entered under Quantity Cookery.

see also Caterers and Catering; Quantity Cookery; Restaurants, Lunchrooms, Etc.

Morgan, William J., Jr. Supervision & Management of Quantity Preparation. 2nd, rev ed. LC 80-83876. (Illus.). 1981. price not set (ISBN 0-8211-1254-6); text ed. price not set. McCutchan.

Mutkoski, Stephen A. & Schurer, Marcia L. Meat & Fish Management for Food Service. 1981. text ed. 17.95 (ISBN 0-534-00907-7, Breton Pubs). Wadsworth Pub.

North, Hallie B. Commercial Food Patents, U.S. Nineteen-Eighty. (Illus.). 1981. lib. bdg. 30.00 (ISBN 0-87055-371-2). AVI.

Terrell, M. E. Professional Food Preperation. 2nd ed. 741p. 1979. 24.50 (ISBN 0-471-85202-3). Wiley.

Van Egmond-Pannell, Dorothy. School Foodservice. (Illus.). 1981. pap. text ed. 17.00 (ISBN 0-87055-378-X). AVI.

FOOD SERVICE-VOCATIONAL GUIDANCE

Cavallaro, Ann. Careers in Food Services. 160p. (YA) 1981. 9.95 (ISBN 0-525-66698-2). Elsevier-Nelson.

FOOD STAMP PLAN

see Food Relief

FOOD SUPPLY

see also Agriculture-Statistics; Famines; Food-Preservation; Food Consumption; Food Industry and Trade; Meat Industry and Trade

Barnett, A. Doak. China & the World Food System. LC 79-87912. (Monographs: No. 12). 128p. 1979. 5.00 (ISBN 0-686-28683-9). Overseas Dev Council.

Caldwell, Malcolm. Wealth of Some Nations. 192p. 1977. 10.00 (ISBN 0-905762-01-0); pap. 6.00. Lawrence Hill.

Report of the Fifteenth FAO Regional Conference for Asia & the Pacific. 97p. 1981. pap. 6.00 (ISBN 92-5-100963-5, F2084, FAO). Unipub.

Report on the Second FAO-UNFPA Expert Consultation on Land Resources for Populations of the Future. 369p. 1981. pap. 20.25 (ISBN 92-5-100925-2, F2073, FAO). Unipub.

Valdes, Alberto, ed. Food Security for Developing Countries. 350p. 1981. lib. bdg. 25.00x (ISBN 0-86531-071-8). Westview.

Woods, Richard G., ed. Future Dimensions of World Food & Populations. (Winrock Ser.). 425p. 1981. lib. bdg. 22.50x (ISBN 0-86531-160-9). Westview.

World Food Programme: Report of the Eighth Session of the UN - FAO Committee on Food Aid Policies & Programmes. 55p. 1980. pap. 7.50 (ISBN 92-5-100895-7, F1967, FAO). Unipub.

World Food Programme: Report of the Ninth Session. 53p. 1981. pap. 6.00 (ISBN 92-5-100953-8, F2092, FAO). Unipub.

FOOD TRADE

see Farm Produce-Marketing; Food Industry and Trade

FOODS, CONTAMINATED

see Food Contamination

FOOT

see also Podiatry

Bateman & Trott. The Foot & Ankle. 1980. 32.00. Thieme Stratton.

Montagne. Atlas of Foot Radiology. 1981. price not set (ISBN 0-89352-097-7). Masson Pub.

Neale, Donald. Common Foot Disorders. (Illus.). 224p. 1981. lib. bdg. 24.00 (ISBN 0-443-01938-X). Churchill.

Rutt. Surgery of the Leg & Foot. (Hackenbroch Ser.). 1980. text ed. write for info. (ISBN 0-7216-4446-5). Saunders.

FOOT RACING

see Running

FOOT TRAILS

see Trails

FOOTBALL

see also Football Coaching; Rugby Football; Soccer

Aaseng, Nathan. Football's Cunning Coaches. LC 80-29252. (The Sports Heroes Library). (Illus.). (gr. 4 up). 1981. PLB 5.95 (ISBN 0-8225-1065-0). Lerner Pubns.

--Football's Steadiest Kickers. LC 80-28868. (Sports Heroes Library). (Illus.). (gr. 4 up). 1981. PLB 5.95 (ISBN 0-8225-1069-3). Lerner Pubns.

--Football's Toughest Tight Ends. LC 80-27803. (Sports Heroes Ser.). (Illus.). (gr. 4 up). 1981. PLB 5.95 (ISBN 0-8225-1070-7). Lerner Pubns.

Heard, Robert. Oklahoma Vs. Texas: When Football Becomes War. LC 80-82909. (Illus.). 544p. 1980. 25.00 (ISBN 0-937642-00-2). Honey Hill.

Holst, Art. Sunday Zebras. 1980. 10.00 (ISBN 0-9605118-0-6). Forest Pub.

FOOTBALL-BIOGRAPHY

see also names of individual players, e.g. Bellino, Joseph Michael

Blair, Sam. Earl Campbell: The Driving Force. 1980. 8.95 (ISBN 0-8499-0259-2). Word Bks.

Bleier, Rocky & O'Neil, Terry. Fighting Back. rev. ed. LC 75-12865. (Illus.). 240p. 1980. 12.95 (ISBN 0-8128-2767-8). Stein & Day.

Diles, Dave L. & Bradshaw, Terry. Terry Bradshaw: Man of Steel. 224p. 1980. pap. 4.95 (ISBN 0-310-39461-9, 12025P). Zondervan.

McIntyre, Bill. Grambling: Cradle of the Pros. Woolfolk, Doug, ed. (Illus.). 110p. 1980. 12.50 (ISBN 0-86518-015-6). Moran Pub Corp.

Tatum, Jack & Kushner, Bill. They Call Me Assassin. 1980. pap. 2.95 (ISBN 0-380-52480-5, 52480). Avon.

FOOTBALL-HISTORY

Batty, Eric G., et al, eds. International Football Book, No. 22. (Illus.). 142p. (YA) 1980. text ed. 17.50x (ISBN 0-285-62445-8, SpS). Soccer.

Florence, Mal. Trojan Heritage: A Pictorial History of USC Football. LC 80-84556. (Illus.). 184p. 1980. 16.95 (ISBN 0-938694-01-4). JCP Corp VA.

FOOTBALL-JUVENILE LITERATURE

Swenson, John. The Eagles. (Headliners Ser.). 192p. (Orig.). (gr. 4 up). 1981. pap. 2.25 (ISBN 0-448-17174-0, Tempo). G&D.

FOOTBALL-OFFENSE

Poff, Mike. Coaches' Guide to Offensive Line Fundamentals & Techniques. LC 80-83977. (Illus.). 160p. (Orig.). 1981. pap. text ed. 5.95 (ISBN 0-918438-62-4). Leisure Pr.

FOOTBALL-TRAINING

Kearin, Timothy. Year Around Conditioning for Army Football. LC 80-82965. (Illus.). 128p. (Orig.). 1980. pap. text ed. 4.95 (ISBN 0-918438-60-8). Leisure Pr.

FOOTBALL COACHING

McIntyre, Bill. Grambling: Cradle of the Pros. Woolfolk, Doug, ed. (Illus.). 110p. 1980. 12.50 (ISBN 0-86518-015-6). Moran Pub Corp.

Sandusky, Jerry. Developing Linebackers the Penn State Way. LC 80-84214. (Fitness America Ser.). (Illus.). 160p. (Orig.). 1981. pap. text ed. 5.95 (ISBN 0-918438-64-0). Leisure Pr.

Storey, Edward J. How to Kick a Football. (Illus.). 160p. (Orig.). 1981. pap. text ed. 5.95 (ISBN 0-918438-61-6). Leisure Pr.

FOOTBALL SCOUTING

Dienhart. Football Scouting Workbook. write for info. (ISBN 0-392-07843-0). Soccer.

FOOTBALL STORIES

see also American Wit and Humor-Sports and Games

Good Times with Football. (Illus.). 24p. (gr. 3-4). 1976. 4.50 (ISBN 0-912122-05-6); pap. 1.89 (ISBN 0-912122-06-4). Football Hobbies.

FOOTE, SAMUEL, 1720-1777

Murray, Grace A. Personalities of the Eighteenth Century: (Samuel Foote, Christopher Smart, William Hazlitt) 230p. 1980. Repr. of 1927 ed. lib. bdg. 25.00 (ISBN 0-8495-3772-X). Arden Lib.

FOOTPATHS

see Trails

FORCE AND ENERGY

see also Dynamics; Mechanics; Pressure; Quantum Theory

Aho, Arnold J. Materials, Energies & Environmental Design. 1981. lib. bdg. 28.50 (ISBN 0-8240-7178-6). Garland Pub.

Learning Achievement Corporation. Multiplication & Energy & Construction: Division & Medicine. Zak, Therese A., ed. (MATCH Ser.). (Illus.). 144p. 1980. text ed. 5.28 (ISBN 0-07-037112-1, G). McGraw.

Miller, David H. Energy at the Surface of the Earth. 1981. 49.50 (ISBN 0-12-497150-4). Acad Pr.

Nelson, Robert V. Understanding Basic Energy Terms. Ide, Arthur F., ed. LC 79-9940. (E Equals MC Squared Ser.). (Illus.). 60p. 1980. 9.00 (ISBN 0-86663-806-7); pap. 6.25 (ISBN 0-86663-807-5). Ide Hse.

Rider, Don K. Energy: Hydrocarbon Fuels & Chemical Resources. 600p. 1981. 40.00 (ISBN 0-471-05915-3, Pub. by Wiley-Interscience). Wiley.

Slattery, John C. Momentum, Energy, & Mass Transfer in Continua. 2nd ed. LC 80-22746. 700p. 1980. text ed. 32.50 (ISBN 0-89874-212-9). Krieger.

FORCE PUMPS

see Pumping Machinery

FORD, HENRY, 1863-1947

Gelderman, Carol. Henry Ford: The Wayward Capitalist. (Illus.). 416p. 1981. 14.95 (ISBN 0-8037-3436-0). Dial.

FORD, HENRY, 1917-

Lasky, Victor. Never Complain, Never Explain. 338p. 1981. 15.00 (ISBN 0-399-90104-3). Marek.

FORD AUTOMOBILE

see Automobiles-Types-Ford

FORECASTING

Levenbach, Hans & Cleary, James P. The Forecasting Process for the Beginning Forecaster. (Illus.). 350p. 1981. text ed. 29.95 (ISBN 0-534-97975-0). Lifetime Learn.

Lindsey, Hal. The Nineteen Eighties Countdown to Armageddon. 192p. 1981. pap. 6.92 (ISBN 0-553-01303-3). Bantam.

Morgan, Chris. Future Man: An Optimistic Look at What the Future Holds for Mankind. 208p. 1981. pap. 6.95 (ISBN 0-686-28897-1). Lewis Pub Co.

Theobald, Robert. Beyond Despair: Directions for America's Third Century. rev. ed. 208p. 1981. 11.95 (ISBN 0-932020-04-6); pap. 7.95 (ISBN 0-932020-05-4). Seven Locks Pr.

Wollaston, Thomas A. The Incredible Conditions of the World in the Year 2000: An Astonishing Forecast. (Illus.). 131p. 1981. 67.85 (ISBN 0-930008-74-X). Inst Econ Pol.

FORECASTING, BUSINESS

see Business Forecasting

FORECASTING, ECONOMIC

see Economic Forecasting

FORECASTING, TECHNOLOGICAL

see Technological Forecasting

FORECASTING, WEATHER

see Weather Forecasting

FOREIGN AFFAIRS

see International Relations;

see subdivisions Foreign Relations under names of countries

FOREIGN AID PROGRAM

see Technical Assistance

FOREIGN AUTOMOBILES

see Automobiles, Foreign

FOREIGN COMMERCE

see Commerce

FOREIGN ECONOMIC RELATIONS

see International Economic Relations

FOREIGN EXCHANGE

see also Sterling Area

Coninx, Raymond G. Foreign Exchange Dealer's Manual. 168p. 1980. 30.00x (ISBN 0-85941-152-4, Pub. by Woodhead-Faulkner England). State Mutual Bk.

Drummond, Ian. The Floating Pound & the Sterling Area, 1931-1939. LC 80-14539. 352p. Date not set. 37.50 (ISBN 0-521-23165-5). Cambridge U Pr.

McRae, R. & Walker, D. Foreign Exchange Management. 1981. 36.00 (ISBN 0-13-325357-0). P-H.

Underwood, Trevor, ed. Foreign Exchange Yearbook 1981. 264p. 1980. 60.00x (Pub. by Woodhead-Faulkner England). State Mutual Bk.

Walker, Townsend. A Guide for Using the Foreign Exchange Market. 360p. 1981. 20.95 (ISBN 0-471-06254-5). Ronald Pr.

FOREIGN EXCHANGE PROBLEM-GREAT BRITAIN

Carse, Stephen, et al. The Financing Procedures of British Foreign Trade. LC 79-18146. 160p. 1980. 24.95 (ISBN 0-521-22534-5). Cambridge U Pr.

FOREIGN INCOME, TAXATION OF

see Income Tax-Foreign Income

FOREIGN INVESTMENTS

see Investments, Foreign

FOREIGN NEWS

Boyd-Barrett, Oliver. The International News Agencies. LC 80-51779. (Communication & Society Ser.: Vol. 13). (Illus.). 284p. 1980. 25.00 (ISBN 0-8039-1511-X); pap. 12.50 (ISBN 0-8039-1512-8). Sage.

FOREIGN OPINION OF THE UNITED STATES

see United States-Foreign Opinion

FOREIGN POLICY

see International Relations

FOREIGN POPULATION

see Emigration and Immigration

FOREIGN RELATIONS

see International Relations

FOREIGN STUDY

Cohen, Gail A., ed. The Learning Traveler Vol. 1: U. S. College-Sponsored Programs Abroad: Academic Year. rev. ed. 186p. 1981. pap. text ed. 8.00 (ISBN 0-87206-108-6). Inst Intl Educ.

FOREIGN TRADE

see Commerce

FOREIGN TRADE POLICY

see Commercial Policy

FOREIGN TRADE REGULATION

see also Commercial Treaties; Import Quotas

Olnek, Jay I. The Invisible Hand. 1980. 14.95 (ISBN 0-938538-00-4). N Stonington.

FOREIGN TRADE ZONES

see Free Ports and Zones

FOREIGNERS

see Aliens; Naturalization

FORENSIC MEDICINE

see Medical Jurisprudence

FORENSIC PSYCHIATRY

Here are entered works on psychiatry as applied in courts of law. Works on the legal status of persons of unsound mind are entered under the heading Insanity-Jurisprudence.

Bjerre, Andreas. The Psychology of Murder: A Study in Criminal Psychology. Classen, E., tr. from Swedish. (Historical Foundations of Forensic Psychiatry & Psychology Ser.). 164p. 1980. Repr. lib. bdg. 19.50 (ISBN 0-306-76067-3). Da Capo.

Bose, Prabodh C. Introduction to Juristic Psychology. (Historical Foundations of Forensic Psychiatry & Psychology Ser.). 426p. 1980. Repr. of 1917 ed. lib. bdg. 39.50 (ISBN 0-686-68561-X). Da Capo.

Brown, M. Ralph. Legal Psychology. (Historical Foundations of Forensic Psychiatry & Psychology Ser.). (Illus.). 346p. 1980. Repr. of 1926 ed. lib. bdg. 35.00 (ISBN 0-306-76065-7). Da Capo.

Davey, Herbert. The Law Relating to the Mentally Defective. (Historical Foundations of Forensic Psychiatry & Psychology Ser.). 568p. 1980. Repr. of 1914 ed. lib. bdg. 49.50 (ISBN 0-306-76070-3). Da Capo.

Goodwin, John C. Insanity & the Criminal. (Historical Foundations of Forensic Psychiatry & Psychology Ser.). 308p. 1980. Repr. of 1924 ed. lib. bdg. 29.50 (ISBN 0-306-76061-4). Da Capo.

Hoag, Ernest B. & Williams, Edward H. Crime, Abnormal Minds & the Law. (Historical Foundations of Forensic Psychiatry & Psychology Ser.). 405p. 1980. Repr. of 1923 ed. lib. bdg. 35.00 (ISBN 0-306-76060-6). Da Capo.

Hollander, Bernard. The Psychology of Misconduct, Vice, & Crime. (Historical Foundations of Forensic Psychiatry & Psychology Ser.). 220p. 1980. Repr. lib. bdg. 25.00 (ISBN 0-306-76063-0). Da Capo.

McCarty, Dwight G. Psychology for the Lawyer. (Historical Foundations of Forensic Psychiatry & Psychology Ser.). Date not set. lib. bdg. 49.50 (ISBN 0-306-76068-1). Da Capo.

Mercier, Charles. Criminal Responsibility. (Historical Foundations of Forensic Psychiatry & Psychology Ser.). 256p. 1980. Repr. of 1931 ed. lib. bdg. 25.00 (ISBN 0-306-76064-9). Da Capo.

Smith, Selwyn M. & Koranyi, Erwin K. Self-Assessment of Current Knowledge in Forensic & Organic Psychiatry. 1978. spiral bdg. 15.00 (ISBN 0-87488-235-4). Med Exam.

White, W. A. Insanity & the Criminal Law. (Historical Foundations of Forensic Psychiatry & Psychology Ser.). 281p. 1980. Repr. of 1923 ed. lib. bdg. 25.00 (ISBN 0-306-76069-X). Da Capo.

Wright, Fred, et al, eds. Forensic Psychology & Psychiatry. LC 80-17982. (N.Y. Academy of Sciences Annals: Vol. 347). 364p. 1980. 58.00 (ISBN 0-89766-084-6). NY Acad Sci.

FORENSIC PSYCHOLOGY

see Psychology, Forensic

FOREORDINATION

see Predestination

FOREST CONSERVATION

see also Forest Products

Cleveland, Harlan, ed. The Management of Sustainable Growth. LC 80-24162. (Pergamon Policy Studies on International Development). 386p. 1981. 40.00 (ISBN 0-08-027171-5). Pergamon.

FOREST ECOLOGY

see also Woody Plants

A Review-Tropical Woodlands & Forest Ecosystems, Nineteen Eighty. (UNEP Report Ser.: No. 4). 84p. 1980. pap. 9.00 (UNEP 030, UNEP). Unipub.

FOREST ECONOMICS

see Forests and Forestry-Economic Aspects

FOREST ENTOMOLOGY

see Entomology

FOREST FLORA

see Forest Ecology; Forests and Forestry

FOREST MANAGEMENT

see Forests and Forestry

FOREST PLANTING

see Forests and Forestry

FOREST PRODUCTS

see also Lumber Trade; Rubber; Timber; Wood

Forest Products Prices 1960-1978. (FAO Forestry Paper Ser.: No. 18). 79p. 1980. pap. 7.50 (ISBN 92-5-000881-3, F1955, FAO). Unipub.

FOREST PROTECTION

see also Plants, Protection of

Smith, W. H. Air Pollution & Forests. (Springer Series on Environmental Management). (Illus.). 400p. 1981. 39.80 (ISBN 0-387-90501-4). Springer-Verlag.

FOREST RANGERS

Glassman, Henry S. Lead the Way, Rangers - Fifth Ranger Bn. (Illus.). 104p. 1980. pap. 5.95 (ISBN 0-934588-03-1). Ranger Assocs.

Signy, F. C. History of the Queen's Park Rangers. 10.00x (ISBN 0-392-07910-0, SpS). Soccer.

FOREST REPRODUCTION

see Forests and Forestry

FOREST VALUATION

see Forests and Forestry-Economic Aspects

FORESTALLING

see Monopolies

FORESTATION

see Forests and Forestry

FORESTRY EDUCATION

see Forestry Schools and Education

FORESTRY SCHOOLS AND EDUCATION
Report of the Eighth Session of FAO Advisory Committee on Forestry Education. 47p. 1980. pap. 7.50 (ISBN 92-5-100480-3, F1968, FAO). Unipub.
FORESTS AND FORESTRY
see also Botany–Ecology; Flood Control; Landscape Gardening; Lumber Trade; Lumbering; Pruning; Trees; Wood
Anderson, David & Smith William, A., eds. Forest & Forestry. 3rd ed. (gr. 10-12). 1981. 14.00 (ISBN 0-8134-2169-1); text ed. 10.50x. Interstate.
Clarkson, Roy B., et al. Forest Plants of the Monangahela National Forest. 1980. pap. 8.95 (ISBN 0-910286-82-5). Boxwood.
Collins, Bobby & White, Fred. Elementary Forestry. 1981. text ed. 15.95 (ISBN 0-8359-1647-2); instr's. manual free (ISBN 0-8359-1646-4). Reston.
Economic Analysis of Forestry Projects. (FAO Forestry Paper Ser.: No. 17, Suppl. 1). 243p. 1980. pap. 13.00 (ISBN 92-5-100830-2, F1959, FAO). Unipub.
Khatib, Ahmad. Chihabi's Dictionary of Agricultural & Forestry Terms: English-Arabic. 1978. 40.00x. Intl Bk Ctr.
Oregon State University Biology Colloquium, 40th. Forests: Fresh Perspectives from Ecosystems Analysis. Proceedings. Waring, Richard H., ed. LC 80-14883. (Illus.). 210p. 1980. pap. 12.00 (ISBN 0-87071-179-2). Oreg St U Pr.
Sonnenfeld, Jeffrey A. Corporate Views of the Public Interest: The Perceptions of the Forest Products Industry. 200p. 1981. 19.95 (ISBN 0-86569-060-X). Auburn Hse.
FORESTS AND FORESTRY–ECOLOGY
see Forest Ecology
FORESTS AND FORESTRY–ECONOMIC ASPECTS
State Taxation of Forest & Land Resources: Symposium Proceedings. (Lincoln Institute Monograph: No. 80-6). 149p. 1980. pap. text ed. 12.00. Lincoln Inst Land.
FORESTS AND FORESTRY–STUDY AND TEACHING
see Forestry Schools and Education
FORESTS AND FORESTRY–ASIA
Bamboo Research in Asia. 228p. 1981. pap. 15.00 (ISBN 0-88936-267-X, I*O*R*C 159, IDRC). Unipub.
FORESTS AND FORESTRY–NORTH AMERICA
Daniel, Glenda & Sullivan, Jerry. A Sierra Club Naturlist's Guide to the North Woods of Michigan, Wisconsin, & Minnesota. (Naturalist's Guide Ser.). (Illus.). 384p. 1981. 24.95 (ISBN 0-87156-248-0); pap. 9.95 (ISBN 0-87156-277-4). Sierra.
FORGETFULNESS
see Memory
FORGIVENESS OF SIN
see also Penance
Augsberger, tr. Livre Para Perdoar. (Portuguese Bks.). 1979. 1.30 (ISBN 0-8297-0735-2). Life Pubs Intl.
Augsburger, David. Caring Enough to Forgive. LC 80-50545. 1981. pap. 4.95 (ISBN 0-8307-0749-2). Regal.
Keysor, Charles W. Forgiveness Is a Two-Way Street. 132p. 1981. pap. 3.95 (ISBN 0-88207-338-9). Victor Bks.
FORM (ESTHETICS)
Williams, Christopher. Origins of Form. (Illus.). 160p. (Orig.). 1980. pap. 12.00 (ISBN 0-8038-5394-7). Hastings.
FORM IN BIOLOGY
see Morphology
FORM LETTERS
Minnick, Sally. Dear World: A Collection of Form Letters for You to Use & Enjoy. 1981. 7.95. Green Hill.
FORM PERCEPTION
Holmes, Kenneth. Basic Shapes...Plus. (Illus.). 24p. (gr. k-3). 1980. pap. 3.95 (ISBN 0-933358-63-6). Enrich.
Magarian, Judith A. Measurement Comparisons. (Illus.). 24p. (gr. k-3). 1980. pap. 3.95 (ISBN 0-933358-64-4). Enrich.
Shape & Colors, No. 1. (Shapes & Colors Ser.). 1980. 1.95 (ISBN 0-8431-0165-2). Price Stern.
Shapes & Colors, No. 3. (Shapes & Colors Ser.). 1980. 1.95 (ISBN 0-8431-0167-9). Price Stern.
Shapes & Colors, No. 4. (Shapes & Colors Ser.). 1980. 1.95 (ISBN 0-8431-0168-7). Price Stern.
FORMAL LANGUAGES
Book, Ronald V., ed. Formal Language Theory: Perspectives & Open Problems. 1980. 25.00 (ISBN 0-12-115350-9). Acad Pr.
Milner, R. A Calculus of Communicating Systems. (Lecture Notes in Computer Science Ser.: Vol. 92). 260p. 1981. pap. 11.80 (ISBN 0-387-10235-3). Springer-Verlag.
FORMAT OF BOOKS
see Books–Format
FORMOSA
see Taiwan
FORMS (LAW)
Here are entered works on and collections of legal forms in general. Forms relating to special topics or branches of law are entered under the specific heading.
see also Legal Composition
McNutt, Robert D. West's Book of Legal Forms. 200p. 1981. pap. text ed. 3.96 (ISBN 0-8299-0516-2). West Pub.
Mattox. Minnesota Legal Forms-Criminal Law. 1981. ring binder 15.00 (ISBN 0-917126-84-X). Mason Pub.
Miller, John M. Minnesota Legal Forms-Commercial Real Estate. Mason Publishing Staff, ed. 150p. 1981. ring binder 15.00 (ISBN 0-917126-89-0). Mason Pub.
Stoneking, Gary E. Minnesota Legal Forms-Personal Injury. Mason Publishing Staff, ed. 150p. 1981. ring binder 15.00 (ISBN 0-917126-93-9). Mason Pub.
Wagner, Michael P. Minnesota Legal Forms: Bankruptcy. Mason Publishing Staff, ed. 150p. 1981. ring binder 15.00 (ISBN 0-917126-92-0). Mason Pub.
FORMS, AUTOMORPHIC
see Automorphic Forms
FORMULA TRANSLATION (COMPUTER PROGRAM LANGUAGE)
see FORTRAN (Computer Program Language)
FORMULARIES
see Medicine–Formulae, Receipts, Prescriptions
FORSTER, EDWARD MORGAN, 1879-1970
Cecil, David. Poets & Story-Tellers. 201p. 1980. Repr. of 1968 ed. lib. bdg. 30.00 (ISBN 0-8495-0852-5). Arden Lib.
Devlin, Laura K. Looking Inward: Studies in James Joyce, E.M. Forster, & the Twentieth Century Novel. 1980. lib. bdg. 59.95 (ISBN 0-87700-269-X). Revisionist Pr.
Sahni, Chaman L. E. M. Forster: The Religious Dimension. 160p. 1981. text ed. write for info. (ISBN 0-391-02201-6). Humanities.
Shahane, Vasant A. Approaches to E. M. Forester. 1981. 10.25 (ISBN 0-391-02200-8). Humanities.
FORTIFICATION
see also Castles
also subdivision Defenses under countries, e.g. Great Britain–Defenses; also names of specific forts, e.g. Fort Ticonderoga
Hart, Herbert M. Tour Guide to Old Forts of New Mexico, Arizona, Nevada, Utah, Colorado, Vol. 2. (Illus.). 65p. (Orig.). 1981. pap. 3.95 (ISBN 0-87108-581-X). Pruett.
--Tour Guide to Old Forts of Oregon, Idaho, Washington, California, Vol. 3. (Illus.). 65p. (Orig.). 1981. pap. 3.95 (ISBN 0-87108-582-8). Pruett.
--Tour Guide to Old Forts of Texas, Kansas, Nebraska, Oklahoma, Vol. 4. (Illus.). 65p. (Orig.). 1981. pap. 3.95 (ISBN 0-87108-583-6). Pruett.
FORTRAN (COMPUTER PROGRAM LANGUAGE)
see also GASP (Computer Program Language)
Bent, Robert J. & Sethares, George C. Fortran. LC 80-28581. 448p. (Orig.). 1981. pap. text ed. 16.95 (ISBN 0-8185-0436-6). Brooks-Cole.
Boillot, Michel. Understanding FORTRAN. 2nd ed. (Illus.). 500p. 1981. pap. text ed. 11.16 (ISBN 0-8299-0355-0). West Pub.
Burkhard, R. E. & Derigs, U. Assignment & Matching Problems: Solution Methods with FORTRAN-Programs. (Lecture Notes in Economics & Mathematical Systems Ser.: Vol. 184). 148p. 1981. pap. 15.00 (ISBN 0-387-10267-1). Springer-Verlag.
Cress, P., et al. Strucured FORTRAN with Watfiv-S. 1980. pap. 13.95 (ISBN 0-13-854752-1). P-H.
Didday, Richard & Page, Rex. Fortran for Humans. 3rd ed. (Illus.). 450p. 1981. pap. text ed. 10.36 (ISBN 0-8299-0356-9). West Pub.
Duchane, Emma, ed. User's Manual, Advanced Fortran IV Utilities for Data General Computers. (Illus.). viii, 223p. 1980. pap. 20.00 (ISBN 0-938876-03-1). Entropy Ltd.
Friedman, Frank & Koffman, Elliot. Problem Solving & Structured Programming in Fortran. 2nd ed. LC 80-20943. (First Course in Computers Ser.). 450p. 1981. pap. text ed. 11.95 (ISBN 0-201-02461-6). A-W.
Friedmann, J., et al. Fortran Four. 2nd ed. (Wiley Self Teaching Guide Ser.). 544p. 1980. pap. 10.95 (ISBN 0-471-07771-2). Wiley.
Hill, Louis A., Jr. Structured Programming in FORTRAN. (Illus.). 512p. 1981. text ed. 13.95 (ISBN 0-13-854612-6). P-H.
Honess, Brian C. Structured Business Problem Solving with Fortran. 300p. 1981. text ed. 13.95 (ISBN 0-205-07332-8); free (ISBN 0-205-07328-X). Allyn.
Nanney, T. Ray. Computing: A Problem-Solving Approach Using FORTRAN Seventy-Seven. (Illus.). 432p. 1981. text ed. 17.95 (ISBN 0-13-165209-5). P-H.
Petersen, T. M. Elementary FORTRAN. (Illus.). 176p. 1976. pap. text ed. 10.95x (ISBN 0-7121-0548-4, Pub. by Macdonald & Evans England). Intl Ideas.
SAS Institute Inc., ed. SAS Programmer's Guide, Nineteen Eighty-One Edition. (SAS Programmer's Guide). 208p. (Orig.). 1980. pap. 9.95. SAS Inst.
Schmidt, B. GPSS Fortran. (Computing Ser.). 544p. 1981. write for info. (ISBN 0-471-27881-5, Pub. by Wiley-Interscience). Wiley.
Seeds, Harice L. Structured Fortran Seventy-Seven for Business & General Applications. 496p. 1981. text ed. 15.95 (ISBN 0-471-07836-0). Wiley.
FORTS
see Fortification
FORTUNES
see Income; Wealth
FOSSIL BOTANY
see Paleobotany
FOSSIL MAN
Weiner, J. S. The Piltdown Forgery. (Illus.). 240p. 1981. pap. 4.00 (ISBN 0-486-24075-4). Dover.
FOSSILS
see Paleontology
FOSTER DAY CARE
see Day Care Centers
FOSTER HOME CARE
see also Adoption
Cautley, Patricia W. New Foster Parents. 288p. 1980. 19.95 (ISBN 0-87705-495-9). Human Sci Pr.
Felker, Evelyn. Raising Other People's Kids: Successful Child-Rearing in the Restructured Family. 160p. (Orig.). 1981. pap. 4.95 (ISBN 0-8028-1868-4). Eerdmans.
Hubbell, Ruth. Foster Care & Families: Conflicting Values & Policies. (Family Impact Seminar Ser.). 200p. 1981. 15.00x (ISBN 0-87722-206-1). Temple U Pr.
FOUNDATIONS
see also Concrete; Masonry; Piling (Civil Engineering); Soil Mechanics; Walls
Institute of Civil Engineers. Diaphragm Walls & Anchorages. 234p. 1980. 79.00x (ISBN 0-7277-0005-7, Pub. by Telford England). State Mutual Bk.
FOUNDATIONS (ENDOWMENTS)
see Charitable Uses, Trusts and Foundations
FOUNDING
see also Die Casting; Metal-Work; Pattern-Making; Type and Type-Founding
Information Sources on the Foundry Industry. rev. ed. (UNIDO Guides to Information Sources Ser.: No.5). 87p. pap. 4.00 (UN). Unipub.
Longden, E. Densening & Chilling in Foundary Work. 178p. 1954. 10.95x (ISBN 0-85264-040-4, Pub. by Griffin England). State Mutual Bk.
FOUNDRY PRACTICE
see Founding
FOWLS
see Poultry
FOX INDIANS
see Indians of North America–Northwest, Old
FRACTIONS
Gregorich, Barbara & Odom, Clark. Fractions. LC 79-730045. (Illus.). 1978. 99.00 (ISBN 0-89290-094-6, A510-SATC). Soc for Visual.
Learning Achievement Corporation. Fractions & Food: Fractions, Decimals & Electronic Communications. Zak, Therese A., ed. (MATCH Ser.). (Illus.). 144p. Date not set. text ed. 5.28 (ISBN 0-07-037113-X, G). McGraw.
Mick, Beverly J. Multiplication Facts & Basic Fractions. (gr. 5-12). 1981. Set. price not set (ISBN 0-932786-04-9); Bk. 1. 4.25 (ISBN 0-932786-05-7); Bk. 2. 4.25 (ISBN 0-932786-06-5). Bellefontaine.
FRACTIONS–PROGRAMMED INSTRUCTION
Gatje, Charles T. & Gatje, John F. A MAP for Fractions. Marcos, Rafael, tr. (Orig., Span.). (gr. 5 up). 1981. pap. text ed. 1.75 (ISBN 0-937534-07-2). G & G Pubs.
Sorracco, Lionel J., Jr. Math House Proficiency Review Tapes: Operations with Whole Numbers & Fractions, Unit A. (YA) (gr. 7 up). 1980. manual & cassettes 159.95 (ISBN 0-917792-03-3). Math Hse.
FRACTIONS, CONTINUED
Jones, William B. & Thron, W. J. Continued Fractions: Analytic Theory & Applications. (Encyclopedia of Mathematics & Applications Ser.: Vol. II). (Illus.). 450p. 1980. cancelled (ISBN 0-201-13510-8). A-W.
FRACTURE MECHANICS
see also Materials–Fatigue; Metals–Fracture
Garrett, G. G. & Marriott, D. L., eds. Engineering Applications of Fracture Analysis: Proceeedings of the First National Conference on Fracture Held in Johannesburg, South Africa, 7-9 November 1979. LC 80-41074. (International Ser. on the Strength & Fractures of Materials & Structures). (Illus.). 440p. 1980. 60.00 (ISBN 0-08-025437-3). Pergamon.
FRACTURE OF METALS
see Metals–Fracture
FRACTURE OF SOLIDS
see Fracture Mechanics
FRACTURES
see also Surgery; X-Rays
also subdivision Fracture or Wounds and injuries under particular bones etc, e.g. Skull–Wounds and Injuries
Connolly, John F., ed. DePalma's the Management of Fractures & Dislocations: An Atlas, 2 vols. 3rd ed. (Illus.). 2000p. Date not set. Set. text ed. price not set (ISBN 0-7216-2666-1); Vol. 1. price not set (ISBN 0-7216-2702-1); Vol. 2. price not set (ISBN 0-7216-2703-X). Saunders.
Francois, D. Advances in Fracture Research: Proceedings of the 5th International Conference on Fracture, 1981, Cannes, France. LC 80-41879. (International Series on the Strength & Fracture of Materials & Structures). 3000p. 1981. 450.00 (ISBN 0-08-025428-4); pap. 375.00 (ISBN 0-08-024776-8). Pergamon.
Letournel, E. & Judet, R. Fracture to the Acetabulum. (Illus.). 420p. 1981. 162.00 (ISBN 0-387-09875-5). Springer-Verlag.
Mears, Dana C. External Skeletal Fixation. (Illus.). 584p. 1981. write for info. (5900-9). Williams & Wilkins.
Sarmiento, A. & Latta, L. Closed Functional Treatment of Fractures. (Illus.). 650p. 1981. 148.00 (ISBN 0-387-10384-8). Springer-Verlag.
FRAMING OF PICTURES
see Picture Frames and Framing
FRANCE–BIOGRAPHY
Gold, Arthur & Fizdale, Robert. Misia: The Life of Misia Sert. (Illus.). 340p. 1981. Repr. pap. price not set (ISBN 0-688-00391-5, Quill). Morrow.
Lafranche, Gaston M. The Intimate Memoirs of Louise Renee De Kerouālle, Duchess of Portsmouth & Aubigny. (The Great Women of History Library). (Illus.). 94p. 1981. 19.85 (ISBN 0-89266-275-1). Am Classical Coll Pr.
FRANCE–COMMERCE
Franko, Lawrence & Stephenson, Sherry. French Export Behavior in Third World Markets, Vol. II. LC 80-66695. (Significant Issues Ser.: No. 6). 96p. 1980. 4.00. CSI Studies.
FRANCE–COURT AND COURTIERS
Petersen-Dyggve, Holgern. Trouveres et Protecteurs De Trouveres Dans les Cours Seigneuriales De France. LC 80-2168. 1981. Repr. of 1942 ed. 41.50 (ISBN 0-404-19032-4). AMS Pr.
FRANCE–DESCRIPTION AND TRAVEL
Eliot, John. The Survey, or Topographical Description of France. with a New Mappe. LC 79-84104. (English Experience Ser.: No. 923). (Illus.). 116p. 1979. Repr. of 1592 ed. lib. bdg. 11.50 (ISBN 90-221-0923-2). Walter J Johnson.
Lanier, Alison R. Update -- France. (Country Orientation Ser.). 1980. pap. text ed. 25.00 (ISBN 0-933662-41-6). Intercult Pr.
FRANCE–DESCRIPTION AND TRAVEL–GUIDEBOOKS
Bristow, Philip. Through the French Canals. 200p. 1980. 18.00 (ISBN 0-245-53403-2, Pub. by Nautical England). State Mutual Bk.
French Pilot, Vol.1. 224p. 1980. 30.00x (Pub. by Nautical England). State Mutual Bk.
Robson, Malcom. French Pilot, Vol. 2. 256p. 1980. 33.00x (ISBN 0-245-53382-6, Pub. by Nautical England). State Mutual Bk.
FRANCE–ECONOMIC CONDITIONS
Merriman, John, ed. French Cities in the Nineteenth Century. 256p. 1981. text ed. 28.50x (ISBN 0-8419-0464-2). Holmes & Meier.
FRANCE–ECONOMIC POLICY
French Export Behaviour in Third World Markets. (Significant Issues Ser.: Vol. II, No. 6). 96p. 1980. pap. 7.50 (ISBN 0-89206-021-2, CSIS014, CSIS). Unipub.
FRANCE–FOREIGN RELATIONS
French Export Behaviour in Third World Markets. (Significant Issues Ser.: Vol. II, No. 6). 96p. 1980. pap. 7.50 (ISBN 0-89206-021-2, CSIS014, CSIS). Unipub.
FRANCE–HISTORY
Bernier, Olivier. Pleasure & Privilege: Life in France, Naples & America. LC 79-6174. (Illus.). 304p. 1981. 14.95 (ISBN 0-385-15780-0). Doubleday.
Blaze, Francois H. L' Academie Imperiale De Musique: Histoire Litteraire, Musicale, Politique et Galant De Ce Theatre, De 1645 a 1855, 2 vols. LC 80-2258. 1981. Repr. of 1855 ed. 95.00 (ISBN 0-404-18804-4). AMS Pr.
Chenon, Emile. Etude sur l'Histoire des Alleux en France avec une Carte des Pays Allodiaux. LC 80-2036. 1981. Repr. of 1888 ed. 33.00 (ISBN 0-404-18557-6). AMS Pr.
Lot, Ferdinand. L' Impot Foncier et la Capitation Personnelle Sous le Bas-Empire et a l'epoque Franque. LC 80-2018. 1981. Repr. of 1928 ed. 21.50 (ISBN 0-404-18576-2). AMS Pr.
Wright, Gordon. France in Modern Times. 3rd ed. 500p. 1981. 24.95 (ISBN 0-393-95153-7); 12.95 (ISBN 0-393-95153-7). Norton.
--France in Modern Times. 3rd ed. 1981. 24.95 (ISBN 0-393-01455-X). Norton.
FRANCE–HISTORY–TO 987
see also Latin Empire, 1204-1261
Dhondt, Jan. Etudes Sur la Naissance Des Principautes Territoriales En France, IXe-IXe Siecle. LC 80-2033. 1981. Repr. of 1948 ed. 38.50 (ISBN 0-404-18560-6). AMS Pr.
Lewis, Archibald R. The Development of Southern French & Catalan Society Seven Eighteen to Ten Fifty. LC 80-2019. 1981. Repr. of 1965 ed. 47.50 (ISBN 0-404-18575-4). AMS Pr.
FRANCE–HISTORY–CAPETIANS, 987-1328
Here are entered works on the period from The Capetians to 1328 as a whole, as well as those on any part of the period.
Newman, William M. Le Domaine Royal Sous les Premiers Capetiens (987-1180) LC 80-2014. 1981. Repr. of 1937 ed. 36.00 (ISBN 0-404-18581-9). AMS Pr.
FRANCE–HISTORY–MEDIEVAL PERIOD, 987-1515
Here are entered works on the medieval period as whole as well as those on any part of this period.
Didier, Noel. Le Droit Des Fiefs Dans la Coutume De Hainaut Au Moyen Age. LC 80-2032. 1981. Repr. of 1945 ed. 29.50 (ISBN 0-404-18561-4). AMS Pr.
Rose, J. H. The Revolutionary & Napoleonic Era. 387p. 1980. Repr. of 1894 ed. lib. bdg. 40.00 (ISBN 0-89760-737-6). Telegraph Bks.

FRANCE–HISTORY–BOURBONS, 1589-1789
Here are entered works on the history of France from 1589 to 1789 as a whole as well as those on any portion of it. For books about individual kings, etc. see under the names of kings etc. e.g. Louis 12th King of France; Richelieu.
Golden, Richard. The Godly Rebellion: Parisian Cures & the Religious Fronde, 1652-1662. LC 80-25282. 264p. 1981. 22.50x (ISBN 0-8078-1466-0). U of NC Pr.
• McLynn, Francis. France & the Jacobite Rising of Seventeen Forty-Five. 256p. 1981. 26.50x (ISBN 0-85224-404-5, Pub. by Edinburgh U Pr Scotland). Columbia U Pr.
FRANCE–HISTORY–17TH CENTURY
see France–History–Bourbons, 1589-1789
FRANCE–HISTORY–1789-1815
Phillips, Roderick. Family Breakdown in Late Eighteenth Century France: Divorces in Rouen 1792-1803. (Illus.). 288p. 1980. 55.00 (ISBN 0-19-822572-5). Oxford U Pr.
FRANCE–HISTORY–1789-1900
Agulhon, Maurice. Marianne into Battle: Republican Imagery & Symbolism in France, 1789-1880. Lloyd, Janet, tr. (Co-Publication with the Maison Des Sciences De L'homme). (Illus.). 224p. Date not set. price not set (ISBN 0-521-23577-4); pap. price not set (ISBN 0-521-28224-1). Cambridge U Pr.
FRANCE–HISTORY–REVOLUTION, 1789-1799
Doyle, William. Origins of the French Revolution. 272p. 1981. 37.50 (ISBN 0-19-873020-9); pap. 14.95 (ISBN 0-19-873021-7). Oxford U Pr.
Jordan, David P. The King's Trial: Louis XVI Vs. the French Revolution. 1981. pap. 5.95 (ISBN 0-520-04399-5, CAL 497). U of Cal Pr.
Manceron, Claude. The French Revolution: Their Gracious Pleasure, Vol. III. LC 80-36724. (Illus.). 480p. 1981. 19.95 (ISBN 0-394-50155-1). Knopf.
FRANCE–HISTORY–REVOLUTION, 1789-1799–CAUSES AND CHARACTER
Doyle, William. Origins of the French Revolution. 272p. 1981. 37.50 (ISBN 0-19-873020-9); pap. 14.95 (ISBN 0-19-873021-7). Oxford U Pr.
FRANCE–HISTORY–REVOLUTION, 1789-1799–PHILOSOPHY
see France–History–Revolution, 1789-1799–Causes and Character
FRANCE–HISTORY–SECOND REPUBLIC, 1848-1852
Forstenzer, Thomas R. French Provincial Police & the Fall of the Second Republic: Social Fear & Counterrevolution. LC 80-8549. 384p. 1981. 25.00x (ISBN 0-691-05318-9). Princeton U Pr.
FRANCE–HISTORY–CRIMEAN WAR, 1853-1856
see Crimean War, 1853-1856
FRANCE–HISTORY–THIRD REPUBLIC, 1870-1940
Kennan, George F. The Decline of Bismarck's European Order: Franco-Russian Relations, 1875-1890. LC 79-83997. (Illus.). 478p. (Orig.). 1981. pap. 6.95 (ISBN 0-691-00784-5). Princeton U Pr.
FRANCE–HISTORY–COMMUNE, 1871
see Paris–History–Commune, 1871
FRANCE–HISTORY–1914-1940
Andrew, Christopher M. & Kanya-Forstner, A. S. The Climax of French Imperial Expansion, 1914-1924. (Illus.). 304p. 1981. 29.50x (ISBN 0-8047-1101-1). Stanford U Pr.
FRANCE–INTELLECTUAL LIFE
Debray, Regis. Teachers, Writers, Celebrities: The Intellectuals of Modern France. 300p. 1981. 17.50 (ISBN 0-8052-7086-8, Pub. by NLB England). Schocken.
FRANCE–JUVENILE LITERATURE
Goldstein, Frances. Children's Treasure Hunt Travel to Belgium & France. LC 80-85012. (Children's Treasure Hunt Travel Guide Ser.). (Illus.). 230p. (Orig.). (gr. k-12). 1981. pap. 4.95 (ISBN 0-933334-02-8). Paper Tiger Pap.
FRANCE–KINGS AND RULERS
Newman, William M. The Kings, the Court & Royal Power in France in the Eleventh Century. LC 80-2030. 1981. Repr. of 1929 ed. 24.50 (ISBN 0-404-18582-7). AMS Pr.
FRANCE–LAWS, STATUTES, ETC.
Kroell, Maurice. L Immunite Franque. LC 80-2021. 1981. Repr. of 1910 ed. 39.50 (ISBN 0-404-18573-8). AMS Pr.
FRANCE–MAPS
Eliot, John. The Survey, or Topographical Description of France. with a New Mappe. LC 79-84104. (English Experience Ser.: No. 923). (Illus.). 116p. 1979. Repr. of 1592 ed. lib. bdg. 11.50 (ISBN 90-221-0923-2). Walter J Johnson.
FRANCE–MILITARY POLICY
Martin, Michel L. Warriors to Managers: The French Military Establishment Since 1945. LC 79-28114. (Illus.). 424p. 1981. 21.00x (ISBN 0-8078-1421-0). U of NC Pr.
FRANCE–NOBILITY
Balon, Joseph. Etudes Franques, I: Aux Origines De la Noblesse. LC 80-2202. 1981. Repr. of 1963 ed. 16.50 (ISBN 0-404-18551-7). AMS Pr.
Lafranche, Gaston M. The Intimate Memoirs of Louise Renee De Kerouaille, Duchess of Portsmouth & Aubigny. (The Great Women of History Library). (Illus.). 94p. 1981. 19.85 (ISBN 0-89266-275-1). Am Classical Coll Pr.
FRANCE–PARLEMENT (PARIS)
Stone, Bailey S. Parlement of Paris, 1774-1789. LC 79-27732. xi, 227p. 1981. 19.00x (ISBN 0-8078-1442-3). U of NC Pr.
FRANCE–POLITICS AND GOVERNMENT
Jacobs, Dan N., et al. Comparative Politics: Introduction to the Politics of Britain, France, Germany, & the Soviet Union. pap. 9.95 (ISBN 0-934540-05-5). Chatham Hse Pubs.
Stone, Bailey S. Parlement of Paris, 1774-1789. LC 79-27732. xi, 227p. 1981. 19.00x (ISBN 0-8078-1442-3). U of NC Pr.
FRANCE–POLITICS AND GOVERNMENT–1328-1589
Seyssel, Claude De. The Monarchy of France. Hexter, J. H. & Kelley, Donald H., trs. from Fr. LC 80-23554. 1981. text ed. 16.95x (ISBN 0-300-02516-5). Yale U Pr.
FRANCE–POLITICS AND GOVERNMENT–1870-
Singer, Barnett. Modern France: Mind, Politics, Society, 1870-1970. LC 80-24177. 212p. 1981. 16.95 (ISBN 0-686-69480-5). U of Wash Pr.
FRANCE–POLITICS AND GOVERNMENT–20TH CENTURY
Kuisel, Richard F. Capitalism & the State in Modern France: Renovation & Economic Management in the Twentieth Century. 352p. Date not set. price not set (ISBN 0-521-23474-3). Cambridge U Pr.
FRANCE–SOCIAL LIFE AND CUSTOMS
Singer, Barnett. Modern France: Mind, Politics, Society, 1870-1970. LC 80-24177. 212p. 1981. 16.95 (ISBN 0-686-69480-5). U of Wash Pr.
FRANCESCO D'ASSISI, SAINT, 1182-1226
Garner, Robert H. The Way of St. Francis. 1981. 6.95 (ISBN 0-8062-1605-0). Carlton.
FRANCESCO D'ASSISI, SAINT, 1182-1226–JUVENILE LITERATURE
De Paola, Tomie. St. Francis of Assisi. (Illus.). 48p. (ps). 1981. PLB 10.95 (ISBN 0-8234-0435-8). Holiday.
FRANCHISE
see Elections
FRANCHISES (RETAIL TRADE)
Green, Michael L., ed. Franchise Handbook. rev. ed. Date not set. 12.00 (ISBN 0-89552-027-3); pap. text ed. 7.95 (ISBN 0-89552-026-5). DMR Pubns.
Head, Victor. Sponsorship: The Newest Marketing Skill. 160p. 1980. 39.00x (ISBN 0-85941-151-6, Pub. by Woodhead-Faulkner England). State Mutual Bk.
Hicks, Tyler G. Franchise Riches Success Kit. 2nd ed. 876p. 1981. pap. 99.50 (ISBN 0-914306-40-5). Intl Wealth.
FRANCHISES, TAXATION OF
see Corporations–Taxation
FRANCIS OF ASSISI, SAINT
see Francesco D'Assisi, Saint, 1182-1226
FRANCISCANS–MISSIONS
Dawson, Christopher. Mission to Asia. (Medieval Academy Reprints for Teaching Ser.). 228p. 1981. pap. 6.00x (ISBN 0-8020-6436-1). U of Toronto Pr.
FRANCISCANS–SECOND ORDER
see Poor Clares
FRANCO-ENGLISH WAR, 1755-1763
see United States–History–French and Indian War, 1755-1763
FRANCS-TIREURS
see Guerrillas
FRANKFURTER, FELIX, 1882-1965
Hirsch, H. N. The Enigma of Felix Frankfurter. LC 80-68184. 320p. 1981. 14.95 (ISBN 0-465-01979-X). Basic.
FRANKLIN, BENJAMIN, 1706-1790
Conner, Paul W. Poor Richard's Politicks: Benjamin Franklin & His New American Order. LC 80-21490. xiv, 285p. 1980. Repr. of 1965 ed. lib. bdg. 27.50x (ISBN 0-313-22695-4, COPRP). Greenwood.
Lokken, Roy N., ed. Meet Dr. Franklin. 2nd ed. 295p. 1981. 20.00 (ISBN 0-89168-035-7). Franklin Inst Pr.
Zall, Paul M., ed. Ben Franklin Laughing: Anecdotes from Original Sources by & About Benjamin Franklin. 216p. 1981. 12.95 (ISBN 0-520-04026-0). U of Cal Pr.
FRANKLIN, BENJAMIN, 1706-1790–JUVENILE LITERATURE
Franklin, Benjamin. The Autobiography & Selected Writings. Lemisch, Jesse, ed. & intro. by. Date not set. pap. 2.50 (ISBN 0-451-51463-7, CJ1332, Sig Classics). NAL.
FRATERNAL BENEFIT SOCIETIES
see Friendly Societies
FRATERNAL ORGANIZATIONS
see Friendly Societies
FRAUD
see also Impostors and Imposture
Bigelow, Melville M. The Law of Fraud & the Procedure Pertaining to the Redress Thereof. lix, 696p. 1981. Repr. of 1877 ed. lib. bdg. 45.00x (ISBN 0-8377-0317-4). Rothman.
Roberts, David. Great Exploration Hoaxes. Michaelman, Herbert, ed. 1981. 12.95 (ISBN 0-517-54075-4, Michaelman Books). Crown.
Thomas, John L. Law of Lotteries, Frauds & Obscenity in the Mails. xviii, 358p. 1980. Repr. of 1903 ed. lib. bdg. 32.50x (ISBN 0-8377-1202-5). Rothman.
FREAKS
see Monsters
FREDHOLM'S EQUATION
see Integral Equations
FREE AGENCY
see Free Will and Determinism
FREE COINAGE
see Silver Question
FREE HARBORS
see Free Ports and Zones
FREE MATERIAL
Free Stuff Editors, ed. Free Stuff for Home & Garden. (Illus.). 120p. (Orig.). 1981. pap. 2.95 (ISBN 0-915658-27-5). Meadowbrook Pr.
--Free Stuff for Travelers. 120p. (Orig.). 1981. pap. 2.95 (ISBN 0-915658-29-1). Meadowbrook Pr.
FREE PORTS AND ZONES
Waldmann, Raymond J., ed. U S Foreign Trade Zones. (Orig.). 1981. pap. 45.00 (ISBN 0-933678-02-9). Transnatl Invest.
FREE SPEECH
see Liberty of Speech
FREE THOUGHT
see also Bible–Evidences, Authority, Etc.
Cohen, Chapman. Essays in Freethinking, Vol. 1. 1980. pap. 4.00. Am Atheist.
FREE TRADE AREAS
see Customs Unions
FREE WILL AND DETERMINISM
see also Freedom (Theology); Responsibility
Schuller, Robert H. Discover Freedom. (Orig.) 1978. pap. 1.25 (ISBN 0-89081-155-5). Harvest Hse.
FREE ZONES
see Free Ports and Zones
FREEBOOTERS
see Buccaneers; Pirates
FREED SLAVES
see Freedmen
FREEDMEN
Morris, Robert C. Reading, 'Writing, & Reconstruction: The Education of Freedmen in the South, 1861-1870. LC 80-25370. (Illus.). 1981. lib. bdg. price not set (ISBN 0-226-53928-8). U of Chicago Pr.
FREEDMEN IN THE UNITED STATES
see Freedmen
FREEDOM
see Liberty
FREEDOM (THEOLOGY)
Brown, Delwin. To Set at Liberty: Christian Faith & Human Freedom. LC 80-21783. 144p. (Orig.). 1981. pap. 6.95 (ISBN 0-88344-501-8). Orbis Bks.
Martin, Everett D. Liberty. 307p. 1981. Repr. of 1930 ed. lib. bdg. 20.00. Arden Lib.
FREEDOM OF SPEECH
see Liberty of Speech
FREEDOM OF SPEECH IN THE CHURCH
see Liberty of Speech in the Church
FREEDOM OF TEACHING
see Teaching, Freedom Of
FREEDOM OF THE PRESS
see Liberty of the Press
FREEDOM OF THE WILL
see Free Will and Determinism
FREEHOLD
see Land Tenure; Real Property
FREEMAN'S FARM, BATTLE OF, 1777
see Saratoga Campaign, 1777
FREEMASONS
Coil, Henry W. Conversation on Freemasonry. 1980. Repr. soft cover 12.50 (ISBN 0-686-68272-6). Macoy Pub.
Denslow, William R. Ten Thousand Famous Freemasons, 4 vols. 1979. Repr. Set. pap. 29.95 slip cover (ISBN 0-686-68268-8). Macoy Pub.
McCoy, Winston. Fellow-Crafts Ritual. 1981. 4.95 (ISBN 0-8062-1608-5). Carlton.
Makrakis, Apostolos. Freemasonry Known by the Masonic Diploma. Cummings, Denver, tr. 135p. (Orig.). 1956. pap. 3.00x (ISBN 0-938366-42-4). Orthodox Chr.
FREESIAS
Smith, Denis. Freesias. 90p. 1980. pap. 9.95 (ISBN 0-901361-25-9, Pub. by Grower Bks England). Intl Schol Bk Serv.
FREEZE-DRYING
Sunset Editors. Canning, Freezing & Drying. 2nd ed. LC 80-53480. (Illus.). 128p. 1981. pap. 4.95 (ISBN 0-376-02213-2, Sunset Books). Sunset-Lane.
FREEZING
see Refrigeration and Refrigerating Machinery
FREEZING OF FOOD
see Food, Frozen
FREIGHT AND FREIGHTAGE
see also Breakage, Shrinkage, etc. (Commerce)
Reebie Associates, et al. Transguide: A Guide to Sources of Freight Transportation Information. LC 80-53144. 392p. 1980. 40.00 (ISBN 0-9604776-0-8). Reebie Assoc.
FREIGHT HANDLING
see Freight and Freightage
FREIGHT PLANES
see Transport Planes
FREIGHT RATES
see Freight and Freightage
FREIGHT SHIPS
see Cargo Ships
FREIGHT VESSELS
see Cargo Ships
FREIGHTERS
see Cargo Ships
FRENCH AND INDIAN WAR, 1755-1763
see United States–History–French and Indian War, 1755-1763
FRENCH ART
see Art, French
FRENCH AUTHORS
see Authors, French
FRENCH-CANADIAN LITERATURE
Bouchard, Rene, ed. Culture Populaire et Litteratures Au Quebec. (Stanford French & Italian Studies: Vol. 19). 308p. (Fr.). 1980. pap. 20.00 (ISBN 0-915838-20-6). Anma Libri.
FRENCH DRAMA–HISTORY AND CRITICISM
Cook, Albert. French Tragedy: The Power of Enchantment. LC 80-39611. 136p. 1981. 12.00x (ISBN 0-8040-0548-6). Swallow.
Gossip, C. J. An Introduction to French Classical Tragedy. 1981. 29.50x (ISBN 0-389-20163-4). B&N.
Hobson, Harold. French Theatre Since Eighteen Thirty. 1979. 17.95 (ISBN 0-7145-3650-4). Riverrun NY.
FRENCH DRAWINGS
see Drawings, French
FRENCH FICTION–HISTORY AND CRITICISM
Hicks, Benjamin E. Plots & Characters in Classic French Fiction. (Plots & Characters Ser.). 1981. 27.50 (ISBN 0-208-01703-8, Archon). Shoe String.
Minogue, Valerie. Nathalie Sarraute: The War of the Words. 156p. 1981. 21.00x (ISBN 0-85224-405-3, Pub. by Edinburgh U Pr Sctland). Columbia U Pr.
FRENCH LANGUAGE
L'Universelle Bordas, 10 vols. (Fr.). 1976. 495.00 set. Pergamon.
Rudman, Jack. French. (Undergraduate Program Field Test Ser.: UPFT-9). (Cloth bdg. avail. on request). pap. 9.95 (ISBN 0-8373-6009-9). Natl Learning.
Stern, A. Z. & Reif, Joseph A., eds. Useful Expressions in French. (Useful Expressions Ser.). 64p. (Orig.). 1980. pap. 1.50 (ISBN 0-86628-006-5). Ridgefield Pub.
FRENCH LANGUAGE–ABBREVIATIONS
see Abbreviations
FRENCH LANGUAGE–CONVERSATION AND PHRASE BOOKS
Arnold, Julius. Student's Guide to Basic French. 2nd ed. 184p. (gr. 9-11). 1980. pap. text ed. 5.50 (ISBN 0-88334-021-6). Ind Sch Pr.
FRENCH LANGUAGE–DIALECTS
Bouchard, Rene, ed. Culture Populaire et Litteratures Au Quebec. (Stanford French & Italian Studies: Vol. 19). 308p. (Fr.). 1980. pap. 20.00 (ISBN 0-915838-20-6). Anma Libri.
FRENCH LANGUAGE–DICTIONARIES–ARABIC
Saisse, Louis. Dictionnaire Francais-Arabe. 1980. pap. 7.95x. Intl Bk Ctr.
FRENCH LANGUAGE–DICTIONARIES–ENGLISH
Cruikshank, Eleanor P. French-English Instant Vocabulary Francais-Anglais. 88p. 1980. pap. 4.00 (ISBN 0-9605284-0-7). Cruikshank.
Gieber, Robert L. An English-French Glossary of Educational Terminology. LC 80-5652. 212p. 1980. lib. bdg. 18.00 (ISBN 0-8191-1344-1); pap. text ed. 9.25 (ISBN 0-8191-1345-X). U Pr of Amer.
FRENCH LANGUAGE–GRAMMAR
Coffman, Mary. Schaum's Outline of French Grammar. (Schaum's Outline Ser.). 288p. 1980. pap. 4.95 (ISBN 0-07-011553-2, SP). McGraw.
Donaldson-Evans, Lancelot K. Love's Fatal Glance: A Study of Eye Imagery in the Poets of the Ecole lyonnaise. LC 80-10415. (Romance Monographs: No. 39). 155p. 1980. 14.50 (ISBN 84-499-3694-2). Romance.
FRENCH LANGUAGE–HISTORY
Mackenzie, Fraser, et al, eds. Studies in French Language Literature & History. 258p. 1980. Repr. of 1949 ed. lib. bdg. 50.00 (ISBN 0-89760-736-8). Telegraph Bks.
FRENCH LANGUAGE–STUDY AND TEACHING
Adler-Golden, Rachel & Gordon, Debbie. Beginning French with Preschoolers: A Montessori Handbook. LC 80-83136. (Illus.). 85p. 1980. pap. text ed. 6.00 (ISBN 0-915676-04-4). Montessori Wkshps.
Foreign Service Institute. Advanced French, 2 pts. 567p. 1980. Pt. A. text & cassettes 170.00x (ISBN 0-88432-067-7, Audio-Forum); Pt. B. text & cassettes 160.00 (ISBN 0-88432-068-5). J Norton Pubs.
FRENCH LANGUAGE–WORDS–HISTORY
Kirk-Greene, C. W. E. French False Friends. 272p. 1981. 18.95 (ISBN 0-7100-0741-8). Routledge & Kegan.
FRENCH LITERATURE (COLLECTIONS)
Here are entered collections of French Literature in French. For translations into English see subdivision Translations into English.
see also French-Canadian Literature
Artaud, Antonin. Artaud: Four Texts. Eshleman, Clayton, tr. from Fr. (Illus.). 80p. 1981. 9.95 (ISBN 0-915572-57-5); pap. 4.50 (ISBN 0-915572-56-7). Panjandrum.

FRENCH LITERATURE (COLLECTIONS)–TO 1500

Gauthier, J. D., ed. French Twenty Bibliography: Provencal Upplement No. 1, Critical & Biographical References to Provencal Literature Since 1850. (Orig.). 1976. pap. 12.00 (ISBN 0-933444-32-X). French Inst.

FRENCH LITERATURE–BIBLIOGRAPHY

Alden, Douglas W., ed. French Twenty Bibliography: Critical & Bibliographical References for the Study of French Literature Since 1885, No. 32. LC 77-648803. (Orig.). 1981. pap. 42.00 (ISBN 0-933444-37-0). French Inst.

FRENCH LITERATURE–HISTORY AND CRITICISM

Aldington, Richard. A Book of Characters from Theophrastus Joseph Hall, Sir Thomas Overbury, Nicolas Breton, John Earle, Thomas Fuller, & Other English Authors; Jean De la Bruyere, Vauvenargues, & Other French Authors. 559p. 1980. Repr. of 1924 ed. lib. bdg. 50.00 (ISBN 0-8482-0049-7). Norwood Edns.

Baker, Susan R. Collaboration et Originalite Chez la Rochefoucauld. LC 79-21085. (U. of Fla. Humanities Monographs: No. 48). 135p. (Orig.). 1980. pap. 9.00 (ISBN 0-8130-0657-0). U Presses Fla.

Boissier, Gaston. Great French Writers: Madame De Sevigne. 154p. 1980. Repr. of 1887 ed. lib. bdg. 25.00 (ISBN 0-8495-0476-7). Arden Lib.

Busby, Keith. Gauvain in Old French Literature. (Degre Second Ser.: No. 2). 425p. 1980. pap. text ed. 48.50x (ISBN 90-6203-831-X). Humanities.

Fairlie, Alison. Imagination & Language. LC 80-40307. (Illus.). 400p. Date not set. 72.00 (ISBN 0-521-23291-0). Cambridge U Pr.

Glidden, Hope H. The Storyteller As Humanist: The Serees of Guillaume Bouchet. (French Forum Monographs: No. 25). 200p. (Orig.). 1981. pap. 11.50 (ISBN 0-917058-24-0). French Forum.

Kerr, Cynthia B. L' Amour, L'Amitie et Laa Fourberie: Une Etude Des Premieres Comedies De Corneille. (Stanford French & Italian Studies: Vol. 20). 152p. (Fr.). 1980. pap. 20.00 (ISBN 0-915838-19-2). Anma Libri.

Mackenzie, Fraser, et al, eds. Studies in French Language Literature & History. 258p. 1980. Repr. of 1949 ed. lib. bdg. 50.00 (ISBN 0-89760-736-8). Telegraph Bks.

O'Connell, David. The Instructions of Saint Louis: A Critical Text. (Romance Language Ser.). 104p. 1980. pap. 8.00 (ISBN 0-8078-9216-5). U of NC Pr.

FRENCH LITERATURE–HISTORY AND CRITICISM–TO 1500

Brereton, Georgine E. & Ferrier, Janet M., eds. Le Menagier De Paris: A Critical Edition. 600p. 1981. 99.00 (ISBN 0-19-815748-7). Oxford U Pr.

FRENCH LITERATURE–HISTORY AND CRITICISM–19TH CENTURY

Allen, James S. Popular French Romanticism: Authors, Readers, & Books in the Nineteenth Century. LC 80-27129. (Illus.). 304p. 1981. 20.00x (ISBN 0-8156-2232-5). Syracuse U Pr.

--Popular French Romantieism: Authors, Readers, & Books in the 19th Century. (Illus.). 1980. 20.00 (ISBN 0-8156-2232-5). Syracuse U Pr.

FRENCH LITERATURE–HISTORY AND CRITICISM–20TH CENTURY

O'Rourke, Brian. The Conscience of the Race: Sex & Religion in Irish & French Novels 1941-1973. 72p. 1981. 10.00x (ISBN 0-906127-22-X, Pub. by Irish Academic Pr Ireland). Biblio Dist.

Robinson, Christopher. French Literature in the Twentieth Century. (Comparative Literature Ser.). 288p. 1981. 15.00x (ISBN 0-389-20121-9). B&N.

FRENCH LITERATURE–CANADA

see French-Canadian Literature

FRENCH MUSIC

see Music, French

FRENCH PAINTINGS

see Paintings, French

FRENCH PHILOSOPHY

see Philosophy, French

FRENCH POETRY–HISTORY AND CRITICISM

Donaldson-Evans, Lancelot K. Love's Fatal Glance: A Study of Eye Imagery in the Poets of the Ecole lyonnaise. LC 80-10415. (Romance Monographs: No. 39). 155p. 1980. 14.50 (ISBN 84-499-3694-2). Romance.

Personnages Historiques Figurant Dans la Poesie Lyrique Francaise Des XII et XIIIe Siecles. LC 80-2166. 1981. 67.50 (ISBN 0-404-19031-6). AMS Pr.

FRENCH POETRY–TRANSLATIONS INTO ENGLISH

Aspinwall, Dorothy B. French Poems in English Verse, Eighteen Fifty to Nineteen Seventy. LC 73-1782. 113p. 1973. lib. bdg. 10.00 (ISBN 0-8108-0599-5). Scarecrow.

FRENCH REVOLUTION

see France–History–Revolution, 1789-1799

FRENCH SCULPTURE

see Sculpture–France

FRENCH SONGS

see Songs, French

FREQUENCIES OF OSCILLATING SYSTEMS

MacFarlane, A. G., ed. Frequency: Response Methods in Control Systems. LC 79-90572. 1979. 39.95 (ISBN 0-87942-125-8). Inst Electrical.

FREQUENCY ANALYSIS (DYNAMICS)

see Frequencies of Oscillating Systems

FREQUENCY OF OSCILLATION

see Frequencies of Oscillating Systems

FRESH WATER

see Drinking Water; Saline Waters–Demineralization

FRESH-WATER BIOLOGY

see also Aquariums; Aquatic Plants; Fresh-Water Fauna; Fresh-Water Flora; Limnology

Barica, J. & Mur, L., eds. Hypertrophic Ecosystems. (Developments in Hydrobiology Ser.: No. 2). 330p. 1981. PLB 87.00 (ISBN 90-6193-752-3, Pub. by Dr. W. Junk). Kluwer Boston.

FRESH-WATER ECOLOGY

Moss, Brian. The Ecology of Fresh Waters. 360p. 1980. pap. 29.95x (ISBN 0-470-26942-1). Halsted Pr.

Ogden, C. G. An Atlas of Freshwater Testate Amoebae. (Illus.). 228p. 1980. text ed. 49.50x (ISBN 0-19-858502-0). Oxford U Pr.

FRESH-WATER FAUNA

see also Aquariums

Ogden, C. G. An Atlas of Freshwater Testate Amoebae. (Illus.). 228p. 1980. text ed. 49.50x (ISBN 0-19-858502-0). Oxford U Pr.

FRESH-WATER FLORA

Magee, Dennis W. Freshwater Wetlands: A Guide to Common Indicator Plants of the Northeast. LC 80-26876. (Illus.). 240p. 1981. lib. bdg. 17.50x (ISBN 0-87023-316-5); pap. text ed. 7.95x (ISBN 0-87023-317-3). U of Mass Pr.

FREUD, SIGMUND, 1856-1939

Engelman, Edmund. Berggasse Nineteen: Sigmund Freud's Home & Offices, Vienna, 1938; the Photographs of Edmund Engelman. LC 80-23056. 1981. pap. 15.00 (ISBN 0-226-20847-8). U of Chicago Pr.

Grunfeld, Frederic V. Prophets Without Honor: A Background to Freud, Kafka, Einstein & Their World. 1980. 5.95x (ISBN 0-07-025087-1). McGraw.

Jahoda, Marie. Freud & the Dilemmas of Psychology. LC 80-17140. vi, 186p. 1981. pap. 4.50x (ISBN 0-8032-7553-6, BB 759, Bison). U of Nebr Pr.

Lewis, Helen B. Freud & Modern Psychology: The/Emotional Basis of Mental Illness, Vol. 1. (Emotions Personality & Psychotherapy Ser.). 240p. 1981. 19.50 (ISBN 0-306-40525-3, Plenum Pr). Plenum Pub.

Meisel, Perry. Freud: A Collection of Critical Essays. (Twentieth Century Views Ser.). 256p. 1981. 13.95 (ISBN 0-13-331405-7, Spec); pap. 5.95 (ISBN 0-13-331397-2). P-H.

Nye, Robert D. Three Psychologies: Perspectives from Freud, Skinner & Rogers. 2nd ed. LC 80-25716. 170p. (Orig.). 1981. pap. text ed. 7.95 (ISBN 0-8185-0438-2). Brooks-Cole.

Shebar, Jonathan & Shebar, Sharon. Sigmond. (gr. 3-6). 1981. write for info. (ISBN 0-671-34003-4). Messner.

Sulloway, Frank J. Freud, Biologist of the Mind: Beyond the Psychoanalytic Legend. 20.00 (ISBN 0-686-68084-7). Basic.

Wollheim, Richard. Sigmund Freud. 316p. Date not set. pap. price not set (ISBN 0-521-28385-X). Cambridge U Pr.

FRICTION

see also Lubrication and Lubricants; Rolling Contact

Kragelsky, I. V., et al. Friction & Wear: Calculation Methods. LC 80-41669. (Illus.). 450p. 1981. 75.00 (ISBN 0-08-025461-6); pap. 60.00 (ISBN 0-08-027320-3). Pergamon.

FRIEDEL-CRAFTS REACTION

Roberts. A Century of Friedel-NCrafts Alkylations & Re-Arrangements. Date not set. price not set (ISBN 0-8247-6433-1). Dekker.

FRIENDLINESS

see Friendship

FRIENDLY SOCIETIES

Pratt, John T. The Law Relating to Friendly Societies. Berkowitz, David S. & Thorne, Samuel E., eds. LC 77-86656. (Classics of English Legal History in the Modern Era Ser.: Vol. 40). 160p. 1979. lib. bdg. 40.00 (ISBN 0-8240-3089-3). Garland Pub.

FRIENDS, SOCIETY OF

Sykes, Marjorie. Quakers in India. (Illus.). 176p. 1980. 12.95 (ISBN 0-04-275003-2, 2585). Allen Unwin.

FRIENDS, SOCIETY OF–DOCTRINAL AND CONTROVERSIAL WORKS

Bruyn, Sevpryn. Quaker Testimonies & Economic Alternatives. LC 80-80915. 35p. pap. 1.25 (ISBN 0-87574-231-9). Pendle Hill.

FRIENDS, SOCIETY OF–HISTORY

Reynolds, Reginald. The Wisdom of John Woolman: With a Selection from His Writings As a Guide to the Seekers of Today. LC 79-8724. xii, 178p. 1981. Repr. of 1948 ed. lib. bdg. 22.50x (ISBN 0-313-22190-1, REJW). Greenwood.

FRIENDSHIP

see also Love; Sympathy

Inrig, Gary. Quality Friendship. 192p. (Orig.). 1981. pap. 2.95 (ISBN 0-8024-2891-6). Moody.

Oxenbury, Helen. Friends. (Baby Board Bks.). (Illus.). 12p. (ps). Date not set. boards 3.50 (ISBN 0-671-42111-5, Little Simon). S&S.

Reader, Dennis J. Coming Back Alive. LC 79-5147. (Illus.). 256p. (gr. 7 up). 1981. 8.95 (ISBN 0-686-68070-7); PLB 8.99 (ISBN 0-686-68071-5). Random.

Reisman, John M. Anatomy of a Friendship. 260p. 1981. pap. 6.95 (ISBN 0-86616-004-3). Lewis Pub Co.

Ripple, Paula. Called to Be Friends. LC 80-67402. 160p. (Orig.). 1980. pap. 3.95 (ISBN 0-87793-212-3). Ave Maria.

FRINGE BENEFITS

see Non-Wage Payments

FRINGILLIDAE

see Finches

FRISBEE (GAME)

Poynter, Margaret. Frisbee Fun. (Illus.). (gr. 3-6). 1978. pap. 1.25 (ISBN 0-671-29885-2). PB.

Roddick, D. Frisbee Disc Basics. 1980. 8.95 (ISBN 0-13-331322-0). P-H.

FRISBIE (GAME)

see Frisbee (Game)

FROEBEL SYSTEM OF EDUCATION

see Kindergarten

FROGS

Sonntag, Linda. Frogs. (The Leprechaun Library). (Illus.). 64p. 1981. 3.95 (ISBN 0-399-12611-2). Putnam.

FROGS–JUVENILE LITERATURE

Dallinger, Jane. Frogs & Toads. (Lerner Natural Science Bks.). (Illus.). (gr. 4-10). 1981. PLB 7.95 (ISBN 0-8225-1454-0). Lerner Pubns.

FRONTIER AND PIONEER LIFE

see also Cowboys; Indians of North America–Captivities; Ranch Life

Cochran, Alice C. Miners, Merchants & Missionaries: The Roles of Missionaries & Pioneer Churches in the Colorado Gold Rush & Its Aftermath, 1858-1870. LC 80-16895. (ATLA Monographs: No. 15). x, 287p. 1980. 15.00 (ISBN 0-8108-1325-4). Scarecrow.

Hochbaum, H. Albert. Canvasback on a Prairie Marsh. LC 80-22699. (Illus.). xx, 208p. 1981. 15.95x (ISBN 0-8032-2300-5); pap. 5.95 (ISBN 0-8032-7200-6, BB 681, Bison). U of Nebr Pr.

Hum-Ishu-ma. Coge-we-a, the Half-Blood: A Depiction of the Great Montana Cattle Range. xvii, 320p. 1981. 17.95x (ISBN 0-8032-3069-9, BB 754, Bison); pap. 6.25 (ISBN 0-8032-8110-2). U of Nebr Pr.

Logan, Bob. Denim & Dogwood. (Illus.). 96p. 1981. 5.95 (ISBN 0-89962-049-3). Todd & Honeywell.

Rasmussen, Linda, et al, eds. A Harvest Yet to Reap: A History of Prairie Women. (Illus.). 240p. 1976. pap. 12.50 (ISBN 0-88961-050-9). U of Nebr Pr.

Reid, Agnes J. Letters of Long Ago. (Utah, the Mormons & the West Ser.: No. 2). 93p. 1973. 9.50 (ISBN 0-87480-158-3, Tanner). U of Utah Pr.

Utley, Robert M. Frontiersmen in Blue: The United States Army & the Indian, 1848-1865. LC 80-27796. (Illus.). xvi, 384p. 1981. 23.50x (ISBN 0-8032-4550-5, BB 769, Bison); pap. 9.95 (ISBN 0-8032-9550-2). U of Nebr Pr.

FRONTIER AND PIONEER LIFE–JUVENILE LITERATURE

Lyons, Grant. Mustangs, Six-Shooters & Barbed Wire. (Illus.). 96p. (gr. 3-5). 1981. PLB 7.29 (ISBN 0-686-69299-3). Messner.

FRONTIER AND PIONEER LIFE–NEW MEXICO

French, William. Further Recollections of a Western Ranchman: New Mexico 1883-1889, Vol. II. (Illus.). 1965p. 20.00 (ISBN 0-87266-011-7). Argosy.

Poe, Sophie A. Buckboard Days. Cunningham, Eugene, ed. (Illus.). 304p. 1981. pap. write for info. (ISBN 0-8263-0572-5); pap. price not set (ISBN 0-8263-0573-3). U of NM Pr.

FRONTIER AND PIONEER LIFE–TEXAS

Poe, Sophie A. Buckboard Days. Cunningham, Eugene, ed. (Illus.). 304p. 1981. pap. write for info. (ISBN 0-8263-0572-5); pap. price not set (ISBN 0-8263-0573-3). U of NM Pr.

FRONTIER AND PIONEER LIFE–THE WEST

Clarke, Mary W. The Slaughter Ranches & Their Makers. (Illus.). Date not set. 12.95. Jenkins.

Gard, Wayne. Frontier Justice. (Illus.). 324p. 1981. 17.50 (ISBN 0-8061-0194-6); pap. 8.95 (ISBN 0-8061-1755-9). U of Okla Pr.

Robinson, Chandler A. J. Evetts Haley: Passing of the Old West. Date not set. 12.50 (ISBN 0-8363-0160-9). Jenkins.

The Saturday Evening Post Saga of the American West. LC 80-67057. (Illus.). 1980. 13.95 (ISBN 0-89387-043-9). Sat Eve Post.

Schaefer, Jack. Monte Walsh. LC 80-25036. x, 442p. 1981. 21.50x (ISBN 0-8032-4124-0); pap. 7.50 (ISBN 0-8032-9121-3, BB 755, Bison). U of Nebr Pr.

FROST, ROBERT, 1874-1963

Bober, Natalie S. A Restless Spirit: The Story of Robert Frost. LC 80-23930. (Illus.). 224p. (gr. 6 up). 1981. PLB 10.95 (ISBN 0-689-30801-9). Atheneum.

Evans, William R. Robert Frost & Sidney Cox: Forty Years of Friendship. 310p. 1981. 15.00 (ISBN 0-87451-195-X). U Pr of New Eng.

Frost, Robert. Robert Frost: Farm-Poultryman--the Story of Robert Frost's Carreer As a Breeder & Fancier of Hens. Thompson, Lawrance & Lathem, Edward C., eds. LC 64-638. 116p. 1981. pap. 5.00 (ISBN 0-87451-202-6). U Pr of New Eng.

FROST

see also Refrigeration and Refrigerating Machinery

Killian, H. Cold & Frost Injuries: Rewarming Damages. (Disaster Medicine: Vol. 3). (Illus.). 260p. 1981. pap. 49.60 (ISBN 0-387-08991-8). Springer-Verlag.

FROZEN ASSETS

see Liquidity (Economics)

FROZEN FOOD

see Food, Frozen

FROZEN FOOD COOKERY

see Cookery (Frozen Foods)

FRUIT

see also Berries; Citrus Fruits; Cookery (Fruit); Fruit-Culture

also particular fruits, e.g. Apple, Orange

Ceres. Herbs & Fruit for Dieting. LC 80-53452. (Everybodys Home Herbal Ser.). 64p. 1981. pap. 1.95 (ISBN 0-394-74837-9). Shambhala Pubns.

FRUIT-CULTURE

see also Berries; Dwarf Fruit Trees; Nurseries (Horticulture); Olive Industry and Trade; Plant Propagation; Pruning

also names of fruits

Edwards, Ray. Growing Soft Fruits. 1980. pap. 4.50 (ISBN 0-7153-7903-8). David & Charles.

Gilbert, Zoe. Fruit Growing in Southern Africa. 1980. 25.00x (Pub. by Bailey & Swinton South Africa). State Mutual Bk.

Ramos, David. Prune Orchard Management. (Illus.). 144p. (Orig.). Date not set. pap. text ed. price not set (ISBN 0-931876-45-1). AG Sci Pubns.

FRUIT TRADE

see also Citrus Fruit Industry; Olive Industry and Trade

Report of the Seventh Session of the Intergovernmental Group on Bananas. 17p. 1981. pap. 6.00 (ISBN 92-5-100950-3, F2091, FAO). Unipub.

FRUITS

see Fruit

FRUSTRATION

see also Control (Psychology)

Schuller, Robert H. Discover Your Opportunities. (Orig.). 1978. pap. 1.25 (ISBN 0-89081-142-3). Harvest Hse.

FRYING

The Sunbeam Frypan Cookbook. 1981. 8.95 (ISBN 0-916752-43-7). Green Hill.

FUCHSIA

Proudley, Brian & Proudley, Valerie. Fuchsias in Color. (Illus.). 206p. 1981. 12.95 (ISBN 0-7137-0754-2, Pub. by Blandford Pr England). Sterling.

FUEL

see also Biomass Energy; Coal; Heating; Liquid Fuels; Petroleum As Fuel; Synthetic Fuels; Wood As Fuel

Klass, Donald L., ed. Biomass As a Nonfossil Fuel Source. LC 80-26044. (ACS Symposium Ser.: No. 144). 1981. 42.00 (ISBN 0-8412-0599-X). Am Chemical.

FUEL OIL

see Petroleum As Fuel

FUGITIVE SLAVES IN THE UNITED STATES

see Slavery in the United States–Fugitive Slaves

FUGUES

see Canons, Fugues, etc.

FULFILLMENT (ETHICS)

see Self-Realization

FULL EMPLOYMENT POLICIES

see also Government Spending Policy; Labor Supply; Public Works; Unemployed

Pierson, Frank C. The Minimum Level of Unemployment & Public Policy. 194p. 1980. text ed. 8.50 (ISBN 0-911558-76-4); pap. text ed. 5.50 (ISBN 0-911558-75-6). Upjohn Inst.

FULTON, ROBERT, 1765-1815

Hutcheon, Wallace S., Jr. Robert Fulton: Pioneer of Undersea Warfare. 192p. 1981. 15.95 (ISBN 0-87021-547-7). Naval Inst Pr.

FUNCTION TESTS (MEDICINE)

see also Heart Function Tests

Mellerowicz, Harald. Ergometry: Basics of Medical Exercise Testing. Smodlaka, Vojin N., ed. Rice, Allan L., tr. from Ger. 1981. text ed. write for info. (ISBN 0-8067-1241-4). Urban & S.

FUNCTIONAL ANALYSIS

see also Approximation Theory; Digital Filters (Mathematics); Integral Equations; Perturbation (Mathematics); Vector Spaces

Kantorovich, L. V. & Akilov, G. P. Functional Analysis. 2nd ed. 800p. 1981. 100.00 (ISBN 0-08-023036-9); pap. 35.00 (ISBN 0-08-026486-7). Pergamon.

Limaye, B. V. Functional Analysis. LC 80-84533. 400p. 1981. 17.95 (ISBN 0-470-26933-2). Halsted Pr.

FUNCTIONAL CALCULUS

see Functional Analysis

FUNCTIONALS

see Functional Analysis

FUNCTIONS

see also Calculus

Iooss, G. & Joseph, D. Elementary Stability & Bifurcation Theory. (Undergraduate Texts in Mathematics Ser.). (Illus.). 286p. 1981. 22.00 (ISBN 0-387-90526-X). Springer-Verlag.

Rivlin, Theodore J. An Introduction to the Approximation of Functions. 160p. 1981. pap. price not set (ISBN 0-486-64069-8). Dover.

Siegel, C. L. Topics in Complex Function Theory, 3 vols. Incl. Vol. 1. Elliptical Functions & Uniformization Theory. 1969. 26.95 (ISBN 0-471-79070-2); Vol. 2. Automorphic Functions & Abelian Integrals. 1972. 26.95 (ISBN 0-471-79080-X); Vol. 3. Abelian Functions & Modular Functions of Several Variables. Tretkoff, M. & Gottschling, E., trs. 244p. 1973. 29.95 (ISBN 0-471-79090-7). LC 69-19931. (Pure & Applied Mathematics Ser., Pub. by Wiley-Interscience). Wiley.

FUNCTIONS, ANALYTIC
see Analytic Functions

FUNCTIONS, BETA
Pearson, K. Tables of the Incomplete Beta-Function. 505p. 1968. 60.00x (ISBN 0-85264-704-2, Pub. by England Griffin). State Mutual Bk.

FUNCTIONS, GAMMA
Pearson, K. Tables of the Incomplete Gamma-Function. 164p. 1965. 30.00x (ISBN 0-85264-703-4, Pub. by Griffin England). State Mutual Bk.

FUNCTIONS, HOLOMORPHIC
see Analytic Functions

FUNCTIONS, MONOGENIC
see Analytic Functions

FUNCTIONS, POTENTIAL
see Differential Equations, Partial; Potential, Theory Of

FUNCTIONS, RECURSIVE
see Recursive Functions

FUNCTIONS, REGULAR
see Analytic Functions

FUNCTIONS, SYMMETRIC
see Symmetric Functions

FUND RAISING
Darnbrough, Ann & Kinrade, Derek. Fund-Raising & Grant-Aid: A Practical & Legal Guide for Charities & Voluntary Organisations. 160p. 1980. 24.00x (ISBN 0-85941-075-7, Pub. by Woodhead-Faulkner England). State Mutual Bk.
Hicks, Tyler G. Raising Money from Grants & Other Sources Success Kit. 2nd ed. 496p. 1981. pap. 99.50 (ISBN 0-914306-45-6). Intl Wealth.
Longacre, Paul. Fund-Raising Projects with a World Hunger Emphasis. LC 80-83771. 72p. 1980. pap. 1.95 (ISBN 0-8361-1940-1). Herald Pr.
Pendleton, Niel. Fundraising: A Guide for Non-Profit Organizations. (Illus.). 192p. 1981. 13.95 (ISBN 0-13-332163-0, Spec); pap. 6.95 (ISBN 0-13-332155-X). P-H.
Porter, Robert, ed. United Arts Fundraising: Nineteen Eighty Campaign Analysis. (Illus., Orig.). 1980. pap. 9.95 (ISBN 0-915400-29-4). Am Council Arts.

FUNDAMENTAL THEOLOGY
see Apologetics

FUNDS
see Finance

FUNDUS OCULI
Nover, Arno & Blodi, Frederick C. The Ocular Fundus: Methods of Examination & Typical Findings. 4th ed. (Illus.). 212p. 1981. text ed. write for info. (ISBN 0-8121-0709-8). Lea & Febiger.

FUNERAL RITES AND CEREMONIES
Weever, John. Ancient Funerall Monuments Within the United Monarchie of Great Britaine, Ireland & the Islands Adjacent. LC 79-84145. (Engilsh Experience Ser.). 910p. 1979. Repr. of 1631 ed. lib. bdg. 125.00 (ISBN 90-221-0961-5). Walter J Johnson.

FUNERAL SERMONS
Coniaris, A. M. Sixty-One Talks for Orthodox Funerals. 1969. pap. 4.95 (ISBN 0-937032-02-6). Light & Life Pub Co MN.

FUNGAL TOXINS
see Mycotoxins

FUNGI
see also Ascomycetes; Bacteriology; Gasteromycetes; Lichens; Molds (Botany); Mushrooms; Soil Micro-Organisms
The Coelomycetes. 694p. 1981. 115.00 (ISBN 0-85198-446-0, CAB 7, CAB). Unipub.
Cole, G. T. & Kendrick, B. Biology of Conidial Fungi, 2 vols. 1981. Vol. 1. write for info. (ISBN 0-12-179501-2); Vol. 2. write for info. (ISBN 0-12-179502-0). Acad Pr.
Dube, H. C. An Introduction to Fungi. 400p. 1980. 24.00x (Pub. by Croom Helm England). State Mutual Bk.
Meinhardt, F. Untersuchungen Zur Genetik Des Fortpflanzungsverhaltens und der Fruchtkoerper-und Antibiotikabbildung Des Basidiomyceten Agrocybe Aegerita. (Bibliotheca Mycologica: No. 75). (Illus.). 128p. (Ger.). 1981. pap. text ed. 20.00x (ISBN 3-7682-1275-0). Lubrecht & Cramer.
Miller, Orson & Miller, Hope. Mudhrooms in Color: How to Know Them, Where to Find Them, & What to Avoid. 11.95 (ISBN 0-686-69507-0, Hawthorn). Dutton.
Petrak, F. & Sydow, H. Die Gattungen der Pyrenomyceten, Sphaeropsideen und Melanconieen, Pt. 1. (Feddes Repertorium: Beiheft 27). 551p. (Ger.). 1979. Repr. of 1926 ed. lib. bdg. 97.20x (ISBN 3-87429-071-9). Lubrecht & Cramer.
Smith, John E. & Berry, David, eds. Filamentous Fungi. Incl. Vol. 1. Industrial Mycology. LC 75-2101. 340p. 59.00 (ISBN 0-470-80187-5); Vol. 2. Biosynthesis & Metabolism. LC 75-41613. 79.50 (ISBN 0-470-15005-X); Vol. 3. Developmental Mycology. LC 75-2101. 54.95 (ISBN 0-470-99352-9). (Filamentous Fungi Ser.: Vols. 1-3). 1975-78. Halsted Pr.
Watling, Roy & Gregory, Norma. Census Catalogue of World Members of the Bolbitiaceae. (Bibliotheca Mycologica). 300p. 1981. lib. bdg. 40.00x (ISBN 3-7682-1279-3, Pub. by Cramer Germany). Lubrecht & Cramer.

FUNGI–BIBLIOGRAPHY
Watling, Roy, ed. A Literature Guide to the Identification of Mushrooms. 120p. (Orig.). 1980. pap. 6.75. Mad River.

FUNGI–EUROPE
Telleria, M. T. Contribucion Al Estudio De los Aphyllophorales Espanoles: With Key to Species in English. (Bibliotheca Mycologica: No. 74). (Illus.). 474p. (Span.). 1981. lib. bdg. 50.00x (ISBN 3-7682-1274-2, Pub. by Cramer Germany). Lubrecht & Cramer.

FUNGI, EDIBLE
see Mushrooms, Edible
Miller, Orson & Miller, Hope. Mudhrooms in Color: How to Know Them, Where to Find Them, & What to Avoid. 11.95 (ISBN 0-686-69507-0, Hawthorn). Dutton.

FUNGI, PHYTOPATHOGENIC
Mace, M. E. & Bell, A. A., eds. Fungal Wilt Diseases of Plants. 1981. price not set (ISBN 0-12-464450-3). Acad Pr.

FUNGICIDES
Page, B. G. & Thomson, W. T. The Nineteen Eighty-One Insecticide, Herbicide, Fungicide Quick Guide. 140p. 1981. pap. 11.00 (ISBN 0-913702-11-0). Thomson Pub Ca.

FUNGUS DISEASES OF PLANTS
see Fungi, Phytopathogenic

FUNNIES
see Comic Books, Strips, etc.

FUR SEAL
see Sealing

FURNACES
Reed, Robert D. Furnace Operations. 3rd ed. 230p. 1981. 18.95 (ISBN 0-87201-301-4). Gulf Pub.
Trinks, W. Industrial Furnaces, 2 vols. Incl. Vol. 1. Principals of Design & Operation. 5th ed. 1961 (ISBN 0-471-89034-0); Vol. 2. Fuels, Furnace Types & Furnace Equipment: Their Selection & Influence Upon Furnace Operation. 4th ed. 1967 (ISBN 0-471-89068-5). LC 61-11493. 39.95 ea. (Pub. by Wiley-Interscience). Wiley.

FURNITURE
see also Home Workshops; Interior Decoration; Upholstery; Wood-Carving
Garner, Philippe. Twentieth Century Furniture. 224p. 1980. 24.95 (ISBN 0-442-25421-0). Van Nos Reinhold.
Philip, P. & Atterbury, P. World Furniture. (Illus.). Date not set. 30.00 (ISBN 0-686-68700-0). Mayflower Bks.

FURNITURE–BUILDING
see Furniture Making

FURNITURE–COLLECTORS AND COLLECTING
Blundell, Peter S. Marketplace Guide to Oak Furniture Styles & Values. (Illus.). 1980. 17.95 (ISBN 0-89145-141-2). Collector Bks.

FURNITURE–HISTORY
Schwarz, Marvin, et al. Furniture of John Henry Belter & the Rococo Revival. 1981. 24.95 (ISBN 0-525-93170-8). Dutton.

FURNITURE–REPAIRING
see also Furniture Finishing
Editors of Time-Life Books. Repairing Furniture. (Home Repair & Improvement). (Illus.). 128p. 1981. 10.95 (ISBN 0-8094-2438-X). Time-Life.
Family Handyman Magazine, ed. Complete Book of Furniture Repair & Refinishing. (Illus.). 288p. 1981. 14.95 (ISBN 0-684-16839-1, ScribT). Scribner.
Kinney, Ralph. Complete Book of Furniture Repair & Refinishing. rev. ed. LC 73-162743. (Illus.). 1981. 20.00x (ISBN 0-684-16839-1, ScribT). Scribner.

FURNITURE–RESTORATION
see Furniture–Repairing; Furniture Finishing

FURNITURE–UNITED STATES
Cathers, David M. Furniture of the American Arts & Crafts Movement: Stickley & Roycroft Mission Oak. 1981. 9.95 (ISBN 0-453-00397-4, H397). NAL.
Hanks, David. Innovative Furniture in America: From 1800 to the Present. (Illus.). 250p. 1981. text ed. 30.00 (ISBN 0-8180-0450-9). Horizon.
Shea, John C. The Pennsylvania Dutch & Their Furniture. 240p. 1980. 19.95 (ISBN 0-442-27546-3). Van Nos Reinhold.

FURNITURE BUILDING
see Furniture Making

FURNITURE FINISHING
Editors of Time-Life Books. Repairing Furniture. (Home Repair & Improvement). (Illus.). 128p. 1981. 10.95 (ISBN 0-8094-2438-X). Time-Life.

FURNITURE MAKING
see also Cabinet-Work; Furniture–Repairing; Furniture; Upholstery
Schmultzhart, Berthold. The Handmade Furniture Book. (Illus.). 144p. 1981. 13.95 (ISBN 0-13-383638-X); pap. 5.95 (ISBN 0-13-383620-7). P-H.

FURNITURE MAKING–AMATEURS' MANUALS
Makepeace, John, et al. The Art of Making Furniture. LC 80-52623. (Illus.). 192p. 1981. 21.95 (ISBN 0-8069-5426-4); lib. bdg. 18.39 (ISBN 0-8069-5427-2). Sterling.

FUSARIUM
Palti, Josef. Toxigenic Fusaria, Their Distribution & Significance As Causes of Disease in Animal & Man. (Acta Phytomedica Ser.: Vol. 6). (Illus.). 112p. (Orig.). 1978. pap. text ed. 24.00 (ISBN 3-489-60326-5). Parey Sci Pubs.

FUSED SALTS
Inman, Douglas & Lovering, David G., eds. Ionic Liquids. 445p. 1981. 49.50 (ISBN 0-306-40412-5, Plenum Pr). Plenum Pub.

FUSION
CIAMDA Eighty: An Index to the Literature on Atomic & Molecular Collision Data Relevant to Fusion Research. 498p. 1980. pap. 31.25 (ISBN 92-0-039080-3, ISP550, IAEA). Unipub.
Teller, Edward, ed. Fusion-Magnetic: Magnetic, Vol. 1. 1981. Pt.a. write for info. (ISBN 0-12-685201-4); Pt. B. write for info. (ISBN 0-12-685241-3). Acad Pr.

FUSION OF CORPORATIONS
see Consolidation and Merger of Corporations

FUSULINIDAE
White, M. P. Some Texas Fusulinidae. (Illus.). 106p. 1932. 0.75 (BULL 3211). Bur Econ Geology.

FUTILITY
see Frustration

FUTURE ESTATES
see Future Interests

FUTURE INTERESTS
Partridge, Ernest, ed. Responsibilities to Future Generations: Environmental Ethics. 275p. (Orig.). 1981. 17.95 (ISBN 0-87975-153-3); pap. text ed. 8.95 (ISBN 0-87975-142-8). Prometheus Bks.
Powers, Mark J. & Vogel, David J. Inside the Financial Futures Markets. 260p. 1980. 23.95 (ISBN 0-471-08136-1). Ronald Pr.

FUTURE LIFE
see also Eschatology; Eternity; Immortality; Resurrection; Soul
Battle, Dennis M. Life After Death? (Illus.). 52p. 1981. pap. 2.00 (ISBN 0-933464-13-4). D M Battle Pubns.
Bowers, Laverne E. Sterile. 1981. 6.95 (ISBN 0-533-04732-3). Vantage.
Harner, Philip B. Everlasting Life in Biblical Thought. 1981. 6.95 (ISBN 0-8062-1611-5). Carlton.
Osis, Karlis & Haraldsson, Erlendur. At the Hour of Death. 1980. pap. 3.95 (ISBN 0-686-69250-0, 49486, Discus). Avon.
Riggle, H. M. Beyond the Tomb. 288p. 4.00. Faith Pub Hse.
Seu Futuro Esta Nas Maos De Deus. 1980. pap. 1.30 (ISBN 0-686-69354-X). Vida Pubs.
Van Dorn, Charles H. Six Things Everyone Should Know. 201p. 1980. 7.95 (ISBN 0-533-03707-7). Vantage.

FUTURE LIFE–CASE STUDIES
Beard, Paul. Living on: How Consciousness Continues & Evolves After Death. 212p. 1981. 12.95 (ISBN 0-8264-0036-1); pap. 5.95 (ISBN 0-8264-0037-X). Continuum.

FUTURES
see Commodity Exchanges

G

GAELIC LANGUAGE
Aitken, A. J., et al, eds. A Dictionary of the Older Scottish Tongue: From the Twelfth Century to the End of the Seventeenth, Founded on the Collections of Sir Wm Craigie, Pt. 30. 1981. pap. price not set (ISBN 0-226-11721-9, Copub with Oxford). U of Chicago Pr.
Dorian, Nancy. Language Death: A Case of Study at a Gaelic-Speaking Community. 1980. text ed. 25.00x (ISBN 0-8122-7785-6); pap. text ed. 11.95x (ISBN 0-8122-1111-1). U of Pa Pr.

GAELS
see Celts

GAGING
Roth, Edward S., ed. Gaging: Practical Design & Application. LC 80-53424. (Manufacturing Update Ser.). (Illus.). 289p. 1981. 29.00 (ISBN 0-87263-064-1). SME.

GAINSBOROUGH, THOMAS, 1727-1788
Lindsay, Jack. Thomas Gainsborough: His Life & Art. LC 80-54397. (Illus.). 248p. 1981. 25.00 (ISBN 0-87663-352-1, Pica Pr). Universe.

GALAPAGOS ISLANDS
Beebe, William. The Arcturus Adventure. (Nature Library Ser.). 450p. 1981. pap. 5.95 (ISBN 0-06-090846-7, CN 846, CN). Har-Row.

GALAXIES
see also Milky Way
Hodge, Paul W. Atlas of the Andromeda Galaxy. (Illus.). 80p. 1981. 50.00 (ISBN 0-295-95795-6). U of Wash Pr.
Jones, Kenneth G., ed. Webb Society Deep-Sky Oberver's Handbook: Galaxies, Vol. 4. 296p. 1981. pap. 14.95 (ISBN 0-89490-050-1). Enslow Pubs.

GALAXY (MILKY WAY)
see Milky Way

GALBRAITH, JOHN KENNETH, 1908-
Galbraith, John K. A Life in Our Times. 576p. 1981. 15.95 (ISBN 0-686-69050-8). HM.

GALES
see Winds

GALILEE
Freyne, Sean V. Galilee from Alexander the Great to Hadrian, 323 B. C. E. to 135 C. E. 27.50 (ISBN 0-89453-099-2). M. Glazier.

GALILEO (GALILEO GALILEI), 1564-1642
Drake, Stillman. Galileo. (Pastmasters Ser.). 1981. 7.95 (ISBN 0-8090-4850-7); pap. 2.95 (ISBN 0-8090-1416-5). Hill & Wang.
--Galileo at Work: His Scientific Biography. LC 78-5239. xxiv, 536p. 1981. pap. 9.95 (ISBN 0-226-16227-3). U of Chicago Pr.

GALL-BLADDER–CALCULI
see Calculi, Biliary

GALL-STONES
see Calculi, Biliary

GALLERIES (ART)
see Art Museums

GALVANISM
see Electricity

GALVEZ, BERNARDO DE, 1746-1786
De Galvez, Bernardo. Diario. 52p. 1966. pap. 5.00. South Pass Pr.
Woodward, Ralph L., Jr., ed. Tribute to Don Bernardo De Galvez. LC 80-116160. (Illus.). xxviii, 148p. 1979. 14.95x (ISBN 0-917860-04-7). Historic New Orleans.

GAMBLING
see also Blackjack (Game); Cards; Lotteries; Probabilities
Casino Management. 384p. 1981. 75.00 (ISBN 0-8184-0311-X). Lyle Stuart.
Charles, R. H. Gambling & Betting: Their Origin & Their Relation to Morality & to Religion. 3rd ed. 92p. 1928. text ed. 2.95 (ISBN 0-567-22066-4). Attic Pr.
Feinman, Jeffrey. Casino Gambling. 128p. (Orig.). 1981. pap. 2.95 (ISBN 0-668-05172-8, 5172). Arco.
Hamilton, Ross. Greyhound Betting for Profit. 64p. 1980. pap. 2.95 (ISBN 0-89650-725-4). Gamblers.
Marshall, Edward. How to Use ESP to Win the American Daily Lottery. LC 80-69615. (Illus.). 64p. (Orig.). 1981. price not set (ISBN 0-938284-00-2). Inner Circle.
Moore, Robin. Compulsion: The True Story of an Addictive Gambler. LC 78-20028. 384p. 1981. 12.95 (ISBN 0-385-13322-7). Doubleday.
Selvidge, James N. Hold Your Horses. 2nd ed. (Illus.). 176p. 1976. pap. 6.95. Jacada Pubns.
Sklansky, David. Sklansky on Poker Theory. rev. ed. 176p. 1980. pap. 5.95 (ISBN 0-89650-918-4). Gamblers.
Skolnick. House of Cards: Legalization & Control of Casino Gambling. (Orig.). 1981. pap. text ed. 7.95 (ISBN 0-316-79708-1). Little.
Tredd, William E. Dice Games New & Old. (Oleander Games & Pastimes Ser.: Vol. 3). (Illus.). 64p. 1981. 9.95 (ISBN 0-906672-00-7); pap. 4.75 (ISBN 0-906672-01-5). Oleander Pr.

GAMBLING PROBLEM (MATHEMATICS)
see Games of Chance (Mathematics)

GAME AND GAME-BIRDS–AFRICA
Robins, Eric. Secret Eden: Africa's Enchanted Wilderness. (Illus.). 128p. 1981. 27.00 (ISBN 0-241-10423-8, Pub. by Hamish Hamilton England). David & Charles.

GAME MANAGEMENT
see Wildlife Management

GAME PROTECTION–AFRICA
Robins, Eric. Secret Eden: Africa's Enchanted Wilderness. (Illus.). 128p. 1981. 27.00 (ISBN 0-241-10423-8, Pub. by Hamish Hamilton England). David & Charles.

GAMES
see also Amusements; Bible Games and Puzzles; Board Games; Cards; Kindergarten; Mathematical Recreations; Olympic Games; Play; Puzzles; Sports also specific games, e.g. Baseball, Contract Bridge, Tennis
Ansara, Michael. Games for Two. (Illus.). 224p. 1981. pap. 8.95 (ISBN 0-906071-26-7). Proteus Pub NY.
Beall, Pamela & Nipp, Susan. Wee Sing & Play. (Illus.). 64p. (Orig.). 1981. pap. 2.25 (ISBN 0-8431-0391-4). Price Stern.
Donnelly, R. H., et al. Active Games & Contests. 2nd ed. 672p. 1958. 17.50 (ISBN 0-471-07088-2). Wiley.
Evans, Larry. Gnomes Games. (Illus.). 64p. 1980. pap. 4.50 (ISBN 0-89844-020-3). Troubador Pr.
Featherman, Buzz. The Fun & Fantasy Book. new ed. (Illus.). 1980. 6.95 (ISBN 0-932238-03-3). Word Shop.
Gamec, Hazel S. The Disappearing ABC Game Book. (Illus.). 12p. write for info. (ISBN 0-938042-02-5). Printek.
--Looking Out of the Window. (Illus.). 12p. 1980. write for info. (ISBN 0-938042-01-7). Printek.
--The Magic Pencil Counting Book. (Illus.). 12p. 1980. write for info. (ISBN 0-938042-00-9). Printek.

Garden, Nancy. The Kid's Code & Cipher Book. LC 80-10434. (Illus.). 176p. (gr. 5 up). 1981. 10.95 (ISBN 0-03-053856-4); pap. 4.95 (ISBN 0-03-059267-4). HR&W.

Gault, C. & Gault, G. Harlem Globetrotters Funniest Games. (ps-3). pap. 0.95 (ISBN 0-590-03000-0, Schol Pap). Schol Bk Serv.

Hagstrom, Julie. Traveling Games for Babies: A Handbook of Games for Infants to Five-Year-Olds. (Illus.). 96p. 1981. pap. 4.95 (ISBN 0-89104-203-2). A & W Pubs.

Latta, Richard. Games for Travel, No. 3. 48p. (Orig.). 1981. pap. 1.75 (ISBN 0-8431-0312-4). Price Stern.

Levmore, Saul. Super Strategies: Games & Puzzles for Strategy Training. (Illus.). 168p. 1981. 10.95 (ISBN 0-385-17165-X). Doubleday.

Lombardy, Dana, ed. The Gamesmaster Catalog. (Illus., Orig.). 1980. pap. 6.95 (ISBN 0-933168-02-0). Boynton & Assoc.

Minter, James F. Pencil Pastimes, No. 9. 128p. 1981. pap. 2.50 (ISBN 0-89104-172-9). A & W Pubs.

Razzi, Jim. Encyclopedia Brown's Fourth Book of Games & Puzzles. 64p. (gr. 4-6). 1981. pap. 1.50 (ISBN 0-553-15110-X). Bantam.

--Encyclopedia Brown's Third Book of Games & Puzzles. 64p. (Orig.). (gr. 4-6). 1981. pap. 1.50 (ISBN 0-553-15077-4). Bantam.

Sternlict, Manny & Hurwitz, Abraham. Games Children Play: Instructive & Creative Play Activities for the Mentally Retarded & Developmentally Disabled Child. 128p. 1980. 12.95 (ISBN 0-442-25857-7). Van Nos Reinhold.

Stuart, Sally E. The All-Occasion Game Book. (Illus.). 64p. (Orig.). 1981. pap. 2.95 (ISBN 0-87239-444-1, 2798). Standard Pub.

Wiswell, Phil. I Hate Charades & Forty-Nine Other New Games. LC 80-54341. (Illus.). 128p. 1981. 5.95 (ISBN 0-8069-4582-6); lib. bdg. 6.69 (ISBN 0-8069-4583-4). Sterling.

Zechlin, Katharina. Making Games in Wood. LC 80-54353. (Illus.). 80p. 1981. pap. 6.95 (ISBN 0-8069-8996-3). Sterling.

GAMES–COMPUTER PROGRAMS

Sagan, Hans. Beat the Odds: Microcomputer Simulations of Casino Games. 192p. 1980. pap. 7.95 (ISBN 0-8104-5181-6). Hayden.

GAMES, OLYMPIC

see Olympic Games

GAMES, RHYTHMIC

see Games with Music

GAMES OF CHANCE

see Gambling

GAMES OF CHANCE (MATHEMATICS)

see also Monte Carlo Method

Eigen, Manfred & Winkler, Ruthild. Laws of the Game: How the Principles of Nature Govern Chance. LC 79-3494. (Illus.). 384p. 1981. 17.95 (ISBN 0-394-41806-9). Knopf.

GAMES WITH MUSIC

Ward, David. Sing a Rainbow: Musical Activities with Mentally Handicapped Children. (Illus.). 64p. (Orig.). 1979. pap. text ed. 8.95x (ISBN 0-19-317416-2). Oxford U Pr.

GAMING

see Gambling

GAMMA FUNCTIONS

see Functions, Gamma

GANDHI, INDIRA (NEHRU), 1917-

Mashruwala, K. G. Gandhi & Marx. 119p. (Orig.). 1981. pap. 1.50 (ISBN 0-934676-30-5). Greenlf Bks.

Singh, Khushwant. Indira Gandhi Returns. 1980. 10.00x (ISBN 0-8364-0655-9, Pub. by Vision India). South Asia Bks.

GANDHI, MOHANDAS KARAMCHAND, 1869-1948

Chaudhuri, Haridas & Frank, Leonard R. Mahatma Gandhi. (Orig.). 1969. pap. 1.00 (ISBN 0-89744-993-2, Pub. by Cultural Integration). Auromere.

De Jong, Constance & Glass, Philip. Satyagraha: M. K. Gandhi in South Africa, 1893-1914. (Illus., Orig.). 1980. pap. 5.00 (ISBN 0-918746-04-3). Standard Edns.

Shirer, William. Gandhi: A Memoir. 1981. 6.95 (ISBN 0-671-25080-9, Touchstone). S&S.

Shirer, William L. Ghandhi: A Memoir. 1981. pap. 4.95 (ISBN 0-671-25080-9, Touchstone Bks). S&S.

GANGLIA, NERVOUS

see Nerves

GAOLS

see Prisons

GARAGES

Russell, James E. Garages & Carports. Horowitz, Shirley M., ed. (Illus.). 144p. (Orig.). 1981. pap. 6.95 (ISBN 0-932944-32-9). Creative Homeowner.

GARBAGE

see Refuse and Refuse Disposal

GARDEN ARCHITECTURE

see Architecture, Domestic; Landscape Gardening

Fleming, Laurence & Gore, Alan. The English Garden. (Illus.). 256p. 1981. 26.00 (ISBN 0-7181-1816-2). Merrimack Bk Serv.

GARDEN FARMING

see Truck Farming

GARDEN POOLS

see Water Gardens

GARDEN WALKS

Russell, James E. Walks, Walls & Fences. Horowitz, Shirley M. & Auer, Marilyn M., eds. (Illus., Orig.). 1981. pap. 6.95 (ISBN 0-932944-36-1). Creative Homeowner.

GARDENING

Here are entered general works. For works dealing with gardening in specific countries see the geographic subdivisions which follow. Works dealing with specific areas of the United states, e.g. Southern States are entered under the subdivision United States.

see also Aquatic Plants; Climbing Plants; Flower Gardening; Fruit-Culture; Greenhouses; Herbs; Horticulture; House Plants; Landscape Gardening; Nurseries (Horticulture); Organic Gardening; Plant Propagation; Plants, Ornamental; Plants, Potted; Pruning; Truck Farming; Vegetable Gardening; Weeds

Bartholomew, Mel. Square Foot Gardening: A New Way to Garden in Less Space with Less Work. Halpin, Anne, ed. (Illus.). 288p. 1981. 13.95 (ISBN 0-87857-340-2); pap. 9.95 (ISBN 0-87857-341-0). Rodale Pr Inc.

Berrisford, Judith. Gardening on Chalk, Lime & Clay. 1979. 14.95 (ISBN 0-571-10952-7, Pub. by Faber & Faber); pap. 6.95 (ISBN 0-571-11129-7). Merrimack Bk Serv.

Boland, Maureen & Boland, Bridget. Old Wives' Lore for Gardeners. (Illus.). Date not set. pap. 3.25 (ISBN 0-374-51639-1). FS&G.

Carr, David. The Gardener's Handbook, 3 bks. Incl. Vol. 1. Broad-Leaved Trees. (Illus.). 144p. 24.00 (ISBN 0-7134-1306-9); pap. 14.50 o.p. (ISBN 0-7134-1306-9); Vol. 2. Conifers. (Illus.). 144p. 24.00 (ISBN 0-7134-1307-7); pap. 14.95 o.p. (ISBN 0-7134-1308-5); Vol. 3. Shrubs. (Illus.). 144p. 23.95 o.p. (ISBN 0-7134-1882-6); pap. 13.95 o.p. (ISBN 0-686-61986-2); Growing Fruit & Nuts. Carr, David. (Illus.). 1980. 23.95 o.p. (ISBN 0-7134-1883-4, Pub. by Batsford England); pap. 14.50 (ISBN 0-7134-1896-6). David & Charles. (Illus.). 1980 (Pub. by Batsford England). David & Charles.

Doscher, Paul, et al. Intensive Gardening Round the Year. (Illus.). 224p. 1981. pap. 15.00 (ISBN 0-8289-0399-9). Greene.

Fish, Margery. A Flower for Every Day. 208p. 1981. pap. 9.95 (ISBN 0-571-11738-4, Pub. by Faber & Faber). Merrimack Bk Serv.

Foster, Lee. Backyard Farming. (Urban Life Practical Solutions to the Challenges of the 80's Ser.). 96p. (Orig.). pap. 4.95 (ISBN 0-87701-224-5). Chronicle Bks.

Garrison, Juanita B. Piedmont Garden: How to Grow by the Calendar. LC 80-23218. 1981. pap. text ed. 4.95 mechanical (ISBN 0-87249-403-9). U of SC Pr.

Halpin, Anne, ed. Gourmet Gardening. (Illus.). 256p. 1981. pap. 9.95 (ISBN 0-87857-349-6). Rodale Pr Inc.

Hill, Lewis. Successful Cold Climate Gardening. 288p. (Orig.). 1981. 14.95 (ISBN 0-8289-0421-9). Greene.

Hill, Thomas. The Art of Gardening. LC 79-84117. (English Experience Ser.: No. 936). 276p. 1979. Repr. of 1608 ed. lib. bdg. 26.00. Walter J Johnson.

Hostage, Jacqueline. Jackie's Indoor-Outdoor Gardening Charts. (Illus.). 128p. (Orig.). 1981. pap. 5.95 plastic comb bdg. (ISBN 0-932620-07-8). Betterway Pubns.

Kramer. Your Trellis Garden. Date not set. 1.49 (ISBN 0-517-31432-0). Bonanza.

Kramer, Jack. Once-a-Week Indoor Gardening Guide. (Orig.). pap. 1.75 (ISBN 0-515-04475-X). Jove Pubns.

--Victorian Gardens: How to Plan, Plant, & Enjoy Nineteenth Century Beauty Today. LC 80-8342. (Illus.). 160p. 1981. 14.95 (ISBN 0-06-250480-0, HarpR); pap. 9.95 (ISBN 0-06-250481-9). Har-Row.

Langhans, Robert W., ed. A Growth Chamber Manual: Environmental Control for Plants. LC 77-90906. (Illus.). 240p. 1978. 19.50x (ISBN 0-8014-1169-6). Comstock.

McDonald, Elvin. Easy Gardens. 1981. 8.95 (ISBN 0-916752-20-8). Green Hill.

--Making Your Lawn & Garden Grow. 7.95 (ISBN 0-916752-07-0). Green Hill.

Mittleider, Jacob R. Gardening by the Foot. LC 80-84564. 150p. 1981. pap. 4.95 (ISBN 0-88290-175-3, 4026). Horizon Utah.

The Old Farmers's Almanac Gardner's Companion. (Illus.). 144p. 1980. pap. 1.50 (ISBN 0-911658-99-8). Yankee Bks.

Proktor, Noel J. Simple Propagation: Propagation by Seed, Division, Layering, Cuttings, Budding & Grafting. (Illus.). 246p. 1981. pap. 8.95 (ISBN 0-571-11707-4, Pub. by Faber & Faber). Merrimack Bk Serv.

Reynolds, Bruford S. Money Saving Recipes Through Sprouting & Gardening. pap. 4.95 (ISBN 0-89036-134-7). Hawkes Pub Inc.

Schumann, Donna N. Living with Plants: A Guide to the Practical Application of Botany. (Illus.). 328p. (Orig.). 1980. pap. 14.20 (ISBN 0-916422-20-8). Mad River.

Seymour, John. The Self-Sufficient Gardener: A Complete Guide to Growing & Preserving All Your Own Food. LC 78-19223. 1979. pap. write for info (ISBN 0-385-14671-X, Dolp). Doubleday.

Shewell-Cooper, W. E. Complete Vegetable Grower. 1973. pap. 5.50 (ISBN 0-571-04797-1, Pub. by Faber & Faber). Merrimack Bk Serv.

Smyser, Carol A. Nature's Design: A Practical Guide to Natural Landscaping. (Illus.). 416p. Date not set. 16.95 (ISBN 0-87857-343-7). Rodale Pr Inc.

Solomon, Steve. The Complete Guide to Organic Gardening West of the Cascades. 192p. 1981. pap. 9.95 (ISBN 0-914718-58-4). Pacific Search.

Southern Living Gardening Staff & Floyd, John A., Jr. Southern Living Garden Guide: Your Answer Book to Garden Questions. LC 80-84409. (Illus.). 224p. 1981. 17.95 (ISBN 0-8487-0518-1). Oxmoor Hse.

Sunset Editors. Basic Gardening: Introduction to. 3rd ed. LC 80-53478. (Illus.). 160p. 1981. pap. 5.95 (ISBN 0-376-03075-5, Sunset Bks). Sunset-Lane.

--Garden Color: Annuals & Perennials. LC 80-53479. (Illus.). 96p. 1981. pap. 3.95 (ISBN 0-376-03154-9, Sunset Bks). Sunset-Lane.

White, Katherine S. Onward & Upward in the Garden. White, E. B., ed. 1981. pap. 6.95 (ISBN 0-374-51629-4). FS&G.

Whitehead, George. Growing for Showing. (Illus.). 176p. 1981. pap. 7.95 (ISBN 0-571-11706-6, Pub. by Faber & Faber). Merrimack Bk Serv.

Wright, Michael, ed. Complete Book of Gardening. 1980. pap. 9.95 (ISBN 0-446-87239-3). Warner Bks.

GARDENING–JUVENILE LITERATURE

Guidetti, Geri. A Seneca Garden. (Illus.). 26p. (Orig.). (gr. 2-8). 1981. pap. 3.95 (ISBN 0-938928-00-7). KMG Pubns OR.

Paul, Aileen. Kids' Indoor Gardening. (gr. 4-7). pap. 0.75 (ISBN 0-671-29608-6). PB.

Springstubb, Tricia. Growing Things. 228p. (gr. 6). 1981. 8.95 (ISBN 0-686-69141-5, Pub. by Atlantic). Little.

Swenson, Allan A. My Own Herb Garden. (Children's Collection Ser.). (Illus.). 72p. 1976. 6.95 (ISBN 0-87857-129-9). Rodale Pr Inc.

GARDENING–UNITED STATES

Webster, Bob. The South Texas Garden Book. 140p. (Orig.). 1980. pap. 10.95 (ISBN 0-931722-03-9). Corona Pub.

GARDENS–CHINA

Soochow Gardens. 1980. 85.00 (ISBN 0-8351-0696-9). China Bks.

GARDENS–GREAT BRITAIN

British Tourist Authority. Discovering Gardens in Britain. (Illus.). 80p. Date not set. pap. price not set (ISBN 0-85263-456-0, Pub. by Auto Assn-British Tourist Authority England). Merrimack Bk Serv.

Clark, H. F. The English Landscape Garden. (Illus.). 128p. 1980. text ed. 16.50x (ISBN 0-904387-38-0). Humanities.

Lemmon, Kenneth. The Gardens of Britain, Five: Yorkshire & Humberside. 1979. 24.00 (ISBN 0-7134-1743-9, Pub. by Batsford England). David & Charles.

MacLean, Theresa. Medieval English Gardens. LC 79-56277. (Illus.). 288p. 1981. 25.00 (ISBN 0-670-46482-1). Viking Pr.

GARDENS–JAPAN

Treib, Marc & Herman, Ron. A Guide to the Gardens of Kyoto. 216p. 1980. pap. text ed. 9.95 (ISBN 0-89955-312-5, Pub. by Shufunotomo Japan). Intl Schol Bk Serv.

GARFIELD, JAMES ABRAM, PRES. U. S., 1831-1881

Doenecke, Justus D. The Presidencies of James A. Garfield & Chester A. Arthur. LC 80-18957. (The American Presidency Ser.). 232p. 1981. 15.00x (ISBN 0-7006-0208-9). Regents Pr KS.

GARIBALDI, GIUSEPPE, 1807-1882

Abba, Giuseppe C. The Diary of One of Garibaldi's Thousand. Vincent, E. R., tr. from Ital. LC 80-24181. (Oxford Library of Italian Classics). (Illus.). xxi, 166p. 1981. Repr. of 1962 ed. lib. bdg. 18.75x (ISBN 0-313-22446-3, ABDO). Greenwood.

GARRICK, DAVID, 1717-1779

Stein, Elizabeth P. David Garrick, Dramatist. 315p. 1980. Repr. of 1937 ed. lib. bdg. 40.00 (ISBN 0-89760-827-5). Telegraph Bks.

GAS

see also Gases; Petroleum

Davis, J. A. High Cost Oil & Gas Resources. 240p. 1981. 40.00x (ISBN 0-85664-588-5, Pub. by Croom Helm LTD England). Biblio Dist.

GAS–ANALYSIS

see Gases–Analysis

GAS, NATURAL

see also Boring

Ikoku, Chi. Natural Gas Engineering. 776p. 1980. 45.00 (ISBN 0-87814-141-3). Pennwell Pub.

GAS AND OIL ENGINES–CARBURETORS

see Carburetors

GAS BEARINGS

see Gas-Lubricated Bearings

GAS CHROMATOGRAPHY

Drucker, D. B. Microbiological Applications of Gas Chromatography. LC 80-40447. 300p. Date not set. price not set (ISBN 0-521-22365-2). Cambridge U Pr.

Jennings. Applications of Glass Capilary Gas Chromatography. Date not set. price not set (ISBN 0-8247-1223-4). Dekker.

GAS DISTRIBUTION

see also Gases, Compressed

ASME Guide for Gas Transmission & Distribution Piping System: Includes All Addenda Through December 1982. 1980. pap. 125.00 (ISBN 0-685-67491-6, AX3080). ASME.

GAS DYNAMICS

see also Aerodynamics

Klinzing, George E. Gas-Solid Transport. (Chemical Engineering Ser.). (Illus.). 358p. 1981. text ed. 28.50 (ISBN 0-07-035047-7, C). McGraw.

GAS LIQUID CHROMATOGRAPHY

see Gas Chromatography

GAS-LUBRICATED BEARINGS

Gross, William & Matsch, Lee A. Fluid Film Lubrication. Vohr, John H. & Wildman, Manfred, eds. LC 80-36889. 773p. 1980. 35.00 (ISBN 0-471-08357-7, Pub. by Wiley-Interscience). Wiley.

International Gas Bearings Symposium, 5th. Proceedings. 1969. lib. bdg. 29.00. BHRA Fluid.

International Gas Bearings Symposium, 2nd. Proceedings. 1965. 26.00. BHRA Fluid.

Papers Presented at the Eighth International Gas Bearing Symposium. (Orig.). 1981. pap. 60.00 library ed. (ISBN 0-686-69308-6). BHRA Fluid.

GAS-PIPES

ASME Guide for Gas Transmission & Distribution Piping System: Includes All Addenda Through December 1982. 1980. pap. 125.00 (ISBN 0-685-67491-6, AX3080). ASME.

GAS-TURBINES

Harman, R. T. Gas Turbine Engineering Applications Cycles & Characteristics. LC 80-21003. 304p. 1981. 29.95 (ISBN 0-470-27065-9). Halsted Pr.

Whittle, Frank. Gas Turbine Aero-Thermodynamics: With Special Reference to Aircraft Propulsion. LC 80-41372. 240p. 1981. 30.00 (ISBN 0-08-026719-X); pap. 17.50 (ISBN 0-08-026718-1). Pergamon.

GAS-TURBINES, AIRCRAFT

see. Airplanes–Turbojet Engines

GAS WELDING

see Oxyacetylene Welding and Cutting

GASDYNAMICS

see Gas Dynamics

GASEOUS PLASMA

see Plasma (Ionized Gases)

GASES

Dymond, J. H. & Smith, E. B. The Second Virial Coefficients of Pure Gases & Mixtures: A Critical Compilation. (Oxford Science Research Papers Ser.). (Illus.). 534p. 1980. pap. text ed. 69.00x (ISBN 0-19-855361-7). Oxford U Pr.

International Gas Research Conference, 1st, 1980. Proceedings. LC 80-83454. 1016p. 1980. 43.50 (ISBN 0-86587-085-3). Gov Insts.

GASES–ABSORPTION AND ADSORPTION

Touloukian, Y. S. & Ho, C. Y. Thermal Accommodation & Adsorption Coefficients of Gases, Vol. Ii-1. 1st ed. (McGraw-Hill CINDAS Data Ser. on Material Properties). 448p. (Orig.). 1980. 42.50 (ISBN 0-07-065031-4). McGraw.

GASES–ANALYSIS

Meek, J. M. & Craggs, J. D. Electrical Breakdown of Gases. 878p. 1978. 139.50 (ISBN 0-471-99553-3). Wiley.

Touloukian, Y. S. & Ho, C. Y. Thermal Accommodation & Adsorption Coefficients of Gases, Vol. Ii-1. 1st ed. (McGraw-Hill CINDAS Data Ser. on Material Properties). 448p. (Orig.). 1980. 42.50 (ISBN 0-07-065031-4). McGraw.

GASES–LIQUEFACTION

see also Hydrogen

Touloukian, Y. S. & Ho, C. Y. Properties of Nonmetallic Fluid Elements, Vol. III. (M-H-CINDAS Data Series on Material Properties). 224p. 1981. text ed. 33.50 (ISBN 0-07-065033-0). McGraw.

GASES–SPECTRA

Murcray, David G., ed. Handbook of High Resolution Infrared Spectra of Gases of Atmospheric Interest. 304p. 1981. 49.95 (ISBN 0-8493-2950-7). CRC Pr.

GASES, COMPRESSED

Compressed Gas Association. Handbook of Compressed Gases. 2nd ed. 1981. text ed. 44.50 (ISBN 0-442-25419-9). Van Nos Reinhold.

GASES IN THE BLOOD

see Blood Gases

GASP (COMPUTER PROGRAM LANGUAGE)

Horn, Carin & Poirot, James. Computer Literacy: Problem-Solving with Computers. (Illus.). 215p. (Orig.). (gr. 7 up). 1981. pap. 10.95 (ISBN 0-88408-133-8). Sterling Swift.

GASTEROMYCETES

Burk, W. R. A Bibliography of North American Gasteromycetes I: Phalales. 200p. 1981. pap. text ed. 20.00x (ISBN 3-7682-1262-9, Pub. by Cramer Germany). Lubrecht & Cramer.

GASTEROPODA

see also Snails

Farmer, Wesley M. Sea-Slug Gastropods. (Illus.). 177p. (Orig.). 1980. pap. 10.00 (ISBN 0-937772-00-3). Farmer Ent.

GASTON, A. G.

Gaston, A. G. Green Power: The Successful Way of A. G. Gaston. (Illus.). 1977. Repr. of 1968 ed. 8.95 (ISBN 0-916624-09-9). TSU Pr.

--Green Power: The Successful Way of A. G. Gaston. (Illus.). 1978. pap. 2.95 (ISBN 0-916624-10-2). TSU Pr.

GASTRIC DISEASES

see Stomach–Diseases

GASTRITIS
see Stomach–Diseases
GASTROENTEROLOGY
see also Intestines
Baron, J. H. & Moody, F., eds. Gastroenterology: Foregut, Vol. 1. (Butterworth International Medical Reviews). 1981. text ed. price not set (ISBN 0-407-02287-2). Butterworth.
The Epidemiology & Control of Gastrointestinal Parasites of Sheep in Australia. 153p. pap. 11.00 (ISBN 0-643-00301-0, CO21, CSIRO). Unipub.
Hawker, Ross W. Notebook of Medical Physiology: Gastroenterology. (Notebooks of Medical Physiology Ser.). (Illus.). 256p. (Orig.). 1981. pap. text ed. 12.50 (ISBN 0-443-02144-9). Churchill.
Okolicsanyi, L. Familial Hyperbilirubinemia: Proceedings of the Workshop on Familial Disorders of Hepatic Bilirubin Metabolism Held in Venice, Italy 23rd-24th May 1980. 250p. 1981. 42.00 (ISBN 0-686-69369-8, Pub. by Wiley-Interscience). Wiley.
Performing G. I. Procedures. (Nursing Photobook Ser.). (Illus.). 1981. 12.95 (ISBN 0-916730-31-X). Intermed Comm.
Powell, L. W. & Piper, D. W., eds. Fundamentals of Gastroenterology: With Self-Assessment Workbook. 3rd ed. (Illus.). 222p. 1980. pap. text ed. 17.50 incl. wkbk. (ISBN 0-909337-26-8); wkbk. avail. ADIS Pr.
Walker & Smith. Practical Approach to Gastroenterology & Procedures in Childhood. (Postgraduate Pediatric Ser.). 1981. text ed. price not set. Butterworth.
Yardley & Goldman. Mucosal Biopsies in Gastroenterology. 1981. text ed. write for info. (ISBN 0-443-08059-3). Churchill.
GASTROINTESTINAL TRACT
see Alimentary Canal
GASTROMYCETES
see Gasteromycetes
GASTROPODA
see Gasteropoda
GATT
see Contracting Parties to the General Agreement on Tariffs and Trade
GAUDIER-BRZESKA, HENRI, 1891-1915
Ede, H. S. Savage Messiah. 1972. 6.95 (ISBN 0-87690-081-3). Dutton.
GAUGING
see Gaging
GAZETTEERS
see Geography–Dictionaries
GEESE
Owen, Myrfyn. Wild Geese of the World. (Illus.). 236p. 1981. 45.00 (ISBN 0-686-69428-7, Pub. by Batsford England). David & Charles.
GELS
see Colloids
GEM CUTTING
Hunt, Henry. Lapidary Carving for Creative Jewelry. LC 80-67509. (Illus.). 144p. (Orig.). 1981. 17.95 (ISBN 0-937764-01-9); pap. 12.95 (ISBN 0-937764-02-7). Desert Pr.
Perry, Nance & Perry, Ron. Practical Gemcutting. (Illus.). 96p. (Orig.). 1980. pap. 13.50 (ISBN 0-589-50192-5, Pub. by Reed Bks Australia). C E Tuttle.
GEMMATION (BOTANY)
see Plants–Reproduction
GEMS
Here are entered books on engraved stones and jewels, interesting from the point of view of antiquities or art. Works on mineralogical interest are entered under Precious Stones.
see also Jewelry
St. Maur, Suzan & Streep, Norbert. The Jewelry Book. (Illus.). 198p. 1981. 9.95 (ISBN 0-312-44230-0). St Martin.
GEMSTONE COLLECTING
see Mineralogy–Collectors and Collecting
GEMSTONES
see Precious Stones
GENEALOGICAL RESEARCH
see Genealogy
GENEALOGY
see also Biography; Heraldry; Kings and Rulers–Genealogy; Wills
also names of families, e.g. Adams Family; and names of places with or without the subdivision Genealogy, e.g. United States - Genealogy
Bradley, Edward J. The Child & Family Genealogy Reporting System. 2nd ed. 1979. 9.95 (ISBN 0-935202-01-3). Child & Family Ent.
Lee, Helen B. Joy Supplement, Two: Descendants of Thomas Joy, Pt.2. LC 76-45277. (Illus.). 1980. pap. write for info. (ISBN 0-87106-075-2). Globe Pequot.
GENEALOGY–BIBLIOGRAPHY
Mayhew, Catherine M. Genealogical Periodical Annual Index, Nineteen Seventy Eight, Vol.17. Towle, Laird C., ed. xii, 167p. 1980. 12.50 (ISBN 0-917890-23-X). Heritage Bk.
Parker, J. Carlyle, ed. Library Service for Genealogists. LC 80-26032. (The Gale Genealogy & Local History Ser.: Vol. 15). 285p. 1981. 30.00 (ISBN 0-8103-1489-4). Gale.
GENEALOGY–JUVENILE LITERATURE
Barnes, Kathleen & Pearce, Virginia. You & Yours. (Illus.). 41p. (Orig.). (gr. 3-6). 1980. pap. 2.95 (ISBN 0-87747-823-6). Deseret Bk.
Wubben, Pamela G. Genealogy for Children. 65p. (ps-7). 1981. pap. 7.95 (ISBN 0-935442-03-0). One Percent.
GENEALOGY–RESEARCH
see Genealogy
GENERAL AGREEMENT ON TARIFFS AND TRADE
see Contracting Parties to the General Agreement on Tariffs and Trade
GENERAL PRACTICE (MEDICINE)
see Family Medicine
GENERAL PROBLEM SOLVER (COMPUTER PROGRAM)
see GPS (Computer Program Language)
GENERAL PROPERTY TAX
see Property Tax
GENERAL SLOCUM (STEAMBOAT)
Rust, Claude. The Burning of the General Slocum. (Illus.). 160p. (YA) 1981. 8.95 (ISBN 0-525-66715-6). Elsevier-Nelson.
GENERAL WARRANTS
see Warrants (Law)
GENERALS
Kinchen, Oscar A. General Bennet H. Young. 1981. 8.95 (ISBN 0-8158-0404-0). Chris Mass.
GENERATION
see Reproduction
GENERATIVE ORGANS
see also Genito-Urinary Organs; Reproduction
Korting. Practical Dermatology of the Genital Region. 1981. text ed. price not set (ISBN 0-7216-5498-3). Saunders.
GENERATIVE ORGANS–SURGERY
Copenhaver, Edward H. Surgery of the Vulva & Vagina: A Practical Guide. (Illus.). 100p. 1981. text ed. write for info. (ISBN 0-7216-2718-8). Saunders.
GENERATIVE ORGANS, FEMALE
see also Gynecology; Obstetrics;
also names of individual organs
Gibbs, Ronald S. Antibiotic Therapy in Obstetrics & Gynecology. 224p. 1981. 16.50 (ISBN 0-471-06003-8, Pub. by Wiley Med). Wiley.
Morrow, C. Paul & Townsend, Duane E. Synopsis of Gynecologic Oncology. 500p. 1981. 29.50 (ISBN 0-471-06504-8, Pub. by Wiley-Med). Wiley.
GENES
see Heredity
GENETIC COUNSELING
Capron, Alexander M., et al, eds. Genetic Counseling: Fact, Values & Norms. LC 79-1736. (Alan R. Liss Ser.: Vol. 15, No. 2). 1979. write for info. (ISBN 0-8451-1025-X). March of Dimes.
Epstein, Charles J., ed. Risk, Communication, & Decision Making in Genetic Counseling. LC 79-5120. (Alan R. Liss Ser.: Vol. 15, No. 5c). 1979. 36.00 (ISBN 0-8451-1030-6). March of Dimes.
GENETIC ENGINEERING
see also Cloning
Alberts, Bruce & Fox, C. Fred, eds. Mechanistic Studies of DNA Replication & Genetic Recombination. (ICN-UCLA Symposia on Molecular & Cellular Biology Ser.: Vol. XIX). 1980. 48.00 (ISBN 0-12-048850-7). Acad Pr.
Blank, Robert H. The Political Implications of Human Genetic Technology. (Special Studies in Science, Technology, & Public Policy). 209p. (Orig.). 1981. lib. bdg. 24.00x (ISBN 0-89158-975-9); pap. text ed. 12.00x (ISBN 0-86531-193-5). Westview.
Cripps, Yvonne M. Controlling Technology: Genetic Engineering & the Law. 170p. 1980. 20.95 (ISBN 0-03-056806-4). Praeger.
Rotter, Jerome I., et al, eds. The Genetics & Heterogeneity of Common Gastrointestinal Disorders. 1980. 35.00 (ISBN 0-12-598760-9). Acad Pr.
Skamene, Emil, ed. Genetic Control of Natural Resistance to Infection & Malignancy. (Perspectives in Immunology Ser.). 1980. 33.00 (ISBN 0-12-647680-2). Acad Pr.
GENETIC SURGERY
see Genetic Engineering
GENETICS
see also Adaptation (Biology); Behavior Genetics; Biology; Chemical Genetics; Chromosomes; Cytogenetics; Evolution; Heredity; Human Genetics; Natural Selection; Population Genetics
Ayala, Francisco & Kiger, John. Solutions Manual for Modern Genetics. 1980. pap. 2.95 (ISBN 0-8053-0313-8, 800F00). Benjamin Cummings.
Bulmer, M. G. The Mathematical Theory of Quantitative Genetics. (Illus.). 220p. 1980. 74.00 (ISBN 0-19-857530-0). Oxford U Pr.
Cottle, Thomas J. Like Fathers, Like Sons: Portraits of Intimacy & Strain. 300p. 1981. price not set (ISBN 0-89391-054-6). Ablex Pub.
Davern, Cedric I., intro. by. Genetics: Readings from Scientific American. LC 80-25208. (Illus.). 1981. text ed. 17.95x (ISBN 0-7167-1200-8); pap. text ed. 8.95x (ISBN 0-7167-1201-6). W H Freeman.
Desnick, Robert J., ed. Enzyme Therapy in Genetic Diseases: Part 2. LC 79-48026. (Alan R. Liss Ser.: Vol. 16, No. 1). 1980. 64.00. March of Dimes.
Falconer, D. S. Introduction to Qualitative Genetics. 2nd ed. (Illus.). 1981. pap. text ed. 25.00x (ISBN 0-582-44195-1). Longman.
Glass, Robert E. Gene Function: E. coli & Its Heritable Elements. 450p. 1980. 60.00x (Pub. by Croom Helm England). State Mutual Bk.
Glover, S. W. & Hopwood, D. A., eds. Genetics As a Tool in Microbiology. (Society for General Microbiology Symposium: No. 31). (Illus.). 450p. Date not set. text ed. price not set (ISBN 0-521-23748-3). Cambridge U Pr.
Korochkin, L. I. Gene Interactions in Development. (Monographs on Theoretical & Applied Genetics: Vol. 4). (Illus.). 340p. 1980. 59.80 (ISBN 0-387-10112-8). Springer-Verlag.
Merrell, David J. Ecological Genetics. (Illus.). 570p. 1981. 25.00x (ISBN 0-8166-1019-3). U of Minn Pr.
Morton, N. E. Outline of Genetic Epidemiology. (Illus.). x, 250p. 1981. pap. 25.75 (ISBN 3-8055-2269-X). S Karger.
An Overview: Genetic Resources, 1980. (UNEP Ser.: No. 5). 132p. 1980. pap. 12.00 (UNEP 034, UNEP). Unipub.
Pai, Anna C. & Marcue-Roberts, Helen. Genetics: Its Concepts & Implications. (Illus.). 736p. 1981. text ed. 24.95 (ISBN 0-13-351007-7). P-H.
Schulman, Joseph D. & Simpson, Joe L., eds. Genetic Diseases in Pregnancy: Maternal Effects & Fetal Outcome. 1981. write for info. (ISBN 0-12-630940-X). Acad Pr.
Straub, W., ed. Current Genetical, Clinical & Morphological Problems. (Developments in Ophthalmology: Vol. 3). (Illus.). 1981. 66.00 (ISBN 3-8055-2000-X). S Karger.
Suzuki, David T. & Griffiths, Anthony J. F. Introduction to Genetic Analysis. 2nd ed. LC 80-24522. (Illus.). 1981. text ed. price not set (ISBN 0-7167-1263-6); instrs.' guide avail.; solutions manual avail. W H Freeman.
Symposium in Honor of the Jackson Laboratory's Fiftieth Anniversary, Bar Harbor, Maine, July 1979. Mammalian Genetics & Cancer: Proceedings. Russell, Elizabeth S., ed. 1981. 42.00x (ISBN 0-8451-0045-9). A R Liss.
Tamarin. Principles of Genetics. 608p. 1981. text ed. 21.95 (ISBN 0-87872-281-5). Duxbury Pr.
Watson, James D. & Tooze, John, eds. Recombinant DNA: A Scrapbook Edited by James D. Watson & John Tooze. (Illus.). 1981. text ed. price not set (ISBN 0-7167-1292-X). W H Freeman.
Woods, R. A. Biochemical Genetics. 2nd ed. LC 79-41695. 80p. 1980. pap. 5.95 (ISBN 0-412-13160-9, 6340). Methuen Inc.
GENITO-URINARY ORGANS
see also Generative Organs
Johnson, Thomas H. Genitourinary Radiology Case Studies. 1980. pap. 16.75 (ISBN 0-87488-090-4). Med Exam.
GENITO-URINARY ORGANS–SURGERY
McDougal, W. Scott. Traumatic Injuries of the Genitourinary System. (Illus.). 139p. 1980. 26.95. Williams & Wilkins.
GENOA
Miluck, Michael, ed. The Genoa-Carson Valley Book, 1981-82. (Illus.). 96p. 1981. pap. 3.00 (ISBN 0-686-28841-6). Dragon Ent.
GENOCIDE
see also Holocaust, Jewish (1939-1945)
Baum, Rainer C. Genocide & National Suicide. 1981. 25.00x (ISBN 0-8476-6970-X). Rowman.
GENRE PAINTING
Schatborn, Peter & Van Hasselt, Carlos. Dutch Genre Drawings. LC 72-86013. (Illus.). 162p. (Orig.). 1972. pap. 7.50. Intl Exhibit Foun.
GEOBOTANY
see Phytogeography
GEOCHEMISTRY
see also Geothermal Resources; Mineralogy, Determinative; Rocks–Analysis
Douglas, A G. & Maxwell, J. R., eds. Advances in Organic Geochemistry 1979: Proceedings of the 9th International Meeting on Organic Geochemistry Held at Newcastle-Upon-Tyne, England, Sept. 1979. LC 80-41078. (International Ser. in Earth Sciences: Vol. 36). (Illus.). 750p. 1980. 150.00 (ISBN 0-08-024017-8). Pergamon.
Jensen, M. L. & Bateman, A. M. Economic Mineral Deposits. 3rd rev. ed. 608p. 1981. text ed. 24.95 (ISBN 0-471-09043-3). Wiley.
Mineralogical Society Geochemistry Group, November 1 & 2, 1978. The Evidence of Chemical Heterogeneity in the Earth's Mantle. Bailey, D. K., et al, eds. (Illus.). 357p. 1980. text ed. 100.00x (ISBN 0-85403-144-8, Pub. by Royal Soc London). Scholium Intl.
GEODYNAMICS
see also Earthquakes; Rock Mechanics
Uyeda, S., et al, eds. Geodynamics of the Western Pacific. (Advances in Earth & Planetary Sciences Ser.: Pt. 6). 592p. 1980. 49.50x (ISBN 0-89955-315-X, Pub. by JSSP Japan). Intl Schol Bk Serv.
GEOGNOSY
see Geology
GEOGRAPHICAL ATLASES
see Atlases
GEOGRAPHICAL DICTIONARIES
see Geography–Dictionaries
GEOGRAPHICAL DISTRIBUTION OF ANIMALS
see Zoogeography
GEOGRAPHICAL DISTRIBUTION OF ANIMALS AND PLANTS
see also Forest Ecology; Phytogeography; Zoogeography;
also subdivisions Geographical Distribution or Migration under names of organisms, e.g. Fishes–Geographical Distribution; Birds–Migration
Nelson, Gareth & Platnick, Norman I. Systematics & Biogeography: Cladistics & Vicariance. LC 80-20828. (Illus.). 592p. 1981. text ed. 35.00x (ISBN 0-231-04574-3). Columbia U Pr.
GEOGRAPHICAL DISTRIBUTION OF DISEASES
see Medical Geography
GEOGRAPHICAL DISTRIBUTION OF MAN
see Anthropo-Geography; Ethnology; Man–Migrations
GEOGRAPHICAL DISTRIBUTION OF PLANTS
see Phytogeography
GEOGRAPHICAL DISTRIBUTION OF PLANTS AND ANIMALS
see Geographical Distribution of Animals and Plants
GEOGRAPHICAL PATHOLOGY
see Medical Geography
GEOGRAPHY
see also Anthropo-Geography; Atlases; Discoveries (In Geography); Ethnology; Man–Influence of Environment; Maps; Medical Geography; Physical Geography; Voyages and Travels
also subdivision Description and Travel under names of countries, e.g. France–Description and Travel; and subdivision Description, Geography under names of countries of antiquity, e.g. Greece–Description, Geography; and subdivision Maps under names of places, e.g. France–Maps
Cohen, Chester G. Shtetl Finder. 1980. pap. 8.25. Periday.
Cole. USSR Geography. 1981. text ed. price not set. Butterworth.
Enyedi, Gyorgy & Meszaros, Julia, eds. Development of Settlement Systems. (Studies in Geography in Hungary: 15). (Illus.). 265p. 1980. 27.50x (ISBN 963-05-1898-8). Intl Pubns Serv.
Geography. 1981. text ed. 25.85 (ISBN 0-06-318186-X, Pub. by Har-Row Ltd England); pap. text ed. 13.10 (ISBN 0-06-318187-8). Har-Row.
Hardy, A. V. The British Isles. 2nd ed. (Geography of the British Isles Ser.). (Illus.). 160p. Date not set. pap. price not set (ISBN 0-521-22258-3). Cambridge U Pr.
Pocock, Douglas, ed. Humanistic Geography & Literature: Essays on the Experience of Place. 224p. 1981. 27.00x (ISBN 0-389-20158-8). B&N.
Rowles, Graham D. Prisoners of Space? Exploring the Geographical Experience of Older People. (Replica Edition Ser.). 216p. 1980. pap. text ed. 10.00x (ISBN 0-86531-072-6). Westview.
Rudman, Jack. Geography. (Undergraduate Program Field Test Ser.: UPFT-10). (Cloth bdg. avail. on request). pap. 9.95 (ISBN 0-8373-6010-2). Natl Learning.
Shapiro, William, ed. Lands & Peoples, 6 vols. LC 80-84474. (Illus.). 1981. write for info. (ISBN 0-7172-8008-X). Grolier Ed Corp.
Statham, Ian & Finlayson, Brian. Hillslope Analysis. LC 80-40564. (Sources & Methods in Geography Ser.). 176p. 1980. pap. text ed. 8.95 (ISBN 0-408-10622-0). Butterworths.
Vincentius, Bellovacensis. Hier Begynneth the Table of the Rubrices of This Presente Volume Namde the Myrrour of the Worlde or Thymage of the Same. Caxton, William, tr. from Fr. LC 79-84143. (English Experience Ser.: No. 960). 204p. (Eng.). 1979. Repr. of 1481 ed. lib. bdg. 30.00 (ISBN 90-221-0960-7). Walter J Johnson.
Wrigley, Neil & Bennett, Robert J., eds. Quantitative Geography in Britain: Retrospect & Prospect. 448p. 1981. price not set (ISBN 0-7100-0731-0). Routledge & Kegan.
GEOGRAPHY–ATLASES
see Atlases
GEOGRAPHY–BIBLIOGRAPHY
Goddard. Information Sources in Geographical Science. (Butterworths Guides to Information Sources Ser.). 1981. text ed. price not set (ISBN 0-408-10690-5). Butterworth.
Hoggart, Keith. Geography & Local Administration: A Bibliography. (Public Administration Ser.: Bibliography P-530). 84p. 1980. pap. 9.00. Vance Biblios.
GEOGRAPHY–DICTIONARIES
Forster, Klaus. Pronouncing Dictionary of English-Place Names. 308p. 1981. 30.00 (ISBN 0-7100-0756-6). Routledge & Kegan.
GEOGRAPHY–GAZETTEERS
see Geography–Dictionaries
GEOGRAPHY–HISTORY
see also Discoveries (In Geography)
Stoddart, D. R., ed. Geography, Ideology & Social Concern. (Illus.). 1981. 26.50x (ISBN 0-389-20207-X). B&N.
GEOGRAPHY–PICTORIAL WORKS
see also Views
America: An Aerial View. Date not set. 5.95 (ISBN 0-517-25701-7). Aerial Photo.
GEORGRAPHY–STATISTICS
see Geography–Tables, Etc.
GEOGRAPHY–STUDY AND TEACHING
Jay, L. J. Geography Teaching with a Little Latitude. (Classroom Close-Ups Ser.: No. 7). (Illus.). 160p. 1981. text ed. 17.95x (ISBN 0-04-371077-8, 2606); pap. text ed. 8.95x (ISBN 0-04-371078-6, AU 461). Allen Unwin.

GEOGRAPHY–TABLES, ETC.
Clark, Isobel. Practical Geostatistics. 1979. 28.50x (ISBN 0-85334-843-X). Intl Ideas.
GEOGRAPHY–VIEWS
see Views
GEOGRAPHY, AGRICULTURAL
see Agricultural Geography
GEOGRAPHY, BIBLICAL
see Bible–Geography
GEOGRAPHY, ECONOMIC
see also Agricultural Geography
also subdivision Economic Conditions under names of countries
O'Sullivan, Patrick. Geographical Economics. 195p. 1981. 24.95 (ISBN 0-470-27122-1). Halsted Pr.
Staff of World Bank. World Tables: 1980. LC 79-3649. (World Bank Occasional Paper Ser.). (Illus.). 480p. 1980. text ed. 27.50x (ISBN 0-8018-2389-7); pap. text ed. 10.95x (ISBN 0-8018-2390-0). Johns Hopkins.
GEOGRAPHY, ECONOMIC–MAPS
French, Brian & Squire, Stan. Human & Economic Geography. (Illus.). 216p. (Orig.). 1973. pap. text ed. 4.50x (ISBN 0-19-519769-0). Oxford U Pr.
GEOGRAPHY, HISTORICAL
Mellor. Geography of Two Germanies. 1978. 20.40 (ISBN 0-06-318066-9, IntlDept). Har-Row.
Mintz, Leigh W. Historical Geology: The Science of a Dynamic Earth. 3rd ed. (Illus.). 576p. 1981. text ed. 20.95 (ISBN 0-675-08028-2); tchr's. ed. 3.95 (ISBN 0-686-69492-9). Merrill.
GEOGRAPHY, HISTORICAL–MAPS
Chambers Atlas of World History. 136p. 1980. 25.00x (ISBN 0-550-14001-8, Pub. by W & R Chambers Scotland). State Mutual Bk.
GEOGRAPHY, MEDICAL
see Medical Geography
GEOGRAPHY, PHYSICAL
see Physical Geography
GEOGRAPHY, POLITICAL
see also Cities and Towns; Geopolitics
Burnett, Alan D. & Taylor, Peter J. Political Studies from Spatial Perspectives: Anglo-American Essays on Political Geography. 1981. price not set (ISBN 0-471-27909-9, Pub. by Wiley-Interscience); pap. price not set (ISBN 0-471-27910-2). Wiley.
Paxton, John, ed. Statesman's Year-Book World Gazetteer. 2nd ed. (Illus.). 800p. 1980. 25.00x (ISBN 0-312-76126-0). St. Martin.
GEOGRAPHY, SOCIAL
see Anthropo-Geography
GEOGRAPHY, URBAN
see Cities and Towns
GEOLOGICAL CHEMISTRY
see Geochemistry
GEOLOGICAL EROSION
see Erosion
GEOLOGICAL OCEANOGRAPHY
see Submarine Geology
GEOLOGICAL PHYSICS
see Geophysics
GEOLOGY
see also Caves; Creation; Crystallography; Earth; Earthquakes; Erosion; Geophysics; Glaciers; Hydrogeology; Mineralogy; Mountains; Natural History; Oceanography; Paleontology; Petroleum–Geology; Petrology; Physical Geography; Rocks; Sedimentation and Deposition; Speleology; Submarine Geology; Volcanoes
Beck, A. E. Physical Principles of Exploration Methods: An Introduction Text for Geology & Geophysics Students. 256p. 1981. 39.95 (ISBN 0-470-27124-8); pap. 18.95 (ISBN 0-470-27128-0). Halsted Pr.
Costa, J. & Baker, V. Surficial Geology: Building with the Earth. LC 80-22644. 1981. write for info. (ISBN 0-471-03229-8). Wiley.
Costa, John E. & Baker, Victor R. Surficial Geology Building with the Earth. 608p. 1981. text ed. 19.95 (ISBN 0-471-03229-8). Wiley.
Eastern Kentucky University, Dept. of Geology. Principles of Physical Geology Laboratory Manual. 80p. 1980. pap. text ed. 5.50 (ISBN 0-8403-2285-2). Kendall-Hunt.
Giode TP Classification in Geology. LC 80-41094. (Geology Ser.). 120p. 1981. 34.95 (ISBN 0-470-27090-X). Halsted Pr.
McLeod, G. C. Georges Bank: Past, Present, & Future. (Special Studies on Natural Resources & Energy Management). 225p. 1981. lib. bdg. 22.00x (ISBN 0-86531-199-4). Westview.
Manual of Applied Geology for Engineers. 414p. 1980. pap. 75.00x (ISBN 0-7277-0038-3, Pub. by Telford England). State Mutual Bk.
Mathewson, Christopher C. Engineering Geology. (Illus.). 416p. 1981. text ed. 24.95 (ISBN 0-675-08032-0). Merrill.
Mitchell-Thome, Raoul C. Geology of the South Atlantic Islands. (Beitraege zur regionalen Geologie der Erde: Vol. 10). (Illus.). 366p. 1970. lib. bdg. 90.05x (ISBN 3-443-11010-X, Pub by Gebrueder Borntraeger Germany). Lubrecht & Cramer.
Morey, G. B. & Hanson, Gilbert N., eds. Selected Studies of Archean Gneisses & Lower Proterozoic Rocks: Southern Canadian Shield. LC 80-67113. (Special Paper Ser.: No. 182). (Illus., Orig.). 1980. pap. write for info. (ISBN 0-8137-2182-2). Geol Soc.
Nuke, Susan. Processes of the Earth's Surface. 96p. 1980. lab manual 6.95. Mountain Pr.
Read, H. H. & Watson, Janet. Introduction & Geology, 2 vols. Incl. Vol. 1. Principles. 2nd ed. LC 76-50637. 1977. 27.95 (ISBN 0-470-99031-7); Vol. 2, 2 pts. LC 75-501. 1975; Pt. 1. Early Stages of Earth History. 221p. 19.95 (ISBN 0-470-71165-5); Pt. 2. Later Stages of Earth History. 371p. 24.95 (ISBN 0-470-71166-3). Halsted Pr.
Riban, David M. Introduction to Physical Science. (Illus.). 656p. 1981. text ed. 21.95 (ISBN 0-07-052140-9, C); instr's manual 4.95 (ISBN 0-07-052141-7). McGraw.
Rudman, Jack. Geology. (Undergraduate Program Field Test Ser.: UPFT-11). (Cloth bdg. avail. on request). pap. 9.95 (ISBN 0-8373-6011-0). Natl Learning.
Sanders, John E. Principles of Physical Geology. 608p. 1981. text ed. 19.95 (ISBN 0-471-08424-7). Wiley.
Visser, W. A., ed. Geological Nomenclature. 568p. 1980. lib. bdg. 95.00 (ISBN 90-247-2403-1). Kluwer Boston.
GEOLOGY–EXAMINATIONS, QUESTIONS, ETC.
Savage, E. Lynn & Biren, Helen A. A Study Guide to Putnam's Geology. 208p. (Orig.). 1978. pap. text ed. 6.95x (ISBN 0-19-502385-4). Oxford U Pr.
GEOLOGY–HISTORY
Skinner, Brian J., ed. Earth's History, Structure, & Materials. (The Earth & Its Inhabitants: Selected Readings from American Scientist Ser.). (Illus.). 184p. (Orig.). 1980. pap. 8.95 (ISBN 0-913232-89-0). W Kaufmann.
Tynan, Eugene J. & Cain, J. Allen. Geology: A Synopsis Part 2 Historical Geology. LC 79-92086. 192p. 1981. pap. text ed. 7.95 (ISBN 0-8403-2306-9). Kendall-Hunt.
GEOLOGY–STATISTICAL METHODS
Koch, George S., Jr. & Link, Richard F. Statistical Analysis of Geological Data. 850p. 1981. pap. 12.50 (ISBN 0-486-64040-X). Dover.
GEOLOGY–ALASKA
Clark, David L. Stratigraphy & Glacial-Marine Sediments of the Amerasian Basin,Central Arctic Ocean. LC 80-65270. (Special Paper Ser.: No. 181). (Illus., Orig.). 1980. pap. 13.00 (ISBN 0-8137-2181-4). Geol Soc.
GEOLOGY–ASIA
Kobayashi, T., et al. Geology & Palaeontology of Southeast Asia, Vol. XXI. 381p. 1980. 52.00x (ISBN 0-86008-263-6, Pub. by U of Tokyo Pr Japan). Intl Schol Bk Serv.
GEOLOGY–AUSTRALIA
Lands of the Alligator Rivers Area, Northern Territory. (Land Research Ser.: No. 38). 171p. 1976. pap. 13.50 (ISBN 0-643-00208-1, CO19, CSIRO). Unipub.
GEOLOGY–EUROPE
Ager, Derek V. The Geology of Europe. 576p. 1980. 44.95x (ISBN 0-470-26990-1). Halsted Pr.
GEOLOGY–GREAT BRITAIN
Anderson, J. G. & Owen, T. R. The Structure of the British Isles. 2nd ed. LC 80-41075. (Illus.). 242p. 1980. 28.00 (ISBN 0-08-023998-6); pap. 13.50 (ISBN 0-08-023997-8). Pergamon.
GEOLOGY–LATIN AMERICA
Weyl, Richard. Geology of Central America, Vol. 15. 2nd ed. (Beitraege Zur Regionalen Geologie der Erde). (Illus.). 371p. 1980. lib. bdg. 88.85x (ISBN 3-443-11015-0). Lubrecht & Cramer.
GEOLOGY–NORTH AMERICA
Asano, Shuzo, ed. Structure of the Transition Zone. (Advances in Earth & Planetary Sciences Ser.: No. 8). 184p. 1980. lib. bdg. 26.50 (ISBN 90-277-1149-6, Pub. by D. Reidel). Kluwer Boston.
Hamblin, W. Kenneth. Atlas of Stereoscopic Aerial Photographs & Landsat Imagery of North America. LC 79-91239. (Illus.). 208p. (Orig.). 15.95 (ISBN 0-935698-00-0). Tasa Pub Co.
GEOLOGY–NORWAY
Fortey, R. A. The Ordovician Trilobites of the Spitsbergen. (Norsk Polarinstitutt Skrifter: Vol. 171). (Illus.). 163p. 1980. pap. text ed. 18.00x (ISBN 82-00-29189-8). Universitet.
Geological Survey of Norway, No. 360, Bulletin 57. (Illus.). 200p. 1981. pap. 24.00x (ISBN 82-00-31397-2). Universitet.
Lock, B. E., et al. The Geology of Edgeoya & Barentsoya: Svalbard. (Norsk Polarinstitutt Skrifter: Vol. 168). (Illus.). 64p. 1980. pap. text ed. 7.50x. Universitet.
Rowell, Unni H. Geological Survey of Norway, No. 361, Bulletin 58. 1981. pap. 12.00x (ISBN 82-00-31430-8). Universitet.
Sturt, B. A., et al. Geological Survey of Norway, No. 358, Bulletin 55. (Illus.). 60p. 1981. pap. 14.00x. Universitet.
Wielens, J. B., et al. Geological Survey of Norway, No. 359, Bulletin 56. (Illus.). 60p. 1981. pap. 14.00x. Universitet.
Winsnes, Thore S., ed. The Geological Development of Svalbard During the Precambrian, Lower Palaeozoic, & Devonian. (Norsk Polarinstitutt Skrifter: Vol. 167). (Illus.). 323p. 1980. pap. text ed. 30.00x (ISBN 82-90307-03-9). Universitet.
GEOLOGY–UNITED STATES
Here are entered works on the geology of the United States as a whole, together with works on individual states or specific areas.
Adkins, W. S. & Arick, M. B. Geology of Bell County, Texas. (Illus.). 92p. 1930. 1.00 (BULL 3016). Bur Econ Geology.
Barnes, V. E. & Schofield, D. A. Potential Low-Grade Iron Ore & Hydraulic-Fracturing Sand in Cambrian Sandstones, Northwestern Llano Region, Texas. (Illus.). 58p. 1964. 2.00 (RI 53). Bur Econ Geology.
Barnes, V. E., et al. Geology of the Llano Region & Austin Area. rev. ed. 154p. 1976. Repr. of 1972 ed. 1.50 (GB 13). Bur Econ Geology.
Bernard, H. A., et al. Recent Sediments of Southeast Texas-A Field Guide to the Brazos Alluvial & Deltaic Plains & the Galveston Barrier Island Complex. 132p. 1970. Repr. 5.00 (GB 11). Bur Econ Geology.
Brand, J. P. Cretaceous of Llano Estacado of Texas. (Illus.). 59p. 1953. 0.70 (RI 20). Bur Econ Geology.
Brown, L. F., et al. Pennsylvanian Depositional Systems in North-Central Texas: A Guide for Interpreting Terrigenous Clastic Facies in a Cratonic Basin. (Illus.). 122p. 1973. Repr. 3.50 (GB 14). Bur Econ Geology.
Brown, T. E., et al. Field Excursions, East Texas: Clay, Glauconite, Ironstone Deposits. (Illus.). 48p. 1969. 1.00 (GB 9). Bur Econ Geology.
Bullard, F. M. The Geology of Grayson County, Texas. (Illus.). 72p. 1931. 0.50 (BULL 3125). Bur Econ Geology.
Caughey, C. A. Depositional Systems in the Paluxy Formation (Lower Cretaceous) Northeast Texas-Oil, Gas, & Ground-Water Resources. (Illus.). 59p. 1977. 2.00 (GC 77-8). Bur Econ Geology.
Dietrich, J. W. & Lonsdale, J. T. Mineral Resources of the Colorado River Industrial Development Association Area. (Illus.). 84p. 1958. 1.50 (RI 37). Bur Econ Geology.
Dutton, S. P., et al. Geology & Geohydrology of the Palo Duro Basin, Texas Panhandle: A Report on the Progress of Nuclear Waste Isolation Feasibility Studies. (Illus.). 99p. 1979. 2.50 (GC 79-1). Bur Econ Geology.
Eargle, D. H., et al. Uranium Geology & Mines, South Texas. (Illus.). 59p. 1971. 1.75 (GB 12). Bur Econ Geology.
Ellison, S. P., Jr. Sulfur in Texas. (Illus.). 1971. 2.00 (HB 2). Bur Econ Geology.
Evans, T. J. Bituminous Coal in Texas. (Illus.). 65p. 1974. 2.00 (HB 4). Bur Econ Geology.
Fisher, W. L. Rock & Mineral Resources of East Texas. (Illus.). 439p. 1965. 5.00 (RI 54). Bur Econ Geology.
Fisher, W. L. & McGowen, J. H. Depostional Systems in the Wilcox Group of Texas & Their Relationship to Occurrence of Oil & Gas. 125p. 1967. Repr. 1.00 (GC 67-4). Bur Econ Geology.
Fisher, W. L. & Rodda, P. U. Lower Cretaceous Sands of Texas: Stratigraphy & Resources. (Illus.). 116p. 1967. 1.75 (RI 59). Bur Econ Geology.
Folk, R. L., et al. Field Excursion, Central Texas: Tertiary Bentonites of Central Texas. 53p. 1973. Repr. of 1961 ed. 1.25 (GB 3). Bur Econ Geology.
Frey, Robert W., ed. Excursions in Southeastern Geology: Field Trip Guidebooks, 2 vols. Incl. Vol. I. Field Trips-1-13. pap. 25.00 (ISBN 0-913312-48-7); Vol. II. Field Trips-14-23. pap. 25.00 (ISBN 0-913312-49-5). (Illus., Orig.). 1980. Set. pap. 40.00 (ISBN 0-913312-50-9). Am Geol.
Galloway, W. E., et al. South Texas Uranium Province, Geologic Perspective. (Illus.). 81p. 1979. 3.00 (GB 18). Bur Econ Geology.
Girard, R. M. Texas Rocks & Minerals: An Amateur's Guide. (Illus.). 109p. 1964. Repr. 2.00 (GB 6). Bur Econ Geology.
Graces, R. W., Jr. Geology of Hood Spring Quadrangle, Brewster County, Texas. (Illus.). 51p. 1954. 2.25 (RI 21). Bur Econ Geology.
Henderson, G. G. Geology of Tom Green County. (Illus.). 116p. 1928. 0.50 (BULL 2807). Bur Econ Geology.
King, P. B. The Geology of the Glass Mountains, Texas: Part I, Descriptive Geology. (Illus.). 167p. 1930. 2.50 (BULL 3038). Bur Econ Geology.
King, P. B. & Flawn, P. T. Geology & Mineral Deposits of Pre-Cambrian Rocks of the Van Horn Area, Texas. (Illus.). 218p. 1953. 5.75 (PUB 5301). Bur Econ Geology.
King, R. E. The Geology of the Glass Mountains, Texas: Part Ii, Faunal Summary & Correlation of the Permian Formations with Description of Brachiopoda. (Illus.). 146p. 1930. 2.50 (BULL 3042). Bur Econ Geology.
McGowen, J. H. & Brewton, J. L. Historical Changes & Related Coastal Processes, Gulf & Mainland Shorelines, Matagorda Bay Area, Texas. (Illus.). 72p. 1975. 6.00. Bur Econ Geology.
McGowen, J. H., et al. Geochemistry of Bottom Sediments Matagorda Bay System, Texas. (Illus.). 64p. 1979. 1.50 (GC 79-2). Bur Econ Geology.
Matthews, W. H. The Geologic Story of Longhorn Cavern. 50p. 1963. 1.00 (GB 4). Bur Econ Geology.
--The Geologic Story of Palo Duro Canyon. (Illus.). 51p. 1969. 1.00 (GB 8). Bur Econ Geology.
--Texas Fossils: An Amateur Collector's Handbook. (Illus.). 123p. 1960. Repr. 1.00 (GB 2). Bur Econ Geology.
Maxwell, R. A. Mineral Resources of South Texas: Region Served Through the Port of Corpus Christi. (Illus.). 140p. 1962. 3.50 (RI 43). Bur Econ Geology.
Myers, D. A., et al. Geology of the Late Paleozoic Horseshoe Atoll in West Texas. (Illus.). 113p. 1956. 2.00 (PUB 5607). Bur Econ Geology.
Nash, J. P., et al. Road Building Materials in Texas. (Illus.). 159p. 1918. 0.50 (BULL 1839). Bur Econ Geology.
Patton, L. T. The Geology of Potter County. (Illus.). 180p. 1923. 0.50 (BULL 2330). Bur Econ Geology.
--The Geology of Stonewall County, Texas. (Illus.). 77p. 1930. 0.50 (BULL 3027). Bur Econ Geology.
Plummer, F. B. The Carboniferous Rocks of the Llano Region of Central Texas. (Illus.). 170p. 1943. 2.00 (PUB 4329). Bur Econ Geology.
Plummer, F. B. & Sargent, E. C. Underground Waters & Subsurface Temperatures of the Woodbine Sand in Northeast Texas. (Illus.). 178p. 1931. 1.00 (BULL 3138). Bur Econ Geology.
Reed, L. C. & Longnecker, O. M., Jr. The Geology of Hemphill County, Texas. (Illus.). 98p. 1932. price not set (BULL 3231). Bur Econ Geology.
Sellards, E. H., et al. The Geology of Texas: Vol.I, Stratigraphy. (Illus.). 1007p. 1978. Repr. of 1932 ed. 8.00 (BULL 3232). Bur Econ Geology.
Slaughter, B. H., et al. The Hill-Shuler Local Faunas of the Upper Trinity River, Dallas & Denton Counties, Texas. (Illus.). 75p. 1962. 2.50 (RI 48). Bur Econ Geology.
Stenzel, H. B. The Geology of Henrys Chapel Quadrangle, Northeastern Cherokee County, Texas. (Illus.). 119p. 1953. 3.50 (PUB 5305). Bur Econ Geology.
Walton, A. W. & Henry, C. D., eds. Cenzoic Geology of the Trans-Pecos Volcanic Field of Texas. 202p. 1979. write for info. (GB 19). Bur Econ Geology.
Wiese, B. R. & White, W. A. Padre Island National Seashore-a Guide to the Geology, Natural Environments & History of a Texas Barrier Island. Date not set. price not set (GB 17). Bur Econ Geology.
Winton, W. M. & Adkins, W. S. The Geology of Tarrant County. (Illus.). 122p. 1919. 0.50 (BULL 1931). Bur Econ Geology.
GEOLOGY, CHEMICAL
see Geochemistry; Mineralogy, Determinative; Rocks–Analysis
GEOLOGY, DYNAMIC
see Geodynamics
GEOLOGY, HISTORICAL
see Geology, Stratigraphic; Paleontology
GEOLOGY, STRATIGRAPHIC
see also Glacial Epoch; Oil Well Logging; Paleontology
Ager, D. V. Nature of the Stratigraphical Record. 2nd ed. 136p. 1981. 17.95 (ISBN 0-470-27052-7). Halsted Pr.
Rayner, D. Stratigraphy of the British Isles. 2nd ed. LC 79-8523. (Illus.). 400p. Date not set. price not set (ISBN 0-521-23452-2); pap. price not set (ISBN 0-521-29961-6). Cambridge U Pr.
GEOLOGY, STRATIGRAPHIC–CAMBRIAN
Vugrinovich, R. G. Precambrian Geochronology of North America: An Annotated Bibliography,1951-1977. LC 80-68063. (Special Paper Ser.: No. 11). 1980. 4.00x (ISBN 0-8137-6011-9). Geol Soc.
GEOLOGY, STRATIGRAPHIC–CARBONIFEROUS
Muir-Wood, Helen M. Malayan Lower Carboniferous Fossils & Their Bearing on the Visean Palaeogeography of Asia. (Illus.). 118p. 1948. 11.50x (ISBN 0-565-00374-7, Pub. by Brit Mus Nat Hist England). Sabbot-Natural Hist Bks.
GEOLOGY, STRATIGRAPHIC–CENOZOIC
Armentrout, John M., ed. Pacific Northwest Cenozoic Biostratigraphy. LC 80-82937. (Special Paper Ser.: No. 184). (Illus., Orig.). 1980. pap. write for info. (ISBN 0-8137-2184-9). Geol Soc.
Pomerol, C. Cenozoic Era. 280p. 1981. 74.95 (ISBN 0-470-27140-X). Halsted Pr.
GEOLOGY, STRUCTURAL
see also Geomorphology; Mountains; Plate Tectonics
Belousov, V. V. Geotectonics. (Illus.). 330p. 1981. 29.80 (ISBN 0-387-09173-4). Springer-Verlag.
GEOLOGY, SUBMARINE
see Submarine Geology
GEOLOGY AND RELIGION
see Religion and Science
GEOMANCY
Von Hartmann, Frank. The Techniques of Astrological Geomancy. (Illus.). 137p. 1981. 47.85 (ISBN 0-89920-019-2). Am Inst Psych.
GEOMETRY
see also Angle; Surfaces; Topology; Trigonometry
Abelson, Harold & DiSessa, Andrea. Turtle Geometry: The Computer As a Medium for Exploring Mathematics. (Illus.). 576p. 1981. text ed. 35.00 (ISBN 0-262-01063-1). MIT Pr.
Baues, Hans J. Geometry of Loop Spaces & the Cobar Construction. LC 80-12430. (Memoirs of the American Mathematical Society Ser.). 1980. 6.40 (ISBN 0-8218-2230-6, MEMO-230). Am Math.

Beem. The Lorentzian Distance Function & Global Lorentzian Geometry. Date not set. price not set (ISBN 0-8247-1369-9). Dekker.
Faux, I. D. & Pratt, M. J. Computational Geometry for Designing & Manufacture. LC 78-40637. 329p. 1980. pap. 22.95 (ISBN 0-470-27069-1). Halsted Pr.
Hermann, Robert. Cartanian Geometry, Nonlinear Waves, & Control Theory, Pt. B. Ackerman, Michael, tr. (Interdisciplinary Mathematics Ser.: Vol. 21). 585p. 1980. text ed. 60.00x (ISBN 0-915692-29-5, QA649.H46). Math Sci Pr.
Hsiang, W., et al, eds. The Chern Symposium Nineteen Seventy Nine. (Illus.). 259p. 1981. 29.50 (ISBN 0-387-90537-5). Springer-Verlag.
Learning Achievement Corporation. Geometry & Design & Maintenance: Ratio, Proportion, Reading Graphs & Data. Zak, Therese A., ed. (MATCH Ser.). (Illus.). 128p. 1981. text ed. 5.28 (ISBN 0-07-037115-6, G). McGraw.
McLeod, Robin J. & Wachspress, Eugene L., eds. Frontiers of Applied Geometru: Proceedings of Symposium. Les Cruces, New Mexico, January 1980. 128p. 1980. pap. 23.40 (ISBN 0-08-026487-5). Pergamon.
Schutz, B. Geometrical Methods of Mathematical Physics. LC 80-40211. (Illus.). 300p. 1980. 39.95 (ISBN 0-521-23271-6); pap. 16.95 (ISBN 0-521-29887-3). Cambridge U Pr.
Vaisman. Foundations of Three Dimensional Euclidean Geometry. Date not set. 35.00 (ISBN 0-8247-6901-5). Dekker.

GEOMETRY, ALGEBRAIC
see also Curves, Algebraic; Geometry, Analytic; Surfaces; Topology
Mumford, D. Algerbraic Geometry I: Complex Projective Varieties, I. (Grundlehren der Mathematischen Wissenschaften: Vol. 221). (Illus.). 200p. 1981. 18.90 (ISBN 0-387-07603-4). Springer-Verlag.
Slodowy, P. Simple Singularities & Simple Algebraic Groups. (Lecture Notes in Mathematics: Vol. 815). 175p. 1980. pap. 11.80 (ISBN 0-387-10026-1). Springer-Verlag.

GEOMETRY, ANALYTIC
see also Surfaces
Borsuk, Karol. Multidimensional Analytic Geometry. 1969. 19.25 (ISBN 0-02-841690-2). Hafner.
Dadourian, H. M. Introduction to Analytic Geometry & the Calculus. 256p. 1981. Repr. of 1949 ed. lib. bdg. price not set (ISBN 0-89874-267-6). Krieger.
Gillet, Philip. Calculus & Analytic Geometry. 928p. 1981. text ed. 28.95 (ISBN 0-669-00641-6); instr's. guide avail. (ISBN 0-669-02702-2); solutions guide vol. 1 6.95 (ISBN 0-669-00642-4); solutions guide vol. 2 6.95 (ISBN 0-669-03212-3); solutions guides vol. 3 6.95 (ISBN 0-669-03213-1). Heath.

GEOMETRY, DIFFERENTIAL
see also Calculus of Tensors; Coordinates; Surfaces
Hurt, Norman & Hermann, R. Quantum Statistical Mechanics & Lie Group Harmonic Analysis, Pt. A. (Lie Groups; History, Frontiers & Applications: Vol. X). 1980. text ed. 30.00x (ISBN 0-915692-30-9, QC174.8.H87). Math Sci Pr.
Poor, Walter A. Differential Geometric Structures. (Illus.). 320p. 1981. text ed. 44.95 (ISBN 0-07-050435-0, C). McGraw.

GEOMETRY CONCEPT
Piaget, Jean, et al. The Child's Conception of Geometry. Lunzer, E. A., tr. 432p. 1981. pap. 8.95 (ISBN 0-393-00057-5). Norton.

GEOMORPHOLOGY
see also Erosion; Landforms; Physical Geography
Coates, Donald, ed. Coastal Geomorphology. (Binghamton Symposia in Geomorphology International Ser.: No. 3). (Illus.). 416p. 1980. text ed. 20.00x (ISBN 0-04-551038-5, 2506). Allen Unwin.
Coates, Donald R., ed. Environmental Geomorphology & Landscape Conservation, 3 vols. Incl. Vol. 1. Prior to 1900. 1972. 43.50 (ISBN 0-12-786241-2); Vol. 2. Urban Areas. 464p. 1974. 39.00 (ISBN 0-12-786242-0); Vol. 3. Non-Urban Regions. 496p. 1973. 43.50 (ISBN 0-12-786243-9). LC 72-77882. (Benchmark Papers in Geology Ser.). (Illus.). Acad Pr.
--Geomorphology & Engineering. (Binghamton Symposia in Geomorphology: International Ser.: No. 7). (Illus.). 384p. 1980. text ed. 30.00x (ISBN 0-04-551040-7, 2584). Allen Unwin.
Doehring, Donald O., ed. Geomorphology in Arid Regions. (Binghamton Symposia in Geomorphology: International Ser.: No. 8). (Illus.). 276p. 1980. text ed. 20.00x (ISBN 0-04-551041-5, 2508). Allen Unwin.
Embleston, C. & King, C. A. Glacial & Periglacial Morphology, 2 vols. 2nd ed. Incl. Vol. 1. Glacial Geomorphology. LC 75-14188. pap. 19.95 (ISBN 0-470-23893-3); Vol. 2. Periglacial Geomorphology. LC 75-14187. pap. 13.95 (ISBN 0-470-23895-X). 1975. Halsted Pr.
Geomorphological Map of Papua New Guinea. (Land Research Ser.: No. 33). (Illus.). 23p. 1979. 9.00 (ISBN 0-643-00092-5, CO17, CSIRO). Unipub.
Gouldie, Andrew, ed. Geomorphological Techniques. (Illus.). 320p. 1981. text ed. 60.00x (ISBN 0-04-551042-3, 2632-3); pap. text ed. 29.95x (ISBN 0-04-551043-1). Allen Unwin.

GEOPHYSICAL PROSPECTING
see Prospecting–Geophysical Methods

GEOPHYSICAL RESEARCH
Gronlie, Gisle. Geophysical Studies in the Norwegian-Greenland Sea. (Norsk Polarinstitutt Skrifter: Vol. 170). (Illus.). 117p. 1980. pap. text ed. 10.00 (ISBN 82-90307-05-5). Universitet.

GEOPHYSICS
see also Geodynamics; Geology; Geophysical Research; Magnetism; Magnetohydrodynamics; Meteorology; Oceanography; Plate Tectonics; Prospecting–Geophysical Methods; Seismology
Beck, A. E. Physical Principles of Exploration Methods: An Introduction Text for Geology & Geophysics Students. 256p. 1981. 39.95 (ISBN 0-470-27124-8); pap. 18.95 (ISBN 0-470-27128-0). Halsted Pr.
Kovacs, William D. & Holtz, Robert D. An Introduction to Geotechnical Engineering. (Illus.). 720p. 1981. text ed. 28.95 (ISBN 0-13-484394-0). P-H.

GEOPOLITICS
see also Anthropo-Geography; Demography; World Politics
Szuprowicz, Bohdan O. Strategic Materials Geopolitics: How to Avoid Shortages, Cartels, Embargoes, & Supply Disruptions. 336p. 1981. 18.95 (ISBN 0-471-07843-3, Pub. by Wiley-Interscience). Wiley.

GEORGE, HENRY, 1839-1897
George, Henry, Jr. Henry George. Aaron, Daniel, ed. (American Men & Women of Letters Ser.). Orig. Title: The Life of Henry George. 640p. 1981. pap. 8.95 (ISBN 0-87754-164-7). Chelsea Hse.

GEORGIA
see also Names of specific cities, counties, etc in Georgia
Fradin, Dennis. Georgia: In Words & Pictures. LC 80-26768. (Young People's Stories of Our States Ser.). (Illus.). 48p. (gr. 2-5). 1981. PLB 8.65g (ISBN 0-516-03910-5, Time Line). Childrens.

GEORGIA–DESCRIPTION AND TRAVEL
Harper, Francis & Presley, Delma E. Okefinokee Album. LC 80-14220. (Illus.). 235p. 1981. 14.95 (ISBN 0-8203-0530-8). U of Ga Pr.

GEORGIA–GENEALOGY
Brunson, Marion B. Our Bailey & Staggers History & Genealogy. 1980. 10.00 (ISBN 0-916620-51-4). Portals Pr.
Gwinnett County, Georgia, Families Eighteen Eighteen to Nineteen Sixty-Eight. LC 80-52845. 662p. 1980. 30.00 (ISBN 0-87797-053-X). Cherokee.
Mitchell, Lizzie R. History of Pike County, Georgia, 1822-1932. LC 80-23352. x, 162p. 1980. Repr. 15.00 (ISBN 0-87152-345-0). Reprint.

GEORGIA–HISTORY
Mitchell, Lizzie R. History of Pike County, Georgia, 1822-1932. LC 80-23352. x, 162p. 1980. Repr. 15.00 (ISBN 0-87152-345-0). Reprint.
Vanstory, Burnette. Georgia's Land of the Golden Isles. LC 80-28565. (Illus.). 225p. 1981. 15.00 (ISBN 0-8203-0557-X); pap. 8.95 (ISBN 0-8203-0558-8). U of Ga Pr.

GEORGIA–POLITICS AND GOVERNMENT
Chanin, Leah F. Reference Guide to Georgia Legal History & Legal Research. 175p. 1980. 20.00 (ISBN 0-87215-315-0). Michie.
Hepburn, Lawrence R. State Government in Georgia. 200p. (Orig.). (gr. 8-12). 1981. pap. text ed. 10.00 (ISBN 0-89854-067-4). U of GA Inst Govt.
Hepburn, Mary A., et al. City Government in Georgia. LC 79-24128. 150p. (Orig.). (gr. 8-12). 1980. pap. 7.50 (ISBN 0-89854-052-6). U of GA Inst Govt.
Jackson, Edwin L. Handbook for Georgia Legislators. 8th ed. 220p. 1980. pap. 10.00x (ISBN 0-89854-069-0). U of GA Inst Govt.
Sentell, Perry R. The Law of Municipal Tort Liability in Georgia. 3rd ed. LC 79-24276. 184p. 1980. pap. text ed. 15.00x (ISBN 0-89854-053-4). U of GA Inst Govt.

GEOSCIENCE
see Earth Sciences

GEOTECHNIQUE
see Rock Mechanics; Soil Mechanics

GEOTECTONICS
see Geology, Structural

GEOTHERMAL RESOURCES
Goldin, Augusta. Geothermal Energy: A Hot Prospect. LC 80-8800. (Illus.). (gr. 7 up). 1981. 10.95 (ISBN 0-15-230662-5, HJ). HarBraceJ.
Rinehart, J. S. Geysers & Geothermal Energy. (Illus.). 223p. 1980. 19.80 (ISBN 0-387-90489-1). Springer-Verlag.
Strub, A. S. & Ungemach, P., eds. Advances in European Geothermal Research. 1096p. 1980. lib. bdg. 63.00 (ISBN 90-277-1138-0, Pub. by D. Reidel). Kluwer Boston.

GERBILS
Paradise, Paul. Gerbils. (Illus.). 96p. 1980. 2.95 (ISBN 0-87666-757-4, KW-037). TFH Pubns.

GERIATRIC NURSING
Burnside, Irene M. Nursing & the Aged. 2nd ed. (Illus.). 736p. 1980. text ed. 17.95 (ISBN 0-07-009211-7, HP). McGraw.
Hogstel, Mildred O. Nursing Care of the Older Adult. 650p. 1981. 16.95 (ISBN 0-471-06022-4, Pub. by Wiley Med). Wiley.
Welter, Paul R. The Nursing Home: A Caring Community Staff Manuel. 96p. 1981. pap. 2.95 (ISBN 0-8170-0935-3). Judson.
--The Nursing Home: A Caring Community-Trainers' Manual. 176p. 1981. pap. 9.95 (ISBN 0-8170-0934-5). Judson.
Yurick, Ann G., et al. The Aged Person & the Nursing Process. 550p. 1980. text ed. 16.95 (ISBN 0-8385-0082-X). ACC.

GERIATRIC PSYCHIATRY
Horton, Arthur M., Jr., ed. Psychotherapeutic Treatment Approaches for the Aging. 320p. 1981. 24.95 (ISBN 0-89789-007-8). J F Bergin.

GERIATRICS
see also Aged–Care and Hygiene; Aged–Medical Care
Bressler, Rubin & Conrad, Kenneth. Drug Therapy for the Elderly. (Illus.). 300p. 1981. pap. text ed. 13.95 (ISBN 0-8016-0782-5). Mosby.
Caldwell, Esther & Hegner, Barbara. Geriatrics: A Study of Maturity. 3rd ed. LC 79-55313. (Practical Nursing Ser.). (Illus.). 288p. 1981. pap. text ed. 8.80 (ISBN 0-8273-1935-5); instr's. guide 1.50 (ISBN 0-8273-1934-7). Delmar.
Coakley, Davis. Acute Geriatric Medicine. 290p. 1981. pap. 27.50 (ISBN 0-88416-354-7). PSG Pub.
Coakley, Davis, ed. Acute Geriatric Medicine. 256p. 1980. 30.00 (Pub. by Croom Helm England). State Mutual Bk.
Elkowitz, Edward B. Geriatric Medicine for the Primary Care Practitioner. 1981. text ed. price not set (ISBN 0-8261-3230-8); pap. text ed. price not set (ISBN 0-8261-3231-6). Springer Pub.
Haug, Marie. Elderly Patients & Their Doctors. 1981. text ed. price not set (ISBN 0-8261-3570-6). Springer Pub.
Helfand, Arthur E. Clinical Podogeriatrics. (Illus.). 248p. 1981. write for info. (3951-2). Williams & Wilkins.
Jarvik, L. F., et al, eds. Clinical Pharmacology & the Aged Patient. (Aging Ser.: Vol. 16). 256p. 1981. text ed. 25.00 (ISBN 0-89004-340-X). Raven.
Kane, Robert L., et al. Geriatrics in the United States: Manpower Projections & Training Considerations. LC 80-8840. (Illus.). write for info. (ISBN 0-669-04386-9). Lexington Bks.
Levenson, Alvin J. & Tollett, Susan M., eds. Multidisciplinary Assessment of the Geriatric Patient. 1981. text ed. price not set (ISBN 0-89004-492-9). Raven.
Mummah, Hazel & Smith, Marsella. The Geriatric Assistant. (Illus.). 320p. 1980. pap. text ed. 11.95 (ISBN 0-07-044015-8, HP). McGraw.
O'Hara-Deveraux, Mary, et al, eds. Eldercare: A Practical Guide to Clinical Geriatrics. 1980. write for info. (ISBN 0-8089-1285-2). Grune.
Somers, Anne R. & Fabian, Dorothy R. The Geriatric Imperative: An Introduction to Gerontology & Clinical Geriatrics. 320p. 1981. pap. 14.95 (ISBN 0-686-69606-9). ACC.

GERM THEORY OF DISEASE
see also Bacteriology; Diseases–Causes and Theories of Causation
McLaren, Anne. Germ Cells & Soma: A New Look at Old Problem. LC 80-54221. (Silliman Lectures: No. 5). (Illus.). 128p. 1981. 15.00 (ISBN 0-300-02694-3). Yale U Pr.

GERMAN ART
see Art, German

GERMAN AUTHORS
see Authors, German

GERMAN DRAMA (COLLECTIONS)
Here are entered collections of dramas in German. For translations into English, see subdivision Translations into English.
Raabe, Paul. Era of German Expressionism. 1980. 25.00 (ISBN 0-7145-0698-2); pap. 8.95 (ISBN 0-7145-0699-0). Riverrun NY.

GERMAN LANGUAGE
Rudman, Jack. German. (Undergraduate Program Field Test Ser.: UPFT-12). (Cloth bdg. avail. on request). pap. 9.95 (ISBN 0-8373-6012-9). Natl Learning.
Stern, A. Z. & Reif, Joseph A., eds. Useful Expressions in German. (Useful Expressions Ser.). 64p. (Orig.). 1980. pap. 1.50 (ISBN 0-86628-007-3). Ridgefield Pub.

GERMAN LANGUAGE–CONVERSATION AND PHRASE BOOKS
Crean, John E., et al. Deutsche Sprach und Landeskunde. Incl. Ratyck, Joanna. wkbk. 6.95 (ISBN 0-394-32649-0); Crean, John E. lab manual 6.95 (ISBN 0-394-32650-4). 608p. 1981. text ed. 17.95 (ISBN 0-394-32648-2). Random.

GERMAN LANGUAGE–DICTIONARIES–ENGLISH
Pheby, John. The Oxford-Duden Pictorial German-English Dictionary. The Dudenredaktion & German Section of Oxford Pr Dictionary Department, eds. (Illus.). 776p. 1980. text ed. 24.95x (ISBN 0-19-864135-4). Oxford U Pr.
Traupman, John C., ed. The Bantam New College German & English Dictionary. 768p. (Orig.). (gr. 7-12). 1981. pap. 2.50 (ISBN 0-553-14155-4). Bantam.

GERMAN LITERATURE–BIBLIOGRAPHY
German Books in Print, Nineteen Eighty to Eighty-One: Authors-Titles-Keywords, 4 vols. 10th ed. Set. 250.00 (ISBN 3-7657-0862-3, Dist by Gale Research Co.). K G Saur.
German Books in Print, Nineteen Eighty to Eighty-One: ISBN Register. 637p. 1980. 95.00 (ISBN 3-7657-0986-7, Dist. by Gale Research Co.). K G Saur.
German Books in Print, Nineteen Eighty to Eighty-One: Subject Guide, 3 vols. 3rd ed. 1980. Set. 240.00 (Dist. by Gale Research Co.). K G Saur.
Heidtmann, Frank, et al, eds. German Photographic Literature, Eighteen Thirty-Nine to Nineteen Seventy-Eight: Theory, Technology, Visual. A Classified Bibliography of German-Language Photographic Publications. 690p. 1980. 85.00 (ISBN 3-598-10026-4, Dist. by Gale Research Co.). K G Saur.

GERMAN LITERATURE–HISTORY AND CRITICISM
Anderson, Walter E. The German Enigma: The Elitist Tradition in German Literature. LC 79-66491. 225p. 1981. 9.95 (ISBN 0-533-04398-0). Vantage.
Gross, David. The Writer & Society: Heinrich Mann & Literary Politics in Germany, 1890-1940. 316p. 1980. text ed. 15.00x (ISBN 0-391-00972-9). Humanities.
Jennings, Lee B. Justinus Kerners Weg Nach Weinsberg 1809-1819: Die Entpolitisierung eines Romantikers. LC 80-69125. (Studies in German Literature, Linusitics, & Culture: Vol. 3). (Illus.). 160p. 1981. text ed. 17.00x (ISBN 0-938100-00-9). Camden Hse.
Scherer, W., et al. A History of German Literature: From the Accession of Frederick the Great to the Death of Goethe. Muller, F. M., ed. Conybeare, Mrs. F. C., tr. 335p. 1980. Repr. of 1981 ed. lib. bdg. 45.00 (ISBN 0-8495-4898-5). Arden Lib.

GERMAN LITERATURE–HISTORY AND CRITICISM–19TH CENTURY
Stern, J. P. Re-Interpretations: Seven Studies in Nineteenth Century German Literature. 370p. Date not set. price not set (ISBN 0-521-23983-4); pap. price not set (ISBN 0-521-28366-3). Cambridge U Pr.

GERMAN LITERATURE–TRANSLATIONS INTO ENGLISH
Glaser, Hermann, ed. The German Mind of the Nineteenth Century: A Literary & Historical Anthology. 416p. 1981. 19.50 (ISBN 0-8264-0041-8); pap. 8.95 (ISBN 0-8264-0044-2). Continuum.
Willson, A. L., ed. Dimension: A Reader of German Literature Since Nineteen Sixty-Eight. 320p. 1981. 9.95 (ISBN 0-8264-0042-6). Continuum.

GERMAN MUSIC
see Music, German

GERMAN OCCUPATION OF DENMARK, 1940-1945
see Denmark–History

GERMAN PHILOSOPHY
see Philosophy, German

GERMAN POETRY–HISTORY AND CRITICISM
Baumann, Cecilia C. Wilhelm Muller: The Poet of the Schubert Song Cycles. LC 80-12806. (Studies in German Literature). (Illus.). 208p. 1981. 17.50x (ISBN 0-271-00266-2). Pa St U Pr.
Bernd, Clifford A. German Poetic Realism. (World Authors Ser.: No. 605). 1981. lib. bdg. 12.95 (ISBN 0-8057-6447-X). Twayne.

GERMAN PORCELAIN
see Porcelain

GERMANS
Evans, Richard & Lee, W. R., eds. The German Family. 224p. 1981. 27.50x (ISBN 0-389-20101-4). B&N.

GERMANY–ARMY
Bender, Roger J. & Odegard, Warren W. Uniforms, Organization & History of the Panzertruppe. (Illus.). 336p. 1980. 24.95 (ISBN 0-912138-18-1). Bender Pub CA.

GERMANY–CHURCH HISTORY
Matheson, Peter. The Third Reich & the Christian Churches. LC 80-26767. 112p. (Orig.). 1981. pap. 5.95 (ISBN 0-8028-1873-0). Eerdmans.

GERMANY–COMMERCE
Reihlen, H., intro. by. Export Directory of German Industries, 1980. 27th ed. LC 57-16210. 1332p. (Orig.). 1980. pap. 55.00x (ISBN 0-8002-2695-X). Intl Pubns Serv.

GERMANY–DESCRIPTION AND TRAVEL
Honnef, Klaus, et al. Eisenstaedt: Germany. (Illus.). 112p. (Orig.). 1981. pap. 12.50 (ISBN 0-87474-530-6). Smithsonian.
Lanier, Alison R. Update -- Germany. (Country Orientation Ser.). 1980. pap. text ed. 25.00 (ISBN 0-933662-40-8). Intercult Network.
Schuster, H. J. Analyse und Bewertung Von Pflanzengesell-Schaften Im Noerdliche Frankenjura - ein Beitrag Zum Problem der Quantifizierung Unter-Schiedlich Anthropogen Beeinflusster Oekosystems. (Dissertationes Botanicae: No. 53). (Illus.). 482p. (Ger.). 1981. pap. text ed. 40.00x (ISBN 3-7682-1264-5, Pub. by Cramer Germany). Lubrecht & Cramer.

GERMANY–DESCRIPTION AND TRAVEL–GUIDEBOOKS
Bristow, Philip. Through the German Waterways. 168p. 1980. 15.00x (ISBN 0-245-51000-1, Pub. by Nautical England). State Mutual Bk.

GERMANY–FOREIGN RELATIONS
Arnold, Hans. Foreign Cultural Policy: A Survey from a German Point of View. 1979. pap. 18.50 (ISBN 0-85496-210-7). Dufour.

GERMANY–FOREIGN RELATIONS–UNITED STATES
Trefousse, Hans L., ed. Germany & America: Essays on Problems of International Relations & Immigration. 270p. 1981. 23.00x (ISBN 0-930888-06-5). Brooklyn Coll Pr.

GERMANY–GEHEIME STAATSPOLIZEI
see Germany–Secret Police

GERMANY–HISTORICAL GEOGRAPHY
Mellor. Geography of Two Germanies. 1978. 20.40 (ISBN 0-06-318066-9, IntlDept). Har-Row.

GERMANY–HISTORY
Tellenbach, Gerd. Konigtum & Stamme in der Werdezeit Des Deutschen Reiches. LC 80-2002. 1981. Repr. of 1939 ed. 18.50 (ISBN 0-404-18600-9). AMS Pr.

GERMANY–HISTORY–1789-1900
Here are entered works in the period between 1789 and 1900 either as a whole or in part, except those subdivisions immediately below.
Sagarra, Eda. An introduction to Nineteenth Century Germany. (Illus.). 1981. text ed. 14.95x (ISBN 0-582-35138-3); pap. text ed. 6.95x (ISBN 0-582-35137-5). Longman.

GERMANY–HISTORY–1871-1918
Steenson, Gary P. Not One Man! Not One Penny! German Social Democracy, 1863-1914. LC 80-54058. (Illus.). 336p. 1981. 19.95 (ISBN 0-8229-3440-X); pap. 8.95 (ISBN 0-8229-5329-3). U of Pittsburgh Pr.

GERMANY–HISTORY–20TH CENTURY
Berghahn, Volker & Kitchen, Martin. Germany in the Age of Total War. 272p. 1981. 25.00x (ISBN 0-389-20186-3). B&N.
Chotjewitz, Peter O. The Thirty Years Peace. Kimber, Robert & Kimber, Rita, trs. from Ger. LC 80-24472. 256p. 1981. 11.95 (ISBN 0-394-50182-9). Knopf.
Hillgruber, Andreas. Germany & the Two World Wars. Kirby, William C., tr. LC 80-27036. 144p. 1981. text ed. 14.50 (ISBN 0-674-35321-8). Harvard U Pr.
Mosse, George L. The Crisis of German Ideology: Intellectual Origins of the Third Reich. LC 78-19126. vill, 373p. 1981. Repr. of 1964 ed. 27.50x (ISBN 0-86527-036-8). Fertig.
--The Crisis of Germany Ideology: Intellectual Origins of the Third Reich. 384p. 1981. Repr. of 1964 ed. pap. text ed. 7.95 (ISBN 0-8052-0669-8). Schocken.
Speier, Hans. From the Ashes of Disgrace: A Journal from Germany, 1945-1955. LC 80-21599. 336p. 1981. lib. bdg. 20.00x (ISBN 0-87023-135-9). U of Mass Pr.

GERMANY–HISTORY–1933-1945
Lang, Daniel. A Backward Look: Germans Remember. (Illus.). 144p. (Orig.). 1981. pap. 4.95 (ISBN 0-07-036241-6). McGraw.
Leuner, H. D. When Compassion Was a Crime: Germany's Silent Heroes, 1933-1945. 1978. pap. 12.95 (ISBN 0-85496-138-0). Dufour.
Speer, Albert. Infiltration: The SS & German Armament. Neugrosschel, Joachim, tr. 604p. 1981. 15.00 (ISBN 0-02-612800-4). Macmillan.
--Inside the Third Reich. (Illus.). 624p. 1981. 8.95 (ISBN 0-02-037500-X). Macmillan.
Zilbert, Edward R. Albert Speer & the Nazi Ministry of Arms: Economic Institutions & Industrial Production in the German War Economy. LC 76-17030. 304p. 1981. 19.50 (ISBN 0-686-69379-5). Fairleigh Dickinson.

GERMANY–HISTORY, MILITARY
Bender, Roger J. & Odegard, Warren W. Uniforms, Organization & History of the Panzertruppe. (Illus.). 336p. 1980. 24.95 (ISBN 0-912138-18-1). Bender Pub CA.

GERMANY–INTELLECTUAL LIFE
Mosse, George L. The Crisis of Germany Ideology: Intellectual Origins of the Third Reich. 384p. 1981. Repr. of 1964 ed. pap. text ed. 7.95 (ISBN 0-8052-0669-8). Schocken.

GERMANY–MILITARY POLICY
Feist, Uwe. Aero Armor Series, Vol. 13. 52p. 1981. pap. 3.95 (ISBN 0-8168-2046-5). Aero.

GERMANY–POLITICS AND GOVERNMENT
Bracher, Karl D. The German Dictatorship: The Origins, Structure, and Effects of National Socialism. Steinberg, Jean, tr. from German. LC 70-95662. Orig. Title: Die Deutsche Diktatur: Enstehung, Struktur, & Folgen Des Nationalsozialismus. 553p. 1972. pap. text ed. 8.95x. Praeger.
Jacobs, Dan N., et al. Comparative Politics: Introduction to the Politics of Britain, France, Germany, & the Soviet Union. pap. 9.95 (ISBN 0-934540-05-5). Chatham Hse Pubs.

GERMANY–POLITICS AND GOVERNMENT–1871-1918
Guttsman, W. L. The German Social Democratic Party 1875-1933. (Illus.). 1981. text ed. 40.00x (ISBN 0-04-943024-6, 2613). Allen Unwin.

GERMANY–POLITICS AND GOVERNMENT–20TH CENTURY
Broszat, Martin. The Hitler State: The Foundation & Development of the Internal Structure of the Third Reich. Hiden, John, tr. from Ger. (Illus.). 400p. 1981. text ed. 22.00x (ISBN 0-582-49200-9); pap. text ed. 12.95x (ISBN 0-582-48997-0). Longman.

GERMANY–POLITICS AND GOVERNMENT–1918-1933
Abraham, David. The Collapse of the Weimar Republic: Political Economy & Crisis. LC 80-8533. 550p. 1981. 30.00x (ISBN 0-691-05322-7); pap. 12.50x (ISBN 0-691-10118-3). Princeton U Pr.
Breitman, Richard. German Socialism & Weimar Democracy. LC 80-21412. 296p. 1981. 20.00x (ISBN 0-8078-1462-8). U of NC Pr.
Guttsman, W. L. The German Social Democratic Party 1875-1933. (Illus.). 1981. text ed. 40.00x (ISBN 0-04-943024-6, 2613). Allen Unwin.

GERMANY–POLITICS AND GOVERNMENT–1933-1945
Mosse, George L. The Crisis of German Ideology: Intellectual Origins of the Third Reich. LC 78-19126. vill, 373p. 1981. Repr. of 1964 ed. 27.50x (ISBN 0-86527-036-8). Fertig.
Prittie, Terence. The Velvet Chancellors: A History of Post-War Germany. (Illus.). 286p. 1981. text ed. 26.00x (ISBN 0-8419-6750-4). Holmes & Meier.
Shirer, William. The Rise & Fall of the Third Reich. 1981. price not set (ISBN 0-671-42813-6, Touchstone). S&S.
Wahle, Kent O. W. Don't Forget, Don't Forgive, Don't Hate. 1981. 6.95 (ISBN 0-533-04495-2). Vantage.

GERMANY–POLITICS AND GOVERNMENT–1945-
Erdstein, Erich & Bean, Barbara. Inside the Fourth Reich. pap. 1.95 (ISBN 0-515-04897-6). Jove Pubns.

GERMANY–SECRET POLICE
Cobler, Sebastian. A Policeman's Utopia: An Interview with the Director of the West German FBI, with an Essay by Hans Magnus Enzensberger. Taubes, Tonia & Wilkins, Sophie, trs. from Ger. (Orig.). 1981. pap. 4.95 (ISBN 0-89396-044-6). Urizen Bks.
Stieber, Wilhelm J. The Chancellor's Spy: The Revelations of the Chief of Bismarck's Secret Service. Van Heurck, Jan, tr. from German. LC 79-52090. Orig. Title: Spion Des Kanzlers. 272p. 1981. 12.50 (ISBN 0-394-50869-6). Grove.

GERMANY, DEMOCRATIC REPUBLIC OF
see Germany, East

GERMANY, EAST
Here are entered works on the present Democratic Republic, and works on the eastern part of the former jurisdiction, Germany.
Krisch, Henry. The German Democratic Republic: A Profile. (Nations of Contemporary Eastern Europe Ser.). 128p. 1981. lib. bdg. 16.50x (ISBN 0-89158-850-7). Westview.

GERMANY, EASTERN
see Germany, East

GERMANY, WEST–FOREIGN RELATIONS
Krippendorff, Ekkehart & Rittberger, Volker, eds. The Foreign Policy of West Germany: Formation & Contents. LC 80-40149. (German Political Studies: Vol. 4). (Illus.). 372p. 1980. 20.00 (ISBN 0-8039-9818-X); pap. 9.95 (ISBN 0-8039-9819-8). Sage.

GERMICIDES
see Fungicides

GERMS
see Bacteria; Bacteriology; Germ Theory of Disease; Micro-Organisms

GERONTOLOGY
see Aged; Geriatrics; Old Age

GESTALT THERAPY
Kogan, Jerry. Gestalt Therapy Resources. 3rd ed. 44p. 1980. pap. 5.00 (ISBN 0-930162-03-X). Transform Berkeley.

GESTAPO
see Germany–Secret Police

GESTATION
see Pregnancy

GESTURE LANGUAGE
see Deaf–Means of Communication

GHANA–ECONOMIC CONDITIONS
Atta, Jacob K. A Macroeconometric Model of a Developing Economy: Ghana (Simulations & Policy Analysis) LC 80-67178. 346p. (Orig.). 1981. pap. text ed. 12.50 (ISBN 0-8191-1504-5). U Pr of Amer.

GHANA–RELIGION
Appiah-Kubi, Kofi. Healing & Religion in Rural Ghana. (Orig.). 1981. pap. 10.95 (ISBN 0-377-00114-7). Friend Pr.
--Healing & Religion in Rural Ghana: A Sociological Study of Health Care Among the Akans. (Illus.). 224p. 1981. text ed. 25.00 (ISBN 0-86598-011-X). Allanheld.
Wyllie, Robert W. The Spirit Seekers: New Religious Movements in Southern Ghana. Cherry, Conrad, ed. LC 79-20486. (Studies in Religion: No. 21). 139p. 13.50 (ISBN 0-89130-355-3); pap. 9.00 (ISBN 0-89130-356-1). Scholars Pr CA.

GHANA–SOCIAL CONDITIONS
Appiah-Kubi, Kofi. Healing & Religion in Rural Ghana: A Sociological Study of Health Care Among the Akans. (Illus.). 224p. 1981. text ed. 25.00 (ISBN 0-86598-011-X). Allanheld.

GHANDI, MAHATMA
see Gandhi, Mohandas Karamchand, 1869-1948

GHOST TOWNS
see Cities and Towns, Ruined, Extinct, etc.

GHOSTS
see also Apparitions; Demonology; Psychical Research; Superstition
Cohen, Daniel. Real Ghosts. (Illus.). (gr. 4 up). 1979. pap. 1.50 (ISBN 0-671-29908-5). PB.
McBain, Ed. Ghosts. (Large Print Bks.). 1980. lib. bdg. 12.95 (ISBN 0-8161-3128-7). G K Hall.
Scott, Beth & Norman, Michael. Haunted Wisconsin. LC 80-22151. (Illus.). 256p. (Orig.). 1980. pap. 9.95 (ISBN 0-88361-082-5). Stanton & Lee.

GIANNUZZI'S SEMILUNAR BODIES
see Salivary Glands

GIANTS
Goldstein, Sam. Goliath to Gog: A Gallery of Giants from Fable, Fact, Fiction & Folklore. (Odd Books for Odd Moments Ser.). (Illus.). 72p. (Orig.). 1980. pap. 3.95 (ISBN 0-938338-00-5). Winds World Pr.
Hoke. Giants, Giants, Giants. (gr. 7 up). 1980. PLB 7.90 (ISBN 0-531-04172-7, E41). Watts.

GIBBON, EDWARD, 1737-1794
Gossman, Lionel. The Empire Unpossess'd: An Essay on Gibbon's "Decline & Fall of the Roman Empire". LC 80-24008. (Illus.). 176p. Date not set. price not set (ISBN 0-521-23453-0). Cambridge U Pr.
Mowat, R. B. Gibbon. 282p. 1980. Repr. of 1936 ed. lib. bdg. 30.00 (ISBN 0-8495-3827-0). Arden Lib.

GIBRALTAR–HISTORY
McGuffie, T. H. The Seige of Gibraltar, 1779-1783. (Illus.). 1965. 6.95 (ISBN 0-8023-1074-5). Dufour.

GIBRAN, KAHLIL, 1883-1931
Kahlil Gibran: Collection of His Famous Works. 19.00x. Intl Bk Ctr.

GIDE, ANDRE PAUL GUILLAUME, 1869-1951
Schlumberger, Jean. Madeleine & Andre Gide. Akeroyd, Richard H., tr. (Illus.). 1980. 12.00 (ISBN 0-916620-45-X). Portals Pr.

GIFT OF TONGUES
see Glossolalia

GIFT TAX
see Gifts–Taxation

GIFTED CHILDREN
see also Children as Artists
Sellin, Don & Birch, Jack. Nature & Needs of the Gifted Child. 350p. 1981. text ed. price not set (ISBN 0-89443-362-8). Aspen Systems.
The American Association for Gifted Children. The Gifted Child, the Family & the Community. LC 80-54030. 228p. 1981. 17.50 (ISBN 0-8027-0673-8). Walker & Co.
Willings, David. The Creatively Gifted: Recognising & Developing the Creative Personality. 184p. 30.00x (ISBN 0-85941-120-6, Pub. by Woodhead-Faulkner England). State Mutual Bk.

GIFTED CHILDREN–EDUCATION
Corrigan, Dean C. & Howey, Kenneth R., eds. Special Education in Transition: Concepts to Guide the Education of Experienced Teachers with Implications for PL 94-142. LC 80-68281. 208p. 1980. pap. 12.95 (ISBN 0-86586-109-9). Coun Exc Child.
Gallagher, James J. Study Guide for Educating Exceptional Children. 3rd ed. (Illus.). 208p. 1980. pap. text ed. write for info. (ISBN 0-395-28690-5). HM.
Hasazi, Susan E. Under One Cover: Implementing the Least Restrictive Environment Concept. LC 80-68096. 208p. 1980. pap. 11.25 (ISBN 0-86586-106-4). Coun Exc Child.
Jordan, June B. & Grossi, John A., eds. An Administrator's Handbook on Designing Programs for the Gifted & Talented. LC 80-68984. 144p. 1980. pap. 9.75 (ISBN 0-86586-112-9). Coun Exc Child.
Keyes, Fenton. Exploring Careers for the Gifted. (Careers in Depth Ser.). (Illus.). 160p. (gr. 7-12). 1981. lib. bdg. 5.97 (ISBN 0-8239-0533-0). Rosen Pr.
Lamkin, Jill S. Getting Started: Career Education Activities for Exceptional Students. 144p. 1980. pap. 5.50 (ISBN 0-86586-113-7). Coun Exc Child.
Maker, June. Curiculum Development for the Gifted. 375p. 1981. text ed. price not set (ISBN 0-89443-347-4). Aspen Systems.
Male, Robert A. & Perrone, Philip. The Development Education & Guidance of Talented Learners. 350p. 1981. text ed. price not set (ISBN 0-89443-359-8). Aspen Systems.
Renzulli, Joseph S. & Stoddard, Elizabeth P., eds. Under One Cover: Gifted & Talented Education in Perspective. LC 80-68284. 248p. 1980. pap. 11.25 (ISBN 0-86586-108-0). Coun Exc Child.

GIFTS–TAXATION
Federal Taxation of Estates, Gifts, & Trusts. 3rd ed. 645p. 1980. 55.00 (ISBN 0-686-28716-9, T118C). ALI-ABA.

GIFTS, SPIRITUAL
see also Glossolalia; Prophecy (Christianity)
Edvarsen, Aril, tr. Les Dons Spirituels. (French Bks.). (Fr.). 1979. 2.10 (ISBN 0-686-28819-X). Life Pubs Intl.
Horton, Harold, tr. Os Don. Do Espirito Santo. (Portuguese Bks.). 1979. 1.35 (ISBN 0-8297-0837-5). Life Pubs Intl.

GILL, ERIC, 1882-1940
Brady, Elizabeth. Eric Gill: Twentieth Century Book Designer. rev. ed. LC 73-18453. 150p. 1974. lib. bdg. 10.00 (ISBN 0-8108-0640-1). Scarecrow.

GIPSIES
Nickels, Steven. The Gypsy Season. Date not set. 10.95 (ISBN 0-87949-187-6). Ashley Bks.

GIRAFFES
Dagg, Anne I & Foster, J. Bristol. The Giraffe: Its Biology, Behavior, & Ecology. 210p. 1980. Repr. of 1976 ed. text ed. write for info. (ISBN 0-89874-275-7). Krieger.

GIRLS–EDUCATION
see Education of Women

GIRLS–EMPLOYMENT
see Children–Employment; Education of Women; Youth–Employment

GIRLS–RELIGIOUS LIFE
Kapp, Ardeth G. Miracles in Pinafores & Bluejeans. LC 77-4268. 81p. pap. 1.50 (ISBN 0-87747-741-8). Deseret Bk.

GIVE-AWAYS
see Free Material

GIVING, CHRISTIAN
see Stewardship, Christian

GLACIAL EPOCH
Denton, G. H. & Hughes, T. J. The Last Great Ice Sheets. LC 79-27808. 1980. write for info. (ISBN 0-471-06006-2, Pub. by Wiley-Interscience). Wiley.

GLACIERS
see also Erosion
Embleston, C. & King, C. A. Glacial & Periglacial Morphology, 2 vols. 2nd ed. Incl. Vol. 1. Glacial Geomorphology. LC 75-14188. pap. 19.95 (ISBN 0-470-23893-3); Vol. 2. Periglacial Geomorphology. LC 75-14187. pap. 13.95 (ISBN 0-470-23895-X). 1975. Halsted Pr.

GLACIOLOGY
see Glaciers

GLADNESS
see Happiness

GLADSTONE, WILLIAM EWART, 1809-1898
Stansky, Peter. Gladstone: A Progress in Politics. 224p. 1981. pap. 4.95 (ISBN 0-393-00037-0). Norton.

GLAND OF INTERNAL SECRETION
see Endocrine Glands

GLANDS
see also Endocrine Glands
also particular glands, e.g. Carotid Gland, Kidneys
Reiter, Russel J., ed. The Pineal Gland: Volume 1, Anatomy & Biochemistry. 288p. 1981. 72.95 (ISBN 0-8493-5714-4). CRC Pr.

GLANDS, DUCTLESS
see Endocrine Glands

GLANDS, LACRIMAL
see Lacrimal Organs

GLANDS, SALIVARY
see Salivary Glands

GLASS
Journal of Glass Studies: Nineteen Seventy-Two, Vol. 22. (Illus.). 165p. 1980. 15.00x (ISBN 0-87290-022-3). Corning.
New Glass Review 1. (Illus.). 16p. pap. 8.00 (ISBN 0-87290-074-6). Corning.
Zerwick, Chloe. A Short History of Glass. (Illus.). 95p. 1981. pap. price not set (ISBN 0-486-24158-0). Dover.

GLASS–JUVENILE LITERATURE
Nord, Barry & Nord, Elaine. The Child's Book of Glass. (Illus.). 64p. (Orig.). (gr. 7-9). Date not set. pap. price not set (101E). Chrome Yellow.

GLASS–RESEARCH
see Glass Research

GLASS, STAINED
see Glass Painting and Staining

GLASS BLOWING AND WORKING
see also Bottles
Littleton, Harvey. Glassblowing: A Search for Form. 136p. 1980. pap. 9.95 (ISBN 0-442-24341-3). Van Nos Reinhold.

GLASS MANUFACTURE
see also Glass Blowing and Working; Optical Instruments
Duffy, J. I., ed. Glass Technology: Developments Since 1978. LC 80-26045. (Chmical Tech. Rev. Ser.: 184). (Illus.). 323p. 1981. 48.00 (ISBN 0-8155-0838-7). Noyes.
Filigree Architecture: Metal & Glass Construction. (Illus.). 216p. (Eng. Fr. & Ger.). 1980. text ed. 19.00 (ISBN 0-89192-298-9). Interbk Inc.

GLASS PAINTING AND STAINING
Giorgi, Louis P. The Windows of Saint Justin Martyr. LC 80-67119. (Illus.). 128p. 1981. 25.00 (ISBN 0-87982-034-9). Art Alliance.
Nord, Barry & Nord, Elaine. Glass Etching-Pattern Book I: Fruit, Flowers, & Birds. (Illus.). 50p. (Orig.). 1980. pap. 3.95 (ISBN 0-935656-02-2, 101C). Chrome Yellow.
--Glass Etching-Pattern Book II: Wildlife, Alphabets, Geometrics. (Illus.). 50p. (Orig.). 1980. pap. 3.95 (ISBN 0-935656-03-0, 101D). Chrome Yellow.
Sibbett, Ed, Jr. Easy-to-Make Stained Glass Lightcatchers: Sixty-Seven Designs for Small Ornaments, with Full-Size Templates. (Illus., Orig.). 1981. pap. price not set (ISBN 0-486-24081-9). Dover.
Sowers, Robert. The Language of Stained Glass. (Illus.). 220p. 1981. 24.95 (ISBN 0-917304-61-6, Pub. by Timber Pr). Intl Schol Bk Serv.
Wallach, Joel L. Beginning Stained Glass Patterns, Bk. 1. (Illus.). 48p. (Orig.). 1980. pap. 4.95x (ISBN 0-934280-04-5). Glass Works.
--Beginning Stained Glass Patterns, Bk. 2. (Illus.). 48p. (Orig.). 1980. pap. 4.95x (ISBN 0-934280-05-3). Glass Works.

Winterbotham, Ann V. Treasury of Traditional Stained Glass Designs. (Illus.). 80p. (Orig.). 1981. pap. price not set (ISBN 0-486-24084-3). Dover.

Wood, Paul W. Working with Stained Glass. LC 80-54350. (Illus.). 104p. 1981. 9.95; lib. bdg. 9.29 (ISBN 0-8069-5441-8); pap. 5.95 (ISBN 0-8069-8966-1). Sterling.

GLASS RESEARCH

Duffy, J. I., ed. Glass Technology: Developments Since 1978. LC 80-26045. (Chmical Tech. Rev. Ser.: 184). (Illus.). 323p. 1981. 48.00 (ISBN 0-8155-0838-7). Noyes.

GLASSWARE–COLLECTORS AND COLLECTING

Corning Museum of Glass. New Glass: A Worldwide Survey. (Illus.). 286p. 1981. pap. price not set (ISBN 0-486-24156-4). Dover.

Edwards, Bill. Imperial Carnival Glass. (Illus.). 1980. pap. 9.95 (ISBN 0-89145-138-2). Collector Bks.

Hollingworth, June. Collecting Decanters. (The Christies International Collectors Ser.). (Illus.). 128p. 1980. 14.95 (ISBN 0-8317-2161-8). Mayflower Bks.

Iness, Lowell, intro. by. M'kee & Bros. Victorian Glass: Five Complete Glass Catalogues from 1859 - 60, 71. (Illus.). 160p. 1981. pap. price not set (ISBN 0-486-24121-1). Dover.

Lalique, Rene. Latique Glass: The Complete Illustrated Catalogue for 1932. (Illus.). 160p. 1981. pap. price not set (ISBN 0-486-24122-X). Dover.

Revi, Albert C. American Art Nouveau Glass. LC 68-18778. (Illus.). 476p. 1981. Repr. 40.00 (ISBN 0-916838-40-4). Schiffer.

Suomen Lasi-Finnish Glass. 68p. 1980. pap. 5.95x (ISBN 0-904461-56-4, Pub. by Ceolfrith Pr England). Intl Schol Bk Serv.

Weiss, Jeffrey. Cornerstone's Collector's Guide to Glass. 128p. 1981. 7.95 (ISBN 0-346-12534-0). Cornerstone.

GLAUCOMA

Josephson, Emanuel. Glaucoma & Its Medical Treatment with Cortin: Myopia Its Cause & Prevention. (Natural Health Ser.). 92p. (Orig.). 1937. pap. text ed. 6.95 (Pub. by Chedney). Alpine Ent.

New Orleans Academy of Ophthalmology. Symposium on Glaucoma. (Illus.). 536p. 1981. text ed. 57.95 (ISBN 0-8016-3667-1). Mosby.

GLEES, CATCHES, ROUNDS, ETC.

Taylor, Mary & Dyk, Carol. Book of Rounds. 1977. pap. 14.95 (ISBN 0-87690-182-8). Dutton.

GLIDERS (AERONAUTICS)

see also Gliding and Soaring

Morrow, Linda & Morrow, Ray. Go Fly a Sailplane. LC 80-65995. (Illus.). 192p. 1981. 10.95 (ISBN 0-689-11080-4). Atheneum.

Wills, Maralys. Manbirds: Hang Gliders & Hang Gliding. 320p. 1981. 17.95 (ISBN 0-13-551101-1). P-H.

GLIDING AND SOARING

see also Gliders (Aeronautics); Hang Gliding

Knauff, Thomas. Glider Basics from Frist Flight to Solo. Northcut, Allan & Northcut, Debbie, eds. LC 80-81375. (Illus.). 155p. 1980. text ed. 12.95. Knauff.

Piggott, Derek. Going Solo: A Simple Guide to Soaring. (Illus.). 112p. 1978. pap. 8.95x. B&N.

GLOBAL SATELLITE COMMUNICATIONS SYSTEMS

see Artificial Satellites in Telecommunication

GLOBULAR PROTEINS

see Proteins

GLOBULIN

Poulik, M. D., ed. Beta Two-Microglobulin: Its Significance in Clinical Medicine. (Journal: Vox Sanguinis: Vol. 38, No. 6). (Illus.). 1980. soft cover 19.75 (ISBN 3-8055-1560-X). S Karger.

GLOSSOLALIA

Bouterse, Wesley. Scriptural Light on Speaking in Tongues. 1980. pap. 0.85 (ISBN 0-86544-010-7). Salvation Army.

Welborn, Don. On the Subject of Tongues: From the New Testament. 56p. pap. 0.35 (ISBN 0-937396-48-6). Walterick Pubs.

GLOUCESTER, EARLS OF

Frankland, Noble. Prince Henry: Duke of Gloucester. (Illus.). 343p. 1980. 25.00x (ISBN 0-297-77705-X, Pub. by Weidenfeld & Nicolson England). Biblio Dist.

GLOUCESTER, ENGLAND

Herbert, N. M., ed. A History of the County of Gloucester, Vol 7. (Victoria History of the Counties of England Ser.). (Illus.). 250p. 1980. 149.00 (ISBN 0-19-722755-4). Oxford U Pr.

GLUCK, CHRISTOPH WILLIBALD, RITTER VON, 1714-1787

Howard, Patricia. C. W. von Gluck: Orfeo. (Cambridge Opera Handbooks Ser.). (Illus.). 200p. Date not set. price not set (ISBN 0-521-22827-1); pap. price not set (ISBN 0-521-29664-1). Cambridge U Pr.

GLUTAMIC ACID

Mora, Jaime & Palacios, Rafael, eds. Glutamine: Metabolism, Enzymology & Regulation. 1980. 28.00 (ISBN 0-12-506040-8). Acad Pr.

GLYNDEBOURNE FESTIVAL OPERA COMPANY

Hughes, Spike. Glyndebourne: A History of the Festival Opera. LC 80-70705. (Illus.). 400p. 1981. 27.50 (ISBN 0-7153-7891-0). David & Charles.

GNOMES

see Fairies

GNOMONICS

see Sun-Dials

GO-KART RACING

see Karting

GOATS

Goats, Rabbits, & Chickens. (Country Home Ser.). 96p. 2.95 (ISBN 0-88453-006-X). Berkshire Traveller.

Mackenzie, David. Goat Husbandry. 4th ed. Laing, Jean, ed. (Illus.). 375p. 1981. 23.00 (ISBN 0-571-18024-8, Pub. by Faber & Faber); pap. 9.95 (ISBN 0-571-11322-2). Merrimack Bk Serv.

Salmon, Jill. The Goatkeeper's Guide. LC 80-69354. (Illus.). 152p. 1981. 14.95 (ISBN 0-7153-8055-9). David & Charles.

GOBBLEDYGOOK

see Languages, Mixed

GOBLINS

see Fairies

GOD

see also Atheism; Causation; Christianity; Creation; Free Thought; Holy Spirit; Jesus Christ; Metaphysics; Myth; Mythology; Natural Theology; Providence and Government of God; Religion; Theism; Theology; Trinity

Adams, James E. Liberacion: El Evangelo de Dios. 1980. pap. 2.45. Banner of Truth.

Adams, Walter E. Who Is God??? God Is Love!!! 115p. (Orig.). 1981. pap. 2.95 (ISBN 0-937408-02-6). Gospel Pubns Fl.

Ammerman, Thomas J. God, If You Exist, Prove It to Me. 1981. 6.95 (ISBN 0-8062-1595-X). Carlton.

Angeles, Peter, ed. Critiques of God. pap. 7.00 (ISBN 0-87980-349-5). Wilshire.

Anselm Of Canterbury. Anselm of Canterbury: Why God Became Man. Hopkins, Jasper & Richardson, Herbert, eds. 105p. 1980. cover 4.950soft (ISBN 0-88946-009-4). E Mellen.

Belleggia, Sr. Concetta. God & the Problem of Evil. 1980. 3.75 (ISBN 0-8198-3007-0); pap. 2.50 (ISBN 0-8198-3008-9). Dghtrs St Paul.

Bernard De Clairvaux, Saint. On Loving God, & Selections from Sermons by St. Bernard of Clairvaux. Martin, Hugh, ed. LC 79-8706. (A Treasury of Christian Books). 125p. 1981. Repr. of 1959 ed. lib. bdg. 17.50x (ISBN 0-313-20787-9, BEOL). Greenwood.

Cheney, Lois A. God Is No Fool. (Orig.). pap. 1.50 (ISBN 0-89129-251-9). Jove Pubns.

Griffiths, Rees. God in Idea & Experience: The Apriori Elements of Religious Consciousness; an Epistemological Study. 316p. Repr. of 1931 ed. text ed. 4.95 (ISBN 0-567-02128-9). Attic Pr.

Guest, Dean. Discovering, the Word of God. 64p. (Orig.). 1980. Repr. pap. 1.95 (ISBN 0-89841-011-8). Zoe Pubns.

Haughton, Rosemary. The Passionate God. 308p. 1981. pap. 11.95 (ISBN 0-8091-2383-5). Paulist Pr.

Ilon. The Supremacy of God. LC 80-66408. 1980. pap. 3.00 (ISBN 0-9600958-6-1). Birth Day.

Kesler, Jay & Stafford, Tim. Breakthrough! Questions for Youth About God. (Campus Life Bk.). 176p. (Orig.). 1981. pap. 4.95 (ISBN 0-310-43371-1). Zondervan.

Kuhlman, Kathryn. Nothing Is Impossible with God. (Orig.). pap. 1.75 (ISBN 0-89129-084-2). Jove Pubns.

MacIntosh, H. R. The Highway of God. (Scholar As Preacher Ser.). 263p. Repr. of 1931 ed. text ed. 7.75 (ISBN 0-567-04424-6). Attic Pr.

Neill, Stephen. The Christians' God. 1980. 1.25 (ISBN 0-686-28774-6). Forward Movement.

Rice, Richard. Openness of God. (Horizon Ser.). 96p. 1981. pap. write for info. (ISBN 0-8127-0303-0). Southern Pub.

Rizzuto, Ana-Maria. The Birth of the Living God: A Psychoanalytic Study. LC 78-10475. x, 246p. 1981. pap. 6.50 (ISBN 0-226-72102-7). U of Chicago Pr.

Spicer, Jack. Fifteen False Propositions About God. 1974. pap. 2.50 (ISBN 0-686-28709-6). Man-Root.

Thompson, Bert. Theistic Evolution. pap. 5.50 (ISBN 0-89315-300-1). Lambert Bk.

Watson, David. Is Anyone There? Answers About God. 120p. 1981. pap. 3.50 (ISBN 0-87788-395-5). Shaw Pubs.

GOD–ATTRIBUTES

see also Providence and Government of God

Synan, J. A. The Trinity, or the Tri-Personal Being of God. pap. 2.95 (ISBN 0-911866-00-0). Advocate.

GOD–BIBLICAL TEACHING

Gray, John. The Biblical Doctrine of the Reign of God. 414p. Repr. of 1979 ed. text ed. 21.50x (ISBN 0-567-09300-X). Attic Pr.

GOD–IMMANENCE

see Immanence of God

GOD–JUVENILE LITERATURE

Hein, Lucille E. Thank You, God. (Illus.). 32p. 1981. pap. 3.50 (ISBN 0-8170-0912-4). Judson.

Hutson, Joan. I Think...I Know: A Poster Book About God. (Illus.). 32p. (Orig.). (gr. 2-4). 1979. pap. 1.95 (ISBN 0-87793-186-0). Ave Maria.

GOD–KNOWABLENESS

Synan, J. A. The Trinity, or the Tri-Personal Being of God. pap. 2.95 (ISBN 0-911866-00-0). Advocate.

GOD–LOVE

Here are entered works on God's love toward man. Works on the love and worship which man accords to God are entered under the heading God–Worship and Love.

Hagin, Kenneth E. El Shaddai. 1980. pap. 1.25 (ISBN 0-89276-401-5). Hagin Ministries.

Newlands, George. Theology of the Love of God. LC 80-22547. 224p. 1981. 12.50 (ISBN 0-8042-0726-7); pap. 6.95 (ISBN 0-8042-0727-5). John Knox.

GOD–OMNIPOTENCE

Wilkerson, Gwen, tr. Par Sa Force. (French Bks.). (Fr.). 1979. 1.85 (ISBN 0-8297-0927-4). Life Pubs Intl.

GOD–PROMISES

Deffner, Donald. You Promised Me God. LC 12-2792. (Illus.). 1981. pap. 4.95 (ISBN 0-570-03827-8). Concordia.

El Testimonio De Dios. 1980. pap. 1.35 (ISBN 0-686-69355-8). Vida Pubs.

GOD–PROOF

Philaretos, S. D. The Idea of Being. Orthodox Christian Educational Society, ed. Cummings, D., tr. from Hellenic. 287p. 1963. 3.00x (ISBN 0-938366-09-2). Orthodox Chr.

GOD–PROVIDENCE AND GOVERNMENT

see Providence and Government of God

GOD–WORSHIP AND LOVE

Coniaris, A. M. Making God Real in the Orthodox Christian Home. 1977. pap. 4.95 (ISBN 0-937032-07-7). Light & Life Pub Co MN.

GOD AND MAN, MYSTICAL UNION OF

see Mystical Union

Bernard de Clairvaux, St. On Loving God: Selections from Sermons by St. Bernard of Clairvaux. Martin, Hugh, ed. LC 79-8706. (A Treasury of Christian Books). 125p. 1981. Repr. of 1959 ed. lib. bdg. 17.50x (ISBN 0-313-20787-9, BEOL). Greenwood.

GOD TRANSCENDENCE

see Transcendence of God

GODS

see also Myth; Mythology; Religions

Heschel, Abraham J. Man's Quest for God: Studies in Prayer & Symbolism. LC 54-10371. (Hudson River Edition Ser.). 1981. 15.00x (ISBN 0-684-16829-4, ScribT). Scribner.

Hillman, et al. Facing the Gods. Hillman, James, ed. 171p. (Orig.). 1980. pap. text ed. 8.50 (ISBN 0-88214-312-3). Spring Pubns.

Love, Jeff. The Quantum Gods. 1979. pap. 7.95 (ISBN 0-87728-476-8). Weiser.

Monaghan, Patricia. The Book of Goddesses & Heroines. 1981. pap. 9.95 (ISBN 0-525-47664-4). Dutton.

GOETHE, JOHANN WOLFGANG VON, 1749-1832

Enright, Dennis J. Commentary on Goethe's Faust. 158p. 1980. Repr. of 1949 ed. lib. bdg. 20.00 (ISBN 0-8414-1916-7). Folcroft.

Gearey, John. Goethes's Faust: The Making of Part I. LC 80-5826. 256p. 1981. 19.00x (ISBN 0-300-02571-8). Yale U Pr.

Metchnikoff, Elias. Optimism & Pessimism in Goethe's Life. (Illus.). 113p. 1981. Repr. of 1908 ed. 41.85 (ISBN 0-89901-025-3). Found Class Reprints.

Moore, Charles L. Incense & Iconoclasm. 343p. 1980. Repr. of 1915 ed. lib. bdg. 30.00 (ISBN 0-89987-573-4). Century Bookbindery.

Robson-Scott, W. D. The Younger Goethe & the Visual Arts. (Angelica Germanica Ser.). 200p. 49.50 (ISBN 0-521-23321-6). Cambridge U Pr.

Steiner, Rudolf. The Theory of Knowledge Implicit in Goethe's World Conception. 2nd ed. Wannamaker, Olin D., tr. from Ger. LC 70-76994. Orig. Title: Grundlinien Einer Erkenntnistheorie der Goetheschen Weltanschauung. 133p. 1978. 6.95 (ISBN 0-910142-94-7); pap. 3.95 (ISBN 0-910142-85-8). Anthroposophic.

Sternfeld, Frederick. Goethe & Music. (Music Reprint Ser.). 176p. 1979. Repr. of 1954 ed. 19.50 (ISBN 0-306-79515-9). Da Capo.

Wahr, Frederick B. Emerson & Goethe. 197p. 1980. Repr. of 1915 ed. lib. bdg. 25.00 (ISBN 0-8492-2979-0). R West.

GOGH, VINCENT VAN

see Van Gogh, Vincent, 1853-1890

GOGOL, NIKOLAI VASILEVICH, 1809-1852

Gippius, V. V. Gogol. Maguire, R., tr. 1981. 17.50 (ISBN 0-88233-612-6). Ardis Pubs.

Trahan, Elizabeth, ed. Gogol's "Overcoat". An Anthology of Critical Essays. 1981. 15.00 (ISBN 0-88233-614-2). Ardis Pubs.

GOITER

Lewis, Alan E. Graves' Disease. LC 80-15624. (Discussions in Patient Management Ser.). 1980. pap. 12.00 (ISBN 0-87488-870-0). Med Exam.

GOITER, EXOPHTHALMIC

see Graves' Disease

GOLD

see also Alchemy; Coinage; Gold Mines and Mining; Jewelry; Money; Quantity Theory of Money; Silver Question

Branson, Oscar T. What You Need to Know About Your Gold & Silver. (Illus.). 56p. (Orig.). 1980. pap. 4.95 (ISBN 0-918080-44-4). Treasure Chest.

Gladson, Deek. The Midas Manual. 1981. pap. 4.00 (ISBN 0-89316-623-5); plastic bdg. 6.00 (ISBN 0-89316-624-3). Exanimo Pr.

GOLD CURE

see Alcoholism–Treatment

GOLD MINES AND MINING

see also California–Gold Discoveries; Hydraulic Mining

Gerrick, David J. Gold Prospecting in Ohio. 84p. 1980. pap. 5.95 (ISBN 0-686-68570-9). Dayton Labs.

Miller, Tron. Gold Rocker Handbook. 1980. pap. 4.00 (ISBN 0-89316-619-7); plastic bdg. 6.00. Exanimo Pr.

Neese, Harvey, ed. Gold Mining for Recreation. (Illus., Orig.). 1981. pap. 4.95 (ISBN 0-87701-182-6). Chronicle Bks.

Santschi, R. J. Treasure Trails. (Doodlebug Edition Ser.). 1974. plastic bag 6.00 (ISBN 0-89316-612-X); pap. 4.00 (ISBN 0-89316-601-4). Exanimo Pr.

Van Mueller, Karl. Gold Panner's Handbook. 1981. pap. 4.00 (ISBN 0-89316-621-9); plastic bdg 6.00 (ISBN 0-686-69464-3). Exanimo Pr.

Von Mueller, Karl. Gold Dredger's Handbook. 2nd ed. 1980. pap. 4.00 (ISBN 0-89316-609-X); plastic bdg. 6.00 (ISBN 0-89316-610-3). Exanimo Pr.

--Placer Miner's Manual, Vol. 1. 1980. pap. 5.00 (ISBN 0-89316-611-1); plastic bdg. 7.50 (ISBN 0-89316-612-X). Exanimo Pr.

--Placer Miner's Manual, Vol. 2. 1980. pap. 5.00 (ISBN 0-89316-613-8); plastic bdg 7.50 (ISBN 0-89316-614-6). Exanimo Pr.

--Placer Miner's Manual, Vol. 3. 1980. pap. 5.00 (ISBN 0-89316-615-4); plastic bdg. 7.50 (ISBN 0-89316-616-2). Exanimo Pr.

--Vibrating Gold Concentrators. 1980. pap. 4.00 (ISBN 0-89316-617-0); plastic bdg. 6.00 (ISBN 0-89316-618-9). Exanimo Pr.

GOLD MINES AND MINING–NEW GUINEA

O'Neill, Jack. Up from the South: A Prospector in New Guinea, Nineteen Thirty-One to Nineteen Thirty-Seven. Sinclair, James, ed. (Illus.). 224p. 1979. text ed. 23.50x (ISBN 0-19-550567-0). Oxford U Pr.

GOLDFISH

Coborn. Goldfish: Their Care & Breeding. (Illus.). 96p. 1981. 3.95 (ISBN 0-903264-24-2, 5215-5, Pub. by K & R Bks England). Arco.

Hervey, George F. & Hems, Jack. The Goldfish. rev. ed. (Illus.). 284p. 1981. pap. 9.50 (ISBN 0-571-11611-6, Pub. by Faber & Faber). Merrimack Bk Serv.

Wolburg, H. Axonal Transport, Degeneration, & Regeneration in the Visual System of the Goldfish. (Advances in Anatomy, Embryology & Cell Biology Ser.: Vol. 67). (Illus.). 100p. 1981. pap. 28.50 (ISBN 0-387-10336-8). Springer-Verlag.

GOLF

see also Putting (Golf); Swing (Golf)

De Monte, John R. The King James' Versions of the Games of Golfe. (Illus.). 82p. (Orig.). 1980. pap. 3.50 (ISBN 0-9605176-0-X). Raycol Prods.

Geiberger, Al & Dennis, Larry. Tempo (Golf's Master Key: How to Find It, How to Keep It) LC 79-52550. (Illus.). 160p. 1980. 9.95 (ISBN 0-914178-34-2). Golf Digest Bks.

McCormack, Mark H. Dunhill Golf Yearbook 1980. 448p. 1980. 18.95 (ISBN 0-385-14942-5); pap. 10.95 (ISBN 0-385-14943-3). Doubleday.

Metz, Richard. The Graduated Swing Method. (Illus.). 128p. 1981. 12.95 (ISBN 0-684-16868-5, ScribT). Scribner.

Mulvoy, Mark. Sports Illustrated Golf. LC 80-8692. (Illus.). 192p. 1981. 8.95 (ISBN 0-06-014871-3, HarpT); pap. 5.95 (ISBN 0-06-090868-8, CN868). Har-Row.

Nicklaus, Jack. Play Better Golf. (Orig.). 1981. pap. price not set (ISBN 0-671-83624-2). PB.

Nicklaus, Jack & Bowden, Ken. Jack Nicklaus' Lesson Tee. LC 76-46733. (Illus.). 160p. 1977. 10.95 (ISBN 0-914178-11-3). Golf Digest Bks.

--Jack Nicklaus' Playing Lessons. (Illus.). 144p. 1981. 12.95 (ISBN 0-914178-42-3, 42901-9). Golf Digest Bks.

PGA Tour. Official PGA Tour Media Guide Nineteen Eighty-One. 240p. 1981. pap. 5.95 (ISBN 0-89480-142-2). Workman Pub.

Player, Gary. Gary Player's Golf Clinic. LC 81-65104. (Illus.). 160p. 1981. pap. 6.95 (ISBN 0-910676-23-2, 6036). DBI.

Seitz, Nick. Improve Your Game (and Learn About) the Superstars of Golf. 192p. 1981. pap. 4.95 (ISBN 0-346-12477-8). Cornerstone.

--Quick Tips from the Golf Spot. (Illus.). 208p. 1981. pap. 6.95 (ISBN 0-914178-43-1, 42903-5). Golf Digest Bks.

Simek, Thomas C. & O'Brien, Richard M. Total Golf: A Behavioral Approach to Lowering Your Score & Getting More Out of Your Game. LC 79-6086. (Illus.). 192p. 1981. 14.95 (ISBN 0-385-15404-6). Doubleday.

Stanley, Louis. Pelham Golf Year. 448p. 1981. 19.95 (ISBN 0-7207-1290-4). Merrimack Bk Serv.

Wagenvoord, James. Golf Diary. (Illus.). 160p. 1981. 6.95 (ISBN 0-312-33806-6). St Martin.

GOLF–PSYCHOLOGICAL ASPECTS

Wiren, Gary, et al. The New Golf Mind. 164p. 1981. pap. 4.95 (ISBN 0-346-12478-6). Cornerstone.

GONGORA Y ARGOTE, LUIS DE, 1561-1627

Beverley, John. Aspects of Gongora's Soledades. (Purdue University Monograhs in Romance Languages: No. 1). 1981. text ed. 23.00x (ISBN 90-272-1711-4). Humanities.

GOOD AND EVIL

see also Providence and Government of God

Conn, Charles W. The Anatomy of Evil. 1981. 7.95 (ISBN 0-8007-1177-7). Revell.
Davis, Stephen T., ed. Encountering Evil: Live Options in Theodicy. LC 80-84647. 1981. pap. 7.95 (ISBN 0-686-69554-2). John Knox.
Sanford, John A. Evil: The Shadow Side of Reality. 176p. 1981. 10.95 (ISBN 0-8245-0037-7). Crossroad NY.
Zappulli, Cesare. The Power of Goodness. 1980. 3.00 (ISBN 0-8198-5800-5); pap. 2.00 (ISBN 0-8198-5801-3). Dghtrs St Paul.

GOOD SAMARITAN (PARABLE)
see Jesus Christ–Parables

GOOD WORKS (THEOLOGY)
Rogers, Dale E. Angel Unaware. (Orig.). pap. 1.50 (ISBN 0-515-05325-2). Jove Pubns.

GOOSE
see Geese

GOREY, EDWARD, 1925-
Gorey, Edward. Gorey Posters. 1979. pap. 8.95 (ISBN 0-8109-2179-0). Abrams.

GORKHALI LANGUAGE
see Nepali Language

GORKI, MAXIM, 1868-1936
Gorki, Maxim. Reminiscences of My Youth. 334p. 1980. Repr. of 1924 ed. lib. bdg. 25.00 (ISBN 0-8492-4961-9). R West.

GORKY, ARSHILE, 1904-1948
Rand, Harry. Arshile Gorky: The Implication of Symbols. LC 77-25046. (Illus.). 256p. 1981. text ed. 40.00 (ISBN 0-8390-0209-2). Allanheld & Schram.

GOTHIC ARCHITECTURE
see Architecture, Gothic

GOTHIC LITERATURE
Brauchli, Jakob. Der Englische Schauerroman um 1880 unter Berucksichtigung der unbekannten Bucher. Bleiler, E. F., ed. LC 78-60913. (The Fiction of Popular Culture Ser.: Vol. 2). 260p. 1979. lib. bdg. 26.00 (ISBN 0-8240-9666-5). Garland Pub.
Radcliffe, Elsa J. Gothic Novels of the Twentieth Century: An Annotated Bibliography. LC 78-24357. 291p. 1979. lib. bdg. 13.00 (ISBN 0-8108-1190-1). Scarecrow.
Skarda, Patricia L. & Jaffe, Nora C. The Evil Image: Two Centuries of Gothic Short Fiction & Poetry. (Illus.). 1981. pap. 7.95 (ISBN 0-452-00549-3, F549, Meridan Bks). NAL.
Tarr, Sr. Mary. Catholicism in Gothic Fiction. Bleiler, E. F., ed. LC 78-60815. (The Fiction of Popular Culture Ser.: Vol. 16). 148p. 1979. lib. bdg. 15.00 (ISBN 0-8240-9652-5). Garland Pub.

GOURMONT, REMY DE, 1858-1915
Jacob, Paul E. Remy de Gourmont. 176p. 1980. Repr. of 1931 ed. lib. bdg. 25.00 (ISBN 0-89984-260-7). Century Bookbindery.

GOVERNMENT
see Civics; Political Science;
also subdivision Politics and Government under names of countries, states, etc., e.g. United States–Politics and government; New York (state) State Politics and Government

GOVERNMENT, COMPARATIVE
see Comparative Government

GOVERNMENT, RESISTANCE TO
see also Civil War; Coups D'Etat; Revolutions
Kaiser, Leo, ed. The Seven Against Thebes. Thoreau, Henry D. LC 80-2522. (Emerson Society Quarterly No. Seventeen Nineteen Fifty Nine,1-30). 1981. Repr. of 1959 ed. 14.00 (ISBN 0-404-19070-7). AMS Pr.
Lakey, George. Manifesto for a Nonviolent Revolution. 1980. staple back bdg. 1.75 (ISBN 0-86571-004-X). Movement New Soc.
Madden, Edward H. Civil Disobedience & Moral Law in Nineteenth-Century American Philosophy. LC 68-11043. 222p. 1970. pap. 2.95 (ISBN 0-295-95070-6). U of Wash Pr.

GOVERNMENT AGENCIES
see Administrative Agencies

GOVERNMENT AND BUSINESS
see Industry and State

GOVERNMENT BUSINESS ENTERPRISES
see also Government Ownership
Hamilton, Neil W. & Hamilton, Peter R. Governance of Public Enterprise: A Case Study of Urban Mass Transit. LC 80-5349. 1981. 18.95. Lexington Bks.
Horn, Richard J., ed. Studies in the Management of Government Enterprise. (Social Dimensions of Economics Ser.: Vol. 1). 1981. lib. bdg. price not set (ISBN 0-89838-052-9, Pub. by Martinus Nijhoff). Kluwer Boston.

GOVERNMENT COMPETITION
see also Government Business Enterprises
Winter, Ralph K. Government & the Corporation. 1978. pap. 4.25 (ISBN 0-8447-3313-X). Am Enterprise.

GOVERNMENT DOCUMENTS
see Government Publications

GOVERNMENT EMPLOYEE STRIKES
see Strikes and Lockouts–Civil Service

GOVERNMENT EMPLOYEES
see Civil Service

GOVERNMENT EXECUTIVES
Silvan, Matthew. Lazarus, Come Out! The Story of My Life. Moran, Hugh, ed. Giannini, Vera, tr. from It. LC 80-82599. Orig. Title: Quella Violenza Di Dio. 224p. (Orig.). 1981. pap. 5.95 (ISBN 0-911782-36-2). New City.

GOVERNMENT EXPENDITURES
see Expenditures, Public

GOVERNMENT HOUSING
see Public Housing

GOVERNMENT IMMUNITY
see Government Liability

GOVERNMENT INFORMATION
Hiebert, Ray, et al. Informing the People: A Public Information Handbook. (Longman Public Communication Ser.). (Illus.). 512p. 1981. 24.95 (ISBN 0-582-28200-4). Longman.
The Market for Government Data Bases Sold Through Commercial Firms. 1980. 950.00 (ISBN 0-686-28893-9, A829). Frost & Sullivan.

GOVERNMENT INFORMATION SERVICES
see Government Publicity

GOVERNMENT INVESTIGATIONS
see Governmental Investigations

GOVERNMENT JOBS
see Civil Service Positions

GOVERNMENT LIABILITY
Perez, Ramon A. Liability Risk Management for Local Governments. 1981. spiral bdg. 25.00 (ISBN 0-88406-148-5). GA St U Busn Pub.

GOVERNMENT OWNERSHIP
see also Government Competition
Winter, Ralph K. Government & the Corporation. 1978. pap. 4.25 (ISBN 0-8447-3313-X). Am Enterprise.

GOVERNMENT POSITIONS
see Civil Service Positions

GOVERNMENT PUBLICATIONS
see also Government Publicity
also subdivision Government Publications under names of countries, states, counties, cities, etc., e.g. United States–Government Publications
Research Libraries of the New York Public Library & the Library of Congress. Bibliographic Guide to Government Publications - Foreign: 1980. (Library Catalogs-Bib. Guides Ser.). 1981. lib. bdg. 195.00 (ISBN 0-8161-6886-5). G K Hall.

GOVERNMENT PUBLICITY
see also Government Publications; Radio Broadcasting
Hiebert, Ray, et al. Informing the People: A Public Information Handbook. (Longman Public Communication Ser.). (Illus.). 512p. 1981. 24.95 (ISBN 0-582-28200-4). Longman.

GOVERNMENT REGULATION OF COMMERCE
see Commercial Policy; Industrial Laws and Legislation; Industry and State; Interstate Commerce; Trade Regulation

GOVERNMENT REGULATION OF RAILROADS
see Interstate Commerce

GOVERNMENT RESPONSIBILITY
see Government Liability

GOVERNMENT SECRECY
see Government Information

GOVERNMENT SPENDING POLICY
see also Expenditures, Public; Public Works;
also subdivision Appropriations and Expenditures under names of countries (for descriptive and statistical works on government spending)
Anton, Thomas J., et al. Moving Money: An Empirical Analysis of Federal Expenditure Patterns. LC 80-21700. 272p. 1980. text ed. 20.00 (ISBN 0-89946-066-6). Oelgeschlager.
Gramlich, Edward M. Benefit-Cost Analysis of Government Programs. (Illus.). 304p. 1981. text ed. 15.95 (ISBN 0-13-074757-2). P-H.
Mieszlowski, Peter & Oakland, William, eds. Fiscal Federalism & Grants-in-Aid. (Papers on Public Economics Ser.: Vol.1). 166p. (Orig.). 1979. pap. text ed. 5.50 (26300). Urban Inst.
Schick, Allen. Congress & Money: Budgeting, Spending & Taxing. LC 80-53322. 600p. 1980. 27.50 (ISBN 0-87766-278-9). Urban Inst.
Wildavsky, Aaron. How to Limit Government Spending. 197p. 1980. 8.95 (ISBN 0-686-69040-0). U of Cal Pr.

GOVERNMENT SURVEYS
see Surveys

GOVERNMENTAL INVESTIGATIONS
see also Criminal Investigation; Police
Greene, Robert W. The Sting Man. (Illus.). 256p. 1981. 12.95 (ISBN 0-525-20985-9). Dutton.

GOVERNORS–UNITED STATES
Pierce, Walter M. Oregon Cattleman, Governor, Congressman: Memoirs & Times of Walter M. Pierce. Bone, Arthur H., ed. LC 80-81718. (Illus.). 528p. 1981. pap. 14.95 (ISBN 0-87595-071-X). Oreg Hist Soc.
Smith, Marion J. General William King. LC 79-67417. (Illus.). 182p. 1980. 11.95 (ISBN 0-89272-072-7). Down East.

GPS (COMPUTER PROGRAM LANGUAGE)
Schmidt, B. GPSS Fortran. (Computing Ser.). 544p. 1981. write for info. (ISBN 0-471-27881-5, Pub. by Wiley-Interscience). Wiley.

GRACE (THEOLOGY)
see also Covenants (Theology)
Jones, Michael, ed. Prayers & Graces. 1980. 5.50 (ISBN 0-903540-33-9, Pub. by Flores Books). St George Bk Serv.
Riggle, H. M. The Two Works of Grace. 56p. pap. 0.40; pap. 1.00 3 copies. Faith Pub Hse.
Teasley, D. O. The Double Cure, or Redemption Twofold. 160p. pap. 1.50 large print. Faith Pub Hse.
Vogel, Arthur A. The Gift of Grace. 1980. 1.50 (ISBN 0-686-28778-9). Forward Movement.

GRACE, GIFTS OF
see Gifts, Spiritual

GRACE AT MEALS
Simons, Thomas G. Blessings: A Reappraisal of Their Nature, Purpose, & Celebration. 1981. pap. 12.95 (ISBN 0-686-69223-3). Resource Pubns.

GRACKLES
see Blackbirds

GRADE LABELING
see Labels

GRADED SCHOOLS
see Grading and Marking (Students)

GRADING AND MARKING (STUDENTS)
Colligan. The A Plus Guide to Good Grades. (gr. 7-12). 1980. pap. 1.50 (ISBN 0-590-30001-6, Schol Pap). Schol Bk Serv.
Rowntree, Derek. Assessing Students. 1980. pap. text ed. 11.50 (ISBN 0-06-318145-2, IntlDept). Har-Row.

GRADUATE WORK
see Universities and Colleges–Graduate Work

GRAFFITI
Haan, Marina N. & Hammerstrom, Richard B. Graffiti in the Big Ten. 164p. (Orig.). 1980. pap. 3.95 (ISBN 0-9604534-0-7). Brown Hse Gall.

GRAFT (IN POLITICS)
see Corruption (In Politics)

GRAFTING OF SKIN
see Skin-Grafting

GRAIN
IMCO Grain Rules. 35p. 1977. 7.00 (IMCO). Unipub.
Post-Harvest Prevention of Waste & Loss of Food Grains. 358p. 1974. 11.75 (APO54, APO). Unipub.
Report of the Twentieth Session of the Intergovernmental Group on Grains to the Committee on Commodity Problems. 30p. 1980. pap. 6.00 (ISBN 92-5-100919-8, F1953, FAO). Unipub.

GRAIN–DISEASES AND PESTS
Jenkyn, J. F. & Plumb, R. T. Strategies for the Control of Cereal Disease: Organized by the British Plant Pathologist, Vol. 2. 250p. 1981. 47.50 (ISBN 0-470-27049-7). Halsted Pr.
Shurtleff, M. C. Compendium of Corn Diseases. 2nd ed. (Compendium Ser.: No. 1). (Illus.). 124p. 1980. 11.00 (ISBN 0-89054-029-2). Am Phytopathol Soc.

GRAIN–STORAGE
Midwest Plan Service Engineers. Structures & Environment Handbook. 10th, rev. ed. Midwest Plan Service Staff, ed. LC 76-27983. (Illus.). 490p. 1980. pap. 10.00 (ISBN 0-686-68276-9, MWPS-1). Midwest Plan Serv.
Post-Harvest Prevention of Waste & Loss of Food Grains. 358p. 1974. 11.75 (APO54, APO). Unipub.

GRAIN PESTS
see Grain–Diseases and Pests

GRAIN SORGHUM
see Sorghum

GRAIN TRADE
Ainsworth, Ralph M. Profitable Grain Trading. LC 80-53316. 256p. 1980. Repr. of 1933 ed. text ed. 25.00 (ISBN 0-934380-04-X). Traders Pr.

GRAMMAR
see Grammar, Comparative and General;
also subdivision Grammar under names of languages, e.g. English Language–Grammar

GRAMMAR, COMPARATIVE AND GENERAL
see also Language and Languages
Bowers, John S. The Theory of Grammatical Relations. LC 80-21018. 304p. 1981. 24.50x (ISBN 0-8014-1079-7). Cornell U Pr.
Bresnan, Joan, ed. The Mental Representation of Grammatical Relations. (Cognitive Theory & Mental Representation Ser.: Vol. 1). 700p. 1981. text ed. 35.00x (ISBN 0-262-02158-7). MIT Pr.

GRAMMAR, COMPARATIVE AND GENERAL–SYNTAX
Brown, E. K. & Miller, J. E. Syntax: A Linguistic Introduction to Sentence Structure. 394p. 1981. text ed. 33.75x (ISBN 0-686-69131-8, Hutchinson U Lib); pap. text ed. 15.50x (ISBN 0-686-69132-6). Humanities.
Kimball, John P. & Tedesch, Philip, eds. Syntax & Semantics, Vol. 14: Tense & Aspect. 1981. price not set (ISBN 0-12-613514-2). Acad Pr.
Kimball, John P., et al. Syntax & Semantics, 13 vols. Incl. Vol. 1. Studies in Language. 260p. 1973. 30.50 (ISBN 0-12-785421-5); Vol. 2. 1973. 30.50 (ISBN 0-12-785422-3); Vol. 3. 1975. 31.00 (ISBN 0-12-785423-1); Vol. 4. 1975. 35.00 (ISBN 0-12-785424-X); Vol. 5. Japanese Generative Grammar. 1975. 45.50 (ISBN 0-12-785425-8); Vol. 6. 1976. 42.50 (ISBN 0-12-785426-6); Vol. 7. 1976. 30.00 (ISBN 0-12-613507-X); Vol. 8. 1976. 30.00 (ISBN 0-12-613508-8); Vol. 9. Pragmatics. 1978. 27.00 (ISBN 0-12-613509-6); Vol. 10. 1979. 38.00 (ISBN 0-12-613510-X); Vol. 11. Presupposition. 1979. 35.00 (ISBN 0-12-613511-8); Vol. 12. Discourse & Syntax. 1979. 43.00 (ISBN 0-12-613512-6); Vol. 13. Current Approaches to Syntax. 1980. write for info. (ISBN 0-12-613513-4). Acad Pr.

GRAMMAR SCHOOLS
see Public Schools

GRAMOPHONE
see Phonograph

GRAND CANYON
Babbitt, Bruce. Grand Canyon: An Anthology. LC 78-58470. (Illus.). 276p. 1980. pap. 8.95 (ISBN 0-87358-275-6). Northland.
Berkowitz, Alan. A Guide to the Bright Angel Trail. 1979. pap. 1.00 (ISBN 0-938216-09-0). GCNHA.
--A Guide to the North Kaibab Trail. 1980. pap. 1.00 (ISBN 0-938216-10-4). GCNHA.
Hughes, Donald. In the House of Stone & Light. LC 77-93502. 137p. 1978. pap. 7.50 (ISBN 0-938216-00-7). GCNHA.
McAdams, Cliff. The Grand Canyon: Guide & Reference Book. (Illus.). 100p. (Orig.). 1981. pap. 5.95 (ISBN 0-87108-577-1). Pruett.
Morris, Larry A. Hiking the Grand Canyon & Havasupai. (Illus.). 96p. 1981. pap. 4.95 (ISBN 0-89404-053-7). Aztex.
Thybony, Scott. Guide to Inner Canyon Hiking: Grand Canyon National Park. rev. ed. (Illus.). pap. 1.75 (ISBN 0-938216-12-0). Grand Canyon.

GRANDPARENTS
Amstutz, Beverly. I Love My Foster Grandparents. (Illus.). 204p. (gr. k-7). 1981. pap. 2.50 (ISBN 0-937836-06-0). Precious Res.
Dodson. How to Grandparent. 1981. 8.95 (ISBN 0-686-69161-X). Lippincott & Crowell.
Dodson, Fitzhugh & Ruben, Paula. How to Grandparent. LC 80-7849. 304p. 1981. 12.95 (ISBN 0-690-01874-6, HarpT). Har-Row.
Kornhaber, Arthur & Woodward, Kenneth L. Grandparents - Grandchildren: The Vital Connection. LC 79-6083. (Illus.). 312p. 1981. 11.95 (ISBN 0-385-15577-8, Anchor Pr). Doubleday.

GRANT, ULYSSES SIMPSON, PRES. U. S., 1822-1885
Cadawallader, Sylvanus. Three Years with Grant: As Recalled by War Correspondent Sylvanus Cadwallader. Thomas, Benjamin P., ed. LC 80-21191. (Illus.). xiv, 361p. 1980. Repr. of 1955 ed. lib. bdg. 28.75x (ISBN 0-313-22576-1, CATY). Greenwood.

GRANTS
see Subsidies

GRANTS-IN-AID
Darnbrough, Ann & Kinrade, Derek. Fund-Raising & Grant-Aid: A Practical & Legal Guide for Charities & Voluntary Organisations. 160p. 1980. 24.00x (ISBN 0-85941-075-7, Pub. by Woodhead-Faulkner England). State Mutual Bk.
Foundation Center. COMSEARCH: Geographic. (COMSEARCH Printouts). (Orig.). 1980. write for info. (ISBN 0-87954-030-3); pap. write for info. (ISBN 0-87954-033-8). Foundation Ctr.
--COMSEARCH: Special Topics. (COMSEARCH Printouts). (Orig.). 1980. pap. 12.00 (ISBN 0-87954-031-1); microfiche 4.00 (ISBN 0-87954-034-6). Foundation Ctr.
--Comsearch: Subjects. (COMSEARCH Printouts). (Orig.). 1980. pap. 12.00 (ISBN 0-87954-029-X); microfiche 4.00 (ISBN 0-87954-032-X). Foundation Ctr.
--The Foundation Center National Data Book, 2 vols. 840p. (Orig.). 1981. pap. 45.00 (ISBN 0-87954-039-7). Foundation Ctr.
--The Foundation Grants Index Nineteen Eighty. LC 72-76018. 540p. (Orig.). 1981. pap. 30.00 (ISBN 0-87954-040-0). Foundation Ctr.
Lee, Lawrence. The Grants Game: How to Win the First Time You Play. 224p. (Orig.). 1981. 11.95 (ISBN 0-936602-18-X); pap. 7.95 (ISBN 0-686-69117-2). Harbor Pub CA.
--The Grants Game: How to Win the First Time You Play. 224p. 1981. 11.95 (ISBN 0-936602-18-X); pap. 7.95 (ISBN 0-936602-03-1). Harbor Pub CA.
Mieszlowski, Peter & Oakland, William, eds. Fiscal Federalism & Grants-in-Aid. (Papers on Public Economics Ser.: Vol.1). 166p. (Orig.). 1979. pap. text ed. 5.50 (26300). Urban Inst.
Reagan, Michael D. & Sanzone, John G. The New Federalism. 2nd ed. 208p. 1981. pap. text ed. 3.95x (ISBN 0-19-502772-8). Oxford U Pr.
Sith, Craig & Skjei, Eric. Getting Grants: A Creative Guide to the Grants System: How to Find Funders, Write Convincing Proposals, & Make Your Grants Work. LC 78-20187. 288p. pap. 4.95 (ISBN 0-06-090834-3, CN 834, CN). Har-Row.
Sulz, Harry. Grantwriting for Health Professionals. 1981. pap. price not set (ISBN 0-316-82196-9). Little.
Van Spiva, Ulysses. How to Get a Grant for Your Own Special Project. 1980. 7.75. TIS Inc.
Wilson, William K. & Wilson, Betty L., eds. Directory of Research Grants, 1981. 360p. 1981. pap. 37.50 (ISBN 0-912700-92-0). Oryx Pr.

GRAPES
Major Wine Grape Varieties of Australia. 61p. 1979. pap. 6.50 (ISBN 0-643-02517-0, CO12, CSIRO). Unipub.
Nuts, Berries & Grapes. (Country Home Ser.). 96p. 2.95 (ISBN 0-88453-009-4). Berkshire Traveller.
Some Wine Grape Varieties for Australia. 50p. 1976. pap. 5.00 (ISBN 0-643-00180-8, CO09, CSIRO). Unipub.

GRAPH THEORY
see also Network Analysis (Planning)
Brown, William G., ed. Reviews in Graph Theory, 4 vols. 1980. Set. 200.00 (ISBN 0-8218-0214-3); Vol. 1. 68.00 (ISBN 0-8218-0210-0); Vol. 2. 68.00 (ISBN 0-8218-0211-9); Vol. 3. 68.00 (ISBN 0-8218-0212-7); Vol. 4. 40.00 (ISBN 0-8218-0213-5). Am Math.

GRAPHIC ARTS
see also Bookbinding; Commercial Art; Drawing; Engraving; Painting; Printing; Prints
Atterbury, Paul. Berthold Wolpe. (Illus.). 96p. 1981. 22.00 (ISBN 0-571-11655-8, Pub. by Faber & Faber). Merrimack Bk Serv.
Biesele, Igildo. Graphic Design Education. (Illus.). 190p. 1981. 67.50 (ISBN 0-8038-2712-1, Visual Communication). Hastings.
Carter, Judith Q. & Carter, Richard D., eds. Herbert L. Fink: Graphic Artist. (Illus.). Date not set. price not set (ISBN 0-8093-1016-3). S Ill U Pr.
Graphic Arts Green Book: 1981 Midwest Edition. 500p. 1981. pap. 50.00 (ISBN 0-910880-09-3). Lewis.
Kinneir, Jock. Words & Buildings. 192p. 1981. 32.50 (ISBN 0-8230-7487-0, Whitney Lib). Watson-Guptill.
Sawamura, Kaichi, ed. Graphic Arts Japan, Vol. 21, 1979-80. LC 64-43886. (Illus.). 190p. (Orig.). 1980. pap. 35.00x (ISBN 0-8002-2728-X). Intl Pubns Serv.
Stevens, Peter S. A Handbook of Regular Patterns: An Introduction to Symmetry in Two Dimensions. (Illus.). 384p. 1981. 37.50 (ISBN 0-262-19188-1). MIT Pr.
GRAPHIC ARTS-DICTIONARIES
Crawford, Tad & Kopelman, Arie. Selling Your Graphic Design & Illustration. 272p. 1981. 13.95 (ISBN 0-312-71252-9). St Martin.
GRAPHIC ARTS-TECHNIQUE
Gill, Bob. Forget All the Rules You Ever Learned About Graphic Design: Including the Ones in This Book. 168p. 1981. 22.50. Watson-Guptill.
Watson, Ernest W. & Watson, Aldren A. The Watson Drawing Book. 1981. pap. 9.95 (ISBN 0-442-20054-4). Van Nos Reinhold.
GRAPHIC ARTS-YEARBOOKS
Goodacre, Clive, ed. Penrose 1980-1981: International Review of the Graphic Arts, Vol.73. (Illus.). 200p. 1981. 59.50 (ISBN 0-8038-5892-2, Visual Communication). Hastings.
Graphic Arts Trade Journal Intl Inc. Export Grafics USA 1980-81. Humphrey, G. A. & Miura, Lydia, eds. (Illus.). 94p. (Orig.). 1980. pap. 10.00 (ISBN 0-910762-06-6). Graph Arts Trade.
GRAPHIC DATA PROCESSING
see Computer Graphics
GRAPHIC DIFFERENTIATION
see Numerical Integration
GRAPHIC METHODS
Lefferts, Robert. Elements of Graphics: How to Prepare Charts & Graphs for Effective Reports. LC 80-8209. (Illus.). 192p. 1981. 12.95 (ISBN 0-06-012578-0, HarpT). Har-Row.
Muller-Brockmann, Josef. Grid Systems in Graphic Design: A Visual Communications Manual. (Visual Communications Bks.). (Illus.). 176p. (Eng. & Ger.). 1981. 45.00 (ISBN 0-8038-2711-3). Hastings.
GRAPHICS, COMPUTER
see Computer Graphics
GRAPHICS, ENGINEERING
see Engineering Graphics
GRAPHOLOGY
Hearns, Rudolf S. Self-Portraits in Autographs. 1981. 7.95 (ISBN 0-8062-1550-X). Carlton.
Hill, Barbara. Graphology. (Illus.). 143p. 1981. 9.95 (ISBN 0-686-69111-3). St Martin.
Lester, David. The Psychological Basis of Handwriting Analysis: The Relationship of Handwriting to Personality & Psychopathology. LC 79-23957. 192p. 1981. text ed. 18.95 (ISBN 0-88229-533-0). Nelson-Hall.
Ruiz, Mary S. & Amend, Karen. The Complete Book of Handwriting Analysis. LC 80-8672. (Illus.). 196p. 1980. Repr. of 1980 ed. lib. bdg. 17.95 (ISBN 0-89370-650-7). Borgo Pr.
GRAPHOPHONE
see Phonograph
GRAPHS
see Graphic Methods
GRASS PARAKEET
see Budgerigars
GRASSES
see also Grasslands; Pastures
also names of grasses
Grounds, Roger. Ornamental Grasses. 216p. 1981. 16.95 (ISBN 0-442-24707-9). Van Nos Reinhold.
Smith, J. P., Jr. A Key to the Genera of Grasses of the Conterminous United States. 1981. pap. price not set. Mad River.
GRASSHOPPERS
see Locusts
GRASSLAND ECOLOGY
African Pastureland Ecology. (FAO Pasture & Fodder Crop Studies: No. 7). 203p. 1981. pap. 11.00 (ISBN 92-5-100873-6, F2099, FAO). Unipub.
GRASSLANDS
Management & the Use of Grasslands, Democratic Republic of the Congo. 152p. 1966. pap. 8.00 (F1918, FAO). Unipub.
The Role of Nitrogen in Intensive Grassland Production. 171p. 1981. pap. 30.00 (ISBN 90-220-0734-0, PDC 214, Pudoc). Unipub.
GRATEFUL DEAD
Harrison, Hank. The Dead. LC 79-56661. (Illus.). 336p. (Orig.). 1980. 14.95 (ISBN 0-89087-282-1); pap. 9.95 (ISBN 0-89087-300-3). Celestial Arts.
GRATES
see Furnaces
GRAVES
see Burial; Funeral Rites and Ceremonies; Sepulchral Monuments
GRAVES' DISEASE
see also Goiter
Lewis, Alan E. Graves' Disease. LC 80-15624. (Discussions in Patient Management Ser.). 1980. pap. 12.00 (ISBN 0-87488-870-C). Med Exam.
GRAVESTONES
see Sepulchral Monuments
GRAVEYARDS
see Cemeteries
GRAVIMETRIC ANALYSIS
see Chemistry, Analytic-Quantitative
GRAVITATION
Here are entered theoretical works on the phenomenon of gravitation. Works relating to measurement of the intensity and direction of the earth's force of attraction are entered under the heading Gravity.
see also Potential, Theory of; Relativity (Physics)
Murdeshwar, M. G. General Topology. LC 80-18434. 480p. 1981. 19.95 (ISBN 0-470-26916-2). Halsted Pr.
GRAVITY
Applewhite, James. Following Gravity. LC 80-21578. 1981. 7.95x (ISBN 0-8139-0885-X). U Pr of Va.
Wald, Robert M. Space, Time, & Gravity. LC 77-4038. viii, 132p. 1981. pap. 3.95 (ISBN 0-226-87031-6). U of Chicago Pr.
GRAY, THOMAS, 1716-1771
Martin, Roger. Essai Sur Thomas Gray. 458p. 1980. Repr. of 1934 ed. lib. bdg. 100.00 (ISBN 0-89984-335-2). Century Bookbindery.
GRAY MARKET
see Black Market
GREASE
see Lubrication and Lubricants; Oils and Fats
GREAT BARRIER REEF, AUSTRALIA
Gillett, Keith. The Australian Great Barrier Reef in Colour. rev. ed. (Illus.). 96p. 1980. Repr. of 1968 ed. 11.95 (ISBN 0-589-50199-2, Pub. by Reed Books Australia). C E Tuttle.
GREAT BRITAIN
see also Commonwealth of Nations; England;
also names of cities, districts, and geographical areas in Great Britain
Yeadon, David. Hidden Corners of Britain. (Illus.). 1981. 19.95 (ISBN 0-393-01460-6). Norton.
GREAT BRITAIN-ANTIQUITIES
Hodgetts, J. Frederick. Olden England, 2 vols. 413p. 1981. Repr. of 1884 ed. Set. lib. bdg. 200.00 (ISBN 0-89987-364-2). Darby Bks.
Jope, E. M. & Jacobsthal, P. Early Celtic Art in the British Isles, 2 vols. (Illus.). 392p. 1980. text ed. 99.00x (ISBN 0-19-817318-0). Oxford U Pr.
Muir, Richard. Riddles in the British Landscape. (Illus.). 200p. 1981. 17.95 (ISBN 0-500-24108-2). Thames Hudson.
GREAT BRITAIN-ARMED FORCES
Geraghty, Tony. Inside the SAS. (Elite Unit Ser.: No. 2). (Illus.). 249p. 1981. 17.95 (ISBN 0-89859-039-7). Battery Pr.
Owen, David L. Providence Their Guide: The Story of the Long Range Desert Group 1940-1945. (Elite Unit Ser.: No. 3). (Illus.). 238p. 1981. 19.95 (ISBN 0-89839-040-0). Battery Pr.
GREAT BRITAIN-BIOGRAPHY
Bailey, Anthony. America, Lost & Found. 1981. 9.95 (ISBN 0-394-51088-7). Random.
Bullied, H. A. The Aspinall Era. 17.95x (ISBN 0-392-07597-0, SpS). Soccer.
Cope, Esther. The Life of a Public Man: Edward, First Baron Montego of Boughton. LC 79-54279. (Memoirs Ser.: Vol. 142). 1980. 9.50 (ISBN 0-87169-142-6). Am Philos.
De Selincourt, Aubrey. Six Great Englishmen. 221p. 1980. lib. bdg. 20.00 (ISBN 0-8482-3652-1). Norwood Edns.
Emden, Paul H. Regency Pageant. 295p. 1980. Repr. of 1936 ed. lib. bdg. 35.00 (ISBN 0-89987-204-2). Darby Bks.
Fane, Julian. Gentleman's Gentleman. 148p. 1981. 14.95 (ISBN 0-241-10434-3, Pub. by Hamish Hamilton England). David & Chalres.
Frankland, Noble. Prince Henry: Duke of Gloucester. (Illus.). 343p. 1980. 25.00x (ISBN 0-297-77705-X). Biblio Dist.
Kirk-Greene, Anthony. A Biographical Dictionary of the British Colonial Governor: Volume I, Africa. LC 80-81949. 256p. 1980. 31.95 (ISBN 0-8179-2611-9). Hoover Inst Pr.
Ormond, Richard. Early Victorian Portraits, 2 vol. (Illus.). 900p. 1980. Set. 160.00 (ISBN 0-312-22480-X). St Martin.
Porchey. Ermine Tales: More Memoirs of the Earl of Carnarvon. (Illus.). 158p. 1980. 14.50x (ISBN 0-297-77763-7, Pub. by Weidenfeld & Nicolson England). Biblio Dist.
--No Regrets: Memoirs of the Earl of Carnarvon. (Illus.). 227p. 1980. Repr. 17.00x (ISBN 0-297-77246-5, Pub. by Weidenfeld & Nicolson England). Biblio Dist.
Richmond, C. John Hopton. (Illus.). 280p. Date not set. price not set (ISBN 0-521-23434-4). Cambridge U Pr.
GREAT BRITAIN-CHURCH HISTORY-ANGLO-SAXON PERIOD, 449-1066
Hugh The Chantor, pseud. The History of the Church of York, 1066-1127. Johnson, Charles, tr. from Lat. & intro. by. LC 80-2227. 1981. Repr. of 1961 ed. 34.50 (ISBN 0-404-18764-1). AMS Pr.
Soames, Henry. The Anglo-Saxon Church: Its History, Revenues & General Character. 4th ed. LC 80-2212. 1981. Repr. of 1856 ed. 39.50 (ISBN 0-404-18786-2). AMS Pr.
GREAT BRITAIN-CIVILIZATION
Hughes, Ann, ed. Seventeenth-Century England: A Changing Culture, Primary Sources, Vol. 1. 1981. 28.50x (ISBN 0-389-20168-5). B&N.
Owens, W. R., ed. Seventeenth-Century England: A Changing Culture, Modern Studies, Vol. 2. 1981. 28.50x (ISBN 0-389-20169-3). B&N.
GREAT BRITAIN-COLONIES-HISTORY
Morgan, D. J. The Official History of Colonial Development, 5 vols. Incl. Vol. 1. The Origins of British Aid Policy 1924-1945. 253p (ISBN 0-391-01684-9); Vol. 2. Developing British Colonial Resources 1945-1951. 398p (ISBN 0-391-01685-7); Vol. 3. Reassessment of British Aid Policy 1951-1965. 334p (ISBN 0-391-01686-5); Vol. 4. Changes in British Aid Policy 1951-1970. 275p (ISBN 0-391-01687-3); Vol. 5. Guidance Towards Self-Government on British Colonies 1941-1971. 382p (ISBN 0-391-01688-1). 1980. text ed. 37.50x ea. Humanities.
GREAT BRITAIN-COMMERCE
Carl, George E. First Among Equals: Great Britain & Venezuela, 1810-1910. Robinson, David J., ed. LC 80-17481. (Dellplain Latin American Studies: No. 5). (Illus.). 188p. (Orig.). 1980. pap. 17.75 (ISBN 0-8357-0574-9, SS-00142, Pub. by Syracuse U Dept Geog). Univ Microfilms.
Sell's British Exporters 1980. LC 75-640255. (Illus.). 230p. (Orig.). 1980. pap. 32.50x (ISBN 0-85499-547-1). Intl Pubns Serv.
Sell's Directory of Products & Services 1980, 2 vols. 95th ed. LC 73-640793. (Orig., Vol. 1, 452pp. Vol. 2, 479 pp.). 1980. Set. pap. 42.50x (ISBN 0-85499-527-7). Intl Pubns Serv.
GREAT BRITAIN-CONSTITUTIONAL HISTORY
see also Great Britain-Parliament
Filmer, Sir Robert. A Disclosure Whether It May Be Lawful to Take Use for Money. Berkowitz, David S. & Thorne, Samuel E., eds. LC 77-89250. (Classics of English Legal History in the Modern Era Ser.: Vol. 79). 166p. 1979. lib. bdg. 40.00 (ISBN 0-8240-3179-2). Garland Pub.
Gneist, Rudolph. The History of the English Constitution, 2 vols. Ashworth, Philip A., tr. from Ger. 1980. Repr. of 1886 ed. Set. lib. bdg. 75.00x (ISBN 0-8377-0613-0). Rothman.
Hargrave, Francis. Collectanea Juridica: Consisting of Tracts Relative to the Law & Constitution of England, 2 vols. 1981. Repr. of 1791 ed. lib. bdg. 75.00x (ISBN 0-8377-0632-7). Rothman.
GREAT BRITAIN-CONSTITUTIONAL HISTORY-SOURCES
De Lolme, Jea L. The Rise & Progress of the English Constitution, 2 vols. Berkowitz, David S. & Thorne, Samuel E., eds. LC 77-86589. (Classics of English Legal History in the Modern Era Ser.: Vol. 20). 1322p. 1979. lib. bdg. 80.00 (ISBN 0-8240-3069-9). Garland Pub.
Pulton, Ferdinand. De Pace Regis et Regni. Berkowitz, David S. & Thorne, Samuel E., eds. LC 77-86638. (Classics of English Legal History in the Modern Era Ser.: Vol.29). 574p. 1979. lib. bdg. 40.00 (ISBN 0-8240-3078-8). Garland Pub.
GREAT BRITAIN-CONSTITUTIONAL LAW
Hayward, C. The Courtesan: The Part She Has Played in Classical & Modern Literature & in Life. Winick, Charles, ed. LC 78-60872. (Prostitution Ser.: Vol. 7). (Illus.). 492p. 1979. lib. bdg. 40.00 (ISBN 0-8240-9721-1). Garland Pub.
GREAT BRITAIN-DEFENSES
Freedman, Lawrence. Britain & Nuclear Weapons. 1981. text ed. 27.50x (ISBN 0-333-30494-2). Humanities.
GREAT BRITAIN-DESCRIPTION AND TRAVEL
see also England-Description and Travel; Scotland-Description and Travel; Wales-Description and Travel
Automobile Association. AA Guesthouses & Inns in Britain. rev. ed. (Illus.). 264p. 1981. pap. write for info. (ISBN 0-86145-042-6, Pub. by Auto Assn-British Tourist Authority England). Merrimack Bk Serv.
--AA Guesthouses, Farmhouses & Inns in Europe. rev. ed. (Illus.). 256p. 1981. pap. write for info. (Pub. by Auto Assn-British Tourist Authority England). Merrimack Bk Serv.
--AA Hotels & Restaurants in Britain. rev. ed. (Illus.). 600p. 1981. pap. write for info. (ISBN 0-86145-040-X, Pub. by Auto Assn-British Tourist Authority England). Merrimack Bk Serv.
--AA Self Catering in Britain. rev. ed. (Illus.). 272p. 1981. pap. write for info. (ISBN 0-86145-043-4, Pub. by Auto Assn-British Tourist Authority England). Merrimack Bk Serv.
--AA Stately Homes, Museums, Castles & Gardens. rev. ed. (Illus.). 272p. 1981. pap. price not set (ISBN 0-86145-044-2, Pub. by Auto Assn-British Tourist Authority England). Merrimack Bk Serv.
--AA The Motorists' Atlas of Western Europe. (Illus.). Date not set. pap. price not set (ISBN 0-86145-029-9, Pub. by Auto Assn-British Tourist Authority England). Merrimack Bk Serv.
Automobile Association & British Tourist Authority. AA -BTA Where to Go in Britain. (Illus.). 224p. 1981. write for info. (ISBN 0-86145-028-0, Pub. by Auto Assn-British Tourist Authority England). Merrimack Bk Serv.
--Britain: Four Countries, One Kingdom. (Illus.). 64p. Date not set. pap. price not set (ISBN 0-85122-188-2, Pub. by Auto Assn-British Tourist Authority England). Merrimack Bk Serv.
British Tourist Authority. Discovering Cathedrals. (Illus.). 80p. 1981. pap. write for info. (ISBN 0-85263-472-2, Pub. by Auto Assn-British Tourist Authority England). Merrimack Bk Serv.
--Discovering English Customs & Traditions. (Illus.). 80p. Date not set. pap. price not set (Pub. by Auto Assn-British Tourist Authority). Merrimack Bk Serv.
--Discovering Gardens in Britain. (Illus.). 80p. Date not set. pap. price not set (ISBN 0-85263-456-0, Pub. by Auto Assn-British Tourist Authority England). Merrimack Bk Serv.
--Discovering Preserved Railways. (Illus.). 72p. Date not set. pap. price not set (ISBN 0-85263-515-X, Pub. by Auto Assn-British Tourist Authority England). Merrimack Bk Serv.
--East Anglia. rev. ed. (Illus.). 114p. Date not set. pap. price not set (ISBN 0-86143-044-1, Pub. by Auto Assn-British Tourist Authority England). Merrimack Bk Serv.
--East Midlands. rev. ed. (Illus.). 66p. Date not set. pap. price not set (ISBN 0-86143-042-5, Pub. by Auto Assn-British Tourist Authority England). Merrimack Bk Serv.
--English Lakeland: Cumbria. rev. ed. (Illus.). 114p. 1981. pap. write for info. (ISBN 0-86143-037-9, Pub. by Auto Assn-British Tourist Authority England). Merrimack Bk Serv.
Chapman, Geoff & Young, Bob. Box Hill. (Illus., Orig.). 1979. pap. 7.95 (ISBN 0-9504143-1-X). Bradt Ent.
Lanier, Alison R. Update -- Britain. (Country Orientation Ser.). 1980. pap. text ed. 25.00 (ISBN 0-933662-35-1). Intercult Network.
Lemmon, Kenneth. The Gardens of Britain, Five: Yorkshire & Humberside. 1979. 24.00 (ISBN 0-7134-1743-9, Pub. by Batsford England). David & Charles.
Muir, Richard. The English Village. (Illus.). 208p. 1980. 19.95 (ISBN 0-500-24106-6). Thames Hudson.
Oldale, Adrienne & Oldale, Peter. Navigating Britain's Coastline: Portland to Dover. LC 80-68901. (Illus.). 88p. 1981. 18.50 (ISBN 0-7153-7960-7). David & Charles.
GREAT BRITAIN-DESCRIPTION AND TRAVEL-GUIDEBOOKS
see also Restaurants, Lunchrooms, etc.-Great Britain
Automobile Association. AA Camping & Caravanning in Britain. rev. ed. (Illus.). 256p. 1981. pap. write for info. (ISBN 0-86145-041-8, Pub. by Auto Assn-British Tourist Authority England). Merrimack Bk Serv.
Automobile Association & British Tourist Authority. Guide to Outdoor Britain: North of England. (Illus.). 160p. 1981. pap. write for info. (ISBN 0-7099-0385-5, Pub. by Auto Assn-British Tourist Authority England). Merrimack Bk Serv.
Bellamy, Rex. The Peak District Companion: A Walker's Guide. LC 80-70294. (Illus.). 208p. 1981. 24.00. David & Charles.
British Tourist Authority. Bed & Breakfast Stops Nineteen Eighty-One. (Illus.). 96p. 1981. pap. write for info. (Pub. by Auto Assn-British Tourist Authority England). Merrimack Bk Serv.
--Heart of England: Shakespeare Country. rev. ed. (Illus.). 122p. 1981. pap. write for info. (ISBN 0-86143-041-7, Pub. by Auto Assn-British Tourist Authority England). Merrimack Bk Serv.
--North West England. rev. ed. (Illus.). 74p. 1981. pap. write for info. (ISBN 0-86143-039-5, Pub. by Auto Assn-British Tourist Authority England). Merrimack Bk Serv.
--Northumbria. rev. ed. (Illus.). 82p. 1981. pap. write for info. (ISBN 0-86143-038-7, Pub. by Auto Assn-British Tourist Authority England). Merrimack Bk Serv.
--Seeing Britain on a Budget. (Illus.). 1981. pap. write for info. (ISBN 0-906318-07-6, Pub. by Auto Assn-British Tourist Authority England). Merrimack Bk Serv.
--South East England. rev. ed. (Illus.). 114p. 1981. pap. write for info. (ISBN 0-86143-048-4, Pub. by Auto Assn-British Tourist Authority England). Merrimack Bk Serv.
--South of England. rev. ed. (Illus.). 114p. 1981. pap. write for info. (ISBN 0-86143-047-6, Pub. by Auto Assn-British Tourist Authority). Merrimack Bk Serv.
--Thames & Chilterns. rev. ed. (Illus.). 66p. 1981. pap. write for info. (ISBN 0-86143-043-3, Pub. by Auto Assn-British Tourist Authority England). Merrimack Bk Serv.
--West Country. rev. ed. (Illus.). 274p. 1981. pap. write for info. (ISBN 0-86143-046-8, Pub. by Auto Assn-British Tourist Authority England). Merrimack Bk Serv.

--Yorkshire & Humberside. rev. ed. (Illus.). 106p. 1981. pap. write for info. (ISBN 0-86143-040-9, Pub. by Auto Assn-British Tourist Authority England). Merrimack Bk Serv.

Eagle, Dorothy & Carnell, Hilary, eds. The Oxford Illustrated Literary Guide to Great Britain & Ireland. (Illus.). 352p. 1981. 19.95 (ISBN 0-19-869125-4). Oxford U Pr.

Hoskins, W. G. Leicestershire: A Shell Guide. 1970. 9.95 (ISBN 0-571-09467-8, Pub. by Faber & Faber). Merrimack Bk Serv.

Ronay, Egon. Egon Ronay's Lucasa Guide 1981: To Hotels, Resturants, Inns in Great Britain & Ireland & Guide to 740 Furnished Apartments in London. rev. ed. LC 74-644899. (Illus.). 830p. 1981. pap. 12.95 (ISBN 0-03-058958-4). HR&W.

GREAT BRITAIN–DIRECTORIES

The Times One Thousand, Nineteen Eighty to Nineteen Eighty One. 360p. 1980. 47.50x (ISBN 0-930466-31-4). Meckler Bks.

GREAT BRITAIN–ECONOMIC CONDITIONS

Appleby, Joyce O. Economic Thought & Ideology in Seventeenth-Century England. LC 77-85527. 304p. 1980. pap. 4.95 (ISBN 0-691-00779-9). Princeton U Pr.

Bosanquet, Helen. The Strength of the People: A Study in Social Economics, London Nineteen Three. 2nd ed. LC 79-56950. (The English Working Class Ser.). 1980. lib. bdg. 30.00 (ISBN 0-8240-0104-4). Garland Pub.

Bowley, A. L. & Burnett-Hurst, A. R. Livelihood & Poverty: A Study in the Economic Conditions of Working-Class Households in Northampton, Warrington, Stanley, & Reading, London, 1915. LC 79-59651. (The English Working Class Ser.). 1980. lib. bdg. 22.00 (ISBN 0-8240-0105-2). Garland Pub.

Chappell, D. J. An Economic History of England. 320p. 1980. pap. 12.95x (ISBN 0-7121-0587-5). Intl Ideas.

Johnston, William. England As It Is: Political, Social & Industrial in the Middle of the Nineteenth Century, 2 vols. (The Development of Industrial Society Ser.). 721p. 1980. 60.00x (ISBN 0-7165-1774-4, Pub. by Irish Academic Pr). Biblio Dist.

Kirby, M. W. The Decline of British Economic Power Since Eighteen Seventy. 216p. 1981. text ed. 24.95x (ISBN 0-04-942169-7, 2614). Allen Unwin.

Lester, C. Edwards. The Glory & Shame of England, 2 vols. (The Development of Industrial Society Ser.). 905p. 1980. Repr. 36.00x (ISBN 0-7165-1789-2, Pub. by Irish Academic Pr). Biblio Dist.

Money, L. C. Chiozza. Riches & Poverty: London Nineteen Six. LC 79-56955. (The English Working Class Ser.). 1980. lib. bdg. 30.00. Garland Pub.

Morris, Derek, ed. The Economic System in the United Kingdom. 2nd ed. 1977. 34.95x (ISBN 0-19-877141-X). Oxford U Pr.

Murray, Bruce K. The People's Budget Nineteen Hundred & Nine to Nineteen Hundred & Ten: Lloyd George & Liberal Politics. 360p. 1980. 49.95 (ISBN 0-19-822626-8). Oxford U Pr.

Offer, Avner. Property & Politics Eighteen-Seventy to Nineteen-Fourteen: Landownership, Law, Ideology & Urban Development in England. LC 80-41010. (Illus.). 480p. Date not set. price not set (ISBN 0-521-22414-4). Cambridge U Pr.

Parry, Edward A. The Law & the Poor: London, Nineteen Fourteen. LC 79-56966. (The English Working Class Ser.). 1980. lib. bdg. 30.00 (ISBN 0-8240-0117-6). Garland Pub.

Pember-Reeves, M. S. Round About a Pound a Week: London, Ninetee Thirteen. LC 79-56968. (The English Working Class Ser.). 1980. lib. bdg. 25.00 (ISBN 0-8240-0119-2). Garland Pub.

Peston, M. H. The British Economy. 224p. 1980. 30.00x (ISBN 0-86003-014-8, Pub. by Allan Pubs England); pap. 19.95x (ISBN 0-86003-115-2). State Mutual Bk.

Rountree, B. Seebohm. Poverty: A Study of Town Life, London Nineteen Ten. 2nd ed. LC 79-56969. (The English Working Class Ser.). 1980. lib. bdg. 38.00 (ISBN 0-8240-0120-6). Garland Pub.

Rountree, B. Seebohm & Lasker, Bruno. Unemployment: A Social Study, London, 1911. LC 79-56970. (The English Workinh Class Ser.). 1980. lib. bdg. 28.00 (ISBN 0-8240-0121-4). Garland Pub.

Rountree, B. Seebohm & Pigou, A. C. Lectures on Housing, Manchester, 1914. LC 79-56971. (The English Working Class Ser.). 1980. lib. bdg. 12.00 (ISBN 0-8240-0122-2). Garland Pub.

Walker, J. British Economic & Social History. 2nd ed. 448p. (Orig.). 1979. pap. text ed. 18.95x (ISBN 0-7121-0266-3, Pub. by Macdonald & Evans England). Intl Ideas.

Williams, Karel. From Pauperism to Poverty. 500p. 1981. 60.00 (ISBN 0-7100-0698-5). Routledge & Kegan.

GREAT BRITAIN–ECONOMIC CONDITIONS–1945-

Black, John. The Economics of Modern Britain: An Introduction to Macroeconomics. 2nd ed. 256p. 1981. 24.50x (ISBN 0-686-28828-9, Pub. by Martin Robertson England); pap. 9.95x (ISBN 0-686-28829-7). Biblio Dist.

Jordan, Bill. Automatic Poverty: The Ricardo Phenomenon. 208p. 1981. price not set (ISBN 0-7100-0824-4); pap. price not set (ISBN 0-7100-0825-2). Routledge & Kegan.

GREAT BRITAIN–ECONOMIC POLICY

Chappell, D. J. An Economic History of England. 320p. 1980. pap. 12.95x (ISBN 0-7121-0587-5). Intl Ideas.

Chrystal, K. A. Controversies in British Macroeconomics. 1979. 21.00x (ISBN 0-86003-022-9, Pub. by Allan Pubs England); pap. 10.50x (ISBN 0-86003-123-3). State Mutual Bk.

Creedy. The Economics of Unemployment in Britain. 1981. text ed. price not set (ISBN 0-408-10703-0). Butterworth.

Farquhar, J. D. The National Economy. 184p. 1975. 18.00x (ISBN 0-86003-008-3, Pub. by Allan Pubs England); pap. 9.00x (ISBN 0-86003-109-8). State Mutual Bk.

Floud, R. & McCloskey, D., eds. The Economic History of Britain Since Seventeen Hundred: Volume 2: 1860 to the 1970s. LC 79-41645. (Illus.). 504p. Date not set. price not set (ISBN 0-521-23167-1); pap. text ed. price not set (ISBN 0-521-29843-1). Cambridge U Pr.

Stamp, A. H. A Social & Economic History of England from Seventeen Hundred to Nineteen Seventy. 334p. 1980. 22.50x (ISBN 0-7050-0070-2, Pub. by Skilton & Shaw England). State Mutual Bk.

GREAT BRITAIN–FOREIGN RELATIONS

Brailsford, Henry N. The War of Steel & Gold: A Study of the Armed Peace. 3rd ed. (The Development of the Industrial Society Ser.). 340p. 1980. Repr. 25.00x (ISBN 0-7165-1767-1, Pub. by Irish Academic Pr). Biblio Dist.

White, Carol. The New Dark Ages Conspiracy: Britain's Plot to Destroy Civilization. LC 80-23546. (Illus.). 400p. (Orig.). 1980. pap. 4.95 (ISBN 0-933488-05-X). New Benjamin.

GREAT BRITAIN–FOREIGN RELATIONS–20TH CENTURY

Wilson, Keith. The Policy of the Entente: The Determinants of British Foreign Policy, 1904-1914. 1981. text ed. 15.00 (ISBN 0-391-02198-2). Humanities.

GREAT BRITAIN–FOREIGN RELATIONS–EUROPE

Butler, David & Marquand, David. European Elections & British Politics. 208p. 1981. text ed. 25.00 (ISBN 0-582-29528-9); pap. text ed. 11.95 (ISBN 0-582-29529-7). Longman.

GREAT BRITAIN–FOREIGN RELATIONS–NEAR EAST

Kimche, Jon & Kimche, David. Both Sides of the Hill: Britain & the Palestine War. (Return to Zion Ser.). (Illus.). 287p. 1981. Repr. of 1960 ed. lib. bdg. 20.00x (ISBN 0-87991-145-X). Porcupine Pr.

GREAT BRITAIN–GENEALOGY

Dewhurst, Jack. Royal Confinements. 198p. 1981. 12.95 (ISBN 0-312-69466-0). St Martin.

Versailles, Elizabeth S. Hathaways Twelve Hundred to Nineteen-Eighty. 621p. (YA) 1980. lib. bdg. write for info. Versailles.

GREAT BRITAIN–HISTORY

Here are entered works on the history of Great Britain as a whole. For works on specific periods see the period subdivisions.

see also Great Britain–History–Juvenile Literature

Brailsford, Henry N. The War of Steel & Gold: A Study of the Armed Peace. 3rd ed. (The Development of the Industrial Society Ser.). 340p. 1980. Repr. 25.00x (ISBN 0-7165-1767-1, Pub. by Irish Academic Pr). Biblio Dist.

Ereira, Alan. The People's England. (Illus.). 288p. 1981. 24.95 (ISBN 0-7100-0596-2). Routledge & Kegan.

Lester, C. Edwards. The Glory & Shame of England, 2 vols. (The Development of Industrial Society Ser.). 905p. 1980. Repr. 36.00x (ISBN 0-7165-1789-2, Pub. by Irish Academic Pr). Biblio Dist.

Martin, Margaret. Colleagues or Competitors. 103p. 1969. pap. text ed. 5.00x (ISBN 0-7135-1538-4, Pub. by Bedford England). Renouf.

Mather, F. C., ed. Chartism & Society. LC 80-15587. 488p. 1980. text ed. 45.00x (ISBN 0-8419-0625-4). Holmes & Meier.

Neale, R. S. Class in English History: 1680-1850. 1981. 28.50x (ISBN 0-389-20177-4). B&N.

Nobbs, Douglas. England & Scotland, 1560-1707. LC 80-25749. xxi, 173p. 1981. Repr. of 1952 ed. lib. bdg. 19.75x (ISBN 0-313-22773-X, NOES). Greenwood.

Ovennell, Marjorie & Ovennell, C. H. A History of Everyday Things in England, 5 vols. Incl. Volume I, 1066-1499. 1969 (ISBN 0-7134-1650-5); Volume II, 1500-1799. 1976 (ISBN 0-7134-1651-3); Volume III, 1733-1851. 1977 (ISBN 0-7134-1652-1); Volume IV, 1851-1914. 1976 (ISBN 0-7134-1653-X); Volume V, 1914-1968. Ellan, S. E. 1977 (ISBN 0-7134-1654-8). 17.95 ea. (Pub. by Batsford England). David & Charles.

Parry, Keith. Trans-Pennine Heritage: People & Transport. LC 80-68691. (Illus.). 1981. 19.95 (ISBN 0-7153-8019-2). David & Charles.

Perkin, Harold. The Structured Crowd: Essays in English Social History. 224p. 1981. 28.50x (ISBN 0-389-20116-2). B&N.

Ramsay, James H. The Foundations of England: Or, Twelve Centuries of British History. 2 vols. LC 80-2215. 1981. Repr. of 1898 ed. Set. 125.00 (ISBN 0-404-18780-3). Vol. 1 (ISBN 0-404-18781-1). Vol. 2 (ISBN 0-404-18782-X). AMS Pr.

Randle, John. Understanding Britain: A History of the British People & Their Culture. (Illus.). 288p. 1981. 25.00x (ISBN 0-631-12471-3, Pub. by Basil Blackwell England); pap. 8.95x (ISBN 0-631-12883-2). Biblio Dist.

Rowlands, Richard. A Restitution of Decayed Intelligence: In Antiquities, Concerning the...English Nation. by the Studie & Travaile of R. Verstagen. Dedicated Unto the Kings Most Excellent Majestie. LC 79-84134. (English Experience Ser.: No. 952). 380p. 1979. Repr. of 1605 ed. lib. bdg. 35.00 (ISBN 90-221-0952-6). Walter J Johnson.

Sheppard, F. H., ed. Grosvenor Estate in Mayfair: The Buildings, Pt. 2. (Survey of London Ser.: Vol. 40). 429p. 1980. text ed. 143.00x (ISBN 0-485-48240-1, Athlone Pr). Humanities.

Smith, Lacey B. & Smith, Jean R., eds. The Past Speaks: Sources & Problems in English History to 1688. 368p. 1981. pap. text ed. 7.95 (ISBN 0-669-02920-3). Heath.

Stamp, A. H. A Social & Economic History of England from Seventeen Hundred to Nineteen Seventy. 334p. 1980. 22.50x (ISBN 0-7050-0070-2, Pub. by Skilton & Shaw England). State Mutual Bk.

GREAT BRITAIN–HISTORY–JUVENILE LITERATURE

Clarke, Amanda. Growing up in Ancient Britain. (Growing up Ser.). (Illus.). 72p. (gr. 6 up). 1981. 14.95 (ISBN 0-7134-3557-7, Pub. by Batsford England). David & Charles.

Lane, Peter. Georgian England. (Visual Sources Ser.). (Illus.). 96p. (gr. 7-9). 1981. 16.95 (ISBN 0-7134-3358-2, Pub. by Batsford England). David & Charles.

GREAT BRITAIN–HISTORY–OUTLINES, SYLLABI, ETC.

Marwick, Arthur, et al, eds. The Illustrated Dictionary of British History. (Illus.). 320p. 1981. 19.95 (ISBN 0-500-25072-3). Thames Hudson.

GREAT BRITAIN–HISTORY–ANGLO-SAXON PERIOD, 449-1066

Here are entered works on the Anglo-Saxon period whether as a whole or portions of the period. For works on specific rulers of this period see the name of the ruler.

Ballard, Adolphus, ed. British Borough Charters, 1042-1216. LC 80-2236. 1981. Repr. of 1913 ed. 49.50 (ISBN 0-404-18750-1). AMS Pr.

Brown, R. Allen, ed. Proceedings of the Battle Conference on Anglo-Norman Studies II: 1979. (Illus.). 210p. 1980. 49.50x (ISBN 0-8476-3455-8). Rowman.

Clemoes, Peter A., ed. Anglo-Saxon England, 8 vols. Incl. Vol. 1. 320p. 1972. 47.50 (ISBN 0-521-08557-8); Vol. 2. 300p. 1973. 47.50 (ISBN 0-521-20218-3); Vol. 3. 320p. 1974. 47.50 (ISBN 0-521-20574-3); Vol. 4. 270p. 1975. 47.50 (ISBN 0-521-20868-8); Vol. 5. 1976. 47.50 (ISBN 0-521-21270-7); Vol. 6. 1977. 47.50 (ISBN 0-521-21701-6); Vol. 7. 1979. 47.50 (ISBN 0-521-22164-1); Vol. 8. 1980. 57.50 (ISBN 0-521-22788-7). LC 78-19043. (Illus.). Cambridge U Pr.

Hugh The Chantor, pseud. The History of the Church of York, 1066-1127. Johnson, Charles, tr. from Lat. & intro. by. LC 80-2227. 1981. Repr. of 1961 ed. 34.50 (ISBN 0-404-18764-1). AMS Pr.

Lappenberg, Johann M. A History of England Under the Anglo-Saxon Kings, 2 vols. Thorpe, Benjamin, rev. by. & tr. LC 80-2209. 1981. Repr. of 1845 ed. 97.50 (ISBN 0-404-18740-4). AMS Pr.

Turner, Sharon. The History of the Anglo-Saxons from the Earliest Period to the Norman Conquest, 3 vols. 7th ed. LC 80-2207. 1981. Repr. of 1852 ed. 160.00 (ISBN 0-404-18790-0). AMS Pr.

GREAT BRITAIN–HISTORY–MEDIEVAL PERIOD, 1066-1485

Here are entered works on the Medieval period as a whole as well as those on parts of the period.

Ballard, Adolphus, ed. British Borough Charters, 1042-1216. LC 80-2236. 1981. Repr. of 1913 ed. 49.50 (ISBN 0-404-18750-1). AMS Pr.

Bigelow, Melville M. History of Procedure in England from the Norman Conquest: The Norman Period (1066-1204) LC 80-2235. 1981. Repr. of 1880 ed. 44.50 (ISBN 0-404-18752-8). AMS Pr.

Chew, Helena M. The English Ecclesiastical Tenants-in-Chief & Knight Service, Especially in the Thirteenth & Fourteenth Centuries. LC 80-2310. 1981. Repr. of 1932 ed. 32.50 (ISBN 0-404-18558-4). AMS Pr.

Dupont, Etienne. La Participation De la Bretagne a la Conquete De l'Angleterre Par les Normands. LC 80-2229. 1981. Repr. of 1911 ed. 17.50 (ISBN 0-404-18758-7). AMS Pr.

Historical Association, London. Social Life in Early England: Historical Association Essays. Barraclough, Geoffrey, ed. LC 79-16998. (Illus.). xi, 264p. 1980. Repr. of 1960 ed. lib. bdg. 34.50x (ISBN 0-313-21298-8, HASL). Greenwood.

Holmes, George A. The Estates of the Higher Nobility in Fourteenth-Century England. LC 80-2024. 1981. Repr. of 1957 ed. 25.00 (ISBN 0-404-18570-3). AMS Pr.

Lennard, Reginald V. Rural England, Ten Eighty-Six to Eleven Thirty-Five: A Study of Social & Agrarian Conditions. LC 80-2222. 1981. Repr. of 1959 ed. 49.50 (ISBN 0-404-18767-6). AMS Pr.

Sanders, Ivor J. Feudal Military Service in England: A Study of the Constitutional & Military Powers of the Barones in Medieval England. LC 80-23778. (Oxford Historical Ser., British Ser.). xv, 173p. 1980. Repr. of 1956 ed. lib. bdg. 19.25x (ISBN 0-313-22725-X, SAFM). Greenwood.

GREAT BRITAIN–HISTORY–TUDORS–1485-1603

Here are entered works on the period between 1485 and 1603 as a whole, as well as those on any part except the reign of Elizabeth, for which see Great Britain–History–Elizabeth–1558-1603.

Brown, Daniel P. The Protectorate & The Northumberland Conspiracy: Political Intrigue in the Reign of Edward VI. LC 80-65156. (European History: Ser. I-1001). (Illus.). 60p. (Orig.). (gr. 11-12). 1980. pap. 3.15 (ISBN 0-930860-02-0). Golden West Hist.

Munday, Anthony. The English Roman Life. Ayres, Phillip J., ed. (Studies in Tudor & Stewart Literature Ser.). (Illus.). 142p. 1980. 22.00 (ISBN 0-19-812635-2). Oxford U Pr.

GREAT BRITAIN–HISTORY–16TH CENTURY

see Great Britain–History–Tudors–1485-1603

GREAT BRITAIN–HISTORY–ELIZABETH, 1558-1603

Greaves, Richard L. Society & Religion in Elizabethan England. 832p. 1981. 32.50x (ISBN 0-8166-1030-4). U of Minn Pr.

MacCaffrey, Wallace T. Queen Elizabeth & the Making of Policy, 1572-1588. LC 80-8564. 536p. 1981. 40.00x (ISBN 0-691-05324-3); pap. 15.00x (ISBN 0-691-10112-4). Princeton U Pr.

GREAT BRITAIN–HISTORY–17TH CENTURY

see Great Britain–History–Stuarts, 1603-1714

GREAT BRITAIN–HISTORY–STUARTS, 1603-1714

Here are entered works on England in the Stuart period as a whole or in part, except for the subdivisions listed immediately below.

Appleby, Joyce O. Economic Thought & Ideology in Seventeenth-Century England. LC 77-85527. 304p. 1980. pap. 4.95 (ISBN 0-691-00779-9). Princeton U Pr.

Ashley, Maurice. England in the Seventeenth Century. new ed. 273p. 1980. 20.00x; pap. 9.95. B&N.

Hughes, Ann, ed. Seventeenth-Century England: A Changing Culture, Primary Sources, Vol. 1. 1981. 28.50x (ISBN 0-389-20168-5). B&N.

Macfarlane, Alan. The Justice & the Mare's Ale: Law & Disorder in Seventeenth-Century England. (Illus.). 225p. Date not set. 19.95 (ISBN 0-521-23949-4). Cambridge U Pr.

Munday, Anthony. The English Roman Life. Ayres, Phillip J., ed. (Studies in Tudor & Stewart Literature Ser.). (Illus.). 142p. 1980. 22.00 (ISBN 0-19-812635-2). Oxford U Pr.

Owens, W. R., ed. Seventeenth-Century England: A Changing Culture, Modern Studies, Vol. 2. 1981. 28.50x (ISBN 0-389-20169-3). B&N.

Spenser, Benjamin. Vox Civitatis, or Londons Complaint Against Her Children in the Countrey. LC 79-84137. (English Experience Ser.: No. 954). 52p. (Eng.). 1979. Repr. of 1625 ed. lib. bdg. 8.00 (ISBN 90-221-0954-2). Walter J Johnson.

Weston, Corin & Greenberg, Janelle R. Subjects & Sovereigns: The Grand Controversy Over Legal Sovereignty in Stuart England. LC 80-40588. 400p. Date not set. 39.50 (ISBN 0-521-23272-4). Cambridge U Pr.

GREAT BRITAIN–HISTORY–PURITAN REVOLUTION, 1642-1660

Childs, John. The Army, James II & the Glorious Revolution. 25.00 (ISBN 0-312-04949-8). St Martin.

GREAT BRITAIN–HISTORY–CIVIL WAR, 1642-1649

see Great Britain–History–Puritan Revolution, 1642-1660

GREAT BRITAIN–HISTORY–1689-1714

Arnstein, Walter, ed. The Past Speaks: Sources & Problems in British History Since 1688. 448p. 1981. pap. text ed. 7.95 (ISBN 0-669-02919-X). Heath.

Garrett, Jane. The Triumphs of Providence. (Illus.). 250p. 1981. 19.50 (ISBN 0-521-23346-1). Cambridge U Pr.

GREAT BRITAIN–HISTORY–18TH CENTURY

Frost, Alan. Convicts & Empire: A Naval Question Seventeen Seventy-Six-Eighteen Eleven. (Illus.). 280p. 1980. 39.50 (ISBN 0-19-554261-4). Oxford U Pr.

Jones, Thomas M. Ward of the Generations: The Revolt of 1173-4. LC 80-18411. (Sponsor Ser.). 242p. (Orig.). 1980. pap. 18.50 (ISBN 0-8357-0528-5, SS-00141). Univ Microfilms.

Riely, John C. The Age of Horace Walpole in Caricature: An Exhibition of Satirical Prints & Drawings from the Collection of W. S. Lewis. 48p. 1981. pap. text ed. 5.00x (ISBN 0-300-03509-8, 73-88450). Yale U Pr.

GREAT BRITAIN–HISTORY–1714-1837

Here are entered works on the period between 1714 and 1837 as a whole or in part.

Arnstein, Walter, ed. The Past Speaks: Sources & Problems in British History Since 1688. 448p. 1981. pap. text ed. 7.95 (ISBN 0-669-02919-X). Heath.

Cook, Chris, et al. British Historical Facts Seventeen Sixty to Eighteen Thirty. ix, 197p. 1980. 32.50 (ISBN 0-208-01868-9, Archon). Shoe String.
Floud, R. & McCloskey, D., eds. The Economic History of Britain Since Seventeen Hundred: Volume 2: 1860 to the 1970s. LC 79-41645. (Illus.). 504p. Date not set. price not set (ISBN 0-521-23167-1); pap. text ed. price not set (ISBN 0-521-29843-1). Cambridge U Pr.
Frost, Alan. Convicts & Empire: A Naval Question, 1776-1811. (Illus.). 280p. 1980. 45.00 (ISBN 0-19-554261-4). Oxford U Pr.

GREAT BRITAIN–HISTORY–19TH CENTURY

Here are entered works on the nineteenth century as a whole or any part except the reign of Victoria, for which see Great Britain–History–Victoria, 1837-1901.

Baily, F. E. The Perfect Age. 187p. 1981. Repr. of 1946 ed. lib. bdg. 30.00 (ISBN 0-89987-064-3). Darby Bks.
Martineau, Harriet. A History of the Thirty Years' Peace 1816-1846, 4 vols. (The Development of Industrial Society Ser.). 2007p. 1980. Repr. 160.00x (ISBN 0-7165-1753-1, Pub. by Irish Academic Pr). Biblio Dist.
Turner, Frank M. Greek Heritage in Victorian Britain. LC 80-24013. (Illus.). 512p. 1981. text ed. 30.00x (ISBN 0-300-02480-0). Yale U Pr.
Wiener, Martin. English Culture & the Decline of the Industrial Spirit, 1850-1980. (Illus.). 256p. Date not set. 15.95 (ISBN 0-521-23418-2). Cambridge U Pr.

GREAT BRITAIN–HISTORY–VICTORIA, 1837-1901

Arnstein, Walter, ed. The Past Speaks: Sources & Problems in British History Since 1688. 448p. 1981. pap. text ed. 7.95 (ISBN 0-669-02919-X). Heath.
Harris, B. E., ed. A History of the County of Chester, Vol. 3. (Victoria History of the Counties of England Ser.). (Illus.). 260p. 1980. 149.00 (ISBN 0-19-722754-6). Oxford U Pr.
McCloskey, Donald N. Enterprise & Trade in Victorian Britain: Essays in Historical Economics. (Illus.). 240p. 1981. text ed. 35.00x (ISBN 0-04-942170-0, 2617-8); pap. text ed. 14.95x (ISBN 0-04-942171-9). Allen Unwin.
Martineau, Harriet. A History of the Thirty Years' Peace 1816-1846, 4 vols. (The Development of Industrial Society Ser.). 2007p. 1980. Repr. 160.00x (ISBN 0-7165-1753-1, Pub. by Irish Academic Pr). Biblio Dist.
Mingay, G. E., ed. The Victorian Countryside, 2 vols. (Illus.). 370p. 1981. 45.00 (ISBN 0-7100-0734-5); 45.00 (ISBN 0-7100-0735-3); Set. price not set (ISBN 0-7100-0736-1). Routledge & Kegan.
Ormond, Richard. Early Victorian Portraits, 2 vol. (Illus.). 900p. 1980. Set. 160.00 (ISBN 0-312-22480-X). St Martin.

GREAT BRITAIN–HISTORY–CRIMEAN WAR, 1853-1856

see Crimean War, 1853-1856

GREAT BRITAIN–HISTORY–20TH CENTURY

Arnstein, Walter, ed. The Past Speaks: Sources & Problems in British History Since 1688. 448p. 1981. pap. text ed. 7.95 (ISBN 0-669-02919-X). Heath.
Holland. Britain & the Commonwealth Alliance 1918-1939. 1979. text ed. 52.00x (ISBN 0-333-27295-1). Humanities.
Pitt, Barrie. Churchill & His Generals. 224p. 1981. pap. 2.50 (ISBN 0-553-14610-6). Bantam.
Wiener, Martin. English Culture & the Decline of the Industrial Spirit, 1850-1980. (Illus.). 256p. Date not set. 15.95 (ISBN 0-521-23418-2). Cambridge U Pr.
Wilson, Keith. The Policy of the Entente: The Determinants of British Foreign Policy, 1904-1914. 1981. text ed. 15.00 (ISBN 0-391-02198-2). Humanities.

GREAT BRITAIN–HISTORY, LOCAL

Finn, F. C. History of Chelsea. 10.00x (ISBN 0-392-07888-0, SpS). Soccer.

GREAT BRITAIN–HISTORY, MILITARY

Frey, Sylvia R. The British Soldier in America: A Social History of Military Life in the Revolutionary Period. 240p. 1981. text ed. 25.00x (ISBN 0-292-78040-0). U of Tex Pr.
Halpenny, Bruce B. Action Stations Two: Military Airfields of Lincolnshire & the East Midlands. (Illus.). 232p. 1981. 37.95 (ISBN 0-85059-484-7). Aztex.

GREAT BRITAIN–HISTORY, NAVAL

see also Armada, 1588

Ballard, G. A. The Black Battlefleet. 264p. 1980. 66.00x (ISBN 0-245-53030-4, Pub. by Nautical England). State Mutual Bk.

GREAT BRITAIN–INDUSTRY

Jordan, Bill. Automatic Poverty: The Ricardo Phenomenon. 208p. 1981. price not set (ISBN 0-7100-0824-4); pap. price not set (ISBN 0-7100-0825-2). Routledge & Kegan.
Favitt, Keith. Technical Innovation & British Economic Performance. 353p. 1981. text ed. 50.00x (ISBN 0-333-26225-5, Pub. by Macmillan, England). Humanities.
Pryke, Richard. The Nationalised Industries: Policies & Performance. 282p. 1981. 32.50x (ISBN 0-85520-241-6, Pub. by Martin Robertson England); pap. 12.95x (ISBN 0-85520-242-4). Biblio Dist.
Sell's British Exporters 1980. LC 75-640255. (Illus.). 230p. (Orig.). 1980. pap. 32.50x (ISBN 0-85499-547-1). Intl Pubns Serv.
Sell's Directory of Products & Services 1980, 2 vols. 95th ed. LC 73-640793. (Orig., Vol. 1, 452pp. Vol. 2, 479 pp.). 1980. Set. pap. 42.50x (ISBN 0-85499-527-7). Intl Pubns Serv.
The Times One Thousand, Nineteen Eighty to Nineteen Eighty One. 360p. 1980. 47.50x (ISBN 0-930466-31-4). Meckler Bks.

GREAT BRITAIN–INDUSTRY–HISTORY

Beveridge, W. H. Unemployment: A Problem of Industry, London 1912. LC 79-59646. (The English Workinh Class Ser.). 1980. lib. bdg. 35.00 (ISBN 0-8240-0101-X). Garland Pub.
Falconer, Keith. Guide to England's Industrial Heritage. LC 80-8027. (Illus.). 270p. 1980. text ed. 29.50x (ISBN 0-8419-0646-7). Holmes & Meier.
Howarth, Edward G. & Wilson, Mona. West Ham: A Study in Social & Industrial Problems, London, 1907. LC 79-56958. (The English Working Class Ser.). 1980. lib. bdg. 35.00 (ISBN 0-8240-0111-7). Garland Pub.
Roberts, Kenneth D. Some Nineteenth Century English Woodworking Tools. (Illus.). 496p. 1980. text ed. 40.00x (ISBN 0-913602-40-X). K Roberts.
Rountree, B. Seebohm & Lasker, Bruno. Unemployment: A Social Study, London, 1911. LC 79-56970. (The English Workinh Class Ser.). 1980. lib. bdg. 28.00 (ISBN 0-8240-0121-4). Garland Pub.
Stanley Rule & Level, Eighteen Ninety-Two Price List Revised to Eighteen Ninety-Seven, Abbrigment. 1980. pap. 3.00 (ISBN 0-913602-36-1). K Roberts.
Underhill Edge Tool Co., Eighteen Fifty-Nine Price List Axes & Mechanics' Tools. 1980. pap. 3.00 (ISBN 0-913602-37-X). K Roberts.
William Chapple: Eighteen Seventy-Six Revised Price List Planes. 1980. pap. 2.50 (ISBN 0-913602-35-3). K Roberts.
Williams, Alfred. Life in a Railway Factory: London Nineteen Fifteen. LC 79-56941. 1980. lib. bdg. 28.00 (ISBN 0-8240-0126-5). Garland Pub.

GREAT BRITAIN–INTELLECTUAL LIFE

Hewison, Robert. In Anger: British Culture in the Cold War, 1945-60. (Illus.). 212p. 1981. 19.95 (ISBN 0-19-520238-4). Oxford U Pr.
Willey, Basil. Nineteenth-Century Studies; Coleridge to Matthew Arnold. LC 80-40634. 288p. 1981. pap. 9.95 (ISBN 0-521-28066-4). Cambridge U Pr.

GREAT BRITAIN–KINGS AND RULERS

Barlow, Frank, ed. The Life of King Edward Who Rests at Westminster: Attributed to a Monk of St. Bertin. Barlow, Frank, tr. LC 80-2170. 1981. Repr. of 1962 ed. 34.50 (ISBN 0-404-18751-X). AMS Pr.
British Tourist Authority. Discovering Kings & Queens. (Illus.). 88p. 1981. pap. write for info. (ISBN 0-85263-439-0, Pub. by Auto Assn-British Tourist Authority England). Merrimack Bk Serv.
Henry the Lion: The Lothian Historical Essay for 1912. LC 80-2008. 1981. Repr. of 1912 ed. 18.50 (ISBN 0-404-18586-X). AMS Pr.

GREAT BRITAIN–MAPS

Harley, J. B. Maps for the Local Historian- a Guide to the British Sources. 86p. 1972. pap. text ed. 4.90x (ISBN 0-7199-0834-5, Pub. by Bedford England). Renouf.

GREAT BRITAIN–NATIONAL HEALTH SERVICE

Haywood, Stuart & Alaszewski, Andy. Crisis in the Health Service: The Politics of Management. 154p. 1980. 30.00x (ISBN 0-7099-0013-9, Pub. by Croom Helm Ltd England). Biblio Dist.

GREAT BRITAIN–NAVY–HISTORY

Cooper, Richard & Uden, Grant. British Ships & Seamen. (Illus.). 591p. 1981. lib. bdg. 40.00x (ISBN 0-312-20028-5). St Martin.
Davies, E. L. & Grove, E. J. Dartmouth: The Royal Naval College, Seventy-Five Years in Pictures. (Illus.). 96p. 1980. 14.95 (ISBN 0-85997-462-6). McCartan & Root.
Winton, John. Find, Fix & Strike! The Fleet Air Arm at War 1939-45. (Illus.). 192p. 1981. 28.50 (ISBN 0-7134-3488-0, Pub. by Batsford England). David & Charles.

GREAT BRITAIN–NOBILITY

Frankland, Noble. Prince Henry: Duke of Gloucester. (Illus.). 343p. 1980. 25.00x (ISBN 0-297-77705-X). Biblio Dist.

GREAT BRITAIN–PARLIAMENT

Acherley, Roger. Free Parliaments. Berkowitz, David S. & Thorne, Samuel E., eds. LC 77-89218. (Classics of English Legal History in the Modern Era Ser.: Vol. 65). 334p. 1979. lib. bdg. 40.00 (ISBN 0-8240-3164-4). Garland Pub.
Jacob, Giles, et al. Laws of Liberty & Property. Berkowitz, David. S. & Thorne, Samuel E., eds. LC 77-89197. (Classics of English Legal History in the Modern Era Ser.: Vol. 56). 325p. 1979. lib. bdg. 40.00 (ISBN 0-8240-3156-3). Garland Pub.
Morgan, Janet, ed. The Backbench Diaries of Richard Crossman. 1072p. 1981. text ed. 35.00 (ISBN 0-8419-0686-6). Holmes & Meier.
Pettus, Sir John. The Constitution of Parliaments in England. Berkowitz, David S. & Thorne, Samuel E., eds. LC 77-89214. (Classics of English Legal History in the Modern Era Ser.: Vol. 63). 446p. 1979. lib. bdg. 40.00 (ISBN 0-8240-3162-8). Garland Pub.
Pulton, Ferdinand. De Pace Regis et Regni. Berkowitz, David S. & Thorne, Samuel E., eds. LC 77-86638. (Classics of English Legal History in the Modern Era Ser.: Vol.29). 574p. 1979. lib. bdg. 40.00 (ISBN 0-8240-3078-8). Garland Pub.
Rush, Michael. Parliamentary Government in Britain. 260p. 1981. pap. text ed. 30.00x (ISBN 0-8419-0680-7). Holmes & Meier.
Smith, J. Berwick, intro. by. Dod's Parliamentary (Pocket) Companion. 161st ed. LC 6-7438. (Illus.). 653p. 1980. 57.50x (ISBN 0-905702-04-2). Intl Pubns Serv.
Toland, John, et al. Anglia Libera. Berkowitz, David S. & Thorne, Samuel E., eds. LC 77-89231. (Classics of English Legal History in the Modern Era Ser.: Vol. 71). 400p. 1979. lib. bdg. 40.00 (ISBN 0-8240-3171-7). Garland Pub.

GREAT BRITAIN–PARLIAMENT–HOUSE OF COMMONS

Flegmann, Vilma. Called to Account: The Public Accounts Committee of the House of Commons. 328p. 1980. text ed. 31.50x (ISBN 0-566-00371-6, Pub. by Gower Pub Co England). Renouf.
Norton, Philip. Dissension in the House of Commons: Nineteen Seventy-Four to Nineteen Seventy-Nine. (Illus.). 560p. 1980. text ed. 79.00x (ISBN 0-19-827430-0). Oxford U Pr.
The Times Guide to the House of Commons. (Illus.). 350p. 1980. 45.00x (ISBN 0-930466-29-2). Meckler Bks.

GREAT BRITAIN–POLITICS AND GOVERNMENT

see also Great Britain–Parliament

Anderson, I. G., ed. Councils, Committees & Boards: A Handbook of Advisory, Cunsultative, Executive & Similar Bodies in British Public Life. 4th ed. 409p. 1980. 100.00x (ISBN 0-900246-32-4). Intl Pubns Serv.
Harrington, James. The Political Writings of James Harrington: Representative Selections. Blitzer, Charles, ed. LC 80-21163. (The Library of Liberal Arts: No. 38). xlii, 165p. 1980. Repr. of 1955 ed. lib. bdg. 22.50x (ISBN 0-313-22670-9, HAWR). Greenwood.
Jacobs, Dan N., et al. Comparative Politics: Introduction to the Politics of Britain, France, Germany, & the Soviet Union. pap. 9.95 (ISBN 0-934540-05-5). Chatham Hse Pubs.
Randall, F. British Government & Politics. (Illus.). 288p. (Orig.). 1979. pap. text ed. 12.95x (ISBN 0-7121-0247-7, Pub. by Macdonald & Evans England). Intl Ideas.
Rees, Philip. Fascism in Britain: An Annotated Bibliography. 1978. text ed. 27.50x (ISBN 0-391-00908-7). Humanities.
Rhodes, Gerald. Inspectorates in British Government. (Royal Institute of Public Administration Ser.). (Illus.). 276p. 1981. text ed. 34.00x (ISBN 0-04-351056-6, 2596). Allen Unwin.
Rush, Michael. Parliamentary Government in Britain. 260p. 1981. pap. text ed. 30.00x (ISBN 0-8419-0680-7). Holmes & Meier.
Wade, John. The Extraordinary Black Book. 2nd ed. (The Development of Industrial Society Ser.). 576p. 1980. Repr. 35.00x (ISBN 0-7165-1588-1, Pub. by Irish Academic Pr). Biblio Dist.

GREAT BRITAIN–POLITICS AND GOVERNMENT–1485-1603

Hicks, Michael. False Fleeting Perjur'd Clarence. (Illus.). 272p. 1980. text ed. 22.00x (ISBN 0-904387-44-5). Humanities.

GREAT BRITAIN–POLITICS AND GOVERNMENT–18TH CENTURY

McCrea, Brian. Henry Fielding & the Poliitics of Mid-Eighteenth-Century England. LC 80-14711. (South Atlantic Modern Language Association Award Study, 1979). 328p. 1981. 20.00x (ISBN 0-8203-0531-6). U of Ga Pr.

GREAT BRITAIN–POLITICS AND GOVERNMENT–19TH CENTURY

Barker, Ernest. Political Thought in England, Eighteen Forty-Eight to Nineteen Fourteen. 2nd ed. LC 80-19766. (Home University Library of Modern Knowledge: 104). 256p. 1980. Repr. of 1928 ed. lib. bdg. 22.50x (ISBN 0-313-22216-9, BAPL). Greenwood.
Johnson, Nancy E., ed. The Diary of Gathorne Hardy, Later Lord Cranbook, 1866-1892: Political Selections. 650p. 1981. 144.00 (ISBN 0-19-822622-5). Oxford U Pr.

GREAT BRITAIN–POLITICS AND GOVERNMENT–20TH CENTURY

Barker, Ernest. Political Thought in England, Eighteen Forty-Eight to Nineteen Fourteen. 2nd ed. LC 80-19766. (Home University Library of Modern Knowledge: 104). 256p. 1980. Repr. of 1928 ed. lib. bdg. 22.50x (ISBN 0-313-22216-9, BAPL). Greenwood.
Bell, David S., ed. Labour into the Eighties. 168p. 1980. 25.00x (ISBN 0-7099-0443-6, Pub. by Croom Helm Ltd England). Biblio Dist.
Ceadel, Martin. Pacifism in Britain Nineteen Fourteen to Nineteen Forty Five: The Defining of a Faith. 352p. 1980. 37.50x (ISBN 0-19-821882-6). Oxford U Pr.
Clark, David. Colne Valley: Radicalism to Socialism. (Illus.). 240p. text ed. 27.00 (ISBN 0-582-50293-4). Longman.
Kennedy, Thomas C. The Hound of Conscience: A History of the No-Conscription Fellowship, 1914-1919. 304p. 1981. text ed. 22.00x (ISBN 0-938626-01-9). U of Mo Pr.
Smith, Brian C. & Stanyer, Jeffrey. Administering Britain: A Guidebook to Administrative Institutions. 288p. 1981. pap. 9.95x (ISBN 0-85520-374-9, Pub. by Martin Robertson England). Biblio Dist.
Stannage, Tom. Baldwin Thwarts the Opposition: The British General Election of 1935. 320p. 1980. 50.00x (ISBN 0-7099-0341-3, Pub. by Croom Helm Ltd England). Biblio Dist.
Stanyer, Jeffrey. Understanding Local Government. 320p. 1981. pap. 9.95x (ISBN 0-85520-373-0, Pub. by Martin Robertson England). Biblio Dist.

GREAT BRITAIN–POLITICS AND GOVERNMENT–1945-

Castle, Barbara. Castle Diaries Nineteen Seventy-Four to Seventy-Six. 788p. 1981. text ed. 40.00 (ISBN 0-8419-0689-0). Holmes & Meier.
Heren, Louis. Alas, Alas for England: What Went Wrong with Britain. 192p. 1981. 22.50 (ISBN 0-241-10538-2, Pub. by Hamish Hamilton England). David & Charles.
Norton, Philip. Dissension in the House of Commons: Nineteen Seventy-Four to Nineteen Seventy-Nine. (Illus.). 560p. 1980. text ed. 79.00x (ISBN 0-19-827430-0). Oxford U Pr.
Rose, Richard. Do Parties Make a Difference? pap. 8.95 (ISBN 0-934540-08-X). Chatham Hse Pubs.
The Times Guide to the House of Commons. (Illus.). 350p. 1980. 45.00x (ISBN 0-930466-29-2). Meckler Bks.

GREAT BRITAIN–RELIGION

Calderwood, David. A Solution of Doctor Resolutus, His Resolutions for Kneeling. LC 79-84093. (English Experience Ser.: No. 913). 60p. 1979. Repr. of 1619 ed. lib. bdg. 8.00 (ISBN 90-221-0913-5). Walter J Johnson.
Cowling, M. Religion & Public Doctrine in Modern England. (Cambridge Studies in the History & Theory of Politics). 498p. 1981. 49.50 (ISBN 0-521-23289-9). Cambridge U Pr.
Greaves, Richard L. Society & Religion in Elizabethan England. 832p. 1981. 32.50x (ISBN 0-8166-1030-4). U of Minn Pr.
Hick, John. God Has Many Names. 108p. 1981. text ed. 20.00x (ISBN 0-333-27747-3, Pub. by Macmillan, England); pap. text ed. 7.50 (ISBN 0-333-27758-9). Humanities.

GREAT BRITAIN–ROYAL AIR FORCE

Glubb, John B. War in the Desert: An R. A. F. Frontier Campaign. LC 80-1929. 1981. Repr. of 1961 ed. 38.00 (ISBN 0-404-18964-4). AMS Pr.

GREAT BRITAIN–ROYAL HOUSEHOLD

Dewhurst, Jack. Royal Confinements. 198p. 1981. 12.95 (ISBN 0-312-69466-0). St Martin.
Packard, Jerrold. Queen & Her Court. (Illus.). 256p. 1981. 12.50 (ISBN 0-684-16796-4, ScribT). Scribner.
Packard, Jerrold M. The Queen & Her Court: A Guide to the British Monarchy Today. 256p. 1981. 14.95 (ISBN 0-684-16796-4, ScribT). Scribner.

GREAT BRITAIN–RURAL CONDITIONS

Johnston, William. England As It Is: Political, Social & Industrial in the Middle of the Nineteenth Century, 2 vols. (The Development of Industrial Society Ser.). 721p. 1980. 60.00x (ISBN 0-7165-1774-4, Pub. by Irish Academic Pr). Biblio Dist.
Lester, C. Edwards. The Glory & Shame of England, 2 vols. (The Development of Industrial Society Ser.). 905p. 1980. Repr. 36.00x (ISBN 0-7165-1789-2, Pub. by Irish Academic Pr). Biblio Dist.
Mingay, G. E., ed. The Victorian Countryside, 2 vols. (Illus.). 370p. 1981. 45.00 (ISBN 0-7100-0734-5); 45.00 (ISBN 0-7100-0735-3); Set. price not set (ISBN 0-7100-0736-1). Routledge & Kegan.

GREAT BRITAIN–SOCIAL CONDITIONS

Allen, Eleanor. Victorian Children. (Junior Reference Ser.). (Illus.). 64p. (gr. 7 up). 7.95 (ISBN 0-7136-1324-6). Dufour.
Besant, Walter. East London: London, Nineteen One. LC 79-56945. (The English Working Class Ser.). 1980. lib. bdg. 32.00 (ISBN 0-8240-0100-1). Garland Pub.
Black, Clementina. Married Women's Work: Being the Report of an Inquiry Undertaken by the Women's Industrial Council, London Nineteen Fifteen. LC 79-56947. (The Englishworking Class Ser.). 1980. lib. bdg. 25.00 (ISBN 0-8240-0102-8). Garland Pub.
Bosanquet, Helen. The Strength of the People: A Study in Social Economics, London Nineteen Three. 2nd ed. LC 79-56950. (The English Working Class Ser.). 1980. lib. bdg. 30.00 (ISBN 0-8240-0104-4). Garland Pub.
Bowley, A. L. & Burnett-Hurst, A. R. Livelihood & Poverty: A Study in the Economic Conditions of Working-Class Households in Northampton, Warrington, Stanley, & Reading, London, 1915. LC 79-59651. (The English Working Class Ser.). 1980. lib. bdg. 22.00 (ISBN 0-8240-0105-2). Garland Pub.
Bray, Reginald A. Boy Labour & Apprenticeship, London Nineteen Eleven. LC 79-56952. (The English Working Class Ser.). 1980. lib. bdg. 22.00 (ISBN 0-8240-0106-0). Garland Pub.

Brown, Muriel & Baldwin, Sally, eds. The Year Book of Social Policy in Britain 1979. 272p. (Orig.). 1980. pap. 45.00 (ISBN 0-7100-0690-X). Routledge & Kegan.

Butler, C. V. Domestic Service, London, Nineteen Sixteen. LC 79-56953. (The English Working Class Ser.). 1980. lib. bdg. 15.00 (ISBN 0-8240-0107-9). Garland Pub.

Cadbury, Edward, et al. Women's Work & Wages: London, Nineteen Nine. LC 79-56954. (The English Working Class). 1980. lib. bdg. 30.00 (ISBN 0-8240-0108-7). Garland Pub.

Howarth, Edward G. & Wilson, Mona. West Ham: A Study in Social & Industrial Problems, London, 1907. LC 79-56958. (The English Working Class Ser.). 1980. lib. bdg. 35.00 (ISBN 0-8240-0111-7). Garland Pub.

Hutchins, B. L. Women in Modern Industry: London Nineteen Fifteen. LC 79-56959. (The English Working Class Ser.). 1980. lib. bdg. 28.00 (ISBN 0-8240-0112-5). Garland Pub.

Jones, Catherine. Immigration & Social Policy in Britain. 275p. 1977. pap. 9.95 (ISBN 0-422-74680-0, 6363). Methuen Inc.

Kay, Joseph. The Social Condition & Education of the People in England & Europe, 2 vols. (The Development of Industrial Society Ser.). 1156p. 1980. Repr. 50.00x (ISBN 0-7165-1565-2, Pub. by Irish Academic Pr). Biblio Dist.

Loane, M. From Their Point of View: London Nineteen Eight. LC 79-56961. (The English Working Class Ser.). 1980. lib. bdg. 27.00 (ISBN 0-8240-0113-3). Garland Pub.

Macdonald, J. Ransay, ed. Women in the Printing Trades: A Sociological Study, London Nineteen Four. LC 79-56961. (The English Working Class Ser.). 1980. lib. bdg. 18.00 (ISBN 0-8240-0114-1). Garland Pub.

Masterman, C. F. From the Abyss. Of Its Inhabitants by One of Them, London, 1903. LC 79-56963. (The English Working Class Ser.). 1980. lib. bdg. 12.00 (ISBN 0-8240-0115-X). Garland Pub.

Money, L. C. Chiozza. Riches & Poverty: London Nineteen Six. LC 79-56955. (The English Working Class Ser.). 1980. lib. bdg. 30.00. Garland Pub.

Mudie-Smith, Richard, ed. Handbook of the Daily News Sweated Industries Exhibition: Nineteen Six. LC 79-56964. (The English Working Class Ser.). 1980. lib. bdg. 16.00 (ISBN 0-8240-0116-8). Garland Pub.

Parry, Edward A. The Law & the Poor: London, Nineteen Fourteen. LC 79-56966. (The English Working Class Ser.). 1980. lib. bdg. 30.00 (ISBN 0-8240-0117-6). Garland Pub.

Paterson, Alexander. Across the Bridges or Life by the South London River-Side, London Nineteen Eleven. LC 79-56967. (The English Working Class Ser.). 1980. lib. bdg. 25.00 (ISBN 0-8240-0118-4). Garland Pub.

Perkin, Harold. The Structured Crowd: Essays in English Social History. 224p. 1981. 28.50x (ISBN 0-389-20116-2). B&N.

Randle, John. Understanding Britain: A History of the British People & Their Culture. (Illus.). 288p. 1981. 25.00x (ISBN 0-631-12471-3, Pub. by Basil Blackwell England); pap. 8.95x (ISBN 0-631-12883-2). Biblio Dist.

Rountree, B. Seebohm & Lasker, Bruno. Unemployment: A Social Study, London, 1911. LC 79-56970. (The English Workinh Class Ser.). 1980. lib. bdg. 28.00 (ISBN 0-8240-0121-4). Garland Pub.

Russell, C. E. Social Problems of the North: London & Oxford, 1913. LC 79-56944. (The English Working Class Ser.). 1980. lib. bdg. 20.00 (ISBN 0-8240-0123-0). Garland Pub.

Solly, Henry. Working Men's Social Clubs & Educational Institutes: London Nineteen Four. LC 79-56943. (The English Working Class Ser.). 1980. lib. bdg. 22.00 (ISBN 0-8240-0124-9). Garland Pub.

Urwick, E. J., ed. Study of Boy Life in Our Cities: London, 1904. LC 79-56942. (The English Working Class Ser.). 1980. lib. bdg. 28.00 (ISBN 0-8240-0125-7). Garland Pub.

Walker, J. British Economic & Social History. 2nd ed. 448p. (Orig.). 1979. pap. text ed. 18.95x (ISBN 0-7121-0266-3, Pub. by Macdonald & Evans England). Intl Ideas.

GREAT BRITAIN–SOCIAL LIFE AND CUSTOMS
see also England–Social Life and Customs

Bott, Alan. Our Fathers (Eighteen Seventy to Nineteen Hundred) 249p. 1980. Repr. lib. bdg. 35.00 (ISBN 0-89987-061-9). Darby Bks.

Cooke, Alistair. The English: Commentaries by Alistair Cooke from Masterpiece Theatre. LC 80-2701. (Illus.). 240p. 1981. cancelled (ISBN 0-394-51907-8). Knopf.

Evans, Eric J. & Richards, Jeffrey. A Social History of Britain in Postcards, 1870 to 1930. 151p. (Orig.). 1981. 23.00 (ISBN 0-582-50292-6). Longman.

Halsey, Albert H. & Heath, Anthony F. Origins & Destinations: Family, Class & Education in Modern Britain. (Illus.). 250p. 1980. text ed. 29.50x (ISBN 0-19-827224-3); pap. 12.95x (ISBN 0-19-827249-9). Oxford U Pr.

Lambert, Anthony J. Victorian & Edwardian Country House Life. (Illus.). 120p. 1981. 21.20x (ISBN 0-8419-0684-X). Holmes & Meier.

Maplet, John. A Greene Forest, or a Naturall Historie. LC 79-84122. (English Experience Ser.: No.941). 244p. 1979. Repr. of 1567 ed. lib. bdg. 18.00 (ISBN 90-221-0941-0). Walter J Johnson.

Marshall, Sybil, ed. Fenland Chronicle. LC 66-21652. 1981. pap. 10.95 (ISBN 0-521-28043-5). Cambridge U Pr.

Molloy, J. Fitzgerald. Court Life Below Stairs: or London Under the Last Georges. 427p. 1980. Repr. of 1897 ed. lib. bdg. 50.00 (ISBN 0-89984-337-9). Century Bookbindery.

Stamp, A. H. A Social & Economic History of England from Seventeen Hundred to Nineteen Seventy. 334p. 1980. 22.50x (ISBN 0-7050-0070-2, Pub. by Skilton & Shaw England). State Mutual Bk.

Turner, Frank M. Greek Heritage in Victorian Britain. LC 80-24013. (Illus.). 512p. 1981. text ed. 30.00x (ISBN 0-300-02480-0). Yale U Pr.

GREAT BRITAIN–SPECIAL OPERATIONS EXECUTIVE

Masterman, J. C. The Double Cross System. 4.95 (ISBN 0-686-28851-3). Academy Chi Ltd.

GREAT LAKES

Mason, Ronald J. Great Lakes Archaeology. LC 80-2340. (New World Archaeological Record Ser.). 1981. price not set (ISBN 0-12-477850-X). Acad Pr.

GREAT LAKES REGION–DESCRIPTION AND TRAVEL–GUIDEBOOKS

Morris, Robert. Country Inns of the Great Lakes: A Guide to Inns, Lodges, & Historic Hostelries of the Upper Midwest. 180p. (Orig.). 1981. pap. 4.95 (ISBN 0-89286-165-7). One Hund One Prods.

GREAT PLAINS

Creigh, Dorothy W. Adams County, 2 vols. Incl. A Study of the Great Plains. 1972. 25.00 (ISBN 0-934858-00-4); The/People. 1971. 25.00 (ISBN 0-934858-01-2). (Illus.). Set. 45.00 (ISBN 0-934858-02-0). Adams County.

GREAT PLAINS–DESCRIPTION AND TRAVEL–GUIDEBOOKS

Clark, Tom. A Short Guide to the High Plains, For Ed Dorn. Miller, Jeffrey, ed. 1981. signed limited ed. 15.00 (ISBN 0-932274-18-8); pap. 3.50 (ISBN 0-932274-17-X). Cadmus Eds.

GREAT SCHISM
see Schism–Eastern and Western Church

GREAT SMOKY MOUNTAINS

Doane, Jim. Great Smoky Mountains Picture Book. Castaldo, George, ed. (Color Pictorial of Great Smoky Mountains Ser.: No. 1). (Illus.). 72p. (Orig.). 1981. price not set (ISBN 0-936672-13-7); pap. price not set (ISBN 0-936672-14-5). Aerial Photo.

GREAT WESTERN RAILWAY (GREAT BRITAIN)

Casserly, Johnston. Locomotives at the Grouping, Great Western Railway. 14.95x (ISBN 0-392-08054-0, SpS). Soccer.

Macdermat, Clinker. History of the Western Railway 1863-1921. 19.25x (ISBN 0-392-07907-0, SpS). Soccer.

Riley, R. C. Great Western Album. 14.50x (ISBN 0-392-07860-0, SpS). Soccer.

GRECO-ROMAN ART
see Art, Greco-Roman

GRECO-ROMAN SCHISM
see Schism–Eastern and Western Church

GREECE–ANTIQUITIES

Snodgrass, Anthony. Archaic Greece: The Age of Experiment. (Orig.). 1981. pap. price not set (ISBN 0-520-04373-1, CAL 505). U of Cal Pr.

Woodford, Susan. The Parthenon. (Cambridge Introduction to the History of Mankind Ser.). Date not set. pap. price not set (ISBN 0-521-22629-5). Cambridge U Pr.

GREECE–CIVILIZATION
see Civilization, Greek

GREECE–HISTORY

Amos, H. D. & Lang, A. G. These Were the Greeks. (Illus.). 224p. 1980. 12.95 (ISBN 0-7175-0789-0). Dufour.

Emlyn-Jones, C. J. The Ionians & Hellenism: A Study of the Cultural Achievement of the Early Greek Inhabitants of Asia Minor. (States & Cities of Ancient Greece Ser.). (Illus.). 256p. 1980. 30.00 (ISBN 0-7100-0470-2). Routledge & Kegan.

Harrison, Jane. Prolegomena to the Study of Greek Religion. 682p. 1981. text ed. 26.00x (ISBN 0-85036-262-8, Pub. by Merlin, England); pap. 13.25x. Humanities.

Jones, A. H. The Greek City from Alexander to Justinian. 404p. (Orig.). 1979. pap. text ed. 22.00x (ISBN 0-19-814842-9). Oxford U Pr.

Legon, Ronald P. Megara: The Political History of a Greek City-State to 336 B. C. LC 80-69828. (Illus.). 344p. 1981. 25.00x (ISBN 0-8014-1370-2). Cornell U Pr.

Levi, Peter. Atlas of Greek World. 239p. 1981. 29.95 (ISBN 0-87196-448-1). Facts on File.

Topping, Peter. Studies on Latin Greece A. D. 1205-1715. 400p. 1980. 60.00x (ISBN 0-86078-012-0, Pub. by Variorum England). State Mutual Bk.

Walbank, F. W. A Historical Commentary on Polybius: Vol. 1, Commentary Books I-IV, Vol. 1. (Illus.). 804p. 1957. text ed. 49.00x (ISBN 0-19-814152-1). Oxford U Pr.

GREECE–POLITICS AND GOVERNMENT

Jones, A. H. The Greek City from Alexander to Justinian. 404p. (Orig.). 1979. pap. text ed. 22.00x (ISBN 0-19-814842-9). Oxford U Pr.

GREECE–RELIGION

Harrison, Jane. Prolegomena to the Study of Greek Religion. 682p. 1981. text ed. 26.00x (ISBN 0-85036-262-8, Pub. by Merlin, England); pap. 13.25x. Humanities.

GREECE, MEDIEVAL

Cheetham, Nicholas. Mediaeval Greece. LC 80-13559. 352p. 1981. 27.50x (ISBN 0-300-02421-5). Yale U Pr.

GREECE, MODERN–DESCRIPTION AND TRAVEL–GUIDEBOOKS

Harrison, John & Harrison, Shirley. Greece. LC 80-50995. (Rand McNally Pocket Guide Ser.). (Illus.). 1980. pap. 3.95 (ISBN 0-528-84307-9). Rand.

GREEK ANTIQUITIES
see Classical Antiquities

GREEK ARCHITECTURE
see Architecture, Greek

GREEK ART
see Art, Greek

GREEK CIVILIZATION
see Civilization, Greek; Hellenism

GREEK DRAMA–HISTORY AND CRITICISM

Bond, Godfrey W., ed. Euripides: Heracles: With Introduction & Commentary. 448p. 1981. 45.00 (ISBN 0-19-814012-6). Oxford U Pr.

GREEK DRAMA–PRESENTATION, ANCIENT
see Theater–Greece

GREEK LANGUAGE
see also Hellenism

Foulkes, Irene. Griego Del Nuevo Testamento: Texto Programado, Tomo III. 220p. (Span.). 1973. pap. text ed. 7.00 (ISBN 0-89922-054-1). Edit Caribe.

--Griego Del Nuevo Testamento: Texto Programado, Tomo II. 203p. (Span.). 1973. pap. 7.00 (ISBN 0-89922-053-3). Edit Caribe.

--Griego Del Nuevo Testamento: Texto Programado, Tomo I. 194p. (Span.). 1973. pap. 7.00 (ISBN 0-89922-052-5). Edit Caribe.

GREEK LANGUAGE–CONVERSATION AND PHRASE BOOKS

Stern, A. Z. & Reif, Joseph A., eds. Useful Expressions in Greek. (Useful Expressions Ser.). 64p. (Orig.). 1980. pap. 1.50 (ISBN 0-86628-008-1). Ridgefield Pub.

GREEK LANGUAGE, BIBLICAL
Comprises the language of the Septuagint and the New Testament.

Walther, James A. New Testament Greek Workbook: An Inductive Study of the Complete Text of the Gospel of John. LC 80-23762. (Illus.). 1981. lib. bdg. 12.00x (ISBN 0-226-87239-4). U of Chicago Pr.

GREEK LANGUAGE, BIBLICAL–DICTIONARIES

Abbott-Smith, G. A Manual Greek Lexicon of the New Testament. 3rd ed. 528p. 1977. text ed. 20.00 (ISBN 0-567-01001-5). Attic Pr.

Cremer, Hermann. Biblico-Theological Lexicon of New Testament Greek. 4th ed. 960p. Repr. of 1895 ed. text ed. 32.00x (ISBN 0-567-01004-X). Attic Pr.

GREEK LANGUAGE, BIBLICAL–GRAMMAR

Marshall, Alfred. New Testament Greek Primer. 176p. (Orig.). 1981. pap. 5.95 (ISBN 0-310-20401-1). Zondervan.

Moulton, J. H., et al. A Grammar of New Testament Greek: Accidence & Word Formation, Vol. 2. 572p. 1979. text ed. 17.50x (ISBN 0-567-01012-0). Attic Pr.

--A Grammar of New Testament Greek: Syntax, Vol. 3. 438p. 1963. text ed. 17.50x (ISBN 0-567-01013-9). Attic Pr.

--A Grammar of New Testament Greek: The Prolegomena, Vol. I. 3rd ed. 320p. 1978. write for info. (ISBN 0-567-01011-2). Attic Pr.

GREEK LANGUAGE, BIBLICAL–READERS

Kohlenberger, John R., ed. The NIV Triglot Old Testament. 1334p. 1981. 49.95 (ISBN 0-310-43820-9). Zondervan.

GREEK LANGUAGE, BIBLICAL–SYNTAX

Burton, E. Syntax of Moods & Tenses of New Testament Greek. 3rd ed. 240p. 1898. text ed. 11.50x (ISBN 0-567-01002-3). Attic Pr.

GREEK LANGUAGE, MODERN

Elefteriades, Olga. Modern Greek Reference Grammar. (Orig.). 1981. pap. text ed. 10.00x (ISBN 0-87840-173-3). Georgetown U Pr.

GREEK LETTERS

Bailey, D. R., ed. Cicero: Epistulae Ad Quintum Fratrem et M. Brutum. (Cambridge Classical Texts & Commentaries Ser.: No. 22). 300p. Date not set. 49.50 (ISBN 0-521-23053-5). Cambridge U Pr.

GREEK LITERATURE–HISTORY AND CRITICISM

Dover, Kenneth. Ancient Greek Literature. 196p. 1980. 15.50 (ISBN 0-19-219137-3); pap. 6.95 (ISBN 0-19-289124-3). Oxford U Pr.

Eckstein, Jerome. The Death of Socrates: Living, Dying & Immortality--the Theater of Ideas in Plato's Phaedo. 288p. 1981. 18.00 (ISBN 0-914366-19-X). Columbia Pub.

Kessels, A. H. Studies on the Dream in Greek Literature. 280p. 1980. pap. text ed. 34.25x (ISBN 90-6194-491-0). Humanities.

GREEK LITERATURE, HELLENISTIC–HISTORY AND CRITICISM

Dover, Kenneth. Ancient Greek Literature. 196p. 1980. 15.50 (ISBN 0-19-219137-3); pap. 6.95 (ISBN 0-19-289124-3). Oxford U Pr.

GREEK MATHEMATICS
see Mathematics, Greek

GREEK MYTHOLOGY
see Mythology, Greek

GREEK PAPYRI
see Manuscripts (Papyri)

GREEK PHILOSOPHY
see Philosophy, Ancient

GREEK POETRY–HISTORY AND CRITICISM

De Almeida, Hermione. Byron & Joyce Through Homer: Don Juan & Ulysses. 256p. 1981. 20.00x (ISBN 0-231-05092-5). Columbia U Pr.

White, Heather. Essays in Hellenistic Poetry. (London Studies in Classical Philology: Vol. 5). 81p. 1981. pap. text ed. 17.25x (ISBN 90-70265-52-4, Pub. by Gieben Holland). Humanities.

GREEK POTTERY
see Pottery, Greek

GREEK VASES
see Vases–Greece

GREEN, THOMAS HILL 1836-1882

Greengarten, I. M. Thomas Hill Green & the Social Assumptions of Liberal-Democratic Thought. 194p. 1981. 25.00x (ISBN 0-8020-5503-6). U of Toronto Pr.

GREENAWAY, KATE, 1846-1901

Callery, Bernadette, et al. Kate Greenaway: Catalogue of an Exhibition of Original Artworks & Related Materials Selected from the Frances Hooper Collection at the Hunt Institute. Mosimann, Elizabeth, compiled by. (Illus.). 112p. 1981. 22.00x (ISBN 0-913196-33-9). Hunt Inst Botanical.

GREENE, GRAHAM, 1904-

Greene, Graham. Ways of Escape. Date not set. 12.95 (ISBN 0-671-41219-1). S&S.

GREENHEAD
see Striped Bass

GREENHOUSES

Beckett, Kenneth A. Amateur Greenhouse Gardening. 1980. 14.95 (ISBN 0-8464-0991-7). Beekman Pubs.

Boodley, James W. The Commerical Greenhouse Handbook. 544p. 1981. 24.95 (ISBN 0-442-23146-6). Van Nos Reinhold.

Nelson, Paul. Greenhouse Operation & Management. 2nd ed. 520p. 1981. text ed. 16.95 (ISBN 0-8359-2576-5); instr's. manual free (ISBN 0-8359-2577-3). Reston.

GREEN'S THEOREM
see Potential, Theory Of

GREETING CARDS

Sandman, Larry, ed. A Guide to Greeting Card Writing. LC 80-19737. 256p. 1980. 10.95 (ISBN 0-89879-022-0). Writers Digest.

GREW, JOSEPH CLARK, 1880-1965

Heinrichs, Waldo H., Jr. American Ambassador: Joseph C. Grew & the Development of the United States Diplomatic Tradition. Freidel, Frank, ed. LC 78-66536. (The History of the United States Ser.: Vol. 7). 474p. 1979. lib. bdg. 35.00 (ISBN 0-8240-9705-X). Garland Pub.

GREYHOUNDS
see Dogs–Breeds–Greyhounds

GRIDDLE CAKES
see Pancakes, Waffles, etc.

GRIEF
see also Consolation

Coniaris, A. M. Christ's Comfort for Those Who Sorrow. 1978. pap. 2.95 (ISBN 0-937032-00-X). Light & Life Pub Co MN.

Howard, Donald. Christians Grieve Too. 1980. pap. 1.45 (ISBN 0-85151-315-8). Banner of Truth.

Marshall, George. Facing Death & Grief. 250p. 1981. 15.95 (ISBN 0-87975-140-1). Prometheus Bks.

Miller, Jolanda. You Can Become Whole Again: A Guide to Healing for Christians in Grief. LC 80-84652. 1981. pap. 5.00 (ISBN 0-8042-1156-6). John Knox.

Novak, Michael, ed. Democracy & Mediating Structures: A Theological Inquiry. 1980. 13.25 (ISBN 0-8447-2175-1); pap. 7.25 (ISBN 0-8447-2176-X). Am Enterprise.

GRIEVANCE PROCEDURES

American Arbitration Association. Lawyers' Arbitration Letters, 1970 to 1979. 1981. 15.95 (ISBN 0-02-900570-1). Free Pr.

GRIFFIN, WALTER BURLEIGH, 1876-1937

Johnson, Donald. Canberra & Walter Burley Griffin: A Bibliography of Eighteen Seventy-Six to Nineteen Seventy-Six & a Guide to Published Sources. (Illus.). 128p. (Orig.). 1980. pap. 6.50x (ISBN 0-19-554203-7). Oxford U Pr.

GRILLPARZER, FRANZ, 1791-1872

Yates, Douglas. Franz Grillparzer, a Critical Biography. 188p. 1980. Repr. of 1946 ed. lib. bdg. 22.50 (ISBN 0-8482-3111-2). Norwood Edns.

GRIMALDI, JOSEPH, 1779-1837

Neville, Giles. Incidents in the Life of Joseph Grimaldi. (Illus.). 64p. 1981. 10.95 (ISBN 0-224-01869-8, Pub. by Chatto-Bodley-Jonathan). Merrimack Bk Serv.

GRIMOND, JOSEPH

Jo Grimond: Memoirs. (Illus.). 316p. 1980. text ed. 27.50x (ISBN 0-8419-6106-9). Holmes & Meier.

GROCERIES–PACKAGING
see Food–Packaging

GROCERY TRADE
see also Supermarkets
Book Div. Research Staff. SN Distribution Study of Grocery Store Sales - 1981. 250p. 1981. pap. 30.00 (ISBN 0-87005-370-1). Fairchild.
GROOMING, PERSONAL
see Beauty, Personal
GROOMING FOR WOMEN
see Beauty, Personal
GROS VENTRE INDIANS
see Indians of North America–The West
GROSVENOR FAMILY
Sheppard, F. H., ed. Grosvenor Estate in Mayfair: The Buildings, Pt. 2. (Survey of London Ser.: Vol. 40). 429p. 1980. text ed. 143.00x (ISBN 0-485-48240-1, Athlone Pr). Humanities.
GROTTOES
see Caves
GROUND-EFFECT MACHINES
see also Helicopters
Instrumentation for Ground Vibration & Earthquakes. 176p. 1980. pap. 65.00x (ISBN 0-7277-0052-9, Pub. by Telford England). State Mutual Bk.
GROUND PROXIMITY MACHINES
see Ground-Effect Machines
GROUND-RENT
see Rent
GROUND WATER
see Water, Underground
GROUP DISCUSSION
see Discussion
GROUP DYNAMICS
see Social Groups
GROUP INDENTITY, ETHNIC
see Ethnicity
GROUP INSURANCE
see Insurance, Group
GROUP MEDICAL PRACTICE
see also Health Maintenance Organizations
Sampson, Edward E. & Sampson, Marya. Group Process for the Health Professions. 2nd ed. 352p. 1981. pap. 12.95 (ISBN 0-471-08279-1, Pub. by Wiley Med). Wiley.
GROUP MEDICAL PRACTICE, PREPAID
see Health Maintenance Organizations
GROUP PSYCHOANALYSIS
see also Group Psychotherapy
Bion, W. R. Experiences in Groups. LC 61-7884. 1981. text ed. 12.95x (ISBN 0-465-02174-3). Basic.
Hamilton, David L., ed. Cognitive Processes in Stereotyping & Intergroup Behavior. 384p. 1981. prof. - refer. 24.95 (ISBN 0-89859-081-7). L Erlbaum Assocs.
GROUP PSYCHOTHERAPY
see also Family Psychotherapy; Group Psychoanalysis; Psychodrama
Agazarian, Yvonne & Peters, Richard. The Visible & Invisible Group: Two Perspectives on Group Psychotherapy & Group Process. (Illus.). 304p. 1981. 27.50 (ISBN 0-7100-0692-6). Routledge & Kegan.
Dyer, William G. Modern Theory & Method in Group Training. 256p. 1981. Repr. of 1972 ed. text ed. write for info. (ISBN 0-89874-280-3). Krieger.
GROUP REPRESENTATION (MATHEMATICS)
see Representations of Groups
GROUP THEATER
Chinoy, Helen K., ed. Reunion: A Self Portrait of the Group Theatre. 77p. 1976. Repr. 4.00; AA members 3.00. Am Theatre Assoc.
GROUPS, ETHNIC
see Ethnic Groups
GROUPS, REPRESENTATION THEORY OF
see Representations of Groups
GROUPS, SOCIAL
see Social Groups
GROUPS, THEORY OF
see also Finite Groups; Lattice Theory; Matrix Groups; Representations of Groups
Mennicke, J. L., ed. Burnside Groups. (Lecture Notes in Mathematics: Vol. 806). 274p. 1980. pap. 16.80 (ISBN 0-387-10006-7). Springer-Verlag.
Napier, Rodney & Gershenfeld, Matti. Groups: Theory & Experience. 2nd ed. (Illus.). 448p. 1981. text ed. write for info. (ISBN 0-395-29703-6). HM.
Stillwell, J. Classical Topology & Combinatorial Group Theory. (Graduate Texts in Mathematics Ser.: Vol. 72). (Illus.). 301p. 1980. 32.00 (ISBN 0-387-90516-2). Springer-Verlag.
Van Der Waerden, B. L. Group Theory & Quantum Mechanics. (Grundlehren der Mathematischen Wissenschaften Ser.: Vol. 214). (Illus.). 211p. 1981. 39.00 (ISBN 0-387-06740-X). Springer-Verlag.
Zieschang, H., et al. Surfaces & Planar Discontinuous Groups: Revised & Expanded Translation. (Lecture Notes in Mathematics Ser.: Vol. 835). 334p. 1981. pap. 19.50 (ISBN 0-387-10024-5). Springer-Verlag.
GROWTH
see also Developmental Biology; Growth (Plants)
also subdivision Growth under subjects, e.g. Bone–Growth; cities and towns - growth
Becker, Robert O. Mechanisms of Growth Control. (Illus.). 377p. write for info. (ISBN 0-398-04469-4). C C Thomas.
Carter, Nicholas, ed. Development, Growth, & Aging. 176p. 1980. 25.00x (ISBN 0-85664-861-2, Pub. by Croom Helm England). State Mutual Bk.
Ritzen, Martin, et al, eds. Biology of Normal Human Growth. Date not set. price not set. Raven.
Tanner, J. M. A History of Studies of Human Growth. (Illus.). 500p. Date not set. price not set (ISBN 0-521-22488-8, 40485). Cambridge U Pr.
GROWTH (PLANTS)
see also Growth Promoting Substances; Plant Hormones
Skoog, F., ed. Plant Growth Substances, Nineteen Seventy-Nine: Proceedings. (Proceedings in Life Sciences Ser.). (Illus.). 580p. 1981. 57.90 (ISBN 0-387-10182-9). Springer-Verlag.
Wareing, P. F. & Phillips, I. D. Growth & Diffentiation in Plants. 3rd ed. Orig. Title: The Control of Growth & Differentiation in Plants. (Illus.). 176p. 1981. 38.00 (ISBN 0-08-026351-8); pap. 19.00 (ISBN 0-08-026350-X). Pergamon.
GROWTH PROMOTING SUBSTANCES
see also Plant Hormones
Leffert, H. L., ed. Growth Regulation by Ion Fluxes. LC 80-13986. (N.Y. Academy of Sciences Annals: Vol. 339). 340p. 60.00x (ISBN 0-89766-049-8). NY Acad Sci.
GRYPHONS
see Animals, Mythical
GUARDIAN AND WARD
see also Adoption; Custody of Children; Executors and Administrators; Parent and Child (Law)
Field, G. W. The Legal Relations of Infants, Parent & Child, & Guardian & Ward: And a Particular Consideration of Guardianship in the State of New York. xx, 376p. 1981. Repr. of 1888 ed. lib. bdg. 28.50x (ISBN 0-8377-0537-1). Rothman.
GUATEMALA–SOCIAL CONDITIONS
Tedlock, Barbara. Time & the Highland Maya. (Illus.). 288p. 1981. 27.50 (ISBN 0-8263-0577-6). U of NM Pr.
GUERILLAS
see Guerrillas
GUERRILLAS
Clutterbock, Richard. Guerillas & Terrorists. 1977. 10.95 (ISBN 0-571-11027-4, Pub. by Faber & Faber). Merrimack Bk Serv.
Clutterbuck, Richard. Guerrillas & Terrorists. LC 80-83219. 125p. 1980. 12.00x (ISBN 0-8214-0590-X); pap. 5.95x (ISBN 0-8214-0592-6). Ohio U Pr.
GUESTS
see Entertaining; Etiquette
GUIDANCE, STUDENT
see Personnel Service in Education; Vocational Guidance
GUIDANCE, VOCATIONAL
see Vocational Guidance
GUIDANCE IN EDUCATION
see Personnel Service in Education
GUIDANCE SYSTEMS (FLIGHT)
Here are entered works on systems for supervising the navigation of aircraft and space vehicles from one location to another.
Gysbers, N. & Moore, E. Improving Guidance Programs. 1981. 12.95 (ISBN 0-13-452656-2). P-H.
GUIDE-BOOKS
see Voyages and Travels–Guidebooks
GUIDE DOGS
Curtis, Patricia. Cindy, a Hearing Ear Dog. LC 80-24487. (Illus.). (gr. 3-5). 1981. PLB 9.95 (ISBN 0-525-27950-4). Dutton.
GUIDE-POSTS
see Signs and Signboards
GUIDEBOOKS
see Travel
GUIDED MISSILES
see also Ballistic Missiles
also names of specific missiles
Slow to Take Offense: Bombers, Cruise Missles & Prudent Deterrence. 136p. 1980. pap. 15.00 (ISBN 0-89206-015-8, CSIS017, CSIS). Unipub.
GUINEA-BISSAU
Goulet, Denis. Looking at Guinea-Bissau: A New Nation's Development Strategy. LC 78-55460. (Occasional Papers: No. 9). 72p. 1978. 2.50 (ISBN 0-686-28695-2). Overseas Dev Council.
GUINEA-PIGS
Hutchinson. Guinea Pigs: Their Care & Breeding. (Illus.). 104p. 1981. 3.95 (ISBN 0-903264-21-8, 5213-9, Pub. by K & R Bks England). Arco.
GUITAR
Tyler, James. The Early Guitar: A History & Handbook. (Early Music Ser.). (Illus.). 176p. (Orig.). 1980. pap. text ed. 22.95x (ISBN 0-19-323182-4). Oxford U Pr.
GUITAR MUSIC
Green Note Music Publications Staff. Country Rock Guitar, Vol. 2. (Guitar Transcription Ser.). 1980. pap. 7.25 (ISBN 0-912910-10-0). Green Note Music.
--Improvising Blues Guitar, Vol. 2. (Guitar Transcription Ser.). 1980. pap. 7.25 (ISBN 0-912910-11-9). Green Note Music.
--Improvising Rock Guitar, Vol. 2. (Guitar Transcription Ser.). 1980. pap. 7.25 (ISBN 0-912910-08-9). Green Note Music.
--Improvising Rock Guitar, Vol. 3. (Guitar Transcription Ser.). 1980. pap. 7.25 (ISBN 0-912910-09-7). Green Note Music.
Tyler, James. The Early Guitar: A History & Handbook. (Early Music Ser.). (Illus.). 176p. (Orig.). 1980. pap. text ed. 22.95x (ISBN 0-19-323182-4). Oxford U Pr.
Wade, Graham. Traditions of the Classical Guitar. 1981. 25.00 (ISBN 0-7145-3794-2). Riverrun NY.
GUITAR MUSIC–DISCOGRAPHY
Rezits, Joseph. Guitar Music in Print. LC 80-84548. 1000p. (Orig.). 1981. pap. 50.00 (ISBN 0-8497-7802-6, Pub. by Kjos West). Kjos.
GUJRI LANGUAGE
see Urdu Language
GUM ELASTIC
see Rubber
GUMBRIN
see Bentonite
GUN CONTROL
see Firearms–Laws and Regulations
GUN DOGS
see Hunting Dogs
GUNNING
see Hunting; Shooting
GUNS
see Firearms; Rifles; Shot-Guns
GUNSMITHING
Traister, John. Clyde Baker's Modern Gunsmithing. (Illus.). 544p. 1981. 19.95 (ISBN 0-8117-0983-3). Stackpole.
GURJARI LANGUAGE
see Urdu Language
GUSTON, PHILIP, 1912-
Feld, Ross. Philip Couston. LC 79-27425. (Illus.). 152p. 1980. 25.00 (ISBN 0-8076-0962-5); pap. 11.95 (ISBN 0-8076-0962-5). Braziller.
Hess, Thomas B. & Feldman, Morton. Six Painters: Mondrian, DeKooning, Guston, Kline, Pollock, Rothko. LC 67-30452. (Illus.). 1968. pap. 3.00 (ISBN 0-914412-22-1). Inst for the Arts.
GUYANA
Sukedo, Iris D. The Sociology of Racial Intergration in Guyana. 224p. 1981. 9.50 (ISBN 0-682-49686-3). Exposition.
GYMNASTICS
see also Acrobats and Acrobatism; Callisthenics; Exercise; Gymnastics for Women; Physical Education and Training
Guraedy, Ila. Illustrated Gymnastics Dictionary for Young People. (Illus., Orig.). pap. 2.50 (ISBN 0-13-450932-3). P-H.
Mazzei, George. Shaping up: The Complete Guide to a Customized Fitness Program. (Orig.). 1981. pap. 7.95 (ISBN 0-345-29471-8). Ballantine.
Sands, Bill. Beginning Gymnastics. (Illus.). 1981. 14.95 (ISBN 0-8092-5948-6); pap. 6.95 (ISBN 0-8092-5947-8). Contemp Bks.
Warren, Meg. The New Book of Gymnastics. 8rev. ed. (Illus.). 120p. 1980. 13.50x (ISBN 0-213-16772-7, Pub. by Weidenfeld & Nicolson England). Biblio Dist.
--The New Book of Gymnastics. (Illus.). 120p. 1980. 13.50x (ISBN 0-213-16772-7). Biblio Dist.
GYMNASTICS–JUVENILE LITERATURE
Olney, Ross R. Gymnastics. 1980. pap. 1.75 (ISBN 0-380-49213-X, 49213, Camelot). Avon.
GYMNASTICS–STUDY AND TEACHING
Kaneko, Akitomo. Olympic Gymnastics. LC 76-1171. (Illus.). 256p. 1980. pap. 7.95 (ISBN 0-8069-8926-2). Sterling.
GYMNASTICS, MEDICAL
see Exercise Therapy
GYMNASTICS FOR WOMEN
Bowers, Carolyn O., et al. Judging & Coaching Women's Gymnastics. 2nd ed. 360p. 1981. pap. text ed. price not set (ISBN 0-87484-391-X). Mayfield Pub.
GYNECOLOGIC ENDOCRINOLOGY
see Endocrine Gynecology
GYNECOLOGIC NURSING
Dean, Patricia G. Self-Assessment of Current Knowledge in Gynecologic Nursing & Women's Health Care. LC 79-92917. 1980. pap. 9.50 (ISBN 0-87488-268-0). Med Exam.
GYNECOLOGY
see also Endocrine Gynecology; Gynecologic Nursing
Ahrens, Uwe, et al. Birth. LC 77-2603. (Illus.). 176p. 1981. pap. 9.95 (ISBN 0-06-090867-X, CN 867, CN). Har-Row.
Bradley, Robert A. Husband Coached Childbirth. 3rd ed. LC 80-8683. (Illus.). 256p. 1981. 9.95 (ISBN 0-06-014850-0, HarpT). Har-Row.
Cohen, Arnold W. Emergencies in Obstetrics & Gynecology. (Clinics in Emergency Medicine Ser.). (Illus.). 224p. 1981. lib. bdg. 20.00 (ISBN 0-443-08130-1). Churchill.
Dean, Patricia G. Self-Assessment of Current Knowledge in Gynecologic Nursing & Women's Health Care. LC 79-92917. 1980. pap. 9.50 (ISBN 0-87488-268-0). Med Exam.
Dilts, P. V., Jr., et al. Core Studies in Obstetrics & Gynecology. 3rd ed. (Illus.). 248p. 1981. write for info. softcover (2572-4). Williams & Wilkins.
Dreher, E., ed. Schweizerische Gesellschaft Fuer Gynaekologie Bericht Ueber Die Jahresversammlung, St. Gallen. June 1980. (Journal: Gynaekologische Rundschau: Vol. 20, No. 1). (Illus.). iv, 144p. 1980. pap. write for info. (ISBN 3-8055-2126-X). S Karger.
Elder, M. G. & Hendricks, C. H. Obstetrics & Gynecology: Preterm Labor, Vol. 1. (Butterworths International Medical Reviews Ser.). 1981. text ed. price not set (ISBN 0-407-02300-3). Butterworths.
Goldhirsch, A., ed. Mammakarzinom: Neue Aspekte Fuer Die Praxis, 1981. (Journal: Gynaekologische Rundschau: Vol. 21, No. 1). (Illus.). 68p. 1981. pap. write for info. (ISBN 3-8055-2188-X). S Karger.
Hibbard, Lester T. Infections in Obstetrics & Gynecology. LC 80-18670. (Discussions in Patient Management Ser.). 1980. pap. 8.00 (ISBN 0-87488-896-4). Med Exam.
Jones, Howard, Jr. & Jones, Georgeanna S. Novak's Textbook of Gynecology. 3rd, student ed. (Illus.). 450p. 1981. write for info. softcover (4467-2). Williams & Wilkins.
Keller, Paul J. Hormornal Disorders in Gynecology. (Illus.). 113p. 1981. pap. 16.50 (ISBN 0-387-10341-4). Springer-Verlag.
Page, Ernest W., et al. Human Reproduction: Essentials of Obstetrics, Gynecology, & Reproductive Medicine. 1981. text ed. price not set (ISBN 0-7216-7053-9). Saunders.
Reinhold, E., ed. Jahrestagung der Oesterreichischen Gesellschaft fur Gynaekologie und Geburtshilfe, Juni 1980, Krems. (Gynaekologische Rundschau: Vol. 20, Suppl. 2, 1981). (Illus.). vi, 294p. 1981. pap. 39.75 (ISBN 3-8055-2191-X). S Karger.
Reinold, E., ed. Jahrestagung der Oesterreichischen Gesellschaft Fur Gynaekologie und Geburtshilfe, Juni 1980, Krems. (Journal: Gynaekologische Rundschau: Vol. 20, Suppl. 2). 300p. 1980. pap. write for info. (ISBN 3-8055-2191-X). S Karger.
Robinson, Aletha. The Lao Handbook of Maternal & Child Health. 1980. pap. 0.50 (ISBN 0-9602790-1-6). The Garden.
Stewart, Felicia & Hatcher, Robert. My Body, My Health. 592p. 1981. pap. 9.95 (ISBN 0-553-01299-1). Bantam.
Van Nagell, John R., Jr. & Barber, Hugh R., eds. Modern Concepts of Gynecological Oncology. 350p. 1981. text ed. 30.00 (ISBN 0-88416-268-0). PSG Pub.
Wynn, Ralph M., ed. Obstetrics & Gynecology Annual 1980. (Obstetrics & Gynecology Ser.). 390p. 1980. 29.50x (ISBN 0-8385-7186-7). ACC.
--Obstetrics & Gynecology Annual, 1981. (Obstetrics & Gynecology Annual Series). 1981. 33.50 (ISBN 0-8385-7188-3). ACC.
GYNECOLOGY, OPERATIVE
Schaefer, George & Graber, Edward A., eds. Complications in Obstetric & Gynecologic Surgery. (Illus.). 650p. 1981. text ed. write for info. (ISBN 0-06-142330-0, Harper Medical). Har-Row.
GYPSIES
see Gipsies
GYRODYNAMICS
see Rotational Motion

H

HABITS OF ANIMALS
see Animals, Habits and Behavior Of
HABSBURG, HOUSE OF
Kann, Robert A. A History of the Hapsburg Empire, 1526-1918. 2nd ed. 662p. 1981. pap. 10.95x (ISBN 0-520-04206-9, CAMPUS 265). U of Cal Pr.
HACKS (CARRIAGES)
see Carriages and Carts
HADES
see Future Life; Hell
HADRIAN, EMPEROR OF ROME, 76-138
Benario, Herbert W. A Commentary on the Vita Hadriana in the Historia Augusta. LC 80-11953. (American Classical Studies: No. 7). 1980. 13.50x (ISBN 0-89130-391-X, 400407); pap. 9.00x. Scholars Pr CA.
HAENDEL, GEORG FRIEDRICH, 1685-1759
Eisenschmitt, Joachim. Die Szenische Darstellung der Opern G. F. Haendels Auf der Londoner Buhne Seiner Zeit, 2 vols. in 1. LC 80-2275. 1981. Repr. of 1940 ed. 29.50 (ISBN 0-404-18843-5). AMS Pr.
HAGUE–INTERNATIONAL COURT OF JUSTICE
Rosenne, S. Documents in International Court Justice. 2nd ed. 1979. 50.00 (ISBN 0-379-20460-6). Oceana.
Sumanpouw, Mathilde. Les Nouvelles Conventions De la Haye: Leur Application Par les Juges Nationaux, Vol. II. 260p. (Fr.). 1980. 45.00x (ISBN 90-286-0870-2). Sijthoff & Noordhoff.
Syatauw, J. Decisions of the International Court of Justice, a Digest. 1963. 12.00 (ISBN 0-379-00187-X). Oceana.
HAIDA INDIANS
see Indians of North America–Northwest, Pacific
HAIKU
see also Senryu
Andrews, J. David. Oh, My Comet, Shine! Found Haiku and Senryu, Based on "Thought Forms" by Mirtala Bentov. 60p. (Orig.). 1979. pap. 5.00; pap. text ed. 5.00. Planetary Pr.
HAIR
Gignac, Louis & Warsaw, Jacqueline. Everything You Need to Know to Have Great Looking Hair. LC 80-51999. (Illus.). 144p. 1981. 14.95 (ISBN 0-670-30040-3). Viking Pr.
Law, Donald. How to Keep Your Hair On. 70p. 1968. pap. 4.00x (ISBN 0-8464-1025-7). Beekman Pubs.
Margo. Growing New Hair! How to Keep What You Have & Fill in Where It's Thin, by Margo, for Men Only. LC 80-66699. (Illus.). 112p. 1980. 7.95 (ISBN 0-394-51417-3). Autumn Pr.
Savage, John. The Biodynamics of Hair Growth. 88p. 1977. pap. 6.50x (ISBN 0-8464-0996-8). Beekman Pubs.

Vallis, Charles P. Hair Transplantation for the Treatment of Male Pattern Baldness. (Illus.). 608p. 46.75 (ISBN 0-398-04165-2). C C Thomas.

HAIRDRESSING
see also Costume

Colletti, Anthony B. Cosmetology Instructor's Guide, No. 1. (Keystone Publications' Audio-Visual Program Ser.). 88p. 1976. 7.10 (ISBN 0-912126-16-7). Keystone Pubns.
--Cosmetology Instructor's Guide, No. 2. (Keystone Publications' Audio-Visual Program Ser.). 80p. 1976. 7.10311 (ISBN 0-912126-17-5). Keystone Pubns.
--Cosmetology Instructor's Guide, No. 3. (Keystone's Publications' Audio-Visual Program Ser.). 136p. 1976. 7.10 (ISBN 0-912126-18-3). Keystone Pubns.
--Cosmetology Instructor's Guide, No. 4. (Keystone Publications' Audio-Visual Program Ser.). 112p. 7.10 (ISBN 0-912126-19-1). Keystone Pubns.
--Twenty-Four Practice Hairstyles. rev. ed. 1981. pap. text ed. 5.00 (ISBN 0-912126-47-7, 1265-00). Keystone Pubns.

Michael, George & Lindsay, Ray. George Michael's Secrets for Beautiful Hair. LC 79-7693. (Illus.). 256p. 1981. 19.95 (ISBN 0-385-15465-8). Doubleday.

Noella. Decedent Hair Styling: Desairology Manual. LC 82-330. (Illus.). 100p. 1980. 17.95x (ISBN 0-9604610-0-0); pap. 11.95x (ISBN 0-9604610-1-9). JJ Pub FL.

HAITI–DESCRIPTION AND TRAVEL

Courlander, Harold. The Drum & the Hoe: Life & Lore of the Haitian People. (California Library Reprint Ser.: No. 31). (Illus.). 436p. 1981. Repr. of 1973 ed. 25.00x (ISBN 0-520-02364-1). U of Cal Pr.

HAITI–HISTORY

Telemaque, Eleanor W. Haiti Through Its Holidays. LC 79-52858. (Illus.). 64p. (gr. 4-6). 1980. 7.50 (ISBN 0-914110-12-8). Blyden Pr.

HAITI–SOCIAL LIFE AND CUSTOMS

Courlander, Harold. The Drum & the Hoe: Life & Lore of the Haitian People. (California Library Reprint Ser.: No. 31). (Illus.). 436p. 1981. Repr. of 1973 ed. 25.00x (ISBN 0-520-02364-1). U of Cal Pr.

HALACHA
see Jewish Law; Talmud

HALFWAY HOUSES

Apte, Robert Z. Halfway Houses. 125p. 1968. pap. text ed. 5.00x (ISBN 0-7135-1522-8, Pub. by Bedford England). Renouf.

Mulligan, Elizabeth. Hoodlum's Priest. 174p. 1979. 9.95 (ISBN 0-86629-000-1). Sunrise MO.

HALIBURTON, THOMAS CHANDLER, 1796-1865

Haliburton, Thomas C. Sam Slick. Baker, Ray P., ed. 420p. 1981. Repr. of 1923 ed. lib. bdg. 45.00 (ISBN 0-8495-2373-7). Arden Lib.

HALIDES

Wilcox. Lead Tin Telluride, Silver Halides & Czochralski Growth. Date not set. price not set (ISBN 0-8247-1354-0). Dekker.

HALLUCINOGENIC DRUGS

Grinspoon, Lester & Bakalar, James B. Psychedelic Drugs Reconsidered. 1981. pap. 7.95 (ISBN 0-465-06451-5). Basic.

HAMBURGER
see Cookery (Beef)

HAMMERED STRINGED INSTRUMENTS
see Stringed Instruments

HAMMETT, DASHIELL, 1894-1961

Layman, Richard. The Shadow Man: A Documentary Life of Dashiell Hammett. 300p. 1981. 14.95 (ISBN 0-15-181459-7). HarBraceJ.

HAND

Blauth, W. & Schneider-Sickert, F. R. Congenital Deformities of the Hand: An Atlas of Their Surgical Treatment. (Illus.). 394p. 1980. 259.60 (ISBN 0-387-10084-9). Springer-Verlag.

HAND–JUVENILE LITERATURE

Rasch, Gerald. Hands Are Handy. 20p. (Orig.). 1981. pap. 3.50 (ISBN 0-86629-011-7). Sunrise MO.

HAND–SURGERY

Blauth, W. & Schneider-Sickert, F. R. Congenital Deformities of the Hand: An Atlas of Their Surgical Treatment. (Illus.). 394p. 1980. 259.60 (ISBN 0-387-10084-9). Springer-Verlag.

Dellon, A. Lee. Evaluation of Sensibility & Reeducation of Sensation of the Hand. (Illus.). 140p. 1981. write for info. (2427-2). Williams & Wilkins.

HAND–WOUNDS AND INJURIES

Beasley. Hand Injuries. (Illus.). 320p. 1981. text ed. write for info. (ISBN 0-7216-1607-0). Saunders.

HAND-TO-HAND FIGHTING
see also Self-Defense

Campbell, Sid. Falcon Claw: The Motion Picture. Morales, Mahi, ed. 115p. 1980. pap. 7.50 (ISBN 0-937610-01-1). Dimond Pubs.

Hayes, Stephen K. The Ninja & Their Secret Fighting Art. LC 81-50105. (Illus.). 160p. 1981. 13.50 (ISBN 0-8048-1374-4). C E Tuttle.

HAND WEAVING

Gilmurray, Susan. Weaving Tricks. 128p. 1981. 12.95 (ISBN 0-442-26132-2). Van Nos Reinhold.

HANDBOOKS, VADE-MECUMS, ETC.

The Forgotten Arts, Book Four. (Illus.). 64p. 1979. 3.95 (ISBN 0-911658-02-5). Yankee Bks.

Hohman, Edward J. & Leary, Norma E. The Greeting Card Handbook. (Barnes & Noble Everyday Handbooks). (Illus.). 160p. (Orig.). 1981. pap. 4.95 (ISBN 0-06-463532-5, EH532, BN). Har-Row.

HANDEL, GEORG FRIEDRICH, 1685-1759
see Haendel, Georg Friedrich, 1685-1759

HANDICAPPED
see also Disability Evaluation; Mentally Handicapped; Physically Handicapped; Sick; Socially Handicapped

Boy Scouts of America & Boys Scout of America. Handicapped Awareness. (Illus.). 48p. (gr. 6-12). 1981. pap. 0.70x (ISBN 0-8395-3370-5, 3370). BSA.

Burgdorf, Robert L., ed. The Legal Rights of Handicapped Persons: Cases, Materials, & Text. 1178p. 1980. 24.50 (ISBN 0-933716-01-X). P H Brookes.

Campling, Jo, ed. Image of Ourselves: Women with Disabilities Talking. 160p. 1981. price not set (ISBN 0-7100-0821-X); pap. price not set (ISBN 0-7100-0822-8). Routledge & Kegan.

Darnbrough, Ann & Kinrade, Derek. Directory for the Disabled: A Handbook of Information & Opportunities for Disabled & Handicapped People. 2nd ed. 208p. 1980. 27.00x (ISBN 0-85941-106-0, Pub. by Woodhead-Faulkner England); pap. 12.00x (ISBN 0-85941-108-7). State Mutual Bk.

Morris, Robert. Allocating Health Resources for the Aged & Disabled: Technology Versus Politics. 1981. price not set (ISBN 0-669-04329-X). Lexington Bks.

Orlansky, Michael D. & Heward, William L. Voices: Interviews with Handicapped People. (Special Education Ser.). (Illus.). 352p. (Orig.). Date not set. pap. text ed. price not set (ISBN 0-675-08024-X). Merrill.

Reddoch, Mildred L. So White, the Lilies. 1981. 5.95 (ISBN 0-8062-1629-8). Carlton.

Roth, William. The Handicapped Speak. LC 80-20297. 240p. 1981. lib. bdg. write for info (ISBN 0-89950-022-6). McFarland & Co.

Sainsbury, Sally. Measuring Disability. 125p. 1973. pap. text ed. 6.25x (ISBN 0-7135-1899-5, Pub. by Bedford England). Renouf.
--Registered As Disabled. 205p. 1970. pap. text ed. 6.25x (ISBN 0-7135-1619-4, Pub. by Bedford England). Renouf.

Sargent, Jean V. An Easier Way: A Handbook for the Elderly & Handicapped. (Illus.). 216p. 1981. pap. 9.95 (ISBN 0-686-69403-1). Iowa St U Pr.

Shaw, Ann M. & Stevens, C. J., eds. Drama, Theatre & the Handicapped. 121p. 1979. 6.95; ATA members 4.95. Am Theatre Assoc.

Topliss, Eda & Gould, Bryan. Charter for the Disabled: The Chronically Sick & Disabled Persons Act 1970. (Aspects of Social Policy Ser.). 160p. 1981. 19.95x (ISBN 0-631-12833-6, Pub. by Basil Blackwell England). Biblio Dist.

HANDICAPPED–BIOGRAPHY

Giddings, Robert. You Should Se Me in Pyjamas. 192p. 1981. 27.00 (ISBN 0-241-10534-X, Pub. by Hamish Hamilton England). David & Charles.

Meyers, Jeff. One of a Kind: The Legend of Carl Joseph. 200p. 1980. pap. 6.95 (ISBN 0-86629-028-1); 11.95 (ISBN 0-86629-025-7). Sunrise MO.

Russell, Harold & Ferullo, Dan. The Best Years of My Life. (Illus.). 224p. 1981. 12.95 (ISBN 0-8397-1026-7). Eriksson.

HANDICAPPED–EDUCATION

Eaton, Peggy & Eiring, Leslie. Joy of Learning. (Illus.). 10.50 (ISBN 0-86575-027-0, 106). Dormac.

Kissinger, Ellen M. A Sequential Curriculum for the Severely & Profoundly Mentally Retarded-Multi-Handicapped. 216p. 1981. pap. 22.75 spiral (ISBN 0-398-04145-8). C C Thomas.

Lazarus, Mitchell. Educating the Handicapped: Where We've Been, Where We're Going. 1980. pap. 11.95 (ISBN 0-87545-019-9). Natl Sch PR.

Lufburrow, Bill. The Most Honest People. LC 80-69253. (Illus., Orig.). 1980. pap. 4.95 (ISBN 0-918464-23-4). D Armstrong.

McLoughlin, James & Lewis, Rena. Assessing Special Students. (Special Education Ser.). (Illus.). 640p. 1981. text ed. 17.95 (ISBN 0-675-08151-3). Merrill.

Pasanella, Anne L. & Volkmor, Cara B. Teaching Handicapped Students in the Mainstream: Coming Back...or Never Leaving. 2nd ed. (Special Education Ser.). (Illus.). 384p. 1981. pap. text ed. 10.95 (ISBN 0-675-08026-6). Merrill.

Popovich, Dorothy & Laham, Sandra L. The Adaptive Behavior Curriculum (ABC) Prescriptive Behavior Analyses for Moderately, Severely, & Profoundly Handicapped Persons, Vol. 1. 336p. (Orig.). 1980. pap. text ed. 13.95 (ISBN 0-933716-13-3). P H Brookes.
--The Adaptive Behavior Curriculum: Thirty-Five Hundred Prescriptive Behavior Analyses for Moderately, Severely, & Profoundly Handicapped Students. 230p. 1980. pap. 13.95 (ISBN 0-933716-13-3). P H Brookes.

Wiegerink, Ronald & Pelosi, John W., eds. Developmental Disabilities: The DD Movement. 182p. 1979. pap. 10.50 (ISBN 0-933716-02-8). P H Brookes.

HANDICAPPED–EMPLOYMENT

Darnbrough, Ann & Kinrade, Derek. Directory for the Disabled: A Handbook of Information & Opportunities for Disabled & Handicapped People. 2nd ed. 208p. 1980. 27.00x (ISBN 0-85941-106-0, Pub. by Woodhead-Faulkner England); pap. 12.00x (ISBN 0-85941-108-7). State Mutual Bk.

Institute for Information Studies, et al. Financial Resources for Disabled Individuals. Vash, Carolyn & Crane, Marjorie Boyer, eds. LC 80-84166. 70p. 1980. pap. write for info. (ISBN 0-935294-06-6). Inst Info Stud.

Lufburrow, Bill. The Most Honest People. LC 80-69253. (Illus., Orig.). 1980. pap. 4.95 (ISBN 0-918464-23-4). D Armstrong.

Rabby, Rami. Locating, Recruiting, & Hiring the Disabled. 1981. pap. 3.95 (ISBN 0-87576-095-3). Pilot Bks.

Wehman, Paul. Competitive Employment: New Horizons for Severely Disabled Individuals. 210p. 1980. pap. 13.95 (ISBN 0-933716-12-5). P H Brookes.

Zimmer, A. B. Employing the Handicapped: A Practical Compliance Manual. 530p. 1981. 19.95 (ISBN 0-8144-5525-5). Am Mgmt.

HANDICAPPED–RECREATION

Clark, Cynthia & Chadwick, Donnacompiled by. Clinically Adapted Instruments for the Multiply Handicapped: A Sourcebook. rev. ed. 1980. Repr. of 1979 ed. 12.95 (ISBN 0-918812-13-5). Magnamusic.

Lane, Jim & Schaaf, Dick. Wheelchair Bowling: A Complete Guide to Bowling for the Handicapped. LC 78-24103. (Illus.). 96p. (Orig.). 1980. pap. 7.95 (ISBN 0-9605306-0-6). Wheelchair Bowlers.

HANDICAPPED–REHABILITATION
see Rehabilitation; Vocational Rehabilitation

HANDICAPPED CHILDREN
see also Aphasia; Mentally Handicapped Children

Baumgartner, Diane. Melissa. (Orig.). 1980. pap. 4.95 (ISBN 0-89191-233-9). Cook.

Bondo, Ulla. Ida: Life with My Handicapped Child. (Illus.). 128p. 1981. 23.00 (ISBN 0-571-11589-6, Pub. by Faber & Faber); pap. 8.95 (ISBN 0-571-11590-X). Merrimack Bk Serv.

Hawley, Gloria H. Laura's Psalm. 1981. pap. 4.95 (ISBN 0-86608-000-7, 14014P). Impact Tenn.

Prensky, Arthur L. & Palkes, Helen. Care of the Neurologically Handicapped Child. (Illus.). 350p. 1981. text ed. 18.95x (ISBN 0-19-502917-8). Oxford U Pr.

Wexler, Susan S. The Story of Sandy. rev. ed. 176p. (RL 10). Date not set. pap. 1.50 (ISBN 0-451-08102-1, W8102, Sig). NAL.

HANDICAPPED CHILDREN–EDUCATION

Adler, Sol, et al. An Interdisciplinary Language Intervention Program for the Moderately & Profoundly Language-Retarded Child. 1980. 19.50 (ISBN 0-8089-1301-8). Grune.

Corrigan, Dean C. & Howey, Kenneth R., eds. Special Education in Transition: Concepts to Guide the Education of Experienced Teachers with Implications for PL 94-142. LC 80-68281. 208p. 1980. pap. 12.95 (ISBN 0-86586-109-9). Coun Exc Child.

Federlin, Anne C. Play in Preschool Mainstreamed & Handicapped Settings. LC 80-65612. 135p. 1981. perfect bdg. 10.50 (ISBN 0-86548-035-4). Century Twenty One.

Hasazi, Susan E. Under One Cover: Implementing the Least Restrictive Environment Concept. LC 80-68096. 208p. 1980. pap. 11.25 (ISBN 0-86586-106-4). Coun Exc Child.

Hayden, Torey L. Somebody Else's Kids. 384p. 1981. 11.95 (ISBN 0-399-12602-3). Putnam.

Moore, Mary H. Parent Partnership Training Program, 8 bks. Incl. Bk. 1. Introductory Guide. LC 78-68013. 128p. pap. text ed. 12.90 (ISBN 0-8027-9053-4); Bk. 2. Parent's Manual. 192p. pap. text ed. 17.80 (ISBN 0-8027-9054-2); Bk. 3. Basic Communications Skills. LC 78-68015. 288p. pap. text ed. 39.10 (ISBN 0-8027-9055-0); Bk. 4. Developing Social Acceptability. LC 78-62918. 216p. pap. text ed. 29.70 (ISBN 0-8027-9056-9); Bk. 5. Developing Responsible Sexuality. LC 78-62919. 160p. pap. text ed. 19.50 (ISBN 0-8027-9057-7); Bk. 6. Light Housekeeping & In-Home Assistance. LC 78-61387. 272p. pap. text ed. 32.60 (ISBN 0-8027-9058-5); Bk. 7. Heavy Duty Cleaning & Yards & Ground Care. LC 78-62939. 240p. pap. text ed. 32.60 (ISBN 0-8027-9059-3); Bk. 8. Skills of Daily Living. LC 78-62940. 304p. pap. text ed. 29.80 (ISBN 0-8027-9060-7). (For use with K-12 handicapped). 1979. Walker Educ.

Popovich, Dorothy. Effective Educational & Behavioral Programming for Severely & Profoundly Handicapped Students. (Illus.). 300p. (Orig.). 1981. pap. text ed. 14.95 (ISBN 0-933716-14-1). P H Brookes.

Popovich, Dorothy & Laham, Sandra L. The Adaptive Behavior Curriculum (ABC) Prescriptive Behavior Analyses for Moderately, Severely, & Profoundly Handicapped Persons, Vol. 1. 336p. (Orig.). 1980. pap. text ed. 13.95 (ISBN 0-933716-13-3). P H Brookes.

Shearer, Ann. Handicapped Children in Residential Care: A Study of Policy Failure. 114p. 1980. pap. text ed. write for info. (ISBN 0-7199-1035-8, Pub. by Bedford England). Renouf.

HANDICAPPED CHILDREN–REHABILITATION

Batshaw, Mark L. & Perret, Yvonne M. Children with Handicaps: A Medical Primer. (Illus.). 300p. 1981. price not set (ISBN 0-933716-16-8). P H Brookes.

Elder, Jerry O. & Magrab, Phyllis R., eds. Coordinating Services to Handicapped Children: A Handbook for Interagency Collaboration. 272p. 1980. pap. 13.95 (ISBN 0-933716-11-7). P H Brookes.

HANDICRAFT
see also Artisans; Basket Making; Bookbinding; Candlemaking; Creative Activities and Seatwork; Decoration and Ornament; Design, Decorative; Embroidery; Folk Art; Furniture; Glass Painting and Staining; Home Workshops; Industrial Arts; Jewelry; Lace and Lace Making; Metal-Work; Modeling; Models and Modelmaking; Mosaics; Needlework; Occupational Therapy; Paper Work; Pottery; Rugs; Sand Craft; Stencil Work; Tapestry; Wood-Carving

Allen, Dorothy S. Plaster Art: Step by Step. Cole, Tom, ed. LC 80-70317. (Illus.). 130p. (Orig.). (gr. 5). 1981. 15.95 (ISBN 0-686-28860-2); pap. 12.95 (ISBN 0-686-28861-0). Dots Pubns.

Better Homes & Gardens Books Editors, ed. Easy Bazaar Crafts. (Illus.). 96p. 1981. 4.95 (ISBN 0-696-00665-0). Meredith Corp.

Biddle, Maureen. Fifty Craft Projects with Bible Verses & Patterns. LC 80-53872. (Illus.). 64p. (Orig.). 1981. pap. 3.50 (ISBN 0-87239-428-X, 2148). Standard Pub.

Chinese Folk Toys & Ornaments. 1980. pap. 4.95 (ISBN 0-8351-0735-3). China Bks.

Davis, Katrina. Toothpick Building Illustrated. (Illus.). 48p. (Orig.). 1980. pap. 3.95 (ISBN 0-937242-04-7). Scandia Pubs.

Gleason, Norma. Cryptograms & Spygrams. 128p. (Orig.). 1981. pap. price not set. Dover.

Grogg, Evelyn. Kindergarten Pattern Book. Eberle, Sarah, rev. by. (Illus.). 48p. (Orig.). 1981. pap. 3.95 (ISBN 0-87239-431-X, 2159). Standard Pub.

Hall, Carolyn V. Soft Sculpture. LC 80-67546. (Illus.). 112p. 1981. 14.95 (ISBN 0-87192-129-4). Davis Mass.

Higginbotham, Bill. Living Country Characters: Step-by-Step Instructions for Eighteen Projects. (Illus., Orig.). 1981. pap. price not set (ISBN 0-486-24135-1). Dover.

Kicklighter, Clois E. & Baird, Ronald J. Crafts, Illustrated Designs & Techniques. LC 79-23955. (Illus.). 384p. 1980. text ed. 14.64 (ISBN 0-87006-298-0). Goodheart.

Lewis, Ralph. Making & Managing an Art & Craft Shop. LC 80-68685. (Making & Managing Ser.). (Illus.). 128p. 1981. 16.95 (ISBN 0-7153-8065-6). David & Charles.

Rabineau, Phyllis. Feather Arts: Beauty, Wealth, & Spirit from Five Continents. Williams, Patricia, ed. LC 78-774595. (Illus.). 88p. (Orig.). 1979. pap. 7.95 (ISBN 0-914868-08-X). Field Mus.

Reader's Digest. Back to Basics. (Illus.). 1981. 19.95 (ISBN 0-89577-086-5, Pub. by Reader's Digest). Norton.
--Crafts & Hobbies: A Step-by-Step Guide to Creative Skills. Date not set. 19.95 (ISBN 0-686-69221-7). Readers Digest Pr.

Reese, Loretta. Fifty Craft Ideas with Patterns. LC 80-53363. (Illus.). 64p. (Orig.). pap. 3.50 (ISBN 0-87239-427-1, 2144). Standard Pub.

Rome, John, ed. The Blandford Book of Traditional Handicrafts. (Illus.). 240p. 1981. 22.50 (ISBN 0-7137-0951-0, Pub. by Blandford Pr England). Sterling.

Saurman, Judith & Pierce, Judith. Ready-to-Use Marbelized Papers. 1979. pap. 3.50 (ISBN 0-486-23901-2). Dover.

Schomas, Rhonda. My Book of Gospel Treasures. (Illus.). 63p. (Orig.). 1980. pap. 3.95 (ISBN 0-87747-839-2). Deseret Bk.

Sibley, Hi. One Hundred Two Birdhouses Feeders You Can Make. (Illus.). 96p. 1980. pap. text ed. 4.80 (ISBN 0-87006-304-9). Goodheart.

Stalberg, Roberta & Nesi, Ruth. China's Crafts: The Story of How They're Made & What They Mean. 1980. pap. 10.95 (ISBN 0-8351-0740-X). China Bks.

Stringer, Leslea & Bowman, Lea. Crafts Handbook for Children's Church: Graded Activities for Ages 3-7. (Teaching Help Ser.). (Orig.). 1981. pap. 6.95 (ISBN 0-8010-8197-1). Baker Bk.

HANDICRAFT–JUVENILE LITERATURE

Arts & Crafts Discovery Units: Arts & Crafts Discovery Units. Incl. Crayon (ISBN 0-87628-523-X); Mobiles (ISBN 0-87628-524-8); Paper (ISBN 0-87628-525-6); Papier Mache (ISBN 0-87628-526-4); Printing (ISBN 0-87628-527-2); Puppets (ISBN 0-87628-528-0); Tempera (ISBN 0-87628-529-9); Tissue (ISBN 0-87628-530-2); Watercolor (ISBN 0-87628-531-0); Weaving (ISBN 0-87628-532-9). (ps-2). 1974. 5.95x ea. Ctr Appl Res.

Holz, Loretta. The Christmas Spider: A Puppet Play from Poland & Other Traditional Games, Crafts & Activities. (gr. 3-7). 5.95 (ISBN 0-399-20754-6); lib. bdg. 5.99g (ISBN 0-399-61164-9). Philomel.

Lawson. Terrific Gifts to Make & Give. (gr. 7-12). 1980. pap. 1.25 (ISBN 0-590-30885-8, Schol Pap). Schol Bk Serv.

HANDLING OF BULK SOLIDS
see Bulk Solids-Handling

HANDLING OF FOOD
see Food Handling

HANDLING OF MATERIALS
see Materials Handling

HANDWRITING
see Graphology; Penmanship; Writing

Hagin, Rosa. Write Right-or Left. (gr. k-3). 1981. Set Of 6. 18.50 (ISBN 0-8027-9140-9); 4.20 ea. (ISBN 0-8027-9120-4). Walker & Co.

HANG GLIDING

Mrazek, James. Hang Gliding. rev. ed. (Illus.). 160p. 1981. 17.95 (ISBN 0-312-35912-8). St Martin.

HANKS, NANCY, 1784-1818
see Lincoln, Nancy (Hanks), 1784-1818

HANNIBAL, 247-183 B.C.

Bath, Tony. Hannibal's Campaigns. (Illus.). 160p. 1981. 31.95 (ISBN 0-85059-492-8). Aztex.

HANUKKAH (FEAST OF LIGHTS)

Greene, Jacqueline. A Classroom Hanukah. (Illus., Orig.). (gr. k-4). 1980. pap. 3.00x (ISBN 0-938836-01-3). Pascal Pubs.

HANUKKAH (FEAST OF LIGHTS)-JUVENILE LITERATURE

Stuhlman, Daniel D. My Own Hanukah Story. (Illus., Orig.). (ps-1). 1980. pap. 3.95 (ISBN 0-934402-07-8); decorations 1.00 (ISBN 0-934402-08-6). BYLS Pr.

HAPPINESS
see also Joy and Sorrow; Mental Health

Da Free, John. What to Remember to Be Happy. (Illus.). pap. 4.95 (ISBN 0-913922-36-6). Dawn Horse Pr.

Edwards, John F. How to Quit the Rat Race - Successfully! LC 80-82676. (Illus.). 159p. (Orig.). 1981. 9.95 (ISBN 0-937590-00-2, Dist. by Caroline Hse.); pap. 5.95 (ISBN 0-937590-01-0). New Era.

Greenwald, Harold. The Happy Person. LC 80-6154. 192p. 1981. 10.95 (ISBN 0-8128-2783-X). Stein & Day.

Gutridge, D. Foster, II. Your Secret Power: Creating Harmony with Others, Vol. 4. 96p. (Orig.). 1981. pap. 5.95 (ISBN 0-938014-04-8, 301D). Freedom Unltd.

Houston, John. The Pursuit of Happiness. 1981. pap. text ed. 7.95x (ISBN 0-673-15421-1). Scott F.

Johnson, Spencer. Precious Present. LC 80-46478. (Illus.). 80p. 1981. 7.95 (ISBN 0-89087-286-4). Celestial Arts.

Keyes, Ken, Jr. Prescriptions for Happiness. LC 80-84855. (Illus.). 132p. 1981. pap. 2.00 (ISBN 0-915972-02-6); pocketbook edition 0.95 (ISBN 0-915972-03-4). Living Love.

Maybaum, Ignaz. Happiness Outside the State. 128p. 1980. 25.00 (ISBN 0-85362-183-7). Routledge & Kegan.

Zodhiates, Spiros. Formula for Happiness. 256p. (Orig.). 1980. pap. 8.75 (ISBN 0-89957-046-1). AMG Pubs.

HAPSBURG, HOUSE OF
see Habsburg, House Of

HAPTICS
see Touch

HARBORS
see also Docks; Free Ports and Zones; Pilots and Pilotage

Bruun, Per. Port Engineering. 3rd ed. 750p. 1981. text ed. 50.00 (ISBN 0-87201-739-7). Gulf Pub.

Cornick, H. F. Dock & Harbour Engineering: The Design of Docks, Vol. 1. 338p. 80.00x (ISBN 0-85264-037-4, Pub. by Griffin England). State Mutual Bk.

Dock & Harbour Engineering: The Design of Harbours, Vol. 2. 352p. 1969. 80.00x (ISBN 0-85264-041-2, Pub. by Griffin England). State Mutual Bk.

Facilities in Ports for the Reception of Oil Residues: Results of an Enquiry Made in 1972. 145p. 1973. 16.50 (IMCO). Unipub.

Facilities in Ports for the Reception of Oil Residues: Results of an Enquiry Made in 1972, Supplement 1976. 27p. 1976. 7.00 (I MCO). Unipub.

Guidelines on the Provision of Adequate Reception Facilities in Ports: Oily Wastes, Pt. 1. 16p. 1976. 7.00 (IMCO) Unipub.

Guidelines on the Provision of Adequate Reception Facilities in Ports: Sewage, Pt. 3. 27p. 1978. 7.00 (IMCO). Unipub.

Guidelines on the Provision of Adequate Reception Facilities in Ports: Garbage, Pt. 4. 27p. 1978. 7.00 (IMCO). Unipub.

HARBORS-CHINA

Tai, En-Sai. Treaty Ports in China: A Study in Diplomacy. (Studies in Chinese History & Civilization). 202p. 1977. 17.50 (ISBN 0-89093-083-X). U Pubns Amer.

HARD OF HEARING CHILDREN
see Children, Deaf

HARDING, WARREN GAMALIEL, PRES. U. S., 1865-1923

Mee, Charles L., Jr. The Ohio Gang: The World of Warren G. Harding. Katz, Herbert M., ed. 250p. 1981. 12.95 (ISBN 0-87131-340-5). M Evans.

HARDWARE
see also Knives; Tools

Schiffer, Herbert F. Early Pennsylvania Hardware. (Illus.). 64p. 1966. pap. 3.75 (ISBN 0-916838-42-0). Schiffer.

HARDY, EMMA LAVINIA (GIFFORD) 1840-1912

Hardy, Godfrey H. The Collected Papers of G. H. Hardy: Theory of Series, Vol. 6. London Mathematical Society Committee, ed. 1974. 49.00 (ISBN 0-19-853340-3). Oxford U Pr.

HARDY, THOMAS, 1840-1928

Gardner, W. H. Some Thoughts on the Mayor of Casterbridge. 52p. 1980. Repr. of 1930 ed. lib. bdg. 6.00 (ISBN 0-8492-4959-7). R West.

Orel, Harold, ed. Thomas Hardy's Personal Writings. 295p. 1981. text ed. 10.00x (ISBN 0-333-05493-8, Pub. by Macmillan, England). Humanities.

Page, Norman. Thomas Hardy. 212p. (Orig.). 1981. pap. price not set (ISBN 0-7100-8615-6). Routledge & Kegan.

Purdy, Richard Little & Millgate, Michael, eds. The Collected Letters of Thomas Hardy: Vol. 2 1893-1901. (Illus.). 320p. 1980. 49.95 (ISBN 0-19-812619-0). Oxford U Pr.

Summer, Rosemary. Thomas Hardy, Psychologist Novelist. 19.95 (ISBN 0-312-80161-0). St Martin.

HARELIP

Melnick, Michael & Bixler, David, eds. Etiology of Cleft Lip & Cleft Palate. (Progress in Clinical & Biological Research: Vol. 46). 566p. 1980. 40.00 (ISBN 0-8451-0046-7). A R Liss.

HARLEM, NEW YORK (CITY)

Lewis, David L. When Harlem Was in Vogue. LC 80-2704. (Illus.). 400p. 1981. 17.95 (ISBN 0-394-49572-1). Knopf.

HARMONY, KEYBOARD

Pelz, William. Basic Keyboard Skills: An Introduction to Accompaniment Improvisation, Transposition & Modulation, with an Appendix on Sight Reading. LC 80-22820. vii, 173p. 1981. Repr. of 1963 ed. PLB 23.50x (ISBN 0-313-22882-5, PEBK). Greenwood.

HARNESS MAKING AND TRADE

Fitz-Gerald, William. The Harness Maker's Illustrated Manual. 15.00. Green Hill.

HARNESS RACING

Ainsley, Tom. Ainsley's New Complete Guide to Harness Racing. rev. ed. 1981. Repr. of 1971 ed. 17.95 (ISBN 0-671-25257-7). S&S.

Evans, Donald P. & Pikelny, Philip S. Rambling Willie: The Horse That God Loved. LC 80-26884. (Illus.). 240p. 1981. 8.95 (ISBN 0-498-02542-X). A S Barnes.

HAROLD, KING OF ENGLAND, 1022-1066

Birch, William D., ed. Vita Haroldi: The Romance of the Life of Harold, King of England. Birch, William D., tr. LC 80-2232. 1981. Repr. of 1885 ed. 32.50 (ISBN 0-404-18753-6). AMS Pr.

HAROLD, PRESTON

Babcock, Winifred. Jung, Harold, Hesse: Contributions of C. G. Jung, Preston Harold & Hermann Hesse Toward a Spiritual Psychology. 275p. 1981. 12.95 (ISBN 0-686-68720-5). World Authors.

HARPER'S FERRY, WEST VIRGINIA

Conway, Martin. Harpers Ferry: Time Remembered. Mehrkam, Deborah, ed. 160p. 1980. 13.95 (ISBN 0-938634-00-3). Carabelle.

HASIDISM

Green, Arthur. Tormented Master: A Life of Rabbi Nahman of Bratslav. LC 80-14668. 408p. 1981. pap. 11.95 (ISBN 0-8052-0663-9). Schocken.

HASTINGS, BATTLE OF, 1066

Korner, Sten. The Battle of Hastings, England & Europe, 1035-1066. LC 80-2221. 1981. Repr. of 1964 ed. 38.00 (ISBN 0-404-18765-X). AMS Pr.

HATHA YOGA
see Yoga, Hatha

HATS
see also Millinery

Couldridge, Alan & Dowell, Celia. The Hat Book. 128p. 1981. 16.95 (ISBN 0-13-384222-3, Spec); pap. 8.95 (ISBN 0-13-384214-2). P-H.

Tomlinson, Jill. Lady Bee's Bonnets. 1971. pap. 2.95 (ISBN 0-571-11133-5, Pub. by Faber &Faber). Merrimack Bk Serv.

HAUNTED HOUSES
see Ghosts

HAVASUPAI INDIANS
see Indians of North America-Southwest, New

HAWAII

Twain, Mark, pseud. Mark Twain in Hawaii. Jones, William R., ed. (Illus.). 96p. 1981. pap. 4.95 (ISBN 0-89646-070-3). Outbooks.

HAWAII-BIOGRAPHY

De Varigny, Charles. Fourteen Years in the Sandwich Islands. Korn, Alfons L., tr. LC 80-26141. (Illus.). 320p. (Fr.). 1981. 24.95 (ISBN 0-8248-0709-X). U Pr of Hawaii.

HAWAII-DESCRIPTION AND TRAVEL

Davis, Lynn. Na Pa'i Ki'i: The Photographers in the Hawaiian Islands, 1900-1945. LC 80-70100. (Special Publication Ser.: No. 69). (Illus.). 48p. Date not set. pap. 5.50 (ISBN 0-910240-29-9). Bishop Mus.

Martin, Henry B. The Polynesian Journal of Henry Byam Martin. Dodd, Edward, ed. (Illus.). 200p. 1981. write for info. (ISBN 0-87577-060-6). Peabody Mus Salem.

Smith, Robert. Hiking Hawaii. Winnett, Thomas, ed. LC 79-93247. (Wilderness Press Trail Guide Ser.). (Illus.). 112p. (Orig.). 1981. write for info. (ISBN 0-89997-000-1). Wilderness Pr.

HAWAII-DESCRIPTION AND TRAVEL-GUIDEBOOKS

Bone, Robert W. Maverick Guide to Hawaii: 1981 Edition. LC 80-25076. (Illus.). 437p. (Orig.). 1981. pap. 8.95 (ISBN 0-88289-277-0). Pelican.

Johnson, Rubellite K. & Mahelona, John. Na Inoa Hoku: A Catalogue of Hawaiian & Pacific Star Names. LC 75-23889. 1975. pap. 4.95 (ISBN 0-914916-09-2). Topgallant.

HAWAII-HISTORY

Martin, Henry B. The Polynesian Journal of Henry Byam Martin. Dodd, Edward, ed. (Illus.). 200p. 1981. write for info. (ISBN 0-87577-060-6). Peabody Mus Salem.

HAWAII-HISTORY-BIBLIOGRAPHY

Swindler, W. F. Chronology & Documentary Handbook of the State of Hawaii. 1978. 8.50 (ISBN 0-379-16136-2). Oceana.

HAWAII-JUVENILE LITERATURE

Rublowsky, John. Born in Fire: A Geological History of Hawaii. LC 79-2001. (Illus.). 96p. (gr. 5 up). 1981. 9.95 (ISBN 0-06-025088-7, HarpJ); PLB 9.89g (ISBN 0-06-025089-5). Har-Row.

HAWAII-RELIGION

Nau, Erika S. Self-Awareness Through Huna- Hawaii's Ancient Wisdom. Grunwald, Stefan, ed. (Orig.). 1981. pap. write for info. (ISBN 0-89855-099-2, Unilaw). Donning Co.

HAWAIIAN POETRY-TRANSLATIONS INTO ENGLISH

Roes, Carol. Mahalo Nui Translations. 1980. pap. 3.00 (ISBN 0-930932-20-X). M. Loke.

HAWAIIAN SONGS
see Songs, Hawaiian

HAWKING
see Falconry

HAWTHORNE, NATHANIEL, 1804-1864

Levin, Harry. The Power of Blackness: Hawthorne, Poe, Melville. LC 80-83221. xxii, 263p. 1980. pap. 6.95x (ISBN 0-8214-0581-0). Ohio U Pr.

Woodberry, George E. Nathaniel Hawthorne, 30 vols. LC 80-23480. (American Men & Women of Letters Ser.). 304p. 1981. pap. 4.95 (ISBN 0-87754-154-X). Chelsea Hse.

HAY-FEVER

Frompovich, Catherine J. Attacking Hay Fever & Winning. Koppenhaver, April M., ed. (Orig.). 1981. pap. 2.00. C J Frompovich.

Knight, Allan. Asthma, Hay Fever & Other Allergies. LC 80-22839. (Positive Health Guides Ser.). (Illus.). 112p. 1981. 9.95 (ISBN 0-668-04675-9); pap. 5.95 (ISBN 0-668-04681-3). Arco.

HAYDN, JOSEPH, 1732-1809

Landon, H. C. Chronicle & Works, 5 vols. Incl. Haydn: The Early Years, 1732-1765. Vol. 1 Haydn: the Early Years, 1732-1765. 640p. 1980. 75.00x (ISBN 0-253-37001-9); Vol. 2. Haydn at Eszterhaza; 1766-1790. 820p. 1978. 60.00x (ISBN 0-253-37002-7); Vol. 3. Haydn in England, 1791-1795. 640p. 1976. 55.00x (ISBN 0-253-37003-5); Vol. 4. Haydnn: the Years of "The Creation" 1796-1800. 640p. 1976. 55.00x (ISBN 0-253-37004-3); Vol. 5. Haydn: the Late Years, 1801-1809. 496p. 1977. 55.00x (ISBN 0-253-37005-1). Set. 300.00x. Ind U Pr.

Larsen, Jens P., et al, eds. Haydn Studies. 1981. 29.95 (ISBN 0-393-01454-1). Norton.

HAYWARD, SUSAN

Linet, Beverly. Susan Hayward: Portrait of a Survivor. LC 80-66003. 1980. 12.95 (ISBN 0-686-68614-4). Atheneum.

HAZARDOUS SUBSTANCES

A Guide for Control & Cleanup of Hazardous Materials. 1975. 0.75. AASHTO.

Institute of Civil Engineers, UK. Transport of Hazardous Materials. 160p. 1980. 39.00x (ISBN 0-7277-0058-8, Pub. by Telford England). State Mutual Bk.

Pelnar, Premysl U. Health Effects of Asbestos & of Some Other Minerals & Fibres As Reflected in the World Literature: A Compendium of References, 1906-1979. 1981. 25.00 set (ISBN 0-930376-25-0). Pathotox Pubs.

Scottish Schools Science Equipment Research Centre, ed. Hazardous Chemicals: A Manual for Schools & Colleges. 1979. pap. 12.95xlab. manual (ISBN 0-05-003204-6). Longman.

Watson, Thomas, et al. R C R A-Hazardous Waste Handbook. 850p. 1980. 65.00 (ISBN 0-86587-086-1). Gov Insts.

Weiss, G., ed. Hazardous Chemicals Data Book. LC 80-21634. (Environmental Health Review: No. 4). 1188p. 1981. 64.00 (ISBN 0-8155-0831-X). Noyes.

HAZLITT, WILLIAM, 1778-1830

Murray, Grace A. Personalities of the Eighteenth Century: (Samuel Foote, Christopher Smart, William Hazlitt) 230p. 1980. Repr. of 1927 ed. lib. bdg. 25.00 (ISBN 0-8495-3772-X). Arden Lib.

Ready, Robert. Hazlitt at Table. LC 79-22811. 128p. 1981. 13.50 (ISBN 0-8386-2414-6). Fairleigh Dickinson.

HEAD-GEAR
see Costume; Hats; Millinery

HEAD-HUNTERS

Curtis, Edward S. In the Land of Head-Hunters. (Illus.). Date not set. 7.95 (ISBN 0-913668-48-6); pap. 3.95 (ISBN 0-913668-47-8). Ten Speed Pr.

HEADACHE

Critchley, Macdonald, et al, eds. International Headache Congress, 1980. 1980. write for info. Raven.

Hanington, Edda. The Headache Book. LC 80-52621. (Illus.). 226p. 1980. 12.50 (ISBN 0-87762-292-2). Technomic.

Kudrow, Lee. Cluster Headache: Mechanisms & Management. (Illus.). 200p. 1981. 29.50 (ISBN 0-19-261169-0). Oxford U Pr.

--Cluster Headache: Mechanisms & Management. (Illus.). 200p. 1980. text ed. 29.50x (ISBN 0-19-261169-0). Oxford U Pr.

HEADDRESS
see Hairdressing

HEADINGS, SUBJECT
see Subject Headings

HEALING (IN RELIGION, FOLK-LORE, ETC.)
see also Faith-Cure

Ripley, John W. & Richmind, Robert W., eds. A Century of Healing Arts-Eighteen Fifty to Nineteen Fifty. (Illus.). 176p. 1980. pap. 5.95. Shawnee County Hist.

HEALING, MENTAL
see Mental Healing

HEALING, PSYCHIC
see Mental Healing

HEALTH
Here are entered works on optimal physical, mental, and social well-being, as well as how to achieve and preserve it. Works on personal body care and cleanliness are entered under Hygiene. Works on muscular efficiency and physical endurance are entered under Physical fitness.
see also Diet; Environmental Health; Executives-Health Programs; Exercise; Health Education; Hygiene; Longevity; Mental Health; Nutrition; Physical Fitness; Public Health; Relaxation; Sleep; Temperance
also subdivision Care and Hygiene under parts of the body, or under age groups dependent on the assistance of others, e.g. Eye-Care and Hygiene; Infants-Care and Hygiene; and subdivision Health and Hygiene under classes of persons or ethnic groups, e.g. Students-Health and Hygiene; Afro-Americans-Health and Hygiene

Allen, Robert & Linde, Shirley. Lifegain: The Exciting New Program That Will Change Your Health - & Your Life. (Appleton Consumerhealth Guides). 288p. 1981. 12.95 (ISBN 0-8385-5671-X). ACC.

Avon Products. Looking Good, Feeling Beautiful. 14.95 (ISBN 0-671-25224-0). S&S.

Barton, John & Barton, Margaret. How to Take Care of Yourselves Naturally. 4th ed. LC 77-80393. Orig. Title: Flow Lines to Health. (Illus.). 158p. 1980. pap. 8.00 (ISBN 0-937216-04-6). J & M Barton.

Beebe, Brooke, et al. Nutrition & Good Health. LC 78-731300. (Illus.). 1978. pap. text ed. 99.00 (ISBN 0-89290-099-7, A576-SATC). Soc for Visual.

Beenstock, Michael. Health, Migration & Development. 192p. 1980. text ed. 27.75x (ISBN 0-566-00369-4, Pub. by Gower Pub Co England). Renouf.

Bennett, Hal Z. The Doctor Within. (Illus.). 160p. 1981. 11.95 (ISBN 0-517-54178-5); pap. 5.95 (ISBN 0-517-54299-4). Potter.

Bieliauskas, Linas A. The Influence of Indiviual Differences in Health & Illness. (Behavioral Sciences for Health Care Professionals). 128p. (Orig.). 1981. lib. bdg. 15.00x (ISBN 0-86531-004-1); pap. text ed. 6.00x (ISBN 0-86531-005-X). Westview.

Breyfogle, Newell D. The Common Sense Medical Guide & Outdoor Reference. McGraw, Robert P., ed. (Illus.). 416p. 1981. text ed. 11.95 (ISBN 0-07-007672-3, HP); pap. text ed. 6.95 (ISBN 0-07-007673-1). McGraw.

Bricklin, Mark & Claessens, Charon. Natural Healing Cookbook: Over Four Hundred Fifty Delicious Ways to Get Better & Stay Healthy. (Illus.). 416p. 1981. 16.95 (ISBN 0-87857-338-0). Rodale Pr Inc.

Bronwen, Meredith. Natural Health & Beauty. (Illus.). 304p. 1981. 19.95 (ISBN 0-03-057976-7). HR&W.

Caplan, Arthur L., et al. Concepts of Health & Disease: Interdisciplinary Perspectives. 608p. 1981. pap. text ed. write for info. (ISBN 0-201-00973-0). A-W.

Carroll, Walter J., ed. Hospital-Health Care Training Media Profiles, Vol. 8. 1981. 85.00 (ISBN 0-88367-206-5). Olympic Media.

Clark, Carolyn C. Enhancing Wellness. 1981. text ed. 26.95 (ISBN 0-8261-2950-1); pap. text ed. 16.95 (ISBN 0-8261-2951-X). Springer Pub.

Corder, Brice W., et al. Health: Current Perspectives. 3rd ed. 403p. 1981. pap. text ed. write for info. (ISBN 0-697-07388-2); instructor's manual avail. (ISBN 0-697-07389-0). Wm C Brown.

Cox, Anthony & Groves, Philip. Design for Health. (Newnes-Butterworth Design Ser.). 1981. text ed. price not set (ISBN 0-408-00389-8, Newnes-Butterworth). Butterworth.

Cox, Stafford G., et al. Wellness R. S. V. P. Your Personal Invitation. 1980. pap. 3.95 (ISBN 0-8053-2304-X, 800100). Benjamin Cummings.

Dalet, Roger. How to Safeguard Your Health & Beauty with the Simple Pressure of a Finger. LC 80-5497. (Illus.). 160p. 1981. 10.95 (ISBN 0-8128-2742-2). Stein & Day.

Day, Stacey B., et al. Biopsychosocial Health. 225p. 1980. pap. 10.50 (ISBN 0-934314-02-0). Intl Found Biosocial Dev.

Derbyshore, Caroline. The New Woman's Guide to Health & Medicine. (Appleton Consumer Health Guides). (Illus.). 316p. 1980. 12.95 (ISBN 0-8385-6759-2); pap. 5.95 (ISBN 0-8385-6758-4). ACC.

Dinaburg & Akel. Nutrition Survival Kit. (Orig.). pap. 1.75 (ISBN 0-515-04654-X). Jove Pubns.

Dupont, Herbert & Dupont, Margaret. Travel with Health. (Appleton Consumer Health Guides). 195p. 1981. 13.95 (ISBN 0-8385-9009-8); pap. 7.95 (ISBN 0-8385-9008-X). ACC.

Easter, Jade. The Healing Handbook. (Illus.). 128p. (Orig.). 1981. pap. 6.95 (ISBN 0-913300-15-2). Unity Pr.

Ehrlich, David & Wolf, George. The Bowel Book: A Practical Guide to Good Health. LC 80-54140. 192p. 1981. 12.95x (ISBN 0-8052-3763-1); pap. 5.95 (ISBN 0-8052-0673-6). Schocken.

Eliopoulos, Nicholas C. Thine Health. Phistiklakis, Nicholas G., ed. (Orig.). 1980. pap. text ed. 12.00 (ISBN 0-9605396-2-X). Phystiklakis & Eliopoulos.

Essentials of Life & Health. 3rd ed. 485p. 1981. pap. text ed. 12.95 (ISBN 0-394-32570-2). Random.

Fodor, John T. & Dalis, Gus T. Health Instruction: Theory & Application. 3rd ed. LC 80-24484. (Illus.). 150p. 1981. text ed. write for info. (ISBN 0-8121-0776-4). Lea & Febiger.

Forbes, Alec. Try Being Healthy. 184p. 1976. pap. 5.50x (ISBN 0-8464-1057-5). Beekman Pubs.

Gilbert, Mitchell. An Owner's Manual for the Human Being. 1980. pap. 4.95 (ISBN 0-686-69316-7). Weiser.

Gimbel, Theo. Healing Through Colour. 108p. 1980. 23.95x (ISBN 0-8464-1017-6). Beekman Pubs.

Gish, Oscar. Doctor Migration & World Health. 151p. 1971. pap. text ed. 6.90x (ISBN 0-7135-1611-9, Pub. by Bedford England). Renouf.

Haas, Elson. Staying Healthy with the Seasons. LC 80-69469. (Illus.). 192p. (Orig.). 1981. pap. 9.95 (ISBN 0-89087-306-2). Celestial Arts.

Hall, Dorothy. The Herb Tea Book. LC 80-84436. (Pivot Original Health Bk.). (Illus.). 120p. 1981. pap. 2.25 (ISBN 0-87983-248-7). Keats.

Heller, Alfred L. Your Body, His Temple. 192p. 1981. pap. 4.95 (ISBN 0-8407-5769-7). Nelson.

Hepner, J. O. Case Studies in Health Administration, 2 vols. Incl. Vol. 1. Health Planning for Emergency Multi-Hospital Systems. LC 77-17008. (Illus.). 1978. pap. text ed. 15.95 (ISBN 0-8016-2156-9); Vol. 2. Hospital Administrator-Physician Relationships. LC 80-16073. 1980. pap. text ed. 21.95 (ISBN 0-8016-2158-5). Mosby.

Huber, Helen, et al. Homemaker-Home Health Aide. LC 78-66616. 1980. pap. 8.80 (ISBN 0-8273-1704-2); instr's. guide 1.50 (ISBN 0-8273-1705-0). Delmar.

Jensen, William E. & Winters, Donna. Keep Healthy Keep Active. 1979. pap. 1.95 (ISBN 0-910286-73-6). Boxwood.

Lawson-Wood, D. & Lawson-Wood, J. Glowing Health Through Diet & Posture. 62p. 1973. pap. 2.50x (ISBN 0-686-68110-X). Beekman Pubs.

Leichtman, Robert R. & Japikse, Carl. The Way to Health. (The Art of Living). 90p. Date not set. pap. 3.00 (ISBN 0-89804-037-X). Ariel Pr.

Leonard, George. The Silent Pulse. 208p. 1981. pap. 2.95 (ISBN 0-553-14368-9). Bantam.

Leonard, Jon N., et al. Live Longer Now. 236p. 1981. pap. 2.50 (ISBN 0-441-48516-2). Charter Bks.

Lindegren, Carl C. The Theory & Practice of Natural Healing. LC 80-50132. 1981. 7.95 (ISBN 0-533-04595-9). Vantage.

London, Mel. Easy Going: A Guide to Good Health & Good Spirits on Your Journey Away from Home. (Illus.). 320p. (Orig.). 1981. 12.95 (ISBN 0-87857-331-3); pap. 9.95 (ISBN 0-87857-345-3). Rodale Pr Inc.

McMillen, S. I. None of These Diseases. (Orig.). pap. 1.50 (ISBN 0-515-04604-3). Jove Pubns.

Malasanos, Lois. Health Assessment. 2nd ed. (Illus.). 753p. 1981. text ed. 26.95 (ISBN 0-8016-3073-8). Mosby.

Mellor, Constance. How to Be Healthy, Wealthy & Wise. 112p. 1976. pap. 6.00x (ISBN 0-8464-1023-0). Beekman Pubs.

Ott, John N. The Dynamics of Color & Light: How They Affect Human Health & Behavior. (Illus.). 256p. 1981. 10.00 (ISBN 0-8159-5314-3). Devin.

Parkhill, Joe. Health, Beauty & Happiness. spiral 5.95 (ISBN 0-88427-014-9). Green Hill.

Pearson, Durk. Life Extension: Adding Years to Your Life & Life to Your Years, a Practical Approach. (Orig.). 1981. 12.95 (ISBN 0-446-51229-X). Warner Bks.

A Pocketguide to Health & Health Problems in School Physical Activities. 1981. pap. 3.00 (ISBN 0-917160-13-4). Am Sch Health.

Powell, Eric F. Health from the Kitchen. 64p. 1969. pap. 2.50x (ISBN 0-8464-1018-4). Beekman Pubs.

Reid, George. Sound of the Trumpet. (Horizon Ser.). 224p. 1981. price not set (ISBN 0-8127-0328-6); pap. price not set (ISBN 0-8127-0321-9). Southern Pub.

Rhodes, Helen. Doctor, What Can I Do? (Horizon Ser.). 128p. 1981. pap. price not set (ISBN 0-8127-0327-8). Southern Pub.

Rudman, Jack. Health Restoration: Area I. (ACT Proficiency Examination Program Ser.: PEP-51). pap. 9.95 (ISBN 0-8373-5901-5). Natl Learning.

--Health Restoration: Area II. (ACT Proficiency Examination Program Ser.: PEP-52). (Cloth bdg. avail. on request). pap. 9.95 (ISBN 0-8373-5902-3). Natl Learning.

Rudy, Ellen & Gray, Ruth. Handbook of Health Assessment. (Illus.). 184p. 1981. pap. text ed. 9.95 (ISBN 0-87619-843-4). R J Brady.

Rutter, M., et al, eds. Education, Health & Behavior. 390p. 1981. Repr. of 1970 ed. text ed. price not set (ISBN 0-89874-268-4). Krieger.

Ryan, Regina S. & Travis, John W. Wellness Workbook: A Guide to Attaining High Level Wellness. 15.95 (ISBN 0-89815-033-7); pap. 9.95 (ISBN 0-89815-032-9). Ten Speed Pr.

Salk, Lee. Dear Dr. Salk: Answers to Your Questions About Your Family. 1980. pap. 2.50 (ISBN 0-446-91486-X). Warner Bks.

Salloway, J. C. Introduction to Social Epidemiology. (Behavioral Science for Health Care Professionals Ser.). 128p. (Orig.). 1981. lib. bdg. 15.00x (ISBN 0-86531-014-9); pap. text ed. 6.00x (ISBN 0-86531-015-7). Westview.

Saxon, Edgar J. A Sense of Wonder. 64p. 1980. pap. 3.25x (ISBN 0-8464-1048-6). Beekman Pubs.

Schuller, Robert H. Discover Health & Happiness. (Orig.). 1978. pap. 1.25 (ISBN 0-89081-143-1). Harvest Hse.

Speight, Phyllis. Before Calling the Doctor. 1976. pap. 3.00x (ISBN 0-8464-0994-1). Beekman Pubs.

Spontaneous Images: Relationship Between Psyche & Soma. (Illus.). 123p. (Orig., Eng.-Fr. & Ger.). 1980. pap. text ed. 16.00 (ISBN 0-89192-311-X). Interbk Inc.

Sprug, Joseph. Index to Nutrition & Health. (Useful Reference Ser. of Library Books: Vol. 119). 1981. write for info. (ISBN 0-87305-125-4). Faxon.

Stewart, Andrew. Live to Ninety & Stay Young. 184p. 1968. 5.25x (ISBN 0-8464-1029-X). Beekman Pubs.

Tansley, David V. Dimensions of Radionics. 224p. 1977. 18.95x (ISBN 0-8464-1005-2). Beekman Pubs.

--Radionics & the Subtle Anatomy of Man. 1980. 5.50 (ISBN 0-8464-1044-3). Beekman Pubs.

--Radionics Interface with the Ether Fields. 112p. 1979. pap. text ed. 10.95x (ISBN 0-8464-1045-1). Beekman Pubs.

Tomlinson, H. The Divination of Disease. 1980. 9.50x (ISBN 0-8464-1006-0). Beekman Pubs.

Von Furstenberg, Ira. Young at Any Age. (Illus.). 208p. 1981. 12.95 (ISBN 0-02-622100-4). Macmillan.

Watson, John. The Massage & Bodywork Resource Guide. (Illus.). 360p. (Orig.). 1981. pap. 6.95 (ISBN 0-913300-13-6). Unity Pr.

HEALTH–AUTHORSHIP

see Medical Writing

HEALTH–BIBLIOGRAPHY

Rees, Alan M. & Young, Blanche A. Consumer Health Information Source Book. (Consumer Health Information Publications Program Ser.). 480p. 1981. 32.50 (ISBN 0-8352-1336-6). Bowker.

HEALTH–DICTIONARIES

Consumer Health Guides Display, 30 bks. 1980. prepack 178.50 (ISBN 0-8385-0199-0). ACC.

HEALTH–JUVENILE LITERATURE

Anderson, James L. & Cohen, Martin. The West Point Fitness & Diet Book. 1978. pap. 3.95 (ISBN 0-380-01894-2, 37342). Avon.

Good Thing Inc. & Burstein, John. Slim Goodbody: Your Health & Feelings. (gr. 1-3). 1978. pap. text ed. 125.00 (ISBN 0-89290-098-9, CM-43). Soc for Visual.

HEALTH–STUDY AND TEACHING

see Health Education

HEALTH, COMMUNITY

see Public Health

HEALTH, INDUSTRIAL

see Industrial Health

HEALTH, MENTAL

see Mental Health

HEALTH, PUBLIC

see Public Health

HEALTH, PUBLIC–ADMINISTRATION

see Public Health Administration

HEALTH, RURAL

Tyrrell, D. A., et al. More Technologies for Rural Health. (Proceedings of the Royal Society, Series B.: Vol. 209). 186p. 1980. text ed. 30.00x (ISBN 0-85403-148-0, Pub. by Royal Soc London). Scholium Intl.

HEALTH ADMINISTRATION

see Public Health Administration

HEALTH CARE

see Medical Care

HEALTH CARE ADMINISTRATION

see Public Health Administration

HEALTH CARE DELIVERY ORGANIZATIONS, COMPREHENSIVE

see Health Maintenance Organizations

HEALTH COMMUNICATION

see Communication in Medicine

HEALTH ECONOMICS

see Medical Economics

HEALTH EDUCATION

see also School Health

Cowley, J. Health Education in Schools. 1981. text ed. 21.00 (ISBN 0-06-318178-9, Pub. by Har-Row England Ltd); pap. text ed. 11.90 (ISBN 0-06-318179-7). Har-Row.

Curriculum Guide for Health Education: Nutrition. 112p. 1975. 12.50. Natl Cath Educ.

Health Instruction II: Guidelines for Planning Health Education Programs K-12. 1981. 4.00 (ISBN 0-917160-14-2). Am Sch Health.

Litwack, Lawrence, et al. Health Counseling. 290p. 1980. 13.50 (ISBN 0-8385-3665-4). ACC.

Meeks, Linda B., et al. Teaching Health Science in Middle & Secondary Schools. 400p. write for info (ISBN 0-697-07392-0). Wm C Brown.

Wigmore, Ann. New Naturama: Living Textbook. 400p. pap. text ed. 12.95. Hippocrates.

HEALTH FACILITIES

see also Halfway Houses

Broyles, Robert. Financial & Managerial Accounting in Health Care Facilities. 600p. Date not set. text ed. price not set (ISBN 0-89443-340-7). Aspen Systems.

Wasserman, Paul, ed. Health Organizations of the United States & Canada: A Directory of Voluntary Associations, Professional Societies & Other Groups Concerned with Health & Related Fields. 5th ed. 500p. 1981. 36.00 (ISBN 0-8103-0466-X). Gale.

HEALTH FOOD

see Food, Natural

HEALTH INSURANCE

see Insurance, Health

HEALTH MAINTENANCE ORGANIZATIONS

Goldsmith, Seth. Health Care Management: Perspectives for Today. 300p. 1981. text ed. price not set (ISBN 0-89443-336-9). Aspen Systems.

Salus: Low Cost Rural Health Care & Health Manpower Training, Vol. 6. 157p. 1980. pap. 10.00 (ISBN 0-88936-249-1, IDRC153, IDRC). Unipub.

HEALTH OF CHILDREN

see Children–Care and Hygiene

HEALTH OF INFANTS

see Infants–Care and Hygiene

HEALTH OF WOMEN

see Women–Health and Hygiene

HEALTH OF WORKERS

see Industrial Health

HEALTH OFFICERS

Salus: Low Cost Rural Health Care & Health Manpower Training, Vol. 6. 157p. 1980. pap. 10.00 (ISBN 0-88936-249-1, IDRC153, IDRC). Unipub.

HEALTH PROFESSIONS

see Medical Personnel

HEALTH RECORDS

see Medical Records

HEALTH SCIENCES ADMINISTRATION

see Public Health Administration

HEALTH SERVICES

see Public Health

HEALTH THOUGHTS

see Mental Healing

HEALTHS, DRINKING OF

see Drinking Customs

HEARING

see also Audiometry; Deafness; Ear

Brown, R. Don & Daigneault, Ernest A. Pharmacology of Hearing: Experimental & Clinical Bases. 360p. 1980. 45.00 (ISBN 0-471-05074-1, Pub. by Wiley-Interscience). Wiley.

Gelfand. Hearing Science. Date not set. price not set (ISBN 0-8247-1189-0). Dekker.

Gelfano. Hearing. 392p. Date not set. 29.75 (ISBN 0-8247-1189-0). Dekker.

International Symposium on Hearing, Fifth, Noordwijkerhout, the Netherlands, April 8-12, 1980. Psychophysical Physiological & Behavioral Studies in Hearing: Proceedings. Van den Brink, G. & Bilsen, F. A., eds. 480p. 1980. 42.50x (ISBN 90-286-0780-3). Sijthoff & Noordhoff.

Ptacek, Paul H., et al. Index to Speech, Language & Hearing Journal Titles, 1954-78. LC 79-20058. 328p. 1979. text ed. 25.00 (ISBN 0-933014-54-6). College-Hill.

Schubert, E. D. Hearing: Its Function & Dysfunction. (Disorders of Human Communications: Vol. 1). (Illus.). 200p. 1980. 29.50 (ISBN 0-387-81579-1). Springer-Verlag.

Zemlin, W. R. Speech & Hearing Science. 2nd ed. (Illus.). 704p. 1981. text ed. 23.95 (ISBN 0-13-827378-2). P-H.

HEARING–JUVENILE LITERATURE

Rosner, Jerome. Auditory Analysis Skillsbook. (gr. k-3). 1981. 17.50 (ISBN 0-8027-9127-1). Walker & Co.

HEARING–TESTING

see Audiometry

HEARING AIDS

Levitt, H., et al, eds. Sensory Aids for the Hearing Impaired. LC 76-28875. 1980. 46.95 (ISBN 0-87942-133-9). Inst Electrical.

Loavenbruck, Angela M. & Madell, Jane, eds. Hearing Aid Dispensing for Audiologists: A Guide for Clinical Service. 1980. 16.50 (ISBN 0-8089-1323-9). Grune.

HEARING DISORDERS

see also Deafness

Barrager, Diane & Perkins, Rodney. The Hearing Book. Orig. Title: Come Again, Please... (Illus.). 128p. 1980. pap. 8.95 (ISBN 0-89106-016-2, 7274). Consulting Psychol.

Gerber, Sanford E. & Mencher, George T. Auditory Dysfunction. (Illus.). 256p. 1980. text ed. 19.95 (ISBN 0-933014-60-0). College-Hill.

Mencher, George T. & Gerber, Sanford. Early Management of Hearing Loss. 1980. write for info. (ISBN 0-8089-1346-8). Grune.

Paparella, Michael M., et al. Sensorineural Hearing Loss, Vertigo & Tinnitus: International Symposium. 232p. 1981. write for info. (6750-8). Williams & Wilkins.

Yeates, Sybil. Development of Hearing. (Studies in Developmental Pediatrics Ser.: Vol. 2). 240p. 1981. text ed. 17.50 (ISBN 0-88416-378-4). PSG Pub.

HEARING DISORDERS IN CHILDREN

see also Children, Deaf

Keith, Robert W., ed. Central Auditory & Language Disorders in Children. (Illus.). 264p. 1981. text ed. 29.00 (ISBN 0-933014-61-9). College-Hill.

HEARING-IMPAIRED CHILDREN

see Children, Deaf

HEARST, PATRICIA, 1954-

Chaney, Lindsay & Ciepi, Michael. The Hearst: Family & Empire, the Later Years. 1981. 14.95 (ISBN 0-671-24765-4). S&S.

HEARST, WILLIAM RANDOLPH, 1863-1951

Chaney & Cieply. The Hearsts. 1981. 16.95 (ISBN 0-671-24765-4). S&S.

Chaney, Lindsay & Ciepi, Michael. The Hearst: Family & Empire, the Later Years. 1981. 14.95 (ISBN 0-671-24765-4). S&S.

Littlefield, Roy E., III. William Randolph Hearst: His Role in American Progressivism. LC 80-5729. 405p. 1980. lib. bdg. 22.75 (ISBN 0-8191-1320-4); pap. text ed. 13.75 (ISBN 0-8191-1321-2). U Pr of Amer.

HEART

see also Blood–Circulation; Cardiography

Fisher, Arthur. The Healthy Heart. Time-Life Bks. Eds., ed. (Library of Health). (Illus.). 176p. 1981. 11.95 (ISBN 0-8094-3750-3). Time-Life.

Heyden, Siegfried. Keep Your Heart in Shape. 96p. (Orig.). 1981. pap. 1.95 (ISBN 0-8326-2249-4, 7446). Delair.

Hurst, J. Willis. The Heart. (Update Ser.: No. 5). (Illus.). 352p. 1981. text ed. 30.00 (ISBN 0-07-031495-0, HP). McGraw.

HEART–ABNORMITIES

Anderson & Becker. Pathology of Congenital Heart Disease. 1981. text ed. price not set. Butterworth.

HEART–DISEASES

see also Cardiacs; Cardiology

Bonchek, Lawrence I. & Brooks, Harold L. Medical & Surgical Management of Heart Disease: A Concise Guide for Non-Cardiologists. 1981. text ed. price not set. Little.

Dalen, James E. & Alpert, Joseph E. Valvular Heart Disease. 1981. text ed. price not set. Little.

Eglash, Albert, ed. Psychogenesis of Coronary Heart Disease: A Syllabus for Medical Researchers. (Bibliographies in Psychosomatic Medicine Ser.: No. 1, Myocardial Infraction). (Illus.). 110p. (Orig.). 1980. lib. bdg. 20.00 (ISBN 0-935320-20-2). Quest Pr.

Goldberger, Emanuel. A Textbook of Clinical Cardiology. (Illus.). 934p. 1981. text ed. 35.00 (ISBN 0-8016-1864-9). Mosby.

Grandis, Sue L. Instrumentation for Coronary Care. (Techniques of Measurement in Medicine: No. 5). (Illus.). 150p. Date not set. price not set (ISBN 0-521-23548-0); pap. price not set (ISBN 0-521-28024-9). Cambridge U Pr.

Halhuber, M. J. & Siegrist, J., eds. Myocardial Infarction & Psychosocial Risks. (Illus.). 152p. 1981. pap. 22.50 (ISBN 0-387-10386-4). Springer-Verlag.

Mo, Sam. Why Heart Attack? 1981. 6.95 (ISBN 0-8062-1546-1). Carlton.

Roberts, William C., et al. Cardiology: 81. (Illus.). 400p. 1981. text ed. 35.00 (ISBN 0-914316-22-2). Yorke Med.

Thomson, James C. Your Heart. Thomson, C. Leslie, ed. 80p. 1974. pap. 3.50x (ISBN 0-8464-1058-3). Beekman Pubs.

Wheatley, David, ed. Stress & the Heart. 2nd ed. 430p. 1981. 39.50 (ISBN 0-89004-520-8). Raven.

HEART–DISEASES–DIAGNOSIS

see also Cardiography; Electrocardiography

Bloomfield, Dennis A. & Simon, Hansjorg. Cardio Active Drugs: Pharmachlogical Basis for Practice. 1981. price not set. Urban & S.

Gruberg, Edward & Raymond, Stephen. Beyond Cholesterol. 208p. 1981. 9.95 (ISBN 0-312-07779-3). St Martin.

Haft, Jacob I., ed. Differential Diagnosis of Chest Pain & Other Cardiac Symptoms. LC 80-68061. (Advances in the Management of Clinical Heart Disease Monograph: Vol. 4). (Illus.). 230p. 1980. 26.50 (ISBN 0-87993-150-7). Futura Pub.

New York Heart Association. Nomenclature & Criteria for Diagnosis of Diseases of the Heart & Great Vessels. 8th ed. LC 78-71219. 349p. 1979. text ed. 14.95 (ISBN 0-316-60536-0); pap. text ed. 11.95 (ISBN 0-316-60537-9). Little.

Tardos,., et al, eds. Pharmacological Control of Heart & Circulation: Proceedings of the Third Congress of the Hungarian Pharmacological Society, Budapest, 1979. LC 80-41281. (Advances in Pharmacological Research & Practice Ser.: Vol. I). 445p. 1981. 84.00 (ISBN 0-08-026386-0). Pergamon.

HEART–DISEASES–PERSONAL NARRATIVES

Singh, John R. A Coronary Experience. 2nd ed. LC 80-82823. (Illus.). 128p. (Orig.). 1980. text ed. 9.95 (ISBN 0-9604672-0-3); pap. text ed. 4.95 (ISBN 0-9604672-1-1). Mid Am Pr.

HEART-DISEASES-PREVENTION

Kavanagh, Terence. The Healthy Heart Program. 328p. 1981. pap. 6.95 (ISBN 0-442-29768-8). Van Nos Reinhold.

Murray, Frank. Program Your Heart for Health. 368p. (Orig.). 1977. pap. 2.95 (ISBN 0-915962-20-9). Larchmont Bks.

HEART-INFARCTION

Greenbaum, Dennis & Gianelli, Stanley, Jr. Acute Cardiovascular Failure. (Clinics in Critical Care Medicine Ser.). (Illus.). 224p. 1981. lib. bdg. 22.50 (ISBN 0-443-08111-5). Churchill.

HEART-SURGERY

Aspinall, Mary Jo. Aortic Arch Surgery. (Surgical Aspects of Cardiovasculardisease: Nursing Intervention Series). 100p. 1980. pap. 6.95 (ISBN 0-686-69603-4). ACC.

Harlan, B. J., et al. Manual of Cardiac Surgery, Vol. I. (Comprehensive Manuals of Surgical Specialities Ser.). (Illus.). 204p. 1980. 140.00 (ISBN 0-387-90393-3). Springer-Verlag.

HEART ATTACK

see Coronary Heart Disease; Heart-Diseases; Heart-Infarction

HEART FUNCTION TESTS

see also Function Tests (Medicine)

Mullins, L. J. Ion Transport in Heart. 125p. 1981. 15.00 (ISBN 0-89004-645-X). Raven.

HEART PATIENTS

see Cardiacs

HEAT

see also Combustion; Entropy; Gases-Liquefaction; High Temperatures; Thermodynamics; Thermography (Copying Process)

Chapple, M. A Level Physics: Mechanics & Heat, Vol. 1. 2nd ed. (Illus.). 336p. (Orig.). 1979. pap. text ed. 10.95x (ISBN 0-7121-0154-3, Pub. by Macdonald & Evans England). Intl Ideas.

United Nations Economic Commission for Europe. Combined Production of Electric Power & Heat: Proceedings of a Seminar Organized by the Committee on Electric Power of the United Nations Economic Commission for Europe, Hamburg, FR Germany, 6-9 November 1978. LC 80-755. (Illus.). 150p. 32.00 (ISBN 0-08-025677-5). Pergamon.

HEAT-PHYSIOLOGICAL EFFECT

Mazumdar, N. C. Indices of Heat Stress. 132p. 1980. 4.95x (ISBN 0-89955-318-4, Pub. by Interprint India). Intl Schol Bk Serv.

HEAT-TRANSMISSION

see also Heat Exchangers

Bankoff, S. George, et al, eds. Heat Transfer in Nuclear Reactor Safety: Proceedings of the International Centre for Heat & Mass Transfer. (International Centre for Heat & Mass Transfer). (Illus.). 1981. text ed. 95.00 (ISBN 0-89116-223-2). Hemisphere Pub.

Collier, J. G. Convective Boiling & Condensation. 2nd ed. (Illus.). 460p. 1981. text ed. 59.50 (ISBN 0-07-011798-5). McGraw.

Eckert, E. R. Heat & Mass Transfer. 2nd ed. LC 81-359. 344p. 1981. Repr. lib. bdg. price not set (ISBN 0-89874-332-X). Krieger.

French, Henri, ed. Heat Transfer & Fluid Flow in Nuclear Systems. 300p. 1981. 30.01 (ISBN 0-08-027181-2). Pergamon.

Holman, J. P. Heat Transfer. 5th ed. (Illus.). 672p. 1981. text ed. 27.95x (ISBN 0-07-029618-9, C); solutions manual 8.95 (ISBN 0-07-029619-7). McGraw.

Irvine, Thomas F., Jr. & Hartnett, James P., eds. Advances in Heat Transfer, 14 vols. Incl. Vol. 1. 1964. 51.00 (ISBN 0-12-020001-5); Vol. 2. 1965. 51.00 (ISBN 0-12-020002-3); Vol. 3. 1966. 51.00 (ISBN 0-12-020003-1); Vol. 4. 1967. 51.00 (ISBN 0-12-020004-X); Vol. 5. 1968. 55.25 (ISBN 0-12-020005-8); Vol. 6. 1970. 55.25 (ISBN 0-12-020006-6); Vol. 7. 1970. 51.00 (ISBN 0-12-020007-4); Vol. 8. 1972. 51.00 (ISBN 0-12-020008-2); Vol. 9. 1973. 51.00 (ISBN 0-12-020009-0); Vol. 10. 1974. 51.00 (ISBN 0-12-020010-4); Vol. 11. 1975. 59.00 (ISBN 0-12-020011-2); lib. bdg. 75.50 (ISBN 0-12-020074-0); microfiche 42.25 (ISBN 0-12-020075-9); Vol. 12. 1976. 49.00 (ISBN 0-12-020012-0); lib. bdg. 63.00 (ISBN 0-12-020076-7); microfiche 55.50 (ISBN 0-12-020077-5); Vol. 13. 1977. 49.00 (ISBN 0-12-020013-9); lib. bdg. 63.00 (ISBN 0-12-020078-3); microfiche 35.50 (ISBN 0-12-020079-1); Vol. 14. 1979. 43.00 (ISBN 0-12-020014-7); lib. bdg. 55.00 (ISBN 0-12-020080-5); microfiche 31.00 (ISBN 0-12-020081-3). Acad Pr.

Jones, Owen C., ed. Nuclear Reactor Safety Heat Transfer: Proceedings of the International Centre for Heat & Mass Transfer. (International Centre for Heat & Mass Trans Transfer Ser.). (Illus.). 1981. text ed. 99.00 (ISBN 0-89116-224-0). Hemisphere Pub.

Lewis, R. W. & Morgan, K. Numerical Methods in Heat Transfer. Zienkiewicz, O. C., ed. (Numerical Methods in Engineering Ser.). 1981. price not set (ISBN 0-471-27803-3, Pub. by Wiley-Interscience). Wiley.

HEAT BARRIER

see High Temperatures

HEAT EXCHANGERS

Chisholm, D., ed. Developments in Heat Exchanger Technology - One. (Illus.). x, 288p. 1980. 65.00x (ISBN 0-85334-913-4). Burgess-Intl Ideas.

Kakac, Sadik, et al, eds. Heat Exchangers - Thermohydraulic Fundamentals & Design, 2 vols. (Illus.). 1000p. 1981. Set. text ed. 95.00 (ISBN 0-89116-225-9). Hemisphere Pub.

HEAT INSULATING MATERIALS

see Insulation (Heat)

HEAT PUMPS

Von Cube, Hans L. & Staimle, Fritz. Heat Pump Technology. Goodall, E. G., tr. 1981. text ed. price not set (ISBN 0-408-00497-5, Newnes-Butterworth). Butterworth.

HEAT SENSITIVE COPYING PROCESSES

see Thermography (Copying Process)

HEAT STRESS (BIOLOGY)

see Heat-Physiological Effect

HEAT TRANSFER

see Heat-Transmission

HEAT TRANSFER IMAGES

see Thermography (Copying Process)

HEATHENISM

see Paganism

HEATING

see also Boilers; Fuel; Furnaces; Insulation (Heat); Solar Heating; Stoves; Ventilation

Bronthon. Heating Service Design. 1981. text ed. 53.95 (ISBN 0-408-00380-4). Butterworth.

Gay, Larry. Central Heating with Wood & Coal. (Illus.). 128p. 1980. write for info. (ISBN 0-8289-0419-7); pap. write for info. (ISBN 0-8289-0420-0). Greene.

Havrella, Raymond. Heating, Ventilating & Air Conditioning Fundamentals. LC 80-17155. (Contemporary Construction Ser.). (Illus.). 288p. (gr. 10-12). 1981. text ed. 16.95x (ISBN 0-07-027281-6, G); wkbk. avail. (ISBN 0-07-027283-2). McGraw.

Industrial Heating Equipment Assn. The Directory of Industrial Heat Processing & Combustion Equipment: U. S. Manufacturers, 1981-1982. 3rd biennial ed. 224p. (Orig.). 1981. pap. write for info. (ISBN 0-931634-05-9). Info Clearing House.

Orchard, W. R. & Sherratt, A. F. Combined Heat & Power Whole City Heating Planning: Tomorrows Energy Economy. LC 80-41444. 234p. 1980. 59.95 (ISBN 0-470-27088-8). Halsted Pr.

Schneider, Raymond K. HVAC Control Systems. 400p. 1981. text ed. 19.95 (ISBN 0-471-05180-2). Wiley.

HEAVEN

see also Angels; Future Life

Carothers, Merlin, tr. El Cielo Baja Al Infierno. (Spanish Bks.). (Span.). 1978. 1.75 (ISBN 0-8297-0766-2). Life Pubs Intl.

Mullen, E. Theodore, Jr. The Assembly of the Gods: The Divine Council in Canaanite & Hebrew Literature. LC 80-10128. (Harvard Semitic Museum Monographs: No. 24). 10.50x (ISBN 0-89130-380-4, 04 00 24). Scholars Pr CA.

Thompson, Fred, Jr. What the Bible Says About Heaven & Hell. (What the Bible Says Ser.). 400p. 1981. 13.50 (ISBN 0-89900-081-9). College Pr Pub.

HEBREW ART

see Art, Jewish

HEBREW LANGUAGE

Fish, Sidney M. Reshith Binah: A Hebrew Primer. 1976. pap. 2.50x (ISBN 0-8197-0035-5). Bloch.

Haden, Peter. Elementary Knowledge: A Story of the Creation of the Hebrew Alaphabet. (Illus.). 68p. 1981. 22.50 (ISBN 0-87663-357-2). Universe.

Kugel, James L. The Idea of Biblical Poetry: Parallelism & Its History. LC 80-25227. 320p. 1981. 27.50x (ISBN 0-300-02474-6). Yale U Pr.

HEBREW LANGUAGE-CONVERSATION AND PHRASE BOOKS

Benjamin, Ben A. Let's Talk Hebrew. 1961. 4.00 (ISBN 0-914080-01-6). Shulsinger Sales.

Stern, A. Z. & Reif, Joseph A., eds. Useful Expressions in Hebrew. (Useful Expressions Ser.). 64p. (Orig.). 1980. pap. 1.50 (ISBN 0-86628-009-X); cassette 4.50 (ISBN 0-86628-014-6). Ridgefield Pub.

HEBREW LANGUAGE-GRAMMAR

Davidson, A. B. An Introductory Hebrew Grammar, with Progressive Exercises in Reading & Writing. 26th ed. Mauchline, John, ed. 336p. 1966. text ed. 14.50x (ISBN 0-567-01005-8). Attic Pr.

Mauchline, John. A Key to the Exercises in the Introductory Hebrew Grammar. 146p. Repr. of 1967 ed. 10.95x (ISBN 0-567-01006-6). Attic Pr.

Simon, Ethelyn, et al. The First Hebrew Primer for Adults. (Orig.). 1981. pap. text ed. 12.95 (ISBN 0-939144-01-8). EKS Pub Co.

HEBREW LANGUAGE-READERS

Kohlenberger, John R., ed. The NIV Triglot Old Testament. 1334p. 1981. 49.95 (ISBN 0-310-43820-9). Zondervan.

HEBREW LANGUAGE-SYNTAX

Davidson, A. B. Hebrew Syntax. 3rd ed. 248p. pap. text ed. 12.00x (ISBN 0-567-21007-3). Attic Pr.

HEBREW LAW

see Jewish Law

HEBREW LITERATURE-HISTORY AND CRITICISM

Burke, David G., ed. The Poetry of Baruch: A Reconstruction & Analysis of the Original Hebrew Text of Baruch 3: 9-5: 9. LC 80-10271. (Society of Biblical Literature, Septuagint & Cognate Studies: No. 10). 22.50x (ISBN 0-89130-381-2, 06 04 10); pap. 18.00x (ISBN 0-89130-382-0). Scholars Pr CA.

Mullen, E. Theodore, Jr. The Assembly of the Gods: The Divine Council in Canaanite & Hebrew Literature. LC 80-10128. (Harvard Semitic Museum Monographs: No. 24). 10.50x (ISBN 0-89130-380-4, 04 00 24). Scholars Pr CA.

Pardee, Dennis. Handbook of Ancient Hebrew Letters. LC 79-22372. (Society of Biblical Literature, Sources for Biblical Study: 15). Date not set. 15.00x (ISBN 0-89130-359-6, 060315); pap. 10.50x (ISBN 0-89130-360-X). Scholars Pr CA.

HEBREW POETRY

Carmi, T. The Penguin Book of Hebrew Verse. 1981. 25.00 (ISBN 0-670-36507-6). Viking Pr.

HEBREW POETRY-HISTORY AND CRITICISM

Kugel, James L. The Idea of Biblical Poetry: Parallelism & Its History. LC 80-25227. 320p. 1981. 27.50x (ISBN 0-300-02474-6). Yale U Pr.

HEBRIDES-SOCIAL LIFE AND CUSTOMS

Brown, Jean. A Song to Sing & a Tale to Tell. 174p. 1980. 14.95 (ISBN 0-906191-43-2, Pub. by Thule Pr England). Intl Schol Bk Serv.

HEDGES

see also Fences; Shrubs

Howland, Joseph E. How to Select & Care for Shrubs & Hedges. Ortho Books Editorial Staff, ed. LC 80-66346. (Illus.). 96p. (Orig.). 1981. pap. 4.95 (Ortho Bks). Chevron Chem.

HEGEL, GEORG WILHELM FRIEDRICH, 1770-1831

Elder, Crawford. Appropriating Hegel. Brennan, Andrew & Lyons, William, eds. (Scots Philosophical Monographs: Vol. 3). 116p. 1980. 12.00 (ISBN 0-08-025729-1). Pergamon.

Laffleur, Mark H. Anti-Hegelianism & the Theory of the Infinite. (Illus.). 131p. 1981. 31.45 (ISBN 0-89266-281-6). Am Classical Coll Pr.

Lamb, David. Hegel: From Foundation to System. (Martinus Nijjoff Philosophy Library: No. 1). 252p. 1980. lib. bdg. 34.50 (ISBN 90-247-2359-0, Martinus Niijoff Pubs). Kluwer Boston.

Steinhauer, Kurt, ed. Hegel: Bibliography. 894p. 1980. 129.50 (ISBN 3-598-03184-X). Bowker.

Toews, John E. Hegelianism: The Path Toward Dialectic Humanism, 1805 to 1841. LC 80-16370. 512p. Date not set. 39.50 (ISBN 0-521-23048-9). Cambridge U Pr.

Verne, Donald P., ed. Hegel's Social & Political Thought: The Philosophy of Objective Spirit. Proceedings of the 1976 Hegel Society of America Conference. 250p. 1980. text ed. 17.50x (ISBN 0-391-00543-X). Humanities.

HEIDEGGER, MARTIN, 1889-1976

Bindeman, Steven L. Heidegger & Wittgenstein: The Poetics of Silence. LC 80-6066. 159p. 1980. lib. bdg. 15.75 (ISBN 0-8191-1350-6); pap. text ed. 7.50 (ISBN 0-8191-1351-4). U Pr of Amer.

Sternberger, Adolf. Der Verstandene Tod: Eine Untersuchung Zu Martin Heideggers Existenzialontologie. Natanson, Maurice, ed. LC 78-66753. (Phenomenology Ser.: Vol. 14). 165p. 1979. lib. bdg. 17.00 (ISBN 0-8240-9556-1). Garland Pub.

HEIDELBERG CATECHISM

Heidelberg Catechism with Scripture Texts. (Orig.). 1981. write for info. (ISBN 0-933140-21-5). Bd of Pubns CRC.

HELICOPTERS

Aviation Mechanincs Journal. Nineteen Eighty Aircraft & Helicopter Digest. (Illus.). 204p. 1980. text ed. 13.25 (ISBN 0-89100-184-0, E*A-184-0). Aviation Maintenance.

Brown, E. M. The Helicopter in Civil Operations. 208p. 1981. 17.95 (ISBN 0-442-24528-9). Van Nos Reinhold.

Taylor, John W., ed. Jane's Pocket Book of Helicopters. (Illus.). 260p. 1981. pap. 8.95 (ISBN 0-686-69548-8, Collier). Macmillan.

HELICOPTERS-PILOTING

Federal Aviation Administration. Basic Helicopter Handbook. 3rd ed. (Pilot Training Ser.). (Illus.). 111p. 1978. pap. 3.75 (ISBN 0-89100-162-X, E*A-A*C61-13B). Aviation Maintenance.

HELICOPTERS, USED

see Used Aircraft

HELL

Carothers, Merlin, tr. El Cielo Baja Al Infierno. (Spanish Bks.). (Span.). 1978. 1.75 (ISBN 0-8297-0766-2). Life Pubs Intl.

Thompson, Fred, Jr. What the Bible Says About Heaven & Hell. (What the Bible Says Ser.). 400p. 1981. 13.50 (ISBN 0-89900-081-9). College Pr Pub.

HELLENISM

Makrakis, Apostolos. Hellenism & the Unfinished Revolution. Orthodox Christian Educational Society, ed. Stephanou, Archimandrite E., tr. from Hellenic. 191p. (Orig.). 1968. pap. 3.00x (ISBN 0-938366-26-2). Orthodox Chr.

Toynbee, Arnold J. Hellenism: The History of a Civilization. LC 80-27772. xii, 272p. 1981. Repr. of 1959 ed. lib. bdg. 25.00x (ISBN 0-313-22742-X, TOHM). Greenwood.

HELMETS

Curtis, Howard M. Two Thousand Five Hundred Years of European Helmets. LC 76-20423. 346p. 1978. 19.75 (ISBN 0-917714-06-7). Beinfeld Pub.

HELVETIUS, CLAUDE ADRIEN, 1715-1771

Smith, D. W., et al, eds. Correspondance generale d'helvetius, Vol. I: 1737-1756. (Romance Ser.). 384p. 1981. 35.00x (ISBN 0-8020-5517-6). U of Toronto Pr.

HEMATOLOGY

see also Blood

Baum, S. J., et al, eds. Experimental Hematology Today: 1980. (Illus.). xii, 290p. 1980. 84.50 (ISBN 3-8055-1705-X). S Karger.

--Experimental Hematology Today 1981. (Illus.). xiv, 240p. 1981. 84.50 (ISBN 3-8055-2255-X). S Karger.

Bowring, C. S. Radionuclide Tracer Techniques in Hematology. 1981. text ed. price not set (ISBN 0-407-00183-2). Butterworth.

Cline, Martin, ed. Leukocyte Function. (Methods in Hematology). (Illus.). 224p. 1981. lib. bdg. 25.00 (ISBN 0-686-28872-6). Churchill.

Figueroa, William G. Hematology: UCLA Postgraduate Medicine for the Internist. (Illus.). 1981. price not set (ISBN 0-89289-377-X). HM.

Ross, D. W., et al, eds. Automation in Hematology: What to Measure & Why. (Illus.). 730p. 1981. pap. 46.00 (ISBN 0-387-10225-6). Springer-Verlag.

Spivak, Jerry L. Fundamentals of Clinical Hematology. (Illus.). 405p. 1980. 25.00 (ISBN 0-06-142465-X, Harper Medical). Har-Row.

HEMATOPHILA

see Hemophilia

HEMATOPOIETIC SYSTEM

see also Marrow

Lieberman, Philip H. & Good, Robert A., eds. Diseases of Hematopoietic System. (Anatomic Pathology Slide Seminar Ser.). (Illus.). 137p. 1981. pap. text ed. 18.00 (ISBN 0-89189-085-8); slides 85.00 (ISBN 0-686-69528-3). Am Soc Clinical.

HEMIC CELLS

see Blood Cells

HEMINGWAY, ERNEST, 1899-1961

Baker, Carlos, ed. Ernest Hemingway: Selected Letters. 960p. 1981. 25.00 (ISBN 0-684-16765-4, ScribT). Scribner.

Laurence, Frank M. Hemingway & the Movies. LC 79-1437. 336p. 1980. 20.00 (ISBN 0-87805-115-5). U Pr of Miss.

HEMODIALYSIS

Levy, Norman B., ed. Psychonephrology One: Psychological Factors in Hemodialysis & Transplantation. 280p. 1981. 25.00 (ISBN 0-306-40586-5, Plenum Pr). Plenum Pub.

HEMOGLOBIN

Fairbanks, Virgil. Hemoglobinopathies & Thalassemias. 1980. 32.50. Thieme Stratton.

HEMOPHILIA

Hilgartner. Hemophilia in the Child. Date not set. price not set. Masson Pub.

HEMORRHAGE, UTERINE

Robertson, W. B. The Endometrium. (Postgraduate Pathology Ser.). 1981. text ed. 52.95 (ISBN 0-407-00171-9). Butterworth.

HEMORRHAGIC DIATHESIS

see Hemophilia

HEMOSTATICS

Pia, H. W., et al, eds. Spontaneous Intracerebral Haematomas: Advances in Diagnosis & Therapy. (Illus.). 500p. 1981. 116.90 (ISBN 0-387-10146-2). Springer Verlag.

HENRY 7TH, KING OF ENGLAND, 1457-1509

Chrimes, S. B., ed. Henry VII. (English Monarch Ser.). 1981. pap. 8.95 (ISBN 0-520-04414-2, CAL 506). U of Cal Pr.

HENRY, JOSEPH, 1797-1878

Reingold, Nathan, ed. The Papers of Joseph Henry: The Princeton Years, January 1838-1840, Vol. 4. LC 72-2005. (The Papers of Joseph Henry Ser.). (Illus.). 432p. 1981. text ed. 30.00x (ISBN 0-87474-792-9). Smithsonian.

HENRY FRANCIS DUPONT WINTERTHUR MUSEUM

Yuletide at Winterthur. (Illus.). 1980. pap. 3.50 (ISBN 0-912724-09-9). Winterthur.

HENS

see Poultry

HEORTOLOGY

see Church Calendar; Fasts and Feasts

HEPATITIS ASSOCIATED ANTIGEN

Melnick, J. L. & Maupas, P., eds. Hepatitis B Virus & Primary Liver Cancer. (Progress in Medical Virology Ser.: Vol. 27). (Illus.). 250p. 1981. 90.00 (ISBN 3-8055-1784-X). S Karger.

HEPATITIS B ANTIGEN

see Hepatitis Associated Antigen

HERALDRY

see also Emblems; Genealogy; Seals (Numismatics)

Grosswirth, Marvin. The Heraldry Book: A Guide to Designing Your Own Coat of Arms. LC 78-22321. (Illus.). 240p. 1981. 11.95 (ISBN 0-385-14157-2). Doubleday.

Guillim, John. A Display of Heraldrie. LC 79-84115. (English Experience Ser.: No. 934). 308p. 1979. Repr. of 1611 ed. lib. bdg. 46.00 (ISBN 90-221-0934-8). Walter J Johnson.

Johnson, David P. Heraldry: The Armiger's News, 1979-1980. LC 80-70043. (Illus.). 55p. 1980. pap. 9.95 (ISBN 0-9605668-0-5). Am Coll Heraldry.

HERB GARDENING

Bonar, Ann & MacCarthy, Daphne. How to Grow & Use Herbs. (Orig.). 1980. pap. 6.95x (ISBN 0-8464-1024-9). Beekman Pubs.

Lathrop, Norma J. Herbs. (Orig.). 1981. pap. 7.95 (ISBN 0-89586-077-5). H P Bks.
Simmons, Adelma. Herb Gardens Delight. 1979. pap. 4.95 (ISBN 0-8015-3403-8, Hawthorn). Dutton.
Verey, Rosemary. The Herb Growing Book. (Illus.). 48p. (gr. 5 up). 1981. 9.95 (ISBN 0-316-89974-7). Little.

HERBAGE
see Grasses

HERBALS
see Botany, Medical; Herbs; Materia Medica, Vegetable; Medicine, Medieval

HERBERT, GEORGE, 1593-1633
Asals, A. Heather. Equivocal Predication: George Herbert's Way to God. 152p. 1981. 25.00x (ISBN 0-8020-5536-2). U of Toronto Pr.
Edgecombe, Rodney. Sweetness Readie Penn'd Imagery, Syntax & Metric in the Poetry of George Herbert. (Elizabethan Studies). 1980. pap. text ed. 25.00x (ISBN 0-391-02185-0). Humanities.
Slights, Camille W. The Casuistical Tradition in Shakespeare, Donne, Herbert, & Milton. LC 80-8576. 352p. 1981. 26.50x (ISBN 0-691-06463-6). Princeton U Pr.

HERBICIDES
Ashton, Floyd M. & Crafts, Alden S. Mode of Action of Herbicides. 2nd ed. 464p. 1981. 42.50 (ISBN 0-471-04847-X, Pub. by Wiley-Interscience). Wiley.
Newton, Michael. Chemicals in the Forest. 160p. 1980. pap. 10.95 (ISBN 0-917304-25-X, Pub. by Timber Pr). Intl Schol Bk Serv.
Page, B. G. & Thomson, W. T. The Nineteen Eighty-One Insecticide, Herbicide, Fungicide Quick Guide. 140p. 1981. pap. 11.00 (ISBN 0-913702-11-0). Thomson Pub Ca.
Que Hee, Shane S. & Sutherland, Ronald G. The Phenoxyalkanoic Herbicides: Volume I-Chemistry, Analysis & Environmental Pollution. 272p. 1981. 62.95 (ISBN 0-8493-5851-5). CRC Pr.
Thomson, W. T. Agricultural Chemicals, Book 2: Herbicides. rev. ed. 260p. 1981. pap. 13.50 (ISBN 0-913702-12-9). Thomson Pub Ca.

HERBS
see also Botany, Medical; Cookery (Herbs and Spices); Materia Medica, Vegetable; Medicine, Medieval
Beckett, Sarah. Herbs for Feminine Ailments. LC 80-53449. (Everybody's Home Herbal Ser.). (Illus.). 63p. (Orig.). 1981. pap. 1.95 (ISBN 0-394-74836-0). Shambhala Pubn.
--Herbs to Soothe Your Nerves. LC 80-53448. (Everybody's Home Herbal Ser.). (Illus.). 64p. (Orig.). 1981. pap. 1.95 (ISBN 0-394-74835-2). Shambhala Pubn.
Brother Aloysius. Comfort to the Sick: A Recipe Book of Medicinal Herbs. 416p. 1981. pap. 8.95 (ISBN 0-87728-525-X). Weiser.
Brownlow, Margaret. Herbs & the Fragrant Garden. 1980. 30.00x (ISBN 0-232-51396-1, Pub. by Darton-Longman-Todd England). State Mutual Bk.
Ceres. Herbs & Fruit for Dieting. LC 80-53452. (Everybodys Home Herbal Ser.). 64p. 1981. pap. 1.95 (ISBN 0-394-74837-9). Shambhala Pubns.
--Herbs for First-Aid & Minor Ailments. LC 80-53453. (Everybodys Home Herbal Ser.). (Illus.). 64p. 1981. pap. 1.95 (ISBN 0-394-74925-1). Shambhala Pubns.
--Herbs for Indigestion. LC 80-53451. (Everybody's Home Herbal Ser.). (Illus.). 63p. (Orig.). 1981. pap. 1.95 (ISBN 0-394-74833-6). Shambhala Pubn.
Challem, Jack & Challem, Renate. What Herbs Are All About. LC 80-82913. 150p. (Orig.). 1980. pap. 2.95 (ISBN 0-87983-242-8). Keats.
Day, Ivan. Perfumery with Herbs. 1980. 30.00x (ISBN 0-232-51414-3, Pub. by Darton-Longman-Todd England). State Mutual Bk.
De Waal, M. Medicinal Herbs in the Bible. Meijlink, Jane, ed. 96p. 1981. pap. 4.95 (ISBN 0-87728-527-6). Weiser.
Farwell, Edith F. A Book of Herbs. 1980. 5.95 (ISBN 0-935720-01-4). Green Hill.
Frompovich, Catherine J. & Hays, Joanne M. Everyday Herbs for Cooking & Healing. 1980. 100 frame filmstrips, cassette, text 15.00 (ISBN 0-935322-11-6). C J Frompovich.
Gosling, Nalda. Herbs for Colds & Flu. LC 80-53450. (Everybodys Home Herbal Ser.). (Illus.). 64p. (Orig.). 1981. pap. 1.95 (ISBN 0-394-74834-4). Shambhala Pubn.
Grounds, Roger. Growing Vegetables & Herbs. (Orig.). 1980. pap. 6.95x (ISBN 0-8464-1016-8). Beekman Pubs.
Hall, Dorothy. The Herb Tea Book. LC 80-84436. (Pivot Original Health Bk.). (Illus.). 120p. 1981. pap. 2.25 (ISBN 0-87983-248-7). Keats.
Hamilton, Geoff. Herbs: How to Grow Them. 1980. pap. 4.50 (ISBN 0-7153-7897-X). David & Charles.
Harris, Ben C., ed. The Compleat Herbal. LC 77-185615. 243p. (Orig.). 1972. pap. 1.75 (ISBN 0-915962-15-2). Larchmont Bks.
Heffern, Richard. The Herb Buyers Guide. (Orig.). pap. 1.50 (ISBN 0-515-04635-3). Jove Pubns.
Jones, George. In a Herb Garden. (Illus.). 98p. 1977. 12.95 (ISBN 0-85475-049-5). Dufour.
Meyer, Joseph E. The Herbalist. (Illus.). 304p. 1981. 10.95 (ISBN 0-8069-3902-8); lib. bdg. 9.89 (ISBN 0-8069-3903-6). Sterling.
Muenscher, Walter C. & Rice, Myron A. Garden Spice & Wild Pot-Herbs: An American Herbal. LC 78-56899. (Illus.). 218p. 1978. pap. 7.95 (ISBN 0-8014-9174-6). Comstock.
Neblekopf, Ethan. The Herbal Connection. 1980. 12.95 (ISBN 0-89557-048-3). Bi World Indus.
Rowland, Lorna. Growing Herbs. (Practical Gardening Ser.). (Illus.). 112p. (Orig.). 1979. pap. 10.50 (ISBN 0-589-01244-4, Pub. by Reed Bks Australia). C E Tuttle.
Stark, Raymond. Indian Herbs. Campbell, Margaret, ed. (Illus.). 50p. 1981. pap. 4.95 (ISBN 0-88839-077-7). Hancock Hse.
Weiner, Michael. The People's Herbal. (Orig.). 1981. pap. 8.95 (ISBN 0-446-97574-5). Warner Bks.

HERBS-THERAPEUTIC USE
see Botany, Medical; Materia Medica, Vegetable; Medicine, Medieval

HEREDITARY DISEASES
see Medical Genetics

HEREDITARY METABOLIC DISORDERS
see Metabolism, Inborn Errors of

HEREDITY
see also Biometry; Chromosomes; Evolution; Hybridization; Genetics; Natural Selection; Population Genetics; Prenatal Influences
Galton, Francis. Natural Inheritance. Bd. with Darwinism. (Contributions to the History of Psychology Ser., Vol. IV, Pt. D: Comparative Psychology). 1978. Repr. of 1889 ed. 30.00 (ISBN 0-89093-173-9). U Pubns Amer.
Glass, Robert E. Gene Function: E. coli & Its Heritable Elements. 450p. 1980. 60.00x (Pub. by Croom Helm England). State Mutual Bk.
M. D. Anderson Symposia on Fundamental Cancer Research, 33rd. Genes, Chromosomes, & Neoplasia. Arrighi, Frances E., et al, eds. 550p. 1981. 49.50 (ISBN 0-89004-532-1). Raven.

HEREDITY, HUMAN
see also Human Genetics
Sen Gupta, N. N. Heredity in Mental Traits. 207p. 1980. Repr. of 1941 ed. lib. bdg. 50.00 (ISBN 0-89984-409-X). Century Bookbindery.

HEREDITY OF DISEASE
see Medical Genetics

HERESIES AND HERETICS
For general descriptive and historical works. Works on heresy in the abstract are entered under the heading Heresy.
Meyer, Samuel. The Deacon & the Jewess: Adventures in Heresy. LC 80-84734. 1981. 10.00 (ISBN 0-8022-2379-6). Philos Lib.

HERMAPHRODITISM
Lepori, N. G. Sex Differentiation, Hermaphroditism & Intersexuality in Vertebrates Including Man. (Illus.). 372p. 1980. text ed. 49.50x (ISBN 88-212-0747-1, Pub. by Piccin Italy). J K Burgess.
McDougall, Richard, tr. Herculine Barbin: Being the Recently Discovered Memoirs of a Nineteenth-Century Hermaphrodite. Foucault, Michel, intro. by. 1980. 8.95 (ISBN 0-394-50821-1); pap. 4.95 (ISBN 0-394-73862-4). Pantheon.

HERMENEUTICS
Bryant, Darrol & Foster, Durwood, eds. Hermeneutics & Unification Theology. LC 80-66201. (Conference Ser.: No. 5). (Illus., Orig.). 1980. pap. 7.95 (ISBN 0-932894-05-4). Unif Theol Seminary.
Lund, A. & Luce, A., trs. Hermeneutica. (Portuguese Bks.). 1979. 1.20 (ISBN 0-8297-0825-1). Life Pubs Intl.
O'Hara, Daniel T. Tragic Knowledge: Yeat's Autobiography & Hermeneutics. LC 80-26825. 224p. 1981. 20.00x (ISBN 0-231-05204-9). Columbia U Pr.
Thompson, J. B. Critical Hermeneutics: A Study in the Thought of Paul Ricoeur & Jurgen Habermas. LC 80-41935. 238p. Date not set. price not set (ISBN 0-521-23932-X). Cambridge U Pr.
Winquist, Charles E. Practical Hermeneutics. LC 79-22848. (Scholars Press General Ser.: No. 1). 12.00x (ISBN 0-89130-363-4); pap. 7.50x (ISBN 0-89130-364-2). Scholars Pr CA.

HERMENEUTICS, BIBLICAL
see Bible-Hermeneutics

HERMETIC ART AND PHILOSOPHY
see Alchemy; Astrology; Magic; Occult Sciences

HERMITAGES
see Monasteries

HERO-WORSHIP
see Heroes

HEROES
see also Courage; Martyrs; Mythology; Saints also particular civilian and military awards, e.g. Nobel Prizes, Medal of Honor
Garmo, Murshed. School of Heroes. (Arabic.). pap. 12.00x. Intl Bk Ctr.

HEROES IN LITERATURE
Galloway, David D. The Absurd Hero in American Fiction: Updike, Styron, Bellow, Salinger. 2nd, rev. ed. 288p. 1981. text ed. 22.50x (ISBN 0-292-70356-2); pap. text ed. 8.95x (ISBN 0-292-70355-4). U of Tex Pr.
Welsh, Alexander. Reflections on the Hero As Quixote. LC 80-8584. 256p. 1981. 15.00x (ISBN 0-691-06465-2). Princeton U Pr.

HEROIN
Sowder, Barbara J. & Burt, Marvin R. Children of Heroin Addicts. 200p. 1980. 18.95 (ISBN 0-03-057033-6). Praeger.

HEROINES
see Women; Women in Literature; Women in the Bible

HEROISM
see Courage; Heroes

HERRESHOFF, NATHANAEL GREENE, 1848-1938
Herreshoff, L. F. Capt. Nat Herreshoff: The Wizard of Bristol. LC 80-28519. (Illus.). 350p. 1981. Repr. of 1953 ed. 17.50 (ISBN 0-911378-32-4). Sheridan.

HERSCHEL, WILLIAM, SIR, 1738-1822
Sime, James. William Herschel & His Work. 272p. 1900. text ed. 3.50 (ISBN 0-567-04521-8). Attic Pr.

HERTZEN, ALEKSANDR IVANOVICH, 1812-1870
Carr, Edward H. The Romantic Exiles. 392p. 1981. pap. 8.95 (ISBN 0-262-53040-6). MIT Pr.

HERTZIAN WAVES
see Microwaves

HESSE, HERMANN, 1877-1962
Babcock, Winifred. Jung, Harold, Hesse: Contributions of C. G. Jung, Preston Harold & Hermann Hesse Toward a Spiritual Psychology. 275p. 1981. 12.95 (ISBN 0-686-68720-5). World Authors.

HESSIANS IN THE AMERICAN REVOLUTION
see United States-History-Revolution, 1775-1783-German Mercenaries

HETEROCERA
see Moths

HETEROCYCLIC COMPOUNDS
Berdy, Janos. Heterocyclic Antibiotics. (CRC Handbook of Antibiotic Compounds: Vol. 5). 640p. 1981. 62.95 (ISBN 0-8493-3456-X). CRC Pr.
Finley, K. T. Triazoles. (Chemistry of Heterocyclic Compounds, Series of Monographs: Vol. 39). 368p. 1980. write for info (ISBN 0-471-07827-1). Wiley.
Katritzky, A. R., ed. Advances in Heterocyclic Chemistry, Vol. 28. (Serial Publication Ser.). 1981. write for info. (ISBN 0-12-020628-5); lib. ed. (ISBN 0-12-020730-3); microfiche ed. (ISBN 0-12-020731-1). Acad Pr.
Penczek, S., et al. Cationic Ring-Opening Polymerization of Heterocyclic Monomers. (Advances in Polymer Science Ser.: Vol. 37). (Illus.). 156p. 1981. 46.00 (ISBN 0-387-10209-4). Springer-Verlag.
Preston, P. N. Benzimidazoles & Congeneric Tricyclic Compounds, Pt. 1, Vol. 40. (Chemistry of Heterocyclic Compounds Ser.). 848p. 1981. write for info. (ISBN 0-471-03792-3, Pub. by Wiley-Interscience). Wiley.
Temple, Carroll. Triazoles, One, Two, Four. (Monographs). 752p. 1980. 175.00 (ISBN 0-471-04656-6, Pub. by Wiley-Interscience). Wiley.

HEXAPODA
see Insects

HEYDRICH, REINHARD, 1904-1942
Deschner, Gunther. Reinhard Heydrich. LC 80-6263. 376p. 1981. 16.95 (ISBN 0-8128-2809-7). Stein & Day.

HI-FI SYSTEMS
see High-Fidelity Sound Systems

HIDATSA INDIANS
see Indians of North America-The West

HIGH BLOOD PRESSURE
see Hypertension

HIGH-FIBER DIET
Theander & James. The Analysis of Dietary Fiber in Food. 288p. 1981. 35.00 (ISBN 0-8247-1192-0). Dekker.

HIGH-FIDELITY SOUND SYSTEMS
see also Stereophonic Sound Systems
Johnson, Kenneth W. & Walker, Willard C. Understanding Audio. (Illus.). 256p. 1980. pap. text ed. 5.75 (ISBN 0-8403-2216-X). Kendall-Hunt.

HIGH-FREQUENCY RADIO
see Radio, Short Wave

HIGH INTRAOCULAR PRESSURE
see Glaucoma

HIGH LICENSE
see Liquor Problem

HIGH PRESSURE (TECHNOLOGY)
Isaacs, Neil S. Liquid Phase High Pressure Chemistry. 384p. 1981. 100.00 (ISBN 0-471-27849-1, Pub. by Wiley-Interscience). Wiley.

HIGH-RESIDUE DIET
see High-Fiber Diet

HIGH SCHOOL EQUIVALENCY EXAMINATION
Lanzano, Susan & Abreu, Rosendo. Preparacion Para el Examen de Equivalencia de la Escuela Superior. 3rd ed. Ringel, Martin & Banks, William K., eds. LC 80-17685. 368p. (Span.). 1981. pap. 6.95 (ISBN 0-668-05095-0, 50950). Arco.
Rockowitz, et al. Barron's How to Prepare for the High School Equivalency Exam (GED) rev. ed. (gr. 10-12). 1978. pap. text ed. 6.95 (ISBN 0-8120-0645-3). Barron.

HIGH SCHOOL LIBRARIES
see School Libraries (High School)

HIGH SCHOOL STUDENTS
Jennings, M. K. High School Seniors Cohort Study, Nineteen Sixty-Five & Nineteen Seventy-Three. 1980. 14.00 (ISBN 0-89138-964-4). ICPSR.

HIGH SEAS, JURISDICTION OVER
see Maritime Law

HIGH-SPEED DATA PROCESSING
see Real-Time Data Processing

HIGH TEMPERATURES
Zemansky, Mark W. Temperatures Very Low & Very High. 144p. 1981. pap. price not set (ISBN 0-486-24072-X). Dover.

HIGH TEMPERATURES-PHYSIOLOGICAL EFFECT
see Heat-Physiological Effect

HIGH TREASON
see Treason

HIGH VACUUM TECHNIQUE
see Vacuum

HIGHER EDUCATION
see Education, Higher

HIGHER EDUCATION AND STATE
Gaffney, Edward M. & Moots, Philip R. Government & Campus: Federal Regulation of Religiously Affiliated Higher Education. LC 80-53164. 210p. 1981. text ed. 15.95 (ISBN 0-268-01003-X); pap. text ed. 8.95 (ISBN 0-268-01005-6). U of Notre Dame Pr.

HIGHER LAW
see Government, Resistance To

HIGHLAND CLANS
see Clans and Clan System

HIGHWAY ENGINEERING
see Highway Research; Road Construction; Roads; Traffic Engineering

HIGHWAY LAW
see Cycling

HIGHWAY RESEARCH
Wells, G. R. Highway Planning Techniques: The Balance of Cost & Benefit. 150p. 1971. 35.00x (ISBN 0-85264-196-6, Pub. by Griffin England). State Mutual Bk.

HIGHWAY SAFETY
see Traffic Safety

HIGHWAY TRANSPORTATION
see Transportation, Automotive

HIGHWAYMEN
see Brigands and Robbers

HIGHWAYS
see Roads

HIKING
see also Backpacking; Mountaineering; Orientation; Trails; Walking
Bluestein, Sheldon. Hiking Trails of Southern Idaho. LC 79-52543. (Illus.). 235p. (Orig.). 1981. pap. 7.95 (ISBN 0-87004-280-7). Caxton.
Dannen, Donna & Dannen, Kent. Walks with Nature in Rocky Mountain National Park. LC 80-26665. (Illus.). 64p. 1981. pap. 3.95 (ISBN 0-914788-38-8). East Woods.
Hoffman, Carolyn. Fifty Hikes in Eastern Pennsylvania. (Illus., Orig.). 1981. pap. price not set (ISBN 0-89725-018-4). NH Pub Co.
McKinney, John. A Day Hiker's Guide to Southern California. 160p. (Orig.). 1981. pap. 8.85 (ISBN 0-88496-163-X). Capra Pr.
Maughan, Jackie J. & Puddicombe, Ann. Hiking the Back Country. 224p. (Orig.). 1981. pap. 9.95 (ISBN 0-8117-2170-1). Stackpole.
Mazel, David. Arizona Trails. Winnett, Thomas, ed. LC 80-53682. (Wilderness Press Trail Guide Ser.). (Illus.). 192p. (Orig.). 1981. pap. 7.95 (ISBN 0-89997-003-6). Wilderness Pr.
Morris, Larry A. Hiking the Grand Canyon & Havasupai. (Illus.). 96p. 1981. pap. 4.95 (ISBN 0-89404-053-7). Aztex.
Rutstrum, Calvin. Hiking Back to Health. LC 80-19803. (Illus.). 136p. (Orig.). 1980. pap. 5.95 (ISBN 0-934802-06-8). Ind Camp Supply.
Smith, Robert. Hiking Hawaii. Winnett, Thomas, ed. LC 79-93247. (Wilderness Press Trail Guide Ser.). (Illus.). 112p. (Orig.). 1981. write for info. (ISBN 0-89997-000-1). Wilderness Pr.
--Hiking Oahu. 2nd ed. LC 80-53464. 122p. 1980. pap. 4.95 (ISBN 0-89997-006-0). Wilderness Pr.

HILBERT SPACE
Fuhrmann, Paul A. Linear Systems & Operators in Hilbert Space. 336p. 1981. text ed. 44.95 (ISBN 0-07-022589-3). McGraw.

HILLBILLY MUSICIANS
see Country Musicians

HIMMLER, HEINRICH, 1900-1945
Reider, Frederic. Hitler's S.S. (Illus.). 256p. 1981. 24.95 (ISBN 0-89404-061-8). Aztex.

HINDI LANGUAGE
see also Urdu Language
Dwivedi, S. Hindi on Trial. 250p. 1980. text ed. 25.00x (ISBN 0-7069-1210-1, Pub by Vikas India). Advent Bk.
Kachru, Yamuna, ed. Aspects of Hindi Grammar. 1980. 12.50x (ISBN 0-8364-0666-4, Pub. by Manohar India). South Asia Bks.

HINDU LITERATURE
Alston, A. J. Devotional Poems of Mirabai. 144p. 1980. text ed. 13.50 (ISBN 0-8426-1643-8). Verry.
Caland, W. Sankhyana Srauta Sutra. Chandra, L., tr. 483p. 1980. text ed. 45.00x (ISBN 0-8426-1646-2). Verry.

HINDU MEDICINE
see Medicine, Hindu

HINDU MUSIC
see Music, Indic

HINDU MYTHOLOGY
see Mythology, Hindu

HINDU SECTS
Bhagowalia, Urmila. Vaisnavism & Society in Northern India. 1980. 22.00x (ISBN 0-8364-0664-8, Pub. by Intellectual India). South Asia Bks.

HINDUISM
see also Caste-India; Hindu Sects; Karma; Vedanta; Women in Hinduism; Yoga

Bhatt, Kjmarila. Anthology of Kumarila Bhatt's Works. Sharma, P. S., ed. 96p. 1980. text ed. 9.00x (ISBN 0-8426-1647-0). Verry.
Bijalwan, C. D. Hindu Omens. 176p. 1980. 8.95x (ISBN 0-89955-321-4, Pub. by Interprint India). Intl Schol Bk Serv.
Chennakesvan, Sarasvati. A Critical Study of Hinduism. 1980. 12.50x (ISBN 0-8364-0614-1). South Asia Bks.
Dye, Joseph M. Ways to Shiva: Life & Ritual in Hindu India. LC 80-25113. (Illus.). 94p. (Orig.). 1980. pap. 4.95 (ISBN 0-87633-038-3). Phila Mus Art.
O'Neal, L. Thomas. Maya in Sankara: Measuring the Immeasurable. 1980. 16.00x (ISBN 0-8364-0611-7). South Asia Bks.
Organ, Troy W. Hindu Quest for the Perfection of Man. LC 73-81450. x, 439p. 1981. pap. 10.00x (ISBN 0-8214-0575-6). Ohio U Pr.
Patel, Satyavrata. Hinduism: Religion & Way of Life. 165p. 1980. text ed. 21.00x (ISBN 0-8426-1661-6). Verry.
Radhakrishnan, S. Hindu View of Life. (Unwin Paperbacks Ser.). 92p. 1980. pap. 4.95 (ISBN 0-04-294045-1, 9048). Allen Unwin.
Sharma, Arvind. The Hindu Scriptural Value System & the Economic Development of India. x, 113p. 1980. text ed. 15.00x (ISBN 0-86590-004-3). Apt Bks.
Vidyarthi, L. P. The Sacred Complex in Hindu Gaya. 2nd ed. 264p. 1980. pap. text ed. 11.25x (ISBN 0-391-02214-8). Humanities.
Vishnu Purana, 2 vols. Wilson, H. H., tr. from Sanskrit. 965p. 1980. 36.00 (ISBN 0-89744-995-9, Pub. by Orient Reprint India). Auromere.

HINDUISM–SECTS
see Hindu Sects

HIP JOINT
Aho, Arnold J. Materials, Energies & Environmental Design. 1981. lib. bdg. 28.50 (ISBN 0-8240-7178-6). Garland Pub.
Chung, Stanley M., ed. Hip Disorders in Infants & Children. (Illus.). 450p. 1981. text ed. price not set (ISBN 0-8121-0706-3). Lea & Febiger.
Hip Society. The Hip Society: The Hip, 8 vols. Incl. Vol. 1. 1973. text ed. 25.00 (ISBN 0-8016-0019-7); Vol. 2. 1974. text ed. 35.00 (ISBN 0-8016-0020-0); Vol. 3. 332p. 1975. text ed. 39.50 (ISBN 0-8016-0035-9); Vol. 4. Evarts, C. M., ed. 1976. text ed. 32.50 (ISBN 0-8016-0036-7); Vol. 5. 1977. text ed. 34.50 (ISBN 0-8016-0038-3); Vol. 6. 1978. text ed. 34.50 (ISBN 0-8016-0041-3); Vol. 7. 1979. text ed. 39.50 (ISBN 0-8016-0033-2); Vol. 8. 336p. 1980. text ed. 44.50 (ISBN 0-8016-0049-9). LC 73-7515. (Illus.). Mosby.
McArdle, J. Functional Morphology of the Hip & Thigh of the Lorisiformes. (Contributions to Primatology Ser.: Vol. 17). (Illus.). 148p. 1981. pap. 19.25 (ISBN 3-8055-1767-X). S Karger.
Tachdjian, M. Congenital Dislocation of the Hip: 0congenital Dislocation of the Hip. Date not set. text ed. price not set (ISBN 0-443-08069-0). Churchill.

HIPPOLOGY
see Horses

HIRUNDINIDAE
see Swallows

HISPANIC CIVILIZATION
see Civilization, Hispanic

HISPANO-AMERICAN WAR, 1898
see United States–History–War of 1898

HISPANOS
see Mexican Americans

HISS, ALGER, 1904-
Rabinowitz, Victor. In Re Alger Hiss, Vol. 2. Tiger, Edith, ed. 1981. pap. 9.95 (ISBN 0-8090-0150-0). Hill & Wang.

HISTOCOMPATIBILITY
see also Immunological Tolerance
International Convocation on Immunology, 7th, Niagra Falls, N. Y., July 1980, et al. Immunbiology of the Major Histocompatibility Complex. Zaleski, M. B. & Kano, K., eds. (Illus.). xii, 390p. 1981. 90.00 (ISBN 3-8055-1896-X). S Karger.

HISTOLOGY
see also Botany–Anatomy; Cells; Microscope and Microscopy; Tissues
also names of particular tissues or organs, e.g. Muscle, Nerves
Germain, Jocelyn P. & Turvey, David J. Preparatory Techniques in Histology. 1981. text ed. price not set. Butterworth.
Krause, William J. & Cutts, J. Jarry. Concise Text of Histology. (Illus.). 175p. 1981. write for info. soft cover (4784-1). Williams & Wilkins.
Leeson, Thomas S. & Leeson, C. Roland. Histology. 1981. text ed. price not set (ISBN 0-7216-5704-4). Saunders.
Robertson, W. B. The Endometrium. (Postgraduate Pathology Ser.). 1981. text ed. 52.95 (ISBN 0-407-00171-9). Butterworth.

HISTOLOGY, PATHOLOGICAL
Rywlin, Arkadi M. Histopathology of the Bone Marrow. LC 75-41570. (Series in Laboratory Medicine). 229p. 1976. text ed. 22.50 (ISBN 0-316-76369-1). Little.

HISTOLOGY, VEGETABLE
see Botany–Anatomy

HISTORIANS
see also Archaeologists
Sterns, Indrikis. The Greater Medieval Historians: An Interpretation & a Bibliography. LC 80-5850. 260p. 1980. lib. bdg. 18.75 (ISBN 0-8191-1327-1); pap. text ed. 10.50 (ISBN 0-8191-1328-X). U Pr of Amer.
Wilson, A. N. The Laird of Abbotsford: A View of Sir Walter Scott. 214p. 1980. text ed. 24.95x (ISBN 0-19-211756-4). Oxford U Pr.

HISTORIANS–CORRESPONDENCE, REMINISCENCES, ETC.
Clough, Shepard B. The Life That I've Lived. LC 80-5503. 297p. 1981. lib. bdg. 19.75 (ISBN 0-8191-1116-3); pap. text ed. 10.75 (ISBN 0-8191-1117-1). U Pr of Amer.

HISTORIANS–GREAT BRITAIN
Morton, S. Fiona, ed. A Bibliography of Arnold J. Toynbee. 300p. 1980. 74.00 (ISBN 0-19-215261-0). Oxford U Pr.

HISTORIANS–UNITED STATES
Cutright, Paul R. & Brodhead, Michael J. Elliott Coues: Naturalist & Frontier Historian. LC 80-12424. (Illus.). 510p. 1981. 28.95 (ISBN 0-252-00802-2). U of Ill Pr.

HISTORIC BUILDINGS
see also Historic Sites
also specific kinds of historic buildings according to use, e.g. Churches; Hotels, Taverns, etc.; and subdivision Buildings under names of cities, e.g. New York (city)–Buildings
Fitch, James M. Historic Preservation. (Illus.). 448p. 1981. 24.95 (ISBN 0-07-021121-3, P&RB). McGraw.
Historic House Association of America. Historic Property Owner's Handbook. 2nd ed. (Illus.). 96p. (Orig.). 1981. pap. 7.95 (ISBN 0-89133-094-1). Preservation Pr.
National Trust for Historic Preservation. American Landmarks: Properties of the National Trust for Historic Preservation. (Illus.). 72p. (Orig.). 1980. pap. 5.95 (ISBN 0-89133-093-3). Preservation Pr.

HISTORIC HOUSES, ETC.
see Historic Buildings

HISTORIC SITES
see also Historic Buildings
Fitch, James M. Historic Preservation. (Illus.). 448p. 1981. 24.95 (ISBN 0-07-021121-3, P&RB). McGraw.
Milley, John. Treasures of Independence. (Illus.). 224p. 1980. 25.00 (ISBN 0-8317-8593-4). Mayflower Bks.
Ramati, Racquel & Urban Design Group of the Department of City Planning, New York. How to Save Your Own Street. LC 78-14709. (Illus.). 176p. 1981. pap. 19.95 (ISBN 0-385-14814-3, Dolp). Doubleday.

HISTORICAL ATLASES
see Geography, Historical–Maps

HISTORICAL CRITICISM
see Historiography

HISTORICAL FICTION
see also subdivision Fiction under names of countries, cities, etc., and under names of historical events and characters
Lascelles, Mary. The Story-Teller Retrieves the Past: Historical Fiction & Fictitious History in the Art of Scott, Stevenson, Kipling, & Some Others. 116p. 1980. 29.50x (ISBN 0-19-812802-9). Oxford U Pr.

HISTORICAL FICTION–BIBLIOGRAPHY
Gerhardstein, Virginia B. Dickinson's American Historical Fiction. 4th ed. LC 80-23450. 328p. 1981. 15.00 (ISBN 0-8108-1362-9). Scarecrow.

HISTORICAL GEOGRAPHY
see Geography, Historical

HISTORICAL GEOLOGY
see also Geology, Stratigraphic; Paleontology
Dott, Robert H. & Batten, Roger L. Evolution of the Earth. 3rd ed. (Illus.). 576p. 1980. text ed. 22.95 (ISBN 0-07-017625-6, C); write for info. McGraw.

HISTORICAL RECORD PRESERVATION
see Archives

HISTORICAL SITES
see Historic Sites

HISTORICAL SOCIETIES
Schiffer, Peter B. The Chester County Historical Society. (Illus.). 70p. 1970. pap. 3.50. Schiffer.

HISTORIOGRAPHY
see also Historians
also subdivision Historiography under names of countries, e.g. United States–History–Historiography
Blundeville, Thomas. The True Order & Method of Wryting & Reading Hystories. LC 79-84088. (English Experience Ser.: No. 908). 68p. (Eng.). 1979. Repr. of 1574 ed. lib. bdg. 7.00 (ISBN 90-221-0908-9). Walter J Johnson.
Ladurie, Emmanuel L. The Mind & Method of the Historian. Reynolds, Sian & Reynolds, Ben, trs. 224p. 1981. price not set (ISBN 0-226-47326-0). U of Chicago Pr.
Stone, Lawrence. The Past & the Present. 288p. 1981. 15.95 (ISBN 0-7100-0628-4). Routledge & Kegan.

HISTORY
Here are entered general works about history, its methods, philosophy, etc. For works on the history of specific places or periods, see World History; History, Ancient; History, modern, etc.
see also Anthropo-Geography; Archaeology; Battles; Biography; Church History; Civilization; Constitutional History; Coups d'Etat; Culture; Diplomacy; Discoveries (In Geography); Ethnology; Genealogy; Geography, Historical; Heraldry; Heroes; Historians; Historic Sites; Historical Fiction; Man–Migrations; Medals; Migrations of Nations; Military History; Naval History; Numismatics; Political Science; Revolutions; Riots; Seals (Numismatics); Social History; Society, Primitive; Treaties
also subdivisions Antiquities, Foreign Relations, History and Politics and Government under names of countries, states, cities, etc.
Boochever, Florence & Jackson, Raymond, eds. Writings from the Beaver Trail. (Illus.). 312p. (Orig.). 1979. pap. 5.50 (ISBN 0-9605090-0-3). Albany Pub Lib.
Gilbert, Lynn & Moore, Gaylen. Who Shaped Our Time. Southern, Carol, ed. 1981. 17.95 (ISBN 0-517-54371-0). Potter.
Rudman, Jack. History. (Undergraduate Program Field Test Ser.: UPFT-13). (Cloth bdg. avail. on request). pap. 9.95 (ISBN 0-8373-6013-7). Natl Learning.

HISTORY–ADDRESSES, ESSAYS, LECTURES
Wedgwood, C. V. Velvet Studies. 159p. 1980. Repr. of 1946 ed. lib. bdg. 15.00 (ISBN 0-89987-861-X). Darby Bks.

HISTORY–ATLASES
see Geography, Historical–Maps

HISTORY–BIBLIOGRAPHY
Francois, Michel, et al, eds. International Bibliography of Historical Sciences: 1976-1977, Vols. 45-46. 492p. 1980. 58.00 (ISBN 3-598-20402-7, Dist. by Gale Research Co.). K G Saur.

HISTORY–CRITICISM
see Historiography

HISTORY–HISTORIOGRAPHY
see Historiography

HISTORY–PHILOSOPHY
see also Civilization
also subdivision History–Philosophy under names of countries, e.g. United States–History–Philosophy
Langley, Ray A. Basic Patterns of Historical Action in the Chematized Analysis of the Philosophy of History. (The Major Currents in Contemporary World History Library). (Illus.). 129p. 1981. 49.25 (ISBN 0-930008-84-7). Inst Econ Pol.
Walsh, W. H. An Introduction to Philosophy of History. 1981. pap. text ed. 9.75x (ISBN 0-391-02163-X, Hutchinson U Lib). Humanities.

HISTORY–STUDY AND TEACHING
Schlereth, Thomas J. Artifacts & the American Past: Techniques for the Teaching Historian. 300p. 1981. pap. 13.95 (ISBN 0-910050-47-3). AASLH.

HISTORY–YEARBOOKS
Facts on File Staff. FOF Yearbook, 1980. 1200p. 1981. lib. bdg. 65.00 (ISBN 0-87196-039-7). Facts on File.
Keeton, George W. & Schwarzenberger, Georg, eds. The Year Book of World Affairs, 1981. 285p. 1981. lib. bdg. 40.00x (ISBN 0-86531-150-1). Westview.
Paneth, Donald. News Dictionary 1980. 400p. 1981. 14.95 (ISBN 0-87196-111-3). Facts on File.

HISTORY, ANCIENT
see also Archaeology; Civilization, Ancient; Numismatics
also names of ancient races and peoples, e.g. Indo-Europeans; hittites; Mediterranean Race; and names of countries of antiquity
The Annals of Tacitus, Books One to Six, Vol. 2. (Cambridge Classical Texts & Commentaries: No. 23). 576p. Date not set. price not set (ISBN 0-521-20213-2). Cambridge U Pr.
Edwards, I. E., et al, eds. Cambridge Ancient History. Incl. Vol. 1, Pt. 1. Prolegomena & Prehistory. pap. 29.50 (ISBN 0-521-29821-0); Vol. 1, Pts. 2A & 2B. Early History of the Middle East. pap. 34.50 (ISBN 0-521-29822-9); Vol. 2, Pt. 1. The Middle East & the Aegean Region, c 1800-1380 B.C. pap. 29.50 (ISBN 0-521-29823-7); Vol. 2, Pts. 2A & 2B. The Middle East & the Aegean Region, c 1380-1000 B.C. pap. 34.50 (ISBN 0-521-29824-5). LC 75-85719. (Illus.). Date not set. Cambridge U Pr.
Melko, Matthew & Weigel, Richard D. Peace in the Ancient World. LC 80-20434. 225p. 1981. lib. bdg. 15.95x (ISBN 0-89950-020-X). McFarland & Co.
Thomas, Gwynne E. H. Political History of the Ancient World. 1981. 7.95 (ISBN 0-8062-1680-8). Carlton.

HISTORY, ANCIENT–JUVENILE LITERATURE
Unstead, R. J. How They Lived in Cities Long Ago. (Illus.). 80p. (gr. 6 up). 1981. 9.95 (ISBN 0-668-05188-4, 5188). Arco.

HISTORY, BIBLICAL
see Bible–History of Biblical Events

HISTORY, CHURCH
see Church History

HISTORY, CONSTITUTIONAL
see Constitutional History

HISTORY, ECCLESIASTICAL
see Church History

HISTORY, ECONOMIC
see Economic History

HISTORY, MEDIEVAL
see Middle Ages–History

HISTORY, MILITARY
see Military History

HISTORY, MODERN–JUVENILE LITERATURE
Cheney, Cora. Vermont: The State with the Storybook Past. 2nd ed. (Illus.). 256p. (gr. 3-6). 1981. pap. 9.95 (ISBN 0-8289-0440-5). Greene.

HISTORY, MODERN–PHILOSOPHY
see History–Philosophy

HISTORY, MODERN–16TH CENTURY
Munday, Anthony. The English Roman Life. Ayres, Phillip J., ed. (Studies in Tudor & Stewart Literature Ser.). (Illus.). 142p. 1980. 22.00 (ISBN 0-19-812635-2). Oxford U Pr.

HISTORY, NATURAL
see Natural History

HISTORY, NAVAL
see Naval History

HISTORY, PHILOSOPHY OF
see History–Philosophy

HISTORY, UNIVERSAL
see World History

HISTORY AND SCIENCE
see Science and Civilization

HISTORY AND SEX
see Sex and History

HISTORY, MODERN–YEARBOOKS
see History–Yearbooks

HISTRIONICS
see Acting; Theater

HITLER, ADOLF, 1889-1945
The Diary of Adolf Hitler. 225p. 1980. 14.95 (ISBN 0-9605224-1-7); pap. 8.88 (ISBN 0-9605224-0-9). Ancient Age.
People's Court, Munich & Hitler, Adolph. Hitler Trial: Before the People's Court in Munich. Freniere, H. Francis, et al, trs. 1976. 130.00 (ISBN 0-89093-050-3). U Pubns Amer.
Toland, John. Adolf Hitler. 1056p. 1981. pap. 9.95 (ISBN 0-345-29470-X). Ballantine.

HOAXES
see Impostors and Imposture

HOBBIES
see also Home Workshops
Ambrose, Mike & Walker, Nora S. Captain Mike's Complete Guide to Grunion Hunting. (Illus.). 93p. (Orig.). 1981. pap. 3.95 (ISBN 0-916392-70-8). Oak Tree Pubns.
Davis, William. The Best of Everything. 224p. 1981. 9.95 (ISBN 0-312-07713-0). St Martin.
Wagenvoord, James. Oak Alley, 4 vols. (Illus.). 160p. 1981. 166.80 (ISBN 0-312-58050-9). St Martin.

HOBOES
see Tramps

HOCKEY
Liss, Howard. Hockey Talk. (gr. 4-6). pap. 0.95 (ISBN 0-686-68482-6). PB.
Moriarty, Tim & Bereswell, Joe. The Dynamic Islanders: From Cellar to Stanley Cup. (Illus.). 144p. 1981. pap. 9.95 (ISBN 0-385-17489-6). Doubleday.

HOCKEY–BIOGRAPHY
Plimpton, George. Open Net. 300p. 1981. 11.95 (ISBN 0-399-12558-2). Putnam.

HODGKIN'S DISEASE
Coltman, Charles A., Jr. & Golomb, Harvey, eds. Hodgkin's Disease & Non-Hodgkin's Lymphomas. (Seminars in Oncology Ser.). 1980. write for info. (ISBN 0-8089-1354-9). Grune.
Taylor, Cliver R. Hodgkin's Disease & the Lymphomas. Horrobin, D. F., ed. LC 78-300154. (Annual Reviews Ser.: Vol. 4). 374p. 1980. 38.00 (ISBN 0-88831-089-7). Eden Med Res.

HOFFMAN, ABBIE
Hoffman, Abbie. Soon to Be a Major Motion Picture. 1980. 13.95 (ISBN 0-686-68806-6, Perigee); pap. 6.95 (ISBN 0-686-68807-4). Putnam.

HOGARTH, WILLIAM, 1697-1764
Bindman, David. Hogarth. (World of Art Ser.). (Illus.). 288p. 1981. 17.95 (ISBN 0-19-520239-2); pap. 9.95 (ISBN 0-19-520240-6). Oxford U Pr.

HOGS
see Swine

HOKKU
see Haiku

HOLIDAYS–JUVENILE LITERATURE
Haas, Carolyn, et al. Backyard Vacation: Outdoor Fun in Your Own Neighborhood. (Illus.). 116p. (gr. 3-6). 1980. 9.95 (ISBN 0-316-33686-6); pap. 5.95 (ISBN 0-316-33685-8). Little.
Lobel. A Holiday for Mr. Muster. (gr. 2-3). 1980. pap. 3.50 incl. record (ISBN 0-590-24003-X, Schol Pap). Schol Bk Serv.

HOLIDAYS, JEWISH
see Fasts and Feasts–Judaism

HOLINESS
see also Perfection; Sanctification
Dieter, Melvin E. The Holiness Revival of the Nineteenth Century. LC 80-17259. (Studies in Evangelicalism: No. 1). 366p. 1980. 17.50 (ISBN 0-8108-1328-9). Scarecrow.

HOLISM
Albright, Peter & Albright, Bets P. Body, Mind & Spirit: The Journey Toward Wholeness. 2nd ed. (Illus.). 320p. 1981. pap. 9.95 (ISBN 0-8289-0386-7). Greene.

Barton, John & Barton, Margaret. Biokinesiology: Vol II Neurovasculars. 3rd ed. (Encyclopedia of Mind & Body). (Illus.). 110p. (Orig.). 1980. pap. 10.00 (ISBN 0-937216-05-4). J&M Barton.
--Flow Lines to Health. 4th ed. (Illus.). 158p. 1980. pap. 8.00 (ISBN 0-937216-04-6). J&M Barton.
Blattner, Barbara. Holistic Nursing. (Illus.). 400p. 1981. text ed. 15.95 (ISBN 0-13-392571-4); pap. text ed. 12.95 (ISBN 0-686-68605-5). P-H.
Buess, Lynn M. Synergy Session. LC 80-67932. (Illus.). 113p. (Orig.). 1980. pap. 4.95 (ISBN 0-87516-427-7). De Vorss.
Hames, Carolyn C. & Joseph, Dayle. Basic Concepts of Helping: A Wholistic Approach. 260p. 1980. pap. text ed. 9.50x (ISBN 0-8385-0558-9). ACC.
Hippchen, Leonard. Holistic Approaches to Offender Rehabilitation. 400p. 1981. price not set (ISBN 0-398-04448-1). C C Thomas.
Holistic Mental Health for Tomorrow's Children: For Teachers & Mental Health Workers. write for info. (ISBN 0-398-04472-4). C C Thomas.
Rose-Neil, Sidney. Acupuncture & the Life Energies. 160p. 1981. pap. 8.95 (ISBN 0-88231-121-2). ASI Pubs Inc.
Van Nuys, Kelvin. A Holist Pilgrimage. LC 80-84738. 1981. 19.95 (ISBN 0-8022-2383-4). Philos Lib.
Wigmore, Ann. Why Suffer? (Illus.). 173p. pap. text ed. 2.95. Hippocrates.

HOLLYWOOD, CALIFORNIA

Carpozi, George, Jr. That's Hollywood: Beautiful & Special People, No. 7. (Orig.). 1980. pap. 1.95 (ISBN 0-532-23281-X). Manor Bks.
--That's Hollywood: The Clossal Cowboys, No. 6. (Orig.). 1980. pap. 1.95 (ISBN 0-532-23222-4). Manor Bks.
Cini, Zelda, et al. Hollywood: Land & Legend. (Illus.). 192p. 1980. 19.95 (ISBN 0-87000-486-7). Arlington Hse.
Fitzmaurice, Victor. Bel-Heirs. 1981. 9.95 (ISBN 0-533-04875-3). Vantage.
Owens, Fred. Making It in Hollywood: An Actor's Guide. 96p. (Orig.). 1980. pap. 5.00 (ISBN 0-936182-01-6). Diamond Heights.
Samuels, M. Screen Greats: Hollywood Nostalgia. 1980. pap. 2.00 (ISBN 0-931064-30-9). O'Quinn Studio.
Strauss, David P. & Worth, Fred L. Hollywood Trivia. 352p. (Orig.). 1981. pap. 2.75 (ISBN 0-446-95492-6). Warner Bks.
Wallace, Irving. Special People, Special Times. 192p. (Orig.). 1981. pap. 2.25 (ISBN 0-523-41480-3). Pinnacle Bks.

HOLMES, OLIVER WENDELL, 1809-1894

Hayakawa, S. I. & Jones, Howard M., eds. Oliver Wendell Holmes. 472p. 1980. Repr. of 1939 ed. lib. bdg. 40.00 (ISBN 0-8495-2351-6). Arden Lib.

HOLOCAUST, JEWISH (1939-1945)

America & the Holocaust. (American Jewish History Ser.: Vol. 68, Pt. 3). 1979. 6.00. Am Jewish Hist Soc.
Brennan, William. Medical Holocausts I: Exterminative Medicine in Nazi Germany & Contemporary America. LC 80-82305. (The Nordland Series in Contemporary American Social Problems). 375p. 1980. pap. 12.95 (ISBN 0-913124-39-7). Nordland Pub.
--Medical Holocausts II: The Language of Exterminative Medicine in Nazi Germany & Contemporary America. LC 80-82305. (The Nordland Series in Contemporary American Social Problems). 320p. 1980. pap. 12.95 (ISBN 0-913124-40-0). Nordland Pub.
Cohen, Arthur A. The Tremendum: A Theological Interpretation of the Holocaust. 144p. 1981. 9.95 (ISBN 0-8245-0006-7). Crossroad NY.
Crawford, Fred R. The Seventy-First Came...to Gunskirchen Lager. LC 79-51047. (Witness to the Holocaust: No. 1). (Illus.). 1979. pap. 1.00 (ISBN 0-89937-027-6). Ctr Res Soc Chg.
Eisenberg, Azriel. Witness to the Holocaust. 649p. 1981. 17.95 (ISBN 0-8298-0432-3). Pilgrim NY.
Laqueur, Walter. The Terrible Secret. 276p. 1980. 12.95 (ISBN 0-316-51474-8). Little.
Lorit, Sergius C. The Last Days of Maximilian Kolbe. Moran, Hugh, tr. from Ital. LC 80-82418. Orig. Title: Kolbe: Cronaca Degli Ultimi Giorni. 144p. 1980. pap. 2.95 (ISBN 0-911782-35-4). New City.
Neusner, Jacob. Strangers at Home: Essays on "The Holocaust", Zionism, & American Judaism. LC 80-19455. 1981. 15.00 (ISBN 0-226-57628-0). U of Chicago Pr.
Parker, Grant. Mayday: The History of a Village Holocaust. LC 80-83408. 260p. (Orig.). 1980. pap. 5.95 (ISBN 0-9604958-0-0). Libty Pr MI.
Rothchild, Sylvia, ed. Voices from the Holocaust. 1981. 14.95 (ISBN 0-453-00396-6, H396). NAL.
Trunk, Isaiah. Jewish Responses to Nazi Persecution. LC 78-6378. 384p. 1981. pap. 9.95 (ISBN 0-8128-6103-5). Stein & Day.
Zyskind, Sara. Stolen Years. (Adult & Young Adult Bks.). 192p. (gr. 4 up). 1981. PLB 9.95 (ISBN 0-8225-0766-8). Lerner Pubns.

HOLOGRAPHY

Kock, Winston E. Lasers & Holography: An Introduction to Coherent Optics. 2nd, rev. ed. (Illus.). 128p. 1981. pap. price not set (ISBN 0-486-24041-X). Dover.
Yaroslavskii, L. P. & Merzlyakov, N. S. Methods of Digital Holography. 250p. 1980. 45.00 (ISBN 0-306-10963-8, Consultants). Plenum Pub.

HOLY GHOST

see Holy Spirit

HOLY HOUR

see Jesus Christ–Passion

HOLY OFFICE

see Inquisition

HOLY ORDERS

see Clergy–Office

HOLY ORTHODOX EASTERN CATHOLIC AND APOSTOLIC CHURCH

see Orthodox Eastern Church

HOLY ROMAN EMPIRE

Falco, Giorgio. The Holy Roman Republic: A Historic Profile of the Middle Ages. Kent, K. V., tr. from Italian. LC 80-19696. Orig. Title: La Santa Romana Republica. 336p. 1980. Repr. of 1965 ed. lib. bdg. 35.00x (ISBN 0-313-22395-5, FAHR). Greenwood.

HOLY ROMAN EMPIRE–CONSTITUTIONAL LAW

Walker, Mack. Johann Jakob Moser & the Holy Roman Empire of the German Nation. LC 79-27720. 352p. 1980. 26.00x (ISBN 0-8078-1441-5). U of NC Pr.

HOLY SEE

see Papacy

HOLY SPIRIT

see also Church–Foundation; Gifts, Spiritual; Pentecost; Spirit; Trinity

Bennett, Dennis & Bennett, Rita, trs. El Espiritu Santo y Tu. (Spanish Bks.). (Span.). 1978. 1.95 (ISBN 0-8297-0439-6). Life Pubs Intl.
Bogorodskii, N. The Doctrine of St. John Damascene on the Procession of the Holy Spirit. LC 80-2351. 1981. Repr. of 1879 ed. 28.50 (ISBN 0-404-18903-2). AMS Pr.
Goodwin, Thomas. Holy Spirit in Salvation. 1979. 12.95 (ISBN 0-85151-279-8). Banner of Truth.
Green, Michael. Creo en el Espiritu Santo. Vilela, Ernesto S., tr. from Eng. LC 77-164. (Serie Creo). 267p. (Orig., Span.). 1977. pap. 3.95 (ISBN 0-89922-090-8). Edit Caribe.
Hembree, Charles R., tr. Fruto Do Espirito. (Portuguese Bks.). 1979. 1.50 (ISBN 0-8297-0652-6). Life Pubs Intl.
The Holy Spirit. (Aglow Bible Study Bk: No. E-3). (Illus.). 64p. (Orig.). 1980. pap. 1.95 (ISBN 0-930756-57-6, 4220-E3). Women's Aglow.
Lockyer, Herbert. The Holy Spirit of God. 1981. 9.95 (ISBN 0-8407-5234-2). Nelson.
Morgan, G. Campbell. The Spirit of God. (Morgan Library). 240p. 1981. pap. 3.95 (ISBN 0-8010-6119-9). Baker Bk.
St. Basil the Great on the Holy Spirit. Anderson, David, tr. from Greek. LC 80-25502. 1980. pap. 3.95 (ISBN 0-913836-74-5). St Vladimirs.
St. Basil The Great. On the Holy Spirit. Anderson, David, tr. from Gr. (Orig.). 1980. pap. 3.95 (ISBN 0-913836-74-5). St Vladimirs.
Smeaton, George. Doctrine of the Holy Spirit. 1980. 12.95 (ISBN 0-85151-187-2). Banner of Truth.
Stephens, John F. Spirit Filled Family, No. 11. 48p. (Orig.). 1980. pap. 1.50 (ISBN 0-89841-008-8). Zoe Pubns.
Stott, John R. Sed Llenos del Espiritu Santo. rev. ed. Cook, David A., tr. from Eng. LC 77-162. 112p. (Orig., Span.). 1977. pap. 2.50 (ISBN 0-89922-084-3). Edit Caribe.
Teasley, D. O. The Holy Spirit & Other Spirits. 192p. pap. 1.75. Faith Pub Hse.

HOLY SPIRIT ASSOCIATON FOR THE UNIFICATION OF WORLD CHRISTIANITY

Bryant, Darrol, ed. Proceedings of the Virgin Islands' Seminar on Unification Theology. LC 80-52594. (Conference Ser.: No. 6). (Illus.). xv, 323p. (Orig.). 1980. pap. text ed. 9.95 (ISBN 0-932894-06-2). Unif Theol Sem.
Durham, Deanna. Life Among the Moonies: Three Years in the Unification Church. (Orig.). 1981. pap. 2.95 (ISBN 0-88270-496-6). Logos.

HOME

see also Family; Family Life Surveys; Home Economics; Marriage

Morris, Willie. The Ghosts of Old Miss, & Other Essays on Home. 165p. 1981. 9.95. Yoknapatawpha.

HOME AND SCHOOL

see also Parent-Teacher Relationships

Berger, Eugenia H. Parents As Partners in the Educational Process. (Illus.). 360p. 1981. pap. text ed. 11.95 (ISBN 0-8016-0637-3). Mosby.
Sinclair, Robert L., ed. A Two-Way Street: Home-School Cooperation in Curriculum Decisionmaking. 92p. (Orig.). 1980. pap. 6.00 (ISBN 0-917754-16-6). Inst Responsive.

HOME APPLIANCES

see Household Appliances

HOME BUYING

see House Buying

HOME CONSTRUCTION

see House Construction

HOME DECORATION

see Interior Decoration

HOME DESIGN

see Architecture, Domestic

HOME ECONOMICS

see also Consumer Education; Cookery; Cost and Standard of Living; Dairying; Entertaining; Food; Food Service; Fuel; Furniture; Heating; House Furnishings; Housewives; Interior Decoration; Laundry; Needlework; Servants; Sewing; Ventilation

Aslett, Don. Is There Life After Housework. (Illus.). 109p. (Orig.). 1980. pap. 4.50. Article One.
Cleaning & Repairing Books: A Practical Home Manual. LC 80-21244. (Illus.). 112p. 1980. pap. 7.95 (ISBN 0-914046-00-4). R L Shep.
Ewart, Nei. Unsafe As Houses: A Guide to Home Safety. (Illus.). 160p. 1981. 12.50 (ISBN 0-7137-1090-X, Pub. by Blandford Pr England). Sterling.
Ginsberg, Linda. Family Financial Survival. LC 80-70436. (Illus.). 192p. (Orig.). 1981. pap. 8.95 (ISBN 0-89087-315-1). Celestial Arts.
Goodspeed. This Is the Life. (gr. 7-12). 1981. text ed. price not set. Bennett Co.
Heloise. Help! from Heloise. LC 80-70543. (Illus.). 500p. 1981. 12.95 (ISBN 0-87795-318-X). Arbor Hse.
Laird, Jean. Homemaker's Book of Time & Money Savers. 1980. pap. 2.50 (ISBN 0-446-91562-9). Warner Bks.
Leckie, Jim, et al. More Other Homes & Garbage: Designs for Self-Sufficient Living. (Illus.). 416p. 1981. pap. 14.95 (ISBN 0-87156-274-X). Sierra.
Maher, Marina. Marina Maher's Terrific Tips. (Orig.). Date not set. pap. 4.95 (ISBN 0-440-58369-1, Dell Trade Pbks). Dell.
Masnick, George & Bane, Mary Jo. The Nation's Families: 1960-1990. LC 80-20531. (Illus.). 200p. (Orig.). 1980. 17.95 (ISBN 0-86569-050-2); pap. 10.00 (ISBN 0-86569-051-0). Auburn Hse.
Olaitan, Samson O. & Agusiobo, Obiora N. Introduction to the Teaching of Home Economics. 320p. 1981. write for info. (ISBN 0-471-27807-6, Pub. by Wiley-Interscience); pap. write for info. (ISBN 0-471-27806-8). Wiley.
Oppenheimer, Lillian & Epstein, Natalie. Decorative Napkin Folding for Beginners. (Illus.). 1980. pap. 1.75 (ISBN 0-486-23797-4). Dover.
Reader's Digest. Back to Basics. (Illus.). 1981. 19.95 (ISBN 0-89577-086-5, Pub. by Reader's Digest). Norton.
Snyder, Laura. Homemaking Executive. pap. 3.95 (ISBN 0-89036-140-1). Hawkes Pub Inc.
Stanaford, Penny. Contributing to Family Living: A Guide to Household Management. (Illus.). 99p. 1980. 7.95 (ISBN 0-9604850-1-5). Postscript.
Torjesen, Hakon. It's a New Day: Reflections of a House Husband. 1981. 7.95 (ISBN 0-9602790-6-7). The Garden.

HOME ECONOMICS–ACCOUNTING

Huber, Roger, ed. Where My Money Is Going: Income & Expense Budget. (Orig.). 1980. pap. 10.00x (ISBN 0-918300-00-2); wkbk. 10.00. Lankey.

HOME ECONOMICS–JUVENILE LITERATURE

Allen, Eleanor. Home Sweet Home: A History of Housework. (Junior Reference Ser.). (Illus.). 64p. (gr. 7 up). 7.95 (ISBN 0-7136-1927-9). Dufour.

HOME EDUCATION

see Self-Culture

HOME FURNISHINGS

see House Furnishings

HOME NURSING

see also Practical Nursing

Rosenbaum, Ernest H., et al. Going Home: A Home Care Training Program. (Illus.). 160p. 1980. 12.00 (ISBN 0-915950-49-9); three ring binder 12.00 (ISBN 0-915950-48-0). Bull Pub.

HOME OWNERSHIP

see also House Buying

Warner, Ralph E. Protect Your Home with a Declaration of Homestead. 3rd ed. (Illus.). 80p. 1978. pap. 4.95 (ISBN 0-917316-02-9). Nolo Pr.

HOME PURCHASE

see House Buying

HOME REMODELING

see Dwellings–Remodeling

HOME REPAIRS

see Dwellings–Maintenance and Repair

HOME STUDY COURSES

see Self-Culture

HOME WORKSHOPS

Gingery, David J. The Milling Machine. LC 80-66142. (Build Your Own Metal Working Shop from Scrap Ser.: Bk. 4). (Illus.). 96p. (Orig.). 1981. pap. 7.95 (ISBN 0-9604330-3-1). D J Gingery.
Ruhe-Schoen, Janet. Organizing & Operating Profitable Workshop Classes. LC 80-25466. 1981. pap. 2.50 (ISBN 0-87576-092-9). Pilot Bks.

HOMEMAKERS

see Housewives

HOMEOPATHY

Borland, D. M. Homeopathy in Practice. Priestman, Kathleen, ed. 230p. 1980. 25.00x (Pub. by Beaconsfield England). State Mutual Bk.
Boyd, Hamish. Introduction to Homeopathic Medicine. 240p. 1980. 49.00x (Pub. by Beaconsfield England). State Mutual Bk.
Clarke, John H. Clinical Repertory. 346p. 1979. text ed. 24.95x (ISBN 0-8464-1000-1). Beekman Pubs.
--The Prescriber. 11th ed. 382p. 1972. 11.95x (ISBN 0-8464-1041-9). Beekman Pubs.
A Dictionary of Practical Materia Medica, 3 vols. 2585p. 1980. text ed. 119.95x (ISBN 0-8464-1004-4). Beekman Pubs.
Donhoffer, Sz. Homeothermia of the Brain. (Illus.). 140p. (Orig.). 1980. pap. 13.50x (ISBN 963-05-2405-8). Intl Pubns Serv.
Hamlyn, E. C. Healing Art of Homeopathy. 111p. 1980. 15.00x (Pub. by Beaconsfield England). State Mutual Bk.
Julian, O. A. Materia Medica of New Homoeopathic Remedies. 637p. 1980. 60.00x (Pub. by Beaconsfield England). State Mutual Bk.
Maury, E. A. Drainage in Homoeopathy. 1980. text ed. 4.00x (ISBN 0-8464-1007-9). Beekman Pubs.
Nelson, A. C. The Homeopathic Handbook. (Orig.). Date not set. 9.95 (ISBN 0-87983-239-8); pap. 6.95 (ISBN 0-87983-240-1). Keats.
Pratt, Noel. Homoeopathic Prescribing. 96p. 1980. 25.00x (Pub. by Beaconsfield England). State Mutual Bk.
Roberts, Herbert A. The Principles & Art of Cure by Homoeopathy. 286p. 1942. 14.95x (ISBN 0-8464-1042-7). Beekman Pubs.
Sheperd, Dorothy. Homeopathy for the First Aider. 1980. text ed. 4.75x (ISBN 0-8464-1021-4). Beekman Pubs.
--The Magic of the Minimum Dose. 214p. 1964. text ed. 15.50x (ISBN 0-8464-1030-3). Beekman Pubs.
Shepherd, D. Essentials of Homoeopathic Prescribing. 78p. 1970. pap. 3.00x (ISBN 0-8464-1008-7). Beekman Pubs.
Shepherd, Dorothy. More Magic of the Minimum Dose. 1980. text ed. 7.00x (ISBN 0-8464-1033-8). Beekman Pubs.
Speight, Phyllis. A Comparison of the Chronic Miasms. 56p. 1977. text ed. 15.50x (ISBN 0-8464-1002-8). Beekman Pubs.
--A Study Course in Homeopathy. 145p. 1979. text ed. 23.95x (ISBN 0-8464-1052-4). Beekman Pubs.
Tyler, Margaret L. Homeopathic Drug Pictures. 885p. 1952. text ed. 29.95x (ISBN 0-8464-1020-6). Beekman Pubs.
Whiiler, C. E. & Kenyon, J. D. An Introduction to the Principles & Practice of Homoeopathy. 371p. 1957. 17.95x (ISBN 0-8464-1027-3). Beekman Pubs.

HOMEOSTASIS

Biro, Z., et al, eds. Homeostasis in Injury & Shock: Proceedings of a Satellite Symposium of the 28th International Congress of Physiological Sciences, Budapest, Hungary, 1980. LC 80-42104. (Advances in Physiological Sciences: Vol. 26). (Illus.). 360p. 1981. 40.00 (ISBN 0-08-027347-5). Pergamon.

HOMER

Griffin, Jasper. Pastmasters Series: Homer. 1981. 7.95 (ISBN 0-8090-5523-6); pap. 2.95 (ISBN 0-8090-1413-0). Hill & Wang.

HOMES

see Dwellings

HOMES (INSTITUTIONS)

see Asylums; Old Age Homes

HOMES, MOBILE

see Mobile Homes

HOMESTEADING

see Frontier and Pioneer Life

HOMILETICAL ILLUSTRATIONS

see also Bible–Homiletical Use; Legends; Parables; Short Stories; Tales

Junior Surprise Sermons with Handmade Objects, 2 bks. Set. pap. 6.00; No. 1. pap. 3.00 (ISBN 0-915398-18-4); No. 2. pap. 3.00 (ISBN 0-915398-19-2). Visual Evangels.

HOMILETICS

see Preaching

HOMILIES

see Sermons

HOMING PIGEONS

see Pigeons

HOMOEOPATHY

see Homeopathy

HOMOPTERA

Ghauri, M. S. The Morphology & Taxonomy of Male Scale Insects (Homoptera: Coccoidea) (Illus.). vii, 221p. 1962. 19.50x (ISBN 0-565-00580-4, Pub. by British Mus Nat Hist England). Sabbot-Natural Hist Bks.

HOMOSEXUALITY

see also Lesbianism

Bayer, Ronald. Homosexuality & American Psychiatry: The Politics of Diagnosis. LC 80-68182. (Illus.). 224p. 1980. 12.95 (ISBN 0-465-03048-3). Basic.
Camus, Renaud. Tricks: Twenty-Five Encounters. 252p. 1981. pap. 10.95 (ISBN 0-312-81823-8). St Martin.
Heger, Heinz. The Men with the Pink Triangle. Fernbach, David, tr. LC 80-69205. (Illus.). 120p. (Orig.). 1980. pap. 4.95 (ISBN 0-932870-06-6). Carrier Pigeon.
Kleinberg, Seymour. Alienated Affections. 320p. 1981. 13.95 (ISBN 0-312-01857-6). St Martin.
Licata, Salvatore J. & Petersen, Robert, eds. Historical Perspectives on Homosexuality. LC 80-6262. 240p. 1981. 14.95 (ISBN 0-8128-2810-0). Stein & Day.
Marotta, Toby. The Politics of Homosexuality. 384p. 1981. 15.00 (ISBN 0-686-69057-5). HM.
Plummer, Kenneth, ed. The Making of the Modern Homosexual. 1980. 22.50x (ISBN 0-389-20159-6). B&N.
Russo, Vito. The Celluloid Closet: Homosexuality in the Movies. LC 79-1682. (Illus.). 256p. 1981. 15.00 (ISBN 0-06-013704-5, HarpT). Har-Row.

--The Celluloid Closet: Homosexuality in the Movies. LC 79-1682. (Illus.). 256p. 1981. pap. 7.95 (ISBN 0-06-090871-8, CN). Har-Row.

Silverstein, Charles. Man to Man: Gay Couples in America. LC 80-23566. 384p. 1981. 12.95 (ISBN 0-688-00041-X). Morrow.

HOMOSEXUALITY AND CHRISTIANITY

Leon, Jorge A. Lo Que Todos Debemos Saber Sobre la Homosexualidad. LC 76-19206. 136p. (Orig., Span.). 1976. pap. 2.95 (ISBN 0-89922-071-1). Edit Caribe.

HOMOTOPY THEORY

Neisendorfer, Joseph. Primary Homotopy Theory. LC 80-12109. (Memoirs of the American Mathematical Society Ser.). 1980. 4.00 (ISBN 0-8218-2232-2, MEMO-232). Am Math.

HONDA AUTOMOBILE

see Automobiles, Foreign–Types–Honda

HONDA MOTORCYCLE

Scott, Ed. Honda CB Seven Fifty DOHC Fours: 1979-1980. Jorgensen, Eric, ed. (Illus.). 318p. (Orig.). 1980. pap. text ed. 9.95 (ISBN 0-89287-304-3, M337). Clymer Pubns.

HONECKER, ERICH E., 1912-

Honecker, Erich. From My Life. LC 80-41162. (Leaders of the World Ser.: Vol. 3). (Illus.). 500p. 1980. 24.00 (ISBN 0-08-024532-3). Pergamon.

HONESTY

see also Business Ethics

Moncure, Jane B. Honesty. rev. ed. LC 80-39571. (What Is It? Ser.). (Illus.). 32p. (gr. k-3). 1981. PLB 5.50 (ISBN 0-89565-203-X). Childs World.

HONEY

see also Bee Culture; Cookery (Honey)

Crane, Eva. Honey: A Comprehensive Survey. LC 74-14447. 1975. 52.50x (ISBN 0-8448-0062-7). Crane-Russak Co.

Mellor, Isha. Honey. (Illus.). 80p. 1981. 6.95 (ISBN 0-312-92306-6). St Martin.

--Honey: A Consideration. (Illus.). 80p. 1981. 6.95 (ISBN 0-312-92306-6). Congdon & Lattes.

Parkhill, Joe. Wonderful World of Honey. 6.95 (ISBN 0-936744-01-4). Green Hill.

HONGKONG–DESCRIPTION AND TRAVEL

Lanier, Alison R. Update -- Hong Kong. (Country Orientation Ser.). 1980. pap. 25.00 (ISBN 0-933662-38-6). Intercult Pr.

HONGKONG–HISTORY

Lindsay, Oliver. At the Going Down of the Sun: Hong Kong & South East Asia, 1914-45. (Illus.). 250p. 1981. 25.00 (ISBN 0-241-10542-0, Pub. by Hamish Hamilton England). David & Charles.

Salaff, Janet W. Working Daughters of Hong Kong: Female Piety or Power in the Family? LC 80-23909. (ASA Rose Monographs). (Illus.). 304p. Date not set. price not set (ISBN 0-521-23679-7); pap. price not set (ISBN 0-521-28148-2). Cambridge U Pr.

HONGKONG–POLITICS AND GOVERNMENT

Wesley-Smith, P. The Unequal Treaty Eighteen Ninety-Seven to Nineteen Ninety-Seven. (East Asian Historical Monographs). (Illus.). 296p. 26.00 (ISBN 0-19-580436-8). Oxford U Pr.

HONI HA-MEAGGEL, 1ST CENTURY B.C.

Gershator, Phillis. Honi & His Magic Circle. (Illus.). (gr. k-4). 1979. 6.95 (ISBN 0-8276-0167-0). Jewish Pubn.

HONORARY DEGREES

see Degrees, Academic

HOOKED RUGS

see Rugs, Hooked

HOOVER, HERBERT CLARK, PRES. U. S., 1874-1964

Myers, William S. The Foreign Policies of Herbert Hoover, 1929-1933. Freidel, Frank, ed. LC 78-66558. (The History of the United States Ser.: Vol. 14). 272p. 1979. lib. bdg. 20.00 (ISBN 0-8240-9699-1). Garland Pub.

Warren, Harris G. Herbert Hoover & the Great Depression. LC 80-19603. x, 372p. 1980. Repr. of 1970 ed. lib. bdg. 28.75x (ISBN 0-313-22659-8, WAHO). Greenwood.

HOOVER DAM

Maxon, James C. Lake Mead-Hoover Dam: The Story Behind the Scenery. DenDooven, Gweneth R., ed. LC 79-87573. (Illus.). 1980. 7.95 (ISBN 0-916122-62-X); pap. 3.00 (ISBN 0-916122-61-1). K C Pubns.

HOPE

Goff, James & Goff, Margaret. In Every Person Who Hopes... (Orig.). 1980. pap. 3.75 (ISBN 0-377-00096-5). Friend Pr.

HOPI INDIANS

see Indians of North America–Southwest, New

HOPKINS, GERARD MANLEY, 1844-1889

Ritz, Jean-Georges. Le Poete Gerard Manley Hopkins, S. J. (1844-1889) 726p. 1980. Repr. of 1963 ed. lib. bdg. 100.00 (ISBN 0-8492-7748-5). R West.

Walhout, Donald. Send My Roots Rain: A Study of Religious Experience in the Poetry of Gerard Manley Hopkins. LC 80-23549. 210p. 1981. 14.95x (ISBN 0-8214-0565-9). Ohio U Pr.

HOPKINS, SAMUEL, 1721-1803

Conforti, Joseph. Samuel Hopkins & the New Divinity Movement: Calvinism, the Congregational Ministry, & Reform in New England Between the Great Awakenings. 240p. (Orig.). 1981. pap. 12.95 (ISBN 0-8028-1871-4). Eerdmans.

HOPPED-UP MOTORS

see Automobiles, Racing–Motors

HORACE (QUINTUS HORATIUS FLACCUS)

Fraenkel, Eduard. Horace. 478p. 1981. pap. 23.95 (ISBN 0-19-814376-1). Oxford U Pr.

Fuchs, Jacob, tr. Horace's Satires & Epistles. 1980. pap. 3.95 (ISBN 0-393-04479-3). Norton.

HORIZONTAL PROPERTY

see Condominium (Housing)

HORMONAL STEROIDS

see Steroid Hormones

HORMONE RESEARCH

Blecher, Melvin & Barr, Robert S. Receptors & Human Disease. (Illus.). 350p. 1981. write for info. (0609-6). Williams & Wilkins.

Greep, Roy, ed. Recent Progress in Hormone Research, Vol. 37. (Serial Publication). 1981. price not set (ISBN 0-12-571137-9). Acad Pr.

HORMONE THERAPY

Van Wimersma Greidanus, T. B. & Rees, L. H., eds. ACTH & LPH in Health & Disease. (Frontiers of Hormone Research Ser.: Vol. 8). (Illus.). 200p. 1981. 60.00 (ISBN 3-8055-1977-X). S Karger.

HORMONES

see also Endocrine Glands; Endocrinology; Hormone Research; Hormone Therapy; Hormones, Sex; Peptide Hormones; Plant Hormones; Steroid Hormones also names of hormones

Blecher, Melvin & Barr, Robert S. Receptors & Human Disease. (Illus.). 350p. 1981. write for info. (0609-6). Williams & Wilkins.

Horrobin, David F. Prolactin, Vol. 8. (Annual Research Reviews Ser.). 152p. 1981. 24.00 (ISBN 0-88831-093-5). Eden Med Res.

Keller, Paul J. Hormornal Disorders in Gynecology. (Illus.). 113p. 1981. pap. 16.50 (ISBN 0-387-10341-4). Springer-Verlag.

Li, Choh H., ed. Hormonal Proteins & Peptides, 7 vols. Incl. Vol. 1. 1973. 31.00 (ISBN 0-12-447201-X); Vol. 2. 1973. 37.50 (ISBN 0-12-447202-8); Vol. 3. 1975. 43.00 (ISBN 0-12-447203-6); Vol. 4. 1977. 33.00 (ISBN 0-12-447204-4); Vol. 5. Lipotropin & Related Peptides. 1978. 29.00 (ISBN 0-12-447205-2); Vol. 6. Thyroid Hormones. 1978. 48.50 (ISBN 0-12-447206-0); Vol. 7. Hypothalmic Hormones. 1979. 32.50 (ISBN 0-12-447207-9). LC 78-5444. Acad Pr.

Litwack, G., ed. Biochemical Actions of Hormones, Vol. 8. 1981. write for info. (ISBN 0-12-452808-2). Acad Pr.

Litwack, Gerald, ed. Biochemical Actions of Hormones, 7 vols. Incl. Vol. 1. 1970. 52.75 (ISBN 0-12-452801-5); Vol. 2. 1972. 52.75 (ISBN 0-12-452802-3); Vol. 3. 1975. 51.50 (ISBN 0-12-452803-1); Vol. 4. 1977. 47.00 (ISBN 0-12-452804-X); Vol. 5. 1978. 42.50 (ISBN 0-12-452805-8); Vol. 6. 1979. 42.50 (ISBN 0-12-452806-6); Vol. 7. 1980. 45.00 (ISBN 0-12-452807-4). LC 70-107567. Acad Pr.

Mori, K., et al. Synthetic Chemistry of Insect Phermones & Juvenile Hormones. (Recent Developments in the Chemistry of Natural Carbon Compounds: Vol. 9). (Illus.). 420p. 1979. 40.00x (ISBN 963-05-1632-2). Intl Pubns Serv.

Munson, P. L., et al, eds. Vitamins & Hormones, Vol. 38. (Serial Publication Ser.). 1981. write for info. (ISBN 0-12-709838-0). Acad Pr.

The Ontogeny & Phylogeny of Hormone Receptors. (Monographs in Developmental Biology). (Illus.). 200p. 1981. pap. 72.00 (ISBN 3-8055-2174-X). S Karger.

Verandakis, A. Hormones in Development & Aging. Date not set. text ed. price not set (ISBN 0-89335-140-7). Spectrum Pub.

HORMONES (PLANTS)

see Plant Hormones

HORMONES, SEX

see also names of hormones, e.g. Androgens, Testosterone

Kilshaw. Steroids & Non-Steroid Hormones. 1981. text ed. price not set. Butterworth.

HOROSCOPES

George, Llewellyn. The A to Z Horoscope Maker & Delineator. 13th, rev. ed. Bytheriver, Marylee, ed. (Illus.). 600p. (Orig.). 1981. 17.95 (ISBN 0-87542-263-2). Llewellyn Pubns.

Goodman, Linda. Linda Goodman's Love Signs: A New Approach to the Human Heart. (Illus.). 1980. pap. 7.95 (ISBN 0-449-90043-6, Columbine). Fawcett.

Jay, Michael. Gay Love Signs. (Orig.). 1980. pap. 6.95 (ISBN 0-345-28774-6). Ballantine.

Schulman, Martin. Celestial Harmony: A Guide to Horoscope Interpretation. 1980. pap. 7.95 (ISBN 0-87728-495-4). Weiser.

HOROSCOPY

see Astrology

HORROR FILMS

Adkinson, A. Wyle & Fry, N., eds. The House of Horror: The Story of Hammer Films. LC 74-76299. 1974. 6.95 (ISBN 0-89388-163-5). Okpaku Communications.

HORROR TALES

Canning. Fifty Great Horror Stories. Date not set. 4.98 (ISBN 0-517-13671-6). Bonanza.

HORROR TALES–HISTORY AND CRITICISM

Tymn, Marshall B. Horror & Supernatural Literature. 320p. 1981. 22.50 (ISBN 0-8352-1341-2). Bowker.

HORS D'OEUVRES

see Cookery (Appetizers)

HORSE

see Horses

HORSE-BREAKING

see Horse-Training

HORSE BREEDING

Blakely, James. Horses & Horse Sense: The Practical Science of Horse Husbandry. 1981. 17.95 (ISBN 0-8359-2887-X); text ed. 14.95 (ISBN 0-8359-2887-X); instr's. manual free (ISBN 0-8359-2888-8). Reston.

Feeding the Horse. Date not set. lib. bdg. 10.75 (ISBN 0-936032-04-9). Thoroughbred Own & Breed.

Names in Pedigrees. Date not set. lib. bdg. 11.00. Thoroughbred Own & Breed.

Thoroughbred Owners & Breeders Association. The Breeder's Guide for 1980. 1981. 57.50 (ISBN 0-936032-41-3). Thoroughbred O.

--Thoroughbred Broodmare Records, 1980. 1981. text ed. 66.75 (ISBN 0-936032-42-1); leather bdg. 77.75 (ISBN 0-936032-43-X). Thoroughbred O.

Wharton, Mary E. & Bowen, Edward L. The Horse World of the Bluegrass, Vol. 1. Denbo, Bruce F. & Wharton, Mary E., eds. 246p. 1980. 30.00 (ISBN 0-934554-00-5). Host Assoc.

HORSE-RACING

see also Harness Racing; Steeplechasing

Blood-Horse Editors. Principal Winners Abroad of 1980. (Annual Supplement of the Blood-Horse). (Orig.). 1981. pap. 10.00 (ISBN 0-936032-38-3). Thoroughbred Own & Breed.

--Sires of Runners, 1980. 1981. pap. 10.00 (ISBN 0-936032-37-5). Thoroughbred Own & Breed.

--Stakes Winners of 1980. (Annual Supplement of the Blood-Horse). 1981. lib. bdg. 20.00 (ISBN 0-936032-39-1); pap. 10.00 (ISBN 0-936032-40-5). Thoroughbred Own & Breed.

Churchill, Peter. Horse Racing. (Illus.). 168p. 1981. 12.95 (ISBN 0-7137-1016-0, Pub. by Blandford Pr England); pap. 6.95 (ISBN 0-7137-1115-9). Sterling.

Savitt, Sam. One Horse, One Hundred Miles, One Day: The Story of the Tevis Cup Endurance Ride. LC 80-2777. (Illus.). 96p. (gr. 7 up). 1981. PLB 7.95 (ISBN 0-396-07935-0). Dodd.

A Second Quarter Century of American Racing. Date not set. 27.25 (ISBN 0-936032-08-1). Thoroughbred Own & Breed.

Shaefer, Jack. Great Endurance Horse Race. (Illus.). 112p. (Orig.). 1981. pap. 6.95 (ISBN 0-88496-165-6). Capra Pr.

HORSE-SHOWS

see also Rodeos

Blood-Horse Editors. Auctions of 1980. (Annual Supplement of the Blood-Horse). (Illus.). 190p. (Orig.). 1981. pap. 10.00 (ISBN 0-936032-36-7). Thoroughbred Own & Breed.

HORSE TRAILS

see Trails

HORSE-TRAINING

Burch. Training Thoroughbred Horses. 2nd rev. ed. 1973. lib. bdg. 10.75 (ISBN 0-936032-29-4). Thoroughbred Own & Breed.

Rabinowitz, Sandy. How I Trained My Colt. LC 79-3162. (Reading-on-My-Own Bk.). (Illus.). 64p. (gr. 2). 1981. 4.95a (ISBN 0-385-15423-2); PLB (ISBN 0-385-15424-0). Doubleday.

Sautter, Frederic J. & Glover, John A. Behavior, Development & Training of the Horse: A Primer of Equine Psychology. LC 80-23654. 176p. 1980. lib. bdg. 9.95 (ISBN 0-668-04809-3, 4809). Arco.

HORSEMANSHIP

see also Rodeos

Brandl, Albert. Modern Riding. (EP Sports Ser.). (Illus.). 142p. 1981. 12.95 (ISBN 0-8069-9133-X, Pub. by EP Publishing England). Sterling.

Burn, Barbara. Complete Guide to Riding People's Horses. (Illus.). 256p. 1981. pap. 5.95 (ISBN 0-312-15746-0). St Martin.

Evans, J. Warren. Horses: A Guide to Their Care & Enjoyment. LC 80-29070. (Illus.). 1981. text ed. price not set (ISBN 0-7167-1253-9). W H Freeman.

Flandorffer, Tamas & Hajas, Jozsef. The Horse & Horsemanship. Kortvelyessy, Eniko, tr. (Illus.). 184p. 1979. 12.50x (ISBN 963-13-3701-4). Intl Pubns Serv.

Fry, Joan & Denby-Wrightson, Kathryn. The Beginning Dressage Book: A Guide to the Basics for Horse & Rider. LC 80-16950. (Illus.). 224p. 1981. 10.95 (ISBN 0-668-04969-3, 4969). Arco.

Ingram, Patricia & Hollander, Lewis. Successful Endurance Riding: The Ultimate Test of Horsemanship. 192p. 1981. 11.95 (ISBN 0-8289-0423-5). Greene.

Starkey, Jane, ed. Horse Sense: Buying & Looking After Your First Horse. (Illus.). 128p. 1981. 9.95 (ISBN 0-8069-3746-7); lib. bdg. 9.29 (ISBN 0-8069-3747-5). Sterling.

Wright, Gordon, frwd. by. George H. Morris Teaches Beginners How to Ride: A Clinic for Instructors, Parents, & Students. LC 79-7224. (Illus.). 144p. 1981. 10.95 (ISBN 0-385-14226-9). Doubleday.

HORSEMANSHIP–DICTIONARIES

Vansteenwyk, E. Illustrated Horseback Riding Dictionary for Young People. 1980. pap. 2.50 (ISBN 0-13-450908-0). P-H.

HORSEMANSHIP–JUVENILE LITERATURE

Thomas, Art & Blackburn, Emily. Horseback Riding Is for Me. (Sports for Me Bks.). (Illus.). (gr. 2-5). 1981. PLB 5.95 (ISBN 0-8225-1092-8). Lerner Pubns.

Van Steenwyk, Elizabeth. Illustrated Riding Dictionary for Young People. LC 80-81789. (Illustrated Dictionaries). (Illus.). 128p. (gr. 5 up). 1981. PLB 6.89 (ISBN 0-8178-0015-8). Harvey.

Wheatley, George. The Young Rider's Companion. (Adult & Young Adult Bks.). (Illus.). 120p. (gr. 4 up). 1981. PLB 14.95 (ISBN 0-8225-0767-6). Lerner Pubns.

HORSES

Blakely, James. Horses & Horse Sense: The Practical Science of Horse Husbandry. 1981. 17.95 (ISBN 0-8359-2887-X); text ed. 14.95 (ISBN 0-8359-2887-X); instr's. manual free (ISBN 0-8359-2888-8). Reston.

Blood-Horse Editors. Auctions of 1980. (Annual Supplement of the Blood-Horse). (Illus.). 190p. (Orig.). 1981. pap. 10.00 (ISBN 0-936032-36-7). Thoroughbred Own & Breed.

Bowen. Thoroughbreds of 1976. Date not set. 46.25 (ISBN 0-936032-14-6). Thoroughbred Own & Breed.

--Thoroughbreds of 1978. Date not set. 36.25 (ISBN 0-936032-15-4). Thoroughbred Own & Breed.

Bradley, Melvin. Horses: A Pactical & Scientific Approach. (Illus.). 560p. 1980. text ed. 19.95x. McGraw.

Evans, J. Warren. Horses: A Guide to Their Care & Enjoyment. LC 80-29070. (Illus.). 1981. text ed. price not set (ISBN 0-7167-1253-9). W H Freeman.

Feeding the Horse. Date not set. lib. bdg. 10.75 (ISBN 0-936032-04-9). Thoroughbred Own & Breed.

Flandorffer, Tamas & Hajas, Jozsef. The Horse & Horsemanship. Kortvelyessy, Eniko, tr. (Illus.). 184p. 1979. 12.50x (ISBN 963-13-3701-4). Intl Pubns Serv.

Martin, George A. The Family Horse. 12.50 (ISBN 0-88427-020-3). Green Hill.

Names in Pedigrees. Date not set. lib. bdg. 11.00. Thoroughbred Own & Breed.

The Pleasure Horse. 96p. 2.95 (ISBN 0-88453-004-3). Berkshire Traveller.

Stallion Register, 1980. Date not set. lib. bdg. 20.00 (ISBN 0-936032-27-8); pap. 10.00 (ISBN 0-936032-28-6). Thoroughbred Own & Breed.

Thoroughbred Broodmare Records, Nineteen Seventy-Eight. Date not set. 66.75 (ISBN 0-936032-11-1). Thoroughbred Own & Breed.

Thoroughbred Owner & Breeder Directory, 1976. Date not set. 97.50. Thoroughbred Own & Breed.

Thoroughbred Owner & Breeder Directory, 1978. Date not set. 27.50 (ISBN 0-936032-13-8). Thoroughbred Own & Breed.

HORSES–ANATOMY

Bradley, Melvin. Horses: A Pactical & Scientific Approach. (Illus.). 560p. 1980. text ed. 19.95x. McGraw.

HORSES–BREEDING

see Horse Breeding

HORSES–EXHIBITIONS

see Horse-Shows

HORSES–HISTORY

Denhardt, Robert M. The Horse of the Americas. LC 74-5955. (Illus.). 343p. 1981. pap. 8.95 (ISBN 0-8061-1724-9). U of Okla Pr.

Hart, Edward. The Heavy Horse at Work. (Illus.). 64p. 1981. pap. 5.95 (ISBN 0-7134-3805-3, Pub. by Batsford England). David & Charles.

HORSES–JUVENILE LITERATURE

Brown, Fern. Behind the Scenes at the Horse Hospital. Tucker, Kathleen, ed. (Behind the Scenes Ser.). (Illus.). 48p. (gr. 3-9). 1981. 7.50 (ISBN 0-8075-0610-9). A Whitman.

Cole, Joanna. A Horse's Body. LC 80-28147. (Illus.). 48p. (gr. k-3). 1981. 6.95 (ISBN 0-688-00362-1); PLB 6.67 (ISBN 0-688-00363-X). Morrow.

Patent, Dorothy H. Horses & Their Wild Relatives. LC 80-23559. (Illus.). 128p. (gr. 5 up). 1981. 8.95 (ISBN 0-8234-0383-1). Holiday.

Radlauer, Ed & Radlauer, Ruth. Horse Mania. LC 80-21550. (Mania Bks). (Illus.). 32p. (gr. k-5). 1981. PLB 7.95g (ISBN 0-516-07784-8, Elk Grove Bks). Childrens.

Thelwell, Norman. Pony Birthday Book. (Illus.). 192p. 1979. 6.95 (ISBN 0-684-16235-0). Scribner.

HORSES–TRAINING

see Horse-Training

HORTICULTURE

see also Agricultural Pests; Fruit-Culture; Greenhouses; Landscape Gardening; Mushroom Culture; Nurseries (Horticulture); Plant Propagation; Plants, Potted; Pruning; Truck Farming; Vegetable Gardening

Janick, Jules, ed. Horticultural Reviews, Vol 3. (Illus.). 1981. lib. bdg. 33.00 (ISBN 0-87055-383-6). AVI.

Schumann, Donna N. Living with Plants: A Guide to the Practical Application of Botany. (Illus.). 328p. (Orig.). 1980. pap. 14.20 (ISBN 0-916422-20-8). Mad River.

HORTICULTURE–BIBLIOGRAPHY

Everett, T. H. The New York Botanical Garden Illustrated Encyclopedia of Horticulture, 10 vols. 1980. Set. lib. bdg. 525.00 (ISBN 0-8240-7222-7). Garland Pub.

HOSPITAL ADMINISTRATION

see Hospitals–Administration

HOSPITAL ATTENDANTS

see Hospitals–Staff

HOSPITAL CARE
see also Coronary Care Units; Intensive Care Units; Monitoring (Hospital Care)
American Hospital Association. Hospital Literature Index: 1978, Vol. 34. 350p. 75.00 (ISBN 0-87258-347-3, 1389). Am Hospital.
Carroll, Walter J., ed. Hospital-Health Care Training Media Profiles, Vol. 8. 1981. 85.00 (ISBN 0-88367-206-5). Olympic Media.
Dunlap, Alice, et al, eds. Hospital Literature Index: 1980 Cumulative Annual, Vol. 36. 704p. 1981. 72.00 (ISBN 0-87258-348-1). Am Hospital.
Laufman, Harold. Hospital Special Care Facilities: Planning for User Needs. (Clinical Engineering Ser.). 1981. price not set (ISBN 0-12-437740-8). Acad Pr.
Lewis, Frank. Average Length of Stay on Short-Stay Hospitals United States, 1977. Shipp, Audrey, ed. (Ser. 13-50). 50p. 1980. pap. text ed. 1.75 (ISBN 0-8406-0198-0). Natl Ctr Health Stats.
National Society of Patient Representatives of the American Hospital Association. Assessing the Patient Representative Program in Hospitals. LC 80-28949. (Illus., Orig.). 1981. pap. 8.00 (ISBN 0-87258-334-1, 1082). Am Hospital.
Ratliff, Bascom W. Leaving the Hospital: Discharge Planning for Total Patient Care. 176p. 1981. 19.75 (ISBN 0-398-04146-6). C C Thomas.
Skillicorn, Stanley A. Quality & Accountability: A New Era in American Hospitals. (Illus.). 143p. 1980. 14.00 (ISBN 0-917636-03-1). Edit Consult.
Society of Paitent Representatives of the American Hospital Association. Essentials of Patient Representative Programs in Hospitals. LC 78-26889. 1978. pap. 8.75 (ISBN 0-87258-255-8, 1251). Am Hospital.
Thompson, Richard A. & Stanford, Gene. Child Life in Hospitals. 1981. write for info (ISBN 0-398-04445-7). C C Thomas.
HOSPITAL CARE, COST OF
see Hospitals–Rates
HOSPITAL CHARGES
see Hospitals–Rates
HOSPITAL EMPLOYEES
see Hospitals–Staff
HOSPITAL MANAGEMENT
see Hospitals–Administration
HOSPITAL MEDICAL RECORDS
see Medical Records
HOSPITAL PERSONNEL
see Hospitals–Staff
HOSPITAL PHARMACIES
Hassan, William E., Jr. Hospital Pharmacy. 4th ed. LC 80-20700. (Illus.). 525p. 1981. text ed. write for info. (ISBN 0-8121-0772-1). Lea & Febiger.
HOSPITAL RATES
see Hospitals–Rates
HOSPITAL SOCIAL WORK
see Medical Social Work
HOSPITAL TRAINING SCHOOLS
see Nursing Schools
HOSPITAL WORKERS
see Hospitals–Staff
HOSPITALERS
Gervers, Michael, ed. The Cartulary of the Order of St. John of Jerusalem (Hospitalers) in England. (Records of Social & Economic History Ser.). 618p. 1980. 169.00 (ISBN 0-19-725996-0). Oxford U Pr.
HOSPITALS
see also Hospital Care; Hospital Pharmacies; Hospitalers; Medical Centers; Medicine, Clinical; Nurses and Nursing; Nursing Homes; Psychiatric Hospitals
also subdivision Hospitals under names of cities, e.g. New York (City)–Hospitals
Barocci, Thomas A. Non-Profit Hospitals: Their Structure, Human Resources, & Economic Importance. LC 80-22075. (Illus.). 224p. 1980. 19.95 (ISBN 0-86569-054-5). Auburn Hse.
Hamill, Charlotte M. The Day Hospital: Organization & Management. LC 80-607802. 192p. 1981. text ed. write for info. (ISBN 0-8261-3040-2). Springer Pub.
Minnesota Hospital Association, compiled by. The Changing Role of the Hospital: Options for the Future. 336p. (Orig.). 1980. pap. 35.00 (ISBN 0-87258-310-4, 1186). Am Hospital.
Siafaca, Ekaterini. Investor-Owned Hospitals & Their Role in the Changing U. S. Health Care System. (Health Care Economics & Technology Ser.). 192p. 1981. 32.95x (ISBN 0-86621-000-8). F&S Pr.
Skillicorn, Stanley A. Quality & Accountability: A New Era in American Hospitals. (Illus.). 143p. 1980. 14.00 (ISBN 0-917636-03-1). Edit Consult.
Snook, Donald. Hospitals: What They Are & How They Work. 250p. 1981. text ed. price not set (ISBN 0-89443-339-3). Aspen Systems.
Strahan, Geneviene W. Inpatient Health Facilities Statistics United States, 1978. Olmsted, Mary, ed. (Ser. 14, No. 24). 50p. 1980. pap. text ed. 1.75 (ISBN 0-8406-0204-9). Natl Ctr Educ Broker.
HOSPITALS–ACCOUNTING
American Medical Record Association. Glossary of Hospital Terms. 2nd rev. ed. 128p. 1974. 5.75 (ISBN 0-686-68577-6, 14911). Hospital Finan.
AUPHA Task Force on Financial Management. Financial Management of Health Care Organizations: A Referenced Outline & Annotated Bibliography. 237p. 1978. 8.00 (ISBN 0-686-68588-1, 14921). Hospital Finan.
Berman, Howard W. & Weeks, Lewis E. The Financial Management of Hospitals. 3rd ed. (Illus.). 585p. 1976. 17.50 (ISBN 0-686-68573-3, 1496). Hospital Finan.
Budgeting Procedures for Hospitals. 88p. 1971. 8.25 (ISBN 0-686-68590-3, 1130). Hospital Finan.
Chart of Accounts for Hospitals. 157p. 1976. 10.75 (ISBN 0-686-68594-6, 2830). Hospital Finan.
Cleverley, William O. Financial Management of Health Care Facilities. 394p. 1976. 18.75 (ISBN 0-686-68581-4, 14915). Hospital Finan.
Hall, B. T. Auditing the Modern Hospital. 256p. 1977. 32.95 (ISBN 0-686-68587-3, 14920). Hospital Finan.
Internal Control & Internal Auditing for Hospitals. 66p. 1969. 8.00 (ISBN 0-686-68592-X, 2025). Hospital Finan.
Kinzer, David M. Health Controls Out of Control. 194p. 9.75 (ISBN 0-686-68584-9, 14918). Hospital Finan.
Lipson, Stephen H. & Hensel, Mary D. Hospital Manpower Budget Preparation Manual. 200p. 1975. 12.00 (ISBN 0-686-68583-0, 14917). Hospital Finan.
Mehta, Nitin H. & Maher, Donald J. Hospital Accounting Systems & Controls. 272p. 1977. 32.95 (ISBN 0-686-68586-5, 14919). Hospital Finan.
Salkever, David & Bice, Thomas. Hospital Certificate-of-Need Controls: Impact on Investment, Costs, & Use. 1979. pap. 5.25 (ISBN 0-8447-3325-3). Am Enterprise.
Silvers, John B. & Prahalad, C. K. Financial Management of Health Institutions. 339p. 1974. 17.95 (ISBN 0-686-68576-8, 14910). Hospital Finan.
HOSPITALS–ADMINISTRATION
American Hospital Association. Hospital Computer Systems Planning: Preparation of Request for Proposal. LC 80-18002. 124p. 1980. 25.00 (1445). Am Hospital.
--Organizing a Cost Containment Committee in the Hospital. LC 76-26173. 104p. 1979. 15.00 (ISBN 0-87258-272-8, 1450). Am Hospital.
American Society for Hospital Food Service Administrators of the American Hospital Association. Preparation of a Hospital Food Service Department Budget. LC 78-24399. 56p. 1978. pap. 9.50 (ISBN 0-87258-254-X, 1615). Am Hospital.
Block, Lee F., ed. Marketing for Hospitals in Hard Times. 200p. 1981. text ed. 17.95 (ISBN 0-931028-16-7); pap. 13.95 (ISBN 0-931028-15-9). Teach'em.
Dixon, Nancy, et al. Quality, Trending, & Management for the Eighties (QTM-80) 236p. 1980. pap. 40.00 (ISBN 0-87258-345-7, 1377). Am Hospital.
Gardocki, Gloria J. & Pokras, Robert. Utilization of Short-Stay Hospitals by Persons with Heart Disease & Malignant Neoplasms. Shipp, Audrey, ed. (Ser. Thirteen: No. 52). 50p. 1981. pap. 1.75 (ISBN 0-8406-0214-6). Natl Ctr Health Stats.
The Hospital Admitting Department. 90p. 1977. 9.50 (ISBN 0-87258-200-0, 1855). Hospital Finan.
Hospital Costs Containment Operations Management. 201p. 1979. 37.50 (ISBN 0-686-68595-4, 2435). Hospital Finan.
Hospital Financial Management Association. Cost Effectiveness Notebook: Nineteen Seventy-Nine Update. 1979. looseleaf 4.00 (ISBN 0-930228-12-X). Hospital Finan.
Kozak, Lola J. The Status of Hospital Discharge Data, in Denmark, Scotland, West Germany, & the United States. Cox, Klaudia, ed. (Ser. Two: No. 88). 55p. 1981. pap. 1.75 (ISBN 0-8406-0211-1). Natl Ctr Health Stats.
Larson, Gene F. The Unforgettable. rev. ed. 1978. 10.00 (ISBN 0-686-68574-1, 1491). Hospital Finan.
Minnesota Hospital Association, compiled by. The Changing Role of the Hospital: Options for the Future. 336p. (Orig.). 1980. pap. 35.00 (ISBN 0-87258-310-4, 1186). Am Hospital.
Modern Hospital: International Planning Practices. (Illus.). 682p. 1980. text ed. 69.95 (ISBN 0-89443-355-5). Aspen Systems.
National Society of Patient Representatives of the American Hospital Association. Assessing the Patient Representative Program in Hospitals. LC 80-28949. (Illus., Orig.). 1981. pap. 8.00 (ISBN 0-87258-334-1, 1082). Am Hospital.
The Practice of Planning in Health Care Institutions. 100p. 1973. 11.25 (ISBN 0-686-68593-8, 2765). Hospital Finan.
Salkever, David & Bice, Thomas. Hospital Certificate-of-Need Controls: Impact on Investment, Costs, & Use. 1979. pap. 5.25 (ISBN 0-8447-3325-3). Am Enterprise.
Society for Hospital Social Work Directors of the American Hospital Association. Reporting System for Hospital Social Work. LC 78-5696. 1978. pap. 8.75 (ISBN 0-87258-237-X, 1562). Am Hospital.
HOSPITALS–ATTENDANTS
see Hospitals–Staff
HOSPITALS–CHARGES
see Hospitals–Rates
HOSPITALS–DESIGN AND CONSTRUCTION
Sarkissian, Wendy, et al. The Design of Medical Environments for Children & Adolescents: An Annotated Bibliography. (Archtecture Ser.: Bibliography A-261). 65p. 1980. pap. 7.00. Vance Biblios.
HOSPITALS–EMPLOYEES
see Hospitals–Staff
HOSPITALS–HYGIENE
Castle, M. Hospital Infection Control: Principles & Practices. LC 80-13424. 1980. 16.95 (ISBN 0-471-05395-3). Wiley.
HOSPITALS–JUVENILE LITERATURE
Holmes, Burnham. Early Morning Rounds: A Portrait of a Hospital. LC 80-69995. (Illus.). 128p. (gr. 7 up). 1981. 9.95 (ISBN 0-590-07611-6, Four Winds). Schol Bk Serv.
HOSPITALS–MANAGEMENT AND REGULATION
see Hospitals–Administration
HOSPITALS–NURSES
see Hospitals–Staff; Nurses and Nursing
HOSPITALS–OUTPATIENT SERVICES
Access to Home Care. 1980. 3.00. Comm Coun Great NY.
Rosenbaum, Ernest H., et al. Going Home: A Home Care Training Program. (Illus.). 160p. 1980. 12.00 (ISBN 0-915950-49-9); three ring binder 12.00 (ISBN 0-915950-48-0). Bull Pub.
HOSPITALS–PHARMACEUTICAL SERVICES
see Hospital Pharmacies
HOSPITALS–PHARMACY DEPARTMENTS
see Hospital Pharmacies
HOSPITALS–PSYCHIATRIC SERVICES
see Psychiatric Hospitals
HOSPITALS–RATES
American Hospital Association. Organizing a Cost Containment Committee in the Hospital. LC 76-26173. 104p. 1979. 15.00 (ISBN 0-87258-272-8, 1450). Am Hospital.
Cost Finding & Rate Setting for Hospitals. 103p. 1968. 9.25 (ISBN 0-686-68591-1, 1365). Hospital Finan.
Hospital Costs Containment Operations Management. 201p. 1979. 37.50 (ISBN 0-686-68595-4, 2435). Hospital Finan.
Hospital Financial Management Association. Cost Effectiveness Notebook: Nineteen Seventy-Nine Update. 1979. looseleaf 4.00 (ISBN 0-930228-12-X). Hospital Finan.
Hospital Regulation Through State Rate Review: Mandated Interference or a Noble Intrusion. 116p. 1978. 7.90 (ISBN 0-686-68585-7, 14922). Hospital Finan.
Ward, Richard A. The Economics of Health Resources. 150p. 1975. 10.25 (ISBN 0-686-68580-6, 14914). Hospital Finan.
HOSPITALS–SAFETY MEASURES
Colling, Russell L. Hospital Security. 2nd ed. 1981. text ed. price not set. Butterworths.
Stanley, Paul E., ed. Handbook of Hospital Safety. 416p. 1981. 59.95 (ISBN 0-8493-0751-1). CRC Pr.
HOSPITALS–STAFF
American Hospital Association. Technology Evaluation & Acquisition Methods (TEAM) for Hospitals. LC 79-21859. (Illus.). 212p. 1979. 200.00 (ISBN 0-87258-293-0, 1288). Am Hospital.
Massachusetts General Hospital Department of Nursing, et al, eds. Manual of Nursing Procedures. 1980. text ed. write for info. (ISBN 0-316-54958-4); pap. text ed. price not set (ISBN 0-316-54958-4). Little.
Record, Jane C. Staffing Primary Care in Nineteen Ninety: Physician Replacement & Cost Savings. (Health Care & Society Ser.: No. 6). 1981. text ed. 23.50 (ISBN 0-8261-3370-3); pap. text ed. cancelled (ISBN 0-8261-3371-1). Springer Pub.
Society for Hospital Social Work Directors of the American Hospital Association. Social Work Staff Development for Health Care. LC 76-41793. 1976. pap. 7.25 (ISBN 0-87258-322-8, 2550). Am Hospital.
HOSPITALS, INSANE
see Psychiatric Hospitals
HOSPITALS, PSYCHIATRIC
see Psychiatric Hospitals
HOST-PARASITE RELATIONSHIPS
McKelvey, John J., Jr., et al, eds. Vectors of Disease Agents: Interactions with Plants, Animals, & Men. 350p. 1980. 34.95 (ISBN 0-03-056887-0). Praeger.
HOSTILITIES
see War
HOSTILITY (PSYCHOLOGY)
Sumrall, Lester. Hostility. 1981. pap. 3.95 (ISBN 0-8407-5765-4). Nelson.
HOT CAKES
see Pancakes, Waffles, etc.
HOT-HOUSES
see Greenhouses
HOT RODS
see Automobiles, Racing; Automobiles, Racing–Motors
HOTEL ADMINISTRATION
see Hotel Management
HOTEL MANAGEMENT
Coffman, C. DeWitt. Hospitality for Sale: Techniques of Promoting Business for Hospitality Establishments. LC 79-28567. (Illus.). 339p. 1980. 17.56x (ISBN 0-86612-000-9); text ed. 21.95 (ISBN 0-686-28892-0). Educ Inst Am Hotel.
Eyster, James J. The Negotiation & Administration of Hotel Management Contracts. 2nd, rev. ed. (Illus.). 209p. 1980. text ed. 22.95 (ISBN 0-937056-04-9). Cornell U Sch Hotel.
Stokes, Arch. The Collective Bargaining Handbook for Hotels, Restaurants & Institutions. (The Stokes Employee Relations Ser.). 352p. 1981. spiral bdg. 39.95 (ISBN 0-8436-2149-4). CBI Pub.
HOTELS, TAVERNS, ETC.
see also Hotel Management; Restaurants, Lunchrooms, etc.
also names of individual hotels and restaurants
Brown, Robert L. Saloons of the American West. (Illus.). 144p. 16.50 (ISBN 0-913582-24-7). Sundance.
Crossette, Barbara. America's Wonderful Little Hotels & Inns. (Illus.). 400p. 1981. 14.95 (ISBN 0-312-92016-4); pap. 8.95 (ISBN 0-312-92016-4). St Martin.
Crossette, Barbara, ed. America's Wonderful Little Hotels & Inns: New, Revised 1981-82 Edition. (Illus.). 400p. 1981. 14.95 (ISBN 0-312-92016-4); pap. 8.95 (ISBN 0-312-92017-2). Congdon & Lattes.
Melcher, Joan. Watering Hole: A User's Guide to Montana Bars. 128p. 1980. pap. text ed. 6.95 (ISBN 0-938314-00-9). MT Mag.
Romantik Hotels. Romantik Hotels & Restaurants. 160p. 1981. 4.98 (ISBN 0-912944-66-3). Berkshire Traveller.
Ross, Corinne M. The Southern Guest House Book. (Illus.). 192p. 1981. pap. 6.95 (ISBN 0-914788-35-3). East Woods.
Simpson, Norman T. Country Inns & Back Roads, North America. 16th ed. (Illus.). 450p. (Orig.). 1981. pap. 8.95 (ISBN 0-912944-65-X). Berkshire Traveller.
Wrigley's Hotel Directory, 1980. 70th ed. 272p. (Orig.). 1980. vinyl cover 19.00x (ISBN 0-8002-2698-4). Intl Pubns Serv.
HOTELS, TAVERNS, ETC.–MANAGEMENT
see Hotel Management
HOTELS, TAVERNS, ETC.–CANADA
Simpson, Norman T. Country Inns & Back Roads, North America. 16th ed. (Illus.). 450p. (Orig.). 1981. pap. 8.95 (ISBN 0-912944-65-X). Berkshire Traveller.
HOTELS, TAVERNS, ETC.–EUROPE
Rubenstein, Hilary. Europe's Wonderful Little Hotels & Inns. (Illus.). 512p. 1981. 12.95 (ISBN 0-312-92188-8); pap. 8.95 (ISBN 0-312-92189-6). St Martin.
Rubinstein, Hilary, ed. Europe's Wonderful Little Hotels & Inns. 3rd rev. ed. (Illus.). 512p. 1981. 14.95 (ISBN 0-86553-038-6); pap. 8.95 (ISBN 0-312-92189-6). Congdon & Lattes.
HOTELS, TAVERNS, ETC.–GREAT BRITAIN
Automobile Association. AA Hotels & Restaurants in Britain. rev. ed. (Illus.). 600p. 1981. pap. write for info. (ISBN 0-86145-040-X, Pub. by Auto Assn-British Tourist Authority England). Merrimack Bk Serv.
Automobile Association & British Tourist Authority. London: Hotels & Restaurants Incl. Budget Accom. rev. ed. (Illus.). 146p. 1981. pap. write for info. (ISBN 0-7095-0576-0, Pub. by Auto Assn-British Tourist Authority England). Merrimack Bk Serv.
Ronay, Egon. Egon Ronay's Nineteen Eighty-One Pub Guide. rev. ed. (Illus.). 1981. pap. price not set (ISBN 0-14-005813-3, Pub. by Auto Assn-British Tourist Authority England). Merrimack Bk Serv.
Scottish Tourist Board. Scotland: Bed & Breakfast. rev. ed. (Illus.). 252p. 1981. pap. price not set (ISBN 0-85419-170-4, Pub. by Auto Assn-British Tourist Authority England). Merrimack Bk Serv.
--Scotland: Hotels & Guesthouses. rev. ed. (Illus.). 328p. 1981. pap. price not set (ISBN 0-85419-169-0, Pub. by Auto Assn-British Tourist Authority England). Merrimack Bk Serv.
HOTLINES (PSYCHIATRY)
see Crisis Intervention (Psychiatry)
HOURS (TIME)
see Sun-Dials
HOUSE BUYING
see also Home Ownership
Hammond, David. The Home Ownership Game & How to Win It. LC 80-68693. (Illus.). 112p. 1981. 13.50 (ISBN 0-7153-7710-8). David & Charles.
Harrison, Henry S. & Leonard, Margery B. Home Buying: The Complete Illustrated Guide. Berlin, Helene, ed. (Illus.). 500p. (Orig.). 1980. pap. 14.95 (ISBN 0-913652-18-0, BK128). Realtors Natl.
Hess, Nancy R. The Home Buyer's Guide. (Illus.). 224p. 1981. pap. 5.95 (ISBN 0-13-392647-8, Spec). P-H.
Howell, Yvonne & Miller, Harry. Selling the Solar Home: California Edition. 93p. 1981. pap. 10.00 (ISBN 0-89934-081-4). Solar Energy Info.
Jacobe, Dennis & Kendall, James N. How to Get the Money to by Your New Home. 200p. 1981. 10.95 (ISBN 0-87094-258-1). Dow Jones-Irwin.

Kravitol, R. Buying, Owning & Selling a Home in the Nineteen Eighties. 1981. pap. 9.95 (ISBN 0-13-109504-8). P-H.
Murphy, Michael C. How to Buy a Home While You Can Still Afford to. LC 79-91390. (Illus.). 160p. 1981. 12.95 (ISBN 0-8069-7154-1); lib. bdg. 9.89 (ISBN 0-8069-7155-X); pap. 6.95 (ISBN 0-8069-8912-2). Sterling.
Phelon, Sheldon, & Masar, Inc., ed. Sheldon's Retail & Phelon's Resident Byers Book. 97th ed. 1981. pap. 70.00 (ISBN 0-686-28951-X). P S & M Inc.
Watkins, Art. How to Avoid the Ten Biggest Home Buying Traps. 1979. pap. 4.50 (ISBN 0-8015-3895-5, Hawthorn). Dutton.

HOUSE CONSTRUCTION
see also Dwellings–Maintenance and Repair; Dwellings–Remodeling; House Painting
Barton, Byron. Building a House. LC 80-22674. (Illus.). 32p. (ps-1). 1981. 7.95 (ISBN 0-688-80291-5); PLB 7.63 (ISBN 0-688-84291-7). Greenwillow.
Farmer, W. D. Homes for Pleasant Living. 35th ed. (Illus., Orig.). 1980. pap. 2.50 (ISBN 0-931518-12-1). W D Farmer.
--Homes for Pleasant Living. 36th ed. (Illus.). 72p. (Orig.). 1980. pap. 3.50 (ISBN 0-931518-13-X). W D Farmer.
Feldheym, Len. Pole House Construction. 224p. (Orig.). 1981. pap. 15.75 (ISBN 0-910460-85-X). Craftsman.
Kern, Ken. Owner-Built Pole Frame House. (Illus.). 192p. 1981. 14.95 (ISBN 0-684-16767-0, ScribT). Scribner.
Kravitol, R. Buying, Owning & Selling a Home in the Nineteen Eighties. 1981. pap. 9.95 (ISBN 0-13-109504-8). P-H.
Martindale, David. Earth Shelters: The New Way to Live. (Illus.). 160p. 1981. 18.95 (ISBN 0-525-93199-6); pap. 10.95 (ISBN 0-525-93200-3). Dutton.
Vila, Robert & Stephen, George. Bob Vila's This Old House. 1981. 20.00 (ISBN 0-525-93192-9); pap. 13.95 (ISBN 0-525-47670-9). Dutton.
Woodframe Houses: Construction & Maintenance. (Illus.). 223p. 1981. pap. 7.95 (ISBN 0-8069-7512-1). Sterling.

HOUSE DECORATION
see Interior Decoration

HOUSE DRAINAGE
see Plumbing; Sewerage

HOUSE-FLIES
see Flies

HOUSE FURNISHINGS
see also Carpets; Clocks and Watches; Furniture; Household Appliances; Interior Decoration; Kitchen Utensils; Pottery; Rugs; Silverwork
Tornborg, Pat. Spring Cleaning. (Sesame Street Early Bird Bks). (Illus.). (ps). 1981. 3.50 (ISBN 0-307-11601-8, Golden Pr). Western Pub.

HOUSE PAINTING
Goodier, J. H. Dictionary of Painting & Decorating. 308p. 1974. 39.50x (ISBN 0-85264-224-5, Pub. by Griffin England). State Mutual Bk.
Gundrey, Elizabeth. Painting & Decorating. (Orig.). 1980. pap. 6.95x (ISBN 0-8464-1036-2). Beekman Pubs.
Hurst, A. E. & Goodier, J. M. Painting & Decorating. 620p. 1980. 75.00x (ISBN 0-85264-243-1, Pub. by Griffin England). State Mutual Bk.

HOUSE PLANS
see Architecture, Domestic–Designs and Plans

HOUSE PLANTS
see also Plants, Potted
also names of plants or classes of plants used as house plants, e.g., African Violets; Cactus; Succulent Plants
Fitch, Charles M. The Complete Book of Houseplants. (Illus.). 320p. 1980. pap. 7.95 (ISBN 0-8015-1660-9, Hawthorn). Dutton.
Kramer, Jack. Indoor Trees. 1980. 25.00x (ISBN 0-232-51399-6, Pub. by Darton-Longman-Todd England). State Mutual Bk.
--Once-a-Week Indoor Gardening Guide. (Orig.). pap. 1.75 (ISBN 0-515-04475-X). Jove Pubns.
Kurtz, Regina & Van Gieson, Susan. Interior Planting Line Art. (Illus.). 1980. pap. text ed. 25.00 (ISBN 0-918436-13-3). Environ Design.
Olson, Craig. Craig Olson's Decorating with Plants. Grooms, Kathe, ed. (Illus.). 110p. 1981. pap. 2.95 (ISBN 0-915658-31-3). Meadowbrook Pr.
Pliner, Robert. The Lazy Indoor Gardener. 1976. pap. 3.95 (ISBN 0-394-73160-3). Random.
Robinette, Gary O. Planting Details. 200p. 1980. pap. text ed. 20.00 (ISBN 0-918436-14-1). Environ Design.
Scrivens, Steven. Interior Planting in Large Buildings: A Handbook for Architects Interior Designers & Horticulturists. LC 80-23565. 200p. 1981. 44.95 (ISBN 0-470-27067-5). Halsted Pr.

HOUSE PURCHASING
see House Buying

HOUSE SELLING
Kravitol, R. Buying, Owning & Selling a Home in the Nineteen Eighties. 1981. pap. 9.95 (ISBN 0-13-109504-8). P-H.

HOUSEHOLD APPLIANCES
Advice About Household Appliances, Cooking, Entertaining. (Home Adviser Ser.). 80p. (Orig.). 1981. pap. 1.95 (ISBN 0-8326-2403-9, 7052). Delair.

HOUSEHOLD EXPENSES
see Cost and Standard of Living; Home Economics–Accounting

HOUSEHOLD GOODS
see House Furnishings; Household Appliances; Kitchen Utensils

HOUSEHOLD MANAGEMENT
see Home Economics

HOUSEHOLD MOVING
see Moving, Household

HOUSEHOLD UTENSILS
see Kitchen Utensils

HOUSEHOLD WORKERS
see Servants

HOUSEKEEPING
see Home Economics

HOUSEMAIDS
see Servants

HOUSES
see Architecture, Domestic; Dwellings

HOUSES, APARTMENT
see Apartment Houses

HOUSES, DEMOUNTABLE
see Buildings, Prefabricated

HOUSES, PREFABRICATED
see Buildings, Prefabricated

HOUSEWIVES
see also Mothers; Wives
Andre, Rae. Homemakers: The Forgotten Workers. LC 80-21258. 1981. 15.00not set (ISBN 0-226-01993-4). U of Chicago Pr.
Coyle, Neva. Living Free. 160p. 1981. pap. 3.95 (ISBN 0-87123-346-0, 210346). Bethany Fell.
Lopata, Helena Z. Occupation: Housewife. LC 80-23658. (Illus.). xvi, 387p. 1980. Repr. of 1971 ed. lib. bdg. 25.00x (ISBN 0-313-22697-0, LOOH). Greenwood.

HOUSING
see also Aged–Dwellings; Home Ownership; Housing, Rural; Mobile Homes; Public Housing
Bourne, Larry S. Geography of Housing. (Scripta Series in Geography). 290p. 1981. 27.95 (ISBN 0-470-27058-6); pap. 19.95 (ISBN 0-470-27059-4). Halsted Pr.
Compendium of Housing Statistics Nineteen Seventy-Five to Nineteen Seventy-Seven. 354p. 1980. pap. 31.00 (UN80/17/4, UN). Unipub.
Golany, Gideon. Housing in Arid Lands Design & Planning. LC 80-41108. 257p. 1980. 104.95 (ISBN 0-470-27055-1). Halsted Pr.
Johnson, M. Bruce, ed. Resolving the Housing Crisis. (Pacific Institute on Public Policy Research Ser.). 1981. price not set professional reference (ISBN 0-88410-381-1). Ballinger Pub.
Koenigsberger, O. H., et al, eds. Work of Charles Abrams: Housing & Urban Renewal in the U. S. A. & the Third World. (Illus.). 264p. 1980. 55.00 (ISBN 0-08-026111-6). Pergamon.
McConnell, Stephen R. & Usher, Carolyn E. Intergenerational House-Sharing. LC 80-67436. (Andrus Papers). 52p. 1980. pap. 3.25 (ISBN 0-88474-098-6). USC Andrus Geron.
McGuire, Chester C. International Housing Policies: A Comparative Analysis. LC 80-8815. 1981. price not set (ISBN 0-669-04385-0). Lexington Bks.
Mandelker, Daniel R. & Montgomery, Roger. Housing in America: Problems & Perspectives. 2nd ed. 600p. pap. 19.50 (ISBN 0-672-83699-8). Bobbs.
Newman, Oscar. Community of Interest. (Illus.). 368p. 1981. pap. 8.95 (ISBN 0-385-11124-X, Anch). Doubleday.
Principles & Recommendations for Population & Housing Censuses. (Statistical Papers Ser.: No. 67). 330p. 1980. pap. 20.00 (UN80/17/8, UN). Unipub.
Stryk, Raymond J. & Bendick, Mark, Jr., eds. Housing Vouchers for the Poor: Lessons from a National Experiment. 1981. 25.00 (ISBN 0-87766-280-0). Urban Inst.

HOUSING–FINANCE
McConnell, Stephen R. & Usher, Carolyn E. Intergenerational House-Sharing. LC 80-67436. (Andrus Papers). 52p. 1980. pap. 3.25 (ISBN 0-88474-098-6). USC Andrus Geron.
Stegman, Michael. Housing Investment in the Inner City: The Dynamics of Decline: a Study of Baltimore Maryland, 1968-1970. 320p. 1972. 18.00 (ISBN 0-262-19103-2). MIT Pr.

HOUSING–LAW AND LEGISLATION
Weicher, John C. Housing: Federal Policies & Programs. 1980. pap. 6.25 (ISBN 0-8447-3378-4). Am Enterprise.

HOUSING–AFRICA
Lewin, A. C. Housing Cooperatives in Developing Countries: A Manual for Self-Help in Low Cost Housing Schemes. 192p. 1981. 35.75 (ISBN 0-471-27820-3, Pub. by Wiley-Intrscience); pap. write for info. (ISBN 0-471-27819-X). Wiley.

HOUSING–EUROPE
Goldenberg, Leon & Weese, Harry. Housing for the Elderly: New Trends in Europe. 1981. lib. bdg. 29.50 (ISBN 0-8240-7139-5). Garland Pub.

HOUSING–GREAT BRITAIN
Burke, Gill. Housing & Social Justice. 240p. 1981. pap. text ed. 12.95x (ISBN 0-582-29514-9). Longman.

HOUSING–NEAR EAST
Hardoy, Jorge E. & Satterthwaite, David. Shelter - Need & Response: Housing, Land & Settlement Policies in Seventeen Third World Nations. 1981. price not set (ISBN 0-471-27919-6, Pub. by Wiley-Interscience). Wiley.

HOUSING, RURAL
see also Cottages; Country Homes
Jones, Alwyn. Rural Housing. 76p. 1975. pap. text ed. 5.00x (ISBN 0-7135-1887-1, Pub. by Bedford England). Renouf.

HOUSING FOR THE AGED
see Aged–Dwellings

HOUSING PROJECTS, GOVERNMENT
see Public Housing

HOUSMAN, ALFRED EDWARD, 1859-1936
Graves, Perceval. A. E. Housman: The Scholar-Poet. 15.95 (ISBN 0-684-16106-0). Scribner.

HOUSTON, TEXAS
Hargrove, Jim, et al. Five Hundred Things to Do in Houston for Free. 140p. Date not set. pap. 3.95 (ISBN 0-695-81563-6). Follett.
Wilson, Ann Q. Houston: A Pictorial History. Friedman, Donna R., ed. (Illus.). 205p. Date not set. pap. price not set (ISBN 0-89865-087-9). Donning Co.

HOUSTON FOOTBALL CLUB (AMERICAN LEAGUE)
Rothaus, Jim. Houston Oilers. (NFL Today Ser.). (gr. 3-12). 1980. PLB 6.45 (ISBN 0-87191-796-3); pap. 2.95 (ISBN 0-89812-248-1). Creative Ed.

HOVERCRAFT
see Ground-Effect Machines

HUALAPAI INDIANS
see Indians of North America–Southwest, New

HUDSON, WILLIAM HENRY, 1841-1922
Hudson, W. H. Far Away & Long Ago. 350p. 1981. 14.95 (ISBN 0-8180-0251-4). Horizon.

HUDSON RIVER AND VALLEY
O'Brien, Raymond J. American Sublime: Landscape & Scenery of the Lower Hudson Valley. (Illus.). 336p. 1981. 19.95 (ISBN 0-686-69182-2). Columbia U Pr.

HUGHES, HOWARD ROBARD, 1905-1976
Irving, Clifford. The Hoax. 380p. 1981. 14.95 (ISBN 0-932966-14-4). Permanent Pr.

HUGHES, LANGSTON, 1902-1967
Larson, Norita D. Langston Hughes, Poet of Harlem. Redpath, Ann, ed. (People to Remember Ser.). (Illus.). 32p. (gr. 5-9). 1981. PLB 5.95 (ISBN 0-87191-798-X). Creative Ed.
Myers, Elisabeth P. Langston Hughes. (gr. k-6). Date not set. pap. price not set (ISBN 0-440-44723-2, YB). Dell.

HUGUENOTS IN FRANCE
Gray, Janet G. The French Huguenots. 200p. (Orig.). 1981. pap. 6.95 (ISBN 0-8010-3758-1). Baker Bk.

HULL, ENGLAND
Gillett, Edward & MacMahon, Kenneth A., eds. A History of Hull. (Illus.). 448p. 1980. 45.00x (ISBN 0-19-713436-X). Oxford U Pr.

HUMAN ABNORMALITIES
see Abnormalities, Human

HUMAN ANATOMY
see Anatomy, Human

HUMAN BEHAVIOR
see also Behavior Modification; Psychobiology; Psychology, Comparative
Barraclough, Norman. Preology: The Scientific Study of the Planning of Human Development. LC 80-40600. 265p. 1980. pap. 13.25 (ISBN 0-08-026083-7). Pergamon.
Bateson, P. P. & Klopfer, Peter H., eds. Perspectives in Ethology: Advantages of Diversity, Vol. 4. 230p. 1980. 25.00 (ISBN 0-306-40511-3, Plenum Pr). Plenum Pub.
Bufford, Rodger K. The Human Reflex: Behavioral Psychology in Biblical Perspective. LC 80-8900. (Illus.). 256p. 1981. 12.95 (ISBN 0-06-061165-0). Har-Row.
Counte, Michael A. & Christman, Luther. Interpersonal Behavior & Health Care. (Behavioral Sciences for the Health Care Professional Ser.). 128p. (Orig.). 1981. lib. bdg. 15.00x (ISBN 0-86531-008-4); pap. text ed. 6.00x (ISBN 0-86531-009-2). Westview.
Crook, John H. The Evolution of Human Consciousness. (Illus.). 462p. 1980. 39.00x (ISBN 0-19-857174-7). Oxford U Pr.
Davis, Keith. Human Behavior at Work. 6th ed. (Management Ser.). (Illus.). 576p. 1981. text ed. 18.95x (ISBN 0-07-015516-X, C); instrs'. manual & test file avail. (ISBN 0-07-015517-8); study guide avail. (ISBN 0-07-015535-6) (ISBN 0-686-68262-9). McGraw.
Davis, Keith & Newstrom, John. Organizational Behavior: A Book of Readings. 6th ed. (Illus.). 468p. Date not set. text ed. price not set (ISBN 0-07-015500-3, C). McGraw.
Garfinkel, Alan. Forms of Explanation: Rethinking the Questions in Social Theory. LC 80-2341. 192p. 1981. 16.00x (ISBN 0-300-02136-4). Yale U Pr.
Harrison, Paul D. The Truth of Human Nature. (Illus.). 300p. (Orig.). Date not set. 14.95 (ISBN 0-938058-25-8); pap. 11.95 (ISBN 0-938058-26-6). Wrightwill Pub.
Hayes, Harold. Three Levels of Time. 1981. 12.95 (ISBN 0-525-21853-X). Dutton.
Hofer, Myron. The Roots of Human Behavior: An Introduction to the Psychobiology of Early Development. LC 80-28377. (Psychology Ser.). (Illus.). 1981. text ed. price not set (ISBN 0-7167-1277-6); pap. text ed. price not set (ISBN 0-7167-1278-4). W H Freeman.
Kierkegaard, Soren A. The Internal Development of Man in Dynamio Representational Expressions. Karlweiss, Joseph R., ed. (Illus.). 107p. 1981. 49.75 (ISBN 0-89266-273-5). Am Classical Coll Pr.
Lombardi, Thomas P. Career Adaptive Behavior Inventory Activity Book. Preston, J. B., ed. 88p. (Orig.). 1980. pap. text ed. 10.00x (ISBN 0-87562-066-3). Spec Child.
Merikangas, James R. Brain-Behavior Relationships. LC 79-2075. 240p. 1981. 23.95x (ISBN 0-669-03082-1). Lexington Bks.
Milton, Charles R. Human Behavior in Organizations. (Illus.). 432p. 1981. text ed. 18.95x (ISBN 0-13-444596-1). P-H.
Moore, John. Zeluco: Various Views of Human Nature Taken from Life and Manners, Foreign and Domestic, 2 vols. in 1. LC 80-2492. 1981. Repr. of 1789 ed. 89.50 (ISBN 0-404-19126-6). AMS Pr.
Persinger, Michael A. Weather Matrix & Human Behavior. LC 80-18422. 300p. 1980. 27.95 (ISBN 0-03-057731-4). Praeger.
Russell, Hugh & Black, Kenneth. Understanding & Influencing Human Behavior. (Illus.). 240p. 1981. text ed. 12.95 (ISBN 0-13-936674-1, Spec). P-H.
Rutter, M., et al, eds. Education, Health & Behavior. 390p. 1981. Repr. of 1970 ed. text ed. price not set (ISBN 0-89874-268-4). Krieger.
Sierles, Frederick. Clinical Behavioral Science. 1981. text ed. write for info. (ISBN 0-89335-131-8). Spectrum Pub.
Singleton, W. T., et al, eds. The Analysis of Social Skill. (NATO Conference Ser., Series III, Human Factors: Vol. II). 350p. 1980. 35.00 (ISBN 0-306-40337-4). Plenum Pub.
Statt, D. Dictionary of Human Behavior. 1981. text ed. 15.70 (ISBN 0-686-69149-0, Pub. by Har-Row Ltd England). Har-Row.
Stein, R. Incest & Human Love. LC 73-82641. 1973. 8.95 (ISBN 0-89388-090-6). Okpaku Communications.
Stevenson, Leslie, ed. The Study of Human Nature. 352p. 1981. pap. text ed. 7.95x (ISBN 0-19-502827-9). Oxford U Pr.
Williams, Terrell G. Consumer Behavior: Concepts & Strategies. 600p. pap. text ed. 14.36 (ISBN 0-8299-0420-4). West Pub.

HUMAN BEINGS ON OTHER PLANETS
see Life on Other Planets

HUMAN BIOLOGY
see also Physical Anthropology
Bliss. Bliss Bibliography, Second Class H: Anthropology, Human Biology & Health Sciences. 1981. price not set (ISBN 0-408-70828-X). Butterworth.
Borek, Ernest. The Atoms Within Us. rev. ed. LC 80-19010. 272p. 1980. text ed. 20.00x (ISBN 0-231-04386-4); pap. text ed. 6.00x (ISBN 0-231-04387-2). Columbia U Pr.
Carter, Nicholas, ed. Development, Growth & Aging. 169p. 1980. 27.50x (ISBN 0-85664-861-2, Pub. by Croom Helm Ltd England). Biblio Dist.
East, Edward M., ed. Biology in Human Affairs. 399p. 1980. Repr. of 1931 ed. lib. bdg. 30.00 (ISBN 0-8495-1348-0). Arden Lib.
Weiss & Mann. Human Biology & Behavior. 3rd ed. 1981. text ed. 16.95 (ISBN 0-316-92891-7); training manual free (ISBN 0-316-92892-5). Little.

HUMAN BODY
see Body, Human

HUMAN CHROMOSOMES
Boyce, A. J. Chromosome Variation in Human Evolution, Vol. 14. 131p. 1975. 24.95 (ISBN 0-470-09330-7). Wiley.

HUMAN ECOLOGY
see also Anthropo-Geography; Community Life; Environmental Policy; Man–Influence of Environment; Man–Influence on Nature; Population; Social Psychology; Sociology
Benoit, Emile. Progress & Survival: An Essay on the the Future of Mankind. Gohn, Jack B., ed. 144p. 1980. 17.95 (ISBN 0-03-056911-7). Praeger.
Bham, Thamsanqa E. The Will to Live. LC 79-66395. 115p. 1980. 6.95 (ISBN 0-533-04383-2). Vantage.
Golden-Wolfe, Malka. Malka - A Total Celebration (a survival manual) LC 80-53000. (Illus., Orig.). 1980. pap. 5.85 (ISBN 0-937946-00-1). Univ Goddess.
Hayes, Harold. Three Levels of Time. 1981. 12.95 (ISBN 0-525-21853-X). Dutton.
Henderson, M. A. The Survival Resource Book. (Illus.). 180p. 1981. pap. 8.95 (ISBN 0-312-77951-8). St Martin.
Jochim, Michael. Strategies for Survival: Cultural Behavior in an Ecological Context. 1981. price not set (ISBN 0-12-385460-1). Acad Pr.
Odum, Howard T. & Odum, Elisabeth C. Energy Basis for Man & Nature. 2nd ed. (Illus.). 352p. 1981. text ed. 19.50 (ISBN 0-07-047511-3, C); pap. text ed. 12.95 (ISBN 0-07-047510-5, C); instrs'. manual avail. McGraw.

Polgar, Steven, ed. Culture & Population: A Collection of Current Studies. LC 80-20070. (Carolina Population Center, Monograph: 9). vi, 195p. 1980. Repr. of 1971 ed. lib. bdg. 19.75x (ISBN 0-313-22620-2, POCP). Greenwood.

HUMAN ENGINEERING

see also Human Information Processing; Man-Machine Systems

DECHEMA, Deutsche Gesellschaft Fuer Chemisches Apparatewesen E. V., ed. Biotechnology: Proceedings of the First European Congress on Biotechnology. (Dechema Monographs: Vol. 82). 304p. 1979. pap. text ed. 37.50 (ISBN 3-527-10765-7). Verlag Chemie.

HUMAN ENVIRONMENT

see Human Ecology

HUMAN EVOLUTION

see also Fossil Man; Sociobiology

Boyce, A. J. Chromosome Variation in Human Evolution, Vol. 14. 131p. 1975. 24.95 (ISBN 0-470-09330-7). Wiley.

Darwin, Charles. The Descent of Man & Selection in Relation to Sex. LC 80-8679. (Illus.). 935p. 1981. 30.00x (ISBN 0-691-08278-2); pap. 8.95 (ISBN 0-691-02369-7). Princeton U Pr.

Kierkegaard, Soren A. The Internal Development of Man in Dynamio Representational Expressions. Karlweiss, Joseph R., ed. (Illus.). 107p. 1981. 49.75 (ISBN 0-89266-273-5). Am Classical Coll Pr.

Sigmon, Becky A. & Cybulski, Jerome S., eds. Homo Erectus: Essays in Honor of Davidson Black. 336p. 1981. 30.00x (ISBN 0-8020-5511-7). U of Toronto Pr.

Steele, E. J. Somatic Selection & Adaptive Evolution. 100p. 1980. 30.00x (Pub. by Croom Helm England). State Mutual Bk.

HUMAN EXPERIMENTATION IN MEDICINE

Jones, James H. Bad Blood: The Tuskegee Syphilis Experiment. LC 80-69281. (Illus.). 1981. 12.95 (ISBN 0-02-916670-5). Free Pr.

HUMAN GENETICS

see also Genetic Counseling; Genetics; Human Chromosomes

Bergsma, Daniel, ed. Human Gene Mapping 4, Vol. 4. LC 78-61294. (S. Karger Ser.: Vol. 14, No. 4). 1978. 50.00. March of Dimes.

--An International System for Human Cytogenetic Namenclature. LC 78-61295. (S. Karger Ser.: Vol. 14, No. 8). 1978. 10.00. March of Dimes.

Blank, Robert H. The Political Implications of Human Genetic Technology. (Special Studies in Science, Technology, & Public Policy). 209p. (Orig.). 1981. lib. bdg. 24.00x (ISBN 0-89158-975-9); pap. text ed. 12.00x (ISBN 0-86531-193-5). Westview.

Capron, Alexander M., et al, eds. Genetic Counseling: Fact, Values & Norms. LC 79-1736. (Alan R. Liss Ser.: Vol. 15, No. 2). 1979. write for info. (ISBN 0-8451-1025-X). March of Dimes.

Epstein, Charles J., ed. Risk, Communication, & Decision Making in Genetic Counseling. LC 79-5120. (Alan R. Liss Ser.: Vol. 15, No. 5c). 1979. 36.00 (ISBN 0-8451-1030-6). March of Dimes.

Ohta, T. Evolution & Variation of Multigene Families. (Lecture Notes in Biomathematics: Vol. 37). 131p. 1980. pap. 9.80 (ISBN 0-387-09998-0). Springer-Verlag.

Reed, Sheldon, ed. Counseling in Medical Genetics. 246p. 1980. 26.00 (ISBN 0-8451-0208-7). A R Liss.

HUMAN GEOGRAPHY

see Anthropo-Geography

HUMAN INFORMATION PROCESSING

Cassel, Don & Jackson, Martin. Introduction to Computers & Information Processing: Language Free Editon. 1981. text ed. 17.95 (ISBN 0-8359-3155-2); study guide 7.95 (ISBN 0-8359-3157-9); instrs'. manual avail. (ISBN 0-8359-3156-0). Reston.

Howell, William C. & Fleishman, Edwin A., eds. Information Processing & Decision Making. (Human Performance & Productivity Ser.: Vol. 2). 1981. professional ref. text 19.95 (ISBN 0-89859-090-6). L Erlbaum Assocs.

Pavlidis, Theo. Computer Graphics & Pictorial Information Processing. (Illus.). 1981. text ed. price not set (ISBN 0-914894-65-X). Computer Sci.

HUMAN INTERACTION

see Social Interaction

HUMAN OPERATORS (SYSTEMS ENGINEERING)

see Man-Machine Systems

HUMAN PALEONTOLOGY

see Fossil Man

HUMAN PARASITOLOGY

see Medical Parasitology

HUMAN RELATIONS

see Interpersonal Relations

HUMAN RESOURCE DEVELOPMENT

see Manpower Policy

HUMAN RIGHTS

see Civil Rights; Civil Rights (International Law)

HUMAN SCIENCE

see Anthroposophy

HUMAN SUBSYSTEMS (SYSTEMS ENGINEERING)

see Man-Machine Systems

HUMANE SOCIETIES

see Animals, Treatment Of; Child Welfare

HUMANE TREATMENT OF ANIMALS

see Animals, Treatment of

HUMANISM

see also Civilization; Culture; Hellenism; Humanities; Learning and Scholarship; Philosophical Anthropology; Renaissance

Ehrenfeld, David. The Arrogance of Humanism. (A Galaxy Bk.: No. 637). 304p. 1981. pap. 5.95 (ISBN 0-19-502890-2). Oxford U Pr.

Hirsch, Rudolf. The Printed Word: Its Impact & Diffusion (Primarily in the 15th & 16th Centuries) 338p. 1980. 70.00x (ISBN 0-86078-026-0, Pub. by Variorum England). State Mutual Bk.

Rothman, David, et al. Humanitarianism or Control? A Symposium on Nineteenth-Century Social Reform in Britain & America. Wiener, Martin, ed. (Rice University Studies: Vol. 67, No. 1). (Orig.). 1981. pap. 5.50x (ISBN 0-89263-248-8). Rice Univ.

HUMANISM–20TH CENTURY

Miller, Ronald B., ed. Black American Literature & Humanism. LC 80-5179. 122p. 1981. price not set (ISBN 0-8131-1436-5). U Pr of Ky.

HUMANISM, RELIGIOUS

Baker, Derek, ed. Religion & Humanism. (Studies in Church History: Vol. 17). 500p. 1981. 36.00x (ISBN 0-631-18050-8, Pub. by Basil Blackwell). Biblio Dist.

HUMANISTIC PSYCHOLOGY

Child, Irvin L. Humanistic Psychology & the Research Tradition: Their Several Virtues. 220p. 1981. Repr. of 1973 ed. text ed. write for info. (ISBN 0-89874-277-3). Krieger.

Pollio, Howard. Behavior & Existence: An Introduction to Empirical Humanistic Psychology. 512p. 1981. text ed. 18.95 (ISBN 0-8185-0425-0). Brooks-Cole.

HUMANISTS

Kurtz, Paul, ed. A Secular Humanist Declaration. 40p. 81. pap. 1.95 (ISBN 0-87975-149-5). Prometheus Bks.

Lennon, Colm. Richard Stanihurst the Dubliner Fifteen Forty-Seven-Sixteen Eighteen. 200p. 1981. 27.50x (Pub. by Irish Academic Pr Ireland). Biblio Dist.

HUMANITARIANISM (RELIGION)

see Humanism–20th Century; Jesus Christ–Divinity; Positivism; Socinianism; Trinity; Unitarianism

HUMANITIES

Arthos, John. The Status of the Humanities. LC 80-84732. 1981. 12.50 (ISBN 0-686-68870-8). Philos Lib.

Cross, Neal M., et al. The Search for Personal Freedom, Vol. 1. 6th ed. 500p. 1981. pap. write for info. (ISBN 0-697-03121-7). Vol. 2 (ISBN 0-697-03122-5). Wm C Brown.

Patton, Peter C. & Holoien, Renee A., eds. Computing in the Humanities. LC 79-3185. 1981. price not set (ISBN 0-669-03397-9). Lexington Bks.

Rademaker, C. S. Life & Work of Gerardus Joannes Vossius (1577-1659) (Respublica Literaria Neerlandica). 472p. 1980. text ed. 48.50x (ISBN 90-232-1785-3). Humanities.

U R T A-A T A Humanities & the Theatre, 2 vols. Set. 5.00; ATA members 3.00. Am Theatre Assoc.

HUMANITIES–BIBLIOGRAPHY

Library Association (London) British Humanities Index 1979. LC 63-24940. 744p. 1980. 190.00x (ISBN 0-85365-583-9). Intl Pubns Serv.

Magill, Frank N., ed. Magill Books Index. LC 80-53597. 800p. 1980. 35.00 (ISBN 0-89356-200-9). Salem Pr.

HUMANITIES–STUDY AND TEACHING

Spann, Sylvia & Culp, Mary B., eds. Thematic Units in Teaching English & the Humanities. 2nd ed. (Orig.). (gr. 6-12). 1980. pap. text ed. 6.00 (ISBN 0-8141-5376-3). NCTE.

Trzyna, Thomas N., et al, eds. Careers for Humanities - Liberal Arts Majors: A Guide to Programs & Resources. LC 80-50352. 188p. (Orig.). 1980. pap. 22.50x (ISBN 0-9604078-0-4). Weatherford.

HUMBUG

see Impostors and Imposture

HUME, DAVID, 1711-1776

Beauchamp, Tom L. & Rosenberg, Alexander. Hume & the Problem of Causation. 352p. 1981. 22.50. Oxford U Pr.

Botwinick, Aryeh. Ethics, Politics & Epistemology: A Study in the Unity of Hume's Thought. LC 80-5809. 197p. 1980. lib. bdg. 17.50 (ISBN 0-8191-1288-7); pap. text ed. 9.00 (ISBN 0-8191-1289-5). U Pr of Amer.

Stroud, Barry. Hume. (Arguments of the Philosophers Ser.). 292p. 1981. pap. 10.00 (ISBN 0-7100-0667-5). Routledge & Kegan.

HUMOR

see Wit and Humor

HUMORISTS

see also Satirists

Nutt, Grady. So Good, So Far. LC 79-90248. 152p. 1981. pap. 4.95 (ISBN 0-914850-68-7). Impact Tenn.

HUMOROUS ILLUSTRATIONS

see Caricatures and Cartoons; Wit and Humor, Pictorial

HUNGARIAN LANGUAGE–DICTIONARIES

Orszagh, Laszlo. Hungarian-English - English-Hungarian Dictionary, 2 vols. 11th, rev. ed. 1977. Set. 15.00 (ISBN 0-686-68937-2). Vol. 1, Hung.-Eng., 464pp (ISBN 963-05-1255-6). Vol. 2, Eng.-Hung., 608pp (ISBN 963-05-1256-4). Heinman.

HUNGARIAN LITERATURE–HISTORY AND CRITICISM

Nyerges, Anton N. Babits & Psychoanalysis Christiana. 100p. (Orig.). 1981. pap. price not set (ISBN 0-9600954-2-X). Nyerges.

HUNGARY

Volgyes, Ivan. Hungary: A Profile. (Nations of Contemporary Eastern Europe). (Illus.). 128p. 1981. lib. bdg. 16.50x (ISBN 0-89158-929-5). Westview.

HUNGARY–DESCRIPTION AND TRAVEL

Enyedi, Gyorgy & Meszaros, Julia, eds. Development of Settlement Systems. (Studies in Geography in Hungary: 15). (Illus.). 265p. 1980. 27.50x (ISBN 963-05-1898-8). Intl Pubns Serv.

HUNGARY–HISTORY

Kosztolnyik, Z. J. Five Eleventh Century Hungarian Kings: Their Policies & Their Relations with Rome. (East European Monographs: No. 79). 288p. 1981. text ed. 20.00x (ISBN 0-914710-73-7). East Eur Quarterly.

Seton-Watson, Hugh & Seton-Watson, Christopher. The Making of a New Europe: R. W. Seton-Watson & the Last Years of Austria-Hungary. 528p. 1981. 50.00 (ISBN 0-295-95792-1). U of Wash Pr.

HUNGARY–POLITICS AND GOVERNMENT

Malyusz, Edith C. The Theatre & National Awakening. Szendrey, Thomas, tr. LC 79-89134. 349p. 1980. write for info. (ISBN 0-914648-10-1). Hungarian Cultural.

HUNGER

Ball, Nicole. World Hunger: A Guide to the Economic & Political Dimensions. Burns, Richard D., ed. (War-Peace Bibliography Ser.: No. 15). (Illus.). 1981. lib. bdg. price not set (ISBN 0-87436-308-X). ABC-Clio.

HUNT, WILLIAM MORRIS, 1824-1879

Ruskin, John. The Art of England: Lectures Given in Oxford by John Ruskin During His Second Tenure of the Slade Professorship. Freedberg, Sydney J., ed. LC 77-25769. (Connosseurship, Criticism, & Art History Ser.: Vol. 23). 292p. 1979. lib. bdg. 21.00 (ISBN 0-8240-3281-0). Garland Pub.

HUNTING

see also Camping; Decoys (Hunting); Falconry; Dogs also headings beginning with names of animals and birds hunted, e.g. Deer Hunting, Duck Shooting, Fox Hunting, Moose Hunting

Danziger, Jeff & Davis, Tom. Unofficial Hunting Rules. (Illus.). 64p. (Orig.). 1980. pap. 3.95 (ISBN 0-9603900-5-7). Lanser Pr.

Elman, Robert, ed. The Complete Book of Hunting. (Illus.). 320p. 1981. 49.95 (ISBN 0-89659-174-3); pap. 16.95 (ISBN 0-89659-150-6). Abbeville Pr.

Lingertwood, Kenneth. Huntsman of Our Time. 15.00x (ISBN 0-392-07938-0, SpS). Soccer.

HUNTING–ANECDOTES, FACETIAE, SATIRE, ETC.

see Hunting Stories

HUNTING–BIBLIOGRAPHY

Glogan, Joseph. Sportsmans Book of U.S. Records. (Illus.). 96p. (Orig.). 1980. pap. text ed. 2.50 (ISBN 0-937328-00-6). NY Hunting.

HUNTING–HISTORY

Hobusch, Erich. Fair Game: A History of Hunting, Shooting & Animal Conservation. Michaelis-Jena, Ruth & Murray, Patrick, trs. from Ger. LC 80-19008. (Illus.). 280p. 1981. 29.95 (ISBN 0-668-05101-9, 5101). Arco.

HUNTING DOGS

Moxon, Peter. Gundogs: Questions & Answers. (Illus.). 96p. (Orig.). 1980. pap. 7.50x (ISBN 0-85242-734-4). Intl Pubns Serv.

HUNTING LEOPARDS

see Cheetahs

HUNTING STORIES

see also American Wit and Humor–Sports and Games

McManus, Patrick. They Shoot Canoes, Don't They? 228p. 1981. 10.95 (ISBN 0-03-058646-1). HR&W.

HUSBAND AND WIFE

see also Divorce; Support (Domestic Relations)

Cothren, Paige. Let None Deal Treacherously. 224p. (Orig.). 1981. pap. 4.95 (ISBN 0-937778-03-6). Fulness Hse.

Durkin, Henry P. Forty-Four Hours to Change Your Life: Marriage Encounter. (Orig.). pap. 1.25 (ISBN 0-89129-139-3). Jove Pubns.

Merrill, Dean, tr. Manual Del Esposo. (Spanish Bks.). (Span.). 1979. 1.90 (ISBN 0-8297-0891-X). Life Pubs Intl.

HUSBANDRY

see Agriculture

HUSSERL, EDMUND, 1859-1938

Dreyfus, Hubert L. & Hall, Harrison, eds. Husserl, Intentionality & Cognitive Science. 1981. text ed. write for info. (ISBN 0-89706-010-5). Bradford Bks.

Lapointe, Francois. Edmund Husserl & His Critics: An International Bibliography (1894-1979) (Bibliographies of Famous Philosophers: Vol. 4). 352p. 1980. 27.50 (ISBN 0-912632-42-9). Philos Document.

McCormick, Peter & Elliston, Frederick A., eds. Husserl: Shorter Works. LC 80-53178. 440p. 1981. text ed. 26.00 (ISBN 0-268-01703-4); pap. text ed. 10.95 (ISBN 0-268-01077-3). U of Notre Dame Pr.

HUTCHINSON, ANNE (MARBURY), 1590-1643

Williams, Selma R. Divine Rebel: The Life of Anne Marbury Hutchinson. LC 80-20109. 256p. 1981. 12.95 (ISBN 0-03-055846-8). HR&W.

HUXLEY, ALDOUS LEONARD, 1894-1963

Leighton, Gerald. Huxley: His Life & Work. 94p. 1980. Repr. lib. bdg. 15.00 (ISBN 0-8492-1649-4). R West.

HUYGENS, CHRISTIAAN, 1629-1695

Symposium on the Life and Work of Christiaan Huygens, Amsterdam, 22-25 August 1979. Studies on Christiaan Huygens: Invited Papers. Bos, H. J., et al, eds. 1980. text ed. 34.25 (ISBN 90-265-0333-4, Pub. by Swets Pub Serv Holland). Swets North Am.

HYBRIDIZATION

see also Genetics

Protides of the Biological Fluids, Colloquium 28: Proceedings of the 28th Colloquium on Protides of the Biological Fluids, Brussels, 5-8 May 1980. LC 58-5908. (Illus.). 600p. 1980. 120.00 (ISBN 0-08-026370-4). Pergamon.

HYDRAULIC CEMENT

see Cement

HYDRAULIC CONVEYING

Stephens, H. S. & Gittins, L., eds. Hydrotransport Seven: Papers Presented at the Seventh International Conference on the Hydraulic Transport of Solids in Pipes. (Illus., Orig.). 1980. pap. 112.00. BHRA Fluid.

HYDRAULIC ENGINEERING

see also Boring; Channels (Hydraulic Engineering); Flood Control; Hydraulic Machinery; Hydraulic Measurements; Hydraulic Mining; Hydraulics; Hydrodynamics; Irrigation; Offshore Structures; Pumping Machinery; Reclamation of Land; Rivers; Water-Supply Engineering; Wells

Hwang, Ned H. Fundamentals of Hydraulic Systems. (P-H Ser. in Environmental Sciences). (Illus.). 352p. 1981. text ed. 28.95 (ISBN 0-13-340000-X). P-H.

Naudascher, E. & Rockwell, D., eds. Practical Experiences with Flow-Induced Vibrations: Symposium Proceedings. (International Association for Hydraulic Research - International Union of Theoretical & Applied Mechanics). (Illus.). 850p. 1980. 82.60 (ISBN 0-387-10314-7). Springer-Verlag.

Sharp, J. J. Hydraulic Modelling. 1981. text ed. price not set (ISBN 0-408-00482-7). Butterworth.

HYDRAULIC MACHINERY

see also Centrifugal Pumps; Pumping Machinery

Mishra, C. B. Hydraulic Machines Through Theory & Examples. x, 318p. (Orig.). 1980. pap. text ed. 10.00x (ISBN 0-210-33860-1). Asia.

HYDRAULIC MEASUREMENTS

Swinney, H. L. & Gollup, J. P., eds. Hydrodynamic Instabilities & the Transition to Turbulence. (Topics in Applied Physics Ser.: Vol. 45). (Illus.). 320p. 1981. 56.60 (ISBN 0-387-10390-2). Springer-Verlag.

HYDRAULIC MINING

see also Gold Mines and Mining

Wilson, Eldred D. Arizona Gold Placers & Placering. (Illus.). 148p. 1980. pap. 5.95 (ISBN 0-89632-003-0). Del Oeste.

HYDRAULIC POWER PLANTS

see Water-Power; Water-Power Electric Plants

HYDRAULICS

see also Channels (Hydraulic Engineering); Fire Extinction; Fluids; Hydraulic Engineering; Hydraulic Measurements

Sharp, J. J. Hydraulic Modelling: Theory & Practice. 1981. text ed. price not set (Fnewnes-Butterworth). Butterworths.

Simon, Andrew L. Practical Hydraulics. 2nd ed. 416p. 1981. text ed. 18.95 (ISBN 0-471-05381-3); tchrs.' ed. 7.50 (ISBN 0-471-07783-6). Wiley.

HYDROAIRPLANES

see Seaplanes

HYDROBIOLOGY

see Fresh-Water Biology; Marine Biology

HYDROBOTANY

see Aquatic Plants

HYDROCARBON RESEARCH

Pucknat, A. W., ed. Health Impacts of Polynuclear Aromatic Hydrocarbons. LC 80-28039. (Environmental Health Review Ser.: No. 5). (Illus.). 271p. 1981. 39.00 (ISBN 0-8155-0840-9). Noyes.

HYDROCARBONS

see also Hydrocarbon Research; Petroleum Products

Jagannath, S. Calculator Programs for the Hydrocarbon Processing Industries, Vol. 2. 1981. 19.95 (ISBN 0-87201-092-9). Gulf Pub.

Norwegian Petroleum Society. Large Scale Flow Measurement of Hydrocarbon Fluids. 173p. 1980. 75.00x (ISBN 82-7270-003-4, Pub. by Norwegian Info Norway). State Mutual Bk.

Pines, Herman. The Chemistry of Catalytic Hydrocarbon Conversions. 1981. price not set (ISBN 0-12-557160-7). Acad Pr.

Pucknat, A. W., ed. Health Impacts of Polynuclear Aromatic Hydrocarbons. LC 80-28039. (Environmental Health Review Ser.: No. 5). (Illus.). 271p. 1981. 39.00 (ISBN 0-8155-0840-9). Noyes.
Rider, Don K. Energy: Hydrocarbon Fuels & Chemical Resources. 600p. 1981. 40.00 (ISBN 0-471-05915-3, Pub. by Wiley-Interscience). Wiley.
HYDROCYCLONES
see Separators (Machines)
HYDRODYNAMICS
see also Channels (Hydraulic Engineering); Hydraulics; Magnetohydrodynamics; Turbulence; Waves
Chandrasekhar, S. Hydrodynamic & Hydromagnetic Stability. (Illus.). 704p. pap. write for info. (ISBN 0-486-64071-X). Dover.
HYDRO-ELECTRIC PLANTS
see Water-Power Electric Plants
HYDROGEN
Hoffman, Peter. The Forever Fuel: The Story of Hydrogen. 250p. 1981. 16.00x (ISBN 0-89158-581-8). Westview.
HYDROGEN BOMB
see also Atomic Bomb
De Volpi, A., et al. Governmental Secrecy & National Security: The Progressive Case. (Pergamon Policy Studies on International Politics). (Illus.). 400p. 1980. 30.00 (ISBN 0-08-025995-2); pap. 15.00 (ISBN 0-08-027529-X). Pergamon.
HYDROGEN NUCLEUS
see Protons
HYDROGENATION
Whitehurst, D. D., ed. Coal Liquefaction Fundamentals. LC 80-20585. (ACS Symposium Ser.: No. 139). 1980. 38.00 (ISBN 0-8412-0587-6). Am Chemical.
HYDROGEOLOGY
Milanovic, Petar. Karst Hydrogeology. 1981. 29.00 (ISBN 0-918334-36-5). WRP.
HYDROGRAPHIC CHARTS
see Nautical Charts
HYDROGRAPHIC SURVEYING
see also Navigation
Norwegian Petroleum Society. Offshore Seismic Data Acquisition & Quality Control. 287p. 1980. 100.00x (ISBN 82-7270-001-8, Pub. by Norwegian Info Norway). State Mutual Bk.
HYDROLOGY
see also Hydrogeology; Oceanography
also headings beginning with the word Water
Applied Modeling of Hydrologic Time Series. 1981. 29.50 (ISBN 0-918334-37-3). WRP.
Casebook of Methods of Computation of Quantitative Changes in the Hydrological Regime of River Basins Due to Human Activities. (Studies & Reports in Hydrology: No. 28). 330p. 1980. pap. 24.25 (ISBN 92-3-101798-5, U1037, UNESCO). Unipub.
Institute of Civil Engineers, UK. Engineering Hydrology Today. 152p. 1980. 65.00x (ISBN 0-7277-0012-X, Pub. by Telford England). State Mutual Bk.
International Hydrological Programme (IHP) Third Session of the Intergovernmental Council Final Report IHP-IC-III. 72p. 1981. pap. 10.00 (ISBN 0-686-69436-8, UNI 1051, UNESCO). Unipub.
Kovacs, G., et al. Subterranean Hydrology. 1981. 45.00 (ISBN 0-918334-35-7). WRP.
HYDROLOGY–DATA PROCESSING
Technical Regulations Hydrology & International Codes. 129p. 1981. pap. 20.00 (ISBN 92-63-10555-3, W477, WMO). Unipub.
HYDROMAGNETIC WAVES
see Magnetohydrodynamics
HYDROMECHANICS
see Fluid Mechanics
HYDROMETRY
see Hydraulic Measurements
HYDROPATHY
see Hydrotherapy
HYDROPHOBIA
see Rabies
HYDROPHYTES
see Algae; Fresh-Water Biology; Fresh-Water Flora; Marine Flora
HYDROTHERAPY
Rhodes, Helen. Doctor, What Can I Do? (Horizon Ser.). 128p. 1981. pap. price not set (ISBN 0-8127-0327-8). Southern Pub.
HYGIENE
Here are entered works on personal body care and cleanliness. Works on optimal physical, mental, and social well-being, as well as how to achieve and preserve it, are entered under Health.
see also Health; Mental Health;
also subdivision Care and hygiene under parts of the body, and under age groups dependent on the assistace of others, e.g. Eye–Care and hygiene; Infants–Care and hygiene; and subdivision Health and hygiene under classes of persons or ethnic groups, e.g. Students–Health and hygiene; Afro-Americans–Health and hygiene
Abrahamson, E. M. & Pezet, A. W. Body, Mind & Sugar. 1977. pap. 3.95 (ISBN 0-380-00903-X, 47415). Avon.
Allen, Eleanor. Wash & Brush up. (Junior Reference Ser.). (Illus.). 64p. (gr. 7 up). 7.95 (ISBN 0-7136-1639-3). Dufour.
Dalet, Roger. How to Safeguard Your Health & Beauty with the Simple Pressure of a Finger. LC 80-5497. (Illus.). 160p. 1981. 10.95 (ISBN 0-8128-2742-2). Stein & Day.
Haas, Elson. Staying Healthy with the Seasons. LC 80-69469. (Illus.). 192p. (Orig.). 1981. pap. 9.95 (ISBN 0-89087-306-2). Celestial Arts.
The Natural Way to Beauty. 3.98. Mayflower Bks.
HYGIENE–ECONOMIC ASPECTS
see Medical Economics
HYGIENE, DENTAL
see Teeth–Care and Hygiene
HYGIENE, PERSONAL
Saffon, M. J. The Fifteen Minute-a-Day Natural Face Lift. 112p. 1981. pap. 3.95 (ISBN 0-446-97788-8). Warner Bks.
HYGIENE, PUBLIC
see Public Health
HYGIENE, RURAL
see Health, Rural
HYGIENE, SOCIAL
see Prostitution; Public Health; Venereal Diseases
HYGIENE, TROPICAL
see Tropical Medicine
HYMNOLOGY
see Hymns
HYMNS
see also Carols; Children's Hymns; Church Music; Religious Poetry
Bausch, Michael & Duck, Ruth. Everflowing Streams. 96p. (Orig.). 1981. pap. 3.95 (ISBN 0-8298-0428-5). Pilgrim NY.
Bennett, Marian, ed. Songs for Preschool Children. LC 80-25091. 96p. 1981. pap. 5.95 (ISBN 0-87239-429-8, 5754). Standard Pub.
Blattner, Elsie & Walker, Luisa, trs. Bosquejos Homileticos. (Spanish Bks.). 1979. 1.75 (ISBN 0-8297-0511-2). Life Pubs Intl.
Evening Light Songs. 512p. 4.50. Faith Pub Hse.
Grieve, Nichol. The Scottish Metrical Psalter (1650) A Revision. 183p. pap. text ed. 2.95 (ISBN 0-567-02127-0). Attic Pr.
Himnos De Gloria y Triunfo. (Spanish Bks.). 1977. 3.75 (ISBN 0-8297-0567-8). Life Pubs Intl.
Himnos De Gloria y Triunfo; Sin Musica. (Spanish Bks.). 1977. 1.40 (ISBN 0-8297-0568-6). Life Pubs Intl.
Hymnos De Gloria; Sin Musica. (Spanish Bks.). 1977. 1.10 (ISBN 0-8297-0566-X). Life Pubs Intl.
Hymnos De Gloria y Triunfo; Sin Musica. (Spanish Bks.). 1977. 1.75 (ISBN 0-8297-0569-4). Life Pubs Intl.
Hymnos De Gloria y Triunfo; Sin Musica. (Spanish Bks.). 1977. 2.60 (ISBN 0-8297-0726-3). Life Pubs Intl.
Mahadevan, T. M. The Hymns of Sankaras. (Illus.). 188p. 1980. text ed. 16.50 (ISBN 0-8426-1652-7). Verry.
Masthay, Carl. Mahican-Language Hymns, Biblical Prose, & Vocabularies from Moravian Sources: With 11 Mohawk Hymns (Transcription & Translation) LC 80-82410. 1980. write for info. Cresset Pubs.
Porter, Ethel & Porter, Hugh. Pilgrim Hymnal. organist's ed. 596p. 8.00. Pilgrim Pr.
Porter, Ethel & Porter, Hugh, eds. Pilgrim Hymnal. 596p. 1931. 6.50 (ISBN 0-8298-0107-3). Pilgrim Pr.
Romero, Juan, tr. Los Himnos De Juan Romero. (Spanish Bks.). (Span.). 1978. 1.60 (ISBN 0-8297-0878-2). Life Pubs Intl.
Shiplett, Gary R. Worship & Hymnody. (Illus.). 122p. (Orig.). 1980. pap. text ed. 5.95 (ISBN 0-916260-08-9). A Meriwether.
HYMNS–CONCORDANCES
Ronander, Albert C. & Porter, Ethel K. Guide to the Pilgrim Hymnal. LC 65-26448. 456p. 1966. 10.95 (ISBN 0-8298-0055-7). Pilgrim Pr.
HYMNS–HISTORY AND CRITICISM
see also Church Music
Colquhoun, Frank. Hymns That Live. 320p. 1981. pap. 6.95 (ISBN 0-87784-473-9). Inter Varsity.
HYMNS, SPANISH
Himnos De Gloria. 150p. pap. 0.75. Faith Pub Hse.
HYPERLIPEMIA
Paoletti, Rodolfo, ed. Hearing on Hypolipidemic Drugs. 1981. text ed. price not set (ISBN 0-89004-649-2). Raven.
HYPERTENSION
Advice About First Aid, High Blood Pressure, Heart Attack. (Home Adviser Ser.). 80p. (Orig.). 1981. pap. 1.95 (ISBN 0-8326-2404-7, 7054). Delair.
Brunner & Gravas. Clinical Hypertension & Hypotension. Date not set. price not set (ISBN 0-8247-1279-X). Dekker.
Buckley, Joseph P. & Ferrario, Carlos, eds. Central Nervous System Mechanisms in Hypertension. 425p. 1981. 39.95 (ISBN 0-89004-545-3). Raven.
Chaithiraphan, S. Current Concept in the Therapy of Hypertension with Beta-Blockers. (Journal: Cardiology Ser.: Vol. 66, Suppl. 1). (Illus.). vi, 62p. 1980. pap. 19.50 (ISBN 3-8055-0912-X). S Karger.
Gant, Norman F. & Worley, Richard. Hypertensions in Pregnancy. 224p. 1980. 18.50x (ISBN 0-8385-4002-3). ACC.
Hutchinson, James C. Hypertension: A Practitioner's Guide to Therapy. 1975. spiral bdg. 13.00 (ISBN 0-87488-709-7). Med Exam.
McDonald. Clinical Kidney Disease & Hypertension. 1980. 32.00. Thieme Stratton.
Murray, Frank. Program Your Heart for Health. 368p. (Orig.). 1977. pap. 2.95 (ISBN 0-915962-20-9). Larchmont Bks.
Philip, T. & Distler, A., eds. Hypertension: Mechanisms & Management. 279p. 1981. pap. 42.00 (ISBN 0-387-10171-3). Springer-Verlag.
Radzialowski. Hypertention Research: Methods & Models. Date not set. price not set (ISBN 0-8247-1344-3). Dekker.
Rosenvold, Lloyd. Drop Your Blood Pressure. 176p. (Orig.). 1980. pap. 2.50 (ISBN 0-515-05721-5). Jove Pubns.
Rowland, Michael. Hypertension of Adults Twenty-Five to Seventy-Four Years of Age: United States, 1971-1975. Shipp, Audrey, ed. (Ser. 11, No. 221). 50p. Date not set. text ed. price not set (ISBN 0-8406-0207-3). Natl Ctr Health Stats.
Sleight, Peter, ed. Arterial Baroreceptors & Hypertension. (Illus.). 380p. 1981. text ed. 67.50x (ISBN 0-19-261259-X). Oxford U Pr.
Villarreal, Herman. Hypertension. (Becker-Perspectives in Nephrology & Hypertension Ser.). 448p. 1981. 35.00 (ISBN 0-471-07900-6, Pub. by Wiley Med). Wiley.
HYPERTHERMIA
see Heat–Physiological Effect
HYPHOMYCETES
see Moniliales
HYPNOSIS
see Hypnotism
HYPNOTISM
see also Mesmerism; Mind and Body; Personality, Disorders of; Psychoanalysis; Rigidity (Psychology)
Clark, Cline. Self-Programming Self-Hypnosis. (Orig.). 1980. pap. text ed. 17.95 (ISBN 0-937798-00-2). Packard Pub.
Copelan, Rachel. How to Hypnotize Yourself & Others. LC 80-70951. 386p. 1981. 10.95 (ISBN 0-8119-0418-0). Fell.
Edmonston, William E. Hypnosis & Relaxation: Modern Verification of an Old Equation. LC 80-22506. (Personality Processes Ser.). 280p. 1981. 21.00 (ISBN 0-471-05903-X, Pub. by Wiley Interscience). Wiley.
Udolf, Roy. Handbook of Hypnosis for Professionals. 384p. 1981. text ed. 24.50 (ISBN 0-442-28881-6). Van Nos Reinhold.
HYPNOTISM–THERAPEUTIC USE
O'Hara, Monica. New Hope Through Hypnotherapy: The Joe Keeton Phenomenon. 150p. 1980. 13.50x (ISBN 0-85626-194-7, Pub. by Abacus Pr England); pap. 7.95x (ISBN 0-85626-194-7). Intl Schol Bk Serv.
Watkins, John G. & Watkins, Helen H. Ego-States & Hidden Observers & the Women in Black & the Lady in White. (Sound Seminars Ser.). 1980. transcript & tapes 29.50x (ISBN 0-88432-066-9, 29400-29401). J Norton Pubs.
HYPOACOUSTIC CHILDREN
see Children, Deaf
HYPOGLYCEMIA
Adams, Ruth & Murray, Frank. Is Blood Sugar Making You a Nutritional Cripple? rev. ed. 174p. (Orig.). 1975. pap. 1.75 (ISBN 0-915962-11-X). Larchmont Bks.
HYPOPHYSIS CEREBRI
see Pituitary Body
HYPOTENSION
see also Blood Pressure
Brunner & Gravas. Clinical Hypertension & Hypotension. Date not set. price not set (ISBN 0-8247-1279-X). Dekker.
HYPOTHALAMUS
Morgane & Panksepp. Physiology of the Hypothalmus, Vol. 2. 672p. 1980. 145.00 (ISBN 0-8247-6904-X). Dekker.
Morgane, Panksepp. Behavioral Studies of the Hypothalmus. 480p. Date not set. 93.50. Dekker.
HYPOTHECATION
see Liens
HYPOXIA
Cowley, R. Adams & Trump, Benjamin F. Pathophysiology of Shock, Anoxia & Ischemia. 600p. 1981. write for info. (2149-4). Williams & Wilkins.
HYSTERIA
see also Demoniac Possession; Witchcraft
Janet, Pierre. The Major Symptoms of Hysteria. 345p. 1980. Repr. of 1920 ed. lib. bdg. 40.00 (ISBN 0-8492-1367-3). R West.
—Mental State of Hystericals. (Contributions to the History of Psychology Ser.: Pt. 2, Medical Psychology). 1978. Repr. of 1901 ed. 30.00 (ISBN 0-89093-166-6). U Pubns Amer.

I

IBERIANS
Carver, Norman. Iberian Villages: Spain & Portugal. 26.95 (ISBN 0-932076-02-5); pap. 17.95 (ISBN 0-932076-03-3). Morgan.
IBSEN, HENRIK, 1828-1906
Durbach, Errol. Ibsen the Romantic: Analogues of Paradise in the Later Plays. 192p. 1981. lib. bdg. 19.00x (ISBN 0-8203-0554-5). U of Ga Pr.
Tammany, Jane E. Henrik Ibsen's Theatre Aesthetic & Dramatic Art. LC 79-92436. (Illus.). 380p. 1980. 22.50 (ISBN 0-8022-2365-6). Philos Lib.
ICE–MANUFACTURE
see Refrigeration and Refrigerating Machinery
ICE AGE
see Glacial Epoch
ICE CARVING
Durocher, Joseph F. Practical Ice Carving. 112p. 1981. pap. text ed. 9.95 (ISBN 0-8436-2206-7). CBI Pub.
ICE HOCKEY
see Hockey
ICE SKATING
see Skating
ICELAND–HISTORY
Gelsinger, Bruce E. Icelandic Enterprise: Economy & Commerce in the Middle Ages. LC 80-26116. (Illus.). 1981. text ed. 19.50 (ISBN 0-87249-405-5). U of SC Pr.
Hood, John C. Icelandic Church Saga. LC 79-8720. (Illus.). xii, 241p. 1981. Repr. of 1946 ed. lib. bdg. 27.50x (ISBN 0-313-22194-4, HOIC). Greenwood.
ICELANDIC AND OLD NORSE LITERATURE–HISTORY AND CRITICISM
Kelchner, Georgia D. Dreams in Old Norse Literature & Their Affinities in Folklore. 154p. 1980. Repr. of 1935 ed. lib. bdg. 30.00 (ISBN 0-8492-1496-3). R West.
ICELANDIC AND OLD NORSE POETRY
Anderson, George K., tr. The Saga of the Volsungs. LC 80-65685. 200p. 1981. 18.00 (ISBN 0-87413-172-3). U Delaware Pr.
ICHTHYOLOGY
see Fishes
ICONOGRAPHY
see Art; Christian Art and Symbolism; Idols and Images; Portraits
ICONS
Brehier, L. L' Art Chretien, son Developement Iconographique des Origines a nos Jours. 2nd ed. (Illus.). 480p. (Fr.). 1981. Repr. of 1928 ed. lib. bdg. 125.00 (ISBN 0-89241-138-4). Caratzas Bros.
IDAHO–DESCRIPTION AND TRAVEL
Bluestein, Sheldon. Hiking Trails of Southern Idaho. LC 79-52543. (Illus.). 235p. (Orig.). 1981. pap. 7.95 (ISBN 0-87004-280-7). Caxton.
Hart, Herbert M. Tour Guide to Old Forts of Oregon, Idaho, Washington, California, Vol. 3. (Illus.). 65p. (Orig.). 1981. pap. 3.95 (ISBN 0-87108-582-8). Pruett.
Lewis, Paul M. Beautiful Idaho. Shangle, Robert D., ed. LC 79-779. 72p. 1979. 14.95 (ISBN 0-915796-93-7); pap. 7.95 (ISBN 0-915796-92-9). Beautiful Am.
IDAHO–HISTORY
Taylor, Dorice. Sun Valley. (Illus.). 264p. 1980. 20.00 (ISBN 0-9605212-0-8). Ex Libris Sun.
Vexler, R. I. Idaho Chronology & Factbook, Vol. 12. 1978. 8.50 (ISBN 0-379-16137-0). Oceana.
IDEAL STATES
see Utopias
IDEALISM
see also Materialism; Pragmatism; Realism; Transcendentalism
Stackelberg, Roderick. Idealism Debased: From Volkisch Ideology to National Socialism. LC 80-84663. (Illus.). 220p. 1981. 18.00x (ISBN 0-87338-252-8). Kent St U Pr.
IDENTIFICATION (RELIGION)
Boom, Corrie T. A Prisoner & Yet. (Orig.). pap. 1.95 (ISBN 0-515-05334-1). Jove Pubns.
Haught, John F. Religion & Self-Acceptance: A Study of the Relationship Between Belief in God & the Desire to Know. LC 80-5872. 195p. 1980. lib. bdg. 17.00 (ISBN 0-8191-1296-8); pap. text ed. 8.75 (ISBN 0-8191-1297-6). U Pr of Amer.
IDENTIFICATION OF DOCUMENTS
see Legal Documents
IDENTIFICATION OF FIREARMS
see Firearms–Identification
IDENTIFICATION OF PLANTS
see Plants–Identification
IDENTITY
see also Reference Groups
Dupreez, Peter. The Politics of Identity. 1980. 25.00 (ISBN 0-312-62697-5). St Martin.
Gerstner, Hugo. Mankind's Quest for Identity. 1981. 22.50 (ISBN 0-930376-23-4). Pathotox Pubs.
IDENTITY, PERSONAL
see Personality
IDEOGRAPHY
see Chinese Language–Writing
IDEOLOGY
Carlsnaes, Walter. The Concept of Ideology & Political Analysis: A Critical Examination of Its Usage by Marx, Lenin, & Mannheim. LC 80-1202. (Contributions in Philosophy Ser.: No. 17). 280p. 1981. lib. bdg. 32.50 (ISBN 0-313-22267-3, CCI/). Greenwood.
Lasswell, Harold D. & Lerner, Daniel, eds. World Revolutionary Elites: Studies in Coercive Ideological Movements. LC 80-21600. xi, 478p. 1980. Repr. of 1965 ed. lib. bdg. 39.75x (ISBN 0-313-22572-9, LAWE). Greenwood.
Therborn, Goran. The Ideology of Power & the Power of Ideology. 144p. 1981. 12.50x (ISBN 0-8052-7095-7, Pub. by NLB England); pap. 5.50 (ISBN 0-8052-7094-9). Schocken.

Zeitlin, Irving M. Ideology & the Development of Sociological Theory. 2nd ed. (P-H Ser. in Sociology). (Illus.). 336p. 1981. text ed. 17.95 (ISBN 0-13-449769-4). P-H.

IDIOPATHIC HEMORRHAGIC SARCOMA
see Kaposi's Sarcoma

IDOLATRY
see Idols and Images

IDOLS AND IMAGES
De Montault, X. Barbier. Traite d'Iconographie Chretienne. (Illus.). 972p. (Fr.). 1981. Repr. of 1890 ed. lib. bdg. 200.00x (ISBN 0-89241-137-6). Caratzas Bros.
L'Orange, H. P. Studies in the Iconography of Cosmic Kingship in the Ancient World. (Illus.). 206p. 1981. Repr. of 1953 ed. lib. bdg. 45.00x (ISBN 0-89241-150-3). Caratzas Bros.

IGNEOUS ROCKS
see Rocks, Igneous

IGNITION DEVICES
see Automobiles–Ignition

IGUANAS
see Lizards

IKONS
see Icons

ILEUS
see Intestines–Obstructions

ILLICIT COINING
see Counterfeits and Counterfeiting

ILLINOIS–BIBLIOGRAPHY
Vexler, R. I. Illinois Chronology & Factbook, Vol. 13. 1978. 8.50 (ISBN 0-379-16138-9). Oceana.

ILLINOIS–DESCRIPTION AND TRAVEL
May, George W. Down Illinois Rivers. (Illus.). 400p. 1981. 16.00 (ISBN 0-9605566-5-6). G W May.

ILLINOIS–HISTORY
Baldwin, Carl R. Echoes of Their Voices. 400p. 1978. 10.95 (ISBN 0-86629-003-6). Sunrise MO.
Cunningham, Eileen S. Lower Illinois Valley, Greene County 1821, Containment: Morgan to 1823, Scott to 1823, Macoupin to 1829, Jersey to 1839. 1980. 98.40 (AU00128); pap. 88.40. E S Cunningham.
--Lower Illinois Valley Limestone Houses. 1976. 17.00 (AU00127); pap. 12.00. E S Cunningham.
Cunningham, Eileen S., ed. Old Settlers Association of Greene County, Illinois: Coda of the Deep Snow of 1830. 1976. 17.00 (AU00122); pap. 12.00. E S Cunningham.
Pease, Theodore C. & Pease, Marguerite J. George Rogers Clark & the Revolution in Illinois, Seventeen Sixty-Three to Seventeen Eighty-Seven. 1929. 3.00 (ISBN 0-912226-12-9). Ill St Hist So.
Pierce, Bess. Moline: A Pictorial History. Friedman, Donna R., ed. (Illus.). 208p. 1981. pap. write for info. (ISBN 0-89865-095-X). Donning Co.
Vexler, R. I. Illinois Chronology & Factbook, Vol. 13. 1978. 8.50 (ISBN 0-379-16138-9). Oceana.

ILLINOIS–POLITICS AND GOVERNMENT
Gove, Samuel K., et al. Illinois Legislature: Structure & Process. LC 76-21238. 208p. 1976. pap. 5.95 (ISBN 0-252-00621-6). U of Ill Pr.

ILLUMINATION
see Lighting

ILLUMINATION OF BOOKS AND MANUSCRIPTS–SPECIMENS, REPRODUCTIONS, ETC.
Narkiss, Bezalel. Hebrew Illuminated Manuscripts in the British Isles: A Catalogue Raisonne, Vol. I; Spanish & Portugese Manuscripts. (Illus.). 492p. 1981. 125.00 (ISBN 0-686-69114-8) (ISBN 0-19-725977-4). Oxford U Pr.

ILLUSTRATION OF BOOKS
see also Drawing; Engraving
also subdivisions illustrations or pictures, illustrations, etc. under specific subjects, e.g. Bible–Pictures, eillustrations, etc.; Shakespeare, William–Illustrations
Brenni, Vito J., compiled by. Book Illustration & Decoration: A Guide to Research. LC 80-1701. (Art Reference Collection Ser.: No. 1). viii, 191p. 1980. lib. bdg. 27.50 (ISBN 0-313-22340-8, BBI/). Greenwood.

ILLUSTRATIONS, HOMILETICAL
see Homiletical Illustrations

ILLUSTRATIONS, HUMOROUS
see Caricatures and Cartoons; Wit and Humor, Pictorial

ILLUSTRATORS
Appelbaum, Stanley & Kelly, Richard, eds. Great Drawings & Illustrations from Punch Eighteen Forty-One to Nineteen Hundred-One: One Hundred Ninety-Two Works by Leech, Keene, du Maurier, May & 21 Others. (Illus.). 144p. (Orig.). 1981. pap. price not set (ISBN 0-486-24110-6). Dover.
Commire, Anne, ed. Something About the Author, Vol. 22. LC 72-27107. (Illus.). 375p. 1981. 38.00 (ISBN 0-8103-0085-0). Gale.
Illustrator Illustrated: Art Directors Index to Illustrators. (Illustrator Illustrated Ser.: No. 2). (Illus.). 1981. 55.00 (ISBN 2-88046-004-2, Pub. by Roto-Vision). Norton.
Weithas, Art, ed. Twenty Years of Award Winners from the Society of Illustrators. (Illus.). 352p. 1981. 45.00 (ISBN 0-8038-7224-0, Visual Communication). Hastings.

IMAGERY (PSYCHOLOGY)
see also Eidetic Imagery
Shepard, Roger N. & Cooper, Lynn A. Mental Images & Their Transformations. (Illus.). 1981. text ed. write for info. (ISBN 0-89706-008-3). Bradford Bks.

IMAGERY, EIDETIC
see Eidetic Imagery

IMAGES AND IDOLS
see Idols and Images

IMAGINARY ANIMALS
see Animal Lore; Animals, Mythical

IMAGINATION
see also Creative Ability; Eidetic Imagery; Fantasy; Imagery (Psychology)
Corbin, Henri. Avicenna & the Visionary Recital. Task, Willard R., tr. from French. 320p. 1980. pap. text ed. 12.50 (ISBN 0-88214-213-5). Spring Pubns.
Engell, James. The Creative Imagination: Enlightenment to Romanticism. 1981. write for info. Harvard U Pr.
LeBoeuf. Imagineering: How to Think & Act Creatively. 88p. Date not set. 9.95 (ISBN 0-07-036952-6). McGraw.

IMAGING SYSTEMS
Clifton, Nancy A. & Simmons, Pamela J. Basic Imaging Procedures in Nuclear Medicine. 192p. 1981. pap. 13.50 (ISBN 0-8385-0578-3). ACC.
Coulam, Craig M. Physical Basis of Medical Imaging. 416p. 1981. 35.00 (ISBN 0-8385-7844-6). ACC.
Putman, Charles E. Diagnostic Imaging in Pulmonary Disease. 1981. 32.50 (ISBN 0-8385-1682-3). ACC.
Sutton, David. Textbook of Radiology & Imaging, 2 vols. 3rd ed. 1981. Vol. 1. text ed. 149.00 (ISBN 0-686-28939-0); Vol. 2. text ed. 175.00 (ISBN 0-686-28940-4). Churchill.
Tanimoto, S. & Klinger, A., eds. Structured Computer Vision: Machine Perception Through Hierarchical Computation Structures. LC 80-14878. 1980. 21.00 (ISBN 0-12-683280-3). Acad Pr.

IMBECILITY
see Mentally Handicapped

IMMANENCE OF GOD
see also Jesus Christ–Mystical Body; Mystical Union; Mysticism; Transcendence of God
Daly, Gabriel. Transcendence & Immanence: A Study in Catholic Modernism & Integralism. 266p. 1980. 34.95x (ISBN 0-19-826652-9). Oxford U Pr.

IMMERSION, BAPTISMAL
see Baptism

IMMIGRATION
see Emigration and Immigration

IMMIGRATION LAW
see Emigration and Immigration Law

IMMORTALITY
Here are entered works on the concept of the survival of the soul after death. For works on the concept of living indefinitely in the flesh, see Immortalism.
see also Eschatology; Future Life; Soul
Reesman, Richard T. Contributions of the Major Philosophers into the Problem of Body Resurrection & Personal Immortality. (Illus.). 117p. 1981. 41.85 (ISBN 0-89920-021-4). Am Inst Psych.

IMMUNE SERUM GLOBULIN
see Immunoglobulins

IMMUNITIES AND PRIVILEGES
see Privileges and Immunities

IMMUNITY
see also Allergy; Communicable Diseases; Serumtherapy; Toxins and Antitoxins
also subdivision Preventive Innoculations under certain diseases, e.g. Tuberculosis–Preventive Innoculations
Blasecki. Mechanisms of Immunity to Virus-Induced Tumors. 376p. 1981. 49.50. Dekker.
Moss, Gordon E. Illness, Immunity & Social Interaction. 298p. 1981. Repr. of 1973 ed. text ed. price not set (ISBN 0-89874-266-8). Krieger.
Steinberg, C. M. & Lefkovits, I., eds. The Immune System: Festschrift in Honor of Niels Kaj Jerne, on the Occasion of His 70th Birthday, Vol. 1. (Illus.). x, 390p. 1981. 118.75 (ISBN 3-8055-3407-8). S Karger.
--The Immune System: Festschrift in Honor of Niels Kaj Jerne, on the Occasion of His 70th Birthday, 2 vols, Vols. 1 & 2. (Illus.). xx, 780p. 1981. 237.50 set (ISBN 3-8055-3409-4). S Karger.
--The Immune System: Festschrift in Honor of Neils Kaj Jerne, on the Occasion of His 70th Birthday, Vol. 2. (Illus.). x, 390p. 1981. 118.75 (ISBN 3-8055-3408-6). S Karger.

IMMUNITY (EXEMPTION)
see Privileges and Immunities

IMMUNITY (PLANTS)
see Plants–Disease and Pest Resistance

IMMUNOGLOBULINS
Glynn, L. E. Structure & Fuction of Antibodies. Steward, M. W., ed. 150p. 1981. pap. 15.00 (ISBN 0-471-27917-X, Pub. by Wiley-Interscience). Wiley.
Glynn, L. E. & Steward, M. W., eds. Antibody Production. 1981. 15.00 (ISBN 0-471-27916-1, Pub. by Wiley-Interscience). Wiley.

IMMUNOLOGICAL DISEASES
see Immunopathology

IMMUNOLOGICAL TOLERANCE
see also Histocompatibility
International Convocation on Immunology, 7th, Niagra Falls, N. Y., July 1980, et al. Immunbiology of the Major Histocompatibility Complex. Zaleski, M. B. & Kano, K., eds. (Illus.). xii, 390p. 1981. 90.00 (ISBN 3-8055-1896-X). S Karger.

IMMUNOLOGY
see also Immunity; Immunological Tolerance; Immunopathology
Alder, William H. & Nordin, Albert A. Immunology of Aging. 240p. 1981. 59.95 (ISBN 0-8493-5809-4). CRC Pr.
Arber, W., et al, eds. Current Topics in Microbiology & Immunology, Vol. 90. (Illus.). 147p. 1980. 51.90 (ISBN 0-387-10181-0). Springer-Verlag.
Bach, Jean F., ed. Immunology. 2nd ed. 950p. 1981. 62.50 (ISBN 0-471-08044-6, Pub. by Wiley Med). Wiley.
Benacerraf, Baruj & Unanue, Emil. Textbook of Immunology. 2nd ed. 300p. 1981. write for info. softcover (0528-6). Williams & Wilkins.
Chedid, L., ed. Immunostimulation. (Illus.). 236p. 1981. 22.50 (ISBN 0-387-10354-6). Springer-Verlag.
Golub, Edward S. The Cellular Basis of the Immune Response. rev. & 2nd ed. LC 80-28080. (Illus.). 325p. 1981. pap. text ed. price not set (ISBN 0-87893-212-7). Sinauer Assoc.
Immunology. 2nd ed. (Illus.). 259p. 1980. text ed. 16.50 (ISBN 0-06-140781-X, Harper Medical). Har-Row.
Larralde, Carlos, et al, eds. Molecules, Cells & Parasites in Immunology. 1980. 19.50 (ISBN 0-12-436840-9). Acad Pr.
Lefkovits, Ivan, ed. Immunological Methods, Vol. 2. 1981. write for info. (ISBN 0-12-442702-2). Acad Pr.
Luderer, Albert & Weetall, Howard, eds. Clinical Cellular Immunology. (Contemporary Immunology Ser.). (Illus.). 1981. 44.50 (ISBN 0-89603-011-3). Humana.
Nakamura, R.., et al, eds. Immunoassays: Clinical Laboratory Techniques for the 1980's. LC 80-21230. (Laboratory & Research Methods in Biology & Medicine: Vol. 4). 482p. 1980. 58.00 (ISBN 0-8451-1653-3). A R Liss.
Rapid Methods & Automation in Microbiology & Immunology: A Bibliography. 250p. 24.00 (ISBN 0-904147-07-X). Info Retrieval.
Skamene, Emil, ed. Genetic Control of Natural Resistance to Infection & Malignancy. (Perspectives in Immunology Ser.). 1980. 33.00 (ISBN 0-12-647680-2). Acad Pr.
Smolensky, M. H. & Reinberg, A., eds. Recent Advances of the Chronobiology of Allergy & Immunology: Symposium on Chronobiology in Allergy & Immunology, Israel, 1979. LC 80-41028. (Illus.). 350p. 1980. 50.00 (ISBN 0-08-025891-3). Pergamon.
Soloman, J. B., ed. Developmental & Comparative Immunology I: First Congress of Developmental & Comparative Immunology, 27 July-1 August 1980, Aberdeen. (Illus.). 580p. 1980. 90.00 (ISBN 0-08-025922-7). Pergamon.
Wilson, J. D. Diagnostic Immunology & Serology: A Clinician's Guide. Simpson, Sandra I., ed. 161p. 1980. pap. text ed. 14.95 (ISBN 0-909337-01-2). ADIS Pr.

IMMUNOLOGY–LABORATORY MANUALS
Rose, N. R. & Friedman, H., eds. Manual of Clinical Immunology. 2nd ed. (Illus.). 1980. 25.00 (ISBN 0-914826-25-5); flexible binding 21.00 (ISBN 0-914826-27-1). Am Soc Microbio.

IMMUNOPATHOLOGY
see also Allergy
Thivolet, J. & Schmitt, D. Cutaneous Immunopathology. (Illus.). 506p. 1978. pap. 19.50 (ISBN 2-85598-175-1). Masson Pub.

IMPEACHMENTS
see also Privileges and Immunities
Impeachment Inquiry Staff of the House Judiciary Committee. Constitutional Grounds for Impeachment. 1.00 (ISBN 0-8183-0129-5). Pub Aff Pr.

IMPERIALISM
see also Militarism
also subdivision Foreign Relations under names of countries
Headrick, Daniel R. The Tools of Empire: Technology & European Imperialism in the Nineteenth Century. 224p. 1981. text ed. 9.95x (ISBN 0-19-502831-7); pap. text ed. 5.95x (ISBN 0-19-502832-5). Oxford U Pr.
Warren, Bill. Imperialism: Pioneer of Capitalism. 296p. 1981. 19.50x (ISBN 0-8052-7089-2, Pub. by NLB England); pap. 8.50 (ISBN 0-8052-7088-4). Schocken.

IMPORT AND EXPORT CONTROLS
see Foreign Trade Regulation

IMPORT QUOTAS
Olnek, Jay I. The Invisible Hand. 1980. 14.95 (ISBN 0-938538-00-4). N Stonington.

IMPORT RESTRICTIONS
see Foreign Trade Regulation; Import Quotas

IMPORTS
see Commerce

IMPOSTORS AND IMPOSTURE
see also Fraud; Quacks and Quackery
Elkanah, Settle. The Compleat Memoirs of the Life of That Notorious Imposter Will Morrell, Alias Bowyer, Alias Wickham,Etc, LC 80-2498. 1981. Repr. of 1694 ed. 47.50 (ISBN 0-404-19134-7). AMS Pr.
Roberts, David. Great Exploration Hoaxes. Michaelman, Herbert, ed. 1981. 12.95 (ISBN 0-517-54075-4, Michaelman Books). Crown.

IMPOTENCE
Carlton, Eric. Sexual Anxiety: A Study of Male Impotence. 197p. 1980. 22.50x. B&N.

IMPREGNATION, ARTIFICIAL
see Artificial Insemination

IMPRESSIONISM (ART)
see also Post-Impressionism (Art)
Blunden, Godfrey & Blunden, Maria. Impressionists & Impressionism. (Illus.). 1980. pap. 14.95 (ISBN 0-686-68748-5). Rizzoli Intl.
Reff, Theodore, ed. Exhibitions of Impressionist Art, Bk. I. (Modern Art in Paris 1855 to 1900 Ser.). 356p. 1981. lib. bdg. 44.00 (ISBN 0-8240-4741-9). Garland Pub.
--Exhibitions of Impressionist Art, Bk. II. (Modern Art in Paris 1855 to 1900 Ser.). 259p. 1981. lib. bdg. 44.00 (ISBN 0-8240-4742-7). Garland Pub.
--Impressionist Group Exhibitions. (Modern Art in Paris 1855 to 1900 Ser.). 157p. 1981. lib. bdg. 44.00 (ISBN 0-8240-4723-0). Garland Pub.

IMPRINTS (IN BOOKS)
Annenberg, Maurice, compiled by. A Typographical Journey Through the Inland Printer. LC 77-89269. 1977. write for info. Maran Pub.

IMPROVISATION (MUSIC)
see also Harmony, Keyboard
Pelz, William. Basic Keyboard Skills: An Introduction to Accompaniment Improvisation, Transposition & Modulation, with an Appendix on Sight Reading. LC 80-22820. vii, 173p. 1981. Repr. of 1963 ed. PLB 23.50x (ISBN 0-313-22882-5, PEBK). Greenwood.

IN-LINE DATA PROCESSING
see on-Line Data Processing

IN-SERVICE TRAINING
see Employees, Training Of

INAUDIBLE SOUND
see Ultrasonics

INBORN ERRORS OF METABOLISM
see Metabolism, Inborn Errors of

INCA MUSIC
see Incas–Music

INCAPACITY, ESTIMATION OF
see Disability Evaluation

INCAS
see also Indians of South America; Peru–Antiquities
Hemming, John. Machu Picchu. Bayrd, Edwin, ed. LC 80-82066. (Illus.). 1981. 16.95 (ISBN 0-88225-302-6). Newsweek.

INCAS–JUVENILE LITERATURE
Lewis, Brenda R. Growing up in Inca Times. (Growing up Ser.). (Illus.). 72p. (gr. 7-9). 1981. 15.95 (ISBN 0-7134-2736-1, Pub. by Batsford England). David & Charles.

INCAS–MUSIC
Stevenson, Robert. Music in Aztec & Inca Territory. (California Library Reprint Ser.: No. 64). 1977. Repr. of 1968 ed. 38.50x (ISBN 0-520-03169-5). UCDLA.

INCEST
Justice, Blair & Justice, Rita. Broken Taboo: Sex in the Family. 304p. 1981. pap. 6.95 (ISBN 0-87705-482-7). Human Sci Pr.

INCINERATORS
Brunner, Calvin. Design of Sewage Sludge Incineration Systems. LC 80-21916. (Pollution Technology Review: No. 71). (Illus.). 380p. 1981. 48.00 (ISBN 0-8155-0825-5). Noyes.

INCOME
see also Capital; Consumption (Economics); Profit; Retirement Income
Collard, David, et al. Income Distribution: The Limits to Redistribution. 267p. 1981. 34.95 (ISBN 0-470-27099-3). Halsted Pr.
Fallick, J. L. & Elliot, R. F., eds. Incomes Policies, Inflation & Relative Pay. (Illus.). 304p. 1981. text ed. 29.95x (ISBN 0-04-331077-X, 2578); pap. text ed. 12.95x (ISBN 0-04-331078-8, 2579). Allen Unwin.
Grimaldi, Paul L. Supplemental Security Income: New Federal Program Aged, Blind, & Disabled. 1980. pap. 5.25 (ISBN 0-8447-3356-3). Am Enterprise.
Webb, Adrian L. Income Redistribution & the Welfare State. 125p. 1971. pap. text ed. 6.25x (Pub. by Bedford England). Renouf.

INCOME–ACCOUNTING
see Income Accounting

INCOME ACCOUNTING
Huber, Roger, ed. Where My Money Is Going: Income & Expense Budget. (Orig.). 1980. pap. 10.00x (ISBN 0-918300-00-2); wkbk. 10.00. Lankey.
James, Simon & Nobes, Christopher. Workbook for the Economics of Taxation. 72p. 1978. pap. 3.00x (ISBN 0-86003-608-1, Pub. by Allan Pubs England). State Mutual Bk.
Ronen, Joshua & Sadan, Simcha. Smoothing Income Numbers: Objectives, Means & Implications. LC 80-21350. (Paperback Series of Accounting). 1981. pap. text ed. 5.95 (ISBN 0-201-06347-6). A-W.

INCOME DISTRIBUTION
see Income

INCOME STATEMENTS
see Financial Statements
INCOME TAX
see also Excess Profits Tax
Brown, C. V. Taxation & the Incentive to Work. (Illus.). 128p. 1980. 29.95 (ISBN 0-19-877134-7); pap. 12.00 (ISBN 0-19-877135-5). Oxford U Pr.
Lasser, S. Jay. Everyone's Income Tax Guide. rev. ed. 192p. 1980. write for info. (ISBN 0-937782-00-9). Hilltop Pubns.
Seidman, J. Seidman's Legislative History of Federal Income & Excess Profits Tax Laws: 1939-1953, 2 vols. 1959. 50.00 (ISBN 0-13-799742-6). P-H.
--Seidman's Legislative History of Federal Income Tax Laws: 1851-1938. 25.00 (ISBN 0-13-799757-1). P-H.
INCOME TAX-AUDITING
see Tax Auditing
INCOME TAX-FOREIGN INCOME
Brownlee, Oswald H. Taxing the Income from U. S. Corporate Investment Abroad. 1979. pap. 3.25 (ISBN 0-8447-3367-9). Am Enterprise.
Owens, Elisabeth A. International Aspects of U. S. Income Taxation: Cases & Materials, Vol. III, Parts Four & Five. LC 80-18605. 512p. 1980. pap. text ed. 12.50x (ISBN 0-915506-24-6). Harvard Law Intl Tax.
INCOME TAX-LAW
Ferguson, M. Carr, et al. Federal Income Taxation of Estates & Beneficiaries. 749p. (Orig.). 1970. text ed. 40.00 (ISBN 0-316-27889-0); text ed. 12.50 1979 supplement (ISBN 0-316-27899-8). 1980 supplement (ISBN 0-316-27900-5). Little.
INCOME TAX-UNITED STATES
Green, Michael L., ed. U. S. Income Tax Guide, 1981. rev. ed. (Buyer's Guide Ser.). 80p. (Orig.). Date not set. pap. 2.50 (ISBN 0-89552-074-5). DMR Pubns.
Greene, Bill. Win Your Personal Tax Revolt. (Illus.). 192p. 1981. 11.95 (ISBN 0-936602-10-4). Harbor Pub CA.
Storrer, Philip & Williams, Brian. The Tax Fighter's Guide 1981. 192p. (Orig.). 1981. pap. 6.95 (ISBN 0-936602-08-2). Harbor Pub CA.
INCOME TAX-UNITED STATES-LAW
Kragen, Adrian A. & McNulty, John K. Cases & Materials on Federal Income Taxation: Taxation of Corporations, Shareholders, Partnerships & Partners, Vol. II. (American Casebook Ser.). 976p. 1981. text ed. 24.95 (ISBN 0-8299-2133-8). West Pub.
Owens, Elisabeth A. International Aspects of U. S. Income Taxation: Cases & Materials, Vol. III, Parts Four & Five. LC 80-18605. 512p. 1980. pap. text ed. 12.50x (ISBN 0-915506-24-6). Harvard Law Intl Tax.
INCURABLE DISEASES
The Healing Art of Clara Walter. 64p. (Orig.). 1981. pap. 2.95 (ISBN 0-932870-08-2). Alyson Pubns.
INDENTURED SERVANTS
Cordasco, Francesco & Pitkin, Thomas M. The White Slave Trade & the Immigrants: A Chapter in American Social History. LC 80-25556. 1981. write for info. (ISBN 0-87917-077-8); pap. write for info. (ISBN 0-87917-076-X). Blaine Ethridge.
INDEPENDENCE
see Autonomy
INDEPENDENT ADMINISTRATIVE AGENCIES
see Independent Regulatory Commissions
INDEPENDENT CONTRACTORS
see Employers' Liability; Liability (Law)
INDEPENDENT REGULATORY COMMISSIONS
Anderson, Douglas D. Regulatory Politics & Electric Utilities. 200p. 1981. 19.95 (ISBN 0-86569-058-8). Auburn Hse.
INDEPENDENT SCHOOLS
see Private Schools
INDEPENDENT STUDY
Powell, James D. & Kelley, C. Aron. Students Resource Manual: Hicks-Gullett Management of Organization. th ed. 368p. Date not set. text ed. price not set (ISBN 0-07-028777-5). McGraw.
INDETERMINISM
see Free Will and Determinism
INDEXES, CARD
see Files and Filing (Documents)
INDEXING, AUTOMATIC
see Automatic Indexing
INDEXING VOCABULARIES
see Subject Headings
INDIA-ANTIQUITIES
Agrawal, D. P. The Archaeology of India. (Scandinavian Institute of Asian Studies Monograph). (Illus.). 320p. 1981. pap. text ed. 23.50 (ISBN 0-7007-0140-0). Humanities.
INDIA-BIOGRAPHY
Abbot, Justin E. Life of Tukaram. 346p. 1980. text ed. 13.50 (ISBN 0-8426-1644-6); pap. text ed 9.00 (ISBN 0-8426-1654-3). Verry.
INDIA-CHURCH HISTORY
Appadurai, Arjun. Worship & Conflict Under Colonial Rule: A South India Case. (Cambridge South Asian Studies: No. 27). (Illus.). 282p. Date not set. price not set (ISBN 0-521-23122-1). Cambridge U Pr.
INDIA-CIVILIZATION
Walimbe, Y. S. Abhinavagupta on Indian Aesthetics. 1980. 9.50x (ISBN 0-8364-0624-9, Pub. by Ajanta). South Asia Bks.
INDIA-COMMERCE
Sharma, T. C. & Continho, O. Economic & Commercial Geography of India. 2nd rev. ed. (Illus.). 400p. 1980. text ed. 22.50 (ISBN 0-7069-0546-6, Pub. by Vikas India). Advent Bk.
INDIA-CONSTITUTIONAL HISTORY
Pylee, M. V. India's Constitution. 3rd rev. ed. (Illus.). ix, 471p. (Orig.). 1980. pap. text ed. 11.95x (ISBN 0-210-33709-5). Asia.
Varadachari, V. K. Governor in the Indian Constitution. 1980. 13.00x (ISBN 0-8364-0658-3, Pub. by Heritage India). South Asia Bks.
INDIA-ECONOMIC CONDITIONS
Bliss, C. J. & Stern, N. H. Palanpur: The Economy of an Indian Village. (Illus.). 464p. 1981. 37.50 (ISBN 0-19-828419-5). Oxford U Pr.
Pillai, S. Devadas, ed. Winners & Losers: Styles of Development & Change in an Indian Region. Baks, C. 407p. 1979. text ed. 36.00 (ISBN 0-8426-1679-9). Verry.
Ray, S. K. Economics of the Black Market. (Replica Edition Ser.). 250p. 1981. lib. bdg. 20.00x (ISBN 0-86531-149-8). Westview.
Rothermund, D., et al, eds. Urban Growth & Rural Stagnation: Studies in the Economy of an Indian Coalfield & Its Hinterland. 1980. 36.00x (ISBN 0-8364-0662-1, Pub. by Manohar India). South Asia Bks.
Sharma, Arvind. The Hindu Scriptural Value System & the Economic Development of India. x, 113p. 1980. text ed. 15.00x (ISBN 0-86590-004-3). Apt Bks.
Sharma, T. C. & Continho, O. Economic & Commercial Geography of India. 2nd rev. ed. (Illus.). 400p. 1980. text ed. 22.50 (ISBN 0-7069-0546-6, Pub. by Vikas India). Advent Bk.
INDIA-ECONOMIC CONDITIONS-1947-
Jha, Prem S. India: A Political Economy of Stagnation. (Illus.). 330p. 1980. 13.95x (ISBN 0-19-561153-5). Oxford U Pr.
Toye, F. J. Public Expenditure & Indian Development Policy Nineteen Sixty to Nineteen Seventy. LC 80-41011. 284p. Date not set. 39.50 (ISBN 0-521-23081-0). Cambridge U Pr.
INDIA-ECONOMIC POLICY
Gupta, Suraj B. Monetary Planning for India. 252p. 1979. text ed. 14.95x (ISBN 0-19-561145-4). Oxford U Pr.
Sastry, K. S. Performance Budgeting for Planned Development. (Illus.). 235p. 1980. text ed. 12.50x (ISBN 0-391-02170-2). Humanities.
Sengupta, Surajit. Business Law in India. 894p. (Orig.). 1979. pap. text ed. 9.95x (ISBN 0-19-560658-2). Oxford U Pr.
INDIA-FOREIGN RELATIONS
Sarhadi, Ajit S. India's Security in Resurgent Asia. viii, 338p. 1980. text ed. 22.50x (ISBN 0-86590-003-5). Apt Bks.
Tharoor, Shashi. Reasons of State. 250p. 1981. text ed. 17.50x (ISBN 0-7069-1275-6, Pub by Vikas India). Advent Bk.
INDIA-FOREIGN RELATIONS-GREAT BRITAIN
Spear, Percival, ed. The Nabobs. 1980. Repr. of 1963 ed. 17.00x (ISBN 0-8364-0659-1, Pub. by Curzon Pr). South Asia Bks.
INDIA-FOREIGN RELATIONS-UNITED STATES
Mehta, Gita. Karma Kola. 1981. pap. 5.95 (ISBN 0-671-25084-1, Touchstone). S&S.
INDIA-HISTORIOGRAPHY
Devahuti. Bias in Indian Historiography. 1980. text ed. write for info. (ISBN 0-391-02174-5). Humanities.
INDIA-HISTORY
Bongard-Levin, G. M. Origin of Aryans: From Scythis to India. Gupta, H. C., tr. 124p. 1980. text ed. cancelled (ISBN 0-8426-1663-2). Verry.
Erskine, William. A History of India Under the Two First Sovereigns of the House of Taimur, Baber & Humayun, 2 vols. 1162p. 1980. Repr. 70.00x (ISBN 0-686-28827-0, Pub. by Irish Academic Pr). Biblio Dist.
Hirschmann, Edwin. The White Mutiny. 1980. 24.00x (ISBN 0-8364-0639-7). South Asia Bks.
Malcolm, John. A Memoir of Central India, Including Malwa, & Adjoining Provinces: With the History, & Copious Illustrations, of the Past & Present Condition of That Country, 2 vols. 3rd ed. 1127p. 1980. Repr. 84.00x (ISBN 0-7165-2129-6, Pub. by Irish Academic Pr). Biblio Dist.
Mehra, Parshotam. The North-East Frontier: A Documentary Study of the Internecine Rivalry Between India, Tibet & China, Vol. 1, 1906-14. 270p. 1979. text ed. 9.95x (ISBN 0-19-561158-6). Oxford U Pr.
Minault, Gail. The Khilafat Movement: Religious Symbolism & Political Mobilization in India. 1981. text ed. 22.50x (ISBN 0-231-05072-0). Columbia U Pr.
Ratnagar, Shereen. Encounters: India's Westerly Trade in the Bronze Age. 240p. 1981. 17.95 (ISBN 0-19-561253-1). Oxford U Pr.
Saletore, R. N. Indian Pirates. 200p. 1980. pap. text ed. 11.25x (ISBN 0-391-02183-4, Pub. by Concept India). Humanities.
Tames, Richard. India & Pakistan in the Twentieth Century. (Twentieth Century World History Ser.). (Illus.). 96p. (gr. 6 up). 1981. 15.95 (ISBN 0-7134-3415-5, Pub. by Batsford England). David & Charles.
INDIA-HISTORY-BRITISH OCCUPATION, 1765-1947
Schact, Joseph. The Origins of Muhammadan Jurisprudence. 364p. 1979. pap. text ed. 12.50x (ISBN 0-19-825357-5). Oxford U Pr.
Tinker, Hugh. The Ordeal of Love: C. F. Andrews & India. (Illus.). 356p. 1979. text ed. 17.95x. Oxford U Pr.
INDIA-HISTORY, MILITARY
Raina, Asoka. Inside R.A.W. The Story of India's Secret Service. 175p. 1981. 12.50x (ISBN 0-7069-1299-3, Pub. by Vikas India). Advent Bk.
Singh, Sukhwant. India's Wars Since Independence: Defence of the Western Front, Vol. II. 350p. 1981. text ed. 35.00 (ISBN 0-7069-1277-2, Pub by Vikas India). Advent Bk.
INDIA-KINGS AND RULERS
Godden, Rumer. Gulbadan: Portrait of a Rose Princess at the Mughal Court. LC 80-51752. (Illus.). 160p. 1981. 14.95 (ISBN 0-670-35756-1, Studio). Viking Pr.
INDIA-LANGUAGES
Shukla, Shaligram. Bhojpuri Grammar. (Bhojpuri.). 1981. text ed. 10.00x (ISBN 0-87840-189-X). Georgetown U Pr.
INDIA-POLITICS AND GOVERNMENT
Karkhanis, Sharad. Indian Politics & the Role of the Press. 224p. 1981. text ed. 20.00x (ISBN 0-7069-1278-0, Pub. by Vikas India). Advent Bk.
Khanna, N. Miracle of Democracy in India. 124p. 1980. 4.50x (ISBN 0-89955-319-2, Pub. by Interprint India). Intl Schol Bk Serv.
Lall, Arthur. The Emergence of Modern India. LC 80-25028. 288p. 1981. 17.95 (ISBN 0-231-03430-X). Columbia U Pr.
Shakir, Moin. Politics of Minorities. 1980. 16.00x (ISBN 0-8364-0622-2, Pub. by Ajanta). South Asia Bks.
Singh, Baljit & Vajpeyi, Dhirendra. Goverment & Politics in India. 130p. (Orig.). 1981. pap. text ed. 8.95 (ISBN 0-86590-006-X). Apt Bks.
--Government & Politics in India. 130p. 1980. text ed. 10.50 (ISBN 0-86590-008-6). Apt Bks.
INDIA-POLITICS AND GOVERNMENT-EARLY TO 1765
Dikshit, D. P. Political History of the Chalukyas of Badami. 1980. 26.00x (ISBN 0-8364-0645-1, Pub. by Abhinav India). South Asia Bks.
Hirschmann, Edwin. The White Mutiny. 1980. 24.00x (ISBN 0-8364-0639-7). South Asia Bks.
Roy, P. C. The Coin Age of Northern India. 1980. 27.50x (ISBN 0-8364-0641-9, Pub. by Abhinav India). South Asia Bks.
Stein, Burton. Peasant State & Society in Medieval South India. (Illus.). 550p. 1980. text ed. 31.00x (ISBN 0-19-561065-2). Oxford U Pr.
INDIA-POLITICS AND GOVERNMENT-1765-1947
Eden, Emily. Up the Country. 1980. Repr. 18.00x (ISBN 0-8364-0660-5, Pub. by Curzon Pr). South Asia Bks.
INDIA-POLITICS AND GOVERNMENT-20TH CENTURY
Gandhi, Mohandas K. Hind Swaraj, or Indian Home Rule. 110p. (Orig.). 1981. pap. 1.50 (ISBN 0-934676-25-9). Greenlf Bks.
INDIA-POLITICS AND GOVERNMENT-1947-
Banerjee, Sumanta. In the Wake of Naxalbari: A History of the Naxalite Movement in India. 436p. 1980. text ed. 22.50 (ISBN 0-8426-1656-X). Verry.
Jha, Prem S. India: A Political Economy of Stagnation. (Illus.). 330p. 1980. 13.95x (ISBN 0-19-561153-5). Oxford U Pr.
Sengupta, Surajit. Business Law in India. 894p. (Orig.). 1979. pap. text ed. 9.95x (ISBN 0-19-560658-2). Oxford U Pr.
Shourie, Arun. Institutions in the Janata Phase. 300p. 1980. text ed. 18.00 (ISBN 0-8426-1678-0). Verry.
INDIA-RELIGION
Dass, Baba Hari. Sweeper to Saint: Stories of the Holy India. Denu, Ma, ed. (Illus.). 200p. (Orig.). 1980. pap. 6.95 (ISBN 0-918100-03-8). Sri Rama.
Jha, Akhileshwar. The Imprisoned Mind: Guru Shisya Tradition in Indian Culture. 1980. 18.50x (ISBN 0-8364-0665-6, Pub. by Ambika India). South Asia Bks.
Sharma, T. N. Religious Thought in India. 1980. 11.00x (ISBN 0-8364-0619-2, Pub. by Ramneek). South Asia Bks.
Srivastava, I. P. Dhrupada: A Study of Its Origin, Historical Development, Structure & Present State. (Illus.). 176p. 1980. text ed. 15.00x (ISBN 0-8426-1648-9). Verry.
Sykes, Marjorie. Quakers in India. (Illus.). 176p. 1980. 12.95 (ISBN 0-04-275003-2, 2585). Allen Unwin.
INDIA-SOCIAL CONDITIONS
Deshpande, C. D., et al. Impact of a Metropolitan City on the Surrounding Region. (Illus.). 167p. 1980. pap. text ed. 8.00x (ISBN 0-391-02206-7). Humanities.
Pillai, S. Devadas, ed. Winners & Losers: Styles of Development & Change in an Indian Region. Baks, C. 407p. 1979. text ed. 36.00 (ISBN 0-8426-1679-9). Verry.
Rothermund, D., et al, eds. Urban Growth & Rural Stagnation: Studies in the Economy of an Indian Coalfield & Its Hinterland. 1980. 36.00x (ISBN 0-8364-0662-1, Pub. by Manohar India). South Asia Bks.
Sinha, R. Social Change in Indian Society. 1980. 11.25 (ISBN 0-391-02184-2). Humanities.
Srinivas, M. N., et al. The Fieldworker & the Field: Problems & Challenges in Sociological Investigation. 300p. 1979. text ed. 13.95x (ISBN 0-19-561118-7). Oxford U Pr.
INDIA-SOCIAL LIFE AND CUSTOMS
Dass, Arvind. Agrarian Relations in India. 1980. 18.50x (ISBN 0-8364-0648-6, Pub. by Manohar India). South Asia Bks.
Deshpande, C. D., et al. Impact of a Metropolitan City on the Surrounding Region. (Illus.). 167p. 1980. pap. text ed. 8.00x (ISBN 0-391-02206-7). Humanities.
Lorrance, Arleen. Hello, Goodbye, I Love You. (Illus., Orig.). 1981. pap. price not set (ISBN 0-916192-18-0). L P Pubns.
Nagarkar, Kiran. Seven Sixes Are Forty-Three. Slee, Shubha, tr. from Marathi. (Asian & Pacific Writing Ser.: No. 14). 213p. 1981. text ed. 15.75 (ISBN 0-7022-1503-1); pap. 8.50 (ISBN 0-7022-1502-3). U of Queensland Pr.
Shingi, P. M., et al. Rural Youth: Education, Occupation & Social Outlook. 1980. 10.00x (ISBN 0-8364-0663-X, Pub. by Abhinav India). South Asia Bks.
Tirtha, Ranjit. Society & Development in Contemporary India. (Illus.). 368p. 1980. 13.50 (ISBN 0-8187-0040-8). Harlo Pr.
Wagle, N. K., ed. Images of Maharashhtra: A Regional Profile in India. 160p. 1980. pap. text ed. 10.50 (ISBN 0-7007-0144-3). Humanities.
INDIA-SOCIAL POLICY
Mishra, Sachida N. Political Socialization in India. (Illus.). 156p. 1980. pap. text ed. 8.75x (ISBN 0-391-02207-5). Humanities.
INDIA-RUBBER
see Rubber
INDIA-RUBBER INDUSTRY
see Rubber Industry and Trade
INDIAN BLANKETS
see Indians of North America-Textile Industry and Fabrics; Indians of South America-Textile Industry and Fabrics
INDIAN CAPTIVITIES
see Indians of North America-Captivities
INDIAN CORN
see Corn
INDIAN FOLK-LORE
see Folk-Lore, Indian
INDIAN LANGUAGES
see Indians of North America-Languages
INDIAN LITERATURE
Benedict, Ruth. Tales of the Cochiti Indians. 256p. 1981. pap. price not set (ISBN 0-8263-0569-5). U of NM Pr.
Kroeber, Karl, ed. Traditional Literatures of the American Indian: Texts & Interpretations. LC 80-18338. x, 162p. 1981. 16.50x (ISBN 0-8032-2704-3, Bison); pap. 5.95 (ISBN 0-8032-7753-9, BB 765). U of Nebr Pr.
Singh, Armitjit, et al, eds. Indian Literature: A Guide to Information Sources. LC 74-11532. (American Literature, English Literature & World Literatures in English Information Guide Ser.: Vol 36). 450p. 1981. 30.00 (ISBN 0-8103-1238-7). Gale.
Vizenor, Gerald. Earthdivers: Tribal Narratives on Mixed Descent. (Illus.). 195p. 1981. 14.95 (ISBN 0-8166-1048-7). U of Minn Pr.
INDIAN LITERATURE (AMERICAN INDIAN)
see Indian Literature
INDIAN LITERATURE (EAST INDIAN)
see Indic Literature
INDIAN MUTINY, 1857-1858
see India-History-British Occupation, 1765-1947
INDIAN OCEAN
Report of the Sixth Session of the Indian Ocean Fishery Commission. (FAO Fisheries Report: No. 234). 35p. 1981. pap. 6.00 (ISBN 92-5-100930-9, F2088, FAO). Unipub.
INDIAN OCEAN REGION
Kerr, Alex, ed. Resources & Development in the Indian Ocean Region. 256p. 1981. lib. bdg. 26.50x (ISBN 0-86531-123-4). Westview.
INDIANA-HISTORY
Vexler, R. I. Indiana Chronology & Factbook, Vol. 14. 1978. 8.50 (ISBN 0-379-16139-7). Oceana.
INDIANA-POLITICS AND GOVERNMENT
Indiana Judges Association. Indiana Pattern Jury Instructions - Criminal. 250p. 1980. 50.00 (ISBN 0-87215-353-3). Michie.
INDIANS
Here are entered works on the aboriginal peoples of the Western Hemisphere, including Eskimos.
Lizot, Jacques. Circle of Fires: Life Among the Yanomami. Simon, Ernest, tr. from Fr. 224p. 1981. 22.50x (ISBN 0-8476-6968-8). Rowman.
INDIANS-ANTIQUITIES
Curtis, Edward S. Indian Days of Long Ago. (Illus.). Date not set. 8.95 (ISBN 0-913668-46-X); pap. 3.95 (ISBN 0-913668-45-1). Ten Speed Pr.
INDIANS-ETHNOLOGY
see Indians; Indians of North America; also indians of South America and similar headings
INDIANS-FOLK-LORE
see Folk-Lore, Indian
INDIANS-LITERATURE
see Indian Literature
INDIANS-MEDICINE
see also Medicine-Man

Krogman, William, et al. Medicine Among the American Indians: CIBA Symposia, 1939, Vol. 1, No. 1. 1981. pap. 4.95 (ISBN 0-686-69101-6). Acoma Bks.

INDIANS–ORIGIN

Kelly, Joyce. The Complete Visitor's Guide to Mesoamerican Ruins. (Illus.). 480p. 1981. 35.00 (ISBN 0-8061-1566-1). U of Okla Pr.

INDIANS IN ART

see subdivision Pictorial Works under Indians; Indians Of North America and similar headings

INDIANS OF CENTRAL AMERICA

American Indian Publishers, ed. Dictionary of Indian Tribes of the Americas, 4 vols. (Illus.). 1980. Set. lib. bdg. 225.00 (ISBN 0-937862-25-8). Am Hist Pubs.

INDIANS OF CENTRAL AMERICA–ETHNOLOGY

see Indians of Central America

INDIANS OF CENTRAL AMERICA–FOLK-LORE

see Folk-Lore, Indian

INDIANS OF CENTRAL AMERICA–ORIGIN

see Indians–Origin

INDIANS OF CENTRAL AMERICA–TEXTILE INDUSTRY AND FABRICS

Auld, Rhoda L. Molas: What They Are; How to Make Them; Ideas They Suggest for Creative Applique. 136p. 1980. pap. 9.95 (ISBN 0-442-20050-1). Van Nos Reinhold.

INDIANS OF MEXICO–FOLK-LORE

see Folk-Lore, Indian

INDIANS OF MEXICO–ORIGIN

see Indians–Origin

INDIANS OF NORTH AMERICA

Here are entered works on the Indians of North America in general. For works of specific tribes or groups of tribes see subdivisions–Eastern States,–Northwest, Pacific,–Southwest, New,–Southwest, Old,–The West.

see also Eskimos

American Indian Publishers, ed. Dictionary of Indian Tribes of the Americas, 4 vols. (Illus.). 1980. Set. lib. bdg. 225.00 (ISBN 0-937862-25-8). Am Hist Pubs.

Axtell, James, ed. The Indian Peoples of Eastern America: A Documentary History of the Sexes. (Illus.). 232p. 1981. text ed. 11.95x (ISBN 0-19-502740-X); pap. text ed. 6.95 (ISBN 0-19-502741-8). Oxford U Pr.

Erdoes, Richard. The Sun Dance People. (Illus.). 241p. Date not set. pap. 1.95 (ISBN 0-394-70803-2, Vin). Random.

INDIANS OF NORTH AMERICA–AGRICULTURE

Carlson, Leonard A. Indians, Bureaucrats, & Land: The Dawes Act & the Decline of Indian Farming. LC 80-1709. (Contributions in Economics & Economic History Ser.: No. 36). 280p. 1981. lib. bdg. 29.95 (ISBN 0-313-22533-8, CDA/). Greenwood.

INDIANS OF NORTH AMERICA–AMUSEMENTS

see Indians of North America–Social Life and Customs

INDIANS OF NORTH AMERICA–ANTIQUITIES

see also Indians of North America–Pottery

also subdivision Antiquities under names of states, e.g. Arizona–Antiquities; also names of places, e.g. Tsura (Indian Settlement)

Alex, Lynn M. Exploring Iowa's Past: A Guide to Prehistoric Archaeology. LC 80-21391. (Illus.). 180p. 1980. pap. 7.95 (ISBN 0-87745-108-7). U of Iowa Pr.

Willoughby, Charles C. Indian Antiquities of the Kennebec Valley. Spiess, Arthur E., ed. (Occasional Publications in Mane Archaeology: No. 1). (Illus.). 160p. 1980. 22.00 (ISBN 0-913764-13-2). Maine St Mus.

--Indian Antiquities of the Kennebec Valley. (Illus.). 1980. 22.00 (ISBN 0-913764-13-2). Maine St Mus.

INDIANS OF NORTH AMERICA–ART

Broder, Patricia J. American Indian Painting & Sculpture. LC 80-66526. (Illus.). 160p. 1981. 29.95 (ISBN 0-89659-147-6). Abbeville Pr.

Kenny, Maurice, ed. From the Center: A Folio of Native American Art & Poetry. (Illus.). 30p. (Orig.). 1981. pap. 7.50 (ISBN 0-936574-03-8). Strawberry Pr NY.

Lee, Georgia. The Portable Cosmos: Effigies, Ornaments & Incised Stone from the Chumash Area. (Ballena Press Anthropological Papers: No. 21). (Illus.). 114p. (Orig.). 1981. pap. 6.95 (ISBN 0-87919-093-0). Ballena Pr.

Philbrook Art Center. Native American Art at Philbrook. LC 80-82374. (Orig.). 1980. pap. 8.00 (ISBN 0-86659-001-3). Philbrook.

INDIANS OF NORTH AMERICA–BEADWORK

see Indians of North America–Textile Industry and Fabrics

INDIANS OF NORTH AMERICA–BIBLIOGRAPHY

Dockstader, Fred J. The American Indian in Graduate Studies: A Bibliolgrapy of Theses & Dissertations, 2 vols, Vol. 25. 1973. Set. pap. 18.00 (ISBN 0-934490-06-6); Vol. 1. pap. 10.00 (ISBN 0-934490-07-4); Vol. 2. pap. 10.00 (ISBN 0-934490-08-2). Mus Am Ind.

Marken, Jack W. & Hoover, Herbert T. Bibliography of the Sioux. LC 80-20106. (Native American Bibliography Ser.: No. 1). 388p. 1980. 17.50 (ISBN 0-8108-1356-4). Scarecrow.

INDIANS OF NORTH AMERICA–BIOGRAPHY

see also names of individual Indians, e.g. Geronimo

Brumble, H. David, III. An Annotated Bibliography of American Indian & Eskimo Autobiographies. LC 80-23449. 190p. 1981. 10.95x (ISBN 0-8032-1175-9). U of Nebr Pr.

Coel, Margaret. Chief Left Hand: Southern Arapaho. LC 80-5940. (The Civilization of the American Indian Ser.: Vol. 159). (Illus.). 482p. 1981. 15.95 (ISBN 0-8061-1602-1). U of Okla Pr.

Todd, Helen. Mary Musgrove: Georgia Indian Princess. LC 80-54424. 147p. (gr. 6-12). 1981. pap. 4.49 (ISBN 0-9605514-0-9). Seven Oaks.

INDIANS OF NORTH AMERICA–BLANKETS

see Indians of North America–Textile Industry and Fabrics

INDIANS OF NORTH AMERICA–CAPTIVITIES

Vaughan, Alden T. & Clark, Edward W., eds. Puritans Among the Indians: Accounts of Captivity & Redemption 1676-1724. (John Harvard Library Ser.). (Illus.). 352p. 1981. text ed. 20.00 (ISBN 0-674-73901-9). Harvard U Pr.

INDIANS OF NORTH AMERICA–CIVILIZATION

see Indians of North America–Culture

INDIANS OF NORTH AMERICA–CULTURE

Here is entered literature dealing with the cultural condition (i.e. arts, industries, religion and mythology, etc.) of the Indian at a given time or period.

Hamilton, Henry W. & Hamilton, Jean T. The Sioux of the Rosebud: A History in Pictures. LC 78-145506. (The Civilization of the American Indian Ser.: Vol. 111). (Illus.). 320p. 1981. pap. 12.50 (ISBN 0-8061-1622-6). U of Okla Pr.

Prakash, B. Aspects of Indian History & Civilization. 1965. 8.50 (ISBN 0-8426-1681-0). Verry.

Vaughan, Alden T. & Richter, Daniel K. Crossing the Cultural Divide: Indians & New Englanders, 1605-1763. 76p. 1980. pap. write for info. (ISBN 0-912296-48-8). Am Antiquarian.

INDIANS OF NORTH AMERICA–CUSTOMS

see Indians of North America–Social Life and Customs

INDIANS OF NORTH AMERICA–ECONOMIC CONDITIONS

Couro, Teo. San Diego County Indians As Farmers & Wage Earners. pap. 1.00 (ISBN 0-686-69102-4). Acoma Bks.

Mongia, J. N. Economics for Administrators. 600p. 1981. text ed. 40.00x (ISBN 0-7069-1293-4, Pub by Vikas India). Advent Bk.

Reno, Philip. Mother Earth, Father Sky, & Economic Development: Navajo Resources & Their Use. (Illus.). 200p. 1981. 12.95x (ISBN 0-8263-0550-4). U of NM Pr.

Talbot, Steve. Roots of Oppression: The American Indian Question. (Orig.). 1981. 14.00 (ISBN 0-7178-0591-3); pap. 4.75 (ISBN 0-7178-0583-2). Intl Pub Co.

INDIANS OF NORTH AMERICA–EDUCATION

see also particular schools, e.g. Carlisle, Pennsylvania. United States Indian School

Morey, Sylvester M. & Gilliam, Olivia L., eds. Respect for Life: The Traditional Upbringing of American Indian Children. LC 80-83371. (Illus.). 202p. 1980. pap. text ed. 4.95 (ISBN 0-913098-34-5). Myrin Institute.

Multicultural Education & the American Indian. 169p. 1979. 5.00 (ISBN 0-686-28733-9). U Cal AISC.

Rosier, Paul & Holm, Wayne. The Rock Point Experience: A Longitudinal Study of a Navajo School Program (Saad Naaki Bee Na'nitin) LC 80-19695. (Bilingual Education Ser.: No. 8). 95p. (Orig.). 1980. pap. text ed. 6.50 (ISBN 0-87281-119-0). Ctr Appl Ling.

INDIANS OF NORTH AMERICA–ETHNOLOGY

see Indians of North America

INDIANS OF NORTH AMERICA–FOLK-LORE

see Folk-Lore, Indian

INDIANS OF NORTH AMERICA–GOVERNMENT RELATIONS

Bee, Robert L. Crosscurrents Along the Colorado: The Impact of Government Policy on the Quechan Indians. 1981. text ed. 20.00x (ISBN 0-8165-0558-6); pap. 9.50x (ISBN 0-686-69385-X). U of Ariz Pr.

Foreman, Richard L. Indian Water Rights. 1980. pap. text ed. 8.95x (ISBN 0-8134-2160-8, 2160). Interstate.

Viola, Herman J. Diplomats in Buckskins: A History of Indian Delegations in Washington City. LC 80-607804. (Illus.). 1981. 17.50 (ISBN 0-87474-944-1). Smithsonian.

INDIANS OF NORTH AMERICA–HISTORY

see also Indians of North America–Wars

Kellogg, Edward P. Roots of the American Indian. LC 79-91921. 1980. text ed. 14.95 (ISBN 0-9603914-0-1). EHUD.

Prakash, B. Aspects of Indian History & Civilization. 1965. 8.50 (ISBN 0-8426-1681-0). Verry.

Wright, J. Leitch, Jr. The Only Land They Knew: The Tragic Story of the American Indians in the Old South. LC 80-1854. (Illus.). 1981. 16.95 (ISBN 0-02-935790-X). Free Pr.

INDIANS OF NORTH AMERICA–HISTORY–SOURCES

Vecsey, Christopher & Venables, Robert W., eds. American Indian Environments: Ecological Issues in Native American History. LC 80-26458. (Illus.). 236p. 1980. text ed. 18.00x (ISBN 0-8156-2226-0); pap. text ed. 9.95x (ISBN 0-8156-2227-9). Syracuse U Pr.

Wilcomb, E., compiled by. The American Indian & the United States: A Documentary History, 4 vols. LC 72-10259. 1973. Set. lib. bdg. 175.00 (ISBN 0-313-20137-4). Greenwood.

INDIANS OF NORTH AMERICA–JUVENILE LITERATURE

Guidetti, Geri. A Seneca Garden. (Illus.). 26p. (Orig.). (gr. 2-8). 1981. pap. 3.95 (ISBN 0-938928-00-7). KMG Pubns OR.

Kloss, Doris. Sarah Winnemucca. LC 81-390. (Story of an American Indian Ser.). (Illus.). (gr. 5 up). 1981. PLB 6.95 (ISBN 0-87518-178-3). Dillon.

McGaw, Jessie B. Chief Red Horse Tells About Custer. (Illus.). 64p. (gr. 4 up). 1981. 8.95 (ISBN 0-525-66713-X). Elsevier-Nelson.

INDIANS OF NORTH AMERICA–LAND TENURE

Carlson, Leonard A. Indians, Bureaucrats, & Land: The Dawes Act & the Decline of Indian Farming. LC 80-1709. (Contributions in Economics & Economic History Ser.: No. 36). 280p. 1981. lib. bdg. 29.95 (ISBN 0-313-22533-8, CDA/). Greenwood.

INDIANS OF NORTH AMERICA–LANGUAGES

see also Algonquian Languages;

also names of languages or group of languages

Bauman, James J. Guide to Issues in Indian Language Retention. 1980. pap. text ed. 5.50 (ISBN 0-87281-132-8). Ctr Appl Ling.

INDIANS OF NORTH AMERICA–LEGAL STATUS, LAWS, ETC.

see also Indians of North America–Land Tenure; Indians of North America–Treaties

Viola, Herman J. Diplomats in Buckskins: A History of Indian Delegations in Washington City. LC 80-607804. (Illus.). 1981. 17.50 (ISBN 0-87474-944-1). Smithsonian.

INDIANS OF NORTH AMERICA–LEGENDS

see also Folk-Lore, Indian

Coffer, William E. Where Is the Eagle? 288p. 1981. 16.95 (ISBN 0-442-26163-2). Van Nos Reinhold.

Palmer, William R. Why the North Star Stands Still: And Other Indian Legends. (Illus.). 118p. 1978. 2.50. Zion.

INDIANS OF NORTH AMERICA–MEDICINE

see also Medicine-Man

Gilmore, Melvin. Notes on the Gynecology & Obstetrics of the Arikara Tribe of Indians, Vol. 14, No. 1. 1980. pap. 2.50 (ISBN 0-686-69103-2). Acoma Bks.

INDIANS OF NORTH AMERICA–MYTHOLOGY

see Folk-Lore, Indian; Indians of North America–Legends; Indians of North America–Religion and Mythology

INDIANS OF NORTH AMERICA–NAMES

Rydjord, John. Indian Place-Names: Their Origin, Evolution, & Meanings, Collected in Kansas from the Siouan, Algonquian, Shoshonean, Caddoan, Iroquoian, & Other Tongues. LC 68-10303. (Illus.). 380p. 1981. 19.95 (ISBN 0-8061-0801-0). U of Okla Pr.

INDIANS OF NORTH AMERICA–ORIGIN

see Indians–Origin

INDIANS OF NORTH AMERICA–PERIODICALS

Murphy, James E. & Murphy, Sharon M. Let My People Know: American Indian Journalism, 1828-1978. LC 80-5941. 300p. 1981. 14.95 (ISBN 0-8061-1623-4). U of Okla Pr.

INDIANS OF NORTH AMERICA–PHILOSOPHY

McNely, James K. Holy Wind in Navajo Philosophy. 1981. text ed. 14.95x (ISBN 0-8165-0710-4); pap. 6.95x (ISBN 0-8165-0724-4). U of Ariz Pr.

INDIANS OF NORTH AMERICA–PICTORIAL WORKS

Curtis, Edward S. Portraits from North American Indian Life. 192p. 1981. pap. 10.95 (ISBN 0-89104-003-X). A & W Pubs.

INDIANS OF NORTH AMERICA–PORTRAITS

see Indians of North America–Pictorial Works

INDIANS OF NORTH AMERICA–POTTERY

Baylor, Byrd. When Clay Sings. (Illus.). 32p. (gr. 1-5). pap. 2.95 (ISBN 0-689-70482-8, A-109, Aladdin). Atheneum.

Dittert, Alfred E., Jr. & Plog, Fred. Generations in Clay: Pueblo Pottery of the American Southwest. LC 80-81831. (Illus.). 168p. 1980. 27.50 (ISBN 0-87358-271-3); pap. 14.95 (ISBN 0-87358-270-5). Northland.

INDIANS OF NORTH AMERICA–RELIGION AND MYTHOLOGY

Gill, Sam D. Sacred Words: A Study of Navajo Religion & Prayer. LC 80-659. (Contributions in Intercultural & Comparative Studies: No. 4). (Illus.). 272p. 1981. lib. bdg. 29.95 (ISBN 0-313-22165-0, GSW/). Greenwood.

INDIANS OF NORTH AMERICA–SCHOOLS

see Indians of North America–Education

INDIANS OF NORTH AMERICA–SOCIAL CONDITIONS

Knack, Martha C. Life Is with People: Household Organization of the Contemporary Paiute Indians. (Anthropological Papers Ser.: No. 19). 106p. (Orig.). 1981. pap. 6.95 (ISBN 0-87919-091-4). Ballena Pr.

Talbot, Steve. Roots of Oppression: The American Indian Question. (Orig.). 1981. 14.00 (ISBN 0-7178-0591-3); pap. 4.75 (ISBN 0-7178-0583-2). Intl Pub Co.

INDIANS OF NORTH AMERICA–SOCIAL LIFE AND CUSTOMS

Axtell, James, ed. The Indian Peoples of Eastern America: A Documentary History of the Sexes. (Illus.). 232p. 1981. text ed. 11.95x (ISBN 0-19-502740-X); pap. text ed. 6.95 (ISBN 0-19-502741-8). Oxford U Pr.

Breton, Raymond & Akian, Gail G. Urban Institutions & People of Indian Ancestry. 52p. 1978. pap. text ed. 3.00x (ISBN 0-920380-14-X, Pub. by Inst Res Pub Canada). Renouf.

Eggan, Fred. The American Indian: Perspectives for the Study of Social Change. LC 80-67926. (Lewis Henry Morgan Lectures). 192p. 1981. 22.50 (ISBN 0-521-23752-1); pap. 6.95 (ISBN 0-521-28210-1). Cambridge U Pr.

Knack, Martha C. Life Is with People: Household Organization of the Contemporary Paiute Indians. (Anthropological Papers Ser.: No. 19). 106p. (Orig.). 1981. pap. 6.95 (ISBN 0-87919-091-4). Ballena Pr.

Margolin, Malcolm. How We Lived: Reminiscences, Stories, Speeches, & Songs of California Indians. 1981. 10.95 (ISBN 0-930588-03-7); pap. 5.95 (ISBN 0-930588-04-5). Heyday Bks.

Morey, Sylvester M. & Gilliam, Olivia L., eds. Respect for Life: The Traditional Upbringing of American Indian Children. LC 80-83371. (Illus.). 202p. 1980. pap. text ed. 4.95 (ISBN 0-913098-34-5). Myrin Institute.

Nabokov, Peter. Indian Running. (Illus.). 160p. (Orig.). 1981. pap. 7.95 (ISBN 0-88496-162-1). Capra Pr.

INDIANS OF NORTH AMERICA–SPORTS

see Indians of North America–Social Life and Customs

INDIANS OF NORTH AMERICA–TEXTILE INDUSTRY AND FABRICS

Rodee, Marian E. Old Navajo Rugs: Their Development from 1900 to 1940. (Illus.). 96p. 1981. price not set (ISBN 0-8263-0566-0); pap. price not set (ISBN 0-8263-0567-9). U of NM Pr.

INDIANS OF NORTH AMERICA–TREATIES

see also Indians of North America–Government Relations

also names of specific treaties

Price, Richard. The Spirit of the Alberta Indian Treaties. 202p. 1979. pap. text ed. 8.95x (ISBN 0-920380-23-9, Pub. by Inst Res Pub Canada). Renouf.

INDIANS OF NORTH AMERICA–WARS

Hedren, Paul L. First Scalp for Custer: The Skirmish at Warbonnet Creek, Nebraska, July 17, 1876. LC 80-68844. (Hidden Springs of Custeriana Ser.: No. V). (Illus.). 106p. 1981. 38.00 (ISBN 0-87062-137-8). A H Clark.

INDIANS OF NORTH AMERICA–WARS–1866-1895

Seymour, Forest W. Sitanka: The Full Story of Wounded Knee. 1981. 9.75 (ISBN 0-8158-0399-0). Chris Mass.

INDIANS OF NORTH AMERICA–WEAVING

see Indians of North America–Textile Industry and Fabrics

INDIANS OF NORTH AMERICA–WOMEN

Axtell, James, ed. The Indian Peoples of Eastern America: A Documentary History of the Sexes. (Illus.). 232p. 1981. text ed. 11.95x (ISBN 0-19-502740-X); pap. text ed. 6.95 (ISBN 0-19-502741-8). Oxford U Pr.

Wolf, Beverly H. The Ways of My Grandmothers. 224p. 1981. pap. 5.95. Morrow.

INDIANS OF NORTH AMERICA–EASTERN STATES

Anderson, Duane C. & Semken, Holmes, eds. The Cherokee Excavations: Holocene Ecology & Human Adaptations in Northwestern Iowa. (Studies in Archaeology). 1980. 23.00 (ISBN 0-12-058260-0). Acad Pr.

Howard, James H. Shawnee: The Ceremonialism of a Native American Tribe & Its Cultural Background. LC 80-23752. (Illus.). xvi, 434p. 1981. 24.95 (ISBN 0-8214-0417-2); pap. 11.95 (ISBN 0-8214-0614-0). Ohio U Pr.

INDIANS OF NORTH AMERICA–NORTHWEST, OLD

Sosin, Jack M. Whitehall & the Wilderness: The Middle West in British Colonial Policy, 1760 to 1775. LC 80-21061. (Illus.). xi, 307p. 1981. Repr. of 1961 ed. lib. bdg. 35.00x (ISBN 0-313-22678-4, SOWW). Greenwood.

INDIANS OF NORTH AMERICA–NORTHWEST, PACIFIC

Ruby, Robert H. & Brown, John A. Indians of the Pacific Northwest: A History. LC 80-5946. (Civilization of the American Indian Ser.: Vol. 158). (Illus.). 400p. 1981. 24.95 (ISBN 0-8061-1731-1). U of Okla Pr.

Wallas, James & Whitaker, Pamela. Kwakiutl Legends. 150p. 1981. text ed. price not set (ISBN 0-88839-094-7). Hancock Hse.
Wolf, Beverly H. The Ways of My Grandmothers. 224p. 1981. pap. 5.95. Morrow.
INDIANS OF NORTH AMERICA–SOUTHWEST, NEW
see also Pueblos
Allen, T. D. Navahos Have Five Fingers. LC 63-17167. (The Civilization of the American Indian Ser.: Vol. 68). (Illus.). 249p. 1981. 13.95 (ISBN 0-8061-0575-5). U of Okla Pr.
Benedict, Ruth. Tales of the Cochiti Indians. 256p. 1981. pap. price not set (ISBN 0-8263-0569-5). U of NM Pr.
Dutton, Bertha P. Indians of the American Southwest. 336p. 1981. 17.50 (ISBN 0-8263-0551-2); pap. 8.95 (ISBN 0-8263-0552-0). U of NM Pr.
Frink, Maurice. Fort Defiance & the Navajos. (Illus.). 150p. (Orig.). 1981. pap. 5.95 (ISBN 0-87108-585-2). Pruett.
Gill, Sam D. Sacred Words: A Study of Navajo Religion & Prayer. LC 80-659. (Contributions in Intercultural & Comparative Studies: No. 4). (Illus.). 272p. 1981. lib. bdg. 29.95 (ISBN 0-313-22165-0, GSW/). Greenwood.
Gracia, Mario T. Desert Immigrants: The Mexican of El Paso, 1880-1920. LC 80-36862. (Western Americana Ser.: No. 32). (Illus.). 328p. 1981. text ed. 23.00x (ISBN 0-300-02520-3). Yale U Pr.
Iverson, Peter. The Navajo Nation. LC 80-1024. (Contributions in Ethnic Studies: No. 3). (Illus.). 312p. 1981. lib. bdg. 25.00 (ISBN 0-313-22309-2, INN/). Greenwood.
Kammer, Jerry. The Second Long Walk: The Navajo-Hopi Land Dispute. 1980. 14.95 (ISBN 0-8263-0549-0). U of NM Pr.
La Lone, Mary. Gabrielino Indians of Southern California: An Annotated Ethnohistoric Bibliography. (Occasional Papers: No. 6). 72p. 1980. pap. 4.50 (ISBN 0-917956-15-X). UCLA Arch.
McNely, James K. Holy Wind in Navajo Philosophy. 1981. text ed. 14.95x (ISBN 0-8165-0710-4); pap. 6.95x (ISBN 0-8165-0724-4). U of Ariz Pr.
INDIANS OF NORTH AMERICA–THE WEST
Haines, Francis. Red Eagles of the Northwest: The Story of Chief Joseph & His People. LC 76-43728. (Illus.). 376p. 1980. Repr. of 1939 ed. 32.50 (ISBN 0-404-15569-3). AMS Pr.
Hamilton, Henry W. & Hamilton, Jean T. The Sioux of the Rosebud: A History in Pictures. LC 78-145506. (The Civilization of the American Indian Ser.: Vol. 111). (Illus.). 320p. 1981. pap. 12.50 (ISBN 0-8061-1622-6). U of Okla Pr.
Irwin, Charles N. The Shoshoni Indians of Inyo County, California. (Ballena Press Publications in Archaeology, Ethnology & History: No. 15). (Illus.). 114p. (Orig.). 1980. pap. 6.95 (ISBN 0-87919-090-6). Ballena Pr.
Read, Ethel M. Lo, the Poor Indian: A Saga of the Suisun Indians of California. LC 80-82306. 580p. (Orig.). 1980. 18.00 (ISBN 0-914330-34-9); pap. 10.00 (ISBN 0-914330-37-3). Panorama West.
INDIANS OF NORTH AMERICA–UNITED STATES
see Indians of North America
INDIANS OF SOUTH AMERICA
see also Ethnology–South America; Incas
American Indian Publishers, ed. Dictionary of Indian Tribes of the Americas, 4 vols. (Illus.). 1980. Set. lib. bdg. 225.00 (ISBN 0-937862-25-8). Am Hist Pubs.
INDIANS OF SOUTH AMERICA–ANTIQUITIES
see also Peru–Antiquities
Hemming, John. Machu Picchu. Bayrd, Edwin, ed. LC 80-82066. (Illus.). 1981. 16.95 (ISBN 0-88225-302-6). Newsweek.
INDIANS OF SOUTH AMERICA–BLANKETS
see Indians of South America–Textile Industry and Fabrics
INDIANS OF SOUTH AMERICA–ETHNOLOGY
see Indians of South America
INDIANS OF SOUTH AMERICA–FOLK-LORE
see Folk-Lore, Indian
INDIANS OF SOUTH AMERICA–ORIGIN
see Indians–Origin
INDIANS OF SOUTH AMERICA–SOCIAL CONDITIONS
Ruby, Robert H. & Brown, John A. The Spokane Indians: Children of the Sun. LC 79-108797. (The Civilization of the American Indian Ser.: Vol. 104). (Illus.). 346p. 1981. 19.95 (ISBN 0-8061-0905-X); pap. 9.95 (ISBN 0-8061-1757-5). U of Okla Pr.
INDIANS OF SOUTH AMERICA–TEXTILE INDUSTRY AND FABRICS
Wasserman, Tamara E. & Hill, Jonathan S. Bolivian Indian Textiles: Traditional Designs & Costumes. (Pictorial Archive Ser.). (Illus.). 64p. (Orig.). 1981. pap. price not set (ISBN 0-486-24118-1). Dover.
INDIANS OF SOUTH AMERICA–WEAVING
see Indians of South America–Textile Industry and Fabrics
INDIANS OF THE UNITED STATES
see Indians of North America
INDIANS OF THE WEST INDIES–ORIGIN
see Indians–Origin
INDIC ART
see Art, Indic
INDIC LANGUAGES
Here are entered works on the languages of India in general, and works not confined to the Indo-Aryan languages, or to any other special group or language.
see also Indo-Aryan Languages
Bongard-Levin, G. M. Origin of Aryans: From Scythis to India. Gupta, H. C., tr. 124p. 1980. text ed. cancelled (ISBN 0-8426-1663-2). Verry.
Venkatacharya, T. Sahityakantakodhara. 96p. 1980. text ed. 10.50 (ISBN 0-8426-1650-0). Verry.
INDIC LITERATURE
Here are entered works dealing with the literature of India in general, works on Indo-Aryan literature, and other works not confined to the literature of a single-language.
Obeyesekere, Ranjini & Fernando, Chitra, eds. An Anthology of Modern Writing from Sri Lanka. (Monographs of the Association for Asian Studies: No. XXXVIII). 1981. text ed. 12.95x (ISBN 0-8165-0702-3); pap. text ed. 6.50x (ISBN 0-8165-0703-1). U of Ariz Pr.
Ramakrishna, D., ed. Indian-English Prose: An Anthology. 1981. text ed. write for info. (ISBN 0-391-02190-7). Humanities.
INDIC LITERATURE–HISTORY AND CRITICISM
Naik, M. K. Aspects of Indian Writing in English. 319p. (Orig.). 1979. pap. text ed. 4.50x (ISBN 0-333-90301-3). Humanities.
Prasad, R. C. Early English Travellers in India. 2nd rev. ed. 391p. 1980. text ed. 27.00 (ISBN 0-8426-1649-7). Verry.
Raghavacharyulu, D. V. The Critical Response: Selected Essays on the American, Commonwealth,Indian & British Traditions in Literature. 1980. 13.50x (ISBN 0-8364-0632-X, Pub. by Macmillan India). South Asia Bks.
INDIC MUSIC
see Music, Indic
INDIC MYTHOLOGY
see Mythology, Indic
INDIC PAINTING
see Painting, Indic
INDIC PHILOSOPHY
see Philosophy, Indic
INDIC SCULPTURE
see Sculpture–India
INDIC SONGS
see Songs, Indic
INDIGNATION
see Anger
INDIRECT COSTS
see Overhead Costs
INDIRECT TAXATION
see Taxation
INDIVIDUALISM
see also Communism; Libertarianism; Socialism
Dallmayr, Fred R. Twilight of Subjectivity: Contributions to a Post-Individualist Theory of Politics. LC 80-23433. 416p. 1981. lib. bdg. 20.00x (ISBN 0-87023-314-9); pap. text ed. 10.00x (ISBN 0-87023-315-7). U of Mass Pr.
Pole, J. R. American Individualism & the Promise of Progress: Inaugural Lecture. (Inaugural Lecture Ser.). 30p. pap. 5.95 (ISBN 0-19-951526-3). Oxford U Pr.
INDO-ARYAN LANGUAGES
Turner, Sir Ralph. A Comparative Dictionary of the Indo-Aryan Languages. 862p. 1966. text ed. 69.00x (ISBN 0-19-713550-1). Oxford U Pr.
INDO-ARYAN LITERATURE
see Indic Literature
INDO-EUROPEANS
see also Celts
Hoddinott, R. F. The Thracians. (Ancient Peoples & Places Ser.). (Illus.). 192p. 1981. 19.95 (ISBN 0-500-02099-X). Thames Hudson.
INDO-GERMANIC PEOPLES
see Indo-Europeans
INDONESIA–ANTIQUITIES
Forman, Bedrich. Borobudur: The Buddhist Legend in Stone. (Illus.). 1980. 16.95. Mayflower Bks.
INDONESIA–DESCRIPTION AND TRAVEL
Lanier, Alison R. Update -- Indonesia. (Counry Orientation Ser.). 1980. pap. text ed. 25.00 (ISBN 0-933662-37-8). Intercult Network.
INDONESIA–HISTORY
Reid, Anthony. The Blood of the People: Revolution & the End of Traditional Rule in Northern Sumatra. (Illus.). 308p. 1979. text ed. 34.50x (ISBN 0-19-580399-X). Oxford U Pr.
INDONESIA–SOCIAL CONDITIONS
Hansen, Gary E., ed. Agricultural & Rural Development in Indonesia. (Special Studies in Social, Political, & Economic Development). 312p. 1981. lib. bdg. 20.00x (ISBN 0-86531-124-2). Westview.
Wertheim, Willem F. Indonesian Society in Transition: A Study of Social Change. LC 80-19660. (Illus.). xiv, 394p. 1980. Repr. of 1959 ed. lib. bdg. 29.75x (ISBN 0-313-22578-8, WEIO). Greenwood.
INDONESIAN TALES
see Tales, Indonesian
INDUCTION (LOGIC)
Christensen, R. Foundations of Inductive Reasoning. xii, 363p. 1964. 39.50 (ISBN 0-686-28748-7, 04-08-01). Entropy Ltd.
Rescher, Nicholas. Induction. LC 80-52598. xii, 225p. 1981. 34.95 (ISBN 0-8229-3431-0). U of Pittsburgh Pr.
INDUSTRIAL ACCIDENTS
see also Disability Evaluation; Employers' Liability; Workmen'S Compensation;
also subdivision Accidents, Safety Appliances, and Safety Measures under particular industries or occupations, e.g. Railroads–Accidents
Ferry, Ted S. Modern Accident Investigation & Analysis: An Executive Guide to Accident Investigation. 350p. 1981. 30.00 (ISBN 0-471-07776-3). Page-Ficklin.
--Modern Accident Investigation & Analysis: An Executive Guide to Accident Investigation. 350p. 1981. 30.00 (ISBN 0-471-07776-3, Pub. by Wiley-Interscience). Wiley.
INDUSTRIAL ACCIDENTS–PREVENTION
see Industrial Safety
INDUSTRIAL ADMINISTRATION
see Industrial Management
INDUSTRIAL ARBITRATION
see Arbitration, Industrial
INDUSTRIAL ARCHAEOLOGY
Here are entered works on the organized study of the physical remains of industries of the 18th and 19th centuries.
Vialls, Christine. Your Book of Industrial Archaeology. (Illus.). 80p. (gr. 4-12). 1981. 9.95 (ISBN 0-571-11633-7, Pub. by Faber & Faber). Merrimack Bk Serv.
INDUSTRIAL ARTS
see also Agriculture; Artisans; Bookbinding; Engineering; Inventions; Machinery in Industry; Mechanical Engineering; Patents; Research, Industrial; Technical Education; Technology
also names of specific industries, arts, trades, etc., e.g. Bookbinding; Printing; Ship-building
Ahlstrand, Alan. Datsun Two Hundred Ten: Nineteen Seventy-Nine to Nineteen Eighty Shop Manual. Jorgensen, Eric, ed. (Illus.). 336p. (Orig.). 1980. pap. text ed. 11.95 (ISBN 0-89287-322-1, A 203). Clymer Pubns.
Ahlstrand, Eric. Datsun F Ten & Three Hundred Ten: Nineteen Seventy-Six to Seventy-Nine Shop Manual. (Illus.). 186p. (Orig.). 1980. pap. text ed. 10.95 (ISBN 0-89287-318-3, A202). Clymer Pubns.
Bishop, Mike. Kawasaki Snowmobiles Nineteen Seventy-Six to Nineteen Eighty: Service, Repair, Maintenance. Jorgensen, Eric, ed. (Illus.). 152p. (Orig.). 1980. pap. text ed. 8.95 (ISBN 0-89287-320-5, X995). Clymer Pubns.
--Yamaha Snowmobiles: Nineteen Seventy-Five to Nineteen Eighty Service, Repair & Maintenance. Jorgensen, Eric, ed. (Illus.). 180p. (Orig.). 1980. pap. text ed. 8.95 (ISBN 0-89287-323-X, X954). Clymer Pubns.
Combs, Jim. BMW Three Hundred Twenty i: Nineteen Seventy-Seven to Nineteen Eighty Shop Manual. Jorgensen, Eric, ed. (Illus.). 248p. (Orig.). 1980. pap. text ed. 10.95 (ISBN 0-89287-326-4, A139). Clymer Pubns.
--Chevy Malibu Chevelle MonteCarlo: 1970-1980 Shop Manual. Jorgensen, Eric, ed. (Illus.). 360p. (Orig.). 1980. pap. text ed. 10.95 (ISBN 0-89287-319-1, A246). Clymer Pubns.
--Oldsmobile Cutlass: Nineteen Seventy to Nineteen Eighty Shop Manual. Jorgensen, Eric, ed. (Illus.). 342p. (Orig.). 1980. pap. text ed. 10.95 (ISBN 0-89287-324-8, A285). Clymer Pubns.
DiPaul, H. Bert. Focusing Industrial Arts on Career Education. LC 79-53500. (Illus.). 143p. (Orig.). (gr. 9-12). 1979. pap. 3.95 (ISBN 0-9605418-0-2). DiPaul.
Sales, David. Suzuki SP-DR Three Hundred Seventy & Four Hundred Singles Nineteen Seventy-Eight to Nineteen Eighty: Service, Repair, Performance. Jorgensen, Eric, ed. (Illus.). 224p. (Orig.). 1980. pap. text ed. 9.95 (ISBN 0-89287-327-2, M374). Clymer Pubns.
Scott, Ed. Yamaha YZ One Hundred to Four Hundred Sixty-Five Monoshock Nineteen Seventy-Five to Nineteen Eighty: Service, Repair, Performance. Jorgensen, Eric, ed. (Illus.). 293p. (Orig.). 1980. pap. text ed. 9.95 (ISBN 0-89287-329-9, M413). Clymer Pubns.
Scott, Edward. Honda Twinstar Nineteen Seventy-Eight to Nineteen Eighty: Service, Repair, Maintenance. Jorgensen, Eric, ed. (Illus.). 242p. (Orig.). 1980. pap. text ed. 9.95 (ISBN 0-89287-325-6, M324). Clymer Pubns.
Vesely, Anton. Kawasaki Nine Hundred & 1000cc Four, 1973-1979: Includes Shaft Drive Service Repair Performance. Jorgensen, Eric, ed. (Illus.). 324p. (Orig.). 1980. pap. text ed. 9.95 (ISBN 0-89287-321-3, M359). Clymer Pubns.
INDUSTRIAL ARTS–EXHIBITIONS
see Exhibitions
INDUSTRIAL BANKING
see Loans, Personal
INDUSTRIAL BUYING
see Industrial Procurement
INDUSTRIAL CHEMISTRY
see Chemical Engineering
INDUSTRIAL COMMUNICATION
see Communication in Management
INDUSTRIAL DESIGN
see Design, Industrial
INDUSTRIAL DISEASES
see Occupational Diseases
INDUSTRIAL DISTRICTS
Here are entered works on self-contained industrial areas within which utilities, transportation, and other general services are offered to a group of companies.
Industrial Estates: A Tool for the Development of Backward Areas. 57p. 1973. 2.75 (APO32, APO). Unipub.
Japanese Industrial Estates for Small Business Development. 32p. 1973. 2.75 (APO37, APO). Unipub.
INDUSTRIAL DRAWING
see Mechanical Drawing
INDUSTRIAL EDUCATION
see Technical Education
INDUSTRIAL ELECTRONICS
Electronic Industries Association & Zbar, Paul B. Industrial Electronics: Atext-Lab Manual. 3rd ed. (Illus.). 320p. Date not set. 12.95x (ISBN 0-07-072793-7, G). McGraw.
INDUSTRIAL ENGINEERING
see also Automation; Human Engineering; Industrial Relations; Production Engineering; Psychology, Industrial; Quality Control; Standardization; Systems Engineering; Work Measurement
Langer, Steven, ed. Compensation of Industrial Engineering. 6th ed. 1981. 60.00 (ISBN 0-916506-63-0). Abbott Langer Assocs.
INDUSTRIAL EQUIPMENT–MAINTENANCE AND REPAIR
see Plant Maintenance
INDUSTRIAL ESTATES
see Industrial Districts
INDUSTRIAL EXHIBITIONS
see Exhibitions
INDUSTRIAL GAMING
see Management Games
INDUSTRIAL HEALTH
see also Industrial Accidents; Occupational Diseases
Beaulieu, Harry J. & Buchan, Roy M. Quantitative Industrial Hygiene. 1981. lib. bdg. 17.50 (ISBN 0-8240-7180-8). Garland Pub.
Burgess, William A. Recognition of Health Hazards in Industry: A Review of Materials & Processes. 372p. 1981. 28.00 (ISBN 0-471-06339-8, Pub. by Wiley-Interscience). Wiley.
Clayton, G. D. & Clayton, F. E. Pattys Industrial Hygiene & Toxicology, 4 vols. 3rd ed. 1981. 305.00 (ISBN 0-471-08431-X). Wiley.
Occupational Exposure to Airborne Substances Harmful to Health. 44p. 1981. pap. 6.50 (ISBN 92-2-102442-3, ILO 152, ILO). Unipub.
Schilling, R. S., ed. Occupational Health Practice. 2nd ed. LC 80-41044. (Illus.). 512p. 1981. text ed. 49.00 (ISBN 0-407-33701-6). Butterworths.
INDUSTRIAL HEALTH ENGINEERING
see Industrial Health
INDUSTRIAL LAWS AND LEGISLATION
Here are entered works of a comprehensive character which deal with laws and legislation regulating industry. Works on the theory of state regulation of industry are entered under Industry and State; Laissez-Faire.
see also Competition, Unfair; Labor Laws and Legislation; Occupations, Dangerous; Patent Laws and Legislation; Trade-Marks; Trade Regulation
Janner, Greville. Janner's Compendium of Employment Law. 759p. 1979. text ed. 45.50x (ISBN 0-220-66363-7, Pub. by Busn Bks England). Renouf.
Klotter, John C., et al. Legal Aspects of Private Security. LC 79-55202. 368p. 1981. text ed. price not set (ISBN 0-87084-488-1). Anderson Pub Co.
Mitchell, Ewan. The Employer's Guide to the Law on Health, Safety & Welfare at Work. 2nd ed. 471p. 1977. text ed. 36.75x (ISBN 0-220-66341-6, Pub. by Busn Bks England). Renouf.
Quirk, Paul J. Industry Influence in Federal Regulatory Agencies. LC 80-8571. 264p. 1981. 18.50x (ISBN 0-691-09388-1); pap. 4.95x (ISBN 0-691-02823-0). Princeton U Pr.
INDUSTRIAL LOCATION
see Industries, Location of
INDUSTRIAL MAINTENANCE
see Plant Maintenance
INDUSTRIAL MANAGEMENT
see also Assembly-Line Methods; Business; Business Consultants; Communication in Management; Controllership; Corporate Planning; Executives; Executives, Training of; Factory Management; Industries, Location of; Industrial Health; Industrial Organization; Industrial Procurement; Industrial Relations; Industrial Sociology; Labor Productivity; Management Audit; Management Games; Managerial Economics; Marketing; Marketing Management; Materials Management; Office Management; Personnel Management; Production Control; Production Management; Production Standards; Sales Management; Shift Systems; Shipment of Goods; Small Business–Management; Technological Innovations
Batty, J., et al. Industrial Administration & Management. 4th ed. (Illus.). 592p. 1979. pap. 16.95x (ISBN 0-7121-0954-4, Pub. by Macdonald & Evans England). Intl Ideas.
Pacifico, Carl R. & Witwer, Daniel B. Practical Industrial Management: Insights for Managers. 550p. 1981. 19.95 (ISBN 0-471-08190-6, Pub. by Wiley-Interscience). Wiley.

Porter, Michael E. Competitive Strategy: Techniques for Analyzing Industries & Competitors. LC 80-65200. (Illus.). 400p. 1980. 14.95 (ISBN 0-02-925360-8). Free Pr.

Woodward, Joan. Industrial Organization: Theory & Practice. 2nd ed. (Illus.). 324p. 1981. 42.00 (ISBN 0-19-874122-7); pap. 20.00 (ISBN 0-19-874123-5). Oxford U Pr.

INDUSTRIAL MANAGEMENT–JAPAN

Sasaki, Naoto. Management & Industrial Structure in Japan. (Illus.). 160p. 1981. 24.00 (ISBN 0-08-024056-9); pap. 13.00 (ISBN 0-08-024057-7). Pergamon.

INDUSTRIAL MATERIALS

see Materials

INDUSTRIAL MICROBIOLOGY

Sebek, O. K. & Laskin, A. I., eds. Genetics of Industrial Microorganisms. (Illus.). 1979. 12.00 (ISBN 0-914826-19-0). Am Soc Microbio.

INDUSTRIAL NOISE

Fader, Bruce. Industrial Noise Control. 320p. 1981. 29.95 (ISBN 0-471-06007-0, Pub. by Wiley Interscience). Wiley.

INDUSTRIAL ORGANIZATION

see also Industrial Management; Industrial Sociology

Martin P. Catherwood Library-Cornell University. Library Catalogue of the Martin P. Catherwood Library of the New York State School of Industrial & Labor Relations: Fourth Supplement. (Library Catalogs & Supplements Ser.). 1980. lib. bdg. 260.00 (ISBN 0-8161-0333-X). G K Hall.

The Stability of Industrial Organisms. 57p. 1981. pap. 12.50 (ISBN 0-85198-470-3, CAB 13, CAB). Unipub.

Woodward, Joan. Industrial Organization: Theory & Practice. 2nd ed. (Illus.). 324p. 1981. 42.00 (ISBN 0-19-874122-7); pap. 20.00 (ISBN 0-19-874123-5). Oxford U Pr.

INDUSTRIAL PARKS

see Industrial Districts

INDUSTRIAL POISONS

see Industrial Toxicology

INDUSTRIAL PROCESS CONTROL

see Process Control

INDUSTRIAL PROCESSING

see Manufacturing Processes

INDUSTRIAL PROCUREMENT

Stumm, David A. Advanced Industrial Selling. 426p. 1981. 17.95 (ISBN 0-8144-5665-0). Am Mgmt.

Zenz, Gary L. Purchasing & the Management of Materials. 5th ed. 600p. 1981. text ed. 21.95 (ISBN 0-471-06091-7); tchrs.' ed. avail. (ISBN 0-471-08935-4). Wiley.

INDUSTRIAL PRODUCTION

see Industry; Supply and Demand

INDUSTRIAL PROPERTY

see also Competition, Unfair; Patent Laws and Legislation; Trade-Marks

Inventive Activity in the Asian & the Pacific Region. 152p. 1981. pap. 26.00 (WIPO66, WIPO). Unipub.

Umbeck, John R. A Theory of Property Rights-with Special Applications to the California Gold Rush. (Illus.). 160p. 1981. text ed. 9.50 (ISBN 0-8138-1675-0). Iowa St U Pr.

Zweigert, Konrad & Kropholler, Jan. Law of Copyright, Competition & Industrial Property. Kolle, Gert & Hallstein, Hans P., eds. (Sources of International Uniform Law Ser.: Vol. III-A First Supplement). 1340p. 1980. 175.00x (ISBN 9-0286-0099-X). Sijthoff & Noordhoff.

INDUSTRIAL PSYCHOLOGY

see Psychology, Industrial

INDUSTRIAL PURCHASING

see Industrial Procurement

INDUSTRIAL RELATIONS

see also Arbitration, Industrial; Collective Bargaining; Grievance Procedures; Industrial Sociology; Labor Laws and Legislation; Personnel Management; Strikes and Lockouts; Trade-Unions

also local subdivisions of countries other than United States, and names of cities, e.g. Industrial Relations–India; Industrial Relations–New York (City)

Abarbanel, Jerome. Redefining the Enviorment. (Key Issues Ser.: No. 9). 1972. pap. 2.00 (ISBN 0-87546-200-6). NY Sch Indus Rel.

Adler, Joseph & Doherty, Robert E., eds. Employment Security in the Public Sector: A Symposium. 1974. pap. 2.00 (ISBN 0-87546-204-9). NY Sch Indus Rel.

Anderson, Howard J. Primer on Labor Relations. 160p. pap. 7.50. BNA.

Coghill, Mary A. Games & Simulatons in Industrial & Labor Relations Training. (Key Issues Ser.: No. 7). 1971. pap. 2.00 (ISBN 0-87546-207-3). NY Sch Indus Rel.

Conciliation & Arbitration Procedures in Labour Disputes. 183p. 1980. pap. 16.00 (ISBN 92-2-102339-7, ILO 151, ILO). Unipub.

East-West Industrial Co-Operation. 122p. 1979. pap. 10.00 (ISBN 0-686-68951-8, UN79/2E25, UN). Unipub.

Employer-Employee Committees & Worker Participaton. (Key Issues Ser.: No. 20). 1976. pap. 3.00 (ISBN 0-87546-221-9). NY Sch Indus Rel.

Fearn, Robert M. Labor Economics: The Emerging Synthesis. 288p. 1981. text ed. 18.95 (ISBN 0-87626-473-9). Winthrop.

Gersuny, Carl. Work Hazards & Industrial Conflict. LC 80-51506. (Illus.). 200p. 1981. 12.00 (ISBN 0-87451-189-5). U Pr of New Eng.

Gohmann, John W. Arbitration & Representation: Applications in Air & Rail Labor Relations. LC 80-84183. 336p. 1981. text ed. 22.50 (ISBN 0-8403-2335-2). Kendall-Hunt.

Goodman, J. F., et al. Ideology & Shopfloor Industrial Relations. 224p. 1981. 37.50x (ISBN 0-7099-0465-7, Pub. by Croom Helm Ltd England). Biblio Dist.

Heib, Elizabeth A., ed. Collection of Employer Contributions Institute, Las Vegas, Nevada, June 15 to 18, 1980: Proceedings. 77p. (Orig.). 1980. pap. 8.00 (ISBN 0-89154-138-1). Intl Found Employ.

Heskes, Deborah. Supportive Services for Disadvantaged Workers & Trainees. (Key Issues Ser.: No. 12). 1973. pap. 2.00 (ISBN 0-87546-225-1). NY Sch Indus Rel.

International Labour Office. Asian Regional Conference, Manila, December 1980, 9th Session: Problems of Rural Workers in Asia & the Pacific, Report III. ii, 104p. (Orig.). 1980. pap. 10.00 (ISBN 92-2-102500-4). Intl Labour Office.

--Ninth Asian Regional Conference, Manila, December, 1980: Report of the Director-General Asian Development in the 1980s-Growth, Employment & Working Conditions, Report I, Pt. 1. iii, 100p. (Orig.). 1980. pap. 10.00 (ISBN 92-2-102497-0). Intl Labour Office.

--Ninth Asian Regional Conference, Manila, December 1980: Report of the Director-General Application of ILO Standards, Report I, Pt. 2. iii, 45p. (Orig.). 1980. pap. text ed. 7.15 (ISBN 92-2-102498-9). Intl Labour Office.

--Programme of Industrial Activities Advisory Committee of Salaried Employees & Professional Workers, 8th Session, Geneva, 1981: The Effects of Technological & Structural Changes on the Employment & Working Conditions of Non-Manual Workers, Report II. iv, 117p. (Orig.). 1980. pap. 8.55 (ISBN 92-2-102557-8). Intl Labour Office.

International Labour Office, Geneva. Technical Guide, 1980: Employment, Unemployment, Hours of Work, Wages, Vol. II. 432p. (Orig.). 1980. pap. 15.70 (ISBN 92-2-102286-2). Intl Labour Office.

Jost, Lee F. & Sutherland, C. Bruce. Guide to Professional Benefit Plan Management & Administration. 405p. (Orig.). 1980. pap. 35.00 (ISBN 0-89154-096-2). Intl Found Employ.

Kovach, Kenneth A. Readings & Cases in Contemporary Labor Relations 1980. LC 80-1429. 359p. 1981. pap. text ed. 12.00 (ISBN 0-8191-1362-X). U Pr of Amer.

Kujawa, D. Employment Effects of Multinational Enterprises: The Case of the United States. International Labour Office, ed. (Research on Employment Effects of Multinational Enterprises. Working Papers Ser.: No. 12). 53p. (Orig.). 1980. pap. 8.55. Intl Labour Office.

Levin, Noel A. Guidelines for Fiduciaries of Taft-Hartley Trusts: An ERISA Manual. 137p. 1980. 25.00 (ISBN 0-89154-135-7). Intl Found Employ.

Muldoon, Joseph A. & Berdie, Mitchell. Effective Employee Assistance: A Comprehensive Guide for the Employer. 1980. 49.95 (ISBN 0-89638-048-3). CompCare.

Poole, Michael & Mansfield. Roger. Managerial Roles in Industrial Relations: Towards a Definitive Survey of Research & Formulation of Models. 1980. text ed. 27.75x (ISBN 0-566-00377-5, Pub. by Gower Pub Co England). Renouf.

Productivity, Quality of Working Life & Labour-Management Relations. 23p. 1976. 2.75 (APO62, APO). Unipub.

Sanchez, Irene, et al. The California Worker's Compensation Rehabilitation System. LC 80-70211. (Illus.). 360p. 1981. 35.00 (ISBN 0-02-927670-5). Macmillan.

Training: Challenge of the 1980s. Offprint of Part 1 of the Report of the Director-General to the International Labour Conference, Geneva, 1980. 50p. (Orig.). 1980. pap. 7.15 (ISBN 92-2-102554-3). Intl Labour Office.

INDUSTRIAL RELATIONS–BIBLIOGRAPHY

Soltow, Martha & Sokkar, Jo A. Industrial Relations & Personnel Management: Selected Information Sources. LC 78-31795. 294p. 1979. lib. bdg. 12.00 (ISBN 0-8108-1203-7). Scarecrow.

INDUSTRIAL RELATIONS–ASIA

Small Industry Bulletin for Asia & the Pacific, No.16. 189p. 1980. pap. 14.00 (UN80-2F4, UN). Unipub.

INDUSTRIAL RELATIONS–EUROPE

Industrial Democracy in Europe (IDE) International Research Group, ed. European Industrial Relations. (Illus.). 256p. 1981. 45.00 (ISBN 0-19-827254-5). Oxford U Pr.

INDUSTRIAL RELATIONS–JAPAN

Sasaki, Naoto. Management & Industrial Structure in Japan. (Illus.). 160p. 1981. 24.00 (ISBN 0-08-024056-9); pap. 13.00 (ISBN 0-08-024057-7). Pergamon.

INDUSTRIAL RELATIONS–LATIN AMERICA

Story, Dale. Sectoral Clash & Industrialization in Latin America. LC 80-28553. (Latin American Foreign & Comparative Studies Program: No. 2). 1981. pap. text ed. 6.00x (ISBN 0-915984-93-8). Syracuse U Foreign Comp.

INDUSTRIAL RESEARCH

see Research, Industrial

INDUSTRIAL REVOLUTION

see Industry–History

INDUSTRIAL SAFETY

see also Industrial Accidents

also subdivisions Safety Appliances and Safety Measures under subjects, e.g. Factories–Safety Appliances

Anderson, C. Richard. OSHA & Accident Control Through Training. LC 74-16444. (Illus.). 225p. 1975. 20.00 (ISBN 0-8311-1094-5). Indus Pr.

Atherly, Gordon. Occupational Health & Safety Concepts. 1978. 22.50x. Intl Ideas.

Beaulieu, Harry J. & Buchan, Roy M. Quantitative Industrial Hygiene. 1981. lib. bdg. 17.50 (ISBN 0-8240-7180-8). Garland Pub.

Browning. The Loss Rate Concept in Safety Engineering. 176p. 1980. 27.50 (ISBN 0-8247-1249-8). Dekker.

Chissick, S. S. & Derricott, R. Occupational Health & Safety Management. LC 80-41218. 720p. 1981. 117.00 (ISBN 0-471-27646-4, Pub. by Wiley-Interscience). Wiley.

Gersuny, Carl. Work Hazards & Industrial Conflict. LC 80-51506. (Illus.). 200p. 1981. 12.00 (ISBN 0-87451-189-5). U Pr of New Eng.

Hazards in Construction. 1980. 60.00x (Pub. by Telford England). State Mutual Bk.

International Labour Office. Safety & Health & the Working Environment: International Labour Conference, 1981, 67th Session. 68p. (Orig.). 1980. pap. 8.55 (ISBN 92-2-102407-5). Intl Labour Office.

Kelman, Steven. Regulating America, Regulating Sweden: A Comparative Study of Occupational Safety & Health Regulations. 320p. 1981. text ed. 19.95x (ISBN 0-262-11076-8). MIT Pr.

Mitchell, Ewan. The Employer's Guide to the Law on Health, Safety & Welfare at Work. 2nd ed. 471p. 1977. text ed. 36.75x (ISBN 0-220-66341-6, Pub. by Busn Bks England). Renouf.

Moran, Robert D. How to Avoid OSHA. (Illus.). 256p. 1981. 49.95 (ISBN 0-87201-652-8). Gulf Pub.

Occupational Exposure to Airborne Substances Harmful to Health. 44p. 1981. pap. 6.50 (ISBN 92-2-102442-3, ILO 152, ILO). Unipub.

Reschenthaler, G. B. Occupational Health & Safety in Canada. 152p. 1979. pap. text ed. 5.00x (ISBN 0-920380-35-2, Pub. by Inst Res Pub Canada). Renouf.

Sanchez, Irene, et al. The California Worker's Compensation Rehabilitation System. LC 80-70211. (Illus.). 360p. 1981. 35.00 (ISBN 0-02-927670-5). Macmillan.

INDUSTRIAL SCHOOLS

see Reformatories

INDUSTRIAL SECURITY MEASURES

see Industry–Security Measures

INDUSTRIAL SOCIOLOGY

Here are entered works on social relations within industry, as distinguished from labor-management relations. Works about the impact of industry on culture and societal changes, and works about the social responsibilities of businessmen are entered under Industry–Social Aspects.

see also Industrial Organization; Industry–Social Aspects

Gardell, Bertil & Johansson, Bunn. Working Life: Social Science Contribution to Work Reform. 352p. 1981. write for info. (ISBN 0-471-27801-7, Pub. by Wiley-Interscience). Wiley.

Leventman, Paula G. Professionals Out of Work. LC 80-1645. (Illus.). 1981. 19.95 (ISBN 0-02-918800-8). Free Pr.

INDUSTRIAL TOXICOLOGY

Occupational Exposure to Airborne Substances Harmful to Health. 44p. 1981. pap. 6.50 (ISBN 92-2-102442-3, ILO 152, ILO). Unipub.

INDUSTRIAL TRAFFIC MANAGEMENT

see Shipment of Goods

INDUSTRIAL UNIONS

see Trade-Unions

INDUSTRIAL WASTES

see Factory and Trade Waste

INDUSTRIAL WORKERS OF THE WORLD

Conlin, Joseph R., ed. At the Point of Production: The Local History of the I.W.W. LC 80-1708. (Contributions in Labor History Ser.: No. 10). 328p. 1981. lib. bdg. 29.95 (ISBN 0-313-22046-8, CPP/). Greenwood.

INDUSTRIALIZATION

see also Technical Assistance; Underdeveloped Areas

The Evolution of Industry in STPI Countries. (Science & Technology for Development: STPI Module 2). 67p. 1981. pap. 5.00 (ISBN 0-88936-257-2, IDRC TS19, IDRC). Unipub.

The Evolution of Science & Technology in STPI Countries. (Science & Technology for Development Ser.: STPI Module 3). 43p. 1981. pap. 5.00 (ISBN 0-88936-255-6, IDRC TS20, IDRC). Unipub.

INDUSTRIES

see Industrial Arts; Industry

also subdivision Industries under names of countries, etc. e.g. United States–Industries; names of particular industries

INDUSTRIES, CHEMICAL

see Chemical Industries

INDUSTRIES, LOCATION OF

see also Factories–Location

Rees, John, et al, eds. Industrial Location & Regional Systems: Spatial Organization in the Economic Sector. (Illus.). 320p. 1981. text ed. 24.95x (ISBN 0-89789-008-6). J F Bergin.

Rowe, James E. Industrial Plant Location. (Public Administation Ser.: Bibliography P-575). 52p. 1980. pap. 5.50. Vance Biblios.

INDUSTRY

see also Businessmen; Entrepreneur; Industrial Management; Industrial Organization; Industrial Relations; Industrialization; Machinery in Industry; Research, Industrial; Small Business

Helleiner, G. H., et al, eds. Protectionism or Industrial Adjustment. (Atlantic Papers Ser.: No. 39). 72p. 1980. write for info. (ISBN 0-916672-79-4). Allanheld.

Vepa, R. K. How to Set up a Small Scale Industry. 250p. 1980. text ed. 25.00 (ISBN 0-7069-1276-4, Pub by Vikas India). Advent Bk.

INDUSTRY–BIBLIOGRAPHY

Davis, John G. & Newman, Phyllis, eds. California Manufacturers Register, 1981. 34th rev. ed. LC 48-3418. 880p. 1981. 85.00 (ISBN 0-911510-83-4). Times-M Pr.

--California Services Register, 1981. 2nd ed. 680p. 1981. 60.00 (ISBN 0-911510-84-2). Times-M Pr.

INDUSTRY–HISTORY

see also Commerce–History; Machinery in Industry

Hammond, J. L. & Hammond, Barbara. The Town Labourer, 1760-1832: The New Civilization. 342p. 1980. Repr. of 1932 ed. lib. bdg. 25.00 (ISBN 0-89984-293-3). Century Bookbindery.

Jeremy, David J. Origins of the Industrial Revolution in the U.S. (Illus.). 544p. 1981. text ed. 32.50x (ISBN 0-262-10022-3). MIT Pr.

Knight, Charles. Passages of a Working Life: During Half a Century with a Prelude of Early Reminiscences, 3 vols. (The Development of Industrial Society Ser.). 1026p. 1980. Repr. 50.00x (ISBN 0-7165-1568-7, Pub. by Irish Academic Pr). Biblio Dist.

McGrain, John W. Good Old Company Towns. (Baltimore County Heritage Publication Ser.). (Illus.). 1981. pap. price not set (ISBN 0-937076-01-5). Baltimore Co Pub Lib.

Mulhall, Michael G. The Progress of the World: In Arts, Agriculture, Century. (The Development of Industrial Society Ser.). 569p. 1980. Repr. 50.00x (ISBN 0-7165-1584-9, Pub. by Irish Academic Pr). Biblio Dist.

INDUSTRY–ORGANIZATION

see Industrial Organization

INDUSTRY–SECURITY MEASURES

O'Block, Robert L. Security & Crime Prevention. c ed. (Illus.). 378p. 1981. pap. text ed. 13.95 (ISBN 0-8016-3738-4). Mosby.

Strauss, Sheryl, ed. Security Problems in a Modern Society. (Illus.). 314p. 1980. text ed. 9.95 (ISBN 0-409-95079-3). Butterworths.

INDUSTRY–SOCIAL ASPECTS

Here are entered works about the impact of industry on culture and societal changes, and works about the social responsibilities of businessmen. Works on social relations within industry, as distinguished from labor-management relations, are entered under Industrial Sociology.

see also Industrial Sociology

Carroll, Archie B. Business & Society: Managing Corporate Social Performance. text ed. 16.95 (ISBN 0-316-13010-9); training manual free (ISBN 0-316-13011-7). Little.

Estes, R. W. Corporate Social Accounting. 166p. 1976. 18.95 (ISBN 0-471-24592-5, Pub. by Wiley-Interscience). Wiley.

Faunce, William. Problems of an Industrial Society. 2nd ed. Munson, Eric M., ed. 256p. 1981. pap. text ed. 8.95 (ISBN 0-07-020105-6, C). McGraw.

INDUSTRY (PSYCHOLOGY)

see Work

INDUSTRY AND STATE

Here are entered works on the relation of Industry and State in general as well as those concerned with the United States. For works on Industry and State in other countries, see local subdivisions below.

see also Commercial Policy; Economic Policy; Full Employment Policies; Government Business Enterprises; Government Competition; Government Ownership; Industrial Laws and Legislation; Labor Laws and Legislation; Public Interest; Subsidies; Trade Regulation; Transportation and State

also specific industries or commercial products

Frenkel, Stephen J., ed. Industrial Action in Australia. 184p. 1981. text ed. 24.95x (ISBN 0-86861-122-0, 2513); pap. text ed. 12.50x (ISBN 0-86861-130-1, 2514). Allen Unwin.

Pinder, John, ed. The International Implications of National Industrial Strategies. 320p. 1981. text ed. 32.50 (ISBN 0-86598-040-3). Allanheld.

Stevenson, Russell B., Jr. Corporations & Information: Secrecy, Access & Disclosure. LC 79-3683. 212p. 1980. text ed. 17.95x (ISBN 0-8018-2344-7). Johns Hopkins.

Winter, Ralph K. Government & the Corporation. 1978. pap. 4.25 (ISBN 0-8447-3313-X). Am Enterprise.

Wolf, Ronald H. & Mund, Vernon A. Business & Government. 1980. text ed. 19.95 (ISBN 0-89894-006-0). Advocate Pub Group.

INDUSTRY AND STATE–GERMANY

Abraham, David. The Collapse of the Weimar Republic: Political Economy & Crisis. LC 80-8533. 550p. 1981. 30.00x (ISBN 0-691-05322-7); pap. 12.50x (ISBN 0-691-10118-3). Princeton U Pr.

INDUSTRY AND STATE–GREAT BRITAIN

Beckett, J. V. Coal & Tobacco. (Illus.). 280p. 1981. 47.50 (ISBN 0-521-23486-7). Cambridge U Pr.

Redwood, John. Public Enterprise in Crisis: The Future of the Nationalised Industries. 211p. 1981. 19.50x (ISBN 0-631-12582-5, Pub. by Basil Blackwell England). Biblio Dist.

Saham, Junid. British Industrial Investment in Malaysia, Nineteen Sixty-Three to Nineteen Seventy-One. (East Asian Social Science Monographs). 366p. 1981. 37.00 (ISBN 0-19-580418-X). Oxford U Pr.

INDUSTRY AND STATE–INDIA

Sharma, K. L. & Singh, Harnek. Entrepreneurial Growth & Development Programmes in Northern India: A Sociological Analysis. 1980. 12.50x (ISBN 0-8364-0649-4, Pub. by Abhinav India). South Asia Bks.

INDUSTRY AND STATE–MALAYSIA

Saham, Junid. British Industrial Investment in Malaysia, Nineteen Sixty-Three to Nineteen Seventy-One. (East Asian Social Science Monographs). 366p. 1981. 37.00 (ISBN 0-19-580418-X). Oxford U Pr.

INEBRIATES

see Alcoholics

INEBRIETY

see Alcoholism

INEQUALITY

see Equality

INFALLIBILITY OF THE POPE

see Popes–Infallibility

INFANT EDUCATION

see Education, Preschool

INFANT MORTALITY

see Infants–Mortality

INFANT PSYCHOLOGY

Anderson, Gene C. & Raff, Beverly, eds. Newborn Behavioral Organization: Nursing Research &Implications. LC 79-2597. (Alan R. Liss Ser.: Vol. 15, No. 7). 1979. 24.00 (ISBN 0-8451-1032-2). March of Dimes.

Lipsitt, Lewis P., ed. Advances in Infancy Research. 300p. 1981. price not set (ISBN 0-89391-045-7). Ablex Pub.

INFANTICIDE

see also Abortion

Hoffer, Peter C. & Hull, N. E. Murdering Mothers: Infanticide in England & New England, 1558-1803. (NYU School of Law Ser. in Anglo-American Legal History). 208p. 1981. text ed. 22.50x (ISBN 0-8147-3412-X). NYU Pr.

INFANTS

see also Children; Infant Psychology

Lipsitt, Lewis P., ed. Advances in Infancy Research. 300p. 1981. price not set (ISBN 0-89391-045-7). Ablex Pub.

INFANTS–CARE AND HYGIENE

see also Baby Sitters; Nurseries; Prenatal Care

Aukema, Susan & Kostick, Marilyn. The Curity Baby Book. 7.95 (ISBN 0-916752-06-2). Green Hill.

Beebe, Brooke. Best Bets for Babies. (Orig.). pap. 4.95 (ISBN 0-440-50453-8, Dell Trade Pbks). Dell.

Brewer, Gail S. & Greene, Janice P. Right from the Start: Meeting the Challenges of Mothering Your Unborn & Newborn Baby. Gerras, Charlie, ed. (Illus.). 256p. (Orig.). 1981. pap. 11.95 (ISBN 0-87857-273-2). Rodale Pr Inc.

Cohen, Jean P. & Goirand, Roger. Your Baby: Pregnancy, Delivery, & Infant Care. (Illus.). 304p. 1981. 16.95 (ISBN 0-13-978130-7, Spec); pap. 8.95 (ISBN 0-13-978122-6). P-H.

Pillitteri, Adele. Maternal-Newborn Nursing: Care of the Growing Family. 2nd ed. 1981. text ed. write for info. (ISBN 0-316-70792-9). Little.

Stoutt, Glen R., Jr. The First Month of Life: A Parent's Guide to Care of the Newborn. 1981. pap. 1.95 (ISBN 0-451-09613-4, J9613, Sig). NAL.

INFANTS–DISEASES

Milunsky, Aubrey, et al, eds. Advances in Perinatal Medicine, Vol. 1. 450p. 1981. 35.00 (ISBN 0-306-40482-6, Plenum Pr). Plenum Pub.

INFANTS–GROWTH

see Children–Growth

INFANTS–LAW

see Children–Law

INFANTS–MORTALITY

Borg, Susan O. & Lasker, Judith. When Pregnancy Fails: Families Coping with Miscarriage, Stillbirth & Infant Death. LC 80-68167. 224p. 1981. 12.95 (ISBN 0-8070-3226-3, BP 613); pap. 6.95 (ISBN 0-8070-3227-1). Beacon Pr.

INFANTS–NUTRITION

see also Breast Feeding

Bond, Jenny T., et al, eds. Infant & Child Feeding. (Nutrition Foundation Ser.). 1981. write for info. (ISBN 0-12-113350-8). Acad Pr.

Castle, Sue. The Complete New Guide to Preparing Baby Foods. rev. ed. LC 79-6099. (Illus.). 336p. 1981. 12.95 (ISBN 0-385-15884-X). Doubleday.

Pipes, Peggy L. Nutrition in Infancy & Childhood. 2nd ed. (Illus.). 288p. 1981. pap. text ed. 11.95 (ISBN 0-8016-3941-7). Mosby.

INFANTS–PSYCHOLOGY

see Infant Psychology

INFANTS (NEWBORN)

Anderson, Gene C. & Raff, Beverly, eds. Newborn Behavioral Organization: Nursing Research &Implications. LC 79-2597. (Alan R. Liss Ser.: Vol. 15, No. 7). 1979. 24.00 (ISBN 0-8451-1032-2). March of Dimes.

Ewy, Donna & Ewy, Rodger. The Cycle of Life. (Illus.). 384p. 1981. 17.95 (ISBN 0-525-93181-3). Dutton.

Jenkins, G. Curtis & Newton, R. The First Year of Life. (Library of General Practice). (Illus.). 260p. 1981. pap. text ed. 18.00 (ISBN 0-443-01717-4). Churchill.

Korones, Sheldon B. High Risk Newborn Infants. 3rd ed. (Illus.). 350p. 1981. text ed. 16.95 (ISBN 0-8016-2738-9). Mosby.

Wille, Lutz & Obladen, Michael. Neonatal Intensive Care: Principles & Guidelines. (Illus.). 300p. 1981. pap. 28.40 (ISBN 0-387-10462-3). Springer-Verlag.

INFANTS (NEWBORN)–DISEASES

Avery, Mary E., et al. The Lung & Its Disorders in the Newborn Infant. 4th ed. (Major Problems in Clinical Pediatrics: Vol. 1). (Illus.). 560p. 1981. text ed. price not set (ISBN 0-7216-1462-0). Saunders.

Colen, B. D. Born at Risk. (Illus.). 240p. 1981. 9.95 (ISBN 0-312-09291-1). St Martin.

Lauersen, Neils H. & Hochberg, Howard. Clinical Perinatal Biochemical Monitoring. 271p. 1981. write for info. (1901-1). Williams & Wilkins.

Stern. Intensive Care in the Newborn, Vol. III. 1981. write for info (ISBN 0-89352-114-0). Masson Pub.

INFANTS (NEWBORN)–MORTALITY

see Infants–Mortality

INFANTS, FOOD FOR

see Infants–Nutrition

INFECTION

see also Communicable Diseases

Castle, M. Hospital Infection Control: Principles & Practices. LC 80-13424. 1980. 16.95 (ISBN 0-471-05395-3). Wiley.

Controlling Infection. (Nursing Photobook Ser.). (Illus.). 160p. 1981. text ed. 12.95 (ISBN 0-916730-35-2). Intermed Comm.

Dixon, Richard E., ed. Nosocomial Infections. (Illus.). 500p. 1981. text ed. price not set (ISBN 0-914316-24-9). Yorke Med.

Hibbard, Lester T. Infections in Obstetrics & Gynecology. LC 80-18670. (Discussions in Patient Management Ser.). 1980. pap. 8.00 (ISBN 0-87488-896-4). Med Exam.

Infection & the Compromised Host: Clinical Correlations & Therapeutic Approaches. 2nd ed. (Illus.). 281p. 1981. 29.00 (ISBN 0-686-69563-1, 0072-1). Williams & Wilkins.

Watts, J. McK., et al. Infection in Surgery: Basic & Clinical Aspects. (Symposium Ser.). (Illus.). 488p. 1981. lib. bdg. 65.00 (ISBN 0-443-02246-1). Churchill.

INFECTIOUS ABORTION

see Brucellosis in Cattle

INFECTIOUS DISEASES

see Communicable Diseases

INFERTILITY

see Sterility

INFINITESIMAL CALCULUS

see Calculus

INFIRMARIES

see Hospitals

INFLAMMATION

Weissmann, Gerald, ed. Advances in Inflammation Research, Vol. 2. 1981. text ed. price not set (ISBN 0-89004-582-8). Raven.

INFLATION (FINANCE)

see also Paper Money; Wage-Price Policy

Benge, Eugene J. How to Lick Inflation Before It Licks You. LC 80-70954. 204p. 1981. 9.95 (ISBN 0-8119-0342-7). Fell.

Bethell, Tom. Television Evening News Covers Inflation: Nineteen Seventy-Eight to Seventy-Nine. Media Institute, ed. (Illus.). 52p. (Orig.). 1980. pap. 5.00 (ISBN 0-937790-00-1). Media Inst.

Case, John. Understanding Inflation. (Illus.). 224p. 1981. 9.95 (ISBN 0-688-00399-0). Morrow.

Corden, W. M. Inflation, Exchange Rates, & the World Economy: Lectures on International Monetary Economics. (Business & Society Studies). 1980. pap. write for info. (ISBN 0-226-11584-4). U of Chicago Pr.

Croom, George E., Jr. & Van Der Wal, John. Now You Can Profit from Inflation. 264p. 1981. 14.95 (ISBN 0-442-25397-4). Van Nos Reinhold.

Davidson, John. The Way to End Inflation. 1980. 7.95 (ISBN 0-533-04736-6). Vantage.

Ellis, Howard S. Notes on Stagflation. 1978. pap. 2.25 (ISBN 0-8447-3323-7). Am Enterprise.

Fallick, J. L. & Elliot, R. F., eds. Incomes Policies, Inflation & Relative Pay. (Illus.). 304p. 1981. text ed. 29.95x (ISBN 0-04-331077-X, 2578); pap. text ed. 12.95x (ISBN 0-04-331078-8, 2579). Allen Unwin.

Jefferson, Michael, et al. Inflation. 1979. 11.95 (ISBN 0-7145-3539-7); pap. 4.95 (ISBN 0-7145-3547-8). Riverrun NY.

Morley. Inflation & Unemployment. 2nd ed. 1979. pap. 6.95 (ISBN 0-03-041016-9). Dryden Pr.

Muller, Fred. America's Coming Nightmare Inflation, Economic Collapse & Crime Revolution. 120p. 1980. 10.00 (ISBN 0-686-68648-9). State Ptg.

Shulman, Morton. How to Invest Your Money & Profit from Inflation. 1981. pap. 2.50 (ISBN 0-345-29740-7). Ballantine.

Tylecote, Andrew. The Causes of the Present Inflation: An Interdisciplinary Explanation Centered on Britain, Germany & the United States. 180p. 1980. text ed. 24.95x (ISBN 0-470-26953-7). Halsted Pr.

Wolfgang, Marvin E. & Lambert, Richard D., eds. Social Effects of Inflation. (The Annals of the American Academy of Political & Social Science: No. 456). 250p. 1981. 7.50 (ISBN 0-87761-264-1); pap. 6.00 (ISBN 0-87761-265-X). Am Acad Pol Soc Sci.

INFORMATION, GOVERNMENT

see Government Information

INFORMATION CENTERS

see Information Services

INFORMATION DISPLAY SYSTEMS

see also Cathode Ray Tubes

Leondes, C. T., ed. Advances in Control & Dynamic Systems: Theory & Application, Vol. 17. (Serial Publication). 1981. price not set (ISBN 0-12-012717-2). Acad Pr.

Thomas, Harry. Handbook of Information Display Devices. 1981. 24.95 (ISBN 0-8359-2743-1). Reston.

INFORMATION NETWORKS, LIBRARY

see Library Information Networks

INFORMATION PROCESSING, HUMAN

see Human Information Processing

INFORMATION SCIENCE

see also Electronic Data Processing; Information Services; Information Storage and Retrieval Systems; Library Science

Duffy, Neil & Assad, Mike. Information Management: An Executive Approach. (Illus.). 224p. 1981. 34.50 (ISBN 0-19-570190-9). Oxford U Pr.

Miller, Mara. Where to Go for What: How to Research, Organize & Present Your Information. (Illus.). 240p. 1981. 11.95 (ISBN 0-13-957217-1, Spec); pap. 5.95 (ISBN 0-13-957209-0). P-H.

Schatz, Anne E. & Funk, Beverley M. Transcription Skills for Information Processing, Module 2. 112p. 1981. pap. text ed. 2.92 (ISBN 0-07-055201-0). McGraw.

Schatz, Anne E. & Funk, Beverley M. Transcription Skills for Information Processing, Module 1. 96p. 1981. pap. text ed. 2.92 (ISBN 0-07-055200-2). McGraw.

Slamecka, V. & Borka, H., eds. Planning & Organisation of National Research Programs in Information Science. (Illus.). 83p. 1980. pap. 27.50 (ISBN 0-08-026472-7). Pergamon.

Thompson, Gordon B. Memo from Mercury: Information Technology Is Different. 62p. 1979. pap. text ed. 3.00x (ISBN 0-920380-29-8, Pub. by Inst Res Pub Canada). Renouf.

Vickery, B. C. & Vickery, A. Information Science: Theory & Practice. 1981. text ed. price not set. Butterworth.

Vidyasagar, M. Input-Output Analysis of Large-Scale Interconnected Systems. (Lecture Notes in Control & Information Sciences Ser.: Vol. 29). 225p. 1981. pap. 16.50 (ISBN 0-387-10501-8). Springer-Verlag.

INFORMATION SCIENCE–STUDY AND TEACHING

Lassia, Margaret R. Games for Information Skills. 80p. 1980. pap. text ed. 8.58x (ISBN 0-931510-06-6). Hi Willow.

INFORMATION SERVICES

see also Archives; Information Storage and Retrieval Systems; Libraries; Reference Services (Libraries); Research

Bailey, Martha J. Supervisory & Middle Managers in Libraries. LC 80-23049. 218p. 1981. 12.00 (ISBN 0-8108-1400-5). Scarecrow.

Boaz, Martha. Strategies for Meeting the Information Needs of Society in the Year 2000. 250p. 1981. lib. bdg. price not set (ISBN 0-87287-249-1). Libs Unl.

Chartrand, Robert Lee & Morentz, James W., Jr., eds. Information Technology Serving Society. 1979. 25.00 (ISBN 0-08-021979-9). Chartrand.

Warnken, Kelly, ed. The Directory of Fee-Based Information Services 1980-81. LC 76-55469. 1980. pap. 6.95 (ISBN 0-936288-00-0). Info Alternative.

INFORMATION SERVICES, GOVERNMENT

see Government Publicity

INFORMATION STORAGE AND RETRIEVAL SYSTEMS

see also Automatic Indexing; Computers; Data Base Management; Electronic Data Processing; Libraries–Automation

Brooke, Rosalind. Information & Advice Services. 181p. 1972. pap. text ed. 5.65x (ISBN 0-7135-1709-3, Pub. by Bedford England). Renouf.

Casley, D. J. & Lury, D. A. Data Collection in Developing Countries. (Illus.). 1981. 45.00 (ISBN 0-19-877123-1); pap. 14.95 (ISBN 0-19-877124-X). Oxford U Pr.

Chartrand, Robert Lee & Morentz, James W., Jr., eds. Information Technology Serving Society. 1979. 25.00 (ISBN 0-08-021979-9). Chartrand.

Fenichel, Carol & Hogan, Thomas. Online Searching: A Primer. 130p. 1981. text ed. 12.95x (ISBN 0-938734-01-6). Learned Info.

Hawkins, Donald. Online Information Retrieval Bibliography 1964-1979. 175p. 1980. 25.00x (ISBN 0-938734-00-8). Learned Info.

International Cooperative Information Systems. 111p. 1980. pap. 10.00 (ISBN 0-88936-252-1, IDRC156, IDRC). Unipub.

Lucas, Henry C., Jr. Implementation: The Key to Successful Information Systems. LC 80-27009. 224p. 1981. 30.00x (ISBN 0-231-04434-8). Columbia U Pr.

Martin, J. Viewdata & Information Society. 1981. 29.95 (ISBN 0-13-941906-3). P-H.

Meadow, Charles T. & Atherton, Pauline. Basics of Online Searching. (Information Science Ser.). 200p. 1981. 14.95 (ISBN 0-471-05283-3, Pub. by Wiley-Interscience). Wiley.

Norback, Craig T. The Computer Invasion. 304p. 1981. text ed. 18.95 (ISBN 0-442-26121-7). Van Nos Reinhold.

Sundburg, M. & Goldkuhl, G. Information Systems Developement: A Systematic Approach. 1981. 24.50 (ISBN 0-13-464677-0). P-H.

Terminological Data Banks. (Infoterm Ser.). 1980. 45.00 (Dist. by Gale Research Co.). K G Saur.

INFORMATION STORAGE AND RETRIEVAL SYSTEMS–AGRICULTURE

Lilley. Information Sources in Agriculture & Food Science. (Butterworths Guides to Information Sources Ser.). 1981. text ed. price not set (ISBN 0-408-10612-3). Butterworth.

INFORMATION STORAGE AND RETRIEVAL SYSTEMS–BUSINESS

Kalthoff, Robert J. & Lee, Leonard S. Productivity & Records Automation. (Illus.). 400p. 1981. text ed. 24.95 (ISBN 0-13-725234-X). P-H.

INFORMATION STORAGE AND RETRIEVAL SYSTEMS–ENGINEERING

Shuchman, Hedvah L. Information Transfer in Engineering. (Illus.). 300p. (Orig.). 1981. pap. 45.00 (ISBN 0-9605196-0-2). Futures Group.

INFORMATION STORAGE AND RETRIEVAL SYSTEMS–MEDICINE

Duncan, Karen, ed. Information Technology & Health Care: The Critical Issues. 200p. 1980. write for info. (ISBN 0-88283-031-7). AFIPS Pr.

INFORMATION THEORY

see also Automatic Control; Data Transmission Systems; Language and Languages; Semantics; Signal Theory (Telecommunication); Telecommunication

Flavin, Matthew. Fundamental Concepts of Information Modeling. (Yourdon Press Monograph). (Illus.). 104p. (Orig.). 1981. pap. 10.00 (ISBN 0-917072-22-7). Yourdon.

Pierce, J. R. An Introduction to Information Theory: Symbols, Signals & Noise. 2nd, rev. ed. 320p. pap. write for info. (ISBN 0-486-24061-4). Dover.

INFORMATION THEORY IN PSYCHOLOGY

see also Human Information Processing

Uttal, William R. A Taxonomy of Visual Processes. LC 80-18262. 802p. 1981. text ed. 45.00 (ISBN 0-89859-075-2). L Erlbaum Assocs.

INFRA-RED TECHNOLOGY

Keyes, R. J., ed. Optical & Infrared Detectors. 2nd ed. (Topics in Applied Physics Ser.: Vol. 19). (Illus.). 325p. 1981. pap. 24.80 (ISBN 0-387-10176-4). Springer-Verlag.

INHALATION THERAPY

Dekornfeld, Thomas J., ed. Selected Papers in Respiratory Therapy. 2nd ed. 1979. pap. 24.00 (ISBN 0-87488-525-6). Med Exam.

Wojniechowski, William V. & Neff, Paula E. Comprehensive Review of Respiratory Therapy. 400p. 1981. 15.95 (ISBN 0-471-08408-5, Pub. by Wiley Med). Wiley.

INHERITANCE (BIOLOGY)

see Heredity

INHERITANCE AND TRANSFER TAX

see also Gifts–Taxation

Engelbrecht, Ted D., et al. Federal Taxation of Estates, Gifts, & Trusts. (Illus.). 528p. 1981. 32.95. P-H.

Federal Taxation of Estates, Gifts, & Trusts. 3rd ed. 645p. 1980. 55.00 (ISBN 0-686-28716-9, T118C). ALI-ABA.

Michaelson, Arthur M. Income Taxation of Estates & Trusts. 11th ed. LC 80-83758. 220p. 1980. text ed. 35.00 (ISBN 0-686-69169-5, J1-1434). PLI.

INHERITANCE AND TRANSFER TAX–GREAT BRITAIN

Berkowitz, David S. & Thorne, Samuel E., eds. British Liberties. LC 77-89201. (Classics of English Legal History in the Modern Era Ser.: Vol. 57). 486p. 1979. lib. bdg. 40.00 (ISBN 0-8240-3156-3). Garland Pub.

INHERITANCE TAX

see Inheritance and Transfer Tax

INHIBITORS, ENZYME

see Enzyme Inhibitors

INITIAL TEACHING ALPHABET

Azarian, Mary. A Farmer's Alphabet. (gr. 1-4). 1981. 10.95 (ISBN 0-87923-394-X); pap. 6.95 (ISBN 0-87923-397-4). Godine.

Mitsumasa, Anno. Anno's Magical ABC: An Anamorphic Alphabet. (Illus.). 64p. 1981. 15.95 (ISBN 0-399-20788-0). Philomel.

INJURIES

see Accidents; First Aid in Illness and Injury; Sports–Accidents and Injuries; Traumatism; Wounds

INJURIES (LAW)

see Accident Law; Employers' Liability; Medical Jurisprudence

INLAND SHIPPING

see Inland Water Transportation

INLAND WATER TRANSPORTATION
Block, Richard A., ed. Understanding T-Boat Regulations. (Illus.). 143p. 1979. pap. text ed. 12.00 (ISBN 0-934114-22-6). Marine Educ.
INNOVATIONS, TECHNOLOGICAL
see Technological Innovations
INNOVATIONS IN EDUCATION
see Educational Innovations
INNS
see Hotels, Taverns, etc.
INNUIT
see Eskimos
INORGANIC CHEMISTRY
see Chemistry, Inorganic
INPUT-OUTPUT ANALYSIS
see Linear Programming; Recursive Programming
INQUISITION
see also Persecution; Torture
Guiraud, Jean. The Medieval Inquisition. Messenger, E. C., tr. LC 78-63181. (Hereseis 2 Ser.). 216p. 1980. Repr. of 1929 ed. 19.00 (ISBN 0-404-16222-3). AMS Pr.
Hamilton, Bernard. Medieval Inquisition: Foundations of Medieval History. LC 80-27997. 110p. (Orig.). 1981. pap. text ed. 13.00x (ISBN 0-8419-0695-5). Holmes & Meier.
INSANE-CARE AND TREATMENT
see Mentally Ill-Care and Treatment
INSANE-LEGAL STATUS, LAWS, ETC.
see Insanity-Jurisprudence; Mental Health Laws
INSANE HOSPITALS
see Psychiatric Hospitals
INSANITY
Here are entered works on the legal aspects of mental disorders. Popular works and works on regional or social aspects of mental disorders are entered under Mental Illness. Systematic descriptions of mental disorders are entered under Psychology, pathological. Works on clinical aspects of mental disorders, including therapy, are entered under Psychiatry.
see also Depression, Mental; Hysteria; Manic-Depressive Psychoses; Mental Illness; Neuroses; Personality, Disorders Of; Psychiatry; Psychology, Pathological; Psychoses; Schizophrenia; Suicide
Brydall, John & Highmore, Anthony. Non Compos Mentis. Berkowitz, David S. & Thorne, Samuel E., eds. LC 77-86669. (Classics of English Legal History in the Modern Era Ser.: Vol. 46). 471p. 1979. lib. bdg. 40.00 (ISBN 0-8240-3095-8). Garland Pub.
Conolly, John. On Some of the Forms of Insanity. Bd. with Inquiry Concerning the Indications of Insanity. (Contributions to the History of Psychology Ser.). 1980. Repr. of 1850 ed. 30.00 (ISBN 0-89093-315-4). U Pubns Amer.
Pinel, Philippe. Treatise on Insanity. Davis, D. D.; tr. from Fr. Bd. with Responsibility in Mental Disease. (Contributions to the History of Psychology Ser., Vol. III, Pt. C: Medical Psychology). 1978. Repr. of 1806 ed. 30.00 (ISBN 0-89093-167-4). U Pubns Amer.
INSANITY-JURISPRUDENCE
Here are entered works on the legal status of persons of unsound mind. Works on the law affecting the welfare of the insane are entered under the heading Mental Health Laws. Works on psychiatry as applied in courts of law are entered under the heading Forensic Psychiatry.
see also Forensic Psychiatry; Liability (Law)
Prichard, James. On the Different Forms of Insanity in Relation to Jurisprudence. Bd. with Suggestions for the Future Provision of Criminal Lunatics. Hood, W. C; Statistics of Insanity. Hood, W. C. (Contributions to the History of Psychology Ser., Vol. III, Pt. E: Insanity & Jurisprudence). 1980. Repr. of 1842 ed. 30.00 (ISBN 0-89093-328-6). U Pubns Amer.
Wexler, David B. Mental Health Law: Major Issues. 265p. 1981. 25.00 (ISBN 0-306-40538-5, Plenum Pr). Plenum Pub.
INSANITY-JURISPRUDENCE-GREAT BRITAIN
Smith, Roger. Trial by Medicine: The Insanity Defense in Victorian England. 280p. 1981. 33.00x (ISBN 0-85224-407-X, Pub.by Edinburgh U Pr Scotland). Columbia U Pr.
INSANITY, DELUSIONAL
see Paranoia
INSANITY, HYSTERICAL
see Hysteria
INSECT BEHAVIOR
see Insects-Behavior
INSECT SOCIETIES
Hermann, Henry R. Social Insects, Vol. 2. 1981. write for info. (ISBN 0-12-342202-7). Acad Pr.
INSECTICIDES
Page, B. G. & Thomson, W. T. The Nineteen Eighty-One Insecticide, Herbicide, Fungicide Quick Guide. 140p. 1981. pap. 11.00 (ISBN 0-913702-11-0). Thomson Pub Ca.
Thomson, W. T. Agricultural Chemicals, Book 1: Insecticides. rev. ed. 240p. 1981. pap. 13.50 (ISBN 0-913702-13-7). Thomson Pub Ca.
Wegler, R., ed. Insecticides: Biochemical & Biological Methods, Natural Products. (Chemie der Pflanzenschutz und Schaedlingsbekaempfungsmittel). 500p. 1981. 152.30 (ISBN 0-387-10307-4). Springer-Verlag.
INSECTS
see also Diptera; Entomology; Fertilization of Plants; Insect Societies; Larvae-Insects also Ants; Butterflies; Moths; Wasps; and similar headings
Anderson, Margaret M. Insect Friends & Enemies. (Illus.). 64p. 1981. 7.50 (ISBN 0-682-49689-8). Exposition.
Blackman, R. L., et al. Insect Cytogenetics. (Royal Entomological Society of London Symposium Ser.). 272p. 1981. 69.95 (ISBN 0-470-27126-4). Halsted Pr.
Fabre, J. Henri. The Insect World of J. Henri Fabre. Teale, Edwin W., ed. (Nature Library Ser.). 352p. (Orig.). 1981. pap. 5.95 (ISBN 0-06-090806-8, CN 806, CN). Har-Row.
Ferris, Clifford D. & Brown, F. Martin, eds. Butterflies of the Rocky Mountain States. LC 80-22274. (Illus.). 500p. 1981. 35.00 (ISBN 0-8061-1552-1); pap. 15.95 (ISBN 0-8061-1733-8). U of Okla Pr.
Hennig, Willi. Insect Phylogeny. 528p. 1981. price not set (ISBN 0-471-27848-3, Pub. by Wiley-Interscience). Wiley.
Shepherd, Walter. Let's Look at Insects. Date not set. price not set (ISBN 0-392-08023-0, SpS). Soccer.
INSECTS-BEHAVIOR
see also Insect Societies
Stein, R. Incest & Human Love. LC 73-82641. 1973. 8.95 (ISBN 0-89388-090-6). Okpaku Communications.
INSECTS-EMBRYOLOGY
see Embryology-Insects
INSECTS-JUVENILE LITERATURE
Little, Brown Editors, ed. Insects: East Coast Edition. (Explorer's Notebooks). (Illus.). 32p. (Orig.). (gr. 5 up). 1981. pap. 1.95 (ISBN 0-316-52771-8). Little.
--Insects: West Coast Edition. (Explorer's Notebooks). (Illus.). 32p. (Orig.). (gr. 5 up). 1980. pap. 1.95 (ISBN 0-316-52772-6). Little.
World Book-Childcraft International Staff. The Bug Book. (Illus.). 304p. (gr. k-6). 1981. price not set (ISBN 0-7166-0681-X). World Bk-Childcraft.
INSECTS-LARVAE
see Larvae-Insects
INSECTS-HAWAII
Hardy, D. Elmo. Insects of Hawaii: Diptera: Cyclorrhapha IV, Vol. 14. LC 48-45482. (Illus.). 500p. (Orig.). 1981. pap. 35.00x (ISBN 0-686-69434-1). U Pr of Hawaii.
INSECTS, SOCIAL
see Insect Societies
INSEMINATION, ARTIFICIAL
see Artificial Insemination
INSIGNIA
see also Emblems
Patrick, Derrick. Fetch Felix. (Illus.). 192p. 1981. 22.50 (ISBN 0-241-10371-1, Pub. by Hamish Hamilton England). David & Charles.
INSOLVENCY
see Bankruptcy
INSOLATION
see Solar Radiation
INSOMNIA
see also Narcotics; Sleep
Kellerman, Henry. Sleep Disorders: Insomnia & Narcolepsy. 250p. 1981. 17.50 (ISBN 0-87630-264-9). Brunner-Mazel.
Maxman, Jerrold S. A Good Night's Sleep: A Step-by-Step Program for Overcoming Insomnia & Other Sleep Problems. (Illus.). 1981. 14.95 (ISBN 0-393-01437-1). Norton.
INSPECTION OF FOOD
see Food Adulteration and Inspection
INSPECTION OF MEAT
see Meat Inspection
INSPECTION OF SCHOOLS
see School Management and Organization
INSPIRATION
see also Creation (Literary, Artistic, etc.); Creative Ability; Enthusiasm; Revelation
Barnard, Jerry. Something Worse Than Hell & Better Than Heaven. 1979. pap. 1.95 (ISBN 0-917726-31-6). Hunter Bks.
Baumann, Dan. Which Way to Happiness. 160p. 1981. pap. price not set (ISBN 0-8307-0773-5). Regal.
Bernard De Clairvaux, Saint. On Loving God, & Selections from Sermons by St. Bernard of Clairvaux. Martin, Hugh, ed. LC 79-8706. (A Treasury of Christian Books). 125p. 1981. Repr. of 1959 ed. lib. bdg. 17.50x (ISBN 0-313-20787-9, BEOL). Greenwood.
Giniger, Ken S., compiled by. Compact Treasury of Inspiration. (Orig.). pap. 1.95 (ISBN 0-89129-229-2). Jove Pubns.
Hobe, Phyllis, compiled by. Fragile Moments. 1980. 14.95 (ISBN 0-8007-1176-9). Revell.
Hunter, Charles. Follow Me! 1975. pap. 1.95 (ISBN 0-917726-35-9). Hunter Bks.
Hunter, Charles & Hunter, Frances. Angels on Assignment. 1979. pap. 3.50 (ISBN 0-917726-33-2). Hunter Bks.
--The Two Sides of a Coin. 1973. pap. 1.95 (ISBN 0-917726-36-7). Hunter Bks.
Hunter, Frances. Come Alive. 1975. pap. 2.95 (ISBN 0-917726-34-0). Hunter Bks.
--A Confession a Day Keeps the Devil Away. 1980. pap. 3.95 (ISBN 0-917726-37-5). Hunter Bks.
Hunter, Frances & Hunter, Charles. Since Jesus Passed by. 1973. pap. 1.95 (ISBN 0-917726-38-3). Hunter Bks.
Inrig, Gary. Quality Friendship. 192p. (Orig.). 1981. pap. 2.95 (ISBN 0-8024-2891-6). Moody.
Jackson, Clyde O. Come Like the Benediction. (Illus.). 1981. 7.00 (ISBN 0-682-49723-1). Exposition.
Kesler, Harold. Comfort One Another with These Words. 1981. pap. 0.95 (ISBN 0-937396-11-7). Walterick Pubs.
Lehman, James. The Old Brethren. (Orig.). 1976. pap. 2.45 (ISBN 0-89129-155-5). Jove Pubns.
Lopez, Barry. Winter Count. (Illus.). 96p. 1981. 9.95 (ISBN 0-684-16817-0, ScribT). Scribner.
McWhirter, David. Millenial Harbinger - Index. LC 81-65031. (Millenial Harbinger Ser.). 864p. 1981. 19.95 (ISBN 0-89900-228-5). College Pr Pub.
Marshall, Catherine. Meeting God at Every Turn. (Illus.). 250p. 1981. 9.95 (ISBN 0-912376-61-9). Chosen Bks Pub.
Sit, Amy. Sing It! 1979. pap. 2.95 (ISBN 0-917726-39-1). Hunter Bks.
Walters, Dottie, ed. Here Is Genius. (Illus.). 402p. 1980. 11.95 (ISBN 0-8119-0351-6). Fell.
Whiting, Thomas A. Be Good to Yourself. LC 80-27304. 128p. 1981. 6.95 (ISBN 0-687-02800-0). Abingdon.
INSTINCT
see also Animal Intelligence; Psychology, Comparative
Bernard, L. L. Instinct: A Study in Social Psychology. 550p. 1980. Repr. of 1924 ed. lib. bdg. 40.00 (ISBN 0-89760-046-0). Telegraph Bks.
INSTITUTIONAL CHURCH
see Church Work
INSTITUTIONAL ECONOMICS
Schotter, Andrew. The Economic Theory of Social Institutions. (Illus.). 240p. Date not set. 29.50 (ISBN 0-521-23044-6). Cambridge U Pr.
INSTITUTIONS, ASSOCIATIONS, ETC.
see Associations, Institutions, etc.
INSTITUTIONS, ECCLESIASTICAL
see Religious and Ecclesiastical Institutions
INSTITUTIONS, INTERNATIONAL
see International Agencies; International Cooperation
INSTRUCTION
see Education; Teaching;
also subdivision Instruction and Study under Music and under names of musical instruments
INSTRUCTIONAL MATERIALS
see Teaching-Aids and Devices
INSTRUCTIONAL MATERIALS CENTERS
Dyer, Esther & Berger, Pam, eds. Public School & Academic Media Centers: A Guide to Information Sources. LC 74-11554. (Books, Publishing & Libraries Information Guide Ser.: Vol. 3). 350p. 1980. 30.00 (ISBN 0-8103-1286-7). Gale.
Martin, Betty & Carson, Ben. The Principal's Handbook on the School Media Center. 212p. 1981. pap. 12.50x (ISBN 0-208-01912-X, Lib Prof Pubns). Shoe String.
INSTRUCTIONAL OBJECTIVES
see Education-Aims and Objectives
INSTRUCTIONAL SYSTEMS ANALYSIS
see Educational Statistics
INSTRUCTIONAL TECHNOLOGY
see Educational Technology
INSTRUCTIONS TO JURIES
Calhoun, Marcus B., et al, eds. Suggested Pattern Jury Instructions: Civil Cases, Vol. 1. LC 80-14282. 335p. 1980. ring bind 35.000 (ISBN 0-89854-060-7). U of GA Inst Govt.
Model Jury Instructions in Virginia: Civil, 2 vols. 1980. Set. 90.00 (ISBN 0-87215-284-7); Vol. I. (ISBN 0-87215-282-0). Vol. II. Michie.
Thompson, Seymour D. Charging the Jury: A Monograph. 196p. 1980. Repr. lib. bdg. 20.00x (ISBN 0-8377-2628-X). Rothman.
INSTRUCTIVE GAMES
see Educational Games
INSTRUMENTAL MUSIC-INSTRUCTION AND STUDY
see also names of specific musical instruments with or without the subdivision Instruction and Study
Kusel, George. The Martial Musician's Mentor: A Complete Course of Instruction for the Fife, Pt. 1. rev., 2nd ed. (Illus.). 52p. (gr. 6 up). 1979. pap. 4.95 (ISBN 0-9604476-1-X). Kusel.
Saucier, Gene A. Woodwinds: Fundamental Performance Techniques. LC 80-5223. (Illus.). 300p. 1981. pap. text ed. 12.95 (ISBN 0-02-872300-7). Schirmer Bks.
INSTRUMENTS, AERONAUTICAL
see Aeronautical Instruments
INSTRUMENTS, ELECTRIC
see Electric Apparatus and Appliances
INSTRUMENTS, MEDICAL
see Medical Instruments and Apparatus
INSTRUMENTS, MUSICAL
see Musical Instruments
INSTRUMENTS, NEGOTIABLE
see Negotiable Instruments
INSTRUMENTS, OPTICAL
see Optical Instruments
INSTRUMENTS, SCIENTIFIC
see Scientific Apparatus and Instruments
INSTRUMENTS, SURGICAL
see Surgical Instruments and Apparatus
INSULATING MATERIALS
Business Communications Co. Substitutes for Asbestos, Gb-061: What-Who-How Much. 1980. 850.00 (ISBN 0-89336-277-8). BCC.
INSULATION (HEAT)
Turner, William C. & Malloy, John F. Thermal Insulation Handbook. 624p. 1981. 62.50 (ISBN 0-07-039805-4). McGraw.
INSULIN
see also Hypoglycemia
Gueriguian, J. L., et al, eds. Insulins, Growth Hormone, & Recombinant DNA Technology. 250p. 1981. 25.00 (ISBN 0-89004-544-5). Raven.
INSURANCE
see also Insurance Companies; Risk (Insurance); Saving and Thrift
Advice About Insurance, Credit, Budgeting. (Home Adviser Ser.). 80p. (Orig.). 1981. pap. 1.95 (ISBN 0-8326-2407-1, 7051). Delair.
Athearn, James L. Risk & Insurance. 4th ed. (Illus.). 550p. 1981. text ed. 15.96 (ISBN 0-8299-0298-8). West Pub.
Wassell, Richard. A Textbook of Reinsurance. 224p. 1980. 27.00x (ISBN 0-85941-166-4, Pub. by Woodhead-Faulkner England). State Mutual Bk.
INSURANCE-DATA PROCESSING
Life Office Management Association, ed. Readings for the Information Systems Specialty. (FLMI Insurance Education Program Ser.). (Illus.). 186p. (Orig.). 1980. pap. text ed. 10.00x (ISBN 0-915322-39-0). Loma.
INSURANCE-RISK
see Risk (Insurance)
INSURANCE-STATE SUPERVISION
see also Friendly Societies; Insurance Law
Broadwell, Martin M. & Simpson, William F. New Insurance Supervisor. 168p. 1981. pap. text ed. cancelled (ISBN 0-201-00568-9). A-W.
INSURANCE-STUDY AND TEACHING
Clews, Roderick. A Textbook of Insurance Broking. 224p. 1980. 27.00x (ISBN 0-85941-121-4, Pub. by Woodhead-Faulkner England). State Mutual Bk.
INSURANCE, AUTOMOBILE
Cockerell, H. A. & Dickinson, G. M. Motor Insurance & the Consumer. 192p. 1980. 30.00x (ISBN 0-85941-146-X, Pub. by Woodhead-Faulkner England). State Mutual Bk.
Council on Law Related Studies. No-Fault Auto Insurance. 1977. 24.00 (ISBN 0-379-00391-0). Oceana.
INSURANCE, BUSINESS
Cushman, Robert F., et al. The Business Insurance Handbook. 600p. 1981. 37.50 (ISBN 0-87094-237-9). Dow Jones-Irwin.
Life Office Management Association, ed. Readings in Management Principles. (FLMI Insurance Education Program Ser.). 68p. (Orig.). 1980. pap. text ed. 5.00x (ISBN 0-915322-37-4). Loma.
INSURANCE, CASUALTY
see also Insurance, Automobile; Insurance, Property
Siver, Edward W. A Management Guide to Casualty & Property Insurance. 1981. write for info. (ISBN 0-87251-049-2). Crain Bks.
Snouffer, Gary H. Property & Casuality Insurance Agent. 224p. (Orig.). 1981. pap. 8.00 (ISBN 0-668-04308-3, 4308). Arco.
INSURANCE, CORPORATE
see Insurance, Business
INSURANCE, DISABILITY
Meyer, Charles W. Social Security Disability Insurance: Problems of Unexpected Growth. 1979. pap. 4.25 (ISBN 0-8447-3365-2). Am Enterprise.
INSURANCE, GROUP
Here are entered works on group insurance in general and on group life insurance. Works on group insurance in other specific fields are entered under Insurance, Casualty; Insurance, Hospitalization etc.
Life Office Management Association, ed. Readings for the Group Insurance Specialty. (FLMI Insurance Education Program Ser.). (Orig.). 1980. pap. 3.75 (ISBN 0-915322-40-4). Loma.
INSURANCE, HEALTH
see also Health Maintenance Organizations; Medical Care; Workmen's Compensation
Comanor, William S. National Health Insurance in Ontario: Effects of a Policy Cost Control. 1980. pap. 4.25 (ISBN 0-8447-3379-2). Am Enterprise.
Feder, J., et al, eds. National Health Insurance: Conflicting Goals & Policy Choices. LC 80-80045. 721p. 1980. text ed. 25.00x; pap. 12.50 (ISBN 0-87766-271-1). Urban Inst.
Fordney, Marilyn T. Insurance Handbook for the Medical Office. 2nd ed. (Illus.). 475p. 1981. pap. text ed. price not set (ISBN 0-7216-3814-7). Saunders.
Gaines, Price, ed. Who Writes What: Nineteen Eighty-One Edition. LC 76-6787. 498p. 1980. pap. 10.50 (ISBN 0-87218-013-1). Natl Underwriter.
Pauly, Mark V., ed. National Health Insurance: What Now, What Later, What Never? 1980. 16.95 (ISBN 0-8447-2184-0); pap. 8.25 (ISBN 0-8447-2185-9). Am Enterprise.
Silverman, Milton, et al. Pills & the Public Purse. 300p. 1981. 14.95 (ISBN 0-520-04381-2). U of Cal Pr.
INSURANCE, LIFE
see also Insurance, Group; Probabilities
Consumer Reports Editors. The Consumers Union Report on Life Insurance: A Guide to Planning & Buying the Protection You Need. 384p. 1981. 14.95 (ISBN 0-03-059109-0); pap. 7.95 (ISBN 0-03-059108-2). HR&W.
Gaines, Price, ed. Interest-Adjusted Index: Nineteen Eighty-One Edition. LC 76-6788. 410p. 1980. pap. 18.00 (ISBN 0-87218-012-3). Natl Underwriter.
--Who Writes What: Nineteen Eighty-One Edition. LC 76-6787. 498p. 1980. pap. 10.50 (ISBN 0-87218-013-1). Natl Underwriter.

Grossman, Eli A. Life Reinsurance. 79p. (Orig.). 1980. pap. text ed. 4.50 (ISBN 0-915322-38-2). Loma.
Huebner, A. & Black, K. Life Insurance. 10th ed. 1981. 22.95 (ISBN 0-13-535799-3). P-H.
Munch. Life Insurance in Estate Planning. 1981. text ed. price not set (ISBN 0-316-58930-6). Little.
Nontax & Tax Aspects of Life Insurance. 53p. 1980. pap. 10.00 (T182). ALI-ABA.
VanCaspel, Venita. Life Insurance: The Great National Consumer Dilemma. 1980. pap. 1.50 (ISBN 0-8359-4022-5). Reston.

INSURANCE, LIFE–ACCOUNTING
Life Office Management Association, ed. Student Guide to Accounting for Life Insurance Companies. (FLMI Insurance Education Program Ser.). 97p. (Orig.). 1980. wkbk. 4.00x (ISBN 0-915322-42-0). Loma.

INSURANCE, MARINE
see also Salvage
Lambeth, R. J. Templeman on Marine Insurance: Its Principles & Practice. 5th ed. 500p. 1981. 48.00x (ISBN 0-7121-1395-9). Sheridan.

INSURANCE, MUTUAL
see Insurance

INSURANCE, PHYSICIANS'
see Physicians–Insurance Requirements

INSURANCE, POSTAL LIFE
see Insurance, Life

INSURANCE, PROPERTY
see also Insurance, Casualty; Insurance, Marine
Siver, Edward W. A Management Guide to Casualty & Property Insurance. 1981. write for info. (ISBN 0-87251-049-2). Crain Bks.
Snouffer, Gary H. Property & Casualty Insurance Agent. 224p. (Orig.). 1981. pap. 8.00 (ISBN 0-668-04308-3, 4308). Arco.

INSURANCE, SICKNESS
see Insurance, Health

INSURANCE, SOCIAL
see Social Security

INSURANCE, STATE AND COMPULSORY
see Social Security

INSURANCE, TRANSPORTATION
see Insurance, Marine

INSURANCE, UNEMPLOYMENT
see also Supplemental Unemployment Benefits
Becker, Joseph M. Unemployment Benefits: Should There Be a Compulsory Federal Standard? 1980. pap. 4.25 (ISBN 0-8447-3389-X). Am Enterprise.

INSURANCE, WORKING-MEN'S
see Social Security

INSURANCE COMPANIES
Bawcutt, Paul. Captive Insurance Companies. 160p. 1980. 54.00x (ISBN 0-85941-077-3, Pub. by Woodhead-Faulkner England). State Mutual Bk.

INSURANCE LAW
Anderson, Ronald T. Agent's Legal Responsibility. LC 80-83690. 168p. 1980. text ed. 12.75 (ISBN 0-87218-307-6). Natl Underwriter.
Garon, Phillip A., ed. Insurance Law Anthology, Vol. 1. (National Law Anthology Ser.). 1981. text ed. 59.95. Intl Lib.

INSURRECTIONS
see Revolutions

INTANGIBLE PROPERTY
see Copyright; Licenses; Patents; Trade-Marks

INTEGRAL EQUATIONS
see also Functional Analysis
Ramm, A. Theory & Applications of Some New Classes of Integral Equations. 344p. 1981. pap. 18.80 (ISBN 0-387-90540-5). Springer-Verlag.

INTEGRALS
Kral, J. Integral Operators in Potential Theory. (Lecture Notes in Mathematics Ser.: Vol. 823). 171p. 1981. pap. 11.80 (ISBN 0-387-10227-2). Springer-Verlag.
Nielsen. Direct Integrel Theory. 184p. 1980. 23.50 (ISBN 0-8247-6971-6). Dekker.

INTEGRATED CIRCUITS
Comer, David J. Electronic Design with Integrated Circuits. LC 80-23365. (Electrical Engineering Ser.). (Illus.). 416p. 1981. text ed. 24.95 (ISBN 0-201-03931-1). A-W.
Dooley, D. J., ed. Conversion Integrated Circuits. LC 80-10541. 1980. 26.95 (ISBN 0-87942-131-2). Inst Electrical.
Fredericksen, Thomas M. Intuitive IC Electronics: A Sophisticated Primer for Engineers & Technicians. (Illus.). 208p. 1981. 18.50 (ISBN 0-07-021923-0, P&RB). McGraw.
Gray, P. R., et al, eds. Analog MOS Integrated Circuits. LC 80-22116. 1980. 30.95 (ISBN 0-87942-141-X). Inst Electrical.
Gray, Paul. Analog MOS Integrated Circuits. 400p. 1980. 28.00 (ISBN 0-471-08966-4, Pub. by Wiley-Interscience); pap. 18.00 (ISBN 0-471-08964-8). Wiley.
Heiserman, David L. Beginner's Handbook of IC Projects. (Illus.). 272p. 1981. 18.95 (ISBN 0-13-074229-5). P-H.
Kahng, D., ed. Advances in Applied Solid State Science, Supplement, 2A: Silicon Integrated Circuits. (Serial Publication). 1981. price not set (ISBN 0-12-002954-5); price not set lib. ed. (ISBN 0-12-002955-3); price not set microfiche ed. (ISBN 0-12-002956-1). Acad Pr.
Kahng, Dawon, ed. Advances in Solid State Science, Supplement 2B: Silicon Integrated Circuits. (Serial Publication). 1981. price not set (ISBN 0-12-002957-X); price not set lib. ed. (ISBN 0-12-002958-8); microfiche ed. (ISBN 0-12-002959-6). Acad Pr.
Smith, J. E., ed. Integrated Injection Logic. LC 80-18841. 1980. 34.95 (ISBN 0-87942-137-1). Inst Electrical.
Sonde, B. S. Introduction to System Design Using Integrated Circuits. 261p. 1981. 24.95 (ISBN 0-470-27110-8). Halsted Pr.
Texas Instruments, Inc. Engineering Staff. The Line Driver & Line Receiver Data Book for Design Engineers Nineteen Eighty One. rev. ed. LC 80-54794. 296p. 1981. pap. write for info. (ISBN 0-89512-106-9, LCCJ290A). Tex Instr Inc.
--The Peripheral Driver Data Book for Design Engineers, Nineteen Eighty One. rev. ed. LC 80-54795. 144p. 1981. pap. write for info. (ISBN 0-89512-107-7, LCC4280A). Tex Instr Inc.
Young, Thomas. Linear Integrated Circuits. (Kosow Electrical Ser.). 464p. 1981. text ed. 18.95 (ISBN 0-471-97941-4). Wiley.

INTEGRATED DATA PROCESSING
see Electronic Data Processing

INTEGRATION, NUMERICAL
see Numerical Integration

INTEGRATION, RACIAL
see Race Relations

INTEGRATION IN EDUCATION
see Articulation (Education); School Integration

INTEGRITY
see Self-Respect

INTEGUMENT (SKIN)
see Skin

INTELLECT
see also Age and Intelligence; Creation (Literary, Artistic, etc.); Imagination; Intelligence Tests; Knowledge, Theory of; Logic; Memory; Perception; Reason; Reasoning (Psychology); Senses and Sensation; Thought and Thinking; Wisdom
Bain, Alexander. Senses & the Intellect. (Contributions to the History of Psychology Ser.: No. 4, Pt. A Orientations). 1978. Repr. of 1855 ed. 30.00 (ISBN 0-89093-153-4). U Pubns Amer.
Doman, Glenn & Armentrout, J. Michael. The Universal Multiplication of Intelligence. (The Gentle Revolution Ser.). 223p. 1980. 12.50 (ISBN 0-936676-02-7). Better Baby.
Formanek, Ruth & Gurian, Anita. Charting Intellectual Development: A Practical Guide to Piagetian Tasks. 2nd ed. write for info. (ISBN 0-398-04476-7). C C Thomas.
Rosenzweig, Mark R. & Brown, T. A., eds. Intelligence & Affectivity: Their Relationship During Child Development. Brown, T. A. & Kaegi, C. E., trs. (Illus.). 1981. 8.00 (ISBN 0-8243-2901-5). Annual Reviews.
Stewart, Rosemarie, ed. East Meets West: The Transpersonal Approach. LC 80-53952. 202p. 1981. pap. 5.25 (ISBN 0-8356-0544-2). Theos Pub Hse.
Taine, Hippolyte A. On Intelligence. (Contributions to the History of Psychology Ser.). 1978. 30.00 (ISBN 0-89093-152-6). U Pubns Amer.

INTELLECT AND AGE
see Age and Intelligence

INTELLECTRONICS
see Artificial Intelligence; Bionics

INTELLECTUAL FREEDOM
see Liberty of Speech; Teaching, Freedom of

INTELLECTUALS
see also Professions;
also subdivision Intellectual Life under names of countries, cities, etc., e.g. France–Intellectual Life
Bruce-Briggs, B. New Class. 252p. 1981. pap. 5.95 (ISBN 0-07-008573-0). McGraw.

INTELLIGENCE
see Intellect

INTELLIGENCE, ARTIFICIAL
see Artificial Intelligence

INTELLIGENCE LEVELS–TESTING
see Intelligence Tests

INTELLIGENCE OF ANIMALS
see Animal Intelligence; Instinct; Psychology, Comparative

INTELLIGENCE SERVICE
see also Espionage; Secret Service
Harger, Richard. The Scourge of Secrecy: A/Personal Testimony & Appeal. LC 80-50239. 218p. 1980. pap. 6.80 (ISBN 0-936472-00-6). Gordy Pr.

INTELLIGENCE TESTING
see Intelligence Tests

INTELLIGENCE TESTS
Flynn, James R. Race, IQ, & Jensen. 320p. 1980. 27.50 (ISBN 0-7100-0651-9). Routledge & Kegan.
Jensen, Arthur R. Straight Talk About Mental Tests. LC 80-83714. (Illus.). 1981. 12.95 (ISBN 0-02-916440-0). Free Pr.
Scarr, Sandra W. IQ: Race, Social Class & Individual Differences. 500p. 1981. profess. & reference 30.00 (ISBN 0-89859-055-8). L Erlbaum Assocs.
Stern, William L. Psychological Methods of Testing Intelligence. Whipple, G. M., tr. from Ger. Bd. with Selected Essays. Binet, Alfred, et al.. (Contributions to the History of Psychology Ser., Vol. IV, Pt. B: Psychometrics & Educational Psychology). 1978. Repr. of 1914 ed. 30.00 (ISBN 0-89093-164-X). U Pubns Amer.

INTELLIGENT MACHINES
see Artificial Intelligence

INTEMPERANCE
see Alcoholism; Liquor Problem; Temperance

INTENSION (PHILOSOPHY)
see Semantics (Philosophy)

INTENSIVE CARE UNITS
see also Coronary Care Units
Colen, B. D. Born at Risk. (Illus.). 240p. 1981. 9.95 (ISBN 0-312-09291-1). St Martin.
Oh, T. Intensive Care Manual. (Illus.). 200p. 1980. text ed. 29.95 (ISBN 0-409-31380-7). Butterworths.
Stern. Intensive Care in the Newborn, Vol. III. 1981. write for info (ISBN 0-89352-114-0). Masson Pub.
Tinker, Jack & Porter, Susan W. A Course in Intensive Therapy Nursing. 294p. 1980. 30.00x (ISBN 0-7131-4347-9, Pub. by Arnold Pubs England). State Mutual Bk.
Turner, Phyllis S. Self-Assessment of Current Knowledge in Intensive Care Nursing. 1980. pap. 9.75 (ISBN 0-87488-227-3). Med Exam.
Vestal, Katherine W. Pediatric Critical Care Nursing. 464p. 1981. 17.95 (ISBN 0-471-05674-X, Pub. by Wiley Med). Wiley.

INTERACTION, SOCIAL
see Social Interaction

INTERCHANGE OF STUDENTS
see Students, Interchange Of

INTERCHANGE OF TEACHERS
see Teachers, Interchange Of

INTERCOMMUNION
see also Church Membership
Ware, K. Communion & Intercommunion. 1980. pap. 1.95 (ISBN 0-937032-20-4). Light&Life Pub Co MN.

INTERCULTURAL COMMUNICATION
Dawson, J. L. & Blowers, G. H., eds. Perspectives in Asian Cross-Cultural Psychology: Selected Papers of the First Asian Regional Conference of the IACCP, March 19-23, 1979. 1981. pap. write for info. (ISBN 90-265-0359-8). Swets North Am.
Samovar, Larry A., et al. Understanding Intercultural Communication. 240p. 1980. pap. text ed. 8.95x (ISBN 0-534-00862-3). Wadsworth Pub.

INTERCULTURAL EDUCATION
see also Race Awareness
Hamnett, Michael P., ed. Research in Culture Learning: Language & Conceptual Studies. Brislin, Richard W. LC 80-21761. 195p. 1980. pap. 10.00x (ISBN 0-8248-0738-3). U Pr of Hawaii.

INTERCULTURAL RELATIONS
see Cultural Relations

INTEREST AND USURY
Fetter, Frank A. Capital, Interest, & Rent: Essays in the Theory of Distribution. Rothbard, Murray N., ed. & intro. by. 1977. write for info. NYU Pr.
Karr, Frederic H. Interest on Third Party Accounts: A Desk Top Primer. 160p. 1980. 18.95 (ISBN 0-03-058024-2). Praeger.
Pring, Martin J. How to Forecast Interest Rates: A Guide to Profits for Consumers, Managers & Investors. 192p. 1981. 14.95 (ISBN 0-07-050865-8, P&RB). McGraw.

INTEREST AND USURY–PROBLEMS, EXERCISES, ETC.
Filmer, Sir Robert. A Disclosure Whether It May Be Lawful to Take Use for Money. Berkowitz, David S. & Thorne, Samuel E., eds. LC 77-89250. (Classics of English Legal History in the Modern Era Ser.: Vol. 79). 166p. 1979. lib. bdg. 40.00 (ISBN 0-8240-3179-2). Garland Pub.

INTERFACES, CHEMISTRY OF
see Surface Chemistry

INTERFERONS
Friedman, Robert M. Interferons: A Primer. 1981. price not set (ISBN 0-12-268280-7). Acad Pr.
Vilcek, Jan, et al, eds. Regulatory Functions of Interferons. new ed. LC 80-25207. (Vol. 350). 641p. 1980. 124.00 (ISBN 0-89766-089-7). NY Acad Sci.
--Regulatory Functions of Interferons, Vol. 350. LC 80-25207. 641p. 1980. 124.00x (ISBN 0-89766-089-7); pap. write for info. (ISBN 0-89766-090-0). NY Acad Sci.

INTERGOVERNMENTAL FISCAL RELATIONS
see also Grants-In-Aid
Marlin, John T. Revenue Sharing Renewal. (COMP Papers Ser.). 52p. pap. 7.50 (ISBN 0-916450-36-8). Coun on Municipal.
Reagan, Michael D. & Sanzone, John G. The New Federalism. 2nd ed. 208p. 1981. pap. text ed. 3.95x (ISBN 0-19-502772-8). Oxford U Pr.

INTERIOR DECORATION
see also Furniture; House Furnishings; Lighting; Lighting, Architectural and Decorative; Tapestry; Upholstery; Wall-Paper
Banov, Abel & Lytle, Marie-Jeanne. Successful Wallcoverings & Decoration. 2nd ed. Case, Virginia A., ed. (Successful Ser.). (Illus.). 136p. 1981. 17.95 (ISBN 0-89999-021-5); pap. 7.95 (ISBN 0-89999-022-3). Structures Pub.
Bradford, Barbara T. Luxury Designs for Apartment Living. LC 77-16899. (Illus.). 352p. 1981. 29.95 (ISBN 0-385-12769-3). Doubleday.
Burden, Ernest. Entourage: A Tracing File for Architecture & Interior Design Drawing. (Illus.). 256p. 1981. 15.95 (ISBN 0-07-008930-2). McGraw.
Hines, Millie, ed. Crafty Ideas for the Home. (Illus.). 96p. (Orig.). 1980. pap. 2.00 (ISBN 0-918178-20-7). Simplicity.
--Easy Ways to Decorate Your Kitchen. (Illus.). 96p. (Orig.). 1981. pap. 2.00 (ISBN 0-918178-24-X). Simplicity.
Hurst, A. E. & Goodier, J. M. Painting & Decorating. 620p. 1980. 75.00x (ISBN 0-85264-243-1, Pub. by Griffin England). State Mutual Bk.
Kleeman, Walter. The Challenge of Interior Design. 304p. 1981. 19.95 (ISBN 0-8436-0133-7). CBI Pub.
Knackstedt, Mary V. Interior Design for Profit. Haney, Laura J., ed. 1980. 17.00 (ISBN 0-9604676-0-2). Kobro Pubns.
Lindahl, Judy. Energy Saving Decorating. new ed. (Illus.). 128p. (Orig.). 1981. pap. 4.95 (ISBN 0-9603032-3-5). Lindahl.
McClellan, Brenda. Successful Home Decorating. Case, Virginia A., ed. (Successful Ser.). (Illus.). 136p. 1981. 18.95 (ISBN 0-89999-021-5); pap. 7.95 (ISBN 0-89999-022-3). Structures Pub.
Maier, Manfred. Basic Principles of Design. 392p. 1981. pap. 35.00 (ISBN 0-442-21206-2). Van Nos Reinhold.
Morrison, Alex. Photofinish. 144p. 1981. 16.95 (ISBN 0-442-21262-3). Van Nos Reinhold.
Murphy, Dennis G. The Materials of Interior Design. Murphy, Gladys N., ed. (Interior Furnishings & Products Ser.). (Illus.). 208p. (Orig.). 1978. 10.50 (ISBN 0-938614-00-2, 211-196). Stratford Hse.
Orr, Monica, ed. Special Rooms: Louisville, Kentucky. LC 80-83167. 72p. (Orig.). 1980. pap. 9.95 (ISBN 0-937246-01-8). Hawley Cooke Orr.
Scrivens, Steven. Interior Planting in Large Buildings: A Handbook for Architects Interior Designers & Horticulturists. LC 80-23565. 200p. 1981. 44.95 (ISBN 0-470-27067-5). Halsted Pr.
Seale, William. A Tasteful Interlude: American Interiors Through the Camera's Eye, 1860 to 1917. (Illus.). 288p. 1981. pap. 12.95 (ISBN 0-910050-49-X). AASLH.
Trupp, Beverly. Color It Home: A Builder's Guide to Interior Design & Merchandising. (Illus.). 240p. 1981. 34.95 (ISBN 0-8436-0136-1). CBI Pub.
Weiss, Jeffery. Great Kitchens. 96p. 1981. pap. 9.95 (ISBN 0-312-34605-0). St Martin.
Weiss, Jeffrey. Great Bathrooms. 96p. 1981. pap. 9.95 (ISBN 0-312-34486-4). St Martin.

INTERIOR DECORATION–BIBLIOGRAPHY
Vance, Mary. Interior Design & Decoration: A Bibliography of Books. (Architecture Ser.: Bibliography A-257). 75p. 1980. pap. 8.00. Vance Biblios.

INTERIOR DECORATION–ENCYCLOPEDIAS, YEARBOOKS
Goodier, J. H. Dictionary of Painting & Decorating. 308p. 1974. 39.50x (ISBN 0-85264-224-5, Pub. by Griffin England). State Mutual Bk.

INTERIOR DECORATION–HANDBOOKS, MANUALS, ETC.
Frazier, Alton E. Good Taste Begins with You. Ide, Arthur F., ed. LC 79-9441. (Illus., Orig.). 1980. pap. 39.00x set (ISBN 0-86663-250-6). Ide Hse.
Stramesi, Annette. Creative Home Decorating. 7.95 (ISBN 0-916752-14-3). Green Hill.

INTERIOR DECORATION–HISTORY
Ball, V. K. Architecture & Interior Design: A Basic History of the Eighteenth Through Twentieth Centuries, 2 vol. set. 1980. Set. 80.00 (ISBN 0-471-08721-1, Pub. by Wiley-Interscience); Set. pap. 50.00 (ISBN 0-471-08720-3); pap. 27.50 (ISBN 0-471-08722-X). Wiley.
--Architecture & Interior Design: A Basic History of the Eighteenth Through Twentieth Centuries. 464p. 1980. pap. 27.50 (ISBN 0-471-08722-X, Pub. by Wiley-Interscience). Wiley.
From the Pages of Interiors Magazine. The Interiors Book of Shops & Restaurants. 144p. 1981. 25.00 (ISBN 0-8230-7284-3, Whitney Lib). Watson-Guptill.

INTERIOR DECORATION–GREAT BRITAIN
Ayres, James. The Shell Book of the Home in Britain: Decoration, Design & Construction of Vernacula Interiors, 1500-1850. (Shell Book Ser.). (Illus.). 240p. 1981. 25.00 (ISBN 0-571-11625-6, Pub. by Faber & Faber). Merrimack Bk Serv.

INTERMENT
see Burial

INTERMITTENT FEVER
see Malaria

INTERMUNICIPAL LAW
see Conflict of Laws

INTERNAL MEDICINE
see also Cardiology; Endocrinology; Gastroenterology; Hematology; Nephrology
Blackshear, P. J. Key References in Internal Medicine. 1981. pap. text ed. write for info. (ISBN 0-443-08079-8). Churchill.

INTERNAL MIGRATION
see Migration, Internal

INTERNAL SECURITY
Fernandez, Eduardo B., et al. Database Security & Integrity. LC 80-15153. (IBM Systems Programming Ser.). (Illus.). 288p. 1981. text ed. 18.95 (ISBN 0-201-14467-0). A-W.

INTERNATIONAL ADMINISTRATION
see International Agencies; International Organization

INTERNATIONAL AGENCIES
Here are entered works on public international organizations and agencies of international government. Particular organizations are entered under their respective names.
see also International Officials and Employees; International Organization
Broad Terms for United Nations Programmes & Activities, 1979. 186p. 1980. pap. 13.00 (ISBN 0-686-68945-3, UN79/0/1, UN). Unipub.
Jutte, Rudiger. The Future of International Organization. 1981. 22.50 (ISBN 0-312-31476-0). St Martin.
INTERNATIONAL AGREEMENTS
see Treaties
INTERNATIONAL AGRICULTURAL COOPERATION
D'A. Shaw, Robert. Jobs & Agricultural Development. LC 79-145446. (Monographs: No. 3). 84p. 1970. 1.00 (ISBN 0-686-28692-8). Overseas Dev Council.
INTERNATIONAL ARBITRATION
see Arbitration, International
INTERNATIONAL BANKING
see Banks and Banking, International
INTERNATIONAL BUSINESS ENTERPRISES
see also Investments, Foreign
Crosswell, C. Legal Aspects of International Business. 1980. 40.00 (ISBN 0-379-20683-8). Oceana.
International Business Transactions in a Nutshell. (Nutshell Ser.). 400p. 1981. pap. text ed. 7.95 (ISBN 0-8299-2119-2). West Pub.
Joyner's Guide to Official Washington for Doing Business Overseas. 364p. 1981. 95.00 (ISBN 0-08-025108-0, JOY 3, Joyner's). Unipub.
Kujawa, D. Employment Effects of Multinational Enterprises: The Case of the United States. International Labour Office, ed. (Research on Employment Effects of Multinational Enterprises. Working Papers Ser.: No. 12). 53p. (Orig.). 1980. pap. 8.55. Intl Labour Office.
Kumar, Krishna & McLeod, Maxwell G., eds. Multinationals from Developing Countries. LC 80-8531. 1981. write for info. (ISBN 0-669-04113-0). Lexington Bks.
Lall, Sanjaya. The Multinational Corporation. 224p. 1980. 32.50 (ISBN 0-8419-5083-0). Holmes & Meier.
Madsen, Axel. Private Power: Multinational Corporations for the Survival of Our Planet. LC 80-19372. 256p. 1980. 12.95 (ISBN 0-688-03735-6). Morrow.
Mason, R. Hal, et al. International Business. 2nd ed. (Management & Administration Ser.). 500p. 1981. text ed. 21.95 (ISBN 0-686-69162-8). Wiley.
Policy Instructions to Build up an Infrastructure for the Generation of Technology. (Science & Technology for Development Ser.: STPI Module 5). 57p. 1981. pap. 5.00 (ISBN 0-88936-263-7, IDRC TS26, IDRC). Unipub.
Simmonds, K. Multinational Corporations Law, Vols. 1-2. 1979. Set. 75.00 (ISBN 0-379-20373-1). Oceana.
--Multinational Corporations Law, Release 3. 1980. 50.00. Oceana.
Surrey, Walter S. & Wallace, Don, Jr., eds. A Lawyer's Guide to International Business Transactions, Pt. IV. 471p. 1980. 55.00 (ISBN 0-686-28717-7, B96B4). ALI-ABA.
Walker, Townsend. A Guide for Using the Foreign Exchange Market. 360p. 1981. 20.95 (ISBN 0-471-06254-5). Ronald Pr.
Wood, Douglas & Byrne, James. International Business Finance. LC 80-23951. 400p. 1981. text ed. 47.50x (ISBN 0-8419-0663-7). Holmes & Meier.
INTERNATIONAL BUSINESS ENTERPRISES-ACCOUNTING
Giannotti, John B. & Smith, Richard W. International Treasury Management for the 1980's: A Practical Approach to Treasury Management in the Multinatioanl Corporation. 600p. 1981. 39.50 (ISBN 0-471-08062-4, Pub. by Wiley Interscience). Wiley.
OECD. Accounting Practices in OECD Member Countris. (International Investment & Multinational Enterprises). (Illus.). 250p. (Orig.). 1980. pap. text ed. 13.50x (ISBN 92-64-12076-9). OECD.
INTERNATIONAL CIVIL SERVICE
see International Officials and Employees
INTERNATIONAL COMPETITION
see Competition, International
INTERNATIONAL CONFERENCES, CONGRESSES AND CONVENTIONS
see Congresses and Conventions
INTERNATIONAL COOPERATION
Here are entered general works on international cooperative activities with or without the participation of governments.
see also Agriculture, Cooperative; Arbitration, International; Congresses and Conventions; International Agencies; International Education; International Organization; Technical Assistance
Coomer, James C., ed. Quest for a Sustainable Society. LC 80-24158. (Pergamon Policy Studies on International Development). 230p. 1981. 24.01 (ISBN 0-08-027168-5). Pergamon.
Fischer. A Collection of International Concessions & Related Instruments, Vols. 9-10. 1980. 45.00 ea. Vol. 9 (ISBN 0-379-10084-3). Vol. 10 (ISBN 0-379-10085-1). Oceana.
NATO: The Next Thirty Years. (Significant Issues Ser.: Vol. I, No. 6). 25p. 1979. pap. 5.00 (ISBN 0-89206-012-3, CSIS007, CSIS). Unipub.
Shaffer, Stephen M. & Shaffer, Lisa R. The Politics of International Cooperation: A Comparison of U. S. Experience in Space & in Security. (Monograph Series in World Affairs). 73p. Date not set. pap. 4.00 (ISBN 0-87940-063-3). U of Denver Intl.
INTERNATIONAL COOPERATION IN EDUCATION
see Educational Exchanges
INTERNATIONAL COOPERATION IN SCIENCE
see Science–International Cooperation
INTERNATIONAL COURT OF JUSTICE
see Hague–International Court of Justice
INTERNATIONAL CRIMINAL COURT (PROPOSED)
Ferencz, Benjamin. An International Criminal Court: A Step Toward World Peace, 2 vols. LC 80-10688. 1212p. 1980. Vol. 1. lib. bdg. 37.50 ea. (ISBN 0-379-20389-8). Vol. 2 (ISBN 0-379-20390-1). Oceana.
INTERNATIONAL CRIMINAL LAW
see International Offenses
INTERNATIONAL ECONOMIC INTEGRATION
see also Customs Unions;
also names of international organizations established to integrate the economies of various countries, e.g. European Economic Community
Corea, Gamani. Need for Change: Towards the New International Economic Order. LC 80-40800. 350p. 1980. 25.00 (ISBN 0-08-026095-0). Pergamon.
Llewellyn, David T. International Financial Integration: The Limits of Sovereignty. 200p. 1980. 29.95x (ISBN 0-470-26960-X). Halsted Pr.
INTERNATIONAL ECONOMIC RELATIONS
see also Commercial Policy; International Business Enterprises; International Economic Integration; International Finance; Investments, Foreign; Technical Assistance
also subdivision Foreign Economic Relations under names of countries, e.g. United States–Foreign Economic Relations
Anell, Lars & Nygren, Birgitta. The Developing Countries & the World Economic Order. 208p. 1980. pap. 8.95 (ISBN 0-416-74630-6, 2002). Methuen Inc.
Atimono, Emiko. Law & Diplomacy in Commodity Economics. 200p. 1981. text ed. 57.95x (ISBN 0-8419-5080-6). Holmes & Meier.
Azzam, Salem, frwd. by. The Muslim World & the Future Economic Order. 383p. 1980. 29.95x (ISBN 0-906041-10-4, Pub. by Islamic Council of Europe England); pap. 14.95x (ISBN 0-906041-09-0). Intl Schol Bk Serv.
Balassa, Bela. The Newly Industrialized Countries in the World Economy. LC 80-20787. 450p. 1981. 42.50 (ISBN 0-08-026336-4); pap. 15.00 (ISBN 0-08-026335-6). Pergamon.
Batchelder, Alan & Haitani, Kanji. International Economics: Theory & Practice. LC 70-21770. (Economics Ser.). 420p. 1981. text ed. 20.95 (ISBN 0-88244-231-7). Grid Pub.
Bhagwati, Jagdish N. Amount & Sharing of Aid. LC 73-123777. (Monographs: No. 2). 208p. 1970. 1.50 (ISBN 0-686-28693-6). Overseas Dev Council.
Brown, Lester R. The Interdependence of Nations. (Development Papers: No. 10). 70p. 1972. pap. 1.00 (ISBN 0-686-28679-0). Overseas Dev Council.
Buckley, Peter J. & Roberts, Brian R. European Direct Investment in the U.S.A. Before World War I. 1981. 25.00 (ISBN 0-312-26940-4). St Martin.
Carlson, Jack & Graham, Hugh. The Economic Importance of Exports to the United States, Vol. Ii. LC 80-66694. (Significant Issues Ser.: No. 6). 128p. 1980. 5.95 (ISBN 0-89206-019-0). CSI Studies.
Cline, William R., ed. Policy Alternatives for a New International Economic Order: An Economic Analysis. LC 79-87553. 410p. 1979. pap. 7.95 (ISBN 0-03-049466-4). Overseas Dev Council.
Cole, J. P. The Development Gap: A Spatial Analysis of World Poverty & Inequality. LC 80-40284. 1981. write for info. (ISBN 0-471-16477-1). Wiley.
De Saint Phalle, Thibaut. U. S. Productivity & Competitiveness in International Trade, Vol. II. LC 80-68434. (Significant Issues Ser.: No. 12). 115p. 1980. 5.95 (ISBN 0-89206-028-X). CSI Studies.
Erb, Guy F. Negotiations on Two Fronts: Manufactures & Commodities. LC 78-57199. (Development Papers: No. 25). 80p. 1978. pap. 1.50 (ISBN 0-686-28674-X). Overseas Dev Council.
Erlanger, George C. The International Monetary Chaos & a Positive Plan for the Monetary Reconstruction of the World. (Illus.). 127p. 1981. 67.85 (ISBN 0-918968-90-9). Inst Econ Finan.
Faaland, Just, ed. Aid & Influence: The Case of Bangladesh. LC 80-13481. 1980. 25.00 (ISBN 0-312-01492-9). St Martin.
Finger, Seymour M. & Harbert, Joseph R., eds. U. S. Policy in International Institutions: Defining Reasonable Options in an Unreasonable World. rev. & updated ed. (Special Studies in International Relations). 200p. (Orig.). 1981. lib. bdg. 20.00x (ISBN 0-86531-105-6); pap. 8.50x (ISBN 0-86531-106-4). Westview.
Flammang, Robert. U. S Programs That Impede U. S. Export Competitveness: The Regulatory Environment, Vol. II. LC 80-80933. (Significant Issues Ser.: No. 3). 45p. 1980. 5.95 (ISBN 0-89206-017-4). CSI Studies.
Fordwor, Kwame D. The African Development Bank: Problems of International Cooperation. LC 80-24607. (Pergamon Policy Studies on International Development). 300p. 1980. 30.00 (ISBN 0-08-026339-9). Pergamon.
Ghatak, Subrata. Monetary Economics in Developing Countries. Date not set. 25.00 (ISBN 0-312-54418-9). St Martin.
Hansen, Roger D. Beyond the North-South Stalemate. LC 78-10607. 348p. 1979. pap. 5.95 (ISBN 0-07-026049-4). Overseas Dev Council.
Hansen, Roger D. & Overseas Development Council Staff. The U. S. & World Development: Agenda for Action, 1976. LC 76-4936. (Agenda Ser.). 240p. 1976. pap. 4.95 (ISBN 0-275-85670-4). Overseas Dev Council.
Howe, James W. & Overseas Development Council Staff. The U. S. & the Developing World: Agenda for Action, 1974. LC 74-4234. (Agenda Ser.). 228p. 1974. pap. 3.95 (ISBN 0-686-28670-7). Overseas Dev Council.
--The U. S. & World Development: Agenda for Action, 1975. LC 75-11641. (Agenda Ser.). 288p. 1975. pap. 4.95 (ISBN 0-275-89310-3). Overseas Dev Council.
Hunter, Robert E. & Overseas Development Council Staff. The United States & the Developing World: Agenda for Action, 1973. LC 73-76292. (Agenda Ser.). 172p. 1973. pap. 2.50 (ISBN 0-686-28671-5). Overseas Dev Council.
ILO International Labour Office, ed. Employment, Growth & Basic Needs: A One-World Problem. LC 77-70278. 256p. 1977. pap. 3.95 (ISBN 0-686-28705-3). Overseas Dev Council.
Katz, Samuel I., ed. U. S.-European Monetary Relations. 1979. 13.25 (ISBN 0-8447-2150-6); pap. 7.25 (ISBN 0-8447-2149-2). Am Enterprise.
Laffer & Miles. International Economics: In an Integrated World. 416p. 1981. pap. write for info. (ISBN 0-8302-4028-4). Goodyear.
Laszlo, Ervin & Kurtzman, Joel, eds. The Structure of the World Economy & Economic Order: Prospects for a New International. LC 79-23350. 1980. 16.50 (ISBN 0-686-64334-8). Pergamon.
Laudicina, Paul A. World Poverty & Development: A Survey of American Opinion. LC 73-89873. (Monographs: No. 8). 126p. 1973. 2.50 (ISBN 0-686-28687-1). Overseas Dev Council.
McLaughlin, Martin M. & Overseas Development Council Staff. The United States & World Development: Agenda 1979. LC 78-71589. (Agenda Ser.). 280p. 1979. pap. 5.95 (ISBN 0-686-28666-9). Overseas Dev Council.
Magdoff, Harry & Sweezy, Paul M. The Deepening Crisis of U.S. Capitalism: Essays by Harry Magdoff & Paul M. Sweezy. LC 80-8935. 256p. 1981. 16.00 (ISBN 0-85345-573-2); pap. 6.50 (ISBN 0-85345-574-0). Monthly Rev.
Mahbub ul Haq. The Third World & the International Economic Order. (Development Papers: No. 22). 54p. 1976. pap. 1.50 (ISBN 0-686-28676-6). Overseas Dev Council.
Malmgren, Harald B. Trade for Development. LC 76-152712. (Monographs: No. 4). 88p. 1971. 1.00 (ISBN 0-686-28691-X). Overseas Dev Council.
Mason, R. Hal, et al. International Business. 2nd ed. (Management & Administration Ser.). 500p. 1981. text ed. 21.95 (ISBN 0-686-69162-8). Wiley.
Mathieson, John A. The Advanced Developing Countries: Emerging Actors in the World Economy. LC 79-91996. (Development Papers: No. 28). 72p. 1979. pap. 3.00 (ISBN 0-686-28672-3). Overseas Dev Council.
Mikesell, Raymond F. & Farah, Mark G. U. S. Export Competitiveness in Manufactures in Third World Countries, Vol. II. LC 80-67711. (Significant Issues Ser.: No. 9). 144p. 1980. 5.95 (ISBN 0-89206-026-3). CSI Studies.
Mundell, Robert A. & Swoboda, Alexander K., eds. Monetary Problems of the International Economy. pap. write for info. (ISBN 0-226-55066-4). U of Chicago Pr.
Njoku, John E. Analyzing Nigerian-Americans Under a New Economic Order. LC 80-5916. 128p. (Orig.). 1981. pap. text ed. 7.50 (ISBN 0-8191-1448-0). U Pr of Amer.
OAS General Secretariat Department of Publications, ed. Boletin Estadistico De la OEA. (Periodical-Quarterly Ser.). 207p. 4.00 (ISBN 0-686-68291-2). OAS.
OECD. National Accounts of OECD Countries, Vol. II. (Illus.). 284p. 1980. pap. 18.00x (ISBN 92-64-02094-2, 30-80-03-3). OECD.
Olson, Robert K. U. S. Foreign Policy & the New International Economic Order. (Special Studies in International Relations). 184p. 1981. lib. bdg. 20.00x (ISBN 0-86531-125-0). Westview.
Ramesh, Jairam & Weiss, Charles, Jr., eds. Mobilizing Technology for World Development. LC 79-5349. 240p. 1979. pap. 6.95 (ISBN 0-03-055451-9). Overseas Dev Council.
Sewell, John & Overseas Development Council Staff. The United States & World Development: Agenda 1977. LC 76-30725. (Agenda Ser.). 272p. 1977. pap. 4.95. Overseas Dev Council.
Sewell, John W. The United States & World Development: Agenda 1980. 256p. 1980. 24.95 (ISBN 0-03-058993-2); pap. 6.95 (ISBN 0-03-058992-4). Praeger.
Smith, Gordon W. The External Public Debt Prospects of the Non-Oil-Exporting Developing Countries. LC 77-90866. (Monographs: No. 10). 64p. 1977. 4.00 (ISBN 0-686-28685-5). Overseas Dev Council.
The Royal Institute of International Affairs, ed. The Chatham House Annual Review: International Economic & Monetary Issues, Vol. 1. (PPS on International Politics). (Illus.). 200p. 1981. 20.00 (ISBN 0-08-027532-X). Pergamon.
Twitchett, Carol C. A Framework for Development: The EEC & the ACP. 160p. 1981. text ed. 28.50x (ISBN 0-04-338094-8, 2592). Allen Unwin.
United Nations. World Economic Survey, 1979-80. LC 48-1401. 116p. (Orig.). 1980. pap. 10.00x (ISBN 0-8002-1108-1). Intl Pubns Serv.
Van Meerhaeghe, Marcel A. A Handbook of International Economic Institutions. 472p. 1980. lib. bdg. 76.50 (ISBN 90-247-2357-4, Pub. by Martinus Nijhoff). Kluwer Boston.
Weiss, Leonard. Trade Liberalization & the National Interest, Vol. II. LC 80-80932. (Significant Issues Ser.: No. 2). 60p. 1980. 5.95 (ISBN 0-89206-016-6). CSI Studies.
Whiting, D. P. International Trade & Payments. (Illus.). 160p. 1978. pap. 11.95x (ISBN 0-7121-0952-8). Intl Ideas.
World Economic Survey 1978 - Current Trends in the World Economy. 125p. 1980. pap. 10.00 (ISBN 0-686-68980-1, UN80/2C1, UN). Unipub.
World Trade Annual Supplement, 1978, 5 vols. 110.00 ea.; Set. 550.00. Vol. 1 (ISBN 0-8027-5969-6). Vol. 2 (ISBN 0-8027-5971-8). Vol. 3 (ISBN 0-8027-5972-6). Vol. 4 (ISBN 0-8027-5973-4). Vol. 5 (ISBN 0-8027-5974-2). Walker & Co.
World Trade Annual, 1978, 5 vols. 50.00 ea.; Set. 250.00 (ISBN 0-8027-5977-7). Vol. 1 (ISBN 0-8027-5963-7). Vol. 2 (ISBN 0-8027-5964-5). Vol. 3 (ISBN 0-8027-5965-3). Vol. 4 (ISBN 0-8027-5966-1). Vol. 5 (ISBN 0-8027-5968-8). Walker & Co.
INTERNATIONAL EDUCATION
Here are entered works on education for international understanding, world citizenship, etc.
see also Students, Interchange Of; Teachers, Interchange Of
Council on International Educational Exchange. The Whole World Handbook: A Guide to Study, Travel, & Work Abroad. 352p. 1981. pap. 5.95 (ISBN 0-525-93171-6). Dutton.
Morrissett, Irving, ed. International Perspectives on Social-Political Education. 1980. pap. write for info. (ISBN 0-89994-253-9). Soc Sci Ed.
Pierce, Lucia & Pierce, Lucia. International Training. 1981. pap. 7.95x (ISBN 0-915432-81-1). NE Conf Teach Foreign.
INTERNATIONAL EDUCATIONAL EXCHANGES
see Educational Exchanges
INTERNATIONAL EXCHANGE
see Foreign Exchange
INTERNATIONAL EXCHANGE OF STUDENTS
see Students, Interchange of
INTERNATIONAL EXHIBITIONS
see Exhibitions
INTERNATIONAL FEDERATION
see International Organization
INTERNATIONAL FINANCE
see also Banks and Banking, International; Foreign Exchange
Argy, Victor. The Post War International Money Crisis: An Analysis. 472p. (Orig.). 1981. text ed. 38.95x (ISBN 0-04-332075-9, 2576); pap. text ed. 17.50x (ISBN 0-04-332076-7, 2577). Allen Unwin.
Baldwin & Richardson. International Trade & Finance. 2nd ed. 1981. pap. text ed. 8.95 (ISBN 0-316-07922-7). Little.
Casey, Douglas. The International Man. 19.95 (ISBN 0-932496-01-6). Green Hill.
Coombs, C. A. The Arena of International Finance. 1976. 22.95 (ISBN 0-471-01513-X, Pub. by Wiley-Interscience). Wiley.
International Center for Settlement of Investment Disputes. Investment Laws of the World, Binder 10. 1979. 75.00 (ISBN 0-379-00650-2). Oceana.
Llewellyn, David T. International Financial Integration: The Limits of Sovereignty. 200p. 1980. 29.95x (ISBN 0-470-26960-X). Halsted Pr.
Lomax, D. F. & Gutmann, P. T. The Euromarkets & International Financial Policies. 275p. 1980. 29.95x (ISBN 0-470-26923-5). Halsted Pr.
Murphy, J. Carter. International Monetary System: Beyond the First Stage of Reform. 1979. pap. 7.25 (ISBN 0-8447-3362-8). Am Enterprise.
Willett, Thomas D. International Liquidity Issues. 1980. pap. 5.25 (ISBN 0-8447-3388-1). Am Enterprise.
Wionczek, Miguel S. International Indebtedness & World Economic Stagnation. 135p. 1981. 17.50 (ISBN 0-08-024702-4). Pergamon.

Wood, Douglas & Byrne, James. International Business Finance. LC 80-23951. 400p. 1981. text ed. 47.50x (ISBN 0-8419-0663-7). Holmes & Meier.

INTERNATIONAL FISCAL RELATIONS

see Intergovernmental Fiscal Relations

INTERNATIONAL INSTITUTIONS

see International Cooperation

INTERNATIONAL LAW

see also Aliens; Arbitration, International; Asylum, Right of; Atomic Weapons (International Law); Autonomy; Civil Rights (International Law); Civil War; Diplomats; Extradition; Fishery Law and Legislation; International Cooperation; International Offenses; International Organization; Maritime Law; Naturalization; Neutrality; Pirates; Refugees, Political; Salvage; Slave-Trade; Sovereignty; Treaties also subdivisions Laws and Legislation and Laws and Regulations under topics of international concern

Australian Yearbook of International Law 1970-1973, Vol. 1. 1975. 30.00 (ISBN 0-379-00482-8). Oceana.

Di Marzo, Luigi. Component Units of Federal States & International Agreement. LC 80-83265. 272p. 1980. 45.00x (ISBN 90-286-0330-1). Sijthoff & Noordhoff.

Fulbecke, William. The Pandectes of the Law of Nations. LC 79-84109. (English Experience Ser.: No.928). 192p. 1979. Repr. of 1602 ed. lib. bdg. 18.00 (ISBN 90-221-0928-3). Walter J Johnson.

Glassner, Martin I. Bibliography on Land-Locked States. LC 80-51737. 60p. 1980. 20.00x (ISBN 90-286-0290-9). Sijthoff & Noordhodf.

Gorove, Stephen. Legal Aspects of International Investment. (L. Q. C. Lamar Society of International Law, University of Mississippi Law Center, Monograph: No. 1). viii, 79p. (Orig.). 1977. pap. text ed. 10.00x (ISBN 0-8377-0607-6). Rothman.

Livermore, Sarah, et al, eds. The American Bar - The Canadian Bar - The International Bar: 1981. 63rd ed. LC 18-21110. 3062p. 1981. 130.00 (ISBN 0-931398-06-1). R B Forster.

McWhinney, Edward. Conflict & Compromise: International Law & World Order in a Revolutionary Age. LC 80-29045. 152p. 1981. text ed. 14.00x (ISBN 0-8419-0694-7); pap. text ed. 8.75x (ISBN 0-8419-0696-3). Holmes & Meier.

OAS General Secretariat, Dept. of Publications. Sexto Curso de Derecho Internationsl Organizado Por el Comite Juridico Interamericano: Julio-Agosto de 1979, Conferencias e Informes. 630p. (Span.). 1979. pap. text ed. 25.00 (ISBN 0-8270-1144-X). OAS.

OAS General Secretariat Office of Development & Codification of International Law. Actas Y Documentos Segunda Conferencia Especializada Interamerica Sobre Derecho Internacional Privado, Vol. 1. (International Law). 455p. 1980. lib. bdg. 25.00 (ISBN 0-8270-1113-X). OAS.

OAS General Secretariat Office of Development & Codification of Inernational Law. Actas Y Documentos Segunda Conferencia Especializada Interamericana Sobre Derecho Internacional Privado, Vol. 3. (International Law Ser.). 469p. 1980. text ed. 25.00 (ISBN 0-8270-1115-6). OAS.

OAS General Secretatiat Office of Development & Codification of International Law. Actas Y Documentos Segunda Conferencia Especializada Interamericana Sobre Derecho Internacional Privado, Vol. 2. (International Law Ser.). 450p. 1980. text ed. 25.00 (ISBN 0-8270-1114-8). OAS.

Royal Institute of International Affairs. British Yearbook of Internaional Law. Incl. Vol. 3. 1965. 15.95x (ISBN 0-19-214625-4); Vol. 7. 1965. 15.95x (ISBN 0-19-214629-7); Vol. 39, 1963. Waldock, H. & Jennings, R. Y., eds. 1965. 24.95x (ISBN 0-19-214622-X); Vol. 40, 1964. Waldock, H. & Jennings, R. Y., eds. 1966. 24.95x (ISBN 0-19-214623-8); Vol. 41, 1965-66. Waldock, H. & Jennings, R. Y., eds. 1968. 24.95x (ISBN 0-19-214657-2); Waldock, H. & Jennings, R. Y., eds. 1969. 24.95x (ISBN 0-19-214658-0); Vol. 44. Waldcock, H. & Jennings, R. Y., eds. 1970. 24.95x (ISBN 0-19-214660-2); Vol. 45. Waldock, H. & Jennings, R. Y., eds. 1973. 59.50x (ISBN 0-19-214661-0). (Royal Institute of International Affairs Ser.). Oxford U Pr.

Seidl-Hohenveldern. American-Austrian Private International Law. 1963. 9.00 (ISBN 0-379-11411-9). Oceana.

Simmonds, K. Multinational Corporations Law, Vols. 1-2. 1979. Set. 75.00 (ISBN 0-379-20373-1). Oceana.

--Multinational Corporations Law, Release 3. 1980. 50.00. Oceana.

Tabory, Mala. Multilingualism in International Law & Institutions. LC 80-51742. 304p. 1980. 32.50x (ISBN 90-286-0210-0). Sijthoff & Noordhoff.

Third United Nations Conference on the Law of the Sea: Official Records, Vol. IX. 191p. 1979. pap. 14.00 (ISBN 0-686-68976-3, UN79/5/3, UN). Unipub.

INTERNATIONAL LAW–ADDRESSES, ESSAYS, LECTURES

Bassiouni, M. Cherif. International Criminal Law: A Draft International Criminal Code. LC 80-50452. 286p. 1980. 50.00x (ISBN 90-286-0130-9). Sijthoff & Noordhoff.

Kalshoven, Frits, et al, eds. Essays on the Development of the International Legal Order: In Memory of Haro F. van Panhuys. 240p. 1980. 50.00x (ISBN 90-286-0360-3). Sijthoff & Noordhoff.

Lerner, Natan. U. N. Convention on the Elimination of Al Forms of Racial Discrimination. LC 80-51738. 278p. 1980. 37.50x (ISBN 90-286-0160-0). Sijthoff & Noordhoff.

Moskowitz, Moses. The Roots & Reaches of United Nations Actions & Decisions. LC 80-51741. 220p. 1980. 28.50x (ISBN 90-286-0140-6). Sijthoff & Noordhoff.

Mosler, Hermann. The International Society As a Legal Community. LC 80-50454. (Collected Courses the Hague Academy of International Law: Vol. 140, 1974-IV). 327p. 1980. pap. 27.50x (ISBN 90-286-0080-9). Sijthoff & Noordhoff.

Sumanpouw, Mathilde. Les Nouvelles Conventions De la Haye: Leur Application Par les Juges Nationaux, Vol. II. 260p. (Fr.). 1980. 45.00x (ISBN 90-286-0870-2). Sijthoff & Noordhoff.

Van Dijk, P. Judicial Review of Governmental Action & the Requirement of an Interest to Sue. LC 80-51740. 618p. 1980. 100.00x (ISBN 90-286-0120-1). Sijthoff & Noordhoff.

INTERNATIONAL LAW–CASES

Deak, Francis. American International Law Cases: 1971-1978, Vols. 1-20. 45.00 ea. Oceana.

International Institute for the Unification of Private Law. Digest of Legal Activities of International & Other Institutions, Release 1. 4th ed. 1980. 85.00 (ISBN 0-379-00545-X). Oceana.

Ruddy, F. American International Law Cases, Vols. 21-22. 1980. 45.00 ea. (ISBN 0-379-20400-2). Vol. 21. Vol. 22 (ISBN 0-379-20401-0). Oceana.

INTERNATIONAL LAW–YEARBOOKS

Bouchez, L. J., et al, eds. Netherlands Yearbook of International Law: State Immunity from Attachment & Execution, Vol. X. 650p. 1980. 40.00x (ISBN 90-286-0710-2). Sijthoff & Noordhoff.

Centre National De la Recherche Scientifique, ed. Annuaire Francais De Droit International, Vol. 25. LC 57-28515. 1288p. 1979. 125.00x (ISBN 2-222-02737-3). Intl Pubns Serv.

Jennings, R. Y. & Brownlie, Ian. The British Year Book of International Law 1979, Vol. 50. 464p. 1981. 98.00 (ISBN 0-19-825360-5). Oxford U Pr.

Matthews, James M., ed. Kime's International Law Directory for 1980. 88th ed. 809p. 1981. 52.50x (ISBN 0-900503-12-2). Intl Pubns Serv.

The Work of the International Law Commission. 325p. 1980. pap. 16.00 (UN80-5-11, UN). Unipub.

Yearbook of the International Law Commission Nineteen Seventy-Eight: Part One of Documents of the Thirtieth Session, Vol. 2. 289p. 1979. pap. 18.00 (UN79-5-6(PT.1), UN). Unipub.

Yearbook of the International Law Commission: Nineteen Seventy-Nine, Vol.1. 247p. 1980. pap. 17.00 (UN80-5-4, UN). Unipub.

INTERNATIONAL LAW, PRIVATE

see Conflict of Laws

INTERNATIONAL MONETARY FUND

Erlanger, George C. The International Monetary Chaos & a Positive Plan for the Monetary Reconstruction of the World. (Illus.). 127p. 1981. 67.85 (ISBN 0-918968-90-9). Inst Econ Finan.

INTERNATIONAL NEWS

see Foreign News

INTERNATIONAL OFFENSES

see also Genocide; Terrorism

Bassiouni, M. Cherif. International Criminal Law: A Draft International Criminal Code. LC 80-50452. 286p. 1980. 50.00x (ISBN 90-286-0130-9). Sijthoff & Noordhoff.

INTERNATIONAL OFFICIALS AND EMPLOYEES

Plantley. The International Civil Service: Law & Management. 1981. write for info. (ISBN 0-89352-103-5). Masson Pub.

INTERNATIONAL ORGANIZATION

Here are entered works on theories and efforts leading toward worldwide or regional political organization of nations.

see also International Agencies; International Cooperation; International Law; International Officials and Employees; Security, International; World Politics also names of specific organizations, e.g. United Nations, Pan American Union

Ramos, Alberto G. The New Science of Organizations: A Reconceptualization of the Wealth of Nations. 224p. 1981. 25.00 (ISBN 0-8020-5527-3). U of Toronto Pr.

Thomas, Harold. The World Power Foundation: Its Goals & Platform. 1980. pap. 6.95. Loompanics.

INTERNATIONAL ORGANIZATIONS

see International Agencies

INTERNATIONAL POLITICS

see World Politics

INTERNATIONAL PRIVATE LAW

see Conflict of Laws

INTERNATIONAL RELATIONS

Here are entered works dealing with the theory of international intercourse. Historical accounts are entered under the headings World Politics; United States–Politics and Government; etc. Works dealing with foreign relations from the point of view of an individual state are entered under the name of the state with subdivision Foreign Relations.

see also Arbitration, International; Competition, International; Congresses and Conventions; Cultural Relations; Detente; Diplomacy; Diplomatic Negotiations in International Disputes; Diplomats; Disarmament; Foreign News; Geography, Political; Geopolitics; Intergovernmental Fiscal Relations; International Cooperation; International Economic Relations; International Law; International Organization; Nationalism; Peace; Refugees, Political; Security, International; Treaties; World Politics also subdivision Foreign Relations under names of countries, e.g. France–Foreign Relations; also names of international alliances, congresses, treaties, etc. e.g. Holy Alliance; Versailles, Treaty of, 1918

Andren, Nils & Birnbaum, Karl E. Belgrade & Beyond: The CSCE Process in Perspective. (East West Perspectives: No. 5). 27.50x (ISBN 90-286-0250-X). Sijthoff & Noordhoff.

Beer, Francis A. Peace Against War: The Ecology of International Violence. LC 80-27214. (International Relations Ser.). (Illus.). 1981. text ed. 18.95x (ISBN 0-7167-1250-4); pap. text ed. 9.95x (ISBN 0-7167-1251-2). W H Freeman.

Beres, Louis R. People, States, & World Order. LC 80-83099. 300p. 1981. pap text ed. 7.95 (ISBN 0-87581-267-8). Peacock Pubs.

Clark, Ronald W. The Greatest Power on Earth: The International Race for Supremacy. LC 80-7899. (Illus.). 352p. 1981. 12.95 (ISBN 0-06-014846-2, HarpT). Har-Row.

Cohen, Bernard C. Political Process & Foreign Policy: The Making of the Japanese Peace Settlement. LC 80-19832. x, 293p. 1980. Repr. of 1957 ed. lib. bdg. 37.50x (ISBN 0-313-22715-2, COPF). Greenwood.

Consensus & Peace. 231p. 1981. pap. 20.75 (ISBN 92-3-101851-5, U1055, UNESCO). Unipub.

Davison, W. Phillips, et al. News from Abroad & the Foreign Policy Public. LC 80-68024. (Headline Ser.: No. 250). (Illus.). 64p. (Orig.). 1980. pap. 2.00 (ISBN 0-87124-063-7). Foreign Policy.

Dolman, Anthony J. & Ettinger, Jan Van, eds. Partners in Tomorrow: Strategies for a New International Order. 1978. 9.95 (ISBN 0-87690-294-8). Dutton.

Fedder, Edwin H., ed. Defense Politics of the Atlantic Alliance. 180p. 1980. 21.95 (ISBN 0-03-058018-8). Praeger.

Ferraris, Luigi V., ed. Report on a Negotiation: Helsinki-Geneva-Helsinki Nineteen Seventy-Two to Nineteen Seventy-Five. Barber, Marie-Claire, tr. from Italian. (Collections De Relations Internationales Ser.). 439p. 1980. 46.00x (ISBN 9-0286-0779-X). Sijthoff & Noordhoff.

Hare, A. Paul & Blumberg, Herbert H. A Search for Peace & Justice: Reflections of Michael Scott. (Illus.). 255p. 1980. 13.50x. Rowman.

Henry, Clement M. Politics & International Relations in the Middle East: An Annotated Bibliography. 114p. (Orig.). 1980. pap. 4.00 (ISBN 0-932098-18-5). Ctr for NE & North Aafrican Stud.

Hinshaw. Domestic Goals in an Interdependent World: The Frankfurt Dialogue. Date not set. 25.00 (ISBN 0-8247-6999-6). Dekker.

Hoskins, Halford. Atlantic Pact. 5.00 (ISBN 0-8183-0229-1). Pub Aff Pr.

Institute for the Study of Conflict, ed. Annual of Power & Conflict Nineteen Seventy-Nine to Nineteen Eighty. 465p. 1980. 50.00x (ISBN 0-8448-1386-9). Crane-Russak Co.

International Affairs Nineteen Thirty-Nine to Nineteen Seventy-Nine. LC 80-22312. 1981. text ed. 24.00 (ISBN 0-8419-0677-7); pap. 12.00 (ISBN 0-8419-0678-5). Holmes & Meier.

LaRouche, Lyndon H., Jr. Why Revival of "SALT" Won't Stop War. 118p. (Orig.). 1980. pap. 3.95 (ISBN 0-933488-08-4). New Benjamin.

Lebow, Richard N. Between War & Peace: The Nature of International Crisis. LC 80-21982. 410p. 1981. text ed. 24.50 (ISBN 0-8018-2311-0). Johns Hopkins.

McGinn, Charles. Bet on Yourself. (Illus.). 153p. (Orig.). 1980. pap. 2.95 (ISBN 0-89260-193-0). Hwong Pub.

McHenry, Donald F. Ethics & Foreign Policy. LC 80-68410. (Distinguished Cria Lecture on Morality & Foreign Policy Ser.). 1980. pap. 4.00 (ISBN 0-87641-220-7). Coun Rel & Intl.

Martell, John. Twentieth Century World. 3rd ed. (Illus.). 1981. pap. 13.95x. Intl Ideas.

Morgan, Patrick M. Theories & Approaches to International Politics. 3rd ed. 302p. 1981. 24.95 (ISBN 0-87855-350-9); text ed. 24.95 (ISBN 0-686-68062-6); pap. 9.95 (ISBN 0-87855-791-1); pap. text ed. 9.95 (ISBN 0-686-68063-4). Transaction Bks.

Multilateral Treaties in Respect of Which the Secretary General Performs Depository Functions. 677p. 1980. pap. 34.00 (ISBN 0-686-68960-7, UN80/5/10, UN). Unipub.

Narayanan, K. R. & Misra, K. P., eds. Nonalignment in Contemporary International Relations. 275p. 1981. text ed. 27.50x (ISBN 0-7069-1286-1, Pub by Vikas India). Advent Bk.

Ofoegbu, Ray. A Foundation Course in International Relations for African Students. 224p. (Orig.). 1980. pap. text ed. 10.50x (ISBN 0-04-327058-1, AU448). Allen Unwin.

Pettman, Ralph. The Biopolitics of International Relations. LC 80-22926. (Pergamon Policy Studies on Biopolitics). 200p. 1981. 20.00 (ISBN 0-08-026329-1); pap. 9.95 (ISBN 0-08-026328-3). Pergamon.

Posses, F. The Art of International Negotiation. 195p. 1978. text ed. 23.50x (ISBN 0-220-66315-7, Pub. by Busn Bks England). Renouf.

Serfaty, Simon. The United States, Western Europe, & the Third World: Allies & Adversaries, Vol. II. LC 80-50588. (Significant Issues Ser.: No. 4). 53p. 1980. 5.95 (ISBN 0-89206-018-2). CSI Studies.

Shaping Accelerated Development & International Changes. 45p. 1980. pap. 3.00 (ISBN 0-686-68971-2, UN80/2A4, UN). Unipub.

Simpson, William G. Which Way Western Man? LC 79-91738. 758p. 1980. pap. 7.00 (ISBN 0-937944-01-7). Natl Alliance.

Spiegel, Steven L. Dominance & Diversity: The International Hierarchy. LC 80-8295. 317p. 1980. lib. bdg. 19.00 (ISBN 0-8191-1331-X); pap. text ed. 10.50 (ISBN 0-8191-1332-8). U Pr of Amer.

Streeten, Paul. Recent Issues in World Developement: A Collection of Survey Articles. (Illus.). 450p. 1981. 115.00 (ISBN 0-08-026812-9). Pergamon.

Stuart, Douglas T. & Tow, William T., eds. China, the Soviet Union & the West: Strategic & Political Dimensions for the Nineteen Eighties. (Special Studies in International Relations). 320p. (Orig.). 1981. lib. bdg. 27.50x (ISBN 0-86531-091-2); pap. text ed. 12.50x (ISBN 0-86531-168-4). Westview.

Watson, Adam. Toleration in Religion & Politics. LC 80-65746. (Second Annual Distinguished Cria Lecture on Morality & Foreign Policy Ser.). 1980. pap. 4.00 (ISBN 0-87641-218-5). Coun Rel & Intl.

Watt, D. C., ed. Greenwich Forum V: Europe & the Sea: the Cause for & Against a New International Regime for the North Sea and Its Approaches. 1980. text ed. 52.00 (ISBN 0-86103-039-7). Butterworths.

West, Robert H. The Invisible World. 275p. 1980. Repr. of 1939 ed. lib. bdg. 30.00 (ISBN 0-8482-7063-0). Norwood Edns.

Ziegler. War, Peace & International Relations. 2nd ed. 1981. pap. text ed. 8.95 (ISBN 0-316-98493-0). Little.

INTERNATIONAL RELATIONS–ADDRESSES, ESSAYS, LECTURES

Stack, John F., Jr., ed. Ethnic Identities in a Transnational World. LC 80-1199. (Contributions in Political Science Ser.: No. 52). 264p. 1981. lib. bdg. 27.50 (ISBN 0-313-21088-8, SEI/). Greenwood.

INTERNATIONAL RELATIONS–STUDY AND TEACHING

Herz, Martin F. How the Cold War Is Taught: Six American History Textbooks Examined. 82p. 1978. pap. 3.00 (ISBN 0-89633-009-5). Ethics & Public Policy.

INTERNATIONAL RELATIONS–YEARBOOKS

ACP States Yearbook, 1980 to 1981. 670p. 1981. pap. 257.25 (ISBN 2-8029-0014-5, ED13, Edns Delta). Unipub.

INTERNATIONAL SALES

see Export Sales

INTERNATIONAL SECURITY

see Security, International

INTERNATIONAL SYSTEM OF UNITS

see Metric System

INTERNATIONAL TRADE

see Commerce

INTERNATIONAL TRADE REGULATION

see Foreign Trade Regulation

INTERNMENT CAMPS

see Concentration Camps

INTERNS (EDUCATION)

see also Student Teaching

Polking, Kirk, ed. Internships Nineteen Hundred Eighty-One. (Orig.). 1981. pap. 6.95 (ISBN 0-89879-036-0). Writers Digest.

INTEROCEANIC CANALS

see Canals

INTERPERSONAL COMMUNICATION

Bach, George R. & Wyden, Peter. The Intimate Enemy: How to Fight Fair in Love & Marriage. 384p. 1981. pap. 2.95 (ISBN 0-380-00392-9, 54452). Avon.

Forrest, Mary & Olson, Margot. Exploring Speech Communication: An Introduction. 320p. 1981. pap. text ed. 9.56 (ISBN 0-8299-0381-X). West Pub.

Gaw. It Depends: Appropriate Interpersonal Communication. 1981. 9.95 (ISBN 0-88284-124-6). Alfred Pub.

Gilmore, Susan K. & Fraleigh, Patrick W. Communication at Work. LC 80-69467. (Illus.). 150p. (Orig.). 1980. 6.95 (ISBN 0-938070-00-2). Friendly Pr.

Hargie, Owen & Dickson, David. Social Skills in Interpersonal Communication. 208p. 1981. 28.00x (ISBN 0-7099-0279-4, Pub. by Croom Helm LTD England). Biblio Dist.

Tubbs, Stewart L. & Moss, Sylvia. Interpersonal Communication. 2nd ed. 299p. 1981. pap. text ed. 10.95 (ISBN 0-394-32684-9). Random.
Weaver, Richard L., II. Understanding Interpersonal Communication. 2nd ed. 1981. pap. text ed. 10.95x (ISBN 0-673-15436-X). Scott F.

INTERPERSONAL PERCEPTION
see Social Perception

INTERPERSONAL RELATIONS
see also Interpersonal Communication; Teacher-Student Relationships
Beardsley, Lou. Mother-in-Laws Can Be Fun. LC 80-84763. 1981. pap. 4.95 (ISBN 0-89081-281-0). Harvest Hse.
Bell, Gary & Seay, Davin R. Lost but Not Forever. LC 80-81472. 1981. pap. 4.95 (ISBN 0-89081-253-5). Harvest Hse.
Berenson, F. M. Understanding Persons: Personal & Impersonal Relations. 19.95 (ISBN 0-312-83154-4). St Martin.
Blank, Raymond. Playing the Game: A Psychopolitical Strategy for Your Career. (Illus.). 224p. 1981. 10.95 (ISBN 0-688-00354-0). Morrow.
Bramson, Robert M. Coping with Difficult People. 240p. 1981. 11.95 (ISBN 0-385-17362-8, Anchor Pr). Doubleday.
Brenton, Myron. Lasting Relationships: How to Recognize the Man or Woman Who's Right for You. 224p. 1981. 10.95 (ISBN 0-89479-078-1). A & W Pubs.
Carlson, Dwight L. Overcoming Hurts & Anger. LC 80-83852. 1981. pap. 4.95 (ISBN 0-89081-277-2). Harvest Hse.
DuBrin, Andrew. Human Relations: A Job-Oriented Approach. 2nd ed. 300p. 1981. text ed. 16.95 (ISBN 0-8359-3002-5); cancelled (ISBN 0-8359-3006-8); instr's. manual avail. (ISBN 0-8359-3003-3). Reston.
Eisler, Richard M. & Frederiksen, Lee W. Perfecting Social Skills: A Guide to Interpersonal Behavior Development. (Applied Clinical Psycholgy Ser.). 225p. 1981. 18.95 (ISBN 0-306-40592-X, Plenum Pr). Plenum Pub.
Gordon, Leonard V. Measurement of Interpersonal Values. LC 74-22623. 122p. (Orig.). 1975. text ed. 12.00 (ISBN 0-574-72770-1); pap. text ed. 8.20 (ISBN 0-574-72764-7). SRA.
Hamersma, Richard J. & Mark, Robert A. The Seven-Pillared Relationship. LC 79-20450. 192p. 1981. 13.95 (ISBN 0-88229-443-1). Nelson-Hall.
Henderson, George. Human Relations: From Theory to Practice. LC 73-19387. (Illus.). 450p. 1981. pap. 9.95 (ISBN 0-8061-1709-5). U of Okla Pr.
Irish, Richard K. How to Live Separately Together: A Guide for Working Couples. LC 78-22637. 264p. 1981. 11.95 (ISBN 0-385-14650-7, Anchor Pr). Doubleday.
Jewett, Paul K. El Hombre como Varon y Hembra. Vilela, Ernesto S., tr. from Eng. 205p. (Orig., Span.). 1979. pap. 4.95 (ISBN 0-89922-132-7). Edit Caribe.
Jones, John E. & Pfeiffer, J. William, eds. The Annual Handbook for Group Facilitators 1981. (Ser. in Human Relations Training). 290p. (Orig.). 1981. pap. 20.00 (ISBN 0-686-69076-1). Univ Assocs.
Kardos, Lajos, ed. Attitudes, Interaction & Personality. Dajka, B., et al, trs. (Illus.). 149p. 1980. 10.50x (ISBN 963-05-2088-5). Intl Pubns Serv.
Kristy, Norton F. Staying in Love: Reinventing Marriage & Other Realationships. (Orig.). pap. 2.75 (ISBN 0-515-05089-X). Jove Pubns.
Kvols-Riedler, Bill & Kvols-Riedler, Kathy. Understanding Yourself & Others. (Illus.). 222p. (Orig.). 1981. pap. 6.95 (ISBN 0-933450-01-X). RDIC Pubns.
Langone, John. Like, Love, Lust: A View of Sex & Sexuality. 144p. 1981. pap. 2.25 (ISBN 0-380-54189-0; 54189). Avon.
Littauer, Florence. The Pursuit of Happiiness. LC 80-85333. 1981. pap. 4.95 (ISBN 0-89081-284-5). Harvest Hse.
Mitchelson, Marvin. Living Together. 1981. 10.95 (ISBN 0-671-24981-9). S&S.
Nouwen, Henri J. M. Intimacy. LC 80-8906. 160p. 1981. pap. 3.95 (ISBN 0-06-066323-5, HarpR). Har-Row.
Ogilvie, Lloyd J. The Beauty of Caring. LC 80-80464 1981. pap. 4.95 (ISBN 0-89081-244-6). Harvest Hse.
--The Beauty of Sharing. LC 80-8880. (Orig.). 1981. pap. 4.95 (ISBN 0-89081-246-2). Harvest Hse.
Orthner, Dennis K. Intimate Relationships: An Introduction to Marriage & the Family. LC 80-21527. (Sociology Ser.). (Illus.). 496p. 1981. text ed. 16.95 (ISBN 0-201-05519-8). A-W.
Pfeiffer, J. William & Jones, John E., eds. A Handbook of Structured Experiences for Human Relations Training, Vol. VIII. LC 73-92840. (Ser. in Human Relations Training). 154p. (Orig.). 1981. pap. 9.50 (ISBN 0-88390-048-3). Univ Assocs.
Sarraute, Nathalie. Between Life & Death. Jolas, Maria, tr. from Fr. 1980. pap. 11.95 (ISBN 0-7145-0122-0); pap. 4.95 (ISBN 0-7145-0123-9). Riverrun NY.
Schickel, Richard. Singled Out. LC 80-54080. 128p. 1981. 9.95 (ISBN 0-670-64710-1). Viking Pr.
Stephens, Ken. Study Guide for Discipleship Evangelism. 1981. pap. 2.50 (ISBN 0-89081-286-1). Harvest Hse.
Taylor, Anita & Taylor, Robert. Couples: The Art of Staying Together. rev. ed. 1980. 4.95 (ISBN 0-87491-403-5). Acropolis.
Timmons, Tim. Loneliness Is Not a Disease. LC 80-83845. 1981. pap. 4.95 (ISBN 0-89081-264-0). Harvest Hse.
Weber, Eric. How to Pick up Girls. 1981. 4.95 (ISBN 0-914094-00-9). Green Hill.
Worchel, S. & Goethals, G. Adjustment & Human Relations. 592p. 1981. text ed. 16.95 (ISBN 0-394-32226-6); wkbk. 6.95 (ISBN 0-394-32737-3). Knopf.

INTERPRETATION
see Hermeneutics

INTERPRETATION, BIBLICAL
see Bible–Criticism, Interpretation, etc.

INTERPRETATION, PHOTOGRAPHIC
see Photographic Interpretation

INTERPRETING AND TRANSLATING
see Translating and Interpreting

INTERPRETIVE DANCING
see Modern Dance

INTERSEXUALITY
see Hermaphroditism

INTERSTATE COMMERCE
see also Restraint of Trade; Trade Regulation
Kitch, Edmund W. Regulation, Federalism, and Interstate Commerce. Tarlock, A. Dan, ed. LC 80-23166. 176p. 1981. lib. bdg. 20.00 (ISBN 0-89946-065-8). Oelgeschlager.

INTERURBAN RAILROADS
see Street-Railroads

INTESTINAL OBSTRUCTIONS
see Intestines–Obstructions

INTESTINES
Bottone, Edward J., ed. Yersinia Enterocolitica. 240p. 1981. 69.95 (ISBN 0-8493-5545-1). CRC Pr.

INTESTINES–DISEASES
see Constipation; Digestive Organs–Diseases
Breckman, Brigid. Stoma Care. 230p. 1980. 40.00x (Pub. by Beaconsfield England). State Mutual Bk.

INTESTINES–OBSTRUCTIONS
Morson, B. C. Histological Typing of Intestinal Tumours. LC 70-101520. (International Histological Classification of Tumours (World Health Organization) Ser.). (Illus.). 69p. 1976. text ed. 53.00 (ISBN 92-4-176015-X); text & slides 142.00. Am Soc Clinical.

INTOXICANTS
see Alcohol; Alcoholic Beverages; Liquors

INTOXICATION
see Alcoholism; Liquor Problem; Narcotic Habit; Temperance

INTRAMURAL SPORTS
Coulbourn, Tyler. Intramural Director's Guide to Program Evaluation. 104p. (Orig.). 1981. pap. price not set (ISBN 0-918438-67-5). Leisure Pr.

INTRAOCULAR PRESSURE, HIGH
see Glaucoma

INTRAUTERINE CONTRACEPTIVES
see also Birth Control; Contraception
Kolbe, Helen K. Intrauterine Devices Abstracts: A Guide to the Literature, 1976-1979. (Population Information Library Ser.: Vol. 1). 575p. 1980. 75.00 (ISBN 0-306-65191-2, IFI). Plenum Pub.

INTROSPECTION (THEORY OF KNOWLEDGE)
see Self-Knowledge, Theory of

INVALID COOKERY
see Cookery for the Sick

INVALIDS–RECREATION
see Handicapped–Recreation

INVARIANTS
Grace, John A. & Young, Alfred. The Algebra of Invariants. LC 65-11860. 1965. 13.95. Chelsea Pub.

INVASION OF PRIVACY
see Privacy, Right of

INVENTIONS
see also Creation (Literary, Artistic, etc.); Inventors; Patents; Research, Industrial; Technological Innovations; Technology Transfer
Brown, Mike. The New Nineteen Eighty Suppressed Inventions & How They Work. 2nd ed. 106p. 1974. pap. 11.95. Madison Pub.
Cohen, Randy & Anderson, Alexandra. Why Didn't I Think of That. (Illus.). 1980. pap. 5.95 (ISBN 0-449-90037-1, Columbine). Fawcett.
Cook, Charles L. Inventor's Guide in a Series of Four Parts: How to Protect, Search, Compile Facts & Sell Your Invention. (Illus.). 1979. 11.95 (ISBN 0-9604670-0-9). C L Cook.
Cook, Chester L. Inventor's Guide in a Series of Four Parts: How to Protect, Search, Compile Facts & Sell Your Invention. rev. ed. (Illus.): 52p. 1981. Repr. of 1979 ed. saddle stitch 11.95 (ISBN 0-9604670-1-7). C L Cook.
Goff, Harry. Inventions Wanted. 1981. 5.95 (ISBN 0-914960-24-5). Green Hill.
Shuldner, Herbert. The Popular Science Guide to Ingenious Devices. Michaelman, Herbert, ed. Date not set. 12.95 (ISBN 0-517-54280-3, Michelman Books). Crown.

INVENTIONS–HISTORY
Daumas, Maurice, ed. A History of Technology & Invention Progress Through the Ages, Vol. 1: The Origins of Technological Civilization to 1450. 520p. 1980. 40.00x (ISBN 0-7195-3730-4, Pub. by Murray Pubs England). State Mutual Bk.
--A History of Technology & Invention Progress Through the Ages, Vol. 3: The Expansion of Mechanization 1725-1860. 700p. 1980. 40.00x (ISBN 0-7195-3732-0, Pub. by Murray Pubs England). State Mutual Bk.
--A History of Technology & Invention Through the Ages, Vol. 2: The First Stages of Mechanization 1450-1725. 694p. 1980. 40.00x (ISBN 0-7195-3731-2, Pub. by Murray Pubs England). State Mutual Bk.

INVENTIONS–JUVENILE LITERATURE
Klein, Aaron E. & Klein, Cynthia L. The Better Mousetrap: A Miscellany of Gadgets, Labor-Saving Devices, & Inventions That Intrigue. (Illus.). 192p. (gr. 6 up). 1981. 10.95 (ISBN 0-8253-0030-4). Beaufort Bks NY.
Wulffson, Don L. The Invention of Ordinary Things. LC 80-17498. (Illus.). 96p. (gr. 3 up). 1981. 6.95 (ISBN 0-688-41978-X); PLB 6.67 (ISBN 0-688-51978-4). Morrow.

INVENTORS
see also Engineers
Faussig, F. W. Psychology of Inventors & Money-Makers. (Illus.). 103p. 1981. 43.25 (ISBN 0-89920-020-6). Am Inst Psych.

INVENTORY CONTROL
see also Materials Management
Atkinson, Chuck. Inventory Management for Small Computers. 140p. 1981. pap. 16.95 (ISBN 0-918398-48-7). Dilithium Pr.
Thomas, Adin B. Stock Control in Manufacturing Industries. 2nd ed. 240p. 1980. text ed. 29.50 (ISBN 0-566-02140-4, Pub. by Gower Pub Co England). Renouf.

INVENTORY MANAGEMENT
see Inventory Control

INVERTEBRATES
see also Arthropoda; Coelenterata; Crustacea; Insects; Mollusks; Myriapoda; Protozoa; Worms
Autrum, H., ed. Comparative Physiology & Evolution of Vision in Invertebrates B: Invertebrate Visual Centers & Behavior I. (Handbook of Sensory Physiology: Vol. VII, Pt. 6B). (Illus.). 650p. 1980. 159.30 (ISBN 0-387-08703-6). Springer-Verlag.
Blackman, Rodger. Aphids. (Invertebrate Types Ser.). (Illus.). 176p. 1981. pap. 12.00 (ISBN 0-08-025943-X). Pergamon.
Clyne, Densey. The Garden Jungle. 184p. 1980. 27.95x (ISBN 0-00-216411-6, Pub. by W Collins Australia). Intl Schol Bk Serv.
Davidson, Elizabeth W., ed. Pathogenesis of Invertebrate Microbial Diseases. 500p. 1981. text ed. 40.00 (ISBN 0-86598-014-4). Allanheld.
Gosner, K. L. Guide to Identification of Marine & Estuarine Invertebates: From Cape Hatteras to the Bay of Fundy. 693p. 1971. pap. 22.50 (ISBN 0-471-31901-5). Wiley.

INVESTIGATIONS
see also Criminal Investigation; Governmental Investigations
Grau, Joseph J. Criminal & Civil Investigation Handbook. (Illus.). 1088p. 1982. 39.50 (ISBN 0-07-024130-9). McGraw.
Mouzakis. Investigative Guidelines & Procedures, No. 1. 1981. text ed. 43.95 (ISBN 0-409-95016-5). Butterworth.

INVESTIGATIONS, GOVERNMENTAL
see Governmental Investigations

INVESTMENT AND SAVING
see Saving and Investment

INVESTMENT IN REAL ESTATE
see Real Estate Investment

INVESTMENTS
see also Bonds; Capital Investments; Loans; Real Estate Investment; Saving and Thrift; Securities; Stock-Exchange; Stocks
Brennan, Mary E. & Heib, Elizabeth A., eds. Investment Institute Hollywood, Florida, April 27 to 30, 1980: Proceedings. 137p. 1980. pap. 10.00 (ISBN 0-89154-134-9). Intl Found Employ.
Casey, Douglas R. International Investing. 1981. pap. 9.95. Everest Hse.
Coleman, David. For the Long Term Investor. 12.95 (ISBN 0-930726-05-7). Green Hill.
Croom, George E., Jr. & Van Der Wal, John. Now You Can Profit from Inflation. 264p. 1981. 14.95 (ISBN 0-442-25397-4). Van Nos Reinhold.
Fabozzi, Frank J. & Zarb, Frank G. The Handbook of Financial Markets: Securities, Options and Futures. 920p. 1981. 37.50 (ISBN 0-87094-216-6). Dow Jones-Irwin.
Geczi, Mike. Futures: The Anti-Inflation Investment. 1980. pap. 2.95 (ISBN 0-686-69239-X, 75713, Discus). Avon.
Gorove, Stephen. Legal Aspects of International Investment. (L. Q. C. Lamar Society of International Law, University of Mississippi Law Center, Monograph: No. 1). viii, 79p. (Orig.). 1977. pap. text ed. 10.00x (ISBN 0-8377-0607-6). Rothman.
Hefferlin, Jonathon. Making Inflation Pay: Jonathon's Guide to Financial Success in the 1980's. 224p. 1981. 10.95 (ISBN 0-936602-09-0). Harbor Pub CA.
Hicks, Tyler G. Sixty Day Fully Financed Fortune. 2nd ed. 150p. 1981. pap. 29.50 (ISBN 0-914306-54-5). Intl Wealth.
Huang, Stanley. Investment Analysis & Management. (Illus.). 500p. 1981. text ed. 19.95 (ISBN 0-87626-453-4). Winthrop.
Kaufman, S. L. Investors Legal Guide. 2nd ed. 1979. 5.95 (ISBN 0-379-11126-8). Oceana.
Levitt, Arthur, Jr. How to Make Your Money Make Money. LC 80-70617. 220p. 1981. 11.95 (ISBN 0-87094-236-0). Dow Jones-Irwin.
Love & Brealy. Modern Development in Invest. Mngt. 2nd ed. 1978. pap. 15.95 (ISBN 0-03-040716-8). Dryden Pr.
McLendon, Gordon. Get Really Rich in the Coming Super Metals Boom. 1981. pap. 4.95 (ISBN 0-671-43202-8). PB.
Merton, Henry. Your Gold & Silver. (Illus.). 96p. 1981. 4.95 (ISBN 0-02-077410-9, Collier). Macmillan.
Nagan, Peter. Fail Safe Investing: How to Make Money with Less Than Ten Thousand Dollars...Without Losing Sleep. 192p. 1981. 9.95 (ISBN 0-399-12616-3). Putnam.
Pratt, Shannon. Valuing a Business: The Analysis & Appraisal of Closely Held Companies. 500p. 1981. 42.50 (ISBN 0-87094-205-0). Dow Jones-Irwin.
Roalman, A. R. Investor Relations That Work. 148p. 1981. 34.95 (ISBN 0-8144-5620-0). Am Mgmt.
Schultz, Harry. Bear Market Investment Strategies. LC 80-70618. 235p. 1981. 13.95 (ISBN 0-87094-224-7). Dow Jones-Irwin.
Sharpe, W. Investments. 2nd ed. 1981. 19.95 (ISBN 0-13-504613-0). P-H.
Silver, A. David. The Radical New Road to Wealth. rev. ed. 1981. pap. 15.00 (ISBN 0-914306-53-7). Intl Wealth.
Smith, Milton. Money Today, More Tomorrow. 320p. 1981. 14.95 (ISBN 0-87626-593-X); pap. text ed. 9.95 (ISBN 0-87626-592-1). Winthrop.
Tobias, Andrew. The Only Investment Guide You'll Ever Need. 200p. 1981. pap. 2.75 (ISBN 0-553-14481-2). Bantam.
Trester, Kenneth R. The Complete Option Player. (Illus.). 316p. 1977. 20.00 (ISBN 0-9604914-0-6). Investrek.
Tuccille, Jerome. Dynamic Investing: The System for Automatic Profits -- No Matter Which Way the Market Goes. 1981. pap. 9.95 (H398). NAL.
VanCaspel, Venita. Energizing Your Investments. 1980. pap. 1.50 (ISBN 0-8359-1678-2). Reston.
Wyckoff, Richard D. The Fundamental Rules of Successful Investing. (Illus.). 121p. 1981. 57.85 (ISBN 0-918968-85-2). Inst Econ Finan.

INVESTMENTS, FOREIGN
see also Technical Assistance
Casey, Douglas. The International Man. 19.95 (ISBN 0-932496-01-6). Green Hill.
Montavon, Remy, et al. The Role of Multinational Companies in Latin America: A Case Study in Mexico. 124p. 1980. 27.50 (ISBN 0-03-057973-2). Praeger.
Robinson, Richard D., et al. Foreign Investment in the Third World: A Comparative Study of Selected Developing Country Investment Promotion Programs. 1980. 10.00 (6005). Chamber Comm US.
Singer, Stuart R. & Weiss, Stanley. Foreign Investment in the United States: 1980 Course Handbook. LC 79-92658. 617p. 1980. pap. text ed. 25.00 (ISBN 0-686-68824-4, B4-6531). PLI.
Zupnick, Elliot. Foreign Investment in the U. S. Costs & Benefits. LC 80-66684. (Headline Ser.: No. 249). (Illus.). 80p. (Orig.). 1980. pap. 2.00 (ISBN 0-87124-061-0). Foreign Policy.

INVISIBLE WORLD
see Spirits

IODIDES
Biological Separations in Iodinated Density-Gradient Media. 205p. 12.00 (ISBN 0-904147-02-9). Info Retrieval.

IONS
see also Anions; Cations; Electrolysis; Electrons; Metal Ions; Plasma (Ionized Gases); Thermionic Emission
Dobler, Max. Ionophores & Their Structure. 350p. 1981. 35.00 (ISBN 0-471-05270-1, Pub. by Wiley-Interscience). Wiley.
Leffert, H. L., ed. Growth Regulation by Ion Fluxes. LC 80-13986. (N.Y. Academy of Sciences Annals: Vol. 339). 340p. 60.00x (ISBN 0-89766-049-8). NY Acad Sci.
Luebbers, D. W., ed. Progress in Enzyme & Ion-Selective Electrodes. (Illus.). 240p. 1981. pap. 34.30 (ISBN 0-387-10499-2). Springer-Verlag.
Mullins, L. J. Ion Transport in Heart. 125p. 1981. 15.00 (ISBN 0-89004-645-X). Raven.
Papovych, Orest. Tetraphenylborates. (IUPAC Solubility Data Ser.: Vol. 18). 260p. 1981. 100.00 (ISBN 0-08-023928-5). Pergamon.

IOWA–ANTIQUITIES
Alex, Lynn M. Exploring Iowa's Past: A Guide to Prehistoric Archaeology. LC 80-21391. (Illus.). 180p. 1980. pap. 7.95 (ISBN 0-87745-108-7). U of Iowa Pr.

IOWA–BIBLIOGRAPHY
Vexler, R. I. Iowa Chronology & Factbook, Vol. 15. 1978. 8.50 (ISBN 0-379-16140-0). Oceana.

IOWA–HISTORY
Kirkpatrick, Inez E. Tavern Days in the Hawkeye State. (Illus.). 370p. (Orig.). (gr. 7 up). Date not set. pap. price not set (ISBN 0-916170-15-2). J B Pubs.

Sopp, LaVerne. Personal Name Index to the Eighteen Fifty-Six City Directories of Iowa. (Genealogy & Local History Ser.: Vol. 13). 400p. 1980. 30.00 (ISBN 0-8103-1486-X). Gale.
Vexler, R. I. Iowa Chronology & Factbook, Vol. 15. 1978. 8.50 (ISBN 0-379-16140-0). Oceana.

IOWA–POLITICS AND GOVERNMENT
Larew, James C. A Party Reborn: The Democrats of Iowa, 1950-1974. LC 80-51855. (Illus.). 216p. 1980. 12.00x (ISBN 0-89033-002-6); pap. 6.00. State Hist Iowa.

IRAN–DESCRIPTION AND TRAVEL
Helms, Cynthia. An Ambassador's Wife in Iran. LC 80-25090. (Illus.). 284p. 1981. 9.95 (ISBN 0-396-07881-8). Dodd.

IRAN–ECONOMIC CONDITIONS
Mahdi, Ali-Akbar. A Selected Bibliography on Political Economy of Iran. (Public Administration Ser.: Bibliography P-598). 104p. 1980. pap. 15.25. Vance Biblios.
Mossavar-Rahmane, Bijan. Energy Policy in Iran: Domestic Choices & International Implications. LC 80-27995. (PPS on Science & Technnology Ser.). (Illus.). 160p. 1981. 15.00 (ISBN 0-08-026293-7). Pergamon.

IRAN–HISTORY
Bosworth, C. E. The Medieval History of Iran, Afghanistan & Central Asia. 374p. 1980. 75.00x (ISBN 0-86078-000-7, Pub. by Variorum England). State Mutual Bk.
Cambridge History of Iran. Incl. Vol. 1. The Land of Iran. Fisher, W. B., ed. 1968. 62.00 (ISBN 0-521-06935-1); Vol. 4. Frye, R. N., ed. 1975. 62.00 (ISBN 0-521-20093-8); Vol. 5. The Saljug & Mongol Periods. Boyle, J. A., ed. LC 67-12845. 1968. 62.00 (ISBN 0-521-06936-X). LC 67-12845. (Illus.). Cambridge U Pr.
Frye, Richard N. Islamic Iran & Central Asia (7th-12th Centuries) 380p. 1980. 75.00x (ISBN 0-86078-044-9, Pub. by Variorum England). State Mutual Bk.
Lambton, A. K. Theory & Practice in Medieval Persian Government. 332p. 1980. 75.00x (ISBN 0-86078-067-8, Pub. by Variorum England). State Mutual Bk.
Minorsky, Vladimir. The Turks, Iran & the Caucasus in the Middle Ages. 368p. 1980. 69.00x (ISBN 0-86078-028-7, Pub. by Variorum England). State Mutual Bk.
Ross, E. Denison, Jr. The Persians. 142p. 1980. Repr. lib. bdg. 30.00 (ISBN 0-89987-713-3). Darby Bks.
Sterling, Martie & Sterling, Robin. Last Flight from Iran. 272p. (Orig.). 1981. pap. 2.50 (ISBN 0-553-20005-4). Bantam.

IRAN–HISTORY–TO 640
Cambridge History of Iran. Incl. Vol. 1. The Land of Iran. Fisher, W. B., ed. 1968. 62.00 (ISBN 0-521-06935-1); Vol. 4. Frye, R. N., ed. 1975. 62.00 (ISBN 0-521-20093-8); Vol. 5. The Saljug & Mongol Periods. Boyle, J. A., ed. LC 67-12845. 1968. 62.00 (ISBN 0-521-06936-X). LC 67-12845. (Illus.). Cambridge U Pr.

IRAN–POLITICS AND GOVERNMENT
Albert, David H. Tell the American People: Perspectives on the Iranian Revolution. rev. ed. LC 80-83577. 1980. 14.95 (ISBN 0-86571-001-5); pap. 4.95 (ISBN 0-86571-003-1). Movement New Soc.
Albert, David H., ed. Tell the American People: Perspectives on the Iranian Revolution. LC 80-82242. 1980. pap. text ed. 3.80 (ISBN 0-86571-000-7). Movement New Soc.
Keddie, Nikki R. Iran: Religion, Politics & Society--Collected Essays. 243p. 1980. pap. 9.95x (ISBN 0-7146-4031-X, F Cass Co). Biblio Dist.
Lambton, A. K. Theory & Practice in Medieval Persian Government. 332p. 1980. 75.00x (ISBN 0-86078-067-8, Pub. by Variorum England). State Mutual Bk.
Mahdi, Ali-Akbar. A Selected Bibliography on Political Economy of Iran. (Public Administration Ser.: Bibliography P-598). 104p. 1980. pap. 15.25. Vance Biblios.
Singh, K. R. Iran: Quest for Security. 421p. 1980. text ed. 37.50x (ISBN 0-7069-1259-4, Pub. by Vikas India). Advent Bk.

IRAN–SOCIAL CONDITIONS
Kazemi, Farhad. Poverty & Revolution in Iran: The Migrant Poor, Urban Marginality & Politics. 180p. 1981. text ed. 17.50x (ISBN 0-8147-4576-8). NYU Pr.

IRAN–SOCIAL LIFE AND CUSTOMS
Abbot, John. The Iranians: How They Live & Work. 168p. 1978. text ed. 8.95 (ISBN 0-03-042496-8, HoltC). HR&W.
Sarkissian, Henry A. Tales of One Thousand & One Iranian Days. 1981. 8.95 (ISBN 0-533-04476-6). Vantage.

IRANIAN CIVILIZATION
see Civilization, Iranian

IRANIAN LANGUAGES
see Kurdish Language

IRAQ–ANTIQUITIES
Adams, Robert M. Heartland of Cities: Surveys of Ancient Settlement & Land Use on the Central Floodplain of the Euphrates. LC 80-13995. (Illus.). 384p. 1981. lib. bdg. 35.00x (ISBN 0-226-00544-5). U of Chicago Pr.
Heyerdahl, Thor. The Tigris Expedition: In Search of Our Beginnings. LC 80-1862. 360p. 1981. 17.95 (ISBN 0-385-17357-1). Doubleday.
Perkins, Ann L. The Comparative Archeology of Early Mesopotamia. LC 49-10748. (Studies in Ancient Oriental Civilization: No. 25). (Illus.). xx, 201p. (Orig.). 1977. pap. text ed. 14.00x (ISBN 0-226-62396-3). Oriental Inst.

IRAQ–POLITICS AND GOVERNMENT
Edmonds, Cecil J. Kurds, Turks, & Arabs: Politics, Travel, & Research in North-Eastern Iraq, 1919-1925. LC 80-1930. 1981. Repr. of 1957 ed. 49.50 (ISBN 0-404-18960-1). AMS Pr.
Khadduri, Majid. Independent Iraq, Nineteen Thirty-Two to Nineteen Fifty-Eight: A Study in Iraqi Politics. 2nd ed. LC 80-1919. 1981. Repr. of 1960 ed. 41.50 (ISBN 0-404-18972-5). AMS Pr.
--Republican Iraq: A Study in Iraqi Politics Since the Revolution of 1958. LC 80-1923. 1981. Repr. of 1969 ed. 37.00 (ISBN 0-404-18973-3). AMS Pr.

IRELAND–BIOGRAPHY
Barrington, George. The Life, Times, & Adventures of George Barrington, the Celebrated Thief & Pickpocket. Bd. with The Memoirs of George Barrington, Containing Every Emarkable Circumstance, from His Birth to the Present Time. LC 80-2470. 1981. 29.50 (ISBN 0-404-19102-9). AMS Pr.
Buckland, Patrick. James Craig. (Gill's Irish Lives Ser.). 143p. 1980. 20.00 (ISBN 0-7171-1078-8, Pub. by Gill & Macmillan Ireland); pap. 6.50 (ISBN 0-7171-0984-4). Irish Bk Ctr.

IRELAND–CIVILIZATION
Scherman, Katharine. The Flowering of Ireland: Saints, Scholars & Kings. (Illus.). 320p. 1981. 15.95 (ISBN 0-316-77284-4). Little.

IRELAND–DESCRIPTION AND TRAVEL
Atlas of Ireland. (Illus.). 112p. 1980. lib. bdg. 99.50. St Martin.
Reilly, Cyril & Reilly, Renee. I Am of Ireland. (Illus.). 60p. (Orig.). 1981. pap. 6.95 (ISBN 0-03-059058-2). Winston Pr.

IRELAND–DESCRIPTION AND TRAVEL–GUIDEBOOKS
Automobile Association. AA Ireland: Where to Go, What to Do. (Illus.). 204p. 1981. pap. write for info. (ISBN 0-86145-035-3, Pub. by Auto Assn-British Tourist Authority England). Merrimack Bk Serv.
Eagle, Dorothy & Carnell, Hilary, eds. The Oxford Illustrated Literary Guide to Great Britain & Ireland. (Illus.). 352p. 1981. 19.95 (ISBN 0-19-869125-4). Oxford U Pr.
Ronay, Egon. Egon Ronay's Lucasa Guide 1981: To Hotels, Resturants, Inns in Great Britain & Ireland & Guide to 740 Furnished Apartments in London. rev. ed. LC 74-644899. (Illus.). 830p. 1981. pap. 12.95 (ISBN 0-03-058958-4). HR&W.

IRELAND–ECONOMIC CONDITIONS
Smith, Elizabeth. The Irish Journals of Elizabeth Smith Eighteen Forty to Eighteen Fifty. Thomson, David & McGusty, Moyra, eds. (Illus.). 352p. 1980. 29.00x (ISBN 0-19-822471-0). Oxford U Pr.

IRELAND–FOREIGN RELATIONS
Fuller, R. Buckminster. Critical Path. 448p. 1981. 15.95 (ISBN 0-312-17488-8). St Martin.
Whitlock, Dorothy, et al, eds. Ireland in Early Medieval Europe. LC 80-40325. (Studies in Memory of Kathleen Hughes). (Illus.). 400p. Date not set. price not set (ISBN 0-521-23547-2). Cambridge U Pr.

IRELAND–HISTORY
DeBreffny. Heritage of Ireland. Date not set. 12.98 (ISBN 0-517-53809-1). Bonanza.
Drudy, P. J. Irish Studies, Vol. 1. LC 80-40084. 192p. Date not set. 27.50 (ISBN 0-521-23336-4). Cambridge U Pr.
Hickey, Denis & Doherty, James. Dictionary of Irish History Since 1800. 615p. 1980. 38.50x (ISBN 0-389-20160-X). B&N.
Hinton, Edward M. Ireland Through Tudor Eyes. 111p. 1980. Repr. of 1935 ed. lib. bdg. 22.50 (ISBN 0-89987-362-6). Darby Bks.
Landon, Michael L. Erin & Britannia: The Historical Backround to a Modern Tragedy. LC 79-27005. (Illus.). 288p. 1981. text ed. 18.95 (ISBN 0-88229-643-4); pap. text ed. 8.95 (ISBN 0-88229-766-X). Nelson-Hall.
Lyons, F. S. & Hawkins, R. A., eds. Ireland Under the Union: Varieties of Tension. (Illus.). 348p. 1980. 42.00x (ISBN 0-19-822469-9). Oxford U Pr.
McCormack, W. J. Sheridan le Fanu & Victorian Ireland. (Illus.). 334p. 1980. text ed. 36.00x (ISBN 0-19-812629-8). Oxford U Pr.
O'Ballance, Edgar. Terror in Ireland: The Heritage of Hate. (Illus.). 280p. 1981. 14.95 (ISBN 0-89141-100-3). Presidio Pr.
Whitlock, Dorothy, et al, eds. Ireland in Early Medieval Europe. LC 80-40325. (Studies in Memory of Kathleen Hughes). (Illus.). 400p. Date not set. price not set (ISBN 0-521-23547-2). Cambridge U Pr.

IRELAND–POLITICS AND GOVERNMENT
Beyond Orange & Green: The Political Eonomy of the Northern Ireland Crisis. 176p. 1978. 12.95 (ISBN 0-905762-16-9, Pub. by Zed Pr); pap. 6.95 (ISBN 0-905762-17-7). Lawrence Hill.
Fuller, R. Buckminster. Critical Path. 448p. 1981. 15.95 (ISBN 0-312-17488-8). St Martin.
Heslinga, M. R. The Irish Border As a Cultural Divide: A Contribution of the Study of Regionalism in the British Isles. 1980. pap. text ed. 18.75x (ISBN 90-232-0864-1). Humanities.
Lyons, F. S. & Hawkins, R. A., eds. Ireland Under the Union: Varieties of Tension. (Illus.). 348p. 1980. 42.00x (ISBN 0-19-822469-9). Oxford U Pr.
O'Ballance, Edgar. Terror in Ireland: The Heritage of Hate. (Illus.). 280p. 1981. 14.95 (ISBN 0-89141-100-3). Presidio Pr.
O'Dowd, Liam, et al. Northern Ireland: Between Civil Rights & Civil War. 224p. 1980. text ed. 26.00x (ISBN 0-906336-18-X); pap. text ed. 19.50x (ISBN 0-906336-19-8). Humanities.
Pearse, P. H. The Letters of P. H. Pearse. O'Buachalla, Seamas, ed. 528p. 1980. text ed. 31.25x (ISBN 0-391-01678-4). Humanities.
Smith, Elizabeth. The Irish Journals of Elizabeth Smith Eighteen Forty to Eighteen Fifty. Thomson, David & McGusty, Moyra, eds. (Illus.). 352p. 1980. 29.00x (ISBN 0-19-822471-0). Oxford U Pr.

IRELAND–SOCIAL CONDITIONS
Fuller, R. Buckminster. Critical Path. 448p. 1981. 15.95 (ISBN 0-312-17488-8). St Martin.
Heslinga, M. R. The Irish Border As a Cultural Divide: A Contribution of the Study of Regionalism in the British Isles. 1980. pap. text ed. 18.75x (ISBN 90-232-0864-1). Humanities.

IRELAND–SOCIAL LIFE AND CUSTOMS
Reilly, Cyril & Reilly, Renee. I Am of Ireland. (Illus.). 60p. (Orig.). 1981. pap. 6.95 (ISBN 0-03-059058-2). Winston Pr.

IRENICS
see Christian Union

IRISH ARCHITECTURE
see Architecture–Ireland

IRISH ART
see Art, Irish

IRISH AUTHORS
see Authors, Irish

IRISH DRAMA (ENGLISH)
Feeney, William, ed. Lost Plays of the Irish Renaissance, Vol. 2. 10.00 (ISBN 0-912262-70-2). Proscenium.

IRISH FICTION (ENGLISH)–HISTORY AND CRITICISM
Wolff, Robert L. William Carleton, Irish Peasant Novelist: A Preface to His Fiction. LC 79-4399. 200p. 1980. lib. bdg. 18.00 (ISBN 0-8240-3527-5). Garland Pub.

IRISH LITERATURE–HISTORY AND CRITICISM
Hall, Wayne E. Shadowy Heroes: Irish Literature of the 1890's. LC 80-21383. (Irish Studies). (Illus.). 1980. 20.00x (ISBN 0-8156-2231-7). Syracuse U Pr.
Harper. Critical Edition of Yeats' A Vision. 1980. text ed. 42.50x (ISBN 0-333-21299-1). Humanities.
Moore, George. Hail & Farewell. Cave, Richard, ed. (Illus.). 774p. 1980. text ed. 35.00x (ISBN 0-7705-1467-7). Humanities.
Schleifer, Ronald, ed. The Genres of the Irish Literary Revival. 190p. 1980. 16.95 (ISBN 0-937664-53-7). Pilgrim Bks OK.

IRISH LITERATURE (ENGLISH)
Lyons, F. S. & Hawkins, R. A., eds. Ireland Under the Union: Varieties of Tension. (Illus.). 348p. 1980. 42.00x (ISBN 0-19-822469-9). Oxford U Pr.

IRISH LITERATURE (ENGLISH)–HISTORY AND CRITICISM
De Almeida, Hermione. Byron & Joyce Through Homer: Don Juan & Ulysses. 256p 1981. 20.00x (ISBN 0-231-05092-5). Columbia U Pr.
O'Rourke, Brian. The Conscience of the Race: Sex & Religion in Irish & French Novels 1941-1973. 72p. 1981. 10.00x (ISBN 0-906127-22-X, Pub. by Irish Academic Pr Ireland). Biblio Dist.

IRISH POETRY–HISTORY AND CRITICISM
Welch, Robert. Irish Poetry from Mocre to Yeats. 248p. 1980. text ed. 23.25x (ISBN 0-901072-93-1). Humanities.

IRISH POETRY (ENGLISH) (COLLECTIONS)
Hoagland, Kathleen, ed. One Thousand Years of Irish Poetry. 832p. 1981. 12.95 (ISBN 0-517-34295-2). Devin.

IRISH TALES
see Tales, Irish

IRON ALLOYS
Touloukian, Y. S. & Ho, C. Y. Properties of Selected Ferrous Alloying Elements, Vol. III. (M-H-CINDAS Data Series on Material Properties). 288p. 1981. text ed. 33.50 (ISBN 0-07-065034-9). McGraw.

IRON AND STEEL SHIPS
see Ships, Iron and Steel

IRON IN THE BODY
see also Iron Metabolism
Cook, James D. Iron. (Methods in Hematology Ser.: Vol. 1). (Illus.). 224p. 1980. 32.00 (ISBN 0-443-08118-2). Churchill.

IRON INDUSTRY AND TRADE–GREAT BRITAIN
Roepke, Howard G. Movememts of the British Iron & Steel Industry, 1720 to 1951, Vol. 36. LC 80-23128. (Illinois Studies in the Social Sciences). (Illus.). vii, 198p. 1981. Repr. of 1956 ed. lib. bdg. 25.00x (ISBN 0-8371-9096-7, ROMB). Greenwood.

IRON METABOLISM
Cook, James D. Iron. (Methods in Hematology Ser.: Vol. 1). (Illus.). 224p. 1980. 32.00 (ISBN 0-443-08118-2). Churchill.

IRON ORES
Brown, T. E., et al. Field Excursions, East Texas: Clay, Glauconite, Ironstone Deposits. (Illus.). 48p. 1969. 1.00 (GB 9). Bur Econ Geology.

IRONWORK
see Architectural Ironwork; Blacksmithing; Welding

IRONY IN LITERATURE
O'Hara, Daniel T. Tragic Knowledge: Yeat's Autobiography & Hermeneutics. LC 80-26825. 224p. 1981. 20.00x (ISBN 0-231-05204-9). Columbia U Pr.
Wilde, Alan. Horizons of Assent: Modernism, Postmodernism, & the Ironic Imagination. LC 80-22576. 224p. 1981. text ed. 15.00x (ISBN 0-8018-2449-4). Johns Hopkins.

IROQUOIS INDIANS
see Indians of North America–Eastern States

IRRADIATION
see also Radioactivation Analysis
Kreuzer, Rudolf, ed. Freezing & Irradiation of Fish. (Illus.). 548p. 41.25 (ISBN 0-85238-008-9, FN). Unipub.

IRREVERSIBLE COMA
see Brain Death

IRRIGATION
see also Arid Regions; Dams; Reservoirs; Windmills
Carruthers, Ian, ed. Social & Economic Perspectives on Irrigation. 100p. 1980. pap. 22.00 (ISBN 0-08-026780-7). Pergamon.
The Contribution of Varietal Tolerance for Problem Soils to Yield Stability in Rice. (IRRI Research Paper Ser.: No. 43). 15p. 1979. pap. 5.00 (R083, IRRI). Unipub.
Denitrification Loss of Fertilizer Nitrogen in Paddy Soils - Its Recognition & Impact. (IRRI Research Paper Ser.: No. 37). 10p. 1979. pap. 5.00 (R077, IRRI). Unipub.
Irrigation Policy & Management in Southeast Asia. 198p. 1978. pap. 16.00 (R009, IRRI). Unipub.
Sole, William C. History of Irrigation in Adams County. 1969. pap. 1.95 (ISBN 0-934858-07-1). Adams County.

IRVING, WASHINGTON, 1783-1859
Bowden, Mary W. Washington Irving. (United States Authors Ser.: No. 397). 1981. lib. bdg. 9.95 (ISBN 0-8057-7314-2). Twayne.
Hedges, William L. Washington Irving: An American Study, 1802-1832. LC 80-23564. (The Goucher College Ser.). xiv, 274p. 1980. Repr. of 1965 ed. lib. bdg. 27.50x (ISBN 0-313-21159-0, HEWI). Greenwood.
Kime, Wayne. Washington Irving Miscellaneous Writings, 1803-1859. (Critical Editions Program). 1981. lib. bdg. 75.00 (ISBN 0-8057-8520-5). Twayne.

ISAIAH, THE PROPHET
Alexander, Joseph A. Commentaries on the Prophecies of Isaiah. 10th ed. 1980. 19.95 (ISBN 0-310-20000-8, 6526). Zondervan.

ISCHEMIA, CEREBRAL
see Cerebral Ischemia

ISCHEMIC HEART DISEASE
see Coronary Heart Disease

ISLAM
see also Civilization, Islamic; Dervishes; Koran; Muslims
also special headings with Islam added in parentheses; subdivision Islam under special topics, e.g. Marriage–Islam; headings beginning with the words Islamic and Muslim
Ahmad, Khurshid, ed. Islam: Its Meaning & Message. 279p. 1980. 17.50 (ISBN 0-86037-002-X, Pub. by Islamic Council of Europe England); pap. 8.95x (ISBN 0-86037-000-3). Intl Schol Bk Serv.
Arberry, Arthur J. Revelation and Reason in Islam. LC 80-1936. 1981. Repr. of 1957 ed. 20.00 (ISBN 0-404-18952-0). AMS Pr.
Brown, Marguerite. Magnificent Muslims. 1981. write for info. (ISBN 0-911026-10-X). New World Press NY.
Carra de Vaux, Bernard. Les Penseurs de l'Islam, 5 vols. LC 80-2197. 1981. Repr. of 1926 ed. Set. 200.00 (ISBN 0-404-18990-3). AMS Pr.
Donaldson, Dwight M. The Shi'ite Religion: A History of Islam in Persia & Irak. LC 80-1933. 45.00 (ISBN 0-404-18959-8). AMS Pr.
Esposito, John L., ed. Islam & Development: Religion and Sociopolitical Change. 1980. 18.00x (ISBN 0-8156-2229-5); pap. 9.95 (ISBN 0-8156-2230-9). Syracuse U Pr.
Gauhar, Altaf, ed. The Challenge of Islam. 393p. 1980. 35.00x (ISBN 0-906041-02-3, Pub. by Islamic Council of Europe England); pap. 14.95x (ISBN 0-906041-03-1). Intl Schol Bk Serv.
Huaain, Ashfaque. The Spirit of Islam: A Summary of the Commentary of Maulana Abul Kalam Azad on A-Fateha, the First Chapter of the Quran. 3rd ed. 95p. 1980. text ed. 12.00 (ISBN 0-8426-1664-0). Verry.
Humayun, Kabir. Science, Democracy, and Islam: And Other Essays. LC 80-2195. 1981. Repr. of 1955 ed. 20.00 (ISBN 0-404-18967-9). AMS Pr.
Kedourie, Elie. Islam in the Modern World. 336p. 1981. 16.95 (ISBN 0-686-69288-8). HR&W.

Le Journeau, Roger. L' Islam Contemporain. LC 80-1922. 1981. Repr. of 1950 ed. write for info. (ISBN 0-404-18975-X). AMS Pr.
Minai, Naila. Women in Islam. LC 80-52405. 320p. 1981. 11.95 (ISBN 0-87223-666-8). Seaview Bks.
O'Leary, De Lacy. Islam at the Cross Roads: A Brief Survey of the Present Position and Problems of the World of Islam. LC 80-1916. 1981. Repr. of 1923 ed. 26.50 (ISBN 0-404-18983-0). AMS Pr.
Peretz, Don, et al. Islam: Legacy of the Past, Challenge of the Future. 1981. 9.95 (ISBN 0-88427-048-3). Green Hill.
Quasem, M. A. Al-Ghazali on Islamic Guidance. 124p. 1980. 9.95x (ISBN 0-89955-208-0, Pub. by M A Quasem Malaysia); pap. 6.95x (ISBN 0-89955-209-9). Intl Schol Bk Serv.

ISLAM–HISTORY
Bosworth, C. E. The Islamic Dynasties. 245p. 1980. pap. 9.00x (ISBN 0-85224-402-9, Pub. by Edinburgh U Pr Scotland). Columbia U Pr.
Esposito, John L., ed. Islam & Development: Religion & Sociopolitical Change. LC 80-25119. (Contemporary Issues in the Middle East Ser.). 292p. 1980. text ed. 22.00x (ISBN 0-8156-2229-5); pap. text ed. 9.95x (ISBN 0-8156-2230-9). Syracuse U Pr.
Frye, Richard N. Islamic Iran & Central Asia (7th-12th Centuries) 380p. 1980. 75.00x (ISBN 0-86078-044-9, Pub. by Variorum England). State Mutual Bk.
Holt, P. M., et al, eds. Cambridge History of Islam. Incl. Vol. 1A. Central Islamic Lands from Pre-Islamic Times to the First World War. 59.00 (ISBN 0-521-21946-9); pap. 19.95 (ISBN 0-521-29135-6); Vol. 1B. Central Islamic Lands Since 1918. 42.00 (ISBN 0-521-21947-7); pap. 14.95 (ISBN 0-521-29136-4); Vol. 2A. The Indian Subcontinent, Southeast Asia, Africa & the Muslim West. 48.00 (ISBN 0-521-21948-5); pap. 18.50 (ISBN 0-521-29137-2); Vol. 2B. Islamic Society & Civilization. 59.00 (ISBN 0-521-21949-3); pap. 21.95 (ISBN 0-521-29138-0). 1977-78. Set. 178.00 (ISBN 0-521-22310-5); Set. pap. 62.00 (ISBN 0-521-08755-4). Cambridge U Pr.
Huaain, Ashfaque. The Spirit of Islam: A Summary of the Commentary of Maulana Abul Kalam Azad on A-Fateha, the First Chapter of the Quran. 3rd ed. 95p. 1980. text ed. 12.00 (ISBN 0-8426-1664-0). Verry.
Kister, M. J. Studies in Jahiliyya & Early Islam. 360p. 1980. 75.00x (ISBN 0-86078-068-6, Pub. by Variorum England). State Mutual Bk.
Lewis, Bernard. Studies in Classical & Ottoman Islam (7th-16th Centuries) 414p. 1980. 68.00x (ISBN 0-902089-97-8, Pub. by Variorum England). State Mutual Bk.
Moore, G. F. History of Religions: Judaism, Christianity, Mohammedanism, Vol. II. (International Theological Library). 568p. 1920. text ed. 13.95x (ISBN 0-567-07203-7). Attic Pr.
Peretz, Don, et al. Islam: Legacy of the Past, Challenge of the Future. 160p. 1981. 9.95 (ISBN 0-88427-048-3, Dist. by Caroline Hse). North River.
Sabini, John. Armies in the Sand: The Struggle for Mecca & Medina. (Illus.). 224p. 1981. 16.95 (ISBN 0-500-01246-6). Thames Hudson.

ISLAM–RELATIONS
Bury, George W. Pan-Islam. LC 80-1938. 1981. Repr. of 1919 ed. 30.00 (ISBN 0-404-18956-3). AMS Pr.
Hassan, Farooq. The Concept of State & Law in Islam. LC 80-69038. 321p. (Orig.). 1981. lib. bdg. 20.75 (ISBN 0-8191-1426-X); pap. text ed. 11.75 (ISBN 0-8191-1427-8). U Pr of Amer.
Procler, Jesse H., ed. Islam & International Relations. LC 80-1914. 1981. Repr. of 1965 ed. 27.50 (ISBN 0-404-18969-5). AMS Pr.

ISLAM–TURKEY
Lewis, Bernard. Studies in Classical & Ottoman Islam (7th-16th Centuries) 414p. 1980. 68.00x (ISBN 0-902089-97-8, Pub. by Variorum England). State Mutual Bk.

ISLAMIC ARCHITECTURE
see Architecture, Islamic

ISLAMIC ART
see Art, Islamic

ISLAMIC CIVILIZATION
see Civilization, Islamic

ISLAMIC COUNTRIES–HISTORY
Holt, P. M., et al, eds. Cambridge History of Islam. Incl. Vol. 1A. Central Islamic Lands from Pre-Islamic Times to the First World War. 59.00 (ISBN 0-521-21946-9); pap. 19.95 (ISBN 0-521-29135-6); Vol. 1B. Central Islamic Lands Since 1918. 42.00 (ISBN 0-521-21947-7); pap. 14.95 (ISBN 0-521-29136-4); Vol. 2A. The Indian Subcontinent, Southeast Asia, Africa & the Muslim West. 48.00 (ISBN 0-521-21948-5); pap. 18.50 (ISBN 0-521-29137-2); Vol. 2B. Islamic Society & Civilization. 59.00 (ISBN 0-521-21949-3); pap. 21.95 (ISBN 0-521-29138-0). 1977-78. Set. 178.00 (ISBN 0-521-22310-5); Set. pap. 62.00 (ISBN 0-521-08755-4). Cambridge U Pr.

ISLAMIC COUNTRIES–POLITICS
Watt, W. M. Islamic Political Thought. 186p. 1980. pap. 6.50x (ISBN 0-85224-403-7, Pub. by Edinburgh U Pr Scotland). Columbia U Pr.

ISLAMIC EMPIRE–HISTORY
Ibn Al-Titaka. Al-Fakhr: On the Systems of Government and the Moslem Dynasties. Whitting, C. E., tr. LC 80-2201. 1981. Repr. of 1947 ed. 35.00 (ISBN 0-404-18968-7). AMS Pr.

ISLAMIC EMPIRE–POLITICS
Ibn Al-Titaka. Al-Fakhr: On the Systems of Government and the Moslem Dynasties. Whitting, C. E., tr. LC 80-2201. 1981. Repr. of 1947 ed. 35.00 (ISBN 0-404-18968-7). AMS Pr.

ISLAMIC LITERATURE–HISTORY AND CRITICISM
DeLamotte, Roy C. Jalaluddin Rumi: Songbird of Sufism. LC 80-5884. 187p. 1980. lib. bdg. 16.75 (ISBN 0-8191-1286-0); pap. text ed. 8.75 (ISBN 0-8191-1287-9). U Pr of Amer.

ISLAMIC PAINTING
see Painting, Islamic

ISLAMIC SOCIOLOGY
see Sociology, Islamic

ISLAMIC THEOLOGY
Cook, M. Early Muslim Dogma. 256p. Date not set. 49.50 (ISBN 0-521-23379-8). Cambridge U Pr.

ISLAMIC WOMEN
see Women, Muslim

ISLANDS OF THE PACIFIC
see also Micronesia
Waldo, Myra. Myra Waldo's Travel Guide to the South Pacific, 1981. (Illus.). 360p. 1981. pap. 8.95 (ISBN 0-02-098920-2, Collier). Macmillan.

ISLE OF WIGHT
Kitchenside, G. M. Isle of Wight Album. 15.95x (ISBN 0-392-07972-0, SpS). Soccer.

ISOENZYMES
Rattazzi, Mario C., et al, eds. Isozymes: Current Topics in Biological & Medical Research, Vol. 4. LC 77-12288. 218p. 1980. 26.00 (ISBN 0-8451-0253-2). A R Liss.
Wolf, P., ed. Tumor Associated Markers: The Importance of Identification in Clinical Medicine. LC 79-87540. (Illus.). 208p. 1979. 25.50 (ISBN 0-89352-065-9). Masson Pub.

ISOPERIMETRICAL PROBLEMS
see Calculus of Variations

ISOTOPIC INDICATORS
see Radioactive Tracers

ISOZYMES
see Isoenzymes

ISRAEL
see also Palestine
Bazak Guide to Israel 1981-1982. LC 66-1422. (Illus.). 500p. (Orig.). 1981. pap. 7.95 (ISBN 0-06-090847-5, CN 847, CN). Har-Row.
Impe, Jack Van & Campbell, Roger F. Israel's Final Holocaust. 1980. pap. 3.95 (ISBN 0-8407-9400-2). Nelson.

ISRAEL–DESCRIPTION AND TRAVEL
Harris, Bill. Israel. (Illus.). 1980. 24.95 (ISBN 0-686-68761-2). Mayflower Bks.

ISRAEL–DESCRIPTION AND TRAVEL–GUIDEBOOKS
Finegan, Jack. Discovering Israel: A Popular Guide to the Holy Land. LC 80-26952. (Illus.). 176p. 1981. pap. 7.95 (ISBN 0-8028-1869-2). Eerdmans.
Vilnay, Zev. The Guide to Israel 1980. 21st ed. LC 66-33490. (Illus.). 662p. 1979. 10.00x (ISBN 0-8002-2713-1). Intl Pubns Serv.

ISRAEL–ECONOMIC CONDITIONS
Davis, Uri. Israel: Utopia Incorporated. 182p. 1977. 10.00 (ISBN 0-905762-12-6, Pub. by Zed Pr); pap. 6.00 (ISBN 0-905762-13-4). Lawrence Hill.
Flink, Salomon J. Israel: Chaos & Challenge: Politics vs. Economics. 265p. 1980. 18.00x (ISBN 965-20-0027-2, Pub. by Turtledove Pr Israel). Intl Schol Bk Serv.

ISRAEL–HISTORY
Bright, John. A History of Israel. 3rd ed. LC 80-22774. Date not set. price not set (ISBN 0-664-21381-2). Westminster.
Knox, D. E. The Making of a New Eastern Question: British Palestine Policy & the Origins of Israel, 1917-1925. 1981. 17.95 (ISBN 0-8132-0555-7). Cath U Pr.
Ramsey, George W. Quest for the Historical Israel. LC 80-82188. 208p. (Orig.). 1981. pap. 12.50 (ISBN 0-8042-0187-0). John Knox.
Smith, James E. Divided We Fall. LC 79-67439. 96p. (Orig.). 1980. pap. 1.95 (ISBN 0-87239-381-X, 40086). Standard Pub.

ISRAEL–POLITICS AND GOVERNMENT
Isaac, Rael J. Party & Politics in Israel: Three Visions of a Jewish State. (Professional Ser.). 256p. 1980. lib. bdg. 19.50 (ISBN 0-582-28196-2). Longman.
Rafael, Gideon. Destination Peace: Three Decades of Israeli Foreign Policy. LC 80-9060. 400p. 1981. 16.95 (ISBN 0-8128-2812-7). Stein & Day.
Sharkansky, Ira. Wither the State? Politics & Public Enterprise in Three Countries. 9.95 (ISBN 0-934540-01-2); pap. 7.95 (ISBN 0-934540-00-4). Chatham Hse Pubs.

ISRAEL–RELIGION
Harrelson, Walter J. From Fertility Cult to Worship. LC 66-14929. (Scholars Press Reprint Ser.: No. 4). pap. 9.00x (ISBN 0-89130-379-0, 00 07 04). Scholars Pr CA.

ISRAEL–SOCIAL LIFE AND CUSTOMS
Rein, Natalie. Daughters of Rachel: Women in Israel. 1980. pap. 4.95 (ISBN 0-14-005731-5). Penguin.

ISRAEL-ARAB BORDER CONFLICTS, 1949-
Schuster, Robert L. Israel, The Middle East & the Moral Conscience of the Western World. (The Major Currents in Contemporary World History). (Illus.). 133p. 1981. 47.85 (ISBN 0-89266-301-4). Am Classical Coll Pr.

ISRAEL-ARAB WAR, 1967–DIPLOMATIC HISTORY
Bradley, C. Paul. The Camp David Peace Process: A Study of Carter Administration Policies (1977-1980) LC 81-50100. (Illus.). viii, 79p. 1981. pap. text ed. 4.50 (ISBN 0-936988-03-7). Tompson & Rutter.

ISRAEL-ARAB WAR, 1973
Kraut, Florence R. From My Israel Journal. LC 80-80528. 56p. (Orig.). 1980. pap. 2.95 (ISBN 0-686-28879-3). Preston St Pr.
Maghroori, Ray & Gorman, Stephen M. The Yom Kippur War: A Case Study in Crisis Decision Making in American Foreign Policy. LC 80-5811. 98p. 1981. lib. bdg. 14.75 (ISBN 0-8191-1373-5); pap. text ed. 6.75 (ISBN 0-8191-1374-3). U Pr of Amer.

ISRAELI NATIONAL CHARACTERISTICS
see National Characteristics, Israeli

ISTANBUL–HISTORY
see also Crusades–Fourth, 1202-1204
Downey, Glanville. Constantinople in the Age of Justinian. LC 60-13473. (The Centers of Civilization Ser.: Vol. 3). (Illus.). 181p. 1981. pap. 3.95 (ISBN 0-8061-1708-7). U of Okla Pr.
Godfrey, John. Twelve Hundred & Four - the Unholy Crusade. (Illus.). 256p. 1980. 28.50 (ISBN 0-19-215834-1). Oxford U Pr.
Wolff, Robert L. Studies in the Latin Empire of Constantinople. 412p. 1980. 60.00x (ISBN 0-902089-99-4, Pub. by Variorum England). State Mutual Bk.

ISTANBUL (PATRIARCHATE)–HISTORY
Downey, Glanville. Constantinople in the Age of Justinian. LC 60-13473. (The Centers of Civilization Ser.: Vol. 3). (Illus.). 181p. 1981. pap. 3.95 (ISBN 0-8061-1708-7). U of Okla Pr.

I.T.A
see Initial Teaching Alphabet

ITALIAN AMERICANS
Caso, Adolph. Lives of the Italian Americans: Fifty Illustrated Biographies. (Illus.). 175p. 1980. 12.50 (ISBN 0-937832-00-6). Dante Univ Bkshlf.

ITALIAN ART
see Art, Italian

ITALIAN AUTHORS
see Authors, Italian

ITALIAN FOLK-LORE
see Folk-Lore, Italian

ITALIAN LANGUAGE–DICTIONARIES
Dizionario Comleto Italiano-Portoghese (Brasiliano)--Portoghese (Brasiliano)-Italiano: Con L'etimologia Delle Voci Itaiane e Portoghesi (Brasiliane), la Loro Esatta Traduzione, Frasi e Modi Di Dire, 2 vols. 1978. Set. 82.00; Vol. 1, 920 Pp. (ISBN 88-203-1010-4); Vol. 2, 1052pp. (ISBN 88-203-0216-0). S F Vanni.
Il Nuovissimo Melzi: Dizionario Enciclopedico Italiano, 2 vols. 2970p. 1979. Set. 89.00x (ISBN 0-913298-53-0). S F Vanni.

ITALIAN LANGUAGE–DICTIONARIES–ENGLISH
Denti, Renzo. Dizionario Tecnico Italiano-Inglese--Inglese-Italiano. 9th rev. ed. 1811p. 1979. 44.00x (ISBN 88-203-1052-X). S F Vanni.
Lucchesi, Mario. Dizionario Medico Ragionato Inglese-Italiano: Termini, Abbreviazioni, Sigle, Eponimi e Sinonimi Medici, Medico-Biologici e Delle Specializzazionni Mediche. 1490p. 1978. 98.00x (ISBN 0-913298-52-2). S F Vanni.
Motta, Giuseppe. Dizionario Commerciale Inglese-Italiano--Italiano-Inglese: Economia, Legge, Finanza, Banca, Etc. 1051p. 1978. 40.00x (ISBN 0-913298-50-6). S F Vanni.

ITALIAN LANGUAGE–DICTIONARIES–SPANISH
Frisoni, Gaetano. Dizionario Moderno Spagnuolo-Italiano--Italiano-Spagnuolo, 2 vols. 1865p. Set. 44.00x (ISBN 0-913298-51-4). S F Vanni.

ITALIAN LANGUAGE–GRAMMAR
Germano, Joseph & Schmitt, Conrad. Schaum's Outline of Italian Grammar. 2nd ed. (Schaum's Outline Ser.). 288p. 1981. pap. 4.95 (ISBN 0-07-023031-5, SP). McGraw.

ITALIAN LANGUAGE–SELF-INSTRUCTION
Stern, A. Z. & Reif, Joseph A., eds. Useful Expressions in Italian. (Useful Expressions Ser.). 64p. (Orig.). 1980. pap. 1.50 (ISBN 0-86628-010-3). Ridgefield Pub.

ITALIAN LITERATURE–HISTORY AND CRITICISM
Costa, Dennis. Irenic Apocalypse: Some Uses of Apocalyptic in Dante, Petrarch & Rebelais. (Stanford French & Italian Studies: Vol. 21). 160p. 1980. pap. 20.00 (ISBN 0-915838-18-4). Anma Libri.

ITALIAN MUSIC
see Music, Italian

ITALIAN NATIONAL CHARACTERISTICS
see National Characteristics, Italian

ITALIAN PAINTING
see Painting, Italian

ITALIAN PAINTINGS
see Paintings, Italian

ITALIAN POETRY (COLLECTIONS)
Here are entered collections by various authors. For English translations see subdivision Translations into English.
Barkan, Stanley H. & Scammacca, Saverio A., eds. Sicilian Antigruppo. (Illus.). 30p. Date not set. 5.00 (ISBN 0-89304-008-8). Cross Cult.
DeLuca, A. Michael & Giuliano, William. Selections from Italian Poetry. LC 66-10394. (Illus.). 128p. (gr. 9 up). 1966. PLB 5.29 (ISBN 0-8178-3792-2). Harvey.

ITALIAN POETRY–HISTORY AND CRITICISM
Smith, Lawrence R., ed. The New Italian Poetry: Nineteen Forty-Five to the Present. 400p. 1981. 16.95 (ISBN 0-520-03859-2). U of Cal Pr.

ITALIAN SCULPTURE
see Sculpture–Italy

ITALIAN SONGS
see Songs, Italian

ITALIAN TALES
see Tales, Italian

ITALIAN WIT AND HUMOR
Spalding, Henry, ed. Joys of Italian Humor & Folklore. LC 80-13750. 360p. 1980. 16.95 (ISBN 0-8246-0255-2). Jonathan David.

ITALIC WRITING
see Writing, Italic

ITALY–BIOGRAPHY
Silvan, Matthew. Lazarus, Come Out! The Story of My Life. Moran, Hugh, ed. Giannini, Vera, tr. from It. LC 80-82599. Orig. Title: Quella Violenza Di Dio. 224p. (Orig.). 1981. pap. 5.95 (ISBN 0-911782-36-2). New City.

ITALY–DESCRIPTION AND TRAVEL
Porter, J. The Making of the Central Pennines. 160p. 1980. 20.85x (ISBN 0-903485-80-X, Pub. by Allan Pubs England). State Mutual Bk.
Tollinchi, Esteban. Arte y Sensualidad: Cincuenta Imagenes Del Hombre y De la Tierra. LC 79-19403. (Illus.). 710p. 1980. write for info. (ISBN 0-8477-2111-6); pap. write for info. (ISBN 0-8477-2112-4). U of PR Pr.

ITALY–DESCRIPTION AND TRAVEL–GUIDEBOOKS
Bristow, Philip. Round the Italian Coast. 256p. 1980. 15.00x (ISBN 0-245-52648-X, Pub. by Nautical England). State Mutual Bk.
Let's Go, Italy 1980-81. (Illus.). 1981. pap. 5.95 (ISBN 0-525-93145-7). Dutton.

ITALY–ECONOMIC CONDITIONS
Templeman, Donald C. The Italian Economy. 400p. 1981. 26.95 (ISBN 0-03-057612-1). Praeger.

ITALY–HISTORY
Berkeley, C. F. Ialy in the Making, 3 vols. Incl. Vol. 1. Eighteen Fifteen to Eighteen Forty-Six. Repr. of 1932 ed. 38.50 (ISBN 0-521-07427-4); Vol. 2. Eighteen Forty-Six to Eighteen Forty-Eight. Repr. of 1936 ed. 44.50 (ISBN 0-521-07428-2); Vol. 3. January 1, Eighteen Forty-Eight to November 16, Eighteen Forty-Eight. Repr. of 1940 ed. 53.50 (ISBN 0-521-07429-0). (Illus.). 1969. Cambridge U Pr.
Corsten, F. L. The Rise of Facism. 2nd ed. 1980. 18.50 (ISBN 0-520-04307-3). U of Cal Pr.
Krekic, Barisa. Dubrovnik, Italy & the Balkans in the Late Middle Ages. 332p. 1980. 75.00x (ISBN 0-86078-070-8, Pub. by Variorum England). State Mutual Bk.
Voilante, Cinzio. La Societa Milanese Nell'eta Precomunale. LC 80-2000. 1981. Repr. of 1953 ed. 35.00 (ISBN 0-404-18602-5). AMS Pr.

ITALY–POLITICS AND GOVERNMENT
Arthur, William. Italy in Transition. 469p. 1980. Repr of 1860 ed. lib. bdg. 50.00 (ISBN 0-89760-005-3). Telegraph Bks.
Corsten, F. L. The Rise of Facism. 2nd ed. 1980. 18.50 (ISBN 0-520-04307-3). U of Cal Pr.
De Grazia, Victoria. The Culture of Consent: Mass Organization of Leisure in Fascist Italy. LC 80-24361. (Illus.). 304p. Date not set. price not set (ISBN 0-521-23705-X). Cambridge U Pr.

ITALY–SOCIAL CONDITIONS
Arthur, William. Italy in Transition. 469p. 1980. Repr. of 1860 ed. lib. bdg. 50.00 (ISBN 0-89760-005-3). Telegraph Bks.

ITERATIVE METHODS (MATHEMATICS)
Hageman, L. A. & Young, D. M. Applied Iterative Methods. (Computer Science & Applied Mathematics Ser.). 1981. price not set (ISBN 0-12-313340-8). Acad Pr.

IVAN 4TH, THE TERRIBLE, CZAR OF RUSSIA, 1530-1584
Carr, Francis. Ivan the Terrible. 1981. 18.50x (ISBN 0-389-20150-2). B&N.
Skrynnikov, R. G. Ivan the Terrible. Graham, Hugh F., ed. (Russian Ser.: No. 32). 1981. 15.00 (ISBN 0-87569-039-4). Academic Intl.

IVORY CARVING
see Scrimshaws

IVORY COAST
Priovolos, Theophilos. Coffee & the Ivory Coast: An Econometric Study. LC 80-8630. (The Wharton Econometric Studies). (Illus.). 240p. 1981. 24.95 (ISBN 0-669-04331-1). Lexington Bks.

IWW
see Industrial Workers of the World

J

JABOTINSKY, VLADIMIR EUGENEVICH, 1880-1940
Schechtman, Joseph B. Fighter & Prophet: The Vladimir Jabotinsky Story-the Later Years. (Return to Zion Ser.). (Illus.). 643p. 1981. Repr. of 1961 ed. lib. bdg. 35.00x (ISBN 0-87991-142-5). Porcupine Pr.
JACK-RABBITS
see Rabbits
JACKSON, ANDREW, PRES. U. S., 1767-1845-JUVENILE LITERATURE
Harrison, et al. Stonewall Jackson. 35p. (gr. 1-9). 1981. 2.95 (ISBN 0-86575-191-9). Dormac.
JACKSON HOLE NATIONAL MONUMENT
Anderson, Elisabeth, et al. Cabin Comments: A Journal of Life in Jackson Hole. LC 80-53090. (Illus.). 286p. (gr. 7-12). 1980. 14.95 (ISBN 0-933160-08-9); pap. 7.75 (ISBN 0-933160-07-0). Teton Bkshop.
JACOBITE REBELLION, 1745-1746
Lenman, Bruce. The Jacobite Rising in Britain Sixteen Eighty-Nine to Seventeen Forty-Six. 1980. text ed. 34.00x (ISBN 0-8419-7004-1). Holmes & Meier.
JADE
Watt, James C. Chinese Jades from Han to Ch'ing. LC 80-20115. (Illus.). 236p. 1980. 22.50 (ISBN 0-87848-057-9). Asia Soc.
JAGUAR (AUTOMOBILE)
see Automobiles, Foreign-Types-Jaguar
JAILS
see Prisons
JAINISM
Chitrabkanu, Gurudev S. Twelve Facets of Reality: The Jain Path to Freedom. Rosenfeld, Clare, ed. LC 80-16773. 200p. 1980. 8.95 (ISBN 0-396-07902-4). Dodd.
JAMAICA-SOCIAL LIFE AND CUSTOMS
Heuman, Gad J. Between Black & White: Race, Politics, & the Free Coloreds in Jamaica, 1792-1865. LC 80-661. (Contributions in Comparative Colonial Studies: No. 5). (Illus.). 240p. 1981. lib. bdg. 35.00 (ISBN 0-313-20984-7, HBW/). Greenwood.
JAMES 2ND, KING OF GREAT BRITAIN, 1633-1701
Childs, John. The Army, James II & the Glorious Revolution. 25.00 (ISBN 0-312-04949-8). St Martin.
JAMES, HENRY, 1811-1882
Daugherty, Sarah B. The Literary Criticism of Henry James. LC 80-36753. xiv, 232p. 1981. 15.95x (ISBN 0-8214-0440-7). Ohio U Pr.
JAMES, HENRY, 1843-1916
Berland, A. Culture & Conduct in the Novels of Henry James. 225p. Date not set. 39.95 (ISBN 0-521-23343-7). Cambridge U Pr.
Kappeler, Susanne. Writing & Reading in Henry James. LC 80-18181. 242p. 1981. 22.50x (ISBN 0-231-05198-0). Columbia U Pr.
Kirschke, James J. Henry James & Impressionism. LC 80-52732. 357p. 1981. 22.50x (ISBN 0-87875-206-4). Whitston Pub.
JAMES, JESSE WOODSON, 1847-1882
Bradley, Larry C. Jesse James: The Making of a Legend. LC 80-81622. (Illus.). 228p. (Orig.). 1980. pap. 8.95 (ISBN 0-9604370-0-2). Larren Pubs.
JAMES, WILLIAM, 1842-1910
Vanden Burgt, Robert J. The Religious Philosophy of William James. LC 80-22936. 176p. 1981. text ed. 16.95 (ISBN 0-88229-594-2); pap. text ed. 8.95 (ISBN 0-88229-767-8). Nelson-Hall.
JAMMING (RADIO)
see Radio-Interference
JAPAN
see also names of cities, towns, and geographic areas in Japan
Grossberg, Kenneth A., ed. Japan Today. (Illus., Orig.). 1981. 12.95 (ISBN 0-89727-018-5); pap. 5.95 (ISBN 0-89727-019-3). Inst Study Human.
Hoffman, Arthur S., ed. Japan & the Pacific Basin. (Atlantic Papers Ser.: No. 40). 68p. 1980. write for info. (ISBN 0-86598-042-X). Allanheld.
Ike, Nobutake. Japan: The New Superstate, a Portable Stanford. pap. text ed. 4.95x (ISBN 0-393-95011-5). Norton.
Trevor, Hugh. Multi-Channel Japan. 1980. pap. 1.00 (ISBN 0-85363-075-5). OMF Bks.
JAPAN-BIBLIOGRAPHY
Bibliography of European Publications on Japan: Fifteen Forty-Two to Eighteen Fifty-Three. 418p. 1977. Repr. of 1940 ed. 70.00 (ISBN 3-7940-3173-3, Dist. by Gale Research Co). K G Saur.
Japan Directory, 1980, 3 vols. LC 62-46629. 1971p. 1980. Set. 180.00x (ISBN 0-8002-2687-9). Intl Pubns Serv.
JAPAN-BIOGRAPHY
Fujii, Shinichi. Tenno Seiji: Direct Imperial Rule. (Studies in Japanese History & Civilization). 415p. 1979. Repr. of 1944 ed. 30.00 (ISBN 0-89093-263-8). U Pubns Amer.
Hamada, Kengi. Prince Ito. (Studies Injapanese History & Civilzation). 1979. Repr. of 1936 ed. 22.00 (ISBN 0-89093-267-0). U Pubns Amer.
Koichi, Marquis K. Diary of Marquis Kido, Nineteen Thirty-One to Nineteen Forty-Five: Selected Translation Selected Translations into English. 500p. 1980. 34.00 (ISBN 0-89093-273-5). U Pubns Amer.
Tomita, Kokei. Peasant Sage of Japan: The Life & Work of Sontoku Ninomiya. (Studies in Japanese History & Civilization). 1979. Repr. of 1912 ed. 24.00 (ISBN 0-89093-258-1). U Pubns Amer.
JAPAN-CIVILIZATION
Boxer, Charles R. Papers on Portugese, Dutch, & Jesuit Influences in 16th & 17th Century Japan: Studies in Japanese History & Civilization. 1979. 29.50 (ISBN 0-89093-255-7). U Pubns Amer.
--Portuguese Embassy to Japan (1644-1647) Bd. with Embassy of Captain Concalo de Siqueria de Souza to Japan in 1644-7. (Studies in Japanese History & Civilization). 172p. 22.00 (ISBN 0-89093-256-5). U Pubns Amer.
De Becker, Joseph E. Principles & Practice of the Civil Code of Japan: A Complete Theoretical & Practical Exposition of the Motifs of the Japanese Civil Code. (Studies in Japanese Law & Government). 852p. 1979. Repr. of 1921 ed. Set. 60.00 (ISBN 0-89093-216-6). U Pubns Amer.
De Becker, Joseph E., tr. from Japanese. Annotated Civil Code of Japan, 4 vols. (Studies in Japanese Law & Government). 1200p. 1979. 95.00 (ISBN 0-89093-215-8). U Pubns Amer.
Kaibara, Ekiken. Way of Contentment. Bd. with Greater Learning for Women. (Studies in Japanese History & Civilization). 1979. Repr. of 1913 ed. 19.00 (ISBN 0-89093-253-0). U Pubns Amer.
Norman, E. Herbert. Ando Shoeki & the Anatomy of Japanese Feudalism. (Studies in Japanese History & Civilization). 254p. 1979. Repr. of 1949 ed. 26.25 (ISBN 0-89093-224-7). U Pubns Amer.
Stead, Alfred, ed. Japan by the Japanese: A Survey by Its Authorities, 2 vols. (Studies in Japanese History & Civilization). 1979. Repr. of 1904 ed. 55.00 (ISBN 0-89093-264-6). U Pubns Amer.
Wigmore, John H. & Simmons, D. B. Notes on Land Tenure & Local Institutions in Old Japan. (Studies in Japanese History & Civilization). 1979. 21.00 (ISBN 0-89093-223-9). U Pubns Amer.
JAPAN-COMMERCE
Hay, K. A. Friends or Acquaintances? Canada & Japan's Other Trading Partners in the Early 1980's. 52p. 1978. pap. text ed. 3.00x (ISBN 0-920380-15-8, Pub. by Inst Res Pub Canada). Renouf.
JAPAN-CONSTITUTIONAL HISTORY
Fujii, Shinichi. Essentials of Japanese Constitutional Law. (Studies in Japanese Law & Government). 459p. 1979. Repr. of 1940 ed. 32.50 (ISBN 0-89093-214-X). U Pubns Amer.
JAPAN-DESCRIPTION AND TRAVEL
Lanier, Alison R. Update -- Japan. (Country Orientation Ser.). 1980. pap. text ed. 25.00 (ISBN 0-933662-39-4). Intercult Network.
Milward, Peter. Oddities in Modern Japan: Observations of an Outsider. (Illus.). viii, 187p. 1980. pap. 11.50 (ISBN 0-89346-183-0, Pub. by Hokuseido Pr). Heian Intl.
JAPAN-DESCRIPTION AND TRAVEL-GUIDEBOOKS
Watanabe, Masahiro & Rogers, Bruce. Instant Japan. (Illus.). 202p. 1981. pap. 3.95 (ISBN 0-89346-181-4). Heian Intl.
JAPAN-ECONOMIC CONDITIONS
Abegglen, James C. The Japanese Factory. rev. ed. LC 80-52878. 200p. 1981. pap. 6.25 (ISBN 0-8048-1372-8). C E Tuttle.
Allen, C. G. A Short Economic History of Modern Japan. 272p. 1980. 19.95 (ISBN 0-312-71771-7). St Martin.
Clark, Rodney. The Japanese Company. LC 78-65480. 292p. 1981. pap. 7.95 (ISBN 0-300-02646-3). Yale U Pr.
Economic Planning Agency (Govt. of Japan) Economic Survey of Japan, 1978-1979. 28th ed. LC 51-61351. (Illus.). 204p. (Orig.). 1979. pap. 35.00x (ISBN 0-8002-2757-3). Intl Pubns Serv.
Japan Institute of International Affairs, ed. White Papers of Japan: Annual Abstract of Official Reports & Statistics of the Japanese Government 1978-79. LC 72-620531. (Illus.). 228p. (Orig.). 1980. pap. 37.50x (ISBN 0-8002-2734-4). Intl Pubns Serv.
Ministry of Finance, Japan. Guide to the Economic Laws of Japan, 2 vols. (Studies in Japanese Law & Government). 1979. Repr. of 1950 ed. Set. 62.50 (ISBN 0-89093-220-4). U Pubns Amer.
Mizuno, Soji. Early Foundations for Japan's Twentieth Century Economic Emergence. Date not set. 8.95 (ISBN 0-533-04541-X). Vantage.
The Occupation of Japan: Economic Policy & Reform. 382p. pap. 6.00. MacArthur Memorial.
A Selected Bibliography of Socio-Economic Development of Japan: Part B Sixteen Hundred to Nineteen Forty. 156p. 1980. pap. 5.00 (ISBN 92-808-0199-6, TUNU094, UNU). Unipub.
Smith, Neil S. Materials on Japanese Social & Economic History: Tokugawa, Japan. (Studies in Japanese History & Civilization). 176p. 1979. Repr. of 1937 ed. 19.50 (ISBN 0-89093-262-X). U Pubns Amer.
Tsuneta Yano Memorial Society (Tokyo), ed. Nippon: A Chartered Survey of Japan, 1980-81. 25th ed. (Illus.). 347p. 1980. 37.50x (ISBN 0-8002-2748-4). Intl Pubns Serv.
Yoshihara, Kunio. Japanese Economic Development: A Short Introduction. (Illus.). 168p. 1979. text ed. 9.95x (ISBN 0-19-580439-2). Oxford U Pr.
JAPAN-FOREIGN RELATIONS
Akagi, Roy. Japan's Foreign Relations, Fifteen Forty-Two to Nineteen Thirty-Six: A Short History. (Studies in Japanese History & Civilization). (Illus.). 560p. 1979. Repr. of 1936 ed. 36.50 (ISBN 0-89093-260-3). U Pubns Amer.
Boxer, Charles R. Papers on Portugese, Dutch, & Jesuit Influences in 16th & 17th Century Japan: Studies in Japanese History & Civilization. 1979. 29.50 (ISBN 0-89093-255-7). U Pubns Amer.
--Portuguese Embassy to Japan (1644-1647) Bd. with Embassy of Captain Concalo de Siqueria de Souza to Japan in 1644-7. (Studies in Japanese History & Civilization). 172p. 22.00 (ISBN 0-89093-256-5). U Pubns Amer.
Japan Institute of International Affairs, ed. White Papers of Japan: Annual Abstract of Official Reports & Statistics of the Japanese Government 1978-79. LC 72-620531. (Illus.). 228p. (Orig.). 1980. pap. 37.50x (ISBN 0-8002-2734-4). Intl Pubns Serv.
JAPAN-FOREIGN RELATIONS-AUSTRALIA
Crawford, John & Okita, Saburo, eds. Australia & Japan: Issues in the Economic Relationship. (Australia-Japan Economic Relations Research Project Monograph: No. 2). (Illus.). 140p. 1980. pap. text ed. 5.95 (ISBN 0-9596197-1-2). Bks Australia.
JAPAN-FOREIGN RELATIONS-CHINA
Yamada, Yosi-Aki & Eastlake, F. Warrington. Heroic Japan: A History of the War Between China & Japan. (Studies in Japanese History & Civilization). 1979. Repr. of 1897 ed. 40.50 (ISBN 0-89093-291-3). U Pubns Amer.
JAPAN-HISTORY
Boxer, Charles R. Papers on Portugese, Dutch, & Jesuit Influences in 16th & 17th Century Japan: Studies in Japanese History & Civilization. 1979. 29.50 (ISBN 0-89093-255-7). U Pubns Amer.
--Portuguese Embassy to Japan (1644-1647) Bd. with Embassy of Captain Concalo de Siqueria de Souza to Japan in 1644-7. (Studies in Japanese History & Civilization). 172p. 22.00 (ISBN 0-89093-256-5). U Pubns Amer.
Fujii, Shinichi. Tenno Seiji: Direct Imperial Rule. (Studies in Japanese History & Civilization). 415p. 1979. Repr. of 1944 ed. 30.00 (ISBN 0-89093-263-8). U Pubns Amer.
Hall, John C., tr. from Japanese. Japanese Feudal Law. (Studies in Japanese Law & Government). (Illus.). 266p. 1979. Repr. of 1906 ed. 24.50 (ISBN 0-89093-211-5). U Pubns Amer.
Hall, John W. Government & Local Power in Japan: A Study on Bizen Province, 500-1700. LC 65-14307. (Illus.). 446p. 1980. 30.00x. Princeton U Pr.
Huber, Thomas M. The Revolutionary Origins of Modern Japan. LC 79-64214. (Illus.). 288p. 1981. 18.50x (ISBN 0-8047-1048-1). Stanford U Pr.
Ito, Hirobumi. Commentaries on the Constitution of the Empire of Japan. (Studies in Japanese Law & Government). 310p. 1979. Repr. of 1906 ed. 25.00 (ISBN 0-89093-212-3). U Pubns Amer.
Kaibara, Ekiken. Way of Contentment. Bd. with Greater Learning for Women. (Studies in Japanese History & Civilization). 1979. Repr. of 1913 ed. 19.00 (ISBN 0-89093-253-0). U Pubns Amer.
Kinmonth, Earl H. The Self-Made Man in Meija Japanese Thought: From Samurai to Salary Man. (Illus.). 400p. 1981. 22.50x (ISBN 0-520-04159-3). U of Cal Pr.
Kiyohara, Michiko. A Checklist of Monographs & Periodicals on the Japanese Colonial Empire. LC 80-84459. (Special Project Ser.: No. 28). 352p. 1981. pap. 11.95 (ISBN 0-8179-4284-X). Hoover Inst Pr.
Kiyohara, Michiko, compiled by. A Checklist of Monographs & Periodicals on the Japanese Colonial Empire. (Special Project: No.28). 352p. 1981. pap. 11.95 (ISBN 0-8179-4284-X). Hoover Inst Pr.
Lay, Arthur H. Brief Sketch of the History of Political Parties in Japan. Bd. with Political Ideas of Modern Japan: An Interpretation Studies in Japanese Law & Government. Kowakami, Kiyoshi K. 461p. 1979. Repr. of 1902 ed. 22.00 (ISBN 0-89093-222-0). U Pubns Amer.
Mizuno, Soji. Early Foundations for Japan's Twentieth Century Economic Emergence. Date not set. 8.95 (ISBN 0-533-04541-X). Vantage.
Mounsey, Augustus H. Satsuma Rebellion: An Episode of Modern Japanese History. (Studies in Japanese History & Civilization). 1979p. Repr. of 1879 ed. 24.00 (ISBN 0-89093-259-X). U Pubns Amer.
Norman, E. Herbert. Ando Shoeki & the Anatomy of Japanese Feudalism. (Studies in Japanese History & Civilization). 254p. 1979. Repr. of 1949 ed. 26.25 (ISBN 0-89093-224-7). U Pubns Amer.
Ponsonby-Fane, Richard A. Fortunes of the Emperors: Studies in Revolution, Exile, Abdication, Usurpation, & Deposition in Ancient Japan. (Studies in Japanese History & Civilization). 1979. 28.00 (ISBN 0-89093-250-6). U Pubns Amer.
--Imperial Cities: The Capitals of Japan from the Oldest Times Until 1229. (Studies in Japanese History & Civilization). 1979. 21.50 (ISBN 0-89093-251-4). U Pubns Amer.
Pratt, Peter, ed. History of Japan: Compiled from the Records of the English East India Company at the Instance of the Court of Directors, 2 vols. (Studies in Japanese History & Civilization). 1979. Repr. of 1931 ed. Set. 62.00 (ISBN 0-89093-261-1). U Pubns Amer.
Smith, Neil S. Materials on Japanese Social & Economic History: Tokugawa, Japan. (Studies in Japanese History & Civilization). 176p. 1979. Repr. of 1937 ed. 19.50 (ISBN 0-89093-262-X). U Pubns Amer.
Stead, Alfred, ed. Japan by the Japanese: A Survey by Its Authorities, 2 vols. (Studies in Japanese History & Civilization). 1979. Repr. of 1904 ed. 55.00 (ISBN 0-89093-264-6). U Pubns Amer.
Totman, Conrad. Japan Before Perry: A Short History. (Illus.). 275p. 1981. 20.00x (ISBN 0-520-04132-1). U of Cal Pr.
Wigmore, John H. & Simmons, D. B. Notes on Land Tenure & Local Institutions in Old Japan. (Studies in Japanese History & Civilization). 1979. 21.00 (ISBN 0-89093-223-9). U Pubns Amer.
Yamada, Nakaba. Ghenko: The Mongol Invasion of Japan. (Studies in Japanese History & Civilization). 1979. Repr. of 1916 ed. 25.00 (ISBN 0-89093-254-9). U Pubns Amer.
JAPAN-HISTORY-ALLIED OCCUPATION, 1945-1952
The Occupation of Japan: Economic Policy & Reform. 382p. pap. 6.00. MacArthur Memorial.
Redford, Lawrence H., ed. The Occupation of Japan & Its Legacy to the Postwar World. 158p. pap. 4.00. MacArthur Memorial.
--The Occupation of Japan: Impact of Legal Refor, 212p. pap. 5.00. MacArthur Memorial.
JAPAN-HISTORY, MILITARY
Mounsey, Augustus H. Satsuma Rebellion: An Episode of Modern Japanese History. (Studies in Japanese History & Civilization). 1979p. Repr. of 1879 ed. 24.00 (ISBN 0-89093-259-X). U Pubns Amer.
Perrin, Noel. Giving up the Gun: Japan's Reversion to the Sword Fifteen Forty-Three to Eighteen Seventy-Nine. LC 80-50744. (Illus.). 122p. 1980. pap. 4.95 (ISBN 0-394-73949-3). Shambhala Pubns.
JAPAN-INDUSTRIES
Yoshihara, Kunio. Japanese Economic Development: A Short Introduction. (Illus.). 168p. 1979. text ed. 9.95x (ISBN 0-19-580439-2). Oxford U Pr.
JAPAN-INTELLECTUAL LIFE
Center for Academic Publications Japan, ed. Current Contents of Academic Journals in Japan, 1978. 18th ed. LC 72-623679. 392p. (Orig.). 1980. pap. 55.00x (ISBN 0-8002-2740-9). Intl Pubns Serv.
JAPAN-MILITARY POLICY
Perrin, Noel. Giving up the Gun: Japan's Reversion to the Sword Fifteen Forty-Three to Eighteen Seventy-Nine. LC 80-50744. (Illus.). 122p. 1980. pap. 4.95 (ISBN 0-394-73949-3). Shambhala Pubns.
JAPAN-POLITICS AND GOVERNMENT
De Becker, Joseph E. Elements of Japanese Law: Studies in Japanese Law & Government. 1979. Repr. of 1916 ed. 34.00 (ISBN 0-89093-210-7). U Pubns Amer.
--Principles & Practice of the Civil Code of Japan: A Complete Theoretical & Practical Exposition of the Motifs of the Japanese Civil Code. (Studies in Japanese Law & Government). 852p. 1979. Repr. of 1921 ed. Set. 60.00 (ISBN 0-89093-216-6). U Pubns Amer.
De Becker, Joseph E., tr. from Japanese. Annotated Civil Code of Japan, 4 vols. (Studies in Japanese Law & Government). 1200p. 1979. 95.00 (ISBN 0-89093-215-8). U Pubns Amer.
Fujii, Shinichi. Essentials of Japanese Constitutional Law. (Studies in Japanese Law & Government). 459p. 1979. Repr. of 1940 ed. 32.50 (ISBN 0-89093-214-X). U Pubns Amer.
Hall, John C., tr. from Japanese. Japanese Feudal Law. (Studies in Japanese Law & Government). (Illus.). 266p. 1979. Repr. of 1906 ed. 24.50 (ISBN 0-89093-211-5). U Pubns Amer.
Hall, John W. Government & Local Power in Japan: A Study on Bizen Province, 500-1700. LC 65-14307. (Illus.). 446p. 1980. 30.00x. Princeton U Pr.
Hamada, Kengi. Prince Ito. (Studies Injapanese History & Civilzation). 1979. Repr. of 1936 ed. 22.00 (ISBN 0-89093-267-0). U Pubns Amer.
Ito, Hirobumi. Commentaries on the Constitution of the Empire of Japan. (Studies in Japanese Law & Government). 310p. 1979. Repr. of 1906 ed. 25.00 (ISBN 0-89093-212-3). U Pubns Amer.
Japan Institute of International Affairs, ed. White Papers of Japan: Annual Abstract of Official Reports & Statistics of the Japanese Government 1978-79. LC 72-620531. (Illus.). 228p. (Orig.). 1980. pap. 37.50x (ISBN 0-8002-2734-4). Intl Pubns Serv.
Lay, Arthur H. Brief Sketch of the History of Political Parties in Japan. Bd. with Political Ideas of Modern Japan: An Interpretation Studies in Japanese Law & Government. Kowakami, Kiyoshi K. 461p. 1979. Repr. of 1902 ed. 22.00 (ISBN 0-89093-222-0). U Pubns Amer.

McLaren, Walter W. Japanese Government Documents: (of the Meiji Era, 2 vols. (Studies in Japanese History & Civilization). 1979. Repr. of 1914 ed. Set. 52.50 (ISBN 0-89093-265-4). U Pubns Amer.

Matsunami, Niichiro. Japanese Constitution & Politics. (Studies in Japanese Law & Government). 577p. 1979. 38.75 (ISBN 0-89093-217-4). U Pubns Amer.

Military of Justice, Japan. Constitution of Japan & Criminal Statutes. (Studies in Japanese Law & Government). 1979. Repr. of 1957 ed. 38.00 (ISBN 0-89093-221-2). U Pubns Amer.

Mimistry of Finance, Japan. Guide to the Economic Laws of Japan, 2 vols. (Studies in Japanese Law & Government). 1979. Repr. of 1950 ed. Set. 62.50 (ISBN 0-89093-220-4). U Pubns Amer.

Ministry of Labor, Japan. Japan Labor Code, 2 vols. (Studies in Japanese Law & Government). 1979. Repr. of 1953 ed. Set. 56.00 (ISBN 0-89093-217-4). U Pubns Amer.

Ponsonby-Fane, Richard A. Fortunes of the Emperors: Studies in Revolution, Exile, Abdication, Usurpation, & Deposition in Ancient Japan. (Studies in Japanese History & Civilization). 1979. 28.00 (ISBN 0-89093-250-6). U Pubns Amer.

Sebald, William J., tr. Selection of Japan's Emergency Legislation. (Studies in Japanese Law & Government). 177p. 1979. Repr. of 1937 ed. 16.00 (ISBN 0-89093-219-0). U Pubns Amer.

Takane, Masalaki. Political Elites in Japan. (Japan Research Monographs: No.1). 180p. 1981. pap. price not set (ISBN 0-912966-33-5). IEAS Ctr Chinese Stud.

Young, Arthur M. Socialist & Labour Movement in Japan. (Studies in Japanese History & Civilization). 145p. 1979. Repr. of 1921 ed. 18.00 (ISBN 0-89093-268-9). U Pubns Amer.

JAPAN–POLITICS AND GOVERNMENT–1945-

McKean, Margaret A. Environmental Protest & Citizen Politics in Japan. 300p. 1981. 28.50x (ISBN 0-520-04115-1). U of Cal Pr.

Redford, Lawrence H., ed. The Occupation of Japan: Impact of Legal Refor, 212p. pap. 5.00. MacArthur Memorial.

JAPAN–RELATIONS (GENERAL) WITH FOREIGN COUNTRIES

Yoshihara, Kunio. Japanese Economic Development: A Short Introduction. (Illus.). 168p. 1979. text ed. 9.95x (ISBN 0-19-580439-2). Oxford U Pr.

JAPAN–RELIGION

Bunce, William K., ed. Religions in Japan. LC 59-9234. 216p. 1981. pap. 5.25 (ISBN 0-8048-0500-8). C E Tuttle.

Nanjio, Bunyiu, tr. from Japanese. Short History of the Twelve Buddhist Sects. (Studies in Japanese History & Civilization). 1979. Repr. of 1886 ed. 19.75 (ISBN 0-89093-252-2). U Pubns Amer.

Paske-Smith, Montague, ed. Japanese Traditions of Christianity: Being Some Old Translations from the Japanese, with British Consular Reports of the Persecutions of 1868-1872. (Studies in Japanese History & Civilization). 1979. Repr. of 1930 ed. 17.50 (ISBN 0-89093-257-3). U Pubns Amer.

JAPAN–SOCIAL CONDITIONS

Japan Institute of International Affairs, ed. White Papers of Japan: Annual Abstract of Official Reports & Statistics of the Japanese Government 1978-79. LC 72-620531. (Illus.). 228p. (Orig.). 1980. pap. 37.50x (ISBN 0-8002-2734-4). Intl Pubns Serv.

Kinmonth, Earl H. The Self-Made Man in Meija Japanese Thought: From Samurai to Salary Man. (Illus.). 400p. 1981. 22.50x (ISBN 0-520-04159-3). U of Cal Pr.

Lee, Changsoo & DeVos, George. Koreans in Japan: Ethnic Conflict & Accommodation. (Illus.). 448p. 1981. 30.00x (ISBN 0-520-04258-1). U of Cal Pr.

A Selected Bibliography of Socio-Economic Development of Japan: Part B Sixteen Hundred to Nineteen Forty. 156p. 1980. pap. 5.00 (ISBN 92-808-0199-6, TUNU094, UNU). Unipub.

JAPAN–SOCIAL LIFE AND CUSTOMS

Milward, Peter. Oddities in Modern Japan: Obeservations of an Outsider. (Illus.). viii, 187p. 1980. pap. 11.50 (ISBN 0-89346-183-0, Pub. by Hokuseido Pr). Heian Intl.

Smith, Neil S. Materials on Japanese Social & Economic History: Tokugawa, Japan. (Studies in Japanese History & Civilization). 176p. 1979. Repr. of 1937 ed. 19.50 (ISBN 0-89093-262-X). U Pubns Amer.

JAPANESE ARCHITECTURE

see Architecture–Japan

JAPANESE ART

see Art, Japanese

JAPANESE FOLK-LORE

see Folk-Lore, Japanese

JAPANESE FOLK-SONGS

see Folk-Songs, Japanese

JAPANESE IN FOREIGN COUNTRIES

Nakano, Takeo U. & Nakano, Leatrice. Within the Barbed Wire Fence: A Japanese Man's Account of His Internment in Canada. (Illus.). 136p. 1981. 10.00 (ISBN 0-295-95789-1). U of Wash Pr.

JAPANESE IN THE UNITED STATES

Bonacich, Edna & Modell, John. The Economic Basis of Ethnic Solidarity: A Study of Japanese Americans. 1980. 14.50 (ISBN 0-520-04155-0). U of Cal Pr.

JAPANESE LANGUAGE–CONVERSATION AND PHRASE BOOKS

Sivan, Avraham J. & Ikeda, Yutakada, eds. Useful Expressions in Japanese. (Useful Expressions Ser.). (Illus.). 64p. (Orig.). 1980. pap. 1.50 (ISBN 0-86628-011-1). Ridgefield Pub.

Watanabe, Masahiro & Nagashima, Kei. Instant Japanese. (Illus.). 188p. 1981. pap. 3.95 (ISBN 0-89346-182-2). Heian Intl.

JAPANESE LANGUAGE–DICTIONARIES–ENGLISH

Hadamitzky, Wolfgang & Spahn, Mark. Kanji & Kana: A Handbook & Dictionary of the Japanese Writing System. LC 81-50106. 384p. 1981. 11.50 (ISBN 0-8048-1373-6). C E Tuttle.

Kawamoto, Shigeo, et al, eds. The Kodansha Japanese-English Dictionary. Shimizu, Hamoru & Harita, Shigehisa, trs. 1250p. 1980. flexible soft-binding 19.95 (ISBN 0-87011-421-2). Kodansha.

JAPANESE LANGUAGE–GRAMMAR

Clarke, H. D. & Hamamura, Motoko. Colloquial Japanese. (Colloquial Ser.). (Orig.). 1981. pap. price not set (ISBN 0-7100-0595-4). Routledge & Kegan.

JAPANESE LANGUAGE–TEXTBOOKS FOR FOREIGNERS

Clarke, H. D. & Hamamura, Motoko. Colloquial Japanese. (Colloquial Ser.). (Orig.). 1981. pap. price not set (ISBN 0-7100-0595-4). Routledge & Kegan.

JAPANESE PAINTINGS

see Paintings, Japanese

JAPANESE PAPER FOLDING

see Origami

JAPANESE POETRY–HISTORY AND CRITICISM

Levy, Ian H., tr. from Japanese. The Ten Thousand Leaves: A Translation of Man'yoshu, Japan's Premier Anthology of Classical Poetry, Vol. 1. LC 80-8561. (Princeton Library of Asian Translations). (Illus.). 280p. 1981. 20.00x (ISBN 0-691-06452-0). Princeton U Pr.

Stryk, Lucien, et al, trs. from Chinese Japanese. Zen Poems of China & Japan: The Crane's Bill. 208p. 1981. pap. 4.95 (ISBN 0-394-17912-9, BC). Grove.

JAPANESE POETRY–TRANSLATIONS INTO ENGLISH

Sato, Hiroaki & Watson, Burton, eds. From the Country of Eight Islands: An Anthology of Japanese Poetry. 480p. 1981. 17.50 (ISBN 0-295-95798-0). U of Wash Pr.

Stryk, Lucien & Ikemoto, Takashi, eds. The Penguin Book of Zen Poetry. Stryk, Lucien & Ikemoto, Takashi, trs. from Japanese. 1981. pap. 4.95 (ISBN 0-14-042247-1). Penguin.

JAPANESE POTTERY

see Pottery, Japanese

JAPANESE SCIENCE

see Science, Japanese

JARGONS

see Languages, Mixed

JARRELL, RANDALL, 1914-1965

Quinn, Sr. Bernetta. Randall Jarrell. (United States Authors Ser.: No. 398). 1981. lib. bdg. 10.95 (ISBN 0-8057-7266-9). Twayne.

JAVA

Changes in Community Institutions & Income Distribution in a West Java Village. (IRRI Research Paper Ser.: No. 50). 16p. 1981. pap. 5.00 (R131, IRRI). Unipub.

Forman, Bedrich. Borobudur: The Buddhist Legend in Tone. (Illus.). 1980. 16.95. Mayflower Bks.

Hoadley, M. C. & Hooker, M. B. Introduction to Javanese Law. LC 80-26636. (Monographs of the Association for Asian Studies: No. XXXVII). 1981. text ed. 9.95x (ISBN 0-8165-0727-9). U of Ariz Pr.

JAWBONING

see Wage-Price Policy

JAWS

Harnisch, Herbert. Clinical Aspects & Treatment of Cysts of the Jaws. (Illus.). 237p. 1974. 38.00. Quint Pub Co.

Topazian, Richard G. & Goldberg, Morton H. Management of Infections of the Oral & Maxillofacial Regions. (Illus.). 500p. 1981. text ed. price not set (ISBN 0-7216-8879-9). Saunders.

JAZZ MUSIC

see also Blues (Songs, etc.)

Balliett, Whitney. Night Creature: A Journal of Jazz, 1975-1980. (Illus.). 275p. 1981. 15.95 (ISBN 0-19-502908-9). Oxford U Pr.

Charters, Samuel & Kunstadt, Leonard. My Husband Gabrilowitsch: A History of the New York Scene. 27.50 (ISBN 0-306-76055-X). Da Capo.

Giddins, Gary. Riding on a Blue Note: Jazz & American Pop. 275p. 1981. 16.95 (ISBN 0-19-502835-X). Oxford U Pr.

Henry, Robert E. The Jazz Ensemble. (Illus.). 144p. 1981. 15.95 (ISBN 0-13-509992-7, Spec); pap. 7.95 (ISBN 0-13-509984-6). P-H.

Sidran, Ben. Black Talk: Roots of Jazz. xvii, 201p. 1981. Repr. of 1971 ed. lib. bdg. 19.50 (ISBN 0-306-76056-8). Da Capo.

Williams, Martin, ed. The Art of Jazz: Ragtime to Bebop. (Da Capo Quality Paperbacks Ser.). 248p. 1981. pap. 6.95 (ISBN 0-306-80134-5). Da Capo.

JAZZ MUSIC–DISCOGRAPHY

Lyons, Len. The One Hundred One Best Jazz Albums: A History of Jazz on Records. LC 80-20392. (Illus.). 640p. 1980. 17.95 (ISBN 0-688-03720-8). Morrow.

JAZZ MUSICIANS

Kaminsky, Max & Hughes, V. E. Jazz Band: My Life in Jazz. (Da Capo Quality Paperbacks Ser.). (Illus.). 242p. 1981. pap. 6.95 (ISBN 0-306-80135-3). Da Capo.

O'Day, Anita & Eells, George. High Times, Hard Times. 320p. 1981. 12.95 (ISBN 0-399-12505-1). Putnam.

JAZZ MUSICIANS–CORRESPONDENCE, REMINISCENCES, ETC.

see Musicians–Correspondence, Reminiscences, etc.

JEANNE D'ARC, SAINT, 1412-1431

Clemens, Samuel L. Personal Recollections of Joan of Arc by the Sieur Louis De Conte. LC 80-23663. (Illus.). xiv, 461p. 1980. Repr. of 1906 ed. lib. bdg. 45.00x (ISBN 0-313-22373-4, CLPR). Greenwood.

Gies, Frances. Joan of Arc: The Legend & the Reality. LC 80-7900. (Illus.). 256p. 1981. 12.95 (ISBN 0-690-01942-4, HarpT). Har-Row.

Warner, Marina. Joan of Arc: The Image of Female Heroism. LC 80-2720. (Illus.). 1981. 17.95 (ISBN 0-394-41145-5). Knopf.

JEFFERS, ROBINSON, 1887-1962

Scott, Robert I. What Odd Expedients & Other Poems by Robinson Jeffers. 1981. 14.50 (ISBN 0-208-01885-9, Archon). Shoe String.

JEFFERSON, THOMAS, PRES. U. S., 1743-1826

Boorstin, Daniel J. The Lost World of Thomas Jefferson. LC 80-26835. 320p. 1981. pap. 6.95 (ISBN 0-226-06496-4). U of Chicago Pr.

Cunningham, Noble E., Jr. The Image of Thomas Jefferson in the Public Eye: Portraits for the People, 1800-1809. LC 80-22757. (Illus.). 1981. write for info. (ISBN 0-8139-0821-3). U Pr of Va.

Dabney, Virginius. The Jefferson Scandals. (Illus.). 156p. 1981. 8.95 (ISBN 0-396-07964-4). Dodd.

Mayo, Bernard, ed. Thomas Jefferson & His Unknown Brother. LC 80-25272. 1981. price not set (ISBN 0-8139-0890-6). U Pr of Va.

Nichols, Frederick D. & Griswold, Ralph E. Thomas Jefferson, Landscape Architect. LC 77-10601. (Illus.). ix, 196p. 1981. pap. 4.95x (ISBN 0-8139-0899-X). U Pr of Va.

JEFFERSON, THOMAS, PRES. U. S., 1743-1826–JUVENILE LITERATURE

Harrison, et al. Thomas Jefferson. (Illus.). 35p. (gr. 1-9). 2.95 (ISBN 0-86575-187-0). Dormac.

JEHOVAH'S WITNESSES

Giron, Jose, tr. Testigos De Jehova y Sus Doctrinas. (Spanish Bks.). 1978. 1.50 (ISBN 0-8297-0604-6). Life Pubs Intl.

Passantino, Robert, et al. Answer to the Cultist at Your Door. LC 80-83850. 1981. pap. 4.95 (ISBN 0-89081-275-6). Harvest Hse.

JENSEN, POVL BANG, 1909-

Flynn, James R. Race, IQ, & Jensen. 320p. 1980. 27.50 (ISBN 0-7100-0651-9). Routledge & Kegan.

JERUSALEM–DESCRIPTION–GUIDEBOOKS

Har-El, Menashe. This Is Jerusalem. rev. ed. Zeevy, Rechavam, ed. (Illus.). 368p. 1980. pap. 6.95 (ISBN 0-86628-002-2). Ridgefield Pub.

JERUSALEM–HISTORY

Johnson, Alexandra W. Jerusalem Fifteen Hundred. (Illus.). 1981. 12.95 (ISBN 0-930720-66-0). Liberator Pr.

Kraemer, Joel L., ed. Jerusalem: Problems & Prospects. 256p. 1980. 25.95 (ISBN 0-03-057733-0); pap. 9.95 (ISBN 0-03-057734-9). Praeger.

Wight, Fred H. Usos y Costumbres De las Tierras Biblica. 336p. (Span.). 1981. pap. 7.95 (ISBN 0-8024-9043-3). Moody.

JEST BOOKS

see Chap-Books

JESTS

see Wit and Humor

JESUITS

Arnauld, Antoine. The Arrainment of the Whole Societie of Jesuites in Fraunce: Holden-the Twelfth & Thirteenth of July, 1594. LC 79-84084. (English Experience Ser.: No. 904). 68p. 1979. Repr. of 1594 ed. lib. bdg. 8.00. Walter J Johnson.

Mitchell, David. The Jesuits. (Illus.). 320p. 1981. 17.50 (ISBN 0-531-09947-4). Watts.

Peters, F. E. Ours: The Making & Unmaking of a Jesuit. 192p. 1981. 11.95 (ISBN 0-399-90113-2). Marek.

Ronan & Hanisch. Epistolario De Juan Ignacio Molina. (Sp.). 1980. 11.60 (ISBN 0-8294-0360-4). Loyola.

JESUITS IN THE UNITED STATES

Gruenberg, Gladys W. Labor Peacemaker: The Life & Works of Father Leo. C. Brown, S. J. Ganss, George E., ed. (Original Studies Composed in English Ser.: No. 4). (Illus.). 176p. 1981. 7.50 (ISBN 0-912422-54-8); pap. 6.00 smythsewn paperbound (ISBN 0-912422-53-X); pap. 5.00 (ISBN 0-912422-52-1). Inst Jesuit.

JESUS, SOCIETY OF

see Jesuits

JESUS CHRIST

see also Antichrist; Christianity; Lord's Supper; Millennium; Redemption; Salvation; Second Advent; Trinity

Agnew, Joseph. Life's Christ Places. 206p. 1911. text ed. 2.95 (ISBN 0-567-02008-8). Attic Pr.

Davies, Chris, et al, eds. Jesus: One of Us. 148p. 1981. pap. 3.95 (ISBN 0-87784-618-9). Inter Varsity.

Muirhead, L. A. The Times of Christ. (Handbooks for Bible Classes). 179p. 1907. text ed. 3.50 (ISBN 0-567-08133-8). Attic Pr.

Religious Education Staff. Lord & Savior: Friend & Brother, Spirit Masters for The Jesus Book. (To Live Is Christ Ser.). 1979. 10.95 (ISBN 0-697-01692-7). Wm C Brown.

Thomas, W. Griffith. Christianity Is Christ. (Shepherd Illustrated Classics). (Illus.). 200p. Date not set. pap. 5.95 (ISBN 0-87983-238-X). Keats.

--Christianity Is Christ. (Shepherd Illustrated Classics Ser.). (Illus.). 200p. 1979. pap. 5.95 (ISBN 0-87983-238-X). Keats.

Zenos, A. C. The Son of Man. (Short Course Ser.). 145p. Repr. of 1914 ed. 2.95 (ISBN 0-567-08312-8). Attic Pr.

JESUS CHRIST–ASCENSION

Milligan, William. The Acension of Christ. Date not set. 12.50 (ISBN 0-86524-061-2). Klock & Klock.

JESUS CHRIST–BEATITUDES

see Beatitudes

JESUS CHRIST–BIOGRAPHY

Barclay, William. Jesus of Nazareth. 288p. 1981. pap. 10.95 (ISBN 0-8407-5759-X). Nelson.

Barrois, George. Jesus Christ & the Temple. LC 80-19700. 164p. 1980. pap. 5.95. St Vladimirs.

Bock, Janet L. The Jesus Mystery: Of Lost Years & Unknown Travels. LC 80-67420. (Illus.). 231p. (Orig.). 1980. pap. 6.95 (ISBN 0-937736-00-7). Aura Bks.

Conrwall, Judson. Let Us See Jesus. 1981. pap. 4.95 (ISBN 0-8007-5052-7). Revell.

Dickens, Charles. The Life of Our Lord. LC 80-22131. (Illus.). 1981. Repr. of 1934 ed. price not set (ISBN 0-664-21382-0). Westminster.

Ingraham, F. & Anderson, Eric. Prince of the House of David. Orig. Title: Three Years in the Holy City. 363p. 1980. Repr. text ed. 9.95 (ISBN 0-89841-003-7). Zoe Pubns.

Keller, W. Phillip. Rabboni. 1981. pap. 5.95 (ISBN 0-8007-5053-5). Revell.

McConkie, Bruce R. The Mortal Messiah, from Bethlehem to Calvary, Bk. 3. LC 79-19606. 486p. 1980. 11.95 (ISBN 0-87747-825-2). Deseret Bk.

Makrakis, Apostolos. The Human Nature of Christ: Growth & Perfection. Orthodox Christian Educational Society, ed. Cummings, D., tr. from Hellenic. 52p. (Orig.). 1965. pap. 1.00x (ISBN 0-938366-28-9). Orthodox Chr.

Morrison, Mary C. Jesus: Sketches for a Portrait. rev. & enl. ed. 1979. 2.00 (ISBN 0-686-28782-7). Forward Movement.

Ramsey, James. The Education of Jesus Christ. LC 80-84438. (Shepherd Classics Ser.). 130p. 1979. pap. 5.95 (ISBN 0-87983-236-3). Keats.

Sanday, W. Outlines of the Life of Christ. 2nd ed. 285p. Repr. of 1906 ed. 4.95 (ISBN 0-567-02224-2). Attic Pr.

Stalker, J. The Life of Jesus Christ. 2nd ed. (Handbooks for Bible Classes). 157p. 1891. text ed. 8.95 (ISBN 0-567-28130-2). Attic Pr.

Staton, Knofel. Meet Jesus. LC 80-53674. 192p. (Orig.). 1981. pap. 3.50 (ISBN 0-87239-426-3, 40092). Standard Pub.

JESUS CHRIST–BIOGRAPHY–HISTORY AND CRITICISM

Herald. Shining Stranger. 3.95 (ISBN 0-916438-29-5). Univ of Trees.

JESUS CHRIST–BIOGRAPHY–JUVENILE LITERATURE

Robertson, Jennny & Parry, Alan. Jesus in Danger. (Ladybird Bible Ser.). (Illus.). 32p. (ps-4). 1980. Repr. 1.95 (ISBN 0-310-42870-X). Zondervan.

Robertson, Jenny. Jesus, the Child. (Ladybird Bible Ser.). (Illus.). 32p. (ps-4). 1980. Repr. 1.95 (ISBN 0-310-42820-3). Zondervan.

--Jesus, the Leader. (Ladybird Bible Ser.). (Illus.). 32p. (ps-4). 1980. Repr. 1.95 (ISBN 0-310-42830-0). Zondervan.

--Paul Meets Jesus. (Ladybird Bible Ser.). (Illus.). 32p. (ps-4). 1980. Repr. 1.95 (ISBN 0-310-42880-7). Zondervan.

Ronertson, Jenny. Jesus, the Storyteller. (Ladybird Bible Ser.). (Illus.). 32p. (ps-4). 1980. Repr. 1.95 (ISBN 0-310-42840-8). Zondervan.

JESUS CHRIST–BIOGRAPHY–PASSION WEEK

see Jesus Christ–Passion

JESUS CHRIST–BIOGRAPHY–STUDY

Esse, John. The Story of Jesus: An Interpretation. (Illus.). 96p. (Orig.). 1980. pap. 4.95. Pundarika.

Wilkerson, David, tr. Jesucristo, Roca Firme. (Spanish Bks.). (Span.). 1978. 1.60 (ISBN 0-8297-0577-5). Life Pubs Intl.

--Jesus Cristo, a Rocha Firme. (Portuguese Bks.). 1979. 1.40 (ISBN 0-8297-0669-0). Life Pubs Intl.

JESUS CHRIST–BIRTH

see Jesus Christ–Nativity; Virgin Birth

JESUS CHRIST–CHARACTER

Bell, D. Rayford. The Philosophy of Christ. LC 80-67408. 104p. 1980. 6.95 (ISBN 0-9604820-0-8); pap. 4.95 (ISBN 0-9604820-1-6). D R Bell.

Smail, Thomas A. The Forgotten Father. 1981. pap. 5.95 (ISBN 0-8028-1879-X). Eerdmans.

Williams, Morris, tr. La Justicia De Dios. (Spanish Bks.). (Span.). 1977. 2.50 (ISBN 0-8297-0759-X). Life Pubs Intl.

--Publiez Sa Justice. (French Bks.). (Fr.). 1979. 2.50 (ISBN 0-8297-0839-1). Life Pubs Intl.

JESUS CHRIST–CRUCIFIXION

McAllister, Dawson. A Walk with Christ to the Cross. (Discussion Manual Ser.). 150p. 1981. pap. 7.95 (ISBN 0-8024-9193-6). Moody.

Murray, Andrew. The Blood of the Cross. 128p. 1981. pap. 2.50 (ISBN 0-88368-103-X). Whitaker Hse.

Schonfield, Hugh. After the Cross. LC 80-27856. 128p. 1981. 7.95 (ISBN 0-498-02549-7). A S Barnes.

JESUS CHRIST–DEVOTIONAL LITERATURE

Schlink, Basilea. Those Who Love Him. 96p. 1981. pap. 2.50 (ISBN 0-87123-609-5, 210609). Bethany Fell.

JESUS CHRIST–DIVINITY

see also Socinianism; Trinity; Unitarianism

Boom, Corrie T., tr. Na Casa De Meu Pai. (Portuguese Bks.). 1979. 1.50 (ISBN 0-8297-0894-4). Life Pubs Intl.

Brungardt, Helen. The Mystical Meaning of Jesus the Christ: Significant Episodes in the Life of the Master. 4.00 (ISBN 0-686-69472-4). Red Earth.

Ten Boom, Corrie, tr. En la Casa De Mi Padre. (Spanish Bks.). (Span.). 1978. 1.90 (ISBN 0-8297-0547-3). Life Pubs Intl.

JESUS CHRIST–FOUNDATION OF THE CHURCH

see Church–Foundation

JESUS CHRIST–INFLUENCE

Carl, Joseph B. Jesus in Our Affluent Society. 208p. 1981. 9.95 (ISBN 0-938234-01-3); pap. 5.95 (ISBN 0-938234-00-5). Ministry Pubns.

Cramer, Raymond L. Psicologia de Jesus y la Salud Mental. Vargas, Carlos A., tr. from Eng. LC 76-16438. 191p. (Orig., Span.). 1976. pap. 3.25 (ISBN 0-89922-074-6). Edit Caribe.

JESUS CHRIST–JUVENILE LITERATURE

see also Jesus Christ–Biography–Juvenile Literature

Dye, Gerald. Growing in Christ. (Double Trouble Puzzles Ser.). 48p. (Orig.). (gr. 6 up). 1981. pap. 1.25 (ISBN 0-87239-447-6, 2837). Standard Pub.

Jesus Feeds Five Thousand. (Tell-a-Bible Story Ser.). (Illus.). 28p. bds. 0.69 (ISBN 0-686-68645-4, 3689). Standard Pub.

Jesus Is Born. (Tell-a-Bible Story Ser.). (Illus.). 28p. bds. 0.69 (ISBN 0-686-68642-X, 3686). Standard Pub.

The Lost Sheep. (Tell-a-Bible Story Ser.). (Illus.). 28p. bds. 0.69 (ISBN 0-686-68646-2, 3690). Standard Pub.

Maschke, Ruby. Life of Christ Story-N-Puzzle Book. 48p. (Orig.). (gr. 4 up). 1981. pap. 1.25 (ISBN 0-87239-449-2, 2839). Standard Pub.

--Teachings of Christ Story-N-Puzzle Book. 48p. (Orig.). (gr. 4 up). 1981. pap. 1.25 (ISBN 0-87239-451-4, 2842). Standard Pub.

Meu Livro De Jesus. (Portugese Bks.). (Port.). 1979. 3.00 (ISBN 0-8297-0757-3). Life Pubs Intl.

Mi Libro De Jesus. (Spanish Bks.). 1977. 3.50 (ISBN 0-8297-0754-9). Life Pubs Intl.

Schraff, Francis, et al. Learning About Jesus. rev. ed. 80p. (gr. 2-4). 1980. pap. 1.95 (ISBN 0-89243-129-6). Liguori Pubns.

Stifle, J. M. ABC Book About Jesus. 1981. pap. 2.95 (ISBN 0-570-04054-X, 56-1715). Concordia.

Wise Men Visit Jesus. (Tell-a-Bible Story Ser.). (Illus.). 28p. bds. 0.69 (ISBN 0-686-68643-8, 3687). Standard Pub.

Zaccheus Meets Jesus. (Tell-a-Bible Story Ser.). (Illus.). 28p. bds. 0.69 (ISBN 0-686-68647-0, 3691). Standard Pub.

JESUS CHRIST–KINGDOM

see also Jesus Christ–Mystical Body

Newbigin, Lesslie. Sign of the Kingdom. 48p. (Orig.). 1981. pap. 1.95 (ISBN 0-8028-1878-1). Eerdmans.

JESUS CHRIST–LIFE

see Jesus Christ–Biography

JESUS CHRIST–LORD'S SUPPER

see Lord's Supper

JESUS CHRIST–MEDITATIONS

see Jesus Christ–Devotional Literature

JESUS CHRIST–MESSIAHSHIP

Shofner, David. Soul Winning. (Illus.). 96p. (Orig.). 1980. pap. write for info. (ISBN 0-89957-051-8). AMG Pubs.

JESUS CHRIST–MIRACLES

Bruce, A. B. The Miracles of Christ. Date not set. 17.25 (ISBN 0-86524-060-4). Klock & Klock.

Elliot, Elizabeth, tr. Doce Cestas De Mendrugos. (Spanish Bks.). (Span.). 1977. 1.90 (ISBN 0-8297-0804-9). Life Pubs Intl.

JESUS CHRIST–MYSTICAL BODY

see also Church–Foundation; Mystical Union

Baillie, D. M. God Was in Christ. 1977. pap. 6.50 (ISBN 0-571-05685-7, Pub. by Faber & Faber). Merrimack Bk Serv

JESUS CHRIST–NATIVITY

see also Christmas; Virgin Birth

Gromacki, Robert. The Virgin Birth of Christ. 200p. 1981. pap. 5.95 (ISBN 0-8010-3765-4). Baker Bk.

Lidden, H. P. & Orr, J. The Birth of Christ. Date not set. 13.95 (ISBN 0-86524-058-2). Klock & Klock.

Randegart, Lyle J. Mary's Baby. 1981. 6.75 (ISBN 0-8062-1656-5). Carlton.

Richardson, Don, tr. Hijo De Paz. (Spanish Bks.). (Span.). 1977. 2.45 (ISBN 0-8297-0572-4). Life Pubs Intl.

Schrage, Alice. Birth of the King. LC 80-53874. 128p. 1981. pap. 1.95 (ISBN 0-8307-0765-4). Regal.

JESUS CHRIST–NEW THOUGHT INTERPRETATIONS

Vines, Jerry. Interviews with Jesus. 1981. 3.25 (ISBN 0-8054-5180-3). Broadman.

JESUS CHRIST–PARABLES

Brewington, Doyle W. The Parables of the Kingdom. 64p. 1981. 4.95 (ISBN 0-8059-2774-3). Dorrance.

Chekijian, Vartan S. The Strange Dreams. 109p. 1980. 5.95 (ISBN 0-533-03227-X). Vantage.

Michaels, J. Ramsey. Servant & Son: Jesus in Parable & Gospel. LC 80-8465. 1981. pap. 8.95 (ISBN 0-8042-0409-8). John Knox.

The Parables of Christ. Date not set. 12.50 (ISBN 0-86524-059-0). Klock & Klock.

Perkins, Pheme. Hearing the Parables of Jesus. 216p. (Orig.). 1981. pap. 6.95 (ISBN 0-8091-2352-5). Paulist Pr.

JESUS CHRIST–PASSION

see also Lent

Marison, Fiscar, tr. The Passion of Our Lord. 302p. 1980. pap. 3.95 (ISBN 0-911988-37-8). AMI Pr.

JESUS CHRIST–PERSON AND OFFICES

The Doctrine of the Person of Jesus Christ. 2nd ed. (International Theological Library). 560p. Repr. of 1913 ed. pap. text ed. 14.50. Attic Pr.

O'Grady, John F. Models of Jesus. LC 80-1726. 192p. 1981. 10.95 (ISBN 0-385-17320-2). Doubleday.

JESUS CHRIST–PERSONALITY

see Jesus Christ–Character

JESUS CHRIST–PRAYERS

see also Lord's Prayer

Macarthur, John, Jr. Jesus' Pattern of Prayer. 200p. 1981. 7.95 (ISBN 0-8024-4961-1). Moody.

Poinsett, Brenda. When Jesus Prayed. LC 80-67896. 1981. pap. 3.25 (ISBN 0-8054-5179-X). Broadman.

JESUS CHRIST–PROPHECIES

Wallace, Arthur, compiled by. America's Witness for Jesus Christ. 70p. 1978. pap. 1.95 (ISBN 0-937892-04-1). LL Co.

Wilkerson, David. The Pocket Promise Book. gift ed. LC 72-86208. 96p. 1981. imitation leather 3.95 (ISBN 0-8307-0782-4). Regal.

JESUS CHRIST–PROPHETIC OFFICE

Hisis, Richard H. Jesus & the Future: Unsolved Questions on Eschatology. LC 80-82189. 1981. 16.50 (ISBN 0-8042-0341-5); pap. 9.95 (ISBN 0-8042-0340-7). John Knox.

JESUS CHRIST–RESURRECTION

see also Easter

Ladd, George E. Creo en la Resurreccion de Jesus. Blanch, Miguel, tr. from Eng. LC 77-79934. (Serie Creo). 204p. (Orig., Span.). 1977. pap. 3.95 (ISBN 0-89922-091-6). Edit Caribe.

McAllister, Dawson. A Walk with Christ Through the Resurrection. (Discussion Manual Ser.). 150p. 1981. pap. 7.95 (ISBN 0-8024-9192-8). Moody.

McDowell, Josh. The Resurrection Factor. 180p. (Orig.). 1981. 8.95 (ISBN 0-918956-71-4, Dist. by Here's Life Publishers Inc.); pap. 4.95 (ISBN 0-918956-72-2). Campus Crusade.

Moule, H. C. & Orr, J. The Resurrection of Christ. Date not set. 16.95 (ISBN 0-86524-062-0). Klock & Klock.

Nutting, George. Resurrection Is Not a Fairy Tale. 1981. 5.75 (ISBN 0-8062-1649-2). Carlton.

Shaw, J. M. The Resurrection of Jesus Christ. 223p. 1920. text ed. 4.95. Attic Pr.

JESUS CHRIST–SAYINGS

see Jesus Christ–Words

JESUS CHRIST–SECOND ADVENT

see Second Advent

JESUS CHRIST–SERMON ON THE MOUNT

see Sermon on the Mount

JESUS CHRIST–SIGNIFICANCE

Mohr, Victor. The Advent of Christ. 116p. Date not set. pap. 4.95 (ISBN 0-934616-16-7). Valkyrie Pr.

Thomas, Mayor I., tr. Vida Salvadora De Cristo. (Spanish Bks.). (Span.). 1979. 1.90 (ISBN 0-8297-0455-8). Vida Pub.

JESUS CHRIST–TEACHINGS

Bennion, Lowell. Jesus, The Master Teacher. 63p. 1980. 4.95 (ISBN 0-87747-833-3). Deseret Bk.

Boice, James M. The Sermon on the Mount. 328p. (Orig.). 1981. pap. 7.95 (ISBN 0-310-21511-0). Zondervan.

Bruce, F. F. Promise & Fulfilment: Present to Professor S. H. Hooke, by the Society for O. T. Study. 224p. 1963. text ed. 12.95x (ISBN 0-567-02055-X). Attic Pr.

Coniaris, A. M. Christ's Comfort for Those Who Sorrow. 1978. pap. 2.95 (ISBN 0-937032-00-X). Light & Life Pub Co MN.

--The Great I Came's of Jesus. 1980. pap. 5.95 (ISBN 0-686-27069-X). Light&Life Pub Co MN.

--No Man Ever Spoke As This Man. 1969. pap. 3.50 (ISBN 0-937032-18-2). Light&Life Pub Co MN.

Goppelt, Leonard. Theology of the New Testament: Jesus & the Gospels, Vol I. Alsup, John E., tr. LC 80-28947. 316p. 1981. 15.95 (ISBN 0-8028-2384-X). Eerdmans.

Hoeksma, Homer C. Voice of Our Fathers. LC 80-8082. 1980. 18.95 (ISBN 0-8254-2841-6). Kregel.

Lamont, Daniel. Christ & the World of Thought. 2nd ed. 309p. 1935. text ed. 6.50 (ISBN 0-567-02160-2). Attic Pr.

Neil, William. Why Listen? The Difficult Sayings of Jesus. (Orig.). pap. 1.50 (ISBN 0-89129-227-6). Jove Pubns.

JESUS CHRIST–TRIAL

Vassilakos, Aristarchus. The Trial of Jesus Christ. Orthodox Christian Educational Society, ed. 64p. (Orig.). 1950. pap. 2.00x (ISBN 0-938366-47-5). Orthodox Chr.

JESUS CHRIST–WORDS

Brown, John. Discourses & Sayings of Our Lord Jesus Christ, 3 vols. Date not set. Set. 45.00 (ISBN 0-88469-142-X). BMH Bks.

Hills, Christopher. The Christ Book: What Did He Really Say? Hills, Norah, ed. LC 80-5865. (Illus.). 204p. 1980. text ed. 10.95 (ISBN 0-916438-37-6). Univ of Trees.

Rajneesh, Bhagwan S. Words Like Fire: Discourses on Jesus. LC 80-8343. 288p. (Orig.). 1981. pap. 5.95 (ISBN 0-06-066787-7, RD 347, HarpR). Har-Row.

JESUS MOVEMENT

see Jesus People

JESUS PEOPLE

Smail, Thomas A. The Forgotten Father. 1981. pap. 5.95 (ISBN 0-8028-1879-X). Eerdmans.

JET PLANES–MOTORS

see Airplanes–Turbojet Engines

JET PLANES, MILITARY

Arnold, Rhodes. The Republic F-Eighty-Four: From Lead Sled to Super Hawg. (Illus.). 128p. 1981. pap. 9.95 (ISBN 0-89404-054-5). Aztex.

JEWELRY

see also Gems

Laffin, Richard F. Jewelers' Inventory Manual. 1981. 24.95 (ISBN 0-931744-04-0). Jewelers Circular.

Meilach, Dona Z. Ethnic Jewelry: Design & Inspiration for Craftsmen & Collectors. Aymar, Brant, ed. 1981. price not set. Crown.

--Ethnic Jewelry: Design & Inspiration for Craftsmen & Collectors. Aymar, Brandt, ed. (Illus.). 192p. 1981. pap. 19.95 (ISBN 0-517-52974-2, Harmony). Crown.

JEWELRY MAKING

see also Silverwork

Foote, Ted. Jewelry Making: A Guide for Beginners. LC 80-67547. (Illus.). 112p. 1981. 14.95 (ISBN 0-87192-130-8). Davis Mass.

Gibbs, Joan. Jewelry for Everyone: Soft Jewelry to Create at Home from Twine & Wool, Bone & Shell, Fur & Feather, Clay & Leather, Beads, Recyclables, Other Easy-to-Find Materials. (Illus.). 128p. 1981. 15.95 (ISBN 0-916144-74-7); pap. 7.95 (ISBN 0-916144-73-9). Stemmer Hse.

Kallenberg, Lawrence. Modeling in Wax for Jewelry & Sculpture. LC 80-70384. (Illus.). 288p. 1981. 18.50 (ISBN 0-686-69521-6); text ed. 18.50 (ISBN 0-686-69522-4). Chilton.

JEWELS

see Gems; Jewelry; Precious Stones

JEWETT, SARAH ORNE, 1849-1909

Westbrook, Perry D. Acres of Flint: Sarah Orne Jewett & Her Contemporaries. rev. ed. LC 80-20501. 204p. 1981. 12.50 (ISBN 0-8108-1357-2). Scarecrow.

JEWISH-ARAB RELATIONS

see also Israel-Arab Border Conflicts, 1949-

Bonds, Joy, et al. Our Roots Are Still Alive: The Story of the Paliesinian People. LC 77-10952. (Illus.). 182p. pap. 5.45 (ISBN 0-917654-12-9). IISJ.

Peretz, Don. Israel and the Palestine Arabs. LC 80-1915. 1981. Repr. of 1958 ed. 31.00 (ISBN 0-404-18984-9). AMS Pr.

Schuster, Robert L. Israel, The Middle East & the Moral Conscience of the Western World. (The Major Currents in Contemporary World History). (Illus.). 133p. 1981. 47.85 (ISBN 0-89266-301-4). Am Classical Coll Pr.

JEWISH-AFRO-AMERICAN RELATIONS

see Afro-Americans–Relations with Jews

JEWISH ART

see Art, Jewish

JEWISH ART AND SYMBOLISM

see also Symbolism in the Bible

Altman, Alexander. Essays in Jewish Intellectual History. LC 80-54471. 336p. 1981. text ed. 20.00 (ISBN 0-87451-192-5). U Pr of New Eng.

Kanof, Abram. Jewish Ceremonial Art & Religious Observance. 32.50 (ISBN 0-8109-0178-1); pap. 12.50 (ISBN 0-8109-2199-5). Abrams.

JEWISH AUTHORS

see Authors, Jewish

JEWISH CHRISTIANS

Here are entered works dealing with Christians of Jewish antecedence.

Longenecker, Richard N. The Christology of Early Jewish Christianity. (Twin Brooks Ser.). 178p. 1981. pap. 5.95 (ISBN 0-8010-5610-1). Baker Bk.

JEWISH CIVILIZATION

see Jews–Civilization

JEWISH ETHICS

see Ethics, Jewish

JEWISH FASTS AND FEASTS

see Fasts and Feasts–Judaism

JEWISH FOLK-LORE

see Folk-Lore, Jewish

JEWISH HOLIDAYS

see Fasts and Feasts–Judaism

JEWISH HOLOCAUST (1939-1945)

see Holocaust, Jewish (1939-1945)

JEWISH LANGUAGE

see Hebrew Language

JEWISH LAW

see also Commandments, Ten

Fairbairn, Patrick. Revelation of Law in Scripture. Date not set. 15.95 (ISBN 0-88469-135-7). BMH Bks.

Quint, Emanuel B. & Hecht, Neil S. Jewish Jurisprudence: Its Sources & Modern Applications, Vol. II. (Jewish Jurisprudence Ser.). 1981. price not set (ISBN 3-7186-0064-1). Harwood Academic.

Schodde, tr. Book of Jubilees. LC 80-53467. 96p. 1980. pap. 3.00 (ISBN 0-934666-08-3). Artisan Sales.

Sonsino, Rifat. Motive Clauses in Hebrew Law: Biblical Forms & Near Eastern Parallels. LC 79-15024. (Society of Biblical Literature Dissertation Ser.: No. 45). 13.50x (ISBN 0-89130-317-0, 060145); pap. 9.00x. Scholars Pr CA.

JEWISH LITERATURE–HISTORY AND CRITICISM

Bokser, Ben Z. The Jewish Mystical Tradition. 280p. 1981. 14.95 (ISBN 0-8298-0435-8); pap. 9.95 (ISBN 0-8298-0451-X). Pilgrim NY.

JEWISH MIGRATION

see Jews–Migrations

JEWISH PHILOSOPHY

De Segonzac, Catherine. Jewish Yoga: A System of Visualization & Movement Rooted in Genesis. 208p. 1981. pap. 7.95 (ISBN 0-87728-529-2). Weiser.

JEWISH PORTRAITS

see Portraits

JEWISH SYMBOLISM AND ART

see Jewish Art and Symbolism

JEWISH WAY OF LIFE

Unterman, Alan. Jews: Their Religious Beliefs & Practices. (Library of Religious Beliefs & Practices). 288p. 1980. write for info. (ISBN 0-7100-0743-4). Routledge & Kegan.

JEWS–BIBLIOGRAPHY

Eppler, Elizabeth E., ed. International Bibliography on Jewish Affairs: A Selected Annotated List of Books & Articles Published in the Diaspora, 1976-1977. 450p. 1981. lib. bdg. 35.00x (ISBN 0-86531-164-1). Westview.

JEWS–BIOGRAPHY

Friedlander, Saul. When Memory Comes. 1980. pap. 2.75 (ISBN 0-686-69240-3, 50807, Discus). Avon.

Jordan, Ruth. Daughter of the Waves: Memories of Growing up in Pre-War Palestine. LC 80-39526. 224p. 1981. 10.95 (ISBN 0-8008-2120-3). Taplinger.

JEWS–CABALA

see Cabala

JEWS–CIVILIZATION

Soloff, Mordecai, et al. Jewish Life. (Sacred Hebrew Ser.). (Illus.). 112p. (Orig.). 1980. pap. 3.50 (ISBN 0-86628-000-6). Ridgefield Pub.

JEWS–CUSTOMS

see Jews–Social Life and Customs

JEWS–EDUCATION

Goerlick, Sherry. City College & the Jewish Poor: Education in New York, 1880-1924. (Illus.). 256p. 1981. 14.95 (ISBN 0-8135-0905-X). Rutgers U Pr.

JEWS–EMIGRATION AND IMMIGRATION

see Jews–Migrations

JEWS–ETHICS

see Ethics, Jewish

JEWS–FASTS AND FEASTS

see Fasts and Feasts–Judaism

JEWS–FOLK-LORE

see Folk-Lore, Jewish

JEWS–HISTORY

Illustrated History of the Jewish People. LC 72-94297. 1973. 6.95 (ISBN 0-89388-078-7). Okpaku Communications.

JEWS–HISTORY–586 B.C.-70 A.D.

Schurer, Emil. History of the Jewish People in the Age of Jesus Christ (175 B.C.-A.D. 135, 2 vols. Vermes, Geza, et al, eds. Vol. 1, Repr. Of 1973 Ed., 632p. 42.00x (ISBN 0-567-02242-0); Vol. 2, Repr. Of 1979 Ed., 608p. 43.75x (ISBN 0-567-02243-9). Attic Pr.

JEWS–HISTORY–70-1789

Schurer, Emil. History of the Jewish People in the Age of Jesus Christ (175 B.C.-A.D. 135, 2 vols. Vermes, Geza, et al, eds. Vol. 1, Repr. Of 1973 Ed., 632p. 42.00x (ISBN 0-567-02242-0); Vol. 2, Repr. Of 1979 Ed., 608p. 43.75x (ISBN 0-567-02243-9). Attic Pr.

JEWS–LAW

see Jewish Law

JEWS–MIGRATIONS

Jacobs, Dan N. & Paul, Ellen F., eds. Studies of the Third Wave: Recent Migration of Soviet Jews to the United States. (Replica Edition Ser.). 176p. 1981. lib. bdg. 20.00x (ISBN 0-86531-143-9). Westview.

JEWS–MISCELLANEA

Kolatch, Alfred J. Jewish Info. Quiz Book. LC 66-30508. 250p. 1980. 9.95 (ISBN 0-8246-0248-X). Jonathan David.

JEWS–POLITICAL AND SOCIAL CONDITIONS

see also Zionism

Isaac, Rael J. Party & Politics in Israel: Three Visions of a Jewish State. (Professional Ser.). 256p. 1980. lib. bdg. 19.50 (ISBN 0-582-28196-2). Longman.

JEWS–PRAYER-BOOKS AND DEVOTIONS

Soloff, Mordecai, et al. Your Siddur. (Sacred Hebrew Ser.). (Illus.). 175p. 1981. pap. 3.50 (ISBN 0-86628-001-4). Ridgefield Pub.

JEWS–RELATIONS WITH AFRO-AMERICANS
see Afro-Americans–Relations with Jews
JEWS–RELIGION
see Judaism
JEWS–RITES AND CEREMONIES
see also Jewish Way of Life
Israel Ministry. What Is a Jew? 1975. 30.00 (ISBN 0-379-13904-9). Oceana.
Unterman, Alan. Jews: Their Religious Beliefs & Practices. (Library of Religious Beliefs & Practices). 288p. 1980. write for info. (ISBN 0-7100-0743-4). Routledge & Kegan.
JEWS–RITUAL
see Jews–Social Life and Customs
JEWS–SOCIAL CONDITIONS
see Jews–Political and Social Conditions
JEWS–SOCIAL LIFE AND CUSTOMS
see also Jewish Way of Life
Goldberg, M. Hirsh. Just Because They're Jewish: The Incredible, Ironic, Bizarre, Funny, & Provocative in the Way Jews Are Seen by Other People. LC 78-6400. 264p. 1981. pap. 6.95 (ISBN 0-8128-6122-1). Stein & Day.
Unterman, Alan. Jews: Their Religious Beliefs & Practices. (Library of Religious Beliefs & Practices). 288p. 1980. write for info. (ISBN 0-7100-0743-4). Routledge & Kegan.
JEWS–ZIONISM
see Zionism
JEWS IN CHINA
White, William C. Chinese Jews: A Compilation of Matters Relating to the Jews of K'ai-feng Fu. abr., 2nd ed. 9.95 (ISBN 0-8037-1252-9). Dial.
JEWS IN ENGLAND
see Jews in Great Britain
JEWS IN FOLK-LORE
see Folk-Lore, Jewish
JEWS IN GREAT BRITAIN
Webb, Philip C. & Grove, Joseph. The Question Whether a Jew, Born Within the British Dominions, Was, Before the Making of the Late Act of Parliament, a Person Capable by Law, to Purchase & Hold Lands to Him and His Heirs. Berkowitz, David S. & Thorne, Samuel E., eds. LC 77-86671. (Classics of English Legal History in the Modern Era Ser.: Vol. 48). 169p. 1979. lib. bdg. 40.00 (ISBN 0-8240-3097-4). Garland Pub.
JEWS IN LITERATURE
Blackman, Murray. A Guide to Jewish Themes in American Fiction, 1940-1980. LC 80-24953. 271p. 1981. lib. bdg. 15.00 (ISBN 0-8108-1380-7). Scarecrow.
Panitz, Esther L. The Alien in Their Midst: Images of the Jews in English Literature. LC 78-75183. 150p. 1981. 10.50 (ISBN 0-8386-2318-2). Fairleigh Dickinson.
JEWS IN RUSSIA
Frankel, Jonathan. Prophecy & Politics: Socialism, Nationalism, & the Russian Jews, 1862-1917. LC 80-14414. (Illus.). 816p. Date not set. price not set (ISBN 0-521-23028-4). Cambridge U Pr.
Rybakov, Anatoli. Heavy Sand. Shukman, Harold, tr. from Rus. 384p. 1981. 13.95 (ISBN 0-670-36499-1). Viking Pr.
Schneersohn, Y. Y. Notations on the Arrest. Levin, Moshe Chaim, ed. Gurevich, David A., tr. from Hebrew. LC 80-21987. (Illus.). 226p. (Orig.). 1980. 11.75 (ISBN 0-86639-100-2). Friends Refugees.
JEWS IN THE UNITED STATES
Ford, Gertrude. Eighty-One Sheriff Street. 272p. 1981. 10.95 (ISBN 0-8119-0343-5). Fell.
Ginzberg, Eli. American Jews: The Building of a Voluntary Community. (Texts & Studies Ser.). 1980. write for info. Am Jewish Hist Soc.
Jacobs, Dan N. & Paul, Ellen F., eds. Studies of the Third Wave: Recent Migration of Soviet Jews to the United States. (Replica Edition Ser.). 176p. 1981. lib. bdg. 20.00x (ISBN 0-86531-143-9). Westview.
Kaganoff, Nathan M., ed. Solidarity & Kinship: Essays on American Zionism. (Illus.). 1980. 5.00. Am Jewish Hist Soc.
Mitchell, William E. Mishpokhe: A Study of New York City Jewish Family Clubs. 262p. 1980. text ed. 19.95 (ISBN 90-27976-95-3); pap. text ed. 5.95 (ISBN 0-202-01166-6). Aldine Pub.
Orthodox Judaism in America. (American Jewish History Ser.: Vol. 69, Pt. 2). 1979. 6.00. Am Jewish Hist Soc.
Roiphe, Anne. Newcomer. 1981. price not set (ISBN 0-671-41455-0, Linden). S&S.
JEWS IN THE UNITED STATES–HISTORY
Brener, David. The Jews of Lancaster, Pennsylvania: A Story with Two Beginnings. LC 79-21690. (Illus.). 200p. 1979. 18.00 (ISBN 0-686-28857-2); pap. 12.00 (ISBN 0-686-28858-0). Cong Shaarai.
Brener, David A. The Jews of Lancaster, Pennsylvania: A Story with Two Beginnings. (Illus.). 188p. (Orig.). 1981. 18.00 (ISBN 0-9605482-1-1); pap. 12.00 (ISBN 0-9605482-0-3). Shaarai Shomayim.
Howe, Irving & Libo, Kenneth. How We Lived: A Documentary History of Immigrant Jews in America, Eighteen Eighty-Nineteen Thirty. 1981. pap. 6.95 (ISBN 0-452-25269-5, Z5269, Plume Bks). NAL.
JEWS IN THE UNITED STATES–JUVENILE LITERATURE
Butwin, Frances. Jews in America. rev. ed. LC 68-31501. (In America Bks.). (Illus.). (gr. 5-11). 1980. PLB 5.95. Lerner Pubns.
JOAN OF ARC
see Jeanne D'Arc, Saint, 1412-1431
JOB APPLICATIONS
see Applications for Positions
JOB ANALYSIS
see also Job Evaluation
Patterson, T. T. Job Evaluation: A Manual for the Patterson Method, Vol. II. 208p. 1978. text ed. 22.00x (ISBN 0-220-66844-2, Pub. by Busn Bks England). Renouf.
JOB DISCRIMINATION
see Discrimination in Employment
JOB EVALUATION
see also Job Analysis
Bartley, Douglas. Job Evaluation-Wage & Salary Administration. LC 80-21099. 272p. 1981. text ed. 14.95 (ISBN 0-201-00095-4). A-W.
Elizur, Dov. Job Evaluation: A Systematic Approach. 188p. 1980. text ed. 37.25 (ISBN 0-566-02120-X, Pub. by Gower Pub Co England). Renouf.
Patterson, T. T. Job Evaluation: A Manual for the Patterson Method, Vol. II. 208p. 1978. text ed. 22.00x (ISBN 0-220-66844-2, Pub. by Busn Bks England). Renouf.
JOB OPENINGS
see Job Vacancies
JOB PERFORMANCE STANDARDS
see Performance Standards
JOB RATING
see Job Evaluation
JOB RESUMES
see Applications for Positions; Resumes (Employment)
JOB SATISFACTION
Carroll, Bonnie. Job Satisfaction. (Key Issues Ser.: No. 3). 1973. pap. 2.00 (ISBN 0-87546-206-5). NY Sch Indus Rel.
Productivity, Quality of Working Life & Labour-Management Relations. 23p. 1976. 2.75 (APO62, APO). Unipub.
Taylor, Linda K. Not for Bread Alone: An Appreciation of Job Enrichment. 3rd ed. 202p. 1980. pap. 12.25x (ISBN 0-220-67019-6, Pub. by Busn Bks England). Renouf.
JOB TRAINING
see Occupational Training
JOB VACANCIES
O'Callaghan, Dorothy. The Job Catalog: Where to Find That Creative Job in Washington D. C./Baltimore. 2nd ed. LC 80-83443. 1980. pap. 6.00 (ISBN 0-914694-05-7). Mail Order.
Robert Lang Adams Associates, ed. The New York Job Bank: Conprehensive Guide to Major Employers Throughout Greater New York City Including Northern New Jersey, Southwestern Connecticut, Long Island, Southeastern New York State, & All Five Boroughs of New York City. 450p. (Orig.). 1981. pap. 9.95 (ISBN 0-937860-03-4). Adams Inc MA.
JOBS
see Professions
JOGGING
Kreuter, Gretchen. Running the Twin Cities. (Illus.). 95p. 1980. pap. 3.95 (ISBN 0-931714-08-7). Nodin Pr.
JOHN PAUL 2ND, POPE
Castle, Tony, ed. Through the Year with Pope John Paul II: Reading for Every Day of the Year. 288p. 1981. 12.95 (ISBN 0-8245-0041-5). Crossroad NY.
JOHN THE BAPTIST, SAINT, ca. 5 B.C.-ca. 30 A.D.
Battersby, W. J. De la Salle: A Pioneer of Modern Education. 236p. 1981. Repr. of 1949 ed. lib. bdg. 40.00 (ISBN 0-89987-065-1). Darby Bks.
JOINTS
Guyot, J. Atlas of Human Limb Joints. (Illus.). 252p. 1981. 146.30 (ISBN 0-387-10380-5). Springer-Verlag.
JOINTS–DISLOCATIONS
see Dislocations
JOINTS–DISEASES
see also Arthritis
Adams, Ruth & Murray, Frank. All You Should Know About Arthritis. 256p. (Orig.). 1979. pap. 2.25 (ISBN 0-915962-28-4). Larchmont Bks.
Schajowicz, F. Tumors & Tumor Like Lesions of Bone & Joints. (Illus.). 650p. 65.00 (ISBN 0-387-90492-1). Springer-Verlag.
Solberg, William K. & Clark, Glenn T. Temporomandibular Joint Problems: Biological Diagnosis & Treatment. 177p. 1980. 39.00 (ISBN 0-931386-18-7). Quint Pub Co.
JOKES
see Wit and Humor
JONAH, THE PROPHET
Lacocque, Andre & Lacocque, Pierre. Jonah Complex. LC 80-84649. 1981. 14.00 (ISBN 0-8042-0091-2); pap. 7.95 (ISBN 0-8042-0092-0). John Knox.
JONAH, THE PROPHET–JUVENILE LITERATURE
Jonah & the Big Fish. (Tell-a-Bible Story Ser.). (Illus.). 28p. bds. 0.69 (ISBN 0-686-68641-1, 3685). Standard Pub.
JONES, JAMES, 1921-
Giles, James R. James Jones. (United States Authors Ser.: No. 366). 1981. lib. bdg. 9.95 (ISBN 0-8057-7293-6). Twayne.
JONGLEURS
see Troubadours; Trouveres
JONSON, BEN, 1573-1637
Dunn, Esther C. Ben Jonson's Art. 159p. 1980. Repr. of 1925 ed. lib. bdg. 30.00 (ISBN 0-8495-1122-4). Arden Lib.
Peterson, Richard S. Imitation & Praise in the Poems of Ben Jonson. LC 80-26261. (Illus.). 280p. 1981. 18.50x (ISBN 0-300-02586-6). Yale U Pr.
JOSEPH, CHIEF OF THE NEZ PERCES, 1840-1904
Haines, Francis. Red Eagles of the Northwest: The Story of Chief Joseph & His People. LC 76-43728. (Illus.). 376p. 1980. Repr. of 1939 ed. 32.50 (ISBN 0-404-15569-3). AMS Pr.
JOSEPH 1ST, EMPEROR OF GERMANY, 1678-1711
In Quest & Crisis: Emperor Joseph I & the Habsburg Monarchy. LC 77-88358. 278p. 1979. 12.95 (ISBN 0-911198-53-9). Purdue.
JOSEPH, SAINT
Life & Glories of St. Joseph. LC 80-53744. 1980. pap. write for info. (ISBN 0-89555-161-6). Tan Bks Pubs.
The Story of Joseph. 79p. pap. 0.50. Faith Pub Hse.
JOURNALISM
see also Crime and the Press; Editing; Editorials; Foreign News; Liberty of the Press; News-Letters; Newspaper Court Reporting; Newspaper Layout and Typography; Newspaper Publishing; Newspapers; Periodicals; Press; Television Broadcasting of News
April, Koral. Headlines & Deadlines. 64p. (gr. 4-7). 1981. write for info. Messner.
Golding, Elliot. Making the News. (Illus.). 241p. 1979. text ed. 35.00x (ISBN 0-582-50460-0). Longman.
Hellmann, John. Fables of Fact: The New Journalism As New Fiction. LC 80-23881. 175p. 1981. 11.95 (ISBN 0-252-00847-2). U of Ill Pr.
Krawiec, T. S., ed. A Road Not Taken: The Editorial Opinions of Frederick C. Thorne. 1981. pap. 11.95 (ISBN 0-88422-013-3). Clinical Psych.
Lendvai, Paul. The Bureaucracy of Truth. 350p. 1981. lib. bdg. 20.00x (ISBN 0-86531-142-0). Westview.
Long, Joan & Long, Ronald. Writer's & Photographer's Guide to Newspaper Markets. 2nd ed. 175p. 1981. pap. price not set (ISBN 0-936940-01-8). Helm Pub.
Ross, Lillian. Reporting. 442p. 1981. 12.94 (ISBN 0-396-07948-2); pap. 8.95 (ISBN 0-396-07949-0). Dodd.
Spencer, M. Lyle. News Writing. 357p. 1980. Repr. of 1917 ed. lib. bdg. 30.00 (ISBN 0-89760-828-3). Telegraph Bks.
Wall, C. Edward, et al, eds. Media Review Digest, Vol. 10, 1980. 1980. 120.00 (ISBN 0-87650-129-3). Pierian.
JOURNALISM–BIOGRAPHY
see Journalists
JOURNALISM–HANDBOOKS, MANUALS, ETC.
Holley, Frederick S., ed. Los Angeles Times Stylebook: A Manual for Writers, Editors, Journalists & Students. 1981. pap. 6.95 (ISBN 0-452-00552-3, F552, Mer). NAL.
Romero, Donald G. A Handbook on Professional Magazine Article Writing. 1975. 3.95 (ISBN 0-87543-127-5). Lucas.
JOURNALISM–HISTORY
Diprima, Richard. Headline History of the Sixties. LC 80-71081. 73p. (Orig.). (gr. 6-12). pap. text ed. write for info. (ISBN 0-86652-011-2). Educ Indus.
JOURNALISM–JUVENILE LITERATURE
Jaspersohn, William. A Day in the Life of a Television News Reporter. (Illus.). 96p. (gr. 5 up). 1981. 9.95 (ISBN 0-316-45813-9). Little.
JOURNALISM–POLITICAL ASPECTS
De Volpi, A., et al. Governmental Secrecy & National Security: The Progressive Case. (Pergamon Policy Studies on International Politics). (Illus.). 400p. 1980. 30.00 (ISBN 0-08-025995-2); pap. 15.00 (ISBN 0-08-027529-X). Pergamon.
JOURNALISM–STUDY AND TEACHING
Metzler, Ken. Newswriting Exercises. (Illus.). 288p. 1981. pap. text ed. 11.95 (ISBN 0-13-617803-0). P-H.
JOURNALISM–COMMUNIST COUNTRIES
Lendvai, Paul. The Bureaucracy of Truth. 350p. 1981. lib. bdg. 20.00x (ISBN 0-86531-142-0). Westview.
Mickiewicz, Ellen. Media & the Russian Public. 170p. 1981. 19.95 (ISBN 0-03-057681-4); pap. 8.95 (ISBN 0-03-057679-2). Praeger.
JOURNALISM–GREAT BRITAIN
Osborn, George. The Role of the British Press in the 1976 Presidential Election. 64p. 1981. 10.00 (ISBN 0-682-49667-7). Exposition.
JOURNALISM–JAPAN
Asano, Osamu & Ishiwata, Mutsuko, eds. The Japanese Press, 1980. 32nd ed. Henshu-sha, Century E. & Higashi, Shinbu, trs. from Japanese. LC 49-25552. (Illus.). 172p. (Orig.). 1980. pap. 25.00x (ISBN 0-8002-2699-2). Intl Pubns Serv.
Kim, Young C. Japanese Journalists & Their World. LC 80-25720. 1981. price not set (ISBN 0-8139-0877-9). U Pr of Va.
JOURNALISM–UNITED STATES
Campbell, Georgetta M. Extant Collections of Early Black Newspapers: A Research Guide to the Black Press, 1880-1915, with an Index to the Boston Guardian, 1902-1904. LC 80-51418. 433p. 1981. 28.50x (ISBN 0-87875-197-1). Whitston Pub.
Hellmann, John. Fables of Fact: The New Journalism As New Fiction. LC 80-23881. 175p. 1981. 11.95 (ISBN 0-252-00847-2). U of Ill Pr.
Kerby, William F. A Proud Profession: Memoirs of a Wall Street Journal Reporter, Editor & Publisher. 200p. 1981. 12.95 (ISBN 0-87094-235-2). Dow Jones-Irwin.
Lowitt, Richard & Beasley, Maurine, eds. One Third of a Nation: Lorena Hickok Reports on the Great Depression. (Illus.). 450p. 1981. 18.95 (ISBN 0-252-00849-9). U of Ill Pr.
Murphy, James E. & Murphy, Sharon M. Let My People Know: American Indian Journalism, 1828-1978. LC 80-5941. 300p. 1981. 14.95 (ISBN 0-8061-1623-4). U of Okla Pr.
Schlesinger, Arthur M. Prelude to Independence: The Newspaper War on Britain 1764-1776. LC 80-22830. 340p. 1980. pap. text ed. 8.95x (ISBN 0-930350-13-8). NE U Pr.
Schudson, Michael. Discovering the News: A Social History of American Newspapers. LC 78-54997. 288p. 1981. pap. 5.95 (ISBN 0-465-01666-9). Basic.
Tinney, James S. & Rector, Justine J. Issues & Trends in Afro-American Journalism. LC 80-6074. 371p. 1980. lib. bdg. 20.75 (ISBN 0-8191-1352-2); pap. text ed. 12.50 (ISBN 0-8191-1353-0). U Pr of Amer.
JOURNALISM, AFRO-AMERICAN
see Afro-American Press
JOURNALISTIC PHOTOGRAPHY
see Photography, Journalistic
JOURNALISTS
Aaseng, Nathan. Walter Cronkite. (The Achievers Ser.). (Illus.). (gr. 4-9). 1981. PLB 5.95 (ISBN 0-8225-0486-3). Lerner Pubns.
Erlanger, Ellen. Dan Rather. (The Achievers Ser.). (Illus.). (gr. 4-9). 1981. PLB 5.95 (ISBN 0-8225-0487-1). Lerner Pubns.
Ethridge, Willie S. Mark Ethridge: The Life & Times of a Great Newspaperman. (Illus.). 484p. 1981. 20.00 (ISBN 0-8149-0852-7). Vanguard.
Hess, Stephen. The Washington Reporters. LC 80-70077. 275p. 1981. 17.95 (ISBN 0-8157-3594-4); pap. 6.95 (ISBN 0-8157-3593-6). Brookings.
International Portrait Gallery: Vol. 11, Second Media People Supplement. (Illus.). 64p. 1981. 35.00 (ISBN 0-686-69447-3, IPG-11). Gale.
Metcalf, Pricilla. James Knowles: Victorian Editor & Architect. (Illus.). 414p. 1980. 44.00x (ISBN 0-19-812626-3). Oxford U Pr.
Tyrrell, Robert. Work of the Television Journalist. 2nd ed. LC 80-41970. 200p. 1981. 22.95 (ISBN 0-240-51051-8). Focal Pr.
Waugh, Evelyn. A Little Order: A Selection from His Journalism. Gallagher, Donat, ed. 224p. 1981. 12.95 (ISBN 0-316-92633-7). Little.
Wheeler, Leslie, ed. Loving Warriors: Selected Letters of Lucy Stone & Henry B. Blackwell, 1853-1893. (Illus.). 1981. 19.95. Dial.
JOURNALISTS–CORRESPONDENCE, REMINISCENCES, ETC.
see also subdivision Personal Narratives under names of Wars, e.g. World War, 1939-1945–Personal Narratives
Cousins, Norman. The Human Option: An Autobiographical Notebook. (Illus.). 1981. 9.95 (ISBN 0-393-01430-4). Norton.
Demaitre, Edmund. Eyewitness: A Journalist Covers the Twentieth Century. (Illus.). 450p. 1981. 17.50 (ISBN 0-8044-1218-9). Ungar.
Grant, Ian. Cameraman at War. (Illus.). 200p. 1981. 31.95 (ISBN 0-85059-489-8). Aztex.
Noble, Gil. Black Is the Color of My TV Tube. (Illus.). 1981. 10.00 (ISBN 0-8184-0297-0). Lyle Stuart.
Rutstrum, Calvin. A Columnist Looks at Life. 133p. (Orig.). 1981. pap. 5.95 (ISBN 0-931714-10-9). Nodin Pr.
Stingley, James. Mother, Mother. 224p. 1981. 11.95 (ISBN 0-312-92543-3). St Martin.
Weinberg, Steve. The Secrets of Washington Journalists. 1981. 12.50 (ISBN 0-87491-424-8). Acropolis.
JOURNEYS
see Voyages and Travels
JOY AND SORROW
see also Happiness
Derrick, Christopher. Joy Without a Cause: Selected Essays. 9.95 (ISBN 0-89385-007-1). Green Hill.
Evans, Colleen T. A New Joy. (Orig.). pap. 1.50 (ISBN 0-89129-015-X). Jove Pubns.
Joy. 186p. 1980. 6.95 (ISBN 0-87747-819-8). Deseret Bk.
Powell, Paul W. Why Me, Lord? 120p. 1981. pap. 3.95 (ISBN 0-89693-007-6). Victor Bks.
JOYCE, JAMES, 1882-1941
Allt, Peter. Some Aspects of the Life & Works of James Augustine Joyce. 50p. 1980. Repr. of 1942 ed. lib. bdg. 7.50 (ISBN 0-89987-026-0). Darby Bks.
Bauerle, Ruth. A Word List to James Joyce's "Exiles". LC 80-8487. 240p. 1981. lib. bdg. 40.00 (ISBN 0-8240-9500-6). Garland Pub.

Bowen, Zack, ed. Irish Renaissance Annual II. 192p. 1981. 12.00 (ISBN 0-87413-185-5). U Delaware Pr.

Cope, Jackson I. Joyce's Cities: Archaeologies of the Soul. LC 80-8056. 176p. 1981. text ed. 12.95x (ISBN 0-8018-2543-1). Johns Hopkins.

Costello, Peter. James Joyce. (Gill's Irish Lives Ser.). 135p. 1980. 20.00 (ISBN 0-7171-1077-X, Pub. by Gill & Macmillan Ireland); pap. 6.50 (ISBN 0-7171-0986-0). Irish Bk Ctr.

Devlin, Laura K. Looking Inward: Studies in James Joyce, E.M. Forster, & the Twentieth Century Novel. 1980. lib. bdg. 59.95 (ISBN 0-87700-269-X). Revisionist Pr.

Ellmann, Richard. The Consciousness of Joyce. 160p. 1981. pap. 3.95 (ISBN 0-19-502898-8, GB 636, OPB). Oxford U Pr.

Lyons, John L. James Joyce's Miltonic Affliction. 52p. 1980. Repr. of 1973 ed. lib. bdg. 7.50 (ISBN 0-8492-1632-X). R West.

O'Brien, Edna. James & Nora: A Portrait of Joyce's Marraige. 50p. 1981. limited signed edition 35.00 (ISBN 0-935716-09-2). Lord John.

Tindall, William. A Readers' Guide to James Joyce. 304p. 1959. pap. 5.95 (ISBN 0-374-50112-2). FS&G.

JOYS FAMILY

Lee, Helen B. Joy Supplement, Two: Descendants of Thomas Joy, Pt.2. LC 76-45277. (Illus.). 1980. pap. write for info. (ISBN 0-87106-075-2). Globe Pequot.

JUDAISM

Here are entered works on Jewish faith and practice in which the main stream of orthodox Judaism is treated and no cleavage is stressed.

see also Cabala; Commandments, Ten; Fasts and Feasts–Judaism; Sabbath

Acceptanc: Establishing the Covenant, Vol. 8. 250p. Date not set. 11.95. Maznaim.

American Jewish Year Book, 1981, Vol. 81. LC 99-4040. 1980. 20.00 (ISBN 0-8276-0185-9). Am Jewish Comm.

Haskelevich, B., tr. from Hebrew. The Disputation of Nachmanides: With Introduction & Commentaries. (Rus.). 1981. pap. 3.75 (ISBN 0-938666-00-2). CHAMH.

Karta, Neturei. Judaism & Zionism: Principles & Definitions. 1980. lib. bdg. 59.95 (ISBN 0-686-68745-0). Revisionist Pr.

Latner, Helen. The Book of Modern Jewish Etiquette: A Guide to All Occasions. LC 80-22537. (Illus.). 416p. 19.95 (ISBN 0-8052-3757-7). Schocken.

Neusner, Jacob. The Life of Torah: Readings in the Jewish Religious Experience. 1974. pap. text ed. 7.95x (ISBN 0-8221-0124-6). Dickenson.

JUDAISM–CEREMONIES AND PRACTICES

see Jews–Rites and Ceremonies

JUDAISM–DEVOTIONAL EXERCISES

see Jews–Prayer-Books and Devotions

JUDAISM–EDUCATION

see Jews–Education

JUDAISM–HISTORY

Moore, G. F. History of Religions: Judaism, Christianity, Mohammedanism, Vol. II. (International Theological Library). 568p. 1920. text ed. 13.95x (ISBN 0-567-07203-7). Attic Pr.

Sigal, Phillip. Emergence of Contemporary Judaism: The Foundation of Judaism from Biblical Origins to the Sixth Century A. D, Vol. 1, Pts. 1 & 2. Incl. Pt. 1. From the Origins to the Separation of Christianity. (Pittsburgh Theological Monographs: No. 29). pap. text ed. 17.50 (ISBN 0-686-64852-8); Pt. 2. Rabbinic Judaism. (Pittsburgh Theological Monographs: No. 29a). pap. text ed. 15.75 (ISBN 0-915138-46-8). 1980. pap. text ed. 31.25 set (ISBN 0-915138-46-8). Pickwick.

JUDAISM–RITUALS

see Jews–Rites and Ceremonies

JUDAISM AND CHRISTIANITY

see Christianity and Other Religions–Judaism

JUDGES

see also Courts; Judgments; Judicial Process; Justice, Administration of

Berkson, Larry C. & Vandenberg, Donna, eds. National Roster of Women Judges, 1980. 120p. (Orig.). 1980. pap. 2.95 (8563). Am Judicature.

Flory, Thomas. Judge & Jury in Imperial Brazil, 1808-1871: Social Control & Political Stability in the New State. 288p. 1981. text ed. 25.00x (ISBN 0-292-74015-8). U of Tex Pr.

JUDGES–CORRESPONDENCE, REMINISCENCES, ETC.

Williams, Dakin. The Bar Bizarre. 270p. 1980. write for info. (ISBN 0-86629-009-5). Sunrise MO.

JUDGMENT

Keeney, Barnaby C. Judgment by Peers. LC 80-2023. 1981. Repr. of 1949 ed. 25.00 (ISBN 0-404-18571-1). AMS Pr.

Sherif, Muzafer & Hovland, Carl I. Social Judgment: Assimilation & Contrast Effects in Communication & Attitude Change. LC 80-21767. (Yale Studies in Attitude & Communication: Vol. 4). xii, 218p. 1981. Repr. of 1961 ed. lib. bdg. 25.00x (ISBN 0-313-22438-2, SHSO). Greenwood.

JUDGMENT (ETHICS)

Hudson, Donald. A Century of Moral Philosophy. 1980. 18.95 (ISBN 0-312-12777-4). St Martin.

JUDGMENTS

see also Jurisdiction; Sentences (Criminal Procedure)

Black, Charles L., Jr. Decision According to Law: Nineteen Seventy-Nine Holmes Lectures. 1981. 12.95 (ISBN 0-393-01452-5). Norton.

JUDGMENTS BY PEERS

see Jury

JUDICIAL BEHAVIOR

see Judicial Process

JUDICIAL DECISION-MAKING

see Judicial Process

JUDICIAL INVESTIGATIONS

see Governmental Investigations

JUDICIAL OFFICERS

see Courts–Officials and Employees

JUDICIAL PROCESS

see also Evidence (Law); Judgments

Black, Charles L., Jr. Decision According to Law: Nineteen Seventy-Nine Holmes Lectures. 1981. 12.95 (ISBN 0-393-01452-5). Norton.

Carbon, Susan B. & Berkson, Larry C. Judicial Retention Elections in the United States. LC 80-69565. 96p. (Orig.). 1980. pap. 4.00 (8566). Am Judicature.

Chian, Nancy & Berkson, Larry. Literature on Judicial Selection. LC 80-69415. 112p. (Orig.). 1980. pap. 4.00 (8564). Am Judicature.

Starr, Isidore. Great Ideas in the Law-Justice: Due Process of Law. 300p. 1981. pap. text ed. 6.50 (ISBN 0-8299-1020-4). West Pub.

Tesitor, Irene A. & Sinks, Dwight B. Judicial Conduct Organization. 2nd ed. 96p. 1980. pap. 3.75 (8567). Am Judicature.

Zerman, Melvyn B. Beyond a Reasonable Doubt: Understanding the American Jury System. 9.95 (ISBN 0-690-04094-6). T y Crowell.

JUDICIARY

see Courts

JUDO

see also Karate

Clark, Buddy. Alone, Unarmed but Safe--the Woman's Judo Defense Book. (Illus.). 128p. 1981. 8.00 (ISBN 0-682-49712-6); pap. 6.00 (ISBN 0-682-49711-8). Exposition.

JUGENDSTIL

see Art Nouveau

JUNG, CARL GUSTAV, 1875-1961

Babcock, Winifred. Jung, Harold, Hesse: Contributions of C. G. Jung, Preston Harold & Hermann Hesse Toward a Spiritual Psychology. 275p. 1981. 12.95 (ISBN 0-686-68720-5). World Authors.

Brome, Vincent. Jung: Man & Myth. LC 80-25159. 327p. 1981. pap. 6.95 (ISBN 0-689-70588-3). Atheneum.

Corbin, et al. Spring '80: An Annual of Archetypal Psychology & Jungian Thought. Hillman, James, ed. 196p. (Orig.). 1980. pap. text ed. 10.00 (ISBN 0-88214-015-9). Spring Pubns.

Hillman, et al. Spring 'seventy-Six: An Annual of Archetypal Psychology & Jungian Thought. Hillman, James, ed. 218p. (Orig.). 1976. pap. text ed. 12.00 (ISBN 0-88214-011-6). Spring Pubns.

Nichols, Sallie. Jung & Tarot: An Archetypal Journey. 1980. 25.00 (ISBN 0-87728-480-6); pap. 9.95 (ISBN 0-87728-515-2). Weiser.

JUNIOR COLLEGES

see also Community Colleges

The Community, Technical, & Junior College in the United States. 96p. 1978. 3.50 (IIE). Unipub.

JURIDICAL PSYCHOLOGY

see Psychology, Forensic

JURISDICTION

see also Conflict of Laws; Judgments

Ault, Warren O. Private Jurisdiction in England. LC 80-1998. 1981. Repr. of 1923 ed. 37.00 (ISBN 0-404-18550-9). AMS Pr.

JURISPRUDENCE–HISTORY

Ullmann, Walter. Jurisprudence in the Middle Ages. 390p. 1980. 75.00x (ISBN 0-86078-065-1, Pub. by Variorum England). State Mutual Bk.

JURISPRUDENCE, COMPARATIVE

see Comparative Law

JURISPRUDENCE, MEDICAL

see Medical Jurisprudence

JURISTIC PSYCHOLOGY

see Law–Psychology; Psychology, Forensic

JURISTS

see Lawyers

JURY

see also Instructions to Juries

Zerman, Melvyn B. Beyond a Reasonable Doubt: Understanding the American Jury System. 9.95 (ISBN 0-690-04094-6). T y Crowell.

JUSTICE

Gard, Wayne. Frontier Justice. (Illus.). 324p. 1981. 17.50 (ISBN 0-8061-0194-6); pap. 8.95 (ISBN 0-8061-1755-9). U of Okla Pr.

JUSTICE, ADMINISTRATION OF

see also Courts; Criminal Justice, Administration of; Governmental Investigations; Judges

Fogel, David & Hudson, Joe, eds. Justice As Fairness: Perspectives on the Justice Model. 300p. 1981. pap. text ed. price not set (ISBN 0-87084-287-0). Anderson Pub Co.

Hensley, Thomas R. The Kent State Incident: Impact of Judicial Process on Public Attitudes. LC 80-1712. (Contributions in Political Science Ser.: No. 56). 224p. 1981. lib. bdg. 27.50 (ISBN 0-313-21220-1, HKS/). Greenwood.

Nelson, William E. Dispute & Conflict Resolution in Plymouth County, Massachusetts, 1725 - 1825. LC 80-17403. (Studies in Legal History). 240p. 1980. 19.50x (ISBN 0-8078-1454-7). U of NC Pr.

Perelman, Chaim. Justice, Law & Argument: Essays on Moral & Legal Reasoning. (Synthese Library: No. 142). 175p. 1980. lib. bdg. 28.50 (ISBN 90-277-1089-9, Pub. by D. Reidel); pap. 10.50 (ISBN 90-277-1090-2). Kluwer Boston.

Posner, Richard A. The Economics of Justice. LC 80-25075. (Illus.). 448p. 1981. text ed. 25.00 (ISBN 0-674-23525-8). Harvard U Pr.

JUSTICE, ADMINISTRATION OF–CHINA

Kaplan, John. The Trial of the Kaohsiung Defendants. (Research Papers & Policy Studies: No. 2). 100p. 1981. pap. price not set (ISBN 0-912966-35-1). IEAS Ctr Chinese Stud.

JUVENAL (DECIMUS JUNIUS JUVENALIS)

Courtney, E. A Commentary on the Satires of Juvenal. 650p. 1981. text ed. 75.00x (ISBN 0-485-11190-X, Athlone Pr). Humanities.

Tengstrom, Emin. A Study of Juvenal's Tenth Satire. 1981. pap. text ed. 14.00x (ISBN 91-7346-089-3). Humanities.

JUVENILE COURTS

see also Probation

Blomberg, Thomas G. Juvenile Court Reform: Widening the Social Control Net. 256p. 1981. lib. bdg. 20.00 (ISBN 0-89946-087-9). Oelgeschlager.

Dawson, Robert O. Standards Relating to Adjudication. (Juvenile Justice Standards Project Ser.). 1980. softcover 7.95 (ISBN 0-88410-809-0); casebound 12.50 (ISBN 0-88410-236-X). Ballinger Pub.

Grisso, Thomas. Juveniles Waiver of Righs: Legal & Psychological Competence. (Perspectives in Law & Psychology Ser.: Vol. 3). 285p. 1981. 32.50 (ISBN 0-306-40526-1, Plenum Pr). Plenum Pub.

Senna & Siegel. Cases & Comments on Juvenile Law. (Criminal Justice Ser.). 600p. 1976. pap. text ed. 17.95 (ISBN 0-8299-0629-0). West Pub.

JUVENILE DELINQUENCY

see also Child Welfare; Juvenile Courts; Juvenile Detention Homes; Reformatories

Altman, Michael L. Standards Relating to Juvenile Records & Information Systems. (Juvenile Justice Standards Project Ser.). 1980. softcover 7.95 (ISBN 0-88410-819-8); casebound 16.50 (ISBN 0-88410-247-5). Ballinger Pub.

Areen, Judith. Standards Relating to Youth Service Agencies. (Juvenile Justice Standards Project Ser.). 1980. softcover 7.95 (ISBN 0-88410-804-X); casebound 16.50 (ISBN 0-88410-756-6). Ballinger Pub.

Bing, Stephen & Brown, Larry. Standards Relating to Monitoring. (Juvenile Justice Standards Project Ser.). 1980. softcover 7.95 (ISBN 0-88410-805-8); casebound 16.50 (ISBN 0-88410-753-1). Ballinger Pub.

Bittner, Egon & Krantz, Sheldon. Standards Relating to Police Handling of Juvenile Problems. (Juvenile Justice Standards Project Ser.). 1980. softcover 7.95 (ISBN 0-88410-806-6); final casebound 16.50 (ISBN 0-88410-755-8). Ballinger Pub.

Buckle, Leonard & Buckle, Suzann. Standards Relating to Planning for Juvenile Justice. (Juvenile Justice Standards Project Ser.). 1980. softcover 7.95; final casebound 16.50 (ISBN 0-88410-754-X). Ballinger Pub.

Evans, David J. Geographical Perspectives in Juvenile Delinquency. 144p. 1980. text ed. 27.75x (ISBN 0-566-00351-1, Pub. by Gower Pub Co England). Renouf.

Gittler, Josephine. Standards Relating to Juvenile Probation Function: Intake & Predisposition Investigative Services. (Juvenile Justice Standards Project Ser.). 1980. softcover 7.95 (ISBN 0-88410-828-7); casebound 14.50 (ISBN 0-88410-248-3). Ballinger Pub.

Gough, Aidan. Standards Relating to Non-Criminal Misbehavior. (Juvenile Justice Standards Project Ser.). Date not set. softcover 6.95 (ISBN 0-88410-832-5). Ballinger Pub.

Jensen, Gary F. & Rojek, Dean G. Readings in Juvenile Delinquency. 448p. 1981. pap. text ed. 9.95 (ISBN 0-669-03763-X). Heath.

Junker, John M. Standards Relating to Juvenile Delinquency & Sanctions. (Juvenile Justice Standards Project Ser.). 1980. softcover 5.95 (ISBN 0-88410-829-5); casebound 12.50 (ISBN 0-88410-235-1). Ballinger Pub.

Langer, Sidney. Scared Straight: Fear in the Deterrence of Delinquency. LC 80-5859. 141p. 1981. lib. bdg. 15.50 (ISBN 0-8191-1494-4); pap. text ed. 6.75 (ISBN 0-8191-1495-2). U Pr of Amer.

LeShan, Eda. The Roots of Crime: What You Need to Know About Crime & What You Can Do About It. LC 80-69999. 192p. (gr. 7 up). 1981. 8.95 (ISBN 0-590-07532-2, Four Winds). Schol Bk Serv.

Lewis, Dorothy O., ed. Psychobiological Vulnerabilities to Delinquency. 1981. text ed. write for info. (ISBN 0-89335-136-9). Spectrum Pub.

Moore, Jim. Flip Line. 300p. (Orig.). 1981. pap. 2.95. Tuppence.

Ravielli, Anthony. What Are Street Games? LC 80-22657. 1981. 10.95 (ISBN 0-689-30838-8). Atheneum.

Siegel, Larry J. & Senna, Joseph J. Juvenile Delinquency: Theory, Practice & Law. (Criminal Justice Ser.). (Illus.). 550p. 1981. text ed. 17.95 (ISBN 0-8299-0414-X). West Pub.

JUVENILE DETENTION HOMES

Hood, Roger. Homeless Borstal Boys. 103p. 1966. pap. text ed. 5.00x (Pub. by Bedford England). Renouf.

JUVENILE DRINKING

see Alcohol and Youth

JUVENILE LITERATURE

see Children's Literature (Collections); also subdivisions under Children's Literature

K

KABBALA

see Cabala

KAFIR WARS

see South Africa–History

KAFKA, FRANZ, 1883-1924

Albright, Daniel. Representation & the Imagination: Beckett, Kafka, Nabokov, & Schoenberg. LC 80-26975. (Chicago Originals Ser.). 256p. 1981. lib. bdg. 20.00x (ISBN 0-226-01252-2). U of Chicago Pr.

Grunfeld, Frederic V. Prophets Without Honor: A Background to Freud, Kafka, Einstein & Their World. 1980. 5.95x (ISBN 0-07-025087-1). McGraw.

KALAHARI DESERT

Silberbauer, G. B. Hunter & Habitat in the Central Kalahari Desert. LC 80-16768. (Illus.). 288p. Date not set. 39.50 (ISBN 0-521-23578-2); pap. 14.95 (ISBN 0-521-28135-0). Cambridge U Pr.

KALAM

see Islamic Theology

KANSAS

see also names of cities, towns, counties, etc. in Kansas

Richmond, Robert. Kansas a Land of Contrast. rev ed. LC 74-77390. 1979. pap. text ed. 10.95x. Forum Pr MO.

KANSAS–DESCRIPTION AND TRAVEL

Hart, Herbert M. Tour Guide to Old Forts of Texas, Kansas, Nebraska, Oklahoma, Vol. 4. (Illus.). 65p. (Orig.). 1981. pap. 3.95 (ISBN 0-87108-583-6). Pruett.

KANSAS–HISTORY

Bird, Roy. Topeka: A Pictorial History. Friedman, Donna R., ed. (Illus.). 208p. 1981. pap. price not set (ISBN 0-89865-114-X). Donning Co.

Stockwell, Nancy. Out Somewhere & Back Again: The Kansas Stories. 1978. pap. write for info. (ISBN 0-9601714-0-1). Medusa.

Vexler, R. I. Kansas Chronology & Factbook, Vol. 16. 1978. 8.50 (ISBN 0-379-16141-9). Oceana.

KANSAS CITY, MISSOURI

Unell, Barbara. Kansas City Catalog. 96p. (Orig.). (gr. 4 up). 1980. pap. 7.00 (ISBN 0-8309-0286-4). Independence Pr.

KANSAS-NEBRASKA BILL

Wolff, Gerald. Kansas-Nebraska Bill: Party, Section, & the Origin of the Civil War. 1980. lib. bdg. 69.95 (ISBN 0-87700-255-X). Revisionist Pr.

KANT, IMMANUEL, 1724-1804

Bernstein, John A. Shaftsbury, Rousseau & Kant: An Introduction to the Conflict Between Aesthetic & Moral Values in Modern Thought. LC 78-75190. 192p. 1980. write for info. (ISBN 0-8386-2351-4). Fairleigh Dickinson.

Wilm, Emil C. Immanuel Kant, Seventeen Hundred Twenty-Four to Nineteen Twenty-Four. 88p. 1980. Repr. of 1925 ed. lib. bdg. 20.00 (ISBN 0-8482-7062-2). Norwood Edns.

Zeldin, Mary-Barbara. Freedom & the Critical Undertaking: Essays on Kant's Later Critiques. LC 80-17553. (Sponsor Ser.). 346p. (Orig.). 1980. pap. 21.75 (ISBN 0-8357-0525-0, SS-00143). Univ Microfilms.

KAPOSI'S SARCOMA

Olweny, Ch. L., et al, eds. Kaposi's Sarcoma. (Antibodies & Chemotherapy: Vol. 29). (Illus.). 200p. 1981. 72.00 (ISBN 3-8055-2076-X). S Karger.

KARATE

see also T'ai Chi Ch'Uan

Chow, David & Spangler, Richard. Kung Fu, History, Philosophy, & Techniques. LC 73-14043. (Illus.). 220p. 1980. pap. 10.95 (ISBN 0-86568-011-6). Unique Pubns.

Hassell, Randall G. The Karate Experience: A Way of Life. LC 80-53429. 110p. 1981. 9.95 (ISBN 0-8048-1348-5). C E Tuttle.

Kozuki, Russel. Junior Karate. (Illus.). (gr. 4-6). 1977. pap. 1.50 (ISBN 0-686-68483-4). PB.

Kubota, Takayuki. Gosoku Ryu Karate: Kumite I. LC 80-53036. (Illus.). 160p. (Orig.). 1980. pap. 6.95 (ISBN 0-86568-010-8). Unique Pubns.

KARMA

see also Anthroposophy

Hanson, Virginia, ed. Karma. 2nd rev. ed. Stewart, Rosemarie. 200p. 1980. pap. write for info. (ISBN 0-8356-0543-4). Theos Pub Hse.

KARTING

Martin, Gary. Competitive Karting. LC 80-83189. (Illus.). 144p. 1980. pap. 9.95 (ISBN 0-9605068-0-2). Martin Motorsports.

KATHMANDU–DESCRIPTION

Ripley, S. Dillon. A Naturalist's Adventure in Nepal: Search for the Spiny Babbler. (Illus.). 301p. 1981. Repr. of 1953 ed. 12.50 (ISBN 0-87474-810-0). Smithsonian.

KATYN FOREST MASSACRE, 1940

Zawodny, J. K. Death in the Forest: The Story of the Katyn Forest Massacre. LC 62-16639. (Illus.). 235p. 1980. text ed. 14.00 (ISBN 0-268-00849-3); pap. text ed. 7.95 (ISBN 0-268-00850-7). U of Notre Dame Pr.

KAVANAGH, PATRICK

Kavanagh, Peter. Sacred Keeper: A Biography of Patrick Kavanagh. (Illus.). 404p. 1980. text ed. 21.00x (ISBN 0-904984-48-6). Humanities.

KAYAKS

see Canoes and Canoeing

KEATON, BUSTER, 1895-1966

Dardis, Tom. Keaton: The Man Who Wouldn't Lie Down. 1980. pap. 4.95 (ISBN 0-14-005701-3). Penguin.

KEATS, JOHN, 1795-1821

Dello Buono, Carmen J. Rare Early Essays on John Keats. 208p. 1980. lib. bdg. 17.50 (ISBN 0-8482-3675-0). Norwood Edns.

Gillham, D. G. Keats-Poems of Eighteen Twenty. 224p. 1969. pap. text ed. 9.95x (ISBN 0-7121-0141-1, Pub. by Macdonald & Evans England). Intl Ideas.

Park, Robert, ed. Selected Letters of John Keats. pap. 1.95 (ISBN 0-451-50697-9, CJ697, Sig Classics). NAL.

KEELEY CURE

see Alcoholism–Treatment

KELP

Powell, Eric F. Kelp the Health Giver. 1980. 2.25 (ISBN 0-8464-1028-1). Beekman Pubs.

KEMBLE, FRANCES ANNE, 1809-1893

Wister, Fanny K. Fanny, the American Kemble: Her Journals & Unpublished Letters. LC 72-80474. 227p. 1972. 10.00x (ISBN 0-932068-00-6). South Pass Pr.

KENNEBEC RIVER AND VALLEY

Willoughby, Charles C. Indian Antiquities of the Kennebec Valley. Spiess, Arthur E., ed. (Occasional Publications in Mane Archaeology: No. 1). (Illus.). 160p. 1980. 22.00 (ISBN 0-913764-13-2). Maine St Mus.

--Indian Antiquities of the Kennebec Valley. (Illus.). 1980. 22.00 (ISBN 0-913764-13-2). Maine St Mus.

KENNEDY, EDWARD MOORE, 1932-

Willis, Larryanne. Chappaquiddick Decision. (Illus., Orig.). 1980. pap. 2.95 (ISBN 0-937980-00-5). Better Bks.

KENNEDY, JOHN FITZGERALD, PRES. U. S., 1917-1963

John -- the Man Who Would Be President. LC 79-93341. 1979. 9.95 (ISBN 0-89387-040-4). Sat Eve Post.

KENNEDY, JOHN FITZGERALD, PRES. U. S., 1917-1963–ASSASSINATION

Bales, James. Communism Killed Kennedy but Did America Learn? 3.95 (ISBN 0-89315-015-0). Lambert Bk.

Kantor, Seth. The Ruby Cover Up. 1980. pap. 2.95 (ISBN 0-89083-680-9, Kable News Co). Zebra.

Lattimer, John K. Lincoln & Kennedy: Medical & Ballistic Comparisons of Their Assassinations. 1980. 19.95 (ISBN 0-15-152281-2). HarBraceJ.

Meagher, Sylvia & Owens, Gary. Master Index to the J. F. K. Assassination Investigation: The Reports & Supporting Volumes of the House Select Committee on Assassinations & the Warren Commission. LC 80-17494. xii, 435p. 1980. 20.00 (ISBN 0-8108-1331-9). Scarecrow.

Summers, Anthony. Conspiracy. (Illus.). 656p. 1981. pap. 8.95 (ISBN 0-07-062400-3). McGraw.

KENNEDY, JOHN PENDLETON, 1795-1870

Tuckerman, Henry T. The Life of John Pendleton Kennedy. 490p. 1980. lib. bdg. 65.00 (ISBN 0-89987-813-X). Darby Bks.

KENT, ENGLAND–HISTORY

Sandys, Charles. A History of Gavelkind & Other Remarkable Customs in the County of Kent. xvi, 352p. 1981. Repr. of 1851 ed. lib. bdg. 35.00x (ISBN 0-8377-1117-7). Rothman.

KENTUCKY–DESCRIPTION AND TRAVEL

Wharton, Mary E. & Bowen, Edward L. The Horse World of the Bluegrass, Vol. 1. Denbo, Bruce F. & Wharton, Mary E., eds. 246p. 1980. 30.00 (ISBN 0-934554-00-5). Host Assoc.

KENTUCKY–GENEALOGY

Davis, Elsie S. Descendants of Jacob Young of Shelby County, Kentucky: Including President Harry S. Truman. LC 80-70981. (Illus.). 171p. (Orig.). 1980. 16.00 (ISBN 0-9605618-1-1); pap. 9.00 (ISBN 0-9605618-0-3). E S Davis.

Roberts, Leonard. Sang Branch Settlers: Tales & Songs of an Eastern Kentucky Family. text ed. 12.00 (ISBN 0-933302-05-3); pap. text ed. 7.95 (ISBN 0-933302-06-1). Pikeville Coll.

KENTUCKY–HISTORY

Fuson, Henry H. Ballads of the Kentucky Highlands. 219p. 1980. Repr. of 1931 ed. text ed. 25.00 (ISBN 0-8492-4706-3). R West.

Roberts, Leonard. South from Hell-Fer Sartin. 287p. 1964. pap. 2.95. Pikeville Coll.

Scalf, Henry P. Kentucky's Last Frontier. 565p. 1972. Repr. of 1966 ed. 12.00. Pikeville Coll.

Vexler, R. I. Kentucky Chronology & Factbook, Vol. 17. 1978. 8.50 (ISBN 0-379-16142-7). Oceana.

KENTUCKY–JUVENILE LITERATURE

Fradin, Dennis. Kentucky: In Words & Pictures. LC 80-25810. (Young People's Stories of Our States Ser.). 48p. (gr. 2-5). 1981. PLB 8.65g (ISBN 0-516-03917-2, Time Line). Childrens.

KENYA

Wa-Githumo, Mwangi. Land & Nationalism: The Impact of Land Expropriation & Land Grievances Upon the Rise & Development of Nationalist Movements in Kenya, 1885-1939. LC 80-5589. 502p. 1981. lib. bdg. 24.50 (ISBN 0-8191-1491-X); pap. text ed. 15.50 (ISBN 0-8191-1492-8). U Pr of Amer.

KENYA–ECONOMIC CONDITIONS

Bigsten, Arne. Regional Inequality & Development: A Case Study of Kenya. 200p. 1980. text ed. 44.00x (ISBN 0-566-00382-1, Pub. by Gower Pub Co England). Renouf.

Norcliffe, Glen, ed. Planning African Development: The Kenya Experience. Pinfold, Tom. 224p. 1981. lib. bdg. 25.00x (ISBN 0-86531-161-7). Westview.

KENYA–HISTORY

Gregoy, Robert G., et al. The Guide to the Kenya National Archives. (Foreign & Comparative Studies-Eastern African Bibliographic Ser.: No. 3). 452p. 1969. 16.00. Syracuse U Foreign Comp.

KENYA–POLITICS AND GOVERNMENT

Kassam, Shirin, et al. A Bibliography on Kenya. (Foreign & Comparative Studies-Eastern African Bibliographic Ser.: No. 2). 461p. 1967. pap. 8.00x. Syracuse U Foreign Comp.

KENYA–SOCIAL CONDITIONS

Cooper, Frederick. From Slaves to Squatters: Plantation Labor & Agriculture in Zanibar & Coastal Kenya, 1890-1925. LC 80-5391. (Illus.). 352p. 1981. text ed. 25.00 (ISBN 0-300-02454-1). Yale U Pr.

Hyden, Goran, et al. Development Administration: The Kenyon Experience. (Illus.). 384p. 1970. text ed. 12.95x. Oxford U Pr.

Potholm, Christian P. & Fredland, Richard A., eds. Integration & Disintegration in East Africa. LC 80-5914. 229p. 1980. lib. bdg. 17.75 (ISBN 0-8191-1298-4); pap. text ed. 9.75 (ISBN 0-8191-1299-2). U Pr of Amer.

KERAMICS

see Ceramics

KERESAN INDIANS

see Indians of North America–Southwest, New

KERN, JEROME, 1885-1945

Freedland, Michael. Jerome Kern: A Biography. LC 80-6160. 200p. 1981. 12.95 (ISBN 0-8128-2776-7). Stein & Day.

KEROUAC, JOHN, 1922-1969

Blouet, Brian W. & Stitcher, Teresa L., eds. The Origins of Academic Geography in the United States. 1981. 37.50 (ISBN 0-208-01881-6, Archon). Shoe String.

Hunt, Tim. Kerouacs Crooked Road: Development of a Fiction. 288p. 1981. 19.50 (ISBN 0-208-01871-9, Archon). Shoe String.

Milewski, Robert J., et al. Jack Kerouac: An Annotated Bibliography of Secondary Sources, 1944-1979. LC 80-24477. (Author Bibliographies Ser.: No. 52). 237p. 1981. 12.50 (ISBN 0-8108-1378-5). Scarecrow.

KEY DEER

see White-Tailed Deer

KEYBOARD HARMONY

see Harmony, Keyboard

KHAS LANGUAGE

see Nepali Language

KICKAPOO INDIANS

see Indians of North America–The West

KIDNEY FAILURE

see Renal Insufficiency

KIDNEYS

see also Nephrology; Urine

also headings beginning with the word Renal

Eisenbach, G. M. & Brod, J., eds. Kidney & Pregnancy. (Contributions to Nephrology Ser.: Vol. 25). (Illus.). vi, 144p. 1981. pap. 54.00 (ISBN 3-8055-1798-X). S Karger.

Jamison, Rex L. & Kriz, Wilhelm. Urinary Concentrating Mechanism: Structure & Function. (Illus.). 425p. 1981. text ed. 35.00x (ISBN 0-19-502801-5). Oxford U Pr.

Lubec, G., ed. The Glomerular Basement Membrane. (Renal Physiology: Vol. 3, No. 1-6). (Illus.). viii, 434p. 1981. pap. write for info. (ISBN 3-8055-2398-X). S Karger.

Rector, Barry M. & Rector, Floyd C., eds. The Kidney, 2 vols. 2nd ed. 1981. Vol. 1. text ed. write for info. (ISBN 0-7216-1967-3); Vol. 2. text ed. write for info. (ISBN 0-7216-1968-1); Set. text ed. write for info. (ISBN 0-7216-1969-X). Saunders.

Silbernagel, S., ed. Abstracts of the International Conference on Renal Transport of Organic Substances Held in Innsbruck, July, 1980. (Journal: Renal Physiology: Vol. 2, No. 3). (Illus.). 62p. 1980. pap. 17.00 (ISBN 3-8055-1641-X). S Karger.

KIDNEYS–DISEASES

see also Renal Insufficiency

Buckalew, Vardaman M. & Moore, Micahel A. Renal Tubular Dysfunction. LC 79-92915. (Discussions in Patient Management Ser.). 1980. pap. 13.50 (ISBN 0-87488-889-1). Med Exam.

Cheigh, Jhoong S., et al, eds. Manual of Clinical Nephrology of the Rogosin Kidney Center. (Developments in Nephrology: No. 1). (Illus.). 470p. 1981. PLB 65.00 (ISBN 90-247-2397-3, Pub. by Martinus Nijhoff). Kluwer Boston.

Hook, Jerry B., ed. Toxicology of the Kidney. (Target Organ Toxicity Ser.). 275p. 1981. 27.50 (ISBN 0-89004-475-9). Raven.

Laszlo, F. A. Renal Cortical Necrosis. (Contributions to Nephrology Ser.: Vol. 28). (Illus.). vi, 210p. 1981. pap. 45.00 (ISBN 3-8055-2109-X). S Karger.

McDonald. Clinical Kidney Disease & Hypertension. 1980. 32.00. Thieme Stratton.

Pathophysiology of Renal Disease. (Contributions to Nephrology Ser.: Vol. 23). (Illus.). vi, 234p. 1980. pap. 58.75 (ISBN 3-8055-0943-X). S Karger.

Schreiner, G. E. Controversies in Nephrology. (Illus.). 722p. 1979. 49.50. Masson Pub.

KIDNEYS–DISEASES–DIAGNOSIS

Valenzuela, Rafael & Deodhar, Sharad D. Interpretation of Immunofluorescent Patterns in Renal Diseases. (Illus.). 144p. 1981. text ed. 45.00 (ISBN 0-89189-079-3, 16-A-003-00); atlas & slides 140.00 (ISBN 0-89189-098-X, 15-A-003-00). Am Soc Clinical.

KIDNEYS–TRANSPLANTATION

Hamburger, Jean, et al. Renal Transplantation: Theory & Practice. 2nd ed. (Illus.). 375p. 1981. write for info. (3872-9). Williams & Wilkins.

KIERKEGAARD, SOREN AABYE, 1813-1855

Elrod, John W. Kierkegaard & Christendom. LC 80-8547. 384p. 1981. 22.50x (ISBN 0-691-07261-2). Princeton U Pr.

Mullen, John D. Kierkegaard's Philosophy: Self-Deception & Cowardice in the Present Age. (Orig.). 1981. pap. 2.95 (ISBN 0-451-61945-5, ME1945, Ment). NAL.

Smith, Joseph H., ed. Kierkegaard's Truth: The Disclosure of the Self. LC 80-27055. (Psychiatry & the Humanities: Vol. 5). (Illus.). 456p. 1981. 36.50x (ISBN 0-300-02621-8). Yale U Pr.

KILLING, MERCY

see Euthanasia

KINDERGARTEN

see also Creative Activities and Seatwork; Education, Preschool; Nursery Schools

Forte, Imogene. Think About It-Kindergarten. LC 80-84619. (Think About It Ser.). (Illus.). 80p. (ps-k). 1981. pap. text ed. 5.95 (ISBN 0-913916-96-X, IP-96X). Incentive Pubn.

Massey, James O. Readiness for Kindergarten. 1975. pap. 1.25 (ISBN 0-89106-014-6, 1281). Consulting Psychol.

KINDERGARTEN–METHODS AND MANUALS

Barbe, Walter B. Resource Book for the Kindergarten Teacher. (Illus.). 1980. 34.95 (ISBN 0-88309-103-8). Zaner-Bloser.

Barbe, Walter B., et al. Basic Skills in Kindergarten: Foundations for Formal Learning. 1980. 10.00 (ISBN 0-88309-104-6). Zaner-Bloser.

Lucas, Virginia H., et al. Kindergarten Program. (Illus.). 1980. pupil bk. 2.97 (ISBN 0-88309-101-1); tchr's guide 4.97 (ISBN 0-88309-102-X). Zaner-Bloser.

KINDERGARTEN–MUSIC

see also Games with Music; Nursery Schools–Music

Cradock, Eveline. Musical Appreciation in an Infant School. (Illus.). 50p. (Orig.). 1977. pap. text ed. 6.75 (ISBN 0-19-321055-X). Oxford U Pr.

Zeitlin, Patty. A Song Is a Rainbow: Body Movement, Music, & Rythym Instruments in the Nursery School & Kindergarten. 336p. (Orig.). pap. 12.95 (ISBN 0-8302-8196-7). Goodyear.

KINDNESS TO ANIMALS

see Animals, Treatment Of

KINEMATICS OF MACHINERY

see Machinery, Kinematics of

KINESIOLOGY

see also Motor Ability

Schotland, Donald L. Diseases of the Motor Unit. (Illus.). 1981. price not set (ISBN 0-89289-410-5). HM.

KINESIOTHERAPY

see Exercise Therapy

KINETICS

see Dynamics

KINETICS, CHEMICAL

see Chemical Reaction, Rate Of

KING, MARTIN LUTHER, 1929-1968–JUVENILE LITERATURE

Clayton, Ed. Martin Luther King: The Peaceful Warrior. (gr. 4-6). 1969. pap. 1.50 (ISBN 0-671-29932-8). PB.

KINGDOM OF GOD

see also Covenants (Theology)

Hunter, A. M. Christ & the Kingdom: What Scripture Says About Living in the Kingdom of God. 120p. 1980. pap. 3.95 (ISBN 0-89283-092-1). Servant.

Talese, Gay. The Kingdom & the Power. 1981. pap. 3.25 (ISBN 0-440-14397-7). Dell.

KINGS AND RULERS–GENEALOGY

Sturluson, Snorri. Heims Kringla, History of the Kings of Norway. Hollander, Lee M., tr. from Old Norse. LC 64-10460. (Illus.). 1977. Repr. of 1964 ed. 27.50x (ISBN 0-89067-040-4). Am Scandinavian.

KINGSLEY, CHARLES, 1819-1875

Harris, Styron. Charles Kingsley: A Reference Book. (Reference Books Ser.). 1981. 26.00 (ISBN 0-8161-8166-7). G K Hall.

KINO, EUSBIUS FRANCISCO, 1644-1711

Kelly, Annamaria. Kino Alla Conquista Dell 'America. LC 80-53508. (Illus.). 148p. (Orig.). 1980. pap. 6.50 (ISBN 0-915076-05-5). SW Mission.

KINSHIP

see also Clans and Clan System; Family

Fortes, Meyer. Kinship & the Social Order: The Legacy of Lewis Henry Morgan. LC 80-67927. (Lewis Henry Morgan Lectures). 368p. Date not set. cancelled; pap. cancelled (ISBN 0-521-28211-X). Cambridge U Pr.

KIOWA INDIANS

see Indians of North America–The West

KISSING

Richey, David. The Small-Boat Handbook. LC 78-3315. 224p. pap. 3.95 (ISBN 0-06-463535-X, EH 535, EH). Har-Row.

KISSINGER, HENRY ALFRED, 1923-

Statement of the Honorable Henry A. Kissinger with Respect to the Treaty on Strategic Arms Limitation Before the Committee on Foreign Relations of the U. S. Senate, July 31, 1979. (Significant Issues Ser.: Vol. 1, No. 4). 35p. 1979. pap. 5.00 (ISBN 0-686-68798-1, CSIS005, CSIS). Unipub.

KISWAHILI LANGUAGE

see Swahili Language

KITCHEN-GARDENS

see Vegetable Gardening

KITCHEN UTENSILS

see also Food Processor Cookery

Heckmann, Manfred. Corkscrews: An Introduction to Their Appreciation. Sullivan, Maurice, ed. (Illus.). 124p. 1981. 12.95 (ISBN 0-686-69566-6). Wine Appreciation.

KITCHENS

Hines, Millie, ed. Easy Ways to Decorate Your Kitchen. (Illus.). 96p. (Orig.). 1981. pap. 2.00 (ISBN 0-918178-24-X). Simplicity.

Weiss, Jeffery. Great Kitchens. 96p. 1981. pap. 9.95 (ISBN 0-312-34605-0). St Martin.

Yarwood, Doreen. The British Kitchen. (Illus.). 192p. 1981. 28.95 (ISBN 0-7134-1430-8, Pub. by Batsford England). David & Charles.

KLEIST, HEINRICH VON, 1777-1811

Miller, Philip B., ed. An Abyss Deep Enough: The Letters of Heinrich Von Kleist with a Selection of Essays & Anecdotes. 288p. 1981. 16.95 (ISBN 0-525-05479-0). Dutton.

KLINE, FRANZ

Hess, Thomas B. & Feldman, Morton. Six Painters: Mondrian, DeKooning, Guston, Kline, Pollock, Rothko. LC 67-30452. (Illus.). 1968. pap. 3.00 (ISBN 0-914412-22-1). Inst for the Arts.

KNEE

American Academy of Orthopaedic Surgeons. Symposium on Reconstructive Surgery of the Knee. LC 78-6486. (Illus.). 1978. 52.50 (ISBN 0-8016-0132-0). Mosby.

KNEIPP CURE

see Hydrotherapy

KNITTING

American School of Needlework. The Great Afghan Book. Thomas, Mary, ed. (Illus.). 160p. 1981. 16.95 (ISBN 0-8069-5444-2, Columbia Hse). Sterling.

Drysdale, Rosemary. Miniature Crocheting & Knitting for Dollhouses. (Illus.). 50p. 1981. pap. 2.00 (ISBN 0-486-23964-0). Dover.

Wright, Mary. Cornish Guernsey & Knit-Frocks. 72p. 1980. 10.00x (ISBN 0-906720-05-2, Pub. by Hodge England). State Mutual Bk.

KNITTING–PATTERNS

Bindingarmynstur, Foroysk. Faroese Knitting Patterns. 60p. 1980. pap. 10.95 (ISBN 0-906191-17-3, Pub. by Thule Pr England). Intl Schol Bk Serv.

KNIVES

Barney, Richard W., et al. How to Make Knives. Beinfeld, Wallace, ed. 182p. 1977. 13.95 (ISBN 0-917714-13-X). Beinfeld Pub.

Hughes, B. R. Modern Handmade Knives. Date not set. price not set (ISBN 0-913150-44-4). Pioneer Pr.

Ingber-Irvin, Beth. Knifemakers Guild Directory. (Illus.). 200p. 1981. pap. 12.95 (ISBN 0-917714-32-6). Beinfeld Pub.

Schreier, Konrad F., Jr. Marbles, Knives & Axes. LC 78-15942. 70p. 1978. pap. 4.50 (ISBN 0-917714-19-9). Beinfeld Pub.

KNOWABLENESS OF GOD

see God–Knowableness

KNOWLEDGE, BOOKS OF

see Encyclopedias and Dictionaries

KNOWLEDGE, CLASSIFICATION OF

see Classification

KNOWLEDGE, REFLEXIVE

see Self-Knowledge, Theory of

KNOWLEDGE, THEORY OF

see also Belief and Doubt; Cognition; Identity; Ideology; Intellect; Judgment; Perception; Pragmatism; Reality; Self-Knowledge, Theory of; Senses and Sensation; Truth; Values

Berger, Gaston. Recherches Sur les Conditions De la Connaissance Essai D'une Theoretique Pure. Natanson, Maurice, ed. LC 78-66755. (Phenomenology Ser.: Vol. 1). 194p. 1979. lib. bdg. 20.00 (ISBN 0-8240-9569-3). Garland Pub.

Dretske, Fred I. Knowledge & the Flow of Information. LC 81-21633. (Illus.). 288p. 1981. text ed. 18.50 (ISBN 0-89706-009-1). Bradford Bks.
Firsoff, V. Axel. At the Crossroads of Knowledge. 146p. 8.95 (ISBN 0-86025-812-2). Ross-Erikson.
Haldane, Viscount. The Reign of Relativity. 434p. 1981. Repr. lib. bdg. 35.00 (ISBN 0-8495-2354-0). Arden Lib.
Hamlyn, D. W. The Theory of Knowledge. (Modern Introductions to Philosophy Ser.). 308p. 1980. pap. text ed. cancelled (ISBN 0-333-11548-1). Humanities.
Lakatos, Imre. Philosophical Papers: Mathematics, Science & Epistemology, Vol. 2. Worrall, J. & Currie, G., eds. LC 77-14374. 295p. 1980. pap. 13.50 (ISBN 0-521-28030-3). Cambridge U Pr.
Schwartz, Barry. Vertical Classification: A Study in Structuralism & the Sociology of Knowledge. LC 80-24207. (Chicago Original Paperback Ser.). 232p. 1981. lib. bdg. 17.00x (ISBN 0-226-74208-3). U of Chicago Pr.
Sweeeney, Francis, ed. The Knowledge Explosion: Liberation & Limitations. 249p. 1969. 4.95 (ISBN 0-374-18204-3). FS&G.
Tennessen, Herman. Problems of Knowledge. 88p. 1980. pap. text ed. 10.25x (ISBN 90-232-1762-4). Humanities.
Valle, Ronald S. & Eckartsberg, Rolf Von, eds. The Metaphors of Consciousness. 500p. 1981. 25.00 (ISBN 0-306-40520-2, Plenum Pr). Plenum Pub.

KNOWLEDGE OF GOD
see God-Knowableness

KNOWLEDGE OF SELF, THEORY OF
see Self-Knowledge, Theory of

KNOX, JOHN, 1505-1572
Murray, Iain. John Knox. 1976. pap. 0.50. Banner of Truth.

KOASATI INDIANS
see Indians of North America-Eastern States

KOHLBERG, ALFRED, 1887-1960
Hersh, Richard H., et al. Promoting Moral Growth: From Piaget to Kohlberg. LC 78-19945. 256p. 1979. pap. text ed. write for info. Longman.

KOLS
see Mundas

KORAN
Jeffery, Arthur. The Qur'an As Scripture. LC 80-1924. 1981. Repr. of 1952 ed. 18.00 (ISBN 0-404-18970-9). AMS Pr.
Quasem, M. A. The Jewels of the Qur'an: Al-Ghazali's Theory. 244p. 1980. 13.95x (ISBN 0-89955-204-8, Pub. by M A Quasem Malaysia); pap. 7.95x (ISBN 0-89955-205-6). Intl Schol Bk Serv.
--The Recitation & Interpretation of the Qur'an. 121p. 1980. 9.95x (ISBN 0-89955-206-4, Pub. by M A Quasem Malaysia); pap. 6.95x (ISBN 0-89955-207-2). Intl Schol Bk Serv.

KOREA
Korea Annual 1980. 17th ed. LC 64-6162. (Illus.). 732p. 1980. pap. 30.00x (ISBN 0-8002-2733-6). Intl Pubns Serv.

KOREA-DESCRIPTION AND TRAVEL
Lanier, Alison R. Update -- South Korea. (Country Orientation Ser.). 1980. pap. text ed. 25.00 (ISBN 0-933662-33-5). Intercult Network.

KOREA-ECONOMIC CONDITIONS
Korean Traders Association. Korean Trade Directory, 1979 to 1980. 21st ed. LC 60-45910. 579p. 1979. 35.00x (ISBN 0-8002-2520-1). Intl Pubns Serv.

KOREA-FOREIGN RELATIONS
Stueck, William W., Jr. The Road to Confrontation: American Policy Toward China & Korea, 1947 - 1950. LC 80-11818. (Illus.). 337p. 1981. 22.00x (ISBN 0-8078-1445-8); pap. 10.00x (ISBN 0-8078-4080-7). U of NC Pr.

KOREA-SOCIAL LIFE AND CUSTOMS
Kim, Young-Pyoung. A Strategy for for Rural Development: Saemaeul Undong in Korea. 1980. pap. 5.00 (ISBN 0-89249-032-2). Intl Development.

KOREAN LANGUAGE
Grant, Bruce K. A Guide to Korean Characters: Reading & Writing Hangul & Hanja. 400p. 1979. 15.50 (ISBN 0-930878-13-2). Hollym Intl.

KOREAN POTTERY
see Pottery, Korean

KOREAN WAR, 1950-1953
Cumings, Bruce. The Origins of the Korean War: Liberation & the Emergence of Separate Regimes. LC 80-8543. (Illus.). 552p. 1981. 35.00x (ISBN 0-691-09383-0); pap. 14.50x (ISBN 0-691-10113-2). Princeton U Pr.

KOREANS IN FOREIGN COUNTRIES
Lee, Changsoo & DeVos, George. Koreans in Japan: Ethnic Conflict & Accommodation. (Illus.). 448p. 1981. 30.00x (ISBN 0-520-04258-1). U of Cal Pr.

KRIEGSSPIEL
see War Games

KRISHNA
Singer, Milton B., ed. Krishna: Myths, Rites, & Attitudes. LC 80-29194. xvii, 277p. 1981. Repr. of 1966 ed. lib. bdg. 27.50x (ISBN 0-313-22822-1, SIKR). Greenwood.

KU KLUX KLAN
Cooke, Fred J. Ku Klux Klan: America's Recurring Nightmare. (Illus.). 160p. (YA) (gr. 7 up). 1980. PLB 8.29 (ISBN 0-671-34055-7). Messner.
Sims, Patsy. The Klan. LC 77-2335. (Illus.). 384p. 1981. pap. 8.95 (ISBN 0-8128-6096-9). Stein & Day.

KUNDALI YOGA
see Yoga, Hatha

KUNG, HANS, 1928-
Nowell, Robert. A Passion for Truth: Hans Kung & His Theology. 376p. 1981. 17.50 (ISBN 0-8245-0039-3). Crossroad NY.

KUNG-FU
see Karate

KURDISH LANGUAGE
Mokri, M. Al-Hadiyati 'l-Hamidiyah: Kurdish-Arabic Dictionary. 1975. 18.00x. Intl Bk Ctr.

KURMANJI LANGUAGE
see Kurdish Language

KUTENAI INDIANS
see Indians of North America-Northwest, Pacific

KUWAIT, ARABIA (STATE)
Al-Sabah, Y. S. F. The Oil Economy of Kuwait. 176p. 1981. write for info. (ISBN 0-7103-0003-4). Routledge & Kegan.
Karam, N. H., tr. Banking Laws of Kuwait. 275p. 1979. 22.00x (ISBN 0-86010-139-8, Pub.by Graham & Trotman England). State Mutual Bk.
Lanier, Alison R. Update -- Kuwait. (Country Orientation Ser.). 1980. pap. text ed. 25.00 (ISBN 0-933662-29-7). Intercult Network.
Oliver, R. A. & Lewis, D. G. The Content of Sixth-Form General Studies. 144p. 1974. 12.00x (ISBN 0-7190-0586-8, Pub. by Manchester U Pr England). State Mutual Bk.

KWAKIUTAL INDIANS
see Indians of North America-Northwest, Pacific

L

LABELS
Bracken, Carolyn. Super Stickers for Kids: One Hundred & Twenty-Eight Fun Labels. (Illus.). 16p. (Orig.). 1981. pap. price not set (ISBN 0-486-24092-4). Dover.

LABOR (OBSTETRICS)
see also Childbirth; Obstetrics
Elder, M. G. & Hendricks, C. H. Obstetrics & Gynecology: Preterm Labor, Vol. 1. (Butterworths International Medical Reviews Ser.). 1981. text ed. price not set (ISBN 0-407-02300-3). Butterworths.

LABOR, COOLIE
see Chinese in Foreign Countries

LABOR, DIVISION OF
see Division of Labor

LABOR, MIGRANT
see Migrant Labor

LABOR, ORGANIZED
see Trade-Unions

LABOR AND CAPITAL
see Industrial Relations

LABOR AND LABORING CLASSES
see also Apprentices; Arbitration, Industrial; Artisans; Capital; Children-Employment; Collective Bargaining; Contract Labor; Cost and Standard of Living; Discrimination in Employment; Division of Labor; Employees, Rating of; Friendly Societies; Industrial Relations; Job Satisfaction; Machinery in Industry; Migrant Labor; Old Age Pensions; Poor; Professions; Servants; Slave Labor; Socialism; Strikes and Lockouts; Sunday Legislation; Supplementary Employment; Trade-Unions; Unemployed; Wages; Women-Employment; Youth-Employment
also classes of laborers, e.g. Coal-Miners, Railroads-Employees; subdivisions Economic Conditions and Social Conditions under names of countries, cities, etc., e.g. U. S.-Economic Conditions
Abarbanel, Jerome. Redefining the Enviorment. (Key Issues Ser.: No. 9): 1972. pap. 2.00 (ISBN 0-87546-200-6). NY Sch Indus Rel.
Adlam, Diana, et al, eds. Politics & Power: Problems in Labour Politics. (Politics & Power Ser.). 220p. (Orig.). 1981. pap. price not set (ISBN 0-7100-0716-7). Routledge & Kegan.
International Labour Office, ed. Equal Opportunities & Equal Treatment for Men & Women Workers: Workers with Family Responsibilities, Report V (1) 84p. (Orig.). 1980. pap. 10.00 (ISBN 92-2-102405-9). Intl Labour Office.
Labour Administration: A General Introduction. 88p. 1980. pap. 12.75 (ISBN 92-2-102350-8, ILO145, ILO). Unipub.
Manpower Assessment & Planning Projects in the Arab Region - Current Issues & Perspectives. 31p. 1980. pap. 6.50 (ISBN 92-2-102173-4, ILO146, ILO). Unipub.
Maurer, Harry. Not Working. 1981. pap. 6.95 (ISBN 0-452-25272-5, Z5272, Plume). NAL.
Parnes, Herbert S. From Mid-Career Through Retirement: Longitudinal Studies of the Male Work Force. (Illus.). 352p. 1981. text ed. 27.50x (ISBN 0-262-16079-X). MIT Pr.
Portes, Alejandro & Walton, John. Labor, Class, & the International System. 1981. price not set (ISBN 0-12-562020-9). Acad Pr.
Seaton, Douglas P. Catholics & Radicals: The Association of Catholic Trade Unionists & the American Labor Movement, from Depression to Cold War. 300p. 1981. 18.50 (ISBN 0-8387-2193-1). Bucknell U Pr.
Thornton, William T. On Labour: Its Wrongful Claims & Rightful Dues: Its Actual Present & Possible Future. 2nd ed. (The Development of Industrial Society Ser.). 499p. 1980. Repr. 35.00x (ISBN 0-7165-1788-4, Pub. by Irish Academic Pr). Biblio Dist.
Zipser, Arthur. Working Class Giant: The Life of William Z. Foster. (Orig.). 1981. 11.00 (ISBN 0-7178-0590-5); pap. 4.25 (ISBN 0-7178-0582-4). Intl Pub Co.

LABOR AND LABORING CLASSES-ACCIDENTS
see Industrial Accidents

LABOR AND LABORING CLASSES-CHILD LABOR
see Children-Employment

LABOR AND LABORING CLASSES-EDUCATION
Doeringer, Peter B., ed. Workplace Perspectives on Education & Training. (Boston Studies in Applied Economics). 184p. 1981. lib. bdg. 17.50 (ISBN 0-89838-054-5, Pub. by Martinus Nijhoff). Kluwer Boston.

LABOR AND LABORING CLASSES-HISTORY
Here are entered general works and works dealing with the United States in particular. Works dealing with the history of labor and laboring classes in other specific areas will be found in the geographical subdivisions which follow.
Aronowitz, Stanley. Class, Politics, & Culture. 256p. 1981. 25.95 (ISBN 0-03-059031-0). Praeger.
Meier, August & Rudwick, Elliott. Black Detroit & the Rise of the Uaw. (Illus.). 304p. 1981. pap. 6.95 (ISBN 0-19-502895-3, GB 632, OPB). Oxford U Pr.
Milton, David. The Politics of U. S. Labor: From the Great Depression to the New Deal. LC 80-8934. 352p. 1981. 18.00 (ISBN 0-85345-569-4). Monthly Rev.
Montgomery, David. Beyond Equality: Labor & the Radical Republicans, 1862-1872. LC 80-24434. 550p. 1981. pap. 9.95 (ISBN 0-252-00869-3). U of Ill Pr.
--Workers' Control in America: Studies in History of Work, Technology, & Labor Struggles. 1980. 5.95 (ISBN 0-521-28006-0). Cambridge U Pr.
Rule, John. The Experience of Labour in Eighteenth Century Industry. 1980. 25.00 (ISBN 0-312-27664-8). St Martin.

LABOR AND LABORING CLASSES-INSURANCE
see Insurance, Health; Old Age Pensions; Insurance, Unemployment

LABOR AND LABORING CLASSES-MEDICAL CARE
see also Nurses and Nursing; Occupational Diseases
Goldstone, Robert, ed. Health Care & Industrial Relations: Costs, Conflicts & Controversy. 120p. 1981. price not set (ISBN 0-89215-112-9). U Cal LA Indus Rel.

LABOR AND LABORING CLASSES-WAGES
see Wages

LABOR AND LABORING CLASSES-1914-
Botsch, Robert E. We Shall Not Overcome: Populism & Southern Blue-Collar Workers. LC 80-11567. 312p. 1981. 19.50x (ISBN 0-8078-1444-X). U of NC Pr.

LABOR AND LABORING CLASSES-AFRICA
The Conditions of the Black Worker. 298p. (Orig.). 1975. pap. text ed. 6.00 (ISBN 0-89192-067-6). Interbk Inc.
Cooper, Frederick. From Slaves to Squatters: Plantation Labor & Agriculture in Zanibar & Coastal Kenya, 1890-1925. LC 80-5391. (Illus.). 352p. 1981. text ed. 25.00 (ISBN 0-300-02454-1). Yale U Pr.

LABOR AND LABORING CLASSES-ASIA
Labour Market Information in Asia: Present Issues & Tasks for the Future. 116p. 1980. pap. 6.50 (ISBN 92-2-102168-8, ILO147, ILO). Unipub.

LABOR AND LABORING CLASSES-AUSTRALASIA
Miller, John. The Workingman's Paradise. Wilding, Michael, ed. 272p. 1980. 18.50x (ISBN 0-424-00057-1, Pub.by Sydney U Pr Australia). Intl Schol Bk Serv.

LABOR AND LABORING CLASSES-AUSTRALIA
Ebbels, R. N. The Australian Labor Movement: Eighteen Fifty to Nineteen Seven. 15.00x (ISBN 0-392-07633-0, SpS). Soccer.

LABOR AND LABORING CLASSES-CHINA
Chan, Ming K. Historiography of the Chinese Labor Movement. LC 80-8323. (Bibliographical Ser.: No. 60). 1981. 35.00 (ISBN 0-8179-2601-1). Hoover Inst Pr.
Lowe, Chuan-Hua. Facing Labor Issues in China. (Studies in Chinese History & Civilization). 1977. Repr. of 1938 ed. 17.50 (ISBN 0-89093-082-1). U Pubns Amer.
Ridker, Ronald. Employment in South Asia: Problems, Prospects & Prescriptions. (Occasional Papers: No. 1). 74p. 1971. 1.00 (ISBN 0-686-28697-9). Overseas Dev Council.
Turner, H. A. The Last Colony: But Whose?; a Study of the Labour Movement, Labour Market & Labour Relations in Hong Kong. LC 80-41112. (Department of Applied Economics Papers in Industrial Relations & Labour: No. 5). (Illus.). 1981. 24.95 (ISBN 0-521-23701-7). Cambridge U Pr.

LABOR AND LABORING CLASSES-EUROPE
Wallerstein, Immanual, ed. On the European Workers' Movements and Eurocommunism. 100p. 1980. pap. 5.001311. Synthesis Pubns.

LABOR AND LABORING CLASSES-FRANCE
Chevalier, Luois. Laboring Classes & Dangerous Classes in Paris During the First Half of the Nineteenth Century. Jellinek, Frank, tr. from Fr. LC 80-8678. 520p. (Orig.). 1981. pap. 8.95 (ISBN 0-691-00783-7). Princeton U Pr.

LABOR AND LABORING CLASSES-GREAT BRITAIN
Black, Clementina. Married Women's Work: Being the Report of an Inquiry Undertaken by the Women's Industrial Council, London Nineteen Fifteen. LC 79-56947. (The Englishworking Class Ser.). 1980. lib. bdg. 25.00 (ISBN 0-8240-0102-8). Garland Pub.
Bray, Reginald A. Boy Labour & Apprenticeship, London Nineteen Eleven. LC 79-56952. (The English Working Class Ser.). 1980. lib. bdg. 22.00 (ISBN 0-8240-0106-0). Garland Pub.
Butler, C. V. Domestic Service, London, Nineteen Sixteen. LC 79-56953. (The English Working Class Ser.). 1980. lib. bdg. 15.00 (ISBN 0-8240-0107-9). Garland Pub.
Cadbury, Edward, et al. Women's Work & Wages: London, Nineteen Nine. LC 79-56954. (The English Working Class). 1980. lib. bdg. 30.00 (ISBN 0-8240-0108-7). Garland Pub.
Freeman, Arnold. Boy Life & Labour: The Manufacture of Inefficiency, London Nineteen Fourteen. LC 79-56956. (The English Working Class Ser.). 1980. lib. bdg. 25.00 (ISBN 0-8240-0110-9). Garland Pub.
Hutchins, B. L. Women in Modern Industry: London Nineteen Fifteen. LC 79-56959. (The English Working Class Ser.). 1980. lib. bdg. 28.00 (ISBN 0-8240-0112-5). Garland Pub.
Jordan, Bill. Automatic Poverty: The Ricardo Phenomenon. 208p. 1981. price not set (ISBN 0-7100-0824-4); pap. price not set (ISBN 0-7100-0825-2). Routledge & Kegan.
Loane, M. From Their Point of View: London Nineteen Eight. LC 79-56961. (The English Working Class Ser.). 1980. lib. bdg. 27.00 (ISBN 0-8240-0113-3). Garland Pub.
Macdonald, J. Ransay, ed. Women in the Printing Trades: A Sociological Study, London Nineteen Four. LC 79-56961. (The English Working Class Ser.). 1980. lib. bdg. 18.00 (ISBN 0-8240-0114-1). Garland Pub.
Mudie-Smith, Richard, ed. Handbook of the Daily News Sweated Industries Exhibition: Nineteen Six. LC 79-56964. (The English Working Class Ser.). 1980. lib. bdg. 16.00 (ISBN 0-8240-0116-8). Garland Pub.
Paterson, Alexander. Across the Bridges or Life by the South London River-Side, London Nineteen Eleven. LC 79-56967. (The English Working Class Ser.). 1980. lib. bdg. 25.00 (ISBN 0-8240-0118-4). Garland Pub.
Pember-Reeves, M. S. Round About a Pound a Week: London, Ninetee Thirteen. LC 79-56968. (The English Working Class Ser.). 1980. lib. bdg. 25.00 (ISBN 0-8240-0119-2). Garland Pub.
Rountree, B. Seebohm. Poverty: A Study of Town Life, London Nineteen Ten. 2nd ed. LC 79-56969. (The English Working Class Ser.). 1980. lib. bdg. 38.00 (ISBN 0-8240-0120-6). Garland Pub.
Routh, Guy. Occupation & Pay in Great Britain. 2nd, rev. ed. 269p. 1981. text ed. 37.50x (ISBN 0-333-28417-8, Pub. by Macmilla, England); pap. text ed. 20.00x (ISBN 0-333-28653-7). Humanities.
Urwick, E. J., ed. Study of Boy Life in Our Cities: London, 1904. LC 79-56942. (The English Working Class Ser.). 1980. lib. bdg. 28.00 (ISBN 0-8240-0125-7). Garland Pub.
Williams, Alfred. Life in a Railway Factory: London Nineteen Fifteen. LC 79-56941. 1980. lib. bdg. 28.00 (ISBN 0-8240-0126-5). Garland Pub.

LABOR AND LABORING CLASSES-INDIA
Aziz, Abdul. Organizing Agricultural Labourers in India. 1980. 7.50x (ISBN 0-8364-0651-6, Pub. by Minerva India). South Asia Bks.

LABOR AND LABORING CLASSES-ITALY
Griffiths, Trevor. Occupations. new ed. 74p. 1981. pap. 7.50 (ISBN 0-571-11667-1, Pub. by Faber & Faber). Merrimack Bk Serv.

LABOR AND LABORING CLASSES-JAPAN
Ministry of Labor, Japan. Japan Labor Code, 2 vols. (Studies in Japanese Law & Government). 1979. Repr. of 1953 ed. Set. 56.00 (ISBN 0-89093-217-4). U Pubns Amer.
Young, Arthur M. Socialist & Labour Movement in Japan. (Studies in Japanese History & Civilization). 145p. 1979. Repr. of 1921 ed. 18.00 (ISBN 0-89093-268-9). U Pubns Amer.

LABOR AND LABORING CLASSES-RUSSIA
Koenker, Diane. Moscow Workers & the Nineteen Seventeen Revolution. LC 80-8557. (Studies of the Russian Institute, Columbia University). (Illus.). 456p. 1981. 30.00x (ISBN 0-691-05323-5). Princeton U Pr.
McAulay, Alastair. Women's Work & Wages in the Soviet Union. 248p. 1981. text ed. 28.50x (ISBN 0-04-339020-X, 2605). Allen Unwin.
Schapiro, Leonard & Godson, Joseph, eds. The Soviet Worker: Illusion & Realities. Date not set. price not set (ISBN 0-312-74923-6). St Martin.

LABOR ARBITRATION
see Arbitration, Industrial
LABOR COLONIES
see Agricultural Colonies
LABOR ECONOMICS
see also Industrial Relations; Labor and Laboring Classes
Appleton, J. D. Labour Economics. 2nd ed. (Illus.). 240p. 1979. pap. text ed. 9.95 (ISBN 0-7121-1246-4, Pub. by Macdonald & Evans England). Intl Ideas.
Helfgott, Roy B. Labor Economics. 2nd ed. 674p. 1981. text ed. 19.95 (ISBN 0-394-32325-4). Random.
LABOR FORCE
see Labor Supply
LABOR GRIEVANCES
see Grievance Procedures
LABOR LAWS AND LEGISLATION
see also Children–Employment; Mining Law; Strikes and Lockouts; Sunday Legislation; Trade-Unions; Workmen's Compensation
also subdivision Legal Status, Laws, etc. under names of professions, e.g. Teachers–Legal Status, Laws, etc.
Aboud, Grace S. & Doherty, Robert E. Practices & Procedures Under the Taylor Law: A Practical Guide in Narrative Form. 1974. pap. 2.00 (ISBN 0-87546-203-0). NY Sch Indus Rel.
Ewing, David. Freedom Inside the Organization: Bringing Civil Liberties to the Workplace. 1977. 10.00 (ISBN 0-87690-249-2). Dutton.
Janner, Greville. Janner's Compendium of Employment Law. 759p. 1979. text ed. 45.50x (ISBN 0-220-66363-7, Pub. by Busn Bks England). Renouf.
--Janner's Employment Forms. 397p. 1979. text ed. 61.25x (ISBN 0-220-67027-7, Pub. by Busn Bks England). Renouf.
MacKenzie, Susan T. Group Legal Services. (Key Issues Ser.: No. 18). 1975. pap. 3.00 (ISBN 0-87546-231-6). NY Sch Indus Rel.
LABOR LAWS AND LEGISLATION–RUSSIA
McAulay, Alastair. Women's Work & Wages in the Soviet Union. 248p. 1981. text ed. 28.50x (ISBN 0-04-339020-X, 2605). Allen Unwin.
LABOR-MANAGEMENT RELATIONS
see Industrial Relations
LABOR MARKET
see Labor Supply
LABOR NEGOTIATIONS
see Arbitration, Industrial; Collective Bargaining
LABOR ORGANIZATIONS
see Trade-Unions
LABOR OUTPUT
see Labor Productivity
LABOR PARTY (GREAT BRITAIN)
see Labour Party (Great Britain)
LABOR PRODUCTIVITY
see also Machinery in Industry; Production Standards
Blake, Robert R. & Mouton, Jane S. Productivity & Creativity: A Social Dynamics Approach. 143p. 1981. 9.95 (ISBN 0-8144-5692-8). Am Mgmt.
Knox, Frank M. Managing Paperwork: The Key to Productivity. LC 80-19685. 1980. 16.95 (ISBN 0-444-00452-1, Thomond Pr). Elsevier.
Mackenzie, Susan T. Noise & Office Work. (Key Issues Ser.: No. 19). 1975. pap. 3.00 (ISBN 0-87546-232-4). NY Sch Indus Rel.
Productivity, Quality of Working Life & Labour-Management Relations. 23p. 1976. 2.75 (APO62, APO). Unipub.
Rosow, James M., ed. Productivity: Prospects for Growth. (Work in America Ser.). 288p. 1981. text ed. 19.95 (ISBN 0-442-29326-7). Van Nos Reinhold.
Ross, Joe. Productivity, People & Profits. 150p. 1981. text ed. 17.95 (ISBN 0-8359-5473-0); pap. 10.95 (ISBN 0-8359-5472-2). Reston.
Wage Increases & Labour Productivity in Japanese Smaller Business. 34p. 1972. 2.75 (APO11, APO). Unipub.
LABOR PRODUCTIVITY–ACCOUNTING
see Productivity Accounting
Greiner, John & Hatry, Harry. Productivity & Motivation: A Review of State & Local Government Initiatives. LC 80-53981. 1981. 18.00 (ISBN 0-87766-283-5, 29600). Urban Inst.
LABOR RELATIONS
see Industrial Relations
LABOR SUPPLY
see also Children–Employment; Job Vacancies; Manpower; Manpower Policy; Unemployed; Youth–Employment
Berg, Ivar, ed. Sociological Perspectives on Labor Markets. (Quantitative Studies in Social Relations). 1981. price not set. Acad Pr.
Berg, Mark R., et al. Jobs & Energy in Michigan: The Next Twenty Years. LC 80-24884. (Illus.). 262p. 1981. 17.95 (ISBN 0-87944-264-6); pap. 11.95 (ISBN 0-87944-263-8). U of Mich Soc Res.
Brown, C. V. Taxation & the Incentive to Work. (Illus.). 128p. 1980. 29.95 (ISBN 0-19-877134-7); pap. 12.00 (ISBN 0-19-877135-5). Oxford U Pr.
Keeley, Michael C. Labor Supply & Public Policy: A Critical Review. (Studies in Labor Economics Ser.). 1981. price not set (ISBN 0-12-403920-0). Acad Pr.
LABOR SUPPLY–JAPAN
Abegglen, James C. The Japanese Factory. rev. ed. LC 80-52878. 200p. 1981. pap. 6.25 (ISBN 0-8048-1372-8). C E Tuttle.
LABOR-UNIONS
see Trade-Unions
LABORATORIES
see also Medical Laboratories
Archenhold, W. F., et al. Social Science Laboratories: A Handbook of Design, Management & Organisation. 303p. 1980. 35.00x (ISBN 0-7195-3436-4, Pub. by Murray Pubs England). State Mutual Bk.
LABORATORIES, MEDICAL
see Medical Laboratories
LABORATORY ANIMALS
Animal Welfare Institute. Humane Biology Projects. 3rd ed. (Illus.). 57p. 1977. pap. text ed. 2.00 (ISBN 0-938414-05-4). Animal Welfare.
Sperlinger, David. Animals in Research: New Perspectives in Animal Experimentation. 384p. 1980. 49.50 (ISBN 0-471-27843-2, Pub. by Wiley-Interscience). Wiley.
LABORATORY TECHNICIANS
see also Medical Technologists
Oppenheim, Irwin A. Textbook for Laboratory Assistants. 3rd ed. (Illus.). 190p. 1981. pap. text ed. 12.95 (ISBN 0-8016-3722-8). Mosby.
LABORERS
see Labor and Laboring Classes
LABOUR PARTY (GREAT BRITAIN)
Haseler, Stephen. The Tragedy of Labour. (Mainstream Ser.). 249p. 1980. 19.50x (ISBN 0-631-11341-X, Pub. by Basil Blackwell). Biblio Dist.
Jenkins, Hugh. Rank & File. 181p. 1980. 25.00x (ISBN 0-7099-0331-6, Pub by Croom Helm Ltd England). Biblio Dist.
Perelman, Chaim. Justice, Law & Argument: Essays on Moral & Legal Reasoning. (Synthese Library: No. 142). 175p. 1980. lib. bdg. 28.50 (ISBN 90-277-1089-9, Pub. by D. Reidel); pap. 10.50 (ISBN 90-277-1090-2). Kluwer Boston.
LA BRUYERE, JEAN DE, 1645-1696
Koppisch, Michael S. The Dissolution of Character: Changing Perspectives in La Bruyere's Caracteres. (French Forum Monographs: No.24). 120p. (Orig.). 1981. pap. 10.50 (ISBN 0-917058-23-2). French Forum.
LACE AND LACE MAKING
see also Macrame
Kliot, Jules & Kliot, Kaethe. Honiton Bobbin Lace: Designs for Prickling from Traditional Pieces. 1979. pap. 8.95 (ISBN 0-916896-16-1). Lacis Pubns.
Kliot, Jules & Kliot, Kaethe, eds. Needle Lace: Battenberg, Point & Reticella. (Illus.). 1981. pap. 5.95 (ISBN 0-916896-18-8). Lacis Pubns.
Stillwell, Alexandra. Teneriffe Lace. (Illus.). 144p. 1980. 16.95 (ISBN 0-8231-5056-9). Branford.
LACERTILIA
see Lizards
LACKAWANNA VALLEY, PENNSYLVANIA
Folsom, Burton W., Jr. Urban Capitalists: Entrepreneurs & City Growth in the Lackawanna & Lehigh Valleys, 1800-1920. LC 80-8864. (Studies in Industry & Society: No. 1). (Illus.). 208p. 1981. text ed. 16.50x (ISBN 0-8018-2520-2). Johns Hopkins.
LACRIMAL ORGANS
see also Aqueous Humor
Yamaguchi. Recent Advances on the Lacrimal System. Date not set. 47.50 (ISBN 0-89352-140-X). Masson Pub.
LACROSSE
James, Stuart. Lacrosse for Beginners. (Illus.). 128p. (gr. 7 up). 1981. PLB price not set. Messner.
LACY FAMILY
Wightman, Wilfred E. The Lacy Family in England & Normandy, 1066-1194. LC 80-2206. 1981. Repr. of 1966 ed. 37.50 (ISBN 0-404-18794-3). AMS Pr.
LAETRILE
Markle, Gerald E. & Petersen, James C., eds. The Laetrile Phenomenon: Politics, Science, & Cancer. LC 80-13466. 208p. 1980. 20.00 (ISBN 0-89158-854-X); pap. 9.75 (ISBN 0-86531-046-7). Westview.
LAFAYETTE, MARIE JOSEPH PAUL YVES ROCH GILBERT DU MOTIER, MARQUIS DE, 1757-1834
Idzerda, Stanley J., et al, eds. Lafayette in the Age of the American Revolution: Selected Letters & Papers, 1776-1790 Vol. III: April 27, 1780-March 29, 1781. LC 76-50268. (The Lafayette Papers). (Illus.). 584p. 1981. 35.00x (ISBN 0-8014-1335-4). Cornell U Pr.
--Lafayette in the Age of the American Revolution, Selected Letters & Papers, 1776-1790: April 1, 1781-December 23, 1781, Vol. IV. LC 76-50268. (The Lafayette Papers Ser.). (Illus.). 1981. 38.50 (ISBN 0-8014-1335-4). Cornell U Pr.
LAKE CHAMPLAIN
see Champlain, Lake
LAKES
see also Limnology
also names of lakes e.g. Superior Lake
Dokulil, M., et al, eds. Shallow Lakes: Contributions to Their Limnology. (Developmrnts in Hydrobiology Ser.: No. 3). 218p. 1981. PLB 59.50 (ISBN 0-686-28842-4, Pub. by W. Junk). Kluwer Boston.
Hakanson, Lars. A Manual of Lake Morphometry. (Illus.). 100p. 1981. pap. 13.90 (ISBN 0-387-10480-1). Springer-Verlag.
Preston, William L. Vanishing Landscapes: Land & Life in the Tulare Lake Basin. (Illus.). 290p. 1981. 15.95 (ISBN 0-520-04053-8). U of Cal Pr.
LAMAISM
Avedon, John F. An Interview with the Dalai Lama. LC 80-83015. (Illus.). 83p. (Orig.). 1980. pap. 6.95 (ISBN 0-937896-00-4). Littlebird.
LAMB, CHARLES, 1775-1834
Baily, F. E. The Perfect Age. 187p. 1981. Repr. of 1946 ed. lib. bdg. 30.00 (ISBN 0-89987-064-3). Darby Bks.
Fulton, Maurice G. Charles Lamb in Essays & Letters. 349p. 1980. Repr. of 1930 ed. lib. bdg. 30.00 (ISBN 0-89984-203-8). Century Bookbindery.
Marns, Edwin W., Jr., ed. The Letters of Charles & Mary Lamb, 3 vols. 40.00 ea. Vol. I, 1975 (ISBN 0-8014-0930-6). Vol. II-1976 (ISBN 0-8014-0977-2). Vol. III-1978 (ISBN 0-8014-1129-7). Cornell U Pr.
North, Ernest D. The Wit & Wisdom of Charles Lamb. 267p. 1980. Repr. of 1892 ed. lib. bdg. 25.00 (ISBN 0-8495-4109-3). Arden Lib.
LAMB, MARY ANN, 1764-1847
Baily, F. E. The Perfect Age. 187p. 1981. Repr. of 1946 ed. lib. bdg. 30.00 (ISBN 0-89987-064-3). Darby Bks.
Marns, Edwin W., Jr., ed. The Letters of Charles & Mary Lamb, 3 vols. 40.00 ea. Vol. I, 1975 (ISBN 0-8014-0930-6). Vol. II-1976 (ISBN 0-8014-0977-2). Vol. III-1978 (ISBN 0-8014-1129-7). Cornell U Pr.
LAMELLIBRANCHIATA
Stenzel, H. B., et al. Pelecypoda from the Type Locality of the Stone City Beds (Middle Eocene) of Texas. (Illus.). 237p. 1957. 3.75 (PUB 5704). Bur Econ Geology.
LANCASTER (BOMBERS)
Franklin, Neville, compiled by. Lancaster Photo Album. (Illus.). 96p. 1981. pap. 17.95 (ISBN 0-85059-477-4). Aztex.
LAND
see Land Use
LAND–VALUATION
see Real Property–Valuation
LAND, CONDEMNATION OF
see Eminent Domain
LAND, RECLAMATION OF
see Reclamation of Land
LAND FORMS
see Landforms
LAND QUESTION
see Land Tenure
LAND RECLAMATION
see Reclamation of Land
LAND SETTLEMENT
see also Agricultural Colonies; Colonization; Migration, Internal
Ashmore, Wendy, ed. Lowland Maya Settlement Patterns. (School of American Research Advanced Seminar Ser.). 464p. 1980. 30.00x (ISBN 0-8263-0556-3). U of NM Pr.
Lonsdale, Richard E. & Holmes, John H., eds. Settlement Systems in Sparsely Populated Regions: The United States & Australia. LC 80-27278. (Pergamon Policy Studies on Urban Affairs; Comparative Rural Transformation Ser.). (Illus.). 360p. 1981. 40.00 (ISBN 0-08-023111-X). Pergamon.
LAND SURVEYING
see Surveying
LAND TAX
see Land Value Taxation; Real Property Tax
LAND TENURE
see also Agricultural Colonies; Elections; Mayors; Municipal Government; Public Administration; Villages
Currie, J. M. The Economic Theory of Agricultural Land Tenure. LC 80-41114. (Illus.). Date not set. price not set (ISBN 0-521-23634-7). Cambridge U Pr.
Kammer, Jerry. The Second Long Walk: The Navajo-Hopi Land Dispute. 1980. 14.95 (ISBN 0-8263-0549-0). U of NM Pr.
Ortiz, Roxanne D. Roots of Resistance: Land Tenure in New Mexico, Sixteen Eighty to Nineteen Eighty. LC 80-18935. 202p. (Orig.). 1980. 14.95 (ISBN 0-89551-050-2); pap. 9.95 (ISBN 0-89551-050-2). UCLA Chicano Stud.
Wa-Githumo, Mwangi. Land & Nationalism: The Impact of Land Expropriation & Land Grievances Upon the Rise & Development of Nationalist Movements in Kenya, 1885-1939. LC 80-5589. 502p. 1981. lib. bdg. 24.50 (ISBN 0-8191-1491-X); pap. text ed. 15.50 (ISBN 0-8191-1492-8). U Pr of Amer.
Wolf, Peter. Land: Power & Wealth. (Illus.). 1981. 17.95 (ISBN 0-394-50437-2). Pantheon.
LAND TENURE–LAW
see also Landlord and Tenant; Leases; Real Property
Johnson, A. H. The Disappearance of the Small Landowner. LC 79-14625. (Illus.). xiii, 164p. 1979. Repr. of 1909 ed. lib. bdg. 13.50x (ISBN 0-678-08077-1). Kelley.
Libecap, Gary. Locking up the Range: Federal Land Controls & Grazing. (Pacific Institute for Public Policy Research Ser.). 1981. price not set professional reference (ISBN 0-88410-382-X). Ballinger Pub.
LAND TENURE–ASIA
Rahman, Mushtaqur & Iowa State University Research Foundation. Agrarian Egalitarianism, Land Tenures & Land Reforms in South Asia. 224p. 1980. pap. text ed. 9.95 (ISBN 0-8403-2343-3). Kendall-Hunt.
Wigmore, John H. & Simmons, D. B. Notes on Land Tenure & Local Institutions in Old Japan. (Studies in Japanese History & Civilization). 1979. 21.00 (ISBN 0-89093-223-9). U Pubns Amer.
LAND USE
see also Agriculture; Eminent Domain; Feudalism; Real Estate Business; Real Property; Reclamation of Land; Rent
Ellickson, Robert C. & Tarlock, A. Dan. Land Use Controls. 1239p. 1981. price not set (ISBN 0-316-23299-8). Little.
Haimes, Y. & Kindler, J., eds. Water & Related Land Resource Systems: Proceedings of the IFAC Symposium, Cleveland, Ohio, U. S. A., 28-31 May 1980. LC 80-41690. (IFAC Proceedings Ser.). (Illus.). 550p. 1981. 120.00 (ISBN 0-08-027307-6). Pergamon.
Lefcoe, George, ed. Respective Roles of State & Local Governments in Land Policy & Taxation. (Lincoln Institute Monograph: No. 80-7). 271p. 1980. write for info. Lincoln Inst Land.
Mandelker, Daniel R. Environment & Equity: A Regulatory Challenge. (Regulation of American Business & Industry (RABI) Ser.). 240p. 1981. 24.95 (ISBN 0-07-039864-X, P&RB). McGraw.
O'Mara, W. Paul, et al. Adaptive Use. LC 78-56054. (Illus.). 246p. 1978. 26.25 (ISBN 0-87420-582-4). Urban Land.
Popper, Frank. The Politics of Land-Use Reform. 312p. 1981. 20.00 (ISBN 0-299-08530-9); pap. text ed. 7.50 (ISBN 0-299-08534-1). U of Wis Pr.
LAND USE–BIBLIOGRAPHY
Bernard, Michael M., ed. Annotated Bibliography on Taxation As an Instrument of Land Planning Policy. (Lincoln Institute Monograph: No. 80-8). 90p. 1980. pap. text ed. 4.00. Lincoln Inst Land.
LAND USE–TAXATION
see Land Value Taxation; Real Property Tax
LAND USE–AFRICA
Third Meeting of the Eastern African Sub Committee for Soil Correlation & Land Evaluation. (World Soil Resources Report: No. 51). 170p. 1981. pap. 9.25 (ISBN 92-5-100902-3, F2082, FAO). Unipub.
LAND USE–NEW GUINEA
Lands of the Ramu-Mandang Area, Papua New Guinea. (Land Research Ser.: No. 37). (Illus.). 135p. 1976. pap. 13.50 (ISBN 0-643-00175-1, CO18, CSIRO). Unipub.
LAND USE–UNITED STATES
Chapman, Jeffrey I. Proposition Thirteen & Land Use: A Case Study of Fiscal Limits in California. LC 79-3749. 1981. 22.95x (ISBN 0-669-03471-1). Lexington Bks.
Jackson, Richard H. Land Use in America. LC 80-20184. (Scripta Ser. in Geography). 224p. 1981. 29.95 (ISBN 0-470-27063-2). Halsted Pr.
LAND USE, URBAN–PLANNING
see City Planning
LAND VALUATION
see Real Property–Valuation
LAND VALUE TAXATION
Bernard, Michael M., ed. Annotated Bibliography on Taxation As an Instrument of Land Planning Policy. (Lincoln Institute Monograph: No. 80-8). 90p. 1980. pap. text ed. 4.00. Lincoln Inst Land.
Brown, Harry G. Selected Articles by Harry Gunnison Brown: The Case for Land Value Taxation. 320p. 1980. 12.50x (ISBN 0-911312-50-1). Schalkenbach.
Proposition Thirteen: A First Anniversary Assessment. (Lincoln Institute Monograph: No. 880-5). (Illus.). 1980. pap. text ed. 5.00. Lincoln Inst Land.
State Taxation of Forest & Land Resources: Symposium Proceedings. (Lincoln Institute Monograph: No. 80-6). 149p. 1980. pap. text ed. 12.00. Lincoln Inst Land.
LANDFORMS
see also names of topographical features e.g. Mountains; Plains
Melhorn, W. N. & Flemal, R. C., eds. Theories of Landform Development. (Binghamton Symposia in Geomorphology: International Ser.: No. 6). (Illus.). 312p. 1980. text ed. 20.00x (ISBN 0-04-551039-3, 2507). Allen Unwin.
LANDLORD AND TENANT
see also Apartment Houses; Leases; Rent
Partington, Martin. Landlord & Tenant: Text & Materials on Housing & Law. 2nd ed. (Law in Context Ser.). xxxviii, 554p. 1981. 54.00x (ISBN 0-297-77790-4, Pub. by Weidenfeld & Nicolson England). Rothman.
Robinson, Leigh. Landlording: A Handy Manual for Scrupulous Landlords & Landladies How Do It Themselves. 3rd ed. 272p. 1980. pap. text ed. 15.00 (ISBN 0-932956-01-7); pap. text ed. 17.50 canadian edition. Express.
Schoshinski, Robert. American Law of Landlords & Tenant, Vol. 1. LC 80-81653. 1980. 60.00. Lawyers Co-Op.

LANDLORD AND TENANT–GREAT BRITAIN

Greve, John. Private Landlords in England. 54p. 1965. pap. text ed. 3.75x (Pub. by Bedford England). Renouf.

LANDOR, WALTER SAVAGE, 1775-1864

Colvin, Sidney. English Men of Letters, Walter Savage Landor. Morley, John, ed. 224p. 1980. Repr. of 1881 ed. lib. bdg. 15.00 (ISBN 0-89760-117-3). Telegraph Bks.

LANDSCAPE

Vance, Mary. Landscape, Landscape Architecture & Landscape Gardening: A Selective List of Books. (Architecture Ser.: Bibliography A-197). 61p. 1980. pap. 6.50. Vance Biblios.

LANDSCAPE ARCHITECTURE

see also Decks (Architecture, Domestic); Garden Walks; Landscape Gardening; Parks; Patios; Plants, Ornamental; Shrubs; Trees; Woody Plants

Anderson, Paul. Regional Landscape Analysis. LC 80-6837. 1980. pap. 19.50 (ISBN 0-918436-11-7). Environ Des VA.

Ferguson, Bruce K. Landscape Literature of the Twentieth Century Books Reviewed in "Landscape Architecture" Magazine, 1910-1979. (Architecture Ser.: Bibliography A-259). 84p. 1980. pap. 9.00. Vance Biblios.

Hannenbaum, L. Landscape Design: A Practical Approach. 1981. text ed. 16.95 (ISBN 0-8359-5577-X); instr's. manual free (ISBN 0-8359-5578-8). Reston.

Jakle, John A. & Oliver, Virginia. Past Landscapes: A Bibliography for Historic Preservationists. rev. ed. (Architecture Ser.: Bibliography A-314). 68p. 1980. pap. 7.50. Vance Biblios.

Kerr, Kathleen W., et al. Cost Data for Landscape Construction: 1981 Edition. rev. ed. (Cost Data for Landscape Construction Ser.). (Illus.). 200p. 1981. pap. 24.95 (ISBN 0-937890-01-4). Kerr Assoc.

Landscape Architecture Magazine. Home Landscape Nineteen Eighty-One. Clay, Grady & Johnson, Norman, eds. (Landscape Architecture Magazine Ser.). 168p. 1981. 7.95 (ISBN 0-07-036193-2). McGraw.

Moffat, Anne & Schiller, Marc. Landscape Design That Saves Energy. (Illus.). 224p. 1981. 17.95 (ISBN 0-688-00031-2, Quill); pap. 9.95 (ISBN 0-688-00395-8). Morrow.

Morris, Robert & King County Arts Commision, eds. Earthworks: Land Reclamation As Sculture. 71p. 1980. pap. text ed. 5.95 (ISBN 0-932216-04-8). Seattle Art.

Smith, Michael A. Landscapes 1975-1979, 2 vols. (Illus.). 120p. 1981. Set. 275.00 (ISBN 0-9605646-0-8). Vol. I (ISBN 0-9605646-1-6). Vol. II (ISBN 0-9605646-2-4). Lodima.

Vance, Mary. Landscape, Landscape Architecture & Landscape Gardening: A Selective List of Books. (Architecture Ser.: Bibliography A-197). 61p. 1980. pap. 6.50. Vance Biblios.

LANDSCAPE GARDENING

see also Landscape Architecture

Grounds, Roger. Ornamental Grasses. 216p. 1981. 16.95 (ISBN 0-442-24707-9). Van Nos Reinhold.

Smith, Ken. Southern Home Landscaping. (Gardening Ser.). (Orig.). 1981. pap. 7.95 (ISBN 0-89586-063-5). H P Bks.

Vance, Mary. Landscape, Landscape Architecture & Landscape Gardening: A Selective List of Books. (Architecture Ser.: Bibliography A-197). 61p. 1980. pap. 6.50. Vance Biblios.

LANDSCAPE IN ART

Novak, Barbara. Nature & Culture: American Landscape & Painting 1825-1875. (Illus.). 336p. 1981. pap. 18.95 (ISBN 0-19-502935-6, OPB). Oxford U Pr.

LANDSCAPE PAINTING

Kautzky, Ted. Painting Trees & Landscapes in Watercolor. 1981. pap. 9.95 (ISBN 0-442-21918-0). Van Nos Reinhold.

Novak, Barbara. Nature & Culture: American Landscape & Painting 1825-1875. (Illus.). 336p. 1981. pap. 18.95 (ISBN 0-19-502935-6, OPB). Oxford U Pr.

Reff, Theodore, ed. Exhibitions of Barbizon & Landscape Art. (Modern Art in Paris 1855 to 1900 Ser.). 449p. 1981. lib. bdg. 44.00 (ISBN 0-8240-4737-0). Garland Pub.

LANDSCAPE PAINTING–TECHNIQUE

Hayes, Colin. A Practical Guide to Landscape Painting. 120p. 1981. 15.95 (ISBN 0-8230-0322-1). Watson-Guptill.

Kinstler, Everett R. Painting Faces, Figures & Landscapes. 144p. 1981. 22.50 (ISBN 0-8230-3625-1). Watson-Guptill.

LANDSCAPE PAINTING–GREAT BRITAIN

Wark, Robert R. British Landscape Drawings & Watercolors, Nineteen-Fifty to Eighteen-Fifty: Twenty-Four Examples from the Huntington Collection. (Illus.). 64p. write for info. (ISBN 0-87328-116-0). Huntington Lib.

LANDSCAPE PHOTOGRAPHY

see Photography–Landscapes

LANFRANC, ABP. OF CANTERBURY, 1005-1089 DECRETA

Macdonald, Allan J. Lanfranc, a Study of His Life, Work & Writing. LC 80-2223. 1981. Repr. of 1926 ed. 37.50 (ISBN 0-404-18768-4). AMS Pr.

LANGUAGE, LEGAL

see Law–Language

LANGUAGE, PHILOSOPHY OF

see Languages–Philosophy

LANGUAGE, PSYCHOLOGY OF

see Psycholinguistics

LANGUAGE ACQUISITION

see Children–Language

LANGUAGE AND LANGUAGES

Here are entered works on language in general, works on the origin and history of language, and surveys of languages; Works dealing with the scientific study of human speech, including phonetics, phonemics, morphology and syntax, are entered under Linguistics. Works on the philosophy and psychology of language are entered under Languages–Philosophy, and Languages–Psychology, respectively.

see also Bilingualism; Children–Language; Communication; Formal Languages; Judgment; Languages–Philosophy; Linguistic Research; Linguistics; Literature; Multilingualism; Programming Languages (Electronic Computers); Psycholinguistics; Rhetoric; Semantics; Semantics (Philosophy); Sociolinguistics; Speech; Translating and Interpreting; Voice; Writing

also names of particular languages or groups of cognate languages, e.g. English Language, Semitic Languages

Chapey, Roberta. Language Intervention Strategies in Adult Aphasia. (Illus.). 381p. 1981. 32.00 (ISBN 0-686-69565-8, 1511-7). Williams & Wilkins.

Conversation Starters for Speech & Language Therapy. 1981. pap. 2.75 (ISBN 0-8134-2186-1, 2186). Interstate.

Cressey, William W. & Napoli, Donna J., eds. Linguistic Symposium on Romance Languages, No. 9. (Orig.). 1981. pap. text ed. 8.95x (ISBN 0-87840-081-8). Georgetown U Pr.

Dodge, James W., ed. Other Words, Other Worlds: Language in Culture. 1972. pap. 7.95x (ISBN 0-915432-72-2). NE Conf Teach.

Elliot, Alison J. Child Language. (Cambridge Textbooks in Linguistics). 180p. Date not set. text ed. price not set (ISBN 0-521-22518-3); pap. text ed. price not set (ISBN 0-521-29556-4). Cambridge U Pr.

Esau, Helmut, et al. Language & Communication. 1980. pap. 8.75. Hornbeam Pr.

Ferguson, C. A., et al, eds. Language in the U. S. A. 650p. Date not set. price not set (ISBN 0-521-23140-X); pap. price not set (ISBN 0-521-29834-2). Cambridge U Pr.

Flowers, Ann M. Big Book of Language Through Sounds. 2nd ed. LC 79-92515. 1980. pap. text ed. 6.95x (ISBN 0-8134-2114-4, 2114). Interstate.

Gans, Eric. The Origin of Language: A Formal Theory of Representation. 1981. 19.95x (ISBN 0-520-04202-6). U of Cal Pr.

Gochnour, Elizabeth A. & Smith, Theresa B. Language of Life. 2nd ed. (Illus.). 1981. pap. 6.50x (ISBN 0-8134-2162-4, 2162). Interstate.

Goodenough, Ward. Culture, Language & Society. 1981. 9.95; pap. 5.95. Benjamin-Cummings.

Lehmann, Winfred P., et al. Introduction to Scholarship in Modern Languages & Literatures. Gibaldi, Joseph, ed. 160p. 1981. 10.50x (ISBN 0-87352-092-0); pap. 6.00x (ISBN 0-87352-093-9). Modern Lang.

Miller, George A. Language & Speech. LC 80-27018. (Illus.). 1981. text ed. price not set (ISBN 0-7167-1297-0); pap. text ed. price not set (ISBN 0-7167-1298-9). W H Freeman.

Nalimov, V. V. In the Labyrinths of Language: A Mathematician's Journey. Colodny, Robert G., ed. (Illus.). 246p. 1981. 22.50 (ISBN 0-89495-007-X). ISI Pr.

Pierce, Joe E. A Theory of Language, Culture & Human Behavior. 161p. 1972. pap. 7.95. Hapi Pr.

Ptacek, Paul H., et al. Index to Speech, Language & Hearing Journal Titles, 1954-78. LC 79-20058. 328p. 1979. text ed. 25.00 (ISBN 0-933014-54-6). College-Hill.

Salomaa, Arto. Jewels of Formal Language Theory. (Illus.). 1981. text ed. 24.95 (ISBN 0-914894-69-2). Computer Sci.

Tursi, Joseph A., ed. FLs & the 'new' Student. 1970. pap. 7.95x (ISBN 0-915432-70-6). NE Conf Teach.

Wells, Gordon, et al. Learning Through Interaction. LC 80-41113. (Language at Home & at School Ser.: Vol. 1). (Illus.). 200p. Date not set. text ed. 39.50 (ISBN 0-521-23774-2); pap. text ed. 10.95 (ISBN 0-521-28219-5). Cambridge U Pr.

LANGUAGE AND LANGUAGES–ADDRESSES, ESSAYS, LECTURES

Gaburo, Kenneth, et al, eds. Allos: 41 Writings by 41 Writers. LC 80-80809. (Illus.). 448p. 1980. softcover 20.95. Lingua Pr.

Grace, George. An Essay on Language. 1981. write for info.; pap. price not set. Hornbeam Pr.

Grimshaw, Allen D. Language As a Social Resource: Essays by Allen D. Grimshaw. (Language Science & National Development). 400p. 1981. text ed. 18.75x (ISBN 0-8047-1108-9). Stanford U Pr.

Kramarae, Cheris, ed. The Voices & Words of Women & Men. 195p. 1981. 28.80 (ISBN 0-08-026106-X). Pergamon.

LANGUAGE AND LANGUAGES–DATA PROCESSING

see Linguistics–Data Processing

LANGUAGE AND LANGUAGES–DICTIONARIES

Stark, Frederick. Phrase Dictionaries for the American Tourist, 6 bks. Incl. German for the American Tourist. pap. (ISBN 0-8326-2409-8, 6570); Spanish for the American Tourist. pap. (ISBN 0-8326-2410-1, 6571); French for the American Tourist. pap. (ISBN 0-8326-2411-X, 6572); Italian for the American Tourist. pap. (ISBN 0-8326-2412-8, 6573); Greek for the American Tourist. pap. (ISBN 0-8326-2413-6, 6574); Russian for the American Tourist. pap. (ISBN 0-8326-2414-4, 6575). 128p. (Orig.). 1981. pap. 1.95 ea. Delair.

Urdang, Laurance, ed. Allusions: Cultural, Literary, Biblical, & Historical: A Thematic Dictionary. 1980. 45.00 (ISBN 0-8103-1124-0). Gale.

LANGUAGE AND LANGUAGES–ETYMOLOGY

see also Names;

also subdivision Etymology under names of languages

Train, John. Remarkable Words: With Astonishing Origins. Remarkable Ser. (Clarkson N. Potter Bks.). 1980. 5.95 (ISBN 0-517-54185-8). Crown.

LANGUAGE AND LANGUAGES–EXAMINATIONS, QUESTIONS, ETC.

Thorum, Arden R. Language Assessment Instruments: Infancy Through Adulthood. 320p. 1980. text ed. 19.75 (ISBN 0-398-04107-5). C C Thomas.

LANGUAGE AND LANGUAGES–GRAMMAR, COMPARATIVE

see Grammar, Comparative and General

LANGUAGE AND LANGUAGES–JUVENILE LITERATURE

Schwartz, Alvin. The Cat's Elbow & Other Secret Languages. (Illus.). 96p. (gr. 3 up). Date not set. 8.95 (ISBN 0-374-31224-9). FS&G.

LANGUAGE AND LANGUAGES–PHILOSOPHY

see Languages–Philosophy

LANGUAGE AND LANGUAGES–PSYCHOLOGY

see Psycholinguistics

LANGUAGE AND LANGUAGES–RESEARCH

see Linguistic Research

LANGUAGE AND LANGUAGES–STUDY AND TEACHING

see also Linguistic Research

Born, Warren C., ed. The Foreign Language Teacher in Today's Classroom Environment. 1979. pap. 7.95x (ISBN 0-915432-79-X). NE Conf Teach.

Clark, Raymond C. Language Teaching Techniques. LC 80-84109. (Pro Lingua Language Resource Handbook Ser.). (Illus.). 128p. (Orig.). 1980. pap. 5.50 (ISBN 0-86647-000-X). Pro Lingua.

Geno, Thomas H., ed. Foreign Languages & International Studies 1981: Toward Cooperation & Integration. LC 55-34379. 200p. 1981. pap. 7.95 (ISBN 0-915432-81-1). NE Conf Teach Foreign.

--Our Profession: Present Status & Future Directions. 1980. pap. 7.95x (ISBN 0-915432-80-3). NE Conf Teach.

Gibaldi, Joseph & Mirollo, James V., eds. Teaching Apprentice Programs in Language & Literature. (Options for Teaching Ser.: No. 4). 160p. (Orig.). 1981. pap. 7.00x (ISBN 0-87352-303-2). Modern Lang.

Lind, Carolyn P., pseud. One Hundred Four Ideas for Improving Your Young Child's Language Skills. (Illus.). 80p. (Orig.). 1980. pap. 10.00 (ISBN 0-9604940-0-6). Lindell Pubs.

Mandel, Barrett J., ed. Three Language-Arts Curriculum Models: Pre-Kindergarten Through College. 1980. pap. 8.50 (ISBN 0-8141-5458-1). NCTE.

Pierce, Joe E. Languages & Linguistics. 2nd ed. 188p. 1980. pap. 11.95 (ISBN 0-913244-23-6). Hapi Pr.

--A Linguistic Method of Teaching Second Languages. 145p. 1973. pap. 6.95 (ISBN 0-913244-05-8). Hapi Pr.

Rivers, Wilga M. Teaching Foreign Language Skills. 2nd, rev. ed. LC 80-24993. 1981. lib. bdg. 22.00x (ISBN 0-226-72098-5); pap. 12.50x (ISBN 0-226-72097-7). U of Chicago Pr.

Ross, Dorothea M. & Ross, Sheila A. Fundamental Skills & Concepts 1: Language Arts Lessons for Grades 1-3. (Makemaster Bk.). 1980. pap. 14.95 (ISBN 0-8224-0291-2). Pitman Learning.

--Fundamental Skills & Concepts 2: Arithmetic Lessons for Grades 1-3. (Makemaster Bk.). 1980. pap. 14.95 (ISBN 0-8224-0292-0). Pitman Learning.

Wood, Barbara S. Children & Communication: Verbal & Nonverbal Language Development. 2nd ed. (Illus.). 320p. 1981. text ed. 15.95 (ISBN 0-13-131920-5). P-H.

LANGUAGE AND LANGUAGES–TESTING

see Language and Languages–Examinations, Questions, etc.

LANGUAGE AND LOGIC

see Logical Positivism

LANGUAGE AND SOCIETY

see Sociolinguistics

LANGUAGE ARTS

see also Communication; English Language; Literature–Study and Teaching; Reading; Speech

Blatt, Gloria T. It's Your Move: Expressive Movement in the Language Arts Reading Class. (Orig.). 1981. pap. 8.95 (ISBN 0-8077-2640-0). Tchrs Coll.

Canario, Jack. The Big Hassle: Getting Along with Authority. (Read on! - Write on! Ser.). (Illus.). 64p. (gr. 6-12). 1980. 2.85 (ISBN 0-915510-38-3). Janus Bks.

--The Put-Down Pro: Getting Along with Friends. (Read on! - Write on! Ser.). (Illus.). 64p. (gr. 6-12). 1980. 2.85 (ISBN 0-915510-39-1). Janus Bks.

Cole, Martha L. & Cole, Jack T. Language Training for the Nonverbal-Language Delayed Child. 275p. 1981. text ed. price not set (ISBN 0-89443-344-X). Aspen Systems.

Milton, Octavia. Assist Three: For Consonant Blends of L, R, & S. 50p. 1981. pap. text ed. 13.00 (ISBN 0-88450-729-7). Communication Skill.

Webber, Margaret S. Language Skills for Exceptional Learners. 275p. 1981. text ed. write for info. (ISBN 0-89443-343-1). Aspen Systems.

Yawkey, Thomas D., et al. Language Arts & the Young Child. LC 80-52447. 270p. 1981. pap. text ed. 7.50 (ISBN 0-87581-263-5). Peacock Pubs.

LANGUAGE ARTS–STUDY AND TEACHING

see Language Arts

LANGUAGE ARTS (ELEMENTARY)

Foster, Lawrence J., et al. Teaching Preschool Language Arts. (Illus.). 272p. 1981. pap. text ed. 15.95 (ISBN 0-8425-1933-5). Brigham.

Reynell, Joan. Language Developement & Assessment. (Studies in Developmental Pediatrics Ser.: Vol. 1). 178p. 1980. text ed. 16.50 (ISBN 0-88416-377-6). PSG Pub.

LANGUAGE DATA PROCESSING

see Linguistics–Data Processing

LANGUAGES–PHILOSOPHY

see also Analysis (Philosophy)

Boretz, Benjamin. Language, As a Music: Six Marginal Pretexts for Composition. LC 80-80807. (Illus.). 88p. 1980. lib. bdg. 15.75. Lingua Pr.

Botwinick, Aryeh. Wittgenstein & Historical Understanding. LC 80-5968. 65p. (Orig.). 1981. pap. text ed. 5.00 (ISBN 0-8191-1431-6). U Pr of Amer.

Chappell, V. C., ed. Ordinary Language: Essays in Philosophical Method. 128p. 1981. pap. 2.75 (ISBN 0-486-24082-7). Dover.

LANGUAGES–PSYCHOANALYSIS

see Psycholinguistics

LANGUAGES–PSYCHOLOGY

see Psycholinguistics

LANGUAGES–SOCIOLOGICAL ASPECTS

see Sociolinguistics

LANGUAGES, MIXED

see also Creole Dialects

Brown, Jason W., ed. Jargonaphasia. (Perspectives in Neurolinguistics & Psycholinguistics Ser.). 1981. price not set (ISBN 0-12-137580-3). Acad Pr.

LANGUAGES, MODERN–STUDY AND TEACHING

Trim, J. L. Developing a Unit-Credit Scheme of Adult Language Learning. LC 80-40756. (Council of Europe Modern Languages Project). 96p. 1980. pap. 10.00 (ISBN 0-08-024596-X). Pergamon.

LANGUE D'OIL

see French Language

LAOS

Lafont, Pierre-Bernard, ed. Bibliographie Du Laos. 2nd ed. Incl. Vol. 1. 1666-1961. 269p; Vol. 2. 1962-1975. 413p. LC 65-53527. (Orig., Fr.). 1978. pap. 55.00x. Intl Pubns Serv.

LAPAROTOMY

see Abdomen–Surgery

LAPIDARY ART

see Gem Cutting

LAPLANDERS

see Lapps

LAPPS

Irwin, John L. The Finns & the Lapps: How They Live & Work. 171p. 1973. text ed. 8.95 (ISBN 0-03-030206-4, HoltC). HR&W.

LARGE PRINT BOOKS

see Large Type Books

LARGE TYPE BOOKS

Auchincloss, Louis. The House of the Prophet. (Large Print Bks.). 1980. lib. bdg. 14.95 (ISBN 0-8161-3133-3). G K Hall.

Benchley, Nathaniel. Sweet Anarchy. (Large Print Bks.). 1980. lib. bdg. 15.50 (ISBN 0-8161-3134-1). G K Hall.

Camuti, Louis J., et al. All My Patients Under the Bed. 1980. lib. bdg. 14.50 (ISBN 0-8161-3170-8, Large Print Bks). G K Hall.

Christman, Elizabeth. Flesh & Spirit. 1980. pap. 2.25 (ISBN 0-686-69260-8, 52142). Avon.

Clark, Mary H. The Cradle Will Fall. (Large Print Bks.). 1980. lib. bdg. 13.95 (ISBN 0-8161-3121-X). G K Hall.

Corman, Avery. The Old Neighborhood. 1980. lib. bdg. 12.95 (ISBN 0-8161-3146-5, Large Print Bks). G K Hall.

Courtney, Caroline. Dangerous Engagement. 1980. lib. bdg. 12.95 (ISBN 0-8161-3094-9, Large Print Bks). G K Hall.

--Guardian of the Heart. (Large Print Bks.). 1980. lib. bdg. 11.95 (ISBN 0-8161-3095-7). G K Hall.

Darcy, Clare. Letty. (Large Print Bks.). 1980. lib. bdg. 12.95 (ISBN 0-8161-3127-9). G K Hall.

Demetz, Hana. The House on Prague Street. 1980. lib. bdg. 12.95 (ISBN 0-8161-3143-0, Large Print Bks). G K Hall.

Di Donato, Georgia. Woman of Justice. (Large Print Bks.). 1980. lib. bdg. 15.95 (ISBN 0-8161-3132-5). G K Hall.

Dreyfack, Raymond. The Complete Book of Walking. LC 80-26185. (Illus.). 288p. 1981. pap. 5.95 (ISBN 0-668-05167-1, 5167). Arco.

Ferrars, E. X. Witness Before the Fact. (Large Print Bks.). 1980. lib. bdg. 11.95 (ISBN 0-8161-3126-0). G K Hall.

Gardner, Erle S. The Case of the Ice Cold Hands. 1980. lib. bdg. 11.95 (ISBN 0-8161-3174-0, Large Print Bks). G K Hall.

Grey, Zane. The Westerner. (Large Print Bks.). 1980. lib. bdg. 10.95 (ISBN 0-8161-3125-2). G K Hall.

Haldeman, Linda. Star of the Sea. 176p. 1981. pap. 2.25 (ISBN 0-380-54114-9, 54114). Avon.

Hale, Arlene. The Winds of Summer. 1980. lib. bdg. 13.50 (ISBN 0-8161-3168-6, Large Print Bks). G K Hall.

Hogan, Ray. The Proving Gun. 1980. lib. bdg. 10.95 (ISBN 0-8161-3172-4, Large Print Bks). G K Hall.

Holt, Victoria. The Mask of the Enchantress. 1980. lib. bdg. 16.95 (ISBN 0-8161-3142-2, Large Print Bks). G K Hall.

James, P. D. An Unsuitable Job for a Woman. 1980. lib. bdg. 13.95 (ISBN 0-8161-6788-5, Large Print Bks). G K Hall.

L'Amour, Louis. Bendigo Shafter. 1980. lib. bdg. 15.95 (ISBN 0-8161-3144-9, Large Print Bks). G K Hall.

Large Print Book Catalog. LC 76-48929. 322p. 1976. 8.00 (ISBN 0-913578-13-4). Inglewood Ca.

Lindau, Joan. Hrs. Cooper's Boardinghouse. 1980. lib. bdg. write for info. (Large Print Bks). G K Hall.

McBain, Ed. Ghosts. (Large Print Bks.). 1980. lib. bdg. 12.95 (ISBN 0-8161-3128-7). G K Hall.

Patten, Lewis B. The Trail of the Apache Kid. (Large Print Bks.). 1980. lib. bdg. 10.95 (ISBN 0-8161-3130-9). G K Hall.

Paul, Barbara. To Love a Stranger. 1980. lib. bdg. 14.95 (ISBN 0-8161-3169-4, Large Print Bks). G K Hall.

Reed, Barry. The Verdict. 1980. lib. bdg. 14.95 (ISBN 0-8161-3175-9, Large Print Bks). G K Hall.

Sayers, Dorothy L. Have His Carcase. (Large Print Bks.). 1980. lib. bdg. 17.95 (ISBN 0-8161-3043-4). G K Hall.

--Strong Poison. (Large Print Bks.). 1980. lib. bdg. 15.95 (ISBN 0-8161-3042-6). G K Hall.

Segal, Erich. Man, Woman & Child. (Large Print Bks.). 1980. lib. bdg. 10.95 (ISBN 0-8161-3124-4). G K Hall.

Singer, Isaac B. Old Love. 1980. pap. 2.50 (ISBN 0-449-24343-5, Crest). Fawcett.

Subject Guide to Large Print Book Catalog. LC 76-30595. 110p. 1976. 5.00 (ISBN 0-913578-15-0). Inglewood Ca.

Thane, Elswyth. Ever After. (Williamsburg Ser.: No. 3). 1981. lib. bdg. 17.95 (ISBN 0-8161-3165-1, Large Print Bks). G K Hall.

--Homing. (Williamsburg Ser.: No. 7). 1981. lib. bdg. 15.95 (ISBN 0-8161-3164-3, Large Print Bks). G K Hall.

--Kissing Kin. (Williamsburg Ser.: No. 5). 1981. lib. bdg. 16.95 (ISBN 0-686-69444-9, Large Print Bks). G K Hall.

--The Light Heart. (Williamsburg Ser.: No. 4). 1981. lib. bdg. 17.95 (ISBN 0-8161-3163-5, Large Print Bks). G K Hall.

Truman, Margaret. Murder in the White House. 1980. lib. bdg. 13.95 (ISBN 0-8161-3171-6, Large Print Bks). G K Hall.

Turnbull, Agnes S. The Two Bishops. 1980. lib. bdg. 14.95 (ISBN 0-8161-3173-2, Large Print Bks). G K Hall.

Tyler, Anne. Morgan's Passing. (Large Print Bks.). 1980. lib. bdg. 16.95 (ISBN 0-8161-3131-7). G K Hall.

LARVAE–INSECTS

Hinton, H. E. Biology of Insect Eggs, 3 vols. LC 77-30390. (Illus.). 1500p. 1980. Set. 350.00 (ISBN 0-08-021539-4). Pergamon.

LARYNGECTOMY

Keith, Robert L. & Darley, Frederic L., eds. Laryngectomee Rehabilitation. LC 79-91246. (Illus.). 533p. 1980. text ed. 24.50 (ISBN 0-933014-56-2). College-Hill.

Kelly, Dan H. & Welborn, Peggy. The Cover-Up: Neckwear for the Laryngectomee & Other Neck Breathers. LC 80-65470. (Illus.). 98p. 1980. pap. text ed. 14.95 (ISBN 0-933014-55-4). College-Hill.

Shedd, Donald P. & Weinberg, Bernd. Surgical-Prosthetic Approaches to Speech Rehabilitation. (Medical Publications Ser.). 1980. lib. bdg. 32.50 (ISBN 0-8161-2186-9). G K Hall.

LARYNX

see also Voice

Cotton & Seid. Laryngl Disease in Children. 1981. text ed. write for info. (ISBN 0-443-08054-2). Churchill.

Silver, C. E. Surgery for Cancer of the Larynx. 1981. text ed. write for info. (ISBN 0-443-08064-X). Churchill.

Tucker. Surgery for Phonatory Disorders. 1981. text ed. write for info. (ISBN 0-443-08058-5). Churchill.

LASER PHOTOGRAPHY

see Holography

LASER SPECTROSCOPY

Demtroeder, W. Laser Spectrosopy: Basic Concepts & Instrumentation. (Springer Series in Chemical Physics: Vol. 5). (Illus.). 700p. 1981. 35.00 (ISBN 0-387-10343-0). Springer-Verlag.

Omenetto, N. Analytical Laser Spectroscopy, Vol. 50. 550p. 1979. 47.50 (ISBN 0-471-65371-3, 1-075). Wiley.

LASERS

see also Nonlinear Optics

Butler, J. K., ed. Semiconductor Injection Lasers. LC 79-91615. 1980. 36.95 (ISBN 0-87942-129-0). Inst Electrical.

Hora, Heinrich. Physics of Laser Driven Plasmas. 325p. 1981. 30.00 (ISBN 0-471-07880-8, Pub. by Wiley-Interscience). Wiley.

Kock, Winston E. Lasers & Holography: An Introduction to Coherent Optics. 2nd, rev. ed. (Illus.). 128p. 1981. pap. price not set (ISBN 0-486-24041-X). Dover.

Sixth European Conference on Optical Communication. (IEE Conference Publication Ser.: No. 190). (Illus.). 466p. (Orig.). 1980. soft cover 73.00 (ISBN 0-85296-223-1). Inst Elect Eng.

Steinfeld, Jeffrey I., ed. Laser-Induced Chemical Processes. 255p. 1981. 32.50 (ISBN 0-306-40587-3, Plenum Pr). Plenum Pub.

Verdeyen, Joseph T. Laser Electronics. (Illus.). 480p. 1981. 32.50 (ISBN 0-13-485201-X). P-H.

LASERS IN MEDICINE

Hieftje, Gary, et al, eds. Lasers in Chemical Analysis. LC 80-84082. (Contemporary Instrumentation & Analysis). (Illus.). 352p. 1981. price not set (ISBN 0-89603-027-X). Humana.

Pratesi, R. & Sacchi, C. A., eds. Lasers in Photomedicine & Photobiology: Proceedings. (Springer Series in Optical Sciences: Vol. 22). (Illus.). 235p. 1980. 29.50 (ISBN 0-387-10178-0). Springer-Verlag.

Schwarz, H. J., et al, eds. Laser Interaction & Related Plasma Phenomena, Vol. 5. 800p. 1981. 75.00 (ISBN 0-306-40545-8, Plenum Pr). Plenum Pub.

LASSEN VOLCANIC NATIONAL PARK

Schaffer, Jeffrey P. Lassen Volcanic National Park. Winnett, Thomas, ed. LC 80-53681. (Illus.). 224p. (Orig.). 1981. pap. 9.95 (ISBN 0-89997-004-4). Wilderness Pr.

LAST SUPPER

Here are entered works on the final meal of Christ with his apostles when the sacrament of the Lord's Supper was instituted.

see also Lord's Supper

Marshall, I. Howard. Last Supper & Lord's Supper. (Orig.). 1981. pap. price not set (ISBN 0-8028-1854-4). Eerdmans.

LAST WORDS

Coppock, Thomas. The Genuine Dying Speech of the Reverend Parson Coppock, Pretended Bishop of Carlisle: Who Was Drawn, Hanged & Quartered There, Oct. 18, 1746, for High Treason & Rebellion, Etc. LC 80-2477. 1981. Repr. of 1746 ed. 23.50 (ISBN 0-404-19109-6). AMS Pr.

LATIN AMERICA

see also names of Latin-American countries and geographic areas of Latin America, e.g. Brazil; Caribbean Area; South America; names of cities, towns, and geographic areas in specific countries

Paddington Press. Latin America Business Travel Guide. 448p. 1981. 19.95 (ISBN 0-87196-339-6); pap. 11.95 (ISBN 0-87196-345-0). Facts on File.

LATIN AMERICA–BIBLIOGRAPHY

Martin, Dolores M., ed. Handbook of Latin American Studies: No. 42, Humanities. 720p. 1981. text ed. 55.00x (ISBN 0-292-73016-0). U of Tex Pr.

The Library of Congress & the University of Texas Library (Austin) Bibliographic Guide to Latin American Studies: 1980. (Library Catalogs Bib. Guides). 1981. lib. bdg. 275.00 (ISBN 0-686-69556-9). G K Hall.

LATIN AMERICA–BIOGRAPHY

Robinson, David J. Studying Latin America: Essays in Honor of Preston E. James. LC 80-12413. (Dellplain Latin American Studies: No. 4). 290p. (Orig.). 1980. pap. 19.25 (ISBN 0-8357-0515-3, SS-00135, Pub. by Syracuse U Dept Geog). Univ Microfilms.

LATIN AMERICA–COMMERCE

Orosz, Arpad. The Foreign Trade Turnover of Latin America Until 1970 & Its Prospective Development up to 1980. LC 77-369256. (Studies on Developing Countries). 130p. (Orig.). 1976. pap. 8.50x (ISBN 0-8002-0494-8). Intl Pubns Serv.

LATIN AMERICA–DESCRIPTION AND TRAVEL

Wilhelm, R. Dwight. Two Ways to Look South: A Guide to Latin America. (Orig.). 1980. pap. 2.25 (ISBN 0-377-00098-1). Friend Pr.

LATIN AMERICA–ECONOMIC CONDITIONS

Bradford, Colin I., Jr. Forces for Change in Latin America: U. S. Policy Implications. LC 70-181831. (Monographs: No. 5). 80p. 1971. 2.00 (ISBN 0-686-28690-1). Overseas Dev Council.

Economic Survey of Latin America 1977. 536p. 1979. pap. 22.00 (ISBN 0-686-68952-6, UN79/2G1, UN). Unipub.

Foxley, Alejandro & Whitehead, Laurence, eds. Economic Stabilization in Latin America: Political Dimensions. 120p. 1980. pap. 16.50 (ISBN 0-08-026788-2). Pergamon.

Montavon, Remy, et al. The Role of Multinational Companies in Latin America: A Case Study in Mexico. 124p. 1980. 27.50 (ISBN 0-03-057973-2). Praeger.

OAS General Secretariat Planning & Statistics. Synthesis Fo Economic Performance in Latin America During 1979. (Statistics Ser.). 40p. 1979. pap. 3.00 (ISBN 0-686-68295-5). OAS.

Orosz, Arpad. The Foreign Trade Turnover of Latin America Until 1970 & Its Prospective Development up to 1980. LC 77-369256. (Studies on Developing Countries). 130p. (Orig.). 1976. pap. 8.50x (ISBN 0-8002-0494-8). Intl Pubns Serv.

Pollitt, Ernesto. Poverty & Malnutrition in Latin America: Early Childhood Intervention Programs. LC 80-18811. 150p. 1980. 21.95 (ISBN 0-03-058031-5). Praeger.

United Nations. Economic Survey of Latin America 1977. LC 50-3616. 536p. (Orig.). 1978. pap. 22.00x (ISBN 0-8002-1067-0). Intl Pubns Serv.

LATIN AMERICA–HISTORY

Nesheim, Margaret. Wet Landing-Dry Landing. (Illus.). 192p. 1981. 10.00 (ISBN 0-682-49673-1). Exposition.

Robinson, H. Latin America. 4th ed. (Illus.). 544p. 1977. pap. text ed. 17.95x (Pub. by Macdonald & Evans England). Intl Ideas.

Wiarda, Howard J. Corporatism & National Development in Latin America. (Replica Edition Ser.). 325p. 1981. lib. bdg. 27.00x (ISBN 0-86531-031-9). Westview.

LATIN AMERICA–JUVENILE LITERATURE

Hoey, Mary. Journey South: Discovering the Americas. (gr. 4-6). 1980. pap. 3.50 (ISBN 0-377-00099-X). Friend Pr.

LATIN AMERICA–POLITICS AND GOVERNMENT

Conniff, Michael, ed. Latin American Populism in Comparative Perspective. (Illus.). 272p. 1981. 19.95 (ISBN 0-8263-0580-6); pap. 9.95 (ISBN 0-8263-0581-4). U of NM Pr.

Dahlin, Therrin C., et al. The Catholic Left in Latin America: A Comprehensive Bibliography. (Reference Bks.). 1981. lib. bdg. 35.00 (ISBN 0-8161-8396-1). G K Hall.

Szekely, A. Latin America & the Law of the Sea, Release 1. 1980. 32.50 (ISBN 0-379-10180-7). Oceana.

LATIN AMERICA–SOCIAL CONDITIONS

Arroyo, Anita. Narrativa Hispanoamericana Actual: America y Sus Problemas. LC 79-19468. (Mente y Palabra Ser.). v, 517p. 1980. 20.00 (ISBN 0-8477-0563-3); pap. 15.00 (ISBN 0-8477-0563-3). U of PR Pr.

Butterworth, Douglas & Chance, John K. Latin American Urbanization. LC 80-18486. (Urbanization in Developing Countries Ser.). (Illus.). 320p. 1981. text ed. 29.95 (ISBN 0-521-23713-0); pap. text ed. 8.95 (ISBN 0-521-28175-X). Cambridge U Pr.

Dixon, Marlene & Jonas, Susanne, eds. Strategies for the Class Struggle in Latin America. (Contemporary Marxism Ser.). (Illus.). 104p. (Orig.). 1980. pap. 5.00 (ISBN 0-89935-010-0). Synthesis Pubns.

Pollitt, Ernesto. Poverty & Malnutrition in Latin America: Early Childhood Intervention Programs. LC 80-18811. 150p. 1980. 21.95 (ISBN 0-03-058031-5). Praeger.

LATIN AMERICA–STATISTICS

Statistical Yearbook for Latin America 1978. 471p. 1980. pap. 32.00 (ISBN 0-686-68973-9, UN79/2G3, UN). Unipub.

Statistical Yearbook for Latin America: Nineteen Seventy-Eight. 471p. 1980. pap. 32.00 (UN79-2G3, UN). Unipub.

United Nations. Statistical Yearbook for Latin America, 1978. 471p. 1979. pap. 32.00x (ISBN 0-8002-1087-5). Intl Pubns Serv.

Wilkie, James W., ed. Statistical Abstract of Latin America 1981, Vol. 21. LC 56-63569. 1981. lib. bdg. price not set (ISBN 0-87903-239-1). UCLA Lat Am Ctr.

LATIN-AMERICAN ART

see Art, Latin-American

LATIN-AMERICAN FICTION–HISTORY AND CRITICISM

Janes, Regina. Gabriel Garcia Marquez: Revolution in Wonderland. 136p. 1981. text ed. 9.00x (ISBN 0-8262-0337-X). U of Mo Pr.

LATIN-AMERICAN LITERATURE–HISTORY AND CRITICISM

Ardura, Ernesto. America En el Horizonte: Una Perspectiva Cultural. LC 79-54965. (Coleccion De Estudios Hispanicos: Hispanic Studies Collection). (Illus.). 161p. (Orig., Span.). Date not set. pap. 9.95 (ISBN 0-89729-240-5). Ediciones.

LATIN-AMERICAN POETRY (COLLECTIONS)

Armand, Octavio, ed. Contemporary Latin American Poetry. 300p. (Orig.). 1981. price not set (ISBN 0-937406-09-0); pap. price not set (ISBN 0-937406-08-2); price not limited ed. (ISBN 0-937406-10-4). Logbridge-Rhodes.

LATIN-AMERICAN POETRY–HISTORY AND CRITICISM

Garcia-Barron, Carlos. Cancionero De la Hisapno-Peruana De 1866. LC 79-51156. (Coleccion De Estudios Hispanicos: Hispanic Studies Collection). (Illus.). 226p. (Span.). 1980. pap. 12.95 (ISBN 0-89729-225-1). Ediciones.

LATIN EMPIRE, 1204-1261

see also Crusades–Fourth, 1202-1204

Wolff, Robert L. Studies in the Latin Empire of Constantinople. 412p. 1980. 60.00x (ISBN 0-902089-99-4, Pub. by Variorum England). State Mutual Bk.

LATIN LANGUAGE–ABBREVIATIONS

see Abbreviations

LATIN LANGUAGE–DICTIONARIES

Freytag, George W. Lexicon Arabico-Latimun. 70.00x. Intl Bk Ctr.

LATIN LANGUAGE–DICTIONARIES–ENGLISH

Glare, P. G., ed. Oxford Latin Dictionary: Fascicle VII. 256p. (Orig.). 1980. pap. 49.50x (ISBN 0-19-864220-2). Oxford U Pr.

LATIN LANGUAGE–READERS

Echols, Edvardus C. Freddus Elephantus et Horatius Porcus Saltans Cincinnatis. 129p. (Orig., Latin). (gr. 10-11). 1980. pap. text ed. 3.50x (ISBN 0-88334-139-5). Ind Sch Pr.

LATIN LANGUAGE–VERB

Bolkestein, A. M. Problems in the Description of Modal Verbs: An Investigation of Latin. (Studies in Greek & Latin Linguistics). 180p. 1980. pap. text ed. 21.00x (ISBN 90-232-1764-0). Humanities.

LATIN LANGUAGE, POPULAR

see Latin Language, Vulgar

LATIN LANGUAGE, VULGAR

Duran, Richard P., ed. Latino Language & Communicative Behavior, Vol. 6. 384p. 1981. 29.50 (ISBN 0-89391-038-4). Ablex Pub.

LATIN LITERATURE–BIBLIOGRAPHY

Valk, Barbara G., ed. Hispanic American Periodicals Index 1978. LC 75-642408. 1981. lib. bdg. price not set (ISBN 0-87903-404-1). UCLA Lat Am Ctr.

LATTER-DAY SAINTS

see Mormons and Mormonism

LATTICE THEORY

Gierz, G., et al. A Compendium of Continuous Lattices. 380p. 1980. 19.80 (ISBN 0-387-10111-X). Springer-Verlag.

LAUGHING GAS

see Nitrous Oxide

LAUNDRY

Cox, M. E. Practical Laundrywork. 147p. 1961. 11.50x (ISBN 0-85264-080-3, Pub. by Griffin England). State Mutual Bk.

LAUREL, STANLEY

Guiles, Fred L. Stan: The Life of Stan Laurel. LC 80-5806. (Illus.). 272p. 1980. 12.95 (ISBN 0-8128-2762-7). Stein & Day.

LAW

see also Courts; Jurisdiction; Justice; Justice, Administration Of; Lawyers; Legal Ethics; Legislation; Statutes

also names of legal systems, e.g. Canon Law, Common Law, Roman Law; special branches of law, e.g. Constitutional Law, Criminal Law, Maritime Law; specific legal topics, e.g. Contracts, Mortgages, Sanctions (Law); subdivision Laws and Legislation under subjects, e.g. Postal Service–Law

Dell, Susanne. Silent in Court. 64p. 1971. pap. text ed. 5.00x (ISBN 0-7135-1576-7, Pub. by Bedford England). Renouf.

Harris, Phil. An Introduction to Law. (Law in Context Ser.). 288p. 1980. 31.00x (ISBN 0-297-77826-9, Pub. by Weidenfeld & Nicolson England). Rothman.

Hayek, F. A. Law, Legislation, & Liberty: Rules & Order. 15.00 (ISBN 0-226-32080-4). U of Chicago Pr.

--Law, Legislation, & Liberty: The Political Order of a Free People. pap. write for info. (ISBN 0-226-32090-1). U of Chicago Pr.

Pelton, Robert W. Loony Laws: You Never Knew You Were Breaking. LC 80-54814. (Illus.). 160p. 1981. 9.95 (ISBN 0-8027-0687-8); pap. 4.95 (ISBN 0-8027-7174-2). Walker & Co.

Redish, Martin H. Federal Jurisdiction: Tensions in the Allocation of Judicial Power. 370p. 1980. 25.00 (ISBN 0-672-84196-7). Michie.

Sirkin, Gerald, ed. Lexeconics: The Interaction of Law & Economics. (Social Dimensions of Economics, CCNY Ser.: Vol. 2). 272p. 1981. lib. bdg. 17.50 (ISBN 0-89838-053-7, Pub. by Martinus Nijhoff). Kluwer Boston.

Striker, John M. & Shapiro, Andrew. Power Plays. 1981. pap. 2.95 (ISBN 0-440-17203-9). Dell.

Zander, Michael. The Law-Making Process. (Law in Context Ser.). 332p. 1980. 40.00x (ISBN 0-297-77750-5, Pub. by Weidenfeld & Nicolson England). Rothman.

LAW–ADDRESSES, ESSAYS, LECTURES

Thomas, John L. The Law of Constructive Contempt: The Shepherd Case Reviewed. 270p. 1980. Repr. of 1904 ed. lib. bdg. 24.00x (ISBN 0-8377-1203-3). Rothman.

LAW–BIBLIOGRAPHY

see also Legal Literature

The Research Libraries of He New York Public Library & the Library of Congress. Bibliographic Guide to Law: 1980. (Library Catalogs Bib. Guides Ser.). 1981. lib. bdg. 125.00 (ISBN 0-8161-6889-X). G K Hall.

Tseng, Henry P. Complete Guide to Legal Materials in Microforms: 1980 Supplement. 1980. perfect bdg. 25.00 (ISBN 0-686-68702-7). AMCO Intl.

LAW–BIOGRAPHY

see also Judges; Lawyers

Davis, Deane C. Justice in the Mountains: Stories & Tales by a Vermont Country Lawyer. LC 80-82866. (Illus.). 192p. 1980. 9.95 (ISBN 0-933050-05-4); pap. 6.95 (ISBN 0-933050-06-2). New Eng Pr VT.

LAW–DICTIONARIES

Curzon, L. B. A Dictionary for Law. 384p. 1979. pap. 14.95x (ISBN 0-7121-0380-5, Pub. by Macdonald & Evans England). Intl Ideas.

Rothenberg, Robert. The Plain-Language Law Dictionary. 1981. pap. 7.95 (ISBN 0-14-051109-1). Penguin.

LAW–EXAMINATIONS
see Law Examinations

LAW–HISTORY AND CRITICISM
see also Comparative Law

Bott, Edmund. A Collection of Decisions of the Court of the King Bench Upon the Poor Laws. Berkowitz, David S. & Thorne, Samuel E., eds. LC 77-89222. (Classics of English Legal History in the Modern Era: Vol. 67). 399p. 1979. lib. bdg. 40.00 (ISBN 0-8240-3166-0). Garland Pub.

Chitty, Joseph. A Treatise on the Game Laws & on Fisheries, 2 vols. Berkowitz, David S. & Thorne, Samuel E., eds. LC 77-86657. (Classics of English Legal History in the Modern Era Ser.: Vol. 41). 1662p. 1979. lib. bdg. 80.00 (ISBN 0-8240-3090-7). Garland Pub.

Curzon, L. B. English Legal History. 2nd ed. 352p. 1979. pap. 12.95x (ISBN 0-7121-0578-6, Pub. by Macdonald & Evans England). Intl Ideas.

Giraldus Cambrensis. Speculum Duorum: Or, a Mirror of Two Men. (University of Wales, History & Law Ser.: No. 27). 1974. 25.00 (ISBN 0-7083-0544-X). Verry.

Jacob, Giles, et al. Laws of Liberty & Property. Berkowitz, David. S. & Thorne, Samuel E., eds. LC 77-89197. (Classics of English Legal History in the Modern Era Ser.: Vol. 56). 325p. 1979. lib. bdg. 40.00 (ISBN 0-8240-3156-3). Garland Pub.

Marks, Marlene A. The Suing of America. LC 80-52412. 256p. 1981. 11.95 (ISBN 0-87223-658-7). Seaview Bks.

LAW–JEWS
see Jewish Law

LAW–LANGUAGE

Bander, Edward J. Dictionary of Legal Terms & Maxims, Vol. 58. 2nd ed. 1979. 5.95 (ISBN 0-379-11119-5). Oceana.

LAW–LITERARY HISTORY
see Jurisprudence–History

LAW–PERIODICALS

Oxbridge Communications, Inc. Legal Periodicals Directory. 150p. 1981. lib. bdg. 35.00 (ISBN 0-87196-335-3). Facts on File.

LAW–PHILOSOPHY
see also Free Will and Determinism

Feinberg, Joel & Gross, Hyman. Philosophy of Law. 2nd ed. 656p. 1980. text ed. 20.95x (ISBN 0-534-00835-6). Wadsworth Pub.

Kim, Hyung I. Fundamental Legal Concepts of China & the West: A Comparative Study. (National University Publications, Multidisciplinary Studies in the Law). 1981. 17.50 (ISBN 0-8046-9275-0). Kennikat.

Wilkin, Robert N. The Spirit of the Legal Profession. viii, 178p. 1981. Repr. of 1938 ed. lib. bdg. 18.50x (ISBN 0-8377-1308-0). Rothman.

LAW–POPULAR WORKS

Hanna, John P. Complete Layman's Guide to the Law. (Illus.). 544p. pap. 8.95 (ISBN 0-13-161224-7, Spec). P-H.

LAW–PRACTICE
see Procedure (Law)

LAW–PSYCHOLOGY
see also Criminal Psychology; Judicial Process; Psychology, Forensic

Robinson, Daniel N., ed. Seminal Cases & Contemporary Commentaries: England. (Contributions to the History of Psychology Ser.: Insanity & Jurisprudence). 1980. 30.00 (ISBN 0-89093-331-6). U Pubns Amer.

--Seminal Cases & Contemporary Commentaries: The United States. (Insanity & Jurisprudence). 1980. 30.00 (ISBN 0-89093-330-8). U Pubns Amer.

LAW–RELIGIOUS ASPECTS
see Religion and Law

LAW–SANCTION
see Sanctions (Law)

LAW–SOCIOLOGY
see Sociological Jurisprudence

LAW–STUDY AND TEACHING
see also Law Examinations

Roth, George J. Slaying the Law School Dragon. LC 80-16974. 284p. 1980. 10.95 (ISBN 0-396-07880-X); pap. 7.95 (ISBN 0-396-07879-6). Dodd.

LAW–AFRICA

Introduction to Law in Contemporary Africa. 100p. 1976. pap. 15.00 (ISBN 0-914970-18-6, CM 002, Conch Mag). Unipub.

LAW–ASIA

Hoadley, M. C. & Hooker, M. B. Introduction to Javanese Law. LC 80-26636. (Monographs of the Association for Asian Studies: No. XXXVII). 1981. text ed. 9.95x (ISBN 0-8165-0727-9). U of Ariz Pr.

LAW–AUSTRALIA

Golding, J., et al, eds. Access to Law: The Second Seminar on Australian Lawyers & Social Change. 336p. (Orig.). 1980. pap. text ed. 16.95 (ISBN 0-7081-1305-2, 0581). Bks Australia.

LAW–CANADA

Livermore, Sarah, et al, eds. The American Bar - The Canadian Bar - The International Bar: 1981. 63rd ed. LC 18-21110. 3062p. 1981. 130.00 (ISBN 0-931398-06-1). R B Forster.

Millar, Perry S. & Baar, Carl. Judicial Administration in Canada. (Institute of Public Administration of Canada, Ipac Ser.). (Illus.). 550p. 1981. 35.95x (ISBN 0-7735-0367-6); pap. 18.95x (ISBN 0-7735-0368-4). McGill-Queens U Pr.

LAW–CHINA

Republic of China. Laws, Ordinances, Regulations, & Rules Relating to the Judicial Administration of the Republic of China. (Studies in Chinese Government & Law). 364p. 1977. Repr. of 1923 ed. 24.00 (ISBN 0-89093-062-7). U Pubns Amer.

Wang, Joseph E., ed. Selected Legal Documents of the People's Republic of China. LC 76-5167. (Studies in Chinese Government & Law). 564p. 1979. 32.50 (ISBN 0-89093-067-8). U Pubns Amer.

--Selected Legal Documents of the People's Republic of China: Volume II. LC 76-5167. (Studies in Chinese Government & Law). 564p. 1979. 32.50 (ISBN 0-89093-241-7). U Pubns Amer.

LAW–EUROPE

Giljstra, D. J., et al, eds. Legal Isssues of European Integration 1979. 2nd ed. 130p. 1980. pap. 21.50 (ISBN 90-2681-178-0, Pub. by Kluwer Law & Taxation). Kluwer Boston.

Merryman, J. H. Law & Social Change in Mediterranean Europe & Latin America: A Handbook of Legal & Social Indicators for Comparative Study. 1980. 47.50 (ISBN 0-379-20700-1). Oceana.

LAW–FRANCE

New Code of Civil Procedure in France, Bk. 1. 1978. 32.50 (ISBN 0-379-20266-2). Oceana.

LAW–GREAT BRITAIN

Brydall, John & Highmore, Anthony. Non Compos Mentis. Berkowitz, David S. & Thorne, Samuel E., eds. LC 77-86669. (Classics of English Legal History in the Modern Era Ser.: Vol. 46). 471p. 1979. lib. bdg. 40.00 (ISBN 0-8240-3095-8). Garland Pub.

Chitty, Joseph, Jr. A Practical Treatise on the Law of Contracts. Berkowitz, David S. & Thorne, Samuel E., eds. LC 77-86636. (Classics of English Legal History in the Modern Era Ser.: Vol. 25). 807p. 1979. lib. bdg. 40.00 (ISBN 0-8240-3074-5). Garland Pub.

Cross, Rupert. The Precedent in English Law. 3rd ed. 252p. 1977. pap. 11.95x (ISBN 0-19-876073-6). Oxford U Pr.

Fonblanque, John. A Treatise of Equity. Ballow, Henry, et al, eds. LC 77-86649. (Classics of English Legal History in the Modern Era Ser.: Vol. 34). 775p. 1979. lib. bdg. 40.00 (ISBN 0-8240-3083-4). Garland Pub.

Hargrave, Francis. Collectanea Juridica: Consisting of Tracts Relative to the Law & Constitution of England, 2 vols. 1981. Repr. of 1791 ed. lib. bdg. 75.00x (ISBN 0-8377-0632-7). Rothman.

Hawkins, William. A Treatise on the Pleas of the Crown, 2 vols. Berkowitz, David S. & Thorne, Samuel E., eds. LC 77-86643. (Classics of English Legal History in the Modern Era Ser.: Vol. 30). 874p. 1979. lib. bdg. 80.00 (ISBN 0-8240-3079-6). Garland Pub.

Mantell, Walter, et al. Short Treatise of the Laws of England. Berkowitz, David S. & Thorne, Samuel E., eds. LC 77-86578. (Classics of English Legal History in the Modern Era Ser.: Vol. 17). 351p. 1979. lib. bdg. 40.00 (ISBN 0-8240-3066-4). Garland Pub.

Nelson, William. Lex Testamentaria. Berkowits, David S. & Thorne, Samuel E., eds. LC 77-89254. (Classics of English Legal History in the Modern Era Ser.: Vol. 81). 552p. 1979. lib. bdg. 40.00 (ISBN 0-8240-3180-6). Garland Pub.

Pulton, Ferdinand. De Pace Regis et Regni. Berkowitz, David S. & Thorne, Samuel E., eds. LC 77-86638. (Classics of English Legal History in the Modern Era Ser.: Vol.29). 574p. 1979. lib. bdg. 40.00 (ISBN 0-8240-3078-8). Garland Pub.

Staunford, William & Romilly, Samuel. Les Plees Del Coron. Berkowitz, David S. & Thorne, Samuel E., eds. LC 77-86634. (Classics of English Legal History in the Modern Era Ser.: Vol. 28). 484p. 1979. lib. bdg. 40.00 (ISBN 0-8240-3077-X). Garland Pub.

Webb, Philip C. & Grove, Joseph. The Question Whether a Jew, Born Within the British Dominions, Was, Before the Making of the Late Act of Parliament, a Person Capable by Law, to Purchase & Hold Lands to Him and His Heirs. Berkowitz, David S. & Thorne, Samuel E., eds. LC 77-86671. (Classics of English Legal History in the Modern Era Ser.: Vol. 48). 169p. 1979. lib. bdg. 40.00 (ISBN 0-8240-3097-4). Garland Pub.

Zander, Michael. Cases & Materials on the English Legal System. 3rd ed. (Law in Context Ser.). xxvii, 476p. 1980. 47.95x (ISBN 0-297-77822-6, Pub. by Weidenfeld & Nicholson England). Rothman.

LAW–GREAT BRITAIN–HISTORY AND CRITICISM

Arnold, Morris S., et al, eds. On the Laws & Customs of England: Essays in Honor of Samuel E. Thorne. LC 80-11909. (Studies in Legal History). xx, 426p. 1981. 25.00x (ISBN 0-8078-1434-2). U of NC Pr.

Buller, Francis. An Introduction to the Law Relative to Trials at Nisi Prius. Berkowitz, David S. & Thorne, Samuel E., eds. LC 77-89211. (Classics of English Legal History in the Modern Era Ser.: Vol. 60). 670p. 1979. lib. bdg. 40.00 (ISBN 0-8240-3159-8). Garland Pub.

Clerk, William. An Epitome of Certaine Late Aspersions Cast at Civilians. LC 79-84095. (English Experience Ser.: No.915). 56p. 1979. Repr. of 1631 ed. lib. bdg. 7.00 (ISBN 90-221-0915-1). Walter J Johnson.

Glanville, Ranulph de. Translation of Glanville: (A Treatise on the Laws & Customs of the Kingdom of England) Beames, John, tr. from Latin. xl, 362p. 1980. Repr. of 1812 ed. lib. bdg. 30.00x (ISBN 0-8377-0313-1). Rothman.

Hammond, Henry. The Lawfull Magistrate Upon Colour of Religion. Berkowitz, David S. & Thorne, Samuel E., eds. LC 77-89203. (Classics of English Legal History in the Modern Era Ser.: Vol. 58). 1979. lib. bdg. 40.00 (ISBN 0-8240-3157-1). Garland Pub.

Pratt, John T. The Law Relating to Friendly Societies. Berkowitz, David S. & Thorne, Samuel E., eds. LC 77-86656. (Classics of English Legal History in the Modern Era Ser.: Vol. 40). 160p. 1979. lib. bdg. 40.00 (ISBN 0-8240-3089-3). Garland Pub.

Robertson, A. J., ed. The Laws of the Kings of England from Edmund to Henry I. LC 80-2210. 1981. Repr. of 1925 ed. 52.50 (ISBN 0-404-18784-6). AMS Pr.

Somers, John & Jacob, Giles. Judgment of Whole Kingdoms & Nations. Berkowitz, David S. & Thorne, Samuel E., eds. LC 77-86589. (Classics of English Legal History in the Modern Era Ser.: Vol. 19). 467p. 1979. lib. bdg. 40.00 (ISBN 0-8240-3069-9). Garland Pub.

Williams, Thomas & Somers, John. Excellency & Praeheminence of the Law of England. Berkowitz, David S. & Thorne, Samuel E., eds. LC 77-86674. (Classics of English Legal History in the Modern Era Ser.: Vol. 50). 357p. 1979. lib. bdg. 40.00 (ISBN 0-8240-3099-0). Garland Pub.

LAW–INDIA

Indian Law Institute. Indian Legal System. 1979. 28.00 (ISBN 0-379-20368-5). Oceana.

LAW–JAPAN

Ministry of Labor, Japan. Japan Labor Code, 2 vols. (Studies in Japanese Law & Government). 1979. Repr. of 1953 ed. Set. 56.00 (ISBN 0-89093-217-4). U Pubns Amer.

LAW–KOREA

Chun, Bong D., et al. Traditional Korean Legan Attitudes. (Korean Research Monographs: No. 2). 101p. 1980. pap. 8.00 (ISBN 0-912966-30-0). IEAS Ctr Chinese Stud.

Kwun Sup Chung, et al. Modernization & Its Impact Upon Korean Law. (Korea Research Monographs: No. 3). 150p. 1981. pap. 12.50 (ISBN 0-686-69422-8). IEAS Ctr Chinese Stud.

Shaw, William. Legal Norms in a Confucian State. (Korea Research Monographs: No. 5). write for info. (ISBN 0-912966-32-7). IEAS Ctr Chinese Stud.

LAW–LATIN-AMERICA

Merryman, J. H. Law & Social Change in Mediterranean Europe & Latin America: A Handbook of Legal & Social Indicators for Comparative Study. 1980. 47.50 (ISBN 0-379-20700-1). Oceana.

LAW–NEAR EAST

Butler, William J. & Levasseur, Georges. Human Rights & the Legal System in Iran. 80p. (Orig.). 1976. pap. text ed. 2.50 (ISBN 0-89192-084-6). Interbk Inc.

Glover, J. N. Laws of the Turks & Caicos, Vol. 7. 1980. 47.50 (ISBN 0-379-12707-5). Oceana.

Khadduri, Majid & Liebesny, Herbert J., eds. Law in the Middle East: Origin & Development of Islamic Law, Vol. 1. LC 80-1921. 1981. Repr. of 1955 ed. 41.50 (ISBN 0-404-18974-1). AMS Pr.

LAW–RUSSIA

Hazard, J. N. Soviet Legal System. 3rd ed. 1977. 20.00. Oceana.

LaFave, Wayne R., ed. Law in the Soviet Society. LC 65-19109. 297p. 1965. pap. 1.95 (ISBN 0-252-72524-7). U of Ill Pr.

LAW–TURKEY

Glover, J. N. Laws of the Turks & Caicos, Vol. 7. 1980. 47.50 (ISBN 0-379-12707-5). Oceana.

LAW–UNITED STATES

Annual Survey of American Law, 1979. 1980. 26.00 (ISBN 0-379-12238-3). Oceana.

Chanin, Leah F. Reference Guide to Georgia Legal History & Legal Research. 175p. 1980. 20.00 (ISBN 0-87215-315-0). Michie.

Cowan, Z. Individual Liberty & the Law. 1977. 10.00 (ISBN 0-379-00597-2). Oceana.

Fein, Bruce E. Significant Decisions of the Supreme Court: 1978-1979 Term. 1980. pap. 6.25 (ISBN 0-8447-3387-3). Am Enterprise.

Gordon, Gary J. Product Liability Litigation. 200p. 1980. pap. 24.50 (ISBN 0-917126-20-3). Mason Pub.

Lieberman, Jethro. The Litigious Society. LC 80-68181. 256p. 1980. 13.95 (ISBN 0-465-04134-5). Basic.

Livermore, Sarah, et al, eds. The American Bar - The Canadian Bar - The International Bar: 1981. 63rd ed. LC 18-21110. 3062p. 1981. 130.00 (ISBN 0-931398-06-1). R B Forster.

Mietus, Norbert J. & West, Bill W. Personal Law. 2nd ed. 512p. 1981. text ed. 16.95 (ISBN 0-574-19505-X, 13-2505); instr's. guide avail. (ISBN 0-574-19506-8, 13-2506). Sci Res Assoc Coll.

Miles, John G., Jr., et al. The Law Officer's Pocket Manual: 1980-81 Edition. 128p. 1980. 5.00 (ISBN 0-686-68899-6). BNA.

Schwartz, Bernard. The American Heritage History of the Law in America. LC 74-8264. (Illus.). 379p. 1981. pap. 12.95 (ISBN 0-8281-0426-3, Dist. by Scribner). Am Heritage.

Whitinger, Robert G. Indiana Small Claims. 180p. 1980. 20.00 (ISBN 0-87215-326-6). Michie.

LAW–UNITED STATES–BIBLIOGRAPHY

Foster, Lynn & Boast, Carol. Subject Compilations of State Laws: Research Guide & Annotated Bibliography. LC 80-1788. 480p. 1981. lib. bdg. 45.00 (ISBN 0-313-21255-4, FOS). Greenwood.

LAW–UNITED STATES–EXAMINATIONS, QUESTIONS, ETC.

Multistate Bar Exam V. 1980. 2.50 (ISBN 0-87543-162-3). Lucas.

LAW–UNITED STATES–HISTORY AND CRITICISM

Johnson, John W. American Legal Culture, 1908-1940. LC 80-1027. (Contributions in Legal Studies: No. 16). 192p. 1981. lib. bdg. 23.95 (ISBN 0-313-22337-8, JAM/). Greenwood.

Reid, John P., ed. The Briefs of the American Revolution. (NYU School of Law Ser. in Anglo-American Legal History). 176p. 1981. text ed. 22.50x (ISBN 0-8147-7384-2). NYU Pr.

LAW, ACCIDENT
see Accident Law

LAW, ADMINISTRATIVE
see Administrative Law

LAW, ADVERTISING
see Advertising Laws

LAW, AGRICULTURAL
see Agricultural Laws and Legislation

LAW, ANGLO-AMERICAN
see Law–Great Britain; Law–United States

LAW, BANKING
see Banking Law

LAW, BUILDING
see Building Laws

LAW, BURIAL
see Burial Laws

LAW, BUSINESS
see Business Law

LAW, CHARITY
see Charity Laws and Legislation

LAW, CIVIL
see Civil Law

LAW, COMMERCIAL
see Commercial Law

LAW, COMPARATIVE
see Comparative Law

LAW, CONSTITUTIONAL
see Constitutional Law

LAW, CORPORATION
see Corporation Law

LAW, CRIMINAL
see Criminal Law

LAW, ECCLESIASTICAL
see Ecclesiastical Law

LAW, EDUCATIONAL
see Educational Law and Legislation

LAW, EMIGRATION
see Emigration and Immigration Law

LAW, FISHERY
see Fishery Law and Legislation

LAW, FOOD
see Food Law and Legislation

LAW, HEBREW
see Jewish Law

LAW, IMMIGRATION
see Emigration and Immigration Law

LAW, INDUSTRIAL
see Industrial Laws and Legislation; Industry and State; Labor Laws and Legislation

LAW, INSURANCE
see Insurance Law

LAW, INTERNATIONAL
see International Law

LAW, JEWISH
see Jewish Law

LAW, LABOR
see Labor Laws and Legislation

LAW, MARTIAL
see Martial Law

LAW, MARITIME
see Maritime Law

LAW, MEDICAL
see Medical Laws and Legislation

LAW, MERCHANT
see Commercial Law

LAW, MINING
see Mining Law

LAW, MOSAIC
see Jewish Law

LAW, PATENT
see Patent Laws and Legislation

LAW, PROBATE
see Probate Law and Practice

LAW, ROMAN
see Roman Law

LAW, SEMITIC
see Jewish Law

LAW, SUNDAY
see Sunday Legislation

LAW, WATER
see Water–Laws and Legislation

LAW AND CHRISTIANITY
see Religion and Law
LAW AND MENTAL ILLNESS
see Insanity–Jurisprudence; Mental Health Laws
LAW AND RELIGION
see Religion and Law
LAW AND SEX
see Sex and Law
LAW AND SOCIETY
see Sociological Jurisprudence
LAW BOOKS
see Law–Bibliography; Legal Literature
LAW ENFORCEMENT

Johnson, David. American Law Enforcement: A History. LC 80-68814. (Orig.). 1981. text ed. 15.95x (ISBN 0-88273-271-4). Forum Pr MO.

Klotter, John C. & Kanovitz, Jacqueline R. Constitutional Law. 4th ed. (Justice Administration Legal Ser.). 900p. Date not set. price not set (ISBN 0-87084-492-X). Anderson Pub Co.

More, Harry, ed. Critical Issues in Law Enforcement. 3d ed. LC 79-55205. 352p. 1981. pap. text ed. price not set (ISBN 0-87084-582-9). Anderson Pub Co.

San Diego Police Dept. Police Tactics in Hazardous Situations. (Criminal Justice Ser.). 1976. pap. text ed. 8.95 (ISBN 0-8299-0628-2). West Pub.

LAW EXAMINATIONS
see also Law Schools–Entrance Examinations

Gruber, et al. The Multistate Bar Examination. rev. ed. (Exam Prep. Ser.). 256p. 1981. pap. text ed. 6.95 (ISBN 0-671-18965-4). Monarch Pr.

Reburn, Rockne. How to Pass the California Bar Exam. (Illus.). 141p. (Orig.). 1980. 14.00 (ISBN 0-9605672-0-8). Bar-None.

LAW IN THE BIBLE
see Jewish Law
LAW OF NATIONS
see International Law
LAW OF SUPPLY AND DEMAND
see Supply and Demand
LAW OF THE SEA
see Maritime Law
LAW REPORTS, DIGESTS, ETC.

UN Law Reports, Vol. 15: Sept. 1980 to Aug. 1981. 1981. 50.00. Walker & Co.

LAW SCHOOLS

Knott, A. E., et al. Australian Schools & the Law. 2nd ed. (Educational Organization & Administration Ser.). 180p. (Orig.). 1981. pap. text ed. 10.25 (ISBN 0-7022-1549-X). U of Queensland Pr.

Roth, George J. Slaying the Law School Dragon. LC 80-16974. 284p. 1980. 10.95 (ISBN 0-396-07880-X); pap. 7.95 (ISBN 0-396-07879-6). Dodd.

LAW SCHOOLS–ENTRANCE EXAMINATIONS

Candrilli, Alfred J., et al. Law School Admission Test. rev. ed. LC 80-22181. 448p. 1981. lib. bdg. 10.95 (ISBN 0-668-05146-9); pap. 6.95 (ISBN 0-686-69096-6). Arco.

LAWBOOKS
see Law–Bibliography; Legal Literature
LAWN TENNIS
see Tennis
LAWNS
see also Grasses

McDonald, Elvin. Making Your Lawn & Garden Grow. 7.95 (ISBN 0-916752-07-0). Green Hill.

LAWRENCE, DAVID HENRY

Hamalian, Leo. D. H. Lawrence in Italy. 224p. 1981. 10.95 (ISBN 0-8008-4572-2). Taplinger.

LAWRENCE, DAVID HERBERT, 1885-1930

Ben-Ephraim, Gavriel. The Moon's Dominion: Narrative Dichotomy & Female Dominance in the First Five Novels of D. H. Lawrence. LC 78-75172. 300p. 1981. 18.50 (ISBN 0-8386-2266-6). Fairleigh Dickinson.

LAWRENCE, MASSACHUSETTS–FOREIGN POPULATION

Cole, Donald B. Immigrant City: Lawrence, Massachusetts Eighteen Forty Five to Nineteen Twenty One. LC 63-39156. 257p. 1980. Repr. of 1963 ed. 13.50x (ISBN 0-8078-0876-8). U of NC Pr.

LAWYERS
see also Bar Associations; Judges; Legal Ethics

Danielle, T. The Lawyers. 1976. 17.50 (ISBN 0-379-00593-X). Oceana.

Digby, K. H. Lawyer in the Wilderness, Data Paper No. 114. 150p. 1980. 5.75 (ISBN 0-87727-114-3). Cornell SE Asia.

Dvorkin, Elizabeth & Himmelstein, Jack. Becoming a Lawyer: A Humanistic Perspective on Legal Education, Professionalism. 200p. 1981. pap. text ed. 17.95 (ISBN 0-8299-2126-5). West Pub.

Prest, Wilfrid, ed. Lawyers in Early Modern Europe & America. LC 80-22574. 224p. 1981. text ed. 27.50x (ISBN 0-8419-0679-3). Holmes & Meier.

Rogers, R. Vashon, Jr. The Law & Medical Men. xiii, 214p. 1981. Repr. of 1884 ed. lib. bdg. 22.00x (ISBN 0-8377-1032-4). Rothman.

Ward, Robert E. & Ward, Catherine C. The Letters of Charles O'connor of Belanagare, Seventeen Seventy-Two to Seventeen Ninety, Vol. II. LC 80-11602. (Sponsor Ser.). 341p. 1980. 24.75 (ISBN 0-8357-0535-8, SS-00145, Pub. by Monograph). Univ Microfilms.

LAWYERS–CORRESPONDENCE, REMINISCENCES, ETC.

Tomkins, D. Michael. Trial & Error. LC 80-39757. 1981. 9.95 (ISBN 0-396-07944-X). Dodd.

LAY LEADERSHIP
see Christian Leadership
LAYOUT
see Printing–Layout and Typography
LAYOUT AND TYPOGRAPHY, ADVERTISING
see Advertising Layout and Typography
LAYOUT AND TYPOGRAPHY, NEWSPAPER
see Newspaper Layout and Typography
LAZARUS, SAINT

North, Brownlow. The Rich Man & Lazarus. 1979. pap. 2.45 (ISBN 0-85151-121-X). Banner of Truth.

LEAD

Kolisko, E. Lead & the Human Organism. 1980. pap. 3.95x (ISBN 0-906492-31-9, Pub. by Kolisko Archives). St George Bk Serv.

LEAD-POISONING

Kolisko, E. Lead & the Human Organism. 1980. pap. 3.95x (ISBN 0-906492-31-9, Pub. by Kolisko Archives). St George Bk Serv.

LEADERSHIP
see also Christian Leadership; Community Leadership; Discussion; Meetings; Recreation Leadership

Betz, Don. Cultivating Leadership: An Approach. LC 80-69039. 120p. (Orig.). 1981. pap. text ed. 4.95 (ISBN 0-8191-1441-3). U Pr of Amer.

Boles, Harold W. Leaders, Leading, & Leadership. LC 80-65616. 170p. 1981. cancelled (ISBN 0-86548-023-0). Century Twenty One.

Flores, Ernest Y. The Mini-Guide to Leadership. LC 80-83627. 90p. 1981. perfect bdg. 5.50 (ISBN 0-86548-037-0). Century Twenty One.

--The Nature of Leadership for Hispanics & Other Minorities. LC 80-69239. 140p. 1981. perfect bdg. 10.95 (ISBN 0-86548-036-2). Century Twenty One.

Hodges, Melvin, tr. Desarrollo Del Varon De Dios. (Spanish Bks.). (Span.). 1978. 0.80 (ISBN 0-8297-0528-7). Life Pubs Intl.

Maude, Barry. Leadership in Management. 240p. 1978. text ed. 29.50x (ISBN 0-220-66361-0, Pub. by Busn Bks England). Renouf.

Solomon, Ben & Bowers, Ethel M. You Can Be a Leader. 140p. (Orig.). 1981. pap. 4.95 (ISBN 0-936626-03-8). Leadership Pr.

Tramel, Mary E. & Reynolds, Helen. Executive Leadership: How to Get It - & Make It Work. (Illus.). 272p. 1981. 13.95 (ISBN 0-13-294132-5, Spec); pap. 6.95 (ISBN 0-686-69280-2). P-H.

Yukl, Gary. Leadership in Organizations. (Illus.). 336p. 1981. text ed. 16.95 (ISBN 0-13-527176-2). P-H.

LEAN, DAVID, 1908-

Castelli, Louis & Cleeland, Caryn L. David Lean: A Guide to References & Resources. 1980. lib. bdg. 18.50 (ISBN 0-8161-7933-6). G K Hall.

LEARNED INSTITUTIONS AND SOCIETIES
see also Societies

Zils, Michael, ed. World Guide to Scientific Associations & Learned Societies. 3rd ed. (Handbook of International Documentation & Information Ser.: Vol. 13). 400p. 1981. 150.00 (ISBN 3-598-20517-1, Dist. by Gale Research). K G Saur.

LEARNING, ART OF
see Study, Method of
LEARNING, PSYCHOLOGY OF
see also Learning Ability; Learning Disabilities; Perceptual-Motor Learning; Praise

Ameican Psychological Association. Social Influences on Behavior: Teachers Handbook. (Human Behavior Curriculum Project Ser.). 48p. (Orig.). (gr. 9-12). 1981. pap. 9.95 (ISBN 0-8077-2620-6). Tchrs Coll.

American Psychological Association. Conditioning & Learning: Student Booklet. (Human Behavior Curriculum Project Ser.). 64p. (gr. 9-12). 1981. pap. text ed. 3.95 (ISBN 0-8077-2623-0). Tchrs Coll.

--Conditioning & Learning: Teachers Handbook & Duplication Masters. (Human Behavior Curriculum Project Ser.). 48p. (gr. 9-12). 1981. 9.95 (ISBN 0-8077-2624-9). Tchrs Coll.

--Social Influences on Behavior: Student Booklet. (Human Behavior Curriculum Project Ser.). 64p. (Orig.). (gr. 9-12). 1981. pap. text ed. 3.95x (ISBN 0-8077-2619-2). Tchrs Coll.

Clifford, Margaret M. & Grandgenett, Myrna. Activities & Readings in Learning & Development. LC 80-84892. (Illus.). 256p. 1981. pap. text ed. price not set (ISBN 0-395-29924-1). HM.

Estes, W. K., ed. Handbook of Learning & Cognitive Processes, 6 vols. Incl. Vol. 1. Introduction to Concepts & Issues. LC 75-20113. 303p. 1975. o.p. (ISBN 0-470-24585-9); Vol. 2. Conditioning & Behavior Therapy. LC 75-20113. 350p. 1975. 18.50 (ISBN 0-470-24586-7); Vol. 3. Approaches to Human Learning & Motivation. LC 76-15010. 1976. 18.50 (ISBN 0-470-15121-8); Vol. 4. Attention & Memory. LC 76-26002. 1976. o.p. (ISBN 0-470-98908-4); Vol. 5. Human Information Processing. LC 78-3847. 1978. 26.50 (ISBN 0-470-26310-5); Vol. 6. Linguistic Functions in Cognitive Theory. 1978. 18.00 (ISBN 0-470-26311-3). Halsted Pr.

Magnusson, David. Toward a Psychology of Situations. 488p. 1981. ref. ed. 24.95 (ISBN 0-89859-061-2). L Erlbaum Assocs.

Taylor, John L. & Walford, Rex. Learning & the Stimulation Game. LC 78-21338. (Illus.). 228p. 1979. 17.50 (ISBN 0-8039-1207-2). Sage.

LEARNING ABILITY
see also Learning, Psychology Of; Learning Disabilities

Kahn, Norma. More Learning in Less Time. 80p. 1979. pap. 3.90 (ISBN 0-8104-6043-2). Hayden.

Rosner, Jerome. Helping Children Overcome Learning Difficulties: A Step-by-Step Guide for Parents & Teachers. 2nd, rev. ed. (Illus.). 377p. pap. 98.95 (ISBN 0-8027-7178-5). Walker & Co.

LEARNING AND SCHOLARSHIP
see also Culture; Education; Humanism; Learned Institutions and Societies; Professional Education; Research; Wisdom

Lyman, Thomas G. New, Tested Techniques for Independent Learning. (Human Development Library Bk). (Illus.). 131p. 1981. 27.85 (ISBN 0-89266-291-3). Am Classical Coll Pr.

Steffen, Jerome O., ed. The American West: New Perspectives, New Dimensions. LC 78-58097. 238p. 1981. pap. 6.95 (ISBN 0-8061-1744-3). U of Okla Pr.

Taylor, John L. & Walford, Rex. Learning & the Stimulation Game. LC 78-21338. (Illus.). 228p. 1979. 17.50 (ISBN 0-8039-1207-2). Sage.

LEARNING DISABILITIES
see also Reading Disability

Bley, Nancy S. & Thornton, Carol A. Teaching Mathematics to the Learning Disabled. 350p. 1981. text ed. price not set (ISBN 0-89443-357-1). Aspen Systems.

Chapman, James W. & Boersma, Frederic J. Affective Correlates of Learning Disabilities. (Modern Approaches to the Diagnosis & Instruction of Multihandicapped Children Ser.: Vol. 15). 108p. 1980. text ed. 22.50 (ISBN 90-265-0341-5, Pub. by Swets Pub Serv Holland). Swets North Am.

Chicoral Index to Reading & Learning Disabilities: Books, 1978 Annual, Vol. 14A. 400p. 1980. 85.00 (ISBN 0-934598-09-6). Am Lib Pub Co.

Chicorel Abstracts to Reading & Learning Disabilities: Periodicals, 1978 Annual, Vol. 19. 400p. 1979. 85.00 (ISBN 0-934598-16-9). Am Lib Pub Co.

Chicorel Abstracts to Reading & Learning Disabilities: Periodicals, 1979 Annual, Vol. 19. 400p. 1980. 85.00 (ISBN 0-934598-10-X). Am Lib Pub Co.

Cole, Martha L. & Cole, Jack T. Language Training for the Nonverbal-Language Delayed Child. 275p. 1981. text ed. price not set (ISBN 0-89443-344-X). Aspen Systems.

Gearheart, Bill. Learning Disabilities: Educational Strategies. 3rd ed. (Illus.). 345p. 1981. text ed. 17.95 (ISBN 0-8016-1768-5). Mosby.

Greene, Roberta M. A Question in Search of an Answer: Learning Disability in Jewish Education. LC 8-18059. (Illus.). 262p. 1981. pap. 5.95 (ISBN 0-8074-0029-7). UAHC.

Hallahan, D. & Cruickshank, W. Psychoeducational Foundations of Learning Disabilities. 1979. 8.95 (ISBN 0-13-734285-3). P-H.

Jacobs, Wilma J. Any Love Notes Today? LC 76-48409. 143p. (Orig.). 1976. pap. 4.95 (ISBN 0-89146-002-0). Learn Pathways.

Johnson, Clark. The Diagnosis of Learning Disabilities. 400p. 1981. text ed. 15.00x (ISBN 0-87108-236-5). Pruett.

Keith, Robert L. Graduated Language Training: For Patients with Aphasia & Children with Language Deficiencies. LC 79-91245. (Illus.). 320p. 1980. clinical test 24.95 (ISBN 0-933014-57-0). College-Hill.

Lerner, Janet W. Learning Disabilities: Theories, Diagnosis, & Teaching Strategies. (Illus.). 560p. 1981. text ed. 17.95 (ISBN 0-395-29710-9); write for info. set study guide (ISBN 0-395-30371-0); write for info. instr's manual (ISBN 0-395-29711-7). HM.

Mercer, Cecil & Mercer, Ann. Teaching Students with Learning Problems. (Orig.). 1981. pap. text ed. 14.95 (ISBN 0-675-08040-1). Merrill.

Sabatino, David, et al. Learning Disabilities: Systemizing Teaching & Service Delivery. 350p. 1981. text ed. price not set (ISBN 0-89443-361-X). Aspen Systems.

Webber, Margaret S. Language Skills for Exceptional Learners. 275p. 1981. text ed. write for info. (ISBN 0-89443-343-1). Aspen Systems.

LEARNING DISORDERS
see Learning Disabiiities
LEASE AND RENTAL SERVICES

Davey, Patrick J. Leasing: Experiences & Expectations, Report No. 791. (Illus.). v, 58p. (Orig.). 1980. pap. 15.00 (ISBN 0-8237-0222-7). Conference Bd.

LEASES
see also Landlord and Tenant

Baker, C. R. & Hayes, R. S. Lease Financing: A Practical Guide. 256p. 1981. 17.95 (ISBN 0-471-06040-2, Pub. by Wiley Interscience). Wiley.

LEATHER

Information Sources on Leather & Leather Products Industries. (UNIDO Guides to Information Sources Ser.: No. 3). 85p. 1980. pap. 4.00 (UNID 226, UN). Unipub.

Thomas, Bill & Stebel, Sid. Shoe Leather Treatment... LC 79-56300. (Illus.). 1979. 11.95 (ISBN 0-312-90861-X). J P Tarcher.

LEATHER INDUSTRY AND TRADE
see also Bookbinding; Harness Making and Trade

Information Sources on Leather & Leather Products Industries. (UNIDO Guides to Information Sources Ser.: No. 3). 85p. 1980. pap. 4.00 (UNID 226, UN). Unipub.

Lingwood, Rex. Leather in Three Dimensions. 144p. 1980. pap. 12.95 (ISBN 0-442-29733-5). Van Nos Reinhold.

LEBANON

Khairallah, Shereen. Lebanon. (World Bibliographical Ser.: No. 2). 154p. 1979. 25.25 (ISBN 0-903450-10-0). ABC-Clio.

Who's Who in Lebanon 1980-1981. 821p. 1980. 60.00 (ISBN 2-903188-01-7, PUB5, Publitec). Unipub.

LECTIONARIES

Allen, Horace T., Jr. A Handbook for the Lectionary. LC 80-19735. pap. 8.95. Geneva Pr.

LECTURES AND LECTURING
see also Oratory; Public Speaking
also subdivision Addresses, Essays, Lectures, under specific subjects, e.g. Art–Addresses, Essays, Lectures

Joshi, Aravind, et al. Elements of Discourse Understanding. LC 80-29393. (Illus.). 352p. Date not set. price not set (ISBN 0-521-23327-5). Cambridge U Pr.

LEDOUX, CLAUDE NICHOLAS, 1736-1806

Lemagny, J. C. & De Menil, Dominiqueintro. by. Visionary Architects: Boullee, Ledoux, Lequeu. (Illus.). 1968. pap. 8.00 (ISBN 0-914412-21-3). Inst for the Arts.

LEE, ARTHUR, 1740-1792

Potts, Louis W. Arthur Lee: A Virtuous Revolutionary. LC 80-21831. (Southern Biography Ser.). 320p. 1981. 25.00x (ISBN 0-8071-0785-9). La State U Pr.

LEE, HENRY, 1756-1818

Royster, Charles. Light-Horse Harry Lee: The Legacy of the American Revolution. LC 80-2706. (Illus.). 320p. 1981. 15.00 (ISBN 0-394-51337-1). Knopf.

LEE, JOHN DOYLE

Measeles, Evelyn B. Lee's Ferry: A Crossing on the Colorado. (Illus.). 150p. 1981. 12.95 (ISBN 0-87108-576-3). Pruett.

LE FANU, JOSEPH SHERIDAN, 1814-1873

McCormack, W. J. Sheridan le Fanu & Victorian Ireland. (Illus.). 334p. 1980. text ed. 36.00x (ISBN 0-19-812629-8). Oxford U Pr.

LEG
see also Femur

Rutt. Surgery of the Leg & Foot. (Hackenbroch Ser.). 1980. text ed. write for info. (ISBN 0-7216-4446-5). Saunders.

LEGACIES, TAXATION OF
see Inheritance and Transfer Tax
LEGAL AID

Garth, Bryant. Neighborhood Law Firms for the Poor: A Comparative Study of Recent Developments in Legal Aid & in the Legal Profession. LC 80-51739. 282p. 1980. 40.00x (ISBN 90-286-0180-5). Sijthoff & Noordhoff.

LEGAL ASSISTANTS

Larbalestrier, D. Paralegal Practice & Procedure: A Practical Guide for the Legal Assistant. 1979. pap. 9.95 (ISBN 0-13-648691-6). P-H.

LEGAL BIBLIOGRAPHY
see Law–Bibliography; Legal Research
LEGAL CHARITIES
see Legal Aid
LEGAL COMPOSITION
see also Briefs; Forms (Law)

Dickerson, F. Reed. Materials on Legal Drafting. (American Casebook Ser.). 407p. 1981. text ed. 14.95. West Pub.

LEGAL DOCUMENTS

Dickerson, F. Reed. Materials on Legal Drafting. (American Casebook Ser.). 407p. 1981. text ed. 14.95. West Pub.

LEGAL EDUCATION
see Law–Study and Teaching
LEGAL ESSAYS
see Law–Addresses, Essays, Lectures
LEGAL ETHICS

Pimsleur, Meira G. Opinions: Committees on Professional Ethics: the Association of the Bar of the City of New York, the New York County Lawyer's Association, New York State Bar Association. LC 80-14204. 1000p. 1980. Set. looseleaf bdg. 150.00 (ISBN 0-379-20670-6). Oceana.

Warvelle, Geo W. Essays in Legal Ethics. xiii, 234p. 1980. Repr. of 1902 ed. lib. bdg. 22.50x (ISBN 0-8377-1305-6). Rothman.

LEGAL FORMS
see Forms (Law)
LEGAL HISTORY
see Law–History and Criticism
LEGAL LANGUAGE
see Law–Language
LEGAL LITERATURE
see also Law–Bibliography

Gopen, George D. Writing from a Legal Perspective. 250p. 1981. text ed. 11.95 (ISBN 0-8299-2123-0). West Pub.

LEGAL MEDICINE
see Medical Jurisprudence
LEGAL PROCEDURE
see Procedure (Law)
LEGAL PROFESSION
see Lawyers
LEGAL PSYCHOLOGY
see Law–Psychology; Psychology, Forensic

LEGAL RESEARCH

Foster, Lynn & Boast, Carol. Subject Compilations of State Laws: Research Guide & Annotated Bibliography. LC 80-1788. 480p. 1981. lib. bdg. 45.00 (ISBN 0-313-21255-4, FOS). Greenwood.

LEGAL RESPONSIBILITY

see Liability (Law)

LEGAL STATUS OF WOMEN

see Women–Legal Status, Laws, etc.

LEGAL STYLE

see Law–Language

LEGENDS

see also Chansons De Geste; Fairy Tales; Folk-Lore; Mythology; Saints

also subdivisions Legends under special subjects, e.g. Mary, Virgin–Legends

Dobie, J. Frank, et al, eds. In the Shadow of History. (Texas Folklore Society Publication Ser.: No. 25). 192p. 1980. Repr. of 1939 ed. 6.95 (ISBN 0-87074-173-X). SMU Press.

LEGENDS–HISTORY AND CRITICISM

Kris, Ernst & Kurz, Otto. Legend, Myth, & Magic in the Image of the Artist: A Historical Experiment. LC 78-24024. (Illus.). 175p. 1981. pap. 5.95 (ISBN 0-300-02669-2). Yale U Pr.

LEGENDS–JUVENILE LITERATURE

see also Legends, American, French, etc. for other juvenile works

Guard, David. Deirdre: A Celtic Legend. LC 80-69774. (Illus.). 118p. (gr. 6). 1981. Repr. of 1977 ed. 9.95 (ISBN 0-89742-047-0). Dawne-Leigh.

--Hale-Ano: A Legend of Hawaii. LC 80-69773. (Illus.). 118p. (gr. 6). 1981. 9.95 (ISBN 0-89742-048-9). Dawne-Leigh.

Ross, Harriet, compiled by. Heroes & Heroines of Many Lands. (Illus.). 160p. 1981. PLB 7.95 (ISBN 0-87460-214-9). Lion.

LEGENDS, AMERICAN

Ainsworth, Catherine H. Legends of New York State. LC 78-54873. (Folklore Bks.). vi, 96p. 1980. 4.00 (ISBN 0-933190-05-0). Clyde Pr.

Helm, Mike. Ghosts, Monsters, & Wild Men: Legends of the Oregon Country. (Illus.). 1981. write for info. (ISBN 0-931742-03-X). Rainy Day Oreg.

LEGENDS, INDIAN

see Indians of North America–Legends

LEGENDS, NORSE

Snorri. Heimskringla: From the Sagas of the Norse Kings. Monsen, Erling, tr. (Illus.). 398p. 1980. 35.00 (ISBN 0-906191-39-4, Pub. by Thule Pr England). Intl Schol Bk Serv.

LEGERDEMAIN

see Conjuring; Magic

LEGISLATION

see also Governmental Investigations; Law; Legislative Bodies; Parliamentary Practice

also legislation on particular subjects; e.g. Factory Laws and Legislation

Kernochan, John M. The Legislative Process. abr. ed. 64p. 1980. pap. text ed. write for info. (ISBN 0-88277-023-3). Foundation Pr.

Neilson, W. A. & MacPherson, J. C. The Legislative Process in Canada: The Need for Reform. 328p. 1978. pap. text ed. 12.95x (ISBN 0-920380-11-5, Pub. by Inst Res Pub Canada). Renouf.

Shannon, W. Wayne. Party, Constituency & Congressional Voting: A Study of Legislative Behavior in the United States House of Representatives. LC 80-25798. (Louisiana State University Studies, Social Science Ser.: No. 14). (Illus.). xii, 202p. 1981. Repr. of 1968 ed. lib. bdg. 23.50x (ISBN 0-313-22771-3, SHPV). Greenwood.

LEGISLATION, COMPARATIVE

see Comparative Law

LEGISLATIVE BODIES

see also Legislators; Parliamentary Practice; Right and Left (Political Science)

Compendium of Legislative Authority: Vol. 1, Suppl. 1, 1978. 66p. 1979. pap. 7.50 (UNEP 39, UNEP). Unipub.

LEGISLATIVE BODIES–RULES AND PRACTICE

see Parliamentary Practice

LEGISLATIVE INVESTIGATIONS

see Governmental Investigations

LEGISLATORS

Cohen, William. Roll Call. 1981. 14.95 (ISBN 0-671-25142-2). S&S.

Elliot, Jeffrey M. & Reginald, R. The Analytical Congressional Directory. (Borgo Reference Library: Vol. 12). 256p. (Orig.). 1981. lib. bdg. 19.95 (ISBN 0-89370-141-6); pap. text ed. 9.95 (ISBN 0-89370-241-2). Borgo Pr.

Hayes, Michael J. Lobbyists & Legislators: A Theory of Political Markets. 256p. 1981. 18.00 (ISBN 0-8135-0910-6). Rutgers U Pr.

Javits, Jacob K. & Steinberg, Rafael. Javits: The Autobiography of a Public Man. (Illus.). 1981. 16.95 (ISBN 0-395-29912-8). HM.

Pierce, Walter M. Oregon Cattleman, Governor, Congressman: Memoirs & Times of Walter M. Pierce. Bone, Arthur H., ed. LC 80-81718. (Illus.). 528p. 1981. pap. 14.95 (ISBN 0-87595-071-X). Oreg Hist Soc.

LEGUMES

Here are entered works on those plants belonging to the family Leguminosae, the pods or seeds of which are edible for man or domestic animals, e.g. peas, beans, lentils, etc., treated collectively.

see also names of luguminous plants

Mineral Nutrition of Legumes in Tropical & Subtropical Soils. 415p. 1978. 29.00 (ISBN 0-643-00311-8, CO14, CSIRO). Unipub.

Plant Relations in Pastures. 475p. 1980. pap. 45.00 (ISBN 0-643-00264-2, CO05, CSIRO). Unipub.

LEICESTERSHIRE, ENGLAND

Hoskins, W. G. Leicestershire: A Shell Guide. 1970. 9.95 (ISBN 0-571-09467-8, Pub. by Faber & Faber). Merrimack Bk Serv.

LEICHHARDT, LUDWIG, 1813-1848–JUVENILE LITERATURE

Webster, E. M. Whirlwinds in the Plain: Ludwig Leichardt - Friends, Foes & History. 484p. 1980. 40.00x (ISBN 0-522-84181-3, Pub. by Melbourne U Pr Australia). Intl Schol Bk Serv.

LEISURE

see also Hobbies; Recreation; Retirement; Time Allocation

Murphy, James F. Concepts of Leisure. 2nd ed. (Illus.). 192p. 1981. text ed. 13.95 (ISBN 0-13-166512-X). P-H.

LENDING

see Loans

LENIN, VLADIMIR ILICH, 1870-1924

Lane, David. Leninism: A Sociological Interpretation. (Themes in the Social Sciences Ser.). (Illus.). 176p. Date not set. price not set (ISBN 0-521-23855-2); pap. price not set (ISBN 0-521-28259-4). Cambridge U Pr.

Weber, Gerda & Weber, Herman. Lenin Chronology. 226p. 1981. lib. bdg. 22.50 (ISBN 0-87196-515-1). Facts on File.

LENINGRAD

Blue Guide - Moscow & Leningrad. 1980. 29.95 (ISBN 0-528-84611-6); pap. 24.95 (ISBN 0-528-84607-8). Rand.

LENINGRAD–HERMITAGE MUSEUM

Suslov, Vitaly. Treasures of the Hermitage. LC 80-81382. (Illus.). 1980. 19.95 (ISBN 0-88225-301-8). Newsweek.

LENSES, PHOTOGRAPHIC

Gaunt, Leonard. Zoom & Special Lenses. LC 80-41245. (Illus.). 128p. 1981. pap. 9.95 (ISBN 0-240-51069-0). Focal Pr.

LENSLESS PHOTOGRAPHY

see Holography

LENT

see also Easter

Sullivan, Barbara. A Page a Day for Lent Nineteen Eighty-One. 100p. 1981. pap. 2.50 (ISBN 0-8091-2340-1). Paulist Pr.

LENT–PRAYER BOOKS AND DEVOTIONS

Adams, John. The Lenten Psalms. (Short Course Ser.). 124p. Repr. of 1912 ed. text ed. 2.95 (ISBN 0-567-08304-7). Attic Pr.

Elberfeld, Katie. Jordan to Jerusalem: A Lenten Pilgrimage. 1979. 1.20 (ISBN 0-686-28783-5). Forward Movement.

LENTEN SERMONS

Here are entered sermons preached during the season of Lent. If they are limited in their scope to the passion of Jesus Christ, entry is made under Jesus Christ–Passion–Sermons.

Burrell, D. J. In the Upper Room. (Short Course Ser.). 146p. 1913. text ed. 2.95 (ISBN 0-567-08317-9). Attic Pr.

LEONARDO DA VINCI, 1452-1519

Bax, Clifford. Leonardo Da Vinci. 160p. 1980. Repr. of 1932 ed. lib. bdg. 27.50 (ISBN 0-8495-0464-3). Arden Lib.

Pedretti, Carlo. Leonardo Da Vinci Nature Studies from the Royal Library at Windsor Castle. (Illus.). 95p. (Orig.). 1980. pap. 10.00 (ISBN 0-384-32298-0). J P Getty Mus.

Popham, A. E. The Drawings of Leonardo da Vinci. (Illus.). 320p. 1981. 15.95 (ISBN 0-224-00909-5, Pub. by Chatto-Bodley-Jonathan). Merrimack Bk Serv.

LEQUEU, JEAN JACQUES, 1757-1825?

Lemagny, J. C. & De Menil, Dominiqueintro. by. Visionary Architects: Boullee, Ledoux, Lequeu. (Illus.). 1968. pap. 8.00 (ISBN 0-914412-21-3). Inst for the Arts.

LERMONTOV, MIKHAIL IUREVICH, 1814-1841

Eikhenbaum, Boris. Lermontov: An Essay in Literary Historical Evaluation. Parrott, Ray & Weber, Harry, trs. 1981. 16.50. Ardis Pubs.

Michailoff, Helen. Mikhail Lermontov: Magic & Mystery. 1981. 20.00. Ardis Pubs.

LESBIANISM

Bulkin, Elly & Larkin, Joan, eds. Lesbian Poetry: An Anthology. (Orig.). 1981. pap. price not set (ISBN 0-930436-08-3). Persephone.

Faderman, Lillian. Surpassing the Love of Men: Love Between Women from the Renaissance to the Present. Guarnaschelli, Maria, ed. LC 80-24482. (Illus.). 488p. 1981. 15.95 (ISBN 0-688-03733-X) (ISBN 0-688-00396-6). Morrow.

--Surpassing the Love of Men: Love Between Women from the Renaissance to the Present. Guarnaschelli, Maria, ed. (Illus.). 488p. 1981. pap. 10.95 (ISBN 0-688-00396-6, Quill). Morrow.

Grahn, Judy, ed. Lesbians Speak Out. (Illus.). 1974. pap. 5.00 (ISBN 0-88447-028-8). Diana Pr.

Rule, Jane. Outlander. LC 80-84221. 220p. (Orig.). 1981. pap. 6.95 (ISBN 0-930044-17-7). Naiad Pr.

LESS DEVELOPED COUNTRIES

see Underdeveloped Areas

LESSING, DORIS MAY, 1919-

Carlson, Edgar M. The Church & the Public Conscience. LC 79-8710. xii, 104p. 1981. Repr. of 1956 ed. lib. bdg. 17.50x (ISBN 0-313-22195-2, CACH). Greenwood.

LESSON PLANNING

Emmers, Amy P. After the Lesson Plan: Realities of High School Teaching. 1981. pap. 7.95 (ISBN 0-8077-2605-2). Tchrs Coll.

Weaver, Horace R., ed. The International Lesson Annual 1981-1982. 448p. (Orig.). 1981. pap. 4.50 (ISBN 0-687-19145-9). Abingdon.

LETTER-WRITING

see also Commercial Correspondence; Form Letters

Altman, Janet. Epistolarity: Approaches to a Form. 1981. write for info. (ISBN 0-8142-0313-2). Ohio St U Pr.

LETTERING

see also Alphabets; Sign Painting

Hewitt, Graily. Lettering. (Illus.). 336p. 1981. pap. 9.95 (ISBN 0-8008-4728-8, 76-26844). Taplinger.

LETTERS

see also English Letters

Harelson, Randy. SWAK: The Complete Book of Mail Fun for Kides. LC 80-54624. (Illus.). 160p. (gr. 3-7). 1981. pap. 3.95 (ISBN 0-89480-150-3). Workman Pub.

John W. Campbell Letters, 3 vols. Incl. Vol. 1. Hay, George, ed. write for info. (ISBN 0-931150-02-7); pap. write for info (ISBN 0-931150-03-5); lib. bdg. write for info. (ISBN 0-931150-04-3); Vol 2. Chapdelaine, Perry A., Sr., ed. write for info; pap. write for info (ISBN 0-931150-06-X); lib. bdg. write for info (ISBN 0-931150-07-8); Vol. 3. Vogt, A. E., ed. write for info (ISBN 0-931150-08-6); pap. write for info (ISBN 0-931150-09-4); lib. bdg. write for info (ISBN 0-931150-10-8). 1981. Authors Co Op.

Lucas, E. V. The Gentlest Art. 422p. 1981. Repr. of 1913 ed. lib. bdg. 25.00 (ISBN 0-89987-509-2). Darby Bks.

Netanyahu, Benjamin & Netanyahu, Iddo, eds. Self-Portrait of a Hero: The Letters of Jonathan Netanyahu (1963-1976) 1981. 12.95 (ISBN 0-394-51376-2). Random.

Philpot, Joseph C. Letters & Memoir of Joseph Charles Philpot. (Giant Summit Ser.). 568p. 1981. pap. 9.95 (ISBN 0-8010-7060-0). Baker Bk.

Selections from the Letters of Abdu'l-Baha. 309p. (Persian.). 1980. 10.00 (ISBN 0-87743-157-4, 7-89-46); pap. 5.00 (ISBN 0-87743-158-2, 7-89-47). Baha'i.

LETTERS OF THE ALPHABET

see Alphabet

LEUCEMIA

see Leukemia

LEUCOCYTES

see also Lymphocytes

Cline, Martin, ed. Leukocyte Function. (Methods in Hematology). (Illus.). 224p. 1981. lib. bdg. 25.00 (ISBN 0-686-28872-6). Churchill.

LEUCODYSTROPHY

Kretschmer, V. Leukozytenseparation und Transfusion. (Beitraege Zu Infusionstherapie und Klinische Ernaehrung Ser.: Vol. 6). (Illus.). viii, 200p. 1981. 18.00 (ISBN 3-8055-1946-X). S Karger.

LEUKEMIA

Catovsky, Daniel. The Leukemic Cell. (Methods in Haematology). (Illus.). 230p. 1981. lib. bdg. 35.00 (ISBN 0-443-01911-8). Churchill.

LEUKEMIA–PERSONAL NARRATIVES

Bloch, Alice. Lifetime Guarantee. (Orig.). 1981. pap. price not set (ISBN 0-930436-09-1). Persephone.

LEVANT–DESCRIPTION AND TRAVEL

Zouche, Robert C. Visits to Monasteries in the Levant. LC 80-2200. 1981. Repr. of 1916 ed. 45.00 (ISBN 0-404-18989-X). AMS Pr.

LEVI-STRAUSS, CLAUDE

Clarke, Simon. Foundations of Structuralism: A Critique of Levi-Strauss & the Structuralist Movement. 224p. 1981. 26.50x (ISBN 0-389-20156-1). B&N.

LEVY ON CAPITAL

see Capital Levy

LEWIS, CLIVE STAPLES, 1898-1963

Derrick, Christopher. C.S. Lewis & the Church of Rome. LC 80-83049. (Orig.). 1981. pap. price not set (ISBN 0-89870-009-4). Ignatius Pr.

Glover, Donald E. C. S. Lewis: The Art of Enchantment. LC 80-21421. xii, 235p. 1981. 15.00x (ISBN 0-8214-0566-7); pap. 6.95 (ISBN 0-8214-0609-4). Ohio U Pr.

Hannay, Margaret P. C. S. Lewis. LC 80-53700. (Modern Literature Ser.). 350p. 1981. 13.50 (ISBN 0-8044-2341-5). Ungar.

Kilby, Clyde & Mead, Marj, eds. Brothers & Friends: An Intimate Portrait of C. S. Lewis; the Diaries of Major Warren Hamilton Lewis. LC 80-7756. (Illus.). 1981. 14.95 (ISBN 0-06-065244-6, HarpR). Har-Row.

Lindskoog, Kay. C. S. Lewis: Mere Christian. rev. ed. 192p. 1981. pap. 5.95 (ISBN 0-87784-466-6). Inter-Varsity.

Smith, Robert H. Patches of Godlight: The Pattern of Thought of C. S. Lewis. LC 80-14132. 287p. 1981. 18.00x (ISBN 0-8203-0528-6). U of Ga Pr.

LEWIS, WYNDHAM, 1884-1957

Jameson, Fredric. Fables of Aggression: Wyndham Lewis, the Modernist As Facist. 1981. pap. 5.95 (ISBN 0-520-04398-7, CAL 496). U of Cal Pr.

LIABILITY (LAW)

see also Employers' Liability; Government Liability; Negligence

Noel, Dix & Phillips, Jerry J. Products Liability in a Nutshell. 2nd ed. (Nutshell Ser.). 353p. 1981. pap. text ed. 6.95 (ISBN 0-8299-2121-4). West Pub.

LIABILITY, EMPLOYERS'

see Employers' Liability

LIABILITY FOR NUCLEAR DAMAGES

Sills, David L., et al, eds. Accident at Three Mile Island: The Human Dimensions. 200p. (Orig.). 1981. lib. bdg. 20.00x (ISBN 0-86531-165-X); pap. text ed. 12.00x (ISBN 0-86531-187-0). Westview.

LIABILITY OF THE STATE

see Government Liability

LIBEL AND SLANDER

see also Liberty of Speech; Liberty of the Press; Privacy, Right Of

Lawhorne, Clifton O. The Supreme Court & Libel. (New Horizons in Journalism Ser.). 1981. 19.95 (ISBN 0-8093-0998-X). S Ill U Pr.

Sack, Robert D. Libel, Slander, & Related Problems. 700p. 1980. text ed. 50.00 (ISBN 0-686-68826-0, G1-0658). PLI.

LIBEL AND SLANDER–GREAT BRITAIN

Berkowitz, David S. & Thorne, Samuel E., eds. An Enquiry into the Doctrine Concerning Libels, Warrants, & the Seizure of Papers. LC 77-86678. (Classics of English Legal History in the Modern Era Ser.: Vol. 52). 99p. 1979. lib. bdg. 40.00 (ISBN 0-8240-3151-2). Garland Pub.

LIBERAL THEOLOGY

see Liberalism (Religion)

LIBERALISM

Holsworth, Robert D. Public Interest Liberalism & the Crisis of Affluence: Reflections on Nader, Environmentalism, & the Politics of a Sustainable Society. (Reference Bks.). 1980. lib. bdg. 17.50 (ISBN 0-8161-9032-1). G K Hall.

Mises, Ludwig Von. Liberlaism: A Socio-Economic Exposition. 1978. write for info. NYU Pr.

LIBERALISM (RELIGION)

McCann, Dennis P. Christian Realism & Liberation Theology: Practical Theologies in Conflict. LC 80-23163. 256p. (Orig.). 1981. pap. 9.95 (ISBN 0-88344-086-5). Orbis Bks.

LIBERIA–POLITICS AND GOVERNMENT

Republic of Liberia, Liberia Supreme Court Records. 35.00 ea. Vol. 24, March Term 1975 To October Term 1975 (ISBN 0-8014-1197-1). Vol. 25, March Term 1976 To October Term 1976 (ISBN 0-8014-1272-2). Cornell U Pr.

LIBERTARIANISM

see also Anarchism and Anarchists; Individualism; Liberty

Strauss, Erwin S. The Case Against a Libertarian Political Party. 1980. pap. 4.50. Loompanics.

LIBERTY

see also Anarchism and Anarchists; Civil Rights; Conformity; Equality; Liberalism; Libertarianism; Political Rights; Teaching, Freedom Of

Archer, Peter & Lord Reay. Freedom at Stake. LC 67-15647. (Background Ser.). 1967. 6.25 (ISBN 0-8023-1118-0). Dufour.

Bennett, J. F. The Way to Be Free. 1980. pap. 6.95 (ISBN 0-87728-491-1). Weiser.

Clifton, Merritt. Freedom Comes from Human Beings. 80p. (Orig.). 1980. pap. 4.00 (ISBN 0-686-28738-X). Samisdat.

Cowan, Z. Individual Liberty & the Law. 1977. 10.00 (ISBN 0-379-00597-2). Oceana.

Haksar, Vinit. Equality, Liberty & Perfectionism. (Clarendon Library of Logic & Philosophy Ser.). 310p. 1979. text ed. 24.95x (ISBN 0-19-824418-5). Oxford U Pr.

Hayek, F. A. Law, Legislation, & Liberty: Rules & Order. 15.00 (ISBN 0-226-32080-4). U of Chicago Pr.

--Law, Legislation, & Liberty: The Political Order of a Free People. pap. write for info. (ISBN 0-226-32090-1). U of Chicago Pr.

Hazell, Robert. Conspiracy & Civil Liberties. 128p. 1974. pap. text ed. 6.25x (ISBN 0-7135-1909-6, Pub. by Bedford England). Renouf.

Richmond, Bruce L. The Pattern of Freedom. 266p. 1980. Repr. of 1911 ed. lib. bdg. 25.00 (ISBN 0-8492-7732-9). R West.

Ten, C. L. Mill on Liberty. 464p. 1981. 31.00 (ISBN 0-19-824643-9); pap. 14.95 (ISBN 0-19-824644-7). Oxford U Pr.

LIBERTY (THEOLOGY)

see Freedom (Theology)

LIBERTY OF SPEECH

see also Libel and Slander; Liberty of the Press

Blount, Charles, et al. A Just Vindication of Learning. Berkowitz, David S. & Thorne, Samuel E., eds. LC 77-86655. (Classics of English Legal History in the Modern Era Ser.: Vol. 39). 109p. 1979. lib. bdg. 40.00 (ISBN 0-8240-3088-5). Garland Pub.

LIBERTY OF SPEECH IN THE CHURCH

Rahner, Karl. Free Speech in the Church. LC 79-8717. Orig. Title: Das Freie Wort in der Kirche. 112p. 1981. Repr. of 1959 ed. lib. bdg. 17.50x (ISBN 0-313-20849-2, RAFS). Greenwood.

LIBERTY OF THE PRESS

see also Libel and Slander; Press; Public Opinion

Rips, Geoffrey. The Campaign Against the Underground Press in the United States: 1960-1979. 80p. 1981. pap. 2.50 (ISBN 0-87286-127-9). City Lights.

LIBERTY OF THE PRESS–GREAT BRITAIN

Blount, Charles, et al. A Just Vindication of Learning. Berkowitz, David S. & Thorne, Samuel E., eds. LC 77-86655. (Classics of English Legal History in the Modern Era Ser.: Vol. 39). 109p. 1979. lib. bdg. 40.00 (ISBN 0-8240-3088-5). Garland Pub.

LIBERTY OF THE WILL

see Free Will and Determinism

LIBRARIANS

O'Reilly, Robert C. & O'Reilly, Marjorie I. Librarians & Labor Relations: Employment Under Union Contracts. LC 80-1049. (Contributions in Librarianship & Information Science Ser.: No. 35). 208p. 1981. lib. bdg. 25.00 (ISBN 0-313-22485-4, OLL/). Greenwood.

Thomas, Diana M., et al. The Effective Reference Librarian. (Library & Information Science). 1981. write for info. (ISBN 0-12-688720-9). Acad Pr.

LIBRARIANSHIP

see Library Science

LIBRARIES

see also Archives; Audio-Visual Library Service; Information Services

Bowker Annual of Library & Book Trade Information 1981. 26th ed. LC 55-12434. (Illus.). 600p. 1981. 32.50 (ISBN 0-8352-1343-9). Bowker.

Woolard, Wilma L. Combined School - Public Libraries: A Survey with Conclusions & Recommendations. LC 80-36742. 204p. 1980. 11.00 (ISBN 0-8108-1335-1). Scarecrow.

LIBRARIES–ACCESSION DEPARTMENTS

see Acquisitions (Libraries)

LIBRARIES–ACCOUNTING

see Library Finance

LIBRARIES–ADMINISTRATION

see Library Administration; Library Science

LIBRARIES–ARRANGEMENT OF BOOKS ON SHELVES

see Classification–Books

LIBRARIES–AUTOMATION

see also Information Storage and Retrieval Systems

Matthews, Joseph R. Choosing an Automated Library System: A Planning Guide. LC 80-17882. 128p. 1980. 11.00 (ISBN 0-8389-0310-X). ALA.

LIBRARIES–BRANCHES, DELIVERY STATIONS, ETC.

Branch Library Service. LC 77-17557. 66p. 1977. 5.00 (ISBN 0-913578-17-7). Inglewood Ca.

LIBRARIES–CATALOGS

see Library Catalogs

LIBRARIES–CIRCULATION, LOANS

see also Libraries–Branches, Delivery Stations, etc.

Circulation Procedures. 2nd ed. 75p. 1972. 3.00. Inglewood Ca.

LIBRARIES–CLASSIFICATION

see Classification–Books

LIBRARIES–HANDBOOKS, MANUALS, ETC.

Corcoran, Eileen. Gaining Skills in Using the Library. (Illus.). 1980. pap. 2.25x (ISBN 0-88323-158-1, 247). Richards Pub.

Wolf, Carolyn & Wolf, Richard. Basic Library Skills: A Short Course. 110p. 1981. lib. bdg. write for info (ISBN 0-89950-018-8). McFarland & Co.

LIBRARIES–HISTORY

Clark, John W. The Care of Books: An Essay on the Development of Libraries & Their Fittings, from the Earliest Times to the End of the 18th Century. 442p. 1980. 50.00x (ISBN 0-902089-78-1, Pub. by Variorum England). State Mutual Bk.

Compton, Charles H., et al. Twenty-Five Crucial Years of the St. Louis Public Library, 1927 to 1952. 1953. write for info. (ISBN 0-937322-00-8). St Louis Pub Lib.

Peebles, Margaret & Howell, J. B., eds. History of Mississippi Libraries. 437p. 1975. 10.00 (ISBN 0-88289-190-1). Pelican.

LIBRARIES–INFORMATION NETWORKS

see Library Information Networks

LIBRARIES–ORDER DEPARTMENT

see Acquisitions (Libraries)

LIBRARIES–ORGANIZATION

see Libraries; Library Administration; Library Science

LIBRARIES–PUBLIC RELATIONS

see Public Relations–Libraries

LIBRARIES–REFERENCE BOOKS

see Reference Books

LIBRARIES–SECURITY MEASURES

Gandert, Slade R. Protecting Your Collection: A Handbook, Survey, & Guide for the Security of Rare Books, Manuscripts, Archives, Works of Art, & the Circulating Library Collection. (Library & Archival Security Ser.: No. 4). 192p. 1981. text ed. 19.95 (ISBN 0-917724-78-X). Haworth Pr.

LIBRARIES–SPECIAL COLLECTIONS

Here are entered works on the methods used to acquire, process and maintain special collections in libraries. Works describing the resources and special collections in libraries which are available for research in various fields are entered under Library Resources.

Library Service to the Spanish Speaking. LC 77-22847. 51p. 1977. 5.00 (ISBN 0-913578-16-9). Inglewood Ca.

Parker, J. Carlyle, ed. Library Service for Genealogists. LC 80-26032. (The Gale Genealogy & Local History Ser.: Vol. 15). 285p. 1981. 30.00 (ISBN 0-8103-1489-4). Gale.

LIBRARIES–GERMANY

Union List of Conference Proceedings in Libraries of the Federal Republic of Germany Including Berlin (West, 2 vols. 907p. 1978. Set. 375.00 (ISBN 3-7940-3004-4, Dist by Gale Research Co). K G Saur.

LIBRARIES, ARCHITECTURAL

see Architectural Libraries

LIBRARIES, BRANCH

see Libraries–Branches, Delivery Stations, etc.

LIBRARIES, CHURCH

Brown, Charles C. Small Church Library. 1980. 0.75 (ISBN 0-686-28794-0). Forward Movement.

Walls, Francine E. The Church Library Workbook. 152p. 1980. pap. 4.95 (ISBN 0-89367-048-0). Light & Life.

LIBRARIES, COLLEGE

see Libraries, University and College

LIBRARIES, EDUCATION

see Education Libraries

LIBRARIES, HIGH-SCHOOL

see School Libraries (High School)

LIBRARIES, MEDICAL

see Medical Libraries

LIBRARIES, MUSIC

see Music Libraries

LIBRARIES, PARISH

see Libraries, Church

LIBRARIES, SCHOOL

see School Libraries

LIBRARIES, SCIENTIFIC

see Scientific Libraries

LIBRARIES, SPECIAL

see also Libraries–Special Collections

also types of special libraries, e.g. Music Libraries

Gibson, Robert W., ed. The Special Library Role in Networks: Proceedings of a Conference. spiral bdg. 10.50 (ISBN 0-87111-279-5). SLA.

Jackson, Eugene B., ed. Special Librarianship: A New Reader. LC 80-11530. 773p. 1980. 27.50 (ISBN 0-8108-1295-9). Scarecrow.

Young, Margaret Labash & Young, Harold C., eds. Subject Directory of Special Libraries & Information Centers, 5 vol. set. 6th ed. 1981. Set. 350.00 (ISBN 0-8103-0305-1). Gale.

--Subject Directory of Special Libaries and Information Centers: Education & Information Science Libraries, Including Audiovisual, Picture, Publishing, Rare Book, & Recreational Libaries, Vol. 2. 6th ed. 1981. 80.00 (ISBN 0-8103-0307-8). Gale.

--Subject Directory of Special Libaries & Information Services: Science & Technology Libraries, Including Agriculture, Energy, Environment-Conservation & Food, Vol. 5. 6th ed. 1981. 80.00 (ISBN 0-8103-0309-4). Gale.

--Subject Directory of Special Libraries & Information Centers: Health Science Libraries, Including All Aspects of Basic & Pplied Medical Sciences, Vol. 3. 6th ed. 1981. 80.00 (ISBN 0-8103-0308-6). Gale.

Young, Margaret Labash & Ypung, Harold C., eds. Subject Directory of Special Libraries & Info. Centers: Business & Law Libaries, Vol. 1. 6th ed. 1981. 80.00 (ISBN 0-8103-0306-X). Gale.

Young, Margarey Labash & Young, Harold C., eds. Subject Directory of Special Libaries & Information Centers: Social Sciences & Humanities Libraries, Including Area-Ethic, Art, Geography-Map, History, Music, Religion, Theology, Theatre, Urban-Regional Planning Libraries, Vol. 4. 6th ed. 1981. 80.00 (ISBN 0-8103-0309-4). Gale.

LIBRARIES, TECHNICAL

see Technical Libraries

LIBRARIES, UNIVERSITY AND COLLEGE

Miller, William & Rockwood, D. Stephen, eds. College Librarianship. LC 80-25546. 290p. 1981. 15.00 (ISBN 0-8108-1383-1). Scarecrow.

Stevens, Norman D., ed. Essays from the New England Academic Librarians' Writing Seminar. LC 80-21502. 230p. 1980. 12.50 (ISBN 0-8108-1365-3). Scarecrow.

LIBRARIES AND COMMUNITY

see also Public Relations–Libraries

Library Association-the Working Party on Community Information, ed. Community Information: What Libraries Can Do. 1980. pap. 9.25x (ISBN 0-85365-872-2, Pub. by Lib Assn England). Oryx Pr.

Library Community Services. LC 77-28184. 98p. 1977. 6.00 (ISBN 0-913578-18-5). Inglewood Ca.

LIBRARIES AND READERS

Corcoran, Eileen. Gaining Skills in Using the Library. (Illus.). 1980. pap. 2.25x (ISBN 0-88323-158-1, 247). Richards Pub.

Library Service to the Spanish Speaking. LC 77-22847. 51p. 1977. 5.00 (ISBN 0-913578-16-9). Inglewood Ca.

Tancer, Jack. Our Reader. (Illus.). 1964. pap. 1.50x (ISBN 0-88323-060-7, 158). Richards Pub.

LIBRARIES AND SOCIETY

Library Community Services. LC 77-28184. 98p. 1977. 6.00 (ISBN 0-913578-18-5). Inglewood Ca.

LIBRARIES AND STUDENTS

Sutherland, Zena, ed. Children in Libraries: Patterns of Access to Materials & Services in Schools & Public Libraries. LC 80-53135. (Studies in Library Science). 128p. 1981. lib. bdg. 10.00x (ISBN 0-226-78063-5). U of Chicago Pr.

LIBRARIES AND THE PHYSICALLY HANDICAPPED

Thomas, Carol H. & Thomas, James L. Academic Library Services for Handicapped Students in the U. S. 350p. 1981. text ed. 45.00x (ISBN 0-912700-95-5). Oryx Pr.

LIBRARY ACQUISITIONS

see Acquisitions (Libraries)

LIBRARY ADMINISTRATION

Bailey, Martha J. Supervisory & Middle Managers in Libraries. LC 80-23049. 218p. 1981. 12.00 (ISBN 0-8108-1400-5). Scarecrow.

Gandert, Slade R. Protecting Your Collection: A Handbook, Survey, & Guide for the Security of Rare Books, Manuscripts, Archives, Works of Art, & the Circulating Library Collection. (Library & Archival Security Ser.: No. 4). 192p. 1981. text ed. 19.95 (ISBN 0-917724-78-X). Haworth Pr.

Lundy, Kathryn R. Women View Librarianship: Nine Perspectives. LC 80-23611. (ACRL Publications in Librarianship: No. 41). 108p. 1980. pap. 7.00 (ISBN 0-8389-3251-7). ALA.

Stueart, Robert D. & Eastlick, John T. Library Management. 2nd ed. LC 80-22895. (Library Science Text Ser.). 292p. 1980. text ed. 22.50x (ISBN 0-87287-241-6); pap. text ed. 14.50x (ISBN 0-87287-243-2). Libs Unl.

LIBRARY ARCHITECTURE

Lushington, Nolan & Mills, Willis N., Jr. Libraries Designed for Users: A Planning Handbook. (Illus.). 1980. 24.50 (ISBN 0-208-01888-3, Lib Prof Pubns). Shoe String.

Miletich, John J. Employee Absenteeism in Both the Public & Private Sectors: An Annotated Bibliography to 1979. (Public Administration Ser.: Bibliographies: P-639). 53p. 1981. pap. 8.25. Vance Biblios.

Weis, Ina J. The Design of Library Areas & Buildings. (Architecture Ser.: Bibliography: A-413). 80p. 1981. pap. 12.00. Vance Biblios.

LIBRARY AUTOMATION

see Libraries–Automation

LIBRARY BUILDINGS

see Library Architecture

LIBRARY CATALOGS

see also Catalogs, Subject; Catalogs, Union

Junior High School Library Catalog. 4th ed. 1980. 62.00 (ISBN 0-8242-0652-5). Wilson.

Name Authority Control for Card Catalogs in the General Libraries. (Contributions to Librarianship Ser.: No. 5). 1980. pap. 10.00 (ISBN 0-930214-07-2). U TX Austin Gen Libs.

LIBRARY CATALOGS–UNION CATALOGS

see Catalogs, Union

LIBRARY CLASSIFICATION

see Classification–Books

LIBRARY EDUCATION

Gardner, Richard K. Library Collections: Their Origin, Selection, & Development. (Library Education Ser.). 384p. 1981. text ed. 17.95 (ISBN 0-07-022850-7, C). McGraw.

Miller, William & Rockwood, D. Stephen, eds. College Librarianship. LC 80-25546. 290p. 1981. 15.00 (ISBN 0-8108-1383-1). Scarecrow.

What Shall I Read? 2nd ed. 1978. 12.95x (ISBN 0-85365-560-X, Pub. by Lib Assn England). Oryx Pr.

LIBRARY EXTENSION

Library Service to the Spanish Speaking. LC 77-22847. 51p. 1977. 5.00 (ISBN 0-913578-16-9). Inglewood Ca.

LIBRARY FINANCE

see also Taxation, Exemption From

Compton, Charles H., et al. Twenty-Five Crucial Years of the St. Louis Public Library, 1927 to 1952. 1953. write for info. (ISBN 0-937322-00-8). St Louis Pub Lib.

Drake, Miriam A. User Fees: A Practical Perspective. 120p. 1981. lib. bdg. 15.00x (ISBN 0-87287-244-0). Libs Unl.

Koenig, Michael, ed. Budgeting Techniques for Libraries & Information Centers. (Professional Development Ser.: No. 1). 1980. pap. write for info. (ISBN 0-87111-278-7). SLA.

LIBRARY INFORMATION NETWORKS

Brelsford, William M. & Relles, Daniel A. Statlib: A Statistical Computing Library. 448p. 1981. text ed. 17.50 (ISBN 0-13-846220-8). P-H.

LIBRARY NETWORKS

see Library Information Networks

LIBRARY OF CONGRESS CLASSIFICATION

see Classification, Library of Congress

LIBRARY PUBLICITY

see Public Relations–Libraries

LIBRARY RESEARCH

see Library Science–Research

LIBRARY RESOURCES

Here are entered works describing the resources and special collections in libraries which are available for research in various fields. Works describing the resources and special collections in a particular field are entered under the subject with subdivision Library Resources, e.g. Africa–Library Resources. Works on the methods used to acquire, process, and maintain special collections in libraries are entered under Libraries–Special Collections.

Baker, Robert K. Doing Library Research: An Introduction for Community College Students. (Westview Guides to Library Research Ser.). 260p. 27.50x (ISBN 0-89158-778-0). Westview.

Branyon, Brenda. Outstanding Women Who Promoted the Concept of the Unified School Library & Audio Visual Program. 375p. 1981. 20.00 (ISBN 0-686-69458-9). Hi Willow.

Handbook of West European Archival & Library Resources. 1981. 75.00 (ISBN 0-686-69415-5, Dist. by Gale Research). K G Saur.

Upon the Objectives to Be Attained by the Establishment of a Public Library: Report of the Trustees of the Public Library of the City of Boston, 1852. Repr. 3.50. Boston Public Lib.

Wiemers, Eugene. Materials Availability Handbook. (Occasional Papers Ser.: No. 149). 1981. pap. 3.00 (ISBN 0-686-69450-3). U of Ill Lib Sci.

LIBRARY SCHOOL EDUCATION

see Library Education

LIBRARY SCIENCE

see also Audio-Visual Library Service; Bibliography; Cataloging; Classification–Books; Information Storage and Retrieval Systems

also headings beginning with the word Library

Branyon, Brenda. Outstanding Women Who Promoted the Concept of the Unified School Library & Audio Visual Program. 375p. 1981. 20.00 (ISBN 0-686-69458-9). Hi Willow.

Briquet de Limos, Antonio A. Librarianship in Developing Societies. (Occasional Papers: No. 148). 1981. pap. 3.00 (ISBN 0-686-69073-7). U of Ill Lib Sci.

Carpenter, Michael A. Corporate Authorship: Its Role in Library Cataloging. LC 80-1026. (Contributions in Librarianship & Information Science Ser.: No. 34). 248p. 1981. lib. bdg. 27.50 (ISBN 0-313-22065-4, CAU/). Greenwood.

Carter, Jane R. Public Librarianship: A Reader. 400p. 1981. lib. bdg. price not set (ISBN 0-87287-246-7). Libs Unl.

Clark, John W. The Care of Books: An Essay on the Development of Libraries & Their Fittings, from the Earliest Times to the End of the 18th Century. 442p. 1980. 50.00x (ISBN 0-902089-78-1, Pub. by Variorum England). State Mutual Bk.

Comaromi, John P. Book Numbers: A Historical Study & Practical Guide to Their Use. 250p. 1981. lib. bdg. price not set (ISBN 0-87287-251-3). Libs Unl.

Fenner, Peter. Researching Science Information. 250p. (Orig.). 1981. pap. 7.95 (ISBN 0-86576-010-1). W Kaufmann.

Gover, Harvey R. Keys to Library Research on the Graduate Level: A Guide to Guides. LC 80-5841. 75p. 1981. pap. text ed. 5.75 (ISBN 0-8191-1370-0). U Pr of Amer.

Harris, Michael J. & Voight, Melvin J., eds. Advances in Librarianship, 8 vols. Incl. Vol. 1. 294p. 1970. 37.50 (ISBN 0-12-785001-5); Vol. 2. 388p. 1971. 37.50 (ISBN 0-12-785002-3); Vol. 3. 275p. 1972. 37.50 (ISBN 0-12-785003-1); Vol. 4. 1974. 37.50 (ISBN 0-12-785004-X); Vol. 5. 1975. 37.50 (ISBN 0-12-785005-8); lib ed. 48.00 (ISBN 0-12-785012-0); microfiche 27.50 (ISBN 0-12-785013-9); Vol. 6. 1976. 28.50 (ISBN 0-12-785006-6); lib ed. 35.50 (ISBN 0-12-785014-7); microfiche 21.00 (ISBN 0-12-785015-5); Vol. 7. 1977. lib ed. 45.00 (ISBN 0-12-785016-3); 35.50 (ISBN 0-12-785007-4); microfiche 25.50 (ISBN 0-12-785017-1); Vol. 8. 25.50 (ISBN 0-12-785008-2); lib. ed. 32.50 (ISBN 0-12-785018-X); microfiche 19.00 (ISBN 0-12-785019-8). LC 79-88675. Acad Pr.

Harrison, C. & Oakes, R. Basics of Librarianship. 1980. pap. 12.50x (Pub. by Lib Assn England). Oryx Pr.

INIS: Authority List for Corporate Entries & Report Number Prefixes. 472p. 1980. pap. 29.75 (ISBN 92-0-178280-2, IN6-R13, IAEA). Unipub.

INIS: Descriptive Cataloguing Rules. 72p. 1980. pap. 5.50 (ISBN 92-0-178180-6, IAEA). Unipub.

Kirkendall, Carolyn A., ed. Directions for the Decade: Library Instruction in the 1980's. (Library Orientation Ser.: No. 12). 1980. 10.00. Pierian.

Library Objectives, Goals, & Activities. LC 73-22178. 105p. 1973. 5.00 (ISBN 0-913578-05-3). Inglewood Ca.

Preksto, Peter W., Jr. Library Skills. (Basic Skills Library). (Illus.). (gr. 4 up). 1979. PLB 5.95 (ISBN 0-87191-714-9). Creative Ed.

Ruoss, Martin. A Policy & Procedure Manual for Church & Synagogue Libraries: A Do-It-Yourself Guide. LC 79-28676. 1980. pap. 3.75 (ISBN 0-915324-17-2). CSLA.

Seminar on Aacr-Two, Univ. of Nottingham, 1979. Proceedings. 1980. pap. 17.50x (ISBN 0-85365-593-6, Pub. by Lib Assn England). Oryx Pr.

Stevens, Norman D., ed. Essays from the New England Academic Librarians' Writing Seminar. LC 80-21502. 230p. 1980. 12.50 (ISBN 0-8108-1365-3). Scarecrow.

Swanson, Don R. & Bookstein, Abraham, eds. Operations Research: Implications for Libraries (35th Annual Conference of the Graduate Library School, August 2-4, 1971) LC 73-185760. (University of Chicago Studies in Library Science). (Illus.). 160p. 1972. lib. bdg. 10.00 (ISBN 0-226-78466-5). U of Chicago Pr.

LIBRARY SCIENCE–BIBLIOGRAPHY

Busha, Charles H., ed. A Library Science Research Reader & Bibliographic Guide. 210p. 1981. lib. bdg. 18.50 (ISBN 0-87287-237-8). Libs Unl.

Johann Gottfried Herder Institute. Alphabetischer Katalog der Bibliothek Des Johann Gottfried Herder - Instituts: Second Supplement. (Library Catalogs-Supplements Ser.). 1981. lib. bdg. 350.00 (ISBN 0-8161-0277-5). G K Hall.

Lengenfelder, Helga, ed. International Bibliography of the Book Trade & Librarianship 1976-79. (Handbook of International Documentation & Information Ser.: Vol. 2). 800p. 1981. 95.00 (ISBN 3-598-20504-X, Dist. by Gale Research). K G Saur.

Research Libraries of the New York Public Library & the Library of Congress. Bibliographic Guide to Conference Publication: 1980. (Library Catalogs-Bib. Guides Ser.). 1981. lib. bdg. 130.00 (ISBN 0-8161-6884-9). G K Hall.

LIBRARY SCIENCE–DATA PROCESSING

Brelsford, William M. & Relles, Daniel A. Statlib: A Statistical Computing Library. 448p. 1981. text ed. 17.50 (ISBN 0-13-846220-8). P-H.

Clinic on Library Applications of Data Processing, 1980. Public Access to Library Automation: Proceedings. Divilbiss, J. L., ed. 1981. 10.00 (ISBN 0-87845-065-3). U of Ill Lib Sci.

LIBRARY SCIENCE–PERIODICALS

Meder, Marylouise D., ed. Library School Review, Vol. 18. 1979. pap. 2.00. Sch Lib Sci.

LIBRARY SCIENCE–RESEARCH

Baker, Robert K. Doing Library Research: An Introduction for Community College Students. (Westview Guides to Library Research Ser.). 260p. 27.50x (ISBN 0-89158-778-0). Westview.

Busha, Charles H., ed. A Library Science Research Reader & Bibliographic Guide. 210p. 1981. lib. bdg. 18.50 (ISBN 0-87287-237-8). Libs Unl.

Gover, Harvey R. Keys to Library Research on the Graduate Level: A Guide to Guides. LC 80-5841. 75p. 1981. pap. text ed. 5.75 (ISBN 0-8191-1370-0). U Pr of Amer.

LIBRARY SCIENCE–STUDY AND TEACHING

see Library Education

LIBRARY SERVICE TO THE PHYSICALLY HANDICAPPED

see Libraries and the Physically Handicapped

LIBRARY SKILLS

see Libraries–Handbooks, Manuals, etc.; Libraries and Readers

LIBYA

Waddams, Frank C. The Libyan Oil Industry. LC 80-13939. (Illus.). 352p. 1980. text ed. 30.00x (ISBN 0-8018-2431-1). Johns Hopkins.

LIBYA–BIBLIOGRAPHY

Schuter, Hans & Magar, Kurt. Index Libycus: A Cumlative Index to Bibliography of Libya,Nineteen Fifteen to Nineteen Seventy-Five. (Reference Books Ser.). 1981. 25.00 (ISBN 0-8161-8534-4). G K Hall.

LICE

Cendrars, Blaise. Lice. LC 80-9058. 189p. 1981. 12.95 (ISBN 0-8128-2815-1). Stein & Day.

LICENSED BEVERAGE INDUSTRY

see Distilling Industries

LICENSED PRACTICAL NURSES

see Practical Nursing

LICENSES

see also Business Tax

Brazell, D. Edmunds. Licensing Check Lists. 49p. (Orig.). 1981. pap. 12.50x (ISBN 0-911378-36-7). Sheridan.

LICHENS

Vobis, G. Bau und Entwicklung der Flechtenpycnidien und Ihrer Goniedien. (Bibliotheca Lichenologica: No. 14). 200p. (Ger.). 1981. pap. text ed. 25.00x (ISBN 3-7682-1270-X, Pub. by Cramer Germany). Lubrecht & Cramer.

LICHTENSTEIN, ROY, 1923-

Cowart, Jack. Roy Lichtenstein: 1970-1980. LC 80-28348. (Illus.). 192p. 1981. 35.00 (ISBN 0-933920-14-8); pap. 16.00 (ISBN 0-933920-15-6). Hudson Hills.

Glenn, Constance W. Roy Lichtenstein Ceramic Sculpture. (Illus.). 64p. (Orig.). 1977. pap. 8.00 (ISBN 0-936270-05-5). Art Mus Gall.

LIE ALGEBRAS

Slodowy, P. Simple Singularities & Simple Algebraic Groups. (Lecture Notes in Mathematics: Vol. 815). 175p. 1980. pap. 11.80 (ISBN 0-387-10026-1). Springer-Verlag.

LIENS

NACM, ed. Mechanics Lien Laws & Federal Tax Lien Law. 1981. pap. 4.50 (ISBN 0-686-69391-4). NACM.

LIFE

see also Conduct of Life; Death; Ethics; Old Age; Philosophical Anthropology

Bichat, Xavier. Physiological Researches on Life & Death. Gold, F., tr. from Fr. Bd. with Outlines of Phrenology; Phrenology Examined. (Contributions to the History of Psychology, Vol. II, Pt. E: Physiological Psychology). 1978. Repr. of 1827 ed. 30.00 (ISBN 0-89093-175-5). U Pubns Amer.

Dobschiner, Johanna R., tr. Destinada a Viver. (Portugese Bks.). (Port.). 1979. 1.60 (ISBN 0-8297-0655-0). Life Pubs Intl.

Hendren, Bob. Life Without End. LC 80-54164. (Journey Bks.). 144p. (Orig.). 1981. pap. 2.35 (ISBN 0-8344-0118-5). Sweet.

Klemke, E. D., ed. The Meaning of Life. 288p. 1981. pap. text ed. 6.95x (ISBN 0-19-502871-6). Oxford U Pr.

Zaner, Richard M. The Context of Self: A Phenomenological Inquiry Using Medicine As a Clue. LC 80-18500. (Continental Thought Ser.: Vol. 1). (Illus.). xiv, 282p. 1981. 16.95x (ISBN 0-8214-0443-1); pap. 8.95x (ISBN 0-8214-0600-0). Ohio U Pr.

LIFE (BIOLOGY)

see also Biology; Genetics; Longevity; Old Age; Reproduction

Corliss, William R. Incredible Life: A Handbook of Biological Mysteries. LC 80-53971. (Illus.). 1050p. 1981. 22.50 (ISBN 0-915554-07-0). Sourcebook.

LIFE, FUTURE

see Future Life

LIFE, JEWISH WAY OF

see Jewish Way of Life

LIFE, SPIRITUAL

see Spiritual Life

LIFE AFTER DEATH

see Future Life; Immortality

LIFE-BOATS

Block, Richard A., ed. Able Seaman & Lifevoatman: All Grades. rev. ed. (Illus.). 338p. 1978. pap. 21.00 (ISBN 0-934114-04-8). Marine Educ.

LIFE INSURANCE

see Insurance, Life

LIFE-LONG EDUCATION

see Adult Education

LIFE ON OTHER PLANETS

Here are entered works on the question of life in outer space. Works on the biology of man or other earth life while in outer space are entered under Space Biology.

Trefil, James & Rood, Robert. Are We Alone? (Illus.). 224p. 1981. 10.95 (ISBN 0-684-16826-X, ScribT). Scribner.

Woodrew, Greta. On a Slide of Light. 224p. 1981. 12.95 (ISBN 0-02-631390-1). Macmillan.

LIFE ON OTHER PLANETS–JUVENILE LITERATURE

Moche. The Star Wars Question & Answer Book About Space. (Illus.). (gr. 4). Date not set. pap. cancelled (ISBN 0-590-30065-2, Schol Pap). Schol Bk Serv.

LIFE-SAVING

see also Search and Rescue Operations; Survival (After Airplane Accidents, Shipwrecks, etc.)

Lifesaving. 64p. (gr. 6-12). 1980. pap. 0.70x. BSA.

U. S. U. L. A. Lifesaving & Marine Safety. 1981. price not set (Assn Pr). Follett.

LIFE SCIENCE ENGINEERING

see Bioengineering

LIFE SCIENCES

see also Agriculture; Biology; Medicine

Burghes, D. N. Mathematical Models in the Social, Management & Life Sciences. LC 79-40989. 287p. 1980. pap. 19.95 (ISBN 0-470-27073-X). Halsted Pr.

Claflin, William E. Collecting, Culturing, & Caring for Living Materials: A Guide for the Teacher, Student & Hobbyist. LC 80-69329. 110p. 1981. perfect bdg. 8.50 (ISBN 0-86548-026-5). Century Twenty One.

Kosterlitz, H. W. & Terenius, L. Y., eds. Pain & Society. (Dahlem Workshop Reports, Life Sciences Research Report Ser.: No. 17). (Illus.). 523p. (Orig.). 1980. pap. text ed. 39.40 (ISBN 0-89573-099-5). Verlag Chemie.

Lewis, R., ed. Computers in Life Sciences. 128p. 1980. 25.00x (Pub. by Croom Helm England). State Mutual Bk.

Poti, S. J. Quantitive Studies in Life Science. 250p. 1980. text ed. 25.00x (ISBN 0-7069-1247-0, Pub by Vikas India). Advent Bk.

R. B Uleck Associates. Life Sciences Jobs Handbook. (Illus., Orig.). 1979. pap. 9.95 (ISBN 0-937562-01-7). Uleck Assoc.

LIFE SPAN PROLONGATION

see Longevity

LIGAND FIELD THEORY

Figgis, B. N. Introduction to Ligand Fields. 351p. 1966. 33.95 (ISBN 0-470-25880-2). Wiley.

LIGHT

see also Color; Lasers; Luminescence; Optics; Photobiology; Photons; Radiation; Refraction; Spectrum Analysis; X-Rays

Babbitt, Edwin D. Principles of Light & Color. (Illus.). 578p. Date not set. 20.00 (ISBN 0-89540-060-X). Sun Pub.

Light & Color: Images from New Mexico. (Illus.). 1980. pap. 12.95 (ISBN 0-89013-134-1). Museum NM Pr.

Ott, John N. The Dynamics of Color & Light: How They Affect Human Health & Behavior. (Illus.). 256p. 1981. 10.00 (ISBN 0-8159-5314-3). Devin.

Warren, Eugene. Geometries of Light. (The Wheaton Literary Ser.). 80p. (Orig.). 1981. pap. 3.95 (ISBN 0-87788-300-9). Shaw Pubs.

LIGHT–CHEMICAL ACTION

see Photochemistry

LIGHT–JUVENILE LITERATURE

Crews, Donald. Light. LC 80-20273. (Illus.). 32p. (ps-1). 1981. 7.95 (ISBN 0-688-00303-6); lib. bdg. 7.63 (ISBN 0-688-00310-9). Greenwillow.

LIGHT, ELECTROMAGNETIC THEORY OF

see Electromagnetic Theory

LIGHT, WAVE THEORY OF

see also Electromagnetic Theory

Chapple, M. A Level Physics: Wave Motion-Sound & Light, Vol. 2. 2nd ed. (Illus.). 240p. (Orig.). 1979. pap. text ed. 10.95x (ISBN 0-7121-0155-1, Pub. by Macdonald & Evans England). Intl Ideas.

LIGHT AMPLIFICATION BY STIMULATED EMISSION OF RADIATION

see Lasers

LIGHT PRODUCTION IN ANIMALS AND PLANTS

see Bioluminescence

LIGHT QUANTUM

see Photons

LIGHTHOUSES

Gibbs, James A. West Coast Lighthouses. Pfeiffer, Douglas A., ed. (Illus.). 96p. (Orig.). 1981. pap. 5.95 (ISBN 0-912856-72-6). Graphic Arts Ctr.

Holland, Francis R., Jr. America's Lighthouses. rev. ed. (Illus.). 240p. 1981. pap. 19.95 (ISBN 0-8289-0441-3). Greene.

Jones, Stephen. Harbor of Refuge. (Illus.). 1981. 16.95 (ISBN 0-393-01417-7). Norton.

Munro, William. Scottish Lighthouses. (Illus.). 240p. 1980. 22.50 (ISBN 0-906191-32-7, Pub. by Thule Pr England). Intl Schol Bk Serv.

LIGHTING

see also Lighting, Architectural and Decorative; Stage Lighting

Boyce, P. R. Human Factors in Lighting. (Illus.). xiii, 420p. 1981. 52.00x (ISBN 0-686-28903-X). Burgess-Intl Ideas.

Lyons. Handbook of Industrial Lighting. 1981. text ed. price not set. Butterworth.

LIGHTING, ARCHITECTURAL AND DECORATIVE

Early Twentieth Century Lighting Fixtures. (Illus.). 1980. pap. 11.95 (ISBN 0-89145-143-9). Collector Bks.

Frazier, A. Eugene. Glamorize with Lighting. Ide, Arthur F., ed. LC 79-9441. (Good Taste Begins with You Ser.). (Illus.). iii, 50p. 1980. Repr. of 1969 ed. pap. text ed. 5.00 (ISBN 0-86663-224-7). Ide Hse.

Kaufman, John E., ed. IES Lighting Handbook-1981: Application Volume. 5th ed. (Illus.). 532p. 1981. 50.00 (ISBN 0-87995-008-0). Illum Eng.

--IES Lighting Handbook-1981: Reference Volume. 5th ed. (Illus.). 488p. 1981. 50.00 (ISBN 0-87995-007-2). Illum Eng.

LIGHTING, DECORATIVE

see Lighting, Architectural and Decorative

LIGHTS, FEAST OF

see Hanukkah (Feast of Lights)

LIGNIN

Crawford, Ronald L. Lignin Biodegradation & Transformation. 192p. 1981. 22.50 (ISBN 0-471-05743-6, Pub. by Wiley-Interscience). Wiley.

LILLY, BENJAMIN VERNON, 1856-1936

Dobie, J. Frank. The Ben Lilly Legend. (Illus.). 253p. 1981. pap. 6.95x (ISBN 0-292-70728-2). U of Tex Pr.

LIMBS (ANATOMY)

see Extremities (Anatomy)

LIMERICKS

Billington, Ray A. Limericks Historical & Hysterical: Plagiarized, Arranged, Annotated & Some Written by Ray Allen Billington. 1981. 9.95 (ISBN 0-393-01453-3). Norton.

Hart, Harold H., compiled by. Limericks Lewd & Lusty. 352p. 1981. pap. 3.95 (ISBN 0-89104-196-6). A & W Pubs.

Potz, Veronica & Babin, Lawrence J. Limericks for Children. (See-Hear-Color Me Book Ser.). 1981. 6.95 (ISBN 0-912492-15-5). Pyquag.

LIMERICKS–JUVENILE LITERATURE

Potz, Veronica. Umericks for Children. (See-Hear-Color Me Bk). 1981. 8.95 (ISBN 0-912492-15-5). Pyquag.

LIMESTONE

Rodda, P. U., et al. Limestone & Dolomite Resources: Lower Cretaceous Rocks, Texas. (Illus.). 286p. 1966. 4.50 (RI 56). Bur Econ Geology.

LIMITATION OF ARMAMENT

see Disarmament

LIMITATIONS (LAW)

see Estates (Law); Real Property

LIMITATIONS, CONSTITUTIONAL

see Constitutional Law

LIMITATIONS, CONTRACTUAL

see Contracts

LIMITED COMPANIES

see Corporations

LIMITS (MATHEMATICS)

see Calculus

LIMNOLOGY

see also Fresh-Water Biology; Water Chemistry

Hutchinson, G. Evelyn. A Treatise on Liminology, 3 vols. Incl. Vol. 1, 2 pts. 1975. Set. 29.95 (ISBN 0-471-42567-2); Pt. 1. Geography & Physics of Lakes. 672p. 17.95 (ISBN 0-471-42567-2); Pt. 2. Chemistry of Lakes. 474p. 16.50 (ISBN 0-471-42569-9); Vol. 2. Introduction to Lake Biology & the Limnoplankton. 1957. 79.50 (ISBN 0-471-42572-9); Vol. 3. Limnological Biology. 704p. 1975. 43.50 (ISBN 0-471-42574-5). LC 57-8888 (Pub. by Wiley-Interscience). Wiley.

McLusky, Donald S. Estuarine Ecosystem. (Tertiary Level Biology Ser.). 176p. 1981. 34.95 (ISBN 0-470-27127-2). Halsted Pr.

LIMU

see Algae; Mosses

LINCOLN, ABRAHAM, PRES. U. S., 1809-1865

Angle, Paul M., ed. The Lincoln Reader. LC 80-25663. (Illus.). xii, 564p. 1981. Repr. of 1947 ed. lib. bdg. 49.50x (ISBN 0-313-22757-8, ANLR). Greenwood.

Donald, David H. Lincoln Reconsidered: Essays on the Civil War Era. LC 80-22804. (Illus.). xiii, 200p. 1981. Repr. of 1956 ed. lib. bdg. 23.50x (ISBN 0-313-22575-3, DOLR). Greenwood.

Lewis, Joseph. Lincoln the Atheist. 1979. pap. 3.00. Am Atheist.

Neely, Mark E., Jr. The Abraham Lincoln Encyclopedia. (Illus.). 448p. 1981. write for info (ISBN 0-07-046145-7, P&RB). McGraw.

Randall, James G. Lincoln & the South. LC 80-22084. (The Walter Lynwood Fleming Lectures in Southern History, L. S. U.). (Illus.). viii, 161p. 1980. Repr. of 1946 ed. lib. bdg. 18.75x (ISBN 0-313-22843-4, RALS). Greenwood.

LINCOLN, ABRAHAM, PRES. U. S., 1809-1865–ASSASSINATION

Buckingham, J. E., Sr. Reminiscences & Souvenirs of the Assassination of Abraham Lincoln. LC 80-128964. (Illus.). 89p. 22.50 (ISBN 0-686-28744-4); pap. 17.50 (ISBN 0-686-28745-2). J L Barbour.

Lattimer, John K. Lincoln & Kennedy: Medical & Ballistic Comparisons of Their Assassinations. 1980. 19.95 (ISBN 0-15-152281-2). HarBraceJ.

McCarty, Burke. The Suppressed Truth About the Assassination of Abraham Lincoln. 255p. 1960. Repr. of 1870 ed. 10.00 (Pub. by Chedney). Alpine Ent.

LINCOLN, NANCY (HANKS), 1784-1818

Wilson, Dorothy C. Lincoln's Mothers. LC 80-950. 432p. 1981. 13.95 (ISBN 0-385-15146-2, Galilee). Doubleday.

LINCOLN, SARAH (BUSH) JOHNSTON, MRS., 1788-1869

Wilson, Dorothy C. Lincoln's Mothers. LC 80-950. 432p. 1981. 13.95 (ISBN 0-385-15146-2, Galilee). Doubleday.

LINE-ENGRAVING

see Engraving

LINEAR ALGEBRAS

see Algebras, Linear

LINEAR DIGITAL FILTERS (MATHEMATICS)

see Digital Filters (Mathematics)

LINEAR PERSPECTIVE

see Perspective

LINEAR PROGRAMMING

see also Recursive Programming

Bonini, Charles P. Computer Models for Decision Analysis. (Illus.). 148p. (Orig.). 1980. pap. text ed. 13.50x (ISBN 0-89426-042-1); tchrs'. ed. 12.50x (ISBN 0-89426-043-X). Scientific Pr.

Cambanis, S. & Miller, Grady. Linear Problems in P-th Order & Stable Processes. 49p. 1980. pap. 1.60 (1272). U of NC Pr.

Rothnberg, Ronald I. Linear Programming. 1979. 22.95 (North Holland). Elsevier.

Schrage, Linus. Linear Programming Models: With Illustrations Using LINDO. (Illus.). 288p. (Orig.). 1981. pap. text ed. 16.00x (ISBN 0-89426-031-6); tchrs'. ed. 16.00x (ISBN 0-89426-033-2). Scientific Pr.

LINEAR SPACES

see Vector Spaces

Fuhrmann, Paul A. Linear Systems & Operators in Hilbert Space. 336p. 1981. text ed. 44.95 (ISBN 0-07-022589-3). McGraw.

LINEAR SYSTEM THEORY

see System Analysis

LINEAR TOPOLOGICAL SPACES

Graves, William H. Conference on Integration, Topology and Geometry in Linear Spaces: Proceedings, Vol. 2. LC 80-25417. (Contemporary Mathematics Ser.). 1980. 14.00 (ISBN 0-8218-5002-4). Am Math.

LINEAR VECTOR SPACES

see Vector Spaces

LINGUA FRANCA

see Languages, Mixed

LINGUISTIC ANALYSIS

see Analysis (Philosophy)

LINGUISTIC RESEARCH

Brame, Michael. Essays on Binding & Fusion. (Linguistics Research Monograph: Vol. 4). 1981. text ed. 32.00 (ISBN 0-932998-04-6). Noit Amrofer.

LINGUISTICS

Here are entered works dealing with the scientific study of human speech, including phonetics, phonemics, morphology, and syntax. Works dealing with language in general, the origin and history of language and surveys of languages, are entered under the heading Language and Languages.

see also Grammar, Comparative and General; Phonetics; Sociolinguistics

Adler, Melvin J. A Pragmatic Logic for Commands. (Pragmatics & Beyond Ser.: No.3). 139p. 1980. pap. text ed. 17.25x (ISBN 90-272-2501-X). Humanities.

Arlotto, Anthony. Introduction to Historical Linguistics. LC 80-6309. 284p. 1981. lib. bdg. 19.75 (ISBN 0-8191-1459-6); pap. text ed. 10.25 (ISBN 0-8191-1460-X). U Pr of Amer.

Crane, et al. An Introduction to Linguistics. 320p. (Orig.). 1981. pap. text ed. 11.95 (ISBN 0-316-16015-6). Little.

Donaldson, T. Ngiyambaa: The Language of the Wangaaybuwan. LC 79-7646. (Cambridge Studies in Linguistics: No. 29). (Illus.). 320p. 1980. 59.50 (ISBN 0-521-22524-8). Cambridge U Pr.

Falk, Julia S. Language & Linguistics: Bases for a Curriculum. (Language in Education Ser.: No. 10). 1978. pap. text ed. 2.95 (ISBN 0-87281-088-7). Ctr Appl Ling.

Ferre, Frederick. Language, Logic, & God: With a New Preface. viii, 184p. 1981. pap. text ed. 6.50x (ISBN 0-226-24456-3). U of Chicago Pr.

Fortescue, Michael D. A Discourse Production Model for Twenty Queations. (Pragmatics & Beyond Ser.: No.2). 145p. 1980. pap. text ed. 17.25x (ISBN 90-272-2505-2). Humanities.

Goospeed, Robert C. From Greek to Graffiti. (Illus.). 288p. (Orig.). 1981. 15.00 (ISBN 0-682-49696-0, University); pap. 10.00 (ISBN 0-682-49706-1, University). Exposition.

Kress, Gunther. Language As Ideology. 1981. pap. price not set (ISBN 0-7100-0795-7). Routledge & Kegan.

Kruijsen, Joep, ed. Liber Amicorum Weijnen: A Collection on Essays Presented to Professor Dr. A. Weijnen on the Occasion of His Seventieth Birthday. 396p. 1980. pap. text ed. 42.75 (ISBN 90-232-1749-7). Humanities.

Ladefoged, Peter. Preliminaries to Linguistic Phonetics. pap. 5.00 (ISBN 0-226-46787-2). U of Chicago Pr.

Leech, G. N. & Short, M. H. Style in Fiction. (English Language Ser.). 384p. 1981. text ed. 32.00 (ISBN 0-582-29102-X); pap. text ed. 16.95 (ISBN 0-582-29103-8). Longman.

Leib, Hans-Heinrich. International Linguistics: Volume 5, Morphology & Morphosemant-Tics. (Current Issues in Linguistic Theory Ser.: No. 17). 250p. 1981. text ed. 27.50x (ISBN 90-272-3508-2). Humanities.

Maquet, J., ed. On Linguistic Anthropology: Essays in Honor of Harry Hoijer, 1979. LC 80-50214. (Other Realities Ser.: Vol. 2). 140p. text ed. 12.00; pap. text ed. 9.00. Undena Pubns.

Martin, Laura. Papers in Mayan Linguistics. 6.00. Lucas.

Moulton, Janice & Robinson, George M. Organization of Language. LC 80-19052. 400p. Date not set. 42.50 (ISBN 0-521-23129-9); pap. 14.95 (ISBN 0-521-29851-2). Cambridge U Pr.

Nemoianu, Anca M. The Boat's Gonna Leave: A Study of Children Learning a Second Language from Conversations with Other Children. (Pragmatics & Beyond: No.13). 122p. 1980. pap. text ed. 17.25x (ISBN 90-272-2507-9). Humanities.

Pierce, Joe E. Development of Linguistic System in English Speaking American Children, Vol. 2. 185p. (Orig.). 1981. pap. 8.95 (ISBN 0-913244-51-1). Hapi Pr.

--A Theory of Language, Culture & Human Behavior. 161p. 1972. pap. 7.95. Hapi Pr.

Prideaux, G. Experimental Linguistics: Integration of Theories & Applications. (Story-Scientia Linguistics Ser.: No. 3). 1980. text ed. 57.75x (ISBN 90-6439-164-5). Humanities.

Queneau, Raymond. Exercises in Style. 2nd ed. Wright, Barbara, tr. from Fr. LC 80-26102. Orig. Title: Exercises De Style. (Illus.). 208p. 1981. 12.95 (ISBN 0-8112-0803-6); pap. 4.95 (ISBN 0-8112-0789-7, ND513). New Directions.

Sturtevant, E. H. Linguistic Change. 183p. 1980. Repr. of 1942 ed. lib. bdg. 30.00 (ISBN 0-89987-765-6). Darby Bks.

Tavakolian, Susan, ed. Language Acquisition & Linguistic Theory. (Illus.). 336p. 1981. text ed. 19.95x (ISBN 0-262-20039-2). MIT Pr.

Vershueren, Jef. On Speech Act Verbs. (Pragmatics & Beyond: No.4). 91p. 1980. pap. text ed. 17.25x (ISBN 90-272-2508-7). Humanities.

Weijnen, A., ed. Atlas Linguarum Europae-Ale. 216p. 1980. text ed. 22.50 (ISBN 90-232-1697-0). Humanities.

LINGUISTICS–ADDRESSES, ESSAYS, LECTURES

Transactions of the Philological Society 1980. 224p. 1981. 35.00x (ISBN 0-631-12574-4, Pub. by Basil Blackwell). Biblio Dist.

LINGUISTICS–DATA PROCESSING

Kolers, Paul A., et al, eds. Processing of Visible Language, Vol. 2. 620p. 1980. 49.50 (ISBN 0-306-40576-8, Plenum Pr). Plenum Pub.

LINGUISTICS–PROGRAMMED INSTRUCTION

Stork, F. C. & Widdowson, J. D. Learning About Linguistics. 1980. pap. text ed. 8.50x (ISBN 0-09-118061-9, Hutchinson U Lib). Humanities.

LIONS

Overbeck, Cynthia. Lions. (Lerner Natural Science Bks.). (Illus.). (gr. 4-10). 1981. PLB 7.95 (ISBN 0-8225-1463-X). Lerner Pubns.

LIPAN INDIANS

see Indians of North America–Southwest, New

LIPID METABOLISM

Christie, W. W., ed. Lipid Metabolism in Ruminant Animals. (Illus.). 464p. 1981. 70.00 (ISBN 0-08-023789-4). Pergamon.

LIPIDOSIS

Schwandt, Med P. Preventing Arterial Lipidoses. 300p. 1981. 27.50 (ISBN 0-87527-232-0). Green.

LIPIDS

see also Lipid Metabolism; Lipoproteins; Steroids

Weete, John D. & Weber, Darrell J. Lipid Biochemistry of Fungi & Other Organisms. 400p. 1980. 45.00 (ISBN 0-306-40570-9, Plenum Pr). Plenum Pub.

LIPOIDOSIS

see Lipidosis

LIPOPROTEINS

Scanu, Angelo M. & Landsberger, Frank R., eds. Lipoprotein Structure. (N.Y. Academy of Sciences Annals: Vol. 348). 436p. 1980. 76.00x (ISBN 0-89766-082-X). NY Acad Sci.

LIP-READING

see Deaf–Means of Communication

LIQUEFACTION OF GASES

see Gases–Liquefaction

LIQUID ASSETS

see Liquidity (Economics)

LIQUID CHROMATOGRAPHY

Horvath, Csaba, ed. High Performance Liquid Chromatography: Advances & Perspectives, Vol. 2. 1980. lib ed 39.50 (ISBN 0-12-312202-3). Acad Pr.

Kabra, Pokar & Marton, Laurence J., eds. Liquid Chromotography in Clinical Analysis. LC 80-84083. (Biological Methods Ser.). 352p. 1981. 49.50 (ISBN 0-89603-026-1). Humana.

Knox, John H. High Performance Liquid Chromatography. 205p. 1981. pap. 17.00x (ISBN 0-85224-383-9, Pub. by Edinburgh U Pr Scotland). Columbia U Pr.

Runser, Dennis J. Maintaining & Troubleshooting HPLC Systems: A Users Guide. 208p. 1981. 22.50 (ISBN 0-471-06479-3, Pub. by Wiley Interscience). Wiley.

LIQUID CRYSTALS

Bata, L., ed. Advances in Liquid Crystal Research & Applications: Proceedings of the Third Liquid Crystal Conference of the Socialist Countries, Budapest, 27-31 August 1979. 1000p. 1981. 170.00 (ISBN 0-08-026191-4). Pergamon.

Helfreich, W. & Heppke, G. Liquid Crystals of One- & Two-Dimensional Order: Proceedings. (Springer Series in Chemical Physics: Vol. 11). (Illus.). 416p. 1981. 39.50 (ISBN 0-387-10399-6). Springer-Verlag.

LIQUID FUELS

see also Petroleum As Fuel; Petroleum Products

Stewart, G. A., et al. The Potential for Liquid Fuels from Agriculture & Forestry in Australia. 147p. 1980. pap. 7.50 (ISBN 0-643-00353-3, Pub. by SIRO Australia). Intl Schol Bk Serv.

LIQUID METALS

see also Mercury

Luscher, E. & Coufal, H., eds. Liquid & Amorphous Metals: Mechanics of Plastic Solids. (NATO-Advanced Study Institute Ser.). 672p. 1980. 75.00x (ISBN 9-0286-0680-7). Sijthoff & Noordhoff.

Ubbelohde, A. R. The Molten State of Matter: Melting & Crystal Structure. LC 77-28300. 454p. 1979. 68.95 (ISBN 0-471-99626-2). Wiley.

LIQUIDITY (ECONOMICS)

see also Monetary Policy

Willett, Thomas D. International Liquidity Issues. 1980. pap. 5.25 (ISBN 0-8447-3388-1). Am Enterprise.

LIQUOR INDUSTRY

see Distilling Industries

LIQUOR INDUSTRY AND TRADE

see also Hotels, Taverns, Etc.

Shanken, Marvin R. The Impact American Beer Market Review & Forecast: Nineteen-Eighty-One Edition. 2nd ed. (Illus.). 60p. 1981. pap. price not set (ISBN 0-918076-15-3). Tasco.

--The Impact American Distilled Spirits Market Review & Forecast: Nineteen-Eighty-One Edition. 6th ed. (Illus.). 60p. 1981. pap. price not set (ISBN 0-918076-14-5). Tasco.

--The Impact American Wine Market Review & Forecast: Nineteen-Eighty-One Edition. 7th ed. (Illus.). 60p. 1981. pap. price not set (ISBN 0-918076-13-7). Tasco.

LIQUOR PROBLEM

see also Alcohol and Youth; Alcoholics; Alcoholism; Hotels, Taverns, etc.; Prohibition; Temperance

Fairchild, Daniel, et al. Everything You Always Wanted to Know About Drinking Problems & Then a Few Things You Didn't Want to Know. 7.50 (ISBN 0-932194-04-4). Green Hill.

LIQUORS

see also Distillation

also names of liquors, e.g. Brandy

Stewart, Hilary. Wild Teas, Coffees, & Cordials. (Illus.). 128p. 1981. 7.95 (ISBN 0-295-95804-9). U of Wash Pr.

LISTENING

Wakefield, Norman. Listening. 1981. pap. 4.95 (ISBN 0-8499-2920-2). Word Bks.

LISTERIOSIS

Seeliger, Heinz P. Listeriosis. 2nd ed. 1961. 15.50 (ISBN 0-02-852020-3). Hafner.

LITERARY CHARACTERS

see Characters and Characteristics in Literature

LITERARY CRITICISM

see Criticism

LITERARY PROPERTY

see Copyright

LITERARY SKETCH

see Essay

LITERARY STYLE

see Style, Literary

LITERARY TERMS

see Literature–Terminology

LITERATURE

Here are entered works dealing with literature in general, not limited to Esthetics, Philosophy, history or any one aspect.

see also Anthologies; Authorship; Autobiography; Biography (As a Literary Form); Books and Reading; Children's Literature (Collections); College Readers; Copyright; Creation (Literary, Artistic, etc.); Criticism; Drama; Essays; Fairy Tales; Fiction; Folk Literature; Gothic Literature; Humanism; Legends; Letters; Poetry; Prose Literature; Quotations; Realism in Literature; Religious Literature; Romanticism; Style, Literary; Tales; Wit and Humor

also Bible in Literature; Children in Literature; Love in Literature; Trees in Literature; and similar headings; also national literatures, e.g. English Literature

Handicrafts of India. 60.00 (ISBN 0-7069-0735-3, Pub. by Vikas India). Advent Bk.

Hartman, Geoffrey H. Saving the Texts: Literature-Derrida-Philosophy. LC 80-21748. (Illus.). 190p. 1981. text ed. 12.95x (ISBN 0-8018-2452-4). Johns Hopkins.

Lehmann, Winfred P., et al. Introduction to Scholarship in Modern Languages & Literatures. Gibaldi, Joseph, ed. 160p. 1981. 10.50x (ISBN 0-87352-092-0); pap. 6.00x (ISBN 0-87352-093-9). Modern Lang.

Rudman, Jack. Literature. (Undergraduate Program Field Test Ser.: UPFT-14). (Cloth bdg. avail. on request). pap. 9.95 (ISBN 0-8373-6014-5). Natl Learning.

LITERATURE–ADDRESSES, ESSAYS, LECTURES

see also Literature–History and Criticism

Fothergwill, Brian, ed. Essays by Divers Hands: Being the Transactions of the Royal Society of Literature. (New Series: Vol. XLI). 147p. 1980. 22.50x (ISBN 0-8476-3530-9). Rowman.

Oates, Joyce C. Contraries: Essays. 192p. 1981. 15.00 (ISBN 0-19-502884-8). Oxford U Pr.

LITERATURE–ANTHOLOGIES

see Anthologies

LITERATURE–BIBLIOGRAPHY

Erdman, David V., et al, eds. The Romantic Movement: A Selective & Critical Bibliography for Nineteen Seventy-Nine. LC 80-8494. 350p. 1980. lib. bdg. 35.00 (ISBN 0-8240-9512-X). Garland Pub.

Grimes, Janet & Daims, Diva. Novels in English by Women, 1891 to 1920: A Preliminary Checklist. Robinson, Doris, ed. LC 79-7911. 800p. 1981. lib. bdg. 75.00 (ISBN 0-8240-9522-7). Garland Pub.

Magill, Frank N., ed. Magill Books Index. LC 80-53597. 800p. 1980. 35.00 (ISBN 0-89356-200-9). Salem Pr.

Radcliffe, Elsa J. Gothic Novels of the Twentieth Century: An Annotated Bibliography. LC 78-24357. 291p. 1979. lib. bdg. 13.00 (ISBN 0-8108-1190-1). Scarecrow.

Terry, Garth M. East European Languages & Literatures: A Subject & Name Index to Articles in English-Language Journals, 1900-1977. 275p. 1978. 47.50. ABC-Clio.

Welch, Jeffrey. Liturature & Film: An Annotated Bibliography, 1900 to 1977. LC 80-8509. 350p. 1981. lib. bdg. 40.00 (ISBN 0-8240-9478-6). Garland Pub.

Worthington, Greville. A Bibliography of the Waverly Novels. 143p. 1980. Repr. of 1931 ed. lib. bdg. 30.00 (ISBN 0-8495-5655-4). Arden Lib.

LITERATURE–BIOGRAPHY

see Authors

LITERATURE–COLLECTIONS

Here are entered general collections. For collections limited to specific periods see subdivisions below, e.g. Literature, Medieval; Literature, Modern.

Bain, Carl E., et al, eds. The Norton Introduction to Literature. 3rd ed. 1536p. 1981. pap. text ed. 11.95x (ISBN 0-393-95146-4); classroom guide avail. (ISBN 0-393-95158-8). Norton.

Hrabal, Bohmil. Closely Watched Trains. (Writers from the Other Europe Ser.). 1981. pap. 3.95 (ISBN 0-14-005808-7). Penguin.

Kimmey, John & Brown, Ashley, eds. The World of Tragedy. 1981. pap. 3.95 (ISBN 0-451-61991-9, ME1991, Ment). NAL.

Plimpton, George, ed. Writers at Work, Vol. 5. (Writers at Work Ser.). 416p. 1981. pap. 8.95 (ISBN 0-14-005818-4). Penguin.

Sklar, Morty, intro. by. Cross-Fertilization: The Human Spirit As Place. (Contemporary Anthology Ser.: No. 3). (Illus.). 64p. 1980. pap. 2.50 (ISBN 0-930370-10-4) (ISBN 0-930370-10-4). Spirit That Moves.

LITERATURE–ESTHETICS

see also Style, Literary

Falk, Eugene H. The Poetics of Roman Ingarden. LC 79-29655. 272p. 1980. 20.00x (ISBN 0-8078-1436-9); pap. 11.00x (ISBN 0-8078-4068-8). U of NC Pr.

LITERATURE–EVALUATION

see Bibliography–Best Books; Books and Reading; Criticism; Literature–History and Criticism

LITERATURE–HISTORY AND CRITICISM

see also Authors; Literature–Addresses, Essays, Lectures

Anozie, Sunday O. Structural Models & African Poetics: Towards a Pragmatic View of Literature. 220p. 1981. 37.50 (ISBN 0-7100-0467-2). Routledge & Kegan.

Barnet, et al. An Introduction to Literature. 7th ed. 1981. pap. text ed. 9.95 (ISBN 0-316-08211-2); tchrs'. manual free (ISBN 0-316-08212-0). Little.

Binion, Rudolph. Soundings. 275p. 1981. 18.95 (ISBN 0-914434-16-0); pap. 8.95 (ISBN 0-914434-17-9). Psychohistory Pr.

Birnbaum, Henrik & Eekman, Thomas. Fiction & Drama in Eastern & Southeastern Europe: Evolution & Experiment in the Postwar Period. (UCLA Slavic Studies: Vol. 1). ix, 463p. 1980. 24.95 (ISBN 0-89357-064-8). Slavica.

Croce, Benedetto. Benedetto Croce's Poetry & Literature: An Introduction to the Criticism & History of Poetry & Literature. Gullace, Giovanni, tr. from Ital. & intro. by. LC 80-19511. 1981. 24.95x (ISBN 0-8093-0982-3). S Ill U Pr.

Davis, Robert C., ed. The Fictional Father: Lacanian Readings of the Text. LC 80-26222. 240p. 1981. lib. bdg. 15.00x (ISBN 0-87023-111-1). U of Mass Pr.

Di Girolamo, Costanzo. A Critical Theory of Literature. 1981. 15.00 (ISBN 0-299-08120-6). U of Wis Pr.

Florida State University Conference on Literature & Films, Fourth. Ideas of Order in Literature & Film: Selected Papers. Ruppert, Peter, et al, eds. LC 80-2601. xiii, 135p. (Orig.). 1981. pap. 8.00 (ISBN 0-8130-0699-6). U Presses Fla.

Forastieri-Braschi, Eduardo & Guiness, Gerald. On Text & Context: Methodological Approaches to the Context of Literature. LC 79-18001. 1980. pap. write for info. (ISBN 0-8477-3194-4). U of PR Pr.

Frane, Jeff. Fritz Leiber. (Starmont Reader's Guide Ser.: No. 8). 64p. 1980. lib. bdg. 9.95 (ISBN 0-89370-039-8). Borgo Pr.

Garvin, Harry, ed. Romanticism, Modernism, Postmodernism: Vol. 25, No. 2. LC 79-50103. (Bucknell Review Ser.). 192p. 1980. 12.00 (ISBN 0-8387-5004-4). Bucknell U Pr.

Graff, Gerald. Literature Against Itself: Literary Ideas in Modern Society. LC 78-9879. x, 250p. 1981. pap. 5.95 (ISBN 0-226-30598-8). U of Chicago Pr.

Hall, Sharon, ed. Twentieth-Century Literary Criticism. (Twentieth-Century Literary Criticism Ser.: Vol. 4). 650p. 1981. 58.00 (ISBN 0-8103-0178-4). Gale.

Halle, Louis J. The Search for an Eternal Norm: As Represented by Three Classics. LC 80-5793. 220p. 1981. lib. bdg. 18.75 (ISBN 0-8191-1444-8); pap. text ed. 9.75 (ISBN 0-8191-1445-6). U Pr of Amer.

Holdom, Lynne. Capsule Reviews. LC 80-20445. 51p. 1980. Repr. of 1977 ed. lib. bdg. 9.95 (ISBN 0-89370-056-8). Borgo Pr.

Kazin, Alfred. Contemporaries, from the Nineteenth Century to the Presen. rev. ed. 500p. 1981. 17.95 (ISBN 0-8180-1131-9); pap. 9.95 (ISBN 0-8180-1132-7). Horizon.

Lodge, David. Working with Structuralism: Essays & Reviews on Nineteenth & Twentieth-Century Literature. 240p. 1981. 30.00 (ISBN 0-7100-0658-6). Routledge & Kegan.

Lutyens, David B. The Creative Encounter. 200p. 1980. Repr. of 1960 ed. lib. bdg. 30.00 (ISBN 0-89987-506-8). Darby Bks.

Marble, Annie R. Pen Names & Personalities. 256p. 1980. Repr. of 1930 ed. lib. bdg. 30.00 (ISBN 0-89987-563-7). Century Bookbindery.

Martin, Graham. The Architecture of Experience. 256p. 1981. 26.50x (ISBN 0-85224-409-6, Pub. by Edinburgh U Pr Scotland). Columbia U Pr.

Martinez-Bonati, Felix. Fictive Discourse & the Structures of Literature: A Phenomenological Approach. rev. exp. ed. Silver, Philip W., tr. from Span. (Illus.). 200p. 1981. 15.00x (ISBN 0-8014-1308-7). Cornell U Pr.

New Writing & Writers, Vol. 17. 1980. pap. 5.95 (ISBN 0-7145-3695-4). Riverrun NY.

Porter, Carolyn. Seeing & Being: The Plight of the Participant-Observer in Emerson, Jones, Adams, Faulkner. 400p. 1981. 22.50x (ISBN 0-8195-5054-X). Wesleyan U Pr.

Ratliff, William F. Creaciones y Creadores: A Basic Literary Reader. 128p. 1981. pap. text ed. 7.95 (ISBN 0-394-32654-7). Random.

Seyler & Wilan. Introduction to Literature. 1981. 10.95 (ISBN 0-88284-113-0). Alfred Pub.

Torgovnick, Marianna. Closure in the Novel. LC 80-8581. 272p. 1981. 16.50x (ISBN 0-691-06464-4). Princeton U Pr.

LITERATURE–MORAL AND RELIGIOUS ASPECTS

see Religion and Literature

LITERATURE–SELECTIONS

see Literature–Collections

LITERATURE–STORIES, PLOTS, ETC.

Kolar, Carol K., compiled by. Plot Summary Index. 2nd rev. & enl. ed. LC 80-27112. 544p. 1981. 25.00 (ISBN 0-8108-1392-0). Scarecrow.

LITERATURE–STUDY AND TEACHING

Gibaldi, Joseph & Mirollo, James V., eds. Teaching Apprentice Programs in Language & Literature. (Options for Teaching Ser.: No. 4). 160p. (Orig.). 1981. pap. 7.00x (ISBN 0-87352-303-2). Modern Lang.

LITERATURE-STYLE
see Style, Literary
LITERATURE-TERMINOLOGY
Scott, A. F., ed. Current Literary Terms. 324p. Repr. of 1980 ed. lib. bdg. 14.95x (ISBN 0-312-17956-1). St Martin.
LITERATURE-TRANSLATING
see Translating and Interpreting
LITERATURE, ANCIENT-HISTORY AND CRITICISM
Ullman, Berthold L. Ancient Writing & Its Influence. (Medieval Academy Reprints for Teaching Ser.). 260p. 1981. pap. 7.50x (ISBN 0-8020-6435-3). U of Toronto Pr.
LITERATURE, APOCALYPTIC
see Apocalyptic Literature
LITERATURE, COMIC
see Comedy
LITERATURE, COMPARATIVE
Comparative Literature Symposium, No. 12. Shakespeare's Art from a Comparative Perspective: Proceedings. Aycock, Wendell M., ed. (Proceedings of the Comparative Literature Symposium). (Illus.). 197p. (Orig.). 1981. pap. write for info. (ISBN 0-89672-081-0). Tex Tech Pr.
LITERATURE, COMPARATIVE-THEMES, MOTIVES
see also Fairy Tales-Classification; Folk Literature-Themes, Motives;
also specific subjects in Literature e.g. Negroes in Literature; Social Problems in Literature; names of literary themes, e.g. Perceval (Romances, etc.)
Hayward, C. The Courtesan: The Part She Has Played in Classical & Modern Literature & in Life. Winick, Charles, ed. LC 78-60872. (Prostitution Ser.: Vol. 7). (Illus.). 492p. 1979. lib. bdg. 40.00 (ISBN 0-8240-9721-1). Garland Pub.
LITERATURE, COMPARATIVE-ENGLISH AND CHINESE
Deeney, John J., ed. Chinese-Western Comparative Literature & Strategy. 220p. 1981. 17.50 (ISBN 0-295-95810-3, Pub. by Chinese Univ Hong Kong). U of Wash Pr.
LITERATURE, LEGAL
see Legal Literature
LITERATURE, MEDIEVAL
Wallace-Hadrill, J. M., tr. The Fourth Book of the Chronicle of Fredegar with Its Continuations. LC 80-28086. (Medieval Classics Ser.). (Illus.). lxvii, 137p. 1981. Repr. of 1960 ed. lib. bdg. 27.50x (ISBN 0-313-22741-1, WAFRE). Greenwood.
LITERATURE, MEDIEVAL-HISTORY AND CRITICISM
Bakere, Jane A. The Cornish Ordinalia: A Critical Study. 191p. 1980. text ed. 50.00x (ISBN 0-7083-0745-0). Verry.
Benson, Larry D & Leyerle, John, eds. Chivalric Literature: Essays on Relations Between Literature and Life in the Later Middle Ages. LC 80-17514. (Studies in Medieval Culture: XIV). (Illus.). 176p. (Orig.). 1980. pap. 10.80 (ISBN 0-918720-09-5). Medieval Inst.
Knapp, Peggy A. & Stugrin, Michael A., eds. Assays: Critical Approaches to Medieval & Renaissance Texts, Vol. 1. LC 80-54059. 200p. 1981. 15.95x (ISBN 0-8229-3439-6). U of Pittsburgh Pr.
LITERATURE, MODERN (COLLECTIONS)
Beckett, Samuel, et al. New Writing & Writers Thirteen. 1980. pap. 6.00 (ISBN 0-7145-3541-9). Riverrun NY.
Boll, Heinrich, et al. New Writing & Writers Fifteen. 1980. pap. 6.00 (ISBN 0-7145-3561-3). Riverrun NY.
Burroughs, William, et al. New Writing & Writers Sixteen. 1980. pap. 6.00 (ISBN 0-7145-3638-5). Riverrun NY.
Varady, Tibor, et al. New Writing & Writers Eighteen. 1980. pap. 6.00 (ISBN 0-7145-3815-9). Riverrun NY.
LITERATURE, MODERN (COLLECTIONS)-15TH AND 16TH CENTURIES
Kullen, Patrick & Roche, Thomas P., Jr., eds. Spenser Studies: A Renaissance Poetry Annual, Vol. II. (Illus.). 320p. 1981. 20.95x (ISBN 0-8229-3433-7). U of Pittsburgh Pr.
Travitsky, Betty, compiled by. The Paradise of Women: Writings by Englishwomen of the Renaissance. LC 80-1705. (Contributions in Women's Studies: No. 22). 312p. 1981. lib. bdg. 29.95 (ISBN 0-313-22177-4, TPW/). Greenwood.
LITERATURE, MODERN (COLLECTIONS)-20TH CENTURY
Sklar, Morty & Mulac, Jim, eds. Editor's Choice: Literature & Graphics from the U. S. Small Press, 1965-1977. LC 79-64861. (Contemporary Anthology Ser.: No. 2). (Illus.). 501p. 1980. 14.50 (ISBN 0-930370-05-8); pap. 9.50 (ISBN 0-930370-04-X); signed, numbered ed. 25.00 (ISBN 0-930370-06-6). Spirit That Moves.
LITERATURE, MODERN-DICTIONARIES, INDEXES, ETC.
Klein, Leonard S., ed. Encyclopedia of World Literature in the Twentieth Century. 2nd rev. ed. (Illus.). Date not set. 75.00 (ISBN 0-8044-3135-3). Ungar.
LITERATURE, MODERN-HISTORY AND CRITICISM
see also Baroque Literature-History and Criticism
Bartlett, Lee. The Beats: Essays in Criticism. LC 80-28179. 250p. 1981. lib. bdg. write for info (ISBN 0-89950-026-9). McFarland & Co.
Madden, David & Powers, Richard. Writers' Revisions: An Annotated Bibliography of Articles & Books About Writers' Revisions & Their Comments on the Creative Process. LC 80-22942. 254p. 1981. 13.50 (ISBN 0-8108-1375-0). Scarecrow.
LITERATURE, MODERN-HISTORY AND CRITICISM-15TH AND 16TH CENTURIES
Knapp, Peggy A. & Stugrin, Michael A., eds. Assays: Critical Approaches to Medieval & Renaissance Texts, Vol. 1. LC 80-54059. 200p. 1981. 15.95x (ISBN 0-8229-3439-6). U of Pittsburgh Pr.
LITERATURE, MODERN-HISTORY AND CRITICISM-20TH CENTURY
see also Dadaism
Bond, et al. New Writing & Writers, No. 14. text ed. 13.00x. Humanities.
Duhamel, P. Albert. After Strange Fruit: Changing Literary Tastes in Post-World-War II Boston. write for info. Boston Public Lib.
Klein, Leonard S., ed. Encyclopedia of World Literature in the Twentieth Century. 2nd rev. ed. (Illus.). Date not set. 75.00 (ISBN 0-8044-3135-3). Ungar.
LITERATURE, PRIMITIVE
see Folk Literature
LITERATURE AND MUSIC
see Music and Literature
LITERATURE AND PSYCHOANALYSIS
see Psychoanalysis and Literature
LITERATURE AND RELIGION
see Religion and Literature
LITERATURE AND SOCIETY
Ziff, Larzer. Literary Democracy: The Declaration of Cultural Independence in America 1837-1861. 1981. 17.95 (ISBN 0-670-43026-9). Viking Pr.
LITERATURE AS A PROFESSION
see Authors; Authorship; Journalism; Journalists
LITHIUM
Berner, P., et al, eds. Aktuelle Perspektiven der Lithiumprophylaxe: Current Perspectives in Lithium Prophilaxis. (Bibliotheca Psychiatrica: No. 161). (Illus.). vi, 294p. 1981. pap. 90.00 (ISBN 3-8055-1753-X). S Karger.
Rossof, Arthur H. & Robinson, William A., eds. Lithium Effects of Granulopiesis & Immune Function. (Advances in Experimental Medicine & Biology Ser.: Vol. 127). 470p. 1980. 47.50 (ISBN 0-306-40359-5). Plenum Pub.
LITHOGRAPHS
Leiris, Michael & Mourlot, Fernand. Joan Miro, Lithographs, Vol. 1. (Illus.). 231p. 1972. 150.00x (ISBN 0-8148-0494-2, Pub. by Tudor). Hennessey.
LITHOGRAPHY
see also Offset Printing
Faux, Ian. Modern Lithography. (Illus.). 352p. 1978. pap. 15.95x (ISBN 0-7121-1294-4, Pub. by Macdonald & Evans England). Intl Ideas.
Hird. Introduction to Photo-Offset Lithography. 1981. text ed. price not set (ISBN 0-87002-336-5). Bennett Co.
LITHOLOGY
see Petrology
LITHOPRINTING
see Offset Printing
LITTLE, MALCOLM, 1925-1965
Wolfenstein, Eugene V. The Victims of Democracy: Malcolm X & the Black Revolution. 600p. 1981. 20.00 (ISBN 0-520-03903-3). U of Cal Pr.
LITTLE BIG HORN, BATTLE OF THE, 1876
Kain, Robert C. In the Valley of the Little Big Horn. rev. ed. (Illus.). 117p. 1978. 7.95 (ISBN 0-917714-16-4). Beinfeld Pub.
McGaw, Jessie B. Chief Red Horse Tells About Custer. (Illus.). 64p. (gr. 4 up). 1981. 8.95 (ISBN 0-525-66713-X). Elsevier-Nelson.
Masters, Joseph G. Shadows Fall Across the Little Horn: Custer's Last Stand. 62p. 1951. 20.00. South Pass Pr.
LITTLE LEAGUE BASEBALL, INC
Shirts, Morris A. Warm up for Little League Baseball. (Illus.). (gr. 3-6). 1977. pap. 1.75 (ISBN 0-671-41135-7). PB.
--Warm up for Little League Baseball. Date not set. pap. 1.95 (ISBN 0-671-42422-X). Archway.
LITTLE'S DISEASE
see Cerebral Palsy
LITURGICAL MOVEMENT
Here are entered works dealing with the revived interest in liturgical matters, which began about 1890 in Catholic circles and spread over to Protestantism.
Largo, Gerald A. Community & Liturgy: An Historical Overview. LC 80-1434. 151p. 1980. lib. bdg. 16.25 (ISBN 0-8191-1302-6); pap. text ed. 7.75 (ISBN 0-8191-1303-4). U Pr of Amer.
LITURGICS
see also Christian Art and Symbolism; Church Music; Fasts and Feasts; Liturgical Movement
Liturgy of St. John Chrysostom. (Eng. & Arab.). 1978. pap. 3.00 (ISBN 0-911726-39-X). Alleluia Pr.
Searle, Mark, ed. Liturgy & Social Justice. 1980. pap. write for info (ISBN 0-8146-1209-1). Liturgical Pr.
LITURGIES
see also Hymns; Liturgies; Mass; Ritual
also subdivision Liturgy and Ritual, or name of ritual, under names of churches, e.g. Catholic Church-Liturgy and Ritual; Church of England-Book of Common Prayer
Huse, Dennis & Watson, Geralyn. Speak Lord, I'm Listening. LC 80-70851. 176p. 1981. pap. 7.95 perfect bnd. (ISBN 0-87793-220-4). Ave Maria.
LITURGY
see Liturgics
LIVE POLIOVIRUS VACCINE
see Poliomyelitis Vaccine
LIVER-DISEASES
Berk, Paul D. & Chalmers, Thomas C., eds. Frontiers in Liver Disease. (Illus.). 300p. 1981. text ed. 35.00 (ISBN 0-86577-017-4). Thieme-Stratton.
Grases, Pedro J. & Beker G., Simon. Color Atlas of Liver Biopsy: A Clinical Pathological Guide. Orig. Title: Guia Practica De Biopsia Hepatica En el Adulto. (Illus.). 125p. 1981. write for info. (ISBN 0-8451-0209-5). A R Liss.
Koff, Raymond S. Liver Disease in Primary Care Medicine. 256p. 1980. 19.95x (ISBN 0-8385-5678-7). ACC.
Melnick, J. L. & Maupas, P., eds. Hepatitis B Virus & Primary Liver Cancer. (Progress in Medical Virology Ser.: Vol. 27). (Illus.). 250p. 1981. 90.00 (ISBN 3-8055-1784-X). S Karger.
Orr, Marsha E. Acute Pancreatic & Hepatic Dysfunction. Percy, R. Craig, ed. (The Fleschner Series in Critical Care Nursings). (Illus.). 175p. (Orig.). 1981. pap. text ed. 9.95 (ISBN 0-937878-04-9). Fleschner.
LIVER-SURGERY
Castaing, D., et al. Hepatic & Portal Surgery in the Rat. (Illus.). 184p. 1980. 37.50 (ISBN 0-89352-101-9). Masson Pub.
LIVESTOCK
see also Cattle; Goats; Horses; Pastures; Sheep
also headings beginning with the word Livestock
Fraser, Alistair & Thear, Katie, eds. Small Farmer's Guide to Raising Livestock & Poultry. (Illus.). 240p. 1981. 25.00 (ISBN 0-668-04687-2). Arco.
Gasser, J. K., et al, eds. Effluents from Livestock. (Illus.). v, 712p. 1980. 80.00x (ISBN 0-85334-895-2). Burgess-Intl Ideas.
Merkel, James A. Managing Livestock Wastes. (Illus.). 1981. text ed. 22.50 (ISBN 0-87055-373-9). AVI.
LIVESTOCK-DISEASES
see Veterinary Medicine
LIVING, COST OF
see Cost and Standard of Living
LIVINGSTONE, DAVID, 1813-1873
David Livingstone. (Ladybird Ser.). 1.49. Chr Lit.
LIZARDS
Hopf, Alice L. Biography of a Komodo Dragon. (A Nature Biography Book). (Illus.). 64p. (gr. 7-11). 1981. PLB 6.99 (ISBN 0-399-61140-1). Putnam.
LOAN SHARKING
see Interest and Usury; Loans, Personal
LOANS
see also Interest and Usury; Investments; Loans, Personal
Cohen, Benjamin & Basagni, Fabio, eds. Private Lending for Balance of Payments Purpose. (Atlantic Institute for International Affairs Ser.: No. 4). 265p. 1981. text ed. 31.50 (ISBN 0-86598-038-1). Allanheld.
Financing Goods. LC 57-7094. 609p. 1957. text ed. 20.00 (ISBN 0-9605500-0-3). A G Sweetser.
Mathis, F. John, ed. Offshore Lending by U. S. Commercial Banks. 2nd ed. LC 80-83082. (Illus.). 344p. 1980. 18.00 (ISBN 0-936742-01-1). R Morris Assocs.
Sweetser, Albert G. Bank Loans Secured by Field-Warehouse Receipts. LC 57-7980. 112p. (Orig.). 1957. pap. 5.00 (ISBN 0-9605500-1-1). A G Sweetser.
LOANS, PERSONAL
Wood, Oliver G., Jr. & Barksdale, William C. How to Borrow Money. 144p. 1981. text ed. 13.95 (ISBN 0-442-25204-8). Van Nos Reinhold.
LOBBYING
Ashworth, William. Under the Infulence: Congress, Lobbies, & the American Park Barreling System. 1981. pap. 7.95 (ISBN 0-8015-5929-4, Hawthorn). Dutton.
Dekieffer, Donald. How to Lobby Congress: A Guide for the Citizen Lobbyist. 228p. 1981. 12.95 (ISBN 0-396-07965-2); pap. 7.95 (ISBN 0-396-07969-5). Dodd.
Hayes, Michael J. Lobbyists & Legislators: A Theory of Political Markets. 256p. 1981. 18.00 (ISBN 0-8135-0910-6). Rutgers U Pr.
LOBSTERS
Stewart, Robert. A Living from Lobsters. 2nd ed. (Illus.). 70p. 9.75 (ISBN 0-85238-099-2, FN). Unipub.
LOCAL ADMINISTRATION
see Local Government
LOCAL ELECTIONS
see Elections
LOCAL GOVERNMENT
Here are entered works which deal with local government of districts, counties, townships, etc. Works dealing with government of municipalities only are entered under Municipal Government; those dealing with government of counties only are entered under County Government.
see also Cities and Towns; County Government; Elections; Mayors; Municipal Government; Public Administration; Villages
Baine, Sean. Community Action & Local Government. 96p. 1975. pap. text ed. 8.75x (ISBN 0-7135-1842-1, Pub. by Bedford England). Renouf.
Bryan, Frank M. Politics in Rural America: People, Parties, & Policy. (Special Study Ser.). 320p. (Orig.). lib. bdg. 26.50x (ISBN 0-89158-561-3); pap. text ed. 10.00x (ISBN 0-89158-984-8). Westview.
Burns, James M., et al. State & Local Politics: Government by the People. 3rd ed. (Illus.). 1981. 9.95f (ISBN 0-13-843516-2). P-H.
Davidson, Jeffrey L. Political Partnerships: Neighborhood Residents & Their Council Members. LC 79-13107. (City & Society Ser.: Vol. 5). (Illus.). 231p. 1979. pap. 8.95 (ISBN 0-8039-1051-7); pap. 8.95 (ISBN 0-8039-1051-7). Sage.
Foster, C. D., et al. Local Government Finance in a Unitary State. (Illus.). 640p. 1980. text ed. 60.00x (ISBN 0-04-336066-1, 2473). Allen Unwin.
Greenwood, Royston, et al. Patterns of Management in Local Government. (Government & Administration Ser.). 192p. 1981. 27.50x (ISBN 0-85520-244-0, Pub. by Martin Robertson England). Biblio Dist.
Hoggart, Keith. Geography & Local Administration: A Bibliography. (Public Administration Ser.: Bibliography P-530). 84p. 1980. pap. 9.00. Vance Biblios.
Jones, George, ed. New Approaches to the Study of Central-Local Government Relationships. 200p. 1980. text ed. 38.00x (ISBN 0-566-00332-5, Pub. by Gower Pr England). Renouf.
Kemp, Roger L. Coping with Proposition Thirteen. LC 80-8188. 1980. 21.95x (ISBN 0-669-03974-8). Lexington Bks.
Lefcoe, George, ed. Respective Roles of State & Local Governments in Land Policy & Taxation. (Lincoln Institute Monograph: No. 80-7). 271p. 1980. write for info. Lincoln Inst Land.
Peterson, Paul E. City Limits. 288p. 1981. lib. bdg. price not set (ISBN 0-226-66292-6); pap. price not set (ISBN 0-226-66293-4). U of Chicago Pr.
Rubinfeld, Daniel, ed. Essays on the Law & Economics of Local Governments. (Papers on Public Econmics Ser.: Vol. 3). 253p. (Orig.). 1980. pap. text ed. 7.50 (ISBN 0-87766-262-2, 27200). Urban Inst.
Zimmerman, Joseph F. State & Local Government. 3rd ed. (Illus., Orig.). pap. 4.95 (ISBN 0-06-460181-1, CO 181, COS). Har-Row.
LOCAL GOVERNMENT BONDS
see Municipal Bonds
LOCAL JUNIOR COLLEGES
see Community Colleges
LOCAL OFFICIALS AND EMPLOYEES
see also Municipal Officials and Employees
Davidson, Jeffrey L. Political Partnerships: Neighborhood Residents & Their Council Members. LC 79-13107. (City & Society Ser.: Vol. 5). (Illus.). 231p. 1979. pap. 8.95 (ISBN 0-8039-1051-7); pap. 8.95 (ISBN 0-8039-1051-7). Sage.
LOCAL TAXATION
Dworak, Robert J. Taxpayers, Taxes, & Government Spending: Perspectives on the Taxpayers Revolt. 272p. 1980. 24.95 (ISBN 0-03-056111-6); pap. 9.95 (ISBN 0-03-056109-4). Praeger.
Quindry, Kenneth E. & Schoening, Niles. State & Local Tax Performance Nineteen Seventy-Eight. rev. ed. 1980. pap. 3.00. S Regional Ed.
LOCAL TRANSIT
see also Street-Railroads; Subways
Hamilton, Neil W. & Hamilton, Peter R. Governance of Public Enterprise: A Case Study of Urban Mass Transit. LC 80-5349. 1981. 18.95. Lexington Bks.
OECD, ed. Urban Public Transport: Evaluation of Performance. (Road Research Ser.). (Illus.). 76p. 1980. pap. 5.50 (ISBN 9-2641-2127-7, 77-80-04-1). OECD.
Vuchic, Vukan. Urban Public Transportation. (Illus.). 672p. 1981. text ed. 38.95 (ISBN 0-13-939496-6). P-H.
LOCALIZATION OF CEREBRAL FUNCTIONS
see Brain-Localization of Functions
LOCATION OF FACTORIES
see Factories-Location
LOCATION OF INDUSTRIES
see Industries, Location Of
LOCKE, JOHN, 1632-1704
Locke, John. The Correspondence of John Locke: Vol. 5, Letters 1702-2198 Covering the Years 1694-1697. DeBeer, E. S., ed. 808p. 1979. text ed. 89.00x (ISBN 0-19-824562-9). Oxford U Pr.
LOCKHART, JOHN GIBSON, 1794-1854
Lockhead, Marian. John Gibson Lockhart. 324p. 1980. lib. bdg. 30.00 (ISBN 0-8482-1621-0). Norwood Edns.
LOCKOUTS
see Strikes and Lockouts

LOCOMOTION
see also Automobiles; Boats and Boating; Cycling; Horsemanship; Navigation; Transportation
Pauwels, F. Biomechanics of the Locomotor Apparatus. (Illus.). 520p. 1980. 175.90 (ISBN 0-387-09131-9). Springer-Verlag.
LOCOMOTIVE DIESELS
see Diesel Locomotives
LOCOMOTIVES
see also Diesel Locomotives
Ahron, E. L. British Steam Railway Locomotive: Volume I, 1825-1925. 29.50x (ISBN 0-392-07695-0, SpS). Soccer.
British Locomotive Names of the 20th Century. 15.95x (ISBN 0-392-07681-0, SpS). Soccer.
Halcroft, H. Locomotive Adventure, Vol. 2. 17.75x (ISBN 0-392-08040-0, SpS). Soccer.
LOCOMOTIVES–HISTORY
Articulated Locomotives of North America. 45.00. Chatham Pub CA.
Evans, Martin. Evening Star. (Illus.). 224p. (Orig.). 1980. pap. 16.50x (ISBN 0-85242-634-8). Intl Pubns Serv.
Hilton, George W. Monon Route. LC 78-52512. (Illus.). 468p. 1978. Repr. of 1978 ed. 30.00 (ISBN 0-8310-7115-X). Howell-North.
Koenig, Karl R. Virginia & Truckee Locomotives. LC 80-67819. (Illus.). 88p. 1980. pap. 14.00 (ISBN 0-89685-102-8). Chatham Pub CA.
Tuplin, W. A. The Steam Locomotive. 1980. text ed. 20.75 (ISBN 0-239-00198-2). Humanities.
LOCOMOTIVES–PICTORIAL WORKS
LeMassena, Robert A. Articulated Steam Locomotives of North America: A Catalogue of "Giant Steam". (Illus.). 416p. 45.00 (ISBN 0-913582-26-3). Sundance.
LOCUSTS
Dallinger, Jane. Grasshoppers. (Lerner Natural Science Bks.). (Illus.). (gr. 4-10). 1981. PLB 7.95 (ISBN 0-8225-1455-9). Lerner Pubns.
LOG CABINS
Goodall, Harrison & Friedman, Renee. Log Structures, Preservation & Problem-Solving. 120p. 1980. pap. 10.95 (ISBN 0-910050-46-5). AASLH.
LOGGING
see Lumbering
LOGGING RAILROADS
Last of the Three-Foot Loggers. 14.95. Chatham Pub CA.
They Felled the Redwoods. 15.00. Chatham Pub CA.
LOGIC
see also Identity; Induction (Logic); Knowledge, Theory Of; Logical Positivism; Modality (Logic); Probabilities; Reasoning; Thought and Thinking
Butrick, Richard. Deduction & Analysis. rev. ed. LC 80-6177. 121p. 1981. lib. bdg. 15.75 (ISBN 0-8191-1410-3); pap. text ed. 6.75 (ISBN 0-8191-1411-1). U Pr of Amer.
Finocchiaro, Maurice A. Galileo & the Art of Reasoning: Rhetorical Foundations of Logic & Scientific Method. (Philosophy of Science Studies: No. 61). 463p. 1980. lib. bdg. 42.00 (ISBN 90-277-1094-5, Pub. by D. Reidel); pap. 21.00 (ISBN 90-277-1095-3). Kluwer Boston.
Jeffrey, Richard C. Formal Logic: Its Scope & Limits. 2nd ed. (Illus.). 256p. 1981. text ed. 17.95 (ISBN 0-07-032321-6, C); instr's manual 5.95 (ISBN 0-07-032322-4). McGraw.
Longley, Peter. Contemporary Logic. LC 80-1443. 178p. (Orig.). 1981. pap. text ed. 8.75 (ISBN 0-8191-1458-8). U Pr of Amer.
Makrakis, Apostolos. Logic: An Orthodox Christian Approach. Orthodox Christian Educational Society, ed. Cummings, Denver, tr. from Hellenic. (The Logos & Holy Spirit in the Unity of Christian Thought Ser.: Vol. 3). 200p. 1977. pap. 3.50x (ISBN 0-938366-04-1). Orthodox Chr.
Peirce, Charles S. Chance, Love & Logic. 317p. 1980. Repr. of 1923 ed. lib. bdg. 50.00 (ISBN 0-89984-386-7). Century Bookbindery.
Russell, Bertrand. Mysticism & Logic & Other Essays. 2nd ed. 1980. pap. 5.95x. B&N.
Smith, J. E., ed. Integrated Injection Logic. LC 80-18841. 1980. 34.95 (ISBN 0-87942-137-1). Inst Electrical.
Volpe, Galvano D. Logic As a Positive Science. 288p. 1981. 19.95 (ISBN 0-8052-7096-5, Pub. by NLB England). Schocken.
LOGIC, DEDUCTIVE
see Logic
LOGIC, INDUCTIVE
see Induction (Logic)
LOGIC, SYMBOLIC AND MATHEMATICAL
see also Constructive Mathematics; Machine Theory; Probabilities; Reasoning; Recursive Functions; Science–Methodology; Semantics (Philosophy)
Halmos, Paul R. Algebraic Logic. LC 61-17955. 1962. 9.95 (ISBN 0-8284-0154-3). Chelsea Pub.
Hao, Wang. Popular Lectures on Mathematical Logic. 286p. 1981. text ed. 24.95 (ISBN 0-442-23109-1). Van Nos Reinhold.
Logic Colloquim '79 Leeds, August 1979, et al. Recursion Theory: Its Generalisations & Applications; Proceedings. Drake, F. R. & Wainer, S. S, eds. (London Mathematical Society Lecture Notes Ser.: No. 45). 300p. 1980. pap. 24.50 (ISBN 0-521-23543-X). Cambridge U Pr.
LOGIC AND FAITH
see Faith and Reason
LOGIC AND LANGUAGE
see Logical Positivism
LOGIC OF MATHEMATICS
see Mathematics–Philosophy
LOGICAL ANALYSIS
see Analysis (Philosophy)
LOGICAL POSITIVISM
see also Analysis (Philosophy); Semantics (Philosophy)
Hanfling, Oswald, ed. Essential Readings in Logical Positivism. 320p. 1981. pap. 14.95x (ISBN 0-631-12566-3, Dist. by Basil Blackwell). Biblio Dist.
LOGISTICS, INDUSTRIAL
see Shipment of Goods
LONDON–ANTIQUITIES
Marsden, Peter. Roman London. (Illus.). 224p. 1981. 19.95 (ISBN 0-500-25073-1). Thames Hudson.
LONDON–BIOGRAPHY
Swinnerton, Frank. The Bookman's London. (Illus.). 161p. 1980. Repr. of 1951 ed. lib. bdg. 30.00 (ISBN 0-8492-8129-6). R West.
LONDON–DESCRIPTION
Crookston, Peter. Village London. 190p. 1979. pap. 4.95 (ISBN 0-500-27150-X). Thames Hudson.
LONDON–DESCRIPTION–GUIDEBOOKS
Automobile Association & British Tourist Authority. A-Z Visitors' London Atlas & Guide. (Illus.). 96p. 1981. pap. write for info. (ISBN 0-85039-107-5, Pub. by Auto Assn-British Tourist Authority England). Merrimack Bk Serv.
British Tourist Authority. Discovering London's Villages. (Illus.). 72p. 1981. pap. write for info. (ISBN 0-85263-451-X, Pub. by Auto Assn-British Tourist Authority England). Merrimack Bk Serv.
LONDON–DIRECTORIES
Woodhead-Faulkner, ed. The City Directory 1980-81: An Investors Chronicle Guide to Financial & Professional Services Allied to the City of London. 432p. 1980. 45.00x (ISBN 0-85941-135-4, Pub. by Woodhead-Faulkner England); pap. 36.00x (ISBN 0-85941-136-2). State Mutual Bk.
LONDON–ECONOMIC CONDITIONS
Woodhead-Faulkner, ed. The City Directory 1980-81: An Investors Chronicle Guide to Financial & Professional Services Allied to the City of London. 432p. 1980. 45.00x (ISBN 0-85941-135-4, Pub. by Woodhead-Faulkner England); pap. 36.00x (ISBN 0-85941-136-2). State Mutual Bk.
LONDON–HISTORY
Crookston, Peter. Village London. 190p. 1979. pap. 4.95 (ISBN 0-500-27150-X). Thames Hudson.
McClure, Ruth K. Coram's Children: The London Foundling Hospital in the Eighteenth Century. LC 80-21375. (Illus.). 336p. 1981. text ed. 27.50 (ISBN 0-300-02465-7). Yale U Pr.
Samuel, Raphael, ed. East End Underworld, Vol. 2: The Life of Arthur Harding. (History Workshop Ser.). (Illus.). 400p. 1981. price not set (ISBN 0-7100-0725-6); pap. price not set (ISBN 0-7100-0726-4). Routledge & Kegan.
LONDON–HOSPITALS
McClure, Ruth K. Coram's Children: The London Foundling Hospital in the Eighteenth Century. LC 80-21375. (Illus.). 336p. 1981. text ed. 27.50 (ISBN 0-300-02465-7). Yale U Pr.
LONDON–MAPS
Automobile Association British Tourist Authority. A-Z London Map. (Illus.). 1981. pap. write for info. (ISBN 0-85039-021-4, Pub. by Auto Assn-British Tourist Authority England). Merrimack Bk Serv.
LONDON–PLAGUE
see Plague–London
LONDON–SOCIAL CONDITIONS
Greve, John. London's Homeless. 76p. 1964. pap. text ed. 3.75x (Pub. by Bedford England). Renouf.
Land, Hilarly. Large Families in London. 154p. 1969. pap. text ed. 6.25x (ISBN 0-7135-1577-5, Pub. by Bedford England). Renouf.
LONELINESS
see also Consolation
Cruz, Nicky & Harris, Madalene. Lonely, but Never Alone. 192p. (Orig.). 1981. pap. 5.95 (ISBN 0-310-43361-4). Zondervan.
Schmidt, Jay H. & Neimark, Paul. Good-Bye Loneliness. LC 77-16766. (Illus.). 192p. 1981. pap. 6.95 (ISBN 0-8128-6095-0). Stein & Day.
Wellington, Paul A., ed. Loneliness. 1980. pap. 2.50 (ISBN 0-8309-0287-2). Herald Hse.
Wright, Norman. An Answer to Loneliness. (Orig.). pap. 1.25 (ISBN 0-89081-077-X). Harvest Hse.
LONGEVITY
see also Aging; Middle Age; Old Age
Georgakas, Dan. The Methuselah Factors: Living Long & Living Well. 1981. 14.95 (ISBN 0-671-24064-1). S&S.
McQuade, Walter & Aikman, Ann. The Longevity Factor. 1981. pap. 2.95 (ISBN 0-671-81611-X). PB.
Moral Responsibility in Prolonging Life Decisions. 200p. (Orig.). 1981. pap. text ed. price not set (ISBN 0-935372-08-3). Pope John Ctr.
Parkinson, C. Northcote & LeCompte, Herman. The Law of Longer Life. (Illus.). 1980. 10.95 (ISBN 0-916624-31-5). TSU Pr.
LOOPS, PHASE-LOCKED
see Phase-Locked Loops
LOPE DE VEGA
see Vega Carpio, Lope Felix De, 1562-1635
LORD'S DAY
see Sabbath
LORD'S PRAYER
Bouley, Alan. From Freedom to Formula: The Evolution of the Eucharistic Prayer from Oral Improvisation to Written Text. (Studies in Christian Antiquity: Vol. 21). 288p. 1980. 25.00x (ISBN 0-8132-0554-9, Pub. by Cath U of America Pr). Intl Schol Bk.
Keller, Phillip, tr. Meditacoes De Um Leigo. (Portugese Bks.). (Port.). 1979. write for info. (ISBN 0-8297-0788-3). Life Pubs Intl.
Keller, Phillis, tr. Un Laico Examina el Padrenuestro. (Spanish Bks.). (Span.). 1978. 1.80 (ISBN 0-8297-0770-0). Life Pubs Intl.
Rommel, Kurt. Our Father Who Art in Heaven. Cooperrider, Edward A., tr. from Ger. LC 80-2373. 64p. 1981. pap. price not set (ISBN 0-8006-1448-8, 1-1448). Fortress.
Watson, Thomas. Lord's Prayer. 1973. 9.95 (ISBN 0-85151-145-7). Banner of Truth.
LORD'S PRAYER–JUVENILE LITERATURE
Lucy, Reda, pseud. The Lord's Prayer for Children. (Illus.). 24p. (Orig.). (ps-3). 1981. pap. 1.95 (ISBN 0-87516-437-4). De Vorss.
LORD'S SUPPER
see also Last Supper; Mass; Sacraments
Castro, Carol C. Welcoming Jesus: Adult Resource Book. 30p. (Orig.). 1979. pap. 1.05 adult resource bk.; Set. tchr's manual 0.75 (ISBN 0-697-01738-9). Wm C Brown.
Consultation on Church Union. World Bread Cup. 1978. 0.85 (ISBN 0-686-28801-7). Forward Movement.
Pope John Paul. Brazill - Journey in the Light of the Eucharist. 1980. write for info. (ISBN 0-8198-1102-5); pap. write for info. (ISBN 0-8198-1103-3). Dghtrs St Paul.
Riggle, H. M. Christian Baptism, Feet Washing & the Lord's Supper. 264p. 3.50. Faith Pub Hse.
LORD'S SUPPER–HISTORY
Marshall, I. Howard. Last Supper & Lord's Supper. (Orig.). 1981. pap. price not set (ISBN 0-8028-1854-4). Eerdmans.
LORIES
see Parrots
LORRIES (MOTOR VEHICLES)
see Motor-Trucks
LOS ANGELES–DESCRIPTION
Bullock, Paul, ed. Directory of Community Services Organizations in Greater Los Angeles. 255p. 1980. 6.50 (ISBN 0-89215-106-4). U Ca LA Indus Rel.
Burnett, William, ed. Views of Los Angeles. rev. ed. (Illus.). 1979. 24.95 (ISBN 0-9602274-1-5); pap. 14.95 (ISBN 0-9602274-0-7). Portriga Pubns.
Peck, David & Fine, David. L. A. Culture Quiz. (Illus.). 96p. (Orig.). 1981. 5.95 (ISBN 0-935232-07-9); pap. 3.95 (ISBN 0-935232-06-0). Deep River Pr.
Robert Lang Adams & Associates, ed. The Los Angeles Job Bank: A Comprehensive Guide to Major Employers Throughout Greater Los Angeles. (Job Bank Ser.). 300p. (Orig.). 1981. pap. 9.95 (ISBN 0-937860-04-2). Adams Inc MA.
LOS ANGELES–DESCRIPTION–GUIDEBOOKS
MacConaugha, Carol. Five Hundred Things to Do in Los Angeles for Free. 140p. 1981. pap. 3.95 (ISBN 0-695-81562-8). Follett.
Stokell, Marjorie. A Visitor's Guide to L.A. Harper, Susan, ed. LC 80-67475. (Illus.). 224p. (Orig.). 1981. pap. 6.95 (ISBN 0-89395-06[illegible]-0). Cal Living Bks.
LOS ANGELES–HISTORY
Burnett, William, ed. Views of Los Angeles. rev. ed. (Illus.). 1979. 24.95 (ISBN 0-9602274-1-5); pap. 14.95 (ISBN 0-9602274-0-7). Portriga Pubns.
Steiner, Rodney. Los Angeles: The Centrifugal City. 224p. 1981. pap. text ed. 12.95 (ISBN 0-8403-2333-6). Kendall-Hunt.
LOTTERIES
Thomas, John L. Law of Lotteries, Frauds & Obscenity in the Mails. xviii, 358p. 1980. Repr. of 1903 ed. lib. bdg. 32.50x (ISBN 0-8377-1202-5). Rothman.
LOUIS 14TH, KING OF FRANCE, 1638-1715–FICTION
Auchincloss, Louis. The Cat & the King. 192p. 1981. 9.95 (ISBN 0-395-30225-0). HM.
LOUIS 16TH, KING OF FRANCE, 1754-1793
Jordan, David P. The King's Trial: Louis XVI Vs. the French Revolution. 1981. pap. 5.95 (ISBN 0-520-04399-5, CAL 497). U of Cal Pr.
LOUISIANA–DESCRIPTION AND TRAVEL
Skeen, C. Edward, ed. Description of Louisiana by Thomas Jefferys: From His "Natural & Civil History of the French Dominions in North & South America". (Mississippi Valley Collection Bulletin, No. 6). (Illus.). 50p. 1973. pap. 5.95x facsimile ed. (ISBN 0-87870-082-X). Memphis St Univ.
Thomson, Bailey, ed. Historic Shreveport. LC 80-54715. (Illus.). 128p. (Orig.). 1980. pap. 6.95 (ISBN 0-939042-00-2). Shreveport Pub.
LOUISIANA–HISTORY
Ditto, Tanya. The Longest Street: A History of Lafourche Parish & Grandlsle. Woolfolk, Doug, ed. (Illus.). 136p. 1980. 13.00 (ISBN 0-86518-013-X). Moran Pub Corp.
Edmonds, David C. Yankee Autumn in Acadiana: A Narrative of the Great Texas Overland Expedition Through Southwestern Louisiana. 2nd ed. LC 79-67333. (Illus.). 512p. 1980. Repr. 15.95 (ISBN 0-937614-01-7). Acadiana Pr.
Skeen, C. Edward, ed. Description of Louisiana by Thomas Jefferys: From His "Natural & Civil History of the French Dominions in North & South America". (Mississippi Valley Collection Bulletin, No. 6). (Illus.). 50p. 1973. pap. 5.95x facsimile ed. (ISBN 0-87870-082-X). Memphis St Univ.
Valentine, Orpha. Lafayette: A Historical Perspective. Woolfolk, Doug, ed. (Illus.). 120p. 1980. 12.50 (ISBN 0-86518-014-8). Moran Pub Corp.
Vexler, R. I. Louisiana Chronology & Factbook, Vol. 18. 1978. 8.50 (ISBN 0-379-16143-5). Oceana.
Winters, John D. The Civil War in Louisiana. LC 63-9647. 552p. 1979. 25.00 (ISBN 0-8071-0834-0). La State U Pr.
LOUISIANA–JUVENILE LITERATURE
Fradin, Dennis. Louisiana: In Words & Pictures. (Young People's Stories of Our States Ser.). (Illus.). 48p. (gr. 2-5). 1981. PLB 8.65g (ISBN 0-516-03918-0, Time Line). Childrens.
LOUSE
see Lice
LOVE
see also Courtly Love; Courtship; Friendship; Marriage
Boom, Corrie T. Amazing Love. (Orig.). pap. 1.50 (ISBN 0-515-04898-4). Jove Pubns.
Bride's Magazine Editors & Calderone, Mary. Questions & Answers About Love & Sex. 144p. (Orig.). 1980. pap. 1.95 (ISBN 0-380-52977-7, 52977). Avon.
Delfiore, Clarence T. Purity & the Carnal Element in Love: The Story of a Concrete Case. (Intimate Life of Man Library). (Illus.). 111p. 1981. 39.75 (ISBN 0-89266-298-0). Am Classical Coll Pr.
Greene, Liz. Star Signs for Lovers. LC 80-5890. (Illus.). 480p. 1980. 14.95 (ISBN 0-8128-2765-1). Stein & Day.
Guidepost Associates. Guideposts Treasury of Love. (Illus.). 352p. 1981. 12.95 (ISBN 0-385-14973-5). Doubleday.
Gutridge, D. Foster, II. Your Secret Power: Creating Love, Vol. 3. (Your Secret Power Ser.). 96p. (Orig.). 1981. pap. 5.95 (ISBN 0-938014-03-X, 2001C). Freedom Unltd.
Jampolsky, Gerald. Love Is Letting Go of Fear. 144p. 1981. pap. 2.50 (ISBN 0-553-14651-3). Bantam.
Kristy, Norton F. Staying in Love: Reinventing Marriage & Other Realationships. (Orig.). pap. 2.75 (ISBN 0-515-05089-X). Jove Pubns.
Langone, John. Like, Love, Lust: A View of Sex & Sexuality. 144p. 1981. pap. 2.25 (ISBN 0-380-54189-0, 54189). Avon.
Lasswell, Marcia & Lobsenz, Norman. Styles of Loving: Why You Love the Way You Do. 192p. 1981. pap. 2.50 (ISBN 0-345-29228-6). Ballantine.
Leavenworth, Carol. Love & Commitment: You Don't Have to Settle for Less. (Illus.). 192p. 1981. 10.95t (ISBN 0-13-540971-3, Spec); pap. 5.95b (ISBN 0-13-540963-2). P-H.
Mayer, Eve R. Let's Stay Lovers. 1981. 7.95 (ISBN 0-533-04917-2). Vantage.
Peirce, Charles S. Chance, Love & Logic. 317p. 1980. Repr. of 1923 ed. lib. bdg. 50.00 (ISBN 0-89984-386-7). Century Bookbindery.
Raudsepp, Eugene. Love & Loving. (Best Thoughts Ser.). (Illus.). 80p. 1981. pap. 2.50 (ISBN 0-8431-0389-2). Price Stern.
--Love & Sexuality. (Best Thoughts Ser.). (Illus.). 80p. 1981. pap. 2.50 (ISBN 0-8431-0387-6). Price Stern.
Sheed, Charlie. How to Know If You're Really in Love. 1981. pap. 2.25 (ISBN 0-671-82841-X). PB.
Strange de Jim. The Strange Experience: How to Become the World's Second Greatest Lover. LC 80-69868. (Illus.). 94p. (Orig.). 1980. perfect bdg. 6.95 (ISBN 0-9605308-1-9). Ash-Kar Pr.
Whiston, Lionel. Through the Eyes of Love. 1981. pap. 4.95 (ISBN 0-8499-2929-6). Word Bks.
LOVE (THEOLOGY)
see also God–Love; God–Worship and Love; Identification (Religion); Self-Love (Theology)
Bernard, Mary. How to Find Real Love & Keep It. Date not set. 8.50 (ISBN 0-533-04684-X). Vantage.
Cardenal, Ernesto. Love. 160p. (Span.). 1981. pap. 4.95 (ISBN 0-8245-0043-1). Crossroad NY.
De Coppens, Peter R. Spiritual Perspective II: The Spiritual Dimension & Implications of Love, Sex, & Marriage. LC 80-6302. 175p. (Orig.). 1981. pap. text ed. 8.75 (ISBN 0-8191-1512-6). U Pr of Amer.
Dodson, Rita. Life, Love & God. Date not set. 4.95 (ISBN 0-533-04647-5). Vantage.
Dorita, la Nina Que Nadie Amaba. 1980. pap. 1.60 (ISBN 0-686-69359-0). Vida Pubs.
Evans, Colleen T. Love Is an Everyday Thing. (Orig.). pap. 1.50 (ISBN 0-89129-243-8). Jove Pubns.
Kelsey, Morton T. Caring: How Can We Love Each Other? 192p. (Orig.). 1981. pap. 6.95 (ISBN 0-8091-2366-5). Paulist Pr.
Lin, Jan. Living Out God's Love. 128p. 1981. pap. 4.95 (ISBN 0-8170-0897-7). Judson.
Merchant, Jane. The Greatest of These. (Orig.). pap. 1.25 (ISBN 0-89129-175-X). Jove Pubns.

Moncure, Jane B. Love. rev. ed. LC 80-27479. (What Is It? Ser.). (Illus.). 32p. (gr. k-3). 1981. PLB 5.50 (ISBN 0-89565-205-6). Childs World.

Morris, Leon. Testaments of Love: A Study of Love in the Bible. (Orig.). 1981. pap. price not set (ISBN 0-8028-1874-9). Eerdmans.

Newlands, George. Theology of the Love of God. LC 80-22547. 224p. 1981. 12.50 (ISBN 0-8042-0726-7); pap. 6.95 (ISBN 0-8042-0727-5). John Knox.

Perkins, Dorothy. Separation & Suffering: Hindu & Christian Views of Love. (Orig.). 1980. pap. 3.00 (ISBN 0-9604742-0-X). D J Perkins.

Tully, Mary Jo & Hirstein, Sandra J. Focus on Loving. (Light of Faith Ser.). (Orig.). (gr. 1). 1981. pap. text ed. 2.65 (ISBN 0-697-01763-X); tchrs' ed. 7.60 (ISBN 0-697-01763-X). Wm C Brown.

LOVE (THEOLOGY)–MEDITATIONS

Elliot, Elisabeth. Love Has a Price Tag. LC 79-50944. 148p. 1981. pap. 5.95 (ISBN 0-915684-87-X). Christian Herald.

LOVE, COURTLY

see Courtly Love

LOVE, PERFECT

see Perfection

LOVE OF SELF (THEOLOGY)

see Self-Love (Theology)

LOVE POETRY–HISTORY AND CRITICISM

Donaldson-Evans, Lancelot K. Love's Fatal Glance: A Study of Eye Imagery in the Poets of the Ecole lyonnaise. LC 80-10415. (Romance Monographs: No. 39). 155p. 1980. 14.50 (ISBN 84-499-3694-2). Romance.

LOVECRAFT, HOWARD PHILLIPS, 1890-1937

Derleth, August W. Some Notes on H. P. Lovecraft. 50p. 1980. Repr. of 1959 ed. lib. bdg. 10.00 (ISBN 0-8495-1059-7). Arden Lib.

LOW-CALORIE DIET

see also Cookery–Reducing Recipes; Low Carbohydrate Diet; Sugar-Free Diet

Better Homes & Gardens Editors. Better Homes & Gardens Calorie Counter's Cookbook. 176p. 1981. pap. 2.50 (ISBN 0-553-14267-4). Bantam.

Consumer Guide Editors. The Dieter's Complete Guide to Calories, Carbohydrates, Sodium, Fats & Cholesterol. 192p. (Orig.). 1981. pap. 5.95 (ISBN 0-449-90050-9, Columbine). Fawcett.

Kraus, Barbara. Calories & Carbohydrates. 4th, rev. ed. 1981. pap. 5.95 (Z5267, Plume). NAL.

--Calories & Carbohydrates. 4th, rev. ed. (Orig.). 1981. pap. 3.50 (ISBN 0-451-09774-2, E9774, Sig). NAL.

LOW CARBOHYDRATE DIET

see also Sugar-Free Diet

Consumer Guide Editors. The Dieter's Complete Guide to Calories, Carbohydrates, Sodium, Fats & Cholesterol. 192p. (Orig.). 1981. pap. 5.95 (ISBN 0-449-90050-9, Columbine). Fawcett.

Kraus, Barbara. Calories & Carbohydrates. 4th, rev. ed. 1981. pap. 5.95 (Z5267, Plume). NAL.

--Calories & Carbohydrates. 4th, rev. ed. (Orig.). 1981. pap. 3.50 (ISBN 0-451-09774-2, E9774, Sig). NAL.

LOW-FAT DIET

see also Cookery–Reducing Recipes

Consumer Guide Editors. The Dieter's Complete Guide to Calories, Carbohydrates, Sodium, Fats & Cholesterol. 192p. (Orig.). 1981. pap. 5.95 (ISBN 0-449-90050-9, Columbine). Fawcett.

LOW INCOME HOUSING

see Housing; Public Housing

LOW SODIUM DIET

see Salt-Free Diet

LOW SUGAR DIET

see Sugar-Free Diet

LOW TEMPERATURE ENGINEERING

see also Gases–Liquefaction; Refrigeration and Refrigerating Machinery

Law, Beverly, ed. Cryogenics Handbook. 1980. text ed. 39.00 (ISBN 0-86103-021-4). Butterworths.

LOW TEMPERATURES

see also Low Temperature Engineering

Zemansky, Mark W. Temperatures Very Low & Very High. 144p. 1981. pap. price not set (ISBN 0-486-24072-X). Dover.

LOWELL, AMY, 1874-1925

Moore, Charles L. Incense & Iconoclasm. 343p. 1980. Repr. of 1915 ed. lib. bdg. 30.00 (ISBN 0-89987-573-4). Century Bookbindery.

LOWELL, JAMES RUSSELL, 1819-1891

Commemoration of the Centenary of the Birth of James Russell Lowell: Poet, Scholar, Diplomat. 88p. 1980. Repr. of 1919 ed. lib. bdg. 35.00 (ISBN 0-8495-3349-X). Arden Lib.

LOYALTY

Here are entered general works on loyalty as a virtue. Works on loyalty to the state are entered under the heading Allegiance.

MacDonald, William. To What Should We Be Loyal. 55p. pap. 0.75 (ISBN 0-937396-47-8). Walterick Pubs.

LUBRICATION AND LUBRICANTS

see also Fluid Film Bearings; Metal-Working Lubricants; Oils and Fats; Petroleum Products also names of lubricants

Cheng, H. S. & Keer, L. M., eds. Solid Contact & Lubrication. (AMD: Vol. 39). 248p. 1980. 30.00 (G00172). ASME.

Gross, William & Matsch, Lee A. Fluid Film Lubrication. Vohr, John H. & Wildman, Manfred, eds. LC 80-36889. 773p. 1980. 35.00 (ISBN 0-471-08357-7, Pub. by Wiley-Interscience). Wiley.

Rohde, S. M. & Cheng, H. S., eds. Surface Roughness Effects in Hydrodynamic & Mixed Lubrication. 211p. 1980. 30.00 (G00193). ASME.

LUDICROUS, THE

see Wit and Humor

LUMBER–TRANSPORTATION

see Logging Railroads

LUMBER TRADE

see also Lumbering; Timber; Woodwork

Amigo, Eleanor & Neuffer, Mark. Beyond the Adirondacks: The Story of St. Regis Paper Company. LC 80-1798. (Contributions in Economics & Economic History: No. 35). (Illus.). xi, 219p. 1980. lib. bdg. 22.95 (ISBN 0-313-22735-7, AFN/). Greenwood.

Hanft, Robert M. Red River: Paul Bunyan's Own Lumber Company & Its Railroads. LC 79-53190. (Illus.). 304p. 32.50 (ISBN 0-9602894-5-3). CSU Ctr Busn Econ.

Van Syckle, Edwin. They Tried to Cut It All; Grays Harbor: Turbulent Years of Greed & Greatness. LC 80-16469. (Illus.). 308p. 1980. 17.95 (ISBN 0-9605152-0-8); pap. 9.95 (ISBN 0-9605152-1-6). Friends Aberdeen.

LUMBERING

see also Lumber Trade; Woodworking Machinery

Knights of the Broadax. LC 79-57239. (Illus.). 154p. (Orig.). 1981. pap. 6.95 (ISBN 0-87004-283-1). Caxton.

Reports of the FAO-Norway Training Course on Logging Operations. 110p. 1980. pap. 6.50 (ISBN 0-686-68194-0, F1937, FAO). Unipub.

LUMBERMEN

Knights of the Broadax. LC 79-57239. (Illus.). 154p. (Orig.). 1981. pap. 6.95 (ISBN 0-87004-283-1). Caxton.

LUMINESCENCE

see also Bioluminescence

Dunitz, J. D., et al, eds. Luminescence & Energy Transfer. (Structure & Bonding Ser.: Vol. 42). (Illus.). 133p. 1981. 40.00 (ISBN 0-387-10395-3). Springer-Verlag.

Hurtubise. Solid Surface Luminescence Analysis. 288p. Date not set. 37.50. Dekker.

LUNATIC ASYLUMS

see Psychiatric Hospitals

LUNCH ROOMS

see Restaurants, Lunchrooms, etc.

LUNGS–CANCER

Greco, F. Anthony, et al. Small Cell Lung Cancer. (Clinical Oncolgy Monograph). 1981. write for info. (ISBN 0-8089-1345-X). Grune.

Livingston, Robert B., ed. Lung Cancer. (Cancer Treatment & Research Ser.: No. 1). (Illus.). 320p. 1981. PLB 47.50 (ISBN 90-247-2394-9, Pub. by Martinus Nijhoff). Kluwer Boston.

LUNGS–DISEASES

see also Lungs–Dust Diseases; Tuberculosis

Avery, Mary E., et al. The Lung & Its Disorders in the Newborn Infant. 4th ed. (Major Problems in Clinical Pediatrics: Vol. 1). (Illus.). 560p. 1981. text ed. price not set (ISBN 0-7216-1462-0). Saunders.

Kehrer, James B. Oxygen Induced Lung Damage: The Chemistry of Oxygen Reduction. (Lectures in Toxicology: No. 4). (Illus.). 1981. 28.00 (ISBN 0-08-025706-2). Pergamon.

Kirby & Smith. Mechanical Ventilation of the Lungs. 1981. text ed. write for info. (ISBN 0-443-08063-1). Churchill.

Miller, Warren C. Chronic Obstructive Pulmonary Disease. LC 79-91977. (Discussions in Pateint Managemenrt Ser.). 1980. pap. 12.00 (ISBN 0-87488-872-7). Med Exam.

Parkes, W. Raymond. Occupational Lung Disorders. 2nd ed. 1981. text ed. price not set (ISBN 0-407-33731-8). Butterworth.

Putman, Charles E. Diagnostic Imaging in Pulmonary Disease. 1981. 32.50 (ISBN 0-8385-1682-3). ACC.

Sackner. Diagnostic Techniques in Pulmonary Disease, Pt. 1. 746p. 1980. 49.50 (ISBN 0-8247-1059-2). Dekker.

Sharnoff, J. G. The Prevention of Venous Thrombosis & Pulmonary Thromboembolism. (Medical Publicatons Ser.). 1980. lib. bdg. 25.00 (ISBN 0-8161-2223-7). G K Hall.

Stone, Daniel J., et al. Practical Points in Pulmonary Diseases. 1978. spiral bdg. 14.00 (ISBN 0-87488-724-0). Med Exam.

LUNGS–DUST DISEASES

Berton, Alberta D., compiled by. Asbestosis: A Comprehensive Bibliography. (Biomedical Information Guides Ser.: Vol. 1). 395p. 1980. 85.00 (ISBN 0-306-65176-9, IFI). Plenum Pub.

LUTE MUSIC

Dowland, Robert. Varietie of Lute-Lessons. LC 79-84102. (English Experience Ser.: No. 921). 76p. 1979. Repr. of 1610 ed. lib. bdg. 14.00 (ISBN 90-221-0921-6). Walter J Johnson.

LUTHER, MARTIN, 1483-1546

Hendrix, Scott H. Luther & the Papacy: Stages in a Reformation Conflict. LC 80-2393. 224p. 1981. 14.95 (ISBN 0-8006-0658-2, 1-658). Fortress.

Siggins, Ian. Luther & His Mother. LC 80-2386. 96p. (Orig.). 1981. pap. 4.95 (ISBN 0-8006-1498-4, 1-1498). Fortress.

Steinmetz, David C. Luther & Staupitz: An Essay in the Intellectual Origins of the Protestant Reformation. LC 80-23007. (Duke Monographs in Medieval & Renaissance Studies: No. 4). 1981. 16.75 (ISBN 0-8223-0447-3). Duke.

LUTHERAN CHURCH

Empie, Paul C. Lutherans & Catholics in Dialogue: Personal Notes for a Study. LC 80-69754. (Orig.). 1981. pap. 3.95 (ISBN 0-8006-1449-6, 1-1449). Fortress.

LUTHERAN CHURCH–MISSOURI SYNOD

see Evangelical Lutheran Synod of Missouri, Ohio and other states

LUTHERAN CHURCH IN THE UNITED STATES

Groh, John E. & Smith, Robert H., eds. The Lutheran Church in North American Life: 1776-1976, 1580-1980. LC 78-71233. 1979. 5.95 (ISBN 0-915644-17-7, Clayton). Luth Acad.

LUTHERANS IN NORTH AMERICA

Groh, John E. & Smith, Robert H., eds. The Lutheran Church in North American Life: 1776-1976, 1580-1980. LC 78-71233. 1979. 5.95 (ISBN 0-915644-17-7, Clayton). Luth Acad.

LUXATIONS

see Dislocations

LYMPHATIC SYSTEM

see Lymphatics

LYMPHATICS

see also Hodgkin's Disease

Weiss, Leonard, et al. Lymphatic System Metastasis. (Medical Publications Ser.). 1980. lib. bdg. 55.00 (ISBN 0-8161-2142-7). G K Hall.

LYMPHOCYTES

De Sousa, Maria. Lymphocyte Circulation: Experimental & Clinical Aspects. 316p. 1981. 57.00 (ISBN 0-471-27854-8, Pub. by Wiley-Interscience). Wiley.

De Weck, A. L., ed. Differentiated Lymphocyte Functions & Their Ontogeny. (Progress in Allergy Ser.: Vol. 28). (Illus.). 250p. 1981. 90.00 (ISBN 3-8055-1834-X). S Karger.

Stewart, William E. & Hadden, John, eds. The Lymphokines. LC 80-85521. (Contemporary Immunology Ser.). (Illus.). 1981. 59.50 (ISBN 0-89603-012-1). Humana.

LYMPHOMA

see also Hodgkin's Disease

Lennert, K. Histopathology of Non-Hodgkin Lymphomas: Kiel Classification. (Illus.). 130p. 1981. 46.00 (ISBN 0-387-10445-3). Springer-Verlag.

Stuart, A. E., et al, eds. Lymphomas Other Than Hodgkin's Disease. (Illus.). 75p. 1981. text ed. 30.00x (ISBN 0-19-261296-4). Oxford U Pr.

LYMPHOSARCOMA

see Hodgkin's Disease

LYMPHOID TISSUE

Glick. Human Lymphoid Cell Cultures: The Fundamentals. Date not set. 22.50 (ISBN 0-8247-6988-0). Dekker.

LYRIC DRAMA

see Opera

LYRIC POETRY

see Poetry

LYSOSOMES

Daems, W. T., et al, eds. Cell Biological Aspects of Disease: The Plasma Membrane & Lysosomes. (Boerhaave Series for Postgraduate Medical Education: No. 19). 330p. 1981. PLB 68.50 (ISBN 90-6021-466-8, Pub. by Leiden U Pr). Kluwer Boston.

LYSSA

see Rabies

M

MACARONI WHEAT

see Wheat

MACAULAY, THOMAS BABINGTON MACAULAY, 1ST BARON, 1800-1859

Pinney, T., ed. The Letters of Thomas Babington Macaulay, Vol. 5. LC 73-75860. (Illus.). 425p. Date not set. 85.00 (ISBN 0-521-22749-6). Cambridge U Pr.

--The Letters of Thomas Babington Macaulay, Vol. 6. LC 73-75860. (Illus.). 350p. Date not set. price not set (ISBN 0-521-22750-X). Cambridge U Pr.

MACCABEES, FEAST OF THE

see Hanukkah (Feast of Lights)

MCCARTHY, EUGENE J., 1916-

McCarthy, Eugene. Frankly McCarthy. Rinzler, Carol E., ed. 1.00 (ISBN 0-8183-0169-4). Pub Aff Pr.

MCCARTHY, JOSEPH RAYMOND, 1909-1957

Days, G. D., ed. Threshold of the McCarthy Era & the McCarthy Era - Beginning of the End. 60p. 1980. pap. 19.95 includes cassettes (ISBN 0-918628-54-7, 54/7). Congeros Pubns.

MCCOSH, JAMES, 1811-1894

Hoeveler, J. David, Jr. James McCosh & the Scottish Intellectual Tradition: From Glasgow to Princeton. (Illus.). 384p. 1981. 25.00x (ISBN 0-691-04670-0). Princeton U Pr.

MACEDONIA

Bompois, H. F. Examen Chronologique des Monnais Frappes par la Communaute des Macedoniens Avant, Pendant et Apes la Conquete Romaine. (Illus.). 102p. (Fr.). 20.00 (ISBN 0-916710-77-7). Obol Intl.

MACHINE DATA STORAGE AND RETRIEVAL SYSTEMS

see Information Storage and Retrieval Systems

MACHINE DESIGN

see Machinery–Design

MACHINE EMBROIDERY

see Embroidery

MACHINE INDUSTRY

see Machinery–Trade and Manufacture

MACHINE INTELLIGENCE

see Artificial Intelligence

MACHINE LANGUAGE

see Programming Languages (Electronic Computers)

MACHINE PARTS

Collins, J. A. Failure of Materials in Mechanical Design: Analysis, Prediction, Prevention. 700p. 1981. 25.00 (ISBN 0-471-05024-5, Pub. by Wiley-Interscience). Wiley.

MACHINE QUILTING

see Quilting

MACHINE-SHOP PRACTICE

Amiss, John M. & Jones, Franklin D. The Use of Handbook Tables & Formulas. 21st ed. Ryffel, Henry H., ed. LC 75-10949. (Illus.). 224p. 8.00 (ISBN 0-8311-1131-3). Indus Pr.

Moltrecht, K. H. Machine Shop Practice. 2nd ed. (Illus.). 1981. Vol. 1, 512 Pp. 19.95 (ISBN 0-8311-1126-7); Vol. 2, 528 Pp. 19.95 (ISBN 0-8311-1132-1). Indus Pr.

MACHINE THEORY

see also Artificial Intelligence; Automata; Control Theory; Computers; Formal Languages; Sequential Machine Theory

Milner, R. A Calculus of Communicating Systems. (Lecture Notes in Computer Science Ser.: Vol. 92). 260p. 1981. pap. 11.80 (ISBN 0-387-10235-3). Springer-Verlag.

MACHINE-TOOLS

see also Manufacturing Processes also specific machine tools, e.g. Planning Machines

Dixon, Robert G. Benchwork. 2nd ed. LC 80-66607. (Machine Trades - Machine Shop Ser.). (Illus.). 208p. 1981. pap. text ed. 7.40 (ISBN 0-8273-1743-3); instr's. guide 1.10 (ISBN 0-8273-1744-1). Delmar.

Equipment Guide-Book Co. Machine Tool Value Guide: Grinding Machines, Vol. III. Husek, Jiri, ed. 600p. 1981. pap. 50.00 (ISBN 0-89692-104-2). Equipment Guide.

MACHINE-TOOLS, AUTOMATIC

see Machine-Tools

MACHINE TRADE

see Machinery–Trade and Manufacture

MACHINERY–DESIGN

see also Human Engineering; Machinery–Models

Collins, J. A. Failure of Materials in Mechanical Design: Analysis, Prediction, Prevention. 700p. 1981. 25.00 (ISBN 0-471-05024-5, Pub. by Wiley-Interscience). Wiley.

Leyer, Albert. Machine Design. 1974. 19.95x (ISBN 0-216-87457-2). Intl Ideas.

Walker, J. H. Large Synchronous Machines: Design, Manufacture & Operation. (Monographs in Electrical & Electronic Engineering). (Illus.). 250p. 1981. 59.00 (ISBN 0-19-859364-3). Oxford U Pr.

MACHINERY–HISTORY

Roberts, Verne L. Machine Guarding: A Historical Perspective. LC 80-84798. (Illus.). 282p. 1980. text ed. 59.95 (ISBN 0-938830-00-7). Inst Product.

MACHINERY–MANUFACTURE

see Machinery–Trade and Manufacture

MACHINERY–MODELS

Atteberry, Pat H. Power Mechanics. LC 80-20581. (Illus.). 112p. 1980. text ed. 4.40 (ISBN 0-87006-307-3). Goodheart.

MACHINERY–TRADE AND MANUFACTURE

Equipment Guide-Book Co. Machine Tool Value Guide: Grinding Machines, Vol. III. Husek, Jiri, ed. 600p. 1981. pap. 50.00 (ISBN 0-89692-104-2). Equipment Guide.

Walker, J. H. Large Synchronous Machines: Design, Manufacture & Operation. (Monographs in Electrical & Electronic Engineering). (Illus.). 250p. 1981. 59.00 (ISBN 0-19-859364-3). Oxford U Pr.

MACHINERY, KINEMATICS OF

see also Rolling Contact

Martin, George H. Kinematics & Dynamics of Machines. 2nd ed. (Illus.). 544p. 1982. text ed. 28.95x (ISBN 0-07-040657-X, C); write for info. solutions manual (ISBN 0-07-040658-8). McGraw.

Szuladzinski, Gregory. Dynamics of Structures & Machinery: Problems & Solutions. 700p. 1981. 50.00 (ISBN 0-471-09027-1, Pub. by Wiley Interscience). Wiley.

MACHINERY AND CIVILIZATION

see Technology and Civilization

MACHINERY IN INDUSTRY

see also Automation; Division of Labor; Labor Productivity; Technocracy; Technological Innovations; Technology–Philosophy; Unemployment, Technological

Land, Charles. Land's Industrial Machinery & Equipment Pricing Guide. 1980. pap. text ed. 29.95 (ISBN 0-442-28820-4). Van Nos Reinhold.

MACHINING OF METALS
see Metal-Work

MCKENNEY, THOMAS LORAINE, 1785-1859
Viola, Herman J. Thomas L. McKenney, Architect of America's Early Indian Policy: 1816-1830. LC 74-18075. (Illus.). xii, 365p. (Orig.). 1981. pap. 8.95x (ISBN 0-8040-0669-5, SB). Swallow.

MACKENZIE RIVER
Aquilina, Alfred P. The Mackenzie Today. Campbell, Margaret, ed. (Illus.). 50p. (Orig.). 1981. pap. 4.00 (ISBN 0-88839-082-3). Hancock Hse.
--The Mackenzie: Yesterday & Beyond. (Illus.). pap. 6.95 (ISBN 0-88839-083-1). Hancock Hse.

MACKINAC-ANTIQUITIES
Armour, David A. & Widder, Keith R. Michilimackinac: A Handbook to the Site. 1st ed. (Illus.). 48p. (Orig.). 1980. pap. 1.50 (ISBN 0-911872-39-6). Mackinac Island.

MACKINAC-HISTORY
Armour, David A. & Widder, Keith R. Michilimackinac: A Handbook to the Site. 1st ed. (Illus.). 48p. (Orig.). 1980. pap. 1.50 (ISBN 0-911872-39-6). Mackinac Island.

MCKINLEY, MOUNT
Moore, Terris. Mt. McKinley: The Pioneer Climbs. (Illus.). 224p. 1981. pap. 8.95 (ISBN 0-89886-021-0). Mountaineers.

MACMILLAN, HAROLD, 1894-
Hutchinson, George. The Last Edwardian at Number Ten: An Impression of Harold Macmillian. (Illus.). 160p. 1980. 12.95 (ISBN 0-7043-2232-3, Pub. by Quartet England). Horizon.

MACRAME
Dodge, Jane. New Macreme. (Step by Step Craft Ser.). Date not set. pap. 2.95 (ISBN 0-307-42023-X, Golden Pr). Western Pub.
Harvey, Virginia I. Color & Design in Macrame. LC 80-25748. (Illus.). 104p. (gr. 11-12). 1980. pap. 9.95 (ISBN 0-914842-55-2). Madrona Pubs.
--Color & Design in Macrame. (Illus.). 104p. 1980. pap. 9.95 (ISBN 0-914842-55-2). Madrona Pubs.

MACROECONOMICS
Barro, Robert J. Money, Expectations & Business Cycles: Essays in Macroeconomics. (Economic Theory, Econometrics & Mathematical Economic Ser.). 1981. write for info. (ISBN 0-12-079550-7). Acad Pr.
Chisholm, Roger & McCarty, Marilu. Principles of Macroeconomics. 2nd ed. 1981. pap. text ed. 10.95x (ISBN 0-673-15493-9). Scott F.
Chrystal, K. A. Controversies in British Macroeconomics. 1979. 21.00x (ISBN 0-86003-022-9, Pub. by Allan Pubs England); pap. 10.50x (ISBN 0-86003-123-3). State Mutual Bk.
Close, Frank A., et al. Study Guide to Accompany Principles of Macroeconomics. 2nd ed. 1981. pap. text ed. 4.95x (ISBN 0-673-15496-3). Scott F.
--Study Guide to Accompany Principles of Microeconomics. 2nd ed. 1981. pap. text ed. 4.95x (ISBN 0-673-15495-5). Scott F.
Frazer, William. Expectations, Forecasting & Control--a Provisional Textbook of Macroeconomics: Volume II, Prices, Market & Turning Points. LC 80-1361. 439p. 1980. lib. bdg. 25.50 (ISBN 0-8191-1290-9); pap. text ed. 16.25 (ISBN 0-8191-1291-7). U Pr of Amer.
Gordon, Robert J. Macroecomomics. 2nd ed. 1981. text ed. 16.95 (ISBN 0-316-32125-7); wkbk. 6.95 (ISBN 0-316-32127-3). Little.
Kelly, William A., Jr. Macroeconomics. (Illus.). 496p. 1981. text ed. 17.95 (ISBN 0-13-542761-4). P-H.
Leijonhufvud, Axel. Information & Coordination: Essays in Macroeconomic Theory. (Illus.). 320p. 1981. text ed. 15.95x (ISBN 0-19-502814-7); pap. text ed. 9.95x (ISBN 0-19-502815-5). Oxford U Pr.
McClelland, Peter D., ed. Introductory Macroeconomics, 1980-81: Readings on Contemporary Issues. LC 80-66907. (Illus.). 224p. (Orig.). 1980. pap. 8.95x (ISBN 0-8014-9873-2). Cornell U Pr.
Okun, Arthur M. Prices & Quantities: A Macroeconomic Analysis. 400p. 1981. 19.95 (ISBN 0-8157-6480-4); pap. 7.95 (ISBN 0-8157-6479-0). Brookings.
Peston, M. H. Theory of Macroeconomic Policy. 224p. 1974. pap. 19.50x (ISBN 0-86003-113-6, Pub. by Allan Pubs England). State Mutual Bk.
Poindexter. Macroeconomics. 1976. 18.95 (ISBN 0-03-089419-0). Dryden Pr.
Poindexter, J. Carl, Jr. Macroeconomics. 2nd ed. LC 79-51107. 560p. 1981. text ed. 17.95 (ISBN 0-03-050271-3). Dryden Pr.
Reekie, W. Duncan. Macroeconomics for Managers. 160p. 1980. 18.00x (ISBN 0-86003-510-7, Pub. by Allan Pubs England); pap. 9.00x (ISBN 0-86003-610-3). State Mutual Bk.
Sanderson, Allen R., ed. DRI-McGraw-Hill Readings in Macroeconomics. (Illus.). 480p. 1981. pap. text ed. 7.95 (ISBN 0-07-054659-2). McGraw.
Wykoff, Frank C. Macroeconomics: Theory, Evidence & Policy. 2nd ed. (Illus.). 640p. 1981. 19.95 (ISBN 0-13-543967-1). P-H.

MACROMOLECULES
Dillon, Lawrence S. Ultrastructure,Macromolecules, & Evolution. 750p. 1981. 69.50 (ISBN 0-306-40528-8, Plenum Pr). Plenum Pub.
Spragg, S. P. The Physical Behavior of Macromolecules with Biological Functions. (Biophysics & Biochemistry Monographs). 208p. 1981. write for info. (ISBN 0-471-27784-3, Pub. by Wiley-Interscience). Wiley.

MACROPHOTOGRAPHY
White, William, Jr., ed. A Laboratory Handbook of Photomacrography. 1981. write for info. Franklin Inst Pr.

MADISON, JAMES, PRES. U. S., 1751-1836
Meyers, Marvin. The Mind of the Founder: Sources of the Political Thought of James Madison. rev. ed. 400p. 1981. 12.50 (ISBN 0-87451-201-8). U Pr of New Eng.

MADONNA
see Mary, Virgin

MAFIA
Hanna, David. The Mafia: Two Hundred Years of Terror. (Orig.). 1980. pap. 2.25 (ISBN 0-532-23131-7). Manor Bks.
Kwitny, Jonathan. Vicious Circles: The Mafia in the Marketplace. 432p. 1981. pap. 6.95 (ISBN 0-393-00029-X). Norton.

MAGAZINES
see Periodicals

MAGIC
Here are entered works dealing with occult science (supernatural arts). Works on modern parlor magic, legerdemain, prestidigitation, etc. are entered under the heading Conjuring.
see also Alchemy; Cabala; Conjuring; Idols and Images; Occult Sciences; Symbolism of Numbers; Witchcraft
Bias, Clifford, compiled by. Ritual Book of Magic. 160p. 1981. pap. 6.95 (ISBN 0-87728-532-2). Weiser.
Bode, Carl. Practical Magic: Poems. LC 80-17597. 52p. 1981. 8.95 (ISBN 0-8040-0362-9); pap. 4.95 (ISBN 0-8040-0373-4). Swallow.
Bronowski, Jacob. Magic, Science & Civilization. (Bamptom Lectures in America Ser.: No. 20). 104p. 1981. pap. 4.95 (ISBN 0-231-04485-2). Columbia U Pr.
Fisher, John. Body Magic. LC 78-6387. (Illus.). 158p. 1980. pap. 6.95 (ISBN 0-8128-6088-8). Stein & Day.
FitzSimons, Raymund. Death & the Magician. LC 80-21071. 1981. 10.95 (ISBN 0-689-11122-3). Atheneum.
Houdini, Harry. Miracle Mongers & Their Methods: A Complete Expose. LC 80-84404. (Skeptic's Bookshelf Ser.). 240p. 1981. Repr. of 1920 ed. 13.95 (ISBN 0-87975-143-6). Prometheus Bks.
Hugard, Jean & Braue, Frederick. Royal Road to Card Magic. 1949. 9.50 (ISBN 0-571-11399-0, Pub. by Faber & Faber). Merrimack Bk Serv.
Kaufman, Hal & Schroeter, Bob. Hocus-Focus. (Orig.). 1981. pap. 1.50 (ISBN 0-451-09781-5, J9781, Sig). NAL.
Kris, Ernst & Kurz, Otto. Legend, Myth, & Magic in the Image of the Artist: A Historical Experiment. LC 78-24024. (Illus.). 175p. 1981. pap. 5.95 (ISBN 0-300-02669-2). Yale U Pr.
Weinstein, Marion. Positive Magic. rev. ed. (Illus.). 320p. 1981. pap. 5.95 (ISBN 0-919345-00-X). Cerridwen & Co.

MAGIC-HISTORY
Barnouw, Erik. The Magician & the Cinema. (Illus.). 112p. 1981. 12.95 (ISBN 0-19-502918-6). Oxford U Pr.
A History of White Magic. 1979. pap. 6.95 (ISBN 0-87728-482-2). Weiser.
Levi, Eliphas. History of Magic. 1980. pap. 7.95 (ISBN 0-87728-077-0). Weiser.
--The Key of the Mysteries. 1980. pap. 6.95 (ISBN 0-87728-078-9). Weiser.
Vetter, George B. Magic & Religion: Their Origins & Consequences. LC 73-82103. 1958. 6.00 (ISBN 0-8022-1776-1). Philos Lib.

MAGIC-JUVENILE LITERATURE
Boyar, Jay. Be a Magician! How to Put on a Magic Show & Mystify Your Friends. (Illus.). 160p. (gr. 7 up). 1981. PLB price not set (ISBN 0-671-42273-1). Messner.
Shalit, Nathan. Science Magic Tricks: Over 50 Fun Tricks That Mystify & Dazzle. LC 79-18645. (Illus.). 128p. (gr. 4-7). 1981. 8.95 (ISBN 0-03-047116-8); pap. 3.95 (ISBN 0-03-059269-0). HR&W.
Sleator, William. That's Silly. LC 80-21902. (Illus.). (gr. k-3). 1981. 7.95 (ISBN 0-525-40981-5). Dutton.
Stoddard, Edward. The First Book of Magic. 1980. pap. 1.75 (ISBN 0-380-49221-0, 49221, Camelot). Avon.

MAGISTRATES
see Judges

MAGNETIC DOMAIN
see Domain Structure

MAGNETIC HEALING
see also Mesmerism
Burke, Abbot G. Magnetic Therapy: Healing in Your Hands. LC 80-22941. (Illus.). 86p. (Orig.). 1980. pap. text ed. 4.95 (ISBN 0-932104-04-5). St George Pr.

MAGNETIC MATERIALS
Koenig, E. G. Magnetic Properties of Coordination & Organometallic Transition Metal Compounds: Supplement Three, (1971, 1972) (Landolt-Boernstein-Numerical Data & Functional Relationships in Science & Technology: Group II, Vol. 11 (Supplement to Vol. 2)). (Illus.). 800p. 1980. 702.10 (ISBN 0-387-09908-5). Springer-Verlag.
Magnetism & Magnetic Materials Digest. Incl. 1965. White, R. L. & Wickersheim, K. A., eds. 1965. 29.50 (ISBN 0-12-747150-2); 1966. Haas, Warren C. & Jarrett, H. S., eds. 1968. 43.50 (ISBN 0-12-312750-5); 1967. Doyle, W. D. & Harris, A. B., eds. 1967. 41.00 (ISBN 0-12-221550-8); 1968. Chang, H. & McGuire, T. R., eds. 1968. 43.50 (ISBN 0-12-170450-5). Acad Pr.

MAGNETIC RECORDERS AND RECORDING
see also Video Tape Recorders and Recording
Dolan, Edward F., Jr. It Sounds Like Fun: How to Use & Enjoy Your Tape Recorder & Stereo. (Illus.). 192p. 1981. PLB price not set (ISBN 0-671-34053-0). Messner.

MAGNETIC RESONANCE
see also Electron Paramagnetic Resonance; Nuclear Magnetic Resonance
DePasquale, Nicholas P. & Bruno, Michael S. Cardiology Case Studies. 2nd ed. LC 79-91847. 1980. pap. 15.00 (ISBN 0-87488-001-7). Med Exam.
Fraissard, Jacques P. & Resing, Henry A., eds. Magnetic Resonance in Colloid & Interface Science. (NATO Advanced Study Institutes C. Mathematical & Physical Sciences Ser.: No. 61). 710p. 1980. lib. bdg. 76.00 (ISBN 90-277-1153-4, Pub. by D. Reidel). Kluwer Boston.
Joint ISMAR-AMPERE International Conference on Magnetic Resonance. Proceedings. Smidt, J., ed. 1981. 60.00. Franklin Inst Pr.
Poole, C. P., Jr. & Farach, H. A. The Theory of Magnetic Resonance. 452p. 1972. 31.95 (ISBN 0-471-69383-9). Wiley.
Simmons, Frank G. & Coombes, Susan E. Cardiopulmonary Technology Examination Review Book, Vol. 1. 1980. pap. 12.50 (ISBN 0-87488-473-X). Med Exam.

MAGNETIC RESONANCE, NUCLEAR
see Nuclear Magnetic Resonance

MAGNETISM
see also Electricity; Electromagnetic Theory; Electromagnetism; Ferromagnetism; Nuclear Magnetism; Spin-Lattice Relaxation
also headings beginning with the word Magnetic
Magnetism & Magnetic Materials Digest. Incl. 1965. White, R. L. & Wickersheim, K. A., eds. 1965. 29.50 (ISBN 0-12-747150-2); 1966. Haas, Warren C. & Jarrett, H. S., eds. 1968. 43.50 (ISBN 0-12-312750-5); 1967. Doyle, W. D. & Harris, A. B., eds. 1967. 41.00 (ISBN 0-12-221550-8); 1968. Chang, H. & McGuire, T. R., eds. 1968. 43.50 (ISBN 0-12-170450-5). Acad Pr.
Sprott, Julien C. Introduction to Modern Electronics. 512p. 1981. text ed. 22.95 (ISBN 0-471-05840-8). Wiley.

MAGNETOHYDRODYNAMICS
see also Plasma Dynamics
Chandrasekhar, S. Hydrodynamic & Hydromagnetic Stability. (Illus.). 704p. pap. write for info. (ISBN 0-486-64071-X). Dover.

MAGNETO-OPTICS
see also Electromagnetic Theory; Electrons
Devreese, J. T., ed. Theoretical Aspects & the New Developments in Megneto-Optics. (NATO Advanced Study Institutes Ser.: B Physics: Vol. 60). 635p. 1981. 69.50 (ISBN 0-306-40555-5, Plenum Pr). Plenum Pub.

MAGRITTE, RENE, 1898-1967
Breton, Andre. Magritte. (Illus.). 1964. pap. 3.50 (ISBN 0-914412-24-8). Inst for the Arts.

MAH JONG
Li, Tze-Chung. Mah Jong: The Rules to Play the Chinese Game. 1981. write for info. (ISBN 0-937256-02-1). Chinese Culture.

MAHOMET THE PROPHET
see Mohammed, the Prophet, 570-632

MAIDEN AUNTS
see Single Women

MAIL BOATS
see Packets

MAIL-ORDER BUSINESS
Brandell, Raymond J. & Brandell, Raymond E. The Dynamics of Making a Fortune in Mail Order. (Illus.). 360p. 1980. 19.95 (ISBN 0-8119-0325-7). Fell.
Direct Mail Databook. 3rd ed. 288p. 1980. text ed. 65.00x (ISBN 0-566-02177-3, Pub. by Pub Co England). Renouf.
Hicks, Tyler G. Directory of High-Discount Merchandise & Product Sources for Distributors & Mail-Order Wealth Builders. 2nd ed. 150p. 1981. pap. 17.50 (ISBN 0-914306-58-8). Intl Wealth.
--How to Make a Fortune Through Export Mail-Order Riches. 2nd ed. 150p. 1981. pap. 17.50 (ISBN 0-914306-57-X). Intl Wealth.
--Mail Order Riches Success Kit. 2nd ed. 927p. 1981. pap. 99.50 (ISBN 0-914306-41-3). Intl Wealth.

MAIL PLANES
see Transport Planes

MAIL SERVICE
see Postal Service

MAILING LISTS
The IRRI Computerized List System. (IRRI Research Paper Ser.: No. 51). 37p. 1981. pap. 5.00 (R134, IRRI). Unipub.

MAILLOL, ARISTIDE JOSEPH BONAVENTURE, 1861-1944
Maillol, Aristide, illus. Maillol Nudes: Thirty-Five Lithographs by Aristide Maillol. (Dover Art Library). Orig. Title: The Dialogues of the Courtesans. (Illus.). 1980. pap. 2.00 (ISBN 0-486-24000-2). Dover.

MAINE
Maine Register: Nineteen Eighty to Nineteen Eighty-One. 1980. 65.00 (ISBN 0-89442-013-5). Tower Pub Co.
Pullen, John. The Twentieth Maine. 1980. 17.50 (ISBN 0-686-68805-8). Pr of Morningside.

MAINE-ANTIQUITIES
Willoughby, Charles C. Indian Antiquities of the Kennebec Valley. Spiess, Arthur E., ed. (Occasional Publications in Mane Archaeology: No. 1). (Illus.). 160p. 1980. 22.00 (ISBN 0-913764-13-2). Maine St Mus.

MAINE-DESCRIPTION AND TRAVEL
DeLorme, David, ed. The Maine Atlas & Gazetteer. 2nd ed. (Illus.). 96p. 1978. pap. 6.95 (ISBN 0-89933-003-7). DeLorme Pub.
Hakola, John W. Legacy of a Lifetime: The Story of Baxter State Park in Maine. (Illus.). 448p. Date not set. 16.00 (ISBN 0-931474-18-3). TBW Bks.
Huber, J. Parker. Thoreau's Travels in Maine. (Illus.). 200p. 1981. pap. 8.95 (ISBN 0-686-69095-8). Appalach Mtn.
McLane, Charles B. Islands of the Mid-Maine Coast: Penobscot & Blue Hill Bays. (Illus.). 576p. 1981 35.00 (ISBN 0-933858-00-0, Pub by Kennebec River Pr); signed & numbered limited ed 100.00 (ISBN 0-933858-01-9). TBW Bks.
Smith, Clyde. Portrait of Maine. Pfeiffer, Douglas, ed. (Portrait of America Ser.). (Illus.). 80p. (Orig.). 1981. pap. 5.95 (ISBN 0-912856-71-8). Graphic Arts Ctr.

MAINE-HISTORY
Bennett, Dean B. & Young, Barbara E., eds. Maine Dirigo: I Lead. LC 80-68242. (Maine Studies Curriculum Project). (Illus.). 300p. 1980. text ed. 13.50 (ISBN 0-89272-103-0). Down East.
McLane, Charles B. Islands of the Mid-Maine Coast: Penobscot & Blue Hill Bays. (Illus.). 576p. 1981. 35.00 (ISBN 0-933858-00-0, Pub by Kennebec River Pr); signed & numbered limited ed 100.00 (ISBN 0-933858-01-9). TBW Bks.
Reid, John G. Acadia, Maine, & New Scotland: Marginal Colonies in the Seventeenth Century. 320p. 1981. 27.50x (ISBN 0-8020-5508-7). U of Toronto Pr.
Vexler, R. I. Maine Chronology & Factbook. 1978. 8.50 (ISBN 0-379-16144-3). Oceana.

MAINSTREAMING IN EDUCATION
Rodrigues, Raymond J. & White, Robert H. Mainstreaming the Non-English Speaking Student. (Theory & Research into Practice Ser.). (Orig.). 1981. write for info. (ISBN 0-8141-3036-4, 30364) NCTE.
Special Learning Corporation. Readings in Mainstreaming. rev. ed. Sullivan, John M., ed. (Special Education Ser.). (Illus.). 224p. 1981. pap. text ed. 9.95 (ISBN 0-89568-293-1). Spec Learn Corp.

MAINTENANCE
see also Plant Maintenance; Repairing
Bell, Clinton C. Maintenance Mechanics Qualification Program. (Illus.). 56p. 1981. pap. write for info. (ISBN 0-89852-389-3). TAPPI.
The Design of a Maintainance System. (Productivity Ser.: No. 14). 50p. 1979. pap. 8.25 (ISBN 92-833-1704-1, APO92, APO). Unipub.
Heintzelman, John. The Complete Handbook of Maintenance Management. 336p. pap. 9.95 (ISBN 0-13-160986-6, Reward). P-H.

MAINTENANCE (DOMESTIC RELATIONS)
see Support (Domestic Relations)

MAIZE
see Corn

MAJOR ORDERS
see Bishops; Clergy

MAKAH INDIANS
see Indians of North America-Northwest, Pacific

MAKE-UP (COSMETICS)
see Cosmetics

MAKE-UP, THEATRICAL
see also Masks
Liszt, Rudolph. The Last Word in Make-up: A Practical Illustrated Handbook. rev. ed. (Illus.). 1980. 6.00 (ISBN 0-686-68849-X). Dramatists Play.

MALACOLOGY
see Mollusks

MALADJUSTED CHILDREN
see Problem Children

MALARIA
Harrison, Gordon. Mosquitoes, Malaria & Man: A History of the Hostilities Since 1880. 320p. 1980. 40.00x (ISBN 0-7195-3580-8, Pub. by Murray Pubs England). State Mutual Bk.

MALARIAL FEVER
see Malaria

MALAWI

Brown, Edward F., et al. A Bibliography of Malawi. (Foreign & Comparative Studies-Eastern African Bibliographic Ser.: No. 1). 161p. 1965. pap. 3.50x. Syracuse U Foreign Comp.

MALAY LITERATURE–HISTORY AND CRITICISM

Sweeney, Amin. Authors & Audiences in Traditional Malay Literature. (Monograph: No. 20). 86p. 1981. pap. 7.00x (Pub by Northern Ill Univ Ctr S E Asian Stud). Cellar.

MALAYA–HISTORY

Butcher, John G. The British in Malaya, Eighteen Eighty to Nineteen Forty-One: The Social History of a European Community in Colonial South-East Asia. (Illus.). 314p. 1979. 34.95x (ISBN 0-19-580419-8). Oxford U Pr.

Sidhu, Jagjit S. Administration in the Federated Malay States: Eighteen Ninety-Six-Nineteen Twenty. (East Asian Historical Monographs). 250p. 1980. 25.00 (ISBN 0-19-580432-5). Oxford U Pr.

MALAYA–POLITICS AND GOVERNMENT

Sidhu, Jagjit S. Administration in the Federated Malay States: Eighteen Ninety-Six-Nineteen Twenty. (East Asian Historical Monographs). 250p. 1980. 25.00 (ISBN 0-19-580432-5). Oxford U Pr.

MALAYSIA

Gullick, John. Malaysia: Economic Expansion & National Unity. (Illus.). 272p. 1980. lib. bdg. 25.00x (ISBN 0-86531-089-0). Westview.

Mazumdar, Dipak. Urban Labor Market & Income Distribution in Peninsular Malaysia. (World Bank Research Publications Ser.). (Illus.). 456p. 1981. 18.95 (ISBN 0-19-520213-9); pap. 7.95 (ISBN 0-19-520214-7). Oxford U Pr.

Young, Kevin, et al. Malaysia: Growth & Equity in a Multiracial Society. LC 79-3677. (A World Bank Country Economic Report Ser.). (Illus.). 368p. 1980. text ed. 25.00 (ISBN 0-8018-2384-6); pap. text ed. 7.95 (ISBN 0-8018-2385-4). Johns Hopkins.

MALAYSIA–POLITICS AND GOVERNMENT

Norris, M. W. Local Government in Peninsular Malaysia. 121p. 1980. text ed. 27.00x (ISBN 0-566-00283-3, Pub. by Gower Pr England). Renouf.

Vasil, Raj K. Ethnic Politics in Malaysia. (Illus.). 234p. 1980. text ed. 16.00x (ISBN 0-391-01770-5). Humanities.

MALCOLM X

see Little, Malcolm, 1925-1965

MALE NURSES

see Men Nurses

MALE PHOTOGRAPHY

see Photography of Men

MALE SEX HORMONE

see Hormones, Sex

MALE STERILITY

see Sterility, Male

MALFORMATIONS, CONGENITAL

see Abnormalities, Human

MALINOWSKI, BRONISLAW, 1884-1942

Firth, Raymond, ed. Man & Culture: An Evaluation of the Work of Bronislaw Malinouski. 292p. 1980. 27.50x (ISBN 0-7100-1376-0, Pub. by Routledge England). Humanities.

MALLARME, STEPHANE, 1842-1898

Mallarme, Stephane. Stephane Mallarme. 159p. 1980. Repr. of 1927 ed. lib. bdg. 20.00 (ISBN 0-8492-6835-4). R West.

MALNUTRITION

Pollitt, Ernesto. Poverty & Malnutrition in Latin America: Early Childhood Intervention Programs. LC 80-18811. 150p. 1980. 21.95 (ISBN 0-03-058031-5). Praeger.

MALPRACTICE

Furrow, Barry R. Malpractice in Psychotherapy. LC 79-3253. 192p. 1980. 18.95x (ISBN 0-669-03399-5). Lexington Bks.

Hutzler, Laurie H. Attorney's Malpractice Prevention Manual. 4th ed. (Illus.). 1979. 29.95x (ISBN 0-937542-00-8); pap. 15.00x (ISBN 0-937542-01-6). Legal Mgmt Serv.

Meisel, David J. Attorney Malpractice: Law & Procedure, Vol.1. LC 79-89562. 1980. 47.50. Lawyers Co-Op.

Pegalis, Steven & Wachsman, Harvey. American Law of Medical Malpactice, 2 vols. LC 79-90712. 1980. 95.00. Lawyers Co-Op.

Smith, Jeffery M. Preventing Legal Malpractice. 160p. 1981. pap. text ed. 7.95 (ISBN 0-8299-2118-4). West Pub.

Speiser, Stuart & Krause, Charles. Aviation Tort Law, 3 vols. LC 78-55326. 1980. 180.00. Lawyers Co-Op.

Van Bieryliet, Alan & Sheldon-Wildgen, Jan. Liability Issues in Community-Based Programs: Legal Principles, Problem Areas & Rdcommendations. 136p. 1980. pap. 10.95 (ISBN 0-933716-08-7). P H Brookes.

MALT

Breweries & Malsters in Europe, 1980. 69th ed. LC 46-33153. Orig. Title: Brauereien und Malzereien in Europa 1980. 610p. (Orig., Eng, Fr. & Ger.). 1980. 92.50x (ISBN 3-8203-0034-1). Intl Pubns Serv.

MALTHUS, THOMAS ROBERT, 1766-1834

Gamon, Richard Louis. The Thoughts of Thomas Robert Malthus As They Apply to the Economic Complexities of Our Present Age. (The Living Thoughts of the Great Economists Ser.). (Illus.). 97p. 1981. 17.55 (ISBN 0-918968-87-9). Inst Econ Finan.

MAMELUKES

Ayalon, David. The Mamluk Military Society. 364p. 1980. 69.00x (Pub. by Variorum England). State Mutual Bk.

--Studies on the Mamluks of Egypt. 360p. 1980. 60.00x (ISBN 0-86078-006-6, Pub. by Variorum England). State Mutual Bk.

MAMMALS

see also Marine Mammals; Primates; Rodentia

also names of families, genera, species, etc.

Fowler, Charles W. & Smith, Tim D. Dynamics of Large Mammal Populations. 525p. 1981. 40.00 (ISBN 0-471-05160-8, Pub.by Wiley Interscience). Wiley.

Godin, Alfred J. Wild Mammals of New England: Field Guide Edition. rev. ed. Vanderweide, Harry, ed. (Illus.). 200p. 1981. pap. 6.95 (ISBN 0-89933-012-6). DeLorme Pub.

Gubernick, David J. & Klopfer, Peter H., eds. Parental Care in Mammals. 460p. 1981. 39.50 (ISBN 0-306-40533-4, Plenum Pr). Plenum Pub.

Hamilton, William J., Jr. & Whitaker, John O., Jr. Mammals of the Eastern United States. 2nd ed. LC 79-12920. (HANH Ser.). (Illus.). 368p. 1979. 19.95x (ISBN 0-8014-1254-4). Comstock.

Mammals in the Seas, Vol. II: Pinniped Species Summaries & Report on Sirenians. (FAO Fisheries Ser.: No. 5, Vol. II). 151p. 1979. 20.25 (ISBN 92-5-100512-5, F2102, FAO). Unipub.

Taglianti, Augusto V. The World of Mammals. Gilbert, John, tr. LC 80-69173. (Abbeville Press Encyclopedia of Natural Science). (Illus.). 256p. 1980. 13.95 (ISBN 0-89659-183-2); pap. 7.95 (ISBN 0-89659-184-0). Abbeville Pr.

MAMMALS–PHYSIOLOGY

Moore, W. J. The Mammalian Skull. (Biological Structure & Function Ser.: No. 8). (Illus.). 400p. Date not set. 85.00 (ISBN 0-521-23318-6). Cambridge U Pr.

Papageorgiou, Nikolaos. Population Energy Relationships of the Agrimi (Capra Aegagrus Cretica) on Theodorou Island, Greece. (Illus.). 56p. (Orig.). pap. text ed. 14.10 (ISBN 3-490-21518-4). Parey Sci Pubs.

MAMMALS–AFRICA

Frame, George & Frame, Lory. Swift & Enduring: Cheetahs & Wild Dogs of the Serengeti. 1981. 15.95 (ISBN 0-525-93060-4). Dutton.

MAMMALS–NORTH AMERICA

Schwartz, Charles W. & Schwartz, Elizabeth R. Wild Mammals of Missouri. rev. ed. 384p. 1981. text ed. 35.00 (ISBN 0-8262-0324-8). U of Mo Pr.

Wallmo, Olof C., ed. Mule & Black-Tailed Deer of North America. LC 80-20128. (Illus.). xvii, 650p. 1981. 29.95 (ISBN 0-8032-4715-X). U of Nebr Pr.

MAN

see also Anthropology; Anthropometry; Craniology; Creation; Ethnology; Heredity; Human Biology; Philosophical Anthropology; Women

Alexander, Jason. In Praise of the Common Man. 86p. (Orig.). 1981. pap. price not set (ISBN 0-931826-02-0). Sitnalta Pr.

Collins, Gary. Hombre in Transicion. Ingledew, Roberto, tr. from Eng. 220p. (Orig., Span.). 1978. pap. 4.50 (ISBN 0-89922-124-6). Edit Caribe.

Haughton, Rosemary. Transformation of Man. rev. ed. 1980. pap. 6.95 (ISBN 0-87243-127-4). Templegate.

Johannes, Walter & Stein. Man & His Place in History. 1980. pap. 4.25x (ISBN 0-906492-35-1, Pub. by Kolisko Archives). St George Bk Serv.

Kruger, Maximilian. The Maximal Problems of Philosophy. (Illus.). 137p. 1981. 39.45 (ISBN 0-89266-274-3). Am Classical Coll Pr.

Ong, Walter J. Fighting for Life: Contest, Sexuality, & Consciousness. LC 80-66968. (Illus.). 240p. 1981. 14.95 (ISBN 0-8014-1342-7). Cornell U Pr.

Petacchi, Donald. Work for Being in the Machine Age. LC 80-82646. 1980. 12.50 (ISBN 0-8022-2376-1). Philos Lib.

Tarneja, Sukh R. Nature, Spirituality & Science. 240p. 1980. text ed. 27.50x (ISBN 0-7069-1203-9, Pub by Vikas India). Advent Bk.

Wallimann, Isidor. Estrangement: Marx's Conception of Human Nature & the Division of Labor. LC 80-929. (Contributions in Philosophy: No. 16). 240p. 1981. lib. bdg. 29.95 (ISBN 0-313-22096-4, WAE/). Greenwood.

MAN–ATTITUDE AND MOVEMENT

see also Posture

Tel Ngandong Fossil Hominids: A Comparative Study of a Far Eastern Homo Erectus Group. LC 80-50035. (Publications in Anthropology: No. 78). 1980. pap. 13.50. Yale U Anthro.

MAN–FOOD HABITS

see Food Habits

MAN–INFLUENCE OF CLIMATE

Kavanagh, P. J. People & Weather. 1980. pap. 5.95 (ISBN 0-7145-3666-0). Riverrun NY.

MAN–INFLUENCE OF ENVIRONMENT

see also Anthropo-Geography; Environmental Health

Coelho, George V., et al, eds. Uprooting & Development--Dilemmas of Coping with Modernization. (Current Topics in Mental Health Ser.). 500p. 1980. 27.50 (ISBN 0-306-40509-1, Plenum Pr). Plenum Pub.

Langfeldt, Steffen. The Energy to Prosper. 138p. (Orig.). 1980. pap. 6.95x (ISBN 0-935190-04-X). AM Books CA.

Winkler, Franz E. Man: The Bridge Between Two Worlds. LC 80-82064. 268p. 1980. pap. 4.95 (ISBN 0-913098-32-9). Myrin Institute.

MAN–INFLUENCE ON NATURE

see also Environmental Policy; Pollution

Dobyns, Henry F. From Fire to Flood: Historic Human Destruction of Sonoran Desert Riverine Oases. (Anthropological Papers Ser.: No. 20). (Illus.). 222p. (Orig.). 1981. pap. 11.95 (ISBN 0-87919-092-2). Ballena Pr.

Human Influences in African Pastureland Environments. 89p. 1981. pap. 6.00 (ISBN 92-5-100874-4, F2076, FAO). Unipub.

Limbrey, Susan & Evans, J. G., eds. The Effect of Man on the Landscape: The Lowland Zone. 160p. 1980. pap. 29.95x (ISBN 0-900312-60-2, Pub. by Council Brit Arch England). Intl Schol Bk Serv.

Winkler, Franz E. Man: The Bridge Between Two Worlds. LC 80-82064. 268p. 1980. pap. 4.95 (ISBN 0-913098-32-9). Myrin Institute.

MAN–MIGRATIONS

see also Migration, Internal; Migrations of Nations

Baker, Robin, ed. The Mystery of Migration. LC 80-16839. (Illus.). 256p. 1981. 29.95 (ISBN 0-670-50286-3). Viking Pr.

MAN–PARASITES

see Medical Parasitology

MAN (PHILOSOPHY)

see Philosophical Anthropology

MAN (THEOLOGY)

see also Humanism, Religious; Identification (Religion); Sex (Theology); Soul

Getz, Gene, tr. Vers la Stature Parfaite De Jesus-Christ. (French Bks.). (Fr.). 1979. 1.95 (ISBN 0-8297-0820-0). Vida Pub.

McDonald, H. D. The Doctrine of Man. (Foundations for Faith Ser.). 5.95 (ISBN 0-89107-217-9). Good News.

MAN, DOCTRINE OF

see Man (Theology)

MAN, ERECT POSITION OF

see Man–Attitude and Movement; Posture

MAN, FOSSIL

see Fossil Man

MAN, PREHISTORIC

see also Fossil Man; Glacial Epoch

also subdivision Antiquities under names of countries, cities, etc., e.g. Rome (City)–Antiquities

Reader, John. Missing Links & the Men Who Found Them. (Illus.). 181p. 1981. 19.95 (ISBN 0-316-73590-6). Little.

MAN, PREHISTORIC–ASIA

Institute of Vertebrate Paleontology & Paleoanthropology of the Chinese Academy of Sciences. Atlas of Primitive Man in China. (Illus.). 200p. 1980. text ed. 52.50 (ISBN 0-442-20013-7, Pub. by Sci Pr China). Van Nos Reinhold.

MAN, PREHISTORIC–MEXICO

Parsons, Jeffrey R. Prehistoric Settlement Patterns in the Southern Valley of Mexico: The Chalco-Xochimilco Region. (Memoir Ser.: No. 14). (Orig.). 1981. pap. write for info. (ISBN 0-932206-88-3). U Mich Mus Anthro.

MAN AND WIFE

see Husband and Wife

MAN-MACHINE CONTROL SYSTEMS

see Man-Machine Systems

MAN-MACHINE SYSTEMS

Petacchi, Donald. Work for Being in the Machine Age. LC 80-82646. 1980. 12.50 (ISBN 0-8022-2376-1). Philos Lib.

MAN-MADE LAKES

see Reservoirs

MAN ON OTHER PLANETS

see Life on Other Planets

MAN POWER

see Manpower

MAN-TO-MAN COMBAT

see Hand-To-Hand Fighting

MANAGEMENT

see also Business; Computer Programming Management; Credit Management; Executive Ability; Executives; Factory Management; Farm Management; Hospitals–Administration; Industrial Management; Office Management; Organization; Organizational Change; Personnel Management; Planning; School Management and Organization; Work Measurement

also subdivision management under specific subjects, e.g. Railroads–Management

Albers, Henry H. Management: The Basic Concepts. 336p. 1981. Repr. of 1972 ed. lib. bdg. price not set (ISBN 0-89874-312-5). Krieger.

Albrecht, Karl. Executive Tune-Up: Personal Effectiveness Skills for Business & Professional People. (Illus.). 224p. 1981. text ed. 13.95 (ISBN 0-13-294215-1, Spec); pap. text ed. 6.95 (ISBN 0-13-294207-0, Spec). P-H.

Allsopp, Michael. Management in the Professions: Guidelines to Improved Professional Performance. 201p. 1979. text ed. 29.50x (ISBN 0-220-67011-0, Pub. by Busn Bks England). Renouf.

Arabinda, Ray. The Manager Beyond the Organization. 1980. 9.50x (ISBN 0-8364-0636-2, Pub. by Macmillan India). South Asia Bks.

Arnold, John. Shooting the Executive Rapids: The First Year in a New Assignment. Newton, William R., ed. (Illus.). 288p. 1981. price not set (ISBN 0-07-002312-3, P&RB). McGraw.

Auxiliary Gift & Coffee Shop Management. 2nd ed. 136p. 1976. 16.25 (ISBN 0-686-68589-X, 1122). Hospital Finan.

Baehler, James R. The New Manager's Guide to Success. 160p. 1980. 19.95 (ISBN 0-03-058014-5). Praeger.

Batty, J. The Board & the Presentation of Financial Information to Management. 340p. 1978. text ed. 36.75x (ISBN 0-220-66352-1, Pub. by Busn Bks England). Renouf.

Belasco, James A. & Hampton, David R. Managemant Today. 2nd ed. 550p. 1981. text ed. 18.95 (ISBN 0-471-08579-0); write for info. tchr's. ed. (ISBN 0-471-08934-6). Wiley.

Bellaschi, Jules. To Lead & Manage. LC 80-83869. 70p. (Orig.). 1980. pap. 4.95 (ISBN 0-9605144-0-6). MJ Pubns.

Betts, Peter W. The Board & Administrative Management: Management for the Board. 192p. 1977. text ed. 23.50x (ISBN 0-220-66338-6, Pub. by Busn Bks England). Renouf.

Blagrove, Luanna C. Management for Proprietors & Partnerships. (Illus.). 165p. 1981. text ed. 24.95 (ISBN 0-9604466-7-2). Blagrove Pubns.

Blake, Robert R., et al. The Academic Administrator Grid: A Guide to Developing Effective Management Teams. LC 80-8908. (Higher Education Ser.). 1981. text ed. price not set (ISBN 0-87589-492-5). Jossey-Bass.

Block, Peter. Fifty-Fifty Consultation: A Guide to Getting Your Expertise Used. (Illus.). 200p. 1981. text ed. price not set (ISBN 0-89384-052-1). Learning Concepts.

Bobrow, Jerry & Covino, William A. GMAT (Graduate Management Admissions Test) Date not set. pap. text ed. cancelled. Cliffs.

Brownstone, D. L. How to Run a Successful Speccialty Food Store. 124p. 1978. pap. 5.95 (ISBN 0-471-04031-2). Wiley.

Buffa, Elwood S. Elements of Production-Operations Management. 256p. 1981. pap. text ed. 10.95 (ISBN 0-471-08532-4). Wiley.

Bullock, G. William, Jr. & Conrad, Clifton F. Management: Perspectives from the Social Sciences. LC 80-6097. 343p. 1981. lib. bdg. 19.75 (ISBN 0-8191-1466-9); pap. text ed. 11.00 (ISBN 0-8191-1467-7). U Pr of Amer.

Burghes, D. N. Mathematical Models in the Social, Management & Life Sciences. LC 79-40989. 287p. 1980. pap. 19.95 (ISBN 0-470-27073-X). Halsted Pr.

Chambers, Harry T. The Management of Small Offset Print Departments. 2nd ed. 217p. 1979. text ed. 22.00x (ISBN 0-220-67007-2, Pub. by Busn Bks England). Renouf.

Chandler, Alfred D., Jr. The Visible Hand: The Managerial Revolution in American Business. 1980. pap. 8.95 (ISBN 0-674-94052-0). Harvard U Pr.

Chao, Lincoln & Rodich, G. Study Guide for Stat. for Management. 272p. 1980. pap. text ed. 7.95 (ISBN 0-8185-0409-9). Brooks-Cole.

Coleman, David. Management of the Firm. 13.95; pap. 9.95 (ISBN 0-930726-02-2). Green Hill.

Company Administration Handbook. 4th ed. 832p. 1980. text ed. 69.75x (ISBN 0-566-02154-4, Pub. by Gower Pub Co England). Renouf.

Cook, Thomas M. & Russell, Robert A. Introduction to Management Science. 2nd ed. (Illus.). 640p. 1981. text ed. 22.95 (ISBN 0-13-486092-6). P-H.

Crix, Frederick C. Reprographic Management Handbook. 2nd ed. 332p. 1979. text ed. 30.75x (ISBN 0-220-67010-2, Pub. by Busn Bks England). Renouf.

Croft, David. Applied Statistics for Management Studies. 2nd ed. (Illus.). 304p. (Orig.). 1976. pap. text ed. 15.95x (ISBN 0-7121-0136-5, Pub. by Macdonald & Evans England). Intl Ideas.

Dannebring, David D. & Starr, Martin K. Management Science: An Introduction. (Quantitative Methods in Management Ser.). 1981. text ed. 22.00 (ISBN 0-07-015352-3, C); write for info study guide (ISBN 0-07-015353-1); write for info instrs.' manual (ISBN 0-07-015354-X). McGraw.

Davis, Keith. Human Behavior at Work. 6th ed. (Management Ser.). (Illus.). 576p. 1981. text ed. 18.95x (ISBN 0-07-015516-X, C); instrs'. manual & test file avail. (ISBN 0-07-015517-8); study guide avail. (ISBN 0-07-015535-6) (ISBN 0-686-68262-9). McGraw.

Denyer, J. C. Office Management. 5th ed. (Illus.). 528p. 1980. pap. text ed. 17.95x (ISBN 0-7121-1525-0). Intl Ideas.

Diamond, Susan Z. Preparing Administrative Manuals. 199p. 1981. 17.95 (ISBN 0-8144-5631-6). Am Mgmt.

Doctors, Samuel, et al. Curriculum Development for Public Management Innovation. LC 80-39481. 160p. 1981. text ed. 20.00 (ISBN 0-89946-079-8). Oelgeschlager.

Drucker, Peter F. Toward the Next Economics & Other Essays. LC 80-8370. 256p. 1981. 11.95 (ISBN 0-06-014828-4, HarpT). Har-Row.

Elkins, Arthur & Callaghan, Dennis W. Managerial Odyssey: Problems in Business & Its Enviroment. 600p. 1981. text ed. 17.50 (ISBN 0-201-03962-1). A-W.
Evered, James F. Shirt-Sleeves Management. 273p. 1981. 12.95 (ISBN 0-8144-5636-7). Am Mgmt.
Federico, Pat A., et al. Management Information Systems & Organizational Behavior. Brun, Kim & McCalla, Douglas B., eds. LC 80-15174. 204p. 1980. 20.95 (ISBN 0-03-057021-2). Praeger.
Flaherty, John E. Managing Change: Today's Challenge to Management. 12.50 (ISBN 0-8424-0115-6). Green Hill.
Frean, David. The Board & Management Development. 188p. 1980. text ed. 30.75x (ISBN 0-220-66304-1, Pub. by Busn Bks England). Renouf.
Galley, J. N. The Board & Computer Management. 185p. 1978. text ed. 23.50x (ISBN 0-220-67000-5, Pub. by Busn Bks England). Renouf.
Gautschi, Theodore F. Management Forum. (Illus.). 271p. 1979. pap. 16.00 (ISBN 0-536-03096-0). Herman Pub.
Gellerman. Manager & Subordinates. 1976. 13.95 (ISBN 0-03-089928-1). Dryden Pr.
Glaser, Rollin & Glaser, Christine. Managing by Design. LC 80-22455. 192p. 1981. text ed. 9.95 (ISBN 0-201-02717-8). A-W.
Glueck. Managing Essentials. 1979. 13.95 (ISBN 0-03-045416-6). Dryden Pr.
Hall, Jay. The Competence Process. LC 80-51211. (Illus.). 1980. text ed. 17.95 (ISBN 0-937932-01-9). Teleometrics.
Handern, Geoff. Business Organisation & Management. 1978. 22.50x (ISBN 0-86003-023-7, Pub. by Allan Pubs England); pap. 11.25x (ISBN 0-86003-124-1). State Mutual Bk.
Harris, Roy D. & Gonzalez, Richard F. The Operations Manager. (Illus.). 450p. 1981. text ed. 14.36 (ISBN 0-8299-0332-1). West Pub.
Heller, Frank A. Competence & Power in Managerial Decision-Making. Wilpert, Bernhard, ed. 256p. 1981. 34.50 (ISBN 0-471-27837-8, Pub. by Wiley-Interscience). Wiley.
Heneman, Herbert G., III, et al. Managing Personnel & Human Resources: Strategies & Programs. 350p. 1981. 15.95 (ISBN 0-87094-234-4). Dow Jones-Irwin.
Hodgetts, Richard M. Management Fundamentals. LC 80-65800. 464p. 1981. text ed. 17.95 (ISBN 0-03-058104-4). Dryden Pr.
Hunter, David M. Supervisory Management: Skill Building Techniques. 300p. 1981. text ed. 16.95 (ISBN 0-8359-7155-4); pap. text ed. 12.95 (ISBN 0-8359-7156-2); instr's. manual free (ISBN 0-8359-7157-0). Reston.
Hutzler, Laurie H. The Regulatory & Paperwork Maze. Incl. A Guide for Association Executives. pap. (ISBN 0-937542-03-2); A Guide for Government Personnel. pap. (ISBN 0-937542-04-0); A Guide for Small Business. pap. (ISBN 0-937542-02-4). (Illus.). 1980. pap. 10.00 ea. Legal Mgmt Serv.
--The Regulatory & Paperwork Maze: A Guide for Small Business, New 1981 "Reagan" Edition. 2nd ed. (Illus.). 1981. pap. 15.00 (ISBN 0-937542-06-7). Legal Mgmt Serv.
International Business & Management Institute. Little Known Business Secrets & Shortcuts for Entrepreneurs & Managers. (Illus.). 110p. (Orig.). pap. 25.00 (ISBN 0-935402-03-9). Intl Comm Serv.
International Business Management. 2nd ed. 1978. 20.95 (ISBN 0-03-040181-X). Dryden Pr.
Kivenko. Managing Work in Process. Date not set. price not set (ISBN 0-8247-1268-4). Dekker.
Krentzman, Harvey C. Successful Management Strategies for Small Business. (Illus.). 208p. 1981. (Spec); pap. text ed. 6.95 (ISBN 0-13-863118-2, Spec). P-H.
Lee, Sang M. Management by Multiple Objective. (Illus.). 240p. 1981. 20.00 (ISBN 0-89433-083-7). Petrocelli.
Leenders, Michael R., et al. Purchasing & Materials Management. 7th ed. 1980. 21.50x (ISBN 0-256-02374-3). Irwin.
Leontiades, Milton. Management Policy: Strategies & Plans. 680p. 1981. text ed. 18.95 (ISBN 0-316-52104-3); tchrs'. manual free (ISBN 0-316-52105-1). Little.
Lewis, C. D. Operations Management in Practice. 304p. 1980. 36.00x (ISBN 0-86003-511-5, Pub. by Allan Pubs England); pap. 18.00x (ISBN 0-86003-611-1). State Mutual Bk.
Littlechild, S. C. Operational Research for Managers. 256p. 1977. 33.00x (ISBN 0-86003-504-2, Pub. by Allan Pubs England); pap. 16.50 (ISBN 0-86003-604-9). State Mutual Bk.
Longenecker, Justin G. & Pringle, Charles D. Management. 5th ed. (Illus.). 544p. 1981. text ed. 19.95 (ISBN 0-675-08061-4); tchr's. manual avail.; study guide 6.95 (ISBN 0-675-09995-1). Merrill.
Love, Barbara, ed. Handbook of Circulation Management. 1980. 49.95 (ISBN 0-918110-02-5). Folio.
The Management of the Family Company. 19p. 1973. 2.75 (APO43, APO). Unipub.
Manning, Frank V. Managerial Dilemmas & Executive Growth. 1981. text ed. 17.95 (ISBN 0-8359-4231-7). Reston.
Margolis, Diane R. The Managers: Corporate Life in America. 312p. 1981. pap. 5.95 (ISBN 0-688-00351-6, Quill). Morrow.
Mason, Richard H. & Swanson, E. Burton. Measurement for Management Decision. (Computer Science: Decision Support). (Illus.). 448p. 1981. text ed. 15.95 (ISBN 0-201-04646-6). A-W.
Matteson, Michael & Ivancevich, John. Management Classics. 2nd ed. 1981. pap. text ed. write for info. (ISBN 0-8302-5469-2). Goodyear.
Maude, Barry. Leadership in Management. 240p. 1978. text ed. 29.50x (ISBN 0-220-66361-0, Pub. by Busn Bks England). Renouf.
Morell, R. W. & Henry, M. Daniel. The Practice of Management. LC 80-8136. 510p. 1981. lib. bdg. 26.00 (ISBN 0-8191-1489-8); pap. text ed. 16.75 (ISBN 0-8191-1490-1). U Pr of Amer.
Morris, Ralph. Computer Basics for Managers. 241p. 1980. text ed. 23.50x (ISBN 0-09-141570-5, Pub. by Busn Bks England). Renouf.
Murphy, Thomas P., et al. Contemporary Public Administration: A Study in Emerging Realities. LC 80-83377. 517p. 1981. text ed. 14.95 (ISBN 0-87581-269-4). Peacock Pubs.
Olm, et al. Management Decisions & Organizational Policy. 3rd ed. 560p. 1981. text ed. 21.95 (ISBN 0-205-07215-1, 0872156); free tchr's ed. (ISBN 0-205-07216-X). Allyn.
Porter, Michael E. Competitive Strategy: Techniques for Analyzing Industries & Competitors. (Illus.). 1980. 15.95 (ISBN 0-02-925360-8). Macmillan.
Pray, Thomas & Strong, Daniel. Decide: A Managerial Decision Game to Accompany Principles of Management by Kurtz & Boone. 120p. 1981. pap. text ed. 6.95 (ISBN 0-394-32698-9). Random.
Radde, Paul O. The Supervision Decision! Employee Guide. (Illus.). 150p. 1981. price not set vinyl binder (ISBN 0-89384-060-2); price not set wkbk. (ISBN 0-89384-061-0). Learning Concepts.
Radford, K. J. Modern Managerial Decision Making. 1981. text ed. 17.95 (ISBN 0-8359-4571-5); instr's. manual avail. (ISBN 0-8359-4229-5). Reston.
Reekie, W. Duncan. Macroeconomics for Managers. 160p. 1980. 18.00x (ISBN 0-86003-510-7, Pub. by Allan Pubs England); pap. 9.00x (ISBN 0-86003-610-3). State Mutual Bk.
--Managerial Economics. 440p. 1975. 45.00x (ISBN 0-86003-007-5, Pub. by Allan Pubs England); pap. 22.50x (ISBN 0-86003-108-X). State Mutual Bk.
Reinfeld, Nyles. Survival Management for Industry. 1981. text ed. 17.95 (ISBN 0-8359-7410-3); instr's. manual free (ISBN 0-8359-7411-1). Reston.
Rolichek. Management Fin. Inst. 2nd ed. 1976. 22.95 (ISBN 0-03-089912-5). Dryden Pr.
Sargent, Alice G. The Androgynous Manager. 240p. 1981. 12.95 (ISBN 0-8144-5568-9). Am Mgmt.
Sethi, S. P. & Thompson, G. L. Optimal Control Theory: Applications to Management Science. (International Series in Management Science - Operations Research: Vol. 1). 1981. lib. bdg. 25.00 (ISBN 0-89838-061-8, Pub. by Martinus Nijhoff). Kluwer Boston.
Shorris, Earl. The Oppressed Middle: The Politics of Middle Management. LC 80-717. 408p. 1981. 13.95 (ISBN 0-385-14564-0, Anchor Pr). Doubleday.
Shtogren, John A., ed. Models for Management: The Structure of Competence. LC 79-93291. (Illus.). 1981. pap. 17.95 (ISBN 0-937932-00-0). Teleometrics.
Silver, Gerald A. Introduction to Management. (Illus.). 525p. 1981. text ed. 16.95 (ISBN 0-8299-0415-8). West Pub.
Singer, Edwin J. Effective Management Coaching. 2nd ed. (Management in Perspective Ser.). 212p. 1979. pap. 11.50x (ISBN 0-85292-248-5). Intl Pubns Serv.
Sloma, Richard S. No-Nonsense Management. 176p. 1981. pap. 3.50 (ISBN 0-553-20035-6). Bantam.
Swift, Eric. Managing Your Export Office. 150p. 1977. text ed. 22.00x (ISBN 0-220-66310-6, Pub. by Busn Bks England). Renouf.
Taylor, Bernard & Hussey, David, eds. The Realities of Planning. (Illus.). 224p. 1981. 36.00 (ISBN 0-08-022226-9). Pergamon.
Taylor, W. J. & Watling, T. F. The Basic Arts of Management. 207p. 1977. text ed. 22.00x (ISBN 0-220-66812-4, Pub. by Busn Bks England). Renouf.
Tedeschi, James T., ed. Impression Management Theory & Social Psychological Research. 1981. price not set (ISBN 0-12-685180-8). Acad Pr.
Thomas, Adin B. Stock Control in Manufacturing Industries. 2nd ed. 240p. 1980. text ed. 29.50 (ISBN 0-566-02140-4, Pub. by Gower Pub Co England). Renouf.
Thompson, Ann M. & Wood, Marcia D. Management Strategies for Women: Or, Now That I'm Boss, How Do I Run This Place? 1981. 10.95 (ISBN 0-671-25476-6). S&S.
Thompson, Arthur A., Jr. & Strickland, A. J., III. Strategy & Policy. 1978. text ed. 19.95 (ISBN 0-256-02083-3). Business Pubns.
Tsurumi, Yoshi. Multinational Management: Business Strategy & Government Policy. 622p. 1976. write for info. (ISBN 0-88410-297-1). Ballinger Pub.
Vervalin, Charles H., ed. Management Handbook for the Hydrocarbon Processing Industries. 242p. 1981. pap. text ed. 15.95 (ISBN 0-87201-480-0). Gulf Pub.
Watson, Charles E. Managing for Results: How to Effecttively Get Things Done. LC 80-24047. 208p. 1981. pap. text ed. price not set. A-W.
Webber, Ross. Mangement Pragmatics. 1979. pap. 10.50x (ISBN 0-256-02232-1). Irwin.
Webber, Ross D. To Be a Manager. 1981. 18.95x (ISBN 0-256-02520-7). Irwin.
Welsh, A. N. The Skills of Management. 247p. 1981. 14.95 (ISBN 0-8144-5670-7). Am Mgmt.
Whitmore, D. A. & Ibbetson, J. The Management of Motivation & Renumeration. 230p. 1977. text ed. 29.50x (ISBN 0-220-66319-X, Pub. by Busn Bks England). Renouf.
Wilings, David R. Understanding Management. 320p. 1979. text ed. 14.35 (ISBN 0-7715-5728-0); instr's. manual 7.41 (ISBN 0-7715-5730-2). Forkner.
Wilson, J. P. Inflation, Deflation, Reflation: Managemnent & Accounting in Economic Uncertainty. 345p. 1980. text ed. 36.75x (ISBN 0-220-67015-3, Pub. by Busn Bks England). Renouf.
Winter, M. Mind Your Own Business, Be Your Own Boss. 1980. 12.95 (ISBN 0-13-583468-6); pap. 6.95 (ISBN 0-13-583450-3). P-H.
Wise, Sheldon. Essentials of Management. LC 79-88238. (The ALA ESP Ser.). (Illus.). v, 110p. (Orig.). 1979. pap. text ed. 6.25 (ISBN 0-934270-06-6). Am Lang Acad.
Young, Jerrald F. Decision Making for Small Business Management. 256p. 1981. Repr. of 1977 ed. lib. bdg. price not set (ISBN 0-89874-346-X). Krieger.

MANAGEMENT–CASE STUDIES
Davis, Keith & Newstrom, John. Organizational Behavior: A Book of Readings. 6th ed. (Illus.). 468p. text ed. 11.95 (ISBN 0-07-015500-3). McGraw.
Raymond, Corey E., et al. Problems in Marketing. 6th ed. (Illus.). 832p. 20.95 (ISBN 0-07-013141-4); instrs'. 4.95 (ISBN 0-07-013142-2). McGraw.
Werther, William & Davis, Keith. Personnel Management. (Illus.). 528p. (Orig.). text ed. 18.95x (ISBN 0-07-069436-2); instructor's manual & test bank. write for info. (ISBN 0-07-069437-0). McGraw.

MANAGEMENT–STUDY AND TEACHING
Leeds, C. S., et al. Management & Business Studies. 2nd ed. 448p. 1978. pap. text ed. 16.95x (ISBN 0-7121-1298-7, Pub. by Macdonald & Evans England). Intl Ideas.

MANAGEMENT, GAME
see Wildlife Management

MANAGEMENT, INDUSTRIAL
see Industrial Management

MANAGEMENT, MARKETING
see Marketing Management

MANAGEMENT, PRODUCT
see Product Management

MANAGEMENT, SALES
see Sales Management

MANAGEMENT, WILDLIFE
see Wildlife Management

MANAGEMENT ACCOUNTING
see Managerial Accounting

MANAGEMENT AUDIT
Smith, Billy E. Managing the Information Systems Audit: A Case Study-Policies, Procedures, & Guidelines. (Illus.). 65p. 1980. pap. text ed. 22.50 (ISBN 0-89413-086-2); avail. wkbk. (ISBN 0-89413-087-0). Inst Inter Aud.

MANAGEMENT AUDITING
see Management Audit

MANAGEMENT CONSULTANTS
see Business Consultants

MANAGEMENT GAMES
Crosby, Philip B. The Art of Getting Your Own Sweet Way. 2nd ed. (Illus.). 224p. 1981. 12.95 (ISBN 0-07-014515-6). McGraw.
Patz, Alan. Strategic Decision Analysis: A Managerial Approach to Policy. 1981. text ed. 18.95 (ISBN 0-316-69400-2); tchrs'. manual free (ISBN 0-316-69401-0). Little.

MANAGEMENT INFORMATION SYSTEMS
Ein-Dor, Phillip & Segev, Eli. A Paradigm for Management Information Systems. 232p. 1980. 22.95 (ISBN 0-03-058017-X). Praeger.
Federico, Pat A., et al. Management Information Systems & Organizational Behavior. Brun, Kim & McCalla, Douglas B., eds. LC 80-15174. 204p. 1980. 20.95 (ISBN 0-03-057021-2). Praeger.
Lucas, Henry & Gibson, Cyrus. Casebook for Management Information Systems. 2nd ed. (Management Information Systems Ser.). (Illus.). 480p. 1980. pap. text ed. 10.95 (ISBN 0-07-038939-X, C) (ISBN 0-686-68691-8). McGraw.

MANAGEMENT MARKETING
see Marketing Management

MANAGEMENT OF FACTORIES
see Factory Management

MANAGERIAL ACCOUNTING
see also Cost Accounting
Davidson, et al. Managerial Accounting. 1978. 20.95 (ISBN 0-03-017416-3). Dryden Pr.
Francia, Arthur J. & Strawser, Robert H. Managerial Accounting. 3rd ed. (Illus.). 565p. 1980. pap. text ed. 18.95 (ISBN 0-931920-20-5); practice problems 4.95x; study guide 5.95x; work papers 6.95x. Dame Pubns.
Horngren, Charles T. Introduction to Management Accounting. 5th ed. (Ser. in Accounting). (Illus.). 848p. 1981. text ed. 21.00 (ISBN 0-13-487652-0); wkbk. by Dudley W. Curry 8.95 (ISBN 0-13-487785-3). P-H.
Nelson & Miller. Modern Management Accounting. 2nd ed. 640p. 1981. write for info. (ISBN 0-8302-5904-X). Goodyear.
Newton, Grant W. CMA, 6 vols. Incl. Vol. 1. Economics & Business. 177p. pap. text ed. 18.50 scp (ISBN 0-06-453723-4); Vol. 2. Organization & Behavior, Including Ethical Considerations. 123p. pap. text ed. 14.95 scp (ISBN 0-06-453729-3); Vol. 3. Public Reporting Standards & Auditing. 201p. pap. text ed. 18.50 scp (ISBN 0-06-453730-7); Vol. 4. Periodic Reporting for Internal & External Purposes. 260p. pap. text ed. 18.50 scp (ISBN 0-06-453731-5); Vol. 5. Decision Analysis, Including Modeling & Information Systems. 246p. pap. text ed. 19.50 scp (ISBN 0-06-453732-3); Vol. 6. Taxes Current Pronouncements, & Updated CMA Questions. 1980. pap. text ed. 18.50 scp (ISBN 0-06-453742-0). pap. (HarpC). Har-Row.
O'Connor, Dennis J. & Bueso, Alberto T. Managerial Finance: Theory & Techniques. (Illus.). 528p. 1981. text ed. 21.00 (ISBN 0-13-550269-1); pap. 8.95 study guide (ISBN 0-13-550293-4). P-H.
Reekie, W. Duncan. Managerial Economics. 440p. 1975. 45.00x (ISBN 0-86003-007-5, Pub. by Allan Pubs England); pap. 22.50x (ISBN 0-86003-108-X). State Mutual Bk.
Shank, John K. Contemporary Managerial Accounting: A Casebook. (Illus.). 352p. 1981. 14.95 (ISBN 0-13-170357-9). P-H.
Simpson, L. Management Accounting: Techniques for Non-Financial Mangers. 246p. 1979. pap. 12.25x (ISBN 0-220-67023-4, Pub. by Busn Bks England). Renouf.
Thacker, Ronald & Ellis, Loudell. Student Guide to Management Accounting: Concepts & Applications. 336p. 1980. pap. text ed. 8.95 (ISBN 0-8359-4196-5). Reston.
Weston, J. Fred & Brigham, Eugene F. Managerial Finance. 7th ed. LC 80-65811. 1088p. 1981. text ed. 20.95 (ISBN 0-03-058186-9). Dryden Pr.

MANAGERIAL ECONOMICS
Carrol, Frieda. Survival Handbook for Small Business. LC 80-70496. 73p. 1980. 16.95 (ISBN 0-9605246-4-9); pap. 12.95. Biblio Pr GA.
O'Connor, Dennis J. & Bueso, Alberto T. A Self-Correcting Approach to Managerial Finance: Theory & Techniques. (Illus.). 320p. 1981. pap. text ed. 9.95 (ISBN 0-13-803189-4). P-H.
Pappas, James L. & Brigham, Eugene F. Fundamentals of Managerial Economics. LC 79-51063. 560p. 1981. text ed. 17.95 (ISBN 0-03-040841-5). Dryden Pr.
Papper. Managerial Economics. 3rd ed. 1979. 21.95 (ISBN 0-03-045126-4). Dryden Pr.
Trower-Subira, George. Black Folks' Guide to Making Big Money in America. 184p. 1980. 11.00 (ISBN 0-9605304-0-1). VSBE.
Watts, B. K. Elements of Finance for Managers. (Illus.). 256p. 1976. pap. 12.95x (ISBN 0-7121-0551-4, Pub. by Macdonald & Evans England). Intl Ideas.

MANAGERS
see Executives

MANATEES
Mammals in the Seas, Vol. II: Pinniped Species Summaries & Report on Sirenians. (FAO Fisheries Ser.: No. 5, Vol. II). 151p. 1979. 20.25 (ISBN 92-5-100512-5, F2102, FAO). Unipub.

MANCHESTER, ENGLAND
Chaloner, W. H. The Movement for the Extension of Owens College, Manchester, Eighteen Sixty-Three to Seventy-Three. 136p. 1973. 9.00x (ISBN 0-7190-0552-3, Pub by Mancherster U Pr England). State Mutual Bk.
Slugg, J. T. Reminiscences of Manchester Fifty Years Ago. (The Development of Industrial Society Ser.). 355p. 1980. Repr. 24.00x (ISBN 0-7165-1771-X, Pub. by Irish Academic Pr). Biblio Dist.
White, H. P. The Continuing Conurbation: Change & Development in Greater Manchester. 224p. 1980. text ed. 30.75x (ISBN 0-566-00248-5, Pub. by Gower Pub Co England). Renouf.

MANDAN INDIANS
see Indians of North America–The West

MANGER IN CHRISTIAN ART AND TRADITION
see Crib in Christian Art and Tradition

MANIA
see Psychoses

MANIC-DEPRESSIVE PSYCHOSES
see also Depression, Mental; Psychology, Pathological
Ross, Harvey. Fighting Depression. 221p. (Orig.). 1975. pap. 1.95. Larchmont Bks.

MANIFOLDS (MATHEMATICS)
Bishop, Richard & Goldberg, Samuel. Tensor Analysis on Manifolds. (Illus.). 1980. pap. 6.00 (ISBN 0-486-64039-6). Dover.

MANIKINS
see Models, Fashion

MANNED UNDERSEA RESEARCH STATIONS
Talkington. Undersea Work Systems. 240p. 1981. write for info. (ISBN 0-8247-1226-9). Dekker.

MANNEQUINS
see Models, Fashion

MANPOWER

see also Labor Supply; Military Service, Compulsory; also such headings as Agricultural Laborers, Chemists, etc.

Ross, Joe. Productivity, People & Profits. 150p. 1981. text ed. 17.95 (ISBN 0-8359-5473-0); pap. 10.95 (ISBN 0-8359-5472-2). Reston.

Stahel, Walter R. The Potential for Substituting Manpower for Energy. Date not set. 12.50 (ISBN 0-533-04799-4). Vantage.

MANPOWER DEVELOPMENT AND TRAINING

see Occupational Training

MANPOWER POLICY

see also Full Employment Policies; Labor Supply

Cascio, Wayne F. & Awad, Elias M. Human Resources Management: An Information Systems Approach. 450p. 1981. text ed. 19.95 (ISBN 0-8359-3008-4); student activities guide 7.95 (ISBN 0-8359-3010-6); instr's. manual avail. (ISBN 0-8359-3009-2). Reston.

Employment After CETA: Outcomes of Recent Research. 1980. 4.00. Comm Coun Great NY.

Gellerman. Management of Human Resources. 1976. 10.95 (ISBN 0-03-080485-X). Dryden Pr.

Guidelines for the Development of Employment & Manpower Information Programmes in Developing Countries. 87p. 1980. pap. 8.00 (ISBN 92-2-102176-9, ILO148, ILO). Unipub.

Karlins, Marvin. The Human Use of Human Resources. 1st ed. (Illus.). 208p. (Orig.). 11.95 (ISBN 0-07-033298-3); pap. text ed. 6.95 (ISBN 0-07-033297-5). McGraw.

Kinlaw, Dennis C. Helping Skills for Human Resource Development: A Facilitator's Package. 100p. (Orig.). 1980. pap. write for info. (ISBN 0-88390-163-3). Univ Assocs.

McBeath, Gordon. Manpower Planning & Control. 218p. 1978. text ed. 24.50x (ISBN 0-220-66348-3, Pub. by Busn Bks England). Renouf.

Schuler, Randall S. Personnel & Human Resource Management. (Management Ser.). (Illus.). 600p. 1981. text ed. 15.96 (ISBN 0-8299-0406-9). West Pub.

Schuler, Randall S., et al. Applied Readings in Personnel & Human Resource Management. (Management Ser.). (Illus.). 300p. 1981. pap. text ed. 6.36 (ISBN 0-8299-0408-5). West Pub.

Snider, Patricia J., ed. Human Resources Planning: A Guide to Data. 2nd ed. LC 80-67468. 392p. 1980. pap. 21.00 (ISBN 0-937856-00-2). Equal Employ.

MANPOWER TRAINING PROGRAMS

see Occupational Training

MANPOWER UTILIZATION

see Manpower Policy

MANSLAUGHTER

see Assassination; Murder

MANUAL ALPHABETS

see Deaf–Means of Communication

MANUAL SKILL

see Motor Ability

MANUFACTURES–CATALOGS

Stanley Rule & Level, Eighteen Ninety-Two Price List Revised to Eighteen Ninety-Seven, Abbrigment. 1980. pap. 3.00 (ISBN 0-913602-36-1). K Roberts.

Underhill Edge Tool Co., Eighteen Fifty-Nine Price List Axes & Mechanics' Tools. 1980. pap. 3.00 (ISBN 0-913602-37-X). K Roberts.

William Chapple: Eighteen Seventy-Six Revised Price List Planes. 1980. pap. 2.50 (ISBN 0-913602-35-3). K Roberts.

William Marples & Sons Price List of American Tools & Hardware, Nineteen Hundred Nine. 1980. pap. 4.50 (ISBN 0-913602-41-8). K Roberts.

MANUFACTURES–DIRECTORIES

Davis, John G. & Newman, Phyllis, eds. California Manufacturers Register, 1981. 34th rev. ed. LC 48-3418. 880p. 1981. 85.00 (ISBN 0-911510-83-4). Times-M Pr.

--California Services Register, 1981. 2nd ed. 680p. 1981. 60.00 (ISBN 0-911510-84-2). Times-M Pr.

MANUFACTURING ENGINEERING

see Production Engineering

MANUFACTURING MANAGEMENT

see Production Management

MANUFACTURING PROCESSES

see also Assembly-Line Methods; Finishes and Finishing; Machine-Tools; Materials; Metal-Work; Process Control; Woodwork

Beebe, William, intro. by. Autofact West Proceedings, Vol. 1. LC 80-53423. (Illus.). 939p. 1980. pap. 55.00 (ISBN 0-87263-065-X). SME.

Burnham, Don, intro. by. Manufacturing Productivity Solutions II. LC 80-54415. (Illus.). 161p. 1980. pap. text ed. 20.00 (ISBN 0-87263-106-0). SME.

Energy Policy for the Manufacturing Sector. 155p. 1980. pap. 13.25 (ISBN 92-833-1459-X, APO 90, APO). Unipub.

Harris. Manufacturing Technology, No. 3. 1981. text ed. price not set (ISBN 0-408-00493-2). Butterworth.

Link, Albert N. Research & Development in U.S. Manufacturing. 124p. 1981. 18.95 (ISBN 0-03-057677-6). Praeger.

McCarty, Frank, intro. by. Autofact West Proceedings, Vol. 2. LC 80-53423. (Illus.). 842p. 1980. pap. 55.00 (ISBN 0-87263-066-8). SME.

Pressman, R. S. & Williams, J. E. Numerical Control & Computer-Aided Manufacturing. 310p. 1977. text ed. 24.95 (ISBN 0-471-01555-5). Wiley.

--Numerical Control & Computer-Aided Manufacturing. 310p. 1977. 24.95 (ISBN 0-471-01555-5). Wiley.

Smith, Donald, et al. CAD-CAM International Delphi Forecast. LC 80-53001. (Illus.). 181p. 1980. pap. 24.00 (ISBN 0-87263-062-5). SME.

Taraman, Khalil S., ed. CAD-CAM, Meeting Today's Productivity Challenge. LC 80-69006. (Manufacturing Update Ser.). (Illus.). 281p. 1980. 29.00 (ISBN 0-87263-063-3). SME.

MANUMISSION OF SLAVES

see Slavery–Emancipation

MANURES

see Fertilizers and Manures

MANUSCRIPT DEPOSITORIES

see Archives

MANUSCRIPTS

see also Music–Manuscripts

Brown, John H. & Grant, Steven A. The Russian Empire & Soviet Union: A Guide to Manuscripts & Archival Materials in the United States. (Libary Catalogs Supplement). 1981. lib. bdg. 75.00 (ISBN 0-8161-1300-9). G K Hall.

Hughes, Andrew. Medieval Manuscripts for Mass & Office: A Guide to Their Organization & Terminology. 496p. 1981. 45.00x (ISBN 0-8020-5467-6). U of Toronto Pr.

Meiss, Millard. The De Levis Hours & the Bedford Workshop. 73p. 1981. text ed. 10.00x (ISBN 0-300-03507-1). Yale U Pr.

Turyn, Alexander. Dated Greek Manuscripts of the Thirteenth & Fourteenth Centuries in the Libraries of Great Britian. LC 80-81547. (Dumbarton Oaks Studies: Vol. 17). (Illus.). 198p. 1980. 65.00 (ISBN 0-88402-077-0, Ctr Byzantine). Dumbarton Oaks.

MANUSCRIPTS–CATALOGS

The Card Catalog of the Manuscript Collections of the Archives of American Art, 10 vols. LC 80-53039. 5000p. 1981. lib. bdg. 595.00 (ISBN 0-8420-2174-4). Scholarly Res Inc.

Edinburgh University Library. First Supplement to Manuscripts, Edinburgh University Library. (Library Catalogs-Supplements). lib. bdg. 115.00 (ISBN 0-8161-0319-4). G K Hall.

Edwards, A. S. & Pearsall, Derek, eds. Middle English Prose: Essays on Bibliographical Problems. LC 80-8595. 150p. 1981. lib. bdg. 25.00 (ISBN 0-8240-9453-0). Garland Pub.

Pigeaud, Theodore G. Literature of Java: Supplement Catalogue Raisonne of Javanese Manuscripts in the Library of the University of Leiden & Other Public Collections in the Netherlands. (Codices Manuscript Ser.: No. XX). (Illus.). 390p. 1980. pap. 64.10 (ISBN 90-6021-453-6, Pub. by Leiden University Press). Kluwer Boston.

MANUSCRIPTS–EXHIBITIONS

see also Bibliographical Exhibitions

Agrawal, O. P. Paintings & MS. of Southeast Asia. 1981. text ed. price not set. Butterworths.

MANUSCRIPTS (PAPYRI)

McCarren, Vincent P. Michigan Papyri XIV. (American Studies in Papyrology: No. 22). 15.00x (ISBN 0-89130-295-6). Scholars Pr CA.

Schuman, Verne B. Washington University Papyri I: Non-Literary Texts, Nos. 1-16. LC 79-14199. (American Society of Papyrologists Ser.: No. 17). 15.00 (ISBN 0-89130-286-7). Scholars Pr CA.

MAO TSE-TUNG, 1893-1976

Bloodworth, Dennis & Ching Ping. Heirs Apparent: What Happens When Mao Dies? 272p. 1973. 7.95 (ISBN 0-374-16898-9). FS&G.

Chou, Eric. Mao Tse-Tung: The Man & the Myth. LC 80-22758. 304p. 1981. 16.95 (ISBN 0-8128-2769-4). Stein & Day.

MAOISM

see Communism

MAP READING

see Maps

MAPS

see also Atlases; Nautical Charts; World Maps

Brown, Lloyd A. The Story of Maps. LC 79-52395. (Illus.). 417p. 1980. Repr. of 1949 ed. 11.95 (ISBN 0-938164-00-7). Vintage Bk Co.

Numerology Map - Interstate System. 1978. 1.00. AASHTO.

MAPS–BIBLIOGRAPHY

Research Libraries of the New York Public Library & the Library of Congress. Bibliographic Guide to Maps & Atlases: 1980. (Library Catalogs-Bib. Guides Ser.). 1981. lib. bdg. 95.00 (ISBN 0-8161-6890-3). G K Hall.

MAPS, HISTORICAL

see Geography, Historical–Maps

MAPS, METEOROLOGICAL

see Meteorology–Charts, Diagrams, etc.

MAPS, WORLD

see World Maps

MARATHON RUNNING

Bloom, Marc. The Marathon: What It Takes to Go the Distance. LC 80-18859. (Illus.). 304p. 1981. 15.95 (ISBN 0-03-052476-8); pap. 8.95 (ISBN 0-686-69124-5). HR&W.

Sullivan, George. Marathon: The Longest Race. LC 80-6776. (Illus.). (gr. 5-8). 1980. PLB 9.95 (ISBN 0-664-32671-4). Westminster.

MARCHING BANDS

see Bands (Music)

MARCONI COMPANY LTD.

Marconi's International Register: 81st Annual Edition. 81th, rev. ed. 1980. lib. bdg. 60.00 (ISBN 0-916446-06-9). Tele Cable.

MARCUS AURELIUS

see Aurelius Antoninus, Marcus, Emperor of Rome, 121-180

MARENZIO, LUCA, 1553-1599

Marenzio, Luca. Il Settimo Libro de, Madrigali a Cinque Voci 1595: Luca Marenzio, the Secular Works, 14. Myers, Patricia, tr. (Illus.). xxxv, 224p. 1980. 35.00x (ISBN 0-8450-7114-9). Broude.

--Madrigali a Quattr Cinque e Sei Vodi, Libro Primo 1588: Luca Marenzio, the Secular Works, No. 7. Ledbetter, Steven, ed. xxvi, 167p. 1977. lib. bdg. 25.00 (ISBN 0-8450-7107-6). Broude.

MARI LANGUAGE

see Cheremissian Language

MARICOPA INDIANS

see Indians of North America–Southwest, New

MARIHUANA

Anderson, Patrick. High in America. LC 80-51772. 360p. 1981. 13.95 (ISBN 0-670-11990-3). Viking Pr.

Bauman, Carl E. Predicting Adolescent Drug Use: Utility Structure & Marijuana. 192p. 1980. 22.95 (ISBN 0-03-050636-0). Praeger.

Clarke, Robert C. Marijuana Botany. (Illus.). 224p. 1981. pap. 7.95 (ISBN 0-915904-45-4). And-or Pr.

Tobias, Ann. Pot -- What It Is, What It Does. LC 78-10817. (Read-Alone Bk.). (Illus.). 48p. (gr. 1-3). 1981. PLB 2.95 (ISBN 0-688-00463-6). Greenwillow.

MARII LANGUAGE

see Cheremissian Language

MARIJUANA

see Marihuana

MARINE AIDS

see Aids to Navigation

MARINE AQUARIUMS

Reed, Don C. Notes from an Underwater Zoo. (Illus.). 1981. 11.95. Dial.

MARINE ARCHITECTURE

see Naval Architecture; Ship-Building

MARINE BIOLOGY

see also Marine Aquariums; Marine Ecology; Marine Fauna; Marine Flora; Marine Microbiology; Marine Resources; Marine Sediments; Sedimentation and Deposition; Shells

Barica, J. & Mur, L., eds. Hypertrophic Ecosystems. (Developments in Hydrobiology Ser.: No. 2). 330p. 1981. PLB 87.00 (ISBN 90-6193-752-3, Pub. by Dr. W. Junk). Kluwer Boston.

Barnes, Margaret & Barnes, Harold, eds. Oceanography & Marine Biology: An Annual Review, Vol. 18. (Illus.). 528p. 1980. 84.00 (ISBN 0-08-025732-1). Pergamon.

Dumont, H. J. & Green, J., eds. Rotatoria. (Developments in Hydrobiology Ser.: No. 1). 268p. 1980. lib. bdg. 79.00 (ISBN 90-6193-754-X, Pub. by Dr. W. Junk). Kluwer Boston.

Falkowski, Paul G., ed. Primary Productivity in the Sea: Environmental Science Research Ser. (Vol. 19). 335p. 1980. 49.50 (ISBN 0-306-40623-3). Plenum Pub.

McLusky, Donald S. Estuarine Ecosystem. (Tertiary Level Biology Ser.). 176p. 1981. 34.95 (ISBN 0-470-27127-2). Halsted Pr.

Oceanography & Marine Biology: An Annual Review, Vol. 18. 1980. 95.00. Taylor Carlisle.

MARINE BOILERS

see Steam-Boilers

MARINE DEPOSITION

see Sedimentation and Deposition

MARINE DIESEL MOTORS

Lamb, John. Running & Maintenance of the Marine Diesel Engine. 722p. 1977. 57.95x (ISBN 0-85264-105-2, Pub. by Griffin England). State Mutual Bk.

Lamb's Questions & Answers on the Marine Diesel Engine. 466p. 1978. 35.95x (ISBN 0-85264-248-2, Pub. by Griffin England). State Mutual Bk.

Woodward, John B. Low Speed Marine Diesel. (Ocean Engineering: a Wiley Ser.). 368p. 1981. 33.50 (ISBN 0-471-06335-5, Pub.by Wiley-Interscience). Wiley.

MARINE DISASTERS

see Shipwrecks

MARINE ECOLOGY

Flint, R. Warren & Rabalais, Nancy N., eds. Environmental Studies of a Marine Ecosystem: South Texas Outer Continental Shelf. (Illus.). 272p. 1981. text ed. 35.00x (ISBN 0-292-72030-0). U of Tex Pr.

Hart, Paul & Pitcher, Tony. Fisheries Ecology. 224p. 1980. 35.00x (ISBN 0-85664-894-9, Pub. by Croom Helm England). State Mutual Bk.

Tait, R. V. Elements of Marine Ecology. 3rd ed. (Illus.). 304p. 1981. pap. write for info. (ISBN 0-408-71054-3). Butterworth.

Thomas Telford Ltd. Editorial Staff. The Marine Environment & Oil Facilities. 168p. 1980. 69.00x (ISBN 0-7277-0075-8, Pub. by Telford England). State Mutual Bk.

Vernberg, F. J. & Vernberg, W. B., eds. Functional Adaptations of Marine Organisms. (Physiological Ecology Ser.). 1981. price not set (ISBN 0-12-718280-2). Acad Pr.

MARINE ENGINEERING

see also Electricity on Ships; Marine Engines; Steam-Boilers

Timm, Simon, ed. Directory of Shipowners, Shipbuilders & Marine Engineers 1980. 78th ed. LC 25-4199. 1514p. 1980. 55.00x (ISBN 0-617-00301-7). Intl Pubns Serv.

Watson. Marine Electrical Practice. 5th ed. 1981. text ed. price not set (ISBN 0-408-00498-3). Butterworth.

MARINE ENGINES

see also Diesel Motor; Marine Diesel Motors; Steam-Boilers

Donat, Hans. Practical Points on Boat Engines. 204p. 1980. 8.00x (ISBN 0-245-53333-8, Pub. by Nautical England). State Mutual Bk.

Durham, Bill, ed. Steamboats & Modern Steam Launches. (Illus.). 631p. 1981. Repr. of 1963 ed. 25.00. A S Barnes.

MARINE FAUNA

see also Fishes; Marine Aquariums; Marine Mammals

Aspects of Brackish Water Fish & Crustacean Culture in the Mediterranean. 135p. 1981. pap. 7.25 (ISBN 92-5-000964-X, F2103, FAO). Unipub.

Fotheringham, Nick. Beachcomber's Guide to Gulf Coast Marine Life. LC 80-10607. (Illus.). 1980. pap. 6.95 (ISBN 0-88415-496-3). Pacesetter Pr.

Reed, Don C. Notes from an Underwater Zoo. (Illus.). 1981. 11.95. Dial.

Vernberg, F. J. & Vernberg, W. B., eds. Functional Adaptations of Marine Organisms. (Physiological Ecology Ser.). 1981. price not set (ISBN 0-12-718280-2). Acad Pr.

MARINE FLORA

see also Marine Aquariums

Hartley, L. P. Shrimp & Anemone. 1963. pap. 2.95 (ISBN 0-571-07061-2, Pub. by Faber & Faber). Merrimack Bk Serv.

MARINE GEOLOGY

see Submarine Geology

MARINE INSURANCE

see Insurance, Marine

MARINE LAW

see Maritime Law

MARINE MAMMALS

Kooyman, Gerald L. Weddell Seal, Consummate Diver. LC 80-18794. (Illus.). 176p. Date not set. price not set (ISBN 0-521-23657-6). Cambridge U Pr.

MARINE MICROBIOLOGY

Wood, E. J. The Living Ocean. 250p. 1980. 29.00x (ISBN 0-85664-026-3, Pub. by Croom Helm England). State Mutual Bk.

MARINE PAINTING

Betts, Edward. Creatice Seascape Painting. 160p. 1981. 19.15 (ISBN 0-8230-1113-5). Watson-Guptill.

Smith, Philip C. More Marine & Drawings in the Peabody Museum. (Illus.). 192p. 1979. 35.00 (ISBN 0-87577-064-9); boxed numbered 50.00 (ISBN 0-686-68319-6). Peabody Mus Salem.

MARINE POLLUTION

see also Oil Pollution of Rivers, Harbors, etc.

Charney, Jonathan I., ed. The New Nationalism & the Use of Common Spaces: Issues in Marine Pollution & the Exploitation of Antarctica. 420p. 1981. text ed. 29.00 (ISBN 0-86598-012-8). Allanheld.

International Conference on Marine Pollution, 1973 - 1977 Edition. 168p. 1977. 13.75 (IMCO). Unipub.

Report of the Symposium on Prevention of Marine Pollution from Ships: Acapulco-1976. 90p. 1976. 12.50 (IMCO). Unipub.

Timagenis. International Control of Marine Pollution, Vols. 1-2. 1980. 37.50 ea. Vol. 1 (ISBN 0-379-20685-4). Vol. 2 (ISBN 0-379-20686-2). Oceana.

MARINE RESOURCES

see also Continental Shelf; Fisheries; Fishery Products; Ocean Engineering

Brin, Andre. Energy & the Oceans. 1981. pap. text ed. write for info. (ISBN 0-86103-024-9, Westbury Hse). Butterworth.

An Overview: Marine Living Resources. (UNEP Report Ser.: No. 7). 73p. 1980. pap. 8.50 (UNEP 035, UNEP). Unipub.

Report of the Thirs Session of the Committee on Resource Managment of the General Fisheries Council for the Mediterranean. (FAO Fisheries Report: No. 240). 20p. 1981. pap. 6.00 (ISBN 92-5-100966-X, F2087, FAO). Unipub.

The Sea: A Select Bibliography on the Legal, Political, Economic & Technological Aspects, 1978-1979. 46p. 1980. pap. 5.00 (ISBN 0-686-68970-4, UN80/16, UN). Unipub.

World List of Aquatic Sciences & Fisheries Serial Titles. (FAO Fisheries Technical Paper: No. 147). 128p. 1980. pap. 7.00 (ISBN 92-5-100904-X, F1946, FAO). Unipub.

World List of Aquatic Sciences & Fisheries Serial Titles. (FAO Fisheries Technical Paper: No. 148). 128p. 1980. pap. 6.00 (ISBN 92-5-000882-1, F1947, FAO). Unipub.

MARINE SAFETY

see Navigation–Safety Measures

MARINE SEDIMENTS

Gray, J. S. The Ecology of Marine Sediments. (Cambridge Studies in Modern Biology: No. 2). (Illus.). 170p. Date not set. price not set (ISBN 0-521-23553-7); pap. price not set (ISBN 0-521-28027-3). Cambridge U Pr.

MARINE SHIPPING

see Shipping

MARINE SIGNALS
see Aids to Navigation
MARINE STRUCTURES
see Offshore Structures
MARINE SURVEYING
see Hydrographic Surveying
MARINE TECHNOLOGY
see Marine Engineering
MARINE TRANSPORTATION
see Shipping
MARINE ZOOLOGY
see Marine Fauna
MARINIDES
see Beni Marin Dynasty
MARIONETTES
see Puppets and Puppet-Plays
MARITAL COUNSELING
see Marriage Counseling
MARITIME DISCOVERIES
see Discoveries (In Geography)
MARITIME HISTORY
see subdivisions Navy or History, Naval under names of countries, e.g. United States–History, Naval and Great Britain–Navy
MARITIME LAW
see also Commercial Law; Free Ports and Zones; Freight and Freightage; Insurance, Marine; Neutrality; Pirates; Salvage; Shipmasters; Ships Papers; Slave-Trade

Amendment Number One to the Fourth Edition of Ship's Routing. 36p. 1979. 11.00 (IMCO). Unipub.

Basic Documents, Vol. 1. 92p. 1979. 16.50 (IMCO). Unipub.

Center for Ocean Management Studies, ed. Comparative Marine Policy. 336p. 1980. 26.95 (ISBN 0-03-058307-1). Praeger.

Code for the Construction & Equipment of Ships Carrying Dangerous Chemicals in Bulk. 86p. 1977. 11.00 (IMCO). Unipub.

Code of Safe Practice for Bulk Cargoes. (Illus.). 137p. 1977. 15.25 (IMCO). Unipub.

Code of Safe Practice for Ships Carrying Timber Deck Cargoes. 31p. 1974. 7.00 (IMCO). Unipub.

Convention on the Inter-Governmental Maritime Consultative Organization. 24p. 1979. 8.25 (IMCO). Unipub.

Durante, F. Western Europe & the Development of the Law of the Sea. 1980. 75.00 (ISBN 0-379-20288-3). Oceana.

Hollick, Ann L. U.S. Foreign Policy & the Law of the Sea. LC 80-8554. 456p. 1981. 27.50x (ISBN 0-691-09387-3); pap. 12.50x (ISBN 0-686-69179-2). Princeton U Pr.

International Conference on Limitation of Liability for Maritime Claims. 46p. 1977. 8.25 (IMCO). Unipub.

Markow, Herbert L. Small Boat Law: Nineteen Seventy-Nine to Nineteen Eighty Supplement. 1981. pap. write for info. (ISBN 0-934108-02-1). H L Markow.

Nordquist, M. New Directions in the Law of the Sea, Vol. 7. 1980. 45.00 (ISBN 0-379-00532-8). Oceana.

OECD. Maritime Transport Nineteen Seventy-Nine. (Illus.). 151p. (Orig.). 1980. pap. text ed. 10.50x (ISBN 92-64-12122-6). OECD.

Procedures for the Control of Ships & Discharges. 22p. 1978. 7.00 (IMCO). Unipub.

Szekely, A. Latin America & the Law of the Sea, Release 1. 1980. 32.50 (ISBN 0-379-10180-7). Oceana.

Third U. N. Conference on the Law of the Sea: Summary Records of Meetings, Documents Resumed Eighth Session, Vol.12. 115p. 1980. pap. 9.00 (UN80-5-12, UN). Uniub.

University of Southampton. World Shipping Law, Release 2. 1980. 80.00 (ISBN 0-379-10168-8). Oceana.

Warren, Gordon H. Fountain of Discontent: The Trent Affair & Freedom of the Seas. LC 80-24499. (Illus.). 366p. 1981. price not set. NE U Pr.

MARITIME LAW–UNITED STATES

Markow, Herbert L. Small Boat Law Supplement 1979-1980. (Orig.). 1981. pap. write for info. (ISBN 0-934108-02-1). H L Markow.

MARITIME SHIPPING
see Shipping
MARITIME SURVEYING
see Hydrographic Surveying
MARKET GARDENING
see Truck Farming
MARKETING
see also Commodity Exchanges; Export Marketing; Merchandising; New Products; Price Policy; Retail Trade; Sales Management; Sales Promotion
also Subdivision Marketing under Names of Commodities, E.g. Farm Produce–Marketing; Fruit–Marketing

Annual Educators Conference Chicago, Illinois, August, 1980. Marketing in the Eighties, Changes & Challenges: Proceedings. Bagozzi, Richard P., et al, eds. LC 80-15934. (No. 46). (Illus., Orig.). 1980. pap. text ed. 30.00 (ISBN 0-87757-141-4). Am Mktg.

Berry, Richard C. Industrial Marketing for Results. LC 80-18222. (Illus.). 144p. 1981. text ed. 19.95 (ISBN 0-201-00075-X). A-W.

Brannen, William H. Practical Marketing for Your Small Retail Business. (Illus.). 272p. 1981. 16.95 (ISBN 0-13-692764-5, Spec); pap. 8.95 (ISBN 0-13-692756-4). P-H.

Business Communications Co. Direct Marketing Business, GB-060: New Perspectives. 1980. cancelled (ISBN 0-89336-276-X). BCC.

Cohen, William A. & Reddick, Marshall E. Successful Marketing for Small Business. 364p. 1981. 17.95 (ISBN 0-8144-5611-1). Am Mgmt.

Enis, Ben M. & Cox, Keith M. Marketing Classics: A Selection of Influential Articles. 4th ed. 528p. 1981. text ed. 13.95 (ISBN 0-205-05715-2); free (ISBN 0-205-07326-3). Allyn.

Fisher, Lawrence. Industrial Marketing: An Analytical Approach to Planning & Execution. 2nd ed. 270p. 1976. text ed. 29.50x (ISBN 0-220-66292-4, Pub. by Busn Bks England). Renouf.

Fisk, George & Nason, Robert W., eds. Macromarketing, Vol. III: New Steps on the Learning Curve. 421p. 1979. 12.00 (ISBN 0-686-69387-6). U CO Busn Res Div.

Fraser, Richard G. Marketing One & Two. 1977. No. 1, 224p. text ed. 13.27 (ISBN 0-7715-0870-0); No. 2, 208p. text ed. 13.27 (ISBN 0-7715-0872-7); tchr's. guide 6.60 (ISBN 0-7715-0871-9). Forkner.

Hafer, George B., ed. A Look Back, a Look Ahead. LC 80-10370. (Proceedings Ser.). (Illus.). 207p. (Orig.). pap. text ed. 10.00 (ISBN 0-87757-134-1). Am Mktg.

Head, Victor. Sponsorship: The Newest Marketing Skill. 160p. 1980. 39.00x (ISBN 0-85941-151-6, Pub. by Woodhead-Faulkner England). State Mutual Bk.

Hemingway, Pamela. Direct Marketing Market Place 1981. 375p. 1981. pap. 40.00 (ISBN 0-934464-02-2). Hilary House Pubs.

Kincaid, William M. Promotion: Products, Servies & Ideas. (Illus.). 360p. 1981. text ed. 19.95 (ISBN 0-675-08082-7); tchr's. manual avail. Merrill.

Kollet, et al. Strategic Marketing. 1972. 20.95 (ISBN 0-03-078770-X). Dryden Pr.

Kurtz, David L. & Boone, Louis E. Marketing. LC 80-65788. 736p. 1981. text ed. 18.95 (ISBN 0-03-057431-5). Dryden Pr.

Larreche, Jean-Claude & Strong, Edward C. Readings in Marketing Strategy. 1981. pap. text ed. 13.50x (ISBN 0-89426-030-8). Scientific Pr.

Mandell, M. & Rosenberg, L. Marketing. 2nd ed. 1981. 21.00 (ISBN 0-13-556225-2); pap. 7.95 study guide (ISBN 0-13-556233-3). P-H.

Mandell, Maurice & Rosenberg, Larry J. Marketing. 2nd ed. (Illus.). 608p. 1981. text ed. 21.00 (ISBN 0-13-556225-2). P-H.

Mas, Janet. Better Brochures, Catalogs & Mailing Pieces. (Illus.). 128p. 1981. 9.95 (ISBN 0-312-07730-0). St Martin.

OECD. Bargain Price Offers & Similar Marketing Practices. (Illus., Orig.). 1980. pap. text ed. 6.00 (ISBN 92-64-12033-5, 24-80-01-1). OECD.

Olshavsky, Richard W. Attitude Research Enters the Eighties. LC 80-20621. (Proceedings Ser.). 196p. 1980. pap. 12.00 (ISBN 0-87757-145-7). Am Mktg.

Rexroad, Robert A. Technical Marketing to the Government. 325p. 1981. 69.50 (ISBN 0-85013-122-7). Dartnell Corp.

Rogers, Robert S. & Chamberlain, V. B., 3rd, eds. National Account Marketing Handbook. 426p. 1981. 24.95 (ISBN 0-8144-5618-9). Am Mgmt.

Rosenbloom. Marketing Channels. 1978. 20.95 (ISBN 0-03-017831-2). Dryden Pr.

Rosenbloom, Bert. Retail Marketing. 470p. 1981. text ed. 20.95 (ISBN 0-394-32191-X). Random.

Ryans, John K., Jr., ed. Marketing Doctoral Dissertation Abstracts, 1979. (Bibliography Ser.: No. 38). 142p. 1980. 15.00 (ISBN 0-87757-146-5). Am Mktg.

Schwerin, Horace S. & Newell, Henry H. Persuasion in Marketing: The Dynamics of Marketing's Great Untapped Resource. 280p. 1981. 23.95 (ISBN 0-471-04554-3, Pub. by Wiley-Interscience). Wiley.

Shapiro, Irving J. Dictionary of Marketing Terms. 4th ed. 276p. 1981. 19.50x (ISBN 0-8476-6967-X). Rowman.

Slater, Charles C. & White, Phillip D., eds. Macromarketing, Vol. II: Distributive Processes from a Societal Perspective, an Elaboration of Issues. 477p. 1978. 10.00 (ISBN 0-686-69388-4). U CO Busn Res Div.

Stanton, William J. Fundamentals of Marketing. 6th ed. (Illus.). 704p. 1981. text ed. 19.95 (ISBN 0-07-060891-1, C); instrs. manual 10.95 (ISBN 0-07-060892-X); study guide 6.95 (ISBN 0-07-060893-8); test file 15.95 (ISBN 0-07-060894-6); transparency masters avail. (ISBN 0-07-060895-4). McGraw.

Terpstra. International Marketing. 2nd ed. 1978. 21.95 (ISBN 0-03-039296-9). Dryden Pr.

Theory Conference, Phoenix, Arizona, February, 1980. Theoretical Developments in Marketing: Proceedings. Lamb, Charles W., Jr. & Dunne, Patrick M., eds. LC 80-12436. (Illus.). 269p. (Orig.). 1980. pap. text ed. 24.00 (ISBN 0-87757-138-4). Am Mktg.

Trueman, R. Introduction Quant. Meth. Dec. Marketing. 2nd ed. 1977. 19.95 (ISBN 0-03-018391-X). Dryden Pr.

Udell, Jon G. & Laczniak, Gene R. Marketing in an Age of Change. (Marketing Ser.). 650p. 1981. text ed. 19.95 (ISBN 0-471-08169-8); tchrs.' ed. avail. (ISBN 0-471-08184-1); test file avail. (ISBN 0-471-08187-6). Wiley.

Walsh, L. S. International Marketing. 272p. 1978. pap. text ed. 11.95x (ISBN 0-7121-0943-9, Pub. by Macdonald & Evans England). Intl Ideas.

Whitehead, Harold. Administration of Marketing & Selling. 19.50x (ISBN 0-392-07566-0, SpS). Soccer.

Willsmer, Ray L. The Basic Arts of Marketing. 230p. 1976. text ed. 22.00x (ISBN 0-220-66307-6, Pub. by Busn Bks England). Renouf.

Yarker, K. A. International Marketing. 178p. 1976. text ed. 23.50x (ISBN 0-220-66298-3, Pub. by Busn Bks England). Renouf.

MARKETING–BIBLIOGRAPHY

Gardner, David M. & Belk, Russell W. A Basic Bibliography on Experimental Design in Marketing. LC 80-19563. (Bibliography Ser.: No. 37). 59p. 1980. pap. 6.00 (ISBN 0-87757-142-2). Am Mktg.

MARKETING–CASE STUDIES

Adler, Roy D. Marketing & Society: Cases & Commentaries. (Illus.). 528p. 1981. text ed. 14.95 (ISBN 0-13-557074-3). P-H.

Contemporary Cases in Marketing. 2nd ed. 1979. 11.95 (ISBN 0-03-045436-0). Dryden Pr.

Stanton, William J. Fundamentals of Marketing. 6th ed. (Illus.). 704p. 1981. text ed. 19.95 (ISBN 0-07-060891-1, C); instrs. manual 10.95 (ISBN 0-07-060892-X); study guide 6.95 (ISBN 0-07-060893-8); test file 15.95 (ISBN 0-07-060894-6); transparency masters avail. (ISBN 0-07-060895-4). McGraw.

Talarzyk, Wayne. Cases for Analysis in Marketing. 2nd ed. LC 80-65809. 384p. 1981. pap. text ed. 8.95 (ISBN 0-03-058179-6). Dryden Pr.

MARKETING–RESEARCH
see Marketing Research
MARKETING MANAGEMENT
see also Product Management

Berry, Richard C. Industrial Marketing for Results. LC 80-18222. (Illus.). 144p. 1981. text ed. 19.95 (ISBN 0-201-00075-X). A-W.

Hutt, Michael D. & Speh, Thomas W. Industrial Marketing Management. LC 80-65803. 576p. 1981. text ed. 18.95 (ISBN 0-03-052656-6). Dryden Pr.

Langer, Steven. Income in Sales-Marketing Management. 1981. pap. 85.00 (ISBN 0-916506-58-4). Abbott Langer Assocs.

Rothberg, Robert R., ed. Corporate Strategy & Product Innovation. 2nd ed. LC 80-1857. (Illus.). 1981. text ed. 17.95 (ISBN 0-02-927520-2). Free Pr.

Udell, Jon G. & Laczniak, Gene R. Marketing in an Age of Change. (Marketing Ser.). 650p. 1981. text ed. 19.95 (ISBN 0-471-08169-8); tchrs.' ed. avail. (ISBN 0-471-08184-1); test file avail. (ISBN 0-471-08187-6). Wiley.

Wilson, M. T. The Management of Marketing. LC 80-23617. 141p. 1981. 29.95 (ISBN 0-470-27074-8). Halsted Pr.

MARKETING MANAGEMENT–CASE STUDIES

Raymond, Corey E., et al. Problems in Marketing. 6th ed. (Illus.). 832p. 20.95 (ISBN 0-07-013141-4); instrs'. 4.95 (ISBN 0-07-013142-2). McGraw.

MARKETING OF FARM PRODUCE
see Farm Produce–Marketing
MARKETING RESEARCH
see also Motivation Research (Marketing)

Market Research Handbook. 813p. 1980. pap. 46.50 (ISBN 0-686-68837-6, SSC146, SSC). Unipub.

Miller, Thomas E. & Sher, Lisa, eds. Findex: The Dictionary of Market Research Reports, Studies & Surveys. 1981. 125.00 (ISBN 0-931634-07-5). Info Clearing House.

Olshavsky, Richard W., ed. Attitude Research Enters the Eighties. LC 80-20621. (Proceedings Ser.). 196p. 1980. 12.00 (ISBN 0-87757-145-7). Am Mktg.

Powers, Mark J. & Vogel, David J. Inside the Financial Futures Markets. 260p. 1980. 23.95 (ISBN 0-471-08136-1). Ronald Pr.

Proctor, Tony & Stone, Marilyn A. Marketing Research. (Illus.). 192p. 1978. pap. text ed. 9.95x (ISBN 0-7121-1291-X, Pub. by Macdonald & Evans England). Intl Ideas.

MARKETS
see also Commodity Exchanges; Fairs;
also Retail Trade; Grocery Trade, and similar headings

White, Paul. Shops & Markets. (Junior Reference Ser.). (Illus.). 64p. (gr. 7 up). 1971. 7.95 (ISBN 0-7136-1155-3). Dufour.

MARKING (STUDENTS)
see Grading and Marking (Students)
MARKOFF PROCESSES
see Markov Processes
MARKOV CHAINS
see Markov Processes
MARKOV PROCESSES

Stoica, L. Local Operator & Markow Processes. (Lecture Notes in Mathematics: Vol. 816). 104p. 1980. pap. 9.80 (ISBN 0-387-10028-8). Springer-Verlag.

MARKSMANSHIP
see Shooting
MAROONS

Price, Sally & Price, Richard. Afro-American Arts of the Suriname Rain Forest. (Illus.). 240p. 1981. 37.50 (ISBN 0-520-04345-6, CAL 516); pap. 14.95 (ISBN 0-520-04412-6). U of Cal Pr.

MARRANOS
see Maroons
MARRIAGE
see also Celibacy; Courtship; Divorce; Domestic Relations; Family; Family Life Education; Home; Marriage Counseling; Remarriage; Sex; Sex in Marriage; Sexual Ethics; Wives

Adams, Jay E. Marriage, Divorce & Remarriage. 120p. 1981. pap. 3.50 (ISBN 0-8010-0168-4). Baker Bk.

--Marriage, Divorce & Remarriage. 1980. pap. 3.50 (ISBN 0-87552-068-5). Presby & Reformed.

Beller, Anne S. Bed & Board: The Economics of Love, Marriage, & Dependency. 1981. 10.95 (ISBN 0-686-68238-6). FS&G.

Birdsong, Robert E. Soul Mates: The Facts & the Fallacies. (Aquarian Academy Supplementary Lecture Ser.: No. 9). 22p. (Orig.). 1980. pap. 1.25 (ISBN 0-917108-32-9). Sirius Bks.

Brant, Henry & Lamdrum, Phil, trs. Quero Melhorar Meu Casamento. (Portuguese Bks.). 1979. 1.25 (ISBN 0-8297-0669-0). Life Pubs Intl.

Brant, Henry & Landrum, Phil, trs. Quiero Mejorar Mi Matrimonio. (Spanish Bks.). (Span.). 1977. 1.90 (ISBN 0-8297-0778-6). Life Pubs Intl.

Cline, Victor, et al. Between Ring & Temple: A Book for Engaged L.D.S. Couples. 1981. price not set (ISBN 0-913420-87-5). Olympus Pub Co.

Corwin, Sheila. Marriage & the Family & Child-Rearing Practices. Zak, Therese A., ed. (Lifeworks Ser.). (Illus.). 160p. 1981. text ed. 4.56 (ISBN 0-07-013198-8). McGraw.

Cox, Frank D. Human Intimacy: Marriage, the Family & Its Meaning. 2nd ed. (Illus.). 475p. 1981. text ed. 13.56 (ISBN 0-8299-0367-4). West Pub.

Doty, Betty. Marriage Insurance. 8.95 (ISBN 0-930822-01-3). Green Hill.

Garrett, Yvonne. The Newlywed Handbook. 1981. 8.95 (ISBN 0-8499-0276-2). Word Bks.

Getz, Gene A. The Measure of a Marriage Workbook. 96p. 1980. lab manual 5.95 (ISBN 0-8307-0756-5). Regal.

God, Phyllis. God. Date not set. 7.95 (ISBN 0-533-04754-4). Vantage.

Harakas, S. Guidelines for Marriage in the Orthodox Church. 1980. pap. 1.25 (ISBN 0-937032-21-2). Light&Life Pub Co MN.

Kristy, Norton F. Staying in Love: Reinventing Marriage & Other Realationships. (Orig.). pap. 2.75 (ISBN 0-515-05089-X). Jove Pubns.

Lasswell, Marcia & Lobsenz, Norman. Styles of Loving: Why You Love the Way You Do. 192p. 1981. pap. 2.50 (ISBN 0-345-29228-6). Ballantine.

Lederach, John & Lederach, Naomi. Marriage in Today's World: Student Activity Book. 56p. 1980. pap. 2.50 (ISBN 0-8361-1946-0). Herald Pr.

Lederer, William J. Marital Choices: Forecasting, Assesing & Improving a Relationship. 1981. 12.95 (ISBN 0-393-01412-6). Norton.

Loudin, Jo. The Hoax of Romance. (Transformation Ser.). 320p. 1981. 12.95 (ISBN 0-13-392456-4, Spec); pap. 6.95 (ISBN 0-13-392449-1). P-H.

Par Voce, Noiva. (Portuguese Bks.). 1979. 0.75 (ISBN 0-8297-0678-X). Life Pubs Intl.

Parker, D. Coffey. The Divinity of Marriage. 1980. 5.00. D C Parker.

Rivers, Caryl & Lupo, Alan. For Better! for Worse! 256p. 1981. 12.95 (ISBN 0-671-25446-4). Summit Bks.

Shapiro, David S. & Shapiro, Elaine S. The Search for Love & Achievement: Marriage & the Family in a Changing World. 2nd ed. 1980. pap. text ed. 10.95x (ISBN 0-917974-48-4). Waveland Pr.

Sommers, Helen. The Married Single. 1981. 4.95 (ISBN 0-8062-1548-8). Carlton.

Sproul, R. C. Discovering the Intimate Marriage. 160p. 1981. pap. 2.95 (ISBN 0-87123-118-2, 200118). Bethany Fell.

Steinmetz, Urban G. Strangers, Lovers, Friends. LC 80-69479. (Illus.). 176p. (Orig.). 1981. pap. 3.95 (ISBN 0-87793-217-4). Ave Maria.

Thatcher, Floyd & Thatcher, Harriett. Long Term Marriage. 1980. 8.95 (ISBN 0-8499-0096-4). Word Bks.

Thomas, Terry C. Adios, Amor Mio. Bautista, Sara, tr. from Eng. LC 77-79933. 202p. (Orig., Span.). 1977. pap. 2.50 (ISBN 0-89922-089-4). Edit Caribe.

Von Hildebrand, D. Man & Woman. 1981. pap. 3.95 (ISBN 0-89526-883-3). Regnery-Gateway.

Weed, James A. National Estimates of Marriage Dissolution & Suvivorship. Cox, Klaudia, ed. (Ser. 3, No. 19). 50p. 1980. pap. text ed. 1.75 (ISBN 0-8406-0196-4). Natl Ctr Health Stats.

Women's Co-Operative Guild. Maternity: Letters from Working-Women, Collected by the Women's Co-Operative Guild with a Preface by the Right Hon. Herbert Samuel, M.P., London 1915. LC 79-56940. (The English Working Class Ser.). 1980. lib. bdg. 20.00 (ISBN 0-8240-0127-3). Garland Pub.

MARRIAGE–CATHOLIC CHURCH
see also Marriage (Canon Law)

Hiesberger, Jean M., ed. Marriage Enrichment Manual. (Paths of Life Ser.). 1980. cancelled (ISBN 0-8091-9187-3). Paulist Pr.

MARRIAGE–ORTHODOX EASTERN CHURCH
Constantelos, D. J. Marriage, Sexuality & Celibacy: A Greek Orthodox Perspective. 1975. pap. 3.95 (ISBN 0-937032-15-8). Light&Life Pub Co MN.
MARRIAGE (CANON LAW)
Muggeridge, Malcolm, et al. Christian Married Love: Five Contributions. Englund, Sergia & Leiva, Erasmo, trs. 150p. (Orig.). 1981. pap. price not set (ISBN 0-89870-008-6). Ignatius Pr.
MARRIAGE, MIXED
Here are entered works on marriage between persons of different religions, or person of different denominations within christianity. Works on marriage between persons of different races are entered under the heading Miscegenation.
DeGrave, Louise. From This Day Forward: Staying Married When No One Else Is & Other Reckless Acts. 228p. 1981. 10.95 (ISBN 0-316-17930-2). Little.
MARRIAGE COUNSELING
Barber, Aldyth & Barber, Cyril. Your Marriage Has Possibilities. 200p. (Orig.). 1981. pap. 4.95 (ISBN 0-89840-012-0). Heres Life.
Bustanoby, Andre & Bustanoby, Fay. Just Talk to Me. 192p. (Orig.). 1981. pap. text ed. 5.95 (ISBN 0-310-22181-1). Zondervan.
Cook, et al. Family Mediation Workbook. Polk, Donice, ed. 90p. (Orig.). 1980. pap. 10.00. D Polk.
Durkin, Mary G. & Anzia, Joan M. Marital Intimacy. 92p. 1980. pap. 6.95 (ISBN 0-8362-3601-7). Andrews & McMeel.
Erdahl, Lowell & Erdahl, Carol. Be Good to Each Other: An Open Letter on Marriage. LC 80-8893. 96p. 1981. pap. 3.95 (ISBN 0-06-062248-2, HarpR). Har-Row.
Greene, Bernard L. A Clinical Approach to Marital Problems: Diagnosis, Prevention & Treatment. 2nd ed. (Illus.). 528p. 1981. text ed. 53.75 (ISBN 0-398-04138-5). C C Thomas.
Haynes, John M. Divorce Mediation: A/Practical Guide for Therapists & Counselors. LC 80-25065. 1981. text ed. 17.95 (ISBN 0-8261-2590-5); pap. text ed. price not set (ISBN 0-8261-2591-3). Springer Pub.
Kreitler, Peter, et al. Affair Prevention. 256p. 1981. 10.95 (ISBN 0-02-566710-6). Macmillan.
Le Peau, Phyllis J. & Le Peau, Andrew T. One Plus One Equals One. 96p. (Orig.). 1981. pap. 2.95 (ISBN 0-87784-803-3). Inter-Varsity.
Merrill, Dean. How to Really Love Your Wife. 196p. 1980. pap. 4.95 (ISBN 0-310-35321-1, 10685). Zondervan.
Miller, Andrew S. Marital Expectations: What to Do When They Go Unmet. 125p. (Orig.). 1980. pap. 3.50 (ISBN 0-937442-00-3). Bibl Based Develop.
No Credentials, but Credible Counseling. 61p. (Orig.). 1981. pap. 7.00 (ISBN 0-686-28928-5). Mor Mac.
Sholerar, G. P. Marriage Is a Family Affair. Date not set. text ed. price not set (ISBN 0-89335-120-2). Spectrum Pub.
Swain, Clark. A Tuneup for Partners in Love. LC 80-84568. 250p. 1981. 7.95 (ISBN 0-88290-171-0, 2015). Horizon Utah.
Wallis, Booker. Marriage Counselling. 17.95x (ISBN 0-392-08121-0, SpS). Soccer.
Woolfolk, Joanna. Honeymoon for Life: How to Live Happily Ever After. LC 77-15966. 252p. 1981. pap. 6.95 (ISBN 0-8128-6102-7). Stein & Day.
Wright, H. Norman. Marital Counseling: A Biblical Behavioral Cognitive Approach. 370p. 1981. 16.95 (ISBN 0-938786-00-8). Chr Marriage.
MARRIAGE CUSTOMS AND RITES
Fielding, William J. Strange Customs of Courtship & Marriage. 315p. 1980. Repr. of 1942 ed. lib. bdg. 25.00 (ISBN 0-89987-259-X). Darby Bks.
Nordtvedt, Matilda & Steinkuehler, Pearl. Something Old, Something New. (Orig.). 1981. pap. 1.95 (ISBN 0-8024-0927-X). Moody.
Scher, Paula. The Honeymoon Book: A Tribute to the Last Ritual of Sexual Innocence. Graver, Fred, ed. (Illus.). 200p. (Orig.). 1981. pap. 9.95 (ISBN 0-87131-339-1). M Evans.
MARRIAGE GUIDANCE
see Marriage Counseling
Lee, Mark W. How to Have a Good Marriage. LC 78-56794. 1981. pap. 5.95 (ISBN 0-915684-89-6). Christian Herald.
MARRIED PEOPLE–PRAYER-BOOKS AND DEVOTIONS
Durkin, Henry P. Forty-Four Hours to Change Your Life: Marriage Encounter. (Orig.). pap. 1.25 (ISBN 0-89129-139-3). Jove Pubns.
MARROW
Rywlin, Arkadi M. Histopathology of the Bone Marrow. LC 75-41570. (Series in Laboratory Medicine). 229p. 1976. text ed. 22.50 (ISBN 0-316-76369-1). Little.
MARSHALL, GEORGE CATLETT, 1880-1959
Marshall, George C. Marshall's Mission to China: The Report & Appended Documents. 1976. Set. 60.00 (ISBN 0-89093-115-1). U Pubns Amer.
MARSHALL, JOHN, 1755-1835
Stites, Frances N. John Marshall: Defender of the Constitution. (Library of American Biography). (Orig.). 1981. 11.95 (ISBN 0-316-81669-8); pap. text ed. 4.95 (ISBN 0-316-81667-1). Little.
Stites, Francis. John Marshall: Defender of the Constitution. 208p. 1980. 11.95 (ISBN 0-316-81669-8). Little.
MARSHALL PLAN
see Economic Assistance, American
MARTIAL (MARTIALUS, MARCUS VALERIUS)
Pott, J. A. & Wright, F. A., trs. Martial, the Twelve Books Epigrams. 402p. 1981. Repr. lib. bdg. 65.00 (ISBN 0-89987-566-1). Darby Bks.
MARTIAL LAW
Elliott. Thailand: Origins of Military Rule. 190p. 1978. 11.95 (ISBN 0-905762-10-X); pap. 5.95 (ISBN 0-905762-11-8). Lawrence Hill.
MARTINEZ RUIZ, JOSE, 1873-
Glenn, Kathleen M. Azorin. (World Authors Ser: No. 604). 1981. lib. bdg. 14.95 (ISBN 0-8057-6446-1). Twayne.
MARTYRDOM
see also Martyrs
Frend, W. H. Martydom & Persecution in the Early Church. (Twin Brooks Ser.). 645p. 1981. pap. 12.95 (ISBN 0-8010-3502-3). Baker Bk.
MARTYRS
see also Martyrdom
Foxe, John. Foxe's Book of Martyrs. 400p. 1981. pap. 2.95 (ISBN 0-686-69320-5). Whitaker Hse.
Marmorstein, Emil. The Murder of Jacob De Haan by the Zionists: A Martyr's Message. 1980. lib. bdg. 59.95 (ISBN 0-686-68747-7). Revisionist Pr.
Schroetter, Hilda N. Foxe's Book of English Martyrs. 360p. 1981. 10.95 (ISBN 0-8499-0152-9). Word Bks.
MARX, KARL, 1818-1883
Bulgakov, Sergei. Karl Marx: As a Religious Type. Lang, Virgil, ed. Barna, Luba, tr. from Rus. LC 78-78117. 200p. 1980. 12.50 (ISBN 0-913124-34-6). Nordland Pub.
Carlsnaes, Walter. The Concept of Ideology & Political Analysis: A Critical Examination of Its Usage by Marx, Lenin, & Mannheim. LC 80-1202. (Contributions in Philosophy Ser.: No. 17). 280p. 1981. lib. bdg. 32.50 (ISBN 0-313-22267-3, CCI/). Greenwood.
Gilbert, Alan. Marx's Politics: Communists & Citizens. 320p. 1981. 19.00 (ISBN 0-8135-0903-3). Rutgers U Pr.
Hazelkorn, Ellen. Marx & Engels: On Ireland - an Annotated Checklist. (Bibliographical Ser.: No. 15). 1981. 2.00 (ISBN 0-89977-031-2). Am Inst Marxist.
Karl Marx-Frederick Engels: Collected Works, Vol. 16. (Illus.). 8.50 (ISBN 0-7178-0516-6). Intl Pub Co.
Rubel, Macmillan. Marx Chronology. 226p. 1981. lib. bdg. 22.50 (ISBN 0-87196-516-X). Facts on File.
Rubel, Maximilien. Rubel on Karl Marx: Five Essays. O'Malley, Joseph & Algozin, Keith, eds. LC 80-21734. 272p. Date not set. price not set (ISBN 0-521-23839-0); pap. price not set (ISBN 0-521-28251-9). Cambridge U Pr.
Rubenstein, David. Marx & Wittgenstein. 240p. 1981. write for info. (ISBN 0-7100-0688-8). Routledge & Kegan.
Wallimann, Isidor. Estrangement: Marx's Conception of Human Nature & the Division of Labor. LC 80-929. (Contributions in Philosophy: No. 16). 240p. 1981. lib. bdg. 29.95 (ISBN 0-313-22096-4, WAE/). Greenwood.
Wood, Allen. Karl Marx. (The Arguments of the Philosophers Ser.). 280p. 1981. 25.00 (ISBN 0-7100-0672-1). Routledge & Kegan.
MARXIAN ECONOMICS
Burger, et al. Marxism, Science & the Movement of History. (Philosophical Currents Ser.: No. 27). 1981. pap. text ed. 34.25x. Humanities.
Caldwell, Malcolm. Wealth of Some Nations. 192p. 1977. 10.00 (ISBN 0-905762-01-0); pap. 6.00. Lawrence Hill.
Heller, Agnes. The Theory of Need in Marx. (Allison & Busby Motive Ser.). 136p. 1981. pap. 7.95 (ISBN 0-8052-8075-8, Pub. by Allison & Busby England). Schocken.
Mashruwala, K. G. Gandhi & Marx. 119p. (Orig.). 1981. pap. 1.50 (ISBN 0-934676-30-5). Greenlf Bks.
Negri, Antonio. Marx Beyond Marx: Notebooks on the Grundrisse. Orig. Title: Marx Oltre Marx. 232p. 1981. 21.95x (ISBN 0-89789-018-3). J F Bergin.
Prybyla, Jan S. Issues in Socialist Economic Modernization. 140p. 1980. 19.95 (ISBN 0-03-057962-7). Praeger.
Roemer, John. Analytical Foundations of Marxian Economic Theory. LC 80-22646. (Illus.). 224p. Date not set. price not set (ISBN 0-521-23047-0). Cambridge U Pr.
MARXISM
see Communism; Socialism
MARY, VIRGIN
Breig, James. Hail Mary: Woman, Wife, Mother of God. (Today Paperback Ser.). (Illus.). 40p. (Orig.). 1980. pap. 1.95 (ISBN 0-89570-197-9). Claretian Pubns.
MARY, VIRGIN–ART
see also Icons
Hurlington, Vincent J. Great Art Madonnas Classed According to Their Significance As Types of Impressive Motherhood. (The Great Art Masters Library Bk.). (Illus.). 143p. 1981. 37.45 (ISBN 0-930582-97-7). Gloucester Art.
MARY, VIRGIN–ICONOGRAPHY
see Mary, Virgin–Art
MARY MAGDALENE, SAINT
Branick, Vincent. Mary, the Spirit & the Church. LC 80-82856. 128p. (Orig.). 1981. pap. 4.95 (ISBN 0-8091-2343-6). Paulist Pr.
MARYLAND–BIOGRAPHY
Haw, James, et al. Stormy Patriot: The Life of Samuel Chase. LC 80-83807. (Illus.). 305p. 1980. 14.95 (ISBN 0-938420-00-3). Md Hist.
MARYLAND–HISTORY
Vexler, R. I. Maryland Chronology & Factbook, Vol. 20. 1978. 8.50 (ISBN 0-379-16145-1). Oceana.
MASAI
Shachtman, Tom. Growing up Masai. LC 80-25017. (Illus.). 56p. (gr. 3-6). 1981. PLB 8.95 (ISBN 0-02-782550-7). Macmillan.
MASCULINITY (PSYCHOLOGY)
Bertels, Frank. The First Book on Male Liberation. (Illus.). 300p. 1980. lib. bdg. 11.00 (ISBN 0-932574-05-X). Brun Pr.
--The First Book on Male Liberation & Six Equality. (Illus.). 352p. 1981. lib. bdg. 25.00 (ISBN 0-932574-05-X); pap. 15.00 (ISBN 0-932574-06-8). Brun Pr.
Conway, Sally. You & Your Husband's Mid-Life Crisis. (Orig.). 1980. pap. 4.95 (ISBN 0-89191-318-1). Cook.
Lewis, Robert A., ed. Men in Difficult Times: Masculinity Today & Tomorrow. (Illus.). 352p. 1981. 14.95 (ISBN 0-13-574418-0, Spectrum); pap. 7.95 (ISBN 0-13-574400-8). P-H.
Terman, Lewis M. & Miles, Catherine C. Sex & Personality. 600p. 1980. Repr. of 1936 ed. lib. bdg. 50.00 (ISBN 0-89987-811-3). Darby Bks.
MASERS
Atwater, Harry A. Introduction to Microwave Theory. rev. ed. Repr. of 1962 ed. lib. bdg. write for info. (ISBN 0-89874-192-0). Krieger.
MASERS, OPTICAL
see Lasers
MASKS
Alkema, Chester J. Mask-Making. LC 80-54343. (Illus.). 96p. 8.95 (ISBN 0-8069-7038-3); lib. bdg. 8.29 (ISBN 0-8069-7039-1). Sterling.
MASOCHISM
Shapiro, David. Autonomy & Rigid Character. LC 80-68953. 167p. 1981. 12.95x (ISBN 0-465-00567-5). Basic.
MASONIC ORDERS
see Freemasons
MASONRY
see also Bricklaying; Cement; Concrete; Foundations; Plastering; Stone-Cutting; Walls
Burch, Monte. Masonry & Concrete. Horowitz, Shirley & Kummings, Gail, eds. (Illus.). 144p. (Orig.). 1981. pap. 6.95 (ISBN 0-932944-30-2). Creative Homeowner.
Dalzell, J. Ralph. Simplified Concrete Masonry Planning & Building. 2nd, rev. ed. Merritt, Frederick S., rev. by. LC 81-385. 398p. 1981. Repr. of 1972 ed. lib. bdg. price not set (ISBN 0-89874-278-1). Krieger.
Masonry. (Illus.). 64p. (gr. 6-12). 1980. pap. 0.70x. BSA.
Nolan, Kenneth. Masonry Contractors Handbook. 256p. (Orig.). 1981. pap. 13.50 (ISBN 0-910460-81-7). Craftsman.
Scharff, Robert. Successful & Masonry. Case, Virginia A., ed. (Successful Ser.). 144p. 1981. 18.95 (ISBN 0-89999-023-1); pap. 8.95 (ISBN 0-89999-024-X). Structures Pub.
Sunset Editors. Basic Masonry Illustrated. LC 80-53484. (Illus.). 96p. (Orig.). 1981. pap. 4.95 (ISBN 0-376-01360-5, Sunset Bks.). Sunset-Lane.
MASONS (SECRET ORDER)
see Freemasons
MASORAH
Yeivin, Israel. Introduction to the Tiberian Masorah. LC 79-24755. (Society of Biblical Literature Masoretic Studies: No. 5). pap. 10.50x (ISBN 0-89130-374-X, 06 05 05). Scholars Pr Ca.
MASS
see also Lord's Supper
Junemann, Joseph. The Mass of the Roman Rite. 25.00 (ISBN 0-87061-054-6). Chr Classics.
MASS CASUALTIES–TREATMENT
see Emergency Medical Services
MASS COMMUNICATION
see Communication; Mass Media; Telecommunication
Lent, John A. Caribbean Mass Communications: A Comprehensive Bibliography. (Archival & Bibliographic Ser.). 152p. 1981. pap. 20.00 (ISBN 0-918456-39-8). African Studies Assn.
MASS FEEDING
see Food Service
MASS MEDIA
see also Moving-Pictures; Newspapers; Radio Broadcasting; Television Broadcasting
Davis, Dennis K. & Baran, Stanley J. Mass Communication & Everyday Life: A Perspective on Theory & Effects. 240p. 1980. pap. text ed. 7.95x (ISBN 0-534-00883-6). Wadsworth Pub.
Davison, W. Phillips & Boylan, James. Mass Media: Systems & Effects. LC 74-31000. 245p. 1976. pap. text ed. 10.95x (ISBN 0-03-038896-1). Praeger.
Debray, Regis. Teachers, Writers, Celebrities: The Intellectuals of Modern France. 300p. 1981. 17.50 (ISBN 0-8052-7086-8, Pub. by NLB England). Schocken.
Hachten, William A. The World News Prism: Changing Media, Clashing Ideologies. 120p. 1981. pap. text ed. 6.50 (ISBN 0-8138-1580-0). Iowa St U Pr.
McAnany, Emile, et al, eds. Structure & Communication: Critical Studies in Mass Media Research. 260p. 1981. 20.95 (ISBN 0-03-057954-6). Praeger.
Patterson, Thomas E. The Mass Media: How Americans Choose Their President. 220p. 1980. 21.95 (ISBN 0-03-057728-4); pap. 8.95 (ISBN 0-03-057729-2). Praeger.
Sobel, Lester A., ed. Media Controversies. 1980. 17.50 (ISBN 0-87196-242-X, Checkmark). Facts on File.
Wall, Edward C., et al, eds. Media Review Digest, Vol. 9. 1979. 120.00 (ISBN 0-87650-101-3). Pierian.
MASS MEDIA–LAW AND LEGISLATION
Pember, Don R. Mass Media Law. 2nd ed. 500p. 1981. text ed. write for info. (ISBN 0-697-04347-9). Wm C Brown.
MASS MEDIA–SOCIAL ASPECTS
Baeher, Helen, ed. Women & Media. LC 80-41424. (Illus.). 150p. 1980. 14.25 (ISBN 0-08-026061-6). Pergamon.
Lee, Chin-Chuan. Media Imperialism Reconsidered: The Homogenizing of Television Culture. LC 80-16763. (People & Communication Ser.: Vol. 10). (Illus.). 276p. 1980. 20.00 (ISBN 0-8039-1495-4). Sage.
--Media Imperialism Reconsidered: The Homogenizing of Television Culture. LC 80-16763. (People & Communication Ser.: Vol. 10). (Illus.). 276p. 1980. pap. 9.95 (ISBN 0-8039-1496-2). Sage.
Rubin, Bernard, ed. Small Voices & Great Trumpets: Minorities & the Media. 295p. 1980. 24.95 (ISBN 0-03-056973-7); pap. 9.95 (ISBN 0-03-056972-9). Praeger.
Said, Edward. Covering Islam: How the Media & the Experts Determine How We See the Rest of the World. 1981. 10.95 (ISBN 0-394-51319-3); pap. 3.95 (ISBN 0-394-74808-5). Pantheon.
Tunstall, Jeremy & Walker, David. Media Made in California: Hollywood, Politics, & the News. (Illus.). 224p. 1981. 15.95 (ISBN 0-19-502922-4). Oxford U Pr.
MASS MEDIA–RUSSIA
Mickiewicz, Ellen. Media & the Russian Public. 170p. 1981. 19.95 (ISBN 0-03-057681-4); pap. 8.95 (ISBN 0-03-057679-2). Praeger.
MASS PSYCHOLOGY
see Social Psychology
MASS TRANSFER
Eckert, E. R. Heat & Mass Transfer. 2nd ed. LC 81-359. 344p. 1981. Repr. lib. bdg. price not set (ISBN 0-89874-332-X). Krieger.
Satterfield, Charles N. Mass Transfer in Heterogeneous Catalysis. LC 80-23432. 286p. 1981. Repr. of 1970 ed. text ed. write for info. (ISBN 0-89874-198-X). Krieger.
MASS TRANSIT
see Local Transit
MASSACHUSETTS–DESCRIPTION AND TRAVEL
More Massachusetts Broadsides. (Massachusetts Historical Society Picture Book Ser.). 1981. price not set. Mass Hist Soc.
MASSACHUSETTS–GENEALOGY
Boyer, Carl, 3rd, et al. Brown Families of Bristol Counties, Massachusetts & Rhode Island & Descendants of Jared Talbot. LC 80-68755. (New England Colonial Families: Vol. 1). 219p. 1980. 18.35 (ISBN 0-936124-04-0). C Boyer.
MASSACHUSETTS–HISTORY
Jones, Douglas L. Village & Seaport: Migration & Society in Eighteenth-Century Massachusetts. LC 80-54469. (Illus.). 240p. 1981. 15.00x (ISBN 0-87451-200-X). U Pr of New Eng.
Moody, Robert E., ed. Papers of Leverett Saltonstall, 1816-1845. (Collections of the Massachusetts Historical Society Ser.). (Illus.). Vol. 1, 1978. 25.00 ea. Vol. 2, 1981. Mass Hist Soc.
Pencak, William. War, Politics, & Revolution in Provincial Massachusetts. (Illus.). 276p. 1980. write for info. (ISBN 0-930350-10-3). NE U Pr.
MASSACHUSETTS–HISTORY–COLONIAL PERIOD, ca. 1600-1775
Chadwich, Philip & Smith, Foster, eds. Seafaring in Colonial Massachusetts. LC 80-51256. (Illus.). xvii, 240p. 1981. 25.00x (ISBN 0-8139-0897-3, Colonial Soc MA). U Pr of Va.
MASSACHUSETTS–JUVENILE LITERATURE
Fradin, Dennis. Massachusetts: In Words & Pictures. LC 80-26161. (Young People's Stories of Our States Ser.). (Illus.). 48p. (gr. 2-5). 1981. PLB 8.65g (ISBN 0-516-03921-0, Time Line). Childrens.
MASSACHUSETTS–POLITICS AND GOVERNMENT
Hindus, Michael S., et al. The Files of the Massachusetts Superior Court, 1859-1959: An Analysis & a Plan for Action. (Reference Publications Ser.). 1980. lib. bdg. 50.00 (ISBN 0-8161-9037-2). G K Hall.
Howland, Gerald. You're in the Driver's Seat. 128p. (Orig.). 1980. pap. write for info. (ISBN 0-8289-0418-9). Greene.
MASSAGE
see also Chiropractic; Shiatsu

Becker, Paul & Wood, Elizabeth C. Beard's Massage. 1981. pap. price not set (ISBN 0-7216-9592-2). Saunders.

Lawrence, Paul A. Lomi-Lomi Hawaiian Massage. LC 80-83756. (Positive Health Ser.). (Illus.). 80p. 1981. 12.95 (ISBN 0-938034-01-4); pap. 5.95 (ISBN 0-938034-02-2). PAL Pr.

Lawson-Wood, D. & Lawson-Wood, J. Five Elements of Acupuncture & Chinese Massage. 96p. 1976. 8.95x (ISBN 0-8464-1010-9). Beekman Pubs.

Strange de Jim. The Strange Experience: How to Become the World's Second Greatest Lover. LC 80-69868. (Illus.). 94p. (Orig.). 1980. perfect bdg. 6.95 (ISBN 0-9605308-1-9). Ash-Kar Pr.

MASSAI

see Masai

MASTERS, EDGAR LEE, 1869-1950

Primeau, Ronald. Beyond "Spoon River". The Legacy of Edgar Lee Masters. 208p. 1981. text ed. 22.50x (ISBN 0-292-70731-2). U of Tex Pr.

MASTERS GOLF TOURNAMENT

Tyalor, Dawson, ed. The Masters: Profiles of a Tournament. 3rd rev. ed. (Illus.). 192p. 1981. 19.95 (ISBN 0-498-01661-7). A S Barnes.

MASTERS OF SHIPS

see Shipmasters

MATERIA MEDICA

see also Anesthetics; Aphrodisiacs; Drugs; Drugs–Dosage; Materia Medica, Dental; Materia Medica, Vegetable; Medicine–Formulae, Receipts, Prescriptions; Pharmacology; Pharmacy; Poisons; Therapeutics

also names of drugs

Challem, Jack & Challem, Renate. What Herbs Are All About. LC 80-82913. 150p. (Orig.). 1980. pap. 2.95 (ISBN 0-87983-242-8). Keats.

Marchetti, Albert. Common Cures for Common Ailments: A Doctor's Guide to Nonprescription, Over-the-Counter Medicines & His Recommendations for Their Use. LC 77-16114. 368p. 1981. pap. 8.95 (ISBN 0-8128-6107-8). Stein & Day.

Meyer, Clarence. Vegetarian Medicines. Meyer, David C., ed. (Illus.). 96p. (Orig.). 1981. pap. 5.95 (ISBN 0-916638-06-5). Meyerbooks.

Meyer, George G., et al. Folk Medicine & Herbal Healing. write for info. (ISBN 0-398-04470-8). C C Thomas.

Meyer, Joseph E. The Herbalist. (Illus.). 304p. 1981. 10.95 (ISBN 0-8069-3902-8); lib. bdg. 9.89 (ISBN 0-8069-3903-6). Sterling.

The Old Herb Doctor. 1981. pap. 6.95 (ISBN 0-87877-052-6). Newcastle Pub.

Smith, William. Wonders in Weeds. 187p. 1977. 13.00x (ISBN 0-8464-1062-1). Beekman Pubs.

MATERIA MEDICA, DENTAL

Requa-Clark, Barbara & Holroyd, Sam V. Applied Pharmacology for the Dental Hygienists. 427p. 1981. pap. 11.95 (ISBN 0-8016-2239-5). Mosby.

MATERIA MEDICA, VEGETABLE

see also Botany, Medical; Herbs; Medicine, Medieval

Harris, Ben C., ed. The Compleat Herbal. LC 77-185615. 243p. (Orig.). 1972. pap. 1.75 (ISBN 0-915962-15-2). Larchmont Bks.

MATERIAL HANDLING

see Materials Handling

MATERIAL SCIENCE

see Materials

MATERIALISM

see also Idealism; Realism

Williams, Raymond. Problems in Materialism & Culture: Selected Essays. 288p. 1981. 19.50x (ISBN 0-8052-7093-0, Pub. by NLB England); pap. 8.75 (ISBN 0-8052-7092-2). Schocken.

MATERIALS

see also Biomedical Materials; Building Materials; Composite Materials; Finishes and Finishing; Manufacturing Processes; Materials Management; Slurry; Strategic Materials

Beer, Ferdinand P. & Johnston, E. Russell, Jr. Mechanics of Materials. (Illus.). 672p. 1981. text ed. 26.95x (ISBN 0-07-004284-5, C); write for info solutions manual (ISBN 0-07-004291-8). McGraw.

Chalmers, B., ed. Progress in Materials Science, Vol. 23. 280p. 1980. 85.00 (ISBN 0-08-024846-2). Pergamon.

Crilly, Eugene R. Material & Process Applications: Land, Sea, Air, Space. (The Science of Advanced Materials & Process Engineering Ser.). 1981. price not set. Soc Adv Material.

Evans, L. S. Chemical & Process Plant: A Guide to the Selection of Engineering Materials. 2nd ed. LC 80-20355. 190p. 1981. 34.95 (ISBN 0-470-27064-0). Halsted Pr.

Flinn, Richard A. & Trojan, Paul K. Engineering Materials & Their Applications. 2nd ed. (Illus.). 753p. 1981. text ed. 22.95 (ISBN 0-395-29645-5); write for info. instr's manual (ISBN 0-395-29646-3). HM.

Interim Specifications - Materials. 1980. 6.00. AASHTO.

Olsen, G. Elements of Mechanics of Materials. 4th ed. 1981. 23.95 (ISBN 0-13-267013-5). P-H.

Sittig, Marshall, ed. Metal & Inorganic Waste Reclaiming Encyclopedia. LC 80-21669. (Pollution Tech. Rev. 70; Chem. Tech. Rev. 175). (Illus.). 591p. (Orig.). 1981. 54.00 (ISBN 0-8155-0823-9). Noyes.

Smith, M. J. Materials & Structures. 2nd ed. (Illus.). 180p. 1980. pap. text ed. 13.95x (ISBN 0-7114-5639-9). Intl Ideas.

Waseda, Yoshio. The Structure of Non-Crystalline Materials. (Illus.). 304p. 1980. text ed. 44.50 (ISBN 0-07-068426-X, C). McGraw.

MATERIALS–FATIGUE

see also Fracture Mechanics;

also subdivision Fatigue under specific subjects, e.g. Metals–Fatigue

Manson, S. S. Thermal Stress & Low-Cycle Fatigue. 416p. 1981. lib. bdg. price not set (ISBN 0-89874-279-X). Krieger.

Osgood, Carl C. Fatigue Design. 2nd ed. (International Series on the Strenth & Fracture of Materials & Structures). 500p. 1981. 65.00 (ISBN 0-08-026167-1); pap. 33.00 (ISBN 0-08-026166-3). Pergamon.

MATERIALS–HANDLING AND TRANSPORTATION

see Materials Handling

MATERIALS–STRENGTHENING MECHANISMS

see Strengthening Mechanisms in Solids

MATERIALS, MAGNETIC

see Magnetic Materials

MATERIALS, STRENGTH OF

see Strength of Materials

MATERIALS HANDLING

see also Bulk Solids Handling; Cargo Handling; Conveying Machinery; Freight and Freightage; Hydraulic Conveying; Motor-Trucks; Pallets (Shipping, Storage, etc.)

Leenders, Michael R., et al. Purchasing & Materials Management. 7th ed. 1980. 21.50x (ISBN 0-256-02374-3). Irwin.

Murphy, G. J. Transport & Distribution. 2nd ed. 300p. 1978. text ed. 24.50x (ISBN 0-220-66321-1, Pub. by Busn Bks England). Renouf.

--The Transport Operators Guide to Professional Competence. 314p. 1980. pap. 21.00x (ISBN 0-09-141591-8, Pub. by Busn Bks England). Renouf.

MATERIALS MANAGEMENT

see also Purchasing

Compton, H. K. Supplies & Materials Management. 2nd ed. (Illus.). 512p. 1979. text ed. 45.00x (ISBN 0-7121-1964-7, Pub. by Macdonald & Evans England). Intl Ideas.

Leenders, Michael R., et al. Purchasing & Materials Management. 7th ed. 1980. 21.50x (ISBN 0-256-02374-3). Irwin.

Zenz, Gary L. Purchasing & the Management of Materials. 5th ed. 600p. 1981. text ed. 21.95 (ISBN 0-471-06091-7); tchrs.' ed. avail. (ISBN 0-471-08935-4). Wiley.

MATERNAL DEPRIVATION

Rutter, Michael. Maternal Deprivation Reassessed. rev. ed. 1981. pap. 3.95 (ISBN 0-14-080561-3). Penguin.

MATERNITY NURSING

see Obstetrical Nursing

MATHEMATICAL ANALYSIS

see also Algebra; Algebras, Linear; Calculus; Combinatorial Analysis; Engineering Mathematics; Functions; Mathematical Optimization; Nonlinear Theories; Numerical Analysis; Programming (Electronic Computers)

Arya, Jagdish C. & Lardner, Robin W. Mathematical Analysis for Business & Economics. (Illus.). 768p. 1981. text ed. 19.95 (ISBN 0-13-561019-2). P-H.

Dieudonne, J. A. Treatise on Analysis, 6 vols. Incl. Vol. 1. 1960. 22.95 (ISBN 0-12-215550-5); Vol. 2. rev. ed. 1970. 44.50 (ISBN 0-12-215502-5); Vol. 3. 1972. 48.50 (ISBN 0-12-215503-3); Vol. 4. 1974. 49.00 (ISBN 0-12-215504-1); Vol. 5. 1977. 34.50 (ISBN 0-12-215505-X); Vol. 6. 1978. 32.00 (ISBN 0-12-215506-8). (Pure & Applied Mathematics Ser.). Acad Pr.

Maybee, John & Greenberg, Harvey, eds. Computer-Assisted Analysis & Model Simplification. 1981. price not set (ISBN 0-12-480720-8). Acad Pr.

Nachbin, Leopoldo, ed. Mathematical Analysis & Applications. (Advances in Mathematics Supplementary Studies: Vol. 7). 1981. Pt. A. write for info. (ISBN 0-12-512801-0); Pt. B. write for info. (ISBN 0-12-512802-9). Acad Pr.

Stromberg, Karl. Introduction to Classical Real Analysis. (Wadsworth International Mathematics Ser.). 576p. 1981. text ed. 29.95x (ISBN 0-686-69568-2). Wadsworth Pub.

Theory of Numbers, Mathematical Analysis & Their Applications. LC 79-20552. (Proceedings of the Steklov Institute). 1979. 60.00 (ISBN 0-8218-3042-2, STEKLO 142). Am Math.

Yosida, K. Functional Analysis. 6th ed. (Grundlehren der Mathemtischen Wissenschaften Ser.: Vol. 123). 501p. 1980. 39.00 (ISBN 0-387-10210-8). Springer-Verlag.

MATHEMATICAL ANALYSIS–PROBLEMS, EXERCISES, ETC.

Christensen, R. Mathematical Analysis of Bluffing in Poker. 60p. 1981. 9.50 (ISBN 0-686-28920-X). Entropy Ltd.

MATHEMATICAL DRAWING

see Mechanical Drawing

MATHEMATICAL ECONOMICS

see Economics, Mathematical

MATHEMATICAL LOGIC

see Logic, Symbolic and Mathematical

MATHEMATICAL MACHINE THEORY

see Machine Theory

MATHEMATICAL MEASUREMENTS

Budlong, John P. Sky & Sextant. 232p. 1981. pap. text ed. 10.95 (ISBN 0-442-20460-4). Van Nos Reinhold.

Math House Proficiency Review Tapes: Applications Involving Measurement, Unit C. (YA) (gr. 7 up). 1980. manual & cassettes 159.95 (ISBN 0-917792-05-X). Math Hse.

MATHEMATICAL MODELS

see also Digital Computer Simulation; Machine Theory; Monte Carlo Method; Programming (Electronic Computers); System Analysis

also subdivision Mathematical Models under specific subjects, e.g. Human Behavior–Mathematical Models

Ditlevsen, Ove. Uncertainty Modeling: With Applications to Multidimensional Civil Engineering. (Illus.). 448p. 1980. text ed. 69.50 (C). McGraw.

Frauenthal, J. C. Mathematical Modeling in Epidemiology. (Universitexts Ser.). 118p. 1980. pap. 16.80 (ISBN 0-387-10328-7). Springer-Verlag.

Maybee, John & Greenberg, Harvey, eds. Computer-Assisted Analysis & Model Simplification. 1981. price not set (ISBN 0-12-480720-8). Acad Pr.

Reason, Peter & Rowan, John. Human Inquiry: A Sourcebook of New Paradigm Research. 1981. price not set (ISBN 0-471-27936-6, Pub. by Wiley Interscience). Wiley.

Saaty, Thomas L. & Alexander, Joyce M. Thinking with Models: Mathematical Models in the Physical, Biological & Social Sciences. (I S Modern Applied Mathematics & Computer Science: Vol. 2). (Illus.). 208p. 1981. 35.00 (ISBN 0-08-026475-1); pap. 20.00 (ISBN 0-08-026474-3). Pergamon.

MATHEMATICAL OPTIMIZATION

see also Decision-Making–Mathematical Models; Experimental Design; Programming (Mathematics); System Analysis

Mital, K. V. Optimization Methods in Operations Research & Systems Analysis. 259p. 1980. pap. 8.95 (ISBN 0-470-27081-0). Halsted Pr.

Sherali, H. D. & Shetty, C. M. Optimization with Disjunctive Constraints. (Lecture Notes in Economics & Mathematical Systems: Vol. 181). (Illus.). 156p. 1980. pap. 15.00 (ISBN 0-387-10228-0). Springer-Verlag.

MATHEMATICAL PHYSICS

see also Dimensional Analysis; Elasticity; Electricity; Engineering Mathematics; Existence Theorems; Hydrodynamics; Magnetism; Nonlinear Theories; Perturbation (Mathematics); Potential, Theory of; Sound; System Analysis; Thermodynamics

Novikov, S. O., ed. Mathematical Physics Review, Vol.i. (Soviet Scietific Reviews Ser.). 218p. 1980. 44.50 (ISBN 3-7186-0019-6). Harwood Academic.

Reed, Michael & Simon, Barry. Methods of Modern Mathematical Physics, 4 vols. Incl. Vol. 1. Functional Analysis. 1972. 24.95 (ISBN 0-12-585001-8); Vol. 2. Fourier Analysis Self-Adjointness. 1975. 34.50 (ISBN 0-12-585002-6); Vol. 3. Scattering Theory. 1979. 42.00 (ISBN 0-12-585003-4); Vol. 4. 1978. 34.00 (ISBN 0-12-585004-2). Acad Pr.

MATHEMATICAL RECREATIONS

see also Chess

Christensen, R. Mathematical Analysis of Bluffing in Poker. 60p. 1981. 9.50 (ISBN 0-686-28920-X). Entropy Ltd.

Crouch. Coordinated Cross Number Puzzle Books, 8 bks. Incl. Bks. A1 & A2. (gr. 1-2). pap. 1.64 ea. worktexts; Bk. A1, Gr. 1. pap. (ISBN 0-8009-0722-1); Bk. A2, Gr. 2. pap. (ISBN 0-8009-0725-6); spirit masters 15.32 ea. Bk. A1 (ISBN 0-8009-0746-9). Bk. A2 (ISBN 0-8009-0748-5). ans. keys. Bk. A1 (ISBN 0-8009-0764-7). Bk. A2 (ISBN 0-8009-0766-3); Bks. A-F. (gr. 3-8). Bk. A, Gr. 3. pap. (ISBN 0-8009-0727-2); Bk. B, Gr. 4. pap. (ISBN 0-8009-0729-9); Bk. C, Gr. 5. pap. (ISBN 0-8009-0735-3); Bk. D, Gr. 6. pap. (ISBN 0-8009-0739-6); Bk. E, Gr. 7. pap. (ISBN 0-8009-0742-6); Bk. F, Gr. 8. pap. (ISBN 0-8009-0744-2). (gr. 1-8). 1979. Bks. A-F. pap. 1.76 ea. worktexts; spiritmasters for Bks. A-F 16.68 ea.; ans. keys for Bks. A1, A2, A-F 3.32 ea. McCormick-Mathers.

Devi, Sahkuntala. Figuring. 160p. 1981. pap. 3.95 (ISBN 0-06-463530-9, EH). Har-Row.

MATHEMATICAL SEQUENCES

see Sequences (Mathematics)

MATHEMATICAL STATISTICS

see also Biometry; Multivariate Analysis; Nonparametric Statistics; Probabilities; Regression Analysis; Statistics; Time-Series Analysis

Huntsberger & Billingsley. Elements of Statistical Inference. 5th ed. 416p. 1981. text ed. 15.95 (ISBN 0-205-07305-0, 5673054); free tchr's ed. (ISBN 0-205-07306-9); free student's guide (ISBN 0-205-07307-7). Allyn.

Medhi, J. P. An Introduction to Stochastic Processes. 320p. 1981. 19.95 (ISBN 0-470-27000-4). Halsted Pr.

Morris, Carl & Rolph, John. Introduction to Data Analysis & Statistical Inference. (Illus.). 416p. 1981. pap. text ed. 13.95. P-H.

Reason, Peter & Rowan, John. Human Inquiry: A Sourcebook of New Paradigm Research. 1981. price not set (ISBN 0-471-27936-6, Pub. by Wiley Interscience). Wiley.

Sen, P. K. Sequential Nonparametrics: Invariance Principles & Statistical Inference. (Probability & Mathematical Statistics Ser.). 350p. 1981. 30.00 (ISBN 0-471-06013-5, Pub. by Wiley-Interscience). Wiley.

MATHEMATICAL SYMBOLS

see Abbreviations

MATHEMATICIANS

Klarner, David A., ed. The Mathematical Gardiner. 382p. 1980. 19.95x (ISBN 0-534-98015-5). Wadsworth Pub.

Morgan, Bryan. Men & Discoveries in Mathematics. 235p. 1980. 15.00x (ISBN 0-7195-2587-X, Pub. by Murray Pubs England). State Mutual Bk.

MATHEMATICS

see also Algebra; Arithmetic; Biomathematics; Business Mathematics; Calculus; Coordinates; Dynamics; Economics, Mathematical; Engineering Mathematics; Fractions; Functions; Geometry; Graphic Methods; Groups, Theory of; Logic, Symbolic and Mathematical; Maxima and Minima; Mensuration; Metric System; Numbers, Theory of; Numeration; Potential, Theory of; Probabilities; Sequences (Mathematics); Statics; Trigonometry; Vector Analysis

also headings beginning with the word Mathematical

Ablon, Leon, et al. The Steps in Mathematics, 5 modules. 1981. softbound 3.95 ea. Module 1 (ISBN 0-8053-0131-3). Module 2 (ISBN 0-8053-0132-1). Module 3 (ISBN 0-8053-0133-X). Module 4. Module 5 (ISBN 0-8053-0135-6). Benjamin-Cummings.

Acosta, Antonio A. & Calvo, Joraida. Matematicas: Repaso Para el Examen De Equivalencia De la Escuela Superior En Espanol. rev. ed. LC 80-25182. 256p. (Orig.). 1981. pap. 5.00 (ISBN 0-668-04821-2, 4821-2). Arco.

Ali, N., et al. Transactions of the Moscow Mathematical Society, 1975. LC 65-4713. 1977. 37.20 (ISBN 0-8218-1632-2, MOSCOW-32). Am Math.

Angel, Allen R. & Porter, Stuart R. Survey of Mathematics: With Applications. LC 80-19471. (Mathematics Ser.). (Illus.). 576p. 1981. text ed. write for info. (ISBN 0-201-00045-8). A-W.

Bird & May. Mathematics Two: Checkbook. 1981. text ed. price not set (ISBN 0-408-00610-2). Butterworths.

Bird, May. Mathematics Two Checkbook. 1981. text ed. price not set (ISBN 0-408-00633-1); pap. text ed. price not set (ISBN 0-408-00609-9). Butterworths.

Brown, Walter C. Basic Mathematics. rev. ed. 128p. 1981. pap. text ed. 4.80 (ISBN 0-87006-317-0). Goodheart.

Cooperstein, Bruce & Mason, Geoffrey, eds. Proceedings of Symposia in Pure Mathematics, Vol. 37. 1981. cancelled (ISBN 0-8218-1440-0). Am Math.

Daintith, John, ed. The Facts on File Dictionary of Mathematics. 224p. 1981. prepub. 14.95 (ISBN 0-87196-512-7). Facts on File.

Davis, Morton. Mathematically Speaking. 484p. 1980. text ed. 16.95 (ISBN 0-686-68334-X, HC); instr's guide avail. HarBraceJ.

Dieudonne, J. A. Treatise on Analysis, 6 vols. Incl. Vol. 1. 1960. 22.95 (ISBN 0-12-215550-5); Vol. 2. rev. ed. 1970. 44.50 (ISBN 0-12-215502-5); Vol. 3. 1972. 48.50 (ISBN 0-12-215503-3); Vol. 4. 1974. 49.00 (ISBN 0-12-215504-1); Vol. 5. 1977. 34.50 (ISBN 0-12-215505-X); Vol. 6. 1978. 32.00 (ISBN 0-12-215506-8). (Pure & Applied Mathematics Ser.). Acad Pr.

Dieudonne, Jean. A Panorama of Pure Mathematics: As Seen by N. Bourbaki. Macdonald, I., tr. LC 80-2330. (Pure & Applied Mathematics Ser.). 1981. write for info. (ISBN 0-12-215560-2). Acad Pr.

Dressler, Isidore. Preliminary Mathematics. (gr. 8). 1981. text ed. 17.92 (ISBN 0-87720-243-5). AMSCO Sch.

Edwards, Barry. The Readable Maths & Statistics Book. (Illus.). 336p. (Orig.). 1980. text ed. 34.95x (ISBN 0-04-310007-4, 2550); pap. text ed. 13.50x (ISBN 0-04-310008-2, 2551). Allen Unwin.

Edwards, R. A Formal Background to Mathematics: Pt. II, A & B. (Universitext). 1170p. 1980. pap. 39.80 (ISBN 0-387-90513-8). Springer-Verlag.

Eicholz, Robert E., et al. Mathematics in Our World. 2nd ed. Incl. Bk. 1. (gr. k). student ed. 3.92 (ISBN 0-201-16000-5); tchr's ed. 11.76 (ISBN 0-201-16001-3); (gr. 1). pap. 6.08 student ed. (ISBN 0-201-16010-2); tchr's ed. 16.00 (ISBN 0-201-16011-0); wkbk. 2.76 (ISBN 0-201-16013-7); tchr's ed. wkbk. 3.00 (ISBN 0-201-16014-5); (gr. 2). student ed. 6.08 (ISBN 0-201-16020-X); tchr's ed. 16.00 (ISBN 0-201-16021-8); wkbk. 2.76 (ISBN 0-201-16023-4); tchr's ed. wkbk. 3.00 (ISBN 0-201-16024-2); (gr. 3). student ed. 10.24 (ISBN 0-201-16030-7); tchr's ed. 16.00 (ISBN 0-201-16031-5); wkbk. 3.52 (ISBN 0-201-16033-1); tchr's ed. wkbk. 4.16 (ISBN 0-201-16034-X); consumable ed. 7.20 (ISBN 0-201-16009-9); (gr. 4). student ed. 10.24 (ISBN 0-201-16040-4); tchr's ed. 16.00 (ISBN 0-201-16041-2); wkbk. 3.52 (ISBN 0-201-16043-9); tchr's ed. wkbk. 4.16 (ISBN 0-201-16044-7); (gr. 5). student ed. 10.24 (ISBN 0-201-16050-1); tchr's ed. 16.00 (ISBN 0-201-16051-X); wkbk. 3.52 (ISBN 0-201-16053-6); tchr's ed. wkbk. 4.16 (ISBN 0-201-16054-4); (gr. 6). student ed. 10.24 (ISBN 0-201-16060-9); tchr's ed. 16.00 (ISBN 0-201-16061-1); wkbk. 3.52 (ISBN 0-201-16063-3); tchr's ed. wkbk. 4.16 (ISBN 0-201-16064-1); (gr. 7). student ed. 12.32 (ISBN 0-201-16070-6); tchr's ed. 16.00 (ISBN 0-201-16071-4); wkbk. 3.52 (ISBN 0-201-16073-0); tchr's ed. wkbk. 4.16 (ISBN 0-201-16074-9); (gr. 8). student ed. 12.32 (ISBN 0-201-16080-3); tchr's ed. 16.00 (ISBN 0-201-16081-1); wkbk. 3.52 (ISBN 0-201-16083-8); tchr's ed. wkbk. 4.16 (ISBN 0-201-16084-6). (gr. 1-8). 1981 (Sch Div). A-W.

Evyatar, A. & Rosenbloom, P. Motivated Mathematics. LC 80-40491. (Illus.). 250p. Date not set. price not set (ISBN 0-521-23308-9). Cambridge U Pr.

Fennell, Francis M. Elementary Mathematics Diagnosis & Correction Kit. 1980. pap. 17.95x comb-bound (ISBN 0-87628-295-8). Ctr Appl Res.

Fineberg, Marjorie. Everyday Math: Tables, Graphs, & Scale. LC 79-730692. (Illus.). 1979. pap. text ed. 99.00 (ISBN 0-89290-129-2, A514-SATC). Soc for Visual.

Foley, et al. Building Math Skills. Incl. Level 1. text ed. 8.32 (ISBN 0-201-13350-4); tchr's manual with ans. 6.00 (13359); test & practice dupl. masters avail.; Level 2. text ed. 8.32; tchr's manual with ans. 6.00 (13379); test & practice dupl. masters avail.. (Gr. 7-12 Basal, Gr. 9-12 Remedial, Gr. 7-12 Supplemental). 1981. A-W.

Gabbay, S. M. Elementary Mathematics for Basic Chemistry & Physics. 128p. (Orig.). 1980. pap. 9.95 (ISBN 0-9604722-0-7). Basic Science Prep Ctr.

Gafney, Leo & Beers, John C. Essential Math Skills. Devine, Peter, ed. 224p. 1980. pap. text ed. 5.20 (ISBN 0-07-010260-0, W); tchr's ed. 6.08 (ISBN 0-07-010261-9); Webstermasters tests 4.52 (ISBN 0-07-010262-7). McGraw.

Gibbons. Basic Math, 9 bks. Incl. Gr. K. pap. text ed. 2.92 (ISBN 0-8009-1401-5); tchr's. ed. 4.40 (ISBN 0-8009-1403-1); Gr. 1 & 2. pap. text ed. 4.64 ea.; Gr. 1. pap. text ed. (ISBN 0-8009-1406-6); Gr. 2. pap. text ed. (ISBN 0-8009-1410-4); tchr's. eds. 6.16 ea. Gr. 1 (ISBN 0-8009-1408-2). Gr. 2 (ISBN 0-8009-1412-0); Gr. 3-6. Gr. 3. pap. text ed. 4.64 (ISBN 0-8009-1414-7); Gr. 4. pap. text ed. 4.64 (ISBN 0-8009-1425-2); Gr. 5. 4.64 (ISBN 0-8009-1433-3); Gr. 6. tchr's. eds. 6.16 ea. (ISBN 0-8009-1443-0); tchr's. ed. gr. 3 6.16 (ISBN 0-8009-1416-3); tchr's. ed. gr. 4 6.16 (ISBN 0-8009-1427-9); tchr's. ed. gr. 5 6.16 (ISBN 0-8009-1437-6); tchr's. ed. gr. 6 6.16 (ISBN 0-8009-1445-7); tests for gr. 3-6 1.12 ea.; Gr. 7 & 8. pap. text ed. 5.08 ea.; Gr. 7. pap text ed. (ISBN 0-8009-1462-7); Gr. 8. pap. text ed. (ISBN 0-8009-1472-4); tchr's. eds. 6.60 ea. Gr. 7 (ISBN 0-8009-1464-3). Gr. 8 (ISBN 0-8009-1474-0). tests for gr. 7-8 1.12 ea. Gr. 7 (ISBN 0-8009-1468-6). Gr. 8 (ISBN 0-8009-1476-7). (gr. k-8). 1977-78. McCormick-Mathers.

Hatcher, William S. The Logical Foundations of Mathematics. LC 80-41253. (Foundations & Philosophy of Science & Technology Ser.). 400p. 1981. 48.00 (ISBN 0-08-025800-X). Pergamon.

Hinchey, Fred A. Introduction to Applicable Mathematics: Elementary Analysis, Vol. 1. LC 80-18569. 290p. 1981. 19.95 (ISBN 0-470-27041-1). Halsted Pr.

Kim & Roush. Introduction to Mathematical Concensus Theory. 192p. 1980. 25.00 (ISBN 0-8247-1001-0). Dekker.

Lapwood, E. R. & Usami, T. Free Oscillations of the Earth. (Cambridge Monographs on Mechanics & Applied Mathematics). (Illus.). 168p. Date not set. price not set (ISBN 0-521-23536-7). Cambridge U Pr.

Maher, Carolyn A., et al. Math, No. 1. Gafney, Leo, ed. (General Math Ser.). (Illus.). (gr. 7-9). 1981. text ed. write for info pupil's ed. (ISBN 0-07-039591-8, W); tchr's ed., 448 p. 13.20 (ISBN 0-07-039592-6); wkbk. to pupils ed. 4.80 (ISBN 0-07-039593-4); wkbk. to tchrs. ed. 5.20 (ISBN 0-07-039594-2). McGraw.

--General Math. Gafney, Leo, ed. 160p. 1980. pupil's ed. 4.80 (ISBN 0-07-039593-4, W); tchrs. ed. 5.20 (ISBN 0-07-039594-2). McGraw.

Mahoney, Susan & Gregorvich, Barbara. Math Word Problems. LC 79-730247. (Illus.). 1979. pap. text ed. 99.00 (ISBN 0-89290-130-6, A515-SATC). Soc for Visual.

Meserve, Bruce E. & Sobel, Max A. Contemporary Mathematics. 3rd ed. (Illus.). 688p. 1981. text ed. 18.95 (ISBN 0-13-170076-6). P-H.

Miller, Mary K. Mathematics for Nurses with Clinical Applications. LC 80-26040. 385p. (Orig.). 1981. pap. text ed. 14.95 (ISBN 0-8185-0429-3). Brooks-Cole.

Nachman, L. J. Fundamental Mathematics. 657p. 1978. 20.95 (ISBN 0-471-62815-8). Wiley.

Newby, J. C. Mathematics for the Biological Sciences: From Graph Through Calculus to Differential Equations. (Illus.). 250p. 1980. 59.00 (ISBN 0-19-859623-5); pap. 27.00 (ISBN 0-19-859624-3). Oxford U Pr.

Nickel, Karl L. Interval Mathematics: 1980. LC 80-25009. 1980. lib ed 29.50 (ISBN 0-12-518850-1). Acad Pr.

Oxtoby, J. C. Measure & Category. 2nd ed. (Graduate Texts in Mathematics: Vol. 2). 106p. 1980. 19.80 (ISBN 0-387-90508-1). Springer-Verlag.

Plumpton, C. & Macilwaine, P. S. New Tertiary Mathematics: Further Pure Mathematics, Vol. 2, Pt. 1. LC 79-41454. (Illus.). 408p. 1981. 42.00 (ISBN 0-08-025033-5); pap. 16.75 (ISBN 0-08-021644-7). Pergamon.

Rallis, Stephen & Schiffmann, Gerard. Weil Representation I: Intertwining Distributions & Discrete Spectrum. LC 80-12191. (Memoirs of the American Mathematical Society Ser.). 1980. 6.40 (ISBN 0-8218-2231-4, MEMO-231). Am Math.

Robinson, R. W., et al. Combinatorial Mathematics VII: Proceedings. (Lecture Notes in Mathematics Ser.: Vol. 829). (Illus.). 256p. 1981. pap. 16.80 (ISBN 0-387-10254-X). Springer-Verlag.

Rudman, Jack. Mathematics. (Undergraduate Program Field Test Ser.: UPFT-15). (Cloth bdg. avail. on request). pap. 9.95 (ISBN 0-8373-6015-3). Natl Learning.

St. John, Michael. From Arithmetic to Algebra. 132p. (Orig.). 1980. pap. text ed. 4.50 (ISBN 0-937354-00-7, TX-334-207). Delta Systems.

St. Paul Technical Vocational Institute Curriculum Commitee. Mathematics for Careers: Measurement & Geometry. LC 80-67549. (General Mathematics Ser.). 176p. 1981. pap. text ed. 7.40 (ISBN 0-8273-2058-2); price not set instr's. guide (ISBN 0-8273-2059-0). Delmar.

Smale, S. The Mathematics of Time. (Illus.). 151p. 1981. pap. 16.00 (ISBN 0-387-90519-7). Springer-Verlag.

Smith, Robert. Applied General Mathematics. LC 79-51586. (General Mathematics Ser.). (Illus.). 480p. 1981. text ed. price not set (ISBN 0-8273-1674-7); price not set instr's. guide (ISBN 0-8273-1675-5). Delmar.

Staszkow, Ronald. Developmental Mathematics: Basic Arithmetic with a Brief Introduction to Algebra. 384p. 1980. pap. text ed. 14.95 (ISBN 0-8403-2213-5). Kendall-Hunt.

Stromberg, Karl. Introduction to Classical Real Analysis. (Wadsworth International Mathematics Ser.). 576p. 1981. text ed. 29.95x (ISBN 0-686-69568-2). Wadsworth Pub.

Vincent, Thomas L. & Grantham, Walter J. Optimality in Parametric Systems. 250p. 1981. 30.00 (ISBN 0-471-08307-0, Pub. by Wiley-Interscience). Wiley.

Wepner, Gabriella. Basic Mathematics. 1981. write for info. Franklin Inst Pr.

Wheeler, Ruric. Modern Mathematics: An Elementary Approach, Alternative Edition. 585p. 1981. text ed. 18.95 (ISBN 0-8185-0413-7). Brooks-Cole.

Wheeler, Ruric E. Modern Mathematics: An Elementary Approach. 5th ed. 625p. 1981. text ed. 19.95 (ISBN 0-8185-0430-7). Brooks-Cole.

Whimbey, Arthur & Lochhead, Jack. Developing Mathematical Skills. (Illus.). 448p. 1981. text ed. 11.95 (ISBN 0-07-069517-2, C). McGraw.

MATHEMATICS–ADDRESSES, ESSAYS, LECTURES

Abikoff, W. The Real Analytic Theory of Teichmueller Space. (Lecture Notes in Mathematics Ser.: Vol. 820). (Illus.). 144p. 1981. pap. 11.80 (ISBN 0-387-10237-X). Springer-Verlag.

Dlab, V. & Gabriel, P., eds. Representation Theory I. (Lecture Notes in Mathematics Ser.: Vol. 831). 373p. 1981. pap. 22.00 (ISBN 0-387-10263-9). Springer-Verlag.

--Representation Theory II. (Lecture Notes in Mathematics: Vol. 832). 673p. 1981. pap. 40.20 (ISBN 0-387-10264-7). Springer-Verlag.

Index of Mathematical Papers. Incl. Vol. 1. July-December, 1970. 1972. 30.00 (ISBN 0-8218-4001-0, IMP-1); Vol. 2, 2 pts. 1972. Set. 60.00 (IMP-2); Jan-June, 1971 (ISBN 0-8218-4002-9); July-Dec., 1971 (ISBN 0-8218-4003-7); Vol. 3, 2 pts. 1973. Set. 80.00 (IMP-3); Jan.-June, 1972 (ISBN 0-8218-4004-5); July-Dec., 1972 (ISBN 0-8218-4005-3); Vol. 4, 2 pts. 1973-74. Set. 80.00 (IMP-4); Jan.-June, 1973 (ISBN 0-8218-4006-1); July-Dec., 1973 (ISBN 0-8218-4007-X); Vol. 5. Index to Mathematical Reviews for 1973. Date not set. 80.00 (ISBN 0-8218-4008-8, IMP-5); Vol. 6. Index to Mathematical Reviews for 1974. 80.00 (ISBN 0-8218-4009-6, IMP-6); Vol. 7. Index to Mathematical Reviews for 1975. 95.00 (ISBN 0-8218-4010-X, IMP-7); Vol. 8. Index to Mathematical Reviews for 1976. 120.00 (ISBN 0-8218-4011-8, IMP-8); Vol. 11. Index to Mathematical Reviews for 1979. 120.00 (ISBN 0-8218-4014-2, IMP-11); Cumulative Index (Author & Subject Index of Mathematical Reviews, 1973-1979) 1070.00 (ISBN 0-8218-0035-3, MREVIN-73-79). Am Math.

Power Computation Conference, 7th, Lausanne, Switzerland, July 12-17, 1980. Procedings. 1981. text ed. price not set (ISBN 0-86103-025-7). Butterworth.

Weizsaecker, C. C. Barriers to Entry: A Theoretical Treatment. (Lecture Notes in Economics & Mathematical Systems Ser.: Vol. 185). (Illus.). 220p. 1981. pap. 19.00 (ISBN 0-387-10272-8). Springer-Verlag.

MATHEMATICS–BIBLIOGRAPHY

Mathematical Reviews Cumulative Index: 1973-1979. Date not set. cancelled (ISBN 0-8218-0035-3). Am Math.

MATHEMATICS–DATA PROCESSING

Rau, Nicholas. Matrices & Mathematical Prgramming: An Introduction for Economists. 1980. 18.50 (ISBN 0-312-52299-1). St Martin.

MATHEMATICS–EXAMINATIONS, QUESTIONS, ETC.

Allasio, John, et al. RCT Mathematics: A Workbook. 168p. (gr. 9-12). 1980. pap. 5.95 (ISBN 0-937820-00-8); ans. key 1.00 (ISBN 0-937820-01-6). Westsea Pub.

Hockett, Shirley. Barron's How to Prepare for Advanced Placement in Mathematics. rev. ed. (gr. 10-12). 1981. pap. text ed. 8.50 (ISBN 0-8120-2071-5). Barron.

Moran, Deborah, et al. GED Mathematics Test Preparation Guide: High School Equivalency Examination. (Cliffs Test Preparation Ser.). 182p. (gr. 10 up). 1981. pap. 3.95 (ISBN 0-8220-2016-5). Cliffs.

MATHEMATICS–HANDBOOKS, MANUALS, ETC.

Lloyd, E. Handbook of Applicable Mathematics: Probability, Vol. 2. (Handbook of Applicable Mathematics Ser.). 444p. 1980. 32.50 (ISBN 0-471-27821-1, Pub. by Wiley-Interscience). Wiley.

Research & Education Association Staff. Handbook of Mathematical Formulas, Tables, Functions, Graphs, Transforms. LC 80-52490. (Illus.). 800p. (Orig.). pap. text ed. 16.85x (ISBN 0-87891-521-4). Res & Educ.

MATHEMATICS–HISTORY

see also Mathematics, Chinese; Mathematics, Greek, and similar headings

Clagett, Marshall. Studies in Medieval Physics & Mathematics. 366p. 1980. 75.00x (ISBN 0-86078-048-1, Pub. by Variorum England). State Mutual Bk.

Dauben, Joseph W., ed. Mathematical Actives: Essays on Mathematics & Its Historical Development. LC 80-1781. 1981. write for info. (ISBN 0-12-204050-3). Acad Pr.

Heath, Thomas L. A History of Greek Mathematics, 2 vols. (Illus.). 1058p. 1981. pap. price not set. Vol. I (ISBN 0-486-24073-8). Vol. II (ISBN 0-486-24074-6). Dover.

Kline, Morris. Mathematics & the Physical World. (Illus.). 496p. 1981. pap. price not set (ISBN 0-486-24104-1). Dover.

Morgan, Bryan. Men & Discoveries in Mathematics. 235p. 1980. 15.00x (ISBN 0-7195-2587-X, Pub. by Murray Pubs England). State Mutual Bk.

Newton, Isaac. The Mathematical Papers of Isaac Newton: Vol. 8, 1697-1722. Whiteside, D. T., ed. LC 65-11203. (Illus.). 750p. Date not set. price not set (ISBN 0-521-20103-9). Cambridge U Pr.

MATHEMATICS–JUVENILE LITERATURE

Barson, Alan. Motivational Games for Mathematics. (Illus.). 40p. (gr. 3-7). 1981. pap. 6.00 (ISBN 0-937138-02-9). Fabmath.

Clark, Clara E. A Tangram Diary. (Illus.). 64p. (Orig.). (gr. 3-6). 1980. pap. 4.95 (ISBN 0-934734-05-4). Construct Educ.

Clark, Clara E. & Sternberg, Betty J. Math in Stride, Bk. 1. (Illus.). 166p. (Orig.). (gr. k-2). 1980. pap. 5.65 (ISBN 0-934734-06-2). Construct Educ.

--Math in Stride, Bk. 2. (Illus.). 203p. (Orig.). (gr. 1-3). 1980. pap. 5.80 (ISBN 0-934734-07-0). Construct Educ.

--Math in Stride, Bk. 3. (Illus.). 219p. (Orig.). (gr. 2-4). 1980. pap. 5.95 (ISBN 0-934734-08-9). Construct Educ.

Earle, Vana. Numbers Workbook Four (with the Scarecrow from Oz) (Funny Face Activity Bks.). (Illus.). 48p. (ps-1). 1981. pap. 1.95 saddle-stitched (ISBN 0-394-84670-2). Random.

Rohm, Robert. Guinness World Records Math Learning Module. LC 79-730909. (Illus.). (gr. 6-7). 1979. pap. text ed. 175.00 (ISBN 0-89290-091-1, CM-73). Soc for Visual.

Svendson, May. Numbers Workbook Three (with Daring Dog) (Funny Face Activity Bks.). (Illus.). 48p. (ps-1). 1981. pap. 1.95 saddle-stitched (ISBN 0-394-84458-0). Random.

MATHEMATICS–PHILOSOPHY

see also Semantics (Philosophy)

Beller, A., et al. Coding the Universe. (London Mathematical Society Lecture Notes: No. 47). 300p. Date not set. price not set (ISBN 0-521-28040-0). Cambridge U Pr.

Lakatos, Imre. Philosophical Papers: Mathematics, Science & Epistemology, Vol. 2. Worrall, J. & Currie, G., eds. LC 77-14374. 295p. 1980. pap. 13.50 (ISBN 0-521-28030-3). Cambridge U Pr.

Wilder, Raymond I. Mathamatics As a Cultural System. (Foundations & Philosophy of Science & Technology Ser.). 170p. 1981. 25.00 (ISBN 0-08-025796-8). Pergamon.

MATHEMATICS–PROBLEMS, EXERCISES, ETC.

DeVore, Russell B. Practical Problems in Mathematics for Heating & Cooling Technicians. LC 79-57141. (Practical Problems in Mathematics Ser.). 175p. 1981. pap. text ed. 6.60 (ISBN 0-8273-1682-8); instr's. guide 2.10 (ISBN 0-8273-1683-6). Delmar.

MATHEMATICS–STATISTICAL METHODS

see Mathematical Statistics

MATHEMATICS–STUDY AND TEACHING

see also Mathematical Models

Bley, Nancy S. & Thornton, Carol A. Teaching Mathematics to the Learning Disabled. 350p. 1981. text ed. price not set (ISBN 0-89443-357-1). Aspen Systems.

Howson, A. G., et al. Curriculum Development in Mathematics. 200p. Date not set. price not set (ISBN 0-521-23767-X). Cambridge U Pr.

Lindquist, Mary M., ed. Selected Issues in Mathematics Education. LC 80-82903. 250p. 1981. write for info. (ISBN 0-8211-1114-0); text ed. write for info. McCutchan.

Santos, Mary G. Math Can Be Easy. 90p. (Orig.). 1980. pap. 6.00 (ISBN 0-914562-10-X). Merriam-Eddy.

Silbert, Jerry, et al. Direct Instruction Mathematics. (Illus., Orig.). 1981. pap. text ed. write for info. (ISBN 0-675-08047-9). Merrill.

Souviney, Randall. Solving Problems Kids Care About. (Illus.). 176p. (Orig.). 1981. pap. 10.95 (ISBN 0-8302-8653-5). Goodyear.

Underhill, Robert G. Teaching Elementary School Mathematics. 3rd ed. 1981. write for info; instr's. manual 3.95 (ISBN 0-686-69502-X). Merrill.

MATHEMATICS–STUDY AND TEACHING–AUDIO-VISUAL AIDS

Math House Proficiency Review Tapes: Applications Involving Measurement, Unit C. (YA) (gr. 7 up). 1980. manual & cassettes 159.95 (ISBN 0-917792-05-X). Math Hse.

Soracco, Lionel J., Jr. Math House Proficiency Review Tapes: Applications Involving Money, Unit D. (YA) (gr. 7 up). 1980. manual & cassettes 159.95 (ISBN 0-917792-06-8). Math Hse.

--Math House Proficiency Review Tapes: Operations with Decimals & Percent, Unit B. (YA) (gr. 7 up). 1980. manual & cassettes 159.95 (ISBN 0-917792-04-1). Math Hse.

Sorracco, Lionel J., Jr. Math House Proficiency Review Tapes: Operations with Whole Numbers & Fractions, Unit A. (YA) (gr. 7 up). 1980. manual & cassettes 159.95 (ISBN 0-917792-03-3). Math Hse.

MATHEMATICS–STUDY AND TEACHING (ELEMENTARY)

Blum, Peter. Everybody Counts: A T. A. Self-Help Book for Math Aversion. 54p. (Orig.). 1981. pap. 6.95 (ISBN 0-9605756-0-X). Math Counsel Inst.

Choat, E. Mathematics & the Primary School Curriculum. 128p. 1980. pap. text ed. 18.75x (ISBN 0-85633-206-2, NFER). Humanities.

Dacey, John. Where the World Is, Teaching Basic Skills Outdoors. (Illus.). 192p. (Orig.). 1981. pap. 10.95 (ISBN 0-8302-9605-0). Goodyear.

Dubisch, Roy. Basic Concepts of Mathematics for Elementary Teachers. 2nd ed. LC 80-19446. (Mathematics Ser.). (Illus.). 483p. 1981. write for info. (ISBN 0-201-03170-1). A-W.

Lerch, Harold H. Active Learning Experiences for Teaching Elementary School Mathematics. (Illus.). 592p. 1981. pap. text ed. price not set (ISBN 0-395-29764-8). HM.

--Teaching Elementary School Mathematics: An Active Learning Approach. (Illus.). 416p. 1981. text ed. price not set (ISBN 0-395-29762-1); price not set instr's. manual (ISBN 0-395-29763-X). HM.

Smith, Douglas B. & Topp, William R. Activity Approach to Elementary Concepts of Mathematics. (Mathematics Ser.). (Illus.). 150p. 1981. pap. text ed. price not set (ISBN 0-201-07694-2). A-W.

MATHEMATICS–STUDY AND TEACHING (SECONDARY)
Miklos, Mary O. Mathematical Ideas. LC 80-5871. 344p. 1980. pap. text ed. 11.50 (ISBN 0-8191-1099-X). U Pr of Amer.
Posamentier, Alfred. Teaching Mathematics in the Secondary School. 1981. pap. text ed. 15.95 (ISBN 0-675-08033-9). Merrill.
Rosier, M. J. Changes in Secondary School Mathematics in Australia, 1964-1978. (ACER Research Monographs: No. 8). 1980. pap. 20.00 (ISBN 0-85563-208-9). Verry.
MATHEMATICS–TABLES, ETC.
see also Integrals
Allen, Edward S. Six-Place Tables. 256p. 1981. Repr. of 1922 ed. lib. bdg. price not set (ISBN 0-89874-287-0). Krieger.
MATHEMATICS–1961-
Crown, J. Conrad & Bittinger, Marvin L. Finite Mathematics: A Modeling Approach. 2nd ed. LC 80-19472. (Mathematics Ser.). (Illus.). 480p. 1981. text ed. 15.95 (ISBN 0-201-03145-0). A-W.
MATHEMATICS, BUSINESS
see Business Mathematics
MATHEMATICS, CONSTRUCTIVE
see Constructive Mathematics
MATHEMATICS, GREEK
Heath, Thomas L. A History of Greek Mathematics, 2 vols. (Illus.). 1058p. 1981. pap. price not set. Vol. I (ISBN 0-486-24073-8). Vol. II (ISBN 0-486-24074-6). Dover.
MATHEMATICS, LOGIC OF
see Mathematics–Philosophy
MATHEMATICS OF FINANCE
see Business Mathematics
MATHER, COTTON 1663-1728
West, Mae. Goodness Had Nothing to Do with It. (A Belvedere Bk.). 312p. 1981. pap. 6.95 (ISBN 0-87754-301-1). Chelsea Hse.
MATISSE, HENRI, 1869-1954
Matisse, Herni. Matisse Line Drawings & Prints. (Illus.). 1980. pap. 2.00 (ISBN 0-486-23877-6). Dover.
MATRICES
see also Linear Programming; Matrix Groups; Multivariate Analysis
Rau, Nicholas. Matrices & Mathematical Prgramming: An Introduction for Economists. 1980. 18.50 (ISBN 0-312-52299-1). St Martin.
MATRIMONIAL REGIME
see Husband and Wife
MATRIMONY
see Marriage
MATRIX GROUPS
Graham, Alexander. Matrix Theory & Applications for Engineers & Mathematicians. LC 79-40988. (Mathematics & Its Applications). 295p. 1980. pap. 24.95 (ISBN 0-470-27072-1). Halsted Pr.
Rogers. Matrix Derivatives. 224p. 1980. 27.50 (ISBN 0-8247-1176-9). Dekker.
MATRIX MECHANICS
see also Quantum Statistics; Quantum Theory; Wave Mechanics
Crouch, T. Matrix Methods Applied to Engineering Rigid Body Mechanics. LC 80-41186. 385p. 1980. 45.00 (ISBN 0-08-024245-6); pap. 18.00 (ISBN 0-08-024246-4). Pergamon.
MATTERHORN
Whymper, Edward. Scrambles Amongst the Alps in the Years Eighteen Sixty to Eighteen Sixty-Nine. (Illus.). 176p. 1981. pap. 5.95 (ISBN 0-89815-043-4). Ten Speed Pr.
MATURITY, EMOTIONAL
see Emotional Maturity
MAUGHAM, WILLIAM SOMERSET, 1874-1965
Morgan, Ted. Maugham. 1981. pap. 9.95 (ISBN 0-671-42811-X, Touchstone). S&S.
MAUROIS, ANDRE, 1885-1967
Larg, David G. Andre Maurois. 239p. 1980. Repr. of 1931 ed. lib. bdg. 25.00 (ISBN 0-8492-1633-8). R West.
MAUSOLEUMS
see Sepulchral Monuments
MAVAR (ELECTRONICS)
see Parametric Amplifiers
MAXIMA AND MINIMA
see also Calculus of Variations; Mathematical Optimization
Sperb, Rene. Maximum Principles & Their Applications. (Mathematics in Science & Engineering). 1981. price not set (ISBN 0-12-656880-4). Acad Pr.
MAXIMUS, SAINT, BP. OF TURIN, d. ca. 420
Thunberg, Lars. Microcosm & Mediator: The Theological Anthropology of Maximus the Confessor. Allchin, A. L., rev. by. LC 80-2368. 1981. Repr. of 1965 ed. 58.00 (ISBN 0-404-18917-2). AMS Pr.
MAYA ART
see Mayas–Art
MAYA LANGUAGE
Martin, Laura. Papers in Mayan Linguistics. 6.00. Lucas.
MAYA MYTHOLOGY
see Mayas–Religion and Mythology
MAYAN LANGUAGES
see also Maya Language
Furbee, Louanna, ed. Mayan Texts III. LC 76-15159. (International Journal of American Linguistics Native American Texts Ser.: No. 5). 122p. (Orig.). 1980. pap. 10.75 (ISBN 0-8357-0567-6, IS-00115, Pub. by U of Chicago Pr). Univ Microfilms.
Martin, Laura. Papers in Mayan Linguistics. 6.00. Lucas.
MAYAS–ANTIQUITIES
Ashmore, Wendy, ed. Lowland Maya Settlement Patterns. (School of American Research Advanced Seminar Ser.). 464p. 1980. 30.00x (ISBN 0-8263-0556-3). U of NM Pr.
MAYAS–ART
Coe, Michael D. & Benson, Elizabeth P. Three Maya Relief Panels at Dumbarton Oaks. LC 66-30016. (Studies in Pre-Columbian Art & Archaeology: No. 2). (Illus.). 1966. pap. 2.00 (ISBN 0-88402-079-7, Ctr Pe-Columbian). Dumbarton Oaks.
MAYAS–RELIGION AND MYTHOLOGY
Bricker, Victoria R. The Indian Christ, the Indian King: The Historical Substrate of Maya Myth & Ritual. (Illus.). 624p. 1981. text ed. 45.00x (ISBN 0-292-73824-2). U of Tex Pr.
Colby, Benjamin N. & Colby, Lore M. The Daykeeper: The Life & Discource of As IXII Deliver. (Illus.). 352p. 1981. text ed. 25.00 (ISBN 0-674-19409-8). Harvard U Pr.
Tedlock, Barbara. Time & the Highland Maya. (Illus.). 288p. 1981. 27.50 (ISBN 0-8263-0577-6). U of NM Pr.
MAYER, LOUIS B., 1885-1957
Carey, Gary. All the Stars in Heaven: The Story of Louis B. Mayer & Metro-Goldwyn-Mayer. (Illus.). 1980. 15.00 (ISBN 0-525-05245-3). Dutton.
MAYFLOWER (SHIP)
Heaton, Vernon. The Mayflower. (Illus.). 200p. 1980. 19.95 (ISBN 0-8317-5745-0). Mayflower Bks.
Simon, Phillip J. Log of the Mayflower. LC 56-9513. 208p. 1980. pap. 7.95 (ISBN 0-911180-02-8). Priam Pr.
MAYORS
FitzGerald, Kathleen W. Brass: Jane Byrne & the Pursuit of Power. 1981. 11.95 (ISBN 0-8092-7006-4). Contemp Bks.
MAZDA AUTOMOBILE
see Automobiles, Foreign–Types–Mazda
MAZE PUZZLES
Evans, Larry. Three-Dimensional Maze Art. (Illus.). 64p. 1980. pap. 4.95 (ISBN 0-89844-012-2). Troubador Pr.
Koziakin, Vladimir. Science Fiction Mazes. 128p. (gr. 4 up). pap. 1.50 (ISBN 0-448-17259-3, Tempo). G&D.
MAZUT
see Petroleum As Fuel; Petroleum Products
MEAD, MARGARET, 1901-1978
Frevert, Patricia D. Margaret Mead Herself. Redpath, Ann, ed. (People to Remember Ser.). (Illus.). 32p. (gr. 5-9). 1981. PLB 5.95 (ISBN 0-87191-799-8). Creative Ed.
MEALS FOR SCHOOL CHILDREN
see School Children–Food
MEANING (PHILOSOPHY)
Powell, Robert. Return to Meaningfulness. LC 80-54613. 180p. 1981. pap. text ed. 7.95 (ISBN 0-932238-07-6). Word Shop.
MEASUREMENT, MENTAL
see Psychometrics
MEASUREMENTS, OPTICAL
see Optical Measurements
MEASUREMENTS, PHYSICAL
see Physical Measurements
MEASUREMENT, PSYCHOLOGICAL
see Psychometrics
MEASURES
see Weights and Measures
MEASURING
see Mensuration
MEAT
see also Cookery (Meat)
Mutkoski, Stephen A. & Schurer, Marcia L. Meat & Fish Management for Food Service. 1981. text ed. 17.95 (ISBN 0-534-00907-7, Breton Pubs). Wadsworth Pub.
Richards, Michael E. Meat for Your Freezer. 1974. 6.95 (ISBN 0-571-10223-9, Pub. by Faber & Faber). Merrimack Bk Serv.
Simoons, Frederick J. Eat Not This Flesh: Food Avoidances in the Old World. LC 80-22232. (Illus.). xiii, 241p. 1981. Repr. of 1967 ed. lib. bdg. 29.75x (ISBN 0-313-22772-1, SIEN). Greenwood.
MEAT–INSPECTION
see Meat Inspection
MEAT CONSUMPTION
see Meat Industry and Trade
MEAT INDUSTRY AND TRADE
see also Cattle Trade; Meat Inspection; Pork Industry and Trade; Slaughtering and Slaughter-Houses
Minish & Lidvall. Fundamentals of Meat Animal Evaluation. 1981. text ed. 15.95 (ISBN 0-8359-2137-9); instr's. manual free (ISBN 0-8359-2138-7). Reston.
MEAT INSPECTION
Guide to Meat Inspection in the Tropics. 95p. 1981. pap. 22.50 (ISBN 0-85198-456-8, CAB 10, CAB). Unipub.
Minish & Lidvall. Fundamentals of Meat Animal Evaluation. 1981. text ed. 15.95 (ISBN 0-8359-2137-9); instr's. manual free (ISBN 0-8359-2138-7). Reston.
MEAT PACKING INDUSTRY
see Meat Industry and Trade
MEATLESS MEALS
see Vegetarianism
MECCA
Asad, Muhammad. The Road to Mecca. LC 80-1937. 1981. Repr. of 1954 ed. 42.00 (ISBN 0-404-18953-9). AMS Pr.
MECHANIC ARTS
see Industrial Arts
Fremon, George & Fremon, Suzanne. Your First Car. (Illus.). 176p. (Orig.). 1981. pap. 3.95 (ISBN 0-89709-024-1). Liberty Pub.
MECHANICAL ARITHMETIC
see Calculating-Machines
MECHANICAL BRAINS
see Cybernetics
MECHANICAL DRAWING
see also Architectural Drawing; Blue-Prints; Design, Industrial; Drawing-Room Practice; Engineering Graphics; Graphic Methods; Lettering
Lieblich, Jerome H., ed. Drawing Requirement Manual. 4th ed. 624p. 1981. lib. bdg. 21.95x perfect bdg (ISBN 0-912702-02-8). Global Eng.
Nelson, John A. Handbook of Drafting Technology. 368p. 1981. text ed. 22.95 (ISBN 0-442-28661-9); pap. text ed. 14.95 (ISBN 0-442-28662-7). Van Nos Reinhold.
Problems in Engineering Drawing for Design & Communications. 8th ed. pap. 8.95 ea. Vol. 1 (ISBN 0-13-716373-8). Vol. 2 (ISBN 0-13-716381-9). P-H.
Shawki, G. S. A. & Metwalli, S. M., eds. Current Advances in Mechanical Design & Production: Proceedings of the First International Conference, Cairo University, 27-29 December 1979. LC 80-41666. (Illus.). 500p. 1981. 75.00 (ISBN 0-08-027294-0). Pergamon.
Stirling, Norman. Technical Drawing: An Introduction Metric. Edition. 370p. 1981. 18.95 (ISBN 0-442-23151-2). Van Nos Reinhold.
Walker, John R. Exploring Metric Drafting. LC 79-24019. (Illus.). 320p. 1980. text ed. 10.96 (ISBN 0-87006-289-1). Good Heart.
MECHANICAL DRAWING–PROBLEMS, EXERCISES, ETC.
Renton, Bruce A. Drafting Projects for Today. 1975. pap. 8.80 (ISBN 0-8273-1926-6). Delmar.
Weaver, Rip. Structural Drafting Workbook. (Illus.). 112p. 1980. pap. text ed. 9.95. Gulf Pub.
MECHANICAL DRAWINGS
Muir, John. The Velvet Monkey Wrench. rev. ed. LC 72-96736. (Illus.). 247p. 1980. pap. 6.00 (ISBN 0-912528-02-8). John Muir.
MECHANICAL ENGINEERING
Here are entered works relating to the application of the principles of mechanics to the design construction and operation of machinery.
see also Chemical Engineering; Diaphragms (Mechanical Devices); Electric Engineering; Electromechanical Devices; Marine Engineering; Mechanical Movements; Mechanics, Applied; Power (Mechanics); Production Engineering
Ahlstrand, Alan. Datsun Two Hundred Ten: Nineteen Seventy-Nine to Nineteen Eighty Shop Manual. Jorgensen, Eric, ed. (Illus.). 336p. (Orig.). 1980. pap. text ed. 11.95 (ISBN 0-89287-322-1, A 203). Clymer Pubns.
Ahlstrand, Eric. Datsun F Ten & Three Hundred Ten: Nineteen Seventy-Six to Seventy-Nine Shop Manual. (Illus.). 186p. (Orig.). 1980. pap. text ed. 10.95 (ISBN 0-89287-318-3, A202). Clymer Pubns.
Alexander, J. M. Strength of Materials: Fundamentals, Vol. 1. 190p. 1981. 47.95 (ISBN 0-470-27119-1). Halsted Pr.
Bacon & Stephens. Mechanical Science for Higher Technicians, Nos. 4-5. 1981. text ed. price not set (ISBN 0-408-00570-X). Butterworth.
Bishop, Mike. Kawasaki Snowmobiles Nineteen Seventy-Six to Nineteen Eighty: Service, Repair, Maintenance. Jorgensen, Eric, ed. (Illus.). 152p. (Orig.). 1980. pap. text ed. 8.95 (ISBN 0-89287-320-5, X995). Clymer Pubns.
--Yamaha Snowmobiles: Nineteen Seventy-Five to Nineteen Eighty Service, Repair & Maintenance. Jorgensen, Eric, ed. (Illus.). 180p. (Orig.). 1980. pap. text ed. 8.95 (ISBN 0-89287-323-X, X954). Clymer Pubns.
Bolton, W. Mechanical Science for Technicians, No. 3. (Technician Ser.). (Illus.). 128p. 1980. pap. text ed. 12.50. Butterworths.
Combs, Jim. BMW Three Hundred Twenty i: Nineteen Seventy-Seven to Nineteen Eighty Shop Manual. Jorgensen, Eric, ed. (Illus.). 248p. (Orig.). 1980. pap. text ed. 10.95 (ISBN 0-89287-326-4, A139). Clymer Pubns.
--Chevy Malibu Chevelle MonteCarlo: 1970-1980 Shop Manual. Jorgensen, Eric, ed. (Illus.). 360p. (Orig.). 1980. pap. text ed. 10.95 (ISBN 0-89287-319-1, A246). Clymer Pubns.
--Oldsmobile Cutlass: Nineteen Seventy to Nineteen Eighty Shop Manual. Jorgensen, Eric, ed. (Illus.). 342p. (Orig.). 1980. pap. text ed. 10.95 (ISBN 0-89287-324-8, A285). Clymer Pubns.
Crouch, T. Matrix Methods Applied to Engineering Rigid Body Mechanics. LC 80-41186. 385p. 1980. 45.00 (ISBN 0-08-024245-6); pap. 18.00 (ISBN 0-08-024246-4). Pergamon.
Dickie, D. E. & Short, Douglas. Lifting Tackle Manual. 1981. text ed. price not set (ISBN 0-408-00446-0, Fnewnes-Butterworth). Butterworth.
Sales, David. Suzuki SP-DR Three Hundred Seventy & Four Hundred Singles Nineteen Seventy-Eight to Nineteen Eighty: Service, Repair, Performance. Jorgensen, Eric, ed. (Illus.). 224p. (Orig.). 1980. pap. text ed. 9.95 (ISBN 0-89287-327-2, M374). Clymer Pubns.
Scott, Ed. Yamaha YZ One Hundred to Four Hundred Sixty-Five Monoshock Nineteen Seventy-Five to Nineteen Eighty: Service, Repair, Performance. Jorgensen, Eric, ed. (Illus.). 293p. (Orig.). 1980. pap. text ed. 9.95 (ISBN 0-89287-329-9, M413). Clymer Pubns.
Scott, Edward. Honda Twinstar Nineteen Seventy-Eight to Nineteen Eighty: Service, Repair, Maintenance. Jorgensen, Eric, ed. (Illus.). 242p. (Orig.). 1980. pap. text ed. 9.95 (ISBN 0-89287-325-6, M324). Clymer Pubns.
Sinclair, Bruce. A Centennial History of the American Society of Mechanical Engineers: 1880-1980. 256p. 1980. text ed. 15.00 (H0175H); pap. text ed. 10.00 (H0175P). ASME.
Sirohi, R. S. Mechanical Measurements. LC 80-27233. 210p. 1981. 13.95 (ISBN 0-470-27107-8). Halsted Pr.
Vesely, Anton. Kawasaki Nine Hundred & 1000cc Four, 1973-1979: Includes Shaft Drive Service Repair Performance. Jorgensen, Eric, ed. (Illus.). 324p. (Orig.). 1980. pap. text ed. 9.95 (ISBN 0-89287-321-3, M359). Clymer Pubns.
MECHANICAL ENGINEERING–CONTRACTS AND SPECIFICATIONS
Towill, Denis R. Coefficient Plane Models for Control System Analysis & Design. (Mechanical Engineering Research Studies: Vol. 1). 260p. 1981. 44.50 (ISBN 0-471-27955-2, Pub. by Wiley-Interscience). Wiley.
MECHANICAL ENGINEERING–DICTIONARIES
Shvarts, V. V. The Concise Illustrated Russian-English Dictionary of Mechanical Engineering. (Illus.). 224p. 1981. pap. 30.00 (ISBN 0-08-027574-5). Pergamon.
MECHANICAL ENGINEERING–EXAMINATIONS, QUESTIONS, ETC.
Gladstone, John. Air Conditioning & Mechanical Trades: Preparing for the Contractor's License Examination. LC 74-18258. (Illus.). 425p. 1980. pap. 18.95 (ISBN 0-930644-04-2). Engineers Pr.
MECHANICAL ENGINEERING–HANDBOOKS, MANUALS, ETC.
Atteberry, Pat H. Power Mechanics. LC 80-20581. (Illus.). 112p. 1980. text ed. 4.40 (ISBN 0-87006-307-3). Goodheart.
MECHANICAL ENGINEERING–PROBLEMS, EXERCISES, ETC.
Szuladzinski, Gregory. Dynamics of Structures & Machinery: Problems & Solutions. 700p. 1981. 50.00 (ISBN 0-471-09027-1, Pub. by Wiley Interscience). Wiley.
MECHANICAL ENGINEERS
Mechanical Engineers in America Born Prior to 1861: A Biographical Dictionary. 350p. 1980. 20.00 (H00176). ASME.
MECHANICAL HANDLING
see Materials Handling
MECHANICAL MODELS
see Machinery–Models
MECHANICAL MOVEMENTS
see also Automata; Machinery, Kinematics Of
Frank, Adolph F. Animated Scale Models Handbook. LC 80-22858. (Illus.). 160p. 1981. lib. bdg. 10.00 (ISBN 0-668-05118-3, 5118). Arco.
Martin, George H. Kinematics & Dynamics of Machines. 2nd ed. (Illus.). 544p. 1982. text ed. 28.95x (ISBN 0-07-040657-X, C); write for info. solutions manual (ISBN 0-07-040658-8). McGraw.
MECHANICAL PERSPECTIVE
see Perspective
MECHANICAL QUADRATURE
see Numerical Integration
MECHANICAL SHOCK
see Shock (Mechanics)
MECHANICAL SPEECH RECOGNIZER
see Automatic Speech Recognition
MECHANICS
see also Biomechanics; Deformations (Mechanics); Dynamics; Elastic Solids; Elasticity; Engineering; Fluids; Force and Energy; Friction; Gases; Hydraulics; Hydrodynamics; Mathematical Physics; Mechanical Movements; Potential, Theory of; Power (Mechanics); Rock Mechanics; Shock (Mechanics); Soil Mechanics; Statics; Statistical Mechanics; Steam-Engines; Strains and Stresses; Strength of Materials; Thermodynamics; Vibration; Wave Mechanics; Wave-Motion, Theory of
Chapple, M. A Level Physics: Mechanics & Heat, Vol. 1. 2nd ed. (Illus.). 336p. (Orig.). 1979. pap. text ed. 10.95x (ISBN 0-7121-0154-3, Pub. by Macdonald & Evans England). Intl Ideas.
Geradin, M. B. M. Fraeijs De Veubeke Memorial Volume of Selected Papers. 79p. 1980. 57.50x (ISBN 90-286-0900-8). Sijthoff & Noordhoff.
Nemat-Nasser, S., ed. Mechanics Today, Vol. 6. LC 80-41699. (Illus.). 225p. 1981. 50.00 (ISBN 0-08-024749-0); pap. 40.00 (ISBN 0-08-027318-1). Pergamon.
Olsen, G. Elements of Mechanics of Materials. 4th ed. 1981. 23.95 (ISBN 0-13-267013-5). P-H.

Shawki, G. S. A. & Metwalli, S. M., eds. Current Advances in Mechanical Design & Production: Proceedings of the First International Conference, Cairo University, 27-29 December 1979. LC 80-41666. (Illus.). 500p. 1981. 75.00 (ISBN 0-08-027294-0). Pergamon.

Tauchert, Theodore R. Energy Principles in Structural Mechanics. 394p. 1981. Repr. of 1974 ed. lib. bdg. price not set (ISBN 0-89874-309-5). Krieger.

MECHANICS–PROBLEMS, EXERCISES, ETC.

Federal Aviation Administration. A&P Mechanics Powerplant Written Examination Questions. (Aviation Maintenance Training Course Ser.). (Illus.). 99p. 1979. pap. 3.75 (ISBN 0-89100-159-X, EA-AC65-22). Aviation Maintenance.

MECHANICS, APPLIED

see also Mechanical Engineering

Heriam, J. L. Engineering Mechanics, 2 vols. Incl. Vol. 1. Statics: SI Version. text ed. 18.95 (ISBN 0-471-05558-1); Arabic ed. (ISBN 0-471-06312-6); Vol. 2. Dynamics: SI Version. text ed. 17.95 (ISBN 0-471-05559-X); Arabic ed. (ISBN 0-471-06311-8). LC 79-11173. 1980. Wiley.

--Engineering Mechanics, 2 vols. Incl. Vol. 1. Statics. text ed. 18.95x (ISBN 0-471-59460-1); Vol. 2. Dynamics. text ed. 19.95x (ISBN 0-471-59461-X). LC 77-24716. 1978. Wiley.

Heriman, J. L. ARA Engineering Mechanics, 2 vols. Incl. Vol. 1. SI Statics (ISBN 0-471-06312-6); Vol. 2. SI Dynamics (ISBN 0-471-06311-8). 1980. 18.95 ea. Wiley.

Smith, Charles E. Applied Mechanics. Incl. Dynamics (ISBN 0-471-80178-X); Statics (ISBN 0-471-80460-6). 1976. text ed. 18.95x ea. Wiley.

MECHANICS, FRACTURE

see Fracture Mechanics

MECHANICS, NONLINEAR

see Nonlinear Mechanics

MECHANICS OF CONTINUA

see Continuum Mechanics

MECHANISMS (MACHINERY)

see Mechanical Movements

MECHANIZATION OF LIBRARY PROCESSES

see Libraries–Automation

MECHANIZED INFORMATION STORAGE AND RETRIEVAL SYSTEMS

see Information Storage and Retrieval Systems

MEDALS

Lawrence, Richard H. The Paduans, Medals by Giovanni Cavino. (Illus.). pap. 5.00 (ISBN 0-916710-74-2). Obol Intl.

MEDIA CENTERS (EDUCATION)

see Instructional Materials Centers

MEDICAL ANTHROPOLOGY

see also Folk Medicine; Paleopathology

Bletzer, Keith V. Selected References in Medical Anthropology. (Public Administration Ser.: Bibliography P-551). 59p. 1980. pap. 6.50. Vance Biblios.

MEDICAL APPARATUS

see Medical Instruments and Apparatus

MEDICAL ASSISTANTS

see Medical Technologists

MEDICAL BOTANY

see Botany, Medical

MEDICAL CARE

see also Dental Care; Health Maintenance Organizations; Hospital Care; Insurance, Health; Medical Social Work

Blum, Richard, et al. Pharmaceuticals & Health Policy: International Perspectives on Provision & Control of Medicine. 1981. write for info. (ISBN 0-312-60402-5). St Martin.

Braverman, Jordan. A Consumer's Book of Health: Advice on Stretching Your Health Care Dollar. LC 80-53186. 256p. (Orig.). 1981. 11.95 (ISBN 0-7216-1930-4); pap. 6.95 (ISBN 0-7216-1935-5). Saunders.

Caldwell, Esther & Hegner, Barbara. Health Assistant. 288p. 1981. text ed. 13.95 (ISBN 0-442-21850-8). Van Nos Reinhold.

Callahan, James J., Jr. & Wallack, Stanley S., eds. Reforming the Long-Term-Care System: Financial & Organizational Options. LC 80-8366. (The University Health Policy Consortium Ser.). 272p. 1981. 24.95x (ISBN 0-669-04040-1). Lexington Bks.

Counte, Michael A. & Christman, Luther. Interpersonal Behavior & Health Care. (Behavioral Sciences for the Health Care Professional Ser.). 128p. (Orig.). 1981. lib. bdg. 15.00x (ISBN 0-86531-008-4); pap. text ed. 6.00x (ISBN 0-86531-009-2). Westview.

Drummond, M. F. Principles of Economic Appraisal in Health Care. (Illus.). 130p. 1980. pap. 12.95 (ISBN 0-19-261273-5). Oxford U Pr.

Flavell, John & Ross, Lee, eds. Social Cognitive Development: Frontiers & Possible Futures. (Illus.). 336p. Date not set. price not set (ISBN 0-521-23687-8); pap. price not set (ISBN 0-521-28156-3). Cambridge U Pr.

Gap Committee on Preventive Psychiatry. Mental Health & Primary Medical Care, Vol. 10. LC 80-19016. (Publication Ser.: No. 105). pap. 4.00 (105, Mental Health Materials Center). Adv Psychiatry.

Goldstone, Robert, ed. Health Care & Industrial Relations: Costs, Conflicts & Controversy. 120p. 1981. price not set (ISBN 0-89215-112-9). U Cal LA Indus Rel.

Hadden, Wilbur C. Basic Data on Health Care Needs of Adults 25-74 Years of Age: United States, 1971-75. Cox, Klaudia, ed. (Ser. 11, No. 218). 50p. 1980. pap. text ed. 1.75 (ISBN 0-8406-0197-2). Natl Ctr Health Stats.

Hingson, Ralph, et al. In Sickness & in Health: Social Dimensions of Medical Care. 300p. 1981. pap. text ed. 12.50 (ISBN 0-8016-4411-9). Mosby.

Kron, Thora. The Management of Patient Care: Putting Leadership Skills to Work. (Illus.). 247p. 1981. pap. text ed. 9.95 (ISBN 0-7216-5529-7). Saunders.

McEwan, Peter J., ed. Second Special Conference Issue: Sixth International Conference on Social Science & Medicine, Amsterdam 1979. 80p. 1980. pap. 14.40 (ISBN 0-08-026763-7). Pergamon.

Mackie, Dustin & Decker, Douglas. A Guide to Group & IPA HMO's. 250p. 1981. text ed. price not set (ISBN 0-89443-341-5). Aspen Systems.

Miller, Alfred E. & Miller, Maria G. Options in Health & Health Care. (Health Medicine & Society Ser.). 512p. 1981. 27.50 (ISBN 0-471-60409-7, Pub. by Wiley-Interscience). Wiley.

Roemer. Roemer Healthcare Systems & Comparative Manpower Policies. Date not set. price not set (ISBN 0-8247-1389-3). Dekker.

Rubright, Bob & MacDonald, Dan. Marketing Human Services. 300p. 1981. text ed. price not set (ISBN 0-89443-338-5). Aspen Systems.

Savitt, Todd L. Medicine & Slavery: The Health Care of Blacks in Antebellum Virginia. LC 78-8520. (Blacks in the New World Ser.). (Illus.). 321p. 1981. pap. 7.50 (ISBN 0-252-00874-X). U of Ill Pr.

Smith, Mickey C. & Knapp, David A. Pharmacy, Drugs & Medical Care. 3rd ed. 345p. 1981. write for info. softcover (7761-9). Williams & Wilkins.

Thompson, Frank J. Policy, Bureaucracy, & the Public's Health. 288p. 1981. text ed. 19.95x (ISBN 0-262-20041-4). MIT Pr.

Towell, D. & Harries, C. Innovations in Patient Care. 224p. 1980. 30.00x (ISBN 0-85664-692-X, Pub. by Croom Helm England). State Mutual Bk.

MEDICAL CARE–ADMINISTRATION

see Public Health Administration

MEDICAL CARE–RESEARCH

see Medical Research

MEDICAL CARE–GREAT BRITAIN

Cule, John. A Doctor for the People: 2000 Years of General Practice in Britain. (Illus.). 1981. PLB 38.70 (ISBN 0-906141-29-X, Pub. by Update Books Ltd). Kluwer Boston.

MEDICAL CARE, AMBULATORY

see Ambulatory Medical Care

MEDICAL CARE, COST OF

see also Hospitals–Rates

American Medical Record Association. Glossary of Hospital Terms. 2nd rev. ed. 128p. 1974. 5.75 (ISBN 0-686-68577-6, 14911). Hospital Finan.

AUPHA Task Force on Financial Management. Financial Management of Health Care Organizations: A Referenced Outline & Annotated Bibliography. 237p. 1978. 8.00 (ISBN 0-686-68588-1, 14921). Hospital Finan.

Berman, Howard W. & Weeks, Lewis E. The Financial Management of Hospitals. 3rd ed. (Illus.). 585p. 1976. 17.50 (ISBN 0-686-68573-3, 1496). Hospital Finan.

Brandt, A., et al. Cost-Sharing in Health Care: Proceedings. (Illus.). 184p. 1981. pap. 22.50 (ISBN 0-387-10325-2). Springer-Verlag.

Buchanan, Robert J. Health-Care Finance: An Analysis of Cost & Utilization Issues. LC 80-8362. 1981. write for info. (ISBN 0-669-04035-5). Lexington Bks.

Cleverley, William O. Financial Management of Health Care Facilities. 394p. 1976. 18.75 (ISBN 0-686-68581-4, 14915). Hospital Finan.

Hartunian, Nelson S., et al. The Incidence & Economic Costs of Major Health Impairments: A Comparative Analysis of Cancer, Motor-Vehicle Injuries, Coronary Heart Disease, & Stroke. LC 80-8189. 1981. price not set (ISBN 0-669-03975-6). Lexington Bks.

Keintz, Rita M., ed. Health Care Costs & Financing: A Guide to Information Sources. LC 80-23862. (Health Affairs Information Guide Ser.: Vol. 6). 400p. 1981. 30.00 (ISBN 0-8103-1482-7). Gale.

Kinzer, David M. Health Controls Out of Control. 194p. 9.75 (ISBN 0-686-68584-9, 14918). Hospital Finan.

Maxwell, Robert. Health & Wealth: An International Study of Health-Care Spending. LC 80-8472. 1981. 22.95 (ISBN 0-669-04109-2). Lexington Bks.

Mumford, James G. How to Cut Your Children's Medical Costs. LC 79-67043. 54p. 1980. 5.95 (ISBN 0-533-04430-8). Vantage.

Silvers, John B. & Prahalad, C. K. Financial Management of Health Institutions. 339p. 1974. 17.95 (ISBN 0-686-68576-8, 14910). Hospital Finan.

Topics in Health Care Financing. Incl. Vol. 6, No. 2. Uniform Reporting (ISBN 0-912862-97-1); Vol. 6, No. 3. Employee Wage & Benefit Administration; Vol. 6, No. 4. Management Contracts (ISBN 0-912862-99-8); Vol. 7, No. 1. Financial Career Opportunities (ISBN 0-89443-175-7). 1979-80. write for info. Aspen Systems.

Waller, Kal. How to Recover Your Medical Expenses. 96p. 1981. pap. 5.95 (ISBN 0-02-098940-7, Collier). Macmillan.

Ward, Richard A. The Economics of Health Resources. 150p. 1975. 10.25 (ISBN 0-686-68580-6, 14914). Hospital Finan.

MEDICAL CARE, INDUSTRIAL

see Labor and Laboring Classes–Medical Care

MEDICAL CARE FOR THE AGED

see Aged–Medical Care

MEDICAL CENTERS

see also Hospitals; Medical Colleges

also names of medical centers, e.g. Mayo Clinic; Hunterdon Medical Center

Caruana, Russell A. A Guide to Organizing a Health Care Fiscal Services Division with Job Descriptions for Key Functions. 2nd ed. 80p. 1981. pap. write for info. (ISBN 0-930228-13-8). Hospital Finan.

MEDICAL CHEMISTRY

see Chemistry, Medical and Pharmaceutical

MEDICAL COLLEGES

see also Medicine–Study and Teaching

Bullock, Mary B. An American Transplant: The Rockefeller Foundation & Peking Union Medical College. LC 77-83098. 280p. 1981. 17.50x (ISBN 0-520-03559-3). U of Cal Pr.

Fogel, Marvin & Walker, Mort. How to Get into Medical School: A Comprehensive Guide. 196p. 1981. pap. 6.95 (ISBN 0-8015-3670-7, Hawthorn). Dutton.

Shugar, Gershon J., et al. How to Get into Medical & Dental School. rev. ed. LC 80-23397. 160p. 1981. lib. bdg. 8.00 (ISBN 0-668-05105-1); pap. 6.00 (ISBN 0-668-05112-4). Arco.

MEDICAL COMMUNICATION

see Communication in Medicine

MEDICAL COOPERATION

see Group Medical Practice; Medical Social Work

MEDICAL COSTS

see Medical Care, Cost of; Medical Economics

MEDICAL DEVICES

see Medical Instruments and Apparatus

MEDICAL DIAGNOSIS

see Diagnosis

MEDICAL ECONOMICS

see also Group Medical Practice; Medical Care, Cost of

Rubright, Bob & MacDonald, Dan. Marketing Human Services. 300p. 1981. text ed. price not set (ISBN 0-89443-338-5). Aspen Systems.

MEDICAL EMERGENCIES

see also Accidents; Emergency Medical Services; Emergency Nursing; First Aid in Illness and Injury

Hardy, R. H. Accidents & Emergencies: A Practical Handbook for Personal Use. 3rd ed. (Illus.). 240p. 1981. text ed. 14.95x (ISBN 0-19-261321-9). Oxford U Pr.

McRae, James T. Emergency Medicine Case Studies. LC 79-88721. 1979. pap. 15.50 (ISBN 0-87488-002-5). Med Exam.

MEDICAL ENGINEERING

see Biomedical Engineering

MEDICAL ETHICS

see also Euthanasia; Human Experimentation in Medicine; Malpractice; Nursing Ethics; Pastoral Medicine; Social Medicine

Abrams, Natalie & Buckner, Michael. Medical Ethics: A Clinical Textbook & Reference for the Health Care Professions. 1981. text ed. write for info. (ISBN 0-89706-012-1); pap. text ed. write for info. (ISBN 0-89706-013-X). Bradford Bks.

Basson, Marc D., ed. Rights & Responsibilities in Modern Medicine: The Second Volume in a Series on Ethics, Humanism, & Medicine. (Progress in Clinical & Biological Research: Vol. 50). 250p. 1980. write for info. A R Liss.

Brody, Howard. Ethical Decisions in Medicine. 2nd ed. 1981. pap. text ed. write for info (ISBN 0-316-10899-5). Little.

Childress, James F. Priorities in Biomedical Ethics. (Orig.). 1981. pap. price not set (ISBN 0-664-24368-1). Westminster.

Duncan, A. S., et al, eds. Dictionary of Medical Ethics. 496p. 1981. 24.50 (ISBN 0-8245-0038-5). Crossroad NY.

Jones, James H. Bad Blood: The Tuskegee Syphilis Experiment. LC 80-69281. (Illus.). 1981. 12.95 (ISBN 0-02-916670-5). Free Pr.

Purtilo, Ruth B. & Cassel, Christine K. Ethical Dimensions in the Health Professions. 200p. 1981. text ed. price not set (ISBN 0-7216-7411-9). Saunders.

Shapiro, Michael H. & Spece, Roy G., Jr. Problems, Cases & Materials on Bioethics & Law. (American Casebook Ser.). 915p. 1981. text ed. 23.95 (ISBN 0-8299-2134-6). West Pub.

MEDICAL EXAMINATIONS

see Diagnosis

MEDICAL EXPERIMENTS ON HUMANS

see Human Experimentation in Medicine

MEDICAL FOLK-LORE

see Folk Medicine

MEDICAL FORMULARIES

see Medicine–Formulae, Receipts, Prescriptions

MEDICAL GENETICS

see also Genetic Counseling; Metabolism, Inborn Errors of

Desnick, Robert J., ed. Enzyme Therapy in Genetic Diseases: Part 2. LC 79-48026. (Alan R. Liss Ser.: Vol. 16, No. 1). 1980. 64.00. March of Dimes.

O'Donnell, James J. & Hall, Bryan D., eds. Penetrance & Variability in Malformation Syndromes. LC 79-5115. (Alan R. Liss Ser.: Vol. 15, No. 5b). 1979. 42.00 (ISBN 0-8451-1029-2). March of Dimes.

MEDICAL GEOGRAPHY

see also Epidemics; Tropical Medicine

Dutt, Ashok K., ed. Contemporary Perspectives on the Medical Geography of South & Southeast Asia. (Illus.). 78p. 1980. pap. 20.00 (ISBN 0-08-026762-9). Pergamon.

MEDICAL GROUP PRACTICE

see Group Medical Practice

MEDICAL GYMNASTICS

see Exercise Therapy

MEDICAL INSPECTION IN SCHOOLS

see School Health

MEDICAL INSTRUMENTS AND APPARATUS

see also Lasers in Medicine; Surgical Instruments and Apparatus

Ferris, Clifford D. Guide to Medical Laboratory Instruments. LC 80-80585. 260p. 1980. text ed. 14.95 (ISBN 0-316-28127-1). Little.

Shoup, T. E., ed. International Conference on Medical & Sports Devices. 270p. 1980. 30.00 (H00160). ASME.

Tischler, Morris. Experiments in General & Biomedical Instrumentation. Haas, Mark, ed. (Illus.). 176p. 1980. pap. text ed. 8.95x (ISBN 0-07-064781-X, G). McGraw.

Traister, Robert. Principles of Biomedical Instrumentation & Monitoring. 300p. 1981. text ed. 24.95 (ISBN 0-8359-5611-3). Reston.

MEDICAL JURISPRUDENCE

see also Forensic Psychiatry; Medical Laws and Legislation; Poisons; Psychology, Forensic

also subdivision Jurisprudence under subjects to which medical jurisprudence is applicable, e.g. Insanity–Jurisprudence

Oliver, John S., ed. Forensic Toxicology. 320p. 1980. 50.00x (Pub. by Croom Helm England). State Mutual Bk.

MEDICAL LABORATORIES

Ferris, Clifford D. Guide to Medical Laboratory Instruments. LC 80-80585. 260p. 1980. text ed. 14.95 (ISBN 0-316-28127-1). Little.

Hersh, Leroy, ed. New Developments in Clinical Instrumentation. 192p. 1981. 49.95 (ISBN 0-8493-5305-X). CRC Pr.

MEDICAL LABORATORY TECHNICIANS

see Medical Technologists

MEDICAL LABORATORY TECHNOLOGY

see Medical Technology

MEDICAL LAWS AND LEGISLATION

see also Medical Jurisprudence; Public Health Laws

Chayet, Neil L. Legal Implications of Emergency Care. 1981. pap. 12.50 (ISBN 0-686-69605-0). ACC.

Grad, Frank P. & Marti, Noelia. Physicians' Licensure & Discipline. LC 79-21925. 471p. 1980. lib. bdg. 45.00 (ISBN 0-379-20463-0). Oceana.

Huttman, Barbara. The Patient's Advocate. 416p. 1981. pap. 8.95 (ISBN 0-14-046492-1). Penguin.

Research Group & Gingerich, Duane, eds. Medical Products Liability: A Comprehensive Guide & Sourcebook. (Health Care Economics & Technology Ser.). 500p. 1981. 59.50x (ISBN 0-86621-001-6). F&S Pr.

Van Bieryliet, Alan & Sheldon-Wildgen, Jan. Liability Issues in Community-Based Programs: Legal Principles, Problem Areas & Rdcommendations. 136p. 1980. pap. 10.95 (ISBN 0-933716-08-7). P H Brookes.

Ziegler, A. Doctor's Administrative Program, 6 vols. Incl. Dap 1. Patient Contract & Public Relations (ISBN 0-87489-150-7); Dap 2. Bookkeeping & Tax Reports (ISBN 0-87489-151-5); Dap 3. Insurance & Third-Party-Payable Claims (ISBN 0-87489-152-3); Dap 4. Correspondence (ISBN 0-87489-153-1); Billing & Collections; Dap 6. Patient Records Control (ISBN 0-87489-155-8). 1978. Set. write for info. (ISBN 0-87489-158-2); Ea. Vol. write for info.

MEDICAL LIBRARIES

see also Information Storage and Retrieval Systems–Medicine

Rees, Alan M. & Crawford, Susan, eds. Directory of Health Sciences Libraries in the United States. LC 80-65893. 356p. 1980. 25.00. Med Lib Assn.

Young, Margaret Labash & Young, Harold C., eds. Subject Directory of Special Libraries & Information Centers: Health Science Libraries, Including All Aspects of Basic & Pplied Medical Sciences, Vol. 3. 6th ed. 1981. 80.00 (ISBN 0-8103-0308-6). Gale.

MEDICAL LITERATURE SEARCHING

see Information Storage and Retrieval Systems–Medicine

MEDICAL MANPOWER

see Medical Personnel; Public Health Personnel

MEDICAL MATHEMATICS

see Medicine–Mathematics

MEDICAL MICROBIOLOGY

Boyd, Robert R. & Hoerl, Bryan G. Basic Medical Microbiology. 2nd ed. 1981. text ed. write for info (ISBN 0-316-10433-7). Little.

--Laboratory Manual to Accompany Basic Medical Microbiology. 1981. write for info. lab manual (ISBN 0-316-10434-5). Little.
Davidson, Elizabeth W., ed. Pathogenesis of Invertebrate Microbial Diseases. 500p. 1981. text ed. 40.00 (ISBN 0-86598-014-4). Allanheld.
Lennette, E. H., et al, eds. Manual of Clinical Microbiology. 3rd ed. (Illus.). 1980. 25.00 (ISBN 0-914826-24-7). Am Soc Microbio.
Microbial Aspects of Dental Caries, 3 vols. 1976. Set. 40.00 (ISBN 0-917000-01-3). Info Retrieval.
Pelczar, Michael, Jr. & Chan, E. C. S. Elements of Microbiology. 1st ed. (Illus.). 704p. (Orig.). text ed. 19.95 (ISBN 0-07-049240-9, C); 10.95 (ISBN 0-07-049241-7); instrs'. 5.50 (ISBN 0-07-049230-1). McGraw.
Schrader, B. & Meier, W., eds. Raman-IR Atlas of Organic Compounds. 1974-1976. Set. 467.70. Vol. 1,345p (ISBN 3-527-25539-7). Vol. 2,386p (ISBN 3-527-25541-9). Vol. 3,507p (ISBN 3-527-25542-7). Verlag Chemie.
Smith, Alice L. Microbiology Laboratory Manual & Workbook. 5th ed. (Illus.). 179p. 1981. paper perfect 9.95 (ISBN 0-8016-4707-X). Mosby.
--Principles of Microbiology. 9th ed. (Illus.). 816p. 1981. text ed. 19.95 (ISBN 0-8016-4682-0). Mosby.

MEDICAL MICROSCOPY
see Microscopy, Medical

MEDICAL PARASITOLOGY
see also Lice
Markell, Edward K. & Voge, Marietta. Medical Parasitology. 5th ed. (Illus.). 400p. 1981. text ed. price not set (ISBN 0-7216-6082-7). Saunders.
Reifsnyder, David N. Parasitic Diseases Case Studies. LC 80-81733. 1980. pap. 18.50 (ISBN 0-87488-049-1). Med Exam.

MEDICAL PERSONNEL
see also Medicine–Vocational Guidance; Physicians; Public Health Personnel
also similar headings
Nassif, Janet Z. Health Professions in Medicine's New Technology. LC 80-22030. (Illus.). 256p. 1981. pap. 5.95 (ISBN 0-668-04436-5, 4436). Arco.

MEDICAL PHYSICS
Damask, Arthur. Medical Physics: External Senses, Vol. 2. 1981. write for info. (ISBN 0-12-201202-X). Acad Pr.

MEDICAL PROFESSION
see Medicine; Physicians

MEDICAL RADIOGRAPHY
see Radiography, Medical

MEDICAL RADIOLOGY
see Radiology, Medical

MEDICAL RECORDS
Society of Paitent Representatives of the American Hospital Association. Essentials of Patient Representative Programs in Hospitals. LC 78-26889. 1978. pap. 8.75 (ISBN 0-87258-255-8, 1251). Am Hospital.

MEDICAL REGISTRATION AND EXAMINATION
see Medical Laws and Legislation

MEDICAL RESEARCH
see also Cancer Research; Human Experimentation in Medicine; Laboratory Animals; Medicine, Experimental; Pharmaceutical Research; Psychosomatic Research
Goldstein, Gerald. A Clinician's Guide to Research Design. LC 79-18818. 288p. 1981. text ed. 24.95 (ISBN 0-88229-340-0). Nelson-Hall.
Zwar, Desmond. The Bio-Adventures: The Drama of Medical Research. LC 80-6168. 288p. 1981. 14.95 (ISBN 0-8128-2807-0). Stein & Day.

MEDICAL RESEARCH ETHICS
see Medical Ethics

MEDICAL SCHOOLS
see Medical Colleges

MEDICAL SERVICES
see Medical Care

MEDICAL SOCIAL WORK
see also Psychiatric Social Work
Society for Hospital Social Work Directors of the American Hospital Association. Quality & Quantity Assurance for Social Workers in Health Care: A Training Manual. LC 80-26488. (Illus.). 96p. (Orig.). 1980. manual 27.50 (ISBN 0-87258-325-2, 2100). Am Hospital.
Stambaugh, Harriett, ed. Social Work on Pediatric Settings. (Social Work in Health Care Ser.: Vol. 1). 350p. 1981. text ed. 22.95 (ISBN 0-917724-29-1). Haworth Pr.

MEDICAL SOCIOLOGY
see Social Medicine

MEDICAL STATISTICS
Danchik, Kathleen M. & Schoenborn, Charlotte A. Highlights: National Survey of Personal Health Practices & Consequences, United States, 1979. Olmsted, Mary, ed. (Ser. 10: No. 137). 50p. 1981. pap. 1.75 (ISBN 0-8406-0218-9). Natl Ctr Health Stats.
Jack, Susan S. & Ries, Peter W. Current Estimates from the Health Interview Survey: United States-1979. Cox, Klaudia, ed. (Ser. 10: No. 136). 55p. 1981. pap. text ed. 1.75 (ISBN 0-8406-0219-7). Natl Ctr Health Stats.

MEDICAL TECHNOLOGISTS
Mummah, Hazel & Smith, Marsella. The Geriatric Assistant. (Illus.). 320p. 1980. pap. text ed. 11.95 (ISBN 0-07-044015-8, HP). McGraw.

MEDICAL TECHNOLOGY
see also Medicine, Clinical
American Hospital Association. Technology Evaluation & Acquisition Methods (TEAM) for Hospitals. LC 79-21859. (Illus.). 212p. 1979. 200.00 (ISBN 0-87258-293-0, 1288). Am Hospital.
Banta, David. Toward Rational Technology in Medicine: Considerations for Health Policy. (Health Care & Society Ser.: No. 5). 1981. text ed. 28.50 (ISBN 0-8261-3200-6); pap. text ed. cacelled (ISBN 0-8261-3201-4). Springer Pub.
Wagner, G., et al, eds. Technology & Health: Man & World Proceedings. (Lecture Notes in Medical Informatics Ser.: Vol. 7). 243p. 1981. pap. 20.70 (ISBN 0-387-10230-2). Springer Verlag.

MEDICAL TOPOGRAPHY
see Medical Geography

MEDICAL ULTRASONICS
see Ultrasonics in Medicine

MEDICAL VIROLOGY
see Virus Diseases

MEDICAL WRITING
Davis, P. Medical Dictation & Transcription. 2nd ed. 400p. 1981. pap. 12.95 (ISBN 0-471-06023-2, Pub. by Wiley Med). Wiley.
Davis, Phyllis. Medical Shorthand. 2nd ed. 275p. 1981. pap. 11.95 (ISBN 0-471-06024-0). Wiley.
Pearce, G. H. The Medical Report & Testimony. 104p. 1980. 35.00x (Pub. by Beaconsfield England). State Mutual Bk.
Robinson, Alice M. & Notter, Lucille. Clinical Writing for Health Professionals. (Illus.). 128p. (Orig.). 1981. pap. price not set (ISBN 0-87619-893-0). R J Brady.

MEDICARE
see Insurance, Health

MEDICATION, ORAL
see Oral Medication

MEDICI, HOUSE OF
Acton, Harold. The Last Medici. rev. ed. (Illus.). 416p. 1980. Repr. of 1958 ed. 22.50 (ISBN 0-500-25074-X). Thames Hudson.
Canfield, Cass. Outrageous Fortunes: The Story of the Medici, the Rothschilds, & J. Pierpont Morgan. (Illus.). 1981. 10.95 (ISBN 0-15-170513-5). HarBraceJ.

MEDICINAL PLANTS
see Botany, Medical

MEDICINE
see also Abnormalities, Human; Anatomy; Aviation Medicine; Bacteriology; Biomedical Engineering; Botany, Medical; Chemistry, Medical and Pharmaceutical; Chiropractic; Dentistry; Diseases–Causes and Theories of Causation; Family Medicine; Folk Medicine; Health; Histology; Homeopathy; Hospitals; Hypnotism; Materia Medica; Mind and Body; Nurses and Nursing; Pathology; Pharmacology; Pharmacy; Physiology; Podiatry; Quacks and Quackery; Surgery; Tropical Medicine; Women in Medicine
also headings beginning with the word Medical
Beeson, Paul B., et al. Cecil Textbook of Medicine, 2 vols. 15th ed. (Illus.). 2478p. 1979. Single Vol. Ed. 49.00 (ISBN 0-7216-1663-1); Two Vol. Set. 60.00 (ISBN 0-7216-1667-4); Vol. 1. 30.00 (ISBN 0-7216-1664-X); Vol. 2. 30.00 (ISBN 0-7216-1666-6). Saunders.
Bursztajn, Harold, et al. Medical Choices, Medical Chances: Decision Making for Patients, Families, & Physicians. 1981. 14.95 (ISBN 0-440-05750-7, Sey Lawr). Delacorte.
Firestein, Gary S. & Harrell, Robert A. The Effective Scutboy. LC 80-25057. (Illus.). 96p. 1981. pap. text ed. 6.00 (ISBN 0-668-05159-0, 5159). Arco.
Gerrick, David J. Footnotes to Medicine. 172p. 1980. 10.95 (ISBN 0-686-68569-5). Dayton Labs.
Horrobin, David. Medical Hubris: A Reply to Ivan Illich. LC 80-66836. 146p. 1980. 9.95 (ISBN 0-88831-080-3); pap. 6.95 (ISBN 0-88831-086-2). Eden Med Res.
Rudman, Jack. Medical Sciences Knowledge Profile Examination (MSKP) (Admission Test Ser.: AT-86). (Cloth bdg. avail. on request). pap. 17.95 (ISBN 0-686-68260-2). Natl Learning.
Studying a Study & Testing a Test: How to Read the Medical Literature. 1981. pap. text ed. price not set (ISBN 0-316-74518-9). Little.
University of Montpellier Faculty of Medicine. Polyphonie Du XIIIe Siecle, 4 vols. LC 80-2191. (Illus.). 1981. Repr. of 1939 ed. 365.00 (ISBN 0-404-19040-5). AMS Pr.
Wasco, James E. Not for Doctors Only: Breakthrough Reports from the Medical Front. 12.95 (ISBN 0-201-08297-7); pap. 7.95 (ISBN 0-201-08298-5). A-W.

MEDICINE–APPARATUS
see Medical Instruments and Apparatus

MEDICINE–AUTHORSHIP
see Medical Writing

MEDICINE–BIBLIOGRAPHY
see also Information Storage and Retrieval Systems–Medicine
Adams, Scott. Medical Bibliography in an Age of Discontinuity. 256p. 1981. 21.50 (ISBN 0-912176-09-1). Med Lib Assn.
Brodman, Estelle. The Development of Medical Bibliography. 226p. 1981. Repr. of 1954 ed. 8.25 (ISBN 0-912176-00-8). Med Lib Assn.
Dunlap, Alice, et al, eds. Hospital Literature Index: 1980 Cumulative Annual, Vol. 36. 704p. 1981. 72.00 (ISBN 0-87258-348-1). Am Hospital.
Medical Books & Serials in Print, 1981. 10th ed. 1650p. 1981. 52.00 (ISBN 0-8352-1356-0). Bowker.
Philbrook, Marilyn M., compiled by. Medical Books for the Layperson: An Annotated Bibliography, Supplement. 1978. pap. 2.00 (ISBN 0-89073-060-1). Boston Public Lib.

MEDICINE–BIOGRAPHY
see also Health Officers; Nurses and Nursing; Physicians
Hodgson, Francis. International Medical Who's Who, 2 vols. 1300p. 1980. Set. text ed. 180.00x (ISBN 0-582-90107-3). Churchill.

MEDICINE–COST OF MEDICAL CARE
see Medical Care, Cost Of

MEDICINE–DATA PROCESSING
Computer Information Services, Chicago Hospital Council. Shared Hospital Computer Services Evaluation. 165p. 1975. 15.00 (ISBN 0-686-68578-4, 14912). Hospital Finan.
Computers in Radiotherapy: 1968 2nd International Conference. 1980. 9.00x (Pub. by Brit Inst Radiology England). State Mutual Bk.
Computers in the Control of Treatment Units: Applications of Modern Technology in Radiotherapy. 1980. 10.00x (Pub. by Brit Inst Radiology England). State Mutual Bk.
DuBoulay, G. H., ed. Considerations About the Use of Computers in Radiodiagnostic Departments. 1980. 45.00x (Pub. by Brit Inst Radiology England). State Mutual Bk.
Herman, G. T. & Natterer, F., eds. Mathematical Aspects of Computerized Tomography: Proceedings. (Lecture Notes in Medical Information Ser.: Vol. 8). 309p. 1981. pap. 28.10 (ISBN 0-387-10277-9). Springer-Verlag.
Park, W. M. & Reece, B. L. Fundamental Aspects of Medical Thermography. 1980. 18.00x (Pub. by Brit Inst Radiology England). State Mutual Bk.
Spohr, Mark. Physician's Guide to Microcomputers. 1981. 18.95 (ISBN 0-8359-5548-6). Reston.

MEDICINE–DICTIONARIES
Duncan, A. S., et al, eds. Dictionary of Medical Ethics. 496p. 1981. 24.50 (ISBN 0-8245-0038-5). Crossroad NY.
Lucchesi, Mario. Dizionario Medico Ragionato Inglese-Italiano: Termini, Abbreviazioni, Sigle, Eponimi e Sinonimi Medici, Medico-Biologici e Delle Specializzazionni Mediche. 1490p. 1978. 98.00x (ISBN 0-913298-52-2). S F Vanni.
Mills, Dorothy H. & Martinez, Jorge C. Dictionary for the Health Professional: English-Spanish-Spanish-English. LC 79-90820. (Illus.). 250p. 1981. pap. 21.20 (ISBN 0-935356-03-7). Mills Pub Co.
New Webster's Medical Dictionary. (Handy Reference Bks.). (Orig.). 1981. pap. 3.50 (ISBN 0-8326-0057-1, 6483). Delair.
Thomas, Clayton L., ed. Taber's Cyclopedic Medical Dictionary. 14th ed. (Illus.). 1796p. 1981. text ed. write for info. (ISBN 0-8036-8307-3); Thumb-indexed Edition. text ed. write for info. (ISBN 0-8036-8306-5). Davis Co.
Urdang. Urdang Dictionary of Current Medical Terms. 464p. 1981. 12.95 (ISBN 0-471-05853-X, Pub. by Wiley Med). Wiley.

MEDICINE–EXAMINATIONS, QUESTIONS, ETC.
Baker, Michael A., ed. Medicine. 7th ed. (Medical Examination Review Ser.: Vol. 2). 1980. pap. 8.50 (ISBN 0-87488-102-1). Med Exam.
McCaulley, Mary H. Application of the Myers-Briggs Type Indicator to Medicine & Other Health Professions, 2 vols. Incl. Monograph I. 554p. 1978. pap. 20.00 (ISBN 0-935652-03-5); Monograph II. 288p. 1977. pap. 15.00 (ISBN 0-935652-04-3). (Illus.). 842p. (Orig.). Set. pap. 30.00 (ISBN 0-935652-05-1). Ctr Applications Psych.
Young, K., et al, eds. The MRCGP Study Book. 150p. 1981. PLB 36.90 (ISBN 0-906141-13-3, Pub. by Update Books Ltd); pap. 31.50 (ISBN 0-686-28845-9). Kluwer Boston.

MEDICINE–FORMULAE, RECEIPTS, PRESCRIPTIONS
see also Pharmacy
U. S. Pharmacopeial Convention. The Physicians' & Pharmacists' Guide to Your Medicines. 544p. (Orig.). 1981. pap. 9.95 (ISBN 0-345-29635-4). Ballantine.

MEDICINE–HANDBOOKS, MANUALS, ETC.
Berkowitz, Richard L., et al. Handbook for Prescribing Medications During Pregnancy. 1981. pap. text ed. write for info (ISBN 0-316-09173-1). Little.
Carding, David K., ed. Family Medical Handbook. 2nd ed. 226p. 1981. 14.95 (ISBN 0-571-18027-2). Merrimack Bk Serv.
U. S. Pharmacopeial Convention. The Physicians' & Pharmacists' Guide to Your Medicines. 544p. (Orig.). 1981. pap. 9.95 (ISBN 0-345-29635-4). Ballantine.
World Book-Childcraft International, Inc. The World Book Illustrated Home Medical Encyclopedia, 4 vols. LC 79-56907. (Illus.). 1038p. 1980. write for info. (ISBN 0-7166-2060-X). World Bk-Childcraft.

MEDICINE–HISTORY
see also Medicine, Medieval
also similar headings
Gordon, Maurice R. Aesculapius Comes to the Colonies. LC 70-101590. (Illus.). 1969. Repr. of 1949 ed. 17.50. Argosy.
Haller, John S., Jr. American Medicine in Transition, 1840-1910. LC 80-14546. (Illus.). 334p. 1981. 27.95 (ISBN 0-252-00806-5). U of Ill Pr.
Reiser, Stanley J. Medicine & the Reign of Technology. LC 77-87389. (Illus.). 317p. (Orig.). 1981. pap. 8.95 (ISBN 0-521-28223-3). Cambridge U Pr.

MEDICINE–INFORMATION SERVICES
Beardsley, Rick, ed. The Videolog in the Health Sciences. 1980-81 ed. (Videolog Ser.). 1981. pap. 49.50 (ISBN 0-88432-069-3). J Norton Pubs.

MEDICINE–INSTRUMENTS
see Medical Instruments and Apparatus; Surgical Instruments and Apparatus

MEDICINE–LAWS AND LEGISLATION
see Medical Laws and Legislation

MEDICINE–MATHEMATICS
Medications & Mathematics for the Nurse. 288p. 1981. text ed. 13.95 (ISBN 0-442-21882-6). Van Nos Reinhold.
Murrell, Sandra & Olsen, Paul. Mathematics for the Health Sciences. (Developmental & Precalculus Math Ser.). (Illus.). 432p. 1981. pap. text ed. 13.95 (ISBN 0-201-04647-4). A-W.

MEDICINE–MISCELLANEA
Ziegler, A. Doctor's Administrative Program, 6 vols. Incl. Dap 1. Patient Contract & Public Relations (ISBN 0-87489-150-7); Dap 2. Bookkeeping & Tax Reports (ISBN 0-87489-151-5); Dap 3. Insurance & Third-Party-Payable Claims (ISBN 0-87489-152-3); Dap 4. Correspondence (ISBN 0-87489-153-1); Billing & Collections; Dap 6. Patient Records Control (ISBN 0-87489-155-8). 1978. Set. write for info. (ISBN 0-87489-158-2); Ea. Vol. write for info.

MEDICINE–MORAL AND RELIGIOUS ASPECTS
see Medical Ethics

MEDICINE–PHILOSOPHY
Murphy, Edmond A. Skepsis, Dogma, & Belief: Uses & Abuses in Medicine. LC 80-8870. 176p. 1981. text ed. 14.95x (ISBN 0-8018-2510-5). Johns Hopkins.
Pellegrino, Edmund D. & Thomasma, David C. A Philosophical Basis of Medical Practice: Toward a Philosophy & Ethic of the Healing Professions. (Illus.). 368p. 1981. 19.95x (ISBN 0-19-502790-6). Oxford U Pr.
--A Philosophical Basis of Medical Practice: Toward a Philosophy & Ethic of the Healing Professions. (Illus.). 368p. 1981. text ed. 11.95x (ISBN 0-19-502789-2). Oxford U Pr.

MEDICINE–POPULAR WORKS
see Medicine, Popular

MEDICINE–PRACTICE
see also Children–Diseases; Communicable Diseases; Diagnosis; Group Medical Practice; Gynecology; Hydrotherapy; Infants–Diseases; Malpractice; Massage; Nurses and Nursing; Obstetrics; Therapeutics
also names of diseases and groups of diseases, e.g. Bronchitis, Fever, Nervous System–Diseases
Cousins, Norman. Anatomy of an Illness As Perceived by the Patient. 176p. 1981. pap. 4.95 (ISBN 0-553-01293-2). Bantam.
Houston, J. C., et al. Short Textbook of Medicine. 6th ed. (Illus., Orig.). 1980. pap. 14.75 (ISBN 0-397-58266-8). Lippincott.
Isselbacher, Kurt J., et al. Harrison's Principles of Internal Medicine. 400p. 1981. text ed. 30.00 (ISBN 0-07-032131-0). McGraw.
Meislin, Harvey W. & Dresnick, Stephen J. Skills & Procedures of Emergency & General Medicine. 250p. 1982. text ed. 29.95 (ISBN 0-8359-7009-4). Reston.

MEDICINE–RESEARCH
see Medical Research

MEDICINE–SOCIAL ASPECTS
see Social Medicine

MEDICINE–STUDY AND TEACHING
Abrams, Robert, et al. FLEX Review. LC 80-83395. 1980. pap. 21.50 (ISBN 0-87488-158-7). Med Exam.
Shugar, Gershon J., et al. How to Get into Medical & Dental School. rev. ed. LC 80-23397. 160p. 1981. lib. bdg. 8.00 (ISBN 0-668-05105-1); pap. 6.00 (ISBN 0-668-05112-4). Arco.

MEDICINE–TERMINOLOGY
Angela. Daffy Definitions of Medical Terms. Date not set. 5.95 (ISBN 0-533-04834-6). Vantage.
Bernthal, Patricia J. & Spiller, James D. Understanding the Language of Medicine: A Programmed Learning Text. (Illus.). 300p. 1981. pap. text ed. 11.95x (ISBN 0-19-502879-1). Oxford U Pr.
Birmingham, Jacqueline J. Medical Terminology: A Self-Learning Module. (Illus.). 448p. 1981. pap. text ed. 11.95 (ISBN 0-07-005386-3, HP). McGraw.
Chabner, Davi-Ellen. The Language of Medicine: A Write-in Text Explaining Medical Terms. 2nd ed. (Illus.). 600p. 1981. text ed. 16.95 (ISBN 0-7216-2479-0). Saunders.
Kinn, Mary E. Review of Medical Terminology. 1980. 7.50. Thieme Stratton.
Manuila, A., ed. Progress in Medical Terminology. (Illus.). vi, 118p. 1981. pap. 30.00 (ISBN 3-8055-2112-X). S Karger.

Smith, G. L. & Davis, P. E. Medical Terminology. 4th ed. 300p. 1980. pap. 11.95 (ISBN 0-471-05827-0, Pub. by Wiley Med). Wiley.
Spatola, Anthony L. Mastering Medical Language. (Illus.). 464p. 1981. pap. text ed. 15.95 (ISBN 0-13-560151-7). P-H.
Urdang. Urdang Dictionary of Current Medical Terms. 464p. 1981. 12.95 (ISBN 0-471-05853-X, Pub. by Wiley Med). Wiley.

MEDICINE–TROPICS
see Tropical Medicine

MEDICINE–VOCATIONAL GUIDANCE
Klein, Kenneth. You Might Save Someone's Life Someday. 324p. 1981. 11.95 (ISBN 0-316-49838-6). Little.

MEDICINE–AFRICA
Appiah-Kubi, Kofi. Healing & Religion in Rural Ghana: A Sociological Study of Health Care Among the Akans. (Illus.). 224p. 1981. text ed. 25.00 (ISBN 0-86598-011-X). Allanheld.
Segall, Marshall & Ulin, Priscilla, eds. Traditional Health Care Delivery in Contemporary Africe. (Foreign & Comparative Studies - African Ser.: No. 35). 100p. 1980. pap. 8.00x (ISBN 0-915984-57-1). Syracuse U Foreign Comp.

MEDICINE–ASIA
Dutt, Ashok K., ed. Contemporary Perspectives on the Medical Geography of South & Southeast Asia. (Illus.). 78p. 1980. pap. 20.00 (ISBN 0-08-026762-9). Pergamon.
Robinson, Aletha. The Lao Handbook of Maternal & Child Health. 1980. pap. 0.50 (ISBN 0-9602790-1-6). The Garden.

MEDICINE–CANADA
Shortt, S. E., ed. Medicine in Canadian Society: Historical Perspectives. 400p. 1981. 23.95x (ISBN 0-7735-0356-0); pap. 11.95 (ISBN 0-7735-0369-2). McGill-Queens U Pr.

MEDICINE–CHINA
Bullock, Mary B. An American Transplant: The Rockefeller Foundation & Peking Union Medical College. LC 77-83098. 280p. 1981. 17.50x (ISBN 0-520-03559-3). U of Cal Pr.
Fulder, Stephen. Tao of Medicine. (Illus.). 1981. pap. 8.95. Inner Tradit.
Kaptchuk, Ted J. The Web That Has No Weaver: Understanding Chinese Medicine. (Illus.). 304p. 1981. 15.00 (ISBN 0-312-92932-3). Congdon & Lattes.

MEDICINE–GREAT BRITAIN
Lancaster, Arnold. Nursery & Midwifery Sourcebook. 304p. 1980. 25.00x (Pub. by Beaconsfield England). State Mutual Bk.
Mencher, Samuel. Private Practice in Britain. 95p. 1967. pap. text ed. 5.00x (Pub. by Bedford England). Renouf.
Wade, Lord. Europe & the British Health Service. 94p. 1974. pap. text ed. 2.50x (ISBN 0-7199-0890-6, Pub. by Bedford England). Renouf.

MEDICINE–INDIA
Dash, Bhagan & Kashyap, Lalitesh. Basic Principles of Ayurveda. 655p. 1980. 37.00x (ISBN 0-391-02208-3). Humanities.

MEDICINE–JAPAN
Bowers, John Z. When the Twain Meet: The Rise of Western Medicine in Japan. LC 80-22356. (Henry E. Sigerist Supplement to the Bulletin of the History of Medicine Ser.: No. 5). 192p. 1981. text ed. 14.00x (ISBN 0-8018-2432-X). Johns Hopkins.

MEDICINE–LATIN AMERICA
Moll, Aristides A. Aesculapius in Latin America. LC 76-101589. (Illus.). 1969. Repr. of 1944 ed. 17.50. Argosy.

MEDICINE–RUSSIA
Knaus, William A. Inside Russian Medicine. 1981. 14.95. Everest Hse.

MEDICINE–TIBET
Clifford, Terry. The Diamond Healing: Tibetan Buddhist Medicine & Psychiatry. 196p. 1981. pap. 7.95 (ISBN 0-87728-528-4). Weiser.

MEDICINE–UNITED STATES
Haller, John S., Jr. American Medicine in Transition, 1840-1910. LC 80-14546. (Illus.). 334p. 1981. 27.95 (ISBN 0-252-00806-5). U of Ill Pr.

MEDICINE, CHINESE
Ware, James R., tr. from Chinese. Alchemy, Medicine, & Religion in the China of A. D. 320: The Nei P'ien of Ko Hung (Pao-p'u tzu) 416p. 1981. pap. price not set (ISBN 0-486-24088-6). Dover.

MEDICINE, CLERICAL
see Pastoral Medicine

MEDICINE, CLINICAL
see also Clinical Enzymology; Diagnosis; Medical Laboratories; Medical Technologists; Medical Technology; Pathology; Radioactivation Analysis
Baughman, Kenneth L. & Greene, Bruce M. Clinical Diagnostic Manual for the House Officer. 110p. 1981. write for info. soft cover (3553-3). Williams & Wilkins.
Buss, David H., et al. Clinical Pathology Continuing Education Review. LC 79-91972. 1980. pap. 14.75 (ISBN 0-87488-320-2). Med Exam.
Delp, Mahlon H. & Manning, Robert T. Major's Physical Diagnosis: An Introduction to the Clinical Process. 9th ed. (Illus.). 650p. 1981. text ed. write for info. (ISBN 0-7216-3002-2). Saunders.
Essex, B. J. Diagnostic Pathways in Clinical Medicine. (Medicine in the Tropics Ser.). (Illus.). 208p. 1981. pap. text ed. 17.00 (ISBN 0-443-02059-0). Churchill.
Essex, Benjamin J. Diagnostic Pathways in Clinical Medicine. 2nd ed. (Medicine in the Tropics Ser.). (Illus.). Date not set. pap. text ed. 19.00 (ISBN 0-443-02059-0). Churchill.
Mason, Stuart & Swash, Michael. Hutchinson's Clinical Methods. 17th ed. (Illus.). 495p. 1980. 14.50 (ISBN 0-397-58270-6). Lippincott.
--Hutchinson's Clinical Methods. 17th ed. 495p. 1980. 14.50 (ISBN 0-397-58270-6). Lippincott.
Miller, Alfred E. Challenges & Strategies in Health: The Coming of Post-Clinical Medicine. (Health, Medicine, & Society Ser.). 504p. 1981. 27.50 (ISBN 0-471-60409-7, Pub. by Wiley-Interscience). Wiley.
Schlierf, G. Langzeitstudie zum Ernaehrungs- und Gesundheitszustand einer Repraesentativen Stichprobe Heidelberger Frauen und Maenner. (Beitraege zu Infusionstherapie und Klinische Ernaehrung: Band 7). viii, 250p. 1981. pap. 18.00 (ISBN 3-8055-2384-X). S Karger.
Zakus, Sharron. Clinical Skills & Assisting Techniques for the Medical Assistant. (Illus.). 536p. 1981. pap. text ed. 15.95 (ISBN 0-8016-5672-9). Mosby.

MEDICINE, COMMUNICATION IN
see Communication in Medicine

MEDICINE, DENTAL
see Teeth–Diseases

MEDICINE, EXPERIMENTAL
see also Human Experimentation in Medicine; Medical Research
Sperlinger, David. Animals in Research: New Perspectives in Animal Experimentation. 384p. 1980. 49.50 (ISBN 0-471-27843-2, Pub. by Wiley-Interscience). Wiley.

MEDICINE, FORENSIC
see Medical Jurisprudence

MEDICINE, HINDU
Rationality, Theory, & Experimentation in Ayurvedic Medicine. 35p. 1980. pap. 5.00 (ISBN 92-808-0106-6, TUNU097, UNU). Unipub.

MEDICINE, INTERNAL
see Internal Medicine; Medicine–Practice

MEDICINE, LEGAL
see Medical Jurisprudence

MEDICINE, MEDIEVAL
see also Herbs
Kealey, Edward J. Medieval Medicus: A Social History of Anglo-Norman Medicine. LC 80-21870. (Illus.). 208p. 1981. text ed. 16.95x (ISBN 0-8018-2533-4). Johns Hopkins.

MEDICINE, NAVAL
see also First Aid in Illness and Injury
Counter, R. T. The Yachtsman's Doctor. 148p. 1980. 27.00 (ISBN 0-245-53425-3, Pub. by Nautical England). State Mutual Bk.
Wallett, Tim. Shark Attack & Treatment of Victims in Southern African Waters. 1980. 25.00x (Pub. by Bailey & Swinton South Africa). State Mutual Bk.

MEDICINE, ORTHOMOLECULAR
see Orthomolecular Medicine

MEDICINE, PASTORAL
see Pastoral Medicine

MEDICINE, POPULAR
see also Folk Medicine; Medicine–Dictionaries
Biviano, Ronald S. Medical Conditions & Terms Made Simple. LC 80-68397. 100p. (Orig.). 1981. pap. 10.00 (ISBN 0-9605476-0-6). Biviano.
Brown, Warren J., ed. Patients' Guide to Medicine: From the Drugstore Through the Hospital. 9th ed. 1981. pap. 7.95 (ISBN 0-912522-71-2). Aero-Medical.

MEDICINE, PREVENTIVE
see also Bacteriology; Immunity; Pathology; Public Health; Serumtherapy
Bruce, Nigel. Teamwork for Preventive Care, Vol. 1. (Social Policy Research Monographs). 264p. 1980. 55.00 (ISBN 0-471-27883-1, Pub. by Wiley-Interscience). Wiley.
Clark, L. Roy & Locke, Sam. How to Survive Your Doctor's Care. (Illus.). 96p. 1981. pap. 4.95 (ISBN 0-87786-005-X). Gold Penny.
The Healing Art of Clara Walter. 64p. (Orig.). 1981. pap. 2.95 (ISBN 0-932870-08-2). Alyson Pubns.
Isacson, Peter. Public Health & Preventive Medicine Continuing Education Review. 1980. pap. 15.00 (ISBN 0-87488-348-2). Med Exam.
Scopes, Nigel, ed. Pest & Disease Control Handbook. 250p. 1979. 35.00x (ISBN 0-901436-42-9, Pub. by Brit Crop Protection England). Intl Schol Bk Serv.

MEDICINE, PSYCHOSOMATIC
see also Enuresis; Pediatrics–Psychosomatic Aspects also subdivision Diseases–Psychosomatic Aspects under names of organs and regions of the body, e.g. Skin–Diseases–Psychosomatic Aspects
Simons, Richard C. & Pardes, Herbert. Understanding Human Behavior in Health & Illness. 2nd ed. (Illus.). 760p. 1981. write for info. (7740-6). Williams & Wilkins.

MEDICINE, SOCIAL
see Social Medicine

MEDICINE, TROPICAL
see Tropical Medicine

MEDICINE, VETERINARY
see Veterinary Medicine

MEDICINE AND PSYCHOLOGY
see also Medicine, Psychosomatic; Psychiatry
Sierles, Frederick. Clinical Behavioral Science. 1981. text ed. write for info. (ISBN 0-89335-131-8). Spectrum Pub.

MEDICINE AND SPORTS
see Sports Medicine

MEDICINE-MAN
see also Shamanism
Mails, Thomas E. Fool's Crow. 1980. pap. 3.50 (ISBN 0-686-69256-X, 52175, Discus). Avon.

MEDICINES, PHYSIOLOGICAL EFFECT OF
see Pharmacology

MEDIEVAL ART
see Art, Medieval

MEDIEVAL CIVILIZATION
see Civilization, Medieval

MEDIEVAL HISTORY
see Middle Ages–History

MEDIEVAL LITERATURE
see Literature, Medieval

MEDIEVAL PHILOSOPHY
see Philosophy, Medieval

MEDIEVAL POETRY
see Poetry, Medieval

MEDITATION
Here are entered works on meditation or mental prayer as a method of promoting the spiritual life. Works that contain collections of meditations are entered under the heading Meditations.
see also Contemplation; Retreats; Transcendental Meditation
Chaudhuri, Haridas. Philosophy of Meditation. 2nd ed. 88p. 1974. pap. 3.50 (ISBN 0-89744-994-0, Pub. by Cultural Integration). Auromere.
Eknath, Easwaran. Instrucciones En la Meditacion. 1980. pap. 1.00 (ISBN 0-915132-23-0). Nilgiri Pr.
Helleberg, Marilyn. Beyond T.M. A Practical Guide to the Lost Tradition of Christian Meditation. LC 80-82811. 144p. (Orig.). 1981. pap. 6.95 (ISBN 0-8091-2325-8). Paulist Pr.
Hills, C., ed. The Secrets of Spirulina. LC 80-22087. 1980. 6.95 (ISBN 0-916438-38-4). Univ of Trees.
Humphries, Christmas. Concentration & Meditation. 343p. 1981. pap. 10.00 (ISBN 0-89540-068-5). Sun Pub.
Kravette, Steve. Complete Meditation. Dodge, Plunkett, tr. (Illus.). 356p. (Orig.). 1981. pap. 9.95 (ISBN 0-914918-28-1). Para Res.
Massy, Robert. You Are What You Breathe. 1980. 1.00 (ISBN 0-916438-41-4). Univ of Trees.
Pearce, Joseph C. The Bond of Power. 1981. 10.95 (ISBN 0-525-06950-X). Dutton.
Swami Muktananda. Meditate. (Transpersonal & Humanistic Psychology Ser.). 9.95 (ISBN 0-87395-497-1). State U NY Pr.

MEDITATION (BUDDHISM)
Guenther, Herbert V. Philosophy & Psychology in the Abhidharma. LC 75-40259. 282p. 1981. pap. 6.95 (ISBN 0-87773-081-4). Great Eastern.
Gyatso, Geshe. Meaningful to Behold. Landaw, Jonathan, ed. Norbu, Tenzin, tr. from Tibetan. 365p. (Orig.). 1981. pap. 12.95 (ISBN 0-86171-003-7). Great Eastern.
Kontrul, Jamgon. The Torch of Certainty. Hanson, Judith, tr. from Tibetan. LC 76-53359. (Illus.). 179p. (Orig.). 1981. pap. 7.95 (ISBN 0-87773-101-2). Great Eastern.
Mountain, Marian. The Zen Environment: The Impact of Zen Meditation. 288p. 1981. 10.95 (ISBN 0-688-00350-8). Morrow.

MEDITATIONS
Here are entered works containing thoughts or reflections on spiritual truths. Works on the nature of meditation are entered under the heading Meditation.
see also Devotional Calendars; Devotional Literature; Jesus Christ–Devotional Literature
also subdivisions Meditations under Bible, Jesus Christ, Lord's Supper, and similar headings
Brenneman, Helen G. Morning Joy. LC 80-26449. 80p. 1981. pap. 3.95 (ISBN 0-8361-1942-8). Herald Pr.
Graham, Munir & De La Torre Bueno, Laura, eds. Index to the Sayings of Hazrat Inayat Khan. (The Collected Works of Hazrat Inayat Khan). 144p. (Orig.). 1981. pap. 3.95 (ISBN 0-930872-23-1, 1009P). Sufi Order Pubns.
Hazrat Inayat Khan. Aphorisms. (The Collected Works of Hazrat Inayat Khan). 128p. (Orig.). 1981. pap. 4.95 (ISBN 0-930872-22-3, 1008P). Sufi Order Pubns.
--The Bowl of Saki. (The Collected Works of Hazrat Inayat Khan). 144p. (Orig.). 1981. pap. 4.95 (ISBN 0-930872-20-7, 1007P). Sufi Order Pubns.
Kung, Hans. The Church-Maintained in Truth: A Theological Meditation. 87p. 1980. 6.95 (ISBN 0-8164-0454-2). Crossroad NY.
Makrakis, Apostolos. Orthodox Christian Meditations (Spiritual Discourses for the Orthodox Christians) Orthodox Christian Educational Society, ed. Cummings, Denver, tr. from Hellenic. 143p. (Orig.). 1965. pap. 2.00x (ISBN 0-938366-22-X). Orthodox Chr.
Sechrist, Elsie. Meditation: Der Weg Zum Licht. Kronberger, Helge F., tr. from Eng. (Illus.). 53p. (Ger.). 1980. pap. 6.00 (ISBN 0-87604-131-4). ARE Pr.
Shepherd, J. Barrie. A Diary of Prayer: Daily Meditations on the Parables of Jesus. (Orig.). 1981. pap. 5.95 (ISBN 0-664-24352-5). Westminster.
The Mother. Prayers & Meditations. rev. ed. Aurobindo, Sri, tr. from Fr. 380p. (Orig.). 1979. pap. 10.00 (ISBN 0-89744-998-3, Sri Aurobindo Ashram Trust India). Auromere.
Upper Room Disciplines 1981. (Orig.). 1980. pap. 3.25x (ISBN 0-8358-0391-0). Upper Room.
Wolf, William J., compiled by. Thomas Traherne's Centuries of Meditation. 1980. 1.60 (ISBN 0-686-28796-7). Forward Movement.

MEDITERRANEAN DISEASE
see Thalassemia

MEDITERRANEAN REGION
Aspects of Brackish Water Fish & Crustacean Culture in the Mediterranean. 135p. 1981. pap. 7.25 (ISBN 92-5-000964-X, F2103, FAO). Unipub.
Williams, Ann, ed. Prophecy & Millenarianism. (Illus.). 1981. text ed. 60.00 (ISBN 0-582-36136-2). Longman.

MEDITERRANEAN REGION–ANTIQUITIES
Wells, P. S. Culture Contact & Culture Change. LC 80-40212. (New Studies in Archaeology). (Illus.). 195p. 1981. 24.95 (ISBN 0-521-22808-5). Cambridge U Pr.

MEDITERRANEAN REGION–DESCRIPTION AND TRAVEL
Bristow, Philip. Down the Spanish Coast. 196p. 1980. 12.00x (ISBN 0-245-52935-7, Pub. by Nautical England). State Mutual Bk.

MEDULLA OSSIUM
see Marrow

MEETINGS
see also Discussion; Leadership; Parliamentary Practice
Doyle, Micheal & Straus, Davis. How to Make Meetings Work. 240p. 1981. pap. 2.50 (ISBN 0-87216-614-7). Playboy Pbks.
Jorgensen, James D., et al. Solving Problems in Meetings. LC 79-21782. 112p. 1981. 8.95 (ISBN 0-88229-521-7). Nelson-Hall.
Lord, Robert W. Running Conventions, Conferences & Meetings. 400p. 1981. 21.95 (ISBN 0-8144-5643-X). Am Mgmt.
O'Connor, Rochelle. Company Planning Meetings, Report No. 788. (Illus.). v, 50p. (Orig.). 1980. pap. 15.00 (ISBN 0-8237-0224-3). Conference Bd.

MEGAVITAMIN THERAPY
see Orthomolecular Medicine

MEHER BABA, 1894-1969
Craske, Margaret. The Dance of Love: My Life with Meher Baba. LC 80-53859. 180p. 1980. pap. 6.95 (ISBN 0-913078-40-9). Sheriar Pr.
Kalchuri, Bhau. Let's Go to Meherabad. 100p. 1981. price not set. Meher Baba Info.

MEIR, GOLDA (MABOVITZ), 1898-
Davidson, Margaret. The Golda Meir Story. rev. ed. (Illus.). 240p. (gr. 3-7). 1981. 9.95 (ISBN 0-684-16877-4). Scribner.

MELANOMA
Ariel, Irving M. Malignant Melanoma. 544p. 1981. 42.50 (ISBN 0-8385-6114-4). ACC.

MELODRAMA
Gerould, Daniel, ed. Melodrama. LC 79-52615. (New York Literary Forum Ser.). (Illus.). 296p. (Orig.). 1980. pap. 12.50x (ISBN 0-931196-06-X). NY Lit Forum.

MELVILLE, HERMAN, 1819-1891
Boswell, Jeanetta. Herman Melville & the Critics: A Checklist of Criticism, 1900-1978. LC 80-25959. (Author Bibliographies Ser.: No. 53). 259p. 1981. 13.50 (ISBN 0-8108-1385-8). Scarecrow.
Heffernan, Thomas F. Stove by a Whale: Owen Chase & the Essex. 256p. 1981. 19.95 (ISBN 0-8195-5052-3). Wesleyan U Pr.
Hillway, Tyrus. Herman Melville. LC 78-11937. (Twayne's U. S. Authors Ser.). 177p. 1979. pap. text ed. 4.95 (ISBN 0-672-61504-5). Bobbs.
Levin, Harry. The Power of Blackness: Hawthorne, Poe, Melville. LC 80-83221. xxii, 263p. 1980. pap. 6.95x (ISBN 0-8214-0581-0). Ohio U Pr.

MELVILLE, HERMAN, 1819-1891–BIBLIOGRAPHY
Boswell, Jeanetta. Herman Melville & the Critics: A Checklist of Criticism, 1900-1978. LC 80-25959. (Author Bibliographies Ser.: No. 53). 259p. 1981. 13.50 (ISBN 0-8108-1385-8). Scarecrow.

MEMBERSHIP CORPORATIONS
see Corporations, Nonprofit

MEMBRANES (BIOLOGY)
see also Plasma Membranes
Bittar, E. Edward. Membrane Structure & Function, Vol. 4. (Membrane Structure & Function Ser.). 200p. 1980. 24.50 (ISBN 0-471-08774-2, Pub. by Wiley-Interscience). Wiley.
Hendy, Bruce. Membrane Physiology & Cell Excitation. 160p. 1980. 30.00x (Pub. by Croom Helm England). State Mutual Bk.
Methods in Membrane Biology, Vols. 1-10. Incl. Vol. 1. 241p. 1974. 27.50 (ISBN 0-686-65013-1); Vol. 2. 363p. 1974. 32.50 (ISBN 0-306-36802-1); Vol. 3. Plasma Membranes. 246p. 1975. 24.50 (ISBN 0-306-36803-X); Vol. 4. Biophysical Approaches. 298p. 1975. 27.50 (ISBN 0-306-36804-8); Vol. 5. Transport. 199p. 1975. 25.00 (ISBN 0-306-36805-6); Vol. 6. 248p. 1976. 29.50 (ISBN 0-306-36806-4); Vol. 7. 267p. 1976. 32.50 (ISBN 0-306-36807-2); Vol. 8. 368p. 1977. 32.50 (ISBN 0-306-36808-0); Vol. 9. 406p. 1978. 35.00 (ISBN 0-306-36809-9); Vol. 10. 227p. 1979. 29.50 (ISBN 0-306-40126-6). LC 73-81094. (Illus., Plenum Pr). Plenum Pub.

Salanki, J., et al, eds. Physiology of Excitable Membranes: Proceedings of the 28th International Congress of Physiological Sciences, Budapest, 1980. LC 80-41853. (Advances in Physiological Sciences: Vol. 4). (Illus.). 350p. 1981. 40.00 (ISBN 0-08-026816-1). Pergamon.

MEMOIRS

see Autobiography; Biography;
also subdivision Correspondence, Reminiscences, etc. under classes of people, e.g. Actors–Correspondence, reminiscenses, etc.; subdivision History–Sources under names of countries; subdivision Personal Narratives under names of wars, diseases, etc. e.g. World War, 1939-1945–Personal Narratives

MEMORIAL TABLETS

see Sepulchral Monuments

MEMORY

see also Eidetic Imagery

Ribot, Theodule A. Diseases of Memory. Smith, W. H. & Snell, M. M., trs. Bd. with Diseases of Personality. Repr. of 1891 ed; Diseases of the Will. Repr. of 1894 ed. (Contributions to the History of Psychology, Vol. I, Pt. C: Medical Psychology). 1978. Repr. of 1882 ed. 30.00 (ISBN 0-89093-165-8). U Pubns Amer.

Torda, C. Memory & Dreams: A Modern Physics Approach. (Illus.). 453p. 1980. 24.95. Walters.

Young, Chester V. The Magic of a Powerful Memory. rev. & abr. ed. LC 80-70955. 254p. 1981. Repr. of 1971 ed. 10.95 (ISBN 0-8119-0416-4). Fell.

MEMORY TRAINING

see Mnemonics

MEN–PHOTOGRAPHY

see Photography of Men

MEN–SEXUAL BEHAVIOR

Bertels, Frank. The First Book on Male Liberation & Six Equality. (Illus.). 352p. 1981. lib. bdg. 25.00 (ISBN 0-932574-05-X); pap. 15.00 (ISBN 0-932574-06-8). Brun Pr.

Friday, Nancy. Men in Love, Male Sexual Fantasies: The Triump of Love Over Rage. 1981. pap. 3.50 (ISBN 0-440-15404-9). Dell.

MEN NURSES

Brown, R. G. The Male Nurse. 139p. 1973. pap. text ed. 5.00x (ISBN 0-7135-1878-2, Pub. by Bedford England). Renouf.

MENDING

see Repairing; Sewing

MENNONITE COOKERY

see Cookery, American

MENNONITES–HISTORY

Dyck, C. J. An Introduction to Mennonite History. 400p. 1981. pap. 9.95 (ISBN 0-8361-1955-X). Herald Pr.

Hertzler, Daniel. From Germantown to Steinbach. 248p. 1981. pap. 7.95 (ISBN 0-8361-1949-5). Herald Pr.

MENOMINEE INDIANS

see Indians of North America–Northwest, Old

MENOPAUSE

Clausen, Muriel C. Menopause: Vitamins & You. 105p. (Orig.). 1980. pap. 4.75 (ISBN 0-9603664-1-5). M C Clausen.

Gray, Madeline. The Changing Years: The Menopause Without Fear. rev. ed. LC 77-16917. 280p. 1981. 12.95 (ISBN 0-385-12635-2). Doubleday.

MENSTRUAL CYCLE

see Menstruation

MENSTRUATION

see also Menopause

Maddux, Hilary C. Menstruation. 1981. pap. 2.50 (ISBN 0-440-05582-2). Dell.

MENSURATION

see also Gaging; Physical Measurements; Surveying; Weights and Measures
also subdivision Measurement under special subjects, e.g. Altitudes–Measurement

Mikhail, Edward M. & Gracie, Gordon. Analysis & Adjustment of Survey Measurements. 368p. 1980. text ed. 28.50 (ISBN 0-442-25369-9). Van Nos Reinhold.

MENSURATION–JUVENILE LITERATURE

Bowden, Joan C. My Measuring Book. (Golden Play & Learn Bk). (Illus.). 14p. (ps). 1980. pap. 2.95 (ISBN 0-307-10729-9). Western Pubs OH.

MENTAL ABILITY AND AGE

see Age and Intelligence

MENTAL DEFICIENCY

see also Mentally Handicapped

Simmons, Harold. The Psychosocial Origins of Mental Retardation. 1980. pap. 5.95 (ISBN 0-87312-011-6). Gen Welfare.

MENTAL DEPRESSION

see Depression, Mental

MENTAL DISEASES

see Mental Illness; Psychology, Pathological; Psychoses

MENTAL HEALING

see also Christian Science; Faith-Cure; Mind and Body; Psychotherapy

Bartow, Donald W. The Adventures of Healing: How to Use New Testament Practices & Receive New Testament Results. rev. ed. 371p. 1981. pap. 5.95 (ISBN 0-938736-02-7). Life Enrich.

Blauer, Stephen. Rejuvenation: Dr. Ann Wigmore's Complete Diet & Health Program. 197p. pap. 4.95. Hippocrates.

Folz, Joe. Psychic Healers of the Philippines. 1981. pap. 2.95 (ISBN 0-88270-508-3). Logos.

Hagin, Kenneth E. Laying on of Hands. 1980. pap. 0.50 mini bk. (ISBN 0-89276-250-0). Hagin Ministries.

Heidenreich, Alfred. Healings in the Gospels. 1980. pap. 7.25 (ISBN 0-903540-36-3, Pub. Floris Books). St George Bk Serv.

Holzer, Hans. Psychic Healing. (Orig.). 1979. pap. 2.25 (ISBN 0-532-23123-6). Manor Bks.

Hunt, Roland. The Seven Keys to Colour Healing. 124p. 1971. 7.25x (ISBN 0-8464-1063-X). Beekman Pubs.

King, Serge. Imagineering for Health. LC 80-53949. 154p. (Orig.). 1980. pap. 4.95 (ISBN 0-8356-0546-9, Quest). Theos Pub Hse.

Kingston, Beryl. Lifting the Curse. 1980. 17.50x (ISBN 0-85223-176-8, Pub. by Telford England). State Mutual Bk.

Kligman, Gail. Calus: Symbolic Transformation in Romanian Ritual. LC 80-21372. (Chicago Originals Ser.). (Illus.). 240p. 1981. lib. bdg. 12.00x (ISBN 0-226-44221-7). U of Chicago Pr.

Kraft, Dean. Portrait of a Psychic Healer. 192p. 1981. 10.95 (ISBN 0-686-69592-5). Putnam.

Los, Pieter. An Entire New Healing Approach. 1981. 8.95 (ISBN 0-533-04361-1). Vantage.

Wagner, James K. Blessed to Be a Blessing. LC 80-52615. 144p. (Orig.). 1980. pap. 4.50 (ISBN 0-8358-0410-0). Upper Room.

Wigmore, Ann. Spiritual Diet. (Health Digest Ser.: No. 152). 64p. pap. 1.50. Hippocrates.

MENTAL HEALTH

see also Community Mental Health Services; Emotions; Happiness; Mental Health Personnel; Mental Health Services; Mental Illness; Personality; Psychiatry; Psychology; Psychology, Pathological; Relaxation; Self-Actualization (Psychology); Stress (Psychology); Success

Crawford, Fred R., ed. Exploring Mental Health Parameters, Vol. III. LC 80-67929. (Orig.). 1980. pap. 8.00 (ISBN 0-89937-030-6). Ctr Res Soc Chg.

Day, Stacey B., et al. Biopsychosocial Health. 225p. 1980. pap. 10.50 (ISBN 0-934314-02-0). Intl Found Biosocial Dev.

Di Bella, Geoffrey A., et al. Day Treatment & Other Partial Hospitals: A Comprehensive Guide. 450p. 1981. 30.00 (ISBN 0-87630-270-3). Brunner-Mazel.

Fromme, Allan. The Book for Normal Neurotics. 1981. 10.95 (ISBN 0-374-11544-3). FS&G.

Richardson, Herbert W., ed. New Religions & Mental Health: A Guide to the Issues. (Symposium Ser.: Vol. 6). (Orig.). 1980. soft cover 11.95x (ISBN 0-88946-910-5). E Mellen.

Silverman, Wade H. Community Mental Health: A Sourcebook for Professionals & Advisors. 450p. 1981. 39.95 (ISBN 0-03-057006-9). Praeger.

Sourcebook on Mental Health. 2nd ed. 660p. 1981. price not set (ISBN 0-8379-4802-9). Marquis.

Stein, Laszlo K., et al. Deafness & Mental Health. 1981. write for info. (ISBN 0-8089-1347-6). Grune.

Veroff, Joseph, et al. Mental Health in America, 1957-1976. LC 80-68959. 1981. 37.50x (ISBN 0-465-04479-4). Basic.

MENTAL HEALTH–BIBLIOGRAPHY

Chicorel Index to Mental Health Book Reviews: 1977 Annual, Vol. 26. 400p. 1978. 85.00 (ISBN 0-934598-77-0). Am Lib Pub Co.

Chicorel Index to Mental Health Book Reviews: 1978 Annual, Vol. 26. 400p. 1980. 85.00 (ISBN 0-934598-08-8). Am Lib Pub Co.

MENTAL HEALTH LAWS

see also Insanity–Jurisprudence

Greenland, Cyril. Mental Illness & Civil Liberty. 126p. 1970. pap. text ed. 5.00x (ISBN 0-7135-1826-X, Pub. by Bedford England). Renouf.

Haavik, Sarah F. & Menninger, Karl A., 2nd. Sexuality, Law, & the Developmentally Disabled Person: Legal & Clinical Aspects of Marriage, Parenthood, & Sterilization. 210p. (Orig.). 1981. pap. text ed. 13.95 (ISBN 0-933716-21-4). P H Brookes.

Maggio, Elio. The Psychiatry-Law Dilemma. 1980. 13.95 (ISBN 0-533-04795-1). Vantage.

MENTAL HEALTH LAWS–GREAT BRITAIN

Wexler, David B. Mental Health Law: Major Issues. 265p. 1981. 25.00 (ISBN 0-306-40538-5, Plenum Pr). Plenum Pub.

MENTAL HEALTH PERSONNEL

see also Clinical Psychology; Psychiatric Nursing; Psychiatric Social Work

Cherniss, Cary. Staff Burnout: Job Stress in the Human Services. LC 80-19408. (Sage Studies in Community Mental Health: Vol. 2). (Illus.). 200p. 1980. 20.00 (ISBN 0-8039-1338-9); pap. 9.95 (ISBN 0-8039-1339-7). Sage.

Grace, Helen K. & Camilleri, Dorothy. Mental Health Nursing: A Socio-Psychological Approach. 2nd ed. 592p. 1981. text ed. write for info. (ISBN 0-697-05517-5); instrs.' manual avail. (ISBN 0-697-05518-3). Wm C Brown.

Kahn, Marvin W. Basic Methods for Mental Health Practitioners. 350p. Date not set. ref. ed. 15.95. Winthrop.

Neal, Margo C. & Cohen, Patricia F. Nursing Care Planning Guides for Psychiatric & Mental Health. 1980. pap. 15.95 (ISBN 0-935236-15-5). Nurseco.

MENTAL HEALTH RESEARCH

see Psychiatric Research

MENTAL HEALTH SERVICES

see also Community Mental Health Services; Halfway Houses; Psychiatric Hospitals

Gap Committee on Preventive Psychiatry. Mental Health & Primary Medical Care, Vol. 10. LC 80-19016. (Publication Ser.: No. 105). pap. 4.00 (105, Mental Health Materials Center). Adv Psychiatry.

Ryback, Ralph S., et al. The Problem-Oriented Record in Psychiatry & Mental Health Care. 2nd ed. 1981. write for info. (ISBN 0-8089-1308-5). Grune.

MENTAL HOSPITALS

see Psychiatric Hospitals

MENTAL HYGIENE

see Mental Health

MENTAL ILLNESS

Here are entered popular works and works on regional or social aspects of mental disorders. Works on the legal aspects of mental illness are entered under Insanity. Systematic descriptions of mental disorders are entered under Psychology, Pathological. Works on clinical aspects of mental disorders, including therapy, are entered under Psychiatry.

see also Mental Deficiency; Mental Health; Paranoia; Psychiatry; Psychology, Pathological

Beers, Clifford W. A Mind That Found Itself. 5th ed. LC 80-5256. (Contemporary Communities Health Ser). 232p. 1981. 14.95 (ISBN 0-8229-3442-6); pap. 6.95 (ISBN 0-8229-5324-2). U of Pittsburgh Pr.

Butterworth, C. A. & Skidmore, D. Caring for the Mentally Ill in the Community. 160p. 1980. 27.00x (Pub by Croom Helm England). State Mutual Bk.

Cockerham, William C. Sociology of Mental Disorder. (Ser. in Sociology). (Illus.). 300p. 1981. text ed. 17.95 (ISBN 0-13-820886-7). P-H.

Hannah, Gerald T., et al, eds. Preservation of Client Rights: A Handbook for Practitioners Providing Therapeutic, Educational, & Rehabilitative Services. LC 80-1644. (Illus.). 1981. 22.95 (ISBN 0-02-913820-5). Free Pr.

Lewis, Helen B. Freud & Modern Psychology: The/Emotional Basis of Mental Illness, Vol. 1. (Emotions Personality & Psychotherapy Ser.). 240p. 1981. 19.50 (ISBN 0-306-40525-3, Plenum Pr). Plenum Pub.

Maudsley, Henry. Responsibility in Mental Disease. Bd. with Treatise on Insanity. (Contributions to the History of Psychology Ser., Vol. III, Pt. C: Medical Psychology). 1978. Repr. of 1876 ed. 30.00 (ISBN 0-89093-167-4). U Pubns Amer.

Smith, Selwyn M. & Koranyi, Erwin K. Self-Assessment of Current Knowledge in Forensic & Organic Psychiatry. 1978. spiral bdg. 15.00 (ISBN 0-87488-235-4). Med Exam.

Snyder, Solomon H. Biological Aspects of Mental Disorder. (Illus.). 272p. 1981. pap. 8.95x (ISBN 0-19-502888-0). Oxford U Pr.

MENTAL ILLNESS–PERSONAL NARRATIVES

Cameron, Doug. How to Survive Being Committed to a Mental Hospital. LC 79-66488. 143p. 1980. 7.95 (ISBN 0-533-04399-9). Vantage.

MENTAL ILLNESS–RESEARCH

see Psychiatric Research

MENTAL ILLNESS AND LAW

see Insanity–Jurisprudence

MENTAL INSTITUTIONS

see Mentally Handicapped–Institutional Care; Psychiatric Hospitals

MENTAL-MOTOR RELATIONSHIP IN EDUCATION

see Perceptual-Motor Learning

MENTAL PRAYER

see Meditation

MENTAL RETARDATION

see Mental Deficiency

MENTAL TESTS

see Educational Tests and Measurements; Intelligence Tests

MENTALLY HANDICAPPED

see also Mental Deficiency

De La Cruz, F. & LaVeck, G. D., eds. Human Sexuality & the Mentally Retarded. LC 72-92057. 1973. 12.50 (ISBN 0-87630-063-8). Brunner-Mazel.

Dickerson, Martha U. Social Work Practice with the Mentally Retarded. Turner, Francis J. & Strean, Herbert S., eds. LC 80-2316. (Fields of Practice Ser.). 1981. text ed. 14.95 (ISBN 0-02-907430-4). Free Pr.

McCormack. Prevention of Mental Retardation & Other Developmental Disabilities. 680p. 1980. 49.75 (ISBN 0-8247-6950-3). Dekker.

Malin, Nigel, et al. Services for the Mentally Handicapped in Britain. 266p. 1980. boards 30.00x (ISBN 0-85664-869-8, Pub. by Croom Helm Ltd England). Biblio Dist.

Readings in Mental Handicaps. rev. ed. Venn, John, ed. (Special Education Ser.). (Illus.). 224p. pap. text ed. write for info. (ISBN 0-89568-195-1). Spec Learn Corp.

Special People...Getting to Know Them: Resources in Mental Retardation. 1.00. Boston Public Lib.

Wortis, Joseph, ed. Mental Retardation & Developmental Disabilities, Vol. XII. LC 73-647002. 200p. 1981. 20.00 (ISBN 0-87630-263-0). Brunner-Mazel.

MENTALLY HANDICAPPED–EDUCATION

Kissinger, Ellen M. A Sequential Curriculum for the Severely & Profoundly Mentally Retarded-Multi-Handicapped. 216p. 1981. pap. 22.75 spiral (ISBN 0-398-04145-8). C C Thomas.

Payne, James S. & Patton, James R. Mental Retardation. (Special Education Ser.). (Illus.). 480p. 1981. text ed. 24.95 (ISBN 0-675-08027-4); write for info. Merrill.

Payne, James S., et al. Strategies for Teaching the Mentally Retarded. 2nd ed. (Special Education Ser.). 368p. 1981. text ed. 17.95 (ISBN 0-675-08067-3). Merrill.

Salvia, John & Ysseldyke, James E. Assessment in Special & Remedial Education. 2nd ed. (Illus.). 576p. 1981. text ed. write for info. (ISBN 0-395-29694-3). HM.

MENTALLY HANDICAPPED–INSTITUTIONAL CARE

see also Psychiatric Hospitals

Hannah, Gerald T., et al, eds. Preservation of Client Rights: A Handbook for Practitioners Providing Therapeutic, Educational, & Rehabilitative Services. LC 80-1644. (Illus.). 1981. 22.95 (ISBN 0-02-913820-5). Free Pr.

MENTALLY HANDICAPPED–LAWS AND LEGISLATION

see Mental Health Laws

MENTALLY HANDICAPPED–REHABILITATION

Crain, Cynthia D. Movement & Phythmic Activities for the Mentally Retarded. 1981. write for info. (ISBN 0-398-04174-1). C C Thomas.

Haavik, Sarah F. & Menninger, Karl A., 2nd. Sexuality, Law, & the Developmentally Disabled Person: Legal & Clinical Aspects of Marriage, Parenthood, & Sterilization. 210p. (Orig.). 1981. pap. text ed. 13.95 (ISBN 0-933716-21-4). P H Brookes.

Heshusius, Lous. Meaning in Life As Experienced by Persons Labeled Retarded in a Group Home: Their Quest to Be. (Illus.). 176p. 1980. 19.50 (ISBN 0-398-04064-8); pap. 15.75 (ISBN 0-398-04079-6). C C Thomas.

Raynes, Norma V., et al. Organisational Structure & the Care of the Mentally Retarded. 192p. 1980. 25.00x (ISBN 0-85664-532-X, Pub. by Croom Helm England). State Mutual Bk.

MENTALLY HANDICAPPED CHILDREN

see also Mentally Ill Children
also names of particular institutions

Wilkin, David. Caring for the Mentally Handicapped Child. 192p. 1980. 30.00x (ISBN 0-85664-648-2, Pub. by Croom Helm England). State Mutual Bk.

MENTALLY HANDICAPPED CHILDREN–EDUCATION

Blackhurst & Berdine. An Introduction to Special Education. 1981. text ed. 15.95 (ISBN 0-316-09060-3); tchrs'. manual free (ISBN 0-316-09061-1). Little.

Champlin, John & Champlin, Connie. Books, Puppets & the Mentally Retarded Student. (Illus.). 162p. (Orig.). 1981. pap. 9.95 (ISBN 0-938594-00-1). Spec Lit Pr.

Cunningham, Cliff & Sloper, Patricia. Helping Your Exceptional Baby: A Practical & Honest Approach to Raising a Mentally Handicapped Child. (Illus.). 1981. pap. 6.95 (ISBN 0-394-73867-5). Pantheon.

Gillham, Bill. The First Words Language Programme. 96p. 1980. 20.00x (Pub. by Beaconsfield England). State Mutual Bk.

Gold, Marc. Try Another Way Training Manual. LC 80-52142. 105p. (Orig.). 1980. pap. 5.95 (ISBN 0-87822-222-7, 2227). Res Press.

Mithang, Dennis E. Prevocational Training for Retarded Students. (Illus.). 304p. 1981. text ed. 29.50 (ISBN 0-398-04111-3). C C Thomas.

Ward, David. Sing a Rainbow: Musical Activities with Mentally Handicapped Children. (Illus.). 64p. (Orig.). 1979. pap. text ed. 8.95x (ISBN 0-19-317416-2). Oxford U Pr.

MENTALLY ILL–CARE AND TREATMENT

Gordon, Richard E. & Gordon, Katherine. Systems of Treatment for the Mentally Ill: Filling the Gaps. 1981. price not set (ISBN 0-8089-1338-7). Grune.

Morrison, James R. Your Brother's Keeper: A Guide for Families of the Mentall Ill. LC 79-27810. 352p. 1981. 20.95 (ISBN 0-88229-563-2). Nelson-Hall.

MENTALLY ILL–CASES, CLINICAL REPORTS, STATISTICS

Estroff, Sue E. Making It Crazy: An Ethnography of Psychiatric Clients in an American Community. 338p. 1981. 19.95 (ISBN 0-520-03963-7). U of Cal Pr.

MENTALLY ILL–HOSPITALS

see Psychiatric Hospitals

MENTALLY ILL–LEGAL STATUS, LAWS, ETC.

see Insanity–Jurisprudence; Mental Health Laws

MENTALLY ILL–PERSONAL NARRATIVES

see Mental Illness–Personal Narratives

MENTALLY ILL–REHABILITATION

Mithang, Dennis E. Prevocational Training for Retarded Students. (Illus.). 304p. 1981. text ed. 29.50 (ISBN 0-398-04111-3). C C Thomas.

MENTALLY ILL CHILDREN

Frederic, Helene & Malinsky, Martine. Martin. McGreal, John & Lipshitz, Susan, trs. from Fr. Orig. Title: Martin: un Enfant Battait Sa Mere. 108p. 1981. price not set (ISBN 0-7100-0814-7). Routledge & Kegan.

MENTALLY RETARDED
see Mentally Handicapped
MENTALLY RETARDED CHILDREN
see Mentally Handicapped Children
MENUS
see also Breakfasts; Caterers and Catering; Dinners and Dining
Groff, Betty & Wilson, Jose. Betty Groff's Country Goodness Cookbook. LC 80-1093. (Illus.). 336p. 1981. 17.95 (ISBN 0-385-12120-2). Doubleday.
Long, John, et al, eds. Menus of the Valley's Finest Restaurants: Nineteen Eighty-One Edition. 176p. 1980. pap. 5.95 (ISBN 0-930380-12-6, 0148-4133). Quail Run.
MEPHITIS
see Skunks
MERCANTILE LAW
see Commercial Law
MERCHANDISE
see Commercial Products
MERCHANDISING
Fulkerson, Katherine. The Merchandise Buyers' Game. 1981. pap. text ed. 2.95 (ISBN 0-933836-13-9). Simtek.
Troxell, Mary D. & Stone, Elaine. Fashion Merchandising. 3rd ed. LC 80-25077. (Gregg McGraw-Hill Marketing Ser.). (Illus.). 480p. 16.50 (ISBN 0-07-065280-5). McGraw.
MERCHANT MARINE-LAW
see Maritime Law
MERCHANT MARKS
see Trade-Marks
MERCHANT SHIPS
see also Cargo Ships; Packets; Steamboats and Steamboat Lines; Tankers
Taylor, D. A. Merchant Ship Construction. (Illus.). 240p. 1980. text ed. 39.95 (ISBN 0-408-00408-8). Butterworths.
MERCHANT SHIP'S PAPERS
see Ships Papers
MERCHANTMEN
see Merchant Ships
MERCURY
Data Profile on Mercury. (IRPTC Data Profile Ser.: No. 3). 198p. 1981. pap. 20.00 (ISBN 0-686-69541-0, UNEP 42, UNEP). Unipub.
Kelkar, S. A. Occupational Exposure to Mercury. xi, 112p. 1980. text ed. 15.95x (ISBN 0-86590-001-9). Apt Bks.
MERCY DEATH
see Euthanasia
MEREDITH, GEORGE, 1828-1909
Henderson, M. Sturge. George Meredith. 324p. 1980. Repr. of 1907 ed. lib. bdg. 30.00. Darby Bks.
Lynch, Hannah. George Meredith. 170p. 1980. Repr. of 1891 ed. lib. bdg. 10.00 (ISBN 0-8495-3335-X). Arden Lib.
MERGER OF CORPORATIONS
see Consolidation and Merger of Corporations
MERINIDES
see Beni Marin Dynasty
MERISTEM
see Growth (Plants)
MERRIMACK RIVER AND VALLEY
Karabatsos, James. A Word-Index to a Week on the Concord & Merrimack Rivers. LC 80-2510. 1981. Repr. of 1971 ed. 18.50 (ISBN 0-404-19058-8). AMS Pr.
MERTON, THOMAS, 1915-1968
Cashen, Richard A. Solitude in the Thought of Thomas Merton. (Cistercian Studies: No. 40). 208p. 1981. 15.50 (ISBN 0-87907-840-5); pap. 5.50 (ISBN 0-87907-940-1). Cistercian Pubns.
Hart, Patrick, ed. The Message of Thomas Merton. (Cistercian Studies: No. 42). 1981. price not set (ISBN 0-87907-842-1). Cistercian Pub.
Nouwen, Henri J. Thomas Merton: Contemplative Critic. LC 80-8898. 176p. 1981. pap. 3.95 (ISBN 0-06-066324-3, HarpR). Har-Row.
MESMERISM
see also Hypnotism; Mental Healing; Mind and Body
Elliotson, John. Numerous Cases of Surgical Operations Without Pain in the Mesmeric State. Bd. with Mesmerism in India; Philosophy of Sleep. (Contributions to the History of Psychology Ser., Vol. X, Pt. A: Orientations). 1978. Repr. of 1843 ed. 30.00 (ISBN 0-89093-159-3). U Pubns Amer.
Esdaile, James. Mesmerism in India. Bd. with Numerous Cases of Surgical Operations; The Philosophy of Sleep. (Contributions to the History of Psychology Ser., Vol. X, Pt. A: Orientations). 1978. Repr. of 1846 ed. 30.00 (ISBN 0-89093-159-3). U Pubns Amer.
MESOPOTAMIAN ART
see Art, Mesopotamian
MESOPOTAMIAN POTTERY
see Pottery, Ancient
METABOLIC DISORDERS
see Metabolism, Disorders of
METABOLIC INHIBITORS
see Enzyme Inhibitors
METABOLISM
see also Bioenergetics; Calcium Metabolism; Carbohydrate Metabolism; Carbohydrates in the Body; Drug Metabolism; Energy Metabolism; Iron Metabolism; Lipid Metabolism; Mineral Metabolism; Nutrition; Plants-Metabolism; Protein Metabolism; Vitamin Metabolism
Beers, Roland F. & Bassett, Edward G., eds. Nutritional Factors: Modulating Effects on Metabolic Processes. (Miles International Symposium Ser.: Vol. 13). 1981. text ed. price not set (ISBN 0-89004-592-5). Raven.
Mora, Jaime & Palacios, Rafael, eds. Glutamine: Metabolism, Enzymology & Regulation. 1980. 28.00 (ISBN 0-12-506040-8). Acad Pr.
Stoddart, R. W. Polysaccharide Metabolism. 224p. 1980. 35.00x (ISBN 0-85664-807-8, Pub. by Croom Helm England). State Mutual England.
METABOLISM, DISORDERS OF
see also Diabetes; Metabolism, Inborn Errors of; Obesity
W., tr. Metabolic Disorders, Methods of Examination. (Developments in Ophthalmology: Vol. 4). (Illus.). 1981. 78.00 (ISBN 3-8055-2014-X). S Karger.
METABOLISM, INBORN ERRORS OF
Ellis, Roland, ed. Inborn Errors of Metabolism. 112p. 1980. 30.00x (Pub. by Croom Helm England). State Mutual Bk.
METAL CORROSION
see Corrosion and Anti-Corrosives
METAL CURTAIN WALLS
see Walls
METAL ENGRAVERS
see Engravers
METAL INDUSTRIES
see Metal-Work; Mineral Industries
METAL IONS
Sigel. Metal Ions in Biological Systems, Vol. II. 448p. 1980. 55.00 (ISBN 0-8247-1004-5). Dekker.
Spiro, Thomas G. Copper Proteins. (Metal Ions in Biology Ser.: Vol. 3). 356p. 1981. 37.50 (ISBN 0-471-04400-8, Pub. by Wiley Interscience). Wiley.
METAL OXIDES
see Metallic Oxides
METAL-WORK
see also Founding; Home Workshops; Metal-Working Lubricants; Metals-Finishing; Sheet-Metal Work; Silverwork; Welding
Filigree Architecture: Metal & Glass Construction. (Illus.). 216p. (Eng. Fr. & Ger.). 1980. text ed. 19.00 (ISBN 0-89192-298-9). Interbk Inc.
Flood, Charles R. Welding & Metal Fabrication. 1981. text ed. price not set (ISBN 0-408-00448-7). Butterworths.
Gingery, David J. The Dividing Head & Deluxe Accessories. LC 80-66142. (Build Your Own Metal Working Shop from Scrap: Bk. 6). (Illus.). 112p. (Orig.). 1981. pap. 7.95 (ISBN 0-9604330-5-8). D J Gingery.
Graham, Gregory S. Metalworking: An Introduction. 1980. text ed. write for info. (ISBN 0-534-00843-7, Breton Pubs). Wadsworth Pub.
Squires, William T. The Metal Craftsman Handbook. 1981. 7.95 (ISBN 0-89606-050-0). Green Hill.
Trainer, Glynnis. The Metalworking Industry. 200p. 1981. cancelled (ISBN 0-86569-062-6). Auburn Hse.
METAL-WORK-HISTORY
Nicholson, Susan M. Catalogue of the Prehistoric Metalwork in Merseyside County Museum, No. 2. (Worknotes Ser.). (Illus.). 148p. (Orig.). 1981. pap. 12.50x (ISBN 0-87474-675-2). Smithsonian.
METAL-WORKING LUBRICANTS
Kalpakjian, S. & Jain, S. C., eds. Metalworking Lubrication. 259p. 1980. 40.00 (H00159). ASME.
METALLIC ALLOYS
see Alloys
METALLIC OXIDES
Agajanian, A. H., ed. MOSFET Technology--a Comprehensive Bibliography. 305p. 1980. 95.00 (ISBN 0-306-65193-9). IFI Plenum.
METALLOGRAPHY
Einspruch, Norman G., ed. Microstructure Science & Engineering, 2 vols. 1981. Vol. 1. write for info. (ISBN 0-12-234101-5); Vol. 2. write info. (ISBN 0-12-234102-3). Acad Pr.
METALLOIDS
see Semimetals
METALLOORGANIC COMPOUNDS
see Organometallic Compounds
METALLURGY
see also Alloys; Chemical Engineering; Metals; Powder Metallurgy; Refractory Materials
also names of metals, with or without the subdivision Metallurgy
Birau, N. & Schlott, W., eds. Melatonin - Current Status & Perspectives: Proceedings of an International Symposium on Melatonin, Held in Bremen, F. R. Germany, September 18-30, 1980. (Advances in the Biosciences Ser.: Vol. 29). (Illus.). 420p. 1981. 65.00 (ISBN 0-08-026400-X). Pergamon.
Brown, Donald. Basic Metallurgy. LC 80-68584. (Mechanical Ser.). (Illus.). 272p. (Orig.). 1981. pap. text ed. 10.40 (ISBN 0-8273-1769-7); price not set instr's. guide (ISBN 0-8273-1770-0). Delmar.
Gaskell, David R. Metallurgical Thermodynamics. 2nd ed. (Materials Engineering Ser.). 560p. 1981. text ed. 29.95 (ISBN 0-07-022946-5). McGraw.
Leslie, William C. The Physical Metallurgy of Steels. (M-H Materials Science & Engineering Ser.). 368p. 1981. text ed. 29.50 (ISBN 0-07-037780-4). McGraw.
Moore. Principles of Chemical Metallurgy. 1981. text ed. price not set (ISBN 0-408-00567-X); pap. text ed. price not set (ISBN 0-408-00430-4). Butterworth.
Taubenblat, Pierre W. Copper Base Powder Metallurgy. LC 80-81464. (New Perspectives in Powder Metallurgy Ser.: Vol. 7). (Illus.). 232p. 1980. 42.00 (ISBN 0-918404-47-9). Metal Powder.
Waseda, Yoshio. The Structure of Non-Crystalline Materials. (Illus.). 304p. 1980. text ed. 44.50 (ISBN 0-07-068426-X, C). McGraw.
METALLURGY, POWDER
see Powder Metallurgy
METALORGANIC COMPOUNDS
see Organometallic Compounds
METALS
see also Alloys; Assaying; Earths, Rare; Liquid Metals; Metallic Oxides; Metallography; Mineralogy; Nonferrous Metals; Precious Metals; Semimetals; Transition Metals
also particular metals and metal groups, e.g. Iron
Chisholm, Malcolm, ed. Reactivity of Metal-Metal Bonds. (ACS Symposium Ser.: No. 155). 1981. price not set (ISBN 0-8412-0624-4). Am Chemical.
Sittig, Marshall, ed. Metal & Inorganic Waste Reclaiming Encyclopedia. LC 80-21669. (Pollution Tech. Rev. 70; Chem. Tech. Rev. 175). (Illus.). 591p. (Orig.). 1981. 54.00 (ISBN 0-8155-0823-9). Noyes.
Suryanarayana, C., compiled by. Rapidly Quenched Metals--a Bibliography: 1973-1979. 310p. 1980. 75.00 (ISBN 0-306-65194-7). IFI Plenum.
METALS-ANALYSIS
Harrison, P. M. & Hoare, R. J. Metals in Biochemistry. LC 79-41813. 80p. 1980. pap. 5.95 (ISBN 0-412-13160-9, 6361). Methuen Inc.
METALS-CORROSION
see Corrosion and Anti-Corrosives
METALS-FAILURE
see Metals-Fracture
METALS-FINISHING
Duffy, J. I., ed. Electroless & Other Nonelectrolytic Plating Techniques: Recent Developments. LC 80-19494. (Chemical Tech. Rev. 171). (Illus.). 366p. 1981. 45.00 (ISBN 0-8155-0818-2). Noyes.
METALS-FRACTURE
Collins, J. A. Failure of Materials in Mechanical Design: Analysis, Prediction, Prevention. 700p. 1981. 25.00 (ISBN 0-471-05024-5, Pub. by Wiley-Interscience). Wiley.
METALS-MICROSCOPIC STRUCTURE
see Metallography
METALS-TOXICOLOGY
Williams, D. F., ed. Systemic Aspects of Biocompatibility. 1981. Vol. 1. 69.95 (ISBN 0-8493-5585-0); Vol. 2. 59.95 (ISBN 0-8493-5589-3). CRC Pr.
METALS, NONFERROUS
see Nonferrous Metals
METALS, TRANSMUTATION OF
see Alchemy
METALS IN THE BODY
Williams, D. F., ed. Systemic Aspects of Biocompatibility. 1981. Vol. 1. 69.95 (ISBN 0-8493-5585-0); Vol. 2. 59.95 (ISBN 0-8493-5589-3). CRC Pr.
METALWORK
see Metal-Work
METAPHOR
Larson, Kay. Artists' Vehicles & Metaphorical Machinery. (Illus.). 1980. pap. 8.00 (ISBN 0-904540-26-X). U of Pa Contemp Art.
METAPHYSICS
see also Causation; Cosmology; God; Knowledge, Theory Of; Space and Time; Values
Braden, Charles S. Spirits in Rebellion: The Rise & Development of New Thought. LC 63-13245. 584p. 1980. Repr. of 1963 ed. 10.00 (ISBN 0-87074-025-3). SMU Press.
Brungardt, Helen. Contemplation: The Activity of Mystical Consciousness. 2nd ed. 72p. 1980. pap. 3.00 (ISBN 0-87707-220-5). Red Earth.
Collingwood, Robin G. An Essay on Metaphysics. 364p. 1940. 24.95x (ISBN 0-19-824121-6). Oxford U Pr.
Connelly, R. J. Whitehead Vs. Hartshorne: Basic Metaphysical Issues. LC 80-69053. 172p. (Orig.). 1981. lib. bdg. 17.75 (ISBN 0-8191-1420-0); pap. text ed. 9.00 (ISBN 0-8191-1421-9). U Pr of Amer.
Esposito, Joseph L. Evolutionary Metaphysics: The Development of Peirce's Theory of Catagories. LC 80-15736. (Illus.). x, 152p. 1980. 15.00x (ISBN 0-8214-0551-9). Ohio U Pr.
Hegel, Georg W. The Metaphysics of the Jewish, the Aegyptian & the Assyrian Spirit. (Illus.). 109p. 1981. 41.75 (ISBN 0-89266-280-8). Am Classical Coll Pr.
Kant, Immanuel. Grounding for the Metaphysics of Morals. Ellington, James W., tr. from Ger. (HPC Philosophical Classics Ser.). 125p. 1981. lib. bdg. 12.50 (ISBN 0-915145-01-4); pap. text ed. 2.75 (ISBN 0-915145-00-6). Hackett Pub.
Lord Easu. Book of Revelations for the Aquarian Age. Rodehaver, Gladys K., compiled by. (Illus., Orig.). 1980. pap. 6.95 (ISBN 0-930208-19-6). Mangan Bks.
Reuscher, John A. Essays on the Metaphysical Foundation of Personal Identity. LC 80-6067. 111p. 1981. lib. bdg. 16.50 (ISBN 0-8191-1471-5); pap. text ed. 7.25 (ISBN 0-8191-1472-3). U Pr of Amer.
St. John, Gladys. Listening Across the Border. 1981. 8.95 (ISBN 0-533-04797-8). Vantage.
Tuala. Tuala Speaks. Tamalelagi, Jeanne, ed. LC 80-67870. 220p. (Orig.). 1980. pap. 8.95 (ISBN 0-87516-425-0). De Vorss.
METAPHYSICS-DICTIONARIES
Yott, Donald H. Man & Metaphysics. 1980. pap. 5.95 (ISBN 0-87728-488-1). Weiser.
METAPSYCHOLOGY
see Psychical Research
METEORITES
Berger, Melvin. Comets, Meteors & Asteroids. (Illus.). 64p. (gr. 10 up). 1981. PLB 6.99 (ISBN 0-399-61148-7). Putnam.
Keil, Klaus & Gomes, Celso P. Brazilian Stone Meteorites. LC 80-5333. (Illus.). 192p. 1981. 20.00x (ISBN 0-8263-0543-1). U of NM Pr.
Lunar & Planetary Institute, compiled by. Proceedings: Eleventh Lunar & Planetary Science Conference, Houston, Texas, March 17-21, 1980, 3 vols. (Geochimica & Cosmochimica Acta: Suppl. 14). 3000p. 1981. Set. 200.00 (ISBN 0-08-026314-3). Pergamon.
METEOROLOGICAL MAPS
see Meteorology-Charts, Diagrams, etc.
METEOROLOGISTS
Compton, Grant. What Does a Meteorologist Do? (What Do They Do Ser.). (Illus.). 80p. (gr. 5 up). 1981. PLB 5.95 (ISBN 0-396-07931-8). Dodd.
METEOROLOGY
see also Atmosphere; Atomic Energy and Meteorology; Climatology; Droughts; Floods; Rain and Rainfall; Solar Radiation; Sun-Spots; Weather; Weather Control; Weather Forecasting; Winds
also headings beginning with the word Meteorological
Cole, Alan. Introduction to the Atmosphere Lab Manual. 1980. loose leaf shrink wrapped 4.75 (ISBN 0-88252-110-1). Paladin Hse.
Kellogg, William W. & Schware, Robert. Climate Change & Society: Consequences of Increasing Atmospheric Carbon Dioxide. (Special Study Ser.). 170p. (Orig.). 1981. lib. bdg. 15.00x (ISBN 0-86531-179-X); pap. 8.00x (ISBN 0-86531-180-3). Westview.
Murphy, Allan H. & Katz, Richard W., eds. Probability, Statistics, & Decision Making in Meterology. 450p. (Orig.). 1981. lib. bdg. 28.50x (ISBN 0-86531-152-8); pap. text ed. 15.00x (ISBN 0-86531-153-6). Westview.
METEOROLOGY-CHARTS, DIAGRAMS, ETC.
Conversion of Grid-Point Data into Meteorological Maps with a Mini-Computer System. (World Weather Watch Report: No. 37). 27p. 1980. pap. 5.00 (ISBN 0-686-68191-6, W469, WMO). Unipub.
METEOROLOGY-DATA PROCESSING
Conversion of Grid-Point Data into Meteorological Maps with a Mini-Computer System. (World Weather Watch Report: No. 37). 27p. 1980. pap. 5.00 (ISBN 0-686-68191-6, W469, WMO). Unipub.
Manual on the Global Data-Processinng System, Vol. II: Regional Aspects. 74p. 1981. pap. 7.00 (W475, WMO). Unipub.
METEOROLOGY-INTERNATIONAL COOPERATION
World Meteorological Congress, Eighth. Proceedings. 261p. 1980. pap. 30.00 (ISBN 92-63-10547-2, W472, WMO). Unipub.
METEOROLOGY, AGRICULTURAL
see also Crops and Climate
The Economic Value of Agrometeorological Information & Advice. (Technical Note Ser.: No. 164). 52p. 1981. pap. 10.00 (ISBN 92-63-10526-X, W478, WMO). Unipub.
METEOROLOGY AND ATOMIC ENERGY
see Atomic Energy and Meteorology
METEOROLOGY IN AERONAUTICS
Dabberdt, Walter F. The Whole Air Weather Guide. (Illus.). 1976. pap. 3.50 (Pub. by Solstice). Aviation.
Federal Aviation Administration. Aviation Weather. 2nd ed. (Pilot Training Ser.). (Illus.). 219p. 1975. pap. 7.00 (ISBN 0-89100-160-3, E*A-A*C61-006A). Aviation Maintenance.
--Aviation Weather Services. 3rd ed. (Pilot Training Ser.). (Illus.). 123p. 1979. pap. 4.50 (ISBN 0-89100-161-1, E*A-A*C61-0045B). Aviation Maintenance.
Goldfarb, Leo. The Weather Book for Pilots. (Illus.). Date not set. spiral bdg. 8.95 (ISBN 0-911721-72-X, Pub. by Weather Book). Aviation.
METER
see Versification
METER (STANDARD OF LENGTH)
see Metric System
METHOD OF STUDY
see Study, Method Of
METHOD OF WORK
see Work
METHODIST CHURCH
Smith, Warren T. Harry Hosier: United Methodist Circuit Rider. LC 80-54008. 64p. 1980. pap. 2.95x (ISBN 0-8358-0422-4). Upper Room.
METHODIST CHURCH-CLERGY
Bauman, Mark K. Warren Akin Candler: The Conservative As Idealist. LC 80-22230. 290p. 1981. 16.00 (ISBN 0-8108-1368-8). Scarecrow.
METHODOLOGY
see also Analysis (Philosophy); Problem Solving; Research

also subdivision Methodology under special subjects, e.g. Science–methodology; Theology–Methodology
Zallen, Harold & Zellen, Eugenia M. Ideas Plus Dollars: Research Methodology & Funding. 2nd ed. LC 79-55737. (Illus.). 1980. 12.95. Academic World.
METOPOSCOPY
see Physiognomy
METRIC SYSTEM
see also Weights and Measures
Mahoney, Susan & Mills, Richard G. Metric Measurement. LC 76-731369. (Illus.). 1976. pap. text ed. 60.00 (ISBN 0-89290-128-4, 507-SAR-SATC). Soc for Visual.
Managing Metrication in Business & Industry. 203p. 1976. 37.00 (ISBN 0-8247-6469-2). Am Natl.
Metric Conversion in the Construction Industries: Planning, Coordination & Timing. 62p. 1980. 15.00. Am Natl.
Metrication: The Australian Experience. 210p. 1975. 4.00. Am Natl.
Quinn, Daniel & Cook, Emilie C. Beginning Metric Measurement Learning Module. 1974. pap. text ed. 124.00 (ISBN 0-89290-132-2, CM-53). Soc for Visual.
Sohns, Marvin L. & Buffington, Audrey V. El Libro De Medicion. (Illus.). 212p. (Span.). 1980. pap. 9.95 (ISBN 0-86582-029-5). Enrich.
Steinke, Don C. Thirty Days to Metric Mastery: For People Who Hate Math. (Illus., Orig.). 1981. pap. 9.00x (ISBN 0-9605344-0-7). Hse of Charles.
Stevens, B. Teaching the Metric System in the Foreign Language Classroom. (Language in Education Ser.: No. 32). 1980. pap. 4.95 (ISBN 0-87281-131-X). Ctr Appl Ling.
Walker, John R. Exploring Metric Drafting. LC 79-24019. (Illus.). 320p. 1980. text ed. 10.96 (ISBN 0-87006-289-1). Good Heart.
METRICS
see Versification
METRO-GOLDWYN-MAYER, INC.
Carey, Gary. All the Stars in Heaven: The Story of Louis B. Mayer & Metro-Goldwyn-Mayer. (Illus.). 1980. 15.00 (ISBN 0-525-05245-3). Dutton.
METROLOGY
see Mensuration; Weights and Measures
METROPOLITAN AREAS
see also Suburbs; Urban Renewal
also names of metropolitan areas, e.g. Chicago Metropolitan Area
Fiser, Webb S. Mastery of the Metropolis. LC 80-23244. x, 168p. 1981. Repr. of 1962 ed. lib. bdg. 17.50x (ISBN 0-313-22732-2, FIMAM). Greenwood.
METROPOLITAN OPERA
see New York (City)–Metropolitan Opera
METS (BASEBALL CLUB)
see New York Baseball Club (National League, Mets)
MEXICAN AMERICANS
Here are entered works on American citizens of Mexican descent or works concerned with Mexican American minority groups. Works on immigration from Mexico, braceros, etc. are entered under Mexicans in the United States.
see also Mexicans in the United States
Davis, James A. Do People Like Me Have Any Control Over Politics? A Study of the Locus of Political Control As Perceived by Mexican-American Adolescents of South Texas. LC 80-65614. 140p. 1981. perfect bdg. 11.50 (ISBN 0-86548-029-X). Century Twenty One.
De Tevis, Rose, et al, eds. El Oro y el Futuro del Pueblo. (Illus.). 155p. 1979. pap. 5.00 (ISBN 0-918358-11-6). Pajarito Pubns.
Elsasser, Nan, et al. Las Mujeres: Conversations from an Hispanic Community. (Women's Lives - Women's Work Ser.). (Illus.). 192p. (gr. 11-12). 1981. 14.95 (ISBN 0-912670-84-3); pap. 4.95 (ISBN 0-912670-70-3). Feminist Pr.
Mirande, Alfredo & Enriquez, Evangelina. La Chicana: The Mexican-American Woman. LC 79-13536. (Illus.). x, 284p. 1981. pap. 6.95 (ISBN 0-226-53160-0). U of Chicago Pr.
Rosenbaum, Robert J. Mexicano Resistance in the Southwest: The Sacred Right of Self-Preservation. (Illus.). 245p. 1981. text ed. 14.95x (ISBN 0-292-77562-8). U of Tex Pr.
MEXICAN ART
see Art, Mexican
MEXICAN FOLK-LORE
see Folk-Lore, Mexican
MEXICAN LITERATURE
Steiner, Stan & Valdez, Luis, eds. Aztlan: An Anthology of Mexican-American Literature. 416p. Date not set. pap. 3.45 (ISBN 0-394-71770-8, Vin). Random.
MEXICAN LITERATURE–HISTORY AND CRITICISM
Leeder, Ellen L. Justo Sierra Y el Mar. LC 78-58669. (Coleccion Polymita Ser.). 83p. (Orig., Span.). 1979. pap. 6.95 (ISBN 0-89729-202-2). Ediciones.
MEXICAN WAR, 1845-1848
see United States–History–War with Mexico, 1845-1848
MEXICANS IN THE UNITED STATES
see also Mexican Americans
Hansen, Niles. The Border Economy: Regional Development in the Southwest. (Illus.). 208p. 1981. text ed. 17.95x (ISBN 0-292-75061-7); pap. text ed. 8.95x (ISBN 0-292-75063-3). U of Tex Pr.
Pinchot, Jane. Mexicans in America. rev. ed. (In America Bks.). (Illus.). 104p. (gr. 5-11). PLB 5.95. Lerner Pubns.
MEXICO
see also provinces, cities and towns, etc. in Mexico
Unibook Staff. Mexico: The Macmillan Concise Illustrated Encyclopedia. Rubio, Pascal O., 3rd, ed. (Illus.). 416p. 1981. 21.95 (ISBN 0-02-620910-1). Macmillan.
MEXICO–ANTIQUITIES
Parsons, Jeffrey R. Prehistoric Settlement Patterns in the Southern Valley of Mexico: The Chalco-Xochimilco Region. (Memoir Ser.: No. 14). (Orig.). 1981. pap. write for info. (ISBN 0-932206-88-3). U Mich Mus Anthro.
MEXICO–BIOGRAPHY
Babb, Jewel. Border Healing Woman: The Story of Jewel Babb. 152p. 1981. text ed. 14.95 (ISBN 0-292-70729-0); pap. 5.95 (ISBN 0-292-70730-4). U of Tex Pr.
MEXICO–DESCRIPTION AND TRAVEL
Baxter, Robert. Baxter's Mexico. 1981. 9.95 (ISBN 0-913384-42-9). Rail-Europe-Baxter.
Lanier, Alison R. Update -- Mexico. (Country Orientation Ser.). 150p. (Orig.). 1980. pap. text ed. 25.00 (ISBN 0-933662-25-4). Intercult Pr.
Miller, Tom. On the Border: Portraits of America's Southwestern Frontier. LC 79-2631. 224p. 1981. 10.95 (ISBN 0-06-013039-3, HarpT). Har-Row.
Shawcross, Mike. San Cristobal de las Casas, Chiapas: City & Area Guide. 3rd ed. (Illus.). 74p. 1980. pap. 4.95 (ISBN 0-933982-16-X). Bradt Ent.
MEXICO–ECONOMIC CONDITIONS
Solis, Leopoldo. Economic Policy Reform in Mexico: A Case Study for Developing Countries. LC 80-26937. (Pergamon Press Series on International Development). 225p. 1981. 25.00 (ISBN 0-08-026330-5). Pergamon.
Tenkte, Adriann & Wallace, Robert B. Protection & Development in Mexico. 1980. 35.00 (ISBN 0-312-65217-8). St Martin.
MEXICO–HISTORY
Lieuwen, Edwin. Mexican Militarism: The Political Rise & Fall of the Revolutionary Army, 1910-1940. LC 80-28937. (Illus.). xiii, 194p. 1981. Repr. of 1968 ed. lib. bdg. 23.50x (ISBN 0-313-22911-2, LIMM). Greenwood.
Powell, T. G. Mexico & the Spanish Civil War. 240p. 1981. 17.50x (ISBN 0-8263-0546-6). U of NM Pr.
Quirk, Robert E. The Mexican Revolution, Nineteen Fourteen to Nineteen Fifteen: The Convention of Aquascalientes. LC 80-28130. 325p. 1981. Repr. of 1960 ed. lib. bdg. 27.50x (ISBN 0-313-22894-9, QUMR). Greenwood.
Rodman, Selden. A Short History of Mexico. rev. ed. LC 80-6151. 264p. 1981. 14.95 (ISBN 0-8128-2808-9). Stein & Day.
MEXICO–HISTORY–FICTION
Leonard, Irving A. Baroque Times in Old Mexico: Seventeenth-Century Persons, Places, & Practices. LC 80-29256. (Illus.). xi, 260p. 1981. Repr. of 1978 ed. lib. bdg. 25.50x (ISBN 0-313-22826-4, LEBT). Greenwood.
MEXICO–HISTORY–TO 1519
Bandelier, Adolph F. The Discovery of New Mexico by the Franciscan Monk Friar Marcos de Niza in 1539. Rodack, Madeleine T., tr. from Fr. LC 80-25083. 1981. 10.95x (ISBN 0-8165-0717-1). U of Ariz Pr.
MEXICO–HISTORY–WAR WITH UNITED STATES, 1845-1848
see United States–History–War with Mexico, 1845-1848
MEXICO–POPULATION
Cook, Sherburne F. & Borah, Woodrow. Essays in Population History, 3 vols. Incl. Vols. 1 & 2. Mexico & the Caribbean. 1971. 27.50x ea. Vol. 1 (ISBN 0-520-01764-1). Vol. 2 (ISBN 0-520-02272-6); Vol. 3. Mexico & California. 1979. 25.00x (ISBN 0-520-03560-7). U of Cal Pr.
Silvers, Arthur & Crosson, Pierre R. Rural Development & Urban Bound Migration in Mexico. LC 80-8024. (Resources for the Future Research Ser.: Paper R-17). (Illus.). 160p. (Orig.). 1980. pap. text ed. 6.95x (ISBN 0-8018-2493-1). Johns Hopkins.
MEXICO–SOCIAL CONDITIONS
Vanderwood, Paul J. Disorder & Progress: Bandits, Police, & Mexican Development. LC 80-22345. (Illus.). xx, 269p. 1981. 19.95x (ISBN 0-8032-4651-X, Bison); pap. 7.95 (ISBN 0-8032-9600-2, BB 767). U of Nebr Pr.
MEXICO–SOCIAL LIFE AND CUSTOMS
Calvert, Peter. The Mexicans: How They Live & Work. LC 74-17467. 168p. 1975. text ed. 8.95 (ISBN 0-03-029696-X, HoltC). HR&W.
Oehler, Mike. One Mexican Sunday. LC 80-82949. (Illus.). 112p. 1980. 8.50 (ISBN 0-9604464-1-9). Mole Pub Co.
MEXICO (CITY)–DESCRIPTION
Carlson, Loraine. The TraveLeer Guide to Mexico City. 2nd ed. LC 80-26850. (Illus.). 220p. 1981. pap. 4.50 (ISBN 0-932554-02-4). Upland Pr.
MEYERBEER, GIACOMO, 1791-1864
Blaze De Bury, Ange H. Meyerbeer et Son Temps. LC 80-2257. 1981. Repr. of 1865 ed. 40.50 (ISBN 0-404-18813-3). AMS Pr.
MIAMI
Blum, Ethel. Miami Alive. 1981. pap. 5.95 (ISBN 0-935572-09-0). Alive Pubns.
MIAMI INDIANS
see Indians of North America–Eastern States
MICE–LEGENDS AND STORIES
Baker, Betty. Danby & George. LC 80-15707. (Illus.). 64p. (gr. 3-5). 1981. 7.95 (ISBN 0-688-80289-3); PLB 7.63 (ISBN 0-688-84289-5). Greenwillow.
MICHELANGELO (BUONARROTI, MICHELANGELO), 1475-1564
Hickey, Dave, et al, eds. Michelangelo Pistoletto. (Illus.). 1980. pap. 5.00. Inst for the Arts.
Phillips, Evelyn M. The Illustrated Guidebook to the Frescoes in the Sistine Chapel. (Illus.). 124p. 1981. Repr. of 1901 ed. 49.85 (ISBN 0-89901-029-6). Found Class Reprints.
MICHELANGELO (BUONARROTI, MICHELANGELO), 1475-1564–FICTION
Michelangelo. Life Drawings of Michelangelo. (Dover Art Library). (Illus.). 1980. pap. 2.00 (ISBN 0-486-23876-8). Dover.
MICHIGAN
see also names of cities, counties, etc. in Michigan
Meek, Forrest B. Michigan's Heartland. Date not set. 14.50 (ISBN 0-9602472-0-3). Edgewood.
MICHIGAN–DESCRIPTION AND TRAVEL
Cook, Louis & Shangle, Robert D. Beautiful: Michigan Country. (Illus.). 72p. 1980. 14.95 (ISBN 0-89802-203-7); pap. 7.95 (ISBN 0-89802-204-5). Beautiful Am.
Daniel, Glenda & Sullivan, Jerry. A Sierra Club Naturlist's Guide to the North Woods of Michigan, Wisconsin, & Minnesota. (Naturalist's Guide Ser.). (Illus.). 384p. 1981. 24.95 (ISBN 0-87156-248-0); pap. 9.95 (ISBN 0-87156-277-4). Sierra.
MICHIGAN–ECONOMIC CONDITIONS
Michigan Statistical Abstract: 1980. 15th ed. LC 56-62855. (MSU Business Studies). 1980. pap. 10.95. Mich St U Busn.
MICHIGAN–HISTORY
Boyum, Burton H., ed. The Mather Mine, Negaunee & Ishpeming Michigan. LC 79-89638. 1979. 18.95 (ISBN 0-938746-04-9). Marquette Cnty.
Meek, Forrest B. Michigan's Timber Battleground. 2nd ed. 483p. lib. bdg. 9.95 softcover sewn binding (ISBN 0-9602472-1-1). Edgewood.
MICHIGAN–JUVENILE LITERATURE
Parker, Lois & McConnell, David. A Little Peoples' Beginning on Michigan. (Illus.). 32p. (Orig.). (gr. 1-2). 1981. pap. 2.75 (ISBN 0-910726-06-X). Hillsdale Educ.
MICRO COMPUTERS
see Microcomputers
MICROBES
see Bacteria; Bacteriology; Germ Theory of Disease; Micro-Organisms; Viruses
MICROBIAL DISEASES IN ANIMALS
see Veterinary Microbiology
MICROBIAL DISEASES IN MAN
see Medical Microbiology
MICROBIAL DRUG RESISTANCE
see Drug Resistance in Micro-Organisms
MICROBIAL ENERGY CONVERSION
see Biomass Energy
MICROBIAL GENETICS
see also Drug Resistance in Micro-Organisms
Bainbridge, Brian W. The Genetics of Microbes. (Tertiary Level Biology Ser.). 204p. 1980. pap. 30.95x (ISBN 0-470-26995-2). Halsted Pr.
MICROBIOLOGY
see also Bacteriology; Industrial Microbiology; Marine Microbiology; Micro-Organisms; Microscope and Microscopy; Veterinary Microbiology; Virology
Arber, W., et al, eds. Current Topics in Microbiology & Immunology, Vol. 90. (Illus.). 147p. 1980. 51.90 (ISBN 0-387-10181-0). Springer-Verlag.
Brenner, S., et al, eds. New Horizons in Industrial Microbiology: Philosophical Transactions of the Royal Society, 1980. rev. ed. (Ser. B: Vol. 290). (Illus.). 152p. text ed. 47.50x (ISBN 0-85403-146-4, Pub. by Dechema Germany). Scholium Intl.
Buffaloe, Neal D. & Ferguson, Dale V. Microbiology. 2nd ed. (Illus.). 752p. 1981. text ed. 20.95 (ISBN 0-395-29649-8); write for info. lab manual (ISBN 0-395-29652-8); write for info. instr's manual (ISBN 0-395-29650-1); write for info. set study guide (ISBN 0-395-29651-X). HM.
Christensen, Mary L. Microbiology for Nursing & Allied Health Students. (Illus.). 624p. write for info. (ISBN 0-398-04176-8). C C Thomas.
Collins, C. H. Microbiology Hazards. 1981. text ed. price not set (ISBN 0-408-10650-6). Butterworth.
Daumeister, W., ed. Electron Microscopy at Molecular Dimensions. (Proceedings in Life Sciences). (Illus.). 300p. 1980. 57.90 (ISBN 0-387-10131-4). Springer-Verlag.
Davis, Bernard D. Microbiology. (Illus.). 1274p. 1980. 39.50 (ISBN 0-06-140691-0, Harper Medical). Har-Row.
DECHMA, Deutsche Gesellschaft Fuer Chemisches Apparatewesen E. V., ed. Microbiology Applied to Technology: Proceedings XIIth International Congress of Microbiology. (DECHEMA Monographs: Vol. 83). 230p. (Orig.). 1979. pap. text ed. 25.80 (ISBN 3-527-10766-5). Verlag Chemie.
Erlich. Geomicrobiology. Date not set. price not set (ISBN 0-8247-1183-1). Dekker.
Glover, S. W. & Hopwood, D. A., eds. Genetics As a Tool in Microbiology. (Society for General Microbiology Symposium: No. 31). (Illus.). 450p. Date not set. text ed. price not set (ISBN 0-521-23748-3). Cambridge U Pr.
Norton, Cynthia F. Microbiology. LC 80-23350. (Life Sciences Ser.). (Illus.). 850p. 1981. text ed. 19.95 (ISBN 0-201-05304-7). A-W.
OAS Gerneral Secretariat Department of Scientific & Technological Affairs. Principios Generales De Microbiologia: Serie De Biologia No. 7. 2nd ed. (Biology Ser.: No. 7). 143p. 1980. text ed. 2.00 (ISBN 0-8270-1097-4). OAS.
Pelczar, Michael, Jr. & Chan, E. C. S. Elements of Microbiology. 1st ed. (Illus.). 704p. (Orig.). text ed. 19.95 (ISBN 0-07-049240-9, C); 10.95 (ISBN 0-07-049241-7); instrs'. 5.50 (ISBN 0-07-049230-1). McGraw.
Perlman, D. & Laskin, A. I., eds. Advances in Applied Microbiology, Vol. 27. (Serial Publication). 1981. 26.00 (ISBN 0-12-002627-9). Acad Pr.
Rapid Methods & Automation in Microbiology & Immunology: A Bibliography. 250p. 24.00 (ISBN 0-904147-07-X). Info Retrieval.
Reed, Gerald. Prescott & Dunn's Industrial Microbiology. 4th ed. (Illus.). 1981. lib. bdg. 59.00 (ISBN 0-87055-374-7). AVI.
Schlessinger, David, ed. Microbiology Nineteen Eighty. (Illus.). 1980. text ed. 22.00 (ISBN 0-914826-23-9). Am Soc Microbio.
--Microbiology, Nineteen Eighty-One. (Illus.). 1981. 22.00 (ISBN 0-914826-31-X). Am Soc Microbio.
--Microbiology Nineteen Seventy-Nine. (Illus.). 1979. text ed. 22.00 (ISBN 0-914826-20-4). Am Soc Microbio.
Seeley, Harry W., Jr. & VanDemark, Paul J. Selected Exercises from Microbes in Action: A Laboratory Manual of Microbiology. 3rd ed. (Illus.). 1981. price not set (ISBN 0-7167-1260-1). W H Freeman.
MICROBIOLOGY–LABORATORY MANUALS
Seeley, Harry W., Jr. & VanDemark, Paul J. Microbes in Action: A Laboratory Manual of Microbiology. 3rd ed. (Illus.). 1981. write for info. (ISBN 0-7167-1259-8); instrs'. manual avail. W H Freeman.
Segel, W. & Wheelis, M. Laboratory Manual to Introduction to the Microbial World. 1980. pap. 8.95 (ISBN 0-13-488031-5). P-H.
MICROBIOLOGY–TECHNIQUES
Brenner, S., et al, eds. New Horizons in Industrial Microbiology: Philosophical Transactions of the Royal Society, 1980. rev. ed. (Ser. B: Vol. 290). (Illus.). 152p. text ed. 47.50x (ISBN 0-85403-146-4, Pub. by Dechema Germany). Scholium Intl.
MICROBIOLOGY, MEDICAL
see Medical Microbiology
MICROCIRCULATION
Advances in Diagnosis & Therapy, Muenchen, November 1980. Congress on Microcirculation & Ischemic Vascular Diseases. Messmer, K. & Fagrell, B., eds. (Illus.). 240p. 1981. pap. 24.00 (ISBN 3-8055-2417-X). S Karger.
Effros, Richard, et al, eds. The Microcirculation: Current Concepts. 1981. write for info. (ISBN 0-12-232560-5). Acad Pr.
Gaehtgens, P., ed. Recent Advances in Microcirculatory Research. (Bibliotheca Anatomica Ser.: No. 20). (Illus.). xiv, 746p. 1980. soft cover 149.25 (ISBN 3-8055-2272-X). S Karger.
MICROCOMPUTERS
Bursky, Dave. Components for Microcomputer System Design. 272p. 1980. pap. 11.95 (ISBN 0-8104-0975-5). Hayden.
Clark, James H. Take AIM, Vol. 1. 416p. (Orig.). pap. text ed. 16.95 (ISBN 0-686-69549-6). Matrix Pubns.
Computerist Inc. All of Micro Vol. 2: The 6502 Journal No. 7-12 Oct-Nov 78 - May 79. Tripp, Robert M., ed. (Illus.). 8.00 (ISBN 0-938222-01-5). Computerist.
--The Best of Micro, Vol. 1. Tripp, Robert M., et al, eds. (Illus.). 176p. (Orig.). 1978. pap. 6.00 (ISBN 0-938222-00-7). Computerist.
Electronics Magazine. Microprocessors & Microcomputers: One-Chip Controllers to High-End Systems. Capece, Raymond P. & Posa, John G., eds. LC 80-11816. (Illus.). 484p. 1980. 24.50 (ISBN 0-07-019141-7, R-011); pap. text ed. 14.95 (ISBN 0-07-606670-3). McGraw.
Freiberger, Stephen & Chew, Paul, Jr. A Consumer's Guide to Personal Computing & Microcomputers. 2nd ed. 208p. 1980. pap. 8.95 (ISBN 0-8104-5116-6). Hayden.
Kraft, George D. & Toy, Wing N. Microprogrammed Control & Reliable Design of Small Computers. (Illus.). 248p. 1981. text ed. 21.95 (ISBN 0-13-581140-6). P-H.
Micro Ink, Inc. The Best of Micro: June 1979 to May 1980, Vol. 3. Tripp, Robert M., ed. (The Best of Micro Ser.). (Illus.). 320p. (Orig.). 1980. pap. 10.00 (ISBN 0-938222-03-1). Computerist.
--The Best of Micro: June 1980 to May 1981, Vol.4. Tripp, Robert M., ed. (The Best of Micro Ser.). (Illus.). Date not set. pap. price not set (ISBN 0-938222-04-X). Computerist.
--The Best of Micro: Vol. 2, Oct-Nov 78 to May 79. Tripp, Robert M., ed. (Illus.). 224p. (Orig.). pap. 8.00 (ISBN 0-938222-02-3). Computerist.

Osborne, A., et al. Micro Systems in Business. (Micro Monograph Ser.: No. 1). 122p. 1980. pap. text ed. 27.00x (ISBN 0-903796-63-5, Pub. by Online Conferences England). Renouf.
Poirot, James L. Microcomputer Systems & Applied BASIC. (Illus.). 150p. (Orig.). (gr. 6-12). 1980. pap. 8.95 (ISBN 0-88408-136-2). Sterling Swift.
Spohr, Mark. Physician's Guide to Microcomputers. 1981. 18.95 (ISBN 0-8359-5548-6). Reston.
Wakerly, John F. Microcomputer Architecture & Programming. 600p. 1981. text ed. 23.95 (ISBN 0-471-05232-9). Wiley.
Weber, J. R. How to Use Your Apple II Computer. LC 80-70465. (IDM's How to Use Your Microcomputer Ser.). 250p. (gr. 10-12). 1981. 19.95 (ISBN 0-938862-02-2); pap. 14.95 (ISBN 0-938862-03-0). Five Arms Corp.
--How to Use Your PET Computer. (IDM's How to Use Your Microcomputer Ser.). 250p. (gr. 10-12). 1981. 14.95 (ISBN 0-9604892-7-4); pap. 12.95 (ISBN 0-9604892-8-2). Five Arms Corp.
--How to Use Your TRS-80 Model II Computer. LC 80-70467. (IDM's How to Use Your Microcomputer Ser.). 250p. (gr. 10-12). 1981. 19.95 (ISBN 0-938862-00-6); pap. 14.95 (ISBN 0-938862-01-4). Five Arms Corp.
Wordsworth, Nat. Understanding Microcomputers & Small Computer Systems. (Da Capo Quality Paperbacks Ser.). (Illus.). 312p. 1981. pap. 8.95 (ISBN 0-306-80143-4). Da Capo.

MICROECONOMICS
see also Managerial Economics
Chisholm, Roger & McCarty, Marilu. Principles of Microeconomics. 2nd ed. 1981. pap. text ed. 10.95x (ISBN 0-673-15402-5). Scott F.
De Meza, David & Osborne, Michael. Problems in Price Theory. LC 80-16597. (Illus.). xiv, 302p. 1980. lib. bdg. 25.00 (ISBN 0-226-14293-0). U of Chicago Pr.
Farquhar, J. D. & Heidensohn, K. The Market Economy. 160p. 18.00x (ISBN 0-86003-004-0, Pub. by Allan Pubs England); pap. 9.00x (ISBN 0-86003-103-9). State Mutual Bk.
Fels, et al. Casebook of Economic, Microeconomic Problems & Policies: Practice in Thinking. 4th ed. 112p. 1978. 5.95 (ISBN 0-8299-0479-4); staff notes avail. West Pub.
Gisser, Micha. Intermediate Price Theory: Analysis, Issues & Applications. (Illus.). 608p. 1981. text ed. 17.95 (ISBN 0-07-023312-8, C); instructor's manual 4.95 (ISBN 0-07-023313-6). McGraw.
Gravelle, H. & Rees, R. Microeconomics. 2nd ed. (Modern Economic Series). (Illus.). 1981. pap. text ed. 25.00 (ISBN 0-582-44075-0). Longman.
Heilbroner, R. & Thorou, L. Understanding Microeconomics. 5th ed. 1981. pap. 10.95 (ISBN 0-13-936567-2); pap. 7.95 study guide (ISBN 0-13-233296-5). P-H.
Mahanty, Aroop K. Intermediate Microeconomics with Applications. 1980. 17.95 (ISBN 0-12-465150-X). Acad Pr.
Nicholson. Microeconomic Theory. 2nd ed. 1978. 21.95 (ISBN 0-03-020831-9). Dryden Pr.
Redman, John C. & Redman, Barbara J. Microeconomics: Resource Allocation & Price Theory. (Illus.). 1981. text ed. 17.50 (ISBN 0-87055-367-4). AVI.
Watson, Donald S. & Getz, Malcolm. Price Theory in Action. 4th ed. 448p. 1981. pap. text ed. 9.95 (ISBN 0-395-30058-4); write for info. instr's manual (ISBN 0-395-30057-6). HM.

MICROELECTRONICS
see also Integrated Circuits; Miniature Electronic Equipment
Berting, Jan, et al, eds. The Socio-Economic Impact of Microelectronics: International Conference on Socio-Economic Problems & Potentialities of Microelectronics, Sept. 1979, Zandvoort, Netherlands. LC 80-49810. (Vienna Centre Ser.). (Illus.). 263p. 1980. 50.00 (ISBN 0-08-026776-9). Pergamon.
Bessant, J. R., et al. The Impact of Microelectronics: A Review of the Literature. LC 80-54414. (Illus.). 174p. 1981. text ed. 25.00 (ISBN 0-87663-729-2, Pica Special Studies). Universe.
Green, K. & Coombs, Rod. The Effects of Microelectronic Technologies on Employment Prospects. 240p. 1980. text ed. 36.75x (ISBN 0-566-00418-6, Pub. by Gower Pub Co England). Renouf.
Jowett, C. E. Application of Engineering in Microelectronic Industries. 184p. 1975. text ed. 22.00x (ISBN 0-220-66278-9, Pub. by Busn Bks England). Renouf.
McLean, J. Michael. The Impact of the Microelectronics Industry on the Structure of the Canadian Economy. 50p. 1979. pap. text ed. 3.00x (ISBN 0-920380-22-0, Pub. by Inst Res Pub Canada). Renouf.
Norman, Colin. Microelectronics at Work: Productivity & Jobs in the World Economy. LC 80-53425. (Worldwatch Papers). 1980. pap. 2.00 (ISBN 0-916468-38-0). Worldwatch Inst.
Swords-Isherwood, N. Microelectronics of the Engineering Industry. 300p. 1980. 32.50x (ISBN 0-89397-094-8). Nichols Pub.
Vears. Microelectronics Systems One: Checkbook. 1981. text ed. price not set (ISBN 0-408-00552-1). Butterworth.

MICROELEMENTS
see Trace Elements

MICROFILMS
Baumann, Roland & Wallace, Diane S. Guide to the Microfilm Collections in the Pennsylvania State Archives. 117p. 1980. pap. 5.00 (ISBN 0-89271-013-6). Pa Hist & Mus.
Index to the Guide to the Microfilm of the Records of Pennsylvania's Revolutionary Governments. 77p. 1980. pap. 3.50 (ISBN 0-89271-012-8). Pa Hist & Must.

MICROFORMS
see also Microfilms
Bahr, Alice H. Microforms: The Librarians' View, 1980-1981. 3rd ed. (Professional Librarian Ser.). (Illus.). 135p. 1981. pap. text ed. 24.50 (ISBN 0-914236-70-9). Knowledge Indus.

MICROGRAPHIC ANALYSIS
see Metallography; Microscope and Microscopy

MICROMINIATURIZATION (ELECTRONICS)
see Microelectronics; Miniature Electronic Equipment

MICRONESIA
Waldo, Myra. Myra Waldo's Travel Guide to the South Pacific, 1981. (Illus.). 360p. 1981. pap. 8.95 (ISBN 0-02-098920-2, Collier). Macmillan.

MICRO-ORGANISMS
see also Bacteria; Fungi; Microbiology; Microscope and Microscopy; Protozoa; Soil Micro-Organisms; Viruses
O'Day, D. H. & Horgen, P. A., eds. Sexual Interactions in Eukaryotic Microbes. LC 80-39593. (Cell Biology Ser.). 1981. 45.00 (ISBN 0-12-524160-7). Acad Pr.
Sebek, O. K. & Laskin, A. I., eds. Genetics of Industrial Microorganisms. (Illus.). 1979. 12.00 (ISBN 0-914826-19-0). Am Soc Microbio.

MICROPHONE
Eargle, John. The Microphone Handbook. 1980. write for info. Elar Pub Co.

MICROPROCESSORS
Auslander, David & Sagues, Paul. Microprocessors for Measurement & Control. 300p. (Orig.). 1981. pap. 15.99 (ISBN 0-931988-57-8). Osborne-McGraw.
Banerji, Dilip & Raymond, Jacque. Elements of Microprogramming. (Illus.). 416p. 1981. text ed. 24.50 (ISBN 0-13-267146-8). P-H.
Brunner, Herb. Introduction to Microprocessors. 1981. text ed. 17.95 (ISBN 0-8359-3247-8); instr's. manual free (ISBN 0-8359-3248-6). Reston.
Bursky, Dave. Microprocessor Systems Design & Applications. 192p. pap. 9.95 (ISBN 0-8104-0976-3). Hayden.
Chattergy, Rahul & Pooch, Udo. Sixteen-Bit Microprocessors. 256p. 1982. text ed. 19.95 (ISBN 0-8359-7003-5). Reston.
Coffron, James W. Practical Troubleshooting for Microprocessors. (Illus.). 256p. 1981. text ed. 19.95 (ISBN 0-13-694273-3). P-H.
Davis, Thomas. Experimentation with Microprocessor Applications. (Orig.). 1980. pap. text ed. 9.95 (ISBN 0-8359-1812-2). Reston.
Electronics Magazine. Microprocessors & Microcomputers: One-Chip Controllers to High-End Systems. Capece, Raymond P. & Posa, John G., eds. LC 80-11816. (Illus.). 484p. 1980. 24.50 (ISBN 0-07-019141-7, R-011); pap. text ed. 14.95 (ISBN 0-07-606670-3). McGraw.
Fiore, Vito, et al. Sixty-Eight Hundred Family Book. 1982. text ed. 14.95 (ISBN 0-8359-7005-1). Reston.
Ghani, Noordin & Farrell, Edward. Microprocessor System Debugging. (Computer Engineering Ser.). 160p. 1981. 28.00 (ISBN 0-471-27860-2, Pub. by Wiley-Interscience). Wiley.
Gilmore, Charles M. Introduction to Microprocessors. LC 80-26115. (Basic Skills in Electricity & Electronics). 320p. 1981. pap. 14.96. McGraw.
--Introduction to Microprocessors: Activities Manual. (Basic Skills in Electricity & Electronics Ser.). 96p. 1981. lab manual 8.96 (ISBN 0-07-023302-0). McGraw.
Gise, Peter. Microprocessor Interfacing. 288p. 1982. text ed. 19.95 (ISBN 0-8359-4364-X). Reston.
Hall, Douglas V. & Hall, Marybelle B. Experiments in Microprocessors & Digital Systems. (Illus.). 176p. 1981. 7.95x (ISBN 0-07-025576-8, G). McGraw.
Kraft, George D. & Toy, Wing N. Microprogrammed Control & Reliable Design of Small Computers. (Illus.). 248p. 1981. text ed. 21.95 (ISBN 0-13-581140-6). P-H.
Morse, Stephen P. The Eighty Eighty-Six Primer: An Introduction to Its Architecture, System Design & Programming. 224p. 1980. pap. 9.95 (ISBN 0-8104-5165-4). Hayden.
Muchow, Kenneth & Deem, Bill. Microprocessor Principles, Programming & Interfacing. 1982. text ed. 18.95 (ISBN 0-8359-4383-6); instrs.' manual avail. (ISBN 0-8359-4384-4). Reston.
National Computing Centre. High-Level Languages for Microprocessor Projects. Taylor, David & Morgan, Lyndon, eds. (Illus.). 279p. (Orig.). 1980. pap. 37.50x (ISBN 0-85012-233-3). Intl Pubns Serv.
Nichols, K. G. Microprocessors: Theory & Practice. (Computer Systems Engineering Ser.). 1981. text ed. price not set (ISBN 0-8448-1384-2). Crane-Russak Co.
Olesky, J. & Rutkowski, G. Microprocessors & Digital Computer Technology. 1981. 22.95 (ISBN 0-13-581116-3). P-H.
Osborne, Adam. The Osborne Four & Eight Bit Microprocessor Handbook. 600p. 1981. pap. text ed. 19.95 (ISBN 0-931988-42-X). Osborne-McGraw.
--The Osborne Sixteen-Bit Microprocessor Handbook. 500p. 1981. pap. 19.95 (ISBN 0-931988-43-8). Osborne-McGraw.
--The Sixty-Eight Thousand Microprocessor Handbook. 200p. (Orig.). 1981. pap. 6.99 (ISBN 0-931988-41-1). Osborne-McGraw.
Rutkowski, George B. & Olesky, Jerome E. Microprocessor & Digital Computer Technology. (Illus.). 416p. 1981. text ed. 22.95 (ISBN 0-13-581116-3). P-H.
Schindler, Max. Microprocessor Software Design. 304p. 1980. pap. 13.25 (ISBN 0-8104-5190-5). Hayden.
Streitmatter, Gene. Microprocessor Software: Programming Concepts & Techniques. (Illus.). 400p. 1981. text ed. 17.95 (ISBN 0-8359-4375-5). Reston.
Taub, Herbert. Digital Circuits & Microprocessors. (Electrical Engineering Ser.). (Illus.). 608p. 1981. text ed. 26.95x (ISBN 0-07-062945-5, C); solutions manual 12.95 (ISBN 0-07-062946-3). McGraw.
Weisbecker, Joe. Home Computers Can Make You Rich. 1980. pap. 6.50 (ISBN 0-8104-5177-8). Hayden.

MICROPUBLICATIONS
see Microforms

MICRORADIOGRAPHY
Mueller, G. Mikroradiographische Untersuchungen Zur Mineralisation der Knochen Fruehgeborener und Junger Saeuglinge, 1980. (Journal: Acta Anatomica: Vol. 108, Suppl. 64). (Illus.). iv, 44p. 1980. pap. 27.00 (ISBN 3-8055-1719-X). S Karger.

MICROSCOPE AND MICROSCOPY
see also Electron Microscope; Histology; Microbiology; Microscopy, Medical; X-Ray Microscope
American Microscopical Society Symposium, 1980. Artificial Substrates: Proceedings. Cairns, John, Jr., ed. 1981. text ed. price not set. Ann Arbor Science.
Becker, R. P. & Johari, O. Scanning Electron Microscopy 1980, No. II. LC 72-626068. (Illus.). xiv, 658p. 50.00 (ISBN 0-931288-12-6). Scanning Electron.
Craig, James R. & Vaughan, David J. Ore Microscopy. 325p. 1981. 32.95 (ISBN 0-471-08596-0, Pub. by Wiley-Interscience). Wiley.
Hall, Cecil E. Introduction to Electron Microscopy. 2nd ed. LC 80-39788. 410p. 1981. Repr. of 1966 ed. lib. bdg. price not set (ISBN 0-89874-302-8). Krieger.
Johari, Om & Becker, R. P., eds. Scanning Electron Microscopy 1980, No. III. LC 72-62608. (Illus.). xx, 670p. 50.00 (ISBN 0-931288-13-4). Scanning Electron.
Loquin & Langeron. Microscopy Handbook. 1981. text ed. price not set. Butterworth.
Marmasse, Claude. Microscopes & Their Uses. 329p. 1980. 20.00 (ISBN 0-677-05510-2). Gordon.
Stoiber, Richard E. & Morse, Stearns A. Microscopic Identification of Crystals. 286p. 1981. Repr. of 1972 ed. lib. bdg. 16.50 (ISBN 0-89874-276-5). Krieger.
Turner, Gerard L. Collecting Microscopes. (The Christies International Collectors Ser.). (Illus.). 128p. 1980. 14.95 (ISBN 0-8317-5950-X). Mayflower Bks.
Wischnitzer, Saul. Introduction to Electron Microscopy. 3rd ed. LC 80-15266. 320p. 1980. 19.75 (ISBN 0-08-026298-8). Pergamon.

MICROSCOPIC ANALYSIS
see Metallography; Microscope and Microscopy

MICROSCOPIC ANATOMY
see Histology

MICROSCOPIC ORGANISMS
see Micro-Organisms

MICROSCOPY, MEDICAL
see also Microsurgery
Electron Microscopy in Human Medicine, Vol. 7: Digestive System. (Electron Microscopy in Human Medicine Ser.). 250p. 1980. 58.00 (ISBN 0-07-032507-3, HP). McGraw.

MICROSURGERY
Peerless, S. & McCormick, C. W., eds. Microsurgery for Cerebral Ischemia. (Illus.). 362p. 1981. 89.80 (ISBN 0-387-90495-6). Springer-Verlag.

MICROWAVE AMPLIFICATION BY STIMULATED EMISSION OF RADIATION
see Masers

MICROWAVE AMPLIFICATION BY VARIABLE REACTANCE
see Parametric Amplifiers

MICROWAVE COOKERY
Chalpin, Lila. A New Look at Microwave Cooking. 1981. 8.95 (ISBN 0-916752-04-6). Green Hill.
Clark, Diane. Diane Clark's Microwave Cookbook. 1981. 14.95 (ISBN 0-8015-2023-1, Hawthorn). Dutton.
Farm Journal Food Editors. Farm Journal's Country-Style Microwave Cookbook. 128p. (Orig.). 1980. pap. 3.50x. Farm Journal.
Favorite Recipes from the Microwave Times. (Illus.). 1980. 6.95 (ISBN 0-918620-20-1). Recipes Unltd.
Litton. Microwave Cooking on a Diet. 160p. 1981. 10.95 (ISBN 0-442-24526-2). Van Nos Reinhold.
Sabin, A. Ross, ed. Range Service (Gas, Electric, Microwave) (Illus.). 253p. (gr. 11). 1979. 20.00 (ISBN 0-938336-06-1). Whirlpool.
Schur, Sylvia. The Tappan Creative Cookbook for Microwave Ovens & Ranges. 1981. pap. 2.95 (ISBN 0-451-09742-4, Sig). NAL.
Sunset Editors. Microwave Cook Book. 2nd ed. LC 80-53481. (Illus.). 1981. pap. 3.95 (ISBN 0-376-02504-2, Sunset Books). Sunset-Lane.
Wheeler, Grace. Microwave Cooking My Way. new ed. LC 80-53591. 240p. 1980. 7.95 (ISBN 0-914488-25-2). Rand-Tofua.
--Microwave Cooking My Way: It's a Matter of Time. Rand, Elizabeth, ed. LC 80-53591. (Illus.). 240p. 1981. plastic comb bound 7.95 (ISBN 0-914488-25-2). Rand-Tofua.

MICROWAVE DEVICES
see also Masers; Parametric Amplifiers
Fox, J., ed. Microwave Research Institute Symposia. Incl. Vol. 1. Modern Network Synthesis. 1952. 19.95 (ISBN 0-470-27093-4); Vol. 4. Modern Advances in Microwave Techniques. LC 55-12897. 1955. o.p. (ISBN 0-470-27192-2); Vol. 5. Modern Network Synthesis. LC 56-2590. 1956. o.p. (ISBN 0-470-27225-2); Vol. 6. Nonlinear Circuit Analysis. LC 55-3575. 1956. o.p. (ISBN 0-470-27258-9); Vol. 9. Millimeter Waves. LC 60-10073. 1960. o.p. (ISBN 0-470-27357-7); Vol. 11. Electromagnetics & Fluid Dynamics of Gaseaous Plasma. LC 62-13174. 1962. 25.95 (ISBN 0-470-27423-9); Vol. 13. Optical Lasers. LC 63-22084. o.p. (ISBN 0-470-27428-X); Vol. 15. System Theory. LC 65-28522. 1965. 26.50 (ISBN 0-470-27430-1); Vol. 17. Modern Optics. LC 67-31757. 1967. o.p. (ISBN 0-470-27433-6); Vol. 19. Computer Processing in Communications. LC 77-122632. 1970. o.p. (ISBN 0-471-27436-4); Vol. 20. Submillimeter Waves. 1971. o.p. (ISBN 0-471-27437-2); Vol. 21. Computers & Automata. 1972. 33.95 (ISBN 0-471-27438-0); Vol. 22. Computer Communications. 1972. 37.95 (ISBN 0-471-27439-9); Vol. 24. Computer Software Engineering. 1977. 44.95 (ISBN 0-470-98948-3). Pub. by Wiley-Interscience). Wiley.
Gandhi, Om P. Microwave Engineering & Applications. (Illus.). 543p. 1981. 60.00 (ISBN 0-08-025589-2); pap. 24.50 (ISBN 0-08-025588-4). Pergamon.
Tri T. Ha. Solid-State Microwave Amplifier Design. 350p. 1981. 30.00 (ISBN 0-471-08971-0). Wiley.

MICROWAVE RADIO
see Radio, Short Wave

MICROWAVES
see also Microwave Devices
Business Communications Co. The Microwave Industry, G-020: Trends, Developments. 1981. 825.00 (ISBN 0-89336-275-1). BCC.
Fox, J., ed. Microwave Research Institute Symposia. Incl. Vol. 1. Modern Network Synthesis. 1952. 19.95 (ISBN 0-470-27093-4); Vol. 4. Modern Advances in Microwave Techniques. LC 55-12897. 1955. o.p. (ISBN 0-470-27192-2); Vol. 5. Modern Network Synthesis. LC 56-2590. 1956. o.p. (ISBN 0-470-27225-2); Vol. 6. Nonlinear Circuit Analysis. LC 55-3575. 1956. o.p. (ISBN 0-470-27258-9); Vol. 9. Millimeter Waves. LC 60-10073. 1960. o.p. (ISBN 0-470-27357-7); Vol. 11. Electromagnetics & Fluid Dynamics of Gaseaous Plasma. LC 62-13174. 1962. 25.95 (ISBN 0-470-27423-9); Vol. 13. Optical Lasers. LC 63-22084. o.p. (ISBN 0-470-27428-X); Vol. 15. System Theory. LC 65-28522. 1965. 26.50 (ISBN 0-470-27430-1); Vol. 17. Modern Optics. LC 67-31757. 1967. o.p. (ISBN 0-470-27433-6); Vol. 19. Computer Processing in Communications. LC 77-122632. 1970. o.p. (ISBN 0-471-27436-4); Vol. 20. Submillimeter Waves. 1971. o.p. (ISBN 0-471-27437-2); Vol. 21. Computers & Automata. 1972. 33.95 (ISBN 0-471-27438-0); Vol. 22. Computer Communications. 1972. 37.95 (ISBN 0-471-27439-9); Vol. 24. Computer Software Engineering. 1977. 44.95 (ISBN 0-470-98948-3). Pub. by Wiley-Interscience). Wiley.

MIDDLE AGE
see also Aging; Longevity; Old Age
Barks, Herb. Prime Time. 144p. 1981. pap. 3.95 (ISBN 0-8407-5768-9). Nelson.
Eichorn, Dorothy, et al, eds. Present & Past in Middle Life. 1981. price not set (ISBN 0-12-233680-1). Acad Pr.
Girdano, Daniel A. Better Late Than Never: How Men Can Avoid a Midlife Fitness Crisis. (Illus.). 256p. 1981. 12.95t (ISBN 0-13-074773-4, Spec); pap. 5.95b (ISBN 0-13-074765-3). P-H.
Hickman, Martha W. The Growing Season. LC 80-68983. 128p. (Orig.). 1980. pap. write for info. (ISBN 0-8358-0411-9). Upper Room.
Utlan. Your Middle Years: A Doctor's Guide for Today's Woman. 12.95 (ISBN 0-8385-9938-9). P-H.
Weaver, Peter. Strategies for the Second Half of Life. 1981. pap. 3.50 (ISBN 0-451-09814-5, E9814, Signet Bks). NAL.

MIDDLE AGE AND EMPLOYMENT
see Age and Employment

MIDDLE AGES
see also Art, Medieval; Church History–Middle Ages, 600-1500; Civilization, Medieval; Literature, Medieval; Renaissance

Clogan, Paul M. Medievalia et Humanistica: Studies in Medieval & Renaissance Culture. (New Ser.: No. 10). 1981. 25.00x (ISBN 0-8476-6944-0). Rowman.

MIDDLE AGES–BIBLIOGRAPHY

Phillips, Jill. Annus Mirabilis: A Bibliography of Medieval Times. (Bibliographies for Librarians Ser.). 1980. lib. bdg. 75.00 (ISBN 0-8490-1398-4). Gordon Pr.

MIDDLE AGES–HISTORY

see also Civilization, Medieval; Crusades; Europe–History–476-1492; Feudalism; Holy Roman Empire; Migrations of Nations; Monasticism and Religious Orders

Ashton, Eliyahu. Studies on the Levantine Trade in the Middle Ages. 372p. 1980. 60.00x (ISBN 0-86078-020-1, Pub. by Variorum England). State Mutual Bk.

Bullough, Vern & Brundage, James. Sex in a Medieval Europe. (New Concepts in Human Sexuality Ser.). 250p. 1981. text ed. 17.95 (ISBN 0-87975-141-X); pap. text ed. 9.95 (ISBN 0-87975-151-7). Prometheus Bks.

Bullough, Vern & Brundage, James, eds. Sex in the Middle Ages. LC 80-85227. (New Concepts in Human Sexuality Ser.). 250p. 1980. 17.95 (ISBN 0-87975-141-X); pap. 9.95 (ISBN 0-87975-151-7). Prometheus Bks.

Delbruck, Hans. Das Mittelalter. LC 80-2677. 1981. Repr. of 1907 ed. 63.50 (ISBN 0-404-18559-2). AMS Pr.

Falco, Giorgio. The Holy Roman Republic: A Historic Profile of the Middle Ages. Kent, K. V., tr. from Italian. LC 80-19696. Orig. Title: La Santa Romana Republica. 336p. 1980. Repr. of 1965 ed. lib. bdg. 35.00x (ISBN 0-313-22395-5, FAHR). Greenwood.

Genicot, Leopold. L' Economie Rurale Namuroise au Bas Moyen Age (1199-1429, 2 vols. LC 80-2028. 1981. Repr. of 1943 ed. Set. 79.50 (ISBN 0-404-18565-7). Vol. 1 (ISBN 0-404-18566-5). Vol. 2 (ISBN 0-404-18567-3). AMS Pr.

Lot, Ferdinand. L Art Militaire et les Armees Au Moyen Age En Europe et Dans le Proche Orient, 2 vols. LC 80-2017. 1981. Repr. of 1946 ed. 90.00 (ISBN 0-686-28932-3). AMS Pr.

Lot, Ferdinand Vols., ed. Histoire Des Institutions Francaises Au Moyen Age, Publiee Sous la Direction De Ferdinand Lot et Robert Fawtier. LC 80-2204. 1981. Repr. of 1957 ed. 110.00 (ISBN 0-404-18606-8). AMS Pr.

Minorsky, Vladimir. The Turks, Iran & the Caucasus in the Middle Ages. 368p. 1980. 69.00x (ISBN 0-86078-028-7, Pub. by Variorum England). State Mutual Bk.

Moss, Henry S. The Birth of the Middle Ages, Three Ninety-Five to Eight Fourteen. LC 80-24038. (Illus.). xvi, 291p. 1980. Repr. of 1964 ed. lib. bdg. 29.75x (ISBN 0-313-22708-X, MOBM). Greenwood.

Piltz, Anders. The World of Medieval Learning. Jones, Davis, tr. (Illus.). 1981. 30.00x (ISBN 0-389-20206-1). B&N.

Poole, Austin L. Obligations of Society in the Turlfth & Thirteenth Centuries: The Ford Lectures Delivered in the University of Oxford in Michaelmas Term. LC 80-2007. 1981. Repr. of 1946 ed. 18.50 (ISBN 0-404-18587-8). AMS Pr.

Rice, Edward. The High Middle Ages. 128p. 1963. 2.95 (ISBN 0-374-29520-4). FS&G.

See, Henri E. Les Classes Rurales et le Regime Domanial En France Au Moyen Age. LC 80-2003. 1981. Repr. of 1901 ed. 61.50 (ISBN 0-404-18594-0). AMS Pr.

Ullmann, Walter. Jurisprudence in the Middle Ages. 390p. 1980. 75.00x (ISBN 0-86078-065-1, Pub. by Variorum England). State Mutual Bk.

--The Papacy & Political Ideas in the Middle Ages. 408p. 1980. 60.00x (ISBN 0-902089-87-0, Pub. by Variorum England). State Mutual Bk.

MIDDLE ENGLISH

see English Language–Middle English, 1100-1500; English Literature (Collections)–Middle English (1100-1500)

MIDDLE WEST

Andrews, Clarence. Growing up in the Midwest. 168p. 1981. 11.25 (ISBN 0-8138-0250-4). Iowa St U Pr.

Reid, Loren. Finally It's Friday: School & Work in Mid-America, 1921-1933. 288p. 1981. 19.95 (ISBN 0-8262-0330-2). U of Mo Pr.

MIDDLE WEST–DESCRIPTION AND TRAVEL

Nash, Linda & Nash, Steve. Chicago & Beyond: Twenty-Six Bike Tours. 224p. 1981. pap. 6.95 (ISBN 0-695-81561-X). Follett.

Whitman, John. The Best Free Attractions in the Midwest. Grooms, Kathe, ed. (The Best Free Attractions Ser.). (Illus.). 200p. 1981. pap. 3.95 (ISBN 0-915658-37-2). Meadowbrook Pr.

MIDGES

see Diptera

MIDRASH–FOLK-LORE

see Folk-Lore, Jewish

MIDWESTERN STATES

see Middle West

MIDWIFERY

see Obstetrics

MIGRANT LABOR

see also Migration, Internal

Daniel, Cletus E. Bitter Harvest: A History of California Farmworkers, 1879-1941. LC 80-25664. 368p. 1981. 19.50x (ISBN 0-8014-1284-6). Cornell U Pr.

Goldfarb, Ronald L. Migrant Farm Workers: A Culture of Despair. 232p. 1981. text ed. 16.00 (ISBN 0-8138-1790-0). Iowa St U Pr.

MIGRANT LABOR–AFRICA

Murray, Colin. Families Divided: The Impact of Migrant Labour in Lesotho. (African Studies: No. 29). (Illus.). 236p. Date not set. price not set (ISBN 0-521-23501-4). Cambridge U Pr.

MIGRATION, INTERNAL

see also Emigration and Immigration; Land Settlement; Rural-Urban Migration

Beenstock, Michael. Health, Migration & Development. 192p. 1980. text ed. 27.75x (ISBN 0-566-00369-4, Pub. by Gower Pub Co England). Renouf.

Burnley, I. H., et al, eds. Mobility & Community Change in Australia. (Studies in Society & Culture). (Illus.). 286p. 1981. text ed. 30.25x (ISBN 0-7022-1446-9). U of Queensland Pr.

Greenwood, Michael. Migration & Economic Growth in the United States: National, Regional & Metropolitan Perspectives. (Studies in Urban Economics). 1981. price not set (ISBN 0-12-300650-3). Acad Pr.

Jones, Douglas L. Village & Seaport: Migration & Society in Eighteenth-Century Massachusetts. LC 80-54469. (Illus.). 240p. 1981. 15.00x (ISBN 0-87451-200-X). U Pr of New Eng.

Raymond, Ronald R., Jr., et al. Grow Your Roots Anywhere, Anytime. Date not set. 12.95. Wyden.

Recommendations on Statistics of International Migration. (Statistical Papers Ser. M: No. 58). 73p. 1979. pap. 6.00 (ISBN 0-686-68967-4, UN79/17/18, UN). Unipub.

Trends & Characteristics of International Migrations Since 1950. (Demographic Studies: No. 64). 172p. 1979. pap. 12.00 (ISBN 0-686-68977-1, UN78/13/5, UN). Unipub.

MIGRATION, JEWISH

see Jews–Migrations

MIGRATION, RURAL-URBAN

see Rural-Urban Migration

MIGRATION OF ANIMALS

see Animal Migration

MIGRATION OF PLANTS

see Plants–Migration

MIGRATIONS OF MAN

see Man–Migrations

MIGRATIONS OF NATIONS

see also Jews–Migrations; Man–Migrations

Clastres, Helene. The Land Without Evil: Tupi-Guarani Prophetism. Grenez-Brovender, Jacqueline, tr. 160p. 1981. 18.50x (ISBN 0-8476-6271-3). Rowman.

Smith, T. E. Commonwealth Migration: Flows & Policies. 1980. text ed. 40.00x (ISBN 0-333-27898-4). Humanities.

MIGRATORY WORKERS

see Migrant Labor

MILITARISM

see also Disarmament; Imperialism; Military Service, Compulsory

Johnson, John J., ed. The Role of the Military in Underdeveloped Countries: Papers of a Conference Sponsored by the Rand Corp. at Santa Monica, Calif. in August 1959. LC 80-25808. viii, 423p. 1981. Repr. of 1967 ed. lib. bdg. 39.75x (ISBN 0-313-22784-5, JORM). Greenwood.

MILITARISM–CHINA

Wilson, Andrew. Ever-Victorious Army: A History of the Chinese Campaign Under Lt. Col. C. G. Gordon & of the Suppression of the T'ai P'ing Rebellion. (Studies in Chinese History & Civilization). 395p. 1977. 24.75 (ISBN 0-89093-078-3). U Pubns Amer.

MILITARISM–NEAR EAST

Pipes, Daniel. Slave Soldiers & Islam: The Genesis of a Military System. LC 80-23969. 272p. 1981. text ed. 25.00x (ISBN 0-300-02447-9). Yale U Pr.

Wolpin, Miles D. Militarism & Social Revolution in the Third World. 256p. 1981. text ed. 25.00 (ISBN 0-86598-021-7). Allanheld.

MILITARY AERONAUTICS

see Aeronautics, Military

MILITARY AIR BASES

see Air Bases

MILITARY AIRPLANES

see Airplanes, Military

MILITARY ART AND SCIENCE

see also Aeronautics, Military; Air Warfare; Armaments; Armies; Arms and Armor; Atomic Warfare; Attack and Defense (Military Science); Battles; Chemical Warfare; Disarmament; Fortification; Naval Art and Science; Psychological Warfare; Soldiers; Spies; Strategy; Tank Warfare; Veterans; War; War Games

also headings beginning with the word Military

Candler. Atlas of African Military Strategy. 102p. Date not set. 29.95 (ISBN 0-02-905750-7). Macmillan.

Cooling, Benjamin F., ed. War, Business, & World Military-Industrial Complexes. (National University Publications, Political Science Ser.). 1981. 19.50 (ISBN 0-8046-9276-9). Kennikat.

Hoeber, Frank. Slow to Take Offense: Bombers, Cruise Missiles, & Prudent Deterrence. LC 80-80662. (CSIS Monograph). 137p. 1980. pap. text ed. 6.95. CSI Studies.

Laird, Melvin R. & Korb, Lawrence J. Problem of Military Readiness. 1980. pap. 3.75 (ISBN 0-8447-1087-3). Am Enterprise.

Sarkesian, Sam C., ed. Combat Effectiveness: Cohesion, Stress, & the Volunteer Military. LC 80-17486. (Sage Research Progress Ser. on War, Revolution, & Peacekeeping: Vol. 9). (Illus.). 305p. 1980. 20.00 (ISBN 0-8039-1440-7). Sage.

--Combat Effectiveness: Cohesion, Stress, & the Volunteer Military. LC 80-17486. (Sage Research Progress Ser. on War, Revolution, & Peacekeeping: Vol. 9). (Illus.). 305p. 1980. pap. 9.95 (ISBN 0-8039-1441-5). Sage.

Slow to Take Offense: Bombers, Cruise Missles & Prudent Deterrence. 136p. 1980. pap. 15.00 (ISBN 0-89206-015-8, CSIS017, CSIS). Unipub.

Wylie, Joseph C. Military Strategy: A General Theory of Power Control. LC 80-36885. vii, 111p. 1980. Repr. of 1967 ed. lib. bdg. 17.50x (ISBN 0-313-22679-2, WYMS). Greenwood.

MILITARY ART AND SCIENCE–HISTORY

Kendall, Paul M. The Story of Land Warfare. LC 74-3764. (Illus.). x, 194p. 1981. Repr. of 1957 ed. lib. bdg. 21.75x (ISBN 0-8371-7463-5, KELW). Greenwood.

Lot, Ferdinand. L Art Militaire et les Armees Au Moyen Age En Europe et Dans le Proche Orient, 2 vols. LC 80-2017. 1981. Repr. of 1946 ed. 90.00 (ISBN 0-686-28932-3). AMS Pr.

MILITARY AVIATION

see Aeronautics, Military

MILITARY BALLOONS

see Balloons

MILITARY BASES

Mattern, Carolyn J. Soldiers When They Go: The Story of Camp Randall, 1861-1865. LC 80-26238. (Illus.). 156p. 1981. 4.95x (ISBN 0-87020-206-5). State Hist Soc Wis.

MILITARY-CIVIL RELATIONS

see Militarism; Military Policy

MILITARY COSTUME

see Uniforms, Military

MILITARY DEPENDENTS

see Air Force Wives

MILITARY DRAFT

see Military Service, Compulsory

MILITARY ENGINEERING

see also Electronics in Military Engineering; Fortification

Liblich, Garnet Mills, ed. Qualified Products List & Sources. 60th ed. 300p. 1981. lib. bdg. 65.00 perfect bdg (ISBN 0-912702-03-6). Global Eng.

MILITARY EQUIPMENT, SUPPLIES, ETC.

see Uniforms, Military;

also subdivisions Commissariat, Equipment, Supplies and stores, Uniforms under armies

MILITARY EXPLOSIVES

see Explosives

MILITARY FAMILIES

see Air Force Wives

MILITARY HISTORY

see also Battles; Military Art and Science–History; Military Policy; Naval History

also subdivisions History, or History, military under names of countries, e.g. United States–History, Military; particuliar wars, battles, sieges, etc.; also France–Army; United States–Army, and similar headings

Beck, Phillip. Oratour: Village of the Dead. 124p. 1979. 15.00. Shoe String.

Kendall, Paul M. The Story of Land Warfare. LC 74-3764. (Illus.). x, 194p. 1981. Repr. of 1957 ed. lib. bdg. 21.75x (ISBN 0-8371-7463-5, KELW). Greenwood.

MILITARY INSTALLATIONS

see Military Bases

MILITARY LIFE

see Soldiers

MILITARY PERSONNEL

see Soldiers

MILITARY POLICY

see also Deterrence (Strategy); Militarism; Strategic Materials

also subdivision Military Policy under names of countries, e.g. United States–Military Policy

Abbiatico, Mario. Grandi Incisioni Su Armi D'Bagi. (Illus.). Repr. of 1976 ed. 30.00. Arma Pr.

Hoeber, Frank. Slow to Take Offense: Bombers, Cruise Missiles, & Prudent Deterrence. LC 80-80662. (CSIS Monograph). 137p. 1980. pap. text ed. 6.95. CSI Studies.

MILITARY POWER

see Armies; Disarmament; Military Art and Science; Sea-Power

MILITARY SCIENCE

see Military Art and Science

MILITARY SERVICE, COMPULSORY

see also Conscientious Objectors;

also subdivisions Recruiting, etc. under armies, e.g. United States–Army–Recruiting, etc.

Davis, James W., Jr. & Dolbeare, Kenneth M. Little Groups of Neighbors: The Selective Service System. LC 80-25861. xv, 276p. 1981. Repr. of 1968 ed. lib. bdg. 35.00x (ISBN 0-313-22777-2, DALN). Greenwood.

Johnson, R. Charles & Sherman, Charles E. Don't Sit in the Draft. 240p. (Orig.). 1980. pap. 6.95 (ISBN 0-917316-32-0). Nolo Pr.

MILITARY SERVICE, VOLUNTARY

see also subdivision Recruting, enlistment, etc. under armies, navies, etc., e.g. United States-Army-Recruiting, enlistment, etc.

Gottlieb, David. Babes in Arms: Youth in the Army. LC 80-15830. (Illus.). 173p. 1980. 14.95 (ISBN 0-8039-1499-7). Sage.

Sarkesian, Sam C. American Military Professionalism. LC 80-27027. (Pergamon Policy Studies on International Politics). 1981. 25.00 (ISBN 0-08-027178-2). Pergamon.

Underhill, Lonnie E. Genealogy Records of the First Arizona Volunteer Infantry Regiment. LC 80-24778. (Illus.). iv, 124p. 1980. pap. 18.50 (ISBN 0-933234-02-3). Roan Horse.

MILITARY SOCIOLOGY

see Sociology, Military

MILITARY STRATEGY

see Military Art and Science; Strategy

MILITARY TRAINING, UNIVERSAL

see Military Service, Compulsory

MILITARY UNIFORMS

see Uniforms, Military

MILITARY VEHICLES

see Vehicles, Military

MILK PRODUCTS

see Dairy Products

MILKY WAY

Bok, Bart J. & Bok, Priscilla F. The Milky Way. 5th ed. LC 80-22544. (Harvard Books on Astronomy Ser.). (Illus.). 384p. 1981. text ed. 20.00 (ISBN 0-674-57503-2). Harvard U Pr.

MILL, JOHN STUART, 1806-1873

Laine, Michael. Checklist of Works on John Stuart Mill. 176p. 1981. 25.00x (ISBN 0-686-69479-1). U of Toronto Pr.

MILLENNIUM

see also Dispensationalism; Second Advent

Seyer, Herman D. Millenialism. 68p. 1979. pap. 1.50. H D Seyer.

MILLER, HENRY, 1827-1916

Perkins, Dorothy. The Passionate Wisdom of Henry Miller: The Religious Dimension of His Life & Art. (Orig.). 1980. pap. 3.00 (ISBN 0-9604742-1-8). D J Perkins.

MILLER, HENRY, 1891-1980

Thiebaud, Twinka, ed. Henry Miller Dinner Chats. (Illus.). 128p. (Orig.). 1981. pap. 6.95 (ISBN 0-88496-166-4). Capra Pr.

Treadwell, Edward F. The Cattle King. (Illus.). xii, 375p. 1981. pap. 6.95 (ISBN 0-934136-10-6). Western Tanager.

MILLINERY

see also Artificial Flowers; Hats

Tomlinson, Jill. Lady Bee's Bonnets. 1971. pap. 2.95 (ISBN 0-571-11133-5, Pub. by Faber &Faber). Merrimack Bk Serv.

MILLING MACHINERY

Here are entered works on machinery used in the process of grinding, etc.

Lewis, Gaspar J. Cabinetmaking, Patternmaking, & Millwork. 448p. 1981. 18.95 (ISBN 0-442-24785-0). Van Nos Reinhold.

MILLIONAIRES

see also Wealth

Lemann, Nicholas. The Fast Track: Texans & Other Strivers. 1981. 12.95 (ISBN 0-393-01436-3). Norton.

MILTON, JOHN, 1608-1674

Bailey, John C. Milton. 256p. 1980. Repr. of 1945 ed. lib. bdg. 20.00 (ISBN 0-8495-0463-5). Arden Lib.

Hunter, John. Milton's Samson Agonistes & Lycidas. 92p. 1980. Repr. of 1872 ed. text ed. 17.50 (ISBN 0-8492-5271-7). R West.

Ivimey, Joseph. John Milton, His Life & Times, Religious & Political Opinions. 397p. 1980. Repr. of 1833 ed. lib. bdg. 40.00 (ISBN 0-8495-2619-1). Arden Lib.

Keightley, Thomas. An Account of the Life, Opinions, & Writings of John Milton. 484p. 1980. Repr. of 1855 ed. lib. bdg. 50.00 (ISBN 0-8492-1495-5). R West.

Slights, Camille W. The Casuistical Tradition in Shakespeare, Donne, Herbert, & Milton. LC 80-8576. 352p. 1981. 26.50x (ISBN 0-691-06463-6). Princeton U Pr.

MILTON, JOHN, 1608-1674–CRITICISM AND INTERPRETATION

Candy, Hugh C. Milton, the Individualist in Metre. 49p. 1980. Repr. lib. bdg. 8.50 (ISBN 0-89987-112-7). Darby Bks.

Fiore, Peter A. Milton & Augustine: Patterns of Augustinian Thought in Milton's Paradise Lost. LC 80-17854. 144p. 1981. 14.50x (ISBN 0-271-00269-7). Pa St U Pr.

Prince, F. T. The Italian Element in Milton's Verse. 183p. 1980. Repr. of 1954 ed. lib. bdg. 30.00 (ISBN 0-8492-2191-9). R West.

Visak, Edward H. Milton Agonistes: A Metaphysical Criticism. 104p. 1980. Repr. of 1923 ed. lib. bdg. 17.50 (ISBN 0-8492-2834-4). R West.

MILTON, JOHN, 1608-1674–DICTIONARIES, INDEXES, ETC.

Le Comte, Edward. Dictionary of Puns in Milton's English Poetry. 240p. 1981. text ed. 25.00x (ISBN 0-231-05102-6). Columbia U Pr.

MILTON, JOHN, 1608-1674–RELIGION AND ETHICS
Empson, W. Milton's God. LC 80-40109. 320p. Date not set. pap. 15.95 (ISBN 0-521-29910-1). Cambridge U Pr.

MILWAUKEE–HISTORY
Anderson, Byron. A Bibliography of Master's Theses & Doctoral Dissertations on Milwaukee Topics, 1911-1977. LC 80-27261. 136p. (Orig.). 1981. pap. 3.95x (ISBN 0-87020-202-2). State Hist Soc Wis.
Korn, Bernhard C. The Story of Bay View. LC 80-83069. (Illus.). 136p. (gr. 6-12). 1980. 5.00 (ISBN 0-938076-05-1). Milwaukee County.

MIND
see Intellect; Psychology

MIND AND BODY
see also Body, Human; Consciousness; Dreams; Faith-Cure; Hypnotism; Medicine, Psychosomatic; Mental Healing; Nervous System; Personality, Disorders of; Psychoanalysis; Psychology, Pathological; Psychology, Physiological; Self; Sleep; Temperament
Brandreth, Gyles. Amazing Facts About the Body. LC 80-1088. (Amazing Facts Books Ser.). (Illus.). 32p. (gr. 5-8). 1981. pap. 2.95. Doubleday.
Cousins, Norman. Anatomy of an Illness As Perceived by the Patient. 176p. 1981. pap. 4.95 (ISBN 0-553-01293-2). Bantam.
Fortune, Dion. The Machinery of the Mind. 1980. pap. 4.95 (ISBN 0-87728-505-5). Weiser.
Macleod, William M. & Macleod, Gael S. M. I. N. D Over Weight: "How to Stay Slim the Rest of Your Life". LC 80-21001. 1981. 7.95 (ISBN 0-13-583385-X). P-H.
Verny, Thomas & Kelly, John. The Secret Life of the Unborn Child. 256p. 1981. 12.95 (ISBN 0-671-25312-3). Summit Bks.

MIND-CURE
see Christian Science; Faith-Cure; Mental Healing; Mind and Body

MIND-DISTORTING DRUGS
see Hallucinogenic Drugs

MINERAL COLLECTING
see Mineralogy–Collectors and Collecting

MINERAL INDUSTRIES
see also Ceramics; Metallurgy; Mines and Mineral Resources; Mining Industry and Finance
also specific types of mines and mining, e.g. Coal Mines and Mining
Boyum, Burton H., ed. The Mather Mine, Negaunee & Ishpeming Michigan. 87p. 1980. 18.95. Longyear Res.
Mular, A. L. & Bhappu, R. B., eds. Mineral Processing Plant Design. 2nd ed. LC 79-57345. (Illus.). 958p. 1980. text ed. 27.00x (ISBN 0-89520-269-7). Soc Mining Eng.
Somasundaran, P., ed. Fine Particles Processing, 2 vols. LC 79-57344. (Illus.). 1865p. 1980. text ed. 45.00x (ISBN 0-89520-275-1). Soc Mining Eng.

MINERAL LANDS
see Mines and Mineral Resources; Mining Law

MINERAL METABOLISM
Adams, Ruth & Murray, Frank. Minerals: Kill or Cure. rev. ed. 366p. (Orig.). 1974. pap. 1.95 (ISBN 0-915962-16-0). Larchmont Bks.

MINERAL OILS–LAW AND LEGISLATION
see Petroleum Law and Legislation

MINERAL RESOURCES
see Mines and Mineral Resources

MINERALOGY
see also Crystallography; Gems; Meteorites; Petrology; Precious Stones; Rocks
also names of minerals, e.g. Feldspar, Quartz
Dana, J. D., et al. Systems of Minerology, 3 vols. 7th ed. Incl. Vol. 1. Elements, Sulfides, Sulfosalts, Oxides. 1944. 46.50 (ISBN 0-471-19239-2); Vol. 2. Halides, Nitrates, Borates, Carbonates, Sulfates, Phosphates, Arsenates, Tungstates, Molybdates. 1951. 42.95 (ISBN 0-471-19272-4); Vol. 3. Silica Minerals. 1962. 23.95 (ISBN 0-471-19287-2). Pub. by Wiley-Interscience). Wiley.
Girard, R. M. Texas Rocks & Minerals: An Amateur's Guide. (Illus.). 109p. 1964. Repr. 2.00 (GB 6). Bur Econ Geology.
In Situ Investigation in Soils & Rocks. 328p. 1980. 80.00x (ISBN 0-901948-30-6, Pub. by Telford England). State Mutual Bk.
Jensen, M. L. & Bateman, A. M. Economic Mineral Deposits. 3rd rev. ed. 608p. 1981. text ed. 24.95 (ISBN 0-471-09043-3). Wiley.
Johnson, Wesley M. & Maxwell, John A. Rock & Mineral Analysis. 584p. 1981. 40.00 (ISBN 0-471-02743-X, Pub. by Wiley-Interscience). Wiley.
Touloukian, U. S. & Ho, C. Y. Physical Properties of Rocks & Minerals, Vol. II. (M-H-CINDAS Data Series on Material Properties). (Illus.). 576p. 1981. text ed. 44.50 (ISBN 0-07-065032-2). McGraw.

MINERALOGY–COLLECTING OF SPECIMENS
see Mineralogy–Collectors and Collecting

MINERALOGY–COLLECTORS AND COLLECTING
Baldwin, Charles. Colorado Gem & Mineral Collecting Localities. pap. 4.95 (ISBN 0-933472-08-0). Johnson Colo.
Touloukian, U. S. & Ho, C. Y. Physical Properties of Rocks & Minerals, Vol. II. (M-H-CINDAS Data Series on Material Properties). (Illus.). 576p. 1981. text ed. 44.50 (ISBN 0-07-065032-2). McGraw.

MINERALOGY, DETERMINATIVE
see also Assaying; Chemistry, Analytic
Shelby, C. A. Heavy Minerals in the Wellborn Formation, Lee & Burleson Counties, Texas. (Illus.). 54p. 1965. 1.25 (RI 55). Bur Econ Geology.

MINERALS
see Mineralogy; Mines and Mineral Resources

MINERALS IN PLANTS
see Plants–Assimilation

MINERALS IN THE BODY
see also Mineral Metabolism
Adams, Ruth & Murray, Frank. Minerals: Kill or Cure. rev. ed. 366p. (Orig.). 1974. pap. 1.95 (ISBN 0-915962-16-0). Larchmont Bks.
Flodin, Nestor W. Vitamin-Trace Mineral-Protein Interactions, Vol. 3. Horribin, David F., ed. (Annual Research Reviews). 362p. 1980. 38.00 (ISBN 0-88831-085-4). Eden Med Res.
Kolisko, E. Lead & the Human Organism. 1980. pap. 3.95x (ISBN 0-906492-31-9, Pub. by Kolisko Archives). St George Bk Serv.
Mervyn, Len. Minerals & Your Health. LC 80-84442. 144p. 1981. Repr. 9.95 (ISBN 0-686-69376-0). Keats.

MINERS
Gardner, James A. Lead King: Moses Austin. 256p. 1980. 9.95 (ISBN 0-86629-004-4). Sunrise MO.

MINES AND MINERAL RESOURCES
see also Mineralogy; Mining Industry and Finance; Mining Law; Precious Metals
also specific types of mines and mining, e.g. Coal Mines and Mining, Gold Mines and Mining
Dawson, J. B. Kimberlites & Their Xenoliths. (Minerals & Rocks: Vol. 15). (Illus.). 252p. 1980. 47.25 (ISBN 0-387-10208-6). Springer-Verlag.
Fischman, Leonard L. World Mineral Trends & U. S. Supply Problems. LC 80-8025. (Resources for the Future, Inc. Research Paper R-20). (Illus.). 576p. (Orig.). 1981. pap. text ed. 15.00x (ISBN 0-8018-2491-5). Johns Hopkins.
International Mine Ventilation Congress, 2nd. Proceedings. Mousset-Jones, Pierre, ed. LC 80-52943. (Illus.). 864p. 1980. 34.00x (ISBN 0-89520-271-9). Soc Mining Eng.
Littlefield, Charles W. Man, Minerals, & Masters. (Illus.). 140p. 1980. pap. 5.50 (ISBN 0-89540-059-6). Sun Pub.
Mining Journal Editors. Mining Annual Review 1980. 200p. 1980. 60.00x (Pub. by Mining Journal England). State Mutual Bk.
Rapid Excavation & Tunneling Conference, 1979. R E T C Proceedings, 2 vols. Hustrulid, William A. & Maevis, Alfred C., eds. LC 79-52280. (Illus.). 1819p. 1979. 55.00x (ISBN 0-89520-266-2). Soc Mining Eng.
Sideri, S. & Johns, S., eds. Mining for Development in the Third World: Multinationals, State Enterprises & the International Economy. LC 80-20930. (Pergamon Policy Studies on International Development). 376p. 1980. 35.00 (ISBN 0-08-026308-9). Pergamon.
Skinner, Brian J., ed. Earth's Energy & Mineral Resources. (The Earth & Its Inhabitants: Selected Readings from American Scientist Ser.). (Illus.). 200p. 1980. pap. 8.95 (ISBN 0-913232-90-4). W Kaufmann.
Sullivan, George. The Gold Hunter's Handbook. LC 80-5718. 208p. 1981. 14.95 (ISBN 0-8128-2788-0). Stein & Day.

MINES AND MINERAL RESOURCES–LAW
see Mining Law

MINES AND MINERAL RESOURCES–TAXATION
Resource Materials: Domsetic Taxation of Hard Minerals. 254p. 1980. pap. 30.00 (T159). ALI-ABA.

MINES AND MINERAL RESOURCES–ASIA
How Japan's Metal Mining Industries Modernized. 65p. 1980. pap. 5.00 (ISBN 92-808-0083-3, TUNU089, UNU). Unipub.
Technology & Labour in Japanese Coal Mining. 65p. 1980. pap. 5.00 (ISBN 92-808-0082-5, TUNU090, UNU). Unipub.

MINES AND MINERAL RESOURCES–AUSTRALIA
Prider, Rex T. Mining in Western Australia. 328p. 1980. 22.50x (ISBN 0-85564-153-3, Pub. by U of West Australia Pr Australia). Intl Schol Bk Serv.

MINES AND MINERAL RESOURCES–GREAT BRITAIN
Handy, L. J. Wage Policy in the British Coalmining Industry. LC 80-40229. (Department of Applied Economics Monograph: No. 27). 312p. Date not set. price not set (ISBN 0-521-23535-9). Cambridge U Pr.
Morrison, T. A. Cornwall's Central Mines: The Northern District, 1810-1895. 400p. 1980. 40.00x (ISBN 0-906720-10-9, Pub. by Hodge England). State Mutual Bk.

MINES AND MINERAL RESOURCES–UNITED STATES
Arizona Industrial Minerals. 1975. 15.80. Minobras.
Barnes, V. E. & Schofield, D. A. Potential Low-Grade Iron Ore & Hydraulic-Fracturing Sand in Cambrian Sandstones, Northwestern Llano Region, Texas. (Illus.). 58p. 1964. 2.00 (RI 53). Bur Econ Geology.
Boyum, Burton H., ed. The Mather Mine, Negaunee & Ishpeming Michigan. LC 79-89638. 1979. 18.95 (ISBN 0-938746-04-9). Marquette Cnty.
Colorado & Utah Industrial Minerals. 1974. 15.50. Minobras.
Dietrich, J. W. & Lonsdale, J. T. Mineral Resources of the Colorado River Industrial Development Association Area. (Illus.). 84p. 1958. 1.50 (RI 37). Bur Econ Geology.
Eargle, D. H., et al. Uranium Geology & Mines, South Texas. (Illus.). 59p. 1971. 1.75 (GB 12). Bur Econ Geology.
Fisher, W. L. Rock & Mineral Resources of East Texas. (Illus.). 439p. 1965. 5.00 (RI 54). Bur Econ Geology.
Galloway, W. E., et al. South Texas Uranium Province, Geologic Perspective. (Illus.). 81p. 1979. 3.00 (GB 18). Bur Econ Geology.
Idaho Industrial Minerals. 1975. 14.50. Minobras.
Lord, Eliot. Comstock Miners & Mining. (Illus.). 578p. 1981. Repr. of 1959 ed. 20.00 (ISBN 0-8310-7008-0). Howell-North.
Maxwell, R. A. Mineral Resources of South Texas: Region Served Through the Port of Corpus Christi. (Illus.). 140p. 1962. 3.50 (RI 43). Bur Econ Geology.
Montana Industrial Minerals. 1975. 15.20. Minobras.
Nevada Industrial Minerals. 1973. 13.40. Minobras.
Rodda, P. U., et al. Limestone & Dolomite Resources: Lower Cretaceous Rocks, Texas. (Illus.). 286p. 1966. 4.50 (RI 56). Bur Econ Geology.
Southern Calif. Industrial Minerals. 1973. 14.70. Minobras.
Uranium Deposits of Arizona, California & Nevada. 1978. 40.30. Minobras.
Uranium Deposits of the Northern U. S. Region. 1977. 37.10. Minobras.
Uranium Guidebook for Wyoming. 1976. xerox copy 40.00. Minobras.
Uranium Resources of the Central & Southern Rockies. 1979. 33.80. Minobras.
Wyoming Industrial Minerals. 1975. 14.00. Minobras.

MINES AND MINING
see Mineral Industries; Mines and Mineral Resources; Mining Industry and Finance

MINHAGIM
see Jews–Rites and Ceremonies

MINI COMPUTERS
see Minicomputers

MINIATURE COMPUTERS
see Minicomputers

MINIATURE ELECTRONIC EQUIPMENT
see also Microelectronics; Minicomputers
Comer, David J. Electronic Design with Integrated Circuits. LC 80-23365. (Electrical Engineering Ser.). (Illus.). 416p. 1981. text ed. 24.95 (ISBN 0-201-03931-1). A-W.

MINIATURE LAMPS–CATALOGS
Smith, Frank & Smith, Ruth. Miniature Lamp. (Illus.). 288p. 1981. Repr. of 1968 ed. 18.95 (ISBN 0-916838-44-7). Schiffer.

MINIATURE OBJECTS
see also Machinery–Models; Models and Modelmaking; Ship Models; Toys
also subdivision Models under names of objects, e.g. Airplanes–Models
Merrill, Virginia & Richardson, Susan M. Reproducing Period Furniture & Accessories in Miniature. Ayman, Brant, ed. 1981. 25.00 (ISBN 0-517-53816-4). Crown.

MINIATURIZATION (ELECTRONICS)
see Miniature Electronic Equipment

MINICOMPUTERS
see also Microcomputers; Microprocessors
Brandon, Dick H. & Siegelstein, Sidney. The Business User's Guide to Minicomputers. 300p. 1980. 50.00 (ISBN 0-932648-18-5). Boardroom.
Canning, Richard G. & Leeper, Nancy C. So You Are Thinking About a Small Business Computer. (Computing in Your Business Ser.). (Illus.). 100p. (Orig.). 1980. pap. 12.50 (ISBN 0-938516-01-9). Canning Pubns.
Gotlieb, C. C. Computers in the Home. 65p. 1978. pap. text ed. 3.00x (ISBN 0-920380-10-7, Pub. by Inst Res Pub Canada). Renouf.
Healey, Martin & Hebditch, David. Minicomputers in on-Line Systems. (Computer Systems Ser.). (Illus.). 352p. 1981. text ed. 22.95 (ISBN 0-87626-579-4). Winthrop.
Moschytz, G. S. Active Filter Design Handbook: For Use with Programmable Pocket Calculators & Minicomputers. 296p. 1981. 49.95 (ISBN 0-471-27850-5, Pub. by Wiley-Interscience). Wiley.
Osborne, Adam. A Business System Buyer's Guide. 600p. (Orig.). 1981. pap. 7.95 (ISBN 0-931988-47-0). Osborne-McGraw.
Poole, Lon. The Apple II User's Guide. 500p. 1981. pap. 15.00 (ISBN 0-931988-46-2). Osborne-McGraw.
Rinder, Robert M. A Practical Guide to Small Computers for Business & Professional Use. 288p. 1981. pap. 6.95 (ISBN 0-671-09259-6). Monarch Pr.
Warren, Jim C., Jr., ed. National Computer Conference '78 Personal Computing Digest. (Illus.). iv, 425p. 1978. pap. 12.00 (ISBN 0-88283-011-2). AFIPS Pr.

MINIMA
see Maxima and Minima

MINIMAX APPROXIMATION
see Chebyshev Approximation

MINIMUM WAGE
see Wages–Minimum Wage

MINING
see Mineral Industries; Mines and Mineral Resources; Mining Industry and Finance

MINING INDUSTRY AND FINANCE
see also Mines and Mineral Resources; Mines and Mineral Resources–Taxation
Conrad, Robert, ed. Taxation of Mineral Resources. Hool, Bryce. LC 80-8392. (Lincoln Institute of Land Policy Book). 1980. 14.95x (ISBN 0-669-04104-1). Lexington Bks.

MINING LAW
see also Petroleum Law and Legislation
Organization of American States. Mining & Petroleum Legislation, Release 1. 1980. 35.00 (ISBN 0-379-20381-2). Oceana.

MINISTERS OF STATE
see Cabinet Officers

MINISTERS OF THE GOSPEL
see Clergy

MINISTRY
see Church Work; Clergy–Office; Pastoral Theology

MINNESOTA–DESCRIPTION AND TRAVEL
Daniel, Glenda & Sullivan, Jerry. A Sierra Club Naturlist's Guide to the North Woods of Michigan, Wisconsin, & Minnesota. (Naturalist's Guide Ser.). (Illus.). 384p. 1981. 24.95 (ISBN 0-87156-248-0); pap. 9.95 (ISBN 0-87156-277-4). Sierra.
Thoreau, Henry D. Thoreaus Minnesota Journey: Two Documents. Harding, Walter, ed. LC 80-2524. 1981. Repr. of 1962 ed. 18.50 (ISBN 0-404-19072-3). AMS Pr.
Wechsler, Charles. Minnesota: State of Beauty. (Illus.). 96p. 1981. pap. 10.95 (ISBN 0-931714-12-5). Nodin Pr.
Will, Robin. Beautiful Minnesota. 72p. 1978. write for info. (ISBN 0-915796-61-9); pap. write for info. (ISBN 0-915796-60-0). Beautiful Am.

MINNESOTA–DESCRIPTION AND TRAVEL–GUIDEBOOK
Buchanan, James W. Minnesota Walk Book: A Guide to Hiking & Cross-Country Skiing in the Pioneer Region. (Minnesota Walk Book Ser.: Vol. 5). (Illus.). 59p. (Orig.). 1979. pap. 4.50 (ISBN 0-931714-07-9). Nodin Pr.

MINNESOTA–HISTORY
Lass, William E. Minnesota's Boundary with Canada: Its Evolution Since 1783. LC 80-21644. (Minnesota Public Affairs Center Publication Ser.). 141p. 1980. 16.50 (ISBN 0-87351-147-6); pap. 8.75 (ISBN 0-87351-153-0). Minn Hist.

MINNESOTA–POLITICS AND GOVERNMENT
McLean, Daniels. Minnesota Legal Forms-Family Law. Mason Publishing Company Staff, ed. (Minnesota Legal Forms 1981 Ser.). 150p. 1981. ring binder 15.00 (ISBN 0-917126-85-8). Mason Pub.
Roer, Kathleen. Minnesota Legal Forms-Real Estate. Mason Publishing Company Staff, ed. (Minnesota Legal Forms 1981 Ser.). 150p. 1981. ring binder 15.00 (ISBN 0-917126-86-6). Mason Pub.

MINOR PLANETS
see Planets, Minor

MINOR PROPHETS
see Prophets

MINORESSES
see Poor Clares

MINORITIES
see also Discrimination; Nationalism; Race Discrimination; Race Relations; Self-Determination, National
also names of individual races of peoples, e.g. Chinese in Foreign Countries; Germans in the United States; also subdivisions Foreign Population and Race relations under names of countries, cities, etc.
Bernardo, Stephanie. The Ethnic Almanac. LC 78-14694. (Illus.). 576p. 1981. 19.95 (ISBN 0-385-14143-2). Doubleday.
--The Ethnic Almanac. LC 80-14694. (Illus.). 576p. 1981. pap. 10.95 (ISBN 0-385-14144-0, Dolp). Doubleday.
Claerbaut, David, ed. New Directions in Ethnic Studies: Minorities in America. LC 80-69329. 115p. 1981. perfect bdg. 8.50 (ISBN 0-86548-026-5). Century Twenty One.
Curry, Ann. Teaching About the Other Americans: Minorities in United States History. LC 80-69120. 110p. 1981. perfect bdg. 8.95 (ISBN 0-86548-028-1). Century Twenty One.
Foster, Charles R., ed. Nations Without a State: Ethnic Minorities of Western Europe. 304p. 1980. 22.95 (ISBN 0-03-056807-2). Praeger.
Higham, John. Strangers in the Land: Patterns of American Nativism, 1860 to 1925. LC 80-22204. (Illus.). xiv, 431p. 1981. Repr. of 1963 ed. lib. bdg. 35.50x (ISBN 0-313-22459-5, HISL). Greenwood.
Rubin, Bernard, ed. Small Voices & Great Trumpets: Minorities & the Media. 295p. 1980. 24.95 (ISBN 0-03-056973-7); pap. 9.95 (ISBN 0-03-056972-9). Praeger.
Wirsing, Robert G., ed. Protection of Ethnic Minorities: Comparative Perspectives. LC 80-25618. (Pergamon Policy Studies on International Politices Ser.). 350p. 1981. 39.50 (ISBN 0-08-025556-6). Pergamon.

MINORITIES–EMPLOYMENT
see also Affirmative Action Programs
Pepper. Affirmative Action Plan Workbook for Federal Contractors. 2nd ed. 1979. pap. 45.00 (ISBN 0-917386-31-0). Exec Ent.

Reid, Peter. Affirmative Action Compliance Kit: Eed Dictionary. 1980. pap. 10.00 (ISBN 0-917386-35-3). Exec Ent.
--Affirmative Action Compliance Kit: Reference Guide. 1980. pap. 15.00 (ISBN 0-917386-34-5). Exec Ent.
--Affirmative Action Compliance Kit: Working Manual. 1980. pap. 75.00 (ISBN 0-917386-33-7). Exec Ent.
Rosen, Doris B. Employment Testing & Minority Groups. (Key Issues Ser.: No. 6). 1970. pap. 2.00 (ISBN 0-87546-239-1). NY Sch Indus Rel.
Simmons. California Prsonnel Managers Guide to EEO Laws. 1980. pap. 25.00 (ISBN 0-917386-40-X). Exec Ent.
Solving EEO Problems. 1980. pap. 9.95 (ISBN 0-917386-36-1). Exec Ent.

MINORS (LAW)
see Children–Law

MINSTREL SHOWS
see Musical Revues, Comedies, etc.

MINTS
see also Coinage
Hudgeons. The Official Price Guide to Mint Errors & Varieties. 3rd ed. (Collector Ser). (Illus.). 182p. 1981. pap. 4.95 (167-05). Hse of Collectibles.

MIRACLE-PLAYS
see Mysteries and Miracle-Plays

MIRACLES
see also Jesus Christ–Miracles; Saints–Legends
Burns, R. M. The Great Debate on Miracles: From Joseph Glanvill to David Hume. LC 78-75197. 300p. 1981. 20.00 (ISBN 0-8387-2378-0). Bucknell U Pr.
Johnston, Francis. Fatima. (The Great Sign). 1980. Repr. of 1979 ed. write for info. Tan Bks Pubs.
Milagros De la Oracion. (Spanish Bks.). 1977. 1.75 (ISBN 0-8297-0443-4). Life Pubs Intl.
Robertson, Pat, tr. Milagro Del Amor Agape. (Spanish Bks.). (Span.). 1978. 1.90 (ISBN 0-8297-0914-2). Life Pubs Intl.
Schuller, Robert H. Discover the Miracles in Your Life. (Orig.). 1978. pap. 1.25 (ISBN 0-89081-136-9). Harvest Hse.

MIRO, JOAN, 1893-
Leiris, Michael & Mourlot, Fernand. Joan Miro, Lithographs, Vol. 1. (Illus.). 231p. 1972. 150.00x (ISBN 0-8148-0494-2, Pub. by Tudor). Hennessey.

MISCARRIAGE
see Abortion

MISCONDUCT IN OFFICE
see Corruption (In Politics); Government Liability

MISDEMEANORS (LAW)
see Criminal Law

MISREPRESENTATION (LAW)
see Fraud

MISSILES, GUIDED
see Guided Missiles

MISSING PERSONS
Cohen, Daniel. Missing Stories of Strange Disappearances. (Illus.). 1980. pap. write for info. (ISBN 0-671-56052-2). PB.
Olsen, Jack. Missing Persons. LC 80-69375. 1981. 12.95 (ISBN 0-689-11133-9). Atheneum.

MISSIOLOGY
see Missions–Theory

MISSION OF THE CHURCH
Here are entered works on the chief objective and responsibility of the church as viewed in its entirety. Works on missionary work are entered under Missions.
see also Church and the World; Missions
Collins, Sheila D. & Collins, John A. In Your Midst: Perspectives on Christian Mission. (Orig.). 1980. pap. 3.25 (ISBN 0-377-00101-5). Friend Pr.

MISSIONARIES
Kung, Andres. Bruce Olson: Missionary of American Colonizer? LC 80-69309. 1981. pap. 5.95 (ISBN 0-915684-83-7). Christian Herald.
Taylor, Hudson & Thompson, Phyllis. God's Adventurer. (Illus.). 1978. pap. 2.25 (ISBN 0-85363-094-1). OMF Bks.
Wilson, Samuel, ed. Mission Handbook: North American Protestant Ministries Overseas. 1980. 22.50 (ISBN 0-912552-34-4). MARC.

MISSIONARIES–CORRESPONDENCE, REMINISCENCES, ETC.
Culpepper, Robert H. God's Calling: A Missionary Autobiography. LC 80-68643. 1981. 4.95 (ISBN 0-8054-6323-2). Broadman.
Fife, Eric S. Against the Clock: The Story of Ray Buker, Sr., Olympic Runner & Missionary Statesman. (Illus.). 224p. (Orig.). 1981. pap. 5.95 (ISBN 0-310-24351-3). Zondervan.

MISSIONARY STORIES
Kendrick, Bv. Ben. Battle for Yanga. LC 80-20643. 127p. 1980. pap. 3.95 (ISBN 0-87227-074-2). Reg Baptist.

MISSIONS
see also Communication (Theology); Evangelistic Work; Missionaries
also subdivision Missions under names of churches, denominations, religious orders, etc. e.g. Church of England–Missions; Jesuits–Missions; Lutheran Church–Missions; Spanish Missions of California
Anderson, Gerald H. & Stransky, Thomas F., eds. Mission Trends No. Five: Faith Meets Faith. (Mission Trends Ser.). 320p. (Orig.). 1981. pap. 3.95 (ISBN 0-8028-1821-8). Eerdmans.
--Mission Trends No.5: Faith Meets Faith, No. 5. (Orig.). 1981. pap. 3.95 (ISBN 0-8091-2356-8). Paulist Pr.
Forbes, William R. Engaging in Mission: A Study-Action Guide. (Orig.). 1980. pap. 2.25 (ISBN 0-377-00102-3). Friend Pr.
Kane, J. Herbert. The Christian World Mission: Today & Tomorrow. 240p. 1981. 9.95 (ISBN 0-8010-5426-5). Baker Bk.
McFadyen, J. F. The Missionary Idea in Life & Religion. 194p. Repr. of 1926 ed. text ed. 3.50 (ISBN 0-567-02180-7). Attic Pr.
Starkes, M. Thomas. The Foundation for Missions. LC 80-67460. 1981. pap. 4.95 (ISBN 0-8054-6325-9). Broadman.
Wilson, Samuel, ed. Mission Handbook: North American Protestant Ministries Overseas. 1980. 22.50 (ISBN 0-912552-34-4). MARC.

MISSIONS–HISTORY
Hefley, James & Hefley, Marti. Unstilled Voices. LC 80-70116. 224p. 1981. 8.95 (ISBN 0-915684-85-3). Christian Herald.

MISSIONS–THEORY
Newbigin, Lesslie. Sign of the Kingdom. 48p. (Orig.). 1981. pap. 1.95 (ISBN 0-8028-1878-1). Eerdmans.

MISSIONS–AFRICA, EAST
Healey, Joseph G. A Fifth Gospel: The Experience of Black Christian Values. LC 80-25033. (Illus.). 320p. (Orig.). 1981. pap. 7.95 (ISBN 0-88344-013-X). Orbis Bks.

MISSIONS–ASIA
Wagner, C. Peter & Dayton, Edward R. Unreached Peoples, Eighty-One. (Orig.). 1981. pap. 8.95 (ISBN 0-89191-331-9). Cook.

MISSIONS–LATIN AMERICA
Materne, Yves, ed. Indian Awakening in Latin America. (Orig.). 1980. pap. 5.95 (ISBN 0-377-00097-3). Friend Pr.

MISSIONS–OCEANICA
Wiltgen, R. M. The Founding of the Roman Catholic Church in Oceania 1825-1850. LC 78-74665. (Illus.). 610p. 1980. text ed. 36.95 (ISBN 0-7081-0835-0, 0572). Bks Australia.

MISSIONS–UNITED STATES
Cochran, Alice C. Miners, Merchants & Missionaries: The Roles of Missionaries & Pioneer Churches in the Colorado Gold Rush & Its Aftermath, 1858-1870. LC 80-16895. (ATLA Monographs: No. 15). x, 287p. 1980. 15.00 (ISBN 0-8108-1325-4). Scarecrow.
Mathieson, Moira. Shepherds of the Delectable Mountains: The Story of the Washington County Mission. 1979. 2.00 (ISBN 0-686-28792-4). Forward Movement.

MISSIONS, CITY
see City Missions

MISSISSIPPI–HISTORY
Ray, William, ed. Conversations: Reynolds Price & William Ray. (Mississippi Collection Bulletin, No. 9). (Illus.). 82p. 1976. pap. 5.95x (ISBN 0-87870-086-2). Memphis St Univ.

MISSISSIPPI RIVER–DESCRIPTION AND TRAVEL
Schwaig, Robert. Odessy of the Blithe Spirit II. 200p. (Orig.). pap. 6.95 (ISBN 0-86629-024-9). Sunrise MO.

MISSISSIPPI RIVER–JUVENILE LITERATURE
Cooper, Kay. Journeys on the Mississippi. (Illus.). 96p. (gr. 4-6). 1981. PLB 7.29 (ISBN 0-686-69304-3). Messner.

MISSOURI
see also names of cities, regions, etc. in Missouri, e.g. St. Louis, Platte County
Christensen, Parrish, et al. Missouri Heart of the Nation. LC 80-66209. 1980. text ed. 16.95x (ISBN 0-88273-237-4). Forum Pr MO.

MISSOURI–HISTORY
Kremer, et al. Missouri's Black Heritage. LC 79-54887. (Orig.). 1980. pap. text ed. 6.95x (ISBN 0-88273-115-7). Forum Pr MO.
Terry, Dickson. There's a Town in Missouri. 136p. (Orig.). 1980. pap. 4.95 (ISBN 0-86629-016-8). Sunrise MO.

MISTAKES
see Errors, Popular

MITHRAISM
Speidel, Michael P. Mithras-Orion: Greek Hero & Roman Army God. (Illus.). 56p. 1980. pap. text ed. 16.00x (ISBN 90-04-06055-3). Humanities.

MITRAL VALVE–DISEASES
see Heart–Diseases

MIXED CYCLOIDS (CHEMISTRY)
see Heterocyclic Compounds

MIXED LANGUAGES
see Languages, Mixed

MIXED MARRIAGE
see Marriage, Mixed

MNEMONICS
see also Memory
Mackinnon, Lillias. Music by Heart. LC 80-26551. xi, 141p. 1981. Repr. of 1954 ed. lib. bdg. 17.50x (ISBN 0-313-22810-8, MAMB). Greenwood.
Suid, Murray. Demonic Mnemonics. LC 80-82982. 1981. pap. 5.50 (ISBN 0-8224-6464-0). Pitman Learning.

MO-PEDS
see Mopeds

MOBILE HOMES
Raskhodoff, Nicholas M. The Complete Mobile Home Book: The Guide to Manufactured Homes. LC 80-5798. 240p. 1981. 19.95 (ISBN 0-8128-2781-3). Stein & Day.

MOBILITY
see Migration, Internal; Social Mobility

MODALITY (LOGIC)
Bellugi, U. & Studdert-Kennedy, M., eds. Signed & Spoken Language: Biological Constraints on Linguistic Form. (Dahlem Workshop Reports, Life Science Research Report Ser.: No. 19). (Illus.). 379p. (Orig.). 1980. pap. 35.70 (ISBN 0-89573-034-0). Verlag Chemie.

MODEL AIRPLANES
see Airplanes–Models

MODEL CARS
see Automobiles–Models

MODEL CITIES
see City Planning

MODEL-MAKING
see Models and Modelmaking

MODEL RAILROADS
see Railroads–Models

MODEL SAMPLING
see Monte Carlo Method

MODELING
see also Sculpture–Technique
Olson, Lynn. Sculpting with Cement: Direct Modeling in a Permanent Medium. (Illus.). 106p. (Orig.). (gr. 11-12). 1981. pap. price not set (ISBN 0-9605678-0-1). Steelstone.

MODELING IN WAX
see Wax Modeling

MODELS, FASHION
Tiegs, Cheryl. The Way to Natural Beauty. (Illus.). 1980. 12.95 (ISBN 0-686-68753-1, 24894). S&S.

MODELS, MECHANICAL
see Machinery–Models

MODELS AND MODELMAKING
see also Pattern-Making; Simulation Methods
also subdivision Models under names of objects, e.g. Automobiles–Models; and Machinery–Models; Surfaces, Models of
Chaney, Charles & Skee, Stanley. Plaster Mold & Model Making. 144p. 1981. Repr. of 1973 ed. text ed. write for info. (ISBN 0-89874-282-X). Krieger.
Frank, Adolph F. Animated Scale Models Handbook. LC 80-22858. (Illus.). 160p. 1981. lib. bdg. 10.00 (ISBN 0-668-05118-3, 5118). Arco.
Himmelblau, David M. Process Analysis & Simulation: Deterministic Systems. (Illus.). 333p. 1980. pap. text ed. 29.95 (ISBN 0-88408-132-X). Sterling Swift.
Jackson, Albert & Day, David. The Modelmaker's Handbook. LC 80-2702. (Illus.). 352p. 1981. 19.95 (ISBN 0-394-50788-6). Knopf.
Laming, Roy. Fun with Building Models. (Learning with Fun Ser.). (Illus.). 64p. 1980. text ed. 11.50x (ISBN 0-7182-1322-X, SpS). Soccer.
Lamit, Gary. Industrial Model Building. (Illus.). 528p. 1981. text ed. 38.00 (ISBN 0-13-461566-2). P-H.
Sansweet, Stephen. Science Fiction Toys & Models, Vol. I. 1980. pap. 3.95 (ISBN 0-931064-27-9). O'Quinn Studio.

MODELS AND MODELMAKING–RADIO CONTROL SYSTEMS
Laidlaw-Dickson, D. J. Radio Control Model Cars Manual. (Illus.). 128p. (Orig.). 1979. pap. 10.00x (ISBN 0-906958-00-8). Intl Pubns Serv.
Siposs, George G. Building & Racing Radio Control Cars & Motorcycles. Angle, Burr, ed. LC 80-84853. (Illus.). 80p. (Orig.). 1981. pap. price not set (ISBN 0-89024-556-8). Kalmbach.

MODERN ART
see Art, Modern–20th Century

MODERN DANCE
Haselbach, Barbara. Improvisation, Dance, & Movement. Murray, Margaret, tr. from Ger. Orig. Title: Improvisation, Tanz, Bewegung. 1980. Repr. of 1976 ed. pap. 19.00 (ISBN 0-918812-15-1). Magnamusic.
McDonagh, Don. Rise & Fall & Rise of Modern Dance. 1970. 7.95 (ISBN 0-87690-013-9). Dutton.

MODERN LITERATURE
see Literature, Modern (Collections)

MODERN MUSIC
see Music–History and Criticism–20th Century

MODERN PHILOSOPHY
see Philosophy, Modern

MODERN POETRY
see Poetry, Modern (Collections)

MODERNISM–CATHOLIC CHURCH
Daly, Gabriel. Transcendence & Immanence: A Study in Catholic Modernism & Integralism. 266p. 1980. 34.95x (ISBN 0-19-826652-9). Oxford U Pr.

MODOC INDIANS
see Indians of North America–Northwest, Pacific

MODULAR ARITHMETIC
Negus, Robert W. Fundamentals of Finite Mathematics. 416p. 1981. Repr. of 1974 ed. text ed. price not set (ISBN 0-89874-270-6). Krieger.

MOGOLLON INDIANS
see Indians of North America–Southwest, New

MOHAMMED, THE PROPHET, 570-632
Bermann, Richard A. The Mahdi of Alah: The Story of the Dervish, Mohammed Ahmed. John, Robin, tr. LC 80-1935. 1981. Repr. of 1932 ed. 36.00 (ISBN 0-404-18955-5). AMS Pr.
Narayan, B. K. Mohammed: The Prophet of Islam, a Flame in the Desert. 250p. 1980. text ed. 27.50x (ISBN 0-8426-1662-4). Verry.

MOHAMMEDAN
see headings beginning with the word Islamic or Muslim

MOHAMMEDANISM
see Islam

MOHAMMEDANS
see Muslims

MOHAVE DESERT, CALIFORNIA
Abbey, Edward. Desert Solitaire. rev. ed. (Literature of the American Wilderness). (Illus.). 296p. 1981. Repr. of 1968 ed. 12.50 (ISBN 0-87905-070-5). Peregrine Smith.

MOHAVE INDIANS
see Indians of North America–Southwest, New

MOHEGAN INDIANS
see Indians of North America–Eastern States

MOLD (BOTANY)
see Molds (Botany)

MOLD, VEGETABLE
see Soils

MOLDING (CLAY, PLASTER, ETC.)
see Modeling; Prosthesis; Sculpture–Technique

MOLDING (PLASTIC)
see Plastics–Molding

MOLDS (BOTANY)
see also Fungi
Malloch, David. Moulds: Their Isolation, Cultivation, & Identification. 88p. 1981. 12.95x (ISBN 0-8020-2418-1). U of Toronto Pr.

MOLECULAR BIOLOGY
Cohn, Waldo E., ed. Progress in Nucleic Acid Research & Molecular Biology, Vol. 25. (Serial Publication). 1981. 29.50 (ISBN 0-12-540025-X); lib. bdg. 38.50 (ISBN 0-12-540094-2); microfiche ed. 20.00 (ISBN 0-12-540095-0). Acad Pr.
Dodson, Guy, et al, eds. Structural Studies on Molecules of Biological Interest: A Volume in Honour of Professor Dorothy Hodgkin. (Illus.). 400p. 1981. 115.00 (ISBN 0-19-855362-5). Oxford U Pr.
Fermi, G. & Perutz, M. F. Haemoglobin & Myoglobin. (Atlas of Molecular Structures in Biology Ser.: No. 2). (Illus.). 100p. 1981. text ed. 45.00x (ISBN 0-19-854706-4). Oxford U Pr.
Hahn, F. E., et al, eds. Progress in Molecular & Subcellular Biology, Vol. 7. (Illus.). 260p. 1980. 50.80 (ISBN 0-387-10150-0). Springer-Verlag.
Jope, Charlene A. Cellular & Molecular Laboratory Manual. 64p. 1981. pap. text ed. 5.95 (ISBN 0-8403-2353-0). Kendall-Hunt.
Meister, Alton, ed. Advances in Enzymology & Related Areas of Molecular Biology. Vol. 45, 1977. 36.50 (ISBN 0-471-02726-X, Pub. by Wiley-Interscience); Vol. 46, 1978. 41.50 (ISBN 0-471-02993-9); Vol. 47, 1978. 42.50 (ISBN 0-471-04116-5); Vol. 51, 1980, 225p. 29.50 (ISBN 0-471-05653-7). Wiley.
Noble, D. & Blundell, T. L., eds. Progress in Biophysics & Molecular Biology, Vol. 35. (Illus.). 206p. 1981. 62.50 (ISBN 0-08-027122-7). Pergamon.
Price, F. W. Basic Molecular Biology. 497p. 1979. 25.95 (ISBN 0-471-69729-X). Wiley.

MOLECULAR PHYSIOLOGY
see Biological Physics

MOLECULAR STRUCTURE
Wheatley, P. J. Determination of Molecular Structure. 2nd, rev. ed. 264p. 1981. pap. 5.00 (ISBN 0-486-64068-X). Dover.

MOLECULES
see also Macromolecules; Molecular Structure
CIAMDA Eighty: An Index to the Literature on Atomic & Molecular Collision Data Relevant to Fusion Research. 498p. 1980. pap. 31.25 (ISBN 92-0-039080-3, ISP550, IAEA). Unipub.
Ratajczak, H. & Orville-Thomas, W. J. Molecular Interactions. Vol. 1, 448 Pp. 78.00 (ISBN 0-471-27664-2, 1-500); Vol. 2. write for info. (ISBN 0-471-27681-2). Wiley.

MOLLUSKS
see also Gasteropoda; Lamellibranchiata; Shells; Snails
Byrne, John H. & Koester, John, eds. Molluscan Nerve Cells: From Biophysics to Behavior. (Cold Spring Harbor Reports in the Neurosciences Ser.: Vol. 1). 250p. 1980. 26.00x (ISBN 0-87969-135-2). Cold Spring Harbor.
Walne, Peter R. Culture of Bivalve Molluscs: Fifty Years' Experience at Conwy. (Illus.). 190p. 16.25 (ISBN 0-85238-063-1, FN). Unipub.

MOLTEN METALS
see Liquid Metals

MOLTEN SALTS
see Fused Salts

MOLYBDENUM
Sutulor, Alexander, ed. International Molybdenum Encyclopedia, 3 vols. Incl. Vol. 1. Resources & Production. 402p. 1978; Vol. 2. Metallurgy & Processing. 375p. 1979; Vol. 3. Products, Uses & Trade. 341p. 1980. (Illus.). Set. text ed. 330.00 (ISBN 0-87930-098-1). Miller Freeman.

MOMBASA
Freeman-Grenville, G. S. The Mombasa Rising Against the Portuguese, Sixteen Thirty-One: From Sworn Evidence. (British Academy-Fontes Historiae Africanae). (Illus.). 224p. 98.00x (ISBN 0-19-725992-8). Oxford U Pr.

MONACHISM
see Monasticism and Religious Orders
MONASTERIES
see also Monasticism and Religious Orders
Braunfels, Wolfgang. Monasteries of Western Europe: The Architecture of the Orders. LC 73-2472. (Illus.). 263p. 1980. 35.00x; pap. 15.00x (ISBN 0-691-00313-0). Princeton U Pr.
Prip-Moller, Johannes. Chinese Buddhist Monasteries. (Illus.). 410p. 1981. 65.00 (ISBN 0-85656-034-0). Great Eastern.
Zouche, Robert C. Visits to Monasteries in the Levant. LC 80-2200. 1981. Repr. of 1916 ed. 45.00 (ISBN 0-404-18989-X). AMS Pr.
MONASTIC AND RELIGIOUS LIFE
see also Celibacy; Spiritual Direction
Bale, John. The First Two Partes of the Acts or Unchaste Examples of the Englyshe Votaryes. LC 79-84086. (English Experience Ser.: No. 906). 540p. 1979. Repr. of 1560 ed. lib. bdg. 40.00 (ISBN 90-221-0906-2). Walter J Johnson.
MONASTICISM AND RELIGIOUS ORDERS
see also Benedictines; Hospitalers; Jesuits; Monasteries; Monastic and Religious Life; Retreats; Trappists
Bharati, Agahananda. The Ochre Robe: An Autobiography. 2nd ed. 300p. 1980. 14.95 (ISBN 0-915520-40-0); pap. 7.95. Ross-Erikson.
Guigo II. Guigo II: The Ladder of Monks & Twelve Meditations. Colledge, Edmund & Walsh, James, trs. (Cistercian Studies: No. 48). 1981. pap. write for info. (ISBN 0-87907-748-4). Cistercian Pubns.
Veilleux, Armand, tr. Pachomian Koinonia I: The Life of St. Pachomius. (Cistercian Studies: No. 45). 524p. (Coptic Greek.). 1981. write for info.; pap. price not set (ISBN 0-87907-945-2). Cistercian Pubns.
MONASTICISM AND RELIGIOUS ORDERS–EGYPT
Ward, Benedicta & Russell, Norman, trs. from Gr. The Lives of the Desert Fathers: The Historia Monachorum in Aegypto. (Cistercian Studies: No. 34). 1981. price not set (ISBN 0-87907-834-0); pap. price not set (ISBN 0-87907-934-7). Cistercian Pubns.
MONASTICISM AND RELIGIOUS ORDERS, ORTHODOX EASTERN
Chetverikov, Sergii. Starets Paisii Velichkovskii: His Life, Teachings & Influence on Orthodox Monasticism. Janov, Carol, ed. Lickwar, Vasily & Lisenko, Alexander I., trs. from Rus. LC 75-29632. 340p. (Orig.). 1980. pap. 35.00 (ISBN 0-913124-22-2). Nordland Pub.
MONETARY POLICY
see also Credit
Griffiths, Brian, ed. Monetary Targets. Wood, Geoffrey E. 27.50 (ISBN 0-312-54421-9). St Martin.
Hamberg, Daniel. The U. S. Monetary System: Money, Banking, & Financial Markets. 1981. text ed. 16.95 (ISBN 0-316-34096-0). Little.
Hanson, J. L. Monetary Theory & Practice. 6th ed. (Illus.). 352p. 1978. pap. text ed. 13.95x (ISBN 0-7121-1293-6, Pub. by Macdonald & Evans England). Intl Ideas.
--An Outline of Monetary Theory. 4th ed. 160p. 1980. pap. text ed. 9.95x (ISBN 0-7121-1533-1). Intl Ideas.
MONETARY POLICY–INDIA
Gupta, Suraj B. Monetary Planning for India. 252p. 1979. text ed. 14.95x (ISBN 0-19-561145-4). Oxford U Pr.
MONETARY QUESTION
see Money
MONEY
see also Banks and Banking; Barter; Capital; Coinage; Coins; Counterfeits and Counterfeiting; Credit; Finance; Finance, Public; Foreign Exchange; Gold; Inflation (Finance); Mints; Paper Money; Precious Metals; Quantity Theory of Money; Silver; Silver Question; Tokens; Wealth
also names of coins, e.g. Dollar
Dennis, G. E. Monetary Economics. (Modern Economic Ser.). (Illus.). 320p. (Orig.). 1981. pap. text ed. 18.95x (ISBN 0-582-45573-1). Longman.
Hudgeons. Hewitt-Donln Catalog of U. S. Small Size Paper Money. 14th ed. (Collector Ser.). (Illus.). 192p. 1981. pap. 3.50 (ISBN 0-87637-112-8, 112-08). Hse of Collectibles.
--The Official Guide to Detecting Altered Counterfeit Coins & Currency. (Collector Ser.). (Illus.). 160p. (Orig.). 1981. pap. 4.95 (ISBN 0-87637-169-1, 169-01). Hse of Collectibles.
--The Official Investors Guide to Buying & Selling Gold, Silver & Diamonds. (Collector Ser.). (Illus.). 160p. (Orig.). 1981. pap. 4.95 (ISBN 0-87637-171-3, 171-03). Hse of Collectibles.
Leijonhufvud, Axel. Information & Coordination: Essays in Macroeconomic Theory. (Illus.). 320p. 1981. text ed. 15.95x (ISBN 0-19-502814-7); pap. text ed. 9.95x (ISBN 0-19-502815-5). Oxford U Pr.
Moore, William G., Sr. Basic Business Facts: Evaluating Money Resources. 1980. pap. text ed. 1.99 (ISBN 0-934488-02-9). Williams Ent.
Radford, Charles D. What No One, but Absolutely No One Knows About Money. (Illus.). 127p. 1981. 31.25 (ISBN 0-89266-284-0). Am Classical Coll Pr.
Spadone, Frank G. Major Variety & Oddity Guide of U. S. Coins. 8th ed. LC 80-84159. (Collector Ser.). (Illus.). 128p. 1981. pap. 4.95 (ISBN 0-87637-162-4, 162-04). Hse of Collectibles.
You Are a Money Brain. Drollinger, William C. Jr. 1981. write for info. (ISBN 0-914244-07-8). Epic Pubns.
MONEY–JUVENILE LITERATURE
German, Joan W. The Money Book. (Illus.). 32p. (ps-2). 1981. 5.95 (ISBN 0-525-66726-1). Elsevier-Nelson.
MONEY–PROGRAMMED INSTRUCTION
Soracco, Lionel J., Jr. Math House Proficiency Review Tapes: Applications Involving Money, Unit D. (YA) (gr. 7 up). 1980. manual & cassettes 159.95 (ISBN 0-917792-06-8). Math Hse.
MONEY–GREAT BRITAIN
Dennis, G. E. Monetary Economics. (Modern Economic Ser.). (Illus.). 320p. (Orig.). 1981. pap. text ed. 18.95x (ISBN 0-582-45573-1). Longman.
MONEY, QUANTITY THEORY OF
see Quantity Theory of Money
MONEY RAISING
see Fund Raising
MONEY SUPPLY
see Money
MONGOLIA–HISTORY
Boyle, J. A. The Mongol World Empire, 1206-1370. 316p. 1980. 60.00x (ISBN 0-86078-002-3, Pub. by Variorum England). State Mutual Bk.
Ewing, Thomas E. Between the Hammer & the Anvil? Chinese & Russian Policies in Outer Mongolia, 1911-1921. (Indiana University Uralic & Altaic Ser.). iv, 300p. 1980. text ed. 19.50 (ISBN 0-933070-06-3). Ind U Res Inst.
--Between the Hammer & the Anvil? Chinese & Russian Policies in Outer Mongolia, 1911-1921. (Indiana University Uralic & Altaic Ser.: Vol. 138). 300p. 1980. 20.00 (ISBN 0-933070-06-3). Ind U Res Inst.
MONGOLIAN LANGUAGE
Poppe, Nicholas. Mongolian Language Handbook. LC 72-125673. (Language Handbook Ser.). 1970. pap. text ed. 5.00 (ISBN 0-87281-003-8). Ctr Appl Ling.
MONGOLS–HISTORY
Boyle, J. A. The Mongol World Empire, 1206-1370. 316p. 1980. 60.00x (ISBN 0-86078-002-3, Pub. by Variorum England). State Mutual Bk.
Moses, Larry W. The Political Role of Mongol Buddhism. (Indiana University Uralic & Altaic Ser.: Vol. 133). x, 299p. 1977. 14.95 (ISBN 0-933070-01-2). Ind U Res Inst.
Pelliot, Paul. Les Mongols et la Papaute, 3 pts. in 1 vol. LC 80-2365. 1981. Repr. of 1923 ed. 34.50 (ISBN 0-404-18913-X). AMS Pr.
MONILIALES
Tubaki, K. Hyphomycetes: Their Perfect-Imperfect Connexions. 300p. 1981. lib. bdg. 20.00x (ISBN 3-7682-1267-X). Lubrecht & Cramer.
MONITORING (HOSPITAL CARE)
see also Hospital Care
Chertow, Bruce S., et al. Patient Management Problems: Exercises in Decision Making & Problem Solving. 336p. 1979. pap. 28.95x (ISBN 0-8385-7769-5). ACC.
Huch, Albert, et al, eds. Continous Transcutaneous Blood Gas Monitorin. LC 79-2586. (Alan R. Liss Ser.: Vol. 15, No. 4). 1979. 68.00 (ISBN 0-8451-1027-6). March of Dimes.
Lauersen, Neils H. & Hochberg, Howard. Clinical Perinatal Biochemical Monitoring. 271p. 1981. write for info. (1901-1). Williams & Wilkins.
MONKS
see Monasticism and Religious Orders
MONOGENIC FUNCTIONS
see Analytic Functions
MONOLOGUE
Westrom, Robert. Monologues for the Actor. 60p. (Orig.). 1978. pap. 2.50 (ISBN 0-938230-02-6). Westrom.
MONOPOLIES
see also Competition; Corporation Law; Restraint of Trade
Spelling, Thomas C. A Treatise on Trusts & Monopolies, Containing an Exposition of the Rule of Public Policy Against Contracts & Combinations in Restraint of Trade, & a Review of Cases, Ancient & Modern. xxvii, 274p. 1981. Repr. of 1893 ed. lib. bdg. 27.50x (ISBN 0-8377-1116-9). Rothman.
MONROE, MARILYN, 1926-1962
Samuels, M. Screen Greats: Monroe. 1980. pap. 2.95 (ISBN 0-931064-32-5). O'Quinn Studio.
MONSOONS
Lighthill, J. & Pearce, R. P., eds. Monsoon Dynamics. LC 78-72091. (Illus.). 700p. Date not set. 130.00 (ISBN 0-521-22497-7). Cambridge U Pr.
MONSTERS
see also Abnormalities, Human
De Menil, Dominique, intro. by. Constant Companions: An Exhibition of Mythological Animals, Demons, & Monsters. (Illus.). 1964. pap. 6.00 (ISBN 0-914412-19-1). Inst for the Arts.
Mank, Gregory W. It's Alive: The Classic Cinema Saga of Frankenstein. LC 80-26625. (Illus.). 176p. 1981. 15.00 (ISBN 0-498-02473-3). A S Barnes.
MONSTERS–JUVENILE LITERATURE
Cohen, Daniel. Everything You Need to Know About Monsters & Still Be Able to Get to Sleep. LC 79-6589. (Illus.). 128p. (gr. 4 up). 1981. 7.95a (ISBN 0-385-15803-3); PLB (ISBN 0-385-15804-1). Doubleday.
--Greatest Monsters in the World. (Illus.). (gr. 4 up). 1977. pap. 1.50 (ISBN 0-671-29990-5). PB.
Dynamite Monster Hall of Fame. (gr. 3-5). pap. 1.50 (ISBN 0-590-11806-4, Schol Pap). Schol Bk Serv.
MONTAIGNE, MICHEL EYQUEM DE, 1533-1592
Frame, Donald M. & McKinley, Mary B., eds. Columbia Montaigne Conference: Papers. (French Forum Monographs: No. 27). 120p. (Orig.). 1981. pap. 11.50 (ISBN 0-917058-26-7). French Forum.
McKinley, Mary B. Words in a Corner: Studies in Montaigne's Latin Quotations. (French Forum Monogaraphs: No. 26). 120p. (Orig.). 1981. pap. 9.50 (ISBN 0-917058-25-9). French Forum.
MONTANA
see also cities, counties, towns, etc. in montana
Cook, Lewis. Beautiful Montana Country. Shangle, Robert D., ed. (Illus.). 72p. 1980. 12.95 (ISBN 0-89802-205-3); pap. 6.95 (ISBN 0-89802-206-1). Beautiful Am.
Fradin, Dennis. Montana: In Words & Pictures. LC 80-25023. (Young People's Stories of Our States Ser.). (Illus.). 48p. (gr. 2-5). 1981. PLB 8.65g (ISBN 0-516-03926-1, Time Line). Childrens.
Melcher, Joan. Watering Hole: A User's Guide to Montana Bars. 128p. 1980. pap. text ed. 6.95 (ISBN 0-938314-00-9). MT Mag.
Peterson, Martin L. The Complete Montana Travel Guide. LC 79-88126. (Illus.). 224p. 1980. pap. 5.95 (ISBN 0-686-28763-0). Lake County.
MONTANA–HISTORY
Lang, William. Montana: Our Land & People. (Illus.). 1981. pap. 11.95 (ISBN 0-87108-586-0). Pruett.
Randolph, Edmund. Beef, Leather & Grass. LC 80-18818. (Illus.). 304p. 1981. 14.95 (ISBN 0-8061-1517-3). U of Okla Pr.
Whitehead, Bruce & Whitehead, Charlotte. Montana Bound: An Activity Approach to Teaching Montana History. (Illus.). 180p. (gr. 5-6). 1980. pap. text ed. 7.95x (ISBN 0-87108-235-7). Pruett.
MONTE CARLO METHOD
Habib, Muhammad K. Sampling Representations & Approximations for Certain Functions & Stochastic Processes. 100p. 1980. pap. 3.15 (1260). U of NC Pr.
Rubenstein, Reuven Y. Simulation & the Monte Carlo Method. (Probability & Mathematical Statistics Ser.). 300p. 1981. 30.00 (ISBN 0-471-08917-6, Pub. by Wiley-Interscience). Wiley.
MONTEREY, CALIFORNIA
Hicks, John & Hicks, Regina. Monterey. (A Pictorial History: No. 2). (Illus.). 64p. 1973. pap. 3.95 (ISBN 0-914606-02-6). Creative Bks.
MONTEREY, CALIFORNIA–DESCRIPTION–VIEWS
Cannery Row, a Pictorial History. Date not set. price not set. Creative Bks.
Monterey, a Pictorial History. Date not set. price not set. Creative Bks.
MONTEVERDI, CLAUDIO, 1567-1643
Stevens, Denis. Letters of Claudio Monteverdi. LC 80-66219. 432p. 1980. 45.00 (ISBN 0-521-23591-X). Cambridge U Pr.
MONTREAL–HISTORY
Marsan, Jean C. Montreal in Evolution: Historical Analysis of the Development of Montreal Architecture & Urban Environment. (Illus.). 488p. 1981. 27.50x (ISBN 0-7735-0339-0). McGill-Queens U Pr.
Mouton, Claude. The Montreal Canadiens. 256p. 1981. 19.95 (ISBN 0-442-29634-7). Van Nos Reinhold.
Senior, Elinor K. British Regulars in Montreal: An Imperial Garrison, 1832-1854. (Illus.). 300p. 1981. 29.95 (ISBN 0-7735-0372-2). McGill-Queens U Pr.
MONUMENTAL THEOLOGY
see Bible–Antiquities; Christian Antiquities
MONUMENTS, SEPULCHRAL
see Sepulchral Monuments
MOONLIGHTING
see Supplementary Employment
MOORE, HENRY SPENCER, 1898-
Teague, Edward H. Henry Moore: Bibliography & Reproductions Index. LC 80-28048. (Illus.). 185p. 1981. lib. bdg. 21.00x (ISBN 0-89950-016-1). McFarland & Co.
MOORE, THOMAS, 1779-1852
Gywnn, Stephen L. Thomas Moore. 204p. 1980. Repr. of 1905 ed. lib. bdg. 22.50 (ISBN 0-8495-2045-2). Arden Lib.
MOORE, THOMAS STURGE, 1870-1944
Gwynn, Frederick L. Sturge Moore & the Life of Art. 159p. 1980. Repr. of 1952 ed. lib. bdg. 30.00 (ISBN 0-89984-249-6). Century Bookbindery.
MOORISH ARCHITECTURE
see Architecture, Islamic
MOORISH ART
see Art, Islamic
MOORISH LANGUAGE (INDIA)
see Urdu Language
MOPEDS
Consumer Guide Editors, ed. Complete Book of Mopeds. 1977. pap. 1.95 (ISBN 0-446-89475-3). Warner Bks.
MORAL CONDITIONS
see also Sex Customs
also subdivision Moral Conditions under names of countries, cities, etc., e.g. United States–Moral Conditions
Gewirth, Alan. Reason & Morality. pap. 9.95 (ISBN 0-226-28876-5). U of Chicago Pr.
Kohlberg, Lawrence. The Philosophy of Moral Development: Essays in Moral Development, Vol. 1. LC 80-8902. 256p. 1981. 17.95 (ISBN 0-06-064760-4). Har-Row.
MORAL EDUCATION
see also Christian Education; Religious Education
Cochrane, Don & Manley-Casimir, Michael, eds. Development of Moral Reasoning: Practical Approaches. LC 80-17141. 352p. 1980. 27.95 (ISBN 0-03-056209-0). Praeger.
Johnson, Henry C., Jr. The Public School & Moral Education. (The Education of the Public & the Public School Ser.). 96p. (Orig.). 1981. pap. 3.95 (ISBN 0-8298-0420-X). Pilgrim NY.
MORAL JUDGMENT
see Judgment (Ethics)
MORAL PHILOSOPHY
see Ethics
MORAL THEOLOGY
see Christian Ethics
MORAL VIRTUES
see Virtue and Virtues
MORALITY AND RELIGION
see Religion and Ethics
MORALS
see Conduct of Life; Ethics; Moral Conditions
MORALS AND WAR
see War and Morals
MORAN, THOMAS, 1837-1926
Priehs, Timothy J. Thomas Moran: The Grand Canyon Sketches. 1978. 2.95 (ISBN 0-938216-07-4). GCNHA.
MORAVIAN INDIANS
see Indians of North America–Eastern States
MORBID ANATOMY
see Anatomy, Pathological
MORE, THOMAS, SIR, SAINT, 1478-1535
Sargent, Daniel. Thomas More. 299p. 1980. Repr. of 1933 ed. lib. bdg. 30.00 (ISBN 0-89984-412-X). Century Bookbindery.
MORGAN, JOHN PIERPONT, 1837-1913
Canfield, Cass. Outrageous Fortunes: The Story of the Medici, the Rothschilds, & J. Pierpont Morgan. (Illus.). 1981. 10.95 (ISBN 0-15-170513-5). HarBraceJ.
Sinclair, Andrew. Corsair: The Life of J. Pierpont Morgan. 1981. 15.00 (ISBN 0-316-79240-3). Little.
MORMON TRAIL
Richards, Aurelia. The Mormon Trail: In Story Form. pap. 5.95 (ISBN 0-89036-137-1). Hawkes Pub Inc.
MORMONS AND MORMONISM
see also Church of Jesus Christ of Latter-Day Saints
Black, William T. Mormon Athletes. (Illus.). 6.95 (ISBN 0-87747-842-2). Deseret Bk.
Coleman, Gary J. A Look at Mormonism. pap. 3.95 (ISBN 0-89036-142-8). Hawkes Pub Inc.
Fluckiger, W. Lynn. Unique Advantages of Being a Mormon. pap. 3.95 (ISBN 0-89036-138-X). Hawkes Pub Inc.
Hansen, Klaus J. Mormonism & the American Experience. LC 80-19312. (History of American Religion Ser.). 224p. 1981. 15.00 (ISBN 0-226-31552-5). U of Chicago Pr.
Kern, Louis J. An Ordered Love: Sex Roles & Sexuality in Victorian Utopias--the Shakers, the Mormons, & the Oneida Community. LC 80-10763. xv, 430p. 1981. 24.00x (ISBN 0-8078-1443-1); pap. 12.50x (ISBN 0-8078-4074-2). U of NC Pr.
Le Grand Richards. A Marvelous Work & a Wonder. 424p. 14.00 (ISBN 0-87747-686-1); pap. 1.50 (ISBN 0-87747-614-4). Deseret Bk.
Miner, Caroline E. & Kimball, Edward L. Camilla. LC 80-69723. (Illus.). 1980. 5.95 (ISBN 0-87747-845-7). Deseret Bk.
Petersen, Mark E. The Great Prologue. LC 75-14997. 136p. 1976. pap. 1.50. Deseret Bk.
Richards, Aurelia. The Mormon Trail: In Story Form. pap. 5.95 (ISBN 0-89036-137-1). Hawkes Pub Inc.
Sturlaugson, Mary F. A Soul So Rebellious. 88p. 1980. 5.95 (ISBN 0-87747-841-4). Deseret Bk.
Taylor, Bill. A Tale of Two Cities: The Mormons-Catholics. 1981. pap. 4.00 (ISBN 0-933046-02-2). Little Red Hen.
Wallace, Arthur. Can Mormonism Be Proved Experimentally? 2nd rev. ed. 170p. 1973. 4.00 (ISBN 0-937892-00-9); pap. 3.00 (ISBN 0-937892-01-7). LL Co.
Wallace, Arthur, compiled by. L. D. S. Children's Comments, Vol. 1. 60p. 1978. pap. 1.95 (ISBN 0-937892-03-3). LL Co.
Widtsoe, John A. Discourses of Brigham Young. 497p. pap. 2.50 (ISBN 0-87747-788-4). Deseret Bk.
MORMONS AND MORMONISM–HISTORY
Long, E. B. The Saints & the Union: Utah Territory During the Civil War. LC 80-16775. (Illus.). 292p. 1981. 17.95 (ISBN 0-252-00821-9). U of Ill Pr.
Reay, Lee. Incredible Journey: Through the Hole-in-the-Rock. Hechtle, Ranier, ed. (Illus.). 128p. (Orig.). 1981. 5.95 (ISBN 0-934826-05-6); pap. 3.95 (ISBN 0-934826-06-4). Meadow Lane.

Roberts, B. H. Comprehensive History of the Church of Jesus Christ of Latter-Day-Saints, 6 vols. 1978. pap. 9.95 set (ISBN 0-8425-1275-6). Brigham.

Roberts, B. H., intro. by. History of the Church, 7 vols. Incl. Vol. 1 (1820-1834) 511p. 1974 (ISBN 0-87747-074-X); Vol. 2 (1834-1837) 543p. 1974 (ISBN 0-87747-075-8); Vol. 3 (1834-1839) 478p (ISBN 0-87747-076-6); Vol. 4 (1839-1842) 620p (ISBN 0-87747-077-4); Vol. 5 (1842-1843) 563p (ISBN 0-87747-078-2); Vol. 6 (1843-1844) 641p (ISBN 0-87747-079-0); Vol. 7 (period 2, The Apostolic Interregnum) 640p (ISBN 0-87747-080-4). 9.95 ea.; index 9.95 (ISBN 0-87747-291-2). Deseret Bk.

MORMONS AND MORMONISM–MISSIONS

Dennison, Mark A. Preparing for the Greatest Two Years of Your Life. pap. 3.95 (ISBN 0-89036-128-2). Hawkes Pub Inc.

Passantino, Robert, et al. Answer to the Cultist at Your Door. LC 80-83850. 1981. pap. 4.95 (ISBN 0-89081-275-6). Harvest Hse.

MORMONS AND MORMONISM–SERMONS

Russon, Robb. Letters to a New Elder: The Melchizedek Priesthood, Its Duty Fulfillment. pap. 2.95 (ISBN 0-89036-144-4). Hawkes Pub Inc.

MORMONS AND MORMONISM IN MEXICO

Palmer, David S. In Search of Cumorah. LC 80-83866. (Illus.). 300p. 1981. 7.75 (ISBN 0-88290-169-9, 1063). Horizon Utah.

MOROCCO–DESCRIPTION AND TRAVEL

Kininmonth, Christopher. The Travellers' Guide to Morocco. rev. ed. (Illus.). 356p. 1981. pap. 10.95 (ISBN 0-224-01897-3, Pub. by Chatto-Bodley-Jonathan). Merrimack Bk Serv.

MOROCCO–HISTORY

see also Beni Marin Dynasty

Cigar, Norman, ed. Muhammad Al-Qadiris Nashr Al Mathani: The Chronicles. (Fontes Historiae Africanae Ser.). (Illus.). 400p. 1980. 89.00 (ISBN 0-19-725994-4). Oxford U Pr.

Spencer, William. Historical Dictionary of Morocco. LC 80-21328. (African Historical Dictionaries: No. 24). 195p. 1980. 11.00 (ISBN 0-8108-1362-9). Scarecrow.

MORONS

see Mentally Handicapped

MORPHOGENESIS

see also Botany–Morphology; Cell Differentiation; Morphology

Connelly, Thomas G., et al, eds. Morphogenesis & Pattern Formation. 325p. 1981. 29.50 (ISBN 0-89004-635-2). Raven.

Gorlin, Robert J., ed. Morphogenesis & Malformation of the Ear. LC 80-18892. (Alan R. Liss: Vol. 16,No. 4). 1980. 44.00 (ISBN 0-8451-1038-1). March of Dimes.

Rosenquist, Glenn C. & Bergsma, Daniel, eds. Morphogenesis & Malinformation of the Cardiovascular System. LC 78-14527. (Alan R. Liss Ser.: Vol. 14, No. 7). 1978. 46.00 (ISBN 0-8451-1023-3). March of Dimes.

MORPHOLOGY

see also Abnormalities, Human; Morphogenesis

McArdle, J. Functional Morphology of the Hip & Thigh of the Lorisiformes. (Contributions to Primatology Ser.: Vol. 17). (Illus.). 148p. 1981. pap. 19.25 (ISBN 3-8055-1767-X). S Karger.

Shipley, Kenneth G. & Banis, Carolyn S. Teaching Morphology Developmentally: Methods & Materials for Teaching Bound Morphology. 1981. manual 50.00 (ISBN 0-88450-728-9). Communication Skill.

Straub, W., ed. Current Genetical, Clinical & Morphological Problems. (Developments in Ophthalmology: Vol. 3). (Illus.). 1981. 66.00 (ISBN 3-8055-2000-X). S Karger.

MORPHOLOGY (PLANTS)

see Botany–Morphology

MORTALITY

see also Infants–Mortality

Alderson, Michael. International Mortality Statistics. 380p. 1981. lib. bdg. 55.00 (ISBN 0-87196-514-3). Facts on File.

Conde, Julien, et al. Mortality in Developing Countries. OECD Deveopment Centre, ed. (Development Centre Studies). (Orig.). 1980. Tome 1 & 2, 1266p. pap. 85.00 (ISBN 9-2640-2097-7, 41-80-05-3); Tome 3, 550p. pap. 30.00 (ISBN 9-2640-2120-5, 41-80-06-1). OECD.

MORTAR

Gutcho, M. H., ed. Cement & Mortar Technology & Additives: Developments Since 1977. LC 80-19343. (Chemical Tech. Rev. 173). 540p. (Orig.). 1981. 54.00 (ISBN 0-8155-0822-0). Noyes.

MORTUARY CUSTOMS

see Burial; Funeral Rites and Ceremonies

MORTUARY LAW

see Burial Laws

MORTUARY STATISTICS

see Infants–Mortality; Mortality

MOSAIC LAW

see Jewish Law

MOSAICS

DiFederico, Frank. The Mosaics of the National Shrine of the Immaculate Conception. (Illus.). 96p. 1981. 16.95 (ISBN 0-916276-09-0). Decatur Hse.

MOSCOW–DESCRIPTION

Blue Guide - Moscow & Leningrad. 1980. 29.95 (ISBN 0-528-84611-6); pap. 24.95 (ISBN 0-528-84607-8). Rand.

MOSES

Offner, Hazel. Moses: A Man Changed by God. 72p. (Orig.). 1981. pap. 2.95 (ISBN 0-87784-617-0). Inter-Varsity.

MOSES–JUVENILE LITERATURE

Baby Moses in a Basket. (Tell-a-Bible Story Ser.). (Illus.). 28p. bds. 0.69 (ISBN 0-686-68638-1, 3682). Standard Pub.

MOSLEM

see headings beginning with the word Islamic or Muslim

MOSLEMS

see Muslims

MOSQUES

Turanszky, Ilona. Azerbaijan: Mosques, Turrets, Palaces. Boros, Laszlo, tr. (Illus.). 184p. 1979. 22.50x (ISBN 963-13-0321-7). Intl Pubns Serv.

MOSSES

Taylor, Ronald J. & Leviton, Alan E., eds. Mosses of North America. 170p. (Orig.). 1980. 11.95 (ISBN 0-934394-02-4). AAASPD.

MOTHER AND CHILD

Friday, Nancy. My Mother, Myself. 1981. pap. 3.25 (ISBN 0-440-15663-7). Dell.

Hawley, Gloria H. Laura's Psalm. 1981. pap. 4.95 (ISBN 0-86608-000-7, 14014P). Impact Tenn.

Mandell, Dale. Early Feminine Development: Current Psychoanalytic Views. 1981. text ed. write for info. (ISBN 0-89335-135-0). Spectrum Pub.

Olsen, Paul. Sons & Mothers: Why Men Behave As They Do. Graver, Fred, ed. 300p. 1981. 11.95 (ISBN 0-87131-338-3). M Evans.

MOTHER GOOSE

Decker, Marjorie A. The Christian Mother Goose Treasury: Part II of the Original Christian Mother Goose Book. LC 80-69167. (Three Part Series: Vol. II). (Illus.). 112p. (gr. k-4). 1980. PLB 10.95 (ISBN 0-933724-01-2). CMG Prods.

MOTHER THERESA

Gonzalez-Balado, Jose. Always the Poor: Mother Teresa, Her Life & Message. Diaz, Olimpia, Sr., tr. from Span. 112p. (Orig.). 1980. pap. 2.50 (ISBN 0-89243-134-2). Liguori Pubns.

Lee, Betsy. Mother Teresa: Caring for All God's Children. LC 80-20286. (Taking Part Ser.). (Illus.). 48p. (gr. 3 up). 1981. PLB 6.95 (ISBN 0-87518-205-4). Dillon.

MOTHERS

see also Grandparents; Housewives; Maternal Deprivation; Prenatal Care; Stepmothers

Lessin, Roy. Moms Are God's Idea. (God's Idea Books Ser.). (Illus.). 32p. (ps-4). 1981. pap. 1.25 (ISBN 0-87123-175-1, 210175). Bethany Fell.

Seidman, Theodore R. & Albert, Marvin H. Becoming a Mother. 240p. 1980. pap. 1.95 (ISBN 0-686-69184-9, Crest). Fawcett.

MOTHERS (IN RELIGION, FOLKLORE, ETC.)

see Women (In Religion, Folklore, etc.)

MOTHERS, UNMARRIED

see Unmarried Mothers

MOTHS

Bradley, J. D., et al. British Tortricoid Moths. Incl. Vol.1. Cochylidae & Tortricidae: Tortricinae. viii, 251p. 1973. 50.00x (ISBN 0-903874-01-6); Vol. 2. Tortrkidae: Olethreutinae. viii, 336p. 1979. 100.00x (ISBN 0-903874-06-7). (Illus., Pub. by Brit Mus Nat Hist England). Sabbot-Natural Hist Bks.

DeTreville, Susan & DeTreville, Stan. Butterflies & Moths. (Illus.). 32p. (Orig.). 1981. pap. 3.50 (ISBN 0-89844-026-2). Troubador Pr.

Treat, Asher E. Mites of Moths & Butterflies. LC 75-7147. (Illus.). 368p. 1975. 45.00x (ISBN 0-8014-0878-4). Comstock.

Watson, A., et al. The Generic Names of Moths of the World. Vol. II. Noctuoidea: Arctiidae, Ctenuchidae, Dioptidae, Lymantriidae, Notodontidae, Thaumetopoeidae & Thyretidae. Nye, I. W., ed. (Illus.). xiv, 228p. 1980. 58.00x (ISBN 0-565-00811-0). Sabbot-Natural Hist Bks.

MOTILITY OF CELLS

see Cells–Motility

MOTION-PICTURE CAMERAS

see Moving-Picture Cameras

MOTION PICTURES

see Moving-Pictures

MOTION STUDY

see Time and Motion Study

MOTIVATION (PSYCHOLOGY)

see also Achievement Motivation; Motivation Research (Marketing); Self-Actualization (Psychology)

Eims, Leroy. Be a Motivation Leader. 144p. 1981. pap. 3.95 (ISBN 0-89693-008-4). Victor Bks.

Flowers, John H., ed. Nebraska Symposium on Motivation, 1980: Human Cognition. LC 53-11655. (Nebraska Symposium on Motivation: Vol. 28). 264p. 1981. 16.50x (ISBN 0-8032-0620-8); pap. 9.95x (ISBN 0-8032-0621-6). U of Nebr Pr.

Shinn, George. The Miracle of Motivation. 1981. text ed. 8.95 (ISBN 0-8423-4353-9). Tyndale.

Whitmore, D. A. & Ibbetson, J. The Management of Motivation & Renumeration. 230p. 1977. text ed. 29.50x (ISBN 0-220-66319-X, Pub. by Busn Bks England). Renouf.

MOTIVATION IN SPORTS

see Sports–Psychological Aspects

MOTIVATION RESEARCH (MARKETING)

Guder, Robert F. Managing for Productivity: Motivating Employees. Reilly, Harry, ed. 100p. 1980. binder 110.00 (ISBN 0-89290-090-3, SUB 111); participant 45.00 (ISBN 0-89290-089-X). Soc for Visual.

MOTOR ABILITY

see also Kinesiology

Capon, Jack. Successful Movement Challenges: Movement Activities for the Developing Child. Alexander, Frank & Alexander, Diane, eds. (Illus.). 129p. 1981. pap. 7.95 (ISBN 0-915256-07-X). Front Row.

Glaser, G. Temporal Lobe Psychomotor Seizures. 1981. pap. text ed. write for info. (ISBN 0-443-08000-3). Churchill.

Hall, Tom. Academic Ropes: A Perceptual-Motor Academic Program. Alexander, Frank & Alexander, Diane, eds. (Illus.). 89p. (Orig.). 1981. pap. 5.95 (ISBN 0-915256-08-8). Front Row.

--Classroom-Made Movement Materials: A Perceptual-Motor Program with Classroom-Made Materials. Alexander, Frank & Alexander, Diane, eds. (Illus., Orig.). 1981. pap. 5.95 (ISBN 0-915256-09-6). Front Row.

Jones, Barbara S. Movement Themes: Topics for Early Childhood Learning Through Creative Movement. LC 80-65608. 115p. 1981. perfect bdg. 8.50 (ISBN 0-86548-042-7). Century Twenty One.

Landers, Daniel & Roberts, Glyn, eds. Psychology of Motor Behavior & Sport 1980. 1981. text ed. 12.00x (ISBN 0-931250-19-6). Human Kinetics.

Schotland, Donald L. Diseases of the Motor Unit. (Illus.). 1981. price not set (ISBN 0-89289-410-5). HM.

MOTOR-BOATS

Block, Richard A., ed. Motorboat Operator License Preparation Course. rev. ed. (Illus.). 269p. 1980. pap. text ed. 18.00 (ISBN 0-934114-29-3). Marine Educ.

MOTOR-CARS

see Automobiles

MOTOR CYCLES

see Motorcycles

MOTOR DEXTERITY

see Motor Ability

MOTOR HOMES

see Campers and Coaches, Truck

MOTOR LEARNING

see also Perceptual-Motor Learning

Fiorentino, Mary R. A Basis for Sensorimotor Development-Normal & Abnormal: The Influence of Primitive, Postural Reflexes on the Development & Distribution of Tone. (Illus.). 184p. 1981. text ed. 14.75 (ISBN 0-398-04179-2). C C Thomas.

MOTOR SCOOTERS

see also names of motor scooters e.g. Vespa Motor Scooter

Edmonds, I. G. Minibikes & Minicycles for Beginners. (Illus.). (gr. 5-7). pap. 1.25 (ISBN 0-671-29783-X). PB.

MOTOR SKILL

see Motor Ability

MOTOR TRANSPORTATION

see Transportation, Automotive

MOTOR-TRUCKS

see also Campers and Coaches, Truck; Materials Handling; Vans

Arrow & D-Fifty Pick-Ups 1979-81. LC 80-70343. (Illus.). 192p. pap. 8.95. Chilton.

Green, Michael, ed. Truck Facts Buyer's Guide, 1981. rev. ed. 96p. (Orig.). write for info. DMR Pubns.

Green, Michael L., ed. New Truck & Van Prices, 1981. rev. ed. (Buyer's Guide Ser.). 96p. (Orig.). Date not set. pap. 2.50 (ISBN 0-89552-070-2). DMR Pubns.

--Used Truck & Van Prices. rev. ed. (Buyer's Guide Ser.). 96p. (Orig.). Date not set. pap. 2.25 (ISBN 0-89552-066-4). DMR Pubns.

Kennett, Pat. World Trucks: Berliet, No. 11. (Illus.). 88p. 1981. 19.95 (ISBN 0-85059-449-9). Aztex.

--World Trucks: International, No. 12. (Illus.). 88p. 1981. pap. 19.95 (ISBN 0-85059-503-7). Aztex.

Montville, John B. The Packard Truck: Ask the Man Who Owns One. (Illus.). 128p. 1981. pap. 14.95 (ISBN 0-89404-052-9). Aztex.

Quackenbush, Robert. City Trucks. Tucker, Kathleen, ed. (Illus.). 40p. (ps-4). 1981. 6.95 (ISBN 0-8075-1163-3). A Whitman.

Toyota Pick-Ups Nineteen Seventy to Eighty-One. LC 80-70344. (Illus.). 224p. 1980. pap. 8.95. Chilton.

MOTOR-TRUCKS–JUVENILE LITERATURE

Mann, Philip, ed. Camiones. Kreps, Georgian, tr. from Eng. (Shape Board Play Book). Orig. Title: Trucks. (Illus.). 14p. (Span.). (ps-3). 1981. bds. 3.50 plastic comb bdg (ISBN 0-89828-200-4, 5004SP). Tuffy Bks.

MOTOR VEHICLES

see also Automobiles; Ground-Effect Machines; Motorcycles

Newton. Motor Vehicle. 10th ed. 1981. text ed. price not set. Butterworth.

MOTOR VEHICLES–RECREATIONAL USE

Woodall's RV How to Guide. Date not set. pap. 4.95 (ISBN 0-671-25520-7). Woodall.

MOTORCYCLE RACING

Motocourse 1980-1981, No. 5. 208p. 1981. 36.95 (ISBN 0-905138-14-7). Motorbooks Intl.

MOTORCYCLES

see also Mopeds; Motor Scooters; Motorcycling; also names of motorcycles, e.g. B.S.A. motorcycle, Honda motorcycle

Caddell, Laurie & Winfield, Mike. Superbikes. (Orig.). 1981. pap. 9.95 (ISBN 0-89586-067-8). H P Bks.

Louis, Harry & Curry, Bob. The Story of Triumph Motorcycles. 3rd ed. (Illus.). 144p. 1981. 37.95 (ISBN 0-85059-480-4). Aztex.

Rich, Mark. Custom Cycles. LC 80-26659. (On the Move Ser.). (Illus.). 48p. (gr. 3-6). 1981. PLB 9.25 (ISBN 0-516-03887-7). Childrens.

Sparks, James C. Mini & Trail Bikes: How to Build Them Yourself. (Illus.). 1976. 9.95 (ISBN 0-87690-184-4); pap. 5.95 (ISBN 0-87690-190-9). Dutton.

Woollett, Mick. Lightweight Bikes. (Illus.). 64p. 1981. pap. 5.95 (Pub. by Batsford England). David & Charles.

MOTORCYCLING

Bishop, George. The Encyclopedia of Motorcycling. (Illus.). 1980. 16.95 (ISBN 0-686-68350-1). Putnam.

Jackson, Bob. Street Biking: How to Ride to Save Your Hide. 1980. pap. 5.95 (ISBN 0-89586-081-3). H P Bks.

Smith, Don. Trials Bike Riding. (EP Sports Ser.). (Illus.). 112p. 1981. 12.95 (ISBN 0-8069-9050-3, Pub. by EP Publishing England). Sterling.

MOTORS

see also Automobiles–Motors; Diesel Motor; Electric Motors

also subdivision Motors under subjects, e.g. Automobiles–Motors

Braymer, Daniel H. & Roe, A. C. Rewinding Small Motors. 3rd ed. LC 80-29580. 432p. 1981. Repr. of 1949 ed. lib. bdg. price not set (ISBN 0-89874-291-9). Krieger.

Brewster, Albert H., Jr. How to Convert Salvage Auto Starter to Powerful DC Motor. 2nd ed. (Illus.). 1981. pap. 6.00x (ISBN 0-918166-04-7). Amonics.

MOULAGE

see Prosthesis

MOULD (BOTANY)

see Molds (Botany)

MOUNT MCKINLEY

see McKinley, Mount

MOUNT VERNON

Bourne, Miriam A. The Children of Mount Vernon: A Guide to George Washington's Home. LC 80-974. (Illus.). 64p. (gr. 4-6). 1981. PLB 8.95 (ISBN 0-385-15535-2); pap. 4.95 (ISBN 0-385-15534-4). Doubleday.

MOUNTAIN CLIMBING

see Mountaineering

MOUNTAIN FLORA

see Alpine Flora

MOUNTAINEERING

see also Rock Climbing; Trails

Lee, Chip. Progressions in Climbing. (Illus.). 250p. 1981. pap. price not set (ISBN 0-910146-35-7). Appalach Mtn.

Loughman, Michael. Learning to Rock Climb. (Outdoor Activities Guides). (Illus.). 192p. (Orig.). 1981. 14.95 (ISBN 0-87156-281-2); pap. 9.95 (ISBN 0-87156-279-0). Sierra.

MacInnes, Hamish. High Drama. (Illus.). 224p. 1981. 11.95 (ISBN 0-89886-031-8). Mountaineers.

Marty, Sid. Men for the Mountains. (Illus.). 272p. 1981. Repr. of 1978 ed. pap. 6.95 (ISBN 0-89886-027-X). Mountaineers.

Messner, Reinhold. K Two: Mountain of Mountains. (Illus.). 176p. 1981. 35.00 (ISBN 0-19-520253-8). Oxford U Pr.

Moore, Terris. Mt. McKinley: The Pioneer Climbs. (Illus.). 224p. 1981. pap. 8.95 (ISBN 0-89886-021-0). Mountaineers.

Renouf, Jane & Hulse, Stewart. First Aid for Hill Walkers & Climbers. (Illus.). 169p. 1978. pap. 5.95 (ISBN 0-14-046293-7). Bradt Ent.

Whymper, Edward. Scrambles Amongst the Alps in the Years Eighteen Sixty to Eighteen Sixty-Nine. (Illus.). 176p. 1981. pap. 5.95 (ISBN 0-89815-043-4). Ten Speed Pr.

MOUNTAINS

see also Geology, Structural; Mountaineering; Volcanoes; Watersheds

Crouter, George. Colorado's Highest: The Magestic Fourteeners. (Illus.). 144p. 16.50 (ISBN 0-913582-22-0). Sundance.

Prater, Yvonne. Snoqualmie Pass: From Indian Trail to Interstate. Earnest, Rebecca, ed. (Illus.). 120p. (Orig.). 1981. pap. 6.95 (ISBN 0-89886-015-6). Mountaineers.

A Review-Mountain Ecosystems, Nineteen Eighty. (UNEP Report Ser.: No. 2). 38p. 1980. pap. 6.00 (UNEP 031, UNEP). Unipub.

Tianshan Mountains. 1980. 20.00 (ISBN 0-8351-0738-8). China Bks.

MOUNTBATTEN, LOUIS MOUNTBATTEN, EARL, 1900-1979

Hough, Richard. Mountbatten. 1981. 15.00 (ISBN 0-394-51162-X). Random.

Smith, Charles. Lord Mountbatten: His Butler's Story. LC 80-51787. (Illus.). 224p. 1980. 12.95 (ISBN 0-8128-2751-1). Stein & Day.

MOUTH–DISEASES

see also Oral Manifestations of General Diseases

Smith, Roy M., et al. Atlas of Oral Pathology. (Illus.). 204p. 1981. text ed. 24.95 (ISBN 0-8016-4684-7). Mosby.

Topazian, Richard G. & Goldberg, Morton H. Management of Infections of the Oral & Maxillofacial Regions. (Illus.). 500p. 1981. text ed. price not set (ISBN 0-7216-8879-9). Saunders.

MOVE GAMES
see Board Games

MOVEMENT, ECUMENICAL
see Ecumenical Movement

MOVIE CAMERAS
see Moving-Picture Cameras

MOVING, HOUSEHOLD
Neuman, Patricia O. Moving: The What, When, Where, & How of It. (Illus.). 128p. 1981. pap. 5.95 (ISBN 0-89651-450-1). Icarus.

MOVING-PICTURE ACADEMY AWARDS
see Academy Awards (Moving-Pictures)

MOVING-PICTURE ACTORS AND ACTRESSES
Cooper, Jackie & Kleiner, Dick. Please Don't Shoot My Dog: The Autobiography of Jackie Cooper with Dick Kleiner. (Illus.). 288p. 12.95 (ISBN 0-688-03659-7). Morrow.
Pickard, Roy. Who Played Who in the Movies. LC 80-26546. 304p. 1981. 14.95 (ISBN 0-8052-3766-6); pap. 5.95 (ISBN 0-8052-0676-0). Schocken.
Samuels, M. Screen Greats: Bogart. 1980. pap. 2.95 (ISBN 0-931064-31-7). O'Quinn Studio.
--Screen Greats: Hollywood Nostalgia. 1980. pap. 2.00 (ISBN 0-931064-30-9). O'Quinn Studio.
--Screen Greats: Monroe. 1980. pap. 2.95 (ISBN 0-931064-32-5). O'Quinn Studio.

MOVING-PICTURE ADAPTATIONS
see Film Adaptations

MOVING-PICTURE AUTHORSHIP
Caughie, John, ed. Theories of Authorship. (B. F. I. Readers in Film Studies). (Illus.). 320p. 1981. 28.00 (ISBN 0-7100-0649-7); pap. 14.00 (ISBN 0-7100-0650-0). Routledge & Kegan.
Schwartz, Nancy & Schwartz, Sheila. The Hollywood Writers' Wars. LC 80-2728. (Illus.). 448p. 1981. 16.95 (ISBN 0-394-41140-4). Knopf.

MOVING-PICTURE CAMERAS
Eastman Kodak, ed. Cinematographer's Field Guide, (H-2) 3rd rev. ed. (Illus.). 100p. Date not set. text ed. 6.95 (ISBN 0-87985-276-3). Eastman Kodak.

MOVING-PICTURE CARTOONS
see also Animation (Cinematography)
Stephenson, Ralph. The Animated Film. LC 72-1785. 208p. 1981. pap. 5.95 (ISBN 0-498-01202-6). A S Barnes.

MOVING-PICTURE CRITICISM
Here are entered works dealing with the concept and technique of moving-picture reviews.
see also Moving-Pictures–Evaluation
Florida State University Conference on Literature & Films, Fourth. Ideas of Order in Literature & Film: Selected Papers. Ruppert, Peter, et al, eds. LC 80-2601. xiii, 135p. (Orig.). 1981. pap. 8.00 (ISBN 0-8130-0699-6). U Presses Fla.
Grierson, John. Grierson on the Movies. Hardy, H. Forsyth, ed. 200p. 1981. 22.00 (ISBN 0-571-11665-5, Pub. by Faber & Faber). Merrimack Bk Serv.

MOVING-PICTURE DIRECTION
see Moving-Pictures–Production and Direction

MOVING-PICTURE EDITING
see Moving-Pictures–Editing

MOVING-PICTURE FILM EDITING
see Moving-Pictures–Editing

MOVING-PICTURE INDUSTRY
see also Moving-Pictures–Production and Direction
Zucker, Ralph. Filmrow: The Executive BlackBook of the Theatrical Motion Picture Marketing Business. 400p. (Orig.). 1981. write for info. Filmrow Pubns.

MOVING-PICTURE INDUSTRY–BIOGRAPHY
see Moving-Pictures–Biography

MOVING-PICTURE MUSIC
Bazelon, Irwin. Knowing the Score: Notes on Film Music. LC 80-24925. (Illus.). 352p. 1981. pap. 6.95 (ISBN 0-668-05132-9, 5132). Arco.
Limbacher, James L. Keeping Score: Film Music 1972-1979. LC 80-26474. 519p. 1981. 22.50 (ISBN 0-8108-1390-4). Scarecrow.

MOVING-PICTURE PLAYS
see also Film Adaptations; Moving-Pictures–Plots, Themes, etc.
Esenwein, J. Berg & Leeds, Arthur. Writing the Photoplay. 425p. 1980. Repr. of 1913 ed. lib. bdg. 35.00 (ISBN 0-8495-1350-2). Arden Lib.

MOVING-PICTURE PLOTS
see Moving-Pictures–Plots, Themes, etc.

MOVING-PICTURE PRODUCERS AND DIRECTORS
Bogdanovich, Peter. Allan Dwan. (A Belvedere Bk.). 220p. 1981. pap. 5.95 (ISBN 0-87754-320-8). Chelsea Hse.
Bordwell, David. The Films of Carl-Theodor Dreyer. 1981. 23.50 (ISBN 0-520-03987-4). U of Cal Pr.
Houseman, John. Front & Center. 1981. pap. 6.95 (ISBN 0-671-41391-0, Touchstone Bks). S&S.
--Run-Through. 1981. pap. 6.95 (ISBN 0-671-41391-0, Touchstone Bks). S&S.
International Portrait Gallery: Vol. 10, Film Directors & Producers Supplement. (Illus.). 64p. 1981. 35.00 (ISBN 0-686-69446-5, IPG-10). Gale.
Korda, Michael. Charmed Lives. 560p. 1981. pap. 3.50 (ISBN 0-380-53017-1, 53017). Avon.
Rainsberger, Todd. Eloquent Light: The Cinematography of James Wong Howe. LC 80-26542. (Illus.). 218p. 1981. 17.50 (ISBN 0-498-02405-9). A S Barnes.

MOVING-PICTURE PRODUCTION
see Moving-Pictures–Production and Direction

MOVING-PICTURE STARS
see Moving-Picture Actors and Actresses

MOVING-PICTURE THEATERS
Batschelet, Ralph J. The Flick & I. 176p. 1981. 9.00 (ISBN 0-682-49717-7). Exposition.

MOVING-PICTURE WRITING
see Moving-Picture Authorship

MOVING-PICTURES
Here are entered general works on moving-pictures. Works on organization and management in the motion picture field are entered under Moving-Picture Industry. Works on photographic processes are entered under Cinematography.
see also Cinematography; Horror Films; Sex in Moving-Pictures; Stunt Men; War Films; Western Films
Academy of Motion Pictures Arts & Sciences. Annual Index to Motion Picture Credits, 1980: Nineteen Eighty. LC 79-644761. 450p. 1981. lib. bdg. 150.00 (ISBN 0-313-20952-9, AN80). Greenwood.
Giannetti, Louis. The American Cinema: The Art, the Industry, the Audience, the Artists. 255p. 1981. text ed. 17.95 (ISBN 0-13-024687-5); pap. text ed. 11.95 (ISBN 0-13-024679-4). P-H.
Hirsh, Foster. The Dark Side of the Screen: Film Noir. LC 80-28955. (Illus.). 192p. 1981. 14.95 (ISBN 0-498-02234-X). A S Barnes.
Monaco, James. How to Read a Film: The Art, Technology, Language, History, & Theory of Film & Media. rev. ed. (Illus.). 576p. 1981. 25.00 (ISBN 0-19-502802-3); pap. 11.95 (ISBN 0-19-502806-6). Oxford U Pr.
Pickard, Roy. The Award Movies: A Complete Guide from A to Z. LC 80-54142. (Illus.). 354p. 1981. 14.95 (ISBN 0-8052-3767-4); pap. 6.95 (ISBN 0-8052-0677-9). Schocken.
Salz, Kay, compiled by. Film Service Profiles. LC 80-10394. 56p. (Orig.). 1980. pap. 5.00 (ISBN 0-935654-00-3, Pub. by Ctr for Arts Info). Pub Ctr Cult Res.
The Saturday Evening Post Movie Book. LC 77-85389. (Illus.). 1977. 10.95 (ISBN 0-89387-013-7); pap. 7.95 (ISBN 0-89387-013-7). Sat Eve Post.

MOVING-PICTURES–ACADEMY AWARDS
see Academy Awards (Moving-Pictures)

MOVING-PICTURES–BIBLIOGRAPHY
Essoe, Gabe. The Offical Book of Movie Lists. (Illus.). 256p. 1981. 12.95 (ISBN 0-87000-496-4). Arlington Hse.
Welch, Jeffrey. Liturature & Film: An Annotated Bibliography, 1900 to 1977. LC 80-8509. 350p. 1981. lib. bdg. 40.00 (ISBN 0-8240-9478-6). Garland Pub.

MOVING-PICTURES–BIOGRAPHY
see also Moving-Picture Actors and Actresses; Moving-Picture Producers and Directors
O'Leary, Liam. Rex Ingram: Master of the Silent Cinema. (Illus.). 224p. 1980. 28.50. B&N.
Pickard, Roy. Who Played Who in the Movies. LC 80-26546. 304p. 1981. 14.95 (ISBN 0-8052-3766-6); pap. 5.95 (ISBN 0-8052-0676-0). Schocken.

MOVING-PICTURES–CATALOGS
Ottoson, Robert. A Reference Guide to the American Film Noir: 1940-1958. LC 80-23176. 290p. 1981. 15.00 (ISBN 0-8108-1363-7). Scarecrow.
Weiss, Ken. The Movie Collector's Catalog. (Illus.). 160p. (Orig.). 1977. pap. 5.95 (ISBN 0-938350-50-1). Cummington Pub.

MOVING-PICTURES–COLLECTORS AND COLLECTING
Weiss, Ken. The Movie Collector's Catalog. (Illus.). 160p. (Orig.). 1977. pap. 5.95 (ISBN 0-938350-50-1). Cummington Pub.

MOVING-PICTURES–COSTUME
see Costume

MOVING-PICTURES–CRITICISM
see Moving-Picture Criticism

MOVING-PICTURES–DIRECTION
see Moving-Pictures–Production and Direction

MOVING-PICTURES–DIRECTORIES
Educational Film Locator: Of the Consortium of University Film Centers & R. R. Bowker. 2nd ed. 2500p. 1980. 50.00 (ISBN 0-8352-1295-5). Bowker.

MOVING-PICTURES–EDITING
Jenkins, Philip. Focal Guide to Movie Tilting. (Focal Guide Ser.). (Illus.). 160p. 1981. pap. 7.95 (ISBN 0-240-51011-9). Focal Pr.

MOVING-PICTURES–EVALUATION
Kael, Pauline. Deeper into Movies. 1980. pap. 2.95 (ISBN 0-446-93525-5). Warner Bks.
Wead, George & Lellis, Geore. Film: Form & Function. LC 80-82804. (Illus.). 512p. 1981. pap. text ed. 12.95 (ISBN 0-395-29740-0). HM.

MOVING-PICTURES–FILM EDITING
see Moving-Pictures–Editing

MOVING-PICTURES–HISTORY
Barnouw, Erik. The Magician & the Cinema. (Illus.). 112p. 1981. 12.95 (ISBN 0-19-502918-6). Oxford U Pr.
Brosnan, John. James Bond in the Cinema. 2nd rev. ed. LC 80-26573. (Illus.). 200p. 1981. 9.95 (ISBN 0-498-02546-2). A S Barnes.
Champlin, Charles. The Movies Grow up, Nineteen Forty to Nineteen Eighty. rev. ed. Orig. Title: The Flicks; or Whatever Became of Andy Hardy? (Illus.). 300p. 1981. 19.95 (ISBN 0-8040-0363-7); pap. 10.00 (ISBN 0-8040-0364-5). Swallow.
Dooley, Roger. From Scarface to Scarlett: American Films in the 1930s. (Illus.). 700p. 1981. 25.00 (ISBN 0-15-133789-6). HarBraceJ.
Florida State University Conference on Literature & Films, Fourth. Ideas of Order in Literature & Film: Selected Papers. Ruppert, Peter, et al, eds. LC 80-2601. xiii, 135p. (Orig.). 1981. pap. 8.00 (ISBN 0-8130-0699-6). U Presses Fla.
Higham, Charles & Greenberg, Joel. Hollywood in the Forty's. 192p. 1981. pap. 5.95 (ISBN 0-498-06928-1). A S Barnes.
Hochman, Stanley, ed. From Quasimodo to Scarlett O'Hara: A National Board of Review Anthology. LC 80-53695. (Ungar Film Library). 400p. 1981. 25.00 (ISBN 0-8044-2381-4); pap. 10.95 (ISBN 0-8044-6274-7). Ungar.
Keyser, Les. Hollywood in the Seventies. LC 78-75313. (Illus.). 172p. 1981. pap. 5.95 (ISBN 0-498-02545-4). A S Barnes.
Koszarski, Richard, et al. The Rivals of D.W. Griffith: Alternate Auteurs, 1913 to 1918. (Illus.). 58p. (Orig.). 1980. pap. 4.95 (ISBN 0-918432-32-4). Ny Zoetrope.
Mast, Gerald. A Short History of the Movies. LC 80-18024. (Illus.). 516p. 1980. pap. text ed. 13.95 (ISBN 0-672-61521-5). Bobbs.
Robinson, David. The History of World Cinema. rev. ed. LC 80-51767. (Illus.). 512p. 1981. 14.95 (ISBN 0-8128-2747-3). Stein & Day.
Schulberg, Budd. Moving Pictures: Memories of a Hollywood Prince. LC 80-9055. 448p. 1981. 16.95 (ISBN 0-8128-2817-8). Stein & Day.
Torrence, Bruce. Those Fabulous Film Factories: The History of Motion Picture Studios in California. (Illus.). 240p. Date not set. price not set (ISBN 0-87905-086-1). Peregrine Smith.

MOVING-PICTURES–JUVENILE LITERATURE
Aylesworth, Thomas G. Monsters from the Movies. 160p. (gr. 4-6). pap. 1.95 (ISBN 0-553-15091-X, Skylark). Bantam.
Edelson, Edward. Great Movies Spectaculars. (Illus.). (YA) (gr. 7-9). 1977. pap. 1.50 (ISBN 0-671-29994-8). PB.

MOVING-PICTURES–MONTAGE
see Moving-Pictures–Editing

MOVING-PICTURES–MORAL AND RELIGIOUS ASPECTS
see also Sex in Moving-Pictures
Martin, Thomas M. Images & the Imageless: A Study in Religious Consciousness & Film. LC 79-57611. 200p. 1981. 20.00 (ISBN 0-8387-5005-2). Bucknell U Pr.

MOVING-PICTURES–MUSICAL ACCOMPANIMENT
see Moving-Picture Music

MOVING-PICTURES–PICTORIAL WORKS
Hochman, Stanley, ed. From Quasimodo to Scarlett O'Hara: A National Board of Review Anthology. LC 80-53695. (Ungar Film Library). 400p. 1981. 25.00 (ISBN 0-8044-2381-4); pap. 10.95 (ISBN 0-8044-6274-7). Ungar.
Lacy, Madison S. & Morgan, Don. Leg Art: Sixty Years of Hollywood Cheesecake. (Illus.). 256p. 1981. 24.95 (ISBN 0-8065-0734-9). Citadel Pr.
Skogsberg, Bertil. Wings on the Screen. Bisset, George, tr. from Swedish. (Illus.). 192p. 1981. 25.00 (ISBN 0-498-02495-4). A S Barnes.

MOVING-PICTURES–PLAY-WRITING
see Moving-Picture Authorship

MOVING-PICTURES–PLOTS, THEMES, ETC.
Films on specific topics are entered under specific headings, e.g. Horror Films; War Films; Children in Motion Pictures; Death in Motion Pictures.
see also Film Adaptations
Haddad-Garcia, George. The Films of Jane Fonda. (Illus.). 256p. 1981. 16.95 (ISBN 0-8065-0752-7). Citadel Pr.
Henry, Marilyn & DeSourdis, Ron. The Films of Alan Ladd. (Illus.). 256p. 1981. 16.95 (ISBN 0-8065-0736-5). Citadel Pr.
Ottoson, Robert. A Reference Guie to the American Film Noir: 1940-1958. LC 80-23176. 290p. 1981. 15.00 (ISBN 0-8108-1363-7). Scarecrow.
Russo, Vito. The Celluloid Closet: Homosexuality in the Movies. LC 79-1682. (Illus.). 256p. 1981. 15.00 (ISBN 0-06-013704-5, HarpT). Har-Row.

MOVING-PICTURES–PRODUCTION AND DIRECTION
see also Moving-Picture Producers and Directors
Burch, Noel. Theory of Film Practice. Lane, Helen R., tr. from French. LC 80-8676. (Illus.). 172p. 1981. 18.50x (ISBN 0-691-03962-3); pap. 5.95 (ISBN 0-691-00329-7). Princeton U Pr.
Hutchison, David. Special Effects, Vol. II. 1980. pap. 7.95 (ISBN 0-931064-22-8). O'Quinn Studio.
Koszarski, Richard, et al. The Rivals of D.W. Griffith: Alternate Auteurs, 1913 to 1918. (Illus.). 58p. (Orig.). 1980. pap. 4.95 (ISBN 0-918432-32-4). Ny Zoetrope.
Prats, A. J. The Autonomous Image: Cinematic Narration & Humanism. xvi, 171p. 1981. price not set (ISBN 0-8131-1406-3). U Pr of Ky.
Slide, Anthony. The Kindergarten of the Movies: A History of the Fine Arts Company. LC 80-20391. 246p. 1980. 13.50 (ISBN 0-8108-1358-0). Scarecrow.
Tuska, Jon, et al, eds. Close-Up: The Contemporary Director. LC 80-23551. 437p. 1981. 22.50 (ISBN 0-8108-1366-1). Scarecrow.

MOVING-PICTURES–SETTING AND SCENERY
see also Scene Painting; Theaters–Stage-Setting and Scenery
Hutchison, David. Special Effects, Vol. II. 1980. pap. 7.95 (ISBN 0-931064-22-8). O'Quinn Studio.
Ritsko, Alan J. Lighting for Location Motion Pictures. 224p. 1980. pap. 8.95 (ISBN 0-442-23136-9). Van Nos Reinhold.

MOVING-PICTURES–SOCIAL ASPECTS
Short, Kenneth, ed. Feature Films As History. LC 80-28715. 192p. 1981. price not set (ISBN 0-87049-314-0). U of Tenn Pr.
Wead, George & Lellis, Geore. Film: Form & Function. LC 80-82804. (Illus.). 512p. 1981. pap. text ed. 12.95 (ISBN 0-395-29740-0). HM.
Woll, Allen L. The Latin Image in American Film. rev. ed. LC 80-620041. (Latin American Studies: Vol. 50). 1981. pap. price not set (ISBN 0-87903-050-X). UCLA Lat Am Ctr.

MOVING-PICTURES–TITLING
see Moving-Pictures–Editing

MOVING-PICTURES–YEARBOOKS
Gertner, Richard, ed. Motion Picture Almanac, 1981, Vol. 52. 716p. 1981. 38.00 (ISBN 0-900610-23-9). Quigley Pub Co.

MOVING-PICTURES–AUSTRALIA
Reade, Eric. History & Heartburn: The Saga of Australian Film, 1896-1978. 353p. 1980. 40.00 (ISBN 0-8386-3082-0). Fairleigh Dickinson.

MOVING-PICTURES–ITALY
Prats, A. J. The Autonomous Image: Cinematic Narration & Humanism. xvi, 171p. 1981. price not set (ISBN 0-8131-1406-3). U Pr of Ky.

MOVING-PICTURES–LATIN AMERICA
Johnson, Randal & Stam, Robert. Brazilian Cinema. LC 80-66323. (Illus.). 260p. 1981. 20.00 (ISBN 0-8386-3078-2). Fairleigh Dickinson.

MOVING-PICTURES, DOCUMENTARY
see also Moving-Pictures–Evaluation
Alexander, William. Film on the Left: American Documentary Film from 1931 to 1942. LC 80-8534. (Illus.). 364p. 1981. 27.50x (ISBN 0-691-04678-6); pap. 12.50x (ISBN 0-691-10111-6). Princeton U Pr.

MOVING-PICTURES, SILENT
Weaver, John T. Twenty Years of Silents, Nineteen Hundred & Eight to Nineteen Twenty-Eight. LC 73-157729. 514p. 1971. lib. bdg. 20.50 (ISBN 0-8108-0299-6). Scarecrow.

MOVING-PICTURES AND RELIGION
see Moving-Pictures–Moral and Religious Aspects

MOVING-PICTURES IN EDUCATION
see also Moving-Pictures–Evaluation
CUFC: Educational Film Locator 1980. 2nd ed. 1980. 50.00 (ISBN 0-8352-1295-5). Bowker.

MOZAMBIQUE
Mittelman, James H. Underdevelopment & the Transition to Socialism: Mozambique & Tanzania. (Studies in Social Discontinuity Ser.). 1981. price not set (ISBN 0-12-500660-8). Acad Pr.
Vail, Leroy & White, Landeg. Capitalism & Colonialism in Mozambique: A Study of the Quelimane District. LC 80-22702. (Illus.). 424p. 1981. 45.00x (ISBN 0-8166-1039-8). U of Minn Pr.

MOZART, JOHANN CHRYSOSTOM WOLFGANG AMADEUS, 1756-1791
Davenport, Marcia. Mozart. 1979. pap. 3.50 (ISBN 0-380-45534-X, 45534, Discus). Avon.
King, Alec H. Mozart Wind & String Concertos. LC 75-27957. (BBC Music Guides: No. 35). (Illus.). 64p. (Orig.). 1978. pap. 2.95 (ISBN 0-295-95478-7). U of Wash Pr.
Liebner, Janos. Mozart on the Stage. 1980. pap. 4.95 (ISBN 0-7145-1070-X). Riverrun NY.
Milnes, John, et al. The Magic Flute: Mozart. Beasch, Anthony & Besch, Anthony, trs. 1980. pap. 4.95 (ISBN 0-7145-3768-3). Riverrun NY.
Radcliffe, Philip. Mozart Piano Concertos. LC 75-27958. (BBC Music Guides: No. 34). (Illus.). 64p. (Orig.). 1978. pap. 2.95 (ISBN 0-295-95477-9). U of Wash Pr.

MUCHA, ALPHONSE MARIE, 1860-1939
Bowers, Q. David & Martin, Mary L. The Postcards of Alphonse Mucha. (Illus.). 100p. 1980. 9.95 (ISBN 0-911572-18-X). Vestal.
Mucha, Alphonse. The Art Nouveau Style Book of Alphonse Mucha. (Illus.). 80p. 1980. pap. 7.95 (ISBN 0-486-24044-4). Dover.

MUCOUS MEMBRANE
see also Endometrium
Strassburg, M. & Knolie, G. Disease of the Oral Mucosa: A Color Atlas. (Illus.). 270p. 1972. 58.00. Quint Pub Co.

MUELLER, GEORGE, 1805-1898
Muller, George. Autobiography of George Muller. Wayland, H. Lincoln, ed. (Giant Summit Books Ser.). 490p. 1981. pap. 8.95 (ISBN 0-8010-6105-9). Baker Bk.

MUGGERIDGE, MALCOLM, 1903-
Hunter, Ian. Malcolm Muggeridge: A Life. 1980. 13.95 (ISBN 0-8407-4084-0). Nelson.

MUHAMMAD THE PROPHET
see Mohammed, the Prophet, 570-632

MUHAMMADANISM
see Islam

MUHAMMADANS
see Muslims

MUIR, EDWIN, 1887-

Noble, Andrew, ed. Selected Literary Criticism of Edwin Muir. (Barnes & Noble Critical Studies). 208p. 1981. 27.50x (ISBN 0-389-20202-9). B&N.

MUIR, JOHN, 1838-1914

Fox, Stephen R. John Muir & His Legacy: The American Conservation Movement. (Illus.). 416p. 1981. 16.95 (ISBN 0-316-29110-2). Little.

Watkins, T. H. John Muir's America. (Illus.). 160p. 1981. pap. 12.95 (ISBN 0-912856-64-5). Graphic Arts Ctr.

MULE DEER

Wallmo, Olof C., ed. Mule & Black-Tailed Deer of North America. LC 80-20128. (Illus.). xvii, 650p. 1981. 29.95 (ISBN 0-8032-4715-X). U. of Nebr Pr.

MULLER, GEORGE

see Mueller, George, 1805-1898

MULTICOMPONENT FLOW

see Multiphase Flow

MULTI-FAMILY HOUSING

see Apartment Houses

MULTILINGUALISM

see also Bilingualism

Tabory, Mala. Multilingualism in International Law & Institutions. LC 80-51742. 304p. 1980. 32.50x (ISBN 90-286-0210-0). Sijthoff & Noordhoff.

Teller, Virginia & White, Sheila J., eds. Studies in Child Language & Multilingualism. LC 80-16810. 187p. 1980. 28.00x (ISBN 0-89766-078-1). NY Acad Sci.

MULTINATIONAL CORPORATIONS

see International Business Enterprises

MULTIPHASE FLOW

see also Two-Phase Flow

Bajura, R. A., ed. Polyphase Flow & Transport Technology. 270p. 1980. 40.00 (H00158). ASME.

MULTI-PHASE MATERIALS

see Composite Materials

MULTIPLE EMPLOYMENT

see Supplementary Employment

MULTIPLE HEMORRHAGIC SARCOMA

see Kaposi's Sarcoma

MULTIPLE SCLEROSIS

Boese, A., ed. Search for the Cause of Multiple Sclerosis & Other Chronic Diseases of the Central Nervous System. (Illus.). 516p. (Orig.). pap. text ed. 55.00 (ISBN 3-527-25875-2). Verlag Chemie.

MULTIPLICATION

Hunt, R. Multiplication & Division. LC 78-730962. 1978. pap. text ed. 99.00 (ISBN 0-89290-093-8, A509-SATC). Soc for Visual.

Learning Achievement Corporation. Multiplication & Energy & Construction: Division & Medicine. Zak, Therese A., ed. (MATCH Ser.). (Illus.). 144p. 1980. text ed. 5.28 (ISBN 0-07-037112-1, G). McGraw.

Mick, Beverly J. Multiplication Facts & Basic Fractions. (gr. 5-12). 1981. Set. price not set (ISBN 0-932786-04-9); Bk. 1. 4.25 (ISBN 0-932786-05-7); Bk. 2. 4.25 (ISBN 0-932786-06-5). Bellefontaine.

--Multiplication Facts, Decimals, & Percents, 2 bks. (gr. 5-12). 1981. Set. price not set (ISBN 0-932786-04-9); Bk. 1. 4.25 (ISBN 0-932786-05-7); Bk. 2. 4.25 (ISBN 0-932786-06-5). Bellefontaine.

Quinn, Daniel & Mills, Richard G. Multiplication Learning Module. 1975. pap. text ed. 225.00 (ISBN 0-89290-133-0). Soc for Visual.

MULTIVARIATE ANALYSIS

Armstrong. ORACLS: A Design System for Linear Multivariable Control. 256p. 1980. 35.00 (ISBN 0-8247-1239-0). Dekker.

Chou, E. Statistical Analysis. 2nd ed. 1975. 24.95. Dryden Pr.

Christiensen, Ronald, ed. Entropy Minimax Sourcebook. (Entropy Minimax Sourcebook Ser.: Vol. IV). 1981. lib. bdg. 59.50 (ISBN 0-938876-07-4). Entropy Ltd.

Green, P. & Barban. Analyzing Multivariate Data. 1978. 28.95 (ISBN 0-03-020786-X). Dryden Pr.

Overall, John E. & Klett, C. James. Applied Multivariate Analysis. 522p. 1981. Repr. of 1972 ed. lib. bdg. price not set (ISBN 0-89874-325-7). Krieger.

MUNDAS

Sachchidananda. The Changing Munda. 1979. text ed. 25.00x (ISBN 0-391-01932-5). Humanities.

MUNICH

Time-Life Books Editors & Bailey, George. Munich. (The Great Cities Ser.). (Illus.). 200p. 1981. 14.95 (ISBN 0-8094-3120-3). Time-Life.

MUNICIPAL ADMINISTRATION

see Municipal Government

MUNICIPAL BONDS

Amdursky, Robert S., ed. Basics for Municipal Bond Lawyers: Course Handbook. LC 80-82474. (Nineteen Seventy-Nine to Nineteen Eighty Corporate Law & Practice Course Handbook Ser.). 887p. 1980. pap. 25.00 (ISBN 0-686-69164-4, B4-6551). PLI.

Mussa, Michael L. & Kormendi, Roger G. Taxation of Municipal Bonds: An Economic Appraisal. 1979. pap. 7.25 (ISBN 0-8447-3331-8). Am Enterprise.

MUNICIPAL CIVIL SERVICE

see Municipal Officials and Employees

MUNICIPAL ELECTIONS

see Elections

MUNICIPAL EMPLOYEES

see Municipal Officials and Employees

MUNICIPAL FINANCE

see also Finance, Public; Licenses; Local Taxation; Municipal Bonds

Burton, John C. A Revised Financial Reporting Model for Municipalities. (Government Auditing Ser.). 1980. pap. 6.00. Coun on Municipal.

Foster, C. D., et al. Local Government Finance in a Unitary State. (Illus.). 640p. 1980. text ed. 60.00x (ISBN 0-04-336066-1, 2473). Allen Unwin.

Mathewson, Kent & Neenan, William B., eds. Financing the Metropolis. 352p. 1980. 29.95 (ISBN 0-03-056886-2). Praeger.

Municipal Accounting & Auditing: Where We Are Now, Where We Should Be Going. (COMP Papers Ser.). 170p. 1980. pap. 18.00 (ISBN 0-916450-41-4). Coun on Municipal.

Municipal Securities Regulation: A Public Perspective, 10 vols. Incl. Vol. 1 & 2. Certain Legal Considerations, Vol. II: An Introduction, Vol. 1. (Bound & sold together with Vol. II). 1977. price of 2 vols. 50.00. Vol. 1 (ISBN 0-916450-08-2). Vol. 2, 129 Pages; Vol. III. Self-Regulation: Is It Working? 148p. 1977. 40.00 (ISBN 0-916450-10-4); Vol. IV. Summary of Publications & Hearings. 264p. 1977. 70.00 (ISBN 0-916450-11-2); Federal Legislative Background Vol. V; Four Legal Memoranda, Vol. VI. 224p. (Vols. V & VI are bound & sold together). 1978. price of 2 vols. 65.00. Vol. V (ISBN 0-916450-12-0). Vol. VI; Vol. VII. Municipal Disclosure Standards Sourcebook. 199p. 1978. 60.00 (ISBN 0-916450-18-X); Vol. VIII. State Laws. 204p. 1978. 50.00 (ISBN 0-916450-19-8); Vol. IX. Disclosure Guidelines. 1979. 40.00; Vol. X. The Way Back: Toward Accountability in America's Cities. 231p. 1979. 25.00 (ISBN 0-916450-21-X). Set. 270.00. Coun on Municipal.

Rousmaniere, Peter F. State Level Disclosure Guidelines. (Municipal Securities Regulation Ser.). 233p. 1980. pap. 40.00 (ISBN 0-916450-20-1). Coun on Municipal.

--The Way Back: Toward Accountability in America's Cities. (Municipal Securities Regulation Ser.). 231p. 1979. pap. 25.00x (ISBN 0-916450-21-X). Coun on Municipal.

Rousmaniere, Peter F. K, et al. Selling Your City: A Primer for Government Officials on Communicating with the Investment Community. 70p. 1978. pap. 8.00 (ISBN 0-916450-22-8). Coun on Municipal.

Securities Regulation Series, 10 vols. Incl. Vol. 1. An Introduction. Marlin, John T. & Rousmaniere, Peter F. 36p; Vol. 2. Certain Legal Considerations. Chadbourne, et al. 129p. (Vols. 1 & 2 bound together) (ISBN 0-916450-09-0); Vol. 3. Self Regulation: Is It Working? Rousmaniere, Peter F. 148p (ISBN 0-916450-10-4); Vol. 4. Summary of Publications & Hearings. Chadbourne, et al. 264p; Vol. 5. Federal Legislative Background. Chadbourne, et al.; Vol. 6. Four Legal Memoranda. Chadbourne, et al. (Vols. 5 & 6 bound together, 122p.) (ISBN 0-916450-13-9); Vol. 7. Municipal Disclosure Standards Sourcebook. Anderson, Kay. 199p (ISBN 0-916450-18-X); Vol. 8. State Laws. Chadbourne, et al. 204p (ISBN 0-916450-19-8); State Level Disclosure Guidelines. Rousmaniere, Peter F. 233p (ISBN 0-916450-20-1); Vol. 10. The Way Back: Toward Accountability in America's Cities. Rousmaniere, Peter F. 231p (ISBN 0-916450-21-X). 1977-80. Set. 300.00. Coun on Municipal.

MUNICIPAL GOVERNMENT

see also Elections; Local Government; Mayors; Municipal Finance; Municipal Officials and Employees; Public Administration

also subdivision Politics and Government under names of cities, e.g. San Francisco–Politics and Government

Arkes, Hadley. The Philosopher in the City: The Moral Dimensions of Urban Politics. LC 80-8536. 496p. 1981. 27.50x (ISBN 0-691-09356-3); pap. 6.95x (ISBN 0-691-02822-2). Princeton U Pr.

Brecher, Charles & Horton, Raymond D., eds. Setting Municipal Priorities, Nineteen Eighty-One. LC 80-67392. 212p. 1981. text ed. 25.00 (ISBN 0-86598-010-1). Allanheld.

Feldman, Lionel D. & Graham, Katherine A. Bargaining for Cities, Municipalities & Intergovernmental Relations: An Assessment. 143p. 1979. pap. text ed. 10.95x (ISBN 0-920380-21-2, Pub. by Inst Res Pub Canada). Renouf.

Harlow, LeRoy F. Servants of All. (Illus.). 384p. 1981. 19.95 (ISBN 0-8425-1892-4). Brigham.

Harrigan. Political Change in the Metropolis. 2nd ed. 1981. pap. text ed. 9.95 (ISBN 0-316-34744-2); training manual free (ISBN 0-316-34745-0). Little.

Horton, Raymond D. & Brecher, Charles, eds. Setting Municipal Priorities, Nineteen Eighty. LC 79-88261. 224p. 1979. text ed. 24.00 (ISBN 0-916672-37-9). Allanheld.

Poole, Robert, Jr. Cutting Back City Hall. LC 79-6411. 224p. 1981. pap. 5.95 (ISBN 0-87663-557-5). Universe.

Sentell, Perry R. The Law of Municipal Tort Liability in Georgia. 3rd ed. LC 79-24276. 184p. 1980. pap. text ed. 15.00x (ISBN 0-89854-053-4). U of GA Inst Govt.

MUNICIPAL INCORPORATION

Miller, Gary J. Cities by Contract: The Politics of Municipal Incorporation. 256p. 1981. text ed. 22.50x (ISBN 0-262-13164-1). MIT Pr.

MUNICIPAL JUNIOR COLLEGES

see Community Colleges

MUNICIPAL OFFICIALS AND EMPLOYEES

Gross, Ernest, et al. New Jersey Police & Fire Arbitration Databook, 1980. 2 vols. 2000p. 1980. Set. 100.00. Inst Mgmt & Labor.

MUNICIPAL SERVICES WITHIN CORPORATE LIMITS

see Municipal Government

MUNICIPAL TAXATION

see Local Taxation

MUNICIPAL TRANSIT

see Local Transit

MUNICIPAL UTILITIES

see Public Utilities

MUNICIPALITIES

see Cities and Towns; Municipal Government

MURDER

see also Assassination; Infanticide; Poisoning; Trials (Murder)

Carpozi, George, Jr. Great Crimes of the Century: Murderers Leave Clues, No. 8. (Orig.). 1980. pap. 1.95 (ISBN 0-532-23130-9). Manor Bks.

--Great Crimes of the Century: The Savage Killers, No. 7. (Orig.). 1980. pap. 1.95 (ISBN 0-532-23129-5). Manor Bks.

Pearson, Edmund. More Studies in Murder. 317p. 1980. Repr. of 1936 ed. lib. bdg. 30.00 (ISBN 0-89760-715-5). Telegraph Bks.

MURDER TRIALS

see Trials (Murder)

MURRAY, ANDREW, 1828-1917

Douglas, W. M. Andrew Murray & His Message. (Christian Biography Ser.). 336p. 1981. pap. 3.95 (ISBN 0-8010-2908-2). Baker Bk.

MUSCLE

see also Contractility (Biology)

Ebashi, S., et al, eds. Muscle Contraction: Its Regulatory Mechanism. 549p. 1981. 64.00 (ISBN 0-387-10411-9). Springer-Verlag.

Grinnell, Alan D., et al, eds. The Regulation of Muscle Contraction: Excitation-Contraction Coupling. (UCLA Forum in Medical Sciences: Vol. 22). 1981. price not set (ISBN 0-12-303780-8). Acad Pr.

Varga, E., et al, eds. Molecular & Cellular Aspects of Muscle Function: Proceedings of the 28th International Congress of Physiological Sciences, Budapest 1980 (Including Proceedings of the Satellite Symposium on Membrane Control of Skeletal Muscle Function) LC 80-42101. (Advances in Physiological Sciences: Vol. 5). (Illus.). 320p. 1981. 40.00 (ISBN 0-08-026817-X). Pergamon.

MUSCLE STRENGTH

Weider, Joe. The Best of Joe Weider's Muscle & Fitness Training Tips & Routines. (Illus.). 1981. 12.95 (ISBN 0-8092-5911-7); pap. 5.95 (ISBN 0-8092-5910-9). Contemp Bks.

--The Best of Joe Weider's Muscle & Fitness: The Worlds's Leading Bodybuilders Answer Your Questions. (Illus.). 1981. 12.95 (ISBN 0-8092-5914-1); pap. 5.95 (ISBN 0-8092-5912-5). Contemp Bks.

Wong, Harry. Dynamic Tension. LC 80-53545. (Illus.). 144p. 1980. pap. 5.95 (ISBN 0-86568-013-2). Unique Pubns.

MUSCLE TISSUE

see Muscle

MUSCLES

Here are entered works on the gross anatomy and movements of muscles. Works on the histology and physiological properties of muscular tissue are entered under the heading Muscle.

see also Muscle Strength

also names of muscles

Goldspink, D. F., ed. The Development & Specialisation of Skeletal Muscle. (Society for Experimental Biology Seminar Ser.: No. 7). (Illus.). 200p. Date not set. 45.00 (ISBN 0-521-23317-8); pap. 19.95 (ISBN 0-521-29907-1). Cambridge U Pr.

MUSCULAR COORDINATION

see Motor Ability

MUSEUM CURATORSHIP AS A PROFESSION

see Museum Work As a Profession

MUSEUM WORK AS A PROFESSION

Girouard, Mark. Alfred Waterhouse & the Natural History Museum. LC 80-53742. (Illus.). 1981. 12.95x (ISBN 0-300-02578-5). Yale U Pr.

MUSEUMS

see also Art Museums; Museum Work As a Profession; Zoological Specimens–Collection and Preservation

also subdivision Galleries and Museums under names of cities, e.g. new york (City)–Galleries and Museums; names of individual museums; and subdivision Collection and Preservation under Insect, Zoological Specimens and similar headings

Albin, Edgar A., et al. Selections from the Permanent Collection of the Springfield Art Museum. Landwehr, William C., ed. LC 80-53333. 100p. (Orig.). 1980. pap. text ed. 9.95 (ISBN 0-934306-03-6). Springfield.

Girouard, Mark. Alfred Waterhouse & the Natural History Museum. LC 80-53742. (Illus.). 1981. 12.95x (ISBN 0-300-02578-5). Yale U Pr.

Hunt, David C. Guide to Oklahoma Museums. LC 80-5939. (Illus.). 250p. 1981. 17.50 (ISBN 0-8061-1567-X); pap. 9.95 (ISBN 0-8061-1752-4). U of Okla Pr.

Rose, Roger G. A Museum to Instruct & Delight. LC 80-69203. (Special Publication Ser.: No. 68). (Illus.). 96p. Date not set. pap. 6.50 (ISBN 0-910240-28-0). Bishop Mus.

Sloan, Blanche C. & Swinburne, Bruce R. Campus Art Museums & Galleries: A Profile. LC 80-23418. 64p. (Orig.). 1981. pap. price not set (ISBN 0-8093-1005-8). S Ill U Pr.

White, Anne. Visiting Museums. 1968. 6.50 (ISBN 0-571-08741-8, Pub. by Faber & Faber). Merrimack Bk Serv.

MUSEUMS–DIRECTORIES

Hanauer, Gary. Small Museums of the West. Vandenburgh, Jane, ed. LC 80-67476. (Illus.). 288p. (Orig.). 1981. pap. 9.95 (ISBN 0-89395-051-3). Cal Living Bks.

Harnik, Tema. Wherewithal: A Guide to Resources for Museums & Historical Societies. 120p. (Orig.). 1981. pap. write for info. (ISBN 0-935654-01-1, Pub. by Ctr for Arts Info). Pub Ctr Cult Res.

Museums of the World. 3rd ed. 1981. 185.00 (ISBN 0-686-69416-3, Dist. by Gale Research). K G Saur.

MUSHROOM CULTURE

Watling, Roy. How to Identify Mushrooms to Genus V. Using Cultural & Developmental Features. 1981. pap. price not set. Mad River.

MUSHROOMS

see also Fungi; Mushroom Culture

Rice, Miriam C. How to Use Mushrooms for Color. rev. ed. (Illus.). 145p. 1980. pap. 7.95 (ISBN 0-916422-19-4). Mad River.

Watling, Roy, ed. A Literature Guide to the Identification of Mushrooms. 120p. (Orig.). 1980. pap. 6.75. Mad River.

MUSHROOMS–CULTURE

see Mushroom Culture

MUSHROOMS, EDIBLE

see also Mushroom Culture

Christensen, Clyde M. Edible Mushrooms. 2nd, rev. ed. (Illus.). 136p. 1981. 12.95 (ISBN 0-8166-1049-5); pap. 6.95 (ISBN 0-8166-1050-9). U of Minn Pr.

Mushroom Terms: Polyglot on Research & Cultivation of Edible Fungi. 312p. 1981. pap. 83.00 (ISBN 90-220-0673-5, PDC 211, Pudoc). Unipub.

MUSIC

see also Chamber Music; Choral Music; Church Music; Composition (Music); Computer Music; Electronic Music; Improvisation (Music); Jazz Music; Kindergarten–Music; Melodrama; Moving-Picture Music; Opera; Orchestral Music; Singing; Songs; Sound; Voice

also subdivision Songs and Music under specific subjects, classes of persons, names of individuals, institutions, societies, etc; also other headings beginning with the words Music and Musical

Baird. Using Media in the Music Program. write for info. (ISBN 0-87628-211-7). Ctr Appl Res.

Carlton, Joseph R. Carlton's Complete Reference Book of Music. LC 44-181. (Illus.). 729p. 1980. PLB 40.00 (ISBN 0-937348-00-7). Carlton Pubns CA.

Daniels. Performing for Others. write for info. (ISBN 0-87628-215-X). Ctr Appl Res.

Dearling, Robert, et al. Music Facts & Feats. rev. ed. (Illus.). 288p. 1981. 19.95 (ISBN 0-8069-9250-6, Pub. by Guinness Superlatives England). Sterling.

Downes, Edward. The Guide to Symphonic Music. LC 76-13813. Orig. Title: The New York Philharmonic Guide to the Symphony. (Illus.). 1058p. pap. 14.95 (ISBN 0-8027-7178-5). Walker & Co.

Elley, Derek, ed. International Music Guide, 1981. (Illus.). 1981. pap. 8.95 (ISBN 0-686-69099-0). A S Barnes.

Johnson, Roger, commentary by. Scores: An Anthology of New Music. LC 80-53302. (Illus.). 450p. 1981. pap. text ed. 12.95 (ISBN 0-02-871190-4). Schirmer Bks.

Kusel, George. The Marching Drummer's Companion. 2nd ed. 52p. 1981. pap. 4.95 (ISBN 0-9604476-0-1). Kusel.

Nye, Robert E. & Bergethon, Bjorner. Basic Music: Functional Musicianship for the Non-Music Major. 5th ed. (Illus.). 240p. 1981. pap. text ed. 11.95 (ISBN 0-13-065672-0). P-H.

Rudman, Jack. Music. (Undergraduate Program Field Test Ser.: UPFT-16). (Cloth bdg. avail. on request). pap. 9.95 (ISBN 0-8373-6016-1). Natl Learning.

Taylor, Deems. Of Men & Music. LC 80-2305. 1981. Repr. of 1937 ed. 36.00 (ISBN 0-404-18873-7). AMS Pr.

Thompson, Oscar. How to Understand Music. 347p. 1980. Repr. of 1935 ed. lib. bdg. 30.00 (ISBN 0-89984-453-7). Century Bookbindery.

MUSIC–ACOUSTICS AND PHYSICS

see also Electro-Acoustics; Sound

Levarie, Siegmund & Levy, Ernst. Tone: A Study in Musical Acoustics. 2nd ed. LC 80-29383. (Illus.). xvii, 256p. 1981. Repr. of 1980 ed. lib. bdg. 27.50x (ISBN 0-313-22499-4, LETO). Greenwood.

Wood, Alexander. The Physics of Music. 7th ed. Bowsher, J. M., ed. LC 80-20967. (Illus.). xiv, 258p. 1981. Repr. of 1975 ed. lib. bdg. 28.50x (ISBN 0-313-22644-X, WOPM). Greenwood.

MUSIC–ADDRESSES, ESSAYS, LECTURES

Noblitt, Thomas, ed. Music East & West: Essays in Honor of Walter Kaufman. (Festschrift Ser.: No. 3). (Illus.). x, 386p. 1981. lib. bdg. 36.00 (ISBN 0-918728-15-0). Pendragon NY.

MUSIC–ANALYSIS, APPRECIATION

Cope, David H. New Directions in Music. 3rd ed. 286p. 1981. pap. text ed. price not set (ISBN 0-697-03448-8). Wm C Brown.

Courtney, Elise & Celeste, Emily. How to Find Music Easily for Good Times in Harmony. LC 80-51888. (Illus.). 317p. (Orig.). 1980. pap. 6.00 (ISBN 0-686-28899-8). Merk.

Jenkins, David & Visocchi, Mark. Portraits in Music I. 66p. 1980. 6.00 (ISBN 0-19-321400-8). Oxford U Pr.

Krenek, Ernst. Exploring Music. 1980. pap. 4.95 (ISBN 0-7145-0226-X). Riverrun NY.

Nadeau, Roland & Tesson, William. Listen: A Guide to the Pleasures of Music. 3rd ed. 544p. 1980. pap. text ed. 14.95 (ISBN 0-8403-2332-8). Kendall-Hunt.

Schonberg, Harold C. Facing the Music. 1981. 14.95 (ISBN 0-671-25406-5). Summit Bks.

Seashore, Carl E. In Search of Beauty in Music: A Scientific Approach to Musical Esthetics. LC 80-25447. (Illus.). xvi, 389p. 1981. Repr. of 1947 ed. lib. bdg. 29.50x (ISBN 0-313-22758-6, SEIS). Greenwood.

Seyer, Philip & Harmon, Paul. What Makes Music Work? Novick, Allan, ed. (Wiley Self-Teaching Guide Ser.). 300p. 1981. pap. text ed. 9.85 (ISBN 0-471-35192-X). Wiley.

Stravinsky, Igor & Craft, Robert. Expositions & Developments. (Orig.). 1981. pap. 4.95 (ISBN 0-520-04403-7, CAL 503). U of Cal Pr.

--Memories & Commentaries. (Orig.). 1981. pap. 4.95 (ISBN 0-520-04402-9, CAL 502). U of Cal Pr.

MUSIC–ANALYSIS, APPRECIATION–AUDIO-VISUAL AIDS

Gaburo, Virginia. Notation. LC 77-75432. (Illus.). 176p. 1977. soft-cover 14.45. Lingua Pr.

MUSIC–APPRECIATION

see Music–Analysis, Appreciation

MUSIC–BIBLIOGRAPHY

see also Music–Discography; Music–Manuscripts; Music Libraries

Catalogue of Printed Music in the British Library to 1980, 62 vols. 1980. Set. 1200.00 (ISBN 0-85157-900-0, Dist. by Gale Research Co.). K G Saur.

Research Libraries of the New York Public Library & the Library of Congress. Bibliographic Guide to Music: 1980. (Libraries Catalogs-Bib. Guides Sew.). 1981. lib. bdg. 90.00 (ISBN 0-8161-6891-1). G K Hall.

MUSIC–BIO-BIBLIOGRAPHY

Rogal, Samuel J. Sisters of Sacred Song: Selected Listing of Women Hymnodists in Great Britain & America. LC 80-8482. 180p. 1981. lib. bdg. 22.00 (ISBN 0-8240-9482-4). Garland Pub.

MUSIC–BIOGRAPHY

see Composers; Conductors (Music); Music–Bio-Bibliography; Musicians; Singers

MUSIC–COMPOSITION

see Composition (Music)

MUSIC–DISCOGRAPHY

Allen, Daniel. Bibliography of Discographies: Jazz, Vol. II. 200p. 1981. 35.00 (ISBN 0-8352-1342-0). Bowker.

Rezits, Joseph. Guitar Music in Print. LC 80-84548. 1000p. (Orig.). 1981. pap. 50.00 (ISBN 0-8497-7802-6, Pub. by Kjos West). Kjos.

MUSIC–ECONOMIC ASPECTS

see also Music Trade

Biederman, Donald E. Legal & Business Aspects of the Music Industry: Music, Videocassettes & Records, Course Handbook. LC 80-81531. (Patents, Copyrights, Trademarks & Literary Property 1979-80 Course Handbook Ser.). 736p. 1980. pap. text ed. 25.00 (ISBN 0-686-68825-2, G4-3676). PLI.

MUSIC–ESTHETICS

see Music–Philosophy and Esthetics

MUSIC–HISTORY AND CRITICISM

Abbey, Lester. A History of Music for Those Who Don't Want to Know Too Much About Music History. LC 80-124026. 1981. pap. 3.00. RWS Bks.

Harter, Jim. Music: A Pictorial Archive of Woodcuts & Engravings. (Pictorial Archive Ser.). (Illus.). 155p. (Orig.). 1981. pap. 6.00 (ISBN 0-486-24002-9). Dover.

Laurence, Dan H., ed. Shaw's Music: The Complete Musical Criticism, 3 vols. LC 80-1113. 1981. Boxed Set. 150.00 (ISBN 0-686-69572-0). Vol. 1 (ISBN 0-396-07960-1). Vol. 2 (ISBN 0-396-07961-X). Vol. 3 (ISBN 0-396-07962-8). Dodd.

McCusker, Honor. Fifty Years of Music in Boston. 3.00. Boston Public Lib.

Rossi, Nick & Rafferty, Sadie. Music Through the Centuries. LC 80-9066. (Illus.). 760p. 1981. lib. bdg. 27.00 (ISBN 0-8191-1498-7); pap. text ed. 16.75 (ISBN 0-8191-1499-5). U Pr of Amer.

Shapiro, Nat, ed. An Encyclopedia of Quotations About Music. (Da Capo Quality Paperbacks Ser.). 1981. pap. 7.95 (ISBN 0-306-80138-8). Da Capo.

Silet, Charles L. The Writings of Paul Rosenfeld: An Annotated Bibliography. LC 79-7931. 250p. 1981. lib. bdg. 35.00 (ISBN 0-8240-9532-4). Garland Pub.

Stucky, Steven. Lutoslawski & His Music. (Illus.). 300p. Date not set. price not set (ISBN 0-521-22799-2). Cambridge U Pr.

MUSIC–HISTORY AND CRITICISM–400-1500

Fenlon, Iain. Music in Medieval & Early Modern Europe: Patronage, Sources & Texts. LC 80-40490. (Illus.). 290p. Date not set. price not set (ISBN 0-521-23328-3). Cambridge U Pr.

Hughes, Andrew. Medieval Manuscripts for Mass & Office: A Guide to Their Organization & Terminology. 496p. 1981. 45.00x (ISBN 0-8020-5467-6). U of Toronto Pr.

MUSIC–HISTORY AND CRITICISM–16TH CENTURY

Fenlon, Iain. Music & Patronage in Sixteenth Century Mantua. LC 79-41377. (Cambridge Studies in Music). (Illus.). 350p. Date not set. 57.50 (ISBN 0-521-22905-7). Cambridge U Pr.

Price, D. C. Patrons & Musicians of the English Renaissance. LC 80-40054. (Cambridge Studies in Music). (Illus.). 250p. Date not set. 55.00 (ISBN 0-521-22806-9). Cambridge U Pr.

MUSIC–HISTORY AND CRITICISM–17TH CENTURY

Marais, Marin. Pieces a une et a Deux Violes, 1686-89: The Instrumental Works, Vol. 1. Hsu, John, ed. xxvii, 191p. 1980. lib. bdg. 67.50x (ISBN 0-8450-7201-3). Broude.

Price, D. C. Patrons & Musicians of the English Renaissance. LC 80-40054. (Cambridge Studies in Music). (Illus.). 250p. Date not set. 55.00 (ISBN 0-521-22806-9). Cambridge U Pr.

MUSIC–HISTORY AND CRITICISM–18TH CENTURY

Larsen, Jens P., et al, eds. Haydn Studies. 1981. 29.95 (ISBN 0-393-01454-1). Norton.

MUSIC–HISTORY AND CRITICISM–19TH CENTURY

Dahlhaus, Carl. Between Romanticism & Modernism: Four Studies in the Music of the Later Nineteenth Century. Kerman, Joseph, ed. Whittall, Mary, tr. from Ger. LC 78-54793. (California Studies in 19th Century Music). 100p. 1980. 10.00x (ISBN 0-520-03679-4). U of Cal Pr.

MUSIC–HISTORY AND CRITICISM–20TH CENTURY

see also Jazz Music

Cope, David H. New Directions in Music. 3rd ed. 200p. 1981. pap. text ed. 7.50x (ISBN 0-697-03448-8). Wm C Brown.

De Falla, Manue. On Music & Musicians. 136p. 1981. pap. 7.95 (ISBN 0-7145-2735-1, Pub. by M. Boyars). Merrimack Bk Serv.

Dunn, David. Sky Drift. LC 80-80806. (Illus.). 90p. 1979. soft wrap-around cover 15.95. Lingua Pr.

Gaburo, Virginia. Who Is Bruce Simonds. 44p. 1978. saddle-sticed 13.95, soft cover, lP recording. Lingua Pr.

Griffiths, Paul. Modern Music: The Avant Garde Since 1945. (Illus.). 308p. 1981. 37.50x (ISBN 0-460-04365-X, Pub. by J. M. Dent England). Biblio Dist.

Yates, Peter. Twentieth Century Music: Its Evolution from the End of the Harmonic Era into the Present Era of Sound. LC 80-23310. xv, 367p. 1981. Repr. of 1967 ed. lib. bdg. 28.75x (ISBN 0-313-22516-8, YATC). Greenwood.

MUSIC–INSTRUCTION AND STUDY

see also Composition (Music); Instrumental Music–Instruction and Study; Kindergarten–Music; Music–Manuals, Text-Books, Etc.; Musical Accompaniment; Singing–Instruction and Study

also subdivision Instruction and Study under names of musical instruments, e.g. Piano–Instruction and Study

Batcheller. Music in Early Childhood. write for info. (ISBN 0-87628-212-5). Ctr Appl Res.

Cradock, Eveline. Musical Appreciation in an Infant School. (Illus.). 50p. (Orig.). 1977. pap. text ed. 6.75 (ISBN 0-19-321055-X). Oxford U Pr.

Crews, Katherine. Music & Perceptual Motor Development. (Classroom Music Enrichment Units Ser.). (Illus.). 1974. pap. text ed. 5.95x (ISBN 0-87628-213-3). Ctr Appl Res.

Hochheimer, Laura. A Sequential Sourcebook for Elementary School Music. 2nd ed. 1980. pap. 12.95 (ISBN 0-918812-12-7). Magnamusic.

Mackinnon, Lillias. Music by Heart. LC 80-26551. xi, 141p. 1981. Repr. of 1954 ed. lib. bdg. 17.50x (ISBN 0-313-22810-8, MAMB). Greenwood.

Mulligan. Integrating Music with Other Studies. write for info. (ISBN 0-87628-218-4). Ctr Appl Res.

Music in Open Education. write for info. (ISBN 0-87628-214-1). Ctr Appl Res.

Regelski, Thomas A. General Music Methods. LC 80-5561. (Illus.). 448p. 1981. text ed. 12.95 (ISBN 0-02-872070-9). Schirmer Bks.

--Teaching General Music: Action Learning for Middle & Secondary Schools. LC 80-5561. (Illus.). 448p. 1981. text ed. 12.95 (ISBN 0-02-872070-9). Schirmer Bks.

Rosen, Charles. Arnold Shoenberg. LC 80-8773. 113p. (Orig.). 1981. pap. 4.95 (ISBN 0-691-02706-4). Princeton U Pr.

Swanson, Bessie R. Music in the Education of Children. 4th ed. 448p. 1980. text ed. 18.95x (ISBN 0-534-00880-1). Wadsworth Pub.

MUSIC–JUVENILE LITERATURE

see also Musical Instruments–Juvenile Literature

Crane, William. Oom-Pah. LC 80-18404. 204p. (gr. 5-9). 1981. PLB 9.95 (ISBN 0-689-30804-3). Atheneum.

MUSIC–KINDERGARTEN

see Kindergarten–Music

MUSIC–MANUALS, TEXT-BOOKS, ETC.

Wingell. Experiencing Music. 1981. 15.95 (ISBN 0-88284-116-5); instr's. manual free (ISBN 0-88284-131-9); wkbk. 4.95 (ISBN 0-88284-117-3); record set 30.00 (ISBN 0-88284-132-7). Alfred Pub.

MUSIC–MANUSCRIPTS

Catalogue of Printed Music in the British Library to 1980, 62 vols. 1980. Set. 1200.00 (ISBN 0-85157-900-0, Dist. by Gale Research Co.). K G Saur.

MUSIC–NURSERY SCHOOLS

see Nursery Schools–Music

MUSIC–PHILOSOPHY AND ESTHETICS

Le Huray, Peter & Day, James. Music & Aesthetics in the Eighteenth & Early Nineteenth Centuries. (Cambridge Studies in Music: Readings in the Literature of Music). (Illus.). 700p. Date not set. price not set (ISBN 0-521-23426-3). Cambridge U Pr.

MUSIC–POETRY

Brun, Herbert & Gaburo, Kenneth. Collaboration One. 24p. 1976. soft cover saddle-stitched 15.00. Lingua Pr.

MUSIC–PROGRAMMED INSTRUCTION

Wingell. Experiencing Music. 1981. 15.95 (ISBN 0-88284-116-5); instr's. manual free (ISBN 0-88284-131-9); wkbk. 4.95 (ISBN 0-88284-117-3); record set 30.00 (ISBN 0-88284-132-7). Alfred Pub.

MUSIC–PSYCHOLOGY

see also Music Therapy

Mackinnon, Lillias. Music by Heart. LC 80-26551. xi, 141p. 1981. Repr. of 1954 ed. lib. bdg. 17.50x (ISBN 0-313-22810-8, MAMB). Greenwood.

Seashore, Carl E. In Search of Beauty in Music: A Scientific Approach to Musical Esthetics. LC 80-25447. (Illus.). xvi, 389p. 1981. Repr. of 1947 ed. lib. bdg. 29.50x (ISBN 0-313-22758-6, SEIS). Greenwood.

MUSIC–READING

see Score Reading and Playing

MUSIC–STUDY AND TEACHING

see Music–Instruction and Study

MUSIC–THEORY

see also Composition (Music); Music–Acoustics and Physics; Music–Philosophy and Esthetics

Benward, Bruce. Music in Theory & Practice. 2nd ed. 1980. 13.95 (ISBN 0-697-03423-2). Wm C Brown.

MUSIC–THERAPEUTIC USE

see Music Therapy

MUSIC, AFRO-AMERICAN

see Afro-American Music

MUSIC, AMERICAN

Bristow, George. Rip Van Winkle. (Early American Music Ser.: No. 25). 297p. 1980. 39.50. Da Capo.

Foote, Arthur. Suite in E, Serenade in E. (Early American Music Ser.: No. 60). 60p. 1980. 18.50. Da Capo.

Herndon, Marcia. Native American Music. new ed. 233p. 1980. lib. bdg. 20.00 (ISBN 0-8482-4475-3). Norwood Edns.

Kaufman, Charles H. Music in New Jersey, 1655-1860. LC 78-75180. 400p. 1981. 35.00 (ISBN 0-8386-2270-4). Fairleigh Dickinson.

Krummel, D. W., et al, eds. Resources of American Music History: A Directory of Source Materials from Colonial Times to World War II. LC 80-14873. (Music in American Life Ser.). 500p. 1981. lib. bdg. 44.95 (ISBN 0-252-00828-6). U of Ill Pr.

Williams, Martin, ed. The Art of Jazz: Ragtime to Bebop. (Da Capo Quality Paperbacks Ser.). 248p. 1981. pap. 6.95 (ISBN 0-306-80134-5). Da Capo.

MUSIC, APPRECIATION OF

see Music–Analysis, Appreciation

MUSIC, AUSTRIAN

Landon, H. C. Chronicle & Works, 5 vols. Incl. Haydn: The Early Years, 1732-1765. Vol. 1 Haydn: the Early Years, 1732-1765. 640p. 1980. 75.00x (ISBN 0-253-37001-9); Vol. 2. Haydn at Eszterhaza; 1766-1790. 820p. 1978. 60.00x (ISBN 0-253-37002-7); Vol. 3. Haydn in England, 1791-1795. 640p. 1976. 55.00x (ISBN 0-253-37003-5); Vol. 4. Haydnn: the Years of "The Creation", 1796-1800. 640p. 1976. 55.00x (ISBN 0-253-37004-3); Vol. 5. Haydn: the Late Years, 1801-1809. 496p. 1977. 55.00x (ISBN 0-253-37005-1). Set. 300.00x. Ind U Pr.

MUSIC, BAROQUE

Rangel-Ribeiro, Victor. Baroque Music: A Practical Guide for the Performer. LC 80-5222. (Illus.). 260p. 1981. 15.00 (ISBN 0-02-871980-8). Schirmer Bks.

MUSIC, BRITISH

see also Music, English

Fennell, Frederick. Basic Band Repertory: British Band Classics from the Conductor's Point of View. 1980. pap. 6.00. Instrumental Co.

Senelick, Laurence, et al. British Music Hall 1840-1923: A Bibliography & Guide to Sources with a Supplement on European Music-Hall. (Archon Books on Popular Entertainments Ser.). 1981. 37.50 (ISBN 0-208-01840-9, Archon). Shoe String.

MUSIC, BRITISH–HISTORY AND CRITICISM

Price, D. C. Patrons & Musicians of the English Renaissance. LC 80-40054. (Cambridge Studies in Music). (Illus.). 250p. Date not set. 55.00 (ISBN 0-521-22806-9). Cambridge U Pr.

MUSIC, CANADIAN

Kallmann, Helmut, et al, eds. Encyclopedia of Music in Canada. 1504p. 1981. 45.00 (ISBN 0-8020-5509-5). U of Toronto Pr.

MUSIC, CHORAL

see Choral Music

MUSIC, DRAMATIC

see Music in Theaters; Musical Revue, Comedy, Etc.; Opera

MUSIC, EFFECT OF

see Music Therapy

MUSIC, ELECTRONIC

see Electronic Music

MUSIC, ENGLISH

see also Music, British

Dutka, JoAnna. Music in the English Mystery Plays. (Early Drama, Art, & Music Ser.). (Illus.). 171p. 1980. 18.80 (ISBN 0-918720-10-9); 11.801321. Medieval Inst.

MUSIC, FRENCH

Blaze, Francois H. L' Academie Imperiale De Musique: Histoire Litteraire, Musicale, Politique et Galant De Ce Theatre, De 1645 a 1855, 2 vols. LC 80-2258. 1981. Repr. of 1855 ed. 95.00 (ISBN 0-404-18804-4). AMS Pr.

Chouquet, Gustave. Histoire de la Musique Dramatique en Frane Depuis Ses Origines Jusqua Nos Jours. LC 80-2265. 1981. Repr. of 1873 ed. 45.00 (ISBN 0-404-18818-4). AMS Pr.

Crozet, Felix. Revue De la Musique Dramatique En France. Bd. with Supplement a la Revue De la Musique Dramatique En France. LC 80-2270. 1981. 48.50 (ISBN 0-404-18833-8). AMS Pr.

Durey De Noinville, Jacques B. Histoire Du Theatre De l'Academie Royale De Musique En France, Depuis Son Etablissement Jusqu' a Present, 2 vols. in 1. 2nd ed. 1981. Repr. of 1757 ed. 47.50 (ISBN 0-404-18838-9). AMS Pr.

Schwan, Eduard. Die Altfranzosischen Liederhandschriften Ihr Verhaltniss, Ihre/Entstehung & Ihre Bestimmung. LC 80-2169. Repr. of 1886 ed. 39.50 (ISBN 0-404-19033-2). AMS Pr.

Spanke, Hans, ed. Eine Altfranzosische Liedersammlung, Deranonyme Teil der Liederhandschriften Knpx. LC 80-2161. 1981. Repr. of 1925 ed. 54.50 (ISBN 0-404-19025-1). AMS Pr.

Van Duesen, Nancy. Music at Nevers Cathedral: Principal Sources of Mediaeval Chant. (Musicological Studies). 430p. 1980. lib. bdg. 55.00 pt. 1 (ISBN 0-912024-34-8); lib. bdg. 55.00 pt. 2 (ISBN 0-912024-33-X). Inst Mediaeval.

MUSIC, GERMAN

Adorno, Theodor. In Search of Wagner. 160p. 1981. 14.50 (ISBN 0-8052-7087-6, Pub. by NLB England). Schocken.

Perle, George. Serial Compositon & Atonality: An Introduction to the Music of Schoenberg, Berg, & Webern. 5th ed. 1981. 16.50x (ISBN 0-520-04365-0). U of Cal Pr.

Schiedermair, Ludwig. Die Deutche Oper: Grundzuge Ihres Werdens & Wesens. LC 80-2299. 1981. Repr. of 1930 ed. 38.50 (ISBN 0-404-18868-0). AMS Pr.

Schultze, Walter. Die Quellen der Hamburger Oper Sixteen Seventy Eight to Seventeen Thirty Eight. LC 80-2300. 1981. Repr. of 1938 ed. 25.50 (ISBN 0-404-18869-9). AMS Pr.

MUSIC, INCA

see Incas–Music

MUSIC, INDIC

Kuppuswamy, Gowry, ed. Indian Music: A Perspective. 1980. 32.50x (ISBN 0-8364-0629-X, Pub. by Sundeep). South Asia Bks.

MUSIC, ITALIAN

Barbezieux, Rigaut De. Le Canzoni: Testi E Commento a Cura Di Mauro Braccini. LC 80-2188. 1981. Repr. of 1960 ed. 26.00 (ISBN 0-404-19017-0). AMS Pr.

Corte, Andrea D., ed. Canto E Bel Canto P.F. Tosi: Opinioni De Cantori Antchi E Moderni Seventeen Twenty Three. LC 80-2268. 1981. Repr. of 1933 ed. 31.50 (ISBN 0-404-18823-0). AMS Pr.

Liuzzi, Fernando. La Lauda e i Primordi Della Melodia Italiana, 2 vols. LC 80-2238. 1981. Repr. of 1935 ed. 185.00 (ISBN 0-404-19037-5). AMS Pr.

MUSIC, MEDIEVAL

see Music–History and Criticism–400-1500

MUSIC, ORIENTAL

Dauvillier, Jean. Le Mariage En Droit Canonique Oriental. LC 80-2357. 1981. Repr. of 1936 ed. 35.00 (ISBN 0-404-18905-9). AMS Pr.

MUSIC, PHYSICAL EFFECT OF

see Music Therapy

MUSIC, POLISH

Houghtby, Natalie. The Music of Szymanowski. LC 80-51747. 120p. 1981. 11.95 (ISBN 0-8008-7539-7, Crescendo). Taplinger.

MUSIC, POPULAR (SONGS, ETC.)–BIBLIOGRAPHY

Brooks, Elston. I've Heard Those Songs Before: The Weekly Top Ten Tunes from 1930 Through 1980. 448p. (Orig.). Date not set. 12.95 (ISBN 0-688-00379-6). Morrow.

MUSIC, POPULAR (SONGS, ETC.)–HISTORY AND CRITICISM

Brooks, Elston. I've Heard Those Songs Before: The Weekly Top Ten Tunes from 1930 Through 1980. 448p. (Orig.). Date not set. 12.95 (ISBN 0-688-00379-6). Morrow.

Smith, Joseph C. The Day the Music Died. LC 80-8914. 464p. 1981. 12.95 (ISBN 0-394-51951-5). Grove.

MUSIC, RELIGIOUS

see Church Music

MUSIC, SACRED

see Church Music

MUSIC, SCOTTISH

Macdonell, Margaret. Songs of Highland Emigrants in North America. 208p. 1981. 18.95x (ISBN 0-8020-5469-2). U of Toronto Pr.

MUSIC, SPANISH

Barcelona, Biblioteca Central, Seccion De Musica. La Musica De la Cantigas De Santa Maria del Rey Alfonso el Sabio, 4 pts. in 3 vols. LC 80-2193. 1981. Set. 375.00 (ISBN 0-404-19046-4). Vol. 1 (ISBN 0-404-19047-2). Vol. 2 (ISBN 0-404-19048-0). Vol. 3 (ISBN 0-404-19049-9). AMS Pr.

Snow, Robert J. The Extant Music of Rodrigo De Ceballos & Its Sources. LC 78-70024. (Detroit Studies in Music Bibliography Ser.: No. 44). 1980. 17.50 (ISBN 0-89990-001-1). Info Coord.

--The Sixteen-Thirteen Print of Juan Esquivel Barahona. LC 78-70021. (Detroit Monographs in Musicology: No. 7). 1978. 11.00 (ISBN 0-911772-92-8). Info Coord.

Subira, Jose. Historia De la Musica Teatral en Espana. LC 80-2304. 1981. Repr. of 1945 ed. 27.50 (ISBN 0-404-18871-0). AMS Pr.

Tinnell, Roger D. An Annotated Discography of Music in Spain Before 1650. 146p. 1980. 12.00. Hispanic Seminary.

MUSIC, THEATRICAL

see Music in Theaters; Musical Revue, Comedy, etc.; Opera

MUSIC AND LITERATURE

see also Music–Poetry

Kelly, James W. The Faust Legend in Music. LC 74-75893. (Detroit Reprints in Music). 1976. 10.00 (ISBN 0-911772-81-2). Info Coord.

Louis, Louise. The Dervish Dance. 40p. 1971. Repr. of 1958 ed. text ed. 4.95. Pen-Art.

Winn, James A. Unsuspected Eloquence: A History of the Relations Between Poetry & Music. LC 80-27055. 384p. 1981. 18.95x (ISBN 0-300-02615-3). Yale U Pr.

MUSIC BOX

Chapuis, Alfred. History of the Musical Box & of Mechanical Music. Fitch, Howard M. & Fitch, Helen F., eds. Roesch, Joseph E., tr. from Fr. LC 80-12449. (Illus.). xvi, 304p. 1980. 27.50 (ISBN 0-915000-01-6). Musical Box Soc.

MUSIC CONDUCTORS

see Conductors (Music)

MUSIC FESTIVALS

Rabin, Carol. Guide to Music Festivals in North America. rev., enl. ed. LC 78-74201. 260p. 1981. 6.95 (ISBN 0-912944-67-6). Berkshire Traveller.

MUSIC-HALLS

Senelick, Laurence, et al. British Music Hall 1840-1923: A Bibliography & Guide to Sources with a Supplement on European Music-Hall. (Archon Books on Popular Entertainments Ser.). 1981. 37.50 (ISBN 0-208-01840-9, Archon). Shoe String.

MUSIC IN THEATERS

Here are entered works on music as an adjunct to theatrical productions.

Chouquet, Gustave. Histoire de la Musique Dramatique en Frane Depuis Ses Origines Jusqua Nos Jours. LC 80-2265. 1981. Repr. of 1873 ed. 45.00 (ISBN 0-404-18818-4). AMS Pr.

Dutka, JoAnna. Music in the English Mystery Plays. (Early Drama, Art, & Music Ser.). (Illus.). 171p. 1980. 18.80 (ISBN 0-918720-10-9); 11.801321. Medieval Inst.

Maillot, Antoine L. La Musique au Theatre. LC 80-2288. 1981. Repr. of 1863 ed. 44.00 (ISBN 0-404-18856-7). AMS Pr.

MUSIC LIBRARIES

Catalogue of Printed Music in the British Library to 1980, 62 vols. 1980. Set. 1200.00 (ISBN 0-85157-900-0, Dist. by Gale Research Co.). K G Saur.

MUSIC PUBLISHERS

see Publishers and Publishing

MUSIC READING

see Score Reading and Playing

MUSIC THERAPY

Clark, Cynthia & Chadwick, Donnacompiled by. Clinically Adapted Instruments for the Multiply Handicapped: A Sourcebook. rev. ed. 1980. Repr. of 1979 ed. 12.95 (ISBN 0-918812-13-5). Magnamusic.

Ruud, Even. Music Therapy & Its Relationship to Current Treatment Theories. rev ed. 1980. pap. 6.50 (ISBN 0-918812-14-3). Magnamusic.

Ward, David. Sing a Rainbow: Musical Activities with Mentally Handicapped Children. (Illus.). 64p. (Orig.). 1979. pap. 8.95x (ISBN 0-19-317416-2). Oxford U Pr.

MUSIC TRADE

see also Music–Economic Aspects

Biederman, Donald E. Legal & Business Aspects of the Music Industry: Music, Videocassettes & Records, Course Handbook. LC 80-81531. (Patents, Copyrights, Trademarks & Literary Property 1979-80 Course Handbook Ser.). 736p. 1980. pap. text ed. 25.00 (ISBN 0-686-68825-2, G4-3676). PLI.

Van Ryzin, Lani. Cutting a Record in Nashville, No. 3. (Hi Lo Ser.). 96p. (YA) (gr. 6 up). 1981. pap. 1.50 (ISBN 0-553-14620-3). Bantam.

MUSICAL ACCOMPANIMENT

see also Moving-Picture Music

Pelz, William. Basic Keyboard Skills: An Introduction to Accompaniment Improvisation, Transposition & Modulation, with an Appendix on Sight Reading. LC 80-22820. vii, 173p. 1981. Repr. of 1963 ed. PLB 23.50x (ISBN 0-313-22882-5, PEBK). Greenwood.

MUSICAL BOX

see Music Box

MUSICAL COMEDIES

see Musical Revues, Comedies, etc.

MUSICAL COMEDY

see Musical Revue, Comedy, Etc.

MUSICAL COMPOSITION

see Composition (Music)

MUSICAL EDUCATION

see Music–Instruction and Study

MUSICAL FESTIVALS

see Music Festivals

MUSICAL INSTRUCTION

see Music–Instruction and Study

MUSICAL INSTRUMENTS

Clark, Cynthia & Chadwick, Donnacompiled by. Clinically Adapted Instruments for the Multiply Handicapped: A Sourcebook. rev. ed. 1980. Repr. of 1979 ed. 12.95 (ISBN 0-918812-13-5). Magnamusic.

Montagu, Jeremy. The World of Romantic & Modern Musical Instruments. LC 80-26106. (Musical Instruments Ser.). (Illus.). 136p. 1981. pap. 27.95 (ISBN 0-87951-126-5). Overlook Pr.

Walls, Jerry G. Conchs, Tibias, & Harps. (Illus.). 192p. 1980. 9.95 (ISBN 0-87666-629-2, S-103). TFH Pubns.

MUSICAL INSTRUMENTS–CONSTRUCTION

Farrell, Susan C. Directory of Contemporary Musical Instrument Makers. LC 80-24924. 320p. 1981. text ed. 24.00x (ISBN 0-8262-0322-1). U of Mo Pr.

Walther, Tom. Make Mine Music: How to Make & Play Instruments & Why They Work. (Brown Paper School Ser.). (Illus.). 128p. (Orig.). (gr. 3 up). 1981. 9.95 (ISBN 0-316-92111-4); pap. 5.95 (ISBN 0-316-92112-2). Little.

MUSICAL INSTRUMENTS–INDUSTRY AND TRADE

see Music Trade

MUSICAL INSTRUMENTS–INSTRUCTION AND STUDY

see Instrumental Music–Instruction and Study

MUSICAL INSTRUMENTS–JUVENILE LITERATURE

Walther, Tom. Make Mine Music: How to Make & Play Instruments & Why They Work. (Brown Paper School Ser.). (Illus.). 128p. (Orig.). (gr. 3 up). 1981. 9.95 (ISBN 0-316-92111-4); pap. 5.95 (ISBN 0-316-92112-2). Little.

Wiseman, Ann. Making Musical Things. (Illus.). 64p. (gr. 2 up). 1979. 8.95 (ISBN 0-684-16114-1). Scribner.

MUSICAL INSTRUMENTS (MECHANICAL)

see also Automata; Music Box

Reblitz, Arthur A. & Bowers, Q. David. Treasures of Mechanical Music. (Illus.). 634p. 1981. 25.00 (ISBN 0-911572-20-1). Vestal.

MUSICAL REVUE, COMEDY, ETC.

For descriptive or historical material. Scores are entered under the heading Musical, Revues, Comedies, etc.

Chouquet, Gustave. Histoire de la Musique Dramatique en Frane Depuis Ses Origines Jusqua Nos Jours. LC 80-2265. 1981. Repr. of 1873 ed. 45.00 (ISBN 0-404-18818-4). AMS Pr.

MUSICAL REVUES, COMEDIES, ETC.

Engel, Lehman. The Musical Theater Workshop. (Sound Seminars Ser.). bk., tapes, listening guide 350.00x (ISBN 0-88432-065-0, 11500). J Norton Pubs.

Hodgins, Gordon W. The Broadway Musical: A Complete LP Discography. LC 80-18911. 188p. 1980. 10.00 (ISBN 0-8108-1343-2). Scarecrow.

MUSICAL THERAPY

see Music Therapy

MUSICIANS

see also Composers; Conductors (Music); Country Musicians; Jazz Musicians; Music–Bio-Bibliography; Rock Musicians; Singers; Women Musicians

Douglass, Fenner. Cavaille-Coll & the Musicians. (Illus.). 48p. 78.00 (ISBN 0-915548-09-7). Sunbury Pr.

Klein, Hermann. Musicians & Mummers. LC 80-2284. (Illus.). 1981. Repr. of 1925 ed. 38.50 (ISBN 0-404-18850-8). AMS Pr.

Scobie, Stephen. Leonard Cohen. 294p. (Orig.). 1978. pap. 4.95 (ISBN 0-295-95686-0, Pub. by Douglas & McIntyre Canada). U of Wash Pr.

Snow, Robert J. The Extant Music of Rodrigo De Ceballos & Its Sources. LC 78-70024. (Detroit Studies in Music Bibliography Ser.: No. 44). 1980. 17.50 (ISBN 0-89990-001-1). Info Coord.

--The Sixteen-Thirteen Print of Juan Esquivel Barahona. LC 78-70021. (Detroit Monographs in Musicology: No. 7). 1978. 11.00 (ISBN 0-911772-92-8). Info Coord.

Tomlin, Pinky. The Object of My Affection: An Autobiography. LC 80-5938. (Illus.). 300p. 1981. 12.50 (ISBN 0-8061-1719-2). U of Okla Pr.

MUSICIANS–CORRESPONDENCE, REMINISCENCES, ETC.

Gambaccini, Peter. Bill Joel: A Photo Biography. 192p. (Orig.). 1980. pap. 2.50 (ISBN 0-515-05317-1). Jove Pubns.

Hawes, Hampton & Asher, Don. Raise up off Me: A Portrait of Hampton Hawes. 180p. 1979. pap. 5.95 (ISBN 0-686-68925-9). Da Capo.

MUSICIANS–POETRY

see Music–Poetry

MUSICIANS, AFRO-AMERICAN

see Afro-American Musicians

MUSICIANS, WOMEN

see Women Musicians

MUSLIM ARCHITECTURE

see Architecture, Islamic

MUSLIM ART

see Art, Islamic

MUSLIM CIVILIZATION

see Civilization, Islamic

MUSLIM PAINTING

see Painting, Islamic

MUSLIM SOCIOLOGY

see Sociology, Islamic

MUSLIM THEOLOGY

see Islamic Theology

MUSLIM WOMEN

see Women, Muslim

MUSLIMISM

see Islam

MUSLIMS

Azzam, Salem, frwd. by. The Muslim World & the Future Economic Order. 383p. 1980. 29.95x (ISBN 0-906041-10-4, Pub. by Islamic Council of Europe England); pap. 14.95x (ISBN 0-906041-09-0). Intl Schol Bk Serv.

Brown, Marguerite. Magnificent Muslims. 1981. write for info. (ISBN 0-911026-10-X). New World Press NY.

DeLamotte, Roy C. Jalaluddin Rumi: Songbird of Sufism. LC 80-5884. 187p. 1980. lib. bdg. 16.75 (ISBN 0-8191-1286-0); pap. text ed. 8.75 (ISBN 0-8191-1287-9). U Pr of Amer.

Donia, Robert J. Islam Under the Double Eagle: The Muslims of Bosnia & Hercegovina, 1878-1914. (East Europan Monographs: No. 78). 256p. 1981. text ed. 17.50x (ISBN 0-914710-72-9). East Eur Quarterly.

MUSLIMS–WOMEN

see Women, Muslim

MUSLIMS IN THE UNITED STATES

Richardson, E. Allen. Muslims in America. 96p. (Orig.). 1981. pap. 4.95 (ISBN 0-8298-0449-8). Pilgrim NY.

MUSSELMEN

see Muslims

MUSSOLINI, BENITO, 1883-1945

Creighton, Warren S. The Contributions of Mussolini to the Civilization of Mankind. (Illus.). 137p. 1981. 51.55 (ISBN 0-89266-282-4). Am Classical Coll Pr.

Skipper, G. C. Benito Mussolini: A Dictator Dies. LC 80-25345. (World at War Ser.). (Illus.). 48p. (gr. 3-8). 1981. PLB 7.95 (ISBN 0-516-04790-6). Childrens.

MUSSULMANISM

see Islam

MUTAGENESIS

Hollaender, Alexander & De Serres, Frederick J., eds. Chemical Mutagens: Principles & Methods for Their Detection, 5 vols. Incl. Vol. 1. 310p. 1971. 27.50 (ISBN 0-306-37101-4); Vol. 2. 300p. 1971. 27.50 (ISBN 0-306-37102-2); Vol. 3. 304p. 1973. 27.50 (ISBN 0-306-37103-0); Vol. 4. 364p. 1976. 35.00 (ISBN 0-306-37104-9); Vol. 5. 348p. 1978. 27.50 (ISBN 0-306-37105-7). LC 73-128505. (Illus., Plenum Pr). Plenum Pub.

MUTILATION

Albers, Michael D. The Terror. (Orig.). 1980. pap. 2.25 (ISBN 0-532-23311-5). Manor Bks.

Summers, Ian & Kagan, Dan. Cattle Mutilations. 288p. (Orig.). 1981. pap. 2.95. Bantam.

MUTISM

Here are entered works on the inability to speak whether from any functional or physical cause other than deafness. Works on the lack of sense of hearing, including the lack combined with the inability to speak, i.e. deaf-mutism, are entered under Deafness.

Kratochwill, Thomas R. Selective Mutism: Implications for Research & Treatment. LC 80-18631. 224p. 1981. profess. & reference 19.95 (ISBN 0-89859-064-7). L Erlbaum Assocs.

MUTUAL BENEFIT ASSOCIATIONS

see Friendly Societies

MUTUAL INSURANCE

see Insurance

MYASTHENIA GRAVIS

Josephson, Emanuel. The Thymus Manganese, & Myasthenia Gravis. (Natural Health Ser.). 124p. 12.00 (Pub. by Chedney); pap. 6.00. Alpine Ent.

MYCENAEAN ART

see Art, Mycenaean

MYCENAEAN POTTERY

see Pottery, Greek

MYCOTOXINS

Cole, Richard J. & Cox, Richard H., eds. Handbook of Toxic Fungal Metabolites. 1981. write for info. (ISBN 0-12-179760-0). Acad Pr.

Hayes, A. Wallace. Mycotoxin Teratogenicity & Mutagenicity. 160p. 1981. 59.95 (ISBN 0-8493-5651-2). CRC Pr.

Perspective on Mycotoxins. (FAO Food & Nutrition Paper Ser.: No. 13). 171p. 1980. pap. 9.25 (ISBN 92-5-100870-1, F1957, FAO). Unipub.

MYELIN

Hashim, George, ed. Myelin: Chemistry & Biology. LC 80-22305. (Progress in Clinical & Biological Research: Vol. 49). 130p. 1980. price not set (ISBN 0-8451-0049-1). A R Liss.

MYODYNAMICS

see Muscles

MYOLOGY

see Muscles

MYRIAPODA

see also Centipedes

Morris, S. F. Catalogue of Type & Figured Fossil Crustacea (Exc. Ostracoda), Chelicerata & Myriapoda in the British Museum (Natural History) (Illus.). 56p. 1980. pap. 13.00x (ISBN 0-565-00828-5). Sabbot-Natural Hist Bks.

MYSTERIES (DRAMATIC)

see Mysteries and Miracle-Plays

MYSTERIES, RELIGIOUS

see also Rites and Ceremonies

Daniken, Erich. Unsolved Mysteries of the Past. 189p. 1981. 28.50 (ISBN 0-686-68311-0). Porter.

MYSTERIES AND MIRACLE-PLAYS

Christie, Agatha. The Mirror Crack'd. 1980. pap. 2.50. PB.

MYSTERIES AND MIRACLE-PLAYS, ENGLISH

Davidson, Clifford, ed. A Middle English Treatise on the Playing of Miracles. LC 81-40028. 93p. 1981. lib. bdg. 14.75 (ISBN 0-8191-1514-2); pap. text ed. 6.75 (ISBN 0-8191-1515-0). U Pr of Amer.

Dutka, JoAnna. Music in the English Mystery Plays. (Early Drama, Art, & Music Ser.). (Illus.). 171p. 1980. 18.80 (ISBN 0-918720-10-9); 11.801321. Medieval Inst.

MYSTERY STORIES

see Adventure and Adventurers; Detective and Mystery Stories (Collections)

MYSTICAL BODY OF CHRIST

see Jesus Christ–Mystical Body

MYSTICAL THEOLOGY

see Mysticism

MYSTICAL UNION

Here are entered works dealing with the indwelling of the Triune God, or of any person of the trinity, in the hearts of believers and conversely, works dealing with the union between man and the Triune God, especially between man and Jesus Christ. Works dealing with the church as the mystical body of Christ are entered under the heading Jesus Christ–Mystical Body.

see also Contemplation

Baker, Robert J. I'm Listening Lord, Keep Talking. 200p. 1981. pap. 6.95 (ISBN 0-8361-1953-3). Herald Pr.

Blumenthal, Warren B. The Creator & Man. LC 80-5843. 139p. 1980. lib. bdg. 15.75 (ISBN 0-8191-1340-9); pap. text ed. 7.50 (ISBN 0-8191-1341-7). U Pr of Amer.

Brand, Paul & Yancey, Phillip. Fearfully & Wonderfully Made. 224p. 8.95 (ISBN 0-310-35450-1). Zondervan.

Camp, Norman. Pensando Con Dios. 128p. (Span.). 1981. pap. 1.95 (ISBN 0-8024-6593-5). Moody.

Carlson, Edgar M. The Church & the Public Conscience. LC 79-8710. xii, 104p. 1981. Repr. of 1956 ed. lib. bdg. 17.50x (ISBN 0-313-22195-2, CACH). Greenwood.

Como Me Sacaras De Este Apuro, Senor? 1979. pap. 1.75 (ISBN 0-686-69350-7). Vida Pubs.

Dobson, James, tr. Dr. Dobson Fala Sobre Amor, Ira. (Portugese Bks.). (Port.). 1979. write for info. (ISBN 0-8297-0674-7). Life Pubs Intl.

Foglio, Frank, tr. Ei, Deus. (Portuguese Bks.). 1979. 1.25 (ISBN 0-8297-0791-3). Life Pubs Intl.

--Oye Dios. (Spanish Bks.). (Span.). 1978. 1.65 (ISBN 0-8297-0588-0). Life Pubs Intl.

Harper, Michael. Live by the Spirit: How to Grow in Your Relationship with God. 154p. 1980. pap. 2.25 (ISBN 0-89283-094-8). Servant.

Haught, John F. Religion & Self-Acceptance: A Study of the Relationship Between Belief in God & the Desire to Know. LC 80-5872. 195p. 1980. lib. bdg. 17.00 (ISBN 0-8191-1296-8); pap. text ed. 8.75 (ISBN 0-8191-1297-6). U Pr of Amer.

Kuhlman, Kathryn, tr. Dios Quiere Sanarte y Revolucionar Tu Vida. (Spanish Bks.). (Span.). 1977. 2.25 (ISBN 0-8297-0751-4). Life Pubs Intl.

Murray, Andrew, tr. La Palabra Irresistible. (Spanish Bks.). (Span.). 1979. 1.95 (ISBN 0-8297-0520-1). Life Pubs Intl.

Ogilvie, Lloyd. Congratulations - God Believes in You. 128p. 1980. 5.95 (ISBN 0-8499-0197-9). Word Bks.

Palms, Roger C., tr. Dios Guia Tu Futuro. (Spanish Bks.). (Span.). 1977. 1.60 (ISBN 0-8297-0767-0). Life Pubs Intl.

Parrott, Bob W. Ontology of Humor. 1981. 10.95 (ISBN 0-8022-2387-7). Philos Lib.

Pentecost, D., tr. Dieu Repond-Problemes-Hommes. (French Bks.). (Fr.). 1979. write for info. Life Pubs Intl.
Van Zweden, J. God's Sovereignty in the Lives of Twin Brothers. pap. 1.95. Reiner.
Weatherhead, Leslie D. Time for God. 1981. pap. 1.75 (ISBN 0-687-42113-6). Abingdon.
Wilkerson, Gwen, tr. En Su Fuerza. (Spanish Bks.). (Span.). 1979. 1.50 (ISBN 0-8297-0910-X). Life Pubs Intl.
Woods, Richard. Mysterion. 372p. 1981. 14.95 (ISBN 0-88347-127-2). Thomas More.

MYSTICISM
see also Cabala; Christian Art and Symbolism; Contemplation; Enthusiasm; Immanence of God; Perfection; Rosicrucians; Symbolism of Numbers
Balthasar, Hans Urs Von. A First Glance at Adrienne Von Speyr. Lawry, Antje & Englund, Sr. Sergia, trs. from Ger. LC 79-91933. Orig. Title: Erster Blick Auf Adrienne Von Speyr. 220p. (Orig.). 1981. pap. 6.95 (ISBN 0-89870-003-5). Ignatius Pr.
Corbin, Henri. Avicenna & the Visionary Recital. Task, Willard R., tr. from French. 320p. 1980. pap. text ed. 12.50 (ISBN 0-88214-213-5). Spring Pubns.
Dupre, Louis. The Deeper Self: A Meditation on Christian Mysticism. 128p. (Orig.). 1981. pap. 4.50 (ISBN 0-8245-0007-5). Crossroad NY.
Ghose, Sisirkumar. The Mystic As a Force for Change. rev. ed. LC 80-53954. 144p. 1980. pap. 4.75 (ISBN 0-8356-0547-7, Quest). Theos Pub Hse.
Macfarlane, Claire. The Mystic Experience & Other Essays. 2 vols. 460p. 1981. Set. 12.95 (ISBN 0-936632-07-0); Vol. 1. 6.50 (ISBN 0-936632-08-9); Vol. 2. 6.50 (ISBN 0-936632-09-7). Mann Pubs.
Rowlands, Henry. Mona Antiqua Restaurata. Feldman, Burton & Richardson, Robert D., eds. LC 78-60894. (Myth & Romanticism Ser.: Vol. 21). 399p. 1979. lib. bdg. 60.00 (ISBN 0-8240-3570-4). Garland Pub.
Russell, Bertrand. Mysticism & Logic & Other Essays. 2nd ed. 1980. pap. 5.95x. B&N.
Schutz, Albert. Call Adonoi: Manual of Practical Cabalah & Gestalt Mysticism. 114p. 1980. pap. 8.95. Ross-Erikson.
Stavropoulos, C. Partakers of Divine Nature. 1976. pap. 3.50 (ISBN 0-937032-09-3). Light & Life Pub Co MN.
Wright, J. Stafford. La Mente y lo Desconocido. Gilchrist, James S., tr. from Eng. LC 76-9906. 228p. (Orig., Span.). 1976. pap. 3.50 (ISBN 0-89922-070-3). Edit Caribe.

MYSTICISM-MIDDLE AGES, 600-1500
Glasscoe, Marion, ed. The Medieval Mystical Tradition in England. 249p. 1981. pap. 12.00x (Pub. by U Exeter, England). Humanities.
Riehle, Wofgang. The Middle English Mystics. 256p. 1981. 32.50 (ISBN 0-7100-0612-8). Routledge & Kegan.

MYSTICISM-HISTORY
Fairweather, William. Among the Mystics: The Development of Mysticism from Its Rise in the East. 161p. Repr. of 1936 ed. 3.50 (ISBN 0-567-02104-1). Attic Pr.

MYSTICISM-GREAT BRITAIN
Glasscoe, Marion, ed. The Medieval Mystical Tradition in England. 249p. 1981. pap. 12.00x (Pub. by U Exeter, England). Humanities.

MYTH
see also Mythology
Carrabino, Victor, ed. The Power of Myth in Literature & Film. LC 80-21998. (A Florida State University Bk.). 136p. 1980. 12.25 (ISBN 0-8130-0673-2, IS-00116, Pub. by U Presses Fla). Univ Microfilms.
Kris, Ernst & Kurz, Otto. Legend, Myth, & Magic in the Image of the Artist: A Historical Experiment. LC 78-24024. (Illus.). 175p. 1981. pap. 5.95 (ISBN 0-300-02669-2). Yale U Pr.
Steinberg, Stephen. The Ethnic Myth: Race, Ethnicity & Class in America. LC 80-69377. 1981. 12.95 (ISBN 0-689-11151-7). Atheneum.

MYTHICAL ANIMALS
see Animals, Mythical

MYTHOLOGY
see also Animals, Mythical; Art and Mythology; Folk-Lore; Gods; Heroes; Myth; Religion, Primitive; Symbolism
also Bull (Cats, Death, Kings and Rulers, Moon) (In Religion, Folk-Lore, etc.); and similar headings as listed in references under Religion, Primitive; also subdivision Religion, Primitive; also subdivision Religion and Mythology under Indians, Indians of North America (South America, etc.)
Campbell, J. F. & Henderson, George. The Celtic Dragon Myth. (The Newcastle Mythology Library: Vol. 4). 1981. pap. 5.95 (ISBN 0-87877-048-8). Newcastle Pub.
Henderson, George. Thhe Celtic Dragon Myth. (Newcastle Mythology Library: Vol. 4). 160p. 1981. Repr. lib. bdg. 12.95 (ISBN 0-89370-648-5). Borgo Pr.
London, Herbert I. & Weeks, Albert. Myths That Rule America. LC 80-5866. 176p. 1981. lib. bdg. 13.50 (ISBN 0-8191-1446-4); pap. text ed. 6.95 (ISBN 0-8191-1447-2). U Pr of Amer.

MYTHOLOGY-DICTIONARIES
Hendricks, Rhoda A. Mythologies of the World: A Concise Encyclopedia. Shapiro, Max S., ed. 240p. 1981. pap. 4.95 (ISBN 0-07-056421-3). McGraw.

MYTHOLOGY-JUVENILE LITERATURE
see also subdivision Juvenile Literature under Mythology, Classical, Mythology, Greek, and similar headings.
Espeland, Pamela. The Story of Baucis & Philemon. LC 80-27674. (A Myth for Modern Children Ser.). (Illus.). 32p. (gr. 1-4). 1981. PLB 5.95 (ISBN 0-87614-140-8). Carolrhoda Bks.
--Theseus & the Road to Athens. LC 80-27713. (Myths for Modern Children Ser.). (Illus.). 32p. (gr. 1-4). 1981. PLB 6.95 (ISBN 0-87614-141-6). Carolrhoda Bks.
Ross, Harriet, compiled by. Heroes & Heroines of Many Lands. (Illus.). 160p. 1981. PLB 7.95 (ISBN 0-87460-214-9). Lion.

MYTHOLOGY, AFRICAN
Ananikian, Mardiros H. Armenian Mythology & African Mythology. (Mythology of All Races Ser.: Vol. VII). Repr. of 1932 ed. 23.50 (ISBN 0-8154-0011-X). Cooper Sq.

MYTHOLOGY, ARMENIAN
Ananikian, Mardiros H. Armenian Mythology & African Mythology. (Mythology of All Races Ser.: Vol. VII). Repr. of 1932 ed. 23.50 (ISBN 0-8154-0011-X). Cooper Sq.

MYTHOLOGY, BRAHMAN
see Mythology, Hindu

MYTHOLOGY, CANAANITE
Gibson, John C. Canaanite Myths and Legends. 2nd ed. 208p. 1978. text ed. 32.00x (ISBN 0-567-02351-6). Attic Pr.

MYTHOLOGY, CLASSICAL
see also Gods; Heroes; Mythology, Greek
also names of mythological persons and objects
Aycock, Wendell M. & Klein, Theodore M., eds. Classical Mythology in Twentieth-Century Thought & Literature. (Proceedings of the Comparative Literature Symposium). (Illus.). 221p. (Orig.). 1980. pap. 12.00 (ISBN 0-89672-079-9). Tex Tech Pr.

MYTHOLOGY, CLASSICAL-DICTIONARIES
see Mythology-Dictionaries

MYTHOLOGY, GREEK
Gordon, R. L., ed. Myth, Religion & Society: Structuralist Essays by M. Detienne, L. Gernet, J. P. Vernant & P. Vidal-Naquet. (Illus.). 250p. Date not set. text ed. price not set (ISBN 0-521-22780-1); pap. text ed. price not set (ISBN 0-521-29640-4). Cambridge U Pr.
Lines, Kathleen, ed. Faber Book of Greek Legends. 1973. 9.95 (ISBN 0-571-09830-4, Pub. by Faber & Faber). Merrimack Bk Serv.
Spretnak, Charlene. Lost Goddesses of Early Greece: A Collection of Pre-Hellenic Mythology. LC 80-68169. (Illus.). 132p. 1981. pap. 5.95 (ISBN 0-8070-3239-5, BP 617). Beacon Pr.

MYTHOLOGY, GREEK-JUVENILE LITERATURE
Wise, William. Monster Myths of Ancient Greece. (Illus.). 48p. (gr. 7-11). 1981. PLB 6.99 (ISBN 0-399-61143-6). Putnam.

MYTHOLOGY, HINDU
see also Symbolism of Numbers
MacFie, J. M. Myths & Legends of India: An Introduction to the Study of Hinduism. 357p. Repr. of 1924 ed. pap. text ed. 4.95 (ISBN 0-567-22181-4). Attic Pr.

MYTHOLOGY, INDIAN (AMERICAN INDIAN)
see Indians of North America-Religion and Mythology

MYTHOLOGY, INDIC
Vidyarthi, L. P. The Sacred Complex in Hindu Gaya. 2nd ed. 264p. 1980. pap. text ed. 11.25x (ISBN 0-391-02214-8). Humanities.

MYTHOLOGY, MAYA
see Mayas-Religion and Mythology

MYTHOLOGY, NEAR EASTERN
see Mythology, Oriental

MYTHOLOGY, ORIENTAL
Picano, Felice. An Asian Minor: The True Story of Ganymede. (Illus.). 80p. 1981. 19.95 (ISBN 0-933322-07-0); pap. 5.95 (ISBN 0-933322-06-2). Sea Horse.

MYTHOLOGY, VEDIC
see Mythology, Hindu

MYTHOLOGY IN ART
see Art and Mythology

MYTHS
see Mythology

N

NABOKOV, VLADIMIR VLADIMIROVICH, 1899-
Albright, Daniel. Representation & the Imagination: Beckett, Kafka, Nabokov, & Schoenberg. LC 80-26975. (Chicago Originals Ser.). 256p. 1981. lib. bdg. 20.00x (ISBN 0-226-01252-2). U of Chicago Pr.
Quennell, Peter, ed. Vladimir Nabokov: A Tribute. (Illus.). 150p. 1981. pap. 5.95. Morrow.
Rowe, W. Woodin. Nabokov's Spectral Dimension. 1981. 15.00 (ISBN 0-88233-641-X). Ardis Pubs.

NAILS (ANATOMY)
Hyde, Judy. Nail Biter's Handbook. (Illus.). 24p. (Orig.). 1980. pap. 2.95 (ISBN 0-930380-11-8). Quail Run.

NAIPALI LANGUAGE
see Nepali Language

NAMES
see also Code Names
Devitt, Michael. Designation. LC 80-26471. 304p. 1981. 22.50x (ISBN 0-231-05126-3). Columbia U Pr.
Name Authority Control for Card Catalogs in the General Libraries. (Contributions to Librarianship Ser.: No. 5). 1980. pap. 10.00 (ISBN 0-930214-07-2). U TX Austin Gen Libs.

NAMES, CODE
see Code Names

NAMES, FICTICIOUS
see Anonyms and Pseudonyms

NAMES, GEOGRAPHICAL-INDIAN
see Indians of North America-Names

NAMES, GEOGRAPHICAL-UNITED STATES
Newton, Charles H. The Reasons Why Place Names in Arizona Are So Named. 48p. pap. 1.95 (ISBN 0-915030-25-X). Tecolote Pr.
Wood, Bryce. San Juan Island: Coastal Place Names & Cartographic Nomenclature. LC 80-17728. (Sponsor Ser.). 280p. (Orig.). 1980. pap. 20.75 (ISBN 0-8357-0526-9, SS-00132). Univ Microfilms.

NAMES, INDIAN
see Indians of North America-Names

NANTUCKET, MASSACHUSETTS
McCalley, John. Natucket Yesterday & Today. (Illus.). 176p. (Orig.). 1981. pap. price not set (ISBN 0-486-24059-2). Dover.

NANTUCKET, MASSACHUSETTS-HISTORY
Hinchman, Lydia S., compiled by. The Early Settlers of Nantucket: Sixteen Fifty-Nine to Eighteen Fifty. LC 80-54078. (Illus.). 346p. 1981. Repr. of 1926 ed. 35.00 (ISBN 0-8048-1354-X). C E Tuttle.

NAPLES
Bernier, Olivier. Pleasure & Privilege: Life in France, Naples & America. LC 79-6174. (Illus.). 304p. 1981. 14.95 (ISBN 0-385-15780-0). Doubleday.

NAPOLEON 1ST, EMPEROR OF THE FRENCH, 1769-1821
Charles-Roux, Francois. Bonaparte: Governor of Egypt. Dickes, E. W., tr. LC 80-1932. (Illus., Fr.). 1981. Repr. of 1937 ed. 47.50 (ISBN 0-404-18958-X). AMS Pr.
Gray, Daniel S. In the Words of Napoleon. LC 77-71468. 1977. pap. 8.50 (ISBN 0-916624-07-2). TSU Pr.
Sloane, William M. The Life of Napoleon Bonaparte, 4 vols. 1980. Repr. of 1910 ed. Set. lib. bdg. 125.00 (ISBN 0-8492-8128-8). R West.

NAPOLEON 1ST, EMPEROR OF THE FRENCH, 1769-1821-CAMPAIGNS
see also Waterloo, Battle of, 1815
Ellis, Geoffrey. Napoleon's Continental Blockade: The Case of Alsace. (Oxford Historical Monographs). (Illus.). 368p. 1981. 49.95 (ISBN 0-19-821881-8). Oxford U Pr.

NAPOLEONIC WARS
see Europe-History-1789-1815; France-History-Revolution, 1789-1799

NARCISSISM
Mandell, Dale. Early Feminine Development: Current Psychoanalytic Views. 1981. text ed. write for info. (ISBN 0-89335-135-0). Spectrum Pub.
Schall, Maxine. Limits. Southern, Carol, ed. 320p. 1981. 11.95 (ISBN 0-517-54143-2). Potter.

NARCOTIC ADDICTION
see Narcotic Habit

NARCOTIC HABIT
see also Opium Habit
Richter, Derek, ed. Addiction & Brain Damage. 320p. 1980. 45.00x (Pub. by Croom Helm England). State Mutual Bk.

NARCOTICS
see also Heroin; Sedatives
Comparative Statement of Estimates & Statistics on Narcotic Drugs for 1978. 42p. 1980. pap. 4.00 (ISBN 0-686-68946-1, UN80/6/5, UN). Unipub.
Estimated World Requirements of Narcotic Drugs in 1980. 60p. 1980. pap. 6.00 (ISBN 0-686-68954-2, UN80/11/1, UN). Unipub.
Report of the International Narcotics Board for 1979. 39p. 1980. pap. 5.00 (ISBN 0-686-68968-2, UN80/XI/2, UN). Unipub.
Statistics on Narcotic Drugs for 1978. 99p. 1980. pap. 9.00 (ISBN 0-686-68974-7, UN80/11/4, UN). Unipub.

NARRAGANSETT BAY-DESCRIPTION
Hale, Stu. Narragansett Bay: A Friend's Perspective. (Marine Bulletin Ser.: No. 42). 7.00 (ISBN 0-938412-19-1). URI MAS.
Olsen, Steve, et al. An Interpretive Atlas of Narragansett Bay. (Marine Bulletin Ser.: No. 40). 1980. 2.00 (ISBN 0-938412-16-7). URI MAS.

NARRATION (RHETORIC)
Berne, Stanley & Zekowski, Arlene. A First Book of the Neo-Narrative. 1954. 75.00 (ISBN 0-913844-09-8). Am Canadian.
Dowling, William C. Language & Logos in Boswell's Life of Johnson. LC 80-8545. (Essays in Literature Ser.). 232p. 1981. 15.00x (ISBN 0-691-06455-5). Princeton U Pr.
Parshall, Linda B. The Art of Narration in Wolfram's "Parzival" & Albrecht's "Jungerer Titurel". LC 79-21146. (Anglica Germanica Ser.: No. 2). 380p. Date not set. price not set (ISBN 0-521-22237-0). Cambridge U Pr.

NARRATIVE POETRY-HISTORY AND CRITICISM
Doorn, Willem V. Theory & Practice of English Narrative Verse Since Eighteen Thirty-Three. 253p. 1980. Repr. of 1833 ed. lib. bdg. 25.00 (ISBN 0-8492-4220-7). R West.

NARRATIVE WRITING
see Narration (Rhetoric)

NASCIMENTO, EDSON ARANTES DO, 1940-
Hahn, James & Hahn, Lynn. Pele'! Edson do Nascimento. Schroeder, Howard, ed. (Sports Legends Ser.). (Illus.). 48p. (Orig.). (gr. 3-5). 1981. PLB 5.95 (ISBN 0-89686-125-2); pap. text ed. 2.95 (ISBN 0-89686-140-6). Crestwood Hse.

NASH, PAUL, 1889-1946
Causey, Andrew. Paul Nash. (Illus.). 532p. 1980. 98.00x (ISBN 0-19-817348-2). Oxford U Pr.

NASSAU COUNTY, NEW YORK
Weidman, Bette S. & Martin, Linda B. Nassau County, Long Island, in Early Photographs, 1869-1940. (Illus.). 144p. (Orig.). 1981. pap. price not set (ISBN 0-486-24136-X). Dover.

NATCHEZ INDIANS
see Indians of North America-Eastern States

NATION-STATE
see National State

NATIONAL CHARACTERISTICS, AUSTRALIAN
Learmonth, Nancy. The Australians: How They Live & Work. LC 72-89452. 166p. 1973. text ed. 8.95 (ISBN 0-03-029571-8, HoltC). HR&W.

NATIONAL CHARACTERISTICS, ISRAELI
Dicks, Brian. The Israelis: How They Live & Work. LC 74-30350. 156p. 1975. text ed. 8.95 (ISBN 0-03-029706-0, HoltC). HR&W.

NATIONAL CHARACTERISTICS, ITALIAN
Bryant, Andrew. The Italians: How They Live & Work. LC 75-27493. 164p. 1976. text ed. 8.95 (ISBN 0-03-028511-9, HoltC). HR&W.

NATIONAL EMBLEMS
see Emblems

NATIONAL FOOTBALL LEAGUE
NFL Public Relations Dept. NFL Nineteen Eighty-One Media Information Book. (Illus.). 130p. 1981. pap. 7.95 (ISBN 0-89480-148-1). Workman Pub.

NATIONAL HEALTH SERVICE, GREAT BRITAIN
see Great Britain-National Health Service

NATIONAL LABOR RELATIONS BOARD
see United States-National Labor Relations Board

NATIONAL PARKS AND RESERVES
see also United States-National Park Service; Wilderness Areas
also names of national parks, e.g. Yellowstone National Park
Albright, Horace M. & Taylor, Frank J. Oh, Ranger! rev. 14th ed. Jones, William R., ed. (Illus.). 176p. pap. 6.95 (ISBN 0-89646-068-1). Outbooks.
Frome, Michael. The National Parks. rev.. ed. (Illus.). 160p. (Orig.). 1981. pap. 9.95 (ISBN 0-528-88045-4). Rand.
Hakola, John W. Legacy of a Lifetime: The Story of Baxter State Park in Maine. (Illus.). 448p. Date not set. 16.00 (ISBN 0-931474-18-3). TBW Bks.
Milley, John. Treasures of Independence. (Illus.). 224p. 1980. 25.00 (ISBN 0-8317-8593-4). Mayflower Bks.
Umhoefer, Jim. Guide to Wisconsin's State Parks, Forests, & Trails. (Illus.). 160p. (Orig.). 1981. pap. 7.95 (ISBN 0-915024-26-8). Tamarack Edns.
Villagran, M. C. Vegetationsgeschichtliche und Pflanzensoziologische Untersuchungen Im Vicente Perez Nationalpark: Chile. (Dissertationes Botanicae: No. 54). (Illus.). 166p. (Ger.). 1981. pap. text ed. 25.00x (ISBN 3-7682-1265-3). Lubrecht & Cramer.

NATIONAL PARKS AND RESERVES-GREAT BRITAIN
Waugh, Mary. The Shell Book of Country Parks. LC 80-68695. (Illus.). 224p. 1981. 19.95 (ISBN 0-7153-7963-1). David & Charles.

NATIONAL PLANNING
see Economic Policy; Social Policy

NATIONAL PSYCHOLOGY
see Ethnopsychology

NATIONAL SELF-DETERMINATION
see Self-Determination, National

NATIONAL SOCIALISM
see also Socialism
Pauley, Bruce. Hitler & the Forgotten Nazis. LC 80-17006. 360p. 1981. 19.00x (ISBN 0-8078-1456-3). U of NC Pr.

NATIONAL SOCIALIST WORKERS PARTY
see Nationalsozialistische Deutsche Arbeiter-Partei

NATIONAL STATE
Banks, Arthur S. Cross-Polity Time-Series Data. 328p. 1971. 50.00 (ISBN 0-262-02071-8). MIT Pr.

NATIONALDEMOKRATISCHE PARTEI DEUTSCHLANDS-GERMANY (FEDERAL REPUBLIC, 1949-)
Aycoberry, Pierre. The Nazi Question. 1981. price not set. Pantheon.
Infield, Glenn B. Secrets of the SS. LC 80-5434. 304p. 1981. 14.95 (ISBN 0-8128-2790-2). Stein & Day.
Mosse, George L. Nazi Culture. LC 80-26608. 432p. 1981. pap. 8.95 (ISBN 0-8052-0668-X). Schocken.

Reider, Frederic. Hitler's S.S. (Illus.). 256p. 1981. 24.95 (ISBN 0-89404-061-8). Aztex.

NATIONALISM

see also Minorities; National State; Nationalism and Socialism; Self-Determination, National

Farmer, Kenneth C. Ukrainian Nationalism in the Post-Stalin Era: Myth, Symbols & Ideology in Soviet Nationalities Policy. (Studies in Contemporary History: Vol. 4). 253p. 1980. lib. bdg. 36.50 (ISBN 90-247-2401-5, Pub. by Martinus Nijhoff). Kluwer Boston.

Luxemburg, Rosa. The National Question: Selected Writings by Rosa Luxembourg. Davis, Horace B., ed. LC 74-2148. (Illus.). 320p. 1981. pap. 7.00 (ISBN 0-85345-577-5). Monthly Rev.

Mitchison, Rosalind. The Roots of Nationalism: Studies in Northern Europe. 175p. 1980. text ed. 31.25x (ISBN 0-85976-058-8). Humanities.

NATIONALISM–EUROPE

Armstrong, John A. Ukranian Nationalism. 2nd ed. LC 79-25529. 361p. 1980. Repr. of 1963 ed. 30.00x (ISBN 0-87287-193-2). Libs Unl.

Tudjman, Franjo. Nationalism in Contemporary Europe. (East European Monographs: No. 76). 352p. 1981. text ed. 21.50x (ISBN 0-914710-70-2). East Eur Quarterly.

NATIONALISM AND SOCIALISM

Vajda, Mihaly. The State & Socialism. (Allison & Busby Motive Ser.). 160p. 1981. pap. 7.95 (Pub. by Alison & Busby, England). Schocken.

NATIONALITY (CITIZENSHIP)

see Citizenship

NATIONALIZATION

see Government Ownership

NATIONALSOZIALISTISCHE DEUTSCHE ARBEITER-PARTEI

Moczarski, Kazimierz. Conversations with an Executioner. (Illus.). 256p. 1981. 12.95 (ISBN 0-13-171918-1). P-H.

NATIONALSOZIALISTISCHE DEUTSCHE ARBEITER-PARTEI, SCHUTZSTAFFEL

Reider, Federic. Hitler's S. S. (Illus.). 256p. 1981. 24.95 (ISBN 0-89404-061-8). Aztex.

Speer, Albert. Infiltration: The SS & German Armament. Neugrosschel, Joachim, tr. 604p. 1981. 15.00 (ISBN 0-02-612800-4). Macmillan.

NATIONS, LAW OF

see International Law

NATIONS, MIGRATIONS OF

see Migrations of Nations

NATIVE RACES

see also Ethnology; Indians of North America–Government Relations;

also subdivision Native Races under names of continents, countries, etc. e.g. Africa–Native Races

Huffer, Virginia, et al. The Sweetness of the Pig: Aboriginal Women in Transition. LC 80-21658. (Illus.). 244p. 1981. 15.00 (ISBN 0-295-95790-5). U of Wash Pr.

NATIVITY OF CHRIST

see Jesus Christ–Nativity

NATO

see North Atlantic Treaty Organization

NATURAL CALAMITIES

see Natural Disasters

NATURAL DISASTERS

see also Floods

International Conference Held in Bangkok, Jan. 7-9, 1980 & Karasudhi, Pisidhi. Engineering for Protection from Natural Disasters: Proceedings. Kanok-Nukulchai, Worsak, ed. 1980. write for info. (ISBN 0-471-27895-5, Pub. by Wiley-Interscience). Wiley.

Whittow, John. Disasters: The Anatomy of Environmental Hazards. LC 79-5236. (Illus.). 405p. 1981. pap. 9.95 (ISBN 0-8203-0542-1). U of Ga Pr.

NATURAL FOOD

see Food, Natural

NATURAL FOOD COOKERY

see Cookery (Natural Foods)

NATURAL GARDENING

see Organic Gardening

NATURAL GAS

see Gas, Natural

NATURAL HISTORY

see also Animal Lore; Aquariums; Biology; Botany; Geographical Distribution of Animals and Plants; Geology; Marine Biology; Mineralogy; Paleontology; Plant Lore; Zoology

Kolisko, Eugen. Natural History. 1980. pap. 3.25x (ISBN 0-906492-21-1, Pub. by Kolisko Archives). St George Bk Serv.

Scandone, Thomas. Emphasis: Natural History. 1979. coil binging 12.95 (ISBN 0-88252-098-9). Paladin Hse.

Slauson, Nedra, ed. Index to Illustrations of the Natural World: Where to Find Pictures of the Living Things of North America. 265p. 1981. 29.95 (ISBN 0-208-01911-1, Lib Prof Pubns). Shoe String.

NATURAL HISTORY–BIBLIOGRAPHY

Munz, Lucille T. & Slauson, Nedra. Index to Illustrations of the Natural World Outside of North America. 1980. write for info. (ISBN 0-208-01857-3, Archon). Shoe String.

NATURAL HISTORY–DICTIONARIES

Khatib, Ahmad. Dictionary of the Natural Environment: English-Arabic. 1979. pap. 5.95. Intl Bk Ctr.

NATURAL HISTORY–STORIES

see Nature Stories

NATURAL HISTORY–AUSTRALIA

Breeden, Stanley & Breeden, Kay. Australia's North. (A Natural History of Australia Ser.: No. 3). 208p. 1980. 34.95x (ISBN 0-00-211441-0, Pub. by W Collins Australia). Intl Schol Bk Serv.

NATURAL HISTORY–CANADA

Janes, Robert. The Great Canadian Outback. (Illus.). 1979. 19.95 (ISBN 0-295-95678-X, Pub. by Douglas & McIntyre Canada). U of Wash Pr.

NATURAL HISTORY–UNITED STATES

Power, Dennis M., ed. The California Islands: Proceedings of a Multidisciplinary Symposium. LC 80-463. 787p. (Orig.). 1980. pap. text ed. 20.00 (ISBN 0-936494-01-8). Santa Barbara Mus Nat Hist.

Watkins, T. H. John Muir's America. (Illus.). 160p. 1981. pap. 12.95 (ISBN 0-912856-64-5). Graphic Arts Ctr.

NATURAL HISTORY, BIBLICAL

see Bible–Natural History

NATURAL RELIGION

see Natural Theology

NATURAL RESOURCES

see also Commercial Products; Conservation of Natural Resources; Fisheries; Forests and Forestry; Geothermal Resources; Marine Resources; Mines and Mineral Resources; Power Resources; Reclamation of Land; Water-Power; Water Resources Development; Water-Supply; Wind Power

Gilbert, Douglas L. Natural Resources & Public Relations. LC 76-143896. (Illus.). 320p. 1971. 8.00 (ISBN 0-933564-03-1). Wildlife Soc.

Hicks, C. S. Man & Natural Resources: An Agricultural Perspective. 250p. 1980. 29.00x (Pub. by Croom Helm England). State Mutual Bk.

Little, Dennis L., et al, eds. Renewable Natural Resources: A Management Handbook for the Eighties. (Special Studies in Natural Resources & Energy Management). 375p. (Orig.). 1981. lib. bdg. 19.50x (ISBN 0-89158-665-2). Westview.

Robert Clark, Gillean. Resource Recovery Planning & Management. 1981. text ed. 24.00 (ISBN 0-250-40298-X). Ann Arbor Science.

Siebert, Horst. Economics of the Environment. LC 80-7442. 1981. price not set (ISBN 0-669-03693-5). Lexington Bks.

NATURAL RESOURCES–LAW AND LEGISLATION

see also Water–Laws and Legislation; Wildlife Conservation–Law and Legislation

Arsanjani, Mahnoush H. International Regulation of Internal Resources: A Study of Law & Policy. LC 80-21169. 1981. write for info. (ISBN 0-8139-0879-5). U Pr of Va.

NATURAL RESOURCES–RUSSIA

Gustafson, Thane. Reform in Soviet Politics: The Lessons of Recent Policies on Land & Water. LC 80-24286. (Illus.). 224p. Date not set. price not set (ISBN 0-521-23377-1). Cambridge U Pr.

NATURAL RESOURCES–UNITED STATES–ECONOMIC CONDITIONS

Simon, Julian L. The Ultimate Resource. LC 80-8575. 336p. 1981. 14.50x (ISBN 0-691-09389-X). Princeton U Pr.

NATURAL SCENERY

see Landscape; Views

NATURAL SCIENCE

see Natural History; Physics; Science

NATURAL SELECTION

see also Evolution; Heredity

Darwin, Charles. The Descent of Man & Selection in Relation to Sex. LC 80-8679. (Illus.). 935p. 1981. 30.00x (ISBN 0-691-08278-2); pap. 8.95 (ISBN 0-691-02369-7). Princeton U Pr.

NATURAL THEOLOGY

see also Creation; Philosophy of Nature; Religion and Science

Lincoln, Bruce. Priests, Warriors & Cattle: A Study in the Ecology of Religions. LC 78-68826. (Hermeneutics: Studies in the History of Religions). 240p. 1981. 20.00x (ISBN 0-520-03880-0). U of Cal Pr.

Tholen, Gerald. Massism Vs. Natural Religion. 1980. pap. 3.00. Am Atheist.

NATURAL WATER CHEMISTRY

see Water Chemistry

NATURALISTS

see also Ornithologists; Scientists

Channing, William E. Thoreau the Poet-Naturalist: With Memorial Verses. LC 80-2679. 1981. Repr. of 1873 ed. 37.50 (ISBN 0-404-19073-1). AMS Pr.

Cutright, Paul R. & Brodhead, Michael J. Elliott Coues: Naturalist & Frontier Historian. LC 80-12424. (Illus.). 510p. 1981. 28.95 (ISBN 0-252-00802-2). U of Ill Pr.

NATURALIZATION

see also Aliens; Citizenship

Webster, Prentiss. Law of Naturalization in the United States of America & of Other Countries. xx, 403p. 1981. Repr. of 1895 ed. lib. bdg. 32.50x (ISBN 0-8377-1309-9). Rothman.

NATURE

see also Landscape; Man–Influence on Nature

Amon, Aline. The Earth Is Sore: Native Americans on Nature. LC 80-36854. (Illus.). 96p. 1981. PLB 9.95 (ISBN 0-689-30798-5). Atheneum.

Angier, Bradford. Wilderness Neighbors. LC 76-26303. 228p. 1981. pap. 5.95 (ISBN 0-8128-6100-0). Stein & Day.

Headstrom, Richard. Nature Discoveries with a Hand Lens. (Illus.). 425p. 1981. pap. price not set (ISBN 0-486-24077-0). Dover.

Henderson, M. A. The Survival Resource Book. (Illus.). 180p. 1981. pap. 8.95 (ISBN 0-312-77951-8). St Martin.

Kinkead, Eugene. A Concrete Look at Nature. (Illus.). 242p. 1974. 8.00x (ISBN 0-8129-0471-0). E Kinkead.

--Wildness Is All Around Us. (Illus.). 178p. 1978. pap. 10.00x (ISBN 0-87690-277-8). E Kinkead.

Watkins, William J. Suburban Wilderness. (Illus.). 192p. 1981. 9.95 (ISBN 0-399-12552-3). Putnam.

NATURE–PHILOSOPHY

see Philosophy of Nature

NATURE–STORIES

see Nature Stories

NATURE, EFFECT OF MAN ON

see Man–Influence on Nature

NATURE, PHILOSOPHY OF

see Philosophy of Nature

NATURE CONSERVATION

see also Wildlife Conservation

Frankel, O. H. & Soule, M. E. Conservation & Evolution. LC 80-40528. (Illus.). 300p. Date not set. 49.50 (ISBN 0-521-23275-9); pap. 17.95 (ISBN 0-521-29889-X). Cambridge U Pr.

NATURE IN ORNAMENT

see Decoration and Ornament; Design, Decorative–Plant Forms

NATURE PHOTOGRAPHY

see also Photography of Animals; Photography of Plants

Feininger, Andreas. Nature Close Up: A Fantastic Journey into Reality. rev. ed. (Illus.). 160p. 1981. pap. price not set (ISBN 0-486-24102-5). Dover.

NATURE PROTECTION

see Nature Conservation

NATURE STORIES

Heady, Ray A. Hard Head I & Other Outdoor Stories. LC 80-83551. (Illus.). 312p. 1980. 12.95 (ISBN 0-913504-59-9). Lowell Pr.

NATURE STUDY

see also Animals, Habits and Behavior of; Biology; Botany; Nature Photography; Zoology

Allaby, Michael. A Year in the Life of a Field. LC 80-68681. (Illus.). 192p. 1981. 22.50 (ISBN 0-7153-7889-9). David & Charles.

Bazalgette, Leon. Henry Thoreau Bachelor of Nature. Brooks, Wyck Van, tr. LC 80-2679. 1981. Repr. of 1924 ed. 37.50 (ISBN 0-404-19076-6). AMS Pr.

Brown, Vinson. The Amateur Naturalist's Handbook. (Illus.). 432p. 1980. 15.95 (Spec); pap. 6.95. P-H.

Burroughs, John. Return of the Birds: Selected Nature Essays of John Burroughs, Vol. 1. Bergon, Frank, ed. (Literature of the American Wilderness). 320p. 1981. pap. 4.45 (ISBN 0-87905-081-0). Peregrine Smith.

--A Sharp Lookout: Nature Essays of John Burroughs, Vol. II. Bergone, Frank, ed. (Literature of the American Wilderness) 320p. 1981. pap. 4.45 (ISBN 0-87905-082-9). Peregrine Smith.

--Signs & Seasons. (Nature Library Ser.). 300p. 1981. pap. 5.95 (ISBN 0-06-090840-8, CN 840, CN). Har-Row.

Campbell, A. C. The Larousse Guide to the Seashore & Shallow Seas of Britain & Europe. LC 80-82755. (Larousse Nature Guides Ser.). (Illus.). 320p. (Orig.). 1981. 10.95 (ISBN 0-88332-251-X, 8068). Larousse.

Clapper, Ronald. The Development of Walden: A Genetic Text. LC 80-2503. 1981. 75.00 (ISBN 0-686-28931-5). AMS Pr.

Dorward, Douglas. Wild Australia. (Illus.). 128p. 1980. 20.95x (ISBN 0-00-211446-1, Pub. by W Collins Australia). Intl Schol Bk Serv.

Freethy, Ron. The Making of the British Countryside. LC 80-68688. (Illus.). 192p. 1981. 24.00 (ISBN 0-7153-8012-5). David & Charles.

Hamlet, John N. & Carter, W. Horace. Land That I Love. (Illus.). 295p. 1980. 6.95 (ISBN 0-937866-00-8). Atlantic Pub Co.

Kidney, Dorothy B. Wilderness Journey. (Illus.). 200p. (Orig.). 1980. pap. 7.95 (ISBN 0-930096-10-X). G Gannett.

Lawrence, R. D. The Study of Life: A Naturalist's View. (Illus.). 43p. 1980. pap. 1.50 (ISBN 0-913098-37-X). Myrin Institute.

Lehmberg, Paul. In the Strong Woods. 160p. 1981. pap. 4.95 (ISBN 0-312-41173-1). St Martin.

McDonald, Ralph J. A Down-Home Gallery of American Wildlife. (Illus.). 101p. 1980. 39.95 (ISBN 0-9605428-1-7); signed numbered ed. 95.00 (ISBN 0-9605428-0-9). Countryside Studio.

Milne, Lururus J. & Milne, Margery J. The World of Night. (Nature Library Ser.). (Illus.). 248p. (Orig.). 1981. pap. 5.95 (ISBN 0-06-090839-4, CN 839, CN). Har-Row.

Pedretti, Carlo. Leonardo Da Vinci Nature Studies from the Royal Library at Windsor Castle. (Illus.). 95p. (Orig.). 1980. pap. 10.00 (ISBN 0-384-32298-0). J P Getty Mus.

Pyle, Robert. The Audubon Society Field Guide to North American Butterflies. LC 80-84240. (Illus.). 864p. 1981. 11.95 (ISBN 0-394-51914-0). Knopf.

Raphael, Ray. An Everyday History of Somewhere. (Illus.). 192p. pap. 10.00 (ISBN 0-933280-11-4). Island Pr.

Russell, Franklin. Watchers at the Pond. 1981. pap. 8.95 (ISBN 0-87923-390-7). Godine.

Slauson, Nedra & Thompson, John W., eds. Index to Illustrations of the Natural World: Where to Find Pictures of the Living Things of North America. 265p. 1981. Repr. of 1980 ed. 29.95 (ISBN 0-208-01911-1, Lib Prof Pubns). Shoe String.

White, William M. Sweet Wild World: Thoreau on Birds & Small Creatures. (Illus.). 146p. (Orig.). 1981. 10.00 (ISBN 0-85699-112-0); pap. 6.95 (ISBN 0-85699-115-5). Chatham Pr.

Zwinger, Ann. Beyond the Aspen Grove. (Nature Library). (Illus.). 384p. (Orig.). 1981. pap. 5.95 (ISBN 0-06-090842-4, CN 842, CN). Har-Row.

NATURE STUDY–JUVENILE LITERATURE

Overbeck, Cynthia. Monkeys. (Lerner Natural Science Bks.). (Illus.). (gr. 4-10). 1981. PLB 7.95 (ISBN 0-8225-1464-8). Lerner Pubns.

Rights, Mollie & Solga, Tim. Beastly Neighbors: Or Why Earwigs Make Good Mothers. (Brown Paper School Ser.). (Illus.). 128p. (Orig.). (gr. 3 up). 1981. 9.95 (ISBN 0-316-74576-6); pap. 5.95 (ISBN 0-316-74577-4). Little.

NATUROPATHY

Davis, Ben. Rapid Healing Foods. LC 79-22770. 1980. 10.95 (ISBN 0-13-753137-0, Parker). P-H.

NAUTICAL ASTRONOMY

see also Navigation

Toghill, Jeff. Celestial Navigation for Beginners. (Orig.). 1980. pap. 8.95 (ISBN 0-8464-0998-4). Beekman Pubs.

NAUTICAL CHARTS

Winlund, Edmond. ChartGuide for Southern California 1980-81. rev. ed. LC 74-29812. (Illus.). 138p. (Orig.). 1979. pap. 17.25 (ISBN 0-938206-00-1). ChartGuide.

NAUTICAL SURVEYING

see Hydrographic Surveying

NAUTICAL TERMS

see Naval Art and Science–Dictionaries; Naval Art and Science–Terminology

NAVAHO INDIANS

see Indians of North America–Southwest, New

NAVAL ADMINISTRATION

see Naval Art and Science

NAVAL AERONAUTICS

see Aeronautics, Military

NAVAL AIR BASES

see Air Bases

NAVAL ARCHITECTURE

see also Boat-Building; Electricity on Ships; Marine Engineering; Ship-Building; Ships, Iron and Steel; Stability of Ships; Warships

also types of vessels, e.g. Motor-Boats

Baxter, B. Naval Architecture: Examples & Theory. 450p. 1978. 29.95x (ISBN 0-85264-179-6, Pub. by Griffin England). State Mutual Bk.

NAVAL ART AND SCIENCE

see also Marine Engineering; Military Art and Science; Navigation; Sea-Power; Seamanship; Ship-Building; Warships

Minikin, R. R. Winds, Waves & Maritime Structures. 295p. 1963. 29.75x (ISBN 0-85264-091-9, Pub. by Griffin England). State Mutual Bk.

NAVAL ART AND SCIENCE–DICTIONARIES

Blackburn, Graham. The Overlook Illustrated Dictionary of Nautical Terms. LC 80-39640. (Illus.). 416p. 1981. 19.95 (ISBN 0-87951-124-9). Overlook Pr.

NAVAL ART AND SCIENCE–TERMINOLOGY

Blackburn, Graham. The Overlook Illustrated Dictionary of Nautical Terms. LC 80-39640. (Illus.). 416p. 1981. 19.95 (ISBN 0-87951-124-9). Overlook Pr.

NAVAL ARTILLERY

see Artillery

NAVAL AVIATION

see Aeronautics, Military

NAVAL BATTLES

see also Battles; Naval History;

also subdivision History, Naval under names of countries, e.g. Great Britain–History, Naval; also names of naval battles

Y'Blood, William T. Red Sun Setting: The Battle of the Philippine Sea. 208p. 1981. 18.95 (ISBN 0-87021-532-9). Naval Inst Pr.

NAVAL BIOGRAPHY

see Admirals; Naval History

also subdivision Biography under Navies e.g. United States–Navy–Biography

NAVAL CONSTRUCTION

see Naval Architecture; Ship-Building

NAVAL ENGINEERING

see Marine Engineering

NAVAL HISTORY

Coletta, Paolo E., ed. A Bibliography of American Naval History. 453p. 1981. 14.95 (ISBN 0-87021-105-6). Naval Inst Pr.

Symonds, Craig L., ed. New Aspects of Naval History. 1981. text ed. 32.95 (ISBN 0-87021-495-0). Naval Inst Pr.

NAVAL MEDICINE

see Medicine, Naval

NAVAL POLICY

see Sea-Power;

also subdivision Defenses under names of countries, e.g. United States–Defense; also Great Britain–Navy; United States–Navy and similar headings
Carlisle, Rodney P. Sovereignty for Sale. 336p. 1981. 19.95 (ISBN 0-87021-668-6). Naval Inst Pr.
Transactions, Vol. 88. (Illus.). 400p. 1981. 35.00 (ISBN 0-9603048-2-7). Soc Naval Arch.

NAVAL SCIENCE
see Naval Art and Science

NAVAL SHIPS
see Warships

NAVAL WARFARE
see Naval Art and Science; Naval Battles

NAVIES–MEDICAL SERVICE
see Medicine, Naval

NAVIGATION
see also Aids to Navigation; Coastwise Navigation; Harbors; Hydrographic Surveying; Lighthouses; Nautical Astronomy; Nautical Charts; Naval Art and Science; Pilot Guides; Pilots and Pilotage; Seamanship; Ship-Building; Shipwrecks; Steam-Navigation; Submarines; Winds; Yachts and Yachting
also names of nautical instruments, e.g. Compass, Gyroscope
Moody, Alton B. Navigation Afloat: A Manual for the Seaman. 768p. 1981. 35.00 (ISBN 0-442-25488-1). Van Nos Reinhold.
Randier, Jean. Marine Navigation Instruments. (Illus.). 219p. 1980. text ed. 47.50x (ISBN 0-7195-3733-9). Humanities.
Recommendation on Basic Principles & Operational Guidance Relating to Navigational Watchkeeping. 12p. 1974. pap. 7.75 (ISBN 92-801-1032-2, IMCO 62, IMCO). Unipub.
Schlereth, Hewitt. Commonplace Coastal Navigation. (Illus.). 1981. 18.95 (ISBN 0-393-03224-8). Norton.
Toghill, Jeff. Navigating with Chart & Compass. (Illus.). 96p. (Orig.). 1980. pap. 8.25 (ISBN 0-589-50183-6, Pub. by Reed Bks Australia). C E Tuttle.

NAVIGATION–DICTIONARIES
see Naval Art and Science–Dictionaries

NAVIGATION–SAFETY MEASURES
see also Radio in Navigation
International Conference on Maritime Search & Rescue, 1979. 38p. 1979. 9.25 (IMCO). Unipub.
International Conference on Revision of the International Regulations for Preventing Collisions at Sea. 128p. 1974. 12.50 (IMCO). Unipub.
International Conference on Safety of Fishing Vessels. 204p. 1977. 18.00 (IMCO). Unipub.
International Conference on Tanker Safety & Pollution Prevention. 106p. 1978. 18.00 (IMCO). Unipub.

NAVIGATION, RADAR IN
see Radar in Navigation

NAVIGATION CHARTS
see Nautical Charts

NAVIGATION LAWS
see Maritime Law

NAVIGATORS
see Discoveries (In Geography)

NAVY
see Naval Art and Science; Sea-Power
also subdivision Navy under names of countries, e.g. United States–Navy

NAZI MOVEMENT
see Germany–Politics and Government–1933-1945

NAZI PARTY
see Nationalsozialistische Deutsche Arbeiter-Partei

NAZISM
see National Socialism

NEAR EAST–ANTIQUITIES
Coon, Carleton S. The Seven Caves: Archaeological Explorations in the Middle East. LC 80-24503. (Illus.). xx, 354p. 1981. Repr. of 1957 ed. lib. bdg. 31.50x (ISBN 0-313-22824-8, COSCA). Greenwood.

NEAR EAST–BIBLIOGRAPHY
Matthews, Noel & Wainwrights, Doreen M., eds. A Guide to Manuscrpits & Documents in the British Isles Relating to the Middle East & North Africa. 500p. 1980. 148.00x (ISBN 0-19-713598-6). Oxford U Pr.

NEAR EAST–CIVILIZATION
Bagnole, John W. Cultures of the Islamic Middle East. (America-Mideast Educational & Training Servies, Inc. - Occasional Paper: No. 4). 86p. (Orig.). 1978. pap. text ed. 4.00 (ISBN 0-89192-296-2). Interbk Inc.

NEAR EAST–DESCRIPTION AND TRAVEL
Paddington Press. Middle East Business Travel Guide. 288p. 1981. 19.95 (ISBN 0-87196-343-4); pap. 11.95 (ISBN 0-87196-323-X). Facts on File.
Schiffer, Michael. Lessons of the Road. 1980. 10.95 (ISBN 0-686-68922-4, Kenan Pr). S&S.

NEAR EAST–ECONOMIC CONDITIONS
The Gulf Telephone Directory 1980. 1980. 95.00x (Pub. by Parrish-Rogers England). State Mutual Bk.
The Jeddah Commercial Directory 1980. 1980. 95.00x (Pub. by Parrish-Rogers England). State Mutual Bk.
May, Brian. The Third World Calamity. (Illus.). 272p. 1981. price not set (ISBN 0-7100-0764-7). Routledge & Kegan.
Middle East & North Africa 1980-81. 985p. 1981. 80.00 (ISBN 0-905118-50-2, EUR 23, Europa). Unipub.
The Middle East & North Africa 1980-81. 27th ed. LC 48-3250. (Illus.). 1005p. 1980. 80.00x (ISBN 0-905118-50-2). Intl Pubns Serv.
The Middle East: Life & Work for the Civil Engineer. 85p. 1980. 29.00x (ISBN 0-7277-0064-2, Pub. by Telford England). State Mutual Bk.
Nicholas, David. The Middle East: Its Oil, Economics, & Investment Policies: A Guide to Sources of Financial Information. LC 80-28555. xxiv, 201p. 1981. lib. bdg. 40.00 (ISBN 0-313-22986-4, NME/). Greenwood.
Tames, Richard. The Arab World Today. (Today Ser.). (Illus.). 96p. 1980. text ed. 15.00x (ISBN 0-7182-0461-1, SpS). Soccer.
Trado Asian-African Directory of Exporters-Importers & Manufacturers, 1980. 25th ed. LC 60-41792. 1640p. 1980. 50.00x (ISBN 0-8002-2736-0). Intl Pubns Serv.

NEAR EAST–FOREIGN RELATIONS
Bagnole, John W. Cultures of the Islamic Middle East. (America-Mideast Educational & Training Servies, Inc. - Occasional Paper: No. 4). 86p. (Orig.). 1978. pap. text ed. 4.00 (ISBN 0-89192-296-2). Interbk Inc.
Jureidini, Paul & McLaurin, R. D. Beyond Camp David: Emerging Alignments & Leaders in the Middle East. LC 80-27406. (Contemporary Issues in the Middle East Ser.). 232p. 1981. text ed. 18.00x (ISBN 0-8156-2235-X); pap. text ed. 8.95x (ISBN 0-8156-2236-8). Syracuse U Pr.
Middle East Negotiations: A Conversation with Joseph Sisco. 1980. pap. 3.25 (ISBN 0-8447-3394-6). Am Enterprise.

NEAR EAST–FOREIGN RELATIONS–UNITED STATES
McDonald, John & Burleson, Clyde. Flight from Dhahran: The/True Experiences of an American Businessman Held Hostage in Saudi Arabia. 256p. 1981. 10.95 (ISBN 0-13-322453-8). P-H.

NEAR EAST–HISTORY
Fraser, T. G. The Middle East: 1914-1979. 1980. 19.95 (ISBN 0-312-53181-8). St Martin.
Frye, Richard N. Islamic Iran & Central Asia (7th-12th Centuries) 380p. 1980. 75.00x (ISBN 0-86078-044-9, Pub. by Variorum England). State Mutual Bk.
Mobley, Jonathan H. The Elusive Peace: The Middle East, Oil & the Economic & Political Future of the World. (The Major Currents in Contemprary World History Lib.). (Illus.). 122p. 1981. 46.55 (ISBN 0-930008-79-0). Inst Econ Pol.
Prawer, Joshua. Crusader Institutions. (Illus.). 536p. 1980. 89.00x (ISBN 0-19-822536-9). Oxford U Pr.
Sykes, Cristopher. Orde Wingate. (Return to Zion Ser.). 575p. 1981. Repr. lib. bdg. 35.00x (ISBN 0-87991-146-8). Porcupine Pr.

NEAR EAST–HISTORY–SOURCES
Matthews, Noel & Wainwrights, Doreen M., eds. A Guide to Manuscrpits & Documents in the British Isles Relating to the Middle East & North Africa. 500p. 1980. 148.00x (ISBN 0-19-713598-6). Oxford U Pr.

NEAR EAST–POLITICS AND GOVERNMENT
The Arabian Gulf Government & Public Services Directory 1980-81. 1980. 175.00x (Pub. by Parrish-Rogers England). State Mutual Bk.
Cantori, Louis J. & Harik, Iliya, eds. Local Politics & Development in the Middle East. (Special Studies on the Middle East). 350p. 1981. lib. bdg. 24.50x (ISBN 0-86531-169-2). Westview.
Clarke, Thurston. By Blood & Fire. 288p. 1981. 13.95 (ISBN 0-399-12605-8). Putnam.
Harris, William W. Taking Root: Israeli Settlement in the West Bank, the Golan & Gaza-Sinai, 1967-1980. 256p. 1981. 39.25 (ISBN 0-471-27863-7, Pub. by Wiley-Interscience). Wiley.
Helms, Christine M. The Cohesion of Saudi Arabia: Evolution of Political Identity. LC 80-8026. (Illus.). 320p. 1981. text ed. 28.00x (ISBN 0-8018-2475-3). Johns Hopkins.
Henry, Clement M. Politics & International Relations in the Middle East: An Annotated Bibliography. 114p. (Orig.). 1980. pap. 4.00 (ISBN 0-932098-18-5). Ctr for NE & North Aafrican Stud.
Jureidini, Paul & McLaurin, R. D. Beyond Camp David: Emerging Alignments & Leaders in the Middle East. LC 80-27406. (Contemporary Issues in the Middle East Ser.). 232p. 1981. text ed. 18.00x (ISBN 0-8156-2235-X); pap. text ed. 8.95x (ISBN 0-8156-2236-8). Syracuse U Pr.
McDonald, John & Burleson, Clyde. Flight from Dhahran: The/True Experiences of an American Businessman Held Hostage in Saudi Arabia. 256p. 1981. 10.95 (ISBN 0-13-322453-8). P-H.
May, Brian. The Third World Calamity. (Illus.). 272p. 1981. price not set (ISBN 0-7100-0764-7). Routledge & Kegan.
Middle East & North Africa 1980-81. 985p. 1981. 80.00 (ISBN 0-905118-50-2, EUR 23, Europa). Unipub.
The Middle East & North Africa 1980-81. 27th ed. LC 48-3250. (Illus.). 1005p. 1980. 80.00x (ISBN 0-905118-50-2). Intl Pubns Serv.
Mobley, Jonathan H. The Elusive Peace: The Middle East, Oil & the Economic & Political Future of the World. (The Major Currents in Contemprary World History Lib.). (Illus.). 122p. 1981. 46.55 (ISBN 0-930008-79-0). Inst Econ Pol.
Mroz, John E. Beyond Security: Private Perceptions Among Arabs & Israelis. (Illus.). 230p. 1981. 20.00 (ISBN 0-08-027517-6); pap. 9.95 (ISBN 0-08-027516-8). Pergamon.
Narayan, B. K. Oman & Gulf-Security. 300p. 1980. text ed. 24.00x (ISBN 0-8426-1660-8). Verry.
Petras, James. Class, State & Power in the Third World: With Case Studies on Class Conflict in Latin America. 300p. 1981. text ed. 19.95 (ISBN 0-86598-018-7). Allanheld.
Tames, Richard. The Arab World Today. (Today Ser.). (Illus.). 96p. 1980. text ed. 15.00x (ISBN 0-7182-0461-1, SpS). Soccer.
Traverton, Gregory, ed. Crisis Management & the Super-Powers in the Middle East. LC 80-67837. (Adelphi Library: Vol. 5). 172p. 1981. text ed. 29.50 (ISBN 0-916672-73-5). Allanheld.
Wolpin, Miles D. Militarism & Social Revolution in the Third World. 256p. 1981. text ed. 25.00 (ISBN 0-86598-021-7). Allanheld.

NEAR EAST–RELIGION
Halsell, Grace. Journey to Jerusalem. 256p. 1981. 9.95 (ISBN 0-02-547590-8). Macmillan.

NEAR EAST–SOCIAL CONDITIONS
The Arabian Gulf Government & Public Services Directory 1980-81. 1980. 175.00x (Pub. by Parrish-Rogers England). State Mutual Bk.
Bedouins, Wealth, & Change: A Study of Rural Development in the United Arab Emirates & the Sultanate of Oman. 64p. 1980. pap. 11.75 (TUNU 086, UNU). Unipub.
Clarke, Thurston. By Blood & Fire. 288p. 1981. 13.95 (ISBN 0-399-12605-8). Putnam.
Middle East & North Africa 1980-81. 985p. 1981. 80.00 (ISBN 0-905118-50-2, EUR 23, Europa). Unipub.
Mroz, John E. Beyond Security: Private Perceptions Among Arabs & Israelis. (Illus.). 230p. 1981. 20.00 (ISBN 0-08-027517-6); pap. 9.95 (ISBN 0-08-027516-8). Pergamon.
Tames, Richard. The Arab World Today. (Today Ser.). (Illus.). 96p. 1980. text ed. 15.00x (ISBN 0-7182-0461-1, SpS). Soccer.
Wolpin, Miles D. Militarism & Social Revolution in the Third World. 256p. 1981. text ed. 25.00 (ISBN 0-86598-021-7). Allanheld.

NEAR EAST–SOCIAL LIFE AND CUSTOMS
Bagnole, John W. Cultures of the Islamic Middle East. (America-Mideast Educational & Training Servies, Inc. - Occasional Paper: No. 4). 86p. (Orig.). 1978. pap. text ed. 4.00 (ISBN 0-89192-296-2). Interbk Inc.

NEBRASKA
see also names of cities, counties, towns, etc. in Nebraska
Hart, Herbert M. Tour Guide to Old Forts of Texas, Kansas, Nebraska, Oklahoma, Vol. 4. (Illus.). 65p. (Orig.). 1981. pap. 3.95 (ISBN 0-87108-583-6). Pruett.

NEBRASKA–HISTORY
Johnson, George E., II. The Nebraskan. 240p. 1981. write for info. (ISBN 0-89305-036-9). Anna Pub.

NECROMANCY
see Magic

NECROSIS
Laszlo, F. A. Renal Cortical Necrosis. (Contributions to Nephrology Ser.: Vol. 28). (Illus.). vi, 210p. 1981. pap. 45.00 (ISBN 3-8055-2109-X). S Karger.
Methods of Caries Prediction. 326p. 1977. 15.00 (ISBN 0-917000-05-6). Info Retrieval.
Microbial Aspects of Dental Caries, 3 vols. 1976. Set. 40.00 (ISBN 0-917000-01-3). Info Retrieval.

NEEDLEPOINT CANVAS WORK
see Canvas Embroidery

NEEDLEPOINT EMBROIDERY
see Canvas Embroidery

NEEDLEWORK
see also Dressmaking; Embroidery; Fabric Pictures; Lace and Lace Making; Netting; Patchwork; Quilting; Samplers; Sewing; Tapestry
The Bantam Step by Step Book of Needlecraft. 512p. 1980. pap. 14.95 (ISBN 0-553-01221-5). Bantam.
Foose, Sandra L. More Scrap Savers Stitchery. LC 80-2740. 1981. 12.95 (ISBN 0-385-17526-4). Doubleday.
Howard, Constance. The Constance Howard Book of Stitches. (Illus.). 144p. 1980. 13.75 (ISBN 0-7134-1005-1). Branford.
Merrill, Virginia & Richardson, Susan M. Reproducing Period Furniture & Accessories in Miniature. Aymar, Brant, ed. 1981. 25.00 (ISBN 0-517-53816-4). Crown.
Ryan, Mildred G. The Complete Encyclopedia of Stitchery. 1981. pap. 8.95 (ISBN 0-452-25264-4, Z5264, Plume). NAL.
Schoenfeld, Susan & Beniner, Winifred. Pattern Design for Needlepoint & Patchwork. 200p. 1981. pap. 9.95 (ISBN 0-442-20671-2). Van Nos Reinhold.
Schraffenberger, Nancy, ed. Woman's Day Decorative Needlework for the Home. (Illus.). 176p. 1981. 15.95 (ISBN 0-8069-5442-6, Columbia Hse). Sterling.
Swedish Handcraft Guild. Counted Cross Stitch Patterns & Designs. (Illus.). 72p. 1981. pap. 8.95 (ISBN 0-684-16950-9, ScsribT). Scribner.
Zimikes, Martha R. Iron-on Transfers from a Treasury of Needlework Designs: Ready-to-Use Patterns for Needlepoint & Embroidery. 96p. 1981. pap. 9.95 (ISBN 0-442-23119-9). Van Nos Reinhold.

NEGATIVE IONS
see Anions

NEGLIGENCE
see also Accident Law; Employers' Liability; Occupations, Dangerous
Woods, Henry. The Negligence Case: Comparative Fault, Vol. 1. LC 78-51108. 1978. 47.50. Lawyers Co-Op.

NEGOTIABLE INSTRUMENTS
see also Bonds
Santiago Romero, Basilio. Tratado De Instrumentos Negociables. 2nd, enl.,rev. ed. LC 79-22321. (Illus.). 1980. write for info. (ISBN 0-8477-2636-3). U of PR Pr.
Whaley. Problems & Materials on Negotiable Instruments. Date not set. text ed. price not set (ISBN 0-316-93214-0). Little.

NEGOTIABLE INSTRUMENTS–TAXATION
see Taxation of Bonds, Securities, etc.

NEGOTIATION
see also Arbitration, Industrial; Arbitration, International; Collective Bargaining; Treaties
Kniveton, Bromley & Towers, Brian. Training for Negotiating. 213p. 1978. text ed. 21.00x (ISBN 0-220-66347-5, Pub. by Busn Bks England). Renouf.

NEGOTIATIONS IN INTERNATIONAL DISPUTES
see Diplomatic Negotiations in International Disputes

NEGRO RACE
see Black Race

NEGRO SPIRTUALS
see Spirituals (Songs)

NEHEMIAH
Getz, Gene A. Nehemiah: A Man of Prayer & Persistence. LC 80-53102. 1981. pap. 4.95 (ISBN 0-8307-0778-6). Regal.

NEILL, ALEXANDER SUTHERLAND, 1883-1973
Placzek, Beverley, ed. Record of a Friendship: The Correspondence of Wilhelm Reich and A.S. Neill. 1981. 15.95 (ISBN 0-374-24807-9). FS&G.

NEMATODA
Mai, W. F. & Lyon, H. H. Pictorial Key to Genera of Plant-Parasitic Nematodes. 4th ed. LC 74-14082. (Illus.). 224p. 1975. 14.50x (ISBN 0-8014-0920-9). Comstock.

NEO-EMPIRICISM
see Logical Positivism

NEO-IMPRESSIONISM (ART)
see Impressionism (Art)

NEO-LATIN LANGUAGES
see Romance Languages

NEONATAL DEATH
see Infants–Mortality

NEONATES
see Infants (Newborn)

NEOPLASMS
see Tumors

NEO-POSITIVISM
see Logical Positivism

NEOPRENE
see Rubber, Artificial

NEO-SCHOLASTICISM
Miethe, Terry L. & Bourke, Vernon J., eds. Thomistic Bibliography, 1940-1978. LC 80-1195. xxii, 318p. 1980. lib. bdg. 39.95 (ISBN 0-313-21991-5, MTH/). Greenwood.

NEO-THOMISM
see Neo-Scholasticism

NEPAL
Pratapaditya Pal. Nepal: Where the Gods Are Young. LC 75-769. (Illus.). 136p. 1975. 19.95 (ISBN 0-87848-045-5). Asia Soc.

NEPAL–ECONOMIC CONDITIONS
Blaikie, M. P., et al. The Struggle for Basic Needs in Nepal. (Illus.). 100p. (Orig.). 1980. pap. 6.50 (ISBN 92-64-12101-3). OECD.
Poffenberger, Mark. Patterns of Change in the Nepal Himalaya. 111p. 1981. lib. bdg. 15.50x (ISBN 0-86531-184-6). Westview.

NEPAL–SOCIAL LIFE AND CUSTOMS
Lorrance, Arleen. Hello, Goodbye, I Love You. (Illus., Orig.). 1981. pap. price not set (ISBN 0-916192-18-0). L P Pubns.

NEPALI LANGUAGE
Verma, M. K. & Sharma, T. N. Intermediate Nepali Reader, 2 vols. 1980. Vol.1. write for info. (ISBN 0-8364-0652-4, Pub. by Manohar India); Vol. 2. write for info. (ISBN 0-8364-0653-2); Set. 32.50 (ISBN 0-686-69016-8). South Asia Bks.

NEPHRITE
see Jade

NEPHRITIS
see Kidneys–Diseases

NEPHROLOGY
see also Kidneys
Cheigh, Jhoong S., et al, eds. Manual of Clinical Nephrology of the Rogosin Kidney Center. (Developments in Nephrology: No. 1). (Illus.). 470p. 1981. PLB 65.00 (ISBN 90-247-2397-3, Pub. by Martinus Nijhoff). Kluwer Boston.
Migone, L., ed. Urinary Proteins. (Contributions to Nephrology Ser.: Vol. 26). (Illus.). vi, 150p. 1981. pap. 54.00 (ISBN 3-8055-1848-X). S Karger.
Pascual, J. F. & Calcagno, P. L., eds. Recent Advances in Pediatric Nephrology. (Contributions to Nephrology Ser.: Vol. 27). (Illus.). vi, 150p. 1981. pap. 54.00 (ISBN 3-8055-1851-X). S Karger.
Schreiner, G. E. Controversies in Nephrology. (Illus.). 722p. 1979. 49.50. Masson Pub.

Strauss, Jose, ed. Pediatric Nephrology, Vol. 5. 1979. lib. bdg. 30.00 (ISBN 0-8240-7031-3). Garland Pub.

--Renal Failure. 1978. lib. bdg. 37.50 (ISBN 0-8240-7011-9). Garland Pub.

NERVE-CELLS

see Nerves; Neurons

NERVE TRANSMISSION

see Neural Transmission

NERVES

see also Nervous System; Synapses

also particular nerves, e.g. Olfactory Nerve, Optic Nerve

Proceedings of a Workshop, Palo Alto, California, July 1979, et al. Conduction Velocity Distributions: A Population Approach to Electrophysiology of Nerve. Dorfman, Leslie J. & Cummins, Kenneth L., eds. (Progress in Clinical & Biological Research Ser.: No. 52). 338p. 1981. 30.00x (ISBN 0-8451-0052-1). A R Liss.

NERVES–ANATOMY

see Neuroanatomy

NERVES–DISEASES

see Nervous System–Diseases

NERVES–SECRETIONS

see Neurosecretion

NERVES–SURGERY

see Nervous System–Surgery

NERVOUS SYSTEM

see also Biological Control Systems; Brain; Central Nervous System; Nerves; Neuroanatomy; Neurosecretion; Shock; Spinal Cord

Bradshaw, Ralph & Schneider, Diana, eds. Proteins of the Nervous System. 2nd ed. 407p. 1980. 39.00 (ISBN 0-89004-327-2). Raven.

Cotman, Carl W. & Jenson, Robert. Instructor's Manual for Behavioral Neuroscience: An Introduction. 1979. 3.00 (ISBN 0-12-191655-3). Acad Pr.

Haymaker, Webb & Adams, Raymond D. Histology & Histopathology of the Nervous System, 2 vols. (Illus.). 3520p. 1980. Set. 295.00 (ISBN 0-398-03482-6). C C Thomas.

Jensen, David. The Human Nervous System. 416p. 1980. pap. text ed. 14.95x (ISBN 0-8385-3944-0). ACC.

Millar, R. P., ed. Neuropeptides: Biochemical & Physiological Studies. (Illus.). 368p. 1981. lib. bdg. 55.90 (ISBN 0-443-02265-8). Churchill.

Prochaska, Georg. Dissertation on the Functions of the Nervous System. Laycock, T., tr. Bd. with On the Study of Character. (Contributions to the History of Psychology Ser., Vol. XIV, Pt. A: Orientations). 1980. Repr. of 1851 ed. 30.00 (ISBN 0-89093-316-2). U Pubns Amer.

Sarnat, Harvey B. & Netsky, Martin G. Evolution of the Nervous System. 2nd ed. (Illus.). 425p. 1981. text ed. 19.50x (ISBN 0-19-502775-2); pap. text ed. 13.95x (ISBN 0-19-502776-0). Oxford U Pr.

Sleight, Peter, ed. Arterial Baroreceptors & Hypertension. (Illus.). 380p. 1981. text ed. 67.50x (ISBN 0-19-261259-X). Oxford U Pr.

Weizman Institute of Science, Rehovot, Israel, Feb. 1980 & Littauer, U. Z. Drug Receptors in the Central Nervous System - Based on a Workshop Sponsored by the European Molecular Biology Organization: Proceedings. 350p. 1980. 43.00 (ISBN 0-471-27893-9, Pub. by Wiley-Interscience). Wiley.

NERVOUS SYSTEM–DISEASES

see also Fear; Neurologic Manifestations of General Diseases; Worry

also specific diseases, e.g. Insanity, Neurasthenia, Neuritis

Boese, A., ed. Search for the Cause of Multiple Sclerosis & Other Chronic Diseases of the Central Nervous System. (Illus.). 516p. (Orig.). pap. text ed. 55.00 (ISBN 3-527-25875-2). Verlag Chemie.

Giles, Floyd H., et al. Developing Human Brain: Growth & Epidemiologic Neuropathology. Date not set. write for info. (ISBN 0-88416-254-0). PSG Pub.

Hirano, Asao. A Guide to Neuropathology. LC 80-83980. (Illus.). 1981. 60.00. Igaku-Shoin.

Lierse, W. & Beck, F., eds. Normal & Impaired Differentiation Processes in the Nervous System. (Bibliotheca Anatomica Ser.: No. 19). (Illus.). 1980. soft cover 112.00 (ISBN 3-8055-1039-X). S Karger.

Olson, William H. Practical Neurology for the Primary Care Physician. (Illus.). 360p. 1981. lexotone spiral bdg. 21.75 (ISBN 0-398-04135-0). C C Thomas.

NERVOUS SYSTEM–DISEASES–DIAGNOSIS

see also Clinical Psychology

Brodal, A. Neurological Anatomy in Relation to Clinical Medicine. 3rd ed. (Illus.). 1072p. 1981. 35.00 (ISBN 0-19-502694-2). Oxford U Pr.

NERVOUS SYSTEM–SECRETIONS

see Neurosecretion

NERVOUS SYSTEM–SURGERY

see also Brain–Surgery

Carmel, Peter W. Clinical Neurosurgery, Vol. 27. (Illus.). 600p. 1981. write for info. (2022-6). Williams & Wilkins.

Dellon, A. Lee. Evaluation of Sensibility & Reeducation of Sensation of the Hand. (Illus.). 140p. 1981. write for info. (2427-2). Williams & Wilkins.

Gillingham, F. J. Advances in Stereotactic & Functional Neurosurgery Four: Proceedings. (Acta Neurochirurgica Supplementum: Vol. 30). (Illus.). 444p. 1981. pap. 146.40 (ISBN 0-387-90501-4). Springer-Verlag.

NERVOUS SYSTEM–TUMORS

Chang. Tumors of the Central Nervous System. 1981. write for info. Masson Pub.

NERVOUS SYSTEM–VERTEBRATES

Masterton, R. B., et al, eds. Evolution, Brain & Behavior in Vertebrates, 2 vols. Incl. Vol. 1. Modern Concepts. 29.95 (ISBN 0-470-15045-9); Vol. 2. Persistent Problems. 14.95 (ISBN 0-470-15046-7). LC 76-6499. 1976. Halsted Pr.

NERVOUS SYSTEM, AUTONOMIC

Pickering, I. S. Exercises for the Autonomic Nervous System: You Need Them! (Illus.). 112p. 1981. price not set (ISBN 0-398-04454-6); pap. price not set (ISBN 0-398-04466-X). C C Thomas.

NERVOUS SYSTEM, VEGETATIVE

see Nervous System, Autonomic

NERVOUS TRANSMISSION

see Neural Transmission

NETHERLANDIC LANGUAGE

see Dutch Language

NETHERLANDS–BIOGRAPHY

Tilstra, Albertine J. A Dutchman Bound for Paradise. Van Dolson, Bobbie J., ed. 128p. 1980. pap. write for info. (ISBN 0-8280-0021-2). Review & Herald.

NETHERLANDS–DESCRIPTION AND TRAVEL–GUIDEBOOKS

Arthur Frommer's Guide to Amsterdam - Holland, 1981-82. 224p. Date not set. pap. 2.95 (ISBN 0-671-41427-5). Frommer-Pasmantier.

Bristow, Philip. Through the Dutch Canals. 250p. 1980. 15.00x (Pub. by Nautical England). State Mutual Bk.

NETHERLANDS–HISTORY

Boxer, C. R. The Dutch Seaborne Empire, Sixteen Hundred to Eighteen Hundred. 1980. pap. text ed. 11.75x (ISBN 0-09-131051-2, Hutchinson U Lib). Humanities.

Parker, Geoffrey. The Dutch Revolt. 320p. 1977. 20.00 (ISBN 0-8014-1136-X). Cornell U Pr.

NETHERLANDS–POLITICS AND GOVERNMENT

Eldersvels, Samuel J., et al. Elite Images of Dutch Politics: Accommodation & Conflict. 296p. 1981. text ed. 15.00x (ISBN 0-472-10009-2). U of Mich Pr.

NETTING

Garner, John. How to Make & Set Nets: The Technology of Netting. (Illus.). 96p. 10.00 (ISBN 0-85238-031-3, FN). Unipub.

Klust, Gerhard. Netting Materials for Fishing Gear. (Illus.). 184p. 8.75 (ISBN 0-85238-060-7, FN). Unipub.

Thomson, David. The Seine Net: Its Origin, Evolution & Use. 12.00 (FN). Unipub.

NETWORK ANALYSIS (PLANNING)

Newell, G. F. Traffic Flow on Transportation Networks. (MIT Press Series Intransportation Studies: No. 5). (Illus.). 288p. 1980. 30.00x (ISBN 0-262-14032-2). MIT Pr.

Woodgate, H. S. Planning by Network. 330p. 1977. text ed. 24.50x (ISBN 0-220-66312-2, Pub. by Busn Bks England). Renouf.

NETWORK THEORY

see Electric Networks; System Analysis

NETWORKS, ELECTRIC

see Electric Networks

NETWORKS OF LIBRARIES

see Library Information Networks

NEURAL TRANSMISSION

Hungarian Pharmacological Society, 3rd Congress, Budapest, 1979. Modulation of Neurochemical Transmission: Proceedings. Knoll, J. & Vizi, E. S., eds. LC 80-41281. (Advances in Pharmacological Research & Practice Ser.: Vol. II). (Illus.). 450p. 1981. 84.00 (ISBN 0-08-026387-9). Pergamon.

Kruk, Z. L. & Pycock, C. J. Neurotransmitters & Drug. 160p. 1980. 35.00x (ISBN 0-85664-865-5, Pub. by Croom Helm England). State Mutual Bk.

Szekely, Gy., et al, eds. Neural Communication & Control: Satellite Symposium of the 28th International Congress of Physiological Sciences, Debrechen, Hungary, 1980. (Advances in Physiological Sciences: Vol. 30). (Illus.). 350p. 1981. 35.00 (ISBN 0-08-027351-3). Pergamon.

NEUROANATOMY

Angevine, Jay B. & Cotman, Carl W. Principles of Neuroanatomy. (Illus.). 300p. 1981. text ed. 18.95x (ISBN 0-19-502885-6); pap. text ed. 11.95x (ISBN 0-19-502886-4). Oxford U Pr.

Brodal, A. Neurological Anatomy in Relation to Clinical Medicine. 3rd ed. (Illus.). 1072p. 1981. 35.00 (ISBN 0-19-502694-2). Oxford U Pr.

Dublin, William B. & Dublin, Arthur B. Atlas of Neuroanatomy for Radiologists: Surface & Sectional-with CT Scanning Correlation. (Illus.). 320p. 1981. 37.50 (ISBN 0-87527-204-5). Green.

Garoutte, Bill. A Survey of Functional Neuroanatomy. (Illus.). 240p. 1981. pap. text ed. 9.00x (ISBN 0-930010-04-3). Jones Med.

Nolte, John. Neuroanatomy. (Illus.). 382p. 1981. pap. text ed. 13.50 (ISBN 0-8016-3702-3). Mosby.

NEUROBIOLOGY

Federoff, S. & Hertz, L., eds. Advances in Cellular Neurobiology, Vol. 2. 1981. write for info. (ISBN 0-12-008302-7). Acad Pr.

Lahue, Robert, ed. Methods in Neurobiology. 1981. 50.00 ea.; Set. 89.50 (ISBN 0-686-69459-7); Vol. 1, 640 Pp. for two vol. set 89.50 (ISBN 0-306-40517-2). Vol. Ii, 700 Pp (ISBN 0-306-40518-0). Plenum Pub.

Smythies, John R. & Bradley, Ronald J. International Review of Neurobiology, Vol. 22. (Serial Publication). 1980. write for info. (ISBN 0-12-366822-0). Acad Pr.

Willis, William D., Jr. & Grossman, Robert G. Medical Neurobiology. (Illus.). 611p. 1981. text ed. 29.50 (ISBN 0-8016-5584-6). Mosby.

NEUROCHEMISTRY

Furst, Susanna & Knoll, J., eds. Opiate Receptors & the Neurochemical Correlates of Pain: Proceedings of the Third Congress of the Hungarian Pharmacological Society, Budapest, 1979. LC 80-41281. (Advances in Pharmacological Research & Practice Ser.: Vol. V). 240p. 1981. 45.00 (ISBN 0-08-026390-9). Pergamon.

Hungarian Pharmacological Society, 3rd Congress, Budapest, 1979. Modulation of Neurochemical Transmission: Proceedings. Knoll, J. & Vizi, E. S., eds. LC 80-41281. (Advances in Pharmacological Research & Practice Ser.: Vol. II). (Illus.). 450p. 1981. 84.00 (ISBN 0-08-026387-9). Pergamon.

Siegel, George J., et al. Basic Neurochemistry. 3rd ed. 1981. write for info (ISBN 0-316-79002-8). Little.

Youdim, M. B. & Lovenberg, W., eds. Essays in Neurochemistry & Neuropharmacology, Vol. 5. Sharman, D. F. & Lagnado, J. R., trs. 152p. 1981. 47.00 (ISBN 0-471-27879-3, Pub. by Wiley-Interscience). Wiley.

NEUROCYTE

see Neurons

NEUROENDOCRINOLOGY

Stark, E., et al, eds. Endocrinology, Neuroendocrinology, Neuropeptides- Part 1: Proceedings of the 28th International Congress of Physiological Sciences, Budapest, 1980. LC 80-42047. (Advances in Physiological Sciences: Vol. 13). (Illus.). 350p. 1981. 40.00 (ISBN 0-08-026827-7). Pergamon.

--Endocrinology, Neuroendocrinology, Neuropeptides-Part II: Proceedings of the 28th International Congress of Physiological Sciences, Budapest, 1980. LC 80-42046. (Advances in Physiological Sciences Ser.: Vol. 14). (Illus.). 350p. 1981. 40.00 (ISBN 0-08-026871-4). Pergamon.

NEUROLOGIC MANIFESTATIONS OF GENERAL DISEASES

Bell, William E. & McCormick, William. Neurologic Infections in Children. 2nd ed. (Major Problems in Clinical Pediatrics Ser.: Vol. 12). (Illus.). 600p. 1981. text ed. price not set (ISBN 0-7216-1676-3). Saunders.

NEUROLOGY

see also Electrophysiology; Nervous System; Neurobiology; Neurochemistry; Neuroendocrinology; Neuropsychiatry; Neuro-Psychopharmacology; Psychology, Pathological; Psychology, Physiological

Appel, Stanley H., ed. Current Neurology, Vol. 3. LC 78-68042. (Current Ser.). (Illus.). 545p. 1981. text ed. price not set (ISBN 0-89289-112-2). HM Prof Med Div.

Cervos-Navarro, J. & Fritschka, E., eds. Cerebral Microcirculation & Metabolism. 1981. text ed. price not set (ISBN 0-89004-590-9). Raven.

Claussen, Claus F. & Desa, Joe V. Clinical Study of Human Equilibrium by Electonystagmography & Allied Tests. (Illus.). xiii, 437p. 1980. text ed. 50.00x (ISBN 0-86590-002-7). Apt Bks.

Courjon, Jean, et al, eds. Clinical Applications of Evoked Potentials in Neurology. 1981. text ed. price not set (ISBN 0-89004-619-0). Raven.

Emmers, Raimond. Pain: A Spike-Interval Coded Message in the Brain. 1981. text ed. price not set (ISBN 0-89004-650-6). Raven.

Enna, S. J., et al, eds. Brain Neurotransmitters & Receptors in Aging & Age-Related Disorders. (Aging Ser.). 1981. text-ed. price not set (ISBN 0-89004-643-3). Raven.

Hodson, C. J., et al. The Pathogenesis of Reflux Nephropathy. Maling, T. M. & McManamon, P. J., eds. 1980. 10.00x (Pub. by Brit Inst Radiology). State Mutual Bk.

Katsuki, Yasuji & Sato, Masayasu. Brain Mechanisms of Sensation. 320p. 1981. 28.50 (ISBN 0-471-08148-5, Pub. by Wiley Med). Wiley.

Kaufman, David M. Clinical Neurology for Psychiatrists. 1981. write for info. (ISBN 0-8089-1321-2). Grune.

Lance, James W. & McLeod, James G. A Physiological Approach to Clinical Neurology. 3rd ed. (Illus.). 368p. 1981. text ed. 49.95 (ISBN 0-407-00196-4). Butterworth.

McKay, Ron, et al, eds. Monoclonal Antibodies Against Neural Antigens. (Cold Spring Harbor Reports in the Neurosciences). 300p. 1981. price not set (ISBN 0-87969-138-7). Cold Spring Harbor.

Nikas. Critical Neurological Assessment & Management. 1981. text ed. price not set. Churchill.

Nikas, Diana L. Critical Neurological Surgical Assessment & Management: Contemporary Issues in Critical Care Nursing. (Vol. 2). (Illus.). 224p. 1981. lib. bdg. 20.00 (ISBN 0-443-08158-1). Churchill.

Oehman, R. L. & Axelsson, R. A. Prolactin Responses to Neuroleptics. (Journal of Neural Transmission Supplementum: Vol. 17). (Illus.). 75p. 1981. pap. 16.00 (ISBN 0-387-81605-4). Springer-Verlag.

Pitcoff, Ramsey K. & Powell, Herb. Neuroradiology with Computed Tomography. 575p. 1981. text ed. price not set (ISBN 0-7216-7444-5). Saunders.

Scheinberg, Peritz. Modern Practical Neurology. 2nd ed. 360p. 1981. 26.00 (ISBN 0-89004-521-6); pap. 14.95 (ISBN 0-686-69137-7). Raven.

Seiden, Margaret. Practical Management of Chronic Neurologic Problems. 1981. 25.00 (ISBN 0-8385-7871-3). ACC.

Stalberg. Neurology: Clinical Neurophysiology, Vol. 1. (Butterworths International Medical Reviews Ser.). 1981. text ed. price not set (ISBN 0-407-02294-5). Butterworth.

Strub, Richard L. & Black, F. William. Organic Brain Syndromes: An Introduction to Neurobehavioral Disorders. (Illus.). 500p. 1981. text ed. 25.00 (ISBN 0-8036-8209-3, 8209-3). Davis Co.

Sutherland, John M. Fundamentals of Neurology. 272p. (Orig.). 1980. pap. 23.50 (ISBN 0-909337-29-2). ADIS Pr.

Van Meter, Marie. Neurologic Care: A Guide for Patient Education. (Patient Education Series). 288p. pap. 9.50 (ISBN 0-8385-6706-1). ACC.

Wilder, B. Joseph & Bruni, Joseph. Seizure Disorders: A Pharmacological Approach to Treatment. 1981. text ed. price not set (ISBN 0-89004-539-9). Raven.

Wolf, John K. Practical Clinical Neurology. LC 79-91846. 1980. pap. 13.75 (ISBN 0-87488-728-3). Med Exam.

NEUROLOGY–CONGRESSES

American Neurological Association. Transactions of the ANA, Vol. 105, 1980. 1981. text ed. price not set. Springer Pub.

NEURONS

Roberts, A. & Bush, B. M., eds. Neurones Without Impulses. LC 79-42572. (Society for Experimental Biology Seminar Ser.). (Illus.). 250p. Date not set. 59.50 (ISBN 0-521-23364-X); pap. 19.95 (ISBN 0-521-29935-7). Cambridge U Pr.

NEUROPATHOLOGY

see Nervous System–Diseases

NEUROPHARMACOLOGY

see also Neuro-Psychopharmacology

Giurgea, Corneliu E. Fundamentals to a Pharmacology of the Mind. (American Lectures on Objective Psychiatry). (Illus.). 376p. 1981. text ed. 37.75 (ISBN 0-398-04130-X). C C Thomas.

Klawans, Harold L., ed. Clinical Neuropharmacology, Vol. 5. 1981. text ed. price not set (ISBN 0-89004-648-4). Raven.

Kruk, Z. L. & Pycock, C. J. Neurotransmitters & Drug. 160p. 1980. 35.00x (ISBN 0-85664-865-5, Pub. by Croom Helm England). State Mutual Bk.

Youdim, M. B. & Lovenberg, W., eds. Essays in Neurochemistry & Neuropharmacology, Vol. 5. Sharman, D. F. & Lagnado, J. R., trs. 152p. 1981. 47.00 (ISBN 0-471-27879-3, Pub. by Wiley-Interscience). Wiley.

NEUROPHYSIOLOGY

see also Neural Transmission

Byrne, John H. & Koester, John, eds. Molluscan Nerve Cells: From Biophysics to Behavior. (Cold Spring Harbor Reports in the Neurosciences Ser.: Vol. 1). 250p. 1980. 26.00x (ISBN 0-87969-135-2). Cold Spring Harbor.

Desmedt, J. E., ed. Motor Unit Types, Recruitment Patterns & Plasticity with Usage in Health & Disease. (Progress in Clinical Neurophysiology Ser.: Vol. 9). (Illus.). x, 350p. 1981. 82.75 (ISBN 3-8055-1929-X). S Karger.

Stalberg. Neurology: Clinical Neurophysiology, Vol. 1. (Butterworths International Medical Reviews Ser.). 1981. text ed. price not set (ISBN 0-407-02294-5). Butterworth.

NEUROPSYCHIATRY

see also Neurology; Psychiatry

Smith, Selwyn M. & Koranyi, Erwin K. Self-Assessment of Current Knowledge in Forensic & Organic Psychiatry. 1978. spiral bdg. 15.00 (ISBN 0-87488-235-4). Med Exam.

Taylor, Michael A., ed. The Neuropsychiatric Mental Status Examination: A Phenomenologic Program Text. Date not set. text ed. price not set (ISBN 0-89335-130-X). Spectrum Pub.

Trimble, Michael R. Neuropsychiatry. 304p. 1981. 37.50 (ISBN 0-471-27827-0, Pub. by Wiley-Interscience). Wiley.

NEUROPSYCHOLOGY

Benedikt, Moriz. Anatomical Studies Upon Brains of Criminals. Fowler, E. P., tr. from Ger. (Historical Foundations of Forensic Psychiatry & Psychology Ser.). (Illus.). 185p. 1980. Repr. of 1881 ed. lib. bdg. 22.50 (ISBN 0-306-76071-1). Da Capo.

Golden, Charles A., et al. Interpretation of the Halstead Reitan Neuropsychological Test Battery: A Casebook Approach. 1980. 26.50 (ISBN 0-8089-1298-4). Grune.

Pirozzolo, Francis J. & Wittrock, Merlin C. Neuropsychological & Cognitive Processes in Reading. (Perspectives in Neurolinguistics & Psycholinguistics Ser.). 1981. price not set (ISBN 0-12-557360-X). Acad Pr.

Usdih, Earl & Bunney, William E. Neuroreceptors Basic & Clinical Aspects: Based on Symposia Held at the American College of Neuropsychology Annual Meeting December 1979. 280p. 1981. 60.50 (ISBN 0-686-69370-1, Pub. by Wiley-Interscience). Wiley.

NEURO-PSYCHOPHARMACOLOGY

Angrist, B., et al, eds. Recent Advances in Neuropsychopharmacology: Selected Papers from the 12th Congress of the Collegium Internationale Neuro-Psychopharmacologicum Goteborg, Sweden, 22-26 June, 1980. (Illus.). 422p. 1981. 110.00 (ISBN 0-08-026382-8). Pergamon.

Palmer, Gene C., ed. Neuropharmacology of Central Nervous System & Behavioral Disorders. LC 80-1107. 1981. 59.00 (ISBN 0-12-544760-4). Acad Pr.

NEUROSECRETION

see also Endocrinology

Neurosecretion & Brain Peptides: Implications for Brain Function & Neurological Disease. (Advances in Biochemical Psychopharmacology Ser.: Vol. 28). 725p. 1981. 58.00 (ISBN 0-89004-535-6). Raven.

Snaith, Philip. Clinical Neurosis. 240p. 1981. text ed. 16.95x. Oxford U Pr.

NEUROSES

see also Depression, Mental; Medicine, Psychosomatic; Obsessive-Compulsive Neuroses; Phobias; Psychoses

also particular neuroses, e.g. Anxiety, Hysteria

Caine, Tom, et al. Personal Styles in Neurosis: Implications for Small Group Psychotherapy & Behavior Therapy. (International Library of Group Psychotherapy & Group Process). 224p. write for info. (ISBN 0-7100-0617-9). Routledge & Kegan.

Eysenck, H. J. You & Neurosis. (Illus.). 224p. 1979. 14.95 (ISBN 0-8039-1287-0). Sage.

Fromme, Allan. The Book for Normal Neurotics. 1981. 10.95 (ISBN 0-374-11544-3). FS&G.

Gossop, M. Theories of Neurosis. (Illus.). 261p. 1981. 35.00 (ISBN 0-387-10370-8). Springer-Verlag.

Janov, Arthur. The Primal Scream. 448p. 1981. pap. 6.95 (ISBN 0-399-50537-7, Perigee). Putnam.

Marks, Isaac. Cure & Care of Neuroses: Theory & Practice of Behavioral Psychotherapy. 272p. 1981. 22.50 (ISBN 0-471-08808-0, Pub. by Wiley-Interscience). Wiley.

NEUROSURGERY

see Nervous System–Surgery

NEUROTROPIC DRUGS

see Neuropharmacology

NEUTRALITY

see also Asylum, Right Of

Sigham & Van Dihn, eds. From Bandung to Colombo: Conference of the Non-Aligned Countries. LC 76-162957. 1975. 7.95 (ISBN 0-89388-221-6). Okpaku Communications.

NEUTRON ACTIVATION ANALYSIS

see Radioactivation Analysis

NEUTRONS

see also Atoms; Electrons; Protons

CINDA Eighty: An Index to the Literature on Microscopic Neutron Data. 442p. 1980. pap. 38.75 (ISBN 92-0-039180-X, ICIN77/80, IAEA). Unipub.

NEVADA

see also names of cities, counties, etc. in Nevada

Fletcher, F. N. Early Nevada: The Period of Exploraton Seventeen Seventy-Six to Eighteen Forty-Eight. LC 80-19035. (Vintage Nevada Ser). (Illus.). xi, 195p. 1980. pap. 5.25 (ISBN 0-87417-061-3). U of Nev Pr.

Fradin, Dennis. Nevada: In Words & Pictures. LC 80-24179. (Young People's Stories of Our States Ser.). (Illus.). 48p. (gr. 2-5). 1981. PLB 8.65g (ISBN 0-516-03928-8, Time Line). Childrens.

Mack, Effie M., et al. Nevada Government. 384p. 1953. octavo 5.00. Holmes.

NEVADA–DESCRIPTION AND TRAVEL

Glass, Mary E. Nevada's Turbulent Fifties: Decade of Political & Economic Change. LC 80-25651. (Nevada Studies in History & Political Science: No. 15). (Illus.). ix, 138p. (Orig.). 1981. pap. price not set (ISBN 0-87417-062-1). U of Nev Pr.

Hall, Shawn. A Guide to the Ghost Towns & Mining Camps of Nye County, Nevada. (Illus.). 156p. 1981. 9.95 (ISBN 0-396-07955-5). Dodd.

McDonald, Douglas. Nevada Lost Mines & Buried Treasure. (Illus.). 1981. 6.95. Nevada Pubns.

Will, Robin. Beautiful Nevada. Shangle, Robert D., ed. (Illus.). 72p. 1981. 14.95 (ISBN 0-89802-101-4); pap. 7.95 (ISBN 0-89802-100-6). Beautiful Am.

NEVADA–IMPRINTS

Armstrong, Robert D. Nevada Printing History: A Bibliography of Imprints & Publications, 1858-1880. (Illus.). 540p. 1981. price not set (ISBN 0-87417-063-X). U of Nev Pr.

NEW BRUNSWICK (PROVINCE)

Aunger, Edmund A. In Search of Political Stability: A Comparative Study of New Brunswick & Northern Ireland. 238p. 1981. 21.95x (ISBN 0-7735-0366-8). McGill-Queens U Pr.

NEW ENGLAND

Jennison, Keith. New England in the Off-Color Season. LC 80-67659. (Illus., Orig.). 1980. pap. 5.95 (ISBN 0-911764-23-2). Durrell.

NEW ENGLAND–BIOGRAPHY

Bushman, Claudia L. Harriet Hanson Robinson & Her Family: A Chronicle of Nineteenth-Century New England Life. LC 80-54470. 320p. 1981. 16.50 (ISBN 0-87451-193-3). U Pr of New Eng.

NEW ENGLAND–DESCRIPTION AND TRAVEL

Berrill, Michael & Berrill, Deborah. A Sierra Club Naturalist's Guide to the North Atlantic Coast. (Sierra Club Naturalist's Guides). (Illus.). 512p. (Orig.). 1981. 24.95 (ISBN 0-87156-242-1); pap. 10.95 (ISBN 0-87156-243-X). Sierra.

Ross, Corinne M. & Woodward, Ralph. New England: Off the Beaten Path, a Guide to Unusual Places. (Illus.). 128p. 1981. pap. 4.95 (ISBN 0-914788-40-X). East Woods.

NEW ENGLAND–DESCRIPTION AND TRAVEL–GUIDEBOOKS

Yankee Magazine's Guide to New England. (Illus.). 144p. 1980. pap. 1.95. Yankee Bks.

NEW ENGLAND–ECONOMIC CONDITIONS

Hoy, John C., ed. Higher Education & the New England Economy in the Nineteen-Eighties. 160p. 1981. 10.00x (ISBN 0-87451-197-6). U Pr of New Eng.

NEW ENGLAND–HISTORY

Hoy, John C., ed. Higher Education & the New England Economy in the Nineteen-Eighties. 160p. 1981. 10.00x (ISBN 0-87451-197-6). U Pr of New Eng.

Newman, Alan B., ed. New England Reflections, Eighteen Eighty-Two to Nineteen Seven: Photographs by the Howes Brothers. (Illus.). 1981. 25.00 (ISBN 0-394-51375-4); pap. 12.95 (ISBN 0-394-74912-X). Pantheon.

Vaughan, Alden T. & Richter, Daniel K. Crossing the Cultural Divide: Indians & New Englanders, 1605-1763. 76p. 1980. pap. write for info. (ISBN 0-912296-48-8). Am Antiquarian.

NEW ENGLAND–HISTORY–COLONIAL PERIOD, ca. 1600-1775

Baxter, James P. The Pioneers of New France in New England. 450p. 1980. Repr. of 1894 ed. 20.00 (ISBN 0-917890-20-5). Heritage Bk.

NEW ENGLAND–JUVENILE LITERATURE

Mathieu, Joe. The Olden Days. (Pictureback Ser.). (Illus.). 32p. (ps-3). 1981. PLB 4.99 (ISBN 0-394-94085-7); pap. 1.25 (ISBN 0-394-84085-2). Random.

NEW ENGLAND FOOTBALL TEAM (AMERICAN CONFERENCE)

McGuane, George. New England Patriots: A Pictorial History. LC 80-84555. (Illus.). 176p. 1981. 16.95 (ISBN 0-938694-00-6). JCP Corp VA.

NEW ENGLAND THEOLOGY

Conforti, Joseph. Samuel Hopkins & the New Divinity Movement: Calvinism, the Congregational Ministry, & Reform in New England Between the Great Awakenings. 240p. (Orig.). 1981. pap. 12.95 (ISBN 0-8028-1871-4). Eerdmans.

NEW GUINEA–DESCRIPTION AND TRAVEL

O'Neill, Jack. Up from the South: A Prospector in New Guinea, Nineteen Thirty-One to Nineteen Thirty-Seven. Sinclair, James, ed. (Illus.). 224p. 1979. text ed. 23.50x (ISBN 0-19-550567-0). Oxford U Pr.

NEW GUINEA–HISTORY

Amarshu, Azeem, et al. Development & Dependency: The Political Economy of Papua New Guinea. (Illus.). 306p. 1979. text ed. 28.00x (ISBN 0-19-550582-4). Oxford U Pr.

NEW GUINEA–SOCIAL LIFE AND CUSTOMS

Cook, Edwin A. & O'Brien, Denise, eds. Blood & Semen: Kinship Systems of Highland New Guinea. LC 80-21559. (Anthropology Ser.: Studies in Pacific Anthropology). (Illus.). 532p. (Orig.). 1980. pap. 38.50 (ISBN 0-472-02710-7, IS-00117, Pub. by U of Mich Pr). Univ Microfilms.

NEW HAMPSHIRE

see also names of cities, counties, towns etc. in New Hampshire

Fradin, Dennis. New Hampshire: In Words & Pictures. LC 80-25421. (Young People's Stories of Our States Ser.). (Illus.). 48p. (gr. 2-5). 1981. PLB 8.65g (ISBN 0-686-69455-4, Time Line). Childrens.

New Hampshire Register: Ninteen Eighty to Nineteen Eighty-One. 1980. 65.00 (ISBN 0-89442-018-6). Tower Pub Co.

NEW HAMPSHIRE–DESCRIPTION AND TRAVEL

Lane, Paula, ed. The New Hamshire Atlas & Gazatteer. 2nd ed. 67p. 1979. pap. 6.95 (ISBN 0-89933-004-5). DeLorme Pub.

Preston, Philip. White Mountains - East. (Illus.). 270p. (Orig.). 1981. pap. 8.50 (ISBN 0-9603106-1-4). Waumbek.

NEW HAMPSHIRE–HISTORY

Griffinn, S. G. & Whitcomb, M. A. A History of the Town of Keene (N.H.), Seventeen Thirty-Two to Nineteen Hundred & Four. (Illus.). 792p. (Orig.). 1980. Repr. of 1904 ed. 38.00 (ISBN 0-917890-21-3). Heritage Bk.

Tardiff, Olive. They Paved the Way: A History of N. H. Women. vi, 98p. (gr. 9-12). 1980. pap. text ed. 3.95 (ISBN 0-917890-22-1). Heritage Bk.

NEW JERSEY

see also names of individual cities, counties, towns, etc. in New Jersey

Laccetti, Silvio R., ed. The Outlook on New Jersey. new ed. LC 79-64897. 488p. 1979. 14.95x (ISBN 0-8349-7540-8). W H Wise.

NEW JERSEY–JUVENILE LITERATURE

Murray, Thomas C. & Barnes, Valerie. The Seven Wonders of New Jersey--& Then Some. LC 80-16424. (Illus.). 128p. 1981. pap. 6.95 (ISBN 0-89490-017-X). Enslow Pubs.

NEW LEFT

see Radicalism; Right and Left (Political Science)

NEW MADRID, MISSOURI–EARTHQUAKE, 1811-1812

Ben-Chieh Liu, et al. Earthquake Risk & Damage Functions: Applications to New Madrid. (Special Studies in Earth Sciences). 300p. 1981. lib. bdg. 24.50x (ISBN 0-86531-144-7). Westview.

NEW MEXICO

see also names of cities, towns, counties, etc. in New Mexico

Fradin, Dennis. New Mexico: In Words & Pictures. (Young People's Stories of Our States Ser.). (Illus.). 48p. (gr. 2-5). 1981. PLB 8.65g (ISBN 0-516-03931-8, Time Line). Childrens.

NEW MEXICO–ANTIQUITIES

Lister, Robert H. & Lister, Florence C. Chaco Canyon: Archaeology & Archaeologists. (Illus.). 312p. 1981. 29.95 (ISBN 0-8263-0574-1). U of NM Pr.

NEW MEXICO–BIBLIOGRAPHY

Vexler, R. I. New Mexico Chronology & Factbook, Vol. 31. 1978. 8.50 (ISBN 0-379-16156-7). Oceana.

NEW MEXICO–DESCRIPTION AND TRAVEL

Sinclair, John L. New Mexico: The Shining Land. 224p. 1980. 14.95 (ISBN 0-8263-0548-2). U of NM Pr.

NEW MEXICO–DESCRIPTION AND TRAVEL–GUIDEBOOKS

Hart, Herbert M. Tour Guide to Old Forts of New Mexico, Arizona, Nevada, Utah, Colorado, Vol. 2. (Illus.). 65p. (Orig.). 1981. pap. 3.95 (ISBN 0-87108-581-X). Pruett.

NEW MEXICO–HISTORY

Cordell, Linda S., ed. Tijeras Canyon: Analyses of the Past. (Illus.). 232p. 1980. pap. 9.95 (ISBN 0-8263-0565-2). U of NM Pr.

French, William. Further Recollections of a Western Ranchman: New Mexico 1883-1889, Vol. II. (Illus.). 1965p. 20.00 (ISBN 0-87266-011-7). Argosy.

Vexler, R. I. New Mexico Chronology & Factbook, Vol. 31. 1978. 8.50 (ISBN 0-379-16156-7). Oceana.

NEW MEXICO–POLITICS AND GOVERNMENT

Garcia, F. Chris & Hain, Paul. New Mexico Government. rev. ed. 360p. 1981. 12.95 (ISBN 0-686-68597-0). U of NM Pr.

Roberts, Susan A., et al. Civics for New Mexicans. LC 80-52284. 375p. 1980. 25.00 (ISBN 0-8263-0547-4). U of NM Pr.

NEW MEXICO–SOCIAL LIFE AND CUSTOMS

Kutsche, Paul & Van Ness, John R. Canones: Values, Crisis, & Survival in a Northern New Mexico Village. (Illus.). 280p. 1981. 17.50x (ISBN 0-8263-0570-9). U of NM Pr.

NEW ORLEANS–CARNIVAL

Hardy, Arthur. New Orleans Mardi Gras Guide, Nineteen Eighty One. rev. ed. (Illus.). 82p. 1981. pap. 2.95x (ISBN 0-930892-05-4). A Hardy & Assocs.

NEW ORLEANS–DESCRIPTION

Arthur Frommer's Guide to New Orleans, 1981-82. 224p. Date not set. pap. 2.95 (ISBN 0-671-41437-2). Frommer-Pasmantier.

Costa, Louis, et al. Streetcar Guide to Uptown New Orleans. Swords, David, ed. (Illus.). 136p. (Orig.). 1980. pap. 5.00 (ISBN 0-939108-00-3). Transitour.

NEW PRODUCTS

see also Design, Industrial

Berridge, A. E. Product Innovation & Development. 236p. 1977. text ed. 24.50x (ISBN 0-220-66325-4, Pub. by Busn Bks England). Renouf.

NEW SOUTH WALES

Halliday, James. Wines & Wineries of New South Wales. 165p. 1981. text ed. 10.95x (ISBN 0-7022-1570-8). U of Queensland Pr.

NEW SOUTH WALES–HISTORY

Frost, Alan. Convicts & Empire: A Naval Question Seventeen Seventy-Six-Eighteen Eleven. (Illus.) 280p. 1980. 39.50 (ISBN 0-19-554261-4). Oxford U Pr.

NEW TESTAMENT GREEK

see Greek Language, Biblical

NEW YORK (CITY)

Fried, William & Watson, Edward B. New York in Aerial Views: Eighty-Six Photographs. (Illus.). 176p. (Orig.). 1981. pap. 6.50 (ISBN 0-486-24018-5). Dover.

Lopez, Manuel D. New York: A Guide to Information & Reference Sources. LC 80-18634. x, 307p. 1980. 17.50 (ISBN 0-8108-1326-2). Scarecrow.

NEW YORK (CITY)–BIOGRAPHY

Cappelli, Louis H. Gigi Bread, Gamblers & Friends. LC 79-67322. 195p. 1980. 7.95 (ISBN 0-533-04449-9). Vantage.

Schor, Amy. Line by Line. 256p. 1981. 11.95 (ISBN 0-399-90083-7). Marek.

NEW YORK (CITY)–DESCRIPTION

Peebles Press International & Zabronski, Ann. Cheap & Cheaper Restaurant Guide to Manhattan. 192p. 1980. 8.95 (ISBN 0-13-128421-5, Spec); pap. 3.95 (ISBN 0-13-128413-4). P-H.

Pennell, Joseph & Bryant, Edward. Pennell's New York City Etchings: Ninety-One Prints. (Illus.). 112p. (Orig.). 1981. pap. write for info. (ISBN 0-486-23913-6). Dover.

Simpson, Charles R. Soho: The Artist in the City. LC 80-27083. 352p. 1981. 20.00 (ISBN 0-226-75937-7). U of Chicago Pr.

NEW YORK (CITY)–DESCRIPTION–GUIDEBOOKS

Appleberg, Marilyn, compiled by. The I Love New York Guide, 1981. (Illus.). 208p. 1981. pap. 3.95 (ISBN 0-02-097220-2, Collier). Macmillan.

Peebles Press International & Zabronski, Ann. The Cheap & Cheaper Restaurant Guide to Manhattan. 192p. 1980. 8.95 (ISBN-0-686-69278-0, Spec); pap. 3.95 (ISBN 0-686-69279-9). P-H.

NEW YORK (CITY)–DIRECTORIES

Germano, William P. & Lecyn, Nancy, eds. Directory of Social & Health Agencies of New York City: 1981-1982. 576p. 1981. 32.50x (ISBN 0-231-05134-4); pap. text ed. 24.00x (ISBN 0-231-05135-2). Columbia U Pr.

NEW YORK (CITY)–ECONOMIC CONDITIONS

Grossman, David A. The Future of New York City's Capital Plant. (America's Urban Capital Stock Ser.: Vol. 1). 112p. (Orig.). 1979. pap. text ed. 4.50 (ISBN 0-87766-249-5, 25700). Urban Inst.

Tabb, William K. The Long Default: New York City & the Urban Fiscal Crisis. LC 80-8933. 1981. 16.00 (ISBN 0-85345-571-6). Monthly Rev.

NEW YORK (CITY)–HISTORY

Simpson, Charles R. Soho: The Artist in the City. LC 80-27083. 352p. 1981. 20.00 (ISBN 0-226-75937-7). U of Chicago Pr.

NEW YORK (CITY)–HISTORY–FICTION

Erenberg, Lewis A. Steppin' Out: New York Nightlife & the Transformation of American Culture, 1890-1930. LC 80-930. (Contributions in American Studies Ser.: No. 50). 296p. 1981. lib. bdg. 23.95 (ISBN 0-313-21342-9, EUN/). Greenwood.

NEW YORK (CITY)–METROPOLITAN OPERA

Wright, Helen L. Metropolitan Opera House. 1980. pap. 14.95. Greylock Pubs.

--Metropolitan Opera House. 1979. write for info. Immediate Pr.

NEW YORK (CITY)–MUSIC HALLS (VARIETY-THEATER, CABARETS, ETC.)

Erenberg, Lewis A. Steppin' Out: New York Nightlife & the Transformation of American Culture, 1890-1930. LC 80-930. (Contributions in American Studies Ser.: No. 50). 296p. 1981. lib. bdg. 23.95 (ISBN 0-313-21342-9, EUN/). Greenwood.

NEW YORK (CITY)–SOCIAL CONDITIONS

This Is New York City: Facts & Trends for Social Planning. 1980. 2.00. Comm Coun Great NY.

NEW YORK (CITY)–SOCIAL LIFE AND CUSTOMS

This Is New York City: Facts & Trends for Social Planning. 1980. 2.00. Comm Coun Great NY.

NEW YORK (STATE)

see also names of cities, counties, and geographic areas in New York (State), e.g. Rochester; Dutchess County; Mohawk River and Valley

Lopez, Manuel D. New York: A Guide to Information & Reference Sources. LC 80-18634. x, 307p. 1980. 17.50 (ISBN 0-8108-1326-2). Scarecrow.

NEW YORK (STATE)–BIOGRAPHY

Lape, Fred. A Farm & Village Boyhood. LC 80-17303. (Illus.). 200p. 9.95 (ISBN 0-8156-0162-X, York State Bks). Syracuse U Pr.

Zistel, Eva. Good Companions. large print ed. LC 80-29117. 1981. Repr. of 1980 ed. 7.95 (ISBN 0-89621-265-3). Thorndike Pr.

NEW YORK (STATE)–DESCRIPTION AND TRAVEL

Fowler, Barney. Adirondack Album, No. 2. (Illus.). 200p. (Orig.). 1980. pap. 10.25 (ISBN 0-9605556-0-9). Outdoor Assocs.

NEW YORK (STATE)–DESCRIPTION AND TRAVEL–GUIDEBOOKS

Dumbleton, Susanne & Older, Anne. In & Around Albany: A Guide for Residents, Students & Visitors. (Illus.). 183p. (Orig.). 1980. pap. 4.50 (ISBN 0-9605460-0-6). Wash Park.

NEW YORK (STATE)–ECONOMIC CONDITIONS

McClelland, Peter D. & Magdovitz, Alan L. Crisis in the Making: The Political Economy of New York State Since Nineteen Forty-Five. LC 80-24167. (Studies in Economic History & Policy: the United States in the Twentieth Century). (Illus.). 512p. Date not set. price not set (ISBN 0-521-23807-2). Cambridge U Pr.

NEW YORK (STATE)–HISTORY

Bliven, Bruce, Jr. New York: The States & the Nation. (Illus.). 1981. 12.95 (ISBN 0-393-05665-1). Norton.

Mushkat, Jerome. The Reconstructiom of the New York Democracy, 1861-1874. LC 79-16826. 328p. 1981. 25.00 (ISBN 0-8386-3002-2). Fairleigh Dickinson.

Smith, James H. History of Dutchess County, New York: 1683-1882. 720p. 1980. Repr. of 1882 ed. 35.00 (ISBN 0-932334-35-0). Heart of the Lakes.

NEW YORK (STATE)–HISTORY–BIBLIOGRAPHY

Chronology & Documentary Handbook of the State of New York. 1978. 8.50. Oceana.

NEW YORK (STATE)–HISTORY, LOCAL

Ruttenber, E. M. & Clark, L. H. History of Orange County, New York: 1683-1881, 2 vols. 1112p. 1980. Repr. of 1881 ed. 45.00 (ISBN 0-932334-33-4). Heart of the Lakes.

NEW YORK (STATE)–POLITICS AND GOVERNMENT

League of Women Voters of New York State. New York State: A Citizen's Handbook. Richman, Jeanne, ed. LC 79-24095. (Illus.). 119p. (Orig.). 1979. pap. 2.95 (ISBN 0-938588-03-6). LWV NYS.

--Toward an Evaluation of the Property Tax System in New York State. Amlung, Susan, ed. (Illus.). 125p. (Orig.). 1979. pap. 4.00 (ISBN 0-938588-02-8). LWV NYS.

McClelland, Peter D. & Magdovitz, Alan L. Crisis in the Making: The Political Economy of New York State Since Nineteen Forty-Five. LC 80-24167. (Studies in Economic History & Policy: the United States in the Twentieth Century). (Illus.). 512p. Date not set. price not set (ISBN 0-521-23807-2). Cambridge U Pr.

Mushkat, Jerome. The Reconstruction of the New York Democracy, 1861-1874. LC 78-16826. 328p. 1981. 25.00 (ISBN 0-8386-3002-2, 3002). Fairleigh Dickinson.

NEW YORK (STATE)–SOCIAL LIFE AND CUSTOMS

Erenberg, Lewis A. Steppin' Out: New York Nightlife & the Transformation of American Culture, 1890-1930. LC 80-930. (Contributions in American Studies Ser.: No. 50). 296p. 1981. lib. bdg. 23.95 (ISBN 0-313-21342-9, EUN/). Greenwood.

NEW YORK BASEBALL CLUB (AMERICAN LEAGUE)

Weil, Robert & Fitzgerald, James. The Yankee Quizbook. LC 80-1654. (Illus.). 144p. 1981. pap. 5.95 (ISBN 0-385-17178-1, Dolp). Doubleday.

NEW YORK BASEBALL CLUB (NATIONAL LEAGUE, METS)

D'Agostino, Dennis. This Date in New York Mets History. LC 80-6157. (This Date Ser.). 256p. 1981. pap. 9.95 (ISBN 0-8128-6068-3). Stein & Day.

NEW YORK YANKEES

see New York Baseball Club (American League)

NEW ZEALAND

Grover, R. F. New Zealand. (World Bibliographical Ser.: No. 13). 1981. write for info. (ISBN 0-903450-31-3). ABC-Clio.

NEW ZEALAND–DESCRIPTION AND TRAVEL

Bone, Richard W. Maverick Guide to New Zealand: 1981 Edition. LC 80-25250. (Illus., Orig.). 1981. pap. 9.95 (ISBN 0-88289-269-X). Pelican.

King, Michael. New Zealand: Its Land & Its People. (Illus.). 152p. 1979. Repr. of 1977 ed. 19.95 (ISBN 0-589-01295-9, Pub. by Reed Bks Australia). C E Tuttle.

Momatiuk, Yva & Eastcott, John. High Country. (Illus.). 128p. 1980. 25.00 (ISBN 0-589-01321-1, Pub. by Reed Bks Australia). C E Tuttle.

NEW ZEALAND–POLITICS AND GOVERNMENT

Penniman, Howard R., ed. New Zealand at the Polls: The General Election of 1978. 1980. pap. 7.95 (ISBN 0-8447-3376-8). Am Enterprise.

NEW ZEALAND–SOCIAL CONDITIONS

King, Michael. New Zealand: Its Land & Its People. (Illus.). 152p. 1979. Repr. of 1977 ed. 19.95 (ISBN 0-589-01295-9, Pub. by Reed Bks Australia). C E Tuttle.

NEW ZEALAND–SOCIAL LIFE AND CUSTOMS

Johnston, R. J. The New Zealanders: How They Live & Work. LC 75-34976. 168p. 1976. text ed. 8.95 (HoltC). HR&W.

NEWBORN INFANTS

see Infants (Newborn)

NEWCASTLE-UPON-TYNE, ENGLAND

Pickering, W. S. F. A Social History of the Diocese of Newcastle. (Illus.). 1981. 35.00 (ISBN 0-85362-189-6, Oriel). Routledge & Kegan.

NEWMAN, JOHN HENRY, CARDINAL, 1801-1890

Gornall, Thomas. The Letters & Diaries of John Henry Newman: Liberalism in Oxford, January 1835 to December 1836, Vol. 5. 464p. 1981. 65.00 (ISBN 0-19-920117-X). Oxford U Pr.

Sarolea, Charles. Cardinal Newman & His Influence on Religious Life & Thought. 182p. Repr. of 1908 ed. 3.50 (ISBN 0-567-04523-4). Attic Pr.

NEWPORT, RHODE ISLAND

Boss, Judith A. Newport: A Pictorial History. Friedman, Donna R., ed. (Illus.). 208p. 1981. pap. price not set (ISBN 0-89865-097-6). Donning Co.

NEWS, FOREIGN

see Foreign News

NEWS AGENCIES

see also Foreign News

Boyd-Barrett, Oliver. The International News Agencies. LC 80-51779. (Communication & Society Ser.: Vol. 13). (Illus.). 284p. 1980. 25.00 (ISBN 0-8039-1511-X); pap. 12.50 (ISBN 0-8039-1512-8). Sage.

NEWS BROADCASTS

see Television Broadcasting of News

NEWS-LETTERS

Arth, Marvin & Ashmore, Helen. Newsletter Editor's Desk Book. 2nd rev. ed. LC 80-83042. (Illus.). 168p. (gr. 11-12). 1980. pap. 9.95 (ISBN 0-938270-00-1). Kindinger.

--The Newsletter Editor's Desk Book. 2nd, rev. ed. 168p. (Orig.). 14.95 (ISBN 0-938270-00-1); pap. 8.95 (ISBN 0-686-28910-2). Kindinger.

NEWS PHOTOGRAPHY

see Photography, Journalistic

NEWS SERVICES

see News Agencies

NEWSPAPER COURT REPORTING

see also Contempt of Court; Crime and the Press

Sullivan, Harold W. Contempts by Publication: The Law of Trial by Newspaper. xiv, 230p. 1980. Repr. of 1941 ed. lib. bdg. 24.00x (ISBN 0-8377-1114-2). Rothman.

NEWSPAPER LAYOUT AND TYPOGRAPHY

see also Advertising Layout and Typography

Garcia, Mario R. Contemporary Newspaper Design: A Structural Approach. (Illus.). 240p. 1981. text ed. 25.95 (ISBN 0-13-170381-1); pap. text ed. 12.95 (ISBN 0-13-170373-0). P-H.

NEWSPAPER PUBLISHING

Newsom, D. E. The Newspaper: Everything You Need to Know to Make It in the Newspaper Business. (Illus.). 256p. 1981. 19.95 (ISBN 0-13-616045-X, Spectrum); pap. 10.95 (ISBN 0-13-616037-9). P-H.

Notman, Larry. Community Newspaper Management: Starting Out. 1981. pap. 10.00x (ISBN 0-918488-10-9). Newspaper Serv.

NEWSPAPER STYLE

see Journalism–Handbooks, Manuals, Etc.

NEWSPAPERS

see also Foreign News; Liberty of the Press; News Agencies; Newspaper Layout and Typography; Newspaper Publishing; Periodicals; Press

also names of individual newspapers, e.g. New York Times; Washington Post; American Newspapers, English, etc.

Gregorich, Barbara & Zack, Carol. The Newspaper: Reading Skills. LC 78-730963. (Illus.). 1978. pap. text ed. 99.00 (ISBN 0-89290-114-4, A160). Soc for Visual.

NEWSPAPERS–JUVENILE LITERATURE

Fisher, Leonard E. The Newspapers. LC 80-8812. (A Nineteenth Century America Book). (Illus.). 64p. (gr. 5 up). 1981. PLB 7.95 (ISBN 0-8234-0387-4). Holiday.

NEWSPAPERS–SECTIONS, COLUMNS, ETC.

see also Book Reviewing

Neal, Lois S. Abstracts of Vital Records from Raleigh, North Carolina, Newspapers 1820-1829, Vol. 2. LC 79-13328. (Abstracts of Vital Records from Raleigh, North Carolina, Newspapers 1799-1915 Ser.). (Illus.). 940p. 1980. 50.00 (ISBN 0-87152-296-9). Reprint.

NEWSPAPERS, PUBLISHING OF

see Newspaper Publishing

NEWSREEL

see also Photography, Journalistic

Fielding, Raymond. The American Newsreel, 1911-1967. LC 73-177334. (Illus.). 392p. 1981. pap. 7.95 (ISBN 0-8061-1717-6). U of Okla Pr.

NEWTON, ISAAC, SIR, 1642-1727

Andrade, Edward N. Sir Isaac Newton. LC 79-15162. 140p. 1979. Repr. of 1958 ed. lib. bdg. 14.50x (ISBN 0-313-22022-0). Greenwood.

NEWTON, JOHN, 1725-1807

Pollock, John. Amazing Grace: John Newton's Story. LC 78-3142. 192p. 1980. 9.95 (ISBN 0-06-066653-6). Har-Row.

NEZ PERCE INDIANS

see Indians of North America–The West

NICARAGUA

Booth, John A. The End & the Beginning: The Nicaraguan Revolution. (Special Studies on Latin America & the Caribbean). (Illus.). 225p. (Orig.). 1981. lib. bdg. 20.00x (ISBN 0-89158-939-2); pap. text ed. 10.00x (ISBN 0-86531-148-X). Westview.

Somoza, Anastasio. Nicaragua Traicionada. 1980. pap. 7.95 (ISBN 0-88279-128-1). Western Island.

Walker, Thomas W. Nicaragua: A Profile. (Nations of Contemporary Latin America). 128p. 1981. lib. bdg. 16.50x (ISBN 0-89158-947-3). Westview.

NICARAGUA–HISTORY

Diederich, Bernard. Somoza. 1981. 16.95 (ISBN 0-525-20670-1). Dutton.

Elman, Richard. Cocktails at Somoza's: A Reporter's Sketchbook of Events in Revolutionary Nicaragua. 196p. 1981. 10.95 (ISBN 0-918222-28-1). Apple Wood.

Meiselas, Susan. Nicaragua-June Nineteen Seventy-Eight to July Nineteen Seventy-Nine. (Illus.). 1981. 20.00 (ISBN 0-394-51265-0); pap. 11.95 (ISBN 0-394-73931-0). Pantheon.

Somoza, Anastasio. Nicaragua Betrayed. 1980. 15.00 (ISBN 0-88279-235-0). Western Islands.

NICHOLAS OF CUSA

see Nicolaus Cusanus, Cardinal, 1401-1464

NICKEL

Betteridge, W. Nickel & Its Alloys. (Illus.). 160p. 1977. pap. 12.95x (ISBN 0-7121-0947-1, Pub. by Macdonald & Evans England). Intl Ideas.

NICKEL INDUSTRY

The Nickel Industry & the Developing Countries. 100p. 1980. pap. 8.00 (UN80-2A2, UN). Unipub.

NICKNAMES

Mossman, Jennifer. New Pseudonyms & Nicknames--Supplements: Supplements to Pseudonyms & Nicknames Dictionary. 1981. softbound 45.00 (ISBN 0-8103-0548-8). Gale.

NICOLAUS CUSANUS, CARDINAL, 1401-1464

Hopkins, Jasper. Nicholas of Cusa on Learned Ignorance: A Translation & an Appraisal of De Docta Ignorantia. LC 80-82907. (Illus.). 216p. text ed. 27.00x (ISBN 0-938060-23-6). Banning Pr.

NIEBUHR, REINHOLD, 1892-1971

Odegard, Holtan P. Sin & Science: Reinhold Niebuhr As Political Theologian. 245p. 1956. 13.00 (ISBN 0-9600524-1-0). Advance Planning.

NIEN REBELLION, 1853-1868

Perry, Elizabeth J. Chinese Perspectives on the Nien Rebellion. 150p. 1981. 18.50 (ISBN 0-87332-191-X). M E Sharpe.

NIETZSCHE, FRIEDRICH WILHELM, 1844-1900

Hubbard, Stanley. Nietzche und Emerson. LC 80-2538. 1981. Repr. of 1958 ed. 25.50 (ISBN 0-404-19264-5). AMS Pr.

Richardson, Larry N. The Philosophy of Nietzsche in Dramatic Representational Expressions. (Essence of the Great Philosophers Ser.). (Illus.). 97p. 1981. 19.75 (ISBN 0-89266-277-8). Am Classical Coll Pr.

Silk, M. S. & Stern, J. P. Nietzsche on Tragedy. LC 80-40433. 500p. Date not set. price not set (ISBN 0-521-23262-7). Cambridge U Pr.

Stern, J. P. A Study of Nietzsche. LC 78-54328. (Major European Authors Ser.). Date not set. pap. price not set (ISBN 0-521-28380-9). Cambridge U Pr.

NIGERIA–DESCRIPTION AND TRAVEL

Lanier, Alison R. Update -- Nigeria. (Country Orientation Ser.). 1980. pap. text ed. 25.00 (ISBN 0-933662-27-0). Intercult Network.

NIGERIA–COMMERCE

Okigbo, P. N. Nigeria's Financial System. (Illus.). 320p. 1981. text ed. 25.00x (ISBN 0-582-59733-1). Longman.

NIGERIA–ECONOMIC CONDITIONS

Bienen, Henry & Diejomaoh, V. P., eds. The Political Economy of Income Distribution in Nigeria. LC 80-16860. (The Political Economy of Income Distribution in Developing Countries Ser.: No. 2). 500p. 1981. text ed. 45.00x (ISBN 0-8419-0618-1). Holmes & Meier.

Onoh, J. K., ed. The Foundations of Nigeria's Financial Infrastructure. 318p. 1980. 50.00x (ISBN 0-7099-0448-7, Pub. by Croom Helm Ltd England). Biblio Dist.

NIGERIA–POLITICS AND GOVERNMENT

Adebayo, Augustus. Principles & Practice of Public Administration in Nigeria. 192p. 1981. 27.00 (ISBN 0-471-27897-1, Pub. by Wiley-Interscience); pap. 13.50 (ISBN 0-471-27898-X). Wiley.

NIGHT WORK

see also Children–Employment; Shift Systems

Reinberg, A., et al, eds. Night & Shift Work-Biological & Social Aspects: Proceedings of the Vth International Symposium on Night and Shift Work-Scientific Committee on Shift Work of the Permanent Commission & International Association on Occupational Health (PCIAIH, Rouen, 12-16 May 1980. (Illus.). 516p. 1981. 80.00 (ISBN 0-08-025516-7). Pergamon.

NIGHTINGALE, FLORENCE, 1820-1910

Keele, Mary, ed. Florence Nightingale in Rome: Letters Written 1847 to 1848. 1981. 12.00 (ISBN 0-87169-143-4). Am Philos.

NINETEENTH CENTURY

Willey, Basil. More Nineteenth-Century Studies: A Group of Honest Doubters. LC 80-40635. 304p. 1981. pap. 9.95 (ISBN 0-521-28067-2). Cambridge U Pr.

NINEVEH

Brackman, Arnold C. The Luck of Nineveh. 352p. 1981. pap. 8.95 (ISBN 0-442-28260-5). Van Nos Reinhold.

NIPPUR

Heimerdinger, J. Sumerian Literary Fragments from Nippur. (Occasional Pubns. of the Babylonian Fund Ser.: Vol. 4). 1980. 20.00 (ISBN 0-934718-31-8). Univ Mus of U PA.

NISEI

see Japanese in the United States

NITRATES

Committee on Nitrate Accumulation. Accumulation of Nitrate. vii, 106p. 1972. pap. text ed. 6.00 (ISBN 0-309-02038-7). Natl Acad Pr.

Wilcox. Growth Mechanisms & Silicon Nitride. Date not set. price not set (ISBN 0-8247-1368-0). Dekker.

NITRATION

Schofield, K. Aromatic Nitration. (Illus.). 350p. Date not set. 67.50 (ISBN 0-521-23362-3). Cambridge U Pr.

NITRO COMPOUNDS

Feuer, Henry, ed. The Chemistry of the Nitro & Nitroso Groups: Part 1. LC 80-21491. 996p. 1981. Repr. of 1969 ed. text ed. write for info. (ISBN 0-89874-271-4). Krieger.

--The Chemistry of the Nitro & Nitroso Groups: Part 2. LC 80-21491. 450p. 1981. Repr. text ed. write for info. (ISBN 0-89874-272-2). Krieger.

NITROGEN

see also Nitrogen Fertilizers

Bothe, H. & Trebst, A., eds. Biochemistry & Physiology of Nitrogen & Sulfur Metabolism. (Proceedings in Life Sciences Ser.). (Illus.). 370p. 1981. 49.80 (ISBN 0-387-10486-0). Springer-Verlag.

NITROGEN–FIXATION

Biological Nitrogen Fixation by Epiphytic Microoganisms in Rice Fields. (IRRI Research Paper Ser.: No. 47). 14p. 1981. pap. 5.00 (ISBN 0-686-69532-1, R 117, IRRI). Unipub.

Broughton, W. J. Nitrogen Fixation, Vol. 1: Ecology. (Illus.). 350p. 1981. 59.00 (ISBN 0-19-854540-1). Oxford U Pr.

NITROGEN FERTILIZERS

Denitrification Loss of Fertilizer Nitrogen in Paddy Soils - Its Recognition & Impact. (IRRI Research Paper Ser.: No. 37). 10p. 1979. pap. 5.00 (R077, IRRI). Unipub.

Nitrogen & Rice. 499p. 1979. pap. 32.50 (R026, IRRI). Unipub.

Recent Developements in Research on Nitrogen Fertilizers for Rice. (IRRI Research Paper Ser.: No. 49). 11p. 1981. pap. 5.00 (ISBN 0-686-69535-6, R 119, IRRI). Unipub.

The Role of Nitrogen in Intensive Grassland Production. 171p. 1981. pap. 30.00 (ISBN 90-220-0734-0, PDC 214, Pudoc). Unipub.

Utilization of the Azolla-Anabaena Complex As a Nitrogen Fertilizer for Rice. (IRRI Research Paper Ser.: No. 11). 15p. 1977. pap. 5.00 (R051, IRRI). Unipub.

NITROGEN FIXATION

see Nitrogen–Fixation

NITROUS OXIDE

Delwiche, C. C. Denitrifigation, Nitrification, & Atmospheric Nitrous Oxide. LC 80-22698. 260p. 1981. 27.50 (ISBN 0-471-04896-8, Pub. by Wiley-Interscience). Wiley.

NIXON, RICHARD MILHOUS, PRES. U. S., 1913-

Nixon, Richard. The Memoirs of Richard Nixon, Vol. 1. 736p. 1981. pap. 2.95 (ISBN 0-446-93259-0). Warner Bks.

--The Memoirs of Richard Nixon, Vol. 2. 728p. 1981. pap. 2.95 (ISBN 0-446-93260-4). Warner Bks.

NOAH'S ARK

Noah Builds a Big Boat. (Tell-a-Bible Story Ser.). (Illus.). 28p. bds. 0.69 (ISBN 0-686-68637-3, 3681). Standard Pub.

Spier, Peter. Noah's Ark. 48p. (ps). 1981. pap. 3.95 (ISBN 0-385-17302-4, Zephyr). Doubleday.

NOCTURNAL ANIMALS

Charles-Dominique, P. & Martin, R. D. Behavior & Ecology of Nocturnal Prosimians: Field Studies in Gabon & Madagascar. (Advances in Ethology Ser.: Vol. 9). (Illus.). 91p. (Orig.). 1972. pap. text ed. 23.50. Parey Sci Pubs.

NOISE

see also Industrial Noise; Noise Control

Holmes, Jack K. Coherent Communication with Applications to Pseudo-Noise Spread Spectrum Synchronization. 850p. 1981. 50.00 (ISBN 0-471-03301-4, Pub. by Wiley-Interscience). Wiley.

NOISE CONTROL

Fader, Bruce. Industrial Noise Control. 320p. 1981. 29.95 (ISBN 0-471-06007-0, Pub. by Wiley Interscience). Wiley.

Noise Abatement Policies. 392p. 1980. 16.00 (ISBN 92-64-12084-X). OECD.

NOMENCLATURE

see Names

NOMINATIONS FOR OFFICE

see also Political Conventions; Primaries

Sanford, Terry. Danger of Democracy: The Presidential Nominating Process. 160p. 1981. 15.00 (ISBN 0-86531-159-5). Westview.

NOMS DE PLUME

see Anonyms and Pseudonyms

NON-ALIGNMENT

see Neutrality

NONCONFORMISTS

see Dissenters

NONCONFORMITY

see Conformity

NON-DESTRUCTIVE TESTING

McGonnagle, W., ed. International Advances in Nondestructive Testing, Vol. 7. 348p. 1981. write for info. (ISBN 0-677-15700-2). Gordon.

Stinchcomb, W. W., et al, eds. Mechanics of Nondestructive Testing. 415p. 1980. 47.50 (ISBN 0-306-40567-9). Plenum Pub.

NONFERROUS METALS

Edwards, John & Robbins, Peter, eds. Guide to Non-Ferrous Metals & Their Markets. 2nd ed. 250p. 1980. 43.50x (ISBN 0-89397-096-4). Nichols Pub.

Material Specifications: Nonferrous Materials, 3 pts. Pt. B. (Boiler & Pressure Vessel Code Ser.: Sec. II). 1980. 110.00 (P0002B); loose-leaf 150.00 (V0002B). ASME.

Touloukian, Y. S. & Ho, C. Y. Properties of Selected Ferrous Alloying Elements, Vol. III. (M-H-CINDAS Data Series on Material Properties). 288p. 1981. text ed. 33.50 (ISBN 0-07-065034-9). McGraw.

NON-FORMAL EDUCATION

Dejene, Alemneh. Non-Formal Education As a Strategy in Development: Comparative Analysis of Rural Development Projects. LC 80-5882. 131p. 1980. lib. bdg. 16.25 (ISBN 0-8191-1346-8); pap. text ed. 7.75 (ISBN 0-8191-1347-6). U Pr of Amer.

NONFOSSIL FUELS

see Synthetic Fuels

NONLINEAR DIFFERENTIAL EQUATIONS

see Differential Equations, Nonlinear

NONLINEAR MECHANICS
Noor, A. K. & McComb, H. G., eds. Computational Methods in Nonlinear Structural & Solid Mechanics: Papers Presented at the Symposium on Computational Methods in Nonlinear Structural & Solid Mechanics, 6-8 October 1980. LC 80-41608. 70.00 (ISBN 0-08-027299-1). Pergamon.
NONLINEAR OPTICS
see also Lasers
Feld, M. S. & Letokhov, V. S., eds. Coherent Nonlinear Optics: Recent Advances. (Topics in Current Physics: Vol. 21). (Illus.). 377p. 1980. 44.50 (ISBN 0-387-10172-1). Springer-Verlag.
NONLINEAR PROGRAMMING
Schittkowski, K. Nonlinear Programming Codes. (Lecture Notes in Economics & Mathematical Systems Ser.: Vol. 183). 242p. 1981. pap. 19.00 (ISBN 0-387-10247-7). Springer-Verlag.
NONLINEAR THEORIES
see also Differential Equations, Nonlinear; System Analysis
Stability of Nonlinear Systems. (Control Theory & Applications Studies Ser.). 208p. 1981. 30.00 (ISBN 0-471-27856-4, Pub. by Wiley-Interscience). Wiley.
Zacks, S. Parametric Statistical Inference: Basic Theory & Modern Approaches. LC 80-41715. (I.S. in Nonlinear Mathematics Series; Theory & Applications: Vol. 4). 400p. 1981. 48.00 (ISBN 0-08-026468-9); pap. 19.70 (ISBN 0-08-026467-0). Pergamon.
NON-MAILABLE MATTER
see Postal Service–Laws and Regulations
NONPARAMETRIC STATISTICS
Johnston, Gordon J. Smooth Nonparametric Regression Analysis. 88p. 1979. pap. 2.80 (1253). U of NC Pr.
NONPROFIT CORPORATIONS
see Corporations, Nonprofit
NON-RESISTANCE TO GOVERNMENT
see Government, Resistance to
NONSELFGOVERNING TERRITORIES
see Colonies
NON-SUPPORT
see Support (Domestic Relations)
NON-VASCULAR PLANTS
see Cryptogams
NONVIOLENCE
see also Pacifism; Passive Resistance
Judson, Stephanie, ed. A Manual on Nonviolence & Children. (Illus.). 115p. (Orig.). 1977. pap. 5.00 (ISBN 0-9605062-1-7). Friends Peace Comm.
Merton, Thomas. The Nonviolent Alternative. Date not set. 12.95 (ISBN 0-374-22312-2); pap. 6.95 (ISBN 0-374-51575-1). FS&G.
NON-VIOLENT NON-COOPERATION
see Passive Resistance
NON-WAGE PAYMENTS
see also Labor and Laboring Classes–Medical Care; Old Age Pensions; Profit-Sharing; Social Security
Employee Benefit Plans & the Economy: Learning Guide, CEBS Course IX. 2nd ed. 1980. spiral 13.00 (ISBN 0-89154-132-2). Intl Found Employ.
Employee Benefits & Plans & the Economy: Answers to the Questions on the Subject Matter for the Learning Guide, CEBS Course IX. 2nd ed. 62p. spiral bdg. 13.00 (ISBN 0-89154-132-2); pap. text ed. 10.00 (ISBN 0-89154-133-0). Intl Found Employ.
Fringe Benefits: A Proposal for the Future. 1979. pap. 9.50. Am Inst CPA.
Greenhill, Richard. Employee Remuneration & Profit Sharing. 224p. 1980. 45.00x (ISBN 0-85941-123-0, Pub. by Woodhead-Faulkner England). State Mutual Bk.
Heib, Elizabeth A., ed. Collection of Employer Contributions Institute, Las Vegas, Nevada, June 15 to 18, 1980: Proceedings. 77p. (Orig.). 1980. pap. 8.00 (ISBN 0-89154-138-1). Intl Found Employ.
Jost, Lee F. & Sutherland, C. Bruce. Guide to Professional Benefit Plan Management & Administration. 405p. (Orig.). 1980. pap. 35.00 (ISBN 0-89154-096-2). Intl Found Employ.
Lawson, J. W. & Smith, Ballard. Managements Complete Guide to Employee Benefits. 259p. 1980. 69.50 (ISBN 0-85013-119-7). Dartnell Corp.
Snider, H. Wayne, ed. Employee Benefits Management. 240p. Date not set. price not set (ISBN 0-937802-00-X). Risk & Ins.
Srb, Jozetta H. Communicating with Employees About Pension & Welfare Benefits. (Key Issues Ser.: No. 8). 1971. pap. 2.00 (ISBN 0-87546-244-8). NY Sch Indus Rel.
NONWOVEN FABRICS
Bhatnagar, ViJay M. Nonwovens & Disposables: New Technical-Marketing Developments. 86p. 1978. pap. 25.00 (ISBN 0-87762-256-6). Technomic.
Bhatnagar, ViJay M., ed. Nonwovens & Disposables: Proceedings of the First Canadian Symposium of Nonwovens & Disposables. LC 78-68591. (Illus.). 1978. pap. 25.00 (ISBN 0-87762-268-X). Technomic.
NORFOLK, VIRGINIA
Walker, Carroll. Norfolk: A Pictorial History. 2nd ed. Friedman, Donna R., ed. (Illus.). 208p. 1981. pap. write for info. (ISBN 0-89865-129-8). Donning Co.

NORMANDY
Haskins, Charles H. Norman Institutions. LC 80-2026. 1981. Repr. of 1918 ed. 39.50 (ISBN 0-404-18568-1). AMS Pr.
NORMANDY–HISTORY–MEDIEVAL PERIOD
Chibnall, Marjorie, ed. The Ecclesiastical History of Orderic Vitalis, Vol. 1. (Oxford Medieval Texts Ser.). (Illus.). 416p. 1980. 79.00 (ISBN 0-19-822243-2). Oxford U Pr.
Palgrave, Francis. The History of Normandy & England, 4 vols. LC 80-2218. 1981. Repr. of 1919 ed. 345.00 (ISBN 0-404-18770-6). AMS Pr.
Prentout, Henri. Essai Sur les Origines et la Fondation Du Duche De Normandie. LC 80-2214. 1981. Repr. of 1911 ed. 39.00 (ISBN 0-404-18776-5). AMS Pr.
Rabasse, Maurice. Du Regime Des Fiefs En Normandie Au Moyen Age. LC 80-2006. 1981. Repr. of 1905 ed. 29.50 (ISBN 0-404-18588-6). AMS Pr.
NORMANS IN ENGLAND
Ritchie, Robert L. The Normans in Scotland. LC 80-2216. 1980. Repr. of 1954 ed. 57.50 (ISBN 0-404-18783-8). AMS Pr.
NORSE LEGENDS
see Legends, Norse
NORSEMEN
see Northmen
NORTH AMERICA
Garreau, Joel. Nine Nations of North America. 1981. 14.00 (ISBN 0-395-29124-0). HM.
NORTH AMERICA–DESCRIPTION AND TRAVEL
Hudson, F. S. North America. 4th ed. (Illus.). 464p. 1978. pap. 14.95x (ISBN 0-7121-1410-6, Pub. by Macdonald & Evans England). Intl Ideas.
NORTH AMERICA–DESCRIPTION AND TRAVEL–GUIDEBOOKS
Gousha North American Road Atlas. rev. ed. 1981. pap. 4.50 (ISBN 0-451-82064-9, XE2064, Sig). NAL.
NORTH AMERICA–HISTORY–BIBLIOGRAPHY
The Research Library of the New York Public Library & the Library of Congress. Bibliographic Guide to North American History: 1980. (Library Catalogs Bib.Guides Ser.). 1981. lib. bdg. 85.00 (ISBN 0-8161-6892-X). G K Hall.
NORTH AMERICAN INDIANS
see Indians of North America
NORTH ATLANTIC REGION
Marcus, G. J. The Conquest of the North Atlantic. (Illus.). 256p. 1981. 25.00 (ISBN 0-19-520252-X). Oxford U Pr.
NORTH ATLANTIC TREATY ORGANIZATION
Bray, Frank T. & Moodie, Michael. Defense Technology & the Atlantic Alliance: Competition or Collaboration? LC 77-80297. (Foreign Policy Report Ser.). 5.00 (ISBN 0-89549-000-5). Inst Foreign Policy Anal.
Johnson, U. Alexis & Packard, George R., eds. The Common Security Interests of Japan, the United States, & NATO. 200p. 1981. professional reference 19.50x. Ballinger Pub.
Kaplan, Lawrence S. & Clawson, Robert W. NATO After Thirty Years. LC 80-53885. 250p. 1981. lib. bdg. 19.95 (ISBN 0-8420-2172-8). Scholarly Res Inc.
Mets, David R. NATO: Alliance for Peace. (Illus.). 190p. (gr. 9-12). 1981. PLB price not set (ISBN 0-671-34065-4). Messner.
--Nato: An Alliance for Peace. (Illus.). 1981. write for info. Messner.
NATO: The Next Thirty Years. (Significant Issues Ser.: Vol. I, No. 6). 25p. 1979. pap. 5.00 (ISBN 0-89206-012-3, CSIS007, CSIS). Unipub.
Nato: the Next Thirty Years: A Report of the Conference, Vol. I. LC 79-57250. (Significant Issues Ser.: No. 6). 25p. 1979. 4.00 (ISBN 0-89206-012-3). CSI Studies.
Yost, David S., ed. NATO's Strategic Options: Arms Control & Defense. (Pergamon Policy Studies on International Politics). (Illus.). 275p. 1981. 30.00 (ISBN 0-08-027184-7). Pergamon.
NORTH CAROLINA–DESCRIPTION AND TRAVEL
Aerial Photo. The Blowing Rock: North Carolina. Date not set. 1.50 (ISBN 0-936672-08-0). Aerial Photo.
--Coastal North Carolina Picture Book. Date not set. 2.00 (ISBN 0-936672-10-2). Aerial Photo.
NORTH CAROLINA–GENEALOGY
Leary, Helen F. & Stirewalt, Maurice R., eds. North Carolina Research: Genealogy & Local History. LC 80-50414. (Illus.). 672p. 1980. 21.50 (ISBN 0-936370-00-9). Natl Genealogical.
NORTH CAROLINA–HISTORY
see also Raleigh'S Roanoke Colonies, 1584-1590
Andrews, Melvin B. Carolina Adventures: Brief Sketches of Growing up in Eastern North Carolina at the Turn of the Century (1889-1915) Andrews, J. David, ed. (Illus.). 92p. (Orig.). 1979. pap. 5.00. Planetary Pr.
Billings, Dwight B., Jr. Planters & the Making of a "New South". Class, Politics, & Development in North Carolina, 1865-1900. LC 78-25952. xiii, 284p. 1979. 15.00x (ISBN 0-8078-1315-X). U of NC Pr.
Vexler, R. I. North Carolina Chronology & Factbook, Vol. 33. 1978. 8.50 (ISBN 0-379-16158-3). Oceana.

NORTH CENTRAL STATES
see Middle West
NORTH DAKOTA
see also names of cities, counties, towns etc. in North Dakota
Fradin, Dennis. North Dakota: In Words & Pictures. LC 80-26480. (Young People's Stories of Our States Ser.). (Illus.). 48p. (gr. 2-5). 1981. PLB 8.65g (ISBN 0-516-03934-2, Time Line). Childrens.
Hanson, Nancy E. Bismarck & Mangan: A Pictorial History. (Illus.). 205p. 1981. pap. price not set (ISBN 0-89865-094-1). Donning Co.
--Fargo: A Pictorial History. (Illus.). 205p. 1981. pap. price not set. Donning Co.
Howard, Thomas W., ed. The North Dakota Political Tradition. 192p. 1981. 8.95 (ISBN 0-8138-0520-1). Iowa St U Pr.
Scneider, Bill. The Dakota Image. LC 80-83707. (Illus.). 96p. 1980. 20.00 (ISBN 0-934318-02-6). Falcon Pr MT.
Vexler, R. I. North Dakota Chronology & Factbook, Vol. 34. 1978. 8.50 (ISBN 0-379-16159-1). Oceana.
NORTH EASTERN RAILWAY COMPANY (GREAT BRITAIN)
Locomotive of the North Eastern Railway. 14.95x (ISBN 0-392-08071-0, SpS). Soccer.
Nock, O. S. British Steam Railway Locomotive: Volume 2, 1925-1965. 31.50x (ISBN 0-392-07700-0, SpS). Soccer.
NORTH POLE
see also Arctic Regions
Hunt, Harrison J. North to the Horizon. Thompson, Ruth H., ed. LC 80-69081. (Illus.). 135p. 1981. 11.95 (ISBN 0-89272-080-8). Down East.
Hunt, William R. To Stand at the Pole: The Dr. Cook-Admiral Peary North Pole Controversy. LC 80-6156. 272p. 1981. 14.95 (ISBN 0-8128-2773-2). Stein & Day.
NORTH SEA
Watt, D. C., ed. Greenwich Forum V: Europe & the Sea: the Cause for & Against a New International Regime for the North Sea and Its Approaches. 1980. text ed. 52.00 (ISBN 0-86103-039-7). Butterworths.
NORTHERN IRELAND
Aunger, Edmund A. In Search of Political Stability: A Comparative Study of New Brunswick & Northern Ireland. 238p. 1981. 21.95x (ISBN 0-7735-0366-8). McGill-Queens U Pr.
Beyond Orange & Green: The Political Eonomy of the Northern Ireland Crisis. 176p. 1978. 12.95 (ISBN 0-905762-16-9, Pub. by Zed Pr); pap. 6.95 (ISBN 0-905762-17-7). Lawrence Hill.
Holland, Jack. Too Long a Sacrifice: Life & Death in Northern Ireland Since Nineteen Sixty-Nine. LC 80-27267. (Illus.). 240p. 1981. 8.95 (ISBN 0-686-69573-9). Dodd.
O'Dowd, Liam, et al. Northern Ireland: Between Civil Rights & Civil War. 224p. 1980. text ed. 26.00x (ISBN 0-906336-18-X); pap. text ed. 19.50x (ISBN 0-906336-19-8). Humanities.
NORTHMEN
see also Vikings
Ferguson, Sheila. Growing up in Viking Times. (Growing up Ser.). (Illus.). 72p. (gr. 6 up). 1981. 14.95 (ISBN 0-7134-2730-2, Pub. by Batsford England). David & Charles.
Leirfall, Jon. West Over Sea. 160p. 1980. 14.95 (ISBN 0-906191-15-7, Pub. by Thule Pr England). Intl Schol Bk Serv.
Snorri. Heimskringla: From the Sagas of the Norse Kings. Monsen, Erling, tr. (Illus.). 398p. 1980. 35.00 (ISBN 0-906191-39-4, Pub. by Thule Pr England). Intl Schol Bk Serv.
NORTHWEST, NEW
see Northwestern States
NORTHWEST, OLD–DESCRIPTION AND TRAVEL
Davenport, Marge. Best of the Old Northwest. LC 80-83780. (Illus., Orig.). 1981. pap. 6.95 (ISBN 0-938274-00-7). Paddlewheel.
NORTHWEST, PACIFIC–DESCRIPTION AND TRAVEL
Bingham, Edwin R. & Love, Glen A., eds. Northwest Perspectives: Essays on the Culture of the Pacific Northwest. LC 77-15189. 264p. 1981. pap. 7.95 (ISBN 0-295-95805-7). U of Wash Pr.
NORWAY–DESCRIPTION AND TRAVEL
Ronning, Olaf & Bjaerevoll, Olav. Flowers of Svalbard. (Illus.). 56p. 1981. pap. 14.00x (ISBN 82-00-05398-9). Universitet.
NORWAY–ECONOMIC CONDITIONS
The Norwegian Price & Income Freeze. 1980. 50.00x (Pub. by Norwegian Info Norway). State Mutual Bk.
NORWAY–FOREIGN RELATIONS
Amundsen, Kirsten. Norway, NATO & the Forgotten Soviet Challenge. (Policy Papers in International Affairs: No. 14). (Illus.). iv, 60p. 1981. pap. 2.95x (ISBN 0-87725-514-8). U of Cal Pr.
NORWAY–HISTORY
Sturluson, Snorri. Heims Kringla, History of the Kings of Norway. Hollander, Lee M., tr. from Old Norse. LC 64-10460. (Illus.). 1977. Repr. of 1964 ed. 27.50x (ISBN 0-89067-040-4). Am Scandinavian.

NORWAY–POLITICS AND GOVERNMENT
Royal Norwegian Ministry of Justice, ed. Administration of Justice in Norway. 96p. 1981. pap. 12.00x (ISBN 82-00-05501-9). Universitet.
Sosin, Jack M. Whitehall & the Wilderness: The Middle West in British Colonial Policy, 1760 to 1775. LC 80-21061. (Illus.). xi, 307p. 1981. Repr. of 1961 ed. lib. bdg. 35.00x (ISBN 0-313-22678-4, SOWW). Greenwood.
Urwin, Derek W. From Ploughshare to Ballotbox. 356p. 1981. pap. 30.00x (ISBN 82-00-05394-6). Universitet.
NORWAY–SOCIAL CONDITIONS
Gustavson, Bjorn & Hunius, Gerry. Improving the Quality of Life: The Case of Norway. 112p. 1981. pap. 25.00x (ISBN 82-00-05525-6). Universitet.
NORWEGIAN PRISONERS
see Prisoners, Norwegian
NOTATION (FOR BOOKS IN LIBRARIES)
see Alphabeting
NOTE-TAKING
Brown, Diane. Notemaking. 245p. 1977. text ed. 10.20 (ISBN 0-7715-0858-1). Forkner.
Ziggy's Class Notes. 1980. 2.95 (ISBN 0-8362-1916-3). Andrews & McMeel.
NOVA SCOTIA–DESCRIPTION AND TRAVEL
Armstrong, Bruce. Sable Island. LC 80-2745. (Illus.). 256p. 1981. 19.95 (ISBN 0-385-13113-5). Doubleday.
NOVELISTS
see Authors
NOVELS
see Fiction
NUCLEAR CHEMISTRY
Here are entered works on the application of chemical techniques to the study of the structure and properties of atomic nuclei, their transformations and reactions. Works on the chemical effects of high energy radiation on matter are entered under Radiation chemistry. Works on the chemical properties of radioactive substances and their use in chemical studies are entered under Radiochemistry.
see also Nuclear Physics; Radiochemistry
Friedlander, Gerhart. Nuclear & Radiochemistry. 3rd ed. 650p. 1981. price not set (ISBN 0-471-28021-6, Pub. by Wiley-Interscience). Wiley.
NUCLEAR DAMAGES, LIABILITY FOR
see Liability for Nuclear Damages
NUCLEAR ENERGY
see Atomic Energy
NUCLEAR ENGINEERING
see also Atomic Power; Nuclear Fuels; Nuclear Reactors
Division 1 - Nuclear Power Plant Components: General Requirements. (Boiler & Pressure Vessel Code Ser.: Sec. 3). 1980. 55.00 (P0003R); pap. 80.00 loose-leaf (V0003R). ASME.
Stewart, Hugh B. Transitional Energy Policy 1980-2030: Alternative Nuclear Technologies. (Pergamon Policy Studies on Science & Technology). 266p. 1981. 30.00 (ISBN 0-08-027183-9); pap. 12.50 (ISBN 0-08-027182-0). Pergamon.
NUCLEAR ENGINEERING AS A PROFESSION
Manpower Development for Nuclear Power: A Guidebook. (Technical Reports Ser.: No. 200). 492p. 1980. pap. 58.50 (ISBN 92-0-155080-4, IOC200, IAEA). Unipub.
NUCLEAR FISSION
Physics & Chemistry of Fission, Nineteen Seventy-Nine, Vol. 11. 501p. 1980. pap. 58.75 (ISBN 92-0-030180-0, ISP526-2, IAEA). Unipub.
NUCLEAR FUELS
see also Uranium
Christensen, R. Thermal Mechanical Behavior of VO2 Nuclear Fuel: Multi-Cycle Test Description, Vol. IV. xiv, 325p. Date not set. 49.50. Entropy Ltd.
--Thermal Mechanical Behavior of VO2 Nuclear Fuel: Statistical Analysis of Acoustic Emission Axial Elagation, & Crack Characteristics. xii, 238p. 1981. 34.50. Entropy Ltd.
--Thermal Mechanical Behavior of VO2 Nuclear Fuel: Statistical Analysis of Acoustic Emission, Diametral Expansion,Anrol Elongation & Crash Characteristics. x, 238p. pap. 34.50. Entropy Ltd.
--Thermal Mechanical Behavior of VO2 Nuclear Fuel: Single Cycle Test Discription, Vol. III. x, 308p. Date not set. 46.50. Entropy Ltd.
--Thermal Mechanical Behavior of V02 Nuclear Fuel: Electrothermal Analysis, Vol. II. x, 122p. Date not set. 19.50. Entropy Ltd.

International Nuclear Fuel Cycle Evaluation. Incl. Report of INFCE Working Group 1 - Fuel & Heavy Water Availability. 314p. pap. 40.25 (ISBN 92-0-159180-2, ISP534-1); Report of INFCE Working Group 2 - Enrichment Availability. 157p. pap. 21.00 (ISBN 9-2015-9280-9, ISP534-2); Report of INFCE Working Group 3 - Assurances of Long-Term Supply of Technology, Fuel, & Heavy Water & Services in the Interest of National Needs Consistent with Non-Proliferation. 104p. pap. 14.00 (ISBN 92-0-159380-5, ISP534-3); Report of INFCE Working Group 4 - Reprocessing, Plutonium Handling, Recycle. 300p. pap. 36.25 (ISBN 9-2015-9480-1, ISP534-4); Report of INFCE Working Group 5 - Fast Breeders. 217p. pap. 28.75 (ISBN 92-0159-580-8, ISP534-5); Report of INFCE Working Group 6 - Spent Fuel Management. 113p. pap. 16.00 (ISBN 92-0-159680-4, ISP534-6); Report of INFCE Working Group 7 - Waste Management & Disposal. 287p. pap. 36.75 (ISBN 92-0-159780-0, ISP534-7); Report of INFCE Working Group 8 - Advanced Fuel Cycle & Reactor Concepts. 181p. pap. 23.75 (ISBN 9-2015-9880-7, ISP534-8); INFCE Summary Volume. 285p. pap. 35.00 (ISBN 9-2015-9980-3, ISP534-9). 1980 (IAEA). Unipub.

Occupational Radiation Exposure in Nuclear Fuel Cycle Facilities. 640p. 1980. pap. 79.25 (ISBN 92-0-020080-X, ISP527, IAEA). Unipub.

NUCLEAR MAGNETIC RESONANCE

see also Nuclear Magnetism

Danadian, R., ed. NMR in Medicine. (NMR--Basic Principles & Progress Ser.). (Illus.). 230p. 1981. 57.90 (ISBN 0-387-10460-7). Springer-Verlag.

Mooney, E. F., ed. Annual Reports on NMR Spectroscopy. Incl. Vol. 1. 1968. 49.00 (ISBN 0-12-505350-9); Vol. 5B. 1974. 62.00 (ISBN 0-12-505345-2); Vol. 6, 2 pts. 1976-78. Pt. B. 34.00 (ISBN 0-12-505346-0); Pt. C. 90.00 (ISBN 0-12-505347-9); Vol. 7. 1978. 43.50 (ISBN 0-12-505307-X); Vol. 8. 1978. 71.00 (ISBN 0-12-505308-8); Vol. 9. 1978. 57.50 (ISBN 0-12-505309-6). Acad Pr.

NUCLEAR MAGNETISM

see also Nuclear Magnetic Resonance

Fogedby, Hans C. Theoretical Aspects of Mainly Low Dimensional Magnetic Systems. (Lecture Notes in Physics Ser.: Vol. 131). 163p. 1981. pap. 12.00 (ISBN 0-387-10238-8). Springer Verlag.

NUCLEAR MEDICINE

Ashkar, F. S., ed. Thyroid & Endocrine System Investigations with Radionuclides & Radioassays. (Illus.). 544p. 1979. 40.50 (ISBN 0-89352-070-5). Masson Pub.

Baum, Sheldon, et al. Atlas of Nuclear Medicine Imaging. 432p. 1980. 78.00x (ISBN 0-8385-0447-7). ACC.

Clifton, Nancy A. & Simmons, Pamela J. Basic Imaging Procedures in Nuclear Medicine. 192p. 1981. pap. 13.50 (ISBN 0-8385-0578-3). ACC.

Juge, O. & Donath, A., eds. Neuronuclear Medicine. (Progress in Nuclear Medicine Ser.: Vol. 7). (Illus.). vii, 240p. 1981. 90.00 (ISBN 3-8055-2319-X). S Karger.

Mayneord, W. V. Some Applications of Nuclear Physics to Medicine. 1980. 15.00x (Pub. by Brit Inst Radiology). State Mutual Bk.

Sodee, D. Bruce & Early, Paul J. Mosby's Manual of Nuclear Medicine Procedures. 3rd ed. (Illus.). 574p. 1981. pap. text ed. 34.95 (ISBN 0-8016-4729-0). Mosby.

NUCLEAR MEDICINE–EQUIPMENT AND SUPPLIES

Berton, Alberta D., compiled by. Nuclear Medicine: A Comprehensive Bibliography. (Biomedical Information Guides Ser.: Vol. 2). 355p. 1980. 85.00 (ISBN 0-306-65178-5, IFI). Plenum Pub.

NUCLEAR PARTICLES

see Particles (Nuclear Physics)

NUCLEAR PHYSICS

see also Atomic Energy; Chemistry, Physical and Theoretical; Nuclear Chemistry; Nuclear Engineering; Nuclear Fission; Nuclear Magnetism; Nuclear Reactions; Nuclear Reactors; Nuclear Spin; Particles (Nuclear Physics); Radiobiology; Scattering (Physics)

French, Henri, ed. Heat Transfer & Fluid Flow in Nuclear Systems. 300p. 1981. 30.01 (ISBN 0-08-027181-2). Pergamon.

NUCLEAR PHYSICS–ADDRESSES, ESSAYS, LECTURES

Frampton, P., et al, eds. First Workshop on Grand Unification. (Lie Groups; History, Frontiers & Applications: Vol. XI). 250p. 1980. text ed. 30.00x (ISBN 0-915692-31-7). Math Sci Pr.

NUCLEAR PHYSICS–DICTIONARIES

INIS: Thesaurus. (INIS Ser.: No. 13, Rev. 19). 748p. 1980. pap. 45.00 (ISBN 92-0-178480-5, IN13/R19, IAEA). Unipub.

NUCLEAR POWER

see Atomic Power

NUCLEAR REACTIONS

see also Nuclear Fission; Photonuclear Reactions

Cannata, F. & Ueberall, H. Giant Resonance Phenomena in Intermediate-Energy Nuclear Reactions. (Springer Tracts in Modern Physics: Vol. 89). (Illus.). 112p. 1980. 29.80 (ISBN 0-387-10105-5). Springer-Verlag.

NUCLEAR REACTORS

Bankoff, S. George, et al, eds. Heat Transfer in Nuclear Reactor Safety: Proceedings of the International Centre for Heat & Mass Transfer. (International Centre for Heat & Mass Transfer). (Illus.). 1981. text ed. 95.00 (ISBN 0-89116-223-2). Hemisphere Pub.

Division 2-Code for Concrete Reactor Vessels & Containments. (Boiler & Pressure Vessel Code Ser.: Sec. 3). 1980. 90.00 (P00032); pap. 125.00 loose-leaf (V00032). ASME.

Factors Relevant to the Decommissioning of Land-Based Nuclear Reactor Plants. (Safety Ser.: No. 52). 28p. 1981. pap. 4.75 (ISBN 0-686-69440-6, ISP 541, IAEA). Unipub.

Fast Reactor Physics Nineteen Seventy-Nine, Vol. 1. 2nd ed. 611p. 1980. pap. 71.00 (ISBN 92-0-050180-X, ISP529-1, IAEA). Unipub.

Glasstone, Samuel & Sesonske, Alexander. Nuclear Reactor Engineering. 2nd ed. 800p. 1980. text ed. 39.50 (ISBN 0-442-20057-9). Van Nos Reinhold.

Goodjohn, Albert J. & Pomraning, Gerald C., eds. Reactor Physics in the Resonance & Thermal Regions, 2 vols. Incl. Vol. 1. Neutron Thermalization. 450p (ISBN 0-262-07023-5); Vol. 2. Resonance Absorbtion. 450p (ISBN 0-262-07024-3). 1966. text ed. 30.00x ea. MIT Pr.

International Tokamak Reactor: Zero Phase. (Panel Proceedings Ser.). 650p. 1980. pap. 81.50 (ISBN 92-0-131080-3, ISP556, IAEA). Unipub.

Jones, Owen C., ed. Nuclear Reactor Safety Heat Transfer: Proceedings of the International Centre for Heat & Mass Transfer. (International Centre for Heat & Mass Trans Transfer Ser.). (Illus.). 1981. text ed. 99.00 (ISBN 0-89116-224-0). Hemisphere Pub.

Keck, Otto. Policy-Making in a Nuclear Program: The Case of the West German Fast-Breeder Reactor. LC 79-3831. 1981. write for info. (ISBN 0-669-03519-X). Lexington Bks.

Power Reactors in Member States 1980. 147p. 1980. pap. 19.50 (ISBN 92-0-152080-8, ISP423-80, IAEA). Unipub.

Winterton, R. H. Thermal Design of Nuclear Reactors. LC 80-41187. (Illus.). 200p. 30.00 (ISBN 0-08-024215-4); pap. 15.00 (ISBN 0-08-024214-6). Pergamon.

NUCLEAR REACTORS–FUEL

see Nuclear Fuels

NUCLEAR REACTORS–SAFETY MEASURES

Bressler, M. N., et al. Criteria for Nuclear Safety Related Piping & Component Support Snubbers. (PVP: No. 45). 40p. 1980. 6.00 (H00173). ASME.

Freeman, Leslie J. Nuclear Witnesses: Insiders Speak Out. (Illus.). 1981. 14.95 (ISBN 0-393-01456-8). Norton.

OECD-NEA. Reference Seismic Grond Motions in Nuclear Safety Assessments. (Illus.). 171p. (Orig.). 1980. pap. text ed. 16.00x (ISBN 92-64-12100-5). OECD.

NUCLEAR SCATTERING

see Scattering (Physics)

NUCLEAR SPECTROSCOPY

Axenrod, Theodore & Webb, Graham. Nuclear Magnetic Resonance Spectroscopy of Nuclei Other Than Protons. 424p. Repr. of 1974 ed. lib. bdg. write for info. (ISBN 0-89874-290-0). Krieger.

Mooney, E. F., ed. Annual Reports on NMR Spectroscopy. Incl. Vol. 1. 1968. 49.00 (ISBN 0-12-505350-9); Vol. 5B. 1974. 62.00 (ISBN 0-12-505345-2); Vol. 6, 2 pts. 1976-78. Pt. B. 34.00 (ISBN 0-12-505346-0); Pt. C. 90.00 (ISBN 0-12-505347-9); Vol. 7. 1978. 43.50 (ISBN 0-12-505307-X); Vol. 8. 1978. 71.00 (ISBN 0-12-505308-8); Vol. 9. 1978. 57.50 (ISBN 0-12-505309-6). Acad Pr.

NUCLEAR SPIN

see also Magnetic Resonance; Spin-Lattice Relaxation

Wolf, Dieter. Spin Temperature & Nuclear Spin Relaxation in Matter: Basic Principles & Applications. (International Series of Monographs on Physics). (Illus.). 480p. 1979. text ed. 34.95x (ISBN 0-19-851295-3). Oxford U Pr.

NUCLEAR TRANSFORMATIONS

see Nuclear Reactions

NUCLEAR WARFARE

see Atomic Warfare

NUCLEAR WASTES

see Radioactive Wastes

NUCLEAR WEAPONS

see Atomic Weapons

NUCLEIC ACIDS

Cohn, Waldo E., ed. Progress in Nucleic Acid Research & Molecular Biology, Vol. 25. (Serial Publication). 1981. 29.50 (ISBN 0-12-540025-X); lib. bdg. 38.50 (ISBN 0-12-540094-2); microfiche ed. 20.00 (ISBN 0-12-540095-0). Acad Pr.

--Progress in Nucleic Acid Research & Molecular Biology: DNA: Multiprotein Interactions, Vol. 26. (Serial Publication Ser.). 1981. write for info. (ISBN 0-12-540026-8); lib. ed. (ISBN 0-12-540095-0); microfiche ed. (ISBN 0-12-540096-9). Acad Pr.

The Eighth Symposium on Nucleic Acids Chemistry: Proceedings. (Nucleic Acids Symposium Ser.: No. 8). 198p. 1980. 20.00 (ISBN 0-904147-28-2). Info Retrieval.

International Symposium in Chemical Synthesis of Nucleic Acids, Egestorf, West Germany, May 1980. Nucleic Acid Synthesis: Applications to Molecular Biology & Genetic Engineering. (Nucleic Acids Symposium Ser.: No. 7). 396p. 1980. 40.00 (ISBN 0-904147-26-6). Info Retrieval.

Symposium on Nucleic Acids, Chemistry, 4th, Kyoto, 1976. Proceedings. 156p. 16.00. Info Retrieval.

Symposium on Nucleic Acids Chemistry, 5th, Mishima, Japan, 1977. Proceedings. 190p. 12.00. Info Retrieval.

Symposium on Nucleic Acids Chemistry, 6th, Nagoya, Japan, 1978. Proceedings. 227p. 15.00. Info Retrieval.

Symposium on Nucleic Acids Chemistry, 7th, Okayama, Japan, 1979. Proceedings. 250p. 16.00. Info Retrieval.

Symposium on the Chemistry of Nucleic Acids Components, 3rd, Czechoslovakia, 1975. Proceedings. 183p. 15.00. Info Retrieval.

NUCLEONS

see Particles (Nuclear Physics)

NUCLEUS (CELLS)

see Cell Nuclei; Cells

NUCLEUS OF THE ATOM

see Nuclear Physics

NUDE IN ART

see also Figure Drawing; Figure Painting

Minkkinen, Arno R., ed. New American Nudes. (Illus.). 128p. 1981. pap. 19.95 (ISBN 0-87100-178-0). Morgan.

NUDISM

Smith, Dennis C. The Naked Child: The Long Range Effects of Family & Social Nudity. LC 80-69234. (Illus.). 180p. 1981. perfect bdg. 7.95 (ISBN 0-86548-056-7). Century Twenty One.

NUMBER CONCEPT- JUVENILE LITERATURE

Robinson, Shari. A First Number Book. LC 80-83587. (Illus.). 96p. (gr. k-4). 1981. PLB 11.85 (ISBN 0-448-13922-7); pap. 3.95 (ISBN 0-448-47335-6). Platt.

Winnie-the-Pooh Do-It-Yourself Counting Book. (Golden Play & Learn Bk.). 14p. (ps). Date not set. pap. 2.95 (ISBN 0-307-10727-2, Golden Pr). Western Pub.

NUMBER GAMES

see Mathematical Recreations

NUMBER RHYMES

see Counting-Out Rhymes

NUMBER SYMBOLISM

see Symbolism of Numbers

NUMBER THEORY

see Numbers, Theory of

NUMBERS, THEORY OF

see also Fields, Algebraic; Groups, Theory of; Numeration; Partitions (Mathematics); Recursive Functions

Dickson, Leonard E. On Varients & Theory of Numbers. 1967. pap. 2.00 (ISBN 0-486-61667-3). Dover.

Siegel, C. L. Topics in Complex Function Theory, 3 vols. Incl. Vol. 1. Elliptical Functions & Uniformization Theory. 1969. 26.95 (ISBN 0-471-79070-2); Vol. 2. Automorphic Functions & Abelian Integrals. 1972. 26.95 (ISBN 0-471-79080-X); Vol. 3. Abelian Functions & Modular Functions of Several Variables. Tretkoff, M. & Gottschling, E., trs. 244p. 1973. 29.95 (ISBN 0-471-79090-7). LC 69-19931. (Pure & Applied Mathematics Ser., Pub. by Wiley-Interscience). Wiley.

Theory of Numbers, Mathematical Analysis & Their Applications. LC 79-20552. (Proceedings of the Steklov Institute). 1979. 60.00 (ISBN 0-8218-3042-2, STEKLO 142). Am Math.

Vaughan, R. C. The Hardy-Littlewood Method. (Cambridge Tracts in Mathematics: No. 80). 160p. Date not set. price not set (ISBN 0-521-23439-5). Cambridge U Pr.

NUMERATION

see also Decimal System

McNamara, Terry S. Numeracy & Accounting. (Illus.). 370p. 1979. pap. text ed. 16.95x (ISBN 0-7121-1411-4, Pub. by Macdonald & Evans England). Intl Ideas.

NUMERATION–JUVENILE LITERATURE

Count to Ten. (Block Bk.). (Illus.). (ps). 1981. 2.50 (ISBN 0-686-69367-1, Golden Pr). Western Pub.

Kraus, Robert. Goodnight Little One. (Illus.). 32p. (ps-2). 1981. paper over board 1.95 (ISBN 0-671-41091-1, Pub. by Windmill). S&S.

Mann, Philip. Contando Para Divirtirme. Kreps, Georgian, tr. from Eng. (Shape Board Play Books). Orig. Title: Counting for Fun. (Illus.). 14p. (Span.). (ps-3). 1981. bds. 3.50 plastic com bdg (ISBN 0-89828-203-9, 5003SP). Tuffy Bks.

Rosenburg, Amye, illus. One, Two, Buckle My Shoe. (Floppies Ser.). (Illus.). 6p. (ps-k). Date not set. 3.95 (ISBN 0-671-42532-3, Little Simon). S&S.

Schulz, Charles M., illus. Tubby Book Featuring Snoopy. (Tubby Bks.). (Illus.). 10p. (ps). 1980. vinyl book 2.95 (ISBN 0-671-41335-X, Pub. by Windmill). S&S.

NUMERATION OF BOOKS IN LIBRARIES

see Alphabeting

NUMERICAL ANALYSIS

see also Digital Filters (Mathematics); Finite Element Method; Iterative Methods (Mathematics); Monte Carlo Method; Numerical Integration

Davies, Alan J. The Finite Element Method: A First Approach. (Oxford Applied Mathematics & Computing Science Ser.). (Illus.). 300p. 1980. 49.50x (ISBN 0-19-859630-8); pap. 27.50x (ISBN 0-19-859631-6). Oxford U Pr.

Lewis, R. W. & Morgan, K. Numerical Methods in Heat Transfer. Zienkiewicz, O. C., ed. (Numerical Methods in Engineering Ser.). 1981. price not set (ISBN 0-471-27803-3, Pub. by Wiley-Interscience). Wiley.

Moorhead, Jack, ed. Numerical Control Applications. LC 80-52613. (Manufacturing Update Ser.). (Illus.). 260p. 1980. 29.00 (ISBN 0-87263-058-7). SME.

--Numerical Control Fundamentals. LC 80-52723. (Manufacturing Update Ser.). (Illus.). 242p. 1980. 29.00 (ISBN 0-87263-057-9). SME.

Pressman, R. S. & Williams, J. E. Numerical Control & Computer-Aided Manufacturing. 310p. 1977. text ed. 24.95 (ISBN 0-471-01555-5). Wiley.

NUMERICAL ANALYSIS–DATA PROCESSING

Poirot, James, et al. Practice in Computers & Mathematics. 227p. (Orig.). (gr. 11-12). 1980. pap. text ed. 5.95 (ISBN 0-88408-126-5). Sterling Swift.

NUMERICAL FILTERS

see Digital Filters (Mathematics)

NUMERICAL INTEGRATION

Antoine, Jaen-Pierre & Tirapegui, Enrique, eds. Functional Integration--Theory & Applications. 355p. 1980. 42.50 (ISBN 0-306-40573-3, Plenum Pr). Plenum Pub.

NUMERICAL SEQUENCES

see Sequences (Mathematics)

NUMEROLOGY

see Symbolism of Numbers

NUMISMATICS

see also Medals; Seals (Numismatics)

Beginners Coin Collecting Kit: For U. S. Coins. (gr. 4 up). 1980. 5.95 (ISBN 0-307-09394-8). Western Pubs OH.

Internaional Numismatic Symposium, Warsaw & Budapest, 1976. Proceedings. Niro-Sey, K. & Gedai, I., eds. (Illus.). 221p. 1980. 27.50x (ISBN 963-05-2055-9). Intl Pubns Serv.

The Numismatic Index: (1888-1978, Vol. 1-99. LC 80-69614. 204p. 1980. pap. 4.95 (ISBN 0-89637-001-1). Am Numismatic.

Price, Martin J., ed. Coins: An Illustrated Survey, 650 B.C. to the Present Day. (Illus.). 320p. 1980. slipcased 50.00 (ISBN 0-416-00691-4). Methuen Inc.

NUMISMATICS–COLLECTORS AND COLLECTING

Andrews, Charles J. Fell's United States Coin Book. 9th rev. ed. LC 73-11213. (Illus.). 156p. 1981. 9.95 (ISBN 0-8119-0349-4); pap. 5.95 (ISBN 0-8119-0421-0). Fell.

Badnow, William R., ed. Edmund's United States Coin Prices. (Orig.). 1981. pap. 2.50 (ISBN 0-440-01794-7, Pub. by Edmund). Dell.

Bale, Don, Jr. Fabulous Investment Potental of Singles. 4th, rev. ed. 1980. pap. 5.00. Bale Bks.

--Fabulous Investment Potential of Uncirculated Singles. 4th, rev. ed. 1980. pap. 5.00. Bale Bks.

--Gold Mine in Gold. 4th, rev. ed. 1980. pap. 5.00. Bale Bks.

--Gold Mine in Your Pocket. 4th, rev. ed. 1980. pap. 5.00. Bale Bks.

--How to Find Valuable Old & Scarce Coins. 4th, rev. ed. 1980. pap. 5.00. Bale Bks.

--How to Invest in Singles. 4th, rev. ed. 1980. pap. 5.00. Bale Bks.

--How to Invest in Uncirculated Singles. 4th, rev. ed. 1980. pap. 5.00. Bale Bks.

--Out of Little Coins, Big Fortunes Grow. 4th, rev. ed. 1980. pap. 5.00. Bale Bks.

Bale, Don, Jr., ed. Fabulous Investment Potential of Liberty Walking Half Dollars. 4th, rev. ed. 1980. pap. 5.00. Bale Bks.

Galster, Georg. Sy loge of Coins of the British Isles-National Museum, Copenhagen, Royal Collection of Coins & Medals: Anglo-Saxon Coins, Aethelred II, Vol. 2. 1966. 25.75x (ISBN 0-19-725896-4). Oxford U Pr.

Grierson, Philip. Later Medieval Numismatics (11th-16th Centuries) 1980. 60.00x (ISBN 0-86078-043-0, Pub. by Variorum England). State Mutual Bk.

Hobson, Burton H. Coin Collecting As a Hobby. rev. ed. LC 67-27759. (Illus.). (gr. 6 up). 1980. 7.95 (ISBN 0-8069-6018-3); PLB 7.49 (ISBN 0-8069-6019-1). Sterling.

NUREMBERG TRIAL OF MAJOR GERMAN WAR CRIMINALS, 1945-1946

Smith, Bradley. The Road to Nuremberg. LC 80-68174. 336p. 1980. 13.95 (ISBN 0-465-07056-6). Basic.

Smith, Bradley F. The American Road to Nuremberg: The Documentary Record, 1944-1945. LC 80-83830. 234p. 1981. price not set (ISBN 0-8179-7481-4). Hoover Inst Pr.

NURSE AND PATIENT

Frik, Seigina M., et al. Chronic Care Nursing. 304p. 1981. text ed. price not set (ISBN 0-8261-3010-0); pap. text ed. price not set (ISBN 0-8261-3011-9). Springer Pub.

Gordon, Laura B. Behavioral Intervention in Health Care. (Behavioral Sciences for Health Care Professionals Ser.). 128p. 1981. lib. bdg. 15.00x (ISBN 0-86531-018-1); pap. text ed. 6.00x (ISBN 0-86531-019-X). Westview.

Sundeen, Sandra, et al. Nurse-Client Interaction: Implementing the Nursing Process. (Illus.). 260p. 1981. pap. text ed. 11.95 (ISBN 0-8016-4844-0). Mosby.

NURSE-PATIENT RELATIONSHIP
see Nurse and Patient

NURSERIES

Cohan & Yoshikawa. Nursery Management. 1982. text ed. 16.95 (ISBN 0-8359-5051-4); instr's. manual free (ISBN 0-8359-5052-2). Reston.

NURSERIES (HORTICULTURE)
see also Plant Propagation

Davidson, Harold & Mechlenburg, Roy. Nursery Management: Administration & Culture. (Illus.). 464p. 1981. text ed. 19.95 (ISBN 0-13-627455-2). P-H.

Toogood, Alan & Stanley, John. The Modern Nurseryman. (Illus.). 432p. 1981. 45.00 (ISBN 0-571-11544-6, Pub. by Faber & Faber); pap. 22.00 (ISBN 0-571-11547-0). Merrimack Bk Serv.

NURSERY RHYMES
see also Children's Poetry; Counting-Out Rhymes

De Paola, Tomie. The Comic Adventures of Old Mother Hubbard & Her Dog. LC 80-19270. (Illus.). 32p. (ps-3). 1981. pap. 5.95 (ISBN 0-15-219542-4, VoyB). HarBraceJ.

Hillman, Priscilla. A Merry-Mouse Book of Nursery Rhymes. LC 80-2053. (Illus.). 32p. (gr. k-1). 1981. 4.95a (ISBN 0-385-17102-1); PLB (ISBN 0-385-17103-X). Doubleday.

Howard, Nina. Barber, Barber, Shave a Pig. 16p. (ps-k). 1981. tchr's ed. 4.95 (ISBN 0-917206-13-4). Children Learn Ctr.

Joyful Nursery Rhymes. (Children's Library of Picture Bks.). (Illus.). 10p. (ps). 1979. 1.95 (ISBN 0-89346-179-2, TA63, Froebel-Kan Japan). Heian Intl.

NURSERY SCHOOLS
see also Day Care Centers; Education, Preschool

Clift, Phillip, et al. The Aims, Role & Deployment of Staff in the Nursery. (Report of the National Foundation for Educational Research in England & Wales). 224p. 1980. pap. text ed. 18.75x (ISBN 0-85633-197-X). Humanities.

Eliason, Claudia & Jenkins, Loa T. A Practical Guide to Early Childhood Curriculum. 2nd ed. (Illus.). 330p. 1981. pap. text ed. 12.95 (ISBN 0-8016-1511-9). Mosby.

Taylor, Katharine W. Parents & Children Learn Together: Parent Cooperative Nursery Schools. 3rd ed. 1981. pap. 6.95 (ISBN 0-8077-2638-9). Tchrs Coll.

NURSERY SCHOOLS–MUSIC
see also Games with Music

Zeitlin, Patty. A Song Is a Rainbow: Body Movement, Music, & Rythym Instruments in the Nursery School & Kindergarten. 336p. (Orig.). pap. 12.95 (ISBN 0-8302-8196-7). Goodyear.

NURSES–CORRESPONDENCE, REMINISCENCES, ETC.

Breckinridge, Mary. Wide Neighborhoods: A Story of the Frontier Nursing Service. (Illus.). 400p. 1981. 18.50 (ISBN 0-8131-1453-5); pap. 8.50 (ISBN 0-8131-0149-2). U Pr of Ky.

NURSES' AIDES

Caldwell, Esther & Hegner, Barbara. Health Assistant. 288p. 1981. text ed. 13.95 (ISBN 0-442-21850-8). Van Nos Reinhold.

NURSES AND NURSING
see also Cancer Nursing; Cardiovascular Disease Nursing; Children–Care and Hygiene; Convalescence; Cookery for the Sick; Diet in Disease; Emergency Nursing; First Aid in Illness and Injury; Geriatric Nursing; Gynecologic Nursing; Home Nursing; Hospitalers; Hospitals; Infants–Care and Hygiene; Labor and Laboring Classes–Medical Care; Men Nurses; Nurse and Patient; Nurses' Aides; Obstetrical Nursing; Pediatric Nursing; Practical Nursing; Psychiatric Nursing; School Nursing; Sick; Surgical Nursing
also subdivisions Hospitals, Charities, etc. and Medical and Sanitary Affairs under names of wars, e.g. United States–History–Civil War, 1861-1865–Hospitals, Charities, etc.; World War, 1939-1945–Medical and Sanitary Affairs

Aspinall, Mary Jo & Tanner, Christine. Experiences in Medical Surgical Nursing. 480p. 1981. pap. 14.95 (ISBN 0-8385-2481-8). ACC.

Austin, Eileen K. Guidelines for the Development of Continuing Education Offerings for Nurses. 176p. 1981. pap. 11.00 (ISBN 0-8385-3524-0). ACC.

Block, Gloria & Nolan, Joellen. Health Assessment for Professional Nursing: A Developmental Approach. 496p. 1981. 24.95 (ISBN 0-8385-3660-3). ACC.

Bloom, Arnold. Toohey's Medicine for Nurses. 13th ed. (Illus.). 1981. pap. text ed. 17.50 (ISBN 0-443-02301-1). Churchill.

Bower, F. L. Nursing & the Concept of Loss. 214p. 1980. 10.95 (ISBN 0-471-04790-2). Wiley.

Britton, Frances. Basic Nursing Skills. (Illus.). 224p. 1981. pap. text ed. 7.95 (ISBN 0-87619-921-X). R J Brady.

Brown, Mary L. Occupational Health Nursing. LC 80-21024. 368p. 1981. text ed. 21.95 (ISBN 0-8261-2250-7); pap. text ed. cancelled (ISBN 0-8261-2251-5). Springer Pub.

Brown, R. G. The Male Nurse. 139p. 1973. pap. text ed. 5.00x (ISBN 0-7135-1878-2, Pub. by Bedford England). Renouf.

Cohen, Helen A. The Nurse's Quest for a Professional Identity. 1980. 14.95 (ISBN 0-201-00956-0); pap. 9.95 (ISBN 0-201-01157-3). A-W.

Creighton, Margo N. & Cohen, Patricia F. Nursing Care Planning Guides for Long Term Care. 1980. pap. write for info. (ISBN 0-935236-13-9). Nurseco.

Creighton, Margo N. & Reighley, Joan. Nursing Care Planning Guides, Set 5. 1981. pap. 11.95 (ISBN 0-935236-14-7). Nurseco.

Donnelly, G. F., et al. The Nursing System: Issues, Ethics & Politics. LC 80-12402. 224p. 1980. 10.95 (ISBN 0-471-04441-5). Wiley.

Edwards, Barba J. & Brilhart, John K. Communications in Nursing Practice. (Illus.). 240p. 1981. pap. text ed. 9.95 (ISBN 0-8016-0786-8). Mosby.

Ellis, Janice R. & Nowlis, Elizabeth A. Nursing: A Human Needs Approach. 2nd ed. LC 80-82841. (Illus.). 528p. 1981. text ed. 17.95 (ISBN 0-395-29642-0); price not set instr's. manual (ISBN 0-395-29643-9). HM.

Emanuelsen, Kathy L. & Densmore, Mary J. Acute Respiratory Care. Percy, R. Craig, ed. (The Fleschner Series in Critical Care Nursing). (Illus.). 190p. (Orig.). 1981. pap. text ed. 9.95 (ISBN 0-937878-01-4). Fleschner.

Epstein, Charlotte. Leadership in Nursing. 225p. 1981. text ed. 14.95 (ISBN 0-8359-3970-7); pap. text ed. 12.95 (ISBN 0-8359-3969-3). Reston.

Eriksen, Karin. Human Services Today. 2nd ed. 192p. 1981. text ed. 12.95 (ISBN 0-8359-3004-1). Reston.

Evans, M. L. & Hansen, B. D. Guide to Pediatric Nursing: A Clinical Reference. 284p. 1980. pap. 14.95 (ISBN 0-8385-3533-X). ACC.

Farley, Vepner. Second Level Nursing: Study Modules. LC 80-70482. (Associate Degree Nursing Ser.). (Illus.). 272p. (Orig.). 1981. pap. text ed. price not set (ISBN 0-8273-1876-6); price not set instr's. guide (ISBN 0-8273-1877-4). Delmar.

Freeman, Ruth B. & Heinrich, Janet. Community Health Nursing Practice. 2nd ed. (Illus.). 500p. 1981. text ed. price not set (ISBN 0-7216-3877-5). Saunders.

Friedman, Marilyn M. Family Nursing: Theory & Assessment. 337p. 1981. pap. 16.50 (ISBN 0-8385-2532-6). ACC.

Gerald, Michael C. & O'Bannon, Freda V. Nursing Pharmacology. (Illus.). 544p. 1981. text ed. 22.95 (ISBN 0-13-627505-2). P-H.

Gillies, Dee A. & Alyn, Irene B. Saunders Tests for Self-Evaluation of Nursing Competence. rev. ed. 1980. text ed. write for info. (ISBN 0-7216-4157-1). Saunders.

Glenn, J. Si Units for Nursing. 1981. pap. text ed. 5.15 (ISBN 0-06-318180-0, Pub. by Har-Row Ltd England). Har-Row.

Green, Marilyn L. & Harry, Joann. Nutrition in Contemporary Nursing Practice. 752p. 1981. 17.95 (ISBN 0-471-03892-X, Pub. by Wiley Med). Wiley.

Hagarty, Catherine. Revelations of an Army Nurse. 1981. 6.75 (ISBN 0-8062-1591-7). Carlton.

Hamilton, Ardith J. Critical Care Nursing Skills. 256p. 1981. pap. 12.95 (ISBN 0-8385-1242-9). ACC.

Hart, Laura K. The Arithmetic of Dosages & Solutions. 5th ed. (Illus.). 100p. 1981. spiral bdg. 7.95 (ISBN 0-8016-2076-7). Mosby.

Hockey, Lisbeth, ed. Current Issues in Nursing. (Recent Advances in Nursing Ser.). 200p. 1981. pap. text ed. 14.00 (ISBN 0-443-02186-4). Churchill.

Kernicki, Jeanette & Weiler, Kathi. Electocardiography for Nurses: Physiological Correlates Electrical Disturbances of the Heart. 304p. 1981. 17.95 (ISBN 0-471-05752-5, Pub. by Wiley Med). Wiley.

Kine, R. Carole, et al. Basic Science Nursing Review. LC 80-22950. 208p. (Orig.). 1981. pap. text ed. 8.00 (ISBN 0-668-05133-7, 5133). Arco.

Lancaster, Arnold. Nursery & Midwifery Sourcebook. 304p. 1980. 25.00x (Pub. by Beaconsfield England). State Mutual Bk.

Long, Rosemary. Systematic Nursing Care. (Illus.). 96p. 1981. 21.00 (ISBN 0-571-11615-9, Pub. by Faber & Faber); pap. 7.95 (ISBN 0-686-28936-6). Merrimack Bk Serv.

MacGuire, Jillian. Threshold to Nursing. 271p. 1969. pap. text ed. 5.00x (Pub. by Bedford England). Renouf.

Massachusetts General Hospital Department of Nursing, et al, eds. Manual of Nursing Procedures. 1980. text ed. write for info. (ISBN 0-316-54958-4); pap. text ed. price not set (ISBN 0-316-54958-4). Little.

Masson, VeNeta. International Nursing. 1981. text ed. price not set (ISBN 0-8261-3170-0); pap. text ed. price not set (ISBN 0-8261-3171-9). Springer Pub.

Medications & Mathematics for the Nurse. 288p. 1981. text ed. 13.95 (ISBN 0-442-21882-6). Van Nos Reinhold.

Mirin, Susan R. The Nurses Guide to Writing for Publication. LC 80-84085. (Nursing Dimension Education Ser & Nursing Dimension Administrative Ser.). 180p. 1981. text ed. 14.50 (ISBN 0-913654-71-X). Nursing Res.

Moore, Mary L. The Newborn & the Nurse. 2nd ed. (Illus.). 450p. 1981. text ed. price not set (ISBN 0-7216-6491-1). Saunders.

Neal, Margo C. & Cohen, Patricia F. Nursing Care Planning Guides, Set 2. 2nd ed. 1980. pap. 11.95 (ISBN 0-935236-16-3). Nurseco.

Neal, Margo C. & Cooper, Signe S., eds. Perspectives on Continuing Education in Nursing. 1980. pap. text ed. 11.95 (ISBN 0-935236-12-0). Nurseco.

Notes on Nursing, 2 bks. Incl. Bk. 1. The Science & the Art. Nightingale, Florence. 50p; Bk. 2. What It Is & What It Is Not. Skeet, Muriel. 75p. 1980. Set. 20.00 (ISBN 0-443-02130-9). Churchill.

Nursing Development Conference Group. Concept Formalization in Nursing: Process & Product. 2nd ed. LC 79-88164. 313p. 1979. text ed. 12.95 (ISBN 0-316-61421-1). Little.

Parse. Man-Living-Health: A Theory of Nursing. 192p. 1981. pap. 11.95 (ISBN 0-471-04443-1, Pub. by Wiley Med). Wiley.

Pembrey, Sue. The Ward Sister. (RCN Research Monograph). 184p. 1981. pap. text ed. 10.00 (ISBN 0-443-02411-1). Churchill.

Performing G. I. Procedures. (Nursing Photobook Ser.). (Illus.). 1981. 12.95 (ISBN 0-916730-31-X). Intermed Comm.

Pillitteri, Adele. Child Health Nursing: Care of the Growing Family. 2nd ed. 1981. text ed. write for info (ISBN 0-316-70793-7). Little.

Pomeranz, Ruth. The Lady Apprentices. 144p. 1973. pap. text ed. 5.00x (ISBN 0-7135-1868-5, Pub. by Bedford England). Renouf.

Price, James L. & Mueller, Charles W. Professional Turnover: The Case of Nurses. (Health Systems Management Ser.). 218p. 1980. write for info. (ISBN 0-89335-124-5). Spectrum Pub.

Redman, Barbara K. Issues and Concepts in Patient Education. (The Patient Education Series). 160p. 1981. pap. 11.50 (ISBN 0-8385-4405-3). ACC.

Redman, Barbara K., ed. Patterns for Distribution of Patient Education. (The Patient Education Series). 176p. 1981. pap. 11.50 (ISBN 0-8385-7776-8). ACC.

Riffle, Kathryn L., ed. Rehabilitative Nursing Case Studies. 1979. pap. 9.50 (ISBN 0-87488-035-1). Med Exam.

Roy, Callista & Roberts, Sharon. Theory Construction in Nursing: An Adaptation Model. (Illus.). 352p. 1981. text ed. 17.95 (ISBN 0-13-913657-6). P-H.

Rudman, Jack. Adult Nursing. (College Proficiency Examination Ser.: CLEP-35). (Cloth bdg. avail. on request). pap. 9.95 (ISBN 0-8373-5435-8). Natl Learning.

Seedor, Marie M. Aids to Nursing Diagnosis. 3rd ed. (Nursing Education Monograph: No. 6). 1980. pap. 8.95 (ISBN 0-397-54120-1, Pub. by Columbia U Pr). Lippincott.

--Aids to Nursing Diagnosis: A Programmed Unit in Fundamentals of Nursing. 3rd ed. 378p. (Orig.). 1980. pap. text ed. 8.50 (ISBN 0-8077-2630-3). Tchrs Coll.

Smith, Dorothy W., et al. Survival of Illness: Implications for Nursing. 1981. pap. text ed. 9.95 (ISBN 0-8261-2871-8). Springer Pub.

Spradley, Barbara W. Community Health Nursing: Concepts & Practice. 1981. text ed. price not set (ISBN 0-316-80748-6). Little.

Stewart Conference on Research in Nursing, Sixteenth. Perspectives on Nursing Leadership: Proceedings. Ketefian, Shake, ed. LC 80-27464. (Orig.). 1981. pap. text ed. 10.95 (ISBN 0-8077-2637-0). Tchrs Coll.

Tinker, Jack & Porter, Susan W. A Course in Intensive Therapy Nursing. 294p. 1980. 30.00x (ISBN 0-7131-4347-9, Pub. by Arnold Pubs England). State Mutual Bk.

Trounce, J. R. Clinical Pharmacology for Nurses. 9th ed. (Illus.). 432p. 1981. pap. text ed. 10.00 (ISBN 0-443-02333-6). Churchill.

Vredevoe, Donna L., et al. Concepts of Oncology Nursing. (Illus.). 400p. 1981. text ed. 18.95 (ISBN 0-13-166587-1). P-H.

Yura. Nursing Leadership: Theory & Process. 2nd ed. (Illus.). 1980. pap. 11.95 (ISBN 0-8385-7028-3). ACC.

NURSES AND NURSING–BIBLIOGRAPHY

Strauch, K. P. & Brundage, D. J. Guide to Library Resources for Nursing. 509p. 1980. pap. 12.75 (ISBN 0-8385-3528-3). ACC.

NURSES AND NURSING–EXAMINATIONS, QUESTIONS, ETC.

Riddle, Janet T. & Dinner, Joan. Objective Tests for Nurses, Book 2. (Objective Tests for Nurses Ser.). (Illus.). 112p. 1981. pap. text ed. 6.95 (ISBN 0-443-01740-9). Churchill.

Steele, Bonnie G. Self-Assessment of Current Knowledge in General Surgical Nursing. 1978. spiral bdg. 9.50 (ISBN 0-87488-290-7). Med Exam.

Stoltzfus, Doris. Self-Assessment of Current Knowledge in Mental Health Nursing. 1979. spiral bdg. 9.50 (ISBN 0-87488-264-8). Med Exam.

Turner, Phyllis S. Self-Assessment of Current Knowledge in Intensive Care Nursing. 1980. pap. 9.75 (ISBN 0-87488-227-3). Med Exam.

NURSES AND NURSING–HISTORY

Breckinridge, Mary. Wide Neighborhoods: A Story of the Frontier Nursing Service. (Illus.). 400p. 1981. 18.50 (ISBN 0-8131-1453-5); pap. 8.50 (ISBN 0-8131-0149-2). U Pr of Ky.

Davies, Celia, ed. Rewriting Nursing History. 226p. 1981. 23.50x (ISBN 0-389-20153-7). B&N.

NURSES AND NURSING–LEGAL STATUS, LAWS, ETC.

Young, A. Nursing the Law. 1981. text ed. 19.80 (ISBN 0-06-318181-9, Pub. by Har-Row Ltd England); pap. text ed. 10.45 (ISBN 0-686-69150-4). Har-Row.

NURSES AND NURSING–PROGRAMMED INSTRUCTION

Massachussetts General Hospital. Dept. of Nursing Staff Education Manual. Stetler, Cheryl B., et al, eds. 1981. text ed. 34.95 (ISBN 0-8359-1281-7). Reston.

NURSES AND NURSING–PSYCHOLOGICAL ASPECTS

Reilly, Dorothy. Behavioral Objectives-Evaluation in Nursing. 2nd ed. 200p. 1980. pap. text ed. 11.95 (ISBN 0-8385-0634-8). ACC.

NURSES AND NURSING–RESEARCH
see Nursing Research

NURSES AND NURSING–STUDY AND TEACHING
see also Nursing Schools

Blomquist, Kathleen B., et al. Community Health Nursing Continuing Education Review. 1979. pap. 9.50 (ISBN 0-87488-401-2). Med Exam.

Brill, E. L. & Kilts, D. F. Foundations for Nursing. 813p. 1980. text ed. 24.95 (ISBN 0-8385-2687-X). ACC.

Horsely, Joanne. Structured Preoperative Teaching: Using Research to Improve Clinical Practice. 1980. 9.50 (ISBN 0-8089-1311-5). Grune.

NURSING (INFANT FEEDING)
see Breast Feeding

NURSING ETHICS
see also Medical Ethics

Benjamin, Martin & Curtis, Joy. Ethics in Nursing. 250p. 1981. text ed. 13.95x (ISBN 0-19-502836-8); pap. text ed. 7.95x (ISBN 0-19-502837-6). Oxford U Pr.

NURSING HOMES
see also Geriatric Nursing

Bloom, Barbara. Utilization Patterns and Financial Characteristics of Nursing Homes in the United States: 1977 Nnhs. Shipp, Audrey, ed. (Series Thirteen: No. 53). 50p. 1981. pap. 1.75 (ISBN 0-8406-0215-4). Natl Ctr Health Stats.

Burstein. The Get Well Hotel. 113p. Date not set. lib. bdg. 4.95 (ISBN 0-07-009244-3). McGraw.

Conger, Shirley & Moore, Kay. Social Work in Long-Term Care Facilities. 160p. 1981. 15.95 (ISBN 0-8436-0850-1). CBI Pub.

Creighton, Margo N. & Cohen, Patricia F. Nursing Care Planning Guides for Long Term Care. 1980. pap. write for info. (ISBN 0-935236-13-9). Nurseco.

Davies, Bleddyn & Knapp, Martin. Old People's Homes & the Production of Welfare. (Library of Social Work Ser.). 240p. 1981. 32.50 (ISBN 0-7100-0700-0). Routledge & Kegan.

Foley, Daniel J. Nursing Home Estimates for California, Illinois, Massachusetts, New York & Texas from the 1977 National Nursing Home Survey. Olmsted, Mary, ed. (Ser. 13-48). 50p. 1980. pap. text ed. 1.75 (ISBN 0-8406-0190-5). Natl Ctr Health Stats.

Hing, Ester. Characteristics of Nursing Home Residents Health Status, & Care Received: National Nursing Home Survey, May-December 1977. Cox, Klaudia, ed. 60p. 1981. pap. 1.95 (ISBN 0-8406-0212-X). Natl Ctr Health Stats.

Sirrocco, Al. Employees in Nursing Homes: National Nursing Home Survey, 1977. Cox, Klaudia, ed. (Ser. Fourteen: No. 25). 50p. 1981. pap. text ed. 1.50 (ISBN 0-8406-0213-8). Natl Ctr Health Stats.

Strahan, Geneviene W. Inpatient Health Facilities Statistics United States, 1978. Olmsted, Mary, ed. (Ser. 14, No. 24). 50p. 1980. pap. text ed. 1.75 (ISBN 0-8406-0204-9). Natl Ctr Educ Broker.

Welter, Paul R. The Nursing Home: A Caring Community Staff Manuel. 96p. 1981. pap. 2.95 (ISBN 0-8170-0935-3). Judson.

--The Nursing Home: A Caring Community-Trainers' Manual. 176p. 1981. pap. 9.95 (ISBN 0-8170-0934-5). Judson.

Zappolo, Aurora. Discharge from Nursing Homes: 1977 National Nursing Home Survey. Cox, Klaudia, ed. (Ser. 13: No. 54). 60p. 1981. pap. 1.75 (ISBN 0-8406-0216-2). Natl Ctr Health Stats.

NURSING LAW
see Nurses and Nursing–Legal Status, Laws, etc.

NURSING PSYCHOLOGY
see Nurses and Nursing–Psychological Aspects

NURSING RESEARCH

Fox, D. J. & Leeser, I. Readings on the Research Process in Nursing. 232p. 1981. pap. 16.50 (ISBN 0-686-69604-2). ACC.

Trussell, Patricia, et al. Finding, Reading & Interpreting Nursing Research. LC 80-84150. 225p. 1981. text ed. price not set (ISBN 0-913654-70-1). Nursing Res.

Williamson, Yvonne M. Research Methodology & Its Application to Nursing. 360p. 1981. 13.95 (ISBN 0-471-03313-8, Pub. by Wiley Med). Wiley.

NURSING SCHOOLS

Wold, Susan J. School Nursing: A Framework for Practice. (Illus.). 530p. 1981. pap. text ed. 15.95 (ISBN 0-8016-5611-7). Mosby.

NUT CULTURE
see Nuts

NUTRITION
see also Animal Nutrition; Diet; Feeds; Food; Food Habits; Malnutrition; Metabolism; Minerals in the Body; Vitamins
also subdivision Nutrition under subjects, e.g. Children–Nutrition

Adams, Ruth. Eating in Eden. 196p. (Orig.). 1976. pap. 1.75 (ISBN 0-915962-16-0). Larchmont Bks.
Adams, Ruth & Murray, Frank. All You Should Know About Beverages for Your Health & Well Being. 286p. 1976. pap. 1.75 (ISBN 0-915962-17-9). Larchmont Bks.
--All You Should Know About Health Foods. 352p. pap. 2.50 (ISBN 0-915962-01-2). Larchmont Bks.
--The Good Seeds, the Rich Grains, the Hardy Nuts for a Healthier, Happier Life. rev. ed. 303p. 1973. pap. 1.75 (ISBN 0-915962-07-1). Larchmont Bks.
--Is Blood Sugar Making You a Nutritional Cripple? rev. ed. 174p. (Orig.). 1975. pap. 1.75 (ISBN 0-915962-11-X). Larchmont Bks.
--Megavitamin Therapy. 277p. (Orig.). 1973. pap. 1.95. Larchmont Bks.
--Minerals: Kill or Cure. rev. ed. 366p. (Orig.). 1974. pap. 1.95 (ISBN 0-915962-16-0). Larchmont Bks.
--The New High Fiber Diet. 319p. (Orig.). 1977. pap. 2.25 (ISBN 0-915962-21-7). Larchmont Bks.
Austin, James E., ed. Nutrition Programs in the Third World: Cases & Concepts. LC 80-21083. 464p. 1981. lib. bdg. 27.50 (ISBN 0-89946-024-0). Oelgeschlager.
Austin, James E. & Zeitlin, Marian F., eds. Nutrition Intervention in Developing Countries: An Overview. LC 80-29223. (Nutrition Intervention in Developing Countries Ser.). 256p. 1981. lib. bdg. 20.00 (ISBN 0-89946-077-1). Oelgeschlager.
Beasley, Sonia. The Spirulina Cookbook: Recipes for Rejuvenating the Body. (Illus.). 160p. (Orig.). 1981. pap. 6.95 (ISBN 0-916438-39-2). Univ of Trees.
Beebe, Brooke, et al. Nutrition & Good Health. LC 78-731300. (Illus.). 1978. pap. text ed. 99.00 (ISBN 0-89290-099-7, A576-SATC). Soc for Visual.
Beers, Roland F. & Bassett, Edward G., eds. Nutritional Factors: Modulating Effects on Metabolic Processes. (Miles International Symposium Ser.: Vol. 13). 1981. text ed. price not set (ISBN 0-89004-592-5). Raven.
Bland, Jeffrey. Your Health Under Siege: Using Nutrition to Fight Back. 256p. 1981. 12.95 (ISBN 0-8289-0415-4). Greene.
Borsook, Henry. Vitamins: What They Are. (Orig.). pap. 1.75 (ISBN 0-515-05132-2). Jove Pubns.
Bourne, G. H., ed. Human Nutrition & Diet. (World Review of Nutrition & Dietetics Ser.: Vol. 36). (Illus.). x, 226p. 1980. 115.00 (ISBN 3-8055-1347-X). S Karger.
--World Review of Nutrition & Dietetics, Vol. 37. (Illus.). x, 240p. 1981. 115.00 (ISBN 3-8055-2143-X). S Karger.
Bradley, Richard. The Country Housewife & Lady's Director. 500p. 1980. Repr. of 1736 ed. 37.50x (ISBN 0-907325-01-7, Pub. by Prospect England). U Pr of Va.
Brody, Jane. Jane Brody's Nutrition Book: A Lifetime Guide to Good Eating for Better Health & Weight Conrol by the Personal Health Columnist for the New Yok Times. (Illus.). 1981. 17.95 (ISBN 0-393-01429-0). Norton.
Brown, Jo G. The Good Food Compendium. LC 78-22306. (Illus.). 336p. 1981. pap. 10.95 (ISBN 0-385-13523-8, Dolp). Doubleday.
Cadwallader, Sharon. Whole Earth Cooking for the Eighties. (Illus.). 128p. 1981. 9.95 (ISBN 0-312-87050-7); pap. 5.95 (ISBN 0-312-87051-5). St Martin.
Calabrese, Edward J. Nutrition & Environmental Health: The Influence of Nutritional Status on Pollutant Toxicity & Carcinogenicity, 2 vols. Incl. Vol. 1. The Vitamins. 60.00 (ISBN 0-471-04833-X); Vol. 2. Minerals & Macronutrients. 544p. 35.00 (ISBN 0-471-08207-4). LC 79-21089. (Environmental Science & Technology Ser.). 1980 (Pub. by Wiley-Interscience). Wiley.
Carbohydrates in Human Nutrition. (Food & Nutrition Paper Ser.: No. 15). 82p. 1980. pap. 6.00 (ISBN 92-5-100903-1, F2040, FAO). Unipub.
Chicago Dietetic Association & South Suburban Dietetic Association. Manual of Clinical Dietetics. 1981. text ed. price not set (ISBN 0-7216-2537-1). Saunders.
Clark, Linda. Know Your Nutrition. rev. ed. LC 80-84437. 275p. 1981. pap. 4.95 (ISBN 0-87983-247-9). Keats.
Cox, Beverly & Benois, George. Cellulite: Defeat It Through Diet & Exercise. (Illus.). 192p. 1981. 12.50 (ISBN 0-8149-0845-4); pap. 9.95 (ISBN 0-8149-0846-2). Vanguard.
Cumming, Candy & Newman, Vicky. Eater's Guide: Nutrition Basics for Busy People. (Illus.). 192p. 1981. 11.95 (ISBN 0-13-223057-7); pap. 5.95 (ISBN 0-13-223040-2). P-H.
Dennison, Darwin. The Dine System: For Better Nutrition & Health. 96p. 1981. pap. text ed. 7.95 (ISBN 0-8403-2371-9). Kendall-Hunt.
Dinaburg & Akel. Nutrition Survival Kit. (Orig.). pap. 1.75 (ISBN 0-515-04654-X). Jove Pubns.
Draper, Harold H., ed. Advances in Nutritional Research, Vols. 1-3. Incl. Vol. 1. 362p. 1977. 27.50 (ISBN 0-306-34321-5); Vol. 2. 264p. 1979. 27.50 (ISBN 0-306-40213-0); Vol. 3. 300p. 1980. 32.50 (ISBN 0-306-40415-X). Plenum Pub. (Illus., Plenum Pr). Plenum Pub.
Easter, Jade. The Healing Handbook. (Illus.). 128p. (Orig.). 1981. pap. 6.95 (ISBN 0-913300-15-2). Unity Pr.
Ellenbogen, Leon. Controversies in Nutrition. (Contemporary Issues in Clinical Nutrition Ser.). (Illus.). 224p. 1981. lib. bdg. 20.00 (ISBN 0-443-08127-1). Churchill.
Ellenboren, Leon. Controversies in Nutrition. (Contemporary Issues in Clinical Nutrition Ser.). 1981. text ed. price not set (ISBN 0-443-08127-1). Churchill.
Fabroni, Al G. Miracle of Natural Self-Cure. 1981. 6.00 (ISBN 0-8062-1581-X). Carlton.
Food Price Policies & Nutrition in Latin America. (Food & Nutrition Bulletin Ser.: Suppl. 3). 170p. 1980. pap. 15.00 (ISBN 92-808-0128-7, TUNU087, UNU). Unipub.
Forman, Robert. How to Control Your Allergies. 256p. (Orig.). 1979. pap. 1.95 (ISBN 0-915962-29-2). Larchmont Bks.
Frompovich, Catherine J. Preventing Burnout: The Nutritional Approach. (Illus.). 145p. Date not set. pap. 50.00 course materials (ISBN 0-935322-14-0). C J Frompovich.
Goeltz, Judith. Jet Stress: What It Is & How to Cope with It. Donsbach, Kurt W., ed. LC 79-89366. 350p. 1980. 9.95 (ISBN 0-86664-000-2). Inst Pubs.
Green, Marilyn L. & Harry, Joann. Nutrition in Contemporary Nursing Practice. 752p. 1981. 17.95 (ISBN 0-471-03892-X, Pub. by Wiley Med). Wiley.
Hafen, Brent Q. Nutrition, Food & Weight Control. 320p. 1980. pap. text ed. 9.95 (ISBN 0-205-06826-X, 6268169); tchr's ed. free (ISBN 0-205-06828-6, 6268285). Allyn.
Hartbarger, Janie C. & Hartbarger, Neil J. Eating for the Eighties: A Complete Guide to Vegetarian Nutrition. LC 80-53187. 320p. 12.95 (ISBN 0-7216-4550-X); pap. 6.95 (ISBN 0-7216-4549-6). Saunders.
Hefferren, John J. & Moller, Mary L., eds. Patterns & Effects of Diet & Disease Today. (AAAS Selected Symposium: No. 59). 225p. 1981. lib. bdg. 18.75x (ISBN 0-89158-844-2). Westview.
Howe, Phyllis. Basic Nutrition in Health & Disease: Including Selection & Care of Food. 7th ed. 450p. 1981. pap. text ed. price not set (ISBN 0-7216-4796-0). Saunders.
Karow, Juliette. The Necessary Diet. (Orig.). 1981. pap. 5.95 (ISBN 0-89865-085-2). Donning Co.
Koniecko, Edward S. Nutritional Encyclopedia for the Elderly. 1981. 12.95 (ISBN 0-8062-1676-X). Carlton.
Kraus, Barbara. Calories & Carbohydrates. 4th, rev. ed. 1981. pap. 5.95 (Z5267, Plume). NAL.
--Calories & Carbohydrates. 4th, rev. ed. (Orig.). 1981. pap. 3.50 (ISBN 0-451-09774-2, E9774, Sig). NAL.
Kunin, Richard A. Mega-Nutrition: The New Prescription for Maximum Health,Energy & Longevity. 1981. pap. 6.95 (ISBN 0-452-25271-7, Z5271, Plume Bks). NAL.
Largen, Velda L. Guide to Nutrition. LC 80-25186. (Illus.). 144p. 1981. text ed. 8.96 (ISBN 0-87006-312-X). Goodheart.
Lesser, Michael. Nutrition & Vitamin Therapy. 224p. 1981. pap. 2.50 (ISBN 0-553-14437-5). Bantam.
McMillen, S. I. None of These Diseases. (Orig.). pap. 1.50 (ISBN 0-515-04604-3). Jove Pubns.
Mannerberg, Donald & Roth, Jane. Aerobic Nutrition: The Long-Life Plan for Ageless Health & Vigor. 1981. 14.95 (ISBN 0-8015-0070-2). Dutton.
Muller, H. G. & Tobin, G. Nutrition & Food Processing. 240p. 1980. 35.00x (ISBN 0-85664-540-0, Pub. by Croom Helm England). State Mutual Bk.
Mulliss, Christine. Goodness! Eating Healthily. 64p. 1977. pap. 4.00x (ISBN 0-8464-1014-1). Beekman Pubs.
Nagy, Steven & Attaway, John, eds. Citrus Nutrition & Quality. LC 80-22562. (ACS Symposium Ser.: No. 143). 1980. 36.25 (ISBN 0-8412-0595-7). Am Chemical.
Newell, Guy R. & Ellison, Neil M., eds. Cancer & Nutrition: Etiology & Treatment. 475p. 1981. 45.00 (ISBN 0-89004-631-X). Raven.
Nutrition & Its Disorders. 3rd ed. (Livingston Medical Text Ser.). (Illus.). 1981. pap. text ed. 15.00 (ISBN 0-443-02158-9). Churchill.
O'Bannon, Dan R. The Ecological & Nutritional Treatment of Health Disorders. (Illus.). 240p. 1981. price not set (ISBN 0-398-04455-4). C C Thomas.
Powell, Eric F. A Home Course in Nutrition. 104p. 1978. pap. 7.50x (ISBN 0-8464-1019-2). Beekman Pubs.
Prince, Francine. Diet for Life. 1981. pap. 4.95 (ISBN 0-346-12496-4). Cornerstone.
Protein Supply-Demands: Changing Styles GA-049. 1981. 800.00 (ISBN 0-89336-287-5). BCC.
Rall, Karen. Beautifood: Looking Better Through Nutrition. LC 80-83615. (Illus.). 160p. (Orig.). 1981. pap. 6.95 (ISBN 0-89087-307-0). Celestial Arts.
Report of the Thirteenth Session Codex Alimentarius Commission. 103p. 1981. pap. 6.00 (ISBN 92-5-100912-0, F2071, FAO). Unipub.
Rubinstein, Helena. Food for Beauty. rev. ed. 256p. 1977. pap. 1.95 (ISBN 0-915962-19-5). Larchmont Bks.
Rush, David, et al, eds. Diet in Pregnancy: A Randomized Controlled Trail of Nutritional Supplements. LC 79-3846. (Alan R. Liss Ser.: Vol. 16, No. 3). 1980. 26.00 (ISBN 0-8451-1037-3). March of Dimes.
Shank, et al. Guide to Modern Meals. O'Neill, Martha, ed. (Illus.). 640p. (gr. 10-12). 1980. 17.28 (ISBN 0-07-056416-7, W); tchrs. resource guide avail. (ISBN 0-07-047514-8). McGraw.
Somogyi, J. C. & Varela, G., eds. Nutritional Deficiencies in Industrialized Countries. (Bibliotheca Nutritic et Dieta Ser.: Vol. 30). (Illus.). 1981. soft cover 48.00 (ISBN 3-8055-1994-X). S Karger.
Spiegel, Janet. Stretching the Food Dollar: Practical Solutions to the Challenges of the 80's. (Urban Life Ser.). (Illus.). 96p. (Orig.). 1981. pap. 4.95 (ISBN 0-87701-172-9). Chronicle Bks.
Sprug, Joseph. Index to Nutrition & Health. (Useful Reference Ser. of Library Books: Vol. 119). 1981. write for info. (ISBN 0-87305-125-4). Faxon.
Stevens, Laura J. & Stoner, Rosemary B. How to Improve Your Child's Behavior Through Diet. 1981. pap. 3.50 (ISBN 0-451-09812-9, E9812, Signet Bks). NAL.
Sumner, Margaret. Thought for Food. (Illus.). 129p. 1981. text ed. 13.95x (ISBN 0-19-217690-0); pap. text ed. 6.95 (ISBN 0-19-286003-8). Oxford U Pr.
Vander, Arthur J. Nutrition, Stress & Toxic Chemicals: An Approach to Environmental Health Controversies. 360p. 1981. text ed. 18.00 (ISBN 0-472-09329-0); pap. 9.95 (ISBN 0-472-06329-4). U of Mich Pr.
Wade, Carlson. What's in It for You? The Shoppers' Complete Guide to Health Store Products. rev. ed. LC 80-84443. (Pivot Original Health Bk.). 144p. (Orig.). 1981. pap. 1.95 (ISBN 0-87983-244-4). Keats.
Wallis, Celestina, et al. Anuska's Complete Body Makeover Book. (Illus.). 224p. 1981. 11.95 (ISBN 0-399-12579-5). Putnam.
Weiner, Michael A. The Sceptical Nutritionist. 256p. 1981. 9.95 (ISBN 0-02-625620-7). Macmillan.
Whitney, Eleanor N. & Hamilton, Eva M. Understanding Nutrition. 2nd ed. (Illus.). 650p. 1981. text ed. 18.95 (ISBN 0-8299-0419-0). West Pub.
Williams, Roger J. The Prevention of Alcoholism Through Nutrition. 176p. (Orig.). 1981. pap. 2.50 (ISBN 0-553-14502-9). Bantam.
Williams, Sue R. Nutrition & Diet Therapy. 4th ed. (Illus.). 875p. 1981. text ed. 19.95 (ISBN 0-8016-5554-4). Mosby.
Winber, Gloria K. Better Eating Habits - A Step by Step Approach. (Illus.). 170p. (Orig.). pap. 5.95. Winfoto.
Winick, M. Nutrition & the Killer Diseases. (Current Concepts in Nutrition Ser.: Vol. 10). 200p. 1981. 24.95 (ISBN 0-471-09130-8, Pub. by Wiley-Interscience). Wiley.
Workshop on the Interfaces Between Agriculture, Nutrition, & Food Science, 1977. Proceedings. 143p. 1979. pap. 7.25 (R087, IRRI). Unipub.
World Nutrition & Nutrition Education. 226p. 1981. 50.50 (ISBN 92-3-101736-5, U1057, UNESCO). Unipub.
Worthington, Bonnie & Taylor, Lynda. Nutrition During Pregnancy & Breast Feeding. (Illus.). 1980. pap. 2.50. Budlong.
Worthington-Roberts, Bonnie S., et al. Nutrition in Pregnancy & Lactation. (Illus.). 296p. 1981. pap. text ed. 11.95 (ISBN 0-8016-5626-5). Mosby.
Wright & Sims. Community Nutrition. 1981. pap. text ed. 11.95 (ISBN 0-686-69107-5). Duxbury Pr.
Yudkin, John. Lose Weight, Feel Great. (Illus.). 219p. 1974. pap. 1.75 (ISBN 0-915962-02-0). Larchmont Bks.

NUTRITION–JUVENILE LITERATURE
O'Connell, Lily H., et al. Nutrition in a Changing World. (Illus.). 152p. (Orig.). (gr. 5). 1981. pap. text ed. 11.95 (ISBN 0-8425-1916-5). Brigham.
Simon, Seymour. About the Food You Eat. Date not set. price not set. McGraw.

NUTRITION–STUDY AND TEACHING
World Nutrition & Nutrition Education. 226p. 1981. 50.50 (ISBN 92-3-101736-5, U1057, UNESCO). Unipub.

NUTRITION DISORDERS
Brewster, Marge A. & Naito, Herbert K., eds. Nutritional Elements & Clinical Biochemistry. 450p. 1980. 45.00 (ISBN 0-306-40569-5, Plenum Pr). Plenum Pub.

NUTRITION OF CHILDREN
see Children–Nutrition; Infants–Nutrition

NUTRITION OF PLANTS
see Plants–Nutrition

NUTS
Nuts, Berries & Grapes. (Country Home Ser.). 96p. 2.95 (ISBN 0-88453-009-4). Berkshire Traveller.

NYAMWEZI
Abrahams, R. G. The Nyamwezi Today: A Tenzanian People in the Seventies. LC 80-41012. (Changing Cultures Ser.). (Illus.). 176p. Date not set. price not set (ISBN 0-521-22694-5); pap. price not set (ISBN 0-521-29619-6). Cambridge U Pr.

O

OAKLAND, CALIFORNIA
Bernhardi, Robert. Building of Oakland with a Section on Piedmont. 116p. 1979. 14.95 (ISBN 0-9605472-0-7). Forest Hill.

OAKLEY, ANNIE, 1860-1926
Harrison, et al. Annie Oakley. (Illus.). 35p. (gr. 1-9). 1981. 2.95 (ISBN 0-86575-185-4). Dormac.
Sayers, Isabelle S. Annie Oakley & Buffalo Bill's Wild West: One Hundred & Two Illustrations. (Illus.). 96p. (Orig.). 1981. pap. price not set (ISBN 0-486-24120-3). Dover.

OAS
see Organization of American States

OBEDIENCE
Buerger, Jane. Obedience. rev. ed. LC 80-39520. (What Is It? Ser.). (Illus.). 32p. (gr. k-3). 1981. PLB 5.50 (ISBN 0-89565-206-4). Childs World.
Elliot, Elisabeth. The Liberty of Obedience. (Festival Bks). 1981. pap. 1.50 (ISBN 0-687-21730-X). Abingdon.

OBESITY
Coyle, Neva. Living Free. 160p. 1981. pap. 3.95 (ISBN 0-87123-346-0, 210346). Bethany Fell.
Livingston, Carole. I'll Never Be Fat Again. 224p. 1981. pap. 2.50 (ISBN 0-345-28659-6). Ballantine.
Millman, Marcia. Such a Pretty Face: Being Fat in America. 1981. pap. 2.75 (ISBN 0-425-04849-7). Berkley Pub.
Schwerdtfeger, Don. The Secret Truth About Fat People. LC 80-82369. (Illus.). 204p. Date not set. 11.95 (ISBN 0-8119-0409-1, Pegasus Rex). Fell.
Smith, Anne, ed. Obesity: A Bibliography 1974-1979. 340p. 1980. 55.00 (ISBN 0-904147-17-7). Info Retrieval.

OBITUARIES
The New York Times Obituaries Index II, 1969-1978. 133p. 1980. write for info. (ISBN 0-667-00598-6). Microfilming Corp.

OBJECTS, MINIATURE
see Miniature Objects

OBLIGATION
see Responsibility

OBSCENITY (LAW)
see also Postal Service–Laws and Regulations
Friedman, Leon, ed. Obscenity. 2nd ed. (Oral Arguments Before the Supreme Court Ser.). 365p. 1981. pap. 8.95 (ISBN 0-87754-211-2). Chelsea Hse.

OBSEQUIES
see Funeral Rites and Ceremonies

OBSESSIVE-COMPULSIVE NEUROSES
Shapiro, David. Autonomy & Rigid Character. LC 80-68953. 167p. 1981. 12.95x (ISBN 0-465-00567-5). Basic.

OBSTETRICAL NURSING
Anderson, Barbara & Shapiro, Pamela. Obstetrics for the Nurse. 272p. 1981. text ed. 13.95 (ISBN 0-442-21840-0). Van Nos Reinhold.
Jensen, Margaret D., et al. Maternity Care: The Nurse & the Family. 2nd ed. LC 80-20723. (Illus.). 966p. 1981. text ed. 24.95 (ISBN 0-8016-2492-4). Mosby.
Neeson, Jean D. & Stockdale, Connie R. The Practitioners Handbook of Ambulatory OB-GYN. 400p. 1981. 17.95 (ISBN 0-471-05670-7, Pub. by Wiley Medical). Wiley.
Pillitteri, Adele. Maternal-Newborn Nursing: Care of the Growing Family. 2nd ed. 1981. text ed. write for info. (ISBN 0-316-70792-9). Little.

OBSTETRICS
see also Abortion; Cesarean Section; Childbirth; Labor (Obstetrics); Obstetrical Nursing; Pregnancy
Cohen, Arnold W. Emergencies in Obstetrics & Gynecology. (Clinics in Emergency Medicine Ser.). (Illus.). 224p. 1981. lib. bdg. 20.00 (ISBN 0-443-08130-1). Churchill.
Cosmi, Ermelando V. Obstetric Anesthesia & Perinatology. 500p. 1981. 33.50 (ISBN 0-8385-7196-4). ACC.
Dilts, P. V., Jr., et al. Core Studies in Obstetrics & Gynecology. 3rd ed. (Illus.). 248p. 1981. write for info. softcover (2572-4). Williams & Wilkins.
Elder, M. G. & Hendricks, C. H. Obstetrics & Gynecology: Preterm Labor, Vol. 1. (Butterworths International Medical Reviews Ser.). 1981. text ed. price not set (ISBN 0-407-02300-3). Butterworths.
Hibbard, Lester T. Infections in Obstetrics & Gynecology. LC 80-18670. (Discussions in Patient Management Ser.). 1980. pap. 8.00 (ISBN 0-87488-896-4). Med Exam.
Iffy, Leslie & Langer, Alvin. Perinatology Case Studies. 1978. pap. 18.75 (ISBN 0-87488-043-2). Med Exam.
Lancaster, Arnold. Nursery & Midwifery Sourcebook. 304p. 1980. 25.00x (Pub. by Beaconsfield England). State Mutual Bk.
Martius. Operative Obstetrics. 1980. 16.00. Thieme Stratton.

Niswander, Kenneth R. Obstetrics: Essentials of Clinical Practice. 2nd ed. 1981. pap. text ed. price not set. Little.
Page, Ernest W., et al. Human Reproduction: Essentials of Obstetrics, Gynecology, & Reproductive Medicine. 1981. text ed. price not set (ISBN 0-7216-7053-9). Saunders.
Psychological Aspects of Pregnancy, Birthing, & Bonding. Blum, Barbara L. & Olsen, Paul T., eds. (New Directions in Psychotheraphy Ser.: Vol. IV). 336p. 1980. 25.95 (ISBN 0-87705-210-7). Human Sci Pr.
Scarpelli, Emilie & Cosmi, Ermelando, eds. Reviews in Perinatal Medicine, Vol. 4. 550p. 1981. 39.00 (ISBN 0-89004-364-7). Raven.
Wynn, Ralph M., ed. Obstetrics & Gynecology Annual 1980. (Obstetrics & Gynecology Ser.). 390p. 1980. 29.50x (ISBN 0-8385-7186-7). ACC.
--Obstetrics & Gynecology Annual, 1981. (Obstetrics & Gynecology Annual Series). 1981. 33.50 (ISBN 0-8385-7188-3). ACC.

OBSTETRICS–SURGERY
see also Cesarean Section
Schaefer, George & Graber, Edward A., eds. Complications in Obstetric & Gynecologic Surgery. (Illus.). 650p. 1981. text ed. write for info. (ISBN 0-06-142330-0, Harper Medical). Har-Row.

OBSTETRICS, OPERATIVE
see Obstetrics–Surgery

OBSTRUCTIONS, INTESTINAL
see Intestines–Obstructions

O'CASEY, SEAN, 1884-1964
Hunt, Hugh. Sean O'Casey. (Gillis Irish Lives Ser.). 153p. 1980. 20.00 (ISBN 0-7171-1080-X, Pub. by Gill & Macmillan Ireland); pap. 6.50 (ISBN 0-7171-1034-6). Irish Bk Ctr.
Krause, David & Lowery, Robert G., eds. Sean O'Casey: Centenary Essays. (Irish Literary Studies 7). 257p. 1981. 24.75x (ISBN 0-389-20096-4). B&N.

OCCIDENTAL ART
see Art

OCCIDENTAL CIVILIZATION
see Civilization, Occidental

OCCLUSION (DENTISTRY)
Celenza, Frank V. Occlusal Morphology. 110p. 1980. pap. 18.00 (ISBN 0-931386-33-0). Quint Pub Co.
Celenza, Frank V. & Nasedkin, John N. Occlusion, the State of the Art. (Illus.). 165p. 1978. 32.00 (ISBN 0-931386-00-4). Quint Pub Co.

OCCULT SCIENCES
see also Alchemy; Astrology; Cabala; Conjuring; Demonology; Geomancy; Magic; Occultism in Literature; Prophecies (Occult Sciences); Psychometry (Occult Sciences); Satanism; Superstition; Witchcraft
Ballard, Juliet B. Treasures from Earth's Storehouse. 311p. (Orig.). 1980. pap. 7.95 (ISBN 0-87604-128-4). ARE Pr.
Case, Paul F. The Magical Language. 320p. pap. 9.95 (ISBN 0-87728-526-8). Weiser.
Chinmoy, Sri. Secrets of the Inner World. (Illus.). 54p. (Orig.). 1980. pap. 2.00 (ISBN 0-88497-499-5). Aum Pubns.
Cohen, Daniel. Famous Curses. (gr. 3-6). pap. 1.75 (ISBN 0-671-41867-X). Archway.
Curtiss, H. A. & Curtiss, F. H. The Message of Aquaria. 487p. 1981. pap. 17.50 (ISBN 0-89540-065-0). Sun Pub.
Dawes, Walter A. Light Shines on Mystery Babylon the Great. (Orig.). 1981. pap. price not set (ISBN 0-938792-10-5). New Capernaum.
DeHaan, Richard. El Culto a Satanas. De la Cerda, Rodolfo, tr. from Eng. 136p. (Orig., Span.). 1975. pap. 2.25 (ISBN 0-89922-059-2). Edit Caribe.
Ebon, Martin, ed. World's Greatest Unsolved Mysteries. (Orig.). 1981. pap. 2.25 (ISBN 0-451-09684-3, E9684, Sig). NAL.
Fernie, William T. The Occult & Curative Powers of Precious Stones. LC 80-8894. (The Harper Library of Spiritual Wisdom Ser.). 496p. 1981. pap. 7.95 (ISBN 0-06-062360-8). Har-Row.
French, Michael. Rhythms. 1981. pap. 2.75 (ISBN 0-425-05023-8). Berkley Pub.
Holzer, Hans. Inside Witchcraft. (Orig.). 1980. pap. 2.25 (ISBN 0-532-23220-8). Manor Bks.
--More Than One Life. (Orig.). 1980. pap. 2.25 (ISBN 0-532-23127-9). Manor Bks.
Ingalese, Isabella. Occult Philosophy. 1980. pap. 5.95 (ISBN 0-87877-049-6). Newcastle Pub.
Koch, Kurt E. Occult ABC. 1980. 7.95 (ISBN 0-8254-3031-3). Kregel.
Lloyd, John U. Etidorhpa. 386p. 1981. pap. 15.00 (ISBN 0-89540-004-9). Sun Pub.
Messent, Peter B., ed. Literature of the Occult: A Collection of Critical Essays. (Twentieth Century Views Ser.). 224p. 1981. text ed. 12.95 (ISBN 0-13-537712-9, Spec); pap. text ed. 4.95 (ISBN 0-13-537704-8, Spec). P-H.
Mickaharic, Draja. Spiritual Cleansing. 128p. 1981. pap. 6.95 (ISBN 0-87728-531-4). Weiser.
Puryear, Herbert B. Sex & the Spiritual Path. 225p. (Orig.). 1980. pap. 5.95 (ISBN 0-87604-129-2). ARE Pr.
Rosellemar, Kenneth. How to Master the Art of Spiritual Intercourse. (The Society of Psychic Research Library). (Illus.). 1981. 45.75 (ISBN 0-89920-025-7). Am Inst Psych.
Schulman, Martin. Karmic Relationships. 1981. pap. 6.951311 (ISBN 0-686-69318-3). Weiser.
Shepard, Leslie. Encyclopedia of Occultism & Parapsychology: A Compedium of Information on the Occult Sciences, Magic, Demonology, Superstitions, Spiritism, Mysticism, Metaphysics, Psychical Science & Parapsycholgy. 2nd ed. (Illus.). 400p. 1981. 125.00 (ISBN 0-8103-0196-2). Gale.
Steiger, Brad. Revelation: The Divine Fire. 1981. pap. 2.50 (ISBN 0-425-04615-X). Berkley Pub.
--Unknown Powers. 1981. pap. 2.50 (ISBN 0-425-05005-X). Berkley Pub.
Thomas, Eugene E. Brotherhood of Mr. Shasta. 307p. 1981. pap. 10.00 (ISBN 0-89540-067-7). Sun Pub.
Wright, J. Stafford. La Mente y lo Desconocido. Gilchrist, James S., tr. from Eng. LC 76-9906. 228p. (Orig., Span.). 1976. pap. 3.50 (ISBN 0-89922-070-3). Edit Caribe.

OCCULT SCIENCES–BIOGRAPHY
Allison, Dorothy & Jacobson, Scott. Dorothy Allison: A Psychic Story. (Orig.). 1980. pap. 2.50 (ISBN 0-515-05304-X). Jove Pubns.
Webb, Richard. These Came Back. (Orig.). 1976. pap. 1.75 (ISBN 0-89129-039-7). Jove Pubns.

OCCULTISM
see Occult Sciences; Occultism in Literature

OCCULTISM IN LITERATURE
see also Supernatural in Literature
Tuveson, Ernest L. The Avatars of Thrice Great Hermes: An Approach to Romanticism. LC 78-75206. 280p. 1981. 17.50 (ISBN 0-8387-2264-4). Bucknell U Pr.

OCCUPATION, CHOICE OF
see Vocational Guidance

OCCUPATION TAX
see Business Tax

OCCUPATION THERAPY
see Occupational Therapy

OCCUPATIONAL ACCIDENTS
see Industrial Accidents

OCCUPATIONAL APTITUDE TESTS
see Employment Tests

OCCUPATIONAL CRIMES
see White Collar Crimes

OCCUPATIONAL DISEASES
see also Industrial Toxicology; Lead-Poisoning; Lungs–Dust Diseases; Skin–Diseases; Workmen's Compensation
Parkes, W. Raymond. Occupational Lung Disorders. 2nd ed. 1981. text ed. price not set (ISBN 0-407-33731-8). Butterworth.
Shaw, Charles R., ed. Prevention of Occupational Cancer. 256p. 1981. 72.95 (ISBN 0-8493-5625-3). CRC Pr.

OCCUPATIONAL HEALTH AND SAFETY
see Industrial Safety

OCCUPATIONAL THERAPY
see also Art Therapy; Handicraft; Music Therapy
Pedretti, Lorraine W. Occupational Therapy: Practice Skills for Physical Dysfunction. (Illus.). 676p. 1981. pap. text ed. 23.95 (ISBN 0-8016-3772-4). Mosby.

OCCUPATIONAL TRAINING
Here are entered works on the vocationally oriented process of endowing people with a skill after either completion or termination of their formal education. Works on vocational instruction within the standard educational system are entered under Vocational Education. Works on retraining persons with obsolete vocational skills are entered under Occupational Retraining. Works on training of employees on the job are entered under Employees, Training Of.
see also Non-Formal Education
Human Resource Development Press. The Complete Guide to Packaged Training Programs. Nadler, Leonard, ed. 250p. (Orig.). 1981. book with periodic supplements 65.00x (ISBN 0-914234-52-8). Human Res Dev.
Wasserman, Paul, ed. New Training & Development Organizations: Supplement to Training & Development Organizations Directory, 2nd Edition. 1981. Set. pap. 48.00 (ISBN 0-686-69180-6). Gale.

OCCUPATIONS–DISEASES
see Occupational Diseases

OCCUPATIONS–HYGIENIC ASPECTS
see Industrial Health

OCCUPATIONS–JUVENILE LITERATURE
Rockwell, Anne. When We Grow Up. LC 80-21768. (Illus.). (ps-1). 1981. PLB 10.95 (ISBN 0-525-42575-6). Dutton.

OCCUPATIONS, DANGEROUS
see also Accident Law; Employers' Liability; Industrial Accidents; Lead-Poisoning; Occupational Diseases
Glassman. Dangerous Lives. (gr. 7-12). 1980. pap. 1.25 (ISBN 0-590-30875-0, Schol Pap). Schol Bk Serv.

OCCUPATIONS AND BUSY WORK
see Creative Activities and Seatwork

OCEAN
see also Diving, Submarine; Underwater Exploration; Oceanography;
also names of oceans, e.g. Pacific Ocean
Jones, Lewis. The Ocean. (Newbury Hse Raders Ser.: Stage 4 - Intermediate). (Illus.). 80p. (Orig.). (gr. 7-12). 1981. pap. text ed. 2.95 (ISBN 0-88377-197-7). Newbury Hse.
The Saturday Evening Post Book of the Sea & Ships. LC 78-61519. (Illus.). 1978. 11.95 (ISBN 0-89387-023-4). Sat Eve Post.
Third United Nations Conference on the Law of the Sea: Official Records, Vol. IX. 191p. 1979. pap. 14.00 (ISBN 0-686-68976-3, UN79/5/3, UN). Unipub.

OCEAN–ECONOMIC ASPECTS
see Marine Resources; Shipping

OCEAN–JUVENILE LITERATURE
Noel, Spike. Fish & the Sea. (Junior Reference Ser.). (Illus.). 64p. (gr. 7 up). 1972. 7.95 (ISBN 0-7136-1239-8). Dufour.

OCEAN BIRDS
see Sea Birds

OCEAN ENGINEERING
see also Manned Undersea Research Stations; Offshore Structures
U.S. Dept. of Energy. Ocean Energy Systems Program Summary: Fiscal Year Nineteen Seventy Nine. 285p. 1981. pap. 30.00 (ISBN 0-89934-100-4). Solar Energy Info.

OCEAN FREIGHTERS
see Cargo Ships

OCEAN LIFE
see Marine Biology

OCEAN RESOURCES
see Marine Resources

OCEAN TRANSPORTATION
see Shipping

OCEAN TRAVEL
see also Steamboats and Steamboat Lines; Yachts and Yachting
Fielding's Worldwide Guide to Cruises. 320p. 1981. Fieldingflex 11.95 (ISBN 0-688-00422-9). Morrow.
Maddocks, Melvin. The Atlantic Crossing. Time-Life Books, ed. (The Seafarers Ser.). (Illus.). 176p. 1981. 14.95 (ISBN 0-8094-2726-5). Time Life.
Ship's Routing. 4th ed. 150p. 1978. 55.00 (IMCO). Unipub.
Supplement Relating to the Annex to the Convention on Facilitation of International Maritime Traffic, 1965. 62p. 1979. 9.75 (IMCO). Unipub.

OCEAN WAVES
McCormick, Michael E. Ocean Wave Energy Conversion. (Alternate Energy Ser.). 300p. 1981. 30.00 (ISBN 0-471-08543-X, Pub. by Wiley-Interscience). Wiley.

OCEANARIUMS
see Marine Aquariums

OCEANEERING
see Ocean Engineering

OCEANICA–BIBLIOGRAPHY
Sources of the History of North Africa, Asia, & Oceania in Scandinavia, 2 pts. Incl. Pt. 1. Sources of the History North Africa, Asia, & Oceania in Denmark. lib. bdg. 162.00 (ISBN 3-598-21474-X); Pt. 2. Sources of the History of North Africa, Asia, & Oceania in Finland, Norway, Sweden. lib. bdg. 65.00 (ISBN 3-598-21475-8). (Guides to the Sources for the History of the Nations). 1980 (Dist. by Gale Research Co.). K G Saur.

OCEANICA–HISTORY
Wiltgen, R. M. The Founding of the Roman Catholic Church in Oceania 1825-1850. LC 78-74665. (Illus.). 610p. 1980. text ed. 36.95 (ISBN 0-7081-0835-0, 0572). Bks Australia.

OCEANOGRAPHY
see also Coasts; Diving; Diving, Submarine; Marine Biology; Navigation; Ocean; Ocean Engineering; Ocean Waves; Submarine Geology; Underwater Exploration
Anikouchine, William & Sternberg, Richard. The World Ocean. 2nd ed. (Illus.). 512p. 1981. 19.95 (ISBN 0-13-967778-X). P-H.
Barnes, H., ed. Oceanography & Marine Biology. Incl. Vol. 8. 1970. 40.50 (ISBN 0-02-840940-X); Vol. 10. 1972. 40.50 (ISBN 0-02-840960-4); Vol. 11. 1973. 40.50 (ISBN 0-02-840970-1); Vol. 12. 1974. 40.50 (ISBN 0-02-841010-6); Vol. 13. 1975. 57.75 (ISBN 0-02-841020-3). Hafner.
Barnes, Margaret & Barnes, Harold, eds. Oceanography & Marine Biology: An Annual Review, Vol. 18. (Illus.). 528p. 1980. 84.00 (ISBN 0-08-025732-1). Pergamon.
Hela, Ilmo & Laevastu, Taivo. Fisheries Oceanography. (Illus.). 254p. 22.00 (ISBN 0-85238-009-7, FN). Unipub.
McLeod, G. C. Georges Bank: Past, Present, & Future. (Special Studies on Natural Resources & Energy Management). 225p. 1981. lib. bdg. 22.00x (ISBN 0-86531-199-4). Westview.
Oceanography & Marine Biology: An Annual Review, Vol. 18. 1980. 95.00. Taylor Carlisle.
Sears, M. & Merriman, D., eds. Oceanography: The Past. (Illus.). 812p. 1980. 37.50 (ISBN 0-387-90497-2). Springer-Verlag.
Thurman, Harold V. Introductory Oceanography. 3rd ed. (Illus.). 596p. 1981. text ed. 19.95 (ISBN 0-675-08058-4); tchr's. ed. 3.95 (ISBN 0-686-69493-7). Merrill.

OCEANOGRAPHY, PHYSICAL
see Oceanography

OCEANOLOGY
see Oceanography

OCLC, INC.
Maruskin. OCLC, Inc. Its Goverence, Function, Finance & Technique. 160p. 1980. 22.75 (ISBN 0-8247-1179-3). Dekker.

O'CONNELL, DANIEL, 1775-1847
Life & Speeches of Daniel O'Connell, M.P. 264p. 1980. Repr. of 1878 ed. lib. bdg. 65.00 (ISBN 0-89984-365-4). Century Bookbindery.

OCTOBER MIDDLE EAST WAR, 1973
see Israel-Arab War, 1973

OCULAR FUNDUS
see Fundus Oculi

OCULAR MANIFESTATIONS OF GENERAL DISEASES
Nicholson. Pediatric Ocular Tumors. 1981. price not set (ISBN 0-89352-125-6). Masson Pub.

OCULOMOTOR SYSTEM
see Eye–Movements

ODONATA
see Dragon Flies

ODONTOLOGY
see Teeth

OFFENBACH, JACQUES, 1819-1880
Offenbach, Jacques. Jacques Offenbach. 1981. 29.95 (ISBN 0-7145-3512-5); pap. 11.95 (ISBN 0-7145-3841-8). Riverrun NY.

OFFENDERS, FEMALE
see Female Offenders

OFFENSIVE FOOTBALL
see Football–Offense

OFFICE, ECCLESIASTICAL
see Clergy–Office

OFFICE, NOMINATIONS FOR
see Nominations for Office

OFFICE, TENURE OF
see Civil Service

OFFICE ADMINISTRATION
see Office Management

OFFICE MACHINES
see Electronic Office Machines

OFFICE MANAGEMENT
see also Office Practice; Office Procedures; Personnel Management
Church, Olive. Office Dynamics Company: An Office Services & Temporary Help Practice Set. 250p. 1981. pap. text ed. 6.95 (ISBN 0-205-07136-8); free (ISBN 0-205-07361-1). Allyn.
Forsyth, Patrick. Running an Effective Sales Office. 160p. 1980. text ed. 37.25x (ISBN 0-566-02185-4, Pub. by Gower Pub Co England). Renouf.
Kasavana, Michael L. Effective Front Office Operations. 352p. text ed. 16.95 (ISBN 0-8436-2200-8). CBI Pub.
Walley, B. H. Office Administration Handbook. 470p. 1975. text ed. 25.75x (ISBN 0-220-66281-9, Pub. by Busn Bks England). Renouf.

OFFICE PRACTICE
see also Calculating-Machines; Commercial Correspondence; Electronic Data Processing; Electronic Office Machines; Files and Filing (Documents); Shorthand; Typewriting
Hall, L. Secretarial & Administrative Practice. 3rd ed. (Illus.). 304p. 1978. pap. 10.95 (ISBN 0-7121-1958-2, Pub. by Macdonald & Evans England). Intl Ideas.

OFFICE PRACTICE–AUTOMATION
Day, L. Automation in the Office. 1981. text ed. price not set (ISBN 0-86103-044-3, Westbury Hse). Butterworth.

OFFICE PROCEDURES
Westgate, Douglas G. Office Procedures 2000. 512p. 1977. text ed. 15.27 (ISBN 0-7715-0897-2); tchr's. manual 39.93 (ISBN 0-7715-0898-0). Forkner.

OFFICES
Morris, Norma A. How to Set up a Business Office: The Complete Guide to Locating, Outfitting & Staffing. (Illus.). 210p. 1981. 14.95 (ISBN 0-913864-62-5). Enterprise Del.

OFFICIAL PUBLICATIONS
see Government Publications

OFFICIAL SECRETS
Dynamite Book of Top Secret Information. (gr. 3-5). pap. 1.50 (ISBN 0-590-11804-8, Schol Pap). Schol Bk Serv.
Popov, Dusko. Spy-Counter Spy. 4.95 (ISBN 0-686-28850-5). Academy Chi Ltd.

OFFICIALS AND EMPLOYEES, INTERNATIONAL
see International Officials and Employees

OFFSET PRINTING
Chambers, Harry T. The Management of Small Offset Print Departments. 2nd ed. 217p. 1979. text ed. 22.00x (ISBN 0-220-67007-2, Pub. by Busn Bks England). Renouf.

OFFSHORE INSTALLATIONS
see Offshore Structures

OFFSHORE STRUCTURES
Armen, H. & Stiansen, S. Computational Methods for Offshore Structures. (AMD: Vol. 37). 154p. 1980. 24.00 (G00170). ASME.
Armer, G. S. & Garas, F. K., eds. Offshore Structures: The Use of Physical Models in Their Design. (Illus.). 420p. 1981. 55.00 (ISBN 0-86095-874-4). Longman.
Beudell, Martin, ed. Offshore Oil & Gas Yearbook 1980-81. 500p. 1980. 115.00x (ISBN 0-85038-336-6). Nichols Pub.
Block, Richard A., ed. Engineer-Chief & Assistant Engineer & Oiler: Limited to Service in the Mineral & Oil Industry. rev. ed. (Illus.). 82p. 1975. pap. text ed. 12.00 (ISBN 0-934114-07-2). Marine Educ.
Block, Richard A. & Collins, Charles B., eds. Standard Operations Manual for the Marine Transportation Sector of the Offshore Mineral & Oil Industry. 61p. (Orig.). 1979. pap. text ed. 7.50 (ISBN 0-934114-09-9). Marine Educ.

Norwegian Petroleum Society. Corrosion Problems Related to Electrical, Instrumentation & Automation Components Offshore. 152p. 1980. 75.00x (ISBN 82-7270-007-7, Pub. by Norwegian Info Norway). State Mutual Bk.
--Engineering & Construction of an Oil Production Platform. 1980. 70.00x (ISBN 82-7270-015-8, Pub. by Norwegian Info Norway). State Mutual Bk.
--Marginal Fields-Criteria for Development. 197p. 1980. 60.00x (ISBN 82-7270-006-9, Pub. by Norwegian Info Norway). State Mutual Bk.
--Offshore North Sea 1978, 2 vols. 1980. 165.00x (Pub. by Norwegian Info Norway). State Mutual Bk.
--Quality Assurance Related to Offshore Activities. 336p. 1980. 95.00x (ISBN 82-7270-009-3, Pub. by Norwegian Info Norway). State Mutual Bk.
Thomas Telford Editorial Staff, Ltd. Design & Construction of Offshore Structures. 184p. 1980. 60.00x (ISBN 0-7277-0041-3, Pub. by Telford England). State Mutual Bk.
Thomas Telford Ltd, Editorial Staff. Maintenance of Maritime Structures. 252p. 1980. 40.00x (ISBN 0-7277-0050-2, Pub. by Telford England). State Mutual Bk.
Thomas Telford Ltd. Editorial Staff. The Marine Environment & Oil Facilities. 168p. 1980. 69.00x (ISBN 0-7277-0075-8, Pub. by Telford England). State Mutual Bk.
--Offshore Structures. 208p. 1980. 75.00x (ISBN 0-7277-0008-1, Pub. by Thomas Telford England). State Mutual Bk.

OGLALA INDIANS
see Indians of North America–The West

OHIO–DESCRIPTION AND TRAVEL
Rucker, Marion E. & LaPidus, Anne. Ohio Magazine's Offical Guide to Columbus & Central Ohio. rev. ed. LC 80-53248. (Illus.). 272p. (Orig.). 1980. pap. 5.95 (ISBN 0-938040-00-6). Ohio Mag.

OHIO–ECONOMIC CONDITIONS
Humphrey, N., et al. The Future of Cincinnati's Capital Plant. (America's Urban Capital Stock Ser.: Vol. 3). 66p. (Orig.). 1980. pap. 4.00 (ISBN 0-87766-264-9, 27400). Urban Inst.
--The Future of Cleveland's Capital Plant. (America's Urban Capital Stock Ser.: Vol. 2). 77p. (Orig.). 1979. pap. text ed. 4.00 (ISBN 0-87766-264-9, 26900). Urban Inst.

OHIO–GENEALOGY
Rife, John M. & Rife, W. R. John & Mary J. Rife of Greene County Ohio: Their Ancestors & Descendants. LC 80-83318. 1980. 5.00. Reiff Pr.

OHIO–HISTORY
Daily Nonpareil Office. Sketches of Springfield in 1856. (Annual Monograph Ser.). 96p. 1973. pap. 3.00 facsimile reprint. Clark County Hist Soc.
Miller, Zane L. Suburb: Neighborhood & Community in Forest Park, Ohio, 1935-1976. LC 80-21828. (Twentieth-Century America Ser.). 256p. 1981. 18.50x (ISBN 0-87049-289-6). U of Tenn Pr.
Old Ohio, 2 vols. Incl. Vol. I. Logan & Matthews.; Vol. II. Welch & Matthews.. (Sun Historical Ser.). pap. 3.50 ea. Sun Pub.
Parkinson, Cornelia M. Historical Tales of Old Reynoldsburg: Selections from the First Five Years of the Courier. (Illus.). 152p. (Orig.). 1980. pap. 7.50 (ISBN 0-938404-00-8). Hist Tales.
--History of Reynoldsburg & Truro Township, Ohio. (Illus.). 200p. 1981. 25.00 (ISBN 0-938404-02-4). Hist Tales.
--The Reynoldsburg Book of Lists. (Orig.). 1981. pap. text ed. 7.50 (ISBN 0-938404-03-2). Hist Tales.
Skardon, Mary A., ed. Yester Year in Clark County, Ohio, 2 vols. in one. (Annual Monograph Ser.). 76p. (Repr. of 1947 & 1948 eds.). 1978. pap. 3.00. Clark County Hist Soc.
Vexler, R. I. Ohio Chronology & Factbook, Vol. 35. 1978. 8.50 (ISBN 0-379-16160-5). Oceana.

OIL
see Oils and Fats; Petroleum

OIL AND GAS LAW
see Petroleum Law and Legislation

OIL CONSERVATION
see Petroleum Conservation

OIL FIELD WORKERS
see Petroleum Workers

OIL-PAINTING
see Painting

OIL POLLUTION OF RIVERS, HARBORS, ETC.
International Convention for the Prevention of Pollution of the Sea by Oil, 1954. 25p. 1978. 7.00 (IMCO). Unipub.
International Convention on Civil Liability for Oil Pollution Damage. 20p. 1977. 7.00 (IMCO). Unipub.
Official Records of the Conference on the Establishment of an International Compensation Fund for Oil Pollution Damage, 1971. 742p. 1978. 33.60 (IMCO). Unipub.

OIL POLLUTION OF WATER
see also Oil Pollution of Rivers, Harbors, Etc.
The Bravo Blow-Out. 287p. 1980. 100.00x (ISBN 8-272-70011-5, Pub. by Norwegian Info Norway). State Mutual Bk.
Conference on the Establishment of an International Compensation Fund for Oil Pollution Damage, 1971. 94p. 1972. 11.00 (IMCO). Unipub.
International Convention Relating to Intervention on the High Seas in Cases of Oil Pollution Casualties (1969) 25p. 1977. 7.00 (IMCO). Unipub.
Manual on Oil Pollution, 3 pts. Incl. Pt. 1. Prevention. 1976. pap. 8.25 (ISBN 0-686-64934-6, IMCO 23); Pt. II. Contingency Planning. 1978. pap. 11.00 (ISBN 0-686-64935-4, IMCO 24); Pt. IV. Practical Information on Means of Dealing with Oil Spillages. 1977. Repr. of 1972 ed. pap. 12.00 (ISBN 0-686-64936-2, IMCO 25). IMCO). Unipub.
Norwegina Petroleum Society. Contingency Planning. 223p. 1980. 75.00x (ISBN 8-27270-010-7, Pub. by Norwegian Info Norway). State Mutual Bk.
Recommendations on International Performance & Test Specifications for Oily-Water Separating Equipment & Oil Content Meters. 36p. 1978. 8.25 (IMCO). Unipub.

OIL RESERVOIR ENGINEERING
Facilities in Ports for the Reception of Oil Residues: Results of an Enquiry Made in 1972. 145p. 1973. 16.50 (IMCO). Unipub.
Facilities in Ports for the Reception of Oil Residues: Results of an Enquiry Made in 1972, Supplement 1976. 27p. 1976. 7.00 (I MCO). Unipub.

OIL SEEDS
see Oilseeds

OIL-SHALES
see also Petroleum
Allred, V. Dean, ed. Oil Shale Processing Technology. 208p. 1981. price not set (ISBN 0-86563-001-1). Ctr Prof Adv.
Griest, W. H., et al, eds. Health Effects Investigation of Oil Shale Development. 1981. text ed. 29.50. Ann Arbor Science.
Nowacki, Perry, ed. Oil Shale Technical Data Handbook. LC 80-27547. (Energy Tech. Rev. 63 Ser.: Chemical Tech. Rev. 182). (Illus.). 309p. 1981. 48.00 (ISBN 0-8155-0835-2). Noyes.

OIL TANKERS
see Tankers

OIL WELL BLOWOUTS
Adams, Neal. Workover Well Control. 320p. 1981. 27.50 (ISBN 0-87814-142-1). Pennwell Pub.

OIL WELL LOGGING
Norwegian Petroleum Society. Measuring Accuracy of Parameters Used in Formation Evaluation in the North Sea. 193p. 1980. 75.00x (ISBN 82-7270-002-6, Pub. by Norwegian Info Norway). State Mutual Bk.

OIL WORKERS
see Petroleum Workers

OILS AND FATS
see also Lubrication and Lubricants; Oilseeds; Petroleum
also names of fats and oils
Swern, Daniel. Bailey's Industrial Oil & Fat Products, Vol. II. 4th ed. 675p. 1981. 50.00 (ISBN 0-471-83958-2, Pub. by Wiley-Interscience). Wiley.

OILS AND FATS, EDIBLE
Intergovernmental Group on Oilseeds, Oils & Fats. Report on the Fourteenth Session of the Intergovernmental Group on Oilseeds, Oils & Fats. 14p. 1980. pap. 6.00 (ISBN 92-5-100937-6, F2044, FAO). Unipub.

OILSEEDS
see also Oils and Fats; Seeds
Intergovernmental Group on Oilseeds, Oils & Fats. Report on the Fourteenth Session of the Intergovernmental Group on Oilseeds, Oils & Fats. 14p. 1980. pap. 6.00 (ISBN 92-5-100937-6, F2044, FAO). Unipub.

OKLAHOMA–DESCRIPTION AND TRAVEL
Hart, Herbert M. Tour Guide to Old Forts of Texas, Kansas, Nebraska, Oklahoma, Vol. 4. (Illus.). 65p. (Orig.). 1981. pap. 3.95 (ISBN 0-87108-583-6). Pruett.
Hunt, David C. Guide to Oklahoma Museums. LC 80-5939. (Illus.). 250p. 1981. 17.50 (ISBN 0-8061-1567-X); pap. 9.95 (ISBN 0-8061-1752-4). U of Okla Pr.
McCoy, Doyle. Roadside Trees & Shrubs of Oklahoma. LC 80-5944. (Illus.). 180p. (Orig.). 1981. pap. 9.95 (ISBN 0-8061-1556-4). U of Okla Pr.

OKLAHOMA–HISTORY
Vexler, R. I. Oklahoma Chronology & Factbook, Vol. 36. 1978. 8.50 (ISBN 0-379-16161-3). Oceana.

OKLAHOMA–JUVENILE LITERATURE
Fradin, Dennis. Oklahoma: In Words & Pictures. LC 80-26961. (Young People's Stories of Our States Ser.). (Illus.). 48p. (gr. 2-5). 1981. PLB 8.65g (ISBN 0-516-03936-9, Time Line). Childrens.

OKLAHOMA, UNIVERSITY OF
Cross, George L. The University of Oklahoma & World War II: A Personal Account, 1941-1946. LC 80-16934. (Illus.). 320p. 1980. 15.95 (ISBN 0-8061-1662-5). U of Okla Pr.

OLD AGE
see also Aged; Aging; Geriatrics; Longevity; Middle Age; Old Age Assistance; Old Age Pensions; Retirement
Davis, Richard H., ed. Aging: Prospects & Issues. 3rd rev. ed. LC 80-53413. 427p. 1981. pap. 10.00 (ISBN 0-88474-097-8). USC Andrus Geron.
Kastenbaum, Robert. Old Age on the New Scene. (Springer Series on Adulthood & Aging: No. 9). 1981. pap. text ed. 19.95 (ISBN 0-8261-2361-9). Springer Pub.
Kayser-Jones, Jeanie S. Old, Alone, & Neglected: Care of the Aged in Scotland & in the United States. 160p. 1981. 14.95 (ISBN 0-520-04153-4). U of Cal Pr.

OLD AGE–DISEASES
see Geriatrics

OLD AGE, SURVIVORS AND DISABILITY INSURANCE
see Insurance, Disability; Old Age Pensions; Social Security

OLD AGE AND EMPLOYMENT
see Age and Employment

OLD AGE ASSISTANCE
see also Aged–Medical Care; Old Age Homes; Old Age Pensions
Davis, Lenwood G. The Black Aged in the United States: An Annotated Bibliography. LC 80-1193. xviii, 200p. 1980. lib. bdg. 22.50 (ISBN 0-313-22560-5, DAB/). Greenwood.
Tinker, Anthea. The Elderly in Modern Society. (Social Policy in Modern Britain Ser.). (Illus.). 320p. 1981. pap. text ed. 13.95x (ISBN 0-582-29513-0). Longman.

OLD AGE HOMES
see also Nursing Homes
Profiles of Two Adult Homes & Their Communities: The Need to Bridge the Gap. 1980. 4.00. Comm Coun Great NY.

OLD AGE PENSIONS
see also Civil Service Pensions; Disability Evaluation
also subdivisions Pensions, and Salaries, Pensions, etc. under names of industries, professions, etc. e.g. Teachers–Salaries, Pensions, etc.
Davies, Bleddyn & Knapp, Martin. Old People's Homes & the Production of Welfare. (Library of Social Work Ser.). 240p. 1981. 32.50 (ISBN 0-7100-0700-0). Routledge & Kegan.
Kutza, Elizabeth A. The Benefits of Old Age: Social Welfare Policies for the Elderly. LC 80-24241. 192p. 1981. lib. bdg. 18.00 (ISBN 0-226-46565-9); pap. 5.95 (ISBN 0-226-46566-7). U of Chicago Pr.

OLD AGE, SURVIVORS AND DISABILITY INSURANCE
see Social Security

OLD ENGLISH LANGUAGE
see English Language–Middle English, 1100-1500

OLD ENGLISH LITERATURE
see Anglo-Saxon Literature (Collections); English Literature (Collections)–Middle English (1100-1500)

OLD FRENCH LITERATURE
see French Literature (Collections)–To 1500

OLD STONE AGE
see Paleolithic Period

OLDER WORKERS
see Age and Employment

OLDUVAI GORGE
see Paleontology–Africa

OLFACTORY NERVE
Cagan, Robert H. & Kare, Morley R., eds. Biochemistry of Taste & Olfaction. (Nutrition Foundation Ser.). 1981. write for info. (ISBN 0-12-154450-8). Acad Pr.
International Symposium on Olfaction & Taste, 6th, Gif Sur Yvette, France, 1977. Olfaction & Taste VI: Proceedings. 500p. 25.00 (ISBN 0-904147-08-8). Info Retrieval.
Valonet, Jean. The Practice of Aromatherapy. (Illus.). 1981. pap. 8.95 (ISBN 0-89281-026-2). Inner Tradit.

OLIGOCHAETA
Brinkhurst, Ralph O. & Cook, David G., eds. Aquatic Oligochaete Biology. 530p. 1980. 55.00 (ISBN 0-306-40338-2). Plenum Pub.
Kuhne, Walter G. The Liassic Therapsid Oligokyphus. (Illus.). iii, 150p. 1956. 16.50x (ISBN 0-565-00115-9, Pub. by British Mus Nat Hist England). Sabbot-Natural Hist Bks.

OLIGOPHRENIA
see Mental Deficiency

OLIPHANT, LAURENCE, 1829-1888
Henderson, Philip. The Life of Laurence Oliphant: Traveller, Diplomat & Mystic. 281p. 1981. Repr. of 1956 ed. lib. bdg. 30.00 (ISBN 0-8495-2364-8). Arden Lib.

OLIVE INDUSTRY AND TRADE
China: Development of Olive Production. 163p. 1981. pap. 8.75 (ISBN 92-5-100995-3, F2097, FAO). Unipub.

OLMSTED, FREDERICK LAW, 1822-1903
Beveridge, Charles E. & McLaughlin, Charles C., eds. The Papers of Frederick Law Olmsted: Vol. II: Slavery & the South, 1852-1857. LC 80-8881. (The Papers of Frederick Law Olmsted). (Illus.). 528p. 1981. text ed. 27.50x (ISBN 0-8018-2242-4). Johns Hopkins.

OLSON, CHARLES, 1910-1970
Olson, Charles & Creeley, Robert. Charles Olson & Robert Creeley: The Complete Correspondence, Vol. 3. Butterick, George F., ed. (Illus.). 200p. (Orig.). 1981. 20.00 (ISBN 0-87685-483-8); deluxe ed. 30.00 (ISBN 0-87685-484-6); pap. 7.50 (ISBN 0-87685-482-X). Black Sparrow.

OLYMPIC GAMES
Associated Press & Grolier, eds. The Olympic Story Nineteen Eighty. (Illus.). 256p. 1981. 14.95 (ISBN 0-531-09942-3). Watts.
Booker, Christopher. The Games War: A Moscow Journal. 208p. 1981. 18.50 (ISBN 0-571-11755-4, Pub. by Faber & Faber); pap. 8.95 (ISBN 0-571-11763-5). Merrimack Bk Serv.
Carroll, Walter J., ed. Olympic's Film Finder: Nineteen Eighty-One Business Edition. 1981. 24.00x (ISBN 0-88367-600-1). Olympic Media.
Holum, Dianne. World of Speed Skating. (Illus.). 320p. 1981. 17.50 (ISBN 0-89490-051-X). Enslow Pubs.
Kaneko, Akitomo. Olympic Gymnastics. LC 76-1171. (Illus.). 256p. 1980. pap. 7.95 (ISBN 0-8069-8926-2). Sterling.
Kanin, David B. A Political History of the Olympic Games. (Replica Edition Ser.). 160p. 1981. lib. bdg. 17.00x (ISBN 0-86531-109-9). Westview.
MacAloon, John J. This Great Symbol: Pierre De Courbertin & the Origins of the Modern Olympic Games. LC 80-21898. 1981. lib. bdg. 25.00x (ISBN 0-226-50000-4). U of Chicago Pr.
Olympic Story: Pursuit of Excellence. LC 80-67767. (Illus.). 1980. write for info. (ISBN 0-7172-8158-2). Grolier Ed Corp.
Segrave, Jeffrey & Chu, Donald, eds. Olympism. 1981. text ed. 17.95x (ISBN 0-931250-20-X). Human Kinetics.

OLYMPIC NATIONAL PARK
Leissler, Frederick. Roads & Trails of Olympic National Park. 4th rev. ed. LC 57-3575. (Illus.). 114p. 1981. pap. 6.95 (ISBN 0-295-95819-7). U of Wash Pr.

OMAHA INDIANS
see Indians of North America–The West

OMAN
Clements, F. A. Oman: The Reborn Land. 1981. text ed. 25.00 (ISBN 0-582-78300-3). Longman.

OMELETS
see Cookery (Eggs)

ON-LINE DATA PROCESSING
see also Real-Time Data Processing
Meadow, Charles T. & Atherton, Pauline. Basics of Online Searching. (Information Science Ser.). 200p. 1981. 14.95 (ISBN 0-471-05283-3, Pub. by Wiley-Interscience). Wiley.

ONCOLOGY
see also Cancer; Tumors
Block, Jerome B. Oncology: UCLA Postgraduate Medicine for the Internist. (Illus.). 1981. price not set (ISBN 0-89289-376-1). HM.
Day, Stacey B., et al. Readings in Oncology. LC 80-80708. (Foundation Publication Ser.). (Illus.). 227p. (Orig.). pap. 12.00 (ISBN 0-934314-01-2). Intl Found Biosocial Dev.
Dietz, J. Rehabiltation Oncology. LC 80-22911. 1981. write for info. (ISBN 0-471-08414-X). Wiley.
Mulkerin, Larry E. Practical Points in Radiation Oncology. 1979. spiral bdg. 17.00 (ISBN 0-87488-726-7). Med Exam.
Murphy, Gerald P., ed. International Advances in Surgical Oncology, Vol. 4. LC 78-51119. 365p. 1981. 46.00x (ISBN 0-8451-0503-5). A R Liss.
See-Lasley, Kay & Ignoffo, Robert. Manual of Oncology Therapeutics. 300p. 1981. pap. text ed. 19.95 (ISBN 0-8016-4448-8). Mosby.
Vredevoe, Donna L., et al. Concepts of Oncology Nursing. (Illus.). 400p. 1981. text ed. 18.95 (ISBN 0-13-166587-1). P-H.
Wang, Rosemary Y. & Kelley, Ann M. Self-Assessment of Current Knowledge in Oncology Nursing. 1979. spiral bdg. 10.50 (ISBN 0-87488-236-2). Med Exam.
Yarbro, John & Bornstein, Richard, eds. Oncologic Emergencies. (Clinical Oncology Monographs). 1980. write for info. (ISBN 0-8089-1317-4). Grune.

ONE-ARMED BANDITS
see Slot Machines

ONE-PARENT FAMILY
see Single-Parent Family

ONEIDA COMMUNITY
see also Perfection
Robertson, Constance. Oneida Community: An Autobiography. (Illus.). 1981. pap. 9.95 (ISBN 0-8156-0166-2). Syracuse U Pr.

ONEIDA INDIANS
see Indians of North America–Eastern States

O'NEILL, EUGENE GLADSTONE, 1888-1953
Sinha, C. P. Eugene O'neill's Tragic Vision. 1981. text ed. 16.00 (ISBN 0-391-02203-2). Humanities.

ONEIROMANCY
see Dreams

ONTARIO–DESCRIPTION AND TRAVEL
Hayes, John, ed. Corpus Vasorum Antiquorum Canada: Royal Ontario Museum, Ontario. (Corpus Vasorum Antiquorum Ser.). (Illus.). 64p. 1980. 89.00 (ISBN 0-19-726000-4). Oxford U Pr.

ONTARIO–POLITICS AND GOVERNMENT
Armstrong, Christopher. The Politics of Federalism: Ontario's Relations with the Federal Government 1867-1942. (Ontario Historical Studies). 316p. 1981. 20.00 (ISBN 0-8020-3374-1). U of Toronto Pr.

OPEN-CUT MINING
see Strip Mining

OPEN DOOR POLICY (FAR EAST)
see Eastern Question (Far East)

OPEN-PIT MINING
see Strip Mining

OPERA
see also Ballet; Melodrama
also names of specific opera companies, e.g. New York (City)–Metropolitan Opera
Blaze, Francois H. De l'Opera En France, 2 vols. LC 80-2259. 1981. Repr. of 1820 ed. Set. 82.50 (ISBN 0-404-18810-9). AMS Pr.

--L' Opera-Italien de 1548 a 1856. LC 80-2260. 1981. Repr. of 1856 ed. 52.00 (ISBN 0-686-69547-X). AMS Pr.
Edwards, Henry S. The Lyrical Drama, 2 vols. LC 80-2274. 1981. Repr. of 1881 ed. 67.50 (ISBN 0-404-18840-0). AMS Pr.
Genest, Emile. L' Opera-Comique Connu et Inconnu: Son Histoire Depuis l'origine Jusqu'a Nos Jours. LC 80-2277. 1981. Repr. of 1925 ed. 39.50 (ISBN 0-404-18845-1). AMS Pr.
Krehbiel, Henry E. A Second Book of Operas, Their Histories, Their Plots & Their Music. LC 80-2280. 1981. Repr. of 1917 ed. 36.50 (ISBN 0-404-18852-4). AMS Pr.
Melitz, Leo L. The Opera Goers' Complete Guide. Hackney, Louise W., rev. by. Salinger, Richard, tr. LC 80-2293. 1981. Repr. of 1936 ed. 54.50 (ISBN 0-404-18859-1). AMS Pr.
Pougin, Arthur. Les Vrais Createurs De l'Opera Francais: Perrin et Cambert. LC 80-2296. 1981. Repr. of 1881 ed. 33.50 (ISBN 0-404-18862-1). AMS Pr.
Remond De Saint-Mard, Toussaint. Reflexions Sur l'Opera. LC 80-2294. 1981. Repr. of 1741 ed. 18.50 (ISBN 0-404-18863-X). AMS Pr.
Riemann, Hugo. Opern-Handbuch. LC 80-2295. 1981. 75.00 (ISBN 0-404-18864-8). AMS Pr.
Taubman, Hyman H. Opera: Front & Back. LC 80-2306. 1981. Repr. of 1938 ed. 51.50 (ISBN 0-404-18872-9). AMS Pr.

OPERA–HISTORY AND CRITICISM

Bekker, Paul. The Changing Opera. Mendel, Arthur, tr. LC 80-2256. 1981. Repr. of 1935 ed. 35.50 (ISBN 0-404-18803-6). AMS Pr.
Bordman, Gerald. American Operetta: From H.M.S. Pinafore to Sweeney Todd. (Illus.). 240p. 1981. 15.95 (ISBN 0-19-502869-4). Oxford U Pr.
Colombani, Alfredo. L Opera Italiana Nel Secolo Xix: Dono Agli Abbonati Des Corriere Della Sera. LC 80-2266. 1981. Repr. of 1900 ed. 61.00 (ISBN 0-404-18819-2). AMS Pr.
Corte, Andrea Della. L' Opera Comica Italiana nel Settecento, Studi ed Appunti, 2 vols. LC 80-2269. 1981. Repr. of 1923 ed. Set. 62.50 (ISBN 0-404-18830-3). Vol. 1 (ISBN 0-404-18831-1). Vol. 2 (ISBN 0-404-18832-X). AMS Pr.
Cucuel, Georges. Les Createurs de l'Opera-Comique Francais. LC 80-2271. 1981. Repr. of 1914 ed. 29.50 (ISBN 0-404-18834-6). AMS Pr.
Gatti-Casazza, Guilio. Memories of the Opera. 1980. 19.95 (ISBN 0-7145-3518-4); pap. 9.95 (ISBN 0-7145-3665-2). Riverrun NY.
Hussey, Dyneley. Eurydice: Or, the Nature of Opera. LC 80-2283. 1981. Repr. of 1929 ed. 17.50 (ISBN 0-404-18849-4). AMS Pr.
La Laurencie, Lionel de. Les Createurs De l'Opera Francais. LC 80-2287. 1981. Repr. of 1921 ed. 26.00 (ISBN 0-404-18854-0). AMS Pr.
Martens, Frederick H. The Book of the Opera & the Ballet & the History of the Opera. LC 80-2289. 1981. Repr. of 1925 ed. 22.50 (ISBN 0-404-18857-5). AMS Pr.
L Opera Buffa Napoletana Durante Il Settecento: Storia Letteraria. 2nd ed. LC 80-2298. 1981. Repr. of 1917 ed. 53.50 (ISBN 0-404-18867-2). AMS Pr.
Orrey, Lesley. Opera in the High Baroque. 1981. 27.50 (ISBN 0-7145-3658-X). Riverrun NY.
Planelli, Antonio. Dell'Opera in Musica. LC 80-2292. 1981. Repr. of 1772 ed. 31.50 (ISBN 0-404-18861-3). AMS Pr.
Walsh, T. J. Second Empire Opera. 1981. 35.00 (ISBN 0-7145-3659-8). Riverrun NY.

OPERA–LIBRETTOS

see Operas–Librettos

OPERA–PRODUCTION AND DIRECTION

Marek, George R. Cosima Wagner. LC 80-7591. (Illus.). 256p. 1981. 15.95 (ISBN 0-06-012704-X, HarpT). Har-Row.
Nagler, A. M. Misdirection: Opera Production in the Twentieth Century. 134p. 1981. 15.00 (ISBN 0-208-01899-9, Archon). Shoe String.

OPERA–STORIES, PLOTS, ETC.

see Operas–Stories, Plots, etc.

OPERA–ENGLAND

Forsyth, Cecil. Music & Nationalism: A Study of English Opera. LC 80-2276. 1981. Repr. of 1911 ed. 37.00 (ISBN 0-404-18844-3). AMS Pr.
Hughes, Spike. Glyndebourne: A History of the Festival Opera. LC 80-70705. (Illus.). 400p. 1981. 27.50 (ISBN 0-7153-7891-0). David & Charles.
John, Nicholas, ed. English National Opera Guides: Caida, Generentola, Fidelio, Magic Flute, Vol. I. 1981. 25.00. Riverrun NY.

OPERA–ITALY

Brown, John. Letters Upon the Poetry & Music of the Italian Opera: Addressed to a Friend. LC 80-2261. 1981. Repr. of 1789 ed. 22.50 (ISBN 0-404-18814-1). AMS Pr.
Colombani, Alfredo. L Opera Italiana Nel Secolo Xix: Dono Agli Abbonati Des Corriere Della Sera. LC 80-2266. 1981. Repr. of 1900 ed. 61.00 (ISBN 0-404-18819-2). AMS Pr.
L Opera Buffa Napoletana Durante Il Settecento: Storia Letteraria. 2nd ed. LC 80-2298. 1981. Repr. of 1917 ed. 53.50 (ISBN 0-404-18867-2). AMS Pr.
Schultze, Walter. Die Quellen der Hamburger Oper Sixteen Seventy Eight to Seventeen Thirty Eight. LC 80-2300. 1981. Repr. of 1938 ed. 25.50 (ISBN 0-404-18869-9). AMS Pr.
Weaver, William. The Golden Century of Italian Opera: From Rossini to Puccini. (Illus.). 256p. 1980. 27.50 (ISBN 0-500-01240-7). Thames Hudson.

OPERA, COMIC

see Opera

OPERAS

see also Musical Revues, Comedies, etc.

Abert, Hermann J. Grundprobleme der Operngeschichte. LC 80-2253. 1981. Repr. of 1926 ed. 14.00 (ISBN 0-404-18800-1). AMS Pr.
Auber, Daniel F. La Muette De Portici, 2 vols. Grossett, Philip & Rosen, Charles, eds. LC 76-49211. (Early Romantic Opera Ser.: Vol. 30). 1980. lib. bdg. 82.00 (ISBN 0-8240-2929-1). Garland Pub.
Bellini, Vincenzo. Norma, 2 vols. Rosen, Charles & Gossett, Philip, eds. LC 76-49177. (Early Romantic Opera Ser.: Vol. 4). Date not set. lib. bdg. 82.00 (ISBN 0-8240-2903-8). Garland Pub.
Budden, Julian. The Operas of Verdi, Vol. 3: From Don Carlos to Falstaff. 1981. 39.95 (ISBN 0-19-520254-6). Oxford U Pr.
Chapin, Anna Alice. The Story of the Rhinegold: Der Ring Des Nibelungen. 138p. 1980. Repr. of 1897 ed. lib. bdg. 25.00 (ISBN 0-89760-119-X). Telegraph Bks.
Donizetti, Gaetano. Dom Sebastien, Gaetano Donizetti, 2 vols. Rosen, Charles & Gossett, Philip, eds. LC 76-49210. (Early Romantic Opera Ser.: Vol. 29). 1980. lib. bdg. 82.00 (ISBN 0-8240-2928-3). Garland Pub.
Goslich, Siegfried. Beitrage Zur Geschicte der Deutschen Romantischen Oper Zwischen Spohrs "Faust" und Wagner's "Lohengrin". LC 80-2281. 1981. Repr. of 1937 ed. 31.50 (ISBN 0-404-18846-X). AMS Pr.
Gregor, Joseph. Kulturgeschicte der Oper. 2nd, rev. & enl. ed. LC 80-2282. 1981. Repr. of 1950 ed. 57.50 (ISBN 0-404-18847-8). AMS Pr.
Howard, John T. The World's Great Operas. LC 80-2278. 1981. Repr. of 1948 ed. 49.50 (ISBN 0-404-18848-6). AMS Pr.
Kretzschmar, Hermann. Geschicte der Oper. LC 80-2285. 1981. Repr. of 1919 ed. 33.50 (ISBN 0-404-18853-2). AMS Pr.
Martens, Frederick H. The Book of the Opera & the Ballet & the History of the Opera. LC 80-2289. 1981. Repr. of 1925 ed. 22.50 (ISBN 0-404-18857-5). AMS Pr.
Meyerbeer, Giacomo. Les Huguenots, 2 vols. Rosen, Charles & Gossett, Philip, eds. LC 76-49196. (Early Romantic Opera Ser.: Vol. 20). 1980. lib. bdg. 82.00 (ISBN 0-8240-2919-4). Garland Pub.
--L'africaine, 2 vols. Grossett, Philip & Rosen, Charles, eds. LC 76-49200. (Early Romantic Opera Ser.: Vol. 24). 944p. 1980. lib. bdg. 82.00 (ISBN 0-8240-2923-2). Garland Pub.
Rossini, Gioachino. Moise. Rosen, Charles & Gossett, Philip, eds. LC 76-49190. (Early Romantic Opera Ser.: Vol. 15). 1980. lib. bdg. 82.00 (ISBN 0-8240-2914-3). Garland Pub.
Rushton, Julian. W. A. Mozart: Don Giovanni. (Cambridge Opera Handbooks Ser.). (Illus.). Date not set. price not set (ISBN 0-521-22826-3); pap. price not set (ISBN 0-521-29663-3). Cambridge U Pr.
Schiedermair, Ludwig. Die Deutche Oper: Grundzuge Ihres Werdens & Wesens. LC 80-2299. 1981. Repr. of 1930 ed. 38.50 (ISBN 0-404-18868-0). AMS Pr.
Spontini, Gasparo. Olympie. Grossett, Philip & Rosen, Charles, eds. LC 76-49227. (Early Romantic Opera Ser.: Vol. 44). 1980. lib. bdg. 82.00 (ISBN 0-8240-2943-7). Garland Pub.

OPERAS–LIBRETTOS

see also Operas–Stories, Plots, etc.

Bellini, Vincenzo. Beatrice Di Tenda, 2 vols. Rosen, Charles & Gosset, Philip, eds. LC 76-49178. (Early Romantic Opera Ser.: Vol. 5). 567p. 1980. lib. bdg. 82.00 (ISBN 0-8240-2904-6). Garland Pub.

OPERAS–STORIES, PLOTS, ETC.

Elliott, Donald & Arrowood, Clinton. Lamb's Tales from the Great Operas. 1981. 9.95 (ISBN 0-87645-110-5). Gambit.

OPERATING STATEMENTS

see Financial Statements

OPERATION PLUTO

see Cuba–History–Invasion, 1961

OPERATIONAL ANALYSIS

see Operations Research

OPERATIONAL AUDITING

see Management Audit

OPERATIONAL RESEARCH

see Operations Research

OPERATIONS, SURGICAL–PSYCHOLOGICAL ASPECTS

see Surgery–Psychological Aspects

OPERATIONS AUDITING

see Management Audit

OPERATIONS RESEARCH

see also Mathematical Optimization; Network Analysis (Planning); Queuing Theory; Research, Industrial; Simulation Methods; Systems Engineering

Bonczek, Robert H., et al. Foundations of Decision Support Systems. LC 80-1779. (Operations Research & Industrial Engineering Ser.). 1981. price not set (ISBN 0-12-113050-9). Acad Pr.
Cooper. Introd. Operations Research Models. 1977. 18.95 (ISBN 0-7216-2688-2). Dryden Pr.
Croucher, John S. Operations Research: A First Course. (Illus.). 320p. 1980. 27.00 (ISBN 0-08-024798-9); pap. 13.50 (ISBN 0-08-024797-0). Pergamon.
Lewis, C. D. Operations Management in Practice. 304p. 1980. 36.00x (ISBN 0-86003-511-5, Pub. by Allan Pubs England); pap. 18.00x (ISBN 0-86003-611-1). State Mutual Bk.
Littlechild, S. C. Operational Research for Managers. 256p. 1977. 33.00x (ISBN 0-86003-504-2, Pub. by Allan Pubs England); pap. 16.50 (ISBN 0-86003-604-9). State Mutual Bk.
Moder, Joseph J. & Elmaghraby, Salah E., eds. Handbook of Operations Research, 2 vols. 1978. Vols. 1 & 2. 32.50 ea. Vol. 1 (ISBN 0-442-24595-5). Vol. 2 (ISBN 0-442-24596-3). Vol. 3. 59.50 (ISBN 0-442-24597-1). Van Nos Reinhold.
Morse, Philip M. & Kimball, George E. Methods of Operations Research. (Illus.). 179p. 1980. pap. 14.95 (ISBN 0-932146-03-1). Peninsula.

OPERATIVE DENTISTRY

see Dentistry, Operative

OPERATIVE OBSTETRICS

see Obstetrics–Surgery

OPERATIVE UROLOGY

see Genito-Urinary Organs–Surgery

OPERATORS, DIFFERENTIAL

see Differential Operators

OPERETTA–HISTORY AND CRITICISM

Allen, Reginald. Gilbert & Sullivan in America. LC 79-54098. (Illus.). 26p. 1979. pap. 3.00. Pierpont Morgan.

OPERETTA–STORIES, PLOTS, ETC.

see Operas–Stories, Plots, etc.

OPERETTAS

see Musical Revues, Comedies, etc.; Operas

OPHIDIA

see Snakes

OPHIOLOGY

see Snakes

OPHTHALMOLOGICAL MANIFESTATIONS OF GENERAL DISEASES

see Ocular Manifestations of General Diseases

OPHTHALMOLOGY

see also Eye

Benson, William E. Retinal Detachment Diagnosis & Treatment. (Illus.). 208p. 1980. text ed. 27.50 (ISBN 0-06-140410-1, Harper Medical). Har-Row.
Gailloud, C., ed. Developments in Ophthalmology, Vol. 2. (Illus.). viii, 492p. 1981. 180.00 (ISBN 3-8055-1672-X). S Karger.
Gelatt, Kirk N., ed. Textbook of Veterinary Opthalmology. LC 80-17291. (Illus.). 788p. 1981. text ed. write for info. (ISBN 0-8121-0686-5). Lea & Febiger.
King, John H. & Wadsworth, Joseph A. An Atlas of Ophthalmic Surgery. 3rd ed. 1980. text ed. write for info. (ISBN 0-397-50481-0). Lippincott.
Peyman, Gholam A., et al, eds. Principles & Practice of Ophthalmology, 3 vols. (Illus.). 2000p. Date not set. Set. text ed. 250.00 (ISBN 0-7216-7228-0); Vol. 1. text ed. 82.50 (ISBN 0-7216-7211-6); Vol. 2. text ed. 82.50 (ISBN 0-7216-7212-4); Vol. 3. text ed. 85.00 (ISBN 0-7216-7213-2). Saunders.
Schmoger, E. & Kelsey, J. H., eds. Visual Electrodiagnosis in Systematic Diseases. (Documenta Opthalmologica Ser.: No. 23). 290p. 1980. lib. bdg. 68.50 (ISBN 90-6193-163-0, Pub by Dr. W. Junk). Kluwer Boston.
Straub, W., ed. Current Genetical, Clinical & Morphological Problems. (Developments in Ophthalmology: Vol. 3). (Illus.). 1981. 66.00 (ISBN 3-8055-2000-X). S Karger.

OPIATES

see Narcotics

OPINION, PUBLIC

see Public Opinion

OPINION POLLS

see Public Opinion Polls

OPIUM HABIT

Kroll, Larry J. & Silverman, Manuel S. Opiate Addiction: Theory & Process. LC 80-8283. 199p. 1980. lib. bdg. 17.50 (ISBN 0-8191-1324-7); pap. text ed. 9.00 (ISBN 0-8191-1325-5). U Pr of Amer.

OPIUM WAR, 1840-1842

see China–History–19th Century

OPPANOL

see Rubber, Artificial

OPPENHEIMER, J. ROBERT, 1904-1967

Goodchild, Peter. J. Robert Oppenheimer: Shatterer of Worlds. (Illus.). 320p. 1981. 15.00 (ISBN 0-686-69049-4). HM.

OPTIC THALAMUS

see Thalamus

OPTICAL COMPUTING

see Optical Data Processing

OPTICAL CRYSTALLOGRAPHY

see Crystal Optics

OPTICAL DATA PROCESSING

see also Information Display Systems

Frieden, B. R., ed. The Computer in Optical Research: Methods & Applications. (Topics in Applied Physics: Vol. 41). (Illus.). 400p. 1980. 58.00 (ISBN 0-387-10119-5). Springer-Verlag.
International Workshop on Ergonomic Aspects of Visual Display Terminals, Milan, March 1980. Proceedings. Grandjean, Etienne & Vigliani, E., eds. (Illus.). 300p. 1980. 47.50x (ISBN 0-85066-211-7). Intl Pubns Serv.

OPTICAL INSTRUMENTS

see also Glass; Microscope and Microscopy; Telescope also names of specific instruments, e.g. Spectroscope

Sixth European Conference on Optical Communication. (IEE Conference Publication Ser.: No. 190). (Illus.). 466p. (Orig.). 1980. soft cover 73.00 (ISBN 0-85296-223-1). Inst Elect Eng.

OPTICAL MASERS

see Lasers

OPTICAL MEASUREMENTS

Marcuse, D. Principles of Optical Fiber Measurement. LC 80-2339. 1981. write for info. (ISBN 0-12-470980-X). Acad Pr.

OPTICS

see also Color; Light; Light, Wave Theory Of; Optical Measurements; Perspective; Photochemistry; Radiation; Refraction; Spectrum Analysis
also headings beginning with the word Optical; also Optics, Geometrical; Optics, Physiological; and similar headings

Baltes, H. P., ed. Inverse Scattering Problems in Optics. (Topics in Current Physics: Vol. 20). (Illus.). 313p. 1980. 42.00 (ISBN 0-387-10104-7). Springer-Verlag.
Born, M. & Wolf, E. Principles of Optics: Electromagnetic Theory of Propagation, Interference & Diffraction of Light. 6th ed. (Illus.). 808p. 1980. 50.00 (ISBN 0-08-026482-4); pap. 27.50 (ISBN 0-08-026481-6). Pergamon.
Levi, L. Applied Optics: A Guide to Optical Systems Design, 2 vols. LC 67-29942. (Pure & Applied Optics Ser.): Vol. 1, 1968. 41.95 (ISBN 0-471-53110-3, Pub. by Wiley-Interscience); Vol. 2, 1980. 75.00 (ISBN 0-471-05054-7). Wiley.
Weik, Martin H. Fiber Optics & Lightwave Communications Standard Dictionary. 320p. 1980. text ed. 18.50 (ISBN 0-442-25658-2). Van Nos Reinhold.

OPTICS, FIBER

see Fiber Optics

OPTICS, LINEAR

see Nonlinear Optics

OPTICS, NONLINEAR

see Nonlinear Optics

OPTIMIZATION (MATHEMATICS)

see Mathematical Optimization

OPTIMIZATION THEORY

see Mathematical Optimization

ORAL COMMUNICATION

Here entered works on speaking as a means of communication. Works on the oral production of meaningful sounds in language are entered under Speech.
see also Oral Tradition; Speech

Bourke, S. F., et al. Oracy in Australian Schools. (Australian Council for Educational Research Ser.: No. 9). 258p. 1980. pap. text ed. 21.00x (ISBN 0-85563-212-7). Verry.
Capp, Glenn R., et al. Basic Oral Communication. 3rd ed. (Illus.). 416p. 1981. pap. text ed. 12.95 (ISBN 0-13-065979-7). P-H.
Dickson, W. Patrick, ed. Children's Oral Communication Skills. (Developmental Psychology Ser.). 1981. write for info. (ISBN 0-12-215450-9). Acad Pr.
Forrest, Mary & Olson, Margot. Exploring Speech Communication: An Introduction. 320p. 1981. pap. text ed. 9.56 (ISBN 0-8299-0381-X). West Pub.
Nadeau, Raymond E. Speech Communication: A Career Education Approach. 2nd ed. 1979. text ed. 12.50 (ISBN 0-201-05007-2). A-W.

ORAL CONTRACEPTIVES

Dickey, Richard P. Managing Contraceptive Pill Patients. 2nd rev. ed. (Illus.). 116p. 1980. vinyl 7.95 (ISBN 0-917634-08-X). Creative Infomatics.
Gillebaud, John. The Pill. (Illus.). 196p. 1980. 16.95 (ISBN 0-19-217675-7); pap. 6.95 (ISBN 0-19-286002-X). Oxford U Pr.
Kolbe, Helen K. Oral Contraceptives Abstracts--a Guide to the Literature: 1977-1979. (Population Information Library Ser.: Vol. 2). 565p. 1980. 75.00 (ISBN 0-306-65192-0). IFI Plenum.

ORAL HISTORY

Zimmerman, William. How to Tape Instant Oral Biographies: Instant Oral Biographies. LC 79-56828. (Illus.). 96p. (Orig.). 1981. pap. price not set (ISBN 0-935966-00-5, 100). Guarionex Pr.

ORAL MANIFESTATIONS OF GENERAL DISEASES

Strassburg, M. & Knolie, G. Disease of the Oral Mucosa: A Color Atlas. (Illus.). 270p. 1972. 58.00. Quint Pub Co.

ORAL MEDICATION

Bloomfield, Dennis A. & Simon, Hansjorg. Cardio Active Drugs: Pharmachlogical Basis for Practice. 1981. price not set. Urban & S.
Medications & Mathematics for the Nurse. 288p. 1981. text ed. 13.95 (ISBN 0-442-21882-6). Van Nos Reinhold.

ORAL RADIOLOGY

see Teeth–Radiography

ORAL TRADITION

Shils, Edward. Tradition. LC 80-21643. 320p. 1981. lib. bdg. price not set (ISBN 0-226-75325-5). U of Chicago Pr.

ORANGE-NASSAU, HOUSE OF

Ryskamp, Charles & Vliegenthart, A. W. William & Mary & Their House. (Illus.). 266p. 1980. 59.00x (ISBN 0-19-520185-X). Oxford U Pr.

ORANGUTANS
Wildlife Education, Ltd. Orangutans. (Zoobooks). (Illus.). 20p. (Orig.). 1980. pap. 1.00 (ISBN 0-937934-02-X). Wildlife Educ.
ORATORY
see also Debates and Debating; Lectures and Lecturing; Persuasion (Rhetoric); Public Speaking
Chavez, Moises. Modelo de Oratoria. 144p. (Orig., Span.). 1979. pap. 3.50 (ISBN 0-89922-141-6). Edit Caribe.
ORCHARDS
see Fruit-Culture
ORCHESTRAL MUSIC
see also Band Music; Symphonies
Delalande, Michel-Richard. De Profundis: Grand Motet for Soloists, Chorus, Woodwinds, Strings, & Continuo. Anthony, James R., ed. LC 79-29740. viii, 173p. 1981. write for info. (ISBN 0-8078-1439-3). U of NC Pr.
Sammartini, Giovanni B. Giovanni Batista Sammartini Sonate a Tre Stromenti. Churgin, Bathia D., ed. LC 80-12339. (Early Musical Masterworks Ser.). 80p. 1981. 20.00x (ISBN 0-8078-1446-6). U of NC Pr.
ORCHID CULTURE
Arditti, Joseph, ed. Orchid Biology: Reviews & Perspectives, I. LC 76-25648. (Illus.). 328p. 1977. 35.00x (ISBN 0-8014-1040-1). Comstock.
Kramer, Jack. Growing Orchids at Your Window. 1979. pap. 4.50 (ISBN 0-8015-3175-6, Hawthorn). Dutton.
ORCHIDS
see also Orchid Culture
Anderson, Frank. Orchids. (Abbeville Library of Art Ser.). (Illus.). 112p. 1981. pap. 4.95 (ISBN 0-89659-122-0). Abbeville Pr.
Cady, Leo & Rotherham, E. R. Australian Native Orchids in Colour. (Reed Colourbook Ser.). (Illus.). 112p. 1970. 11.75 (ISBN 0-589-07011-8, Pub. by Reed Bks Australia). C E Tuttle.
Kraenzlin, R. Monographie von Masdevallia Ruiz et Pavon Lothiana Kraenz: Scaphosepalum Pfitzer, Cryptophorantus Bearb, Rodr., Pseudostomeria Kraenzl. (Feddes Repertorium: Beiheft 34). 240p. (Ger.). 1980. Repr. of 1925 ed. lib. bdg. 47.85x (Pub. by Koeltz Germany). Lubrecht & Cramer.
Orchard Handbook. (Country Home Ser.). 96p. 2.95 (ISBN 0-88453-007-8). Berkshire Traveller.
Petrie, W. & Campbell, M. Guide to Orchids of Canada & the United States: Excluding the Tropicals of Florida & Hawaii & the Asiatics of Alaska. (Illus.). 1981. pap. price not set (ISBN 0-88839-089-0). Hancock Hse.
Schelchter, R. Beitraege zur Orchideenkunde von Zentralamerika, 2 vols. in one. (Feddes Repertorium: Beiheft 17 & 18). 402p. (Ger.). 1980. Repr. of 1922 ed. lib. bdg. 70.20x (ISBN 3-87429-181-2, Pub. by Koeltz Germany). Lubrecht & Cramer.
Schlechter, R. Beitraege zur Orchideenkunde von Colombia. (Feddes Repertorium: Beiheft 27). 183p. (Ger.). 1980. Repr. of 1924 ed. lib. bdg. 40.55x (ISBN 3-87429-182-0, Pub. by Koeltz Germany). Lubrecht & Cramer.
--Orchideenflora von Rio Grande do Sul. (Feddes Repertorium: Beiheft 35). 108p. (Ger.). 1980. Repr. of 1925 ed. lib. bdg. 30.70x (ISBN 3-87429-185-5, Pub. by Koeltz Germany). Lubrecht & Cramer.
--Orcidaceae Perrierianae zur Orchideenkunde der Insel Madagascar. (Feddes Repertorium: Beiheft 33). 391p. (Ger.). 1980. Repr. of 1925 ed. lib. bdg. 59.80x (Pub. by Koeltz Germany). Lubrecht & Cramer.
ORDER OF ST. CLARE
see Poor Clares
ORDERS, MAJOR
see Bishops; Clergy
ORDERS, MONASTIC
see Monasticism and Religious Orders
ORDINARY'S COURTS
see Probate Law and Practice
OREGON–DESCRIPTION AND TRAVEL
Blood, Marje. Exploring the Oregon Coast by Car. LC 80-25484. (Illus.). 224p. (Orig.). 1980. pap. 6.95 (ISBN 0-916076-41-5). Writing.
Dart, John O. & Johnson, Daniel M. Oregon: Wet, High, & Dry. 500p. (Orig.). 1981. pap. 18.95x (ISBN 0-913244-53-8). Hapi Pr.
Hart, Herbert M. Tour Guide to Old Forts of Oregon, Idaho, Washington, California, Vol. 3. (Illus.). 65p. (Orig.). 1981. pap. 3.95 (ISBN 0-87108-582-8). Pruett.
Sunset Editors. Oregon: Travel Guide to. 4th ed. LC 80-53486. (Illus.). 128p. 1981. pap. 5.95 (ISBN 0-376-06615-6, Sunset Bks.). Sunset-Lane.
OREGON–HISTORY
Jensen-Worth, Veryl M. Early Days on the Upper Willamette. 2nd, rev ed. (Illus.). 142p. 1981. 17.50; pap. 9.95. Worth Co.
Lockley, Fred. The Lockley Files. Helm, Mike, ed. (Illus.). 300p. (Orig.). 1981. pap. 9.95 (ISBN 0-931742-08-0). Rainy Day Oreg.
McKay, Harvey J. St. Paul, Oregon, Eighteen Thirty to Eighteen Ninety. LC 80-69228. (Illus.). 1980. 15.00 (ISBN 0-8323-0384-4). Binford.
Stein, Harry. Salem: A Pictorial History. (Illus.). 205p. 1981. pap. price not set (ISBN 0-89865-125-5). Donning Co.
Vexler, R. I. Oregon Chronology & Factbook, Vol. 37. 1978. 8.50 (ISBN 0-379-16162-1). Oceana.
OREGON–JUVENILE LITERATURE
Cloutier, James. This Day in Oregon. LC 80-83719. (Illus.). 128p. (gr. 4 up). 1981. pap. 6.95 (ISBN 0-918966-06-X). Image West.
ORES
see also Metallurgy; Metals; Mineralogy; Mines and Mineral Resources
also names of specific ores, e.g. Iron Ores
Craig, James R. & Vaughan, David J. Ore Microscopy. 325p. 1981. 32.95 (ISBN 0-471-08596-0, Pub. by Wiley-Interscience). Wiley.
Muns, George F. Chemical Analysis of Ores & Minerals for Copper, Silver, Gold, & the Platinum Metals. (Illus.). 53p. (Orig.). 1980. pap. 6.50 (ISBN 0-9604924-0-2). Muns.
Wills, B. A. Mineral Processing Technology: An Introcuction to the Practical Aspects of Ore Treatment & Mineral Recovery. 2nd ed. LC 80-41698. (International Series on Materials Science & Technology: Vol. 29). (Illus.). 450p. 1981. 60.00 (ISBN 0-08-027322-X); pap. 20.00 (ISBN 0-08-027323-8). Pergamon.
ORES–ANALYSIS
see Assaying
ORGAN
see also Electronic Organ
Lindow, Ch. W. Historic Organs in France, No.1. Blanchard, Homer D., tr. (The Little Organ Books Ser.). (Illus.). 1980. pap. 21.00 (ISBN 0-930112-03-2). Praestant.
Norman, Herbert & Norman, H. John. The Organ Today. (Illus.). 224p. 1981. 25.00 (ISBN 0-7153-8053-2). David & Charles.
Whitworth, Reginald. The Cinema & Theatre Organ. (Illus.). 144p. 1981. pap. 15.00x (ISBN 0-913746-14-2). Organ Lit.
ORGAN–CONSTRUCTION
Blanchard, Homer D., ed. Organs of Our Time Two. 154p. write for info. Praestant.
Whitworth, Reginald. The Cinema & Theatre Organ: A Comprehensive Description of This Instrument, Its Constituent Parts, & Its Use. (Illus.). 144p. 1981. pap. 15.00x (ISBN 0-913746-14-2). Organ Lit.
ORGAN, ELECTRONIC
see Electronic Organ
ORGAN MUSIC
Blanchard, Homer D. The Bach Organ Book. (The Little Organ Books Ser.: No. 3). (Illus.). Date not set. pap. price not set. Praestant.
Lindow, Ch. W. & Blanchard, Homer D. A Little Organ Lexicon. (The Little Organ Book Ser.: No. 2). 44p. 1981. pap. write for info. Praestant.
ORGAN MUSIC–HISTORY AND CRITICISM
Blanchard, Homer D. The Bach Organ Book. (The Little Organ Books Ser.: No. 3). (Illus.). Date not set. pap. price not set. Praestant.
ORGAN TRADE
see Music Trade
ORGAN TRANSPLANTATION
see Transplantation of Organs, Tissues, Etc.
ORGANIC CHEMISTRY
see Chemistry, Organic
ORGANIC GARDENING
Foster, Catharine O. The Ecological Garden. Ingraham, Erick, tr. (Illus.). 188p. (Orig.). 1981. 12.50 (ISBN 0-8159-5407-7); pap. 6.95 (ISBN 0-8159-5408-5). Devin.
ORGANICALLY GROWN FOOD
see Food, Natural
ORGANICULTURE
see Organic Gardening
ORGANIZATION
see also Industrial Management; Industrial Organization; Management; Planning
Cachenmeyer, Charles. Organizational Politica. (Analysis Ser.). 74p. (Orig.). 1979. pap. text ed. 14.95 (ISBN 0-938526-00-6). Inst Analysis.
Denhardt, Robert B. In the Shadow of Organization. LC 80-23775. 168p. 1981. 17.50x (ISBN 0-7006-0210-0). Regents Pr KS.
England, George, et al. Functioning of Complex Organizations. LC 80-21966. 352p. 1981. lib. bdg. 25.00 (ISBN 0-89946-067-4). Oelgeschlager.
Masi, Dale A. Organizing for Women: Issues, Strategies, & Services. LC 78-19577. (Illus.). 1981. 22.95 (ISBN 0-669-02577-1). Lexington Bks.
Olm, et al. Management Decisions & Organizational Policy. 3rd ed. 560p. 1981. text ed. 21.95 (ISBN 0-205-07215-1, 0872156); free tchr's ed. (ISBN 0-205-07216-X). Allyn.
ORGANIZATION–RESEARCH
see Organizational Research
ORGANIZATION, INDUSTRIAL
see Industrial Organization
ORGANIZATION, INTERNATIONAL
see International Organization
ORGANIZATION DEVELOPMENT
see Organizational Change
ORGANIZATION OF AMERICAN STATES
OAS Department of Publication, ed. Actas y Documentos: Resoluciones Aprobadas. Septimo Periodo Extraordinario de Sesiones. Washington, D.C. 22 de Mayo de 1979. 266p. 1980. pap. text ed. 15.00 (ISBN 0-8270-1171-7). OAS.
OAS General Secretariat. Actas y Documentos Segunda Conferencia Especializada Interamericana Sobre Derecho Internacional Privado, 3 vols. (CIDIP-II Ser.: Vols. 1-3). 1980. Vol. 1, 455p. pap. text ed. 25.00 (ISBN 0-8270-1113-X); Vol. 2, 547p. pap. text ed. 25.00 (ISBN 0-8270-1114-8); Vol. 3, 469p. pap. text ed. 25.00 (ISBN 0-8270-1115-6). OAS.
--Aplicacoes Da Teoria De Grupos Na Espectroscopia De Raman E Do Infravermelho. (Fisica Monografia: No. 14). 102p. 1980. pap. text ed. 2.00 (ISBN 0-8270-1126-1). OAS.
--Decima Primeira Reunino Do Conselho Interamericano De Educacao, Ciencia E Cultura: Relatorio Final. 206p. (Port., 27 de julho a 2 de agosto de 1980, Bogota, Colombia). 1980. pap. text ed. 19.00 (ISBN 0-8270-1199-7). OAS.
--Guia De las Fuentes En Hispanoamerica Para el Estudio De la Administracion Virreinal Espanola En Mexico y En el Peru 1535-1700. 523p. 1980. pap. 15.00 (ISBN 0-8270-1091-5). OAS.
--Manual De Normas Vigentes En Materia De Direitos Humanos: Actualizado Em Julho De 1980. (Human Rights Ser.). 149p. (Port.). 1980. pap. text ed. 4.00 (ISBN 0-8270-1203-9). OAS.
--Onzieme Reunion Du Conseil Interamericain Pour L'education, la Science et la Culture: Rapport Final. 236p. (Fr.). 1980. pap. text ed. 19.00 (ISBN 0-8270-1198-9). OAS.
--Revista Interamericana De Bibliografia: (Inter-American Review of Bibliography) (Vol. XXX, No. 3). 116p. (Engl. & Span.). 1980. pap. text ed. 2.00. OAS.
--Short-Term Economic Reports: Colombia, Vol. 1. 2nd ed. (Short Term Economic Reports Ser.). 77p. 1980. pap. text ed. 5.00 (ISBN 0-8270-1261-6). OAS.
--Sintesis De las Decisiones Tomadas En las Sesiones y Textos De las Resoluciones Aprobadas. (Vol. XXXI Enero-Diciembre De 1978). 174p. 1980. pap. text ed. 3.00 (ISBN 0-8270-6300-8). OAS.
--Trabajos Realizados Por el Comite Juridico Interamericano Durante el Periodo Ordinario De Sesiones. (International Law Ser.). 147p. 1980. text ed. 10.00 (ISBN 0-8270-1156-3). OAS.
--Trabajos Realizados Por el Comite Juridico Interamericano Durante el Periodo Ordinario De Sesiones: Celebrado Del 4 Al 29 De Agosto De 1980. (Comite Juridico Interamericano). 155p. (Span.). 1980. pap. text ed. 10.00 (ISBN 0-8270-1267-5). OAS.
--Trabalhos Realizados Pela Comissao Juridica Interamericana Durante Seu Periodo Ordinario De Sessoes: 30 de Julho a 16 de Agosto de 1979. 165p. (Port.). 1980. pap. text ed. 7.00 (ISBN 0-8270-1146-6). OAS.
--Tratados y Convenciones Interamerianos. (Serie Sobre Tratados: No. 9). 303p. 1980. pap. text ed. 15.00 (ISBN 0-8270-1159-8). OAS.
--Los Virus. (Serie De Biologia: No. 8). 72p. (Orig.). 1980. pap. text ed. 2.00 (ISBN 0-8270-1169-5). OAS.
--Work Accomplished by the Inter-American Juridical Committee During Its Regular Meeting: Held from January 14 to February 9, 1980. 127p. 1980. pap. text ed. 11.00 (ISBN 0-8270-1223-3). OAS.
OAS General Secretariat, ed. Boletin Estadistico de la OEA: Enero-Junio 1980, Vol. 2, Nos. 1-2. 221p. 1980. pap. text ed. 4.00. OAS.
Statements of the Laws of the OAS Member States in Matters Affecting Business. Incl. Brazil. 308p (ISBN 0-8270-5470-X); Colombia. 303p (ISBN 0-8270-5480-7); Dominica; Grenada; St. Lucia; Suriname. 1980. write for info. OAS.
ORGANIZATION OF PETROLEUM EXPORTING COUNTRIES
Johany, Ali D. The Myth of the OPEC Cartel: The Role of Saudi Arabia. 191p. 1981. 34.00 (ISBN 0-471-27864-5, Pub. by Wiley-Interscience). Wiley.
OPEC Official Resolutions & Press Releases 1960-1980. LC 80-41924. 224p. 1980. pap. 40.00 (ISBN 0-08-027335-1). Pergamon.
ORGANIZATIONAL BEHAVIOR
Aldag, Ramon & Brief, Arthur. Managing Organizational Behavior. (Illus.). 500p. 1981. text ed. 15.95 (ISBN 0-8299-0306-2). West Pub.
Blank, Raymond. Playing the Game: A Psychopolitical Strategy for Your Career. (Illus.). 224p. 1981. 10.95 (ISBN 0-688-00354-0). Morrow.
Davis, Keith & Newstrom, John. Organizational Behavior: A Book of Readings. 6th ed. (Illus.). 468p. Date not set. text ed. price not set (ISBN 0-07-015500-3, C). McGraw.
--Organizational Behavior: A Book of Readings. 6th ed. (Illus.). 468p. 1981. text ed. 11.95 (ISBN 0-07-015500-3). McGraw.
Higgins. Organizational Policy: Strat Mgmt. 1979. 21.95 (ISBN 0-03-022186-2). Dryden Pr.
Howe, Roger J. Building Profits Through Organizational Change. 272p. 1981. 17.95 (ISBN 0-8144-5681-2). Am Mgmt.
Luthans, Fred & Thompson, Kenneth R. Contemporary Readings in Organizational Behavior. 3rd ed. (Illus.). 512p. Date not set. text ed. 11.95x (ISBN 0-07-039148-3, C). McGraw.
Schieve, William C. & Allen, Peter M., eds. Self-Organization & Dissipative Structures: Applications in the Physical & Social Sciences. (Illus.). 472p. 1981. text ed. 50.00x (ISBN 0-292-70354-6). U of Tex Pr.
White, Donald D. Contemporary Perspectives in Organizational Behavior. 500p. 1981. price not set (ISBN 0-205-07350-6); free (ISBN 0-205-07351-4). Allyn.
White, Donald D. & Vroman, H. William. Action in Organizations. 500p. 1981. price not set (ISBN 0-205-07353-0); instructor manual free (ISBN 0-205-07354-9). Allyn.
ORGANIZATIONAL CHANGE
Bibeault, Donald. Corporate Turnaround: How Managers Turn Losers into Winners. 416p. 1981. 22.95 (ISBN 0-07-005190-9). McGraw.
Francis, G. James. Organization Development: A Practical Approach. 200p. 1982. text ed. 17.95 (ISBN 0-8359-5301-7). Reston.
Harvey, D. & Brown, H. Experiemntal Approach to Organizational Developement. 2nd ed. 1981. pap. 10.95 (ISBN 0-13-295360-9). P-H.
Jones, Andrew N. & Cooper, Cary L. Combating Managerial Obsolescence. LC 80-16307. 192p. 1980. lib. bdg. 19.95 (ISBN 0-86003-509-3, JCO/). Greenwood.
Lawlor, Edward E., III. Pay & Organization Development. 230p. 1981. pap. text ed. 6.95 (ISBN 0-201-03990-7). A-W.
Michael, Stephen R., et al. Techniques of Organizational Change. (Illus.). 363p. 1981. 16.95 (ISBN 0-07-041775-X). McGraw.
ORGANIZATIONAL RESEARCH
Funk, David A. Group Dynamic Law. LC 80-84733. 1981. 29.50 (ISBN 0-686-68867-8). Philos Lib.
ORGANIZATIONS
see Associations, Institutions, etc.
ORGANIZATIONS, INTERNATIONAL
see International Agencies
ORGANIZED CAMPS
see Camps
ORGANIZED CRIME
see also Gambling; Mafia; Prostitution
Bresler, Fenton. The Chinese Mafia. LC 80-5797. (Illus.). 256p. 1981. 12.95 (ISBN 0-8128-2752-X). Stein & Day.
Hanna, David. The Mafia: Two Hundred Years of Terror. (Orig.). 1980. pap. 2.25 (ISBN 0-532-23131-7). Manor Bks.
Kwitny, Jonathan. Vicious Circles: The Mafia in the Marketplace. 432p. 1981. pap. 6.95 (ISBN 0-393-00029-X). Norton.
ORGANOFLUORINE COMPOUNDS
Ferroelectrics to Fluorine Compounds, Organic, Vol. 10. 962p. 1980. 145.00 (ISBN 0-471-02063-X). Wiley.
ORGANOMETALLIC COMPOUNDS
see also particular organometallic compounds, e.g. Organomagnesium Compounds
Eich, J. J., ed. Organometallic Syntheses: Non-Transitional Compounds, Vol. 2. 1981. write for info. (ISBN 0-12-234950-4). Acad Pr.
ORGANOSULPHUR COMPOUNDS
Freidlina, R. Kh., ed. Organic Sulfer Chemistry: Ninth International Symposium on Organic Sulfur Chemistry, Riga, USSR, 9-14 June 1980. (IUPAC Symposium Ser.). (Illus.). 270p. 1981. 81.00 (ISBN 0-08-026180-9). Pergamon.
ORGANS
see Organ
ORGANS, ARTIFICIAL
see Artificial Organs
ORIENTAL ARCHITECTURE
see Architecture, Oriental
ORIENTAL ART
see Art, Oriental
ORIENTAL MUSIC
see Music, Oriental
ORIENTAL MYTHOLOGY
see Mythology, Oriental
ORIENTAL PHILOSOPHY
see Philosophy, Oriental
ORIENTAL POTTERY
see Pottery, Oriental
ORIENTAL RUGS
see Rugs, Oriental
ORIENTALS
see Asians
ORIENTATION
Brown, Terry & Hunter, Rob. The Concise Book of Orienteering. 1979. pap. 2.95. Vanguard.
ORIENTATION (COLLEGE STUDENTS)
see College Student Orientation
ORIENTATION (STUDENTS)
see Students
ORIENTATION (TEACHERS)
see Teachers, Training of
ORIGAMI
see also Paper Work
Randlett, Samuel. The Best of Origami. (Illus.). 185p. 1981. 12.95 (ISBN 0-571-10275-1, Pub. by Faber & Faber). Merrimack Bk Serv.
Takahama, Toshie. Origami for Displays. (Illus.). 32p. (Orig.). 1979. pap. 3.50 (ISBN 0-8048-1350-7, Pub by Shufunotomo Co. Ltd, Japan). C E Tuttle.
--Origami for Fun: Thirty-One Basic Models. (Illus.). 32p. (Orig.). 1980. Repr. of 1973 ed. pap. 3.50 (ISBN 0-8048-1352-3, Shufuntomo Co Ltd Japan). C E Tuttle.

--Origami Toys: Fifteen Simple Models. (Illus.). 32p. (Orig.). 1979. pap. 3.50 (ISBN 0-8048-1351-5, Pub by Shufunotomo Co. Ltd. Japan). C E Tuttle.

ORKNEY ISLANDS

Brown, George M. Portrait of Orkney. (Illus.). 128p. 1981. 23.00 (ISBN 0-7012-0513-X, Pub. by Chatto-Bodley-Jonathan). Merrimack Bk Serv.

Linklater, Eric. Orkney & Shetland: An Historical, Geographical, Social & Scenic Survey. 3rd ed. Nicolson, James R., rev. by. (Illus.). 285p. 1980. 20.00x (ISBN 0-7091-8142-6). Intl Pubns Serv.

ORNAMENT

see Decoration and Ornament

ORNAMENTAL ALPHABETS

see Alphabets

ORNAMENTAL DESIGN

see Design, Decorative

ORNAMENTAL PLANTS

see Plants, Ornamental

ORNITHOLOGISTS

Cutright, Paul R. & Brodhead, Michael J. Elliott Coues: Naturalist & Frontier Historian. LC 80-12424. (Illus.). 510p. 1981. 28.95 (ISBN 0-252-00802-2). U of Ill Pr.

ORNITHOLOGY

Petrak, Margaret L., ed. Diseases of Cage & Aviary Birds. 2nd ed. (Illus.). 540p. 1981. text ed. price not set (ISBN 0-8121-0692-X). Lea & Febiger.

ORNITHOLOGY, ECONOMIC

see Birds, Injurious and Beneficial

OROGRAPHY

see Mountains

ORPHANS' COURTS

see Probate Law and Practice

ORTHODOX EASTERN CHURCH

Coniaris, A. M. Making God Real in the Orthodox Christian Home. 1977. pap. 4.95 (ISBN 0-937032-07-7). Light & Life Pub Co MN.

--Orthodoxy: A Creed for Today. 1972. pap. 5.95 (ISBN 0-937032-19-0). Light&Life Pub Co MN.

Harakas, S. Guidelines for Marriage in the Orthodox Church. 1980. pap. 1.25 (ISBN 0-937032-21-2). Light&Life Pub Co MN.

--Something Is Stirring in World Orthodoxy. 1978. pap. 2.95 (ISBN 0-937032-04-2). Light & Life Pub Co MN.

Kowalczyk, J. Orthodox View on Abortion. 1979. pap. 1.50 (ISBN 0-686-27070-3). Light&Life Pub Co MN.

Makrakis, Apostolos. The City of Zion--the Human Society in Christ, i.e., the Church Built Upon a Rock. Orthodox Christian Educational Society, ed. Cummings, Denver, tr. from Hellenic. 109p. 1958. pap. 3.00x (ISBN 0-938366-16-5). Orthodox Chr.

--The Holy Orthodox Church. Orthodox Christian Educational Society, ed. Lisney, M. I. & Krick, L., trs. from Hellenic. 298p. (Orig.). 1980. pap. 5.00x (ISBN 0-938366-34-3). Orthodox Chr.

--Memoir of the Nature of the Church of Christ. Orthodox Christian Educational Society, ed. Cummings, Denver, tr. from Hellenic. 175p. 1947. 3.00x (ISBN 0-938366-21-1). Orthodox Chr.

--The Orthodox Definition of Political Science. Orthodox Christian Educational Society, ed. Cummings, Denver, tr. from Hellenic. 163p. 1968. pap. 2.00x (ISBN 0-938366-31-9). Orthodox Chr.

Meyendorff, John. The Orthodox Church: Its Past & Its Role in the World Today. 258p. 1981. pap. write for info. (ISBN 0-913836-81-8). St Vladimirs.

Nissiotis, M. Interpeting Orthodoxy. 1980. pap. 2.45 (ISBN 0-937032-23-9). Light&Life Pub Co MN.

Staniloae, Dumitru. Theology & the Church. Barringer, Robert, tr. from Romanian. LC 80-19313. 240p. (Orig.). 1980. pap. 6.95 (ISBN 0-913836-69-9, BS695.57 230.19498). St Martin.

Winkler, Gabriele. Prayer Attitude in the Eastern Church. 1978. pap. 1.25 (ISBN 0-937032-01-8). Light & Life Pub Co MN.

Zhishman, Joseph. Das Ehrerecht der Orientalischen Kirche. LC 80-2367. 1981. Repr. of 1864 ed. 63.50 (ISBN 0-404-18918-0). AMS Pr.

ORTHODOX EASTERN CHURCH–LITURGY AND RITUAL

Harakas, S. Living the Liturgy. 1974. pap. 3.50 (ISBN 0-937032-17-4). Light&Life Pub Co MN.

Makrakis, Apostolos. Catechesis of the Orthodox Church. rev. ed. Orthodox Christian Educational Society, ed. 239p. 1969. pap. text ed. 4.00x (ISBN 0-938366-14-9). Orthodox Chr.

Ware, K. Communion & Intercommunion. 1980. pap. 1.95 (ISBN 0-937032-20-4). Light&Life Pub Co MN.

ORTHODOX EASTERN CHURCH–RELATIONS–CATHOLIC CHURCH

see also Schism–Eastern and Western Church

Makrakis, Apostolos. The Innovations of the Roman Church. 82p. (Orig.). 1966. pap. 1.50x (ISBN 0-938366-39-4). Orthodox Chr.

ORTHODOX EASTERN CHURCH–RELATIONS–PROTESTANT CHURCHES

Makrakis, Apostolos. An Orthodox Protestant Debate. Cummings, Denver, tr. 1949. pap. 2.00x (ISBN 0-938366-37-8). Orthodox Chr.

ORTHODOX EASTERN CHURCH–SERMONS

Coniaris, A. M. Eighty Talks for Orthodox Young People. 1975. pap. 3.50 (ISBN 0-937032-16-6). Light&Life Pub Co MN.

--Sermons on the Major Holy Days of the Orthodox Church. 1978. pap. 4.95 (ISBN 0-937032-03-4). Light & Life Pub Co MN.

--Sixty-One Talks for Orthodox Funerals. 1969. pap. 4.95 (ISBN 0-937032-02-6). Light & Life Pub Co MN.

ORTHODOX EASTERN MONASTICISM AND RELIGIOUS ORDERS

see Monasticism and Religious Orders, Orthodox Eastern

ORTHOEPY

see Phonetics

ORTHOMOLECULAR MEDICINE

see also Chemotherapy; Nutrition

Applewhite, Philip B. Molecular Gods: How Molecules Determine Our Behavior. (Illus.). 288p. 1981. 10.95 (ISBN 0-13-599530-2). P-H.

ORTHOMOLECULAR THERAPY

see Orthomolecular Medicine

ORTHOPEDIA

see also Orthopedic Surgery; Pediatric Orthopedia also special conditions to which orthopedic methods are applicable, e.g. Hip Joints–Diseases; Spine–Abnormities and Deformities

Hensinger, Robert N. Neonatal Orthapeadics. (Neonatology Ser.). 1981. write for info. (ISBN 0-8089-1355-7). Grune.

Mears, Dana C. External Skeletal Fixation. (Illus.). 584p. 1981. write for info. (5900-9). Williams & Wilkins.

Mubarak, Scott J., et al. Compartment Snydromes & Volkmann's Contracture. (Saunder's Monographs in Clinical Orthopedics: Vol. 3). (Illus.). 200p. 1981. text ed. price not set (ISBN 0-7216-6604-3). Saunders.

Sevitt, Simon. Bone Repair & Fracture Healing in Man. (Current Problems in Orthopaedics Ser.). (Illus.). 300p. 1981. lib. bdg. 62.00 (ISBN 0-443-01806-5). Churchill.

ORTHOPEDIC APPARATUS

Bray, Jean & Wright, Sheila, eds. The Use of Technology in the Care of the Elderly & the Disabled. LC 80-17847. xii, 267p. 1980. lib. bdg. 29.95 (ISBN 0-313-22616-4, BTC/). Greenwood.

ORTHOPEDIC SURGERY

Kopta, Joseph A., et al, eds. Orthopedic Surgery Continuing Education Review. LC 80-80366. 1980. pap. 14.50 (ISBN 0-87488-398-9). Med Exam.

Spear, Curtis V. Self-Assessment of Knowledge in Orthopedic Surgery. LC 80-80368. 1980. pap. 16.50 (ISBN 0-87488-229-X). Med Exam.

ORTHOPTICS

Cashell, G. T. & Durran, I. M. Handbook of Orthoptic Principles. 4th ed. (Illus.). 1981. pap. text ed. 13.75 (ISBN 0-443-02200-3). Churchill.

ORWELL, GEORGE, 1903-1950

Bal, Sant S. George Orwell: The Ethical Imagination. 144p. 1981. text ed. 9.25 (ISBN 0-391-02202-4). Humanities.

Crick, Bernard. George Orwell: A Life. 1981. 19.95 (ISBN 0-316-16112-8). Little.

OSAGE INDIANS

see Indians of North America–The West

OSCARS (MOVING-PICTURES)

see Academy Awards (Moving-Pictures)

OSCILLATIONS

see also Damping (Mechanics); Frequencies of Oscillating Systems

Bolton, W. Waves, Rays & Oscillations, Bk. 6. LC 80-41396. (Study Topics in Physics). 96p. 1980. pap. text ed. write for info. (ISBN 0-408-10657-3). Butterworths.

Mickens, Ronald E. An Introduction to Nonlinear Oscillations. LC 80-13169. (Illus.). 320p. Date not set. text ed. price not set (ISBN 0-521-22208-7). Cambridge U Pr.

OSCILLOSCOPE

see Cathode Ray Oscilloscope

OSMANIC LANGUAGE

see Turkish Language

OSMANLI LANGUAGE

see Turkish Language

OSTEOARTHRITIS

see Arthritis

OSTEOLOGY

see Skeleton

OTARIA

see Seals (Animals)

OTO INDIANS

see Indians of North America–The West

OTOLARYNGOLOGY

Dayal, Vijay S. Clinical Otolaryngology. (Illus.). 304p. 1981. pap. text ed. write for info (ISBN 0-397-50499-3). Lippincott.

Farb, Stanley N. The Ear, Nose, & Throat Book: A Doctor's Guide to Better Health. (Appleton Consumer Health Guides). (Illus.). 158p. 1980. 12.95 (ISBN 0-8385-2021-9); pap. 5.95 (ISBN 0-8385-2020-0). ACC.

Jazbi, Basharat, ed. Pediatric Otorhinolaryngology: A Review of Ear, Nose, & Throat Problems in Children. 320p. 1980. 24.50x (ISBN 0-8385-7799-7). ACC.

Jongkees, L. B. Iatrogenic Problems in Otorlaryngology. 1981. text ed. write for info. (ISBN 0-443-08050-X). Churchill.

McGuirt, W. Frederick, ed. Pediatric Otolaryngology Case Studies. LC 80-80367. 1980. pap. 18.50 (ISBN 0-87488-094-7). Med Exam.

OTOLOGY

see Ear

OTORHINOLARYNGOLOGY

see Otolaryngology

OUT OF THE BODY EXPERIENCES

see Astral Projection

OUTDOOR COOKERY

see Cookery (Wild Foods); Cookery, Outdoor

OUTDOOR EDUCATION

see also Camping; Physical Education and Training

Ford, Phyllis M. Principles & Practices of Outdoor-Environment Education. LC 80-23200. 350p. 1981. text ed. 15.95 (ISBN 0-471-04768-6). Wiley.

Meier, Joel F., et al. High Adventure Outdoor Pursuits: Organization & Leadership. (Brighton Ser. in Recreation & Leisure). (Illus.). 240p. (Orig.). 1980. pap. 9.95 (ISBN 0-89832-019-4). Brighton Pub.

Neimark, Paul. Hiking & Exploring. (Wilderness World Ser.). (Illus.). 64p. (gr. 3 up). 1981. PLB 9.25 (ISBN 0-516-02453-1). Childrens.

Wlson, Renate. Inside Outward Bound. (Illus.). 208p. 1981. pap. 7.95 (ISBN 0-914788-41-8). East Woods.

OUTDOOR LIFE

see also Camping; Country Life; Hiking; Mountaineering; Picnicking; Sports

Anderson, Ken. The Sterno Guide to the Outdoors. 5.95 (ISBN 0-916752-16-X). Green Hill.

Demske, Richard. Year-Round Outdoor Building Projects: An Encyclopedia of Building Techniques & Construction Plans. 304p. 1980. pap. 9.95 (ISBN 0-442-21259-3). Van Nos Reinhold.

Grow, Laurence. The Old House Book of Outdoor Living Places. (Illus., Orig.). 1981. 15.00 (ISBN 0-446-51219-2). Warner Bks.

--The Old House Book of Outdoor Spaces. (Orig.). 1981. 8.95 (ISBN 0-446-97556-7). Warner Bks.

Meck, Charles R., ed. The Great Outdoors Book. LC 81-65103. (Illus.). 256p. (Orig.). 1981. pap. 8.95 (ISBN 0-910676-24-0, 7706). DBI.

Rutstrum, Calvin. Backcountry. LC 80-22052. (Illus.). 200p. 1981. pap. 10.00 (ISBN 0-934802-07-6). Ind Camp Supply.

OUTDOOR RECREATION

see also Camping; Parks; Picnicking; Wildlife Conservation

Alderson, Frederick. Outdoor Games. (Junior Reference Ser.). (Illus.). 64p. (gr. 7 up). 1980. 7.95 (ISBN 0-7136-2031-5). Dufour.

Eathorne, Richard H. The Analysis of Outdoor Recreation Demand: A Review & Annotated Bibliography of the Current State-of-the-Art. (Public Administration Ser.: Bibliography P-563). 93p. 1980. pap. 10.00. Vance Biblios.

Ford, Phyllis M. Principles & Practices of Outdoor-Environment Education. LC 80-23200. 350p. 1981. text ed. 15.95 (ISBN 0-471-04768-6). Wiley.

McManus, Patrick. They Shoot Canoes, Don't They? 228p. 1981. 10.95 (ISBN 0-03-058646-1). HR&W.

Meier, Joel F., et al. High Adventure Outdoor Pursuits: Organization & Leadership. (Brighton Ser. in Recreation & Leisure). (Illus.). 240p. (Orig.). 1980. pap. 9.95 (ISBN 0-89832-019-4). Brighton Pub.

OUTDOOR RELIEF

see Public Welfare

OUTER SPACE–EXPLORATION

O'Leary, Brian. The Fertile Stars. (Illus.). 1981. 12.95. Everest Hse.

OUTER SPACE–EXPLORATION–JUVENILE LITERATURE

Cohen, Daniel. A Close Look at Close Encounters. LC 80-2784. (Illus.). 192p. (gr. 7 up). 1981. PLB 7.95 (ISBN 0-396-07927-X). Dodd.

Furniss, Tim. Man in Space. (Today's World Ser.). (Illus.). 72p. (gr. 7-9). 1981. 15.95 (ISBN 0-7134-3582-8, Pub. by Batsford England). David & Charles.

OUTER SPACE–JUVENILE LITERATURE

DiCerto, Joseph. Star Voyage. Orig. Title: One Hundred Two Questions & Answers About Outer Space. (Illus.). 96p. (gr. 4-7). 1981. PLB price not set (ISBN 0-671-33034-9). Messner.

OUTLAWS

see also Brigands and Robbers

Hutton, Harold. Doc Middleton: Life & Legends of the Notorious Plains Outlaw. LC 67-14260. (Illus.). 290p. 1980. 14.95 (ISBN 0-8040-0532-X, SB). Swallow.

O'Neal, Bill. Henry Brown: The Outlaw-Marshall. (Illus.). 165p. 12.95; leatherbound collector's edition 75.00. Creative Pubns.

Vanderwood, Paul J. Disorder & Progress: Bandits, Police, & Mexican Development. LC 80-22345. (Illus.). xx, 269p. 1981. 19.95x (ISBN 0-8032-4651-X, Bison); pap. 7.95 (ISBN 0-8032-9600-2, BB 767). U of Nebr Pr.

OUTPATIENT SERVICES IN HOSPITALS

see Hospitals–Outpatient Services

OUTPUT STANDARDS

see Production Standards

OVARIES

see also Menstruation

Hutchinson, J. S. The Hypothalamo-Pituitary Control of the Ovary. Horrobin, D. F., ed. (Annual Research Reviews Ser.: Vol. 2). 215p. 1980. 28.00 (ISBN 0-88831-091-9). Eden Med Res.

OVENS

see Stoves

OVERHEAD COSTS

Clark, John M. Studies in the Economics of Overhead Costs. 1980. pap. write for info. (ISBN 0-226-10851-1). U of Chicago Pr.

Heyel, Carl & Naidich, Arnold. Encyclopedia on How to Cut Overhead. 1980. 89.95. Busn Res Pubns.

OVERSIGHT, CONGRESSIONAL (UNITED STATES)

see United States–Congress–Powers and Duties

OVERWEIGHT

see Obesity

OWLS

Strand, Mark. The Owl's Insomnia. LC 73-81724. 1973. pap. 4.95. Atheneum.

OWNERSHIP

see Property

OXFORD UNIVERSITY

Oorthuys, Cas. Oxford in Focus. (Illus.). 144p. 1981. pap. 7.50 (ISBN 0-85181-100-0, Pub. by Faber & Faber). Merrimack Bk Serv.

OXIDATION

West, J. M. Basic Corrosion & Oxidation. 247p. 1981. 69.95 (ISBN 0-470-27080-2). Halsted Pr.

OXYACETYLENE WELDING AND CUTTING

Brightman, Robert. Bernzomatic Torch Tips. 6.95 (ISBN 0-916752-16-X). Green Hill.

Jefferson, Ted B. & Jefferson, D. T. Jefferson's Gas Welding Manual. 4th ed. (Monticello Bks). 140p. 1980. pap. 5.00. Jefferson Pubns.

OXYGEN

Kintzinger, J. P. & Marsmann, H. Oxygen-Seventeen & Silicon-Twenty-Nine. (NMR-Basic Principles & Progress Ser.: Vol. 17). (Illus.). 250p. 1981. 48.00 (ISBN 0-387-10414-3). Springer-Verlag.

OXYGEN THERAPY

Seedor, Marie M. A Nursing Guide to Oxygen Therapy: Unit in Fundamentals of Nursing. 3rd rev. ed. (Nursing Education Monograph: No. 10). (Illus.). 1980. pap. 8.50 (Pub. by Columbia U Pr). Lippincott.

P

P L-ONE (COMPUTER PROGRAM LANGUAGE)

Abel, Peter. Structured PL-One & PL: A Problem Solving Approach. 1981. text ed. 18.95 (ISBN 0-8359-7120-1); pap. text ed. 12.95 (ISBN 0-8359-7119-8); instr's. manual avail. (ISBN 0-8359-7121-X). Reston.

SAS Institute Inc., ed. SAS Programmer's Guide, Nineteen Eighty-One Edition. (SAS Programmer's Guide). 208p. (Orig.). 1980. pap. 9.95. SAS Inst.

PACEMAKER, ARTIFICIAL (HEART)

Sonnenberg, David E. & Birnbaum, Michael. Pacemakers: A Patient's Guide. Groom, Kathe, ed. (Illus.). 200p. 1980. write for info. (ISBN 0-935576-04-5); pap. write for info. (ISBN 0-935576-05-3). Kesend Pub Ltd.

PACIFIC ISLANDS (TER.) CONGRESS OF MICRONESIA

Hoyt, Edwin P. To the Marianas: War in the Central Pacific: 1944. 192p. 1980. deluxe ed. 12.95 (ISBN 0-442-26105-5). Van Nos Reinhold.

PACIFIC SETTLEMENT OF INTERNATIONAL DISPUTES

see Arbitration, International; Diplomatic Negotiations in International Disputes

PACIFIC STATES

United Nations. Statistical Yearbook for Asia & the Pacific, 1978: Annuaire Statistique pour l'asie et le Pacifique. 11th ed. LC 76-641968. (Illus.). 536p. (Orig.). 1979. pap. 28.00x (ISBN 0-8002-1083-2). Intl Pubns Serv.

PACIFISM

see also Conscientious Objectors; Passive Resistance to Government; Peace

Ceadel, Martin. Pacifism in Britain Nineteen Fourteen to Nineteen Forty Five: The Defining of a Faith. 352p. 1980. 37.50x (ISBN 0-19-821882-6). Oxford U Pr.

Gandhi, Mohandas K. For Pacifists. Kumarappa, Bharatan, ed. 130p. (Orig.). 1981. pap. 1.50 (ISBN 0-934676-28-3). Greenlf Bks.

Matheson, Peter. A Just Peace. (Orig.). 1981. pap. 5.95 (ISBN 0-377-00107-4). Friend Pr.

Snow, Mike. Christian Pacifism. 1981. write for info. (ISBN 0-913408-67-0). Friends United.

PACKAGED BUILDINGS

see Buildings, Prefabricated

PACKAGING

see also Aerosols; Containers; Labels; Plastics in Packaging

Paine, F. A. The Packaging Media. 444p. 1978. 43.95 (ISBN 0-470-99369-3). Wiley.

Paulson, Walter G., et al. Planning a Corrugated Container Plant. (Tappi Press Reports). (Illus.). 125p. 1980. 93.95 (ISBN 0-89852-387-7, 01-01-R087). Tappi.

Rich, Susan, ed. Kline Guide to the Packaging Industry. (Illus.). 324p. 1980. pap. 100.00. Kline.

Smith, D. K. Package Conveyors: Design & Estimating. 136p. 1972. 25.00x (ISBN 0-85264-213-X, Pub. by Griffin England). State Mutual Bk.

Stern, Walter. Stern's Handbook of Package Design Research. 704p. 1981. 42.50 (ISBN 0-471-05901-3, Pub. by Wiley-Interscience). Wiley.

PACKETS

Rosner, Roy D. Packet Switching: Tomorrow's Communications Today. (Illus.). 1981. text ed. 31.50. Lifetime Learn.

PACKING (TRANSPORTATION)
see Backpacking
PACKING INDUSTRY
see Meat Industry and Trade
PADDLEBALL
see also Racquetball
Peele, David A., ed. Racket & Paddle Games: A Guide to Information Sources. LC 80-23977. (Sports, Games & Pastimes Information Guide Ser., Part of the Gale Information Guide Library: Vol. 9). 300p. 1980. 30.00 (ISBN 0-8103-1480-0). Gale.
PADDY FIELD CULTURE
see Irrigation
PADEREWSKI, IGNACY JAN, 1860-1941
Duleba, Wladyslaw & Sokolowska, Zofia. Ignacy Paderewski. Litwinski, Wiktor, tr. from Polish. (Library of Polish Studies: Vol. VII). (Illus.). text ed. 8.95 (ISBN 0-917004-14-0). Kosciuszko.
PADRE ISLAND, TEXAS
Wiese, B. R. & White, W. A. Padre Island National Seashore-a Guide to the Geology, Natural Environments & History of a Texas Barrier Island. Date not set. price not set (GB 17). Bur Econ Geology.
PAEDOPHILIA
see Pedophilia
PAGANISM
Jackson, John G. Pagan Origins of the Christ Myth. 1980. pap. 3.00. Am Atheist.
MacMullen, Ramsay. Paganism in the Roman Empire. LC 80-54222. 221p. 1981. 23.00x (ISBN 0-300-02655-2). Yale U Pr.
PAIN
see also Anesthetics; Suffering
Emmers, Raimond. Pain: A Spike-Interval Coded Message in the Brain. 1981. text ed. price not set (ISBN 0-89004-650-6). Raven.
Furst, Susanna & Knoll, J., eds. Opiate Receptors & the Neurochemical Correlates of Pain: Proceedings of the Third Congress of the Hungarian Pharmacological Society, Budapest, 1979. LC 80-41281. (Advances in Pharmacological Research & Practice Ser.: Vol. V). 240p. 1981. 45.00 (ISBN 0-08-026390-9). Pergamon.
Gorsky, Benjamin H. Pain: Origin & Treatment -- Discussions in Patient Management. LC 80-15857. 1980. 18.00 (ISBN 0-87488-448-9); pap. 10.00 (ISBN 0-87488-447-0). Med Exam.
Kosterlitz, H. W. & Terenius, L. Y., eds. Pain & Society. (Dahlem Workshop Reports, Life Sciences Research Report Ser.: No. 17). (Illus.). 523p. (Orig.). 1980. pap. text ed. 39.40 (ISBN 0-89573-099-5). Verlag Chemie.
Perlstein, Israel. How to Relieve or Eliminate Chronic Pains - Discomforts Acquired During Sleep: A Doctor's Solution to Your Sleeping Problems. (Illus.). 64p. (Orig.). 1981. pap. 1.95 (ISBN 0-8326-2252-4, 7445). Delair.
Trieger, Norman. Pain Control. (Illus.). 143p. 1974. 24.00. Quint Pub Co.
PAINE, THOMAS, 1737-1809
Sedgwick, Ellery. Thomas Paine. 150p. 1980. Repr. of 1899 ed. lib. bdg. 20.00 (ISBN 0-8482-6306-5). Norwood Edns.
PAINT
see also Corrosion and Anti-Corrosives; Pigments
Flick, Ernest W. Exterior Water-Based Trade Paint Formulations. LC 80-19212. 349p. 1981. 36.00 (ISBN 0-8155-0820-4). Noyes.
Morgans, W. M. Outlines of Paint Technology, Vol. 1. 1981. 75.00x (ISBN 0-686-68842-2, Pub. by Griffin England). State Mutual Bk.
PAINT MATERIALS
see also Paint; Pigments
Thomas, Anne W. Colors from the Earth. 132p. 1980. 13.95 (ISBN 0-442-25786-4). Van Nos Reinhold.
PAINTED GLASS
see Glass Painting and Staining
PAINTERS
see also Artists
De Menil, Dominique, ed. Jim Love up to Now. LC 80-82000. (Illus.). 1980. pap. 8.00 (ISBN 0-914412-16-7). Inst for the Arts.
Henderson, David, intro. by. Joe Overstreet. LC 72-85404. (Illus.). 1972. pap. 2.25 (ISBN 0-914412-02-7). Inst for the Arts.
PAINTERS–AUSTRALIA
Catalano, Gary. The Years of Hope: Australian Art & Criticism 1959-1968. (Illus.). 224p. 1980. 33.50 (ISBN 0-19-554220-7). Oxford U Pr.
PAINTERS–GERMANY
Marrow, James H. & Shestack, Alan, eds. Hans Baldung Grien: Prints & Drawings. LC 80-52733. (Illus.). xiv, 282p. 1981. lib. bdg. 19.95 (ISBN 0-89467-013-1). Yale Art Gallery.
Radycki, J. Diane, tr. The Letters & Journals of Paula Modersohn-Becker. LC 80-18993. 370p. 1980. 17.50 (ISBN 0-8108-1344-0). Scarecrow.
PAINTERS–ITALY
Okada, Kenzo, et al, illus. Okada, Shinoda, & Tsutaka. LC 79-84887. (Illus.). 50p. (Orig.). 1979. pap. 6.00 (ISBN 0-88397-034-1). Intl Exhibit Foun.
PAINTERS–NETHERLANDS
Sutton, Peter C. Pieter De Hooch: Complete Edition with a Catalogue Raisonne. LC 80-7667. (Illus.). 312p. 1980. slipcased 95.00x (ISBN 0-8014-1339-7). Cornell U Pr.
PAINTERS–UNITED STATES
Kahan, Mitchell D. Roger Brown. LC 80-24063. (Illus.). 96p. (Orig.). 1980. pap. 10.00 (ISBN 0-89280-042-9). Montgomery Mus.
Mc Larty, Barbara L., ed. Charles Heaney: Master of the Oregon Scene. McLarty, Jack, tr. (Illus.). 65p. (Orig.). 1980. pap. 9.50. Image Gallery.
PAINTING
see also Color; Composition (Art); Cubism; Easter Eggs; Figure Painting; Flower Painting and Illustration; Genre Painting; Glass Painting and Staining; Impressionism (Art); Landscape Painting; Marine Painting; Paintings; Perspective; Post-Impressionism (Art); Proportion (Art); Realism in Art; Scene Painting; Stencil Work; Still-Life Painting; Water-Color Painting
Osborne, Roy. Lights & Pigments: Color Principles for Artists. LC 80-8790. (Icon Editions). (Illus.). 176p. (Orig.). 1981. pap. 5.95 (ISBN 0-06-430113-3, HarpT). Har-Row.
PAINTING–HISTORY
see also Painting, French; Painting, Italian, and similar headings
Gottlieb, Carla. From the Window of God to the Vanity of Man: A Study of Window Symbolism in Western Painting. LC 80-53355. (Illus.). 500p. 1980. 35.00 (ISBN 0-9604420-1-4); pap. 25.00 (ISBN 0-9604420-2-2). Boian Bks.
PAINTING–JUVENILE LITERATURE
Klimo, Kate, ed. My Color Book. (Playboards Ser.). (Illus.). 12p. (ps-k). Date not set. boards 2.95 (ISBN 0-671-42529-3, Little Simon). S&S.
PAINTING–TECHNIQUE
see also Airbrush Art
Bearden, Romare & Holty, Carl. The Painter's Mind: A Study of the Relations of Srtructure & Space in Painting a New Printing. LC 80-8527. 240p. 1981. lib. bdg. 25.00 (ISBN 0-8240-9457-3). Garland Pub.
Betts, Edward. Creatice Seascape Painting. 160p. 1981. 19.15 (ISBN 0-8230-1113-5). Watson-Guptill.
Hildebrand, Adolf. The Problem of Form in Painting and Sculpture. Freedberg, Sydney J., ed. LC 77-19375. (Connoisseurship & Art History Ser.: Vol. 11). (Illus.). 141p. 1979. lib. bdg. 20.00 (ISBN 0-8240-3269-1). Garland Pub.
Kinstler, Everett R. Painting Faces, Figures & Landscapes. 144p. 1981. 22.50 (ISBN 0-8230-3625-1). Watson-Guptill.
Marandel, J. Patrice, intro. by. Gray Is the Color: An Exhibition of Grisaille Painting, 13th-20th Centuries. LC 73-92776. (Illus.). 1974. pap. 5.00 (ISBN 0-914412-08-6). Inst for the Arts.
Parramon, J. M. Oils. (Art Ser.). (Orig.). 1980. pap. 4.95 (ISBN 0-89586-073-2). H P Bks.
PAINTING, AMERICAN
Flexner, James T. First Flowers of Our Wilderness: American Painting, the Colonial Period. (History of American Painting Ser.: Vol. 1). (Illus.). 390p. 1980. pap. 5.00 (ISBN 0-486-22180-6). Dover.
PAINTING, CHINESE
Chien-chiu, Chow & Chen-ying, Chow L. Chinese Painting: A Comprehensive Guide. (Illus.). 240p. 1980. 45.00 (ISBN 0-89955-139-4, Pub. by Art Bk Co Taiwan). Intl Schol Bk Serv.
Jorgensen, Gunhild. Techniques of China Painting. 112p. 1980. pap. 7.95 (ISBN 0-442-20176-1). Van Nos Reinhold.
Sullivan, Michael. The Three Perfections: Chinese Painting, Poetry & Calligraphy. LC 80-18189. (Illus.). 64p. 10.00 (ISBN 0-8076-0996-X); pap. 4.95 (ISBN 0-8076-0997-8). Braziller.
PAINTING, DECORATIVE
see Decoration and Ornament
PAINTING, DUTCH
Wilson, William H. The Golden Age: Dutch Seventeenth Century Portraiture. LC 80-53473. (Illus.). 175p. (Orig.). 1980. pap. 8.00 (ISBN 0-916758-03-6). Ringling Mus Art.
PAINTING, EUROPEAN
Sutton, Peter C. Pieter De Hooch: Complete Edition with a Catalogue Raisonne. LC 80-7667. (Illus.). 312p. 1980. slipcased 95.00x (ISBN 0-8014-1339-7). Cornell U Pr.
PAINTING, INDIC
Welsh, Stuart C. Room for Wonder: Indian Painting During the British Period, 1760 to 1880. LC 78-50093. (Illus.). 192p. 1981. pap. 14.95 (ISBN 0-917418-60-3). Agrinde Pubns.
PAINTING, ISLAMIC
Simpson, Marianna S. Arab & Persian Painting in the Fogg Art Museum, Vol. II. Walsh, Peter & Kaliski, Andrea, eds. LC 80-10525. (Fogg Art Museum Handbooks). (Illus.). 125p. 1980. pap. 8.50 (ISBN 0-916724-10-7). Fogg Art.
PAINTING, ITALIAN
Boskovits, Miklos. Italian Panel Painting of the Fourteenth & Fifteenth Centuries. Hoch, Elisabeth, tr. from Hungarian. (Illus.). 70p. 1980. 25.00 (ISBN 0-937832-02-2). Dante Univ Bkshlf.
PAINTING, MUSLIM
see Painting, Islamic
PAINTING, PERSIAN
Azarpay, Guitty. Sogdian Painting: The Pictorial Epic in Oriental Art. 300p. 1981. 50.00x (ISBN 0-520-03765-0). U of Cal Pr.
Simpson, Marianna S. Arab & Persian Painting in the Fogg Art Museum, Vol. II. Walsh, Peter & Kaliski, Andrea, eds. LC 80-10525. (Fogg Art Museum Handbooks). (Illus.). 125p. 1980. pap. 8.50 (ISBN 0-916724-10-7). Fogg Art.
Welch, Stuart C. Wonders of the Age: Masterpieces of Early Safavid Painting, 1501-1576. LC 79-2480. 223p. 1979. pap. 12.95 (ISBN 0-916724-38-7). Fogg Art.
PAINTING, RELIGIOUS
see Christian Art and Symbolism
PAINTINGS
see also Portraits; Water Colors
Ballantine, Betty. Frazetta Four. 96p. 1980. pap. 8.95 (ISBN 0-553-01267-3). Bantam.
PAINTINGS–JUVENILE LITERATURE
Goodall, John S. Victorians Abroad. LC 80-67431. (Illus.). 64p. 1981. 8.95 (ISBN 0-689-50191-9, McElderry Bk). Atheneum.
PAINTINGS–PRIVATE COLLECTIONS
McCaughey, Patrick, ed. Australian Paintings of the Heidelberg School: The Jack Manton Collection. (Illus.). 160p. 1979. text ed. 65.00x (ISBN 0-19-550592-1). Oxford U Pr.
PAINTINGS, ABSTRACT
see Art, Modern–20th Century
PAINTINGS, AMERICAN
Arthur, John. Realism Photo-Realism. LC 80-83113. (Illus.). 123p. 1980. 25.00 (ISBN 0-86659-002-1); pap. 16.50 (ISBN 0-86659-003-X). Philbrook.
Baro, Gene. Robert Gordy: Paintings & Drawings. (Illus.). 1981. pap. price not set (ISBN 0-89494-011-2). New Orleans Mus Art.
Moline, Mary. Norman Rockwell Encylopedia. LC 79-90498. (Illus.). 1979. 15.95 (ISBN 0-89387-032-3). Sat Eve Post.
Norman Rockwell Review. LC 79-90499. (Illus.). 1979. 11.95 (ISBN 0-89387-033-1). Sat Eve Post.
Troyen, Carol. The Boston Tradition: American Paintings from the Museum of Fine Arts, Boston. LC 80-69210. (Illus.). 216p. (Orig.). 1980. pap. 15.95 (ISBN 0-917418-66-2). Am Fed Arts.
PAINTINGS, ASIAN
Agrawal, O. P. Paintings & MS of Southeast Asia. 1981. text ed. price not set. Butterworths.
PAINTINGS, BRITISH
Wark, Robert R. British Landscape Drawings & Watercolors, Nineteen-Fifty to Eighteen-Fifty: Twenty-Four Examples from the Huntington Collection. (Illus.). 64p. write for info. (ISBN 0-87328-116-0). Huntington Lib.
PAINTINGS, CHINESE
Shan-Hse, Cheng. Selected Paintings of Cheng Shan-Shi. 220p. 1980. 39.95 (ISBN 0-89955-140-8, Pub. by Art Bk Co Taiwan). Intl Schol Bk Serv.
PAINTINGS, ENGLISH
see Paintings, British
PAINTINGS, FLEMISH
Crowe, J. A. & Cavalcaselle, G. B. The Early Flemish Painters: Notices of Their Lives & Works. Freedberg, Sydney J., ed. LC 77-18679. (Connoisseurship, Criticism, & Art History Ser.: Vol. 6). 383p. 1979. lib. bdg. 38.00 (ISBN 0-8240-3263-2). Garland Pub.
PAINTINGS, FRENCH
De Fontenelle, Maurice. The Early History of French Painting. (Illus.). 121p. 1981. 39.55 (ISBN 0-930582-93-4). Gloucester Art.
PAINTINGS, GERMAN
Janssen, Horst, illus. Horst Janssen: Master Drawings. LC 79-92751. (Illus.). 50p. (Orig.). 1980. pap. 6.50 (ISBN 0-88397-026-0). Intl Exhibit Foun.
PAINTINGS, ITALIAN
Boskovits, Miklos. Italian Panel Painting of the Fourteenth & Fifteenth Centuries. Hoch, Elisabeth, tr. from Hungarian. (Illus.). 70p. 1980. 25.00 (ISBN 0-937832-02-2). Dante Univ Bkshlf.
PAINTINGS, JAPANESE
Bowie, Henry P. The Techniques & Laws of Japanese Painting. (Illus.). 129p. 1981. 47.45 (ISBN 0-930582-91-8). Gloucester Art.
PAINTINGS, MODERN
see Art, Modern–20th Century
PAINTS
see Paint
PAIUTE INDIANS
see Indians of North America–Southwest, New
PAKISTAN–HISTORY
Gledhill, Alan. Pakistan: The Development of Its Laws & Constitution. LC 80-20180. (The British Commonwealth, the Development of Its Laws & Constitutions: Vol. 8). x, 263p. 1980. Repr. of 1957 ed. lib. bdg. 29.75x (ISBN 0-313-20842-5, GLPA). Greenwood.
Tames, Richard. India & Pakistan in the Twentieth Century. (Twentieth Century World History Ser.). (Illus.). 96p. (gr. 6 up). 1981. 15.95 (ISBN 0-7134-3415-5, Pub. by Batsford England). David & Charles.
PAKISTAN–POLITICS AND GOVERNMENT
Bhutto, Z. My Execution. 1980. 10.00x (ISBN 0-8364-0650-8, Pub. by Muswati India). South Asia Bks.
Khan, Mahmood H. Underdevelopment & Agrarian Structure in Pakistan. (Replica Edition Ser.). 275p. 1981. lib. bdg. 20.00x (ISBN 0-86531-134-X). Westview.
PALACES
see also Castles
Ch'en Chieh-Hsien. Manchu Palace Memorials from the Palace Museum in Taipei. (Indiana University Uralic & Altaic Ser.: Vol. 139). 350p. write for info. Ind U Res Inst.
Turanszky, Ilona. Azerbaijan: Mosques, Turrets, Palaces. Boros, Laszlo, tr. (Illus.). 184p. 1979. 22.50x (ISBN 963-13-0321-7). Intl Pubns Serv.
PALATE, CLEFT
see Cleft Palate
PALEOANTHROPOLOGY
see Man, Prehistoric
PALEOBIOLOGY
see Paleobotany; Paleontology
PALEOBOTANY
Taylor, Thomas N. Paleobotany: An Intro. to Plant Biology. (Illus.). 576p. 1981. text ed. 29.95 (ISBN 0-07-062954-4). McGraw.
PALEOETHNOGRAPHY
see Archaeology; Man, Prehistoric
PALEOGRAPHY–BIBLIOGRAPHY
Ackerman, Robert W. & Ackerman, Gretchen P. Sir Frederic Madden: A Bibliography & Biographical Sketch. LC 78-68237. 150p. 1979. lib. bdg. 18.00 (ISBN 0-8240-9819-6). Garland Pub.
PALEOLITHIC PERIOD
Coon, Carleton S. The Seven Caves: Archaeological Explorations in the Middle East. LC 80-24503. (Illus.). xx, 354p. 1981. Repr. of 1957 ed. lib. bdg 31.50x (ISBN 0-313-22824-8, COSCA). Greenwood.
Roe, Derek A. The Lower & Middle Paleolithic Periods in Britain. (Archaeology in Britain Ser.). (Illus.). 384p. 1981. 95.00 (ISBN 0-7100-0600-4). Routledge & Kegan.
PALEONTOLOGY
see also Extinct Animals; Paleobotany; Sedimentary Structures
also mollusks, Fossil; Vertebrates, Fossil, and similar headings
Beede, J. W. & Kniker, H. T. Species of the Genus Schwagerina & Their Stratigraphic Significance. (Illus.). 96p. 1924. 1.00 (BULL 2433). Bur Econ Geology.
Kobayashi, T., et al. Geology & Palaneontology of Southeast Asia, Vol. XXI. 381p. 1980. 52.00x (ISBN 0-86008-263-6, Pub. by U of Tokyo Pr Japan). Intl Schol Bk Serv.
Leakey, Richard E. The Making of Mankind. (Illus.). 256p. 1981. 25.00 (ISBN 0-525-15055-2). Dutton.
Quinn, J. H. Miocene Equidae of the Texas Gulf Coastal Plain. (Illus.). 102p. 1955. 1.75 (PUB 5516). Bur Econ Geology.
Skinner, Brian J., ed. Paleontology & Paleoenvironments. (The Earth & Its Inhabitants: Selected Readings from American Scientist Ser.). (Illus.). 250p. (Orig.). 1981. pap. 8.95 (ISBN 0-913232-93-9). W Kaufmann.
Slaughter, B. H., et al. The Hill-Shuler Local Faunas of the Upper Trinity River, Dallas & Denton Counties, Texas. (Illus.). 75p. 1962. 2.50 (RI 48). Bur Econ Geology.
Stenzel, H. B., et al. Pelecypoda from the Type Locality of the Stone City Beds (Middle Eocene) of Texas. (Illus.). 237p. 1957. 3.75 (PUB 5704). Bur Econ Geology.
PALEONTOLOGY–BIBLIOGRAPHY
Morris, S. F. Catalogue of Type & Figured Fossil Crustacea (Exc. Ostracoda), Chelicerata & Myriapoda in the British Museum (Natural History) (Illus.). 56p. 1980. pap. 13.00x (ISBN 0-565-00828-5). Sabbot-Natural Hist Bks.
PALEONTOLOGY–AFRICA
Tindell-Hopwood, A. & Hollyfield, J. P. Fossil Mammals of Africa, No. 8: An Annotated Bibliography of the Fossil Mammals of Africa 1742-1950. 194p. 1954. pap. 16.00x (ISBN 0-565-00179-5). Sabbot-Natural Hist Bks.
PALEONTOLOGY–ASIA
Muir-Wood, Helen M. Malayan Lower Carboniferous Fossils & Their Bearing on the Visean Palaeogeography of Asia. (Illus.). 118p. 1948. 11.50x (ISBN 0-565-00374-7, Pub. by Brit Mus Nat Hist England). Sabbot-Natural Hist Bks.
PALEONTOLOGY–NORTH AMERICA
Lucas, Spencer & Rigby, Keith, Jr., eds. Advances in San Juan Basin Paleontology. 440p. 1981. 27.50x (ISBN 0-8263-0554-7). U of NM Pr.
PALEONTOLOGY, BOTANICAL
see Paleobotany
PALEONTOLOGY, ZOOLOGICAL
see Paleontology
PALEOPATHOLOGY
Grundmann, E., ed. Drug Induced Pathology. (Current Topics in Phathology Ser.: Vol. 69). (Illus.). 384p. 1981. 70.00 (ISBN 0-387-10415-1). Springer-Verlag.
PALEOZOOLOGY
see Paleontology
PALESTINE
see also Israel;
also names of cities, regions, etc. in Palestine
Jones, Christina. Friends in Palestine. 1981. write for info. (ISBN 0-913408-62-X). Friends United.
Sakran, Frank. Palestine, Still a Dilemma. 6.95. New World Press NY.
PALESTINE–HISTORY
see also Bible–History of Biblical Events; Bible–History of Contemporary Events, etc.; Crusades; Judaism–History

Frith, Francis. Egypt & the Holy Land in Historic Photographs: Seventy-Seven Views. Van Haaften, Julia, ed. 112p. 1981. pap. 7.00 (ISBN 0-486-24048-7). Dover.

PALESTINE–POLITICS AND GOVERNMENT

Amos, John W., II. Palestinian Resistance: Organization of a Nationalist Movement. LC 80-16134. (Pergamon Policy Studies on International Politics). 496p. 1981. 45.00 (ISBN 0-08-025094-7). Pergamon.

Nakhleh, Emile A. West Bank & Gaza: Toward the Making of a Palestinian State. 1979. pap. 4.25 (ISBN 0-8447-3335-0). Am Enterprise.

Yodfat, Aryeh & Arnon-Ohanna, Yuval. P. L. O. Strategy & Tactics. 1981. write for info. (ISBN 0-312-61761-5). St Martin.

PALESTINE–SOCIAL CONDITIONS

Amos, John W., II. Palestinian Resistance: Organization of a Nationalist Movement. LC 80-16134. (Pergamon Policy Studies on International Politics). 496p. 1981. 45.00 (ISBN 0-08-025094-7). Pergamon.

PALESTINE FOLK-LORE

see Folk-Lore, Palestine

PALESTINIAN ARABS

see also Jewish-Arab Relations

Bonds, Joy, et al. Our Roots Are Still Alive: The Story of the Paliesinian People. LC 77-10952. (Illus.). 182p. pap. 5.45 (ISBN 0-917654-12-9). IISJ.

PALESTINIANS

see Palestinian Arabs

PALLET SYSTEMS

see Pallets (Shipping, Storage, etc.)

PALLETIZED UNIT LOADS

see Pallets (Shipping, Storage, Etc.)

PALLETS (SHIPPING, STORAGE, ETC.)

Powell, Victor G. Warehousing: Analysis for Effective Operations. 240p. 1976. text ed. 29.50x (ISBN 0-220-66301-7, Pub. by Busn Bks England). Renouf.

PALSY, SHAKING

see Paralysis Agitans

PAN-AFRICANISM

Asiwaju, A. I., et al, eds. Tarikh: Pan-Africanism, Vol. 6. (Illus.). 69p. 1980. pap. text ed. 3.25x (ISBN 0-582-60374-9). Humanities.

PANAMA–DESCRIPTION AND TRAVEL

Cheville, Lila R. & Cheville, Richard A. Festivals & Dances of Panama. (Illus.). 187p. (Orig.). 1981. pap. 8.50 (ISBN 0-913714-53-4). Legacy Bks.

PANAMA CANAL

OAS General Secretariat Bureau of Legal Affairs. Tratados Sobre el Canal De Panama Suscritos Entre la Republica De Panama y los Estados Unidos De America. (Serie Sobre Tratados: No. 57 & 57a). 157p. 1979. text ed. 9.00 (ISBN 0-8270-0715-9). OAS.

PAN-AMERICAN UNION

see Organization of American States

PANCAKES, WAFFLES, ETC.

Brooks, Rose-Marie. Sunbeam Great Crepe Recipes. 7.95 (ISBN 0-916752-03-8). Green Hill.

PANCREAS–DISEASES

see also Hypoglycemia

Cohn. Pancreatic Cancer: New Directions in Therapeutic Management. 1981. price not set (ISBN 0-89352-133-7). Masson Pub.

Orr, Marsha E. Acute Pancreatic & Hepatic Dysfunction. Percy, R. Craig, ed. (The Fleschner Series in Critical Care Nursings). (Illus.). 175p. (Orig.). 1981. pap. text ed. 9.95 (ISBN 0-937878-04-9). Fleschner.

PANDAS

The Giant Panda. 1981. text ed. 29.95 (ISBN 0-442-20064-1). Van Nos Reinhold.

PANGENESIS

see Heredity; Reproduction

PANNENBERG, WOLFHART, 1928-

McKenzie, David. Wolfhart Pannenberg & Religious Philosophy. LC 80-8171. 169p. 1980. lib. bdg. 17.50 (ISBN 0-8191-1314-X); pap. text ed. 9.00 (ISBN 0-8191-1315-8). U Pr of Amer.

PAPACY

see also Catholic Church; Church–Foundation

Carlen, Claudia, ed. The Papal Encyclicals, 5 vols. 1981. Set. 400.00 (ISBN 0-8434-0765-4, Consortium). McGrath.

Holmes, D. The Papacy in the Modern World. 288p. 1981. 14.95 (ISBN 0-8245-0047-4). Crossroad NY.

PAPACY–HISTORY

Murphy, Francis X. The Papacy Today. 256p. 1981. lib. bdg. 10.95 (ISBN 0-02-588240-6). Macmillan.

Ullmann, Walter. The Papacy & Political Ideas in the Middle Ages. 408p. 1980. 60.00x (ISBN 0-902089-87-0, Pub. by Variorum England). State Mutual Bk.

PAPAGO INDIANS

see Indians of North America–Southwest, New

PAPAL INFALLIBILITY

see Popes–Infallibility

PAPER

Warren, Alister. Paper. (Illus.). pap. 8.95 (ISBN 0-584-62051-9). Dufour.

PAPER-BOUND EDITIONS

see Bibliography–Paperback Editions

PAPER-CUTTING

see Paper Work

PAPER DOLLS

see Paper Work

PAPER FOLDING

see Paper Work

PAPER FOLDING, JAPANESE

see Origami

PAPER INDUSTRY

see Paper Making and Trade

PAPER MAKING AND TRADE

see also Book Industries and Trade

Amigo, Eleanor & Neuffer, Mark. Beyond the Adirondacks: The Story of St. Regis Paper Company. LC 80-1798. (Contributions in Economics & Economic History: No. 35). (Illus.). xi, 219p. 1980. lib. bdg. 22.95 (ISBN 0-313-22735-7, AFN/). Greenwood.

Cote, Wilfred A., ed. Papermaking Fibers: A Photomicroscopic Atlas. (Renewable Materials Institute Ser.). (Illus.). 200p. 1980. pap. text ed. 12.00x (ISBN 0-8156-2228-7). Syracuse U Pr.

Information Sources on the Utilization of Agricultural Residues for the Production of Panels, Pulp, & Paper. (UNIDO Information Sources Ser.: No.35). 99p. 1980. pap. 4.00 (UN). Unipub.

Projected Pulp & Paper Mills in the World 1979-1989. 132p. 1980. pap. 7.25 (ISBN 92-5-100913-9, F1938, FAO). Unipub.

Pulp & Paper Capacities Survey, 1979-1984. 286p. 1980. pap. 15.25 (ISBN 92-5-000914-3, F1945, FAO). Unipub.

Pulping & Paper-Making Properties of Fast Growing Plantation Wood Species, Vols. 1 & 2. (FAO Forestry Paper Ser.: No. 19). 1980. pap. 46.75 set (ISBN 0-686-68193-2, F1969, FAO); Vol. 1, 486 Pp. pap. 46.75 (ISBN 92-5-100865-5). Vol. 2, 400 Pp (ISBN 92-5-100866-3). Unipub.

Whitney, Roy P. The Story of Paper. (TAPPi Press Reports). (Illus.). 28p. 1980. pap. 9.99 (ISBN 0-89852-385-0, 01-01-R085). Tappi.

PAPER MONEY

Narbeth, Colin, et al. Collecting Paper Money & Bonds. (The Christies International Collectors Ser.). (Illus.). 128p. 1980. 14.95 (ISBN 0-8317-0940-5). Mayflower Bks.

PAPER SCULPTURE

Randlett, Samuel. The Best of Origami. (Illus.). 185p. 1981. 12.95 (ISBN 0-571-10275-1, Pub. by Faber & Faber). Merrimack Bk Serv.

PAPER-WEIGHTS

see Paperweights

PAPER WORK

see also Decoupage; Origami

Antique Dolls Go to a Paper Doll Wedding. 8p. (gr. 8-12). 1978. pap. 3.50 (ISBN 0-914510-09-6). Evergreen.

Howard, Marion. Those Fascinating Paper Dolls: An Illustrated Handbook for Collectors. (Illus.). 320p. 1981. pap. 6.95 (ISBN 0-486-24055-X). Dover.

Nason, Janet. Dolls of the Nineteen Thirties Paper Dolls. 8p. (gr. 8-12). 1978. pap. 3.50 (ISBN 0-914510-08-8). Evergreen.

Rosamond, Peggy J. Antique French Doll Coloring Books. 8p. (gr. 8-12). pap. 3.50 (ISBN 0-914510-06-1). Evergreen.

--Antique French Doll Paper Dolls. 8p. (gr. 8-12). 1976. pap. 3.50. Evergreen.

Young, Mary. Collector's Guide to Paperdolls. (Illus.). 1980. pap. 9.95 (ISBN 0-89145-133-1). Collector Bks.

PAPER WORK–JUVENILE LITERATURE

Bae, Yoong. Paper Robots. (Illus.). 32p. (Orig.). 1981. pap. 3.50 (ISBN 0-686-69425-2). Troubador Pr.

--Paper Rockets. (Illus.). 32p. 1980. pap. 3.50 (ISBN 0-89844-022-X). Troubador Pr.

Grater, Michael. Cut & Fold Paper Spaceships That Fly. (Illus.). 48p. (Orig.). (gr. 1-5). Date not set. pap. price not set (ISBN 0-486-23978-0). Dover.

Swanberg, Nancie. Great Ballet Paper Dolls. (Illus.). 32p. (Orig.). 1981. pap. 3.50 (ISBN 0-89844-027-0). Troubador Pr.

Tierney, Tom. Pavlova & Nijinsky Paper Dolls in Full Color. (Illus.). 32p. (Orig.). 1981. pap. price not set (ISBN 0-486-24093-2). Dover.

PAPERBACKS

see Bibliography–Paperback Editions

PAPERWEIGHTS

Hollister, Paul & Lanmon, Dwight P. Paperweights: Flowers Which Clothe the Meadows. (Illus.). 167p. 1981. pap. price not set. Dover.

Ingold, Gerard. The Art of the Paperweight: Saint Louis. L. H. Selman Ltd., ed. (Illus.). 1981. price not set (ISBN 0-933756-01-1). Paperweight Pr.

Selman, Lawrence H. Collectors' Paperweights-Price Guide & Catalogue. (Illus.). 1981. pap. 5.00 (ISBN 0-933756-02-X). Paperweight Pr.

Selman, Lawrence H. & Pope-Selman, Linda. Paperweights for Collectors. rev. ed. 1981. price not set (ISBN 0-933756-03-8). Paperweight Pr.

PAPUA NEW GUINEA

Amarshu, Azeem, et al. Development & Dependency: The Political Economy of Papua New Guinea. (Illus.). 306p. 1979. text ed. 28.00x (ISBN 0-19-550582-4). Oxford U Pr.

Geomorphological Map of Papua New Guinea. (Land Research Ser.: No. 33). (Illus.). 23p. 1979. 9.00 (ISBN 0-643-00092-5, CO17, CSIRO). Unipub.

Howie-Willis, Ian. A Thousand Graduates: Conflict in University Development in Papua New Guinea, 1961-1976. Fisk, E. K., ed. (Pacific Research Series Monograph: No. 3). 362p. 1980. pap. text ed. 12.95 (ISBN 0-909150-01-X, 0014). Bks Australia.

Land Limitation & Agricultural Land Use Potential Map of Papua New Guinea. (Land Research Ser.: No. 36). (Illus.). 84p. 1975. 9.00 (ISBN 0-643-00164-6, CO16, CSIRO). Unipub.

Lands of the Ramu-Mandang Area, Papua New Guinea. (Land Research Ser.: No. 37). (Illus.). 135p. 1976. pap. 13.50 (ISBN 0-643-00175-1, CO18, CSIRO). Unipub.

Robinson, Neville K. Villagers at War: Some Papua New Guinea Experience in World War II. Fisk, E. K., ed. (Pacific Research Series Monograph: No. 2). 223p. 1980. pap. text ed. 12.95 (0475). Bks Australia.

Vegetation Map of Papua New Guinea. (Land Research Ser.: No. 35). 24p. 1975. 13.50 (ISBN 0-643-00138-7, CSIRO). Unipub.

PAPYRI, EGYPTIAN

see Manuscripts (Papyri)

PAPYRUS MANUSCRIPTS

see Manuscripts (Papyri)

PARABLES

see also Bible–Parables; Jesus Christ–Parables

Carter, James E. People Parables. (Pocket Pulpit Library). 128p. 1981. pap. 2.95 (ISBN 0-8010-2348-3). Baker Bk.

Chekijian, Vartan S. The Strange Dreams. 109p. 1980. 5.95 (ISBN 0-533-03227-X). Vantage.

Groves, Wanda J. Precious Parables for Tiny Tots. 27p. 1980. 4.50 (ISBN 0-533-04417-0). Vantage.

PARABOLE

see Metaphor

PARACLETE

see Holy Spirit

PARAKEET

see Budgerigars; Parrots

Silva, Tony & Kotlar, Barbara. Conures. (Illus.). 96p. 1980. 2.95 (ISBN 0-87666-893-7, KW-121). TFH Pubns.

PARALLELS (GEOMETRY)

Knoedel, W. & Schneider, H. J., eds. Parallel Processes & Related Automata. (Computing Supplementum Ser.: No. 3). 203p. 1981. pap. 59.00 (ISBN 0-387-81606-2). Springer-Verlag.

PARALYSIS, CEREBRAL

see Cerebral Palsy

PARALYSIS AGITANS

Agnoli, A., ed. Sixth Meeting of the Italian League Against Parkinson's Disease & Extrapyramidal Disorders, 1981. (Journal: Pharmacology: Vol. 22, No. 1). (Illus.). 92p. 1981. pap. write for info. (ISBN 3-8055-2322-X). S Karger.

PARAMAGNETIC RESONANCE, ELECTRONIC

see Electron Paramagnetic Resonance

PARAMEDICAL PERSONNEL

see Allied Health Personnel

PARAMETRIC AMPLIFIERS

Kimmich, H. P. Monitoring of Vital Parameters During Extracorporeal Circulation. (Illus.). 1981. soft cover 72.00 (ISBN 3-8055-2059-X). S Karger.

Zacks, S. Parametric Statistical Inference: Basic Theory & Modern Approaches. LC 80-41715. (I.S. in Nonlinear Mathematics Series; Theory & Applications: Vol. 4). 400p. 1981. 48.00 (ISBN 0-08-026468-9); pap. 19.70 (ISBN 0-08-026467-0). Pergamon.

PARANOIA

Gale, June. SNOW: Twice Orphaned-Once Rescued. LC 80-21941. (Illus.). 168p. 1980. 10.00 (ISBN 0-914016-74-1). Phoenix Pub.

Jackson, George A. A Case Study: Mr. Paranoid. 64p. 1981. 4.00 (ISBN 0-682-49692-8). Exposition.

PARAPLEGIA

Eareckson, Joni & Musser, Joe. Joni. (Illus.). 256p. 1980. pap. 2.95 (ISBN 0-310-23982-6). Zondervan.

PARAPSYCHOLOGY

see Psychical Research

PARASITE-HOST RELATIONSHIPS

see Host-Parasite Relationships

PARASITES

see also Agricultural Pests

also names of parasitic orders, classes, etc., e.g. Cestoda, Nemathelminthes, Ticks

The Epidemiology & Control of Gastrointestinal Parasites of Sheep in Australia. 153p. pap. 11.00 (ISBN 0-643-00301-0, CO21, CSIRO). Unipub.

McKelvey, John J., Jr., et al, eds. Vectors of Disease Agents: Interactions with Plants, Animals, & Men. 350p. 1980. 34.95 (ISBN 0-03-056887-0). Praeger.

Reifsnyder, David N. Parasitic Diseases Case Studies. LC 80-81733. 1980. pap. 18.50 (ISBN 0-87488-049-1). Med Exam.

PARASITES–MAN

see Medical Parasitology

PARASITIC DISEASES

see Medical Parasitology

PARASITOLOGY

see also Medical Parasitology; Parasites; Veterinary Medicine

Ash, Lawrence R. & Orihel, Thomas C. Atlas of Human Parasitology. LC 80-25291. (Illus.). 176p. 1980. text ed. 45.00 (ISBN 0-89189-081-5, 16-7-001-00). Am Soc Clinical.

Schmidt, Gerald D. & Roberts, Larry S. Foundations of Parasitology. 2nd ed. (Illus.). 672p. 1981. pap. text ed. 24.95 (ISBN 0-8016-4344-9). Mosby.

PARATHESIS

Toxicological Evaluation of Parathion & Azinphosmethyl in Freshwater Model Ecosystems. (Agricultural Research Reports: No. 898). 112p. 1980. pap. 20.75 (ISBN 90-220-0732-4, PDC210, Pudoc). Unipub.

PARBATE LANGUAGE

see Nepali Language

PARDON

see also Amnesty; Probation

Toland, John, et al. Anglia Libera. Berkowitz, David S. & Thorne, Samuel E., eds. LC 77-89231. (Classics of English Legal History in the Modern Era Ser.: Vol. 71). 400p. 1979. lib. bdg. 40.00 (ISBN 0-8240-3171-7). Garland Pub.

PARENT AND CHILD

see also Adolescence; Adolescent Parents; Child Abuse; Children–Management; Fathers; Maternal Deprivation; Mother and Child; Mothers; Single-Parent Family; Stepchildren; Stepfathers; Stepmothers; Youth

Alquist, Tom. Getting Your Way with Parents. LC 80-68888. 128p. (Orig.). 1981. pap. 2.50 (ISBN 0-89636-065-2). Accent Bks.

Auerbach, Stevanne. The Whole Child: A Sourcebook. (Illus.). 320p. 1981. 17.95 (ISBN 0-399-12364-4). Putnam.

Behrstock, Barry & Trubo, Richard. The Parent's When-Not-to Worry Book: Straight Talk About All Those Myths You've Learned from Your Parents, Friends-- & Even Doctors. LC 80-7894. 256p. 1981. 10.95 (ISBN 0-690-01972-6, HarpT). Har-Row.

Brazelton, T. Berry. On Becoming a Family: The Growth of Attachment. 1981. 14.95 (ISBN 0-440-06712-X, Sey Lawr). Delacorte.

Feuerstein, Phillis & Roberts, Carol. The Not So Empty Nest: How to Live with Your Kids After They've Lived Someplace Else. 256p. 1981. 10.95 (ISBN 0-695-81441-9). Follett.

Gage, Joy P. Broken Boundaries-Broken Lives. 1981. pap. 3.95 (ISBN 0-89636-068-7). Accent Bks.

Henderson, Ronald W., ed. Parent-Child Interaction: Theory, Research & Projects. LC 80-2336. (Educational Psychology Ser.). 1981. write for info. (ISBN 0-12-340620-X). Acad Pr.

Kiley, Dan. Keeping Parents Out of Trouble. (Orig.). 1981. 11.95 (ISBN 0-446-51221-4). Warner Bks.

Kohl, Herbert. Growing with Your Children. 256p. 1981. pap. 2.95 (ISBN 0-553-13923-1). Bantam.

Lenz, Elinor. Once My Child Now My Friend. (Orig.). 1981. 12.95 (ISBN 0-446-51224-9). Warner Bks.

Loader, Anne, compiled by. Pregnancy & Parenthood. (Illus.). 226p. 1980. 16.95 (ISBN 0-19-217684-6); pap. 8.95 (ISBN 0-19-286006-2). Oxford U Pr.

Polansky, Norman A., et al. Damaged Parents: An Anatomy of Child Neglect. LC 80-22793. (Illus.). 288p. 1981. 15.00 (ISBN 0-226-67221-2). U of Chicago Pr.

Sussman, Alan & Guggenheim, Martin. The Rights of Parents. 288p. (Orig.). 1980. pap. 2.50 (ISBN 0-380-76729-5, 76729). Avon.

Wright, Logan. Parent Power. 240p. 1981. pap. 2.95 (ISBN 0-553-14654-8). Bantam.

PARENT AND CHILD (LAW)

see also Adoption; Children–Law; Custody of Children; Stepchildren; Support (Domestic Relations)

Field, G. W. The Legal Relations of Infants, Parent & Child, & Guardian & Ward: And a Particular Consideration of Guardianship in the State of New York. xx, 376p. 1981. Repr. of 1888 ed. lib. bdg. 28.50x (ISBN 0-8377-0537-1). Rothman.

PARENT EDUCATION

Alliance of Perinatal Research & Services, Inc. The Father Book: Pregnancy & Beyond. 1981. 17.50 (ISBN 0-87491-618-6); pap. 8.95 (ISBN 0-87491-422-1). Acropolis.

Brooks, Jane B. The Process of Parenting. (Illus.). 460p. (Orig.). 1981. write for info (ISBN 0-87484-474-6). Mayfield Pub.

Dinkmeyer, Don & McKay, Gary D. Systematic Training for Effective Parenting (STEP) Parent's Handbook. (Illus.). 117p. 1976. pap. text ed. 4.85 (ISBN 0-913476-77-3). Am Guidance.

Harman, David & Brim, Orville G., Jr. Learning to Be Parents: Principles, Programs, & Methods. LC 80-24030. (Illus.). 276p. 1980. 14.95 (ISBN 0-8039-1272-2). Sage.

Hooks, William, et al, eds. The Pleasure of Their Company: How to Have More Fun with Your Children. LC 80-70382. 480p. (Orig.). 1981. pap. 9.95 (ISBN 0-686-69524-0). Chilton.

Kannenberg, Gary D. From Birth to Twelve: How to Be a Successful Parent to Infants & Children. LC 80-69331. 125p. 1981. 7.95 (ISBN 0-86548-043-5). Century Twenty One.

McGinnis, Marilyn. Give Me a Child Until He's Two: Then You Take Him till He's Four! LC 80-54005. 176p. pap. 4.95 (ISBN 0-8307-0785-9). Regal.

Macpherson, Michael C. Family Years: A Guide to Positive Parenting. 146p. (Orig.). 1981. pap. 5.95 (ISBN 0-03-059131-7). Winston Pr.

Marion, Robert. Educators, Parents & Exceptional Children. (Illus.). 275p. 1980. text ed. write for info. (ISBN 0-89443-334-2). Aspen Systems.

Olness, Karen. Parenting Happy Healthy Children. 1981. 9.95 (ISBN 0-9602790-4-0). The Garden.

--Raising Happy Healthy Children. 1981. pap. 3.95 (ISBN 0-9602790-5-9). The Garden.

Pollock, Shirley. Adventures in Being a Parent: Family Enrichment Ideas for Busy Parents. (Orig.). 1981. pap. 3.50 (ISBN 0-87239-458-1, 2971). Standard Pub.

PARENT-TEACHER RELATIONSHIPS
see also Home and School

Berger, Eugenia H. Parents As Partners in the Educational Process. (Illus.). 360p. 1981. pap. text ed. 11.95 (ISBN 0-8016-0637-3). Mosby.

Bush, Catharine S. Workshops for Parents & Teachers. (Language Remediation & Expansion Ser.). 1981. spiral 15.00 (ISBN 0-88450-738-6). Communication Skill.

Moore, Mary H. Parent Partnership Training Program, 8 bks. Incl. Bk. 1. Introductory Guide. LC 78-68013. 128p. pap. text ed. 12.90 (ISBN 0-8027-9053-4); Bk. 2. Parent's Manual. 192p. pap. text ed. 17.80 (ISBN 0-8027-9054-2); Bk. 3. Basic Communications Skills. LC 78-68015. 288p. pap. text ed. 39.10 (ISBN 0-8027-9055-0); Bk. 4. Developing Social Acceptability. LC 78-62918. 216p. pap. text ed. 29.70 (ISBN 0-8027-9056-9); Bk. 5. Developing Responsible Sexuality. LC 78-62919. 160p. pap. text ed. 19.50 (ISBN 0-8027-9057-7); Bk. 6. Light Housekeeping & In-Home Assistance. LC 78-61387. 272p. pap. text ed. 32.60 (ISBN 0-8027-9058-5); Bk. 7. Heavy Duty Cleaning & Yards & Ground Care. LC 78-62939. 240p. pap. text ed. 32.60 (ISBN 0-8027-9059-3); Bk. 8. Skills of Daily Living. LC 78-62940. 304p. pap. text ed. 29.80 (ISBN 0-8027-9060-7). (For use with K-12 handicapped). 1979. Walker Educ.

PARENTAL BEHAVIOR IN ANIMALS

Gubernick, David J. & Klopfer, Peter H., eds. Parental Care in Mammals. 460p. 1981. 39.50 (ISBN 0-306-40533-4, Plenum Pr). Plenum Pub.

PARENTAL CUSTODY
see Custody of Children

PARENTS, ADOLESCENT
see Adolescent Parents

PARENTS AND TEACHERS
see Parent-Teacher Relationships

PARENTS WITHOUT PARTNERS
see Single-Parent Family

PAREXIC ANALYSIS
see Numerical Analysis

PARGETTING
see Plastering

PARIS–DESCRIPTION–GUIDEBOOKS

Corbierre, Anne. Paris. LC 80-50996. (Rand McNally Pocket Guide Ser.). (Illus.). 1980. pap. 3.95 (ISBN 0-528-84308-7). Rand.

De Havenon, Andre, ed. A Touch of Paris: A Selective Guide to Paris in Plain English. (Illus.). 255p. (Orig.). 1981. pap. 9.95 (ISBN 0-933982-14-3). Bradt Ent.

Peebles Press International. Cheap & Cheaper Restaurant Guide to Paris. 192p. 1980. 8.95 (ISBN 0-13-128488-6, Spec); pap. 3.95 (ISBN 0-13-128470-3). P-H.

PARIS–HISTORY

Chevalier, Luois. Laboring Classes & Dangerous Classes in Paris During the First Half of the Nineteenth Century. Jellinek, Frank, tr. from Fr. LC 80-8678. 520p. (Orig.). 1981. pap. 8.95 (ISBN 0-691-00783-7). Princeton U Pr.

Evenson, Norma. Paris, a Century Change Eighteen-Seventy Eight to Nineteen Seventeen Eight. LC 78-10257. (Illus.). 399p. 1981. pap. 12.95 (ISBN 0-300-02667-6). Yale U Pr.

Golden, Richard. The Godly Rebellion: Parisian Cures & the Religious Fronde, 1652-1662. LC 80-25282. 264p. 1981. 22.50x (ISBN 0-8078-1466-0). U of NC Pr.

PARIS–HISTORY–COMMUNE, 1871

Horne, Alistair. The Fall of Paris: The Siege & the Commune 1870-71. 464p. 1981. pap. 2.95 (ISBN 0-14-005210-0). Penguin.

PARIS PEACE CONFERENCE, 1919

Marks, Sally. Innocent Abroad: Belgium at the Paris Peace Conference of 1919. LC 80-13698. (Illus.). 456p. 1980. 26.00x (ISBN 0-8078-1451-2). U of NC Pr.

PARISH LIBRARIES
see Libraries, Church

PARISH MANAGEMENT
see Church Management

PARISH SCHOOLS
see Church Schools

PARKINSON'S DISEASE
see Paralysis Agitans

PARKS
see also Landscape Gardening; National Parks and Reserves; Zoological Gardens

Rutledge, Albert J. A Visual Approach to Park Design. 1981. lib. bdg. 21.50 (ISBN 0-8240-7258-8). Garland Pub.

PARLIAMENTARY PRACTICE

Robert, Henry M. Parliamentary Law. 588p. 1981. pap. 19.95 (ISBN 0-686-28898-X). Lewis Pub Co.

--Parliamentary Practice: An Introduction to Parliamentary Law. 203p. 1981. pap. 4.95 (ISBN 0-86616-008-6). Lewis Pub Co.

Russell, Kenneth L., ed. How in Parlimentary Procedure. 4th ed. (Illus.). (gr. 9-12). 1981. pap. text ed. 1.95 (ISBN 0-8134-2171-3, 2171). Interstate.

PARLIAMENTS
see Legislative Bodies

PARNELL, CHARLES STEWART, 1846-1891

Bew, Paul. C. S. Parnell. (Gill's Irish Lives Ser.). 152p. 1980. 20.00 (ISBN 0-7171-1079-6, Pub. by Gill & Macmillan); pap. 6.50 (ISBN 0-7171-0963-1). Irish Bk Ctr.

PAROCHIAL LIBRARIES
see Libraries, Church

PAROCHIAL SCHOOLS
see Church Schools

PAROLE EVIDENCE
see Evidence (Law)

PARROTS
see also Budgerigars; Cockateels

Decoteau, A. E. The Handbook of Amazon Parrots. (Illus.). 221p. 1980. 12.95 (ISBN 0-87666-892-9, H-1025). TFH Pubns.

PARTI COMMUNIST FRANCAISE
see Communist Party of France

PARTIAL DIFFERENTIAL EQUATIONS
see Differential Equations, Partial

PARTIALLY-SEEING CHILDREN
see Visually Handicapped Children

PARTICLES
see also Colloids; Fluidization

European Federation of Chemical Engineering, European Symposium, Amsterdam, Holland, June 3-5, 1980. Particle Technology Nineteen Eighty: Proceedings, Vols. A & B. Schonert, K., et al, eds. (E FCE Publication Ser.: No. 7). 1232p. 1980. text ed. 79.00x (ISBN 3-921567-27-0, Pub. by Dechema Germany). Scholium Intl.

Guanghou Conference on Theoretical Particle Physics, 1980: Proceedings, 2 vols. 1980. text ed. 89.50 (ISBN 0-442-20273-3). Van Nos Reinhold.

Halliday, Ian & McIntosh, Bruce A., eds. Solid Particles in the Solar System. (International Astronomical Union Symposium: No. 90). 432p. 1980. PLB 49.95 (ISBN 90-277-1164-X, Pub. by D. Reidel); pap. 26.50 (ISBN 90-277-1165-8). Kluwer Boston.

Kaye, Brian H. Direct Characterization of Fine Particles. (Chemical Analysis Ser.). 500p. 1981. 50.00 (ISBN 0-471-46150-4, Pub. by Wiley-Interscience). Wiley.

Lee, T. D. Field Theory & Particle Analysis. (Contemporary Concepts in Physics Ser.). 1981. 35.00 (ISBN 0-686-69595-X); pap. 14.00 (ISBN 0-686-69596-8). Harwood Academic.

Somasundaran, P., ed. Fine Particles Processing, 2 vols. LC 79-57344. (Illus.). 1865p. 1980. text ed. 45.00x (ISBN 0-89520-275-1). Soc Mining Eng.

PARTICLES (NUCLEAR PHYSICS)

Frampton, P., et al, eds. First Workshop on Grand Unification. (Lie Groups; History, Frontiers & Applications: Vol. XI). 250p. 1980. text ed. 30.00x (ISBN 0-915692-31-7). Math Sci Pr.

PARTIES
see Entertaining

PARTIES, POLITICAL
see Political Parties

PARTISANS
see Guerrillas

PARTITIONS (MATHEMATICS)

Andrews, George E. Partitions: Yesterday & Today. 56p. (Orig.). 1980. pap. text ed. 7.95 (ISBN 0-9597579-0-2). Bks Australia.

PARTITO COMMUNISTA ITALIANO
see Communist Party of Italy

PARTNERSHIP
see also Corporation Law

Blagrove, Luanna C. Business Problems & Solutions for Proprietors & Partnerships. 160p. 1981. 24.95; pap. 19.95 (ISBN 0-9604466-9-9). Blagrove Pubns.

--Introduction to Proprietor & Partnership Businesses. 160p. 1981. 24.95; pap. 19.95. Blagrove Pubns.

--The Professional's Business Guide for Proprietor & Partnerships. rev. ed. (Illus.). 185p. 1981. 29.95 (ISBN 0-9604466-5-6). Blagrove Pubns.

Howell, John C. Prepare Your Own Partnership Agreements. 144p. 1980. pap. 5.95 (Spec). P-H.

Wallace, Melvin. Partners in Business. 200p. 1981. 14.95 (ISBN 0-913864-66-8); pap. 7.95 (ISBN 0-913864-67-6). Enterprise Del.

Washburn, Susan. Partners. LC 80-65985. 1981. 11.95 (ISBN 0-689-11103-7). Atheneum.

PARTON, DOLLY

James, Otis. Dolly Parton: A Photo-Bio. (Orig.). pap. 1.95 (ISBN 0-515-05157-8). Jove Pubns.

PARTURITION
see Childbirth; Labor (Obstetrics)

PASCAL, BLAISE, 1623-1662

The Provincial Letters of Blaise Pascal with a Biographical Preface. 324p. 1980. Repr. lib. bdg. 20.00 (ISBN 0-89984-387-5). Century Bookbindery.

PASCAL (COMPUTER PROGRAM LANGUAGE)

Cooper, James W. Introduction to Pascal for Scientists. 304p. 1981. 17.50 (ISBN 0-471-08785-8, Pub. by Wiley-Interscience). Wiley.

Dyck, et al. Computing: An Introduction to Structured Problem Solving Using Pascal. 1981. text ed. 18.95 (ISBN 0-8359-0902-6); instr's. manual free (ISBN 0-8359-0903-4). Reston.

Eisenbach, S. & Sadler, C. PASCAL for Programmers. (Illus.). 225p. 1981. pap. 8.80 (ISBN 0-387-10473-9). Springer-Verlag.

Findlay, William & Watt, David A. Pascal: An Introduction to Methodical Programming. 2nd ed. (Illus.). Date not set. pap. text ed. price not set (ISBN 0-914894-73-0). Computer Sci.

McGregor, Jim & Watt, Alan. Simple Pascal. 1981. text ed. price not set (ISBN 0-914894-72-2). Computer Sci.

PASSIONS
see Emotions

PASSIVE RESISTANCE
see also Nonviolence; War and Religion

Desai, Narayan. Handbook for Satyagrahis. 1980. pap. 3.00 perfect bdg. (ISBN 0-86571-002-3). Movement New Soc.

Lakey, George. Manifesto for a Nonviolent Revolution. 1980. staple back bdg. 1.75 (ISBN 0-86571-004-X). Movement New Soc.

PASSIVE RESISTANCE TO GOVERNMENT
see also Pacifism

Gandhi, Mohandas K. For Pacifists. Kumarappa, Bharatan, ed. 130p. (Orig.). 1981. pap. 1.50 (ISBN 0-934676-28-3). Greenlf Bks.

PASSOVER

Drucker, Malka. Passover: A Season of Freedom. LC 80-8810. (A Jewish Holidays Book). (Illus.). 96p. (gr. 5 up). 1981. PLB 8.95 (ISBN 0-8234-0389-0). Holiday.

PASTERNAK, BORIS LEONIDOVICH, 1890-1960

Rowland, Harry F. & Rowland, Paul. Pasternak's "Doctor Zhivago". (Crosscurrents-Modern Critiques Ser.). 1968. pap. 6.95 (ISBN 0-8093-0293-4). S Ill U Pr.

PASTIMES
see Amusements; Games; Sports

PASTORAL COUNSELING
Here are entered works on the clergyman as the counselor.
see also Counseling; Pastoral Medicine; Pastoral Psychology

Aaen, Bernhard. No Appointment Needed. Van Dolson, Bobbie J., ed. 128p. 1981. pap. write for info. (ISBN 0-8280-0025-5). Review & Herald.

Adams, Jay E., ed. Journal of Practical Practice, Vol. 4, No. 2. 1980. pap. 5.00 (ISBN 0-87552-032-4). Presby & Reformed.

Barr, William D. Counseling with Confidence. (Orig.). 1981. pap. 4.95 (ISBN 0-88270-492-3). Logos.

Bowers, Margaretta K., et al. Counseling the Dying. LC 80-8903. (Harper's Ministers Paperback Library). 208p. 1981. pap. 4.95 (ISBN 0-06-061020-4). Har-Row.

Carr, John C., et al, eds. The Organization & Administration of Pastoral Counseling Centers. LC 80-22416. 304p. 1980. 15.95 (ISBN 0-687-29430-4). Abingdon.

Collins, Gary. Orientacion Sicologica Eficaz. Blanch, Miguel, tr. from Eng. 206p. (Orig., Span.). 1979. pap. 4.50 (ISBN 0-89922-136-X). Edit Caribe.

--Personalidades Quebrantadas. Flores, Jose, tr. from Eng. LC 78-62403. 215p. (Orig., Span.). 1978. pap. 4.50 (ISBN 0-89922-116-5). Edit Caribe.

Leas, Speed & Kittlaus, Paul. The Pastoral Counselor in Social Action. Clinebell, Howard J. & Stone, Howard W., eds. LC 80-8059. (Creative Pastoral Care & Counseling Ser.). 96p. (Orig.). 1981. pap. 3.25 (ISBN 0-8006-0565-9, 1-565). Fortress.

McKenzie, John G. Nervous Disorders & Religion: A Study of Souls in the Making. LC 79-8719. 183p. 1981. Repr. of 1951 ed. lib. bdg. 18.75x (ISBN 0-313-22192-8, MCND). Greenwood.

PASTORAL COUNSELING (JUDAISM)

McKenzie, John G. Nervous Disorders & Religion: A Study of Souls in the Making. LC 79-8719. 183p. 1981. Repr. of 1951 ed. lib. bdg. 18.75x (ISBN 0-313-22192-8, MCND). Greenwood.

PASTORAL LITERATURE–HISTORY AND CRITICISM

Rosenberg, D. N. Oaten Reeds & Trumpets: Pastoral & Epic in Virgil, Spenser, & Milton. LC 80-17974. 288p. 1981. 22.50 (ISBN 0-8387-5002-8). Bucknell U Pr.

PASTORAL MEDICINE

Dayringer, Richard, ed. Pastor & Patient. LC 80-70247. 240p. 1981. 20.00 (ISBN 0-87668-437-1). Aronson.

PASTORAL OFFICE AND WORK
see Pastoral Theology

PASTORAL POETRY–HISTORY AND CRITICISM

Mallette, Richard. Spenser, Milton, & Renaissance Pastoral. LC 78-73154. 224p. 1980. 18.50 (ISBN 0-8387-2412-4). Bucknell U Pr.

PASTORAL PSYCHIATRY
see Pastoral Psychology

PASTORAL PSYCHOLOGY
see also Pastoral Counseling; Pastoral Medicine

McKenzie, John G. Nervous Disorders & Religion: A Study of Souls in the Making. LC 79-8719. 183p. 1981. Repr. of 1951 ed. lib. bdg. 18.75x (ISBN 0-313-22192-8, MCND). Greenwood.

PASTORAL THEOLOGY
see also Church Attendance; Church Work; Clergy; Communication (Theology); Pastoral Counseling; Pastoral Medicine; Pastoral Psychology

Brister, C. W. El Cuidado Pastoral De la Iglesia. Tinao, D., et al, trs. Orig. Title: Pastoral Care in the Church. 226p. (Span.). 1980. pap. 4.75 (ISBN 0-311-42040-0). Casa Bautista.

Cohen, Joe H. Equipped for Good Work: A Guide for Pastorso. 1981. 14.95 (ISBN 0-88289-271-1). Pelican.

Collins, Gary. The Joy of Caring. 192p. 1980. pap. 5.95 (ISBN 0-8499-2928-8). Word Bks.

Hamblin, Douglas H., ed. Problems & Practice of Pastoral Care. 1981. 29.50x (ISBN 0-631-12921-9, Pub. by Basil Blackwell); pap. 10.95x (ISBN 0-631-12931-6). Biblio Dist.

Keating, Charles J. The Pastoral Planning Book. 96p. (Orig.). 1981. pap. 6.95 (ISBN 0-8091-2360-6). Paulist Pr.

PASTORS
see Clergy; Priests

PASTRY

Callen, Anna T. The Savory Pie. Behrman, Marion, ed. 288p. 1981. 15.95 (ISBN 0-517-54380-X). Crown.

Clayton, Bernard. The Complete Book of Pastry. 17.95 (ISBN 0-671-24276-8). S&S.

Time-Life Bks. Eds., ed. Pies & Pastries. (The Good Cook Ser.). (Illus.). 176p. 1981. 12.95 (ISBN 0-8094-2895-4). Time-Life.

PASTURES
see also Grasses

Human Influences in African Pastureland Environments. 89p. 1981. pap. 6.00 (ISBN 92-5-100874-4, F2076, FAO). Unipub.

An Introduction to African Pastureland Production. 192p. 1981. pap. 11.00 (ISBN 92-5-100872-8, F2075, FAO). Unipub.

Management & Utilization of Pastures, East Africa: Kenya, Tanzania, Uganda. (Pasture & Fodder Crop Studies: No. 3). 124p. 1969. pap. 7.75 (ISBN 92-5-100420-X, F1970, FAO). Unipub.

Plant Relations in Pastures. 475p. 1980. pap. 45.00 (ISBN 0-643-00264-2, CO05, CSIRO). Unipub.

PATCHWORK

Brondolo, Barbara. Small Patchwork Projects. (Illus.). 64p. (Orig.). 1981. pap. write for info. (ISBN 0-486-24030-4). Dover.

Marti, Judy. Patchworkbook. 100p. 1981. pap. 9.95 (ISBN 0-9602970-2-2). Moon Over Mntn.

Schoenfeld, Susan & Beniner, Winifred. Pattern Design for Needlepoint & Patchwork. 200p. 1981. pap. 9.95 (ISBN 0-442-20671-2). Van Nos Reinhold.

Solvit, Marie-Janine. Pictures in Patchwork. LC 76-51189. (Illus.). 120p. 1981. pap. 8.95. Sterling.

PATENT LAWS AND LEGISLATION
see also Competition, Unfair; Copyright; Patent Practice; Trade-Marks

Choate, Robert A. & Francis, William H. Cases & Materials on Patent Law, Also Including Trade Secrets - Copyrights - Trademarks. 2nd ed. (American Casebook Ser.). 1100p. 1981. text ed. 23.95 (ISBN 0-8299-2124-9). West Pub.

Directory of Patent Attorneys & Agents. LC 80-23400. 328p. 1980. pap. 11.00 (ISBN 0-08-026343-7). Pergamon.

Inventive Activity in the Asian & the Pacific Region. 152p. 1981. pap. 26.00 (WIPO66, WIPO). Unipub.

Richardson, Robert O. How to Get Your Own Patent. LC 80-54340. (Illus.). 128p. 1981. 16.95 (ISBN 0-8069-5564-3); lib. bdg. 14.99 (ISBN 0-8069-5565-1); pap. 8.95 (ISBN 0-8069-8990-4). Sterling.

Silfen, Martin E. Counseling Clients in the Entertainment Industry 1980, 2 vols. LC 80-80021. (Patents, Copyrights, Trademarks, & Literary Property Course Handbook Ser.). 1433p. 1980. pap. text ed. 25.00 (ISBN 0-686-68822-8, G6-3666). PLI.

PATENT PRACTICE

Directory of Patent Attorneys & Agents. LC 80-23400. 328p. 1980. pap. 11.00 (ISBN 0-08-026343-7). Pergamon.

PATENTS
see also Inventions; Patent Laws and Legislation; Trade-Marks

Sittig, Marshall, ed. Metal & Inorganic Waste Reclaiming Encyclopedia. LC 80-21669. (Pollution Tech. Rev. 70; Chem. Tech. Rev. 175). (Illus.). 591p. (Orig.). 1981. 54.00 (ISBN 0-8155-0823-9). Noyes.

PATENTS–LAWS AND LEGISLATION
see Patent Laws and Legislation

PATER, WALTER HORATIO, 1839-1894

Inman, Billie A. Walter Pater's Reading: A Bibliography of His Library Borrowings & Literary References, 1858 to 1873. LC 78-68284. 390p. 1981. lib. bdg. 40.00 (ISBN 0-8240-9790-4). Garland Pub.

PATERNITY
see also Parent and Child (Law)

Bryant, Neville. Disputed Paternity. 1980. 24.00. Thieme Stratton.

PATHOLOGICAL ANATOMY
see Anatomy, Pathological

PATHOLOGICAL BOTANY
see Plant Diseases

PATHOLOGICAL CHEMISTRY
see Chemistry, Medical and Pharmaceutical

PATHOLOGICAL HISTOLOGY
see Histology, Pathological

PATHOLOGICAL PSYCHOLOGY
see Psychology, Pathological

PATHOLOGY
see also Abnormalities, Human; Anatomy, Pathological; Bacteriology; Chemistry, Clinical; Diagnosis; Diseases–Causes and Theories of Causation; Histology, Pathological; Immunity; Immunopathology; Medicine; Medicine, Preventive; Paleopathology; Therapeutics

Bloor, C. H. Pathology. (Illus.). 1981. pap. text ed. write for info. (ISBN 0-443-08073-9). Churchill.

Buss, David H., et al. Clinical Pathology Continuing Education Review. LC 79-91972. 1980. pap. 14.75 (ISBN 0-87488-320-2). Med Exam.

Cawson, R. A. Aids to Oral Pathology & Diagnosis. (Dental Ser.). (Illus.). 144p. 1981. pap. text ed. 8.75 (ISBN 0-443-01871-5). Churchill.

Govan, et al. Pathology Illustrated. (Illus.). 1981. text ed. 35.00 (ISBN 0-443-01647-X). Churchill.

Govan, Alastair D., et al. Pathology Illustrated. (Illus.). 880p. (Orig.). 1981. pap. text ed. 35.00 (ISBN 0-443-01647-X). Churchill.

Grundmann, E., ed. Drug Induced Pathology. (Current Topics in Phathology Ser.: Vol. 69). (Illus.). 384p. 1981. 70.00 (ISBN 0-387-10415-1). Springer-Verlag.

Hockings, Paul. Sex & Disease in a Mountain Community. 1980. 14.00x (ISBN 0-8364-0625-7, Pub. by Vikas). South Asia Bks.

Introduction to General Pathology. 2nd ed. (Churchill Livingstone Medical Text). (Illus.). 320p. 1981. pap. text ed. 12.50 (ISBN 0-443-01970-3). Churchill.

Pinkus, Herman. A Guide to Dermatohistopathology. 3rd ed. 672p. 1981. 40.00 (ISBN 0-8385-3151-2). ACC.

Riddle, R. M. Pathology of Drug Induced & Tonic Diseases. 1981. text ed. write for info. (ISBN 0-443-08083-6). Churchill.

Rose, Hilarly. Doctors, Patients & Pathology. 79p. 1972. pap. text ed. 5.00x (ISBN 0-7135-1741-7, Pub. by Bedford England). Renouf.

Sommers, Sheldon C. & Rosen, Paul P., eds. Pathology Annual: Cumulative Index 1966-1979. (Pathology Annual Ser.). 208p. 1980. 13.50x (ISBN 0-8385-7766-0). ACC.

--Pathology Annual 1980, Pt. 1. (Pathology Annual Ser.). 482p. 1980. 35.00x (ISBN 0-8385-7761-X). ACC.

--Pathology Annual 1980, Pt. 2. (Pathology Annual Ser.). 432p. 1980. 33.50x (ISBN 0-8385-7762-8). ACC.

--Pathology Annual,1981: Part 1. (Pathology Annual Series). 1981. 35.00 (ISBN 0-8385-7763-6). ACC.

Stefanini, Mario & Benson, Ellis, eds. Progress in Clinical Pathology, Vol. 8. (Serial Publication Ser.). 1981. write for info. (ISBN 0-8089-1310-7). Grune.

PATHOLOGY, CELLULAR

see also Cell Culture

Daems, W. T., et al, eds. Cell Biological Aspects of Disease: The Plasma Membrane & Lysosomes. (Boerhaave Series for Postgraduate Medical Education: No. 19). 330p. 1981. PLB 68.50 (ISBN 90-6021-466-8, Pub. by Leiden U Pr). Kluwer Boston.

PATHOLOGY, DENTAL

see Teeth–Diseases

PATHOLOGY, EXPERIMENTAL

Jasmin, G., ed. Cell Markers. (Methods & Achievements in Experimental Pathology: Vol. 10). (Illus.). vi, 294p. 1981. 90.00 (ISBN 3-8055-1736-X). S Karger.

PATHOLOGY, GEOGRAPHIC

see Medical Geography

PATHOLOGY, SURGICAL

Ali, Majid, et al. Surgical Pathology Case Studies, Vol. 1. 1978. spiral bdg. 19.50 (ISBN 0-87488-068-8). Med Exam.

--Surgical Pathology Case Studies, Vol. 2. 1978. spiral bdg. 19.50 (ISBN 0-87488-089-0). Med Exam.

Fenoglio. Progress in Surgical Pathology, Vol. III. 1981. 54.50 (ISBN 0-89352-122-1). Masson Pub.

Rosai, Juan. Manual of Surgical Pathology Gross Room Procedures. (Illus.). 128p. 1981. 17.95x (ISBN 0-8166-1027-4). U of Minn Pr.

PATHOLOGY, VEGETABLE

see Plant Diseases

PATHS

see Trails

PATHS, GARDEN

see Garden Walks

PATIENT AND NURSE

see Nurse and Patient

PATIENT AND PHYSICIAN

see Physician and Patient

PATIENT CARE RECORDS

see Medical Records

PATIENT MONITORING

see Monitoring (Hospital Care)

PATIENTS

see Sick

PATIOS

see also Decks (Architecture, Domestic)

Hamilton, Geoff. Design & Build a Patio or Terrace. 4.50. David & Charles.

Time-Life Books Editors. Porches & Patios. (Home Repair & Improvement Ser). (Illus.). 128p. 1981. 10.95 (ISBN 0-8094-3474-1). Time-Life.

PATRIARCHS AND PATRIARCHATE

Andreev, K. The Patriarchs of Constantinople Between the Council of Chalcedon & Photius. LC 80-2353. 1981. Repr. of 1895 ed. 38.50 (ISBN 0-404-18901-6). AMS Pr.

PATRIARCHY

see Family

PATRISTICS

see Fathers of the Church

PATTERN-MAKING

see also Design; Founding; Mechanical Drawing; Wood-Carving

Lewis, Gaspar J. Cabinetmaking, Pattermaking, & Millwork. 448p. 1981. 18.95 (ISBN 0-442-24785-0). Van Nos Reinhold.

Shoben, Martin & Ward, Janet. Pattern Cutting & Making up: Vol. 3, The Professional Approach. (Illus.). 192p. 1981. 53.00 (ISBN 0-7134-3561-5, Pub. by Batsford England); pap. 30.00 (ISBN 0-7134-3562-3). David & Charles.

PATTERN PERCEPTION

Fu, K. S., ed. Digital Pattern Recognition. 2nd ed. (Communication & Cybernetics: Vol. 10). (Illus.). 234p. 1980. pap. 29.80 (ISBN 0-387-10207-8). Springer-Verlag.

Varmuza, K. Pattern Recognition in Chemistry. (Lecture Notes in Chemistry Ser.: Vol. 21). (Illus.). 217p. 1981. pap. 21.00 (ISBN 0-387-10273-6). Springer-Verlag.

PAUL, SAINT, APOSTLE

Farrar, F. W. The Life & Work of St. Paul. Date not set. 2 vol. set 43.95 (ISBN 0-86524-055-8). Klock & Klock.

Johnson, Hubert R. Who Then Is Paul? Chevy Chase Manuscripts, ed. LC 80-1406. 272p. 1981. lib. bdg. 19.75 (ISBN 0-8191-1364-6); pap. text ed. 10.75 (ISBN 0-8191-1365-4). U Pr of Amer.

Lincoln, Andrew T. Paradise Now & Not Yet. LC 80-41024. (Society for the New Testament Studies Monographs: No. 43). 240p. Date not set. price not set (ISBN 0-521-22944-8). Cambridge U Pr.

Stalker, J. The Life of Saint Paul. (Handbooks for Bible Classes). 150p. 1967. pap. text ed. 3.50 (ISBN 0-567-28131-0). Attic Pr.

PAUPERISM

see Poor

PAVAROTTI, LUCIANO

Pavarotti, Luciano & Wright, William. Pavarotti: My Own Story. LC 80-1990. (Illus.). 240p. 1981. 14.95 (ISBN 0-385-15340-6). Doubleday.

PAVEMENTS

see also Roads; Streets

Guidelines for Skid Resistant Pavement Design. 1976. 1.50. AASHTO.

Institute of Civil Engineers. Aircraft Pavement Design. 114p. 1980. 79.00x (ISBN 0-901948-04-7, Pub. by Telford England). State Mutual Bk.

PAVING

see Pavements

PAVLOV, IVAN PETROVICH, 1849-1936

Gray, Jeffrey A. Ivan Pavlov. (Modern Masters Ser.). 1981. pap. 3.95. Penguin.

PAVLOVA, ANNA, 1885-1931

Anna Pavlova. (Profiles Ser.). (Illus.). 64p. (gr. 3-6). 1981. 7.95 (ISBN 0-241-10481-5, Pub. by Hamish Hamilton England). David & Charles.

Lazzarini, John & Lazzarini, Roberta. Pavlova: Repertoire of a Legend. LC 80-5560. (Illus.). 1980. 35.00 (ISBN 0-02-871970-0). Schirmer Bks.

PAW

see Foot

PAWNEE INDIANS

see Indians of North America–The West

PAYROLLS

Weber, Jeffrey R. Computerized Payroll System: Manual & Source Code for Microcomputers. (International Data Management Computerized Accouting System Ser.). 144p. 1981. pap. 29.95 (ISBN 0-9604892-3-1). Five Arms Corp.

PAZ, OCTAVIO, 1914-

Chantikian, Kosrof, ed. Octavio Paz: Homage to the Poet. LC 80-82167. 256p. (Orig.). 1981. 15.00 (ISBN 0-916426-03-3); pap. 7.95 (ISBN 0-916426-04-1). Kosmos.

PEACE

see also Arbitration, International; Disarmament; International Education; International Organization; Pacifism; Security, International; Sociology, Military; War

Beer, Francis A. Peace Against War: The Ecology of International Violence. LC 80-27214. (International Relations Ser.). (Illus.). 1981. text ed. 18.95x (ISBN 0-7167-1250-4); pap. text ed. 9.95x (ISBN 0-7167-1251-2). W H Freeman.

Doob, Leonard W. The Pursuit of Peace. LC 80-1201. 376p. 1981. lib. bdg. 29.95 (ISBN 0-313-22630-X, DPO/). Greenwood.

Eller, Vernard. War & Peace from Genesis to Revelation. 232p. 1981. pap. 8.95 (ISBN 0-8361-1947-9). Herald Pr.

Sas, Ted. Human Pax. LC 79-67757. 1981. 5.95 (ISBN 0-533-04481-2). Vantage.

Ziegler. War, Peace & International Relations. 2nd ed. 1981. pap. text ed. 8.95 (ISBN 0-316-98493-0). Little.

PEACE–SONGS AND MUSIC

Bausch, Michael & Duck, Ruth. Everflowing Streams. 96p. (Orig.). 1981. pap. 3.95 (ISBN 0-8298-0428-5). Pilgrim NY.

PEACEFUL COEXISTENCE

see United States–Foreign Relations–Russia; World Politics–1945-

PEACEMAKING

see Reconciliation

PEARSE, PADRAIC, 1879-1916–CRITICISM AND INTERPRETATION

Pearse, P. H. The Letters of P. H. Pearse. O'Buachalla, Seamas, ed. 528p. 1980. text ed. 31.25x (ISBN 0-391-01678-4). Humanities.

PEARY, ROBERT EDWIN, 1856-1920

Hunt, William R. To Stand at the Pole: The Dr. Cook-Admiral Peary North Pole Controversy. LC 80-6156. 272p. 1981. 14.95 (ISBN 0-8128-2773-2). Stein & Day.

PEASANT ART

see Folk Art

PEASANTRY–EUROPE

Sanders, Irwin, et al. East European Presantries: Social Reflections-an Annotated Bibliography of Periodical Articles, Vol.2. (Reference Books Ser.). 1981. 16.00 (ISBN 0-8161-8488-7). G K Hall.

PEASANTRY–LATIN AMERICA

Greenberg, James B. Santiago's Sword: Chatino Peasant Religion & Economics. 250p. 1981. 16.95x (ISBN 0-520-04135-6). U of Cal Pr.

McClintock, Cynthia. Peasant Cooperatives & Political Change in Peru. LC 80-8563. (Illus.). 480p. 1981. 30.00x (ISBN 0-691-07627-8); pap. 7.95x (ISBN 0-691-02202-X). Princeton U Pr.

PEASANTRY–NORWAY

Nodtuedt, Magnus. Rebirth of Norway's Peasantry: Folk Leader Hans Nielsen Hauge. 305p. 1965. octavo 5.95. Holmes.

PEAT BOGS

Godwin, Harry. The Archives of the Peat Bogs. (Illus.). Date not set. price not set (ISBN 0-521-23784-X). Cambridge U Pr.

PEBBLES

see Rocks

PECOS VALLEY

Hughes, Alton. Pecos: A History of the Pioneer West, Vol. 2. (Illus.). 232p. 1981. 16.95 (ISBN 0-933512-34-1). Pioneer Bk Tx.

PEDAGOGICAL LIBRARIES

see Education Libraries

PEDAGOGY

see Education; Teaching

PEDESTRIANISM

see Walking

PEDIATRIC ALLERGY

Berman, Bernard A. & MacDonnell, Kenneth F. Differential Diagnosis & Treatment of Pediatric Allergy. 1981. text ed. write for info (ISBN 0-316-09182-0). Little.

Galant, Stanley P., et al. Pediatric Allergy Case Studies. LC 80-18937. 1980. pap. 14.50 (ISBN 0-87488-195-1). Med Exam.

O'Connell, Edward J., et al. Self-Assessment of Current Knowledge in Pediatric Allergy. LC 79-91200. 1980. pap. 18.00 (ISBN 0-87488-238-9). Med Exam.

PEDIATRIC ANESTHESIA

Gray & Rees. Pediatric Anesthesia. 1981. text ed. price not set (ISBN 0-407-00114-X). Butterworths.

PEDIATRIC CARDIOLOGY

Moller, James H. & Neal, William A. Heart Disease in Infancy. 522p. 1980. 36.50x (ISBN 0-8385-3671-9). ACC.

Rao, P. Syamasundar & Miller, Max D. Pediatric Cardiology. LC 61-66847. (Medical Examination Review Ser.: Vol. 37). 1980. pap. 19.50 (ISBN 0-87488-140-4). Med Exam.

Zuberbuhler, J. R. Clinical Diagnosis in Pediatric Cardiology. (Modern Pediatric Cardiology Ser.). (Illus.). 192p. 1981. text ed. 50.00 (ISBN 0-686-28921-8). Churchill.

--Clinical Diagnosis in Pediatric Cardiology. (Modern Pediatric Cardiology Ser.). (Illus.). 192p. 1981. 50.00 (ISBN 0-443-01889-8). Churchill.

PEDIATRIC DERMATOLOGY

De Bersaques, J., ed. Symposium sur les Tumeurs Cutanees des Enfants. Gent. November 1978. (Journal: Dermatologica: Vol. 161, Suppl. 1, 1980). (Illus.). iv, 160p. 1980. pap. 11.00 (ISBN 3-8055-2238-X). S Karger.

PEDIATRIC ENDOCRINOLOGY

Collu, Robert, et al, eds. Pediatric Endocrinology. (Comprehensive Endocrinology Ser.). 1981. text ed. price not set (ISBN 0-89004-543-7). Raven.

PEDIATRIC NURSING

Azarnoff, Pat & Hardgrove, Carol. The Family in Child Health Care. 240p. 1981. pap. 14.95 (ISBN 0-471-08663-0, Pub. by Wiley-Med). Wiley.

Brunner, L. & Suddarth, D. Pediatric Nursing. 1981. pap. text ed. 18.35 (ISBN 0-06-318183-5, Pub. by Har-Row Ltd England). Har-Row.

Charles-Edwards, Imelda & Nixon, Harold. Nursing Care of the Pediatric Surgical Patient. 1981. text ed. price not set. Butterworth.

Evans, M. L. & Hansen, B. D. Guide to Pediatric Nursing: A Clinical Reference. 284p. 1980. pap. 14.95 (ISBN 0-8385-3533-X). ACC.

Korones, Sheldon B. High Risk Newborn Infants. 3rd ed. (Illus.). 350p. 1981. text ed. 16.95 (ISBN 0-8016-2738-9). Mosby.

Steele. Child Health Nursing: Concepts & Management. 1981. price not set (ISBN 0-89352-035-7). Masson Pub.

Thompson, Eleanor D. Pediatric Nursing: An Introductory Text. 400p. 1981. pap. text ed. price not set (ISBN 0-7216-8843-8). Saunders.

Tudor, Mary J. Child Development. 544p. 1981. text ed. 22.95 (ISBN 0-07-065412-3, HP). McGraw.

Vestal, Katherine W. Pediatric Critical Care Nursing. 464p. 1981. 17.95 (ISBN 0-471-05674-X, Pub. by Wiley Med). Wiley.

Wong, Donna L. & Whaley, Lucille F. Clinical Handbook of Pediatric Nursing. (Illus.). 316p. 1981. pap. text ed. 10.95 (ISBN 0-8016-5545-5). Mosby.

PEDIATRIC ORTHOPEDIA

Ferguson, Albert. Orthopaedic Surgery in Infancy & Childhood. 5th ed. (Illus.). 654p. 1981. write for info. (3167-8). Williams & Wilkins.

PEDIATRIC RADIOLOGY

Lefebvre, Jacques. Clinical Practice in Pediatric Radiology: The Respiratory System, Vol. II. Kaufman, Herbert J., ed. LC 79-83739. 448p. 1979. 65.50 (ISBN 0-89352-066-7). Masson Pub.

PEDIATRIC SURGERY

see Children–Surgery

PEDIATRIC UROLOGY

see also Enuresis

Belman, A. Barry & Kaplan, George W. Urologic Problems in Pediatrics. (Major Problems in Clinical Pediatrics Ser.: Vol. 22). (Illus.). 200p. 1981. text ed. price not set (ISBN 0-7216-1678-X). Saunders.

PEDIATRICS

see also Children–Care and Hygiene; Children–Diseases; Infants–Diseases

Al-Rashid, Rashid A. Pediatric Cancer Chemotherapy. (Medical Outline Ser.). 1979. 26.00 (ISBN 0-87488-685-6); pap. 17.00 (ISBN 0-87488-663-5). Med Exam.

Droske, Susan C. Pediatric Diagnostic Procedures. 272p. 1981. pap. 11.95 (ISBN 0-471-04928-X, Pub. by Wiley Med). Wiley.

Gerbeaux, Jacques. Pediatric Respiratory Disease. 875p. 1981. 45.00 (ISBN 0-471-03456-8, Pub. by Wiley-Med). Wiley.

Ghai, O. P. & Taneja, P. N. Current Topics in Pediatrics: Abstracts of Papers from the International Congress of Pediatrics, New Delhi, India, Oct 23-29 1977. 350p. 1980. pap. 12.50x (ISBN 0-89955-324-9, Pub. by Interprint India). Intl Schol Bk Serv.

Ghai, O. P., ed. New Developments in Pediatric Research, 3 vols. 1330p. 1980. Set. 42.50x (ISBN 0-89955-325-7, Pub. by Interprint India); pap. 25.00x (ISBN 0-89955-326-5). Intl Schol Bk Serv.

--Perspectives in Pediatrics. 158p. 1980. 8.50x (ISBN 0-89955-323-0, Pub. by Interprint India). Intl Schol Bk Serv.

Griffith, H. Winter, et al. Information & Instructions for Pediatric Patients. LC 80-51712. 320p. 1980. 35.00 (ISBN 0-938372-00-9). Winter Pub Co.

Howell, R. Rodney & Simon, Frank A. Patient Management Problems: Pediatrics. LC 80-18503. (Illus.). 160p. 1981. pap. text ed. 9.00 (ISBN 0-668-04780-1, 4780). Arco.

Hull, David. Recent Advances in Paediatrics, No. 6. (Recent Advances Ser.). (Illus.). 300p. 1981. lib. bdg. 42.50 (ISBN 0-443-02208-9). Churchill.

International Congress of Pediatrics, Fifteenth, New Delhi, India, Oct 23-29, 1977. Dictionary of Participants. 148p. 1980. pap. 15.00x (ISBN 0-89955-327-3, Pub. by Interprint India). Intl Schol Bk Serv.

Kalokerinos, Archie. Every Second Child. LC 80-84435. 138p. 1981. pap. 2.95 (ISBN 0-87983-250-9). Keats.

Kretchmer & Brasel. Biomedical & Social Bases of Pediatrics. 1981. write for info. (ISBN 0-89352-093-4). Masson Pub.

Lilly, John R., et al. Pediatric Surgery Case Studies. 1978. spiral bdg. 19.50 (ISBN 0-87488-069-6). Med Exam.

McGuirt, W. Frederick, ed. Pediatric Otolaryngology Case Studies. LC 80-80367. 1980. pap. 18.50 (ISBN 0-87488-094-7). Med Exam.

Nicholson. Pediatric Ocular Tumors. 1981. price not set (ISBN 0-89352-125-6). Masson Pub.

Olness, Karen. Practical Pediatrics in Less-Developed Countries. 1980. pap. 9.95 (ISBN 0-9602790-2-4). The Garden.

--Practical Pediatrics in Less-Developed Countries. 1980. pap. 7.95 (ISBN 0-9602790-2-4). The Garden.

Pagliaro, Louis A., et al, eds. Problems in Pediatric Drug Therapy. LC 78-50204. 313p. 1979. text ed. 19.50 (ISBN 0-914768-29-8, 16). Drug Intl Pubns.

Pascual, J. F. & Calcagno, P. L., eds. Recent Advances in Pediatric Nephrology. (Contributions to Nephrology Ser.: Vol. 27). (Illus.). vi, 150p. 1981. pap. 54.00 (ISBN 3-8055-1851-X). S Karger.

Perez, Rosanne H. Protocols for Perinatal Practice. (Illus.). 450p. 1981. text ed. 19.95 (ISBN 0-8016-3805-4). Mosby.

Pollack, Margaret. Adaptive Development. (Studies in Developmental Pediatrics Ser: Vol. 3). 240p. 1981. text ed. 17.50 (ISBN 0-88416-380-6). PSG Pub.

Rao, P. Syamasundar & Miller, Max D. Pediatric Cardiology. LC 61-66847. (Medical Examination Review Ser.: Vol. 37). 1980. pap. 19.50 (ISBN 0-87488-140-4). Med Exam.

Rickham, P. P. & Hecker, W. C. Management of the Burned Child. (Progress in Pediatric Surgery Ser.: Vol. 14). 1981. write for info. (ISBN 0-8067-1514-6). Urban & S.

Robinson, Aletha. The Lao Handbook of Maternal & Child Health. 1980. pap. 0.50 (ISBN 0-9602790-1-6). The Garden.

Sheldon, Stephen H. Manual of Ambulatory Pediatrics. 275p. 1981. 9.50 (ISBN 0-89004-632-8). Raven.

Smith, David H. & Hokelman, Robert A. Controversies in Child Health & Pediatrics. (Illus.). 480p. 1981. text ed. 29.95 (ISBN 0-07-058510-5, HP). McGraw.

Stalder, G. & Fliegel, C. P., eds. Praeventive Aspekte in der Paediatrie. (Paediatrische Fortbildungskurse Fuer Die Praxis Ser.: Vol. 52). (Illus.). 1981. soft cover 48.00 (ISBN 3-8055-1980-X). S Karger.

Toback, Charles. Pediatrician's Psychological Handbook. LC 79-92916. 1980. pap. 10.50 (ISBN 0-87488-687-2). Med Exam.

PEDIATRICS–PSYCHOSOMATIC ASPECTS

Stambaugh, Harriett, ed. Social Work on Pediatric Settings. (Social Work in Health Care Ser.: Vol. 1). 350p. 1981. text ed. 22.95 (ISBN 0-917724-29-1). Haworth Pr.

PEDIGREES

see Genealogy; Heraldry

PEDOLOGY (CHILD STUDY)

see Children

PEDOLOGY (SOIL SCIENCE)

see Soil Science

PEDOPHILIA

Taylor, Brian. Perspectives in Paedophilia. 160p. 1981. 42.50 (ISBN 0-7134-3718-9, Pub. by Batsford England); pap. 16.95 (ISBN 0-7134-3719-7). David & Charles.

PEIRCE, CHARLES SANTIAGO SANDERS, 1839-1914

Apel, Karl-Otto. Charles Sanders Peirce: From Pragmatism to Pragmaticism. Krois, John M., tr. from Ger. Orig. Title: Der Denkweg Von Charles Sanders Peirce. 336p. 1981. lib. bdg. 20.00x (ISBN 0-87023-177-4). U of Mass Pr.

PEKING

Tun Li-Ch'En. Annual Customs & Festivals in Peking. Bodde, Derk, tr. from Chinese. (Illus.). 175p. 1981. 10.00 (ISBN 0-85656-029-4). Great Eastern.

PELAGIUS

Selected Bibliography on Pelagic Fish Egg & Larva Surveys. (FAO Fisheries Circular: No. 706). 97p. 1980. pap. 6.00 (ISBN 0-686-68187-8, F2023, FAO). Unipub.

PELECYPODA

see Lamellibranchiata

PENAL CODES

see Criminal Law

PENAL INSTITUTIONS

see Prisons; Reformatories

PENAL LAW

see Criminal Law

PENALTIES (CRIMINALS LAW)

see Punishment

PENANCE

see also Church Discipline; Fasting; Forgiveness of Sin

Hamelin, Leonce. Reconciliation in the Church. O'Connell, Matthew J., tr. from Fr. Orig. Title: La Reconciliation en Eglise. 125p. 1981. pap. text ed. 5.50 (ISBN 0-8146-1215-6). Liturgical Pr.

PENDERGAST, THOMAS JOSEPH, 1870-1945

Quigley, Martin. Mr. Blood's Last Night. 167p. 1980. pap. 5.95 (ISBN 0-86629-023-0). Sunrise MO.

PENGUINS–JUVENILE LITERATURE

Johnson, Sylvia A. Penguins. LC 80-2880. (Lerner Natural Science Bks.). (gr. 4-10). 1981. PLB 7.95 (ISBN 0-8225-1453-2). Lerner Pubns.

PENICILLIN

Baddiley, James & Abraham, E. P., eds. Penicillin Fifty Years After Fleming. 2nd ed. (Royal Society Ser.). 378p. 1980. lib. bdg. 62.00x (ISBN 0-85403-140-5, Pub. by Royal Soc London). Scholium Intl.

PENITENTIARIES

see Prisons

PENMANSHIP

see also Alphabets; Calligraphy; Graphology; Lettering; Writing; Writing, Italic

Barbe, Walter B. Zaner-Bloser Handwriting Workbook: Cursive. (Illus.). 1977. 3.95 (ISBN 0-88309-098-8). Zaner-Bloser.

--Zaner-Bloser Handwriting Workbook: Manuscript. (Illus.). 1977. 3.95 (ISBN 0-88309-097-X). Zaner-Bloser.

Barbe, Walter B., et al. Creative Growth with Handwriting. Incl. Readiness (ISBN 0-88309-233-6); Grade One. tchrs.' manual 9.95 (ISBN 0-88309-245-X); consumable (ISBN 0-88309-234-4); non-consumable (ISBN 0-88309-256-5); Grade Two. tchrs.' manual 9.95 (ISBN 0-88309-246-8); consumable (ISBN 0-88309-235-2); non-consumable; Book 2T. tchrs.' manual 9.95 (ISBN 0-88309-247-6); consumable (ISBN 0-88309-235-0); non-consumable (ISBN 0-88309-236-0); Grade 3T. tchrs.' manual 9.95 (ISBN 0-88309-248-4); consumable (ISBN 0-88309-259-X); non-consumable (ISBN 0-88309-237-9); Grade 4. tchrs.' manual 9.95 (ISBN 0-88309-250-6); consumable (ISBN 0-88309-239-5); non-consumable; Grade 5. tchrs.' manual 9.95 (ISBN 0-88309-251-4); consumable (ISBN 0-88309-262-X); non-consumable (ISBN 0-88309-240-9); Grade 6. tchrs.' manual 9.95 (ISBN 0-88309-252-2); consumable (ISBN 0-88309-263-8); non-consumable (ISBN 0-88309-241-7); Grade 7. tchrs.' manual 6.96 (ISBN 0-88309-253-0); consumable (ISBN 0-88309-264-6); non-consumable (ISBN 0-88309-242-5); Grade 8. tchrs.' manual 6.95 (ISBN 0-88309-254-9); consumable; non-consumable. (Illus.). 1979. pupil bk., consumable or non-consumable 1.97 ea. Zaner-Bloser.

Gourdie, Tom. Handwriting Made Easy: A Simple Modern Approach. (Illus.). 64p. 1981. pap. 3.95 (ISBN 0-8008-4597-8). Taplinger.

Jarman, Christopher. The Development of Handwriting Skills: A Book of Resources for Teachers. 150p. 1980. 17.95x (ISBN 0-631-19240-9, Pub. by Basil Blackwell); pap. 9.95x (ISBN 0-631-19230-1). Biblio Dist.

PENMEN

see Calligraphers

PENN, WILLIAM, 1644-1718

Penn, William & Myers, Albert C. William Penn's Own Account of the Lenni Lenape or Delaware Indians. rev. ed. (Illus.). 96p. 1981. pap. 4.95 (ISBN 0-912608-13-7). Mid Atlantic.

PENNSYLVANIA–DESCRIPTION AND TRAVEL

Hoffman, Carolyn. Fifty Hikes in Eastern Pennsylvania. (Illus., Orig.). 1981. pap. price not set (ISBN 0-89725-018-4). NH Pub Co.

PENNSYLVANIA–HISTORY

Arndt, Karl J. Harmony on the Connoquenessing: George Rapp's First American Harmony: 1803-1815. LC 80-828. (Documentary History of Rapp's Harmony Society, 1700-1916 Ser.). (Illus.). 1072p. (Eng. & Ger.). 1981. 38.00 (ISBN 0-937640-01-8). Harmony Soc.

Blockson, Charles L. The Underground Railroad in Pennsylvania. LC 80-69847. (Illus.). 1981. 12.95 (ISBN 0-933184-21-2); pap. 6.95 (ISBN 0-933184-22-0). Flame Intl.

Coode, Thomas H. & Bauman, John F. People, Poverty, & Politics: Pennsylvanians During the Great Depression. LC 78-75198. 280p. 1981. 24.50 (ISBN 0-8387-2320-9). Bucknell U Pr.

Vexler, R. I. Pennsylvania Chronology & Factbook, Vol. 38. 1978. 8.50 (ISBN 0-379-16163-X). Oceana.

Wolf, George D. William Warren Scranton: Pennsylvania Statesman. LC 80-21736. (Illus.). 160p. 1981. 16.50x (ISBN 0-271-00278-6, Keystone Bks). Pa St U Pr.

PENNSYLVANIA DUTCH

see Pennsylvania Germans

PENNSYLVANIA GERMANS

Shea, John C. The Pennsylvania Dutch & Their Furniture. 240p. 1980. 19.95 (ISBN 0-442-27546-3). Van Nos Reinhold.

PENOLOGY

see Prisons; Punishment; Reformatories

PENSIONS

see also Civil Service Pensions; Old Age Pensions; Social Security

also names of professions, industries, etc. or subdivision Salaries, Pensions, etc. under names of professions, etc. e.g. Teachers–Salaries, Pensions, etc.

Clark, Robert L., ed. Retirement Policy in an Aging Society. LC 79-56502. (Illus.). vii, 215p. 1980. 16.75 (ISBN 0-8223-0441-4). Duke.

Cooper, Robert D. & Carlsen, Melody A. Pension Fund Operations & Expenses: The Technical Report. (Illus.). 149p. (Orig.). 1980. pap. 15.00 (ISBN 0-89154-139-X). Intl Found Employ.

Gollin, James. The Star Spangled Retirement Dream: Why It's Going Sour & What You Can Do About It. 224p. 1981. 12.95 (ISBN 0-684-16866-9, ScribT). Scribner.

Logue, Dennis E. Legislative Influences on Corporate Pension Plans. 1979. pap. 5.25 (ISBN 0-8447-3337-7). Am Enterprise.

Lynes, Tony. French Pensions. 163p. 1967. pap. text ed. 5.00x (Pub. by Bedford England). Renouf.

Mariner, Elwyn E. The Massachusetts Retirement Plan. 9th ed. 1977. pap. 2.50. Mariner.

Srb, Jozetta H. Portable Pensions. (Key Issues Ser.: No. 4). 1969. pap. 3.00 (ISBN 0-87546-245-6). NY Sch Indus Rel.

Young, J. M. & Buchanan, N. J. Accounting for Pensions. 160p. 1980. 39.00x (ISBN 0-85941-124-9, Pub. by Woodhead-Faulkner England). State Mutual Bk.

PENSIONS, CIVIL

see Civil Service Pensions

PENTECOST

Tiede, David L. & Kavanagh, Aidan. Pentecost 1. Achtemeier, Elizabeth, et al, eds. LC 79-7377. (Proclamation 2: Aids for Interpreting the Lessons of the Church Year, Ser. A). 64p. (Orig.). 1981. pap. 2.50 (ISBN 0-8006-4096-9, 1-4096). Fortress.

PENTECOST FESTIVAL

Furnish, Victor P. & Thulin, Richard L. Pentecost 3. Achtemeier, Elizabeth, et al, eds. LC 79-7377. (Proclamation 2: Aids for Interpreting the Lessons of the Church Year, Ser. A). 64p. (Orig.). 1981. pap. 2.50 (ISBN 0-8006-4098-5, 1-4098). Fortress.

Minear, Paul S. & Adams, Harry B. Pentecost 2. Achtemeier, Elizabeth, et al, eds. LC 79-7377. (Proclamation 2: Aids for Interpreting the Lessons of the Church Year, Ser. A). 64p. (Orig.). 1981. pap. 2.50 (ISBN 0-8006-4097-7, 1-4097). Fortress.

PENTECOSTALISM

see also Jesus People

Gee, Don A., tr. Pentecostes. (Spanish Bks.). 1979. 1.25 (ISBN 0-8297-0552-X). Life Pubs Intl.

Hoekema, Anthony A. Tongues & Spirit-Baptism. 264p. 1981. pap. 6.95 (ISBN 0-8010-4243-7). Baker Bk.

McDonnell, Kilian. Presence, Power, Praise: Documents on Charismatic Renewal: National Documents, Vol. 2. 1980. 35.00 (ISBN 0-8146-1189-3). Liturgical Pr.

Perkins, Carol. Renewal in Song: No. 2. pap. 3.95 (ISBN 0-88270-333-1). Logos.

Precio Del Pentecostes. (Spanish Bks.). 1979. 2.00 (ISBN 0-686-28806-8). Life Pubs Intl.

Smail, Thomas A. The Forgotten Father. 1981. pap. 5.95 (ISBN 0-8028-1879-X). Eerdmans.

PEOPLE, SINGLE

see Single People

PEOPLE'S TEMPLE

Feinsod, Ethan. Awake in a Nightmare. 1981. 14.95 (ISBN 0-393-01431-2). Norton.

Yee, Min S. & Layton, Thomas N. In My Father's House. 384p. 1981. 13.95 (ISBN 0-03-053396-1). HR&W.

PEPPERS

Bullock, J. Benbow. Vaya Con Dios. (Illus.). 150p. 1981. pap. 6.95 (ISBN 0-937024-02-3). Gourmet Guides.

PEPTIDE HORMONES

Li, Choh H., ed. Hormonal Proteins & Peptides, 7 vols. Incl. Vol. 1. 1973. 31.00 (ISBN 0-12-447201-X); Vol. 2. 1973. 37.50 (ISBN 0-12-447202-8); Vol. 3. 1975. 43.00 (ISBN 0-12-447203-6); Vol. 4. 1977. 33.00 (ISBN 0-12-447204-4); Vol. 5. Lipotropin & Related Peptides. 1978. 29.00 (ISBN 0-12-447205-2); Vol. 6. Thyroid Hormones. 1978. 48.50 (ISBN 0-12-447206-0); Vol. 7. Hypothalmic Hormones. 1979. 32.50 (ISBN 0-12-447207-9). LC 78-5444. Acad Pr.

PEPTIDES

Burgen, Sir Arnold, et al. Neuroactive Peptides. (Proceedings of the Royal & Society, Series B.: Vol. 210). (Illus.). 192p. 1980. text ed. 35.00x (ISBN 0-85403-149-9, Pub. by Royal Soc London). Scholium Intl.

Laszlo, F. A., ed. Recent Results in Peptide Hormone & Androgenic Steroid Research. (Illus.). 325p. 1979. 30.00x (ISBN 963-05-2292-6). Intl Pubns Serv.

Li, Choh H., ed. Hormonal Proteins & Peptides, 7 vols. Incl. Vol. 1. 1973. 31.00 (ISBN 0-12-447201-X); Vol. 2. 1973. 37.50 (ISBN 0-12-447202-8); Vol. 3. 1975. 43.00 (ISBN 0-12-447203-6); Vol. 4. 1977. 33.00 (ISBN 0-12-447204-4); Vol. 5. Lipotropin & Related Peptides. 1978. 29.00 (ISBN 0-12-447205-2); Vol. 6. Thyroid Hormones. 1978. 48.50 (ISBN 0-12-447206-0); Vol. 7. Hypothalmic Hormones. 1979. 32.50 (ISBN 0-12-447207-9). LC 78-5444. Acad Pr.

Millar, R. P., ed. Neuropeptides: Biochemical & Physiological Studies. (Illus.). 368p. 1981. lib. bdg. 55.90 (ISBN 0-443-02265-8). Churchill.

Neurosecretion & Brain Peptides: Implications for Brain Function & Neurological Disease. (Advances in Biochemical Psychopharmacology Ser.: Vol. 28). 725p. 1981. 58.00 (ISBN 0-89004-535-6). Raven.

PEPYS, SAMUEL, 1633-1703

Ponsonby, Arthur. Samuel Pepys. 160p. 1980. Repr. of 1928 ed. lib. bdg. 20.00 (ISBN 0-89760-706-6). Telegraph Bks.

Wilson, Edward M. & Cruickshank, Don W. Samuel Pepys's Spanish Plays. 160p. 1981. 74.00 (ISBN 0-19-721793-1). Oxford U Pr.

PEQUOT INDIANS

see Indians of North America–Eastern States

PERCENTAGE

Burleigh, Robert & Matlak, Raymond. Percent. LC 79-730248. (Illus.). 1979. pap. 99.00 (ISBN 0-89290-096-2, A512-SATC). Soc for Visual.

Learning Achievement Corp. Decimals, Percent & Money: Measurement & Transportation. Zak, Therese A., ed. (MATCH Ser.). (Illus.). 144p. 1981. text ed. 5.28 (ISBN 0-07-037114-8, G). McGraw.

PERCEPTION

see also Cognition; Consciousness; Ideology; Information Theory in Psychology; Social Perception

Bach, Marcus. Power of Perception. 1973. pap. 2.95 (ISBN 0-8015-5976-6, Hawthorn). Dutton.

Carterette, Edward C. & Friedman, Morton P., eds. Handbook of Perception. Incl. Vol. 1. 1974. 40.00 (ISBN 0-12-161901-X); Vol. 2. 1974. 48.00 (ISBN 0-12-161902-8); Vol. 4. Hearing. 1978. 49.50 (ISBN 0-12-161904-4); Vol. 5. 1975. 48.00 (ISBN 0-12-161905-2); Vol. 6, 2 pts. 1978. Pt. A, Testing & Smelling. 30.00 (ISBN 0-686-62060-7); Pt. B, Feeling & Hurting. 30.00 (ISBN 0-12-161922-2); Vol. 7. 1975. 48.00 (ISBN 0-12-161907-9); Vol. 8. Perceptual Coding. 1978. 40.00, by subscription 35.00 (ISBN 0-12-161908-7); Vol. 9. Perceptual Processing. 1978. 31.50, by subscription 25.00 (ISBN 0-12-161909-5); Vol. 10. Perceptual Ecology. 1978. 43.00, by subscription 34.00 (ISBN 0-12-161910-9). Acad Pr.

Levine, Michael W. & Shefner, Jeremy M. Fundamentals of Sensation & Perception. (Psychology Ser.). (Illus.). 480p. 1981. text ed. 19.95 (ISBN 0-201-04339-4). A-W.

PERCEPTION, EXTRASENSORY

see Extrasensory Perception

PERCEPTUAL DEFENSE

see Perception

PERCEPTUAL-MOTOR LEARNING

Crews, Katherine. Music & Perceptual Motor Development. (Classroom Music Enrichment Units Ser.). (Illus.). 1974. pap. text ed. 5.95x (ISBN 0-87628-213-3). Ctr Appl Res.

Dellon, A. Lee. Evaluation of Sensibility & Reeducation of Sensation of the Hand. (Illus.). 140p. 1981. write for info. (2427-2). Williams & Wilkins.

Holding, Dennis H. Human Skills. (Studies in Human Performance Ser.). 304p. 1981. 39.95 (ISBN 0-471-27838-6, Pub. by Wiley-Interscience). Wiley.

Rosner, Jerome. Perceptual Skills Curriculum, 4 programs. Incl. Introductory Guide. LC 73-83888. 96p. tchr's ed. 7.50 (ISBN 0-8027-8025-3); Prog. 1. Visual-Motor Skills. 327p. pap. text ed. 24.90 (ISBN 0-8027-8026-1); Prog. 2. Auditory Motor Skills. 304p. pap. text ed. 15.95 (ISBN 0-8027-8027-X); Prog. 3. General Motor Skills. 144p. pap. text ed. 7.95 (ISBN 0-8027-8028-8); Prog. 4. Introducing Letters & Numerals, Pts. 1 & 2. 562p. pap. text ed. 46.90 (ISBN 0-8027-8029-6). 1973. Walker Educ.

PERCOLATION

Rodriques, A. & Tondeur, D., eds. Percolation Processes: Theory & Applications. (NATO Advanced Study Institute Ser.: Applied Science, No. 33). 594p. 1980. 65.00x (ISBN 90-286-0579-7). Sijthoff & Noordhoff.

PERFECT LOVE

see Perfection

PERFECTION

Cahn, Steven M. Eclipse of Excellence. 1.00 (ISBN 0-8183-0142-2). Pub Aff Pr.

Hornbrook, John F. Glimpse of Perfection. 178p. (Orig.). 1979. pap. 3.95 (ISBN 0-89841-004-5). Zoe Pubns.

PERFECTIONISM

see Perfection

PERFECTIONISTS

see Oneida Community

PERFORMANCE

Swezey, Robert W. Individual Performance Assessment: An Approach to Criterion-Referenced Test Development. 1981. text ed. 16.95 (ISBN 0-8359-3066-1). Reston.

PERFORMANCE BUDGET

see Program Budgeting

PERFORMANCE RATING (OF EMPLOYEES)

see Employees, Rating Of

PERFORMANCE STANDARDS

Jaeger, Richard & Title, Carol K., eds. Minimum Competency Achievement Testing. 487p. 18.25 (ISBN 0-8211-0909-X); institutional price 21.25. Am Educ Res.

Watling, Tom. Plan for Promotion: Advancement & the Manager. 237p. 1977. text ed. 19.75x (ISBN 0-220-66327-0, Pub. by Busn Bks England). Renouf.

PERFORMING ARTISTS

see Entertainers

PERFORMING ARTS

see also Theater

also other art forms performed on stage or screen, e.g. Ballet, Concerts, Opera

Burton, L. & Kuroda, K. Arts Play: Creative Activities in Art, Music, Dance & Drama for Young Children. (ps-3). 1981. write for info. spiral bdg. (ISBN 0-201-00201-9, Sch Div). A-W.

Performing Arts 1876-1981. 1981. 150.00 (ISBN 0-8352-1372-2). Bowker.

Rachow, Louis A., ed. Theatre & Performing Arts Collections. (Special Collections Ser.: Vol. 1, No. 1). 128p. 1981. text ed. 19.95 (ISBN 0-917724-47-X). Haworth Pr.

Wilmeth, Don B. The Language of American Popular Entertainment: A Glossary of Argot, Slang, & Terminology. LC 80-14795. 296p. 1981. lib. bdg. 29.95 (ISBN 0-313-22497-8, WEN/). Greenwood.

PERFORMING ARTS AS A PROFESSION

Waack, William L., ed. Careers & Career Education in the Performing Arts: An Annotated Bibliography. 57p. 3.50. Am Theatre Assoc.

PERFUMES

Wells, F. V. Perfumery Technology. 2nd ed. 400p. 1981. 110.00 (ISBN 0-470-26958-8). Halsted Pr.

PERICOPES

see Lectionaries

PERINEURAL ANESTHESIA

see Conduction Anesthesia

PERIODICALS

Here are entered works on the periodicals of the world, and on special aspects or sections of periodicals, language, or area, e.g. Latin American Periodicals, French Periodicals.

see also Liberty of the Press; Newspapers; Press also American Periodicals, English Periodicals, and similar headings; also subdivision Periodicals under specific subjects, e.g. Music–Periodicals; also names of specific periodicals

Center for Academic Publications Japan, ed. Current Contents of Academic Journals in Japan, 1978. 18th ed. LC 72-623679. 392p. (Orig.). 1980. pap. 55.00x (ISBN 0-8002-2740-9). Intl Pubns Serv.

Rivers, William L. & Smolkin, Shelley. Free-Lancer & Staff Writer: Newspaper Features & Magazine Articles. 3rd ed. 352p. 1980. text ed. 14.95x (ISBN 0-534-00873-9). Wadsworth Pub.

PERIODICALS–ABBREVIATIONS OF TITLES

Alkire, Leland G., Jr., ed. Periodical Title Abbreviations. 3rd ed. 500p. 1981. 50.00 (ISBN 0-8103-0337-X). Gale.

PERIODICALS–BIBLIOGRAPHY

INIS: Authority List for Journal Titles. (INIS-11(Rev.9)). 228p. 1981. pap. 14.00 (ISBN 0-686-69441-4, IN11R9, IAEA). Unipub.

Mendel, Roberta, ed. The Pin Prick Press Annual Index of Serial & Chapbook Publications, 1980. (Orig.). 1981. pap. 3.00 (ISBN 0-936424-07-9, 007). Pin Prick.

Ulrich's International Periodicals Directory 1980. 2200p. 1980. 69.50 (ISBN 0-8352-1297-1). Bowker.

PERIODICALS–BIBLIOGRAPHY–UNION LISTS

Gascoigne, ed. British Union Catalogue of Periodicals 1979. 1980. text ed. 31.50 (ISBN 0-408-70857-3). Butterworths.

PERIODICALS–DIRECTORIES

Ulrich's International Periodicals. 19th ed. 1980. 69.50 (ISBN 0-8352-1297-1). Bowker.

PERIODICALS–INDEXES

Here are entered indexes to groups of periodicals and indexes to specific periodicals of such a general nature that they cannot be classified under a specific subject. For periodicals which deal with special subjects see name of subject with or without the subdivisions Indexes or Periodicals.

African Index to Continental Periodical Literature: Covering 1978, No. 3. 1980. 62.50 (Dist. by Gale Research Co.). K G Saur.

Osborn, Andrew D. Serial Publications. 3rd ed. LC 80-11686. 486p. 1980. 20.00 (ISBN 0-8389-0299-5). ALA.

PERIODICALS–SECTIONS, COLUMNS, ETC.

see Newspapers–Sections, Columns, etc.

PERIODICALS–UNION LISTS

see Periodicals–Bibliography–Union Lists

PERIODICITY IN ORGANISMS

see Biological Rhythms

PERIODONTAL DISEASE

Chaikin, Richard. Elements of Surgical Treatment in the Delivery of Periodontal Therapy. (Illus.). 177p. 1978. 54.00 (ISBN 3-87652-661-2). Quint Pub Co.

Harnisch, Herbert. Apicoectomy. (Illus.). 151p. 1975. 42.00. Quint Pub Co.

Shanley, Diarmuid. Efficacy of Treatment Procedures in Periodontics. 340p. 1980. 68.00 (ISBN 0-931386-43-8). Quint Pub Co.

PERIODONTIUM–DISEASES

see Periodontal Disease

PERIPHERAL CIRCULATION

Jenkins, Dave. Peripherals & Interconnects. 300p. 1982. text ed. 12.95 (ISBN 0-8359-5501-X). Reston.

PERKINS, FRANCES, 1882-1965

Mohr, Lillian H. Frances Perkins: That Woman in FDR's Cabinet. 14.95 (ISBN 0-88427-019-X). Green Hill.

PERLS, FREDERICK S.

Shepard, Martin. Fritz. LC 80-50243. 256p. 1981. Repr. of 1975 ed. 7.95 (ISBN 0-933256-15-9). Second Chance.

PERON, EVA

Fraser, Nicholas & Navarro, Marysa. Eva Peron. (Illus.). 1981. 14.95 (ISBN 0-393-01457-6). Norton.

Taylor, Julie. Eva Peron: The Myths of a Woman. LC 79-19547. x, 176p. 1981. pap. write for info. (ISBN 0-226-79144-0). U of Chicago Pr.

Weber, Andrew & Rice, Tim. Evita: The Lgend of Eva Peron, 1919-1952. 1979. pap. 5.95 (ISBN 0-380-46433-0, 46433). Avon.

PERORAL MEDICATION

see Oral Medication

PERSE, SAINT-JOHN, 1887-

Perse, John. St.-John Perse: Letters. Knodel, Arthur J., ed. LC 79-9080. (Bollingen Ser.: LXXXVII: 2). (Illus.). 712p. 1981. 20.00x (ISBN 0-691-09868-9); pap. 8.50 (ISBN 0-691-01836-7). Princeton U Pr.

PERSECUTION

see also Inquisition; Martyrdom; Martyrs
also names of sects persecuted, e.g. Albigenses, Waldenses

Frend, W. H. Martydom & Persecution in the Early Church. (Twin Brooks Ser.). 645p. 1981. pap. 12.95 (ISBN 0-8010-3502-3). Baker Bk.

PERSIAN ART

see Art, Persian

PERSIAN GULF STATES

Bhutani, Surendra, ed. Contemporary Gulf. 1980. 12.00x (ISBN 0-8364-0667-2, Pub. by Academic India). South Asia Bks.

Hay, Rupert. The Persian Gulf States. LC 80-1926. 1981. Repr. of 1959 ed. 23.50 (ISBN 0-404-18966-0). AMS Pr.

PERSIAN LANGUAGE–DICTIONARIES

Addi, Al-Sayyid. Dictionary of Persian Loan Words in the Arabic Language. 1980. 15.00x. Intl Bk Ctr.

PERSIAN LITERATURE–TRANSLATIONS INTO ENGLISH

Welch, Stuart C. A King's Book of Kings. 200p. 1981. 50.00 (ISBN 0-87099-028-4, 494208). NYGS.

PERSIAN PAINTING

see Painting, Persian

PERSONAL AIRCRAFT

see Airplanes, Private

PERSONAL AIRPLANES

see Airplanes, Private

PERSONAL BEAUTY

see Beauty, Personal

PERSONAL CLEANLINESS

see Hygiene

PERSONAL COMBAT

see Hand-To-Hand Fighting

PERSONAL DEVELOPMENT

see Personality; Success

PERSONAL EFFICIENCY

see Success

PERSONAL FINANCE

see Finance, Personal

PERSONAL HEALTH

see Health

PERSONAL INCOME TAX

see Income Tax

PERSONAL LIBERTY

see Liberty

PERSONAL LOANS

see Loans, Personal

PERSONAL PROPERTY

see also Bailments

Biddle, Arthur. A Treatise on the Law of Warranties in the Sale of Chattels. xx, 308p. 1981. Repr. of 1884 ed. lib. bdg. 30.00x (ISBN 0-8377-0316-6). Rothman.

PERSONAL RADIOTELEPHONE

see Citizens Band Radio

PERSONALITY

see also Character; Charm; Ego (Psychology); Humanistic Psychology; Personality Assessment; Rigidity (Psychology); Self; Soul

Allport, Gordon W. Personality & Social Encounter: Selected Essays. LC 77-13911. x, 388p. 1981. pap. text ed. 17.00x (ISBN 0-226-01494-0). U of Chicago Pr.

American Psychological Association. Studying Personality: Student Booklet. (Human Behavior Curriculum Project Ser.). 64p. (Orig.). (gr. 9-12). 1981. pap. text ed. 3.95x (ISBN 0-8077-2627-3). Tchrs Coll.

--Studying Personality: Teachers Manual & Duplication Masters. (Human Behavior Curriculum Project Ser.). 48p. (Orig.). (gr. 9-12). 1981. pap. 9.95x (ISBN 0-8077-2628-1). Tchrs Coll.

Auld, James. Real Personality. 1981. 7.75 (ISBN 0-8062-1597-6). Carlton.

Bagby, English. The Psychology of Personality. 236p. 1980. Repr. of 1928 ed. lib. bdg. 35.00 (ISBN 0-8492-3590-1). R West.

Binet, Alfred. Alterations of Personality. Baldwin, Helen G., tr. from Fr. Bd. with On Double-Consciousness. Repr. of 1890 ed. (Contributions to the History of Psychology Ser., Vol. V, Pt. C: Medical Psychology). 1978. Repr. of 1896 ed. 30.00 (ISBN 0-89093-169-0). U Pubns Amer.

Coates, C. R. Developing a Commanding Personality. LC 79-23634. 180p. 1981. 14.95 (ISBN 0-88229-414-8). Nelson-Hall.

Easwaran, Eknath. Dialogue with Death: The Spiritual Psychology of the Katha Upanishad. 288p. (Orig.). 1981. pap. 6.00 (ISBN 0-915132-24-9). Nilgiri Pr.

Geis, F. L. Personality Research Manual. 227p. 1978. 10.95 (ISBN 0-471-29519-1). Wiley.

Hillman, et al. Spring 'seventy-Six: An Annual of Archetypal Psychology & Jungian Thought. Hillman, James, ed. 218p. (Orig.). 1976. pap. text ed. 12.00 (ISBN 0-88214-011-6). Spring Pubns.

Kardos, Lajos, ed. Attitudes, Interaction & Personality. Dajka, B., et al, trs. (Illus.). 149p. 1980. 10.50x (ISBN 963-05-2088-5). Intl Pubns Serv.

Kline, Nathan S. From Sad to Glad. 1981. pap. 2.95 (ISBN 0-345-29545-5). Ballantine.

Linton, Ralph. The Cultural Background of Personality. LC 80-29240. xix, 157p. 1981. Repr. of 1945 ed. lib. bdg. 17.50x (ISBN 0-313-22783-7, LICU). Greenwood.

Lucas, Katherine & Lucas, Louise. Hometown, U. S. A. (Illus., Orig.). 1980. pap. 4.95 (ISBN 0-914634-75-5, 8001). DOK Pubs.

Lynn, R., ed. Dimensions of Personality: Essays in Honour of H. J. Eysenck. (Illus.). 490p. 1981. 95.00 (ISBN 0-08-024294-4). Pergamon.

Schuller, Robert H. You Can Become the Person You Want to Be. (Orig.). pap. 2.25 (ISBN 0-515-05970-6). Jove Pubns.

Schultz, Duane. Theories of Personality. 2nd ed. LC 80-26414. 384p. 1981. text ed. 17.95 (ISBN 0-8185-0439-0). Brooks-Cole.

Van Der Hoop, J. H. Conscious Orientation. Hutton, Luara, tr. 352p. 1980. Repr. of 1930 ed. lib. bdg. 50.00 (ISBN 0-89987-875-X). Darby Bks.

Vento, Carla. Of Time & Value. (Illus.). 96p. (Orig.). 1980. tchr's ed 4.95 (ISBN 0-914634-76-3, 8002). DOK Pubs.

Wheeler, Ladd, ed. Review of Personality & Social Psychology: No. 1. (Illus.). 352p. 1980. 20.00 (ISBN 0-8039-1457-1). Sage.

--Review of Personality & Social Psychology: No. 1. (Illus.). 352p. 1980. pap. 9.95 (ISBN 0-8039-1458-X). Sage.

PERSONALITY, DISORDERS OF

see also Autism; Clinical Psychology; Frustration; Hypnotism; Psychoses

Millon, Theodore. Disorders of Personality: DSMIII; AXIS II. 352p. 1981. 27.50 (ISBN 0-471-06403-3, Pub. by Wiley-Interscience). Wiley.

PERSONALITY ASSESSMENT

Krug, Samuel E. A Sixteen PF Codebook. 1981. pap. price not set (ISBN 0-918296-16-1). Inst Personality & Ability.

Yando, Regina & Seitz, Victoria. Intellectual & Personality Characteristics of Children: Social-Class & Ethnic-Group Differences. 136p. 1979. profess./reference text 12.95 (ISBN 0-89859-001-9). Erlbaum Assocs.

PERSONALTY

see Personal Property

PERSONNEL MANAGEMENT

see also Applications for Positions; Communication in Management; Discrimination in Employment; Employees, Rating of; Employees, Training of; Employees, Transfer of; Employment Tests; Executives; Executives, Training of; Factory Management; Grievance Procedures; Industrial Sociology; Job Satisfaction; Psychology, Industrial; Recruiting of Employees; Supervision of Employees; Time and Motion Study
also specific subjects with or without the subdivisions Administration or Personnel Management, e.g. Hospitals–Administration; School Personnel Management

Adams, Sexton & Griffin, Adelaide. Modern Personnel Management. 330p. 1981. 14.95 (ISBN 0-87201-662-5). Gulf Pub.

Basic Requirements for Personnel Monitoring. (Safety Ser.: No. 14). 40p. 1980. pap. 6.00 (ISBN 92-0-123980-7, ISP 559, IAEA). Unipub.

Beatty, Richard W. & Schneier, Craig E. Personnel Administration: An Experiential Skill-Building Approach. 576p. 1981. pap. text ed. 14.95 (ISBN 0-201-00172-1). A-W.

Dessler, Gary. Personnel Management. 2nd ed. 500p. 1981. text ed. 18.95 (ISBN 0-8359-5518-4); study guide 7.95 (ISBN 0-8359-5521-4); instr's. manual free. Reston.

Foulkes, Fred K. Personnel Policies in Nonunion Companies. 350p. 1981. 19.95 (ISBN 0-686-69329-9). P-H.

Karlins, Marvin. The Human Use of Human Resources. 1st ed. (Illus.). 208p. (Orig.). 11.95 (ISBN 0-07-033298-3); pap. text ed. 6.95 (ISBN 0-07-033297-5). McGraw.

Kelley, Nelson L. & Whatley, Arthur A. Personnel Management in Action, Skill Building Experiences. 2nd ed. (West Ser. in Management). 300p. 1981. pap. text ed. 13.95 (ISBN 0-8299-0389-5). West Pub.

Life Office Management Association, ed. Readings for the Personnel Administration Specialty. (FLMI Insurance Education Program Ser.). 95p. (Orig.). 1980. pap. 6.00x (ISBN 0-915322-41-2). Loma.

Mondy & Noe. Personnel: The Management of Human Resources. 750p. 1980. text ed. 20.95 (ISBN 0-205-07217-8, 0872172); free tchr's ed. (ISBN 0-205-07218-6). Allyn.

Nigro, Felix A. & Nigro, Lloyd G. The New Public Personnel Administration. 2nd ed. LC 80-83098. 420p. 1981. text ed. 14.95 (ISBN 0-87581-265-1). Peacock Pubs.

Roseman, Edward. Managing Employee Turnover: A Postive Approach. 241p. 1981. 17.95 (ISBN 0-8144-5585-9). Am Mgmt.

Schuler, Randall S. Personnel & Human Resource Management. (Management Ser.). (Illus.). 600p. 1981. text ed. 15.96 (ISBN 0-8299-0406-9). West Pub.

Schuler, Randall S., et al. Applied Readings in Personnel & Human Resource Management. (Management Ser.). (Illus.). 300p. 1981. pap. text ed. 6.36 (ISBN 0-8299-0408-5). West Pub.

Smith, Jerald R. The Personnel Management Game. 1980. pap. text ed. 4.95 (ISBN 0-933836-14-7). Simtek.

Werther, William & Davis, Keith. Personnel Management. (Illus.). 528p. (Orig.). text ed. 18.95x (ISBN 0-07-069436-2); instructor's manual & test bank. write for info. (ISBN 0-07-069437-0). McGraw.

PERSONNEL MANAGEMENT–BIBLIOGRAPHY

Soltow, Martha & Sokkar, Jo A. Industrial Relations & Personnel Management: Selected Information Sources. LC 78-31795. 294p. 1979. lib. bdg. 12.00 (ISBN 0-8108-1203-7). Scarecrow.

PERSONNEL MANAGEMENT–EXAMINATIONS, QUESTIONS, ETC.

Eckles, Robert W. & Carmichael, Ronald L. Supervisory Management. (Management Ser.). 550p. 1981. text ed. 22.95 (ISBN 0-471-05947-1); tchrs.' ed. avail. (ISBN 0-471-08941-9). Wiley.

PERSONNEL SERVICE IN EDUCATION

see also Counseling; Grading and Marking (Students); Pregnant Schoolgirls; School Social Work; Vocational Guidance

Drapela, Victor J. Guidance & Counseling Around the World. LC 79-64966. 344p. 1981. lib. bdg. 20.50 (ISBN 0-8191-1384-0); pap. text ed. 11.50 (ISBN 0-8191-0777-8). U Pr of Amer.

Roth, Robert A. Individualized Staff Development Programs for Competency Development: A Systematic Approach. LC 80-8258. 123p. 1980. pap. text ed. 7.50 (ISBN 0-8191-1326-3). U Pr of Amer.

PERSONS, SINGLE

see Single People

PERSPECTIVE

see also Drawing; Proportion (Art)

Green, Benjamin. The Basic Guide to Pictorial Perspective. (A Promotion of the Arts Library Book). (Illus.). 97p. 1981. 27.75 (ISBN 0-86650-001-4). Gloucester Art.

Parramon, J. M. Perspective. (Art Ser.). (Orig.). 1981. pap. 4.95 (ISBN 0-89586-082-1). H P Bks.

PERSUASION (PSYCHOLOGY)

see also Propaganda

Schwerin, Horace S. & Newell, Henry H. Persuasion in Marketing: The Dynamics of Marketing's Great Untapped Resource. 280p. 1981. 23.95 (ISBN 0-471-04554-3, Pub. by Wiley-Interscience). Wiley.

PERSUASION (RHETORIC)

see also Oratory

Burgess, John A. & Huber, Robert B. Persuasion in the Courtroom. (Orig.). 1981. text ed. write for info (ISBN 0-316-11635-1). Little.

PERTURBATION (MATHEMATICS)

Kato, T. Perturbation Theory for Linear Operators. 2nd ed. (Grundlehren der Mathematischen Wissenschaften: Vol. 132). (Illus.). 619p. 1980. 72.00 (ISBN 0-387-07558-5). Springer-Verlag.

Kevorkian, J. & Cole, J. D. Perturbation Methods in Applied Mathematics. (Applied Mathematical Sciences Ser.: Vol. 34). (Illus.). 512p. 1981. 42.00 (ISBN 0-387-90507-3). Springer-Verlag.

Meyer, Richard & Parter, Seymour, eds. Singular Perturbations & Syasymptotics. LC 80-24946. 1980. lib ed 22.00 (ISBN 0-12-493260-6). Acad Pr.

Miranker, Willard L. Numerical Methods for Stiff Equations & Singular Perturbation Problems. (Mathematics & Its Applications Ser.: No. 5). 216p. 1980. lib. bdg. 29.95 (ISBN 90-277-1107-0, Pub. by D. Reidel). Kluwer Boston.

PERTURBATION THEORY

see Perturbation (Mathematics)

PERU–ANTIQUITIES

Hemming, John. Machu Picchu. Bayrd, Edwin, ed. LC 80-82066. (Illus.). 1981. 16.95 (ISBN 0-88225-302-6). Newsweek.

MacNeish, Richard S., et al. Prehistory of the Ayacucho Basin, Peru, Vol. II: Excavations & Chronology. LC 80-13960. (Illus.). 368p. 1981. text ed. 45.00 (ISBN 0-472-04907-0). U of Mich Pr.

Moseley, Micheal E. & Day, Kent C., eds. Chan Chan: Andean Desert City. (School of American Research Advanced Seminar Ser.). (Illus.). 440p. 1981. 29.95x (ISBN 0-8263-0575-X). U of NM Pr.

PERU–DESCRIPTION AND TRAVEL

Benson, Elizabeth & Conklin, William. Museums of the Andes. Lafarge, Henry, ed. LC 80-8912. 1981. 16.95 (ISBN 0-88225-306-9). Newsweek.

PERU–POLITICS AND GOVERNMENT

Burkholder, Mark A. Politics of a Colonial Career: Jose Baquijano & the Audencia of Lima. 198p. 1981. 20.00 (ISBN 0-8263-0545-8). U of NM Pr.

PERU–SOCIAL CONDITIONS

Barndt, Deborah. Education & Social Change: A Photographic Study of Peru. 1980. pap. text ed. 19.95 (ISBN 0-8403-2283-6). Kendall-Hunt.

McClintock, Cynthia. Peasant Cooperatives & Political Change in Peru. LC 80-8563. (Illus.). 480p. 1981. 30.00x (ISBN 0-691-07627-8); pap. 7.95x (ISBN 0-691-02202-X). Princeton U Pr.

PERVERSION, SEXUAL

see Sexual Deviation

PEST CONTROL

see also Insect Control; Weed Control; and similar headings; also subdivision Control under names of pests

Elements of Integrated Control of Sorghum Pests. (FAO Plant Production & Protection Ser.: No. 19). 167p. 1980. pap. 9.00 (ISBN 92-5-100884-1, F1943, FAO). Unipub.

Guidelines for Integrated Control of Maize Pests. (FAO Plant Production & Protection Paper Ser.: No. 18). 98p. 1980. pap. 6.00 (ISBN 92-5-100875-2, F1942, FAO). Unipub.

The Methodology for Determining Insect Control Recommendations. (IRRI Research Paper Ser.: No. 46). 31p. 1980. pap. 5.00 (R086, IRRI). Unipub.

Morse, Roger A., ed. Honey Bee Pests, Predators & Diseases. LC 78-58027. (Illus.). 1978. 32.50x (ISBN 0-8014-0975-6). Comstock.

Nordlund, Donald A., et al, eds. Semiochemicals: Their Role in Pest Control. 400p. 1981. 27.50 (ISBN 0-471-05803-3, Pub. by Wiley-Interscience). Wiley.

Pimentel, David, ed. Handbook of Pest Management in Agriculture. 1981. Vol. 1. 69.95 (ISBN 0-8493-3841-7); Vol. 2. 67.95 (ISBN 0-8493-3842-5); Vol. 3. 69.95 (ISBN 0-8493-3843-3). CRC Pr.

Scopes, Nigel, ed. Pest & Disease Control Handbook. 250p. 1979. 35.00x (ISBN 0-901436-42-9, Pub. by Brit Crop Protection England). Intl Schol Bk Serv.

Ware, George W. Complete Guide to Pest Control: With & Without Chemicals. LC 80-52306. 1980. 18.50 (ISBN 0-913702-09-9). Thomson Pub CA.

PEST RESISTANCE OF PLANTS

see Plants–Disease and Pest Resistance

PESTALOZZI, JOHANN HEINRICH, 1746-1827

Pestalozzi, Johann H. Pestalozzi's Educational Writings. Green, John A., tr. from Ger. Bd. with How Gertrude Teaches Her Children. (Contributions to the History of Psychology Ser., Vol. II, Pt. B: Psychometrics). 1978. Repr. of 1898 ed. 30.00 (ISBN 0-89093-163-1). U Pubns Amer.

PESTICIDES

see also Fungicides; Herbicides; Insecticides; Spraying and Dusting Residues in Agriculture

Barons, Keith C. Are Pesticides Really Necessary? 280p. 1981. pap. 6.95 (ISBN 0-89526-888-4). Regnery-Gateway.

Code of Practice for Safe Use of Pesticides. 28p. 1980. pap. 5.00 (ISBN 0-643-00171-9, CO11, CSIRO). Unipub.

Hutson, D. H. & Roberts, T. R. Progress in Pesticide Biochemistry, Vol. 1. 360p. 1981. 71.95 (ISBN 0-471-27920-X, Pub. by Wiley-Interscience). Wiley.
Newton, Michael. Chemicals in the Forest. 160p. 1980. pap. 10.95 (ISBN 0-917304-25-X, Pub. by Timber Pr). Intl Schol Bk Serv.
Recommendations on the Safe Use of Pesticides in Ships. 14p. 1973. 5.50 (IMCO). Unipub.
Recommended Methods for Meausurment of Pest Resistance to Pesticides. (FAO Plant Production & Protection Paper: No. 21). 136p. 1981. pap. 7.25 (ISBN 92-5-100883-3, F2079, FAO). Unipub.
Sittig, Marshall, ed. Pesticide Manufacturing & Toxic Materials Control Encyclopedia. LC 80-19373. (Chemical Tech. Rev. 168; Env. Health Rev. 3; Pollution Tech. Rev. 69). (Illus.). 810p. 1981. 96.00 (ISBN 0-8155-0814-X). Noyes.
Stimmann, Michael. Pesticide Application & Safety Training. rev. ed. (Illus.). 98p. (Orig.). 1980. pap. text ed. 4.00. Ag Sci Pubns.
Worthing, Charles R., ed. The Pesticide Manual. 6th ed. 655p. 1979. 59.95x (ISBN 0-901436-44-5, Pub. by Brit Crop Protection England). Intl Schol Bk Serv.

PESTICIDES-ENVIRONMENTAL ASPECTS
Pesticide Residues in Food 1979. (FAO Plant Production & Protection Paper Ser.: No. 20). 97p. 1980. pap. 6.00 (ISBN 92-5-100922-8, F1936, FAO). Unipub.

PESTICIDES-TOXICOLOGY
Pesticide Residues in Food 1979. (FAO Plant Production & Protection Paper Ser.: No. 20). 97p. 1980. pap. 6.00 (ISBN 92-5-100922-8, F1936 FAO). Unipub.
Pesticide Residues in Food-1979 Evaluations. 568p. 1981. pap. 30.25 (ISBN 92-5-100958-9, F2089, FAO). Unipub.

PESTICIDES AND THE ENVIRONMENT
see Pesticides-Environmental Aspects

PESTILENCES
see Epidemics

PETER, SAINT, APOSTLE
Flynn, Leslie B. From Clay to Rock: Personal Insights into Life from Simon Peter. LC 80-69307. 176p. 1981. pap. 5.95 (ISBN 0-915684-79-9). Christian Herald.

PETER 1ST, THE GREAT, EMPEROR OF RUSSIA, 1672-1725
Soloviev, Sergei M. History of Russia: Peter the Great: the Great Reforms Being, Vol. 16. Papmehl, K. A., tr. 1981. 20.00 (ISBN 0-87569-042-4). Academic Intl.

PETERSBURG, VIRGINIA
Henderson, William D. Gilded Age City: Politics, Life, & Labor in Petersburg, Virginia, 1874-1889. LC 80-1385. (Illus.). 603p. 1980. lib. bdg. 25.50 (ISBN 0-8191-1294-1); pap. text ed. 17.50 (ISBN 0-8191-1295-X). U Pr of Amer.

PETITION, RIGHT OF
Tardu, M. Human Rights: The International Petition System, Release 1. 1980. 35.00 (ISBN 0-379-20252-2). Oceana.

PETRARCH, FRANCESCO (FRANCESCO PETRARCA), 1304-1374
Holloway-Calthrop, H. C. Petrarch His Life & Times. 319p. 1980. Repr. of 1907 ed. lib. bdg. 45.00 (ISBN 0-89984-274-7). Century Bookbindery.

PETROGRAPHY
see Petrology

PETROLEUM
see also Boring; Petroleum Products
Arrow, Kenneth J. & Kalt, Joseph P. Petroleum Price Regulation: Should We Decontrol? 1979. pap. 4.25. Am Enterprise.
Atkinson, G. Origin & Chemistry of Petroleum: Oriceedings of the Third Annual Karcher Symposium, Oklahoma, May 4, 1979. Zuckerman, J. J., ed. (Illus.). 120p. 1981. 24.00 (ISBN 0-08-026179-5). Pergamon.
Davis, J. A. High Cost Oil & Gas Resources. 240p. 1981. 40.00x (ISBN 0-85664-588-5, Pub. by Croom Helm LTD England). Biblio Dist.
Hallwood, C. Paul & Sinclair, Stuart W. Oil Debt & Development: OPEC in the Third World. 208p. 1981. text ed. 29.95x (ISBN 0-04-382027-1, 2580). Allen Unwin.
Herald, F. A., ed. Occurrence of Oil & Gas in West Texas. (Illus.). 456p. 1957. 9.00 (PUB 5716). Bur Econ Geology.
Kaylin, Arleen & Barnett, Laurie, eds. Update 1980. LC 80-21499. (The Great Contemporary Issues Ser.: Group Ii). (Illus.). 320p. 1980. 35.00 (ISBN 0-405-13781-8). Arno.

PETROLEUM-GEOLOGY
see also Oil Well Logging
Hobson, G. D., ed. Developments in Petroleum Geology - Two. (Illus.). 345p. 1980. 70.00x (ISBN 0-85334-907-X). Burgess-Intl Ideas.

PETROLEUM-JUVENILE LITERATURE
Piper, Roger. The Story of Oil. (Junior Reference Ser.). (Illus.). 64p. (gr. 7 up). 7.95 (ISBN 0-7136-1911-2). Dufour.

PETROLEUM-LAW
see Petroleum Law and Legislation

PETROLEUM-PIPE LINES
Crespe, Mary A., ed. Pipeline Rates on Crude Petroleum Oil. 800p. Date not set. 95.00. CSG Pr.

PETROLEUM-TAXATION
see Petroleum Law and Legislation

PETROLEUM-TRANSPORTATION
see also Petroleum-Pipe Lines; Tankers
Block, Richard A., ed. Tankerman: All Grades. rev. ed. (Illus.). 250p. 1981. pap. 21.00 (ISBN 0-934114-30-7). Marine Educ.
Block, Richard A. & Collins, Charles B., eds. The M&O Master's Handbook. (Illus.). 271p. (Orig.). 1979. pap. text ed. 18.00 (ISBN 0-934114-16-1). Marine Educ.
--Standard Operations Manual for the Marine Transportation Sector of the Offshore Mineral & Oil Industry. 61p. (Orig.). 1979. pap. text ed. 7.50 (ISBN 0-934114-09-9). Marine Educ.
Hughes, J. R. The Storage & Handling of Petroleum Liquids. 332p. 1978. 85.00x (ISBN 0-85264-251-2, Pub. by Griffin England). State Mutual Bk.

PETROLEUM AS FUEL
Annual Bulletin of Gas Statistics, Vol. 24. 97p. 1979. pap. 8.00 (ISBN 0-686-68941-0, UN79/2E26, UN). Unipub.

PETROLEUM CHEMICALS
Rudd, Dale F., et al. Petrochemical Technology Assessment. 325p. 1981. 32.95 (ISBN 0-471-08912-5, Pub. by Wiley-Interscience). Wiley.

PETROLEUM CONSERVATION
Odell, Peter R. British Oil Policy: A Radical Alternative. 75p. 1980. 35.00x (ISBN 0-85038-316-1). Nichols Pub.
Odell, Peter R. & Rosing, Kenneth E. Future of Oil: A Simulation Study of the Interrelationships of Resources, Reserves, & Use 1980-2080. 300p. 1980. 47.50x (ISBN 0-89397-097-2). Nichols Pub.

PETROLEUM ENGINEERING
see also Oil Reservoir Engineering; Oil Well Logging; Petroleum-Transportation; Petroleum Industry and Trade
American Petroleum Institute. Manual of Petroleum Measurement Standards. LC 80-67080. (Chapter 11.1 -- Volume Correction Factors Ser.: Vol. I). (Illus.). 678p. 1980. write for info. (ISBN 0-89364-022-0). Am Petroleum.
--Manual of Petroleum Measurement Standards. LC 80-67080. (Chapter 11.1 -- Volume Correction Factors: Vol. II). (Illus.). 592p. 1980. write for info. (ISBN 0-89364-023-9). Am Petroleum.
--Manual of Petroleum Measurement Standards. LC 80-67080. (Chapter 11.1 -- Volume Correction Factors: Vol. III). (Illus.). 563p. 1980. write for info. (ISBN 0-89364-024-7). Am Petroleum.
--Manual of Petroleum Measurement Standards. LC 80-67080. (Chapter 11.1 -- Volume Correction Factors: Vol. IV). (Illus.). 878p. 1980. write for info. (ISBN 0-89364-025-5). Am Petroleum.
--Manual of Petroleum Measurement Standard. LC 80-67080. (Chapter 11.1 --Volume Corrections Factors: Vol. V). (Illus.). 812p. 1980. write for info. (ISBN 0-89364-026-3). Am Petroleum.
--Manual of Petroleum Measurement Standards. LC 80-67080. (Chapter 11.1 -- Volume Correction Factors: Vol. IX). (Illus.). 587p. 1980. write for info. (ISBN 0-89364-032-8). Am Petroleum.
--Manual of Petroleum Measurement Standard. LC 80-67080. (Chapter 11.1 -- Volume Correction Factors: Vol. X). (Illus.). 420p. 1980. write for info. (ISBN 0-89364-033-6). Am Petroleum.
--Manual of Petroleum Measurement Standards. (Chapter 11.1 -- Vol. Correction Factors). (Illus.). 1980. write for info. (ISBN 0-89364-021-2). Am Petroleum.
--Manual of Petroleum Measurement Standards. LC 80-67080. (Chapter 11.1 -- Volume Correction Factors). 1980. write for info. (ISBN 0-89364-035-2). Am Petroleum.
--Manual of Petroleum Measurements Standards. LC 80-67080. (Chapter 11.1 -- Volume Correction Factors: Vol. VII). (Illus.). 958p. 1980. write for info. (ISBN 0-89364-029-8). Am Petroleum.
Block, Richard A., ed. Engineer-Chief & Assistant Engineer & Oiler: Limited to Service in the Mineral & Oil Industry. rev. ed. (Illus.). 82p. 1975. pap. text ed. 12.00 (ISBN 0-934114-07-2). Marine Educ.
Block, Richard A. & Collins, Charles B., eds. The M&O Master's Handbook. (Illus.). 271p. (Orig.). 1979. pap. text ed. 18.00 (ISBN 0-934114-16-1). Marine Educ.
The Bravo Blow-Out. 287p. 1980. 100.00x (ISBN 8-272-70011-5, Pub. by Norwegian Info Norway). State Mutual Bk.
Goins, W. C. & Sheffield, Riley. Blowout Prevention. 2nd ed. 300p. 1981. 19.95 (ISBN 0-87201-073-2). Gulf Pub.
Lynch, Philip F. Downhole Operations. (Basic Petroleum Production Operations Ser.: Vol. 3). (Illus.). 128p. (Orig.). 1981. pap. text ed. 14.95 (ISBN 0-87201-225-5). Gulf Pub.
Norwegian Petroleum Society. Marginal Fields-Criteria for Development. 197p. 1980. 60.00x (ISBN 82-7270-006-9, Pub. by Norwegian Info Norway). State Mutual Bk.
Norwegina Petroleum Society. Contingency Planning. 223p. 1980. 75.00x (ISBN 8-27270-010-7, Pub. by Norwegian Info Norway). State Mutual Bk.
Skinner, David R. An Introduction to Petroleum Production Operations, Vol. 1. 200p. 1981. 12.95 (ISBN 0-87201-767-2). Gulf Pub.
Wheeler, Robert R. & Whited, Maurine. Oil from Prospect to Pipeline. 4th ed. 157p. 1981. pap. 6.95 (ISBN 0-87201-635-8). Gulf Pub.

PETROLEUM GEOLOGY
see Petroleum-Geology

PETROLEUM INDUSTRY AND TRADE
see also Petroleum Products; Petroleum Workers
Beudell, Martin, ed. Offshore Oil & Gas Yearbook 1980-81. 500p. 1980. 115.00x (ISBN 0-85038-336-6). Nichols Pub.
Bullock, James B. No More Dry Holes. LC 80-66936. (Illus.). 150p. 1981. pap. 9.95 (ISBN 0-937024-00-7). Gourmet Guides.
Crespe, Mary A., ed. Pipeline Rates on Crude Petroleum Oil. 800p. Date not set. 95.00. CSG Pr.
Financial Solidarity for Development: Efforts & Institutions of the Members of OPEC 1973-1976 Review, Vol. 1. 117p. 1979. pap. 15.00 (ISBN 0-686-68957-7, 79/2D9, UN). Unipub.
Financial Solidarity for Development: Statistical Annex, Vol. 2. 83p. 1979. pap. 15.00 (ISBN 0-686-68958-5, UN79/2D9, UN). Unipub.
Goins, W. C. & Sheffield, Riley. Blowout Prevention. 2nd ed. 300p. 1981. 19.95 (ISBN 0-87201-073-2). Gulf Pub.
Griest, W. H., et al, eds. Health Effects Investigation of Oil Shale Development. 1981. text ed. 29.50. Ann Arbor Science.
Lynch, Philip F. Downhole Operations. (Basic Petroleum Production Operations Ser.: Vol. 3). (Illus.). 128p. (Orig.). 1981. pap. text ed. 14.95 (ISBN 0-87201-225-5). Gulf Pub.
Rintoul, William. Drilling Ahead. (Illus.). 300p. 1981. 16.95 (ISBN 0-934136-09-2, Valley Pub). Western Tanager.
Schumacher, M. M., ed. Enhanced Recovery of Residual & Heavy Oils. 2nd ed. LC 80-19812. (Energy Tech. Rev. 59; Chemical Tech. Rev. 174). (Illus.). 378p. 1981. 48.00 (ISBN 0-8155-0816-6). Noyes.
Skinner, David R. An Introduction to Petroleum Production Operations, Vol. 1. 200p. 1981. 12.95 (ISBN 0-87201-767-2). Gulf Pub.
Van Poolen, H. K., et al. Fundamentals of Enhanced Oil Recovery. 176p. 1980. 30.00 (ISBN 0-87814-144-8). Pennwell Pub.
Wheeler, Robert R. & Whited, Maurine. Oil from Prospect to Pipeline. 4th ed. 157p. 1981. pap. 6.95 (ISBN 0-87201-635-8). Gulf Pub.

PETROLEUM INDUSTRY AND TRADE-DICTIONARIES
Moureau, Magdaleine & Brace, Gerald, eds. Dictionary of Petroleum Technology-Dictionnaire Dechnique Du Petrol: English-French - French-English. rev. ed. LC 64-56944. (Collection Des Dictionnaires Techniques: No. 1). 975p. 1979. 100.00x (ISBN 2-7108-0361-5). Intl Pubns Serv.

PETROLEUM INDUSTRY AND TRADE-HISTORY
Boatright, Mody C. Folklore of the Oil Industry. LC 63-21186. 228p. 1980. Repr. of 1963 ed. 6.95 (ISBN 0-87074-007-5). SMU Press.
Halbouty, Michel & Clark, James. Spindletop. 336p. 1980. 16.95 (ISBN 0-87201-791-5). Gulf Pub.

PETROLEUM INDUSTRY AND TRADE-LAW
see Petroleum Law and Legislation

PETROLEUM INDUSTRY AND TRADE-AUSTRALIA
Conybeare, C. E. B. Oil Search in Australia. LC 80-65047. (Illus.). 151p. 1980. pap. text ed. 14.95 (ISBN 0-7081-1164-5, 0593). Bks Australia.

PETROLEUM INDUSTRY AND TRADE-CHINA
Carlson, Sevinc. China's Oil: Problems & Prospects. LC 79-92159. (CSIS Monograph). 128p. 1979. 77.00 (ISBN 0-89206-010-7). CSI Studies.

PETROLEUM INDUSTRY AND TRADE-EUROPE
Grayson, L. E. European National Oil Companies. 256p. 1981. price not set (ISBN 0-471-27861-0, Wiley-Interscience). Wiley.
Norwegian Petroleum Society. European Petroleum Related Industries. 109p. 1980. 75.00x (ISBN 82-7270-016-6, Pub. by Norwegian Info Norway). State Mutual Bk.

PETROLEUM INDUSTRY AND TRADE-GREAT BRITAIN
Parsler, Ron & Shapiro, Dan. The Social Impact of Oil in Scotland. 192p. 1980. text ed. 27.75x (ISBN 0-566-00375-9, Pub. by Gower Pub Co England). Renouf.

PETROLEUM INDUSTRY AND TRADE-NEAR EAST
Anderson, Irvine H. Aramco, the United States, & Saudi Arabia: A Study of the Dynamics of Foreign Oil Policy, 1933-1950. LC 80-8535. 288p. 1981. 15.00x (ISBN 0-691-04679-4). Princeton U Pr.
Johany, Ali D. The Myth of the OPEC Cartel: The Role of Saudi Arabia. 191p. 1981. 34.00 (ISBN 0-471-27864-5, Pub. by Wiley-Interscience). Wiley.
Mallakh, Ragaei El. OPEC: Twenty Years & Beyond. 240p. 1981. lib. bdg. 25.00x (ISBN 0-86531-163-3). Westview.
Servan-Schreiber, Jean-Jacques. The World Challenge. 1981. 14.95 (ISBN 0-671-42524-2). S&S.
Waddams, Frank C. The Libyan Oil Industry. LC 80-13939. (Illus.). 352p. 1980. text ed. 30.00x (ISBN 0-8018-2431-1). Johns Hopkins.

PETROLEUM INDUSTRY AND TRADE-NORTH SEA REGION
Norwegian Petroleum Society. Contracts & Taxation in the Norwegian North Sea. 130p. 1980. 75.00x (Pub. by Norwegian Info Norway). State Mutual Bk.
--Development Through Cooperation Between the Scandinavian & Oapec Countries. 296p. 1980. 75.00x (Pub. by Norwegian Info Norway). State Mutual Bk.
--Engineering & Construction of an Oil Production Platform. 1980. 70.00x (ISBN 82-7270-015-8, Pub. by Norwegian Info Norway). State Mutual Bk.
--European Petroleum Related Industries. 109p. 1980. 75.00x (ISBN 82-7270-016-6, Pub. by Norwegian Info Norway). State Mutual Bk.
--Large Scale Flow Measurement of Hydrocarbon Fluids. 173p. 1980. 75.00x (ISBN 82-7270-003-4, Pub. by Norwegian Info Norway). State Mutual Bk.
--Marginal Fields-Criteria for Development. 197p. 1980. 60.00x (ISBN 82-7270-006-9, Pub. by Norwegian Info Norway). State Mutual Bk.
--Measuring Accuracy of Parameters Used in Formation Evaluation in the North Sea. 193p. 1980. 75.00x (ISBN 82-7270-002-6, Pub. by Norwegian Info Norway). State Mutual Bk.
--North Sea Field Development: Experiences & Challenges. 314p. 1980. 95.00x (ISBN 82-7270-012-3, Pub. by Norwegian Info Norway). State Mutual Bk.
--Offshore North Sea 1978, 2 vols. 1980. 165.00x (Pub. by Norwegian Info Norway). State Mutual Bk.
--Quality Assurance Related to Offshore Activities. 336p. 1980. 95.00x (ISBN 82-7270-009-3, Pub. by Norwegian Info Norway). State Mutual Bk.
S. E. Haugan Consulting. Fish Versus Oil. 1980. 50.00x (Pub. by Norwegian Info Norway). State Mutual Bk.

PETROLEUM INDUSTRY AND TRADE-NORWAY
Norwegian Petroleum-Yearbook for the Norwegian Petroleum Society 1979. 211p. 1980. 60.00x (ISBN 82-7270-004-2, Pub. by Norwegian Info Norway). State Mutual Bk.
Norwegian Petroleum Yearbook for the Norwegian Petroleum Society 1980. 218p. 1980. 60.00x (ISBN 82-7270-013-1, Pub. by Norwegian Info Norway). State Mutual Bk.
Scandinavian Institute of Maritime Law. Norwegian Petroleum Law. 500p. 1980. 135.00x (Pub. by Norwegian Info Norway). State Mutual Bk.

PETROLEUM INDUSTRY AND TRADE-UNITED STATES
Anderson, Irvine H. Aramco, the United States, & Saudi Arabia: A Study of the Dynamics of Foreign Oil Policy, 1933-1950. LC 80-8535. 288p. 1981. 15.00x (ISBN 0-691-04679-4). Princeton U Pr.
Halbouty, Michel & Clark, James. Spindletop. 336p. 1980. 16.95 (ISBN 0-87201-791-5). Gulf Pub.
Rintoul, William. Oildorado: Boom Times on the West Side. LC 78-50141. (Illus.). 240p. 1980. pap. 7.95 (ISBN 0-934136-07-6, Valley Calif). Western Tanager.
Williamson, Harold F., et al. The American Petroleum Industry: The Age of Illumination, 1859-1899; the Age of Energy, 1899-1959, 2 vols. LC 80-22253. (Northwestern University Studies in Business History). (Illus.). 1981. Repr. of 1959 ed. Set. lib. bdg. 125.00x (ISBN 0-313-22788-8, WIAC). Greenwood.

PETROLEUM LAW AND LEGISLATION
Arrow, Kenneth J. & Kalt, Joseph P. Petroleum Price Regulation: Should We Decontrol? 1979. pap. 4.25. Am Enterprise.
Organization of American States. Mining & Petroleum Legislation, Release 1. 1980. 35.00 (ISBN 0-379-20381-2). Oceana.
Scandinavian Institute of Maritime Law. Norwegian Petroleum Law. 500p. 1980. 135.00x (Pub. by Norwegian Info Norway). State Mutual Bk.

PETROLEUM PIPE LINES
see Petroleum-Pipe Lines

PETROLEUM POLLUTION OF WATER
see Oil Pollution of Water

PETROLEUM PRODUCTS
see also Lubrication and Lubricants; Petroleum As Fuel; Petroleum
also names of specific products, e.g. Gasoline
Falbe, Jurgen. Chemical Feedstocks from Coal. 730p. 1981. 50.00 (ISBN 0-471-05291-4, Pub. by Wiley-Interscience). Wiley.

PETROLEUM WASTE
see also Oil Pollution of Water
Facilities in Ports for the Reception of Oily Wastes. 202p. 1980. pap. 24.75 (ISBN 92-801-1097-7, IMCO60, IMCO). Unipub.
Guidelines on the Provision of Adequate Reception Facilities in Ports, Part II: Residues & Mixtures Containing Noxious Liquid Substances. 14p. 1980. pap. 6.00 (ISBN 9-2801-1098-5, IMCCO 61, IMCO). Unipub.

PETROLEUM WORKERS
Avery, Ernest. Jungle Oil: Hazardous Times. 1981. 8.95 (ISBN 0-533-04889-3). Vantage.

PETROLOGY
see also Crystallography; Geochemistry; Geology; Mineralogy; Rocks
also varieties of rock, e.g. Quartz
McBride, E. F. Sedimentary Petrology & History of the Haymond Formation (Pennsylvanian), Marathon Basin, Texas. 101p. 1966. 2.50 (RI 57). Bur Econ Geology.

Sood, Mohan K. Modern Igneous Petrology. 250p. 1981. 22.50 (ISBN 0-471-08915-X, Pub. by Wiley-Interscience). Wiley.

PETROLOGY–JUVENILE LITERATURE

see Rocks–Juvenile Literature

PETRONIUS ARBITER

Mitchell, J. M. Petronius Leader of Fashion. 364p. 1981. Repr. of 1922 ed. lib. bdg. 35.00 (ISBN 0-89987-565-3). Darby Bks.

PETS

see also Cage-Birds; Domestic Animals

also particular species of animals, e.g. Cats, Dogs, etc.

Ogelsby, Mac, et al. Pet Games & Recreation. 1981. text ed. 14.95 (ISBN 0-8359-5530-3); pap. 9.95 (ISBN 0-8359-5529-X). Reston.

PETS–JUVENILE LITERATURE

Pet Friends. (Photo Board Bks.). (Illus.). 12p. (ps). 1980. 1.50 (ISBN 0-307-06070-5, Golden Pr). Western Pub.

PEWTER

Scott, Jack L. Pewter Wares from Sheffield. LC 80-68670. (Illus.). 260p. 1980. 28.00 (ISBN 0-937864-00-5). Antiquary Pr.

PHANSIGARS

see Thugs

PHANTOMS

see Apparitions; Ghosts

PHARMACEUTICAL CHEMISTRY

see Chemistry, Medical and Pharmaceutical

PHARMACEUTICAL INDUSTRY

see Drug Trade

PHARMACEUTICAL RESEARCH

Bezold, C. The Future of Pharmaceuticals. 144p. 1980. 12.00 (ISBN 0-471-08343-7, Pub. by Wiley Med). Wiley.

Kecskemeti, Valeria & Knoll, J., eds. Prostanoids: Proceedings of the Third Congress of the Hungarian Pharmacological Society, Budapest, 1979. LC 80-41281. (Advances in Pharmacological Research & Practice Ser.: Vol. VI). 175p. 1981. 34.00 (ISBN 0-08-026391-7). Pergamon.

Vizi, E. S. & Wollemann, Marie, eds. Aminergic & Peptidergic Receptors: Satellite Symposium of the Third Congress of the Hungarian Pharmacological Society, Szeged, 1979. LC 80-41281. (Advances in Pharmacological Research & Practice Ser.: Vol. VII). 220p. 1981. 41.00 (ISBN 0-08-026839-0). Pergamon.

PHARMACEUTICALS, DELAYED-ACTION

see Delayed-Action Preparations

PHARMACISTS–LEGAL STATUS, LAWS, ETC.

see Pharmacy–Laws and Legislation

PHARMACODYNAMICS

see Pharmacology

PHARMACOLOGY

see also Chemistry, Medical and Pharmaceutical; Chemotherapy; Drug Metabolism; Drug Resistance in Micro-Organisms; Drugs; Neuropharmacology; Pharmacy; Psychopharmacology

Adrian, R. H. Reviews of Physiology, Biochemistry, & Pharmacology, Vol. 88. (Illus.). 280p. 1981. 52.00 (ISBN 0-387-10408-9). Springer-Verlag.

Adrian, R. H., ed. Reviews of Physiology, Biochemistry & Pharmacology, Vol. 89. (Illus.). 260p. 1981. 54.30 (ISBN 0-387-10495-X). Springer-Verlag.

Asperheim, Mary K. Pharmacology: An Introduction Text. 5th ed. (Illus.). 272p. 1981. text ed. 10.50 (ISBN 0-7216-1446-9). Saunders.

Asperheim, Mary K. & Eisenhauer, Laurel A. The Pharmacologic Basis of Patient Care. 4th ed. (Illus.). 624p. 1981. text ed. write for info. (ISBN 0-7216-1438-8). Saunders.

Blum, Richard, et al. Pharmaceuticals & Health Policy: International Perspectives on Provision & Control of Medicine. 1981. write for info. (ISBN 0-312-60402-5). St Martin.

Brown, R. Don & Daigneault, Ernest A. Pharmacology of Hearing: Experimental & Clinical Bases. 360p. 1980. 45.00 (ISBN 0-471-05074-1, Pub. by Wiley-Interscience). Wiley.

Comer, Joyce B. Pharmacology in Critical Care. Percy, R. Craig, ed. (The Fleschner Series in Critical Care Nursings). (Illus.). 175p. (Orig.). 1981. pap. text ed. 9.95 (ISBN 0-937878-03-0). Fleschner.

Crossland, James. Lewis's Pharmacology. 5th ed. 960p. 1981. lib. bdg. price not set; pap. text ed. 49.50 (ISBN 0-443-01173-7). Churchill.

DiPalma, Joseph R. Basic Pharmacology in Medicine. 2nd ed. (Illus.). 640p. 1981. text ed. 25.00 (ISBN 0-07-017011-8, HP). McGraw.

Eadie, Mervyn J. & Tyrer, John H. Neurological Clinical Pharmacology. 470p. 1980. text ed. 47.50 (ISBN 0-909337-07-1). ADIS Pr.

Folb, P. I. Safety of Medicines: Evaluation & Prediction. (Illus.). 120p. 1980. pap. 12.90 (ISBN 0-387-10143-8). Springer-Verlag.

Foster, R. W. Twelve Hundred Multiple Choice Questions in Pharmacology. LC 79-42816. (Illus.). 188p. 1980. pap. write for info. Butterworths.

Foster, R. W. & Cox, Barry. Basic Pharmacology. LC 80-49873. (Illus.). 296p. 1980. text ed. 18.95 (ISBN 0-407-00170-0). Butterworths.

Frishman, William H. Clinical Pharmacology of the Beta-Adrenocepter Blocking Drugs. 288p. 1980. 16.95x (ISBN 0-8385-1143-0). ACC.

Gerald, Michael C. Pharmacology: An Introduction to Drugs. (Illus.). 720p. 1981. 19.95 (ISBN 0-13-662098-1). P-H.

Gerald, Michael C. & O'Bannon, Freda V. Nursing Pharmacology. (Illus.). 544p. 1981. text ed. 22.95 (ISBN 0-13-627505-2). P-H.

Jarvik, L. F., et al, eds. Clinical Pharmacology & the Aged Patient. (Aging Ser.: Vol. 16). 256p. 1981. text ed. 25.00 (ISBN 0-89004-340-X). Raven.

Lewis, Peter J. & O'Grady, John M., eds. Clinical Pharmacology of Prostacyclin. 1981. price not set (ISBN 0-89004-591-7). Raven.

Magyar, K., ed. Monoamine Oxidases & Their Selective Inhibition: Proceedings of the Third Congress of the Hungarian Pharmacological Society, Budapest, 1979. LC 80-41281. (Advances in Pharmacological Research Practice Ser.: Vol. IV). 165p. 1981. 30.00 (ISBN 0-08-026389-5). Pergamon.

Marion, Mildred F., et al. Pharmacology Learning Guide. (Illus.). 100p. 1981. pap. text ed. 7.95 (ISBN 0-8016-3109-2). Mosby.

Mathe, G. & Muggia, F. M., eds. Cancer Chemo- & Immunopharmacology, Part I: Chemopharmacology. (Recent Results in Cancer Research Ser.: Vol. 74). (Illus.). 315p. 1981. 66.00 (ISBN 0-387-10162-4). Springer-Verlag.

--Cancer Chemo- & Immunopharmacology, Part II: Immunopharmacology, Relations, & General Problems. (Recent Results in Cancer Research Ser.: Vol. 75). (Illus.). 260p. 1981. 52.00 (ISBN 0-387-10163-2). Springer-Verlag.

Meyers, Frederick H., et al. Review of Medical Pharmacology. 7th, rev. ed. LC 80-82744. (Illus.). 747p. 1980. lexotone cover 17.50 (ISBN 0-87041-153-5). Lange.

Quantitative Aspects of Chemical Pharmacology. 256p. 1980. 80.00x (ISBN 0-85664-892-2, Pub. by Croom Helm England). State Mutual Bk.

Remington's Pharmaceutical Sciences. 16th ed. 1980. 55.00 (ISBN 0-912734-02-7). Mack Pub.

Requa-Clark, Barbara & Holroyd, Sam V. Applied Pharmacology for the Dental Hygienists. 427p. 1981. pap. 11.95 (ISBN 0-8016-2239-5). Mosby.

Schild, H. O. Applied Pharmacology. 12th ed. (Illus.). 500p. 1981. pap. text ed. 32.00 (ISBN 0-443-02199-6). Churchill.

Thomas, John A. Textbook of Endocrine Pharmacology. Date not set. price not set (ISBN 0-8067-1901-X). Urban & S.

Thompson, Emmanuel B. Drug Screening: Fundamentals of Drug Evaluation Techniques in Pharmacology. LC 80-83409. (Illus.). 325p. (Orig.). 1981. text ed. 23.00x (ISBN 0-932126-06-5); pap. text ed. 18.00x (ISBN 0-932126-07-3). Graceway.

Tognoni, Gianni, et al, eds. Frontiers in Therapeutic Drug Monitoring. (Monographs of the Mario Negri Institute for Pharmacological Research). 200p. 1980. text ed. 21.50 (ISBN 0-89004-508-9). Raven.

Trounce, J. R. Clinical Pharmacology for Nurses. 9th ed. (Illus.). 432p. 1981. pap. text ed. 10.00 (ISBN 0-443-02333-6). Churchill.

Trounce, J. R., ed. Clinical Pharmacology for Nurses. 9th ed. (Illus.). Date not set. text ed. price not set (ISBN 0-443-02333-6). Churchill.

Turner, Paul & Shand, David G., eds. Recent Advances in Clinical Pharmacology, No. 2. (Recent Advances Ser.). (Illus.). 178p. 1981. lib. bdg. 40.00 (ISBN 0-443-02183-X). Churchill.

PHARMACOLOGY–DICTIONARIES

Mason, David & Dyller, Fran. Pharmaceutical Dictionary & Reference for Prescription Drugs. LC 80-82854. (Illus.). 256p. 1981. pap. 3.50 (ISBN 0-87216-783-6). Playboy Pbks.

PHARMACOLOGY–RESEARCH

see Pharmaceutical Research

PHARMACY

see also Botany, Medical; Chemistry, Medical and Pharmaceutical; Drugs; Hospitals; Materia Medica; Medicine–Formulae, Receipts, Prescriptions; Pharmacology

Business Systems Research Group. The Pharmacy Computer Handbook. 141p. 1980. 29.95 (ISBN 0-9603584-1-2). Busn Systems Res.

Remington's Pharmaceutical Sciences. 16th ed. 1980. 55.00 (ISBN 0-912734-02-7). Mack Pub.

Smith, Harry A. Principles & Methods of Pharmacy Management. 2nd ed. LC 80-17560. (Illus.). 413p. 1980. text ed. 19.50 (ISBN 0-8121-0765-9). Lea & Febiger.

PHARMACY–LAWS AND LEGISLATION

Helms, Robert, ed. International Supply of Medicines: Implications of U. S. Regulatory Reform. 1980. 14.25 (ISBN 0-8447-2190-5); pap. 6.25 (ISBN 0-8447-2191-3). Am Enterprise.

Smith, Mickey C. & Knapp, David A. Pharmacy, Drugs & Medical Care. 3rd ed. 345p. 1981. write for info. softcover (7761-9). Williams & Wilkins.

PHARMACY–RESEARCH

see Pharmaceutical Research

PHASE-LOCKED LOOPS

Geiger, Dana F. Phaselock Loops for DC Motor Control. 140p. 1981. 22.00 (Pub. by Wiley-Interscience). Wiley.

PHENOMENOLOGY

see also Existentialism

Berger, Gaston. Recherches Sur les Conditions De la Connaissance Essai D'une Theoretique Pure. Natanson, Maurice, ed. LC 78-66755. (Phenomenology Ser.: Vol. 1). 194p. 1979. lib. bdg. 20.00 (ISBN 0-8240-9569-3). Garland Pub.

Celms, Theodor. Der Phanomenologische Idealismus Husserls. Natanson, ed. LC 78-66733. (Phenomenology: Vol. 3). 192p. 1979. lib. bdg. 20.00 (ISBN 0-8240-9567-7). Garland Pub.

Chisholm, Roderick M., ed. Realism & the Background of Phenomenology. vii, 308p. 1981. lib. bdg. 22.00 (ISBN 0-917930-34-7); pap. text ed. 8.50x (ISBN 0-917930-14-2). Ridgeview.

Curtis, Bernard & Mays, Wolfe, eds. Phenomenology & Education: Self-Consciousness & Its Development. 150p. 1978. pap. 9.95 (ISBN 0-416-70960-5, 6368). Methuen Inc.

Dudeck, C. V. Hegel's Phenomenology of Mind: Analysis & Commentary. LC 80-67258. 292p. 1981. lib. bdg. 19.75 (ISBN 0-8191-1406-5); pap. text ed. 10.25 (ISBN 0-8191-1407-3). U Pr of Amer.

Kruger, Dreyer. An Introduction to Phenomenological Psychology. LC 80-29203. 212p. 1981. pap. text ed. 8.95 (ISBN 0-8207-0150-5). Duquesne.

Stavenhagen, Kurt. Absolute Stellungnahmen: Eine Ontologische Untersuchung Uber das Wesen der Religion. Natanson, Maurice, ed. LC 78-66740. (Phenomenology Ser.: Vol. 13). 234p. 1979. lib. bdg. 23.00 (ISBN 0-8240-9557-X). Garland Pub.

PHEROMONES

Mori, K., et al. Synthetic Chemistry of Insect Phermones & Juvenile Hormones. (Recent Developments in the Chemistry of Natural Carbon Compounds: Vol. 9). (Illus.). 420p. 1979. 40.00x (ISBN 963-05-1632-2). Intl Pubns Serv.

PHILADELPHIA–DESCRIPTION

Arthur Frommer's Guide to Philadelphia, 1981-82. 224p. Date not set. pap. 2.95 (ISBN 0-671-41440-2). Frommer-Pasmantier.

PHILADELPHIA–HISTORY

Chandler, Charles L., et al. Philadelphia: Port of History 1609-1837. (Illus.). 82p. 1976. pap. 3.25 (ISBN 0-913346-02-0). Phila Maritime Mus.

Hershberg, Theodore, ed. Philadelphia: Work, Space, Family & Group Experience in the Nineteenth Century. Essays Toward an Interdisciplinary History of the City. (Illus.). 608p. 1981. 29.95 (ISBN 0-19-502752-3). Oxford U Pr.

--Philadelphia: Work, Space, Family & Group Experience in the Nineteenth Century. Essays Toward an Interdisciplinary History of the City. (Illus.). 608p. 1981. pap. 8.95 (ISBN 0-19-502753-1, 619, GB). Oxford U Pr.

Lukacs, John. Philadelphia: Patricians & Philistines 1900-1950. (Illus.). 1981. 15.00 (ISBN 0-374-23161-3). FS&G.

PHILADELPHIA–SOCIAL LIFE AND CUSTOMS

Hershberg, Theodore, ed. Philadelphia: Work, Space, Family & Group Experience in the Nineteenth Century. Essays Toward an Interdisciplinary History of the City. (Illus.). 608p. 1981. 29.95 (ISBN 0-19-502752-3). Oxford U Pr.

--Philadelphia: Work, Space, Family & Group Experience in the Nineteenth Century. Essays Toward an Interdisciplinary History of the City. (Illus.). 608p. 1981. pap. 8.95 (ISBN 0-19-502753-1, 619, GB). Oxford U Pr.

PHILANTHROPISTS

Prochaska, F. K. Women & Philanthropy in Nineteenth-Century England. (Illus.). 312p. 1980. 36.00 (ISBN 0-19-822627-6); pap. 21.00 (ISBN 0-19-822628-4). Oxford U Pr.

PHILANTHROPY

see Social Service

PHILATELY AND PHILATELISTS

see Postage-Stamps–Collectors and Collecting

PHILIP, DUKE OF EDINBURGH, 1921-

Judd, Denis. Prince Philip, Duke of Edinburgh. LC 80-22691. 1981. 16.95 (ISBN 0-689-11131-2). Atheneum.

PHILIP 2ND, KING OF MACEDON, 382-336 B.C.

Andronicos, Manolis, et al. Philip of Macedon. Hatzopoulos, Miltiades B. & Loukopoulos, Louisa D., eds. (Illus.). 254p. 1980. 45.00 (ISBN 0-89241-330-1). Caratzas Bros.

PHILIPPINE ISLANDS–ECONOMIC CONDITIONS

Infante, Jaime T. The Political, Economic, & Labor Climate in the Philippines. LC 80-53988. (Multinational Industrial Relations Ser.: No. 8a). (Illus.). 147p. 1980. pap. 15.00 (ISBN 0-89546-024-6). Indus Res Unit-Wharton.

Spatial Analysis for Regional Development. 44p. 1981. pap. 6.75 (ISBN 92-808-0166-X, TUNU 101, UNU). Unipub.

PHILIPPINE ISLANDS–HISTORY

Constantino, Renato. The History of the Philippines: From the Spanish Colonization to the Second World War. 459p. 1981. pap. 8.95 (ISBN 0-85345-579-1). Monthly Rev.

Ileto, Reynaldo C. Pasyon & Revolution: Popular Movements in the Philippines, 1840-1910. (Illus.). 345p. 1980. 18.75x (ISBN 0-686-28640-5); pap. 13.75x (ISBN 0-686-28641-3). Cellar.

PHILIPPINE ISLANDS–POLITICS AND GOVERNMENT

Infante, Jaime T. The Political, Economic, & Labor Climate in the Philippines. LC 80-53988. (Multinational Industrial Relations Ser.: No. 8a). (Illus.). 147p. 1980. pap. 15.00 (ISBN 0-89546-024-6). Indus Res Unit-Wharton.

PHILIPPINE LANGUAGES

Gonzalez, Andrew B. Language & Nationalism: The Philippine Experience Thus Far. 179p. 1980. 18.25 (ISBN 0-686-28647-2); pap. 11.25x (ISBN 0-686-28648-0). Cellar.

PHILIPPINE LITERATURE

Galdon, Joseph A., ed. Essays on the Philippine Novel in English. 168p. 1980. 17.50x (ISBN 0-686-28638-3); pap. 8.50x (ISBN 0-686-28639-1). Cellar.

PHILLIPS, WENDELL, 1811-1884

Bartlett, Irving H. Windell & Ann Phillips: The Community of Reform 1840-1880. (Illus.). 1981. 17.95 (ISBN 0-393-01426-6). Norton.

PHILO JUDAEUS

Billings, Thomas H. The Platonism of Philo Judaeus. Taran, Leonardo, ed. LC 78-66560. (Ancient Philosophy Ser.: Vol. 3). 117p. 1979. lib. bdg. 13.00 (ISBN 0-8240-9608-8). Garland Pub.

PHILOSOPHERS–BIBLIOGRAPHY

Cohn, Margot & Buber, Rafael, eds. Martin Buber: A Bibliography of His Writings, 1897-1978. 164p. 1980. 35.00 (ISBN 3-598-10146-5, Dist by Gale Research Co.). K G Saur.

PHILOSOPHERS–GREAT BRITAIN

Straaten, Zak Van, ed. Philosophical Subjects: Essays Presented to P. F. Strawson. 304p. 1980. 37.50 (ISBN 0-19-824603-X). Oxford U Pr.

PHILOSOPHERS' STONE

see Alchemy

PHILOSOPHICAL ANALYSIS

see Analysis (Philosophy)

PHILOSOPHICAL ANTHROPOLOGY

see also Humanism; Man (Theology); Mind and Body

Kruger, Maximilian. The Maximal Problems of Philosophy. (Illus.). 137p. 1981. 39.45 (ISBN 0-89266-274-3). Am Classical Coll Pr.

PHILOSOPHICAL THEOLOGY

Foster, Michael B. Mystery & Philosophy. LC 79-8721. (The Library of Philosophy & Theology). 96p. 1980. Repr. of 1957 ed. lib. bdg. 18.75x (ISBN 0-313-20792-5, FOMP). Greenwood.

PHILOSOPHY

see also Act (Philosophy); Analysis (Philosophy); Atomism; Belief and Doubt; Causation; Christianity–Philosophy; Consciousness; Cosmology; Creation; Criticism (Philosophy); Esthetics; Ethics; Fate and Fatalism; Free Will and Determinism; God; Good and Evil; Humanism; Idealism; Ideology; Knowledge, Theory of; Logic; Materialism; Meaning (Philosophy); Metaphysics; Mind and Body; Mysticism; Perception; Platonists; Pluralism; Positivism; Pragmatism; Psychology; Realism; Reality; Soul; Space and Time; Structuralism; Theism; Thought and Thinking; Transcendentalism; Truth; Utilitarianism; Will

Andronis, Constantine. Apostolos Makrakis--An Evaluation of Half A Century. 369p. (Orig.). 1966. pap. 4.00x (ISBN 0-938366-33-5). Orthodox Chr.

Apelt, Otto. Platonis Sophista: Recentsuit, Prolegomenis et Commentariis Instruxit. Taran, Leonardo, ed. LC 78-66612. (Ancent Philosophy Ser.: Vol. 1). 225p. lib. bdg. 20.00 (ISBN 0-8240-9611-8). Garland Pub.

Autobiography of No One. (Illus.). 128p. 1981. 7.95 (ISBN 0-89962-048-5). Todd & Honeywell.

Berkeley, George. Philosophical Works: Including the Works on Vision. 1981. 18.50; pap. 8.75. Rowman.

Billings, Thomas H. The Platonism of Philo Judaeus. Taran, Leonardo, ed. LC 78-66560. (Ancient Philosophy Ser.: Vol. 3). 117p. 1979. lib. bdg. 13.00 (ISBN 0-8240-9608-8). Garland Pub.

Boethius. On the Consolation of Philopsophy. 1981. pap. 3.95 (ISBN 0-89526-885-X). Regnery-Gateway.

Boyer, David L., et al, eds. The Philosopher's Annual 1980, Vol. III. xii, 225p. (Orig.). 1980. lib. bdg. 22.00 (ISBN 0-917930-38-X); pap. text ed. 8.50x (ISBN 0-917930-18-5). Ridgeview.

Brough, John B., ed. Philosophical Knowledge. LC 80-69505. (Proceedings: Vol. 54). 250p. (Orig.). 1981. pap. 8.00 (ISBN 0-918090-14-8). Am Cath Philo.

Cale, David L. The Basics of Consequentialism. LC 80-82228. (Illus.). 160p. 1980. 12.95 (ISBN 0-87012-393-9); pap. 7.95 (ISBN 0-87012-389-0). Laurel Inst.

Campbell, Joseph, ed. Man & Transformation: Papers from the Eranosyears, Vol. 5. Manheim, Ralph, tr. from Fr. LC 72-1982. (Bollingen Ser.: Xxx). (Illus.). 452p. 1980. 20.00x (ISBN 0-691-09733-X); pap. 5.95 (ISBN 0-691-01834-0). Princeton U Pr.

Casares, Angel J. Carso de Filosofia. rev., 2nd ed. 238p. 1980. text ed. write for info. (ISBN 0-8477-2821-8); pap. text ed. write for info. (ISBN 0-8477-2822-6). U of PR Pr.

Cassidy, Laurence L. Existence & Presence: The Dialectics of Divinity. LC 80-5881. 246p. 1981. lib. bdg. 16.50 (ISBN 0-8191-1486-3); pap. text ed. 7.50 (ISBN 0-8191-1487-1). U Pr of Amer.

Chisholm, Roderick. The First Person: An Essay on Reference & Intentionality. LC 80-24910. 192p. 1981. 22.50x (ISBN 0-8166-1045-2). U of Minn Pr.

Clark, Bea. Centrist. 1981. 6.50 (ISBN 0-8062-1577-1). Carlton.

Clarke, Patricia, ed. Paul of Venicē: Logica Magna, Pt. 1, Fascicule 7. (Classical & Medieval Logic Texts Ser.). 232p. 1981. 149.00 (ISBN 0-19-726003-9). Oxford U Pr.

Cobb, John B., Jr. & Schroeder, W. Widick, eds. Process Philosophy & Social Thought. LC 80-70781. (Studies in Religion & Society). 250p. 1981. 19.95x (ISBN 0-913348-18-X). Ctr Sci Study.

Comte, August. The Positive Analysis of Social Phenomena. (The Essential Library of the Great Philosophers). (Illus.). 129p. (Fr.). 1981. 37.85 (ISBN 0-89901-027-X). Found Class Reprints.

Craven, Margaret. Again Calls the Owl. 1981. pap. 2.25 (ISBN 0-440-10074-7). Dell.

Derrida, Jacques. Spurs: Nietzsche's Styles. Harlow, Barbara, tr. from Fr. LC 79-31. vi, 166p. 1981. pap. 4.50 (ISBN 0-226-14333-3). U of Chicago Pr.

Dretske, Fred I. Seeing & Knowing. pap. write for info. (ISBN 0-226-16245-1). U of Chicago Pr.

Edgar, William J. Evidence. LC 80-67262. 471p. 1980. lib. bdg. 22.75 (ISBN 0-8191-1292-5); pap. text ed. 13.75 (ISBN 0-8191-1293-3). U Pr of Amer.

Ellul, Jacques, et al. Jacques Ellul: Interpretive Essays. Christians, Clifford G. & Van Hook, Jay M., eds. LC 80-12342. 340p. 1981. 24.95 (ISBN 0-252-00812-X). U of Ill Pr.

Epaulic. Freedom Through Knowledge. 1981. 5.50 (ISBN 0-8062-1602-6). Carlton.

Feigl, Herbert & Sellars, Wilfrid, eds. Readings in Philosophical Analysis. x, 593p. 1981. lib. bdg. 25.00 (ISBN 0-917930-29-0); pap. text ed. 12.50x (ISBN 0-917930-09-6). Ridgeview.

Ferriz, David. I Realized God Via Mathematics. Norris, Patrick, tr. from Span. 300p. (Orig.). 1980. pap. 5.95 (ISBN 0-89260-191-4). Hwong Pub.

Frost, S. E., Jr. The Basic Teachings of the Philosophers. 314p. 1980. Repr. of 1942 ed. lib. bdg. 25.00 (ISBN 0-89987-256-5). Darby Bks.

George, F. H. The Science of Philosophy. 1981. price not set (ISBN 0-677-05550-1). Gordon.

Grant, Edward. Much Ado About Nothing. LC 80-13876. (Illus.). 545p. Date not set. 59.50 (ISBN 0-521-22983-9). Cambridge U Pr.

Greco, Marshall C. Group Life: The Nature & Treatment of Its Specific Conflicts. 357p. 1980. Repr. of 1950 ed. lib. bdg. 35.00 (ISBN 0-89984-229-1). Century Bookbindery.

Grunfeld, Frederic V. Prophets Without Honor: A Background to Freud, Kafka, Einstein & Their World. 1980. 5.95x (ISBN 0-07-025087-1). McGraw.

Hegel, Georg W. Lectures on the Philosophy of World History: Reason in History. Forbes, D. & Nisbet, H. B., eds. (Cambridge Studies in the History & Theory of Politics). 290p. (Ger.). 1981. pap. 12.95 (ISBN 0-521-28145-8). Cambridge U Pr.

Held, David. Introduction to Critical Theory: Horkheimer to Habermas. 497p. 1980. 32.50x (ISBN 0-520-04121-6); pap. 12.75x (ISBN 0-520-04175-5, CAMPUS 261). U of Cal Pr.

Jan. And Kyroot Said: Contemporary Work Commentaries from a Sanguinary Cosmic Sage. 315p. 1980. 9.00 (ISBN 0-936380-04-7). Chan Shal Imi.

--The Death of Gurdjieff in the Foothills of Georgia: Secret Papers of an American Work Group. 316p. 1980. 9.00 (ISBN 0-936380-03-9). Chan Shal Imi.

--Dialogues of Gurdjieff: An Allegorical Work Adventure, Vol. 1. rev., enl. ed. 314p. 1980. 9.00 (ISBN 0-936380-02-0). Chan Shal Imi.

--Magnus Machina: The Great Machine, (Work Maps of the Inner Terrain of Modern Man) rev., enl. ed. 216p. 1980. 6.00 (ISBN 0-936380-05-5). Chan Shal Imi.

Jones, Abel J. In Search of Truth. 207p. 1980. Repr. of 1946 ed. lib. bdg. 25.00 (ISBN 0-89984-259-3). Century Bookbindery.

Jung, C. G. The Archetypes & the Collective Unconscious: Bollingen Ser. Hull, R. F., tr. from Ger. LC 75-156. (Xx: 9,I). (Illus.). 560p. 1980. 30.00x (ISBN 0-691-09761-5); pap. 9.95 (ISBN 0-691-01833-2). Princeton U Pr.

Kandias, Kostis. Revelations One: Noah's Flood Was a Result of Nuclear War. (Illus.). 256p. 1981. 10.00 (ISBN 0-682-49672-3). Exposition.

Koenig, Alfred E., et al, eds. Philosophy of the Humanistic Society. LC 80-1425. 290p. (Orig.). 1981. lib. bdg. 22.50 (ISBN 0-8191-1414-6); pap. text ed. 11.75 (ISBN 0-8191-1415-4). U Pr of Amer.

Labriola, Antonio. Socialism & Philosophy. LC 79-90007. 223p. 1980. 12.00 (ISBN 0-914386-21-2); pap. 4.50 (ISBN 0-914386-22-0). Telos Pr.

Lachs, John & Scott, Charles E., eds. The Human Search: An Introduction to Philosophy. 528p. 1981. pap. text ed. 10.95x (ISBN 0-19-502675-6). Oxford U Pr.

Leibniz, G. W. New Essays on Human Understanding. Remnant, Peter & Bennett, Jonathan, eds. 610p. Date not set. price not set (ISBN 0-521-23147-7); pap. price not set (ISBN 0-521-29836-9). Cambridge U Pr.

Leichtman, Robert R. & Japikse, Carl. The Art of Living, Vol. 1. 242p. Date not set. pap. 5.00 (ISBN 0-89804-032-9). Ariel Pr.

Lipman, Matthew. El Descubrimiento De Harry Stottlemeier. Marti, Oscar R., tr. from Eng. (Philosophy for Children). 190p. (Orig., Eng. & Span.). (gr. 5-6). pap. 10.00 (ISBN 0-916834-16-6). Inst Adv Philo

--Pixie. (Philosophy for Children). 90p. (Orig.). (gr. 3-4). pap. 6.00 (ISBN 0-916834-17-4). Inst Adv Philo.

MacMurray, John. Interpreting the Universe. 164p. 1980. Repr. lib. bdg. 25.00 (ISBN 0-89987-576-9). Darby Bks.

Makrakis, Apostolos. A New Philosophy & the Philosophical Sciences, 2 vols. Orthodox Christian Educational Society, ed. Cummings, Denver, tr. from Hellenic. Incl. Vol. 1. Introduction to Philosophy, Psychology, Logic, & Theology. 888p; Vol. 2. Introduction to Ethics. 745p. 1940. Repr. of 1890 ed. Set. 20.00x (ISBN 0-938366-01-7). Orthodox Chr.

Ohsawa, George. Jack & Mitie. Rothman, Sandy, ed. Burns, Ken, tr. from Fr. Orig. Title: Jack et Madame Mitie En Occident. 224p. (Orig.). 1981. pap. 9.50 (ISBN 0-918860-36-9). G Ohsawa.

Origen. The Philocalia of Origen. Robinson, J. Armitage, rev. by. & intro. by. LC 80-2359. 1981. Repr. of 1893 ed. 39.50 (ISBN 0-404-18911-3). AMS Pr.

Poplasen, Ilija. The Struggle for the Good, 2 pts. (Illus.). 1981. Repr. of 1978 ed. Pt. I, 61 Pgs. 10.00 (ISBN 0-935352-03-1); Pt. II, 128 Pgs. 20.00 (ISBN 0-935352-04-X). MIR PA.

Rogers, Jack B. & Baird, Forrest. Introduction to Philosophy: A Case Study Approach. LC 80-8344. (Case Study Ser.). 240p. (Orig.). 1981. pap. text ed. 8.95x (ISBN 0-06-066997-7, RD 346, HarpR). Har-Row.

Rousseau, Jean-Jacques. Confessions, 2 vols. 1960. Vol. I. 5.00 ea. (ISBN 0-460-00859-5). Vol. II (ISBN 0-460-00860-9). Dutton.

Rudman, Jack. Philosophy. (Undergraduate Program Field Test Ser.: UPFT-17). (Cloth bdg. avail. on request). pap. 9.95 (ISBN 0-8373-6017-X). Natl Learning.

--Scholastic Philosophy. (Undergraduate Program Field Test Ser.: UPFT-22). (Cloth bdg. avail. on request). pap. 9.95 (ISBN 0-8373-6022-6). Natl Learning.

Tiefenbrun. Signs of the Hidden. 1980. pap. text ed. 28.50x (ISBN 9-0040-3778-0). Humanities.

Wasserstrom, Richard. Philosophy & Social Issues: Five Studies. LC 79-9486. 224p. 1980. pap. text ed. 6.95 (ISBN 0-268-01536-8). U of Notre Dame Pr.

PHILOSOPHY–ADDRESSES, ESSAYS, LECTURES

D'Amico, Robert. Marx & Philosophy of Culture. LC 80-24405. (University of Florida Humanities Monograph: No. 50). viii, 108p. (Orig.). 1981. pap. 7.00 (ISBN 0-8130-0689-9). U Presses Fla.

Gutting, Gary, ed. Paradigms & Revolutions: Appraisals & Applications of Thomas Kuhn's Philosophy of Science. LC 80-20745. 256p. 1980. text ed. 18.95 (ISBN 0-268-01542-2); pap. text ed. 7.95 (ISBN 0-268-01543-0). U of Notre Dame Pr.

Halverson, William H. Concise Readings in Philosophy. 447p. 1981. pap. text ed. 9.95 (ISBN 0-394-32551-6). Random.

Mates, Benson. Skeptical Essays. LC 80-19553. 1981. lib. bdg. 17.00x (ISBN 0-226-50986-9). U of Chicago Pr.

Mellor, D. H., ed. Prospects for Pragmatism. 270p. 1981. 29.50 (ISBN 0-521-22548-5). Cambridge U Pr.

Miller, John W. The Paradox of Cause & Other Essays. 192p. 1981. pap. 5.95 (ISBN 0-393-00032-X). Norton.

Reck, Andrew J., ed. Selected Writings: George Herbert Mead. LC 80-27248. lxxii, 416p. 1981. 24.00x (ISBN 0-226-51672-5); pap. 10.95 (ISBN 0-226-51671-7). U of Chicago Pr.

PHILOSOPHY–COLLECTIONS

Minton, Arthur J. & Shipka, Thomas A. Philosophy: Paradox & Discovery. 2nd ed. 496p. 1982. pap. text ed. 11.95 (ISBN 0-07-042413-6, C). McGraw.

Straaten, Zak Van, ed. Philosophical Subjects: Essays Presented to P. F. Strawson. 304p. 1980. 37.50 (ISBN 0-19-824603-X). Oxford U Pr.

PHILOSOPHY–EXAMINATIONS, QUESTIONS, ETC.

Tiles, J. E. Things That Happen. Brennan, Andrew & Lyons, William E., eds. (Scots Philosophical Monograph: Vol. 1). (Illus.). 157p. 1980. 13.50 (ISBN 0-08-025724-0). Pergamon.

PHILOSOPHY–HISTORY

C. S. Peirce Bicentennial International Congress. Proceedings. Ketner, Kenneth, et al, eds. (Graduate Studies, Texas Tech Univ.: No. 23). 420p. (Orig.). 1981. price not set (ISBN 0-89672-075-6); pap. price not set (ISBN 0-89672-074-8). Tex Tech Pr.

Heller, Agnes. Renaissance Man. LC 80-6192. 490p. 1981. pap. 9.95 (ISBN 0-8052-0674-4). Schocken.

Pinera-Llera, Humberto. Introduccion E Historica De la Filosofia. 3rd ed. LC 89-65885. (Coleccion Textos). (Illus.). 348p. (Span.). 1980. pap. 12.95 (ISBN 0-89729-254-5). Ediciones.

Plott, John C. Global History of Philosophy: The Patristic-Sutra Period, Vol. 3. 1980. 27.00 (ISBN 0-8426-1680-2). Verry.

Riede, David C. & Baker, J. Wayne. The Western Intellectual Tradition: Greece Through the Middle Ages, Vol. 1. 208p. 1980. pap. text ed. 8.50 (ISBN 0-8403-2259-3). Kendall-Hunt.

Wydeville, A. & Rivers, Earl, trs. from Fr. Here Endeth the Book Named the Dictes or Sayengis of the Philosophres. LC 79-84100. (English Experience Ser.: No. 920). 160p. (Eng.). 1979. Repr. of 1477 ed. lib. bdg. 25.00 (ISBN 90-221-0920-8). Walter J Johnson.

PHILOSOPHY–INTRODUCTIONS

Minton, Arthur J. & Shipka, Thomas A. Philosophy: Paradox & Discovery. 2nd ed. 496p. 1982. pap. text ed. 11.95 (ISBN 0-07-042413-6, C). McGraw.

Wolff, Robert P. About Philosophy. 2nd ed. (Illus.). 448p. 1981. text ed. 15.95 (ISBN 0-13-000695-5). P-H.

PHILOSOPHY–METHODOLOGY

see Methodology

PHILOSOPHY, AMERICAN

Kegley, Jacquelyn A., et al. Person & Community in American Philosophy. Kolenda, Konstantin, ed. (Rice University Studies: Vol. 66, No. 4). (Orig.). 1981. pap. 5.50 (ISBN 0-89263-247-X). Rice Univ.

Madden, Edward H. Civil Disobedience & Moral Law in Nineteenth-Century American Philosophy. LC 68-11043. 222p. 1970. pap. 2.95 (ISBN 0-295-95070-6). U of Wash Pr.

Werkmeister, William H. A History of Philosophical Ideas in America. LC 80-24507. xvi, 599p. 1981. Repr. of 1949 ed. lib. bdg. 49.75x (ISBN 0-313-22743-8, WEHI). Greenwood.

PHILOSOPHY, ANALYTICAL

see Analysis (Philosophy)

PHILOSOPHY, ANCIENT

see also Atomism; Platonists; Sophists (Greek Philosophy)

Apostle, H. G. Aristotle's Posterior Analytics. LC 81-80233. (Apostle Translations of Aristotle's Works Ser.: Vol. 4). 350p. (Orig.). 1981. text ed. 19.20x (ISBN 0-9602870-6-X); pap. text ed. 9.60x (ISBN 0-9602870-7-8). Peripatetic.

Banner, William A. Moral Norms & Moral Order. LC 80-24206. x, 111p. 1981. 10.00 (ISBN 0-8130-0661-9). U Presses Fla.

Billings, Grace H. The Art of Transition in Plato. Taran, Leonardo, ed. LC 78-66578. (Ancient Philosophy Ser.: Vol. 2). 110p. 1979. lib. bdg. 13.00 (ISBN 0-8240-9609-6). Garland Pub.

Claus, David B. Toward the Soul: A Inquiry into the Meaning of XUXN Before Plate. LC 80-13559. (Classical Monographs). 232p. 1981. text ed. 17.50x (ISBN 0-300-02096-1). Yale U Pr.

Dombrowski, Daniel A. Plato's Philosophy of History. LC 80-5853. 225p. 1981. lib. bdg. 17.75 (ISBN 0-8191-1356-5); pap. text ed. 9.50 (ISBN 0-8191-1357-3). U Pr of Amer.

Hershbell, Jackson P. Pseudo-Plato, Axiochus. Hershbell, Jackson P., tr. LC 79-20127. (Society of Biblical Literature, Text & Translations: 21). Date not set. price not set (ISBN 0-89130-353-7, 060221); pap. price not set (ISBN 0-89130-354-5). Scholars Pr CA.

North, Helen F., ed. Interpretations of Plato: A Swarthmore Symposium. (Supplement Mnemosyne: No. 50). viii, 112p. 1980. text ed. 21.75x (ISBN 0-391-01138-3). Humanities.

Plato. Gorgias. Irwin, Terence, tr. from Greek. (Clarendon Plato Ser.). 278p. 1979. text ed. 29.00x (ISBN 0-19-872087-4); pap. text ed. 14.95x (ISBN 0-19-872091-2). Oxford U Pr.

PHILOSOPHY, ARAB

O'Leary, De Lacy. Arabic Thought and Its Place in History. rev. ed. LC 80-1917. 1981. Repr. of 1939 ed. 35.00 (ISBN 0-404-18982-2). AMS Pr.

PHILOSOPHY, ASIAN

Kim, Yong C. Oriental Thought: An Introduction to the Philosophical & Religious Thought of Asia. (Littlefield, Adams Quality Paperback Ser.: No. 365). 130p. 1981. pap. 3.95 (ISBN 0-8226-0365-9). Littlefield.

PHILOSOPHY, EAST INDIAN

see Philosophy, Indic

PHILOSOPHY, FRENCH

Descombes, Vincent. Modern French Philosophy. Scott-Fox, L. & Harding, J. M., trs. 240p. Date not set. 32.50 (ISBN 0-521-22837-9); pap. 11.50 (ISBN 0-521-29672-2). Cambridge U Pr.

PHILOSOPHY, GERMAN

Gardiner, Paul B. The Abysmal Failure of the German Philosophers. (Illus.). 157p. 1981. 39.75 (ISBN 0-89266-285-9). Am Classical Coll Pr.

Kierkegaard, Soren. The Corsair Affair & Articles Related to the Writings. Hong, Howard V. & Hong, Edna H., trs. from Danish. LC 80-7538. (Kierkegaards Writings: No. XIII). (Illus.). 380p. 1981. 25.00x (ISBN 0-691-07246-9). Princeton U Pr.

Toews, John E. Hegelianism: The Path Toward Dialectic Humanism, 1805 to 1841. LC 80-16370. 512p. Date not set. 39.50 (ISBN 0-521-23048-9). Cambridge U Pr.

PHILOSOPHY, GREEK

see Philosophy, Ancient

PHILOSOPHY, INDIC

Chennakesavan, Sarasvati. Concepts of Mind in Indian Philosophy. 1980. 14.00x (ISBN 0-8364-0638-9). South Asia Bks.

Jaimini. Karma Mimansa Sutras of Jaimini. 91p. 1980. pap. 5.50. KMS Pr CO.

Sastri, G. A Study in the Dialectics of Sphota. 106p. 1980. text ed. 10.50 (ISBN 0-8426-1653-5). Verry.

PHILOSOPHY, MEDIEVAL

Friedman, John B. The Monstrous Races in Medieval Art & Thought. LC 80-23181. (Illus.). 272p. 1981. text ed. 20.00 (ISBN 0-674-58652-2). Harvard U Pr.

Hopkins, Jasper. Nicholas of Cusa's Debate with John Wenck: A Translation & an Appraisal of De Ignota Litteratura & Apologia Doctae Ignorantiae. LC 80-82908. 1981. 23.00x (ISBN 0-938060-24-4). Banning Pr.

Marenbon, J. From the Circle of Alcuin to the School of Auxerre. (Cambridge Studies in Medieval Life & Thought: Third Ser., Vol. 15). (Illus.). 248p. Date not set. price not set (ISBN 0-521-23428-X). Cambridge U Pr.

Potts, T. C. Conscience in Medieval Philosophy. 180p. 1980. 47.50 (ISBN 0-521-23287-2). Cambridge U Pr.

PHILOSOPHY, MODERN

see also Enlightenment; Evolution; Existentialism; Humanism–20th Century; Humanism, Religious; Neo-Scholasticism; Phenomenology; Philosophy, Renaissance; Positivism; Pragmatism; Semantics (Philosophy); Transcendentalism;

also Philosophy, English; Philosophy, french; and similiar headings

Hesse, Mary B. Forces & Fields. 320p. 1962. 10.00 (ISBN 0-8022-0712-X). Philos Lib.

Kontopoulos, Kyriakos M. Knowledge & Determination: The Transition from Hegel to Marx. 1980. text ed. 23.00x (ISBN 90-6032-125-1). Humanities.

Kristeller, Paul O. Renaissance Thought & Its Sources. Mooney, Michael, ed. 352p. 1981. Repr. 9.50 (ISBN 0-231-04513-1). Columbia U Pr.

Levitt, Morton. Freud & Dewey on the Nature of Man. 1960. 3.75 (ISBN 0-8022-0966-1). Philos Lib.

Motylewski, Leo F. Essene Plan. LC 76-14499. 1976. 8.75 (ISBN 0-8022-2183-1). Philos Lib.

Schweitzer, Albert. Thoughts for Our Times. Anderson, Erica, ed. (Illus.). 64p. 1981. Repr. of 1975 ed. 3.95 (ISBN 0-8298-0448-X). Pilgrim NY.

PHILOSOPHY, MODERN–20TH CENTURY

DeGrood, David. Radical Currents in Contemporary Philosophy, Vol. II. 1981. write for info. Fireside Bks.

PHILOSOPHY, MORAL

see Ethics

PHILOSOPHY, ORIENTAL

Clifford, Terry. The Diamond Healing: Tibetan Buddhist Medicine & Psychiatry. 196p. 1981. pap. 7.95 (ISBN 0-87728-528-4). Weiser.

Kim, Yong C. Oriental Thought: An Introduction to the Philosophical & Religious Thought of Asia. (Littlefield, Adams Quality Paperback Ser.: No. 365). 130p. 1981. pap. 3.95 (ISBN 0-8226-0365-9). Littlefield.

Kim, Yong Choon. Oriental Thought: An Introduction to the Philosophical & Religious Thought of Asia. 130p. 1981. Repr. of 1973 ed. 8.95x (ISBN 0-8476-6972-6). Rowman.

PHILOSOPHY, PATRISTIC

see Fathers of the Church

PHILOSOPHY, RENAISSANCE

Hogg, James. Richard Whytford's the Pype or Tonne of the Lyfe of Perfection, Vol. 4, Pt. 3. (Elizabethan & Renaissance Studies: No. 89). 1979. pap. text ed. 25.00 (ISBN 0-391-01689-X). Humanities.

Hopkins, Jasper. Nicholas of Cusa's Debate with John Wenck: A Translation & an Appraisal of De Ignota Litteratura & Apologia Doctae Ignorantiae. LC 80-82908. 1981. 23.00x (ISBN 0-938060-24-4). Banning Pr.

PHILOSOPHY, ROMAN

see Philosophy, Ancient

PHILOSOPHY, RUSSIAN

Lendvai, Paul. The Bureaucracy of Truth. 350p. 1981. lib. bdg. 20.00x (ISBN 0-86531-142-0). Westview.

PHILOSOPHY AND RELIGION

see also Christianity–Philosophy; Faith and Reason; Religion–Philosophy

Gewirth, Alan. Reason & Morality. 416p. 1981. pap. 9.95x (ISBN 0-226-28876-5). U of Chicago Pr.

Radhakrishnan, S. An Idealist View of Life. (Paperbacks Ser.). 288p. 1980. pap. 6.75 (ISBN 0-04-141009-2, 1614). Allen Unwin.

Smart, Ninian. A Dialogue of Religions. LC 79-8730. (The Library of Philosophy & Theology). 142p. 1981. Repr. of 1960 ed. lib. bdg. 17.50x (ISBN 0-313-22187-1, SMDR). Greenwood.

PHILOSOPHY AND SCIENCE

see Science–Philosophy

PHILOSOPHY OF HISTORY

see History–Philosophy

PHILOSOPHY OF LANGUAGE

see Languages–Philosophy

PHILOSOPHY OF LAW

see Law–Philosophy

PHILOSOPHY OF MEDICINE

see Medicine–Philosophy

PHILOSOPHY OF NATURE

see also Cosmology; Natural Theology

Bass, Robert E. Some Features of Organization in Nature: A Contribution to Philosophy. 1980. 6.00. Print Mail Serv.

PHILOSOPHY OF TEACHING

see Education–Philosophy

PHOBIAS

Goldstein, Sam. What Are You Afraid of? An Illustrated Dictionary of Fearful Words Ending in Phobia. (Weirdictionaries Ser.). (Illus.). 72p. (Orig.). 1981. pap. 3.95 (ISBN 0-938338-05-6). Winds World Pr.

Sutherland, E. Ann & Zalman Amit. Phobia Free. (Orig.). pap. 1.95 (ISBN 0-515-04700-7). Jove Pubns.

Wenrich, Wes W., et al. Self-Directed Systemic Desensitization. LC 76-9019. (Illus.). 95p. (Orig.). 1980. pap. 7.00 (ISBN 0-917472-05-5). F Fournies.

PHOENIX, ARIZONA

Hoffman, Roslyn. Phoenix: A Pictorial History. Friedman, Donna R., ed. (Illus.). 208p. 1981. pap. write for info. (ISBN 0-89865-090-9). Donning Co.

PHONETICS

see also Speech; Voice

also subdivision Phonetics, Phonology, and Pronunciation under names of languages, e.g. English Language–Phonetics

Arnoff, Mark & Kean, Mary-Louise, eds. Juncture. (Studia Linguistica et Philologica: Ovol. 7). 144p. 1980. pap. 25.00 (ISBN 0-915838-46-X). Anma Libri.

Calvert, Donald. Descriptive Phonetics. 1980. 16.00. Thieme Stratton.

Fischer-Jorgensen, ed. International Congress of Phonetic Sciences, 9th Special Lectures. Copenhagen, August 1979. (Journal: Phonetica Ser.: Vol. 37, No 1-2). (Illus.). 108p. 1980. pap. 19.75 (ISBN 3-8055-1414-X). S Karger.

Gussman, Edmund. Studies in Abstract Phonology. (Linguistic Inquiry Monographs). 160p. (Orig.). 1980. 22.50x (ISBN 0-262-07081-2); pap. text ed. 13.50x (ISBN 0-262-57057-2). MIT Pr.

Ladefoged, Peter. Preliminaries to Linguistic Phonetics. pap. 5.00 (ISBN 0-226-46787-2). U of Chicago Pr.

Manoni, Mary H. & Cienkus, Robert. Phonetic Rules in Reading. LC 78-730055. (Illus.). 1978. pap. text ed. 99.00 (ISBN 0-89290-103-9, A329-SATC). Soc for Visual.

Walsh, Harry H., ed. Phonology & Speech Remediation: A Book of Readings. LC 78-32109. (Illus.). 268p. text ed. 18.95 (ISBN 0-933014-52-X). College-Hill.

PHONICS

see Reading (Elementary)–Phonetic Method

PHONODISCS

see Phonorecords

PHONOGRAPH

see also Electro-Acoustics; Phonorecords; Sound-Recording and Reproducing

Proudfoot, Christopher. Collecting Phonographs & Gramophones. (The Christies International Collectors Ser.). (Illus.). 128p. 1980. 14.95 (ISBN 0-8317-3952-5). Mayflower Bks.

PHONOGRAPH RECORDS

see Phonorecords

PHONOGRAPHY

see Shorthand

PHONOLOGY

see Phonetics

also subdivisions Phonetics, Phonology, and Pronunciation under names of languages, e.g. French Language–Phonetics; English Language–Phonology; Italian Language–Pronunciation

Zwirner, E. & Zwirner, K. Phonometrie, Teil 1: Grundfragen der Phonometrie. 3rd ed. Zwirner, E. & Ezawa, K., eds. (Bibliotheca Phonetica Ser.: No. 3). (Illus.). vi, 218p. 1981. pap. 49.75 (ISBN 3-8055-2370-X). S Karger.

PHONORECORDS

see also Music–Discography; Phonotapes

Connelly, Will. The Musician's Guide to Independent Record Production. (Illus.). 1981. 12.95 (ISBN 0-8092-5969-9); pap. 6.95 (ISBN 0-8092-5968-0). Contemp Bks.

Reinhart, Charles. You Can't Do That: Beatles Bootlegs & Novelty Records, 1963-1980. 1981. 11.95 (ISBN 0-87650-128-5). Pierian.

PHONORECORDS–BIBLIOGRAPHY

Chicorel Index to the Spoken Arts on Discs, Tapes, & Cassettes, Vol. TA. 500p. 1974. 85.00. Am Lib Pub Co.

PHONORECORDS–REVIEWS

Carter, Edith. Records in Review Nineteen Eighty, Vol. 25. (Records in Review Nineteen Eighty). 1980. 15.95 (ISBN 0-911656-09-X). Wyeth Pr.

Maleady, Antoinette O. Index to Record & Tape Reviews: A Classical Music Buying Guide for 1979. 1980. 52.50 (ISBN 0-917600-05-3). Chulainn Press.

PHONOTAPES

Maleady, Antoinette O. Index to Record & Tape Reviews: A Classical Music Buying Guide for 1979. 1980. 52.50 (ISBN 0-917600-05-3). Chulainn Press.

PHONOTAPES–BIBLIOGRAPHY

Chicorel Index to the Spoken Arts on Discs, Tapes, & Cassettes, Vol. TA. 500p. 1974. 85.00. Am Lib Pub Co.

PHOSPHORUS

Goldwhite, H. Introduction to Phosphorus Chemistry. LC 79-27141. (Cambridge Texts in Chemistry & Biochemistry). 175p. Date not set. 30.00 (ISBN 0-521-22978-2); pap. text ed. 12.95 (ISBN 0-521-29757-5). Cambridge U Pr.

Holmes, Robert R. Pentacoordinated Phosphorus. Incl. Vol. 1, Structure & Spectroscopy. (No. 175). 92.00 (ISBN 0-8412-0458-6); Vol. 2, Reaction Mechanisms. (No. 176). 52.00 (ISBN 0-8412-0528-0). (ACS Monograph). 1980. Set. 144.00 (ISBN 0-8412-0529-9). Am Chemical.

PHOSPHORYLATION

Biochemical Societies of France, Great Britain, Italy, & the Netherlands. Joint Meeting, Venice, 1976. Phosphorylated Proteins & Related Enzymes: Proceedings. 121p. 1980. 8.00. Info Retrieval.

PHOTIUS, d. 892

Treadgold, W. T. The Nature of the Bibliotheca of Photius. (Dumbarton Oaks Studies: Vol. 18). 1980. write for info. (ISBN 0-88402-090-8, Ctr Byzantine). Dumbarton Oaks.

Treadgold, Warren T. The Nature of the Bibliotheca of Photius. (Dumbarton Oaks Studis: Vol. 18). (Illus.). 201p. 1980. write for info. (ISBN 0-88402-090-8, Ctr Byzantine). Dumbarton Oaks.

PHOTO INTERPRETATION

see Photographic Interpretation

PHOTOBIOLOGY

Smith, Kendric C., ed. Photochemical & Photobiological Reviews, Vols. 1-5. Incl. Vol. 1. 391p. 1976. 39.50 (ISBN 0-306-33801-7); Vol. 2. 329p. 1977. 29.50 (ISBN 0-306-33802-5); Vol. 3. 315p. 1978. 27.50 (ISBN 0-306-33803-3); Vol. 4. 343p. 1979. 35.00 (ISBN 0-306-40225-4); Vol. 5. 375p. 1980. 35.00 (ISBN 0-306-40360-9). LC 75-43689 (Plenum Pr). Plenum Pub.

Tometsko, Andrew M. & Richard, Frederic M., eds. Applications of Photochemistry in Probing Biological Targets. LC 80-15368. (N.Y. Academy of Sciences Annals: Vol. 346). 1980. 88.00x (ISBN 0-89766-080-3); pap. write for info. (ISBN 0-89766-081-1). NY Acad Sci.

PHOTOCHEMISTRY

see also Photobiology

Padwa. Organic Photochemistry. 1981. 65.00. Dekker.

Smith, Kendric C., ed. Photochemical & Photobiological Reviews, Vols. 1-5. Incl. Vol. 1. 391p. 1976. 39.50 (ISBN 0-306-33801-7); Vol. 2. 329p. 1977. 29.50 (ISBN 0-306-33802-5); Vol. 3. 315p. 1978. 27.50 (ISBN 0-306-33803-3); Vol. 4. 343p. 1979. 35.00 (ISBN 0-306-40225-4); Vol. 5. 375p. 1980. 35.00 (ISBN 0-306-40360-9). LC 75-43689 (Plenum Pr). Plenum Pub.

Tometsko, Andrew M. & Richard, Frederic M., eds. Applications of Photochemistry in Probing Biological Targets. LC 80-15368. (N.Y. Academy of Sciences Annals: Vol. 346). 1980. 88.00x (ISBN 0-89766-080-3); pap. write for info. (ISBN 0-89766-081-1). NY Acad Sci.

PHOTOELECTRICITY

see also Photonuclear Reactions

PRC Energy Analysis Co. Design, Installation & Operation of Small, Stand-Alone Photovoltaic Powersystems. 300p. 1981. pap. 34.50 (ISBN 0-89934-092-X). Solar Energy Info.

PHOTOGRAMMETRY

see also Photographic Interpretation

Atkinson, K. B., ed. Developments in Close Range Photogrammetry - One. (Illus.). xii, 220p. 1980. 45.00x (ISBN 0-85334-882-0). Burgess-Intl Ideas.

Auto-Carto IV, 2 vols. 1979. member 17.50; non-member 30.00. ASP.

Complete Index to P. E. & R. S. Nineteen Thirty-Foru to Nineteen Seventy-Nine. member 7.50; non-member 15.00. ASP.

Thermosense II. 1979. member 15.00; non-member 19.50. ASP.

PHOTOGRAPHERS

Hall, James B. Minor White: Rites & Passages. LC 77-80023. (Illus.). 144p. 1981. 25.00 (ISBN 0-89381-069-X); pap. 15.00. Aperture.

Johnson, William S., commentary by. W. Eugene Smith: Master of the Photographic Essay. LC 80-68723. (Illus.). 1981. 35.00 (ISBN 0-89381-070-3). Aperture.

Lassam, Robert. Fox Talbot, Photographer. (Illus.). 94p. 1981. 22.50 (ISBN 0-900193-77-8, Pub. by Compton Pr England); pap. 9.95 (ISBN 0-686-69417-1). Kent St U Pr.

PHOTOGRAPHERS–DIRECTORIES

Roto-Vision Editors. Art Director's Index to Photographers. (Art Directors Index Ser.: No. 7). (Illus.). 1981. 80.00 (ISBN 2-88046-005-0, Pub. by Roto-Vision Switzerland); pap. 17.50. Norton.

PHOTOGRAPHIC APPARATUS AND SUPPLIES

see Photography–Apparatus and Supplies

PHOTOGRAPHIC COMPOSITION

see Composition (Photography)

PHOTOGRAPHIC DARK ROOMS

see Photography–Studios and Dark Rooms

PHOTOGRAPHIC INTERPRETATION

Nagao, Makoto & Matsuyama, Takashi, eds. A Structural Analysis of Complex Aerial Photographs. (Advanced Applications in Pattern Recognition Ser.). 200p. 1980. 32.50 (ISBN 0-306-40571-7, Plenum Pr). Plenum Pub.

PHOTOGRAPHIC LENSES

see Lenses, Photographic

PHOTOGRAPHIC MEASUREMENTS

see Photogrammetry

PHOTOGRAPHIC PROCESSING

see Photography–Processing

PHOTOGRAPHIC SUPPLIES

see Photography–Apparatus and Supplies

PHOTOGRAPHS

Blaisdell, Gus. Park City. LC 80-65768. (Illus.). 252p. 1981. 75.00. Aperture.

Miller, Sylvia R. A Pictoral Memoir. LC 80-81146. (Illus.). 120p. 1980. 20.00 (ISBN 0-913504-57-2). Lowell Pr.

Schwartzman, Steven. Hill Country Women. (Illus., Orig.). 1980. pap. 9.00 (ISBN 0-937710-02-4). SunShine.

--Stereo Infrared Landscapes. (Illus., Orig.). 1980. pap. 9.00 (ISBN 0-937710-01-6). SunShine.

Vogt, Christian. Photographs. 1980. 35.00. Norton.

PHOTOGRAPHS–CATALOGS

Gates, John K. A Touch of Nostalgia: A Glimpse of America's Past. LC 80-84010. (Illus.). 192p. (Orig.). 1980. pap. 14.95 (ISBN 0-9605168-0-8). Photographit.

PHOTOGRAPHS–CONSERVATION AND RESTORATION

Averkamp, Marcella. Preserving Paper & Photographic Materials: A Handbook for Curators & Librarians. LC 80-26028. (Illus.). 88p. (Orig.). 1981. pap. 7.95x (ISBN 0-87020-203-0). State Hist Soc Wis.

PHOTOGRAPHS–EXHIBITIONS

see Photography–Exhibitions

PHOTOGRAPHS–TRIMMING, MOUNTING, ETC.

Morrison, Alex. Photofinish. 144p. 1981. 16.95 (ISBN 0-442-21262-3). Van Nos Reinhold.

PHOTOGRAPHY

see also Cameras; Cinematography; Composition (Photography); Lenses, Photographic; Macrophotography; Nature Photography; Travel Photography

also headings beginning with the word Photographic

Bathes, Roland. Camera Lucida: Reflections on Photography. Howard, Richard, tr. (Illus.). 1981. 11.95 (ISBN 0-8090-3340-2). Hill & Wang.

Bauer, Erwin & Bauer, Peggy. Photographing the West a State-by-State Guide. LC 80-81770. (Illus.). 192p. 1980. 27.50 (ISBN 0-87358-269-1); pap. 14.95 (ISBN 0-87358-268-3). Northland.

Conceptography. Date not set. price not set. Creative Bks.

Eastman Kodak Company. Images, Images, Images: The Book of Programmed Multi-Image Production. rev. ed. (Illus.). 264p. (Orig.). 1980. pap. 19.95 (ISBN 0-87985-285-2, S-12). Eastman Kodak.

--Kodak Guide to Thirty-Five MM Photography. LC 79-54310. (Illus.). 288p. (Orig.). 1980. text ed. 16.50 (ISBN 0-87985-242-9, AC-95H); pap. text ed. 9.95 (ISBN 0-87985-236-4, AC-95S). Eastman Kodak.

Eisenstaedt, Alfred. Eisenstaedt's Guide to Photography. (Illus.). 176p. 1981. pap. 11.95 (ISBN 0-14-046483-2). Penguin.

Haskins, Sam. Photo Graphics. (Illus.). 1981. 30.00 (ISBN 2-88046-016-6, Pub. by Roto-Vision Switzerland). Norton.

Klindt, Steven, ed. New American Photography. (Illus.). 48p. 1981. pap. 10.00 (ISBN 0-932026-06-0). Chicago Contemp Photo.

Malcolm, Janet. Diana & Nikon: Essays on the Aesthetic of Photography. (Illus.). 176p. 1980. pap. 8.95 (ISBN 0-87923-387-7). Godine.

Marincola, Paula. Photography: Made in Philadelphia 4. LC 80-84551. (Illus.). 1979. pap. 4.00 (ISBN 0-88454-059-6). U of Pa Contemp Art.

Photograph A-V Program Directory. LC 80-83469. (Illus.). 224p. 1980. 24.50 (ISBN 0-936524-00-6). PMI Inc.

Roto-Vision Editors. Art Director's Index to Photographer: American Section, No. 7. (Illus., Orig.). 1981. pap. 17.50 (ISBN 2-88046-010-7, Pub. by Roto-Vision Switzerland). Norton.

Upton & Upton. Photography. 2nd ed. 1981. pap. text ed. 15.95 (ISBN 0-316-88747-1). Little.

Wagenvoord, James. Photography Notes. (Illus.). 160p. 1981. 6.95 (ISBN 0-312-60840-3). St Martin.

Webster, Frank. The New Photography. 1981. 29.95 (ISBN 0-7145-3798-5); pap. 14.95 (ISBN 0-7145-3801-9). Riverrun NY.

PHOTOGRAPHY–ANIMATED PICTURES

see Cinematography; Moving-Pictures

PHOTOGRAPHY–APPARATUS AND SUPPLIES

see also Cameras; Lenses, Photographic; Photography–Studios and Dark Rooms

Swedlund, Charles. Photography. (Illus.). 384p. 1981. 25.00 (ISBN 0-686-69125-3). HR&W.

PHOTOGRAPHY–BIBLIOGRAPHY

Barger, M. Susan. Bibliography of Photographic Processes in Use Before 1880: Their Materials, Processing, & Conservation. LC 80-84390. 160p. 1980. pap. 37.50 (ISBN 0-89938-003-4). Graph Arts Res RIT.

Flowers, Damon B., ed. The Photography Index for 1980, Vol. IV. LC 80-640225. 160p. (Orig.). 1981. pap. 8.95 (ISBN 0-934918-03-1). Photo Res.

Heidtmann, Frank, et al, eds. German Photographic Literature, Eighteen Thirty-Nine to Nineteen Seventy-Eight: Theory, Technology, Visual. A Classified Bibliography of German-Language Photographic Publications. 690p. 1980. 85.00 (ISBN 3-598-10026-4, Dist. by Gale Research Co.). K G Saur.

PHOTOGRAPHY–BUSINESS METHODS

Long, Joan & Long, Ronald. Writer's & Photographer's Guide to Newspaper Markets. 2nd ed. 175p. 1981. pap. price not set (ISBN 0-936940-01-8). Helm Pub.

PHOTOGRAPHY–COMPOSITION

see Composition (Photography)

PHOTOGRAPHY–DARKROOM TECHNIQUE

see Photography–Processing

PHOTOGRAPHY–EXHIBITIONS

Baker, Krystyna. Masks. Date not set. price not set (ISBN 0-89672-086-1); price not set ltd. signed ed. (ISBN 0-89672-092-6); pap. price not set (ISBN 0-89672-085-3). Tex Tech Pr.

Glenn, Constance, ed. Kathe Kollwitz - Jake Zeitlin: Jake Zetlin Bookshop & Gallery-1937; The Art Museum & Galleries, California State University, Long Beach-1979. (Illus.). 64p. (Orig.). 1979. pap. 8.00 (ISBN 0-936270-14-4). Art Mus Gall.

Glenn, Constance W. & Rice, Leland. Frances Benjamin Johnston: Women of Class & Station. (Illus.). 96p. (Orig.). 1979. pap. 8.00 (ISBN 0-936270-12-8). Art Mus Gall.

Glenn, Constance W., ed. The Frederick Weisman Company Collection of California Art. 2nd ed. (Illus.). 64p. 1979. pap. 8.00 (ISBN 0-936270-11-X). Art Mus Gall.

Hine, Lewis. Women at Work: One Hundred Fifty Photographs by Lewis Hine. (Illus.). 128p. (Orig.). 1981. pap. price not set (ISBN 0-486-24154-8). Dover.

Lyon, Danny & McCune, Billy. Conversations with the Dead: Photographs of Prison Life. (Illus.). 1970. pap. 0.25 (ISBN 0-914412-00-0). Inst for the Arts.

Papageorge, Tod, ed. Walker Evans & Robert Frank: A Study of Experience. (Illus.). 72p. 1981. pap. write for info. (ISBN 0-89467-015-8). Yale Art Gallery.

PHOTOGRAPHY–EXPOSURE

Gaunt, Leonard. Practical Exposure. LC 80-40793. (Practical Photography Ser.). (Illus.). 192p. 1981. 19.95 (ISBN 0-240-51058-5). Focal Pr.

PHOTOGRAPHY–HANDBOOKS, MANUALS, ETC.

see also Cameras;

also types subdivided for specific cameras, e.g. Cameras–Types–Leica

Bernard, Carl & Norquay, Karen. Practical Effects in Photography. LC 80-40794. (Practical Photography Ser.). (Illus.). 168p. 1981. 19.95 (ISBN 0-240-51082-8). Focal Pr.

Bruck, Axel. Creative Camera Techniques. LC 80-41402. (Illus.). 144p. 1981. 19.95 (ISBN 0-240-51106-9). Focal Pr.

Busselle, Michael. The Complete Book of Photographing People. 1980. 19.95 (ISBN 0-671-41257-4, Kenan Pr). S&S.

Grill, Tom & Scanlon, Mark. Taking Better Pictures with Your 35mm SLR: A Practial Guide--with Special Emphasis on 35mm Automatic Cameras. LC 80-7855. (Illus.). 128p. 1981. 15.95 (ISBN 0-690-01920-3, HarpT). Har-Row.

--Taking Better Pictures with Your 35mm SLR: A Practial Guide--with Special Emphasis on 35mm Automatic Cameras. LC 80-7855. (Illus.). 128p. 1981. pap. 7.95 (ISBN 0-690-01921-1, CN 864, CN). Har-Row.

London, Barbara & Boyer, Richard. Your Automatic Camera Indoors. 1981. pap. 6.95 (ISBN 0-442-21956-3). Van Nos Reinhold.

--Your Automatic Camera Outdoors. 1981. pap. 6.95 (ISBN 0-442-21955-5). Van Nos Reinhold.

Lynch, David. Focalguide to Better Pictures. LC 80-41302. (Focalguide Ser.). 1981. pap. 7.95 (ISBN 0-240-51053-4). Focal Pr.

McKenzie, Peter. Focalguide to Travel Photography. LC 80-41482. (Focalguide Ser.). (Illus.). 136p. 1981. pap. 7.95 (ISBN 0-240-51072-0). Focal Pr.

Wild, Victor. How to Take & Sell Erotic Photographs: Secrets of the Masters. 126p. (Orig.). 1981. pap. 9.95 (ISBN 0-938444-00-X). Wildfire Pub.

PHOTOGRAPHY–HISTORY

Engelman, Edmund. Berggasse Nineteen: Sigmund Freud's Home & Offices, Vienna, 1938; the Photographs of Edmund Engelman. LC 80-23056. 1981. pap. 15.00 (ISBN 0-226-20847-8). U of Chicago Pr.

McCausland, Elizabeth. Eyewitness: The Growth of Photography. Peters, Susan D., ed. (Illus.). 250p. 1981. 22.50 (ISBN 0-8180-1421-0). Horizon.

Swedlund, Charles. Photography. (Illus.). 384p. 1981. 25.00 (ISBN 0-686-69125-3). HR&W.

PHOTOGRAPHY–JUVENILE LITERATURE

Carrier, Rick & Carroll, David. Action! Camera! Super-Eight Cassette Film Making for Beginners. LC 78-162739. (Illus.). 78p. 1972. 7.95 (ISBN 0-684-12490-4). Scribner.

Cooper, Miriam. Snap! Photography. (Illus.). (gr. 4-7). 1981. PLB price not set (ISBN 0-671-34021-2). Messner.

PHOTOGRAPHY–LANDSCAPES

see also Photography, Artistic

Alinder, James, ed. New Landscapes. (Untitled Ser.: No. 24). (Illus.). 56p. 1981. pap. 8.95 (ISBN 0-933286-21-X). Friends Photography.

Duffield, Mary R. & Jones, Warren. Plants for Dry Climates. (Orig.). 1981. pap. 7.95 (ISBN 0-89586-042-2). H P Bks.

Fell, Derek. How to Photograph Flowers, Plants & Landscapes. (Photography Ser.). (Orig.). 1980. pap. 7.95 (ISBN 0-89586-068-6). H P Bks.

Gill, Spencer. Washington Shores. (Illus.). 128p. 1981. 27.50 (ISBN 0-912856-68-8). Graphic Arts Ctr.

Isherwood, Justin. Wisconsin. (Illus.). 128p. 1981. 27.50 (ISBN 0-912856-67-X). Graphic Arts Ctr.
Wamsley, James. Virginia. (Illus.). 128p. 1981. 27.50 (ISBN 0-912856-66-1). Graphic Arts Ctr.
Welsh, Stan. Utah Two. (Illus.). 128p. 1981. 27.50 (ISBN 0-912856-65-3). Graphic Arts Ctr.
Woods, Gerald & Williams, John. Creative Techniques in Landscape Photography. LC 80-8396. (Illus.). 200p. 1981. 18.95 (ISBN 0-06-014835-7, HarpT). Har-Row.

PHOTOGRAPHY–LENSES
see Lenses, Photographic

PHOTOGRAPHY–LIGHTING
see also Photography–Exposure
Adventures in Existing-Light Photography. rev. ed. (Code No. AC-44). (Illus.). 1980. pap. 4.00 (ISBN 0-87985-251-8). Eastman Kodak.
Brooks, David. How to Control & Use Photographic Lighting. (Orig.). 1980. pap. 7.95 (ISBN 0-89586-059-7). H P Bks.

PHOTOGRAPHY–MOVING-PICTURES
see Cinematography; Moving-Pictures

PHOTOGRAPHY–PORTRAITS
see also Photography of Women
Ekman, Paul. The Face of Man: Expressions of Uniersal Emotion in a New Guinea Village. LC 79-12934. 154p. 1980. lib. bdg. 25.00 (ISBN 0-8240-7130-1). Garland Pub.
Gowland, Peter. The Secrets of Photographing Women. Michelman, Herbert, ed. (Illus.). 224p. 1981. 12.95 (ISBN 0-517-54180-7, Michelman Books). Crown.
Hirsch, Julia. Family Photographs: Content, Meaning & Effect. LC 80-25591. (Illus.). 160p. 1981. 12.95 (ISBN 0-19-502889-9). Oxford U Pr.

PHOTOGRAPHY–PROCESSING
Stone, Jim, ed. Darkroom Dynamics: An Introduction to Creative Printing. 208p. 1981. pap. 12.95 (ISBN 0-442-27927-2). Van Nos Reinhold.

PHOTOGRAPHY–STUDIOS AND DARK ROOMS
Here are entered works on the construction and physical layout of studios and dark rooms.
Langford, Michael. The Darkroom Handbook. LC 80-2703. (Illus.). 352p. 1981. 25.00 (ISBN 0-394-51370-3). Knopf.
Stone, Jim, ed. Darkroom Dynamics: An Introduction to Creative Printing. 208p. 1981. pap. 12.95 (ISBN 0-442-27927-2). Van Nos Reinhold.

PHOTOGRAPHY–SUPPLIES
see Photography–Apparatus and Supplies

PHOTOGRAPHY–YEARBOOKS
Photography Year Book 1981. 45th ed. LC 36-13575. (Illus.). 271p. 1980. text ed. 30.00x (ISBN - 085242-732-8). Intl Pubns Serv.

PHOTOGRAPHY, ARTISTIC
Here are entered works on photography as a fine art, including aesthetic theory, as well as books of artistic photographs.
see also Photography–Landscapes; Photography of Men; Photography of Women
Adams, Ansel. The Portfolios of Ansel Adams. 1981. 14.95 (ISBN 0-686-68992-5, 713953). NYGS.
Alinder, James, ed. Discovery & Recognition. (Untitled Ser.: No. 25). 56p. (Orig.). 1981. pap. 9.95 (ISBN 0-933286-24-4). Friends Photography.
Andy Warhol's Exposures. 1980. 12.50 (ISBN 0-448-12658-3). G&D.
Buffalo Fine Arts Academy & Cranbook Academy of Art-Museum. Donald Blumberg. LC 79-50455. (Illus.). Date not set. pap. 8.95 (ISBN 0-914782-24-X). Buffalo Acad.
Burden, Shirley, ed. Presence. (Illus.). 92p. 1981. 20.00 (ISBN 0-89381-075-4). Aperture.
Curtis, Edward S. Portraits from North American Indian Life. 192p. 1981. pap. 10.95 (ISBN 0-89104-003-X). A & W Pubs.
Dean, Roy. The Dean's List. (Illus.). 1980. write for info. Rho-Delta Pr.
Hamilton, David, photos by. The Best of David Hamilton. LC 80-83280. (Illus.). 144p. 1980. pap. 10.95 (ISBN 0-688-00403-2, Quill). Morrow.
--David Hamilton's Private Collection. LC 80-83281. (Illus.). 128p. 1980. pap. 10.95 (ISBN 0-688-00402-4, Quill). Morrow.
Healey, Denis. Healey's Eye. (Illus.). 192p. 1981. 19.95 (ISBN 0-224-01793-4, Pub. by Chatto-Bodley-Jonathan). Merrimack Bk Serv.
Heinzen, Richard H. & Clemons, Neil L. Breaking Through: Photography & Poetry Celebrating the Many Shades of Earthly Joys. (Illus.). 80p. (Orig.). 1980. pap. 10.95 (ISBN 0-686-28881-5, 880). Sunshine Arts WA.
Henes, Donna. Dressing Our Wounds in Warm Clothes. LC 81-65197. (Illus.). 72p. (Orig.). 1981. pap. 9.00 (ISBN 0-937122-02-5). Astro Artz.
Herdeg, Walter, ed. Photographis '81: The International Annual of Advertising, Editorial & Television Photography. (Illus.). 264p. 1981. 59.50 (ISBN 0-8038-5893-0, Visual Communication). Hastings.
Honnef, Klaus, et al. Eisenstaedt: Germany. (Illus.). 112p. (Orig.). 1981. pap. 12.50 (ISBN 0-87474-530-6). Smithsonian.
Hume, Sandy. Western Man: Photographs from the National Western Stock Show. 1980. 18.95 (ISBN 0-933472-48-X); pap. 12.95 (ISBN 0-933472-49-8). Johnson Colo.
Jachna, Joseph. Light Touching Silver: Photographs by Joseph Jachna. Klindt, Steven, ed. (Illus.). 48p. (Orig.). 1980. pap. 5.00 (ISBN 0-932026-05-2). Chicago Contemp Photo.
Kertesz, Andre. From My Window. 1981. 24.95 (ISBN 0-8212-1125-0). NYGS.
Kismaric, Susan. American Children. 1981. 14.95 (ISBN 0-87070-229-7, 037338); pap. 7.95 (ISBN 0-87070-232-7, 037346). NYGS.
--American Children: Photographs in the Collection of the Museum of Modern Art. (Springs Mills Series on the Art of Photography). (Illus.). 80p. 1981. 14.95 (ISBN 0-87070-232-7); pap. 7.95 (ISBN 0-87070-229-7). Museum Mod Art.
Korniss, Peter. Passing Times. (Illus.). 1979. 17.50x (ISBN 963-13-0733-6). Intl Pubns Serv.
LeWitt, Sol. On the Walls of the Lower East Side. (Illus.). 72p. (Orig.). 1981. pap. 20.00 (ISBN 0-9601068-8-X). Agrinde Pubns.
Lyon, Danny. Danny Lyon. 144p. 1981. 35.00 (ISBN 0-89381-073-8). Aperture.
Mark, Mary E. Falkland Road: Prostitutes of Bombay. LC 80-11778. (Illus.). 96p. 1981. 25.00 (ISBN 0-394-50987-0); pap. 12.95 (ISBN 0-394-74000-9). Knopf.
Meyerowitz, Joel. St. Louis & the Arch. 112p. 1981. pap. 29.95 (ISBN 0-8212-1105-6). NYGS.
Morgan, William. Portals & Photographs. 1981. pap. 5.95 (ISBN 0-87233-057-5). Bauhan.
Pfhal, John, photos by. Altered Landscapes. (Untitled 26 Ser.). (Illus.). 56p. (Orig.). 1981. pap. 10.95 (ISBN 0-933286-23-6). Friends Photography.
Pratt, Charles & Maxwell, William. The Garden & the Wilderness. (Illus.). 159p. 1980. 50.00 (ISBN 0-8180-1420-2). Horizon.
Schad, Tennyson & Shapiro, Ira, eds. American Showcase, Vol.1. (Illus.). 226p. pap. 19.95 (ISBN 0-931144-01-9). Am Showcase.
--American Showcase, Vol. 2. (Illus.). 266p. 35.00 (ISBN 0-931144-04-3); pap. 22.50 (ISBN 0-931144-03-5). Am Showcase.
--American Showcase, Vol.4. (Illus.). 40.00 (ISBN 0-931144-08-6); pap. 27.50 (ISBN 0-931144-07-8). Am Showcase.
Seale, William. A Tasteful Interlude: American Interiors Through the Camera's Eye, 1860 to 1917. (Illus.). 288p. 1981. pap. 12.95 (ISBN 0-910050-49-X). AASLH.
Seyl, Susan. The Art Perfected: Portraiture from the Cronise Studio. LC 80-83177. (Illus.). 160p. 1980. pap. text ed. 10.95 (ISBN 0-87595-070-1). Oreg Hist Soc.
Singh, Raghubir, ed. Rajasthan: India's Enchanted Land. 1981. 27.50 (ISBN 0-500-54070-5). Thames Hudson.
Smith, Barbara T. A Log Book. LC 81-65196. (Illus.). 100p. (Orig.). 1981. 15.00 (ISBN 0-937122-03-3). Astro Artz.
Smith, Terry. Images of Rural Texas. LC 80-54842. (Illus.). 128p. 1981. 18.95 (ISBN 0-938898-11-6). Red River.
Solan, Joseph M., et al, eds. A Moment of Vision. LC 80-68991. 80p. (Orig.). 1980. pap. 9.50 (ISBN 0-937968-00-5). Dark Sun.
Vogt, Christian. Christian Vogt: Photographs. (Living Photographers Ser.). (Illus.). 1981. 35.00 (ISBN 0-686-69478-3, Pub. by Roto-Vision). Norton.
Wilson, Charis, ed. Cole Weston: 18 Photographs. (Illus.). 56p. 1981. pap. 19.95 (ISBN 0-87905-084-5). Peregrine Smith.
Witkin, Lee D. & London, Barbara. The Photograph Collector's Guide. 448p. 1981. pap. 19.95 (ISBN 0-8212-1124-2). NYGS.

PHOTOGRAPHY, BIOLOGICAL
see Nature Photography; Photography of Animals; Photography of Plants

PHOTOGRAPHY, DOCUMENTARY
Hamer, Red. Four Seasons of the Chesapeake Bay: Fall-Winter, Vol. II. Hamer, Barbara H., ed. (Illus.). 128p. 1981. 27.50 (ISBN 0-9605400-2-4). Four Seas Bk.
--Four Seasons of the Chesapeake Bay: Spring-Summer, Vol. 1. Hamer, Barbara H., ed. (Illus.). 128p. 1980. 27.50 (ISBN 0-9605400-0-8). Four Seas Bk.

PHOTOGRAPHY, FLASH-LIGHT
Carraher, Ron & Chartier, Colleen. Electronic Flash Photography: A Complete Guide to the Best Equipment & Creative Techniques. 136p. 1980. 24.95 (ISBN 0-442-21463-4); pap. 14.95 (ISBN 0-442-23135-0). Van Nos Reinhold.

PHOTOGRAPHY, JOURNALISTIC
see also Photography of Sports
Grant, Ian. Cameraman at War. (Illus.). 200p. 1981. 31.95 (ISBN 0-85059-489-8). Aztex.
Kobre, Ken. Photojournalism: The Professionals' Approach. (Illus.). 368p. (Orig.). 1980. 24.95 (ISBN 0-930764-16-1); pap. text ed. 15.95 (ISBN 0-930764-15-3). Curtin & London.
Los Angeles Press Photographers. Just One More. (Illus.). 1981. lib. bdg. 14.95 (ISBN 0-912076-41-0); pap. 9.95 (ISBN 0-912076-45-3). ESE Calif.

PHOTOGRAPHY, LENSLESS
see Holography

PHOTOGRAPHY, PICTORIAL
see Photography, Artistic

PHOTOGRAPHY, STEREOSCOPIC
Hamblin, W. Kenneth. Atlas of Stereoscopic Aerial Photographs & Landsat Imagery of North America. LC 79-91239. (Illus.). 208p. (Orig.). 15.95 (ISBN 0-935698-00-0). Tasa Pub Co.

PHOTOGRAPHY AS A PROFESSION
Schwarz, Ted. Careers in Photography. 1981. 12.95 (ISBN 0-8092-7019-6); pap. 5.95 (ISBN 0-8092-7018-8). Contemp Bks.

PHOTOGRAPHY OF ANIMALS
Preston-Mafham, Ken. Practical Wildlife Photography. LC 80-40792. (Practical Photography Ser.). (Illus.). 144p. 1981. 19.95 (ISBN 0-240-51081-X). Focal Pr.

PHOTOGRAPHY OF FLOWERS
see Photography of Plants

PHOTOGRAPHY OF MEN
Hume, Sandy. Western Man: Photographs from the National Western Stock Show. 1980. 18.95 (ISBN 0-933472-48-X); pap. 12.95 (ISBN 0-933472-49-8). Johnson Colo.

PHOTOGRAPHY OF NATURE
see Nature Photography

PHOTOGRAPHY OF PLANTS
Fell, Derek. How to Photograph Flowers, Plants & Landscapes. (Photography Ser.). (Orig.). 1980. pap. 7.95 (ISBN 0-89586-068-6). H P Bks.

PHOTOGRAPHY OF SPORTS
see also Photography, Journalistic; Sports
Eastman Kodak Company, ed. Filming Sports: The How-to Book for Coaches, Sports Information Directors, Motion Picture - Still Sports Photographers (S-65) (Illus.). 288p. (Orig.). 1981. pap. 19.95 (ISBN 0-87985-268-2). Eastman Kodak.
Shay, Arthur. Sports Photography: How to Take Great Action Shots. (Illus.). 1981. 14.95 (ISBN 0-8092-5962-1); pap. 7.95 (ISBN 0-8092-5961-3). Contemp Bks.

PHOTOGRAPHY OF THE MALE
see Photography of Men

PHOTOGRAPHY OF WOMEN
see also Women–Portraits
Gowland, Peter. The Secrets of Photographing Women. Michelman, Herbert, ed. (Illus.). 224p. 1981. 12.95 (ISBN 0-517-54180-7, Michelman Books). Crown.

PHOTOJOURNALISM
see Photography, Journalistic

PHOTOLYSIS (CHEMISTRY)
see Photochemistry

PHOTOMACROGRAPHY
see Macrophotography

PHOTONS
see also Lasers; Photonuclear Reactions
Cochard, G. & Kessler, P., eds. Photon-Photon Collisions: Proceedings. (Lecture Notes in Physics Ser.: Vol. 134). 400p. 1981. pap. 27.70 (ISBN 0-387-10262-0). Springer-Verlag.

PHOTONUCLEAR REACTIONS
see also Photoelectricity
Cochard, G. & Kessler, P., eds. Photon-Photon Collisions: Proceedings. (Lecture Notes in Physics Ser.: Vol. 134). 400p. 1981. pap. 27.70 (ISBN 0-387-10262-0). Springer-Verlag.

PHOTOPLAYS
see Moving-Picture Plays

PHRENOLOGY
see also Brain–Localization of Functions; Mind and Body; Physiognomy
Bain, Alexander. On the Study of Character, Including an Estimate of Phrenology. (Contributions to the History of Psychology Ser.: Orientations). 1980. Repr. of 1861 ed. 30.00 (ISBN 0-89093-316-2). U Pubns Amer.

PHTHISIS
see Tuberculosis

PHYLOGENY
see also Evolution; Paleontology
Jope, Charlene A. Organismic & Environmental Laboratory Manual. 144p. 1981. pap. text ed. 6.95 (ISBN 0-8403-2322-0). Kendall-Hunt.
Wiley, Edward O. Phylogenetics: Theory & Practice of Phylogenetic Systematics. 552p. 1981. price not set (ISBN 0-471-05975-7, Pub. by Wiley-Interscience). Wiley.

PHYLOGENY (BOTANY)
Hennig, Willi. Insect Phylogeny. 528p. 1981. price not set (ISBN 0-471-27848-3, Pub. by Wiley-Interscience). Wiley.
Roy, M. Aaron. Species Identity & Attachment: A Phylogenic Evaluation. 1979. lib. bdg. 37.50 (ISBN 0-8240-7052-6). Garland Pub.

PHYSICAL ANTHROPOLOGY
see also Anthropometry; Children–Growth; Craniology; Fossil Man; Human Behavior; Human Biology; Human Evolution; Human Genetics; Man–Influence of Environment; Primates; Race
Jurmain, et al. Physical Anthropology & Archaeology. (Illus.). 1981. pap. text ed. 11.96 (ISBN 0-8299-0388-7). West Pub.
Poirier, Frank E. In Search of Ourselves: An Introduction to Physical Anthropology. 3rd rev. ed. 1981. pap. text ed. price not set (ISBN 0-8087-1666-2). Burgess.
Steele, E. J. Somatic Selection & Adaptive Evolution. 100p. 1980. 30.00x (Pub. by Croom Helm England). State Mutual Bk.

PHYSICAL CHEMISTRY
see Chemistry, Physical and Theoretical

PHYSICAL CULTURE
see Physical Education and Training

PHYSICAL CULTURE PHOTOGRAPHY
see Photography of Men

PHYSICAL DIAGNOSIS
Holbrook, John H. Physical Diagnosis Review. LC 79-88046. 1979. pap. 8.50 (ISBN 0-87488-135-8). Med Exam.

PHYSICAL EDUCATION AND TRAINING
see also Athletics; Callisthenics; College Sports; Exercise; Games; Gymnastics; Health Education; Nudism; Physical Education for Children; Physical Fitness; Posture; Sports
also names of sports or exercises, e.g. Football; also apparatus used in gymnasiums
Advice About Drugs, Food, Fitness. (Home Adviser Ser.). 80p. (Orig.). 1981. pap. 1.95 (ISBN 0-8326-2408-X, 7050). Delair.
Anderson, James L. & Cohen, Martin. The Competitive Edge: The West Point Guide for the Weekend Athlete. (Illus.). 1981. 14.95. Morrow.
--The West Point Fitness & Diet Book. 256p. 1981. pap. 2.95 (ISBN 0-380-54205-6, 54205). Avon.
Baumgartner, Ted A. & Jackson, Andrew S. Measurement for Evaluation in Physical Education. 2nd ed. (Illus.). 576p. 1981. text ed. write for info. (ISBN 0-395-29623-4); write for info. instr's manual (ISBN 0-395-29637-4). HM.
Brooks, George A., ed. Perspectives on the Academic Discipline of Physical Education. 1981. text ed. 17.95 (ISBN 0-931250-18-8). Human Kinetics.
Consumer Guide, ed. The Consumer Guide Body Fitness & Shaping Program. (Illus.). 384p. 1981. pap. 8.95 (ISBN 0-89104-206-7). A & W Pubs.
Corbin, Charles B. & Dowell, J. Linus. Concepts in Physical Education with Laboratories & Experiments. 4th ed. 350p. 1981. pap. text ed. write for info. (ISBN 0-697-07177-4); instrs.' manual avail. (ISBN 0-697-07178-2). Wm C Brown.
Crowe, Walter C., et al. Priciples & Methods of Adapted Physical Education & Recreation. 4th ed. (Illus.). 602p. 1981. text ed. 20.95 (ISBN 0-8016-0327-7). Mosby.
DeVore, Steven, et al. Sybervision: Muscle Memory Programming for Any Sport. (Illus.). 250p. 1981. 12.95 (ISBN 0-914090-98-4). Chicago Review.
Erickson, Dorie A. How to Firm Flabby Flesh. (Illus.). 35p. (Orig.). 1981. pap. 3.95 (ISBN 0-937242-02-0). Scandia Pubs.
Kruger, Hayes & Kruger, Jane M. Movement & Education in Physical Education: A Guide to Teaching & Planning. 2nd ed. 1981. pap. text ed. 12.95x (ISBN 0-697-07181-2). Wm C Brown.
Rudman, Jack. Physical Education. (Undergraduate Program Field Test Ser.: UPFT-18). (Cloth bdg. avail. on request). pap. 9.95 (ISBN 0-8373-6018-8). Natl Learning.
Schwarsenneger, Arnold. Arnold's Bodybuilding for Men. 1981. 14.95 (ISBN 0-671-25613-0). S&S.
Welch, Paula D. & Lerch, Harold A. Handbook of American Physical Education & Sport. write for info. C C Thomas.
Wiseman, Douglas C. Practical Approach to Adapted Physical Education. (Physical Education Ser.). (Illus.). 544p. 1981. text ed. 17.95 (ISBN 0-201-08347-7). A-W.

PHYSICAL EDUCATION AND TRAINING–JUVENILE LITERATURE
Bershad, Carol & Bernick, Deborah. Bodyworks: The Kids' Guide to Food & Physical Fitness. (Illus.). 240p. (gr. 5-9). 1981. PLB 8.99 (ISBN 0-394-94752-5); pap. 5.95 (ISBN 0-394-84752-0). Random.
Capone. Your 14-Day Total Shape-up Plan. (gr. 7-12). 1980. pap. 1.25 (ISBN 0-590-30913-7, Schol Pap). Schol Bk Serv.

PHYSICAL EDUCATION AND TRAINING–MEDICAL ASPECTS
see Sports Medicine

PHYSICAL EDUCATION AND TRAINING–STUDY AND TEACHING
Mosston, Muska. Teaching Physical Education. 2nd ed. (Illus.). 256p. 1981. pap. text ed. 12.95 (ISBN 0-675-08036-3). Merrill.
Sherrill, Claudine. Adapted Physical Education & Recreation: A Multidisciplinary Approach. 2nd ed. 1981. 15.95x (ISBN 0-697-07176-6). Wm C Brown.

PHYSICAL EDUCATION FOR CHILDREN
Kirchner, Glenn, et al. Physical Education for Elementary School Children. 5th ed. 1981. text ed. 15.95x (ISBN 0-697-07175-8); instrs.' manual 1.00 (ISBN 0-697-07179-0); unit lesson plans avail. (ISBN 0-697-07180-4). Wm C Brown.
A Pocketguide to Health & Health Problems in School Physical Activities. 1981. pap. 3.00 (ISBN 0-917160-13-4). Am Sch Health.

PHYSICAL ENDURANCE
see Physical Fitness

PHYSICAL FITNESS
see also Muscle Strength
Anderson, James L. & Cohen, Martin. The Competitive Edge: The West Point Guide for the Weekend Athlete. LC 80-23535. (Illus.). 352p. 1981. 14.95 (ISBN 0-688-00352-4). Morrow.
--The Competitive Edge: The West Point Guide for the Weekend Athlete. (Illus.). 1981. 14.95. Morrow.

Bar-Khama, Amos, et al. Israeli Fitness Strategy: Based on the Physical Training Program of the Israel Defense Forces. LC 80-17222. (Illus.). 192p. 1980. pap. 5.95 (ISBN 0-688-08628-4, Quill). Morrow.
Better Homes & Gardens Books Editors, ed. Good Food & Fitness. (Illus.). 96p. 1981. 4.95 (ISBN 0-696-00635-9). Meredith Corp.
Broccoletti, Pete. Building up: The Young Athlete's Guide to Weight Training. (Illus.). 160p. 1981. 13.95 (ISBN 0-89651-053-0); pap. 8.95 (ISBN 0-89651-054-9). Icarus.
Clark, Linda. Stay Young Longer. (Orig.). pap. 1.95 (ISBN 0-515-05076-8). Jove Pubns.
Cohen, Lawrence S., et al. Physical Conditioning & Cardiovascular Rehabilitation. 344p. 1981. 25.00 (ISBN 0-471-08713-0, Pub. by Wiley-Med). Wiley.
Friedman, Philip & Eisen, Gail. The Pilates Method of Physical & Mental Conditioning. 1981. pap. 7.95 (ISBN 0-446-97859-0). Warner Bks.
Gilmore, C. P. Exercising for Fitness. Time-Life Books, ed. (Health Ser.). (Illus.). 176p. 1981. 12.95 (ISBN 0-8094-3754-6). Time Life.
Girdano, Daniel A. Better Late Than Never: How Men Can Avoid a Midlife Fitness Crisis. (Illus.). 256p. 1981. 12.95t (ISBN 0-13-074773-4, Spec); pap. 5.95b (ISBN 0-13-074765-3). P-H.
God, Phyllis. God. Date not set. 7.95 (ISBN 0-533-04754-4). Vantage.
Holbrook, Charles & Holbrook, Linda. Run-a-Day Logbook. Groninger, Vicki, ed. (Illus.). 420p. (Orig.). 1980. pap. 8.95 (ISBN 0-9604998-0-6). DCT Ent.
Kelly, Michael B. The Fitness Factor: Practical Body Building for Health. LC 80-20432. (Illus.). 256p. 1981. 11.95 (ISBN 0-668-05115-9, 5115). Arco.
Lorin, Martin I. The Parents' Book of Physical Fitness for Children. LC 78-3151. (Illus.). 290p. 1981. pap. 5.95 (ISBN 0-689-70608-1). Atheneum.
Mazzei, George. Shaping up: The Complete Guide to a Customized Fitness Program. (Orig.). 1981. pap. 7.95 (ISBN 0-345-29471-8). Ballantine.
Mellerowicz, Harald. Ergometry: Basics of Medical Exercise Testing. Smodlaka, Vojin N., ed. Rice, Allan L., tr. from Ger. 1981. text ed. write for info. (ISBN 0-8067-1241-4). Urban & S.
Rawls, Eugene. A Handbook of Yoga for Modern Living. (Orig.). pap. 1.50 (ISBN 0-515-00958-X). Jove Pubns.
Rosenthal, Gary. Spalding Guide to Fitness for the Weekend Athlete. 7.95 (ISBN 0-916752-08-9). Green Hill.
Rutstrum, Calvin. Hiking Back to Health. LC 80-19803. (Illus.). 136p. (Orig.). 1980. pap. 5.95 (ISBN 0-934802-06-8). Ind Camp Supply.
Sprague, Ken. The Athlete's Body. 1981. 10.95 (ISBN 0-87477-140-4); pap. 7.95 (ISBN 0-87477-151-X). J P Tarcher.
Walsh, Barry & Douglas, Peter. Getting Fit the Hard Way. (Illus.). 1981. 12.50 (ISBN 0-7137-1086-1, Pub. by Blandford Pr England). Sterling.
Wassersug, Joseph D. Jarm-How to Jog with Your Arms to Live Longer. 1981. 11.95 (ISBN 0-87949-197-3). Ashley Bks.
Weider, Joe. The Best of Joe Weider's Muscle & Fitness Training Tips & Routines. (Illus.). 1981. 12.95 (ISBN 0-8092-5911-7); pap. 5.95 (ISBN 0-8092-5910-9). Contemp Bks.
--The Best of Joe Weider's Muscle & Fitness: The World's Leading Bodybuilders Answer Your Questions. (Illus.). 1981. 12.95 (ISBN 0-8092-5914-1); pap. 5.95 (ISBN 0-8092-5912-5). Contemp Bks.

PHYSICAL FITNESS–JUVENILE LITERATURE
Hockey, Robert V. Physical Fitness: The Pathway to Healthful Living. (Illus.). 195p. 1981. pap. text ed. 8.95 (ISBN 0-8016-2216-6). Mosby.

PHYSICAL GEOGRAPHY
see also Agricultural Geography; Caves; Climatology; Earth; Earthquakes; Erosion; Geochemistry; Geophysics; Glaciers; Lakes; Landforms; Man–Influence on Nature; Meteorology; Mountains; Ocean; Oceanography; Rivers; Sedimentation and Deposition; Speleology; Volcanoes; Water, Underground; Watersheds; Winds
also Lakes, Mountains, Ocean, Plains, Rivers, Valleys, and other geographical terms
Knapp, B. J., ed. Practical Foundations of Physical Geography. (Illus.). 152p. 1981. pap. text ed. 11.50x (ISBN 0-04-551035-0, 2590); tchr's ed. 13.50x (ISBN 0-04-551034-2, 2589). Allen Unwin.

PHYSICAL MEASUREMENTS
see also Dimensional Analysis; Mensuration; Physics–Laboratory Manuals; Time Measurements
Lunar & Planetary Institute, compiled by. Proceedings: Eleventh Lunar & Planetary Science Conference, Houston, Texas, March 17-21, 1980, 3 vols. (Geochimica & Cosmochimica Acta: Suppl. 14). 3000p. 1981. Set. 200.00 (ISBN 0-08-026314-3). Pergamon.

PHYSICAL OCEANOGRAPHY
see Oceanography

PHYSICAL RESEARCH
see Physics–Research

PHYSICAL STAMINA
see Physical Fitness

PHYSICAL TRAINING
see Physical Education and Training

PHYSICALISM
see Logical Positivism

PHYSICALLY HANDICAPPED
see also Amputees; Deaf
Katz, Irwin. Stigma: A Social Psychological Analysis. LC 80-20765. 180p. 1981. ref. 16.50 (ISBN 0-89859-078-7). L Erlbaum Assocs.
Panckhurst, J. Focus on Physical Handicap. 158p. 1981. pap. text ed. 16.00x (ISBN 0-85633-217-8, NFER). Humanities.

PHYSICALLY HANDICAPPED–PERSONAL NARRATIVES
Knutzleman, Charles T. & Cryderman, Lynx. They Accepted the Challenge. (Illus.). 304p. 1981. 11.95 (ISBN 0-312-79971-3). St Martin.
Shannon, Fred. The Life & Agony of the Elephant Man. (Orig.). 1979. pap. 2.25 (ISBN 0-532-23280-1). Manor Bks.

PHYSICALLY HANDICAPPED–REHABILITATION
see also Cookery for the Physically Handicapped
Bray, Jean & Wright, Sheila, eds. The Use of Technology in the Care of the Elderly & the Disabled. LC 80-17847. xii, 267p. 1980. lib. bdg. 29.95 (ISBN 0-313-22616-4, BTC/). Greenwood.

PHYSICALLY HANDICAPPED AND LIBRARIES
see Libraries and the Physically Handicapped

PHYSICIAN AND PATIENT
Bille, Donald A. Practical Approaches to Patient Teaching. 1981. pap. text ed. write for info (ISBN 0-316-09498-6). Little.
Clark, L. Roy & Locke, Sam. How to Survive Your Doctor's Care. (Illus.). 96p. 1981. pap. 4.95 (ISBN 0-87786-005-X). Gold Penny.
Goen, Ted, Jr. Smile or I'll Kick Your Bed. (Illus.). 1981. 12.95 (ISBN 0-393-01433-9). Norton.
Gordon, Laura B. Behavioral Intervention in Health Care. (Behavioral Sciences for Health Care Professionals Ser.). 128p. 1981. lib. bdg. 15.00x (ISBN 0-86531-018-1); pap. text ed. 6.00x (ISBN 0-86531-019-X). Westview.
Huttmann, Barbara. The Patient's Advocate, the Complete Handbook of Patient's Rights: How to Get Them & How to Use Them to Save Your Time, Your Money, & Your Life. LC 80-52005. 400p. 1981. 16.95 (ISBN 0-670-54273-3). Viking Pr.
Mendelson, Robert S. Male Practice: How Doctors Manipulate Women. 1981. 10.95 (ISBN 0-8092-5974-5). Contemp Bks.
Physician-Patient Communication: Readings & Recommendations. write for info (ISBN 0-398-04465-1). C C Thomas.
Romfh, Richard F. Patients' Guide to Doctors: How to Hire & Fire Your Doctor to Save Your Life. Date not set. 15.95 (ISBN 0-87949-199-X). Ashley Bks.
Simpson, Peter & Levitt, Ruth. Going Home. (Illus.). 400p. 1981. pap. text ed. 20.00 (ISBN 0-443-01839-1). Churchill.
Ziegler, A. Doctor's Administrative Program, 6 vols. Incl. Dap 1. Patient Contract & Public Relations (ISBN 0-87489-150-7); Dap 2. Bookkeeping & Tax Reports (ISBN 0-87489-151-5); Dap 3. Insurance & Third-Party-Payable Claims (ISBN 0-87489-152-3); Dap 4. Correspondence (ISBN 0-87489-153-1); Billing & Collections; Dap 6. Patient Records Control (ISBN 0-87489-155-8). 1978. Set. write for info. (ISBN 0-87489-158-2); Ea. Vol. write for info.

PHYSICIANS
see also Public Relations–Physicians; Women Physicians
Fine, Carla. Married to Medicine. LC 80-69372. 1981. 11.95 (ISBN 0-689-11128-2). Atheneum.
Gish, Oscar. Doctor Migration & World Health. 151p. 1971. pap. text ed. 6.90x (ISBN 0-7135-1611-9, Pub. by Bedford England). Renouf.
Rogers, R. Vashon, Jr. The Law & Medical Men. xiii, 214p. 1981. Repr. of 1884 ed. lib. bdg. 22.00x (ISBN 0-8377-1032-4). Rothman.
Rose, Hilarly. Doctors, Patients & Pathology. 79p. 1972. pap. text ed. 5.00x (ISBN 0-7135-1741-7, Pub. by Bedford England). Renouf.
Salloway, J. C. Health Care Delivery Systems. (Behavioral Sciences for Health Care Professionals Ser.). 128p. (Orig.). 1981. lib. bdg. 15.00x (ISBN 0-86531-016-5); pap. text ed. 6.00x (ISBN 0-86531-017-3). Westview.

PHYSICIANS–BIOGRAPHY
Bowers, Garvey B. My Brother Will Take the Blame. 1981. 10.00 (ISBN 0-533-04929-6). Vantage.
De Wiest, Roger J. Night Flight to Brussels. LC 80-84739. 1981. 15.00 (ISBN 0-686-68869-4). Philos Lib.
Hes-Swartenberg, Hindle S. Jewish Physicians in the Netherlands Sixteen Hundred to Nineteen-Forty. (Illus.). 1980. pap. text ed. 17.75x (ISBN 90-237-1743-0). Humanities.
Siraisi, Nancy G. Taddeo Alderotti & His Pupils: Two Generations of Italian Medical Learning. LC 80-7554. 488p. 1981. 32.00x (ISBN 0-691-05313-8). Princeton U Pr.

PHYSICIANS–INSURANCE REQUIREMENTS
Klass, Richard A. The Physician's Business Manual. 400p. 1980. 23.50x (ISBN 0-8385-7850-0). ACC.
Ziegler, A. Doctor's Administrative Program, 6 vols. Incl. Dap 1. Patient Contract & Public Relations (ISBN 0-87489-150-7); Dap 2. Bookkeeping & Tax Reports (ISBN 0-87489-151-5); Dap 3. Insurance & Third-Party-Payable Claims (ISBN 0-87489-152-3); Dap 4. Correspondence (ISBN 0-87489-153-1); Billing & Collections; Dap 6. Patient Records Control (ISBN 0-87489-155-8). 1978. Set. write for info. (ISBN 0-87489-158-2); Ea. Vol. write for info.

PHYSICIANS–LEGAL STATUS, LAWS, ETC.
see Medical Laws and Legislation

PHYSICIANS–LICENSES
Grad, Frank P. & Marti, Noelia. Physicians' Licensure & Discipline. LC 79-21925. 471p. 1980. lib. bdg. 45.00 (ISBN 0-379-20463-0). Oceana.

PHYSICIANS–SALARIES, PENSIONS, ETC.
Klass, Richard A. The Physician's Business Manual. 400p. 1980. 23.50x (ISBN 0-8385-7850-0). ACC.

PHYSICIANS–GREAT BRITAIN
Abel-Smith, Brian. British Doctors at Home & Abroad. 63p. 1964. pap. text ed. 3.75x (Pub. by Bedford England). Renouf.

PHYSICIANS, WOMEN
see Women Physicians

PHYSICIANS IN LITERATURE
Yearsley, Percival M. Doctors in Elizabethan Drama. 128p. 1980. Repr. of 1933 ed. lib. bdg. 20.00 (ISBN 0-8495-6101-9). Arden Lib.

PHYSICIANS' INSURANCE
see Physicians–Insurance Requirements

PHYSICISTS
An Inventory of Published Letters to & from Physicists: 1900-1950. LC 80-51581. (Berkeley Papers in History of Science: No. VI). (Orig.). 1981. pap. write for info. (ISBN 0-918102-06-5). U Cal Hist Sci Tech.

PHYSICS
see also Agricultural Physics; Astrophysics; Biological Physics; Chemistry, Physical and Theoretical; Dynamics; Elasticity; Electricity; Electrons; Field Theory (Physics); Force and Energy; Friction; Gases; Geophysics; Gravitation; Heat; Hydraulics; Ions; Light; Magnetism; Magnetohydrodynamics; Mathematical Physics; Mechanics; Medical Physics; Meteorology; Music–Acoustics and Physics; Optics; Quantum Theory; Radiation; Solid State Physics; Sound; Statics; Thermodynamics; Weights and Measures
Beiser, Arthur. Concepts of Modern Physics. 3rd ed. (Illus.). 512p. 1981. text ed. 22.50 (ISBN 0-07-004382-5, C). McGraw.
Blaquiere, A., et al, eds. Dynamical Systems & Microphysics. (CISM - International Centre for Mechanical Sciences Courses & Lectures: Vol. 261). (Illus.). ix, 412p. 1980. pap. 39.00 (ISBN 0-387-81533-3). Springer-Verlag.
Blicher, Adolph. Field-Effect & Bipolar Power Transistor Physics. 1981. write for info. (ISBN 0-12-105850-6). Acad Pr.
Boardman, A. D. Physics Programs. Incl. Applied Physics. LC 80-40121. 136p (ISBN 0-471-27740-1); Magnetism. LC 80-40124. 106p (ISBN 0-471-27733-9); Optics. LC 80-40123. 134p (ISBN 0-471-27729-0); Solid State Physics. LC 80-40125. 144p (ISBN 0-471-27734-7). 1980. 13.50 ea. Wiley.
Cohen, I. Bernard. The Birth of the New Physics. LC 78-25792. (Illus.). 200p. 1981. Repr. of 1960 ed. lib. bdg. 19.75x (ISBN 0-313-20773-9, COBN). Greenwood.
Cullen, William. First Lines for the Practice of Physic. Bd. with Physiology. Peart, E. (Contributions to the History of Psychology Ser., Vol. XII, Pt. A: Orientations). 1980. Repr. of 1822 ed. 30.00 (ISBN 0-89093-314-6). U Pubns Amer.
Eisberg, Robert M. & Lerner, Lawrence S. Physics, Foundations & Applications, Vol. I. 720p. 1981. text ed. 21.95x (ISBN 0-07-019091-7, C); write for info study guide (ISBN 0-07-019111-5). McGraw.
--Physics: Foundations & Applications, Vol. II. (Illus.). 864p. 1981. text ed. 21.95 (ISBN 0-07-019092-5, C); solutions maual avail. (ISBN 0-07-019119-0); numerical calculations, suppl. avail. (ISBN 0-07-019120-4). McGraw.
--Physics: Foundations & Applications, Combined Vol. (Illus.). 1552p. 1981. text ed. 28.95x (ISBN 0-07-019110-7, C); price not set instrs'. manual (ISBN 0-07-019110-7); price not set numerical calculation supplement (ISBN 0-07-019120-4). McGraw.
Gabbay, S. M. Elementary Mathematics for Basic Chemistry & Physics. 128p. (Orig.). 1980. pap. 9.95 (ISBN 0-9604722-0-7). Basic Science Prep Ctr.
Guanghou Conference on Theoretical Particle Physics, 1980: Proceedings, 2 vols. 1980. text ed. 89.50 (ISBN 0-442-20273-3). Van Nos Reinhold.
Jeans, James. Physics & Philosophy. 232p. 1981. pap. price not set (ISBN 0-486-24117-3). Dover.
Khalatnikov, I. M. Physics Reviews Vol.III. (Soviet Scientific Reviews Ser.). 484p. 1980. 98.00 (ISBN 0-686-69597-6). Harwood Academic.
Kumakhov, M. Energy Losses & Ion Ranges in Solids. 1981. cancelled (ISBN 3-7186-0059-5). Harwood Academic.
Kursunoglu, Behram, et al, eds. Recent Developments in High-Energy Physics. (Studies in the Natural Sciences Ser.: Vol. 17). 320p. 1980. 39.50 (ISBN 0-306-40565-2, Plenum Pr). Plenum Pub.
McGregor, Donald R. The Inertia of the Vacuum: A New Foundation for Theoretical Physics. 96p. 1981. 6.00 (ISBN 0-682-49722-3). Exposition.
Marion, Jerry. Physics in the Modern World. 2nd ed. 1980. 20.95 (ISBN 0-12-472280-6). Acad Pr.
--Study Guide to Physics in the Modern World. 2nd ed. 1980. 5.95 (ISBN 0-12-472284-9). Acad Pr.
Metcalf, Harold J. Air Track Physics: A First Semester Laboratory Manual. 49p. 1980. pap. text ed. 4.95 (ISBN 0-8403-2286-0). Kendall-Hunt.
Nolan, Peter J. & Bigliani, Raymond E. Experiments in Physics. 1981. pap. text ed. price not set (ISBN 0-8087-1446-5). Burgess.
Nussbaumer, H. Fast Fourier Transform & Convoution Algorithms. (Springer Series in Information Sciences: Vol. 2). (Illus.). 330p. 1981. 36.60 (ISBN 0-387-10159-4). Springer-Verlag.
O'Dwyer, John J. College Physics. 752p. 1980. text ed. 22.95x (ISBN 0-534-00827-5). Wadsworth Pub.
Okebe, P. N. Preliminary Practical Physics. 1981. price not set (ISBN 0-471-27852-1, Pub. by Wiley-Interscience); pap. price not set (ISBN 0-471-27851-3). Wiley.
Park, David. The Image of Eternity: Roots of Time in the Physical World. 1981. pap. 5.95 (ISBN 0-452-00551-5, F551, Mer). NAL.
Pasachoff, Jay M. & Kutner, Marc L. Invitation to Physics. 1980. text ed. 16.95x (ISBN 0-393-95164-2); tchr's manual & test bank free (ISBN 0-393-95167-7). Norton.
Phillips, W. A., ed. Amorphous Solids. (Topics in Current Physics Ser.: Vol. 24). (Illus.). 190p. 1981. 32.00 (ISBN 0-387-10330-9). Springer-Verlag.
Prigogine, I. & Rice, Stuart A. Advances in Chemical Physics, Vol. 48. (Advances in Chemical Physics Ser.). 530p. 1981. 53.00 (ISBN 0-471-08294-5, Pub. by Wiley-Interscience). Wiley.
Prigogine, I. & Rice, Stuart A., eds. Advances in Chemical Physics, Vols. 27, 31-37, 43-44 & 46. Incl. Vol. 27. 50.50 (ISBN 0-471-69932-2); Vol. 31. 45.50 (ISBN 0-471-69933-0); Vol. 32. 35.95 (ISBN 0-471-69934-9); Vol. 33. 41.95 (ISBN 0-471-69935-7); Vol. 34. 41.50 (ISBN 0-471-69936-5); Vol. 35. 42.50 (ISBN 0-471-69937-3); Vol. 36. 52.50 (ISBN 0-471-02274-8); Vol. 37. 40.50 (ISBN 0-471-03459-2); Vol. 43. 1980. 36.50 (ISBN 0-471-05741-X); Vol. 44. 1980. 65.00 (ISBN 0-471-06025-9); Vol. 46. 432p. 1980. 42.50 (ISBN 0-471-08295-3). LC 58-9935 (Pub. by Wiley-Interscience). Wiley.
Reed, Michael & Simon, Barry. Methods of Modern Mathematical Physics, 4 vols. Incl. Vol. 1. Functional Analysis. 1972. 24.95 (ISBN 0-12-585001-8); Vol. 2. Fourier Analysis Self-Adjointness. 1975. 34.50 (ISBN 0-12-585002-6); Vol. 3. Scattering Theory. 1979. 42.00 (ISBN 0-12-585003-4); Vol. 4. 1978. 34.00 (ISBN 0-12-585004-2). Acad Pr.
Riban, David M. Introduction to Physical Science. (Illus.). 656p. 1981. text ed. 21.95 (ISBN 0-07-052140-9, C); instr's manual 4.95 (ISBN 0-07-052141-7). McGraw.
Rindler, W. Essential Relativity. rev. ed. (Texts & Monographs in Physics). (Illus.). 284p. 1980. pap. 19.80 (ISBN 0-387-10090-3). Springer-Verlag.
Robertson, Barry C. Modern Physics for Applied Science. 368p. 1981. text ed. 20.95 (ISBN 0-471-05343-0). Wiley.
Rochstrasser, R. M., et al, eds. Picosecond Phenomena II: Proceedings. (Springer Series in Chemical Physics: Vol. 14). (Illus.). 382p. 1981. 38.00 (ISBN 0-387-10403-8). Springer-Verlag.
Roller, Duane & Blum, Ronald. Fundamental Physics, 2 vols. Incl. Vol. 1. Mechanics, Waves & Thermodynamics; Vol. 2. Electricity, Magnetism, Light & Modern Physics. (Illus.). 1981. text ed. 22.95 ea.; text ed. 28.95 (ISBN 0-8162-7282-4); wkbk. & sol. manual avail. Holden-Day.
Rudman, Jack. Physics. (Undergraduate Program Field Test Ser.: UPFT-19). (Cloth bdg. avail. on request). pap. 9.95 (ISBN 0-8373-6019-6). Natl Learning.
Stafleu. Time & Again: A Systematic Analysis of the Foundations of Physics. 1981. 19.95x (ISBN 0-88906-108-4). Radix Bks.
Wilson, Jerry D. Physics: Concepts & Aplications. 2nd ed. (Illus.). 884p. 1981. text ed. 22.95 (ISBN 0-669-03373-1); instr's guide avail. (ISBN 0-669-01948-8); student guide 7.95 (ISBN 0-669-03362-6); lab guide 12.95 (ISBN 0-669-01947-X). Heath.

PHYSICS–ADDRESSES, ESSAYS, LECTURES
Guangzhou Conference on Theoretical Particle Physics 1980. Proceedings, Vols. 1 & 2. 1980. text ed. 89.50 (ISBN 0-442-20273-3, Pub. by Sci Pr China). Van Nos Reinhold.
Harnad, J. P. & Shnider, S., eds. Geometrical & Topological Methods in Gauge Theories: Proceedings. (Lecture Notes in Physics: Vol. 129). 155p. 1980. pap. 14.00 (ISBN 0-387-10010-5). Springer-Verlag.

PHYSICS–DICTIONARIES
Daintith, John, ed. The Facts on File Dictionary of Physics. 248p. 1981. 14.95 (ISBN 0-87196-511-9). Facts on File.

PHYSICS–EXPERIMENTS
Marton, Claire, ed. Methods of Experimental Physics: Fluid Dynamics, Vol. 18B. 1981. write for info. (ISBN 0-12-475956-4). Acad Pr.

PHYSICS–HISTORY

Clagett, Marshall. Studies in Medieval Physics & Mathematics. 366p. 1980. 75.00x (ISBN 0-86078-048-1, Pub. by Variorum England). State Mutual Bk.

Heilbron, J. L. & Wheaton, B. R. Literature on the General History of Physics in the First Half of the 20th Century. LC 80-51580. (Berkeley Papers in the History of Science: No. V). (Orig.). 1981. pap. write for info. (ISBN 0-918102-05-7). U Cal Hist Sci Tech.

PHYSICS–LABORATORY MANUALS

Bernard, C. H. & Epp, C. D. Laboratory Experiments in College Physics. 5th ed. 1981. 13.50 (ISBN 0-471-05441-0). Wiley.

PHYSICS–RESEARCH

Kumakhov, M. & Komarov, F. Energy Losses & Ion Ranges in Solids. 400p. 1981. price not set (ISBN 0-677-21220-8). Gordon.

PHYSICS–STUDY AND TEACHING

Marion, Jerry. Instructor's Manual for Physics in the Modern World. 2nd ed. 1980. 2.00 (ISBN 0-12-472282-2). Acad Pr.

PHYSICS, ASTRONOMICAL

see Astrophysics

PHYSICS, BIOLOGICAL

see Biological Physics

PHYSICS, NUCLEAR

see Nuclear Physics

PHYSICS, TERRESTRIAL

see Geophysics

PHYSICS RESEARCH

see Physics–Research

PHYSIOGNOMY

Bella, Leopold & Baker, Samm S. Reading Faces. LC 80-19235. (Illus.). 160p. 1981. 9.95 (ISBN 0-03-057869-8). HR&W.

PHYSIOGRAPHY

see Geology; Geomorphology; Physical Geography

PHYSIOLOGICAL ACOUSTICS

see Hearing; Music–Acoustics and Physics

PHYSIOLOGICAL ASPECTS OF READING

see Reading–Physiological Aspects

PHYSIOLOGICAL EFFECT OF CHEMICALS

see Pharmacology

PHYSIOLOGICAL PSYCHOLOGY

see Psychology, Physiological

PHYSIOLOGICAL STRESS

see Stress (Physiology)

PHYSIOLOGY

see also Anatomy; Blood–Circulation; Cells; Electrophysiology; Growth; Health; Homeostasis; Lymphatics; Metabolism; Muscles; Nervous System; Neurophysiology; Nutrition; Old Age; Pregnancy; Psychology, Physiological; Reproduction; Respiration; Rheology; Senses and Sensation

also names of organs and secretions, e.g. Heart, Kidneys, Bile, Gastric Juice

Adrian, R. H. Reviews of Physiology, Biochemistry, & Pharmacology, Vol. 88. (Illus.). 280p. 1981. 52.00 (ISBN 0-387-10408-9). Springer-Verlag.

Adrian, R. H., ed. Reviews of Physiology, Biochemistry & Pharmacology, Vol. 89. (Illus.). 260p. 1981. 54.30 (ISBN 0-387-10495-X). Springer-Verlag.

Burnside, John. Adams' Physical Diagnosis. 16th ed. (Illus.). 275p. 1981. write for info. soft cover (1137-5). Williams & Wilkins.

Feher, O. & Joo, F., eds. Cellular Analogues of Conditioning & Neural Plasticity: Proceedings of a Satellite Symposium of the 28th International Congress of Physiological Sciences, Szeged, Hungary, 1980. LC 80-41992. (Advances in Physiological Sciences: Vol. 36). (Illus.). 300p. 1981. 40.00 (ISBN 0-08-027372-6). Pergamon.

Gravitational Physiology: Proceedings of the 28th International Congress of Physiological Sciences, Budapest, 1980. LC 80-42103. (Advances in Physiological Sciences: Vol. 19). (Illus.). 350p. 1981. 40.00 (ISBN 0-08-027340-8). Pergamon.

Hainsworth, F. Reed. Animal Physiology: Adaptations in Function. (Life Sciences Ser.). (Illus.). 600p. 1981. text ed. 19.95 (ISBN 0-201-03401-8). A-W.

Hawker, Ross W. Notebook of Medical Physiology: Gastroenterological. (Illus.). 1981. pap. text ed. 12.50 (ISBN 0-443-02144-9). Churchill.

Heller, Lois J. & Mohrman, David E. Cardiovascular Physiology. Mixter, Richard W., ed. (Illus.). 176p. 1980. pap. text ed. 9.95 (ISBN 0-07-027973-X). McGraw.

Kovach, A. G. B., et al, eds. Cardiovascular Physiology, Microcirculation & Capillary Exchange: Proceedings of the 28th International Congress of Physiological Sciences, Budapest, 1980. LC 80-41873. (Advances in Physiological Sciences: Vol. 7). (Illus.). 400p. 1981. 50.00 (ISBN 0-08-026819-6). Pergamon.

--Cardiovascular Physiology, Heart, Peripheral Circulation & Methodology: Proceedings of the 28th International Congress of Physiological Sciences, Budapest, Hungary, 1980. LC 80-41875. (Advances in Physiological Sciences). (Illus.). 400p. 1981. 50.00 (ISBN 0-08-026820-X). Pergamon.

--Cardiovascular Physiology-Neural Control Mechanisms: Proceesings of the 28th International Congress of Physiological Sciences, Budapest, 1980. LC 80-41927. (Advances in Physiological Sciences: Vol. 9). (Illus.). 400p. 1981. 50.00 (ISBN 0-08-026821-8). Pergamon.

Magendie, Francois. Elementary Treatise on Human Physiology. Revere, John, tr. from Fr. Bd. with Mind & the Brain. Binet, Alfred; An Essay. Huxley, T. H. (Contributions to the History of Psychology, Vol. IV, Pt. E: Physiological Psychology). 1978. Repr. of 1844 ed. 30.00 (ISBN 0-89093-177-1). U Pubns Amer.

Obal, F. & Benedek, G., eds. Environmental Physiology: Proceedings of the 28th International Congress of Physiological Sciences, Budapest, 1980 (Including the Satellite Symposium on Sports Physiology) LC 80-42102. (Advances in Physiological Sciences: Vol. 18). (Illus.). 375p. 1981. 40.00 (ISBN 0-08-027339-4). Pergamon.

Rudman, Jack. Anatomy & Physiology. (College Proficiency Examination Ser.: CLEP-37). (Cloth bdg. avail. on request). pap. 9.95 (ISBN 0-8373-5437-4). Natl Learning.

Salanki, J., et al, eds. Physiology of Non-Excitable Cells: Proceedings of the 28th International Congress of Physiological Sciences, Budapest, 1980. LC 80-41874. (Advannces in Physiological Sciences: Vol. 3). (Illus.). 350p. 1981. 40.00 (ISBN 0-08-026815-3). Pergamon.

--Physiology of Excitable Membranes: Proceedings of the 28th International Congress of Physiological Sciences, Budapest, 1980. LC 80-41853. (Advances in Physiological Sciences: Vol. 4). (Illus.). 350p. 1981. 40.00 (ISBN 0-08-026816-1). Pergamon.

Sturkie, P. D., ed. Basic Physiology. (Illus.). 350p. 1981. 19.80 (ISBN 0-387-90485-9). Springer-Verlag.

Szelenyi, Z & Szekely, M. Contributions to Thermal Physiology: Proceedings of a Satellite Symposium of the 28th International Congress of Physiological Sciences, Budapest, 1980. LC 80-41854. (Advances in Physiological Sciences Ser.: Vol. 32). (Illus.). 560p. 1981. 60.00 (ISBN 0-08-027354-8). Pergamon.

PHYSIOLOGY–LABORATORY MANUALS

Erskine, Irene. Laboratory Guide for Anatomy & Physiology. 176p. 1980. pap. text ed. 8.95 (ISBN 0-8403-2350-6). Kendall-Hunt.

PHYSIOLOGY, COMPARATIVE

see also Laboratory Animals

also Birds, Animals, and similar headings with or without the subdivision Physiology

Brendel, W. & Zink, R. A., eds. High Altitude Physiology & Medicine I: Physiology of Adaptation. (Topics in Environmental Physiology & Medicine Ser.). (Illus.). 190p. 1981. 39.80 (ISBN 0-387-90482-4). Springer-Verlag.

Pethes, G. & Frenyo, V. L. Advances in Animal & Comparative Physiology: Proceedings of the 28th International Congress of Physiological Sciences, Budapest, 1980. LC 80-41894. (Advances in Physiological Sciences: Vol. 20). (Illus.). 400p. 1981. 50.00 (ISBN 0-08-027341-6). Pergamon.

PHYSIOLOGY, MOLECULAR

see Biological Physics

PHYSIOLOGY OF PLANTS

see Plant Physiology

PHYSIQUE PHOTOGRAPHY

see Photography of Men

PHYTOCHEMISTRY

see Botanical Chemistry

PHYTOGEOGRAPHY

see also Plants–Migration

Stott, Philip. Historical Plant Geography. (Illus.). 192p. 1981. text ed. 30.00x (ISBN 0-04-580010-3, 2641-2); pap. text ed. 14.95x (ISBN 0-04-580011-1). Allen Unwin.

PHYTOGRAPHY

see Botany

PHYTOHORMONES

see Plant Hormones

PHYTOLOGY

see Botany

PHYTOPATHOGENIC FUNGI

see Fungi, Phytopathogenic

PHYTOPATHOLOGY

see Plant Diseases

PHYTOPHTORA

Zentmyer, George A., ed. Phytophthora Cinna Moni & the Diseases It Causes. (Monograph Ser.: No. 10). 96p. 1980. 8.00 (ISBN 0-89054-030-6). Am Phytopathol Soc.

PHYTOSOCIOLOGY

see Plant Communities

PHYTOTHERAPY

see Materia Medica, Vegetable

PIAGET, JEAN, 1896-

Boden, Margaret A. Jean Piaget. (The Modern Masters Ser.). 1980. pap. 4.95 (ISBN 0-14-005327-1). Penguin.

Furth, Hans G. Piaget & Knowledge: Theoretical Foundations. LC 80-26284. (Illus., Orig.). 1981. pap. price not set (ISBN 0-226-27420-9). U of Chicago Pr.

Hersh, Richard H., et al. Promoting Moral Growth: From Piaget to Kohlberg. LC 78-19945. 256p. 1979. pap. text ed. write for info. Longman.

Sigel, I. E., et al, eds. New Directions in Piagetian Theory & Practice. 320p. 1981. ref. 19.95 (ISBN 0-89859-072-8). L Erlbaum Assocs.

PIANISTS–CORRESPONDENCE, REMINISCENCES, ETC.

see Musicians–Correspondence, Reminiscences, Etc.

PIANO–HISTORY

Colt, C. F. & Miall, Anthony. The Early Piano. (Illus.). 160p. 1981. 75.00x (ISBN 0-389-20187-1). B&N.

PIANO–INSTRUCTION AND STUDY

see also Harmony, Keyboard; Musical Accompaniment

Chase, Mildred P. Just Being at the Piano. LC 80-8999. 112p. (Orig.). 1981. 9.95 (ISBN 0-915238-44-6); pap. 5.95 (ISBN 0-915238-45-4). Peace Pr.

Dallen. Piano Study for Beginners. 1981. pap. 14.95 (ISBN 0-13-675603-4). P-H.

Oestereich, James & Pennington, Earl. Improving & Arranging on the Keyboard. (Illus.). 208p. 1981. 16.95 (ISBN 0-13-453563-4, Spec); pap. 7.95 (ISBN 0-13-453555-3). P-H.

Ortmann, Otto. The Physiological Mechanics of Piano Technique. (Music Ser.). (Illus.). xvi, 396p. 1981. Repr. of 1929 ed. lib. bdg. 39.50 (ISBN 0-306-76058-4). Da Capo.

Singletary, Dasie. Parents: The Child's First Piano Teacher. (Illus.). 32p. (gr. k-4). 1980. PLB 5.95 (ISBN 0-89962-042-6). Todd & Honeywell.

PIANO–METHODS

Cooper, Peter. Style in Piano Playing. 1980. 11.95 (ISBN 0-7145-3512-5). Riverrun NY.

PIANO AND VIOLONCELLO MUSIC

see Violoncello and Piano Music

PIANO MUSIC

Anderson, Leroy. Leroy Anderson: Twenty-Five Melodies for Piano Solo. Orig. Title: Leroy Anderson (Almost Complete) (Illus.). 1980. pap. 6.95. Dover.

Chopin, Frederic. Waltzes for Piano. (Carl Fischer Music Library: No. 309). 80p. (gr. 9-12). 1902. pap. 3.00 (ISBN 0-686-64064-0, L 309). Fischer Inc NY.

Peters, C. F. Complete String Quartets Transcribed for Four-Hand Piano, 2 series. unabr. ed. Ser. 1, 320p. pap. 7.95 (ISBN 0-486-23974-8); Ser. 2, 256p. pap. 6.95 (ISBN 0-486-23975-6). Dover.

PIANO TRADE

see Music Trade

PICASSO, PABLO, 1881-1973

Frevert, Patricia D. Pablo Picasso, Twentieth Century Genius. Redpath, Ann, ed. (People to Remember Ser.). (Illus.). 32p. (gr. 5-9). 1981. PLB 5.95 (ISBN 0-87191-800-5). Creative Ed.

Rubin, William, ed. Pablo Picasso: A Retrospective. (Illus.). 1981. pap. 25.00 (ISBN 0-686-69217-9). NYGS.

Russell, Frank D. Picasso's Guernica: The Labyrinth of Narrative and Vision. LC 79-52472. 350p. 1980. text ed. 35.00 (ISBN 0-8390-0243-2). Allanheld.

PICKLING

see Canning and Preserving

PICKUP CAMPERS

see Campers and Coaches, Truck

PICNICKING

see also Cookery, Outdoor

Chatfield-Taylor, Joan. Picnics. LC 79-64872. (Illus.). 1980. pap. 4.95 (ISBN 0-394-73760-1). Taylor & NG.

PICTORIAL PHOTOGRAPHY

see Photography, Artistic

PICTURE-BOOKS FOR CHILDREN

Aylesworth, Jim. Tonight's the Night. Fay, Ann, ed. (Self-Starter Bks.). (Illus.). 32p. (ps-1). 1981. 6.50 (ISBN 0-8075-8020-1). A Whitman.

Barber, Phyllis. Smiley Snake's Adventure. Jordan, Alton, ed. (Buppet Series). (Illus.). (gr. k-3). 1981. PLB 4.50 (ISBN 0-89868-098-0, Read Res); pap. text ed. 1.95 (ISBN 0-89868-109-X). ARO Pub.

Batherman, Muriel. Before Columbus. (gr. k-3). 1981. 8.95 (ISBN 0-395-30088-6). HM.

Beers, V. Gilbert. With Mini & Maxi in Muffkinland. (Muffin Family Adventure Ser.). 79p. (gr. k-4). 1981. text ed. 8.95 (ISBN 0-8024-4063-0). Moody.

Big Birds B Book. (Wipe off Bks.). 9p. (ps). Date not set. 2.39 (ISBN 0-307-01842-3, Golden Pr). Western Pub.

Blume, Judy. The One in the Middle Is the Green Kangaroo. (Illus.). 40p. (ps-3). 1981. 7.95 (ISBN 0-87888-182-4). Bradbury Pr.

Brothers Grimm. The Seven Ravens. Crawford, Elizabeth D., tr. from Ger. LC 80-25365. (Illus.). 24p. (gr. k-3). 1981. 8.95 (ISBN 0-688-00371-0); PLB 8.59 (ISBN 0-688-00372-9). Morrow.

De Paola, Tomie. The Comic Adventures of Old Mother Hubbard & Her Dog. LC 80-19270. (Illus.). 32p. (ps-3). 1981. 11.95 (ISBN 0-15-219541-6, HJ). HarBraceJ.

De Papp Severo, Emoke. The Good-Hearted Youngest Brother. (Illus.). 32p. (gr. k-3). 1981. 9.95 (ISBN 0-87888-141-7). Bradbury Pr.

Dewey, Ariane. The Thunder God's Son. LC 80-16325. (Illus.). 32p. (gr. k-4). 1981. 7.95 (ISBN 0-688-80295-8); PLB 7.63 (ISBN 0-688-84295-X). Greenwillow.

Enderle, Judith A. Good Junk. (Illus.). 32p. (ps-3). 1981. 5.95 (ISBN 0-525-66720-2). Elsevier-Nelson.

Ernie & Bert Present Finish the Story. (Wipe off Bks.). 9p. (ps). 2.39 (ISBN 0-307-01844-X, Golden Pr). Western Pub.

Ford, Barbara. Black Bear. (gr. 7 up). 1981. 8.95 (ISBN 0-395-30444-X). HM.

Four Golden Learning Bee Books. Date not set. pap. 2.95 boxed set (ISBN 0-307-13638-8, Golden Pr). Western Pub.

Freeman, Don. Norman the Doorman. (Picture Puffins Ser.). (Illus.). (ps-3). 1981. pap. 1.95 (ISBN 0-14-050288-2, Puffin). Penguin.

Friedman, Joy T. The Important Thing About. LC 80-83936. (Illus.). 96p. (gr. k-2). 1981. PLB 10.15 (ISBN 0-448-13947-2); pap. 3.95 (ISBN 0-448-14754-8). G&D.

Fujikawa, Gyo. Come Out & Play. (Gyo Fujikawa Tiny Board Books). (Illus.). 14p. (ps-k). 1981. 1.95 (ISBN 0-448-15115-4). G&D.

--Fairyland. (Gyo Fujikawa Tiny Board Books). (Illus.). 14p. (ps-k). 1981. 1.95 (ISBN 0-448-15139-1). G&D.

--Make-Believe. (Gyo Fujikawa Tiny Board Books). (Illus.). 14p. (ps-k). 1981. 1.95 (ISBN 0-448-15127-8). G&D.

--Mother Goose. (Gyo Fujikawa Tiny Board Books). (Illus.). 14p. (ps-k). 1981. 1.95 (ISBN 0-448-15091-3). G&D.

Graig, M. J. The Man Whose Name Was Not Thomas. (Illus.). 32p. (gr. k-3). 1981. 7.95a (ISBN 0-385-15064-4); PLB (ISBN 0-385-15065-2). Doubleday.

Grover Presents Finish the Picture. (Wipe-off Bks). 9p. (ps). 2.39 (ISBN 0-307-01841-5, Golden Pr). Western Pub.

Hoban, Tana. Take Another Look. LC 80-21342. (Illus.). 32p. (ps-3). 1981. 7.95 (ISBN 0-688-80298-2); PLB 7.63 (ISBN 0-688-84298-4). Greenwillow.

Holl, Adelaide. My Weekly Reader Picture Word Book. (Illus.). 128p. (ps-k). Date not set. pap. 5.95 (ISBN 0-671-42542-0, Little Simon). S&S.

Izawa, T. & Hijkata, S., illus. What Time Is It? (Puppet Storybooks). (Illus.). 18p. (gr. k-2). 1981. 3.50 (ISBN 0-448-09753-2). G&D.

Janosch. The Trip to Panama. (Illus.). 48p. (ps-3). 1981. 8.95 (ISBN 0-316-45766-3, Atlantic). Little.

Jeschke, Susan. Perfect the Pig. LC 80-39998. (Illus.). 48p. (gr. k-3). 1981. 9.95 (ISBN 0-03-058622-4). HR&W.

Krahn, Fernando. Here Comes Alex Pumpernickel. (Illus.). 32p. (ps up). 1981. 7.95 (ISBN 0-316-50311-8, Atlantic). Little.

Kraus, Robert. The Old-Fashioned Raggedy Ann ABC Book. Kraus, Pam, ed. (Illus.). 32p. (ps-2). 1980. 4.95 (ISBN 0-671-42552-8). Windmill Bks.

Marie, Geraldine. The Magic Box. (Illus.). 32p. (ps-3). 1981. 5.95 (ISBN 0-525-66721-0). Elsevier-Nelson.

Marshall, James. The Guest. (gr. k-3). 1981. pap. 3.45x (ISBN 0-395-31127-6). HM.

Moncure, Jane B. No! No! Word Bird. LC 80-29491. (Word Birds for Early Birds Ser.). (Illus.). 32p. (gr. k-2). 1981. PLB 5.50 (ISBN 0-89565-161-0). Childs World.

Most, Bernard. There's an Ape Behind the Drape. LC 80-24280. (Illus.). 32p. (gr. k-3). 1981. 6.95 (ISBN 0-688-00380-X); PLB 6.67 (ISBN 0-688-00381-8). Morrow.

My Word Book. LC 80-83586. (Illus.). 80p. (gr. k-3). 1981. PLB 11.85 (ISBN 0-448-13494-2); pap. 4.95 (ISBN 0-448-11548-4). G&D.

Nister, Ernest. Magic Windows: An Antique Revolving Picture Book. (Illus.). 14p. (ps up). 1981. 6.95 (ISBN 0-399-20773-2). Philomel.

Pape, Donna L. The Mouse at the Show. (Illus.). 32p. (ps-2). 1981. 5.95 (ISBN 0-525-66722-9). Elsevier-Nelson.

Provensen, Alice & Provensen, Martin, illus. A Peaceable Kingdom: The Shaker Abecedarius. (Picture Puffins Ser.). (Illus.). (gr. k-3). pap. 2.95 (ISBN 0-14-050370-6, Puffin). Penguin.

Reese, Bob. Who's a Silly Egg? Jordan, Alton, ed. (Buppet Series). (Illus.). (gr. k-3). 1981. PLB 4.50 (ISBN 0-89868-092-1, Read Res); pap. text ed. 1.95 (ISBN 0-89868-103-0). ARO Pub.

Reese, Bob, et al. Buppet Character Book Set, 10 bks. Jordan, Alton, ed. (Illus.). (gr. k-3). 1981. Set. PLB 45.00 (ISBN 0-89868-088-3, Read Res); pap. 19.50 set (ISBN 0-89868-099-9). ARO Pub.

Sans Souci, Robert & Sans Souci, Daniel. Song of Sedna. LC 80-627. (Illus.). 32p. (gr. 3). 1981. 8.95a (ISBN 0-385-15866-1); PLB (ISBN 0-385-15867-X). Doubleday.

Selman, LaRue. Boots, Two. Jordan, Alton, ed. (Buppet Series). (Illus.). (gr. k-3). 1981. PLB 4.50 (ISBN 0-89868-094-8, Read Res); pap. text ed. 1.95 (ISBN 0-89868-105-7). ARO Pub.

--The Hero, Two. Jordan, Alton, ed. (Buppet Series). (Illus.). (gr. k-3). 1981. PLB 4.50 (ISBN 0-89868-089-1, Read Res); pap. text ed. 1.95 (ISBN 0-89868-100-6). ARO Pub.

--JD & the Bee. Jordan, Alton, ed. (Buppet Series). (Illus.). (gr. k-3). 1981. PLB 4.50 (ISBN 0-89868-093-X, Read Res); pap. text ed. 1.95 (ISBN 0-89868-104-9). ARO Pub.

--Rain Frog. Jordan, Alton, ed. (Buppet Series). (Illus.). (gr. k-3). 1981. PLB 4.50 (ISBN 0-89868-091-3, Read Res); pap. text ed. 1.95 (ISBN 0-89868-102-2). ARO Pub.

--Sammy Skunk Plays the Clown. Jordan, Alton, ed. (Buppet Series). (Illus.). (gr. k-3). 1981. PLB 4.50 (ISBN 0-89868-097-2, Read Res); pap. text ed. 1.95 (ISBN 0-89868-108-1). ARO Pub.

Simon, Norma. Nobody's Perfect. Tucker, Kathleen, ed. (Concept Bks.). (Illus.). 32p. (gr. k-3). 1981. 6.50 (ISBN 0-8075-5707-2). A Whitman.

Six Looney Tunes Golden Shape Books, 6 bks. 144p. 1980. Set. pap. 3.50 (ISBN 0-307-13625-6). Western Pubs OH.

Smith, Glenna C. The Little Mouse Was a Grouch. Jordan, Alton, ed. (Buppet Series). (Illus.). (gr. k-3). 1981. PLB 4.50 (ISBN 0-89868-095-6, Read Res); pap. text ed. 1.95 (ISBN 0-89868-106-5). ARO Pub.

Stanek, Muriel. Starting School. Fay, Ann, ed. (Self-Starter Bks.). (Illus.). 32p. (ps-1). 1981. 6.50 (ISBN 0-8075-7617-4). A Whitman.

Stevenson, James. The Wish Card Ran Out! (Illus.). 32p. (gr. k-4). 1981. 7.95 (ISBN 0-688-80305-9); PLB 7.63 (ISBN 0-688-84305-0). Greenwillow.

Tax, Meredith. Families. (Illus.). 32p. (ps-3). 1981. 7.95 (ISBN 0-316-83240-5, Pub. by Atlantic). Little.

Taylor, Jody. A Child's Very Own First Book. (Gingerbread Bks.). (Illus.). (ps-2). 1980. 2.50 (ISBN 0-525-69035-2, Gingerbread); PLB 5.95 (ISBN 0-525-69036-0, Gingerbread). Dutton.

--My Favorite Toys. (Illus.). (ps). 1979. 2.50 (ISBN 0-525-69501-X, Gingerbread). Dutton.

Thayer, Jane. Clever Raccoon. LC 80-23119. (Junior Bks.). (Illus.). 32p. (gr. k-3). 1981. 7.95 (ISBN 0-688-00238-2); PLB 7.63 (ISBN 0-688-00239-0). Morrow.

Tong. Gary Tong's Crazy Cut-Outs. (ps-3). pap. 1.50 (ISBN 0-590-05738-3, Schol Pap). Schol Bk Serv.

Wilkin, Eloise, illus. Baby Listens. (Baby's First Golden Bks.). (Illus.). 8p. (ps). Date not set. 1.25 (ISBN 0-307-10754-X, Golden Pr). Western Pub.

--Baby Looks. (Baby's First Golden Bks.). (Illus.). 8p. (ps). Date not set. 1.25 (ISBN 0-307-10753-1, Golden Pr). Western Pub.

Willard, Nancy. The Marzipan Moon. LC 80-24221. (Illus.). 48p. (ps-3). 1981. pap. 4.95 (ISBN 0-15-252963-2, VoyB). HarBraceJ.

Winder, Jack. What Are Faces for? Jordan, Alton, ed. (Buppet Series). (Illus.). (gr. k-3). 1981. PLB 4.50 (ISBN 0-89868-096-4, Read Res); pap. text ed. 1.95 (ISBN 0-89868-107-3). ARO Pub.

Winnie-the-Pooh Every Day Is Special. (Wipe-off Bks.). 9p. (ps). 2.39 (ISBN 0-307-01845-8, Golden Pr). Western Pub.

Wolf, Aline D. A Book About Anna: For Children & Their Parents. (Illus.). 56p. (Orig.). 1981. pap. write for info. (ISBN 0-9601016-4-0). Parent-Child Pr.

PICTURE FRAMES AND FRAMING

Cantore, William J. & Cantore, Virginia B. Creative Picture Framing. (Illus.). 128p. 1981. 12.95 (ISBN 0-13-190645-3, Spec); pap. 6.95 (ISBN 0-13-190637-2). P-H.

PICTURE POST CARDS

see Postal Cards

PICTURE POSTERS

see Posters

PICTURES

see also Caricatures and Cartoons; Paintings; Portraits also engravings, Etchings, Paintings, and similar headings; and subdivision Pictorial works under various subjects, e.g. Natural history–Pictorial works

Mayor, A Hyatt. Prints & People: A Social History of Printed Pictures. rev. ed. LC 80-7817. (Illus.). 496p. 1980. 37.50x; pap. 12.50. Princeton U Pr.

PICTURES, HUMOROUS

see Caricatures and Cartoons; Wit and Humor, Pictorial

PIDGIN LANGUAGES

see Languages, Mixed

PIES

see Pastry

PIG

see Swine

PIGEONS

Aerts, Jan. Pigeon Racing. 1973. 14.95 (ISBN 0-571-08287-4, Pub. by Faber & Faber). Merrimack Bk Serv.

--Pigeon Racing: Advanced Techniques. (Illus.). 192p. 1981. pap. 7.95 (ISBN 0-571-11572-1, Pub. by Faber & Faber). Merrimack Bk Serv.

Goodwin, Derek. Pigeons & Doves of the World. 2nd ed. LC 76-55484. (Illus.). 464p. 1977. 32.50x (ISBN 0-8014-1100-9). Comstock.

Rotondo, Joe, ed. Rotondo on Racing Pigeons. (Illus.). 330p. 1981. 35.00. North Am Fal Hunt.

PIGMENTS

see also Dyes and Dyeing; Paint also names of pigments

Gutcho, M. H., ed. Inorganic Pigments: Manufacturing Processes. LC 80-16319. (Chemical Technology Review No. 166). 488p. 1980. 54.00 (ISBN 0-8155-0811-5). Noyes.

Thomas, Anne W. Colors from the Earth. 132p. 1980. 13.95 (ISBN 0-442-25786-4). Van Nos Reinhold.

PIGS

see Swine

PILATE, PONTIUS, 1ST CENTURY

Babb, Charles. Pontius Pilate, Vol. 2. 1981. 9.75 (ISBN 0-8062-1564-X). Carlton.

PILES (CIVIL ENGINEERING)

see Piling (Civil Engineering)

PILING (CIVIL ENGINEERING)

Institute of Civil Engineers. Behaviour of Piles. 244p. 1980. 75.00x (ISBN 0-901948-07-1, Pub. by Telford England). State Mutual Bk.

--Numerical Methods in Offshore Piling. 224p. 1980. 69.00x (ISBN 0-7277-0086-3, Pub. by Telford England). State Mutual Bk.

--Piles in Weak Rock. 244p. 1980. 35.00x (ISBN 0-7277-0034-0, Pub. by Telford England). State Mutual Bk.

Institute of Civil Engineers, ed. Large Bored Piles. 160p. 1980. 40.00x (ISBN 0-901948-67-5, Pub. by Telford England). State Mutual Bk.

Institute of Civil of Engineers. Recent Developments in the Design & Construction of Piles. 380p. 1980. 80.00x (ISBN 0-7277-0082-0, Pub. by Telford England). State Mutual Bk.

PILOT CHARTS

see Nautical Charts

PILOT GUIDES

French Pilot, Vol.1. 224p. 1980. 30.00x (Pub. by Nautical England). State Mutual Bk.

Robson, Malcolm. Channel Island Pilot. 176p. 1980. 27.00 (ISBN 0-245-53413-X, Pub. by Nautical England). State Mutual Bk.

Robson, Malcom. French Pilot, Vol. 2. 256p. 1980. 33.00x (ISBN 0-245-53382-6, Pub. by Nautical England). State Mutual Bk.

Winner, Walter, ed. Airman's Information Manual: Nineteen Eighty-One. 304p. 1981. pap. 5.50 (ISBN 0-911721-86-X). Aviation.

PILOTLESS AIRCRAFT

see Guided Missiles

PILOTS (AERONAUTICS)

see Air Pilots

PILOTS AND PILOTAGE

see also Navigation; Pilot Guides

Aviation Maintenance Publishers. Pilot Logbook. 72p. 1979. text ed. 3.95 (ISBN 0-89100-112-3, E*A-P*L*O-2). Aviation Maintenance.

Block, Richard A., ed. Ocean & Inland Operator License Preparation Course. rev. ed. (Illus.). 499p. 1979. pap. text ed. 42.00 (ISBN 0-934114-21-8). Marine Educ.

Federal Aviation Administration. Airline Transport Pilot: Airplane (Air Carrier) Written Test Guide. (Pilot Training Ser.). (Illus.). 189p. 1979. pap. 5.95 (ISBN 0-89100-199-9, EA-AC-61-87). Aviation Maintenance.

--Airman's Information Manual. (Pilot Training Ser.). (Illus.). 327p. 1980. pap. 4.95 (ISBN 0-89100-149-2, EA-149-2). Aviation Maintenance.

--Aviation Instructor's Handbook. (Pilot Training Ser.). 170p. 1977. pap. 3.75 (ISBN 0-89100-170-0, E*A-A*C60-14). Aviation Maintenance.

--Commercial Pilot Flight Test Guide. 2nd ed. (Pilot Training Ser.: Pilot Training Ser.). 70p. 1975. pap. 1.75 (ISBN 0-89100-172-7, E*A-A*C61-55A). Aviation Maintenance.

--Commercial Pilot Written Test Guide. 3rd ed. (Pilot Training Ser.). (Illus.). 141p. 1979. pap. 4.75 (ISBN 0-89100-110-7, E*A-A*C61-71B). Aviation Maintenance.

--Federal Aviation Regulations Handbook for Pilots. 2nd ed. (Pilot Training Ser.). (Illus.). 448p. 1980. pap. 6.95 (ISBN 0-89100-185-9, E*A-R*P-1A). Aviation Maintenance.

--Flight Instructor Written Test Guide. 3rd ed. (Pilot Training Ser.). (Illus.). 138p. 1979. pap. 6.00 (ISBN 0-89100-137-9, E*A-A*C61-72B). Aviation Maintenance.

--Instrument Flying Handbook. 3rd ed. (Pilot Training Ser.). (Illus.). 274p. 1971. pap. 6.00 (ISBN 0-89100-164-6, E*A-A*C61-27B). Aviation Maintenance.

--Instrument Rating Written Test Guide. 5th ed. (Pilot Bks.). (Illus.). 200p. 1977. pap. 3.75 (ISBN 0-89100-169-7, E*A-A*C61-8D). Aviation Maintenance.

--Pilot's Handbook of Aeronautical Knowledge. 2nd ed. (Pilot Training Ser.). (Illus.). 207p. 1971. pap. 7.50 (ISBN 0-89100-100-X, E*A-A*C61-23A). Aviation Maintenance.

--Private Pilot-Airplane Written Test Guide. 4th ed. (Pilot Training Ser.). (Illus.). 148p. 1979. pap. 3.00 (ISBN 0-89100-166-2, E*A-A*C61-32C). Aviation Maintenance.

--Private Pilot Flight Test Guide. 2nd ed. (Pilot Training Ser.). 92p. 1975. pap. 1.35 (ISBN 0-89100-171-9, E*A-A*C61-54A). Aviation Maintenance.

King, John & King, Martha. Answers & Explanations to Commercial Pilot Written Test Guide. (Pilot Training Ser.). (Illus.). 68p. 1979. pap. 6.95 (ISBN 0-89100-153-0, E*A-61-71-B*G). Aviation Maintenance.

--Answers & Explanations to Private Pilot - Airplane Written Test Guide. (Pilot Training Ser.). 58p. 1979. pap. 6.95 (ISBN 0-89100-104-2, E*A-61-32C*G). Aviation Maintenance.

--Combined Commercial Pilot Written Test Questions, Answers & Explanations Book. (Pilot Training Ser.). (Illus.). 210p. 1979. pap. 10.95 (ISBN 0-89100-167-0, EA-A C61-71 B-1). Aviation Maintenance.

--Flight Instructor's Written Test Questions, Answers & Explanations. combined ed. (Pilot Training Ser.). 1980. pap. 13.95 (ISBN 0-89100-200-6, E*A-A*C61-72B-1). Aviation Maintenance.

--Fundamentals of Instruction. (Pilot Training Ser.). 1979. pap. 2.95 (ISBN 0-89100-134-4, E*A-A*C61-90). Aviation Maintenance.

--Instrument Pilot Airplane Written Test Guide, Including Answers & Explanations. (Pilot Training Ser.). (Illus.). 290p. 1978. pap. 10.95 (ISBN 0-89100-196-4, E*A-A*C61-8D*G-1). Aviation Maintenance.

--Private Pilot - Airplane Written Test Questions Including Answers & Explanations. combined ed. (Pilot Training Ser.). (Illus.). 206p. 1979. pap. 8.95 (ISBN 0-89100-197-2, E*A-A*C61-32C-1). Aviation Maintenance.

King, Martha & King, John. Flight Instructor Written Test Answers & Explanations. (Pilot Training Ser.). 1980. pap. 8.95 (ISBN 0-89100-191-3, E*A-61-72B*G). Aviation Mainenance.

Robson, Malcolm. Channel Island Pilot. 176p. 1980. 27.00 (ISBN 0-245-53413-X, Pub. by Nautical England). State Mutual Bk.

Taylor, S. E. & Parmar, H. A. Ground Studies for Pilots. Incl. Vol. I. Radio Aids. 3rd ed. 200p. 1979. text ed. 26.50x (ISBN 0-246-11169-0); Vol. II. Plotting & Flight Planning. 130p. 1976. text ed. 19.95x (ISBN 0-246-11176-3); Vol. III. Navigation General. 232p. 1979. text ed. 26.50x (ISBN 0-246-11177-1). Pub. by Granada England). Renouf.

PIMA INDIANS

see Indians of North America–Southwest, New

PINCHOT, GIFFORD, 1865-1946

McGeary, M. Nelson. Gifford Pinchot: Forester-Politician. Freidel, Frank, ed. LC 78-66552. (The History of the United States Ser.: Vol. 12). 481p. 1979. lib. bdg. 36.00 (ISBN 0-8240-9700-9). Garland Pub.

PINDAR, 522-443 B.C.

Gerber, Douglas E. Pindar's Olympian I: A Commentary. (Phoenix Supplementary Volumes Ser.). 264p. 1981. 47.50 (ISBN 0-8020-5507-9). U of Toronto Pr.

PINE

see also individual species, e.g. Yellow Pine

Lanner, Ronald M. The Pinon Pine: A Natural & Cultural History. (Illus.). 160p. 1981. price not set (ISBN 0-87417-065-6). U of Nev Pr.

PINEAL BODY

Reiter, Russel J., ed. The Pineal Gland: Volume 1, Anatomy & Biochemistry. 288p. 1981. 72.95 (ISBN 0-8493-5714-4). CRC Pr.

Vollrath, L. E. The Pineal Organ. (Hanbuch der Mikroskopischen Anatomie: Vol. VI-7). (Illus.). 600p. 1981. 259.60 (ISBN 0-387-10313-9). Springer-Verlag.

PINKERTON, ALLAN, 1819-1884

Anderson, Lavere. Allan Pinkerton. (gr. k-6). Date not set. pap. price not set (ISBN 0-440-40210-7, YB). Dell.

PINTER, HAROLD, 1930-

Hinchliffe, Arnold P. Harold Pinter. rev. ed. (English Authors Ser.: No. 51). 1981. lib. bdg. 9.95 (ISBN 0-8057-6784-3). Twayne.

PIPE

see also Pipe-Fitting; Pipe Lines; Water-Pipes

Burkholder, Lloyd, Sr. Basic Pipe Estimating. 224p. (Orig.). 1981. pap. 15.50 (ISBN 0-910460-84-1). Craftsman.

International Conference on Internal & External Protection of Pipes, 1st. Proceedings. 1976. 60.00 (ISBN 0-900983-46-9). BHRA Fluid.

PIPE-WELDING

Kimbro, Ralph H. The Art of Pipewelding. 1981. 10.00 (ISBN 0-8062-1633-6). Carlton.

PIPE-FITTING

see also Plumbing

Engineering Industry Training Board. Training for Pipe Fitters, 23 vols. 1976. 41.95x. Intl Ideas.

PIPE LINES

see also Pipe; also subdivision Pipe Lines under special subjects, e.g. Petroleum–Pipe Lines

Marks, Alex. Oceanic Pipeline Computations. 560p. 1980. 75.00 (ISBN 0-87814-143-X). Pennwell Pub.

Shuldener, Henry L. & Fullman, James B. Water & Piping Problems: A Troubleshooter's Guide for Large & Small Buildings. 275p. 1981. 19.95 (ISBN 0-471-08082-9, Pub. by Wiley-Interscience). Wiley.

Welding Institute of Canada, Toronto, Ontario, ed. Pipeline & Energy Plant Piping--Design & Construction: Proceedings of the International Conference on Pipeline & Energy Plant Piping, Calgary, Alberta, Nov. 10-13, 1980. (Illus.). 360p. 1980. 40.00 (ISBN 0-08-025368-7). Pergamon.

PIPE-ORGAN

see Organ

PIRATES

see also Buccaneers

Saletore, R. N. Indian Pirates. 200p. 1980. pap. text ed. 11.25x (ISBN 0-391-02183-4, Pub. by Concept India). Humanities.

PISCICULTURE

see Fish-Culture

PITCH

Ellis, Alexander J. & Mendel, Arthur. Studies in the History of Musical Pitch. (Music Ser.). 238p. 1981. lib. bdg. 22.50 (ISBN 0-306-76020-7). Da Capo.

PITCHING (BASEBALL)

Shaw, Bob. Pitching. (Illus.). 1981. pap. 6.95 (ISBN 0-8092-5913-3). Contemp Bks.

PITTSBURGH FOOTBALL CLUB (NATIONAL LEAGUE)

Livinston, Pat. The Pittsburgh Steelers: A Pictorial History. LC 79-91292. 198p. 1980. 14.95 (ISBN 0-918908-11-6). Jordan & Co.

PITUITARY BODY

Bonneville, J. F., et al. Radiology of the Sella Turcica. (Illus.). 262p. 1981. 116.80 (ISBN 0-387-10319-8). Springer-Verlag.

PITUITARY BODY–DISEASES

Sheline, Glenn E., et al. Pituitary Adenomas. (Oncologic Multidisciplinary Decisions in Onology Ser.). (Illus.). 248p. 1981. pap. 50.00 (ISBN 0-08-027463-3). Pergamon.

PITUITARY HORMONES

Beardwell, C. Clinical Endocrinology: Pituitary, Vol. 1. (Butterworths International Medical Reviews Ser.). 1981. text ed. price not set (ISBN 0-407-02272-4). Butterworth.

PL-ONE (COMPUTER PROGRAM LANGUAGE)

see P L-One (Computer Program Language)

PLACER MINING

see Hydraulic Mining

PLACES OF RETIREMENT

see Retirement, Places of

PLAGUE

London College of Physicians. Certain Necessary Directions Aswell for the Cure of the Plague As for Preventing the Infection: Also Certaine Select Statutes. LC 79-84120. (English Experience Ser.: No. 939). 148p. 1979. Repr. of 1636 ed. lib. bdg. 14.00 (ISBN 90-221-0939-9). Walter J Johnson.

PLAGUE–LONDON

Lodge, Thomas. A Treatise of the Plague: Containing the Nature, Signes, & Accidents of the Same. LC 79-84119. (English Experience Ser.: No. 938). 92p. 1979. Repr. of 1603 ed. lib. bdg. 10.50 (ISBN 90-221-0938-0). Walter J Johnson.

PLAINS, THE GREAT

see Great Plains

PLANETOIDS

see Planets, Minor

PLANETS, MINOR

Berger, Melvin. Comets, Meteors & Asteroids. (Illus.). 64p. (gr. 10 up). 1981. PLB 6.99 (ISBN 0-399-61148-7). Putnam.

PLANNED PARENTHOOD

see Birth Control

PLANNING

see also Curriculum Planning; Economic Policy; Educational Planning; Lesson Planning; Regional Planning; Social Policy also subdivision Planning under facilities and services e.g. Cities and Towns–Planning

Bapat, Meera. Shelter for the Poor: The Case of Poona. (Progress in Planning Ser.: Vol. 15, Pt. 3). 85p. 1981. pap. 13.50 (ISBN 0-08-026811-0). Pergamon.

Diamond, D. R. & McLoughlin, J. B., eds. Progress in Planning, Vol. 12. 224p. 1980. 47.00 (ISBN 0-08-026100-0). Pergamon.

Ellis, Darryl J. & Pekar, Peter P. Planning for Non-Planners. 1981. 12.95 (ISBN 0-8144-5593-X). Am Mgmt.

The Limits of Planning. (Analysis Ser.). 1980. pap. 14.95 (ISBN 0-938526-02-2). Inst Analysis.

Reinharth, Leon, et al. The Practice of Planning: Strategic, Administrative, Operational. 352p. 1980. text ed. 19.95. Van Nos Reinhold.

Wilson, A. G. & Kirby, M. J. Mathematics for Geographers & Planners. 2nd ed. (Contemporary Problems in Geography Ser.). (Illus.). 424p. 1980. text ed. 36.00x (ISBN 0-19-874114-6); pap. text ed. 19.95x (ISBN 0-19-874115-4). Oxford U Pr.

PLANNING, CITY

see City Planning

PLANNING, CORPORATE

see Corporate Planning

PLANS

see Architectural Drawing; Maps; Mechanical Drawing

PLANT ANATOMY

see Botany–Anatomy

PLANT AND EQUIPMENT INVESTMENTS

see Capital Investments

PLANT ASSIMILATION

see Plants–Assimilation

PLANT ASSOCIATIONS

see Plant Communities

PLANT CHEMISTRY

see Botanical Chemistry

PLANT CLASSIFICATION

see Botany–Classification

PLANT COMMUNITIES

see also Botany–Ecology

Gehu, J. M., ed. Colloques Phytosociologiques VII: Lille 1978, le Vegetation Des Sois Tourbeux. 556p. (Fr.). 1981. lib. bdg. 75.00x (ISBN 3-7682-1260-2, Pub. by Cramer Germany). Lubrecht & Cramer.

PLANT DISEASES

see also Fungi, Phytopathogenic; Plants–Disease and Pest Resistance; Rusts (Fungi) also subdivision Disease and Pests under particular subjects, e.g. Trees–Diseases and Pests

Ainsworth, G. C. Introduction to the History of Plant Pathology. LC 80-40476. 220p. Date not set. price not set (ISBN 0-521-23032-2). Cambridge U Pr.

An Atlas of Sulphur Deficiency in Commercial Plants. 18p. 1978. pap. 5.00 (ISBN 0-643-00210-3, CO03, CSIRO). Unipub.

Ingram, D. S. & Helgeson, J. P. Tissue Culture Methods for Plant Pathologists: Organized by the British Plant Pathologists, Vol. 2. 250p. 1981. 47.50 (ISBN 0-470-27048-9). Halsted Pr.

Littlefield, Larry J. Biology of the Plant Rusts: An Introduction. (Illus.). 112p. 1981. text ed. 9.00. Iowa St U Pr.

Mace, M. E. & Bell, A. A., eds. Fungal Wilt Diseases of Plants. 1981. price not set (ISBN 0-12-464450-3). Acad Pr.
Maramorosch, Karl & Harris, Kerry. Plant Diseases & Vectors: Ecology & Epidemiology. 1981. price not set (ISBN 0-12-470240-6). Acad Pr.
Matthews, R. E. Plant Virology. 2nd ed. 1981. write for info. (ISBN 0-12-480560-4). Acad Pr.
Muentzig, Arne. Triticale: Results & Problems. (Advances in Plant Breeding Ser.: Vol. 10). (Illus.). 103p. (Orig.). 1979. pap. text ed. 35.00 (ISBN 3-489-76210-X). Parey Sci Pubs.

PLANT DISTRIBUTION
see Phytogeography

PLANT ECOLOGY
see Botany–Ecology

PLANT ENGINEERING
see also Factory and Trade Waste; Industrial Safety; Materials Handling; Plant Maintenance
Polimeros, George. Energy Cogeneration Handbook: Criteria for Central Plant Design. 264p. 1981. 39.50 (ISBN 0-8311-1130-5). Indus Pr.

PLANT FORMS IN DESIGNS
see Design, Decorative–Plant Forms

PLANT GENETICS
Nitzsche, Werner & Wenzel, Gerhard. Haploids in Plant Breeding. (Advances in Plant Breeding Ser.). (Illus.). 101p. 1977. pap. text ed. 28.00 (ISBN 3-489-75010-1). Parey Sci Pubs.
Roebbelen, Gerhard & Sharp, Eugene L. Mode of Inheritance, Interaction & Application of Genes Conditioning Resistance to Yellow Rust. (Advances in Plant Breeding Ser.: Vol. 9). (Illus.). 88p. (Orig.). 1978. pap. text ed. 25.00 (ISBN 3-489-71110-6). Parey Sci Pubs.

PLANT GEOGRAPHY
see Phytogeography

PLANT GROWTH
see Growth (Plants)

PLANT HORMONES
Macmillan, J., ed. Hormonal Regulation of Development I: Molcular Aspects of Plant Hormones. (Encyclopedia of Plant Physiology Ser.: Vol. 9). (Illus.). 681p. 1981. 134.60 (ISBN 0-387-10161-6). Springer-Verlag.
Went, R. W., et al. Phytohormones. (Landmark Reprint in Plant Science Ser.). 1937. text ed. 22.50 (ISBN 0-86598-004-7). Allanheld.

PLANT INVESTMENTS
see Capital Investments

PLANT LOCATION
see Industries, Location of

PLANT LORE
Henslow, G. The Plants of the Bible. 294p. 1981. Repr. of 1900 ed. lib. bdg. 75.00 (ISBN 0-8495-2375-3). Arden Lib.
Stokes, Donald. The Natural History of Wild Shrubs & Vines. LC 80-8219. (Illus.). 256p. 1981. 12.95 (ISBN 0-06-014163-8, HarpT). Har-Row.

PLANT MAINTENANCE
Information Resources on Industrial Maintenence & Repair. (UNIDO Guides to Information Sources Ser.: No.36). 86p. 1980. pap. 4.00 (UNID-236, UN). Unipub.
Lyons. Handbook of Industrial Lighting. 1981. text ed. price not set. Butterworth.

PLANT MIGRATION
see Plants–Migration

PLANT MORPHOLOGY
see Botany–Morphology

PLANT NUTRITION
see Plants–Nutrition

PLANT PATHOLOGY
see Plant Diseases

PLANT PHYSIOLOGY
see also Epiphytes; Fertilization of Plants; Growth (Plants); Plants–Assimilation; Plants–Metabolism; Plants–Nutrition; Plants–Reproduction
Briggs, W. R., et al, eds. Annual Review of Plant Physiology, Vol 32. (Illus.). 1981. text ed. 20.00 (ISBN 0-8243-0632-5). Annual Reviews.
Galston, Arthur. Green Wisdom. LC 80-68183. 1981. 12.95 (ISBN 0-465-02712-1). Basic.
Johnson, Christopher B. Physiological Processes Limiting Plant Productivity. 1981. text ed. price not set (ISBN 0-408-10649-2). Butterworth.
Osmond, C. B., et al. Physiological Processes in Plant Ecology: Towards a Synthesis with Atriplex. (Ecololgical Studies: Vol. 36). (Illus.). 500p. 1980. 49.80 (ISBN 0-387-10060-1). Springer-Verlag.

PLANT PROPAGATION
see also Seeds
Toogood, Alan. Propagation. LC 80-6164. (Illus.). 336p. 1981. 13.95 (ISBN 0-8128-2772-4). Stein & Day.

PLANT REPRODUCTION
see Plants–Reproduction

PLANT SOCIETIES
see Plant Communities

PLANT TAXONOMY
see Botany–Classification

PLANTATION CROPS
see Tropical Crops

PLANTATION LIFE
Hermann, Janet S. The Pursuit of a Dream. (Illus.). 288p. 1981. 17.50 (ISBN 0-19-502887-2). Oxford U Pr.
Smedes, Susan D. Memorials of a Southern Planter. Green, Fletcher M., ed. 408p. pap. 8.95 (ISBN 0-87805-132-5). U Pr of Miss.

PLANTING
see Agriculture; Gardening; Landscape Gardening; Trees

PLANTS
see also Alpine Flora; Aquatic Plants; Botany; Climbing Plants; Cryptogams; Fertilization of Plants; Flowers; Gardening; Growth (Plants); House Plants; Paleobotany; Succulent Plants; Tropical Plants; Weeds also names of individual plants, and headings beginning with the word Plant
Martin, W. C. & Hutchins, R. Flora of New Mexico, 2 vols. (Illus.). 3000p. 1980. Set. lib. bdg. 160.00x (ISBN 3-7682-1263-7, Pub. by Cramer Germany); Vol. 1. lib. bdg. 80.00x (ISBN 3-7682-1283-1); Vol. 2. lib. bdg. 8.00x (ISBN 3-7682-1284-X). Lubrecht & Cramer.
Pyenson, Louis L. Healthy Plant Handbook. (Illus.). 1981. lib. bdg. 15.00 (ISBN 0-87055-377-1). AVI.
Raven, Peter H., et al. Biology of Plants. 3rd ed. 1981. text ed. write for info. (ISBN 0-87901-132-7); write for info. lab manual (ISBN 0-87901-142-4); prep guide avail. (ISBN 0-87901-143-2). Worth.
Ross-Craig, Stella. Drawings of British Plants, 8 vols. Incl. Vol. 1 (ISBN 0-7135-1137-0); Vol. 2 (ISBN 0-7135-1138-9); Vol. 3 (ISBN 0-7135-1139-7); Vol. 4; Vol. 5 (ISBN 0-7135-1141-9); Vol. 6 (ISBN 0-7135-1142-7); Vol. 7 (ISBN 0-7135-1143-5); Vol. 8. (Illus.). 1980. 256.25 set (ISBN 0-7135-1110-9); 32.50 ea. Lubrecht & Cramer.

PLANTS–ANATOMY
see Botany–Anatomy

PLANTS–ASSIMILATION
Zinc Deficiency in Rice: A Review of Research at the International Rice Research Institute. (IRRI Research Paper Ser.: No. 9). 17p. 1977. pap. 5.00 (R049, IRRI). Unipub.

PLANTS–CLASSIFICATION
see Botany–Classification

PLANTS–DISEASE AND PEST RESISTANCE
Pest Resistance to Pesticides in Agriculture. 38p. 1970. pap. 6.00 (F1984, FAO). Unipub.
Recommended Methods for Meausurment of Pest Resistance to Pesticides. (FAO Plant Production & Protection Paper: No. 21). 136p. 1981. pap. 7.25 (ISBN 92-5-100883-3, F2079, FAO). Unipub.

PLANTS–DISEASES
see Plant Diseases

PLANTS–ECOLOGY
see Botany–Ecology

PLANTS–GENETICS
see Plant Genetics

PLANTS–GEOGRAPHICAL DISTRIBUTION
see Phytogeography

PLANTS–GROWTH
see Growth (Plants)

PLANTS–IDENTIFICATION
McGuire, Diane K., ed. Beatrix Farrand's Plant Book for Dumbarton Oaks. LC 80-12169. (Illus.). 1980. 20.00x (ISBN 0-88402-095-9, Ctr Landscape Arch); pap. 10.00x. Dumbarton Oaks.
Shaw, Richard J. & On, Danny. Plants of Waterton-Glacier National Parks & the Northern Rockies. Orig. Title: Plants of Waterton-Glacier National Parks. 160p. 1981. pap. 6.95 (ISBN 0-87842-137-8). Mountain Pr.

PLANTS–IMMUNITY
see Plants–Disease and Pest Resistance

PLANTS–METABOLISM
Richter, Gerhard. Plant Metabolism. 450p. 1980. 60.95x (ISBN 0-85664-955-4, Pub. by Croom Helm England). State Mutual Bk.
Wexler, Jerome. Secrets of the Venus's Fly Trap. LC 80-2775. (Illus.). 64p. (gr. 2-5). 1981. PLB 6.95 (ISBN 0-396-07941-5). Dodd.

PLANTS–MIGRATION
Baker, Robin, ed. The Mystery of Migration. LC 80-16839. (Illus.). 256p. 1981. 29.95 (ISBN 0-670-50286-3). Viking Pr.

PLANTS–MORPHOLOGY
see Botany–Morphology

PLANTS–NUTRITION
Food for Plants. (Discovering Soils Ser.: No. 6). 33p. 1978. pap. 5.00 (ISBN 0-643-02170-1, CO13, CSIRO). Unipub.
Holmes, M. R. Nutrition of the Oilseed Rape Crop. (Illus.). xii, 148p. 1980. 25.00x (ISBN 0-85334-900-2). Burgess-Intl Ideas.

PLANTS–PATHOLOGY
see Plant Diseases

PLANTS–PEST RESISTANCE
see Plants–Disease and Pest Resistance

PLANTS–REPRODUCTION
see also Fertilization of Plants
Johnson, Christopher B. Physiological Processes Limiting Plant Productivity. 1981. text ed. price not set (ISBN 0-408-10649-2). Butterworth.
Nitzsche, Werner & Wenzel, Gerhard. Haploids in Plant Breeding. (Advances in Plant Breeding Ser.). (Illus.). 101p. 1977. pap. text ed. 28.00 (ISBN 3-489-75010-1). Parey Sci Pubs.

PLANTS, CULTIVATED
see also Flowers; Gardening; Plants, Edible; Plants, Ornamental; Tropical Plants
Anderson, Frank J. Cultivated Flowers. (Abbeville Library of Art Ser.). (Illus.). 112p. (Orig.). 1981. pap. 4.95 (ISBN 0-89659-182-4). Abbeville Pr.
Benzing, David H. Biology of the Bromeliads. 300p. (Orig.). 1980. pap. write for info (ISBN 0-916422-21-6). Mad River.

PLANTS, EDIBLE
see also Mushrooms, Edible
Heiser, Charles B., Jr. The Sunflower. LC 74-15906. (Illus.). 198p. 1981. pap. 5.95 (ISBN 0-8061-1743-5). U of Okla Pr.
Kavasch, E. Barrie. Wild Edibles of the Northeast. (Northeast Color Ser.). (Illus.). 64p. (Orig.). 1981. pap. 4.95 (ISBN 0-686-69148-2). Hancock Hse.
Richardson, Joan. Wild Edible Plants of New England: A Field Guide, Including Poisonous Plants Often Encountered. (Illus.). 256p. (Orig.). 1981. pap. 9.95 (ISBN 0-89933-009-6). DeLorme Pub.

PLANTS, EFFECT OF AIR POLLUTION ON
Grace, J., et al. Plants & Their Atmospheric Enviroment. (British Ecological Society Symposia Ser.). 428p. 1981. 89.95 (ISBN 0-470-27125-6). Halsted Pr.

PLANTS, FOLK-LORE OF
see Plant Lore

PLANTS, FOSSIL
see Paleobotany

PLANTS, MEDICINAL
see Botany, Medical

PLANTS, ORNAMENTAL
Olson, Craig. Craig Olson's Decorating with Plants. Grooms, Kathe, ed. (Illus.). 110p. 1981. pap. 2.95 (ISBN 0-915658-31-3). Meadowbrook Pr.

PLANTS, PHOTOGRAPHY OF
see Photography of Plants

PLANTS, POTTED
Tarsky, Sue. The Potted Plant Book. (Illus.). 48p. (gr. 5 up). 1981. 9.95 (ISBN 0-316-83206-5). Little.

PLANTS, PROTECTION OF
see also National Parks and Reserves
Littlefield, Larry J. Biology of the Plant Rusts: An Introduction. (Illus.). 112p. 1981. text ed. 9.00. Iowa St U Pr.
Sill, Webster H., Jr. Integrated Plant Protection. (Illus.). 328p. 1981. text ed. 25.00. Iowa St U Pr.

PLANTS, SEX IN
see Plants–Reproduction

PLANTS AND ANIMALS, GEOGRAPHIC DISTRIBUTION OF
see Geographical Distribution of Animals and Plants

PLASMA (IONIZED GASES)
see also Exploding Wire Phenomena; Plasma Dynamics
Hora, Heinrich. Physics of Laser Driven Plasmas. 325p. 1981. 30.00 (ISBN 0-471-07880-8, Pub. by Wiley-Interscience). Wiley.
Pozhela, J. Plasma & Current Instabilities in Semiconductors. Germogenova, O. A., tr. (International Series in the Science of the Solid State: Vol. 18). (Illus.). 314p. 1981. 54.00 (ISBN 0-08-025048-3). Pergamon.
Schwarz, H. J., et al, eds. Laser Interaction & Related Plasma Phenomena, Vol. 5. 800p. 1981. 75.00 (ISBN 0-306-40545-8, Plenum Pr). Plenum Pub.
Veprek, S. & Venugopalan, M., eds. Plasma Chemistry: Volume III. (Topics in Current Chemistry: Vol. 94). (Illus.). 160p. 1980. 42.50 (ISBN 0-387-10166-7). Springer-Verlag.

PLASMA DYNAMICS
see also Magnetohydrodynamics
Leontovich, M. A., ed. Reviews of Plasma Physics, Vol. 8. 425p. 1980. 42.50 (ISBN 0-306-17068-X, Consultants Bureau). Plenum Pub.
Sitenko, A. G. Fluctuations & Non-Linear Wave Interactions in Plasmas. Kocherga, O. D., tr. (International Series in Natural Philosophy: Vol. 107). (Illus.). 250p. 1981. 42.00 (ISBN 0-08-025051-3). Pergamon.

PLASMA MEMBRANES
Daems, W. T., et al, eds. Cell Biological Aspects of Disease: The Plasma Membrane & Lysosomes. (Boerhaave Series for Postgraduate Medical Education: No. 19). 330p. 1981. PLB 68.50 (ISBN 90-6021-466-8, Pub. by Leiden U Pr). Kluwer Boston.

PLASTER CASTS
Chaney, Charles & Skee, Stanley. Plaster Mold & Model Making. 144p. 1981. Repr. of 1973 ed. text ed. write for info. (ISBN 0-89874-282-X). Krieger.

PLASTERING
Taylor, J. B. Plastering: A Practical Handbook. 3rd ed. (Illus.). 1980. 27.50x. Intl Ideas.

PLASTIC COATING
Gillies, M. T., ed. Solventless & High Solids Industrial Finishes: Recent Developments. LC 80-21553. (Chemical Technology Review: No. 179). (Illus.). 342p. 1981. 48.00 (ISBN 0-8155-0828-X). Noyes.

PLASTIC MATERIALS
see Plastics

PLASTIC MOLDING
see Plastics–Molding

PLASTIC PACKAGING
see Plastics in Packaging

PLASTIC PRODUCTS
see Plastics

PLASTIC SURGERY
see Surgery, Plastic

PLASTICITY
see also Plastics; Rheology
Gollin, Eugene S., ed. Developmental Plasticity: Behavioral & Biological Aspects of Variations in Development. (Developmental Psychology Ser.). 1981. write for info. (ISBN 0-12-289620-3). Acad Pr.

PLASTICS
see also Chemistry, Organic–Synthesis; Condensation Products (Chemistry); Plasticity; Rubber, Artificial also names of plastics, e.g. Nylon
Baker, John & Heyman, J. Plastic Design of Frames, 2 vols. Incl. Vol. 1. Fundamentals. 32.95 (ISBN 0-521-07517-3); pap. 15.95 (ISBN 0-521-29778-8); Vol. 2. Applications. 33.95 (ISBN 0-521-07984-5). LC 69-19370. (Illus.). 1969-1971. Cambridge U Pr.
Business Communications Co. Plastics Vs. Other Pipes, P-043R. 1980. 750.00 (ISBN 0-89336-270-0). BCC.
Dubois, J. Harry. Plastics. 6th ed. 480p. 1981. text ed. 32.00 (ISBN 0-442-26263-9). Van Nos Reinhold.
Grandilli, Peter A. Technician's Handbook of Plastics. 272p. 1981. text ed. 19.95 (ISBN 0-442-23870-3). Van Nos Reinhold.
Pritchard, G., ed. Developments in Reinforced Plastics, No. 1. (Illus.). xii, 283p. 1981. 62.00x (ISBN 0-85334-919-3). Intl Ideas.
U.S. Foamed Plastics Markets & Directory. LC 63-59134. 100p. 1979. pap. 25.00 (ISBN 0-87762-277-9). Technomic.

PLASTICS–DICTIONARIES
Whittington, Lloyd R. Whittington's Dictionary of Plastics. 2nd rev. ed. LC 78-73776. 1978. 25.00 (ISBN 0-87762-267-1). Technomic.

PLASTICS–MOLDING
Design & Manufacture of Plastic Injection Moulds. (Productivity Ser.: No. 13). 70p. 1979. pap. 8.25 (ISBN 92-833-1703-3, APO 93, APO). Unipub.

PLASTICS IN PACKAGING
Rich, Susan, ed. Kline Guide to the Packaging Industry. (Illus.). 324p. 1980. pap. 100.00. Kline.

PLATE TECTONICS
Geophysics Research Board. Continental Tectonics. (Studies in Geophysics). xii, 197p. 1980. pap. text ed. 13.50 (ISBN 0-309-02928-7). Natl Acad Pr.
Ollier, C. D. Tectonics & Landforms. (Geomorphology Texts Ser.). (Illus.). 304p. 1981. text ed. 50.00 (ISBN 0-582-30032-0). Longman.
Weyman, Darrell. Tectonic Processes. (Process in Physical Geography Ser.: No. 4). (Illus.). 128p. (Orig.). 1981. pap. text ed. 8.95x (ISBN 0-04-551044-X, 2653). Allen Unwin.

PLATING
see Metals–Finishing

PLATO, 427?-347 B.C.
Dombrowski, Daniel A. Plato's Philosophy of History. LC 80-5853. 225p. 1981. lib. bdg. 17.75 (ISBN 0-8191-1356-5); pap. text ed. 9.50 (ISBN 0-8191-1357-3). U Pr of Amer.
Jordan, Nehemiah. The Wisdom of Plato: An Attempt at an Outline, 2 vols. LC 80-1409. (Orig.). 1981. Set. lib. bdg. 47.50 (ISBN 0-8191-1408-1); Set. pap. text ed. 33.00 (ISBN 0-8191-1409-X). Vol. I, 544p. Vol. 2, 536p. U Pr of Amer.
Mackenzie, Mary M. Plato on Punishment. 272p. 1981. 22.50x (ISBN 0-520-04169-0). U of Cal Pr.
Rightridge, Allan. Plato & the Metaphysics of the State. (The Most Meaningful Classics in World Culture). (Illus.). 108p. 1981. 43.75 (ISBN 0-89266-297-2). Am Classical Coll Pr.
Vlastos, Gregory. Platonic Studies. 2nd ed. LC 80-8732. 520p. 1981. 35.00x; pap. 12.50. Princeton U Pr.
Zaslavsky, Robert. Platonic Myth & Platonic Writing. LC 80-5563. 306p. 1981. lib. bdg. 20.50 (ISBN 0-8191-1381-6); pap. text ed. 11.50 (ISBN 0-8191-1382-4). U Pr of Amer.

PLATO, 427?-347 B.C.–BIBLIOGRAPHY
Billings, Grace H. The Art of Transition in Plato. Taran, Leonardo, ed. LC 78-66578. (Ancient Philosophy Ser.: Vol. 2). 110p. 1979. lib. bdg. 13.00 (ISBN 0-8240-9609-6). Garland Pub.

PLATONISTS
Billings, Thomas H. The Platonism of Philo Judaeus. Taran, Leonardo, ed. LC 78-66560. (Ancient Philosophy Ser.: Vol. 3). 117p. 1979. lib. bdg. 13.00 (ISBN 0-8240-9608-8). Garland Pub.

PLAY
see also Amusements; Drama in Education; Games; Hobbies; Recreation; Sports
Cheska, Alyce T. Play As Context. (Illus., Orig.). 1981. pap. text ed. 12.95 (ISBN 0-918438-66-7). Leisure Pr.
Hans, James S. The Play of the World. LC 80-39630. 224p. 1981. lib. bdg. 15.00x (ISBN 0-87023-324-6); pap. 7.95 (ISBN 0-87023-325-4). U of Mass Pr.
Oxenbury, Helen. Playing. (Baby Board Bks.). (Illus.). 12p. (ps-k). Date not set. boards 3.50 (ISBN 0-671-42109-3, Little Simon). S&S.
Smith, P. K. & Connolly, K. J. The Ecology of Preschool Behaviour. LC 79-42647. (Illus.). 400p. Date not set. 49.50 (ISBN 0-521-22331-8). Cambridge U Pr.
Sternlict, Manny & Hurwitz, Abraham. Games Children Play: Instructive & Creative Play Activities for the Mentally Retarded & Developmentally Disabled Child. 128p. 1980. 12.95 (ISBN 0-442-25857-7). Van Nos Reinhold.

PLAY–THERAPEUTIC USE
see Play Therapy

PLAY DIRECTION (THEATER)
see Theater–Production and Direction

PLAY PRODUCTION (THEATER)
see Theater–Production and Direction

PLAY THERAPY

The Child & Play. (Educational Studies & Documents: No. 34). 68p. 1980. pap. 4.00 (ISBN 92-3-101658-X, U1030, UNESCO). Unipub.

Schaeffer, Charles E., ed. Therapeutic Use of Child's Play. LC 75-9556. 684p. 1981. Repr. of 1977 ed. 30.00 (ISBN 0-87668-209-3). Aronson.

PLAYBOY

Brady, Frank. Playboy's Hefner. 230p. 1980. 28.50 (ISBN 0-686-68307-2). Porter.

PLAYGROUND BALL

see Softball

PLAYING-CARDS

see Cards

PLAYS

see Drama

PLAYS, CHRISTMAS

see Christmas Plays

PLAYS, MEDIEVAL

see Mysteries and Miracle-Plays

PLAYS, TELEVISION

see Television Plays

PLAYS FOR CHILDREN

see Children's Plays

PLAYWRIGHTS

see Dramatists

PLECTRAL INSTRUMENTS

see Stringed Instruments

PLOTINUS, d. 270 A.D.

Helleman-Elgersma, W. Soul Sisters: A/Commentary on Enneads IV 3(27), 1-8 of Plotinus. 485p. 1980. pap. text ed. 51.50x (ISBN 90-6203-931-6, Pub. by Rodopi Holland). Humanities.

PLOVERS

Vaughan, Richard. Plovers. 160p. 1980. 25.00x (ISBN 0-900963-36-0, Pub. by Terence Dalton England). State Mutual Bk.

PLUMBING

see also Pipe-Fitting; Sanitary Engineering; Sewerage; Water-Pipes

D'Arcangelo, B. F., et al. Mathematics for Plumbers & Pipefitters. 3rd rev. ed. (Applied Mathematics Ser.). (Illus.). 210p. 1981. pap. text ed. price not set (ISBN 0-8273-1291-1); price not set instr's. guide. Delmar.

Lambrecht, Ann. Step-by-Step Plumbing. (Step-by-Step Home Repair Ser.). (Illus.). 96p. 1981. 4.95 (ISBN 0-696-00575-1). Meredith Corp.

Nielsen, Louis S. Standard Plumbing Engineering Design. (Illus.). 384p. 1981. 21.50 (ISBN 0-07-046541-X). McGraw.

Thiesse, James L. Plumbing Fundamentals. (Contemporary Construction Ser.). (Illus.). 192p. (gr. 10-12). 1981. 16.95x (ISBN 0-07-064191-9, G). McGraw.

Wilson, Scott. The Plumber's Bible. LC 76-42420. (Homeowner's Bible Ser.). (Illus.). 160p. 1981. pap. 4.95 (ISBN 0-385-11211-4). Doubleday.

PLUMBING-ESTIMATES

Massey, Howard C. Plumbing Estimators Handbook. 256p. (Orig.). 1981. pap. 15.25 (ISBN 0-910460-82-5). Craftsman.

PLUMBISM

see Lead-Poisoning

PLUNDER OF THE ARTS

see Art Thefts

PLURALISM

see also Atomism; Reality

Ehrlich, Stanislaw & Wooton, Graham, eds. Three Faces of Pluralism: Political, Ethnic, & Religious. 232p. 1980. 18.95x (ISBN 0-566-00313-9, 03274-3, Pub. by Gower Pub Co England). Lexington Bks.

Foote, Nancy, et al. Drawings: The Pluralist Decade. LC 80-83653. (Illus.). 1979. pap. 8.00 (ISBN 0-88454-057-X). U of Pa Contemp Art.

McClain, William B. Travelling Light. (Orig.). 1981. pap. 3.75 (ISBN 0-377-00109-0). Friend Pr.

Stack, John F., Jr., ed. Ethnic Identities in a Transnational World. LC 80-1199. (Contributions in Political Science Ser.: No. 52). 264p. 1981. lib. bdg. 27.50 (ISBN 0-313-21088-8, SEI/). Greenwood.

Wm. C. Brown Education Division Staff. Pluralism, Similarities, & Contrast: Aids to Understanding Religion in North America. (To Live Is Christ Ser.). 28p. (Orig.). 1979. wkbk. 10.95 (ISBN 0-697-01735-4). Wm C Brown.

PLURILINGUALISM

see Multilingualism

PLUTO, OPERATION

see Cuba-History-Invasion, 1961

PLYMOUTH AUTOMOBILE

see Automobiles-Types-Plymouth

PNEUMA

see Soul; Spirit

PNEUMATIC MACHINERY

Patrick, Dale R. Instrumentation Training Course: Electronic Instruments, 2 vols, Vol. 2. 2nd ed. LC 79-63866. 1979. pap. 11.95 (ISBN 0-672-21580-2, 21580); pap. 24.95 set (ISBN 0-672-21581-0). Sams.

Patrick, Dale R. & Patrick, Stephen. Instrumentation Training Course: Pneumatic Instruments, Vol. 1. 2nd ed. LC 79-63866. 1979. pap. 13.95 (ISBN 0-672-21579-9, 21579). Sams.

PNEUMATOLOGY (THEOLOGY)

see Spirit

PNEUMOCONIOSIS

see Lungs-Dust Diseases

PNEUMOGASTRIC NERVE

see Vagus Nerve

PNEUMOMASSAGE

see Massage

POCKET BATTLESHIPS

see Warships

POCKET COMPANIONS

see Handbooks, Vade-Mecums, etc.

PODIATRY

Clarke, Theodore H., ed. Yearbook of Podiatric Medicine & Surgery 1981. (Illus.). 512p. 1980. 49.00 (ISBN 0-87993-129-9). Futura Pub.

Gerbert, Joshua, ed. Textbook of Bunion Surgery. LC 80-68895. (Illus.). 300p. 1981. monograph 24.50 (ISBN 0-87993-153-1). Futura Pub.

Helfand, Arthur E. Clinical Podogeriatrics. (Illus.). 248p. 1981. write for info. (3951-2). Williams & Wilkins.

POE, EDGAR ALLAN, 1809-1849

Benton, Richard. Bedlam Patterns: Love & the Idea of Madness in Poe's Fiction. 1979. pap. 2.75 (ISBN 0-910556-13-X). Enoch Pratt.

Buranelli, Vincent, ed. Edgar Allan Poe. LC 77-7265. (Twaynes's U. S. Authors Ser.). 166p. 1977. pap. text ed. 4.95 (ISBN 0-672-61502-9). Bobbs.

Dameron, J. Lasley. Popular Literature: Poe's Not So Soon Forgotten Lore. Kadis, Averil J., ed. 1980. pap. 2.50 (ISBN 0-910556-16-4). Enoch Pratt.

Ewers, Hanns H. Edgar Allan Poe. 55p. 1980. Repr. of 1917 ed. lib. bdg. 10.00 (ISBN 0-8495-1347-2). Arden Lib.

Hammond, J. A. An Edgar Allan Poe Companion. (Companion Ser.). (Illus.). 1981. 27.50x (ISBN 0-389-20172-3). B&N.

Levin, Harry. The Power of Blackness: Hawthorne, Poe, Melville. LC 80-83221. xxii, 263p. 1980. pap. 6.95x (ISBN 0-8214-0581-0). Ohio U Pr.

Poe, Edgar Allan. Letters & Documents in the Enoch Pratt Free Library. Bd. with Merun & Recollections of Edgar A. Poe. Wilmer, Lambert A. LC 41-10640. 30.00x (ISBN 0-8201-1199-6). Schol Facsimiles.

Saliba, David R. A Psychology of Fear: The Nightmare Formula of Edgar Allan Poe. LC 80-8267. 277p. 1980. lib. bdg. 18.50 (ISBN 0-8191-1269-0); pap. text ed. 10.25 (ISBN 0-8191-1270-4). U Pr of Amer.

Whitman, Sarah H. P. Edgar Poe & His Critics. LC 80-26202. 105p. Repr. of 1949 ed. 9.00x (ISBN 0-686-69559-3). Gordian.

POETESSES

see Women Poets

POETICS

Here are entered treatises on the art of poetry (technique and philosophy) Works limited to the philosophy of poetry are entered under the heading Poetry.

see also Poetry-Authorship; Rhythm; Versification

James, David G. Scepticism & Poetry: An Essay on the Poetic Imagination. LC 80-21749. 274p. 1980. Repr. of 1960 ed. lib. bdg. 25.00x (ISBN 0-313-22840-X, JASP). Greenwood.

Jerome, Judson. The Poet's Handbook. LC 80-17270. 88p. 1980. 10.95 (ISBN 0-89879-021-2). Writers Digest.

Lindemann. Arnoldwesker Als Gesellschaftskritiker. (Poetic Drama & Poetic Theory Ser.). 1980. pap. text ed. 25.00x. Humanities.

Rajnath. T. S. Eliot's Theory of Poetry. 1980. text ed. 12.50x (ISBN 0-391-01755-1). Humanities.

Vowel & Dipthong Tones. 1977. pap. 1.95. Primary Pr.

POETRY

see also Ballads; Children'S Poetry; Epigrams; Hymns; Limericks; Nursery Rhymes; Religious Poetry; Sonnets; War Poetry

also English Poetry, French Poetry, etc. and subdivision Poetry under particular subjects and names of famous persons, e.g. Christmas-Poetry, Lincoln, Abraham-Poetry

Aldan, Daisy. The Art & Craft of Poetry. 96p. 1981. 7.95 (ISBN 0-88427-047-5, Dist. by Caroline Hse). North River.

Gage, John T. In the Arresting Eye: The Rhetoric of Imagism. LC 80-24893. 208p. 1981. 17.95x (ISBN 0-8071-0790-5). La State U Pr.

Ward, J. P. Poetry & the Sociological Idea. 256p. 1981. 23.50x (ISBN 0-389-20188-X). B&N.

POETRY-ADDRESSES, ESSAYS, LECTURES

Proffer, Carl, ed. Modern Russian Poets on Poetry. 1976. 15.00 (ISBN 0-88233-185-X). Ardis Pubs.

Rothenberg, Jerome. Pre-Faces & Other Writings. LC 80-24031. 224p. 1981. 14.95 (ISBN 0-8112-0785-4); pap. 6.95 (ISBN 0-8112-0786-2, NDP511). New Directions.

White, Heather. Essays in Hellenistic Poetry. (London Studies in Classical Philology: Vol. 5). 81p. 1981. pap. text ed. 17.25x (ISBN 90-70265-52-4, Pub. by Gieben Holland). Humanities.

POETRY-AUTHORSHIP

Andrews, J. David. Choosing the Best Form for Your Poem: An Illustrated Guide to Fifteen Noteworthy Verse Forms. 92p. (gr. 6-12). 1979. pap. 6.50; pap. text ed. 5.50. Planetary Pr.

POETRY-COLLECTIONS

see also the poetry of specific nationalities, e.g. English Poetry, French Poetry

Ashbery, John, et al. Apparitions. 60p. ltd. signed ed. 50.00 (ISBN 0-935716-10-6). Lord John.

Barkan, Stanley H., ed. Five Contemporary Turkish Poets. Sait, Talat, tr. (Cross-Cultural Review No. 6). 48p. (Turkish & Eng.). 1980. 10.00 (ISBN 0-89304-610-8); pap. 4.00 (ISBN 0-89304-611-6). Cross Cult.

Bisbee Press Collective, ed. The Bisbee Anthology Nineteen Eighty: Poetry. 62p. (Orig.). 1980. pap. 5.00 (ISBN 0-938196-00-6). Bisbee Pr.

Bulkin, Elly & Larkin, Joan, eds. Lesbian Poetry: An Anthology. (Orig.). 1981. pap. price not set (ISBN 0-930436-08-3). Persephone.

Carman, Bliss, ed. The World's Best Poetry, Vol. I: Home & Friendship. new ed. LC 80-84498. (The Granger Anthology Ser.: Ser. I). 480p. 1981. Repr. of 1904 ed. lib. bdg. 29.95x (ISBN 0-89609-202-X). Granger Bk.

Chase, Nan E., ed. Bountiful: A Poetry Digest. (First Annual Ser.). (Illus.). 53p. pap. 4.25 (ISBN 0-938512-00-5). Brigadoon.

Cunningham, J. V. Collected Poems and Epigrams. LC 71-132578. 142p. 1971. pap. 8.95 (ISBN 0-8040-0517-6). Swallow.

Curry, Georgene & Pearson, Larry, eds. The Poets Tree. (Anthology Ser.: Vol. 1). (Illus.). 104p. (Orig.). 1980. pap. 4.50. Pikes Peak.

Dobrin, Arthur, ed. Lace: Poetry from the Poor, the Homeless, the Aged, the Physically & Emotionally Disabled. 96p. 15.00 (ISBN 0-89304-036-3); pap. 7.95 (ISBN 0-89304-037-1). Cross Cult.

Ehrlich, Gretel. To Touch the Water. Trusky, Tom, ed. LC 80-69276. (Modern & Contemporary Poets of the West Ser.). 60p. (Orig.). 1981. pap. 2.50 (ISBN 0-916272-16-8). Ahsahta Pr.

Golden, Dean W. & Wright, A. J. Dancing in Your Ear: Poems of Protest, Humor & Love. (Doctor Jazz Press Chapbook Ser.: No. 1). (Illus.). 40p. (Orig.). 1980. pap. 2.50 (ISBN 0-934002-00-2). Doctor Jazz.

Halman, Talat S. & Barkan, Stanley H., eds. Cross-Cultural Review: Five Contemporary Turkish Poets, No. 6. 48p. 10.00 (ISBN 0-89304-610-8); pap. 4.00 (ISBN 0-89304-611-6). Cross Cult.

Hartnett, Michael. Poems in English. 1977. text ed. 15.75x (ISBN 0-85105-313-0, Dolmen Pr). Humanities.

Hayes, Michael. Supernatural Poetry. 1980. 10.95 (ISBN 0-7145-3697-0). Riverrun NY.

Holton, George S. Metamorphosis of a Poet. 1981. 7.95 (ISBN 0-533-04886-9). Vantage.

Kwiatkowski, Diana, ed. The Poet Pope. 67p. 1981. 9.50 (ISBN 0-933906-16-1); pap. 4.50 (ISBN 0-933906-15-3). Gusto Pr.

Laughlin, J., et al, eds. New Directions Forty-Two: Anthology. LC 37-1751. 192p. 1981. 15.95 (ISBN 0-8112-0783-8); pap. 5.95 (ISBN 0-8112-0784-6, NDP510). New Directions.

Lewis, Janet. Poems Old & New, Nineteen Eighteen to Nineteen Seventy-Eight. LC 80-26209. xvi, 112p. 1981. 11.00 (ISBN 0-8040-0371-8); pap. 5.95 (ISBN 0-8040-0372-6). Swallow.

Louis, Louise. Consulate of One. (Illus.). 16p. 1977. lib. bdg. 1.99. Pen-Art.

--Perennial Promise: First Lillibook Anthology. 48p. pap. 3.95. Pen-Art.

Luhan, Mabel L., et al. Three Fates in Taos. Moore, Harry T., ed. (Illus.). 228p. 1981. 20.00x (ISBN 0-933806-10-8). Black Swan CT.

Pater, Alan F., ed. Nineteen Eighty One Anthology of Magazine Verse & Yearbook of American Poetry. 650p. lib. bdg. write for info. (ISBN 0-917734-05-X); lib. bdg. price not set (ISBN 0-917734-05-X). Monitor.

Reiser, Virginia S. Favorite Poems in Large Print. 1981. lib. bdg. 17.95 (ISBN 0-8161-3160-0, Large Print Bks). G K Hall.

Robson, E. & Wimp, J., eds. Against Infinity. 1979. 17.00; pap. 8.95. Primary Pr.

Schutz, Susan P., ed. I Promise You My Love. (Illus.). 64p. (Orig.). 1981. pap. 4.95 (ISBN 0-88396-129-6). Blue Mtn Pr CO.

Stryk, Lucien, ed. Prairie Voices: A Collection of Illinois Poets. 64p. 1980. pap. 4.00 (ISBN 0-933180-21-7). Spoon Riv Poetry.

Van de Warsenburg, Hans, compiled by. Cross-Cultural Review: Five Contemporary Flemish Poets, No. 3. Holmes, James S., et al, trs. Barkan, Stanley H., ed. 48p. 10.00 (ISBN 0-89304-604-3); pap. 4.00 (ISBN 0-89304-605-1). Cross Cult.

Vincent, Stephen & Zweig, Ellen, eds. The Poetry Reading. 1981. lib. bdg. 20.00 (ISBN 0-917672-36-4); pap. 7.95 (ISBN 0-917672-35-6). Momos.

Whitman, Ruth. An Anthology of Modern Yiddish Poetry. LC 66-25551. 141p. 1979. pap. 4.95. Workmen's Circle.

World's Best Poems. Adams, R. L., ed. 1981. 28.50 (ISBN 0-686-68313-7). Porter.

POETRY-DICTIONARIES, INDEXES, ETC.

Morris, Helen. Where's That Poem? rev & enl ed. 287p. 1980. pap. 10.50x (ISBN 0-631-11791-1, Pub. by Basil Blackwell). Biblio Dist.

POETRY-HISTORY AND CRITICISM

Caws, Mary A. The Eye in the Text: Essays on Perception, Mannerist to Modern. LC 80-8540. (Princeton Essays on the Arts Ser.: No. 11). (Illus.). 334p. 1981. 17.50x (ISBN 0-691-06453-9); pap. 6.95x (ISBN 0-691-01377-2). Princeton U Pr.

Croce, Benedetto. Benedetto Croce's Poetry & Literature: An Introduction to the Criticism & History of Poetry & Literature. Gullace, Giovanni, tr. from Ital. & intro. by. LC 80-19511. 1981. 24.95x (ISBN 0-8093-0982-3). S Ill U Pr.

Davison, Edward. Some Modern Poets & Other Critical Essays. 255p. 1980. Repr. lib. bdg. 35.00 (ISBN 0-89987-157-7). Century Bookbindery.

De Croome, D. Empaytaz. Albor: Mediaeval & Renaissance Dawn-Songs in the Iberian Peninsula. LC 80-23767. (Sponsor Ser.). 106p. (Orig.). 1980. pap. 12.75 (ISBN 0-8357-0531-5, SS-00144). Univ Microfilms.

Gilby, Thomas. Poetic Experience. 114p. 1980. Repr. of 1934 ed. lib. bdg. 20.00 (ISBN 0-8492-4976-7). R West.

Hagin, Peter. The Epic Hero & the Decline of Heroic Poetry. 182p. 1980. Repr. of 1964 ed. lib. bdg. 25.00 (ISBN 0-89987-361-8). Darby Bks.

Hirschberg, Stuart. Myth in the Poetry of Ted Hughes. 1980. 22.50x. B&N.

Lourie, Margaret A., ed. William Morris's "the Defence of Guenevere", & Other Poems. LC 80-83223. 275p. 1981. lib. bdg. 33.00 (ISBN 0-8240-9452-2). Garland Pub.

McKinnon, Karen. Spiralings: A Journal into Poems. (Illus.). 48p. (Orig.). 1980. pap. 5.00 (ISBN 0-88235-041-2). San Marcos.

Perloff, Marjorie. Poetry After Symbolism: Rimbaud to Cage. LC 80-8569. (Illus.). 360p. 1981. 20.00x (ISBN 0-691-06462-8). Princeton U Pr.

Poetry As a Performance Art on & off the Page. 1976. pap. 1.95. Primary Pr.

Rothstein, Eric. Restoration & Eighteenth-Century Poetry 1660-1780. (Routledge Histort of English Poetry Ser.). 350p. 1981. price not set (ISBN 0-7100-0660-8). Routledge & Kegan.

Toliver, Harold. The Past That Poets Make. LC 80-18825. 304p. 1981. text ed. 24.00 (ISBN 0-674-65676-8). Harvard U Pr.

White, Heather. Essays in Hellenistic Poetry. (London Studies in Classical Philology: Vol. 5). 81p. 1981. pap. text ed. 17.25x (ISBN 90-70265-52-4, Pub. by Gieben Holland). Humanities.

Zukofsky, Louis. A Test of Poetry. 1981. 12.95 (ISBN 0-393-01446-0); pap. 4.95 (ISBN 0-393-00050-8). Norton.

POETRY-PHILOSOPHY

see Poetry

POETRY-SELECTIONS

see Poetry-Collections

POETRY-STUDY AND TEACHING

Aldan, Daisy. The Art & Craft of Poetry: A Guide for Students & Teachers. 7.95 (ISBN 0-88427-050-5). Green Hill.

Talarico, Ross. Pits Exercises: A Manual-Anthology for Teachers & Students. (Poetry in the Schools Programs). 64p. (Orig.). (gr. 10-12). 1981. pap. 3.95 (ISBN 0-933362-05-6). Assoc Creative Writers.

Tickle, Phyllis A. On Beyond Koch. (Illus.). 160p. 1981. pap. 2.95 (ISBN 0-918518-20-2). St Luke TN.

POETRY-TECHNIQUE

see Poetics

POETRY, MEDIEVAL

Dragonetti, Roger. La Technique Poetique Des Trouveres Dans la Chanson Courtoise: Contribution a l'etude De la Rhetorique Medievale. LC 80-2163. 1981. Repr. of 1960 ed. 76.00 (ISBN 0-404-19029-4). AMS Pr.

POETRY, MEDIEVAL-HISTORY AND CRITICISM

Greenfield, Concetta C. Humanist & Scholastic Poetics, 1250-1500. LC 76-49779. 341p. 1981. 22.50 (ISBN 0-8387-1991-0). Bucknell U Pr.

Napolski, Max von. Leben und Werke Des Trobadors Ponz De Capduoill. LC 80-2183. 1981. Repr. of 1879 ed. 26.50 (ISBN 0-404-19009-X). AMS Pr.

POETRY, MODERN (COLLECTIONS)

Hunter, Jim. Modern Poets Five. 160p. 1981. pap. 8.95 (ISBN 0-571-11567-5, Pub. by Faber & Faber). Merrimack Bk Serv.

POETRY AND MUSIC

see Music and Literature

POETRY FOR CHILDREN

see Children's Poetry; Nursery Rhymes

POETRY OF PLACES-SOUTH AMERICA

Curet de De Anda, Miriam. Le Poesia De Jose Gautier Benitez. LC 80-17629. (Coleccion Mente y Palabra Ser.). (Illus.). 232p. Date not set. 6.25 (ISBN 0-8477-0570-6); pap. 5.00 (ISBN 0-8477-0571-4). U of PR Pr.

POETS

see also Dramatists; Troubadours; Trouveres; Women Poets

Baumann, Cecilia C. Wilhelm Muller: The Poet of the Schubert Song Cycles. LC 80-12806. (Studies in German Literature). (Illus.). 208p. 1981. 17.50x (ISBN 0-271-00266-2). Pa St U Pr.

Davison, Edward. Some Modern Poets & Other Critical Essays. 255p. 1980. Repr. of 1928 ed. lib. bdg. 35.00 (ISBN 0-89760-149-1). Telegraph Bks.

De Selincourt, Ernest. English Poets & the National Ideal. 119p. 1980. Repr. of 1916 ed. text ed. 20.00 (ISBN 0-8492-4226-6). R West.

Lyne, R. O. The Latin Love Poets from Catullus to Horace. 320p. 1981. 37.50 (ISBN 0-19-814453-9); pap. 15.95 (ISBN 0-19-814454-7). Oxford U Pr.

Pagan, Juan A. Lorca En la Lirica Puertorriquena. LC 80-17628. (Mente y Palabra Ser.). (Illus.). 486p. 1980. 6.25 (ISBN 0-8477-0574-9); pap. 5.00 (ISBN 0-8477-0575-7). U of PR Pr.
Ray, David, ed. From A to Z: 200 Contemporary American Poets. LC 80-27328. xi, 243p. 1981. 16.95 (ISBN 0-8040-0369-6); pap. 8.95 (ISBN 0-8040-0370-X). Swallow.
Scobie, Stephen. Leonard Cohen. 294p. (Orig.). 1978. pap. 4.95 (ISBN 0-295-95686-0, Pub. by Douglas & McIntyre Canada). U of Wash Pr.
Tomlinson, Charles. Some Americans: A Personal Record. (A Quantum Bk.). 100p. 1981. 10.00 (ISBN 0-520-04037-6). U of Cal Pr.
Vega, Jose L. Cesar Vallejo En Trilce. LC 79-26380. (Coleccion UPREX, 60 Ser.: Estudios Literarios). ix, 132p. Date not set. pap. write for info. (ISBN 0-8477-0060-7). U of PR Pr.
Vinson, James & Kirkpatrick, Daniel, eds. Great Poets. (Great Writers of the English Language Ser.). 1200p. 1979. 45.00x (ISBN 0-312-34640-9). St Martin.
Vinson, Jim & Kirkpatrick, Daniel, eds. Contemporary Poets. 3rd ed. (Contemporary Writers Ser.). 1900p. 1980. lib. bdg. 60.00x (ISBN 0-312-16765-2). St Martin.

POETS–CORRESPONDENCES, REMINISCENCES, ETC.

Alberti, Rafael. The Lost Grove: The Autobiography of a Spanish Poet in Exile. Berns, Gabriel, ed. (Illus.). 331p. 1981. pap. 5.95 (CAL 464). U of Cal Pr.
Perse, John. St.-John Perse: Letters. Knodel, Arthur J., ed. LC 79-9080. (Bollingen Ser.: LXXXVII: 2). (Illus.). 712p. 1981. 20.00x (ISBN 0-691-09868-9); pap. 8.50 (ISBN 0-691-01836-7). Princeton U Pr.

POETS, WOMEN

see Women Poets

POISONERS

see Poisoning

POISONING

Vale, J. A. & Meredith, T. J., eds. Poisoning: Diagnosis & Treatment. (Illus.). 1981. PLB 37.75 (ISBN 0-906141-81-8, Pub. by Update Books Ltd); pap. 30.75 (ISBN 0-906141-82-6). Kluwer Boston.

POISONOUS ANIMALS

see also Poisonous Snakes
also specific poisonous animals, e.g. Rattlesnakes; Spiders

Altmann, Horst. Poisonous Plants & Animals. (Illus.). 144p. 1981. pap. 5.95 (ISBN 0-7011-2526-8, Pub. by Chatto-Bodley-Jonathan). Merrimack Bk Serv.

POISONOUS SNAKES

Phelps, Tony. Poisonous Snakes. (Illus.). 320p. 1981. 27.50 (ISBN 0-7137-0877-8, Pub. by Blanford Pr England). Sterling.
Simon, Seymour. Poisonous Snakes. LC 80-23938. (Illus.). 80p. (gr. 2-6). 1981. 11.95 (ISBN 0-590-07513-6, Four Winds). Schol Bk Serv.

POISONS

see also Medical Jurisprudence; Pesticides; Poisonous Animals; Toxicology; Toxins and Antitoxins
also specific substances, with or without the subdivision Toxicology; names of poisons

Altmann, Horst. Poisonous Plants & Animals. (Illus.). 144p. 1981. pap. 5.95 (ISBN 0-7011-2526-8, Pub. by Chatto-Bodley-Jonathan). Merrimack Bk Serv.

POISONS, ECONOMIC

see Pesticides

POISONS, INDUSTRIAL

see Industrial Toxicology

POKER

Alberts, Ulvis. Poker Face. LC 80-70464. (Illus.). 144p. limited ed. 125.00 (ISBN 0-9605416-0-8); pap. 30.00 (ISBN 0-9605416-1-6). Angel City.
Ankeny, Nesmith. Poker Strategy. LC 80-68177. 272p. 1981. 11.95 (ISBN 0-465-05839-6). Basic.
Christensen, R. Mathematical Analysis of Bluffing in Poker. 60p. 1981. 9.50 (ISBN 0-686-28920-X). Entropy Ltd.
Jacoby, Oswald. Oswald Jacoby on Poker. LC 80-70553. 192p. 1981. pap. 4.95 (ISBN 0-385-17590-6, Dolp). Doubleday.
Sklansky, David. Sklansky on Poker Theory. rev. ed. 176p. 1980. pap. 5.95 (ISBN 0-89650-918-4). Gamblers.
Taetzsch, Lyn. Winning Methods of Bluffing & Betting in Poker. LC 75-36140. (Illus.). 138p. (Orig.). 1981. pap. 6.95. Sterling.
Wallace, Frank R. A B C's of Poker. 1980. pap. cancelled (ISBN 0-911752-31-5). I & O Pub.

POLAND–HISTORY

Fleming, Nicholas. August: 1939. (Illus.). 242p. 1980. 19.50x (ISBN 0-8419-7200-1). Holmes & Meier.
Gross, Jan & Gross, Irena, eds. War Through the Children's Eyes: The Soviet Occupation of Poland & the Deportations, 1939-1941. LC 80-83832. (Publications Ser.: No.247). 300p. 1981. 21.95. Hoover Inst Pr.
Kukiel, Marian. Czartoryski & European Unity: 1770-1861. LC 80-22899. (Poland's Millenium Ser. of the Kosciuszko Foundation). (Illus.). xvii, 354p. 1981. Repr. of 1955 ed. lib. bdg. 35.00x (ISBN 0-313-22511-7, KUCZ). Greenwood.
Kulczycki, John J. School Strikes in Prussian Poland, 1901 to 1907: The Struggle Over Bilingual Education. (East European Monographs: No. 82). 320p. 1981. 21.00x (ISBN 0-914710-76-1). East Eur Quarterly.
Pertek, Jerzy. Poles on the High Seas. Jordan, Alexander, tr. (Library of Polish Studies: Vol. 9). text ed. 8.95 (ISBN 0-917004-13-2). Kosciuszko.
Skurnowicz, Joan S. Romantic Nationalism & Liberalism: Joachim Lelewel & the Polish National Idea. (East European Monographs: No. 83). 224p. 1981. text ed. 16.00x (ISBN 0-914710-77-X). East Eur Quarterly.
Williams, George H. The Polish Brethren. (Harvard Theological Studies: No. 30). 16.00; pap. 11.00 (ISBN 0-89130-201-8). Scholars Pr CA.

POLAND–POLITICS AND GOVERNMENT

Gambit Thirty-Three - Thirty-Four: Polish Issue. 1980. pap. 8.00. Riverrun NY.

POLAR EXPEDITIONS

see Antarctic Regions; Arctic Regions; North Pole
also names of exploring expeditions and explorers

POLAROID LAND (CAMERA)

see Cameras–Types–Polaroid Land

POLEMICS (THEOLOGY)

see Apologetics

POLICE

see also Criminal Investigation; Detectives; Public Relations–Police; Secret Service
also subdivision Police under names of cities, e.g. Boston–Police

Alderson, John. Policing Freedom. 288p. 1979. 22.95x (ISBN 0-7121-1815-2, Pub. by Macdonald & Evans England). Intl Ideas.
Brown, Michael. Working the Street: Police Discretion & the Dilemmas of Reform. LC 80-69175. 380p. 1981. text ed. 15.00 (ISBN 0-87154-190-4). Russell Sage.
Bunyard, R. S. Police: Organisation & Command. (Illus.). 400p. 1978. 21.95x (ISBN 0-7121-1671-0, Pub. by Macdonald & Evans England). Intl Ideas.
Campbell, Don. Police: The Exercise of Power. 128p. 1978. 13.95x (ISBN 0-7121-1678-8, Pub. by Macdonald & Evans Engalnd). Intl Ideas.
Freed, Leonard. Police Work. 1981. 19.95 (ISBN 0-671-25202-X, Touchstone Bks); pap. 9.95 (ISBN 0-671-25203-8). S&S.
Jonnes, J. Merryn. Organisational Aspects of Police Behaviour. 192p. 1980. 34.25x (ISBN 0-566-00402-X, Pub. by Gower Pub Co England). Renouf.
Monahan, Lynn H & Farmer, Richard E. Stress & the Police: A Manual for Prevention. LC 80-83671. 1981. pap. 7.95 (ISBN 0-913530-23-9). Palisades Pubs.
Monkkonen, Eric. Police in Urban America, Eighteen Hundred Sixty to Nineteen Twenty. LC 80-16762. (Interdisciplinary Perspectives on Modern History Ser.). (Illus.). 256p. Date not set. price not set (ISBN 0-521-23454-9). Cambridge U Pr.
Simpson, Keith. Police: The Investigation of Violence. (Illus.). 240p. 1978. 17.95x (ISBN 0-7121-1689-3, Pub. by Macdonald & Evans England). Intl Ideas.
Varwell, D. W. Police & the Public. 128p. 1978. 13.95x (ISBN 0-7121-1683-4, Pub. by Macdonald & Evans England). Intl Ideas.

POLICE–CORRESPONDENCE, REMINISCENCES, ETC.

Riley, Bill & Leake, Laura. History & Events of the Early Nineteen Twenties. LC 79-56202. 1981. 8.95 (ISBN 0-533-04515-0). Vantage.

POLICE–EXAMINATIONS, QUESTIONS, ETC.

Murray, Joseph A. Police Officer. 8th ed. LC 80-24919. 352p. 1981. lib. bdg. 10.00 (ISBN 0-668-05128-0); pap. 6.00 (ISBN 0-668-05130-2). Arco.

POLICE–EUROPE

Cobler, Sebastian. A Policeman's Utopia: An Interview with the Director of the West German FBI, with an Essay by Hans Magnus Enzensberger. Taubes, Tonia & Wilkins, Sophie, trs. from Ger. (Orig.). 1981. pap. 4.95 (ISBN 0-89396-044-6). Urizen Bks.

POLICE–JAPAN

Ames, Walter L. Police & Community in Japan. (Illus.). 300p. 1981. 16.50 (ISBN 0-520-04070-8). U of Cal Pr.

POLICE ADMINISTRATION

Nardulli, Peter F. & Stonecash, Jeffrey M. Politics, Rationality, & the Urban Services: The Police. LC 80-27169. 228p. 1981. lib. bdg. 20.00 (ISBN 0-89946-076-3). Oelgeschlager.
Salerno, Charles. Police at the Bargaining Table. 1981. write for info (ISBN 0-398-04462-7). C C Thomas.

POLICE MANAGEMENT

see Police Administration

POLICE SUPERVISORS

see Supervision of Police Personnel

POLICY SCIENCES

see also Decision-Making

Brigham, John & Brown, Don W., eds. Policy Implementation: Penalties or Incentives? LC 80-16765. (Sage Focus Editions: Vol. 25). (Illus.). 284p. 1980. pap. 9.95 (ISBN 0-8039-1351-6). Sage.
Grumm, John G. & Wasby, Stephen L., eds. The Analysis of Policy Impact. (A Policy Studies Orgnization Bk.). 224p. 1981. 23.95x (ISBN 0-669-03951-9). Lexington Bks.
Meehan, Eugene J. Reasoned Argument in Social Science: Linking Research to Policy Ser. LC 80-1198. (Illus.). 248p. 1981. lib. bdg. 27.50 (ISBN 0-313-22481-1, MRE). Greenwood.
Raven, Bertram H., ed. Policy Studies Review Annual, Vol. 4. LC 77-72938. (Illus.). 768p. 1980. 35.00 (ISBN 0-8039-1119-X). Sage.
Spirey, W. Allen & Wrobleski, William J. Econometric Model Performance in Forecasting & Policy Assessment. 1979. pap. 4.25 (ISBN 0-8447-3327-X). Am Enterprise.

POLIOMYELITIS VACCINE

Hennessen, W. & Van Wezel, A. L., eds. Reassessment of Inactivated Poliomyelitis Vaccine. (Developmentsin Biological Standardization Ser.: Vol. 47). (Illus.). 1981. soft cover 45.00 (ISBN 3-8055-1820-X). S Karger.

POLITENESS

see Etiquette

POLITICAL BEHAVIOR

see Political Psychology

POLITICAL CONVENTIONS

see also Nominations for Office; Political Parties; Primaries

Lord, Robert W. Running Conventions, Conferences & Meetings. 400p. 1981. 21.95 (ISBN 0-8144-5643-X). Am Mgmt.

POLITICAL CORRUPTION

see Corruption (In Politics)

POLITICAL ECONOMY

see Economics

POLITICAL ETHICS

see also Civics; Corruption (In Politics); Government, Resistance To

Bruckner, D. J., ed. Politics & Language: Spanish & English in the United States. (Orig.). 1980. pap. 4.00x (ISBN 0-686-28732-0). U Chi Ctr Policy.
Dallmayr, Fred A. Beyond Dogma & Despair: Toward a Critical Phenomenology of Politics. LC 80-53179. 256p. 1981. text ed. 19.95 (ISBN 0-268-00661-X). U of Notre Dame Pr.
Morrison, Minion K. Ethnicity & Political Integration: Ashanti, Ghana. (Foreign & Comparative Studies Program African Ser.: No. XXXVI). 1981. pap. text ed. price not set (ISBN 0-915984-59-8). Syracuse U Foreign Comp.

POLITICAL GEOGRAPHY

see Geography, Political

POLITICAL MURDER

see Assassination

POLITICAL PARTIES

see also Political Conventions; Politics, Practical; Right and Left (Political Science)
also subvision Politics and Government under names of countries, cities, etc. e.g. United States–Politics and Government; names of political parties, e.g. Democratic Party

Bender, David L. The Political Spectrum: Opposing Viewpoints. (Opposing Viewpoints Ser.). (gr. 12). 1981. lib. bdg. 8.95 (ISBN 0-89908-325-0); pap. text ed. 3.95 (ISBN 0-89908-300-5). Greenhaven.
Janda, Kenneth. Comparative Political Parties Data, Nineteen Fifty to Nineteen Sixty-Two. LC 79-90467. 1980. 14.00 (ISBN 0-89138-966-0). ICPSR.
Nagy, Charles J., Jr. Political Parties & System Flexibility. LC 80-5846. 196p. 1981. lib. bdg. 18.00 (ISBN 0-8191-1453-7); pap. text ed. 9.00 (ISBN 0-8191-1454-5). U Pr of Amer.
Petrocik, John R. Party Coalitions: Realignments & the Decline of the New Deal Party System. LC 80-22212. (Illus.). 1981. lib. bdg. price not set (ISBN 0-226-66378-7). U of Chicago Pr.

POLITICAL PARTIES–CANADA

Smith, David E. The Regional Decline of a National Party: Liberals on the Prairies. (Canadian Government Ser.). 184p. 1981. 14.00x (ISBN 0-8020-2421-1); pap. 6.50 (ISBN 0-8020-6430-2). U of Toronto Pr.

POLITICAL PARTIES–GREAT BRITAIN

Finer, S. E. Changing British Party System 1945-1979. 1980. pap. 7.25 (ISBN 0-8447-3368-7). Am Enterprise.

POLITICAL PARTIES–JAPAN

Lay, Arthur H. Brief Sketch of the History of Political Parties in Japan. Bd. with Political Ideas of Modern Japan: An Interpretation Studies in Japanese Law & Government. Kowakami, Kiyoshi K. 461p. 1979. Repr. of 1902 ed. 22.00 (ISBN 0-89093-222-0). U Pubns Amer.

POLITICAL PARTIES–UNITED STATES

Clubb, Jerome, et al. Partisan Realignment: Voters, Parties, & Government in American History. LC 80-16474. (Sage Library of Social Research: Vol. 108). 320p. 1980. 18.00 (ISBN 0-8039-1445-8); pap. 8.95 (ISBN 0-8039-1446-6). Sage.

POLITICAL PLATFORMS

see Political Parties

POLITICAL PRISONERS

Washburn, Lindy & Van Vactor, Lloyd. Twenty Longest Days. 197p. (Orig.). 1981. pap. 7.95 (ISBN 0-8298-0450-1). Pilgrim NY.

POLITICAL PSYCHOLOGY

see also Political Socialization; Propaganda; Public Opinion

Dallmayr, Fred R. Twilight of Subjectivity: Contributions to a Post-Individualist Theory of Politics. LC 80-23433. 416p. 1981. lib. bdg. 20.00x (ISBN 0-87023-314-9); pap. text ed. 10.00x (ISBN 0-87023-315-7). U of Mass Pr.

POLITICAL REFUGEES

see Refugees, Political

POLITICAL RIGHTS

see also Citizenship

Abernathy, Glenn. The Right of Assembly & Association. 300p. 1981. pap. text ed. 7.95 (ISBN 0-87249-410-1). U of SC Pr.
Bay, Christian. Strategies of Political Emancipation. LC 80-53117. 240p. 1981. text ed. 18.95 (ISBN 0-268-01702-6). U of Notre Dame Pr.
Rousseau, Jean-Jacques. The Social Contract. 227p. 1980. Repr. of 1893 ed. lib. bdg. 30.00 (ISBN 0-89987-716-8). Darby Bks.

POLITICAL SATIRE

see also subdivision History–Humor, Caricatures, etc. under United States and subdivision History, Comic, Satirical, etc. under other countries

Lock, F. P. The Politics of Gulliver's Travels. 166p. 1980. text ed. 22.00x (ISBN 0-19-812656-5). Oxford U Pr.

POLITICAL SCANDALS

see Corruption (In Politics)

POLITICAL SCIENCE

see also Administrative Law; Anarchism and Anarchists; Authoritarianism; Autonomy; Bureaucracy; Church and State; Citizenship; Civics; Civil Rights; Civil Service; Civilization; Clans and Clan System; Communism; Comparative Government; Conservatism; Constitutional History; Constitutional Law; Constitutions; Coups D'Etat; Democracy; Elections; Equality; Executive Power; Federal Government; Geopolitics; Government, Resistance to; Government Ownership; Imperialism; Individualism; International Organization; Legislation; Liberalism; Liberty; Local Government; Municipal Government; Nationalism; Petition, Right of; Political Conventions; Political Ethics; Political Parties; Political Psychology; Politics, Practical; Populism; Power (Social Sciences); Pressure Groups; Public Administration; Public Opinion; Radicalism; Revolutions; Right and Left (Political Science); Social Contract; Socialism; Sovereignty; State, the; State Governments; Taxation; Utopias; World Politics
also subheading Constitution and subdivision Politics and Government under names of countries, states, etc. e.g. United States–Constitution; Massachusetts–Politics and Government

Banks, Arthur S. Cross-Polity Time-Series Data. 328p. 1971. 50.00 (ISBN 0-262-02071-8). MIT Pr.
Barrett, C. Strategy & Society. 161p. 1976. 7.00x (ISBN 0-7190-0627-9, Pub. by Manchester U Pr England). State Mutual Bk.
Bay, Christian. Strategies of Political Emancipation. LC 80-53117. 240p. 1981. text ed. 18.95 (ISBN 0-268-01702-6). U of Notre Dame Pr.
Bender, Lynn D. Perspectivas Politicas, Vol. 1. 2nd, rev. ed. (Illus.). 116p. pap. text ed. 4.55 (ISBN 0-913480-50-9). Inter Am U Pr.
Brown, A. Lee. Rules & Conflicts: An Introduction to Political Life & Its Study. (Illus.). 384p. 1981. pap. text ed. 9.95 (ISBN 0-13-783738-0). P-H.
Buchanan, William. Understanding Political Variables. 3rd ed. LC 80-23707. (Illus.). 1980. pap. text ed. 12.95x (ISBN 0-684-16673-9, ScribC). Scribner.
Curtis, Michael, ed. Great Political Theories, Vol. 1. 1976. pap. 2.50 (ISBN 0-380-00785-1, 40626, Discus). Avon.
--Great Political Theories, Vol. 2. 1976. pap. 2.50 (ISBN 0-380-01235-9, 49858, Discus). Avon.
Danford, John W. Wittgenstein & Political Philosophy: A Reexamination of the Foundations of Social Science. LC 78-6716. xiv, 166p. 1981. pap. 6.95 (ISBN 0-226-13594-2). U of Chicago Pr.
Donovan, John C., et al. People, Power & Politics: An Introduction to Political Science. (Illus.). 384p. 1981. pap. text ed. 11.95 (ISBN 0-201-03246-5). A-W.
Illich, Ivan. Shadow Work. 160p. 1981. 15.00 (ISBN 0-7145-2710-6, Pub. by M. Boyars); pap. 5.95 (ISBN 0-7145-2711-4). Merrimack Bk Serv.
Jacobsen, Gertrude A. & Lipman, Miriam H. Political Science. 2nd ed. (Illus.). 1979. pap. 3.95 (ISBN 0-06-460178-1, CO 178, COS). Har-Row.
Laponce, J. A. Left & Right: The Topography. 284p. 1981. 27.50x (ISBN 0-8020-5533-8). U of Toronto Pr.
Laver, Michael. The Politics of Private Desires. 272p. 1981. pap. 3.95 (ISBN 0-14-022316-9, Pelican). Penguin.
Lipset, Seymour M. Political Man: The Social Bases of Politics. LC 80-8867. 584p. 1981. pap. text ed. 7.50x (ISBN 0-8018-2522-9). Johns Hopkins.
Machiavelli. The Prince. pap. 1.50. Bantam.
New Individualist Review Journal. New Individualist Review. LC 65-35281. 1024p. 1981. 12.00 (ISBN 0-913966-90-8). Liberty Fund.
Nimmo, Dan & Rivers, William L., eds. Watching American Politics. LC 80-23788. (Illus.). 336p. (Orig.). 1981. pap. text ed. 9.95 (ISBN 0-582-28197-0). Longman.
Oppenheim, Felix. Political Concepts: A Reconstruction. LC 80-23846. (Illus.). 1981. lib. bdg. price not set (ISBN 0-226-63184-2). U of Chicago Pr.
Pettman, Ralph. The Biopolitics of International Relations. LC 80-22926. (Pergamon Policy Studies on Biopolitics). 200p. 1981. 20.00 (ISBN 0-08-026329-1); pap. 9.95 (ISBN 0-08-026328-3). Pergamon.
Rasberry, Robert W. The Technique of Political Lying. LC 80-5976. 301p. 1981. lib. bdg. 19.75 (ISBN 0-8191-1482-0); pap. text ed. 11.25 (ISBN 0-8191-1483-9). U Pr of Amer.
Read, Leonard E. Thoughts Rule the World. 128p. 1981. 6.00 (ISBN 0-910614-67-9). Foun Econ Ed.

Rudman, Jack. Political Science. (Undergraduate Program Field Test Ser.: UPFT-20). (Cloth bdg. avail. on request). pap. 9.95 (ISBN 0-8373-6020-X). Natl Learning.

The Universal Reference System: 1979 Annual Supplement, 3 vols. 2412p. 1980. Set. 350.00 (ISBN 0-306-69029-2). IFI Plenum.

Vidich, Arthur J. & Glasman, Ronald M., eds. Conflict & Control: Challenge to Legitimacy of Modern Governments. rev. ed. LC 78-19653. (Saga Focus Editions: Vol. 7). (Illus.). 304p. 1979. 18.95 (ISBN 0-8039-0974-8). Sage.

Watson, Thomas E. Handbook of Politics & Economics. (Studies in Populism). 1980. lib. bdg. 75.00 (ISBN 0-686-68879-1). Revisionist Pr.

White, Elliott. Sociobiology & Human Politics. LC 79-3016. 1981. price not set (ISBN 0-669-03602-1). Lexington Bks.

POLITICAL SCIENCE–ADDRESSES, ESSAYS, LECTURES

Adlam, Diana, et al, eds. Politics & Power: Problems in Labour Politics. (Politics & Power Ser.). 220p. (Orig.). 1981. pap. price not set (ISBN 0-7100-0716-7). Routledge & Kegan.

Raphael, David. Justice & Liberty. 1980. text ed. 40.00x (ISBN 0-485-11195-0, Athlone Pr). Humanities.

POLITICAL SCIENCE–BIBLIOGRAPHY

Holler, Frederick L. The Information Sources of Political Science. 3rd, rev. ed. 288p. 1980. 65.00 (ISBN 0-87436-179-6). ABC-Clio.

POLITICAL SCIENCE–BIOGRAPHY

see Political Scientists

POLITICAL SCIENCE–EARLY WORKS TO 1700

Harrington, James. The Political Writings of James Harrington: Representative Selections. Blitzer, Charles, ed. LC 80-21163. (The Library of Liberal Arts: No. 38). xlii, 165p. 1980. Repr. of 1955 ed. lib. bdg. 22.50x (ISBN 0-313-22670-9, HAWR). Greenwood.

POLITICAL SCIENCE–EXAMINATIONS, QUESTIONS, ETC.

Dupreez, Peter. The Politics of Identity. 1980. 25.00 (ISBN 0-312-62697-5). St Martin.

POLITICAL SCIENCE–HISTORY

Curtis, Michael, ed. The Great Political Theories, Vol 1. 464p. 1981. pap. 3.95 (77222, Discus). Avon.

--The Great Political Theories, Vol 2. 496p. 1981. pap. 3.95 (77230, Discus). Avon.

Frederick Of Prussia. The Refutation of Machiavelli's Prince or Anti-Machiavel. Sonnino, Paul, tr. LC 80-15801. viii, 173p. 1981. 13.95x (ISBN 0-8214-0559-4); pap. 5.95 (ISBN 0-8214-0598-5). Ohio U Pr.

Rockwell, Kenneth G. Megalomania & Mediocrity in the Leadership of Nations: The Meaning for the World. (The Major Currents in Contemporary World History Library). (Illus.). 117p. 1981. 39.95 (ISBN 0-89266-292-1). Am Classical Coll Pr.

Schware, Robert. Quantification in the History of Political Thought: Toward a Qualitative Approach. LC 80-1704. (Contributions in Political Science Ser.: No. 55). 184p. 1981. lib. bdg. 25.00 (ISBN 0-313-22228-2, SPT/). Greenwood.

Strauss, Leo & Cropsey, Joseph. History of Political Philosophy. 2nd ed. LC 80-26907. xii, 850p. 1981. pap. text ed. 14.00x (ISBN 0-226-77690-5). U of Chicago Pr.

POLITICAL SCIENCE–HISTORY–EUROPE

Mulier, Eco O. & Haitsma, G. The Myth of Venice & Dutch Republican Thought in the Seventeenth Century. 250p. 1980. pap. text ed. 20.00x (ISBN 90-232-1781-0). Humanities.

POLITICAL SCIENCE–HISTORY–GREAT BRITAIN

Salmon, John H. The French Religious Wars in English Political Thought. LC 80-24621. vii, 202p. 1981. Repr. of 1959 ed. lib. bdg. 22.50x (ISBN 0-313-22221-5, SAFR). Greenwood.

POLITICAL SCIENCE–HISTORY–UNITED STATES

Spitz, David. Patterns of Anti-Democratic Thought: An Analysis & Criticism, with Special Reference to the American Political Mind in Recent Times. LC 80-22640. 347p. 1981. Repr. of 1965 ed. lib. bdg. 27.50x (ISBN 0-313-22392-0, SPPD). Greenwood.

Thompson, Kenneth W., ed. The Virginia Papers of the Presidency, Vol. V: The White Burkett Miller Center Forums, 1981, Pt. 1. 91p. 1981. lib. bdg. 11.75 (ISBN 0-8191-1502-9); pap. text ed. 5.50 (ISBN 0-8191-1503-7). U Pr of Amer.

POLITICAL SCIENCE–RESEARCH

see Political Science Research

POLITICAL SCIENCE–YEARBOOKS

Paxton, John, ed. Statesman's Year Book, 1980-81. 117th ed. 1700p. 1980. 30.00x (ISBN 0-312-76093-0). St Martin.

POLITICAL SCIENCE RESEARCH

Zisk, Betty. Political Research: A Methodological Sampler. 352p. 1981. pap. text ed. 8.95 (ISBN 0-669-02338-8). Heath.

POLITICAL SCIENTISTS

Walker, Mack. Johann Jakob Moser & the Holy Roman Empire of the German Nation. LC 79-27720. 352p. 1980. 26.00x (ISBN 0-8078-1441-5). U of NC Pr.

POLITICAL SOCIALIZATION

Sigel, Roberta S. & Hoskin, Marilyn. The Political Involvement of Adolescents. 320p. 1981. 22.00 (ISBN 0-8135-0897-5). Rutgers U Pr.

POLITICIANS

see Statesmen

POLITICS, PRACTICAL

Here are entered works dealing with practical political methods in general political machines, electioneering, etc.

see also Business and Politics; Corruption (In Politics); Elections; Lobbying; Nominations for Office; Primaries; Voting; Youth–Political Activity

also subdivision Politics and Government under names of countries, states, etc., e.g. Massachusetts–Politics and Government; headings beginning with the word Political

Papworth, Joseph. New Politics. 336p. 1980. text ed. 37.50x (ISBN 0-7069-1273-X, Pub. by Vikas India). Advent Bk.

POLITICS, PRACTICAL–PSYCHOLOGICAL ASPECTS

see Political Psychology

POLITICS AND BUSINESS

see Business and Politics

POLITICS AND CHRISTIANITY

see Christianity and Politics

POLITICS AND YOUNG PEOPLE

see Youth–Political Activity

POLITY, ECCLESIASTICAL

see Church Polity

POLLINATION

see Fertilization of Plants

POLLOCK, JACKSON, 1912-1956

Hess, Thomas B. & Feldman, Morton. Six Painters: Mondrian, DeKooning, Guston, Kline, Pollock, Rothko. LC 67-30452. (Illus.). 1968. pap. 3.00 (ISBN 0-914412-22-1). Inst for the Arts.

POLLS

see Elections; Public Opinion Polls; Voting

POLLUTION

see also Air–Pollution; Environmental Engineering; Factory and Trade Waste; Refuse and Refuse Disposal; Spraying and Dusting Residues in Agriculture; Water–Pollution

also subdivision Pollution under subjects, e.g. Air–Pollution; Water–Pollution

Brown, Michael. Laying Waste: The Poisoning of America by Toxic Chemicals. 1981. pap. 3.50. WSP.

Chemical Trends in Wildlife: An International Cooperative Study. (Illus.). 1980. pap. 7.00 (ISBN 9-2641-2105-6). OECD.

Connon, James. A Clear View - Guide to Industrial Pollution Control. LC 75-15321. 1975. pap. 4.00. Inform.

Duffus, John H. Environmental Toxicology. (An Environmental Science Ser.). 132p. 1981. 15.95 (ISBN 0-470-27051-9). Halsted Pr.

Eisenreich, Steven J. Atmospheric Pollutants in Natural Waters. 1981. text ed. 40.00 (ISBN 0-250-40369-2, Dist. by Butterworths). Ann Arbor Science.

Kiefer, Irene. Poisoned Land: The Problem of Hazardous Waste. LC 80-22120. (Illus.). 96p. (gr. 5-9). 1981. PLB 8.95 (ISBN 0-689-30837-X). Atheneum.

McKean, Margaret A. Environmental Protest & Citizen Politics in Japan. 300p. 1981. 28.50x (ISBN 0-520-04115-1). U of Cal Pr.

Manual on Oil Pollution, 3 pts. Incl. Pt. 1. Prevention. 1976. pap. 8.25 (ISBN 0-686-64934-6, IMCO 23); Pt. II. Contingency Planning. 1978. pap. 11.00 (ISBN 0-686-64935-4, IMCO 24); Pt. IV. Practical Information on Means of Dealing with Oil Spillages. 1977. Repr. of 1972 ed. pap. 12.00 (ISBN 0-686-64936-2, IMCO 25). IMCO). Unipub.

Nader, Ralph, et al, eds. Who's Poisoning America: Corporate Polluters & Their Victims in the Chemical Age. 320p. 1981. 12.95 (ISBN 0-87156-276-6). Sierra.

Norwood, Christopher. At Highest Risk: Protecting Children from Environmental Pollution. 1981. pap. 4.95 (ISBN 0-14-005830-3). Penguin.

Phillips, David J. Quantitative Aquatic Biological Indicators: Their Use to Monitor Trace Metal & Organochlorine Pollution. (Illus.). xii, 460p. 1980. 65.00x (ISBN 0-85334-884-7). Burgess-Intl Ideas.

Teja, A. S. Chemical Engineering & the Environment. (Critical Reports on Applied Chemistry). 115p. 1981. 27.95 (ISBN 0-470-27106-X). Halsted Pr.

Tver, David F. Dictionary of Industrial Pollution, Ecology & Environment. (Illus.). 1981. price not set (ISBN 0-8311-1060-0). Indus Pr.

Walker, Colin. Environmental Pollution by Chemicals. 1980. pap. text ed. 7.75x (ISBN 0-09-123891-9, Hutchinson U Lib). Humanities.

POLLUTION–CONTROL

see Pollution

POLLUTION–PREVENTION

see Pollution

POLLUTION CONTROL EQUIPMENT

Martin, A. E., ed. Emission Control Technology for Industrial Boilers. LC 80-26046. (Pollution Tech. Rev. 74 Ser.: Energy Tech. Rev. 62). (Illus.). 405p. 1981. 48.00 (ISBN 0-8155-0833-6). Noyes.

POLLUTION EQUIPMENT

see Pollution Control Equipment

POLLUTION OF WATER

see Water–Pollution

POLO, MARCO, 1254-1323

Sharp, Marilyn. Marco Polo. 338p. 1981. 12.95 (ISBN 0-399-90106-X). Marek.

POLYAMINES

Caldarera, Claudio M., et al, eds. Advances in Polyamine Research, Vol. 3. 1981. text ed. price not set (ISBN 0-89004-621-2). Raven.

POLYBIUS

Walbank, F. W. A Historical Commentary on Polybius: Vol. 1, Commentary Books I-IV, Vol. 1. (Illus.). 804p. 1957. text ed. 49.00x (ISBN 0-19-814152-1). Oxford U Pr.

POLYCYCLIC COMPOUNDS

Lee, Milton L., et al. Analytical Chemistry of Polycyclic Aromatic Compounds. 1981. write for info. (ISBN 0-12-440840-0). Acad Pr.

POLYELECTROLYTE SOLUTIONS

see Electrolyte Solutions

POLYGLOTTISM

see Multilingualism

POLYMERIZATION

see Polymers and Polymerization

POLYMERS AND POLYMERIZATION

see also Condensation Products (Chemistry); Macromolecules; Plastics

Allen, N. S., ed. Developments in Polymer Photochemistry - One. (Illus.). x, 222p. 1980. 42.50x (ISBN 0-85334-911-8). Burgess-Intl Ideas.

Allen, N. S. & McKellar, J. F., eds. Photochemistry of Dyed & Pigmented Polymers. (Illus.). xii, 296p. 1980. 50.00x (ISBN 0-85334-898-7). Burgess-Intl Ideas.

Bassett, D. C. Principles of Polymer Morphology. (Cambrige Solid State Science Ser.). (Illus.). 220p. Date not set. price not set (ISBN 0-521-23270-8); pap. price not set (ISBN 0-521-29886-5). Cambridge U Pr.

Bely, V. A., et al. Friction & Wear in Polymer-Based Materials. LC 80-41825. (Illus.). 400p. 1981. 85.00 (ISBN 0-08-025444-6). Pergamon.

Berry, G. C. & Sroog, C. E. Rigid Chain Polymers: Synthesis & Properties. (Journal of Polymer Science Symposium Ser.: No. 65). 226p. 1979. 20.50 (ISBN 0-471-05802-5). Wiley.

Cantow, H. J., et al, eds. Polymer Products. (Advances in Polymer Science Ser.: Vol. 39). (Illus.). 230p. 1981. 57.80 (ISBN 0-387-10218-3). Springer-Verlag.

--Polymerization Processes. (Advances in Polymer Sciences Ser.: Vol. 38). (Illus.). 180p. 1981. 46.00 (ISBN 0-387-10217-5). Springer-Verlag.

Dawkins, J. V., ed. Developments in Polymer Characterisation - Two. (Illus.). x, 240p. 1980. 55.00x (ISBN 0-85334-909-6). Burgess-Intl Ideas.

Fettes, E. M. Chemical Reactions of Polymers, Vol. 19. 1304p. 1964. 90.00 (ISBN 0-470-39305-X). Wiley.

Hall, Christopher. Polymer Materials: An Introduction for Technologists & Scientists. LC 80-19341. 250p. 1981. 29.95 (ISBN 0-470-27028-4). Halsted Pr.

Hebeisch, A. & Guthrie, J. T. The Chemistry & Technology of Cellulose Copolymers. (Polymers - Properties & Applications Ser.: Vol. 4). (Illus.). 340p. 1981. 87.30 (ISBN 0-387-10164-0). Springer-Verlag.

International Symposium on Polymers in Concrete. Proceedings. 1978. 22.25 (SP-58); 17.50. ACI.

Jenkins, R., et al. Properties of Polymers. (Advances in Polymer Sciences: Vol. 36). (Illus.). 150p. 1980. 40.20 (ISBN 0-387-10204-3). Springer-Verlag.

Kennedy, Joseph P. & Marechal, Ernest. Carbocationic Polymerization. 675p. 1981. 65.00 (ISBN 0-471-01787-6, Pub. by Wiley-Interscience). Wiley.

Meltzer, Yale L. Water-Soluble Polymers: Developments Since 1978. LC 80-26174. (Chemical Technology Rev. Ser.: 181). (Illus.). 608p. 1981. 54.00 (ISBN 0-8155-0834-4). Noyes.

Scott, Gerald, ed. Developments in Polymer Stabilisation - Two. (Illus.). x, 245p. 1980. 45.00x (ISBN 0-85334-885-5). Burgess-Intl Ideas.

--Developments in Polymer Stabilisation, No. 3. (Illus.). ix, 195p. 1981. 38.00x (ISBN 0-85334-890-1). Intl Ideas.

Stannett, V. & Jenkins, A. D., eds. Progress in Polymer Science, Vol. 6. (Illus.). 266p. 1981. 35.00 (ISBN 0-08-020335-3). Pergamon.

Szycher, Michael & Robinson, William J., eds. Synthetic Biomedical Polymers: Concepts & Applications. LC 80-52137. (Illus.). 235p. 1980. 39.00 (ISBN 0-87762-290-6). Technomic.

Vinogradov, G. V. & Malkin, A. Y. Rheology of Polymers. (Illus.). 468p. 1981. 58.00 (ISBN 0-387-09778-3). Springer-Verlag.

Vogl, O. & Simionescu, C. I. Unsolved Problems of Co- & Graft Polymerization. (Journal of Polymer Science Ser.: Polymer Symposium No. 64). 373p. 1979. 29.95 (ISBN 0-471-05696-0). Wiley.

Woodward, Arthur E. & Bovey, Frank, eds. Polymer Characterization by ESR & NMR. LC 80-21840. (ACS Symposium Ser.: No. 142). 1980. 32.00 (ISBN 0-8412-0594-9). Am Chemical.

POLYNESIA–SOCIAL LIFE AND CUSTOMS

Fornander, Abraham. An Account of the Polynesian Race: Its Origin & Migration, 3 vols. in 1. LC 69-13505. (Illus.). 1980. Repr. of 1878 ed. Set. 37.50 (ISBN 0-8048-0002-2). C E Tuttle.

POLYNESIANS

Fornander, Abraham. An Account of the Polynesian Race: Its Origin & Migration, 3 vols. in 1. LC 69-13505. (Illus.). 1980. Repr. of 1878 ed. Set. 37.50 (ISBN 0-8048-0002-2). C E Tuttle.

POLYNOMIALS

see also Approximation Theory

Green, J. A. Polynomial Representations of GLN. (Lecture Notes in Mathematics: Vol. 830). 118p. 1981. pap. 9.80 (ISBN 0-387-10258-2). Springer-Verlag.

POLYNUCLEOTIDES

see Nucleic Acids

POLYPS

see Coelenterata

POLYSACCHARIDES

see also Cellulose

Brant, David A., ed. Solution Properties of Polysaccharides. (ACS Symposium Ser.: No. 150). 1981. price not set (ISBN 0-8412-0609-0). Am Chemical.

Stoddart, R. W. Polysaccharide Metabolism. 224p. 1980. 35.00x (ISBN 0-85664-807-8, Pub. by Croom Helm England). State Mutual England.

POLYURETHANES

see Urethanes

POMO INDIANS

see Indians of North America–Southwest, New

POMOLOGY

see Fruit; Fruit-Culture

POMPEY, GNAEUS POMPEIUS MAGNUS, 106 B.C.-48 B.C.

Greenhalgh, Peter. Pompey, Vol. I: The Roman Alexander. 288p. 1981. text ed. 23.00 (ISBN 0-8262-0335-3). U of Mo Pr.

POND LIFE

see Fresh-Water Biology

PONY CLUB

Lewis, James K. The Pony Club Book. LC 79-87794. (Illus.). 128p. 1981. 8.95 (ISBN 0-498-02257-9). A S Barnes.

POOR

see also Agricultural Colonies; Asylums; Child Welfare; Cost and Standard of Living; Labor and Laboring Classes; Old Age Pensions; Population; Public Welfare; Tramps; Unemployed

also subdivision Poor under names of cities, e.g. New York (City)–Poor

Abel-Smith, Brian. The Poor & the Poorest. 78p. 1965. pap. text ed. 5.00x (Pub. by Bedford England). Renouf.

In This Boke Are Conteyened These Statutes,...Whiche to Put in Execution, the Justices of Peace...Ware Admonished. LC 79-84105. (English Experience Ser.: No.924). 68p. 1979. Repr. of 1538 ed. lib. bdg. 7.00 (ISBN 90-221-0924-0). Walter J Johnson.

POOR CLARES

Koester, Mary C. Into This Land: Centennial History of the Cleveland Poor Clare Monestary of the Blessed Sacrament. (Illus.). 274p. 1980. write for info. (ISBN 0-934906-03-3); pap. write for info. (ISBN 0-934906-04-1). R J Liederbach.

POOR RELIEF

see Public Welfare

POPE, ALEXANDER, 1688-1744

Bogel, Fredric V. Acts of Knowledge: Pope's Later Poems. LC 78-75194. 285p. 1981. 18.50 (ISBN 0-8387-2380-2). Bucknell U Pr.

POPES–HISTORY

see Papacy–History

POPES–INFALLIBILITY

Makrakis, Apostolos. A Scriptural Refutation of the Pope's Primacy. Cummings, Denver, tr. from Hellenic. 171p. (Orig.). 1952. pap. 2.00x (ISBN 0-938366-40-8). Orthodox Chr.

POPES–PRIMACY

see also Bishops

Makrakis, Apostolos. A Scriptural Refutation of the Pope's Primacy. Cummings, Denver, tr. from Hellenic. 171p. (Orig.). 1952. pap. 2.00x (ISBN 0-938366-40-8). Orthodox Chr.

POPLAR

Poplars & Willows. (Forestry Ser.: No. 10). 328p. 1958. pap. 36.75 (ISBN 92-5-100500-1, F2046, FAO). Unipub.

POPULAR ERRORS

see Errors, Popular

POPULATION

see also Animal Populations; Birth Control; Census; Contraception; Demography; Man–Migrations; Migration, Internal; Mortality

also subdivision Population under names of countries, cities, etc., e.g. United States–Population

And the Poor Get Children: Radical Perspectives on Population Dynamics. LC 80-8932. 288p. 1981. 16.00 (ISBN 0-686-69511-9). Monthly Rev.

Boserup, Ester. Population & Technological Change: A Study of Long-Term Trends. LC 80-21116. (Illus.). 1981. lib. bdg. 17.50x (ISBN 0-226-06673-8). U of Chicago Pr.

Hock, Saw S. Population Control for Zero Growth in Singapore. 250p. 1981. 29.95 (ISBN 0-19-580430-9). Oxford U Pr.

Jain, Sagar C., ed. Management Development in Population Programs. 200p. (Orig.). 1981. pap. 15.00 (ISBN 0-89055-307-6). U of NC Pr.

Lonsdale, Richard E. & Holmes, John H., eds. Settlement Systems in Sparsely Populated Regions: The United States & Australia. LC 80-27278. (Pergamon Policy Studies on Urban Affairs; Comparative Rural Transformation Ser.). (Illus.). 360p. 1981. 40.00 (ISBN 0-08-023111-X). Pergamon.
McNamara, Robert S. Accelerating Population Stabilization Through Social & Economic Progress. (Development Papers: No. 24). 64p. 1977. pap. 1.50 (ISBN 0-686-28675-8). Overseas Dev Council.
Newman, James L., ed. Drought, Famine & Population Movement in Africa. LC 74-25877. (Foreign & Comparative Studies-Eastern African Ser.: No. 17). 144p. 1975. pap. 4.50x (ISBN 0-915984-14-8). Syracuse U Foreign Comp.
Nortman, Dorothy & Hofstatter, Ellen. Population & Family Planning Programs. 10th ed. LC 80-52443. (Illus.). 96p. (Orig.). 1980. pap. 4.50 (ISBN 0-87834-041-6). Population Coun.
Patterns of Urban & Rural Population Growth. (Population Studies: No. 68). 1980. 13.00 (E.79.XIII9). UN.
Paxman, John M., ed. The World Population Crisis: Policy Implications & the Role of Law: Proceedings of the American Society of International Law Regional Meeting & the John Bassett Moore Society of International Law Symposium. LC 80-19753. vi, 179p. 1980. Repr. of 1971 ed. lib. bdg. 22.50x (ISBN 0-313-22619-9, PAWO). Greenwood.
Piotrow, Phyllis T. World Population: The Present & Futues Crisis, No. 251. 1st ed. LC 80-69582. (Headline Ser.: No. 251). (Illus.). 80p. (Orig.). 1980. pap. 2.00 (ISBN 0-87124-064-5). Foreign Policy.
--World Population: The Present & Future Crisis. LC 80-69582. (Headline Ser.: No. 251). (Illus.). 80p. (Orig.). 1980. pap. 2.00 (ISBN 0-87124-064-5). Foreign Policy.
Population Concepts in Home Management Courses. 1979. pap. 7.50 (ISBN 92-5-100847-7, F1965, FAO). Unipub.
Population Education Workshop Proceedings. 62p. 1974. 2.75. Natl Cath Educ.
Principles & Recommendations for Population & Housing Censuses. (Statistical Papers Ser.: No. 67). 330p. 1980. pap. 20.00 (UN80/17/8, UN). Unipub.
Woods, Richard G., ed. Future Dimensions of World Food & Populations. (Winrock Ser.). 425p. 1981. lib. bdg. 22.50x (ISBN 0-86531-160-9). Westview.

POPULATION-RESEARCH
see Population Research

POPULATION-STATISTICS
Patterns of Urban & Rural Population Growth. (Population Studies: No.68). 175p. 1979. pap. 13.00 (UN79-13-9, UN). Unipub.
Snyder, Robert. The Biology of Population Growth. 300p. 1980. 30.00x (Pub. by Croom Helm England). State Mutual Bk.

POPULATION, FOREIGN
see Emigration and Immigration; also subdivision Emigration and Immigration under names of countries, and subdivision Foreign Population under names of countries, cities, etc.

POPULATION GENETICS
Dobzhansky, Theodosius. Dobzhansky's Genetics of Natural Populations: I-XLIII. Lewontin, R. C., et al, eds. 1024p. 1981. 42.50x (ISBN 0-231-05132-8). Columbia U Pr.
Hartl, Daniel L. A Primer of Population Genetics. LC 80-23009. (Illus.). 175p. (Orig.). 1981. pap. text ed. 8.00x (ISBN 0-87893-271-2). Sinauer Assoc.
Wallace, Bruce. Basic Popultaion Genetics. LC 80-39504. (Illus.). 736p. 1981. 25.00x (ISBN 0-231-05042-9). Columbia U Pr.
Wills, Christopher. Genetic Variability. (Illus.). 350p. 1981. text ed. 45.00x (ISBN 0-19-857570-X). Oxford U Pr.

POPULATION RESEARCH
Demographic Transition & Socio-Economic Development. (Population Studies: No. 65). 153p. 1979. pap. 10.00 (ISBN 0-686-68948-8, UN79/13/2, UN). Unipub.
Jones, H. R. Population Geography. 1981. text ed. 25.85 (ISBN 0-06-318188-6, Pub. by Har-Row Ltd England); pap. text ed. 13.10 (ISBN 0-06-318189-4). Har-Row.

POPULATIONS, ANIMAL
see Animal Populations

POPULATIONS, FISH
see Fish Populations

POPULISM
Botsch, Robert E. We Shall Not Overcome: Populism & Southern Blue-Collar Workers. LC 80-11567. 312p. 1981. 19.50x (ISBN 0-8078-1444-X). U of NC Pr.
Conniff, Michael L. Urban Politics in Brazil: The Rise of Populism, 1925-1945. LC 80-54060. (Pitt Latin American Ser.). (Illus.). 280p. 1981. 19.95x (ISBN 0-8229-3438-8). U of Pittsburgh Pr.
Watson, Thomas E. Prose Miscellanies. (Studies in Populism). 1980. lib. bdg. 69.95 (ISBN 0-686-68882-1). Revisionist Pr.
--The Roman Catholic Hierarchy. (Studies in Populism). 1980. lib. bdg. 69.95 (ISBN 0-686-68883-X). Revisionist Pr.
--Sketches: Historical, Literary, Biographical, Economic. (Studies in Populism). 1980. lib. bdg. 75.00 (ISBN 0-686-68884-8). Revisionist Pr.

PORCELAIN
see also Pottery
also names of varieties of porcelain, e.g. Chelsea Porcelain, Dresdan Porcelain
Gompertz, G. M. Korean Pottery & Porcelain of Yi Period. 1968. 33.00 (ISBN 0-571-08404-4, Pub. by Faber & Faber). Merrimack Bk Serv.
Herman, Lloyd. American Porcelain. (Illus.). 150p. 1980. pap. 14.95 (ISBN 0-917304-60-8, Pub. by Timber Pr). Intl Schol Bk Serv.
Rontgen, Robert E. Marks on German Bohemian & Austrian Porcelain, Seventeen Ten to the Present. Rontgen, Robert E., tr. (Illus.). 704p. 1981. 75.00 (ISBN 0-916838-38-2). Schiffer.

PORCELAIN-COLLECTORS AND COLLECTING
Gaston, Mary F. Collector's Encyclopedia of Limoges Porcelain. (Illus.). 1980. 19.95 (ISBN 0-89145-132-3). Collector Bks.
Williams, Petra. Flow Blue China, an Aid to Identification. rev. ed. LC 80-70461. (Illus.). 234p. 1981. 12.95x (ISBN 0-914736-07-8). Fountain Hse East.

PORCELAIN-HISTORY
Azel, Jan & McCready, Karen. Porcelain: Traditions & New Visions. 200p. 1981. 30.00 (ISBN 0-8230-4091-7). Watson-Guptill.

PORCELAIN-PRICES
Worth, Veryl M. Willow Pattern China: With Separate Price Guide. 2nd ed. (Illus.). 1981. pap. 9.95. Worth Co.

PORCELAIN, CHINESE
Schiffer, H., et al. Chinese Export Porcelain: Standard Patterns & Forms, 1780-1880. 256p. 1980. 59.85x (ISBN 0-903485-96-6, Pub. by Allan Pubs England). State Mutual Bk.
Smedley, Margaret. T'ang Pottery & Porcelain. (Illus.). 168p. 1981. 58.00 (ISBN 0-571-10957-8, Pub. by Faber & Faber). Merrimack Bk Serv.

PORK
Jul, Mogens & Zeuthen, Peter. Quality of Pig Meat: Progress of Food & Nutrition Science. (Vol. 4, No. 6). 80p. 1981. 20.00 (ISBN 0-08-026831-5). Pergamon.

PORK INDUSTRY AND TRADE
Jul, Mogens & Zeuthen, Peter. Quality of Pig Meat: Progress of Food & Nutrition Science. (Vol. 4, No. 6). 80p. 1981. 20.00 (ISBN 0-08-026831-5). Pergamon.

PORNOGRAPHY
see also Erotica; Obscenity (Law); Sex in Moving-Pictures
Dworkin, Andrea. Pornography: Men's Graphic Depiction of Whores. 288p. 1981. 12.95 (ISBN 0-399-12619-8, Perigee); pap. 5.95 (ISBN 0-399-50532-6). Putnam.
Griffin, Susan. Pornography & Silence: Culture's Revolt Against Nature. LC 80-8206. 320p. 1981. 11.95 (ISBN 0-06-011647-1, HarpT). Har-Row.
Lederer, Laura, ed. Take Back the Night: Women on Pornography. LC 80-17084. 352p. 1980. 14.95 (ISBN 0-688-03728-3). Morrow.
Shaughnessy, Edward J. & Trebbi, Diana. A Standard for Miller: A Community Response to Pornography. LC 80-5648. (Illus.). 256p. 1980. lib. bdg. 18.75 (ISBN 0-8191-1280-1); pap. text ed. 10.50 (ISBN 0-8191-1281-X). U Pr of Amer.

PORNOGRAPHY IN MOTION PICTURES
see Sex in Moving-Pictures

PORPHYRIN AND PORPHYRIN COMPOUNDS
Dolphin, David, ed. The Porphyrins. Incl. Vol. 1, Pt. A. 59.00 (ISBN 0-12-220101-9); Physical Chemistry. Vol. 3, Pt. A. 71.00 (ISBN 0-12-220103-5); Vol. 4, Pt. B. 50.00 (ISBN 0-12-220104-3); Vol. 5, Pt. C. 57.50 (ISBN 0-12-220105-1). LC 77-14197. 1978-79. Acad Pr.

PORSCHE (AUTOMOBILE)
see Automobiles, Foreign-Types-Porsche

PORT HUDSON, LOUISIANA-SIEGE, 1863
Winters, John D. The Civil War in Louisiana. LC 63-9647. 552p. 1979. 25.00 (ISBN 0-8071-0834-0). La State U Pr.

PORTALS
see Doors and Doorways

PORTER, KATHERINE ANNE, 1894-
Lopez, E. H. Katherine Anne Porter. 352p. 1981. 14.95 (ISBN 0-316-53199-5). Little.

PORTFOLIO
see Investments; Securities

PORTRAITS
see also Caricatures and Cartoons; Photography-Portraits
also subdivision Portraits under local biography, names of wars, and classes of persons, and names of prominent persons
Busselle, Michael. The Complete Book of Photographing People. 1980. 19.95 (ISBN 0-671-41257-4, Kenan Pr). S&S.
Kerslake, John. Early Georgian Portraits, 2 vols. (Illus.). 800p. Set. 160.00 (ISBN 0-312-22476-1). St. Martin.
L'Orange, H. P. Apotheosis in Ancient Portraiture. (Illus.). 156p. 1981. Repr. of 1947 ed. lib. bdg. 40.00x (ISBN 0-89241-149-X). Caratzas Bros.
Oliver, Andrew & Tolles, Bryant F., Jr. Windows on the Past: Portraits at the Essex Institute. (E. I. Museum Booklet Ser.). (Illus.). 60p. (Orig.). 1981. pap. 4.95 (ISBN 0-88389-080-1). Essex Inst.
Rumford, Beatrix T., ed. American Folk Portraits: Paintings & Drawings from the Abbey Aldrich Rockefeller Folk Art Center. 1981. 35.00 (ISBN 0-686-69213-6). NYGS.
Seyl, Susan. The Art Perfected: Portraiture from the Cronise Studio. LC 80-83177. (Illus.). 160p. 1980. pap. text ed. 10.95 (ISBN 0-87595-070-1). Oreg Hist Soc.
Strong, Roy. Tudor & Jacobean Portraits, 2 vol. (Illus.). 700p. 1980. Set. 160.00x (ISBN 0-312-82220-0). St Martin.

PORTRAITS-CATALOGS
Erhart, K. Patricia, et al. Roman Portraits: Aspects of Self & Society. (Illus.). 108p. (Orig.). 1980. pap. 7.75. J P Getty Mus.
Yung, K. K., compiled by. National Portrait Gallery: Complete Illustrated Catalogue. (Illus.). 650p. 1980. 49.50x (ISBN 0-312-15777-0). St Martin.

PORTS
see Harbors

PORTUGAL-FOREIGN RELATIONS
Humbaraci & Mucnik. Portugal's African Wars. LC 72-93676. 1974. 10.00 (ISBN 0-89388-072-8). Okpaku Communications.

PORTUGAL-HISTORY
Freeman-Grenville, G. S. The Mombasa Rising Against the Portuguese, Sixteen Thirty-One: From Sworn Evidence. (British Academy-Fontes Historiae Africanae). (Illus.). 224p. 98.00x (ISBN 0-19-725992-8). Oxford U Pr.
Humbaraci & Mucnik. Portugal's African Wars. LC 72-93676. 1974. 10.00 (ISBN 0-89388-072-8). Okpaku Communications.

PORTUGUESE IN FOREIGN COUNTRIES
Bender, Gerald J. Angola Under the Portuguese: The Myth & the Reality. (Illus.). 315p. 1981. pap. 6.95x (ISBN 0-520-04274-3, CAMPUS 269). U of Cal Pr.
Pap, Leo. The Portuguese-Americans. (Immigrant Heritage of America Ser.). 1981. lib. bdg. 14.95 (ISBN 0-8057-8417-9). Twayne.

PORTUGUESE LANGUAGE-CONVERSATION AND PHRASE BOOKS
Stern, A Z. & Reif, Joseph A. Useful Expressions Portuguese. (Useful Expressions Ser.). 64p. (Orig.). 1981. pap. 1.50 (ISBN 0-86628-022-7). Ridgefield Pub.

PORTUGUESE LANGUAGE-DICTIONARIES
Diziònario Comleto Italiano-Portoghese (Brasiliano)--Portoghese (Brasiliano)-Italiano: Con L'etimologia Delle Voci Itaiane e Portoghesi (Brasiliane), la Loro Esatta Traduzione, Frasi e Modi Di Dire, 2 vols. 1978. Set. 82.00; Vol. 1, 920 Pp. (ISBN 88-203-1010-4); Vol. 2, 1052pp. (ISBN 88-203-0216-0). S F Vanni.

PORTUGUESE LITERATURE-HISTORY AND CRITICISM
Sousa, Ronald W. The Rediscoverers: Major Writers in the Portuguese Literature of National Regeneration. LC 80-21453. (Illus.). 208p. 1981. 17.50x (ISBN 0-271-00300-6). Pa St U Pr.

POSITION ANALYSIS
see Topology

POSITIVE IONS
see Cations

POSITIVISM
see also Idealism; Logical Positivism; Materialism; Pragmatism; Realism
Prater, Arnold. Miracle Living. (Orig.). pap. 2.95 (ISBN 0-89081-125-3). Harvest Hse.
Schuller, Robert H. Discover Courage to Face Your Future. (Orig.). 1978. pap. 1.25 (ISBN 0-89081-156-3). Harvest Hse.
--Discover Freedom. (Orig.). 1978. pap. 1.25 (ISBN 0-89081-155-5). Harvest Hse.
--Discover Health & Happiness. (Orig.). 1978. pap. 1.25 (ISBN 0-89081-143-1). Harvest Hse.
--Discover How Life Can Be Beautiful. (Orig.). 1978. pap. 1.25 (ISBN 0-89081-153-9). Harvest Hse.
--Discover How to Bloom Where You Are Planted. 1978. pap. 1.25 (ISBN 0-89081-154-7). Harvest Hse.
--Discover How to Get Your Priorities Straight. (Orig.). 1978. pap. 1.25 (ISBN 0-89081-137-7). Harvest Hse.
--Discover How to Turn Activity into Energy. (Orig.). 1978. pap. 1.25 (ISBN 0-89081-135-0). Harvest Hse.
--Discover Self-Love. (Orig.). 1978. pap. 1.25 (ISBN 0-89081-134-2). Harvest Hse.
--Discover the Miracles in Your Life. (Orig.). 1978. pap. 1.25 (ISBN 0-89081-136-9). Harvest Hse.
--Discover the Power for Overcoming Defeat. (Orig.). 1978. pap. 1.25 (ISBN 0-89081-141-5). Harvest Hse.
--Discover Your Opportunities. (Orig.). 1978. pap. 1.25 (ISBN 0-89081-142-3). Harvest Hse.
--Discover Your Possibilities. (Orig.). 1980. pap. 2.25 (ISBN 0-89081-214-4). Harvest Hse.
--Discover Your Self-Confidence. (Orig.). 1978. pap. 1.25 (ISBN 0-89081-144-X). Harvest Hse.
Schwanauer, Francis. No Many Is Not a One (For the Case Is a Comparison) LC 80-6173. 66p. (Orig.). 1981. pap. text ed. 5.00 (ISBN 0-8191-1455-3). U Pr of Amer.

POSITIVISM, LOGICAL
see Logical Positivism

POSOLOGY
see Drugs-Dosage

POSSESSION, DEMONIAC
see Demoniac Possession

POST CARDS
see Postal Cards

POST-GRADUATE WORK
see Universities and Colleges-Graduate Work

POST-IMPRESSIONISM (ART)
see also Cubism; Dadaism; Impressionism (Art); Surrealism
Reff, Theodore, ed. Post-Impressionist Group Exhibitions. (Modern Art in Paris Ser.). 302p. 1981. lib. bdg. 44.00 (ISBN 0-8240-4728-1). Garland Pub.

POST-OFFICE
see Postal Service

POST-OPERATIVE CARE
see Postoperative Care

POSTAGE-STAMP COLLECTIONS
see Postage-Stamps-Collectors and Collecting

POSTAGE-STAMPS
Luff, John N. The Postage Stamps of the United States. LC 80-54039. 320p. 1981. Repr. of 1940 ed. lib. bdg. 35.00 (ISBN 0-88000-121-6). Quarterman.

POSTAGE-STAMPS-CATALOGS
Heery, Joseph M., ed. Harris Postage Stamp Catalog: Fall-Winter 1980-1981. (Illus.). 362p. (Orig.). 1980. pap. 2.95 (ISBN 0-937458-02-3). Harris & Co.

POSTAGE-STAMPS-COLLECTORS AND COLLECTING
Bierman, Stanley M. The World's Greatest Stamp Collectors. LC 80-70957. (Illus.). 400p. 1981. 17.95 (ISBN 0-8119-0347-8). Fell.
Crown, Francis, Jr. Confederate Postmaster Provisionals. 1981. lib. bdg. 60.00 (ISBN 0-88000-124-0). Quarterman.
Driscoll, Robert G., intro. by. R & R Catolog & Guide to First Day Cover Collecting: 1980-1981 Edition. (Illus.). 112p. (Orig.). 1980. pap. 1.95 (ISBN 0-937458-05-8). Harris & Co.
Gaines, Arleigh, ed. United Nations Philately. LC 80-53294. (Illus.). 704p. 1980. write for info. looseleaf (ISBN 0-938152-00-9). R & D Pubns.
Heery, Joseph M., ed. Postage Stamp Price Index U. S. & Canada from 1845: 1980-1981 Edition. (Illus.). 192p. (Orig.). 1980. pap. 2.95 (ISBN 0-937458-01-5). Harris & Co.
Mann, Wesley P., intro. by. How to Collect Stamps. rev. ed. (Illus.). 187p. (gr. 4 up). 1980. pap. 2.50 (ISBN 0-937458-00-7). Harris & Co.
Young, Walter J. Stamp Collecting A-Z. LC 80-27181. (Illus.). 150p. 1981. 9.95 (ISBN 0-498-02479-2). A S Barnes.

POSTAL CARDS
Morgan, Hal. Big Time. (Illus.). 80p. 1981. pap. 6.95 (ISBN 0-312-07852-8). St Martin.

POSTAL LAWS AND REGULATIONS
see Postal Service-Laws and Regulations

POSTAL LIFE INSURANCE
see Insurance, Life

POSTAL SERVICE
Adie, Douglas K. An Evaluation of Postal Service Wage Rates. 1977. pap. 3.75 (ISBN 0-8447-3265-6). Am Enterprise.
Tierney, John T. Postal Reorganization: Managing the Public's Business. 200p. 1981. 19.95 (ISBN 0-86569-061-8). Auburn Hse.

POSTAL SERVICE-LAWS AND REGULATIONS
see also Obscenity (Law)
Thomas, John L. Law of Lotteries, Frauds & Obscenity in the Mails. xviii, 358p. 1980. Repr. of 1903 ed. lib. bdg. 32.50x (ISBN 0-8377-1202-5). Rothman.

POSTCARDS
see Postal Cards

POSTERS
see also Commercial Art; Signs and Signboards
The Dynamite 3-D Poster Book. (gr. 3-5). pap. 3.95 (ISBN 0-590-11816-1, Schol Pap). Schol Bk Serv.
Felde, Nathan & Friedman, Julius. Public Works: The Posters of Nathan Felde & Julius Friedman. (Illus.). 64p. pap. 14.95 (ISBN 0-937246-00-X). Chicago Review.
Herdeg, Walter, ed. Graphics Posters '81: The International Annual of Poster Art. (Visual Communications Bks.). (Illus.). 204p. 1981. 59.50 (ISBN 0-8038-2714-8). Hastings.

POSTOPERATIVE CARE
DeLoach, Jane E. General Surgical Nursing. (Nursing Outline Ser.). 1979. pap. 9.50 (ISBN 0-87488-393-8). Med Exam.
Donovan, Kathryn N. General Surgical Nursing Continuing Review. LC 80-81906. 1980. pap. 9.75 (ISBN 0-87488-318-0). Med Exam.
Matsumoto, Teuro. Pre- & Postoperative Evaluation of Surgical Patients. 1979. pap. 15.50 (ISBN 0-87488-735-6). Med Exam.

POSTURE
see also Man-Attitude and Movement; Physical Education and Training; School Health
Lawson-Wood, D. & Lawson-Wood, J. Progressive Vitality & Dynamic Posture. 88p. 1977. 12.00x (ISBN 0-8464-1043-5). Beekman Pubs.

POTABLE WATER
see Drinking Water

POTASSIUM IN THE BODY
Krause, Corinne. How to up Your Potassium. 5.95 (ISBN 0-9604104-0-6). Green Hill.

POTATOES

Cornog, Mary, ed. Growing & Cooking Potatoes. LC 80-52993. 1981. pap. 7.95 (ISBN 0-911658-15-7, 3076). Yankee Bks.

POTAWATOMI INDIANS

see Indians of North America–Eastern States

POTENTIAL, ELECTRIC

see Electric Currents; Potential, Theory Of

POTENTIAL, THEORY OF

Kral, J. Integral Operators in Potential Theory. (Lecture Notes in Mathematics Ser.: Vol. 823). 171p. 1981. pap. 11.80 (ISBN 0-387-10227-2). Springer-Verlag.

POTENTIAL FUNCTIONS

see Differential Equations, Partial; Potential, Theory Of

POTTED PLANTS

see Plants, Potted

POTTER, BEATRIX, 1866-1943

Frevert, Patricia D. Beatrix Potter, Children's Storyteller. Redpath, Ann, ed. (People to Remember Ser.). (Illus.). 32p. (gr. 5-9). 1981. PLB 5.95 (ISBN 0-87191-801-3). Creative Ed.

POTTERY

see also Porcelain; Tiles

also names of varieties of pottery, e.g. Wedgwood Ware; subdivision Pottery under Indians of North America; Indians of Mexico; and similar headings

Birks, Tony. Potter's Companion: The Complete Guide to Pottery Making. (Illus.). 1977. pap. 4.95 (ISBN 0-87690-246-8). Dutton.

Rye, Owen S. Pottery Technology: Principles & Reconstruction. LC 80-53439. (Manuals on Archeology Ser.: No. 4). (Illus.). 1981. 18.00x (ISBN 0-9602822-2-X). Taraxacum.

Zakin, Richard. Electric Kiln Ceramics: A Potter's Guide to Clay & Glazes. LC 80-68274. (Illus.). 256p. 1981. 24.50 (ISBN 0-686-69517-8). Chilton.

POTTERY–COLLECTORS AND COLLECTING

Barnard, Julian. Collecting Victorian Ceramic Tiles. (The Christies International Collectors Ser.). (Illus.). 128p. 1980. 14.95 (ISBN 0-8317-9168-3). Mayflower Bks.

Husford, Sharon & Husford, Bob. Collector's Encyclopedia of Roseville Pottery. (2nd Ser.). (Illus.). 1980. 19.95 (ISBN 0-89145-139-0). Collector Bks.

POTTERY, AMERICAN

Clark, Garth. American Potters: The Work of 20 Modern Masters. 144p. 1981. 24.50 (ISBN 0-8230-0213-6). Watson-Guptill.

Dittert, Alfred E., Jr. & Plog, Fred. Generations in Clay: Pueblo Pottery of the American Southwest. LC 80-81831. (Illus.). 168p. 1980. 27.50 (ISBN 0-87358-271-3); pap. 14.95 (ISBN 0-87358-270-5). Northland.

POTTERY, ANCIENT

see also Pottery, Primitive

Brown, Roxanna M. Legend & Reality: Early Ceramics from South-East Asia. (Oxford in Asia Studies in Ceramics). (Illus.). 246p. 1977. 43.00x (ISBN 0-19-580383-3). Oxford U Pr.

POTTERY, ASIAN

Brown, Roxanna M. Legend & Reality: Early Ceramics from South-East Asia. (Oxford in Asia Studies in Ceramics). (Illus.). 246p. 1977. 43.00x (ISBN 0-19-580383-3). Oxford U Pr.

Frasche, Dean F. Southeast Asian Ceramics: Ninth Through Seventeenth Centuries. LC 76-20204. (Illus.). 144p. 1976. 25.00 (ISBN 0-87848-047-1). Asia Soc.

POTTERY, AUSTRALIAN

Scholes, Paul A. Bendigo Pottery. (Illus.). 281p. 1980. 34.95 (4040, Pub. by Lowden Pub Co Australia). Bks Australia.

POTTERY, CHINESE

Hayashiya, Seizo & Trubner, Henry. Chinese Ceramics from Japanese Collections. LC 77-1654. (Illus.). 136p. 1977. 19.95 (ISBN 0-87848-049-8). Asia Soc.

Smedley, Margaret. T'ang Pottery & Porcelain. (Illus.). 168p. 1981. 58.00 (ISBN 0-571-10957-8, Pub. by Faber & Faber). Merrimack Bk Serv.

POTTERY, GREEK

Bell, Malcolm. Morgantina Studies: Vol. 1, the Terracottas. LC 80-8537. (Illus.). 416p. 1981. 55.00x (ISBN 0-691-03946-1). Princeton U Pr.

POTTERY, JAPANESE

Sanders, Herbert H. & Tomimoto, Kenkichi. The World of Japanese Ceramics. LC 67-16771. (Illus.). 267p. 1981. 27.50 (ISBN 0-87011-042-X). Kodansha.

POTTERY, KOREAN

Gompertz, G. M. Korean Pottery & Porcelain of Yi Period. 1968. 33.00 (ISBN 0-571-08404-4, Pub. by Faber & Faber). Merrimack Bk Serv.

POTTERY, ORIENTAL

Bushell, S. W. Oriental Ceramic Art. (Illus.). 432p. 1980. 35.00 (ISBN 0-517-52581-X). Crown.

POTTERY, PREHISTORIC

see Pottery, Ancient; Pottery, Primitive

POTTERY, PRIMITIVE

see also Pottery, Ancient

Hurley, William M. Prehistoric Cordage: Identification of Impressions on Pottery. (Manuals on Archaeology Ser.: No. 3). (Illus.). xii, 154p. 1979. 18.00x (ISBN 0-9602822-0-3). Taraxacum.

POULTRY

see also Cookery (Chicken); Cookery (Poultry); Geese also names of specific breeds

Fraser, Alistair & Thear, Katie, eds. Small Farmer's Guide to Raising Livestock & Poultry. (Illus.). 240p. 1981. 25.00 (ISBN 0-668-04687-2). Arco.

Goats, Rabbits, & Chickens. (Country Home Ser.). 96p. 2.95 (ISBN 0-88453-006-X). Berkshire Traveller.

POUND, EZRA LOOMIS, 1885-1972

Pound, Ezra. Letters to John Theobald. Pearce, Donald & Schneidau, Herbert, eds. (Illus.). 196p. 1981. 20.00 (ISBN 0-933806-02-7). Black Swan CT.

Read, Forrest. Seventy-Six: One World & the Cantos of Ezra Pound. LC 80-15892. (Illus.). 475p. 1981. 25.00x (ISBN 0-8078-1455-5); pap. 14.00x (ISBN 0-8078-4076-9). U of NC Pr.

POVERTY

see also Poor; Public Welfare

also subdivisions Economic Conditions and Social Conditions under names of countries, e.g. Great Britain–Economic Conditions; Italy–Social Conditions

Fitchen, Janet M. Poverty in Rural America: A Cast Study. (Special Studies in Contemporary Social Issues). 266p. (Orig.). 1981. lib. bdg. 20.00x (ISBN 0-89158-868-X); pap. text ed. 9.50x (ISBN 0-89158-901-5). Westview.

Mitchell, Simon. The Logic of Poverty: The Case of the Brazilian Northeast. (Direct Edition Ser.). 200p. (Orig.). 1981. pap. 18.95 (ISBN 0-7100-0637-3). Routledge & Kegan.

Pollitt, Ernesto. Poverty & Malnutrition in Latin America: Early Childhood Intervention Programs. LC 80-18811. 150p. 1980. 21.95 (ISBN 0-03-058031-5). Praeger.

Williams, Karel. From Pauperism to Poverty. 500p. 1981. 60.00 (ISBN 0-7100-0698-5). Routledge & Kegan.

POWDER METALLURGY

Defense Technology Seminar, Yuma, Arizona, 1979. Powder Metallurgy in Defense Technology: Proceedings, Vol. 5. (Orig.). 1980. pap. text ed. 40.00 (ISBN 0-918404-50-9). Metal Powder.

Lenel, Fritz V. Powder Metallurgy: Principles & Applications. LC 80-81830. (Illus.). 608p. 1980. 55.00 (ISBN 0-918404-48-7). Metal Powder.

National Powder Metallurgy Conferenes, Los Angeles & Cincinnati, 1978 & 1979. Progress in Powder Metallurgy: Proceedings, Vols. 34 & 35. Cebulak, W., et al, eds. (Illus., Orig.). 1980. pap. text ed. 56.00 (ISBN 0-918404-49-5). Metal Powder.

Taubenblat, Pierre W. Copper Base Powder Metallurgy. LC 80-81464. (New Perspectives in Powder Metallurgy Ser.: Vol. 7). (Illus.). 232p. 1980. 42.00 (ISBN 0-918404-47-9). Metal Powder.

POWER (MECHANICS)

see also Force and Energy; Power Resources; Water-Power; Wind Power

Carty, T. & Smith, A. Power & Manoeuvrability. 1978. text ed. 18.25x (ISBN 0-905470-04-4). Humanities.

Wood, Peter. Switching Power Converters. 464p. 1981. text ed. 26.50 (ISBN 0-442-24333-2). Van Nos Reinhold.

POWER (PSYCHOLOGY)

see Control (Psychology)

POWER (SOCIAL SCIENCES)

see also Community Power; Social Status

Jouvenel, Bertrand de. On Power: Its Nature & the History of Its Growth. Huntington, J. F., tr. from Fr. LC 80-24721. xix, 421p. 1981. Repr. of 1949 ed. lib. bdg. 39.75x (ISBN 0-313-22515-X, JOOP). Greenwood.

Therborn, Goran. The Ideology of Power & the Power of Ideology. 144p. 1981. 12.50x (ISBN 0-8052-7095-7, Pub. by NLB England); pap. 5.50 (ISBN 0-8052-7094-9). Schocken.

POWER (THEOLOGY)

see also Authority (Religion)

Sherwood, John R. & Wagner, John C. Sources & Shapes of Power. LC 80-28125. (Into Our Third Century Ser.). (Orig.). 1981. pap. 3.95 (ISBN 0-687-39142-3). Abingdon.

POWER, EXECUTIVE

see Executive Power

POWER-BOATS

see Motor-Boats

POWER DISTRIBUTION, ELECTRIC

see Electric Power Distribution

POWER-PLANTS

Au-Yang, M. K., ed. Flow-Induced Vibration of Power Plant Components. (PVP: No. 41). 176p. 1980. 24.00 (H00168). ASME.

Hall, Lenwood W., et al. Power Plant Chlorination: A Biological & Chemical Assessment. 302p. 1981. text ed. 39.95 (ISBN 0-250-40396-X). Ann Arbor Science.

OECD. Siting Procedures for Major Energy Facilities: Some National Cases. (Illus.). 142p. (Orig.). 1980. pap. text ed. 8.00x (ISBN 92-64-11986-8). OECD.

Polimeros, George. Energy Cogeneration Handbook: Criteria for Central Plant Design. 264p. 1981. 39.50 (ISBN 0-8311-1130-5). Indus Pr.

POWER-PLANTS, ATOMIC

see Atomic Power Plants

POWER RESOURCES

Here are entered works on the available sources of mechanical power in general. Works on the physics and engineering aspects of power are entered under Power (Mechanics).

see also Biomass Energy; Energy Conservation; Solar Energy; Water-Power; Wind Power

also specific legal headings related to individual sources of power, e.g. Gas–Law and Legislation; Petroleum Law and Legislation

Abdulhadi, Hassan T. Energy--a Global Outlook: The Case for Effective International Co-operation. LC 80-41616. (Illus.). 300p. 1980. 40.00 (ISBN 0-08-027292-4); pap. 15.00 (ISBN 0-08-027293-2). Pergamon.

Ackerman, Bruce A. & Hassler, William T. Clean Coal - Dirty Air. (Illus.). 175p. 1981. 20.00x (ISBN 0-300-02628-5); pap. 5.95 (ISBN 0-300-02643-9). Yale U Pr.

Adelman, M. A. & Kaufman, G. M. Estimation of Resources & Reserves. 1981. price not set (ISBN 0-88410-644-6). Ballinger Pub.

Allen, James. From Poverty to Power. 184p. 1980. pap. 5.50 (ISBN 0-89540-061-8). Sun Pub.

American Petroleum Institute. Two Energy Futures: A National Choice for the 80's. LC 80-24004. (Illus.). 166p. (Orig.). 1980. pap. text ed. write for info. (ISBN 0-89364-037-9). Am Petroleum.

Amr, et al. Energy Systems in the United States. Date not set. price not set (ISBN 0-8247-1275-7). Dekker.

Auer, Peter, ed. Energy & the Developing Nations. (Pergamon Policy Studies on Energy). (Illus.). 400p. 1981. 50.00 (ISBN 0-08-027527-3). Pergamon.

Automation Industries. Solar Energy Reports Available from the National Solar Data Program. 50p. 1981. pap. 11.95 (ISBN 0-89934-104-7). Solar Energy Info.

Axelrod, Regina S., ed. Energy & the Urban Environment. LC 79-3523. (Conflict & Resolution). (Illus.). 1981. write for info. (ISBN 0-669-03460-6). Lexington Bks.

Bach, Wilfrid, et al, eds. Interactions of Energy & Climate. 568p. 1980. lib. bdg. 58.00 (ISBN 90-277-1179-8, Pub. by D. Reidel); pap. 26.50 (ISBN 90-277-1177-1). Kluwer Boston.

Barker, Michael, ed. Studies in Renewable Resource Policy, 10 vols, Vol. 1. 1981. pap. write for info. (ISBN 0-934842-74-4). Coun State Plan.

Battelle Columbus Labs. Solar Energy Employment & Requirements: 1978-1983. 200p. 1981. pap. 24.50 (ISBN 0-89934-102-0). Solar Energy Info.

Biogas & Other Rural Energy Resources Workshop, Suva. Proceedings. Bd. with Proceedings: Rural Energy Development Roving Seminar; Bangkok, Manila, Tehran & Jakarta. (Energy Resources Development Ser.: No. 19). 152p. 1979. pap. text ed. 10.00 (79/2F10, UN). Unipub.

Brin, Andre. Energy & the Oceans. 1981. pap. text ed. write for info. (ISBN 0-86103-024-9, Westbury Hse). Butterworth.

Business Communications Co. Staff. Total Energy Systems, E-021, E-021. 1981. 875.00 (ISBN 0-89336-282-4). BCC.

Cafornia Energy Commission. Passive Solar Handbook. 330p. 1981. lib. bdg. 34.50 (ISBN 0-89934-101-2). Solar Energy Info.

Casper, Barry M. & Wellstone, Paul D. Powerline: The First Battle of America's Energy War. 336p. 1981. lib. bdg. 18.50x (ISBN 0-87023-320-3); pap. 7.95 (ISBN 0-87023-321-1). U of Mass Pr.

Cleveland, Harlan, ed. Energy Futures of Developing Countries: The Neglected Victims of the Energy Crisis. 1980. 19.95 (ISBN 0-03-058669-0). Praeger.

Cluett, Christopher, et al. Individual & Community Response to Energy Facility Siting: An Annotated Bibliography. (Public Adminstration Ser.: Bibliography P-493). 50p. 1980. pap. 5.50. Vance Biblios.

Colorado Energy Research Institute, Colorado School of Mines. Water & Energy in Colorado's Future. 330p. 1981. lib. bdg. 25.00x (ISBN 0-86531-118-8). Westview.

Critser, James R., Jr. Energy Systems: Solar, Wind, Water, Geothermal. (Ser. 11-79). 1981. 125.00 (ISBN 0-914428-70-5). Lexington Data.

Crump, Ralph W., ed. The Design Connection: Energy & Technology in Architecture. Harms, Martin J. (Preston Thomas Memorial Series in Architecture). 144p. 1981. text ed. 19.95 (ISBN 0-442-23125-3). Van Nos Reinhold.

Cullen, Jim. How to Be Your Own Power Company: The Low-Voltage Direct-Current, Power-Generating System. 142p. 1980. 16.95 (ISBN 0-442-24340-5); pap. 10.95 (ISBN 0-442-24345-6). Van Nos Reinhold.

Davis, Albert J. & Schubert, Robert P. Alternative Natural Energy Sources in Building Design. 2nd ed. 256p. 1981. 17.95 (ISBN 0-442-23143-1); pap. 9.95 (ISBN 0-442-22008-1). Van Nos Reinhold.

Davy McKee Corp. Plant Conversion Potential to Fuel Alcohol Production. 125p. 1981. pap. 24.50 (ISBN 0-89934-095-4). Solar Energy Info.

Dix, Samuel M. Energy Economics. Date not set. 25.00 (ISBN 0-918998-05-0). Energy Educ.

Eden, R. J., et al. Energy Economics: Growth, Resources & Policies. (Illus.). 445p. Date not set. 34.95 (ISBN 0-521-23685-1). Cambridge U Pr.

Energy Efficient Building Handbook. 1981. 45.00 (ISBN 0-89336-283-2). BCC.

Energy Policy for the Manufacturing Sector. 155p. 1980. pap. 13.25 (ISBN 92-833-1459-X, APO 90, APO). Unipub.

Energy Reserves & Supplies in the ECE Region. 74p. 1980. pap. 7.00 (ISBN 0-686-68953-4, UN79/2E24, UN). Unipub.

Goldin, Augusta. Oceans of Energy: Reservoir of Power for the Future. LC 79-3767. (Illus.). 114p. (gr. 7 up). 8.95 (ISBN 0-15-257688-6, HJ). HarBraceJ.

Gordon, Richard. World Energy Problems: An Economic Analysis. (Illus.). 320p. 1981. text ed. 30.00x (ISBN 0-262-07080-4). MIT Pr.

Hackleman, Michael. Better Use of. LC 80-9000. (Illus.). 144p. 1981. pap. 9.95 (ISBN 0-915238-50-0). Peace Pr.

Hafele, W. & Kirchmayer, L. K., eds. Modeling of Large-scale Energy Systems: Proceedings of the IIASA-IFAC Symposium, Laxenburg, Austria, Feb. 25-29, 1980, Vol. 11. LC 80-41554. (IIASA Proceedings Ser.: Vol 11). 350p. 1980. 70.00 (ISBN 0-08-025696-1). Pergamon.

House, David. The Biogas Handbook. LC 80-8998. Orig. Title: The Compleat Biogas Handbook. (Illus.). 224p. 1981. pap. 10.95 (ISBN 0-915238-47-0). Peace Pr.

Howell, Yvonne & Miller, Harry. Selling the Solar Home: California Edition. 93p. 1981. pap. 10.00 (ISBN 0-89934-081-4). Solar Energy Info.

Jaques Cattell Press, ed. Energy Research Programs. 450p. 1981. 75.00 (ISBN 0-8352-1352-8). Bowker.

Kahan, Michael. Energy. 1981. 16.95 (ISBN 0-936278-00-5). Green Hill.

Kavrakoglu, Ibbrahim, ed. Mathematical Modeling of Energy Systems. (NATO Advanced Study Institute Ser.: Applied Science, No. 37). 490p. 1980. 55.00x (ISBN 90-286-0690-4). Sijthoff & Noordhoff.

Krockover, Gerald & Devito, Alfred. Activities Handbook for Energy Education. (Illus.). 192p. (Orig.). 1981. pap. 10.95 (ISBN 0-8302-2717-2). Goodyear.

Let's Reach for the Sun: Thirty Original Solar & Earth Sheltered Home Designs. rev. ed. (Illus.). 144p. 1981. pap. 9.95 (ISBN 0-9603570-1-7). Space-Time.

Littlefield, Charles W. Man, Minerals, & Masters. (Illus.). 140p. 1980. pap. 5.50 (ISBN 0-89540-059-6). Sun Pub.

McCormick, Michael E. Ocean Wave Energy Conversion. (Alternate Energy Ser.). 300p. 1981. 30.00 (ISBN 0-471-08543-X, Pub. by Wiley-Interscience). Wiley.

McGraw-Hill Book Co. McGraw-Hill Encyclopedia of Energy. 2nd ed. Parker, Sybil P., ed. LC 80-18078. (Illus.). 856p. 1980. 34.50 (ISBN 0-07-045268-7). McGraw.

Manassah, Jamal T., ed. Alternate Energy Sources. 1981. Pt. A. write for info. (ISBN 0-12-467101-2); Pt. B. write for info. (ISBN 0-12-467102-0). Acad Pr.

Morgan, Robert P. & Icerman, Larry J. Renewable Resource Utilization for Development. (PPS on International Development Ser.). 325p. 1981. 35.00 (ISBN 0-08-026338-0). Pergamon.

Mukherjee, J. N. Forward with Nature: An Integrated Approach to World Problems of Technology, Energy & Agriculture. 188p. 1979. text ed. 18.00x (ISBN 0-8426-1676-4). Verry.

Nelson, Robert V. Coal: The New Energy Source. Ide, Arthur F., ed. LC 79-9940. (E Equals M C Squared Ser.). (Illus.). 70p. (Orig.). 1981. 12.00 (ISBN 0-86663-804-0); pap. 7.50 (ISBN 0-86663-805-9). Ide Hse.

Norback, Peter & Norback, Craig. The Consumer's Energy Handbook. 272p. 1981. 19.95 (ISBN 0-442-26066-0); pap. 14.95 (ISBN 0-442-26067-9). Van Nos Reinhold.

OAO Corp. Biomass Energy Systems Program Summary Nineteen Eighty. 220p. 1981. pap. 24.50 (ISBN 0-89934-103-9). Solar Energy Info.

Odum, Howard T. & Odum, Elisabeth C. Energy Basis for Man & Nature. 2nd ed. (Illus.). 352p. 1981. text ed. 19.50 (ISBN 0-07-047511-3, C); pap. text ed. 12.95 (ISBN 0-07-047510-5, C); instrs'. manual avail. McGraw.

OECD & IEA, eds. A Group Strategy for Energy Research, Development & Demonstration. 97p. (Orig.). 1980. pap. 8.00 (ISBN 9-2641-2124-2). OECD.

Office of Technology Assessment. Energy from Biological Processes. 205p. 1981. lib. bdg. 34.50 (ISBN 0-89934-090-3); pap. 22.50 (ISBN 0-89934-107-1). Solar Energy Info.

Oppenheimer, Ernest J. Natural Gas: The New Energy Leader. 156p. (Orig.). 1981. pap. 7.50 (ISBN 0-9603982-2-8). Pen & Podium.

Oxford Energy Seminar, First & Mabro, Robert. World Energy; Issues & Policies: Proceedings. 384p. 1980. 44.00x (ISBN 0-19-920119-6). Oxford U Pr.

Pluta, Joseph E., ed. The Energy Picture: Problems & Prospects. LC 80-68659. 185p. 1980. pap. 6.00. U of Tex Busn Res.

Power for the Use of Man. 128p. 1980. 35.00x (ISBN 0-7277-0067-7, Pub. by Telford England). State Mutual Bk.

PRC Energy Analysis Co. Design, Installation & Operation of Small, Stand-Alone Photovoltaic Powersystems. 300p. 1981. pap. 34.50 (ISBN 0-89934-092-X). Solar Energy Info.

Proceedings of the Workshop on Biogas & Other Rural Energy Resources, Held at Suva, & the Roving Seminar on Rural Energy Development, Held at Bangkok, Manila, Tehran, & Jakarta. (Energy Resources Development Ser.: No.19-1979). 152p. 1979. pap. 10.00 (79-2F10, UN). Unipub.

Public Servie Co. of New Mexico. Technical & Economic Assessment of Solar Hybrid Repowering. 450p. 1981. pap. 39.50 (ISBN 0-89934-083-0). Solar Energy Info.
Raytheon Service Co. Wind Energy Systems Program Summary Nineteen Eighty. 230p. 1981. pap. 19.50 (ISBN 0-89934-108-X). Solar Energy Info.
Ross, D. Energy from the Waves. 2nd rev. ed. LC 80-41076. (Illus.). 160p. 1981. 21.00 (ISBN 0-08-026715-7); pap. 9.00 (ISBN 0-686-68875-9). Pergamon.
Ross, Marc H. & Williams, Robert H. Our Energy-Regaining Control. (Illus.). 320p. 1980. 16.95 (ISBN 0-07-053894-8, P&RB). McGraw.
Rural Energy Systems in the Humid Tropics. 56p. 1980. pap. 8.50 (ISBN 92-808-0093-0, TUNU088, UNU). Unipub.
Schaefer, Elizabeth & Benson, Jim. Energy & Power in Your Community: How to Analyze Where It Comes from, How Much It Costs, & Who Controls It. (Illus.). 140p. (Orig.). 1980. pap. text ed. 6.00 (ISBN 0-937786-03-9). Inst Ecological.
Schnittker Assocs. Ethanol: Farm & Fuel Issues. 160p. 1981. pap. 19.50 (ISBN 0-89934-096-2). Solar Energy Info.
Schwaller, Anthony E. Energy: Sources of Power. LC 79-57017. (Technology Series). (Illus.). 446p. 1980. text ed. 15.95 (ISBN 0-87192-122-7, 000-4). Davis Pubns.
Skinner, Brian J., ed. Earth's Energy & Mineral Resources. (The Earth & Its Inhabitants: Selected Readings from American Scientist Ser.). (Illus.). 200p. 1980. pap. 8.95 (ISBN 0-913232-90-4). W Kaufmann.
Solomon, Lawrence. Energy Shock: After the Oil Runs Out. LC 80-1072. 224p. 1981. 17.95 (ISBN 0-385-17160-9); pap. 9.95 (ISBN 0-385-17161-7). Doubleday.
SRI International. California Energy Futures: Two Alternative Societal Scenarios & Their Energy Implications - Consultant Report. 206p. 1981. pap. 24.50 (ISBN 0-89934-094-6). Solar Energy Info.
Stobaugh, Robert & Yergin, Daniel, eds. Energy Future: The Report of the Energy Project at the Harvard Business School. 1980. pap. 2.95 (ISBN 0-345-29349-5). Ballantine.
Sullivan, Thomas F. & Heavner, Martin L., eds. Energy Reference Handbook. 3rd ed. LC 80-84728. 400p. 1981. 28.50 (ISBN 0-86587-082-9). Gov Insts.
Texas A & M University Library. Energy Bibliography & Index, Vol. 4. 1400p. 1981. 295.00 (ISBN 0-87201-284-0). Gulf Pub.
Timmerhaus, Klaus D., ed. Energy Resources Recovery in Arid Lands. (Illus.). 200p. 1981. price not set (ISBN 0-8263-0582-2); pap. price not set (ISBN 0-8263-0583-0). U of NM Pr.
United Nations Economic Commission for Europe. Combined Production of Electric Power & Heat: Proceedings of a Seminar Organized by the Committee on Electric Power of the United Nations Economic Commission for Europe, Hamburg, FR Germany, 6-9 November 1978. LC 80-755. (Illus.). 150p. 32.00 (ISBN 0-08-025677-5). Pergamon.
University of Oklahoma Science & Public Policy Program. Energy from the West: A Technology Assessment of Western Energy Resource Development. LC 80-5936. (Illus.). 500p. 1981. 25.00 (ISBN 0-8061-1750-8); pap. 9.95 (ISBN 0-8061-1751-6). U of Okla Pr.
Ural, Oktay, ed. Energy Resources & Conservation Related to Built Environment: Proceedings of the International Conference, Dec. 7-12, 1980, Miami Beach, Florida, 2 vols. (Pergamon Policy Studies on International Development). 1290p. 1981. Set. 150.00 (ISBN 0-08-027170-7). Pergamon.
U.S. Dept. of Energy. Ocean Energy Systems Program Summary: Fiscal Year Nineteen Seventy Nine. 285p. 1981. pap. 30.00 (ISBN 0-89934-100-4). Solar Energy Info.
--Solar Energy Program Summary Document Nineteen Eighty One. 375p. 1981. pap. 34.50 (ISBN 0-89934-093-8). Solar Energy Info.
U.S. National Alcohol Fuels Commission. State Initiatives on Alcohol Fuels. 102p. 1981. pap. 15.00 (ISBN 0-89934-105-5). Solar Energy Info.
U.S. National Alcohols Fuels Commission. Fuel Alcohol on the Farm. 50p. 1981. pap. 4.95 (ISBN 0-89934-097-0). Solar Energy Info.
Vogt, Frederick, ed. Energy Conservation & Use of Solar & Other Renewable Energy: Proceedings. (Illus.). 580p. 1981. 100.00 (ISBN 0-08-026866-8). Pergamon.
Working Group Meeting on Energy Planning Program & Committee on Natural Resources, Fifth. Proceedings. (Energy Resources Development Ser.: No. 20). 151p. 1980. pap. 12.00 (ISBN 0-686-68966-6, UN79/2F11, UN). Unipub.

POWER RESOURCES–AUSTRALIA

Saddler, Hugh. Energy in Australia. 215p. 1981. text ed. 19.95x (ISBN 0-86861-298-7, 2646). Allen Unwin.

POWER RESOURCES–GREAT BRITAIN

British Association for the Advancement of Science, ed. Energy in the Balance. 260p. 1980. pap. text ed. 23.40 (ISBN 0-86103-031-1). Butterworths.

POWER SUPPLY

see Power Resources

POWERS (LAW)

see Trusts and Trustees

POWERS (THEOLOGY)

see Spirits

POWERS, CONGRESSIONAL (UNITED STATES)

see United States–Congress–Powers and Duties

PRACTICE (LAW)

see Procedure (Law)

PRACTICAL NURSING

see also Home Nursing

Thompson, Eleanor D. Pediatric Nursing: An Introductory Text. 400p. 1981. pap. text ed. price not set (ISBN 0-7216-8843-8). Saunders.

PRACTICAL POLITICS

see Politics, Practical

PRACTICE TEACHING

see Student Teaching

PRAGMATISM

see also Reality; Truth; Utilitarianism

Cole, Peter, ed. Radical Pragmatics. 1981. price not set (ISBN 0-12-179660-4). Acad Pr.
Mulvaney, Robert J. & Zeltner, Philip M., eds. Pragmatism: Its Sources & Prospects. LC 80-26475. 1981. text ed. 9.95 (ISBN 0-87249-404-7). U of SC Pr.

PRAGUE

Time-Life Books Editors & Moorehouse, Geoffrey. Prague. (The Great Cities Ser.). (Illus.). 200p. 1981. 14.95 (ISBN 0-8094-3116-5). Time-Life.

PRAISE

Collingridge, Ruth & Sekowsky, JoAnne. Introduction to Praise. (Workshop Ser.). (Orig.). 1980. pap. write for info. (ISBN 0-930756-60-6, 4235-PW1). Women's Aglow.
Wilkerson, David, tr. Poder De la Alabanza. (Spanish Bks.). (Span.). 1978. 1.90 (ISBN 0-8297-0444-2). Life Pubs Intl.
--Respuesta a la Alabanza. (Spanish Bks.). (Span.). 1979. 1.80 (ISBN 0-8297-0446-9). Life Pubs Intl.

PRAWNS

see Shrimps

PRAYER

see also Contemplation; Devotional Exercises; Meditation; Prayers; Retreats

Allen, Charles L. All Things Are Possible Through Prayer. (Orig.). pap. 1.95 (ISBN 0-515-05982-X). Jove Pubns.
Baker, Robert J. I'm Listening Lord, Keep Talking. 200p. 1981. pap. 6.95 (ISBN 0-8361-1953-3). Herald Pr.
Beryl & Newman, Michael. A Guide to Prayer for Busy People. (Jubilee Ser.). (Illus.). 48p. (Orig.). 1980. pap. 1.95 (ISBN 0-89570-196-0). Claretian Pubns.
Biehl, Bobb & Hagelganz, James W. Praying: How to Start & Keep Going. 144p. 1981. pap. text ed. 2.50 (ISBN 0-8307-0781-6). Regal.
Bouley, Alan. From Freedom to Formula: The Evolution of the Eucharistic Prayer from Oral Improvisation to Written Text. (Studies in Christian Antiquity: Vol. 21). 288p. 1980. 25.00x (ISBN 0-8132-0554-9, Pub. by Cath U of America Pr). Intl Schol Bk.
Carlson, G. Raymond. Prayer & the Christian's Devotional Life. (Radiant Life Ser.). 128p. (Orig.). 1981. write for info. Gospel Pub.
Clark, Glenn. Living Prayer. 1980. pap. 0.50 (ISBN 0-910924-88-0). Macalester.
Delbene, Ron & Montgomery, Herb. Breath of Life: A Simple Way to Pray. 128p. (Orig.). 1981. pap. 3.95 (ISBN 0-03-059059-0). Winston Pr.
Dull, Elaine & Sekowsky, Jo Anne. Ensenanos a Orar. Fast, Todd H., tr. (Estudio Biblico De Aglow: No. E-2(S)). 64p. (Span.). 1980. pap. 1.95 (ISBN 0-930756-55-X, 4220-E2). Women's Aglow.
Egli, Glenn. Prayer That Releases Power. (Orig.). 1981. pap. 4.95 (ISBN 0-88270-506-7). Logos.
For All God's People: Ecumenical Prayer Cycle. 240p. (Orig.). 1981. pap. cancelled (ISBN 0-88344-012-1). Orbis Bks.
Gibson, Elsie. Honest Prayer. LC 80-39570. (Orig.). 1981. pap. price not set (ISBN 0-664-24348-7). Westminster.
Gipson, Leland F. How to Use the Tremendous Power of Creative Prayer. 120p. (Orig.). 1981. pap. 3.95x (ISBN 0-9605014-0-1). Levada.
Hagin, Kenneth E. The Art of Intercession. 1980. pap. 3.25 (ISBN 0-89276-503-8). Hagin Ministries.
Harakas, S. Melody of Prayer. 1979. pap. 1.45 (ISBN 0-686-27068-1). Light&Life Pub Co MN.
Hill, Jeanne. Secrets of Prayer Joy. 64p. 1981. pap. 2.95 (ISBN 0-8170-0910-8). Judson.
Jones, Michael, ed. Prayers & Graces. 1980. 5.50 (ISBN 0-903540-33-9, Pub. by Flores Books). St George Bk Serv.
Leech, Kenneth. True Prayer: An Invitation to Christian Spirituality. 208p. 1981. 9.95 (ISBN 0-06-065227-6, HarpR). Har-Row.
Lockyer. All the Prayers All the Pomises. Date not set. Set. 24.90 (ISBN 0-686-69347-7, 10089). Zondervan.
Macarthur, John, Jr. Jesus' Pattern of Prayer. 200p. 1981. 7.95 (ISBN 0-8024-4961-1). Moody.
Maloney, George A. Prayer of the Heart. LC 80-69095. 208p. (Orig.). 1981. pap. 3.95 (ISBN 0-87793-216-6). Ave Maria.
Martin, Fay C. Availing Prayer. 120p. pap. 1.00. Faith Pub Hse.
Michaelle. Yoga & Prayer. Cumming, Diane, tr. pap. 6.50 (ISBN 0-87061-059-7). Chr Classics.
Murray, Andrew. The Prayer Life. 160p. 1981. pap. 2.50 (ISBN 0-88368-102-1). Whitaker Hse.
Prose, Mary R. Spiritual Journeying: Directions on the Path for Prayer. LC 79-67513. 94p. 1980. 6.95 (ISBN 0-533-04472-3). Vantage.
Religious Education Staff. The Spirit Alive in Prayer: Spirit Masters. (To Live Is Christ Ser.). 1979. 9.95 (ISBN 0-697-01699-4). Wm C Brown.
Rinker, Rosalind. Conversational Prayer. (Orig.). pap. 1.50 (ISBN 0-89129-210-1). Jove Pubns.
Smith, Chuck. Effective Prayer Life. LC 78-27511. 96p. 1980. pap. 1.95 (ISBN 0-936728-03-5). Word for Today.
Steere, Douglas V. Prayer in the Contemporary World. LC 80-82942. 32p. Repr. of 1966 ed. pap. 1.25 (ISBN 0-87574-907-0). Pendle Hill.
Tileston, Mary W. Great Souls at Prayer. 366p. Repr. of 1898 ed. text ed. 9.50 (ISBN 0-227-67474-X). Attic Pr.
Winkler, Gabriele. Prayer Attitude in the Eastern Church. 1978. pap. 1.25 (ISBN 0-937032-01-8). Light & Life Pub Co MN.

PRAYER–BIBLICAL TEACHING

Barton, Donald W. Training of the Twelve: How to Teach Yourself & Others to Pray. 165p. (Orig.). 1981. pap. 3.95 (ISBN 0-938736-01-9). Life Enrich.

PRAYER–JUVENILE LITERATURE

see also Children–Prayer-Books and Devotions

Todd, Sharon. Adventures in Nameless Valley Ranch. Van Dolson, Bobbie J., ed. 96p. 1981. pap. price not set (ISBN 0-8280-0032-8). Review & Herald.
Touching Incidents & Remarkable Answers to Prayer. 135p. pap. 1.00. Faith Pub Hse.

PRAYER, MENTAL

see Meditation

PRAYERS

see also Bible–Prayers; Children–Prayer-Books and Devotions; Grace at Meals; Lord's Prayer; Meditations; Prayer

also subdivision Prayer-Books and Devotions under religious denominations, classes of persons, etc., e.g. Catholic Church–Prayer-Books and Devotions

Carr, Jo & Sorley, Imogene. Plum Jelly & Stained Glass & Other Prayers. (Festival Bks). 1981. pap. 1.95 (ISBN 0-687-31660-X). Abingdon.
Long, Charles H., ed. Partners in Prayer. 1980. 1.50 (ISBN 0-686-28786-X). Forward Movement.
Miller, William A. Conservations. 96p. 1980. pap. 2.95 (ISBN 0-934104-04-2). Woodland.
Morneau, Robert F. Mantras for the Morning: An Introduction to Holistic Prayer. (Illus.). 120p. 1981. pap. 4.25 (ISBN 0-8146-1210-5). Liturgical Pr.
Nouwen, Henri J. A Cry for Mercy: Prayers from the Genesee. LC 80-2563. 144p. 1981. 9.95 (ISBN 0-385-17507-8). Doubleday.
Ortega, Jose L. Devocionario Biblico Guadalupano. 64p. 1980. pap. 1.50 (ISBN 0-89243-130-X). Liguori Pubns.
Pink, A. W. Effectual Fervent Prayer. White, Donald R., ed. 176p. 1981. 8.95 (ISBN 0-8010-7059-7). Baker Bk.
Prayers for All Occasions. 1951. 0.60 (ISBN 0-686-28788-6). Forward Movement.
Prayers New & Old. 1937. 0.60 (ISBN 0-686-28789-4). Forward Movement.
Stevens, Elliot L., ed. CAR Yearbook: 1979, Vol. 89. 1980. 15.00. Central Conf.
The Mother. Prayers & Meditations. rev. ed. Aurobindo, Sri, tr. from Fr. 380p. (Orig.). 1979. pap. 10.00 (ISBN 0-89744-998-3, Sri Aurobindo Ashram Trust India). Auromere.
White, Mary C., compiled by. Prayers by & for the Elderly. 1979. 0.60 (ISBN 0-686-28787-8). Forward Movement.
Wolf, Mary A. Mom's Tried & True Recipes for Family Prayer. (Illus., Orig.). 1981. pap. 3.25 (ISBN 0-89570-199-5). Claretian Pubns.

PRAYERS, TABLE

see Grace at Meals

PRAYERS AND INSTRUCTIONS

see Instructions to Juries

PRAYERS FOR CHILDREN

see Children–Prayer-Books and Devotions

PRAYERS IN THE PUBLIC SCHOOLS

see Religion in the Public Schools

PREACHING

see also Bible–Homiletical Use; Communication (Theology); Homiletical Illustrations; Sermons

Alan Of Lille. The Art of Preaching. Evans, Gillian R., tr. (Cistercian Fathers Ser.: No. 23). (Orig., Lat.). 1981. pap. price not set (ISBN 0-87907-923-1). Cistercian Pubns.
Bartlett, Gene E. Postscript to Preaching: After Forty Years, How Will I Preach Today? 88p. 1981. pap. 3.95 (ISBN 0-8170-0909-4). Judson.
Benn, J. Solomon. Preaching in Ebony. (Resources for Black Ministries Ser.). 128p. (Orig.). 1981. pap. 3.45 (ISBN 0-8010-0803-4). Baker Bk.
Chartier, Myron R. Preaching As Communication: An Interpersonal Perspective. LC 80-21304. (Abingdon Preacher Library). 128p. (Orig.). 1981. pap. 4.95 (ISBN 0-687-33826-3). Abingdon.
Cohen, Joe H. Equipped for Good Work: A Guide for Pastorso. 1981. 14.95 (ISBN 0-88289-271-1). Pelican.
Cox, James W. & Cox, Patricia P., eds. Twentieth Century Pulpit, Vol. II. 1981. pap. 8.95 (ISBN 0-687-42716-9). Abingdon.
Dabney, Robert L. On Preaching. 1979. 10.95 (ISBN 0-85151-290-9). Banner of Truth.
Lischer, Richard. A Theology of Preaching: The Dynamics of the Gospel. (Preacher's Library). (Orig.). 1981. pap. 4.95 (ISBN 0-687-41570-5). Abingdon.
Philip, D. Frank. Manual of Elocution for the Ministry. 122p. Repr. of 1948 ed. text ed. 3.50 (ISBN 0-567-02207-2). Attic Pr.
Rambisoon, Amar B. The Essentials of Successful Preaching. 1981. 6.50 (ISBN 0-8062-1706-5). Carlton.
Thompson, William D. Preaching Biblically: Exegesis & Interpretation. (Abingdon Preacher's Library). (Orig.). 1981. pap. 4.95 (ISBN 0-687-33840-9). Abingdon.
Turner, J. J. Practical Sermons That Motivate. pap. 2.95 (ISBN 0-89315-211-0). Lambert Bk.
Willimon, William H. Integrative Preaching: The Pulpit at the Center. LC 80-39628. (Abingdon Preacher's Library). 112p. (Orig.). 1981. pap. 4.95 (ISBN 0-687-19129-7). Abingdon.
Wilson, Jim. Go Preach the Kingdom Heal the Sick. 127p. pap. text ed. 4.75 (ISBN 0-227-67659-9). Attic Pr.
Woodworth, Floyd, tr. Escalera De la Predicacion. (Spanish Bks.). 1978. 1.80 (ISBN 0-686-28804-1). Life Pubs Intl.

PRECEDENTS (LAW)

see Forms (Law)

PRECIOUS METALS

see also Gold; Silver

St. Maur, Suzan & Streep, Norbert. The Jewelry Book. (Illus.). 198p. 1981. 9.95 (ISBN 0-312-44230-0). St Martin.

PRECIOUS STONES

Here are entered works of mineralogical or technological interest. Works on engraved stones and jewels from the point of view of antiquities or art are entered under Gems.

see also names of precious stones, e.g. Diamonds, Emeralds

Webster, Robert. Gemmologists' Compendium. 6th rev. ed. Jobbins, Allan, ed. 256p. 1980. 14.95 (ISBN 0-442-23885-1). Van Nos Reinhold.

PRECIOUS STONES–NORTH AMERICA

Baldwin, Charles. Colorado Gem & Mineral Collecting Localities. pap. 4.95 (ISBN 0-933472-08-0). Johnson Colo.

PRECISION OF MEASUREMENT

see Physical Measurements

PRECOCITY

see Gifted Children

PREDESTINATION

see also Free Will and Determinism

Gerstner, John. Predestination Primer. Date not set. pap. 1.95 (ISBN 0-88469-145-4). BMH Bks.

PREFABRICATED BUILDINGS

see Buildings, Prefabricated

PREGNANCY

see also Labor (Obstetrics); Obstetrics; Pregnant Schoolgirls; Prenatal Care

Alliance of Perinatal Research & Services, Inc. The Father Book: Pregnancy & Beyond. 1981. 17.50 (ISBN 0-87491-618-6); pap. 8.95 (ISBN 0-87491-422-1). Acropolis.
Berkowitz, Richard L., et al. A Guide to the Use of Medications During Pregnancy. 1980. pap. write for info. (ISBN 0-316-09173-1). Little.
--Handbook for Prescribing Medications During Pregnancy. 1981. pap. text ed. write for info (ISBN 0-316-09173-1). Little.
Brewer, Gail S. & Greene, Janice P. Right from the Start: Meeting the Challenges of Mothering Your Unborn & Newborn Baby. Gerras, Charlie, ed. (Illus.). 256p. (Orig.). 1981. pap. 11.95 (ISBN 0-87857-273-2). Rodale Pr Inc.
Cohen, Jean P. & Goirand, Roger. Your Baby: Pregnancy, Delivery, & Infant Care. (Illus.). 304p. 1981. 16.95 (ISBN 0-13-978130-7, Spec); pap. 8.95 (ISBN 0-13-978122-6). P-H.
Eisenbach, G. M. & Brod, J., eds. Kidney & Pregnancy. (Contributions to Nephrology Ser.: Vol. 25). (Illus.). vi, 144p. 1981. pap. 54.00 (ISBN 3-8055-1798-X). S Karger.
Ewy, Donna & Ewy, Rodger. The Cycle of Life. (Illus.). 384p. 1981. 17.95 (ISBN 0-525-93181-3). Dutton.
Horos, Carol. Prepared Childbirth. Date not set. pap. 2.25 (ISBN 0-440-07087-2). Dell.
Jimenez, Sherry L. Childbearing: A Guide for Pregnant Parents. (Illus.). 176p. 1980. 12.95 (Spec); pap. 5.95. P-H.
Kenefick, Madeleine. Positively Pregnant. (Illus.). 224p. 1981. pap. 2.75 (ISBN 0-523-41182-0). Pinnacle Bks.
Loader, Anne, compiled by. Pregnancy & Parenthood. (Illus.). 226p. 1980. 16.95 (ISBN 0-19-217684-6); pap. 8.95 (ISBN 0-19-286006-2). Oxford U Pr.
McCauley, Carole S. Pregnancy After Thirty-Five. 1976. 7.95 (ISBN 0-87690-219-0). Dutton.
Psychological Aspects of Pregnancy, Birthing, & Bonding. Blum, Barbara L. & Olsen, Paul T., eds. (New Directions in Psychotheraphy Ser.: Vol. IV). 336p. 1980. 25.95 (ISBN 0-87705-210-7). Human Sci Pr.
Sacks, Elizabeth. Shakespeare's Images of Pregnancy. 1980. 16.95 (ISBN 0-312-71595-1). St Martin.

Women's Co-Operative Guild. Maternity: Letters from Working-Women, Collected by the Women's Co-Operative Guild with a Preface by the Right Hon. Herbert Samuel, M.P., London 1915. LC 79-56940. (The English Working Class Ser.). 1980. lib. bdg. 20.00 (ISBN 0-8240-0127-3). Garland Pub.

Worthington, Bonnie & Taylor, Lynda. Nutrition During Pregnancy & Breast Feeding. (Illus.). 1980. pap. 2.50. Budlong.

PREGNANCY, COMPLICATIONS OF

Janz, D., et al, eds. Epilepsy, Pregnancy, & Child. 1981. text ed. price not set (ISBN 0-89004-654-9). Raven.

Milunsky, Aubrey, et al, eds. Advances in Perinatal Medicine, Vol. 1. 450p. 1981. 35.00 (ISBN 0-306-40482-6, Plenum Pr). Plenum Pub.

Schulman, Joseph D. & Simpson, Joe L., eds. Genetic Diseases in Pregnancy: Maternal Effects & Fetal Outcome. 1981. write for info. (ISBN 0-12-630940-X). Acad Pr.

PREGNANT GIRLS IN THE SCHOOLS

see Pregnant Schoolgirls

PREGNANT SCHOOLGIRLS

Ooms, Theodora. Teenage Pregnancy in a Family Context: Implications for Policy. (Family Impact Seminar Ser.). 350p. 1981. 19.50x (ISBN 0-87722-204-5). Temple U Pr.

Shapiro, Constance H. Adolescent Pregnancy Prevention: School-Community Cooperation. (Illus.). 144p. 1981. price not set (ISBN 0-398-04463-5); pap. price not set (ISBN 0-398-04464-3). C C Thomas.

PREHISTORIC ANIMALS

see Extinct Animals; Paleontology

PREHISTORIC ANTIQUITIES

see Archaeology; Man, Prehistoric

PREHISTORIC FAUNA

see Paleontology

PREHISTORIC MAN

see Man, Prehistoric

PREJUDICES AND ANTIPATHIES

see also Antisemitism; Empathy; Race Awareness; Racism

Higham, John. Strangers in the Land: Patterns of American Nativism, 1860 to 1925. LC 80-22204. (Illus.). xiv, 431p. 1981. Repr. of 1963 ed. lib. bdg. 35.50x (ISBN 0-313-22459-5, HISL). Greenwood.

Katz, Irwin. Stigma: A Social Psychological Analysis. LC 80-20765. 180p. 1981. ref. 16.50 (ISBN 0-89859-078-7). L Erlbaum Assocs.

PRELUDES AND FUGUES

see Canons, Fugues, etc.

PREMARITAL COUNSELING

see Marriage Counseling

PREMIERS

see Prime Ministers

PRENATAL CARE

Fried & Oxern. Smoking for Two: Cigarettes & Pregnancy. 102p. Date not set. 8.95 (ISBN 0-02-910720-2). Macmillan.

Rush, David, et al, eds. Diet in Pregnancy: A Randomized Controlled Trail of Nutritional Supplements. LC 79-3846. (Alan R. Liss Ser.: Vol. 16, No. 3). 1980. 26.00 (ISBN 0-8451-1037-3). March of Dimes.

Schwartz, Leni. The Life of the Unborn: Nurturing Your Child Before Birth. 312p. 1981. 12.95 (ISBN 0-399-90090-X). Marek.

White, D. N. Recent Advances in Perinatal Pathology & Physiology: Ultra Sound in Biomedicine Research Ser, Vol. 4. (Research Studies Press Ser.). 264p. 1981. 54.00 (ISBN 0-471-27925-0, Pub. by Wiley-Interscience). Wiley.

PRENATAL INFLUENCES

see also Heredity, Human

Naeye, Richard L., et al. Perinatal Diseases. (The International Academy of Pathology Monograph: No. 22). (Illus.). 300p. 1981. write for info. (6301-4). Williams & Wilkins.

PRENDERGAST, CHARLES

Wattenmaker, Richard J. The Art of Charles Prendergast. LC 68-9480. (Illus.). 1968. pap. 3.00 (ISBN 0-87846-141-8, Pub. by Mus Fine Arts Boston). C E Tuttle.

PREPAID GROUP MEDICAL PRACTICE

see Health Maintenance Organizations

PREROGATIVE, ROYAL

Chitty, Joseph, Jr. A Treatise on the Law of the Prerogative of the Crown. Berkowitz, David S. & Thorne, Samuel E., eds. LC 77-89235. (Classics of the English Legal History in the Modern Era Ser.: Vol. 72). 515p. 1979. lib. bdg. 40.00 (ISBN 0-8240-3171-7). Garland Pub.

PRESBYTERIAN CHURCH–SERMONS

Gossip, A. J. Experience Worketh Hope. (Scholar As Preacher Ser.). 206p. 1945. text ed. 7.75 (ISBN 0-567-04423-8). Attic Pr.

Leith, John. The Church: A Believing Fellowship. rev. ed. LC 80-82192. 1980. 6.95 (ISBN 0-8042-1813-7). John Knox.

Stewart, James S. The Gates of New Life. (Scholar As Preacher Ser.). 261p. Repr. of 1937 ed. pap. text ed. 10.00 (ISBN 0-567-24426-1). Attic Pr.

--The Strong Name. (Scholar As Preacher). 268p. Repr. of 1940 ed. text ed. 7.75 (ISBN 0-567-04427-0). Attic Pr.

PRESBYTERS

see Elders (Church Officers)

PRESCHOOL EDUCATION

see Education, Preschool

PRESCHOOL READERS

see Readers

PRESCRIPTIONS

see Medicine–Formulae, Receipts, Prescriptions

PRESERVATION OF ART OBJECTS

see Art Objects–Conservation and Restoration

PRESERVATION OF BOOKS

see Books–Conservation and Restoration

PRESERVATION OF FOOD

see Food–Preservation

PRESERVATION OF FORESTS

see Forest Conservation

PRESERVATION OF HISTORICAL RECORDS

see Archives

PRESERVATION OF ORGANS, TISSUES, ETC.

Scott, Russell. The Body As Property. 1981. 14.95 (ISBN 0-670-17743-1). Viking Pr.

PRESERVATION OF PHOTOGRAPHS

see Photographs–Conservation and Restoration

PRESERVATION OF WILDLIFE

see Wildlife Conservation

PRESERVATION OF ZOOLOGICAL SPECIMENS

see Zoological Specimens–Collection and Preservation

PRESERVING

see Canning and Preserving

PRESIDENTIAL PRIMARIES

see Primaries

PRESIDENTS–UNITED STATES

see also Elections–United States; Executive Power also names of Presidents

Bemis, Samuel F. John Quincy Adams & the Foundations of American Foreign Policy. LC 80-23039. (Illus.). xix, 588p. 1981. Repr. of 1949 ed. lib. bdg. 49.75x (ISBN 0-313-22636-9, BEAD). Greenwood.

Brooks, Stewart M. Our Murdered Presidents: The Medical Story. (Illus.). 234p. 1966. 8.95. Fell.

Davis, Vincent, ed. The Post Imperial Presidency. 288p. 1980. 19.95 (ISBN 0-03-055741-0). Praeger.

Grossman, Michael B. & Kumar, Martha J. Portraying the President: The White House & the News Media. 380p. 1981. text ed. 26.50 (ISBN 0-8018-2375-7); pap. 9.95 (ISBN 0-8018-2537-7). Johns Hopkins.

Kearny, Edward. Dimensions of the Modern Presidency. LC 80-68461. (Orig.). 1981. pap. text ed. 7.95x (ISBN 0-88273-268-4). Forum Pr MO.

Lewis, David A. & Hicks, Darryl E. The Presidential Zero-Year Mystery. (Orig.). 1980. pap. 2.95 (ISBN 0-88270-490-7). Logos.

The Presidents. LC 79-57491. (Illus.). 1980. 13.95 (ISBN 0-89387-038-2). Sat Eve Post.

Rose, Richard & Suleiman, Ezra N., eds. Presidents & Prime Ministers. 1980. pap. 8.25 (ISBN 0-8447-3386-5). Am Enterprise.

Sanford, Terry. Danger of Democracy: The Presidential Nominating Process. 160p. 1981. 15.00 (ISBN 0-86531-159-5). Westview.

Washington Post Staff Members. The Pursuit of the Presidency. Harwood, Richard, ed. Date not set. pap. 5.95 (ISBN 0-686-28876-9). Berkley Pub.

PRESIDENTS–UNITED STATES–ELECTION

Patterson, Thomas E. The Mass Media: How Americans Choose Their President. 220p. 1980. 21.95 (ISBN 0-03-057728-4); pap. 8.95 (ISBN 0-03-057729-2). Praeger.

Peirce, Neal R. & Longley, Lawrence D. The People's President: The Electoral College in American History & the Direct Vote Alternative. rev. ed. LC 80-24260. (Illus.). 416p. 1981. text ed. 40.00x (ISBN 0-300-02612-9); pap. 9.95 (ISBN 0-300-02704-4). Yale U Pr.

Ranney, Austin, ed. Presidential Nominating Process: Can It Be Improved? 1980. pap. 3.25 (ISBN 0-8447-3397-0). Am Enterprise.

PRESIDENTS–UNITED STATES–MESSAGES

Wilson, Woodrow. The Papers of Woodrow Wilson, Vol. 18-33. Link, Arthur S., ed. Incl. Vol. 18. 1908-1909. 1974. 30.00x (ISBN 0-691-04631-X); Vol. 19. Jan.-July 1910. 1975. 30.00x (ISBN 0-691-04633-6); Vol. 20. Jauary 12 - July 15, 1910. 1975. 30.00 (ISBN 0-691-04635-2); Vol. 21. July-Nov. 1910. 1976. 30.00 (ISBN 0-691-04636-0); Vol. 22. 1911. 1976-1977. 30.00 (ISBN 0-691-04638-7); Vol. 23. 1911-1912. 1976-1977. 30.00 (ISBN 0-691-04643-3); Vol. 24. January-August, 1912. (Illus.). 1977. text ed. 30.00 (ISBN 0-691-04645-X); Vol. 25. August - November, 1912. (Illus.). 1978. text ed. 30.00 (ISBN 0-691-04650-6); Vol. 26. Contents & Index, Vols. 14-25. 1980. 25.00 (ISBN 0-691-04664-6); Vol. 27. January - June 1913. (Illus.). 1978. 30.00 (ISBN 0-691-04652-2); Vol. 28. 1913. (Illus.). 1978. text ed. 30.00 (ISBN 0-691-04653-0); Vol. 29. 1913-1914. 1979. 30.00x (ISBN 0-691-04659-X); Vol. 30. May - December 1914. 30.00x (ISBN 0-691-04663-8); Vol. 31. September - December 1914. 1979. 30.00x (ISBN 0-691-04666-2); Vol. 32. 1979. 30.00x (ISBN 0-691-04667-0); Vol. 33. April - July 1915. (Illus.). 30.00x (ISBN 0-691-04668-9). LC 66-10880. Princeton U Pr.

PRESIDENTS–UNITED STATES–STATE OF THE UNION MESSAGES

see Presidents–United States–Messages

PRESIDENTS–UNITED STATES–WIVES AND CHILDREN

Robbins, Jhan. Bess & Harry. large print ed. LC 80-27985. 1981. Repr. of 1980 ed. 9.95 (ISBN 0-89621-263-7). Thorndike Pr.

PRESLEY, ELVIS ARON, 1935-1977

Crumbaker, Marge & Tucker, Gabe. Up & Down with Elvis Presley. (Illus.). 320p. 1981. 12.95 (ISBN 0-399-12571-X). Putnam.

Friedman. Meet Elvis Presley. (gr. 7-12). pap. 1.25 (ISBN 0-590-11875-7, Schol Pap). Schol Bk Serv.

PRESS

see also Crime and the Press; Foreign News; Liberty of the Press; News Agencies; Newspapers; Periodicals; Public Opinion

Infa Press & Advertisers Year Book 1979. 17th ed. 318p. 1979. 25.00x (ISBN 0-8002-2737-9). Intl Pubns Serv.

Liebling, A. J. The Press. 1981. pap. 6.95 (ISBN 0-394-74849-2). Pantheon.

Weiner, Richard. News Bureaus in the U. S. 6th ed. LC 80-83995. 186p. 1981. 25.00 (ISBN 0-913046-01-9). Public Relations.

PRESS–AFRICA

Botha, F. M., ed. The Advertising & Press Annual of Sothern Africa, 1980. LC 52-41681. (Illus.). 278p. 1980. 62.50x (ISBN 0-8002-2727-1). Intl Pubns Serv.

Pollak, Richard. Up Against Apartheid: The Role & the Plight of the Press in South Africa. LC 80-22363. (Science & International Affairs Ser.). 160p. 1981. price not set (ISBN 0-8093-1013-9). S Ill U Pr.

PRESS–FRANCE

Freiberg, J. W. The French Press: Class, State, & Ideology. 255p. 1981. 31.95 (ISBN 0-03-058309-8). Praeger.

PRESS, AFRO-AMERICAN

see Afro-American Press

PRESS AND CRIME

see Crime and the Press

PRESS CENSORSHIP

see Liberty of the Press

PRESS CONFERENCES

Ferrell, Robert H., et al. The Talkative President: The off-the-Record Press Conferences of Calvin Coolidge. Freidel, Frank, ed. LC 78-66526. (The History of the United States Ser.: Vol. 6). 287p. 1979. lib. bdg. 23.00 (ISBN 0-8240-9706-8). Garland Pub.

PRESS WORKING OF METAL

see Sheet-Metal Work

PRESSURE

see also Pressure Vessels

Smith, George V., ed. Material-Environment Interactions in Structural & Pressure Containment Service. (MPC: No. 15). 160p. 1980. 30.00 (G00188). ASME.

PRESSURE GROUPS

see also Lobbying

Abraham, David. The Collapse of the Weimar Republic: Political Economy & Crisis. LC 80-8533. 550p. 1981. 30.00x (ISBN 0-691-05322-7); pap. 12.50x (ISBN 0-691-10118-3). Princeton U Pr.

Hayes, Michael J. Lobbyists & Legislators: A Theory of Political Markets. 256p. 1981. 18.00 (ISBN 0-8135-0910-6). Rutgers U Pr.

Martin, Ross M. Tuc: The Growth of a Pressure Group Eighteen Sixty Eight to Nineteen Seventy Six. 408p. 1980. text ed. 42.00x (ISBN 0-19-822475-3). Oxford U Pr.

PRESSURE PACKAGING

see Aerosols

PRESSURE VESSELS

see also Boilers; Steam-Boilers

Boiler & Pressure Vessel Code Ser. (Boiler & Pressure Code Ser.: Sec X). 1980. 55.00 (P00100); pap. 65.00 loose-leaf (V00100). ASME.

Code Cases Book: Boilers & Pressure Vessels. (Boiler & Pressure Vessel Code Ser.). 1980. pap. 100.00 loose-leaf (V00120). ASME.

Code Cases Book: Boilers & Pressure Vessels. (Boilers & Pressure Vessel Code Ser.). 1980. pap. 100.00 loose-leaf (V00120). ASME.

Code Cases Book: Nuclear Components. (Boilers & Pressure Vessel Code Ser.). 1980. pap. 140.00 loose-leaf (V0012N). ASME.

Code Cases Book: Nuclear Components. (Boiler & Pressure Vessel Code Ser.). 1980. loose leaf 140.00 (V0012). ASME.

Companies Holding Boiler & Pressure Vessel Certificates of Authorization for Use of Code Symbol Stamps: 1980 Edition, Three Issues. 1978. 675.00 (EX0052). ASME.

Companies Holding Boiler & Pressure Vessel Certificates of Authorization for Use of Code Symbol Stamps: 1980 Edition-Three Issues, No. EX0052. 1980. 75.00. ASME.

Division 1: Appendices. (Boiler & Pressure Vessel Code Ser.: Sec. 3). 1980. 100.00 (P0003A); pap. 125.00 loose-leaf (V0003A). ASME.

Division 1: Subsection NB-Class 1 Components. (Boiler & Pressure Vessel Code Ser.: Sec. 3). 1980 70.00 (P0003B); pap. 100.00 loose-leaf (V0003B). ASME.

Division 1: Subsection NC-Class 2 Components. (Boiler & Pressure Vessel Code Ser.: Sec. 3). 1980. 70.00 (P0003C); pap. 100.00 loose-leaf (V0003C). ASME.

Division 1: Subsection ND-Class 3 Components. (Boiler & Pressure Vessel Code Ser.: Sec. 3). 1980. 70.00 (P0003D); pap. 100.00 loose-leaf (V0003D). ASME.

Division 1: Subsection NE Class MC Components. (Boiler & Pressure Vessel Code Ser.: Sec. 3). 1980. bound edition 70.00 (P0003E); pap. 100.00 loose-leaf (P0003E). ASME.

Division 1: Subsection NF-Component Supports. (Boiler & Pressure Vessel Code Ser.: Sec. 3). 1980. 55.00 (P0003F); pap. 65.00 loose-leaf (V0003F). ASME.

Division 1: Subsection NG-Core Support Structures. (Boiler & Pressure Vessel Code Ser.: Sec. 3). 1980. 55.00 (P0003G); pap. 65.00 loose-leaf (V0003G). ASME.

Interpreatations of the ASME Boiler & Pressure Vessel Code. 1980. annual subscription 30.00 (E0098); special 3-yr. subscription 70.00. ASME.

Magyesy, Eugene F. Pressure Vessel Handbook. 5th ed. (Illus.). Date not set. 35.00 (ISBN 0-914458-07-8). Pressure.

Material Specifications: Ferrous Materials, 3 pts, Pt. A. (Boiler & Pressure Vessel Code Ser.: Sec II). 1980. 125.00 (P0002A); loose-leaf 172.00 (V0002A). ASME.

Material Specifications: Welding Rods, Electrodes & Filler Metals. (Boiler & Pressure Vessel Code Ser.: Sec II). 1980. 55.00 (P0002C); pap. 70.00 loose-leaf (V0002C). ASME.

Nichols, R. W., ed. Developments in Pressure Vessel Technology: Materials & Fabrication, No. 3. (Illus.). xii, 364p. 1981. 68.00x (ISBN 0-686-69032-X). Intl Ideas.

Thomas Telford Ltd. Editorial Staff. Prestressed Concrete Pressure Vessels. 762p. 1980. 79.00x (ISBN 0-901948-45-4, Pub. by Telford England). State Mutual England.

PRESTIDIGITATION

see Conjuring; Magic

PRESTRESSED CONCRETE

Design Guide Plant Cast Precast & Prestressed Concrete. softcover 17.50 (ISBN 0-937040-17-7). Prestressed Concrete.

PRESTRESSED CONCRETE CONSTRUCTION

Lin, T. Y. & Burns, Ned H. Design of Prestressed Concrete Structures. 3rd ed. 752p. 1981. text ed. 28.95 (ISBN 0-471-01898-8); tchrs.' ed. avail. (ISBN 0-471-08788-2). Wiley.

PRETENDERS

see Impostors and Imposture

PREVENTION OF ACCIDENTS

see Accidents–Prevention

PREVENTION OF CRIME

see Crime Prevention

PREVENTION OF CRUELTY TO ANIMALS

see Animals, Treatment Of

PREVENTION OF DISEASE

see Medicine, Preventive

PREVENTION OF FIRES

see Fire Prevention

PREVENTIVE MEDICINE

see Medicine, Preventive

PREVIN, ANDRE, 1929-

Bookspan, Martin & Yockey, Ross. Andre Previn: A Biography. LC 80-2746. (Illus.). 384p. 1981. 14.95. Doubleday.

PRIBILOF ISLANDS

Jones, Dorothy K. A Century of Servitude: Pribilof Aleuts Under U. S. Rule. LC 80-1407. 198p. 1980. lib. bdg. 17.75 (ISBN 0-8191-1348-4); pap. text ed. 9.00 (ISBN 0-8191-1349-2). U Pr of Amer.

PRICE LABELS

see Labels

PRICE POLICY

see also Competition, Unfair; Restraint of Trade

Gisser, Micha. Intermediate Price Theory: Analysis, Issues & Applications. (Illus.). 608p. 1981. text ed. 17.95 (ISBN 0-07-023312-8, C); instructor's manual 4.95 (ISBN 0-07-023313-6). McGraw.

Leftwich. Price Systems Res. Alloc. 1979. 20.95 (ISBN 0-03-045421-2). Dryden Pr.

Young, Alexander. Pricing Decisions: A Practical Guide to Interdivisional Transfer Pricing Policy. 223p. 1979. text ed. 36.75x (ISBN 0-220-67002-1, Pub. by Busn Bks England). Renouf.

PRICE THEORY

see Microeconomics

PRICE-WAGE POLICY

see Wage-Price Policy

PRICING

see Price Policy

PRIESTESSES

see Priests

PRIESTHOOD

see also Priests

Laity, Edward. Priesthood, Old & New. 1980. 1.95 (ISBN 0-86544-012-3). Salvation Army.

PRIESTS

see also Clergy; Priesthood; also subdivision Clergy under church bodies, e.g. Catholic Church–Clergy; Church of England–Clergy

Covell, Jon Carter & Yamada, Abbot S. Unraveling Zen's Red Thread: Ikkyu's Controversial Way. LC 80-81040. (Illus.). 341p. 1980. 18.50 (ISBN 0-930878-19-1). Hollym Intl.

PRIMACY OF THE POPE

see Popes–Primacy

PRIMARIES

see also Nominations for Office

Ranney, Austin. Federalization of Presidential Primaries. 1978. pap. 3.25 (ISBN 0-8447-3297-4). Am Enterprise.

PRIMARY EDUCATION

see Education, Primary

PRIMATES

see also Apes; Man; Physical Anthropology; Sasquatch

Chivers, David J., ed. Malayan Forest Primates: Ten Years' Study in a Tropical Rain Forest. 375p. 1980. 42.50. Plenum Pub.

MacPhee, R. D. Auditory Regiona of Primates & Eutherian Insectivores. (Contributions to Primatology Ser.: Vol. 18). (Illus.). 280p. 1981. pap. 35.00 (ISBN 3-8055-1963-X). S Karger.

Napier, P. H. Catalogue of Primates in the British Museum (Natural History) & Elsewhere in the British Isles, Part 2: Family Cercopithecidae, Subfamily Cercopthecinae. 120p. 1980. pap. 25.00x (ISBN 0-565-00815-3). Sabbot-Natural Hist Bks.

PRIME MINISTERS

Rose, Richard & Suleiman, Ezra N., eds. Presidents & Prime Ministers. 1980. pap. 8.25 (ISBN 0-8447-3386-5). Am Enterprise.

Walter, James. The Leader: A Political Biography of Gough Whitlam. (Illus.). 295p. 1981. text ed. 18.00x (ISBN 0-7022-1557-0). U of Queensland Pr.

PRIME MINISTERS–GREAT BRITAIN

Thomson, George M. The Prime Ministers. LC 80-83530. (Illus.). 304p. 1981. 15.95 (ISBN 0-688-00432-6). Morrow.

PRIMERS, SPANISH

see Spanish Language–Textbooks for Children

PRIMITIVE LITERATURE

see Folk Literature

PRIMITIVE POTTERY

see Pottery, Primitive

PRIMITIVE RELIGION

see Religion, Primitive

PRIMITIVE SOCIETY

see Society, Primitive

PRINT MAKING

see Prints–Technique

PRINTERS

see also Printing

Atterbury, Paul. Berthold Wolpe. (Illus.). 96p. 1981. 22.00 (ISBN 0-571-11655-8, Pub. by Faber & Faber). Merrimack Bk Serv.

Crutchley, Brooke. To Be a Printer. 200p. 1980. 19.95 (ISBN 0-521-23663-0). Cambridge U Pr.

PRINTERS' IMPRINTS

see Imprints (In Books)

PRINTING

Printing Trades Blue Book: 1981 New York Metropolitan Edition. 1981. pap. 50.00 (ISBN 0-910880-08-5). Lewis.

PRINTING–COMPOSITION

see Type-Setting

PRINTING–HISTORY

Crutchley, Brooke. To Be a Printer. 200p. 1980. 19.95 (ISBN 0-521-23663-0). Cambridge U Pr.

Hirsch, Rudolf. The Printed Word: Its Impact & Diffusion (Primarily in the 15th & 16th Centuries) 338p. 1980. 70.00x (ISBN 0-86078-026-0, Pub. by Variorum England). State Mutual Bk.

Shaw, Graham W. Printing in Calcutta to Eighteen Hundred: A Description & Checklist. (Illus.). 144p. 1981. 79.00 (ISBN 0-19-721792-3). Oxford U Pr.

Twitchett, Denis. Printing & Publishing in Medieval China. (Illus.). 1981. pap. 14.50 (ISBN 0-913720-08-9). Sandstone.

PRINTING–LAYOUT AND TYPOGRAPHY

see also Advertising Layout and Typography; Newspaper Layout and Typography; Type and Type-Founding

Annenberg, Maurice, compiled by. A Typographical Journey Through the Inland Printer. LC 77-89269. 1977. write for info. Maran Pub.

Rels, Herbert. Rules of Printed English. 1980. 25.00x (ISBN 0-232-51038-5, Pub. by Darton-Longman-Todd England). State Mutual Bk.

Ruder, Emil. Typography: A Manual of Design. 2nd ed. (Illus.). 128p. 1981. pap. text ed. 12.95 (ISBN 0-8038-7223-2, Visual Communication). Hastings.

Silver, Gerald A. Graphic Layout & Design. 320p. 1981. 13.95 (ISBN 0-442-26774-6). Van Nos Reinhold.

PRINTING, OFFSET

see Offset Printing

PRINTING INDUSTRY

Palmer, Peggy, ed. An American Original: The Story of Kwik-Kopy Printing. (Illus.). 139p. 1980. text ed. 8.95 (ISBN 0-918464-29-3); pap. text ed. 2.95 (ISBN 0-918464-30-7). D Armstrong.

PRINTMAKING

see Prints–Technique

PRINTS

Calloway, Stephen. English Prints for the Collector. LC 80-19370. (Illus.). 240p. 1981. 50.00 (ISBN 0-87951-120-6). Overlook Pr.

Johnson, Margaret K. & Hilton, Dale K. Japanese Prints Today: Tradition with Innovation. (Illus.). 256p. (Orig.). 1980. pap. 9.95 (ISBN 0-8048-1345-0, Pub. by Shufunotomo Co Ltd Japan). C E Tuttle.

Latham, Robert. Catalogue of the Pepys Library at Magdalene College, Cambridge, Vol. 3: Pt. 1 - Prints & Drawings (General) Aspitall, A., ed. 160p. 1981. 135.00x (ISBN 0-8476-3637-2). Rowman.

Neiman, LeRoy. The Prints of LeRoy Neiman. (Illus.). 364p. 1980. 100.00. Control Data.

Reff, Theodore, ed. Exhibitions of Modern Prints. (Modern Art in Paris 1855 to 1900 Ser.). 339p. 1981. lib. bdg. 44.00 (ISBN 0-8240-4726-5). Garland Pub.

--Exhibitions of the Society of Printmakers. (Modern Art in Paris 1855 to 1900 Ser.). 262p. 1981. lib. bdg. 44.00 (ISBN 0-8240-4729-X). Garland Pub.

Simons, Rosemary. Collecting Original Prints. (The Christies International Collectors Ser.). (Illus.). 128p. 1980. 14.95 (ISBN 0-8317-1499-9). Mayflower Bks.

PRINTS–TECHNIQUE

Griffiths, Antony. Prints & Printmaking: An Introduction to the History & Techniques. 152p. 1981. text ed. 12.95 (ISBN 0-394-32673-3). Knopf.

PRISON ESCAPES

see Escapes

PRISONERS

Alpert, Geoffrey P., ed. Legal Rights of Prisoners. LC 80-17241. (Sage Criminal Justice System Annuals: Vol. 14). (Illus.). 280p. 1980. 20.00 (ISBN 0-8039-1188-2). Sage.

--Legal Rights of Prisoners. LC 80-17241. (Sage Criminal Justice System Annuals: Vol. 14). (Illus.). 280p. 1980. pap. 9.95 (ISBN 0-8039-1189-0). Sage.

Haggart, David. The Life of David Haggert, Alias John Wilson, Alias John Morison, Alias Barney M'Coul, Alias John M'Colgan, Alias Daniel O'Brien, Alias the Switcher: Written by Himself, While Under Sentence of Death. LC 80-2482. 1981. Repr. of 1821 ed. 37.50 (ISBN 0-404-19116-9). AMS Pr.

Krantz, Sheldon. Cases & Materials on the Law of Corrections & Prisoners' Rights. 2nd ed. (American Casebook Ser.). 786p. 1981. text ed. 22.95 (ISBN 0-8299-2127-3). West Pub.

McWhorter, William L. Inmante Society: Legs, Half-Pants & Gunmen, a Study of Inmate Guards. LC 80-69327. 140p. 1981. perfect bdg. 11.95 (ISBN 0-86548-047-8). Century Twenty One.

Ohrwalder, Joseph. Ten Years' Captivity in the Mahdi's Camp, 1882-1892. 13th, rev. & abr. ed. LC 80-2199. (Illus.). 1981. Repr. of 1893 ed. 54.00 (ISBN 0-404-18981-4). AMS Pr.

Richmond, M. S. Prison Profiles. 1965. 9.00 (ISBN 0-379-00238-8). Oceana.

PRISONERS–PERSONAL NARRATIVES

Lyon, Danny & McCune, Billy. Conversations with the Dead: Photographs of Prison Life. (Illus.). 1970. pap. 0.25 (ISBN 0-914412-00-0). Inst for the Arts.

PRISONERS, CHINESE

McKnight, Brian E. The Quality of Mercy: Amnesties & Traditional Chinese Justice. LC 80-26650. 224p. 1981. pap. 15.00x (ISBN 0-8248-0736-7). U Pr of Hawaii.

PRISONERS, NORWEGIAN

Christie, Nils. Limits to Pain. 96p. 1981. pap. 10.00x (ISBN 82-00-05528-0). Universitet.

PRISONERS, POLITICAL

see Political Prisoners

PRISONERS' FAMILIES

Swan, L. Alex. Families of Black Prisoners: Survival & Progress. (University Book Ser.). 1981. 188.95 (ISBN 0-8161-8412-7). G K Hall.

PRISONERS OF WAR

see also Concentration Camps

also subdivision Prisoners and Prisons under individual wars, e.g. United States–History–Revolution, 1775-1783–Prisoners and Prisons

Blair, Joan & Blair, Clay, Jr. Return from the River Kwai. 320p. 1981. pap. 2.75 (ISBN 0-345-29007-0). Ballantine.

Kochan, Miriam. Prisoners of England. 288p. 1980. text ed. 37.50x (ISBN 0-391-01738-1). Humanities.

Nakano, Takeo U. & Nakano, Leatrice. Within the Barbed Wire Fence: A Japanese Man's Account of His Internment in Canada. (Illus.). 136p. 1981. 10.00 (ISBN 0-295-95789-1). U of Wash Pr.

PRISONS

Carothers, Merlin, tr. De la Prision a la Alabanza. (Spanish Bks.). (Span.). 1979. 1.60 (ISBN 0-8297-0447-7). Life Pubs Intl.

Leslie, William. Message from Angola. Date not set. 4.95 (ISBN 0-8062-1654-9). Carlton.

Lyon, Danny & McCune, Billy. Conversations with the Dead: Photographs of Prison Life. (Illus.). 1970. pap. 0.25 (ISBN 0-914412-00-0). Inst for the Arts.

Ten Boom, Corrie, tr. Cartas Da Prisao. (Portugese Bks.). (Port.). 1979. 1.20 (ISBN 0-8297-0734-4). Life Pubs Intl.

PRISONS–GREAT BRITAIN

McConville, Sean. A History of English Prison Administration: 1750-1877. 520p. 1981. price not set (ISBN 0-7100-0694-2). Routledge & Kegan.

PRISONS–RUSSIA

Lapenna, Ivo. Soviet Penal Policy. (Background Ser.). 1968. 6.25 (ISBN 0-8023-1196-2). Dufour.

PRISONS–UNITED STATES

Bender, David L. America's Prisons: Opposing Viewpoints. (Opposing Viewpoints Ser.). 140p. (gr. 12). 1980. lib. bdg. 8.95 (ISBN 0-89908-330-7); pap. text ed. 3.95 (ISBN 0-89908-305-6). Greenhaven.

Freedman, Estelle B. Their Sister's Keepers: Women's Prison Reform in America, 1830-1930. LC 80-24918. (Women & Culture Ser.). 256p. 1981. text ed. 18.50 (ISBN 0-472-10008-4). U of Mich Pr.

Rothman. Conscience & Convenience: The Asylum & Its Alternatives in Progressive America. (Orig.). 1980. pap. text ed. 8.95 (ISBN 0-316-75775-6). Little.

PRIVACY, RIGHT OF

Gross, H. Privacy, Its Legal Protection. rev. ed. 1976. 5.95 (ISBN 0-379-11099-7). Oceana.

Hayden, Trudy & Novik, Jack. Your Rights to Privacy. (ACLU Handbook Ser.). 1980. pap. 2.50 (ISBN 0-686-69238-1, 75895). Avon.

Posner, Richard A. The Economics of Justice. LC 80-25075. (Illus.). 448p. 1981. text ed. 25.00 (ISBN 0-674-23525-8). Harvard U Pr.

PRIVATE AIRPLANES

see Airplanes, Private

PRIVATE HOUSEHOLD WORKERS

see Servants

PRIVATE INTERNATIONAL LAW

see Conflict of Laws

PRIVATE LAW

see Civil Law

PRIVATE RADIOTELEPHONE

see Citizens Band Radio

PRIVATE SCHOOLS

Gaffney, Edward M. & Moots, Philip R. Government & Campus: Federal Regulation of Religiously Affiliated Higher Education. LC 80-53164. 210p. 1981. text ed. 15.95 (ISBN 0-268-01003-X); pap. text ed. 8.95 (ISBN 0-268-01005-6). U of Notre Dame Pr.

PRIVATE SCHOOLS–DIRECTORIES

Private Independent Schools: The Bunting & Lyon Book, 1981. 34th ed. LC 72-122324. (Illus.). 1981. 40.00x (ISBN 0-913094-34-X). Bunting.

PRIVILEGE TAX

see Business Tax

PRIVILEGED DEBTS

see Bankruptcy

PRIVILEGES AND IMMUNITIES

see also Impeachments

Kroell, Maurice. L' Immunite Franque. LC 80-2021. 1981. Repr. of 1910 ed. 39.50 (ISBN 0-404-18573-8). AMS Pr.

PRIZE-FIGHTING

see Boxing

PRIZES (REWARDS)

see Rewards (Prizes, etc.)

PROBABILITIES

see also Chance; Games of Chance (Mathematics); Mathematical Statistics; Reliability (Engineering); Risk; Stochastic Processes; Time-Series Analysis

Barra, Jean-Rene & Herbach, L. Mathematical Basis of Statistics. LC 80-519. (Probability & Mathematical Statistical Ser.). 1981. write for info. (ISBN 0-12-079240-0). Acad Pr.

Cambanis, Stamatis & Simons, Gordon. Probability & Expectation Inequalities. 49p. 1980. pap. 1.60 (1263). U of NC Pr.

Ditlevsen, Ove. Uncertainty Modeling: With Applications to Multidimensional Civil Engineering. (Illus.). 448p. 1980. text ed. 69.50 (C). McGraw.

Fleiss, Joseph L. Statistical Methods for Rates & Proportions. 2nd ed. (Probability & Statistics Ser.: Applied Probability & Statistics). 300p. 1981. 24.95 (ISBN 0-471-06428-9, Pub. by Wiley-Interscience). Wiley.

Gani, J. & Rohatgi, V. K., eds. Contributions to Probability: A Collection of Papers Dedicated to Eugen Lukacs. LC 80-768. 1981. 40.00 (ISBN 0-12-274460-8). Acad Pr.

Sen, P. K. Sequential Nonparametrics: Invariance Principles & Statistical Inference. (Probability & Mathematical Statistics Ser.). 350p. 1981. 30.00 (ISBN 0-471-06013-5, Pub. by Wiley-Interscience). Wiley.

Weron, A., ed. Probability Theory an Vector Spaces II: Proceedings. (Lecture Notes in Mathematics Ser.: Vol. 828). 324p. 1981. pap. 19.50 (ISBN 0-387-10253-1). Springer-Verlag.

PROBATE LAW AND PRACTICE

see also Estates (Law); Executors and Administrators; Inheritance and Transfer Tax; Wills

Grimes, John S. Henry's Probate Law & Practice. 7th ed. 5500p. Date not set. text ed. 125.00 (ISBN 0-672-83934-2). Michie.

PROBATION

see also Juvenile Courts; Pardon

Albanese, Jay S., et al. Is Probation Working: A Guide for Managers & Methodologists. LC 80-6311. 190p. 1981. lib. bdg. 17.75 (ISBN 0-8191-1507-X); pap. text ed. 8.75 (ISBN 0-8191-1508-8). U Pr of Amer.

PROBES (ELECTRONIC INSTRUMENTS)

Heinrich, Kurt F. Electron Beam X-Ray Microanalysis. 608p. 1980. text ed. 42.50 (ISBN 0-442-23286-1). Van Nos Reinhold.

PROBLEM CHILDREN

Here are entered works on children with behavior difficulties due to emotional instability or social environment.

see also Juvenile Delinquency

Gabel, Stewart, ed. Behavioral Problems of Childhood. 1981. price not set (ISBN 0-8089-1336-0). Grune.

PROBLEM CHILDREN–EDUCATION

Brown, Gwen, et al. Educating Adolescents with Behavior Disorders. (Special Education Ser.). 448p. Date not set. text ed. 18.95 (ISBN 0-675-08056-8). Merrill.

Crisci, Elizabeth. What Do You Do with Joe? Problem Pupils & Tactful Teachers. (Illus.). 64p. (Orig.). 1981. pap. 3.50 (ISBN 0-87239-414-X, 3650). Standard Pub.

Gillha, Bill. Problem Behaviour in the Secondary School. 192p. 1981. 26.00x (ISBN 0-7099-0129-1, Pub. by Croom Helm LTD England). Biblio Dist.

PROBLEM SOLVING

see also GASP (Computer Program Language)

Ainsworth-Land, Vaune & Fletcher, Norma. Making Waves with Creative Problem-Solving. (Illus.). 52p. (Orig.). 1979. pap. text ed. 3.95 (ISBN 0-914634-66-6, 7913). DOK Pubs.

Borck, Leslie E. & Fawcett, Stephen B. Learning Counseling & Problem-Solving Skills. 350p. (Orig.). 1981. text ed. 26.00 (ISBN 0-917724-30-5); pap. text ed. 13.95 (ISBN 0-917724-35-6). Haworth Pr.

Eberle, Bob & Standish, Bob. C. P. S. for Kids: A Resource Book for Teaching Creative Problem-Solving to Children. (Illus.). 128p. (Orig.). 1980. tchr's ed 7.95 (ISBN 0-914634-79-8, 8005). DOK Pubs.

Hayes, John R. The Complete Problem Solver. 1981. write for info. Franklin Inst Pr.

Horn, Carin & Poirot, James. Computer Literacy: Problem-Solving with Computers. (Illus.). 215p. (Orig.). (gr. 7 up). 1981. pap. 10.95 (ISBN 0-88408-133-8). Sterling Swift.

King, L. Thomas. Problem Solving in a Project Environment: A Consulting Process. 168p. 1981. 19.95 (ISBN 0-471-08115-9, Pub. by Wiley-Interscience). Wiley.

Mullen, Tom. Mountaintops & Molehills. 1981. 6.95 (ISBN 0-8499-0193-6). Word Bks.

Souviney, Randall. Solving Problems Kids Care About. (Illus.). 176p. (Orig.). 1981. pap. 10.95 (ISBN 0-8302-8653-5). Goodyear.

Van Gundy, Arthur B. Techniques of Structured Problem Solving. 320p. 1981. text ed. 18.95 (ISBN 0-442-21223-2). Van Nos Reinhold.

PROCEDURE (LAW)

see also Administrative Procedure; Appellate Procedure; Civil Procedure; Courts; Criminal Procedure; Equity Pleading and Procedure; Judicial Process; Probate Law and Practice

Berkowitz, David S. & Thorne, Samuel E., eds. British Liberties. LC 77-89201. (Classics of English Legal History in the Modern Era Ser.: Vol. 57). 486p. 1979. lib. bdg. 40.00 (ISBN 0-8240-3156-3). Garland Pub.

Blackstone, Sir William. Commentaries on the Law of England, 4 vols. Berkowitz, David S. & Thorne, Samuel E., eds. LC 77-86570. (Classics of English Legal History in the Modern Era Ser.: Vol. 10). 2025p. 1979. Set. lib. bdg. 160.00 (ISBN 0-8240-3059-1). Garland Pub.

Hale, Matthew & Giles, Jacob. The Analysis of the Law. Berkowitz, David S. & Thorne, Samuel E., eds. LC 77-86566. (Classics of English Legal History in the Modern Era Ser.: Vol. 8). 435p. 1979. lib. bdg. 40.00 (ISBN 0-8240-3057-5). Garland Pub.

Larbalestrier, D. Paralegal Practice & Procedure: A Practical Guide for the Legal Assistant. 1979. pap. 9.95 (ISBN 0-13-648691-6). P-H.

West, Richard, et al. Discourse Concerning Treasons & Bills of Attainder. Berkowitz, David S. & Thorne, Samuel E., eds. LC 77-89246. (Classics of English Legal History in the Modern Era Ser.: Vol. 77). 273p. 1979. lib. bdg. 40.00 (ISBN 0-8240-3176-8). Garland Pub.

PROCEDURE (LAW)–GREAT BRITAIN

Bacon, Francis & Francis, Richard. Examples of a Treatise on Universal Justice or the Fountains of Equity, by Aphorisms. Berkowitz, David S. & Thorne, Samuel E., eds. LC 77-86639. (Classics of English Legal History in the Modern Era Ser.: Vol. 33). 125p. 1979. lib. bdg. 40.00 (ISBN 0-8240-3082-6). Garland Pub.

Berkowitz, David S. & Thorne, Samuel E., eds. Baron & Feme. LC 77-86664. (Classics of English Legal History in the Modern Era Ser.: Vol. 43). 445p. 1979. lib. bdg. 40.00 (ISBN 0-8240-3092-3). Garland Pub.

Bott, Edmund. A Collection of Decisions of the Court of the King Bench Upon the Poor Laws. Berkowitz, David S. & Thorne, Samuel E., eds. LC 77-89222. (Classics of English Legal History in the Modern Era: Vol. 67). 399p. 1979. lib. bdg. 40.00 (ISBN 0-8240-3166-0). Garland Pub.

Chitty, Joseph. A Treatise on the Game Laws & on Fisheries, 2 vols. Berkowitz, David S. & Thorne, Samuel E., eds. LC 77-86657. (Classics of English Legal History in the Modern Era Ser.: Vol. 41). 1662p. 1979. lib. bdg. 80.00 (ISBN 0-8240-3090-7). Garland Pub.

Coke, Edward & Highmore, Anthony, Jr. A Little Treatise on Baile & Maineprize. Berkowitz, David S. & Thorne, Samuel E., eds. LC 77-86576. (Classics of English Legal History in the Modern Era Ser.: Vol. 13). 352p. 1979. lib. bdg. 40.00 (ISBN 0-8240-3062-1). Garland Pub.

Hammond, Henry. The Lawfull Magistrate Upon Colour of Religion. Berkowitz, David S. & Thorne, Samuel E., eds. LC 77-89203. (Classics of English Legal History in the Modern Era Ser.: Vol. 58). 1979. lib. bdg. 40.00 (ISBN 0-8240-3157-1). Garland Pub.
Heale, William & Swinburne, Henry. An Apologie for Women. Berkowitz, David S. & Thorne, Samuel E., eds. LC 77-86658. (Classics of English Legal History in the Modern Era Ser.: Vol. 42). 322p. 1979. lib. bdg. 40.00 (ISBN 0-8240-3091-5). Garland Pub.
Jenkins, David, et al. Lex Terrae. Berkowitz, David S. & Thorne, Samuel E., eds. LC 77-89226. (Classics of English Legal History in the Modern Era Ser.: Vol. 70). 313p. 1979. lib. bdg. 40.00 (ISBN 0-8240-3169-5). Garland Pub.
Littlton, Thomas. Lyttleton: His Treatise of Tenures. Berkowitz, David S. & Thorne, Samuel E., eds. LC 77-89237. (Classics of English Legal History in the Modern Era Ser.: Vol. 73). 727p. 1979. lib. bdg. 40.00 (ISBN 0-8240-3172-5). Garland Pub.
Nelson, William. Lex Testamentaria. Berkowits, David S. & Thorne, Samuel E., eds. LC 77-89254. (Classics of English Legal History in the Modern Era Ser.: Vol. 81). 552p. 1979. lib. bdg. 40.00 (ISBN 0-8240-3180-6). Garland Pub.
Toland, John, et al. Anglia Libera. Berkowitz, David S. & Thorne, Samuel E., eds. LC 77-89231. (Classics of English Legal History in the Modern Era Ser.: Vol. 71). 400p. 1979. lib. bdg. 40.00 (ISBN 0-8240-3171-7). Garland Pub.

PROCESS CONTROL
see also Chemical Process Control
Cheremisinoff, Paul N. & Perlis, Harlan J. Analytical Measurements & Instrumentation for Process & Pollution Control. LC 80-70319. 450p. 1981. text ed. 49.95 (ISBN 0-250-40405-2). Ann Arbor Science.
Cheremisinoff, Paul N. & Perlis, Harlan J., eds. Automatic Process Control. 150p. 1981. text ed. write for info. (ISBN 0-250-40400-1). Ann Arbor Science.
Himmelblau, David M. Process Analysis by Statistical Methods. (Illus.). 471p. 1981. pap. text ed. 29.95 (ISBN 0-88408-140-0). Sterling Swift.
Isermann, R. & Kaltenecker, H. Digital Computer Applications to Process Control: Proceedings of the Sixth IFAC-IFIP Conference, Dusseldorf, Federal Republic of Germany, 14-17 October 1980. LC 80-41343. (IFAC Proceedings). 550p. 1981. 100.00 (ISBN 0-08-026749-1). Pergamon.

PROCESS ENGINEERING
see Production Engineering

PROCESS ENGINEERING (MANUFACTURES)
see Manufacturing Processes

PROCESSING, INDUSTRIAL
see Manufacturing Processes

PROCESSING, PHOTOGRAPHIC
see Photography–Processing

PROCUREMENT, INDUSTRIAL
see Industrial Procurement

PRODIGAL SON (PARABLE)
see Jesus Christ–Parables

PRODUCE
see Farm Produce

PRODUCT MANAGEMENT
see also New Products
Canavan, Michael M. Product Liability for Supervisors & Managers. 1981. text ed. 15.95 (ISBN 0-8359-5630-X). Reston.
Greenwood, Douglas C. Product Engineering Design Manual. (Illus.). 342p. 1981. Repr. text ed. write for info. (ISBN 0-89874-273-0). Krieger.
New, C. C. Managing the Manufacture of Complex Products. 379p. 1977. text ed. 29.50x (ISBN 0-220-66318-1, Pub. by Busn Bks England). Renouf.
Stessin, Lawrence. Product Liability Portfolio. 1977. 39.95. Busn Res Pubns.
Wind, Yoram, et al. New-Product Forecasting: Models & Applications. LC 80-8388. 1981. price not set (ISBN 0-669-04102-5). Lexington Bks.

PRODUCTION, COOPERATIVE
see Cooperation; Cooperative Societies

PRODUCTION CONTROL
see also Inventory Control
Adam, Everett E., Jr. & Hershauer, James C. Productivity & Quality: Measurement As a Basis for Improvement. (Illus.). 192p. 1981. text ed. 18.95 (ISBN 0-13-725002-9). P-H.
Lachenmeyer, Charles. Productive Performance. (Analysis). 51p. (Orig.). 1980. pap. text ed. 14.95 (ISBN 0-938526-01-4). Inst Analysis.

PRODUCTION ENGINEERING
see also Assembly-Line Methods; Manufacturing Processes; Materials Handling
Bailey, Anne M., ed. The Asiatic Mode of Production: Science & Politics. (Illus.). 352p. 1981. price not set (ISBN 0-7100-0737-X) (ISBN 0-7100-0738-8). Routledge & Kegan.
Pelegrin, M. J., et al, eds. Comparison of Automatic & Oprations Research Techniques Applied to Large Systems Analysis. LC 80-40979. (Illus.). 240p. 40.00 (ISBN 0-08-024454-8). Pergamon.

PRODUCTION-LINE METHODS
see Assembly-Line Methods

PRODUCTION MANAGEMENT
Buffa & Newman. Plaid for Production & Operations Management. rev. ed. Date not set. price not set (ISBN 0-256-02222-4, 11-1035-02). Learning Syst.
Buffa, Elwood S. Basic Production Management, 2 vols. Incl. Vol. 1. A Short Course in Managing Day-to-Day Operations. LC 75-27388 (ISBN 0-471-11830-3); Vol. 2. A Short Course in Planning & Designing Productive Systems. LC 75-27389 (ISBN 0-471-11831-1). (Business Administration Ser.). 1975. Set. text ed. 37.90 (ISBN 0-471-11832-X, Pub. by Wiley-Interscience); text ed. 18.95 ea. Wiley.
Fearon, et al. Fundamentals of Production Operations Management. 171p. 1979. pap. text ed. 6.95 (ISBN 0-8299-0269-4); instrs.' manual avail. (ISBN 0-8299-0478-6). West Pub.
Kalthoff, Robert J. & Lee, Leonard S. Productivity & Records Automation. (Illus.). 400p. 1981. text ed. 24.95 (ISBN 0-13-725234-X). P-H.
Olson, Richard F. Performance Appraisal: A Guide to Greater Productivity. (Self-Teaching Guide Ser.). 200p. 1981. pap. text ed. 8.95 (ISBN 0-471-09134-0). Wiley.
Schroeder, R. Operations Management. (Management Ser.). (Illus.). 736p. 1981. text ed. 19.95 (ISBN 0-07-055612-1, C); instr's manual 5.95 (ISBN 0-07-055613-X). McGraw.
Whalley, B. H. Production Management Handbook. 512p. 1980. text ed. 49.25x (ISBN 0-566-02133-1, Pub. by Gower Pub Co England). Renouf.

PRODUCTION STANDARDS
see also Time and Motion Study; Work Measurement
Tucker, Spencer A. & Lennon, Thomas H. Production Standards in Profit Planning. 256p. 1981. 19.95 (ISBN 0-444-00456-4, Thomond). Elsevier.

PRODUCTIVITY ACCOUNTING
Alexander Hamilton Institiue, Inc. Moderne Budgetierungsverfahren. Jenks, James M., ed. (Illus.). 85p. (Orig., Ger.). 1978. pap. 49.50 (ISBN 0-86604-004-8, TX-150-972). Hamilton Inst.
Alexander Hamilton Institute, Inc. The Manual of Modern Budgetary Practices. Jenks, James M., ed. (Illus.). 85p. (Orig.). 1976. pap. 57.25x (ISBN 0-86604-000-5, A783160). Hamilton Inst.
Alexander Hamilton Unstitute, Inc. Measuring Morale: Key to Increased Productivity. (Illus.). 53p. (Orig.). 1976. pap. 53.25x (ISBN 0-86604-010-2, A806007). Hamilton Inst.
Alluisi, Earl A. & Fleishman, Edwin A., eds. Stress & Performance Effectiveness. (Human Performance & Productivity Ser.: Vol.3). 336p. 1981. professional ref. text 19.95 (ISBN 0-89859-091-4). L Erlbaum Assocs.
Burnham, Don, intro. by. Manufacturing Productivity Solutions II. LC 80-54415. (Illus.). 161p. 1980. pap. text ed. 20.00 (ISBN 0-87263-106-0). SME.
Cowing, T. G. & Stevenson, R. E., eds. Productivity Measurement in Regulated Industries. (Economic Theory, Econometrics & Mathematical Economic Ser.). 1981. price not set (ISBN 0-12-194080-2). Acad Pr.
Dogramaci, Ali & Adam, Nabil R. Aggregate & Industry-Level Productivity Analysis. (Productivity Analysis Studies: Vol. 2). 204p. 1981. lib. bdg. 25.00 (ISBN 0-89838-037-5, Pub. by Martinus Nijhoff). Kluwer Boston.
Dunnette, Marvin D. & Fleishman, Edwin A., eds. Human Capability Assessment. (Human Performance & Productivity Ser.: Vol. 3). 336p. 1981. professional ref. text 19.95 (ISBN 0-89859-085-X). L Erlbaum Assocs.
Fallon, Carlos. Value Analysis, Vol. 1. rev., 2nd ed. LC 80-16194. (Illus.). 277p. 1980. text ed. 18.75 (ISBN 0-937144-00-2); pap. 10.75 (ISBN 0-937144-01-0). Triangle Pr.
McClenney, Byron N. Management for Productivity. 126p. (Orig.). 1980. pap. 5.00 (ISBN 0-87117-103-1). Am Assn Comm Jr Coll.
Mercer, James L. & Philips, Ronald J., eds. Public Technology: Key to Improved Government Productivity. 451p. 1981. 24.95 (ISBN 0-8144-5546-8). Am Mgmt.
Olson, Richard F. Performance Appraisal: A Guide to Greater Productivity. (Self-Teaching Guide Ser.). 200p. 1981. pap. text ed. 8.95 (ISBN 0-471-09134-0). Wiley.
Taraman, Khalil S., ed. CAD-CAM, Meeting Today's Productivity Challenge. LC 80-69006. (Manufacturing Update Ser.). (Illus.). 281p. 1980. 29.00 (ISBN 0-87263-063-3). SME.

PRODUCTIVITY OF LABOR
see Labor Productivity

PRODUCTS, BIOLOGICAL
see Biological Products

PRODUCTS, COMMERCIAL
see Commercial Products

PRODUCTS, DAIRY
see Dairy Products

PRODUCTS, NEW
see New Products

PROFESSIONAL BASEBALL CLUBS
see Baseball Clubs

PROFESSIONAL EDUCATION
see also Library Education; Medical Colleges; Technical Education; Universities and Colleges; also subdivision Study and Teaching under specific professions, e.g. Law–Study and Teaching
Martindale, Don. Ideals & Realities of Ph.D Advising. (Intercontinental Series in Sociology: No. 3). 14.95 (ISBN 0-933142-02-1). Intercont Press.

PROFESSIONAL ETHICS
see also Business Ethics; Legal Ethics; Medical Ethics; Nursing Ethics
Begun, James W. Professionalism & Public Interest. (Health & Public Policy Ser.). 176p. 1981. text ed. 17.50x (ISBN 0-262-02156-0). MIT Pr.

PROFESSIONAL LABORATORY EXPERIENCES (EDUCATION)
see Student Teaching

PROFESSIONS
see also College Graduates; Intellectuals; Vocational Guidance
also subdivision Vocational Guidance under specific professions
Career Planning & Decision-Making for College Students. 5.95; instrs'. 7.50. McKnight.
Dobson, Julia M. & Hawkins, Gerald S. Conversation in English: Professional Careers. (Illus.). 108p. (gr. 9-12). 1978. pap. text ed. 3.96 (ISBN 0-278-46440-8). Litton Educ Pub.
Michaels, Allen. Backdoor Guide to Entering a Profession. 60p. (Orig.). 1981. pap. 10.00. Sunrise PA.

PROFIT
see also Capitalism; Entrepreneur; Excess Profits Tax; Income; Risk
Hazel, A. C. & Reid, A. S. Enjoying a Profitable Business. 2nd ed. 251p. 1976. text ed. 18.50x (ISBN 0-220-66287-8, Pub. by Busn Bks England). Renouf.
Rachlin, Robert. Profit Strategies for Business. 144p. 1981. 12.95 (ISBN 0-13-726216-7, Spec); pap. 4.95 (ISBN 0-13-726208-6). P-H.
--Successful Techniques for Higher Profits. 260p. 1981. 16.95 (ISBN 0-938712-02-0). Marr Pubns.
Walley, B. H. Profit Planning Handbook. 325p. 1978. text ed. 29.50x (ISBN 0-220-66342-4, Pub. by Busn Bks England). Renouf.

PROFIT AND LOSS STATEMENTS
see Financial Statements

PROFIT-SHARING
see also Cooperation; Employee Ownership
Greenhill, Richard. Employee Remuneration & Profit Sharing. 224p. 1980. 45.00x (ISBN 0-85941-123-0, Pub. by Woodhead-Faulkner England). State Mutual Bk.

PROGRAM BUDGETING
Sastry, K. S. Performance Budgeting for Planned Development. (Illus.). 235p. 1980. text ed. 12.50x (ISBN 0-391-02170-2). Humanities.

PROGRAMMABLE CALCULATORS
Mullish, Henry & Kochan, Stephen. Programmable Pocket Calculators. 264p. 1980. pap. 9.95 (ISBN 0-8104-5175-1). Hayden.
Weir, Maurice D. Calculator Clout: Programming Methods for Your Programmable. (Illus.). 256p. 1981. text ed. 17.95 (ISBN 0-13-110411-X, Spec); pap. text ed. 8.95 (ISBN 0-13-110403-9, Spec). P-H.

PROGRAMMING (ELECTRONIC COMPUTERS)
see also Computer Programming Management; Computer Programs; Electronic Digital Computers; Programming Languages (Electronic Computers) also names of specific computers, e.g. IBM 1620
Banerji, Dilip & Raymond, Jacque. Elements of Microprogramming. (Illus.). 416p. 1981. text ed. 24.50 (ISBN 0-13-267146-8). P-H.
Controls Over Using & Changing Computer Programs. 1979. pap. 5.00. Am Inst CPA.
David, D. J. Pet Basics. 225p. 1981. pap. 9.95 (ISBN 0-918398-47-9). Dilithium Pr.
Dembrinski, P., ed. Mathematical Foundation of Computer Science: Proceedings. (Lecture Notes in Computer Science: Vol. 88). 723p. 1980. pap. 37.20 (ISBN 0-387-10027-X). Springer-Verlag.
Gorin, Ralph E. Introduction to DECsystem 20: Assembly Language Programming. 1981. pap. 21.00 (ISBN 0-932376-12-6). Digital Pr.
Howe, Hubert S., Jr. TRS-80 Assembly Language. (Illus.). 192p. 1981. text ed. 15.95 (ISBN 0-13-931139-4, Spec); pap. text ed. 6.95 (ISBN 0-13-931121-1, Spec). P-H.
Hughes, Charles E., et al, eds. Advanced Programming Techniques: A Second Course in Programming Using Fortran. 287p. 1978. text ed. 19.95 (ISBN 0-471-02611-5). Wiley.
Hughes, J. K. Structured Programming Using PL-C. 512p. 1981. text ed. 14.95 (ISBN 0-471-04969-7). Wiley.
Lehnen, Robert G. & Forthofer, Ronald N. Program Analysis: The GSK Categorical Data Approach. (Illus.). 225p. 1981. text ed. 25.00 (ISBN 0-534-97974-2). Lifetime Learn.
Marlin, C. D. Coroutines. (Lecture Notes in Computer Science Ser.: Vol. 95). (Illus.). 246p. 1981. pap. 16.80 (ISBN 0-387-10256-6). Springer-Verlag.
Peoples Computer Company. What to Do After You Hit Return. 180p. 1980. 14.95 (ISBN 0-8104-5476-9). Hayden.
Petersen, J. L. Computer Programs for Spelling Correction. (Lecture Notes in Computer Science Ser.: Vol. 96). 213p. 1981. pap. 14.00 (ISBN 0-387-10259-0). Springer-Verlag.
Reynolds, J. Craft of Programming. 1981. 22.95 (ISBN 0-13-188862-5). P-H.
Robinet, B., ed. International Symposium on Programming. (Lecture Notes in Computer Science: Vol. 83). 341p. 1980. pap. 19.50 (ISBN 0-387-09981-6). Springer-Verlag.
Schmid, Hermann. Decimal Computation. 280p. 1981. Repr. of 1974 ed. lib. bdg. write for info. (ISBN 0-89874-318-4). Krieger.
Scott, John. Basic Computer Logic. LC 80-5074. (The Lexington Books Series in Computer Science). 1981. write for info. (ISBN 0-669-03706-0). Lexington Bks.
Tremblay, Jean-Paul & Bunt, Richard B. An Introduction to Computer Science: An Algorithmic Approach, Short Edition. Stewart, Charles E., ed. (Illus.). 432p. 1980. text ed. 16.95 (ISBN 0-07-065167-1, C). McGraw.

PROGRAMMING (MATHEMATICS)
see also Linear Programming
Conference on Mathematical Programming, 3rd, Matrafured, Hungary, 1975. Studies on Mathematical Programming: Proceddings. Prekopa, A., ed. (Mathematical Methods of Operations Research). 200p. 1980. 22.50x (ISBN 963-05-1854-6). Intl Pubns Serv.
De Bakker, M. Mathematical Theory of Program Correctness. 1980. 28.00 (ISBN 0-13-562132-1). P-H.

PROGRAMMING LANGUAGE ONE
see P L-One (Computer Program Language)

PROGRAMMING LANGUAGES (ELECTRONIC COMPUTERS)
see also specific languages, e.g. FORTRAN (Computer Program Language)
Bakker, J. W. & Leeuwen, J. Van, eds. Automata, Languages & Programming: Seventh Colloquim. (Lecture Notes in Computer Sciences: Vol. 85). 671p. 1980. pap. 31.90 (ISBN 0-387-10003-2). Springer-Verlag.
Cherry, George. ADA Programming Structures: With an Introduction to Structured Concurrent Programming. 400p. 1981. text ed. 15.95 (ISBN 0-8359-0151-3). Reston.
Fernandez, Judi & Ashley, Ruth. Introduction to Eighty-Eighty, Eighty Eighty-Five Assembly Language Programming. 300p. 1981. pap. text ed. 8.95 (ISBN 0-471-08009-8). Wiley.
Guido, Raymond. Calculating with Basic. (Da Capo Quality Paperbacks Ser.). (Illus.). 80p. 1981. pap. text ed. 8.95 (ISBN 0-306-80144-2). Da Capo.
Hill, I. D. & Meek, B. L. Programming Language Standardisation: Computer & Their Applications. LC 80-41092. 261p. 1980. 65.00 (ISBN 0-470-27077-2). Halsted Pr.
Katzan, Harry, Jr. Invitation to Forth. (Illus.). 240p. 1981. 17.50 (ISBN 0-89433-173-6). Petrocelli.
Leventhal, Lance. Six Eight Zero Nine Assembly Language Programming. (Assembly Language Programming Ser.: No. 6). 530p. 1980. pap. text ed. 16.99 (ISBN 0-931988-35-7). Osborne-McGraw.
Leventhal, Lance, et al. Z Eight Thousand Assembly Language Programming. (Assembly Language Programming Ser.: No.5). 930p. (Orig.). 1980. pap. text ed. 19.99 (ISBN 0-931988-36-5). Osborne-McGraw.
Lien, David A. The BASIC Handbook: An Encyclopedia of the BASIC Computer Language. 2nd ed. Gunzel, Dave, ed. LC 78-64886. (CompuSoft Learning Ser.). 1981. pap. 19.95 (ISBN 0-932760-00-7). CompuSoft.
Miller, Alan R. Eighty-Eighty - ZEighty Assembly Language: Techniques for Improved Programming. 224p. 1980. pap. text ed. 8.95 (ISBN 0-471-08124-8). Wiley.
Poirot, James L. & Retzlaff, Don A. Microcomputer Workbook: Apple II Ed. 2nd ed. 137p. (gr. 11-12). 1981. pap. text ed. 5.95 (ISBN 0-88408-139-7). Sterling Swift.
Schneider & Bruell. Advanced Programming & Problem Solving with Pascal. 480p. 1981. text ed. 22.95 (ISBN 0-471-07876-X). Wiley.
Schrage, Linus. User's Manual for LINDO. (Orig.). 1981. pap. text ed. 10.00x (ISBN 0-89426-032-4). Scientific Pr.
Tennent, R. Principles of Programming Languages. 1981. 21.00 (ISBN 0-13-709873-1). P-H.
Wood, D. Grammar & L Formas: An Introduction. (Lecture Notes in Computer Science: Vol. 91). 314p. 1980. pap. 19.50 (ISBN 0-387-10233-7). Springer-Verlag.

PROGRAMMING MANAGEMENT (ELECTRONIC COMPUTERS)
see Computer Programming Management

PROGRAMS, COMPUTER
see Computer Programs

PROGRAMS, RADIO
see Radio Programs

PROGRAMS, TELEVISION
see Television Programs

PROGRESS
see also Civilization; Science and Civilization; Social Change
Benoit, Emile. Progress & Survival: An Essay on the the Future of Mankind. Gohn, Jack B., ed. 144p. 1980. 17.95 (ISBN 0-03-056911-7). Praeger.
Edgar, William J. Evidence. LC 80-67262. 471p. 1980. lib. bdg. 22.75 (ISBN 0-8191-1292-5); pap. text ed. 13.75 (ISBN 0-8191-1293-3). U Pr of Amer.
Mitchell, Lee C. Witnesses to a Vanishing America: The Nineteenth-Century Response. LC 80-8567. (Illus.). 288p. 1981. 16.50x (ISBN 0-691-06461-X). Princeton U Pr.
Pole, J. R. American Individualism & the Promise of Progress: Inaugural Lecture. (Inaugural Lecture Ser.). 30p. pap. 5.95 (ISBN 0-19-951526-3). Oxford U Pr.

PROGRESSIVISM (U. S. POLITICS)
Weinstein, James. The Corporate Ideal in the Liberal State: 1900-1918. LC 80-22211. xvii, 263p. 1981. Repr. of 1968 ed. lib. bdg. 25.00x (ISBN 0-313-22709-8, WECI). Greenwood.

PROHIBITED EXPORTS AND IMPORTS
see Foreign Trade Regulation

PROHIBITION
see also Liquor Problem; Temperance
Cashman, Sean D. Prohibition: The Life of the Land. LC 80-1853. (Illus.). 1981. 15.95 (ISBN 0-02-905730-2). Free Pr.
Kivley, Melvin. The Still & I. 1981. 8.95 (ISBN 0-533-04820-6). Vantage.

PROJECT MANAGEMENT
Taylor, W. J. & Watling, T. F. Successful Project Management. 269p. 1979. text ed. 29.50x (ISBN 0-220-67004-8, Pub. by Busn Bks England). Renouf.

PROJECT NETWORKS
see Network Analysis (Planning)

PROJECT RANGER
Day, James M. Captain Clint: Peoples Texas Ranger. 1980. 17.50 (ISBN 0-87244-055-9). Texian.

PROJECTIVE TECHNIQUES
Here are entered works on projection as a testing or diagnostic technique for revealing personality attributes or psychopathological factors.
see also Play Therapy
Rabin, Albert. Assessment with Projective Techniques: A Concise Introduction. 1981. text ed. 22.95 (ISBN 0-8261-3550-1); pap. text ed. cancelled (ISBN 0-8261-3551-X). Springer Pub.

PROLONGATION OF LIFE SPAN
see Longevity

PRONGHORN ANTELOPE
Yoakum, James D., compiled by. American Pronghorn Antelope. LC 79-89207. (Illus.). 244p. (Orig.). 1979. pap. 4.50 (ISBN 0-933564-05-8). Wildlife Soc.

PROPAGANDA
see also Advertising; Government Publicity; Lobbying; Persuasion (Psychology); Press; Psychological Warfare; Public Opinion; Public Relations; Publicity
also subdivision Propaganda under names of wars, e.g. World War, 1939-1945–Propaganda
Thomson, Oliver. Mass Persuasion in History: An Historical Analysis of the Development of Propaganda Techniques. 1977. 14.50 (ISBN 0-8448-1076-2). Crane-Russak Co.

PROPAGANDA, AMERICAN
Chandler, Robert W. War of Ideas: The U. S. Propaganda Compaign in Vietnam. (Westview Special Studies in National Defense & Security Ser.). 301p. 1981. lib. bdg. 25.00x (ISBN 0-86531-082-3). Westview.

PROPAGANDA, RUSSIAN
Hazan, Baruch. Soviet Impregnational Propaganda. 1981. 20.00 (ISBN 0-88233-643-6). Ardis Pubs.

PROPAGATION OF PLANTS
see Plant Propagation

PROPANE
Mother Earth News Staff. How to Convert Your Vehicle to Propane. Hoffman, Robert, ed. 50p. (Orig.). 1981. pap. 7.50 (ISBN 0-938432-01-X). Mother Earth.
Smith, Ross. Propane Conversion of Engines. rev. ed. (Applied Technology Ser.). (Illus.). 76p. 1980. pap. 8.45 (ISBN 0-938260-01-4). Smith & Assoc.
--Propane Conversion of Engines. rev. ed. (Applied Technology Ser.). (Illus.). 76p. 1980. pap. 9.15. Ashford.

PROPER NAMES
see Names

PROPERTY
see also Eminent Domain; Future Interests; Income; Personal Property; Real Property; Wealth
Abrahamsson, Bengt & Brostrom, Anders. The Rights of Labor. LC 80-16233. 301p. 25.00 (ISBN 0-8039-1477-6). Sage.
Boyer, Ralph E. Survey of the Law of Property. 3rd ed. 737p. 1981. text ed. write for info. (ISBN 0-8299-2128-1). West Pub.

PROPERTY–VALUATION
see Valuation

PROPERTY, HORIZONTAL
see Condominium (Housing)

PROPERTY, LITERARY
see Copyright

PROPERTY, PERSONAL
see Personal Property

PROPERTY, REAL
see Real Property

PROPERTY INSURANCE
see Insurance, Property

PROPERTY RIGHTS
see Industrial Property

PROPERTY TAX
Here are entered works on the general property tax, including both real and personal property. Works on the general property tax in individual cities, counties or other local government units are entered under the name of the city, county, etc., with or without the subdivision Taxation.
see also Capital Levy; Real Property Tax
Kaufman, George & Rosen, Kenneth T., eds. The Property Tax Revolt: The Case of Proposition 13. (Real Estate & Urban Economics Ser.). 1981. price not set prof. - refer. (ISBN 0-88410-693-4). Ballinger Pub.

PROPHECIES (OCCULT SCIENCES)
see also Astrology
Lindsay, Gordon. Will Our President Die in Office? (Prophecy Ser.). 1980. 2.25 (ISBN 0-89985-984-4). Christ Nations.
Martin, Bischof. Sunsets into Sunrises. Ozols, Violet, tr. 560p. Date not set. 20.00 (ISBN 0-934616-14-0). Valkyrie Pr.

PROPHECY (CHRISTIANITY)
Battle, Dennis M. America's Future in Symbolic Prophecy. (Illus.). 52p. 1981. pap. 2.50 (ISBN 0-933464-10-X). D M Battle Pubns.
Dasbach, Fernando L. The Father Has Come. 113p. 1981. 10.00. Regenbogen-Verlag.
Ryrie, Charles C. The Best Is Yet to Come. 128p. 1981. pap. 2.95 (ISBN 0-8024-4938-7). Moody.
Warner, D. S. & Riggle, H. M. The Cleansing of the Sanctuary. 541p. Repr. 5.50. Faith Pub Hse.

PROPHETS
Bokser, Ben Z. The Jewish Mystical Tradition. 280p. 1981. 14.95 (ISBN 0-8298-0435-8); pap. 9.95 (ISBN 0-8298-0451-X). Pilgrim NY.
Brickner, Balfour. Searching the Prophets for Values. 1981. 6.95 (ISBN 0-8074-0047-5). UAHC.
Moloney, F. J. Disciples & Prophets. 240p. 1981. 9.95 (ISBN 0-8245-0049-0). Crossroad NY.
Smith, William R. The Prophets of Israel. (Social Science Classics Ser.). 446p. 1982. 19.95 (ISBN 0-87855-318-5); text ed. 19.95 (ISBN 0-686-68059-6); pap. 7.95 (ISBN 0-87855-700-8); pap. text ed. 7.95 (ISBN 0-686-68060-X). Transaction Bks.

PROPORTION (ART)
see also Composition (Art); Perspective
Green, Benjamin. The Basic Guide to Pictorial Perspective. (A Promotion of the Arts Library Book). (Illus.). 97p. 1981. 27.75 (ISBN 0-86650-001-4). Gloucester Art.

PROPRIETARY RIGHTS
see Industrial Property

PROSE LITERATURE
see also Biography (As a Literary Form); Essays; Fiction
Introduction Seven: Stories by New Writers. 256p. 1981. 13.95 (ISBN 0-571-11680-9, Pub. by Faber & Faber). Merrimack Bk Serv.
Swatridge, Colin & Swatridge, Susan. The Biblio File: An Index of Prose Passages. 354p. 1980. 19.50x (ISBN 0-631-92640-2, Pub. by Basil Blackwell); pap. 10.50x (ISBN 0-631-92620-8). Biblio Dist.

PROSODY
see Versification

PROSPECTING–GEOPHYSICAL METHODS
see also Seismic Prospecting
Whiteley, Robert J. Geophysical Case Study of the Woodlawn Orebody, New South Wales Australia. LC 79-42637. (Illus.). xviii, 592p. 1980. 80.00 (ISBN 0-08-023996-X). Pergamon.

PROSTAGLANDIN
Annual Symposium of Basic Medical Sciences, 10th & Piper, Priscilla J. SRS-A & Leukotrienes: Proceedings. (Prostaglandin Research Studies Press Ser.). 304p. 1981. 63.00 (ISBN 0-471-27959-5, Pub. by Wiley-Interscience). Wiley.
Boeynaems, J. M. & Herman, A. G., eds. Prostaglandins, Prostacyclin, Thromboxanes Measurement. (Developments in Pharmacology Ser.: No. 1.). (Illus.). 209p. 1981. PLB 34.00 (ISBN 90-247-2417-1, Pub. by Martinus Nijhoff). Kluwer Boston.
Forster, Werner, et al. Prostaglandins & Thromboxins: Proceedings of the Third International Symposium on Prostaglandins & Thromboxanes in the Cardiovascular System, Hale-Salle, GDR, 5-7 May 1980. LC 80-41802. (Illus.). 500p. 1981. 80.00 (ISBN 0-08-027369-6). Pergamon.
Mehta, Jawahar & Mehta, Paulette, eds. Platelets & Prostaglandins in Cardiovascular Disease. 300p. 1981. write for info. (ISBN 0-87993-089-6). Futura Pub.

PROSTATE GLAND–DISEASES
see also Bladder
Hafez, E. S. & Spring-Mills, E., eds. Prostatic Carcinoma: Biology & Diagnosis. (Clinics in Andrology: No. 6). (Illus.). 200p. 1981. PLB 68.50 (ISBN 0-686-28844-0). Kluwer Boston.

PROSTHESIS
see also Artificial Organs; Pacemaker, Artificial (Heart); Prosthodontics; Vascular Grafts
Critser, James R., Jr. Prosthetics & Contact Lens: Series 10PC - 79. 1981. refer. - ring bdg. 60.00 (ISBN 0-686-69159-8). Lexington Data.

PROSTHODONTICS
Dolder, Eugene J. & Durrer, Gustav T. The Bar Joint Denture. (Illus.). 150p. 1978. 42.00 (ISBN 0-931386-02-0). Quint Pub Co.
Henderson, Davis & Steffel, Victor L. McCracken's Removable Partial Prosthodontics. 6th ed. (Illus.). 516p. 1981. text ed. 28.75 (ISBN 0-8016-2146-1). Mosby.
Johnson, Dean L. & Stratton, Russell J. Fundamentals of Removable Prosthodontics. (Illus.). 500p. 1980. 46.00 (ISBN 0-931386-10-1). Quint Pub Co.
Jumber, Joseph. An Altas of Overdentures & Precision Attachments. (Illus.). 256p. 1981. 60.00. Quint Pub Co.
Matsuo, Shimegi. Screw-Retained Dental Prostheses. 140p. 1981. 42.00 (ISBN 0-931386-35-7). Quint Pub Co.
Miller, Ernest L. & Grasso, Joseph E. Removable Partial Prosthodontics. 2nd ed. 440p. 1981. write for info. (5990-4). Williams & Wilkins.
Passamonti, Gino. Atlas of Complete Dentures. (Illus.). 140p. 1979. 48.00 (ISBN 0-931386-08-X). Quint Pub Co.
Renner. Complete Dentures: A Guide for Patient Treatment. (Monographs in Dentristy: Vol. 3). 1981. 32.50 (ISBN 0-89352-123-X). Masson Pub.
Rudd, Kenneth D., et al. Dental Laboratory Procedures: Removable Partial Dentures, Vol. III. (Illus.). 612p. 1981. text ed. 37.50 (ISBN 0-8016-3516-0). Mosby.
Schillingburg, Herbert, et al. Fundamentals of Fixed Prosthodontics. 2nd ed. (Illus.). 454p. 1981. write for info. Quint Pub Co.
Shillingburg, Herbert. Preparations for Cast Gold Restorations. (Illus.). 168p. 1974. 48.50. Quint Pub Co.
Shillingburg, Herbert, et al. Fundamentals of Fixed Prosthodontics. (Illus.). 339p. 1978. 32.50 (ISBN 3-87652-641-8). Quint Pub Co.
Singer, Fritz & Schon, Fritz. Partial Dentures. (Illus.). 207p. 1973. 42.00. Quint Pub Co.

PROSTITUTION
see also Sex Crimes; Sexual Ethics; Venereal Diseases
Cohen, Bernard. Deviant Street Networks: Prostitution in New York. LC 80-8039. 1980. 19.95 (ISBN 0-669-03949-7). Lexington Bks.
Marchant, James. The Master Problem. Winick, Charles, ed. LC 78-60869. (Prostitution Ser.: Vol. 12). 371p. 1979. lib. bdg. 36.00 (ISBN 0-8240-9716-5). Garland Pub.
Roe, Clifford & Winick, Charles. The Great War on White Slavery or Fighting for the Protection of Our Girls. LC 78-66466. (Prostitution Ser.: Vol. 16). 448p. 1979. lib. bdg. 40.00 (ISBN 0-8240-9712-2). Garland Pub.
Segilman, E. R. The Social Evil, with Special Reference to Conditions Existing in the City of New York. Winick, Charles, ed. LC 78-60871. (Prostitution Ser.: Vol. 3). 188p. 1979. lib. bdg. 20.00 (ISBN 0-8240-9725-4). Garland Pub.

PROSTITUTION–ASIA
DeLeeuw, Hendrik. Cities of Sin. Winick, Charles, ed. LC 78-60861. (Prostitution Ser.: Vol. 5). 297p. 1979. lib. bdg. 30.00 (ISBN 0-8240-9723-8). Garland Pub.

PROSTITUTION–GREAT BRITAIN
Hall, Gladys. Prostitution in the Modern World: Prostitution Ser. Winick, Charles, ed. LC 78-60866. (Vol. 6). 200p. 1979. lib. bdg. 20.00 (ISBN 0-8240-9722-X). Garland Pub.

PROTECTION OF ANIMALS
see Animals, Treatment of

PROTECTION OF CHILDREN
see Child Welfare

PROTECTION OF ENVIRONMENT
see Environmental Protection

PROTECTION OF NATURE
see Nature Conservation

PROTECTION OF PLANTS
see Plants, Protection Of

PROTECTION OF WILDLIFE CONSERVATION
see Wildlife Conservation

PROTECTIVE COATINGS
see also Corrosion and Anti-Corrosives; Paint
Gillies, M. T., ed. Powder Coating: Recent Developments. LC 80-26426. (Chemical Tech. Rev. Ser.: 183). (Illus.). 326p. 1981. 48.00 (ISBN 0-8155-0836-0). Noyes.
Pappas, S. Peter & Winslow, F. H., eds. Photodegradation & Photostabilization of Coatings. (ACS Symposium Ser: No. 151). 1981. price not set (ISBN 0-8412-0611-2). Am Chemical.

PROTEIDS
see Proteins

PROTEIN BIOSYNTHESIS
Koch, Gebhard & Richter, Dietmar. Biosynthesis, Modification & Processing of Cellular & Viral Polyproteins. 1980. 29.00 (ISBN 0-12-417560-0). Acad Pr.
Zimmerman, Morris, et al, eds. Percursor Processing in the Biosynthesis of Proteins. LC 80-16863. 449p. 1980. 79.00x (ISBN 0-89766-072-2). NY Acad Sci.

PROTEIN METABOLISM
see also Protein Biosynthesis
Buttery, P. J. & Lindsay, D. B. Protein Deposition in Animals. 29th ed. LC 80-49869. (Nottingham Easter School Ser.). (Illus.). 320p. 1980. text ed. 64.95 (ISBN 0-408-10676-X). Butterworths.
Koch, Gebhard & Richter, Dietmar. Biosynthesis, Modification & Processing of Cellular & Viral Polyproteins. 1980. 29.00 (ISBN 0-12-417560-0). Acad Pr.

PROTEIN SYNTHESIS
see Protein Biosynthesis

PROTEINS
see also Protein Metabolism
also various protein groups and bodies, e.g. Peptones, Casein
Anfinsen, C. B., et al, eds. Advances in Protein Chemistry, Vol. 34. (Serial Publication). 1981. price not set (ISBN 0-12-034234-0); price not set lib. ed. (ISBN 0-12-034284-7); price not set microfiche. Acad Pr.
Biochemical Societies of France, Great Britain, Italy, & the Netherlands. Joint Meeting, Venice, 1976. Phosphorylated Proteins & Related Enzymes: Proceedings. 121p. 8.00. Info Retrieval.
Bodwell, C. E. & Adkins, J. S. Protein Quality for Humans: Assessment & in Vitro Estimation. (Illus.). 1981. lib. bdg. price not set (ISBN 0-87055-388-7). AVI.
Bradshaw, Ralph & Schneider, Diana, eds. Proteins of the Nervous System. 2nd ed. 407p. 1980. 39.00 (ISBN 0-89004-327-2). Raven.
Cherry, John P., ed. Protein Functionality in Foods. (ACS Symposium Ser.: No. 147). 1981. price not set (ISBN 0-8412-0605-8). Am Chemical.
Frieden, Carl & Nichol, Lawrence. Protein-Protein Interactions. 400p. 1981. 30.00 (ISBN 0-471-04979-4, Pub. by Wiley-Interscience). Wiley.
Li, Choh H., ed. Hormonal Proteins & Peptides, 7 vols. Incl. Vol. 1. 1973. 31.00 (ISBN 0-12-447201-X); Vol. 2. 1973. 37.50 (ISBN 0-12-447202-8); Vol. 3. 1975. 43.00 (ISBN 0-12-447203-6); Vol. 4. 1977. 33.00 (ISBN 0-12-447204-4); Vol. 5. Lipotropin & Related Peptides. 1978. 29.00 (ISBN 0-12-447205-2); Vol. 6. Thyroid Hormones. 1978. 48.50 (ISBN 0-12-447206-0); Vol. 7. Hypothalmic Hormones. 1979. 32.50 (ISBN 0-12-447207-9). LC 78-5444. Acad Pr.
Protein Supply-Demands: Changing Styles GA-049. 1981. 800.00 (ISBN 0-89336-287-5). BCC.
Protides of the Biological Fluids, Colloquium 28: Proceedings of the 28th Colloquium on Protides of the Biological Fluids, Brussels, 5-8 May 1980. LC 58-5908. (Illus.). 600p. 1980. 120.00 (ISBN 0-08-026370-4). Pergamon.

PROTESTANT CHURCHES–RELATIONS–ORTHODOX EASTERN CHURCH
Makrakis, Apostolos. An Orthodox Protestant Debate. Cummings, Denver, tr. 1949. pap. 2.00x (ISBN 0-938366-37-8). Orthodox Chr.

PROTESTANT EPISCOPAL CHURCH IN THE U. S. A.
Kelleran, Marion & Krumm, John M. Denver Crossroads. 1979. 1.60 (ISBN 0-686-28775-4). Forward Movement.

PROTESTANT REFORMATION
see Reformation

PROTESTANTISM
see also Evangelicalism; Reformation
Flew, Robert N. & Davies, Rupert E., eds. The Catholicity of Protestantism: Being a Report Presented to His Grace the Archbishop of Canterbury by a Group of Free Churchmen. LC 80-29108. 159p. 1981. Repr. of 1950 ed. lib. bdg. 17.50x (ISBN 0-313-22825-6, FLCAT). Greenwood.

PROTESTANTISM–HISTORY
Balbani, Niccolo. Newes from Italy of a Second Moses or, the Life of Galeacius Carracciolus the Noble Marquese of Vico. Crashaw, W., tr. LC 79-84085. (English Experience Ser.: No. 905). 92p. 1979. Repr. of 1608 ed. lib. bdg. 10.00 (ISBN 90-221-0905-4). Walter J Johnson.
Becon, Thomas. The Demaundes of Holy Scripture, with Answeres to the Same. LC 79-84087. (English Experience Ser.: No.907). 116p. 1979. Repr. of 1577 ed. lib. bdg. 9.00 (ISBN 90-221-0907-0). Walter J Johnson.
Coverdale, M., tr. from Dutch. The Original & Sprynge of All Sectes & Orders by Whome, Wha or Where (Sic) They Beganne. LC 79-84127. (English Experience Ser.: No. 946). 140p. (Eng.). 1979. Repr. of 1537 ed. lib. bdg. 11.50 (ISBN 90-221-0946-1). Walter J Johnson.
Jacobus, Verheiden. The History of the Moderne Protestant Divines, Containing Their Parents, Countries, Education, with Register of Their Writings. Lupton, D., tr. from Latin. LC 79-84142. (English Experience Ser.: No. 959). 400p. 1979. Repr. of 1637 ed. lib. bdg. 28.00 (ISBN 90-221-0959-3). Walter J Johnson.
Rolte, J., tr. Palatinate - a Full Declaration of the Faith & Ceremonies Professed in the Dominions of Prince Fredericke, 5. Prince Elector Palatine. LC 79-84129. (English Experience Ser.: No. 947). 208p. 1979. Repr. of 1614 ed. lib. bdg. 20.00 (ISBN 90-221-0947-X). Walter J Johnson.
Zwingli, Ulrich. The Acconmpt Rekenynge & Confession of the Faith of Huldrik Zwinglius. Cotsforde, Thomas, tr. from Latin. LC 79-84148. (The English Experience: No. 964). Orig. Title: Swinglische Bekenntuis. 156p. 1979. Repr. of 1555 ed. lib. bdg. 11.50 (ISBN 90-221-0964-X). Walter J Johnson.

PROTESTANTISM, EVANGELICAL
see Evangelicalism

PROTESTANTS IN THE UNITED STATES
Orozco, E. C. Republican Protestantism in Aztlan. 261p. 1980. 22.00 (ISBN 0-686-28883-1); pap. 11.00 (ISBN 0-686-28884-X). Petereins Pr.
Smith, Timothy. Revivalism & Social Reform: American Protestantism on the Eve of the Civil War. LC 80-8114. Orig. Title: Revialism & Social Reform in Mid-Nineteenth Century America. 272p. 1980. pap. text ed. 5.95x (ISBN 0-8018-2477-X). Johns Hopkins.

PROTESTS, DIPLOMATIC
see Diplomacy

PROTONS
see also Atoms; Electrons; Neutrons

Brodsky, William A., ed. Anion & Proton Transport, Vol. 341. new ed. LC 80-15917. 610p. 1980. 107.00 (ISBN 0-89766-070-6). NY Acad Sci.

PROTOPHYTA
see Cryptogams

PROTOZOA
Kolisko, Eugen. Zoology for Everybody, Vol. 4: Protozoa. 1980. pap. 4.25x (ISBN 0-906492-24-6, Pub. by Kolisko Archives). St George Bk Serv.

PROUDHON, PIERRE JOSEPH, 1809-1865
Ritter, Alan. The Political Thought of Pierre-Joseph Proudhon. LC 80-19558. (Illus.). xii, 222p. 1980. Repr. of 1969 ed. lib. bdg. 23.50x (ISBN 0-313-22719-5, RIPT). Greenwood.

PROUST, MARCEL, 1871-1922
Slater, Maya. Humour in the Works of Proust. (Oxford Modern Languages & Literature Monographs). 200p. 1979. text ed. 22.00x (ISBN 0-19-815534-4). Oxford U Pr.
Splitter, Randolph. Proust's "Recherche". A Psychoanalytic Interpretation. 176p. 1981. 20.00 (ISBN 0-7100-0664-0). Routledge & Kegan.
Vogely, Maxine A. A Proust Dictionary. 765p. 1981. 50.00x (ISBN 0-87875-205-6). Whitston Pub.

PROVIDENCE, RHODE ISLAND
Conley, Patrick T. Providence: A Pictorial History. Friedman, Donna R., ed. (Illus.). 205p. 1981. pap. price not set (ISBN 0-89865-128-X). Donning Co.

PROVIDENCE AND GOVERNMENT OF GOD
A Justicia De Deus. 1980. pap. 1.90 (ISBN 0-686-69353-1). Vida Pubs.
Marxhausen, Evelyn. When God Laid Down the Law. LC 59-1259. (Arch Bk.). 1981. pap. 0.79 (ISBN 0-570-06142-3). Concordia.
El Plan De Dios y los Vencedores. 1980. pap. 1.40 (ISBN 0-686-69349-3). Vida Pubs.
Por Que, Senor? 1980. pap. 1.60 (ISBN 0-686-69362-0). Vida Pubs.

PROVIDENCE AND THRIFT
see Saving and Thrift

PROXY
Illustrations of Selected Proxy Information. (Financial Report Survey Ser.: No. 20). 1979. pap. 8.00. Am Inst CPA.

PRUNING
Hill, Lewis. Pruning Simplified: A Complete Guide to Pruning Trees, Shrubs, Bushes, Hedges, Vines, Flowers, Garden Plants, Houseplants & Bonsai. Yepsen, Roger B., ed. (Illus.). 224p. 1981. pap. 9.95 (ISBN 0-87857-249-X). Rodale Pr Inc.

PRUSSIA-HISTORY
Here are entered works on the history of Prussia in general, including the period of the margravate and electorate of Brandenburg. The history of Brandenburg prior to 1640 is entered under Brandenburg-History.
Urban, William. The Prussian Crusade. LC 80-5647. 469p. 1980. lib. bdg. 24.00 (ISBN 0-8191-1278-X); pap. text ed. 15.50 (ISBN 0-8191-1279-8). U Pr of Amer.

PSALTERS
Weitzmann, Kurt. Byzantine Liturgical Psalters & Gospels. 322p. 1980. 200.00x (ISBN 0-86078-064-3, Pub. by Variorum England). State Mutual Bk.

PSEUDOLEUCEMIA
see Hodgkin's Disease

PSEUDOMONAS
Brown, M. Resistance of Pseudomonas Aeruginosa. 335p. 1975. 60.50 (ISBN 0-471-11210-0). Wiley.

PSEUDONYMS
see Anonyms and Pseudonyms

PSEUDOROMANTICISMS
see Romanticism

PSYCHAGOGY
see Psychology, Applied; Psychotherapy

PSYCHEDELIC DRUGS
see Hallucinogenic Drugs

PSYCHIATRIC HOSPITALS
see also Mentally Handicapped-Institutional Care
Freedman, Joel. On Both Sides of the Gate. LC 79-67518. 1981. 6.95 (ISBN 0-533-04466-9). Vantage.
Rothman: Conscience & Convenience: The Asylum & Its Alternatives in Progressive America. (Orig.). 1980. pap. text ed. 8.95 (ISBN 0-316-75775-6). Little.

PSYCHIATRIC NURSING
Burgess, Ann W. & Lazare, Aaron. Psychiatric Nursing in the Hospital & the Community. 3rd ed. (Illus.). 736p. 1981. text ed. 19.95 (ISBN 0-13-731927-4). P-H.
Jalim, M. Psychiatric Nursing Objective Tests. 128p. 1981. pap. 5.95 (ISBN 0-571-11582-9, Pub. by Faber & Faber). Merrimack Bk Serv.
Stoltzfus, Doris. Self-Assessment of Current Knowledge in Mental Health Nursing. 1979. spiral bdg. 9.50 (ISBN 0-87488-264-8). Med Exam.

PSYCHIATRIC PERSONNEL
see Mental Health Personnel

PSYCHIATRIC RESEARCH
see also Psychosomatic Research
Serafetinides, E. A. Psychiatric Research in Practice: Biobehavioral Themes. (Seminars in Psychology Ser.). 1981. 24.50 (ISBN 0-8089-1316-6). Grune.

PSYCHIATRIC SOCIAL WORK
see also Medical Social Work; Pastoral Counseling; Pastoral Psychology
Sunier, A. Dealing with Problem People. 84p. 1980. pap. text ed. 8.50x (ISBN 90-232-1761-6). Humanities.

PSYCHIATRY
Here are entered works on the clinical and therapeutic aspects of psychology. Works on abnormal psychology in general are entered under the heading Psychology, Pathological.
see also Clinical Psychology; Geriatric Psychiatry; Group Psychotherapy; Mental Health; Mental Illness; Neuropsychiatry; Neuroses; Psychology, Pathological; Psychoses; Psychotherapy; Shock Therapy
Arieti, Silvano & Brodie, Keith H. American Handbook of Psychiatry: Advances & New Directions, Vol. VII. LC 80-68960. (American Handbook of Psychiatry Ser.). 784p. 1981. 45.50x (ISBN 0-465-00157-2). Basic.
Bernstein, Jerold G. Handbook of Drug Therapy in Psychiatry. 1981. write for info. (ISBN 0-88416-323-7). PSG Pub.
Darby, John J. & Hecker, Michael, eds. Speech Evaluation in Psychiatry. 1980. 34.00 (ISBN 0-8089-1315-8). Grune.
Dongier, Maurice & Wittkower, Eric D. Divergent Views in Psychiatry. (Illus.). Date not set. text ed. price not set (ISBN 0-06-140695-3, Harper Medical). Har-Row.
Fauman, Beverly J. & Fauman, Michael. Emergency Psychiatry. (Illus.). 150p. 1981. write for info. softcover (3046-9). Williams & Wilkins.
Gabriel, E., ed. Ueber Kie Beeinflussbarkeit Psychiatrischer Krankheitsverlaeufe, 1980, Vol. 13, No. 3-4. (Illus.). iv, 136p. 1981. pap. write for info. (ISBN 3-8055-2336-X). S Karger.
Gaw, Albert, ed. Cross-Cultural Psychiatry. 475p. 1981. text ed. 37.50 (ISBN 0-88416-338-5). PSG Pub.
Giannini, A. James. Psychitric, Psychologenic, & Somatopsychic Disorders Handbook. 1978. pap. 14.50 (ISBN 0-87488-596-5). Med Exam.
Kemali, D., ed. Advances in Biological Psychiatry, Vol. 6. (Illus.). 128p. 1981. pap. 48.00 (ISBN 3-8055-2420-X). S Karger.
Levy. The New Language of Psychiatry: Learning & Using DSM-III. 384p. 1981. text ed. 16.95 (ISBN 0-87626-610-3). Winthrop.
Nahem, Joseph. Psychology & Psychiatry Today: A Marxist View. 1981. 15.00 (ISBN 0-7178-0581-6); pap. 5.50 (ISBN 0-7178-0579-4). Intl Pub Co.
Ryback, Ralph S., et al. The Problem-Oriented Record in Psychiatry & Mental Health Care. 2nd ed. 1981. write for info. (ISBN 0-8089-1308-5). Grune.
Stannard-Friel, Don. Harassment Therapy: A Case Study of Psychiatric Violence. (University Books Ser.). 1981. lib. bdg. 16.95 (ISBN 0-8161-9030-5). G K Hall.
Stapleton, Thomas. The Prevention of Psychiatric Disorders in Children. 244p. 1981. 16.00 (ISBN 0-87527-234-7). Green.
Ziskin, Jay. Coping with Psychiatric & Psychological Testimony, 2 vols. 3rd ed. Incl. Vol. 1. 429p. 50.00 (ISBN 0-9603630-2-5); Vol. 2. 577p. write for info. (ISBN 0-9603630-3-3). 1981. Set. 80.00 (ISBN 0-9603630-4-1). Law & Psych.

PSYCHIATRY-ADDRESSES, ESSAYS, LECTURES
Hall, Richard C., ed. Psychiatry in Crisis. 1981. text ed. write for info. (ISBN 0-89335-133-4). Spectrum Pub.

PSYCHIATRY-BIBLIOGRAPHY
Schizophernia: A Bibliography of Books in English. 146p. 1981. lib. bdg. 22.50 (ISBN 0-8482-7064-9). Norwood Edns.

PSYCHIATRY-CASES, CLINICAL REPORTS, STATISTICS
Reynolds, David K. & Farberow, Norman L. The Family Shadow: Sources of Suicide & Schizophrenia. 188p. 1981. 14.95 (ISBN 0-520-04213-1). U of Cal Pr.

PSYCHIATRY-DICTIONARIES
Campbell, Robert J., ed. Psychiatric Dictionary. 800p. 1981. 29.50 (ISBN 0-19-502817-1). Oxford U Pr.

PSYCHIATRY-RESEARCH
see Psychiatric Research

PSYCHIATRY, FORENSIC
see Forensic Psychiatry

PSYCHIATRY, GERIATRIC
see Geriatric Psychiatry

PSYCHIATRY AND ART
see Art Therapy

PSYCHIATRY IN GENERAL HOSPITALS
see Psychiatric Hospitals

PSYCHIC HEALING
see Mental Healing

PSYCHICAL RESEARCH
see also Apparitions; Astral Projection; Dreams; Extrasensory Perception; Ghosts; Hypnotism; Mind and Body; Personality, Disorders Of; Psychology, Religious; Psychometry (Occult Sciences)
Alcock, James E. Parapsychology-Science or Magic? A Psychological Perspective. (Foundations & Philosophy of Science & Technology Ser.). 300p. 1981. 45.00 (ISBN 0-08-025773-9); pap. 20.00 (ISBN 0-08-025772-0). Pergamon.
Ferguson, Sibyl. The Crystal Ball. 1980. pap. 1.00 (ISBN 0-87728-483-0). Weiser.
Frazier, Kendrick, ed. Borderlands Beyond Science: Skeptical Inquiries into the Paranormal. LC 80-84403. (Critiques of the Paranormal Ser.). 400p. 1981. 19.95 (ISBN 0-87975-147-9); pap. 9.95 (ISBN 0-87975-148-7). Prometheus Bks.
Gardner, Martin. The Buffooneries of Modern Science. LC 80-84405. (Critiques of the Paranormal Ser.). 450p. 1981. 19.95 (ISBN 0-87975-144-4); pap. 9.95 (ISBN 0-87975-145-2). Prometheus Bks.
Hopkins, James K. A Woman to Deliver Her People: Joanna Southcott & English Millenarianism in an Era of Revolution. (Illus.). 320p. 1981. text ed. 22.50x (ISBN 0-292-79017-1). U of Tex Pr.
Kraft, Dean. Portrait of a Psychic Healer. 192p. 1981. 10.95 (ISBN 0-686-69592-5). Putnam.
Oliver, Frederick S. A Dweller on Two Planets: The Dividing of the Way-Phylos the Thibetan. LC 80-8896. (The Harper Library of Spiritual Wisdom Ser.). (Illus.). 432p. 1981. pap. 6.95 (ISBN 0-06-066565-3). Har-Row.
Petschek, Joyce S. The Silver Bird: A Tale for Those Who Dream. LC 80-70049. (Illus.). 192p. 1981. pap. 8.95 (ISBN 0-89087-318-6). Celestial Arts.
Rhea, Kay & O'Leary, Maggie. The Psychic Is You. LC 79-53023. 168p. 1981. pap. 5.95 (ISBN 0-89087-311-9). Celestial Arts.
Robinson, Diana. To Stretch a Plank: A Survey of Psychokinesis. LC 80-12335. 282p. 1981. 15.95 (ISBN 0-88229-404-0). Nelson-Hall.
Rodriguez, Jose C. Eyes of the Mind. 1981. 12.50 (ISBN 0-533-04591-6). Vantage.
Roll, William G., ed. Research in Parapsychology 1979: Abstracts & Papers from the Twenty-Second Annual Convention of the Parapsychological Association. LC 66-2858. 238p. 1980. 12.00 (ISBN 0-8108-1327-0). Scarecrow.
Sargent, Carl L. Exploring Psi in the Ganzfeld. LC 80-82752. (Parapsychological Monograph Ser.: No. 17). (Illus.). 1980. pap. text ed. 6.00 (ISBN 0-912328-33-9). Parapsych Foun.
--Exploring the Ganzfeld. LC 80-82752. (Parapsychological Monograph: No. 17). 1980. pap. 6.00 (ISBN 0-912328-33-9). Parapsych Foun.
Shepard, Leslie. Encyclopedia of Occultism & Parapsychology: A Compedium of Information on the Occult Sciences, Magic, Demonology, Superstitions, Spiritism, Mysticism, Metaphysics, Psychical Science & Parapsycholgy. 2nd ed. (Illus.). 400p. 1981. 125.00 (ISBN 0-8103-0196-2). Gale.
Weiss, Clara. Astrological Keys to Self Realization & Self Actualization. 1980. pap. 4.95 (ISBN 0-87728-509-8). Weiser.
Wolman, Benjamin B. Handbook of Parapsychology. 1070p. 1981. pap. text ed. 17.95 (ISBN 0-442-26479-8). Van Nos Reinhold.
Zondag-Hamaker, Karen. Astro-Psychology. 1980. pap. 7.95 (ISBN 0-87728-465-2). Weiser.

PSYCHOANALYSIS
see also Dreams; Ego (Psychology); Group Psychoanalysis; Hypnotism; Medicine, Psychosomatic; Mind and Body; Psychology; Psychology, Pathological; Psychology, Physiological; Transference (Psychology)
Bernstein, Anne E. & Warner, Gloria. An Introduction to Contemporary Psychoanalysis. LC 80-70246. 300p. 1981. 25.00 (ISBN 0-87668-442-8). Aronson.
Breger, Louis. Freud's Unfinished Journey. 220p. write for info. (ISBN 0-7100-0613-6). Routledge & Kegan.
Burns, David D. Feeling Good. 1981. pap. 3.95 (ISBN 0-451-09804-8, E9804, Signet Bks). NAL.
Edward, Joyce, et al. Separation-Individuation Theory & Clinical Practice. 324p. 1981. text ed. 22.95 (ISBN 0-89876-018-6). Gardner Pr.
Fromm, Erich. To Have or to Be? 256p. 1981. pap. 2.95 (ISBN 0-553-10949-9). Bantam.
Jacobson, Alan M. & Parmelee, Dean X., eds. Psychoanalysis: A Contemporary Appraisal. 250p. 1981. 20.00 (ISBN 0-87630-269-X). Brunner-Mazel.
Klauber, John. Difficulties in the Analytic Encounter. LC 80-69670. 200p. 1981. 25.00 (ISBN 0-87668-430-4). Aronson.
Skura, Meredith A. The Literary Use of the Psychoanalytic Process. LC 80-23390. 288p. 1981. 19.50x (ISBN 0-300-02380-4). Yale U Pr.
Wolberg, Arlene R. The Psychoanalytic Psychotherapy of the Borderline Patient. (Illus.). 350p. 1981. text ed. 30.00 (ISBN 0-86577-022-0). Thieme-Stratton.

PSYCHOANALYSIS-ADDRESSES, ESSAYS, LECTURES
MacCabe, Colin. The Talking Cure: Essays in Psychoanalysis. 1981. 25.00 (ISBN 0-312-78474-0). St Martin.

PSYCHOANALYSIS-BIBLIOGRAPHY
Miller, Glenn E., ed. Chicago Psychoanalytic Literature Index Nineteen Seventy-Five. 1975. write for info. Chicago Psych.
--Chicago Psychoanalytic Literature Index 1980: Chicago Institute for Psychoanalysis. 1981. lib. bdg. 50.00 (ISBN 0-918568-07-2). Chicago Psych.

PSYCHOANALYSIS-HISTORY
Badcock, C. R. The Psychoanalysis of Culture. 264p. 1980. 36.50x (ISBN 0-631-11701-6, Pub. by Basil Blackwell). Biblio Dist.
Fine, Reuben. The Psychoanalytic Vision. LC 80-2154. 1981. 19.95 (ISBN 0-02-910270-7). Free Pr.

PSYCHOANALYSIS AND LITERATURE
Davis, Robert C., ed. The Fictional Father: Lacanian Readings of the Text. LC 80-26222. 240p. 1981. lib. bdg. 15.00x (ISBN 0-87023-111-1). U of Mass Pr.

PSYCHOBIOLOGY
see also Psychology, Physiological
Chertok, Leon. Hypnosis: The Psychobiological Crossroads. 224p. 1981. 36.00 (ISBN 0-08-026793-9); pap. 18.00 (ISBN 0-08-026813-7). Pergamon.
Lewis, Dorothy O., ed. Psychobiological Vulnerabilities to Delinquency. 1981. text ed. write for info. (ISBN 0-89335-136-9). Spectrum Pub.

PSYCHODRAMA
Yablonsky, Lewis. Psychodrama. 300p. Date not set. pap. text ed. 11.95 (ISBN 0-89876-016-X). Gardner Pr.

PSYCHOGENETICS
see Behavior Genetics

PSYCHOGERIATRICS
see Geriatric Psychiatry

PSYCHOLINGUISTICS
see also Children-Language; Speech, Disorders of; Thought and Thinking
Brown, Jason W., ed. Jargonaphasia. (Perspectives in Neurolinguistics & Psycholinguistics Ser.). 1981. price not set (ISBN 0-12-137580-3). Acad Pr.
Leontiev, Aleksei A. Psychology & the Language Learning Process. LC 80-41819. 160p. 1981. 11.95 (ISBN 0-08-024601-X); pap. 5.95 (ISBN 0-08-024600-1). Pergamon.

PSYCHOLOGICAL ANTHROPOLOGY
see Ethnopsychology

PSYCHOLOGICAL ASPECTS OF DISABILITY
see Handicapped

PSYCHOLOGICAL MEASUREMENT
see Psychometrics

PSYCHOLOGICAL RESEARCH
Bachrach, Arthur J. Psychological Research: An Introduction. 4th ed. 205p. 1981. pap. text ed. 6.95 (ISBN 0-394-32288-6). Random.
Greenwood, Larry. How to Search for Information: A Beginner's Guide to the Literature of Psychology. LC 80-53708. (Basic Tools Ser.: No. 1). 50p. (Orig.). 1980. pap. text ed. 3.95 (ISBN 0-938376-00-4). Willowood Pr.
Wood. Fundamentals of Psychological Research. 3rd ed. text ed. 17.95 (ISBN 0-316-95169-2); training manual free (ISBN 0-316-95170-6). Little.

PSYCHOLOGICAL SCALING
see Psychometrics

PSYCHOLOGICAL STATISTICS
see Psychometrics

PSYCHOLOGICAL STRESS
see Stress (Psychology)

PSYCHOLOGICAL TESTING
see Psychometrics

PSYCHOLOGICAL WARFARE
Here are entered general works dealing with methods used to undermine the morale of the civilian population and the military forces of any enemy country.
see also Propaganda;
also subdivision Psychological Aspects under names of wars, e.g. World War, 1939-1945-Psychological Aspects
Chandler, Robert W. War of Ideas: The U. S. Propaganda Compaign in Vietnam. (Westview Special Studies in National Defense & Security Ser.). 301p. 1981. lib. bdg. 25.00x (ISBN 0-86531-082-3). Westview.

PSYCHOLOGY
see also Adjustment (Psychology); Adolescent Psychology; Assertiveness (Psychology); Attitude (Psychology); Behavior Genetics; Behaviorism (Psychology); Belief and Doubt; Body, Human; Child Psychology; Cognition; Consciousness; Control (Psychology); Developmental Psychology; Emotions; Ethnopsychology; Hostility (Psychology); Human Behavior; Humanistic Psychology; Ideology; Imagination; Information Theory in Psychology; Instinct; Intellect; Interpersonal Relations; Judgment; Knowledge, Theory of; Logic; Memory; Mental Health; Motivation (Psychology); Perception; Personality; Physiognomy; Political Psychology; Praise; Problem Solving; Psychical Research; Psychoanalysis; Psychobiology; Reasoning (Psychology); Self-Acceptance; Senses and Sensation; Social Interaction; Social Psychology; Stress (Psychology); Temperament; Thought and Thinking; Values; Will
also subdivision Psychology under specific subjects, e.g. Aeronautics-Psychology
Abma, John S. Introductory Psychology, 7 vols. 2nd ed. Incl. Vol. 1-Introductory to Psychology (ISBN 0-86589-007-2); Vol. 2-Learning (ISBN 0-86589-008-0); Vol. 3-the Physiological Bases of Behavior (ISBN 0-86589-009-9); Vol. 4-Individual Differences & Group Processes (ISBN 0-86589-010-2); Vol. 5-Motivation & Stress (ISBN 0-86589-011-0); Vol. 6-Mental Health (ISBN 0-86589-012-9); Vol. 7-Measurements, Statistics & Analysis (ISBN 0-86589-013-7). 1973. Set. 16.75 (ISBN 0-86589-006-4). Individual Learn.
Bach, George R. & Deutsch, Ronald M. Stop! You're Driving Me Crazy. 1981. pap. 2.95 (ISBN 0-425-04738-5). Berkley Pub.
Broughton, John M. & Freeman-Moir, D. John, eds. The Foundation of Cognitive-Development Psychology: James Mark Baldwin's Theory & Its Contemporary Meaning. 300p. 1981. text ed. price not set (ISBN 0-89391-043-0). Ablex Pub.

Brown, Thomas. Sketch of a System of the Philosophy of the Human Mind. Bd. with Logic of Condillac. (Contributions to the History of Psychology Ser., Pt. A: Orientations). 1978. Repr. of 1820 ed. 30.00 (ISBN 0-89093-150-X). U Pubns Amer.

Cermack, Laird S. Human Memory & Amnesia. 400p. 1981. ref. ed. 24.95 (ISBN 0-89859-095-7). L Erlbaum Assocs.

Corbin, et al. Spring '80: An Annual of Archetypal Psychology & Jungian Thought. Hillman, James, ed. 196p. (Orig.). 1980. pap. text ed. 10.00 (ISBN 0-88214-015-9). Spring Pubns.

Dally, Ann. Understanding. LC 78-66254. 192p. 1981. pap. 6.95 (ISBN 0-8128-6104-3). Stein & Day.

Darley, J. Psychology. 1981. 17.95 (ISBN 0-13-733154-1); pap. 5.95 (ISBN 0-13-733188-6). P-H.

Denmark, Florence L., ed. Psychology: The Leading Edge, Vol. 340. new ed. (N.Y. Academy of Sciences Annals: Vol. 340). 114p. 1980. 20.00 (ISBN 0-89766-068-4); pap. write for info. (ISBN 0-89766-069-2). NY Acad Sci.

Ellis, Robert S. The Psychology of Individual Differences. 533p. 1980. Repr. of 1930 ed. lib. bdg. 45.00 (ISBN 0-89760-204-8). Telegraph Bks.

Endicott, Lane D. Beyond the Rainbow Mists: A Journey That Takes You Out of This World. 1981. 6.50 (ISBN 0-8062-1614-X). Carlton.

Feather, Norman T., ed. Expectations & Actions: Expectancy-Value Models in Psychology. 400p. 1981. professional reference text 24.95 (ISBN 0-89859-080-9). L Erlbaum Assocs.

Froebel, Frederich. Educations of Man. Hailmann, W. N., tr. from German. (Contributions to the History of Psychology B, I: Psychometrics Ser.). 1978. Repr. of 1887 ed. write for info. (ISBN 0-89093-161-5). U Pubns Amer.

Gendlin, Eugene. Focusing. 192p. (Orig.). 1981. pap. 3.50 (ISBN 0-553-14526-6). Bantam.

Gillies, Jerry. Psychological Immortality: Using Your Mind to Extend Your Life. 225p. 1981. 11.95 (ISBN 0-399-90103-5). Marek.

Greenwood, Larry. How to Search for Information: A Beginner's Guide to the Literature of Psychology. LC 80-53708. (Basic Tools Ser.: No. 1). 50p. (Orig.). 1980. pap. text ed. 3.95 (ISBN 0-938376-00-4). Willowood Pr.

Hamaker-Zondag, Karen. Interpretation: Jungian Symbolism & Astrology, Pt. 1. 192p. 1981. 7.95 (ISBN 0-87728-523-3). Weiser.

Harvey, John H. & Weary, Gifford. Perspectives on Attributional Processes. 250p. 1981. pap. text ed. write for info. (ISBN 0-697-06637-1). Wm C Brown.

Harvey, John H., et al, eds. New Directions in Attribution Research, Vol. 3. 512p. 1981. prof. -refer. 29.95 (ISBN 0-89859-098-1). L Erlbaum Assocs.

Herbart, Johann F. Textbook of Psychology. Smith, Margaret K., tr. Bd. with Study of Psychology; Outlines of Psychology. (Contributions to the History of Psychology Ser., Vol. VI, Pt. A: Orientations). 1978. Repr. of 1891 ed. 30.00 (ISBN 0-89093-155-0). U Pubns Amer.

Holland, Henry. Chapters on Mental Physiology. Bd. with On Man's Power Over Himself to Prevent or Control Insanity. Barlow, John. (Contributions to the History of Psychology Ser., Vol. VI, Pt. C: Medical Psychology). 1980. Repr. of 1858 ed. 30.00 (ISBN 0-89093-321-9). U Pubns Amer.

Holland, Morris K. Introductory Psychology. 688p. 1981. text ed. 17.95 (ISBN 0-669-03347-2); instr's. guide with test avail. (ISBN 0-669-03346-4); student guide 5.95 (ISBN 0-669-03347-2). Heath.

Jeeves, Malcolm, ed. Psychology Survey, No. 3. 208p. (Orig.). 1980. text ed. 25.00x (ISBN 0-04-150073-3, 2311); pap. text ed. 11.50 (ISBN 0-04-150074-1, 2312). Allen Unwin.

Kendler, Howard H. Psychology: A Science in Conflict. (Illus.). 416p. 1981. text ed. 19.95x (ISBN 0-19-502900-3); pap. text ed. 9.95x (ISBN 0-19-502901-1). Oxford U Pr.

Kopp, Sheldon. An End to Innocence: Facing Life Without Illusions. 208p. 1981. pap. 2.95 (ISBN 0-553-13327-6). Bantam.

Langs, Robert. Resistances & Interventions. LC 80-69667. 460p. 1981. 30.00 (ISBN 0-87668-433-9). Aronson.

Lloyd, Barbara & Gay, J., eds. Universals of Human Thought. LC 79-41471. (Illus.). 300p. Date not set. 47.50 (ISBN 0-521-22953-7); pap. 14.95 (ISBN 0-521-29818-0). Cambridge U Pr.

McPherson, Ian & Sutton, Andrew. Reconstructing Psychological Practice. 192p. 1981. 26.00x (ISBN 0-7099-0419-3, Pub. by Croom Helm LTD England). Biblio Dist.

Miller, Gordon. Life Choices. 176p. 1981. pap. 2.50 (ISBN 0-553-14154-6). Bantam.

Morris, Janet E. Wind from the Abyss. (New Age Ser.). 352p. (Orig.). 1981. pap. 2.50 (ISBN 0-553-14343-3). Bantam.

Murray, Henry A. Endeavors in Psychology: Selections from the Personology of Henry A. Murray. Shneidman, Edwin S., ed. LC 80-7598. 656p. 1981. 30.00 (ISBN 0-06-014039-9, HarpT). Har-Row.

Nahem, Joseph. Psychology & Psychiatry Today: A Marxist View. 1981. 15.00 (ISBN 0-7178-0581-6); pap. 5.50 (ISBN 0-7178-0579-4). Intl Pub Co.

Naropa Institute Journal of Psychology, Vol. 1. 71p. (Orig.). 1981. pap. 6.00 (ISBN 0-87773-751-7). Great Eastern.

Read, M. K. Juan Huarte de San Juan. (World Authors Ser.: No. 619). 1981. lib. bdg. 14.95 (ISBN 0-8057-6461-5). Twayne.

Research & Education Association Staff. The Psychology Problem Solver. LC 80-53174. (Illus.). 1056p. (Orig.). pap. text ed. 16.85x (ISBN 0-87891-523-0). Res & Educ.

Rokeach, Milton. The Three Christs of Ypsilanti: A Psychological Study. (Morningside Book Ser.). 360p. 1981. pap. 8.00x (ISBN 0-231-05271-5). Columbia U Pr.

Rudman, Jack. National Psychology Boards (NPsyB) (Admission Test Ser.: AT-89). (Cloth bdg. avail. on request). pap. 19.95 (ISBN 0-8373-5089-1). Natl Learning.

--Psychology. (Undergraduate Program Field Test Ser.: UPFT-21). (Cloth bdg. avail. on request). pap. 9.95 (ISBN 0-8373-6021-8). Natl Learning.

Rush, Benjamin. Two Essays on the Mind. 1972. 7.50 (ISBN 0-87630-061-1). Brunner-Mazel.

Sarason, Seymour B. Psychology Misdirected. LC 80-69283. 1981. 16.95 (ISBN 0-02-928100-8). Free Pr.

Schall, Maxine. Limits. Southern, Carol, ed. 320p. 1981. 11.95 (ISBN 0-517-54143-2). Potter.

Schultz, Duane. A History of Modern Psychology. 3rd ed. LC 80-616. 1980. lib ed 18.95 (ISBN 0-12-633060-3); write for info. (ISBN 0-12-633065-4). Acad Pr.

Shedd, Charlie & Shedd, Martha. Celebration in the Bedroom. 128p. 1981. pap. 2.50 (ISBN 0-553-14436-7). Bantam.

Simons, Richard C. & Pardes, Herbert. Understanding Human Behavior in Health & Illness. 2nd ed. (Illus.). 760p. 1981. write for info. (7740-6). Williams & Wilkins.

Spontaneous Images: Relationship Between Psyche & Soma. (Illus.). 123p. (Orig., Eng. Fr. & Ger.). 1980. pap. text ed. 16.00 (ISBN 0-89192-311-X). Interbk Inc.

Springer, Sally P. & Deutsch, Georg. Left Brain, Right Brain. LC 80-25453. (Psychology Ser.). (Illus.). 1981. text ed. 11.95x (ISBN 0-7167-1269-5); pap. text ed. 6.95x (ISBN 0-7167-1270-9). W H Freeman.

Stout, George F. Manual of Psychology. (Contributions to the History of Psychology Ser.: Orientations). 1978. Repr. of 1899 ed. write for info. U Pubns Amer.

Thorndike, E. L. Human Nature & the Social Order. 1019p. 1980. Repr. of 1940 ed. lib. bdg. 100.00 (ISBN 0-89987-812-1). Darby Bks.

Wallon, Henri. Development of the Child. Voyat, Gilbert, ed. LC 80-69666. 260p. 1981. 30.00 (ISBN 0-87668-434-7). Aronson.

Weyand, Clint. Surviving Popular Psychology: Debriefing the Me Degeneration. 148p. (Orig.). 1980. pap. 3.95 (ISBN 0-686-28854-8). Being Bks.

Wheeler, Ladd, ed. Review of Personality & Social Psychology: No. 1. (Illus.). 352p. 1980. pap. 9.95 (ISBN 0-8039-1458-X). Sage.

Wheelwright, Jane. The Death of a Woman. 288p. 1981. 12.95 (ISBN 0-312-18744-0). St Martin.

Wittgenstein, Ludwig. Remarks on the Philosophy of Psychology, Vol. 1. Anscombe, G. E. & Von Wright, G. H., eds. LC 80-52781. 408p. 1980. lib. bdg. 35.00x (ISBN 0-226-90433-4). U of Chicago Pr.

--Remarks on the Philosophy of Psychology, Vol. 2. Von Wright, G. H. & Nyman, Heikki, eds. Luckhardt, C. G. & Aue, A. E., trs. LC 80-52781. 1980. lib. bdg. 27.50x (ISBN 0-226-90434-2). U of Chicago Pr.

Wolman, Benjamin B. & Knapp, Susan. Contemporary Theories & Systems in Psychology. rev., 2nd ed. 690p. 1981. 42.50 (ISBN 0-306-40515-6, Plenum Pr); pap. 17.95 (ISBN 0-306-40530-X). Plenum Pub.

Woodruff, A. Bond. Directed Readings: Introduction to Psychology. 2nd ed. 144p. 1980. pap. text ed. 5.95 (ISBN 0-8403-2243-7). Kendall-Hunt.

Wundt, Wilhelm M. Lectures on Human & Animal Psychology. Creighton, J., tr. from German. (Contributions to the History of Psychology D, I, Comparative Psychology Ser.). 1978. Repr. of 1894 ed. 30.00 (ISBN 0-89093-170-4). U Pubns Amer.

Zanden, James W. Human Development. 2nd ed. 665p. 1981. text ed. 16.95 (ISBN 0-394-32370-X); wkbk. 6.95 (ISBN 0-394-32371-8). Knopf.

Ziskin, Jay. Coping with Psychiatric & Psychological Testimony, 2 vols. 3rd ed. Incl. Vol. 1. 429p. 50.00 (ISBN 0-9603630-2-5); Vol. 2. 577p. write for info. (ISBN 0-9603630-3-3). 1981. Set. 80.00 (ISBN 0-9603630-4-1). Law & Psych.

PSYCHOLOGY–ADDRESSES, ESSAYS, LECTURES

Andreas-Salome, Lou. Selected Essays of Lou Andreas-Salome. Binion, Rudolph, ed. 500p. (Orig.). 1981. price not set (ISBN 0-937406-15-5); pap. price not set (ISBN 0-937406-14-7); price not set limited ed. (ISBN 0-937406-16-3). Logbridge-Rhodes.

Brodie, Benjamin. Psychological Inquiries: A Series of Essays Intended to Illustrate the Mutual Relations of the Physical Organization & the Mental Faculties. Bd. with On Animal Electricity. DuBois-Reymond, E. (Contributions to the History of Psychology Ser., Vol. VI, Pt. E). 1980. Repr. of 1854 ed. 30.00 (ISBN 0-89093-325-1). U Pubns Amer.

Kardos, Lajos & Pleh, Csaba, eds. Problems of the Regulations of Activity. (Illus.). 733p. 1980. write for info. (ISBN 963-05-2447-3). Intl Pubns Serv.

Whytt, Robert. Works of Robert Whytt. Bd. with Memoirs on the Nervous System. Hall, Marshall; Memoirs. Cabanis, Pierre J; Two Essays. Hall, G. S. & DuBois-Reymond, E.. (Contributions to the History of Psychology Ser., Vol. I, Pt. E: Physiological Psychology). 1978. Repr. of 1768 ed. 30.00 (ISBN 0-89093-174-7). U Pubns Amer.

PSYCHOLOGY–BIBLIOGRAPHY

Research Libraries Fo the New York Public Library & the Library of Congress. Bibliographic Guide to Psychology: 1980. (Library Catalogs-Guides Ser.). 1981. lib. bdg. 70.00 (ISBN -08161-6893-8). G K Hall.

Rosenzweig, Mark R. & Porter, Lyman W., eds. Annual Review of Psychology, Vol. 32. LC 50-13143. (Illus.). 1981. text ed. 20.00 (ISBN 0-8243-0232-X). Annual Reviews.

PSYCHOLOGY–CASES, CLINICAL REPORTS, STATISTICS

Revesz, G. The Psychology of a Musical Prodigy. 180p. 1980. Repr. of 1925 ed. lib. bdg. 45.00 (ISBN 0-89987-715-X). Darby Bks.

PSYCHOLOGY–EXAMINATIONS, QUESTIONS, ETC.

Golden, Charles A., et al. Interpretation of the Halstead Reitan Neuropsychological Test Battery: A Casebook Approach. 1980. 26.50 (ISBN 0-8089-1298-4). Grune.

PSYCHOLOGY–HISTORY

Binet, Alfred. Alterations of Personality. Baldwin, Helen G., tr. from Fr. Bd. with On Double-Consciousness. Repr. of 1890 ed. (Contributions to the History of Psychology Ser., Vol. V, Pt. C: Medical Psychology). 1978. Repr. of 1896 ed. 30.00 (ISBN 0-89093-169-0). U Pubns Amer.

Fichte, Johann G. Characteristics of the Present Age. Smith, W., tr. Bd. with Way Towards the Blessed Life. (Contributions to the History of Psychology Ser., Pt. A: Orientations). 1978. Repr. of 1889 ed. 30.00 (ISBN 0-89093-151-8). U Pubns Amer.

Lewes, George H. Study of Psychology. (Contributions to the History of Psychology Ser.: No. 6, Pt. A Orientations). 1978. Repr. of 1879 ed. 30.00 (ISBN 0-89093-155-0). U Pubns Amer.

Lewis, Helen B. Freud & Modern Psychology: The/Emotional Basis of Mental Illness, Vol. 1. (Emotions Personality & Psychotherapy Ser.). 240p. 1981. 19.50 (ISBN 0-306-40525-3, Plenum Pr). Plenum Pub.

Lotze, Hermann. Outlines of Psychology. Ladd, George T., tr. from Ger. (Contributions to the History of Psychology Ser.: Orientations). 1978. Repr. of 1886 ed. 30.00 (ISBN 0-89093-155-0). U Pubns Amer.

Pedagogical Seminary: (Selections) Hall, G. Stanley, ed. (Contributions to the History of Psychology Ser.: Psychometric & Educational Psychology). 1980. 30.00 (ISBN 0-89093-320-0). U Pubns Amer.

Prisco, Salvatore, III. An Introduction to Psychohistory: Theories & Case Studies. LC 80-8245. 190p. 1980. lib. bdg. 17.50 (ISBN 0-8191-1335-2); pap. text ed. 9.00 (ISBN 0-8191-1336-0). U Pr of Amer.

Robinson, Daniel N. Mind Unfolded: Essays on Psychology's Historic Texts. 1978. 24.00 (ISBN 0-89093-207-7); pap. 8.00 (ISBN 0-89093-209-3). U Pubns Amer.

Spalding, D. A., et al. Seminal Research Papers. (Contributions to the History of Psycholgy Ser.: No. 11, Pt. A Orientations). 1978. Repr. of 1873 ed. 30.00 (ISBN 0-89093-160-7). U Pubns Amer.

Wundt, Wilhelm M. Elements of Folk Psychology: Outlines of Psychological History of the Development of Mankind. Schaub, E. L., tr. from German. (Contributions to the History of Psychology Ser.). 1980. Repr. of 1916 ed. 30.00 (ISBN 0-89093-317-0). U Pubns Amer.

PSYCHOLOGY–JUVENILE LITERATURE

Cisek, James D. & George, Anthea, eds. Finding Solutions: Learning How to Deal with Life's Problems & Decisions. (Illus.). (gr. 6-10). 1980. wkbk 3.95 (ISBN 0-9604510-0-5); lab manual 4.95 (ISBN 0-9604510-1-3). Life Skills.

PSYCHOLOGY–MEASUREMENT

see Psychometrics

PSYCHOLOGY–METHODOLOGY

Stone, Gerald L. A Cognitive-Behavioral Approach Psychology: Implications for Practice, Research, & Training. LC 80-21344. 256p. 1980. 21.95 (ISBN 0-03-055926-X). Praeger.

PSYCHOLOGY–RESEARCH

see Psychological Research

PSYCHOLOGY–SCALING

see Psychometrics

PSYCHOLOGY–STATISTICS

see Psychometrics

PSYCHOLOGY, ABNORMAL

see Psychology, Pathological

Hersen, Michel, et al, eds. Progress in Behavior Modification, Vol. 11. 1981. write for info. (ISBN 0-12-535611-0); lib. bdg. write for info. (ISBN 0-12-535694-3); price not set microfiche (ISBN 0-12-535695-1). Acad Pr.

PSYCHOLOGY, APPLIED

Here are entered general works on the application of psychology in various fields such as industry, advertising, military life. Works on applied psychology intended as guides to successful personal development are entered under such headings as Success and Personality.

see also Behavior Modification; Childbirth–Psychology; Clinical Psychology; Counseling; Human Engineering; Interpersonal Relations; Law–Psychology; Negotiation; Pastoral Psychology; Persuasion (Psychology); Psychological Warfare; Psychology, Industrial

also subdivision Psychological Aspects under specific subjects, e.g. Economics–Psychological Aspects

Billingham, Katherine A. Developmental Psychology for the Health Care Professions: Prenatal Through Adolescent Development, Pt. 1. (Behavioral Sciences for Health Care Professionals Ser.). 128p. (Orig.). 1981. lib. bdg. 15.00x (ISBN 0-86531-000-9); pap. text ed. 6.00x (ISBN 0-86531-001-7). Westview.

Hadfield, J. A. Psychology & Morals. 245p. 1980. Repr. of 1926 ed. lib. bdg. 30.00 (ISBN 0-8492-5282-2). R West.

Kaszniak, Alfred W. Developmental Psychology for the Health Care Professions: Young Adult Through Late Aging, Pt. II. (Behavioral Sciences for Health Care Professionals Ser.). 128p. (Orig.). 1981. lib. bdg. 15.00x (ISBN 0-86531-012-2); pap. text ed. 6.00x (ISBN 0-86531-013-0). Westview.

Thorndike, Robert M. Principles of Data Collection. (Gardner Press Ser. on Measurement & Statistics). 350p. 1981. text ed. 22.00 (ISBN 0-89876-022-4). Gardner Pr.

PSYCHOLOGY, CHILD

see Child Psychology

PSYCHOLOGY, CLERICAL

see Pastoral Psychology

PSYCHOLOGY, CLINICAL

see Clinical Psychology

PSYCHOLOGY, COMPARATIVE

see also Animal Intelligence; Animals, Habits and Behavior of; Human Behavior; Instinct; Play; Sociobiology

Lindsay, William L. Mind in the Lower Animal in Health & Disease. (Contributions to the History of Psychology Ser.: Pts. 6 & 7, Comparative Psychology). 1980. Repr. of 1879 ed. 30.00 ea. U Pubns Amer.

Morgan, C. Lloyd. Introduction to Comparative Psychology. (Contributions to the History of Psychology D, II Comparative Psychology Ser.). 1978. Repr. of 1894 ed. 30.00 (ISBN 0-89093-171-2). U Pubns Amer.

Wundt, Wilhelm M. Lectures on Human & Animal Psychology. Creighton, J., tr. from German. (Contributions to the History of Psychology D, I, Comparative Psychology Ser.). 1978. Repr. of 1894 ed. 30.00 (ISBN 0-89093-170-4). U Pubns Amer.

PSYCHOLOGY, CRIMINAL

see Criminal Psychology

PSYCHOLOGY, DEVELOPMENTAL

see Developmental Psychology

PSYCHOLOGY, EDUCATIONAL

see Educational Psychology

PSYCHOLOGY, ETHNIC

see Ethnopsychology

PSYCHOLOGY, EXPERIMENTAL

Conrad, Eva & Maul, Terry. Introduction to Experimental Psychology. 350p. 1981. text ed. 16.95 (ISBN 0-471-06005-4). Wiley.

Harzem, Peter & Zeiler, Michael D. Predictability, Correlation & Contiguity. 400p. 1981. 48.00 (ISBN 0-471-27847-5, Pub. by Wiley-Interscience). Wiley.

Robinson, P., ed. Fundamentals of Experimental Psychology: A Comparative Approach. 2nd ed. 19.95 (ISBN 0-13-339135-3); pap. 5.95 wkbk (ISBN 0-13-339127-2). P-H.

PSYCHOLOGY, FORENSIC

see also Criminal Psychology; Evidence (Law); Forensic Psychiatry

Bjerre, Andreas. The Psychology of Murder: A Study in Criminal Psychology. Classen, E., tr. from Swedish. (Historical Foundations of Forensic Psychiatry & Psychology Ser.). 164p. 1980. Repr. lib. bdg. 19.50 (ISBN 0-306-76067-3). Da Capo.

Bose, Prabodh C. Introduction to Juristic Psychology. (Historical Foundations of Forensic Psychiatry & Psychology Ser.). 426p. 1980. Repr. of 1917 ed. lib. bdg. 39.50 (ISBN 0-686-68561-X). Da Capo.

Brown, M. Ralph. Legal Psychology. (Historical Foundations of Forensic Psychiatry & Psychology Ser.). (Illus.). 346p. 1980. Repr. of 1926 ed. lib. bdg. 35.00 (ISBN 0-306-76065-7). Da Capo.

Davey, Herbert. The Law Relating to the Mentally Defective. (Historical Foundations of Forensic Psychiatry & Psychology Ser.). 568p. 1980. Repr. of 1914 ed. lib. bdg. 49.50 (ISBN 0-306-76070-3). Da Capo.

Goodwin, John C. Insanity & the Criminal. (Historical Foundations of Forensic Psychiatry & Psychology Ser.). 308p. 1980. Repr. of 1924 ed. lib. bdg. 29.50 (ISBN 0-306-76061-4). Da Capo.

Haward, Lionel. Forensic Psychology. 280p. 1981. 45.00 (ISBN 0-7134-2475-3, Pub. by Batsford England). David & Charles.
Hoag, Ernest B. & Williams, Edward H. Crime, Abnormal Minds & the Law. (Historical Foundations of Forensic Psychiatry & Psychology Ser.). 405p. 1980. Repr. of 1923 ed. lib. bdg. 35.00 (ISBN 0-306-76060-6). Da Capo.
Hollander, Bernard. The Psychology of Misconduct, Vice, & Crime. (Historical Foundations of Forensic Psychiatry & Psychology Ser.). 220p. 1980. Repr. lib. bdg. 25.00 (ISBN 0-306-76063-0). Da Capo.
McCarty, Dwight G. Psychology for the Lawyer. (Historical Foundations of Forensic Psychiatry & Psychology Ser.). Date not set. lib. bdg. 49.50 (ISBN 0-306-76068-1). Da Capo.
Mercier, Charles. Criminal Responsibility. (Historical Foundations of Forensic Psychiatry & Psychology Ser.). 256p. 1980. Repr. of 1931 ed. lib. bdg. 25.00 (ISBN 0-306-76064-9). Da Capo.
White, W. A. Insanity & the Criminal Law. (Historical Foundations of Forensic Psychiatry & Psychology Ser.). 281p. 1980. Repr. of 1923 ed. lib. bdg. 25.00 (ISBN 0-306-76069-X). Da Capo.
Wright, Fred, et al, eds. Forensic Psychology & Psychiatry. LC 80-17982. (N.Y. Academy of Sciences Annals: Vol. 347). 364p. 1980. 58.00 (ISBN 0-89766-084-6). NY Acad Sci.

PSYCHOLOGY, INDUSTRIAL
see also Industrial Sociology
Federico, Pat A., et al. Management Information Systems & Organizational Behavior. Brun, Kim & McCalla, Douglas B., eds. LC 80-15174. 204p. 1980. 20.95 (ISBN 0-03-057021-2). Praeger.

PSYCHOLOGY, JURISTIC
see Psychology, Forensic

PSYCHOLOGY, LEGAL
see Law–Psychology; Psychology, Forensic

PSYCHOLOGY, NATIONAL
see Ethnopsychology

PSYCHOLOGY, PASTORAL
see Pastoral Psychology

PSYCHOLOGY, PATHOLOGICAL
see also Aphasia; Clinical Psychology; Criminal Psychology; Depression, Mental; Fantasy; Hysteria; Manic-Depressive Psychoses; Medicine, Psychosomatic; Mental Health; Mental Illness; Narcissism; Neuroses; Personality, Disorders Of; Projective Techniques; Psychiatric Social Work; Psychiatry; Psychoanalysis; Psychology, Forensic; Rigidity (Psychology); Transference (Psychology)
Adams, Henry E. Abnormal Psychology. 750p. Date not set. text ed. price not set. Wm C Brown.
Eisdorfer, C., et al. Conceptual Models for Psychopathology. 1981. text ed. write for info. (ISBN 0-89335-123-7). Spectrum Pub.
Goldstein & Baker. Readings in Abnormal Psychology. (Orig.). 1981. pap. text ed. 8.95 (ISBN 0-316-07830-1). Little.
Guggenbuhl-Craig, Adolf. Eros on Crutches. Hartman, Gary V., tr. from Ger. 126p. (Orig.). 1980. pap. text ed. 7.00 (ISBN 0-88214-315-8). Spring Pubns.
Joffe, Justin M., ed. Prevention Through Political Action & Social Change. (Primary Prevention of Psychopathology Ser.: No. 5). 330p. 1981. 20.00 (ISBN 0-87451-187-9). U Pr of New Eng.
Levy, Norman B., ed. Psychonephrology One: Psychological Factors in Hemodialysis & Transplantation. 280p. 1981. 25.00 (ISBN 0-306-40586-5, Plenum Pr). Plenum Pub.
Prokop, Charles & Bradley, L. A., eds. Medical Psychology: Contributions to Behavioral Medicine. LC 80-1676. 1981. price not set (ISBN 0-12-565960-1). Acad Pr.
Sidis, Boris. Psychopathological Researches. 329p. 1980. Repr. of 1902 ed. lib. bdg. 75.00 (ISBN 0-89984-411-1). Century Bookbindery.
Vingoe, Frank J. Clinical Psychology & Medicine: An Interdisciplnary Approach. (Illus.). 480p. 1981. text ed. 35.00x. Oxford U Pr.
Weintraub, Walter. Verbal Behavior: Adaption & Psychopathology. LC 80-27021. 224p. 1981. text ed. price not set (ISBN 0-8261-2660-X); pap. text ed. price not set (ISBN 0-8261-2661-8). Springer Pub.

PSYCHOLOGY, PHYSIOLOGICAL
see also Behaviorism (Psychology); Brain–Localization of Functions; Emotions; Human Engineering; Hypnotism; Information Theory in Psychology; Memory; Mind and Body; Pain; Psychoanalysis; Psychometrics; Senses and Sensation; Sleep; Temperament
Applewhite, Philip B. Molecular Gods: How Molecules Determine Our Behavior. (Illus.). 288p. 1981. 10.95 (ISBN 0-13-599530-2). P-H.
Bechtereva, N. P., ed. Psychophysiology Today & Tomorrow: Proceedings of International Union of Physiological Sciences Conference on Psychophysiology, 1979. (Illus.). 270p. 1980. 60.00 (ISBN 0-08-025930-8). Pergamon.
Brown, Thomas S. & Wallace, Patricia. Physiological Psychology. 1980. tchrs' ed. 20.95 (ISBN 0-12-136660-X). Acad Pr.
Furnham, A. & Argyle, M., eds. The Psychology of Social Situations: Selected Readings. 350p. 1981. 40.00 (ISBN 0-08-024319-3); pap. 15.70 (ISBN 0-08-023719-3). Pergamon.
Kimball, Chase P. The Biopsychosocial Approach to the Patient. (Illus.). 382p. 1981. softcover 24.00 (ISBN 0-686-69562-3, 9400-9). Williams & Wilkins.
McFarland, Richard A. Physiological Psychology: The Biology of Human Behavior. (Illus.). 600p. 1981. text ed. price not set (ISBN 0-87484-500-9). Mayfield Pub.
Maudsley, Henry. Physiology & Pathology of the Mind. (Contributions to the History of Psychology Ser.: Medical Psychology). 1978. Repr. of 1867 ed. 30.00 (ISBN 0-89093-168-2). U Pubns Amer.
Ward, James. Psychology & Psychological Principles. (Contributions to the History of Psychology Ser.: Vol. 8, Pt. a, Orientations). 1978. 30.00 (ISBN 0-89093-157-7). U Pubns Amer.
Wegener, Bernd, ed. Social Attitudes & Psychophysical Measurement. 432p. 1981. professional reference text 24.95 (ISBN 0-89859-083-3). L Erlbaum Assocs.

PSYCHOLOGY, POLITICAL
see Political Psychology

PSYCHOLOGY, PRACTICAL
see Psychology, Applied

PSYCHOLOGY, RACIAL
see Ethnopsychology

PSYCHOLOGY, RELIGIOUS
see also Enthusiasm; Miracles; Pastoral Psychology; Psychology, Applied
Collins, Gary R. Psychology & Theology. 160p. (Orig.). 1981. pap. 5.95 (ISBN 0-687-34830-7). Abingdon.
Gawryn, Marvin. Reaching High: The Psychology of Spiritual Living. LC 80-24306. 200p. 1981. 11.95 (ISBN 0-938380-00-1); pap. 7.95 (ISBN 0-938380-01-X). Spiritual Renaissance.
Kane, Thomas A. Happy Are You Who Affirm. (Illus.). 144p. 1980. pap. 5.00 (ISBN 0-89571-010-2). Affirmation.
Morningstar, Jim. Spiritual Psychology: A New Age Course for Body, Mind & Spirit. 2nd ed. (Illus.). 119p. Date not set. pap. 8.00 (ISBN 0-9604856-0-0). Morningstar.
Peatling, John H. Religious Education in a Psychological Key. 380p. (Orig.). 1981. pap. price not set (ISBN 0-89135-027-6). Religious Educ.

PSYCHOLOGY, SEXUAL
see Sex (Psychology)

PSYCHOLOGY, SOCIAL
see Social Psychology

PSYCHOLOGY AND RELIGION
see Psychology, Religious

PSYCHOLOGY OF COLOR
see Color–Psychological Aspects

PSYCHOLOGY OF LANGUAGE
see Psycholinguistics

PSYCHOLOGY OF LEARNING
see Learning, Psychology Of

PSYCHOMETRICS
see also Decision-Making–Mathematical Models; Educational Tests and Measurements
Ghiselli, Edwin E., et al. Measurement Theory for the Behavioral Sciences. LC 80-27069. (Psychology Ser.). (Illus.). 1981. text ed. 21.95x (ISBN 0-7167-1048-X); pap. text ed. 13.95 (ISBN 0-7167-1252-0). W H Freeman.
Levine, Gustav. Introductory Statistics for Psychology: The Logic & the Methods. LC 80-81254. 1981. write for info. (ISBN 0-12-445480-1). Acad Pr.
Oltman, Debra. Study Guide for Weinberg, Schumaker & Oltman's Statistics: An Intuitive Approach. 4th ed. 250p. (Orig.). 1981. pap. text ed. 7.95 (ISBN 0-8185-0442-0). Brooks-Cole.
Pagano, Robert R. Understanding Statistics in the Behavioral Sciences. (Illus.). 520p. 1981. text ed. write for info. (ISBN 0-8299-0316-X). West Pub.
Pedagogical Seminary: (Selections) Hall, G. Stanley, ed. (Contributions to the History of Psychology Ser.: Psychometric & Educational Psychology). 1980. 30.00 (ISBN 0-89093-320-0). U Pubns Amer.
Whaley, Donald L. Psychological Testing & the Philosophy of Measurement. 58p. 1973. pap. text ed. 7.00 (ISBN 0-914474-02-2). F Fournies.

PSYCHOMETRY (OCCULT SCIENCES)
Ferguson, Sibyl. The Crystal Ball. 1980. pap. 1.00 (ISBN 0-87728-483-0). Weiser.

PSYCHOMETRY (PSYCHOPHYSICS)
see Psychometrics

PSYCHONEUROSES
see Neuroses

PSYCHOPATHOLOGY
see Psychology, Pathological

PSYCHOPHARMACOLOGY
see also Hallucinogenic Drugs; Neuro-Psychopharmacology; Tranquilizing Drugs
Ban, T. A. & Hollender, M. H. Psychopharmacology for Everyday Practice. vi, 190p. 1981. pap. 19.75 (ISBN 3-8055-2241-X). S Karger.
Burrows & Norman. Pschyotropic Drugs. 528p. 1980. 68.00 (ISBN 0-8247-1009-6). Dekker.
Cautela, Joseph R. Organic Dysfunction Survey Schedules. LC 80-53910. 157p. (Orig.). 1981. pap. text ed. write for info. (ISBN 0-87822-223-5, 2235). Res Press.
Cole, Jonathan O., ed. Psychopharmacology Update. LC 79-48064. 195p. 1980. 14.95 (ISBN 0-669-03695-1). Heath.
Giurgea, Corneliu E. Fundamentals to a Pharmacology of the Mind. (American Lectures on Objective Psychiatry). (Illus.). 376p. 1981. text ed. 37.75 (ISBN 0-398-04130-X). C C Thomas.
Iversen, Susan D. & Iversen, Leslie L. Behavioral Pharmacology. 2nd ed. (Illus.). 288p. 1981. text ed. 17.95 (ISBN 0-19-502778-7); pap. text ed. 10.95 (ISBN 0-19-502779-5). Oxford U Pr.
Janowsky, David S., et al. Psychopharmacology Case Studies. 1978. pap. 12.75 (ISBN 0-87488-052-1). Med Exam.
Rosenblatt, Seymour & Dodson, Reynolds. Beyond Valium: The Brave New World of Psychochemistry. 316p. 1981. 13.95 (ISBN 0-399-12577-9). Putnam.

PSYCHOPHYSICS
see Psychology, Physiological

PSYCHOPHYSIOLOGY
see Psychology, Physiological

PSYCHOSES
see also Neuroses; Senile Psychosis
Waters, Brent G. & Jurek, Mary B., eds. Self-Assessment of Current Knowledge in Psychosis. LC 80-18729. 1980. pap. 18.00 (ISBN 0-87488-233-8). Med Exam.

PSYCHOSOMATIC DENTISTRY
see Dentistry–Psychological Aspects

PSYCHOSOMATIC DISEASES IN CHILDREN
see Pediatrics–Psychosomatic Aspects

PSYCHOSOMATIC MEDICINE
see Medicine, Psychosomatic

PSYCHOSOMATIC RESEARCH
Aitken, C., ed. Psychosomatics & Pleasure: Proceedings of the Twenty-Third Annual Conference of the Society for Psychosomatic Research Held at the Royal College of Physicians, London, 19-20 November 1979. 88p. 1980. pap. 20.00 (ISBN 0-08-026797-1). Pergamon.

PSYCHOTECHNICS
see Psychology, Industrial

PSYCHOTHERAPY
see also Art Therapy; Behavior Therapy; Child Psychotherapy; Gestalt Therapy; Group Psychotherapy; Mental Healing; Psychopharmacology; Sex Therapy
Budman, Simon, ed. Forms of Brief Therapy. 500p. 1981. 25.00 (ISBN 0-89862-608-0). Guilford Pr.
Burns, David D. Feeling Good. 1981. pap. 3.95 (ISBN 0-451-09804-8, E9804, Signet Bks). NAL.
Dubovsky, Steven L. Psychotherapeutics in Primary Care. 1981. price not set (ISBN 0-8089-1337-9). Grune.
Fleshman, Bob & Fryrear, Jerry L. The Arts in Therapy. LC 80-20334. 240p. 1981. text ed. 19.95 (ISBN 0-88229-520-9); pap. text ed. 9.95 (ISBN 0-88229-762-7). Nelson-Hall.
Furrow, Barry R. Malpractice in Psychotherapy. LC 79-3253. 192p. 1980. 18.95x (ISBN 0-669-03399-5). Lexington Bks.
Glasser, William & Powers, William T. Stations of the Mind: New Directions for Reality Therapy. LC 80-8205. (Illus.). 288p. 1981. 11.95 (ISBN 0-06-011478-9, HarpT). Har-Row.
Horton, Arthur M., Jr., ed. Psychotherapeutic Treatment Approaches for the Aging. 320p. 1981. 24.95 (ISBN 0-89789-007-8). J F Bergin.
Janet, Pierre. Principles of Psychotherapy. Guthrie, H. M. & Guthrie, E. R., trs. 322p. 1980. Repr. of 1924 ed. lib. bdg. 40.00 (ISBN 0-8495-2760-0). Arden Lib.
Langs, Robert, ed. International Journal of Psychoanalytic Psychotherapy, Vol. 8. LC 75-648853. 705p. 1980. 35.00 (ISBN 0-87668-428-2). Aronson.
McNiff, Shaun. The Arts & Psychotherapy. (Illus.). 280p. 19.75. C C Thomas.
Murray, J. A. An Introduction to a Christian Psycho-Therapy. 2nd ed. 291p. 1947. text ed. 4.95 (ISBN 0-567-02202-1). Attic Pr.
Olsen, Paul. Comprehensive Psychotherapy. (Vol. 2). 1981. price not set. Gordon.
Olsen, Paul, ed. Comprehensive Psychotherapy, Vol. 2. 1981. price not set. Gordon.
Slipp, Samuel. Curative Factors in Dynamic Psychotherapy. (Illus.). 448p. 1981. 22.95 (ISBN 0-07-058190-8). McGraw.
Storr, Anthony. The Art of Psychotherapy. 204p. 1980. 13.95 (ISBN 0-686-68763-9). S&S.
Whitaker, Carl A. & Malone, Thomas P. The Roots of Psychotherapy. LC 80-24437. (Brunner Mazel Classics in Psychoanalysis & Psychotherapy: No. 9). 272p. 1981. Repr. 17.50 (ISBN 0-87630-265-7). Brunner-Mazel.
Wile, B. Couples Therapy: A Nontraditional Approach. 240p. 1981. 22.50 (ISBN 0-471-07811-5, Pub. by Wiley Interscience). Wiley.
Wolberg, Arlene R. The Psychoanalytic Psychotherapy of the Borderline Patient. (Illus.). 350p. 1981. text ed. 30.00 (ISBN 0-86577-022-0). Thieme-Stratton.

PSYCHOTHERAPY–CASES, CLINICAL REPORTS, STATISTICS
Frederic, Helene & Malinsky, Martine. Martin. McGreal, John & Lipshitz, Susan, trs. from Fr. Orig. Title: Martin: un Enfant Battait Sa Mere. 108p. 1981. price not set (ISBN 0-7100-0814-7). Routledge & Kegan.

PSYCHOTHERAPY–RESEARCH
see Psychiatric Research

PSYCHOTIC CHILDREN
see Mentally Ill Children

PSYCHOTROPIC DRUGS
see Psychopharmacology

PUBLIC ADMINISTRATION
Here are entered works on the principles and techniques involved in the conduct of public business. Works descriptive of governmental machinery are entered under the area concerned, with the subdivision Politics and Government.
see also Administrative Agencies; Administrative Law; Bureaucracy; Civil Service; Government Publicity; Governmental Investigations; Impeachments; Intelligence Service; Personnel Management
also subdivision Politics and Government under names of countries, cities, etc.
Barry, Donald D. & Whitcomb, Howard R. The Legal Foundations of Public Administration. 407p. 1980. text ed. 17.95 (ISBN 0-8299-2120-6). West Pub.
Brigham, John & Brown, Don W., eds. Policy Implementation: Penalties or Incentives? LC 80-16765. (Sage Focus Editions: Vol. 25). (Illus.). 284p. 1980. pap. 9.95 (ISBN 0-8039-1351-6). Sage.
Captor, Renee S. Library Research for the Analysis of Public Policy. (Learning Packages in the Policy Sciences Ser.: No. 19). 36p. 1979. pap. text ed. 3.00 (ISBN 0-936826-08-8). Pol Stud Assocs.
Cutchin, Debbie. Guide to Public Administration. LC 80-84211. 130p. 1981. pap. text ed. 4.95 (ISBN 0-87581-272-4). Peacock Pubs.
Harmon, Michael M. Action Theory for Public Administration. (Longman Professional Studies in Public Administration). 256p. (Orig.). 1981. text ed. 22.50 (ISBN 0-582-28254-3); pap. text ed. 9.95 (ISBN 0-582-28255-1). Longman.
Kebbede, Girma. Basic Geographic Techniques in the Analysis of Public Policy. (Learning Packages in the Policy Sciences Ser.: No. 18). (Illus.). 46p. (Orig.). 1978. pap. text ed. 3.00 (ISBN 0-936826-07-X). Pol Stud Assocs.
Klingner, Donald E., ed. Public Personnel Management: Readings in Contexts & Strategies. (Illus.). 500p. (Orig.). 1981. write for info (ISBN 0-87484-517-3). Mayfield Pub.
Legal Foundation of Public Administration. 407p. 1980. text ed. 17.95 (ISBN 0-8299-2120-6). West Pub.
Levitt, Ruth. Implementing Public Policy. 256p. 1981. 30.00x (ISBN 0-7099-0068-6, Pub. by Croom Helm Ltd England). Biblio Dist.
Lynn, Laurence E., Jr. Managing the Public's Business: The Job of the Government Executive. LC 80-68176. 416p. 1981. 17.50 (ISBN 0-465-04378-X). Basic.
OECD. Strategies for Change & Reform in Public Management. (Public Management Ser.: No. 1). 242p. (Orig.). 1980. pap. text ed. 16.00x (ISBN 92-64-12121-8). OECD.
Rouse, John E., Jr., ed. Public Administration in American Society: A Guide to Information Sources. (American Government & History Information Guide Ser.: Vol. 11). 300p. 1980. 30.00 (ISBN 0-8103-1424-X). Gale.
Samuels, Warren & Wade, Larry, eds. Taxing & Spending Policy. (Orig.). 1980. pap. 5.00 (ISBN 0-918592-41-0). Policy Studies.
Union for Radical Political Economics (URPE), ed. Crisis in the Public Sector: A Reader. LC 80-8936. 1981. pap. 7.50 (ISBN 0-85345-575-9). Monthly Rev.

PUBLIC ADMINISTRATION–BIBLIOGRAPHY
Heaser, Eileen & Kong, Les. The Sacramento Region: Planning, Growth & Development, A Bibliographic Guide. (Public Administration Ser.: Bibliographies: P-673). 61p. 1981. 9.00. Vance Biblios.
Isaacs, Hope L., et al. Public Administration Ser.: Bibliographies, 2 vols. (Public Administration Ser.: Bibliography: P-638). 304p. 1981. pap. 20.00. Vance Biblios.
Stofferahn, Curtis W. & Korsching, Peter F. Communication, Diffusion & Adoption of Innovations: A Bibliographical Update. (Public Administration Ser.: Bibliography P-433). 50p. 1980. pap. 5.50. Vance Biblios.
Vance Bibliographies. Index to Public Administration Series Bibliography: No. P-394 to P-636, Jan. 1980 to Dec. 1980, No. P-394 To P-636, Jan. 1980 To Dec. 1980. (Public Administration Ser.: Bibliography: P-637). 81p. 1981. pap. 7.50. Vance Biblios.

PUBLIC ASSISTANCE
see Public Welfare

PUBLIC COMMUNITY COLLEGES
see Community Colleges

PUBLIC CORPORATIONS
see Corporations

PUBLIC DOCUMENTS
see Government Publications

PUBLIC EMPLOYEE STRIKES
see Strikes and Lockouts–Civil Service

PUBLIC FINANCE
see Finance, Public

PUBLIC HEALTH
see also Burial; Communicable Diseases; Community Health Services; Community Mental Health Services; Environmental Health; Epidemics; Food Adulteration and Inspection; Hospitals; Industrial Health; Meat Inspection; Medical Care; Medicine, Preventive; Mental Health; Noise; Occupational Diseases; Pollution; Refuse and Refuse Disposal; Sanitary Engineering; School Health; Sewage Disposal; Slaughtering and Slaughter-Houses; Social Medicine; Swimming Pools; Water-Supply; Zoonoses

Altenstetter, Christa, ed. Innovation in Health Policy & Service Delivery: A Cross-National Perspective, 3vols, Vol. 3. LC 80-39617. 256p. 1981. lib. bdg. 25.00 (ISBN 0-89946-078-X). Oelgeschlager.

Altman, Stuart & Sapolsky, Harvey M., eds. Federal Health Programs: Improving the Health-Care System? LC 79-48059. (The University Health Policy Consortium Ser.). 1981. 24.95x (ISBN 0-669-03690-0). Lexington Bks.

American Hospital Association. Appropriateness Review of Health Services: Manual for Lawyers, Planners & Hospitals. LC 80-23209. 128p. 1980. pap. 18.75 (ISBN 0-87258-336-8, 1527). Am Hospital.

Bliss. Bliss Bibliography, Second Class H: Anthropology, Human Biology & Health Sciences. 1981. price not set (ISBN 0-408-70828-X). Butterworth.

Breslow, Lester, et al, eds. Annual Review of Public Health, Vol 2. 1981. text ed. 20.00 (ISBN 0-8243-2702-0). Annual Reviews.

Gleason, Herbert P., ed. Getting Better: A Report on Health Care from the Salzbug Seminar. LC 80-23486. 192p. Date not set. text ed. 22.50 (ISBN 0-89946-053-4). Oelgeschlager.

Isacson, Peter. Public Health & Preventive Medicine Continuing Education Review. 1980. pap. 15.00 (ISBN 0-87488-348-2). Med Exam.

Jansen, Elly, ed. The Theraputic Community. 320p. 1980. 35.00x (ISBN 0-85664-967-8, Pub. by Croom Helm England). State Mutual Bk.

Kark, Sidney L. The Practice of Community-Oriented Primary Health Care. 288p. 1980. pap. 13.50x (ISBN 0-8385-7865-9). ACC.

Last, John M., ed. Maxcy-Rosenau Public Health & Preventive Medicine. 11th ed. 1492p. 1980. text ed. 64.50x (ISBN 0-8385-6186-1). ACC.

Lunz, Mary E. Communication in Health Care Organizations. 420p. 1981. text ed. price not set (ISBN 0-914904-69-8). Health Admin Pr.

Marcus, Isabel. Dollars for Reform: The OEO Neighborhood Health Center Experience. LC 78-2198. 1981. 22.95x (ISBN 0-669-03092-9). Lexington Bks.

Milio, Nancy. Promoting Health Through Public Policy. 320p. 1981. text ed. 25.00 (ISBN 0-8036-6177-0, 6177-0). Davis Co.

Neuhauser, Duncan, ed. Quest for Excellence in Health Care Delivery. (Illus.). 180p. 1981. text ed. price not set (ISBN 0-914904-70-1). Health Admin Pr.

Ng, Lorenz K. & Davis, Devra, eds. Strategies for Public Health: Promoting Health & Preventing Disease. 384p. 1980. text ed. 21.95 (ISBN 0-442-24428-2). Van Nos Reinhold.

Society for Hospital Social Work Directors of the American Hospital Association. Quality & Quantity Assurance for Social Workers in Health Care: A Training Manual. LC 80-26488. (Illus.). 96p. (Orig.). 1980. manual 27.50 (ISBN 0-87258-325-2, 2100). Am Hospital.

Spradley, Barbara W. Community Health Nursing: Concepts & Practice. 1981. text ed. price not set (ISBN 0-316-80748-6). Little.

Stokes, Bruce. Men & Family Planning. (Worldwatch Papers Ser.). 1980. pap. 2.00 (ISBN 0-916468-40-2). Worldwatch Inst.

Straetz, Ralph, et al, eds. Critical Perspectives & Issues in Health Policy. (Orig.). 1980. pap. 5.00 (ISBN 0-918592-42-9). Policy Studies.

Suchman, Edward A. Sociology & the Field of Public Health. LC 63-21228. 1963. pap. 2.00 (ISBN 0-87154-864-X). Russell Sage.

PUBLIC HEALTH–AUTHORSHIP
see Medical Writing

PUBLIC HEALTH–LAW AND LEGISLATION
see Public Health Laws

PUBLIC HEALTH–ASIA

Ohnuki-Tierney, Emiko. Illness & Healing Among the Sakhalin Ainu: A Symbolic Interpretation. LC 80-24268. (Illus.). 272p. Date not set. price not set (ISBN 0-521-23636-3). Cambridge U Pr.

PUBLIC HEALTH, RURAL
see Health, Rural

PUBLIC HEALTH, TROPICAL
see Tropical Medicine

PUBLIC HEALTH ADMINISTRATION

Begun, James W. Professionalism & Public Interest. (Health & Public Policy Ser.). 176p. 1981. text ed. 17.50x (ISBN 0-262-02156-0). MIT Pr.

Broyles, Robert & Lay, Colin. Statistics in Health Administration, 2 vols. Incl. Vol. 1. Basic Concepts & Applications. 1979. 47.50 (ISBN 0-89443-153-6); Vol. II. Advanced Concepts & Applications. 1980. 48.00 (ISBN 0-89443-166-8). LC 79-23280. Aspen Systems.

Ching-Chih Chen. Health Sciences Information Sources. 608p. 1981. text ed. 50.00x (ISBN 0-262-03074-8). MIT Pr.

Financial Management Education in Health Administration Programs. 1979. 6.00. Assn Univ Progs Hlth.

Health Services Management in the Health Administration Curriculum. 1978. 5.00. Assn Univ Progs Hlth.

Honigsbaum, Frank. The Struggle for the Ministry of Health. 80p. 1970. pap. text ed. 5.00x (ISBN 0-7135-1836-7, Pub. by Bedford England). Renouf.

Hunter, James. Coping with Uncertainty Policy & Politics in the National Health Service. 320p. 1981. write for info. (ISBN 0-471-27906-4, Pub. by Wiley-Interscience). Wiley.

Kuhl, Ingrid K. The Executive Role in Health Service Delivery Organizations. 1977. 5.00. Assn Univ Progs Hlth.

Rakech. Managing Health Care Org. 1977. 18.95 (ISBN 0-7216-7451-8). Dryden Pr.

Reisman, Arnold. Materials Management for Health Services. LC 79-3524. 1981. 35.95 (ISBN 0-669-03458-4). Lexington Bks.

PUBLIC HEALTH LAWS
see also Health Officers
also specific legal headings related to public health, e.g. Narcotic Laws, Food Laws and Legislation; also subdivisions Laws and Legislation under topics in the field of public health

Conant, Ralph W. Politics of Community Health. 2.00 (ISBN 0-8183-0193-7). Pub Aff Pr.

PUBLIC HEALTH PERSONNEL
see also Health Officers

Society for Hospital Social Work Directors of the American Hospital Association. Social Work Staff Development for Health Care. LC 76-41793. 1976. pap. 7.25 (ISBN 0-87258-322-8, 2550). Am Hospital.

PUBLIC HEALTH SERVICES
see Public Health

PUBLIC HOUSES
see Hotels, Taverns, etc.

PUBLIC HOUSING

Manpower Demonstration Research Group. Tenant Management: Findings from a Three-Year Experiment in Public Housing. 240p. 1981. write for info. (ISBN 0-88410-694-2). Ballinger Pub.

Newman, Oscar. Community of Interest. (Illus.). 368p. 1981. pap. 8.95 (ISBN 0-385-11124-X, Anch). Doubleday.

Struyk, Raymond J. A New System for Public Housing: Salvaging a National Resource. LC 80-53321. 254p. 1980. 20.00 (ISBN 0-87766-279-7). Urban Inst.

PUBLIC HYGIENE
see Public Health

PUBLIC INTEREST

Chasen, Daniel Jack. Up for Grabs: Inquiries into Who Wants What. (Illus.). 133p. 7.95 (ISBN 0-914842-18-8); pap. 4.95 (ISBN 0-914842-17-X). Madrona Pubs.

Sonnenfeld, Jeffrey A. Corporate Views of the Public Interest: The Perceptions of the Forest Products Industry. 200p. 1981. 19.95 (ISBN 0-86569-060-X). Auburn Hse.

PUBLIC JUNIOR COLLEGES
see Community Colleges

PUBLIC LANDS
see Agricultural Colonies; National Parks and Reserves; United States–Public Lands

PUBLIC LAW (CANON LAW)
see Canon Law

PUBLIC OPINION
see also Attitude (Psychology); Press; Propaganda; Public Relations; Publicity
also subdivision Foreign Opinion, or Foreign Public Opinion, under names of countries or certain wars, e.g. France–History–Revolution, 1789-1799–Foreign Public Opinion

Hastings, Elizabeth H. & Hastings, Philip K., eds. Index to International Public Opinion: Nineteen Seventy-Nine to Nineteen Eighty. LC 80-643917. 510p. 1981. lib. bdg. 75.00 (ISBN 0-313-22535-4, IN80). Greenwood.

Hennessy, Bernard C. Public Opinion. 4th ed. LC 80-27733. 350p. (Orig.). 1981. pap. text ed. 12.95 (ISBN 0-8185-0449-8). Brooks-Cole.

Janowitz, Morris & Hirsch, Paul, eds. Reader in Public Opinion & Mass Communication. 3rd ed. LC 80-2444. 448p. 1981. pap. text ed. 10.95 (ISBN 0-02-916020-0). Free Pr.

Luttbeg, Norman R. Public Opinion & Public Policy. 3rd ed. LC 80-52446. 475p. 1981. pap. text ed. 11.95 (ISBN 0-87581-259-7). Peacock Pubs.

Payne, Stanley L. The Art of Asking Questions. 1980 ed. LC 80-7824. 264p. 1980. 22.50x (ISBN 0-691-08104-2); pap. 6.95 (ISBN 0-691-02367-0). Princeton U Pr.

PUBLIC OPINION–RESEARCH
see Public Opinion Polls

PUBLIC OPINION–AFRICA

Jacobs, Sylvia M. The African Nexus: Black American Perspectives on the European Partitioning of Africa, 1880-1920. LC 80-660. (Contributions in Afro-American & African Studies: No. 55). (Illus.). 264p. 1981. lib. bdg. 27.50 (ISBN 0-313-22312-2, JEP/). Greenwood.

PUBLIC OPINION–UNITED STATES

Bryce, James. Public Opinion in the American Commonwealth. 1981. 18.95 (ISBN 0-87923-370-2); pap. 8.95 (ISBN 0-87923-371-0). Godine.

Jacobs, Sylvia M. The African Nexus: Black American Perspectives on the European Partitioning of Africa, 1880-1920. LC 80-660. (Contributions in Afro-American & African Studies: No. 55). (Illus.). 264p. 1981. lib. bdg. 27.50 (ISBN 0-313-22312-2, JEP/). Greenwood.

PUBLIC OPINION POLLS
Here are entered works on the technique of public opinion polls or straw votes.

Gallup, George H., ed. The Gallup Poll: Public Opinion, 1980. LC 79-56557. 320p. 1981. lib. bdg. 49.50 (ISBN 0-8420-2181-7). Scholarly Res Inc.

--The International Gallup Polls: Public Opinion, 1979. LC 79-3844. 350p. 1981. lib. bdg. 49.50 (ISBN 0-8420-2180-9). Scholarly Res Inc.

Lemert, James B. Does Mass Communication Change Public Opinion, After All? A New Approach to Effects Analysis. LC 80-23826. 260p. 1981. text ed. 17.95 (ISBN 0-88229-474-1); pap. text ed. 8.95 (ISBN 0-88229-764-3). Nelson-Hall.

Martin, Elizabeth, et al, eds. Sourcebook of Harris National Surveys: Repeated Questions, 1963-1976. (IRSS Technical Papers). (Illus.). 515p. 1981. pap. write for info. (ISBN 0-89143-091-1). U NC Inst Res Soc Sci.

PUBLIC OWNERSHIP
see Government Ownership

PUBLIC POLICY
see Economic Policy; Environmental Policy; Military Policy; Social Policy

PUBLIC POLICY (LAW)

Brigham, John & Brown, Don W., eds. Policy Implementation: Penalties or Incentives? LC 80-16765. (Sage Focus Editions: Vol. 25). (Illus.). 284p. 1980. 18.95 (ISBN 0-8039-1350-8). Sage.

PUBLIC POLICY (LAW)–GREAT BRITAIN

Rose, Richard. Do Parties Make a Difference? pap. 8.95 (ISBN 0-934540-08-X). Chatham Hse Pubs.

PUBLIC RELATIONS
see also Advertising; Propaganda; Public Opinion; Publicity

Boyle, Charles A. Speak Out with Clout. LC 77-17265. 196p. 1977. 6.95 (ISBN 0-89709-020-9). Liberty Pub.

Cole, Robert S. The Practical Handbook of Public Relations. (Illus.). 224p. 1981. text ed. 18.95 (ISBN 0-13-691162-5, Spec); pap. text ed. 9.95 (ISBN 0-13-691154-4). P-H.

Jefkins, Frank. Public Relations. 232p. 1980. pap. text ed. 11.95x (ISBN 0-7121-1698-2). Intl Ideas.

Voros, Gerald J. & Alvarez, Paul, eds. What Happens in Public Relations. 275p. 1981. 17.95 (ISBN 0-8144-5652-9). Am Mgmt.

PUBLIC RELATIONS–BUSINESS
see Public Relations

PUBLIC RELATIONS–INDUSTRY
see Public Relations

PUBLIC RELATIONS–LIBRARIES

Kohn, Rita & Tepper, Krysta. You Can Do It: A PR Skills Manual for Librarians. LC 80-24217. xii, 232p. 1981. pap. 12.50 (ISBN 0-8108-1401-3). Scarecrow.

Library Community Services. LC 77-28184. 98p. 1977. 6.00 (ISBN 0-913578-18-5). Inglewood Ca.

PUBLIC RELATIONS–PHYSICIANS

Ziegler, A. Doctor's Administrative Program, 6 vols. Incl. Dap 1. Patient Contract & Public Relations (ISBN 0-87489-150-7); Dap 2. Bookkeeping & Tax Reports (ISBN 0-87489-151-5); Dap 3. Insurance & Third-Party-Payable Claims (ISBN 0-87489-152-3); Dap 4. Correspondence (ISBN 0-87489-153-1); Billing & Collections; Dap 6. Patient Records Control (ISBN 0-87489-155-8). 1978. Set. write for info. (ISBN 0-87489-158-2); Ea. Vol. write for info.

PUBLIC RELATIONS–POLICE

Martin, Carol A. Law Enforcement & Community Relations: A Selected Bibliography. (Public Administration Ser.: Bibliography: P-634). 1980. pap. 7.50. Vance Biblios.

PUBLIC RELATIONS–PUBLIC ADMINISTRATION
see Government Publicity

PUBLIC RELIEF
see Public Welfare

PUBLIC SCHOOL FACILITIES
see School Facilities

PUBLIC SCHOOLS
Here are entered works on primary and secondary schools controlled or supported by state and local government, including, in European countries, the higher schools preparatory to the university (Gymnasiem, Lycees, etc.) Works on the public schools of a particular city are entered under the name of the city with subdivision Public Schools, e.g. New York (City)–Public Schools. Works on British privately endowed schools, known as public schools are entered under Public Schools, Endowed (Great Britain.).
see also Religion in the Public Schools; Schools
also headings beginning with the word School

Bitter, John. Practical Public Relations for the Public Schools. LC 77-71467. 1977. text ed. 9.95 (ISBN 0-916624-08-0). TSU Pr.

Johnson, Henry C., Jr. The Public School & Moral Education. (The Education of the Public & the Public School Ser.). 96p. (Orig.). 1981. pap. 3.95 (ISBN 0-8298-0420-X). Pilgrim NY.

PUBLIC SCHOOLS–BUSINESS MANAGEMENT
see also Education–Finance

Everhart, Robert, ed. The Public School Monopoly: Education & State in American Society. (Pacific Institute for Public Policy Research Ser.). 1981. price not set professional reference (ISBN 0-88410-383-8). Ballinger Pub.

Taylor, Irwin. Public Schools: A Treatise on the Rights, Powers, Duties & Liabilities of School Boards, Officers & Teachers. 411p. 1980. Repr. of 1893 ed. lib. bdg. 30.00x (ISBN 0-8377-1204-1). Rothman.

PUBLIC SCHOOLS–FINANCE
see Education–Finance

PUBLIC SCHOOLS–SANITARY AFFAIRS
see School Health

PUBLIC SECTOR STRIKES
see Strikes and Lockouts–Civil Service

PUBLIC SECURITIES
see Municipal Bonds; Securities

PUBLIC SERVICE
see also Public Utilities

Mirengoff, William, et al. Ceta: Assessment of Public Service Employment Programs. xxl, 197p. 1980. pap. text ed. 10.50 (ISBN 0-309-02925-2). Natl Acad Pr.

PUBLIC SERVICE CORPORATIONS
see Public Utilities

PUBLIC SPEAKING
see also Debates and Debating; Lectures and Lecturing; Oratory; Persuasion (Rhetoric); Preaching; Rhetoric; Speeches, Addresses, etc.

Boyle, Charles A. Speak Out with Clout. LC 77-17265. 196p. 1977. 6.95 (ISBN 0-89709-020-9). Liberty Pub.

Faries, Clyde J. Concepts in Public Speaking: Consumer Responsibility. 112p. 1980. pap. text ed. 5.95 (ISBN 0-8403-2239-9). Kendall-Hunt.

Fluharty, George W & Ross, Harold R. Public Speaking. 2nd ed. (Illus.). 416p. (Orig.). 1981. pap. 5.95 (ISBN 0-06-463525-2, EH 525, EH). Har-Row.

Haynes, Judy L. Organizing a Speech: A Programmed Guide. 2nd ed. (Speech Communication Ser.). (Illus.). 192p. 1981. pap. text ed. 9.95 (ISBN 0-13-641530-X). P-H.

Hunt, Gary. Public Speaking. (Illus.). 386p. 1981. text ed. 12.95 (ISBN 0-13-738807-1). P-H.

Klopf, Donald W. & Cambra, Ronald E. Personal & Public Speaking. 208p. 1981. pap. text ed. 8.95 (ISBN 0-89582-042-0). Morton Pub.

Litfin, Duane. Public Speaking: A Handbook for Christians. 400p. (Orig.). 1981. pap. 9.95 (ISBN 0-8010-5605-5). Baker Bk.

Longo, Teodosio. Fundamentals of Singing & Speaking. 112p. 1945. 7.00x (ISBN 0-913298-54-9). S F Vanni.

McCabe & Bender. Speaking Is a Practical Matter. 4th ed. 384p. 1981. pap. text ed. 12.95 (ISBN 0-205-07230-5, 4872304); free tchr's ed. (ISBN 0-205-07231-3). Allyn.

Newman, Edwin. Edwin Newman on Language: Strictly Speaking & a Civil Tongue. 1980. pap. 6.95 (ISBN 0-446-97459-5). Warner Bks.

Oppenheimer, Evelyn. Oral Book Reviewing to Stimulate Reading: A Practical Guide in Technique for Lecture & Broadcast. LC 80-20006. 168p. 1980. 10.00 (ISBN 0-8108-1352-1). Scarecrow.

Stedman, William. A Guide to Public Speaking. 2nd ed. (Illus.). 208p. pap. text ed. 9.95 (ISBN 0-13-370619-2). P-H.

Wasserman, Paul, ed. Speakers & Lecturers: How to Find Them. 2nd ed. 350p. 1981. 68.00 (ISBN 0-8103-0393-0). Gale.

PUBLIC SPEAKING–STUDY AND TEACHING
see Public Speaking

PUBLIC SPENDING POLICY
see Government Spending Policy

PUBLIC TELEVISION
see Television in Education

PUBLIC TRUSTEES
see Trusts and Trustees

PUBLIC TWO-YEAR COLLEGES
see Community Colleges

PUBLIC UTILITIES
Here are entered works on public service or public utility corporation and publications of the commissions controlling them.
see also Corporation Law; Corporations; Government Business Enterprises; Public Service; Railroads; Street-Railroads; Water-Supply

Cowper, Denis A., ed. Public Utilities Law Anthology, 1980-1981, Vol. VI. LC 74-77644. (National Law Anthology Ser.). 1981. text ed. 59.95. Intl Lib.

Sichel, Werner & Gies, Thomas G., eds. Applications of Economic Principles in Public Utility Industries. (Michigan Business Studies: Vol. 2, No. 3). (Illus.). 180p. 1981. price not set (ISBN 0-87712-211-3). U Mich Busn Div Res.

PUBLIC UTILITY REGULATION
see Public Utilities

PUBLIC WELFARE
Here are entered works on tax-supported welfare activities.
see also Asylums; Child Welfare; Community Organizations; Day Care Centers; Disaster Relief; Food Relief; Hospitals; Medical Social Work; Old Age Assistance; Poor; Psychiatric Social Work; Social Medicine; Social Service; Social Workers; Unemployed

also subdivision Charities under names of cities, e.g. New York (City)–Charities; also subdivision Civilian Relief under names of wars, e.g. World War, 1939-1945–Civilian Relief

Brown, Peter G., et al, eds. Income Support: Conceptual & Policy Issues. (Maryland Studies in Public Philosophy Ser.). 400p. 1981. 27.50x (ISBN 0-8476-6969-6). Rowman.

Howard, Anne. Welfare Rights- the Local Authorities Role. 52p. 1978. pap. text ed. 4.40x (ISBN 0-7199-0946-5, Pub. by Bedford England). Renouf.

Pearl, David & Gray, Kevin. A Textbook of Social Welfare Law. 240p. 1981. 31.00x (ISBN 0-85664-644-X, Pub. by Croom Helm LTD England). Biblio Dist.

Plant, Raymond, et al. Political Philosophy & Social Welfare: Essays on the Normative Basis of Welfare Provision. (International Library of Welfare & Philosophy). 280p. 1981. 27.50 (ISBN 0-7100-0611-X); pap. 15.00 (ISBN 0-7100-0631-4). Routledge & Kegan.

Social Welfare & Family Planning: Concepts, Strategies & Methods Report of a U. N. Project, 1971-1978. 107p. 1979. pap. 8.00 (ISBN 0-686-68972-0, UN79/4/6, UN). Unipub.

PUBLIC WELFARE–CANADA

Jones, Andrew & Rutman, Leonard. In the Children's Aid: J. J. Kelso & Child Welfare in Ontario. 256p. 1981. 17.50 (ISBN 0-8020-5491-9). U of Toronto Pr.

Moscovitch, Allan & Drover, Glenn, eds. Inequality: Essays on the Political Economy of Social Welfare. (Studies in the Political Economy of Canada). 408p. 1981. 30.00x (ISBN 0-8020-2403-3); pap. 10.00 (ISBN 0-8020-6426-4). U of Toronto Pr.

PUBLIC WELFARE–EUROPE

Mommsen, Wolfgang J., ed. The Emergence of the Welfare State in Britain & Germany. 350p. 1981. 31.00x (ISBN 0-7099-1710-4, Pub. by Croom Helm LTD England). Biblio Dist.

PUBLIC WELFARE–FRANCE

Stevens, Cindy. Public Assistance in France. 94p. 1973. pap. text ed. 5.00x (ISBN 0-7135-1846-4, Pub. by Bedford England). Renouf.

PUBLIC WELFARE–GREAT BRITAIN

Barker, Anthony. Public Participation in Britain. 192p. 1979. pap. text ed. 17.40x (ISBN 0-7199-1029-3, Pub. by Bedford England). Renouf.

Mommsen, Wolfgang J., ed. The Emergence of the Welfare State in Britain & Germany. 350p. 1981. 31.00x (ISBN 0-7099-1710-4, Pub. by Croom Helm LTD England). Biblio Dist.

PUBLIC WELFARE–RUSSIA

George, Vic & Manning, Nick. Socialism, Social Welfare, & the Soviet Union. (Radical Social Policy Ser.). 224p. (Orig.). 1980. pap. 15.95 (ISBN 0-7100-0608-X). Routledge & Kegan.

PUBLIC WELFARE–UNITED STATES

Cunha, Deborah, ed. Public Welfare Directory: 1980-1981. LC 41-4981. 1980. pap. 35.00x (ISBN 0-910106-11-8). Am Pub Welfare.

Levitan, Sar A. Programs in Aid of the Poor for the 1980's. LC 80-8093. (Policy Studies in Employment & Welfare: No. 1). (Illus.). 166p. 1980. text ed. 11.00 (ISBN 0-8018-2483-4); pap. text ed. 3.95 (ISBN 0-8018-2484-2). Johns Hopkins.

PUBLIC WORKS

see also Government Business Enterprises
also subdivision Public Works under names of countries, cities, etc., e.g. United States–Public Works

Dodge Cost Information Systems Division. Dodge Guide to Public Works & Heavy Construction Costs, 1981. 232p. 1981. 31.80 (ISBN 0-07-017326-5). McGraw.

NACM, ed. Bonds on Public Works. 1981. pap. 4.75 (ISBN 0-934914-38-9). NACM.

PUBLIC WORSHIP

see also Church Attendance; Liturgics; Ritual; Young People'S Meetings (Church Work)

Baynes, Richard W. God's OK -- You're OK? Perspective on Christian Worship. LC 79-67440. 96p. (Orig.). 1981. pap. 1.95 (ISBN 0-87239-382-8, 40088). Standard Pub.

Lawson, LeRoy. The Family of God: The Meaning of Church Membership. LC 80-53497. 64p. (Orig.). 1981. pap. 1.50 (ISBN 0-87239-432-8, 39970). Standard Pub.

PUBLICITY

see also Advertising; Journalism; Press; Propaganda; Public Opinion; Public Relations

Benziger, Barbara F. The Prison of My Mind. LC 80-54811. 184p. 1981. pap. 5.95 (ISBN 0-8027-7172-6). Walker & Co.

Delacorte, Toni, et al. Free Press. 240p. (Orig.). 1981. pap. 9.95 (ISBN 0-936602-15-5). Harbor Pub CA.

--Free Press: A Do It Yourself Guide to Promote Your Interests, Organization or Business. 240p. 1981. 9.95 (ISBN 0-936602-15-5). Harbor Pub CA.

Norback, Craig T. U. S. Publicity Directory, 5 vols. Incl. Vol. 1. Radio-TV (ISBN 0-471-06372-X); Vol. 2. Newspapers (ISBN 0-471-06375-4); Vol. 3. Magazines (ISBN 0-471-06373-8); Vol. 4. Business & Finance (ISBN 0-471-06371-1); Vol. 5. Communication Services (ISBN 0-471-06374-6). 1980. 65.00 ea. (Pub. by Wiley-Interscience); Set. write for info. (ISBN 0-471-06369-X). Wiley.

PUBLICITY, GOVERNMENT

see Government Publicity

PUBLISHERS AND PUBLISHING

see also Book Industries and Trade; Books; Booksellers and Bookselling; Catalogs, Publishers'; Copyright; Newspaper Publishing; Printing

Balkin, Richard. Writer's Guide to Book Publishing. rev. ed. 288p. 1981. 15.95 (ISBN 0-8015-8925-8, Hawthorn); pap. 8.95 (ISBN 0-8015-8926-6, Hawthorn). Dutton.

Directory of Publishing & Bookselling in Brazil. 179p. 1980. 50.00x (ISBN 0-901618-22-5, Pub. by Brit Coun England). State Mutual Bk.

Doty, Betty. Publish Your Own Hardbound Books. 1981. 7.95. Green Hill.

European Publishers' Catalog Annual: 1980. 80000p. 1980. catalog collection 410.00 (ISBN 0-930466-32-2). Meckler Bks.

Folio Magazine Editors, ed. Handbook of Magazine Publishing. 1977. 59.95 (ISBN 0-918110-00-9). Folio.

Geiser, Elizabeth & Brewer, Annie. Book Publishers Directory. 3rd ed. 500p. 1981. 160.00 (ISBN 0-8103-0191-1). Gale.

Huenefeld, John & Wiley, Virginia. Planning & Control Guides & Forms for Small Book Publishers. LC 80-21051. 72p. 1980. 44.00 (ISBN 0-931932-01-7). Huenefeld Co.

Italian Publishing in the Seventies: An Exhibition (Catalog) pap. 3.00. Boston Public Lib.

Jones, H. Kay. Butterworths: History of a Publishing House. 296p. 1980. text ed. 27.00 (ISBN 0-406-17606-X). Butterworths.

Mathieu, Aron. The Book Market: How to Write, Publish & Market Your Book. LC 80-71059. 512p. 1981. 14.95 (ISBN 0-939014-00-9). Andover Pr.

Nineteen Seventy-Eight Supplement to the Handbook of Magazine Publishing. 1978. 20.00 (ISBN 0-918110-03-3). Folio.

Nineteen Seventy-Nine Folio Annual: Supplement to the Handbook of Magazine Publishing. 1979. 20.00 (ISBN 0-918110-04-1). Folio.

Vost, Leon & Voet-Griselle, Jenny. The Plantin Press at Antwerp: 1555-1589. 500p. (Dutch.). 1981. 250.00 ea.; Vol. 1. (ISBN 0-8390-0264-5); Vol. 2. (ISBN 0-8390-0265-3). Allanheld & Schram.

PUBLISHERS AND PUBLISHING–BIBLIOGRAPHY

American Book Publishing Record Annual Cumulative 1980. 1260p. 1981. text ed. 59.00 (ISBN 0-8352-1245-9). Bowker.

Intl. Pubns. Serv. International Publications: An Annual Annotated Subject Bibliography 1980-1981. 4th ed. LC 72-626822. 256p. 1981. pap. 7.50x (ISBN 0-8002-0140-X). Intl Pubns Serv.

Sandhu, Harpreet & Bukkila, Laura. Guide to Publishers & Distributors Serving Minority Languages. rev. ed. 176p. 1980. pap. 4.50 (ISBN 0-89763-051-3). Natl Clearinghse Bilingual Ed.

PUBLISHERS AND PUBLISHING–DIRECTORIES

Ayer Directory of Publications: 1981. rev. ed. LC 80-70115. 1981. 66.00 (ISBN 0-910190-20-8). Ayer Pr.

Found, Peter, ed. International Literary Market Place 1981. 15th ed. LC 77-70295. 500p. 1981. pap. 42.50 (ISBN 0-8352-1345-5). Bowker.

Hicks, Stanley E., ed. Exhibits Directory: 1981. 92p. (Orig.). 1981. pap. 20.00 (ISBN 0-933636-01-6). AAP.

International ISBN Agency, ed. International ISBN Publishers' Directory. edition 1980 ed. 1433p. 1981. 95.00 (ISBN 3-88053-010-6). Bowker.

Who Distributes What & Where. 2nd ed. 1981. 39.00 (ISBN 0-8352-1373-0). Bowker.

Zils, Michael, ed. American Publishers Directory. 2nd ed. 500p. 1980. text ed. 35.00 (ISBN 0-89664-076-0). K G Saur.

PUBLISHERS AND PUBLISHING–CHINA

Twitchett, Denis. Printing & Publishing in Medieval China. (Illus.). 1981. pap. 14.50 (ISBN 0-913720-08-9). Sandstone.

PUBLISHERS AND PUBLISHING–GERMANY

German Books in Print, Nineteen Eighty to Eighty-One: Authors-Titles-Keywords, 4 vols. 10th ed. Set. 250.00 (ISBN 3-7657-0862-3, Dist by Gale Research Co.). K G Saur.

German Books in Print, Nineteen Eighty to Eighty-One: ISBN Register. 637p. 1980. 95.00 (ISBN 3-7657-0986-7, Dist. by Gale Research Co.). K G Saur.

German Books in Print, Nineteen Eighty to Eighty-One: Subject Guide, 3 vols. 3rd ed. 1980. Set. 240.00 (Dist. by Gale Research Co.). K G Saur.

Stark, Gary D. Entrepreneurs of Ideology: Neoconservative Publishers in Germany, 1890-1933. LC 80-14906. 384p. 1981. 26.50x (ISBN 0-8078-1452-0). U of NC Pr.

PUBLISHERS AND PUBLISHING–GREAT BRITAIN

British Publishers' Catalog Annual: 1980. 1980. catalog collection 275.00 (ISBN 0-930466-33-0). Meckler Bks.

Curwen, Peter J. The UK Publishing Industry. (Illus.). 176p. 1981. 24.00 (ISBN 0-08-024081-X). Pergamon.

St. John Thomas, David, ed. Good Books Come from Devon. LC 80-70289. (Illus.). 108p. 1981. pap. 5.95 (ISBN 0-7153-8139-3). David & Charles.

PUBLISHERS' CATALOGS

see Catalogs, Publishers'

PUBLISHERS' IMPRINTS

see Imprints (In Books)

PUBLISHING OF NEWSPAPERS

see Newspaper Publishing

PUDDINGS

Collins, Christine. Perfect Puddings. 1976. 5.95 (ISBN 0-571-10859-8, Pub. by Faber & Faber). Merrimack Bk Serv.

PUEBLO INDIANS

see Indians of North America–Southwest, New

PUEBLOS

Hill, W. W. Ethnography of Santa Clara Pueblo. Lange, Charles H., ed. (Illus.). 550p. 1981. 35.00x (ISBN 0-8263-0555-5). U of NM Pr.

PUERTO RICO–ANTIQUITIES

Ojo & San Juan Excavations. 1981. pap. 14.95 (ISBN 0-89013-135-X). Museum NM Pr.

PUERTO RICO–ECONOMIC CONDITIONS

Tata, Robert J. Structural Changes in Puerto Rico's Economy 1947-1976. LC 80-19080. (Latin America Ser., Ohio University Papers in International Studies). (Illus.). 104p. (Orig.). 1981. pap. 11.95. Ohio U Ctr Intl.

PUERTO RICO–POLITICS AND GOVERNMENT

Munoz Martin, Luis. Mensajes al Pueblo Puertorriqueno: Pronunciados Ante las Camaras Legislativas, 1949-1964. Marin, Gerard P. & Rios, Louis J., eds. 358p. 1980. 15.00 (ISBN 0-913480-47-9); pap. 6.95 (ISBN 0-913480-48-7); Rack Size. 4.95 (ISBN 0-913480-49-5). Inter Am U Pr.

PUERTO RICO–SOCIAL CONDITIONS

Safa, Helen I. Familias De Arrabal: Un Estudio Sobre Desarrollo y Desigualdad. LC 80-19853. ix, 191p. Date not set. pap. price not set (ISBN 0-8477-2455-7). U of PR Pr.

PUFFINS

Friedman, Judi. Puffins, Come Back! LC 80-2786. (Illus.). 80p. (gr. 3-7). 1981. PLB 6.95 (ISBN 0-396-07940-7). Dodd.

PUGILISM

see Boxing

PULMONARY DISEASES

see Lungs–Diseases

PULMONARY TUBERCULOSIS

see Tuberculosis

PULPWOOD

Projected Pulp & Paper Mills in the World 1979-1989. 132p. 1980. pap. 7.25 (ISBN 92-5-100913-9, F1938, FAO). Unipub.

Pulp & Paper Capacities Survey, 1979-1984. 286p. 1980. pap. 15.25 (ISBN 92-5-000914-3, F1945, FAO). Unipub.

Pulping & Paper-Making Properties of Fast Growing Plantation Wood Species, Vols. 1 & 2. (FAO Forestry Paper Ser.: No. 19). 1980. pap. 46.75 set (ISBN 0-686-68193-2, F1969, FAO); Vol. 1, 486 Pp. pap. 46.75 (ISBN 92-5-100865-5). Vol. 2, 400 Pp (ISBN 92-5-100866-3). Unipub.

PULSE FAMILY

see Legumes

PULVERIZERS

see Milling Machinery

PUMPERS, FIRE-DEPARTMENT

see Fire-Engines

PUMPING MACHINERY

see also Centrifugal Pumps; Heat Pumps

Pollak, F. Pump Users' Handbook. 2nd ed. (Illus.). 208p. 1980. 19.95 (ISBN 0-87201-770-2). Gulf Pub.

Pumps-the Developing Needs: Seventh Technical Conference of Thhe BPMA in Conjunction with BHRA. (Orig.). 1981. pap. 71.00 library ed. (ISBN 0-686-69310-8). BHRA Fluid.

Symposium on Jet Pumps & Ejectors, 1st. Proceedings. 1972. 28.00. BHRA Fluid.

PUMPS

see Pumping Machinery

PUMPS, CENTRIFUGAL

see Centrifugal Pumps

PUNCTUATION

see also subdivision Punctuation under names of languages, e.g. English Language–Punctuation

Gregorich, Barbara & Waldowski, Therese F. Punctuation Through Proofreading. LC 78-730056. (Illus.). 1977. pap. text ed. 99.00 (ISBN 0-89290-124-1, A325). Soc for Visual.

Lutgendorf, Philip & Gray, Mary Jane. Punctuation. LC 77-731014. (Illus.). (gr. 7-9). 1977. pap. text ed. 99.00 (ISBN 0-89290-120-9, A149-SAR). Soc for Visual.

PUNISHMENT

see also Amnesty; Capital Punishment; Criminal Law; Discipline of Children; Pardon; Prisons; Probation; Reformatories; Sentences (Criminal Procedure); Torture
also particular forms of punishment

Gross, Hyman & Von Hirsch, Andrew, eds. Sentencing. 416p. 1981. text ed. 19.95x (ISBN 0-19-502763-9); pap. text ed. 9.95x (ISBN 0-19-502764-7). Oxford U Pr.

Mackenzie, Mary M. Plato on Punishment. 272p. 1981. 22.50x (ISBN 0-520-04169-0). U of Cal Pr.

Sadist, Golem N. Cruel & Unusual Punishments: From the Here & the Hereafter. (Odd Books for Odd Moments Ser.). (Illus.). 72p. (Orig.). 1980. pap. 3.95 (ISBN 0-938338-03-X). Winds World Pr.

PUNISHMENT OF CHILDREN

see Discipline of Children

PUNS AND PUNNING

Gordon, Harvey C. Punishment: The Art of Punning. 1980. pap. 2.95 (ISBN 0-446-97263-0). Warner Bks.

PUPIL-TEACHER RELATIONSHIPS

see Teacher-Student Relationships

PUPPETS AND PUPPET-PLAYS

The Art of the Muppets. (Illus.). 1980. pap. 5.95 (ISBN 0-553-01313-0). Bantam.

Brown, Forman. Small Wonder: The Story of the Yale Puppeteers & the Turnabout Theatre. LC 80-17815. 288p. 1980. 12.50 (ISBN 0-8108-1334-3). Scarecrow.

Garsee, Lee. New Dimensions in Puppet Ministry. 1981. pap. write for info. (ISBN 0-89137-607-0). Quality Pubns.

Hanford, Robert T. Complete Book of Puppets & Puppeteering. LC 80-54338. (Illus.). 160p. 1981. 12.95 (ISBN 0-8069-7032-4); lib. bdg. 11.69 (ISBN 0-8069-7033-2); pap. 7.95 (ISBN 0-8069-8970-X). Sterling.

Hunt, Tamara & Renfro, Nancy. Puppetry & Early Childhood Education: Preschool & Primary. Scwalb, Ann W., ed. (Puppetry in Education Ser.). (Illus.). 200p. (Orig.). Date not set. pap. 10.95 (ISBN 0-931044-04-9). Renfro Studios.

Miller, George B., Jr., et al, eds. Property Library: An Annotated Bibliography Based on the Batchelder-McPharlin Collection at the University of New Mexico. LC 80-23474. 200p. 1981. lib. bdg. 29.95 (ISBN 0-313-21359-3, HPL). Greenwood.

PUPPETS AND PUPPET-PLAYS–BIBLIOGRAPHY

Miller, George B., Jr., et al, eds. Puppetry Library: An Annotated Bibliography Based on the Batchelder-McPharlin Collection at the University of New Mexico. Hannaford, William E. Jr. LC 80-23474. 200p. 1981. lib. bdg. 29.95 (ISBN 0-313-21359-3, HPL/). Greenwood.

PUPPETS AND PUPPET-PLAYS–JUVENILE LITERATURE

Zokeisha. Baby Animals. (Puppet Story Board Bks.). (Illus.). 12p. (ps-k). Date not set. boards 2.95 (ISBN 0-671-42645-1, Little Simon). S&S.

--Bedtime Stories. (Puppet Story Board Bks.). (Illus.). 12p. (ps-k). Date not set. boards 2.95 (ISBN 0-671-42644-3, Little Simon). S&S.

--Little Nursery Rhymes. (Puppet Story Board Bks.). (Illus.). 12p. (ps-k). Date not set. boards 2.95 (ISBN 0-671-42642-7, Little Simon). S&S.

--Mother Goose. (Puppet Story Board Bks.). (Illus.). 12p. (ps-k). Date not set. boards 2.95 (ISBN 0-671-42643-5, Little Simon). S&S.

PURBUTTI LANGUAGE

see Nepali Language

PURCELL, HENRY, 1658-1695

Westrup, J. A. Purcell. rev. ed. (The Master Musicians Ser.). (Illus.). 325p. 1980. 19.75 (ISBN 0-460-03177-5, Pub. by J M Dent England). Biblio Dist.

PURCHASING

see also Consumer Education; Consumers; Industrial Procurement; Sales

Leenders, Michael R., et al. Purchasing & Materials Management. 7th ed. 1980. 21.50x (ISBN 0-256-02374-3). Irwin.

Stevens, John. Measuring Purchasing Performance. 254p. 1978. text ed. 23.50x (ISBN 0-220-66331-9, Pub. by Busn Bks England). Renouf.

PURCHASING, AUTOMOBILE

see Automobile Purchasing

PURCHASING, INDUSTRIAL

see Industrial Procurement

PURE FOOD

see Food Adulteration and Inspection; Food Law and Legislation

PURIFICATION OF WATER

see Water–Purification

PURIM (FEAST OF ESTHER)

Stuhlman, Daniel D. My Own Pesach Story. (My Own Holiday Stories: No. 2). (Illus.). 1981. pap. 3.95 (ISBN 0-686-28904-8). BYLS Pr.

PURITY, RITUAL

Fortune, Dion. The Problem of Purity. 1980. pap. 4.95 (ISBN 0-87728-506-3). Weiser.

PURSUIT PLANES

see Airplanes, Military; Fighter Planes

PUSHKIN, ALEKSANDR SERGEEVICH, 1799-1837

Kodjak, Andrej, et al, eds. Alexander Pushkin Symposium II. (New York University Slavic Papers Ser.: Vol. III). (Illus.). 131p. (Orig.). 1980. pap. 8.95 (ISBN 0-89357-067-2). Slavica.

PUTTING (GOLF)

Taylor, Dawson & Smith, Horton. Master's Secrets of Putting. 2nd rev. ed. (Illus.). 200p. 1982. price not set (ISBN 0-498-02513-6). A S Barnes.

PUZZLES

see also Anagrams; Bible Games and Puzzles; Crossword Puzzles; Educational Games; Mathematical Recreations; Tangram (Chinese Puzzle)

Copps, Dale. The Sherlock Holmes Puzzle Book. (Illus.). 160p. 1980. pap. 3.95 (ISBN 0-385-14839-9, Dolp). Doubleday.

Doherty, Linda. Tempo Word Finds: No. 5. (No. 5). 128p. (gr. 6 up). 1981. pap. 1.50 (ISBN 0-448-05567-8, Tempo). G&D.

Gardner, Martin. More Perplexing Puzzles & Teasers. (Illus.). (gr. 3-6). 1977. pap. 1.25 (ISBN 0-671-29832-1). PB.

--Perplexing Puzzles & Tantalizing Teasers. 1981. pap. 1.50 (ISBN 0-686-69007-9). Archway.
--Science Fiction Puzzle Tales. Novograd, Nancy, ed. (Illus.). 128p. 1981. 10.95 (ISBN 0-517-54380-X); pap. 4.95 (ISBN 0-517-54381-8). Potter.
Halperin, Ed, et al. Symbol Simons Too. (Orig.). (gr. 3-7). 1981. pap. 2.50 (ISBN 0-671-42537-4). Wanderer Bks.
Hamilton, B. Brainteasers & Mindbenders. 1981. pap. 4.95 (ISBN 0-13-080945-4); 10.95 (ISBN 0-13-080952-7). P-H.
Levmore, Saul. Super Strategies: Games & Puzzles for Strategy Training. (Illus.). 168p. 1981. 10.95 (ISBN 0-385-17165-X). Doubleday.
Mallett, Jerry J. Reading Skills Activity Puzzles, 6 bks. Incl. Brain-Twisters (ISBN 0-87628-738-0); Comprehension Challengers (ISBN 0-87628-735-6); Dynamite Decoding Puzzles (ISBN 0-87628-733-X); Puzzles for Super Sleuths (ISBN 0-87628-736-4); Thingumajigs for Thinking (ISBN 0-87628-737-2); Word Power (ISBN 0-87628-734-8). (gr. 2-6). 1980. pap. 6.95x ea. Ctr Appl Res.
Minter, James F. Pencil Pastimes, No. 9. 128p. 1981. pap. 2.50 (ISBN 0-89104-172-9). A & W Pubs.
Mohan, Maden & Risko, Victoria. Perception Stimulators. (Illus.). 64p. (Orig.). 1980. tchr's ed. 2.50 (ISBN 0-914634-80-1, 6932). DOK Pubs.
Rafferty, Kathleen. Dell Word Search, No. 20. 1981. pap. 1.95 (ISBN 0-440-12071-3). Dell.
Rafferty, Kathleen, ed. The Big Dell Book of Crosswords & Pencil Puzzles. (Orig.). 1981. pap. 6.95 (ISBN 0-440-50970-X, Dell Trade Pbks). Dell.
Razzi, Jim. Encyclopedia Brown's Fourth Book of Games & Puzzles. 64p. (gr. 4-6). 1981. pap. 1.50 (ISBN 0-553-15110-X). Bantam.
--Encyclopedia Brown's Third Book of Games & Puzzles. 64p. (Orig.). (gr. 4-6). 1981. pap. 1.50 (ISBN 0-553-15077-4). Bantam.
Read, Ronald C. Tangrams: Three Hundred & Thirty Puzzles. 1978. pap. 2.50 (ISBN 0-486-21483-4). Dover.

PUZZLES–JUVENILE LITERATURE
Fellows. Puzzle Blast. (gr. 3-5). pap. 0.95 (ISBN 0-590-11894-3, Schol Pap). Schol Bk Serv.
Gardner, Martin. Perplexing Puzzles & Tantalizing Teasers. (Illus., Orig.). (gr. 3-6). 1971. pap. 1.25 (ISBN 0-671-29927-1). PB.
Rosen. Mummy Jokes & Puzzles. (gr. 3-5). 1980. pap. 1.25 (ISBN 0-590-30052-0, Schol Pap). Schol Bk Serv.
Tallarico, Tony. Search-a-Picture Puzzles. Schneider, Meg, ed. (Puzzlebacks Ser.). 64p. (gr. 3-7). 1981. pap. 1.25 (ISBN 0-671-42656-7, Wanderer). S&S.
--Spooky Haunted House Puzzles. Schneider, Meg, ed. (Puzzlebacks Ser.). 64p. (gr. 3-7). 1981. pap. 1.25 (ISBN 0-671-42655-9, Wanderer). S&S.
Whitney, Susan. Dr. Gloom's Monster Jokes & Puzzles. (Dr. Gloom Activity Ser.). (Illus.). 64p. (gr. 4-6). pap. 1.95 (ISBN 0-15-224223-6, VoyB). HarBraceJ.
--Dr. Gloom's Outer Space Jokes & Puzzles. (Dr. Gloom's Activity Ser.). (Illus.). 64p. (gr. 4-6). pap. 1.95 (ISBN 0-15-224225-2, VoyB). HarBraceJ.

PYNCHON, THOMAS, 1937-
Schaub, Thomas H. Pynchon: The Voice of Ambiguity. LC 80-11944. 175p. 1981. 13.50 (ISBN 0-252-00816-2). U of Ill Pr.

PYRAMIDS
Seiss, Joseph A. The Great Pyramid: A Miracle in Stone. LC 80-8341. (Harper's Library of Spiritual Wisdom). 256p. 1981. pap. 5.95 (ISBN 0-06-067211-0, HarpR). Har-Row.

Q

QABALAH
see Cabala

QATAR
Lanier, Alison R. Update -- Singapore. (Country Orientation Ser.). 1980. pap. text ed. 25.00 (ISBN 0-686-28735-5). Intercult Network.

QUACKS AND QUACKERY
Consumer Reports Editors. Health Quackery: Consumer's Union's Report on False Health Claims, Worthless Remedies & Unproved Therapies. 252p. 1981. 13.95 (ISBN 0-03-058899-5); pap. 6.95x (ISBN 0-03-058898-7). HR&W.

QUADRATURE, MECHANICAL
see Numerical Integration

QUADRUMANA
see Primates

QUAKERS
see Friends, Society Of

QUALIFICATIONS FOR OFFICE
see Nominations for Office

QUALITATIVE ANALYSIS
see Chemistry, Analytic–Qualitative

QUALITY CONTROL
see also Process Control;
also names of specific industries, e.g. Food Industry
Caplen, R. H. A Practical Approach to Quality Control. 3rd ed. 310p. 1978. pap. text ed. 14.75x (ISBN 0-220-66368-8, Pub. by Busn Bks England). Renouf.
Dewar, Donald L. Quality Circle Leader Manual & Instructional Guide. (Quality Circle Member Manual: Quality Circle Handbook). 248p. 1980. pap. 15.00 (ISBN 0-937670-02-2). Quality Circle.
--Quality Circle Member Manual. (Quality Circle Handbook & Quality Circle Leader Manual & Instructional Guide Ser.). (Orig.). 1980. pap. 8.00 (ISBN 0-937670-01-4). Quality Circle.
--Quality Circles: Questions & Answers to 100 Frequently Asked Questions. rev. ed. (Illus.). 1980. pap. 3.25 (ISBN 0-937670-00-6). Quality Circle.
Goldberg, Harold. Extending the Limits of Reliability Theory. 300p. 1981. 30.00 (ISBN 0-471-07799-2, Pub. by Wiley Interscience). Wiley.
Jamieson, Archibald. Introduction to Quality Control. 1981. text ed. 16.95 (ISBN 0-8359-3264-8); instr's. manual free (ISBN 0-8359-3265-6). Reston.
Preparing for Standardization Certification & Quality Control. 298p. 1979. 15.25 (APO80, Apo). Unipub.
Shilling. Acceptance Sampling in Quality Control. Date not set. price not set (ISBN 0-8247-1347-8). Dekker.

QUALITY OF WATER
see Water Quality

QUANTITATIVE ANALYSIS
see Chemistry, Analytic–Quantitative

QUANTITY COOKERY
Here are entered works dealing solely with quantity food preparation. Works on quantity preparation and service of food for outside the home are entered under Food Service.
see also Food Service
American Society for Hospital Food Service Administrators of the American Hospital Association. Preparation of a Hospital Food Service Department Budget. LC 78-24399. 56p. 1978. pap. 9.50 (ISBN 0-87258-254-X, 1615). Am Hospital.
Crusius, Vera C. Principles & Applications of Quantity Food Management. (Orig.). 1981. pap. text ed. pns (ISBN 0-8087-2966-7). Burgess.

QUANTITY SURVEYING
see Building–Estimates

QUANTITY THEORY OF MONEY
Radigan, John D. The Silver Revolution & the New Monetary Order of the World. (Illus.). 129p. 1981. 49.85 (ISBN 0-89266-283-2). Am Classical Coll Pr.

QUANTUM BIOCHEMISTRY
International Symposium on Quantum Biology & Quantum Pharmacology. Proceedings. (International Journal of Quantum Chemistry-Quantum Biology Symposium: No. 5). 472p. 1978. 40.50 (ISBN 0-471-05635-9). Wiley.
Snell, Esmond E., ed. Annual Review of Biochemistry, Vol 50. LC 32-25093. (Illus.). 1218p. 1981. text ed. 21.00 (ISBN 0-8243-0850-6). Annual Reveiws.

QUANTUM CHEMISTRY
see also Chemical Bonds; Quantum Biochemistry
Carsky, P. & Urban, M. Ab Initio Calculations: Methods & Applications in Chemistry. (Lecture Notes in Chemistry: Vol. 16). (Illus.). 247p. 1980. pap. 21.00 (ISBN 0-387-10005-9). Springer-Verlag.
Clementi, E. Computational Aspects for Large Chemical Systems. (Lecture Notes in Chemistry: Vol. 19). (Illus.). 184p. 1980. pap. 17.50 (ISBN 0-387-10014-8). Springer-Verlag.
International Symposium on Quantum Biology & Quantum Pharmacology. Proceedings. (International Journal of Quantum Chemistry-Quantum Biology Symposium: No. 5). 472p. 1978. 40.50 (ISBN 0-471-05635-9). Wiley.
Lowdin, P. O. & Ohrn, Y. Proceedings. (International Journal of Quantum Chemistry-Quantum Chemistry Symposium: No. 12). 550p. 1978. 40.50 (ISBN 0-471-05633-2). Wiley.

QUANTUM DYNAMICS
see Quantum Theory

QUANTUM FIELD THEORY
Streit, L., ed. Quantum Fields-Algebras, Processes. (Illus.). 144p. 1981. 40.20 (ISBN 0-387-81607-0). Springer-Verlag.

QUANTUM MECHANICAL AMPLIFIERS
see Masers

QUANTUM MECHANICS
see Quantum Theory

QUANTUM STATISTICS
see also Matrix Mechanics; Quantum Theory; Statistical Mechanics; Wave Mechanics
Bratteli, O. & Robinson, D. W., eds. Operators Algebra & Quantum Statistical Mechanics, Vol. II: Equilibrium States; Models. (Texts & Monographs in Physics Ser.). 496p. 1981. 46.00 (ISBN 0-387-10381-3). Springer-Verlag.
Hurt, Norman & Hermann, R. Quantum Statistical Mechanics & Lie Group Harmonic Analysis, Pt. A. (Lie Groups; History, Frontiers & Applications: Vol. X). 1980. text ed. 30.00x (ISBN 0-915692-30-9, QC174.8.H87). Math Sci Pr.

QUANTUM THEORY
see also Chemistry, Physical and Theoretical; Force and Energy; Neutrons; Quantum Chemistry; Quantum Field Theory; Radiation; Relativity (Physics); Statistical Thermodynamics; Thermodynamics; Wave Mechanics
Cohen-Tannoudji, Claude, et al. Quantum Mechanics, 2 vols. LC 76-5874. 1978. Vol. 1. 37.50 (ISBN 0-471-16432-1, Pub. by Wiley-Interscience); 34.50 (ISBN 0-471-16434-8); Vol. 1. pap. 21.95 (ISBN 0-471-16433-X); Vol. 2. pap. 20.50 (ISBN 0-471-16435-6). Wiley.
Daudel, Raymond, et al, eds. Quantum Theory of Chemical Reactions: Solvent Effect, Reaction Mechanisms, Photochemical Processes, Vol. 11. 340p. 1980. PLB 42.00 (ISBN 90-277-1182-8). Kluwer Boston.
Hanna, Melvin. Quantum Mechanics in Chemistry. 3rd ed. 1980. pap. text ed. 12.95 (ISBN 0-8053-3705-9, 33708); pap. text ed. 9.95 (33705). Benjamin-Cummings.
Van Der Waerden, B. L. Group Theory & Quantum Mechanics. (Grundlehren der Mathematischen Wissenschaften Ser.: Vol. 214). (Illus.). 211p. 1981. 39.00 (ISBN 0-387-06740-X). Springer-Verlag.

QUASI-JUDICIAL AGENCIES
see Independent Regulatory Commissions

QUEBEC (PROVINCE)–HISTORY
Moniere, Denis. The Development of Ideologies in Quebec. Howard, Richard, tr. from Fr. Orig. Title: Le Developpement Des Ideologies Du Quebec. 320p. 1981. 27.50x (ISBN 0-8020-5452-8); pap. 10.00 (ISBN 0-8020-6358-6). U of Toronto Pr.

QUEBEC (PROVINCE)–SOCIAL CONDITIONS
Moniere, Denis. The Development of Ideologies in Quebec. Howard, Richard, tr. from Fr. Orig. Title: Le Developpement Des Ideologies Du Quebec. 320p. 1981. 27.50x (ISBN 0-8020-5452-8); pap. 10.00 (ISBN 0-8020-6358-6). U of Toronto Pr.

QUEEN BEES
see Bee Culture

QUEENSLAND
Hughes, Colin A. The Government of Queensland. (Governments of the Australian States & Territories Ser.). (Illus.). 322p. 1981. text ed. 36.25x (ISBN 0-7022-1515-5); pap. text ed. 19.25x (ISBN 0-7022-1516-3). U of Queensland Pr.

QUERIES
see Questions and Answers

QUESTION BOXES
see Questions and Answers

QUESTIONNAIRES
Lees-Haley, Paul R. The Questionnaire Design Handbook. LC 80-82969. 150p. (Orig.). 1980. pap. 9.95 (ISBN 0-938124-00-5). Innova Assoc.

QUESTIONS AND ANSWERS
Questions and answers on special subjects are entered under the subject subdivided by Miscellanea, e.g. Theology–Miscellanea. Examination questions on special subjects are entered under the subject subdivided by Examinations, Questions, etc. e.g. Engineering–Examinations, Questions, Etc.
Burgett, Gordon L. The Query Book. LC 80-24144. (Illus.). 120p. (Orig.). 1981. pap. 7.95 (ISBN 0-9605078-0-9). Write to Sell.
Calveley, Christina. The Family Quiz Book. 1981. pap. 2.95 (ISBN 0-14-005507-X). Penguin.
Da Free John. The Four Fundamental Questions. 2nd ed. LC 79-92923. 1980. pap. 1.95 (ISBN 0-913922-49-8). Dawn Horse Pr.
Gilbar, Steven. The Book Book. 224p. 1981. 10.95 (ISBN 0-312-08803-5). St Martin.
Hamilton, B. Brainteasers & Mindbenders. 1981. pap. 4.95 (ISBN 0-13-080945-4); 10.95 (ISBN 0-13-080952-7). P-H.
Wills, Tom T., compiled by. The Giant Quiz Book. 256p. 1981. pap. 6.95 (ISBN 0-89104-207-5). A & W Pubs.

QUEUING THEORY
Gorney, Len. Queueing Theory: A Solving Approach. (Illus.). 300p. 1981. 20.00 (ISBN 0-89433-128-0). Petrocelli.
Kleinrock, Leonard. Queueing Systems, 2 vols. Incl. Vol. 1. Theory. 432p. 30.00 (ISBN 0-471-49110-1); Vol. 2. Computer Applications. 512p. 32.00 (ISBN 0-471-49111-X). LC 74-9846. 1975-76 (Pub. by Wiley-Interscience). Wiley.

QUICHES
see Indians of Central America

QUICKSILVER
see Mercury

QUILTING
Haders, Phyllis. Sunshine & Shadow: The Amish & Their Quilts. LC 76-5094. (Illus.). 72p. 1981. pap. 5.95 (ISBN 0-87663-556-7). Universe.
--The Warner Collectors' Guide to American Quilts. (Orig.). 1981. pap. 9.95 (ISBN 0-446-97636-9). Warner Bks.
James, Michael. The Second Quiltmaker's Handbook. (Creative Handcrafts Ser.). 208p. 1981. 24.95 (ISBN 0-13-797795-6, Spec); pap. 10.95 (ISBN 0-13-797787-5). P-H.
Orbelo, Beverly. A Texas Quilting Primer. 48p. 1980. pap. 5.00 (ISBN 0-931722-07-1). Corona Pub.
Parker, Kay. Quilted Tessellations: Designs from M. C. Escher. (Illus.). 140p. 1981. 16.95 (ISBN 0-89594-045-0); pap. 9.95 (ISBN 0-89594-044-2). Crossing Pr.
Singletary, Milly. Hawaiian Quilting Made Easy. (Illus.). 64p. 1980. pap. 5.00 (ISBN 0-9601256-8-X). Singletary.

QUISLING, VIDKUN, 1887-1945
Knudsen, Franklin. I Was Quisling's Secretary. 192p. 1967. 6.00 (351, Pub. by Britons England). Inst Hist Rev.
--I Was Quisling's Secretary. 192p. 1967. 6.00 (ISBN 0-911038-96-5, 351, Inst Hist Rev). Noontide.

QUIZ BOOKS
see Questions and Answers

QUOTAS, IMPORT
see Import Quotas

QUOTATIONS
see also Last Words
Alexander, E. Curtis. Axioms & Quotations of Yosef Ben-Jochannan. LC 80-70287. (Illus.). 118p. (gr. 8-12). 1980. pap. 6.95 (ISBN 0-938818-01-5). ECA Pub.
Bartlett, John. Bartlett's Familiar Quotations: Fifteenth & 125th Anniversary Edition. rev. & enl. ed. LC 68-15664. 1980. 24.95 (ISBN 0-316-08275-9). Little.
Lewis, Alec. The Quotable Quotations Book. 352p. 1981. pap. 5.95 (ISBN 0-346-12523-5). Cornerstone.
Murphy, Edward. Two Thousand Five Hundred One Line Quotations for Speakers, Writers & Raconteurs. Michaelman, Herbert, ed. 1981. 12.95 (ISBN 0-517-54281-1, Michaelman Books). Crown.
Schneider, A. F. Power Packed Pronouncements. (Anthology of Familiar Quotes Ser.). 88p. (Orig.). 1980. pap. 1.75 (ISBN 0-938784-00-5). Dicul Pub.
Wilding, Gary. Marin County Speaks Out: "Quips-Quotes-Opinions of the 'real' People" 1980. LC 79-93227. 300p. (Orig.). 1980. pap. 5.95 (ISBN 0-936092-02-5, 103). Harbinger Pr.

R

RAABE, WILHELM KARL, 1831-1910
Daemmrich, Horst S. Wilhelm Raabe. (World Authors Ser.: No. 594). 1981. lib. bdg. 13.95 (ISBN 0-8057-6436-4). Twayne.

RABBINICAL LITERATURE–HISTORY AND CRITICISM
Halperin, David. Merkabah in Rabbinic Literature. (American Oriental Ser.: Vol. 62). 1980. 14.00x. Am Orient Soc.

RABBIT AUTOMOBILE
see Automobiles, Foreign–Types–Rabbit

RABBITS
Goats, Rabbits, & Chickens. (Country Home Ser.). 96p. 2.95 (ISBN 0-88453-006-X). Berkshire Traveller.

RABIES
MacDonald, David W. Rabies & Wildlife: A Biologist's Perspective. (Illus.). 160p. 1980. text ed. 38.00x (ISBN 0-19-857567-X); pap. 11.95 (ISBN 0-19-857576-9). Oxford U Pr.

RACE
see also Black Race
Coon, Carleton S., et al. Races: A Study of the Problems of Race Formation in Man. LC 80-24479. (American Lecture Ser.: No. 77). (Illus.). xiv, 153p. 1981. Repr. of 1950 ed. lib. bdg. 19.75x (ISBN 0-313-22878-7, CORA). Greenwood.
Flynn, James R. Race, IQ, & Jensen. 320p. 1980. 27.50 (ISBN 0-7100-0651-9). Routledge & Kegan.
Montagu, Ashley, ed. The Concept of Race. LC 80-21682. xviii, 270p. 1980. Repr. of 1964 ed. lib. bdg. 27.50x (ISBN 0-313-22721-7, MOCR). Greenwood.

RACE AWARENESS
see also Ethnicity; Racism
Sociological Theories: Race & Colonialism. 499p. 1981. pap. 34.00 (ISBN 92-310-1635-0, U1050, UNESCO). Unipub.

RACE DISCRIMINATION
Here are entered works which are limited to overt discriminatory behavior directed against racial or ethnic groups. Works on racism as a attitude as well as works on both attitude and overt discriminatory behavior directed against racial or ethnic groups are entered under Racism. Works on discrimination directed against a particular group are entered under the name of the group with subdivision Social conditions, or similar subdivision, e.g. Civil rights.
see also Discrimination in Education; Discrimination in Employment
also names of racial or ethnic groups, e.g. Mexicans in the United States
Barrera, Mario. Race & Class in the Southwest: A Theory of Racial Inequality. LC 78-62970. 261p. 1980. pap. text ed. 5.95 (ISBN 0-268-01601-1). U of Notre Dame Pr.
Keech, William R. The Impact of Negro Voting: The Role of the Vote in the Quest for Equality. LC 80-26518. (American Politics Research Ser.). ix, 113p. 1981. Repr. of 1968 ed. lib. bdg. 19.75x (ISBN 0-313-22774-8, KEIN). Greenwood.
Lerner, Natan. U. N. Convention on the Elimination of Al Forms of Racial Discrimination. LC 80-51738. 278p. 1980. 37.50x (ISBN 90-286-0160-0). Sijthoff & Noordhoff.
Posner, Richard A. The Economics of Justice. LC 80-25075. (Illus.). 448p. 1981. text ed. 25.00 (ISBN 0-674-23525-8). Harvard U Pr.
Reich, Michael. Racial Inequality: A Political-Economic Analysis. LC 80-8573. 320p. 1981. 20.00x (ISBN 0-691-04227-6); pap. 6.95 (ISBN 0-691-00365-3). Princeton U Pr.

RACE PREJUDICE
see Racism
RACE PROBLEMS
see Race Relations
RACE PSYCHOLOGY
see Ethnopsychology
RACE QUESTION
see Race Relations
RACE RELATIONS
see also Genocide; Intercultural Education; Minorities; Race Discrimination; Racism; United States–Race Relations
also subdivision Race relations under names of regions, countries, cities, etc., e.g. United States–Race relations; subdivision Native races under names of continents and countries, e.g. South Africa–Native races; and names of individual races and ethnic groups with pertinent topical subdivision, e.g. Afro-Americans–Relations with Jews; Indians of North America–Government relations
Hughes, Everett C. & Hughes, Helen M. Where Peoples Meet: Racial & Ethnic Frontiers. LC 80-27901. 204p. 1981. Repr. of 1952 ed. lib. bdg. 19.75x (ISBN 0-313-22785-3, HUWP). Greenwood.
Sukedo, Iris D. The Sociology of Racial Intergration in Guyana. 224p. 1981. 9.50 (ISBN 0-682-49686-3). Exposition.
Van der Merwe, Hendrik & Schrire, Robert A., eds. Race & Ethnicity: South African & International Perspectives. 240p. 1981. pap. 12.95x (ISBN 0-8476-3651-8). Rowman.
RACES OF MAN
see Ethnology
RACING AUTOMOBILES
see Automobiles, Racing
RACING PIGEONS
see Pigeons
RACISM
Here are entered works on racism as an attitude as well as works on both attitude and overt discriminatory behavior directed against racial or ethnic groups. Works which are limited to overt discriminatory behavior directed against racial or ethnic groups are entered under Race discrimination. Works on racism directed against a particular group are entered under the name of the group with subdivision Social conditions, or similar subdivision, e.g. Civil rights.
see also Antisemitism; Genocide; Race Discrimination; Race Relations
Breitman, George. Fighting Racism in World War Ii. 1980. 20.00 (ISBN 0-913460-81-8); pap. 5.95 (ISBN 0-913460-82-6). Monad Pr.
RACQUET BALL
see Racquetball
RACQUETBALL
see also Paddleball
Alsen, Philip E. & Witbeck, Alan R. Racquetball. 3rd ed. 112p. 1980. write for info. (ISBN 0-697-07172-3). Wm C Brown.
Darden, Ellington. Power Racquetball Featuring PST. LC 80-84215. (Illus.). 128p. (Orig.). 1981. pap. text ed. 4.95 (ISBN 0-918438-65-9). Leisure Pr.
Hudson, Toni, et al. Racquetball for Women. pap. 3.00 (ISBN 0-87980-384-3). Wilshire.
Peele, David A., ed. Racket & Paddle Games: A Guide to Information Sources. LC 80-23977. (Sports, Games & Pastimes Information Guide Ser., Part of the Gale Information Guide Library: Vol. 9). 300p. 1980. 30.00 (ISBN 0-8103-1480-0). Gale.
Sauser, Jean & Shay, Arthur. Beginning Racquetball Drills. (Illus., Orig.). 1981. pap. 3.95 (ISBN 0-8092-5928-1). Contemp Bks.
--Intermediate Racquetball Drills. (Illus., Orig.). 1981. pap. 3.95 (ISBN 0-8092-5926-5). Contemp Bks.
RADAR
Ewell, George W. Microwave Radar Transmitters: Systems, Modulators & Devices. (Illus.). 300p. 1981. 21.50 (ISBN 0-07-019843-8, P&RB). McGraw.
Radar Instruction Manual. 2nd ed. (Illus.). 120p. 1979. pap. text ed. 14.55 (ISBN 0-934114-26-9). Marine Educ.
RADAR IN NAVIGATION
Radar Instruction Manual. 2nd ed. (Illus.). 120p. 1979. pap. text ed. 14.55 (ISBN 0-934114-26-9). Marine Educ.
Wilkes, Kenneth. Radio & Radar in Sail & Power Boats. 120p. 1980. 15.00x (ISBN 0-245-53191-2, Pub. by Nautical England). State Mutual Bk.
RADIAL SAWS
DeCristoforo, R. J. The Magic of Your Radial Arm Saw. 1980. text ed. 12.95 (ISBN 0-8359-4183-3). Reston.
RADIATA
see Coelenterata
RADIATION
see also Electromagnetic Waves; Irradiation; Light; Luminescence; Quantum Theory; Radiesthesia; Radiology; Scattering (Physics); Sound; Spectrum Analysis; X-Rays
Lacey, Jim & Keough, Allen. Radiation Curing: A Discussion of Advantages, Features & Applications. LC 80-52815. (Illus.). 89p. (Orig.). 1980. pap. text ed. 8.50 (ISBN 0-87263-060-9). SME.
Lawson, Ken, intro. by. Radiation Curing V: A Look to the 80's. LC 80-52816. (Illus.). 544p. 1980. pap. text ed. 55.00 (ISBN 0-87263-059-5). SME.
Mayneord, W. V. & Clark, R. H. Carcinogenesis & Radiation Risk: A Biomathematical Reconnaissance. 1980. 35.00x (Pub. by Brit Inst Radiology England). State Mutual Bk.
Mulkerin, Larry E. Practical Points in Radiation Oncology. 1979. spiral bdg. 17.00 (ISBN 0-87488-726-7). Med Exam.
Occupational Radiation Exposure in Nuclear Fuel Cycle Facilities. 640p. 1980. pap. 79.25 (ISBN 92-0-020080-X, ISP527, IAEA). Unipub.
Panati, Charles & Hudson, Michael. The Silent Intruder: Surviving the Radiation Age. 224p. 1981. 9.95 (ISBN 0-686-69062-1). HM.
Piesinger, Gregory H. Nuclear Radiation: What It Is, How to Detect It, How to Protect Yourself from It. (Illus.). 150p. (Orig.). 1980. pap. 9.95 (ISBN 0-937224-00-6). Dyco Inc.
RADIATION–DOSAGE
Here are entered works on the radiation dose in general. Works on the measurement of the radiation dose are entered under Radiation Dosimetry. Works on the measurement of radiation parameters and values in general are entered under Radiation–Measurement.
Bates, T. D. & Berry, R. J., eds. High Dose-Rate Afterloading in the Treatment of Cancer of the Uterus. 1980. 90.00x (Pub. by Brit Inst Radiology). State Mutual Bk.
RADIATION–MEASUREMENT
Here are entered works on the measurement of radiation parameters and values in general. Works on the measurement of the radiation dose are entered under Radiation Dosimetry. Works on the radiation dose in general are entered under Radiation–Dosage.
see also Radiation–Dosage; Radiation Dosimetry; Radioactivity–Measurement
Committee on Radioactive Waste Management. Implementation of Long-Term Environmental Radiation Standards? The Issue of Verification. ix, 65p. 1979. pap. text ed. 5.50 (ISBN 0-309-02879-5). Natl Acad Pr.
The Design of Counting Systems for Dynamic Studies & Uptake Measurements. 1980. 10.00 (Pub. by Brit Inst Radiology England). State Mutual Bk.
Moon, Parry & Spencer, Donna E. The Photic Field. 272p. 1981. text ed. 25.00x (ISBN 0-262-13166-8). MIT Pr.
RADIATION–SAFETY MEASURES
Ebert, H., et al, eds. Radiation Protection Optimization--Present Experience & Methods: Proceedings of the European Scientific Seminar, Luxembourg, Oct. 1979. LC 80-41671. (Illus.). 330p. 1980. pap. 50.00 (ISBN 0-08-027291-6). Pergamon.
Langmead, W. A., ed. Manual of Good Practice for Radiation Protection of the Patient: Diagnostic Radiology. 1980. Part 1. 15.00x (Pub. by Brit Inst Radiology). State Mutual Bk.
Thomas, Ralph H. & Perez-Mendez, Victor, eds. Advances in Radiation Protection & Dosimetry. (Ettore Najorana International Science Ser., Life Sciences: Vol. 2). 650p. 1980. 69.50 (ISBN 0-306-40468-0). Plenum Pub.
RADIATION, SOLAR
see Solar Radiation
RADIATION BIOLOGY
see Radiobiology
RADIATION DOSIMETRY
Here are entered works on the measurement of radiation dose. Works on the radiation dose in general are entered under Radiation–Dosage. Works on the measurement of radiation parameters and values in general are entered under Radiation–Measurement.
Thomas, Ralph H. & Perez-Mendez, Victor, eds. Advances in Radiation Protection & Dosimetry. (Ettore Najorana International Science Ser., Life Sciences: Vol. 2). 650p. 1980. 69.50 (ISBN 0-306-40468-0). Plenum Pub.
RADIATION PROTECTION
see Radiation–Safety Measures
RADIATION THERAPY
see Radiotherapy
RADICALISM
Boyer, John W. Political Radicalism in Late Imperial Vienna: Origins of the Christian Social Movement, 1848-1897. LC 80-17302. (Illus.). 1981. lib. bdg. price not set (ISBN 0-226-06957-5). U of Chicago Pr.
Robinson, John A. The Roots of a Radical. 176p. 1981. 9.95 (ISBN 0-8245-0028-8). Crossroad NY.
RADIESTHESIA
Wethered, Vernon D. The Practice of Medical Radiesthesia. 150p. 1977. 9.15x (ISBN 0-8464-1040-0). Beekman Pubs.
RADIO
see also Electro-Acoustics; Radar; Sound-Recording and Reproducing
also subdivision Radio Equipment under subjects, e.g. Automobiles–Radio Equipment; and headings beginning with the word Radio, e.g. Radio Frequency Modulation; Radio In Navigation
Beitman, Hartford. Directory of Antique Radio Collectors & Suppliers. 5th ed. (Orig.). 1980. pap. 3.00x (ISBN 0-938630-00-8); notebook 4.00x (ISBN 0-938630-01-6). Antique Radio.
Danielson. Radio Systems for Technicians, No. 2. 1981. text ed. price not set (ISBN 0-408-00561-0). Butterworth.
RADIO–AMATEURS' MANUALS
Luciani, Vince. Amateur Radio: Super Hobby! LC 80-51260. (Illus.). 144p. 1981. 14.95x (ISBN 0-9602310-2-1); pap. 8.95x (ISBN 0-9602310-1-3). Cologne Pr.
RADIO–BROADCASTING
see Radio Broadcasting
RADIO–DICTIONARIES
Roberts, R. S. Dictionary of Radio, TV & Audio. 1981. text ed. price not set (ISBN 0-408-00339-1, Newnes-Butterworth). Butterworth.
RADIO–HANDBOOKS, MANUALS, ETC.
Ross, John F. Handbook for Radio Engineering Managers. 1000p. 1980. text ed. 94.95 (ISBN 0-408-00424-X). Butterworths.
RADIO–INTERFERENCE
Nelson, William R. Interference Handbook. (Illus.). 240p. 1981. 8.95 (ISBN 0-933616-01-5). Radio Pubns.
RADIO–JAMMING
see Radio–Interference
RADIO–JUVENILE LITERATURE
Radlauer, Ed. Some Basics About Radio-Control Cars. LC 80-22039. (Gemini Bks). 32p. (gr. 4 up). 1981. PLB 8.65g (ISBN 0-516-07691-4, Elk Grove Bks). Childrens.
RADIO–LAWS AND REGULATIONS
Noll, Edward M. First Class Radiotelephone License Handbook. 5th ed. LC 80-52936. 1980. pap. 11.95 (ISBN 0-672-21757-0). Sams.
RADIO–STATIC
see Radio–Interference
RADIO–STATIONS
see Radio Stations
RADIO–TRANSMITTERS AND TRANSMISSION
see also Radio Stations
Ewell, George W. Microwave Radar Transmitters: Systems, Modulators & Devices. (Illus.). 300p. 1981. 21.50 (ISBN 0-07-019843-8, P&RB). McGraw.
RADIO, AUTOMOBILE
see Automobiles–Radio Equipment
RADIO, CITIZENS BAND
see Citizens Band Radio
RADIO, SHORT WAVE
see also Citizens Band Radio; Microwaves
Davey, Gilbert. Fun with Short Wave Radio. rev. ed. Cox, Jack, ed. (Learning with Fun Ser.). (Illus.). 64p. 1980. text ed. 11.50x (ISBN 0-7182-1319-X, Sps). Soccer.
RADIO BROADCASTING
see also Radio–Transmitters and Transmission; Radio Programs; Radio Stations; Television Broadcasting
Becker, Judith, et al. Fine-Tuning: An NCCB Report on Noncommercial Radio. 1980. pap. 3.00 (ISBN 0-9603466-4-3). NCCB.
Clift, Charles, III & Greer, Archie, eds. Broadcast Programming: The Current Perspective. 6th ed. LC 80-8127. 249p. 1981. text ed. 8.50 (ISBN 0-8191-1429-4). U Pr of Amer.
Eastman, Susan T. & Head, Sidney W. Broadcast Programming: Strategies for Winning Television & Radio Audiences. 400p. 1980. text ed. 15.95x (ISBN 0-534-00882-8). Wadsworth Pub.
Jones, Vane A. North American Radio-T.V. Station Guide: TV Station Guide. 14th ed. 1980. pap. 7.95 (ISBN 0-672-21725-2). Sams.
McCarthy, Paul & Duncan, John, eds. Close Radio Catalog. LC 81-65198. (Illus.). 100p. (Orig.). 1981. pap. 5.00 (ISBN 0-937122-01-7). Astro Artz.
McMahon, Michael, ed. Nineteen Eighty-One Radio Contacts. 1981. pap. text ed. 126.00 (ISBN 0-935224-05-X). Larimi Comm.
Wall, C. Edward, et al, eds. Media Review Digest, Vol. 10, 1980. 1980. 120.00 (ISBN 0-87650-129-3). Pierian.
RADIO BROADCASTING–BIBLIOGRAPHY
Glenn, Peter, et al, eds. National Radio Publicity Directory, 1980-81. 10th ed. 400p. 1981. ring-binder 75.00 (ISBN 0-87314-046-X). Peter Glenn.
RADIO BROADCASTING–HISTORY
Face the Nation: The Collected Transcripts from the CBS Radio & Television Broadcasts, 1954-1978, 21 vols. Incl. Vol. 1, 1954-1955. 465p (ISBN 0-03-941431-0); Vol. 2, 1956. 418p (ISBN 0-03-091432-9); Vol. 3, 1957. 443p (ISBN 0-03-091433-7); Vol. 4, 1958. 409p (ISBN 0-03-091434-5); Vol. 5, 1959. 420p (ISBN 0-03-091435-3); Vol. 6, 1960-1961. 499p (ISBN 0-03-091436-1); Vol. 7, 1963-1964. 435p (ISBN 0-03-091437-X); Vol. 8, 1965. 316p (ISBN 0-03-091438-8); Vol. 9, 1966. 344p (ISBN 0-03-091439-6); Vol. 10, 1967. 390p (ISBN 0-03-091440-X); Vol. 11, 1968. 384p (ISBN 0-03-091441-8); Vol. 12, 1969. 353p (ISBN 0-03-091442-6); Vol. 13, 1970. 393p (ISBN 0-03-091443-4); Vol. 14, 1971. 416p (ISBN 0-03-091445-0); Vol. 15, 1972. 418p (ISBN 0-8108-0822-6); Vol. 16, 1973. 398p (ISBN 0-8108-0823-4); Vol. 17, 1974. 375p (ISBN 0-8108-0824-2); Vol. 18, 1975. 382p (ISBN 0-8108-0916-8); Vol. 19, 1976. 382p (ISBN 0-8108-1021-2); Vol. 20, 1977. 371p (ISBN 0-8108-1021-2); Vol. 21, 1978. 365p (ISBN 0-8108-1021-2). 29.50 ea. Microfilming Corp.
Terrace, Vincent. Radio's Golden Years: The Encyclopedia of Radio Programs 1930-1960. (Illus.). 288p. 1981. 15.00 (ISBN 0-498-02393-1). A S Barnes.
RADIO BROADCASTING–LAWS AND LEGISLATION
see Radio–Laws and Regulations
RADIO BROADCASTING–GREAT BRITAIN
Paulu, Burton. Television & Radio in the United Kingdom. 544p. 1981. 39.50x (ISBN 0-8166-0941-1). U of Minn Pr.
RADIO EQUIPMENT, AUTOMOBILE
see Automobiles–Radio Equipment
RADIO IN NAVIGATION
see also Radar in Navigation
Wilkes, Kenneth. Radio & Radar in Sail & Power Boats. 120p. 1980. 15.00x (ISBN 0-245-53191-2, Pub. by Nautical England). State Mutual Bk.
RADIO INTERFERENCE
see Radio–Interference
RADIO JOURNALISTS
see Journalists
RADIO PLAYS–HISTORY AND CRITICISM
Rothel, David. Who Was That Masked Man? The Story of the Lone Ranger. rev. ed. LC 80-27237. (Illus.). 290p. 1981. 19.90 (ISBN 0-498-02538-1). A S Barnes.
RADIO PROGRAMS
Glenn, Peter, et al, eds. National Radio Publicity Directory, 1981. 11th ed. 320p. 1981. 85.00 (ISBN 0-87314-047-8). Peter Glenn.
RADIO STATIONS
see also Radio–Transmitters and Transmission
Bloch, Louis M., Jr. The Gas Pipe Networks: The Early History of College Radio, 1936-1946. (Illus.). 156p. 1981. 12.95 (ISBN 0-914276-02-6). Bloch & Co OH.
RADIO TRANSMISSION
see Radio–Transmitters and Transmission
RADIOACTIVATION ANALYSIS
McKlveen, John W. Fast Neutron Activation Analysis: Elemental Data Base. 306p. 1981. text ed. 39.95 (ISBN 0-250-40406-0). Ann Arbor Science.
RADIOACTIVE INDICATORS
see Radioactive Tracers
RADIOACTIVE SUBSTANCES–SAFETY REGULATIONS
Chicken, J. C. Nuclear Power Hazard Control Policy. LC 80-40992. (Illus.). 300p. 1981. 35.00 (ISBN 0-08-023254-X); pap. 17.50 (ISBN 0-08-023255-8). Pergamon.
RADIOACTIVE SUBSTANCES–TRANSPORTATION
International Legal Conference on Maritime Carriage of Nuclear Subtances, 1971. 39p. 1972. 8.25 (IMCO). Unipub.
RADIOACTIVE TRACERS
see also Nuclear Medicine; Radioisotope Scanning
Bowring, C. S. Radionuclide Tracer Techniques in Hematology. 1981. text ed. price not set (ISBN 0-407-00183-2). Butterworth.
RADIOACTIVE WASTE DISPOSAL
Brawner, Charles O., ed. First International Conference on Uranium Mine Waste Disposal. LC 80-69552. (Illus.). 626p. 1980. 22.00x (ISBN 0-89520-279-4). Soc Mining Eng.
Guide to the Safe Handling of Radioactive Wastes at Nuclear Power Plants. (Technical Reports Ser.: No. 198). 84p. 1980. pap. 12.00 (ISBN 92-0-125080-0, IOC198, IAEA). Unipub.
Jackson, Thomas, ed. Nuclear Waste Management: The Ocean Alternative- Edited Proceedings of a Public Policy Forum Sponsored by the Oceanic Society in the Georgetown University Law Center, DC, February 6, 1980. (Pergamon Policy Studies on Energy). (Illus.). 100p. 15.00 (ISBN 0-08-027204-5). Pergamon.
Separation, Storage & Disposal of Krypton-85. (Technical Reports Ser.: No. 199). 66p. 1980. pap. 9.75 (ISBN 92-0-125180-7, IDC199, IAEA). Unipub.
Simon, R. & Orlowski, S., eds. Radioactive Waste Management & Disposal. 703p. 1980. 82.00 (ISBN 3-7186-0056-0). Harwood Academic.
Underground Disposal of Radioactive Wastes, Vol. II. 613p. 1980. pap. 76.75 (ISBN 92-0-020280-2, ISP528-2, IAEA). Unipub.
Underground Disposal of Radioactive Wastes, Vol. 1. 517p. 1980. pap. 60.75 (ISP 528-1, IAEA). Unipub.
RADIOACTIVE WASTES
see also Radioactive Waste Disposal
High Level Nuclear Waste from Past to Present: Policy & Prophecy. 1980. 3.25. Tech Info Proj.
RADIOACTIVITY–MEASUREMENT
see also Radioactivation Analysis; Radioisotope Scanning
Traceability & Quality Control in the Measurement of Environmental Radioactivity: Seminar Sponsored by the International Committee for Radionuclide Metrology in Braunschweig, June 18-19, 1979. 80p. 1980. pap. 15.00 (ISBN 0-08-026253-8). Pergamon.
RADIOACTIVITY–SAFETY MEASURES
see also Radioactive Waste Disposal
Spear, F. G., ed. Certain Aspects of the Action of Radiation on Living Cells. 1980. 10.00x (Pub. by Brit Inst Radiology England). State Mutual Bk.

Underground Disposal of Radioactive Wastes, Vol. 1. 517p. 1980. pap. 60.75 (ISP 528-1, IAEA). Unipub.

RADIOBIOLOGY

see also Radioactive Tracers; Radioisotopes in the Body

also subdivision Physiological Effects under radiation subjects, e.g. Radiation–Physiological Effects

Chadwick, K. H. & Leenhouts, H. P. The Molecular Theory of Radiation Biology. (Monographs on Theoretical & Applied Genetics: Vol. 5). (Illus.). 450p. 1981. 67.50 (ISBN 0-387-10297-3). Springer-Verlag.

Lett, J. T. & Adler, H. I., eds. Advances in Radiation Biology, Vol. 9. (Serial Publication Ser.). 1981. write for info. (ISBN 0-12-035409-8). Acad Pr.

Radiobiological Equivalents of Chemical Pollutants. 115p. 1980. pap. 14.75 (ISBN 92-0-111180-0, ISP 544, IAEA). Unipub.

RADIOCHEMICAL ANALYSIS

see Radioactivation Analysis

RADIOCHEMISTRY

Here are entered works on the chemical properties of radioactive substances and their use in chemical studies. Works on the chemical effects of high energy radiation on matter are entered under Radiation Chemistry. Works on the application of chemical techniques to the study of the structure and properties of atomic nuclei, their transformations and reactions are entered under Nuclear Chemistry.

see also Nuclear Chemistry; Radioactivation Analysis; Radioactive Tracers

Emeleus, H. J. & Sharpe, A. G., eds. Advances in Inorganic Chemistry & Radiochemistry, Vol. 24. (Serial Publication Ser.). 1981. write for info. (ISBN 0-12-023624-9). Acad Pr.

Friedlander, Gerhart. Nuclear & Radiochemistry. 3rd ed. 650p. 1981. price not set (ISBN 0-471-28021-6, Pub. by Wiley-Interscience). Wiley.

RADIODIAGNOSIS

see Diagnosis, Radioscopic

RADIODONTIA

see Teeth–Radiography

RADIOGRAPHY, MEDICAL

see also Diagnosis, Radioscopic; Tomography

also subdivision Radiography under names of organs e.g. Brain–Radiography

Ryan, Gerald D. Radiographic Positioning of Small Animals. LC 80-26069. (Illus.). 147p. 1981. text ed. write for info. (ISBN 0-8121-0774-8). Lea & Febiger.

Tomlinson, H. Medical Divination. 88p. 1966. 5.50x (ISBN 0-8464-1031-1). Beekman Pubs.

Wethered, Vernon D. Medical Radiesthesia & Radionics: An Introduction. 196p. 1957. 11.95x (ISBN 0-8464-1032-X). Beekman Pubs.

RADIOISOTOPE SCANNING

Leach, K. G. The Physica Aspects of Radioisotopic Organ Imaging. 1980. 10.00x (Pub. by Brit Inst Radiology). State Mutual Bk.

A Survey of Images of a Phanton Produced by Radioisotope Scanners & Cameras 1976. 1980. 10.00x (Pub. by Brit Inst Radiology). State Mutual Bk.

RADIOISOTOPES–LABORATORY MANUALS

Faires, R. A. & Boswell, G. G. Radioisotope Lab Techniques. 4th ed. LC 80-41045. 272p. 1980. text ed. 39.95 (ISBN 0-408-70940-5). Butterworths.

RADIOISOTOPES IN MEDICINE

see Nuclear Medicine

RADIOISOTOPES IN THE BODY

Sowby, F. D., ed. Annals of the ICRP, Vol. 5, No. 1-6. (ICRP Publication: No. 30, Supplement to Part 2). 756p. 1980. 100.00. Pergamon.

RADIOLOGICAL PHYSICS

see Radiology

RADIOLOGY

see also Radiation

Critser, James R., Jr. Radiology. 99p. 1980. 60.00 (ISBN 0-914428-68-3, 10R-79). Lexington Data.

Langmead, W. A., ed. Manual of Good Practice for Radiation Protection of the Patient: Diagnostic Radiology. 1980. Part 1. 15.00x (Pub. by Brit Inst Radiology). State Mutual Bk.

Sutton, David. A Textbook of Radiology & Imaging. 3rd ed. (Illus.). 1392p. 1980. lib. bdg. 149.00 in 1 vol. (ISBN 0-443-01700-X); lib. bdg. 175.00 in 2 vols. (ISBN 0-686-28870-X). Churchill.

Wilks, Robin J. Principles of Radiological Physics. (Illus.). 528p. 1981. pap. text ed. 37.50 (ISBN 0-443-02035-3). Churchill.

RADIOLOGY, MEDICAL

see also Diagnosis, Radioscopic; Nuclear Medicine; Pediatric Radiology; Radiography, Medical; Radiotherapy

Critser, James R., Jr. Clinical Assays. (Ser. 10CA 80). 1981. 80.00 (ISBN 0-914428-78-0). Lexington Data.

Ehrlich, Ruth A. & Givens, Ellen D. Patient Care in Radiography. (Illus.). 230p. 1981. pap. text ed. 12.95 (ISBN 0-8016-1507-0). Mosby.

Johnson, Thomas H. Genitourinary Radiology Case Studies. 1980. pap. 16.75 (ISBN 0-87488-090-4). Med Exam.

Lefebvre, Jacques. Clinical Practice in Pediatric Radiology: The Respiratory System, Vol. II. Kaufman, Herbert J., ed. LC 79-83739. 448p. 1979. 65.50 (ISBN 0-89352-066-7). Masson Pub.

Leonard, William L., ed. Radiologic Technology Examination Review Book, Vol. 1. 4th ed. 1979. pap. 9.50 (ISBN 0-87488-441-1). Med Exam.

Montagne. Atlas of Foot Radiology. 1981. price not set (ISBN 0-89352-097-7). Masson Pub.

Pitcoff, Ramsey K. & Powell, Herb. Neuroradiology with Computed Tomography. 575p. 1981. text ed. price not set (ISBN 0-7216-7444-5). Saunders.

Sutton, David. Textbook of Radiology & Imaging, 2 vols. 3rd ed. 1981. Vol. 1. text ed. 149.00 (ISBN 0-686-28939-0); Vol. 2. text ed. 175.00 (ISBN 0-686-28940-4). Churchill.

The Use of Computers in Therapeutic Radiology: International Conference, 1966. 1980. 10.00x (Pub. by Brit Inst Radiology). State Mutual Bk.

RADIOMETRIC ANALYSIS

see Radioactivation Analysis

RADIOPHARMACEUTICALS

Cox, P. H., ed. Progress in Radiopharmacology. (Progress in Radio Pharmology Ser.: Vol. 1). 1979. 41.50 (ISBN 0-444-80178-2, North Holland). Elsevier.

Guidelines for the Preparation of Radiopharmaceuticals in Hospitals. 1980. 10.00x (Pub. by Brit Inst Radiology). State Mutual Bk.

RADIOSCOPIC DIAGNOSIS

see Diagnosis, Radioscopic

RADIOTELEPHONE

Block, Richard A., ed. Radiotelephone Operator. (Illus.). 70p. Date not set. pap. 9.00 (ISBN 0-934114-27-7). Marine Educ.

RADIOTHERAPY

see also Radiation–Dosage

Berry, R. J., ed. Computerized Tomographic Scanners on Radiotheraopy in Europe. 1980. 20.00x (Pub. by Brit Inst Radiology England). State Mutual Bk.

Cohen, M., et al, eds. Central Axis Depth Dose Data for Use in Radiotherapy. 1980. 25.00x (Pub. by Brit Inst Radiology England). State Mutual Bk.

Computers in Radiotherapy: 1968 2nd International Conference. 1980. 9.00x (Pub. by Brit Inst Radiology England). State Mutual Bk.

Computers in the Control of Treatment Units: Applications of Modern Technology in Radiotherapy. 1980. 10.00x (Pub. by Brit Inst Radiology England). State Mutual Bk.

Deeley, T. J., ed. The Planning of Radiotherapy Departments. 1980. 50.00x (Pub. by Brit Inst Radiology). State Mutual Bk.

Dubois, J. B., ed. Immunopharmacologic Effects of Radiation Therapy. (European Organization for Research on Treatment of Cancer (EORTC) Monographs: Vol. 8). 475p. 1981. 45.00 (ISBN 0-89004-531-3). Raven.

DuBoulay, G. H., ed. Considerations About the Use of Computers in Radiodiagnostic Departments. 1980. 45.00x (Pub. by Brit Inst Radiology England). State Mutual Bk.

Pilapil, F. & Studva, K., eds. Programmed Instruction: Radiation Therapy. 55p. 1979. pap. 6.50 (ISBN 0-89352-099-3). Masson Pub.

Pycock, C. J. & Taberner, P. V., eds. Central Neurotransmitter Turnover. 200p. 1980. 30.00x (Pub. by Croom Helm England). State Mutual Bk.

Stryker, John A., et al. Radiation Therapy Technology Examination Review. LC 80-80369. 1980. pap. 14.00 (ISBN 0-87488-459-4). Med Exam.

Treatment Simulators: Applications of Modern Technology in Radiotherapy-1976. 1980. 10.00x (Pub. by Brit Inst Radiology). State Mutual Bk.

Watkins, B. Radiation Therapy Mold Technology: Principles. Design & Applications. (Illus.). 224p. 1981. 30.00 (ISBN 0-08-025373-3). Pergamon.

RAFFIA WORK

see also Basket Making

Weiss, Jeffrey. Cornerstone Collector's Guide to Wicker. 128p. 1981. 7.95 (ISBN 0-346-12535-9). Cornerstone.

RAGTIME MUSIC

Williams, Martin, ed. The Art of Jazz: Ragtime to Bebop. (Da Capo Quality Paperbacks Ser.). 248p. 1981. pap. 6.95 (ISBN 0-306-80134-5). Da Capo.

RAIL TRANSPORTATION

see Railroads

RAILROAD CONDUCTORS

Green, Elizabeth A. The Modern Conductor. 3rd ed. (Illus.). 288p. 1981. text ed. 18.95 (ISBN 0-13-590216-9). P-H.

RAILROAD CONSTRUCTION

see Railroad Engineering

RAILROAD ENGINEERING

Fiennes, G. F. I Tried to Run a Railway. pap. text ed. 14.95x (ISBN 0-392-07972-0, SpS). Soccer.

RAILROAD MODELS

see Railroads–Models

RAILROADS

see also Eminent Domain; Freight and Freightage; Locomotives; Street-Railroads; Subways

also names of individual railroads

Carter, Ernest. Let's Look at Trains. 17.50x (ISBN 0-392-08037-0, SpS). Soccer.

ECMT for OCED. Scope for Railway Transport in Urban Areas: Scope for Railway Transport in Urban Areas. (ECMT Round Table Ser.: No. 47). (Illus.). 375p. (Orig.). 1980. pap. 20.00x (ISBN 92-821-1063-X, 75-80-06-1). OECD.

Harshaw, Lou. Trains, Tressels, & Tunnels. 1981. 8.95 (ISBN 0-932298-10-9). Green Hill.

Mackay, James. Railway Antiques. (Orig.). 1980. pap. 8.95x (ISBN 0-8464-1046-X). Beekman Pubs.

RAILROADS–CONDUCTORS

see Railroad Conductors

RAILROADS–DICTIONARIES

The Dictionary of Railway Terms. 1033p. (Polyglot.). 1978. 47.50x (ISBN 0-8002-2264-4). Intl Pubns Serv.

RAILROADS–ENGINEERING

see Railroad Engineering

RAILROADS–HISTORY

Balfour, John. The Armoured Train. (Illus.). 168p. 1981. 25.50 (ISBN 0-7134-2547-4, Pub. by Batsford England). David & Charles.

Cook, Roger & Zimmerman, Karl. Western Maryland Railroad. (Illus.). 320p. 1981. 25.00 (ISBN 0-8310-7139-7). Howell-North.

Hattich, William. Tombstone. LC 80-5947. (Illus.). 64p. 1981. 9.95 (ISBN 0-8061-1753-2). U of Okla Pr.

Hewison, Christian H. Shedmaster to Railway Inspectorate. LC 80-68694. (Illus.). 192p. 1981. 19.95 (ISBN 0-7153-8074-5). David & Charles.

Hollingsworth, Brian. Festiniog Adventure: The Festiniog Railway's Deviation Project. LC 80-68683. (Illus.). 160p. 1981. 16.95 (ISBN 0-7153-7956-9). David & Charles.

Lehigh Valley Railroad. 25.00. Chatham Pub CA.

Masterson, V. V. The Katy Railroad & the Last Frontier. (Illus.). 312p. 1981. 12.95 (ISBN 0-8061-0255-1). U of Okla Pr.

Nock, O. S. Railway Archaeology. (Illus.). 160p. 1981. 35.95 (ISBN 0-85059-451-0). Aztex.

Satow, Michael & Desmond, Ray. Railways of the Raj. (Illus.). 120p. 1980. 29.95 (ISBN 0-8147-7816-X). NYU Pr.

Westwood, John. Railways at War. LC 80-25429. 224p. 1981. 17.50 (ISBN 0-8310-7138-9). Howell-North.

Wrottesley, John. Great Northern Railway, Vol. III. (Illus.). 192p. 1981. 30.00 (ISBN 0-7134-3835-5, Pub. by Batsford England). David & Charles.

Zauner, Phyllis. The Train Whistle's Echo: Story of Western Railroading. (Western Mini-Histories Ser.). (Illus.). 64p. (Orig.). 1980. pap. 3.00 (ISBN 0-936914-05-X). Zanel Pubns.

RAILROADS–JUVENILE LITERATURE

see also Railroads–United States–History–Juvenile Literature

Dorin, Patrick C. Yesterday's Trains. (Superwheels & Thrill Sports Bks.). (Illus.). (gr. 4 up). 1981. PLB 6.95 (ISBN 0-8225-0448-0). Lerner Pubns.

Mann, Philip. El Gran Passo en Tren. Kreps, Georgian, tr. from Span. (Shape Board Play Book). Orig. Title: The Great Train Ride. (Illus.). 14p. (Eng.). (ps-3). 1981. bds. 3.50 plastic comb bdg. (ISBN 0-89828-201-2, 5005SP). Tuffy Bks.

RAILROADS–MODELS

Hayden, Bob, ed. Track Planning Ideas from Model Railroader. LC 80-84022. (Illus.). 96p. (Orig.). 1981. pap. 5.95 (ISBN 0-89024-555-X). Kalmbach.

Paust, Gil. Model Railroading: How to Plan, Build, & Maintain Your Trains & Pikes. LC 80-1817. (Illus.). 160p. (gr. 4 up). 1981. 9.95a (ISBN 0-385-13033-3); PLB (ISBN 0-385-13034-1). Doubleday.

Yorkis, Paul G. & Walsh, Jim. Greenberg's Guide to American Flyer's Gauge. 160p. 1980. pap. 19.95 (ISBN 0-442-21209-7). Van Nos Reinhold.

RAILROADS–PICTORIAL WORKS

Digerness, David S. The Mineral Belt: Old South Park-Across the Great Divide, Vol. 2. (Illus.). 416p. 49.00 (ISBN 0-913582-21-2). Sundance.

--The Mineral Belt: Old South Park-Denver to Leadville, Vol. 1. (Illus.). 416p. 49.00 (ISBN 0-913582-20-4). Sundance.

Jackson, W. H. Rocky Mountain Railroad Album: Stream & Steel Cross the Great Divide. (Illus.). 79p. 195.00 (ISBN 0-913582-14-X). Sundance.

LeMassena, Robert. Rio Grande... to the Pacific! (Illus.). 416p. 35.00 (ISBN 0-913582-10-7). Sundance.

LeMassena, Robert A. Articulated Steam Locomotives of North America: A Catalogue of "Giant Steam". (Illus.). 416p. 45.00 (ISBN 0-913582-26-3). Sundance.

McCoy, Dell. The Crystal River Pictorial. (Illus.). 224p. 27.00 (ISBN 0-913582-04-2). Sundance.

McCoy, Dell & Collman, Russell. The Rio Grande Pictorial. (Illus.). 216p. 30.00 (ISBN 0-913582-02-6). Sundance.

Mangan, Terry W. Colorado on Glass: First 50 Years of Glass-Plate Photography in Colorado. (Illus.). 416p. 47.00 (ISBN 0-913582-13-1). Sundance.

Shoemaker, Len. Roaring Fork Valley: An Illustrated Chronicle. (Illus.). 216p. 27.00 (ISBN 0-913582-06-9). Sundance.

RAILROADS–GREAT BRITAIN

British Tourist Authority. Discovering Preserved Railways. (Illus.). 72p. Date not set. pap. price not set (ISBN 0-85263-515-X, Pub. by Auto Assn-British Tourist Authority England). Merrimack Bk Serv.

Glover, John. London's Railways Today. LC 80-70293. (Illus.). 96p. 1981. 17.95 (ISBN 0-7153-8070-2). David & Charles.

Locomotive at the Grouping, London, Midland, & Scottish. 14.95x (ISBN 0-392-08071-0, SpS). Soccer.

RAILROADS–GREAT BRITAIN–HISTORY

Ahron, E. L. British Steam Railway Locomotive: Volume I, 1825-1925. 29.50x (ISBN 0-392-07695-0, SpS). Soccer.

Atthill, Robin. The Somerset & Dorset Railway. LC 80-69344. (Illus.). 224p. 1981. 12.95 (ISBN 0-7153-4164-2). David & Charles.

Bonavia, Michael R. British Rail: The First Twenty-Five Years. LC 80-68687. (Illus.). 208p. 1981. 18.50 (ISBN 0-7153-8002-8). David & Charles.

Cartwright, Ralph & Russell, R. T. The Welshpool & Lanfair Light Railway. LC 80-70290. (Illus.). 208p. 1981. 19.95 (ISBN 0-7153-8151-2). David & Charles.

Marshall, John. Forgotten Railways: North-West England. LC 80-68899. (Illus.). 176p. 1981. 16.95 (ISBN 0-7153-8003-6). David & Charles.

St. John Thomas, David. A Regional History of the Railways of Great Britian: Volume I, The West Country. LC 80-70296. (Illus.). 256p. 1981. 28.00 (ISBN 0-7153-8152-0). David & Charles.

RAILROADS–IRELAND

Middlemass, Tom. Irish Standard Guage Railways. LC 80-68690. (Illus.). 96p. 1981. 16.50 (ISBN 0-7153-8007-9). David & Charles.

RAILROADS–UNITED STATES

Scheller, William G. Train Trips: Exploring America by Rail. (Illus.). 270p. (Orig.). 1981. pap. 6.95 (ISBN 0-914788-34-5). East Woods.

Zlatkovich, Charles P. Texas Railroads: A Record of Construction & Abandonment. (Research Monograph). 100p. (Orig.). 1981. pap. 7.00 (ISBN 0-87755-248-7). U of Tex Busn Res.

RAILROADS–UNITED STATES–HISTORY

Best, Gerald M. Ships & Narrow Gauge Rails: The Story of the Pacific Coast Company. (Illus.). 155p. Date not set. Repr. of 1964 ed. 15.00 (ISBN 0-8310-7042-0). Howell-North.

Coach Cabbage & Caboose. 34.95. Chatham Pub CA.

Digerness, David S. The Mineral Belt: Old South Park-Across the Great Divide, Vol. 2. (Illus.). 416p. 49.00 (ISBN 0-913582-21-2). Sundance.

--The Mineral Belt: Old South Park-Denver to Leadville, Vol. 1. (Illus.). 416p. 49.00 (ISBN 0-913582-20-4). Sundance.

Feagans, Raymond J. The Railroad That Ran by the Tide. (Illus.). 146p. Date not set. Repr. of 1972 ed. 15.00 (ISBN 0-8310-7042-0). Howell-North.

Ferrell, Mallory H. The Colorado & Southern Narrow Gauge. (Illus.). 1981. 34.95 (ISBN 0-87108-534-8). Pruett.

Henry Huntington & the Pacific Electric. pap. 10.00. Chatham Pub CA.

Interurban Railways of the Bay Area. 20.00. Chatham Pub CA.

Jackson, W. H. Rocky Mountain Railroad Album: Stream & Steel Cross the Great Divide. (Illus.). 79p. 195.00 (ISBN 0-913582-14-X). Sundance.

Key System Album. 16.00. Chatham Pub CA.

Langauge of the Railroader. 9.95. Chatham Pub CA.

Last of the Three-Foot Loggers. 14.95. Chatham Pub CA.

Lawson, Archie. Freight Trains West. (Illus.). 150p. (Orig.). 1980. 9.95 (ISBN 0-9604806-0-9); pap. 5.95 (ISBN 0-9604806-1-7). Lucas Pubs CA.

LeMassena, Robert. Rio Grande... to the Pacific! (Illus.). 416p. 35.00 (ISBN 0-913582-10-7). Sundance.

McCoy, Dell. The Crystal River Pictorial. (Illus.). 224p. 27.00 (ISBN 0-913582-04-2). Sundance.

McCoy, Dell & Collman, Russell. The Rio Grande Pictorial. (Illus.). 216p. 30.00 (ISBN 0-913582-02-6). Sundance.

Mangan, Terry W. Colorado on Glass: First 50 Years of Glass-Plate Photography in Colorado. (Illus.). 416p. 47.00 (ISBN 0-913582-13-1). Sundance.

Matches, Flumes & Rails. 17.95. Chatham Pub CA.

Monun Route. 25.00. Chatham Pub CA.

The Mountains. 29.50. Chatham Pub CA.

Myrick, David F. Railroads of Arizona, Vol. 1. (Illus.). 480p. Date not set. Repr. of 1975 ed. 30.00 (ISBN 0-8310-7111-7). Howell-North.

New England Diesels. 28.95. Chatham Pub CA.

Northwestern Pacific Railroad. 22.00. Chatham Pub CA.

Paradise Regained. pap. 5.95. Chatham Pub CA.

Railroad in the Clouds. 28.00. Chatham Pub CA.

Rails That Climb. 24.95. Chatham Pub CA.

Rio Grande. 25.00. Chatham Pub CA.

Rosenberger, Homer T. The Philadelphia & Erie Railroad: Its Place in American Economic History. LC 74-75110. (Illus.). 748p. 1975. lib. bdg. 22.50 (ISBN 0-914932-02-0). Rose Hill.

Shoemaker, Len. Roaring Fork Valley: An Illustrated Chronicle. (Illus.). 216p. 27.00 (ISBN 0-913582-06-9). Sundance.

Southern Pacific Daylight. 59.95. Chatham Pub CA.

Southern Pacific Motive Power Annual, 1966-67. (Illus.). 10.35 (ISBN 0-89685-001-3). Chatham Pub CA.

Southern Pacific Motive Power Annual, 1967-68. (Illus.). 10.35 (ISBN 0-89685-002-1). Chatham Pub CA.

Southern Pacific Motive Power Annual, 1968-69. (Illus.). 10.35 (ISBN 0-89685-003-X). Chatham Pub CA.

Southern Pacific Motive Power Annual, 1970. (Illus.). 10.35 (ISBN 0-89685-004-8). Chatham Pub CA.

Strapal, Joseph A. Southern Pacific Motive Power Annual, 1971. (Illus.). 1971. 9.95 (ISBN 0-89685-005-6). Chatham Pub CA.

They Felled the Redwoods. 15.00. Chatham Pub CA.

Westwood, John. Railways at War. LC 80-25429. 224p. 1981. 17.50 (ISBN 0-8310-7138-9). Howell-North.

Williams, Miller & McPherson, James A. Railroad: Trains & Train People. 1976. pap. 7.95 (ISBN 0-394-73237-5). Random.

RAILROADS–UNITED STATES–HISTORY–JUVENILE LITERATURE

Waitley, Douglas. The Age of the Mad Dragons: Steam Locomotives in North America. LC 80-27242. (Illus.). 192p. (gr. 6 up). 1981. 10.95 (ISBN 0-8253-0029-0). Beaufort Bks NY.

RAILROADS, LOGGING

see Logging Railroads

RAILROADS, STREET

see Street-Railroads

RAILROADS, UNDERGROUND

see Subways

RAILWAY LIENS

see Liens

RAILWAYS

see Railroads

RAIN AND RAINFALL

see also Droughts; Floods; Meteorology

Bassett, Preston R. & Bartlett, Margaret F. Raindrop Stories. LC 80-19036. (Illus.). 40p. (gr. k-3). 1981. 9.95 (ISBN 0-590-07628-0, Four Winds). Schol Bk Serv.

RALEIGH, WALTER, SIR, 1552?-1618

Firth, Charles. Sir Walter Raleigh's History of the World. 49p. 1980. Repr. write for info. (ISBN 0-8492-4707-1). R West.

Thoreau, Henry D. Sir Walter Raleigh. Sanborn, Franklin B., ed. LC 80-2523. 1981. Repr. of 1905 ed. 24.50 (ISBN 0-686-28929-3). AMS Pr.

RALEIGH'S ROANOKE COLONIES, 1584-1590

Durant, David. Ralegh's Lost Colony. LC 80-65992. (Illus.). 320p. 1981. 12.95 (ISBN 0-689-11098-7). Atheneum.

RAMAN SPECTROSCOPY

Eesley, G. L. Coherent Raman Spectroscopy. (Illus.). 150p. 1981. 41.00 (ISBN 0-08-025058-0). Pergamon.

RANA

see Frogs

RANCH LIFE

see also Cowboys

Call, Hughie. Golden Fleece. LC 80-38781. (Illus.). 1981. 17.95x (ISBN 0-8032-1413-8, Bison); pap. 5.25 (ISBN 0-8032-6308-2, BB 760, Bison). U of Nebr Pr.

Cotton, E. J. & Mitchell, Ethel. Buffalo Bud: Adventures of an Alberta Cowboy. (Illus.). 130p. (Orig.). 1981. pap. 9.95 (ISBN 0-88839-095-5). Hancock Hse.

Randolph, Edmund. Beef, Leather & Grass. LC 80-18818. (Illus.). 304p. 1981. 14.95 (ISBN 0-8061-1517-3). U of Okla Pr.

RANCH LIFE–JUVENILE LITERATURE

Bishop, Ann. Annie O'Kay's Riddle Roundup. (Illus.). 40p. (gr. 2-5). 1981. 7.95 (ISBN 0-525-66727-X). Elsevier-Nelson.

Boy Scouts of America. Farm & Ranch Management. (Illus.). 32p. (gr. 6-12). 1980. pap. 0.70x (3348). BSA.

RANDOM PROCESSES

see Stochastic Processes

RANDOM SAMPLING

Lucas, Donna. Towards Reconstruction of an un-Paired Random Sample. 115p. 1979. pap. 3.60 (1252). U of NC Pr.

RANGER PROJECT

see Project Ranger

RANK

see Social Classes

RAPE

Booher, Dianna D. Rape: What Woud You Do If...? 192p. (gr. 7 up). 1981. PLB price not set (ISBN 0-671-42201-4). Messner.

Sussman, Les & Bordwell, Sally. The Rape File. 1981. 12.50 (ISBN 0-87754-094-2). Chelsea Hse.

RAPID READING

Kump, Peter. Breakthrough Rapid Reading. 256p. 1980. 5.95 (ISBN 0-13-081554-3, Reward). P-H.

Kusnetz, Len. Your Child Can Be a Super Reader. LC 79-84790. 128p. 1980. pap. 3.95. Liberty Pub.

Miller, Wanda, et al. Reading Faster & Understanding More Book III. (Illus.). 416p. 1981. pap. text ed. 12.95 (ISBN 0-87626-733-9). Winthrop.

Shefter, Harry. Faster Reading Self-Taught. rev. ed. 1981. pap. write for info. (ISBN 0-671-83230-1). PB.

RAPID TRANSIT

see Local Transit

RAPPAHANNOCK INDIANS

see Indians of North America–Eastern States

RARE ANIMALS

see also Extinct Animals; Rare Birds

Cadieux, Charles. These Are the Endangered. (Illus.). 228p. 1981. 15.00 (ISBN 0-913276-35-9). Stone Wall Pr.

Leen, Nina. Rare & Unusual Animals. (Illus.). 80p. (gr. 3-7). 1981. 8.95 (ISBN 0-03-057478-1). HR&W.

RARE BIRDS

Hendrich, Paula. The Birds Are in Your Hands. (Illus.). 160p. (gr. 5 up). Date not set. 8.95 (ISBN 0-688-00417-2); PLB 8.59 (ISBN 0-688-00418-0). Morrow.

King, Warren B. Endangered Birds of the World: The ICPB Bird Red Data Book. 624p. 1981. text ed. 19.95x (ISBN 0-87474-584-5); pap. text ed. 8.95 (ISBN 0-87474-583-7). Smithsonian.

Ripley, S. Dillon. A Naturalist's Adventure in Nepal: Search for the Spiny Babbler. (Illus.). 301p. 1981. Repr. of 1953 ed. 12.50 (ISBN 0-87474-810-0). Smithsonian.

RARE BOOKS

see Bibliography–Rare Books

RARE EARTH METALS

see Earths, Rare

RARE EARTHS

see Earths, Rare

RARE METALS

see Nonferrous Metals

RASPUTIN, GRIGORII EFIMOVICH, 1871-1916

De Enden, Michel. Rasputin & the Waning of the Russian Monarchy. 300p. (Orig.). 1980. pap. write for info. (ISBN 0-913124-46-X). Nordland Pub.

Rasputin, Maria & Barrham, Patte. Rasputin: The Man Behind the Myth. 328p. 1981. pap. 2.95. Warner Bks.

RAT

see Rats

RATING, JOB

see Job Evaluation

RATING OF EMPLOYEES

see Employees, Rating Of

RATIOCINATION

see Reasoning

RATIONALIZATION OF INDUSTRY

see Industrial Management

RATS

Castaing, D., et al. Hepatic & Portal Surgery in the Rat. (Illus.). 184p. 1980. 37.50 (ISBN 0-89352-101-9). Masson Pub.

RATTLESNAKES

Armstrong, Barry L. & Murphy, James B. The Natural History of Mexican Rattlesnakes. Wiley, E. O. & Collins, Joseph T., eds. (U of KS Museum of Nat. Hist. Special Publication: No. 5). (Illus.). 88p. (Orig.). Date not set. pap. 6.00 (ISBN 0-89338-010-5). U of KS Mus Nat Hist.

Klauber, Laurence M. Rattlesnakes: Their Habits, Life Histories, & Influence on Mankind. abr. ed. (Illus.). 400p. 1981. 14.95 (ISBN 0-520-04038-4). U of Cal Pr.

RAW FOOD

see Food, Raw

RAYMOND 4TH DE SAINT-GILLES, COUNT OF TOULOUSE, d. 1105

Hill, John H. & Hill, Laurita L. Raymond IV, Count of Toulouse. LC 80-11116. (Illus.). viii, 177p. 1980. Repr. of 1962 ed. lib. bdg. 19.50x (ISBN 0-313-22362-9, HIRA). Greenwood.

RAYS, ROENTGEN

see X-Rays

REACTANCE AMPLIFIERS

see Parametric Amplifiers

REACTION RATE (CHEMISTRY)

see Chemical Reaction, Rate Of

REACTIONS, CHEMICAL

see Chemical Reactions

REACTOR FUELS

see Nuclear Fuels

REACTORS (NUCLEAR PHYSICS)

see Nuclear Reactors

REACTORS, CHEMICAL

see Chemical Reactors

READ, HERBERT EDWARD, 1893-1968

Woodcock, George. Herbert Read: The Stream & the Source. 1972. 11.95 (ISBN 0-571-08656-X, Pub. by Faber & Faber). Merrimack Bk Serv.

READABILITY (LITERARY STYLE)

Tompkins, Jane P., ed. Reader-Response Criticism: From Formalism to Post-Structuralism. LC 80-7966. 320p. 1981. text ed. 20.00x (ISBN 0-8018-2400-1); pap. text ed. 6.95x (ISBN 0-8018-2401-X). Johns Hopkins.

READERS

see also College Readers; English Language–Dictionaries, Juvenile

Blockcolsky, Valeda & Frazer, Joan. Star Trails, "CH". 1980. 20.00 (ISBN 0-88450-726-2, 3150-B). Communication Skill.

--Star Trails,"SH". 1980. 20.00 (ISBN 0-88450-727-0, 3140-B). Communication Skill.

--Star Trails,"TH". 1980. 20.00 (ISBN 0-88450-725-4, 3131-B). Communication Skill.

Broad, Delia. Space Adventures Reading Series Sampler. 1980. pap. 19.95 (ISBN 0-88450-723-8, 4520-B). Communication Skill.

Hill, L. A. Elementary Anecdotes in American English. (Anecdotes in American English Ser.). (Illus.). 72p. 1980. 2.50x (ISBN 0-19-502601-2). Oxford U Pr.

Thompson, T. J. Ten Red Rods. LC 80-83135. (Illus.). 16p. (Orig.). (ps-1). 1980. pap. text ed. 1.50 (ISBN 0-915676-02-8). Montessori Wkshps.

Trimmer, Joseph & Hairston, Maxine. The Riverside Reader. LC 80-82759. 544p. 1981. pap. text ed. 7.95 (ISBN 0-395-28940-8); instr's manual 0.75. HM.

READERS–BIBLE

Daily Light on the Daily Path (NIV) 384p. 1981. 8.95 (ISBN 0-310-23110-8); pap. 4.95 (ISBN 0-310-23111-6). Zondervan.

Speck, S. L. & Riggle, H. M., eds. Bible Readings for Bible Students & for the Home & Fireside. 432p. 1902. 5.00. Faith Pub Hse.

READERS (HIGHER EDUCATION)

see College Readers

READERS AND LIBRARIES

see Libraries and Readers

READERS' DIGEST

Reader's Digest. Almanac & Yearbook 1981. (Illus.). 1981. 6.95 (ISBN 0-89577-090-3, Pub. by Reader's Digest). Norton.

READING

see also Readability (Literary Style); Readers

Aukerman, Robert C. The Basal Reader Approach to Reading. 400p. 1981. text ed. 14.95 (ISBN 0-471-03082-1); pap. text ed. 8.95 (ISBN 0-471-09066-2). Wiley.

Bossone, Richard M. & Ashe, Amy E. English Proficiency: Developing Your Reading & Writing Power, Bk. 1. 320p. (gr. 7-9). 1980. 10.32 (ISBN 0-07-006589-6, W); tchrs. manual 6.00 (ISBN 0-07-006590-X). McGraw.

Brower, Reuben A. The Fields of Light: An Experiment in Critical Reading. LC 80-19289. xii, 218p. 1980. Repr. of 1951 ed. lib. bdg. 23.50x (ISBN 0-313-22653-9, BRFI). Greenwood.

Browne, M. Neil & Keely, Stuart M. Asking the Right Questions. 224p. 1981. pap. text ed. 6.95 (ISBN 0-13-049395-3). P-H.

Burleigh, Robert. Basic Learning Skills: Base Words & Word Parts Learning Module. (gr. 2-3). 1978. pap. text ed. 215.00 (ISBN 0-89290-108-X, CM-38D). Soc for Visual.

--Basic Learning Skills: Consonant Sounds Learning Module. (gr. k-2). 1978. pap. text ed. 290.00 (ISBN 0-89290-106-3, CM-38B). Soc for Visual.

--Basic Reading Skills: Reading Readiness Learning Module. (gr. k-1). 1977. pap. text ed. 215.00 (ISBN 0-89290-105-5, CM-38A). Soc for Visual.

Covino, William A. & Coda-Messerle, Margaret. GED Reading Skills Test Preparation Guide: High School Equivalency Examination. (Cliffs Test Preparation Ser.). 105p. (Orig.). (gr. 10 up). 1981. pap. 2.95 (ISBN 0-8220-2014-9). Cliffs.

Davis, Leo G. Ounce of Prevention Is Worth a Pound of Cure. 1981. 6.50 (ISBN 0-8062-1569-0). Carlton.

Forgan, Harry W. & Mangrum, Charles T. Teaching Content Area Reading Skills. 2nd ed. (Illus.). 336p. 1981. pap. text ed. 12.95 (ISBN 0-675-08037-1); instr's. manual 3.75 (ISBN 0-686-69501-1). Merrill.

Frank, Marjorie S. & Hutchins, P. J. Building Language Power with Cloze, Level F. (Skillbooster Ser.). 64p. (gr. 6). 1981. write for info. (ISBN 0-87895-519-4). Modern Curr.

Gillespy, Rosalynne H. Space Wars. LC 78-730966. 1978. pap. text ed. 175.00 (ISBN 0-89290-111-X, CM-31). Soc for Visual.

Gregorich, Barbara & Zack, Carol. The Newspaper: Reading Skills. LC 78-730963. (Illus.). 1978. pap. text ed. 99.00 (ISBN 0-89290-114-4, A160). Soc for Visual.

Hall, Mary A. Teaching Reading As a Language Experience. 3rd ed. (Illus.). 160p. 1981. pap. text ed. 6.95 (ISBN 0-686-69503-8). Merrill.

Hayward, Linda. A Phonic Dictionary. (Illus.). 96p. (gr. k-4). 1981. PLB 11.85 (ISBN 0-448-13923-5); pap. 3.95 (ISBN 0-448-47336-4). Platt.

Heilman, Arthur, et al. Principles & Practices of Teaching Reading. 5th ed. (Illus.). 544p. 1981. text ed. 16.95 (ISBN 0-675-08150-5); instr's. manual 3.75 (ISBN 0-686-69498-8). Merrill.

Hudson & Weaver. Reading, Writing & Speaking: Here & Now. (Illus.). 1980. pap. 2.95x (ISBN 0-88323-160-3, 248). Richards Pub.

Johnson, Barbara. The Critical Difference: Essays in the Contemporary Rhetoric of Reading. LC 80-21533. 176p. 1981. text ed. 12.00x (ISBN 0-8018-2458-3). Johns Hopkins.

Kahan, Jane & Trotter, Gwendolyn. Reading Comprehension Skills. LC 78-730058. (Illus.). 1979. pap. text ed. 99.00 (ISBN 0-89290-104-7, A330-SATC). Soc for Visual.

Kakn, Jane & Trotter, Gwendolyn. Reading in the Content Areas. LC 78-730059. (Illus.). 1978. pap. text ed. 99.00 (ISBN 0-89290-102-0, A328-SATC). Soc for Visual.

Kusnetz, Len. Your Child Can Be a Super Reader. LC 79-84790. 128p. 1980. pap. 3.95. Liberty Pub.

Lesgold, Alan M. & Perfetti, Charles A., eds. Interactive Processes in Reading. LC 80-21048. 448p. 1981. professional reference text 24.95 (ISBN 0-89859-079-5). L Erlbaum Assocs.

Manoni, Mary, et al. Champions in Sports Learning Module. LC 76-731377. 1976. pap. text ed. 175.00 (ISBN 0-89290-112-8, CM-36). Soc for Visual.

Manoni, Mary H. & Cienkus, Robert. Phonetic Rules in Reading. LC 78-730055. (Illus.). 1978. pap. text ed. 99.00 (ISBN 0-89290-103-9, A329-SATC). Soc for Visual.

Miller, Wilma H. The Reading Activities Handbook. 476p. 1980. pap. 15.95 (ISBN 0-03-051371-5). HR&W.

Nessel, Denise D. & Jones, Margaret B. Language-Experience Approach to Reading: A Handbook for Teachers of Reading. (Orig.). 1981. pap. 8.95. Tchrs Coll.

Rosner, Jerome. Basic Decoding Skillsbook. (gr. k-3). 1981. 10.80 (ISBN 0-8027-9128-X). Walker & Co.

Rudman, Jack. Diagnosis & Remediation of Reading Problems. (College Proficiency Examination Ser: CLEP-38). (Cloth bdg. avail. on request). pap. 9.95 (ISBN 0-8373-5438-2). Natl Learning.

Schubert, Delwyn G. & Torgerson, Theodore L. Improving the Reading Program. 5th ed. 1981. pap. text ed. 8.95x (ISBN 0-697-06186-8). Wm C Brown.

Vacca, Richard T. Content Area Reading. 1981. text ed. 14.95 (ISBN 0-316-89488-5). Little.

Waller, T. G. & Mackinnon, G. E., eds. Reading Research: Advances in Theory & Practice, Vol. 2. (Serial Publication). 1981. price not set (ISBN 0-12-572302-4). Acad Pr.

Woods, Mary L. & Moe, Alden J. Analytic Reading Inventory. 2nd ed. (Illus.). 160p. 1981. spiral bdg. 7.95 (ISBN 0-675-08059-2). Merrill.

READING–ABILITY TESTING

Doherty, Cecelia & Ilyin, Donna. Technical Manual for ELSA: English Language Skills Assessment in a Reading Context. (ELSA Tests Ser.). 1981. pap. text ed. 3.95 (ISBN 0-686-69474-0). Newbury Hse.

Garvin, Harry R., ed. Theories of Reading, Looking, & Listening. LC 80-20475. (Bucknell Review Ser.). 192p. 1981. 12.00 (ISBN 0-8387-5007-9). Bucknell U Pr.

READING–EXAMINATIONS, QUESTIONS, ETC.

Lipner, Barbara E. & Fredericks, Robert F. How to Prepare for the Regents Competency Exam in Reading. 340p. (gr. 9-12). 1981. pap. text ed. 6.95 (ISBN 0-8120-2287-4). Barron.

READING–PHYSIOLOGICAL ASPECTS

Pirozzolo, Francis J. & Wittrock, Merlin C. Neuropsychological & Cognitive Processes in Reading. (Perspectives in Neurolinguistics & Psycholinguistics Ser.). 1981. price not set (ISBN 0-12-557360-X). Acad Pr.

READING–REMEDIAL TEACHING

see also Developmental Reading; Rapid Reading

Chicoral Index to Reading & Learning Disabilities: Books, 1978 Annual, Vol. 14A. 400p. 1980. 85.00 (ISBN 0-934598-09-6). Am Lib Pub Co.

Chicorel Abstracts to Reading & Learning Disabilities: Periodicals, 1978 Annual, Vol. 19. 400p. 1979. 85.00 (ISBN 0-934598-16-9). Am Lib Pub Co.

Chicorel Abstracts to Reading & Learning Disabilities: Periodicals, 1979 Annual, Vol. 19. 400p. 1980. 85.00 (ISBN 0-934598-10-X). Am Lib Pub Co.

McInnis, Philip. Decoding Keys for Reading Success. (gr. k-9). 1981. 298.00 (ISBN 0-8027-9129-8); Primary Level. 98.00 (ISBN 0-8027-9130-1); Intermediate Level. 96.00 (ISBN 0-8027-9131-X); Advanced Level. 108.00 (ISBN 0-8027-9132-8); 4.50 (ISBN 0-8027-9133-6). Walker & Co.

Maxwell. Reading Progress from Eight to Fifteen. 1977. pap. text ed. 18.75x (ISBN 0-85633-120-1, NFER). Humanities.

Milligan, Jerry L. Reading Difficulties: Their Analysis & Treatment. 1981. pap. 7.50 (ISBN 0-87562-069-8). Spec Child.

Wilson, Robert M. Diagnostic & Remedial Reading for Classroom & Clinic. 4th ed. (Illus.). 448p. 1981. text ed. 17.95 (ISBN 0-675-08048-7); instr's. manual 3.95 (ISBN 0-686-69489-9). Merrill.

Zintz, Miles V. Corrective Reading. 4th ed. 470p. 1981. text ed. write for info. (ISBN 0-697-06187-6). Wm C Brown.

READING–STUDY AND TEACHING

see Reading; Reading (Elementary); Reading (Secondary Education)

READING (ELEMENTARY)

see also Initial Teaching Alphabet; Reading–Remedial Teaching

Conaway, Judith. Reading Workbook Four (Cowardly Lion's Book) (Funny Face Activity Bks.). (Illus.). 48p. (ps-1). 1981. pap. 1.95 saddle-stitched (ISBN 0-394-84695-8). Random.

--Reading Workbook Three (Rascal Raccoon's Book) (Funny Face Activity Bks.). (Illus.). 48p. (ps-1). 1981. pap. 1.95 saddle stitched (ISBN 0-394-84440-8). Random.

Dacey, John. Where the World Is, Teaching Basic Skills Outdoors. (Illus.). 192p. (Orig.). 1981. pap. 10.95 (ISBN 0-8302-9605-0). Goodyear.

Diehl, Kathryn & Hodenfield, G. K. Johnny Still Can't Read...but You Can Teach Him at Home. 5th ed. (Illus.). 75p. 1979. pap. 2.50 (ISBN 0-9603552-0-0). K Diehl.

Doman, Glenn. How to Teach Your Baby to Read. rev. ed. (The Gentle Revolution Ser.). 166p. 1979. Repr. of 1964 ed. 9.50 (ISBN 0-936676-01-9). Better Baby.

Flesch, Rudolf. Why Johnny Still Can't Read: A New Look at the Scandal of Our Schools. LC 80-8686. 192p. 1981. 10.95 (ISBN 0-06-014842-X, HarpT). Har-Row.

Foreman, Dale I. & Allen, Sally. Reading Skills for Social Studies: Understanding Concepts, Level D. (Skillbooster Ser.). 64p. (gr. 4). 1980. wkbk. 2.80 (ISBN 0-87895-452-X). Modern Curr.

Gracenin, Carolyn T. Thoughts, Troubles & Things About Reading from the Cradle Through Grade Three. LC 80-65611. 180p. 1981. perfect bdg. 14.95 (ISBN 0-86548-038-9). Century Twenty One.

Hillert, Margaret. The Ball Book. (Just Beginning-to-Read Ser.). (Illus.). 32p. (gr. 1-6). 1981. PLB 4.39 (ISBN 0-695-41553-0); pap. 1.50 (ISBN 0-695-31553-6). Follett.

Isakson, Marne & Bradley, Lonnie. Reading with Race Cars. (gr. k-3). 1981. 26.80 (ISBN 0-8027-9079-8). Walker & Co.

Mason, George E. A Primer on Teaching Reading: Basic Concepts & Skills of the Early Elementary Years. LC 80-52458. 234p. 1981. pap. text ed. 7.50 (ISBN 0-87581-262-7). Peacock Pubs.

The Master Blender: Sound-Symbol Skillsbook. (Part of McInnis-Hammondsport Plan Ser.). (gr. k-6). 1981. 16.50 (ISBN 0-8027-9123-9). Walker & Co.

Shangold, Helen. Cloze Stories for Reading Success. (gr. k-3). 1981. 13.50 (ISBN 0-8027-9124-7). Walker & Co.

--Crosswords for Reading Success. (gr. k-3). 1981. 13.60 (ISBN 0-8027-9125-5). Walker & Co.

Williams, Helen E. Independent Reading, K-Three. LC 80-20423. 1980. pap. 17.25 (ISBN 0-87272-089-6). Brodart.

Zinggeler, Jeff, et al, illus. Read & Learn with Beth, the Traveler. (Read & Learn Ser.). (Illus.). 88p. (gr. 3-5). 1979. pap. 2.95 (ISBN 0-675-01056-X). Merrill.

READING (ELEMENTARY)-PHONETIC METHOD

Hailman, Arthur W. Phonics in Proper Perspective. 4th ed. (Illus.). 128p. 1981. pap. text ed. 6.50 (ISBN 0-675-08065-7). Merrill.

Holmes, Paul C. Phonics Guidelines: An Introduction. 320p. 1980. pap. text ed. 12.95 (ISBN 0-8403-2225-9). Kendall-Hunt.

Hull, Marion. Phonics for the Teacher of Reading. 3rd ed. (Illus.). 144p. 1981. pap. text ed. 5.95 (ISBN 0-675-08074-6). Merrill.

Kramer. Phonics Crossword Puzzles Series. Incl. Early Phonics Crossword Puzzle Book. (gr. k). 1974. pap. text ed. 1.60 (ISBN 0-8009-0438-9); tchr's. ed. 3.00 (ISBN 0-8009-0450-8); spirit masters (ISBN 0-8009-0440-0); Bk. A. (gr. 1-2). 1971. pap. text ed. (ISBN 0-8009-0441-9); tchr's. ed. (ISBN 0-8009-0443-5); spirit masters (ISBN 0-8009-0442-7); Bk. B. (gr. 3-4). 1970. pap. text ed. (ISBN 0-8009-0445-1); tchr's. ed. (ISBN 0-8009-0447-8); spirit masters (ISBN 0-8009-0444-3); Bk. C. (gr. 5-6). 1971. pap. text ed. (ISBN 0-8009-0449-4); tchr's. ed. (ISBN 0-8009-0451-6); spirit masters (ISBN 0-8009-0448-6). (gr. k-6). Bks. A-C. pap. text ed. 1.76 ea.; tchr's. eds. Bks. A-C 3.32 ea.; spirit masters Early Phonics-Bk. C 6.88 ea. McCormick-Mathers.

READING (HIGHER EDUCATION)

see also College Readers

Yehl, Joan K. & Bandlow, Richard F. P. O. W. E. R. The Reading - Writing Connection. (Illus.). 320p. 1981. pap. text ed. 8.95 (ISBN 0-675-08064-9); instr's. manual 3.95 (ISBN 0-686-69497-X). Merrill.

Yunker, Mary J. Guinness World Records Comprehension Module Program II. LC 78-730959. (gr. 4-8). 1978. pap. text ed. 175.00 (ISBN 0-89290-110-1, CM-72). Soc for Visual.

READING (SECONDARY EDUCATION)

Johns, Jerry L. A Secondary Reading Inventory. 100p. (gr. 7 up). 1981. write for info. wire coil (ISBN 0-697-06058-6). Wm C Brown.

READING, CHOICE OF

see Bibliography-Best Books; Books and Reading

READING, DEVELOPMENTAL

see Developmental Reading

READING COMPREHENSION

Cushenbery, Donald C. & Meyer, Ronald E. Reading Comprehension Mastery Kits, 6 bks. Incl. Critiical Reading (ISBN 0-87628-701-1); Drawing Conclusions (ISBN 0-87628-698-8); Following Directions (ISBN 0-87628-699-6); Locating Hidden Meaning (ISBN 0-87628-700-3); Recognizing Main Ideas (ISBN 0-87628-697-X); Understanding Details (ISBN 0-87628-696-1). 1980. pap. 6.95x ea. Ctr Appl Res.

Pettit, Neila T. & Cockriel, Irwin W. Petriel Reading Comprehension Test. 1973. 1.00 (ISBN 0-87543-097-X); 0.75 (ISBN 0-87543-091-0). Lucas.

READING DISABILITY

see also Dyslexia

Ekwall, Eldon E. Locating & Correcting Reading Difficulties. 3rd ed. (Illus.). 192p. 1981. pap. text ed. 6.95 (ISBN 0-675-08062-2). Merrill.

READING INTERESTS

see Books and Reading

READING INTERESTS OF CHILDREN

see Books and Reading for Children

READING RETARDATION

see Reading Disability

REAGAN, RONALD

Van Der Linden, Frank. Ronald Reagan. 288p. 1981. 10.95 (ISBN 0-686-69236-5). Morrow.

REAGENTS, CHEMICAL

see Chemical Tests and Reagents

REAL ESTATE

see Real Property

REAL ESTATE BUSINESS

see also Home Ownership; House Buying; House Selling; Industrial Districts; Real Estate Investment

Akerson, Charles B. Capitalization Theory & Techniques Study Guide. 1980. pap. 10.00 (ISBN 0-911780-48-3). Am Inst Real Estate Appraisers.

Cardiff, Gray E. & English, John W. Coming Real Estate Crash. 1980. pap. 2.50 (ISBN 0-446-91575-0). Warner Bks.

Conroy, Kathleen. Valuing the Timeshare Property. 97p. 1981. 15.00 (ISBN 0-911780-50-5). Am Inst Real Estate Appraisers.

Crawford, H. Warren & Rodgers, John F. Maryland Supplement for Modern Real Estate Practice. 3rd ed. 140p. (Orig.). 1981. pap. 7.95 (ISBN 0-88462-267-3). Real Estate Ed Co.

Davey, H. & Mercer, H. Real Estate Principles in California. 4th ed. 1981. 19.95. P-H.

Distress Property: How to Buy It in California. 323p. 1981. 55.00 (ISBN 0-934668-07-8). B Greene.

Driscoll, Donald C. & Davey, Homer C. The Practice of Real Estate in California. (Illus.). 304p. 1981. 18.95 (ISBN 0-13-693606-7). P-H.

Emerson, William M. Tennessee Supplement for Modern Real Estate Practice. 130p. (Orig.). 1981. pap. 7.95 (ISBN 0-88462-338-6). Real Estate Ed Co.

Epley, Donald R. & Rabianski, Joseph. Principles of Real Estate Decisions. LC 80-21354. 1981. text ed. 18.95 (ISBN 0-201-03188-4). A-W.

Esau, Theodore. Complete Real Estate Listings Handbook. 265p. 18.95 (ISBN 0-13-162404-0, Busn). P-H.

Fessler, George R. & Westcott, Ray D. The Advanced Real Estate Primer. 20th ed. 336p. pap. 7.95 (ISBN 0-935810-04-8). Primer Pubs.

--The Real Estate Primer. 35th ed. 298p. pap. 8.95 (ISBN 0-935810-00-5). Primer Pubs.

Fisher, Fred. Brokers Beware: Selling Real Estate Within the Law. 220p. 1981. text ed. 15.95 (ISBN 0-8359-0569-1). Reston.

Floyd, Charles F. Real Estate Principles. 592p. 1981. text ed. 19.95 (ISBN 0-394-32263-0). Random.

Gaddy, Wade & Hart, Robert. Real Estate Fundamentals. 250p. (Orig.). 1981. pap. 13.95 (ISBN 0-88462-425-0). Real Estate Ed Co.

Golden, Edward J. The Art & Science of Real Estate Investment Analysis. 300p. 1980. pap. text ed. 15.00 (ISBN 0-9604532-0-2). Adv Prof Seminars.

Guidelines for Appraisal Office Policies & Procedures. 69p. (Orig.). 1981. pap. 8.00 (ISBN 0-911780-49-1). Am Inst Real Estate Appraisers.

Hicks, Tyler G. How to Borrow Your Way to Real Estate Riches Using Government Money. 2nd ed. 150p. 1981. pap. 15.00 (ISBN 0-914306-52-9). Intl Wealth.

Jackson, F. Scott & Lippman, William J., eds. Condominium & Cooperative Conversions 1980: Course Handbook. LC 80-81527. (Nineteen Seventy-Nine to Nineteen Eighty Real Estate Law & Practice Course Handbook Ser.). 549p. 1981. pap. 25.00 (ISBN 0-686-69166-0, N4-4352). PLI.

Johnsich, John R. Real Estate Mathematics Study Manual & Reference Book. rev. ed. (Illus.). 131p. 1980. pap. 9.95 (ISBN 0-914256-13-0). Real Estate Pub.

Lindeman, Bruce. Real Estate Brokerage. 450p. 1981. text ed. 16.95 (ISBN 0-8359-6517-1); instr's. manual free (ISBN 0-8359-6518-X). Reston.

Lynch, Louise. ABC's of Real Estate Exchanging. 1981. text ed. 12.95 (ISBN 0-8359-0015-0); instrs'. manual avail. (ISBN 0-8359-0016-9). Reston.

Martin, Joseph H. & Jackson, William. New Jersey Supplement for Modern Real Estate Practice. 3rd ed. 130p. (Orig.). 1981. pap. 7.95 (ISBN 0-88462-281-9). Real Estate Ed Co.

Mason, Jess. How to Succeed in Real Estate...in Ten Minutes...Twice a Day! (Illus.). 160p. 1981. 12.50 (ISBN 0-682-49728-2). Exposition.

Miller, John M. Minnesota Legal Forms-Commercial Real Estate. Mason Publishing Staff, ed. 150p. 1981. ring binder 15.00 (ISBN 0-917126-89-0). Mason Pub.

Murrison, Wayne G. Buy or Sell Your Own Home, Lot, or Farm. Orig. Title: Homeowner Sell Your House Yourself. (Illus.). 92p. 1980. pap. text ed. 20.00. Murrison Co.

Myler, Charles E., Jr. Arizona Supplement to Modern Real Estate Practice. 3rd ed. 200p. (Orig.). 1980. pap. 7.95 (ISBN 0-88462-295-9). Real Estate Ed Co.

Nessen, Robert L. The Real Estate Book: A Complete Guide to Acquiring, Financing, & Investing in a Home or Commercial Property. 272p. 1981. 12.95 (ISBN 0-686-69140-7). Little.

O'Donnell. Practice of Real Estate. 1978. 17.95 (ISBN 0-7216-6913-1). Dryden Pr.

Parks, Gerald. Real Estate Profit Power: Managing Your Own Real Estate Office. 1981. text ed. 16.95 (ISBN 0-8359-6595-3); instr's manual free (ISBN 0-8359-6596-1). Reston.

Readings in Highest & Best Use. 224p. (Orig.). 1981. pap. 10.50 (ISBN 0-911780-51-3). Am Inst Real Estate Appraisers.

Readings in the Appraisal of Special Purpose Properties. 280p. 1981. pap. 10.50 (ISBN 0-911780-52-1). Am Inst Real Estate Appraisers.

Real Estate Education Co. & Grubb & Ellis Commercial Brokerage Co. Successful Leasing & Selling of Retail Property. 256p. 1980. binder 49.95 (ISBN 0-695-81503-2). Follett.

Real Estate Education Company Staff & Grubb & Ellis Company. Successful Leasing & Selling of Retail Property. 250p. 1980. 49.95 (ISBN 0-88462-315-7). Real Estate Ed Co.

Reilly, John W. The Language of Real Estate. 585p. (Orig.). 1977. pap. 19.95 (ISBN 0-88462-354-8). Real Estate Ed Co.

Rejnis, Ruth. How to Buy Real Estate Without Getting Burned. LC 81-80094. 288p. (Orig.). 1981. pap. 3.50 (ISBN 0-87216-851-4). Playboy Pbks.

Silverman, Ruth D. Idaho Supplement for Modern Real Estate Practice. 3rd ed. 140p. 1981. pap. 7.95 (ISBN 0-88462-291-6). Real Estate Ed Co.

--North Carolina Supplement for Modern Real Estate Practice. Hetrick, Patrick, ed. 130p. (Orig.). 1981. pap. 7.95 (ISBN 0-88462-301-7). Real Estate Ed Co.

Tosh & Ordway. Real Estate Math Made Easy. 1981. text ed. 15.95 (ISBN 0-8359-6556-2); instr's. manual free (ISBN 0-8359-6557-0). Reston.

VanCaspel, Venita. The Real Rewards of Real Estate. 1980. pap. 1.50 (ISBN 0-8359-6605-4). Reston.

REAL ESTATE BUSINESS-EXAMINATIONS, QUESTIONS, ETC.

Beals, Richard. National Real Estate Examination Study Guide. 1980. pap. text ed. 10.00 (ISBN 0-89764-002-0). Lincoln's Leadership.

Ellis, J. Introduction to the Realestate Profession: Guide to Real Estatelicense Examination. 1981. pap. 8.24 (ISBN 0-13-494005-9). P-H.

REAL ESTATE BUSINESS-LAW AND LEGISLATION

Augustine, Don & Fass, Peter M. Private Real Estate Limited Partnerships 1980: A Course Handbook. LC 80-81320. (Real Estate Law & Practice Course Handbook Ser.). 950p. 1980. pap. text ed. 25.00 (ISBN 0-686-68828-7, N4-4353). PLI.

Jacobus, Charles. Texas Real Estate Law. 2nd ed. 1981. 19.95 (ISBN 0-8359-7571-1); text ed. 15.95 (ISBN 0-686-68878-3); instr's. manual free (ISBN 0-8359-7572-X). Reston.

Roer, Kathleen. Minnesota Legal Forms-Real Estate. Mason Publishing Company Staff, ed. (Minnesota Legal Forms 1981 Ser.). 150p. 1981. ring binder 15.00 (ISBN 0-917126-86-6). Mason Pub.

University of Southern Main - Center for Real Estate Education. An Introduction to Real Estate Law. 250p. (Orig.). 1981. pap. 14.95 (ISBN 0-88462-428-5). Real Estate Ed Co.

Zalaznick, Charles. Real Estate Development & Construction Financing 1980: Course Handbook. LC 80-80907. (Real Estate Law & Practice Course Handgook Ser.). 716p. 1980. pap. text ed. 25.00 (ISBN 0-686-68829-5, N4-4349). PLI.

REAL ESTATE BUSINESS-VOCATIONAL GUIDANCE

Crispen, Margaret. How Any Woman Can Get Rich Fast in Real Estate. 1980. pap. 4.95. Warner Bks.

REAL ESTATE INVESTMENT

see also Real Estate Business

Baker, Ruth. Getting Rich in Real Estate Partnerships. (Orig.). 1981. 11.95 (ISBN 0-446-51222-2). Warner Bks.

Bullock, Paul. How to Profit from Condominium Conversions. 1981. 17.95 (ISBN 0-913864-64-1). Enterprise Del.

Friedman, Jack & Ordway, Nicholas. Income Property Appraisal & Analysis. 300p. 1981. text ed. 17.95 (ISBN 0-8359-3057-2); instr's. manual free (ISBN 0-8359-3058-0). Reston.

Glubetich, Dave. Double Your Money in Real Estate Every Two Years. Moretz, Judy, ed. (Illus.). 232p. 1980. 12.95 (ISBN 0-9601530-4-7). Impact Pub.

Hicks, Tyler G. Fast Financing of Your Real Estate Fortune Success Kit. 2nd ed. 523p. 1981. pap. 99.50 (ISBN 0-914306-46-4). Intl Wealth.

--Real Estate Riches Success Kit. 2nd ed. 466p. 1981. pap. 99.50 (ISBN 0-914306-43-X). Intl Wealth.

Nielsen, Sally E., ed. Investing in Old Buildings. (Illus.). 1980. pap. 3.95. Greater Portland.

Ramsey, Dan. How to Make One Hundred Thousand Dollars a Year Selling Residential Real Estate. 297p. 1980. 14.95 (ISBN 0-13-423582-7, Busn). P-H.

Sirmans, C. F. & Jaffe, Austin J. Complete Real Estate Investment Handbook. (Illus.). 272p. 1981. 17.95 (ISBN 0-13-162321-4, Spectrum); pap. 8.95 (ISBN 0-13-162313-3). P-H.

Snyder, Earl. Before You Invest: Questions & Answers on Real Estate. 1981. text ed. 12.95 (ISBN 0-8359-0453-9). Reston.

Temple, Douglas M. Real Estate Investment for the Eighties: How to Build Financial Security in the Face of Inflation. (Illus.). 1981. 12.95 (ISBN 0-8092-7024-2). Contemp Bks.

REAL ESTATE TAX

see Real Property Tax

REAL PROPERTY

Here are entered treatises on real property in the legal sense, i.e. the law of immovable property, and works on real estate in general, or real estate conditions in any particular place. Works on the buying, selling, and management of real estate are entered under the heading Real Estate Business. For land laws use Land Tenure-(country subdivision) e.g. Land Tenure-Sweden.

see also Condominium (Housing); Eminent Domain; Estates (Law); Land Tenure; Landlord and Tenant; Leases; Mining Law; Real Estate Business-Law and Legislation; Rent

Davenport, Humphrey. An Abridgement of the Lord Coke's Commentary on Littleton. Berkowitz, David S. & Thorne, Samuel E., eds. LC 77-89239. (Classics of English Legal History in the Modern Era Ser.: Vol. 74). 484p. 1979. lib. bdg. 40.00 (ISBN 0-8240-3173-3). Garland Pub.

Davidson, Sara. Real Property. 1981. pap. 2.95 (ISBN 0-671-41269-8). PB.

Gobble, Bill & Harwood, Bruce. North Carolina Real Estate. 1981. text ed. 16.95 (ISBN 0-8359-4951-6). Reston.

Lagoulle, Henri. Essai Sur la Conception Juridique De la Propriete Fonciere Dans le Tres Anciendroit Normand: Premiere Partie, la Conception Feodale. LC 80-2020. 1981. Repr. of 1902 ed. 47.50 (ISBN 0-404-18574-6). AMS Pr.

Littlton, Thomas. Lyttleton: His Treatise of Tenures. Berkowitz, David S. & Thorne, Samuel E., eds. LC 77-89237. (Classics of English Legal History in the Modern Era Ser.: Vol. 73). 727p. 1979. lib. bdg. 40.00 (ISBN 0-8240-3172-5). Garland Pub.

New York Assn. of Realtors & Harwood, Bruce. New York Real Estate. 1981. text ed. 16.95 (ISBN 0-8359-4894-3). Reston.

REAL PROPERTY-TAXATION

see Real Property Tax

REAL PROPERTY-VALUATION

Here are entered works on the general theory and methodology of real property valuation. Works on the valuation of real property for tax purposes are entered under the heading Real Property Tax.

Babcock, Henry. Appraisal Principles & Procedures. 289p. 1980. pap. text ed. 20.00 (ISBN 0-937828-19-X). Am Soc Appraisers.

Baum, Andrew & Mackmin, David. The Income Approach to Property Valuation. rev. ed. 216p. (Orig.). 1981. pap. 14.95 (ISBN 0-7100-0833-3). Routledge & Kegan.

Cook, Charles C., intro. by. Land Valuation Methods: Urban Land. (Lincoln Institute Monograph: No. 80-1). (Illus.). 200p. 1980. pap. text ed. 10.00. Lincoln Inst Land.

Godfrey, Robert S. Appraisal Manual, 1981. 2nd ed. 320p. 1981. pap. 33.00 (ISBN 0-911950-35-4). Means.

Wolf, Peter. Land: Power & Wealth. (Illus.). 1981. 17.95 (ISBN 0-394-50437-2). Pantheon.

REAL PROPERTY-GREAT BRITAIN

Parker, R. A. The Rents of Council Houses. 90p. 1967. pap. text ed. 5.00x (Pub. by Bedford England). Renouf.

REAL PROPERTY TAX

see also Land Value Taxation; Mines and Mineral Resources-Taxation

Lyons, Paul. Real Estate Investor's Tax & Profit Planner. 1981. pap. 12.95 (ISBN 0-8359-6529-5). Reston.

Proposition Thirteen: A First Anniversary Assessment. (Lincoln Institute Monograph: No. 880-5). (Illus.). 1980. pap. text ed. 5.00. Lincoln Inst Land.

REAL-TIME DATA PROCESSING

see also on-Line Data Processing

IFAC - IFIP Workshop, Leibnitz, Austria, April 1980. Real Time Programming, 1980: Proceedings. Haase, V. H., ed. LC 80-49720. (IFAC Proceedings Ser.). 150p. 1980. 40.00 (ISBN 0-08-027305-X). Pergamon.

REALISM

see also Idealism; Materialism; Positivism; Pragmatism

Lukacs, Georg. Essays on Realism. 1980. text ed. 26.00x (ISBN 0-391-02179-6). Humanities.

McCann, Dennis P. Christian Realism & Liberation Theology: Practical Theologies in Conflict. LC 80-23163. 256p. (Orig.). 1981. pap. 9.95 (ISBN 0-88344-086-5). Orbis Bks.

REALISM IN ART

see also Figurative Art; Romanticism in Art

Hedberg, Gregory. German Realism of the Twenties. (Illus.). 1980. 15.00. Minneapolis Inst Arts.

Reff, Theodore, ed. Exhibitions of Later Realist Art. (Modern Art in Paris 1855 to 1900 Ser.). 320p. 1981. lib. bdg. 44.00 (ISBN 0-8240-4740-0). Garland Pub.

--Exhibitions of Realist Art, Bk. I. (Modern Art in Paris 1855 to 1900 Ser.). 518p. 1981. lib. bdg. 44.00 (ISBN 0-8240-4738-9). Garland Pub.

--Exhibitions of Realist Art, Bk. II. (Modern Art in Paris 1855 to 1900 Ser.). 345p. 1981. lib. bdg. 44.00 (ISBN 0-8240-4739-7). Garland Pub.

REALISM IN LITERATURE

see also Romanticism

Levine, George. The Realistic Imagination: English Fiction from Frankenstein to Lady Chatterley. LC 80-17444. 1981. lib. bdg. 25.00x (ISBN 0-226-47550-6). U of Chicago Pr.

REALITY

see also Knowledge, Theory Of; Pluralism; Pragmatism; Relativity

Pearce, Joseph C. The Bond of Power. 1981. 10.95 (ISBN 0-525-06950-X). Dutton.

Vogt, Douglas & Sultan, Gary. Reality Revealed: The Theory of Multidimensional Reality. LC 77-88915. 460p. 1979. 12.95 (ISBN 0-930808-01-0). Ross-Erikson.

REALTY

see Real Property

REASON

see also Faith and Reason; Reasoning; Wisdom

Chakeres, John A. Traces: An Investigation in Reason. LC 76-47816. (Illus., Orig.). 1977. pap. 7.95 (ISBN 0-917924-00-2). Nuance Pr.

Feinberg, Joel. Reason & Responsibility. 5th ed. 640p. 1980. text ed. 17.95x (ISBN 0-534-00924-7). Wadsworth Pub.

Lydgate, John. Reason & Sensuality: Studies & Notes, Vol. 2. Sieper, Ernst, ed. (Early English Text Society Ser.). 1903. 9.95x (ISBN 0-19-722534-9). Oxford U Pr.

REASON AND FAITH
see Faith and Reason

REASONING
see also Induction (Logic); Logic

Finocchiaro, Maurice A. Galileo & the Art of Reasoning: Rhetorical Foundations of Logic & Scientific Method. (Philosophy of Science Studies: No. 61). 463p. 1980. lib. bdg. 42.00 (ISBN 90-277-1094-5, Pub. by D. Reidel); pap. 21.00 (ISBN 90-277-1095-3). Kluwer Boston.

Thomas, Stephen. Practical Reasoning in Natural Language. (Illus.). 352p. 1981. pap. text ed. 9.95 (ISBN 0-13-692137-X). P-H.

REASONING (PSYCHOLOGY)
see also Intellect

Barker, Evelyn M. Everyday Reasoning. (Illus.). 304p. 1981. pap. text ed. 8.95 (ISBN 0-13-293407-8). P-H.

REBELLIONS
see Civil War; Revolutions

REBELS (SOCIAL PSYCHOLOGY)
see Alienation (Social Psychology); Conformity; Dissenters

RECLAMATION OF LAND
see also Irrigation

Hart, John & Orman, Larry. Endangered Harvest: The Future of Bay Area Farmland. (Orig.). 1980. pap. 3.00 (ISBN 0-9605262-0-X). PFOS.

RECONCILIATION

Castro, Carol C. Welcoming God's Forgiveness. 30p. (Orig.). 1978. pap. 1.05 adult resource bk.; pap. 10.25 (ISBN 0-697-01737-0). Wm C Brown.

RECONSTRUCTION
see also Freedmen; Ku Klux Klan

Billings, Dwight B., Jr. Planters & the Making of a "New South". Class, Politics, & Development in North Carolina, 1865-1900. LC 78-25952. xiii, 284p. 1979. 15.00x (ISBN 0-8078-1315-X). U of NC Pr.

Gambill, Edward L. Conservative Ordeal: Northern Democrats & Reconstruction, 1865 to 1868. 208p. 1981. text ed. 13.50 (ISBN 0-8138-1385-9). Iowa St U Pr.

Morris, Robert C. Reading, 'Writing, & Reconstruction: The Education of Freedmen in the South, 1861-1870. LC 80-25370. (Illus.). 1981. lib. bdg. price not set (ISBN 0-226-53928-8). U of Chicago Pr.

RECORD PLAYERS
see Phonograph

RECORDER MUSIC

Duetti Facili per Flauti in Do: Twenty Nine Duets for Recorder & Flute. pap. 1.95 (ISBN 0-916786-45-5). St George Bk Serv.

RECORDS, PHONOGRAPH
see Phonorecords

RECOVERY OF NATURAL RESOURCES
see Recycling (Waste, etc.)

RECREATION
see also Amusements; Community Organizations; Educational Games; Hobbies; Leisure; Outdoor Recreation

Eathorne, Richard H. The Analysis of Outdoor Recreation Demand: A Review & Annotated Bibliography of the Current State-of-the-Art. (Public Administration Ser.: Bibliography P-563). 93p. 1980. pap. 10.00. Vance Biblios.

Napier, Tel L. Outdoor Recreation Planning, Perspectives & Research. 288p. 1981. pap. text ed. 12.95 (ISBN 0-8403-2309-3). Kendall-Hunt.

Willcox, Isobel. Acrobats & Ping-Pong: Young China's Games, Sports, & Amusements. LC 80-22176. (Illus.). 160p. (gr. 4 up). 1981. PLB 8.95 (ISBN 0-396-07917-2). Dodd.

RECREATION-ADMINISTRATION
see also Recreation Leadership

Shivers, Jay S. & Halper, Joseph W. The Crisis in Urban Recreational Services. LC 79-17414. 384p. 1981. 27.50 (ISBN 0-8386-3006-5, 3006). Fairleigh Dickinson.

RECREATION-STUDY AND TEACHING
see Recreation Leadership

RECREATION ADMINISTRATION
see Recreation-Administration

RECREATION AS A PROFESSION
see Recreation Leadership

RECREATION CENTERS

The Activities of Some Centres Engaged in Research & Information Programmes in the Field of Youth. 212p. 1980. pap. 15.00 (UN80-4-2, UN). Unipub.

RECREATION LEADERSHIP
see also Recreation-Administration

Sherrill, Claudine. Adapted Physical Education & Recreation: A Multidisciplinary Approach. 2nd ed. 1981. 15.95x (ISBN 0-697-07176-6). Wm C Brown.

RECREATION MANAGEMENT
see Recreation-Administration

RECREATIONAL FISHING
see Fishing

RECREATIONAL MOTOR VEHICLES
see Motor Vehicles-Recreational Use

RECREATIONS
see Amusements; Games; Hobbies; Play; Sports

RECREATIONS, MATHEMATICAL
see Mathematical Recreations

RECREATIONS, SCIENTIFIC
see Scientific Recreations

RECRUITING OF EMPLOYEES
see also Employment Interviewing
also names of professions with or without subdivision Recruiting

Aboud, Grace. Hiring & Training the Disadvantaged for Public Employment. (Key Issues Ser.: No. 11). 1973. pap. 2.00 (ISBN 0-87546-202-2). NY Sch Indus Rel.

Coghill, Mary A. Lie Detector in Employment. (Key Issues Ser.: No. 2). 1973. pap. 2.00 (ISBN 0-87546-208-1). NY Sch Indus Rel.

Rosen, Doris B. Employment Testing & Minority Groups. (Key Issues Ser.: No. 6). 1970. pap. 2.00 (ISBN 0-87546-239-1). NY Sch Indus Rel.

Stidger, Ruth W. The Compentence Game: How to Find, Use & Keep Competent Employees. LC 80-17657. (Illus.). 160p. 1980. 12.95 (ISBN 0-444-00453-X, Thomond Pr). Elsevier.

RECTIFICATION OF SPIRITS
see Distillation

RECTORS
see Clergy

RECURSIVE FUNCTIONS
see also Machine Theory

Normann, D. Recursion on the Countable Functionals. (Lecture Notes in Mathematics: Vol. 811). 191p. 1980. pap. 11.80 (ISBN 0-387-10019-9). Springer-Verlag.

RECURSIVE PROGRAMMING

Lewis, Harry R. & Papadimitriou, Christos H. Elements of the Theory of Computation. (Software Ser.). (Illus.). 496p. 1981. text ed. 22.50 (ISBN 0-13-273417-6). P-H.

RECYCLING (WASTE, ETC.)
Here are entered works on the processing of waste paper, cans, bottles, etc. Works on the recycling or reuse of specific materials are entered under Wood Waste, Agricultural wastes, etc. Works on reclaiming and reusing equipment or parts are entered under Salvage (Waste, etc.).
see also Energy Conservation

Henstock, M. & Bever, M. B., eds. New & Better Uses of Secondary Resources: Proceedings of the Second Recycling World Congress, Philippine International Conventional Center, Manila, March 1979. 278p. 1980. pap. 40.00 (ISBN 0-08-026245-7). Pergamon.

Holmes, John R. Refuse Recycling & Recovery: A Review of the State of the Art. 168p. 1981. 38.00 (ISBN 0-471-27902-1, Pub. by Wiley-Interscience); pap. 14.00 (ISBN 0-471-27903-X). Wiley.

Kiang. Waste Energy Utilization Technology. 264p. 1981. 29.75 (ISBN 0-8247-1173-4). Dekker.

Mason, Billy, ed. Directory of Recycable Waste, Bk. 2. (Orig.). 1981. pap. 9.95 (ISBN 0-686-28908-0). Kelso.

Sittig, Marshall. Organic & Polymer Waste Reclaiming Encyclopedia. LC 80-26007. (Chem. Tech. Rev. 180 Ser.: Pollution Tech. Rev. 73). (Illus.). 512p. 1981. 54.00 (ISBN 0-8155-0832-8). Noyes.

Sittig, Marshall, ed. Metal & Inorganic Waste Reclaiming Encyclopedia. LC 80-21669. (Pollution Tech. Rev. 70; Chem. Tech. Rev. 175). (Illus.). 591p. (Orig.). 1981. 54.00 (ISBN 0-8155-0823-9). Noyes.

Tin Cans & Trash Recovery: Saving Energy Through Utilizing Municipal Ferrous Waste. 1980. pap. 2.00. Tech Info Proj.

RED BLOOD CORPUSCLES
see Erythrocytes

RED CROSS. U. S. AMERICAN NATIONAL RED CROSS

Gilbo, Patrick F. The American Red Cross--the First Century: A Pictorial History. LC 80-8204. (Illus.). 256p. 1981. 25.00 (ISBN 0-06-011461-4, HarpT). Har-Row.

RED FOX

Zimen, E., ed. The Red Fox: Symposium on Behavior & Ecology. (Biogeographica Ser.: Vol. 18). 286p. 1980. lib. bdg. 73.50 (ISBN 0-686-28665-0, Pub. by Dr. W. Junk). Kluwer Boston.

REDEMPTION
see also Salvation

Kilpatrick, T. B. The Redemption of Man. (Short Course Ser.). 163p. 1920. text ed. 2.95 (ISBN 0-567-08320-9). Attic Pr.

Teasley, D. O. The Double Cure, or Redemption Twofold. 160p. pap. 1.50 large print. Faith Pub Hse.

REDEVELOPMENT, URBAN
see City Planning

REDUCING
see also Low-Calorie Diet

Holt, Robert L. How Women Stay Slim. LC 80-92693. 1980. 12.95x (ISBN 0-930926-04-8); pap. 7.95x (ISBN 0-930926-05-6). Calif Health.

Jones, Lucile. Tony's Tummy. Van Dolson, Bobbie J., ed. 32p. 1981. pap. price not set (ISBN 0-8280-0039-5). Review & Herald.

Livingston, Carole. I'll Never Be Fat Again. 224p. 1981. pap. 2.50 (ISBN 0-345-28659-6). Ballantine.

Macleod, William M. & Macleod, Gael S. M. I. N. D Over Weight: "How to Stay Slim the Rest of Your Life". LC 80-21001. 1981. 7.95 (ISBN 0-13-583385-X). P-H.

Mellin, Laurel. Shapedown: Weight Management Program for Adolescents. LC 80-67385. (Illus.). 186p. (Orig.). (gr. 7-12). 1980. tchr's ed. 10.00 (ISBN 0-935902-02-3); wkbk. 10.00 (ISBN 0-935902-01-5). Balboa Pub.

Netzer, Corinne T. Brand Name Calorie Counter. (Orig.). 1981. pap. 2.75 (ISBN 0-440-10676-1). Dell.

Osman, Jack & Van Dolson, Bobbie J. Thin from Within. 160p. 1981. pap. write for info. (ISBN 0-8280-0027-1). Review & Herald.

Solomon, Neil. Stop Smoking, Lose Weight. 320p. 1981. 11.95 (ISBN 0-399-12600-7). Putnam.

REDUCING DIETS
see also Low-Calorie Diet

Adams, Rex. Doctor's Amazing Speed Reducing Diet. LC 79-11343. 1979. 10.95 (ISBN 0-13-216275-X, Parker). P-H.

Adams, Ruth & Murray, Frank. The New High Fiber Diet. 319p. (Orig.). 1977. pap. 2.25 (ISBN 0-915962-21-7). Larchmont Bks.

Anderson, James L. & Cohen, Martin. The West Point Fitness & Diet Book. 256p. 1981. pap. 2.95 (ISBN 0-380-54205-6, 54205). Avon.

Atkins, Robert. Dr. Atkins Diet Revolution. 336p. 1981. pap. 2.95 (ISBN 0-553-14736-6). Bantam.

Ceres. Herbs & Fruit for Dieting. LC 80-53452. (Everybodys Home Herbal Ser.). 64p. 1981. pap. 1.95 (ISBN 0-394-74837-9). Shambhala Pubns.

Claiborne, Craig. Craig Claiborne's Gourmet Diet. 1981. pap. 2.95 (ISBN 0-345-29579-X). Ballantine.

Consumer-Aid Group. Successful Dieter's Sure-Fire Dieting Tips. Grooms, Kathe, ed. (A Consumer-Aid Bk.). (Illus.). 130p. 1981. pap. 3.95 (ISBN 0-915658-34-8). Meadowbrook Pr.

Consumer Guide Editors. The Dieter's Complete Guide to Calories, Carbohydrates, Sodium, Fats & Cholesterol. 192p. (Orig.). 1981. pap. 5.95 (ISBN 0-449-90050-9, Columbine). Fawcett.

Downing, Frank & Bardoff, O. The Hollywood Emergency Diet. 192p. 1981. 9.95 (ISBN 0-8119-0419-9, Pegasus Rex). Fell.

Hayden, Naura. Hip, High Protein, Low-Cal Easy Does It Cookbook. 1981. pap. price not set (ISBN 0-671-42390-8). PB.

Heffron, Dan. The Million Dollar Diet Plan. (Illus.). 148p. (Orig.). 1980. pap. 10.00 (ISBN 0-9605104-1-9). Heffron Ent.

Jones, Jeanne & Kientzler, Kharma. Fitness First-a-Fourteen-Day Diet & Exercise Program. LC 80-11320. (Illus.). 154p. (Orig.). 1980. pap. 6.95 (ISBN 0-89286-162-2). One Hund One Prods.

Jordan, Henry A. & Berland, Theodore. The Doctor's Calories-Plus Diet: The New Food IQ Way to Weight Loss. 1981. 10.95 (ISBN 0-8092-5939-7). Contemp Bks.

Marshall, Edward. Dr. Marshall's Lifelong Weight Control Program. 132p. 1981. 7.95 (ISBN 0-395-29476-2). HM.

Mazel, Judy. The Beverly Hills Diet: Get As Slim As You Like for the Rest of Your Life. 192p. 1981. 9.95 (ISBN 0-02-582600-X). Macmillan.

Merzer, Meridee. Winning the Diet Wars. LC 79-2765. 1980. 9.95 (ISBN 0-15-196378-9). HarBraceJ.

Omura, Yoshiaki, et al. The Tofu-Miso High Efficiency Diet. 208p. 1981. 10.95 (ISBN 0-668-05178-7); pap. 6.95 (ISBN 0-668-05180-9). Arco.

Parriott, Sara. Calories Don't Count When... LC 79-84900. (Illus.). 96p. 1979. pap. 2.95 (ISBN 0-87477-105-6). J P Tarcher.

Pryor, Nancy. The Amazing Diet Secret of a Desperate Housewife. (Illus.). 180p. 1981. 9.95 (ISBN 0-8119-0420-2, Pegasus Rex). Fell.

Redbook Magazine. Redbook Wise Woman's Diet: All-Time Favorite Recipes. Pomeroy, Ruth, ed. (Illus.). 176p. 1980. 14.95 (ISBN 0-88421-161-4). Butterick Pub.

Siegel, Murray J. & Van Kueren, Dolores. Think Thin. LC 76-151435. 288p. 1981. pap. 9.95 (ISBN 0-8397-7993-3). Eriksson.

Tarnower, Herman & Baker, Samm S. The Complete Scarsdale Medical Diet. 240p. 1981. pap. 2.95 (ISBN 0-553-14446-4). Bantam.

TerHuen, Pat & Smith, Lynda. Being Fat (Has Nothing to Do with Food) A Handbook for the Yo-Yo-Dieter. LC 80-80247. (Illus.). 80p. 1981. pap. 3.95 (ISBN 0-89087-314-3). Celestial Arts.

Vaneven, Maxine T. How to Be Your Own Thin Self. 1981. pap. price not set (ISBN 0-916774-03-1). Tolvan Co.

Vincent, L. M. Competing with the Sylph: Dancers & the Pursuit of the Ideal Body Form. 143p. 1980. pap. 5.95 (ISBN 0-8362-2407-8). Andrews & McMeel.

Yudkin, John. Lose Weight, Feel Great. (Illus.). 219p. 1974. pap. 1.75 (ISBN 0-915962-02-0). Larchmont Bks.

REFERENCE BOOKS
see also Bibliography-Best Books; Encyclopedias and Dictionaries; Reference Services (Libraries)

Balachandran, S. & Balachandran, M., eds. Reference Sources Nineteen Eighty. 1981. 65.00 (ISBN 0-87650-127-7). Pierian.

Cheney, Frances N. & Williams, Wiley J. Fundamental Reference Sources. 2nd ed. 300p. 1980. 12.50 (ISBN 0-8389-0308-8). ALA.

Covey, Alma A. Reviewing Reference Books: An Evaluation of the Efectiveness of Selected Announcement, Review & Index Media in Their Coverage of Reference Books. LC 70-182831. 142p. 1972. lib. bdg. 10.00 (ISBN 0-8108-0456-5). Scarecrow.

Holte, Susan & Wynar, Bohdan S., eds. Best Reference Books, 1970-1980: Titles of Lasting Value Selected from American Reference Books Annual. 450p. 1981. lib. bdg. 30.00x (ISBN 0-87287-255-6). Libs Unl.

Magill, Frank N., ed. Magill Books Index. LC 80-53597. 800p. 1980. 35.00 (ISBN 0-89356-200-9). Salem Pr.

Parish, David W. State Government Reference Publications: An Annotated Bibliography. 2nd ed. 250p. 1981. lib. bdg. price not set (ISBN 0-87287-253-X). Libs Unl.

REFERENCE BOOKS-BIBLIOGRAPHY

Magel, Charles R. A Bibliography on Animal Rights & Related Matters. LC 80-5636. 622p. 1981. lib. bdg. 28.50 (ISBN 0-8191-1488-X). U Pr of Amer.

Wynar, Bohdan S., et al, eds. American Reference Books Annual 1981, Vol. 12. LC 75-12038. 800p. 1981. lib. bdg. 45.00x (ISBN 0-87287-250-5). Libs Unl.

REFERENCE BOOKS, ENGLISH
see Reference Books

REFERENCE GROUPS

Bressoud, David M. Analutical & Combinational Generalizations of the Rogers-Ramanujan Identities. LC 79-27622. (Memoirs Ser.). 1980. 6.00 (ISBN 0-8218-2227-6, MEMO-227). Am Math.

Covey, Alma A. Reviewing Reference Books: An Evaluation of the Efectiveness of Selected Announcement, Review & Index Media in Their Coverage of Reference Books. LC 70-182831. 142p. 1972. lib. bdg. 10.00 (ISBN 0-8108-0456-5). Scarecrow.

REFERENCE SERVICES (LIBRARIES)
see also Information Services

Desk Reference Library. (Orig.). 1981. pap. 9.95 (ISBN 0-8326-0203-5, 6465). Delair.

Kumar, Krishan. Reference Service. 2nd rev. ed. 390p. 1980. text ed. 18.95 (ISBN 0-7069-0637-3, Pub. by Vikas India). Advent Bk.

Thomas, Diana M., et al. The Effective Reference Librarian. (Library & Information Science). 1981. write for info. (ISBN 0-12-688720-9). Acad Pr.

REFERENCE WORK (LIBRARIES)
see Reference Services (Libraries)

REFINISHING, FURNITURE
see Furniture Finishing

REFLECTION (THEORY OF KNOWLEDGE)
see Self-Knowledge, Theory of

REFLUX, VESICO-URETERAL
see Vesico-Ureteral Reflux

REFORM, SOCIAL
see Social Problems

REFORM OF THE CHURCH
see Church Renewal

REFORM SCHOOLS
see Reformatories

REFORMATION
see also Calvinism; Church History-Modern Period, 1500-; Europe-History-1492-1648; Protestantism; Theology, Doctrinal-History-16th Century
also names of religious sects, e.g. Huguenots, Hussites, Waldenses

Cunningham, William. Reformers & the Theology of Reformation. 1979. 15.95 (ISBN 0-85151-013-2). Banner of Truth.

Hillerbrand, Hans J. The World of the Reformation. (Twin Brooks Ser.). 229p. 1981. pap. 6.95 (ISBN 0-8010-4248-8). Baker Bk.

Jensen, De Lamar. Reformation Europe: Age of Reform & Revolution. 480p. 1981. pap. text ed. 10.95 (ISBN 0-669-03626-9). Heath.

Klassen, Peter. The Reformation. LC 79-54030. (Problems in Civilization Ser.). (Orig.). 1980. pap. text ed. 3.95x (ISBN 0-88273-408-3). Forum Pr MO.

Lindsay, T. M. History of the Reformation: In Lands Beyond Germany, Vol. 2. 2nd ed. (International Theological Library). 648p. 1908. text ed. 13.95x (ISBN 0-567-07212-6). Attic Pr.

--The Reformation. (Handbooks for Bible Classes). 224p. 1977. text ed. 8.95. Attic Pr.

Oberman, H. A. Masters of the Reformation: Rival Roads to a New Ideology. Martin, D., tr. from German. 432p. Date not set. price not set (ISBN 0-521-23098-5). Cambridge U Pr.

Thompson, Bard. Renaissance & Reformation. (Texts & Studies in Religion, Vol. 11). (Orig.). 1981. soft cover 24.95x (ISBN 0-88946-915-6). E Mellen.

REFORMATION-GERMANY

Lindsay, T. M. History of the Reformation: In Germany, Vol. 1. 2nd ed. (International Theological Library). 544p. 1907. text ed. 13.95x. Attic Pr.

REFORMATORIES
see also Juvenile Delinquency; Juvenile Detention Homes
also names of reformatories, and subdivision Prisons and Reformatories under names of cities, e.g. London-Prisons and Reformatories

Barnard, Henry. Reformatory Education. 361p. 1980. Repr. of 1857 ed. lib. bdg. 20.00 (ISBN 0-8492-3589-8). R West.

REFORMATORIES FOR WOMEN
Freedman, Estelle B. Their Sister's Keepers: Women's Prison Reform in America, 1830-1930. LC 80-24918. (Women & Culture Ser.). 256p. 1981. text ed. 18.50 (ISBN 0-472-10008-4). U of Mich Pr.
REFRACTION
Safir, Aran. Refraction & Clinical Optics. (Illus.). 565p. 1980. text ed. 37.50 (ISBN 0-06-142318-1, Harper Medical). Har-Row.
REFRACTORIES
see Refractory Materials
REFRACTORY MATERIALS
Duffy, J. L., ed. Refractory Materials: Developments Since 1977. LC 80-21945. (Chemical Technology Review: No. 178). (Illus.). 367p. 1981. 42.00 (ISBN 0-8155-0827-1). Noyes.
REFRACTORY MATERIALS–TABLES, CALCULATIONS, ETC.
Samsonov, Gregory & Vinitskii, I. M. Handbook of Refractory Compounds. 550p. 1980. 75.00 (ISBN 0-306-65181-5). IFI Plenum.
REFRIGERATION AND REFRIGERATING MACHINERY
see also Air Conditioning; Freeze-Drying; Heat Exchangers
Carrico, Clayton H. Refrigeration Licenses: (Contractor-Journeyman-Operator) Unlimited. 1980. text ed. 25.00x (ISBN 0-912524-20-0). Busn News.
Hallowell, Elliott R. Cold & Freezer Storage Manual. 2nd ed. (Illus.). 1980. text ed. 35.00 (ISBN 0-87055-366-6). AVI.
Meredith. Refrigeration Technician's Pocketbook. 1981. text ed. price not set (ISBN 0-408-00545-9). Butterworth.
Progress in Refrigeration Science & Technology, 4 vols. 1980. pap. 275.00 (ISBN 0-686-68835-X, IIR67, IIR). Unipub.
Sabin, A. Ross, ed. Refrigeration, Pt. I. (Illus.). 144p. (gr. 11). 1974. 20.00 (ISBN 0-938336-01-0). Whirlpool.
--Refrigeration, Pt. II. (Illus.). 203p. (gr. 11). 1974. 20.00 (ISBN 0-938336-02-9). Whirlpool.
REFUGEES
see also Refugees, Political
Sherbinin, Michael de, ed. Nineteen Eighty-One World Refugee Survey. (Illus.). 64p. 1981. 5.00 (ISBN 0-936548-02-9). US Comm Refugees.
Stone, Scott C. & McGowan, John E. Wrapped in the Wind's Shawl: The Refugees of Southeast Asia. (Illus.). 138p. (Orig.). 1980. pap. 8.95 (ISBN 0-89141-107-0). Presidio Pr.
Torjesen, Hakon, et al. The Gift of the Refugees: Notes of a Volunteer Family of a Refugee Camp. 1981. 9.95 (ISBN 0-9602790-3-2). The Garden.
REFUGEES, NEGRO
see Freedmen; Slavery in the United States–Fugitive Slaves
REFUGEES, POLITICAL
see also Aliens; Asylum, Right of; Emigration and Immigration Law
also subdivision Refugees under specific wars, e.g. World War, 1939-1945–Refugees
Barron, John. MIG Pilot: The Final Escape of Lieutenant Belenko. 232p. 1981. pap. 2.95 (ISBN 0-380-53868-7). Avon.
Grahl-Madsen, Atle. Territorial Asylum. LC 80-10498. (Monograph in the Uppsala University Swedish Institute of International Law). 231p. 1980. lib. bdg. 28.00 (ISBN 0-379-20706-0). Oceana.
Strong, Jaryl. Escape from Islam. 1981. pap. 3.95 (ISBN 0-8423-0712-5). Tyndale.
REFUGES, WILDLIFE
see Wildlife Refuges
REFUSE AND REFUSE DISPOSAL
see also Factory and Trade Waste; Incinerators; Pollution; Radioactive Waste Disposal; Refuse As Fuel; Sewage Disposal; Water–Pollution
Curi, K. Treatment & Disposal of Liquid & Solid Industrial Wastes: Proceedings of the Third Turkish-German Environmental Engineering Symposium, Istanbul, July 1979. LC 80-40993. (Illus.). 515p. 1980. 75.00 (ISBN 0-08-023999-4). Pergamon.
Dale, Richard. Anti-Dumping Law in a Liberal Trade Order. Date not set. price not set (ISBN 0-312-04373-2). St Martin.
Institute of Civil Engineers, UK. Safety in Sewers & at Sewage Works. 64p. 1980. pap. 12.00x (ISBN 0-901948-12-8, Pub. by Telford England). State Mutual Bk.
World Health Organization. Waste Discharge into the Marine Environment: Principles & Guidelines. LC 80-40899. (Illus.). 544p. 1980. 75.00 (ISBN 0-08-026194-9). Pergamon.
REFUSE AS FUEL
see also Biomass Energy
Hall, Carl. Biomass As an Alternative Fuel. LC 80-84729. 350p. 1981. 35.00 (ISBN 0-86587-087-X). Gov Insts.
OAO Corp. Biomass Energy Systems Program Summary Nineteen Eighty. 220p. 1981. pap. 24.50 (ISBN 0-89934-103-9). Solar Energy Info.
Palz, W. & Chartier, P., eds. Energy from Biomass in Europe. (Illus.). xii, 248p. 1981. 35.00x (ISBN 0-85334-934-7). Intl Ideas.
Robinson, J. S., ed. Fuels from Biomass: Technology & Feasibility. LC 80-23488. (Energy Tech. Re. 61; Chem. Tech. Rev. 176). (Illus.). 377p. 1981. 48.00 (ISBN 0-8155-0824-7). Noyes.

REFUSE INCINERATORS
see Incinerators
REGIONAL ANESTHESIA
see Conduction Anesthesia
REGIONAL PLANNING
see also City Planning; Coastal Zone Management; Social Surveys
Armstrong, Harvey & Taylor, Jim. Regional Economic Policy & Its Analysis. 352p. 1978. 43.50x (ISBN 0-86003-015-6, Pub. by Allan Pubs England); pap. 21.75x (ISBN 0-86003-116-0). State Mutual Bk.
Clout, Hugh D. Regional Development in Western Europe. 432p. 1981. 16.50 (ISBN 0-471-27846-7, Pub. by Wiley-Interscience); pap. 7.50 (ISBN 0-471-27845-9). Wiley.
Portugali, Juval. Distribution, Allocation, Social Structure & Spatial Form: Elements of Planning Theory. (Progress in Planning: Vol. 14, Part 3). (Illus.). 83p. 1980. pap. 13.50 (ISBN 0-08-026808-0). Pergamon.
Stopher, Peter R., et al, eds. New Horizons in Travel-Behavior Research. LC 78-24830. 1981. price not set (ISBN 0-669-02850-9). Lexington Bks.
REGIONAL PLANNING–LAW AND LEGISLATION
see also City Planning and Redevelopment Law
Hoffman, George W., ed. Federalism & Regional Development: Case Studies on the Experience in the United States & the Federal Republic of Germany. (Illus.). 784p. 1981. text ed. 40.00x (ISBN 0-292-73825-0). U of Tex Pr.
REGISTRATION OF TRADE-MARKS
see Trade-Marks
REGISTRATION OF VOTERS
see Voters, Registration Of
REGRESSION ANALYSIS
Lewis-Beck, Michael S. Applied Regression: An Introduction. LC 80-5821. (Quantitative Applications in the Social Sciences Ser.: No. 22). (Illus.). 79p. 1980. pap. 3.50 (ISBN 0-8039-1494-6). Sage.
REGULAR FUNCTIONS
see Analytic Functions
REGULATED INDUSTRIES
see Public Utilities
REGULATION OF TRADE
see Trade Regulation
REGULATORY COMMISSIONS
see Independent Regulatory Commissions
REHABILITATION
see also Exercise Therapy; Occupational Therapy; Vocational Rehabilitation
Ami Sha'Ked. Human Sexuality & Rehabilitation Medicine: Sexual Functioning Following Spinal Cord Injury. (Illus.). 228p. 1981. write for info. (7749-X). Williams & Wilkins.
Hammerman, Susan & Maikowski, Stephen, eds. The Economics of Disability: International Perspectives. (Illus.). 200p. (Orig.). 1981. pap. write for info. (ISBN 0-9605554-0-4). Rehab Intl.
Institute for Information Studies. Rehabilitation Engineering Sourcebook Supplement. Vash, Carolyn, et al, eds. LC 79-24747. (Illus.). 85p. 1981. pap. write for info. (ISBN 0-935294-05-8). Inst Info Stud.
Melluzzo, Paul J. & Nealon, Eleanor. Living with Surgery: Before & After. rev. ed. LC 80-53188. 304p. 1980. pap. 6.95 (ISBN 0-7216-6261-7). Saunders.
Riffle, Kathryn L., ed. Rehabilitative Nursing Case Studies. 1979. pap. 9.50 (ISBN 0-87488-035-1). Med Exam.
Sine, Robert D., et al. Basic Rehabilitation Techniques: A Self-Instructional Guide. 2nd. ed. 250p. 1981. text ed. write for info. (ISBN 0-89443-342-3). Aspen Systems.
Spiegel, Allen D. & Podair, Simon. Rehabilitating People with Disabilities into the Mainstream of Society. LC 80-16497. (Illus.). 350p. 1981. 28.00 (ISBN 0-8155-0839-5). Noyes.
Wiegerink, Ronald & Pelosi, John W., eds. Developmental Disabilities: The DD Movement. 182p. 1979. pap. 10.50 (ISBN 0-933716-02-8). P H Brookes.
Wilkins, Alfred T., Jr. & Dunn, Joseph. The Real Race. LC 80-85152. (Illus.). 210p. 1981. 10.95 (ISBN 0-938694-04-9). Jordan & Co.
Wright, George N. Total Rehabilitation. LC 80-81957. 830p. 1980. text ed. 32.50 (ISBN 0-316-95628-7). Little.
REHABILITATION, RURAL
see also Agricultural Colonies; Community Development
Enyedi, Gyorgy & Volgyes, Ivan, eds. The Effect of Modern Agriculture on Rural Developement. LC 80-25232. (Pergamon Policy Studies on International Developement Comparative Rural Transformations Ser.). (Illus.). 280p. 1981. 32.50 (ISBN 0-08-027179-0). Pergamon.
Evaluating Social Action Projects. 161p. 1981. pap. 9.25 (ISBN 92-3-101807-8, U1052, UNESCO). Unipub.
Kim, Young-Pyoung. A Strategy for for Rural Development: Saemaeul Undong in Korea. 1980. pap. 5.00 (ISBN 0-89249-032-2). Intl Development.
REHABILITATION, VOCATIONAL
see Vocational Rehabilitation

REICH, WILHELM, 1897-1957
Placzek, Beverley, ed. Record of a Friendship: The Correspondence of Wilhelm Reich and A.S. Neill. 1981. 15.95 (ISBN 0-374-24807-9). FS&G.
REID, THOMAS 1710-1796
Reid, Thomas. Thomas Reid's Lectures on Natural Theology (1780) Duncan, Elmer H., ed. LC 80-5964. 177p. 1981. lib. bdg. 19.00 (ISBN 0-8191-1354-9); pap. text ed. 9.00 (ISBN 0-8191-1355-7). U Pr of Amer.
REIGN OF TERROR
see France–History–Revolution, 1789-1799
REINFORCED CONCRETE
Darlison, John L. & Fordyce, M. W. Glass Reinforced Concrete. 1981. text ed. price not set. Butterworth.
Taylor, R. Composite Reinforced Concrete. 104p. 1980. 50.00x (ISBN 0-7277-0077-4, Pub. by Telford England). State Mutual Bk.
REINFORCED CONCRETE CONSTRUCTION
see also Prestressed Concrete Construction
Ferrocement Materials & Applications. 1979. 23.25 (SP-61); 17.75. ACI.
Reinforced Concrete Structures in Seismic Zones. 1977. 25.00 (SP-53). ACC.
Reinforced Concrete Structures Subjected to Wind & Earthquake Forces. 1980. 32.95 (SP-63). ACI.
REINFORCED FIBROUS COMPOSITES
see Fibrous Composites
REINFORCED SOLIDS
see Composite Materials
REJECTION, MATERNAL
see Maternal Deprivation
REKHTA LANGUAGE
see Urdu Language
RELATIONS, RACE
see Race Relations
RELATIVISTIC QUANTUM FIELD THEORY
see Quantum Field Theory
RELATIVITY
Geroch, Robert. General Relativity from A to B. pap. 4.95 (ISBN 0-226-28864-1). U of Chicago Pr.
RELATIVITY (PHYSICS)
see also Gravitation; Quantum Field Theory; Quantum Theory; Space and Time
Geroch, Robert. General Relativity from A to B. (Illus.). 238p. 1981. pap. 4.95 (ISBN 0-226-28864-1). U of Chicago Pr.
Lilley, S. Discovering Relativity for Yourself. LC 80-40263. (Illus.). 425p. Date not set. 49.50; pap. 19.95 (ISBN 0-521-29780-X). Cambridge U Pr.
Rindler, W. Essential Relativity. rev. ed. (Texts & Monographs in Physics). (Illus.). 284p. 1980. pap. 19.80 (ISBN 0-387-10090-3). Springer-Verlag.
RELATIVITY (PHYSICS)–JUVENILE LITERATURE
Apfel, Necia H. It's All Relative: Einstein's Theory of Relativity. LC 80-28188. (Illus.). 144p. (gr. 5 up). 1981. 8.95 (ISBN 0-688-41981-X); PLB 8.59 (ISBN 0-688-51981-4). Morrow.
RELAXATION
Edmonston, William E. Hypnosis & Relaxation: Modern Verification of an Old Equation. LC 80-22506. (Personality Processes Ser.). 280p. 1981. 21.00 (ISBN 0-471-05903-X, Pub. by Wiley Interscience). Wiley.
RELAXATION, SPIN-LATTICE
see Spin-Lattice Relaxation
RELIABILITY (ENGINEERING)
see also Quality Control
Goldberg, Harold. Extending the Limits of Reliability Theory. 300p. 1981. 30.00 (ISBN 0-471-07799-2, Pub. by Wiley Interscience). Wiley.
Tillman. Optimization of Systems Reliability. 328p. 1980. 37.50 (ISBN 0-8247-6989-9). Dekker.
RELIEF (AID)
see Public Welfare
RELIEF, INTERNATIONAL
Roddy, Lee. On Wings of Love. 128p. 1981. pap. 3.95 (ISBN 0-8407-5758-1). Nelson.
RELIGION
see also Atheism; Belief and Doubt; Faith; God; Mysteries, Religious; Mysticism; Myth; Mythology; Natural Theology; Positivism; Psychology, Religious; Religions; Revelation; Satanism; Spiritual Life; Superstition; Theism; Theology; Theosophy; Worship also subdivision Religion, or Religion and Mythology, under names of countries, races, peoples, etc., e.g. Egypt–Religion; Indians of North America–Religion and Mythology; also headings beginning with the word Religious
Bergman, G. Merle. Realtheism: A Religion & Bible for the Humanist Age. 160p. 1981. 10.95 (ISBN 0-938986-03-1); pap. 6.95 (ISBN 0-938986-04-X). Fellowship Pr.
Cohu, J. R. Vital Problems of Religion. 304p. Repr. of 1914 ed. text ed. 2.95 (ISBN 0-567-02077-0). Attic Pr.
Gurdjieff, G. I. Life Is Real Only Then, When "I Am". 1981. 12.95 (ISBN 0-525-14547-8). Dutton.
Kiek, Edward S. The Modern Religious Situation. 227p. Repr. of 1926 ed. 2.95 (ISBN 0-567-02158-0). Attic Pr.
Lenning, Larry G. Blessing in Mosque & Mission. LC 80-25110. 176p. (Orig.). 1980. pap. write for info. (ISBN 0-87808-433-9). William Carey Lib.
Moore, John A. Write for the Religion Market. LC 80-25607. 128p. 1981. 9.95 (ISBN 0-88280-084-1). ETC Pubns.
Shiphorst, Albert. The Hilarious Saints. 1981. 5.75 (ISBN 0-8062-1640-9). Carlton.

Tillich, Paul. The Relation of Religion & Health. 150p. 1981. 15.00 (ISBN 0-913028-81-9); pap. 5.95 (ISBN 0-686-69475-9). North Atlantic.
Wedgwood, James I. The Larger Meaning of Religion. 80p. 1981. pap. text ed. 3.70 (ISBN 0-918980-10-0). St Alban Pr.
RELIGION–BIBLIOGRAPHY
Commenting & Commentaries. (C. H. Spurgeon Library). 1981. pap. 3.95 (ISBN 0-8010-8194-7). Baker Bk.
Wiersbe, Warren W. A Basic Library for Bible Students. (Orig.). 1981. pap. 2.95 (ISBN 0-8010-9641-3). Baker Bk.
RELIGION–HISTORY
Eliade, Mircea. A History of Religious Ideas, Vol. I: From the Stone Age to the Eleusinian Mysteries. Trask, Willard R., tr. from Fr. LC 77-16784. xviii, 490p. 1981. pap. 8.95 (ISBN 0-226-20401-4). U of Chicago Pr.
Hutchison, John A. Paths of Faith. 3rd ed. (Illus.). 608p. Date not set. text ed. 18.95 (ISBN 0-07-031532-9, C). McGraw.
Leuba, James H. The Psychological Origin & the Nature of Religion. 94p. 1980. Repr. of 1909 ed. lib. bdg. 12.50 (ISBN 0-8482-1622-9). Norwood Edns.
Luibheid, Colm. Eusebius of Caesarea & the Arian Crisis. 128p. 1981. 18.50x (ISBN 0-7165-2277-2, Pub. by Irish Academic Pr Ireland). Biblio Dist.
Moore, George F. The Birth & Growth of Religion. 188p. Repr. of 1927 ed. 2.95 (ISBN 0-567-02199-8). Attic Pr.
Rankin, O. S. Israel's Wisdom Literature: Its Bearing on Theology & the History of Religions. LC 36-33127. 288p. Repr. of 1936 ed. text ed. 7.50 (ISBN 0-567-02214-5). Attic Pr.
Vetter, George B. Magic & Religion: Their Origins & Consequences. LC 73-82103. 1958. 6.00 (ISBN 0-8022-1776-1). Philos Lib.
RELIGION–PHILOSOPHY
see also Christianity–Philosophy; Philosophy and Religion
Evans, Donald. Struggle & Fulfillment: The Inner Dynamics of Religion & Morality. LC 80-8050. 256p. 1981. pap. 7.95 (ISBN 0-8006-1426-7, 1-1426). Fortress.
Lecerf, Auguste. An Introduction to Reformed Dogmatics. Leigh-Hunt, S., tr. (Twin Brooks Ser.). 408p. (Orig.). 1981. pap. 9.95 (ISBN 0-8010-5603-9). Baker Bk.
Lisiero, Dario. People Ideology-People Theology: New Perspectives on Religious Dogma. 64p. 1980. 10.95 (ISBN 0-682-49664-2, Banner). Exposition.
RELIGION–PSYCHOLOGY
see Psychology, Religious
RELIGION, COMPARATIVE
see Religions
RELIGION, MIXED
see Marriage, Mixed
RELIGION, PRIMITIVE
see also Birth (In Religion, Folk-Lore, etc.); Idols and Images; Indians of North America–Religion and Mythology; Superstition; Voodooism; Women (In Religion, Folklore, etc.)
also subdivisions Religion or Religion and mythology under names of ethnic groups, e.g. Indians of North America–Religion and Mythology
Bell, John. Bell's New Pantheon, 2 vols. Feldman, Burton & Richardson, Robert D., eds. LC 78-60919. (Myth & Romanticism Ser.: Vol. 4). 809p. 1979. Set. lib. bdg. 120.00 (ISBN 0-8240-3553-4). Garland Pub.
Carmody, Denise L. The Oldest God: Archaic Religion Yesterday & Today. LC 80-25499. 192p. (Orig.). 1981. pap. 6.95 (ISBN 0-687-28813-4). Abingdon.
RELIGION AND EDUCATION
see Church and Education
RELIGION AND ETHICS
see also Christian Ethics; Ethics, Jewish
Hastings, A. W. & Hastings, E., eds. Important Moral Issues. LC 66-78349. 128p. Repr. of 1966 ed. pap. text ed. 4.95 (ISBN 0-567-22302-7). Attic Pr.
Helm, Paul, ed. Divine Commands & Morality. (Readings in Philosophy Ser.). 192p. 1981. pap. 11.50 (ISBN 0-19-875049-8). Oxford U Pr.
RELIGION AND LAW
Burstein, A. Religion, Cults & the Law. 1980. 5.95 (ISBN 0-379-11133-0). Oceana.
Hayward, John. A Reporte of a Discourse Concerning Supreme Power in Affaires of Religion. LC 79-84116. (English Experience Ser.: No. 935). 64p. 1979. Repr. of 1606 ed. lib. bdg. 8.00 (ISBN 90-221-0935-6). Walter J Johnson.
McMillan, Richard C., ed. Education, Religion, & the Supreme Court. LC 78-74196. (Special Studies Ser.: No. 6). 1979. 4.95 (ISBN 0-932180-05-1). Assn Baptist Profs.
Malbin, Michael J. Religion & Politics: The Intentions of the Athors of the First Amendment. 1978. pap. 3.25 (ISBN 0-8447-3302-4). Am Enterprise.
RELIGION AND LITERATURE
Jay, Elisabeth. The Religion of the Heart: Anglican Evangelicalism & the Nineteenth-Century Novel. 1979. write for info. (ISBN 0-19-812092-3). Oxford U Pr.
Luccock, Halford E. Contemporary American Literature & Religion. 300p. 1980. Repr. of 1934 ed. lib. bdg. 30.00 (ISBN 0-89984-324-7). Century Bookbindery.

RELIGION AND PHILOSOPHY
see Philosophy and Religion
RELIGION AND POETRY
see Religion and Literature
RELIGION AND PSYCHOLOGY
see Psychology, Religious
RELIGION AND SCIENCE
see also Bible and Science; Creation; Evolution; Faith and Reason; Natural Theology
Jones, James W. The Texture of Knowledge: An Essay on Religion & Science. LC 80-69036. 112p. 1981. lib. bdg. 15.75 (ISBN 0-8191-1360-3); pap. text ed. 6.75 (ISBN 0-8191-1361-1). U Pr of Amer.
Lea, William S. Faith & Science: Mutual Responsibility for a Human Future. 1979. 1.50 (ISBN 0-686-28776-2). Forward Movement.
McKay, Donald M. Science, Chance & Providence. (Riddell Memorial Lectures Ser.). (Illus.). 78p. 1978. text ed. 13.95x. Oxford U Pr.
Stace, Walter T. Religion & the Modern Mind. LC 80-24093. 285p. 1980. Repr. of 1952 ed. lib. bdg. 22.50x (ISBN 0-313-22662-8, STRM). Greenwood.
Whitehouse, W. A. Creation, Science, & Theology: Essays in Response to Karl Barth. 272p. (Orig.). 1981. pap. 10.95 (ISBN 0-8028-1870-6). Eerdmans.
Zaglits, Oscar. Man, Religion & Science. Date not set. 10.95 (ISBN 0-533-04808-7). Vantage.
RELIGION AND SEX
see Sex and Religion
RELIGION AND SOCIAL PROBLEMS
see Church and Social Problems; Religion and Sociology
RELIGION AND SOCIETY
see Religion and Sociology
RELIGION AND SOCIOLOGY
Works limited to the Christian religion are entered under the heading Sociology, Christian, and related subjects referred to under that heading.
see also Church and Social Problems; Sociology, Christian
Chalfant. Religion in Contemporary Society. 1981. 14.95 (ISBN 0-88284-126-2). Alfred Pub.
Chamie, Joseph. Religion & Fertility: Arab Christian-Muslim Differentials. LC 80-19787. (ASA Rose Monograph Ser.). (Illus.). 176p. Date not set. price not set (ISBN 0-521-23677-0); pap. price not set (ISBN 0-521-28147-4). Cambridge U Pr.
Hopkin, C. Edward. The Not So Good Book: A Resource for the Alienated. 100p. 1981. 5.95 (ISBN 0-8059-2776-X). Dorrance.
Maston, T. B. El Mundo En Crisis. Adams, Bob, tr. from Eng. 224p. (Span.). 1981. pap. write for info. (ISBN 0-311-46084-4). Casa Bautista.
RELIGION AND STATE
see also Church and State
Hayward, John. A Reporte of a Discourse Concerning Supreme Power in Affaires of Religion. LC 79-84116. (English Experience Ser.: No. 935). 64p. 1979. Repr. of 1606 ed. lib. bdg. 8.00 (ISBN 90-221-0935-6). Walter J Johnson.
Schmid, Carol L. Conflict & Consensus in Switzerland. 1981. 18.50x (ISBN 0-520-04079-1). U of Cal Pr.
RELIGION AND WAR
see War and Religion
RELIGION IN LITERATURE
see also Religion and Literature; Religious Poetry; Theater-Moral and Religious Aspects
O'Rourke, Brian. The Conscience of the Race: Sex & Religion in Irish & French Novels 1941-1973. 72p. 1981. 10.00x (ISBN 0-906127-22-X, Pub. by Irish Academic Pr Ireland). Biblio Dist.
RELIGION IN POETRY
see Religion in Literature
RELIGION IN THE PUBLIC SCHOOLS
Spykman, Gordon, et al. Society, State, & Schools: A Case for Structural & Confessional Pluralism. 224p. (Orig.). 1981. pap. 11.95 (ISBN 0-8028-1880-3). Eerdmans.
RELIGION OF HUMANITY
see Positivism
RELIGIONS
Here are entered works on the major world religions. Works on religious groups whose adherents recognize special teachings or practices which fall within the normative bounds of the major world religions are entered under Sects. Works on groups or movements whose system of religious beliefs or practices differs significantly from the major world religions and which are often gathered around a specific deity or person are entered under Cults.
see also Bahaism; Buddhism; Christianity; Cults; Druids and Druidism; Gods; Hinduism; Humanism, Religious; Islam; Judaism; Lamaism; Mythology; Paganism; Positivism; Religion; Sects; Shamanism; Taoism
Hutchison, John A. Paths of Faith. 3rd ed. (Illus.). 608p. Date not set. text ed. 18.95 (ISBN 0-07-031532-9, C). McGraw.
Lewis, Warren, ed. Towards a Global Congress of the World's Religions. LC 80-53764. (Conference Ser.: No. 7). (Illus.). xiv, 78p. (Orig.). 1980. pap. text ed. 3.25x (ISBN 0-932894-07-0). Unif Theol Seminary.
Small, R. Leonard. No Other Name. 190p. 1966. text ed. 4.95 (ISBN 0-567-02257-9). Attic Pr.
Vajpeyi, Kailash. The Science of Mantras: A Manual of Happiness & Prosperity. 128p. 1980. 13.50 (ISBN 0-391-02213-X). Humanities.
Wm. C. Brown Education Division Staff. Mystery, Value & Awareness: Aids for Understanding Religions of the World. (To Live Is Christ Ser.). 28p. (Orig.). 1979. wkbk. 10.95 (ISBN 0-697-01736-2). Wm C Brown.
RELIGIONS-BIOGRAPHY
Coray, Henry W. J. Gresham Machen. 128p. (Orig.). 1981. pap. 4.95 (ISBN 0-8254-2327-9). Kregel.
RELIGIONS-ETHICS
see Religious Ethics
RELIGIONS-HISTORY
Greaves, Richard L. Society & Religion in Elizabethan England. 832p. 1981. 32.50x (ISBN 0-8166-1030-4). U of Minn Pr.
Moore, G. F. History of Religions: China, Japan, Egypt, Babylonia, Assyria, India, Persia, Greece, Rome, Vol. I. (International Theological Library). 654p. 1914. text ed. 13.95x (ISBN 0-567-07202-9). Attic Pr.
RELIGIONS, COMPARATIVE
see Religions
RELIGIONS, MODERN
see Cults; Sects
RELIGIOUS AND ECCLESIASTICAL INSTITUTIONS
see also Mosques; Temples
Directory of Religious Organizations, No. 2. 2nd ed. 500p. 1980. 75.00 (ISBN 0-8434-0757-3, Consortium). McGrath.
RELIGIOUS ART
see Cathedrals; Christian Art and Symbolism; Church Architecture; Idols and Images; Mosques; Temples; also Art, Buddhist; Art, Gothic; Art, Medieval, and similar headings
RELIGIOUS BELIEF
see Belief and Doubt; Faith
RELIGIOUS BIOGRAPHY
see also Christian Biography
Bordeaux, Michael. Evidencia que Condeno a Aida Skripnikova. Vega, Pedro, tr. from Eng. 123p. (Orig., Span.). 1975. pap. 1.50 (ISBN 0-89922-060-6). Edit Caribe.
Isichei, Elizabeth. Entirely for God. (Cistercian Studies: No. 43). 132p. 1980. pap. 11.95 (ISBN 0-87907-943-6). Cistercian Pubns.
Miles, Austin. The Real Ringmaster. Boneck, John & Dudley, Cliff, eds. LC 80-83458. 150p. 1980. 8.95 (ISBN 0-89221-079-6). New Leaf.
Miner, Caroline E. & Kimball, Edward L. Camilla. LC 80-69723. (Illus.). 1980. 5.95 (ISBN 0-87747-845-7). Deseret Bk.
Murray, Iain H., ed. Diary of Kenneth Macrae. (Illus.). 535p. 1980. 16.95 (ISBN 0-85151-297-6). Banner of Truth.
Sturlaugson, Mary F. A Soul So Rebellious. 88p. 1980. 5.95 (ISBN 0-87747-841-4). Deseret Bk.
RELIGIOUS CEREMONIES
see Rites and Ceremonies
RELIGIOUS DENOMINATIONS
see Religions; Sects;
also particular denominations and sects
RELIGIOUS EDUCATION
Here are entered works dealing with instruction in religion in school and private life. Cf. note under Church and Education.
see also Bible-Study; Christian Education; Confirmation-Instruction and Study; Moral Education; Religion in the Public Schools; Sunday-Schools; Teaching, Freedom of; Theology-Study and Teaching
Barber, Lucie W. The Religious Education of Preschool Children. 190p. (Orig.). 1981. pap. write for info. (ISBN 0-89135-026-8). Religious Educ.
Boys, Mary C., ed. Ministry & Education in Conversation. LC 80-53204. 160p. (Orig.). 1981. pap. 6.95 (ISBN 0-88489-126-7). St Mary's.
Bullock, Dorothy. Give Your Child Permission to Unfold. LC 80-70509. 64p. (Orig.). 1981. pap. 2.95 (ISBN 0-87516-438-2). De Vorss.
Fallis, William J. Points for Emphasis, Nineteen Eighty-One to Eighty Two. 1981. pap. 1.95 (ISBN 0-8054-1467-3). Broadman.
--Points for Emphasis, Nineteen Eighty-One T0 Eighty-Two. larger type ed. 1981. pap. 2.75 (ISBN 0-8054-1466-5). Broadman.
Hakes, D. T. The Development of Metalinguistic Abilities in Children. (Springer Series in Language & Communication: Vol. 9). (Illus.). 119p. 1980. 22.50 (ISBN 0-387-10295-7). Springer-Verlag.
Lynn, Robert W. & Wright, Elliott. The Big Little School. 2nd rev. & enl. ed. LC 79-27864. 178p. 1980. pap. 6.95 (ISBN 0-89135-021-7). Religious Educ.
Moran, Gabriel. Interplay: A Theory of Religion & Education. LC 80-53203. 125p. (Orig.). 1981. pap. 5.95 (ISBN 0-88489-125-9). St Mary's.
Rouse, Doris & Waldrop, Sybil. Moral & Spiritual Development for the Young Child. LC 79-55850. 1981. perfect bdg - 3 hole punch 6.95 (ISBN 0-8054-4923-X). Broadman.
Van Eijndhoven, J., ed. Religious Education of the Deaf. (Modern Approaches to the Diagnosis & Instruction of Multi-Handicapped Children Ser.: Vol. 11). 168p. 1973. text ed. 20.25 (ISBN 90-237-4111-0, Pub. by Swets Pub. Ser Holland). Swets North Am.
RELIGIOUS EDUCATION-TEACHER TRAINING
Here are entered works dealing with the systematic instruction of lay teachers to prepare them to give religious instruction.
see also Religious Education As a Profession
Gribbon, R. T. Students, Churches & Higher Education. 128p. 1981. pap. 6.95 (ISBN 0-8170-0931-0). Judson.
Rusbuldt, Richard E. Basic Teacher Skills: Handbook for Church School Teachers. 144p. 1981. pap. 4.95 (ISBN 0-8170-0919-1). Judson.
RELIGIOUS EDUCATION-TEACHING METHODS
Flagel, Clarice. Avoiding Burnout: Time Management for D. R.E.'s. 60p. (Orig.). 1981. pap. 4.95 (ISBN 0-697-01782-6). Wm C Brown.
Gribbon, R. T. Students, Churches & Higher Education. 128p. 1981. pap. 6.95 (ISBN 0-8170-0931-0). Judson.
Rusbuldt, Richard E. Basic Teacher Skills: Handbook for Church School Teachers. 144p. 1981. pap. 4.95 (ISBN 0-8170-0919-1). Judson.
RELIGIOUS EDUCATION-VOCATIONAL GUIDANCE
see Religious Education As a Profession
RELIGIOUS EDUCATION-GERMANY
Terry, W. Clinton, III. Teaching Religion: The Secularization of Religion Instruction in a West German School System. LC 80-5569. 208p. 1981. lib. bdg. 18.50 (ISBN 0-8191-1366-2); pap. text ed. 9.50 (ISBN 0-8191-1367-0). U Pr of Amer.
RELIGIOUS EDUCATION AS A PROFESSION
White, Anne S. All in All. 128p. (Orig.). 1980. pap. 2.50 (ISBN 0-9605178-0-4). Victorious Ministry.
RELIGIOUS EDUCATION OF CHILDREN
Artz, Thomas & Haley, Ruth M. Helping Your Child Appreciate the Mass & the Sacraments. 144p. (Orig.). 1980. pap. 2.95 (ISBN 0-89243-132-6). Liguori Pubns.
Barber, Lucie W. The Religious Education of Preschool Children. LC 80-27623. 190p. (Orig.). 1981. pap. price not set (ISBN 0-89135-026-8). Religious Educ.
Gobbel, A. Roger & Huber, Phillip C. Creative Designs with Children at Worship. LC 80-82225. 96p. (Orig.). 1981. pap. 4.95 (ISBN 0-8042-1526-X). John Knox.
Helping Your Child Know Right from Wrong. LC 79-91138. (Redemptovist Pastoral Publication). (gr. 3-5). 1980. pap. 2.50 (ISBN 0-89243-117-2, 39900). Liguori Pubns.
I Believe in God. 52p. 1975. 3.00. Natl Cath Educ.
Ng, David & Thomas, Virginia. Children in the Worshipping Community. LC 80-84653. (Illus.). 128p. (Orig.). 1981. pap. 6.50 (ISBN 0-8042-1688-6). John Knox.
RELIGIOUS EDUCATION OF PRE-SCHOOL CHILDREN
Archdiocese of Newark. Growing in Faith with Your Child. Ivory, Thomas P., ed. 48p. (Orig.). pap. 2.50 (ISBN 0-697-01693-5). Wm C Brown.
Barnett, Regina R. Create, One. 31p. (Orig.). (ps). 1978. pap. text ed. 4.95 student work pad (ISBN 0-697-01678-1); tchr's manual 10.75 (ISBN 0-697-01677-3). Wm C Brown.
--Create, Two. 31p. (Orig.). (ps). 1979. pap. text ed. 4.95 student work pad (ISBN 0-697-01705-2); tchr's manual 10.75 (ISBN 0-697-01706-0). Wm C Brown.
RELIGIOUS EDUCATION OF YOUNG PEOPLE
Finley, James. Your Future & You. (Illus.). 176p. (Orig.). (gr. 10-12). 1981. pap. 3.50 (ISBN 0-87793-223-9); tchrs. ed. 2.25 (ISBN 0-87793-224-7). Ave Maria.
Hargrove, Barbara. Religion for a Dislocated Generation. 144p. 1981. 9.95 (ISBN 0-8170-0891-8). Judson.
Slover, Luella H. Ministry with Young Adults. 1980. pap. 3.00 (ISBN 0-8309-0283-X). Herald Hse.
RELIGIOUS ETHICS
Manuel, Dino. Paragraph of Life: Killer-Your Friend? 64p. 1981. 5.00 (ISBN 0-682-49724-X). Exposition.
RELIGIOUS FESTIVALS
see Fasts and Feasts
RELIGIOUS HISTORY
see Church History
RELIGIOUS HUMANISM
see Humanism, Religious
RELIGIOUS INSTITUTIONS
see Religious and Ecclesiastical Institutions
RELIGIOUS LIFE
see Christian Life; Monastic and Religious Life
also subdivision Religious Life under classes of persons, e.g. Family-Religious Life
RELIGIOUS LIFE (JUDAISM)
see Jewish Way of Life
RELIGIOUS LITERATURE
see also Buddhist Literature; Hindu Literature; Religious Poetry
Duck, Ruth C. Bread for the Journey. 96p. 1981. pap. 3.95 (ISBN 0-8298-0423-4). Pilgrim NY.
McClintock, John & Strong, James. Cyclopedia of Biblical, Theological, & Ecclesiastical Literature, 12 vols. 12400p. 1961. text ed. 395.00 (ISBN 0-8010-6123-7). Baker Bk.
Moynahan, Michael E. How the Word Became Flesh: Story Dramas for Education & Worship. 1981. pap. 9.95 (ISBN 0-89390-029-X). Resource Pubns.
RELIGIOUS MUSIC
see Church Music
RELIGIOUS MYSTERIES
see Mysteries, Religious
RELIGIOUS ORDERS
see Monasticism and Religious Orders
RELIGIOUS PAINTING
see Christian Art and Symbolism
RELIGIOUS POETRY
see also Hymns
Bracciolini, Francisco, tr. Alceste: The Tradgeie of Alceste & Eliza. LC 79-84082. (English Experience Ser.: No. 902). 80p. 1979. Repr. of 1638 ed. lib. bdg. 9.00 (ISBN 90-221-0902-X). Walter J Johnson.
Kittrell, Beverly. Poems of Faith. 1981. 5.95 (ISBN 0-533-04798-6). Vantage.
Miller, David. A Song of Love. Date not set. 5.95 (ISBN 0-533-04741-2). Vantage.
RELIGIOUS POETRY-HISTORY AND CRITICISM
Lazear, Robert. Maestro de Dolores. (Illus.). 342p. (Orig., Span.). 1979. pap. 4.50 (ISBN 0-89922-138-6). Edit Caribe.
RELIGIOUS PSYCHOLOGY
see Psychology, Religious
RELIGIOUS RITES
see Rites and Ceremonies
RELIGIOUS SCULPTURE
see Christian Art and Symbolism
RELIGIOUS SOCIOLOGY
see Religion and Sociology
RELIGIOUS THOUGHT
see also Theology, Doctrinal-History
Kim, Yong Choon. Oriental Thought: An Introduction to the Philosophical & Religious Thought of Asia. 130p. 1981. Repr. of 1973 ed. 8.95x (ISBN 0-8476-6972-6). Rowman.
Sullivan, John, ed. Spiritual Direction. LC 80-26654. (Carmelite Studies: No. I). 240p. (Orig.). 1980. pap. 6.95x (ISBN 0-9600876-8-0). ICS Pubns.
RELIGIOUS THOUGHT-GREAT BRITAIN
Stein, Gordon. Freethought in the United Kingdom & the Commonwealth: A Descriptive Bibliography. LC 80-1792. 192p. 1981. lib. bdg. 35.00 (ISBN 0-313-20869-7, SFU/). Greenwood.
RELIGIOUS THOUGHT-INDIA
Dada. Towards the Unknown. LC 81-65123. (Illus.). 128p. (Orig.). 1981. pap. 4.95 (ISBN 0-930608-02-X). Dada Ctr.
REMAND HOMES
see Juvenile Detention Homes; Reformatories
REMARRIAGE
Adams, Jay E. Marriage, Divorce & Remarriage. 120p. 1981. pap. 3.50 (ISBN 0-8010-0168-4). Baker Bk.
--Marriage, Divorce & Remarriage. 1980. pap. 3.50 (ISBN 0-87552-068-5). Presby & Reformed.
Lippi, Otty. The Second Time Around: An Honest Widow Reveals Her Intimate & Humorous Experiences in the Dating & Mating Game. LC 80-27189. 1981. 12.95 (ISBN 0-934878-03-X). Dembner Bks.
REMBRANDT, HARMENSZOON VAN RIJN, 1606-1669
Haal, Bob. Rembrandt: His Life, His Work, His Times. 125.00 (ISBN 0-8109-4750-1). Abrams.
REMEDIAL READING
see Reading-Remedial Teaching
REMINGTON, FREDERIC, 1861-1909
Rush, N. Orwin. Diversions of a Westerner: With Emphasis Upon Owen Wister's & Frederic Remington's Books & Libraries. LC 78-53134. (Illus.). 224p. 1979. 10.00 (ISBN 0-932068-05-7). South Pass Pr.
REMODELING OF BUILDINGS
see Buildings-Repair and Reconstruction
REMODELING OF DWELLINGS
see Dwellings-Remodeling
REMOTE SENSING
Lavigne, D. M., et al. Remote Sensing & Ecosystem Management. (Norsk Polarinstitutt Skrifter: Vol. 166). (Illus.). 51p. 1980. pap. text ed. 5.00x. Universitet.
REMOTE TERRAIN SENSING
see Remote Sensing
RENAISSANCE
see also Civilization, Medieval; Humanism; Literature, Medieval; Middle Ages
Clogan, P. M., ed. Medievalia et Humanistica, Vols. 1-3 & 6-9. Incl. Vol. 1. LC 75-32451. 251p. 1976 (ISBN 0-521-21032-1); Vol. 2. Medieval & Renaissance Studies in Review. LC 75-32452. 223p (ISBN 0-521-21033-X); Vol. 3. Social Dimension in Medieval & Renaissance Studies. LC 75-32453. 328p (ISBN 0-521-21034-8); Vol. 6. LC 75-16872. 1979 (ISBN 0-521-20999-4); Vol. 7. Studies in Medieval & Renaissance Culture: Medieval Poetics. LC 76-12914. 1977 (ISBN 0-521-21331-2); Vol. 8. Studies in Medieval & Renaissance Culture Transformation & Continuity. LC 75-32451. 1978 (ISBN 0-521-21783-0); Vol. 9. LC 75-32451. 1979 (ISBN 0-521-22446-2). 36.00 ea. Cambridge U Pr.
Clogan, Paul M. Medievalia et Humanistica: Studies in Medieval & Renaissance Culture. (New Ser.: No. 10). 1981. 25.00x (ISBN 0-8476-6944-0). Rowman.
Jensen, De Lamar. Renaissance Europe: Age of Recovery & Reconciliation. 416p. 1980. pap. text ed. 10.95 (ISBN 0-669-51722-4). Heath.

Letts, Rosa M. The Renaissance. (Cambridge Introduction to the History of Art Ser.: No. 3). (Illus.). 100p. Date not set. 19.95 (ISBN 0-521-23394-1); pap. 6.95 (ISBN 0-521-29957-8). Cambridge U Pr.

Symposium on the Renaissance, University of Wisconsin, 1959. The Renaissance: A Reconsideration of the Theories & Interpretations of the Age. Helton, Tinsley, ed. LC 80-21869. xiii, 160p. 1980. Repr. of 1961 ed. lib. bdg. 19.50x (ISBN 0-313-22797-7, SYRE). Greenwood.

RENAISSANCE–EUROPE
see Renaissance

RENAISSANCE–ITALY
Cochrane, Eric. Historians & Historiography in the Italian Renaissance. LC 80-16097. 1981. lib. bdg. 35.00x (ISBN 0-226-11152-0). U of Chicago Pr.

RENAISSANCE ART
see Art, Renaissance

RENAISSANCE LITERATURE
see Literature, Modern (Collections)–15th and 16th Centuries

RENAISSANCE PHILOSOPHY
see Philosophy, Renaissance

RENAISSANCE SCULPTURE
see Sculpture, Renaissance

RENAL DISEASES
see Kidneys–Diseases

RENAL FAILURE
see Renal Insufficiency

RENAL INSUFFICIENCY
Buckalew, Vardaman M. & Moore, Micahel A. Renal Tubular Dysfunction. LC 79-92915. (Discussions in Patient Management Ser.). 1980. pap. 13.50 (ISBN 0-87488-889-1). Med Exam.

Yuill, G. M. The Treatment of Renal Failure. 214p. 1975. 12.00x (ISBN 0-7190-0628-7, Pub. by Manchester U Pr England). State Mutual Bk.

RENAN, JOSEPH ERNEST, 1823-1890
Espinasse, Francis. Life of Ernest Renan. 242p. 1980. Repr. of 1895 ed. lib. bdg. 15.00 (ISBN 0-89760-205-6). Telegraph Bks.

RENEWAL OF THE CHURCH
see Church Renewal

RENIN
Oparil, Suzanne, et al. Renin. Horrobin, D. F., ed. (Annual Research Reviews Ser.: Vol. 5). 368p. 1980. 38.00 (ISBN 0-88831-092-7). Eden Med Res.

RENT
see also Landlord and Tenant
Gilderbloom, John I., ed. Rent Control: A Source Book. 314p. (Orig.). 1981. pap. 9.95 (ISBN 0-938806-00-9). Foun Natl Prog.

REORGANIZATION OF CORPORATIONS
see Corporate Reorganizations

REPAIRING
see also Buildings–Repair and Reconstruction
also subdivision Repairing under various subjects, e.g. Jewelry–Repairing
Brightman, Robert. Fix It. 7.95 (ISBN 0-916752-18-6). Green Hill.

REPORT CARDS
see Grading and Marking (Students)

REPORT WRITING
see also Business Report Writing; Note-Taking; Technical Writing
Blustein, Lotte & Geary, Rosemary J. Writing the Research Paper. rev. ed. (Illus.). 60p. (gr. 7-12). 1980. pap. text ed. 4.45 (ISBN 0-9605248-2-7). Blustein-Geary.

Gregorich, Barbara & Waldowski, Therese F. The Research Paper. LC 78-730060. (Illus.). 1977. pap. text ed. 99.00 (ISBN 0-89290-124-1, A323). Soc for Visual.

Macrorie, Ken. Searching Writing. 352p. 1980. pap. 8.95x (ISBN 0-8104-6037-8). Hayden.

Russo, William. Secrets of the Research Paper: An Easy Guide to Success. 1980. pap. 1.95 (ISBN 0-931660-03-3). R Oman Pubns.

Strenski, Ellen & Manfred, Madge. The Research Paper Workbook. (English & Humanities Ser.). (Illus.). 283p. (Orig.). pap. text ed. 7.95x (ISBN 0-582-28203-9). Longman.

REPORTS, SCIENTIFIC
see Technical Reports

REPORTS, TECHNICAL
see Technical Reports

REPRESENTATIONS OF GROUPS
Nayrayana. Combinatorics, Representation Theory & Statistical Methods in Groups: Young Day Proceedings. 192p. 1980. 25.00 (ISBN 0-686-68601-2). Dekker.

REPRODUCTION
see also Cells; Embryology; Fertility; Fetus; Generative Organs; Genetics; Menstruation; Plants–Reproduction; Pregnancy; Sex; Sterility
Boyarsky, Saul & Polakoski, Kenneth, eds. Goals in Male Reproductive Research: Proceedings of Conference on Future Goals in Reproductive Medicine & Surgery, 20 September, 1979, Bethesda, Md. 144p. 1981. 30.00 (ISBN 0-08-025910-3). Pergamon.

Buffalo Reproduction & Artificail Insemination. (FAO Animal Production & Health Paper: No. 13). 370p. 1981. pap. 20.00 (ISBN 92-5-100743-8, F2086, FAO). Unipub.

Cytogenetics in Animal Reproduction. (Illus.). 96p. 1981. 45.00 (ISBN 0-85198-444-4, CAB 8, CAB). Unipub.

Flerko, B., et al, eds. Reproduction & Development: Proceedings of the 28th International Congress of Physiological Sciences, Budapest, 1980. LC 80-41877. (Advances in Physiological Sciences: Vol. 15). (Illus.). 200p. 1981. 25.00 (ISBN 0-08-027336-X). Pergamon.

Frajese, G., et al, eds. Oligozoospermia. 1981. text ed. price not set (ISBN 0-89004-589-5). Raven.

Hafez, E. S. Human Reproduction: Conception & Contraception. 2nd ed. (Illus.). 932p. 1980. text ed. 47.50 (ISBN 0-06-141066-7, Harper Medical). Har-Row.

Jagiello, Georgiana & Vogel, Henry J., eds. Bioregulators of Reproduction. (P&S Biomedical Sciences Ser.). 1981. price not set. Acad Pr.

Roberts, Helen. Women, Health & Reproduction. 208p. (Orig.). 1981. pap. 11.95 (ISBN 0-7100-0703-5). Routledge & Kegan.

Sadow, Janet, et al. Human Reproduction. 224p. 1980. 50.00x (ISBN 0-85664-878-7, Pub. by Croom Helm England). State Mutual Bk.

REPRODUCTION–JUVENILE LITERATURE
Newman, Matt & Lemay, Nita K. The Human Reproductive System. (Illus.). (gr. 5-8). 1980. pap. text ed. 88.00 (ISBN 0-89290-101-2, A794-SATC). Soc for Visual.

REPRODUCTION (PSYCHOLOGY)
see also Imagination; Memory; Mnemonics
Roberts, Helen. Women, Health & Reproduction. 208p. (Orig.). 1981. pap. 11.95 (ISBN 0-7100-0703-5). Routledge & Kegan.

REPRODUCTIVE ORGANS
see Generative Organs

REPTILES
see also Lizards; Snakes
Duellman, William E., et al. The South American Herpetofauna: Its Origin, Evolution, & Dispersal. (U of KS Museum of Nat. Hist. Monograph: No. 7). (Illus.). 485p. Date not set. 30.00 (ISBN 0-89338-009-1); pap. 25.00 (ISBN 0-89338-008-3). U of KS Mus Nat Hist.

Radlauer, Ed & Radlauer, Ruth. Reptile Mania. LC 80-21575. (Mania Bks). (Illus.). 32p. (gr. k-5). 1981. PLB 7.95g (ISBN 0-516-07785-6, Elk Grove Bks). Childrens.

Rivero, Juan A. Los Anfibios y Reptils de Puerto Rico. LC 76-11798. (Illus.). 448p. (Orig.). 1976. pap. write for info. (ISBN 0-8477-2317-8). U of PR Pr.

REPTILES–JUVENILE LITERATURE
DeTreville, Susan & DeTreville, Stan. Reptiles & Amphibians. (Illus.). 32p. (Orig.). 1981. pap. 3.50 (ISBN 0-89844-025-4). Troubador Pr.

RESCUE WORK
see also First Aid in Illness and Injury; Life-Saving; Search and Rescue Operations
Beattie, John. Lifeboats to the Rescue. LC 80-70704. (Illus.). 160p. 1981. 17.95 (ISBN 0-7153-8103-2). David & Charles.

RESEARCH
see also Agricultural Research; Botanical Research; Economic Research; Educational Research; Experimental Design; Geophysical Research; Hormone Research; Hydrocarbon Research; Information Services; Intelligence Service; Learning and Scholarship; Legal Research; Linguistic Research; Marketing Research; Medical Research; Methodology; Motivation Research (Marketing); Nursing Research; Operations Research; Organizational Research; Political Science Research; Psychiatric Research; Psychical Research; Psychological Research; Report Writing; Research, Industrial; Sex Research; Social Science Research; Social Science Research; Sociological Research; Universities and Colleges–Graduate Work
also subdivision Research under certain subjects, e.g. Nutrition–Research
Farkas, Janos, ed. Sociology of Science & Research. (Illus.). 503p. 1979. 47.50x (ISBN 963-05-2204-7). Intl Pubns Serv.

Gibson, Jack E. Managing Research Development. 450p. 1981. 35.00 (ISBN 0-471-08799-8, Pub. by Wiley-Interscience). Wiley.

Miller, Mara. Where to Go for What: How to Research, Organize & Present Your Information. (Illus.). 240p. 1981. 11.95 (ISBN 0-13-957217-1, Spec); pap. 5.95 (ISBN 0-13-957209-0). P-H.

Zallen, Harold & Zellen, Eugenia M. Ideas Plus Dollars: Research Methodology & Funding. 2nd ed. LC 79-55737. (Illus.). 1980. 12.95. Academic World.

RESEARCH, BOTANICAL
see Botanical Research

RESEARCH, INDUSTRIAL
see also Highway Research; Inventions; Marketing Research; New Products
Inventive Activity in the Asian & the Pacific Region. 152p. 1981. pap. 26.00 (WIPO66, WIPO). Unipub.

RESEARCH, MEDICAL
see Medical Research

RESEARCH, PSYCHOLOGICAL
see Psychological Research

RESEARCH BUILDINGS
see Laboratories

RESEARCH REPORTS
see Report Writing

RESERVES (ACCOUNTING)
Morrell. The Future of Dollar & World Reserve System. 1981. text ed. price not set (ISBN 0-408-10674-3); pap. text ed. price not set (ISBN 0-408-10675-1). Butterworth.

RESERVOIRS
see also Flood Dams and Reservoirs; Irrigation
Institute of Civil Engineers, UK. Floods & Reservoir Safety: An Engineering Guide. 1980. pap. 25.00x (ISBN 0-7277-0033-2, By Telford England). State Mutual Bk.

Reiss, L. H. Reservoir Engineering Aspects of Fractured Formations. 200p. (Orig.) 1981. pap. text ed. 14.95 (ISBN 0-87201-303-0). Gulf Pub.

RESETTLEMENT
see Land Settlement

RESIDENCES
see Architecture, Domestic; Dwellings

RESIDENT PHYSICIANS
see Hospitals–Staff

RESIDENTIAL CONSTRUCTION
see House Construction

RESIDENTIAL TREATMENT OF DISTURBED CHILDREN
see Child Psychotherapy–Residential Treatment

RESIDUE ARITHMETIC
see Modular Arithmetic

RESIDUES OF AGRICULTURAL CHEMICALS
see Spraying and Dusting Residues in Agriculture

RESISTANCE OF MATERIALS
see Strength of Materials

RESISTANCE OF PLANTS TO DISEASE
see Plants–Disease and Pest Resistance

RESISTANCE TO DRUGS IN MICRO-ORGANISMS
see Drug Resistance in Micro-Organisms

RESISTANCE TO GOVERNMENT
see Government, Resistance To

RESONANCE, MAGNETIC
see Magnetic Resonance

RESOURCE MANAGEMENT
see Conservation of Natural Resources

RESOURCE RECOVERY
see Recycling (Waste, etc.)

RESOURCES, MARINE
see Marine Resources

RESOURCES, NATURAL
see Natural Resources

RESPIRATION
see also Blood Gases; Respiratory Organs; Yoga, Hatha
Hutas, I. & Debreczeni, L. A., eds. Respiration: Proceedings of the 28th International Congress of Physiological Sciences, Budapest 1980. (Advances in Physiological Sciences: Vol. 10). (Illus.). 665p. 1981. 70.00 (ISBN 0-08-026823-4). Pergamon.

Kryer, M. Pathophysiology of Respiration. (Wiley Pathophysiology Ser.). 384p. 1981. 17.50 (ISBN 0-471-05923-4, Pub. by Wiley Med). Wiley.

Sullivan, Colin E., et al, eds. The Control of Breathing During Sleep. (Sleep Ser.: Vol. 3, No. 3-4). 256p. 1981. text ed. 30.00 (ISBN 0-89004-652-2). Raven.

RESPIRATORY DISEASES
see Respiratory Organs–Diseases

RESPIRATORY ORGANS
see also Larynx; Respiration
Melillo, G., et al, eds. Respiratory Allergy. 214p. 26.50. Masson Pub.

Mines, Allan. Respiratory Physiology. (Raven Press Ser. in Physiology). 180p. 1981. 12.50 (ISBN 0-89004-634-4). Raven.

Woolf, Colin R. The Clinical Core of Respiratory Medicine. (Illus.). 224p. 1981. pap. text ed. write for info (ISBN 0-397-50501-9). Lippincott.

RESPIRATORY ORGANS–DISEASES
Brody & Snider. Current Topics in Management of Respiratory Diseases, Vol. 1. 1981. pap. text ed. price not set (ISBN 0-443-08104-2). Churchill.

--Current Topics in Management of Respiratory Diseases, Vol. 2. 1981. pap. text ed. price not set (ISBN 0-443-08103-4). Churchill.

Brody, Jerome S. & Snider, Gordon, eds. Current Topics in the Management of Respiratory Diseases. (Illus.). 200p. 1981. pap. text ed. 12.50 (ISBN 0-443-08104-2). Churchill.

--Current Topics in the Management of Respiratory Disease, Vol II. (Illus.). 200p. 1981. pap. text ed. 12.50 (ISBN 0-443-08103-4). Churchill.

Emanuelsen, Kathy L. & Densmore, Mary J. Acute Respiratory Care. Percy, R. Craig, ed. (The Fleschner Series in Critical Care Nursing). (Illus.). 190p. (Orig.). 1981. pap. text ed. 9.95 (ISBN 0-937878-01-4). Fleschner.

Flenley, D. C., ed. Recent Advances in Respiratory Medicine, No. 2. (Recent Advances Ser.). (Illus.). 272p. 1981. lib. bdg. 42.25 (ISBN 0-443-02012-4). Churchill.

Gerbeaux, Jacques. Pediatric Respiratory Disease. 875p. 1981. 45.00 (ISBN 0-471-03456-8, Pub. by Wiley-Med). Wiley.

O'Brien, Richard J. & Drizd, Terence A. Basic Data on Spirometry in Adults Twenty-Five to Seventy-Four Years of Age: United States 1971-75. Cox, Klaudia, ed. (Ser. 11, No. 222). 50p. Date not set. pap. text ed. 1.75 (ISBN 0-8406-0205-7). Natl Ctr Health Stats.

Springer, Llewellyn W. Emergency Treatment of Accute Respiratory Disease. 3rd ed. (Illus.). 180p. 1981. pap. text ed. 11.95 (ISBN 0-87619-862-0). R J Brady.

Weiner, William J., ed. Respiratory Dysfunction in Neurologic Disease. LC 80-68262. (Illus.). 344p. 1980. monograph 32.50 (ISBN 0-87993-152-3). Futura Pub.

RESPONSIBILITY
see also Free Will and Determinism
Feinberg, Joel. Reason & Responsibility. 5th ed. 640p. 1980. text ed. 17.95x (ISBN 0-534-00924-7). Wadsworth Pub.

RESPONSIBILITY (LAW)
see Liability (Law)

RESPONSIBILITY, LEGAL
see Liability (Law)

RESTAURANT MANAGEMENT
Dyer, Dewey A. So You Want to Start a Restaurant? rev. 2nd ed. 192p. 1981. 12.95 (ISBN 0-8436-2199-0). CBI Pub.

King, Carole. Professional Dining Room Management. (Ahrens Ser.). 160p. 1980. pap. 7.95 (ISBN 0-8104-9471-X). Hayden.

RESTAURANTS, LUNCHROOMS, ETC.
see also Hotels, Taverns, etc.; Restaurant Management also names of restaurants; subdivisions Description or Description–Guidebooks under names of cities
Romantik Hotels. Romantik Hotels & Restaurants. 160p. 1981. 4.98 (ISBN 0-912944-66-8). Berkshire Traveller.

Strang, William A. Restaurant & Food Store Surveys, 1979: Evaluating the Potential for a Small Business Information System in Wisconsin. (Wisconsin Economy Studies: No. 18). (Orig.). 1979. pap. 5.00 (ISBN 0-86603-007-7). Bureau Busn Res U Wis.

Wilkinson, Jule. Three C's of Atmosphere. 1971. pap. 8.95 (ISBN 0-686-69418-X). CBI Pub.

RESTAURANTS, LUNCHROOMS, ETC.–EUROPE
Peebles Press International. Cheap & Cheaper Restaurant Guide to Paris. 192p. 1980. 8.95 (ISBN 0-13-128488-6, Spec); pap. 3.95 (ISBN 0-13-128470-3). P-H.

RESTAURANTS, LUNCHROOMS, ETC.–GREAT BRITAIN
Aoutomobile Association. Nine Hundred Ninety-Nine Places to Eat for Around Five Pounds. rev. ed. (Illus.). 288p. 1981. pap. price not set (ISBN 0-86145-055-8, Pub. by Auto Assn-British Tourist Authority England). Merrimack Bk Serv.

Automobile Association. AA Guesthouses & Inns in Britain. rev. ed. (Illus.). 264p. 1981. pap. write for info. (ISBN 0-86145-042-6, Pub. by Auto Assn-British Tourist Authority England). Merrimack Bk Serv.

--AA Guesthouses, Farmhouses & Inns in Europe. rev. ed. (Illus.). 256p. 1981. pap. write for info. (Pub. by Auto Assn-British Tourist Authority England). Merrimack Bk Serv.

--AA Hotels & Restaurants in Britain. rev. ed. (Illus.). 600p. 1981. pap. write for info. (ISBN 0-86145-040-X, Pub. by Auto Assn-British Tourist Authority England). Merrimack Bk Serv.

British Tourist Authority. Bed & Breakfast Stops Nineteen Eighty-One. (Illus.). 96p. 1981. pap. write for info. (Pub. by Auto Assn-British Tourist Authority England). Merrimack Bk Serv.

Scottish Tourist Board. Scotland: Bed & Breakfast. rev. ed. (Illus.). 252p. 1981. pap. price not set (ISBN 0-85419-170-4, Pub. by Auto Assn-British Tourist Authority England). Merrimack Bk Serv.

RESTAURANTS, LUNCHROOMS, ETC.–UNITED STATES
Beeler, Valerie. Dining in-Cincinnati. (Dining in Ser.). 1981. pap. 7.95 (ISBN 0-89716-079-7). Peanut Butter.

Bogert, John & Bogert, Joan. The Hundred Best Restaurants in the Valley of the Sun: 1981. 4th ed. LC 77-79784. 160p. 1980. pap. 2.25 (ISBN 0-937974-00-5). ADM Co.

Crain, Jim. Historic Country Inns of California. LC 77-727. 170p. 1980. pap. 5.95 (ISBN 0-87701-208-3). Chronicle Bks.

Dining in-Vail. (Dining in Ser.). 1981. pap. 7.95 (ISBN 0-89716-059-2). Peanut Butter.

Finigan, Robert. Robert Finigan's Guide to Discriminating Dining in San Francisco. (Illus.). 192p. (Orig.). 1981. pap. 6.95 (ISBN 0-89141-123-2). Presidio Pr.

Hemingway, Muffet & Armstrong, Russ. Dining in-Sun Valley. (Dining in Ser.). 1981. pap. 7.95 (ISBN 0-89716-078-9). Peanut Butter.

Lesburg, Sandy. Sandy Lesburg's One Hundred Great Restaurants of America. Michaelman, Herbert, ed. 1981. 12.95 (ISBN 0-517-53988-8, Michaelman Books). Crown.

Lords Locator for Fine Restaurants: Northeastern Edition. 2nd ed. 1981. pap. 5.95 vinyl covered (ISBN 0-686-69473-2). C Kerr Ent.

New Vegetarian Restaurant Guide. 288p. pap. 6.95 (ISBN 0-686-28809-2). Daystar Pub Co.

Peebles Press International & Zabronski, Ann. The Cheap & Cheaper Restaurant Guide to Manhattan. 192p. 1980. 8.95 (ISBN 0-686-69278-0, Spec); pap. 3.95 (ISBN 0-686-69279-9). P-H.

--Cheap & Cheaper Restaurant Guide to Manhattan. 192p. 1980. 8.95 (ISBN 0-13-128421-5, Spec); pap. 3,95 (ISBN 0-13-128413-4). P-H.

Tait, Elaine. Best Restaurants Philadelphia & Environs. rev. ed. (Best Restaurants Ser.). (Illus.). 225p. 1981. pap. 3.95 (ISBN 0-89286-189-4). One Hurd One Prods.

Waldo, Myra. Myra Waldo's Restaurant Guide to New York City & Vicinity. 1981. 434p. 1981. pap. 6.95 (ISBN 0-02-098900-8, Collier). Macmillan.

RESTORATION OF ART OBJECTS

see Art Objects–Conservation and Restoration

RESTORATION OF BOOKS

see Books–Conservation and Restoration

RESTORATION OF BUILDINGS

see Architecture–Conservation and Restoration

RESTORATION OF FURNITURE

see Furniture–Repairing; Furniture Finishing

RESTORATION OF PHOTOGRAPHS

see Photographs–Conservation and Restoration

RESTORATIVE DENTISTRY

see Dentistry, Operative

RESTRAINT OF ANIMALS

see Animals, Treatment Of

RESTRAINT OF TRADE

see also Competition, Unfair; Interstate Commerce; Monopolies; Price Policy

Powledge, Fred. Engineering of Restraint. 1.00 (ISBN 0-686-68336-6). Pub Aff Pr.

RESTRICTIVE TRADE PRACTICES

see Restraint of Trade

RESUMES (EMPLOYMENT)

De Prez, Caroline S. & De Prez, Richard J. Resume Manual for the Military: A Complete Job-Hunting Guide for Present & Future Veterans. LC 80-68132. (Illus.). 177p. (Orig.). 1980. pap. 10.95 (ISBN 0-9604728-0-0). Alfa Sierra.

Gray, Ernest. Successful Business Resumes. 265p. 1981. 10.95 (ISBN 0-8436-0771-8). CBI Pub.

Lathrop, Richard. Don't Use a Resume. 1980. pap. 1.95 (ISBN 0-89815-027-2). Ten Speed Pr.

Ulrich, Heinz & Conner, Robert. National Job Finding Guide. LC 79-6182. 336p. 1981. pap. 10.95 (ISBN 0-385-15782-7, Dolp). Doubleday.

RESURRECTION

see also Future Life; Jesus Christ–Resurrection

Reesman, Richard T. Contributions of the Major Philosophers into the Problem of Body Resurrection & Personal Immortality. (Illus.). 117p. 1981. 41.85 (ISBN 0-89920-021-4). Am Inst Psych.

RETAIL ADVERTISING

see Advertising

RETAIL FRANCHISES

see Franchises (Retail Trade)

RETAIL STORES

see Stores, Retail

RETAIL TRADE

see also Advertising; Department Stores; Franchises (Retail Trade); Grocery Trade; Packaging; Salesmen and Salesmanship; Stores, Retail; Supermarkets; Telephone Selling

Bluestone, Barry, et al. The Retail Revolution: Market Transformation, Investment, & Labor in the Modern Department Store. LC 80-26036. (Illus.). 192p. 1980. 19.95 (ISBN 0-86569-052-9). Auburn Hse.

Corbman, B. P. & Krieger, M. Mathematics of Retail Merchandising. 2nd ed. 411p. 1972. 19.95 (ISBN 0-471-06587-0). Wiley.

Larson, C. Basic Retailing. 2nd ed. 1981. 20.95 (ISBN 0-13-068072-9). P-H.

Meyer, Warren G., et al. Retailing Principles & Practices. 7th ed. LC 80-24885. (Illus.). 560p. (gr. 11-12). text ed. 13.48 (ISBN 0-07-041693-1, G). McGraw.

National Retail Merchants Association, ed. Voluntary Standard for the Electronic Purchase Order and Invoice. 1980. 18.75. Natl Ret Merch.

Productivity in General Merchandise Retailing. 1980. pap. 35.00 (G28680). Natl Ret Merch.

RETAIL TRADE–MANAGEMENT

Daykin, Leonard, ed. Loss Prevention: A Management Guide to Improving Retail Security. 1981. 19.50 (ISBN 0-911790-51-9). Prog Grocer.

RETAIL TRADE–GREAT BRITAIN

Guy, Clifford M. Retail Location & Retail Planning in Britain. 208p. 1980. text ed. 30.00x (ISBN 0-566-00270-1, Pub. by Gower Pub Co England). Renouf.

RETARDED CHILDREN

see Mentally Handicapped Children

RETARDED READERS

see Reading Disability

RETENTION (PSYCHOLOGY)

see Memory

RETINA–DISEASES

Benson, William E. Retinal Detachment Diagnosis & Treatment. (Illus.). 208p. 1980. text ed. 27.50 (ISBN 0-06-140410-1, Harper Medical). Har-Row.

Shafer, Donald M. Manual on Retinal Detachment. 150p. 1981. write for info. (1550-8). Williams & Wilkins.

RETIREMENT

see also Aged; Retirement Income

Bradford, Leland P. Preparing for Retirement: A Program for Survival - A Participants Workbook. LC 80-52897. 106p. 1981. pap. write for info. (ISBN 0-88390-160-9). Univ Assocs.

--Preparing for Retirement: A Program for Survival - A Trainers Kit. LC 80-2897. 196p. 1981. looseleaf bdg. 39.95 (ISBN 0-88390-161-7). Univ Assocs.

Clark, Robert L., ed. Retirement Policy in an Aging Society. LC 79-56502. (Illus.). vii, 215p. 1980. 16.75 (ISBN 0-8223-0441-4). Duke.

Disston, Harry. Beginning the Rest of Your Life: A Guide to an Active Retirement. 160p. (Orig.). 1981. pap. 4.95 (ISBN 0-87000-518-9). Arlington Hse.

Downs, Hugh & Roll, Richard J. Hugh Downs' The Best Years Book: How to Plan for Fulfillment, Security, & Happiness in the Retirement Years. 1981. 14.95 (ISBN 0-440-04064-7, E Friede). Delacorte.

Dye, Harold E. No Rocking Chair for Me. 1980. pap. 3.95 (ISBN 0-8054-5286-9). Broadman.

Foner, Anne & Schwab, Karen. Aging & Retirement. LC 80-24765. (Social Gerontology Ser.). 192p. (Orig.). 1981. pap. text ed. 8.95 (ISBN 0-8185-0444-7). Brooks-Cole.

Gordus, Jeanne P. Leaving Early: Perspectives & Problems in Current Retirement Practice & Policy. LC 80-39653. 88p. (Orig.). 1980. pap. text ed. 4.00 (ISBN 0-911558-78-0). Upjohn Inst.

Jessup, L. F. Law of Retirement, Vol. 48. 2nd ed. 1979. 5.95 (ISBN 0-379-11124-1). Oceana.

Martin, Kathryn. A Question of Age: The Dorm & I. 224p. 1981. price not set (ISBN 0-936988-01-0). Tompson & Rutter.

Willing, Jules Z. The Reality of Retirement: The Inner Experience of Becoming a Retired Person. 224p. 1981. 10.95 (ISBN 0-688-00298-6); pap. 6.95 (ISBN 0-688-00394-X). Morrow.

Woodall's Nineteen Eighty-One Sunbelt Retirement Directory. 1981. pap. 6.95 (ISBN 0-671-41536-0). Woodall.

RETIREMENT, PLACES OF

Dickinson, Peter. Retirement Edens. 1981. 14.95 (ISBN 0-525-93173-2); pap. 8.95 (ISBN 0-525-93174-0). Dutton.

RETIREMENT INCOME

see also Old Age Pensions

Colberg, Marshall R. Social Security Retirement Test: Right or Wrong? 1978. pap. 4.25 (ISBN 0-8447-3307-5). Am Enterprise.

Gollin, James. The Star Spangled Retirement Dream: Why It's Going Sour & What You Can Do About It. 224p. 1981. 12.95 (ISBN 0-684-16866-9, ScribT). Scribner.

Mariner, Elwyn E. The Massachusetts Retirement Plan. 9th ed. 1977. pap. 2.50. Mariner.

Smith, Don P. Retired Man's Way to Riches. 330p. 1980. pap. 15.00 (ISBN 0-937514-10-1, New Era). World Merch Import.

Social Security, Savings Plan & Other Retirement Arrangements: Learning Guide CEBS Course III. 1980. spiral 13.00 (ISBN 0-89154-130-6). Intl Found Employ.

Social Security, Savings Plans & Other Retirement Arrangements: Answers to Questions on Subject Matter for Learning Guide CEBS Course III. rev. ed. 101p. (Orig.). 1980. spiral bdg. o.p. 13.00; pap. 10.00 (ISBN 0-89154-131-4). Intl Found Employ.

RETIREMENT PENSIONS

see Civil Service Pensions; Old Age Pensions; Pensions

RETREATS

Here are entered works dealing with periods of retirement for the purpose of meditation and spiritual development.

see also Meditations

Haas, Joseph S. The Northeast Retreat. (Cathedral of the Beechwoods Ser.: No. 1). (Illus.). 102p. (Orig.). 1980. write for info. (ISBN 0-9605552-0-X). Haas Ent NH.

RETRIBUTION

see Future Life; Hell

RETZ, JEAN FRANCOIS PAUL DE GONDI, CARDINAL DE, 1613-1679

Watts, Derek A. Cardinal De Retz: The Ambiguities of a Seventeenth-Century Mind. 308p. 1980. text ed. 39.95x (ISBN 0-19-815762-2). Oxford U Pr.

REUSABLE SPACE VEHICLES

Powers, Robert M. Shuttle: The World's First Spaceship. 1980. pap. 2.75 (ISBN 0-446-95331-8). Warner Bks.

REVELATION

see also Apocalyptic Literature

Maclean, Dorothy. To Hear the Angels Sing. 192p. (Orig.). 1980. pap. text ed. 7.00 (ISBN 0-936878-01-0). Lorian Pr.

REVENUE LAW

see Taxation–Law

REVENUE SHARING

see Intergovernmental Fiscal Relations

REVIEWING (BOOKS)

see Book Reviewing

REVIEWS

see Books–Reviews

REVIVAL (RELIGION)

see Evangelistic Work

REVIVAL OF LETTERS

see Renaissance

REVIVALISTS

see Evangelists

REVIVALS

see also Enthusiasm; Evangelistic Work; Jesus People; Retreats

Dieter, Melvin E. The Holiness Revival of the Nineteenth Century. LC 80-17259. (Studies in Evangelicalism: No. 1). 366p. 1980. 17.50 (ISBN 0-8108-1328-9). Scarecrow.

Sprague, William B. Lectures on Revivals. 1978. 12.95 (ISBN 0-85151-276-3). Banner of Truth.

REVOLUTION, AMERICAN

see United States–History–Revolution, 1775-1783

REVOLUTION, FRENCH

see France–History–Revolution, 1789-1799

REVOLUTION OF 1848 IN FRANCE

see France–History–Second Republic, 1848-1852

REVOLUTION OF 1848 IN HUNGARY

see Hungary–History

REVOLUTIONARY WAR, AMERICAN

see United States–History–Revolution, 1775-1783

REVOLUTIONISTS

Hachey, Thomas & Weber, Ralph E. The Awakening of a Sleeping Giant: Third World Leaders & National Liberation. LC 80-12517. 160p. 1981. pap. text ed. 6.50 (ISBN 0-89874-081-9). Krieger.

Raylor, A. J. Revolutions & Revolutionaries. LC 80-66006. 1980. 12.95 (ISBN 0-689-11069-3). Atheneum.

REVOLUTIONISTS–IRELAND

Pearse, P. H. The Letters of P. H. Pearse. O'Buachalla, Seamas, ed. 528p. 1980. text ed. 31.25x (ISBN 0-391-01678-4). Humanities.

REVOLUTIONISTS–RUSSIA

Toplitsky, Tania S. The Russian Revolution in Nineteen Hundred Five. 164p. 1981. 13.50 (ISBN 0-682-49720-7). Exposition.

REVOLUTIONS

see also Civil War; Coups D'Etat; Europe–History–1815-1871; Government, Resistance to; Revolutionists; Terrorism

also France–History–Revolution, 1789-1799; United States–History–Revolution, 1775-1783, and similar headings

Burton, Anthony. Revolutionary Violence: The Theories. LC 77-83808. 1978. 14.00x (ISBN 0-8448-1262-5). Crane-Russak Co.

Hachey, Thomas & Weber, Ralph E. The Awakening of a Sleeping Giant: Third World Leaders & National Liberation. LC 80-12517. 160p. 1981. pap. text ed. 6.50 (ISBN 0-89874-081-9). Krieger.

Hawke, David. In the Midst of a Revolution. LC 80-23581. 235p. 1980. Repr. of 1961 ed. lib. bdg. 23.50x (ISBN 0-313-22604-0, HAIT). Greenwood.

Leiden, Carl & Schmitt, Karl M. The Politics of Violence: Revolution in the Modern World. LC 80-23161. x, 244p. 1980. Repr. of 1968 ed. lib. bdg. 27.50x (ISBN 0-313-22463-3, LEPV). Greenwood.

Nevinson, Henry W. Essays in Rebellion. 241p. 1980. Repr. of 1913 ed. lib. bdg. 30.00 (ISBN 0-8495-4018-6). Arden Lib.

Raylor, A. J. Revolutions & Revolutionaries. LC 80-66006. 1980. 12.95 (ISBN 0-689-11069-3). Atheneum.

Weiss & Klass. Case Studies in Regulation: Revolution & Reform. 1981. pap. text ed. 9.95 (ISBN 0-316-92893-3). Little.

REVOLVING SYSTEMS

see Rotational Motion

REVUES

see Musical Revues, Comedies, etc.

REWARDS (PRIZES, ETC.)

Collis, Maurice. Raffles. 1970. 4.95 (ISBN 0-571-09227-6, Pub. by Faber & Faber). Merrimack Bk Serv.

Donnelly, R. H., et al. Active Games & Contests. 2nd ed. 672p. 1958. 17.50 (ISBN 0-471-07088-2). Wiley.

REYES, ALFONSO, 1889-

Morales, Jorge Luis. Alfonso Reyes y la Literatural Espanola. (Mante y Palabra Ser.). 193p. (Span.). 1980. 6.25 (ISBN 0-8477-0558-7); pap. 5.00 (ISBN 0-8477-0559-5). U of PR Pr.

RHEOLOGY

see also Colloids; Deformations (Mechanics); Elasticity; Plasticity

Billington, E. W. & Tate, A. The Physics of Deformation & Flow. (Illus.). 720p. 1981. text ed. 59.00 (ISBN 0-07-005285-9, C). McGraw.

Vinogradov, G. V. & Malkin, A. Y. Rheology of Polymers. (Illus.). 468p. 1981. 58.00 (ISBN 0-387-09778-3). Springer-Verlag.

Walters, Kenneth. Rheometry: Industrial Applications. 432p. 1981. write for info. (ISBN 0-471-27878-5, Pub. by Wiley-Interscience). Wiley.

RHEOLOGY (BIOLOGY)

Chmiel, Horst & Walitza, Eckehard. Rheology of Blood & Synovial Fluids. 184p. 1981. 42.00 (ISBN 0-471-27858-0, Pub. by Wiley-Interscience). Wiley.

Fung, Y. C. Biomechanics: Mechanical Properties of Living Tissues. (Illus.). 400p. 1980. 29.80 (ISBN 0-387-90472-7). Springer-Verlag.

Hwang, N. H. & Gross, D. R., eds. Biorheology: Physics of Biological Tissues. (NATO Advanced Study Institute Ser.: Applied Science). 382p. 1980. 42.50x (ISBN 90-286-0950-4). Sijthoff & Noordhoff.

Mueller, W. & Wagenhaeuser, F. J., eds. Die Lumboischialgie. (Fortbildungskurse Fuer Rheumatologie Ser.: Vol. 6). (Illus.). viii, 240p. 1981. pap. 54.00 (ISBN 3-8055-2207-X). S Karger.

RHETORIC

see also Criticism; Debates and Debating; English Language–Rhetoric; Exposition (Rhetoric); Lectures and Lecturing; Letter-Writing; Narration (Rhetoric); Oratory; Persuasion (Rhetoric); Preaching; Public Speaking; Style, Literary

also subdivisions Composition and Exercises, and Rhetoric under names of languages; also figures of speech, e.g. Metaphor

Bramer, George R. & Sedley, Dorothy. Writing for Readers. (Illus.). 500p. 1981. text ed. price not set (ISBN 0-675-08045-2); write for info. tchr's. ed (ISBN 0-675-08038-X); instr's. manual 3.95 (ISBN 0-686-69504-6). Merrill.

Cathcart, Robert. Post Communication: Rhetorical Analysis & Evaluation. LC 80-36842. (Speech Communication Ser.). 144p. 1981. pap. text ed. 5.95 (ISBN 0-672-61520-7). Bobbs.

Dubois, Jacques, et al. A General Rhetoric. Burrell, Paul B. & Slotkin, Edgar M., trs. from Fr. LC 80-24495. (Illus.). 288p. 1981. text ed. 18.95x (ISBN 0-8018-2326-9). Johns Hopkins.

Ferre, John P. & Pauley, Steven E. Rhetorical Patterns: An Anthology of Contemporary Essays. (Illus.). 208p. 1981. pap. text ed. 6.95 (ISBN 0-675-08023-1). Merrill.

Holladay, Sylvia & Brown, Thomas. Options in Rhetoric: Writing & Reading. (Illus.). 416p. 1981. pap. text ed. 8.95 (ISBN 0-13-638254-1). P-H.

Manoni, Mary H. & O'Donnell, Elizabeth L. Rhetoric in Effective Communication. LC 78-730061. (Illus.). 1977. pap. text ed. 99.00 (ISBN 0-89290-122-5, A321). Soc for Visual.

Moody, P. Writing Today: A Rhetoric Handbook. 1981. 10.95 (ISBN 0-13-971556-8); pap. 9.95 wkbk & key (ISBN 0-13-971572-X). P-H.

Provost, Gary. Make Every Word Count. LC 80-23699. 256p. 1980. 10.95 (ISBN 0-89879-020-4). Writers Digest.

Ruszkiewicz, John J. Well-Bound Words: A Rhetoric. 1981. text ed. 11.95x (ISBN 0-673-15355-X). Scott F.

Tibbetts, Charlene & Tibbetts, A. M. Strategies: A Rhetoric & Reader. 1981. pap. text ed. 8.95x (ISBN 0-673-15461-0). Scott F.

RHETORIC–1500-1800

Horner, Winifred B., ed. Historical Rhetoric: An Annotated Bibliography of Selected Sources in English. 1980. lib. bdg. 35.00 (ISBN 0-8161-8191-8). G K Hall.

Murphy, James J. Rhetoric in the Middle Ages: A History of Rhetorical Theory from Saint Augustine to the Renaissance. 1981. pap. 7.95x (ISBN 0-520-04406-1, CAMPUS 277). U of Cal Pr.

RHEUMATIC GOUT

see Rheumatoid Arthritis

RHEUMATIC HEART DISEASE

Weisman, M. H. Rheumatic Disease. 1981. text ed. price not set (ISBN 0-443-08100-X). Churchill.

Weisman, Michael. Rheumetic Disease. (Illus.). 288p. 1981. lib. bdg. 25.00 (ISBN 0-443-08100-X). Churchill.

RHEUMATISM

see also Arthritis; Rheumatoid Arthritis

Ansell, Barbara M. Rheumatic Disorders in Childhood. LC 80-40275. (Postgraduate Paediatrics Ser.). (Illus.). 344p. 1980. text ed. 66.95 (ISBN 0-407-00186-7). Butterworths.

Bohan, Anthony. Rheumatology Continuing Education Review. 1980. spiral bdg. 14.00 (ISBN 0-87488-333-4). Med Exam.

Rosenbaum, Edward E. Rheumatology. (New Directions in Therapy Ser.). 1980. pap. 15.50 (ISBN 0-87488-683-X). Med Exam.

RHEUMATOID ARTHRITIS

Bohan, Anthony. Rheumatology Continuing Education Review. 1980. spiral bdg. 14.00 (ISBN 0-87488-333-4). Med Exam.

Rosenbaum, Edward E. Rheumatology. (New Directions in Therapy Ser.). 1980. pap. 15.50 (ISBN 0-87488-683-X). Med Exam.

RHINOCEROS

The International Trade in Rhinoceros Products. 83p. 1980. pap. 7.50 (ISBN 2-88032-203-0, IUCN-86, IUCN). Unipub.

Schenkel, R. & Schenkel-Hulliger, L. Ecology & Behavior of the Black Rhinoceros (Diceros Bicornis L.) A Field Study. (Illus.). 100p. (Orig.). 1969. pap. text ed. 16.50. Parey Sci Pubs.

RHINOLOPHUS

see Bats

RHODE ISLAND

see also names of cities, etc., in Rhode Island

Fradin, Dennis. Rhode Island: In Words & Pictures. LC 80-22669. (Young People's Stories of Our States Ser.). (Illus.). 48p. (gr. 2-5). 1981. PLB 8.65g (ISBN 0-516-03939-3, Time Line). Childrens.

RHODE ISLAND–GENEALOGY

Boyer, Carl, 3rd, et al. Brown Families of Bristol Counties, Massachusetts & Rhode Island & Descendants of Jared Talbot. LC 80-68755. (New England Colonial Families: Vol. 1). 219p. 1980. 18.35 (ISBN 0-936124-04-0). C Boyer.

RHODE ISLAND–HISTORY

Vexler, R. I. Rhode Island Chronology & Factbook, Vol. 39. 1978. 8.50 (ISBN 0-379-16164-8). Oceana.

RHODESIA

Pollak, Oliver & Pollak, Karen. Rhodesia-Zimbabwe. (World Bibliographical Ser.: No. 4). 197p. 1979. 25.25 (ISBN 0-903450-14-3). ABC-Clio.

RHODESIA–ECONOMIC CONDITIONS
Zimbabwe Directory 1980-81: Including Botswana. 71st ed. LC 38-1460. Orig. Title: Rhodesia Directory. (Illus.). 996p. (Orig.). 1980. pap. 45.00x (ISBN 0-8002-2747-6). Intl Pubns Serv.

RHODODENDRON
Van Veen, Ted. Rhododendrons in America. 2nd ed. LC 77-104390. (Illus.). 1980. pap. 25.00 (ISBN 0-8323-0374-7). Binford.

RHOPALOCERA
see Butterflies

RHYOLITE, NEVADA
Weight, Harold O. & Weight, Lucile. Rhyolite-Death Valley's Ghost City of Golden Dreams. 9th ed. 1980. pap. 1.95. Calico Pr.

RHYS, JEAN
Nebeker, Helen. Jean Rhys: Woman in Passage. 250p. 1981. price not set (ISBN 0-920792-04-9). Eden Women.

RHYTHM
see also Versification
Wilson, Katherine M. The Real Rhythm in English Poetry. 171p. 1980. Repr. of 1929 ed. lib. bdg. 25.00 (ISBN 0-89987-860-1). Darby Bks.

RHYTHM (ART)
see Proportion (Art)

RHYTHMIC GAMES
see Games with Music

RICE
Beyond IR Eight IRRI's Second Decade. 27p. 1980. pap. 20.25 (ISBN 0-686-69538-0, R 113, IRRI). Unipub.
Biological Nitrogen Fixation by Epiphytic Microoganisms in Rice Fields. (IRRI Research Paper Ser.: No. 47). 14p. 1981. pap. 5.00 (ISBN 0-686-69532-1, R 117, IRRI). Unipub.
Descriptors for Rice Oryza Satival. 21p. 1981. pap. 5.00 (ISBN 0-686-69533-X, R 121, IRRI). Unipub.
Intergovernmental Group on Rice. Report of the Twenty-Third Session of the Intergovernmental Group on Rice to the Committee on Commodity Problems. 29p. 1980. pap. 6.00 (ISBN 92-5-100926-0, F2043, FAO). Unipub.
International Bibliography of Azolla. 66p. 1979. pap. 34.50 (R129, IRRI). Unipub.
The International Bibliography of Rice Research: Nineteen Sixty-Seven Supplement. 353p. 1980. pap. 21.50 (ISBN 0-686-69536-4, R 104, IRRI). Unipub.
The International Bibliography of Rice Research 1977: Supplement. 556p. 1978. pap. 100.00 (R122, IRRI). Unipub.
IRRI Annual Report for 1978. 478p. 1979. pap. 43.00 (R128, IRRI). Unipub.
Quality Characteristics of Milled Rice Grown in Different Countries. (IRRI Research Paper Ser.: No. 48). 25p. 1981. pap. 5.00 (ISBN 0-686-69534-8, R 118, IRRI). Unipub.
Recent Developements in Research on Nitrogen Fertilizers for Rice. (IRRI Research Paper Ser.: No. 49). 11p. 1981. pap. 5.00 (ISBN 0-686-69535-6, R 119, IRRI). Unipub.
Rice Improvement in China & Other Asian Countries. 307p. 1980. pap. 19.50 (ISBN 0-686-69537-2, R 116, IRRI). Unipub.
Rice Milling Equipment Operation & Maintenance. (Agricultural Services Bulletin: No. 22). 95p. 1974. pap. 6.00 (F1972, FAO). Unipub.

RICE–DISEASES AND PESTS
A Handbook of Rice Diseases in the Tropics. 58p. 1979. pap. 5.00 (R032, IRRI). Unipub.
Implication of the International Rice Blast Nursery Data to the Genetics of Resistance. (IRRI Research Paper Ser.: No. 40). 19p. 1979. pap. 5.00 (R080, IRRI). Unipub.
Insect Pests of Rice. 68p. 1977. pap. 5.00 (R005, IRRI). Unipub.
Recent Studies on Rice Tungro Disease at IRRI. (IRRI Research Paper Ser.: No. 1). 11p. 1976. pap. 5.00 (R041, IRRI). Unipub.
Research Highlights for 1977. 122p. Date not set. pap. 18.50 (R127, IRRI). Unipub.
Residues of Carbofuran Applied As a Systematic Insecticide in Irrigated Wetland Rice: Implications for Insect Control. (IRRI Research Paper Ser.: No. 17). 28p. 1978. pap. 5.00 (R057, IRRI). Unipub.
Rice Leaf Folder: Mass Rearing & a Proposal for Screening for Varietal Resistance in the Greenhouse. (IRRI Research Paper Ser.: No. 27). 17p. 1979. pap. 5.00 (R067, IRRI). Unipub.
Rice Ragged Stunt Disease in the Phillipines. (IRRI Research Paper Ser.: No. 16). 25p. 1978. pap. 5.00 (R056, IRRI). Unipub.
Rice Virus Diseases. 142p. 1972. pap. 4.00 (R014, IRRI). Unipub.
Screening Rice for Tolerance to Mineral Stresses. (IRRI Research Paper Ser.: No. 6). 20p. 1977. pap. 5.00 (R046, IRRI). Unipub.
Study on Kresek (Wilt) of the Rice Bacterial Blight Syndrome. (IRRI Research Paper Ser.: No. 39). 8p. 1979. pap. 5.00 (R079, IRRI). Unipub.
Transmission of Rice Tungro Virus at Various Temperatures: A Transitory Virus-Vector Interaction. (IRRI Research Paper Ser.: No. 4). 26p. 1977. pap. 5.00 (R044, IRRI). Unipub.
Variation in Varietal Reaction to Rice Tungro Disease: Possible Causes. (IRRI Research Paper Ser.: No. 32). 8p. 1979. pap. 5.00 (R072, IRRI). Unipub.
Zinc Deficiency in Rice: A Review of Research at the International Rice Research Institute. (IRRI Research Paper Ser.: No. 9). 17p. 1977. pap. 5.00 (R049, IRRI). Unipub.

RICE BREEDING
An Agro-Climatic Classification for Evaluating Cropping Systems Potentials in Southeast Asian Rice Growing Regions. 10p. pap. 5.00 (R112, IRRI). Unipub.
Aliways to Rice Garden: A Case Study of the Intensification of Rice Farming in Camarines Sur, Philippines. (IRRI Research Paper Ser.: No. 36). 23p. 1979. pap. 5.00 (R076, IRRI). Unipub.
An Analysis of the Labor-Intensive Continuous Rice Production System. (IRRI Research Paper Ser.: No. 29). 39p. 1979. pap. 5.00 (R069, IRRI). Unipub.
Anatomy of a Peasant Economy. 149p. 1978. pap. 12.50 (R040, IRRI). Unipub.
Barriers to Increased Rice Production in Eastern India. (IRRI Research Search Paper Ser.: No. 25). 23p. 1979. pap. 5.00 (R065, IRRI). Unipub.
Beyond IR Eight IRRI's Second Decade. 27p. 1980. pap. 20.25 (ISBN 0-686-69538-0, R 113, IRRI). Unipub.
A Bibliography of Rice Literature Translations Available in the International Rice Institute Library & Documentation Center. 191p. 1976. pap. 36.00 (R108, IRRI). Unipub.
Biological Constraints to Farmers' Rice Yields in Three Philippine Provinces. (IRRI Research Paper Ser.: No. 30). 69p. 1979. pap. 5.00 (R070, IRRI). Unipub.
Biological Nitrogen Fixation in Paddy Field Studies by SITU Acetylene-Reduction Assays: In Paddy Field Studies by SITU Acetylene-Reduction Assays. (IRRI Research Paper Ser.: No. 3). 16p. 1977. pap. 5.00 (R043, IRRI). Unipub.
Brown Planthopper: Threat to Rice Production in Asia. 369p. 1979. pap. 21.50 (R038, IRRI). Unipub.
Changes in Rice Farming in Selected Areas of Asia. 377p. 1975. pap. 16.00 (R011, IRRI). Unipub.
Changes in Rice Harvesting Systems in Central Luzon & Laguna. (IRRI Research Paper Ser.: No. 31). 24p. 1979. pap. 5.00 (R071, IRRI). Unipub.
Constraints to High Yields on Asian Rice Farms: An Interim Report. 235p. 1977. pap. 11.00 (R010, IRRI). Unipub.
The Contribution of Varietal Tolerance for Problem Soils to Yield Stability in Rice. (IRRI Research Paper Ser.: No. 43). 15p. 1979. pap. 5.00 (R083, IRRI). Unipub.
Descriptors for Rice Oryza Satival. 21p. 1981. pap. 5.00 (ISBN 0-686-69533-X, R 121, IRRI). Unipub.
Determining Superior Cropping Patterns for Small Farms in a Dryland Rice Environment: Test of Methodology. (IRRI Research Paper Ser.: No. 33). 15p. 1979. pap. 5.00 (R073, IRRI). Unipub.
Differential Response of Rice Varieties to the Brown Plant-Hopper in International Screening Tests. (IRRI Research Paper Ser.: No. 52). 13p. 1980. pap. 5.00 (R132, IRRI). Unipub.
Diffusion & Adoption of Genetic Materials Among Rice Breeding Programs in Asia. (IRRI Research Paper Ser.: No. 18). 25p. 1978. pap. 5.00 (R058, IRRI). Unipub.
Drought & Rice Improvement in Perspective. (IRRI Research Paper Ser.: No. 14). 27p. 1978. pap. 5.00 (R054, IRRI). Unipub.
Economic Consequences of the New Rice Technology. 402p. 1978. pap. 20.00 (R012, IRRI). Unipub.
The Effect of the New Rice Technology on Family Labor Utilization in Laguna. (IRRI Research Paper Ser.: No. 42). 17p. 1979. pap. 5.00 (R082, IRRI). Unipub.
Evapotranspiration from Rice Fields. (IRRI Research Paper Ser.: No. 34). 15p. 1979. pap. 5.00 (R074, IRRI). Unipub.
A Farmers Primer on Growing Rice. 221p. 1979. pap. 14.50 (R024, IRRI). Unipub.
Field Problems of Tropical Rice. 95p. 1974. pap. 5.00 (R006, IRRI). Unipub.
The Flowering Response of the Rice Plant to Photoperiod: A Review of the Literature. 75p. 1976. pap. 5.00 (R023, IRRI). Unipub.
Genetic Analysis of Traits Related to Grain Characteristics & Quality in Two Crosses of Rice. (IRRI Research Paper Ser.: No. 35). 14p. 1979. pap. 5.00 (R075, IRRI). Unipub.
Genetic & Sociological Aspects of Rice Breeding in India. (IRRI Research Paper Ser.: No. 10). 31p. 1977. pap. 5.00 (R050, IRRI). Unipub.
Genetic Interrelationships to Improved Rice Varieties in Asia. (IRRI Research Paper Ser.: No. 23). 34p. 1979. pap. 5.00 (R063, IRRI). Unipub.
Germplasm Bank Information Retrieval System. (IRRI Research Paper Ser.: No. 45). 24p. 1979. pap. 5.00 (R085, IRRI). Unipub.
A Handook on the Methodology for an Integrated Experiment-Survey on Rice Yield Constraints. 59p. 1978. pap. 6.00 (R130, IRRI). Unipub.
I R R I Annual Report for Nineteen Seventy-Five. 479p. 1976. pap. 37.50 (R090, IRRI). Unipub.
I R R I Annual Report for Nineteen Seventy-Six. 418p. 1977. pap. 43.00 (R089, IRRI). Unipub.
I R R I Annual Report for Nineteen Seventy-Seven. 548p. 1978. pap. 43.00 (R088, IRRI). Unipub.
Implication of the International Rice Blast Nursery Data to the Genetics of Resistance. (IRRI Research Paper Ser.: No. 40). 19p. 1979. pap. 5.00 (R080, IRRI). Unipub.
International Bibliography of Rice Research Cumulative Indexes Nineteen Seventy-One to Nineteen Seventy-Five. 232p. 1976. pap. 57.50 (R098, IRRI). Unipub.
International Bibliography of Rice Research Cumulative Indexes Nineteen Sixty-Six to Nineteen Seventy. 153p. 1972. pap. 21.50 (R091, IRRI). Unipub.
International Bibliography of Rice Research Nineteen Sixty-Eight Supplement. 348p. 1969. pap. 21.50 (R105, IRRI). Unipub.
International Bibliography of Rice Research Nineteen Seventy-Five Supplement. 452p. 1976. pap. 57.50 (R097, IRRI). Unipub.
International Bibliography of Rice Research Nineteen Seventy-Four Supplement. 386p. 1975. pap. 36.00 (R096, IRRI). Unipub.
The International Bibliography of Rice Research Nineteen Sixty-Nine Supplement. 289p. 1970. pap. 21.50 (R106, IRRI). Unipub.
International Bibliography of Rice Research Nineteen Sixty-One Supplement. 164p. 1963. pap. 21.50 (R100, IRRI). Unipub.
International Bibliography of Rice Research Nineteen Seventy-One Supplement. 282p. 1972. pap. 21.50 (R093, IRRI). Unipub.
International Bibliography of Rice Research Nineteen Seventy Supplement. 1971. pap. 21.50 (R092, IRRI). Unipub.
International Bibliography of Rice Research Nineteen Sixty-Six Supplement. 296p. 1967. pap. 21.50 (R103, IRRI). Unipub.
International Bibliography of Rice Research Nineteen Sixty-Seven Supplement. 143p. 1968. pap. 21.50 (R115, IRRI). Unipub.
International Bibliography of Rice Research Nineteen Seventy-Six Supplement. 470p. 1977. pap. 63.25 (R099, IRRI). Unipub.
International Bibliography of Rice Research Nineteen Sixty-Two Supplement. 164p. 1964. pap. 21.50 (RIOI, IRRI). Unipub.
International Bibliography of Rice Research Nineteen Seventy-Two Supplement. 295p. 1973. pap. 21.50 (R094, IRRI). Unipub.
International Bibliography of Rice Research Nineteen Sixty-Three Supplement. 213p. 1965. pap. 21.50 (R102, IRRI). Unipub.
International Bibliography of Rice Research Nineteen Seventy-Three Supplement. 321p. 1974. pap. 21.50 (R095, IRRI). Unipub.
The International Bibliography of Rice Research 1978: Supplement. 598p. 1979. pap. 106.50 (R123, IRRI). Unipub.
International Bibliography on Cropping Systems Nineteen Seventy-Five. 195p. 1977. pap. 36.00 (R109, IRRI). Unipub.
The International Bibliography on Cropping Systems 1976. 181p. 1977. pap. 36.00 (R124, IRRI). Unipub.
Internatonal Deep-Water Rice Workshop, 1978. Proceedings. 300p. 1979. pap. 15.50 (R037, IRRI). Unipub.
Interpretive Analysis of Selected Papers from Changes in Rice Farming in Selected Areas of Asia. 825p. 1978. pap. 11.00 (R007, IRRI). Unipub.
IR Forty-Two: A Rice Type for Small Farmers of South & Southeast Asia. (IRRI Research Paper Ser.: No. 44). 10p. 1979. pap. 5.00 (R084, IRRI). Unipub.
Laboratory Manual for Physiological Studies of Rice. 83p. 1976. pap. 4.00 (R020, IRRI). Unipub.
Major Research in Upland Rice. 255p. 1975. pap. 11.00 (R021, IRRI). Unipub.
Manual for Field Collectors of Rice. 32p. 1975. pap. 5.00 (R110, IRRI). Unipub.
Matsushima, Seizo. Rice Cultivation for the Million. 350p. 1980. 35.00x (ISBN 0-89955-203-X, Pub. by JSSP Japan). Intl Schol Bk Serv.
Measuring the Economic Benefits of New Technologies to Small Rice Farmers. (IRRI Research Paper Ser.: No. 28). 21p. 1979. pap. 5.00 (R068, IRRI). Unipub.
Methods of Screening Rices for Varietal Resistance to Cercospora Leaf Spot. (IRRI Research Paper Ser.: No. 19). 9p. 1979. pap. 5.00 (R059, IRRI). Unipub.
Multi-Site Tests Environments & Breeding Strategies for New Rice Technology. (IRRI Research Paper Ser.: No. 7). 30p. 1977. pap. 5.00 (R047, IRRI). Unipub.
Parentage of IRRI Crosses IR1-R30,000. 302p. pap. 14.50 (R0120, IRRI). Unipub.
Pearson, Scott R. & Stryker, J. Dirck. Rice in West Africa: Policy & Economics. LC 80-50906. (Illus.). 472p. 1981. 39.00x (ISBN 0-8047-1095-3). Stanford U Pr.
Rainfed Lowland Rice As a Research Priority: An Economist's View. (IRRI Research Paper Ser.: No. 26). 50p. 1979. pap. 5.00 (R066, IRRI). Unipub.
Rainfed Lowland Rice: Selected Papers from the 1978 International Rice Research Conference. 341p. 1979. pap. 19.50 (R029, IRRI). Unipub.
Report of a Rice Cold Tolerance Workshop. 139p. 1979. pap. 16.00 (R001, IRRI). Unipub.
Research Highlights for 1977. 122p. Date not set. pap. 18.50 (R127, IRRI). Unipub.
Residues of Carbofuran Applied As a Systematic Insecticide in Irrigated Wetland Rice: Implications for Insect Control. (IRRI Research Paper Ser.: No. 17). 28p. 1978. pap. 5.00 (R057, IRRI). Unipub.
Rice Blast Workshop. Proceedings. 222p. 1979. pap. 18.50 (R008, IRRI). Unipub.
Rice Breeders in Asia: A Ten Country Survey of Their Backgrounds, Attitudes & Use of Genetic Materials. (IRRI Research Paper Ser.: No. 13). 18p. 1978. pap. 5.00 (R053, IRRI). Unipub.
Rice Breeding. 738p. 1972. pap. 43.00 (R030, IRRI). Unipub.
Rice Improvement. 186p. 1979. pap. 19.50 (R033, IRRI). Unipub.
Rice Improvement in China & Other Asian Countries. 307p. 1980. pap. 19.50 (ISBN 0-686-69537-2, R 116, IRRI). Unipub.
Rice in the Tropics: A Guide to the Development of National Programs. 256p. 1979. pap. 19.50 (R019, IRRI). Unipub.
Rice Production Manual. 382p. 1970. pap. 21.50 (R018, IRRI). Unipub.
Rice Research & Production in China: An IRRI Team's View. 119p. 1978. pap. 7.50 (R016, IRRI). Unipub.
Rice, Science & Man: Papers Presented at the Tenth Anniversary Celebration of the International Rice Research Institute. 163p. 1975. pap. 8.00 (R017, IRRI). Unipub.
Rice: Soil, Water, Land. 185p. 1978. pap. 18.50 (R015, IRRI). Unipub.
Scientific Communication Among Rice Breeders in 10 Asian Nations. (IRRI Research Paper Ser.: No. 12). 15p. 1978. pap. 5.00 (R052, IRRI). Unipub.
Screening Rice for Tolerance to Mineral Stresses. (IRRI Research Paper Ser.: No. 6). 20p. 1977. pap. 5.00 (R046, IRRI). Unipub.
Soils & Rice. 825p. 1978. pap. 40.00 (R002, IRRI). Unipub.
Specific Soil Chemical Characteristics for Rice Production in Asia. (IRRI Research Paper Ser.: No. 2). 18p. 1976. pap. 5.00 (R042, IRRI). Unipub.
Sulfur Nutrition of Wetland Rice. (IRRI Research Paper Ser.: No. 21). 29p. 1979. pap. 5.00 (R061, IRRI). Unipub.
Sympoisum on Cropping Systems Research & Development for the Asian Rice Farmer. Proceedings. 454p. 1977. pap. 18.50 (R004, IRRI). Unipub.
Symposium on Climate & Rice. Proceedings. 565p. 1976. pap. 37.50 (R025, IRRI). Unipub.
Techniques for Field Experiments with Rice. 46p. 1972. pap. 5.00 (R111, IRRI). Unipub.
Training Manual for Rice Production. 140p. 1976. pap. 12.00 (R035, IRRI). Unipub.
Tropical Climate & Its Influence on Rice. (IRRI Research Paper Ser.: No. 20). 25p. 1979. pap. 5.00 (R060, IRRI). Unipub.
Utilization of the Azolla-Anabaena Complex As a Nitrogen Fertilizer for Rice. (IRRI Research Paper Ser.: No. 11). 15p. 1977. pap. 5.00 (R051, IRRI). Unipub.
Weather & Climate Data for Philippine Rice Research. (IRRI Research Paper Ser.: No. 41). 14p. 1979. pap. 5.00 (R081, IRRI). Unipub.
Workshop on Chemical Aspects of Rice Grain Quality. Proceedings. 390p. 1979. pap. 20.50 (R027, IRRI). Unipub.
Workshop on the Genetic Conservation of Rice. Proceedings. 54p. 1978. pap. 7.50 (R034, IRRI). Unipub.
Zinc Deficiency in Rice: A Review of Research at the International Rice Research Institute. (IRRI Research Paper Ser.: No. 9). 17p. 1977. pap. 5.00 (R049, IRRI). Unipub.

RICE TRADE
De Datta, Surajit K. Principles & Practices of Rice Production. 704p. 1981. 40.00 (ISBN 0-471-08074-8, Pub. by Wiley-Interscience). Wiley.

RICH FOOL (PARABLE)
see Jesus Christ–Parables

RICHARD 3RD, KING OF ENGLAND, 1452-1485
Lamb, V. B. The Betrayal of Richard III. 128p. 1980. 9.75x (ISBN 0-7050-0066-4, Pub. by Skilton & Shaw England). State Mutual Bk.

RICHES
see Wealth

RICHMOND–HISTORY
Hoehling, A. A. & Hoehling, Mary. Day Richmond Died. (Illus.). 272p. 1981. 12.95 (ISBN 0-498-02313-3). A S Barnes.

RICHTOFEN, MANFRED ALBRECHT, FREIHERR VON, 1892-1918
Von Richthofen, Manfred. The Red Baron. Ulanoff, Stanley M., ed. Kilduff, Peter, tr. from Ger. LC 80-68107. (Illus.). 241p. 1980. Repr. 12.95 (ISBN 0-8168-7925-7). Aero.

RIDDLES–JUVENILE LITERATURE
Ainsworth, Catherine H. Black & White & Said All Over: Riddles. LC 78-54873. (Folklore Bks.). 36p. 1980. 2.00 (ISBN 0-933190-02-6). Clyde Pr.
Alley, Robert, illus. Riddles. (Look Look Bks). (Illus.). 24p. (ps-3). 1981. pap. 1.25 (ISBN 0-307-11860-6, Golden Pr). Western Pub.
Bishop, Ann. Annie O'Kay's Riddle Roundup. (Illus.). 40p. (gr. 2-5). 1981. 7.95 (ISBN 0-525-66727-X). Elsevier-Nelson.

Doty, Roy. Puns, Gags, Quips, & Riddles & Q's Are Weird O's. (Illus.). (gr. 3-5). 1976. pap. 1.50 (ISBN 0-671-29909-3). PB.

Thaler, Mike. Oinker Away: Pig Riddles, Cartoons, Jokes and Other Amusing Things from the Creator of the Letterman. (Orig.). 1981. pap. 1.50 (ISBN 0-686-69579-8). Archway.

RIDICULOUS, THE
see Wit and Humor

RIDING
see Horsemanship

RIFLES
Brophy, William S. The Krag Rifle. 258p. 1978. 24.95 (ISBN 0-917714-21-0). Beinfeld Pub.

Waite, M. O. & Ernst, Bernard D. Trapdoor Springfield. (Illus.). 300p. 1980. 29.95 (ISBN 0-917714-20-2). Beinfeld Pub.

Womack, Lester. The Commercial Mauser 'ninety-Eight Sporting Rifle. Angevine, Jay B., Jr., ed. (Illus.). 72p. 1981. 20.00x (ISBN 0-9605530-0-2). Womack Assoc.

RIGHT AND LEFT (POLITICAL SCIENCE)
Alexander, Robert J. The Right Opposition: The Lovestoneities & the International Communist Opposition of the 1930's. LC 80-1711. (Contributions in Political Science Ser.: No. 54). 320p. 1981. lib. bdg. 32.50 (AOP/). Greenwood.

RIGHT OF ASYLUM
see Asylum, Right Of

RIGHT OF PETITION
see Petition, Right of

RIGHT OF PRIVACY
see Privacy, Right Of

RIGHTS, CIVIL
see Civil Rights

RIGHTS OF WOMEN
see Women's Rights

RIGIDITY (PSYCHOLOGY)
Shapiro, David. Autonomy & Rigid Character. LC 80-68953. 167p. 1981. 12.95x (ISBN 0-465-00567-5). Basic.

RILKE, RAINER MARIA, 1875-1926
Schwarz, Egon. Poetry & Politics in the Work of Rainer Maria Rilke. Wellbery, David E., tr. from Ger. LC 80-53704. 160p. 1981. 9.95 (ISBN 0-8044-2811-5). Ungar.

RIMBAUD, JEAN NICOLAS ARTHUR, 1854-1891
Hackett, C. A. Rimbaud. LC 80-40455. (Major European Authors Ser.). 250p. Date not set. price not set; pap. price not set (ISBN 0-521-29756-7). Cambridge U Pr.

RINGLING BROTHERS AND BARNUM AND BAILEY CIRCUS
Matthews, Kenneth & McDevitt, Robert. The Unlikely Legacy, the Story of John Ringling: The Circus & Sarasota. 2nd rev. ed. (Illus.). 64p. (Orig.). 1980. 5.95 (ISBN 0-936076-02-X); pap. 3.95 (ISBN 0-936076-00-3). Aaron Pubs.

RINGS (ALGEBRA)
see also Fields, Algebraic
Faith, C. Algebra I: Rings, Modules & Categories. (Grundlehren der Mathematischen Wissenschaften Ser.: Vol. 190). 610p. 1981. 48.00 (ISBN 0-387-05551-7). Springer-Verlag.

Kochman, Stanley O. The Symplectic Cobordism Ring. LC 79-27872. 1980. 9.60 (ISBN 0-8218-2228-4). Am Math.

Montgomery, S. Fixed Rings of Finite Automorphism Groups of Associative Rings. (Lectures Notes in Mathematics Ser.: Vol. 818). 126p. 1981. pap. 9.80 (ISBN 0-387-10232-9). Springer-Verlag.

Van Oystaeyen, F., ed. Ring Theory, Antwerp Nineteen-Eighty: Prooceedings. (Lecture Notes in Mathematics Ser.: Vol. 825). 209p. 1981. pap. 14.00 (ISBN 0-387-10246-9). Springer-Verlag.

RIO GRANDE RIVER AND VALLEY
Maxwell, R. A. The Big Bend of the Rio Grande: A Guide to the Rocks, Landscape, Geologic History & Settlers of the Area of Big Bend National Park. (Illus.). 138p. 1968. Repr. 3.00 (GB 7). Bur Econ Geology.

Miller, Tom. On the Border: Portraits of America's Southwestern Frontier. LC 79-2631. 224p. 1981. 10.95 (ISBN 0-06-013039-3, HarpT). Har-Row.

RIOTS
see also Crowds
also subdivision Riot under names of specific cities, e.g. Los Angeles–Riots, 1965
Salert, Barbara & Sprague, John. The Dynamics of Riots. Hannan, Michael, ed. LC 80-18546. (Methodology Monograph Ser.). (Illus.). 126p. (Orig.). 1980. pap. 9.25 (ISBN 0-89138-956-3, IS-00114, Pub. by ICPSR). Univ Microfilms.

RISK
see also Probabilities; Profit
Coe, Charles. Understanding Risk Management: A Guide for Governments. 70p. (Orig.). 1980. pap. 7.50x. U of GA Inst Govt.

Crockford, Neil. An Introduction to Risk Management. 112p. 1980. 27.00x (ISBN 0-85941-116-8, Pub. by Woodhead-Faulkner England). State Mutual Bk.

Wilson, Richard & Crouch, Edmond. Risk-Benefit Analysis. Date not set. price not set (ISBN 0-88410-667-5). Ballinger Pub.

RISK (INSURANCE)
Athearn, James L. Risk & Insurance. 4th ed. (Illus.). 550p. 1981. text ed. 15.96 (ISBN 0-8299-0298-8). West Pub.

RITES AND CEREMONIES
see also Baptism; Birth (In Religion, Folk-Lore, etc.); Fasts and Feasts; Funeral Rites and Ceremonies; Marriage Customs and Rites; Mysteries, Religious; Purity, Ritual; Ritual; Sacraments
also subdivision Ceremonies and Practices under subjects, e.g. Catholic Church–Ceremonies and Practice
Klauber, Laurence M. Rattlesnakes: Their Habits, Life Histories, & Influence on Mankind. abr. ed. (Illus.). 400p. 1981. 14.95 (ISBN 0-520-04038-4). U of Cal Pr.

MacCormack, Sabine. Art & Ceremony in Late Antiquity. (The Transformation of the Classical Heritage Ser.). (Illus.). 450p. 1981. 35.00x (ISBN 0-520-03779-0). U of Cal Pr.

RITES AND CEREMONIES–JEWS
see Jews–Rites and Ceremonies

RITUAL
see also Liturgics; Liturgies; Rites and Ceremonies; also subdivision Rituals under names of religions and religious denominations, e.g. Buddhism–rituals; and under the heading Secret societies, and names of specific secret societies
Klauber, Laurence M. Rattlesnakes: Their Habits, Life Histories, & Influence on Mankind. abr. ed. (Illus.). 400p. 1981. 14.95 (ISBN 0-520-04038-4). U of Cal Pr.

RITUAL PURITY
see Purity, Ritual

RIVER BASINS
see Watersheds

RIVERS
see also Dams; Erosion; Floods; Hydraulic Engineering; Water–Laws and Legislation; Water–Pollution; Water-Power; Water-Rights; Watersheds also names of specific Rivers, or Rivers and Valleys, e.g. Mississippi River, Rhine River and Valley
McCaffrey, M. Stanislaus. The Dolores: A River Running Guide. 96p. (Orig.). 1981. pap. 4.95 (ISBN 0-87108-578-X). Pruett.

May, George W. Down Illinois Rivers. (Illus.). 400p. 1981. 16.00 (ISBN 0-9605566-5-6). G W May.

RIVERS–POLLUTION
see Water–Pollution

ROAD CONSTRUCTION
Construction Manual for Highway Construction. 1980. 9.00. AASHTO.

Design Guide for Local Roads & Streets: Rural & Urban. 1971. 1.00. AASHTO.

Geometric Design Standards for Highways Other Than Freeways. 1969. 1.00. AASHTO.

Guide Specifications for Highway Construction. 1979. 10.00. AASHTO.

Institute of Civil Engineers, UK. Mechanization for Road & Bridge Construction. 54p. 1980. 55.00x (ISBN 0-901948-58-6, Pub. by Telford England). State Mutual Bk.

ROAD CONSTRUCTION–SAFETY MEASURES
Van Bommel, W. J. & DeBoer, J. B. Road Lighting. (Philips Technical Library). (Illus.). 363p. 1980. text ed. 69.50x (ISBN 0-333-30679-1). Scholium Intl.

ROAD MATERIALS
see also Highway Research
Nash, J. P., et al. Road Building Materials in Texas. (Illus.). 159p. 1918. 0.50 (BULL 1839). Bur Econ Geology.

ROAD RESEARCH
see Highway Research

ROAD SIGNS
see Signs and Signboards

ROAD TRAFFIC
see Traffic Engineering

ROAD TRANSPORTATION
see Transportation, Automotive

ROADS
see also Highway Research; Pavements; Streets; Trails
Institute of Civil Engineers, UK. Highways & the Environment. 1980. pap. 15.00x (ISBN 0-7277-0065-0, Pub. by Telford England). State Mutual Bk.

ROADS–CONSTRUCTION
see Road Construction

ROADS–HISTORY
Cawley, James & Cawley, Margaret. The First New York-Philadelphia Stage Road. LC 78-75175. (Illus.). 120p. 1980. 14.50 (ISBN 0-8386-2331-X). Fairleigh Dickenson.

ROADS–RESEARCH
see Highway Research

ROADS, ROMAN
Sitwell, Nigel. The Roman Roads of Europe. (Illus.). 240p. 1981. 35.00 (ISBN 0-312-69080-0). St Martin.

ROANOKE RIVER AND VALLEY
Manooch, Charles S., III. Spring Comes to the Roanoke. (Illus.). 140p. 1979. 7.95 (ISBN 0-9605270-0-1). Era Davidson.

ROBBERS
see Brigands and Robbers

ROBBERY
see also Brigands and Robbers
Feiden, Doug. The Ten Million Dollar Getaway: The Inside Story of the Lufthansa Heist. (Orig.). pap. 2.50 (ISBN 0-515-05452-6). Jove Pubns.

ROBESON, PAUL
Robeson, Susan. The Whole World in His Hands: A Pictoral Biography of Paul Robeson. (Illus.). 256p. 1981. 17.95 (ISBN 0-8065-0754-3). Citadel Pr.

ROBINSON, ROBERT, 1735-1790
Bowers, Q. David & Bowers, Christine. Robert Robinson: American Illustator. (Illus.). 68p. 1981. pap. 9.95 (ISBN 0-911572-19-8). Vestal.

ROBOTS
see Androids; Automation

ROCK CLIMBING
see also Mountaineering
Hall, Chris. Southern Rock: A Climber's Guide to the South. (Illus.). 192p. 1981. pap. 7.95 (ISBN 0-914788-37-X). East Woods.

Radlauer, Ed. Some Basics About Rock Climbing. LC 80-22053. (Gemini Bks). 32p. (gr. 4 up). 1981. PLB 8.65g (ISBN 0-516-07692-2, Elk Grove Bks). Childrens.

ROCK COLLECTING
see Mineralogy–Collectors and Collecting

ROCK FISH
see Striped Bass

ROCK GARDENS
see also Alpine Gardens
Hamilton, Geoff. Design & Build a Rockery. 4.50. David & Charles.

Schacht, Wilhelm. Rock Gardens. (Illus.). 190p. Repr. 17.50 (ISBN 0-87663-354-8, Pica Pr). Universe.

ROCK MECHANICS
see also Soil Mechanics
Bell, F. G. Engineering Properties of Soils & Rocks. (Illus.). 144p. 1981. pap. text ed. 12.50 (ISBN 0-408-00537-8). Butterworths.

Brown, E. T., ed. Rock Characterization, Testing & Monitoring: ISRM Suggested Methods. LC 80-49711. 200p. 1981. 40.00 (ISBN 0-08-027308-4); pap. 20.00 (ISBN 0-08-027309-2). Pergamon.

Kovaco, W. & Holtz, R. Introduction to Geotechniical Engineering. 1981. 28.95 (ISBN 0-13-484394-0). P-H.

Roberts, A. Applied Geotechnology: A Text for Students & Engineers on Rock Excavation & Related Topics. (Illus.). 416p. 1981. 50.00 (ISBN 0-08-024015-1); pap. 25.00 (ISBN 0-08-024014-3). Pergamon.

ROCK MUSIC
Bianco, David, compiled by. Who's New Wave in Music, 1976 to 1980: A Catalog & Directory. LC 80-21534. 300p. (Orig.). 1981. pap. 5.50 (ISBN 0-938136-00-3). Lunchroom Pr.

Green Note Music Publications Staff. Country Rock Guitar, Vol. 2. (Guitar Transcription Ser.). 1980. pap. 7.25 (ISBN 0-912910-10-0). Green Note Music.

--Improvising Rock Guitar, Vol. 2. (Guitar Transcription Ser.). 1980. pap. 7.25 (ISBN 0-912910-08-9). Green Note Music.

--Improvising Rock Guitar, Vol. 3. (Guitar Transcription Ser.). 1980. pap. 7.25 (ISBN 0-912910-09-7). Green Note Music.

Pollock, Bruce. When Rock Was Young: A Nostalgic Review of the Top Forty Era. LC 80-23460. (Illus.). 224p. 1981. 13.95 (ISBN 0-03-049836-8, Owl Books); pap. 6.95 (ISBN 0-03-049841-4). HR&W.

Schaffner, Nicholas & Schaffner, Elizabeth. Five Hundred & Five Rock & Roll Questions Your Friends Can't Answer. LC 80-54484. 160p. 1981. 9.95 (ISBN 0-8027-0674-6); pap. 5.95 (ISBN 0-8027-7171-8). Walker & Co.

Smith, Joseph C. The Day the Music Died. LC 80-8914. 464p. 1981. 12.95 (ISBN 0-394-51951-5). Grove.

ROCK MUSICIANS
Bennett, H. Stith. On Becoming a Rock Musician. LC 80-5378. 272p. 1981. lib. bdg. 15.00x (ISBN 0-87023-311-4). U of Mass Pr.

Cain, Robert. Whole Lotta Shakin' Goin' on: Jerry Lee Lewis. (Illus.). 1981. pap. 9.95. Dial.

Dewitt, Howard A. Chuck Berry: Rock'n'roll Music. (Illus.). 120p. (Orig.). 1981. 12.95 (ISBN 0-938840-01-0); pap. 5.95 (ISBN 0-938840-00-2). Horizon Bks CA.

Ditlea. Rock Stars. (gr. 7-12). 1980. pap. 1.25 (ISBN 0-590-31206-5, Schol Pap). Schol Bk Serv.

Hopkins, Jerry & Sugerman, Danny. No One Here Gets Out Alive. 400p. (Orig.). 1981. pap. 2.95 (ISBN 0-446-93921-8). Warner Bks.

Myra, Donald. Headliners: Billy Joel. 192p. (Orig.). 1981. pap. 2.25 (ISBN 0-448-17175-9, Tempo). G&D.

Nelson, Paul. Rod Stewart: A Biography. LC 80-8063. (Illus.). 160p. 1980. pap. 8.95 cancelled (ISBN 0-394-17745-2, E 770, BC). Grove.

Schumacher, Craig. Bee Gees. (Rock'n Roll Stars Ser.). 32p. (gr. 4-12). 1979. PLB 5.95 (ISBN 0-87191-697-5); pap. 2.95. Creative Ed.

ROCK SHELTERS
see Caves

ROCKEFELLER FAMILY
Josephson, Emanuel. The Federal Reserve Conspiracy & the Rockefellers: Their Gold Corner. LC 68-29455. (Blacked-Out History Ser.). 374p. 1968. 12.50 (Pub. by Chedney); pap. 8.00. Alpine Ent.

ROCKEFELLER FOUNDATION
Bullock, Mary B. An American Transplant: The Rockefeller Foundation & Peking Union Medical College. LC 77-83098. 280p. 1981. 17.50x (ISBN 0-520-03559-3). U of Cal Pr.

ROCKERIES
see Rock Gardens

ROCKET FLIGHT
see Space Flight

ROCKET SHIPS
see Space Ships

ROCKETS (AERONAUTICS)–MODELS
Pratt, Douglas R. Basics of Model Rocketry. Angle, Burr, ed. LC 80-84580. (Illus., Orig.). 1981. pap. 2.50 (ISBN 0-89024-557-6). Kalmbach.

ROCKFISH
see Striped Bass

ROCKHOUNDS
see Mineralogy–Collectors and Collecting

ROCKS
see also Crystallography; Geochemistry; Geology; Mineralogy; Petrology; Rock Mechanics
also varieties of rock, e.g. Granite, Limestone
Barnes, V. E., et al. Utilization of Texas Serpentine. (Illus.). 52p. 1950. 0.60 (PUB 5020). Bur Econ Geology.

ROCKS–AGE
see Geology, Stratigraphic

ROCKS–ANALYSIS
Brown, E. T., ed. Rock Characterization, Testing & Monitoring: ISRM Suggested Methods. LC 80-49711. 200p. 1981. 40.00 (ISBN 0-08-027308-4); pap. 20.00 (ISBN 0-08-027309-2). Pergamon.

Johnson, Wesley M. & Maxwell, John A. Rock & Mineral Analysis. 584p. 1981. 40.00 (ISBN 0-471-02743-X, Pub. by Wiley-Interscience). Wiley.

ROCKS–JUVENILE LITERATURE
Kehoe, Michael. The Rock Quarry Book. LC 80-28165. (Illus.). 32p. (gr. k-3). 1981. PLB 5.95 (ISBN 0-87614-142-4). Carolrhoda Bks.

ROCKS, IGNEOUS
Fisher, W. L. Rock & Mineral Resources of East Texas. (Illus.). 439p. 1965. 5.00 (RI 54). Bur Econ Geology.

Lunar & Planetary Institute, compiled by. Proceedings: Eleventh Lunar & Planetary Science Conference, Houston, Texas, March 17-21, 1980, 3 vols. (Geochimica & Cosmochimica Acta: Suppl. 14). 3000p. 1981. Set. 200.00 (ISBN 0-08-026314-3). Pergamon.

Plummer, F. B. The Carboniferous Rocks of the Llano Region of Central Texas. (Illus.). 170p. 1943. 2.00 (PUB 4329). Bur Econ Geology.

Sood, Mohan K. Modern Igneous Petrology. 250p. 1981. 22.50 (ISBN 0-471-08915-X, Pub. by Wiley-Interscience). Wiley.

Sutherland, D. S. Igneous Rocks of the British Isles. 560p. 1981. 94.00 (ISBN 0-471-27810-6, Pub. by Wiley-Interscience). Wiley.

ROCKS, SEDIMENTARY
Brand, J. P. Cretaceous of Llano Estacado of Texas. (Illus.). 59p. 1953. 0.70 (RI 20). Bur Econ Geology.

ROCKWELL, NORMAN, 1894-1978
Moline, Mary. Norman Rockwell Encylopedia. LC 79-90498. (Illus.). 1979. 15.95 (ISBN 0-89387-032-3). Sat Eve Post.

Norman Rockwell Review. LC 79-90499. (Illus.). 1979. 11.95 (ISBN 0-89387-033-1). Sat Eve Post.

Rockwell, Norman. Norman Rockwell: My Adventures As an Illustrator. LC 79-55715. (Illus.). 1979. 13.95 (ISBN 0-89387-034-X). Sat Eve Post.

The Saturday Evening Post Norman Rockwell Book. LC 77-12286. (Illus.). 1977. 11.95 (ISBN 0-89387-007-2). Sat Eve Post.

ROCKY MOUNTAINS
Boyarsky, Bill. The Rise of Ronald Reagan. (Illus.). 1981. Repr. of 1964 ed. price not set. Random.

Sprague, Marshall. The Great Gates: The Story of the Rocky Mountain Passes. LC 80-21994. (Illus.). x, 468p. 1981. 23.50x (ISBN 0-8032-4122-4); pap. 8.50 (ISBN 0-8032-9119-1, BB 742, Bison). U of Nebr Pr.

ROCKY MOUNTAINS, CANADIAN
Boyarsky, Bill. The Rise of Ronald Reagan. (Illus.). 1981. Repr. of 1964 ed. price not set. Random.

Sprague, Marshall. The Great Gates: The Story of the Rocky Mountain Passes. LC 80-21994. (Illus.). x, 468p. 1981. 23.50x (ISBN 0-8032-4122-4); pap. 8.50 (ISBN 0-8032-9119-1, BB 742, Bison). U of Nebr Pr.

RODENTIA
see also Rats; Squirrels
Hahn, James & Hahn, Lynn. Hamsters, Gerbils, Guinea Pigs, Pet Mice & Pet Rats. 1980. pap. 1.75 (ISBN 0-380-49239-3, 49231, Camelot). Avon.

RODEOS
Munn, Vella. Rodeo Riders. LC 80-81792. (Illus.). 96p. (gr. 4-9). 1981. PLB 6.59 (ISBN 0-8178-0013-1). Harvey.

ROENTGEN RAYS
see X-Rays

ROENTGENOGRAMS
see X-Rays

ROENTGENOLOGY, DIAGNOSTIC
see Diagnosis, Radioscopic

ROETHKE, THEODORE, 1908-1963
Wolff, George. Theodore Roethke. (United States Authors Ser.: No. 390). 1981. lib. bdg. 9.95 (ISBN 0-8057-7323-1). Twayne.

ROGERS, CARL RANSOM, 1902-
Nye, Robert D. Three Psychologies: Perspectives from Freud, Skinner & Rogers. 2nd ed. LC 80-25716. 170p. (Orig.). 1981. pap. text ed. 7.95 (ISBN 0-8185-0438-2). Brooks-Cole.

ROGUES AND VAGABONDS
see also Brigands and Robbers; Tramps

Head, Richard & Kirkman, Francis. The English Rogue, Described in the Life of Meriton Latroon, a Witty Extravagant: Being a Complete History of the Most Eminent Cheats of Both Sexes. LC 80-2483. 1981. Repr. of 1928 ed. 73.50 (ISBN 0-404-19117-7). AMS Pr.

ROLE, SOCIAL
see Social Role

ROLE PLAYING
Dillow, Jeffery. High Fantasy. 1981. 14.95 (ISBN 0-8359-2827-6). Reston.

ROLLER-SKATING
Cuthbertson, Tom. Anybody's Roller Skating Book. (Illus.). (YA) 1981. 8.95 (ISBN 0-89815-042-6); pap. 4.95 (ISBN 0-89815-040-X). Ten Speed Pr.
Edwards, I. G. Roller Skating: A Beginner'sguide. (Illus.). (gr. 5-7). 1979. pap. 1.95 (ISBN 0-671-43292-3). PB.
Konner. Roller Fever. (gr. 7-12). 1980. pap. 1.50 (ISBN 0-590-30029-6, Schol Pap). Schol Bk Serv.
Moran, Tom. Roller Skating Is for Me. (Sports for Me Bks.). (Illus.). (gr. 2-5). 1981. PLB 5.95 (ISBN 0-8225-1097-9). Lerner Pubns.

ROLLING CONTACT
Browne, A. L. The General Problem of Rolling Contact. Tsai, N. T., ed. (AMD: Vol. 40). 176p. 1980. 28.00 (G00173). ASME.

ROLLING-STOCK
see Locomotives

ROMAIC LANGUAGE
see Greek Language, Modern

ROMAN ALPHABET
see Alphabet

ROMAN ANTIQUITIES
see Classical Antiquities; Roads, Roman; Rome–Antiquities

ROMAN ARCHITECTURE
see Architecture, Roman

ROMAN ART
see Art, Roman

ROMAN CATHOLIC CHURCH
see Catholic Church

ROMAN EMPERORS
DeQuincey, Thomas. The Caesars. (Illus.). 300p. 1981. 12.95 (ISBN 0-8180-0824-5). Horizon.

ROMAN LAW
see also Civil Law
also legal headings with subdivision Roman Law in parentheses, e.g. Sales (Roman Law)
Curzon, L. B. Roman Law. 240p. 1974. pap. 9.95x (ISBN 0-7121-1853-5, Pub. by Macdonald & Evans England). Intl Ideas.

ROMAN PHILOSOPHY
see Philosophy, Ancient

ROMAN ROADS
see Roads, Roman

ROMANCE LANGUAGES
see also languages belonging to the Romance group, e.g. French Language, Italian Language
Danner, Horace C. Words from the Romance Languages. LC 80-82095. (Clavis Ser.). (Illus.). 232p. 1980. pap. 7.00 (ISBN 0-937600-00-8). Imprimis.

ROMANCE LITERATURE–HISTORY AND CRITICISM
Cook, Robert F. Chanson D'Antioche, Chanson De Geste: Le Cycle de la Croisade Estil Epique? (Purdue University Monographs in Romance Languages: No. 2). 115p. 1980. text ed. 17.25x (ISBN 90-272-1712-2, Athlone Pr). Humanities.

ROMANESQUE ART
see Art, Romanesque

ROMANIA
Graham, Lawrence S. Romania: A Profile. (Nations of Contemporary Eastern Europe Ser.). 128p. 1981. lib. bdg. 16.50x (ISBN 0-89158-925-2). Westview.

ROMANIAN ART
see Art, Romanian

ROMANOV, HOUSE OF
Trewin, J. C. The House of Special Purpose: An Intimate Portrait of the Last Days of the Russian Imperial Family. LC 74-30457. 148p. 1981. pap. 8.95 (ISBN 0-8128-6119-1). Stein & Day.
Tsar Alexis, His Reign & His Russia. (Russian Ser.: No. 34). 1981. 15.00 (ISBN 0-87569-040-8). Academic Intl.

ROMANTICISM
see also Realism in Literature
Andrews, William L. Literary Romanticism in America. LC 80-24365. 168p. 1981. 14.95x (ISBN 0-8071-0760-3). La State U Pr.
Morse, David. Perspectives on Romanticism: A Transformational Analysis. 362p. 1981. 29.50x (ISBN 0-389-20164-2). B&N.
--Romanticism: A Structural Analysis. 252p. 1981. 29.50x (ISBN 0-389-20165-0). B&N.

ROMANTICISM–GREAT BRITAIN
De Maar, Harko Gerrit. A History of Modern English Romanticism. 246p. 1980. Repr. of 1924 ed. lib. bdg. 30.00 (ISBN 0-8492-4217-7). R West.
Engell, James. The Creative Imagination: Enlightenment to Romanticism. 1981. write for info. Harvard U Pr.

ROMANTICISM IN ART
see also Realism in Art
Reff, Theodore, ed. Exhibitions of Romantic Art. (Modern Art in Paris 1855 to 1900 Ser.). 340p. 1981. lib. bdg. 44.00 (ISBN 0-8240-4736-2). Garland Pub.

ROMANTICISM IN LITERATURE
see Romanticism

ROME–ANTIQUITIES
Cagnat, R. & Chapot, V. Manuel D'archeologie Romaine, 2 vols. (Illus., Fr.). 1981. Repr. of 1920 ed. lib. bdg. 150.00x (ISBN 0-89241-139-2). Vol. 1. 735p. Vol. 2, 574p. Caratzas Bros.

ROME–BIOGRAPHY
see also Roman Emperors
Bowder, Diana, ed. Who Was Who in the Roman World. LC 80-67821. (Illus.). 256p. 1980. 25.00 (ISBN 0-8014-1358-3). Cornell U Pr.

ROME–HISTORY
Millon, Judith. St. Pauls Within-the-Walls: Rome, a History. 1981. 8.95 (ISBN 0-87233-058-3). Bauhan.
Sherwin-White, A. N. The Roman Citizenship. 2nd ed. 496p. 1980. pap. 24.95x (ISBN 0-19-814847-X). Oxford U Pr.
Tingay & Badcock. These Were the Romans. (Illus.). pap. 8.95 (ISBN 0-7175-0591-X). Dufour.

ROME–HISTORY–EMPIRE, 30 B.C.-476 A.D.
Chapot, Victor. The Roman World. 449p. 1980. Repr. of 1928 ed. lib. bdg. 50.00 (ISBN 0-89760-118-1). Telegraph Bks.
MacMullen, Ramsay. Paganism in the Roman Empire. LC 80-54222. 221p. 1981. 23.00x (ISBN 0-300-02655-2). Yale U Pr.
--Roman Social Relations, 50 B. C to A. D. 284. LC 73-86909. 317p. 1981. pap. 4.95x (ISBN 0-300-02702-8). Yale U Pr.

ROME–SOCIAL CONDITIONS
Hopkins, K. Conquerors & Slaves. LC 77-90209. (Illus.). 272p. 1981. pap. 12.50 (ISBN 0-521-28181-4). Cambridge U Pr.

ROME (CITY)
Harrison, G. B., ed. Anthony Munday: The English Romayne Lyfe. 105p. 1980. Repr. of 1925 ed. lib. bdg. 22.50 (ISBN 0-89760-543-8). Telegraph Bks.

ROME (CITY)–CHURCHES
Phillips, Evelyn M. The Illustrated Guidebook to the Frescoes in the Sistine Chapel. (Illus.). 124p. 1981. Repr. of 1901 ed. 49.85 (ISBN 0-89901-029-6). Found Class Reprints.

ROME (CITY)–DESCRIPTION–GUIDEBOOKS
Willey, David. Rome. LC 80-50997. (Rand McNally Pocket Guide Ser.). (Illus.). 1980. pap. 3.95 (ISBN 0-528-84309-5). Rand.

ROMMEL, ERWIN, 1891-1944
Law, Richard D. & Luther, Craig W. Rommel: A Narrative & Pictorial History. (Illus.). 368p. 1980. 17.95 (ISBN 0-912138-20-3). Bender Pub CA.

ROOD-LOFTS
see Church Architecture

ROOF-TRUSSES
see Roofs; Trusses

ROOFS
see also Decks (Architecture, Domestic)
Meyers, Donald L. Modern Roofing: Care & Repair. Horowitz, Shirley M., ed. (Illus.). 144p. (Orig.). 1981. pap. 6.95 (ISBN 0-686-69553-4). Creative Homeowner.
Sunset Editors. Roofing & Siding. LC 80-53487. (Illus.). 112p. (Orig.). 1981. pap. 4.95 (ISBN 0-376-01490-3, Sunset Bks). Sunset-Lane.

ROOMING HOUSES
see Hotels, Taverns, etc.

ROOSEVELT, ELEANOR (ROOSEVELT), 1884-1962
Berger, Jason. A New Deal for the World: Eleanor Roosevelt & American Foreign Policy, 1920-1962. 240p. 1981. 20.00x (ISBN 0-930888-07-3). Brooklyn Coll Pr.

ROOSEVELT, FRANKLIN DELANO, PRES. U. S., 1882-1945
Dallek, Robert. Franklin D. Roosevelt & American Foreign Policy, 1932-1945. (A Galaxy Book: No. 628). 690p. 1981. pap. 9.95 (ISBN 0-19-502894-5). Oxford U Pr.
Fish, Hamilton. F D R: The Other Side of the Coin. 255p. 1976. pap. 8.00 (ISBN 0-911038-64-7, Inst Hist Rev). Noontide.
Josephson, Emanuel. The Strange Death of Franklin Roosevelt: A History of the Roosevelt-Delano Dynasty: America's Royal Family. (Blacked-Out History Ser.). 284p. 11.00 (Pub. by Chedney); pap. 4.95. Alpine Ent.

ROOSEVELT, FRANKLIN DELANO, PRES. U. S., 1882-1945–JUVENILE LITERATURE
Feinberg, Barbara S. Franklin D. Roosevelt, Gallant President. LC 80-22307. (Illus.). 96p. (gr. 2-6). 1981. 7.50 (ISBN 0-688-00433-4); PLB 7.20 (ISBN 0-688-00434-2). Morrow.

ROOSEVELT, THEODORE, PRES. U. S., 1858-1919
Roosevelt, Kermit. Memories of My Father. (Illus.). 98p. Date not set. Repr. of 1920 ed. 44.85 (ISBN 0-89901-026-1). Found Class Reprints.

ROOSEVELT FAMILY
Josephson, Emanuel. The Strange Death of Franklin Roosevelt: A History of the Roosevelt-Delano Dynasty: America's Royal Family. (Blacked-Out History Ser.). 284p. 11.00 (Pub. by Chedney); pap. 4.95. Alpine Ent.
Parks, Lillian R. & Leighton, Frances S. The Roosevelts: A Family in Turmoil. (Illus.). 300p. 1981. 12.50 (ISBN 0-13-783043-2). P-H.

ROSAECRUCIANS
see Rosicrucians

ROSE, PETER, 1942-
Aaseng, Nathan. Pete Rose. LC 79-27377. (The Achievers Ser.). (Illus.). (gr. 4-9). 1981. PLB 5.95 (ISBN 0-8225-0480-4). Lerner Pubns.

ROSE CULTURE
Ray, Richard & MacCaskey, Michael. Roses. (Gardening Ser.). (Orig.). 1981. pap. 7.95 (ISBN 0-89586-079-1). H P Bks.
Roses Under Glass. 78p. 1980. pap. 9.95 (ISBN 0-901361-36-4, Pub. by Grower Bks England). Intl Schol Bk Serv.

ROSE-COLD
see Hay-Fever

ROSES
see also Cookery (Flowers); Rose Culture
Anderson, Frank. Redoute Roses. (Abbeville Library of Art Ser.). (Illus.). 112p. 1981. pap. 4.95 (ISBN 0-89659-096-8). Abbeville Pr.
Curtis, Henry. Beauties of the Rose. facsimile ed. (Illus.). 120p. 65.00x (ISBN 0-936736-00-3). Sweetbrier.

ROSICRUCIANS
Reff, Theodore, ed. Exhibitions of the Rosicrucian Salon. (Modern Art in Paris 1855 to 1900 Ser.). 354p. 1981. lib. bdg. 44.00 (ISBN 0-8240-4730-3). Garland Pub.

ROSSETTI, CHRISTINA GEORGINA, 1830-1894
Proctor, Ellen A. A Brief Memoir of Christina G. Rossetti. 84p. 1980. Repr. of 1895 ed. lib. bdg. 10.00 (ISBN 0-8495-4391-6). Arden Lib.

ROSSETTI, DANTE GABRIEL, 1828-1882
Rees, Joan. The Poetry of Dante Gabriel Rossetti. 150p. Date not set. 39.95 (ISBN 0-521-23537-5). Cambridge U Pr.
Ruskin, John. The Art of England: Lectures Given in Oxford by John Ruskin During His Second Tenure of the Slade Professorship. Freedberg, Sydney J., ed. LC 77-25769. (Connoisseurship, Criticism, & Art History Ser.: Vol. 23). 292p. 1979. lib. bdg. 21.00 (ISBN 0-8240-3281-0). Garland Pub.

ROSSETTI FAMILY
Hunt, Violet. The Wife of Rossetti. 338p. 1980. Repr. of 1932 ed. lib. bdg. 30.00 (ISBN 0-8492-5283-0). R West.

ROSY CROSS, ORDER OF THE
see Rosicrucians

ROTARY CLUB
Walsh, James P. The First Rotarian. (Illus.). 351p. 1980. 14.95 (ISBN 0-906360-02-1). Scan Pub.

ROTATING SYSTEMS
see Rotational Motion

ROTATIONAL MOTION
Molin, Y. N., et al. Spin Exchange: Principles & Applications in Chemistry & Biology. (Springer Series in Chemical Physics: Vol. 8). (Illus.). 242p. 1980. 39.00 (ISBN 0-387-10095-4). Springer-Verlag.

ROTH, PHILIP
Jones, Judith & Nance, Guinevera. Philip Roth. LC 80-53701. (Modern Literature Ser.). 160p. 1981. 9.95 (ISBN 0-8044-2438-1); pap. 4.95 (ISBN 0-8044-6320-4). Ungar.

ROTHKO, MARK, 1903-1970
Hess, Thomas B. & Feldman, Morton. Six Painters: Mondrian, DeKooning, Guston, Kline, Pollock, Rothko. LC 67-30452. (Illus.). 1968. pap. 3.00 (ISBN 0-914412-22-1). Inst for the Arts.

ROTHSCHILD FAMILY
Canfield, Cass. Outrageous Fortunes: The Story of the Medici, the Rothschilds, & J. Pierpont Morgan. (Illus.). 1981. 10.95 (ISBN 0-15-170513-5). HarBraceJ.

ROUGHAGE IN THE DIET
see High-Fiber Diet

ROUMANIA
see Romania

ROUNDS
see Glees, Catches, Rounds, etc.

ROUSSEAU, JEAN JACQUES, 1712-1778
Bernstein, John A. Shaftsbury, Rousseau & Kant: An Introduction to the Conflict Between Aesthetic & Moral Values in Modern Thought. LC 78-75190. 192p. 1980. write for info. (ISBN 0-8386-2351-4). Fairleigh Dickinson.
Mason, John H. The Indispensable Rousseau. 352p. (Orig.). 1980. 17.50 (ISBN 0-7043-2190-4, Pub. by Quartet England); pap. 7.95 (ISBN 0-7043-3220-5). Horizon.
Misenheimer, Helen E. Rousseau on the Education of Women. LC 80-5857. 109p. 1981. lib. bdg. 15.75 (ISBN 0-8191-1404-9); pap. text ed. 7.50 (ISBN 0-8191-1405-7). U Pr of Amer.
Payne, William H. Rousseau's Emile. 363p. 1980. Repr. of 1911 ed. lib. bdg. 35.00 (ISBN 0-89987-659-5). Darby Bks.

ROUTES OF TRAVEL
see Air Travel; Ocean Travel; Voyages and Travels–Guidebooks

ROYAL BALLET
Bland, Alexander. The Royal Ballet: The First Fifty Years. LC 80-2403. (Illus.). 288p. 1981. 35.00 (ISBN 0-385-17043-2). Doubleday.

ROYAL PREROGATIVE
see Prerogative, Royal

RUBBER
Evans, Colin W., ed. Developments in Rubber & Rubber Composites - One. (Illus.). ix, 184p. 1980. 35.00x (ISBN 0-85334-892-8). Burgess-Intl Ideas.
Solo, Robert. Across the High Technology Threshold: The Case of Synthetic Rubber. 130p. 1980. Repr. of 1959 ed. lib. bdg. 17.50 (ISBN 0-8482-6222-0). Norwood Edns.

RUBBER, ARTIFICIAL
Information Sources on the Natural & Synthetic Rubber Industry. (UNIDO Guides to Information Sources Ser.: No.34). 108p. 1980. pap. 4.00 (UNIDO230, UN). Unipub.

RUBBER INDUSTRY AND TRADE
see also Rubber, Artificial
Grilli, Enzo R., et al. The World Rubber Economy: Structure, Changes, & Prospects. LC 80-554. (World Bank Occasional Papers). (Illus.). 224p. 1981. pap. text ed. 6.50x (ISBN 0-8018-2421-4). Johns Hopkins.
Information Sources on the Natural & Synthetic Rubber Industry. (UNIDO Guides to Information Sources Ser.: No.34). 108p. 1980. pap. 4.00 (UNIDO230, UN). Unipub.

RUBBER-SHEET GEOMETRY
see Topology

RUBENS, PETER PAUL, SIR, 1577-1640
Burckhardt, Jakob. Recollections of Rubens. Freedberg, Sydney J., ed. LC 77-18674. (Connoisseurship Criticism & Art History Ser.: Vol. 4). 374p. 1979. lib. bdg. 33.00 (ISBN 0-8240-3261-6). Garland Pub.
Strong, Roy. Britannia Triumphans: Inigo Jones, Rubens & Whitehall Palace. (Lectures Ser.). (Illus.). 72p. 1981. 10.95 (ISBN 0-500-55012-3). Thames Hudson.

RUBIDOMYCIN
Arcamone, Federico. Doxorubicin. LC 80-1106. (Medicinal Chemistry Ser.). 1981. price not set (ISBN 0-12-059280-0). Acad Pr

RUG MANUFACTURE
see Rugs; Weaving

RUGBY FOOTBALL
see also Football
Smith, David & Williams, Gareth. Fields of Praise: The Official History of the Welsh Rugby Union, 1881-1981. (Illus.). 505p. 1981. text ed. 47.50 (ISBN 0-7083-0766-3). Verry.

RUGGER
see Rugby Football

RUGS
see also Carpets
Knight, Brian. Rugweaving: Technique & Design. (Illus.). 1981. 22.50 (ISBN 0-7134-2582-2, Pub. by Batsford England). David & Charles.
Rodee, Marian E. Old Navajo Rugs: Their Development from 1900 to 1940. (Illus.). 96p. 1981. price not set (ISBN 0-8263-0566-0); pap. price not set (ISBN 0-8263-0567-9). U of NM Pr.

RUGS, HOOKED
Rodmell, Ken. How to Use Type. 120p. 1981. pap. 7.95 (ISBN 0-442-29801-3). Van Nos Reinhold.

RUGS, ORIENTAL
Sarre, Friedrich & Sarre, Trenkwald. Oriental Carpet Designs in Full Color. (Illus.). 1980. pap. 6.00 (ISBN 0-486-23835-0). Dover.

RUINS
see Antiquities; Archaeology
also subdivision Antiquities under names of countries, cities, etc. e.g. Rome–Antiquities

RUIZ, JOSE MARTINEZ
see Martinez Ruiz, Jose, 1873-

RULE MAKING, ADMINISTRATIVE
see Administrative Procedure

RULES OF ORDER
see Parliamentary Practice

RUNES
Elliott, Ralph W. Runes: An Introduction. LC 80-26090. (Illus.). xvi, 124p. 1981. Repr. of 1959 ed. lib. bdg. 21.00x (ISBN 0-313-22870-1, ELRU). Greenwood.
Kempton, Karl. Rune. (Illus.). 100p. 1981. 50.00 (ISBN 0-686-69461-9). Porter.

RUNNING
see also Jogging; Marathon Running; Track-Athletics
Dintiman, George B. How to Run Faster: A Do-It-Yourself Book for Athletes in All Sports. LC 76-54436. (Illus.). 60p. 1979. text ed. 3.25. Champion Athle.
Kreuter, Gretchen. Running the Twin Cities. (Illus.). 95p. 1980. pap. 3.95 (ISBN 0-931714-08-7). Nodin Pr.
Liquori, Marty & Parker, John L. Playboy's Book of Real Running. 1980. 10.95 (ISBN 0-87223-625-0). Playboy.
Lovesey, Peter. Five Fings of Distance. (Illus.). 197p. 1981. 10.95 (ISBN 0-312-29484-0). St Martin.
Nabokov, Peter. Indian Running. (Illus.). 160p. (Orig.). 1981. pap. 7.95 (ISBN 0-88496-162-1). Capra Pr.
Weisenfeld, Murray. Runner's Repair Manual. 192p. 1981. pap. 4.95 (ISBN 0-312-69597-7). St Martin.
Whitley, Craig. Recipes for Runners: A Complete Nutrition Guide for Runners. (Illus.). 272p. 1981. cancelled (ISBN 0-913276-34-0). Stone Wall Pr.

RURAL ARCHITECTURE
see Architecture, Domestic; Cottages; Country Homes

RURAL CONDITIONS
see also Country Life; Farm Life; Rural Poor; Villages

also subdivision Rural Conditions or social conditions under names of countries, states, etc. e.g. United States–Rural Conditions

Czestochowski, Joseph S. John Stewart Curry & Grant Wood: A Portrait of Rural America. 240p. 1981. text ed. 26.00x (ISBN 0-8262-0336-1). U of Mo Pr.

Durand-Drouhin, Jean-Louis & Szwengrub, Lili-Marie, eds. Rural Community Studies in Europe: Trends, Selected & Annotated Bibliographies, Analyses, Vol. I. LC 80-41523. (Publications of the Vienna Centre Ser.). (Illus.). 342p. 1981. 70.50 (ISBN 0-08-021384-7). Pergamon.

Enyedi, Gyorgy & Volgyes, Ivan, eds. The Effect of Modern Agriculture on Rural Developement. LC 80-25232. (Pergamon Policy Studies on International Developement Comparative Rural Transformations Ser.). (Illus.). 280p. 1981. 32.50 (ISBN 0-08-027179-0). Pergamon.

Gall, Donald A., ed. Resource Directory on Rural America. 51p. (Orig.). 1981. pap. 4.95 (ISBN 0-8298-0446-3). Pilgrim NY.

Hansen, Gary E., ed. Agricultural & Rural Development in Indonesia. (Special Studies in Social, Political, & Economic Development). 312p. 1981. lib. bdg. 20.00x (ISBN 0-86531-124-2). Westview.

Hunter, Guy, et al, eds. Policy & Practice in Rural Development. LC 76-15078. 526p. text ed. 19.50 (ISBN 0-86598-002-0). Allanheld.

Imboden, Nicolas & OECD. Managing Information for Rural Development Projects. (Illus.). 87p. (Orig.). 1980. pap. 6.50 (ISBN 92-64-12039-4, 41-80-03-1). OECD.

Moris, Jon R. Managing Induced Rural Development. 1981. pap. 8.00 (ISBN 0-89249-033-0). Intl Development.

United Nations Asian & Pacific Development Inst., ed. Local Level Planning & Rural Development: Alternative Strategies. 409p. 1980. text ed. 20.50x (ISBN 0-391-02171-0, Pub. by Concept India). Humanities.

RURAL ECONOMIC DEVELOPMENT
see Community Development; Rehabilitation, Rural

RURAL EDUCATION
see Education, Rural

RURAL EXODUS
see Rural-Urban Migration

RURAL HEALTH
see Health, Rural

RURAL HOSPITALS
see Hospitals

RURAL HOUSING
see Housing, Rural

RURAL LIFE
see Country Life; Farm Life; Outdoor Life

RURAL POOR

Coombs, Philip H., ed. Meeting the Basic Needs of the Rural Poor: The Integrated, Community-Based Approach. LC 80-19838. (Pergamon Policy Studies on International Development). 828p. 1980. 49.50 (ISBN 0-08-026306-2). Pergamon.

RURAL POPULATION
see also Rural-Urban Migration

Coward, Raymond T. & Smith, William M., eds. The Family in Rural Society. (Special Studies in Contemporary Social Issues). 280p. 1981. lib. bdg. 25.00x (ISBN 0-86531-121-8). Westview.

RURAL POVERTY
see Rural Poor

RURAL SOCIOLOGY
see Sociology, Rural

RURAL-URBAN MIGRATION
see also Urbanization

Kazemi, Farhad. Poverty & Revolution in Iran: The Migrant Poor, Urban Marginality & Politics. 180p. 1981. text ed. 17.50x (ISBN 0-8147-4576-8). NYU Pr.

Silvers, Arthur & Crosson, Pierre R. Rural Development & Urban Bound Migration in Mexico. LC 80-8024. (Resources for the Future Research Ser.: Paper R-17). (Illus.). 160p. (Orig.). 1980. pap. text ed. 6.95x (ISBN 0-8018-2493-1). Johns Hopkins.

Zachariah, K. C. & Conde, Julian. Migration in West Africa: The Demographic Aspects. (World Bank Research Publication Ser.). (Illus.). 256p. 1980. 16.95 (ISBN 0-19-520186-8); pap. 6.95 (ISBN 0-19-520187-6). Oxford U Pr.

RUSKIN, JOHN, 1819-1900

Fitch, Raymond E. The Poison Sky: Myth & Apocalypse in Ruskin. LC 70-122097. (Illus.). 500p. 1981. 25.00x (ISBN 0-8214-0090-8). Ohio U Pr.

Ruskin, John. Letters of John Ruskin to Bernard Quaritch. 125p. 1980. Repr. of 1938 ed. lib. bdg. 25.00 (ISBN 0-8495-4637-0). Arden Lib.

RUSSELL, BERTRAND RUSSELL, 3RD EARL, 1872-1970

Murray, Jon G. An Atheist's Bertrand Russell. 1980. pap. 3.29 (ISBN 0-911826-14-9). Am Atheist.

RUSSIA–ARMED FORCES

Heilbrunn, Otto. The Soviet Secret Services. LC 80-27994. 216p. 1981. Repr. of 1956 ed. lib. bdg. 21.75x (ISBN 0-313-22892-2, HESSE). Greenwood.

Jones, David R., ed. Military-Naval Encyclopedia of Russia & the Soviet Union: Mersu, Vol. 3. 1981. write for info. (ISBN 0-87569-041-6). Academic Intl.

--Soviet Armed Forces Review Annual: Safra, Vol. 4. 1981. 45.00 (ISBN 0-87569-037-8). Academic Intl.

Scott, Harriet F. & Scott, William F. The Armed Forces of the USSR. rev. ed. 440p. 1981. lib. bdg. 27.50x (ISBN 0-86531-194-3); pap. text ed. 12.50x (ISBN 0-86531-087-4). Westview.

RUSSIA–BIBLIOGRAPHY

Brown, John H. & Grant, Steven A. The Russian Empire & Soviet Union: A Guide to Manuscripts & Archival Materials in the United States. (Libary Catalogs Supplement). 1981. lib. bdg. 75.00 (ISBN 0-8161-1300-9). G K Hall.

New York Public Library, Research Libraries & Library of Congress. Bibliographic Guide to Soviet & East European Studies, 1980. (Library Catalogs - Bibliographic Guides Ser.). 1981. lib. bdg. 195.00 (ISBN 0-8161-6894-6). G K Hall.

Thompson, Anthony. Russia - U. S. S. R. (World Bibliographical Ser.: No. 6). 287p. 1979. 34.75 (ISBN 0-903450-18-6). ABC-Clio.

RUSSIA–BIOGRAPHY

Barron, John. MIG Pilot: The Final Escape of Lieutenant Belenko. 232p. 1981. pap. 2.95 (ISBN 0-380-53868-7). Avon.

Bokov, Nikolai. Nobody. Fitzlyon, April, tr. 1979. 9.95 (ISBN 0-7145-0975-2); pap. 4.95 (ISBN 0-7145-3551-6). Riverrun NY.

Call, Paul. Vasily I. Kelsiev: An Encounter Between the Russian Revolutionaries & the Old Believers. LC 78-78270. 350p. 1980. 33.50 (ISBN 0-913124-36-2). Nordland Pub.

Chetverikov, Sergii. Starets Paisii Velichkovskii: His Life, Teachings & Influence on Orthodox Monasticism. Janov, Carol, ed. Lickwar, Vasily & Lisenko, Alexander I., trs. from Rus. LC 75-29632. 340p. (Orig.). 1980. pap. 35.00 (ISBN 0-913124-22-2). Nordland Pub.

De Enden, Michel. Rasputin & the Waning of the Russian Monarchy. 300p. (Orig.). 1980. pap. write for info. (ISBN 0-913124-46-X). Nordland Pub.

Ginzburg, Eugenia. Within the Whirlwind. Boland, Ian, tr. (Helen & Kurt Wolff Bk.). 1981. 14.95 (ISBN 0-15-197517-5). HarBraceJ.

Koulomzin, Sophie. Many Worlds: A Russian Life. LC 80-19332. 368p. 1980. pap. 8.95 (ISBN 0-913836-72-9, BS597 K64A35). St Martin.

--Many Worlds: A Russian Life. LC 80-19332. 368p. 1980. pap. 8.95. St Vladimirs.

Kuschevsky, Ivan. Nikolai Negorev. Costello, Bella, tr. 1980. pap. 4.95 (ISBN 0-7145-0414-9). Riverrun NY.

Osipova, Nonna. Bridges Between Clouds. (Illus.). 100p. (Orig.). 1981. pap. 4.00 (ISBN 0-935500-07-3). Am Samizdat.

Stremooukhoff, D. Vladimir Soloviev & His Messianic Work. Meyendorff, Elizabeth, tr. from Fr. LC 78-78264. 375p. (Orig.). 1980. pap. 37.50 (ISBN 0-913124-37-0). Nordland Pub.

Young, George M., Sr. Nikolai Fedorov: An Introduction. LC 78-78119. 400p. 1980. 29.50 (ISBN 0-913124-29-X). Nordland Pub.

RUSSIA–CONSTITUTIONAL LAW

Butler, W. E. Collected Legislation of the U.S.S.R, Realeases 1 & 2. 1980. Set. looseleaf 300.00 (ISBN 0-379-20450-9). Oceana.

RUSSIA–DESCRIPTION AND TRAVEL

Cole. USSR Geography. 1981. text ed. price not set. Butterworth.

RUSSIA–ECONOMIC CONDITIONS

Adam, Jan, ed. Wage Control & Inflation in the Soviet Bloc Countries. 266p. 1980. 22.95 (ISBN 0-03-057007-7). Praeger.

Bornstein, Morris, ed. The Soviet Economy: Continuity & Change. 532p. (Orig.). 1981. lib. bdg. 26.50x (ISBN 0-89158-958-9); pap. text ed. 12.00x (ISBN 0-89158-959-7). Westview.

Perlo, Ellen & Perlo, Victor. Dynamic Stability: The Soviet Economy Today. (Illus.). 365p. (Orig.). 1981. pap. 4.75 (ISBN 0-7178-0577-8). Intl Pub Co.

Prybyla, Jan S. Issues in Socialist Economic Modernization. 140p. 1980. 19.95 (ISBN 0-03-057962-7). Praeger.

RUSSIA–ECONOMIC POLICY

Schapiro, Leonard & Godson, Joseph, eds. The Soviet Worker: Illusion & Realities. Date not set. price not set (ISBN 0-312-74923-6). St Martin.

Voznesensky, N. A. Economy of the USSR During World War II. 8.00 (ISBN 0-8183-0233-X). Pub Aff Pr.

RUSSIA–FOREIGN RELATIONS

Halliday, Fred. Soviet Policy in the Arc of Crisis. 90p. 1981. pap. 4.95 (ISBN 0-89758-028-1). Inst Policy Stud.

Jahn, Egbert. Soviet Foreign Policy. (Allison & Busby's Motive Ser.). 160p. 1981. pap. 7.95 (ISBN 0-8052-8096-0, Pub. by Allison & Busby England). Schocken.

Naik, J. A. Russia & the Western World. 227p. 1980. text ed. 25.00x (ISBN 0-391-01745-4). Humanities.

Pipes, Richard. U. S. Soviet Relations in the Era of Detente: A Tragedy of Errors. 230p. (Orig.). 1981. lib. bdg. 22.00x (ISBN 0-86531-154-4); pap. text ed. 10.00x (ISBN 0-86531-155-2). Westview.

Saviter, Mark H. The Awakening of Nationalistic Drives & the Tragic Dilemma of the Soviet Leadership. (The Major Currents in Contemporary World History Library). (Illus.). 113p. 1981. 67.75 (ISBN 0-930008-83-9). Inst Econ Pol.

RUSSIA–FOREIGN RELATIONS–1917-1945

Ewing, Thomas E. Between the Hammer & the Anvil? Chinese & Russian Policies in Outer Mongolia, 1911-1921. (Indiana University Uralic & Altaic Ser.: Vol. 138). 300p. 1980. 20.00 (ISBN 0-933070-06-3). Ind U Res Inst.

Stewart, John F., ed. The Crime of Moscow in Vynnytsia. 2nd new ed. (Illus.). 48p. 1980. pap. 3.00 (ISBN 0-911038-90-6, 357). Noontide.

RUSSIA–FOREIGN RELATIONS–1945-

Amundsen, Kirsten. Norway, NATO & the Forgotten Soviet Challenge. (Policy Papers in International Affairs: No. 14). (Illus.). iv, 60p. 1981. pap. 2.95x (ISBN 0-87725-514-8). U of Cal Pr.

Nogee, Joseph L. & Donaldson, Robert H. Soviet Foreign Policy Since World War II. (Pergamon Policy Studies on International Politics). 300p. Date not set. 35.00 (ISBN 0-08-025997-9); pap. 10.95 (ISBN 0-08-025996-0). Pergamon.

Papp, Daniel S. Vietnam: The View from Moscow, Peking, Washington. LC 80-20117. (Illus.). 263p. 1981. lib. bdg. 17.95x (ISBN 0-89950-010-2). McFarland & Co.

RUSSIA–FOREIGN RELATIONS–CHINA–1949-

Stoessinger, John G. Nations in Darkness: China, Russia, & America. 3rd ed. 263p. 1981. pap. text ed. 6.95 (ISBN 0-394-32657-1). Random.

RUSSIA–FOREIGN RELATIONS–TURKEY

Rossos, Andrew. Russia & the Balkans: Inter-Balkan Rivalries & Russian Foreign Policy 1908-1914. 320p. 1981. 35.00x (ISBN 0-8020-5516-8). U of Toronto Pr.

RUSSIA–FOREIGN RELATIONS–UNITED STATES

Balfour, Michael. The Adversaries: America, Russia and the Open World 1941-1962. 224p. 1981. price not set (ISBN 0-7100-0687-X). Routledge & Kegan.

Douglas, Roy. From War to Cold War: 1942-48. 1980. 19.95 (ISBN 0-312-30862-0). St Martin.

Stoessinger, John G. Nations in Darkness: China, Russia, & America. 3rd ed. 263p. 1981. pap. text ed. 6.95 (ISBN 0-394-32657-1). Random.

Swann, Ingo, ed. What Will Happen to You When the Soviets Take Over. LC 80-25438. 244p. (Orig.). 1980. write for info. (ISBN 0-9604946-6-9). Starform.

RUSSIA–HISTORY

De Madariaga, Isabel. Russia in the Age of Catherine the Great. LC 80-21993. (Illus.). 728p. 1981. 40.00x (ISBN 0-300-02515-7). Yale U Pr.

Feodoroff, Nicholas V. The Truth: Cossacks, the Glory of Russia. 1981. 6.75 (ISBN 0-8062-1704-9). Carlton.

Pavlov, A. Pamiatniki Drevnerrusskago Kanonicheskago Prava. LC 80-2366. (Russkaya Istorischeskaya Biblioteka: Vol. 6). 76.00 (ISBN 0-404-18912-1). AMS Pr.

Rauch, Georg von. A History of Soviet Russia. 6th ed. Jacobsohn, Peter & Jacobsohn, Annette, trs. from German. LC 76-185777. 541p. 1972. pap. text ed. 7.95x. Praeger.

Szeftel, Marc. Russian Institutions & Culture up to Peter the Great. 374p. 1980. 60.00x (ISBN 0-902089-80-3, Pub. by Variorum England). State Mutual Bk.

Tsar Alexis, His Reign & His Russia. (Russian Ser.: No. 34). 1981. 15.00 (ISBN 0-87569-040-8). Academic Intl.

Wolfe, Bertram D. Revolution & Reality: Essays on the Origin of the Soviet System. LC 80-16178. (Illus.). 422p. 1981. 19.00x (ISBN 0-8078-1453-9); pap. 11.00x (ISBN 0-8078-4073-4). U of NC Pr.

RUSSIA–HISTORY–BIBLIOGRAPHY

Clendenning, P. H. & Bartlett, R. Eighteenth Century Russia: A Select Bibliography of Works Published Since 1955. (Russian Bibliography Ser.: No. 3). (Illus.). 260p. 1981. 18.00 (ISBN 0-89250-110-3); pap. 8.95 (ISBN 0-89250-111-1). Orient Res Partners.

RUSSIA–HISTORY–TO 1689

Baron, Samuel H. Muscovite Russia. 362p. 1980. 75.00x (ISBN 0-86078-063-5, Pub. by Variorum England). State Mutual Bk.

RUSSIA–HISTORY–1689-1800

Bundesinstitut Fur Ostwissenschaftliche und Internationale Studien. The Soviet Union, Nineteen Seventy-Eight to Nineteen Seventy-Nine. (The Soviet Union Ser.: Vol. 5). 220p. 1980. text ed. 29.50x (ISBN 0-8419-0632-7). Holmes & Meier.

Gleason, Walter J. Moral Idealists, Bureaucracy, & Catherine the Great. 320p. 1981. 21.00 (ISBN 0-8135-0917-3). Rutgers U Pr.

Soloviev, Sergei M. History of Russia: Peter the Great: the Great Reforms Being, Vol. 16. Papmehl, K. A., tr. 1981. 20.00 (ISBN 0-87569-042-4). Academic Intl.

RUSSIA–HISTORY–19TH CENTURY

Avrich, Paul. The Russian Anarchists. LC 80-21590. (Studies of the Russian Institute, Columbia University). (Illus.). vii, 303p. 1980. Repr. of 1967 ed. lib. bdg. 28.50x (ISBN 0-313-22571-0, AVRA). Greenwood.

RUSSIA–HISTORY–20TH CENTURY

Avrich, Paul. The Russian Anarchists. LC 80-21590. (Studies of the Russian Institute, Columbia University). (Illus.). vii, 303p. 1980. Repr. of 1967 ed. lib. bdg. 28.50x (ISBN 0-313-22571-0, AVRA). Greenwood.

D'Encausse, Helene C. Decline of an Empire: The Soviet Socialist Republic in Revolt. LC 80-8402. (Illus.). 304p. 1981. pap. 4.95 (ISBN 0-06-090844-0, CN 844, CN). Har-Row.

RUSSIA–HISTORY–REVOLUTION OF 1905

Toplitsky, Tania S. The Russian Revolution in Nineteen Hundred Five. 164p. 1981. 13.50 (ISBN 0-682-49720-7). Exposition.

RUSSIA–HISTORY–1917-

Medvedev, Roy, ed. Samizdat Reigister Two. 1981. 19.95 (ISBN 0-393-01419-3). Norton.

Rousset, David. The Legacy of the Bolshevik Revolution: A Critical History of the USSR. (Allison & Busby Motive Ser.). 416p. 1981. pap. 12.95 (ISBN 0-8052-8091-X, Pub. by Allison & Busby England). Schocken.

RUSSIA–HISTORY–REVOLUTION–1917-1921
see also name of specific provinces, with or without the subdivision History, e.g. Ukraine

Cockfield, Jamie H., ed. Dollars & Diplomacy: Ambassador David Rowland Francis & the Fall of Tsarism, 1916-17. LC 80-19786. ix, 149p. 1981. 12.75 (ISBN 0-8223-2445-8). Duke.

Kettle, Michael. Russia & the Allies Nineteen Seventeen to Nineteen Twenty, Vol. I: The Allies & the Russian Collapse; March 1917-1918. (Illus.). 300p. 1981. 27.50x (ISBN 0-8166-0981-0). U of Minn Pr.

Koenker, Diane. Moscow Workers & the Nineteen Seventeen Revolution. LC 80-8557. (Studies of the Russian Institute, Columbia University). (Illus.). 456p. 1981. 30.00x (ISBN 0-691-05323-5). Princeton U Pr.

Luxemburg, Rosa. The Russian Revolution, & Leninism or Marxism? LC 80-24374. (Ann Arbor Ser. for the Study of Communism & Marxism). 109p. 1981. Repr. of 1961 ed. lib. bdg. 18.75x (ISBN 0-313-22429-3, LURR). Greenwood.

Trotsky, Leon. History of the Russian Revolution. 1980. pap. 14.95 (ISBN 0-913460-83-4). Monad Pr.

RUSSIA–HISTORY–REVOLUTION, 1917-1921–INFLUENCE

Rousset, David. The Legacy of the Bolshevik Revolution: A Critical History of the USSR. (Allison & Busby Motive Ser.). 416p. 1981. pap. 12.95 (ISBN 0-8052-8091-X, Pub. by Allison & Busby England). Schocken.

RUSSIA–INDUSTRIES

Lendvai, Paul. The Bureaucracy of Truth. 350p. 1981. lib. bdg. 20.00x (ISBN 0-86531-142-0). Westview.

RUSSIA–INTELLECTUAL LIFE

Gleason, Walter J. Moral Idealists, Bureaucracy, & Catherine the Great. 320p. 1981. 21.00 (ISBN 0-8135-0917-3). Rutgers U Pr.

Shatz, Marshall S. Soviet Dissent in Historical Perspective. LC 80-13318. 240p. 1981. 19.95 (ISBN 0-521-23172-8). Cambridge U Pr.

RUSSIA–KOMITET GOSUDARSTVENNOI BEZOPASNOSTI

Rositzke, Harry. KGB: The Eyes of Russia. LC 80-2063. 288p. 1981. 14.95 (ISBN 0-385-15390-2). Doubleday.

RUSSIA–LANGUAGES

Comrie, B. The Languages of the Soviet Union. (Cambridge Language Surveys Ser.: No. 2). (Illus.). 320p. Date not set. price not set (ISBN 0-521-23230-9); pap. price not set (ISBN 0-521-29877-6). Cambridge U Pr.

RUSSIA–MILITARY POLICY

Halliday, Fred. Soviet Policy in the Arc of Crisis. 90p. 1981. pap. 4.95 (ISBN 0-89758-028-1). Inst Policy Stud.

Hanks, Robert J. The Unnoticed Challenge: Soviet Maritime Strategy & the Global Choke Points. LC 80-83751. (Special Report Ser.). 68p. 1980. 6.50 (ISBN 0-89549-025-0). Inst Foreign Policy Anal.

RUSSIA–NAVY

Hanks, Robert J. The Unnoticed Challenge: Soviet Maritime Strategy & the Global Choke Points. LC 80-83751. (Special Report Ser.). 68p. 1980. 6.50 (ISBN 0-89549-025-0). Inst Foreign Policy Anal.

Jones, David R., ed. Military-Naval Encyclopedia of Russia & the Soviet Union: Mersu, Vol. 3. 1981. write for info. (ISBN 0-87569-041-6). Academic Intl.

RUSSIA–POLITICS AND GOVERNMENT

Azbel, Mark Y. Refusenik: Trapped in the Soviet Union. Forbes, Grace P., ed. (Illus.). 528p. 1981. 17.95 (ISBN 0-395-30226-9). HM.

Berdyaev, Nicolas. The Origin of Russian Communism. 239p. 1980. Repr. of 1937 ed. lib. bdg. 30.00 (ISBN 0-89760-047-9). Telegraph Bks.

George, Vic & Manning, Nick. Socialism, Social Welfare, & the Soviet Union. (Radical Social Policy Ser.). 224p. (Orig.). 1980. pap. 15.95 (ISBN 0-7100-0608-X). Routledge & Kegan.

Gleason, Walter J. Moral Idealists, Bureaucracy, & Catherine the Great. 320p. 1981. 21.00 (ISBN 0-8135-0917-3). Rutgers U Pr.

Jacobs, Dan N., et al. Comparative Politics: Introduction to the Politics of Britain, France, Germany, & the Soviet Union. pap. 9.95 (ISBN 0-934540-05-5). Chatham Hse Pubs.

Kosygin, A. N. Selected Speeches & Writings. LC 80-41077. 352p. 1981. 100.00 (ISBN 0-08-023610-3). Pergamon.

Shamsuddin. Politics of Secularization in the USSR. 336p. 1980. text ed. 27.50x (ISBN 0-7069-1274-8, Pub. by Vikas India). Advent Bk.

Simes, Dimitri K., et al. Soviet Succession: Leadership in Transition. LC 78-62798. (Sage Policy Paper Ser.: Vol. 59). 80p. 1978. pap. 3.50 (ISBN 0-8039-1124-6). Sage.

Simons, William B. The Soviet Codes of Law. (Law in Eastern Europe Ser.: No. 23). 1288p. 1980. 92.50x (ISBN 90-286-0810-9). Sijthoff & Noordhoff.

Smith, Gordon B., ed. Public Policy & Administration in the Soviet Union. 240p. 1980. 23.95 (ISBN 0-03-057726-8); pap. 9.95 (ISBN 0-03-057727-6). Praeger.

Smith, Gordon B., et al, eds. Soviet & East European Law & the Scientific-Technical Revolution. (Pergamon Policy Studies on International Politics). (Illus.). 330p. 1981. 34.00 (ISBN 0-08-027195-2). Pergamon.

Thompson, James C. & Vidmer, Richard F. Political Administration in the Soviet Union & the United States. 240p. 1981. 22.95 (ISBN 0-89789-009-4). J F Bergin.

Turchin, Valentin. The Inertia of Fear. Daniels, Guy, tr. from Russian. LC 80-36818. 336p. 1981. 16.95 (ISBN 0-231-04622-7). Columbia U Pr.

Yin, John. The Government of the Soviet Union: A Constitutional Approach, Vol. 1. LC 80-82427. (Orig.). 1980. pap. 29.50 (ISBN 0-913124-41-9). Nordland Pub.

RUSSIA–POLITICS AND GOVERNMENT–1945-

Parrish, Michael. The U S S R in World War II: An Annotated Bibliography of Books Published in the Soviet Union, 1945 to 1975. LC 80-8502. 925p. 1981. lib. bdg. 110.00 (ISBN 0-8240-9485-9). Garland Pub.

Rubinstein, Alvin Z. Soviet Foreign Policy Since World War II: Imperial & Global. (Political Science Ser.). (Illus.). 354p. 1981. text ed. 15.00 (ISBN 0-87626-810-6); pap. text ed. 9.95 (ISBN 0-87626-809-2). Winthrop.

Saviter, Mark H. The Awakening of Nationalistic Drives & the Tragic Dilemma of the Soviet Leadership. (The Major Currents in Contemporary World History Library). (Illus.). 113p. 1981. 67.75 (ISBN 0-930008-83-9). Inst Econ Pol.

Slusser, Robert M. & Ginsburgs, George. A Calendar of Soviet Treaties: 1958-1973. LC 80-50453. 990p. 1980. 125.00x (ISBN 90-286-0609-2). Sijthoff & Noordhoff.

Swann, Ingo, ed. What Will Happen to You When the Soviets Take Over. LC 80-25438. 244p. (Orig.). 1980. write for info. (ISBN 0-9604946-6-9). Starform.

Wittikoff, Douglas. The Desperate Alternatives of the Soviet Leaders in the Face of the Incipient Break-up of the Communist Empire. (The Major Currents in Contemporary World History Library Ser.). (Illus.). 143p. 1981. 69.85 (ISBN 0-930008-81-2). Inst Econ Pol.

RUSSIA–RELATIONS (GENERAL) WITH FOREIGN COUNTRIES

Hanson, Philip. Trade & Technology in Soviet-Western Relations. 300p. 1981. 30.00x (ISBN 0-231-05276-6). Columbia U Pr.

RUSSIA–RELIGION

Fletcher, William. Soviet Believers: The Religious Sector of the Population. LC 80-25495. (Illus.). 276p. 1981. 27.50x (ISBN 0-7006-0211-9). Regents Pr KS.

Florvosky, Georges. Ways of Russian Theology: Pt. 2. Haugh, Richard S., et al, eds. (Collected Works of Georges Florovsky). 400p. (Orig.). 1980. pap. 27.50 (ISBN 0-913124-24-9). Nordland Pub.

Harris, T. L. Unholy Pilgrimage: A Visit to Russia to Find What Twenty Years of Official Atheism Had Done for the Russian People. 195p. Repr. of 1937 ed. text ed. 2.95. Attic Pr.

RUSSIA–RURAL CONDITIONS

Owen, Thomas C. Capitalism & Politics in Russia: A Social History of the Moscow Merchants, 1855 to 1905. LC 80-11279. (Illus.). 352p. Date not set. 35.00 (ISBN 0-521-23173-6). Cambridge U Pr.

RUSSIA–SOCIAL CONDITIONS

Shatz, Marshall S. Soviet Dissent in Historical Perspective. LC 80-13318. 240p. 1981. 19.95 (ISBN 0-521-23172-8). Cambridge U Pr.

Szeftel, Marc. Russian Institutions & Culture up to Peter the Great. 374p. 1980. 60.00x (ISBN 0-902089-80-3, Pub. by Variorum England). State Mutual Bk.

Turchin, Valentin. The Inertia of Fear. Daniels, Guy, tr. from Russian. LC 80-36818. 336p. 1981. 16.95 (ISBN 0-231-04622-7). Columbia U Pr.

RUSSIA–SOCIAL CONDITIONS–1945-

Farmer, Kenneth C. Ukrainian Nationalism in the Post-Stalin Era: Myth, Symbols & Ideology in Soviet Nationalities Policy. (Studies in Contemporary History: Vol. 4). 253p. 1980. lib. bdg. 36.50 (ISBN 90-247-2401-5, Pub. by Martinus Nijhoff). Kluwer Boston.

Medvedev, Roy, ed. Samizdat Reigister Two. 1981. 19.95 (ISBN 0-393-01419-3). Norton.

Mickiewicz, Ellen. Media & the Russian Public. 170p. 1981. 19.95 (ISBN 0-03-057681-4); pap. 8.95 (ISBN 0-03-057679-2). Praeger.

RUSSIA–SOCIAL LIFE AND CUSTOMS

Koulomzin, Sophie. Many Worlds: A Russian Life. LC 80-19332. 368p. 1980. pap. 8.95. St Vladimirs.

Pankhurst, Jerry & Sacks, Michael P., eds. Contemporary Soviet Society: Sociological Perspectives. 310p. 1980. 23.95 (ISBN 0-03-055916-2); pap. 9.95 (ISBN 0-03-055911-1). Praeger.

Parker, W. H. The Russians: How They Live & Work. LC 72-93295. 179p. 1973. text ed. 8.95 (ISBN 0-03-029581-5, HoltC). HR&W.

RUSSIA–STATISTICS

Scherer, John L., ed. U S S R Facts & Figures Annual (UFFA, Vol. 4 1980. 42.50 (ISBN 0-87569-035-1). Academic Intl.

RUSSIAN ARCHITECTURE

see Architecture–Russia

RUSSIAN ART

see Art, Russian

RUSSIAN AUTHORS

see Authors, Russian

RUSSIAN FICTION–HISTORY AND CRITICISM

Clark, Katerina. The Soviet Novel: History As Ritual. LC 80-18758. 1981. lib. bdg. 20.00x (ISBN 0-226-10766-3). U of Chicago Pr.

Rabinowitz, Stanley J. Sologub's Literary Children: Keys to a Symbolist's Prose. (Illus.). 176p. 1980. pap. 9.95 (ISBN 0-89357-069-9). Slavica.

RUSSIAN LANGUAGE–CONVERSATION AND PHRASE-BOOKS

Stern, A. Z. & Reif, Joseph A., eds. Useful Expressions in Russian. (Useful Expressions Ser.). (Illus.). 64p. (Orig.). 1980. pap. 1.50 (ISBN 0-86628-012-X). Ridgefield Pub.

RUSSIAN LANGUAGE–DICTIONARIES

Drummond, David A. & Perkins, G. Dictionary of Russian Obscenities. rev. ed. 79p. (Rus. & Eng.). 1980. pap. text ed. 3.50 (ISBN 0-933884-17-6). Berkeley Slavic.

RUSSIAN LANGUAGE–GRAMMAR

Newman, Lawrence W., ed. The Comprehensive Russian Grammar of A.A. Barsov. lxxxvi, 382p. (Rus. & Eng.). 1980. 24.95 (ISBN 0-89357-072-9). Slavica.

RUSSIAN LANGUAGE–HISTORY

Gardiner, S. C. Old Church Slavonic: An Elementary Grammar. Date not set. price not set (ISBN 0-521-23674-6). Cambridge U Pr.

RUSSIAN LANGUAGE–SYNTAX

Harris, Alice C. Georgian Syntax: A Study in Relational Grammar. (Cambridge Studies in Linguistics: No. 33). (Illus.). 300p. Date not set. price not set (ISBN 0-521-23584-7). Cambridge U Pr.

RUSSIAN LITERATURE (COLLECTIONS)

Aksenov, Vasily P. Ozhog. (Rus.). 1980. 18.50 (ISBN 0-88233-600-2); pap. 10.50 (ISBN 0-88233-601-0). Ardis Pubs.

RUSSIAN LITERATURE–HISTORY AND CRITICISM

Calder, Angus. Revolutionary Empire. 1981. 35.00 (ISBN 0-525-19080-5). Dutton.

Fennell, J. L., et al, eds. Oxford Slavonic Papers, Vol. 13. (Illus.). 128p. 1981. 45.00 (ISBN 0-19-815656-1). Oxford U Pr.

Kodjak, Andrej, et al, eds. The Structural Analysis of Narrative Texts, Conference Papers. (New York University Slavic Papers: Vol. II). (Illus.). 203p. (Orig.). 1980. pap. 10.95 (ISBN 0-89357-071-0). Slavica.

Zoshchenko, Mikhail. Rasskazy, 1921-1930. (Rus.). 1980. pap. 5.00 (ISBN 0-88233-591-X). Ardis Pubs.

RUSSIAN PHILOSOPHY

see Philosophy, Russian

RUSSIAN POETRY

Proffer, Carl, ed. Modern Russian Poets on Poetry. 1976. 15.00 (ISBN 0-88233-185-X). Ardis Pubs.

RUSSIAN POETRY–HISTORY AND CRITICISM

Conant, Roger. The Political Poetry & Ideology of Fyodor Tyutchev. (Ardis Essay Ser.: No. 7). 82p. 1981. text ed. 10.00. Ardis Pubs.

RUSSIAN PROPAGANDA

see Propaganda, Russian

RUSSIAN SCIENCE

see Science, Russian

RUSSIAN SONGS

see Songs, Russian

RUSSIANS IN THE UNITED STATES

Eubank, Nancy. Russians in America. LC 72-3598. (In America Bks.). (Illus.). 96p. (gr. 5-11). 1979. PLB 5.95. Lerner Pubns.

Johnston, Barry V. Russian American Social Mobility: An Analysis of the Achievement Syndrome. LC 80-65609. 145p. 1981. perfect bdg. 10.95 (ISBN 0-86548-041-9). Century Twenty One.

RUSSO-FINNISH WAR, 1939-1940

Erfurth, Waldemar. Last Finnish War. 1979. 22.00 (ISBN 0-89093-205-0). U Pubns Amer.

RUSSO-TURKISH WAR, 1853-1856

see Crimean War, 1853-1856

RUST

see Corrosion and Anti-Corrosives

RUSTLESS COATINGS

see Corrosion and Anti-Corrosives

RUSTS (FUNGI)

Roebbelen, Gerhard & Sharp, Eugene L. Mode of Inheritance, Interaction & Application of Genes Conditioning Resistance to Yellow Rust. (Advances in Plant Breeding Ser.: Vol. 9). (Illus.). 88p. (Orig.). 1978. pap. text ed. 25.00 (ISBN 3-489-71110-6). Parey Sci Pubs.

RUTHENIAN LITERATURE

see Ukrainian Literature

RYE WHISKEY

see Whiskey

S

SABBATH

Here are entered works on the concept of a day of rest, as defined in the Ten Commandments, particularly works on Seventh-Day or Saturday observance. Works on First-Day or Sunday observance are entered under Sunday.

see also Sunday Legislation

O'Sullivan, Patrick. The Sabbath of the New Testament. (Illus.). 52p. 1981. pap. 2.50 (ISBN 0-933464-12-6). D M Battle Pubns.

Riggle, H. M. The Sabbath & the Lord's Day. 160p. pap. 1.50. Faith Pub Hse.

Scherman, Nosson. Siddur: Sabbath Eve Service. 1980. 8.95 (ISBN 0-686-68764-7); pap. 5.95 (ISBN 0-686-68765-5). Mesorah Pubns.

SABBATH–JUVENILE LITERATURE

Hughes, Patti. Sunday Supplement for Kids. (Illus.). 63p. (Orig.). (gr. 3-6). 1980. pap. 3.95 (ISBN 0-87747-848-1). Deseret Bk.

SABIN, FLORENCE RENA, 1871-1953

Downing, Sybil & Barker, Jane V. Florence Rena Sabin. (Illus.). 80p. (Orig.). (gr. 5-6). 1981. pap. 5.50 (ISBN 0-87108-237-3). Pruett.

SACCO-VANZETTI CASE

Joughin, Louis & Morgan, Edmund M. The Legacy of Sacco & Vanzetti. LC 77-92101. 596p. 30.00x (ISBN 0-691-04656-5); pap. 5.95 (ISBN 0-691-00588-5). Princeton U Pr.

SACRAMENT OF THE ALTAR

see Lord's Supper

SACRAMENTS

see also Baptism; Lord's Supper; Marriage; Penance

Coniaris, A. M. These Are the Sacraments. 1981. pap. 5.95 (ISBN 0-686-69400-7). Light & Life.

Pennock, Michael. The Sacraments & You. (Illus.). 272p. (gr. 10-12). 1981. pap. 3.95 (ISBN 0-87793-221-2); teachers ed. 2.25 (ISBN 0-87793-222-0). Ave Maria.

SACRAMENTS–CATHOLIC CHURCH

Martos, Joseph. Doors to the Sacred. LC 80-626. 552p. 1981. 15.95 (ISBN 0-385-15738-X). Doubleday.

SACRED ART

see Christian Art and Symbolism

SACRED MINISTRY

see Clergy–Office

SACRED MUSIC

see Church Music

SACRED NUMBERS

see Symbolism of Numbers

SACRED SONGS

see Hymns

EL SADAT, ANWAR, PRES. EGYPT, 1918-

Kosman, William Y. Sadat's Realistic Peace Initiative. Date not set. 8.95 (ISBN 0-533-04614-9). Vantage.

SADISM

Shapiro, David. Autonomy & Rigid Character. LC 80-68953. 167p. 1981. 12.95x (ISBN 0-465-00567-5). Basic.

SADLER'S WELLS THEATRE BALLET

see Royal Ballet

SAFETY, INDUSTRIAL

see Industrial Safety

SAFETY ENGINEERING

see Industrial Safety

SAFETY MEASURES

see Industrial Safety

SAFETY REGULATIONS

see also Atomic Power–Law and Legislation; Fire Prevention; Firearms–Laws and Regulations

Guy, Edward T. & Merrigan, John J. Forms for Safety & Security Management. 448p. 1980. text ed. 28.95 (ISBN 0-409-95089-0). Butterworths.

SAIBARA

see Folk-Songs, Japanese

SAILING

see also Boats and Boating; Gliders (Aeronautics); Navigation; Yachts and Yachting

Beard, Henry & McKie, Roy. Sailing. LC 80-54621. (Illus.). 96p. 1981. 8.95 (ISBN 0-89480-158-9); pap. 4.95 (ISBN 0-89480-144-9). Workman Pub.

Blyth, Chay & Blyth, Maureen. Innocent Abroad. 196p. 1980. 6.00x (Pub. by Nautical England). State Mutual Bk.

Denk, Roland. Sailing. (Illus.). 140p. 1981. 12.95 (ISBN 0-8069-9144-5, Pub. by EP Publishing England). Sterling.

Faraham, Moulton M. Sailing for Beginners. rev. ed. (Illus.). 272p. 1981. 14.95 (ISBN 0-02-537140-1). Macmillan.

Hinz, Earl. Sail Before Sunset. (Illus.). 244p. 1979. 12.95 (ISBN 0-679-51350-7). Western Marine Ent.

Hiscock, Eric. Cruising Under Sail. rev. ed. (Illus.). 544p. 1981. 35.00 (ISBN 0-19-217599-8). Oxford U Pr.

Lewis, Christa. Boobies on My Bowsprit. 1981. 8.75 (ISBN 0-8062-1598-4). Carlton.

Livingston, Kimball. Sailing the Bay. (Illus.). 128p. (Orig.). 1981. pap. 5.95 (ISBN 0-87701-180-X). Chronicle Bks.

Messora, L. Start Sailing. (Orig.). 1980. pap. 8.95x (ISBN 0-8464-1051-6). Beekman Pubs.

Mulville, Frank. The Death of Schooner Integrity. Campbell, Dennis, ed. (Illus.). 169p. Date not set. 12.95 (ISBN 0-89182-032-9); pap. 7.95 (ISBN 0-89182-033-7). Charles River Bks.

Pettegrove, James P. Sailing with Dr. Summers. Date not set. 6.95 (ISBN 0-533-04668-8). Vantage.

Schwaig, Robert. Odessy of the Blithe Spirit II. 200p. (Orig.). pap. 6.95 (ISBN 0-86629-024-9). Sunrise MO.

Walker, Nicolette M. Introduction to Dinghy Sailing. (Illus.). 104p. 1981. 14.95 (ISBN 0-7153-8022-2). David & Charles.

SAILING–JUVENILE LITERATURE

Vandervoort, Tom. Sailing Is for Me. (Sports for Me Bks.). (Illus.). (gr. 2-5). 1981. PLB 5.95 (ISBN 0-8225-1128-2). Lerner Pubns.

SAILING SHIPS

see also Schooners

Hawkins, Clifford W. The Dhow. 144p. 1980. 57.00x (ISBN 0-245-52655-2, Pub. by Nautical England). State Mutual Bk.

Levi, Renato S. Dhows to Deltas. 255p. 1980. 15.00x (ISBN 0-245-59956-8, Pub. by Nautical England). State Mutual Bk.

Macgregor, David R. Fast Sailing Ships. 316p. 1980. 57.00x (ISBN 0-245-51964-5, Pub. by Nautical England). State Mutual Bk.

SAILING VESSELS

see Sailing Ships

SAILORS' LIFE

see Seafaring Life

SAILPLANES (AERONUTICS)

see Gliders (Aeronautics)

ST. BENEDICT, ORDER OF

see Benedictines

SAINT DENIS, RUTH, 1880-

Shelton, Suzanne. Divine Dancer: Abiography of Ruth St. Denis. LC 80-2442. (Illus.). 312p. 1981. 14.95 (ISBN 0-385-14159-9). Doubleday.

ST. HELENS, MOUNT

Doran, Jeffry W. Search on Mount St. Helens. Pica, George, ed. (Illus.). 96p. (Orig.). pap. 7.95 (ISBN 0-938700-00-6). Imagesmith.

Jones, J. P. & Jones, Betty. Of Smoke & Ash - Mt. St. Helens. (Illus., Orig.). 1980. pap. write for info. (ISBN 0-9604838-0-2). G & BJ's Serv.

Kelso, Linda. Mount St. Helens: Volcano. Shangle, Robert D., ed. (Illus.). 64p. 1980. pap. 7.95 (ISBN 0-89802-209-6). Beautiful Am.

Palmer, Leonard. Mt. Saint Helens, the Volcano Explodes. 15.00; pap. 7.95 (ISBN 0-86519-004-6). Green Hill.

Roberts, Don & Roberts, Diana. Mount St. Helens the Volcano of Our Time. (Illus.). 48p. (Orig.). pap. 5.95 (ISBN 0-936608-10-2). F Amato Pubns.

ST. LOUIS–DESCRIPTION

Schumacher, Claire W. The Whiteside Island Story-Merald Isle of St. Louis Bay. LC 74-29021. 65p. 1980. 2.50 (ISBN 0-917378-04-0). Schumacher Pubns.

ST. LOUIS–ECONOMIC CONDITIONS

Compton, Charles H., et al. Twenty-Five Crucial Years of the St. Louis Public Library, 1927 to 1952. 1953. write for info. (ISBN 0-937322-00-8). St Louis Pub Lib.

ST. LOUIS–HISTORY

Baer, Howard F. St. Louis to Me: 1978. 10.95 (ISBN 0-86629-005-2). Sunrise MO.

Rodabough, John. Frenchtown. 200p. 1981. 19.95 (ISBN 0-86629-021-4). Sunrise MO.

Sunrise Publishing Company Editors, ed. The Greatest of Expositions: St. Louis World's Fair, 1904. rev. ed. 1981. pap. 8.95 (ISBN 0-86629-029-X). Sunrise MO.

Young, Andrew D. & Provenzo, Eugene F., Jr. The History of the St. Louis Car Company. (Illus.). 304p. 1981. Repr. of 1978 ed. 27.50 (ISBN 0-8310-7114-1). A S Barnes.

SAINTS

see also Martyrs

also names of Saints, e.g. Teresa, Saint

Baba Hari Dass. Harikhan Baba--Known, Unknown. LC 75-3838. (Illus.). 93p. (Orig.). 1975. pap. 1.95 (ISBN 0-918100-00-3). Sri Rama.

Dooley, Catherine. The Saints Book. 64p. (Orig.). (gr. k-3). 1981. pap. 2.95 (ISBN 0-8091-6547-3). Paulist Pr.

Gies, Frances. Joan of Arc: The Legend & the Reality. LC 80-7900. (Illus.). 256p. 1981. 12.95 (ISBN 0-690-01942-4, HarpT). Har-Row.

Hayes, Zachary. The Hidden Center: Spirituality & Speculative Christology in St. Bonaventure. 224p. (Orig.). 1981. pap. 7.95 (ISBN 0-8091-2348-7). Paulist Pr.

McBride, Alfred. Saints Are People: Church History Through the Saints. 144p. (Orig.). 1981. pap. 4.00 (ISBN 0-697-01783-4). Wm C Brown.

Young, William, tr. St. Ignatius's Own Story. 1980. Repr. 3.95 (ISBN 0-8294-0359-0). Loyola.

Zekowski, Arlene & Berne, Stanley. Cardinals & Saints. LC 58-11713. 1958. 75.00 (ISBN 0-913844-10-1). Am Canadian.

SAINTS–JUVENILE LITERATURE

Patterson, Yvonne. Doubting Thomas. (Arch Bk.: No. 18). 1981. pap. 0.79 (ISBN 0-570-06144-X, 59-1261). Concordia.

SAINTS–LEGENDS
Saint, Phil, tr. Cataclimo. (Spanish Bks.). (Span.). 1978. 1.00 (ISBN 0-8297-0435-3). Life Pubs Intl.
SAINTS, WOMEN
Lappin, Peter. Halfway to Heaven. 240p. (Orig.). 1980. pap. write for info. (ISBN 0-89944-052-5). D Bosco Pubns.
SALADIN, SULTAN OF EGYPT AND SYRIA, 1137-1193
Lyons, M. & Jackson, D. Saladin: Politics of Holy War. LC 79-13078. (Cambridge University Oriental Publications Ser.). (Illus.). 400p. Date not set. price not set (ISBN 0-521-22358-X). Cambridge U Pr.
SALADS
Gerras, Charles, ed. Rodale's Soups & Salads Cookbook & Kitchen Album. (Illus.). 352p. 1981. 14.95 (ISBN 0-87857-332-1). Rodale Pr Inc.
Matteson, Marilee, ed. Small Feasts: Soups, Salads, & Sandwiches. (Clarkson N. Potter Bks.). 1980. 17.95 (ISBN 0-517-54052-5). Crown.
Nelson, Kay S. The Complete International Salad Book. 304p. 1981. pap. 2.50 (ISBN 0-553-13557-0). Bantam.
Swedlin, Rosalie. A World of Salads. LC 80-18134. (Illus.). 256p. 1981. 17.95 (ISBN 0-03-053391-0); pap. 9.95 (ISBN 0-686-69291-8). HR&W.
SALAMANDERS
Billings, Charlene W. Salamanders. LC 80-21838. (A Skylight Bk.). (Illus.). 48p. (gr. 2-5). 1981. PLB 5.95 (ISBN 0-396-07913-X). Dodd.
SALES
see also Auctions; Export Sales
Marks, Ronald. Personal Selling. 576p. 1981. text ed. 17.95 (ISBN 0-205-07327-1); free (ISBN 0-205-07328-X). Allyn.
Petty, Ryan. How to Make More Money with Your Garage Sale. 96p. 1981. pap. 3.95 (ISBN 0-312-39602-3). St Martin.
Stockton, John M. Sales in a Nutshell. 2nd ed. LC 80-25579. (Nutshell Ser.). 358p. 1980. pap. text ed. write for info. (ISBN 0-8299-2116-8). West Pub.
Ullman, James M. How to Hold a Garage Sale. LC 80-53812. (Illus.). 96p. (Orig.). 1981. pap. 3.95 (ISBN 0-528-88040-3). Rand.
Webster, Jonathan & Webster, Harriet. The Underground Marketplace. LC 80-54401. (Illus.). 208p. 1981. text ed. 12.50x (ISBN 0-87663-348-3); pap. 6.95 (ISBN 0-87663-555-9). Universe.
SALES, INTERNATIONAL
see Export Sales
SALES MANAGEMENT
Allen, P. Sales & Sales Management. 2nd ed. (Illus.). 288p. 1979. pap. 12.95x (ISBN 0-7121-1962-0, Pub. by Macdonald & Evans England). Intl Ideas.
Bellenger, Danny N. & Berl, Robert L. Sales Management: A Review of the Current Literature. (Research Monograph: No. 89). 1981. spiral bdg. 10.00 (ISBN 0-88406-147-7). GA St U Busn Pub.
Cundiff, Edward W., et al. Sales Management. (Illus.). 656p. 1981. text ed. 20.95 (ISBN 0-13-788059-6). P-H.
Fenton, John. The A to Z of Sales Management. 168p. 1981. 14.95 (ISBN 0-8144-5655-3). Am Mgmt.
Forsyth, Patrick. Running an Effective Sales Office. 160p. 1980. text ed. 37.25x (ISBN 0-566-02185-4, Pub. by Gower Pub Co England). Renouf.
Futrell, Charles M. Cases in Sales Management. LC 80-65797. 320p. 1981. pap. text ed. 10.95 (ISBN 0-03-054736-9). Dryden Pr.
--Sales Management. LC 80-65796. 528p. 1981. text ed. 17.95 (ISBN 0-03-049276-9). Dryden Pr.
Langer, Steven. Income in Sales-Marketing Management. 1981. pap. 85.00 (ISBN 0-916506-58-4). Abbott Langer Assocs.
Wilson, M. T. Managing Sales Force. (Illus.). 184p. 1970. 19.50 (ISBN 0-7161-0048-7). Herman Pub.
SALES PROMOTION
see also Advertising; Exhibitions; Salesmen and Salesmanship
Edwards, Charles M., Jr. & Lebowitz, Carl R. Retail Advertising & Sales Promotion. (Illus.). 576p. 1981. text ed. 19.95 (ISBN 0-13-775098-6); pap. 17.95 (ISBN 0-13-775080-3). P-H.
OECD. Bargain Price Offers & Similar Marketing Practices. (Illus., Orig.). 1980. pap. text ed. 6.00 (ISBN 92-64-12033-5, 24-80-01-1). OECD.
SALESMANSHIP
see Salesmen and Salesmanship
SALESMEN AND SALESMANSHIP
see also Advertising; Booksellers and Bookselling; Mail-Order Business; Marketing; Sales Management; Sales Promotion; Telephone Selling
Allen, P. Sales & Sales Management. 2nd ed. (Illus.). 288p. 1979. pap. 12.95x (ISBN 0-7121-1962-0, Pub. by Macdonald & Evans England). Intl Ideas.
Anderson, Bert M. Write True to Yourself So You Sell: 19 Lessons in Folios. write for info. (ISBN 0-917628-02-0). Coraco.
Bell, Michael. The Salesman in the Field: Conditions of Work & Employment of Commercial Travellers & Representatives. International Labour Office, Geneva, ed. viii, 108p. (Orig.). 1980. pap. 8.55 (ISBN 92-2-102308-7). Intl Labour Office.
Hickerson, J. Mel. How I Made the Sale That Did the Most for Me: Fifty Great Sales Stories by Fifty Great Salespeople. 400p. 1981. 10.95 (ISBN 0-471-07769-0, Pub. by Wiley-Interscience). Wiley.
Hyatt, Carole. Woman's Selling Game: How to Sell Yourself & Anything Else. 1980. pap. 4.95 (ISBN 0-446-97195-2). Warner Bks.
Micali, Paul J. Survival Handbook for Salespeople. 160p. 1981. pap. 8.95 (ISBN 0-8436-0853-6). CBI Pub.
Preston, Paul & Nelson, Ralph. Salesmanship: A Contemporary Approach. 1981. 15.95 (ISBN 0-8359-6933-9); instr's manual free. Reston.
Richardson, Linda. Banking & Sales: A Consultative Guide to Cross Selling Financial Products & Services. 165p. 1981. 19.95 (ISBN 0-471-09010-7, Pub. by Wiley-Interscience). Wiley.
Sack, Steven M. & Steinberg, Howard J. The Salesperson's Legal Guide. LC 80-22647. 144p. 1981. 12.95 (ISBN 0-13-788190-8); pap. 5.95 (ISBN 0-13-788182-7). P-H.
The Salesman in the Field. 108p. 1980. pap. 9.50 (ISBN 92-2-102308-7, ILO149, ILO). Unipub.
The Silent Salesman. 2nd ed. 156p. 1973. text ed. 19.50x (ISBN 0-220-66203-7, Pub. by Busn Bks England). Renouf.
Stumm, David A. Advanced Industrial Selling. 426p. 1981. 17.95 (ISBN 0-8144-5665-0). Am Mgmt.
Whitehead, Harold. Administration of Marketing & Selling. 19.50x (ISBN 0-392-07566-0, SpS). Soccer.
Young. Personal Selling. 1978. 19.95 (ISBN 0-03-020836-X). Dryden Pr.
Zintz, Walter. Nova Venturion's Handbook for Non-Salesmen. 1981. softcover 12.50 (ISBN 0-915254-09-3). Nova Venturion.
SALINE WATERS–DEMINERALIZATION
Delyannis, A. E. & Delyannis, E. E. Seawater & Desalting, Vol. 1. 180p. 1980. 34.90 (ISBN 0-387-10206-X). Springer-Verlag.
Scott, Jeanette, ed. Desalination of Seawater by Reverse Osmosis. LC 80-26421. (Pollution Tech. Rev. Ser.: No. 75). 431p. 1981. 39.00 (ISBN 0-8155-0837-9). Noyes.
SALINGER, JEROME DAVID, 1919-
French, Warren, ed. J. D. Salinger. (Twayne's U. S. Authors Ser.). 187p. 1963. pap. text ed. 4.95 (ISBN 0-672-61505-3). Bobbs.
SALISH INDIANS
see Indians of North America–Northwest, Pacific
SALISHAN INDIANS
see Indians of North America–Northwest, Pacific
SALIVARY GLANDS
Zelles, T., ed. Saliva & Salivation: Proceedings of a Satellite Symposium to the 28th International Congress of Physiological Held at Szekesfehervar, Hungary, 1980. LC 80-41878. (Advances in Physiological Sciences: Vol. 28). (Illus.). 500p. 1981. 60.00 (ISBN 0-08-027349-1). Pergamon.
SALK VACCINE
see Poliomyelitis Vaccine
SALMON
McNeil, William J. & Himsworth, Daniel C., eds. Salmonid Ecosystems of the North Pacific. LC 80-17800. (Illus.). 348p. pap. 15.00 (ISBN 0-87071-335-3); pap. text ed. 15.00 (ISBN 0-686-68208-4). Oreg St U Pr.
Roberts, Ronald J. & Shepherd, C. Jonathan. Handbook of Trout & Salmon Diseases. (Illus.). 172p. 21.25 (ISBN 0-85238-066-6, FN). Unipub.
SALMON FISHING
Eaton, Roy. Trout & Salmon Fishing. LC 80-68897. (Illus.). 192p. 1981. 22.50 (ISBN 0-7153-8117-2). David & Charles.
SALOONS
see Hotels, Taverns, etc.; Liquor Industry and Trade
SALT-FREE DIET
Brenner, Eleanor P. Gourmet Cooking Without Salt. LC 79-6856. (Illus.). 416p. 1981. 15.95 (ISBN 0-385-14821-6). Doubleday.
SALT LAKE CITY
Haglund, Karl T. & Notarianni, Philip F. The Avenues of Salt Lake City. LC 80-54105. (Illus.). 176p. 1980. pap. 7.50 (ISBN 0-913738-31-X). Utah St Hist Soc.
SALT-WATER AQUARIUMS
see Marine Aquariums
SALTS, FUSED
see Fused Salts
SALVAGE
see also Shipwrecks
Finnerty, W. Patrick, et al. Community Structure & Trade at Isthmus Cove: A Salvage Excavation on Catalina Island (Calif.) (Pacific Coast Archaeological Society Occasional Papers: No. 1). 81p. 1981. pap. 2.95. Acoma Bks.
SALVATION
see also Covenants (Theology); Redemption; Sanctification
Berry, R. L. Around Old Bethany. 83p. pap. 0.75. Faith Pub Hse.
Byrum, E. E. The Secret of Salvation. 264p. pap. 2.50. Faith Pub Hse.
Gromacki, Robert. Is Salvation Forever? 1981. pap. 4.95 (ISBN 0-8024-7507-8). Moody.
McDonald, H. D. Salvation. (Foundations for Faith). 4.95 (ISBN 0-89107-225-X). Good News.
Spurgeon, C. H. All of Grace. 128p. 1981. pap. 2.50 (ISBN 0-88368-097-1). Whitaker Hse.
Warner, D. S. Salvation, Present, Perfect, Now or Never. 63p. pap. 0.40; pap. 1.00 3 copies. Faith Pub Hse.
Wilson, Ostis B. The Plan of Salvation. 64p. pap. 0.50. Faith Pub Hse.
SALVATION (CATHOLIC CHURCH)
see Salvation
SAMPLERS
Ondori Staff. A Treasury of Embroidery Samples. LC 80-84416. (Illus.). 96p. 1981. pap. 5.95 (ISBN 0-87040-496-2). Japan Pubns.
SAMURAI
Tanaka, Minoru. Brotherhood of Mt. Shasta. 88p. 1981. pap. 4.50 (ISBN 0-89540-009-X). Sun Pub.
Tsunetomo, Yamamoto. The Hagakure: A Code to the Way of the Samurai. Mukoh, Takao, tr. from Japanese. xii, 182p. 1980. pap. 13.50 (ISBN 0-89346-169-5, Pub. by Hokuseido Pr). Heian Intl.
SAN ANTONIO, TEXAS
Bowen, David. Picture Book of San Antonio. 32p. (English & Spanish.). pap. 2.50 (ISBN 0-931722-02-0). Corona Pub.
San Antonio Bicentennial Heritage Committee. San Antonio in the Eighteenth Century. 2nd ed. (Illus.). 154p. 1976. pap. 7.95 (ISBN 0-933164-22-X). U of Tex Inst Tex Culture.
SAN FRANCISCO–BIOGRAPHY
Daniels, Douglas H. Images of Our Roots: Photographic, Oral, & Written Documents of the San Francisco Bay Area's Black Pioneers, 1850-1930. (National History Ser.). (Illus.). 1981. 22.50 (ISBN 0-89482-054-0); pap. 12.50 (ISBN 0-89482-055-9). Stevenson Pr.
SAN FRANCISCO–DESCRIPTION
Porter, Jean & Cahn, Leonard. San Francisco: Cool, Gray City of Love. 1981. 19.95 (ISBN 0-525-93180-5, Hawthorn); pap. 10.95 (ISBN 0-525-47663-6). Dutton.
St. Pierre, Brian & Moose, Mary E. The Flavor of North Beach: The Insider's Guide to San Francisco's Historic Italian District. 160p. (Orig.). 1981. pap. 5.95 (ISBN 0-87701-157-5). Chronicle Bks.
SAN FRANCISCO–DESCRIPTION–GUIDEBOOKS
Anthony, Jill & Anthony, Gene. The Great Cable Car Adventure Book. (Illus.). 192p. (Orig.). 1981. pap. 6.95 (ISBN 0-89141-120-8). Presidio Pr.
Camaro Editors. Official Visitors Guide: San Francisco. 1980. 2.95 (ISBN 0-913290-32-7). Camaro Pub.
Doss, Margot P. The Bay Area at Your Feet: Walks with San Francisco's Margot Patterson Doss. rev. ed. (Illus.). 288p. (Orig.). 1981. pap. 7.95 (ISBN 0-89141-097-X). Presidio Pr.
Finigan, Robert. Robert Finigan's Guide to Discriminating Dining in San Francisco. (Illus.). 192p. (Orig.). 1981. pap. 6.95 (ISBN 0-89141-123-2). Presidio Pr.
Shepard, Susan & Levering, Robert. In the Neighborhoods. (Orig.). 1981. pap. 6.95 (ISBN 0-87701-144-3). Chronicle Bks.
Zobel, Jan, ed. San Francisco Bay Area People's Yellow Pages. 5th ed. (Illus.). 1981. pap. 4.95. SF Bay Area.
SAN FRANCISCO–HISTORY
Mack, Gerstle. Nineteen Hundred Six: Surviving the Great Earthquake & Fire. 96p. (Orig.). pap. 5.95 (ISBN 0-87701-176-1). Chronicle Bks.
Saul, Eric & DeNevi, Don. The Great San Francisco & Fire, 1906. LC 80-83616. (Illus.). 176p. 25.00 (ISBN 0-89087-288-0). Celestial Arts.
Snaer, Seymour. San Francisco Nineteen Thirty-Nine. 1980. pap. 9.95 (ISBN 0-9602462-5-8). Working Pr CA.
Zauner, Phyllis & Zauner, Lou. San Francisco, the Way It Was Then & Now. (Western Mini-Histories Ser.). (Illus.). 64p. (Orig.). 1980. pap. 3.00 (ISBN 0-936914-04-1). Zanel Pubns.
SAN FRANCISCO BAY AND BAY REGION
Foster, Lee. Portrait of the Bay Area. Pfeiffer, Douglas A., ed. (Portrait of America Ser.). (Illus.). 80p. (Orig.). 1981. pap. text ed. 5.95 (ISBN 0-912856-69-6). Graphic Arts Ctr.
SAN JOAQUIN VALLEY, CALIFORNIA
Preston, William L. Vanishing Landscapes: Land & Life in the Tulare Basin. (Illus.). 290p. 1981. 15.95 (ISBN 0-520-04053-8). U of Cal Pr.
SAN JUAN ISLANDS
Pixler, Paul. Hiking Trails of the San Juans. (Illus.). 120p. (Orig.). 1981. pap. 5.95 (ISBN 0-87108-579-8). Pruett.
Wood, Bryce. San Juan Island: Coastal Place Names & Cartographic Nomenclature. LC 80-17728. (Sponsor Ser.). 280p. (Orig.). 1980. pap. 20.75 (ISBN 0-8357-0526-9, SS-00132). Univ Microfilms.
SAN LUIS OBISPO COUNTY, CALIFORNIA
Macdonald, Lachlan P. An Uncommon Guide to San Luis Obispo County California. rev. 2nd ed. LC 75-2794. (Illus.). 1981. pap. 5.95 (ISBN 0-686-69421-X). Padre Prods.
SANCTIFICATION
see also Holiness; Mystical Union; Perfection
Berry, R. L. Adventures in the Land of Canaan. 128p. pap. 1.00. Faith Pub Hse.
Byers, J. W. Sanctification. 96p. 0.75. Faith Pub Hse.
Teasley, D. O. The Double Cure, or Redemption Twofold. 160p. pap. 1.50 large print. Faith Pub Hse.
SANCTIONS (LAW)
Brigham, John & Brown, Don W., eds. Policy Implementation: Penalties or Incentives? LC 80-16765. (Sage Focus Editions: Vol. 25). (Illus.). 284p. 1980. 18.95 (ISBN 0-8039-1350-8). Sage.
SANCTUARIES, WILDLIFE
see Wildlife Refuges
SANCTUARY (LAW)
see Asylum, Right Of
SAND CRAFT
see also Sand Sculpture
Allen, Joseph, et al. Sandcastles. LC 80-1648. (Illus.). 164p. 1981. pap. 8.95 (ISBN 0-385-15931-5, Dolp). Doubleday.
SAND SCULPTURE
Allen, Joseph, et al. Sandcastles. LC 80-1648. (Illus.). 164p. 1981. pap. 8.95 (ISBN 0-385-15931-5, Dolp). Doubleday.
SANDBURG, CARL, 1878-1967
Corwin, Norman. A Date with Sandburg. (Santa Susana Press Ser.). 1981. 17.50 (ISBN 0-937048-30-5). CSUN.
Perry, Lilla S. My Friend Carl Sandburg: The Biography of a Friendship. Perry, E. Caswell, ed. LC 80-21908. 234p. 1981. 12.00 (ISBN 0-8108-1367-X). Scarecrow.
SANDWICHES
Matteson, Marilee, ed. Small Feasts: Soups, Salads, & Sandwiches. (Clarkson N. Potter Bks.). 1980. 17.95 (ISBN 0-517-54052-5). Crown.
Uvezian, Sonia. Complete International Sandwich Cookbook. LC 80-5715. 288p. 1981. 14.95 (ISBN 0-8128-2787-2). Stein & Day.
SANITARY AFFAIRS
see Public Health
SANITARY CHEMISTRY
see Food–Analysis; Food Adulteration and Inspection
SANITARY ENGINEERING
see also Filters and Filtration; Pollution; Refuse and Refuse Disposal; Sewage; Water-Supply
American Society of Civil Engineers, compiled by. Sanitary Landfill, Manual 39. (ASCE Manual & Report on Engineering Practice Ser.: No. 39). 92p. looseleaf binder 27.50 (ISBN 0-87262-215-0). Am Soc Civil Eng.
Anchor, R. D. Design of Liquid-Retaining Concrete Structures. 176p. 1981. 49.95 (ISBN 0-470-27123-X). Halsted Pr.
Metcalf & Eddy, Inc. & Tchobanoglous, George. Pumping & Collection of Wastewater. (Water Resources & Engineering Ser.). (Illus.). 400p. 1981. text ed. 28.95 (ISBN 0-07-041680-X, C); student's manual 4.95 (ISBN 0-07-041681-8). McGraw.
Nielsen, Louis S. Standard Plumbing Engineering Design. (Illus.). 384p. 1981. 21.50 (ISBN 0-07-046541-X). McGraw.
SANITATION, TROPICAL
see Tropical Medicine
SANKEY, IRA DAVID, 1840-1908
Ludwig, Charles. Sankey Still Sings. (Christian Biography Ser.). 176p. 1981. pap. 2.95 (ISBN 0-8010-5601-2). Baker Bk.
SANSKRIT DRAMA–HISTORY AND CRITICISM
Baumer, Rachel & Brandon, James R. Sanskrit Drama in Performance. 1981. 27.50 (ISBN 0-8248-0688-3). U Pr of Hawaii.
--Sanskrit Drama in Performance. (Illus.). 352p. 1981. text ed. 27.50x (ISBN 0-8248-0688-3). U Pr of Hawaii.
SANSKRIT POETRY–(COLLECTIONS)
Pollock, Sheldon. Aspects of Verification in Sanskrit Lyric Poetry. (American Oriental Ser.: Vol. 61). 1977. 11.00. Am Orient Soc.
SANTA BARBARA COUNTY, CALIFORNIA
Gagnon, Dennis R. Exploring the Santa Barbara Backcountry. LC 73-77044. (Illus.). 150p. (Orig.). 1981. pap. 5.95 (ISBN 0-934136-13-0). Western Tanager.
Smth, Clifton F. A Flora of the Santa Barbara Region, California. LC 76-9164. 331p. 1976. pap. text ed. 12.50 (ISBN 0-936494-00-X). Santa Barbara Mus Nat Hist.
SANTA FE, NEW MEXICO
Historic Santa Fe Foundation. Old Santa Fe Today. 3rd. enl. ed. (Illus.). 128p. 1981. pap. price not set (ISBN 0-8263-0562-8). U of NM Pr.
Thompson, Waite & Gottleib, Richard M. The Santa Fe Guide. Hausman, Gerald, ed. LC 80-18575. (Illus.). 64p. (Orig.). 1980. pap. 4.50 (ISBN 0-913270-89-X). Sunstone Pr.
SANTA FE TRAIL
Russell, Marian. Land of Enchantment: Memoirs of Marian Russell Along the Santa Fe Trail. 176p. 1981. write for info. (ISBN 0-8263-0571-7). U of NM Pr.
SANTAYANA, GEORGE, 1863-1952
Lamont, Corliss, ed. Dialogue on George Santayana. 115p. (Orig.). 1981. pap. 4.95 (ISBN 0-8180-1327-3). Horizon.
SARACENIC ARCHITECTURE
see Architecture, Islamic
SARACENIC ART
see Art, Islamic
SARATOGA CAMPAIGN, 1777
Furneaux, Rupert. The Battle of Saratoga. LC 69-17940. 320p. 1981. pap. 7.95 (ISBN 0-8128-6125-6). Stein & Day.
SARCOMA
see Tumors
SARCOMA, KAPOSI'S
see Kaposi's Sarcoma
SARGASSO SEA
Beebe, William. The Arcturus Adventure. (Nature Library Ser.). 450p. 1981. pap. 5.95 (ISBN 0-06-090846-7, CN 846, CN). Har-Row.

SARTRE, JEAN PAUL, 1905-1980
Marill-Alberes, Rene. Jean-Paul Sartre: Philosopher Without Faith. LC 60-15950. 1960. 4.75 (ISBN 0-8022-0015-X). Philos Lib.

SASQUATCH
see also Primates
Hunter, Don & Dahinden, Rene. Sasquatch. 208p. (RL 9). Date not set. pap. 1.95 (ISBN 0-451-09186-8, J9186, Sig). NAL.
Place, Marion T. On the Track of Bigfoot. (Illus.). (gr. 5 up). 1979. pap. 1.75 (ISBN 0-671-29944-1). PB.

SATAN
see Devil

SATANISM
see also Demoniac Possession
Battle, Dennis M. The Beast's Mark & Number: 666. (Illus.). 52p. 1981. pap. 2.50 (ISBN 0-933464-11-8). D M Battle Pubns.

SATELLITE COMMUNICATION SYSTEMS
see Artificial Satellites in Telecommunication

SATELLITES
International Conference on the Establishment of an International Maritime Satellite System, 1975-1976. 102p. 1976. 11.00 (IMCO). Unipub.

SATIRE, ENGLISH–HISTORY AND CRITICISM
Carlson, Leland H. Martin Marprelate, Gentleman. (Illus.). 400p. 1981. price not set (ISBN 0-87328-112-8). Huntington Lib.

SATIRE, POLITICAL
see Political Satire

SATIRISTS
Wood, T. M. George Du Maurier: The Satirist of the Victorians. 198p. 1980. Repr. of 1913 ed. lib. bdg. 35.00 (ISBN 0-89760-913-1). Telegraph Bks.

SATURDAY REVIEW
Cousins, Norman. The Human Option: An Autobiographical Notebook. (Illus.). 1981. 9.95 (ISBN 0-393-01430-4). Norton.

SATURNISM
see Lead-Poisoning

SATYAGRAHA
see Passive Resistance

SAUCERS, FLYING
see Flying Saucers

SAUDI ARABIA
Clements, Frank A. Saudi Arabia. (World Bibliographical Ser.: No. 5). 197p. 1979. 25.25 (ISBN 0-903450-15-1). ABC-Clio.
Helms, Christine M. The Cohesion of Saudi Arabia: Evolution of Political Identity. LC 80-8026. (Illus.). 320p. 1981. text ed. 28.00x (ISBN 0-8018-2475-3). Johns Hopkins.
Kabir, Hasan. Doing Business in Saudi Arabia. 350p. 1980. 49.95 (ISBN 0-89260-187-6). Hwong Pub.
Lanier, Alison R. Update -- Saudi Arabia. (Country Orientation Ser.). 150p. 1980. pap. text ed. 25.00 (ISBN 0-933662-26-2). Intercult Network.
Saudi Arabia & Its Place in the World. (Illus.). cased 45.00. Three Continents.

SAUDI ARABIA–ECONOMIC CONDITIONS
Moliver, Donald M. & Abbondante, Paul J. The Economy of Saudi Arabia. 200p. 1980. 21.95 (ISBN 0-03-057004-2). Praeger.

SAUK INDIANS
see Indians of North America–Northwest, Old

SAUL, KING OF ISRAEL
Petersen, Mark E. Three Kings of Israel. LC 80-36697. 179p. 1980. 6.95 (ISBN 0-87747-829-5). Deseret Bk.

SAVATE
see Boxing

SAVING AND INVESTMENT
see also Investments; Saving and Thrift
Shulman, Morton. How to Invest Your Money & Profit from Inflation. 1981. pap. 2.50 (ISBN 0-345-29740-7). Ballantine.
You Are a Money Brain. Drollinger, William C. Jr. 1981. write for info. (ISBN 0-914244-07-8). Epic Pubns.

SAVING AND THRIFT
see also Cost and Standard of Living; Saving and Investment
McLachlan, Christopher A. Inflation-Wise: How to Do Almost Everything for Less. 1981. pap. 4.95 (ISBN 0-380-76836-4). Avon.

SAXONS
see also Anglo-Saxons
Humble, Richard. The Saxon Kings. (Illus.). 223p. 1980. 17.00x (ISBN 0-297-77784-X, Pub. by Weidenfeld & Nicolson England). Biblio Dist.

SAXOPHONE
Richmond, Stanley. Clarinet & Sax0 Phone Experience. 1980. 25.00x (Pub.by Darton-Longman-Todd England). State Mutual Bk.

SAYBROOK, CONNECTICUT–HISTORY
Holmes, John C. Visitor: Jack Kerouac in Old Saybrook. 1980. limited edition, numbered & signed by the author 8.00 (ISBN 0-934660-04-2). TUVOTI.

SAYERS, DOROTHY LEIGH, 1893-1957
Brabazon, James. Dorothy L. Sayers: A Biography. (Illus.). 320p. 1981. 15.95 (ISBN 0-684-16864-2, ScribT). Scribner.

SAYINGS
see Epigrams; Quotations

SCALDS
see Burns and Scalds

SCALING, PSYCHOLOGICAL
see Psychometrics

SCANDINAVIAN ART
see Art, Scandinavian

SCANDINAVIAN LITERATURE
Budd, John, compiled by. Eight Scandanavian Novelists: Criticism & Reviews in English. LC 80-24895. 192p. 1981. lib. bdg. 25.00 (ISBN 0-313-22869-8, BSN/). Greenwood.

SCARRON, PAUL, 1610-1660
Scarron, Paul. Scarrons Novels. Davies, John, tr. LC 80-2497. 1981. Repr. of 1694 ed. 69.50 (ISBN 0-404-19133-9). AMS Pr.

SCATTERING (PHYSICS)
DaSanto, J. A., ed. Mathematical Methods & Applications of Scattering Theory: Proceedings. (Lecture Notes in Physics: Vol. 130). 331p. 1980. pap. 22.00 (ISBN 0-387-10023-7). Springer-Verlag.
Henderson, Douglas, ed. Theoretical Chemistry: Theory of Scattering: Papers in Honor of Henry Eyring, Vol. 6B. (Serial Publications). 1981. price not set (ISBN 0-12-681907-6). Acad Pr.
Reed, Michael & Simon, Barry. Methods of Modern Mathematical Physics, 4 vols. Incl. Vol. 1. Functional Analysis. 1972. 24.95 (ISBN 0-12-585001-8); Vol. 2. Fourier Analysis Self-Adjointness. 1975. 34.50 (ISBN 0-12-585002-6); Vol. 3. Scattering Theory. 1979. 42.00 (ISBN 0-12-585003-4); Vol. 4. 1978. 34.00 (ISBN 0-12-585004-2). Acad Pr.

SCATTERING OF PARTICLES
see Scattering (Physics)

SCENARIOS
see Moving-Picture Plays; Television Plays

SCENE PAINTING
see also Theaters–Stage-Setting and Scenery
Marker, Frederick J. & Marker, Lise-Lone. Edward Gordon Craig & the Pretenders: A Production Revisited. (Special Issues Ser.). (Illus.). Date not set. price not set (ISBN 0-8093-0966-1). S Ill U Pr.
Roenfeld, Sybil. Georgian Scene Painters & Scene Painting. Date not set. price not set (ISBN 0-521-23339-9). Cambridge U Pr.

SCENERY
see Landscape; Views

SCENERY (STAGE)
see Theaters–Stage-Setting and Scenery

SCHARY, DORE
Schary, Dore. Heyday. 1981. pap. 2.95 (ISBN 0-425-04805-5). Berkley Pub.

SCHEDULED AIRLINES
see Air Lines

SCHIELE, EGON, 1890-1918
Whitford, Frank. Egon Schiele: World of Art. (Illus.). 288p. 1981. 17.95 (ISBN 0-19-520245-7); pap. 9.95 (ISBN 0-19-520246-5). Oxford U Pr.

SCHISM–EASTERN AND WESTERN CHURCH
Makrakis, Apostolos. The Innovations of the Roman Church. 82p. (Orig.). 1966. pap. 1.50x (ISBN 0-938366-39-4). Orthodox Chr.

SCHISTOSOMA JAPONICUM
McLaren, Diane J. Schistosoma Mansoni: The Parasite Surface in Relation to Host Immunity. (Tropical Medicine Research Studies Ser.). 1981. write for info. (ISBN 0-471-27869-6, Pub. by Wiley-Interscience). Wiley.

SCHIZOPHRENIA
see also Schizophrenics
Arieti, Silvano. Understanding & Helping the Schizophrenic: A Guide for Family & Friends. 1981. pap. 4.95 (ISBN 0-671-41252-3, Touchstone Bks). S&S.
Dunham, H. Warren. Social Systems & Schizophrenia: Selected Papers. LC 80-14193. 332p. 1980. 28.95 (ISBN 0-03-056134-5). Praeger.
Schizophernia: A Bibliography of Books in English. 146p. 1981. lib. bdg. 22.50 (ISBN 0-8482-7064-9). Norwood Edns.
Strauss, John S., et al, eds. The Psychotherapy of Schizophrenia. 300p. 1980. 27.50 (ISBN 0-306-40497-4). Plenum Pub.

SCHIZOPHRENICS
Reynolds, David K. & Farberow, Norman L. The Family Shadow: Sources of Suicide & Schizophrenia. 188p. 1981. 14.95 (ISBN 0-520-04213-1). U of Cal Pr.

SCHIZOPHRENICS–PERSONAL NARRATIVES
Fair, Talitha D. The Liberation of Lily. (Orig.). 1981. pap. 4.95 (ISBN 0-89636-059-8). Accent Bks.

SCHOENBERG, ARNOLD, 1874-1951
Albright, Daniel. Representation & the Imagination: Beckett, Kafka, Nabokov, & Schoenberg. LC 80-26975. (Chicago Originals Ser.). 256p. 1981. lib. bdg. 20.00x (ISBN 0-226-01252-2). U of Chicago Pr.
Rognoni, Luigi. Second Vienna School. Mann, Robert, tr. (Illus.). 420p. 1980. lib. bdg. 27.50 (ISBN 0-7145-3528-1). Riverrun NY.
Rosen, Charles. Arnold Shoenberg. LC 80-8773. 113p. (Orig.). 1981. pap. 4.95 (ISBN 0-691-02706-4). Princeton U Pr.

SCHOLARSHIP
see Learning and Scholarship

SCHOLARSHIPS
Brownstein, Samuel C. & Weiner, Mitchel. You Can Win a Scholarship. (gr. 10-12). 1981. pap. text ed. price not set. Barron.
Green, Barry & Green, Alan. The Directory of Athletic Scholarships: Where They Are & How to Get Them. 312p. 1981. 14.95 (ISBN 0-399-12620-1, Perigee); pap. 6.95 (ISBN 0-399-50533-4). Putnam.
Lerner, Craig Alan, ed. Grants Register: Nineteen Eighty-One-Eighty-Three. 7th ed. 800p. 1980. 32.50x (ISBN 0-312-34407-4). St Martin.

SCHOLASTIC APTITUDE TEST
Bennett, Frances C. & Chang, Sung-wen. Page a Day SAT Study Guide. 320p. (Orig.). 1981. pap. 3.95 (ISBN 0-668-05196-5, 5196). Arco.
Bobrow, Jerry & Covino, William A. PSAT (Preliminary Scholastic Aptitute Test) Date not set. pap. text ed. cancelled. Cliffs.
--SAT (Scholastic Apitute Test) Date not set. pap. text ed. cancelled. Cliffs.
Donner, Michael. How to Beat the SAT's. (gr. 11-12). 1981. pap. 3.95 (ISBN 0-89480-154-6). Workman Pub.
Freedman, Gabriel F., et al, eds. Scholastic Aptitude Test (SAT) LC 80-88. 512p. 1981. lib. bdg. 12.00 (ISBN 0-668-04916-2, 4916). Arco.

SCHOLASTIC SUCCESS
see Academic Achievement

SCHONBERG, ARNOLD, 1874-1951
see Schoenberg, Arnold, 1874-1951

SCHOOL ADJUSTMENT
see Student Adjustment

SCHOOL ADMINISTRATION
see School Management and Organization

SCHOOL-AGE PARENTS
see Adolescent Parents

SCHOOL AND COMMUNITY
see Community and School

SCHOOL AND HOME
see Home and School

SCHOOL ATTENDANCE
see also Children–Employment; Educational Law and Legislation; School Children–Transportation
White, Roger. Absent with Cause: Lessons of Truancy. (Routledge Education Bks.). 300p. (Orig.). 1980. pap. 18.00 (ISBN 0-7100-0665-9). Routledge & Kegan.

SCHOOL-BOOKS
see Text-Books

SCHOOL BUSINESS MANAGEMENT
see Public Schools–Business Management

SCHOOL CENSUS
see School Attendance

SCHOOL CHILDREN–FOOD
Parker, Lynn, et al. Frac's Guide to Quality School Lunch & Breakfast Programs. rev. ed. Perry, Cecilia, ed. Orig. Title: Frac's Guide to the School Lunch & Breakfast Programs. 52p. 1980. pap. text ed. 1.00 (ISBN 0-934220-04-2). Food Res Action.

SCHOOL CHILDREN–TRANSPORTATION
see also School Attendance
Langerton, Edward P. The Busing Coverup. LC 75-34839. 182p. 1975. pap. 2.95. Quam Pr.

SCHOOL COSTS
see Education–Costs

SCHOOL EMPLOYEES
see also Teachers
Fawcett, Claude W. School Personnel Systems. LC 78-57240. (Illus.). write for info. (ISBN 0-669-02375-2). Lexington Bks.

SCHOOL ENROLLMENT
see School Attendance

SCHOOL EVALUATION
see Educational Surveys

SCHOOL FACILITIES
Kelley, Edgar A. School Climate. Koerner, Thomas F., ed. 80p. (Orig.). 1981. pap. text ed. 4.00 (ISBN 0-88210-115-3). Natl Assn Principals.

SCHOOL FINANCE
see Education–Finance

SCHOOL FUNDS
see Public Schools

SCHOOL HEALTH
see also Posture; Sports Medicine
School Health in America. 2nd ed. 1979. pap. 1.00 (ISBN 0-917160-12-6). Am Sch Health.

SCHOOL INSPECTION
see School Management and Organization

SCHOOL INTEGRATION
Wilkinson, J. Harvie, ed. From Brown to Bakke: The Supreme Court & School Integration, 1954-1978. (A Galaxy Book: No. 634). 378p. 1981. pap. 6.95 (ISBN 0-19-502897-X). Oxford U Pr.

SCHOOL LAW
see Educational Law and Legislation

SCHOOL LIBRARIES
see also Children's Literature (Collections); Instructional Materials Centers
also subdivisions under Children's Literature
Aaron, Shirley L. A Study of Combined School-Public Libraries. LC 80-19785. 120p. 1980. pap. 7.00 (ISBN 0-8389-3247-9). ALA.
Archenhold, W. F., et al. School Science Laboratories: A Handbook of Design, Management & Organisation. 303p. 1980. 35.00x (ISBN 0-7195-3436-4, Pub. by Murray Pubs England). State Mutual Bk.
Babin, Lawrence J. The School Library. 1981. pap. 1.95 (ISBN 0-912492-17-1). Pyquag.
Fitzgerald, Gregory. Hunting the Yahoos. (Illus.). 100p. (Orig.). 1981. pap. 4.50 (ISBN 0-934996-14-8). Am Stud Pr.
Stuhlman, Daniel D. How to Use the School Library. (Teacher Education Ser.: No. 3). (Orig.). Date not set. pap. 1.25 (ISBN 0-934402-06-X). BYLS Pr.

SCHOOL LIBRARIES (HIGH SCHOOL)
Senior High School Library Catalog: 1980 Supplement to the 11th Ed. 1980. 50.00 (ISBN 0-8242-0619-3). Wilson.

SCHOOL LIFE
see Students

SCHOOL LUNCHES
see School Children–Food

SCHOOL MANAGEMENT AND ORGANIZATION
Here are entered works dealing with the management, organization, supervision, etc. of schools in general, and in the United States as a whole.
see also Articulation (Education); Classroom Management; Public Schools–Business Management; School Attendance; School Employees; School Personnel Management; Teaching
Bryson & Bentley. Ability Grouping of Public School Students: Legal Aspects of Tracking Methods. 300p. 1980. 15.00 (ISBN 0-87215-332-0). Michie.
Click, Phyllis. Administration of Schools for Young Children. 2nd ed. LC 79-55285. (Early Childhood Education Ser.). 176p. 1981. pap. text ed. 10.60 (ISBN 0-8273-1575-9); instr's. guide 1.80 (ISBN 0-8273-1576-7). Delmar.
Davis, Jack & Loveless, E. E. The Administrator & Educational Facilities. LC 80-1445. 272p. 1981. lib. bdg. 19.00 (ISBN 0-8191-1391-3); pap. text ed. 10.50 (ISBN 0-8191-1392-1). U Pr of Amer.
Dull, Lloyd W. Educational Supervision: A Handbook. (Illus.). 504p. 1981. text ed. 18.95 (ISBN 0-675-08060-6). Merrill.
The Economy of Energy Conservation in Educational Facilities. 82p. (Orig.). 1973. pap. text ed. 4.00. Interbk Inc.
Giammatteo, Michael C., et al. Forces on Leadership. 80p. 1981. pap. 4.00 (ISBN 0-88210-116-1). Natl Assn Principals.
Jones, Roy. Primary School Management. 160p. 1980. 14.95 (ISBN 0-7153-7843-0). David & Charles.
Olds, Robert. Managing Your Schools: What's Ahead. 1979. pap. 11.95 (ISBN 0-87545-016-4). Natl Sch PR.
Rioux, William. You Can Improve Your Child's School. 1980. 12.95 (ISBN 0-686-68754-X, 25116). S&S.
Society of Education Officers. Educational Administration. Brooksbank, Kenneth, ed. 300p. (Orig.). 1981. pap. text ed. 16.95 (ISBN 0-900313-65-X). Longman.
Wiles, Jon W. & Bondi, Joseph, Jr. The Essential Middle School. (Illus.). 432p. Date not set. text ed. 16.95 (ISBN 0-675-08086-X). Merrill.

SCHOOL MANAGEMENT AND ORGANIZATION–LAWS AND LEGISLATION
Zerchykov, Ross, et al. Leading the Way: State Mandates for School Advisory Council in California, Florida, & South Carolina. 175p. (Orig.). 1980. pap. 6.00 (ISBN 0-917754-15-8). Inst Responsive.

SCHOOL MANAGEMENT AND ORGANIZATION–GREAT BRITAIN
Dawson, Peter. Making a Comprehensive Work: The Road from Bomb Alley. 160p. 1981. 25.00x (ISBN 0-631-12534-5, Pub. by Basil Blackwell England); pap. 12.50x. Biblio Dist.

SCHOOL NURSING
Kolisko, Eugen. Medical Work in Education. 1980. pap. 1.95x (ISBN 0-906492-38-6, Pub. by Kolisko Archives). St. George Bk Serv.

SCHOOL OPERATION POLICIES
see School Management and Organization

SCHOOL ORGANIZATION
see School Management and Organization

SCHOOL PERSONNEL
see School Employees

SCHOOL PERSONNEL MANAGEMENT
Fawcett, Claude W. School Personnel Systems. LC 78-57240. (Illus.). write for info. (ISBN 0-669-02375-2). Lexington Bks.

SCHOOL PLANTS
see School Facilities

SCHOOL PLAYS
see Children's Plays

SCHOOL SOCIAL WORK
see also Personnel Service in Education
Deshler, Betty, intro. by. School Social Work & the Law. LC 80-83075. (Conference Proceedings Ser.). 192p. (Orig.). pap. text ed. 7.50 (ISBN 0-87101-088-7, CBP-088-C). Natl Assn Soc Wkrs.
School Social Work & the Law. LC 80-83075. (NASW Conference Proceedings Ser.). 192p. 1980. pap. text ed. 7.50x (ISBN 0-87101-088-7, CBP-088-C). Natl Assn Soc Wkrs.

SCHOOL SURVEYS
see Educational Surveys

SCHOOL TAXES
see Education–Finance

SCHOOL TEACHING
see Teaching

SCHOOL TRANSPORTATION
see School Children–Transportation

SCHOOLGIRL PREGNANCY
see Pregnant Schoolgirls

SCHOOLS
see also Church Schools; Education; Forestry Schools and Education; Medical Colleges; Private Schools; Professional Education; Public Schools; Sunday-Schools; Technical Education; Universities and Colleges
also headings beginning with the word School: and subdivision Study and Teaching under subjects, e.g. Mathematics–Study and Teaching
Gleeson, Denis, ed. Identity & Structure. 212p. 1979. 16.50x (ISBN 0-905484-01-0, Pub. by Nafferton England); pap. 9.50x (ISBN 0-905484-06-1). State Mutual Bk.
SCHOOLS–CURRICULA
see Education–Curricula; Universities and Colleges–Curricula
SCHOOLS–FINANCE
see Education–Finance
SCHOOLS–INSPECTION
see School Management and Organization
SCHOOLS–LAW AND LEGISLATION
see Educational Law and Legislation
SCHOOLS–MANAGEMENT AND ORGANIZATION
see School Management and Organization
SCHOOLS–PERSONNEL MANAGEMENT
see School Personnel Management
SCHOOLS–SANITARY AFFAIRS
see School Health
SCHOOLS, COMMERCIAL
see Business Education
SCHOOLS, DENOMINATIONAL
see Church Schools
SCHOOLS, PAROCHIAL
see Church Schools
SCHOOLS OF NURSING
see Nursing Schools
SCHOONERS
Smith, Herbert. Dreams of Natural Places: A New England Schooner Odyssey. LC 80-69529. (Illus.). 102p. 1981. 15.95 (ISBN 0-89272-107-3). Down East.
SCHOPENHAUER, ARTHUR, 1788-1860
Miller, Bruce R. The Philosophy of Schopenhauer in Dramatic Representational Expressions. (Illus.). 101p. 1981. 19.75 (ISBN 0-89266-279-4). Am Classical Coll Pr.
SCHUBERT, FRANZ PETER, 1797-1828
Einstein, Alfred. Shubert: A Musical Portrait. (Music Ser.). ix, 343p. 1981. Repr. of 1951 ed. lib. bdg. 27.50 (ISBN 0-306-76083-5). Da Capo.
Woodford, Peggy. Schubert, His Life & Times. expanded ed. (Illus.). 192p. Repr. of 1978 ed. 19.95 (ISBN 0-87666-640-3). Paganiniana Pubns.
SCIENCE
see also Astronomy; Bacteriology; Biology; Botany; Chemistry; Crystallography; Ethnology; Geology; Life Sciences; Mathematics; Meteorology; Mineralogy; Natural History; Paleontology; Petrology; Physics; Physiology; Space Sciences; Zoology
also headings beginning with the word Scientific
Asimov, Isaac. The Road to Infinity. 256p. 1981. pap. 2.75 (ISBN 0-380-54155-6, 54155). Avon.
Atwood, Beth, et al. Reading About Science, Skills & Concepts, 3 bks. Kane, Joanne E., ed. (Reading About Science, Skills & Concepts Ser.). (Illus.). (gr. 5-7). 1980. Bk. E, 144 Pgs. pap. text ed. 5.04x (ISBN 0-07-002425-1, W); Bk. F, 160 Pgs. pap. text ed. 5.28x (ISBN 0-07-002426-X); Bk. G, 160 Pgs. pap. text ed. 5.28x (ISBN 0-07-002427-8); tchrs. ed. 3.24 (ISBN 0-686-68698-5). McGraw.
Beveridge, W. E. B. Seeds of Discovery. (Illus.). 1981. 12.95 (ISBN 0-393-01444-4). Norton.
Busch, Lawrence, ed. Science & Agricultural Development. 220p. 1981. text ed. 28.00 (ISBN 0-86598-022-5). Allanheld.
Gandy, Richard E., ed. Theories & Observation in Science. vii, 184p. 1980. lib. bdg. 22.00 (ISBN 0-917930-39-8); pap. 7.50x (ISBN 0-917930-19-3). Ridgeview.
General Science Index: June 1979-May 1980. (Sold on service basis). 1980. write for info. Wilson.
Gribbin, John. Death of the Sun. 1981. pap. price not set (ISBN 0-440-51854-7, Delta). Dell.
Mallow, Jeffry. Science Anxiety: Fear of Science & How to Overcome It. 256p. 1981. 9.95 (ISBN 0-444-00457-2, Thomond). Elsevier.
Nicholas, J. W. Psience: A General Theory of Existence. LC 77-11135. pap. 3.95 (ISBN 0-915520-09-5). Ross-Erikson.
Panati, Charles. Breakthroughs. 1981. pap. 3.25 (ISBN 0-425-04925-6). Berkley Pub.
Peacocke, A. R. The Sciences & Theology in the Twentiety Century. (Oxford International Symposia). 320p. 1981. price not set (ISBN 0-85362-188-8). Routledge & Kegan.
The Present Situation of Science & Technology in the STPI Countries. (Science & Technology for Development Ser.: STPI Module 4). 65p. pap. 5.00 (IDRC TS22, IDRC). Unipub.
Science & Technology for Development: A Review of Schools of Thought on Science, Technology, Development, & Technical Change. (STPI Module Ser.: No. 1). 55p. 1980. pap. 5.00 (ISBN 0-88936-215-7, IDRCTS18, IDRC). Unipub.
SCIENCE–ABBREVIATIONS
Anglo-American & German Abbreviations in Science & Technology Supplement. 1981. 52.50 (ISBN 3-598-20512-0). Bowker.
SCIENCE–ADDRESSES, ESSAYS, LECTURES
Gutting, Gary, ed. Paradigms & Revolutions: Appraisals & Applications of Thomas Kuhn's Philosophy of Science. LC 80-20745. 256p. 1980. text ed. 18.95 (ISBN 0-268-01542-2); pap. text ed. 7.95 (ISBN 0-268-01543-0). U of Notre Dame Pr.
Humayun, Kabir. Science, Democracy, and Islam: And Other Essays. LC 80-2195. 1981. Repr. of 1955 ed. 20.00 (ISBN 0-404-18967-9). AMS Pr.
SCIENCE–AUTHORSHIP
see Technical Writing
SCIENCE–DATA PROCESSING
Friend, J. N. Science Data. 4th ed. 120p. 1960. 10.00x (ISBN 0-85264-090-0, Pub. by Griffin England). State Mutual Bk.
SCIENCE–DICTIONARIES
Frick, G. William, ed. Environmental Glossary. LC 80-67274. 225p. 19.50 (ISBN 0-86587-080-2). Gov Insts.
Grolier Incorporated. Encyclopedia Science Supplement, 1981. Kondo, Herbert, ed. LC 64-7603. (Illus.). 1980. write for info. (ISBN 0-7172-1511-3). Grolier Ed Corp.
Kordo, Herbert, ed. New Book of Popular Science, 6 vols. LC 80-83090. (Illus.). 1981. write for info. (ISBN 0-7172-1211-4). Grolier Ed Corp.
SCIENCE–EXPERIMENTS
see also Experimental Design
The Formula. 289p. 1980. pap. 12.95 (ISBN 0-8362-2702-6). Andrews & McMeel.
SCIENCE–EXPERIMENTS–JUVENILE LITERATURE
Brown, Sam E. Bubbles, Rainbows & Worms: Science Experiments for Pre-School Children. LC 80-84598. (Illus.). 1981. pap. 5.95 (ISBN 0-87659-100-4). Gryphon Hse.
Simon, Seymour. Einstein Anderson Makes up for Lost Time. (Einstein Anderson, Science Sleuth Ser.). (Illus.). 96p. (gr. 3-7). 1981. 6.95 (ISBN 0-670-29067-X). Viking Pr.
SCIENCE–HISTORY
Buchdahl, G., ed. Changing Views About the Principles of Scientific Theory Evaluation. 90p. 1980. pap. 16.50 (ISBN 0-08-027408-0). Pergamon.
Kline, Morris. Mathematics & the Physical World. (Illus.). 496p. 1981. pap. price not set (ISBN 0-486-24104-1). Dover.
Wallace, William A. Causality & Scientific Explanation: Classical & Contemporary Science, Vol. 2. 432p. 1981. lib. bdg. 22.75 (ISBN 0-8191-1480-4); pap. text ed. 13.75 (ISBN 0-8191-1481-2). U Pr of Amer.
--Causality & Scientific Explanation: Medieval & Early Classical Science, Vol. 1. 298p. 1981. lib. bdg. 19.25 (ISBN 0-8191-1478-2); pap. text ed. 10.50 (ISBN 0-8191-1479-0). U Pr of Amer.
SCIENCE–HISTORY–UNITED STATES
C. S. Peirce Bicentennial International Congress. Proceedings. Ketner, Kenneth, et al, eds. (Graduate Studies, Texas Tech Univ.: No. 23). 420p. (Orig.). 1981. price not set (ISBN 0-89672-075-6); pap. price not set (ISBN 0-89672-074-8). Tex Tech Pr.
Reingold, Nathan, ed. The Papers of Joseph Henry: The Princeton Years, January 1838-1840, Vol. 4. LC 72-2005. (The Papers of Joseph Henry Ser.). (Illus.). 432p. 1981. text ed. 30.00x (ISBN 0-87474-792-9). Smithsonian.
SCIENCE–INFORMATION SERVICES
Archenhold, W. F., et al. School Science Laboratories: A Handbook of Design, Management & Organisation. 303p. 1980. 35.00x (ISBN 0-7195-3436-4, Pub. by Murray Pubs England). State Mutual Bk.
SCIENCE–INTERNATIONAL COOPERATION
The Collective Self-Reliance of Developing Countries in the Fields of Science & Technology. 23p. 1981. pap. 6.75 (ISBN 92-808-0173-2, T*U*N*U 108, UNU). Unipub.
Report of the First Session of the Joint Scientific Committee. 140p. 1980. pap. 25.00 (W474, WMO). Unipub.
Ritterberger, Volker, ed. Science & Technology in a Changing International Order: The United Nations Conference on Science & Technology for Development. (Special Studies in Social, Political, & Economic Development). 200p. 1981. lib. bdg. 25.00x (ISBN 0-86531-146-3). Westview.
SCIENCE–LABORATORY MANUALS
Gerlovich, Jack A., ed. Better Science Through Safety. 160p. 1981. text ed. 6.00 (ISBN 0-8138-1780-3). Iowa St U Pr.
SCIENCE–METHODOLOGY
see also Experimental Design; Logic
Hilpinen, Risto, ed. Scientific Rationality: Studies in the Foundations of Science & Ethics. (Philosophical Studies in Philosophy: No. 21). 247p. 1980. lib. bdg. 44.75 (ISBN 90-277-1112-7, Pub. by D. Reidel). Kluwer Boston.
SCIENCE–MORAL ASPECTS
see Science and Ethics
SCIENCE–PHILOSOPHY
see also Logical Positivism; Semantics (Philosophy)
Bronowski, Jacob. Magic, Science & Civilization. (Bamptom Lectures in America Ser.: No. 20). 104p. 1981. pap. 4.95 (ISBN 0-231-04485-2). Columbia U Pr.
Buchdahl, G., ed. Changing Views About the Principles of Scientific Theory Evaluation. 90p. 1980. pap. 16.50 (ISBN 0-08-027408-0). Pergamon.
Chant, Colin & Fauvel, John. Darwin to Einstein: Historical Studies in Science & Belief. (Illus.). 352p. 1981. text ed. 25.00 (ISBN 0-582-49156-8). Longman.
Coley, Noel & Hall, Vance, eds. Darwin to Einstein: Primary Sources on Science & Belief. (Illus.). 368p. 1981. text ed. 25.00 (ISBN 0-582-49158-4). Longman.
Collins, Margaret S., et al, eds. Science & the Question of Human Equality. (AAAS Selected Symposium: No. 58). 180p. 1981. lib. bdg. 16.00x (ISBN 0-89158-952-X). Westview.
Grunfeld, Joseph. Science & Values. 210p. 1980. text ed. 23.00x (ISBN 90-6032-018-2). Humanities.
Lakatos, Imre. Philosophical Papers: Mathematics, Science & Epistemology, Vol. 2. Worrall, J. & Currie, G., eds. LC 77-14374. 295p. 1980. pap. 13.50 (ISBN 0-521-28030-3). Cambridge U Pr.
--Philosophical Papers: The Methodology of Scientific Research Programmes, Vol. 1. Worrall, J. & Currie, G., eds. LC 77-71415. 258p. 1980. pap. 12.50 (ISBN 0-521-28031-1). Cambridge U Pr.
Philosophy (Concepts) of Scientific & Technological Development. 17p. 1981. pap. 6.75 (ISBN 92-808-0176-7, T*U*N*U 109, UNU). Unipub.
Skagestad, Peter. The Road of Inquiry: C. S. Pierce's Pragmatic Realism. LC 80-25278. 296p. 1981. 20.00x (ISBN 0-231-05004-6). Columbia U Pr.
Stove, David. Popper & After: Four Modern Irrationalists. 192p. 1981. 20.50 (ISBN 0-08-026792-0); pap. 10.75 (ISBN 0-08-026791-2). Pergamon.
Tweney, Ryan D., et al, eds. On Scientific Thinking. 496p. 1981. 25.00x (ISBN 0-231-04814-9); pap. 12.50x (ISBN 0-231-04815-7). Columbia U Pr.
VanFrassen, B. C. The Scientific Image. (Clarendon Library of Logic & Philosophy Ser.). 248p. 1980. text ed. 45.00x (ISBN 0-19-824424-X). Oxford U Pr.
SCIENCE–RESEARCH
see Research
SCIENCE–SOCIAL ASPECTS
Barman, Charles R., et al. Science & Societal Issues: A Guide for Science Teachers. (Illus.). 152p. 1981. pap. text ed. 9.00 (ISBN 0-8138-0485-X). Iowa St U Pr.
Cole, Jonathan R. & Cole, Stephen. Social Stratification in Science. 1973. pap. 9.00 (ISBN 0-226-11339-6). U of Chicago Pr.
Farkas, Janos, ed. Sociology of Science & Research. (Illus.). 503p. 1979. 47.50x (ISBN 963-05-2204-7). Intl Pubns Serv.
Knorr, Karin D., et al, eds. The Social Process of Scientific Investigation. (Sociology of the Sciences Ser.: No. IV). 356p. 1980. lib. bdg. 34.50 (ISBN 90-277-1174-7, Pub. by D. Reidel); pap. 15.95 (ISBN 90-277-1175-5). Kluwer Boston.
Science & Social Structure: A Festschrift for Robert K. Merton. LC 80-13464. (N.Y. Academy of Sciences Transactions: Vol. 39). 173p. 1980. 15.00x (ISBN 0-89766-043-9). NY Acad Sci.
SCIENCE–STUDY AND TEACHING
see also Nature Study
Doran, Rodney L. Basic Measurement & Evaluation of Science Instruction. (Illus.). 144p. (Orig.). 1980. pap. 3.00 (ISBN 0-87355-016-1). Natl Sci Tchrs.
Esler, William K. & Esler, Mary K. Teaching Elementary Science. 2nd ed. 512p. 1980. text ed. 18.95x (ISBN 0-534-00913-1). Wadsworth Pub.
Linking Science Education to Real Life. 90p. 1981. pap. 7.00 (UB90, UNESCO Regional Office). Unipub.
Solomon, Joan. Science Teaching. 224p. 1981. 25.00x (ISBN 0-7099-2304-X, Pub. by Croom Helm Ltd England). Biblio Dist.
UNESCO Handbook for Science Teachers. 199p. 1980. pap. 14.95 (ISBN 0-89059-006-0, U1029, UNESCO). Unipub.
SCIENCE–TERMINOLOGY
Biddle, Wayne. Coming to Terms: A Lexicon for Science-Watchers. 1981. 8.95 (ISBN 0-670-33092-2). Viking Pr.
--Coming to Terms: Lexicon for the Science Watcher. LC 80-54198. (Illus.). 128p. 1981. 8.95 (ISBN 0-670-33092-2). Viking Pr.
SCIENCE–VOCATIONAL GUIDANCE
Goldreich, Gloria & Goldreich, Esther. What Can She Be? A Scientist. LC 80-25011. (What Can She Be Ser.). (Illus.). 32p. (gr. 3-6). 1981. 7.95 (ISBN 0-03-055671-6). HR&W.
SCIENCE, APPLIED
see Technology
SCIENCE, BRITISH
Hunter, Michael. Science & Society in Restoration England. LC 80-41071. 224p. Date not set. 37.50 (ISBN 0-521-22866-2); pap. 12.95 (ISBN 0-521-29685-4). Cambridge U Pr.
SCIENCE, CHINESE
Volti, Rudi. Science & Technology in China. (Special Studies on China & East Asia). 350p. 1981. lib. bdg. 25.00x (ISBN 0-89158-951-1). Westview.
Xu Liangying & Fan Dianian. Science & Socialist Construction in China. Perrolle, Pierre M., ed. Hsu, John C., tr. from Chinese. 250p. 25.00 (ISBN 0-87332-189-8). M E Sharpe.
SCIENCE, JAPANESE
Gibson, Robert W., Jr. & Kunkel, Barbara K. Japanese Scientific & Technical Literature: A Subject Guide. LC 80-39693. (Illus.). 480p. 1981. lib. bdg. 75.00 (ISBN 0-313-22929-5, GJS/). Greenwood.
SCIENCE, MENTAL
see Psychology
SCIENCE, MORAL
see Ethics
SCIENCE, POLITICAL
see Political Science
SCIENCE, RUSSIAN
Skulachev, V. P., ed. Soviet Scientific Review: Biology Review, Vol. 2, Section D. 1981. write for info. (ISBN 3-7186-0058-7). Harwood Academic.
Vol'Pin, M., ed. Soviet Scientific Reviews 011section B: Chemistry Reviews, Vol.2. (Soviet Scientific Reviews). 480p. 1980. 90.00 (ISBN 3-7186-0018-8). Harwood Academic.
Vol'Pin, M. E., ed. Soviet Scientific Review: Chemistry Review, Vol. 3, Section B. 1981. write for info. (ISBN 3-7186-0057-9). Harwood Academic.
SCIENCE, SOCIAL
see Sociology
SCIENCE AND ART
see Art and Science
SCIENCE AND CIVILIZATION
Here are entered works on the role of science in the history and development of civilization.
Coley, Noel & Hall, Vance, eds. Darwin to Einstein: Primary Sources on Science & Belief. (Illus.). 368p. 1981. text ed. 25.00 (ISBN 0-582-49158-4). Longman.
SCIENCE AND ETHICS
Lakoff, Sanford A., ed. Science & Ethical Responsibility. 1980. pap. text ed. 17.50 (ISBN 0-201-03993-1). A-W.
Singer, Peter. The Expanding Circle: Ethics and Sociobiology. 1981. 10.95 (ISBN 0-374-15112-1). FS&G.
SCIENCE AND HISTORY
see Science and Civilization
SCIENCE AND RELIGION
see Religion and Science
SCIENCE AND SOCIETY
see Science and Civilization
SCIENCE AND SPACE
see Space Sciences
SCIENCE AND THE BIBLE
see Bible and Science
SCIENCE FICTION
Greenberg, Martin H., ed. Astounding Science Fiction, July, Nineteen Thirty-Nine. 184p. 1981. Repr. of 1939 ed. write for info. (ISBN 0-8093-0991-2). S Ill U Pr.
The Immortals of Science Fiction. (Illus.). 120p. 1980. pap. 11.95 (ISBN 0-8317-4880-X). Mayflower Bks.
SCIENCE FICTION (COLLECTIONS)
Asimov, Isaac & Greenberg, Martin H., eds. Isaac Asimov Presents the Great SF Stories, No. 5. 1981. pap. 2.50 (ISBN 0-87997-604-7, UE1604). Daw Bks.
Asimov, Isaac, et al, eds. One Hundred Great Science Fiction Short Short Stories. 1980. pap. 2.50 (ISBN 0-686-69237-3, 50773). Avon.
--Isaac Asimov Presents the Best Science Fiction of the 19th Century. LC 80-27721. 192p. 1981. 9.95 (ISBN 0-8253-0038-X). Beaufort Bks NY.
--The Seven Deadly Sins of Science Fiction. 1980. pap. 2.50 (ISBN 0-449-24349-4, Crest). Fawcett.
Carr, Jayge, et al. Pandora, No. 5. Wickstrom, Lois, ed. (Illus.). 60p. (Orig.). 1980. pap. 2.50 (ISBN 0-916176-10-X). Sproing.
Dozois, Gardner. Best Science Fiction Stories of the Year: Tenth Annual Collection. 256p. 1981. 11.95 (ISBN 0-525-06499-0). Dutton.
Finder, Jan H., ed. Alien Encounters. 256p. 1981. 11.95 (ISBN 0-8008-0168-7). Taplinger.
Gresham, Stephen, et al. SPWAO Showcase. Warren, David, ed. Raney, Ken, tr. (Illus.). 72p. (Orig.). 1981. pap. 3.00 (ISBN 0-916176-14-2). Sproing.
Herbert, Frank, ed. Nebula Winners Fifteen. LC 78-645226. 256p. 1981. 12.95 (ISBN 0-06-014830-6, HarpT). Har-Row.
Howard, Robert E. The Vultures. (Illus.). 1973. 8.50 (ISBN 0-87707-115-2). Fictioneer Bks.
London, Jack. Selected Science Fiction & Fantasy Stories. LC 76-52712. (Illus.). 1979. 8.50 (ISBN 0-934882-03-7). Fictioneer Bks.
Lorrah, Jean, et al. Pandora, No. 6. Wickstrom, Lois, ed. (Illus.). 60p. (Orig.). 1980. pap. 2.50 (ISBN 0-916176-11-8). Sproing.
Nolan, William Fl & Greenberg, Martin H., eds. Science Fiction Origins. 1980. 2.25 (ISBN 0-445-04626-0). Popular Lib.
Nolane, Richard D., ed. Terra SF. 1981. pap. 2.25 (ISBN 0-87997-595-4, UE1595). Daw Bks.
Pronzini, Bill, et al, eds. The Arbor House Treasury of Horror & the Supernatural. LC 80-70220. 512p. (Orig.). 1981. 19.95 (ISBN 0-87795-309-0); pap. 8.95 (ISBN 0-87795-319-8). Arbor Hse.
Rapier, Regina. Tales Out of Time, Vol. 1: The Mad Compactor & Other Science Fiction Short Stories. 1980. 7.50 (ISBN 0-686-69469-4). R C Rapier.
Wollheim, Donald A., ed. The Nineteen Eighty-One Annual World's Best SF. (Science Fiction Ser.). 1981. pap. 2.50 (ISBN 0-87997-617-9, UE1617). DAW Bks.

Zebrowski, George. The Best of Thomas M. Scortia. LC 80-2349. 288p. 1981. 11.95 (ISBN 0-385-14695-7). Doubleday.

SCIENCE FICTION–BIBLIOGRAPHY

Bishop, Gerald. Science Fiction Books Published in Britain, 1972 & 1973. LC 80-20590. 64p. 1980. Repr. of 1975 ed. lib. bdg. 9.95 (ISBN 0-89370-086-X). Borgo Pr.

The Checklist of the Science Fiction Magazines: Through 1980. 112p. (Orig.). 1981. pap. 5.50 (ISBN 0-935064-10-9). H W Hall.

Hall, H. W. SFBRI: Science Fiction Book Review Index, Vol. 11, 1980. LC 72-625320. 54p. (Orig.). 1981. pap. text ed. 5.00 (ISBN 0-935064-06-0). H W Hall.

Reginald, R. X, Y & Z: A List of Those Books Examined in the Course of Compiling Science Fiction & Fantasy Literature, a Checklist, 1700 to 1974, with Contemporary Science Fiction Authors II, Which Were Judged to Fall Outside the Genre of Fantastic Literature; an Anti-Bibliography. LC 80-11697. (Borgo Reference Library: Vol. 10). 160p. 1981. lib. bdg. 19.95x (ISBN 0-89370-809-7); pap. 9.95x (ISBN 0-89370-909-3). Borgo Pr.

Smith, Curtis S. Twentieth Century Science Fiction Writers. (Twentieth Century Writers Ser.). 1600p. 1981. 65.00x (ISBN 0-312-82420-3). St Martin.

SCIENCE FICTION–HISTORY AND CRITICISM

Asimov, Isaac. Asimov on Science Fiction. LC 80-2246. 288p. 1981. 13.95 (ISBN 0-385-17443-8). Doubleday.

Ferman, Edward L. & Greenberg, Martin H., eds. Fantasy & Science Fiction, April Nineteen Sixty-Five. (Alternatives Ser.). 160p. Date not set. price not set (ISBN 0-8093-1007-4). S Ill U Pr.

Frane, Jeff. Reader's Guide to Fritz Leiber. Scholbin, Roger C., ed. LC 80-22107. (Starmont Reader's Guides to Contemporary Science Fiction & Fantasy Authors Ser.: Vol. 8). (Illus.). 1980. pap. text ed. 3.95 (ISBN 0-916732-10-X). Starmont Hse.

Lem, Stanislaw. The Cosmic Carnival of Stanislaw Lem: An Anthology of Entertaining Stories by the Modern Master of Science Fiction. Kandel, Michael, ed. 256p. (Orig.). 1981. pap. 7.95 (ISBN 0-8264-0043-4). Continuum.

Malik, Rex, ed. Future Imperfect: Science Fact & Science Fiction. 219p. 1980. 25.00x (ISBN 0-903804-64-6). Nichols Pub.

Miller, Fred D. & Smith, Nicholas D., eds. Thought Probes: Philosophy Through Science Fiction. (Illus.). 368p. 1981. text ed. 11.95 (ISBN 0-13-920041-X). P-H.

Mogen, David. Wilderness Visions: Science Fiction Westerns, Vol. 1. LC 80-8673. (I. O. Evans Studies in the Philosophy & Criticism of Literature: No. 1). 64p. 1981. lib. bdg. 8.95x (ISBN 0-89370-152-1); pap. text ed. 2.95x (ISBN 0-89370-252-8). Borgo Pr.

Sammons, Martha C. A Guide Through C. S. Lewis' Space Trilogy. LC 80-68329. 1980. pap. 4.95 (ISBN 0-89107-185-7, Cornerstone Bks). Good News.

Schweitzer, Darrell. Science Fiction Voices, No. 5: Interviews with Science-Fiction Writers. (The Milford Series: Popular Writers of Today: Vol. 35). 64p. 1981. lib. bdg. 8.95 (ISBN 0-89370-151-3); pap. text ed. 2.95x (ISBN 0-89370-251-X). Borgo Pr.

SCIENCE FICTION–JUVENILE LITERATURE

Zelazny, Roger. The Courts of Chaos. 1979. pap. 1.75 (ISBN 0-380-47175-2, 47175). Avon.

SCIENCE FICTION–TECHNIQUE

Liebman, Arthur. Science Fiction: Masters of Today. 140p. 1981. lib. bdg. 7.97 (ISBN 0-8239-0537-3). Rosen Pr.

SCIENCE FICTION, AMERICAN

Greenberg, Martin & Olander, Joseph. Science Fiction of the Fifties. 1979. pap. 4.95 (ISBN 0-380-46409-8, 46409). Avon.

SCIENCE FICTION FILMS

Johnson, W. Science Fiction Film: Focus on. 1972. pap. 2.95 (ISBN 0-13-795161-2). P-H.

SCIENCE OF LANGUAGE

see Linguistics

SCIENCE OF SCIENCE

see Science

SCIENCE RESEARCH

see Research

SCIENCE STORIES

see Science Fiction (Collections)

SCIENCES, OCCULT

see Occult Sciences

SCIENCES, SOCIAL

see Social Sciences

SCIENTIFIC APPARATUS AND INSTRUMENTS

see also Electric Apparatus and Appliances; Electronic Apparatus and Appliances; Medical Instruments and Apparatus; Optical Instruments; Surgical Instruments and Apparatus

also names of particular instruments, e.g. Spectroscope

McWane, John W. Introduction to Electronics & Instrumentation. 1981. text ed. 19.95 (ISBN 0-534-00938-7, Breton Pubs). Wadsworth Pub.

SCIENTIFIC ASSOCIATIONS

see Scientific Societies

SCIENTIFIC EDUCATION

see Science–Study and Teaching

SCIENTIFIC INSTITUTIONS

see Scientific Societies

SCIENTIFIC INSTRUMENTS

see Scientific Apparatus and Instruments

SCIENTIFIC LIBRARIES

Young, Margaret Labash & Young, Harold C., eds. Subject Directory of Special Libraries & Information Services: Science & Technology Libraries, Including Agriculture, Energy, Environment-Conservation & Food, Vol. 5. 6th ed. 1981. 80.00 (ISBN 0-8103-0309-4). Gale.

SCIENTIFIC MANAGEMENT

see Industrial Management

SCIENTIFIC METHOD

see Science–Methodology

SCIENTIFIC PROPERTY

see Patent Laws and Legislation

SCIENTIFIC RECREATIONS

see also Mathematical Recreations

Goldstein, Martin & Goldstein, Inge. How We Know. (Da Capo Quality Paperbacks Ser.). (Illus.). 376p. 1981. pap. 8.95 (ISBN 0-306-80140-X). Da Capo.

SCIENTIFIC REPORTS

see Technical Reports

SCIENTIFIC RESEARCH

see Research

SCIENTIFIC SOCIETIES

see also Learned Institutions and Societies

Zils, Michael, ed. World Guide to Scientific Associations & Learned Societies. 3rd ed. (Handbook of International Documentation & Information Ser.: Vol. 13). 400p. 1981. 150.00 (ISBN 3-598-20517-1, Dist. by Gale Research). K G Saur.

SCIENTIFIC WRITING

see Technical Writing

SCIENTISTS

see also Mathematicians; Naturalists; Ornithologists; Physicists; Science–Vocational Guidance; Women Scientists

Medawar, P. B. Advice to a Young Scientist. LC 79-1676. 128p. 1981. pap. 3.95 (ISBN 0-06-090810-6, CN 810, CN). Har-Row.

Shapiro, Stanley J. Exploring Careers in Science. (Careers in Depth Ser.). (Illus.). 140p. 1981. lib. bdg. 5.97 (ISBN 0-8239-0535-7). Rosen Pr.

Shipp, James F. Russian-English Dictionary of Surnames: Important Names from Science & Technology. xvi, 317p. (Orig.). 1981. pap. 30.00x (ISBN 0-917564-10-3). Translation Research.

SCIENTISTS–BIOGRAPHY

Dyson, Freeman. Disturbing the Universe. LC 78-20665. 304p. 1981. pap. 4.95 (ISBN 0-06-090771-1, CN 771, CN). Har-Row.

Gillispie, Charles C., ed. Dictionary of Scientific Biography, 8 vols. 1981. lib. bdg. 595.00 set (ISBN 0-684-16962-2); lib. bdg. 80.00 ea. Scribner.

Moulton, Forest R. & Schifferes, Justus J., eds. The Autobiography of Science. 748p. 1980. 25.00x (ISBN 0-7195-0979-3, Pub. by Murray Pubs England). State Mutual Bk.

Urdang Assoc., ed. Biographical Encyclopedia of Scientists, 2 vols. 1981. lib. bdg. 80.00 (ISBN 0-87196-396-5). Vol. 1, 600p. Vol. 2, 600p. Facts on File.

SCIENTISTS–CORRESPONDENCE, REMINISCENCES, ETC.

Dukas, Helen & Hoffman, Banesh. Albert Einstein, the Human Side: New Glimpses from His Archives. LC 78-70289. 168p. 1981. pap. 3.95 (ISBN 0-691-02368-9). Princeton U Pr.

SCIENTISTS–EMPLOYMENT

Guidelines to Professional Employment for Engineers & Scientists. Date not set. 1.00 (511-78). AAES.

SCLEROSIS, MULTIPLE

see Multiple Sclerosis

SCOLIOSIS

Brooks, H. Leon, ed. Scoliosis & Allied Deformities of the Spine. 1981. write for info. (ISBN 0-88416-270-2). PSG Pub.

SCOOTERS, MOTOR

see Motor Scooters

SCORE READING AND PLAYING

Johnson, Roger, commentary by. Scores: An Anthology of New Music. LC 80-53302. (Illus.). 450p. 1981. pap. text ed. 12.95 (ISBN 0-02-871190-4). Schirmer Bks.

Thomson, William E. Introduction to Music Reading: Concepts & Applications. 2nd ed. 320p. 1980. pap. text ed. 12.95x (ISBN 0-534-00817-8). Wadsworth Pub.

SCORPIONS

Levy, G. & Amitai, P. Scorpiones: Arachnida I, Vol. 3. (Fauna Palestina Ser.). (Illus.). 132p. 1981. text ed. 25.00x (ISBN 0-87474-606-X). Smithsonian.

SCOTCH WHISKEY

see Whiskey

SCOTLAND–ANTIQUITIES

Piggott, Stuart, ed. The Prehistoric Peoples of Scotland. LC 80-27371. (Studies in Ancient History & Archaeology). (Illus.). ix, 165p. 1981. Repr. of 1962 ed. lib. bdg. 25.00x (ISBN 0-313-22916-3, PIPR). Greenwood.

Ritchie, Anna & Ritchie, Graham. Scotland; Archaeology & Early History. (Ancient People & Places Ser.). (Illus.). 192p. 1981. 19.95 (ISBN 0-500-02100-7). Thames Hudson.

SCOTLAND–BIOGRAPHY

Fraser, James F. Dr. Jimmy: Some Reminiscences by James Fowler Fraser 1893-1979. 150p. 1980. pap. 10.90 (ISBN 0-08-025737-2). Pergamon.

Grant, J. F. Along a Highland Road. 208p. 1980. 25.00x (ISBN 0-85683-048-8, Pub. by Shepheard-Walwyn England). State Mutual Bk.

The Scotch Rogue: The Life and Actions of Donald MacDonald, a Highland Scot. LC 80-2491. 1981. Repr. of 1784 ed. 39.50 (ISBN 0-404-19125-8). AMS Pr.

SCOTLAND–DESCRIPTION AND TRAVEL

see also Great Britain–Description and Travel

Fraser, Amy S. Roses in December: Edwardian Recollections. (Illus.). 1981. price not set (ISBN 0-7100-0823-6). Routledge & Kegan.

Hammond, Reginald J. Complete Scotland. 13th ed. Lowther, Kenneth E., ed. (Red Guide Ser.). (Illus.). 449p. 1980. 17.50x (ISBN 0-7063-5905-4). Intl Pubns Serv.

SCOTLAND–DESCRIPTION AND TRAVEL–GUIDEBOOKS

MacInnes, David & MacInnes, Kathleen. Walking Through Scotland. LC 80-68895. (Illus.). 192p. 1981. 19.95 (ISBN 0-7153-8090-7). David & Charles.

Scottish Tourist Board. Scotland: Bed & Breakfast. rev. ed. (Illus.). 252p. 1981. pap. price not set (ISBN 0-85419-170-4, Pub. by Auto Assn-British Tourist Authority England). Merrimack Bk Serv.

--Scotland: Hotels & Guesthouses. rev. ed. (Illus.). 328p. 1981. pap. price not set (ISBN 0-85419-169-0, Pub. by Auto Assn-British Tourist Authority England). Merrimack Bk Serv.

SCOTLAND–HISTORY

see also Jacobite Rebellion, 1745-1746

Anderson, Marjorie C. Kings & Kingship in Early Scotland. 304p. 1981. 20.00x (ISBN 0-7073-0179-3, Pub. by Scottish Academic Pr Scotland). Columbia U Pr.

MacDonald, Donald J. Clan Donald. (Illus.). 437p. 1980. 59.95 (ISBN 0-904265-21-8). Pelican.

Nobbs, Douglas. England & Scotland, 1560-1707. LC 80-25749. xxi, 173p. 1981. Repr. of 1952 ed. lib. bdg. 19.75x (ISBN 0-313-22773-X, NOES). Greenwood.

Piggott, Stuart, ed. The Prehistoric Peoples of Scotland. LC 80-27371. (Studies in Ancient History & Archaeology). (Illus.). ix, 165p. 1981. Repr. of 1962 ed. lib. bdg. 25.00x (ISBN 0-313-22916-3, PIPR). Greenwood.

Shaw, Frances J. The Northern & Western Islands of Scotland in the Seventeenth Century. (Illus.). 275p. 1980. text ed. 39.00x (ISBN 0-85976-059-6). Humanities.

Stevenson, D. Alasdair MacColla & the Highland Problem in the Seventeenth Century. 1980. text ed. 39.00x (ISBN 0-85976-055-3). Humanities.

Webster, Bruce, ed. The Acts of David II, 1329-71. 550p. 1981. 55.00x (ISBN 0-85224-395-2, Pub. by Edinburgh U Pr Scotland). Columbia U Pr.

SCOTLAND–INDUSTRIES

Payne, Peter L. The Early Scottish Limited Companies, Eighteen Fifty-Six to Eighteen Ninety-Five. 144p. 1981. 22.00x (Pub. by Scottish Academic Pr Scotland). Columbia U Pr.

SCOTLAND–POLITICS AND GOVERNMENT

Dickson. Scottish Capitalism. 1980. text ed. 24.75x (ISBN 0-85315-482-1). Humanities.

SCOTLAND–SOCIAL CONDITIONS

Parsler, Ron & Shapiro, Dan. The Social Impact of Oil in Scotland. 192p. 1980. text ed. 27.75x (ISBN 0-566-00375-9, Pub. by Gower Pub Co England). Renouf.

SCOTLAND–SOCIAL LIFE AND CUSTOMS

Walker, John. The Scottish Sketches of R. B. Cunninghame Graham. (Illus.). 232p. 1981. 13.50x (ISBN 0-7073-0288-9, Pub. by Scottish Academic Pr Scotland). Columbia U Pr.

SCOTT, WALTER, SIR, BART., 1771-1832

Hewitt, David. Scott on Himself. 288p. 1981. 15.00x (ISBN 0-7073-0283-8, Pub. by Scottish Academic Pr Scotland). Columbia U Pr.

Reed, James. Sir Walter Scott: Locality & Landscape. 1980. text ed. 40.00x (ISBN 0-485-11197-7, Athlone Pr). Humanities.

SCOTTISH AUTHORS

see Authors, Scottish

SCOTTISH CLANS

see Clans and Clan System

SCOTTISH LANGUAGE

see Gaelic Language

SCOTTISH LITERATURE–HISTORY AND CRITICISM

Lindsay, Maurice. History of Scottish Literature. 1977. 22.50 (ISBN 0-7091-5642-1). Dufour.

SCOTTISH MUSIC

see Music, Scottish

SCOTTISH POETRY–HISTORY AND CRITICISM

Scott, P. H. & Davis, A. C., eds. The Age of MacDiarmid: Essays on Hugh MacDiarmid & His Influence on Contemporary Scotland. 268p. 1981. 22.50x (ISBN 0-389-20199-5). B&N.

SCOUTING, FOOTBALL

see Football Scouting

SCREENPLAYS

see Moving-Picture Plays

SCRIMSHAWS

Gilkerson, William. Maritime Arts by William Gilkerson. (Illus.). 100p. (Orig.). 1981. pap. write for info. (ISBN 0-87577-061-4). Peabody Mus Salem.

SCRIP

see Securities

SCUBA DIVING

Here are entered works on free diving with the use of an aqualung. Works on free diving with the use of mask, fins and snorkel are entered under Skin Diving.

Vallintine, Reginald. Divers & Diving. (Illus.). 176p. 1981. 12.95 (ISBN 0-7137-0855-7, Pub. by Blandford Pr England); pap. 6.95 (ISBN 0-7137-1128-0). Sterling.

SCULPTURE

see also Bronzes; Ice Carving; Modeling; Paper Sculpture; Plaster Casts; Post-Impressionism (Art); Proportion (Art); Sand Sculpture; Wax Modeling; Wood-Carving

Modern Makonde Sculpture Exhibit Catalog. (Foreign & Comparative Studies-African Special Publications: No.5). 103p. 1968. pap. 3.50x. Syracuse U Foreign Comp.

SCULPTURE–EXHIBITIONS

The Minneapolis Institute of Arts. Sculptures from the David Daniels Collection. (Illus.). 1979. 15.00. Minneapolis Inst Arts.

SCULPTURE–HISTORY

Eisler, Colin, ed. Drawings into Sculpture. (Illus.). 108p. (Orig.). 1981. pap. 12.50 (ISBN 0-9601068-7-1). Agrinde Bks.

Haskell, Francis & Penny, Nicholas. Taste & the Antique: The Lure of Classical Sculpture 1500-1900. LC 80-24951. (Illus.). 392p. 1981. 45.00x (ISBN 0-300-02641-2). Yale U Pr.

SCULPTURE–TECHNIQUE

see also Modeling

Hall, Carolyn V. Soft Sculpture. LC 80-67546. (Illus.). 112p. 1981. 14.95 (ISBN 0-87192-129-4). Davis Mass.

Hildebrand, Adolf. The Problem of Form in Painting and Sculpture. Freedberg, Sydney J., ed. LC 77-19375. (Connoisseurship & Art History Ser.: Vol. 11). (Illus.). 141p. 1979. lib. bdg. 20.00 (ISBN 0-8240-3269-1). Garland Pub.

Olson, Lynn. Sculpting with Cement: Direct Modeling in a Permanent Medium. (Illus.). 106p. (Orig.). (gr. 11-12). 1981. pap. price not set (ISBN 0-9605678-0-1). Steelstone.

SCULPTURE–AFRICA

Traditional Sculpture from Upper Volta. (Illus.). 48p. (Orig.). 1978. pap. text ed. 5.00 (ISBN 0-89192-279-2). Interbk Inc.

SCULPTURE–FRANCE

Reff, Theodore, ed. Exhibitions of Sculpture. (Modern Art in Paris 1855 to 1900 Ser.). 394p. 1981. lib. bdg. 44.00 (ISBN 0-8240-4745-1). Garland Pub.

Souchal, Francois. French Sculptors, Vol. 2. (Illus.). 464p. 1981. 200.00 (ISBN 0-85181-063-2, Pub. by Faber & Faber). Merrimack Bk Serv.

SCULPTURE–INDIA

Pathy, T. V. Elura: Art & Culture. (Illus.). 190p. 1980. text ed. 31.00x (ISBN 0-391-01758-6). Humanities.

SCULPTURE–ITALY

Pogany-Balas, Edit. The Influence of Rome's Antique Monumental Sculptures on the Great Master's of the Renaissance. Debreczeni, Arpad, tr. (Illus.). 115p. 1980. 25.00x (ISBN 963-05-1682-9). Intl Pubns Serv.

SCULPTURE–UNITED STATES

Freeman, Robert. Hidden Treasure: Public Sculpture in Providence, Rhode Island. (Illus.). 50p. (Orig.). 1981. pap. 4.95 (ISBN 0-917012-23-2). RI Pubns Soc.

Goossen, C. Herbert Ferber. LC 80-66531. (Illus.). 1981. 75.00 (ISBN 0-89659-148-4). Abbeville Pr.

Mayor, A. Hyatt, intro. by. A Century of American Sculpture: Treasures from Brookgreen Gardens. (Illus.). 128p. 1981. 29.95 (ISBN 0-89659-185-9); pap. 16.95 (ISBN 0-89659-150-6). Abbeville Pr.

SCULPTURE, BAROQUE

Lavin, Irving. Bernini & the Unity of the Visual Arts, 2 vols. (Illus.). 498p. 1980. text ed. 89.00x (ISBN 0-19-520184-1). Oxford U Pr.

SCULPTURE, MODERN–20TH CENTURY

Piene, Otto, et al. Centerbeam. (Illus.). 1980. pap. 15.00 (ISBN 0-262-66047-4). MIT Pr.

SCULPTURE, RELIGIOUS

see Christian Art and Symbolism

SCULPTURE, RENAISSANCE

Pogany-Balas, Edit. The Influence of Rome's Antique Monumental Sculptures on the Great Master's of the Renaissance. Debreczeni, Arpad, tr. (Illus.). 115p. 1980. 25.00x (ISBN 963-05-1682-9). Intl Pubns Serv.

SEA

see Ocean

SEA, DOMINION OF THE

see Maritime Law; Sea-Power

SEA ANIMALS

see Marine Fauna

SEA BIRDS

Auks of the World. (Illus.). 250p. 1981. 30.00 (ISBN 0-88839-084-X). Hancock Hse.

Russell, Franklin. Sea Has Wings. 1973. 10.00 (ISBN 0-87690-097-X). Dutton.

SEA-FISHERIES

see Fisheries

SEA LAWS

see Maritime Law

SEA LIFE

see Seafaring Life

SEA-LIONS

see Seals (Animals)

SEA PLANES
see Seaplanes
SEA-POWER
see also Naval Battles; Naval History; Warships also subdivision History, Naval under names of countries, e.g. Great Britain–History, Naval; United States–Navy; and similar headings
Alford, Jonathan, ed. Sea Power & Influence: Iold Issues & New Challenges. LC 80-67840. (Adelphi Library: Vol. 2). 224p. 1981. text ed. 31.50 (ISBN 0-916672-72-7). Allanheld.
Roskill, Stephen W. The Strategy of Sea Power: Its Development & Application. LC 80-27028. (Lees-Knowles Lecture Ser., Cambridge, 1961). 287p. 1981. Repr. of 1962 ed. lib. bdg. 27.50x (ISBN 0-313-22801-9, ROSSP). Greenwood.
SEA RESOURCES
see Marine Resources
SEA SCOUTS
see Boy Scouts
SEA SHELL COLLECTING
see Shells
SEA SHELLS
see Shells
SEA STORIES
Conrad, Joseph, et al. Fifty Great Sea Stories. 768p. 1980. Repr. lib. bdg. 30.00 (ISBN 0-686-68073-1). Arden Lib.
Fox, Uffa. More Joys of Living. 180p. 1980. 12.00x (ISBN 0-245-50796-5, Pub. by Nautical England). State Mutual Bk.
Tomlinson, H. M., ed. Great Sea Stories of All Nations. 1108p. 1980. Repr. of 1930 ed. 40.00 (ISBN 0-89760-884-4). Telegraph Bks.
SEA TRANSPORTATION
see Shipping
SEA TRAVEL
see Ocean Travel
SEA-URCHINS
Clark, Hubert L. Catalogue of the Recent Sea-Urchins (Echinoidea) in the Collection of the British Museum (Natural History) (Illus.). xxviii, 250p. 1925. 21.00x (ISBN 0-565-00165-5, Pub. by British Mus Nat Hist England). Sabbot-Natural Hist Bks.
SEA WATER–DEMINERALIZATION
see Saline Waters–Demineralization
SEA WAVES
see Ocean Waves
SEAFARING LIFE
Chadwich, Philip & Smith, Foster, eds. Seafaring in Colonial Massachusetts. LC 80-51256. (Illus.). xvii, 240p. 1981. 25.00x (ISBN 0-8139-0897-3, Colonial Soc MA). U Pr of Va.
Mayhall, Carole. Lord of My Rocking Boat. (Orig.). 1981. price not set. NavPress.
SEAL FISHERIES
see Sealing
SEALING
see also Seals (Animals)
Flint, Sue. Let the Seals Live. 192p. 1980. 14.95 (ISBN 0-906191-35-1, Pub. by Thule Pr England). Intl Schol Bk Serv.
SEALING (TECHNOLOGY)
see also Plastics; Welding
Dunitz, J. D., et al. Bonding Problems. (Structure & Bonding Ser.: Vol.43). (Illus.). 240p. 1981. 58.00 (ISBN 0-387-10407-0). Springer-Verlag.
International Conference on Fluid Sealing, 4th. Proceedings. 1969. 29.00 (ISBN 0-900983-04-3). BHRA Fluid.
International Conference on Fluid Sealing, 3rd. Proceedings. 1967. 47.00. BHRA Fluid.
International Conference on Fluid Sealing, 2nd. Proceedings. 1964. 45.00. BHRA Fluid.
International Conference on Fluid Sealing, 1st. Proceedings. 1961. 45.00. BHRA Fluid.
Stephens, H. S. & Stapleton, Mrs. C. A. Papers Presented at the Ninth International Conference on Fluid Sealing. (Illus., Orig.). 1981. pap. 78.00 library ed. (ISBN 0-686-69309-4). BHRA Fluid.
White & Denny. Sealing Mechanisms of Flexible Packings. 1947. 16.00. BHRA Fluid.
SEALS (ANIMALS)
see also Sealing
Brady, Irene. Elephants on the Beach. (Illus.). 32p. (gr. 2-5). 1979. 7.95 (ISBN 0-684-16115-X). Scribner.
Kooyman, Gerald L. Weddell Seal, Consummate Diver. LC 80-18794. (Illus.). 176p. Date not set. price not set (ISBN 0-521-23657-6). Cambridge U Pr.
SEALS (NUMISMATICS)
see also Emblems
Buchanan, Briggs. Early Near Eastern Seals in the Yale Babylonian Collection. Kasten, Ulla, ed. LC 75-43309. (Illus.). 520p. 1981. text ed. 65.00 (ISBN 0-300-01852-5). Yale U Pr.
Lai, T. C. Chinese Seals. LC 76-7789. (Illus.). 224p. 1976. 10.00 (ISBN 0-295-95517-1). U of Wash Pr.
SEAMANSHIP
see also Navigation
Block, Richard A., ed. Able Seaman & Lifevoatman: All Grades. rev. ed. (Illus.). 338p. 1978. pap. 21.00 (ISBN 0-934114-04-8). Marine Educ.
--Motorboat Operator License Preparation Course. rev. ed. (Illus.). 269p. 1980. pap. text ed. 18.00 (ISBN 0-934114-29-3). Marine Educ.
--Ocean & Inland Operator License Preparation Course. rev. ed. (Illus.). 499p. 1979. pap. text ed. 42.00 (ISBN 0-934114-21-8). Marine Educ.
International Conference on Training & Certification of Seafarers, 1978. 146p. 1978. 22.00 (IMCO). Unipub.
Moody, Alton B. Navigation Afloat: A Manual for the Seaman. 768p. 1981. 35.00 (ISBN 0-442-25488-1). Van Nos Reinhold.
SEAPLANES
Frey, Jay J. How to Fly Floats: Seaplane Flying. (Illus.). Date not set. pap. 4.95x (ISBN 0-911721-71-1, Pub. by Edo-Aire). Aviation.
SEAPOWER
see Sea-Power
SEARCH AND RESCUE OPERATIONS
see also Survival (After Airplane Accidents, Shipwrecks, etc.)
Beattie, John. Lifeboats to the Rescue. LC 80-70704. (Illus.). 160p. 1981. 17.95 (ISBN 0-7153-8103-2). David & Charles.
Doran, Jeffry W. Search on Mount St. Helens. Pica, George, ed. (Illus.). 96p. (Orig.). pap. 7.95 (ISBN 0-938700-00-6). Imagesmith.
International Conference on Maritime Search & Rescue, 1979. 38p. 1979. 9.25 (IMCO). Unipub.
Merchant Ship Search & Rescue Manual (MERSAR) (Illus.). 53p. 1977. 8.25 (IMCO). Unipub.
SEARCH WARRANTS
see Warrants (Law)
SEASHORE BIOLOGY–JUVENILE LITERATURE
Monroe, Alex. Barnacle & His Friends. (Illus.). 42p. (Orig.). (gr. 1-6). 1980. pap. 2.75 (ISBN 0-933614-07-1). Peregrine Pr.
SEASHORE BIOLOGY–GREAT BRITAIN
Campbell, A. C. The Larousse Guide to the Seashore & Shallow Seas of Britain & Europe. LC 80-82755. (Larousse Nature Guides Ser.). (Illus.). 320p. (Orig.). 1981. 10.95 (ISBN 0-88332-251-X, 8068). Larousse.
SEASHORE ECOLOGY
A Review-Coastal Ecosystems, Nineteen Eighty. (UNEP Report Ser.: No. 4). 65p. 1980. pap. 7.50 (UNEP 033, UNEP). Unipub.
A Review-Island Ecosystems. (UNEP Report Ser.: No. 3). 34p. 1980. pap. 6.00 (UNEP 032, UNEP). Unipub.
SEASONS–JUVENILE LITERATURE
The Seasons. (Golden Photo Board Bks.). (Illus.). 12p. (ps). 1980. 1.50 (ISBN 0-307-06075-6, Golden Pr). Western Pub.
SEAT WORK
see Creative Activities and Seatwork
SEATTLE–DESCRIPTION
Layman, Earl D. The Sights of Seattle: Downtown. (Illus.). 96p. (Orig.). 1981. pap. 6.95 (ISBN 0-914842-59-5). Madrona Pubs.
SEATTLE–HISTORY
Morgan, Lane & Morgan, Murray C. Seattle: A Pictorial History. (Illus.). 205p. 1981. pap. price not set (ISBN 0-89865-091-7). Donning Co.
SEATTLE FOOTBALL CLUB (AMERICAN LEAGUE)
Rothaus, Jim. Seattle Seahawks. (NFL Today Ser.). (gr. 3-12). 1980. PLB 6.45 (ISBN 0-87191-795-5); pap. 2.95 (ISBN 0-89812-247-3). Creative Ed.
SEAWATER
Delyannis, A. E. & Delyannis, E. E. Seawater & Desalting, Vol. 1. 180p. 1980. 34.90 (ISBN 0-387-10206-X). Springer-Verlag.
Scott, Jeanette, ed. Desalination of Seawater by Reverse Osmosis. LC 80-26421. (Pollution Tech. Rev. Ser.: No. 75). 431p. 1981. 39.00 (ISBN 0-8155-0837-9). Noyes.
SECOND ADVENT
see also Millennium
Duke, David A. Christ's Coming--Satan's Kingdom. 220p. (Orig.). 1981. pap. 2.95 (ISBN 0-9605056-0-1). D A Duke.
Riggle, H. M. Jesus Is Coming Again. 111p. pap. 1.00. Faith Pub Hse.
Robinson, Lafayette. The Second Coming of Christ Is Now. LC 80-83601. (Illus.). 160p. Date not set. pap. price not set (ISBN 0-8187-0041-6). Harlo Pr.
SECONDARY EDUCATION
see Education, Secondary
SECONDARY EMPLOYMENT
see Supplementary Employment
SECONDARY SCHOOLS
see Education, Secondary; Private Schools; Public Schools
SECRECY IN GOVERNMENT
see Official Secrets
SECRET LIENS
see Liens
SECRET SERVICE
see also Detectives; Espionage; Intelligence Service; Spies
Popov, Dusko. Spy-Counter Spy. 4.95 (ISBN 0-686-28850-5). Academy Chi Ltd.
SECRET SERVICE–GREAT BRITAIN
Deacon, Richard. A History of the British Secret Service: Covers the Development of the Intelligence System from the Days of Henry VII to the Present. 6.50 (ISBN 0-686-28849-1). Academy Chi Ltd.
SECRETARIAL PRACTICE
see Office Practice
SECRETARIAL TRAINING
see Business Education; shorthand; Typewriting and allied subjects
SECRETARIES OF STATE
see Cabinet Officers
SECTS
Here are entered works on religious groups whose adherents recognize special teachings or practices which fall within the normative bounds of the major world religions. Works on the major world religions are entered under Religions. Works on groups or movements whose system of religious beliefs or practices differs significantly from the major world religions and which are often gathered around a specific deity or person are entered under Cults.
see also Church History–Modern Period, 1500-; Cults; Eastern Churches
also particular denominations and sects
Richardson, Herbert W., ed. New Religions & Mental Health: A Guide to the Issues. (Symposium Ser.: Vol. 6). (Orig.). 1980. soft cover 11.95x (ISBN 0-88946-910-5). E Mellen.
SECTS, HINDU
see Hindu Sects
SECULARISM
Blamires, Harry. The Secularist Heresy. 160p. 1980. pap. 4.95 (ISBN 0-89283-095-6). Servant.
Kurtz, Paul, ed. A Secular Humanist Declaration. 40p. 81. pap. 1.95 (ISBN 0-87975-149-5). Prometheus Bks.
SECUNDUS, JOANNES NICOLAI, 1511-1536
Endres, Clifford W. Joannes Secundus: The Latin Love Elegy in the Renaissance. 1981. 25.00 (ISBN 0-208-01832-8, Archon). Shoe String.
SECURITIES
see also Bonds; Investments, Foreign; Liquidity (Economics); Municipal Bonds; Stocks
Fleischer, Arthur, Jr., et al, eds. Eleventh Annual Institute on Securities Regulation. LC 70-125178. 593p. 1980. text ed. 50.00 (ISBN 0-686-69167-9, B2-1275). PLI.
Friedman, Howard M. Securities & Commodities Enforcement: Criminal Prosecutions & Civil Injunctions. LC 79-9685. 1981. price not set (ISBN 0-669-03617-X). Lexington Bks.
Municipal Securities Regulation: A Public Perspective, 10 vols. Incl. Vol. 1 & 2. Certain Legal Considerations, Vol. II: An Introduction, Vol. 1. (Bound & sold together with Vol. II). 1977. price of 2 vols. 50.00. Vol. 1 (ISBN 0-916450-08-2). Vol. 2, 129 Pages; Vol. III. Self-Regulation: Is It Working? 148p. 1977. 40.00 (ISBN 0-916450-10-4); Vol. IV. Summary of Publications & Hearings. 264p. 1977. 70.00 (ISBN 0-916450-11-2); Federal Legislative Background Vol. V, Four Legal Memoranda, Vol. VI. 224p. (Vols. V & VI are bound & sold together). 1978. price of 2 vols. 65.00. Vol. V (ISBN 0-916450-12-0). Vol. VI; Vol. VII. Municipal Disclosure Standards Sourcebook. 199p. 1978. 60.00 (ISBN 0-916450-18-X); Vol. VIII. State Laws. 204p. 1978. 50.00 (ISBN 0-916450-19-8); Vol. IX. Disclosure Guidelines. 1979. 40.00; Vol. X. The Way Back: Toward Accountability in America's Cities. 231p. 1979. 25.00 (ISBN 0-916450-21-X). Set. 270.00. Coun on Municipal.
Sametz, Arnold, ed. Securities Activities of Commercial Banks. LC 80-8339. 1981. write for info. (ISBN 0-669-04031-2). Lexington Bks.
Scott, David L. Security Investments. (Illus.). 1981. 17.95x (ISBN 0-8476-6971-8). Rowman.
Securities Regulation Series, 10 vols. Incl. Vol. 1. An Introduction. Marlin, John T. & Rousmaniere, Peter F. 36p; Vol. 2. Certain Legal Considerations. Chadbourne, et al. 129p. (Vols. 1 & 2 bound together) (ISBN 0-916450-09-0); Vol. 3. Self Regulation: Is It Working? Rousmaniere, Peter F. 148p (ISBN 0-916450-10-4); Vol. 4. Summary of Publications & Hearings. Chadbourne, et al. 264p; Vol. 5. Federal Legislative Background. Chadbourne, et al.; Vol. 6. Four Legal Memoranda. Chadbourne, et al. (Vols. 5 & 6 bound together, 122p.) (ISBN 0-916450-13-9); Vol. 7. Municipal Disclosure Standards Sourcebook. Anderson, Kay. 199p (ISBN 0-916450-18-X); Vol. 8. State Laws. Chadbourne, et al. 204p (ISBN 0-916450-19-8); State Level Disclosure Guidelines. Rousmaniere, Peter F. 233p (ISBN 0-916450-20-1); Vol. 10. The Way Back: Toward Accountability in America's Cities. Rousmaniere, Peter F. 231p (ISBN 0-916450-21-X). 1977-80. Set. 300.00. Coun on Municipal.
SECURITIES EXCHANGE
see Stock-Exchange
SECURITY (LAW)
Ricks, Truett A., et al. Principles of Security: An Introduction. (Illus.). 400p. 1981. text ed. price not set (ISBN 0-87084-744-9). Anderson Pub Co.
SECURITY, INTERNAL
see Internal Security
SECURITY, INTERNATIONAL
see also Disarmament; International Organization; Neutrality; Peace
Burt, Richard, ed. Arms Control & Defense Postures in the Nineteen-Eighties. (Special Studies in National Security & Defense Policy Ser.). 220p. 1981. lib. bdg. 24.00x (ISBN 0-86531-162-5). Westview.
Johnson, U. Alexis & Packard, George R., eds. The Common Security Interests of Japan, the United States, & NATO. 200p. 1981. professional reference 19.50x. Ballinger Pub.
SECURITY MEASURES (MILITARY INFORMATION)
see Industry–Security Measures
SECURITY MEASURES, INDUSTRIAL
see Industry–Security Measures
SECURITY SYSTEMS
see also Libraries–Security Measures; Police
Barnard, Robert L. Intrusion Detection Systems. 300p. 1981. text ed. 21.95 (ISBN 0-409-95026-2). Butterworths.
Finneran, Eugene. Security Supervision: A Handbook for Supervisors & Managers. 300p. 1981. text ed. 19.95 (ISBN 0-409-95025-4). Butterworths.
Green, Gion & Farber, Raymond C. Introduction to Security: Principles & Practices. 3rd ed. 1981. text ed. 17.95 (ISBN 0-409-95036-X). Butterworth.
Guy, Edward T. & Merrigan, John J. Forms for Safety & Security Management. 448p. 1980. text ed. 28.95 (ISBN 0-409-95089-0). Butterworths.
Powell, John W. Campus Security & Law Enforcement. 250p. 1981. text ed. 19.95 (ISBN 0-409-95028-9). Butterworth.
Third International Conference. Security Through Science & Engineering: Proceedings. De Vore, R. William & Jackson, J. S., eds. LC 80-83300. (Illus.). 1980. pap. 33.50 (ISBN 0-89779-042-1, UKYBU122); 4.50 (ISBN 0-89779-043-X). OES Pubns.
Trimmer. Understanding & Servicing Alarms. 1981. text ed. price not set. Butterworth.
SEDATIVES
see also Anesthetics; Narcotics; Tranquilizing Drugs
Hamburg, Harold L. Sedation. (Illus.). 198p. 1980. pap. 16.00 (ISBN 0-931386-07-1). Quint Pub Co.
SEDIMENT TRANSPORT
see also Channels (Hydraulic Engineering)
Stelczer, K. Theory & Practice of Bed-Load Transport. 1981. 22.00 (ISBN 0-918334-38-1). WRP.
SEDIMENTARY ROCKS
see Rocks, Sedimentary
SEDIMENTARY STRUCTURES
Bernard, H. A., et al. Recent Sediments of Southeast Texas-A Field Guide to the Brazos Alluvial & Deltaic Plains & the Galveston Barrier Island Complex. 132p. 1970. Repr. 5.00 (GB 11). Bur Econ Geology.
Monty, C., ed. Phanerozoic Stromatolites: Case Histories. (Illus.). 260p. 1981. 52.60 (ISBN 0-387-10474-7). Springer-Verlag.
Reineck, H. E. & Singh, I. B. Depositional Sedimentary Environments with Reference to Terrigenous Clastics. 2nd rev. ed. (Illus.). 549p. 1980. pap. 29.80 (ISBN 0-387-10189-6). Springer-Verlag.
SEDIMENTATION AND DEPOSITION
see also Erosion; Marine Sediments; Rocks, Sedimentary
Beckett Jackson Raeder, Inc. Soil Erosion & Sedimentation Control. (Illus.). 150p. 1980. pap. text ed. 20.00 (ISBN 0-918436-15-X). Environ Design.
Brown, L. F., et al. Pennsylvanian Depositional Systems in North-Central Texas: A Guide for Interpreting Terrigenous Clastic Facies in a Cratonic Basin. (Illus.). 122p. 1973. Repr. 3.50 (GB 14). Bur Econ Geology.
Caughey, C. A. Depositional Systems in the Paluxy Formation (Lower Cretaceous) Northeast Texas-Oil, Gas, & Ground-Water Resources. (Illus.). 59p. 1977. 2.00 (GC 77-8). Bur Econ Geology.
Dutton, S. P., et al. Geology & Geohydrology of the Palo Duro Basin, Texas Panhandle: A Report on the Progress of Nuclear Waste Isolation Feasibility Studies. (Illus.). 99p. 1979. 2.50 (GC 79-1). Bur Econ Geology.
Fisher, W. L. & McGowen, J. H. Depostional Systems in the Wilcox Group of Texas & Their Relationship to Occurrence of Oil & Gas. 125p. 1967. Repr. 1.00 (GC 67-4). Bur Econ Geology.
McBride, E. F. Sedimentary Petrology & History of the Haymond Formation (Pennsylvanian), Marathon Basin, Texas. 101p. 1966. 2.50 (RI 57). Bur Econ Geology.
McGowen, J. H., et al. Geochemistry of Bottom Sediments Matagorda Bay System, Texas. (Illus.). 64p. 1979. 1.50 (GC 79-2). Bur Econ Geology.
SEDIMENTS (GEOLOGY)
see also Clay; Marine Sediments; Sedimentary Structures
Reineck, H. E. & Singh, I. B. Depositional Sedimentary Environments with Reference to Terrigenous Clastics. 2nd rev. ed. (Illus.). 549p. 1980. pap. 29.80 (ISBN 0-387-10189-6). Springer-Verlag.
SEDUM
Clausen, Robert T., ed. Sedum of North America North of the Mexican Plateau. LC 75-6084. (Illus.). 784p. 1975. 80.00x (ISBN 0-8014-0950-0). Comstock.
SEE, HOLY
see Papacy
SEEDS
see also Oilseeds
Advances in Research & Technology of Seeds, Pt. 5. 115p. 1981. pap. 25.00 (ISBN 90-220-0746-4, PDC 215, Pudoc). Unipub.

Breeding for Improved Herbage & Seed Yield in Setaria Sphacelata (Schumach) Stapf & Hubbard Ex Moss. (Agricultural Research Reports: No. 900). 146p. 1981. pap. 29.00 (ISBN 90-220-0738-3, PDC 213, Pudoc). Unipub.

Lubbock, Sir John. A Contribution to Our Knowledge of Seedlings, 2 vols. (Landmark Reprints in Plant Science Ser.). 1978. Vol. 325vol. 2. text ed. 29.50 (ISBN 0-86598-008-X); text ed. 29.50 (ISBN 0-86598-025-X). Allanheld.

Report of the Sixth FAO-SIDA Training Course on Seed Technology. 26p. 1976. pap. 6.00 (F1985, FAO). Unipub.

SEGREGATION IN EDUCATION

see also Discrimination in Education; School Integration

Friedman, Leon, ed. Argument: Brown vs. Board of Education of Topeka, 1925-55, 2 vols. 2nd ed. LC 70-75118. (Oral Arguments Before the Supreme Court Ser.). 610p. 1981. Set. pap. 12.95 (ISBN 0-87754-210-4). Chelsea Hse.

SEGYE KIDOKKYO T'ONGIL SILLYONG HYOPHOE

see Holy Spirit Associaton for the Unification of World Christianity

SEISMIC PROSPECTING

Palmer, Derecke. The Generalized Reciprocal Method of Seismic Refraction Prospecting. Burke, Kenneth B., ed. (Illus.). 112p. 1980. write for info. (ISBN 0-931830-14-1). Soc Exploration.

SEISMOLOGY

see also Earthquakes; Volcanoes

Norwegian Petroleum Society. Offshore Seismic Data Acquisition & Quality Control. 287p. 1980. 100.00x (ISBN 82-7270-001-8, Pub. by Norwegian Info Norway). State Mutual Bk.

OECD-NEA. Reference Seismic Grond Motions in Nuclear Safety Assessments. (Illus.). 171p. (Orig.). 1980. pap. text ed. 16.00x (ISBN 92-64-12100-5). OECD.

Waters, Kenneth H. Reflection Seismology. 2nd ed. 350p. 1981. 34.95 (ISBN 0-471-08224-4, Pub. by Wiley-Interscience). Wiley.

SELECTION, NATURAL

see Natural Selection

SELECTIVE SERVICE

see Military Service, Compulsory

SELENIUM

Spallholz, J. E., et al. Selenium in Biology & Medicine: Second International Symposium. (Illus.). 1981. lib. bdg. 45.00 (ISBN 0-87055-379-8). AVI.

SELF

see also Body, Human; Consciousness; Ego (Psychology); Existentialism; Mind and Body; Personality; Role Playing; Thought and Thinking; Will

Zimmerman, Michael. Eclipse of the Self: The Development of Heidegger's Concept of Authenticity. LC 80-19042. xxx, 331p. 1981. 18.95x (ISBN 0-8214-0570-5); pap. 9.95 (ISBN 0-8214-0601-9). Ohio U Pr.

SELF-ACCEPTANCE

ARE Study Group No. 1. Suche Nach Gott, Bk I. Kronberger, Helge F., tr. from Eng. 135p. (Ger.). 1978. pap. 10.00 (ISBN 0-87604-131-4). ARE Pr.

SELF-ACTUALIZATION (PSYCHOLOGY)

Iwersen, Marguerite. Mind Matters. LC 80-67158. 123p. (Orig.). 1981. pap. 5.50 (ISBN 0-87516-421-8). De Vorss.

SELF-APPRAISAL

see Self-Evaluation

SELF-CONCEPT

see Self-Perception

SELF-CONFIDENCE

see Self-Reliance

SELF-CONTROL

Macleod, William M. & Macleod, Gael S. M. I. N. D Over Weight: "How to Stay Slim the Rest of Your Life". LC 80-21001. 1981. 7.95 (ISBN 0-13-583385-X). P-H.

Shapiro, Lawrence E. Games to Grow On: Activities to Help Children Learn Self-Control. (Illus.). 176p. 1981. text ed. 13.95 (ISBN 0-13-346148-3, Spec); pap. text ed. 5.95 (ISBN 0-13-346130-0, Spec). P-H.

SELF-CULTURE

see also Books and Reading; Mnemonics

Kingsley, Emily P. I Can Do It Myself. (Sesame Street Starter Bks). (Illus.). 32p. (ps). 1981. 3.50 (ISBN 0-307-11604-2, Golden Pr). Western Pub.

Littleton, August V. The Art & Science of Psychomancy with Concrete & Practical Applications. (Library of Scientific Psychology Bk.). (Illus.). 107p. 1981. 29.45 (ISBN 0-89920-022-2). Am Inst Psych.

SELF-DEFENSE

see also Boxing; Hand-To-Hand Fighting; Judo

Baltazzi, Evan S. Self-Protection at Close Quarters & Beyond. (Illus.). 50.00 (ISBN 0-918948-03-7). Evanel.

Hayes, Stephen K. Ninja: Spirit of the Shadow Warrior. Griffeth, Bill, ed. LC 80-84678. 1980. pap. 6.95 (ISBN 0-89750-073-3). Ohara Pubns.

James. Stand Firm: The Teenager's Guide to Self-Defense. (gr. 7-12). 1980. pap. 1.25 (ISBN 0-590-30033-4, Schol Pap). Schol Bk Serv.

Jwing-Ming, Yang. Shaolin Long Fist. (Illus.). 250p. (Orig.). 1981. pap. 7.95 (ISBN 0-86568-020-5). Unique Pubns.

Lee, Chong. Super Dynamic Kicks, Vol. 3. LC 80-84496. 1980. pap. 5.50 (ISBN 0-89750-072-5). Ohara Pubns.

Urquidez, Benny. Training & Fighting Skills. Sobel, Stuart & Farkas, Emil, eds. (Illus.). 200p. (Orig.). 1981. pap. 10.95 (ISBN 0-86568-015-9). Unique Pubns.

SELF-DEFENSE FOR WOMEN

Clark, Buddy. Alone, Unarmed but Safe--the Woman's Judo Defense Book. (Illus.). 128p. 1981. 8.00 (ISBN 0-682-49712-6); pap. 6.00 (ISBN 0-682-49711-8). Exposition.

Tegner & McGrath. Self-Defense & Assault Prevention for Girls & Women. 1980. pap. 2.95 (ISBN 0-87407-026-0). Thor.

SELF-DESTRUCTION

see Suicide

SELF-DETERMINATION, NATIONAL

see also Autonomy; Minorities; Sovereignty

The Right to Self-Determination. 86p. 1979. pap. 8.00 (79-14-5, UN). Unipub.

SELF-EMPLOYED

see also Entrepreneur; Professions; Small Business

Gladson, Deek. The Miser's Manual: A Guide to Frofitable Self-Employment. 1981. pap. 4.00 (ISBN 0-686-69465-1); plastic bdg. 6.00 (ISBN 0-89316-626-X). Exanimo Pr.

Logan, George H. Tax Reduction for Small Business & Self Employed. 1981. pap. 9.95 (ISBN 0-914598-08-2). Padre Prods.

Winter, M. Mind Your Own Business, Be Your Own Boss. 1980. 12.95 (ISBN 0-13-583468-6); pap. 6.95 (ISBN 0-13-583450-3). P-H.

SELF-ESTEEM

see Self-Respect

SELF-EVALUATION

see also Self-Perception

Butler, Pamela E. Talking to Yourself: Learning to Communicate with the Most Important Person in Your Life. LC 80-6161. 192p. 1981. 12.95 (ISBN 0-8128-2779-1). Stein & Day.

Mischel, Theodore, ed. The Self: Psychological & Philosophical Issues. 359p. 1977. pap. 12.00x (ISBN 0-8476-6946-7). Rowman.

Young, James J. Growing Through Divorce. LC 79-90993. (Paths of Life Ser.). 60p. (Orig.). 1979. pap. 2.45 (ISBN 0-8091-2267-7). Paulist Pr.

SELF-EVALUATION OF SCHOOLS

see Educational Surveys

SELF-FULFILLMENT

see Self-Realization

SELF-HELP

see Christian Life; Conduct of Life; Psychology, Applied; Success; Self-Culture; Youth;
also the cross references listed at the beginning of each of these headings, and subdivision Self-Instruction under names of languages and subdivision Programmed Instruction under subjects

SELF-INSTRUCTION

see Self-Culture
also subdivision Self-Instruction under names of languages and subdivision Programmed Instruction under subjects

SELF-KNOWLEDGE, THEORY OF

Stebbing, Rita. The Philosophy of Spiritual Activity As a Path to Self-Knowledge. 1980. pap. 2.95 (ISBN 0-916786-50-1). St George Bk Serv.

Swami Muktananda. Reflections of the Self. LC 80-50391. (Illus., Orig.). 1980. pap. 5.95 (ISBN 0-914602-50-0). SYDA Found.

SELF-KNOWLEDGE IN LITERATURE

Wilkins, Eliza G. Know Thyself in Greek & Latin Literature. Taran, Leonardo, ed. LC 78-66584. (Ancient Philosophy Ser.: Vol. 28). 111p. 1979. lib. bdg. 13.00 (ISBN 0-8240-9572-3). Garland Pub.

SELF-LOVE (PSYCHOLOGY)

see Narcissism; Self-Respect

SELF-LOVE (THEOLOGY)

Price, Eugenia. Just As I Am. (Orig.). 1976. pap. 1.75 (ISBN 0-89129-187-3). Jove Pubns.

SELF-MASTERY

see Self-Control

SELF-PERCEPTION

see also Self-Evaluation

Larson, Bruce. The One & Only You. (Orig.). 1976. pap. 1.50 (ISBN 0-89129-135-0). Jove Pubns.

SELF-RATING

see Self-Evaluation

SELF-REALIZATION

Amman, L. A. Self Liberation. 1981. pap. 6.95 (ISBN 0-87728-511-X). Weiser.

Butler, Pamela E. Self-Assertion for Women. rev. ed. LC 80-8904. (Illus.). 320p. (Orig.). 1981. pap. 7.95 (ISBN 0-06-250121-6, HarpR). Har-Row.

Larson, Bruce. The One & Only You. (Orig.). 1976. pap. 1.50 (ISBN 0-89129-135-0). Jove Pubns.

Prater, Arnold. Miracle Living. (Orig.). pap. 2.95 (ISBN 0-89081-125-3). Harvest Hse.

Romen, A. S. Self-Suggestion & Its Influence on the Human Organism. Lewis, A. S. & Forsky, V., eds. (Illus.). 220p. 1980. 20.00 (ISBN 0-87332-195-2). M E Sharpe.

Schuller, Robert H. Discover How to Get Your Priorities Straight. (Orig.). 1978. pap. 1.25 (ISBN 0-89081-137-7). Harvest Hse.

--Discover Your Self-Confidence. (Orig.). 1978. pap. 1.25 (ISBN 0-89081-144-X). Harvest Hse.

--You Can Become the Person You Want to Be. (Orig.). pap. 2.25 (ISBN 0-515-05970-6). Jove Pubns.

Silo. The Look Within. 1980. pap. 3.95 (ISBN 0-87728-494-6). Weiser.

Weiss, Clara. Astrological Keys to Self Realization & Self Actualization. 1980. pap. 4.95 (ISBN 0-87728-509-8). Weiser.

Young, Ellin. Help Yourself to Understand Nineteen Eighty-One. 1980. pap. 2.95 (ISBN 0-87728-512-8). Weiser.

SELF-REALIZATION (PSYCHOLOGY)

see Self-Actualization (Psychology)

SELF-REALIZATION (RELIGION)

see Identification (Religion)

SELF-RELIANCE

Allaby, Michael & Bunyard, Peter. The Politics of Self-Sufficiency. 208p. 1980. 21.00 (ISBN 0-19-217695-1). Oxford U Pr.

SELF-RESPECT

Bradshaw, Pete. The Management of Self-Esteem: How People Can Feel Good About Themselves & Better About Their Organizations. (Illus.). 368p. 1981. 10.95 (ISBN 0-13-549535-0, Spec); pap. 4.95 (ISBN 0-13-549527-X). P-H.

Hornbrook, John F. & Wolf, Allan C. You Are Somebody Special. 148p. (Orig.). 1980. pap. 3.95 (ISBN 0-89841-005-3). Zoe Pubns.

Mischel, Theodore, ed. The Self: Psychological & Philosophical Issues. 359p. 1977. pap. 12.00x (ISBN 0-8476-6946-7). Rowman.

Raudsepp, Eugene. Essential Self. (Best Thoughts Ser.). (Illus.). 80p. (Orig.). 1981. pap. 2.50 (ISBN 0-8431-0388-4). Price Stern.

Schuller, Robert H. Discover Self-Love. (Orig.). 1978. pap. 1.25 (ISBN 0-89081-134-2). Harvest Hse.

--Self-Love. (Orig.). pap. 1.95 (ISBN 0-515-05829-7). Jove Pubns.

SELLERS, PETER, 1925-

Evans, Peter. Peter Sellers: The Mask Behind the Mask. 1980. pap. 2.50 (ISBN 0-451-09758-0, E9758, Sig). NAL.

SELLING BY TELEPHONE

see Telephone Selling

SEMANTICS

Devitt, Michael. Designation. LC 80-26471. 304p. 1981. 22.50x (ISBN 0-231-05126-3). Columbia U Pr.

Flavin, Matthew. Fundamental Concepts of Information Modeling. (Yourdon Press Monograph). (Illus.). 104p. (Orig.). 1981. pap. 10.00 (ISBN 0-917072-22-7). Yourdon.

Jones, N. D., ed. Semantics-Directed Compiler Generation: Proceedings. (Lecture Notes in Computer Science Ser.: Vol. 94). 489p. 1981. pap. 27.00 (ISBN 0-387-10250-7). Springer-Verlag.

Kimball, John P. & Tedesch, Philip, eds. Syntax & Semantics, Vol. 14: Tense & Aspect. 1981. price not set (ISBN 0-12-613514-2). Acad Pr.

Kimball, John P., et al. Syntax & Semantics, 13 vols. Incl. Vol. 1. Studies in Language. 260p. 1973. 30.50 (ISBN 0-12-785421-5); Vol. 2. 1973. 30.50 (ISBN 0-12-785422-3); Vol. 3. 1975. 31.00 (ISBN 0-12-785423-1); Vol. 4. 1975. 35.00 (ISBN 0-12-785424-X); Vol. 5. Japanese Generative Grammar. 1975. 45.50 (ISBN 0-12-785425-8); Vol. 6. 1976. 42.50 (ISBN 0-12-785426-6); Vol. 7. 1976. 30.00 (ISBN 0-12-613507-X); Vol. 8. 1976. 30.00 (ISBN 0-12-613508-8); Vol. 9. Pragmatics. 1978. 27.00 (ISBN 0-12-613509-6); Vol. 10. 1979. 38.00 (ISBN 0-12-613510-X); Vol. 11. Presupposition. 1979. 35.00 (ISBN 0-12-613511-8); Vol. 12. Discourse & Syntax. 1979. 43.00 (ISBN 0-12-613512-6); Vol. 13. Current Approaches to Syntax. 1980. write for info. (ISBN 0-12-613513-4). Acad Pr.

Urdang, Laurance, ed. Allusions: Cultural, Literary, Biblical, & Historical: A Thematic Dictionary. 1980. 45.00 (ISBN 0-8103-1124-0). Gale.

SEMANTICS (PHILOSOPHY)

see also Analysis (Philosophy); Communication; Meaning (Philosophy)

Falk, Eugene H. The Poetics of Roman Ingarden. LC 79-29655. 272p. 1980. 20.00x (ISBN 0-8078-1436-9); pap. 11.00x (ISBN 0-8078-4068-8). U of NC Pr.

SEMASIOLOGY

see Semantics

SEMEIOTICS

see Semantics (Philosophy); Semiotics; Signs and Symbols

SEMIARID REGIONS

see Arid Regions

SEMICONDUCTORS

see also Microelectronics; Parametric Amplifiers
also particular semiconducting substances, e.g. Germanium, Silicon; and headings beginning with the word Semiconductor

Butler, J. K., ed. Semiconductor Injection Lasers. LC 79-91615. 1980. 36.95 (ISBN 0-87942-129-0). Inst Electrical.

Chapple, M. A-Level Physics: Electricity & Semiconducters, Vol.3. 2nd ed. (Illus.). 288p. (Orig.). 1980. pap. text ed. 11.95x (ISBN 0-7121-0158-6). Intl Ideas.

Gray, Paul. Analog MOS Integrated Circuits. 400p. 1980. 28.00 (ISBN 0-471-08966-4, Pub. by Wiley-Interscience); pap. 18.00 (ISBN 0-471-08964-8). Wiley.

Hodgson, Myra, ed. An American Response to the Foreign Industrial Challenge in High Technology Industries. 175p. (Orig.). 1980. pap. 95.00 (ISBN 0-686-69372-8). W Fraser Pubs.

Howard W. Sams Engineering Staff. Semiconductor General Purpose Replacements. 3rd ed. 1980. pap. 17.95 (ISBN 0-672-21730-9). Sams.

Nozik, Art J., ed. Photoeffects at Semiconductor-Electrolyte Interfaces. LC 80-27773. (Symposium Ser.: No. 146). 1981. 39.00 (ISBN 0-8412-0604-X). Am Chemical.

OAS General Secretariat Department of Scientific & Technological Affairs. Semiconductors. 2nd ed. (Serie De Fisica (Monograph on Physics): No. 6). 63p. 1980. Repr. text ed. 2.00 (ISBN 0-8270-1068-0). OAS.

Willardson, Robert & Beer, A. C., eds. Semiconductors & Semimetals: Contacts, Junctions, Emitters, Vol. 15. 1981. price not set (ISBN 0-12-752115-1). Acad Pr.

Zawadzki, W., ed. Narrow Gap Semiconductors: Physics & Applications. (Lecture Notes in Physics Ser.: Vol. 133). 572p. 1981. pap. 37.20 (ISBN 0-387-10261-2). Springer-Verlag.

SEMIMETALS

Willardson, Robert & Beer, A. C., eds. Semiconductors & Semimetals: Contacts, Junctions, Emitters, Vol. 15. 1981. price not set (ISBN 0-12-752115-1). Acad Pr.

SEMINARIANS

Cohen, Joe H. Equipped for Good Work: A/Guide for Pastorso. 1981. 14.95 (ISBN 0-88289-271-1). Pelican.

George, Denise. How to Be a Seminary Student-& Survive. 1981. pap. 3.95 (ISBN 0-8054-6930-3). Broadman.

SEMINOLE INDIANS

see Indians of North America–Eastern States

SEMIOLOGY (LINGUISTICS)

see Semiotics

SEMIOLOGY (SEMANTICS)

see Semantics

SEMIOTICS

see also Semantics (Philosophy); Signs and Symbols

De George, Richard T., ed. Semiotic Themes. (University of Kansas Humanistic Studies: No. 53). (Illus.). 284p. 1981. pap. 12.00 (ISBN 0-686-28731-2). U of KS Pubns.

Steiner, Wendy, ed. The Sign in Music & Literature. (Illus.). 264p. 1981. text ed. 25.00x (ISBN 0-292-77563-6). U of Tex Pr.

SEMI-PRECIOUS STONES

see Precious Stones

SENECA, LUCIUS ANNAEUS

Strem, George G. The Life & Teaching of Lucius Annaeus Seneca. LC 79-67526. 175p. 1981. 10.00 (ISBN 0-533-04463-4). Vantage.

SENECA INDIANS

see Indians of North America–Eastern States

SENEGAL

Colvin, Lucie G. Historical Dictionary of Senegal. LC 80-25466. (African Historical Dictionaries: No. 23). 355p. 1981. 17.50 (ISBN 0-8108-1369-6). Scarecrow.

SENESCENCE

see Aging; Old Age

SENILE PSYCHOSIS

Fisk, Albert. A New Look at Senility. write for info (ISBN 0-398-04436-8). C C Thomas.

Reisberg, Barry. Brain Failure: An Introduction to Current Concepts of Senility. LC 80-69717. (Illus.). 1981. 19.95 (ISBN 0-02-926260-7). Free Pr.

SENIOR CITIZENS

see Aged

SENRYU

Andrews, J. David. Oh, My Comet, Shine! Found Haiku and Senryu, Based on "Thought Forms" by Mirtala Bentov. 60p. (Orig.). 1979. pap. 5.00; pap. text ed. 5.00. Planetary Pr.

SENSATION

see Senses and Sensation

SENSES AND SENSATION

see also Control (Psychology); Hearing; Ideology; Pain; Taste; Touch; Vision

Bain, Alexander. Senses & the Intellect. (Contributions to the History of Psychology Ser.: No. 4, Pt. A Orientations). 1978. Repr. of 1855 ed. 30.00 (ISBN 0-89093-153-4). U Pubns Amer.

Grastyan, E. & Molnar, P., eds. Sensory Functions: Proceedings of the 28th International Congress of Physiological Sciences, Budapest, 1980. LC 80-41852. (Advances in Physiological Sciences). (Illus.). 350p. 1981. 40.00 (ISBN 0-08-027337-8). Pergamon.

Levine, Michael W. & Shefner, Jeremy M. Fundamentals of Sensation & Perception. (Psychology Ser.). (Illus.). 480p. 1981. text ed. 19.95 (ISBN 0-201-04339-4). A-W.

SENSING, REMOTE

see Remote Sensing

SENSORY MOTOR LEARNING

see Perceptual-Motor Learning

SENTENCES (CRIMINAL PROCEDURE)

Alper, Benedict S. & Nichols, Lawrence T. Beyond the Courtroom: Community Justice & Programs in Conflict Resolution. LC 78-20376. write for info. (ISBN 0-669-02724-3). Lexington Bks.

Campbell, Arthur. Law of Sentencing, Vol.1. LC 78-18626. 1978. 47.50. Lawyers Co-Op.

Gross, Hyman & Von Hirsch, Andrew, eds. Sentencing. 416p. 1981. text ed. 19.95x (ISBN 0-19-502763-9); pap. text ed. 9.95x (ISBN 0-19-502764-7). Oxford U Pr.

SEPARATION (TECHNOLOGY)
see also Adsorption; Chromatographic Analysis; Distillation; Electrophoresis; Emulsions; Flotation; Fluidization; Separators (Machines)
Biological Separations in Iodinated Density-Gradient Media. 205p. 12.00 (ISBN 0-904147-02-9). Info Retrieval.
Weissberger, Arnold & Hsu, Hsien-Wen. Separations by Centrifugal Phenomena. (Techniques of Chemistry Ser.: Vol. 16). 400p. 49.50 (ISBN 0-471-05564-6, Pub. by Wiley-Interscience). Wiley.
SEPARATORS (MACHINES)
see also Filters and Filtration
Recommendations on International Performance & Test Specifications for Oily-Water Separating Equipment & Oil Content Meters. 36p. 1978. 8.25 (IMCO). Unipub.
Stephens, H. S. & Priestley, G., eds. Papers Presented at the International Conference on Hydrocyclones. (Illus.). 247p. (Orig.). 1980. pap. 78.00 (ISBN 0-906085-48-9). BHRA Fluid.
SEPOY REBELLION
see India–History–British Occupation, 1765-1947
SEPULCHRAL MONUMENTS
see also Pyramids
Mihalyka, Jean M., compiled by. Gravestone Inscriptions in Northampton County Virginia. 6.00 (ISBN 0-686-69510-0). Va State Lib.
SEQUENCES (MATHEMATICS)
Smith, Walter L. On the Cumulants of Cumulative Processes. 48p. 1959. pap. 1.60 (1257). U of NC Pr.
Wimp, Jet. Sequence Transformations & Their Applications. LC 80-68564. (Mathematics in Science & Engineering Ser.). 1981. price not set (ISBN 0-12-757940-0). Acad Pr.
SEQUENTIAL MACHINE THEORY
see also Electronic Digital Computers
Booth, Taylor L. Sequential Machines & Automata Theory. 608p. 1981. Repr. of 1967 ed. text ed. price not set (ISBN 0-89874-269-2). Krieger.
Montgomery, S. Fixed Rings of Finite Automorphism Groups of Associative Rings. (Lectures Notes in Mathematics Ser.: Vol. 818). 126p. 1981. pap. 9.80 (ISBN 0-387-10232-9). Springer-Verlag.
SEQUOIA NATIONAL FOREST, CALIFORNIA
Muir, John. Sierra Big Trees. abr. ed. Jones, William R., ed. (Illus.). 80p. 1981. pap. 3.95 (ISBN 0-89646-069-X). Outbooks.
SERAPHIM
see Angels
SERENGETI NATIONAL PARK
Frame, George & Frame, Lory. Swift & Enduring: Cheetahs & Wild Dogs of the Serengeti. 1981. 15.95 (ISBN 0-525-93060-4). Dutton.
SERIALS
see Periodicals
SERMON ON THE MOUNT
see also Beatitudes
Gonsalves, Carol. Sermon on the Mountain. (Arch Bk. Supplement Ser.). 1981. pap. 0.79 (ISBN 0-570-06149-0, 59-1304). Concordia.
Jones, E. Stanley. The Christ of the Mount. (Festival Ser.). 336p. 1981. pap. 2.45 (ISBN 0-687-06925-4). Abingdon.
Wright, T. H. The Sermon on the Mount for to-Day. 298p. Repr. of 1927 ed. 4.95 (ISBN 0-567-02296-X). Attic Pr.
SERMONS
see also Children'S Sermons; Communion Sermons; Funeral Sermons; Lenten Sermons; Preaching
also subdivision Sermons under special subjects, e.g. Beatitudes–Sermons; Easter–Sermons; Missions–Sermons
Benn, J. Solomon. Preaching from the Bible. (Resources for Black Ministries Ser.). 80p. (Orig.). 1981. pap. 2.95 (ISBN 0-8010-0801-8). Baker Bk.
Benn, Solomon J., III. God's Soul Medicine. (Resources for Black Ministries Ser.). 64p. (Orig.). 1981. pap. 2.45 (ISBN 0-8010-0802-6). Baker Bk.
Bernard Of Clairvaux. Bernard of Clairvaux: Sermons I on Conversations; Lenten Sermons on the Psalm "He Who Dwells". Said, Marie-Bernard, tr. (Cistercian Fathers Ser.: No. 25). (Lat.). 1981. price not set (ISBN 0-87907-125-7); pap. price not set (ISBN 0-87907-925-8). Cistercian Pubns.
Blattner, Elsie & Walker, Luisa, trs. Bosquejos Homileticos. (Spanish Bks.). 1979. 1.75 (ISBN 0-8297-0511-2). Life Pubs Intl.
Bolton, Robert. A Discourse About the State of True Happinesse. LC 79-84089. (English Experience Ser.: No. 909). 184p. 1979. Repr. of 1641 ed. lib. bdg. 14.00 (ISBN 90-221-0909-7). Walter J Johnson.
Borras, Jose. El Inmenso Amor De Dios. 96p. (Span.). Date not set. pap. price not set (ISBN 0-311-43038-4). Casa Bautista.
Carpenter, Nathanael. Achitophel, or Toe Picture of a Wicked Politician. LC 79-84094. (English Experience Ser.: No. 914). 76p. 1979. Repr. of 1629 ed. lib. bdg. 9.00 (ISBN 90-221-0914-3). Walter J Johnson.
Coniaris, A. M. Sermons on the Major Holy Days of the Orthodox Church. 1978. pap. 4.95 (ISBN 0-937032-03-4). Light & Life Pub Co MN.
Eavey, C. B. Chapel Talks. (Pocket Pulpit Library). 120p. 1981. pap. 2.95 (ISBN 0-8010-3365-9). Baker Bk.
Ferris, Theodore P. This Is the Day: Selected Sermons. 2nd ed. LC 76-39640. 384p. 1980. pap. 10.00 (ISBN 0-911658-16-5, 3077). Yankee Bks.
Gutierrez, Rolando C. Mensaje De los Salmos, Tomo III. 160p. 1981. pap. write for info. (ISBN 0-311-04028-4). Casa Bautista.
Higdon, Barbara M. Good News for Today. 1981. pap. write for info. (ISBN 0-8309-0298-8). Herald Hse.
Hodge, Charles. Princeton Sermons. 1979. 11.95 (ISBN 0-85151-285-2). Banner of Truth.
Jordan, Jerry M. The Brown Bag: A Bag Full of Sermons for Children. (Illus.). 117p. 1981. pap. 5.95 (ISBN 0-8298-0411-0). Pilgrim NY.
Jowett, John H. The Best of John H. Jowett. (Best Ser.). 256p. (Orig.). 1981. pap. 3.95 (ISBN 0-8010-5142-8). Baker Bk.
Kilpatrick, T. B. Bishop Butler's Three Sermons Upon Human Nature. (Handbooks for Bible Classes Ser.). 123p. 1949. text ed. 3.50 (ISBN 0-567-08142-7). Attic Pr.
King, Martin L., Jr. Strength to Love. LC 80-2374. 160p. 1981. pap. 4.25 (ISBN 0-8006-1441-0, 1-1441). Fortress.
Liptak, David Q. Sacramental & Occasional Homilies. LC 80-29287. 96p. (Orig.). 1981. pap. 4.95 (ISBN 0-8189-0406-2). Alba.
Lorber, Jakob. The Lord's Sermons. Ozols, Violet & Von Koerber, Hildegard, trs. from Ger. LC 80-50280. (Jakob Lorber Ser.). 278p. 1981. 12.95 (ISBN 0-934616-06-X). Valkyrie Pr.
Makrakis, Apostolos. Kyriakodromion (Sunday Sermonary) Orthodox Christian Educational Society, ed. Cummings, D., tr. from Hellenic. 637p. 1951. 8.00x (ISBN 0-938366-20-3). Orthodox Chr.
--Three Great Friday Sermons & Other Theological Discourses. Orthodox Christian Educational Society, ed. Cummings, Denver, tr. from Hellenic. 107p. (Orig.). 1952. pap. 2.00x (ISBN 0-938366-48-3). Orthodox Chr.
Moore, Harvey D. & Moore, Patsie S. The Mysterious Marvelous Snowflake. LC 80-20996. 128p. (Orig.). 1981. pap. 4.95 (ISBN 0-687-27640-3). Abingdon.
Romero, Oscar. A Martyr's Message of Hope: Six Homilies of Oscar Romero. 125p. (Orig.). 1981. pap. 4.95 (ISBN 0-934134-09-X). Natl Cath Reporter.
Sermons for Special Occasions. 1981. pap. 4.95 (ISBN 0-570-03825-1, 12-2790). Concordia.
Smith, Chuck. The Answer for Today, Vol. 1. 72p. (Orig.). 1980. pap. 1.95 (ISBN 0-936728-09-4). Word for Today.
Spray, Russell E. Instant Sermons for Busy Pastors. (Sermon Outline Ser.). (Orig.). 1981. pap. 1.45 (ISBN 0-8010-8192-0). Baker Bk.
Sweeting, George. Special Sermons on the Family. (Special Sermon Ser.). 144p. 1981. pap. 2.95 (ISBN 0-8024-8208-2). Moody.
Turner, J. J. Practical Sermons That Motivate. pap. 2.95 (ISBN 0-89315-211-0). Lambert Bk.
Walsh, Kilian & Edmonds, Irene, trs. Bernard of Clairvaux: Sermons on the Song of Songs, Vol. III. (Cistercian Fathers Ser.: No. 31). 1979. 15.95; pap. 5.00 (ISBN 0-87907-931-2). Cistercian Pubns.
SERMONS–ILLUSTRATIONS
see also Homiletical Illustrations
Junior Surprise Sermons with Handmade Objects, 2 bks. Set. pap. 6.00; No. 1. pap. 3.00 (ISBN 0-915398-18-4); No. 2. pap. 3.00 (ISBN 0-915398-19-2). Visual Evangels.
SERMONS–OUTLINES
Appelman, Hyman. Appelman's Outlines & Illustrations. (Pocket Pulpit Library). 128p. 1981. pap. 2.95 (ISBN 0-8010-0072-6). Baker Bk.
Keiningham, C. W. Sermon Outlines for Funerals. (Sermon Outline Ser.). (Orig.). 1981. pap. 1.45 (ISBN 0-8010-5427-3). Baker Bk.
Lockaby, George W. Sermon Outlines on the Person & Work of Christ. 1981. pap. 2.25 (ISBN 0-8054-2238-2). Broadman.
Mason, H. Lee. Sermon Outlines for Evangelism. (Sermon Outline Ser.). (Orig.). 1981. pap. 1.45 (ISBN 0-8010-6120-2). Baker Bk.
Spray, Russell E. Time-Saving Sermon Outlines. (Sermon Outline Ser.). (Orig.). 1981. pap. 1.45 (ISBN 0-8010-8193-9). Baker Bk.
SERMONS, AMERICAN
Davis, Thomas M. & Davis, Virginia L., eds. Edward Taylor's "Church Record" & Related Sermons. (American Literary Manuscripts Ser.: Vol. 1). 1981. lib. bdg. 35.00 (ISBN 0-8057-9650-9). Twayne.
SERMONS, ANGLO-SAXON
AElfric. AElfric's Catholic Homilies: The Second Series Text. Godden, Malcolm, ed. (Early English Text Soc., Supplementary Ser.: No. 5). (Illus.). 480p. 1979. text ed. 49.50x (ISBN 0-19-722405-9). Oxford U Pr.
SERMONS, ENGLISH
Fisher, John. This Treatise Concernynge the Fruytfull Saynges of Davyd..Was Made & Compyled by..John Fyssher..Bysshop of Rochester. LC 79-84106. (English Experience Ser.: No. 925). 296p. 1979. Repr. of 1509 ed. lib. bdg. 28.00 (ISBN 90-221-0925-9). Walter J Johnson.
SEROLOGY
see also Immunology
Wilson, J. D. Diagnostic Immunology & Serology: A Clinician's Guide. Simpson, Sandra I., ed. 161p. 1980. pap. text ed. 14.95 (ISBN 0-909337-01-2). ADIS Pr.
SERPENTS
see Snakes
SERUM
see also Serum Protein
Wolf. Intrepretation of Electrophoretic Patterns of Serum Proteins, Lipoproteins, Isoenzymes, & Hemoglobins. 1981. price not set (ISBN 0-89352-035-7). Masson Pub.
SERUM PROTEIN
Ward, T. M. Serum Proteins in Clinical Medicine. 1981. text ed. price not set (ISBN 0-407-00161-1). Butterworth.
SERUMTHERAPY
see also Allergy; Immunity; Medicine, Preventive; Toxins and Antitoxins
Wolf. Intrepretation of Electrophoretic Patterns of Serum Proteins, Lipoproteins, Isoenzymes, & Hemoglobins. 1981. price not set (ISBN 0-89352-035-7). Masson Pub.
SERVANTS
see also Apprentices; Indentured Servants
Smith, Charles. Lord Mountbatten: His Butler's Story. LC 80-51787. (Illus.). 224p. 1980. 12.95 (ISBN 0-8128-2751-1). Stein & Day.
SERVICE, COMPULSORY MILITARY
see Military Service, Compulsory
SERVICE BOOKS (MUSIC)
see also subdivision Liturgy and Ritual under denominations
Arango, Tony, tr. Armonias Corales, Vol. 1. 144p. (Orig., Span.). 1977. pap. 4.75 (ISBN 0-89922-082-7). Edit Caribe.
SERVICE RATING
see Employees, Rating Of
SERVICEMEN, MILITARY
see Soldiers
SETTING (STAGE)
see Theaters–Stage-Setting and Scenery
SETTLEMENT OF LAND
see Land Settlement
SEVASTOPOL–SIEGE, 1854-1855
see Crimean War, 1853-1856
SEVENTEENTH CENTURY
Watts, Derek A. Cardinal De Retz: The Ambiguities of a Seventeenth-Century Mind. 308p. 1980. text ed. 39.95x (ISBN 0-19-815762-2). Oxford U Pr.
SEVENTH-DAY ADVENTISTS
Willis, Mary. People of That Book. Van Dolson, Bobbie J., ed. 128p. 1981. pap. price not set (ISBN 0-8280-0033-6). Review & Herald.
SEVERANCE TAX
see Mines and Mineral Resources–Taxation
SEWAGE
Hudson, James F., et al. Pollution-Pricing: Industrial Response to Wastewater Charges. LC 80-8363. 1981. price not set (ISBN 0-669-04033-9). Lexington Bks.
Institute of Civil Engineers, UK. Advanced in Sewage Treatment. 88p. 1980. 60.00x (ISBN 0-901948-70-5, Pub. by Telford England). State Mutual Bk.
Iskander, I. K. Modeling Wastewater Renovation Land Treatment. 343p. 1981. 20.00 (ISBN 0-471-08128-0, Pub. by Wiley-Interscience). Wiley.
Wastewater Treatment & Resource Recovery. 47p. 1980. pap. 5.00 (ISBN 0-88936-260-2, IDRC154, IDRC). Unipub.
SEWAGE–PURIFICATION
Application of Adsorption to Wastewater Treatment. (Illus.). 1981. text ed. 40.00 (ISBN 0-937976-03-2). Enviro Pr.
Culp, Gordon, et al. Wastewater Reuse & Recycling Technology. LC 80-21778. (Pollution Technology Review Ser.: 72). (Illus.). 838p. 1981. 49.00 (ISBN 0-8155-0829-8). Noyes.
Eckenfelder, W. W., Jr., et al. Control, Operation & Management of Activated Sludge Plants. (Series I,Book 3). text ed. 40.00 (ISBN 0-937976-01-6). Enviro Pr.
Grady & Lim. Biological Wastewater Treatment: Theory & Applications. 984p. 1980. 75.00 (ISBN 0-8247-1000-2). Dekker.
Jenkins, S. H. Treatment of Domestic & Industrial Wastewaters in Large Plants: Proceedings of a Workshop Held in Vienna, Austria, Sept. 1979. (Progress in Water Technology: Vol. 12, Nos. 3 & 5). 550p. 1980. 90.00 (ISBN 0-08-026033-0). Pergamon.
Middlebrooks, E. Joe. Water Reuse: State-of-the-Art. 1981. text ed. 40.00 (ISBN 0-250-40359-5). Ann Arbor Science.
Perrich, Jerry R., ed. Congressional Staff Directory, Ltd. 272p. 1981. 69.95 (ISBN 0-8493-5693-8). CRC Pr.
Wastewater Treatment & Resource Recovery. 47p. 1980. pap. 5.00 (ISBN 0-88936-260-2, IDRC154, IDRC). Unipub.
SEWAGE DISPOSAL
see also Refuse and Refuse Disposal; Water–Pollution
Blendermann, Louis. Controlled Storm Water Drainage. LC 78-15080. (Illus.). 200p. 1979. 27.00 (ISBN 0-8311-1123-2). Indus Pr.
Brunner, Calvin. Design of Sewage Sludge Incineration Systems. LC 80-21916. (Pollution Technology Review: No. 71). (Illus.). 380p. 1981. 48.00 (ISBN 0-8155-0825-5). Noyes.
Institute of Civil Engineers, UK. Safety in Sewers & at Sewage Works. 64p. 1980. pap. 12.00x (ISBN 0-901948-12-8, Pub. by Telford England). State Mutual Bk.
Intergovernmental Conference on the Convention on the Dumping of Wastes at Sea. 36p. 1976. 8.25 (IMCO). Unipub.
Jenkins, S. H. Treatment of Domestic & Industrial Wastewaters in Large Plants: Proceedings of a Workshop Held in Vienna, Austria, Sept. 1979. (Progress in Water Technology: Vol. 12, Nos. 3 & 5). 550p. 1980. 90.00 (ISBN 0-08-026033-0). Pergamon.
Recommendations on International Effluent Standards & Guidelines for Performance Tests for Sewage Treatment Plants. 9p. 1977. 5.50 (IMCO). Unipub.
Scott & Smith. Dictionary of Waste & Water Treatment. 1981. text ed. price not set (ISBN 0-408-00495-9). Butterworth.
SEWALL, SAMUEL, 1652-1730
Chamberlain, N. H. Samuel Sewall & the World He Lived in. 319p. 1980. Repr. of 1897 ed. lib. bdg. 30.00 (ISBN 0-89987-110-0). Darby Bks.
SEWERAGE
see also Plumbing; Sewage
Metcalf & Eddy, Inc. & Tchobanoglous, George. Pumping & Collection of Wastewater. (Water Resources & Engineering Ser.). (Illus.). 400p. 1981. text ed. 28.95 (ISBN 0-07-041680-X, C); student's manual 4.95 (ISBN 0-07-041681-8). McGraw.
SEWERS
see Sewerage
SEWING
see also Dressmaking; Embroidery; Needlework; Quilting
Hymer, Dian D. Sew, Recycle, & Save: Practical Solutions to the Challenges of the 80's. (Urban Life Ser.). (Illus.). 96p. (Orig.). 1981. pap. 4.95 (ISBN 0-87701-179-6). Chronicle Bks.
Katz, Ruth. Make It & Wear It. LC 80-54707. (Illus.). 48p. (gr. 5-9). 1981. 7.95 (ISBN 0-8027-6418-5); PLB 8.95 (ISBN 0-8027-6419-3). Walker & Co.
Martensson, Kerstin. Kwik-Sew Method for Easy Sewing. (Illus.). pap. 6.95 (ISBN 0-913212-09-1). Kwik Sew.
Popko, Rhonda. The Book of Basic Sewing. (Illus.). 104p. (Orig.). 1981. pap. 4.95 (ISBN 0-8326-2248-6, 7445). Delair.
Ruggieri, Lorraine. Woman's Day Book of No-Pattern Sewing. 128p. (Orig.). 1981. pap. 6.95 (ISBN 0-449-90053-3, Columbine). Fawcett.
SEX
see also Generative Organs; Homosexuality; Lesbianism; Masochism; Pedophilia; Reproduction; Sadism; Sex Customs
also headings beginning with the word Sexual
Hockings, Paul. Sex & Disease in a Mountain Community. 1980. 14.00x (ISBN 0-8364-0625-7, Pub. by Vikas). South Asia Bks.
Howard, Alan. Sex in the Light of Reincarnation & Freedom. 1980. pap. 4.95 (ISBN 0-916786-48-X). St George Bk Serv.
Kaufman, Sherwin A. Sexual Sabotage: How to Enjoy Sex Inspite of Physical & Emotional Problems. 256p. 1981. 13.95 (ISBN 0-02-560740-5). Macmillan.
Lair, Jess. Sex: If I Didn't Laugh, I'd Cry. 1980. pap. 2.50 (ISBN 0-449-24336-2, Crest). Fawcett.
Lehrman, Nat. Masters & Johnson Explained. rev. ed. LC 76-19839. 272p. 1981. pap. 2.75 (ISBN 0-87216-808-5). Playboy Pbks.
Lorde, Audre. Uses of the Erotic: The Erotic As Power. (Out & Out Pamphlet Ser.). pap. 1.00 (ISBN 0-918314-09-7). Out & Out.
Nass, et al. Sexual Choices: An Introduction to Human Sexuality. (Illus.). 550p. 1981. text ed. 17.95 (ISBN 0-87872-285-8). Duxbury Pr.
Ong, Walter J. Fighting for Life: Contest, Sexuality, & Consciousness. LC 80-66968. (Illus.). 240p. 1981. 14.95 (ISBN 0-8014-1342-7). Cornell U Pr.
Parriott, Sara. Sex Doesn't Count When... LC 79-66310. (Illus.). 96p. 1979. pap. 2.95 (ISBN 0-87477-113-7). J P Tarcher.
Penney, Alexandra. How to Make Love to a Man. Southern, Carol, ed. 160p. 1981. 10.00 (ISBN 0-517-54145-9). Potter.
Raudsepp, Eugene. Love & Sexuality. (Best Thoughts Ser.). (Illus.). 80p. 1981. pap. 2.50 (ISBN 0-8431-0387-6). Price Stern.
Richardson, Laurel W. Readings in Sex & Gender. 416p. 1982. pap. text ed. 12.95 (ISBN 0-669-03370-7). Heath.
Rimbaud, Robert C. What Nobody, but Absolutely Nobody Knows About Sex, or New Discoveries into the Metaphysics of Sex. (Illus.). 113p. 1981. 18.25 (ISBN 0-89266-286-7). Am Classical Coll Pr.
SEX–CAUSE AND DETERMINATION
see also Sex Chromosomes
Lepori, N. G. Sex Differentiation, Hermaphroditism & Intersexuality in Vertebrates Including Man. (Illus.). 372p. 1980. text ed. 49.50x (ISBN 88-212-0747-1, Pub. by Piccin Italy). J K Burgess.
SEX–DICTIONARIES
DeMoya, Armando, et al. The Practical Medical Dictionary of Sex. LC 80-5799. 304p. 1981. 16.95 (ISBN 0-8128-2794-5). Stein & Day.
SEX–PHYSIOLOGICAL ASPECTS
see Sex (Biology)

SEX-PSYCHOLOGICAL ASPECTS
see Sex (Psychology)
De Coppens, Peter R. Spiritual Perspective II: The Spiritual Dimension & Implications of Love, Sex, & Marriage. LC 80-6302 175p. (Orig.). 1981. pap. text ed. 8.75 (ISBN 0-8191-1512-6). U Pr of Amer.
SEX-RESEARCH
see Sex Research
SEX (BIOLOGY)
see also Generative Organs; Reproduction; Sex-Cause and Determination
Hite, Shere. The Hite Report on Male Sexuality. LC 80-2709. 1981. 17.95 (ISBN 0-394-41392-X). Knopf.
Hogan, Rosemarie. Human Sexuality: A Nursing Perspective. 768p. 1980. pap. text ed. 13.95 (ISBN 0-8385-3955-6). ACC.
Nass, et al. Sexual Choices: An Introduction to Human Sexuality. (Illus.). 550p. 1981. text ed. 17.95 (ISBN 0-87872-285-8). Duxbury Pr.
SEX (PHYSIOLOGY)
see Sex (Biology)
SEX (PSYCHOLOGY)
see also Masculinity (Psychology); Sex Role
Bennett, J. G. Sex. 128p. 1981. pap. 5.95 (ISBN 0-87728-533-0). Weiser.
Elskamp, Karen E. & Munzert, Alfred W. Test Your Sex Appeal. LC 80-85277. (Test Yourself Ser.). 64p. 1981. pap. 3.95 (ISBN 0-671-42627-3). Monarch Pr.
Hite, Shere. The Hite Report on Male Sexuality. LC 80-2709. 1981. 17.95 (ISBN 0-394-41392-X). Knopf.
Hogan, Rosemarie. Human Sexuality: A Nursing Perspective. 768p. 1980. pap. text ed. 13.95 (ISBN 0-8385-3955-6). ACC.
Kahan, Jane M., et al. Understanding Your Sexuality. (Illus.). 1980. pap. text ed. 104.00 (ISBN 0-89290-100-4, A793-SATC). Soc for Visual.
Kahn, Sandra & Davis, Jean. Sexual Preferences. 256p. 1981. 9.95 (ISBN 0-312-71351-7). St Martin.
Kaufman, Sherwin A. Sexual Sabotage: How to Enjoy Sex Inspite of Physical & Emotional Problems. 256p. 1981. 13.95 (ISBN 0-02-560740-5). Macmillan.
LaHaye, Tim & LaHaye, Beverly. The Act of Marriage. 316p. 1981. pap. 2.95. Zondervan.
Leman, Kevin. Sex Begins in the Kitchen. LC 80-54004. 144p. 1981. text ed. 7.95 (ISBN 0-8307-0787-5). Regal.
Lorde, Audre. Uses of the Erotic: The Erotic As Power. (Out & Out Pamphlet Ser.). pap. 1.00 (ISBN 0-918314-09-7). Out & Out.
Lydgate, John. Reason & Sensuality: Studies & Notes, Vol. 2. Sieper, Ernst, ed. (Early English Text Society Ser.). 1903. 9.95x (ISBN 0-19-722534-9). Oxford U Pr.
Nass, et al. Sexual Choices: An Introduction to Human Sexuality. (Illus.). 550p. 1981. text ed. 17.95 (ISBN 0-87872-285-8). Duxbury Pr.
Offit, Avodah. Night Thoughts: Reflections of a Sex Therapist. 284p. 1981. 11.95 (ISBN 0-312-92575-1). Congdon & Lattes.
Rosen, Raymond & Rosen, Linda R. Human Sexuality. 576p. 1981. text ed. 17.95 (ISBN 0-394-32028-X). Random.
Yorburg, Betty. Sexual Identity: Sex Roles & Social Change. LC 80-22489. 240p. 1981. Repr. text ed. 8.50 (ISBN 0-89874-265-X). Krieger.
SEX (THEOLOGY)
see also Homosexuality and Christianity
Constantelos, D. J. Marriage, Sexuality & Celibacy: A Greek Orthodox Perspective. 1975. pap. 3.95 (ISBN 0-937032-15-8). Light&Life Pub Co MN.
Sumrall, Lester. Sixty Things God Said About Sex. 144p. 1981. pap. 3.95 (ISBN 0-8407-5756-5). Nelson.
SEX AND HISTORY
Bullough, Vern & Brundage, James. Sex in a Medieval Europe. (New Concepts in Human Sexuality Ser.). 250p. 1981. text ed. 17.95 (ISBN 0-87975-141-X); pap. text ed. 9.95 (ISBN 0-87975-151-7). Prometheus Bks.
Tannahill, Reay. Sex in History. LC 79-15053. 480p. 1981. pap. 8.95 (ISBN 0-8128-6115-9). Stein & Day.
SEX AND LAW
see also Abortion; Birth Control; Domestic Relations; Prostitution; Sex Crimes
Marchant, James. The Master Problem. Winick, Charles, ed. LC 78-60869. (Prostitution Ser.: Vol. 12). 371p. 1979. lib. bdg. 36.00 (ISBN 0-8240-9716-5). Garland Pub.
SEX AND RELIGION
see also Homosexuality and Christianity; Sex (Theology); Sex in the Bible
Evola, Julius. Metaphysics of Sex. Ormrod, J. A., tr. from Ital. (Illus.). 1981. pap. 8.95 (ISBN 0-89281-025-4). Inner Tradit.
Human Sexuality & Personhood. 200p. (Orig.). 1981. pap. price not set (ISBN 0-935372-09-1). Pope John Ctr.
Kern, Louis J. An Ordered Love: Sex Roles & Sexuality in Victorian Utopias--the Shakers, the Mormons, & the Oneida Community. LC 80-10763. xv, 430p. 1981. 24.00x (ISBN 0-8078-1443-1); pap. 12.50x (ISBN 0-8078-4074-2). U of NC Pr.
LaHaye, Tim & LaHaye, Beverly. The Act of Marriage. 316p. 1981. pap. 2.95. Zondervan.
Musser, Harlan C. Sex -- Our Myth Theology? 196p. 1981. pap. 7.95 (ISBN 0-8059-2768-9). Dorrance.
Pierson, Jack D. What a Teenager Ought to Know About Sex & God. (Teenager's Essential Education Library). (Illus.). 147p. 1981. 21.75 (ISBN 0-89266-288-3). Am Classical Coll Pr.
Simmons, Paul D. & Crawford, Kenneth. Mi Desarrollo Sexual. Sabanes De Plou, Dafne, tr. from Eng. (El Sexo En la Vida Cristiana). 96p. (Span.). (gr. 10-12). Date not set. Repr. pap. price not set (ISBN 0-311-46253-7, Edit Mundo). Casa Bautista.
SEX CHROMOSOMES
see also Sex-Cause and Determination
Robinson, Arthur, et al, eds. Sex Chromosome Aneuploidy: Prospective Studies on Children. LC 78-13921. (Alan R. Liss Ser.: Vol. 15, No. 1). 1979. 32.00 (ISBN 0-8451-1024-1). March of Dimes.
SEX CRIMES
see also Adultery; Incest; Prostitution; Sex and Law
Mrazek, Patricia B. & Kempe, C. H. Sexually Abused Children & Their Families. 300p. 1981. 72.01 (ISBN 0-08-026796-3). Pergamon.
Segilman, E. R. The Social Evil, with Special Reference to Conditions Existing in the City of New York. Winick, Charles, ed. LC 78-60871. (Prostitution Ser.: Vol. 3). 188p. 1979. lib. bdg. 20.00 (ISBN 0-8240-9725-4). Garland Pub.
Sexual Abuse of Children: Implications from the Sexual Trauma Treatment Program of Connecticut-Special Report of Two Research Utilization Workshops. 1979. 3.00. Comm Coun Great NY.
SEX CUSTOMS
see also Sex and Religion; Sex in Literature
Antonovsky, Helen F., et al. Adolescent Sexuality: A Study of Attitudes & Behavior. LC 80-8337. 176p. 1980. 18.95 (ISBN 0-669-04030-4). Lexington Bks.
Bride's Magazine Editors & Calderone, Mary. Questions & Answers About Love & Sex. 144p. (Orig.). 1980. pap. 1.95 (ISBN 0-380-52977-7, 52977). Avon.
Bullough, Vern & Brundage, James, eds. Sex in the Middle Ages. LC 80-85227. (New Concepts in Human Sexuality Ser.). 250p. 1980. 17.95 (ISBN 0-87975-141-X); pap. 9.95 (ISBN 0-87975-151-7). Prometheus Bks.
Diagram Group. Sex: A User's Manual. (Illus.). 196p. 1981. 14.95 (ISBN 0-399-12574-4, Perigee); pap. 6.95 (ISBN 0-399-50517-2). Putnam.
Feldman, P. & MacCulloch, M. Human Sexual Behavior. LC 79-41220. 226p. 1980. 34.50 (ISBN 0-471-27676-6, Pub. by Wiley-Interscience). Wiley.
Parkin, Molly. Molly's Manhattan. 200p. Date not set. cancelled (ISBN 0-686-68788-4). Riverrun NY.
Schutz, Albert L. Love & Religion: A Study of Sexual Delusion. Lowenkopf, Anne N., ed. (Illus., Orig.). 1981. 14.50 (ISBN 0-936596-02-3); pap. 9.95 (ISBN 0-936596-02-3). Quantal.
Starr, Bernard D. & Weiner, Marcella B. The Starr-Weiner Report on Sex & Sexuality in the Mature Years. 1981. 12.95 (ISBN 0-8128-2750-3). Stein & Day.
Talese, Gay. Thy Neighbor's Wife. 1981. pap. 3.95 (ISBN 0-440-18689-7). Dell.
SEX DETERMINATION
see Sex-Cause and Determination
SEX DIFFERENCES IN EDUCATION
Sutherland, Margaret B. Sex Bias in Education. (Theory & Practice in Education Ser.: Vol. 2). 208p. 1981. 25.00x (ISBN 0-631-10851-3, Pub. by Basil Blackwell England); pap. 12.50x (ISBN 0-631-12617-1). Biblio Dist.
SEX DIFFERENTIATION
see Sex-Cause and Determination
SEX DISCRIMINATION
Reied, Morton H., ed. Systems of Equality & Inequality in Human Society. 240p. 1981. 20.95 (ISBN 0-89789-012-4). J F Bergin.
Sutherland, Margaret B. Sex Bias in Education. (Theory & Practice in Education Ser.: Vol. 2). 208p. 1981. 25.00x (ISBN 0-631-10851-3, Pub. by Basil Blackwell England); pap. 12.50x (ISBN 0-631-12617-1). Biblio Dist.
Taubenfeld, H. Sex-Based Discrimination, Release 1. 1980. 35.00. Oceana.
SEX DISCRIMINATION AGAINST MEN
see Sex Discrimination
SEX DISCRIMINATION AGAINST WOMEN
see Sex Discrimination
SEX EDUCATION
see Sex Instruction
Lieberman, E. J. & Peck, Ellen. Sex & Birth Control: A Guide for the Young. rev. ed. LC 79-7094. (Illus.). 304p. 1981. 10.95 (ISBN 0-690-01837-1, HarpT). Har-Row.
SEX HORMONES
see Hormones, Sex
SEX IN LITERATURE
see also Sex in the Bible
Atkins, John. Sex in Literature, Vol. 2. 1980. 15.95 (ISBN 0-7145-0919-1); pap. 6.95 (ISBN 0-7145-1138-2). Riverrun NY.
--Sex in Literature, Vol. 3. 1981. 25.00 (ISBN 0-7145-3668-7). Riverrun NY.
O'Rourke, Brian. The Conscience of the Race: Sex & Religion in Irish & French Novels 1941-1973. 72p. 1981. 10.00x (ISBN 0-906127-22-X, Pub. by Irish Academic Pr Ireland). Biblio Dist.
SEX IN MARRIAGE
Grace, Mike & Grace, Joyce. A Joyful Meeting: Sexuality in Marriage. (Illus.). 100p. (Orig.). 1980. pap. 3.00 (ISBN 0-936098-14-7). Natl Marriage.
SEX IN MOVING-PICTURES
see also Moving-Pictures-Moral and Religious Aspects
Solinas, PierNico. Ultimate Porno. LC 80-69871. 1981. 14.95 (ISBN 0-938112-00-7). Eyecontact.
SEX IN THE BIBLE
Morris, Leon. Testaments of Love: A Study of Love in the Bible. (Orig.). 1981. pap. price not set (ISBN 0-8028-1874-9). Eerdmans.
SEX INSTRUCTION
Adler, Alfred. Cooperation Between the Sexes: Writings on Women, Love, Marriage & Its Disorders. LC 76-23804. 480p. 1980. Repr. of 1978 ed. 25.00 (ISBN 0-87668-443-6). Aronson.
Bailey, Alice A. & Khul, Djwhal. A Compilation on Sex. 160p. (Orig.). pap. 5.00 (ISBN 0-85330-136-0). Lucis.
Boyd, Daniel. How to Double Your Sex Drive. 160p. 1980. 12.95 (ISBN 0-917224-09-4). Gregory Pubns.
Brown, Paul & Faulder, Carolyn. Learning to Love: How to Make Bad Sex Good & Good Sex Better. LC 78-52202. 188p. (Orig.). 1981. pap. 4.95 (ISBN 0-87663-559-1, Pica Pr). Universe.
Diagram Group. Sex: A User's Manual. (Illus.). 196p. 1981. 14.95 (ISBN 0-399-12574-4, Perigee); pap. 6.95 (ISBN 0-399-50517-2). Putnam.
Fitzgerald, Peter J. The Basis of Sex Education. 1981. 7.95 (ISBN 0-533-04636-X). Vantage.
Gelinas, Paul. Coping with Sexual Problems. (Coping with Ser.). 140p. 1981. lib. bdg. 7.97 (ISBN 0-8239-0542-X). Rosen Pr.
Kahan, Jane M., et al. Understanding Your Sexuality. (Illus.). 1980. pap. text ed. 104.00 (ISBN 0-89290-100-4, A793-SATC). Soc for Visual.
Kelly, Gary F., ed. Good Sex: The Healthy Man's Guide to Sexual Fulfillment. 1981. pap. 2.95 (ISBN 0-451-09572-3, Sig). NAL.
National Information Center for Special Education Materials (NICSEM) NICSEM Mini-Index to Special Education Materials: Family Life & Sex Education. LC 80-82540. 1980. pap. 16.00 (ISBN 0-89320-043-3). Univ SC Natl Info.
Sex Education Notebook. (Illus.). 59p. (Orig.). 1981. pap. 7.00 (ISBN 0-686-28927-7). Mor Mac.
Shirley, Grace. Shirley's Twentieth Century Lovers' Guide. 160p. (Orig.). 1981. pap. 2.50 (ISBN 0-523-40868-4). Pinnacle Bks.
Solutions for Today's Sex Problems & Prostitution. Date not set. 3.70x (ISBN 0-686-68074-X). C C Brown Pub.
Symons, Donald. The Evolution of Human Sexuality. 368p. 1981. pap. 6.95 (ISBN 0-19-502907-0, GB 638, OPB). Oxford U Pr.
SEX INSTRUCTION-BIBLIOGRAPHY
Darnbrough, Ann & Kinrade, Derek. Directory of Sexual Advisory Services (in Great Britain) 128p. 1980. 24.00x (ISBN 0-85941-162-1, Pub. by Woodhead-Faulkner England); pap. 9.00. State Mutual Bk.
SEX INSTRUCTION FOR CHILDREN AND YOUTH
Bell, Ruth, et al. Changing Bodies, Changing Lives: A Book for Teens on Sex & Relationships. (Illus.). 1981. 14.95 (ISBN 0-394-50304-X); pap. 7.95 (ISBN 0-394-73632-X). Random.
Berenstain, Stan & Berenstain, Jan. How to Teach Your Children About Sex. 1980. pap. 2.95. Ballantine.
Cooney, Nancy H. Sex, Sexuality, & You: A Handbook for Growing Christians. 100p. (Orig.). 1980. pap. text ed. 3.50 (ISBN 0-697-01741-9); tchr's resource guide 0.75 (ISBN 0-697-01742-7). Wm C Brown.
Griffin, Glen C. You Were Smaller Than a Dot. LC 72-90685. 31p. (gr. k-6). 1980. pap. 3.95 (ISBN 0-87747-817-1). Deseret Bk.
Lieberman, E. J. & Peck, Ellen. Sex & Birth Control: A Guide for the Young. rev. ed. LC 79-7094. (Illus.). 304p. 1981. 10.95 (ISBN 0-690-01837-1, HarpT). Har-Row.
Olsen, Arvis J. Sexuality: Guidelines for Teenagers. 80p. (Orig.). 1981. pap. 1.95 (ISBN 0-8010-6674-3). Baker Bk.
Palau, Luis. Sexo y Juventud. 83p. (Orig., Span.). (YA) 1974. pap. 1.95 (ISBN 0-89922-032-0). Edit Caribe.
Pierson, Jack D. What a Teenager Ought to Know About Sex & God. (Teenager's Essential Education Library). (Illus.). 147p. 1981. 21.75 (ISBN 0-89266-288-3). Am Classical Coll Pr.
Shapiro, Constance H. Adolescent Pregnancy Prevention: School-Community Cooperation. (Illus.). 144p. 1981. price not set (ISBN 0-398-04463-5); pap. price not set (ISBN 0-398-04464-3). C C Thomas.
SEX ORGANS
see Generative Organs
SEX PERVERSION
see Sexual Deviation
SEX RESEARCH
Masters, William H., et al, eds. Ethical Issues in Sex Therapy & Research, Vol. 2. 456p. 1980. text ed. 22.50 (ISBN 0-316-54989-4). Little.
SEX ROLE
Howe, Florence & Rothermich, John A., eds. The Sex-Role Cycle: Socialization from Infancy to Old Age. (Women's Lives - Women's Work Ser.). 192p. (Orig.). 1980. pap. text ed. 4.23. Webster-McGraw.
Lewis, Robert A., ed. Men in Difficult Times: Masculinity Today & Tomorrow. (Illus.). 352p. 1981. 14.95 (ISBN 0-13-574418-0, Spectrum); pap. 7.95 (ISBN 0-13-574400-8). P-H.
Lichtenstein, Grace. Machisma: Women & Daring. LC 79-7114. 360p. 1981. 14.95 (ISBN 0-385-15109-8). Doubleday.
Loudin, Jo. The Hoax of Romance. (Transformation Ser.). 320p. 1981. 12.95 (ISBN 0-13-392456-4, Spec); pap. 6.95 (ISBN 0-13-392449-1). P-H.
Nowak, Mariette. Eve's Rib. 272p. 1981. pap. 5.95 (ISBN 0-312-27240-5). St Martin.
Romer, Nancy. The Sex-Role Cycle: Socialization from Infancy to Old Age. (Women's Lives - Women's Work Ser.). (Illus.). 190p. (Orig.). (gr. 11-12). 1981. pap. 5.95 (ISBN 0-912670-69-X). Feminist Pr.
Sanday, Peggy R. Female Power & Male Dominance: On the Origins of Sexual Inequality. LC 80-18461. (Illus.). 256p. Date not set. text ed. price not set (ISBN 0-521-23618-5); pap. text ed. price not set (ISBN 0-521-28075-3). Cambridge U Pr.
Schaffer, Kay R. Sex Roles & Human Behavior. (Psychology Ser.). 448p. 1981. text ed. 14.95 (ISBN 0-87626-807-6). Winthrop.
Yorburg, Betty. Sexual Identity: Sex Roles & Social Change. LC 80-22489. 240p. 1981. Repr. text ed. 8.50 (ISBN 0-89874-265-X). Krieger.
SEX THERAPY
G-Jo Institute. Sexual Pleasure Enhancement Program. 1980. pap. 4.50 (ISBN 0-916878-12-0). Falkynor Bks.
Masters, William H., et al, eds. Ethical Issues in Sex Therapy & Research, Vol. 2. 456p. 1980. text ed. 22.50 (ISBN 0-316-54989-4). Little.
Schiller, Patricia. The Sex Profession. 252p. 1981. pap. 8.00 (ISBN 0-88416-340-7). PSG Pub.
--The Sex Profession: What Sex Therapy Can Do. 250p. (Orig.). 1980. 11.00 (ISBN 0-937532-00-2); pap. 8.00 (ISBN 0-937532-01-0). Chilmark Hse.
SEXUAL BEHAVIOR
see Sex; Sex Customs; Sexual Ethics
SEXUAL BEHAVIOR, PSYCHOLOGY OF
see Sex (Psychology)
SEXUAL CRIMES
see Sex Crimes
SEXUAL DEVIATION
see also Sex Therapy
Barry, Kathleen. Female Sexual Slavery. 336p. 1981. pap. 3.95 (ISBN 0-380-54213-7, 54213, Discus). Avon.
Cox, Daniel J. & Daitzman, Reid J., eds. Exhibitionism Description, Assessment, & Treatment. 1980. lib. bdg. 32.50 (ISBN 0-8240-7033-X). Garland Pub.
Wilson, Glenn & Gosselin, Chris. Sexual Variations: Fetishism, Sadomasochism & Transvestism. 1981. 12.95 (ISBN 0-671-24624-0). S&S.
SEXUAL DISCRIMINATION
see Sex Discrimination
SEXUAL DISEASES
see Venereal Diseases
SEXUAL ETHICS
see also Birth Control; Contraception; Dating (Social Customs); Prostitution; Sex and Religion; Sex Crimes
Langone, John. Like, Love, Lust: A View of Sex & Sexuality. 144p. 1981. pap. 2.25 (ISBN 0-380-54189-0, 54189). Avon.
SEXUAL OFFENSES
see Sex Crimes
SEXUAL ORGANS
see Generative Organs
SEXUAL PERVERSION
see Sexual Deviation
SEXUAL PSYCHOLOGY
see Sex (Psychology)
SHAFTESBURY, ANTHONY ASHLEY COOPER, 3RD EARL OF, 1671-1713
Bernstein, John A. Shaftsbury, Rousseau & Kant: An Introduction to the Conflict Between Aesthetic & Moral Values in Modern Thought. LC 78-75190. 192p. 1980. write for info. (ISBN 0-8386-2351-4). Fairleigh Dickinson.
SHAKERS
Hunez, Jean M., ed. Gifts of Power: The Writings of Rebecca Jackson, Black Visionary, Shaker Eldress. (Illus.). 370p. 1981. lib. bdg. 20.00x (ISBN 0-87023-299-1). U of Mass Pr.
Melcher, Marguerite F. Shaker Adventure. 1980. pap. 6.00 (ISBN 0-937942-08-1). Shaker Mus.
Williams, Richard E. Called & Chosen: The Story of Mother Rebecca Jackson & the Philadelphia Shakers. LC 80-25498. (ATLA Monograph Ser.: No. 17). 193p. 1981. 11.00 (ISBN 0-8108-1382-3). Scarecrow.
SHAKESPEARE, WILLIAM, 1564-1616
Dello Buno, Carmen J. Rare Early Essays on William Shakespeare: Third Series. 206p. 1980. lib. bdg. 17.50 (ISBN 0-8482-3651-3). Norwood Edns.

Ingleby, Clement M. Shakespeare's Bones. 48p. 1980. Repr. of 1883 ed. lib. bdg. 10.00 (ISBN 0-89987-400-2). Darby Bks.

Sykes, Claud W. Alias William Shakespeare? 221p. 1980. Repr. of 1947 ed. lib. bdg. 25.00 (ISBN 0-89987-764-8). Century Bookbindery.

Young, George M. Today & Yesterday: Tennyson, Burke, Thackeray, Shakespeare. 312p. 1980. lib. bdg. 15.00 (ISBN 0-8482-3125-2). Norwood Edns.

SHAKESPEARE, WILLIAM, 1564-1616–ANTONY AND CLEOPATRA

Von Steppat, Michael. The Critical Reception of Shakespeare's "Antony & Cleopatra" from 1607 to 1905. (Bochum Studies in English: No. 9). 619p. 1980. text ed. 45.75x (ISBN 90-6032-188-X). Humanities.

SHAKESPEARE, WILLIAM, 1564-1616–AS YOU LIKE IT

Chaddock, Ron. As You Like It. LC 80-82091. (Understand Ye Shakespeare Ser.). 1980. pap. 8.95 deluxe ed. (ISBN 0-933350-34-1). Morse Pr.

SHAKESPEARE, WILLIAM, 1564-1616–AUTOBIOGRAPHY

see Shakespeare, William, 1564-1616–Biography

SHAKESPEARE, WILLIAM, 1564-1616–BIOGRAPHY

Ewen, Alfred. Bell's Miniature Series of Great Writers: Shakespeare. 128p. 1980. Repr. of 1904 ed. lib. bdg. 20.00 (ISBN 0-89984-178-3). Century Bookbindery.

Schoenbaum, S. William Shakespeare: Records & Images. (Illus.). 316p. 1981. 98.00 (ISBN 0-19-520234-1). Oxford U Pr.

SHAKESPEARE, WILLIAM, 1564-1616–CHARACTERS

Donovan, John A. Dogs in Shakespeare. 9.95 (ISBN 0-87714-074-X). Green Hill.

Kahn, Coppelia. Man's Estate: Masculine Identity in Shakespeare. 200p. 1981. 16.00x (ISBN 0-520-03899-1). U of Cal Pr.

SHAKESPEARE, WILLIAM, 1564-1616–COMEDIES

Felheim, Marvin & Traci, Philip. Realism in Shakespeare's Romantic Comedies: "O Heavenly Mingle". LC 80-5580. 239p. 1980. lib. bdg. 17.55 (ISBN 0-8191-1282-8); pap. text ed. 9.75 (ISBN 0-8191-1283-6). U Pr of Amer.

Makaryk, Irene R. Comic Justice in Shakespeare's Comedies, Vol. 2. (Jacobean Drama Studies: No.91). 259p. 1980. pap. text ed. 25.00 (ISBN 0-391-02197-4). Humanities.

Wheeler, Richard P. Shakespeare's Development & Problem Comedies: Turn & Counter-Turn. 275p. 1981. 18.50x (ISBN 0-520-03902-5). U of Cal Pr.

SHAKESPEARE, WILLIAM, 1564-1616–COMMENTARIES

see Shakespeare, William, 1564-1616–Criticism and Interpretation

SHAKESPEARE, WILLIAM, 1564-1616–CRITICISM AND INTERPRETATION

Bertram, Paul. White Spaces in Shakespeare. 112p. 1981. 12.50x (ISBN 0-934958-01-7); pap. 8.00x (ISBN 0-934958-02-5). Arete Pr.

Cecil, David. Poets & Story-Tellers. 201p. 1980. Repr. of 1968 ed. lib. bdg. 30.00 (ISBN 0-8495-0852-5). Arden Lib.

Comparative Literature Symposium, No. 12. Shakespeare's Art from a Comparative Perspective: Proceedings. Aycock, Wendell M., ed. (Proceedings of the Comparative Literature Symposium). (Illus.). 197p. (Orig.). 1981. pap. write for info. (ISBN 0-89672-081-0). Tex Tech Pr.

Ewen, Alfred. Bell's Miniature Series of Great Writers: Shakespeare. 128p. 1980. Repr. of 1904 ed. lib. bdg. 20.00 (ISBN 0-89984-178-3). Century Bookbindery.

Ford, Harold. Shakespeare, His Ethical Teaching. 112p. 1980. Repr. lib. bdg. 30.00 (ISBN 0-89987-257-3). Century Bookbindery.

French, Marilyn. Shakespeare's Division of Experience. LC 80-23147. 384p. 1981. 15.95 (ISBN 0-671-44865-X). Summit Bks.

Marsh, Derick R., ed. The Recurring Miracle. 208p. 1980. pap. 14.00x (ISBN 0-424-00085-7, Pub. by Sydney U Pr Australia). Intl Schol Bk Serv.

Rabkin, Norman. Shakespeare & the Problem of Meaning. LC 80-18538. 1981. lib. bdg. 16.00x (ISBN 0-226-70177-8). U of Chicago Pr.

Slights, Camille W. The Casuistical Tradition in Shakespeare, Donne, Herbert, & Milton. LC 80-8576. 352p. 1981. 26.50x (ISBN 0-691-06463-6). Princeton U Pr.

Stoll, Edgar E. Shakespeare Studies: Historical & Comparative in Method. 502p. 1980. lib. bdg. 50.00 (ISBN 0-89984-410-3). Century Bookbindery.

SHAKESPEARE, WILLIAM, 1564-1616–HAMLET

Charlton, Henry B. Hamlet. 50p. 1980. Repr. of 1942 ed. lib. bdg. 6.00 (ISBN 0-8492-3865-X). R West.

Granville-Baker, Harley. Preface to Shakespeare: Volume 1, Hamlet. 1977. pap. 10.50 (ISBN 0-7134-2050-2, Pub. by Batsford England). David & Charles.

Venable, Emerson. The Hamlet Problem & Its Solution. 107p. 1980. Repr. of 1912 ed. lib. bdg. 20.00 (ISBN 0-8492-2835-2). R West.

SHAKESPEARE, WILLIAM, 1564-1616–KING LEAR

Colman, E. A., ed. King Lear. (The Challis Shakespeare Ser). 1981. pap. 3.50x (ISBN 0-686-68844-9, Pub. by Sydney U Pr Australia). Intl Schol Bk Serv.

Muir, K., ed. Shakespeare Survey: King Lear, No. 33. LC 49-1639. (Shakespeare Surveys Ser.). (Illus.). 230p. Date not set. 39.50 (ISBN 0-521-23249-X). Cambridge U Pr.

SHAKESPEARE, WILLIAM, 1564-1616–KING LEAR–BIBLIOGRAPHY

Champion, Larry S. King Lear: An Annotated Bibliography. LC 80-8489. (The Garland Shakespeare Bibliographies). 900p. 1980. lib. bdg. 100.00 (ISBN 0-8240-9498-0). Garland Pub.

SHAKESPEARE, WILLIAM, 1564-1616–KNOWLEDGE AND LEARNING

Nutt, Alfred T. The Fairy Mythology of Shakespeare. 49p. 1980. Repr. of 1900 ed. lib. bdg. 10.00 (ISBN 0-8495-4019-4). Arden Lib.

Yearsley, Percival M. Doctors in Elizabethan Drama. 128p. 1980. Repr. of 1933 ed. lib. bdg. 20.00 (ISBN 0-8495-6101-9). Arden Lib.

SHAKESPEARE, WILLIAM, 1564-1616–LANGUAGE

Cercignani, Fausto. Shakespeare's Works & Elizabethan Pronunciation. 448p. 1981. 74.00 (ISBN 0-19-811937-2). Oxford U Pr.

Dent, R. W. Shakespeare's Proverbial Language: An Index. 378p. 1981. 24.50x (ISBN 0-520-03894-0). U of Cal Pr.

SHAKESPEARE, WILLIAM, 1564-1616–LOVE'S LABOUR'S LOST

Chaddick, Ron. Love's Labor Lost. LC 80-82093. (Understand Ye Shakespeare Ser.). 1980. pap. 8.95 deluxe ed. (ISBN 0-933350-35-X). Morse Pr.

SHAKESPEARE, WILLIAM, 1564-1616–MACBETH

Chaddock, Ron. Tragedy of Macbeth. LC 80-82092. (Understand Ye Shaskespeare Ser.). 1980. pap. 8.95 deluxe ed. (ISBN 0-933350-33-3). Morse Pr.

Riemer, A. P., ed. Macbeth. 1980. pap. 3.50x (ISBN 0-424-00081-4, Pub. by Sydney U Pr Australia). Intl Schol Bk Serv.

SHAKESPEARE, WILLIAM, 1564-1616–POETICAL WORKS

Hibbard, G. R. The Making of Shakespeare's Dramatic Poetry. 184p. 1981. 17.50x (ISBN 0-8020-2400-9); pap. 7.50 (ISBN 0-8020-6424-8). U of Toronto Pr.

SHAKESPEARE, WILLIAM, 1564-1616–QUOTATIONS

Dent, R. W. Shakespeare's Proverbial Language: An Index. 378p. 1981. 24.50x (ISBN 0-520-03894-0). U of Cal Pr.

SHAKESPEARE, WILLIAM, 1564-1616–ROMEO AND JULIET

Nickelsen, John R. Romeo & Juliet: A Study Text. LC 79-26683. (Illus.). 1980. pap. text ed. 5.25 (ISBN 0-684-16497-3, SSP 46, ScribC). Scribner.

SHAKESPEARE, WILLIAM, 1564-1616–SONNETS

Smith, Hallett. The Tension of the Lyre: Poetry in Shakespeare's Sonnets. (Illus.). 180p. 1981. price not set (ISBN 0-87328-114-4). Huntington Lib.

SHAKESPEARE, WILLIAM, 1564-1616–STAGE HISTORY

Gurr, A. The Shakespearean Stage, 1574-1642. 2nd ed. LC 80-40085. (Illus.). 220p. 1981. 49.50 (ISBN 0-521-23029-2); pap. 12.95 (ISBN 0-521-29772-9). Cambridge U Pr.

SHAKESPEARE, WILLIAM, 1564-1616–STAGE-SETTING AND SCENERY

see Shakespeare, William, 1564-1616–Stage History

SHAKESPEARE, WILLIAM, 1564-1616–STYLE

Hibbard, G. R. The Making of Shakespeare's Dramatic Poetry. 184p. 1981. 17.50x (ISBN 0-8020-2400-9); pap. 7.50 (ISBN 0-8020-6424-8). U of Toronto Pr.

Sacks, Elizabeth. Shakespeare's Images of Pregnancy. 1980. 16.95 (ISBN 0-312-71595-1). St Martin.

Schmidgall, Gary. Shakespeare & the Courtly Aesthetic. (Illus.). 344p. 1981. 22.50x (ISBN 0-520-04130-5). U of Cal Pr.

SHAKESPEARE, WILLIAM, 1564-1616–TEMPEST

Wilkes, G. A., ed. The Tempest. (The Challis Shakespeare Ser.). 1981. pap. 3.50x (ISBN 0-686-68845-7, Pub. by Sydney U Pr Australia). Intl Schol Bk Serv.

SHAKESPEARE, WILLIAM, 1564-1616–TRAGEDIES

Bayley, John. Shakespeare & Tragedy. 224p. 1981. price not set (ISBN 0-7100-0632-2); pap. price not set (ISBN 0-7100-0607-1). Routledge & Kegan.

Fairchild, Arthur H. Shakespeare & the Tragic Theme. 145p. 1980. Repr. of 1944 ed. lib. bdg. 25.00 (ISBN 0-89987-258-1). Darby Bks.

SHAMANISM

see also Medicine-Man

Huhm, Halla Pai. Kut: Korean Shamanist Rituals. 102p. 1980. 12.50 (ISBN 0-930878-18-3). Hollym Intl.

SHANTUNG, CHINA

Wood, Ge-Zay. Shantung Question: A Study in Diplomacy & World Politics. (Studies in Chinese History Civilization). 1977. 21.50 (ISBN 0-89093-089-9). U Pubns Amer.

SHAPE DISCRIMINATION

see Form Perception

SHAPIRO, KARL JAY, 1913- –BIBLIOGRAPHY

Reino, Joseph. Karl Shapiro. (United States Authors Ser.: No. 404). 1981. lib. bdg. 12.95 (ISBN 0-8057-7333-9). Twayne.

SHARES OF STOCK

see Stocks

SHARKS

Hovey, Eddy. Shark Gourmet Seafood of the Future. Sharp, George, ed. LC 80-52109. (Illus.). 111p. pap. 6.95 (ISBN 0-937496-00-6). Sea Harvest.

SHARKS–JUVENILE LITERATURE

Blumberg, Rhoda. Sharks. 1980. pap. 1.75 (ISBN 0-380-49247-4, 49247, Camelot). Avon.

SHARKS–AFRICA

Wallett, Tim. Shark Attack & Treatment of Victims in Southern African Waters. 1980. 25.00x (Pub. by Bailey & Swinton South Africa). State Mutual Bk.

SHAW, GEORGE BERNARD, 1856-1950

Hamon, Augustin F. The Technique of Bernard Shaw's Plays. 70p. 1980. Repr. of 1912 ed. lib. bdg. 12.50 (ISBN 0-8492-5274-1). R West.

Silver, Arnold. Bernard Shaw: The Darker Side. LC 79-92454. (Illus.). 384p. 1981. text ed. 25.00x (ISBN 0-8047-1091-0). Stanford U Pr.

SHAWNEE INDIANS

see Indians of North America–Eastern States

SHEAR (MECHANICS)

Bradbury, J. S., et al, eds. Turbulent Shear Flows, Two. (Illus.). 480p. 1980. 68.00 (ISBN 0-387-10067-9). Springer-Verlag.

SHEEP

Cattle, Sheep, & Hogs. (Country Home Ser.). 96p. 2.95 (ISBN 0-88453-005-1). Berkshire Traveller.

Juergenson, Elwood M. Approved Practices in Sheep Production. 4th ed. (Illus.). (gr. 9-12). 1981. 13.00 (ISBN 0-8134-2163-2, 2163); text ed. 9.75x. Interstate.

The Management & Diseases of Sheep. 469p. 1981. 85.00 (ISBN 0-85198-451-7, CAB 9, Cab). Unipub.

Prolific Tropical Sheep. (FAO Animal Production & Health Paper Ser.: No. 17). 124p. 1981. pap. 7.00 (ISBN 92-5-100845-0, F2107, FAO). Unipub.

SHEET-METAL WORK

Short Course in Sheet Metal Shop Theory. 128p. 1980. 12.50 (ISBN 0-912914-05-X). Practical Pubns.

SHELL PARAKEET

see Budgerigars

SHELLEY, PERCY BYSSHE, 1792-1822

Cronin, Richard. Shelley's Poetic Thoughts. 1981. 22.50 (ISBN 0-312-71664-8). St Martin.

Dello Buono, Carmen J. Rare Early Essays on Percy Bysshe Shelley. 220p. 1981. lib. bdg. 22.50 (ISBN 0-8482-3653-X). Norwood Edns.

Jack, Adolphus A. Shelley, an Essay. 127p. 1980. Repr. of 1904 ed. lib. bdg. 15.00 (ISBN 0-8492-1368-1). R West.

SHELLFISH

see also Crustacea; Mollusks

Recommended International Code of Hygienic Practice for Molluscan Shellfish. 22p. 1980. pap. 5.25 (ISBN 92-5-100893-0, F1949, FAO). Unipub.

Tedone, David. Complete Shellfisherman's Guide. (Illus.). 200p. 1981. pap. 7.95 (ISBN 0-933614-09-8). Peregrine Pr.

SHELLFISH FISHERIES

Milne, P. H. Fish & Shellfish Farming in Coastal Waters. (Illus.). 208p. 24.75 (ISBN 0-85238-022-4, FN). Unipub.

Nowak, W. S. The Marketing of Shellfish. (Illus.). 280p. 15.25 (ISBN 0-85238-010-0, FN). Unipub.

SHELLS

see also Mollusks

Gordon, Julius & Weeks, Townsend E. Seashells of the S. E. Coast. Campbell, Margaret, ed. (Illus.). 50p. (Orig.). 1981. pap. 4.95 (ISBN 0-88839-080-7). Hancock Hse.

Rehder, Herald A. The Audubon Society Field Guide to North American Seashells. LC 80-84239. 864p. 1981. 9.95 (ISBN 0-394-51913-2). Knopf.

SHELLS (ENGINEERING)

Wilby, C. B. Design Graphs for Concrete Shell Roofs. (Illus.). xii, 148p. 1980. 37.50x (ISBN 0-85334-899-5). Burgess-Intl Ideas.

SHEOL

see Hell

SHERIDAN, RICHARD BRINSLEY BUTLER, 1751-1816

Durant, Jack D. Richard Brinsley Sheridan: A Reference Guide. (Reference Books Ser.). 1981. lib. bdg. 30.00 (ISBN 0-8161-8146-2). G K Hall.

Sigmond, G. G. The Life of the Right Honourable Richard Brinsley Sheridan. 206p. 1980. Repr. of 1848 ed. lib. bdg. 30.00 (ISBN 0-8414-8049-4). Folcroft.

SHERMAN ANTITRUST LAW, 1890

Letwin, William. Law & Economic Policy in America: The Evolution of the Sherman Antitrust Act. LC 80-21868. xi, 304p. 1980. Repr. of 1965 ed. lib. bdg. 27.50x (ISBN 0-313-22651-2, LELE). Greenwood.

SHETLAND ISLANDS

Graham, John. The Shetland Dictionary. 144p. 1980. 13.95x (ISBN 0-906191-33-5, Pub. by Thule Pr England). Intl Schol Bk Serv.

Gronneberg, Roy. Island Futures. 96p. 1980. pap. 5.95 (ISBN 0-686-68846-5, Pub. by Thule Pr England). Intl Schol Bk Serv.

Linklater, Eric. Orkney & Shetland: An Historical, Geographical, Social & Scenic Survey. 3rd ed. Nicolson, James R., rev. by. (Illus.). 285p. 1980. 20.00x (ISBN 0-7091-8142-6). Intl Pubns Serv.

Smith, Hans, intro. by. Second Report of the Commissioners Appointed to Inquire into the Truck System (Shetland), 1892. 1980. pap. 10.95x (ISBN 0-906191-06-8, Pub. by Thule Pr England). Intl Schol Bk Serv.

Spence, David. Shetland's Living Landscape. 160p. 1980. 17.95x (ISBN 0-906191-14-9, Pub. by Thule Pr England). Intl Schol Bk Serv.

SHIATSU

Blake, Michael. Natural Healer's Acupressure Handbook: G-Jo Fingertip Technique. (Illus.). 1977. 9.95 (ISBN 0-916878-06-6). Falkynor Bks.

Lawson-Wood, D. & Lawson-Wood, J. First Aid at Your Fingertips. 56p. 1976. pap. 4.00x (ISBN 0-8464-1009-5). Beekman Pubs.

SHIATZU

see Shiatsu

SHIFT SYSTEMS

Reinberg, A., et al, eds. Night & Shift Work-Biological & Social Aspects: Proceedings of the Vth International Symposium on Night and Shift Work-Scientific Committee on Shift Work of the Permanent Commission & International Association on Occupational Health (PCIAIH, Rouen, 12-16 May 1980. (Illus.). 516p. 1981. 80.00 (ISBN 0-08-025516-7). Pergamon.

SHIP-BUILDING

see also Boat-Building; Marine Engines; Naval Architecture; Ship Building Workers; Ship Models; Ships, Iron and Steel; Warships

also particular types of vessels, e.g. Steamboats, Torpedo-Boats

Code for the Construction & Equipment of Ships Carrying Dangerous Chemicals in Bulk. 86p. 1977. 11.00 (IMCO). Unipub.

Wingrove, Gerald A. The Techniques of Ship Modelling. (Illus.). 133p. 1974. 12.50x (ISBN 0-85242-366-7). Intl Pubns Serv.

SHIP-BUILDING–HISTORY

Brogger, W. W. & Shetelig, Hakon. The Viking Ships. (Illus.). 196p. 1980. 27.50 (ISBN 0-906191-40-8, Pub. by Thule Pr England). Intl Schol Bk Serv.

SHIP BUILDING WORKERS

Timm, Simon, ed. Directory of Shipowners, Shipbuilders & Marine Engineers 1980. 78th ed. LC 25-4199. 1514p. 1980. 55.00x (ISBN 0-617-00301-7). Intl Pubns Serv.

SHIP CAPTAINS

see Shipmasters

SHIP HANDLING

see Boats and Boating; Yachts and Yachting

SHIP MODELS

Powell, James D. Building Plastic Ship Models. (Illus.). 350p. 1981. cancelled (ISBN 0-498-02286-2). A S Barnes.

Wingrove, Gerald A. The Techniques of Ship Modelling. (Illus.). 133p. 1974. 12.50x (ISBN 0-85242-366-7). Intl Pubns Serv.

SHIP PILOTS

see Pilots and Pilotage

SHIP REGISTERS–GREAT LAKES

Greenwood, John O. Namesakes Nineteen Fifty-Six to Ninety Eighty. 1981. casebound 27.00 (ISBN 0-686-69468-6). Freshwater.

SHIP WAKES

see Wakes (Fluid Dynamics)

SHIPMASTERS

Timm, Simon, ed. Directory of Shipowners, Shipbuilders & Marine Engineers 1980. 78th ed. LC 25-4199. 1514p. 1980. 55.00x (ISBN 0-617-00301-7). Intl Pubns Serv.

SHIPMENT OF GOODS

see also Breakage, Shrinkage, etc. (Commerce); Packaging

Kemp, J. F. & Young, P. Notes on Cargo Work. 4th ed. (Kemp & Young Ser.). (Illus., Orig.). 1981. pap. text ed. 9.50x (ISBN 0-540-07332-6). Sheridan.

Supplement Number One to the Nineteen Seventy-Seven Edition of the Code for the Construction & Equipment of Ships Carrying Dangerous Chemicals in Bulk. 24p. 1978. 7.00 (IMCO). Unipub.

Supplement to the Code of Safe Practice for Ships Carrying Timber Deck Cargoes. 18p. 1979. 7.00 (IMCO). Unipub.

Willerton, P. F. Basic Shiphandling for Masters, Mates & Pilots. 152p. 1981. 17.50x (ISBN 0-540-07333-4). Sheridan.

SHIPPING

see also Coastwise Navigation; Free Ports and Zones; Inland Water Transportation; Insurance, Marine; Maritime Law; Steamboats and Steamboat Lines

Amendment Number One to the Fourth Edition of Ship's Routing. 36p. 1979. 11.00 (IMCO). Unipub.

Gold, Edgar. Maritime Transport: The Evolution of International Marine Policy & Shipping Law. LC 80-8641. (Illus.). 1981. write for info. (ISBN 0-669-04338-9). Lexington Bks.

OECD. Maritime Transport Nineteen Seventy-Nine. (Illus.). 151p. (Orig.). 1980. pap. text ed. 10.50x (ISBN 92-64-12122-6). OECD.

Review of Maritime Transport, 1977. 60p. 1979. pap. 7.00 (ISBN 0-686-68969-0, 79/2D7, UN). Unipub.

Watt, D. C. Greenwich Forum VI: Britain & the Sea: the Challenges for Shipping in the 1990's. 1981. text ed. write for info. (ISBN 0-86103-049-4, Westbury Hse). Butterworths.

SHIPPING–HISTORY

Musk, George. Canadian Pacific: The Story of the Famous Shipping Line. (Illus.). 272p. 1981. 45.00 (ISBN 0-7153-7968-2). David & Charles.

Worden, William L. Cargoes: Matson's First Century in the Pacific. 208p. 1981. 12.95 (ISBN 0-8248-0708-1). U Pr of Hawaii.

SHIPPING–LAW

see Maritime Law

SHIPPING–GREAT BRITAIN

Watt, D. C. Greenwich Forum VI: Britain & the Sea: the Challenges for Shipping in the 1990's. 1981. text ed. write for info. (ISBN 0-86103-049-4, Westbury Hse). Butterworths.

SHIPPING–INDIA

Trivedi, H. M. Indian Shipping in Perspective. 540p. 1981. 40.00x (ISBN 0-7069-1202-0, Pub. by Vikas India). Advent Bk.

SHIPPING–PACIFIC OCEAN

Worden, William L. Cargoes: Matson's First Century in the Pacific. 208p. 1981. 12.95 (ISBN 0-8248-0708-1). U Pr of Hawaii.

SHIPPING–UNITED STATES

Sletmo, Gunnar K. & Williams, Ernest W., Jr. Liner Conferences in the Container Age: U. S. Policy at Sea. LC 80-70838. (Studies of the Modern Corporation). (Illus.). 1981. 29.95 (ISBN 0-02-929200-X). Free Pr.

SHIPPING, INLAND WATER

see Inland Water Transportation

SHIPS

see also Boats and Boating; Fishing Boats; Merchant Ships; Navigation; Packets; Sailing; Sailing Ships; Schooners; Seamanship; Steamboats and Steamboat Lines; Submarines; Tankers; Warships; Yachts and Yachting

also names of ships, and headings beginning with the word Ship

The Saturday Evening Post Book of the Sea & Ships. LC 78-61519. (Illus.). 1978. 11.95 (ISBN 0-89387-023-4). Sat Eve Post.

Walton, T. Know Your Own Ship. Baxter, B., ed. 373p. 1970. 28.00x (ISBN 0-85264-151-6, Pub. by Griffin England). State Mutual Bk.

SHIPS–AUTOMATION

Datz, I. Mortimer. Power Transmission & Automation for Ships & Submersibles. (Illus.). 190p. 30.00 (ISBN 0-85238-074-7, FN). Unipub.

SHIPS–CONSTRUCTION

see Ship-Building

SHIPS–FIRES AND FIRE PREVENTION

Recommendation Concerning Fire Safety Requirements for Cargo Ships. 25p. 1976. 7.00 (IMCO). Unipub.

SHIPS–MAINTENANCE AND REPAIR

Thomas, B. E. Management of Shipboard Maintenance. (Illus.). 143p. 1981. 18.50x (ISBN 0-540-07354-7). Sheridan.

SHIPS–OFFICERS

see Shipmasters

SHIPS–PICTORIAL WORKS

Miller, Willam, Jr. The Great Luxury Liners, 1927-1952: A Photographic Record. (Illus.). 160p. Date not set. pap. 6.95 (ISBN 0-486-24056-8). Dover.

SHIPS–RADIO

see Radio in Navigation

SHIPS, CARGO

see Cargo Ships

SHIPS, ELECTRICITY ON

see Electricity on Ships

SHIPS, IRON AND STEEL

Emmerson, George S. SS Great Eastern: The Greatest Iron Ship. LC 80-69345. (Illus.). 216p. 1981. 25.50 (ISBN 0-7153-8054-0). David & Charles.

SHIP'S DOCUMENTS

see Ships Papers

SHIPS PAPERS

Filby, P. William, ed. Bibliography of Ship Passenger Lists (1538-1900) Being a Guide to Published Lists of Immigrants to the United States & Canada. 160p. 1981. 44.00 (ISBN 0-8103-1098-8). Gale.

SHIP'S STABILITY

see Stability of Ships

SHIPWORKERS

see Ship Building Workers

SHIPWRECKS

see also Life-Saving; Survival (After Airplane Accidents, Shipwrecks, etc.);

also names of wrecked vessels, e.g. Titanic (Steamship)

Brown, Walter & Anderson, Norman. Sea Disasters. LC 80-27156. (Illus.). 112p. (gr. 4-7). 1981. PLB 7.95 (ISBN 0-201-09154-2, 9154, A-W Childrens). A-W.

Heffernan, Thomas F. Stove by a Whale: Owen Chase & the Essex. 256p. 1981. 19.95 (ISBN 0-8195-5052-3). Wesleyan U Pr.

Larn, Richard. Shipwrecks of Great Britain & Ireland. LC 80-68898. (Illus.). 1981. 24.00 (ISBN 0-7153-7491-5). David & Charles.

Snow, Edward R. Sea Disasters & Inland Catastrophes. LC 80-23876. (Illus.). 288p. 1980. 9.95 (ISBN 0-396-07908-3). Dodd.

SHIPYARD WORKERS

see Ship Building Workers

SHIRLEY, JAMES, 1596-1666

Armstrong, Ray L. The Poems of James Shirley. 108p. 1980. Repr. of 1941 ed. lib. bdg. 27.50 (ISBN 0-8495-0062-1). Arden Lib.

SHOCK

see also Traumatism

Cowley, R. Adams & Trump, Benjamin F. Pathophysiology of Shock, Anoxia & Ischemia. 600p. 1981. write for info. (2149-4). Williams & Wilkins.

Third Annual Conference on Shock, Lake of the Ozarks, Missouri, June 1980. Advances in Shock Research, Vol. 5: Proceedings, Part One. Lefer, Allan M., ed. LC 79-63007. 150p. 1981. 26.00x (ISBN 0-8451-0604-X). A R Liss.

Third Annual Conference on Shock, Lake of the Ozarks, Missouri, June 1980, et al. Advances in Shock Research, Vol. 6: Proceedings, Part Two. Schumer, William & Spitzer, John J., eds. LC 79-63007. 150p. 1981. 26.00x (ISBN 0-8451-0605-8). A R Liss.

SHOCK (MECHANICS)

Reiff, D. D., ed. Component Support Snubbers: Design, Application & Testing. (PVP: No. 42). 130p. 1980. 10.00 (H00169). ASME.

SHOCK THERAPY

Palmer, Robert L., ed. Electroconvulsive Therapy: An Appraisal. (Illus.). 320p. 1981. text ed. 59.50x (ISBN 0-19-261266-2). Oxford U Pr.

Patterson, Michael M. & Kesner, Raymond P., eds. Electrical Stimulation Research Techniques. (Methods in Physiological Psychology Ser.). 1981. price not set (ISBN 0-12-547440-7). Acad Pr.

SHOE REPAIRING

see Boots and Shoes–Repairing

SHOOTING

Here are entered works on the use of firearms and the technique of shooting. Works on shooting game are entered under the heading Hunting.

see also Archery; Explosives; Firearms

Yochem, Barbara & Shelby, Peggy. Inner Shooting. 128p. 1981. 6.95 (ISBN 0-938826-03-4); pap. 3.95 (ISBN 0-938826-02-6). By by Products.

SHOP MANAGEMENT

see Factory Management

SHOP PRACTICE

see Machine-Shop Practice

SHOPLIFTING

Daykin, Leonard, ed. Loss Prevention: A Management Guide to Improving Retail Security. 1981. 19.50 (ISBN 0-911790-51-9). Prog Grocer.

SHOPPER'S GUIDES

see Consumer Education

SHOPPING CENTERS–GREAT BRITAIN

Bennison, D. J. & Davies, R. L. The Impact of Town Centre Shopping Schemes in Britain: Their Impact on Traditional Retail Environments. (Progress in Planning Ser.: Vol. 14, Part 1). (Illus.). 104p. 1980. pap. 13.50 (ISBN 0-08-026789-0). Pergamon.

SHOPS

see Stores, Retail

SHORE BIRDS

see also Sea Birds

Thiede, Walter. Water & Shore Birds. (Illus.). 144p. 1981. pap. 5.95 (ISBN 0-7011-2527-6, Pub. by Chatto-Bodley-Jonathan). Merrimack Bk Serv.

SHORING AND UNDERPINNING

Institute of Civil Engineers. Diaphragm Walls & Anchorages. 234p. 1980. 79.00x (ISBN 0-7277-0005-7, Pub. by Telford England). State Mutual Bk.

SHORT STORIES

Here are entered collections of short stories by various authors.

Abrahams, William. Prize Stories 1981: The O'henry Awards. 360p. 1981. text ed. 13.95 (ISBN 0-385-15977-3). Doubleday.

Clanton, Bruce. In Season & Out. LC 80-54272. 80p. 1981. pap. 6.25 (ISBN 0-89390-025-7). Resource Pubns.

Jose, Nicholas. The Possession of Amber. 285p. 1981. text ed. 13.25 (ISBN 0-7022-1537-6); pap. 7.25 (ISBN 0-7022-1538-4). U of Queensland Pr.

Kemp, Gene. Dog Days & Cat Naps. (Illus.). 110p. (gr. 2-5). 1981. 11.95 (ISBN 0-571-11595-0, Pub. by Faber & Faber). Merrimack Bk Serv.

Nabokov, Vladimir. Tyrants Destroyed & Other Stories. 252p. 1981. pap. 5.95 (ISBN 0-07-045718-2). McGraw.

Peake, Mervyn. Peake's Progress: Selected Writings & Drawings of Mervyn Peake. Gilmore, Maeve, ed. LC 80-83054. (Illus.). 576p. 1981. 25.00 (ISBN 0-87951-121-4). Overlook Pr.

Pritchett, V. S., ed. The Oxford Book of Short Stories. 750p. 1981. 19.95 (ISBN 0-19-214116-3). Oxford U Pr.

Reader's Digest. Stories Behind Everyday Things. 19.95 (ISBN 0-89577-068-7). Readers Digest Pr.

Robbin, Edward. Thursday's Child No. 2. LC 80-83893. (Anthology of Short Stories Ser.). (Illus.). 200p. (Orig.). 1980. pap. 5.00 (ISBN 0-9603518-2-5). Glen Pr.

Stegner, Wallace. The Women on the Wall. LC 80-22461. x, 277p. 1981. 16.50x (ISBN 0-8032-4111-9); pap. 5.50 (ISBN 0-8032-9110-8, BB-710, Bison). U of Nebr Pr.

West, Ralph E. Sea-Change: An Anthology of Short Stories. 228p. (Orig.). (gr. 11-12). 1980. pap. text ed. 4.50x (ISBN 0-88334-126-3). Ind Sch Pr.

Wilson, Barbara. Taking Sides. (Orig.). 1981. pap. 4.95 (ISBN 0-931188-09-1). Seal Pr WA.

Young, Ian, ed. On the Line: New Gay Fiction. 224p. 1981. 11.95 (ISBN 0-89594-048-5); pap. 5.95 (ISBN 0-89594-049-3). Crossing Pr.

SHORT STORIES–HISTORY AND CRITICISM

see Short Story

SHORT STORIES–JUVENILE LITERATURE

see also Children's Stories

Jameson, Mack & Nist, Al. The Last Good-Bye & Other Stories. Roderman, Winifred H., ed. (Read on - Write on Ser). (Illus.). 64p. (Orig.). (gr. 7-12). 1981. pap. text ed. 2.85 (ISBN 0-915510-55-3); tchrs. ed. free. Janus Bks.

--Time to Change & Other Stories. Roderman, Winifred H., ed. (Read on - Write on Ser.). (Illus.). (gr. 7-12). 1981. pap. text ed. 2.85 (ISBN 0-915510-56-1). Janus Bks.

SHORT STORIES, AFRIKAANS

The Saturday Evening Post Family Album. LC 80-67059. (Illus.). 1980. 15.95 (ISBN 0-89387-047-1). Sat Eve Post.

SHORT STORIES, AMERICAN

see also Western Stories

Alexander Botts: Great Stories from the Saturday Evening Post. LC 77-90937. 1977. 5.95 (ISBN 0-89387-011-0). Sat Eve Post.

The American Story. LC 75-16576. (Illus.). 1975. 9.95 (ISBN 0-89387-000-5). Sat Eve Post.

Charlie Chan: Great Stories from the Saturday Evening Post. LC 77-90936. 1977. 5.95 (ISBN 0-89387-015-3). Sat Eve Post.

Fantasy Voyages: Great Science Fiction from the Saturday Evening Post. LC 79-55717. 1979. 7.95 (ISBN 0-89387-036-6). Sat Eve Post.

Glencannon: Great Stories from the Saturday Evening Post. LC 77-23723. 1977. 5.95 (ISBN 0-89387-017-X). Sat Eve Post.

Great Love Stories from the Saturday Evening Post. LC 76-41559. 1976. 5.95 (ISBN 0-89387-003-X). Sat Eve Post.

Mr. Moto: Great Stories from the Saturday Evening Post. LC 77-90931. 1977. 5.95 (ISBN 0-89387-016-1). Sat Eve Post.

A Treasury of the Saturaday Evening Post. LC 75-16576. (Illus.). write for info. (ISBN 0-89387-029-3). Sat Eve Post.

Tugboat Annie: Great Stories from the Saturday Evening Post. LC 77-78985. 1977. 5.95 (ISBN 0-89387-010-2). Sat Eve Post.

You Be the Judge from The Saturday Evening Post. LC 79-53768. (Illus.). 1979. 5.95 (ISBN 0-89387-035-8). Sat Eve Post.

SHORT STORIES, ENGLISH

Maclean, A. D. Winter's Tales 26. 224p. 1981. 11.95 (ISBN 0-312-88414-1). St Martin.

Sampson, Alistair. Waiting with Abstain. (Illus.). 172p. 1978. 9.95 (ISBN 0-916838-14-5). Schiffer.

SHORT STORIES, ENGLISH–TRANSLATIONS FROM FOREIGN LANGUAGES

Draper, C. G. The Gift of the Magi & Other Stories. (Hewbury House Reader Ser.: Stage 2 - Beginner). (Illus., Orig.). 1981. pap. text ed. 1.95 (ISBN 0-88377-169-1). Newbury Hse.

Pallas, Norvin. Short Short Stories. (Newbury Hse Readers Ser.: Stage 4 - Intermediate Level). (Illus.). (gr. 7-12). 1981. pap. text ed. 2.80 (ISBN 0-88377-198-5). Newbury Hse.

SHORT STORIES, HINDI

Amore, Roy C. & Shinn, Larry D. Lustful Maidens & Ascetic Kings: Buddhist & Hindu Stories of Life. (Illus.). 150p. 1981. 14.95 (ISBN 0-19-502838-4); pap. 5.95 (ISBN 0-19-502839-2). Oxford U Pr.

SHORT STORIES, INDIC

Subramanyam, Ka Naa, ed. Tamil Short Stories. 1981. text ed. 10.50x (ISBN 0-7069-1241-1, Pub by Vikas India). Advent Bk.

SHORT STORIES, IRISH

Forkner, Ben, ed. Modern Irish Short Stories. 1980. pap. 5.95 (ISBN 0-14-005669-6). Penguin.

SHORT STORIES, RUSSIAN

Aksenov, Vasily P. Zolotaia Nasha Zhelezka. (Rus.). 1979. 15.00 (ISBN 0-88233-479-4); pap. 5.00 (ISBN 0-88233-480-8). Ardis Pubs.

SHORT STORIES, RUSSIAN–TRANSLATIONS INTO ENGLISH

Richards, David, ed. The Penguin Book of Russian Short Stories. 1981. pap. 4.50 (ISBN 0-14-004816-2). Penguin.

SHORT STORY

Here are entered works on the theory and art of short story writing. Collections of stories are entered under the heading Short Stories.

Barrett, Charls R. Short Story Writing. 257p. 1981. Repr. lib. bdg. 30.00 (ISBN 0-8495-0465-1). Arden Lib.

Pattee, Fred L., ed. Century Readings in the American Short Story. 562p. 1980. Repr. of 1927 ed. lib. bdg. 40.00 (ISBN 0-89760-708-2). Telegraph Bks.

Smith, Elliott L. & Hart, Andrew W. The Short Story: A Contemporary Looking Glass. 678p. 1981. pap. text ed. 9.95 (ISBN 0-394-32529-X). Random.

SHORT WAVE RADIO

see Radio, Short Wave

SHORTENINGS

see Oils and Fats, Edible

SHORTHAND

see also Abbreviations; Dictation (Office Practice)

Hill, I. C. First Teeline Workbook. 1977. pap. text ed. 4.00x (ISBN 0-435-45341-6). Heinemann Ed.

Zelter, M. Exploring Shorthand. 96p. 1980. text ed. 4.60 (ISBN 0-7715-0735-6). Forkner.

SHORTHAND–EXERCISES FOR DICTATION

Farmer & Anderson. Business Transcription. 192p. 1973. text ed. 10.60 (ISBN 0-7715-0740-2). Section A, Units 1-10 (6 Cassettes (ISBN 0-7715-0742-9). Section B, Units 11-20 (6 Cassettes (ISBN 0-7715-0743-7). Section C, Units 21-30 (6 Cassettes (ISBN 0-7715-0744-5). Forkner.

Farmer & Brown. Dicta-Typing: A Short Course. 72p. 1974. text ed. 4.60 wkbk. (ISBN 0-7715-0861-1); tchr's. manual, 136p. 28.33 (ISBN 0-7715-0862-X). Forkner.

SHORTHAND–PROGRAMMED INSTRUCTION

Salser, Carl W. & Yerian, Theo. Personal Shorthand, 3 pts. Incl. Pt. 1. pap. text ed. 6.85 (ISBN 0-89420-106-9, 241050); Cassette Recordings. 314.05 (ISBN 0-89420-167-0, 241000); Pt. 2. pap. text ed. 7.50 (ISBN 0-89420-107-7); cassette recordings 311.45 (ISBN 0-89420-168-9); Pt. 3. pap. text ed. (ISBN 0-89420-108-5). Cassette Recordings (ISBN 0-89420-169-7). (Personal Shorthand Cardinal Ser.). 1980. Set. text ed. write for info (ISBN 0-89420-105-0). cassette recordings 936.00 (ISBN 0-89420-170-0). Natl Book.

SHOSHONI INDIANS

see Indians of North America–The West

SHOSTAKOVICH, DMITRII DMITRIEVICH, 1906-1975

Ottaway, Hugh. Shostakovich Symphonies. LC 77-82651. (BBC Music Guides: No. 39). (Illus.). 64p. (Orig.). 1978. pap. 2.95 (ISBN 0-295-95573-2). U of Wash Pr.

SHOT-GUNS

Anderson, Robert S., ed. Reloading for Shotgunners. LC 81-65119. (Illus.). 224p. 1981. pap. 7.95 (ISBN 0-910676-25-9, 2606). DBI.

Baer, Larry L. The Parker Gun. rev. ed. LC 77-75333. 196p. 1980. 24.95 (ISBN 0-917714-18-0). Beinfeld Pub.

Brophy, William S. L. C. Smith Shotguns. LC 77-84338. 244p. 1977. 24.95 (ISBN 0-917714-09-1). Beinfeld Pub.

McIntosh, Michael. Best Shotguns Ever Made. (Illus.). 192p. 1981. 12.95 (ISBN 0-684-16825-1, ScribT). Scribner.

SHOULDER

Neer, C. S. Shoulder Reconstruction. (Illus.). 1981. text ed. write for info. Churchill.

SHOW BUSINESS

see Performing Arts

SHOW CARDS

see Posters

SHOW-MEN

see Entertainers

SHREWS

Rathbun, G. B. The Social Structure & Ecology of Elephant-Shrews. (Advances in Ethology Ser.: Vol. 20). (Illus.). 84p. (Orig.). 1979. pap. text ed. 29.50 (ISBN 3-489-60836-4). Parey Sci Pubs.

SHRIMPS

FAO Species Catalogue, Vol. 1: Shrimps & Prawns of the World; an Annotated Catalogue of Species of Interest to Fisheries. (FAO Fisheries Synopsis Ser.: No. 125, Vol. 1). 287p. 1980. pap. 15.50 (ISBN 92-5-100896-5, F1939, FAO). Unipub.

Hartley, L. P. Shrimp & Anemone. 1963. pap. 2.95 (ISBN 0-571-07061-2, Pub. by Faber & Faber). Merrimack Bk Serv.

Recommended International Code of Practice for Shrimps or Prawns. 1980. pap. 5.25 (ISBN 92-5-100915-5, F1950, FAO). Unipub.

Shrimps of the Pacific Coast of Canada. 280p. 1981. 32.50 (ISBN 0-660-10177-7, SSC 148, SSC). Unipub.

SHRINKAGE (COMMERCE)

see Breakage, Shrinkage, etc. (Commerce)

SHRUBS

see also specific shrubs, e.g. Rhododendron

Edwards, Ray. Choosing & Caring for Garden Shrubs. pap. 4.50 (ISBN 0-7153-7902-X). David & Charles.

Howland, Joseph E. How to Select & Care for Shrubs & Hedges. Ortho Books Editorial Staff, ed. LC 80-66346. (Illus.). 96p. (Orig.). 1981. pap. 4.95 (Ortho Bks). Chevron Chem.

Mooberry, F. M. & Scott, Jane H. Grow Native Shrubs in Your Garden. LC 80-69807. 1980. 5.95x. Brandywine Conserv.

Rowland, Lorna. Growing Herbs. (Practical Gardening Ser.). (Illus.). 112p. (Orig.). 1979. pap. 10.50 (ISBN 0-589-01244-4, Pub. by Reed Bks Australia). C E Tuttle.

SHRUBS–GREAT BRITAIN

Bean, W. J., compiled by. Trees & Shrubs: Hardy in the British Isles, 4 vols. 8th ed. Clarke, D. L. & Taylor, George, eds. (Illus.). 850p. 1981. 280.00x set (ISBN 0-312-81742-8). St Martin.

Harz, Kurt. Trees & Shrubs. (Illus.). 144p. 1981. pap. 5.95 (ISBN 0-7011-2542-X, Pub. by Chatto-Bodley-Jonathan). Merrimack Bk Serv.

SHRUBS–UNITED STATES

Stokes, Donald. The Natural History of Wild Shrubs & Vines. LC 80-8219. (Illus.). 256p. 1981. 12.95 (ISBN 0-06-014163-8, HarpT). Har-Row.

SICILY–DESCRIPTION AND TRAVEL

Kininmonth, Christopher. The Travellers' Guide to Sicily. rev. ed. (Illus.). 306p. 1981. pap. 7.95 (ISBN 0-224-01854-X, Pub. by Chatto-Bodley-Jonathan). Merrimack Bk Serv.

SICILY–HISTORY
Rabe, Claire. Sicily Enough. LC 76-28246. 73p. 1980. pap. 3.75 (ISBN 0-88496-070-6). Ross-Erikson.
SICK
see also Cookery for the Sick; Diet in Disease; First Aid in Illness and Injury; Hospitals; Nurses and Nursing
Noonan, Karen A. Coping with Illness. 2nd ed. LC 80-67825. (Practical Nursing Ser.). (Illus.). 288p. 1981. pap. text ed. 8.00 (ISBN 0-8273-1438-8); instr's. guide 1.25 (ISBN 0-8273-1922-3). Delmar.
Schemmer, Kenneth E. Between Faith & Tears. 1981. pap. 3.95 (ISBN 0-8407-5770-0). Nelson.
SICKLE CELL ANEMIA
Cerami & Washington. Sickle Cell Anemia. LC 72-93681. 1973. 8.95 (ISBN 0-89388-068-X). Okpaku Communications.
SICKNESS INSURANCE
see Insurance, Health
SIDE DRUM
see Drum
SIDEREAL SYSTEM
see Stars
SIDEROGRAPHY
see Engraving
SIERRA MADRE MOUNTAINS
Traven, B. El Tesoro De la Sierra Madre. Rodriguez, M., ed. (Span.). 1963. 8.95 (ISBN 0-13-273771-X). P-H.
SIERRA NEVADA MOUNTAINS
Wood, Robert S. Desolation Wilderness. 2nd rev. ed. (Illus.). 256p. 1975. pap. 4.95 (ISBN 0-89815-044-2). Ten Speed Pr.
SIGHT
see Vision
SIGHT-SAVING
see Eye–Care and Hygiene
SIGHT-SAVING BOOKS
see Large Type Books
SIGILLOGRAPHY
see Seals (Numismatics)
SIGN-BOARDS
see Signs and Signboards
SIGN LANGUAGE
see also Deaf–Means of Communication; Signs and Symbols
Bellugi, U. & Studdert-Kennedy, M., eds. Signed & Spoken Language: Biological Constraints on Linguistic Form. (Dahlem Workshop Reports, Life Science Research Report Ser.: No. 19). (Illus.). 379p. (Orig.). 1980. pap. 35.70 (ISBN 0-89573-034-0). Verlag Chemie.
Dirst, Richard D. Sign Language Evaluation Manual for Evaluators. 51p. 1980. pap. text ed. 3.50 (ISBN 0-9602220-3-0). RIFD.
SIGN PAINTING
see also Alphabets; Lettering; Signs and Signboards
Blackistone, Mick & McLendon, Charles. Signage Communication Standards. (Illus.). 192p. 1982. 24.95 (ISBN 0-07-005740-0, P&RB). McGraw.
SIGNAL THEORY (TELECOMMUNICATION)
Digital Signal Processing Committee, ed. Programs for Digital Signal Processing. LC 79-89028. 1979. 35.95; tape version 50.00. Inst Electrical.
Su, Kendall L. A Collection of Solved Problems in Circuits, Electronics, & Signal Analysis, Vol. 1. 96p. 1980. pap. text ed. 5.50 (ISBN 0-8403-2262-3). Kendall-Hunt.
SIGNATURES (WRITING)
see Seals (Numismatics)
SIGNBOARDS
see Signs and Signboards
SIGNETS
see Seals (Numismatics)
SIGNIFICS
see Semantics (Philosophy)
SIGNS
see Signs and Signboards; Signs and Symbols
SIGNS AND SIGNBOARDS
see also Posters; Sign Painting
American Institute of Graphic Arts. Symbol Signs. (Visual Communication Bks). (Illus.). 192p. (Orig.). 1981. pap. 12.95 (ISBN 0-8038-6777-8). Hastings.
Blackistone, Mick & McLendon, Charles. Signage Communication Standards. (Illus.). 192p. 1982. 24.95 (ISBN 0-07-005740-0, P&RB). McGraw.
SIGNS AND SYMBOLS
see also Abbreviations; Ciphers; Cryptography; Emblems; Heraldry; Semiotics; Semantics (Philosophy); Symbolism
Baudrillard, Jean. For a Critique of the Political Economy of the Sign. Levin, Charles, tr. from Fr. lib. bdg. 14.00 (ISBN 0-914386-23-9); pap. 4.50 (ISBN 0-914386-24-7). Telos Pr.
Gustason, G. & Zaevolkow, E., eds. Using Signing Exact English in Total Communication. LC 80-84549. 62p. 1980. 4.50 (ISBN 0-916708-04-7). Modern Signs.
Thompson, Philip & Davenport, Peter, eds. Dictionary of Visual Language. (Illus.). 288p. 1981. 30.00x (ISBN 0-312-20108-7). St Martin.
SIKHISM
Marenco, Ethne K. Transformation of Sikh Society. 342p. pap. 10.95 (ISBN 0-913244-08-2). Hapi Pr.
SIKHS–RELIGION
see Sikhism
SIKHS IN GREAT BRITAIN
Helweg, Arthur W. Sikhs in England: The Development of a Migrant Community. (Illus.). 190p. 1979. text ed. 10.95x (ISBN 0-19-561150-0). Oxford U Pr.
SIKSIKA INDIANS
see Indians of North America–The West
SILICON
Keller & Mulbauer. Floating Zone Silicon. 256p. 1981. 39.75 (ISBN 0-8247-1167-X). Dekker.
Kintzinger, J. P. & Marsmann, H. Oxygen-Seventeen & Silicon-Twenty-Nine. (NMR-Basic Principles & Progress Ser.: Vol. 17). (Illus.). 250p. 1981. 48.00 (ISBN 0-387-10414-3). Springer-Verlag.
SILICOSIS
see Lungs–Dust Diseases
SILK MANUFACTURE AND TRADE
Ming-tse Li, Lillian. China's Silk Trade: A Traditional Industry & the International Market, 1842-1937. (Harvard East Asian Monograph: No. 97). 1981. text ed. 15.00x (ISBN 0-674-11962-2). Harvard U Pr.
SILT
see Sedimentation and Deposition
SILVER
see also Coinage; Money; Silver Question; Silverwork
Branson, Oscar T. What You Need to Know About Your Gold & Silver. (Illus.). 56p. (Orig.). 1980. pap. 4.95 (ISBN 0-918080-44-4). Treasure Chest.
Ensko, Stephen G. & Wenham, Edward. English Silver 1675-1825. rev. ed. (Illus.). 144p. 1980. 24.95x (ISBN 0-938186-00-0). Arcadia Pr.
Jastram, Roy W. Silver: The Restless Metal. 225p. 1981. 23.95 (ISBN 0-471-03912-8, Pub. by Wiley-Interscience). Wiley.
SILVER ARTICLES
see Silverwork
SILVER QUESTION
see also Coinage; Gold; Money; Quantity Theory of Money
Radigan, John D. The Silver Revolution & the New Monetary Order of the World. (Illus.). 129p. 1981. 49.85 (ISBN 0-89266-283-2). Am Classical Coll Pr.
SILVER WORK
see Silverwork
SILVERSMITHING
see Silverwork
SILVERWORK
see also Jewelry; Jewelry Making
Ash, Douglas. How to Identify English Silver Drinking Vessels. 15.00x (ISBN 0-392-07924-0, SpS). Soccer.
Mackie, Carey T., et al. Crescent City Silver. (Illus.). vi, 130p. 1980. pap. 15.00x (ISBN 0-917860-05-5). Historic New Orleans.
SIMON, CLAUDE
Birn, Randi & Gould, Karen, eds. Orion Blinded: Essays on Claude Simon. LC 79-17687. 320p. 1981. 18.50 (ISBN 0-8387-2420-5). Bucknell U Pr.
SIMPSON, O. J., 1947-
Jameson, J. The Picture Life of O. J. Simpson. 1978. pap. 1.75 (ISBN 0-380-01906-X, 51649, Camelot). Avon.
SIMULATION METHODS
see also Artificial Intelligence; Bionics; Mathematical Models; Mathematical Optimization
Herbert-Sturtridge. Simulations. (ELT Guide Ser.: No. 2). 1979. pap. text ed. 14.50x (ISBN 0-85633-192-9, NFER). Humanities.
Law, Averill M. & Kelton, David. Simulation Modeling & Analysis. (Illus.). 416p. 1981. text ed. 25.95 (ISBN 0-07-036696-9). McGraw.
Rubenstein, Reuven Y. Simulation & the Monte Carlo Method. (Probability & Mathematical Statistics Ser.). 300p. 1981. 30.00 (ISBN 0-471-08917-6, Pub. by Wiley-Interscience). Wiley.
UKSC Eighty-One. 1981. text ed. price not set (ISBN 0-86103-041-9, Westbury Hse). Butterworth.
SIN, FORGIVENESS OF
see Forgiveness of Sin
SINAN, QOJA, MI'MAR, 1490-1558
De Osa, Veronica. Sinan: The Turkish Michelangelo. 1981. 10.95 (ISBN 0-533-04655-6). Vantage.
SINATRA, FRANK, 1917-
Carpozi, George, Jr. Frank Sinatra: Is This Man Mafia? (Orig.). 1979. pap. 2.25 (ISBN 0-532-23282-8). Manor Bks.
SINGAPORE
Hock, Saw S. Population Control for Zero Growth in Singapore. 250p. 1981. 29.95 (ISBN 0-19-580430-9). Oxford U Pr.
Time Periodicals Ltd., ed. Straits Times Dictionary of Singapore. 948p. 1980. 58.50x (ISBN 0-8002-2750-6). Intl Pubns Serv.
SINGER, ISAAC BASHEVIS
Singer, Isaac B. Lost in America. LC 79-6037. 1981. 17.95 (ISBN 0-686-69069-9). Doubleday.
SINGERS
Charnace, Guy. A Star of Song: The Life of Christina Nilsson. M., J. C. & C., E., trs. LC 80-2264. 1981. Repr. of 1870 ed. 14.50 (ISBN 0-404-18818-4). AMS Pr.
Davidson, John & Casady, Cort. The Singing Entertainer. LC 79-17183. 227p. 1979. pap. 9.95 (ISBN 0-88284-095-9). Alfred Pub.
Haney, Lynn. Naked at the Feast: A Biography of Josephine Baker. (Illus.). 360p. 1981. 15.00 (ISBN 0-396-07900-8). Dodd.
LeVine, Michael. Johnny Horton-Your Singing Fisherman. Date not set. 10.95 (ISBN 0-533-04802-8). Vantage.
O'Day, Anita & Eells, George. High Times, Hard Times. 320p. 1981. 12.95 (ISBN 0-399-12505-1). Putnam.
Santley, Charles. Student & Singer. 1981. Repr. of 1892 ed. 39.50 (ISBN 0-404-18866-4). AMS Pr.
SINGERS–CORRESPONDENCE, REMINISCENCES, ETC.
see Musicians–Correspondence, Reminiscences, etc.
SINGING
see also Respiration; Voice
Christy, Van A. Foundations in Singing: A Basic Text in the Fundamentals of Teaching & Song Interpretation - Medium-High Voice Edition. 250p. (Orig.). 1981. write for info. plastic comb bind. (ISBN 0-697-03483-6). Wm C Brown.
Longo, Teodosio. Fundamentals of Singing & Speaking. 112p. 1945. 7.00x (ISBN 0-913298-54-9). S F Vanni.
Ottman, R. More Music for Sight Singing. 1981. pap. 11.95 (ISBN 0-13-601211-6). P-H.
SINGING–INSTRUCTION AND STUDY
see also Chants (Plain, Gregorian, etc.)–Instruction and Study
Vennard, William. Singing: The Mechanism & the Technic. rev ed. (Illus.). 275p. 1967. pap. 8.95 (ISBN 0-686-64100-0, 04685). Fischer Inc NY.
Wormhoudt, Pearl S. Building the Voice As an Instrument with a Studio Reference Handbook. (Illus., Orig.). 1981. pap. text ed. 8.95 (ISBN 0-916358-08-9). Wormhoudt.
SINGING–METHODS
see also Bel Canto
Coffin, Berton. Coffin's Overtones of Bel Canto: Phonetic Basis of Artistic Singing with One Hundred Chromatic Vowel-Chart Exercises. LC 80-21958. 254p. 1980. text ed. 20.00 (ISBN 0-8108-1370-X); Accompanying Chart. 7.50; Set. 27.50. Scarecrow.
SINGLE MEN
see Bachelors
SINGLE-PARENT FAMILY
see also Divorcees; Maternal Deprivation; Unmarried Mothers; Widows
Knight, Bryan M. Enjoying Single Parenthood. 176p. 1981. pap. 6.95 (ISBN 0-442-29623-1). Van Nos Reinhold.
SINGLE PEOPLE
see also Bachelors; Divorcees; Single Women
Babin, Lawrence J. Singles Are Suckers. 1981. pap. 6.95 (ISBN 0-912492-16-3). Pyquag.
Staples, Robert. The World of Black Singles: Changing Patterns of Male-Female Relations. LC 80-1025. (Contributions in Afro-American & African Studies: No. 57). 288p. 1981. lib. bdg. 25.00 (ISBN 0-313-22478-1, SBS/). Greenwood.
SINGLE WOMEN
see also Divorcees; Unmarried Mothers; Widows
Peterson, Nancy L. Our Lives for Ourselves: Women Who Have Never Married. 320p. 1981. 13.95 (ISBN 0-399-12476-4). Putnam.
SINHALESE LANGUAGE
Reynolds, C. Sinhalese: An Introductory Course. 1980. 38.00x (ISBN 0-8364-0661-3, Pub. by London U England). South Asia Bks.
Reynolds, C. H. Sinhalese: An Introductory Course. 1980. 38.00x (ISBN 0-8364-0661-3). South Asia Bks.
SINN FEIN REBELLION, 1916
see Ireland–History
SIOUX INDIANS
see Indians of North America–The West
SIRENIA
see Manatees
SISTERS OF ST. CLARE
see Poor Clares
SITWELL, DAME EDITH, 1887-1964
Elborn, Geoffrey. Edith Sitwell: A Biography. LC 80-1985. 312p. 1981. 14.95 (ISBN 0-385-13467-3). Doubleday.
Glendinning, Victoria. Edith Sitwell: A Unicorn Among Lions. LC 80-2721. (Illus.). 384p. 1981. 17.95 (ISBN 0-394-50439-9). Knopf.
SIVA
Kramrisch, Stella. The Presence of Siva. LC 80-8558. (Illus.). 550p. 1981. 37.50x (ISBN 0-691-03964-X); pap. 16.50x (ISBN 0-691-10115-9). Princeton U Pr.
SIZE OF PARTICLES
see Particles
SKATEBOARDS
La Vada, Weir. Skateboards & Skateboarding. (gr. 4-6). 1977. pap. 1.75 (ISBN 0-671-41136-5). PB.
SKATING
see also Roller-Skating
Holum, Dianne. World of Speed Skating. (Illus.). 320p. 1981. 17.50 (ISBN 0-89490-051-X). Enslow Pubs.
SKEES AND SKEE-RUNNING
see Skis and Skiing
SKELETAL REMAINS
see Anthropometry; Man, Prehistoric
SKELETON
see also Anthropometry; Extremities (Anatomy); Joints; Skull; Spine
also names of bones, e.g. Clavicle, Humerus
Green, Stuart A. Complications of External Skeletal Fixation: Causes, Prevention, & Treatment. write for info. (ISBN 0-398-04482-1). C C Thomas.
SKELTON, JOHN, 1460-1529
Edwards, Anthony S. John Skelton. (The Critical Heritage Ser.). 300p. 1981. price not set (ISBN 0-7100-0724-8). Routledge & Kegan.
SKETCH, LITERARY
see Essay
SKETCHING
see Drawing
SKIING
see Skis and Skiing
SKIN
see also Dermatoglyphics; Fingerprints
Litt, Jerome Z. Your Skin & How to Live in It. LC 80-65323. 223p. 1980. pap. 4.95 (ISBN 0-86551-011-3). Corinthian.
Marchesani, O. & Sautter, H. Atlas of the Oscular Fundus. 1959. 80.00 (ISBN 0-02-848820-2). Hafner.
Walzer, Richard A. Skintelligence: How to Be Smart About Skin. (Appleton Consumer Health Guides). 256p. 1981. 12.95 (ISBN 0-8385-8569-8); pap. 6.95 (ISBN 0-8385-8568-X). ACC.
Wertelecki, Wladimir & Plato, Chris C., eds. Dermatoglyphics Fifty Years Later. LC 79-2595. (Alan R. Liss Ser.: Vol. 15, No. 6). 1979. 76.00 (ISBN 0-8451-1031-4). March of Dimes.
SKIN–DISEASES
see also Dermatology
also specific diseases, e.g. Blastomycosis, Eczema, Lupus
Roenigk, Henry H., Jr. Office Dermatology. (Illus.). 340p. 1981. write for info. (7316-8). Williams & Wilkins.
Sneddon, I. B. & Church, R. E. Skin Disorders in Clinical Practice. 3rd ed. 19.50 (ISBN 0-201-07705-1). A-W.
Thivolet, J. & Schmitt, D. Cutaneous Immunopathology. (Illus.). 506p. 1978. pap. 19.50 (ISBN 2-85598-175-1). Masson Pub.
SKIN–PAPILLARY RIDGES
see Dermatoglyphics
SKIN–SURGERY
Salisbury, Roger E. & Bevin, A. Griswold. Atlas of Reconstructive Burn Surgery. 1981. text ed. price not set (ISBN 0-7216-7903-X). Saunders.
SKIN DIVING–JUVENILE LITERATURE
Briggs, Carole S. Skin Diving Is for Me. (Sports for Me Bks.). (Illus.). (gr. 2-5). 1981. PLB 5.95 (ISBN 0-8225-1132-0). Lerner Pubns.
SKIN-GRAFTING
Salisbury, Roger E. & Bevin, A. Griswold. Atlas of Reconstructive Burn Surgery. 1981. text ed. price not set (ISBN 0-7216-7903-X). Saunders.
SKINNER, BURRHUS FREDERIC, 1904-
Nye, Robert D. Three Psychologies: Perspectives from Freud, Skinner & Rogers. 2nd ed. LC 80-25716. 170p. (Orig.). 1981. pap. text ed. 7.95 (ISBN 0-8185-0438-2). Brooks-Cole.
Sagal, Paul T. Skinner's Philosophy. LC 80-5737. 132p. 1981. lib. bdg. 15.75 (ISBN 0-8191-1432-4); pap. text ed. 7.50 (ISBN 0-8191-1433-2). U Pr of Amer.
SKIP TRACERS
see Missing Persons
SKIS AND SKIING
Dicke, Karen & Goeldner, C. R. Colorado Ski Industry Characteristics & Financial Analysis. 1981. 25.00 (ISBN 0-686-69386-8). U CO Busn Res Div.
Goeldner, C. R. & Farwell, Ted. NSAA Economic Analysis of North American Ski Areas (79-80 Season) 139p. 1980. 35.00 (ISBN 0-89478-054-9). U CO Busn Res Div.
Howe, John G. Skiing Mechanics. 1981. 16.95 (ISBN 0-686-28916-1). Poudre Pub Co.
SKIS AND SKIING–DIRECTORIES
Walter, C. Illustrated Skiing Dictionary for Young People. 1980. pap. 2.50 (ISBN 0-13-450858-0). P-H.
SKIS AND SKIING–JUVENILE LITERATURE
Boy Scouts, of America. Skiing. (Illus.). 56p. (gr. 6-12). 1980. pap. 0.70x. BSA.
Walter, Claire. Illustrated Skiing Dictionary for Young People. LC 80-81790. (Illustrated Dictionaries). (Illus.). 128p. (gr. 4 up). 1981. PLB 6.89 (ISBN 0-8178-0017-4). Harvey.
Weir, LaVada. Grass Skiing: A Complete Beginner's Book. (Illus.). 128p. (gr. 4-6). 1981. PLB 7.29 (ISBN 0-686-69301-9). Messner.
SKORZENY, OTTO
Infield, Glenn. Skorzeny: Hitler's Commando. (Illus.). 304p. 1981. 15.95 (ISBN 0-312-72777-1). St Martin.
SKULL
Here are entered anatomical and pathological works.
see also Craniology; Jaws
Moore, W. J. The Mammalian Skull. (Biological Structure & Function Ser.: No. 8). (Illus.). 400p. Date not set. 85.00 (ISBN 0-521-23318-6). Cambridge U Pr.
SKULL–ABNORMITIES AND DEFORMITIES
External Ear Malformations: Epidemiology, Genetics & Natural History. LC 79-2501. (Alan R. Liss Ser.: Vol. 15, No. 9). 1979. 18.00 (ISBN 0-8451-1034-9). March of Dimes.

Gorlin, Robert J., ed. Morphogenesis & Malformation of the Ear. LC 80-18892. (Alan R. Liss: Vol. 16,No. 4). 1980. 44.00 (ISBN 0-8451-1038-1). March of Dimes.

Melnick, Michael & Jorgenson, Ronald, eds. Developmental Aspects of Craniofacial Dysmorphology. LC 79-2487. (Alan R. Liss Ser.: Vol. 15, No. 8). 1979. 16.00 (ISBN 0-8451-1033-0). March of Dimes.

SKULL–RADIOGRAPHY

Du Boulay, G. H. Principles of X-Ray Diagnosis of the Skull. 2nd ed. (Illus.). 384p. 1979. text ed. 115.00x. Butterworths.

Korach. Manual of Radiographic Techniques of the Skull. 1981. write for info (ISBN 0-89352-098-5). Masson Pub.

SKUNKS

Blassingame, Wyatt. Skunks. LC 80-21555. (A Skylight Bk.). (Illus.). 64p. (gr. 2-5). 1981. PLB 5.95 (ISBN 0-396-07909-1). Dodd.

SKY

see Atmosphere

SKY SAILING

see Hang Gliding

SKYSURFING

see Hang Gliding

SLANDER (LAW)

see Libel and Slander

SLANG

Wilmeth, Don B. The Language of American Popular Entertainment: A Glossary of Argot, Slang, & Terminology. LC 80-14795. 296p. 1981. lib. bdg. 29.95 (ISBN 0-313-22497-8, WEN/). Greenwood.

SLAUGHTERING AND SLAUGHTER-HOUSES

see also Meat Inspection

Clarke, Mary W. The Slaughter Ranches & Their Makers. (Illus.). Date not set. 12.95. Jenkins.

SLAVE LABOR

see also Contract Labor; Indentured Servants

Jensen, Marilyn. Phillis Wheatley, Negro Slave of John Wheatley. pap. 9.95. Lion.

SLAVE-TRADE

Collister, Peter. The Sulivans & the Slave Trade. (Illus.). 199p. 1981. 14.95x (ISBN 0-8476-3611-9). Rowman.

SLAVE TRADE–AFRICA

Davidson, Basil. The African Slave Trade. rev. enl. ed. 312p. 1981. 12.50 (ISBN 0-686-69142-3, Pub. by Atlantic Monthly Pr); pap. 6.95 (ISBN 0-686-69143-1). Little.

SLAVERY–EMANCIPATION

Bolt, Christine & Dresher, Seymour. Anti-Slavery, Religion & Reform. 275p. 1980. 27.50 (ISBN 0-208-01783-6, Archon). Shoe String.

SLAVERY AND THE CHURCH

Bolt, Christine & Dresher, Seymour. Anti-Slavery, Religion & Reform. 275p. 1980. 27.50 (ISBN 0-208-01783-6, Archon). Shoe String.

Lesick, Lawrence T. The Lane Rebels: Evangelicalism & Antislavery in Antebellum America. LC 80-24123. (Studies in Evangelicalism: No. 2). 287p. 1980. 15.00 (ISBN 0-8108-1372-6). Scarecrow.

SLAVERY IN AFRICA

Nwulia, Moses D. The History of Slavery in Mauritius & the Seychelles, 1810-1875. LC 79-15363. 280p. 1981. 18.50 (ISBN 0-8386-2398-0). Fairleigh Dickinson.

SLAVERY IN AMERICA

Tushnet, Mark V. The American Law of Slavery, Eighteen Ten-Eighteen Sixty: Considerations of Humanity & Interest. LC 80-8582. 288p. 1981. 20.00x (ISBN 0-691-04681-6); pap. 9.50x (ISBN 0-691-10104-3). Princeton U Pr.

SLAVERY IN CUBA

Murray, David R. Odious Commerce: Britain, Spain & the Abolition of the Cuban Slave Trade. LC 79-52835. (Cambridge Latin American Studies: No. 37). 435p. Date not set. 44.50 (ISBN 0-521-22867-0). Cambridge U Pr.

SLAVERY IN THE UNITED STATES

see also Abolitionists; Freedmen; Kansas-Nebraska Bill; Slave Labor; Slave-Trade; Southern States–History; Underground Railroad

Berlin, Ira. Slaves Without Masters: The Free Negro in the Antebellum South. 446p. 1981. pap. 6.95 (ISBN 0-19-502905-4, GB 629, OPB). Oxford U Pr.

Fehrenbacher, Don E. Slavery, Law, & Politics: The Dred Scott Case in Historical Perspective. (Illus.). 288p. 1981. 16.95 (ISBN 0-19-502882-1). Oxford U Pr.

--Slavery, Law & Politics: The Dred Scott Case in Historical Perspective. (Illus.). 288p. 1981. pap. 6.95 (ISBN 0-19-502883-X, GB639, GB). Oxford U Pr.

Hermann, Janet S. The Pursuit of a Dream. (Illus.). 288p. 1981. 17.50 (ISBN 0-19-502887-2). Oxford U Pr.

Miller, Randall M., ed. The Afro-American Slaves: Community or Chaos? 128p. (Orig.). 1981. pap. 5.50 (ISBN 0-89874-078-9). Krieger.

Moore, W. American Negro Slavery & Abolition. LC 73-148362. 1971. 10.00 (ISBN 0-89388-000-0); pap. 5.95. Okpaku Communications.

SLAVERY IN THE UNITED STATES–ANTI-SLAVERY MOVEMENTS

Lesick, Lawrence T. The Lane Rebels: Evangelicalism & Antislavery in Antebellum America. LC 80-24123. (Studies in Evangelicalism: No. 2). 287p. 1980. 15.00 (ISBN 0-8108-1372-6). Scarecrow.

SLAVERY IN THE UNITED STATES–FUGITIVE SLAVES

Blockson, Charles L. The Underground Railroad in Pennsylvania. LC 80-69847. (Illus.). 1981. 12.95 (ISBN 0-933184-21-2); pap. 6.95 (ISBN 0-933184-22-0). Flame Intl.

SLAVERY IN THE UNITED STATES–HISTORY

Cope, Robert S. Carry Me Back: Slavery & Servitude in Seventeenth Century Virginia. (Illus.). xv, 179p. 1973. 2.00. Pikeville Coll.

SLAVERY IN THE UNITED STATES–LAW

Fehrenbacher, Don E. Slavery, Law, & Politics: The Dred Scott Case in Historical Perspective. (Illus.). 288p. 1981. 16.95 (ISBN 0-19-502882-1). Oxford U Pr.

--Slavery, Law & Politics: The Dred Scott Case in Historical Perspective. (Illus.). 288p. 1981. pap. 6.95 (ISBN 0-19-502883-X, GB639, GB). Oxford U Pr.

SLAVERY IN THE UNITED STATES–LEGAL STATUS OF SLAVES IN FREE STATES

Fehrenbacher, Don E. Slavery, Law, & Politics: The Dred Scott Case in Historical Perspective. (Illus.). 288p. 1981. 16.95 (ISBN 0-19-502882-1). Oxford U Pr.

--Slavery, Law & Politics: The Dred Scott Case in Historical Perspective. (Illus.). 288p. 1981. pap. 6.95 (ISBN 0-19-502883-X, GB639, GB). Oxford U Pr.

SLAVES, EMANCIPATION OF

see Slavery–Emancipation

SLAVIC LANGUAGES

De Bray, Reginald G. Guide to the Slavonic Languages, 2 pts. rev., enl., 3rd ed. Incl. Pt. 1. South. 399p. 24.95 (ISBN 0-89357-060-5); Pt. 2. West. 483p. 27.95 (ISBN 0-89357-061-3). 1980. Slavica.

DeBray, Reginald G. Guide to the Slavonic Languages: Part 2. 3rd rev. ed. 483p. 80. 27.95 (ISBN 0-89357-061-3). Slavica.

De Bray, Reginald G. Guide to the Slavonic Languages: Pt. 1, Guide to the South Slavonic Languages. 3rd rev. ed. 399p. 1980. 24.95 (ISBN 0-89357-060-5). Slavica.

--Guide to the Slavonic Languages: Pt. 3, Guide to the East Slavonic Languages. 3rd rev. ed. 254p. 1980. 22.95 (ISBN 0-89357-062-1). Slavica.

Macedonian-English, English-Macedonian Dictionary, 2 vols. 1978. Set. 20.00. Macedonian-English 476pp. English-Macedonian 422pp. Heinman.

SLAVS IN THE UNITED STATES

Barendse, Michael A. Social Expectations & Perception: The Case of the Slavic Anthracite Workers. LC 80-8610. (Penn State Studies: No. 47). (Illus.). 90p. (Orig.). 1981. pap. text ed. 3.50x (ISBN 0-271-00277-8). Pa St U Pr.

SLEEP

see also Dreams; Insomnia

Kellerman, Henry. Sleep Disorders: Insomnia & Narcolepsy. 250p. 1981. 17.50 (ISBN 0-87630-264-9). Brunner-Mazel.

Macnish, Robert. Philosophy of Sleep. (Contributions to the History of Psycholgy Ser.: Orientations). 1978. Repr. of 1834 ed. 30.00 (ISBN 0-89093-159-3). U Pubns Amer.

Maxman, Jerrold S. A Good Night's Sleep: A Step-by-Step Program for Overcoming Insomnia & Other Sleep Problems. (Illus.). 1981. 14.95 (ISBN 0-393-01437-1). Norton.

Miles, Laughton E. & Dement, William C. Sleep & Aging. (Sleep Ser.: Vol. 3, No. 2). 108p. 1981. text ed. 20.00 (ISBN 0-89004-651-4). Raven.

Orem, J. & Barnes, C. D., eds. Physiology in Sleep. (Research Topics in Physiology Ser.). 1981. write for info. (ISBN 0-12-527650-8). Acad Pr.

SLEEP THERAPY

Fifth European Congress on Sleep Research, Amsterdam, September 1980. Sleep Nineteen Eighty. Koella, W. P., ed. (Illus.). 1981. 108.00 (ISBN 3-8055-2045-X). S Karger.

SLEEPLESSNESS

see Insomnia

SLEIGHT OF HAND

see Conjuring; Magic

SLIDEFILMS

see Filmstrips

SLIME MOLDS

see Acrasiales

SLOCUM, JOSHUA, b. 1844

Slocum, Victor. Capt. Joshua Slocum: The Life & Voyages of America's Best Known Sailor. LC 80-28585. (Illus.). 384p. 1981. Repr. of 1950 ed. 16.50 (ISBN 0-911378-04-9). Sheridan.

SLOT MACHINES

Fey, Marshall. The Slot Machine Story. (Illus.). 1981. 25.00 (ISBN 0-913814-33-4). Nevada Pubns.

SLOVAKIA

Seton-Weston, R. W. A History of the Czechs & Slovaks. 413p. 1980. Repr. of 1943 ed. lib. bdg. 50.00 (ISBN 0-8492-2974-X). R West.

SLOW ELECTRIC COOKERY

see Electric Cookery, Slow

SLUGS

see Tokens

SLUM CLEARANCE

see City Planning; Housing

SLUM CLEARANCE LAW

see City Planning and Redevelopment Law

SLURRY

Gittins, Lavinia. Wear in Slurry Pipelines. (BHRA Information Ser.). (Illus.). 173p. (Orig.). Date not set. pap. 45.00 (ISBN 0-906085-45-4). BHRA Fluid.

SMALL ARMS

see Firearms

SMALL BOAT RACING

see Yacht Racing

SMALL BUSINESS

see also Franchises (Retail Trade)

Alcorn, Pat. Success & Survival in the Family Owned Business. 256p. 1981. 17.95 (ISBN 0-07-000961-9). McGraw.

Brownstone, D. M. Successful Selling Skills for Small Business. 112p. 1978. 4.95 (ISBN 0-471-04029-0). Wiley.

Burstinger, Irving. Run Your Own Retail Store: From Raising the Money to Counting the Profits. (Illus.). 304p. 1981. 19.95 (ISBN 0-13-784017-9, Spec); pap. 12.95 (ISBN 0-13-784009-8). P-H.

Cohen, William A. & Reddick, Marshall E. Successful Marketing for Small Business. 364p. 1981. 17.95 (ISBN 0-8144-5611-1). Am Mgmt.

Delany, George & Delany, Sandra. The No. One Home Business Book. LC 80-84427. (Illus.). 176p. 1981. pap. 4.95 (ISBN 0-89709-022-5). Liberty Pub.

Fiederer, S. M. Easy Money. LC 80-54016. 1981. pap. 14.95 (ISBN 0-938584-00-6, 123058). United Pub NY.

Ford, Ian. Buying & Running Your Own Business. 2nd ed. 210p. 1977. text ed. 21.00x (ISBN 0-220-66336-X, Pub. by Busn Bks England). Renouf.

GAAP for Smaller Businesses. 1976. pap. 2.25. Am Inst CPA.

German, Paul M. How to Win the Small Business Game. (Illus.). 182p. (Orig.). 1981. 16.95 (ISBN 0-9605436-1-9); pap. 12.95 (ISBN 0-9605436-0-0). Small Busn Pubns.

Gupa, Brijen K. & Lopatin, Arthur D. Starting & Succeeding in Small Business: A Guide for the Innercity Businessman. LC 78-58105. iv, 100p. (Orig.). 1978. pap. 15.00 (ISBN 0-936876-14-X). Learn Res Intl Stud.

Gupta, Brijan K. & Lopatin, Arthur D. Small Business Development in the Inner City Areas of Rochester. LC 78-58110. (Illus.). xx, 231p. (Orig.). 1978. pap. 22.50 (ISBN 0-936876-15-8). Learn Res Intl Stud.

Hazel, A. C. & Reid, A. S. Enjoying a Profitable Business. 2nd ed. 251p. 1976. text ed. 18.50x (ISBN 0-220-66287-8, Pub. by Busn Bks England). Renouf.

Hutzler, Laurie H. A Financing Survival Manual for Small Business. (Illus.). 1981. pap. 15.00 (ISBN 0-937542-05-9). Legal Mgmt Serv.

Kirkpatrick, Frank. How to Buy a Country Business. 1981. 11.95 (ISBN 0-8092-5944-3). Contemp Bks.

Lane, Byron. How to Free Yourself in a Business of Your Own. (Illus.). 176p. 1980. 11.95 (Spec); pap. 5.95. P-H.

Lester, Mary. A Woman's Guide to Starting a Small Business. LC 80-24298. pap. 2.50 (ISBN 0-87576-093-7). Pilot Bks.

McQuown, Judith H. Inc. Yourself. 1981. pap. 5.95 (ISBN 0-446-97817-5). Warner Bks.

Scase, Richard & Goffee, Robert. The Real World of the Small Business Owner. 166p. 1980. 27.50x (ISBN 0-7099-0452-5, Pub. by Croom Helm Ltd England). Biblio Dist.

Vice, Fred H. The Armchair Millionaire. 120p. (Orig.). pap. 7.95 (ISBN 0-87364-204-X). Paladin Ent.

Witt, Bud. How to Start a Business in Your Home & Gro. LC 47-332. 208p. (Orig.). (gr. 12). 1980. pap. text ed. 12.00 (ISBN 0-9604932-0-4). B Witt.

Zintz, Walter. Nova Venturion's Bootstrap Venture Manual. 1981. softcover 14.50 (ISBN 0-915254-08-5). Nova Venturion.

SMALL BUSINESS–ACCOUNTING

see Accounting

SMALL BUSINESS–FINANCE

Bannock, Graham. The Economics of Small Firms: Return from the Wilderness. 120p. 1981. 14.50x (ISBN 0-631-11391-6, Pub. by Basil Blackwell). Biblio Dist.

Hicks, Tyler G. Business Borrowers Complete Success Kit. 2nd ed. 596p. 1981. pap. 99.50 (ISBN 0-914306-44-8). Intl Wealth.

--Business Capital Sources. 2nd ed. 150p. 1981. pap. 15.00 (ISBN 0-914306-47-2). Intl Wealth.

--Small Business Investment Company Directory & Handbook. 2nd ed. 150p. 1981. pap. 15.00 (ISBN 0-914306-48-0). Intl Wealth.

Wood, E. G. Bigger Profits for the Smaller Firm. 2nd ed. 211p. 1978. pap. text ed. 12.25x (ISBN 0-220-66350-5, Pub. by Busn Bks England). Renouf.

SMALL BUSINESS–MANAGEMENT

Alcorn, Pat. Success & Survival in the Family Owned Business. 256p. 1981. 17.95 (ISBN 0-07-000961-9). McGraw.

Allsopp, Michael. Survival in Business. 139p. 1977. text ed. 22.00x (ISBN 0-220-66320-3, Pub. by Busn Bks England). Renouf.

Bellavance, Diane. Advertising & Public Relations for a Small Business. (Illus.). 80p. 1980. pap. 5.95 (ISBN 0-9605276-0-5). DBA Bks.

Brannen, William H. Practical Marketing for Your Small Retail Business. (Illus.). 272p. 1981. 16.95 (ISBN 0-13-692764-5, Spec); pap. 8.95 (ISBN 0-13-692756-4). P-H.

Burnstiner, Irving. Run Your Own Store: From Raising the Money to Counting the Profits. (Illus.). 304p. 1981. 19.95 (ISBN 0-13-784017-9, Spectrum); pap. 12.95 (ISBN 0-13-784009-8). P-H.

English, John. How to Organise & Operate a Small Business in Australia. 270p. 1981. text ed. 22.50x (ISBN 0-86861-282-0, 2648). Allen Unwin.

Erskine, Kathryn A. What You Always Wanted to Know About Operating a Small Business but Didn't Know Who to Ask. (Illus.). 69p. (Orig.). 1980. pap. 9.95 (ISBN 0-9605058-0-6). Erskine.

Gladson, Deek. The Miser's Manual: A Guide to Profitable Self-Employment. 1981. pap. 4.00 (ISBN 0-686-69465-1); plastic bdg. 6.00 (ISBN 0-89316-626-X). Exanimo Pr.

Hazel, A. C. & Reid, A. S. Managing the Survival of Smaller Companies. 2nd ed. 159p. 1977. text ed. 18.50x (ISBN 0-220-66328-9, Pub. by Busn Bks England). Renouf.

--Rapid Company Growth: How to Plan & Manage Small Company Expansion. 166p. 1979. pap. 14.75x (ISBN 0-220-67025-0, Pub. by Busn Bks England). Renouf.

Hicks, Tyler G. Financial Broker-Finder-Business Broker-Consultant Success Kit. 2nd ed. 485p. 1981. pap. 99.50 (ISBN 0-686-69033-8). Intl Wealth.

--How to Prepare & Process Export-Import Documents: A Fully Illustrated Guide. 2nd ed. 320p. 1981. pap. 25.00 (ISBN 0-914306-51-0). Intl Wealth.

Justis, Robert T. Managing Your Small Business. (Illus.). 288p. 1981. text ed. 18.95 (ISBN 0-686-68607-1). P-H.

Krentzman, Harvey C. Successful Management Strategies for Small Business. (Illus.). 208p. 1981. (Spec); pap. text ed. 6.95 (ISBN 0-13-863118-2, Spec). P-H.

Logan, George H. Tax Reduction for Small Business & Self Employed. 1981. pap. 9.95 (ISBN 0-914598-08-2). Padre Prods.

Mucciolo, Louis. Small Business: Look Before You Leap; a Catalog of Sources of Information to Help You Start & Manage Your Own Small Business. 256p. 1981. pap. 7.95 (ISBN 0-668-05173-6, 5173). Arco.

Nicholas, Ted. The Ted Nicholas Small Business Course. 500p. (Orig.). 1981. pap. 14.95 (ISBN 0-913864-65-X). Enterprise Del.

Potts, Phil. Survival Is the Bottom Line. 58p. (Orig.). 1980. pap. 2.95 (ISBN 0-89260-182-5). Hwong Pub.

Scalo, James V. The Complete Credits & Collection Starter Success Kit. rev. ed. 150p. 1981. pap. 29.50 (ISBN 0-914306-55-3). Intl Wealth.

Siegel, W. L. People Management for Small Business. 130p. 1978. 5.95 (ISBN 0-471-04030-4, 1-382). Wiley.

Smith, Brian. How to Prosper in Your Own Business: Getting Started & Staying on Course. 352p. 1980. 20.00 (ISBN 0-8289-0408-1). Greene.

SMALL COMPUTERS

see Minicomputers

SMALL LOANS

see Loans, Personal

SMART, CHRISTOPHER, 1722-1771

Murray, Grace A. Personalities of the Eighteenth Century: (Samuel Foote, Christopher Smart, William Hazlitt) 230p. 1980. Repr. of 1927 ed. lib. bdg. 25.00 (ISBN 0-8495-3772-X). Arden Lib.

Vines, Sherard. Georgian Satirists: Edward Young, Christopher Smart, Charles Churchill. 217p. 1980. Repr. of 1934 ed. lib. bdg. 25.00 (ISBN 0-8495-5528-0). Arden Lib.

SMITH, ALFRED EMMANUEL, 1873-1944

Silva, Ruth C. Rum, Religion, & Votes: Nineteen Twenty-Eight Re-Examined. LC 80-24997. ix, 76p. 1981. Repr. of 1962 ed. lib. bdg. 22.50x (ISBN 0-313-22768-3, SIRR). Greenwood.

--Rum, Religion, & Votes: Nineteen Twenty-Eight Re-Examined. LC 80-24997. 85p. 1981. Repr. of 1962 ed. lib. bdg. 22.50 (ISBN 0-313-22768-3, SIRR). Greenwood.

SMITH, BESSIE, 1898-1937

Albertson, Chris. Bessie. LC 79-163353. 253p. 1981. pap. 6.95. Stein & Day.

SMITH, SYDNEY, 1771-1845

Bell, Alan. Sydney Smith. (Illus.). 240p. 1980. 29.95 (ISBN 0-19-812050-8). Oxford U Pr.

SMITH AND WESSON, INC., SPRINGFIELD, MASSACHUSETTS

Jinks, Roy G. History of Smith & Wesson. (Illus.). 290p. 1977. 15.95 (ISBN 0-917714-14-8). Beinfeld Pub.

SMOCKING

Marshall, Beverly. Smocks & Smocking. 1981. 14.95 (ISBN 0-442-28268-0). Van Nos Reinhold.

SMOKED FOODS COOKERY

see Cookery (Smoked Foods)

SMOKING

Bayless, Gordon E. How to (Easily) Eliminate the Smoking Habit. rev. ed. Ide, Arthur F., ed. (Studies in Health). (Illus.). 50p. 1981. pap. 16.95 (ISBN 0-86663-653-6). Ide Hse.

Berton, Alberta D., compiled by. Smoking & Health: A Comprehensive Bibliography. (Biomedical Information Guides Ser.: Vol. 3). 535p. 1980. 95.00 (ISBN 0-306-65184-X, IFI). Plenum Pub.

Eysenck, H. J. & Eaves, L. J. The Causes & Effects of Smoking. LC 79-48085. (Illus.). 400p. 1980. 39.95 (ISBN 0-8039-1454-7). Sage.

Freed, Alvyn M. & Michelson, Herb. Please Keep on Smoking: We Need the Money. (Orig.). 1980. pap. 2.95 saddle stitch (ISBN 0-915190-27-3). Jalmar Pr.

Fried & Oxern. Smoking for Two: Cigarettes & Pregnancy. 102p. Date not set. 8.95 (ISBN 0-02-910720-2). Macmillan.

G-Jo Institute. Stop Smoking Soon. 1980. pap. 4.50 (ISBN 0-916878-09-0). Falknyor Bks.

Hanson, Barbara H. S. T. O. P. Smoking. 100p. (Orig.). 1981. 9.95 (ISBN 0-934400-14-8). Landmark Bks.

Klebba, A. Joan. Mortality from Diseases Associated with Smoking: United States, 1960-77. Shipp, Audrey, ed. (Ser. 20, No. 17). 50p. Date not set. pap. text ed. price not set (ISBN 0-8406-0208-1). Natl Ctr Health Stats.

Lamore, Lee. Stop Trying to Stop Smoking, & Do It This Time: Secrets of a Mad Smoker. LC 80-69207. 112p. pap. 3.95 (ISBN 0-938318-00-4). Britton Pub.

Meftah, Michael. Smoking & Chemical Abuse. 1981. 5.75 (ISBN 0-8062-1616-6). Carlton.

Ogle, Jane. The Stop Smoking Diet. De Kay, George C., ed. 192p. 1981. 8.95 (ISBN 0-87131-337-5). M Evans.

Solomon, Neil. Stop Smoking, Lose Weight. 320p. 1981. 11.95 (ISBN 0-399-12600-7). Putnam.

SMOKING–PHYSIOLOGICAL EFFECT
see Tobacco–Physiological Effect

SMOKY MOUNTAINS
see Great Smoky Mountains

SMOOTHING FILTERS (MATHEMATICS)
see Digital Filters (Mathematics)

SNAILS

Brown, David S. Freshwater Snails of Africa & Their Medical Importance. (Illus.). 450p. 1980. 55.00 (ISBN 0-85066-145-5). Am Malacologists.

SNAKE RIVER AND VALLEY

Nelson, Sharlene & LeMieux, Joan. Cruising the Columbia & Snake Rivers: Eleven Cruises in the Inland Waterway. 192p. 1981. pap. 8.95 (ISBN 0-914718-57-6). Pacific Search.

SNAKES
see also Poisonous Snakes;
also particular kinds of snakes, e.g. Rattlesnakes

Gunther, Albert. Catalogue of Colubrine Snakes in the Collection of the British Museum. xvi, 281p. 1971. Repr. of 1858 ed. 4.50x (ISBN 0-565-00709-2, Pub. by British Mus Nat Hist England). Sabbot-Natural Hist Bks.

Pinney, Roy. The Snake Book. LC 78-68336. (Illus.). 256p. 1981. 12.95 (ISBN 0-385-13547-5). Doubleday.

Tennant, Alan & Werler, John E. The Snakes of Texas: A Field Guide. (Illus.). 384p. 1981. text ed. 19.95 (ISBN 0-292-77559-8); pap. 9.95 (ISBN 0-292-77560-1). U of Tex Pr.

Visser, John & Chapman, David. Snakes & Snakebite. 1980. 30.00x (Pub. by Bailey & Swinton South Africa). State Mutual Bk.

SNARE DRUM
see Drum

SNOW, CHARLES PERCY, SIR, 1905-

Sinha, S. N. The Sequential Novels of C.P. Snow: A Study of the Themes of Power & Morality. 242p. 1979. text ed. 15.00 (ISBN 0-8426-1655-1). Verry.

SNOWPLOW EFFECT
see Plasma Dynamics

SNUFF-BOXES AND BOTTLES

Curtis, Emily B. Reflected Glory in a Bottle: Chinese Snuff Bottle Portraits. (Illus.). 128p. 1980. 25.00 (ISBN 0-9605096-0-7). Soho Bodhi.

SOARING (AERONAUTICS)
see Gliding and Soaring

SOBRIQUETS
see Nicknames

SOCCER

Coombs, Charles. Be a Winner in Soccer. (Illus.). (gr. 5-7). 1980. pap. write for info. (ISBN 0-671-41104-7). PB.

Harris, Paul E., Jr. So You'd Like to Know More About Soccer! A Guide for Parents. 120p. pap. 3.95 (ISBN 0-88839-107-2). Soccer for Am.

Kaatz, Evelyn. Soccer! How One Player Made the Pros. (Illus.). 128p. (gr. 3 up). 1981. 7.95 (ISBN 0-316-47752-4). Little.

Mc Gettigan, James P. Complete Book of Drills for Winning Soccer. 254p. 1980. 10.95 (ISBN 0-13-156356-4, Parker). P-H.

Nelson, Richard L. Soccer for Men. 4th ed. (Physical Education Activities Ser.). 1981. pap. text ed. 3.25x (ISBN 0-697-07094-8). Wm C Brown.

Reeves, John A. & Simon, J. Malcolm. Coaches' Collection of Soccer Drills. LC 80-84212. (Illus.). 96p. (Orig.). 1981. pap. text ed. 4.95 (ISBN 0-918438-63-2). Leisure Pr.

Zabrowski, Edward K. Soccer Statistics Made Easy: A Guide to Rating & Predicting Player & Team Performance. (Illus.). viii, 81p. 1979. 5.95 (ISBN 0-9604994-0-7). Crossbar Ent.

SOCCER–HISTORY

Tischler, Steven. Footballers & Businessmen: The Origin of Professional Soccer in England. 180p. 1981. text ed. 24.00x (ISBN 0-8419-0658-0). Holmes & Meier.

SOCIAL ALIENATION
see Alienation (Social Psychology)

SOCIAL ASPECTS
see subdivision Social Aspects under subjects

SOCIAL CASE WORK
see also Counseling; Family Social Work; Marriage Counseling; Probation; School Social Work; Social Work with Youth; Social Workers

Pippin, James A. Developing Casework Skills. LC 80-18799. (Sage Human Services Guides: No. 15). 160p. 1980. pap. 8.00 (ISBN 0-8039-1503-9). Sage.

SOCIAL CASEWORK–STUDY AND TEACHING
see Social Work Education

SOCIAL CHANGE
Here are entered works on the theory of social change.
see also Community Development; Industry–Social Aspects; Social Evolution

Citizen Monitoring: A Guide for Social Change. 1979. 5.00. Comm Coun Great NY.

Eggan, Fred. The American Indian: Perspectives for the Study of Social Change. LC 80-67926. (Lewis Henry Morgan Lectures). 192p. 1981. 22.50 (ISBN 0-521-23752-1); pap. 6.95 (ISBN 0-521-28210-1). Cambridge U Pr.

Etzioni-Halevy, Eva. Social Change: Moderization & Post-Modernization. 280p. 1981. price not set (ISBN 0-7100-0767-1); pap. price not set (ISBN 0-7100-0768-X). Routledge & Kegan.

Kessler, Ronald & Greenberg, David. Linear Panel Analysis: Quantitative Models of Change. (Quantitative Studies in Social Relations). 1981. price not set (ISBN 0-12-405750-0). Acad Pr.

Merryman, J. H. Law & Social Change in Mediterranean Europe & Latin America: A Handbook of Legal & Social Indicators for Comparative Study. 1980. 47.50 (ISBN 0-379-20700-1). Oceana.

Mitchell, Lee C. Witnesses to a Vanishing America: The Nineteenth-Century Response. LC 80-8567. (Illus.). 288p. 1981. 16.50x (ISBN 0-691-06461-X). Princeton U Pr.

Sinha, R. Social Change in Indian Society. 1980. 11.25 (ISBN 0-391-02184-2). Humanities.

Villoldo, Alberto & Dychtwald, Kenneth, eds. Millenium: Glimpses into the Twenty-First Century. (Illus.). 348p. 1981. 15.00 (ISBN 0-87477-145-5); pap. 8.95 (ISBN 0-87477-166-8). J P Tarcher.

SOCIAL CLASSES

Coleman, Richard P., et al. Social Standing in America: New Dimensions of Class. LC 77-20426. 353p. 1981. pap. 6.95 (ISBN 0-465-07929-6). Basic.

Landecker, Werner S. Class Crystallization. 272p. 1981. 19.00 (ISBN 0-8135-0918-1). Rutgers U Pr.

Portes, Alejandro & Walton, John. Labor, Class, & the International System. 1981. price not set (ISBN 0-12-562020-9). Acad Pr.

SOCIAL COMPACT
see Social Contract

SOCIAL CONDITIONS
see Social History

SOCIAL CONFLICT
see also Social Classes

Abraham, David. The Collapse of the Weimar Republic: Political Economy & Crisis. LC 80-8533. 550p. 1981. 30.00x (ISBN 0-691-05322-7); pap. 12.50x (ISBN 0-691-10118-3). Princeton U Pr.

SOCIAL CONFORMITY
see Conformity

SOCIAL CONTRACT

Barker, Ernest, ed. Social Contract: Essays by Locke, Hume, & Rousseau. LC 80-22006. xliv, 307p. 1980. Repr. of 1947 ed. lib. bdg. 27.50x (ISBN 0-313-22409-9, BACT). Greenwood.

SOCIAL DANCING
see Ballroom Dancing

SOCIAL DEMOCRACY
see Socialism

SOCIAL DEMOCRATIC PARTY OF GERMANY

Breitman, Richard. German Socialism & Weimar Democracy. LC 80-21412. 296p. 1981. 20.00x (ISBN 0-8078-1462-8). U of NC Pr.

SOCIAL DEVIANCE
see Deviant Behavior

SOCIAL ECOLOGY
see Human Ecology

SOCIAL EQUALITY
see Equality

SOCIAL EVOLUTION
see also Social Change; Sociobiology

Dahlberg, Francis, ed. Woman the Gatherer. LC 80-25262. (Illus.). 288p. 1981. text ed. 15.00x (ISBN 0-300-02572-6). Yale U Pr.

Dallmayr, Fred R. Twilight of Subjectivity: Contributions to a Post-Individualist Theory of Politics. LC 80-23433. 416p. 1981. lib. bdg. 20.00x (ISBN 0-87023-314-9); pap. text ed. 10.00x (ISBN 0-87023-315-7). U of Mass Pr.

Glenn, Edmund S. Man & Mankind: Conflict & Communication Between Cultures. 300p. 1981. price not set (ISBN 0-89391-068-6). Ablex Pub.

Markl, H. & Feldman, M., eds. Evolution of Social Behavior: Hypotheses & Empirical Tests. (Dahlem Workshop Reports,Life Sciences Research Report Ser.: No. 18). (Illus.). 261p. (Orig.). 1980. pap. text ed. 22.50 (ISBN 0-89573-033-2). Verlag Chemie.

Villoldo, Alberto & Dychtwald, Kenneth, eds. Millenium: Glimpses into the Twenty-First Century. (Illus.). 348p. 1981. 15.00 (ISBN 0-87477-145-5); pap. 8.95 (ISBN 0-87477-166-8). J P Tarcher.

SOCIAL GROUPS
see also Leadership; Reference Groups; Social Mobility; Social Psychology; Social Values

European Institute & Johnstad, Trygve, eds. Group Dynamics & Society: A Multinational Approach. LC 80-24932. 352p. 1980. text ed. 27.50 (ISBN 0-89946-070-4). Oelgeschlager.

Funk, David A. Group Dynamic Law. LC 80-84733. 1981. 29.50 (ISBN 0-686-68867-8). Philos Lib.

SOCIAL HISTORY
see also Church and Social Problems; Labor and Laboring Classes; Moral Conditions; Poor; Rural Conditions; Social Indicators; Social Mobility; Social Policy; Social Problems; Social Surveys; Technology and Civilization; Urbanization
also subdivision Social Conditions under names of countries, e.g. Italy–Social Conditions

Cary & Weinberg. The Social Fabric: Volume 2. 3rd ed. 1980. pap. text ed. 8.95 (ISBN 0-316-13074-5). Little.

Hobsbawm, E. J. Bandits. (Illus.). 1981. pap. 3.95 (ISBN 0-394-74850-6). Pantheon.

SOCIAL HYGIENE
see Prostitution; Public Health; Venereal Diseases
also related subjects referred to under these headings

SOCIAL INDICATORS

On Social Indicators & Development. 36p. 1981. pap. 10.00 (ISBN 92-808-0147-3, TUNU 107, UNU). Unipub.

SOCIAL INSECTS
see Insect Societies

SOCIAL INSTITUTIONS
Here are entered works on interrelated systems of social roles, norms, or processes organized for the satisfaction of an important social need or function, e.g. family, economy, education.
see also Social Structure

Posner, Richard A. The Economics of Justice. LC 80-25075. (Illus.). 448p. 1981. text ed. 25.00 (ISBN 0-674-23525-8). Harvard U Pr.

Schotter, Andrew. The Economic Theory of Social Institutions. (Illus.). 240p. Date not set. 29.50 (ISBN 0-521-23044-6). Cambridge U Pr.

SOCIAL INSURANCE
see Social Security

SOCIAL INTERACTION

Moss, Gordon E. Illness, Immunity & Social Interaction. 298p. 1981. Repr. of 1973 ed. text ed. price not set (ISBN 0-89874-266-8). Krieger.

SOCIAL MEDICINE

Birenbaum, Arnold. Health Care & Society: Patients, Professions, Programs & Policies. LC 80-67092. 350p. 1981. text ed. 28.50 (ISBN 0-916672-57-3). Allanheld.

Butrym, Zofia. Medical Social Work in Action. 128p. 1968. pap. text ed. 5.00x (Pub. by Bedford England). Renouf.

Downie, R. S. & Telfer, Elizabeth. Caring & Curing: A Philosophy of Medicine & Social Work. LC 80-40246. 180p. 1980. 19.95 (ISBN 0-416-71800-0, 2063). Methuen Inc.

Hingson, Ralph, et al. In Sickness & in Health: Social Dimensions of Medical Care. 300p. 1981. pap. text ed. 12.50 (ISBN 0-8016-4411-9). Mosby.

Morris, Robert. Allocating Health Resources for the Aged & Disabled: Technology Versus Politics. 1981. price not set (ISBN 0-669-04329-X). Lexington Bks.

Society for Hospital Social Work Directors of the American Hospital Association. Documentation by Social Workers in Medical Records. 1978. pap. 6.00 (ISBN 0-87258-256-6, 1085). Am Hospital.

--Reporting System for Hospital Social Work. LC 78-5696. 1978. pap. 8.75 (ISBN 0-87258-237-X, 1562). Am Hospital.

--Social Work Staff Development for Health Care. LC 76-41793. 1976. pap. 7.25 (ISBN 0-87258-322-8, 2550). Am Hospital.

Suchman, Edward A. Sociology & the Field of Public Health. LC 63-21228. 1963. pap. 2.00 (ISBN 0-87154-864-X). Russell Sage.

Wilson, Robert N., et al. Readings in Medical Sociology. 448p. Date not set. text ed. 12.95 (ISBN 0-669-03945-4). Heath.

Wolf, Stewart. Social Environment & Health. LC 80-50868. (The Jessie & John Danz Lecture Ser.). (Illus.). 112p. 1981. 8.95 (ISBN 0-295-95777-8). U of Wash Pr.

SOCIAL MOBILITY
see also Social Classes

Kaelble, Hartmut. Historical Research on Social Mobility. Noakes, Ingrid, tr. 1981. text ed. 22.50x (ISBN 0-231-05274-X). Columbia U Pr.

SOCIAL PERCEPTION
see also Personality Assessment

Gordon, Leonard V. Measurement of Interpersonal Values. LC 74-22623. 122p. (Orig.). 1975. text ed. 12.00 (ISBN 0-574-72770-1); pap. text ed. 8.20 (ISBN 0-574-72764-7). SRA.

SOCIAL PLANNING
see Social Policy

SOCIAL POLICY
see also Economic Policy; Education and State; Welfare Economics
also subdivision Social Policy under names of countries, states, cities, etc.

Benoit, Emile. Progress & Survival: An Essay on the Future of Mankind. Gohn, Jack B., ed. 144p. 1980. 17.95 (ISBN 0-03-056911-7). Praeger.

Bruyn, S. T. The Social Economy: People Transforming Modern Business. 392p. 1977. 29.95 (ISBN 0-471-01985-2). Wiley.

Chance, M. R. & Larsen, R. R. The Social Structure of Attention. 339p. 1976. 46.00 (ISBN 0-471-01573-3). Wiley.

Culyer, A. J. The Political Economy of Social Policy. 1980. 27.50 (ISBN 0-312-62242-2). St Martin.

Dunn, W. Public Policy Analysis: An Introduction. 1981. pap. 18.50 (ISBN 0-13-737957-9). P-H.

Dunn, William, ed. Social Values & Public Policy. (Illus., Orig.). 1981. pap. 5.00 (ISBN 0-918592-44-5). Policy Studies.

Finsterbusch, Kurt. Understanding Social Impacts: Assessing the Effects of Public Projects. LC 80-17586. (Sage Library of Social Research: Vol. 110). (Illus.). 311p. 1980. 18.00 (ISBN 0-8039-1015-0); pap. 8.95 (ISBN 0-8039-1016-9). Sage.

Hill, Michael. Understanding Social Policy. (Aspects of Social Policy Ser.). 272p. 1981. pap. 10.00x (ISBN 0-631-18180-6, Pub. by Basil Blackwell England). Biblio Dist.

Luttbeg, Norman R. Public Opinion & Public Policy. 3rd ed. LC 80-52446. 475p. 1981. pap. text ed. 11.95 (ISBN 0-87581-259-7). Peacock Pubs.

MacLeod, Roy M. Treasury Control & Social Administration. 62p. 1968. pap. text ed. 5.00x (Pub. by Bedford England). Renouf.

Mazmanian, Daniel & Sabatier, Paul A., eds. Effective Policy Implementation. LC 79-3041. (Policy Study Organization Bks.). 1981. 23.95x (ISBN 0-669-03311-1). Lexington Bks.

Palumbo, Dennis J. & Harder, Marvin A. Implementing Public Policy. LC 80-8597. (Policy Studies Organization Bks.). 1981. price not set (ISBN 0-669-04305-2). Lexington Bks.

Palumbo, Dennis J., et al, eds. Evaluating & Optimizing Public Policy. LC 80-8598. (Policy). 1981. price not set (ISBN 0-669-04306-0). Lexington Bks.

Rothman, David & Wheeler, Stanton, eds. Social History & Social Policy. LC 80-1772. (Studies in Social Discontinuity). 1981. price not set (ISBN 0-12-598680-7). Acad Pr.

SOCIAL PROBLEMS
see also Children–Employment; Church and Social Problems; Civilization; Cost and Standard of Living; Crime and Criminals; Discrimination; Divorce; Emigration and Immigration; Housing; Juvenile Delinquency; Liquor Problem; Migrant Labor; Migration, Internal; Old Age Pensions; Poor; Progress; Prostitution; Public Health; Public Welfare; Race Discrimination; Race Relations; Social Surveys; Sociology, Islamic; Suicide; Sunday Legislation; Unemployed

Abel-Smith, Brian. The Poor & the Poorest. 78p. 1965. pap. text ed. 5.00x (Pub. by Bedford England). Renouf.

Anderson, Elijah. A Place on the Corner. LC 78-1879. (Studies of Urban Society). 248p. 1981. pap. 5.50 (ISBN 0-226-01954-3). U of Chicago Pr.

Brickner, Balfour. Searching the Prophets for Values. 1981. 6.95 (ISBN 0-8074-0047-5). UAHC.

Gregory, Peter. Polluted Homes. 64p. 1965. pap. text ed. 3.75x (Pub. by Bedford England). Renouf.

Horton, Paul B. & Leslie, Gerald R. The Sociology of Social Problems. 7th ed. (Illus.). 672p. 1981. text ed. 18.95 (ISBN 0-13-821702-5). P-H.

Leonard, George B. The Transformation. 288p. 1981. pap. 5.95 (ISBN 0-87477-169-2). J P Tarcher.

Paxman, John M., ed. The World Population Crisis: Policy Implications & the Role of Law: Proceedings of the American Society of International Law Regional Meeting & the John Bassett Moore Society of International Law Symposium. LC 80-19753. vi, 179p. 1980. Repr. of 1971 ed. lib. bdg. 22.50x (ISBN 0-313-22619-9, PAWO). Greenwood.

Reasons & Purdue. Ideology of Social Problems. 15.95 (ISBN 0-88284-110-6). Alfred Pub.

Roman, A. The World in Crisis. 1981. 11.95 (ISBN 0-533-04903-2). Vantage.

Rubington, Earl & Weinberg, Martin S., eds. The Study of Social Problems: Five Perspectives. 3rd ed. 256p. 1981. pap. text ed. 7.95x (ISBN 0-19-502825-2). Oxford U Pr.

Sheleff, Leon. Generations Apart: Adult Hostility to Youth. 352p. 1981. 18.95 (ISBN 0-07-056540-6, P&RB). McGraw.

Solly, Henry. Working Men's Social Clubs & Educational Institutes: London Nineteen Four. LC 79-56943. (The English Working Class Ser.). 1980. lib. bdg. 22.00 (ISBN 0-8240-0124-9). Garland Pub.

Wasserstrom, Richard. Philosophy & Social Issues: Five Studies. LC 79-9486. 224p. 1980. pap. text ed. 6.95 (ISBN 0-268-01536-8). U of Notre Dame Pr.

Weinberg, Martin S., et al, eds. The Solution of Social Problems: Five Perspectives. 2nd ed. 240p. 1981. pap. text ed. 7.95x (ISBN 0-19-502787-6). Oxford U Pr.

Weiss & Klass. Case Studies in Regulation: Revolution & Reform. 1981. pap. text ed. 9.95 (ISBN 0-316-92893-3). Little.

Williamson, et al. Social Problems: The Contemporary Debates. 3rd ed. 1981. pap. text ed. 9.95 (ISBN 0-316-94362-2); test bank avail. (ISBN 0-316-94363-0). Little.

SOCIAL PROBLEMS AND THE CHURCH
see Church and Social Problems

SOCIAL PROGRESS
see Progress

SOCIAL PSYCHOLOGY
see also Alienation (Social Psychology); Attitude (Psychology); Crowds; Discrimination; Empathy; Ethnopsychology; Interpersonal Relations; Leadership; Minorities; Political Psychology; Psychological Warfare; Psychology, Applied; Psychology, Forensic; Public Opinion; Social Conflict; Social Interaction; Social Role

American Psychological Association. Changing Attitudes: Student Booklet. (Human Behavior Curriculum Project Ser.). 64p. (Orig.). (gr. 9-12). 1981. pap. text ed. 3.95 (ISBN 0-8077-2621-4). Tchrs Coll.

--Changing Attitudes: Teachers Handbook & Duplication Masters. (Human Behavior Curriculum Project Ser.). 48p. (Orig.). (gr. 9-12). 1981. 9.95 (ISBN 0-8077-2622-2). Tchrs Coll.

Argyle, M., et al. Social Situations. (Illus.). 450p. Date not set. price not set (ISBN 0-521-23260-0); pap. price not set (ISBN 0-521-29881-4). Cambridge U Pr.

Cratty, Bryant J. Social Psychology in Athletics. (Illus.). 320p. 1981. text ed. 15.95 (ISBN 0-13-817650-7). P-H.

Current Trends in Social Psychology. 299p. 1980. Repr. of 1948 ed. lib. bdg. 35.00 (ISBN 0-89984-108-2). Century Bookbindery.

Freedman, Jonathan, et al. Social Psychology. 4th ed. (Illus.). 656p. 1981. text ed. 18.95 (ISBN 0-13-817783-X). P-H.

Hollander, Edwin P. Principles & Methods of Social Psychology. 4th ed. (Illus.). 548p. 1981. text ed. 18.95x (ISBN 0-19-502822-8). Oxford U Pr.

Rosnow, Ralph L. Paradigms in Transition: The Methodology of Social Inquiry. 176p. 1981. text ed. 12.00x (ISBN 0-19-502876-7); pap. text ed. 5.95 (ISBN 0-19-502877-5). Oxford U Pr.

Shaver, Kelly G. Principles of Social Psychology. 2nd ed. (Psychology Ser.). (Illus.). 656p. 1981. text ed. 19.95 (ISBN 0-87626-634-0). Winthrop.

Tedeschi, James T., ed. Impression Management Theory & Social Psychological Research. 1981. price not set (ISBN 0-12-685180-8). Acad Pr.

Vander Zanden, James W. Social Psychology. 2nd ed. 524p. 1981. text ed. 17.95 (ISBN 0-394-32427-7). Random.

Wheeler, Ladd, ed. Review of Personality & Social Psychology: No. 1. (Illus.). 352p. 1980. 20.00 (ISBN 0-8039-1457-1). Sage.

Williamson, Robert C., et al. Social Psychology. LC 80-52451. 550p. 1981. text ed. 14.95 (ISBN 0-87581-264-3). Peacock Pubs.

SOCIAL PSYCHOTECHNICS
see Psychology, Applied

SOCIAL REFORM
see Social Problems

SOCIAL ROLE
see also Role Playing; Sex Role

Rousseau, Jean J. Annotated Social Contract. Sheroner, Charles M., ed. pap. 3.95 (ISBN 0-452-00369-5, FM369, Mer). NAL.

Skjei, Eric & Rabkin, Richard. The Male Ordeal: Role Crisis in a Changing World. 320p. 1981. 13.95 (ISBN 0-399-12575-2, Perigee). Putnam.

SOCIAL SCIENCE
see Social Sciences; Sociology

SOCIAL SCIENCE RESEARCH
see also Communication in the Social Sciences; Sociological Research

Broom, L., et al. Investigating Social Mobility. (ANU Department of Sociology Monograph: No. 1). (Illus.). 220p. (Orig.). 1980. pap. text ed. 11.95 (ISBN 0-909851-32-8, 1561). Bks Australia.

Casanova, Pablo G. The Fallacy of Social Science Research: A Critical Examination & New Qualitative Model. (PPS on Social Policy Ser.). 75p. 1981. 15.00 (ISBN 0-08-027549-4). Pergamon.

Duncan, Ronald J., ed. Investigacion Social En Puerto Rico. LC 80-23445. 350p. 1980. text ed. 13.00 (ISBN 0-913480-45-2); pap. 8.00 (ISBN 0-913480-44-4). Inter Am U Pr.

Duncan, Ronald J., et al. Manual De Tecnicas De Investigacion Social. LC 80-23411. (Illus.). 78p. 1980. 5.00 (ISBN 0-913480-46-0). Inter Am U Pr.

Meehan, Eugene J. Reasoned Argument in Social Science: Linking Research to Policy Ser. LC 80-1198. (Illus.). 248p. 1981. lib. bdg. 27.50 (ISBN 0-313-22481-1, MRE). Greenwood.

SOCIAL SCIENCES
Here are entered general and comprehensive works dealing with sociology, political science, and economics.
see also Civics; Conservatism; Human Behavior; Human Ecology; Liberalism; Power (Social Sciences); Social Change

Bartholomew, David. Guidebook for Social Scientists. 148p. 1981. 34.50 (ISBN 0-471-27932-3, Pub. by Wiley-Interscience); pap. 19.95 (ISBN 0-471-27933-1). Wiley.

Harmon, Michael M. Action Theory for Public Administration. (Longman Professional Studies in Public Administration). 256p. (Orig.). 1981. text ed. 22.50 (ISBN 0-582-28254-3); pap. text ed. 9.95 (ISBN 0-582-28255-1). Longman.

Helfgot, Joseph H. Professional Reforming: Mobilization for Youth & the Failure of Social Science. 240p. 1981. 23.95 (ISBN 0-669-04100-9). Lexington Bks.

Lyon, William & Duke, Bill. Introduction to Human Services. (Illus.). 320p. 1981. pap. text ed. 14.95 (ISBN 0-8359-3216-8). Reston.

MacRae, Duncan, Jr. The Social Function of Social Science. LC 75-32282. 376p. 1981. pap. 7.95 (ISBN 0-300-02670-6). Yale U Pr.

Mannheim, Karl. Man & Society in an Age of Reconstruction. Shils, Edward, tr. from Ger. (Studies in Modern Social Structure). 490p. 40.00 (ISBN 0-7100-1788-X). Routledge & Kegan.

Martindale, Don & Mohan, Raj P. Ideals & Realities: Some Problem Areas of Professional Social Science. (Intercontinental Series in Sociogy: No. 2). 250p. 1980. lib. bdg. 14.95 (ISBN 0-933142-01-3). Intercont Press.

Mehlinger, Howard & Davis, O. L., Jr., eds. The Social Studies. LC 80-83744. (National Society for the Study of Education 80th Yearbooks: Pt. II). 300p. 1981. lib. bdg. 16.00x. U of Chicago Pr.

Pearce, W. Barnett & Cronen, Vernon E. Communication, Action & Meaning: The Creation of Social Realities. 308p. 1980. 29.95 (ISBN 0-03-057611-3). Praeger.

Report of the United Nations University Expert Group on Human & Social Development. 36p. 1980. pap. 5.00 (ISBN 92-808-0145-7, TUNU082, UNU). Unipub.

Rudeng, Erik & Holm, Hans-Henrik, eds. Social Science Research: Prospects & Purposes. 210p. 1981. 36.00x (ISBN 82-00-05521-3). Universitet.

Schusky, Ernest L. Introduction to Social Science. (Illus.). 512p. 1981. pap. text ed. 15.95 (ISBN 0-13-496703-8). P-H.

Singleton, Laurel R., ed. Data Book of Social Studies Materials & Resources, Vol. 6. (Data Bk.). (Orig.). 1981. pap. 10.00 (ISBN 0-89994-254-7). Soc Sci Ed.

Zulke, Frank. Through the Eyes of Social Science. 2nd ed. 336p. 1981. pap. text ed. 7.95x (ISBN 0-917974-54-9). Waveland Pr.

SOCIAL SCIENCES-EXAMINATIONS, QUESTIONS, ETC.

Williams, Paul L. & Moore, Jerry R., eds. Criterion-Referenced Testing for the Social Studies, No. 64. LC 80-84889. (Bulletin Ser.). 1980. pap. write for info. (ISBN 0-87986-034-0). Coun Soc Studies.

SOCIAL SCIENCES-HISTORY

Bergner, Jeffrey T. The Origin of Formalism in Social Science. LC 80-17484. 160p. 1981. lib. bdg. 16.00 (ISBN 0-226-04362-2). U of Chicago Pr.

SOCIAL SCIENCES-MATHEMATICAL MODELS

Burghes, D. N. Mathematical Models in the Social, Management & Life Sciences. LC 79-40989. 287p. 1980. pap. 19.95 (ISBN 0-470-27073-X). Halsted Pr.

Harshbarger, Ronald J. & Reynoldds, James J. Mathematical Applications for Management, Life & Social Studies. 604p. 1981. text ed. 17.95 (ISBN 0-669-03209-3); solutions guide avail. (ISBN 0-669-03211-5). Heath.

SOCIAL SCIENCES-METHODOLOGY
see also Communication in the Social Sciences

Kelley, Truman L. & Krey, A. C. Tests & Measurements in the Social Sciences. 635p. 1980. Repr. of 1934 ed. lib. bdg. 35.00 (ISBN 0-89987-452-5). Century Bookbindery.

Morris, Lynn L. & Fitz-Gibbon, Carol T. How to Deal with Goals & Objectives. rev. ed. LC 78-57012. (Program Evaluation Kit Ser.: Vol. 2). (Illus.). 78p. 1978. pap. 4.50 (ISBN 0-8039-1065-7). Sage.

Sechrest, Lee, et al, eds. Evaluation Studies Review Annual, Vol. 4. rev. ed. LC 76-15865. (Illus.). 766p. 1979. 35.00 (ISBN 0-8039-1329-X). Sage.

SOCIAL SCIENCES-RESEARCH
see Social Science Research

SOCIAL SCIENCES-STATISTICS

Compendium of Social Statistics 1977. (Statistical Papers K Ser.: No. 4). 1325p. 1980. pap. 35.00 (ISBN 0-686-68947-X, UN80/17/6, UN). Unipub.

Fuller, M. F. & Lury, D. A. Statistics Workbook for Social Science Students. 256p. 1977. 30.00x (ISBN 0-86003-016-4, Pub. by Allan Pubs England); pap. 15.00x (ISBN 0-86003-117-9). State Mutual Bk.

SOCIAL SCIENCES-STUDY AND TEACHING

Danbury, Hazel. Teaching Practical Social Work. 85p. 1979. pap. text ed. 7.40x (ISBN 0-7199-0953-8, Pub. by Bedford England). Renouf.

Jones, Kathleen. The Teaching of Social Studies in British Universities. 87p. 1964. pap. text ed. 3.75x (Pub. by Bedford England). Renouf.

SOCIAL SCIENCES-STUDY AND TEACHING (ELEMENTARY)

Ryan. The Social Studies Sourcebook: Ideas for Teaching in the Elementary & Middle School. new ed. 320p. 1980. pap. text ed. 10.45 (ISBN 0-205-06802-4, 2368021). Allyn.

SOCIAL SCIENCES-STUDY AND TEACHING (SECONDARY)

Educational Resources Center. Social Science Skills: Activities for the Secondary Classroom, 7 vols. Incl. American Government Issues (ISBN 0-8077-2649-4); American Lifestyle Issues (ISBN 0-8077-2648-6); Consumer Issues (ISBN 0-8077-2647-8); Economic Issues (ISBN 0-8077-2645-1); Energy Issues (ISBN 0-8077-2646-X); Global Issues (ISBN 0-8077-2643-5); Population Issues (ISBN 0-8077-2644-3); Basic Skills (ISBN 0-8077-2650-8). (Orig.). 1981. price not set. Tchrs Coll.

SOCIAL SCIENCES-VOCATIONAL GUIDANCE

R. B. Uleck Associates. Social & Behavioral Sciences Jobs Handbook. (Illus.). 48p. (Orig.). 1979. pap. 9.95 (ISBN 0-937562-02-5). Uleck Assoc.

Rodgers, Barbara N. The Careers of Social Studies Students. 75p. 1964. pap. text ed. 3.75x (Pub. by Bedford England). Renouf.

SOCIAL SCIENCES-YEARBOOKS

Sechrest, Lee, et al, eds. Evaluation Studies Review Annual, Vol. 4. rev. ed. LC 76-15865. (Illus.). 766p. 1979. 35.00 (ISBN 0-8039-1329-X). Sage.

SOCIAL SCIENCES AND STATE

The Utilisation of the Social Sciences in Policy Making in the United States: Case Studies. 392p. (Orig.). 1980. pap. 20.00 (ISBN 9-2641-2128-5). OECD.

SOCIAL SECURITY
see also Friendly Societies; Insurance, Disability; Insurance, Health; Insurance, Unemployment; Old Age Pensions; Workmen'S Compensation

Campbell, Colin D., ed. Financing Social Securtiy. 1979. 15.25 (ISBN 0-8447-2140-9); pap. 8.25 (ISBN 0-8447-2140-9). Am Enterprise.

Colberg, Marshall R. Social Security Retirement Test: Right or Wrong? 1978. pap. 4.25 (ISBN 0-8447-3307-5). Am Enterprise.

Consumer Guide Editors. Social Security Benefits. 1980. pap. 2.50 (ISBN 0-449-90029-0, Columbine). Fawcett.

Darby, Michael R. Effects of Social Security on Income & the Capital Stock. 1979. pap. 4.25 (ISBN 0-8447-3329-6). Am Enterprise.

Meyer, Charles W. Social Security Disability Insurance: Problems of Unexpected Growth. 1979. pap. 4.25 (ISBN 0-8447-3365-2). Am Enterprise.

Neitzel, James, ed. Our Social Security System: How Can We Make It Sound, Successful, & Solvent. 94p. (Orig.). 1977. pap. 7.50 (ISBN 0-89154-123-3). Intl Found Employ.

Social Security, Savings Plan & Other Retirement Arrangements: Learning Guide CEBS Course III. 1980. spiral 13.00 (ISBN 0-89154-130-6). Intl Found Employ.

SOCIAL SECURITY-AUSTRALIA

Kewley, T. H., ed. Australian Social Security Today. 248p. 1980. 22.50x (ISBN 0-424-00067-9, Pub. by Sydney U Pr Australia). Intl Schol Bk Serv.

SOCIAL SERVICE
see also Church and Social Problems; Community Organizations; Marriage Counseling; Medical Social Work; Psychiatric Social Work; Public Welfare; School Social Work; Social Case Work; Social Workers

Austin, Michael J. Supervisory Management for the Human Services. (P-H Ser. in Social Work Practices). 352p. 1981. text ed. 16.95 (ISBN 0-13-877068-9). P-H.

Baker, Frank & Northman, John E. Helping: Human Services for the 80's. 221p. 1981. pap. text ed. 8.75 (ISBN 0-8016-0424-9). Mosby.

Barnes, Jack. Social Care Research. 163p. 1978. pap. text ed. 8.75x (ISBN 0-7199-0947-3, Pub. by Bedford England). Renouf.

Bruno, Frank J. Trends in Social Work, Eighteen Seventy-Four to Nineteen Fifty-Six: A History Based on the Proceedings of the National Conference of Social Work. 2nd ed. LC 80-19210. xviii, 462p. 1980. Repr. of 1957 ed. lib. bdg. 39.75x (ISBN 0-313-22665-2, BRTI). Greenwood.

Butler, John R. Who Goes Home? 75p. 1970. pap. text ed. 5.00x (ISBN 0-7135-1593-7, Pub. by Bedford England). Renouf.

Chapman, Paul. Unmet Needs & the Delivery of Care. 110p. 1979. pap. text ed. 9.90x (ISBN 0-7199-0962-7, Pub. by Bedford England). Renouf.

Clegg, Joan. Dictionary of Social Services- Policy & Practice. 147p. 1977. text ed. 12.50x (ISBN 0-7199-0932-5, Pub. by Bedford England). Renouf.

Connolly, W. E. Appearance & Reality in Politics. 224p. Date not set. price not set (ISBN 0-521-23026-8). Cambridge U Pr.

Coombs, Philip H., ed. Meeting the Basic Needs of the Rural Poor: The Integrated, Community-Based Approach. LC 80-19838. (Pergamon Policy Studies on International Development). 828p. 1980. 49.50 (ISBN 0-08-026306-2). Pergamon.

Dea, Kay, ed. Perspectives for the Future: Social Work Practice in the 80's. LC 80-83988. (Professional Conference Vols. Ser.). 192p. (Orig.). 1980. pap. text ed. 12.50x (ISBN 0-87101-089-5, CBO-089-C). Natl Assn Soc Wkrs.

Deacon, Alan. In Search of the Scrounger. 110p. 1976. pap. text ed. 7.50x (ISBN 0-7135-1992-4, Pub. by Bedford England). Renouf.

Dubois, Paul M. Modern Administrative Practices in Human Services. 1981. write for info. (ISBN 0-398-04164-4). C C Thomas.

Epstein, Charlotte. An Introduction to the Human Services: Developing Knowledge, Skills, & Sensitivity. (Illus.). 368p. 1981. text ed. 15.95 (ISBN 0-686-69277-2). P-H.

Freeman, Roger. The Wayward Welfare State. (Publications Ser.: No. 249). (Illus.). 415p. 1981. price not set. Hoover Inst Pr.

Gilbert, Neil & Specht, Harry. The Emergence of Social Work. 2nd ed. LC 80-83097. 484p. 1981. pap. text ed. 12.95 (ISBN 0-87581-266-X). Peacock Pubs.

Gladstone, F. J. Voluntary Action in a Changing World. 137p. 1979. pap. text ed. 9.90x (ISBN 0-7199-1033-1, Pub. by Bedford England). Renouf.

Goldstein, Howard. Social Learning & Change: A Cognitive Approach to Human Services. LC 80-23446. 1981. 19.50 (ISBN 0-87249-402-0). U of SC Pr.

Grinnell, Richard. Social Work Research & Evaluation. LC 80-52448. 600p. 1981. text ed. 19.50 (ISBN 0-87581-261-9). Peacock Pubs.

Henry, Sue. Group Skills in Social Work: A Four Dimensional Approach. LC 80-83378. 416p. 1981. text ed. 12.50 (ISBN 0-87581-268-6). Peacock Pubs.

Horejsi, Charles R., et al. Social Work Practice with Parents of Children in Foster Care: A Handbook. write for info. (ISBN 0-398-04471-6). C C Thomas.

Howard, Anne. Welfare Rights- the Local Authorities Role. 52p. 1978. pap. text ed. 4.40x (ISBN 0-7199-0946-5, Pub. by Bedford England). Renouf.

Jenkins, Shirley. The Ethnic Dilemma in Social Services. LC 80-2155. (Illus.). 1981. 14.95 (ISBN 0-02-916400-1). Free Pr.

Jones, Ray & Pritchard, Colin. Social Work with Adolescents. (Library of Social Work). 260p. 1981. 16.95 (ISBN 0-7100-0632-2); pap. write for info. (ISBN 0-7100-0633-0). Routledge & Kegan.

Kamerman, Sheila B. Maternal & Parental Benefits & Leaves: An International Review. LC 80-69763. (Impact on Policy Monograph Ser.: No. 1). (Illus.). 80p. (Orig.). 1980. pap. text ed. 5.00 (ISBN 0-938436-00-7). Columbia U Ctr Soc Sci.

Levitan, Sar A. Programs in Aid of the Poor for the 1980's. LC 80-8093. (Policy Studies in Employment & Welfare: No. 1). (Illus.). 166p. 1980. text ed. 11.00 (ISBN 0-8018-2483-4); pap. text ed. 3.95 (ISBN 0-8018-2484-2). Johns Hopkins.

Marks, Janet. Home Help. 112p. 1975. pap. text ed. 7.50x (ISBN 0-7135-1842-1, Pub. by Bedford England). Renouf.

Martinez-Brawley, Emilia E. Seven Decades of Rural Social Work: From Country Life Commission to Rural Caucus. 275p. 1981. 21.95 (ISBN 0-03-058027-7). Praeger.

Morris, Lynn L. & Fitz-Gibbon, Carol T. How to Measure Program Implementation. LC 78-58655. (Program Evaluation Kit Ser.: Vol. 4). (Illus.). 140p. 1978. pap. 6.95 (ISBN 0-8039-1066-5). Sage.

Moseley, L. G. Research for Social Welfare: Six Case Studies in Cyprus. 143p. 1979. pap. text ed. 9.90x (ISBN 0-7199-0948-1, Pub. by Bedford England). Renouf.

National Conference on Social Welfare, ed. The Social Welfare Forum, 1980. 288p. 1981. 27.50 (ISBN 0-231-05290-1). Columbia U Pr.

Oswin, Maureen. Holes in the Welfare Net. 168p. 1978. text ed. 13.75x (ISBN 0-7199-0939-2, Pub. by Bedford England). Renouf.

Robinson, Tim. In Worlds Apart-Professionals & Their Clients in the Welfare State. 87p. 1978. pap. text ed. 4.90x (ISBN 0-7199-0942-2, Pub. by Bedford England). Renouf.

Sanders. Fundamentals of Social Work Practice. 1981. pap. text ed. price not set. Duxbury Pr.

School of Social Work, Columbia University. Dictionary Catalog of the Whitney M. Young, Jr., Memorial Library of Social Work. (Library Catalogs & Supplements Ser.). 1980. lib. bdg. 1275.00 (ISBN 0-8161-0307-0). G K Hall.

Stein, Herman D., ed. Organization & the Human Services: Cross-Disciplinary Reflections. 275p. 1981. 17.50x (ISBN 0-87722-209-6). Temple U Pr.

Stewart, Rosemary. Continously Under Review. 70p. 1967. pap. text ed. 5.00x (Pub. by Bedford England). Renouf.

Thomas, David N. & Henderson, Paul, eds. Readings in Community Work. 196p. 1981. text ed. 29.50x (ISBN 0-04-361045-5, 2650-1); pap. text ed. 14.95x (ISBN 0-04-361046-3). Allen Unwin.

Watts, Thomas D. The Societal Learning Approach: A New Approach to Social Welfare Policy & Planning in America. LC 80-69231. 140p. 1981. perfect bdg. 11.95 (ISBN 0-86548-058-3). Century Twenty One.

Webb, Adrian L. Income Redistribution & the Welfare State. 125p. 1971. pap. text ed. 6.25x (Pub. by Bedford England). Renouf.

SOCIAL SERVICE–BIBLIOGRAPHY
Germano, William P. & Lecyn, Nancy, eds. Directory of Social & Health Agencies of New York City: 1981-1982. 576p. 1981. 32.50x (ISBN 0-231-05134-4); pap. text ed. 24.00x (ISBN 0-231-05135-2). Columbia U Pr.
SOCIAL SERVICE–CASES
see Social Case Work
SOCIAL SERVICE–STUDY AND TEACHING
see Social Work Education
SOCIAL SERVICE–GREAT BRITAIN
Bolger, Steve, et al, eds. Towards Socialist Welfare Work: Working in the State. (Critical Texts in Social Work & the Welfare State). 176p. 1980. text ed. 32.50x (ISBN 0-333-28905-6); pap. text ed. 10.50x (ISBN 0-333-28906-4). Humanities.
Economic & Social Committee of the European Communities - General Secretariat, ed. Community Advisory Committees for the Representation of Socio-Economic Interest. 240p. 1980. text ed. 24.75x (ISBN 0-566-00328-7, Pub. by Gower Pub Co England). Renouf.
Hazel, Nancy. A Bridge to Independence: The Kent Family Placement Project. (Practice of Social Work Ser.). 208p. 1981. 25.00x (ISBN 0-631-12943-X, Pub. by Basil Blackwell England); pap. 12.50x (ISBN 0-631-12596-5). Biblio Dist.
Packman, Jean. The Child's Generation: Child Care Policy in Britain. 2nd ed. (Aspects of Social Policy Ser.). 200p. 1981. pap. 12.50x (ISBN 0-631-12664-3, Pub. by Basil Blackwell England). Biblio Dist.
Wright, Christopher. The Welfare State. (Illus.). 72p. (gr. 9-12). 1981. 14.95 (ISBN 0-7134-2375-7, Pub. by Batsford England). David & Charles.
SOCIAL SERVICE, MEDICAL
see Medical Social Work
SOCIAL SERVICE, PSYCHIATRIC
see Psychiatric Social Work
SOCIAL SERVICE, SCHOOL
see School Social Work
SOCIAL STATUS
see also Social Classes; Social Role
Landecker, Werner S. Class Crystallization. 272p. 1981. 19.00 (ISBN 0-8135-0918-1). Rutgers U Pr.
Rousseau, Jean J. Annotated Social Contract. Sheroner, Charles M., ed. pap. 3.95 (ISBN 0-452-00369-5, FM369, Mer). NAL.
SOCIAL STRATIFICATION
see Social Classes
SOCIAL STRUCTURE
Chance, M. R. & Larsen, R. R. The Social Structure of Attention. 339p. 1976. 46.00 (ISBN 0-471-01573-3). Wiley.
SOCIAL STUDIES
see Social Sciences
SOCIAL SURVEYS
see also Economic Surveys; Educational Surveys; Family Life Surveys; Public Opinion Polls
Smith, Tom W. & Rich, Guy J. A Compendium of Trends on General Social Survey Questions. (National Opinion Research Center (NORC): No. 129). (Orig.). 1980. pap. text ed. 7.50x (ISBN 0-932132-24-3). NORC.
SOCIAL SYSTEMS
see also Social Institutions
Dunham, H. Warren. Social Systems & Schizophrenia: Selected Papers. LC 80-14193. 332p. 1980. 28.95 (ISBN 0-03-056134-5). Praeger.
SOCIAL VALUES
Dunn, William, ed. Social Values & Public Policy. (Illus., Orig.). 1981. pap. 5.00 (ISBN 0-918592-44-5). Policy Studies.
Hardy, Jean. Values in Social Policy: Nine Contradictions. (Radical Social Policy Ser.). 132p. (Orig.). 1981. pap. price not set (ISBN 0-7100-0782-5). Routledge & Kegan.
SOCIAL WELFARE
see Public Welfare; Social Problems; Social Service
SOCIAL WORK
see Social Service
SOCIAL WORK EDUCATION
Wilson, Suanna J. Recording: Guidelines for Social Workers. LC 79-7636. 241p. 1980. 19.95 (ISBN 0-02-935940-6). Free Pr.
SOCIAL WORK WITH THE AGED
Rowlings, Cherry. Social Work with Elderly People. (Studies in the Personal Social Services: No. 3). 144p. (Orig.). 1981. text ed. 19.95x (ISBN 0-04-362036-1, 2603); pap. text ed. 7.95x (ISBN 0-04-362037-X, 2604). Allen Unwin.
SOCIAL WORK WITH YOUTH
see also Child Welfare; Volunteer Workers in Social Service
Crompton, Margaret. Respecting Children: Social Work with Young People. LC 80-5820. (Illus.). 246p. 1980. 20.00 (ISBN 0-8039-1544-6); pap. 9.95 (ISBN 0-8039-1545-4). Sage.
SOCIAL WORKERS
Borgatta, Edgar F., et al. Social Workers' Perceptions of Clients: A Study of the Caseload of a Social Agency. LC 80-27204. 92p. 1981. Repr. of 1960 ed. lib. bdg. 17.50x (ISBN 0-313-22812-4, BOSW). Greenwood.
Cherniss, Cary. Staff Burnout: Job Stress in the Human Services. LC 80-19408. (Sage Studies in Community Mental Health: Vol. 2). (Illus.). 200p. 1980. 20.00 (ISBN 0-8039-1338-9); pap. 9.95 (ISBN 0-8039-1339-7). Sage.
Rudman, Jack. Certified Professional Social Worker (CPSW) (Admission Test Ser.: AT-88). (Cloth bdg. avail. on request). pap. 17.95 (ISBN 0-8373-5088-3). Natl Learning.
Satyamurti, Carole. Occupational Survival: The Case of the Local Authority Social Worker. (Practice of Social Work Ser.: No. 5). 208p. 1981. 25.00x (ISBN 0-631-12441-1, Pub. by Basil Blackwell England); pap. 12.50x (ISBN 0-631-12595-7). Biblio Dist.
SOCIALISM
see also Anarchism and Anarchists; Christianity and Economics; Church and Social Problems; Communism; Equality; Individualism; Industry and State; Labor and Laboring Classes; Marxian Economics; National Socialism; Nationalism and Socialism; Old Age Pensions; Technocracy; Trade-Unions; Utopias; Women and Socialism
Abrahamsson, Bengt & Brostrom, Anders. The Rights of Labor. LC 80-16233. 301p. 25.00 (ISBN 0-8039-1477-6). Sage.
Burke, John P., et al, eds. Marxism & the Good Society. 224p. Date not set. price not set (ISBN 0-521-23392-5). Cambridge U Pr.
Denitch, Bogdan, ed. Democratic Socialism: The Mass Left in Advanced Industrial Societies. 220p. 1981. text ed. 26.00 (ISBN 0-86598-015-2). Allanheld.
Dixon, Marlene & Jonas, Susanne, eds. Contradictions of Socialist Construction. 100p. (Orig.). 1979. pap. 4.00 (ISBN 0-89935-008-9). Synthesis Pubns.
Eastman, Max. Reflections on the Failure of Socialism. LC 55-7352. 128p. 1981. pap. 4.95 (ISBN 0-8159-6707-1). Devin.
George, Vic & Manning, Nick. Socialism, Social Welfare, & the Soviet Union. (Radical Social Policy Ser.). 224p. (Orig.). 1980. pap. 15.95 (ISBN 0-7100-0608-X). Routledge & Kegan.
Hodges, Donald C. The Bureaucratization of Socialism. LC 80-23253. 240p. 1981. lib. bdg. 15.00x (ISBN 0-87023-138-3). U of Mass Pr.
Labriola, Antonio. Socialism & Philosophy. LC 79-90007. 223p. 1980. 12.00 (ISBN 0-914386-21-2); pap. 4.50 (ISBN 0-914386-22-0). Telos Pr.
Lindsay, Jack. Crisis in Marxism. 1981. 22.50x (ISBN 0-389-20185-5). B&N.
Novak, Michael, ed. Capitalism &Socialism: A Theological Inquiry. 1979. 12.25 (ISBN 0-8447-2153-0); pap. 6.25 (ISBN 0-8447-2154-9). Am Enterprise.
Prior, Mike, ed. The Popular & the Political: Essays on Socialism in the 1980's. 220p. 1981. pap. price not set (ISBN 0-7100-0627-6). Routledge & Kegan.
Semmel, Bernard, ed. Marxism & the Science of War. 288p. 1981. 37.50 (ISBN 0-19-876112-0); pap. 17.95 (ISBN 0-19-876113-9). Oxford U Pr.
Thomas, Jack R. & Patsouras, Louis. Varieties & Problems of Twentieth Century Socialism. LC 79-21450. 214p. 1981. text ed. 15.95 (ISBN 0-88229-444-X); pap. text ed. 8.95 (ISBN 0-88229-743-0). Nelson-Hall.
Watson, Thomas E. Socialists & Socialism. (Studies in Populism). 1980. lib. bdg. 69.95 (ISBN 0-686-68885-6). Revisionist Pr.
SOCIALISM–HISTORY
Bienkowski, W. Theory & Reality: The Development of Social Systems. (Allison & Busby Motive Ser.). 272p. 1981. 17.95x (ISBN 0-8052-8093-6, Pub. by Allison & Busby England); pap. 8.95 (ISBN 0-8052-8092-8). Schocken.
Samuel, Raphael, ed. People's History & Socialist Theory. (History Workshop Ser.). 425p. 1981. price not set (ISBN 0-7100-0765-5); pap. price not set (ISBN 0-7100-0652-7). Routledge & Kegan.
SOCIALISM AND NATIONALISM
see Nationalism and Socialism
SOCIALISM AND WOMEN
see Women and Socialism
SOCIALISM IN AFRICA
Mohiddin, Ahmed. African Socialism in Two Countries. 231p. 1981. 25.00x (ISBN 0-389-20170-7). Barron.
The Most Recent Tendecies in the Socialist Orientation of Various African & Arab Countries. (Dissertationes Orientales: No. 41). 323p. (Orig.). 1979. pap. 6.00x (Pub. by Orient Inst Czechoslovakia). Paragon.
SOCIALISM IN ASIA
Young, Arthur M. Socialist & Labour Movement in Japan. (Studies in Japanese History & Civilization). 145p. 1979. Repr. of 1921 ed. 18.00 (ISBN 0-89093-268-9). U Pubns Amer.
SOCIALISM IN EUROPE
Bahro, Rudolph. The Alternative in Eastern Europe. 464p. 1981. 19.50 (ISBN 0-8052-7056-6, Pub. by NLB England); pap. 9.50 (ISBN 0-8052-7098-1). Schocken.
Bienkowski, W. Theory & Reality: The Development of Social Systems. (Allison & Busby Motive Ser.). 272p. 1981. 17.95x (ISBN 0-8052-8093-6, Pub. by Allison & Busby England); pap. 8.95 (ISBN 0-8052-8092-8). Schocken.
Boyer, John W. Political Radicalism in Late Imperial Vienna: Origins of the Christian Social Movement, 1848-1897. LC 80-17302. (Illus.). 1981. lib. bdg. price not set (ISBN 0-226-06957-5). U of Chicago Pr.
Griffiths, Trevor. Occupations. new ed. 74p. 1981. pap. 7.50 (ISBN 0-571-11667-1, Pub. by Faber & Faber). Merrimack Bk Serv.
SOCIALISM IN GERMANY
Breitman, Richard. German Socialism & Weimar Democracy. LC 80-21412. 296p. 1981. 20.00x (ISBN 0-8078-1462-8). U of NC Pr.
SOCIALISM IN INDIA
Gandhi, Mohandas K. Socialism of My Conception. Hingorani, Anand T., ed. 290p. (Orig.). 1981. pap. 4.00 (ISBN 0-934676-29-1). Greenlf Bks.
SOCIALISM IN RUSSIA
Frankel, Jonathan. Prophecy & Politics: Socialism, Nationalism, & the Russian Jews, 1862-1917. LC 80-14414. (Illus.). 816p. Date not set. price not set (ISBN 0-521-23028-4). Cambridge U Pr.
SOCIALISM IN THE NEAR EAST
The Most Recent Tendecies in the Socialist Orientation of Various African & Arab Countries. (Dissertationes Orientales: No. 41). 323p. (Orig.). 1979. pap. 6.00x (Pub. by Orient Inst Czechoslovakia). Paragon.
SOCIALISTS
Watson, Thomas E. Socialists & Socialism. (Studies in Populism). 1980. lib. bdg. 69.95 (ISBN 0-686-68885-6). Revisionist Pr.
SOCIALIZATION
see also Political Socialization
Romer, Nancy. The Sex-Role Cycle: Socialization from Infancy to Old Age. (Women's Lives - Women's Work Ser.). (Illus.). 190p. (Orig.). (gr. 11-12). 1981. pap. 5.95 (ISBN 0-912670-69-X). Feminist Pr.
SOCIALIZATION, POLITICAL
see Political Socialization
SOCIALIZATION OF INDUSTRY
see Government Ownership
SOCIALIZED MEDICINE
see Insurance, Health
SOCIALLY HANDICAPPED
Aboud, Grace. Hiring & Training the Disadvantaged for Public Employment. (Key Issues Ser.: No. 11). 1973. pap. 2.00 (ISBN 0-87546-202-2). NY Sch Indus Rel.
SOCIALLY HANDICAPPED CHILDREN–EDUCATION
Dixon, Nancy P. Children of Poverty with Handicapping Conditions: How Teachers Can Cope Humanistically. write for info. (ISBN 0-398-04478-3). C C Thomas.
SOCIETIES
see also Agricultural Societies; Associations, Institutions, etc.; Clubs; Cooperative Societies; Friendly Societies; Historical Societies; Learned Institutions and Societies; Scientific Societies; Trade-Unions; Women–Societies and Clubs
Crip, H. & Rudduck, L. The Mothering Years: The Story of the Canberra Mothercraft Society 1926-79. (Illus.). 112p. (Orig.). 1980. pap. text ed. 7.95 (ISBN 0-9595400-0-8, 0584). Bks Australia.
SOCIETIES, BENEFIT
see Friendly Societies
SOCIETIES, COOPERATIVE
see Cooperative Societies
SOCIETY, PRIMITIVE
see also Clans and Clan System; Gipsies; Man, Prehistoric; Religion, Primitive
Dahlberg, Francis, ed. Woman the Gatherer. LC 80-25262. (Illus.). 288p. 1981. text ed. 15.00x (ISBN 0-300-02572-6). Yale U Pr.
Hallpike, Christopher R. The Foundations of Primitive Thought. (Illus.). 530p. 1979. text ed. 49.00x (ISBN 0-19-823196-2). Oxford U Pr.
SOCIETY AND ART
see Art and Society
SOCIETY AND COMMUNISM
see Communism and Society
SOCIETY AND EDUCATION
see Educational Sociology
SOCIETY AND LANGUAGE
see Sociolinguistics
SOCIETY AND LAW
see Sociological Jurisprudence
SOCIETY AND LIBRARIES
see Libraries and Society
SOCIETY AND LITERATURE
see Literature and Society
SOCIETY AND THE CHURCH
see Church and the World
SOCIETY AND THEATER
see Theater and Society
SOCIETY AND WAR
see War and Society
SOCIETY OF JESUS
see Jesuits
SOCINIANISM
see also Jesus Christ–Divinity; Trinity; Unitarianism
Williams, George H. The Polish Brethren. (Harvard Theological Studies: No. 30). 16.00; pap. 11.00 (ISBN 0-89130-201-8). Scholars Pr CA.
SOCIOBIOLOGY
Crook, John H. The Evolution of Human Consciousness. (Illus.). 462p. 1980. 39.00x (ISBN 0-19-857174-7). Oxford U Pr.
Singer, Peter. The Expanding Circle: Ethics and Sociobiology. 1981. 10.95 (ISBN 0-374-15112-1). FS&G.
White, Elliott. Sociobiology & Human Politics. LC 79-3016. 1981. price not set (ISBN 0-669-03602-1). Lexington Bks.
Wittenberger. Animal Social Behavior. (Illus.). 748p. 1981. text ed. price not set (ISBN 0-87872-295-5). Duxbury Pr.
SOCIOLINGUISTICS
Duran, Richard P., ed. Latino Language & Communicative Behavior. Vol. 6. 384p. 1981. 29.50 (ISBN 0-89391-038-4). Ablex Pub.
Fishman, Joshua A. Sociology of Language. 1972. pap. 9.95 (ISBN 0-912066-16-4). Newbury Hse.
Penalosa, Fernando. Introduction to the Sociology of Language. 320p. (Orig.). 1981. pap. text ed. 13.95 (ISBN 0-88377-183-7). Newbury Hse.
SOCIOLOGICAL JURISPRUDENCE
Brigham, John & Brown, Don W., eds. Policy Implementation: Penalties or Incentives? LC 80-16765. (Sage Focus Editions: Vol. 25). (Illus.). 284p. 1980. 18.95 (ISBN 0-8039-1350-8). Sage.
Fryer, Bob, et al, eds. Law, State & Society. Hunt, Alan & McBarret, Doreen. 224p. 1981. 31.00x (ISBN 0-7099-1004-5, Pub. by Croom Helm LTD England). Biblio Dist.
Mungham, Geoff & Bankowski, Zenon, eds. Essays in Law & Society. 216p. (Orig.). 1980. pap. 18.00 (ISBN 0-7100-0489-3). Routledge & Kegan.
Vago, Steven. Law & Society. (Ser. in Sociology). (Illus.). 352p. 1981. text ed. 16.95 (ISBN 0-13-526483-9). P-H.
SOCIOLOGICAL RESEARCH
see also Social Science Research
Dialectical Transformation: A Study of "Dialogue" As a Method for Research & Development in a Rural Milieu. 10p. 1981. pap. 10.00 (ISBN 92-808-0162-7, TUNU 105, UNU). Unipub.
Jackson, David J. & Borgatta, Edgar F., eds. Factor Analysis & Measurement in Sociological Research: A Multi-Dimensional Perspective. (Sage Studies in International Sociology: Vol. 21). 320p. 1981. 20.00 (ISBN 0-8039-9814-7) (ISBN 0-8039-9815-5). Sage.
Payne, Geoff, et al. Sociology & Social Research. (International Library of Sociology). 272p. 1981. price not set (ISBN 0-7100-0626-8). Routledge & Kegan.
Srinivas, M. N., et al. The Fieldworker & the Field: Problems & Challenges in Sociological Investigation. 300p. 1979. text ed. 13.95x (ISBN 0-19-561118-7). Oxford U Pr.
Wagenaar, Theodore C. Readings for Social Research. 336p. 1980. pap. text ed. 10.95x (ISBN 0-534-00740-6). Wadsworth Pub.
SOCIOLOGY
see also Cities and Towns; Civilization; Communication; Communism and Society; Community; Conservatism; Crime and Criminals; Crowds; Educational Sociology; Equality; Ethnopsychology; Family; Government Ownership; Heredity; Human Ecology; Individualism; Industrial Sociology; Labor and Laboring Classes; Leadership; Liquor Problem; Man–Influence of Environment; Poor; Population; Power (Social Sciences); Public Welfare; Race Relations; Social Change; Social Conflict; Social Contract; Social Groups; Social History; Social Institutions; Social Mobility; Social Problems; Social Psychology; Social Surveys; Social Systems; Socialism; Socialization; Society, Primitive; Sociolinguistics; Sociological Jurisprudence; Unemployed; War and Society; Women
Apsler, Alfred. An Introduction to Social Science. 3rd ed. 541p. 1981. text ed. 16.95 (ISBN 0-394-32534-6). Random.
Barry, Kathleen. Female Sexual Slavery. 336p. 1981. pap. 3.95 (ISBN 0-380-54213-7, 54213, Discus). Avon.
Bonnett, Aubrey W. Institutional Adaptation of West Indian Immigrants to America: An Analysis of Rotating Credit Associations. LC 80-69054. 160p. 1981. lib. bdg. 16.50 (ISBN 0-8191-1500-2); pap. text ed. 7.50 (ISBN 0-8191-1501-0). U Pr of Amer.
Boudon, Raymond. The Crisis in Sociology: Problems of Sociological Epistemology. (European Perspectives Ser.). 272p. 1981. 25.00x (ISBN 0-231-05178-6). Columbia U Pr.
Cary & Weinberg. The Social Fabric: Volume 1. 3rd ed. (Orig.). 1980. pap. 8.95 (ISBN 0-316-13078-8). Little.
Dahrendorf, Ralf. Life Changes: Approaches to Social & Political Theory. LC 79-18685. x, 182p. 1981. pap. 5.95 (ISBN 0-226-13443-1). U of Chicago Pr.
DeFleur, Melvin L., et al. Sociology: Human Society. 3rd ed. 1981. text ed. 17.95x (ISBN 0-673-15211-1). Scott F.
Firth, Raymond W. Elements of Social Organization. 3rd ed. LC 80-24763. (Josiah Mason Lectures Ser., 1947). (Illus.). xi, 260p. 1981. Repr. of 1961 ed. lib. bdg. 28.50x (ISBN 0-313-22745-4, FIES). Greenwood.
Ford, P. Social Theory & Social Practice: An Exploration of Experience. (Bibliography on Parliamentary Papers Ser.). 335p. 1968. 24.00x (ISBN 0-7165-0500-2, Pub. by Irish Academic Pr Ireland). Biblio Dist.
Galtung, Johan. The True Worlds: A Transnational Experience. LC 79-7351. (Preferred World for the 1990's Ser.). (Illus.). 469p. 1981. pap. text ed. 9.95 (ISBN 0-02-911070-X). Free Pr.
Gladstone, F. J. Voluntary Action in a Changing World. 137p. 1979. pap. text ed. 9.90x (ISBN 0-7199-1033-1, Pub. by Bedford England). Renouf.
Goldsmid, Charles & Wilson, Everett. Passing on Sociology: The Teaching of Discipline. 448p. 1980. text ed. 21.95x (ISBN 0-534-00914-X). Wadsworth Pub.

Grant, James P. Disparity Reduction Rates in Social Indicators: A Proposal for Measuring & Targeting Progress in Meeting Basic Needs. LC 78-61153. (Monographs: No. 11). 88p. 1978. 3.00 (ISBN 0-686-28684-7). Overseas Dev Council.

Greenblat, Cathy & Dressler, David. An Introduction to Sociology. 4th ed. 592p. 1981. pap. text ed. 15.95 (ISBN 0-394-32656-3); wkbk 6.95 (ISBN 0-394-32711-X). Knopf.

Halmos. The Sociology of Sociology. 1970. pap. text ed. 7.75x. Humanities.

Henslin, James M., ed. Down to Earth Sociology: Society, Structure, & Everyday Life. 3rd ed. LC 80-2315. 1981. pap. text ed. 9.95 (ISBN 0-02-914660-7). Free Pr.

Hollis, F. & Woods, M. E. Casework: A Psychological Therapy. 3rd ed. 552p. 1981. text ed. 16.95 (ISBN 0-394-32368-8). Random.

Hunt, Sonja & Hilton, Jennifer. Individual Development & Social Experience. (Illus.). 296p. 1981. pap. text ed. 12.50x (ISBN 0-04-150077-6, 2623). Allen Unwin.

Lemert, Charles, ed. French Sociology: Rupture & Renewal Since 1968. 528p. 1981. 22.50x (ISBN 0-231-04698-7); pap. 10.00x (ISBN 0-231-04699-5). Columbia U Pr.

Lichtenberger, James P. Development of Social Theory. 482p. 1980. Repr. of 1925 ed. lib. bdg. 45.00 (ISBN 0-89987-508-4). Darby Bks.

MacCormack, Carol & Strathern, Marilyn, eds. Nature, Culture & Gender. (Illus.). 1980. 24.95 (ISBN 0-521-23491-3); pap. 8.95 (ISBN 0-521-28001-X). Cambridge U Pr.

MacIver, R. M. Society. 596p. 1980. Repr. of 1937 ed. lib. bdg. 40.00 (ISBN 0-89984-338-7). Century Bookbindery.

Morgan, Gordon D. Introductory Sociology: Lectures, Readings & Exercises. LC 80-65606. 145p. 1981. perfect bdg. 10.50 (ISBN 0-86548-049-4). Century Twenty One.

Nelson, Harold A. Sociology in Bondage: An Introduction to Graduate Study. LC 80-65605. 145p. 1981. perfect bdg. 9.95 (ISBN 0-86548-051-6). Century Twenty One.

Otten, C. Michael. Power, Values, & Society: An Introduction to Sociology. 1981. pap. text ed. 11.95x (ISBN 0-673-15260-X). Scott F.

Owen, John E. Sociology: Readings on Human Society. 1981. pap. text ed. 7.95x (ISBN 0-673-15265-0). Scott F.

Parsons, Talcott, et al. Working Papers in the Theory of Action. LC 80-24475. 269p. 1981. Repr. of 1953 ed. lib. bdg. 25.00x (ISBN 0-313-22468-4, PAWP). Greenwood.

Payne, Geoff, et al. Sociology & Social Research. (International Library of Sociology). 272p. 1981. price not set (ISBN 0-7100-0626-8). Routledge & Kegan.

Peacock, Carol. Hand-Me-Down-Dreams. LC 80-26048. 192p. 1981. 12.95x (ISBN 0-8052-3761-5); pap. 8.95 (ISBN 0-8052-0678-7). Schocken.

Pearman, William A. & Rotz, Robert A. The Province of Sociology: Selected Profiles. LC 79-17996. 212p. 1981. text ed. 15.95 (ISBN 0-88229-434-2); pap. text ed. 8.95 (ISBN 0-88229-735-X). Nelson-Hall.

Pinto, Diana, ed. Contemporary Italian Sociology: A Reader. (Illus.). 224p. Date not set. price not set (ISBN 0-521-23738-6); pap. price not set (ISBN 0-521-28191-1). Cambridge U Pr.

Reuter, Edward B. Handbook of Sociology. 233p. 1980. Repr. of 1941 ed. lib. bdg. 30.00 (ISBN 0-89987-156-9). Darby Bks.

Rich, William. Smaller Families Through Social & Economic Progress. LC 72-97989. (Monographs: No. 7). 74p. 1973. 2.00 (ISBN 0-686-28688-X). Overseas Dev Council.

Ritzer, George. Towards an Integrated Social Paradigm: The Search for an Exemplar & an Image of the Subject Matter. 300p. 1981. pap. text ed. 13.95 (ISBN 0-205-06721-2). Allyn.

Robertson, Ian. Sociology. 2nd ed. 1981. text ed. write for info. (ISBN 0-87901-134-3); write for info. study guide (ISBN 0-87901-144-0); write for info. reader (ISBN 0-87901-168-8). Worth.

Rudman, Jack. Sociology. (Undergraduate Program Field Test Ser.: UPFT-23). (Cloth bdg. avail. on request). pap. 9.95 (ISBN 0-8373-6023-4). Natl Learning.

Sands, Melissa. The Making of the American Mistress. (Orig.). 1981. pap. 2.50 (ISBN 0-425-04751-2). Berkley Pub.

Scanzoni, Letha D. & Scanzoni, John. Men, Women, & Change. (Illus.). 576p. 1981. 18.95 (ISBN 0-07-055054-9); instr's manual 5.95 (ISBN 0-07-055055-7). McGraw.

Schnabel, John F. Study Guide to Accompany Sociology: Human Society. 3rd ed. 1981. pap. text ed. 4.95x (ISBN 0-673-15479-3). Scott F.

Shepard, Jon M. Sociology. (Illus.). 600p. 1980. text ed. 16.95 (ISBN 0-8299-0412-3). West Pub.

Sherman, H. J. Sociology: Traditional & Radical Perspectives. 1981. pap. text ed. 15.70 (ISBN 0-06-318190-8, Pub. by Har-Row Ltd Eng). Har-Row.

Shils, Edward. Tradition. LC 80-21643. 320p. 1981. lib. bdg. price not set (ISBN 0-226-75325-5). U of Chicago Pr.

Smelser, Neil J. Sociology. (Ser. in Sociology). (Illus.). 640p. 1981. text ed. 18.95 (ISBN 0-13-820829-8). P-H.

Sociological Theories: Race & Colonialism. 499p. 1981. pap. 34.00 (ISBN 92-310-1635-0, U1050, UNESCO). Unipub.

Talese, Gay. Fame & Obscurity. 1981. pap. 3.25 (ISBN 0-440-12620-7). Dell.

--Honor Thy Father. 1981. pap. 3.25 (ISBN 0-440-13668-7). Dell.

Taylor, W. D. Symbiosis Intelligentsia. 224p. 1981. 9.50 (ISBN 0-682-49675-8). Exposition.

Touraine, Alain. The Voice & the Eye: The/Analysis of Social Movements. Duff, Alan, tr. from Fr. Orig. Title: Le Voix et le Regard. Date not set. 37.59 (ISBN 0-521-23874-9); pap. 12.95 (ISBN 0-521-28271-3). Cambridge U Pr.

Van Eys, Jan. Humanity & Personhood: Personal Reaction to a World in Which Children Can Die. write for info. (ISBN 0-398-04467-8). C C Thomas.

Weydemeyer, Winton. A Grange Master's America: In Defense of Freedom. 272p. 1981. 12.50 (ISBN 0-682-49677-4). Exposition.

White, Edmund. States of Desire. 320p. 1981. pap. 3.95 (ISBN 0-553-14544-4). Bantam.

Young, Kimball. Source Book Fro Sociology. 639p. 1980. Repr. of 1935 ed. lib. bdg. 45.00 (ISBN 0-8495-6105-1). Arden Lib.

Zeitlin, Irving M. Ideology & the Development of Sociological Theory. 2nd ed. (P-H Ser. in Sociology). (Illus.). 336p. 1981. text ed. 17.95 (ISBN 0-13-449769-4). P-H.

--The Social Condition of Humanity: An Introduction to Sociology. 432p. 1981. pap. text ed. 11.95x (ISBN 0-19-502734-5). Oxford U Pr.

Zey-Ferrell, Mary & Aiken, Michael. Complex Organizations: Critical Perspectives. pap. text ed. 11.95 (ISBN 0-673-15269-3). Scott F.

SOCIOLOGY–ADDRESSES, ESSAYS, LECTURES

Allport, Gordon W. Personality & Social Encounter: Selected Essays. LC 77-13911. x, 388p. 1981. pap. text ed. 17.00x (ISBN 0-226-01494-0). U of Chicago Pr.

Hebding, Daniel E. & Glick, Leonard. Introduction to Sociology. 2nd ed. (Sociology Ser.). (Illus.). 480p. 1981. pap. text ed. 12.95 (ISBN 0-201-03997-4). A-W.

Nowak, Stefan. Understanding & Prediction. (Synthese Library: No. 94). 482p. 1980. pap. 15.95 (ISBN 90-277-1199-2, Pub. by D. Reidel). Kluwer Boston.

SOCIOLOGY–BIBLIOGRAPHY

Jones, Dorothy M. & Wood, John R. An Aleut Bibliography. LC 74-620054. 192p. 1976. pap. 15.00 (ISBN 0-295-95529-5). U of Wash Pr.

SOCIOLOGY–DICTIONARIES

Bottomore, Tom & Nisbet, Robert, eds. A History of Sociological Analysis. 717p. 1981. pap. text ed. 10.95x (ISBN 0-465-03024-6). Basic.

SOCIOLOGY–HISTORY

Bottomore, Tom & Nisbet, Robert, eds. A History of Sociological Analysis. 717p. 1981. pap. text ed. 10.95x (ISBN 0-465-03024-6). Basic.

Howard, Ronald L. A Social History of American Family Sociology, 1865-1940. Mogey, John H. & Van Leeuwen, Louis Th., eds. LC 80-1790. (Contributions in Family Studies Ser.: No. 4). 168p. 1981. lib. bdg. 22.50 (ISBN 0-313-22767-5, MOA/). Greenwood.

Johnson, Doyle P. Sociological Theory: Classical Founders & Contemporary Perspectives. 600p. 1981. text ed. 16.95 (ISBN 0-471-02915-7); tchrs.' ed. avail. (ISBN 0-471-08958-3). Wiley.

SOCIOLOGY–METHODOLOGY

Jackson, David J. & Borgatta, Edgar F., eds. Factor Analysis & Measurement in Sociological Research: A Multi-Dimensional Perspective. (Sage Studies in International Sociology: Vol. 21). 320p. 1981. 20.00 (ISBN 0-8039-9814-7) (ISBN 0-8039-9815-5). Sage.

Leinhardt, Samuel, ed. Sociological Methodology Nineteen Eighty-One. LC 68-54940. (Social & Behavioral Science Series). 1981. text ed. price not set (ISBN 0-87589-490-9). Jossey-Bass.

SOCIOLOGY–RESEARCH

see Sociological Research

SOCIOLOGY–STATISTICS AND STATISTICAL METHODS

Compendium of Social Statistics, 1977. (Statistical Papers Series K: No. 4). 1325p. 1980. pap. 35.00 (UN80-17-6, UN). Unipub.

SOCIOLOGY, CHRISTIAN

Here are entered works on social theory from a Christian point of view. The relationship of this heading to Church and Social Problems is that of abstract to concrete.

see also Christianity and Economics; Church and Social Problems

Hauerwas, Stanley. A Community of Character: Toward a Constructive Christian Social Ethic. LC 80-53072. 320p. 1981. text ed. 20.00 (ISBN 0-268-00733-0). U of Notre Dame Pr.

SOCIOLOGY, CHRISTIAN–MODERN, 1500-

see Sociology, Christian

SOCIOLOGY, DESCRIPTIVE

see Social History

SOCIOLOGY, EDUCATIONAL

see Educational Sociology

SOCIOLOGY, INDUSTRIAL

see Industrial Sociology

SOCIOLOGY, ISLAMIC

Gellner, Ernest. Muslim Society. LC 80-41103. (Cambridge Studies in Social Anthropology: No. 32). 280p. Date not set. price not set (ISBN 0-521-22160-9). Cambridge U Pr.

SOCIOLOGY, MEDICAL

see Social Medicine

SOCIOLOGY, MILITARY

see also Armed Forces–Political Activity; Militarism; Military Policy; Pacifism; Peace; War and Society

Sarkesian, Sam C. American Military Professionalism. LC 80-27027. (Pergamon Policy Studies on International Politics). 1981. 25.00 (ISBN 0-08-027178-2). Pergamon.

SOCIOLOGY, RELIGIOUS

see Religion and Sociology

SOCIOLOGY, RURAL

see also Community; Community Development; Country Life; Farm Life; Rural Conditions; Urbanization; Villages

Association of Voluntary Agency for Rural Development, India. Block-Level Planning. 128p. 1980. text ed. 18.95x (ISBN 0-7069-1063-X, Pub by Vikas India). Advent Bk.

Carlson & Lassey. Rural Society & Environment in America. (Agricultural Science Ser.). (Illus.). 448p. 1981. text ed. 15.95x (ISBN 0-07-009959-6, C). McGraw.

Dialectical Transformation: A Study of "Dialogue" As a Method for Research & Development in a Rural Milieu. 10p. 1981. pap. 10.00 (ISBN 92-808-0162-7, TUNU 105, UNU). Unipub.

Harley, Johansen & Fugitt, Glen V. The Changing Rural Village of America. 1981. price not set (ISBN 0-88410-692-6). Ballinger Pub.

National Council of Social Service. The Right to Know- a Review of Advice Services in Rural Areas. 71p. 1978. pap. text ed. 1.90x (ISBN 0-7199-0954-6, Pub. by Bedford England). Renouf.

Newby, H. International Perspectives in Rural Sociology. 220p. 1978. 38.25 (ISBN 0-471-99606-8). Wiley.

United Nations Asian & Pacific Development Inst., ed. Local Level Planning & Rural Development: Alternative Strategies. 409p. 1980. text ed. 20.50x (ISBN 0-391-02171-0, Pub. by Concept India). Humanities.

SOCIOLOGY, URBAN

see also Cities and Towns; Community Power; Urban Renewal; Urbanization

Mescon, Michael H. & Bramlette, Carl A., Jr., eds. Individual & the Future of Organizations, Vol. 10. (Franklin Foundation Lecture Ser.). 1981. pap. 3.75 (ISBN 0-88406-144-2). GA St U Busn Pub.

--Individual & the Future of Organizations, Vol. 11. (Franklin Foundation Lecture Ser.). 1981. pap. 3.75 (ISBN 0-88406-145-0). GA St U Busn Pub.

Phillips, E. Barbara & LeGates, Richard T. City Lights: An Introduction to Urban Studies. (Illus.). 608p. 1981. pap. text ed. 14.95x (ISBN 0-19-502797-3). Oxford U Pr.

Saunders, Peter. Social Theory & the Urban Question. LC 80-21654. 302p. 1981. text ed. 28.50x (ISBN 0-8419-0622-X); pap. text ed. 11.95x (ISBN 0-8419-0623-8). Holmes & Meier.

SOCIOLOGY AND ART

see Art and Society

SOCIOLOGY AND LITERATURE

see Literature and Society

SOCIOLOGY AND RELIGION

see Religion and Sociology

SOCIOLOGY OF LANGUAGE

see Sociolinguistics

SOCIOLOGY OF LAW

see Sociological Jurisprudence

SOFISM

see Sufism

SOFT DRINKS

see Beverages

SOFTBALL

see also Baseball

Madison, Arnold. How to Play Girls' Softball. (Illus.). 128p. (gr. 4-6). 1981. PLB 7.29 (ISBN 0-686-69303-5). Messner.

Zolna, Ed & Conklin, Mike. Mastering Softball. (Mastering Ser.). (Illus.). 1981. 12.95 (ISBN 0-8092-7184-2); pap. 5.95 (ISBN 0-8092-7183-4). Contemp Bks.

SOFTCOATED WHEATEN TERRIER

see Dogs–Breeds–Softcoated Wheaten Terrier

SOFTWARE, COMPUTER

see Computer Programs; Programming (Electronic Computers); Programming Languages (Electronic Computers);

also similiar headings

SOIL (ENGINEERING)

see Soil Mechanics

SOIL CHEMISTRY

Stucki, J. W. & Banwart, L., eds. Advanced Chemical Methods for Soil & Clay Minerals Reasearch. 488p. 1980. lib. bdg. 58.00 (Pub. by D. Reidel). Kluwer Boston.

SOIL CONSERVATION

see also Erosion

Beckett Jackson Raeder, Inc. Soil Erosion & Sedimentation Control. (Illus.). 150p. 1980. pap. text ed. 20.00 (ISBN 0-918436-15-X). Environ Design.

Foster, Albert B. Approved Practices in Soil Conservation. 5th ed. (Illus.). 1981. 13.00 (ISBN 0-8134-2170-5, 2170); text ed. 9.75x. Interstate.

SOIL ECOLOGY

Hyams, Edward. Soil & Civilization. 312p. 1980. 15.00x (ISBN 0-7195-3311-2, Pub. by Murray Pubs England). State Mutual Bk.

Jenny, H. The Soil Resource: Origin & Behavior. (Ecological Studies: Vol. 37). (Illus.). 377p. 1981. 29.80 (ISBN 0-387-90543-X). Springer-Verlag.

SOIL ENGINEERING

see Soil Mechanics

SOIL EROSION

see Soil Conservation

SOIL FERTILITY

Priorities for Alleviating Soil-Related Constraints to Food Production in the Tropics. 468p. 1981. pap. 31.50 (R133, IRRI). Unipub.

SOIL FORMATION

Jenny, H. The Soil Resource: Origin & Behavior. (Ecological Studies: Vol. 37). (Illus.). 377p. 1981. 29.80 (ISBN 0-387-90543-X). Springer-Verlag.

SOIL FUNGI

see Soil Micro-Organisms

SOIL MECHANICS

see also Foundations; Rock Mechanics; Structural Engineering; Underground Construction

Bell, F. G. Engineering Properties of Soils & Rocks. (Illus.). 144p. 1981. pap. text ed. 12.50 (ISBN 0-408-00537-8). Butterworths.

Jain, S. K. Fundamental Aspects of the Normality Rule & Their Role in Deriving Constitutive Laws of Soils. (Civil Engineering & Engineering Mechanics Ser.: No. 1). (Illus.). 178p. 1980. 23.50 (ISBN 0-9605004-0-5, 5004-0-5). Eng Pubns.

Kovaco, W. & Holtz, R. Introduction to Geotechniical Engineering. 1981. 28.95 (ISBN 0-13-484394-0). P-H.

Prakash, Shamsher. Soil Dynamics. (Illus.). 432p. 1981. text ed. 26.95 (ISBN 0-07-050658-2, C); student's manual 4.95 (ISBN 0-07-050659-0). McGraw.

A Soil Technological Study on Effectuating & Maintaining Adequate Playing Conditions of Grass Sports Fields. (Agricultural Research Reports Ser.: No. 903). 124p. 1981. pap. 29.50 (ISBN 90-220-0743-X, PDC 220, Pudoc). Unipub.

Sopher, Charles & Baird, Jack. Soils & Soil Management. 2nd ed. 1981. text ed. 16.95 (ISBN 0-8359-7031-0); instr's. manual free (ISBN 0-8359-7032-9). Reston.

Thomas Telford Editorial Staff, Ltd. A Century of Soil Mechanics. 490p. 1980. 35.00x (ISBN 0-901948-15-2, Pub. by Telfor England). State Mutual Bk.

Thomas Telford Ltd. Editorial Staff. Milestones in Soil Mechanics. 338p. 1980. 40.00x (ISBN 0-7277-0010-3, Pub. by Telford England). State Mutual Bk.

SOIL MICRO-ORGANISMS

Verona, O. & Gambogi, P. Genera of Soil Microfungi. Byford, W. J., tr. 320p. 1981. pap. text ed. 25.00x (ISBN 3-7682-1259-9). Lubrecht & Cramer.

SOIL SCIENCE

see also Agriculture

Soils & Rice. 825p. 1978. pap. 40.00 (R002, IRRI). Unipub.

Specific Soil Chemical Characteristics for Rice Production in Asia. (IRRI Research Paper Ser.: No. 2). 18p. 1976. pap. 5.00 (R042, IRRI). Unipub.

SOILS

see also Agricultural Chemistry; Agricultural Physics; Clay; Fertilizers and Manures; Irrigation; Particles; Reclamation of Land

also headings beginning with the word Soil

Priorities for Alleviating Soil-Related Constraints to Food Production in the Tropics. 468p. 1981. pap. 31.50 (R133, IRRI). Unipub.

Sopher, Charles & Baird, Jack. Soils & Soil Management. 2nd ed. 1981. text ed. 16.95 (ISBN 0-8359-7031-0); instr's. manual free (ISBN 0-8359-7032-9). Reston.

SOILS–ANALYSIS

Clayton, P. M. & Tiller, K. G. A Chemical Method for the Determination of the Heavy Metal Content of Soils in Environmental Studies. 1980. 10.00x (ISBN 0-643-00341-X, Pub. by CSJRO Australia). State Mutual Bk.

In Situ Investigation in Soils & Rocks. 328p. 1980. 80.00x (ISBN 0-901948-30-6, Pub. by Telford England). State Mutual Bk.

Kovacs, William D. & Holtz, Robert D. An Introduction to Geotechnical Engineering. (Illus.). 720p. 1981. text ed. 28.95 (ISBN 0-13-484394-0). P-H.

Land Evaluation for Rainfed Agriculture: Report of an Expert Consultation. (World Soil Resources Reports: No. 52). 122p. 1981. pap. 6.50 (ISBN 92-5-100994-5, F2104, FAO). Unipub.

Mineral Nutrition of Legumes in Tropical & Subtropical Soils. 415p. 1978. 29.00 (ISBN 0-643-00311-8, CO14, CSIRO). Unipub.

Physiochemical Properties of Submerged Soils in Relationship to Fertility. (IRRI Research Paper Ser.: No. 5). 32p. 1977. pap. 5.00 (R045, IRRI). Unipub.

A Provisional Methodology for Soil Degradation Assessment. 94p. 1980. pap. 7.50 (ISBN 9-2510-0869-8, F1958, FAO). Unipub.

Soil Nitrogen As Fertilizer or Pollutant. (Panel Proceedings Ser.). 398p. 1980. pap. 50.50 (ISBN 92-0-111080-4, ISP535, IAEA). Unipub.

SOILS–BACTERIOLOGY
see Soil Micro-Organisms

SOILS–MECHANICS
see Soil Mechanics

SOILS–AFRICA
Third Meeting of the Eastern African Sub Committee for Soil Correlation & Land Evaluation. (World Soil Resources Report: No. 51). 170p. 1981. pap. 9.25 (ISBN 92-5-100902-3, F2082, FAO). Unipub.

SOILS–AUSTRALIA
Butler, B. E. A Soil Survey of the Horticultural Soils in the Murrumbidgee Irrigation Areas, New South Wales. 1980. 20.00x (ISBN 0-686-64952-4, Pub. by CSIRO Australia). State Mutual Bk.
Lands of the Alligator Rivers Area, Northern Territory. (Land Research Ser.: No. 38). 171p. 1976. pap. 13.50 (ISBN 0-643-00208-1, CO19, CSIRO). Unipub.

SOILS (ENGINEERING)
see Soil Mechanics

SOLANACEAE
Huber, K. A. Morphologisch und Entwicklungsgeschichtliche Untersuchungen an Blueten und Bluetenstaenden Von Solannaceen und Von Nolana Paradoxa Lindl: Nolanaceae. (Dissertationes Botanicae: No. 55). (Illus.). 486p. (Ger.). 1980. pap. text ed. 50.00x (ISBN 3-7682-1268-8). Lubrecht & Cramer.

SOLAR ACTIVITY
see also Solar Radiation; Sun-Spots
Aatec Publications, compiled by. Solar Census: The Directory for the Eighties. LC 80-68910. 484p. 1980. perfect-bound 45.00 (ISBN 0-937948-00-4). Aatec Pubns.

SOLAR CORONA
see Sun

SOLAR ENERGY
see also Solar Engines; Solar Heating
Allen, James. From Poverty to Power. 184p. 1980. pap. 5.50 (ISBN 0-89540-061-8). Sun Pub.
Asimov, Isaac. How Did We Find Out About Solar Power? (History of Science Ser.). (Illus.). 64p. (gr. 4-7). 1981. 6.95 (ISBN 0-8027-6422-3); PLB 7.85 (ISBN 0-8027-6423-1). Walker & Co.
Automation Industries. Solar Energy Reports Available from the National Solar Data Program. 50p. 1981. pap. 11.95 (ISBN 0-89934-104-7). Solar Energy Info.
Battelle Columbus Labs. Solar Energy Employment & Requirements: 1978-1983. 200p. 1981. pap. 24.50 (ISBN 0-89934-102-0). Solar Energy Info.
Bereny, et al. Baseline Study of U.S. Industry Solar Exports for Nineteen Seventy-Nine. 73p. 1981. Repr. of 1980 ed. 35.00 (ISBN 0-89934-080-6). Solar Energy Info.
Bossong, Ken. Passive Solar Retrofit for Homeowners & Apartment Dwellers. (Illus.). 100p. (Orig.). 1981. pap. text ed. 5.00 (ISBN 0-89988-068-1). Citizens Energy.
Business Communications Co. Tapping Solar Markets in Developing Countries, E-041. 1981. 800.00 (ISBN 0-89336-274-3). BCC.
Caifornia Energy Commission. Passive Solar Handbook. 330p. 1981. lib. bdg. 34.50 (ISBN 0-89934-101-2). Solar Energy Info.
Cole, John. Sun Reflections: Images for a New Solar Age. Posner, Marcy, ed. (Illus.). 208p. 1981. 14.95 (ISBN 0-87857-318-6); pap. 10.95 (ISBN 0-87857-317-8). Rodale Pr Inc.
Cowan, H. J., ed. Solar Energy Applications in the Design of Buildings. (Illus.). x, 325p. 1980. 50.00x (ISBN 0-85334-883-9). Burgess-Intl Ideas.
Ehrenkrantz Group & Mueller Associates Inc. Active Solar Energy System Design Practice Manual: Preliminary Field Experience. 230p. 1981. pap. 24.50 (ISBN 0-89934-091-1). Solar Energy Info.
Flavin, Christopher. Energy & Architecture: The Solar & Conservation Potential. LC 80-54002. (Worldwatch Papers). 1980. pap. 2.00 (ISBN 0-916468-39-9). Worldwatch Inst.
Garrison, A. Joseph. Solar Projects: Working Solar Devices to Cut Out & Assemble. (Illus.). 128p. (Orig.). 1981. lib. bdg. 12.90 (ISBN 0-89471-129-6); pap. 6.95 (ISBN 0-89471-130-X). Running Pr.
Gunn, Anita & Courrier, Kathleen, eds. Shining Examples: Model Projects Using Renewable Resources. LC 80-67831. (Illus.). 210p. 1980. 6.95 (ISBN 0-937446-00-9). Ctr Renewable.
Hoffman, Jim. Rodale Plans: Solar Food Dryer. Wolf, Ray, ed. (Illus.). 64p. (Orig.). 1981. pap. 12.95 (ISBN 0-87857-333-X). Rodale Pr Inc.
Hollon, Jennifer K. Solar Energy for California's Residential Sector: Progress, Problems, & Prospects. LC 80-29096. (IGS Research Report: No. 80-3). 71p. 1980. pap. text ed. 4.50 (ISBN 0-87772-279-X). Inst Gov Stud Berk.
Howell, Yvonne & Miller, Harry. Selling the Solar Home: California Edition. 93p. 1981. pap. 10.00 (ISBN 0-89934-081-4). Solar Energy Info.
Kreider, Jan F. & Kreith, Frank, eds. Solar Energy Handbook. (Illus.). 1099p. 1981. 49.50 (ISBN 0-07-035474-X). McGraw.
Let's Reach for the Sun: Thirty Original Solar & Earth Sheltered Home Designs. rev. ed. (Illus.). 144p. 1981. pap. 9.95 (ISBN 0-9603570-1-7). Space-Time.
Livingstone, Richard. Electricity from the Sun: Photovoltaic Energy. (Energy Systems Bks.). (Illus.). 160p. 1981. pap. 7.95 (ISBN 0-07-038150-X). McGraw.
Palz, W & Steemers, Tc, eds. Solar Houses in Europe: How They Have Worked. LC 80-49715. (Illus.). 320p. 1981. 40.00 (ISBN 0-08-026743-2); pap. 20.00 (ISBN 0-08-026744-0). Pergamon.
Public Servie Co. of New Mexico. Technical & Economic Assessment of Solar Hybrid Repowering. 450p. 1981. pap. 39.50 (ISBN 0-89934-083-0). Solar Energy Info.
Reynoldson, George. Let's Reach for the Sun: 30 Original Solar & Earth Sheltered Home Designs. rev. ed. Erdahl, Jeanne, ed. (Illus.). 144p. 1981. pap. 9.95 (ISBN 0-9603570-1-7). Space-Time.
Rose, Pat R. The Solar Boat Book. LC 80-69217. (Illus.). 266p. (Orig.). 1979. pap. 9.95 (ISBN 0-9604874-0-9). Aqua-Sol Ent.
Schmidt, Werner J. & Philbin, Janis. Solar Installer's Training Program: California Ed. 1981. Repr. of 1980 ed. 35.00 (ISBN 0-89934-084-9). Solar Energy Info.
Smithsonian. Fire of Life: The Smithsonian Book of the Sun. (Illus.). 1981. 24.95 (ISBN 0-89599-006-7). Smithsonian Expo.
Solar Energy & the Consumer Loan: California Ed. (Solarcal Seminar Ser.). 100p. 1981. Repr. of 1979 ed. 25.00 (ISBN 0-89934-082-2). Solar Energy Info.
Solar Energy Research Institute. Solar Energy Information Locator - Nineteen Eighty. 60p. 1981. pap. 3.95 (ISBN 0-89934-089-X). Solar Energy Info.
Stambolis, C., ed. Solar Energy in the Eighties: Conference Proceedings, London, 14-51 Jan 1981. LC 80-41617. (Illus.). 232p. 1981. 60.00 (ISBN 0-08-026123-X). Pergamon.
U.S. Dept. of Energy. Solar Energy Program Summary Document Nineteen Eighty One. 375p. 1981. pap. 34.50 (ISBN 0-89934-093-8). Solar Energy Info.
Vogt, Frederick, ed. Energy Conservation & Use of Renewable Energies in the Bio-Industries: Proceedings of the International Seminar on Energy Conservation & the Use of Solar & Other Renewable Energies in Agriculture, Horticulture & Fishculture, 15-19 September, 1980, Polytechnic of Central London. LC 80-49739. (Illus.). 580p. 1981. 100.00 (ISBN 0-08-026866-8). Pergamon.
--Energy Conservation & Use of Solar & Other Renewable Energy: Proceedings. (Illus.). 580p. 1981. 100.00 (ISBN 0-08-026866-8). Pergamon.

SOLAR ENGINES
Bereny, et al. Baseline Study of U.S. Industry Solar Exports for Nineteen Seventy-Nine. 73p. 1981. Repr. of 1980 ed. 35.00 (ISBN 0-89934-080-6). Solar Energy Info.
Blake, James N. Run Your Car on Sunshine: Using Solar Energy for a Solar Powered Car. LC 80-82734. (Illus.). 64p. 1981. lib. bdg. 12.95 (ISBN 0-915216-64-7); pap. 4.95 (ISBN 0-915216-65-5). Love Street.

SOLAR HEAT
see Solar Heating

SOLAR HEATING
Anderson, Bruce & Wells, Malcolm. Solar Energy: The Homeowners Guide to Natural Heating & Cooling. (Illus., Orig.). 1981. 17.95 (ISBN 0-931790-51-4); pap. 8.95 (ISBN 0-931790-09-3). Brick Hse Pub.
Coxon, Dewayne. Practical Solar Heating Manual Wih Blueprints: For Air & Water Systems. 150p. 1981. text ed. 19.95 (ISBN 0-250-40446-X). Ann Arbor Science.
Kreider, Jan F. The Solar Heating Design Process: Active & Passive. (Illus.). 432p. 1981. 21.50 (ISBN 0-07-035478-2, P&RB). McGraw.
Moselle, Gary. Installing Solar Heating Systems. 224p. (Orig.). 1981. pap. 13.50 (ISBN 0-910460-83-3). Craftsman.
Reif, Daniel K. Solar Retrofit: Adding Solar to Your Home. (Illus.). 200p. 1981. 17.95 (ISBN 0-931790-50-6); pap. 8.95 (ISBN 0-931790-15-8). Brick Hse Pub.
Schubert, R. & Ryan, L. Fundamentals of Solar Heating. 1981. 23.95 (ISBN 0-13-344457-0). P-H.
Tully, Gordon F. Solar Heating Systems: Analysis & Design with the Sun-Pulse Method. (Energy Learning Systems Bks.). (Illus.). 232p. 1981. 23.95 (ISBN 0-07-065441-7). McGraw.

SOLAR PHYSICS
see Sun

SOLAR POWER
see Solar Energy

SOLAR RADIATION
see also Solar Activity; Solar Energy; Sun-Spots
Aatec Publications, compiled by. Solar Census: The Directory for the Eighties. LC 80-68910. 484p. 1980. perfect-bound 45.00 (ISBN 0-937948-00-4). Aatec Pubns.

SOLAR SYSTEM
see also Comets; Earth; Satellites; Sun
also names of individual planets
Skinner, Brian J., ed. The Solar System & Its Strange Objects. (The Earth & Its Inhabitants: Selected Readings from American Scientist Ser.). (Illus.). 200p. (Orig.). 1981. pap. 9.95 (ISBN 0-913232-84-X). W Kaufmann.

SOLDIERS
see also Armies; Generals; Military Art and Science; Veterans
also subdivision Military Life under Armies, e.g. United States–Army–Military Life
Dun, Smith. Memoirs of the Four-Foot Colonel, Data Paper No. 113. 125p. 1980. 6.00 (ISBN 0-87727-113-5). Cornell SE Asia.
Gottlieb, David. Babes in Arms: Youth in the Army. LC 80-15830. (Illus.). 173p. 1980. 14.95 (ISBN 0-8039-1499-7). Sage.
Maginnis, John J. Profile of a Citizen Soldier. (Illus.). 254p. 1981. 9.95 (ISBN 0-89962-046-9). Todd & Honeywell.

SOLDIERS–UNIFORMS
see Uniforms, Military

SOLES
see Flatfishes

SOLICITORS
see Lawyers

SOLID FILM
see Thin Films

SOLID STATE CHEMISTRY
see also Solid State Physics
Solid State Chemistry. 1980. 5.00 (ISBN 0-910362-14-9). Chem Educ.

SOLID STATE ELECTRONICS
Howard W. Sams Engineering Staff. Tube Substitution Handbook. 21st ed. LC 80-13842. 1980. pap. 3.95 (ISBN 0-672-21746-5). Sams.

SOLID STATE PHYSICS
see also Solid State Chemistry; Solids
Barone, Antonio & Paterno, Gianfranco. The Physics & Applications of the Josephson Effect. 450p. 1981. 40.00 (ISBN 0-471-01469-9, Pub. by Wiley-Interscience). Wiley.
Kahng, D., ed. Advances in Applied Solid State Science, Supplement, 2A: Silicon Integrated Circuits. (Serial Publication). 1981. price not set (ISBN 0-12-002954-5); price not set lib. ed. (ISBN 0-12-002955-3); price not set microfiche ed. (ISBN 0-12-002956-1). Acad Pr.
Kahng, Dawon, ed. Advances in Solid State Science, Supplement 2B: Silicon Integrated Circuits. (Serial Publication). 1981. price not set (ISBN 0-12-002957-X); price not set lib. ed. (ISBN 0-12-002958-8); microfiche ed. (ISBN 0-12-002959-6). Acad Pr.
Mott, Nevill, ed. The Beginnings of Solid State Physics. (Royal Society Ser.). 177p. 1980. lib. bdg. 30.00x (ISBN 0-85403-143-X, Pub. by Royal Soc London). Scholium Intl.

SOLID WASTE MANAGEMENT
see Factory and Trade Waste; Refuse and Refuse Disposal

SOLIDS
see also Crystals; Elastic Solids; Solid State Physics; Thin Films
Chalmers, B., ed. Progress in Materials Science, Vol. 23. 280p. 1980. 85.00 (ISBN 0-08-024846-2). Pergamon.
High Solids Coatings Buyer's Guide. 1981. 21.00 (ISBN 0-686-28813-0). Tech Marketing.
International Symposium on Hydrotransport of Solids in Pipes, 4th. Proceedings. 1977. 60.00 (ISBN 0-900983-56-6). BHRA Fluid.
International Symposium on Hydrotransport of Solids in Pipes, 3rd. Proceedings. 1974. 50.00 (ISBN 0-900983-38-8). BHRA Fluid.
International Symposium on Pneumotransport of Solids in Pipes, 3rd. Proceedings. 1977. 60.00 (ISBN 0-900983-52-3). BHRA Fluid.
International Symposium on Pneumotransport of Solids in Pipes, 1st. Proceedings. 1972. 37.00 (ISBN 0-900983-15-9). BHRA Fluid.
I.U.T.A.M Symposium on Optical Methods in Mechanics of Solids. Optical Methods in Mechanics of Solids: Proceedings. Lagarde, Alexis, ed. 692p. 1980. 50.00x (ISBN 90-286-0860-5). Sijthoff & Noordhoff.
Kumakhov, M. Energy Losses & Ion Ranges in Solids. 1981. cancelled (ISBN 3-7186-0059-5). Harwood Academic.
Nemat-Nasser, S. Variational Methods in the Mechanics of Solids: Proceedings of the UUTAM Symposium, Sept. 11-13, 1978. LC 80-41529. (Illus.). 426p. 1981. 100.00 (ISBN 0-08-024728-8). Pergamon.
Phillips, W. A., ed. Amorphous Solids. (Topics in Current Physics Ser.: Vol. 24). (Illus.). 190p. 1981. 32.00 (ISBN 0-387-10330-9). Springer-Verlag.

SOLIDS–FRACTURE
see Fracture Mechanics

SOLIDS–STRENGTHENING MECHANISMS
see Strengthening Mechanisms in Solids

SOLIDS, REINFORCED
see Composite Materials

SOLOMON, KING OF ISRAEL
Petersen, Mark E. Three Kings of Israel. LC 80-36697. 179p. 1980. 6.95 (ISBN 0-87747-829-5). Deseret Bk.

SOLS
see Colloids

SOLUBLE FERMENTS
see Enzymes

SOLUTIONS, ELECTROLYTE
see Electrolyte Solutions

SOLZHENITSYN, ALEKSANDR ISAEVICH, 1918-
Lakshin, Vladimir. Solzhenitsyn, Tvardovsky & Novy Mir. 176p. 1980. 10.00 (ISBN 0-262-12086-0). MIT Pr.

SOMATOLOGY
see Physical Anthropology

SON OF MAN
Higgins, A. J. The Son of Man in the Teaching of Jesus. LC 79-42824. (Society for New Testament Studies Monographs: No. 40). 186p. Date not set. 24.50 (ISBN 0-521-22363-6). Cambridge U Pr.

SONAR
Echo Sounding & Sonar for Fishing. 102p. 1980. pap. 22.50 (ISBN 0-85238-110-7, FN86, FN). Unipub.

SONG BOOKS
see Songs

SONGS
see also Ballads; Carols; Glees, Catches, Rounds, etc. also subdivision Songs and Music under specific subjects, classes of persons, societies, institutions, etc., e.g. Cowboys–Songs and Music
Amauri, Maurice & Decraon, Pierre. Les Chansons Attribuees Aux Seigneurs De Craon. Langfors, Arthur, ed. LC 80-2160. (Societe Neo-Philologique De Helsingfors, Memoires Ser.: Vol. 6). 1981. Repr. of 1917 ed. 17.50 (ISBN 0-404-19020-0). AMS Pr.
Crane, Walter, illus. The Baby's Opera. (Illus.). 56p. (gr. k up). 1981. 4.95 (ISBN 0-671-42551-X, Pub. by Windmill). S&S.
Farmer, John S. Merry Songs & Ballads: Musa Pedestris, 6 vols. Set. 61.50x (ISBN 0-8154-0066-7). Cooper Sq.
Keller, C. Silly Song Book. 1980. pap. 1.95 (ISBN 0-13-809954-5). P-H.
Ord, John. The Bothy Songs & Ballads of Aberdeen. Banff & Moray, Angus & the Mearns. 493p. 1980. Repr. of 1930 ed. lib. bdg. 25.00 (ISBN 0-8492-7307-2). R West.
Wright, Thomas. Songs & Ballads, with Other Short Poems, Chiefly of the Reign of Philip & Mary. 214p. 1980. Repr. of 1860 ed. lib. bdg. 45.00 (ISBN 0-8495-5827-1). Arden Lib.

SONGS, CANADIAN
Creighton, Helen. Songs of Nova Scotia. 1968. pap. 6.00 (ISBN 0-486-21703-5). Dover.

SONGS, ENGLISH–HISTORY AND CRITICISM
Percival, Allen. English Love Songs. (Illus.). 256p. 1980. 27.50x (ISBN 0-389-20147-2). B&N.
Randolph, Henry F., ed. Fifty Years of English Song, 2 vols. (Illus.). 290p. 1981. Repr. of 1888 ed. lib. bdg. 150.00 (ISBN 0-8495-4574-9). Arden Lib.

SONGS, FRENCH
Debussy, Claude. Songs, 1880 to 1904. Benson, Rita, ed. (Orig.). 1981. pap. price not set (ISBN 0-486-24131-9). Dover.
Petersen-Dyggve, Holger N. Chansons Francaises Du XIIIe Siecle. LC 80-2167. 1981. 29.50 (ISBN 0-404-19030-8). AMS Pr.
Schwan, Eduard. Die Altfranzosischen Liederhandschriften Ihr Verhaltniss, Ihre/Entstehung & Ihre Bestimmung. LC 80-2169. Repr. of 1886 ed. 39.50 (ISBN 0-404-19033-2). AMS Pr.
Spanke, Hans, ed. Eine Altfranzosische Liedersammlung, Deranonyme Teil der Liederhandschriften Knpx. LC 80-2161. 1981. Repr. of 1925 ed. 54.50 (ISBN 0-404-19025-1). AMS Pr.

SONGS, HAWAIIAN
Roes, Carol. Mahalo Nui Translations. 1980. pap. 3.00 (ISBN 0-930932-20-X). M. Loke.

SONGS, INDIAN
Cloutier, David. Spirit Spirit: Shaman Songs. rev. enl. ed. (Illus.). 100p. 1980. pap. 4.50 (ISBN 0-914278-30-4). Copper Beech.

SONGS, INDIC
Mojumder, Atindra, tr. from Bengali. The Caryapadas: Tantric Poems of the Eighty-Four Mahasiddhas (Siddhacaryas) 2nd rev. ed. 225p. 1980. text ed. 13.95x (ISBN 0-935548-03-3). Santarasa Pubns.

SONGS, ITALIAN
Barbezieux, Rigaut De. Le Canzoni: Testi E Commento a Cura Di Mauro Braccini. LC 80-2188. 1981. Repr. of 1960 ed. 26.00 (ISBN 0-404-19017-0). AMS Pr.
Corte, Andrea D., ed. Canto E Bel Canto P.F. Tosi: Opinioni De Cantori Antchi E Moderni Seventeen Twenty Three. LC 80-2268. 1981. Repr. of 1933 ed. 31.50 (ISBN 0-404-18823-0). AMS Pr.

SONGS, RUSSIAN
Okudzhava, Bulat. Sixty-Five Songs; Sixty-Five Pesen. Frumkin, V., ed. (Eng. & Rus.). 1980. 18.00 (ISBN 0-88233-637-1); pap. 11.00 (ISBN 0-88233-638-X). Ardis Pubs.

SONIC ENGINEERING
see Acoustical Engineering

SONNETS
Davies, John. Wittes Pilgrimage, (by Poeticall Essaies) Through a World of Amorous Sonnets, Etc. LC 79-84099. (English Experience Ser.: No. 919). 172p. 1979. Repr. of 1605 ed. lib. bdg. 17.00 (ISBN 90-221-0919-4). Walter J Johnson.

SONORA, MEXICO–DESCRIPTION AND TRAVEL
Helms, Christopher L. & DenDooven, Gweneth R., eds. The Sonorar Desert. LC 80-82918. (Illus.). 1980. 8.95 (ISBN 0-916122-72-7); pap. 3.75 (ISBN 0-916122-71-9). K C Pubns.

SOPHISTS (GREEK PHILOSOPHY)
Apelt, Otto. Platonis Sophista: Recentsuit, Prolegomenis et Commentariis Instruxit. Taran, Leonardo, ed. LC 78-66612. (Ancent Philosophy Ser.: Vol. 1). 225p. lib bdg. 20.00 (ISBN 0-8240-9611-8). Garland Pub.
SOPHOCLES, 496?-406 B.C.
Burton, R. W. B. The Chorus in Sopocles Tragedies. 312p. 1980. 48.00x (ISBN 0-19-814374-5). Oxford U Pr.
Segal, Charles. Tragedy & Civilization: An Interpretation of Sophocles. LC 80-19765. (Modern Classical Lectures: No. 26). 544p. 1981. text ed. 30.00 (ISBN 0-674-90206-8). Harvard U Pr.
Sophocles: Dramatist & Philosopher. LC 80-22360. 64p. 1981. Repr. of 1958 ed. lib. bdg. 22.50x (ISBN 0-313-22625-3, KISD). Greenwood.
SOPORIFICS
see Narcotics
SORCERY
see Magic; Witchcraft
SORGHUM
Elements of Integrated Control of Sorghum Pests. (FAO Plant Production & Protection Ser.: No. 19). 167p. 1980. pap. 9.00 (ISBN 92-5-100884-1, F1943, FAO). Unipub.
SORPTION
see Adsorption
SORPTION OF GASES
see Gases–Absorption and Adsorption
SORROW
see Grief; Joy and Sorrow
SOUBRIQUETS
see Nicknames
SOUL
see also Future Life; Immortality; Personality; Psychology; Spirit; Spiritual Life
McHardy, George. The Higher Powers of the Soul. (Short Course Ser.). 142p. Repr. of 1912 ed. text ed. 2.95 (ISBN 0-567-08321-7). Attic Pr.
Purce, Jill. The Mystic Spiral: Journey of the Soul. (Art & Imagination Ser.). (Illus.). 128p. 1980. pap. 8.95 (ISBN 0-500-81005-2). Thames Hudson.
Winslow, Octavius. Personal Declension & Revival of Religion in the Soul. 1978. pap. 2.95 (ISBN 0-85151-261-5). Banner of Truth.
SOUL MUSIC
see Afro-American Music
SOUND
see also Acoustical Engineering; Architectural Acoustics; Electro-Acoustics; Hearing; Music–Acoustics and Physics; Noise; Phonetics; Ultrasonics; Vibration
Chapple, M. A Level Physics: Wave Motion-Sound & Light, Vol. 2. 2nd ed. (Illus.). 240p. (Orig.). 1979. pap. text ed. 10.95x (ISBN 0-7121-0155-1, Pub. by Macdonald & Evans England). Intl Ideas.
Palmer. Sound Exploration & Discovery. write for info. (ISBN 0-87628-217-6). Ctr Appl Res.
SOUND–APPARATUS
see also Magnetic Recorders and Recording; Microphone
Wells, Andy J. Audio Servicing: Text/Lab Manual. 1st ed. (Illus.). 144p. 9.95 (ISBN 0-07-069247-5). McGraw.
--Audio Servicing: Theory & Practice. 1st ed. (Illus.). 240p. (Orig.). pap. text ed. 13.95 (ISBN 0-07-069246-7, G); lab manual 9.95 (ISBN 0-07-069247-5). McGraw.
SOUND–RECORDING AND REPRODUCING
see also High-Fidelity Sound Systems; Magnetic Recorders and Recording; Stereophonic Sound Systems
Alkin, Glyn. Sound Recording & Reproduction. LC 80-41481. (Illus.). 208p. 1981. 24.95 (ISBN 0-240-51070-4). Focal Pr.
Johnson, Kenneth W. & Walker, Willard C. Understanding Audio. (Illus.). 256p. 1980. pap. text ed. 5.75 (ISBN 0-8403-2216-X). Kendall-Hunt.
SOUND ENGINEERING
see Acoustical Engineering
SOUND NAVIGATION AND RANGING
see Sonar
SOUND RECORDING AND REPRODUCING
see Sound–Recording and Reproducing
SOUND RECORDING TAPES
see Phonotapes
SOUND-WAVES–INDUSTRIAL APPLICATIONS
see Acoustical Engineering
SOUNDS
Flowers, Ann M. The Big Book of Sounds. 3rd ed. LC 80-81413. 1980. pap. text ed. 6.95x (ISBN 0-8134-2142-X, 2142). Interstate.
Friedman, Joy T. Sounds All Around. LC 80-83935. Orig. Title: Look Around & Listen. (Illus.). 80p. (gr. k-2). 1981. PLB 10.15 (ISBN 0-448-13945-6); pap. 3.95 (ISBN 0-448-14755-6). G&D.
SOUPED UP MOTORS
see Automobiles, Racing–Motors
SOUPS
Gerras, Charles, ed. Rodale's Soups & Salads Cookbook & Kitchen Album. (Illus.). 352p. 1981. 14.95 (ISBN 0-87857-332-1). Rodale Pr Inc.
Matteson, Marilee, ed. Small Feasts: Soups, Salads, & Sandwiches. (Clarkson N. Potter Bks.). 1980. 17.95 (ISBN 0-517-54052-5). Crown.
Orcutt, Georgia. Soups, Chowders & Stews. Taylor, Sandra, ed. (Flair of New England Ser.). 1981. pap. 8.95 (ISBN 0-911658-17-3, 3078). Yankee Bks.
SOUTH AFRICA–BIBLIOGRAPHY
Musiker, Reuben. South Africa. (World Bibliographical Ser.: No. 7). 194p. 1980. 25.25 (ISBN 0-903450-16-X). ABC-Clio.
State Library, Pretoria, ed. South African National Bibliography, 1977. 972p. 1977. 35.00x. Intl Pubns Serv.
--South African National Bibliography, 1978. 735p. 1978. 35.00x (ISBN 0-8002-2754-9). Intl Pubns Serv.
--South African National Bibliography, 1979. 747p. 1979. 66.50x (ISBN 0-8002-2755-7). Intl Pubns Serv.
SOUTH AFRICA–ECONOMIC CONDITIONS
The Activities of Transnational Corporations in the Industrial, Mining & Military Sectors of Southern Africa. 79p. 1980. pap. 7.00 (ISBN 0-686-68940-2, UN80/2A3, UN). Unipub.
Du Toit, Darcy. Capital & Labour in South Africa. (Monographs from the African Studies Centre, Leiden). 480p. 1981. price not set (ISBN 0-7103-0001-8). Routledge & Kegan.
Marks, Shula & Atmore, Anthony, eds. Economy & Society in Pre-Industrial South Africa. (Illus.). 385p. (Orig.). 1980. pap. 25.00; pap. text ed. 9.95 (ISBN 0-582-64656-1). Longman.
SOUTH AFRICA–FOREIGN RELATIONS
The Activities of Transnational Corporations in the Industrial, Mining & Military Sectors of Southern Africa. 79p. 1980. pap. 7.00 (ISBN 0-686-68940-2, UN80/2A3, UN). Unipub.
SOUTH AFRICA–HISTORY
Frederic, Helene & Malinsky, Martine. Martin. McGreal, John & Lipshitz, Susan, trs. from Fr. Orig. Title: Martin: un Enfant Battait Sa Mere. 108p. 1981. price not set (ISBN 0-7100-0814-7). Routledge & Kegan.
The Old Transvaal, Eighten Thirty-Four to Eighteen Ninety-Nine. 1980. 40.00x (Pub. by Bailey & Swinton South Africa). State Mutual Bk.
SOUTH AFRICA–POLITICS AND GOVERNMENT
Frederic, Helene & Malinsky, Martine. Martin. McGreal, John & Lipshitz, Susan, trs. from Fr. Orig. Title: Martin: un Enfant Battait Sa Mere. 108p. 1981. price not set (ISBN 0-7100-0814-7). Routledge & Kegan.
Van der Merwe, Henrik. South Africa: Morality & Action. (Studies in Quakerism). 60p. (Orig.). 1981. pap. 3.00 (ISBN 0-89670-007-0). Progresiv Pub.
SOUTH AFRICA–RACE QUESTION
Addison, John. Apartheid. (Today's World Ser.). (Illus.). 72p. (gr. 7-9). 1981. 15.95 (ISBN 0-7134-2485-0, Pub. by Batsford England). David & Charles.
Lambley, Peter. The Psychology of Apartheid. LC 80-53595. 312p. 1981. lib. bdg. 16.50x (ISBN 0-8203-0548-0). U of Ga Pr.
Laurence, John C. Race, Propaganda & South Africa: The Manipulation of Western Opinion & Policies by the Forces of White Supremacy. 1981. text ed. 19.25 (ISBN 0-575-02691-X, Pub. by Gollancz England). Humanities.
Van der Merwe, Hendrik & Schrire, Robert A., eds. Race & Ethnicity: South African & International Perspectives. 240p. 1981. pap. 12.95x (ISBN 0-8476-3651-8). Rowman.
SOUTH AFRICA–SOCIAL CONDITIONS
Lambley, Peter. The Psychology of Apartheid. LC 80-53595. 312p. 1981. lib. bdg. 16.50x (ISBN 0-8203-0548-0). U of Ga Pr.
Marks, Shula & Atmore, Anthony, eds. Economy & Society in Pre-Industrial South Africa. (Illus.). 385p. (Orig.). 1980. pap. 25.00; pap. text ed. 9.95 (ISBN 0-582-64656-1). Longman.
Van der Merwe, Henrik. South Africa: Morality & Action. (Studies in Quakerism). 60p. (Orig.). 1981. pap. 3.00 (ISBN 0-89670-007-0). Progresiv Pub.
SOUTH AFRICA–SOCIAL LIFE AND CUSTOMS
February, V. A. The Coloured Image. (Monographs from the African Studies Center, Leiden). 256p. 1981. price not set (ISBN 0-7103-0002-6). Routledge & Kegan.
SOUTH AFRICAN LITERATURE
February, V. A. The Coloured Image. (Monographs from the African Studies Center, Leiden). 256p. 1981. price not set (ISBN 0-7103-0002-6). Routledge & Kegan.
SOUTH AMERICA–DESCRIPTION AND TRAVEL
Miller, Tom. On the Border: Portraits of America's Southwestern Frontier. LC 79-2631. 224p. 1981. 10.95 (ISBN 0-06-013039-3, HarpT). Har-Row.
SOUTH AMERICA–ECONOMIC CONDITIONS
Guidelines for Productivity Measurement & Analysis for APO Member Countries. 52p. 1980. pap. 13.25 (ISBN 92-833-1463-8, APO 87, APO). Unipub.
SOUTH AMERICA–HISTORY
Nesheim, Margaret. Wet Landing-Dry Landing. (Illus.). 192p. 1981. 10.00 (ISBN 0-682-49673-1). Exposition.
SOUTH CAROLINA–BIBLIOGRAPHY
Vexler, R. I. South Carolina Chronology & Factbook, Vol. 40. 1978. 8.50 (ISBN 0-379-16165-6). Oceana.
SOUTH CAROLINA–BIOGRAPHY
Bailey, N. Louise & Cooper, Elizabeth I., eds. Biographical Directory of the South Carolina House of Representatives: Seventeen-Seventy-Five to Seventeen-Ninty, Vol. 3. 780p. 1981. text ed. 14.95 (ISBN 0-87249-406-3). U of SC Pr.
Perry, Benjamin F. The Writings of Benjamin F. Perry. Meats, Stephen & Arnold, Edwin T., eds. Incl. Vol. I. Essays, Public Letters, & Speeches. 640p. 35.00 (ISBN 0-87152-340-X); Vols. II & III. Reminiscences of Public Men. Vol. II, 576p. 35.00 ea. (ISBN 0-87152-341-8); Vol. III, 572p. 35.00 (ISBN 0-87152-342-6). LC 80-19568. (The South Carolina Ser.: Bibliographical & Textual: No. 6). 1980. Repr. Set. 105.00 (ISBN 0-87152-339-6). Reprint.
Richardson, James M. History of Greenville County, South Carolina: Narrative & Biographical. LC 80-23330. 342p. 1980. Repr. of 1930 ed. 22.50 (ISBN 0-87152-343-4). Reprint.
SOUTH CAROLINA–DESCRIPTION AND TRAVEL
Rhyne, Nancy. The Grand Stand: An Uncommon Guide to Myrtle Beach & Its Surroundings. (Illus.). 160p. (Orig.). 1981. pap. 4.95 (ISBN 0-914788-36-1). East Woods.
SOUTH CAROLINA–GENEALOGY
Obear, Katharine T. Through the Years in Old Winnsboro. LC 80-23314. xx, 258p. 1980. Repr. of 1940 ed. write for info. (ISBN 0-87152-344-2). Reprint.
SOUTH CAROLINA–HISTORY
Herd, E. Don, Jr. The South Carolina Upcountry, Fifteen Forty to Nineteen Eighty: Historical & Biographical Sketches, Vol. 1. 1981. pap. 11.95 (ISBN 0-87921-062-1). Attic Pr.
Obear, Katharine T. Through the Years in Old Winnsboro. LC 80-23314. xx, 258p. 1980. Repr. of 1940 ed. write for info. (ISBN 0-87152-344-2). Reprint.
Perry, Benjamin F. The Writings of Benjamin F. Perry. Meats, Stephen & Arnold, Edwin T., eds. Incl. Vol. I. Essays, Public Letters, & Speeches. 640p. 35.00 (ISBN 0-87152-340-X); Vols. II & III. Reminiscences of Public Men. Vol. II, 576p. 35.00 ea. (ISBN 0-87152-341-8); Vol. III, 572p. 35.00 (ISBN 0-87152-342-6). LC 80-19568. (The South Carolina Ser.: Bibliographical & Textual: No. 6). 1980. Repr. Set. 105.00 (ISBN 0-87152-339-6). Reprint.
Richardson, James M. History of Greenville County, South Carolina: Narrative & Biographical. LC 80-23330. 342p. 1980. Repr. of 1930 ed. 22.50 (ISBN 0-87152-343-4). Reprint.
Vexler, R. I. South Carolina Chronology & Factbook, Vol. 40. 1978. 8.50 (ISBN 0-379-16165-6). Oceana.
SOUTH DAKOTA
see also names of cities, towns, etc. in South Dakota
Fradin, Dennis. South Dakota: In Words & Pictures. LC 80-25349. (Young People's Stories of Our States Ser.). (Illus.). 48p. (gr. 2-5). 1981. PLB 8.65g (ISBN 0-516-03941-5, Time Line). Childrens.
Scneider, Bill. The Dakota Image. LC 80-83707. (Illus.). 96p. 1980. 20.00 (ISBN 0-934318-02-6). Falcon Pr MT.
Vexler, R. I. South Dakota Chronology & Factbook, Vol. 41. 1978. 8.50 (ISBN 0-379-16166-4). Oceana.
SOUTH SEAS
see Micronesia
SOUTHERN PACIFIC RAILROAD
Strapac, Joseph A. Southern Pacific Review Nineteen Eighty. (Illus.). 1980. pap. 14.00 (ISBN 0-930742-04-4). Shade Tree.
SOUTHERN STATES–BIOGRAPHY
Thomson, J. S., ed. Personalities of the South. 9th ed. 641p. 1980. 44.95x (ISBN 0-686-28826-2, Pub. by Intl Biog). Biblio Dist.
--Personalities of the South. 10th ed. 634p. 1981. 49.95x (ISBN 0-934544-03-4, Pub. by Intl Biog). Biblio Dist.
SOUTHERN STATES–CIVILIZATION
Fuller, Chet. I Hear Them Calling My Name: A Journey Through the New South. 320p. 1981. 12.95 (ISBN 0-395-30528-4). HM.
SOUTHERN STATES–DESCRIPTION AND TRAVEL–GUIDEBOOKS
Rand McNally & Company & Southern Living Travel Editors. Southern Living Travel South - 1981. (Illus.). 192p. 1981. pap. 9.95 (ISBN 0-686-69039-7). Oxmoor Hse.
Whitman, John. The Best Free Attractions in the South. Grooms, Kathe, ed. (The Best Free Attractions Ser.). (Illus.). 200p. 1981. pap. 3.95 (ISBN 0-915658-38-0). Meadowbrook Pr.
SOUTHERN STATES–ECONOMIC CONDITIONS
Bateman, Fred & Weiss, Thomas. A Deplorable Scarcity: The Failure of Industrialization in the Slave Economy. LC 80-13238. xii, 237p. 1981. 19.00x (ISBN 0-8078-1447-4). U of NC Pr.
SOUTHERN STATES–HISTORY
Clark, Thomas D. & Kirwan, Albert D. The South Since Appomattox: A Century of Regional Change. LC 80-24023. (Illus.). vii, 438p. 1980. Repr. of 1967 ed. lib. bdg. 39.75x (ISBN 0-313-22698-9, CLSS). Greenwood.
Dennis, Frank A., ed. Southern Miscellany: Essays in Honor of Glover Moore. LC 80-20373. 202p. 1981. 15.00 (ISBN 0-87805-129-5). U Pr of Miss.
Hershey, Virginia S. Those Southern Milners: A Collection of Record Abstracts for the Southern States Between 1606 & 1850 with Biographical & Historical Sketches, Family Records, & Genealogies up to 1900. (Illus.). 426p. 1980. 40.00x (ISBN 0-9605320-0-5, TX-578-128). Hershey.
Randall, James G. Lincoln & the South. LC 80-22084. (The Walter Lynwood Fleming Lectures in Southern History, L. S. U.). (Illus.). viii, 161p. 1980. Repr. of 1946 ed. lib. bdg. 18.75x (ISBN 0-313-22843-4, RALS). Greenwood.
SOUTHERN STATES–HISTORY–CIVIL WAR, 1861-1865
see United States–History–Civil War, 1861-1865
SOUTHERN STATES–INDUSTRIES
Bateman, Fred & Weiss, Thomas. A Deplorable Scarcity: The Failure of Industrialization in the Slave Economy. LC 80-13238. xii, 237p. 1981. 19.00x (ISBN 0-8078-1447-4). U of NC Pr.
SOUTHERN STATES–POLITICS AND GOVERNMENT
Black, Merle. Social Science Perspectives of the South, Vol. 1. Reed, John S., ed. 1981. price not set (ISBN 0-677-16260-X). Gordon.
Fuller, Chet. I Hear Them Calling My Name: A Journey Through the New South. 320p. 1981. 12.95 (ISBN 0-395-30528-4). HM.
SOUTHERN STATES–SOCIAL CONDITIONS
Black, Merle. Social Science Perspectives of the South, Vol. 1. Reed, John S., ed. 1981. price not set (ISBN 0-677-16260-X). Gordon.
SOUTHERN STATES–SOCIAL LIFE AND CUSTOMS
see also Plantation Life
Bertelson, David. The Lazy South. LC 80-24033. ix, 284p. 1980. Repr. of 1967 ed. lib. bdg. 25.00x (ISBN 0-313-22696-2, BELS). Greenwood.
Bridenbaugh, Carl. Myths & Realities: Societies of the Colonial South. LC 80-25280. (The Walter Lynwood Fleming Lectures in Southern History Ser., Louisiana State University). x, 208p. 1981. Repr. of 1952 ed. lib. bdg. 19.75x (ISBN 0-313-22770-5, BRMR). Greenwood.
Chandler, Kathleen. Les Belles Lettres. (Illus.). 160p. 1981. 7.95 (ISBN 0-89962-204-6). Todd & Honeywell.
Mayfield, Chris, ed. Growing up Southern: Southern Exposure Looks at Childhood, Then & Now. (Illus.). 1981. 17.95 (ISBN 0-394-50913-7); pap. 7.95 (ISBN 0-394-74809-3). Pantheon.
SOUTHWEST, NEW
Here are entered works on that part of the United States which roughly corresponds to the old Spanish province of New Mexico, including the present Arizona, New Mexico, Southern Colorado, Utah, Nevada and California.
Hansen, Niles. The Border Economy: Regional Development in the Southwest. (Illus.). 208p. 1981. text ed. 17.95x (ISBN 0-292-75061-7); pap. text ed. 8.95x (ISBN 0-292-75063-3). U of Tex Pr.
SOUTHWEST, NEW–ANTIQUITIES
Rosenbaum, Robert J. Mexicano Resistance in the Southwest: The Sacred Right of Self-Preservation. (Illus.). 245p. 1981. text ed. 14.95x (ISBN 0-292-77562-8). U of Tex Pr.
SOVEREIGN IMMUNITY
see Government Liability
SOVEREIGNS
see Roman Emperors
also subdivision Kings and Rulers under names of countries
SOVEREIGNTY
see also Autonomy; Self-Determination, National; Social Contract; State, the
Miller, J. D. The World of States: Connected Essays. 1981. price not set (ISBN 0-312-89240-3). St Martin.
SOVIET-FINNISH WAR, 1939-1940
see Russo-Finnish War, 1939-1940
SOY-BEAN
Oster, Merrill J., et al. Multiply Your Money Trading Soybeans: A Beginner's Guide to Speculating in Soybean Futures. 198p. 1981. 14.95 (ISBN 0-914230-10-7). Investor Pubns.
SOZIALDEMOKRATISCHE PARTEI DEUTSCHLANDS
see Social Democratic Party of Germany
SPACE (ARCHITECTURE)
Cartwright, Richard M. Design of Urban Space: A GLC Manual. 208p. 1981. 44.95 (ISBN 0-470-27066-7). Halsted Pr.
SPACE AND TIME
see also Relativity (Physics)
Sleator, William. The Green Futures of Tycho. LC 80-23020. (gr. 5-9). 1981. PLB 9.95 (ISBN 0-525-31007-X). Dutton.
Wald, Robert M. Space, Time, & Gravity. LC 77-4038. viii, 132p. 1981. pap. 3.95 (ISBN 0-226-87031-6). U of Chicago Pr.
SPACE ENVIRONMENT
see also Solar Radiation
Heppenheimer, T. A. Towards Distant Suns. (Illus.). 1980. pap. 8.95 (ISBN 0-449-90035-5, Columbine). Fawcett.
SPACE EXPLORATION (ASTRONAUTICS)
see Outer Space–Exploration

SPACE FLIGHT
see also Astronautics
Werz, James R., ed. Spacecraft Attitude Determination & Control. (Astrophysics & Space Science Library: No. 73). 858p. 1980. PLB 52.00 (ISBN 90-277-0959-9, Pub. by D. Reidel); pap. 28.95 (ISBN 90-277-1204-2). Kluwer Boston.
SPACE FLIGHT–JUVENILE LITERATURE
Poynter, Margaret & Lane, Arthur. Voyager: The Story of a Space Mission. LC 80-18723. (Illus.). 160p. 1981. 9.95 (ISBN 0-689-30827-2). Atheneum.
SPACE FLIGHT TRAINING
see Flight Training
SPACE LATTICE (MATHEMATICS)
see Lattice Theory
SPACE OF MORE THAN THREE DIMENSIONS
see Space and Time
SPACE RESEARCH
see Outer Space–Exploration; Space Sciences
SPACE ROCKETS
see Space Vehicles
SPACE SCIENCES
see also Astronautics; Astronomy; Geophysics; Space and Time
Hanle, Paul A. & Chamberlain, Von Del, eds. Space Science Comes of Age: Perspectives in the History of the Space Sciences. (Illus.). 220p. 1981. 25.00 (ISBN 0-87474-508-X); pap. 12.50 (ISBN 0-87474-507-1). Smithsonian.
SPACE SHIPS
Powers, Robert M. Shuttle: The World's First Spaceship. 1980. pap. 2.75 (ISBN 0-446-95331-8). Warner Bks.
Zimmerman, Howard. Spaceships. enl. ed. 1980. pap. 7.95 (ISBN 0-931064-23-6). O'Quinn Studio.
SPACE SHUTTLES
see Reusable Space Vehicles
SPACE-TIMES
see Space and Time
SPACE TRAVEL
see Space Flight
SPACE VEHICLES
see also Astronautics; Reusable Space Vehicles; Space Ships
Werz, James R., ed. Spacecraft Attitude Determination & Control. (Astrophysics & Space Science Library: No. 73). 858p. 1980. PLB 52.00 (ISBN 90-277-0959-9, Pub. by D. Reidel); pap. 28.95 (ISBN 90-277-1204-2). Kluwer Boston.
SPACE WEATHER
see Space Environment
SPACECRAFT
see Space Vehicles
SPAIN–BIOGRAPHY
Harter, Hugh A. Gertrudis Gomez De Avellaneda. (World Authors Ser.: No. 599). 1981. lib. bdg. 14.95 (ISBN 0-8057-6441-0). Twayne.
SPAIN–CIVILIZATION
OAS General Secretariat. Guia De las Fuentes En Hispanoamerica Para el Estudio De la Administracion Virreinal Espanola En Mexico y En el Peru 1535-1700. 523p. 1980. pap. 15.00 (ISBN 0-8270-1091-5). OAS.
SPAIN–DESCRIPTION AND TRAVEL
Capek, Karel. Letters from Spain. 192p. 1980. Repr. of 1931 ed. lib. bdg. 25.00 (ISBN 0-8495-0999-8). Arden Lib.
SPAIN–DESCRIPTION AND TRAVEL–GUIDEBOOKS
Bristow, Philip. Down the Spanish Coast. 196p. 1980. 12.00x (ISBN 0-245-52935-7, Pub. by Nautical England). State Mutual Bk.
SPAIN–HISTORY
Here are entered general works on Spanish history, and works on all periods of Spanish history except the Civil War, 1936-1939, which are entered below under Spain–History–Civil War, 1936-1939.
Bar, Antonio. Syndicalism & Revolution in Spain. (History of Anarchism Ser.). 1981. lib. bdg. 69.95 (ISBN 0-8490-3208-3). Gordon Pr.
Eaton, Samuel D. The Forces of Freedom in Spain 1974-1979, P-245. LC 80-8383. (Illus.). 216p. 1981. pap. 11.95 (ISBN 0-8179-7452-0). Hoover Inst Pr.
Lopez-Morrillas, J. The Krausist Movement & Ideological Change in Spain: Eighteen Fifty-Four to Eighteen Seventy-Four. 180p. Date not set. price not set (ISBN 0-521-23256-2). Cambridge U Pr.
Stevens, John, tr. The Spanish Libertines. LC 80-2499. 1981. Repr. of 1707 ed. 83.50 (ISBN 0-404-19135-5). AMS Pr.
SPAIN–HISTORY–WAR OF 1898
see United States–History–War of 1898
SPAIN–HISTORY–CIVIL WAR, 1936-1939
Powell, T. G. Mexico & the Spanish Civil War. 240p. 1981. 17.50x (ISBN 0-8263-0546-6). U of NM Pr.
SPAIN–INTELLECTUAL LIFE
Lopez-Morrillas, J. The Krausist Movement & Ideological Change in Spain: Eighteen Fifty-Four to Eighteen Seventy-Four. 180p. Date not set. price not set (ISBN 0-521-23256-2). Cambridge U Pr.
Procter, Evelyn S. Alfonso X of Castile, Patron of Literature & Learning. LC 80-10508. (Norman Macoll Lectures: 1949). vi, 149p. 1980. Repr. of 1951 ed. lib. bdg. 19.50x (ISBN 0-313-22347-5, PRAL). Greenwood.
SPAIN–POLITICS AND GOVERNMENT
Carr, Raymond. Modern Spain. 256p. 1981. 19.95 (ISBN 0-19-215828-7); pap. 11.50 (ISBN 0-19-289090-5). Oxford U Pr.
SPANISH AMERICA
see Latin America
SPANISH-AMERICAN LITERATURE
see also Mexican Literature
Oberhelman, Harley D. The Presence of Faulkner in the Writings of Garcia Marquez. (Graduate Studies, Texas Tech Univ.: No. 22). (Illus.). 1980. pap. 7.00 (ISBN 0-89672-080-2). Tex Tech Pr.
Schwartz, Ronald. Nomads, Exiles, & Emigres: The Rebirth of the Latin American Narrative, 1960-80. LC 80-20669. 168p. 1980. 10.00 (ISBN 0-8108-1359-9). Scarecrow.
Sommers, J. & Ybarra-Frausto, T. Modern Chicano Writers: A Collection of Critical Essays. 1979. 10.95 (ISBN 0-13-589721-1); pap. 3.45 (ISBN 0-13-589713-0). P-H.
Tapia, John R. The Indian in the Spanish-American Novel. LC 80-6182. 120p. (Orig.). 1981. lib. bdg. 16.25 (ISBN 0-8191-1428-6); pap. text ed. 7.75 (ISBN 0-8191-1438-3). U Pr of Amer.
SPANISH-AMERICAN WAR, 1898
see United States–History–War of 1898
SPANISH AMERICANS IN THE UNITED STATES
De Mundo Lo, Sara. Index to the Spanish American Biography: The Andean Countries, Vol. 1. (Reference Bks.). 1981. lib. bdg. 60.00 (ISBN 0-8161-8181-0). G K Hall.
Howe, Florence & Rothermich, John A., eds. Las Mujeres: Conversations from a Hispanic Community. (Women's Lives - Women's Work Ser.). 192p. (Orig.). 1980. pap. text ed. 4.23 (ISBN 0-07-020445-4). Webster-McGraw.
Wald, Heywood. Lo Paso Bien En los Estados Inidos. (gr. 9-12). 1981. pap. 0.95 (ISBN 0-8120-2318-8). Barron.
SPANISH ARMADA
see Armada, 1588
SPANISH ART
see Art, Spanish
SPANISH CIVILIZATION
see Civilization, Hispanic; Spain–Civilization
SPANISH DRAMA
Visigli, R. El Gesticulador: Pieza Para Demagogos En Tres Actos. Ballinger, R., ed. (Span.). 1963. 8.95 (ISBN 0-13-273771-X). P-H.
SPANISH GUITAR
see Guitar
SPANISH HYMNS
see Hymns, Spanish
SPANISH INQUISITION
see Inquisition
SPANISH LANGUAGE
Andino, Alrto. Frutos De Mi Trasplante. LC 79-52356. (Coleccion Caniqui). 102p. (Span.). 1980. pap. 5.95 (ISBN 0-89729-230-8). Ediciones.
Bruckner, D. J., ed. Politics & Language: Spanish & English in the United States. (Orig.). 1980. pap. 4.00x (ISBN 0-686-28732-0). U Chi Ctr Policy.
Rudman, Jack. Spanish. (Undergraduate Program Field Test Ser.: UPFT-24). (Cloth bdg. avail. on request). pap. 9.95 (ISBN 0-8373-6024-2). Natl Learning.
Schmitt, Conrad J. Espanol: Sigamos, Pupil's Edition. 3rd ed. Chimienti, Teresa, ed. LC 80-13032. (Illus.). 282p. (Span.). (gr. 8). 1980. text ed. 11.64 (ISBN 0-07-055578-8, W); tchrs. ed. 13.16 (ISBN 0-07-055579-6); wkbk. avail. (ISBN 0-07-055575-3); filmstrips 93.92 (ISBN 0-07-098994-X). McGraw.
Turk, Laurel H. & Espinosa, Aurelio M. Foundation Course in Spanish. 5th ed. (Illus.). 439p. 1981. text ed. 16.95 (ISBN 0-669-02637-9); wkbk. 5.95 (ISBN 0-669-02638-7); answer keys with tests avail. (ISBN 0-669-02639-5); tapescript avail. (ISBN 0-669-02640-9); reels set of 15 75.00 (ISBN 0-669-02641-7); cassettes set of 15 75.00 (ISBN 0-669-02643-3); demo tape avail. (ISBN 0-669-02644-1). Heath.
Varela, Beatriz. Lo Chino en el Habla Cubana. LC 79-54025. (Coleccion Polymita). (Illus.). 64p. (Orig., Span.). 1980. pap. 6.95 (ISBN 0-89729-233-2). Ediciones.
SPANISH LANGUAGE–BUSINESS SPANISH
Perez, Roman & Ferrie, Carmen. Introduction to Business Translation: A Handbook in English - Spanish Contrastive Linguistics. LC 80-18052. 196p. 1980. pap. write for info. (ISBN 0-8477-3328-9). U of PR Pr.
Santana, Jorge A. Spanish for the Professions. 256p. 1981. pap. text ed. 7.95 (ISBN 0-394-32652-0). Random.
SPANISH LANGUAGE–CONVERSATION AND PHRASE BOOKS
see also Spanish Language–Textbooks for Children
Andrews, Marta, et al. Platicas: Conversational Spanish. LC 80-84024. 304p. 1981. pap. text ed. 11.95 (ISBN 0-8403-2328-X). Kendall-Hunt.
Kahn, Michel. My Everyday Spanish Word Book. (Illus.). 46p. (gr. 3-9). 1981. 7.95 (ISBN 0-8120-5431-8). Barron.
Knorre, Marty, et al. Puntas de Partida: An Invitation to Spanish. Incl. Arana, Alice & Arana, Oswaldo. 224p. wkbk. 6.95; Yates, Maria S. 196p. lab manual 6.95 (ISBN 0-394-32630-X). 608p. 1981. text ed. 17.95 (ISBN 0-394-32618-0). Random.
Schmitt, Conrad J. Espanol, Comencemos: Pupil's Edition. 3rd ed. Chimienti, Teresa, ed. LC 80-13033. (Illus.). 280p. (Span.). (gr. 7). 1980. text ed. 10.60 (ISBN 0-07-055573-7, W); tchr's ed. 11.96 (ISBN 0-07-055574-5); wkbk. 3.80 (ISBN 0-07-055575-3); tests 66.00 (ISBN 0-07-055576-1); filmstrips 93.32 (ISBN 0-07-098991-5); test replacements 39.60 (ISBN 0-07-055577-X). McGraw.
Stern, A. Z. & Reif, Joseph A., eds. Useful Expressions in Spanish. (Useful Expressions Ser.). 64p. (Orig.). 1980. pap. 1.50 (ISBN 0-86628-013-8). Ridgefield Pub.
Vasi, Susanne & Tomasino, Joseph. Exercises in Spanish. new ed. 200p. 1980. pap. 3.25 (ISBN 0-88345-446-7, 18638); cassettes 25.00. Regents Pub.
SPANISH LANGUAGE–DIALECTS
Canfield, D. Lincoln. Spanish Pronunciation in the Americas. LC 80-23664. (Illus.). 1981. lib. bdg. 15.00x (ISBN 0-226-09262-3). U of Chicago Pr.
SPANISH LANGUAGE–DICTIONARIES
Diccionario Enciclopedico Espasa, 12 vols. (Span.). 1978. Set. 165.00. Pergamon.
Mackenzie, David, ed. A Manual of Manuscript Transcription for the Dictionary of the Old Spanish Language. 2nd ed. (Illus.). 122p. 1981. pap. 15.00. Hispanic Seminary.
Perez, Roman & Ferrie, Carmen. Introduction to Business Translation: A Handbook in English - Spanish Contrastive Linguistics. LC 80-18052. 196p. 1980. pap. write for info. (ISBN 0-8477-3328-9). U of PR Pr.
SPANISH LANGUAGE–DICTIONARIES–ENGLISH
Barcelo, J. R. Spanish-English - English-Spanish Chemical Vocabulary. vii, 111p. (Orig.). 1980. pap. 7.50 (ISBN 84-205-0696-6). Heinman.
Lipton, Gladys & Munoz, Olivia. Diccionario Del Ingles Americano. (Illus.). 368p. (gr. 10-12). 1981. pap. 2.95 (ISBN 0-8120-2319-6). Barron.
New Webster's Quick Reference English-Spanish Dictionary. (Quick Reference Ser.). (Orig.). 1981. pap. 1.95 (ISBN 0-8326-0054-7, 6607). Delair.
SPANISH LANGUAGE–DICTIONARIES–ITALIAN
Frisoni, Gaetano. Dizionario Moderno Spagnuolo-Italiano--Italiano-Spagnuolo, 2 vols. 1865p. Set. 44.00x (ISBN 0-913298-51-4). S F Vanni.
SPANISH LANGUAGE–GRAMMAR
Parisi, Gino. Intermediate Spanish Review Grammar. 336p. Date not set. pap. text ed. 8.95 (ISBN 0-669-02632-8); wkbk. 3.95 (ISBN 0-669-02633-6). Heath.
SPANISH LANGUAGE–PHONETICS
Burt, John R. From Phonology to Philology: An Outline of Descriptive & Historical Spanish Linguistics. LC 80-67212. 208p. 1980. lib. bdg. 17.50 (ISBN 0-8191-1310-7); pap. text ed. 9.50 (ISBN 0-8191-1311-5). U Pr of Amer.
Lombardi, Ronald P. & De Peters, Amalia B. Modern Spoken Spanish: An Interdisciplinary Perspective. LC 80-1442. 507p. (Orig.). 1981. pap. text ed. 16.75 (ISBN 0-8191-1513-4). U Pr of Amer.
SPANISH LANGUAGE–PRONUNCIATION
Canfield, D. Lincoln. Spanish Pronunciation in the Americas. LC 80-23664. (Illus.). 1981. lib. bdg. 15.00x (ISBN 0-226-09262-3). U of Chicago Pr.
SPANISH LANGUAGE–TEXTBOOKS FOR CHILDREN
see also Spanish Language–Conversation and Phrase Books
Fry, Edward B. Sailboat: Barco De Vela, Bk. 3. Gunning, Monica, tr. (Storybooks for Beginners Ser.). (Illus.). 15p. (Eng. & Span.). 1980. pap. 12.50 set (ISBN 0-89061-214-5). Jamestown Pubs.
--Sailboat in the Wind: Barco De Vela En el Viento, Bk. 4. Gunning, Monica, tr. (Storybooks for Beginners Ser.). (Illus.). 15p. (Eng. & Span.). (gr. 1). 1980. pap. 12.50 (ISBN 0-89061-215-3). Jamestown Pubs.
Mountain, Lee. Dragon Don & John: Dragon Donaldo y Juan. Gunning, Monica, tr. (Storybooks for Beginners Ser.). (Illus.). 15p. (Eng. & Span.). 1980. pap. 12.50 set (ISBN 0-89061-213-7). Jamestown Pubs.
--Dragon Don: Dragon Donaldo, Bk. 1. Gunning, Monica, tr. (Storybooks for Beginners Ser.). (Illus.). 15p. 1980. pap. 12.50 set (ISBN 0-89061-212-9). Jamestown Pubs.
SPANISH LANGUAGE–TEXTBOOKS FOR FOREIGNERS
see also Spanish Language–Conversation and Phrase Books
Arsuaga De Vila, Maria. Manual De Espanol. rev. ed. LC 80-36752. 253p. 1980. Set. write for info. (ISBN 0-8477-3177-4). Vol. 1,pt. 1 (ISBN 0-8477-3195-2). Vol. 1,pt. 2 (ISBN 0-8477-3196-0). U of PR Pr.
Vasi, Susanne & Tomasino, Joseph. Exercises in Spanish. 229p. 1981. pap. text ed. 3.25 (ISBN 0-88345-421-1, 18638). Regents Pub.
SPANISH LITERATURE–HISTORY AND CRITICISM
Ilie, Paul. Literature & the Inner Exile: Authoritarian Spain, 1939-1975. LC 80-18281. 208p. 1981. text ed. 14.50x (ISBN 0-8018-2424-9). Johns Hopkins.
Johnson, Roberta. Carmen Laforet. (World Authors Ser: No. 601). 1981. lib. bdg. 14.50 (ISBN 0-8057-6443-7). Twayne.
Salem, Luis. La Nota Biblica en la Literatura Castellana. LC 77-163. 186p. (Orig., Span.). 1977. pap. 3.25 (ISBN 0-89922-086-X). Edit Caribe.
Seminario De Estudios Hispanicos & Onis, Federico de. Luis Llorens Torres En Su Centenario. LC 80-21479. (Coleccion UPREX, 57 Ser.: Estudios Literarios). 1981. pap. write for info. (ISBN 0-8477-0057-7). U of PR Pr.
Weiss, Beno & Perez, Louis C. Juan De la Cueva's los Inventores De las Cosas: A Critical Edition & Study. LC 80-83466. 220p. 1980. text ed. 17.50x (ISBN 0-271-00279-4). Pa St U Pr.
SPANISH MUSIC
see Music, Spanish
SPANISH POETRY (COLLECTIONS)
Here are entered collections in Spanish. For English translations see subdivision Translations into English.
see also Latin-American Poetry (Collections)
Empringham, Toni, ed. Chicano Poetry Anthology. 128p. (Orig.). 1981. pap. 6.50 (ISBN 0-88496-164-8). Capra Pr.
Ismaili, Rashidah, et al. Womanrise (Anthology) Rivera, Louis R., ed. (Illus.). 128p. (Orig.). 1978. pap. 4.25 (ISBN 0-917886-05-4). Shamal Bks.
SPANISH POETRY–HISTORY AND CRITICISM
Inclan, Josefina. Carmen Conde y el Mar - Carmen Conde & the Sea. Santayana, Manuel J., tr. LC 80-69623. (Coleccion Polymita). 81p. (Orig., Span. & Eng.). 1980. pap. 8.95 (ISBN 0-89729-277-4). Ediciones.
McCormick, Robert. The Concept of Happiness in the Spanish Poetry of the Eighteenth Century. LC 80-68000. (Hispanic Studies Collection Ser.). 206p. (Orig.). 1980. pap. 19.95 (ISBN 0-89729-264-2). Ediciones.
SPARRING
see Boxing
SPATIAL ANALYSIS (STATISTICS)
Barlow, I. M. Spatial Dimensions of Urban Government. (Geographical Research Studies Press Ser.). 900p. 1981. 49.00 (ISBN 0-471-27978-1, Pub by Wiley Interscience). Wiley.
Hamilton, F. E. & Linge, G. J. Spatial Analysis, Industry & the Industrial Environment - Progess in Research & Applications: International Industrial Systems, Vol. 2. 1981. price not set (ISBN 0-471-27918-8, Pub. by Wiley-Interscience). Wiley.
Ripley, Brian D. Spatial Statistics. (Probability & Mathematical Statistics Ser.: Applied Probability & Statistics). 352p. 1981. 27.00 (ISBN 0-471-08367-4, Pub. by Wiley-Interscience). Wiley.
Spatial Analysis for Regional Development. 44p. 1981. pap. 6.75 (ISBN 92-808-0166-X, TUNU 101, UNU). Unipub.
Stohr, Walter & Taylor, D. R. Development from Above or Below? A Radical Reappraisal of Spatial Planning in Developing. 448p. 1981. 47.85 (ISBN 0-471-27823-8, Pub.by Wiley-Interscience). Wiley.
Wilson, A. G. & Kirby, M. J. Mathematics for Geographers & Planners. 2nd ed. (Contemporary Problems in Geography Ser.). (Illus.). 424p. 1980. text ed. 36.00x (ISBN 0-19-874114-6); pap. text ed. 19.95x (ISBN 0-19-874115-4). Oxford U Pr.
SPEAKING
see Debates and Debating; Lectures and Lecturing; Oratory; Preaching; Public Speaking; Rhetoric; Voice
SPEAKING WITH TONGUES
see Glossolalia
SPECIAL COLLECTIONS IN LIBRARIES
see Libraries–Special Collections
SPECIAL EDUCATION
see also Exceptional Children–Education
Battle, James. Canadian Self-Esteem Inventories for Children & Adults. 1981. pap. 45.50 for complete battery (ISBN 0-686-69429-5). Spec Child.
DeShong, Barbara. The Special Educator: Stress & Survival. 350p. 1981. text ed. price not set (ISBN 0-89443-358-X). Aspen Systems.
Kniker, Charles R. & Naylor, Natalie A. Teaching Today & Tomorrow. (Special Education Ser.). (Orig.). 1981. pap. text ed. 15.95 (ISBN 0-675-08034-7); instrs'. manual 3.95. Merrill.
Milligan, Jerry L. Reading Difficulties: Their Analysis & Treatment. 1981. pap. 7.50 (ISBN 0-87562-069-8). Spec Child.
National Information Center for Special Education Materials (NICSEM) NICSEM Master Index to Special Education Materials, 3 vols. LC 80-83854. 1980. Set. pap. 106.00 (ISBN 0-89320-049-2). Univ SC Natl Info.
--NICSEM Mini-index to Special Education Materials: Functional Communication Skills. LC 80-82540. 1980. pap. 16.00 (ISBN 0-89320-045-X). Univ SC Natl Info.
--NICSEM Mini-index to Special Education Materials: High Interests, Controlled Vocabulary Supplementary Reading Materials for Adolescents & Young Adults. LC 80-82901. 1980. pap. 16.00 (ISBN 0-89320-047-6). Univ. SC Natl Info.
--NICSEM Mini-index to Special Education Materials: Independent Living Skills for Moderately & Severely Handicapped Students. LC 80-82530. 1980. pap. 16.00 (ISBN 0-89320-044-1). Univ SC Natl Info.
--NICSEM Mini-index to Special Education Materials: Personal & Social Developments for Moderately & Severely Handicapped Students. LC 80-82541. 1980. pap. 16.00 (ISBN 0-89320-046-8). Univ SC Natl Info.

--NICSEM Source Directory. LC 80-83757. 1980. pap. 12.50 (ISBN 0-89320-050-6). Univ SC Natl Info.

SPECIAL LIBRARIES
see Libraries, Special

SPECIALIZED AGENCIES OF THE UNITED NATIONS
see International Agencies

SPECIALTY STORES
see Stores, Retail

SPECIE
see Gold; Money; Silver

SPECIE PAYMENTS
see Finance, Public; Silver Question

SPECIMENS, PRESERVATION OF
see Taxidermy; Zoological Specimens–Collection and Preservation

SPECTACLES
see Eye-Glasses

SPECTERS
see Apparitions; Ghosts

SPECTRA
see Spectrum Analysis

SPECTROCHEMICAL ANALYSIS
see Spectrum Analysis

SPECTROMETER

Boumans, P. W. Line Coincidence Tables for Inductively Coupled Plasma Atomic Emission Spectrometry, 2 vols. LC 80-41344. (Illus.). 941p. 1980. 250.00 set (ISBN 0-08-026243-0). Pergamon.

Vanasse, George A., ed. Spectrometric Techniques, Vol. II. 1981. write for info. (ISBN 0-12-710402-X). Acad Pr.

SPECTROPHOTOMETRY

Sunshine, Irving, ed. CRC Handbook of Spectrophotometric Data of Drugs. 432p. 1981. 62.95 (ISBN 0-8493-3571-X). CRC Pr.

SPECTROSCOPY
see Spectrum Analysis

SPECTROSCOPY, NUCLEAR
see Nuclear Spectroscopy

SPECTROSCOPY, RAMAN
see Raman Spectroscopy

SPECTRUM, ATOMIC
see Atomic Spectra

SPECTRUM ANALYSIS
see also Atomic Spectra; Electron Paramagnetic Resonance; Laser Spectroscopy; Light; Nuclear Spectroscopy; Raman Spectroscopy; X-Ray Spectroscopy
also subdivision Spectra under subjects, e.g. Iron–Spectra; Neon–Spectra; Stars–Spectra

Boumans, P. W. Atomic Absorption Spectroscopy-Past, Present & Future: To Commemorate the 25th Anniversary of Alan Walsh's Landmark Paper in Spectrochimica Acta. 248p. 1981. pap. 32.50 (ISBN 0-08-026267-8). Pergamon.

Chakrabarti, C. L. Progress in Analytical Atomic Spectroscopy, 2 vols. (Illus.). 282p. 1980. 76.00 (ISBN 0-08-027126-X). Pergamon.

Chamberlain, J. The Principals of Interferometric Spectroscopy. LC 78-13206. 360p. 1979. 58.00 (ISBN 0-471-99719-6). Wiley.

Electrical Events Associated with Primary Photosynthetic Reactions in Chloroplast Membranes. (Agricultural Research Reports Ser.: No. 905). 86p. 1981. pap. 16.75 (ISBN 90-220-0756-1, PDC 218, Pudoc). Unipub.

Grell, E., ed. Membrane Spectroscopy. (Molecular Biology, Biochemistry, & Biophysics Ser.: Vol. 31). (Illus.). 512p. 1981. 87.40 (ISBN 0-387-10332-5). Springer-Verlag.

Martin, G. J., et al. N-NMR Spectroscopy. (NMR-Basic Principles & Progress Ser.: Vol. 18). (Illus.). 390p. 1981. 87.30 (ISBN 0-387-10459-3). Springer-Verlag.

Mooney, E. F., ed. Annual Reports on NMR Spectroscopy. Incl. Vol. 1. 1968. 49.00 (ISBN 0-12-505350-9); Vol. 5B. 1974. 62.00 (ISBN 0-12-505345-2); Vol. 6, 2 pts. 1976-78. Pt. B. 34.00 (ISBN 0-12-505346-0); Pt. C. 90.00 (ISBN 0-12-505347-9); Vol. 7. 1978. 43.50 (ISBN 0-12-505307-X); Vol. 8. 1978. 71.00 (ISBN 0-12-505308-8); Vol. 9. 1978. 57.50 (ISBN 0-12-505309-6). Acad Pr.

Silverstein, Robert M. & Bassler, G. Clayton. Spectrometric Indentification of Organic Compounds. 4th ed. Morrill, Terence C., ed. 704p. 1981. text ed. 20.95 (ISBN 0-471-02990-4). Wiley.

Verma, R. N. Spectroscopic References to Polyatomic Molecules. 125p. 1980. 75.00 (ISBN 0-306-65190-4). IFI Plenum.

Willis, R. F., ed. Vibrational Spectroscopy of Adsorbates. (Springer Series in Chemical Physics: Vol. 15). (Illus.). 200p. 1981. 29.50 (ISBN 0-387-10429-1). Springer-Verlag.

SPEECH
Here are entered works on the oral production of meaningful sounds in language. Works on speaking as a means of communication are entered under Oral communication or more specific headings, e.g. Public speaking.
see also Children–Language; Language and Languages; Oral Communication; Phonetics; Speech Therapy; Voice

Ballmer, T. & Brennenstuhl, W. Speech Art Classification. (Springer Series in Language & Communication: Vol. 8). (Illus.). 304p. 1981. 29.50 (ISBN 0-387-10294-9). Springer-Verlag.

Barad, Dianne S. K-Speech News. (gr. 7-12). 1981. manual 15.00. Communication Skill.

Beveridge-Wavering, Agnes & Seibert-Shook, Mavis. Reinforcing Home Activities: Program for Articulation Improvement. 1981. pap. 7.50 (ISBN 0-8134-2158-6, 2158). Interstate.

Byrns, James H. Speak for Yourself. 329p. 1981. pap. text ed. 10.95 (ISBN 0-394-32410-2). Random.

Curtis, Dan B. & Brewer, Robert S. Speaking As a Farmer: Winning FFA Speeches, Principles of Speech Preparation & Presentation. 256p. 1980. pap. text ed. 8.95 (ISBN 0-8403-2248-8). Kendall-Hunt.

Darby, John J. & Hecker, Michael, eds. Speech Evaluation in Psychiatry. 1980. 34.00 (ISBN 0-8089-1315-8). Grune.

Dobkins, David H. & Kneller, Richard. Workbook for Speech Fundamentals. 128p. 1980. pap. text ed. 5.25 (ISBN 0-8403-2257-7). Kendall-Hunt.

Garner, Alan. Conversationally Speaking: Tested New Ways to Increase Your Personal & Social Effectiveness. 164p. (Orig.). 1980. pap. 4.95 (ISBN 0-938044-00-1). Psych Res Assoc.

Hudson & Weaver. Reading, Writing & Speaking: Here & Now. (Illus.). 1980. pap. 2.95x (ISBN 0-88323-160-3, 248). Richards Pub.

Klopf, Donald W. & Cambra, Ronald E. Personal & Public Speaking. 208p. 1981. pap. text ed. 8.95 (ISBN 0-89582-042-0). Morton Pub.

Lillis, B. Lauren. Instant Speaking Course. 1981. pap. 1.50 (ISBN 0-8134-2176-4). Interstate.

Miller, George A. Language & Speech. LC 80-27018. (Illus.). 1981. text ed. price not set (ISBN 0-7167-1297-0); pap. text ed. price not set (ISBN 0-7167-1298-9). W H Freeman.

Newman, Edwin. Edwin Newman on Language: Strictly Speaking & a Civil Tongue. 1980. pap. 6.95 (ISBN 0-446-97459-5). Warner Bks.

Ptacek, Paul H., et al. Index to Speech, Language & Hearing Journal Titles, 1954-78. LC 79-20058. 328p. 1979. text ed. 25.00 (ISBN 0-933014-54-6). College-Hill.

Rudman, Jack. Speech Pathology & Audiology. (Undergraduate Program Field Test Ser.: UPFT-25). (Cloth bdg. avail. on request). pap. 9.95 (ISBN 0-8373-6025-0). Natl Learning.

Spatz, Jacob. The Speaker's Bible. 200p. 1981. 12.95 (ISBN 0-8159-6841-8). Devin.

Subtelny, Joanne D., ed. Speech Assessment & Speech Improvement for the Hearing Impaired. 420p. 1980. pap. text ed. 19.95 (ISBN 0-88200-138-8, A0138). Alexander Graham.

Zemlin, W. R. Speech & Hearing Science. 2nd ed. (Illus.). 704p. 1981. text ed. 23.95 (ISBN 0-13-827378-2). P-H.

SPEECH–PHYSIOLOGICAL ASPECTS

Penfield, Wilder & Roberts, Lamar. Speech & Brain Mechanisms. LC 59-5602. (Illus.). 304p. 1981. 25.00x; pap. 6.95. Princeton U Pr.

SPEECH–PSYCHOLOGY
see Psycholinguistics

SPEECH–STUDY AND TEACHING

Worthley, William J. Sourcebook of Articulation Activities. 1981. pap. text ed. price not set. Little.

SPEECH, DISORDERS OF
see also Aphasia; Communicative Disorders; Speech Disorders in Children; Stuttering

Aronson, Arnold E. Clincal Voice Disorders. 1980. 19.50. Thieme Stratton.

Dedo, Herbert H. & Shipp, Thomas. Spastic Dysphonia: A Surgical & Voice Therapy Treatment Program. LC 80-65193. (Illus.). 96p. 1980. pap. text ed. 12.95 (ISBN 0-933014-58-9). College-Hill.

Stryker, S. Speech After Stroke. 2nd ed. (Illus.). 442p. 1980. pap. 22.75 (ISBN 0-398-04122-9). C C Thomas.

Walsh, Harry H., ed. Phonology & Speech Remediation: A Book of Readings. LC 78-32109. (Illus.). 268p. text ed. 18.95 (ISBN 0-933014-52-X). College-Hill.

SPEECH, LIBERTY OF
see Liberty of Speech

SPEECH COMMUNICATION
see Oral Communication

SPEECH CORRECTION
see Speech Therapy

SPEECH DEFECTS
see Speech, Disorders Of

SPEECH DISORDERS IN CHILDREN

Hubbell, Robert D. Children's Language Disorders: An Integrated Approach. (Illus.). 432p. 1981. text ed. 18.95 (ISBN 0-13-132001-7). P-H.

Pennington, R. Corbin & James, Elizabeth. For Parents of a Child Whose Speech Is Delayed. 2nd ed. 1980. pap. 0.50 (ISBN 0-8134-2137-3, 2137). Interstate.

SPEECH-READING
see Deaf–Means of Communication

SPEECH THERAPY

Brown, Betty B. Speech Therapy: Principles & Practice. (Illus.). 288p. 1981. pap. 15.00 (ISBN 0-443-02099-X). Churchill.

Conversation Starters for Speech & Language Therapy. 1981. pap. 2.75 (ISBN 0-8134-2186-1, 2186). Interstate.

Milton, Octavia. Assist Three: For Consonant Blends of L, R, & S. 50p. 1981. pap. text ed. 13.00 (ISBN 0-88450-729-7). Communication Skill.

Sarno, Martha T. & Hook, Olle, eds. Aphasia: Assessment & Treatment. LC 80-80488. (Illus.). 288p. 1980. 34.50 (ISBN 0-89352-086-1). Masson Pub.

SPEECHES, ADDRESSES, ETC.
see also Lectures and Lecturing; Public Speaking
also subdivision Addresses, Essays, Lectures under particular subjects, e.g. Geology–Addresses, Essays, Lectures; subdivision Addresses, Sermons, etc.; under wars, e.g. United States–History–Civil War, 1861-1865–Addresses, Sermons, etc.

Proceedings of the American Academy & Institute of Arts & Letters. (Second Ser.: No. 31). 100p. 1981. 10.00 (ISBN 0-915974-25-8). Am Acad Inst Arts.

SPEECHLESSNESS
see Mutism

SPEED READING
see Rapid Reading

SPELEOLOGY
see also Caves

Mitchell, Robert W. & Reddell, James R., eds. Studies on the Cavernicole Fauna of Mexico & Adjacent Regions. (Association for Mexican Cave Studies: Bulletin 5). 201p. 1973. 13.00. Speleo Pr.

Reddell, James R. A Preliminary Bibliography of Mexican Cave Biology with a Checklist of Published Records. (Association for Mexican Cave Studies: Bulletin 3). 184p. 1971. 10.00. Speleo Pr.

Reddell, James R., ed. Studies on the Caves & Cave Fauna of the Yucatan Peninsula. (Association for Mexican Cave Studies: Bulletin 6). 296p. 1977. 13.00. Speleo Pr.

Reddell, James R. & Mitchell, Robert W., eds. Studies on the Cavernicole Fauna of Mexico. (Association for Mexican Cave Studies: Bulletin 4). 239p. 1971. 13.00. Speleo Pr.

SPELLING
see English Language–Orthography and Spelling

SPELLS
see Magic

SPENSER, EDMUND, 1552?-1599

Ironic Historian: The Narrator of Books 3 & 4 of the Faerie Queene. (Elizabethan Studies: No. 98). 1980. pap. text ed. 25.00x (ISBN 0-391-02186-9). Humanities.

Kullen, Patrick & Roche, Thomas P., Jr., eds. Spenser Studies: A Renaissance Poetry Annual, Vol. II. (Illus.). 320p. 1981. 20.95x (ISBN 0-8229-3433-7). U of Pittsburgh Pr.

Mallette, Richard. Spenser, Milton, & Renaissance Pastoral. LC 78-73154. 224p. 1980. 18.50 (ISBN 0-8387-2412-4). Bucknell U Pr.

Rix, Herbert D. Rhetoric in Spenser's Poetry. 88p. 1980. Repr. of 1940 ed. lib. bdg. 15.00 (ISBN 0-89987-712-5). Darby Bks.

Roche, Thomas P., Jr. & O'Donnell, C. P., eds. Edmund Spenser: The Faerie Queene. 1247p. 1981. text ed. 40.00x (ISBN 0-300-02705-2); pap. 12.95x (ISBN 0-300-02706-0). Yale U Pr.

SPHRAGISTICS
see Seals (Numismatics)

SPICES
see also Cookery (Herbs and Spices)
also names of spices

Muenscher, Walter C. & Rice, Myron A. Garden Spice & Wild Pot-Herbs: An American Herbal. LC 78-56899. (Illus.). 218p. 1978. pap. 7.95 (ISBN 0-8014-9174-6). Comstock.

SPIDERS

Reed, John R. A Gallery of Spiders: Poems. LC 80-81894. (Ontario Review Press Poetry Ser.). 80p. 1980. 9.95 (ISBN 0-86538-005-8); pap. 4.95 (ISBN 0-86538-006-6). Ontario Rev NJ.

SPIDERS–JUVENILE LITERATURE

Dallinger, Jane. Spiders. (Lerner Natural Science Bks.). (Illus.). (gr. 4-10). 1981. PLB 7.95 (ISBN 0-8225-1456-7). Lerner Pubns.

Ryder, Joanne. The Spiders Dance. LC 78-22495. (Illus.). 48p. (gr. 1-4). 1981. 8.95 (ISBN 0-06-025133-6, HarpJ); PLB 8.79 (ISBN 0-06-025134-4). Har-Row.

SPIDERS–AUSTRALIA

Child, John. Australian Spider. pap. 6.50x (ISBN 0-392-07647-0, SpS). Soccer.

SPIES
see also Espionage; Secret Service

Powers, Thomas. The Man Who Kept the Secrets: Richard Helms & the CIA. 1981. pap. 3.50 (ISBN 0-671-83654-4). PB.

Reilly, Sidney. Britain's Master Spy: The Adventures of Sidney Reilly. 296p. 1980. Repr. of 1933 ed. lib. bdg. 35.00 (ISBN 0-89984-449-9). Century Bookbindery.

Rhoer, Edward Van Der. Many a Secret Place: The Story Ofthe Master Spy Sidney George Reilly. 288p. 1981. 12.50 (ISBN 0-684-16870-7, ScribT). Scribner.

SPIN (DYNAMICS)
see Rotational Motion

SPIN FISHING

Gooch, Bob. Spinning for Trout. (Illus.). 192p. 1981. 12.50 (ISBN 0-684-16843-X, ScribT). Scribner.

SPIN-LATTICE RELAXATION

Wolf, Dieter. Spin Temperature & Nuclear Spin Relaxation in Matter: Basic Principles & Applications. (International Series of Monographs on Physics). (Illus.). 480p. 1979. text ed. 34.95x (ISBN 0-19-851295-3). Oxford U Pr.

SPINAL ANESTHESIA

Greene, Nicholas M. Physiology of Spinal Anesthesia. 3rd ed. 265p. 1981. write for info. (3554-1). Williams & Wilkins.

SPINAL COLUMN
see Spine

SPINAL CORD
see also Nervous System

Schafer, R. C., ed. Chiropractic Physical & Spinal Diagnosis. (Illus.). 578p. 1980. text ed. 30.00 (ISBN 0-936948-00-0). Am Chiro Acad.

SPINAL CORD–RADIOGRAPHY

Calenoff, Leonid. Radiology of Spinal Cord Injury. (Illus.). 500p. 1981. text ed. 42.50 (ISBN 0-8016-1114-8). Mosby.

SPINAL CORD–WOUNDS AND INJURIES

Norris, William C., et al. The Spinal Injury Learning Series. LC 80-26576. (Illus.). 1981. price not set (ISBN 0-87805-131-7). U Pr of Miss.

SPINE

DeGiacomo, F. P. Chiropractic Analysis Through Palpation. McDonnell, James, ed. (Illus.). 192p. 1980. 12.00 (ISBN 0-938470-00-0). NY Chiro Coll.

SPINE–ABNORMITIES AND DEFORMITIES
see also Scoliosis

Bedbrook, G., ed. The Care & Management of Spinal Cord Injuries. (Illus.). 351p. 1981. 39.80 (ISBN 0-387-90494-8). Springer-Verlag.

The Low-Back Patient & Therapeutic Exercise Handouts 1979. Date not set. Set Of 25. 25.00. Masson Pub.

Myrianthopoulos, Ntinos C. & Bergsma, Daniel, eds. Recent Advances in the Developmental Biology of Central Nervous System Malformations. LC 79-4947. (Alan R. Liss Ser.: Vol. 15, No. 3). 1979. 16.00 (ISBN 0-8451-1026-8). March of Dimes.

SPINE–CURVATURE
see Spine–Abnormities and Deformities

SPINE–SURGERY

Jenkins, D. A., et al. A Manual of Spinal Surgery. 1981. text ed. price not set. Butterworth.

SPINE–WOUNDS AND INJURIES

Ami Sha'Ked. Human Sexuality & Rehabilitation Medicine: Sexual Functioning Following Spinal Cord Injury. (Illus.). 228p. 1981. write for info. (7749-X). Williams & Wilkins.

SPINNING

Bolz, Roger W. Multiple Thread Mills. 1950. 18.50 (ISBN 0-930220-02-1). Conquest.

Duncan, Molly. Spin Your Own Wool & Dye It & Weave It. rev. ed. (Illus.). 52p. 1978. 7.50 (ISBN 0-589-00334-8, Pub by Reed Books Australia). C E Tuttle.

Kilbride, Thomas. Spinning & Weaving at Home. (Illus.). 128p. 1981. pap. 5.95 (ISBN 0-8069-9272-7). Sterling.

Mitchell, Lillias. Irish Spinning Dyeing & Weaving. (Illus.). 1978. 12.95 (ISBN 0-85221-101-5). Dufour.

SPINNING (FISHING)
see Spin Fishing

SPINOR ANALYSIS
see also Calculus of Tensors; Vector Analysis

Cartan, Elie. The Theory of Spinors. 160p. 1981. pap. price not set (ISBN 0-486-64070-1). Dover.

SPINSTERS
see Single Women

SPIRIT
Here are entered works limited to the conception of spirit as differentiated from soul.
see also Consciousness; Holy Spirit; Mind and Body; Soul

The Holy Spirit. (Aglow Bible Study: Bk. E-3). 64p. 1980. pap. 1.95 (ISBN 0-930756-57-6, 4220-E). Women's Aglow.

Lull, David J. The Spirit in Galatia: Paul's Interpretation of Pneuma As Divine Power. LC 79-26094. (Society of Biblical Literature Dissertation: No. 49). 13.50x (ISBN 0-89130-367-7, 06-01-49); pap. 9.00x (ISBN 0-89130-368-5). Scholars Pr CA.

Ross-Bryant, Lynn. Imagination & the Life of the Spirit: An Introduction to the Study of Religion & Literature. LC 79-28464. (Scholars Press General Ser.: Vol. 2). 13.50x (ISBN 0-89130-377-4, 00 03 02); pap. 9.00x (ISBN 0-89130-378-2). Scholar Pr CA.

SPIRIT, HOLY
see Holy Spirit

SPIRIT WRITINGS

Roberts, Jane & Butts, Robert F. The Individual & the Nature of Mass Events: A Seth Book. LC 80-22600. 336p. 1981. 11.95 (ISBN 0-13-457259-9). P-H.

SPIRITS
see also Angels; Apparitions; Demonology; Ghosts; Witchcraft

Teasley, D. O. The Holy Spirit & Other Spirits. 192p. pap. 1.75. Faith Pub Hse.

SPIRITUAL DIRECTION

Alexander, Archibald. Thoughts on Religious Experience. 1978. 8.95 (ISBN 0-85151-080-9). Banner of Truth.

Baker, Pat. Giving God What You Are. 1981. pap. 3.95 (ISBN 0-8054-5333-4). Broadman.

Bridge, William. A Lifting up for the Downcast. 1979. pap. 3.95 (ISBN 0-85151-298-4). Banner of Truth.

Carroll, L. Patrick & Dyckman, Katharine M. Inviting the Mystic, Supporting the Prophet: The Dynamics of Spiritual Direction. 128p. (Orig.). 1981. pap. 4.95 (ISBN 0-8091-2378-9). Paulist Pr.

Chinmoy, Sri. The Jewel of Humility. (Illus.). 56p. (Orig.). 1980. pap. 2.00 (ISBN 0-88497-493-6). Aum Pubns.

--Perfection in the Head World. 55p. (Orig.). 1980. pap. 2.00 (ISBN 0-88497-492-8). Aum Pubns.

Coe, Frances & Coe, Ivan. Insearch. 112p. 1981. 6.50 (ISBN 0-682-49713-4). Exposition.

Devers, Dorothy. Faithful Friendship. 1980. 2.00 (ISBN 0-686-28777-0). Forward Movement.

Earl, Gloria. The Book. 1981. 6.75 (ISBN 0-8062-1572-0). Carlton.

Hall, Ruth. Three Steps to Heaven. 1981. 4.95 (ISBN 0-8062-1560-7). Carlton.

MacArthur, John, Jr. The Legacy of Jesus. 1981. text ed. 7.95 (ISBN 0-8024-8524-3). Moody.

Nee, Watchman. The Messenger of the Cross. Kaung, Stephen, tr. (Orig.). 1980. pap. text ed. write for info. (ISBN 0-935008-50-0); pap. 2.95 (ISBN 0-935008-50-0). Christian Fellow Pubs.

Payne, Leanne. The Healing Presence. 176p. 1981. pap. 4.95 (ISBN 0-89107-215-2). Good News.

Religious Education Staff. Man & Woman Spirit Masters. (To Live Is Christ Ser.). 1980. 10.95 (ISBN 0-697-01752-4). Wm C Brown.

--Mystery, Value, & Awareness: Spirit Masters for Religions of the World. (To Live Is Christ Ser.). 1979. 10.95 (ISBN 0-697-01730-3). Wm C Brown.

--Pluralism, Similarities, & Contrast: Spirit Masters for Religion in North America. (To Live Is Christ Ser.). 1979. 10.95 (ISBN 0-697-01735-4). Wm C Brown.

--The Spirit Alive in Service: Spirit Masters. (To Live Is Christ Ser.). 1979. 9.95 (ISBN 0-697-01712-5). Wm C Brown.

--The Spirit Alive in Vocations: Spirit Masters. (To Live Is Christ Ser.). 1980. 9.95 (ISBN 0-697-01755-9). Wm C Brown.

Sullivan, John, ed. Spiritual Direction. LC 80-26654. (Carmelite Studies: No. I). 240p. (Orig.). 1980. pap. 6.95x (ISBN 0-9600876-8-0). ICS Pubns.

Templin, Kevin. Finality Testament: Book of Life. 1981. 5.75 (ISBN 0-8062-1679-4). Carlton.

Thompson, Murray S. Grace & Forgiveness in Ministry. LC 80-23613. 176p. (Orig.). 1981. pap. 6.95 (ISBN 0-687-15680-7). Abingdon.

Twyman, Mary E. Letters to the Pope. 158p. 1981. 6.95 (ISBN 0-934400-15-6). Landmark Bks.

SPIRITUAL GIFTS

see Gifts, Spiritual

SPIRITUAL HEALING

see Faith-Cure

SPIRITUAL LIFE

see also Christian Life; Faith; Monastic and Religious Life; Retreats; Sanctification; Spiritual Direction

Bharti, Ma Satya. Death Comes Dancing: Celebrating Life with Bhagwan Shree Rajneesh. 200p. 1981. pap. 9.95 (ISBN 0-7100-0705-1). Routledge & Kegan.

Bittleston, Adam. Our Spiritual Companions. 1980. pap. 13.50 (ISBN 0-903540-39-8, Pub. by Floris Books). St George Bk Serv.

Chinmoy, Sri. Secrets of the Inner World. (Illus.). 54p. (Orig.). 1980. pap. 2.00 (ISBN 0-88497-499-5). Aum Pubns.

De Lubicz, Isha S. The Opening of the Way. Gleaolow, Rupert, tr. 1981. pap. 8.95 (ISBN 0-89281-015-7). Inner Tradit.

Drijvers, H. J. W. Cults & Beliefs at Edessa. (Illus.). 204p. 1980. text ed. 54.75 (ISBN 90-04-06050-2). Humanities.

Ellwood, Robert S., Jr. Alternative Altars: Unconventional & Eastern Spirituality in America. LC 78-15089. xvi, 192p. 1981. pap. 5.50 (ISBN 0-226-20620-3). U of Chicago Pr.

Evans, Margiad. Ray of Darkness. 1980. 11.50 (ISBN 0-7145-3727-6); pap. 4.95 (ISBN 0-7145-3607-5). Riverrun NY.

Gawryn, Marvin. Reaching High: The Psychology of Spiritual Living. LC 80-24306. 200p. 1981. 11.95 (ISBN 0-938380-00-1); pap. 7.95 (ISBN 0-938380-01-X). Spiritual Renaissance.

Hill, Harold & Harrell, Irene B. How to Live the Bible Like a King's Kid. 1980. pap. 3.95 (ISBN 0-8007-5051-9). Revell.

Jack, LaWant P. All Things in Their Time. pap. 5.95 (ISBN 0-89036-145-2). Hawkes Pub Inc.

Jackson, William J. Sai Krishna Lila. LC 80-67137. 1980. pap. 3.60 (ISBN 0-9600958-7-X). Birth Day.

Johnston, William. The Mirror Mind: Spirituality & Transformation. LC 80-8350. 192p. 1981. 10.95 (ISBN 0-06-064197-5, HarpR). Har-Row.

Kelsey, Morton T. Transcend: A Guide to the Spiritual Quest. 240p. (Orig.). 1981. pap. 5.95 (ISBN 0-8245-0015-6). Crossroad NY.

Mohr, Victor. A Spiritual View of Life. Ozols, Violet, tr. from Ger. (Victor Mohr Ser.). 364p. Date not set. pap. 15.00 (ISBN 0-934616-15-9). Valkyrie Pr.

Nouwen, Henri J. Making All Things New: An Invitation to Life in the Spirit. LC 80-8897. 96p. 1981. 6.95 (ISBN 0-06-066326-X). Har-Row.

Pike, Diane K. A Roadmap for Seekers of the Journey into Self. (Illus., Orig.). 1981. pap. price not set (ISBN 0-916192-17-2). L P Pubns.

Sri Aurobindo. The Life Divine. 1112p. 1980. 18.75 (ISBN 0-89071-290-5, Pub. by Sri Aurobindo Ashram India); pap. 14.00 (ISBN 0-89071-289-1). Matagiri.

Stebbing, Rita. The Philosophy of Spiritual Activity As a Path to Self-Knowledge. 1980. pap. 2.95 (ISBN 0-916786-50-1). St George Bk Serv.

Stuart, Vincent G. Changing Mind. LC 80-53447. 80p. 1981. 5.95 (ISBN 0-394-51791-1). Shambhala Pubns.

Thurston, Mark A. Experiments in Practical Spirituality: Keyed to a Search for God, Book II. (Illus.). 147p. (Orig.). 1980. pap. 4.95 (ISBN 0-87604-122-5). ARE Pr.

SPIRITUAL LIFE–VEDANTA AUTHORS

see Vedanta

SPIRITUAL-MINDEDNESS

see Spirituality

SPIRITUALITY

see also Soul; Spiritual Life

Carlson, G. R., tr. La Dynamique Spirituelle. (French Bks.). (Fr.). 1979. 1.80 (ISBN 0-8297-0777-8). Life Pubs Intl.

Downer, Craig C. Spiritual Evolution. Date not set. 10.00 (ISBN 0-533-04704-8). Vantage.

Easwaran, Eknath. Dialogue with Death: The Spiritual Psychology of the Katha Upanishad. 288p. (Orig.). 1981. pap. 6.00 (ISBN 0-915132-24-9). Nilgiri Pr.

Maestri, William. The God for Every Day. 204p. 1981. 8.95 (ISBN 0-88347-123-X). Thomas More.

Niendorff, John S. Listen to the Light. 96p. 1980. pap. 2.50 (ISBN 0-911336-84-2). Sci of Mind.

Packo, John E. Find and Use Your Spiritual Gifts. 117p. (Orig.). 1980. pap. 2.95 (ISBN 0-87509-293-4); avail. leaders guide 1.25 (ISBN 0-87509-294-2). Chr Pubns.

Pilch, John J. Wellness: Your Invitation to Full Life. Frost, Miriam, ed. Orig. Title: Wellness. 128p. (Orig.). 1981. pap. text ed. 5.95 (ISBN 0-03-059062-0). Winston Pr.

Rice, Joyce G. Love Never Ends. pap. 3.95 (ISBN 0-89036-147-9). Hawkes Pub Inc.

Sujata. Beginning to See. rev., enl. ed. 1980. pap. 4.50 (ISBN 0-913300-06-3). Unity Pr.

Tarneja, Sukh R. Nature, Spirituality & Science. 240p. 1980. text ed. 27.50x (ISBN 0-7069-1203-9, Pub by Vikas India). Advent Bk.

Walsh, James, ed. The Cloud of Unknowing. (Classics of Western Spirituality Ser.). 1981. 11.95 (ISBN 0-8091-0314-1); pap. 7.95 (ISBN 0-8091-2332-0). Paulist Pr.

SPIRITUALS (SONGS)

see also Blues (Songs, Etc.)

Bryan, Ashley. Walk Together Children. (gr. 2 up). pap. 2.95 (ISBN 0-689-70485-2, A-112, Aladdin). Atheneum.

SPITSBERGEN

Fortey, R. A. The Ordovician Trilobites of the Spitsbergen. (Norsk Polarinstitutt Skrifter: Vol. 171). (Illus.). 163p. 1980. pap. text ed. 18.00x (ISBN 82-00-29189-8). Universitet.

SPITZ, MARK

Spitz, Mark & Herskowitz, Mickey. Seven Golds: Mark Spitz' Own Story. LC 80-1694. (Illus.). 256p. 1981. 10.95 (ISBN 0-385-12135-0). Doubleday.

SPOILS SYSTEM

see Corruption (In Politics)

SPOKEN ENGLISH

see English Language–Conversation and Phrase Books; English Language–Spoken English

SPORTING DOGS

see Hunting Dogs

SPORTING GOODS

see also Athletics–Apparatus and Equipment

Shoup, T. E., ed. International Conference on Medical & Sports Devices. 270p. 1980. 30.00 (H00160). ASME.

SPORTS

see also Amusements; Athletes; Athletics; College Sports; Games; Gymnastics; Olympic Games; Outdoor Life; Photography of Sports; Physical Education and Training; Rodeos; Track-Athletics

also names of sports, e.g. Golf

Jackson, John J. Sport Administration. write for info. (ISBN 0-398-04440-6). C C Thomas.

Kelly, Robert. Sports Trivia Puzzler, No. 4. (Orig.). 1981. pap. 1.95 (ISBN 0-440-07807-5). Dell.

Welch, Paula D. & Lerch, Harold A. Handbook of American Physical Education & Sport. write for info. C C Thomas.

SPORTS–ACCIDENTS AND INJURIES

see also Sports Medicine

Reilly, Thomas, ed. Sports Fitness & Sports Injuries. (Illus.). 304p. 1981. 45.00 (ISBN 0-571-11628-0, Pub. by Faber & Faber); pap. 28.00 (ISBN 0-571-11629-9). Merrimack Bk Serv.

Schiavi, Michael R. The Athletic Trainers Guide: Prevention, Care - Treatment of Sports Injuries to Young Athletes. (Illus.). 1981. 11.95 (ISBN 0-87460-317-X). Lion.

SPORTS–BIOGRAPHY

Burchard, S. H. Sports Star: Tommy John. LC 80-8794. (Sports Star Ser.). (Illus.). 64p. (gr. 4-6). pap. 3.95 (ISBN 0-15-278039-4, VoyB). HarBraceJ.

Gutman, Bill. Pro Sports Champions. (Illus.). 192p. 1981. PLB price not set (ISBN 0-671-34028-X). Messner.

Hahn, James & Hahn, Lynn. Patty! Patricia Berg. Schroeder, Howard, ed. (Sports Legends Ser.). (Illus.). 48p. (Orig.). (gr. 3-5). PLB 5.95 (ISBN 0-89686-127-9); pap. text ed. 2.95 (ISBN 0-89686-142-2). Crestwood Hse.

Mule, Marty & Remy, Bob. Louisiana Athletes: The Top Twenty. (Illus.). (gr. 6 up). 1981. 8.95 (ISBN 0-88289-282-7). Pelican.

SPORTS–JUVENILE LITERATURE

Brondfield. Great Sports Photos. (gr. 3-5). 1980. pap. 1.50 (ISBN 0-590-30369-4, Schol Pap). Schol Bk Serv.

Willcox, Isobel. Acrobats & Ping-Pong: Young China's Games, Sports, & Amusements. LC 80-22176. (Illus.). 160p. (gr. 4 up). 1981. PLB 8.95 (ISBN 0-396-07917-2). Dodd.

SPORTS–LAW AND LEGISLATION

Blackman, Martin E. & Hochberg, Phillip R. Representing Professional Athletes & Teams 1980. LC 80-81911. (Real Estate Law & Practice Course Handbook Ser.). 699p. 1980. pap. text ed. 25.00 (ISBN 0-686-68830-9, G4-3678). PLI.

SPORTS–MEDICAL ASPECTS

see Sports Medicine

SPORTS–MISCELLANEA

Maestri, Vic. Little Eva, Baby Doll, & Blondy Ryan. (Orig.). pap. 4.50 (ISBN 0-682-49710-X). Exposition.

Sports Trivia Puzzler, No. 3. 1981. pap. 1.95 (ISBN 0-440-08132-7). Dell.

SPORTS–PHILOSOPHY

Rigauer, Bero. Sport & Work. Guttmann, Allen, ed. 110p. (Eng.). 1981. 12.50x (ISBN 0-231-05200-6). Columbia U Pr.

SPORTS–PHOTOGRAPHY

see Photography of Sports

SPORTS–PSYCHOLOGICAL ASPECTS

Holum, Dianne. World of Speed Skating. (Illus.). 320p. 1981. 17.50 (ISBN 0-89490-051-X). Enslow Pubs.

Landers, Daniel & Roberts, Glyn, eds. Psychology of Motor Behavior & Sport 1980. 1981. text ed. 12.00x (ISBN 0-931250-19-6). Human Kinetics.

Ryan, Frank. Sports & Psychology. 224p. 1981. 9.95 (ISBN 0-13-837856-8). P-H.

SPORTS–RECORDS

Clark, Patrick. Sports Firsts. 320p. 1981. 14.95 (ISBN 0-87196-302-7). Facts on File.

Reichler, Joseph L. The Great All-Time Baseball Record Book: A Unique Sourcebook of Facts, Feats & Figures. (Illus.). 608p. 1981. 19.95 (ISBN 0-02-603100-0). Macmillan.

SPORTS–SOCIAL ASPECTS

Hart, Marie & Birrell, Susan. Sport in the Socio-Cultural Process. 3rd ed. 544p. 1981. pap. text ed. write for info. (ISBN 0-697-07099-9). Wm C Brown.

Holt, Richard. Sport & Society in Modern France. 1980. 25.00 (ISBN 0-208-01887-5, Archon). Shoe String.

Markham, Jesse W. & Teplitz, Paul V. Baseball Economics & Public Policy. LC 79-6032. 1981. write for info. (ISBN 0-669-03607-2). Lexington Bks.

SPORTS–EUROPE

Holt, Richard. Sport & Society in Modern France. 1980. 25.00 (ISBN 0-208-01887-5, Archon). Shoe String.

SPORTS, INJURIES FROM

see Sports–Accidents and Injuries

SPORTS, INTRAMURAL

see Intramural Sports

SPORTS FOR WOMEN

see also Track-Athletics for Women

Lawless, Joann. The Complete Book of Women's Sports. LC 78-22816. (Illus.). 512p. 1981. 17.95 (ISBN 0-385-14175-0, Anchor Pr); pap. 10.95 (ISBN 0-385-17199-4). Doubleday.

Stanek, Carolyn. The Complete Guide to Women's College Athletics. (Illus.). 1981. 14.95 (ISBN 0-8092-5986-9); pap. 7.95 (ISBN 0-8092-5985-0). Contemp Bks.

SPORTS MEDICINE

see also Sports–Accidents and Injuries

Darden, Ellington. The Athlete's Guide to Sports Medicine. (Illus.). 1981. 14.95 (ISBN 0-8092-7160-5); pap. 6.95 (ISBN 0-8092-7159-1). Contemp Bks.

Dominguez, Richard H. Complete Book of Sports Medicine. 1980. pap. 4.95 (ISBN 0-446-97213-4). Warner Bks.

Reilly, Thomas, ed. Sports Fitness & Sports Injuries. (Illus.). 304p. 1981. 45.00 (ISBN 0-571-11628-0, Pub. by Faber & Faber); pap. 28.00 (ISBN 0-571-11629-9). Merrimack Bk Serv.

SPORTS MOTIVATION

see Sports–Psychological Aspects

SPORTS RECORDS

see Sports–Records

SPRAYING AND DUSTING RESIDUES IN AGRICULTURE

Gunther, F. A., ed. Residue Reviews, Vol. 75. (Illus.). 189p. 1981. 29.80 (ISBN 0-387-90534-0). Springer-Verlag.

--Residue Reviews, Vol. 76. (Illus.). 218p. 1981. 29.80 (ISBN 0-387-90535-9). Springer-Verlag.

--Residue Reviews, Vol. 79. (Illus.). 280p. 1981. 39.80 (ISBN 0-387-90539-1). Springer-Verlag.

Huber, J. T. Upgrading Residues & by-Products for Animals. 160p. 1981. 44.95 (ISBN 0-8493-5445-5). CRC Pr.

Residue Reviews, Vol. 74. (Illus.). 150p. 1980. 26.80 (ISBN 0-387-90503-0). Springer-Verlag.

U.S. Dept. of Energy. Anaerobic Fermentation of Agricultural Residue: Potential for Improvement & Implementation. 455p. 1981. pap. 39.50 (ISBN 0-89934-099-7). Solar Energy Info.

SPRING–JUVENILE LITERATURE

Allington, Richard L. & Krull, Kathleen. Spring. LC 80-25093. (Beginning to Learn About Ser.). (Illus.). 32p. (ps-2). 1981. PLB 9.65 (ISBN 0-8172-1342-2). Raintree Child.

SPRINGFIELD RIFLE

Frasca, Albert J. & Hill, Robert H. The Forty Five - Seventy Springfield. Suydam, Charles R., ed. LC 80-51230. (Illus.). 396p. 1980. 49.50 (ISBN 0-937500-11-9); deluxe ed. 9.50 deluxe edition (ISBN 0-937500-10-0). Springfield Pub Co.

SPRINTING

see Running

SPY STORIES

Fox, Anthony. Kingfisher Scream. LC 80-51769. 228p. 1981. 10.95 (ISBN 0-670-41352-6). Viking Pr.

SPYING

see Espionage; Spies

SQUABS

see Pigeons

SQUARE KNOTTING

see Macrame

SQUASH (GAME)

Colburn, Alan. Squash: The Ambitious Player's Guide. (Illus.). 112p. 1981. 19.95 (ISBN 0-571-11657-4, Pub. by Faber & Faber); pap. 8.95 (ISBN 0-571-11658-2). Merrimack Bk Serv.

SQUIDHOUND

see Striped Bass

SQUIRRELS

Horwich, R. H. The Ontogeny of Social Behavior in the Gray Squirrel (Sciurus carolinensis) (Advances in Ethology Ser.: Vol. 8). (Illus.). 103p. (Orig.). 1972. pap. text ed. 23.50. Parey Sci Pubs.

SRI LANKA–DESCRIPTION AND TRAVEL

Zeylancius. Ceylon. 1970. 19.95 (ISBN 0-236-17657-9, Pub. by Paul Elek). Merrimack Bk Serv.

SRIVIJAYA (KINGDOM)

The Art of Srivijaya. 68p. 1980. pap. 36.00 (ISBN 92-3-101656-3, U 1043, UNESCO). Unipub.

STABILITY OF SHIPS

Hind, J. Anthony. Stability & Trim of Fishing Vessels. (Illus.). 120p. 9.50 (FN). Unipub.

STABILITY OF STRUCTURES

see Structural Stability

STABILIZATION, ECONOMIC

see Economic Stabilization

STABLES

Sadler, Julius T., Jr. & Sadler, Jacqueline D. American Stables: An Architectural Tour. 1981. 29.95 (ISBN 0-8212-1105-6). NYGS.

STAGE COSTUME

see Costume

STAGE GUIDES

see Theaters–Stage-Setting and Scenery

STAGE LIGHTING

Ritsko, Alan J. Lighting for Location Motion Pictures. 224p. 1980. pap. 8.95 (ISBN 0-442-23136-9). Van Nos Reinhold.

STAGE-SETTING

see Theaters–Stage-Setting and Scenery

STAGING

see Theaters–Stage-Setting and Scenery

STAINED GLASS

see Glass Painting and Staining

STALIN, JOSEPH (IOSIF STALIN), 1879-1953

O'Seyenko-Antonov, A. V. The Time of Stalin: Portrait of a Tyranny. LC 80-8681. (Illus.). 384p. 1981. 15.00 (ISBN 0-06-010148-2, HarpT). Har-Row.

STAMINA, PHYSICAL

see Physical Fitness

STAMMERING

see Stuttering

STAMP-COLLECTING AND STAMP-COLLECTORS

see Postage-Stamps–Collectors and Collecting

STAMPS, POSTAGE

see Postage-Stamps

STANDARD OF LIVING

see Cost and Standard of Living

STANDARD OF VALUE

see Money; Value

STANDARDIZATION

see also Labels; Production Standards; Quality Control

also subdivision Standards, or Grading and Standardization under subjects

Preparing for Standardization Certification & Quality Control. 298p. 1979. 15.25 (APO80, Apo). Unipub.

STANDARDS

see subdivision Standards under subjects, e.g. Engineering Instruments

STANDARDS OF OUTPUT

see Production Standards

STANLEY, HENRY MORTON, SIR, 1841-1904

Walters, Alphonse J. Stanleys Emin Pasha Expedition. LC 80-1910. (Illus.). 1981. Repr. of 1890 ed. 43.00 (ISBN 0-404-18988-1). AMS Pr.

STANTON, EDWIN MCMASTERS, 1814-1869

Thomas, Benjamin P. & Hyman, Harold M. Stanton: The Life & Times of Lincoln's Secretary of War. LC 80-18970. (Illus.). xvii, 642p. 1980. Repr. of 1962 ed. lib. bdg. 49.50x (ISBN 0-313-22581-8, THSL). Greenwood.

STAR CATALOGS

see Stars–Catalogs

STARS

see also Astrology; Astronomy; Astrophysics; Galaxies; Life on Other Planets; Milky Way; Solar System

also names of individual stars

De Jager, C., ed. The Brightest Stars. (Geophysics & Astrophysics Monographs: No. 19). 472p. 1981. PLB 73.50 (ISBN 90-277-1109-7, Pub. by D. Reidel); pap. 1.50 (ISBN 90-277-1109-7). Kluwer Boston.

Jastrow, Robert. Red Giants & White Dwarfs. 1980. pap. 7.95 (ISBN 0-446-97349-1). Warner Bks.

STARS–ATLASES

Bok, Bart J. & Bok, Priscilla F. The Milky Way. 5th ed. LC 80-22544. (Harvard Books on Astronomy Ser.). (Illus.). 384p. 1981. text ed. 20.00 (ISBN 0-674-57503-2). Harvard U Pr.

Jackson, Joseph H. & Baumert, John H. Pictorial Guide to the Planets. 3rd ed. LC 80-7897. (Illus.). 256p. 1981. 19.95 (ISBN 0-06-014869-1, HarpT). Har-Row.

STARS–CATALOGS

Jones, Kenneth G., ed. Webb Society Deep-Sky Oberver's Handbook: Galaxies, Vol. 4. 296p. 1981. pap. 14.95 (ISBN 0-89490-050-1). Enslow Pubs.

STARS, DOUBLE

Martin, George R. Night Flyers. Bd. with True Names. Vinge, Vernor. (Binary Star: No. 5). (Orig.). 1981. pap. 2.50 (ISBN 0-440-10757-1). Dell.

STATE, THE

see also National State; Political Science; Public Interest

Jouvenel, Bertrand de. On Power: Its Nature & the History of Its Growth. Huntington, J. F., tr. from Fr. LC 80-24721. xix, 421p. 1981. Repr. of 1949 ed. lib. bdg. 39.75x (ISBN 0-313-22515-X, JOOP). Greenwood.

Rightridge, Allan. Plato & the Metaphysics of the State. (The Most Meaningful Classics in World Culture). (Illus.). 108p. 1981. 43.75 (ISBN 0-89266-297-2). Am Classical Coll Pr.

Shennan, J. H. The Origins of the Modern European State, Fourteen Fifty to Seventeen Twenty-Five. 1980. text ed. 14.50x (ISBN 0-09-119030-4, Hutchinson U Pr); pap. text ed. 9.25x (ISBN 0-09-119031-2). Humanities.

Vajda, Mihaly. The State & Socialism. (Allison & Busby Motive Ser.). 160p. 1981. pap. 7.95 (Pub. by Alison & Busby, England). Schocken.

STATE, THE–HISTORY OF THEORIES

see Political Science–History

STATE AND ART

see Art and State

STATE AND CHURCH

see Church and State

STATE AND EDUCATION

see Education and State

STATE AND ENERGY

see Energy Policy

STATE AND ENVIRONMENT

see Environmental Policy

STATE AND HIGHER EDUCATION

see Higher Education and State

STATE AND INDUSTRY

see Industry and State

STATE AND INSURANCE

see Social Security

STATE AND RELIGION

see Religion and State

STATE AND SOCIAL SCIENCES

see Social Sciences and State

STATE AND TECHNOLOGY

see Technology and State

STATE AND TRANSPORTATION

see Transportation and State

STATE BUDGETS

see Budget

STATE GOVERNMENTS

Here are entered works on state governments in general and in the United States. See also geographic subdivisions which follow.

see also Federal Government; Governors–United States; Local Government; Taxation, State

Barker, Michael, ed. Studies in State Development Policy, 9 vols, Vol. 1. 1979. pap. 66.00x (ISBN 0-934842-24-8). Coun State Plan.

Burns, James M., et al. State & Local Politics: Government by the People. 3rd ed. (Illus.). 1981. 9.95f (ISBN 0-13-843516-2). P-H.

Hanus, Jerome J., ed. The Nationalization of State Government. LC 80-8635. (Illus.). 192p. 1981. 19.95x (ISBN 0-669-04334-6). Lexington Bks.

Lefcoe, George, ed. Respective Roles of State & Local Governments in Land Policy & Taxation. (Lincoln Institute Monograph: No. 80-7). 271p. 1980. write for info. Lincoln Inst Land.

Marshall, H. H. From Dependence to Statehood, Vol. 1. 1980. 50.00 (ISBN 0-379-20348-0). Oceana.

Mirchandani, G. G. State Assembly Elections. 240p. 1980. text ed. 22.50x (ISBN 0-7069-1288-8, Pub. by Vikas India). Advent Bk.

Wright, Nancy D. & Allen, Gene P., eds. The National Directory of State Agencies, 1980-1981. 718p. 1975. text ed. 62.50 (ISBN 0-87815-032-3). Info Resources.

Zimmerman, Joseph F. State & Local Government. 3rd ed. (Illus., Orig.). pap. 4.95 (ISBN 0-06-460181-1, CO 181, COS). Har-Row.

STATE LIABILITY

see Government Liability

STATE-LOCAL FISCAL RELATIONS

see Intergovernmental Fiscal Relations

STATE OF THE UNION MESSAGES

see Presidents–United States–Messages

STATE OWNERSHIP

see Government Ownership

STATE PARKS

see Parks

STATE PLANNING

see Economic Policy; Regional Planning; Social Policy

STATE RESPONSIBILITY

see Government Liability

STATE UNIVERSITIES AND COLLEGES

see Universities and Colleges

STATES, IDEAL

see Utopias

STATESMEN

see also Diplomats

Paxton, John, ed. Statesman's Year-Book World Gazetteer. 2nd ed. (Illus.). 800p. 1980. 25.00x (ISBN 0-312-76126-0). St. Martin.

Pragnell, Mervyn O. & Keillor, Jean-Pierre, eds. International Yearbook & Statesman's Who's Who. 28th ed. LC 53-1425. 1454p. 1980. 105.00x (ISBN 0-610-00526-X). Intl Pubns Serv.

Radi, Heather, et al. Biographical Register of the New South Wales Parliament 1901-70. (Australian Parliaments, Biographical Notes: No. 6). 302p. 1979. text ed. 37.95 (ISBN 0-7081-1756-2, 0575, Pub. by ANUP Australia); pap. text ed. 18.95 (ISBN 0-7081-1757-0, 0574). Bks Australia.

STATESMEN–UNITED STATES

Allen, Howard W. Poindexter of Washington: A Study in Progressive Politics. LC 80-20123. 352p. 1981. price not set (ISBN 0-8093-0952-1). S Ill U Pr.

Bailey, N. Louise & Cooper, Elizabeth I., eds. Biographical Directory of the South Carolina House of Representatives: Seventeen-Seventy-Five to Seventeen-Ninty, Vol. 3. 780p. 1981. text ed. 14.95 (ISBN 0-87249-406-3). U of SC Pr.

Perry, Benjamin F. The Writings of Benjamin F. Perry. Meats, Stephen & Arnold, Edwin T., eds. Incl. Vol. I. Essays, Public Letters, & Speeches. 640p. 35.00 (ISBN 0-87152-340-X); Vols. II & III. Reminiscences of Public Men. Vol. II, 576p. 35.00 ea. (ISBN 0-87152-341-8); Vol. III, 572p. 35.00 (ISBN 0-87152-342-6). LC 80-19568. (The South Carolina Ser.: Bibliographical & Textual: No. 6). 1980. Repr. Set. 105.00 (ISBN 0-87152-339-6). Reprint.

STATICS

see also Dynamics; Elastic Solids; Elasticity; Equilibrium; Strains and Stresses

Cerny, Ladislav. Statics & Strength of Materials. (Illus.). 382p. 1981. text ed. 21.95 (ISBN 0-07-010339-9, C). McGraw.

STATISTICAL ANALYSIS

see Multivariate Analysis

STATISTICAL DESIGN

see Experimental Design

STATISTICAL DIAGRAMS

see Statistics–Charts, Tables, etc.; Statistics–Graphic Methods

STATISTICAL INFERENCE

see Mathematical Statistics; Probabilities

STATISTICAL MECHANICS

see also Quantum Statistics; Statistical Thermodynamics

Hurt, Norman & Hermann, R. Quantum Statistical Mechanics & Lie Group Harmonic Analysis, Pt. A. (Lie Groups; History, Frontiers & Applications: Vol. X). 1980. text ed. 30.00x (ISBN 0-915692-30-9, QC174.8.H87). Math Sci Pr.

STATISTICAL THERMODYNAMICS

Kreuzer, H. J. Non-Equilibrium Thermodynamics & Its Statistical Foundations. (Monographs on the Physics & Chemistry of Materials). (Illus.). 500p. 1981. 105.00 (ISBN 0-19-851361-5). Oxford U Pr.

STATISTICS

see also Biometry; Census; Commercial Statistics; Criminal Statistics; Econometrics; Educational Statistics; Experimental Design; Home Economics–Accounting; Mathematical Statistics; Medical Statistics; Probabilities; Regression Analysis

also subdivision Statistics and Statistical Methods under specific subjects, e.g. Agriculture–Statistics; Education–Statistics; and subdivisions Statistics, Medical; Statistics, Vital, etc. under names of countries, cities, etc., e.g. United States–Statistics, Vital

Anderson Sweeney, David R. & Williams, Thomas A. Introduction to Statistics: An Applications Approach. (Illus.). 750p. text ed. 14.36 (ISBN 0-8299-0361-5). West Pub.

Ashton, Gordon C. & McMillan, Ian. A Medley of Statistical Techniques for Researchers. 64p. 1981. pap. 6.25 (ISBN 0-686-69139-3). Kendall-Hunt.

Baltz, Howard B. Fundamentals of Inferential Statistics for Business Analysis. 2nd ed. 416p. 1980. pap. text ed. 18.95 (ISBN 0-8403-2217-8). Kendall-Hunt.

Barra, Jean-Rene & Herbach, L. Mathematical Basis of Statistics. LC 80-519. (Probability & Mathematical Statistical Ser.). 1981. write for info. (ISBN 0-12-079240-0). Acad Pr.

Cochran, William G. & Snedecor, George W. Statistical Methods. 7th ed. 507p. 1980. 21.50 (ISBN 0-8138-1560-6). Iowa St U Pr.

Dickinson, J. P. Statistics for Business, Finance, & Accounting. (Illus.). 328p. 1976. text ed. 21.00x (ISBN 0-7121-1939-6, Pub. by Macdonald & Evans England); pap. text ed. 14.95x (ISBN 0-7121-1948-5). Intl Ideas.

Edwards, Barry. The Readable Maths & Statistics Book. (Illus.). 336p. (Orig.). 1980. text ed. 34.95x (ISBN 0-04-310007-4, 2550); pap. text ed. 13.50x (ISBN 0-04-310008-2, 2551). Allen Unwin.

Groebner, David & Shannon, Patrick. Business Statistics: A Decision-Making Approach. (Illus.). 800p. 1981. text ed. 20.95 (ISBN 0-675-08083-5); tchr's. manual avail.; lab manual avail. (ISBN 0-675-08084-3); test bank avail. Merrill.

Johnston, James O. & Spatz, Chris. Study Guide for Basic Statistics: Tales of Distributions. 2nd ed. 150p. (Orig.). 1981. pap. text ed. 6.95 (ISBN 0-8185-0454-4). Brooks-Cole.

Joint Statistical Papers of J. Neyman & E. S. Pearson. 299p. 1967. 25.00x (ISBN 0-85264-706-9, Pub. by Griffin England). State Mutual Bk.

Koopmans. An Introduction to Contemporary Statistics. (Illus.). 500p. 1981. text ed. 20.95. Duxbury Pr.

Meier & Brudney. Applied Statistics & Analytic Techniques for Public Administrators. 1981. 15.95. Duxbury Pr.

Myers, Buddy L. & Enrick, Norbert L. Statistical Functions & Formulas: A Source of Simplified Derivations Based on Elementary Mathematics. 174p. 1981. Repr. of 1970 ed. text ed. price not set (ISBN 0-89874-286-2). Krieger.

Raktoe, B. L., et al. Factorial Design. (Wiley Series in Probability & Mathematical Statistics). 250p. 1981. 23.95 (ISBN 0-471-09040-9, Pub. by Wiley-Interscience). Wiley.

Runyon, Richard P. How Numbers Lie: A Consumer's Guide to Numerical Hocus Pocus. (Illus.). 192p. 1981. 7.95 (ISBN 0-86616-000-0). Lewis Pub Co.

Thirkettle, G. L. Wheldon's Business Statistics. 8th ed. (Illus.). 256p. 1976. pap. text ed. 11.95x (ISBN 0-7121-2331-8, Pub. by Macdonald & Evans England). Intl Ideas.

Triola, Mario F. Elementary Statistics. 16.95 (ISBN 0-8053-9305-6); pap. text ed. 3.95 (ISBN 0-8053-9307-2). Benjamin-Cummings.

Van Matre, Joseph G. & Gilbreath, Glenn H. Statistics for Business & Economics. 1980. text ed. 19.50x (ISBN 0-256-02276-3). Business Pubns.

Weiss, Neil & Hassett, Matthew. Introductory Statistics. LC 80-23520. (Statistics Ser.). (Illus.). 672p. 1981. text ed. 17.95 (ISBN 0-201-09507-6). A-W.

Wonnacott, Thomas J. & Wonnacott, Ronald J. Statistics: Discovering Its Power. 448p. 1981. text ed. 16.95 (ISBN 0-471-01412-5). Wiley.

STATISTICS–BIBLIOGRAPHY

Ketz, Samuel & Johnson, Norman L. Encyclopedia of Statistical Sciences, 2 vols. 500p. 1981. Vol. 1. 82.50 (ISBN 0-471-05546-8, Pub. by Wiley-Interscience); Vol. 2. 82.50 (ISBN 0-471-05547-6). Wiley.

STATISTICS–CHARTS, TABLES, ETC.

Pearson, E. S. & Hartley, H. O., eds. Biometrika Tables for Statisticians, Vol. 1. 3rd ed. 270p. 1976. lib. bdg. 25.95x. Lubrecht & Cramer.

--Biometrika Tables for Statisticians: Reprint with Corrections, Vol. 2. 385p. 1976. Repr. lib. bdg. 30.50x. Lubrecht & Cramer.

Rohlf, F. James & Sokal, Robert R. Statistical Tables. 2nd ed. 1981. text ed. price not set (ISBN 0-7167-1257-1); pap. text ed. price not set (ISBN 0-7167-1258-X). W H Freeman.

STATISTICS–DATA PROCESSING

Roberts, Harry V. Conversational Statistics. (Data Analysis Series). 256p. 1974. pap. text ed. 15.95 (ISBN 0-07-053135-8, C). McGraw.

Spencer, B. P. Benefit-Cost Analysis of Data Used to Allocate Funds. (Lecture Notes in Statistics: Vol. 3). 296p. 1980. pap. 16.80 (ISBN 0-387-90511-1). Springer-Verlag.

Van Tassel, Dennie. Basic-Pack Statistics Programs. (Ser. in Personal Computing). (Illus.). 240p. 1981. pap. text ed. 16.95 (ISBN 0-13-066381-6). P-H.

STATISTICS–GRAPHIC METHODS

Fleiss, Joseph L. Statistical Methods for Rates & Proportions. 2nd ed. (Probability & Statistics Ser.: Applied Probability & Statistics). 300p. 1981. 24.95 (ISBN 0-471-06428-9, Pub. by Wiley-Interscience). Wiley.

Fu, K. S. & Yu, T. S. Statistical Pattern Classification Using Contextual Information. (Patterns Recognition & Image Processing Ser.). 208p. 1981. write for info. (ISBN 0-471-27859-9, Pub. by Wiley-Interscience). Wiley.

STATISTICS–PROBLEMS, EXERCISES, ETC.

Statistics Prob. Inf. Dec. 2nd ed. 1975. 24.95 (ISBN 0-03-014011-0). Dryden Pr.

STATISTICS, MATHEMATICAL

see Mathematical Statistics

STATISTICS, NONPARAMETRIC

see Nonparametric Statistics

STATUETTES

see Bronzes; Idols and Images; Jade

STATUTES

Here are entered works on statute law, as distinguished from constitutional law and from the law arising from judicial or administrative decisions. Works on the interpretation of statutory law are entered under Law–Interpretation and Construction. Works on the theory or practice of statute making are entered under Legislation or Bill Drafting.

Sedgwick, Theodore. A Treatise on the Rules Which Govern the Interpretation & Construction of Statutory & Constitutional Law. 2nd ed. Pomeroy, John N., ed. xlviii, 692p. 1981. Repr. of 1874 ed. lib. bdg. 49.50x (ISBN 0-8377-1115-0). Rothman.

STAUPITZ, JOHANN VON, 1524

Steinmetz, David C. Luther & Staupitz: An Essay in the Intellectual Origins of the Protestant Reformation. LC 80-23007. (Duke Monographs in Medieval & Renaissance Studies: No. 4). 1981. 16.75 (ISBN 0-8223-0447-3). Duke.

STEAM–TABLES, CALCULATIONS, ETC.

Meyer, C. A., et al. ASME Steam Tables. 4th ed. 1979. pap. text ed. 22.50 (G00038). ASME.

STEAM-BOILERS

see also Feed-Water; Furnaces; Pressure Vessels; Steam-Engines

Milton, J. H. & Leach, R. M. Marine Steam Boilers. 4th ed. (Illus.). 700p. 1980. text ed. 33.75 (ISBN 0-408-00416-9). Butterworths.

STEAM-ENGINES

see also Locomotives; Marine Engines; Steam-Boilers

Durham, Bill, ed. Steamboats & Modern Steam Launches. (Illus.). 631p. 1981. Repr. of 1963 ed. 25.00. Howell-North.

STEAM ENGINES–HISTORY

Tuplin, W. A. The Steam Locomotive. 1980. text ed. 20.75 (ISBN 0-239-00198-2). Humanities.

Watkins, George. The Steam Engine in Industry-One. 128p. 1980. 25.00x (ISBN 0-686-64742-4, Pub. by Moorland England). State Mutual Bk.

STEAM-ENGINES, MARINE

see Marine Engines

STEAM-FITTING

see Pipe-Fitting

STEAM GENERATORS

see Steam-Boilers

STEAM-NAVIGATION

see also Marine Engineering; Navigation; Steamboats and Steamboat Lines

Mackay, J. S. The Analysis of Marine Steam Indicator Diagrams. 130p. 1949. 27.50x (ISBN 0-85264-019-6, Pub. by Griffin England). State Mutual Bk.

STEAM-PUMPS

see Pumping Machinery

STEAMBOATS AND STEAMBOAT LINES

see also Ocean Travel; Steam-Navigation

also names of steamboats, e.g. Lusitania

Best, Gerald M. Ships & Narrow Gauge Rails: The Story of the Pacific Coast Company. (Illus.). 155p. Date not set. Repr. of 1964 ed. 15.00 (ISBN 0-8310-7042-0). Howell-North.

Durham, Bill, ed. Steamboats & Modern Steam Launches. (Illus.). 631p. 1981. Repr. of 1963 ed. 25.00. A S Barnes.

--Steamboats & Modern Steam Launches. (Illus.). 631p. 1981. Repr. of 1963 ed. 25.00. Howell-North.

Morris, Paul C. & Morin, Joseph F. The Island Steamers: A Chronology of Steam Transportation to & from the Offshore Islands of Martha's Vineyard & Nantucket. 2nd ed. Towne, Sumner A., Jr., ed. LC 77-79090. (Illus.). 196p. 1977. pap. 11.95 (ISBN 0-686-28900-5). Nantucket Nautical.

STEEL–JUVENILE LITERATURE

Harter, Walter. Steel: The Metal with Muscle. (Illus.). 96p. (gr. 4-7). 1981. PLB price not set. Messner.

STEEL, STRUCTURAL

Steele, L. E. & Stahlkopf, K. E., eds. Assuring Structural Integrity of Steel Reactor Pressure Vessels. (Illus.). xii, 220p. 1980. 40.00x (ISBN 0-85334-906-1). Burgess-Intl Ideas.

STEEL ALLOYS

Touloukian, Y. S. & Ho, C. Y. Properties of Selected Ferrous Alloying Elements, Vol. III. (M-H-CINDAS Data Series on Material Properties). 288p. 1981. text ed. 33.50 (ISBN 0-07-065034-9). McGraw.

STEEL AND IRON SHIPS

see Ships, Iron and Steel

STEEL-ENGRAVING

see Engraving

STEEL INDUSTRY AND TRADE–GREAT BRITAIN

Roepke, Howard G. Movememts of the British Iron & Steel Industry, 1720 to 1951, Vol. 36. LC 80-23128. (Illinois Studies in the Social Sciences). (Illus.). vii, 198p. 1981. Repr. of 1956 ed. lib. bdg. 25.00x (ISBN 0-8371-9096-7, ROMB). Greenwood.

STEEL INDUSTRY AND TRADE–JAPAN

IE in Japanese Steel Industry. 144p. 1973. 7.75 (APO30, APO). Unipub.

STEEPLECHASING

Curling, Bill. Royal Champion: The Story of Steeplechasing's First Lady. (Illus.). 272p. 1981. 29.95 (ISBN 0-7181-1930-4). Merrimack Bk Serv.

STEGANOGRAPHY

see Cryptography

STEINBECK, JOHN ERNST, 1902-1968
French, Warren, ed. John Steinbeck. (Twayne's U. S. Authors Ser.). 189p. pap. text ed. 4.95 (ISBN 0-672-61501-0). Bobbs.
Lisca, Peter. The Wide World of John Steinbeck. 332p. 1981. Repr. of 1958 ed. 15.00 (ISBN 0-87752-217-0). Gordian.
STEINER, RUDOLF, 1861-1925
Easton, Stewart C. Rudolf Steiner: Herald of a New Epoch. LC 80-67026. (Illus.). 1980. pap. 9.95 (ISBN 0-910142-93-9). Anthroposophic.
Pusch, Hans. Working Together on Rudolf Stein's Mystery Dramas: Steiner's Mystery Dramas. LC 80-67024. (Illus.). 144p. (Orig.). 1980. pap. text ed. 9.95 (ISBN 0-910142-91-2). Anthroposophic.
Spock, Marjorie. Eurythmy. (Illus.). 148p. (Orig.). 1980. pap. 9.95 (ISBN 0-910142-88-2). Anthroposophic.
STEINLEN, THEOPHILE ALEXANDRE, 1859-1923
Steinlen, Theophile-Alexandre. Steinlen Cats. (Illus.). 48p. 1980. pap. 2.00 (ISBN 0-486-23950-0). Dover.
STENCIL WORK
Abbe, Dorothy, compiled by. Stencilled Ornament & Illustration. pap. 15.00 (ISBN 0-89073-064-4). Boston Public Lib.
STENGEL, CASEY
Hahn, James & Hahn, Lynn. Casey! Charles Stengel. Schroeder, Howard, ed. (Sports Legends Ser.). (Illus.). 48p. (Orig.). (gr. 3-5). 1981. PLB 5.95 (ISBN 0-89686-126-0); pap. text ed. 2.95 (ISBN 0-89686-141-4). Crestwood Hse.
STENOGRAPHY
see Shorthand
STEPCHILDREN
see also Stepfathers; Stepmothers
Stenson, Janet S. Now I Have a Step-Parent, & It's Kind of Confusing. 1979. pap. 2.95 (ISBN 0-380-46516-7, 46516). Avon.
Visher, Emily B. & Visher, John S. A Manual for Stepfamilies. 150p. 1981. 10.00 (ISBN 0-87630-268-1). Brunner-Mazel.
STEPFATHERS
see also Stepchildren
Visher, Emily B. & Visher, John S. A Manual for Stepfamilies. 150p. 1981. 10.00 (ISBN 0-87630-268-1). Brunner-Mazel.
STEPMOTHERS
see also Stepchildren
Visher, Emily B. & Visher, John S. A Manual for Stepfamilies. 150p. 1981. 10.00 (ISBN 0-87630-268-1). Brunner-Mazel.
STEREOENCEPHALOTOMY
Riechert, T. Stereotactic Brain Operations: Methods, Clinical Aspects, Indications. (Illus.). 387p. 1980. 120.00 (ISBN 3-456-80457-1, Pub. by Hans Huber). J K Burgess.
STEREOMETRY
see Mensuration
STEREOPHONIC SOUND SYSTEMS
Lyttle, Richard B. Complete Beginner's Guide to Stereo. LC 79-8564. (Illus.). 192p. 1981. 9.95a (ISBN 0-385-15532-8); lib. bdg. (ISBN 0-385-15533-6). Doubleday.
Tarumoto, David H., ed. High-Performance Review: Audio Equipment & Recordings for the Perceptive Listener, Vol. 1. (Illus.). 480p. 1981. pap. 24.00x (ISBN 0-88232-068-8). Delbridge Pub Co.
STEREOPHOTOGRAMMETRY
see Photogrammetry
STEREOSCOPIC PHOTOGRAPHY
see Photography, Stereoscopic
STEREOTAXIC SURGERY
see Stereoencephalotomy
STERIDES
see Steroids
STERILITY
see also Fertility; Fertility, Human
Barwin, B. Norman, et al. Self-Assessment of Current Knowledge in Infertility & Gynecologic Endocrinology. 1979. spiral bdg. 14.50 (ISBN 0-87488-231-1). Med Exam.
University of North Carolina at Chapel Hill, Dept. of OB-GYN. Infertility, a Practical Guide for the Physician. Hammond, Mary G. & Talbert, Luther M., eds. LC 80-84920. (Illus.). 128p. (Orig.). 1981. 14.95x (ISBN 0-938938-00-2, 810-M*O-001). Health Sci Consort.
White, Karol. What to Do When You Think You Can't Have a Baby. LC 80-1730. (Illus.). 216p. 1981. 11.95 (ISBN 0-385-15446-1). Doubleday.
STERILITY, MALE
Cunningham, G. R., et al, eds. Regulation of Male Fertility. (Clinics in Andrology Ser.: No. 5). (Illus.). 245p. 1981. PLB 68.50 (ISBN 90-247-2373-6, Pub. by Martinus Nijhoff). Kluwer Boston.
STERILIZATION
Hodgson, Jane E. Abortion & Sterilization: Medical & Social Aspects. 1981. write for info. (ISBN 0-8089-1344-1). Grune.
STERILIZATION, FEMALE
see Sterilization of Women
STERILIZATION OF WOMEN
Brown, Herbert P. & Schanzer, Stephan N. Female Sterilization by Vaginal Tubal Ligation. 200p. 1981. text ed. 15.00 (ISBN 0-88416-356-3). PSG Pub.

STERLING AREA
Drummond, Ian. The Floating Pound & the Sterling Area, 1931-1939. LC 80-14539. 352p. Date not set. 37.50 (ISBN 0-521-23165-5). Cambridge U Pr.
STEROID HORMONES
see also Hormones, Sex
Gower, D. B. Steroid Hormones. 120p. 1980. 35.00x (ISBN 0-85664-838-8, Pub. by Croom Helm England). State Mutual Bk.
Kilshaw. Steroids & Non-Steroid Hormones. 1981. text ed. price not set. Butterworth.
STEROIDS
see also Lipids; Steroid Hormones
Briggs, M. H. & Christie, G. A., eds. Advances in Steroid Biochemistry & Pharmacology, Vols. 1-7. Incl. Vol. 1. 71.50 (ISBN 0-12-037501-X); Vol. 2. 66.50 (ISBN 0-12-037502-8); Vol. 3. 1972. 35.50 (ISBN 0-12-037503-6); Vol. 4. 1974. 45.00 (ISBN 0-12-037504-4); Vol. 5. 1976. 51.50 (ISBN 0-12-037505-2); Vol. 6. 1978. 24.50 (ISBN 0-12-037506-0); Vol. 7. 1980. 23.00 (ISBN 0-12-037507-9). Acad Pr.
STEVEDORING
see Cargo Handling
STEWARDESSES (AIR LINES)
see Air Lines–Flight Attendants
STEWARDS (AIR LINES)
see Air Lines–Flight Attendants
STEWARDSHIP, CHRISTIAN
see also Christianity and Economics
Marx, Werner. Nuevas Fuerzas. LC 77-243. 166p. (Orig., Span.). 1976. pap. 3.25 (ISBN 0-89922-068-1). Edit Caribe.
Patterson, F. W. Manual De Finanzas Para Iglesias. (Illus.). 118p. 1980. pap. 1.95 (ISBN 0-311-17005-6). Casa Bautista.
STEWS
Orcutt, Georgia. Soups, Chowders & Stews. Taylor, Sandra, ed. (Flair of New England Ser.). 1981. pap. 8.95 (ISBN 0-911658-17-3, 3078). Yankee Bks.
STIEGLITZ, ALFRED, 1864-1946
Seligmann, Herbert J., ed. Alfred Stieglitz Talking: Notes on Some of His Conversations, 1925-1931 with a Foreward. 161p. 1981. text ed. 15.00x (ISBN 0-300-03510-1, 66-20942). Yale U Pr.
STILL-LIFE PAINTING
Kominsky, Nancy. Paint Along with Nancy Kominsky: Still Lifes. (Orig.). 1981. pap. 7.95 (ISBN 0-446-87792-1). Warner Bks.
Sterling, Charles. Still-Life Painting from Antiquity to the Present. rev. ed. LC 78-24827. (Icon Editions Ser.). (Illus.). 320p. 1981. 25.00 (ISBN 0-06-438530-2, HarpT). Har-Row.
STILLWATER, BATTLE OF, 1777
see Saratoga Campaign, 1777
STOCHASTIC ANALYSIS
Rao, M. M. Foundations of Stochastic Analysis. (Probability & Mathematical Statistics Ser.). 1981. price not set (ISBN 0-12-580850-X). Acad Pr.
STOCHASTIC PROCESSES
see also Markov Processes; Monte Carlo Method; Stochastic Analysis
Adler, Robert J. The Geometry of Random Fields. 304p. 1981. 47.50 (ISBN 0-471-27844-0, Pub. by Wiley-Interscience). Wiley.
Bartlett, M. S. Introduction to Stochastic Processes. 3rd ed. LC 76-57094. (Illus.). 404p. Date not set. pap. 17.95 (ISBN 0-521-28085-0). Cambridge U Pr.
Bucy, R. S., et al. Stochastic Differential Equations. McKean, H. P. & Keller, J. B., eds. LC 72-13266. (SIAM-AMS Proceedings). 1973. 22.00 (ISBN 0-8218-1325-0). Am Math.
Crigelionis, B., ed. Stochastic Differential Systems; Filtering & Control: Proceedings. (Lecture Notes in Control & Information Sciences Ser.: Vol. 25). 362p. 1981. pap. 24.20 (ISBN 0-387-10498-4). Springer-Verlag.
Gihman, I. I. & Skorohod, A. V. The Theory of Stochastic Processes, Vol. 1. (Grundlehren der Mathematischen Wissenschaften: Vol. 210). 570p. 1981. 89.00 (ISBN 0-387-06573-3). Springer-Verlag.
Habib, Muhammad K. Sampling Representations & Approximations for Certain Functions & Stochastic Processes. 100p. 1980. pap. 3.15 (1260). U of NC Pr.
Kall, P. & Prekopa, A., eds. Recent Results in Stochastic Programming: Proceedings. (Lecture Notes in Economics & Mathematical Systems: Vol. 179). (Illus.). 256p. 1980. pap. 19.00 (ISBN 0-387-10013-X). Springer-Verlag.
Medhi, J. P. An Introduction to Stochastic Processes. 320p. 1981. 19.95 (ISBN 0-470-27000-4). Halsted Pr.
Prabhu, N. U. Stochastic Storage Processes: Queues, Insurance Risk & Dams. (Applications of Mathematics Ser.: Vol. 15). 140p. 1981. 19.80 (ISBN 0-387-90522-7). Springer Verlag.
Sorenson. Parameter Estimation: Principles & Problems. 400p. 1980. 45.00 (ISBN 0-8247-6987-2). Dekker.
STOCHASTIC SAMPLING
see Monte Carlo Method
STOCK (ANIMALS)
see Livestock
STOCK CONTROL
see Inventory Control

STOCK CORPORATIONS
see Corporations
STOCK-EXCHANGE
Here are entered works on stock trading and speculation and on stock exchanges in general.
see also Bonds; Foreign Exchange; Securities; Stocks; Wall Street
also names of specific exchanges, e.g. New York Stock Exchange
Burns, Joseph M. Treatise on Markets: Spot, Futures, & Options. 1979. pap. 5.25 (ISBN 0-8447-3340-7). Am Enterprise.
Chamberlain, G. H. Trading in Options. 144p. 1980. 30.00x (ISBN 0-85941-168-0, Pub. by Woodhead-Faulkner England). State Mutual Bk.
Dames, Ralph T. The Winning Option. LC 79-23369. 128p. 1981. 14.95 (ISBN 0-88229-527-6). Nelson-Hall.
Ellinger, A. G. & Stewart, T. H. A Post-War History of the Stock Market. 80p. 1980. 30.00x (ISBN 0-85941-153-2, Pub. by Woodhead-Faulkner England). State Mutual Bk.
Elliott, Ralph N. An Elementary Introduction into the Elliott's Wave Theory. (The New Stock Market Reference Library). (Illus.). 91p. 1981. 27.55 (ISBN 0-918968-92-5). Inst Econ Fina.
Elliott, Robert M. The Most Significant Stock Market Chart Patterns & the Amazing Anticipatory Meaning They Contain. (Illus.). 151p. 1981. 49.75 (ISBN 0-918968-89-5). Inst Econ Finan.
Flumiani, C. M. The Physiology & Psychology of Stock Market Charts. (Illus.). 103p. 1981. 47.85 (ISBN 0-918968-84-4). Inst Econ Finan.
--The Wall Street Manual for Teenagers. (Illus.). 99p. 1981. 13.75 (ISBN 0-89266-287-5). Am Classical Coll Pr.
Gann, William D. The Subtle Art of Choosing Early & Late Leaders in the Operations of the Stock Market. (Illus.). 123p. 1981. 49.85 (ISBN 0-918968-97-6). Inst Econ Finan.
Lefevre, Edwin. Reminiscences of a Stock Operator. 1980. Repr. of 1923 ed. flexible cover 12.00 (ISBN 0-87034-058-1). Fraser Pub Co.
Little, Jeffrey B. & Rhodes, Lucien. Understanding Wall Street. LC 78-54787. (Illus.). 220p. 1980. pap. 7.95 (ISBN 0-89709-010-1). Liberty Pub.
Miller, A. T. The Principles & Techniques of Stock Market Manipulation. (The New Stock Market Reference Library Ser.). (Illus.). 117p. 1981. 39.85 (ISBN 0-918968-95-X). Inst Econ Finan.
Mitchell, Lloyd A. How to Make Money in Wall Street Through the Intelligent Use of Price-Earnings Ratios. (The New Stock Market Reference Library). (Illus.). 112p. 1981. 39.45 (ISBN 0-918968-93-3). Inst Econ Fina.
Nagan, Peter. Fail Safe Investing: How to Make Money with Less Than Ten Thousand Dollars...Without Losing Sleep. 192p. 1981. 9.95 (ISBN 0-399-12616-3). Putnam.
Osgood, Arthur F. The Art of Playing Safe in Wall Street: Wall Street Discoveries Capable of Maximizing Your Stock Market Profits & of Practically Eliminating Your Stock Market Potential Losses. (Illus.). 99p. 1981. 23.75 (ISBN 0-918968-88-7). Inst Econ Finan.
Oster, Merrill J., et al. Multiply Your Money Trading Soybeans: A Beginner's Guide to Speculating in Soybean Futures. 198p. 1981. 14.95 (ISBN 0-914230-10-7). Investor Pubns.
Phillips, Susan & Zecher, Richard. The SEC & the Public Interest. (Illus.). 184p. 1981. text ed. 19.95x (ISBN 0-262-16080-3). MIT Pr.
Righetti, Raymond R. Stock Market Strategy for Consistent Profits. LC 79-23006. 176p. 1981. 14.95 (ISBN 0-88229-574-8). Nelson-Hall.
Rubinstein, Mark & Cox, John J. Options Markets. (Illus.). 432p. 1981. 29.95 (ISBN 0-13-638205-3). P-H.
Stewart, Joseph T. Dynamic Stock Option Trading. 184p. 1981. 31.95 (ISBN 0-471-08670-3). Ronald Pr.
Trester, Kenneth R. The Option Players Advanced Guidebook: Turning the Tables on the Options Markets. LC 80-83175. (Illus.). 275p. 1980. 35.00 (ISBN 0-9604914-1-4). Investrek.
Vanderman, Timothy D. The Intelligent Anticipation of Stock Market Reversals for the Maximization of Speculative Profits. (The New Stock Market Reference Library). (Illus.). 116p. 1981. 41.75 (ISBN 0-918968-94-1). Inst Econ Fina.
STOCK MARKET
see Stock-Exchange
STOCK OWNERSHIP FOR EMPLOYEES
see Employee Ownership
STOCKS
see also Bonds; Corporations; Stock-Exchange
Gann, William D. Successful Stock Selecting Methods in Wall Street. (The New Stock Market Reference Library). (Illus.). 118p. 1981. 49.85 (ISBN 0-918968-96-8). Inst Econ Finan.
Tuccille, Jerome. Dynamic Investing: The System for Automatic Profits -- No Matter Which Way the Market Goes. 1981. pap. 9.95 (H398). NAL.
STOCKS–TAXATION
see Taxation of Bonds, Securities, etc.
STOCKTON, FRANK R., 1834-1902
Golemba, Henry L. Frank R. Stockton. (United States Authors Ser.: No. 374). 1981. lib. bdg. 11.95 (ISBN 0-8057-7288-X). Twayne.

STOICHIOMETRY
see Chemistry–Problems, Exercises, etc.; Chemistry, Physical and Theoretical
STOMACH–DISEASES
Rotter, Jerome I., et al, eds. The Genetics & Heterogeneity of Common Gastrointestinal Disorders. 1980. 35.00 (ISBN 0-12-598760-9). Acad Pr.
STOMATOLOGY
see Mouth–Diseases; Teeth; Teeth–Diseases
STONE, LUCY, 1818-1893
Wheeler, Leslie, ed. Loving Warriors: Selected Letters of Lucy Stone & Henry B. Blackwell, 1853-1893. (Illus.). 1981. 19.95. Dial.
STONE, PHILOSOPHERS'
see Alchemy
STONE AGE
see also Archaeology; Man, Prehistoric; Paleolithic Period
McMann, Jean M. Riddles of the Stone Age. LC 79-67658. (Illus.). 160p. 1980. 16.95 (ISBN 0-500-05033-3). Thames Hudson.
STONE-CARVING
see Sculpture
STONE-CUTTING
Kindersley, David & Cardozo, Lida L. Letters Slate Cut. (Illus.). 96p. 1981. pap. 9.95 (ISBN 0-8008-4741-5, Pentalic). Taplinger.
STONE HOUSES
Blaser, Werner. The Rock Is My Home: Structures in Stone. (Illus.). 224p. (Eng., Fr. & Ger.). 1976. text ed. 15.00 (ISBN 0-89192-299-7). Interbk Inc.
STONEWARE
see Pottery
STONEWORK, DECORATIVE
see Sculpture
STONY INDIANS
see Indians of North America–The West
STORAGE
see Warehouses
also names of stored products, e.g. Farm Produce, Coal, etc.
STORAGE DEVICES, COMPUTER
see Computer Storage Devices
STORAGE WAREHOUSES
see Warehouses
STORES, COOPERATIVE
see Cooperative Societies
STORES, DEPARTMENT
see Department Stores
STORES, RETAIL
see also Department Stores
Burstinger, Irving. Run Your Own Retail Store: From Raising the Money to Counting the Profits. (Illus.). 304p. 1981. 19.95 (ISBN 0-13-784017-9, Spec); pap. 12.95 (ISBN 0-13-784009-8). P-H.
White, Paul. Shops & Markets. (Junior Reference Ser.). (Illus.). 64p. (gr. 7 up). 1971. 7.95 (ISBN 0-7136-1155-3). Dufour.
STORIES
see Fiction
STORY, SHORT
see Short Story
STOUT, REX, 1886-
Townsend, Guy, et al. Rex Stout: A Primary & Secondary Bibliography. LC 80-8507. 210p. 1980. lib. bdg. 30.00. Garland Pub.
STOVES
see also Heating
Morrison, James W. The Complete Coalburning Stove & Furnace Guide. (Illus.). 288p. 1981. 11.95 (ISBN 0-668-05097-7, 5097-7). Arco.
Sabin, A. Ross, ed. Range Service (Gas, Electric, Microwave). (Illus.). 253p. (gr. 11). 1979. 20.00 (ISBN 0-938336-06-1). Whirlpool.
STRAINS AND STRESSES
see also Deformations (Mechanics); Elasticity; Engineering Design; Materials–Fatigue; Shells (Engineering); Shock (Mechanics); Strength of Materials; Structural Design; Structural Dynamics; Thermal Stresses
Collins, J. A. Failure of Materials in Mechanical Design: Analysis, Prediction, Prevention. 700p. 1981. 25.00 (ISBN 0-471-05024-5, Pub. by Wiley-Interscience). Wiley.
Richards, T. H. Energy Methods in Stress Analysis. LC 79-29647. (Engineering Science Ser.). 410p. 1980. pap. 26.95 (ISBN 0-470-27068-3). Halsted Pr.
STRATEGIC MATERIALS
Main Trends in World Power: Political Impact of Strategic Weapons. 60p. 1978. pap. 7.50 (ISBN 0-89206-004-2, CSIS001, CSIS). Unipub.
Szuprowicz, Bohdan O. Strategic Materials Geopolitics: How to Avoid Shortages, Cartels, Embargoes, & Supply Disruptions. 336p. 1981. 18.95 (ISBN 0-471-07843-3, Pub. by Wiley-Interscience). Wiley.
STRATEGY
see also Air Warfare; Armies; Atomic Warfare; Deterrence (Strategy); Military Art and Science; Psychological Warfare; Tank Warfare
Bertram, Christoph, ed. Strategic Deterrence in a Changing Environment. LC 80-67841. (Adelphi Library Vol. 6). 200p. 1981. text ed. 29.50 (ISBN 0-916672-75-1). Allanheld.
Candler. Atlas of African Military Strategy. 102p. Date not set. 29.95 (ISBN 0-02-905750-7). Macmillan.

Mason, Richard O. & Mitroff, Ian I. Challenging Strategic Planning Assumptions: Theory, Cases & Techniques. 300p. 1981. 24.95 (ISBN 0-471-08219-8, Pub. by Wiley-Interscience). Wiley.

STRATIFICATION, SOCIAL
see Social Classes

STRATIGRAPHIC GEOLOGY
see Geology, Stratigraphic

STRAUSS, RICHARD, 1864-1949
Hartmann, Rudolf. Richard Strauss: The Staging of His Operas & Ballets. (Illus.). 226p. 1981. 39.95 (ISBN 0-19-520251-1). Oxford U Pr.

STRAW VOTES
see Public Opinion Polls

STRAWBERRIES
Ulrich, Albert, et al. Strawberry Deficiency Symptoms: A Visual & Plant Analysis Guide to Fertilization. LC 79-67379. (Illus.). 58p. pap. text ed. 8.00x (ISBN 0-931876-37-0). Ag Sci Pubns.

STREAKED BASS
see Striped Bass

STREAM POLLUTION
see Water-Pollution

STREAMLINING
see Aerodynamics

STREET-CARS
see Electric Railroads-Cars

STREET CHRISTIANS
see Jesus People

STREET-RAILROADS
see also Subways
Carlson, Norman & Peterson, Arthur, eds. Remember When-Trolley Wires Spanned the Country: Bullentin-119. LC 78-74495. (Illus.). 1980. 30.00 (ISBN 0-915348-20-9). Central Electric.

STREET RAILROADS-CARS
see Electric Railroads-Cars

STREET TRAFFIC
see Traffic Engineering

STREETS
see also Pavements; Roads
Design Guide for Local Roads & Streets: Rural & Urban. 1971. 1.00. AASHTO.

STRENGTH OF MATERIALS
see also Elasticity; Fracture Mechanics; Materials-Fatigue; Strains and Stresses; Strengthening Mechanisms in Solids; Structural Design
Accelerated Strength Testing. 1978. 23.25 (SP-56); 17.25. ACI.
Alexander, J. M. Strength of Materials: Fundamentals, Vol. 1. 190p. 1981. 47.95 (ISBN 0-470-27119-1). Halsted Pr.
Cerny, Ladislav. Statics & Strength of Materials. (Illus.). 382p. 1981. text ed. 21.95 (ISBN 0-07-010339-9, C). McGraw.
Research & Education Association Staff. Problem Solver in Strength of Materials & Mechanics of Solids. LC 80-83305. (Illus.). 896p. (Orig.). pap. text ed. 22.85x (ISBN 0-87891-522-2). Res & Educ.

STRENGTH OF MUSCLES
see Muscle Strength

STRENGTHENING MECHANISMS IN SOLIDS
Research & Education Association Staff. Problem Solver in Strength of Materials & Mechanics of Solids. LC 80-83305. (Illus.). 896p. (Orig.). pap. text ed. 22.85x (ISBN 0-87891-522-2). Res & Educ.

STRESS (PHYSIOLOGY)
Cooper, C. L. & Payne, R. Stress at Work. (Studies in Occupational Stress). 293p. 1978. 36.50 (ISBN 0-471-99547-9, Pub. by Wiley-Interscience). Wiley.
Ellestad, Myrin H. Stress Testing: Principles & Testing. 1980. 35.00 (ISBN 0-8036-3111-1). Davis Co.
Kaufman, Sherwin A. Sexual Sabotage: How to Enjoy Sex Inspite of Physical & Emotional Problems. 256p. 1981. 13.95 (ISBN 0-02-560740-5). Macmillan.
Nathan, Ronald G. & Charlesworth, Edward A. Stress Management: A Conceptual & Procedural Guide. LC 80-70400. (Illus.). 223p. (Orig.). 1980. 19.95 (ISBN 0-938176-01-3). Wendover.
Rechcigl, Miloslav, ed. Handbook of Nutritional Requirements in a Functional Context. 1981. Vol. 1. 72.95 (ISBN 0-686-69343-4); Vol. 2. 77.95 (ISBN 0-8493-3958-8). CRC Pr.
Wheatley, David, ed. Stress & the Heart. 2nd ed. 430p. 1981. 39.50 (ISBN 0-89004-520-8). Raven.

STRESS (PSYCHOLOGY)
see also Anxiety
Ainsworth, Stanley. Positive Emotional Power: How to Manage Your Feelings. (Illus.). 256p. 1981. 12.95 (ISBN 0-13-687616-1); pap. 6.95 (ISBN 0-686-69330-2). P-H.
Alluisi, Earl A. & Fleishman, Edwin A., eds. Stress & Performance Effectiveness. (Human Performance & Productivity Ser.: Vol.3). 336p. 1981. professional ref. text 19.95 (ISBN 0-89859-091-4). L Erlbaum Assocs.
Bergler, Edmund. Tensions Can Be Reduced to Nuisances. 12.95 (ISBN 0-87140-976-3); pap. 3.95 (ISBN 0-87140-976-3). Liveright.
Bieliauskas, Linas A. Stress & Its Relationship to Health & Illness. (Behavioral Sciences for Health Care Professionals Ser.). 128p. (Orig.). 1981. lib. bdg. 15.00x (ISBN 0-86531-002-5); pap. text ed. 6.00x (ISBN 0-86531-003-3). Westview.
Brief, et al. Managing Job Stress. (Orig.). 1981. pap. text ed. 8.95 (ISBN 0-316-10799-9). Little.
Curtis, Jack & Detert, Richard. How to Relax: A Holistic Approach to Stress Management. 190p. (Orig.). 1981. pap. text ed. price not set (ISBN 0-87484-527-0). Mayfield Pub.
Dempcy, Mary & Tihista, Rene. Your Stress Personalities: A Look at Your Selves. (Illus.). 252p. (Orig.). 1981. pap. 8.95 (ISBN 0-89141-077-5). Presidio Pr.
House, James S. Work Stress & Social Support. LC 80-22234. 200p. 1981. pap. text ed. cancelled (ISBN 0-201-03101-9). A-W.
Imber, Steve, ed. Readings in Emotional & Behavioral Disorders. rev. ed. (Special Education Ser.). (Illus.). 224p. pap. text ed. 9.95 (ISBN 0-89568-294-X). Spec Learn Corp.
Kaufman, Sherwin A. Sexual Sabotage: How to Enjoy Sex Inspite of Physical & Emotional Problems. 256p. 1981. 13.95 (ISBN 0-02-560740-5). Macmillan.
Korth, Leslie O. Tensions: A Practical Method for Their Release. 1980. 4.00x (ISBN 0-8464-1053-2). Beekman Pubs.
Levi, Lennart. Occupational Stress: Sources, Management & Prevention. (Occupational Stress Ser.). 143p. 1981. pap. text ed. 6.50 (ISBN 0-201-04317-3). A-W.
Margolis, Clorinda & Shrier, Linda. A Manual of Stress Management. 1981. write for info. Franklin Inst Pr.
Monahan, Lynn H & Farmer, Richard E. Stress & the Police: A Manual for Prevention. LC 80-83671. 1981. pap. 7.95 (ISBN 0-913530-23-9). Palisades Pubs.
Moss, Leonard. Management Stress. (Occupational Stress Ser.). 224p. 1981. pap. text ed. 6.50 (ISBN 0-201-05050-1). A-W.
Nathan, Ronald G. & Charlesworth, Edward A. Stress Management: A Conceptual & Procedural Guide. (Illus.). 223p. (Orig.). 1980. pap. text ed. 19.95 (ISBN 0-938176-01-3). Biobehavioral Pr.
--Stress Management: A Conceptual & Procedural Guide. LC 80-70400. (Illus.). 223p. (Orig.). 1980. 19.95 (ISBN 0-938176-01-3). Wendover.
North, Barbara & Crittenden, Penelope. Anti-Stress Workbook. (Illus.). 79p. (Orig.). 1980. pap. 4.95 (ISBN 0-938480-00-6). Healthworks.
Tubesing, Donald A. Kicking Your Stress Habits: A Do-It-Yourself Guide for Coping with Stress. LC 80-54046. (Orig.). 1981. pap. 10.00 (ISBN 0-938586-00-9). Whole Person.
Van Dijkhuizen, N. From Stressors to Strains: Research into Their Interrelationships. xii, 292p. 1980. pap. text ed. 27.75 (ISBN 90-265-0351-2). Swets North Am.
Veninga, Robert L. & Spradley, James P. The Work-Stress Connection: How to Cope with Job Burnout. 348p. 1981. 12.95 (ISBN 0-316-80747-8). Little.

STRESSES
see Strains and Stresses

STRIKES AND LOCKOUTS
Here are entered works of strikes and lockouts in general. Individual strikes limited in extent to one city or county are entered under the place. Individual strikes of wider extent are entered under their generally accepted name. A strike against a single employer is entered under the name of the employer.
see also Arbitration, Industrial; Collective Bargaining; Trade-Unions
also names of strikes, e.g. Steel Strikes, 1919-1920
Conlin, Joseph R., ed. At the Point of Production: The Local History of the I.W.W. LC 80-1708. (Contributions in Labor History Ser.: No. 10). 328p. 1981. lib. bdg. 29.95 (ISBN 0-313-22046-8, CPP/). Greenwood.
Cooke, Frederick H. The Law of Trade & Labor Combinations As Applicable to Boycotts, Strikes, Trade Conspiracies, Monopolies, Pools, Trusts, & Kindred Topics. xxv, 214p. 1981. Repr. of 1898 ed. lib. bdg. 24.00x (ISBN 0-8377-0430-8). Rothman.

STRIKES AND LOCKOUTS-CIVIL SERVICE
Aboud, Antone & Aboud, Grace S. Right to Strike in Public Employment. (Key Issues Ser.: No. 15). 1974. pap. 2.00 (ISBN 0-87546-201-4). NY Sch Indus Rel.

STRINDBERG, AUGUST, 1849-1912
Strindberg, August. The Chamber Plays. 2nd, rev. ed. Sprinchorn, Evert, et al, trs. from Swedish. 288p. 1981. 15.00 (ISBN 0-8166-1028-2); pap. 6.95 (ISBN 0-8166-1031-2). U of Minn Pr.

STRING QUARTETS-ANALYTICAL GUIDES
Lam, Basil. Beethoven String Quartets, 2 vols. Incl. Vol. 1. (BBC Music Guides Ser.: No. 32). 64p. pap. (ISBN 0-295-95423-X); Vol. 2. (BBC Music Guides Ser.: No. 33). 64p. pap. (ISBN 0-295-95424-8). LC 75-5008. (Illus.). 1975. pap. 1.95 ea. U of Wash Pr.

STRINGED INSTRUMENTS
Here is entered material on instruments employing strings, whether bowed, hammered or plucked.
Lamb, Norman. Guide to Teaching Strings. 3rd ed. (Instrumental Technique Ser.). 225p. 1980. pap. text ed. 7.95 (ISBN 0-697-03603-0). Wm C Brown.

STRIP MINING
Strip-Mineable Coals Guidebook. LC 80-81269. 1980. 103.00. Minobras.

STRIPED BASS
Bennett, D. W. Secrets of Striped Bass Fishing. (N. E. Fishing Ser.). (Illus.). 70p. (Orig.). 1981. pap. 6.95 (ISBN 0-88839-103-X). Hancock Hse.

STROKE PATIENTS
Ancowitz, Arthur M. Strokes & Their Prevention. (Orig.). pap. 2.75 (ISBN 0-515-05723-1). Jove Pubns.
Broida, Helen. Coping with Stroke. LC 79-220. 136p. 1979. text ed. 14.95 (ISBN 0-933014-50-3). College-Hill.
Lubic, Lowell G. & Palkovitz, Harry P. Stroke. (Discussions in Patient Management Ser.). 1979. pap. 9.50 (ISBN 0-87488-893-X). Med Exam.

STRUCTURAL ANALYSIS (MATHEMATICS)
see Lattice Theory

STRUCTURAL DESIGN
see also Building; Strains and Stresses; Strength of Materials
also names of specific structures, with or without the subdivision Design, or Design and Construction, e.g. Bridges; Factories-Design and Construction
Cowan, Henry J. Structural System. (Illus.). 356p. 1981. price not set (ISBN 0-442-21714-5); pap. price not set (ISBN 0-442-21713-7). Van Nos Reinhold.
Lenoe, Edward M., et al, eds. Fibrous Composites in Structural Design. 900p. 1980. 85.00 (ISBN 0-306-40354-4). Plenum Pub.

STRUCTURAL DYNAMICS
see also Earthquakes and Building
Meirovitch, Leonard. Computational Methods in Structural Dynamics. (Mechanics: Dynamical Systems Ser.: No. 4). 450p. 1980. 35.00x (ISBN 90-286-0580-0). Sijthoff & Noordhoff.
Smith, George V., ed. Material-Environment Interactions in Structural & Pressure Containment Service. (MPC: No. 15). 160p. 1980. 30.00 (G00188). ASME.

STRUCTURAL ENGINEERING
see also Foundations; Hydraulic Engineering; Soil Mechanics; Structures, Theory Of
also specific kinds of structures, e.g. Bridges, Buildings; specific structural forms, e.g. Girders; specific systems of construction, e.g. Buildings, Iron and Steel
Cook, Robert D. Concepts & Applications of Finite Element Analysis. 2nd ed. 576p. 1981. text ed. 31.95 (ISBN 0-471-03050-3); price not set tchr's ed (ISBN 0-471-08200-7). Wiley.
Dickinson, Brian. Developing Structured Systems: A Methodology Using Structured Techniques. LC 80-54609. (Illus.). 392p. 1981. 45.00 (ISBN 0-917072-23-5). Yourdon.
Ferguson, Phil M. Reinforced Concrete Fundamentals: SI Version. 4th ed. 736p. 1981. text ed. 28.95 (ISBN 0-471-05897-1). Wiley.
Gjelsvik, Atle. The Theory of Thin Walled Bars. 272p. 1981. 27.95 (ISBN 0-471-08594-4, Pub. by Wiley-Interscience). Wiley.
Gokhfeld, D. A. & Cherniavsky, O. F. Limit Analysis of Structures at Thermal Cycling. (Mechanics of Plastic Solids Ser.: No. 4). 576p. 1980. 110.00x (ISBN 90-286-0455-3). Sijthoff & Noordhoff.
Irvine, H. M. Cable Structures. (Illus.). 304p. 1981. text ed. 50.00x (ISBN 0-686-69224-1). MIT Pr.
Lauer, Kenneth R. Structural Engineering for Architects. (Illus.). 672p. 1981. text ed. 25.95 (ISBN 0-07-036622-5, C). McGraw.
Nichols, R. W., ed. Non-Destructive Examination in Relation to Structural Integrity. (Illus.). x, 286p. 1980. 60.00x (ISBN 0-85334-908-8). Burgess-Intl Ideas.
Schild, Erich, et al. Structural Failure in Residential Buildings, 3 vols. Incl. Vol. 1. Flat Roofs, Roof Terraces & Balconies. 24.50x (ISBN 0-470-26305-9); Vol. 2. External Walls & Openings. 27.95x (ISBN 0-470-26789-5); Vol. 3. 154p. 29.95x (ISBN 0-470-26846-8). LC 77-28647. 1978-80. Set. 85.85x (ISBN 0-470-26898-0). Halsted Pr.
Tuma, Jan J. & Reddy, M. N. Schaum's Outline of Space Structural Analysis. (Illus.). 272p. 1981. pap. 8.95 (ISBN 0-07-065432-8). McGraw.

STRUCTURAL FRAMES-VIBRATION
see Structural Dynamics

STRUCTURAL GEOLOGY
see Geology, Structural

STRUCTURAL MATERIALS
see Building Materials

STRUCTURAL SHELLS
see Shells (Engineering)

STRUCTURAL STABILITY
Smolira, M. Analysis of Structures by the Force-Displacement Method. xii, 389p. 1980. 62.50 (ISBN 0-85334-814-6, Pub. by Applied Science). Burgess-Intl Ideas.

STRUCTURAL STEEL
see Steel, Structural

STRUCTURALISM
Lodge, David. Working with Structuralism: Essays & Reviews on Nineteenth & Twentieth-Century Literature. 240p. 1981. 30.00 (ISBN 0-7100-0658-6). Routledge & Kegan.
Williams, Christopher. Origins of Form. (Illus.). 160p. (Orig.). 1980. pap. 12.00 (ISBN 0-8038-5394-7). Hastings.

STRUCTURE, CHEMICAL
see Chemical Structure

STRUCTURE, MOLECULAR
see Molecular Structure

STRUCTURE (PHILOSOPHY)
see Structuralism

STRUCTURES, ENGINEERING OF
see Structural Engineering

STRUCTURES, OFFSHORE
see Offshore Structures

STRUCTURES, SEDIMENTARY
see Sedimentary Structures

STRUCTURES, THEORY OF
see also Shells (Engineering); Strains and Stresses; Strength of Materials; Structural Design; Structural Engineering; Structural Stability
Kanchi, M. B. Matrix Methods of Structural Analysis. LC 80-18442. 432p. 1981. 17.95 (ISBN 0-470-26945-6). Halsted Pr.
Smith, M. J. Materials & Structures. 2nd ed. (Illus.). 180p. 1980. pap. text ed. 13.95x (ISBN 0-7114-5639-9). Intl Ideas.

STRUCTURES, THEORY OF-DATA PROCESSING
Popkin, Gary S. Introductory Structured COBOL Programming. 496p. 1981. text ed. 18.95 (ISBN 0-442-26771-1). Van Nos Reinhold.

STUART, JESSE, 1907-
Spurlock, John H. He Sings for Us: A Sociolinguistic Analysis of the Appalachian Subculture & of Jesse Stuart As a Major American Author. LC 80-8297. (Illus.). 190p. 1980. lib. bdg. 16.50 (ISBN 0-8191-1271-2); pap. text ed. 8.75 (ISBN 0-8191-1272-0). U Pr of Amer.

STUD FARMS
see Horse Breeding

STUDENT ADJUSTMENT
Mitchell, Scott C. SuperStudent! The Student's High School Handbook. rev. ed. LC 80-84049. (Illus.). 112p. (gr. 9-12). 1981. pap. text ed. 4.95 (ISBN 0-938494-00-7). Kingsfield.

STUDENT ENROLLMENT
see School Attendance

STUDENT EXPENDITURES
see College Costs

STUDENT GUIDANCE
see Personnel Service in Education; Vocational Guidance

STUDENT LIFE AND CUSTOMS
see Students

STUDENT MOVEMENT
see Youth Movement

STUDENT-TEACHER RELATIONSHIPS
see Teacher-Student Relationships

STUDENT TEACHING
see also Interns (Education)
Hevener, Fillmer, Jr. Successful Student Teaching: A Handbook for Elementary & Secondary Student Teachers. LC 80-69332. 125p. 1981. perfect bdg. 8.95 (ISBN 0-86548-040-0). Century Twenty One.
Meyer, D. Eugene. The Student Teacher on the Firing Line. LC 80-69236. 135p. 1981. perfect bdg. 11.95 (ISBN 0-86548-048-6). Century Twenty One.
Olaitan, Samson O. & Augusiobo, Obiora N. Handbook of Practice Teaching. LC 80-40291. 192p. 1981. write for info. (ISBN 0-471-27805-X, Pub. by Wiley-Interscience); pap. write for info. (ISBN 0-471-27804-1). Wiley.

STUDENT TRANSPORTATION
see School Children-Transportation

STUDENTS
see also College Students; Pregnant Schoolgirls
also headings beginning with College or School, e.g. College, Choice of; School Sports; Transfer Students
Brophy, Jere, et al. Student Characteristics & Teaching. (Professional Ser.). 224p. 1981. text ed. 22.50 (ISBN 0-582-28152-0). Longman.
Epstein, Joyce L., ed. The Quality of School Life. LC 80-5350. 1980. write for info. (ISBN 0-669-03869-5). Lexington Bks.

STUDENTS-GRADING AND MARKING
see Grading and Marking (Students)

STUDENTS-PERSONNEL WORK
see Personnel Service in Education

STUDENTS, INTERCHANGE OF
Cohen, Gail A., ed. The Learning Traveler: Vacation Study Abroad, Vol. 2. rev. ed. 186p. 1981. pap. text ed. 8.00 (ISBN 0-87206-107-8). Inst Intl Educ.

STUDY, COURSES OF
see Education-Curricula

STUDY, INDEPENDENT
see Independent Study

STUDY, METHOD OF
see also College Student Orientation; Independent Study; Note-Taking; Self-Culture
also subdivision Study and Teaching under particular subjects, e.g. Art-Study and Teaching
Fenton, Norman. Self-Direction & Adjustment. 121p. 1980. Repr. of 1926 ed. lib. bdg. 22.50 (ISBN 0-89760-225-0). Telegraph Bks.
Hill. Principless of Learning. 1981. 7.95 (ISBN 0-88284-123-8). Alfred Pub.
Karlins, Marvin. The Other Way to Better Grades. 168p. (Orig.). 1981. pap. 4.95 (ISBN 0-449-90046-0, Columbine). Fawcett.
Phipps, Rita. The Successful Student's Handbook: A Step-by-Step Guide to Study Skills. LC 80-54427. (Illus.). 160p. (Orig.). 1981. pap. price not set (ISBN 0-295-95813-8). U of Wash Pr.
Powell, James D. & Kelley, C. Aron. Students Resource Manual: Hicks-Gullett Management of Organization. th ed. 368p. Date not set. text ed. price not set (ISBN 0-07-028777-5). McGraw.

Rich, Dale. How You Can Get Straight A's in College by Beating the System. 123p. (Orig.). 1981. 9.95 (ISBN 0-89896-099-1). Larksdale.

Study Skills Workshop Kit Level I. (gr. 5-9). 1980. pap. 9.95 (ISBN 0-88210-112-9). Natl Assn Principals.

Study Skills Workshop Kit Level II. (gr. 8-10). 1979. pap. 9.95 (ISBN -088210-113-7). Natl Assn Principals.

STUNT MEN

Miklowitz, Gloria D. Movie Stunts & the People Who Do Them. LC 80-7984. (Illus.). 64p. (gr. 4-6). 1980. pap. 3.95 (ISBN 0-15-256039-4, VoyB). HarBraceJ.

STUTTERING

Irwin, Ann. Successful Treatment of Stuttering. 1981. 9.95 (ISBN 0-8027-0671-1). Walker & Co.

Rockey, Denyse. Speech Disorder in Nineteenth Century Britain: The History of Stuttering. 280p. 1980. 50.00x (ISBN 0-85664-809-4, Pub. by Croom Helm Ltd England). Biblio Dist.

STYLE, LEGAL

see Law–Language

STYLE, LITERARY

see also Criticism; Letter-Writing; Literature–Esthetics; Literature–History and Criticism; Rhetoric also subdivision Style under names of languages, e.g. English Language–Style

Murry, John M. The Problem of Style. LC 80-21463. x, 133p. 1980. Repr. of 1960 ed. lib. bdg. 19.50x (ISBN 0-313-22523-0, MUPR). Greenwood.

STYLE IN DRESS

see Costume; Fashion

STYLE MANUALS (AUTHORSHIP)

see Authorship–Handbooks, Manuals, Etc.

STYLE MANUALS (JOURNALISM)

see Journalism–Handbooks, Manuals, Etc.

STYPTICS

see Hemostatics

SUAHELI LANGUAGE

see Swahili Language

SUBJECT CATALOGS

see Catalogs, Subject

SUBJECT CATALOGING, AUTOMATIC

see Automatic Indexing

SUBJECT DICTIONARIES

see Encyclopedias and Dictionaries

SUBJECT HEADINGS

see also Automatic Indexing; Catalogs, Subject; Classification–Books

Wilson, T. D. An Introduction to Chain Indexing. (Library & Information Science Ser.). 107p. 1971. 11.00 (ISBN 0-208-01069-6, Linnet). Shoe String.

SUBMANDIBULAR GLAND

see Salivary Glands

SUBMARINE EXPLORATION

see Underwater Exploration

SUBMARINE GEOLOGY

see also Marine Sediments; Plate Tectonics; Sedimentation and Deposition

Boillot, G. Geology of the Continental Margins. Scarth, Alwyn, tr. from Fr. (Illus.). 160p. 1981. pap. text ed. 14.50 (ISBN 0-582-30036-3). Longman.

SUBMARINE RESEARCH STATIONS, MANNED

see Manned Undersea Research Stations

SUBMARINES

see also Sonar

Beaver, Paul. U-Boats in the Atlantic: World War Two Photo Album. (Illus.). 96p. 1981. pap. 5.95 (ISBN 0-89404-057-X). Aztex.

Datz, I. Mortimer. Power Transmission & Automation for Ships & Submersibles. (Illus.). 190p. 30.00 (ISBN 0-85238-074-7, FN). Unipub.

SUBMAXILLARY GLAND

see Salivary Glands

SUBMINIATURE ELECTRONIC EQUIPMENT

see Miniature Electronic Equipment

SUBSIDIES

Loiry, William S. Winning with Science: Source Book of Grants, Prizes & Awards for Science Competition. (Illus.). 224p. 1981. 11.95 (ISBN 0-87460-355-2). Lion.

SUBSOIL RIGHTS

see Mining Law

SUBSONIC AERODYNAMICS

see Aerodynamics

SUBSTITUTIONS

see Groups, Theory Of

SUBSURFACE CONSTRUCTION

see Underground Construction

SUBTERRANEAN CONSTRUCTION

see Underground Construction

SUBTERRANEAN WATER

see Water, Underground

SUBTRACTION

Lutgendorf, Philip. Addition & Subtraction. LC 79-730038. (Illus.). 1978. pap. text ed. 99.00 (ISBN 0-89290-092-X, A508-SATC). Soc for Visual.

SUBURBAN LIFE

Sussman, Vic. Never Kiss a Goat on the Lips: Tales of a Suburban Homesteader. Stoner, Carol, ed. (Illus.). 288p. 1981. 12.95 (ISBN 0-87857-346-1); pap. 8.95 (ISBN 0-87857-347-X). Rodale Pr Inc.

SUBURBS

see also Suburban Life

Miller, Zane L. Suburb: Neighborhood & Community in Forest Park, Ohio, 1935-1976. LC 80-21828. (Twentieth-Century America Ser.). 256p. 1981. 18.50x (ISBN 0-87049-289-6). U of Tenn Pr.

Muller, Peter O. Contemporary Suburban America. (Illus.). 240p. 1981. pap. 9.95 (ISBN 0-13-170647-0). P-H.

SUBVENTIONS

see Subsidies

SUBWAYS

Steiner, Bradley J. Subway Survival: The Art of Self Defense on American Public Transit Facility. 1980. pap. 7.95. Loompanics.

SUCCESS

see also Academic Achievement; Applications for Positions; Business; Charm; Conduct of Life; Failure (Psychology); Saving and Thrift; Self-Realization

Boddy, Michael & Beckett, Richard. Surviving in the Eighties. (Illus.). 192p. (Orig.). 1980. text ed. 28.50 (ISBN 0-86861-106-9, 2515); pap. text ed. 14.95 (ISBN 0-86861-114-X, 2516). Allen Unwin.

Bolles, R. N. What Color Is Your Parachute? 1981 Ed. (Illus.). 1981. 14.95 (ISBN 0-89815-047-7); pap. 6.95 (ISBN 0-89815-046-9). Ten Speed Pr.

Brownstone, David M. Sell Your Way to Success. 224p. 1981. 12.95 (ISBN 0-471-09257-6); pap. 7.95 (ISBN 0-471-09242-8). Wiley.

Chan, K. C. More Precious Than Rubies. 1981. 8.95 (ISBN 0-533-04287-9). Vantage.

Charell, Ralph. How to Make Things Go Your Way. 192p. 1981. pap. 4.95 (ISBN 0-346-12518-9). Cornerstone.

Charrell, Ralph. The Magic of Thinking Rich. 11.95 (ISBN 0-671-42376-2). S&S.

Davis, Creath, tr. Victoria En la Crisis. (Spanish Bks.). (Span.). 1977. 1.95 (ISBN 0-8297-0785-9). Vida Pub.

De Vos, Richard. Believe! 1981. pap. price not set (ISBN 0-671-41757-6). PB.

Edwards, John F. How to Quit the Rat Race - Successfully! LC 80-82676. (Illus.). 159p. (Orig.). 1981. 9.95 (ISBN 0-937590-00-2, Dist. by Caroline Hse.); pap. 5.95 (ISBN 0-937590-01-0). New Era.

--How to Quit the Rat Race-Successfully. 1981. 9.95 (ISBN 0-937590-00-2). pap. 5.95 (ISBN 0-937590-01-0). Green Hill.

Faussig, F. W. Psychology of Inventors & Money-Makers. (Illus.). 103p. 1981. 43.25 (ISBN 0-89920-020-6). Am Inst Psych.

Feltner, C. E., Jr. Winning Is Everything--Losing Is Nothing! LC 80-68579. 200p. 1981. 9.95 (ISBN 0-87754-066-7). Chelsea Hse.

Fine, Linda. How to Make the Most of the New You. 224p. 1981. 10.95 (ISBN 0-668-04919-7); pap. 6.95 (ISBN 0-668-04923-5). Arco.

Fromme, Allan. The Book for Normal Neurotics. 1981. 10.95 (ISBN 0-374-11544-3). FS&G.

Girard, Joe. How to Sell Yourself. 352p. 1981. pap. 5.95 (ISBN 0-446-97336-X). Warner Bks.

Gutridge, D. Foster, II. Your Secret Power: Creating Happiness, Vol. 2. (Your Secret Power Ser.). 96p. (Orig.). 1981. pap. 5.95 (ISBN 0-938014-02-1, 1001B). Freedom Unltd.

--Your Secret Power: Creating Riches, Vol. 1. LC 80-69710. (Your Secret Power Ser.). 80p. (Orig.). 1980. pap. 5.95 (ISBN 0-938014-01-3, 901A). Freedom Unltd.

Hafen, B., et al. Self Help Handbook. 1980. 14.95 (ISBN 0-13-803304-8); pap. 7.95 (ISBN 0-13-803296-3). P-H.

Haldane, Bernhard. How to Make a Habit of Success. 240p. 1981. pap. 2.50 (ISBN 0-446-91658-7). Warner Bks.

Heverly, Judith. Fratonizing in the Office: The Book the Boss Should Never Have. 1981. 8.95 (ISBN 0-87949-177-9). Ashley Bks.

Hicks, Tyler G. Starting Millionaire Success Kit. 2nd ed. 361p. 1981. pap. 99.50 (ISBN 0-914306-39-1). Intl Wealth.

--Zero Cash Success Techniques Kit. 2nd ed. 876p. 1981. pap. 99.50 (ISBN 0-914306-42-1). Intl Wealth.

Hill, Harold, tr. Comment Vaincre. (French Bks.). (Fr.). 1979. 1.75 (ISBN 0-8297-0814-6). Life Pubs Intl.

--Como Ser un Triunfador. (Spanish Bks.). (Span.). 1977. 1.90 (ISBN 0-8297-0750-6). Life Pubs Intl.

--Como Servencedor. (Portuguese Bks.). 1979. 1.40 (ISBN 0-8297-0824-3). Life Pubs Intl.

--Diez Pasos Para Alcanzar la Victoria. (Spanish Bks.). (Span.). 1978. 1.90 (ISBN 0-8297-0864-2). Life Pubs Intl.

--Pleine Victoire. (French Bks.). (Fr.). 1979. 1.95 (ISBN 0-8297-0942-8). Life Pubs Intl.

--Supreme Victorie. (French Bks.). (Fr.). 1979. 1.95 (ISBN 0-8297-0942-8). Life Pubs Intl.

Jaress, Michael F. Congratulations, You Made It... Again. (Illus.). 288p. (Orig.). 1981. pap. 6.95 (ISBN 0-938320-04-1). Comm Consultants.

Jayne, Fred E. How to Survive Hard Times. pap. 1.95 (ISBN 0-89036-146-0). Hawkes Pub Inc.

Jones, Charlie. Life Is Tremendous. 1981. pap. 2.25 (ISBN 0-8423-2184-5). Tyndale.

Keyon, Rosiam. Being & Alienation. LC 78-61109. 350p. 1981. 10.00 (ISBN 0-686-69333-7). Philos Lib.

LaHaye, Tim, tr. Como Vencer a Depressao. (Portuguese Bks.). 1979. 1.50 (ISBN 0-8297-0648-8). Life Pubs Intl.

--Como Vencer la Depresion. (Spanish Bks.). (Span.). 1978. 1.95 (ISBN 0-8297-0515-5). Life Pubs Intl.

Lake, Joe. What a Way to Go. 1980. 6.95 (ISBN 0-533-04440-5). Vantage.

Landers, Ann. The Ann Landers Encyclopedia A to Z. Date not set. 7.95 (ISBN 0-345-28892-0). Ballantine.

Larson, E. Richard. Sue Your Boss. 1981. 14.95 (ISBN 0-374-27161-5); pap. 6.95 (ISBN 0-374-51608-1). FS&G.

LeBaron, Charles. Gentle Vengeance. 1981. 12.95 (ISBN 0-399-90112-4). Marek.

Lowry, Albert J. How to Become Financially Successful by Owning Your Own Business. 1981. 11.95 (ISBN 0-671-41261-2). S&S.

McKeever, Jim. How You Can Be Prepared. 246p. (Orig.). 1980. 14.95 (ISBN 0-931608-12-0); pap. 12.95 (ISBN 0-931608-13-9). Alpha Omega.

Mallough, Don. You Can Manage Your Life: 16 Keys to Success. 96p. (Orig.). 1981. pap. 3.95 (ISBN 0-8010-6114-8). Baker Bk.

Margerison, Charles. How to Assess Your Managerial Style. 167p. 1981. 12.95 (ISBN 0-8144-5632-4). Am Mgmt.

Mason, Billy. Dollar Making Tips for Survival in the Eighties. 50p. (Orig.). 1981. lib. bdg. 9.95 (ISBN 0-686-28909-9). Kelso.

Miss Piggy. Miss Piggy's Guide to Life. LC 80-2708. (Illus.). 192p. 1981. 12.95 (ISBN 0-394-51912-4). Knopf.

Molloy, John T. Molloy's Live for Success. LC 80-2279. (Illus.). 288p. 1981. 11.95 (ISBN 0-688-00412-1). Morrow.

Moriarty, Larry. The Traveling Salesman: How to Find Answers for Lots of Things for Lots of People Especially Salesman. LC 81-50012. (Illus.). 200p. 1981. 14.95 (ISBN 0-939102-13-7). MLM Pubs.

Mukerjee. The Song of the Self Supreme. Date not set. pap. 7.95 (ISBN 0-913922-14-5). Dawn Horse Pr.

Palmer, Lynne. Prosperity Signs. (Orig.). 1981. pap. 3.25 (ISBN 0-440-17144-X). Dell.

Ramsey, Dan. One Hundred & One Successful Ways to Turn Weekends into Wealth. 216p. 1980. 10.95 (ISBN 0-13-634808-4, Parker). P-H.

Rathgeb, Marlene M. Success Signs. (Illus.). 224p. 1981. 10.95 (ISBN 0-312-77485-0); pap. 5.95 (ISBN 0-312-77486-9). St Martin.

Raudsepp, Eugene. Success & Failure. (Best Thoughts Ser.). (Illus.). 80p. (Orig.). 1981. pap. 2.50 (ISBN 0-8431-0390-6). Price Stern.

Raudsepp, Eugene & Yeager, Joseph C. How to Sell New Ideas: Your Company's & Your Own. (Illus.). 224p. 1981. 15.95 (ISBN 0-13-432427-7, Spec); pap. 6.95. P-H.

Ringer. Restoring the American Dream. 1981. pap. 2.95 (ISBN 0-449-24314-1). Fawcett.

Roalman, A. R. Investor Relations That Work. 148p. 1981. 34.95 (ISBN 0-8144-5620-0). Am Mgmt.

Rusher, William A. How to Win Arguments. LC 79-6874. 264p. 1981. 10.95 (ISBN 0-385-15255-8). Doubleday.

Scheele, Adele M. Skills for Success. 208p. 1981. pap. 2.95 (ISBN 0-345-29484-X). Ballantine.

Schuller, Robert, tr. Pensamento Da Possiblilidade, O. (Portugese Bks.). (Port.). 1979. 1.50 (ISBN 0-8297-0727-1). Life Pubs Intl.

--Seras Lo Que Quieras Ser. (Spanish Bks.). (Span.). 1978. 1.90 (ISBN 0-8297-0514-7). Life Pubs Intl.

Schuller, Robert H. Discover How Life Can Be Beautiful. (Orig.). 1978. pap. 1.25 (ISBN 0-89081-153-9). Harvest Hse.

--Discover How to Bloom Where You Are Planted. 1978. pap. 1.25 (ISBN 0-89081-154-7). Harvest Hse.

--Discover the Power for Overcoming Defeat. (Orig.). 1978. pap. 1.25 (ISBN 0-89081-141-5). Harvest Hse.

--Discover Your Possibilities. (Orig.). 1980. pap. 2.25 (ISBN 0-89081-214-4). Harvest Hse.

Schulman, Janet. The Great Big Dummy. (gr. k-6). Date not set. pap. price not set (ISBN 0-440-43072-0, YB). Dell.

Sherman, Harold & Pollard, Al. Extra Success Potential: The Art of Out-Thinking & Out-Sensing Others in Business & Everyday Life. 200p. 1981. pap. 5.95 (ISBN 0-13-298109-2). P-H.

Shinn, George. The Miracle of Motivation. 1981. text ed. 8.95 (ISBN 0-8423-4353-9). Tyndale.

Siegel, Eli. Self & World. LC 75-44647. 1981. pap. price not set (ISBN 0-910492-27-1); text ed. price not set (ISBN 0-910492-28-X). Definition.

Smith, Don P. Page Systems. (Illus.). 1976. pap. 3.00 (ISBN 0-937514-08-X, New Era). World Merch Import.

Steiner, Claude. The Other Side of Power. LC 80-8921. 192p. 1981. 16.50 (ISBN 0-394-51950-7, Ever); pap. 6.95 (ISBN 0-394-17926-9). Grove.

Stewart, Don. Miracle Success. 1980. pap. text ed. 2.95 (ISBN 0-88270-484-2). Logos.

Tack, Alfred. Sell Your Way to Success. 6th ed. 256p. 1978. pap. 13.50x (ISBN 0-220-66366-1, Pub. by Busn Bks England). Renouf.

Thomas, Virginia R. Flying with Broken Wings. Date not set. 6.95 (ISBN 0-533-04791-9). Vantage.

Uris, Auren. Over Fifty: The Definitive Guide to the Best Years of Your Life. 624p. 1981. pap. 9.95 (ISBN 0-553-01297-5). Bantam.

Vajpeyi, Kailash. The Science of Mantras: A Manual of Happiness & Prosperity. 128p. 1980. 13.50 (ISBN 0-391-02213-X). Humanities.

VanCaspel, Venita. To Win the Money Game. 1980. pap. 1.50 (ISBN 0-8359-8692-6). Reston.

Vice, Fred H. The Armchair Millionaire. 120p. (Orig.). pap. 7.95 (ISBN 0-87364-204-X). Paladin Ent.

Walters, Dottie, ed. The Pearl of Potentiality. LC 79-91548. 296p. 1980. 11.95 (ISBN 0-8119-0338-9, Pub. by Royal CBC). Fell.

--Success Secrets of Successful Women. LC 78-68596. (Illus.). 276p. 1978. 11.95 (ISBN 0-8119-0339-7, Pub. by Royal CBC). Fell.

Williams, Sunnie. The Nomie Book: Growing up from Shy. (Illus.). 104p. (Orig.). (gr. 3-6). 1981. pap. 5.95 (ISBN 0-9605444-0-2). Wee Smile.

Young, Ellin. Help Yourself to Understand Nineteen Eighty-One. 1980. pap. 2.95 (ISBN 0-87728-512-8). Weiser.

SUCCESSION TAXES

see Inheritance and Transfer Tax

SUCCULENT PLANTS

see also Cactus; Sedum

Barkuizen, B. The Succulents of Southern Africa. 1980. 60.00x (Pub. by Bailey & Swinton South Africa). State Mutual Bk.

SUDAN

Worrall, Nick. Sudan. (Illus.). 136p. 1980. 30.00 (ISBN 0-7043-2242-0, Pub. by Quqrtet England). Horizon.

SUDAN (REGION)–HISTORY

Santi, Paul & Hill, Richard, eds. The Europeans in the Sudan Eighteen Thirty Four to Eighteen Seventy Eight. (Illus.). 352p. 1980. 45.00 (ISBN 0-19-822718-3). Oxford U Pr.

SUFFERING

see also Consolation; Good and Evil; Joy and Sorrow; Loneliness; Martyrdom; Pain

Schemmer, Kenneth E. Between Faith & Tears. 1981. pap. 3.95 (ISBN 0-8407-5770-0). Nelson.

SUFISM

see also Dervishes

Corbin, Henry. Creative Imagination in the Sufism of Ibn 'arabi. LC 68-20869. (Bollingen Ser.: XCI). (Illus.). 420p. 1980. pap. 6.95 (ISBN 0-691-01828-6). Princeton U Pr.

SUFISM–POETRY

Shah, Idries. Learning How to Learn: Psychology & Spirituality in the Sufi Way. LC 80-8892. 304p. 1981. pap. 6.95 (ISBN 0-06-067255-2). Har-Row.

SUGAR–MANUFACTURE AND REFINING

Small-Scale Cane Sugar Processing & Residue Utilization. (FAO Agricultural Services Bulletin: No. 19). 56p. 1981. pap. 6.00 (ISBN 92-5-100935-X, F2069, FAO). Unipub.

SUGAR–MANUFACTURING AND REFINING–INDIA

Baviskar, B. S. The Politics of Development: Sugar Cooperatives in Rural Maharashtra. (Illus.). 240p. 1981. 18.95 (ISBN 0-19-561206-X). Oxford U Pr.

SUGAR-CANE

Small-Scale Cane Sugar Processing & Residue Utilization. (FAO Agricultural Services Bulletin: No. 19). 56p. 1981. pap. 6.00 (ISBN 92-5-100935-X, F2069, FAO). Unipub.

SUGAR-FREE DIET

see also Cookery for Diabetics

Martinez, Pam. Sugarless Cooking. 5.95 (ISBN 0-934230-05-6). Green Hill.

SUGAR GROWING

see also Sugar–Manufacture and Refining; Sugar-Cane

Baviskar, B. S. The Politics of Development: Sugar Cooperatives in Rural Maharashtra. (Illus.). 240p. 1981. 18.95 (ISBN 0-19-561206-X). Oxford U Pr.

SUGAR-REFINING

see Sugar–Manufacture and Refining

SUICIDE

Farmer, R. D. & Hirsch, S. R., eds. The Suicide Syndrome. 272p. 1980. 40.00x (ISBN 0-85664-868-X, Pub. by Croom Helm England). State Mutual Bk.

Giovacchini, Peter. The Urge to Die: Why Young People Commit Suicide. LC 80-24435. 256p. 1981. 12.95 (ISBN 0-02-543440-3). Macmillan.

Madison, Arnold. Suicide & Young People. 144p. (gr. 6 up). 1981. pap. 3.95 (ISBN 0-686-69043-5, Clarion). HM.

Maris, Ronald W. Pathways to Suicide: A Survey of Self-Destructive Behaviors. LC 80-24520. (Illus.). 512p. 1981. text ed. 26.50x (ISBN 0-8018-2437-0). Johns Hopkins.

Reynolds, David K. & Farberow, Norman L. The Family Shadow: Sources of Suicide & Schizophrenia. 188p. 1981. 14.95 (ISBN 0-520-04213-1). U of Cal Pr.

Wallace, Samuel E. & Eser, Albin, eds. Suicide & Euthanasia: The Rights of Personhood. LC 80-28799. 176p. 1981. 12.50x (ISBN 0-87049-299-3). U of Tenn Pr.

SULKY RACING

see Harness Racing

SULLIVAN, ARTHUR SEYMOUR, SIR, 1842-1900

Dunhill, Thomas F. Sullivan's Comic Operas: A Critical Appreciation. (Music Ser.). 256p. 1981. Repr. of 1928 ed. lib. bdg. 25.00 (ISBN 0-306-76080-0). Da Capo.

SULPHUR

see also Organosulphur Compounds

An Atlas of Sulphur Deficiency in Commercial Plants. 18p. 1978. pap. 5.00 (ISBN 0-643-00210-3, CO03, CSIRO). Unipub.

Bothe, H. & Trebst, A., eds. Biochemistry & Physiology of Nitrogen & Sulfur Metabolism. (Proceedings in Life Sciences Ser.). (Illus.). 370p. 1981. 49.80 (ISBN 0-387-10486-0). Springer-Verlag.
Business Communications Co. Sulfur Specialty Chemicals, C-031. 1981. 850.00 (ISBN 0-89336-272-7). BCC.
Ellison, S. P., Jr. Sulfur in Texas. (Illus.). 1971. 2.00 (HB 2). Bur Econ Geology.
Stirling, C. J. The Chemistry of Sulphoniom Group, Part 2. (Chemistry of Functional Group Ser.). 1400p. 1981. 130.00 (ISBN 0-471-27770-3, Pub.by Wiley-Interscience); Set. 240.00 (ISBN 0-471-27655-3). Wiley.

SULPHUR ORGANIC COMPOUNDS
see Organosulphur Compounds

SUMATRA
Reid, Anthony. The Blood of the People: Revolution & the End of Traditional Rule in Northern Sumatra. (Illus.). 308p. 1979. text ed. 34.50x (ISBN 0-19-580399-X). Oxford U Pr.

SUMERIAN LANGUAGE–TEXTS
Heimerdinger, J. Sumerian Literary Fragments from Nippur. (Occasional Pubns. of the Babylonian Fund Ser.: Vol. 4). 1980. 20.00 (ISBN 0-934718-31-8). Univ Mus of U PA.

SUMIE
Aubrey, Vickey. Chinese Brush Painting for Children. (Illus.). 32p. (gr. 2 up). 1981. 9.95 (ISBN 0-8149-0851-9). Vanguard.
Rosenfield, John M., ed. Song of the Brush: Japanese Paintings from the Sanso Collection. (Illus.). 87p. 1979. text ed. 22.95 (ISBN 0-932216-02-1); pap. text ed. 14.95 (ISBN 0-932216-03-X). Seattle Art.

SUMMER–JUVENILE LITERATURE
Allington, Richard L. & Krull, Kathleen. Summer. LC 80-25097. (Beginning to Learn About Ser.). (Illus.). 32p. (gr. k-2). 1981. PLB 9.65 (ISBN 0-8172-1341-4). Raintree Child.

SUMMER CAMPS
see Camps

SUN
see also Solar Activity; Solar Radiation; Solar System; Spectrum Analysis; Sun-Spots
also names of solar instruments
Lunar & Planetary Institute, ed. The Ancient Sun: Proceedings of the Conference on the Ancient Sun: Fossil Record in the Earth, Moon & Meteorites, Boulder Colorado, October 16-19, 1979. LC 80-20084. (Geochimica & Cosmochimica Acta: Suppl. 13). 500p. 1980. 56.00 (ISBN 0-08-026324-0). Pergamon.

SUN DECKS (ARCHITECTURE)
see Decks (Architecture, Domestic)

SUN-DIALS
Stoneman, Milton. Easy to Make Wooden Sundials: Instructions & Plans for Five Projects. (Illus.). 64p. (Orig.). 1981. pap. price not set (ISBN 0-486-24141-6). Dover.

SUN-SPOTS
Baer, Steve. Sunspots. write for info. (ISBN 0-88930-062-3); pap. write for info. (ISBN 0-88930-061-5). Zomeworks Corp.

SUN-WORSHIP
Smithsonian. Fire of Life: The Smithsonian Book of the Sun. (Illus.). 1981. 24.95 (ISBN 0-89599-006-7). Smithsonian Expo.

SUNDAY LEGISLATION
Harris, George E. A Treatise on Sunday Laws: The Sabbath–the Lord's Day, Its History & Observance, Civil & Criminal. xxiii, 338p. 1980. Repr. of 1892 ed. lib. bdg. 32.50x (ISBN 0-8377-2232-2). Rothman.

SUNDAY-SCHOOLS
see also Bible–Study; Religious Education
A Escola Dominical. (Portugese Bks.). (Port.). 1979. 1.45 (ISBN 0-8297-0799-9). Life Pubs Intl.
Williams, Ralph, tr. Escuela Dominical, Corazon De la Iglesia. (Spanish Bks.). 1979. 1.30 (ISBN 0-8297-0550-3). Life Pubs Intl.

SUNDAY-SCHOOLS–EXERCISES, RECITATIONS, ETC.
Fehl, James I., ed. Standard Lesson Commentary, 1981-1982: Twenty-Ninth Annual Edition. (Illus.). 456p. 1981. 6.95 (ISBN 0-87239-436-0, 74008); pap. 5.95 (ISBN 0-87239-435-2, 1982). Standard Pub.

SUNDAY-SCHOOLS–HISTORY
Shurden, Walter B. The Sunday School Board: Ninety Years of Service. (Orig.). 1981. soft cover 5.95 (ISBN 0-8054-6558-8). Broadman.
--The Sunday School Board: Ninety Years of Service. (Orig.). pap. 5.95 (ISBN 0-8054-6558-8). Broadman.

SUNKEN CITIES
see Cities and Towns, Ruined, Extinct, etc.

SUNKEN TREASURE
see Treasure-Trove

SUNSPOTS
see Sun-Spots

SUPERCONDUCTORS
Moon, F. C., ed. Mechanics of Superconducting Structures. (AMD: No. 41). 148p. 1980. 24.00 (G00174). ASME.
Suenaga, Masaki & Clark, Alan F., eds. Filamentary A-Fifteen Superconductors. (Cryogenic Materials Ser.). 385p. 1980. 45.00 (ISBN 0-306-40622-5). Plenum Pub.

SUPERIOR CHILDREN
see Gifted Children

SUPERMARKETS
Book Div. Research Staff. SN Distribution Study of Grocery Store Sales - 1981. 250p. 1981. pap. 30.00 (ISBN 0-87005-370-1). Fairchild.

SUPERNATURAL (THEOLOGY)
Korem, Danny & Meier, Paul. The Fakers: Exploding the Myths of the Supernatural. (Illus.). 1981. 8.95 (ISBN 0-8010-5431-1). Baker Bk.

SUPERNATURAL IN LITERATURE
see also Occultism in Literature
Tymn, Marshall B. Horror & Supernatural Literature. 320p. 1981. 22.50 (ISBN 0-8352-1341-2). Bowker.

SUPERREALISM
see Surrealism

SUPERSONICS
see Ultrasonics

SUPERSTITION
see also Alchemy; Animal Lore; Apparitions; Astrology; Demonology; Dreams; Errors, Popular; Fairies; Folk-Lore; Ghosts; Magic; Occult Sciences; Voodooism; Witchcraft
Ainsworth, Catherine H. Superstitions from Seven Towns of the United States. (Folklore Bks.). vi, 58p. 1980. 2.00 (ISBN 0-933190-00-X). Clyde Pr.
Hendricks, George D. Mirrors, Mice, & Mustaches. 110p. 1981. pap. 4.95 (ISBN 0-87074-075-X). SMU Press.
--Roosters, Rhymes, & Railroad Tracks. 200p. 1980. pap. 6.95 (ISBN 0-87074-177-2). SMU Press.
Robbins, R. H., ed. Sir Thomas Browne's Pseudodoxia Epidemica. (Oxford English Texts Ser.). (Illus.). 1000p. 1980. 129.00 (ISBN 0-19-812706-5). Oxford U Pr.

SUPERTANKERS
see Tankers

SUPERVISION OF EMPLOYEES
see also Supervision of Police Personnel; Supervisors
Eckles, Robert W. & Carmichael, Ronald L. Supervisory Management. (Management Ser.). 550p. 1981. text ed. 22.95 (ISBN 0-471-05947-1); tchrs.' ed. avail. (ISBN 0-471-08941-9). Wiley.
Rosenbaum, Bernard L., ed. How to Motivate Today's Workers: Motivational Models for Managers & Supervisors. (Illus.). 192p. 1981. 14.95 (ISBN 0-07-053711-9, P&RB). McGraw.

SUPERVISION OF POLICE PERSONNEL
Garner, Gerald W. Police Supervision: A Common Sense Approach. 296p. 1981. write for info. (ISBN 0-398-04127-X). C C Thomas.

SUPERVISORS
Bailey, Martha J. Supervisory & Middle Managers in Libraries. LC 80-23049. 218p. 1981. 12.00 (ISBN 0-8108-1400-5). Scarecrow.
Trojanowicz, R. Environment of the First Line Supervisors. 1980. 13.95 (ISBN 0-13-282848-0). P-H.

SUPERVISORS, POLICE
see Supervision of Police Personnel

SUPPLEMENTAL UNEMPLOYMENT BENEFITS
Becker, Joseph M. Unemployment Benefits: Should There Be a Compulsory Federal Standard? 1980. pap. 4.25 (ISBN 0-8447-3389-X). Am Enterprise.
Hamermesh, Daniel S. Unemployment: Insurance & the Older American. LC 80-18946. 117p. 1980. 4.00 (ISBN 0-911558-72-1). Upjohn Inst.

SUPPLEMENTARY EMPLOYMENT
Grimaldi, Paul L. Supplemental Security Income: New Federal Program Aged, Blind, & Disabled. 1980. pap. 5.25 (ISBN 0-8447-3356-3). Am Enterprise.

SUPPLY AND DEMAND
see also Competition; Consumption (Economics); Value
Hayes, Michael J. Lobbyists & Legislators: A Theory of Political Markets. 256p. 1981. 18.00 (ISBN 0-8135-0910-6). Rutgers U Pr.

SUPPORT (DOMESTIC RELATIONS)
see also Parent and Child (Law)
Kuchler, F. Law of Support. 3rd ed. 1980. 5.95 (ISBN 0-379-11135-7). Oceana.

SUPREMACY OF THE POPE
see Popes–Primacy

SURF
see Ocean Waves

SURF-BOATS
see Life-Boats

SURF RIDING
see Surfing

SURFACE ACTIVE AGENTS
Bluestein. Amphoteric Surfactants. Date not set. price not set (ISBN 0-8247-1277-3). Dekker.

SURFACE CHEMISTRY
see also Adsorption; Catalysis; Colloids
Kerker, Milton, ed. Colloid & Interface Science, Vols. 2-5. Incl. Vol. 2. Aerosols, Emulsions & Surfactants. 35.00 (ISBN 0-12-404502-2); Vol. 3. Adsorption, Catalysis, Solid Surfaces, Wetting, Surface Tension & Water. 37.50 (ISBN 0-12-404503-0); Vol. 4. Hydrosols & Rheology. 36.50 (ISBN 0-12-404504-9); Vol. 5. Biocolloids, Polymers, Monolayers, Membranes & General Papers. 36.50 (ISBN 0-12-404505-7). 1976. Set. 122.00. Acad Pr.
Landman, Uzi, ed. Aspects of the Kinetics & Dynamics of Surface Reactions. LC 80-68004. (AIP Conference Proceedings: No. 61). 343p. 1980. lib. bdg. 22.25 (ISBN 0-88318-160-6). Am Inst Physics.
Shaw, D. J. Introduction to Colloid & Surface Chemistry. 3rd ed. LC 80-49871. 256p. 1980. text ed. 14.95 (ISBN 0-408-71049-7). Butterworths.
Somorjai, Gabor A. Chemistry in Two Dimensions: Surfaces. LC 80-21443. (George Fisher Baker Non-Resident Lectureship in Chemistry at Cornell University Ser.). (Illus.). 552p. 1981. 48.50 (ISBN 0-8014-1179-3). Cornell U Pr.

SURFACE MINING
see Strip Mining

SURFACES
see also Coordinates; Geometry, Algebraic
Berkeley, R. C., et al. Microbial Adhesion to Surfaces. LC 80-41358. 600p. 1981. 110.00 (ISBN 0-470-27083-7). Halsted Pr.
Feuerbacher, B., et al. Photoemission & the Electronic Properties of Surfaces. 540p. 1978. 61.95 (ISBN 0-471-99555-X). Wiley.
Rohde, S. M. & Cheng, H. S., eds. Surface Roughness Effects in Hydrodymanic & Mixed Lubrication. 211p. 1980. 30.00 (G00193). ASME.

SURFACES (CHEMISTRY)
see Surface Chemistry

SURFACTANTS
see Surface Active Agents

SURFBOARD RIDING
see Surfing

SURFING
Shaw, Stephen M. & Brown, Aileen, eds. Surfboard: How to Build Surfboards & How to Surf. (Illus.). 1980. 8.00 (ISBN 0-912750-03-0). Transmedia.
Winner, Ken & Jones, Roger. Windsurfing with Ken Winner: A Complete Illustrated Guide to a Fast-Growing Sport. LC 80-8399. (Illus.). 136p. (Orig.). 1981. pap. 8.95 (ISBN 0-06-250971-3, CN 4007, CN). Har-Row.

SURGERY
see also Anesthetics; Artificial Organs; Blood–Transfusion; Children–Surgery; Dissection; Fractures; Hypnotism–Therapeutic Use; Microsurgery; Obstetrics–Surgery; Orthopedia; Orthopedic Surgery; Pathology, Surgical; Shock; Skin-Grafting; Transplantation of Organs, Tissues, etc.; Veterinary Surgery; Wounds
also subdivisions Surgery and Wounds and Injuries under names of organs and regions of the body, e.g. Abdomen–Surgery; Chest–Wounds and Injuries
Bosk, Charles L. Forgive & Remember: Managing Medical Failure. LC 78-16596. 248p. 1981. pap. 5.95 (ISBN 0-226-06680-0). U of Chicago Pr.
Caprini, Joseph A., et al. Gallstones. (Discussions in Surgical Management Ser.). 1979. pap. 10.50 (ISBN 0-87488-953-7). Med Exam.
Elliotson, John. Numerous Cases of Surgical Operations Without Pain in the Mesmeric State. Bd. with Mesmerism in India; Philosophy of Sleep. (Contributions to the History of Psychology Ser., Vol. X, Pt. A: Orientations). 1978. Repr. of 1843 ed. 30.00 (ISBN 0-89093-159-3). U Pubns Amer.
Karran, Stephen. Controversies in Surgical Sepsis. 350p. 1980. 38.50. Praeger.
Kra, Siegfried J. & Boltax, Robert S. Is Surgery Necessary. 256p. 1981. 10.95 (ISBN 0-02-566560-X). Macmillan.
Lee, Danise L. Surgery Without Fear. (Illus.). 48p. 1980. pap. 4.95 (ISBN 0-937210-00-5). Time-Lee Pubns.
Libig, Mark C. Surgical Technology: The 70's. 432p. 1981. text ed. 26.50 (ISBN 0-8403-2336-0). Kendall-Hunt.
McSwain, Norman, Jr. & Skelton, Mary B. Surgical Procedures in Emergency Medicine. 300p. 1982. text ed. 29.95 (ISBN 0-8359-7394-8). Reston.
Matsumoto, Teuro. Pre- & Postoperative Evaluation of Surgical Patients. 1979. pap. 15.50 (ISBN 0-87488-735-6). Med Exam.
Melluzzo, Paul J. & Nealon, Eleanor. Living with Surgery: Before & After. LC 80-51388. 320p. (Orig.). 1981. pap. 6.95 (ISBN 0-03-059081-7). HR&W.
--Living with Surgery: Before & After. rev. ed. LC 80-53188. 304p. 1980. pap. 6.95 (ISBN 0-7216-6261-7). Saunders.
Nikas, Diana L. Critical Neurological Surgical Assessment & Management: Contemporary Issues in Critical Care Nursing. (Vol. 2). (Illus.). 224p. 1981. lib. bdg. 20.00 (ISBN 0-443-08158-1). Churchill.
Nyhus, Lloyd M. Surgery Annual, 1981. (Surgery Annual Series). 1981. 27.00 (ISBN 0-8385-8715-1). ACC.
Nyhus, Lloyd M., ed. Surgery Annual 1980. (Surgery Annual Ser.). 512p. 1980. 33.50x (ISBN 0-8385-8713-5). ACC.
Ram, M. D., ed. Self-Assessment of Current Knowledge in Surgery. LC 80-18730. 1980. pap. 16.50 (ISBN 0-87488-223-0). Med Exam.
Rob, Charles & Smith, Rodney, eds. Atlas of General Surgery. LC 80-41016. (Operative Surgery Ser.). (Illus.). 786p. 1980. text ed. 59.95 (ISBN 0-407-00206-5). Butterworths.
Rutt. Surgery of the Leg & Foot. (Hackenbroch Ser.). 1980. text ed. write for info. (ISBN 0-7216-4446-5). Saunders.
Sigel, Bernard. Clinical Simulations in Surgery. Forman, Phillip M., ed. 352p. 1980. pap. 38.50 (ISBN 0-8385-1174-0). ACC.
Simmons, Richard. Surgical Infectious Disease. 1981. 65.00 (ISBN 0-8385-8729-1). ACC.
Stillman, Richard M. Surgery Review & Assessment: Tumor, Trauma, & Specialties. 1981. pap. 12.50 (ISBN 0-686-69608-5). ACC.
Stillman, Richard M. & Sawyer, Philip N. Surgical Resident's Manual. 192p. 1980. pap. 12.50x (ISBN 0-8385-8732-1). ACC.
Tucker. Surgery for Phonatory Disorders. 1981. text ed. write for info. (ISBN 0-443-08058-5). Churchill.

SURGERY–COMPLICATIONS AND SEQUELAE
Watts. Infection in Surgery: Basic & Clinical Aspects. 1981. text ed. 65.00 (ISBN 0-443-02246-1). Churchill.

SURGERY–HISTORY
Ravitch, Mark M. A Century of Surgery: History of the American Surgical Association, 2 vols. (Illus.). 1600p. 1981. Set. 195.00. Lippincott.

SURGERY–INSTRUMENTS
see Surgical Instruments and Apparatus

SURGERY–PSYCHOLOGICAL ASPECTS
Goen, Ted, Jr. Smile or I'll Kick Your Bed. (Illus.). 1981. 12.95 (ISBN 0-393-01433-9). Norton.
Goin, John M. & Goin, Maria K. Changing the Body: Psychological Effects of Plastic Surgery. 240p. 1981. write for info. soft cover (3630-0). Williams & Wilkins.
MacDonald, John A. Facing the Scalpel: What to Expect, What to Beware of When You Have an Operation. (Illus.). 144p. 1981. 10.95 (ISBN 0-13-299198-5); pap. 4.95 (ISBN 0-13-299180-2). P-H.

SURGERY–STUDY AND TEACHING
Burnett, William. Clinical Science for Surgeons. 1981. text ed. price not set (ISBN 0-407-00181-6). Butterworth.

SURGERY, COSMETIC
see Surgery, Plastic

SURGERY, DENTAL
see Dentistry; Dentistry, Operative

SURGERY, EXPERIMENTAL
see also Transplantation of Organs, Tissues, etc.
Castaing, D., et al. Hepatic & Portal Surgery in the Rat. (Illus.). 184p. 1980. 37.50 (ISBN 0-89352-101-9). Masson Pub.

SURGERY, PEDIATRIC
see Children–Surgery

SURGERY, PLASTIC
see also Harelip; Prosthesis; Skin-Grafting
American Society of Plastic & Reconstructive Surgeons & McDowell, Frank. The McDowell Series of Plastic Surgery Indexes: Nineteen Forty-Six to Nineteen Seventy-One the Great Index, Vol. Iv. (Illus.). 1168p. 1981. 225.00 (ISBN 0-686-69564-X, 5767-7). Williams & Wilkins.
Goin, John M. & Goin, Maria K. Changing the Body: Psychological Effects of Plastic Surgery. 240p. 1981. write for info. soft cover (3630-0). Williams & Wilkins.
Miller, Stephen H., et al. Practical Points in Plastic Surgery. LC 79-91201. 1980. pap. 20.00 (ISBN 0-87488-719-4). Med Exam.
Pirruccello, Frank W. Plastic & Reconstructive Surgery of the Face: Cosmetic Surgery. (Illus.). 200p. 1981. write for info. (6891-1). Williams & Wilkins.
Salisbury, Roger E. & Bevin, A. Griswold. Atlas of Reconstructive Burn Surgery. 1981. text ed. price not set (ISBN 0-7216-7903-X). Saunders.

SURGERY, STEREOTAXIC
see Stereoencephalotomy

SURGERY, VETERINARY
see Veterinary Surgery

SURGICAL INSTRUMENTS AND APPARATUS
see also Medical Instruments and Apparatus; Orthopedic Apparatus
also particular instruments
Anderson, Robert M. & Romfh, Richard F. Technique in the Use of Surgical Tools. 208p. 1980. 16.50 (ISBN 0-8385-8843-3). ACC.

SURGICAL NURSING
see also Postoperative Care
Aspinall, Mary Jo & Tanner, Christine. Experiences in Medical Surgical Nursing. 480p. 1981. pap. 14.95 (ISBN 0-8385-2481-8). ACC.
DeLoach, Jane E. General Surgical Nursing. (Nursing Outline Ser.). 1979. pap. 9.50 (ISBN 0-87488-393-8). Med Exam.
Donovan, Kathryn N. General Surgical Nursing Continuing Review. LC 80-81906. 1980. pap. 9.75 (ISBN 0-87488-318-0). Med Exam.
Steele, Bonnie G. Self-Assessment of Current Knowledge in General Surgical Nursing. 1978. spiral bdg. 9.50 (ISBN 0-87488-290-7). Med Exam.

SURGICAL PATHOLOGY
see Pathology, Surgical

SURGICAL SHOCK
see Shock

SURPLUS AGRICULTURAL COMMODITIES
see also Food Relief
Changes in Food Habits in Relation to Increase of Productivity. 370p. 1973. 13.75 (APO14, APO). Unipub.
Principles of Surplus Disposal & Consultative Obligations of Member Nations. 81p. 1981. pap. 6.00 (ISBN 92-5-100899-X, F2078, FAO). Unipub.

SURREALISM
see also Dadaism
Cawa, Mary A. A Metapoetic of the Passage: Architextures in Surrealiam & After. LC 80-54468. 192p. 1981. 12.00x (ISBN 0-87451-194-1). U Pr of New Eng.

SURVEYING
see also Cartography; Hydrographic Surveying

Bourne, William. A Booke Called the Treasure for Travellers. LC 77-25950. (English Experience Ser.: No. 911). 276p. 1979. Repr. of 1578 ed. lib. bdg. 26.00. Walter J Johnson.

Desch, H. E. Structural Surveying. 269p. 1970. 33.95 (ISBN 0-85264-167-2, Pub. by Griffin England). State Mutual Bk.

Dugdale, R. H. Surveying. 3rd ed. (Illus.). 224p. 1980. pap. text ed. 14.95x (ISBN 0-7114-5641-0). Intl Ideas.

Hobbs, F. D. & Doling, J. F. Planning for Engineers & Surveyors. LC 80-41553. (Illus.). 230p. 1980. 30.00 (ISBN 0-08-025459-4); pap. 15.00 (ISBN 0-08-025458-6). Pergamon.

Jackson, J. E. Sphere Spheroid & Projections for Surveyors: Aspects of Modern Land Surveying. LC 80-82507. 138p. 1980. 37.95 (ISBN 0-470-27044-6). Halsted Pr.

Lindeburg, Michael R. Surveying Law for the California Civil Professional Engineering Exam. (Engineering Review Manual Ser.). (Illus.). 154p. 1981. pap. 9.50 (ISBN 0-932276-26-1). Prof Engine.

Mikhail, Edward M. & Gracie, Gordon. Analysis & Adjustment of Survey Measurements. 368p. 1980. text ed. 28.50 (ISBN 0-442-25369-9). Van Nos Reinhold.

Norden, John. The Surveiors Dialogue...for All Men to Peruse, That Have to Do with the Revenues of Land, or the Manurance, Use or Occupation. Third Time Imprinted & Enlarged. LC 79-84126. (English Experience Ser.: No. 945). 280p. 1979. Repr. of 1618 ed. lib. bdg. 26.00 (ISBN 90-221-0945-3). Walter J Johnson.

Willis, Arthur J. & Willis, Christopher J. Practice & Procedure for the Quantity Surveyor. 8th ed. 239p. 1980. text ed. 30.00x (ISBN 0-246-11172-0, Pub. by Granada England); pap. text ed. 16.75x (ISBN 0-246-11242-5, Pub. by Granada England). Renouf.

Wilson, Ramsay J. Land Surveying. 2nd ed. (Illus.). 480p. 1977. pap. 14.95x (ISBN 0-7121-1242-1, Pub. by Macdonald & Evans England). Intl Ideas.

SURVEYING, MARINE
see Hydrographic Surveying

SURVEYS

Burges, Bill. Facts & Figures: A Layman's Guide to Conducting Surveys. 125p. (Orig.). 1976. pap. text ed. 4.25 (ISBN 0-917754-02-6). Inst Responsive.

SURVEYS, CADASTRAL
see Real Property

SURVEYS, ECONOMIC
see Economic Surveys

SURVEYS, EDUCATIONAL
see Educational Surveys

SURVEYS, SOCIAL
see Social Surveys

SURVIVAL (AFTER AIRPLANE ACCIDENTS, SHIPWRECKS, ETC.)
see also Search and Rescue Operations

Angel, Nicholas. Capsize in a Trimaran: A Story of Survival in the North Atlantic. (Illus.). 1981. 15.95 (ISBN 0-393-03264-7). Norton.

Clayton, Bruce D. Life After Doomsday: A Survivalist Guide to Nuclear War & Other Disasters. (Illus.). 192p. 1981. pap. 8.95 (ISBN 0-8037-4752-7). Dial.

Japan Broadcasting Corporation, ed. Unforgettable Fire: Pictures Drawn by Atomic Bomb Survivors. (Illus.). 1981. 15.95 (ISBN 0-394-51585-4); pap. 7.95 (ISBN 0-394-74823-9). Pantheon.

Reader, Dennis J. Coming Back Alive. LC 79-5147. (Illus.). 256p. (gr. 7 up). 1981. 8.95 (ISBN 0-686-68070-7); PLB 8.99 (ISBN 0-686-68071-5). Random.

Stoffel, R. & Lavalla, Patrick. Survival Sense for the Pilot. (Illus.). 160p. (Orig.). 1980. pap. 5.95 (ISBN 0-913724-24-6). Survival Ed Assoc.

SURVIVAL (HUMAN ECOLOGY)
see Human Ecology

SURVIVORS' BENEFITS (OLD AGE PENSIONS)
see Old Age Pensions

SUSPENDED SENTENCE
see Probation

SUSQUEHANNA RIVER AND VALLEY

Roberts, Ellis W. Along the Susquehanna. 128p. 1980. 7.95 (ISBN 0-686-28856-4). Colwyn-Tangno.

SUSSEX, ENGLAND

Drewett, P. L., ed. The Archaeology in Sussex to AD1500. 110p. 1980. pap. 20.95x (ISBN 0-900312-67-X, Pub. by Council Brit Arch England). Intl Schol Bk Serv.

History of the County for Sussex, Vol. 6, Pt. 1. (Victoria History of the Counties of England Ser.). (Illus.). 272p. 1980. 149.00 (ISBN 0-19-722753-8). Oxford U Pr.

SVALBARD
see also Spitsbergen

Lock, B. E., et al. The Geology of Edgeoya & Barentsoya: Svalbard. (Norsk Polarinstitutt Skrifter: Vol. 168). (Illus.). 64p. 1980. pap. text ed. 7.50x. Universitet.

Winsnes, Thore S., ed. The Geological Development of Svalbard During the Precambrian, Lower Palaeozoic, & Devonian. (Norsk Polarinstitutt Skrifter: Vol. 167). (Illus.). 323p. 1980. pap. text ed. 30.00x (ISBN 82-90307-03-9). Universitet.

SW RADIO
see Radio, Short Wave

SWAHILI LANGUAGE

Wilson, Peter. Simplified Swahili. 328p. (Orig.). 1981. pap. text ed. 8.95x (ISBN 0-582-62358-8). Longman.

SWALLOWS

Whittemore, Margaret. Chimney Swifts & Their Relatives. 176p. 1981. pap. 5.95 (ISBN 0-912542-02-0). Nature Bks Pub.

SWAT, PAKISTAN

Barth, Fredrik. Features of Person & Society in Swat-Collected Essays on Pathans: Selected Essays of Frederik Barth, Vol. II. (International Library of Anthropology Ser.). 208p. 1981. 32.00 (ISBN 0-7100-0620-9). Routledge & Kegan.

SWEDEN–HISTORY

Sweden - a Short Survey of the Kingdom of Sweden. LC 79-84139. (English Experience Ser.: No. 956). 116p. 1979. Repr. of 1632 ed. lib. bdg. 11.50 (ISBN 90-221-0956-9). Walter J Johnson.

SWEDISH LITERATURE–HISTORY AND CRITICISM

Strindberg, August. The Chamber Plays. 2nd, rev. ed. Sprinchorn, Evert, et al, trs. from Swedish. 288p. 1981. 15.00 (ISBN 0-8166-1028-2); pap. 6.95 (ISBN 0-8166-1031-2). U of Minn Pr.

SWEDISH POETRY (COLLECTIONS)

Barkan, Stanley H., ed. Four Contemporary Swedish Poets. Fulton, Robin & Hollo, Anselm, trs. (Cross-Cultural Review No.5). 48p. Date not set. 10.00 (ISBN 0-89304-608-6); pap. 4.00 (ISBN 0-89304-609-4). Cross Cult.

Harding, Gunnar & Barkan, Stanley H., eds. Cross-Cultural Review: Four Contemporary Swedish Poets, No. 5. Fulton, Robin & Hollo, Anselm, trs. 48p. 10.00 (ISBN 0-89304-608-6); pap. 4.00 (ISBN 0-89304-609-4). Cross Cult.

SWELL
see Ocean Waves

SWIFT, JONATHAN, 1667-1745

Lock, F. P. The Politics of Gulliver's Travels. 166p. 1980. text ed. 22.00x (ISBN 0-19-812656-5). Oxford U Pr.

Mell, Donald C., et al, eds. Contemporary Studies of Swift's Poetry. LC 79-21610. (Illus.). 216p. 1980. 18.50 (ISBN 0-87413-173-1, 173). U Delaware Pr.

SWIMMING
see also Diving

Katz, Jane & Bruning, Nancy P. Swimming for Total Fitness: A Progressive Aerobic Program. LC 80-708. (Illus.). 380p. 1981. pap. 10.95 (ISBN 0-385-15932-3, Dolp). Doubleday.

Murray, John L. Infaquatics: Teaching Kids to Swim. (Illus.). 224p. 1981. Repr. of 1980 ed. pap. 6.95 (ISBN 0-688-00476-8, Quill). Morrow.

Rajki, Bela. Teaching to Swim, Learning to Swim. Hepp, Ferenc, tr. from Hung. Orig. Title: Uszastanitas--Uszastanulas. (Illus.). 83p. 1980. 12.50x (ISBN 963-13-0957-6). Intl Pubns Serv.

Wetmore, Reagh. Drownproofing Techniques for Floating, Swimming & Open Water Survival. (Illus., Orig.). 1981. pap. 7.95 (ISBN 0-8289-0410-3). Greene.

SWIMMING–JUVENILE LITERATURE

Boy Scouts of America. Swimming. (Illus.). 48p. (gr. 6-12). 1980. pap. 0.70x. BSA.

Gleasner, Diana C. Illustrated Swimming, Diving & Surfing Dictionary for Young People. (Illus.). (gr. 9 up). pap. 2.50 (ISBN 0-13-451195-6). P-H.

SWIMMING POOLS

Derven, Ronald & Nichols, Carol. Sucessful Swimming Pools. 2nd ed. Case, Virginia A., ed. (Successful Ser.). (Illus.). 128p. 1981. 18.95 (ISBN 0-89999-025-8); pap. 8.95 (ISBN 0-89999-026-6). Structures Pub.

Sunset Editors. Swimming Pools. 5th ed. LC 80-53488. (Illus.). 128p. 1981. pap. 4.95 (ISBN 0-376-01607-8, Sunset Bks.). Sunset-Lane.

SWINBURNE, ALGERNON CHARLES, 1837-1909

McSweeney, Kerry. Tennyson & Swinburne As Romantic Naturalists. 240p. 1981. 25.00x (ISBN 0-8020-2381-9). U of Toronto Pr.

SWINE
see also Pork Industry and Trade

Cattle, Sheep, & Hogs. (Country Home Ser.). 96p. 2.95 (ISBN 0-88453-005-1). Berkshire Traveller.

Lavine, Sigmund A. & Scuro, Vincent. Wonders of Pigs. (Wonders Ser.). (Illus.). 80p. (gr. 4 up). 1981. PLB 6.95 (ISBN 0-396-07943-1). Dodd.

Mitchelmore, Peter. The Pigkeeper's Guide. LC 80-68686. (Illus.). 136p. 1981. 14.95 (ISBN 0-7153-7995-X). David & Charles.

Pond, Wilson G. & Houpt, Katherine A. The Biology of the Pig. LC 77-90909. (Illus.). 352p. 1978. 25.00x (ISBN 0-8014-1137-8). Comstock.

Scott, Jack D. The Book of the Pig. (Illus.). 64p. (ps up). 1981. 8.95 (ISBN 0-399-20718-X). Putnam.

SWINE–ANATOMY

Hughes, Paul & Varley, Mike. Reproduction in the Pig. LC 80-40241. 254p. 1980. text ed. 39.95 (ISBN 0-408-70946-4); pap. text ed. 23.95 (ISBN 0-408-70921-9). Butterworths.

SWING (GOLF)

Metz, Richard. The Graduated Swing Method. (Illus.). 128p. 1981. 12.95 (ISBN 0-684-16868-5, ScribT). Scribner.

SWING MUSIC
see Jazz Music

SWITZERLAND–DESCRIPTION AND TRAVEL

Kubly, Herbert. Native's Return. LC 80-5894. 408p. 1981. 14.95 (ISBN 0-8128-2768-6). Stein & Day.

Martin, William. Switzerland. 1971. 11.95 (ISBN 0-236-15402-8, Pub. by Paul Elek). Merrimack Bk Serv.

SWITZERLAND–HISTORY

Steinberg, J. Why Switzerland? LC 75-36024. (Illus.). 225p. 1981. pap. 9.50 (ISBN 0-521-28144-X). Cambridge U Pr.

SWITZERLAND–POLITICS AND GOVERNMENT

Schmid, Carol L. Conflict & Consensus in Switzerland. 1981. 18.50x (ISBN 0-520-04079-1). U of Cal Pr.

SWITZERLAND–SOCIAL LIFE AND CUSTOMS

Kubly, Herbert. Native's Return. LC 80-5894. 408p. 1981. 14.95 (ISBN 0-8128-2768-6). Stein & Day.

SYDNEY, AUSTRALIA

Yeomans, John. The Twenty Best Sights of Sydney. 128p. 1980. pap. 4.95x (ISBN 0-686-68862-7, Pub. by W Collins Australia). Intl Schol Bk Serv.

SYLVICULTURE
see Forests and Forestry

SYMBIOSIS

Batra, Lekh R., ed. Insect Fungus Symbiosis: Nutrition, Mutualism & Commensalism. LC 78-20640. 288p. 1979. text ed. 27.50 (ISBN 0-470-26671-6). Allanheld.

Margulis, Lynn. Symbiosis in Cell Evolution: Life & Its Environment on the Early Earth. LC 80-26695. (Illus.). 1981. text ed. 27.95x (ISBN 0-7167-1255-5); pap. text ed. 13.95x (ISBN 0-7167-1256-3). W H Freeman.

SYMBOLIC AND MATHEMATICAL LOGIC
see Logic, Symbolic and Mathematical

SYMBOLIC LANGUAGE
see ALGOL (Computer Program Language)

SYMBOLIC NUMBERS
see Symbolism of Numbers

SYMBOLICS
see Creeds

SYMBOLISM
see also Christian Art and Symbolism; Ciphers; Cryptography; Emblems; Heraldry; Idols and Images; Jewish Art and Symbolism; Ritual; Semantics (Philosophy); Signs and Symbols
also references under Religion, Primitive

Battle, Dennis M. America's Future in Symbolic Prophecy. (Illus.). 52p. 1981. pap. 2.50 (ISBN 0-933464-10-X). D M Battle Pubns.

Campbell, Florence. Your Days Are Numbered. 21st ed. 246p. 1980. pap. 5.50 (ISBN 0-87516-422-6). De Vorss.

Maldonado, Luis & Power, David, eds. Symbol & Art in Worship, Concilium 132. (New Concilium 1980). 128p. 1980. pap. 5.95 (ISBN 0-8164-4765-9). Crossroad NY.

Schwaller de Lubicz, R. A. Esoterism & Symbol. (Illus.). 1981. 5.95 (ISBN 0-89281-014-9). Inner Tradit.

Weimer, Walter B. & Palermo, David, eds. Cognition & the Symbolic Processes, Vol. 2. 426p. 1981. professional ref. text 24.95 (ISBN 0-89859-066-3). L Erlbaum Assocs.

SYMBOLISM IN ART
see also Christian Art and Symbolism; Jewish Art and Symbolism

Reff, Theodore, ed. Exhibitions of Symbolists & Nabi. (Modern Art in Paris 1855 to 1900 Ser.). 254p. 1981. lib. bdg. 44.00 (ISBN 0-8240-4743-5). Garland Pub.

SYMBOLISM IN THE BIBLE

Edwards, Charles L. Understanding Biblical Symbols. 96p. 1981. 6.00 (ISBN 0-682-49704-5). Exposition.

SYMBOLISM OF NUMBERS

Goodwin, Mathew O. Numerology: The Complete Guide. 1981. Repr. Set. lib. bdg. 33.00 (ISBN 0-89370-999-9); Vol. 1. lib. bdg. 16.95 ea. (ISBN 0-89370-653-1). Vol. 2 (ISBN 0-89370-654-X). Borgo Pr.

Goodwin, Matthew O. Numerology: The Complete Guide. (Orig.). 1981. Set. pap. 17.50 (ISBN 0-87877-999-X); Vol. 1. pap. 8.95 (ISBN 0-87877-053-4); Vol. 2. pap. 8.95 (ISBN 0-87877-054-2). Newcastle Pub.

Sharp, Richard M. & Mitzner, Seymour. Numero Magico, 4 bks. rev. ed. Editorial Turabo, Inc., ed. Incl. Libro Primero. 48p. (gr. 1-3) (ISBN 0-675-01038-1); Libro 2. 48p. (gr. 2-4) (ISBN 0-675-01039-X); Libra 3. 48p. (gr. 3-5) (ISBN 0-675-01040-3); Libra 4. 48p. (gr. 4-6) (ISBN 0-675-01041-1). (Span.). 1979. pap. 1.50 ea. Merrill.

SYMBOLS
see Signs and Symbols

SYMBOLS (IN SCIENCE TECHNOLOGY, ETC.)
see Technology–Abbreviations;
see subdivision Notation under names of sciences, e.g. Chemistry–Notation

SYMMETRIC FUNCTIONS

David, F. N., et al. Symmetric Function & Allied Tables. 278p. 1966. 27.00x (ISBN 0-85264-702-6, Pub. by Griffin England). State Mutual Bk.

SYMMETRIC SPACES

Bucy, R. S., et al. Stochastic Differential Equations. McKean, H. P. & Keller, J. B., eds. LC 72-13266. (SIAM-AMS Proceedings). 1973. 22.00 (ISBN 0-8218-1325-0). Am Math.

Cahen, Michel & Parker, Monique. Pseudo-Riemannian Symmetric Spaces. LC 79-27541. (Memoirs Ser.). 1980. 6.80 (ISBN 0-8218-2229-2, MEMO-229). Am Math.

Namikawa, Y. Toroidal Compactification of Siegel Spaces. (Lecture Notes in Mathematics: Vol. 812). 162p. 1980. pap. 11.80 (ISBN 0-387-10021-0). Springer-Verlag.

SYMMETRY (ART)
see Proportion (Art)

SYMPATHY
see also Empathy

Moncure, Jane B. Caring. rev. ed. LC 80-27506. (What Is It? Ser.). (Illus.). (gr. k-3). 1981. PLB 5.50 (ISBN 0-89565-201-3). Childs World.

SYMPHONIES

Schumann, Robert. Complete Symphonies in Full Score. 1980. pap. 11.95 (ISBN 0-486-24013-4). Dover.

SYMPTOMS
see Diagnosis

SYNANON FOUNDATION

Olin, William. Escape from Utopia: My Ten Years in Synanon. 300p. 1981. 12.95 (ISBN 0-913300-53-5); pap. 6.95 (ISBN 0-913300-54-3). Unity Pr.

SYNAPSES

Brzin, M., et al, eds. Synaptic Constituents in Health & Disease: Proceedings of the Third Meeting of the European Society for Neurochemistry, Bled, August 31st-Sept, 5th, 1980. (Illus.). 760p. 1980. 125.00 (ISBN 0-08-025921-9). Pergamon.

SYNCRETISM (CHRISTIANITY)
see Christianity and Other Religions

SYNGE, JOHN MILLINGTON, 1871-1909

Dublin University. John Millington Synge, Eighteen Seventy-One to Nineteen Hundred & Nine: A Catalogue of an Exhibition Held at Trinity College Library, Dublin on the Occasion of the 50th Anniversary of His Death. 53p. 1980. Repr. of 1959 ed. lib. bdg. 8.50 (ISBN 0-8492-8117-2). R West.

SYNTACTICS
see Semantics (Philosophy)

SYNTAX
see Grammar, Comparative and General–Syntax;
see subdivision Syntax under names of particular languages, e.g. English Language–Syntax

SYNTHESIZER MUSIC
see Electronic Music

SYNTHETIC CHEMISTRY
see Chemistry, Organic–Synthesis

SYNTHETIC FUELS

Bentz, Edward J., Jr. & Salmon, Eliahi J. Synthetic Fuels Technology Overviews with Health & Environmental Impacts. 136p. 1981. text ed. 19.95 (ISBN 0-250-40423-0). Ann Arbor Science.

Business Communications Co. Staff. Synfuels: Equipment, Technology, Supplies, Money, People, E-042. 1981. 875.00 (ISBN 0-89336-281-6). BCC.

Hill, Richard F., et al, eds. Synfuels Industry Opportunities. Boardman, Elliot B. & Heavner, Martin L. LC 80-84730. 256p. 1981. 32.50 (ISBN 0-86587-088-8). Gov Insts.

SYNTHETIC PERFUMES
see Perfumes

SYNTHETIC PRODUCTS
see also Perfumes; Plastics; Rubber, Artificial; Synthetic Fuels

Flavin, Christopher. The Future of Synthetic Materials: The Petroleum Connection. (Worldwatch Papers Ser.). 1980. pap. 2.00 (ISBN 0-916468-35-6). Worldwatch Inst.

Venkataraman, Krishnasami, ed. The Chemistry of Synthethic Dyes, 8 vols. Incl. Vol. 1. 1952. 62.50 (ISBN 0-12-717001-4); Vol. 2. 1952. 62.50 (ISBN 0-12-717001-4); Vol. 3. 1970. 62.50 (ISBN 0-12-717003-0); Vol. 4. 1971. 62.50 (ISBN 0-12-717004-9); Vol. 5. 1972. 68.00 (ISBN 0-12-717005-7); Vol. 6. 1973. 62.50 (ISBN 0-12-717006-5); Vol. 7. 1974. 62.50 (ISBN 0-12-717007-3); Vol. 8. 1978. 62.50 (ISBN 0-12-717008-1). (Organic & Biological Chemistry Ser.). Set. 412.00 (ISBN 0-12-717002-2). Acad Pr.

SYNTHETIC RUBBER
see Rubber, Artificial

SYRIA–HISTORY

Prawer, Joshua. Crusader Institutions. (Illus.). 536p. 1980. 89.00x (ISBN 0-19-822536-9). Oxford U Pr.

SYSTEM ANALYSIS
see also Control Theory; Electric Networks; Mathematical Optimization; Nonlinear Theories; Systems Engineering

Bensoussan, A. & Lions, J. L., eds. Analysis & Optimization of Systems: Proceedings. (Lecture Notes in Control & Information Sciences Ser.: Vol. 28). 999p. 1981. pap. 57.90 (ISBN 0-387-10472-0). Springer-Verlag.

Brethower, Dale M. Behavior Analysis in Business & Industry: A Total Performance System. (Illus.). 130p. (Orig.). 1972. pap. 10.00 (ISBN 0-914474-06-5); instr's. manual avail. F Fournies.

Checkland, P. B. Systems Thinking, Systems Practice. 320p. 1981. 31.95 (ISBN 0-471-27911-0, Pub. by Wiley-Interscience). Wiley.

Clifton, H. D. Systems Analysis for Business Data Processing. 3rd ed. 242p. 1978. text ed. 30.75x (ISBN 0-220-66369-6, Pub. by Busn Bks England). Renouf.

Medina, Barbara F. A Mathematical Approach to Evaluating Systems. 250p. 1981. price not set (ISBN 0-677-05570-6). Gordon.

--Structured System Analysis: A New Technique. 1981. write for info. (ISBN 0-677-05570-6). Gordon.

NATO ASI & AMS Summer Seminar in Applied Mathematics Held at Harvard University, Cambridge, Ma., June 18-29, 1979. Geometrical Methods for Th Theory of Linear Systems: Proceedings. Byrnes, Christopher I. & Martin, Clyde F., eds. (NATO Advanced Study Institutes Series C: Mathematical & Physical Sciences, 62). 313p. 1980. lib. bdg. 39.50 (ISBN 90-277-1154-2, Pub. by D. Reidel). Kluwer Boston.

Smith, Ronald B. How to Plan, Design & Implement a Bad System. (Illus.). 1981. 12.00 (ISBN 0-89433-148-5). Petrocelli.

Stability of Nonlinear Systems. (Control Theory & Applications Studies Ser.). 208p. 1981. 30.00 (ISBN 0-471-27856-4, Pub. by Wiley-Interscience). Wiley.

SYSTEM SIMULATION

see Simulation Methods

SYSTEM THEORY

see System Analysis

SYSTEMATIC BOTANY

see Botany–Classification

SYSTEMATIC THEOLOGY

see Theology, Doctrinal

SYSTEMS, THEORY OF

see System Analysis

SYSTEMS ANALYSIS

see System Analysis

SYSTEMS ENGINEERING

see also Bionics; Man-Machine Systems; Operations Research; Reliability (Engineering); Simulation Methods; Weapons Systems

ICS Nineteen Eighty-One: Proceedings of the International Computing Symposium on Systems Architecture. 1981. pap. text ed. price not set (ISBN 0-86103-050-8, Westbury Hse). Butterworth.

Najim, M & Abdel-Fettah, Y. M., eds. System Approach for Developement: Proceedings of the Third IFAC-IFIP-IFORS Conference, Rabat, Morocco, 24-27 November 1980. LC 80-41530. 600p. 1981. 105.00 (ISBN 0-08-025670-8); pap. 80.00 (ISBN 0-08-027283-5). Pergamon.

SYSTEMS OPTIMIZATION

see Mathematical Optimization

SYSTEMS RELIABILITY

see Reliability (Engineering)

T

TABERNACLE

Blattner, E. F., tr. El Tabernaculo. (Spanish Bks.). 1977. 0.75 (ISBN 0-8297-0601-1). Life Pubs Intl.

Guest, Dean. Tabernacle, God's Dwelling Place. 64p. (Orig.). Date not set. pap. 1.95 (ISBN 0-89841-012-6). Zoe Pubns.

Laity, Edward. Tabernacle Types & Teaching. 1980. pap. 1.25 (ISBN 0-86544-011-5). Salvation Army.

TABLE BLESSINGS

see Grace at Meals

TABLE DECORATION

see Table Setting and Decoration

TABLE SETTING AND DECORATION

see also Flower Arrangement; Pottery

Dlugosch, Sharon. Table Setting Teachers Manual. 1980. 7.00 (ISBN 0-918420-02-4). Brighton Pubns.

Von Bornstedt, Marianne & Prytz, Ulla. Folding Table Napkins. LC 72-81040. (Illus.). 48p. 1981. pap. 4.95 (ISBN 0-8069-8974-2). Sterling.

TABLES (SYSTEMATIC LISTS)

see Statistics–Charts, Tables, etc.

TABLES, MATHEMATICAL

see Mathematics–Tables, etc.

TABLETS, MEMORIAL

see Sepulchral Monuments

TACHYGRAPHY

see Shorthand

TADPOLES

see Frogs

TAE KWON DO

see Karate

TAHITI

Ferdon, Edwin N. Early Tahiti As the Explorers Saw It. LC 80-26469. 1981. text ed. 19.50x (ISBN 0-8165-0708-2); pap. 12.50 (ISBN 0-8165-0720-1). U of Ariz Pr.

TAHLTAN INDIANS

see Indians of North America–Northwest, Pacific

T'AI CHI CH'UAN

Galante, Lawrence. Tai Chi: The Supreme Ultimate. 1981. pap. 8.95 (ISBN 0-87728-497-0). Weiser.

TAI PING REBELLION

see Taiping Rebellion, 1850-1864

TAIPING REBELLION, 1850-1864

Michael, Franz & Chang, Chung-Li. The Taiping Rebellion: Documents & Comments. Incl. Vol. 2. 756p (ISBN 0-295-73959-2); Vol. 3. 1107p (ISBN 0-295-73958-4). LC 66-13538. (Publications on Asia of the Institute for Foreign & Area Studies: No. 14, Pt. 2). 1971. 30.00 ea. U of Wash Pr.

--The Taiping Rebellion: History, Vol. 1. (Publications on Asia of the Institute for Foreign & Area Studies: No. 14, Pt. 1). 256p. 1966. 10.00 (ISBN 0-295-73958-4); pap. 5.95 (ISBN 0-295-95244-X). U of Wash Pr.

TAIWAN

Foley, Frederic J. The Great Formosan Imposter. 126p. 1980. 7.50 (ISBN 0-89955-148-3, Pub. by Mei Ya Pub Taiwan). Intl Schol Bk Serv.

Taiwan Statistical Data Book, 1979. LC 72-219425. (Illus., Orig.). 1979. pap. 12.50x (ISBN 0-8002-2236-9). Intl Pubns Serv.

TAIWAN–DESCRIPTION AND TRAVEL

Lanier, Alison. Update -- Taiwan. (Country Orientation Ser.). 1980. pap. text ed. 25.00 (ISBN 0-933662-30-0). Intercult Network.

TAIWAN–ECONOMIC CONDITIONS

Council for Economic Planning & Development (Republic of China) Taiwan Statistical Data Book, 1980. LC 72-219425. (Illus.). 318p. (Orig.). 1980. pap. 12.50x (ISBN 0-8002-2749-2). Intl Pubns Serv.

Steinhoff, Manfred. Prestige & Profit: The Development of Entrepreneurial Abilities in Taiwan 1880-1972. (Development Studies Centre Monograph: No. 20). (Illus.). 153p. (Orig.). 1980. pap. text ed. 11.95 (ISBN 0-909150-94-X, 0588). Bks Australia.

TAIWAN–POLITICS AND GOVERNMENT

Council for Economic Planning & Development (Republic of China) Taiwan Statistical Data Book, 1980. LC 72-219425. (Illus.). 318p. (Orig.). 1980. pap. 12.50x (ISBN 0-8002-2749-2). Intl Pubns Serv.

Downen, Robert. The Taiwan Pawn in the China Game: Congress to the Rescue, Vol. I. LC 79-88334. (Significant Issues Ser.: No. 1). 80p. 1979. 5.95 (ISBN 0-89206-007-7). CSI Studies.

The Taiwan Pawn in the China Game. 80p. 1979. pap. 7.50 (ISBN 0-89206-007-7, CSIS002, CSIS). Unipub.

TAIWAN–SOCIAL CONDITIONS

Ahern, Emily M., ed. The Anthropology of Taiwanese Society. Gates, Hill. LC 79-64212. 480p. 1981. 30.00x (ISBN 0-8047-1043-0). Stanford U Pr.

TALENTED CHILDREN

see Gifted Children

TALENTS (PARABLE)

see Jesus Christ–Parables

TALES

see also Fairy Tales; Homiletical Illustrations; Legends; Parables; Short Stories

Roberts, Leonard. Old Greasybeard: Tales from the Cumberland Gap. LC 69-20398. (Illus.). 1980. pap. text ed. 7.95 (ISBN 0-933302-04-5). Pikeville Coll.

TALES, AFRICAN

Finnegan, Ruth H. Limba Stories & Story-Telling. LC 80-25904. (Oxford Library of African Literature). xii, 352p. 1981. Repr. of 1967 ed. lib. bdg. 28.75x (ISBN 0-313-22723-3, FILS). Greenwood.

Umobuarie, David. Black Justice. (Three Crown Books Ser.). 204p. (Orig.). 1976. pap. 8.95 (ISBN 0-19-575232-5). Oxford U Pr.

TALES, AMERICAN

Carpenter, Cal. The Walton War & Tales of the Great Smoky Mts. 4.95 (ISBN 0-932298-03-6). Green Hill.

Ellison, Glenn R. More Tales from Slim Ellison. 1981. 17.50 (ISBN 0-8165-0715-5); pap. 9.50 (ISBN 0-8165-0681-7). U of Ariz Pr.

Irving, Washington. Washington Irving's Tales of the Supernatural. Wagenknecht, Edward, ed. (Illus.). 288p. 1981. 14.95 (ISBN 0-916144-64-X); pap. 7.95 (ISBN 0-916144-65-8). Stemmer Hse.

TALES, ARABIC

Atil, Esin. Kalila Wa Dimna: Fables from a Fourteenth Century Arabic Manuscript. (Illus.). 96p. (Orig.). 1981. 17.50 (ISBN 0-87474-216-1); pap. 9.95 (ISBN 0-87474-215-3). Smithsonian.

TALES, BRITISH

Tales from Shakespeare. 1981. 28.50 (ISBN 0-686-68310-2). Porter.

TALES, CHINESE

Link, Perry. Mandarin Ducks & Butterflies: Popular Fiction in the Early Twentieth-Century Chinese Cities. (Illus.). 352p. 1981. 20.00x (ISBN 0-520-04111-9). U of Cal Pr.

TALES, INDONESIAN

Samuel-Hool, Leonie. To All My Grandchildren: Lessons in Indonesian Cooking. Hool, Sherman, ed. LC 80-84766. (Illus.). 120p. 1981. 12.95 (ISBN 0-936016-50-7); pap. 7.95 (ISBN 0-936016-75-2). Liplop.

TALES, IRISH

Temperley, Alan. Tales of Galloway. 319p. 1980. 12.50x (ISBN 0-7050-0076-1, Pub. by Skilton & Shaw England). State Mutual Bk.

TALES, ITALIAN

Ainsworth, Catherine H. Italian-American Folktales. LC 76-52643. (Folklore Bks.). xii, 180p. 1980. 5.00 (ISBN 0-933190-03-4). Clyde Pr.

TALES, SUFI

Shah, Amina. The Tale of Four Dervishes & Other Sufi Tales. LC 80-8895. 288p. (Orig.). 1981. pap. 5.95 (ISBN 0-06-067256-0). Har-Row.

TALES, WELSH

Radford, Ken. Tales of South Wales. 192p. 1980. 12.00x (ISBN 0-7050-0080-X, Pub. by Skilton & Shaw England). State Mutual Bk.

TALL BUILDINGS

Council on Tall Buildings & Urban Habitat. Tall Buildings: Systems & Concepts. LC 80-65692. (Monographs on Planning & Design of Tall Buildings: No. 4). 651p. 1980. text ed. 40.00 (ISBN 0-87262-239-8). Am Soc Civil Eng.

TALMUD

Haskelevich, B., ed. Introduction to the Talmud Study. 400p. (Rus.). 1981. pap. 6.00 (ISBN 0-938666-01-0). CHAMH.

TALMUD–FOLK-LORE

see Folk-Lore, Jewish

TAMAYO, RUFINO, 1900-

Lynch, James B., Jr., intro. by. Rufino Tamayo: Fifty Years of His Painting. LC 78-10760. (Illus.). 90p. 1981. 15.00 (ISBN 0-295-95816-2, Pub. by Phillips); pap. 7.50 (ISBN 0-295-95822-7). U of Wash Pr.

TAMILS

Ramachandran, K. S. Archaeology of South India: Tamilnadu. 1980. 40.00x (ISBN 0-8364-0669-9, Pub. by Sundeep). South Asia Bks.

TANGANYIKA–POLITICS AND GOVERNMENT

Baily, Martin. Union of Tanganyika & Zanzibar-a Study in Political Intergration. (Foreign & Comparative Studies-Eastern African Ser.: No.9). 114p. 1973. pap. 4.50x (ISBN 0-915984-05-9). Syracuse U Foreign Comp.

TANGRAM (CHINESE PUZZLE)

Eiffeis & Schuyt. Tangram: The Ancient Chinese Puzzle. 12.95 (ISBN 0-8109-2174-X). Abrams.

Johnston, Susan. Tangram ABC Kit. 1979. pap. 1.75 (ISBN 0-486-23853-9). Dover.

TANK-CARS

see Petroleum–Transportation

TANK TACTICS

see Tank Warfare

TANK-VESSELS

see Tankers

TANK WARFARE

Quarrie, Bruce. World War Two Photo Album: Panzers in the Balkans & Italy. (Illus.). 96p. 1981. pap. 5.95 (ISBN 0-89404-059-6). Aztex.

TANKERS

see also Petroleum–Transportation

Block, Richard A., ed. Tankerman: All Grades. rev. ed. (Illus.). 250p. 1981. pap. 21.00 (ISBN 0-934114-30-7). Marine Educ.

International Conference on Tanker Safety & Pollution Prevention. 106p. 1978. 18.00 (IMCO). Unipub.

Rutherford, D. L. Tanker Cargo Handling. 128p. 1979. 69.50x (ISBN 0-85264-256-3, Pub. by Griffin England). State Mutual Bk.

TANZANIA

Matthiessen, Peter. Sand Rivers. LC 80-36703. (Illus.). 240p. 1981. 19.95 (ISBN 0-670-61696-6, Studio). Viking Pr.

TANZANIA–INDUSTRIES

Pitblado, J. Roger. The North Mkata Plain, Tanzania: A Study of Land Capability & Land Tenure. (Department of Geography Research Publications Ser.). 200p. 1981. pap. 8.50x (ISBN 0-8020-3378-4). U of Toronto Pr.

Vail, David J. Technology for Ujamaa Village Developement in Tanzania. LC 74-25876. (Foreign & Comparative Studies-Eastern African Ser.: No. 18). 64p. 1975. pap. 3.50x (ISBN 0-915984-15-6). Syracuse U Foreign Comp.

TANZANIA–POLITICS AND GOVERNMENT

Mittelman, James H. Underdevelopment & the Transition to Socialism: Mozambique & Tanzania. (Studies in Social Discontinuity Ser.). 1981. price not set (ISBN 0-12-500660-8). Acad Pr.

TANZANIA–SOCIAL CONDITIONS

Potholm, Christian P. & Fredland, Richard A., eds. Integration & Disintegration in East Africa. LC 80-5914. 229p. 1980. lib. bdg. 17.75 (ISBN 0-8191-1298-4); pap. text ed. 9.75 (ISBN 0-8191-1299-2). U Pr of Amer.

TAOISM

Fulder, Stephen. Tao of Medicine. (Illus.). 1981. pap. 8.95. Inner Tradit.

Maspero, Henri. Taoism & Chinese Religion. Kierman, Frank A., tr. from Fr. LC 80-13444. Orig. Title: Le Taoisme et les religions Chinoises. 656p. 1981. lib. bdg. 32.50x (ISBN 0-87023-308-4). U of Mass Pr.

Ni Hua-Ching, Master & Hua-Ching. The Complete Works of Lao Tzu: Tao Teh Ching & Hua Hu Ching. LC 79-88745. 219p. 1979. pap. text ed. 7.50x (ISBN 0-937064-00-9). Wisdom Garden.

--Tao-the Subtle Universal Law & the Integral Way of Life. LC 79-91720. 166p. 1980. pap. text ed. 7.50 (ISBN 0-937064-01-7). Wisdom Garden.

--The Taoist Inner View of the Universe & the Immortal Realm. LC 79-91720. 218p. 1980. pap. text ed. 12.50x (ISBN 0-937064-02-5). Wisdom Garden.

Welch, et al, eds. Facets of Taoism: Essays in Chinese Religion. LC 77-28034. 307p. 1981. pap. 7.95x (ISBN 0-300-02673-0). Yale U Pr.

TAOS INDIANS

see Indians of North America–Southwest, New

TAP DANCING

Connor, Jim. Ann Miller: Tops in Taps. (Illus.). 224p. (Orig.). 1981. 19.95 (ISBN 0-531-09949-0); pap. 10.95 (ISBN 0-531-09950-4). Watts.

TAPE-RECORDER MUSIC

see Computer Music; Electronic Music

TAPE RECORDERS

see Magnetic Recorders and Recording

TAPE RECORDINGS (SOUND REPRODUCTIONS)

see Phonotapes

TAPES

see Phonotapes

TAPESTRY

see also Fabric Pictures

Jewell, Brian. Conquest & Overlord. (Illus.). 96p. 1981. 25.00 (ISBN 0-686-69381-7, 5209). Arco.

TAPEWORMS

see Cestoda

TARIFF UNIONS

see Customs Unions

TARKENTON, FRANCIS A.

Hahn, James & Hahn, Lynn. Tark! Francis Tarkenton. Schroeder, Howard, ed. (Sports Legends Ser.). (Illus.). 48p. (Orig.). (gr. 3-5). 1981. PLB 5.95 (ISBN 0-89686-121-X); pap. text ed. 2.95 (ISBN 0-89686-136-8). Crestwood Hse.

TAROT

Nichols, Sallie. Jung & Tarot: An Archetypal Journey. 1980. 25.00 (ISBN 0-87728-480-6); pap. 9.95 (ISBN 0-87728-515-2). Weiser.

Nordic, Rolla. The Tarot Shows the Path. 1979. pap. 3.95 (ISBN 0-87728-477-6). Weiser.

Wang, Robert. The Qabalistic Tarot. (Illus.). 320p. 1981. pap. 8.95 (ISBN 0-87728-520-9). Weiser.

TARTAR LANGUAGES

see Turko-Tataric Languages

TARZAN (MOVING-PICTURE SERIES)

Holtsmark, Erling B. Tarzan & Tradition: Classical Myth in Popular Literature. LC 80-1023. (Contributions to the Study of Popular Culture: No. 1). (Illus.). 216p. 1981. lib. bdg. 22.50 (ISBN 0-313-22530-3, HOT/). Greenwood.

TASTE

Cagan, Robert H. & Kare, Morley R., eds. Biochemistry of Taste & Olfaction. (Nutrition Foundation Ser.). 1981. write for info. (ISBN 0-12-154450-8). Acad Pr.

International Symposium on Olfaction & Taste, 6th, Gif Sur Yvette, France, 1977. Olfaction & Taste VI: Proceedings. 500p. 25.00 (ISBN 0-904147-08-8). Info Retrieval.

TASTE (ESTHETICS)

see Esthetics

TAVERNS

see Hotels, Taverns, etc.

TAX ACCOUNTING

Warner, James. Taxation. 8th ed. LC 78-65093. 9.00 (ISBN 0-932788-04-1). Bradley CPA.

TAX AUDITING

Jacobs, Vernon K. & Schoeneman, Charles W. Taxpayer's Audit Survival Manual. 256p. 1980. spiral bdg. 35.00 (ISBN 0-932496-08-3). Alexandria Hse.

--The Taxpayers' Audit Survival Manual. 1981. 35.00 (ISBN 0-932496-08-3). Green Hill.

TAX AVOIDANCE

see Tax Planning

TAX DELINQUENCY

see Tax Evasion

TAX-DODGING

see Tax Evasion

TAX EVASION

Criminal Aspects of Tax Fraud Cases. 3rd ed. 288p. 1980. text ed. 35.00 (ISBN 0-686-28652-9, T057B). ALI ABA.

Owens, Elisabeth A. International Aspects of U. S. Income Taxation: Cases & Materials, Vol. III, Parts Four & Five. LC 80-18605. 512p. 1980. pap. text ed. 12.50x (ISBN 0-915506-24-6). Harvard Law Intl Tax.

TAX EXEMPTION

see Taxation, Exemption from

TAX LAW

see Taxation–Law

TAX PLANNING

see also Estate Planning

Anderson, B. Ray. How You Can Use Inflation to Beat IRS: All the Legal Ways to Keep Your Money for Yourself & Your Family... Without Getting in Trouble with the IRS. LC 80-8429. (Illus.). 416p. 1981. 12.95 (ISBN 0-06-014825-X, HarpT). Har-Row.

Block, Julian. Tax Saving. LC 80-70260. 224p. 1981. 12.95 (ISBN 0-686-69525-9); pap. 7.95 (ISBN 0-686-69526-7). Chilton.

Bracewell-Milnes, Barry. The Economics of International Tax Avoidance: Political Power Versus Economic Law. (International Taxation Ser.: No. 2). 120p. 1980. lib. bdg. 29.00 (ISBN 90-2000-633-9, Pub. by Kluwer Law & Taxation Publishers). Kluwer Boston.

Diogenes. The April Game. 224p. 1981. pap. 2.50 (ISBN 0-87216-784-4). Playboy Pbks.

Drollinger, William C. & Drollinger, William C. Jr. Tax Shelters & Tax-Free Income for Everyone, Vol II. 4th ed. 1981. write for info. (ISBN 0-914244-06-X). Epic Pubns.

Green, Bill. Welcome to the Tax Revolt. (Illus.). 192p. 1981. 11.95 (ISBN 0-936602-10-4). Harbor Pub CA.

Rosenberg, Alan S. Evaluating Tax Shelter Offerings: 1980 Course Handbook. LC 80-80759. 512p. 1980. pap. text ed. 25.00 (ISBN 0-686-68823-6, J4-3477). PLI.

Schain, George M. Estates, Gifts & Fiduciaries: Planning & Taxation. 3rd ed. Gold, Jeffrey S., ed. 444p. 1980. 29.95 (ISBN 0-07-055120-0, P&RB); wkbk. & 10 cassettes 195.00 (ISBN 0-07-079056-6). McGraw.

Sommerfeld, Ray M. The Dow Jones-Irwin Guide to Tax Planning. 3rd ed. 364p. 1981. pap. 9.95 (ISBN 0-87094-233-6). Dow Jones-Irwin.

Starchild, Adam. Everyman's Guide to Tax Havens. 112p. (Orig.). 1980. pap. 6.00 (ISBN 0-87364-203-1). Paladin Ent.

Steiner, Barry R. Pay Less Tax Legally: 1981 Edition. (Orig.). 1980. pap. 3.95 (ISBN 0-451-09522-7, E9522, Sig). NAL.

Storrer, Philip & Williams, Brian. The Nineteen Eighty-One Tax Fighter's Guide. 192p. 1981. pap. 6.95 (ISBN 0-936602-08-2). Harbor Pub CA.

Tax Planning Techniques for Individuals. (Study in Federal Taxation Ser.: No. 2). 1980. pap. 22.50. Am Inst CPA.

Tax Planning Tips from the Tax Adviser. 1980. pap. 16.50. Am Inst CPA.

Whitman, Robert. Simplified Guide to Estate Planning & Administration. 192p. 1981. pap. 6.95 (ISBN 0-671-09136-0). Monarch Pr.

TAX RELATIONS, INTERGOVERNMENTAL

see Intergovernmental Fiscal Relations

TAX RETURNS

VanCaspel, Venita. Avoid the One-Way Trip to Washington. 1980. pap. 1.50 (ISBN 0-8359-0297-8). Reston.

TAX RETURNS–AUDITING

see Tax Auditing

TAX SAVING

see Tax Planning

TAX SHELTERS

see Tax Planning

TAXABLE TRANSFERS

see Inheritance and Transfer Tax

TAXATION

see also Business Tax; Excess Profits Tax; Income Tax; Inheritance and Transfer Tax; Intergovernmental Fiscal Relations; Licenses; Local Taxation; Property Tax; Tax Evasion; Tax Planning; Taxation, State

also subdivision Taxation under specific subjects, e.g. Corporations–Taxation; Land–Taxation

Browning, Edgar K. & Johnson, William R. Distribution of the Tax Burden. 1979. pap. 4.25 (ISBN 0-8447-3349-0). Am Enterprise.

James, Simon & Nobes, Christopher. The Economics of Taxation. 320p. 1978. 33.00x (ISBN 0-86003-507-7, Pub. by Allan Pubs England); pap. 16.50x (ISBN 0-86003-607-3). State Mutual Bk.

Lefcoe, George, ed. Respective Roles of State & Local Governments in Land Policy & Taxation. (Lincoln Institute Monograph: No. 80-7). 271p. 1980. write for info. Lincoln Inst Land.

P-H Staff. Prentice-Hall Federal Tax Course. students ed. Rubin, A., ed. 1981. 21.00 (ISBN 0-13-312488-6); pap. 7.95 study guide (ISBN 0-13-312496-7). P-H.

Samuels, Warren & Wade, Larry, eds. Taxing & Spending Policy. (Orig.). 1980. pap. 5.00 (ISBN 0-918592-41-0). Policy Studies.

TAXATION–ACCOUNTING

see Tax Accounting

TAXATION–EVASION

see Tax Evasion

TAXATION–HISTORY

Seidman, J. Seidman's Legislative History of Excess Profit Tax Laws: 1917-1946. 1959. 15.00. P-H.

--Seidman's Legislative History of Federal Income & Excess Profits Tax Laws: 1939-1953, 2 vols. 1959. 50.00 (ISBN 0-13-799742-6). P-H.

TAXATION–LAW

see also Tax Evasion

Hopkins, Bruce R. The Law of Tax-Exempt Organizations, 1981 Supplement. 3rd ed. 200p. 1981. pap. 15.95 (ISBN 0-471-09351-3, Pub. by Wiley Interscience). Wiley.

Indexation of the Tax Laws for Inflation. (Statement of Tax Policy: No. 6). 1980. pap. 3.00. Am Inst CPA.

Seidman, J. Seidman's Legislative History of Excess Profit Tax Laws: 1917-1946. 1959. 15.00. P-H.

--Seidman's Legislative History of Federal Income & Excess Profits Tax Laws: 1939-1953, 2 vols. 1959. 50.00 (ISBN 0-13-799742-6). P-H.

--Seidman's Legislative History of Federal Income Tax Laws: 1851-1938. 25.00 (ISBN 0-13-799767-1). P-H.

TAXATION–GREAT BRITAIN

Prest, A. R. Value-Added Taxation: The Experience of the United Kingdom. 1980. pap. 4.25 (ISBN 0-8447-3404-7). Am Enterprise.

TAXATION–JAPAN

De Becker, Eric V. Survey of Some Japanese Tax Laws. (Studies in Japanese Law & Government). 182p. 1979. Repr. of 1931 ed. 18.50 (ISBN 0-89093-218-2). U Pubns Amer.

TAXATION–UNITED STATES

Bandy, Dale & Swad, Randy. Federal Income Taxation, 1981. 250p. 1981. pap. text ed. 12.95 (ISBN 0-13-308502-3). P-H.

Greenberg, Samuel. Taxes, Government & You. 58p. 1980. 6.95 (ISBN 0-533-04424-3). Vantage.

Guide to Federal Tax Elections. (Study in Federal Taxation Ser.: No. 3). 1980. pap. 12.50. Am Inst CPA.

Lindholm, Richard W. The Economics of VAT: Preserving Efficiency, Capitalism & Social Progress. LC 80-8428. 1980. 19.95 (ISBN 0-669-04111-4). Lexington Bks.

TAXATION, EVASION OF

see Tax Evasion

TAXATION, EXEMPTION FROM

see also Tax Evasion

Hayden, John L. How to Incorporate in Tax Free Nevada for Only Fifty Dollars. LC 80-85433. 50p. 1981. text ed. 14.95. Newport Beach.

Hopkins, Bruce R. The Law of Tax-Exempt Organizations, 1981 Supplement. 3rd ed. 200p. 1981. pap. 15.95 (ISBN 0-471-09351-3, Pub. by Wiley Interscience). Wiley.

Logan, George H. Tax Reduction for Small Business & Self Employed. 1981. pap. 9.95 (ISBN 0-914598-08-2). Padre Prods.

TAXATION, INCIDENCE OF

see Taxation

TAXATION, LOCAL

see Local Taxation

TAXATION, STATE

Quindry, Kenneth E. & Schoening, Niles. State & Local Tax Performance Nineteen Seventy-Eight. rev. ed. 1980. pap. 3.00. S Regional Ed.

TAXATION OF BONDS, SECURITIES, ETC.

see also Municipal Bonds

Brownlee, Oswald H. Taxing the Income from U. S. Corporate Investment Abroad. 1979. pap. 3.25 (ISBN 0-8447-3367-9). Am Enterprise.

Mussa, Michael L. & Kormendi, Roger G. Taxation of Municipal Bonds: An Economic Appraisal. 1979. pap. 7.25 (ISBN 0-8447-3331-8). Am Enterprise.

TAXATION OF BUSINESS

see Business Tax

TAXATION OF EXCESS PROFITS

see Excess Profits Tax

TAXATION OF FOREIGN INCOME

see Income Tax–Foreign Income

TAXATION OF FRANCHISES

see Corporations–Taxation

TAXATION OF INCOME

see Income Tax

TAXATION OF LAND VALUES

see Land Value Taxation

TAXATION OF LEGACIES

see Inheritance and Transfer Tax

TAXATION OF REAL PROPERTY

see Real Property Tax

TAXATION OF SECURITIES

see Taxation of Bonds, Securities, etc.

TAXATION OF STOCKS

see Taxation of Bonds, Securities, etc.

TAXES

see Taxation

TAXES, SCHOOL

see Education–Finance

TAXIDERMY

see also Zoological Specimens–Collection and Preservation;

also subdivision Collection and Preservation under Zoological Specimens, and Birds, Fishes, Reptiles, and similar headings

Phillips, Archie & Phillips, Bubba. How to Mount Fish. (Illus.). 144p. 1981. 19.95 (ISBN 0-8117-0787-3). Stackpole.

TAXONOMY

see Botany–Classification

TAYLOR, EDWARD, 1642-1729

Davis, Thomas M. & Davis, Virginia L. Edward Taylor Vs. Solomon Stoddard: The Nature of the Lord's Supper, Vol. II. (American Literary Manuscripts Ser.). 1981. lib. bdg. 30.00 (ISBN 0-8057-9653-3). Twayne.

--The Unpublished Writings of Edward Taylor, 3 vols. (American Literary Manuscripts Ser.). 1981. Set. lib. bdg. 90.00 (ISBN 0-8057-9655-X). Twayne.

Davis, Thomas M. & Davis, Virginia L., eds. Edward Taylor's "Church Record" & Related Sermons. (American Literary Manuscripts Ser.: Vol. 1). 1981. lib. bdg. 35.00 (ISBN 0-8057-9650-9). Twayne.

--Edward Taylor's Minor Poetry, Vol. 3. (American Literary Manuscripts Ser.). 1981. lib. bdg. 35.00 (ISBN 0-8057-9654-1). Twayne.

TCHAIKOVSKY, PETER, 1840-1893

Tchaikovsky, Piotr I. Letters to His Family: An Autobiography. Young, Percy M., ed. Von Meck, Galina, tr. LC 80-6162. 576p. 1981. 25.00 (ISBN 0-8128-2802-X). Stein & Day.

TCHEBYCHEFF APPROXIMATION

see Chebyshev Approximation

TCHEREMISSIAN LANGUAGE

see Cheremissian Language

TEA

Hall, Dorothy. The Herb Tea Book. LC 80-84436. (Pivet Original Health Bk.). (Illus.). 120p. 1981. pap. 2.25 (ISBN 0-87983-248-7). Keats.

Stewart, Hilary. Wild Teas, Coffees, & Cordials. (Illus.). 128p. 1981. 7.95 (ISBN 0-295-95804-9). U of Wash Pr.

TEA ROOMS

see Restaurants, Lunchrooms, etc.

TEACH YOURSELF COURSES

see Self-Culture

also subdivision Self-Instruction under names of languages

TEACHER ASSOCIATIONS

see Teachers' Unions

TEACHER AUTONOMY

see Teaching, Freedom of

TEACHER ORGANIZATIONS

see Teachers' Unions

TEACHER-PARENT RELATIONSHIPS

see Parent-Teacher Relationships

TEACHER-STUDENT RELATIONSHIPS

Naylor, Phyllis R. Getting Along with Your Teachers. LC 80-22319. 96p. (gr. 4-6). 1981. 7.50g (ISBN 0-687-14123-0). Abingdon.

TEACHERS

see also Educators; Teachers of the Deaf; Teaching; Teaching As a Profession; Women Teachers

Davis, Ed. Teachers As Curriculum Evaluators. (Classroom & Curriculum in Australia Ser.: No. 4). 180p. 1981. text ed. 21.00x (ISBN 0-86861-090-9, 2517); pap. text ed. 9.95x (ISBN 0-86861-098-4, 2518). Allen Unwin.

Epstein, Joseph, ed. Masters: Portraits of Great Teachers. LC 80-68180. 224p. 1981. 14.95 (ISBN 0-465-04420-4). Basic.

--Masters: Portraits of Sixteen Great Teachers. LC 80-68180. 224p. 1980. 13.95 (ISBN 0-465-04420-4). Basic.

TEACHERS–CERTIFICATION

Woellner, Elizabeth H. Requirements for Certification: Of Teachers, Counselors, Librarians, Administrators for Elementary Schools, Secondary Schools, Junior Colleges, 1981-82. 45th ed. (Illus.). 240p. 1981. lib. bdg. price not set (ISBN 0-226-90466-0, A43-1905). U of Chicago Pr.

TEACHERS–CORRESPONDENCE, REMINISCENCES, ETC.

Japp, Alexander H. Three Great Teachers of Our Own Time. 255p. 1980. Repr. of 1865 ed. lib. bdg. 30.00 (ISBN 0-8492-1281-2). R West.

Johnson, Lois H. Cornflakes. (Illus.). 80p. 1981. 6.00 (ISBN 0-682-49695-2). Exposition.

TEACHERS–HANDBOOKS, MANUALS, ETC.

Crabtree, June. Effective Teaching: Basic Principles & Activities for Individualizing Instruction. rev. ed. 96p. (Orig.). 1981. pap. 5.95 (ISBN 0-87239-454-9, 3653). Standard Pub.

Dinkmeyer, Don, et al. Systematic Training for Effective Teaching: Teacher's Handbook. (Illus.). 291p. (Orig.). 1980. pap. text ed. 12.00 (ISBN 0-913476-75-7). Am Guidance.

UNESCO Handbook for Science Teachers. 199p. 1980. pap. 14.95 (ISBN 0-89059-006-0, U1029, UNESCO). Unipub.

TEACHERS–LEGAL STATUS, LAWS, ETC.

see also Teachers–Certification

Swalls, Fred, et al, eds. Legal Rights & Responsibilities of Indiana Teachers. 4th ed. 1980. pap. text ed. 8.95x (ISBN 0-8134-2152-7, 2152). Interstate.

TEACHERS–PERSONNEL MANAGEMENT

see School Personnel Management

TEACHERS–PSYCHOLOGY

Stones, E. Psychopedagogy: Psychological Theory & the Practice of Teaching. 490p. 1979. 21.95 (ISBN 0-416-71330-0, 2525); pap. 13.95 (ISBN 0-416-71340-8, 6420). Methuen Inc.

TEACHERS, CERTIFICATION OF

see Teachers–Certification

TEACHERS, INTERCHANGE OF

Teaching Abroad. 87p. 1976. 6.00 (IIE). Unipub.

TEACHERS, TRAINING OF

Here are entered works dealing with the history and methods of training teachers in general and in the United states. Works dealing with the training of teachers in other countries are listed under the appropriate subdivisions. Works dealing with the study of education as a science are entered under Education–Study and Teaching and works bearing upon the art and methods of teaching under the heading Teaching.

see also Comparative Education; Interns (Education); Student Teaching; Teachers' Workshops

Dinkmeyer, Don, et al. Systematic Training for Effective Teaching (STET) Teacher's Resource Book: Special Ctivities for Teachers & Students. (Illus.). 161p. (Orig.). 1980. pap. 7.00 (ISBN 0-913476-76-5). Am Guidance.

Hendricks, Gay. The Centered Teacher: Awareness Activities for Teachers & Their Students. (Transformation Ser.). 192p. 1981. 9.95 (ISBN 0-13-122234-1, Spec); pap. 4.95 (ISBN 0-13-122226-0). P-H.

TEACHERS, TRAINING OF–LATIN AMERICA

Caribbean Co-Operation for Curriculum Develoment & Reform in Teacher Training. (Experiments & Innovations in Education Ser.: No. 39). 46p. 1980. pap. 3.50 (U 1041, UNESCO). Unipub.

TEACHERS AND PARENTS

see Parent-Teacher Relationships

TEACHERS OF THE DEAF

Corbett, Edward E. & Jensema, Carl J. Teachers of the Deaf: Descriptive Profiles. xviii, 158p. 1981. 7.95 (ISBN 0-913580-64-3). Gallaudet Coll.

TEACHERS' UNIONS

Angell, George W., ed. Faculty & Teacher Bargaining: The Impact of Unions on Education. LC 80-8769. 1981. write for info. (ISBN 0-669-04360-5). Lexington Bks.

Feiman, Sharon, ed. Teacher Centers: What Place in Education. (Orig.). 1980. pap. 1.50. U Chi Ctr Policy.

TEACHERS' WORKSHOPS

Feiman, Sharon, ed. Teacher Centers: What Place in Education. (Orig.). 1980. pap. 1.50. U Chi Ctr Policy.

TEACHING

see also Audio-Visual Education; Classroom Management; Education; Education Libraries; Education of Children; Educational Psychology; Kindergarten; School Management and Organization; Student Teaching; Study, Method of; Teacher-Student Relationships

also subdivision Instruction and Study or Study and Teaching under various subjects, e.g. Music–Instruction and Study; Science–Study and Teaching

Barzun, Jacques. Teacher in America. LC 80-82370. 496p. 1981. 9.00 (ISBN 0-913966-78-9, Liberty Pr); pap. 4.00 (ISBN 0-913966-79-7). Liberty Fund.

Beechick, Ruth. Teaching Juniors. LC 80-68886. (Teacher Training Ser.). 192p. (Orig.). 1981. pap. 3.95 (ISBN 0-89636-062-8). Accent Bks.

Carkhuff, Robert R. The Skilled Teacher: A System Approach to Teaching Skills. (Illus.). 184p. 1981. pap. 10.95 (ISBN 0-914234-52-8). Human Res Dev Pr.

--Toward Actualizing Human Potential. (Illus.). 184p. 1981. 10.95x (ISBN 0-914234-15-3). Human Res Dev Pr.

Dembo, Myron. Teaching for Learning. 2nd ed. 1981. pap. text ed. write for info. (ISBN 0-8302-8856-2). Goodyear.

Dierenfield, Richard B. Learning to Teach. LC 80-69119. 135p. 1981. perfect bdg. 10.95 (ISBN 0-86548-031-1). Century Twenty One.

Donovan, Timothy R. & McClelland, Ben W. Eight Approaches to Teaching Composition. 160p. 1980. pap. 6.50 (ISBN 0-8141-1303-6). NCTE.

Douglass, Harl R. Modern Methods in High School Teaching. 544p. 1981. Repr. lib. bdg. 25.00 (ISBN 0-8495-1061-9). Arden Lib.

Duck. Teaching with Charisma. 364p. 1980. text ed. 12.95 (ISBN 0-205-07256-9, 2372568). Allyn.

Galloway, David. Teaching & Counselling. 192p. 1981. pap. 13.50 (ISBN 0-582-48987-3). Longman.

Howe, Florence & Rothermich, John A., eds. Women's "True" Profession: Voices from the History of Teaching. (Women's Lives-Women's Work Ser.). 352p. (Orig.). 1981. pap. text ed. 6.45 (ISBN 0-07-020437-3). McGraw.

Jacobsen, David, et al. Methods for Teaching: A Skills Approach. (Illus.). 304p. 1981. pap. text ed. 11.95 (ISBN 0-675-08079-7). Merrill.

Kniker, Charles R. & Naylor, Natalie A. Teaching Today & Tomorrow. (Special Education Ser.). (Orig.). 1981. pap. text ed. 15.95 (ISBN 0-675-08034-7); instrs'. manual 3.95. Merrill.

Knudsen, Charles W. Evaluation & Improvement of Teaching (in Secondary Schools) 538p. 1980. Repr. of 1932 ed. lib. bdg. 30.00 (ISBN 0-89984-302-6). Century Bookbindery.

Kozol, Jonathan. On Being a Teacher. 208p. 1981. 12.95 (ISBN 0-8264-0035-3). Continuum.

McCabe, Colin, ed. Evaluating in-Service Training for Teachers. 129p. 1981. pap. text ed. 22.00x (ISBN 0-85633-205-4, NFER). Humanities.

McFee, June K. & Degge, Rogena M. Art, Culture, & Environment: A Catalyst for Teaching. 416p. 1980. pap. text ed. 13.95 (ISBN 0-8403-2330-1). Kendall-Hunt.

Martin, Robert J. Teaching Through Encouragement: Techniques to Help Students Learn. 208p. 1980. 10.95 (Spec); pap. 4.95. P-H.

Mitchell, Bruce M., et al. Planning for Creative Learning. 2nd ed. 176p. 1981. pap. text ed. 9.95 (ISBN 0-8403-2302-6). Kendall-Hunt.

Noar, Gertrude. Every Child a Winner: Individualized Instruction. 150p. 1981. pap. price not set (ISBN 0-89874-340-0). Krieger.

Pearlman, Myer, tr. Ensenando Con Exito. (Spanish Bks.). 1978. 1.75 (ISBN 0-8297-0548-1). Vida Pubs.

Prizzi, Elaine & Hoffman, Jeanne. Teaching off the Wall. 1980. pap. 6.95 (ISBN 0-8224-6830-1). Pitman Learning.

Robinson, Adjai. Principles & Practice of Teaching. (Illus.). 176p. (Orig.). 1980. pap. text ed. 10.50x (ISBN 0-04-370098-5, AU449). Allen Unwin.

Study Skills Workshop Kit Level I. (gr. 5-9). 1980. pap. 9.95 (ISBN 0-88210-112-9). Natl Assn Principals.

Study Skills Workshop Kit Level II. (gr. 8-10). 1979. pap. 9.95 (ISBN -088210-113-7). Natl Assn Principals.

TEACHING–AIDS AND DEVICES

see also Audio-Visual Education; Bulletin Boards; Creative Activities and Seatwork; Handicraft; Moving-Pictures in Education; Paper Work; Television in Education

Barbe, Walter B. & Swassing, Raymond H. Teaching Through Modality Strengths: Concepts & Practices. LC 79-66953. 1979. 10.00 (ISBN 0-88309-100-3). Zaner-Bloser.

Brotherson, Mary Lound. A Handbook for Aides. 1981. pap. write for info (ISBN 0-8134-2177-2, 2177). Interstate.
Low-Cost Educational Materials - Inventory, Vol. 1. 158p. 1981. pap. 13.75 (UB89, UNESCO Regional Office). Unipub.
Southwest Regional Laboratory for Education Research & Development. Instructional Product Research, 8 vols. Incl. Vol. 1. Classifying & Interpreting Educational Research Studies. pap. text ed. 1.95x (ISBN 0-442-27863-2); Vol. 2. Selecting Variables for Educational Research. pap. text ed. 1.95x (ISBN 0-442-27864-0); Vol. 3. Components of the Educational Research Proposal. pap. text ed. 1.50x (ISBN 0-442-27865-9); Vol. 4. pap. o.p.; Vol. 5. pap. o.p.; Vol. 6. Choosing an Appropriate Statistical Procedure. pap. text ed. 1.95x (ISBN 0-442-27868-3); Vol. 7. The Use of Library Computer Programs for Statistical Analysis. pap. text ed. 1.50x (ISBN 0-442-27869-1); Vol. 8. The Research Report. pap. text ed. 1.95x (ISBN 0-442-27870-5). 1972. Van Nos Reinhold.
Walker, Luisa. Metodos De Ensenanza. (Spanish Bks.). 1979. 1.50 (ISBN 0-8297-0583-X). Life Pubs Intl.
Weaver, Horace R., ed. The International Lesson Annual 1981-1982. 448p. (Orig.). 1981. pap. 4.50 (ISBN 0-687-19145-9). Abingdon.

TEACHING–HISTORY
see Education–History

TEACHING–VOCATIONAL GUIDANCE
see Teaching As a Profession

TEACHING, FREEDOM OF
see also Church and Education
Stelzer, Leigh & Banthin, Joanna. Teachers Have Rights, Too: What Educators Should Know About School Law. (Orig.). 1981. pap. write for info. (ISBN 0-89994-249-0). Soc Sci Ed.

TEACHING AS A PROFESSION
Trowbridge, Leslie, et al. Becoming a Secondary School Science Teacher. 3rd ed. 352p. 1981. pap. text ed. 15.95 (ISBN 0-675-08030-4). Merrill.

TEACHING AUTHORITY OF THE CHURCH
see Catechetics–Catholic Church

TEACHING INTERNSHIP
see Interns (Education)

TEACHING LABORATORIES
see Student Teaching

TEACHING MATERIALS
see Teaching–Aids and Devices

TEACHINGS OF JESUS
see Jesus Christ–Teachings

TEAR SACS
see Lacrimal Organs

TECHNICAL ASSISTANCE
see also Community Development; Industrialization; International Agricultural Cooperation; Investments, Foreign; Underdeveloped Areas
Helleiner, Gerald K. Intra - Firm Trade & the Developing Countries. 1981. 25.00 (ISBN 0-312-42538-4). St Martin.
Riddell, Robert. Ecodevelopment. 1980. 27.50 (ISBN 0-312-22585-7). St Martin.
Townshend, J. R., ed. Terrain Analysis & Remote Sensing. (Illus.). 240p. (Orig.). text ed. 45.00x (ISBN 0-04-551036-9, 2597); pap. text ed. 22.50x (ISBN 0-04-551037-7, 2598). Allen Unwin.

TECHNICAL COMMUNICATION
see Communication of Technical Information

TECHNICAL DICTIONARIES
see Technology–Dictionaries

TECHNICAL DRAWING
see Mechanical Drawing

TECHNICAL EDUCATION
see also Apprentices; Employees, Training of; Forestry Schools and Education; Industrial Arts; Occupational Training; Professional Education; Vocational Education
The Community, Technical, & Junior College in the United States. 96p. 1978. 3.50 (IIE). Unipub.
Engineering & Technology Enrollments, 1979, 2 pts. Incl. Pt. 1. Engineering Enrollments. 45.00; Pt. 2. Technology Enrollments. 45.00. 1980. Set. 75.00. AAES.
Exporting Technical Education. 97p. 1968. 4.50 (ISBN 0-686-68834-1, IIE24, IIE). Unipub.
OAS General Secretariat, Dept. of Educational Affairs. Glosario de Technologia Educativa. (Illus.). 83p. (Span.). 1978. pap. text ed. 3.00 (ISBN 0-8270-1060-5). OAS.

TECHNICAL INFORMATION, COMMUNICATION OF
see Communication of Technical Information

TECHNICAL INNOVATIONS
see Technological Innovations

TECHNICAL INSTITUTES
see Technical Education

TECHNICAL LIBRARIES
Young, Margaret Labash & Young, Harold C., eds. Subject Directory of Special Libaries & Information Services: Science & Technology Libraries, Including Agriculture, Energy, Environment-Conservation & Food, Vol. 5. 6th ed. 1981. 80.00 (ISBN 0-8103-0309-4). Gale.

TECHNICAL REPORTS
Here are entered works on the processing and use of technical and scientific reports. Guides to technical authorship are entered under the heading Technical Writing.
see also Technical Writing
Jones, Paul W. & Keene, Michael L. Writing Scientific Papers-Reports. 8th ed. 365p. 1981. pap. text ed. write for info. (ISBN 0-697-03773-8). Wm C Brown.

TECHNICAL SCHOOLS
see Technical Education

TECHNICAL TERMS
see Technology–Dictionaries

TECHNICAL WRITING
Here are entered guides to authorship in engineering, science, and technology. Similar guides in other fields are entered under a corresponding term if in common usage, e.g. Medical Writing; otherwise under (subject)–authorship.
see also Authorship–Handbooks, Manuals, etc.; Technical Reports
Alred, Gerald J., et al. Business & Technical Writing: An Annotated Bibliography of Books, 1880-1980. LC 80-29211. 249p. 1981. 12.50 (ISBN 0-8108-1397-1). Scarecrow.
Bricq, Ron S. Technically Write! Communicating in a Technological Era. 2nd ed. (Illus.). 448p. 1981. pap. text ed. 11.95 (ISBN 0-13-898700-9). P-H.
Hoover, Hardy. Essentials for the Scientific & Technical Writer. 224p. 1981. pap. 4.00 (ISBN 0-486-24060-6). Dover.
Turner, Barry T. Effective Technical Writing & Speaking. 2nd ed. 220p. 1978. text ed. 22.00x (ISBN 0-220-66344-0, Pub. by Busn Bks England). Renouf.

TECHNICIANS, LABORATORY
see Laboratory Technicians

TECHNOCRACY
see also Technology and Civilization
Putt, A. Putt's Law & the Successful Technocrat. (Illus.). 124p. 1981. 8.00 (ISBN 0-682-49702-9). Exposition.
Ramesh, Jairam & Weiss, Charles, Jr., eds. Mobilizing Technology for World Development. LC 79-5349. 240p. 1979. pap. 6.95 (ISBN 0-03-055451-9). Overseas Dev Council.

TECHNOLOGICAL FORECASTING
see also Technology Transfer
Enk, Gordon A. & Hornick, William F. Value Issues in Technology Assessment. (Special Studies in Science, Technology, & Public Policy). 180p. 1981. lib. bdg. 20.00x (ISBN 0-89158-973-2). Westview.
Knight, Thomas J. Technology's Future: The Hague Congress Technology Assessment. 566p. 1981. Repr. of 1976 ed. text ed. price not set (ISBN 0-89874-283-8). Krieger.

TECHNOLOGICAL INNOVATIONS
see also Machinery in Industry
Boserup, Ester. Population & Technological Change: A Study of Long-Term Trends. LC 80-21116. (Illus.). 1981. lib. bdg. 17.50x (ISBN 0-226-06673-8). U of Chicago Pr.
Das, Ram. Appropriate Technology. 1981. 11.95 (ISBN 0-533-04744-7). Vantage.
Dasgupta, Biplab. The New Agrarian Technology & India. 1980. 17.50x (ISBN 0-8364-0635-4, Pub. by Macmillan India). South Asia Bks.
Development, Environment & Technology: Towards a Technology for Self-Reliance. 51p. 1978. pap. 6.00 (ISBN 0-686-68949-6, UN78/2D11, UN). Unipub.
Halty-Carrere, Maximo. Technological Development Strategies for Developing Countries: A Review for Policy Makers. 155p. 1979. pap. text ed. 12.95x (ISBN 0-920380-24-7, Pub. by Inst Res Pub Canada). Renouf.
Inventive Activity in the Asian & the Pacific Region. 152p. 1981. pap. 26.00 (WIPO66, WIPO). Unipub.
Kingston, William. Innovation. 1979. 11.95 (ISBN 0-7145-3540-0); pap. 4.95 (ISBN 0-7145-3611-3). Riverrun NY.
Morehouse, Ward. Separate, Unequal, but More Autonomous. (Working Papers in the World Order Models Project Ser.). 50p. (Orig.). 1981. pap. 1.50 (ISBN 0-686-28913-7). Transaction Bks.
Mukherjee, J. N. Forward with Nature: An Integrated Approach to World Problems of Technology, Energy & Agriculture. 188p. 1979. text ed. 18.00x (ISBN 0-8426-1676-4). Verry.
Ritterberger, Volker, ed. Science & Technology in a Changing International Order: The United Nations Conference on Science & Technology for Development. (Special Studies in Social, Political, & Economic Development). 200p. 1981. lib. bdg. 25.00x (ISBN 0-86531-146-3). Westview.
Technology Assessment for Development. 166p. 1980. pap. 13.00 (ISBN 0-686-68975-5, UN80/2A1, UN). Unipub.
Watkins; Fincham. Construction Science & Materials for Technicians 2. 1981. text ed. price not set (ISBN 0-408-00488-6). Butterworth.

TECHNOLOGICAL INNOVATIONS–AFRICA
Vail, David J. Technology for Ujamaa Village Developement in Tanzania. LC 74-25876. (Foreign & Comparative Studies-Eastern African Ser.: No. 18). 64p. 1975. pap. 3.50x (ISBN 0-915984-15-6). Syracuse U Foreign Comp.

TECHNOLOGICAL TRANSFER
see Technology Transfer

TECHNOLOGICAL UNEMPLOYMENT
see Unemployment, Technological

TECHNOLOGISTS
see also Laboratory Technicians
Groeg, Otto J., ed. Who's Who in Technology: Austria, Germany, Switzerland, 2 vols. 1055p. 1979. Set. 195.00x (ISBN 3-921220-24-6). Intl Pubns Serv.

TECHNOLOGY
see also Building; Electric Engineering; Engineering; Industrial Arts; Industrial Management; Inventions; Mineral Industries; Railroad Engineering; Technical Education; Technocracy; Technological Innovations; Unemployment, Technological
also names of specific industries, arts trades, etc., e.g. Clock and Watch Making, Printing, Tailoring
Alford, Jonathan, ed. The Impact of New Military Technolgy. LC 80-67839. (Adelphi Library: Vol. 4). 140p. 1981. text ed. 29.50 (ISBN 0-916672-74-3). Allanheld.
Bame, E. Allen & Cummings, Paul. Exploring Technology. (Technology Series). (Illus.). 288p. 1980. text ed. 12.95 (ISBN 0-87192-112-X, 000-3); tchr's. guide 13.25 (ISBN 0-87192-114-6); activity manual 6.95 (ISBN 0-87192-113-8). Davis Pubns.
Bowyer, Jack. Building Technology Three. (Newnes-Butterworths Technician Ser.). 96p. 1980. pap. 9.95 (ISBN 0-408-00411-8). Butterworths.
DeVore, Paul W. Technology: An Introduction. LC 79-53782. (Technology Ser.). (Illus.). 397p. 1980. text ed. 16.95 (ISBN 0-87192-115-4, 000-5). Davis Pubns.
Engineering & Technology Degrees, 1980, 3 pts. Incl. Pt. 1. By Schools. 25.00; Pt. 2. By Minorities. 75.00; Pt. 3. By Curriculum. 25.00. 1981. Set. 100.00 (201-80). AAES.
Heiner, Carol W. & Hendrix, Wayne R. People Create Technology. LC 79-53802. (Technology Series). (Illus.). 256p. (gr. 5-9). 1980. text ed. 12.95 (ISBN 0-87192-109-X, 000-2); tchr's guide 10.60 (ISBN 0-87192-111-1); activity manual 4.95 (ISBN 0-87192-110-3). Davis Pubns.
Nelkin, Dorothy. Controversy: Politics of Technical Decisions. LC 78-21339. (Focus Editions Ser.: Vol. 8). 256p. 1979. 18.95 (ISBN 0-8039-1209-9); pap. 9.95 (ISBN 0-8039-1210-2). Sage.
Peacocke, A. R. The Sciences & Theology in the Twentieth Century. (Oxford International Symposia). 320p. 1981. price not set (ISBN 0-85362-188-8). Routledge & Kegan.
The Placement of Engineering & Technology Graduates. Date not set. 25.00 (210-80). AAES.
The Present Situation of Science & Technology in the STPI Countries. (Science & Technology for Development Ser.: STPI Module 4). 65p. pap. 5.00 (IDRC TS22, IDRC). Unipub.
Schuurman & Egbert. Technology & the Future: A Philosophical Challenge. 1980. 19.95x (ISBN 0-88906-111-4). Radix Bks.
Science & Technology for Development: A Review of Schools of Thought on Science, Technology, Development, & Technical Change. (STPI Module Ser.: No. 1). 55p. 1980. pap. 5.00 (ISBN 0-88936-215-7, IDRCTS18, IDRC). Unipub.
Shipp, James F. Russian-English Dictionary of Surnames: Important Names from Science & Technology. xvi, 317p. (Orig.). 1981. pap. 30.00x (ISBN 0-917564-10-3). Translation Research.
Weatherhead, R. G. FRP Technology. (Illus.). xvii, 460p. 1980. 70.00x (ISBN 0-85334-886-3). Burgess-Intl Ideas.

TECHNOLOGY–ABBREVIATIONS
Anglo-American & German Abbreviations in Science & Technology Supplement. 1981. 52.50 (ISBN 3-598-20512-0). Bowker.

TECHNOLOGY–ADDRESSES, ESSAYS, LECTURES
Johnston, R. & Gummett, P. Directory Technology. 240p. 1980. 30.00x (ISBN 0-85664-740-3, Pub. by Croom Helm England). State Mutual Bk.

TECHNOLOGY–AUTHORSHIP
see Technical Writing

TECHNOLOGY–BIBLIOGRAPHY
The Research Libraries of the New York Public Library & the Library of Congress. Bibliographic Guide to Technology: 1980. (Library Catalogs Bib. Guides). 1981. lib. bdg. 175.00 (ISBN 0-8161-6895-4). G K Hall.

TECHNOLOGY–DICTIONARIES
Denti, Renzo. Dizionario Tecnico Italiano-Inglese--Inglese-Italiano. 9th rev. ed. 1811p. 1979. 44.00x (ISBN 88-203-1052-X). S F Vanni.
Jouklova, Z. Technical Dictionary: English, Czech, English. 510p. (Czech.). 1970. 12.00x (ISBN 0-89918-301-8). Vanous.
Kuznetsov, B., ed. Russian-English Polytechnical Dictionary. LC 80-41193. 900p. 1981. 100.00 (ISBN 0-08-023609-X). Pergamon.

TECHNOLOGY–EXHIBITIONS
see Exhibitions

TECHNOLOGY–HISTORY
see also Industrial Archaeology
Daumas, Maurice, ed. A History of Technology & Invention Progress Through the Ages, Vol. 1: The Origins of Technological Civilization to 1450. 520p. 1980. 40.00x (ISBN 0-7195-3730-4, Pub. by Murray Pubs England). State Mutual Bk.
--A History of Technology & Invention Progress Through the Ages, Vol. 3: The Expansion of Mechanization 1725-1860. 700p. 1980. 40.00x (ISBN 0-7195-3732-0, Pub. by Murray Pubs England). State Mutual Bk.
--A History of Technology & Invention Through the Ages, Vol. 2: The First Stages of Mechanization 1450-1725. 694p. 1980. 40.00x (ISBN 0-7195-3731-2, Pub. by Murray Pubs England). State Mutual Bk.
The Evolution of Science & Technology in STPI Countries. (Science & Technology for Development Ser.: STPI Module 3). 43p. 1981. pap. 5.00 (ISBN 0-88936-255-6, IDRC TS20, IDRC). Unipub.
Headrick, Daniel R. The Tools of Empire: Technology & European Imperialism in the Nineteenth Century. 224p. 1981. text ed. 9.95x (ISBN 0-19-502831-7); pap. text ed. 5.95x (ISBN 0-19-502832-5). Oxford U Pr.

TECHNOLOGY–HISTORY–CHINA
Volti, Rudi. Science & Technology in China. (Special Studies on China & East Asia). 350p. 1981. lib. bdg. 25.00x (ISBN 0-89158-951-1). Westview.

TECHNOLOGY–JUVENILE LITERATURE
Paige, David. Moving a Rocket, a Sub, & the London Bridge. LC 80-22125. (On the Move Ser.). (Illus.). 48p. (gr. 3-6). 1980. PLB 9.25 (ISBN 0-516-03890-7). Childrens.
Whittingham, Richard. Just About Anything Can Be Moved. LC 80-22669. (On the Move Ser.). 48p. (gr. 3-6). 1981. PLB 9.25 (ISBN 0-516-03889-3). Childrens.

TECHNOLOGY–PHILOSOPHY
see also Machinery in Industry; Technology and Civilization
Philosophy (Concepts) of Scientific & Technological Development. 17p. 1981. pap. 6.75 (ISBN 92-808-0176-7, T*U*N*U 109, UNU). Unipub.

TECHNOLOGY–SOCIAL ASPECTS
Here are entered works on the impact of technology on modern society. Works on the role of technology in the history and development of civilization are entered under Technology and Civilization.
Allaby, Michael & Bunyard, Peter. The Politics of Self-Sufficiency. 208p. 1980. 21.00 (ISBN 0-19-217695-1). Oxford U Pr.
Collingridge, David. The Social Control of Technology. 1980. 22.50 (ISBN 0-312-73168-X). St Martin.
Wicklein, John. Electronic Nightmare: The New Communications & Freedom. LC 80-54199. 320p. 1981. 15.95 (ISBN 0-670-50658-3). Viking Pr.

TECHNOLOGY, EDUCATIONAL
see Educational Technology

TECHNOLOGY AND CIVILIZATION
Here are entered works on the role of technology in the history and development of civilization. Works on the impact of technology on modern society are entered under Technology–Social Aspects.
see also Machinery in Industry; Social Problems; Technocracy; Technology–Philosophy
Diffrient, Niels. Humanscale, Vols. 4-9. 1981. Vols. 4-6. 37.50 (ISBN 0-686-69225-X); Vols. 7-9. 50.00 (ISBN 0-262-04061-1). MIT Pr.
Faunce, William. Problems of an Industrial Society. 2nd ed. Munson, Eric M., ed. 256p. 1981. pap. text ed. 8.95 (ISBN 0-07-020105-6, C). McGraw.
McRobie, George. Small Is Possible. LC 79-2634. 256p. 1981. 11.95 (ISBN 0-06-013041-5, CN694, HarpT); pap. 4.95 (ISBN 0-06-090694-4). Har-Row.

TECHNOLOGY AND STATE
see also Industry and State
Hodgson, Myra, ed. An American Response to the Foreign Industrial Challenge in High Technology Industries. 175p. (Orig.). 1980. pap. 95.00 (ISBN 0-686-69372-8). W Fraser Pubs.

TECHNOLOGY ASSESSMENT
Office of Technology Assessment Congress of the United States, ed. Technology & East West Trade. LC 80-26121. 312p. 1981. text ed. 25.00 (ISBN 0-86598-041-1). Allanheld.
Technology & East West Trade: Office of Technology Assessment, Congress of the U. S. LC 80-26121. 312p. 1981. text ed. 25.00 (ISBN 0-86598-041-1). Allanheld.

TECHNOLOGY TRANSFER
see also Technological Forecasting
Fikentscher, Wolfgang. Draft International Code of Conduct on the Transfer of Technology. (IIC Studies: Vol. 4). 211p. (Orig.). 1980. pap. text ed. 23.80 (ISBN 0-89573-030-8). Verlag Chemie.
Gee, Sherman. Technology Transfer, Innovation, & International Competitiveness. 240p. 1980. 21.00 (ISBN 0-471-08468-9, Pub. by Wiley-Interscience). Wiley.
Goulet, Denis. The Uncertain Promise: Value Conflicts in Technology Transfer. LC 77-80314. 324p. 1977. 12.95 (ISBN 0-89021-045-4); pap. 5.95 (ISBN 0-686-28704-5). Overseas Dev Council.
Hanson, Philip. Trade & Technology in Soviet-Western Relations. 300p. 1981. 30.00x (ISBN 0-231-05276-6). Columbia U Pr.
Legal Aspects of the Transfer of Technology in Modern Society. 18p. 1980. pap. 5.00 (ISBN 92-808-0175-9, TUNU099, UNU). Unipub.

Njoku, John E. Analyzing Nigerian-Americans Under a New Economic Order. LC 80-5916. 128p. (Orig.). 1981. pap. text ed. 7.50 (ISBN 0-8191-1448-0). U Pr of Amer.

Perlmutter, Howard V. & Sagafi-Nejad, Tagi. International Technology Transfer: Guidelines, Codes & a Muffled Quadrilogue. (Pergamon Policy Studies on International Developement). (Illus.). 250p. 1981. 27.50 (ISBN 0-08-027519-2). Pergamon.

Sagafi-nejad, Tagi, et al, eds. Controlling International Technology Transfer: Issues, Perspectives, & Policy Implications. LC 80-28329. (PPS on International Development Ser.). 525p. 1981. 55.00. Pergamon.

TECTONICS, PLATE

see Plate Tectonics

TEEN-AGE

see Adolescence

TEEN-AGE PARENTS

see Adolescent Parents

TEEN-AGERS

see Youth

TEEPEE BURNERS

see Incinerators

TEETH

see also Dentistry

Grundler, Horst. The Study of Tooth Shapes: A Systematic Procedure. (Illus.). 104p. 1976. 24.00 (ISBN 3-87652-561-6). Quint Pub Co.

TEETH–CARE AND HYGIENE

Here are entered works on personal dental hygiene for the layman. Works on dental hygiene as practiced by dental hygienists are entered under Dental Hygiene.

see also Dental Hygiene

Cormier, Patricia P. & Levy, Joyce I. Community Oral Health: A Systems Approach for the Dental Health Profession. 240p. 1980. pap. 14.95x (ISBN 0-8385-1184-8). ACC.

Goldberg, Hyman J. Your Mouth Is Your Business: The Dentists' Guide to Better Health. (Appleton Consumer Health Guides). (Illus.). 215p. 1980. 12.95 (ISBN 0-8385-9943-5); pap. 5.95 (ISBN 0-8385-9942-7). ACC.

TEETH–DISEASES

see also Endodontics; Teeth–Radiography

Berns, Joel M. The Story of Impacted Wisdom Teeth Kit. 1980. pap. 24.00 (ISBN 0-931386-14-4). Quint Pub Co.

Bhaskar, S. N. Synopsis of Oral Pathology. 6th ed. (Illus.). 676p. 1981. text ed. 27.50 (ISBN 0-8016-0685-3). Mosby.

Faschlicht, Samuel. Tooth Mutilations & Dentistry in Pre-Columbian Mexico. (Illus.). 152p. 1976. 46.00. Quint Pub Co.

Harvey, Clair & Kelly, James E. Decayed, Missing & Filled Teeth Among Persons One to Seventy-Four: United States, 1971-74, No. 11-223. Shipp, Audrey, ed. 50p. Date not set. pap. text ed. price not set (ISBN 0-8406-0209-X). Natl Ctr Health Stats.

TEETH–DISEASES–DIAGNOSIS

Tyldesley, W. R. Oral Medicine. (Illus.). 225p. 1981. pap. text ed. 22.95x (ISBN 0-19-261275-1). Oxford U Pr.

TEETH–OCCLUSION

see Occlusion (Dentistry)

TEETH–RADIOGRAPHY

Kasle, Myron J. & Langlais, Robert. Basic Principles of Oral Radiography. (Exercises in Dental Radiology Ser.: Vol. 4). (Illus.). 200p. 1981. text ed. price not set (ISBN 0-7216-5291-3). Saunders.

Wuehrmann, Arthur H. & Manson-Hing, Lincoln R. Dental Radiology. 5th ed. (Illus.). 500p. 1981. text ed. 27.50 (ISBN 0-8016-5643-5). Mosby.

TEETH, ARTIFICIAL

see Prosthodontics

TEILHARD DE CHARDIN, PIERRE, 1881-1955

Lukas, Mary & Lukas, Ellen. Teilhard. 360p. 1981. pap. 6.95 (ISBN 0-07-039047-9). McGraw.

TELECOMMUNICATION

see also Artificial Satellites in Telecommunication; Broadcasting; Data Transmission Systems; Phase-Locked Loops; Radio; Signal Theory (Telecommunication); Telephone; Television

Arredondo, Larry A. Getting Started in Telecommunications Management. 1980. softcover 30.00 (ISBN 0-936648-04-X). Telecom Lib.

Bylanski, P. & Ingram, D. G. Digital Transmission Systems. rev. ed. (IEE Telecommunications Ser.). 431p. pap. write for info. (ISBN 0-906048-37-0, Pub. by Peregrinus England). Inst Electrical.

Change Magazine Editors. The Communications Revolution & the Education of Americans. LC 80-66849. 64p. (Orig.). 1980. pap. 6.95 (ISBN 0-915390-24-8). Change Mag.

Chin, Felix. Regulatory Reform of Telecommunications: A Selected Bibliography. (Public Administration Ser.: Bibliography P-521). 50p. 1980. pap. 5.50. Vance Biblios.

Hudson, J. E. Adaptive Arrays. (IEE Electromagnetic Waves Ser.). 1981. price not set (Pub. by Peregrinus England). Inst Electrical.

Moss, Mitchell L. Telecommunications & Productivity. 416p. 1980. text ed. 37.50 (ISBN 0-201-04649-0). A-W.

Newton, Harry. Professional Managemant Via Telecommunications. 1980. softcover 7.50 (ISBN 0-936648-03-1). Telecom Lib.

Pelton, Joseph N. Global Talk. LC 80-83261. 320p. 1980. write for info. (ISBN 90-286-0240-2). Sijthoff & Noordhoff.

Stavroulakis, Peter. Interference Analysis of Communication Systems. 472p. 1980. 38.00 (ISBN 0-471-08674-6, Pub. by Wiley-Interscience); pap. 25.75 (ISBN 0-471-08673-8). Wiley.

Telecommunication Transmission. (IEE Conference Publication). 1981. pap. price not set. Inst Electrica.

Telecommunications Energy. (IEE Conference Publication). (Illus., Orig.). 1981. pap. price not set. Inst Electrical.

TELECOMMUNICATION–DICTIONARIES

Aries. Dictionary of Telecommunication. 1981. text ed. price not set (ISBN 0-408-00328-6). Butterworth.

TELEGONY

see Hybridization

TELEMETRY, BIOLOGICAL

see Biotelemetry

TELENCEPHALON

Braak, H. Architectonics of the Human Telencephalic Cortex. (Studies of Brain Functions: Vol. 4). (Illus.). 147p. 1981. 27.50 (ISBN 0-387-10312-0). Springer-Verlag.

TELEPHONE

see also Radiotelephone; Telephone Selling

Brandon, Belinda B., ed. The Effect of the Demographics of Individual Households on Their Telephone Useage. 432p. 1980. write for info. (ISBN 0-88410-695-0). Ballinger Pub.

Waz, Joseph W., Jr. Reverse the Charges: How to Save Dollars on Your Phone Bill. 1980. pap. 3.50 (ISBN 0-9603466-5-1). NCCB.

TELEPHONE–JUVENILE LITERATURE

Imbo, M. Mi Guia Telefonica. Mann, Philip, ed. Kreps, Georgian, tr. from Eng. (Shape Board Play Book). Orig. Title: My Telephone Book. (Illus.). 14p. (Span.). (ps-3). 1981. bds. 3.50 plastic come bdg. (5009SP). Tuffy Bks.

Klimo, Kate, ed. My Telephone Book. (Playboards Ser.). (Illus.). 12p. (ps-k). Date not set. boards 2.95 (ISBN 0-671-42526-9, Little Simon). S&S.

TELEPHONE–LAW AND REGULATIONS

see also Electric Engineering–Laws and Legislation; Wire-Tapping

Noll, Edward M. First Class Radiotelephone License Handbook. 5th ed. LC 80-52936. 1980. pap. 11.95 (ISBN 0-672-21757-0). Sams.

TELEPHONE–RATES

Strange, Howard. How to Save Lots of Money on Your Phone Bill. 128p. (Orig.). 1981. pap. 1.95 (ISBN 0-345-29373-8). Ballantine.

TELEPHONE, WIRELESS

see Radio

TELEPHONE SELLING

Bury, Charles. Telephone Techniques That Sell. 1980. pap. 4.95 (ISBN 0-446-97453-6). Warner Bks.

TELERADIESTHESIA

see Radiesthesia

TELESCOPE

Bell, Louis. The Telescope. 287p. 1981. pap. price not set (ISBN 0-486-24151-3). Dover.

King, Henry C. The History of the Telescope. LC 79-87811. (Illus.). 480p. 1980. Repr. of 1979 ed. 16.50x (ISBN 0-938164-05-8). Vintage Bk Co.

TELEVISION

Arlen, Michael J. The Camera Age: Essays on Television. 1981. 12.95 (ISBN 0-374-11822-1). FS&G.

Gertner, Richard, ed. Television Almanac, 1981, Vol. 26. 650p. 1981. 38.00 (ISBN 0-900610-25-5). Quigley Pub Co.

TELEVISION–BROADCASTING

see Television Broadcasting

TELEVISION–DICTIONARIES

Roberts, R. S. Dictionary of Radio, TV & Audio. 1981. text ed. price not set (ISBN 0-408-00339-1, Newnes-Butterworth). Butterworth.

TELEVISION–DIRECTION

see Television–Production and Direction

TELEVISION–PRODUCTION AND DIRECTION

Levinson, Richard & Link, William. Stay Tuned. 256p. 1981. 10.95 (ISBN 0-312-76136-8). St Martin.

TELEVISION–STAGE-LIGHTING

see Stage Lighting

TELEVISION–TRANSMITTERS AND TRANSMISSION

Middleton, Robert G. One Hundred & One Ways to Use Your VOM, TVM, DVM. 3rd ed. LC 80-52934. 1980. pap. 9.95 (ISBN 0-672-21756-2). Sams.

TELEVISION ADVERTISING

Arlen, Michael J. Thirty Seconds. 224p. 1981. pap. 2.95 (ISBN 0-14-005810-9). Penguin.

Busch, H. Ted & Landeck, Terry. The Making of a Television Commercial. LC 80-23192. (Illus.). 228p. 1981. 10.95 (ISBN 0-02-518830-5). Macmillan.

TELEVISION AND CHILDREN

Lake, Sara, ed. Children & Television. (Special Interest Resource Guides in Education Ser.). (Orig.). 1981. pap. 8.50x (ISBN 0-912700-87-4). Oryx Pr.

Murray, John P. Television & Youth: Twenty-Five Years of Research & Controversy. 278p. (Orig.). 1980. pap. text ed. 10.00 (ISBN 0-938510-00-2, 010-TV). Boys Town Ctr.

Singer, Dorothy G., et al. Teaching Television: How to Use TV to Your Child's Advantage. (Illus.). 192p. 1981. 10.95 (ISBN 0-8037-8515-1). Dial.

TELEVISION AUDIENCES

Davis, Richard H. Television & the Aging Audience. LC 80-68093. (Illus.). 107p. (Orig.). 1980. 8.50 (ISBN 0-88474-096-X); pap. 6.50 (ISBN 0-686-28656-1). USC Andrus Geron.

TELEVISION BROADCASTING

see also Television–Transmitters and Transmission; Television Advertising; Television Audiences; Television in Education; Television Programs; Video Tape Recorders and Recording

Clift, Charles, III & Greer, Archie, eds. Broadcast Programming: The Current Perspective. 6th ed. LC 80-8127. 249p. 1981. text ed. 8.50 (ISBN 0-8191-1429-4). U Pr of Amer.

Eastman, Susan T. & Head, Sidney W. Broadcast Programming: Strategies for Winning Television & Radio Audiences. 400p. 1980. text ed. 15.95x (ISBN 0-534-00882-8). Wadsworth Pub.

James, Clive. The Crystal Bucket. 192p. 1981. 11.95 (ISBN 0-224-01890-6, Pub. by Chatto-Bodley-Jonathan). Merrimack Bk Serv.

Jones, Vane A. North American Radio-T.V. Station Guide: TV Station Guide. 14th ed. 1980. pap. 7.95 (ISBN 0-672-21725-2). Sams.

Lemay, Harding. Eight Years in Another World. LC 80-69363. 1981. 10.95 (ISBN 0-689-11149-5). Atheneum.

McCavitt, William. Television Studio Operations Manual. rev. ed. 106p. 1980. pap. 4.50 (ISBN 0-935648-05-4). Halldin Pub.

McMahon, Michael, ed. Nineteen Eighty-One Television Contacts. 1981. pap. text ed. 117.00 (ISBN 0-935224-04-1). Larimi Comm.

Rutkowski, Katherine, ed. Videotex Services. (NCTA Executive Seminar Ser.: No. 1). (Orig.). 1980. pap. 40.00 (ISBN 0-686-28867-X). Natl Cable.

Wall, C. Edward, et al, eds. Media Review Digest, Vol. 10, 1980. 1980. 120.00 (ISBN 0-87650-129-3). Pierian.

TELEVISION BROADCASTING–AUDIENCES

see Television Audiences

TELEVISION BROADCASTING–HISTORY

Bergreen, Laurence. Look Now, Pay Later: The Rise of Network Broadcasting. 1981. pap. 3.95 (ISBN 0-451-61966-8, ME1966, Ment). NAL.

Katzman, Natan. Program Decisions in Public Television. 72p. 1976. pap. 3.50 (Pub Telecomm). NAEB.

TELEVISION BROADCASTING–NEWS

see Television Broadcasting of News

TELEVISION BROADCASTING–SOCIAL ASPECTS

Lee, Chin-Chuan. Media Imperialism Reconsidered: The Homogenizing of Television Culture. LC 80-16763. (People & Communication Ser.: Vol. 10). (Illus.). 276p. 1980. 20.00 (ISBN 0-8039-1495-4). Sage.

--Media Imperialism Reconsidered: The Homogenizing of Television Culture. LC 80-16763. (People & Communication Ser.: Vol. 10). (Illus.). 276p. 1980. pap. 9.95 (ISBN 0-8039-1496-2). Sage.

TELEVISION BROADCASTING–GREAT BRITAIN

Paulu, Burton. Television & Radio in the United Kingdom. 544p. 1981. 39.50x (ISBN 0-8166-0941-1). U of Minn Pr.

TELEVISION BROADCASTING OF NEWS

Bethell, Tom. Television Evening News Covers Inflation: Nineteen Seventy-Eight to Seventy-Nine. Media Institute, ed. (Illus.). 52p. (Orig.). 1980. pap. 5.00 (ISBN 0-937790-00-1). Media Inst.

Face the Nation: The Collected Transcripts from the CBS Radio & Television Broadcasts, 1954-1978, 21 vols. Incl. Vol. 1, 1954-1955. 465p (ISBN 0-03-941431-0); Vol. 2, 1956. 418p (ISBN 0-03-091432-9); Vol. 3, 1957. 443p (ISBN 0-03-091433-7); Vol. 4, 1958. 409p (ISBN 0-03-091434-5); Vol. 5, 1959. 420p (ISBN 0-03-091435-3); Vol. 6, 1960-1961. 499p (ISBN 0-03-091436-1); Vol. 7, 1963-1964. 435p (ISBN 0-03-091437-X); Vol. 8, 1965. 316p (ISBN 0-03-091438-8); Vol. 9, 1966. 344p (ISBN 0-03-091439-6); Vol. 10, 1967. 390p (ISBN 0-03-091440-X); Vol. 11, 1968. 384p (ISBN 0-03-091441-8); Vol. 12, 1969. 353p (ISBN 0-03-091442-6); Vol. 13, 1970. 393p (ISBN 0-03-091443-4); Vol. 14, 1971. 416p (ISBN 0-03-091445-0); Vol. 15, 1972. 418p (ISBN 0-8108-0822-6); Vol. 16, 1973. 398p (ISBN 0-8108-0823-4); Vol. 17, 1974. 375p (ISBN 0-8108-0824-2); Vol. 18, 1975. 382p (ISBN 0-8108-0916-8); Vol. 19, 1976. 382p (ISBN 0-8108-1021-2); Vol. 20, 1977. 371p (ISBN 0-8108-1021-2); Vol. 21, 1978. 365p (ISBN 0-8108-1021-2). 29.50 ea. Microfilming Corp.

Glasgow University Media Group. Bad News, Vol.1. 326p. 1981. price not set (ISBN 0-7100-0792-2). Routledge & Kegan.

Golding, Elliot. Making the News. (Illus.). 241p. 1979. text ed. 35.00x (ISBN 0-582-50460-0). Longman.

McMahon, Michael, ed. Nineteen Eighty to Nineteen Eighty-One TV News. 1980. 70.00 (ISBN 0-935224-03-3). Larimi Comm.

Roeh, Itzhak, et al. Almost Midnight: Reforming the Late Night News. LC 80-16991. (People & Communication: Vol. 11). (Illus.). 200p. 1980. 18.50 (ISBN 0-8039-1504-7). Sage.

--Almost Midnight: Reforming the Late Night News. LC 80-16991. (People & Communication: Vol. 11). (Illus.). 200p. 1980. pap. 8.95 (ISBN 0-8039-1505-5). Sage.

TELEVISION COMMERCIALS

see Television Advertising

TELEVISION DIRECTION

see Television–Production and Direction

TELEVISION DRAMA

see Television Plays

TELEVISION IN ADVERTISING

see Television Advertising

TELEVISION IN EDUCATION

Avery, Robert K., et al. Research Index of NAEB Journals, 1957 to 1979. 169p. 1980. pap. 13.50. NAEB.

Beardsley, Rick, ed. The Videolog: General Interest & Education. 1980-81 ed. (Videolog Ser.). 500p. 1981. pap. 34.50 (ISBN 0-88432-071-5). J Norton Pubs.

Chu, Godwin C. & Schramm, Wilbur. Learning from Television: What the Research Says. 116p. 1979. pap. 6.00 (Pub Telecomm). NAEB.

Katzman, Natan. Program Decisions in Public Television. 72p. 1976. pap. 3.50 (Pub Telecomm). NAEB.

Middleton, John. Cooperative School Television & Educational Change. 135p. 1979. pap. 6.95. NAEB.

National Telecommunications & Information Administration, ed. The Nixon Administration Public Broadcasting Papers. 124p. 1979. pap. 5.00. NAEB.

Schramm, Wilbur, et al. Bold Experiment: The Story of Educational Television in American Samoa. LC 79-67777. (Illus.). 264p. 1981. text ed. 17.50x (ISBN 0-8047-1090-2). Stanford U Pr.

TELEVISION JOURNALISM

see Television Broadcasting of News

TELEVISION NEWS

see Television Broadcasting of News

TELEVISION PLAYS

Brandt, George, ed. British Television Drama. LC 80-41031. (Illus.). 300p. Date not set. price not set (ISBN 0-521-22186-2); pap. price not set (ISBN 0-521-29384-7). Cambridge U Pr.

TELEVISION PRODUCTION

see Television–Production and Direction

TELEVISION PROGRAMS

see also Television Audiences; Television Plays

Clavell, James, frwd. by. The Making of James Clavell's Shogun. (Illus.). 1980. pap. 8.95 (ISBN 0-440-55709-7, Delta). Dell.

Essoe, Gabe. The Offical Book of TV Lists. (Illus.). 256p. 1981. 12.95 (ISBN 0-87000-497-2). Arlington Hse.

Gianakos, Larry J. Television Drama Series Programming: A Comprehensive Chronicle, 1947-1959. LC 80-17023. 581p. 1980. 29.50 (ISBN 0-8108-1330-0). Scarecrow.

Hammond, Charles. The Image Decade: Television Documentary 1965-1975. 256p. 1981. 16.95 (ISBN 0-8038-3431-4, Communication Arts); pap. 9.95 (ISBN 0-8038-3432-2). Hastings.

Jeffries, Wendy. That's Incredible, Vol. 1. (That's Incredible TV Show Ser.). 192p. (Orig.). 1981. pap. 2.25 (ISBN 0-515-05807-6). Jove Pubns.

--That's Incredible, Vol. 2. (That's Incredible TV Show Ser.). 192p. (Orig.). 1981. pap. 2.25 (ISBN 0-515-05870-X). Jove Pubns.

--That's Incredible, Vol. 3. (That's Incredible TV Show Ser.). 192p. (Orig.). 1981. pap. 2.25 (ISBN 0-515-05986-2). Jove Pubns.

Lely, James A. Battlestar Galactica. (T. V. & Movie Tie-Ins Ser.). 32p. (gr. 4-12). 1979. PLB 5.95 (ISBN 0-87191-701-7); pap. 2.95 (ISBN 0-89812-033-0). Creative Ed.

--Star Wars. (T.V. & Movie Tie-Ins Ser.). (Illus.). (gr. 4-12). 1979. PLB 5.95 (ISBN 0-87191-700-9); pap. 2.95 (ISBN 0-89812-036-5). Creative Ed.

Linke, Frances. Space Patrol III. (Space Patrol Ser.: No. 3). 205p. 20.00 (ISBN 0-933276-06-0). Nin-Ra Ent.

Norbom, Mary Ann. Richard Dawson & Family Feud. (Illus., Orig.). 1981. pap. 1.95 (ISBN 0-451-09773-4, J9773, Sig). NAL.

Rothel, David. Who Was That Masked Man? The Story of the Lone Ranger. rev. ed. LC 80-27237. (Illus.). 290p. 1981. 19.90 (ISBN 0-498-02538-1). A S Barnes.

Schumacher, Craig. Happy Days. (T.V. & Movie Tie-Ins Ser.). (Illus.). (gr. 4-12). 1979. PLB 5.95 (ISBN 0-87191-702-5); pap. 2.95 (ISBN 0-89812-034-9). Creative Ed.

Star Trek. (T.V. & Movie Tie-in Ser.). (Illus.). (gr. 4-12). 1979. PLB 5.95 (ISBN 0-87191-718-1); pap. 2.95 (ISBN 0-89812-032-2). Creative Ed.

Tennis, Craig. Here's Johnny: A Close-up of Johnny Carson & the Tonight Show. (Illus.). pap. 2.50 (ISBN 0-686-68808-2). PB.

Terrace, Vincent. Complete Encyclopedia of Television Programs 1947-1979. 2nd rev. ed. LC 79-87791. (Illus.). 1200p. 1981. 29.95 (ISBN 0-498-02177-7); pap. 10.95 (ISBN 0-498-02488-1). A S Barnes.

Turner, Mark. Hardy Boys. (T.V. & Movie Tie-Ins Ser.). (gr. 4-12). 1979. PLB 5.95 (ISBN 0-87191-703-3); pap. 2.95 (ISBN 0-89812-035-7). Creative Ed.

Williams, Walter. The Mr. Bill Show. 80p. pap. 2.50 (ISBN 0-671-42039-9). PB.

TELEVISION SCRIPTS

see also Television Plays; Television Programs

Brenner, Alfred. TV Scriptwriter's Handbook. LC 80-23700. 288p. 1980. 10.95 (ISBN 0-89879-024-7). Writers Digest.

TELEVISION TRANSMISSION

see Television–Transmitters and Transmission

TELFORD, THOMAS, 1757-1834

Penfold, Alastair, ed. Thomas Telford: Engineer. 192p. 1980. 40.00x (ISBN 0-7277-0084-7, Pub. by Telford England). State Mutual Bk.

TELLURIUM

Wilcox. Lead Tin Telluride, Silver Halides & Czochralski Growth. Date not set. price not set (ISBN 0-8247-1354-0). Dekker.

TELOMERIZATION

see Polymers and Polymerization

TELSTAR SATELLITES

see Artificial Satellites in Telecommunication

TEMPERAMENT

see also Character; Emotions

Keirsey, David & Bates, Marilyn. Please Understand Me: An Essay on Temperament Styles. 1978. write for info. Prometheus Nemesis.

TEMPERANCE

see also Alcohol–Physiological Effect; Alcohol and Youth; Alcoholics; Alcoholism; Hotels, Taverns, etc.; Liquor Industry and Trade; Liquor Problem; Narcotic Habit; Prohibition

McCarty, Jeanne. The Struggle for Sobriety. (Southwestern Studies: No. 62). 1980. pap. 3.00 (ISBN 0-87404-121-X). Tex Western.

TEMPERATURES, LOW

see Low Temperatures

TEMPLE OF GOD

see also Mosques

Barrois, Georges A. Jesus Christ & the Temple. LC 80-19700. 163p. (Orig.). 1980. pap. 5.95 (ISBN 0-913836-73-7, BS680 T4837). St Martin.

TEMPLES

see also Mosques

Wang, Robert. The Secret Temple. 1980. 15.00 (ISBN 0-87728-490-3); pap. 7.95 (ISBN 0-87728-518-7). Weiser.

Woodford, Susan. The Parthenon. (Cambridge Introduction to the History of Mankind Ser.). Date not set. pap. price not set (ISBN 0-521-22629-5). Cambridge U Pr.

TEMPORAL BONE

Glaser, G. Temporal Lobe Psychomotor Seizures. 1981. pap. text ed. write for info. (ISBN 0-443-08000-3). Churchill.

TEMPTATION

see also Good and Evil

Perryman, F. J. How to Resist the Devil. pap. 0.50. Faith Pub Hse.

TEN COMMANDMENTS

see Commandments, Ten

TENANTS

see Landlord and Tenant

TENNESSEE

see also names of cities, counties, towns, etc. in Tennessee

Livingood, James W. Hamilton County. Dunn, Joy B. & Crawford, Charles W., eds. (Tennessee County History Ser.: No. 33). 144p. 1981. 12.50 (ISBN 0-87870-120-6). Memphis St Univ.

TENNESSEE–GENEALOGY

Wright, Mildred S. William Harper Wright: His Ancestry & Descendants & Allied Lines of Stone's River, Tennessee. LC 80-52849. (Illus.). 183p. 1980. 35.00 (ISBN 0-917016-16-5); accopress 25.00 (ISBN 0-917016-17-3). M S Wright.

TENNESSEE–HISTORY

Corlew, Robert E. Tennessee: A Short History. 2nd ed. LC 80-13553. (Illus.). 568p. 1981. 22.50 (ISBN 0-87049-258-6); pap. text ed. 14.50x (ISBN 0-87049-302-7). U of Tenn Pr.

Holt, Edgar A. Claiborne County. Dunn, Joy B. & Crawford, Charles W., eds. (Tennessee County History Ser.: No. 13). (Illus.). 144p. 1981. 12.50x (ISBN 0-87870-101-X). Memphis St Univ.

Johnson, Charles O. & Jackson, Charles W. City Behind a Fence: Oak Ridge, Tennessee, 1942-1946. LC 80-15897. (Illus.). 272p. 1981. 18.50 (ISBN 0-87049-303-5); pap. 9.50 (ISBN 0-87049-309-4). U of Tenn Pr.

Vexler, R. I. Tennessee Chronology & Factbook, Vol. 42. 1978. 8.50 (ISBN 0-379-16167-2). Oceana.

TENNESSEE–SOCIAL LIFE AND CUSTOMS

Bryant, Carlene F. We're All Kin: A Cultural Study of a Mountain Neighborhood. LC 81-473. 160p. 1981. 9.50x (ISBN 0-87049-312-4). U of Tenn Pr.

TENNESSEE VALLEY AUTHORITY

Selznick, Philip. T. V. A. & the Grass Roots: A Study in the Sociology of Formal Organization. (California Library Reprint Ser.: No. 103). 1980. 18.50x (ISBN 0-520-03979-3). U of Cal Pr.

TENNIS

Ashe, Arthur. Arthur Ashe's Tennis Clinic. LC 80-84951. (Illus.). 144p. 1981. 12.95 (ISBN 0-914178-44-X, 42904-3). Golf Digest Bks.

Assaiante, Paul, ed. Championship Tennis by the Experts. LC 80-83978. (West Point Sports Fitness Ser.: Vol. 13). (Illus.). 208p. (Orig.). 1981. pap. text ed. 6.95 (ISBN 0-918438-23-3). Leisure Pr.

Cambell, Shep. Quick Tips from the Tennis Spot. LC 80-84952. (Illus.). 208p. 1981. pap. 6.95 (ISBN 0-914178-45-8, 42906-X). Golf Digest Bks.

Campbell, Shep. Quick Tips from the CBS Tennis Spot. (Illus.). 208p. (Orig.). 1981. pap. 6.95 (ISBN 0-914178-45-8, 42906-X). Tennis Mag.

Dintiman, George B., et al. Doctor Tennis: A Complete Guide to Conditioning & Injury Prevention for All Ages. LC 80-65623. (Illus.). 106p. (Orig.). 1980. text ed. 4.95 (ISBN 0-938074-00-8). Champion Athlete.

Fox, Allen & Evans, Richard. If I'm the Better Player, Why Can't I Win. LC 79-63332. (Tennis Magazine Bks.). 160p. 1979. 8.95. Golf Digest Bks.

Johnson, Joan D. & Xanthos, Paul. Tennis. 4th ed. (Pysical Education Activities Ser.). 1981. pap. text ed. 3.25x (ISBN 0-697-07174-X). Wm C Brown.

Schwed, Peter. Peter Schwed's Tennis Quiz. (Illus.). 224p. (Orig.). 1981. pap. 8.95 (ISBN 0-914178-46-6, 42907-8). Tennis Mag.

--Test Your Tennis I.Q. LC 80-84954. (Illus.). 224p. 1981. pap. 8.95 (ISBN 0-914178-46-6, 42907-8). Golf Digest Bks.

Smith, Stan, et al. Teach Yourself Tennis! LaMarche, Robert J., ed. LC 80-66688. (Illus.). 224p. Date not set. 12.95 (ISBN 0-914178-39-3). Tennis Mag.

Stove, Betty & Adams, Susan. Tennis. (Burns Sports Ser.). 156p. Date not set. pap. cancelled (ISBN 0-695-81571-7). Follett.

Sullivan, George. Tennis Rules Illustrated. 96p. (Orig.). 1981. pap. 3.95 (ISBN 0-346-12525-1). Cornerstone.

Tennis Magazine Editors. Instant Tennis Lessons. (Tennis Magazine Bks-Instant Lesson Ser.). (Illus.). 191p. 1978. pap. 4.95 (ISBN 0-914178-18-0). Golf Digest Bks.

--The Tennis Player's Handbook. LC 79-65033. (Tennis Magazine Bks). (Illus.). 318p. 1980. pap. 8.95 (ISBN 0-914178-32-6). Golf Digest Bks.

--Tennis Strokes & Strategies. LC 75-14065. (Illus.). 217p. 1975. 10.95 (ISBN 0-671-22073-X). Tennis Mag.

Tennis Magazine Eds. & Instruction Advisory Board. Tennis: How to Play, How to Win. LC 77-92906. (Tennis Magazine Bks.). (Illus.). 222p. 1978. 11.95 (ISBN 0-914178-19-9). Golf Digest Bks.

TENNIS–BIOGRAPHY

Aaseng, Nathan. Winning Men of Tennis. LC 80-28598. (Sports Heroes Library). (Illus.). (gr. 4 up). 1981. PLB 5.95 (ISBN 0-8225-1068-5). Lerner Pubns.

--Winning Women of Tennis. (The Sports Heroes Library). (Illus.). (gr. 4 up). 1981. PLB 5.95 (ISBN 0-8225-1067-7). Lerner Pubns.

TENNYSON, ALFRED TENNYSON, BARON, 1809-1892

Elton, Oliver. Tennyson & Matthew Arnold. 96p. 1980. Repr. of 1924 ed. lib. bdg. 12.50 (ISBN 0-8492-4411-0). R West.

Hair, Donald S. Domestic & Heroic in Tennyson's Poetry. 272p. 1981. 25.00x (ISBN 0-8020-5530-3). U of Toronto Pr.

Lang, Andrew. Modern English Writers, Alfred Tennyson. 233p. 1980. Repr. lib. bdg. 25.00 (ISBN 0-89984-321-2). Century Bookbindery.

McSweeney, Kerry. Tennyson & Swinburne As Romantic Naturalists. 240p. 1981. 25.00x (ISBN 0-8020-2381-9). U of Toronto Pr.

Stanley, Hiram M. Essays on Literary Art: Tennyson, Wordsworth, Jane Austen, Thoreau. 164p. 1980. Repr. of 1897 ed. lib. bdg. 25.00 (ISBN 0-8414-8035-4). Folcroft.

Walker, Hugh. The Age of Tennyson. 309p. 1980. Repr. of 1932 ed. lib. bdg. 25.00 (ISBN 0-89760-914-X). Telegraph Bks.

Walters, J. Cummings. Tennyson, Poet, Philosopher, Idealist. 370p. 1980. Repr. of 1893 ed. lib. bdg. 40.00 (ISBN 0-89984-505-3). Century Bookbindery.

Young, George M. Today & Yesterday: Tennyson, Burke, Thackeray, Shakespeare. 312p. 1980. lib. bdg. 15.00 (ISBN 0-8482-3125-2). Norwood Edns.

TENNYSON, EMILY (SELLWOOD) TENNYSON, BARONESS, 1813-1896

Hoge, James O. & James O., eds. Lady Tennyson's Journal. LC 80-21387. 1981. price not set (ISBN 0-8139-0876-0). U Pr of Va.

TENPINS

see Bowling

TENSION (PSYCHOLOGY)

see Stress (Psychology)

TENSOR ANALYSIS

see Calculus of Tensors

TENT OF MEETING

see Tabernacle

TENURE OF LAND

see Land Tenure

TENURE OF OFFICE

see Civil Service

TERATOLOGY

see Abnormalities, Human; Monsters

TEREZIN (CONCENTRATION CAMP)

Bor, Josef. The Terezin Requiem. 1978. pap. 1.95 (ISBN 0-380-01673-7, 33449, Bard). Avon.

TERMINOLOGY

see Names

TERMS, LITERARY

see Literature–Terminology

TERRACES (ARCHITECTURE)

see Decks (Architecture, Domestic)

TERRAIN SENSING, REMOTE

see Remote Sensing

TERRESTRIAL PHYSICS

see Geophysics

TERROR, REIGN OF

see France–History–Revolution, 1789-1799

TERROR TALES

see Horror Tales

TERRORISM

see also Genocide

Alexander, Yonah, ed. Behavioral & Quantitative Perspectives on Terrorism. Gleason, John M. LC 80-39752. (Pergamon Press Series on International Politics). 300p. 1981. 32.50 (ISBN 0-08-025989-8). Pergamon.

Clutterbock, Richard. Guerillas & Terrorists. 1977. 10.95 (ISBN 0-571-11027-4, Pub. by Faber & Faber). Merrimack Bk Serv.

Clutterbuck, Richard. Guerrillas & Terrorists. LC 80-83219. 125p. 1980. 12.00x (ISBN 0-8214-0590-X); pap. 5.95x (ISBN 0-8214-0592-6). Ohio U Pr.

Cooper, H. H. The Hostage-Takers. 1st ed. (Illus.). 100p. (Orig.). 1981. pap. 12.00 (ISBN 0-87364-209-0). Paladin Ent.

Sloan, Stephen. Simulating Terrorism. LC 80-5937. (Illus.). 200p. 1981. 12.95 (ISBN 0-8061-1746-X); pap. 5.95 (ISBN 0-8061-1760-5). U of Okla Pr.

TEST-BORING

see Boring

TEST PROBES

see Probes (Electronic Instruments)

TESTACEA

see Mollusks

TESTICLE

Bollack, C. G. & Clavert, A., eds. Epididymis & Fertility: Biology & Pathology. (Progress in Reproductive Biology Ser.: Vol. 8). (Illus.). viii, 192p. 1981. 58.75 (ISBN 3-8055-2157-X). S Karger.

TESTIS

see Testicle

TESTS AND MEASUREMENTS IN EDUCATION

see Educational Tests and Measurements

TETON MOUNTAINS, WYOMING

Anderson, Elisabeth, et al. Cabin Comments: A Journal of Life in Jackson Hole. LC 80-53090. (Illus.). 286p. (gr. 7-12). 1980. 14.95 (ISBN 0-933160-08-9); pap. 7.75 (ISBN 0-933160-07-0). Teton Bkshop.

Maughan, Ralph. Beyond the Tetons. (Illus.). 135p. (Orig.). 1981. pap. 5.95 (ISBN 0-87108-580-1). Pruett.

TEWA INDIANS

see Indians of North America–Southwest, New

TEXAS

see also names of cities, towns, regions, etc. in Texas

Wright, Rita & Anderson, Mildred, eds. Texas Trade & Professional Associations (1981 Edition) rev. ed. 75p. (Orig.). 1981. pap. 5.00 (ISBN 0-686-69074-5). U of Tex Busn Res.

TEXAS–ANTIQUITIES

Hester, Thomas R. Digging into South Texas Prehistory. (Illus.). 202p. 1980. 14.00 (ISBN 0-931722-05-5); pap. 8.95 (ISBN 0-931722-04-7). Corona Pub.

Matthews, W. H. Texas Fossils: An Amateur Collector's Handbook. (Illus.). 123p. 1960. Repr. 1.00 (GB 2). Bur Econ Geology.

TEXAS–BIOGRAPHY

Babb, Jewel. Border Healing Woman: The Story of Jewel Babb. 152p. 1981. text ed. 14.95 (ISBN 0-292-70729-0); pap. 5.95 (ISBN 0-292-70730-4). U of Tex Pr.

Baxter, Norman. A Line on Texas. LC 80-15870. (Illus.). 1980. pap. 6.95 (ISBN 0-88415-429-7). Pacesetter Pr.

Hughes, Alton. Pecos: A History of the Pioneer West, Vol. 2. (Illus.). 232p. 1981. 16.95 (ISBN 0-933512-34-1). Pioneer Bk Tx.

King, C. Richard. The Lady Cannoneer: A Biography of Angelina Belle Peyton Eberly, Heroine of Texas, Archives War. (Illus.). 192p. 1981. 12.95 (ISBN 0-89015-280-2). Eakins.

Lemann, Nicholas. The Fast Track: Texans & Other Strivers. 1981. 12.95 (ISBN 0-393-01436-3). Norton.

Murrah, David J. C. C. Slaughter: Rancher, Banker, Baptist. (Illus.). 184p. 1981. 14.95 (ISBN 0-292-71067-4). U of Tex Pr.

Stevens, R. T. Woman of Texas. 1981. pap. 2.95 (ISBN 0-440-19555-1). Dell.

TEXAS–DESCRIPTION AND TRAVEL

Harmon, Jack. Texas Missions & Landmarks. 2nd ed. (Illus.). 57p. 1978. 10.00 (ISBN 0-933164-43-2); pap. 6.95 (ISBN 0-933164-17-3). U of Tex Inst Tex Culture.

Johnson, Lady Bird. Texas: A Roadside View. (Illus.). 51p. 1980. 12.00 (ISBN 0-911536-89-2). Trinity U Pr.

Sheldon, Robert A. Roadside Geology of Texas. (Illus.). 180p. 1980. pap. 6.95. Corona Pub.

Smith, Terry. Images of Rural Texas. LC 80-54842. (Illus.). 128p. 1981. 18.95 (ISBN 0-938898-11-6). Red River.

TEXAS–DESCRIPTION AND TRAVEL–GUIDEBOOKS

Hart, Herbert M. Tour Guide to Old Forts of Texas, Kansas, Nebraska, Oklahoma, Vol. 4. (Illus.). 65p. (Orig.). 1981. pap. 3.95 (ISBN 0-87108-583-6). Pruett.

TEXAS–ECONOMIC CONDITIONS

Farrell, H. Clyde & Kens, Paul. Buying, Renting & Borrowing in Texas: The Rules of the Game. LC 80-52895. (Illus.). 278p. 1980. 10.95 (ISBN 0-937606-00-6); pap. 6.95 (ISBN 0-937606-01-4). Tex Consumer.

Pluta, Joseph E., et al. Texas Fact Book 1981. rev. ed. 200p. (Orig.). 1981. pap. 6.00 (ISBN 0-87755-246-0). U of Tex Busn Res.

TEXAS–HISTORY

Crosby County Historical Commission. A History of Crosby County, 1876-1977. 1978. write for info. Crosby County.

Dobie, J. Frank. Cow People. (Illus.). 317p. 1981. pap. 6.95 (ISBN 0-292-71060-7). U of Tex Pr.

McDonald, Archie & Procter, Ben. Texas Heritage. LC 79-54886. (Orig.). 1980. pap. text ed. 6.95x (ISBN 0-88273-001-0). Forum Pr MO.

McDonald, Archie P., ed. Eastern Texas History: Selections from East Texas Historical Journal. 12.50 (ISBN 0-8363-0159-5). Jenkins.

Texas & the American Revolution. (Illus.). 72p. 1975. pap. text ed. 3.50 (ISBN 0-933164-23-8). U of Tex Inst Tex Culture.

TEXAS–HISTORY–BIBLIOGRAPHY

Vexler, R. I. Texas Chronology & Factbook, Vol. 43. 1978. 8.50 (ISBN 0-379-16168-0). Oceana.

TEXAS–HISTORY, LOCAL

Bronwell, Nancy. Lubbock: A Pictorial History. Friedman, Donna R., ed. (Illus.). 208p. 1980. pap. write for info. (ISBN 0-89865-076-3). Donning Co.

Brough, Walter & Sutton, Michael. Explosion: The Day Texas City Died. 1980. pap. 2.75 (ISBN 0-686-69244-6, 75838). Avon.

Casey, Clifford B. Alpine, Texas: Then & Now. (Illus.). 446p. 1980. 20.00 (ISBN 0-933512-33-3). Pioneer Bk Tx.

Jordan, Terry G., et al. Log Cabin Village: A History & Guide. (Illus.). 1980. 15.00; pap. 6.95 (ISBN 0-87611-050-2). Tex St Hist Assn.

Matthews, W. H. The Geologic Story of Longhorn Cavern. 50p. 1963. 1.00 (GB 4). Bur Econ Geology.

TEXAS–POLITICS AND GOVERNMENT

Dickens, E. Larry, et al. Texas: Lone Star State Government. (Illus.). 152p. (Orig.). 1980. pap. text ed. 6.95 (ISBN 0-88408-135-4). Sterling Swift.

Government & Politics of Texas. 7th ed. 1981. text ed. 9.95 (ISBN 0-316-55422-7); tchrs'. manual free (ISBN 0-316-55423-5). Little.

Lamare, James W. Texas Politics: Economics, Power, & Policy. 225p. 1981. pap. text ed. 7.16 (ISBN 0-8299-0390-9). West Pub.

Maxwell, William E. & Crain, Ernest. Texas Politics Today. 2nd ed. (Illus.). 585p. 1981. pap. text ed. 8.76 (ISBN 0-8299-0395-X). West Pub.

TEXAS RANGERS

Davis, John L. The Texas Rangers: Their First 150 Years. (Illus.). 114p. 1975. 5.95 (ISBN 0-933164-19-X). U of Tex Inst Tex Culture.

Haley, J. Evetts. Jeff Milton: A Good Man with a Gun. (Illus.). 432p. 1981. 19.91 (ISBN 0-8061-0182-2); pap. 9.95 (ISBN 0-8061-1756-7). U of Okla Pr.

TEXT-BOOKS

see also Readers;

also particular branches of study with or without the subdivision Text-Books, e.g. Arithmetic; English Language–Grammar; Geography–Text-Books; also subdivision Text-Books for foreigners under names of languages, e.g. English Language–Text-Books for Foreigners

Council on Interracial Books for Children, Inc. Guidelines for Selecting Bias-Free Textbooks & Storybooks. LC 80-165903. 105p. 1980. pap. 6.95 (ISBN 0-930040-33-3). CIBC.

TEXT-BOOKS–BIBLIOGRAPHY

El-Hi Textbooks in Print 1981. 800p. 1981. 38.00 (ISBN 0-8352-1357-9). Bowker.

TEXTILE DESIGN

Johnston, Meda P. & Kaufman, Glen. Design on Fabrics. 2nd ed. 188p. 1981. 14.95 (ISBN 0-442-26339-2); pap. 9.95 (ISBN 0-442-23145-8). Van Nos Reinhold.

Tana, Pradumna Tana & Tana, Roselba. Traditional Designs from India for Artists & Craftsmen. (Illus.). 112p. (Orig.). 1981. pap. price not set (ISBN 0-486-24129-7). Dover.

TEXTILE FABRICS

see also Carpets; Indians of North America–Textile Industry and Fabrics; Nonwoven Fabrics; Rugs; Tapestry

Constantine, Mildred & Larsen, Jack L. The Art Fabric. 240p. 1981. 39.95 (ISBN 0-442-21638-6). Van Nos Reinhold.

Joseph, Marjory & Gieseking, Audrey G. Illustrated Guide to Textiles. 2nd ed. 1981. 8.95 (ISBN 0-8087-3400-8). Burgess.

TEXTILE FABRICS–INDIA

Tana, Pradumna Tana & Tana, Roselba. Traditional Designs from India for Artists & Craftsmen. (Illus.). 112p. (Orig.). 1981. pap. price not set (ISBN 0-486-24129-7). Dover.

TEXTILE FABRICS–INDONESIA

Gaworski, Michael E. & Warming, Wanda. The World of Indonesian Textiles. LC 80-82526. (Illus.). 280p. 1981. 50.00 (ISBN 0-87011-432-8). Kodansha.

TEXTILES

see Textile Fabrics

THACKERAY, WILLIAM MAKEPEACE, 1811-1863

Young, George M. Today & Yesterday: Tennyson, Burke, Thackeray, Shakespeare. 312p. 1980. lib. bdg. 15.00 (ISBN 0-8482-3125-2). Norwood Edns.

THAILAND-ECONOMIC CONDITIONS

Conservation & Development in Northern Thailand. 114p. 1980. pap. 15.00 (ISBN 92-808-0077-9, TUNU083, UNU). Unipub.

THAILAND-HISTORY

Elliott. Thailand: Origins of Military Rule. 190p. 1978. 11.95 (ISBN 0-905762-10-X); pap. 5.95 (ISBN 0-905762-11-8). Lawrence Hill.

THAILAND-POLITICS AND GOVERNMENT

Elliott. Thailand: Origins of Military Rule. 190p. 1978. 11.95 (ISBN 0-905762-10-X); pap. 5.95 (ISBN 0-905762-11-8). Lawrence Hill.

THALAMUS

Tasker, Ronald R., et al. The Thalmus & the Midbrain of Man: A Physiological Atlas Using Electrical Stimulatiob. (American Lecture Neurosurgery Ser.). (Illus.). 464p. write for info. (ISBN 0-398-04475-9). C C Thomas.

THALASSEMIA

Fairbanks, Virgil. Hemoglobinopathies & Thalassemias. 1980. 32.50. Thieme Stratton.

THALLIUM

Wackers, Frans J., ed. Thallium-201 & Technettium-99m-Pyrophosphate Nyocardial Imaging in the Coronary Care Unit. (Developments in Cardiovascular Medicine Ser.: No. 9). (Illus.). 255p. 1981. PLB 42.00 (ISBN 90-247-2396-5, Pub. by Martinus Nijhoff). Kluwer Boston.

THEATER

Here are entered works which deal with the drama as acted upon the stage, and works treating of the historical, legal, moral, and religious aspects of the theater.

see also Acting; Actors and Actresses; Children'S Plays; Drama; Dramatic Criticism; Melodrama; Music in Theaters; Mysteries and Miracle-Plays; Puppets and Puppet-Plays; Theater and Society

Cohen, Robert. The Theatre. (Illus.). 500p. (Orig.). 1981. pap. text ed. price not set (ISBN 0-87484-459-2). Mayfield Pub.

Isadora, Rachel. Jesse & Abe. LC 80-15584. (Illus.). 32p. (gr. k-4). 1981. 7.95 (ISBN 0-688-80302-4); PLB 7.63 (ISBN 0-688-84302-6). Greenwillow.

Mamet, David. A Life in the Theatre. LC 77-91884. 8.95 (ISBN 0-394-50158-6, GP806). Grove.

O'Donovan, Michael. The Art of the Theatre. 50p. 1980. Repr. of 1947 ed. lib. bdg. 10.00 (ISBN 0-8492-7308-0). R West.

Pickering, Jerry. Theatre: A Contemporary Introduction. 3rd ed. (Illus.). 380p. 1981. pap. text ed. 10.36 (ISBN 0-8299-0403-4). West Pub.

Rudman, Jack. Drama & Theatre. (Undergraduate Program Field Test Ser.: UPFT-5). (Cloth bdg. avail. on request). pap. 9.95 (ISBN 0-8373-6005-6). Natl Learning.

Shaw, Ann M. & Stevens, C. J., eds. Drama, Theatre & the Handicapped. 121p. 1979. 6.95; ATA members 4.95. Am Theatre Assoc.

U R T A-A T A Humanities & the Theatre, 2 vols. Set. 5.00; ATA members 3.00. Am Theatre Assoc.

THEATER-BIBLIOGRAPHY

Brill, Chip & Glenn, Peter, eds. The New York Casting-Survival Guide & Datebook, 1981. 124p. 1980. pap. 10.00 (ISBN 0-87314-036-2). Peter Glenn.

Rachow, Louis A., ed. Theatre & Performing Arts Collections. (Special Collections Ser.: Vol. 1, No. 1). 128p. 1981. text ed. 19.95 (ISBN 0-917724-47-X). Haworth Pr.

S S T A Bibliography. rev. ed. 63p. 1975. 3.50; ATA members 2.50. Am Theatre Assoc.

The Research Libraries of the New York Pubic Library & the Library of Congress. Bibliographic Guide to Theatre Arts: 1980. (Library Catalogs-Bib. Guides Ser.). 1981 (ISBN 0-8161-6896-2). lib. bdg. 75.00 (ISBN 0-686-69557-7). G K Hall.

THEATER-COSTUME

see Costume

THEATER-DIRECTION

see Theater-Production and Direction

THEATER-HISTORY

Arnott, Peter. The Theater in Its Time: An Introduction. 1981. text ed. 15.95 (ISBN 0-316-05194-2). Little.

Booth, Michael R. Victorian Spectacular Theatre, Eighteen Fifty Yo Nineteen Ten. (Theatre Production Studies). (Illus.). 190p. 1981. price not set (ISBN 0-7100-0739-6). Routledge & Kegan.

Esslin, Martin, ed. Illustrated Encyclopedia of World Theater. (Illus.). 320p. 1981. pap. 12.95 (ISBN 0-500-27207-7). Thames Hudson.

Nuttall, Jeff. Performance Art Memoirs, Vol. I. 1981. 13.95 (ISBN 0-7145-3788-8); pap. 6.95 (ISBN 0-7145-3711-X). Riverrun NY.

Patterson, Michael. The Revolution in German Theatre, Nineteen Hundred to Nineteen Thirty-Three. (Illus.). 226p. 1981. price not set (ISBN 0-7100-0659-4). Routledge & Kegan.

THEATER-MORAL AND RELIGIOUS ASPECTS

Barish, Jonas. The Antitheatrical Prejudice. 1981. 20.00 (ISBN 0-520-03735-9). U of Cal Pr.

THEATER-PICTORIAL WORKS

Blum, Daniel. A Pictorial History of the American Theatre 1860-1980. rev. ed. Aymar, Brandt, ed. 464p. 1981. 19.95 (ISBN 0-517-54262-5). Crown.

THEATER-PRODUCTION AND DIRECTION

Greenberg, Jan W. Theatre Facts: From Putting the Show Together Through Opening Night. LC 80-20295. 1981. 10.95 (ISBN 0-03-051451-7). HR&W.

Miles-Brown, John. Directing Drama. (Illus.). 176p. 1980. text ed. 24.75x (ISBN 0-7206-0557-1). Humanities.

Wills, J. Robert. Directing in the Theatre: A Casebook. LC 80-19432. 149p. 1980. 10.00 (ISBN 0-8108-1348-3); instr's manual avail. Scarecrow.

THEATER-SOCIAL ASPECTS

see Theater and Society

THEATER-STAGE LIGHTING

see Stage Lighting

THEATER-STUDY AND TEACHING

Ratliff, Gerald L. The Theatre Student: Learning Scenes. (Theatre Student Ser.) (Illus.). 140p. 1981. lib. bdg. 12.50 (ISBN 0-8239-0531-4). Rosen Pr.

THEATER-VOCATIONAL GUIDANCE

see Theater As a Profession

THEATER-YEARBOOKS

Hughes, Catharine R., ed. Anerican Theatre Annual, 1979-80. (Illus.). 200p. 1981. 35.00 (ISBN 0-8103-0419-8). Gale.

Willis, John. Theatre World: Vol. 36, 1979-80. Aymar, Brandt, ed. (Illus.). 288p. 1981. 18.95 (ISBN 0-517-54264-1). Crown.

THEATER-ASIA

Brandon, James R., ed. Theatre Perspectives One: Asian Theatre. 198p. 1980. 10.00. Am Theatre Assoc.

THEATER-ENGLAND

see Theater-Great Britain

THEATER-EUROPE

Malyusz, Edith C. The Theatre & National Awakening. Szendrey, Thomas, tr. LC 79-89134. 349p. 1980. write for info. (ISBN 0-914648-10-1). Hungarian Cultural.

THEATER-GERMANY

Patterson, Michael. The Revolution in German Theatre, Nineteen Hundred to Nineteen Thirty-Three. (Illus.). 226p. 1981. price not set (ISBN 0-7100-0659-4). Routledge & Kegan.

THEATER-GREAT BRITAIN

Morley, Malcolm. Margate & Its Theatres. 8.95 (ISBN 0-392-08118-0, SpS). Soccer.

Stone, George W., Jr., ed. The Stage & the Page: London's "Whole Show" in the Eighteenth Century Theatre. 1981. 14.95x (ISBN 0-520-04201-8). U of Cal Pr.

Vernon, Frank. The Twentieth-Century Theatre. 159p. 1980. Repr. of 1924 ed. lib. bdg. 30.00 (ISBN 0-89760-927-1). Telegraph Bks.

Wearing, J. P. The London Stage, Nineteen Hundred to Nineteen Nine: A Calendar of Plays & Players, 2 vols. LC 80-28353. 1202p. 1981. Set. 50.00 (ISBN 0-8108-1403-X). Scarecrow.

THEATER-GREECE

Burton, R. W. B. The Chorus in Sopocles Tragedies. 312p. 1980. 48.00x (ISBN 0-19-814374-5). Oxford U Pr.

THEATER-ITALY

Carlson, Marvin. Italian Stage from Goldoni to D'annunzio. LC 80-10554. 225p. 1981. lib. bdg. write for info. (ISBN 0-89950-000-5). McFarland & Co.

THEATER-LATIN AMERICA

Unger, Roni. Poesia in Voz Alta in the Theater of Mexico. 184p. 1981. text ed. 15.00x (ISBN 0-8262-0333-7). U of Mo Pr.

THEATER-POLAND

Drosdowski, Bohdan, ed. Twentieth Century Polish Theatre. Itzin, Cathy, tr. 1980. 16.95 (ISBN 0-7145-3738-1). Riverrun NY.

THEATER-SPAIN

Tapia, John R. The Spanish Romantic Theater. LC 80-5565. 87p. 1980. lib. bdg. 13.75 (ISBN 0-8191-1276-3); pap. text ed. 6.50 (ISBN 0-8191-1277-1). U Pr of Amer.

THEATER-UNITED STATES

Chinoy, Helen K. & Jenkins, Linda W. Women in American Theatre. Michelman, Herber, ed. (Illus.). 384p. 1981. 15.95 (ISBN 0-517-53729-X, Michaelman Books). Crown.

The State Arts Agencies in Nineteen Seventy-Four: All Present & Accounted for. (Report Ser.: No. 8). 160p. pap. 4.50 (Pub. by Ctr Fot Arts Info). Pub Ctr Cult Res.

THEATER-UNITED STATES-HISTORY

Blum, Daniel. A Pictorial History of the American Theatre 1860-1980. rev. ed. Aymar, Brandt, ed. 464p. 1981. 19.95 (ISBN 0-517-54262-5). Crown.

Chinoy, Helen K., ed. Reunion: A Self Portrait of the Group Theatre (1976) 77p. Repr. 4.00. Am Theatre Assoc.

Miller, Tice L. Bohemians & Critics: American Theatre Criticism in the Nineteenth Century. LC 80-24430. x. 190p. 1981. 12.00 (ISBN 0-8108-1377-7). Scarecrow.

THEATER AND SOCIETY

Cornish, Roger & Kase, C. Robert, eds. Senior Adult Theatre: The American Theatre Association Handbook. LC 80-23485. (Illus.). 96p. 1981. 8.95x (ISBN 0-271-00275-1); pap. text ed. 5.95x (ISBN 0-271-00275-1). Pa St U Pr.

Phillips, Henry. The Theatre & Its Critics in Seventeenth-Century France. (Modern Language & Literature Monographs). 272p. 1980. 36.00 (ISBN 0-19-815535-2). Oxford U Pr.

THEATER AS A PROFESSION

see also Acting As a Profession

Brill, Chip & Glenn, Peter, eds. The New York Casting-Survival Guide & Datebook, 1981. 124p. 1980. pap. 10.00 (ISBN 0-87314-036-2). Peter Glenn.

THEATER CRITICISM

see Dramatic Criticism

THEATER IN ART

see Theaters-Stage-Setting and Scenery

THEATERS-STAGE-SETTING AND SCENERY

see also Scene Painting

Booth, Michael R. Victorian Spectacular Theatre, Eighteen Fifty Yo Nineteen Ten. (Theatre Production Studies). (Illus.). 190p. 1981. price not set (ISBN 0-7100-0739-6). Routledge & Kegan.

Marker, Frederick J. & Marker, Lise-Lone. Edward Gordon Craig & the Pretenders: A Production Revisited. (Special Issues Ser.). (Illus.). Date not set. price not set (ISBN 0-8093-0966-1). S Ill U Pr.

Payne, Darwin R. The Scenographic Imagination. (Illus.). 1981. price not set (ISBN 0-8093-1009-0); pap. price not set (ISBN 0-8093-1010-4). S Ill U Pr.

Roenfeld, Sybil. Georgian Scene Painters & Scene Painting. Date not set. price not set (ISBN 0-521-23339-9). Cambridge U Pr.

THEATERS, MOVING-PICTURE

see Moving-Picture Theaters

THEATRICAL COSTUME

see Costume

THEATRICAL MAKE-UP

see Make-Up, Theatrical

THEATRICAL MUSIC

see Music in Theaters; Musical Revue, Comedy, etc.; Opera

THEATRICAL SCENERY

see Theaters-Stage-Setting and Scenery

THEFT

see Thieves

THEFTS, ART

see Art Thefts

THEISM

see also Atheism; Christianity; God

Thompson, Bert. Theistic Evolution. pap. 5.50 (ISBN 0-89315-300-1). Lambert Bk.

THEOCRACY

see War and Religion

THEOLOGIANS

see also Christian Biography;

also subdivisions Biography or Clergy under names of Christian denominations

Eaton, Jeffrey C. The Logic of Theism: An Analysis of the Thought of Austin Farrer. LC 80-67260. 288p. 1980. lib. bdg. 19.25 (ISBN 0-8191-1337-9); pap. text ed. 10.50 (ISBN 0-8191-1338-7). U Pr of Amer.

Hastings, A. W. & Hastings, E., eds. Theologians of Our Time. LC 66-73626. 224p. Repr. of 1966 ed. pap. text ed. 4.95 (ISBN 0-567-22301-9). Attic Pr.

Sykes, S. W. Karl Barth: Studies of His Theological Method. 214p. 1979. text ed. 29.00x (ISBN 0-19-826649-9). Oxford U Pr.

THEOLOGICAL ANTHROPOLOGY

see Man (Theology)

THEOLOGICAL BELIEF

see Faith

THEOLOGICAL EDUCATION

see Religious Education; Theology-Study and Teaching

THEOLOGICAL SEMINARIES, CATHOLIC

Seminaries & Psychology. 70p. 1978. 2.95. Natl Cath Educ.

THEOLOGICAL STUDENTS

see Seminarians

THEOLOGICAL VIRTUES

see Charity; Faith; Virtue and Virtues

THEOLOGY

see also Atheism; Calvinism; Christianity; Church; Church History; Ethics; Free Thought; Natural Theology; Religion; Religion and Science; Secularism; Theism

Alluntis, Felix & Wolter, Allan B., illus. John Duns Scotus: God & Creatures; the Quodlibetal Questions. Orig. Title: Quaestiones Quodlibetales. 548p. Repr. of 1975 ed. write for info. Cath U Pr.

Anderson, Gerald H. & Stransky, Thomas F. Christ's Lordship & Religious Pluralism. LC 80-25406. 256p. (Orig.). 1981. pap. 8.95 (ISBN 0-88344-088-1). Orbis Bks.

Bogorodskii, N. The Doctrine of St. John Damascene on the Procession of the Holy Spirit. LC 80-2351. 1981. Repr. of 1879 ed. 28.50 (ISBN 0-404-18903-2). AMS Pr.

Bradford, John. Writings of Bradford. 1979. Set. 28.95. Banner of Truth.

Brooks, Thomas. Works of Brooks, 6 vols. 1980. Set. 90.00. Banner of Truth.

Cupitt, Don. Taking Leave. 192p. 1981. 9.95 (ISBN 0-8245-0045-8). Crossroad NY.

Davis, John J. Theology Primer. 128p. (Orig.). 1981. pap. 5.95 (ISBN 0-8010-2912-0). Baker Bk.

Florovsky, Georges. Ways of Russian Theology: Pt. 2. Haugh, Richard S., et al, eds. (Collected Works of Georges Florovsky). 400p. (Orig.). 1980. pap. 27.50 (ISBN 0-913124-24-9). Nordland Pub.

Harvey, Van A. The Historian & the Believer: The Morality of Historical Knowledge & Christian Belief. 1981. pap. price not set (ISBN 0-664-24367-3). Westminster.

Hebblethwaite, B. L. The Problems of Theology. LC 79-41812. 176p. 1980. 21.50 (ISBN 0-521-23104-3); pap. 6.95 (ISBN 0-521-29811-3). Cambridge U Pr.

Hill, Brennan & Newland, Mary R., eds. Theologians & Catechists in Dialogue: The Albany Forum. 64p. (Orig.). 1977. pap. 2.25 (ISBN 0-697-01671-4). Wm C Brown.

Hodge, Charles. Way of Life. 1978. pap. 3.95 (ISBN 0-85151-273-9). Banner of Truth.

Hoffecker, W. Andrew. Piety & the Princeton Theologians. (Orig.). 1981. pap. 5.95 (ISBN 0-8010-4253-4). Baker Bk.

Kaiser, Walter C., Jr. Toward an Exegetical Theology. 224p. 1981. 9.95 (ISBN 0-8010-5425-7). Baker Bk.

Kane, G. Stanley. Anselm's Doctrine of Freedom & The Will. (Texts & Studies in Religion, Vol. 10). 1981. soft cover 24.95x (ISBN 0-88946-914-8). E Mellen.

Makrakis, Apostolos. A Revelation of Treasure Hid--Concerning Freedom, Concerning the Motherland, Concerning Justice, Apostolical Canons Respecting Baptism. Orthodox Christian Educational Society, ed. Cummings, Denver, tr. from Hellenic. 80p. (Orig.). 1952. pap. 1.00x (ISBN 0-938366-23-8). Orthodox Chr.

--Theology: An Orthodox Standpoint. Orthodox Christian Educational Society, ed. Cummings, Denver, tr. from Hellenic. (The Logos & Holy Spirit in the Unity of Christian Thought Ser.: Vol. 4). 216p. 1977. pap. 3.50x (ISBN 0-938366-03-3). Orthodox Chr.

O'Collins, Gerald. Fundamental Theology. LC 80-82809. 288p. (Orig.). 1981. pap. 6.95 (ISBN 0-8091-2347-9). Paulist Pr.

Rahner, Karl. Concern for the Church: Theological Investigations Vol. XX. (Theological Investigations Ser.). 272p. (Ger.). 1981. 12.95 (ISBN 0-8245-0027-X). Crossroad NY.

Rankin, O. S. Israel's Wisdom Literature: Its Bearing on Theology & the History of Religions. LC 36-33127. 288p. Repr. of 1936 ed. text ed. 7.50 (ISBN 0-567-02214-5). Attic Pr.

Rousseau, Richard W. Disclosure of the Ultimate: Fundamental Theology Reconsidered. LC 80-8259. 399p. 1980. lib. bdg. 21.50 (ISBN 0-8191-1284-4); pap. 13.25 (ISBN 0-8191-1285-2). U Pr of Amer.

Sibbes, Richard. Works on Sibbes, Vol. 1. 1979. 14.95 (ISBN 0-85151-169-4). Banner of Truth.

Sproule, John A. In Defense of Pretribulationism. 56p. (Orig.). 1980. pap. 2.95 (ISBN 0-88469-133-0). BMH Bks.

Stroup, George W. The Promise of Narrative Theology: Recovering the Gospel in the Church. LC 80-84654. 216p. (Orig.). 1981. pap. 8.50 (ISBN 0-8042-0683-X). John Knox.

--The Promise of Narrative Theology: Recovering the Gospel in the Church. LC 80-84654. pap. 8.50 (ISBN 0-8042-0683-X). John Knox.

Taylor, Michael J., ed. The Sacraments: Readings in Contemporary Theology. LC 80-9534. 274p. (Orig.). 1981. pap. 7.95 (ISBN 0-8189-0406-2). Alba.

Torres, Sergio & Eagleson, John, eds. The Challenge of Basic Christian Communities. Drury, John, tr. 192p. (Orig.). 1981. pap. 7.95 (ISBN 0-88344-503-4). Orbis Bks.

Turner, William B. Theology - the Quintessence of Science. LC 80-82649. 1981. 14.95 (ISBN 0-8022-2375-3). Philos Lib.

Warfield, Benjamin B. The Works of Benjamin B. Warfield, 10 vols. 1981. Repr. of 1932 ed. 149.50 (ISBN 0-8010-9645-6). Baker Bk.

THEOLOGY-BIOGRAPHY

see Theologians

THEOLOGY-COLLECTED WORKS-20TH CENTURY

Staniloae, Dumitru. Theology & the Church. Barringer, Robert, tr. from Romanian. LC 80-19313. 240p. (Orig.). 1980. pap. 6.95 (ISBN 0-913836-69-9, BS695.57 230.19498). St Martin.

THEOLOGY-DICTIONARIES

Bauer, J. B. Encyclopedia of Biblical Theology: The Concise Sacramentum Verbi. 1172p. 1981. 29.50 (ISBN 0-8245-0042-3). Crossroad NY.

McClintock, John & Strong, James. Cyclopedia of Biblical, Theological, & Ecclesiastical Literature, 12 vols. 12400p. 1961. text ed. 395.00 (ISBN 0-8010-6123-7). Baker Bk.

Rahner, Karl & Vorgrimler, Herbert. Dictionary of Theology. 2nd ed. 500p. (Ger.). 1981. 24.50 (ISBN 0-8245-0040-7). Crossroad NY.

THEOLOGY-PHILOSOPHY

see Christianity-Philosophy

THEOLOGY-STUDY AND TEACHING

see also Catechisms; Christian Education; Church and Education; Religious Education; Seminarians; Teaching, Freedom of

Sayre, John L. & Hamburger, Roberta. Tools for Theological Research. 6th ed. 100p. (Orig.). 1981. pap. price not set (ISBN 0-912832-20-7). Seminary Pr.

THEOLOGY–TERMINOLOGY

Stroup, George W. The Promise of Narrative Theology: Recovering the Gospel in the Church. LC 80-84654. 216p. (Orig.). 1981. pap. 8.50 (ISBN 0-8042-0683-X). John Knox.

--The Promise of Narrative Theology: Recovering the Gospel in the Church. LC 80-84654. pap. 8.50 (ISBN 0-8042-0683-X). John Knox.

THEOLOGY–EARLY CHURCH, ca. 30-600

Kelly, J. N. Early Christian Creeds. 3rd ed. 446p. 1979. text ed. 25.00x (ISBN 0-582-48931-8). Longman.

THEOLOGY–20TH CENTURY

Barth, Karl. The Christian Life. Bromiley, Geoffrey W., ed. LC 80-39942. 328p. 1981. 14.95 (ISBN 0-8028-3523-6). Eerdmans.

--Karl Barth Letters: 1961 to 1968. Bromiley, Geoffrey W., tr. LC 80-29140. 288p. 1981. 14.95 (ISBN 0-8028-3536-8). Eerdmans.

Happold, F. C. Religious Faith & Twentieth Century Man. 192p. 1981. 6.95 (ISBN 0-8245-0046-6). Crossroad NY.

Klassen, A. J. A Bonhoeffer Legacy: Essays in Understanding. 186p. (Orig.). 1981. pap. 13.95 (ISBN 0-8028-1744-0). Eerdmans.

Robinson, John A. The Roots of a Radical. 176p. 1981. 9.95 (ISBN 0-8245-0028-8). Crossroad NY.

Stob, Henry. Theologial Reflections. 200p. (Orig.). 1981. pap. 11.95 (ISBN 0-8028-1881-1). Eerdmans.

Whitehouse, W. A. Creation, Science, & Theology: Essays in Response to Karl Barth. 272p. (Orig.). 1981. pap. 10.95 (ISBN 0-8028-1870-6). Eerdmans.

THEOLOGY, BIBLICAL

see Bible–Theology

THEOLOGY, COVENANT

see Covenants (Theology)

THEOLOGY, CRISIS

see Dialectical Theology

THEOLOGY, DEVOTIONAL

see Devotional Exercises; Devotional Literature; Meditations; Prayers

THEOLOGY, DISPENSATIONAL

see Dispensationalism

THEOLOGY, DOCTRINAL

see also Angels; Apologetics; Authority (Religion); Baptism; Bible–Theology; Catechisms; Catholicity; Christian Ethics; Christianity–Philosophy; Covenants (Theology); Creeds; Devil; Dialectical Theology; Dispensationalism; Dogma; Eschatology; Faith; Forgiveness of Sin; Free Will and Determinism; Freedom (Theology); Gifts, Spiritual; God; Good and Evil; Grace (Theology); Heresies and Heretics; Holiness; Holy Spirit; Inspiration; Islamic Theology; Jesus Christ; Lord's Supper; Love (Theology); Man (Theology); Miracles; Mystical Union; Mysticism; New England Theology; Perfection; Power (Theology); Predestination; Providence and Government of God; Resurrection; Revelation; Sacraments; Salvation; Sanctification; Trinity

also subdivision Doctrinal and Controversial Works under names of Christian denominations, e.g. Baptism–Doctrinal and Controversial Works

Barth, Karl. Church Dogmatics. Incl. Vol. 4. Doctrine of Reconciliation, 2 pts. Pt. 3, Repr. Of 1962 Ed., 492p. 23.00x (ISBN 0-567-09044-2); Pt. 4, Repr. Of 1969 Ed., 240p. 12.95x (ISBN 0-567-09045-0); Vol. 5. Index: with Aids to the Preacher. Bromiley, G. W. & Torrance, G. F. 584p. Repr. of 1977 ed. 32.00x (ISBN 0-567-09046-9). Attic Pr.

--Church Dogmatics: The Doctrine of Creation, Vol. III, Pt. I. 440p. 1958. text ed. 23.00x (ISBN 0-567-09031-0). Attic Pr.

--Church Dogmatics: The Doctrine of God, Vol. II, Pt. I. Parker, T. H., et al, trs. from Ger. 710p. 1957. text ed. 23.00x (ISBN 0-567-09021-3). Attic Pr.

--Church Dogmatics: The Doctrine of God, Vol. II, Pt. II. Bromiley, G. W., tr. from Ger. 820p. 1957. text ed. 23.00x (ISBN 0-567-09022-1). Attic Pr.

--Church Dogmatics: The Doctrine of the Word of God (Prolegomena to Church Dogmatics, Vol. 1, Pt. 2. Thomson, G. T. & Knight, Harold, eds. 924p. 1956. text ed. 23.00x (ISBN 0-567-09012-4). Attic Pr.

--Church Dogmatics, Vol. III: The Doctrine of Creation, Pt. 3. 560p. Repr. of 1961 ed. text ed. 23.00x (ISBN 0-567-09033-7). Attic Pr.

--Church Dogmatics Vol. III: The Doctrine of Creation Pt. 4. 720p. Repr. of 1961 ed. text ed. 23.00 (ISBN 0-567-09034-5). Attic Pr.

--Church Dogmatics, Vol IV: The Doctrine of Reconciliation-Part 1. 814p. Repr. of 1956 ed. text ed. 23.00x (ISBN 0-567-09041-8). Attic Pr.

--Church Dogmatics, Vol. IV: The Doctrine of Reconciliation-Part 2. 882p. Repr. of 1958 ed. text ed. 23.00x (ISBN 0-567-09042-6). Attic Pr.

--Church Dogmatics, Vol. IV: The Doctrine of Reconciliation-Part 3, (I) 496p. Repr. of 1961 ed. text ed. 23.00 (ISBN 0-567-09043-4). Attic Pr.

--Church Dogmatics, Vol. 1: The Doctrine of the Word of God (Prolegomena to Church Dogmatics), Pt. 1. 2nd ed. Bromiley, G. W., tr. from Ger. 592p. Repr. of 1975 ed. text ed. 23.00x (ISBN 0-567-09013-2). Attic Pr.

Carson, D. A. Divine Sovereignty & Human Responsibility: Biblical Perspectives in Tension. Toon, Peter & Martin, Ralph, eds. LC 79-27589. (New Foundations Theological Library). 228p. 1981. 18.50 (ISBN 0-8042-3707-7); pap. 9.95 (ISBN 0-8042-3727-1). John Knox.

Carver, C. C. Church of God Doctrines. 180p. 1948. pap. 2.00. Faith Pub Hse.

Church Dogmatics: The Doctrine of Creation, Vol. III, Pt. II. 680p. 1960. text ed. 23.00x (ISBN 0-567-09032-9). Attic Pr.

Clarke, W. N. An Outline of Christian Theology. 498p. 1898. text ed. 9.50x (ISBN 0-567-02069-X). Attic Pr.

Hutton, W. H. A Disciple's Religion. (Scholar As Preacher Ser.). 246p. Repr. of 1911 ed. 7.75 (ISBN 0-567-04410-6). Attic Pr.

Kane, John F. Pluralism & Truth in Religion. Dietrich, Wendell, ed. LC 80-20659. (American Academy of Religion Dissertation Ser.). 1981. write for info. (ISBN 0-89130-413-4); pap. write for info. (ISBN 0-89130-414-2). Scholars Pr CA.

Kung, Hans. Justification: The Doctrine of Karl Barth & a Catholic Reflection. LC 80-26001. 1981. pap. price not set (ISBN 0-664-24364-9). Westminster.

Lewis, Edwin. A Manual of Christian Beliefs. 162p. 1927. text ed. 2.95 (ISBN 0-567-02170-X). Attic Pr.

Luther, Martin. The Bondage of the Will. Packer, J. I. & Johnston, O. R., trs. from Ger. 323p. Repr. of 1957 ed. text ed. 14.95x (ISBN 0-227-67417-0). Attic Pr.

Matheson, Peter. A Just Peace. (Orig.). 1981. pap. 5.95 (ISBN 0-377-00107-4). Friend Pr.

Robinson, H. Wheeler. The Christian Doctrine of Man. 392p. Repr. of 1926 ed. 10.00x (ISBN 0-567-22219-5). Attic Pr.

Saint Augustine. On Christian Doctrine. 1981. pap. 3.95 (ISBN 0-89526-887-6). Regnery-Gateway.

Schleiermacher, Friedrich. On the Glaubenslehre: Two Letters to Dr. Lucke. Massey, James A., ed. Duke, James & Fiorenza, Francis S., trs. from Ger. LC 80-20717. (American Academy of Religion, Texts & Translations Ser.: No. 3). Orig. Title: Sendschreiben Uber Seine Glaubenslehre an Lucke. 1981. write for info. (ISBN 0-89130-419-3); pap. write for info. (ISBN 0-89130-420-7). Scholars Pr CA.

Staniloae, Dumitru. Theology & the Church. Barry, Robert, tr. from Romanian. LC 80-19313. 240p. 1980. pap. 6.95 (ISBN 0-913836-69-9). St Vladimirs.

Wiedekehr, Dietrich. Belief in Redemption: Explorations in Doctrine from the New Testament to Today. Moiser, Jeremy, tr. from Ger. LC 78-24088. Orig. Title: Glaube an Erlosung. 120p. 1981. pap. 5.95 (ISBN 0-8042-0476-4). John Knox.

Will, Paul J., et al. Public Education Religion Studies: An Overview. Taylor, Mark, ed. LC 80-12237. (Aids for the Study of Religion Ser.). 1981. write for info. (ISBN 0-89130-401-0); pap. write for info. (ISBN 0-89130-402-9). Scholars Pr CA.

THEOLOGY, DOCTRINAL–HISTORY

see also Religious Thought

also specific subjects with or without the subdivision History of Doctrines, e.g. Jesus Christ–History of Doctrines

Cunningham, William. Historical Theology, 2 vols. 1979. Set. 31.95; Vol. I. (ISBN 0-85151-286-0); Vol. 2. (ISBN 0-85151-287-9). Banner of Truth.

THEOLOGY, DOCTRINAL–HISTORY–16TH CENTURY

Cunningham, William. Reformers & the Theology of Reformation. 1979. 15.95 (ISBN 0-85151-013-2). Banner of Truth.

THEOLOGY, DOCTRINAL–HISTORY–17TH CENTURY

Cunningham, William. Reformers & the Theology of Reformation. 1979. 15.95 (ISBN 0-85151-013-2). Banner of Truth.

THEOLOGY, DOCTRINAL–POPULAR WORKS

Smith, F. G. The Last Reformation. 256p. 5.00; pap. 3.50. Faith Pub Hse.

THEOLOGY, DOGMATIC

see Theology, Doctrinal

THEOLOGY, ECCLESIASTICAL

see Church

THEOLOGY, ETHICAL

see Christian Ethics

THEOLOGY, FEDERAL

see Covenants (Theology)

THEOLOGY, FUNDAMENTAL

see Apologetics

THEOLOGY, ISLAMIC

see Islamic Theology

THEOLOGY, MORAL

see Christian Ethics

THEOLOGY, MUSLIM

see Islamic Theology

THEOLOGY, MYSTICAL

see Mysticism

THEOLOGY, NATURAL

see Natural Theology

THEOLOGY, NEW ENGLAND

see New England Theology

THEOLOGY, PASTORAL

see Pastoral Theology

THEOLOGY, PRACTICAL

see also Baptism; Canon Law; Catechetics; Christian Art and Symbolism; Christian Education; Christian Life; Church Polity; Church Renewal; Church Work; Clergy; Devotional Exercises; Devotional Literature; Ecclesiastical Law; Evangelistic Work; Fasts and Feasts; Gifts, Spiritual; Hymns; Liturgics; Liturgies; Lord's Supper; Missions; Pastoral Theology; Prayer; Preaching; Religious Education; Revivals; Sacraments; Sermons; Spiritual Life; Sunday-Schools; Worship

Magliato, Joe. The Wall Street Gospel. LC 80-84629. (Orig.). 1981. pap. 4.95 (ISBN 0-89081-279-9). Harvest Hse.

Seldon, Eric. The God of the Present Age. LC 80-26149. 1981. pap. price not set (ISBN 0-8309-0305-4). Herald Hse.

THEOLOGY, SYSTEMATIC

see Theology, Doctrinal

THEORETICAL CHEMISTRY

see Chemistry, Physical and Theoretical

THEORY OF APPROXIMATION

see Approximation Theory

THEORY OF GRAPHS

see Graph Theory

THEORY OF GROUPS

see Groups, Theory of

THEORY OF STRUCTURES

see Structures, Theory of

THEOSOPHY

see also Anthroposophy; Karma; Rosicrucians; Vedanta; Yoga

Theosophical Articles: Articles by Wm. Q. Judge Reprinted from Nineteenth-Century Theosophical Periodicals, 2 vols. 1276p. 1980. Set. 25.00. Theosophy.

THERAPEUTIC EXERCISE

see Exercise Therapy

THERAPEUTICS

see also Bibliotherapy; Chemistry, Medical and Pharmaceutical; Chemotherapy; Diet in Disease; Drugs; Hemodialysis; Hormone Therapy; Inhalation Therapy; Materia Medica; Medicine–Formulae, Receipts, Prescriptions; Narcotics; Nurses and Nursing; Nutrition; Oral Medication; Orthomolecular Medicine; Serumtherapy; Shock Therapy; X-Rays

also names of individual drugs, and names of diseases and groups of diseases, e.g. Bronchitis, Fever, Nervous System–Diseases; also subdivision Therapeutic Use under specific subjects, e.g. Poetry–Therapeutic Use; X-Rays–Therapeutic Use

Civetta, Joseph M. Intensive Care Therapeutics. 400p. 1980. pap. 17.50x (ISBN 0-8385-4305-7). ACC.

Conn, Howard, ed. Current Therapy 1981. (Illus.). 1100p. 1981. pap. write for info. (ISBN 0-7216-2709-9). Saunders.

Cook, Albert M. & Webster, John G., eds. Therapeutic Medical Devices: Application & Design. (Illus.). 656p. 1981. 39.95 (ISBN 0-13-914796-9). P-H.

Critser, James R., Jr. Medical Therapeutic Apparatus-Systems: Series No. 10tas-79. 1981. 60.00 (ISBN 0-914428-69-1). Lexington Data.

Woods, H. F. Topics in Therapeutics, No. 6. 1980. lib. bdg. 25.00 (ISBN 0-8161-2222-9, Hall Medical). G K Hall.

THERMAL ANALYSIS

Winterton, R. H. Thermal Design of Nuclear Reactors. LC 80-41187. (Illus.). 200p. 30.00 (ISBN 0-08-024215-4); pap. 15.00 (ISBN 0-08-024214-6). Pergamon.

THERMAL EQUILIBRIUM

see Heat; Thermodynamics

THERMAL INSULATION

see Insulation (Heat)

THERMAL REPRODUCTIVE PROCESSES

see Thermography (Copying Process)

THERMAL STRESSES

Manson, S. S. Thermal Stress & Low-Cycle Fatigue. 416p. 1981. lib. bdg. price not set (ISBN 0-89874-279-X). Krieger.

THERMAL TRANSFER

see Heat–Transmission

THERMAL WATERS

see Geothermal Resources

THERMIONIC EMISSION

Hatsopoulos, G. N. & Gyftopoulos, E. P. Thermionic Energy Conversion, 2 vols. Incl. Vol. 1. Processes & Duricy. text ed. 25.00x (ISBN 0-262-08060-5); Vol. 2. Theory, Technology & Application. text ed. 35.00x (ISBN 0-262-08059-1). (Illus.). 1979. MIT Pr.

THERMODYNAMICS

see also Entropy; Gas Dynamics; Heat; Heat Pumps; Quantum Theory; Statistical Mechanics; Statistical Thermodynamics; Thermal Analysis

Schmidt, Frank W. & Willmott, A. John. Thermal Energy Storage & Regeneration. (Illus.). 352p. 1981. 35.50 (ISBN 0-07-055346-7). McGraw.

Seely. Elements of Thermal Technology. Date not set. price not set (ISBN 0-8247-1174-2). Dekker.

Thermodynamics of Nuclear Materials, Nineteen Seventy-Nine, Vol. 1. 587p. 1980. pap. 68.25 (ISBN 92-0-040080-9, ISP 520-1, IAEA). Unipub.

Thermodynamics of Nuclear Materials: 1979. 427p. 1981. pap. 54.00 (ISBN 92-0-040180-5, ISP 520, IAEA). Unipub.

Wood, Bernard D. Applications of Thermodynamics. 3rd ed. (Mechanical Engineering Ser.). 1981. text ed. write for info. A-W.

THERMOGRAPHY (COPYING PROCESS)

Park, W. M. & Reece, B. L. Fundamental Aspects of Medical Thermography. 1980. 18.00x (Pub. by Brit Inst Radiology England). State Mutual Bk.

THESAURI, SUBJECT

see Subject Headings

THESIS WRITING

see Report Writing

THIEVES

see also Brigands and Robbers; Rogues and Vagabonds

Garcia, Carlos. Guzman, Hinde & Hannam Outstript: Being a Discovery of the Whole Art, Mistery & Antiquity of Theeves & Theeving. LC 80-2480. 1981. Repr. of 1657 ed. 49.50 (ISBN 0-404-19114-2). AMS Pr.

THIGHBONE

see Femur

THIN FILMS

Dash, J. G. Films on Solid Surfaces. 1975. 42.50 (ISBN 0-12-203350-7). Acad Pr.

Dash, J. G. & Ruvalds, J., eds. Phase Transitions in Surface Films. (NATO Advanced Studies Institutes Ser., Series B- Physical Sciences: Vol. 51). 375p. 1980. 42.50 (ISBN 0-306-40348-X). Plenum Pub.

THIN LAYER CHROMATOGRAPHY

Giddings. Advances in Chromatography, Vol. 19. 336p. Date not set. 39.75. Dekker.

Kirchner, J. G. Techniques of Chemistry: Vol. 14 Thin Layer Chromatography. 2nd ed. 1137p. 1978. 77.00 (ISBN 0-471-93264-7). Wiley.

Touchstone, Joseph C. & Rogers, Dexter. Thin Layer Chromatography: Quantitative Environmental & Clinical Applications. LC 80-36871. 384p. 1980. 27.50 (ISBN 0-471-07958-8, Pub. by Wiley-Interscience). Wiley.

THINKING

see Artificial Intelligence; Thought and Thinking

THIOKOL

see Rubber, Artificial

THIRD WORLD

see Underdeveloped Areas

THOMAS AQUINAS, SAINT, 1225?-1274

Miethe, Terry L. & Bourke, Vernon J., eds. Thomistic Bibliography, 1940-1978. LC 80-1195. xxii, 318p. 1980. lib. bdg. 39.95 (ISBN 0-313-21991-5, MTH/). Greenwood.

THOMAS, JOSHUA, 1776-1853

Blaxland, Gregory. J. H. Thomas: A Life for Unity. 14.95 (ISBN 0-392-07986-0, SpS). Soccer.

THOMISM (MODERN PHILOSOPHY)

see Neo-Scholasticism

THONGA TRIBE

Shewmaker, Stan. Tonga Christianity. 1971. pap. 3.45. William Carey Lib.

THORACIC SURGERY

see Chest–Surgery

THOREAU, HENRY DAVID, 1817-1862

Atkinson, Brooks J. Henry Thoreau the Cosmic Yankee. LC 80-2678. 1981. Repr. of 1927 ed. 22.50 (ISBN 0-404-19075-8). AMS Pr.

Bazalgette, Leon. Henry Thoreau Bachelor of Nature. Brooks, Wyck Van, tr. LC 80-2679. 1981. Repr. of 1924 ed. 37.50 (ISBN 0-404-19076-6). AMS Pr.

Channing, William E. Thoreau the Poet-Naturalist: With Memorial Verses. LC 80-2679. 1981. Repr. of 1873 ed. 37.50 (ISBN 0-404-19073-1). AMS Pr.

Clapper, Ronald. The Development of Walden: A Genetic Text. LC 80-2503. 1981. 75.00 (ISBN 0-686-28931-5). AMS Pr.

The Concord Saunterer. LC 80-2504. 1981. Repr. of 1940 ed. 19.50 (ISBN 0-404-19052-9). AMS Pr.

Deshmukh, D. G. Thoreau and Indian Thought: A Study of the Impact of Indian Thought on the Life of Henry David Thoreau. LC 80-2505. 1981. Repr. of 1974 ed. price not set (ISBN 0-404-19053-7). AMS Pr.

Gozzi, Raymond. Tropes and Figures: A Psychological Study of Henry David Thoreau. LC 80-2506. 1981. 62.50 (ISBN 0-404-19054-5). AMS Pr.

Harding, Walter. Thoreau on the Lecture Platform. LC 80-2681. 1981. 12.50 (ISBN 0-404-19077-4). AMS Pr.

Hovey, Allen B. The Hidden Thoreau. LC 80-2450. 1981. Repr. of 1966 ed. 22.75 (ISBN 0-404-19056-1). AMS Pr.

Huber, J. Parker. Thoreau's Travels in Maine. (Illus.). 200p. 1981. pap. 8.95 (ISBN 0-686-69095-8). Appalach Mtn.

Jones, Samuel A. Pertaining to Thoreau. 171p. 1980. Repr. of 1901 ed. text ed. 20.00 (ISBN 0-8492-1280-4). R West.

Jones, Samuel A., ed. Pertaining to Thoreau. LC 80-2509. 1981. Repr. of 1901 ed. 26.00 (ISBN 0-404-19057-X). AMS Pr.

Krutch, Joseph W. Henry David Thoreau. LC 80-2511. 1981. Repr. of 1948 ed. 34.00 (ISBN 0-404-19059-6). AMS Pr.

Porte, Joel. Emerson & Thoreau: Transcendentalists in Conflict. LC 80-2512. 1981. Repr. of 1966 ed. 29.50 (ISBN 0-404-19060-X). AMS Pr.

Robinson, Kenneth A. Thoreau & the Wild Appetite. LC 90-2682. 1981. Repr. of 1957 ed. 12.50 (ISBN 0-404-19079-0). AMS Pr.

Sanborn, Franklin B. Henry D. Thoreau. LC 80-2515. 1981. Repr. of 1910 ed. 37.50 (ISBN 0-404-19063-4). AMS Pr.

--The Personality of Thoreau. LC 80-2516. 1981. Repr. of 1901 ed. 18.50 (ISBN 0-404-19064-2). AMS Pr.

Sherwin, J. Stephen. A Word Index to Walden, Turth Textual Notes. LC 80-2517. 1981. Repr. of 1960 ed. 24.50 (ISBN 0-404-19065-0). AMS Pr.

Snyder, Helene A. Thoreau's Philosophy of Life, with Special Consideration of the Influence of Hindoo Philosophy. LC 80-2518. 1981. Repr. of 1900 ed. 18.50 (ISBN 0-404-19066-9). AMS Pr.

Stanley, Hiram M. Essays on Literary Art: Tennyson, Wordsworth, Jane Austen, Thoreau. 164p. 1980. Repr. of 1897 ed. lib. bdg. 25.00 (ISBN 0-8414-8035-4). Folcroft.

Thoreau, Henry D. Consciousness in Concord: The Text of Thoreau's Hitherto "Lost Journal," 1840-1841. LC 80-2519. 1981. Repr. of 1958 ed. 29.50 (ISBN 0-404-19067-7). AMS Pr.

--The First & Last Journeys of Thoreau, 2 vols. in 1. Sanborn, Franklin B., ed. LC 80-2520. 1981. Repr. of 1905 ed. 45.00 (ISBN 0-404-19068-5). AMS Pr.

--Some Unpublished Letters of Henry D. & Sophia E. Thoreau: A Chapter in the History of a Still-Born Book. Jones, Samuel A., ed. LC 80-2684. 1981. Repr. of 1899 ed. 15.50 (ISBN 0-404-19078-2). AMS Pr.

--Thoreaus Minnesota Journey: Two Documents. Harding, Walter, ed. LC 80-2524. 1981. Repr. of 1962 ed. 18.50 (ISBN 0-404-19072-3). AMS Pr.

Wagenknecht, Edward. Henry David Thoreau: What Manner of Man? LC 80-23542. (New England Writers Ser.). 224p. 1981. lib. bdg. 12.50x (ISBN 0-87023-136-7); pap. 5.95 (ISBN 0-87023-137-5). U of Mass Pr.

THOREAU, HENRY DAVID, 1817-1862–BIBLIOGRAPHY

Adams, Raymond. The Thoreau Library of Raymond Adams. 24.50 (ISBN 0-686-28930-7). AMS Pr.

THORNWELL, JAMES HENLEY, 1812-1862

Palmer, B. M. Life & Letters of J. H. Thornwell. 1974. 13.95 (ISBN 0-85151-195-3). Banner of Truth.

THOROUGHBRED HORSE

Thoroughbred Owners & Breeders Association. The Breeder's Guide for 1980. 1981. 57.50 (ISBN 0-936032-41-3). Thoroughbred O.

--Thoroughbred Broodmare Records, 1980. 1981. text ed. 66.75 (ISBN 0-936032-42-1); leather bdg. 77.75 (ISBN 0-936032-43-X). Thoroughbred O.

THOROUGHFARES

see Roads; Streets

THORPE, JIM, 1888-1953

Hahn, James & Hahn, Lynn. Thorpe! Jim Thorpe. Schroeder, Howard, ed. (Sports Legends Ser.). (Illus.). 48p. (Orig.). (gr. 3-5). 1981. PLB 5.95 (ISBN 0-89686-123-6); pap. text ed. 2.95 (ISBN 0-89686-138-4). Crestwood Hse.

Wheeler, Robert W. Jim Thorpe: The World's Greatest Athlete. LC 78-58080. (Illus.). 320p. 1981. pap. 5.95 (ISBN 0-8061-1745-1). U of Okla Pr.

THOUGHT, FREE

see Free Thought

THOUGHT AND THINKING

see also Cognition; Ideology; Intellect; Judgment; Logic; Memory; Perception; Psycholinguistics; Reasoning; Reasoning (Psychology); Self

Browne, M. Neil & Keely, Stuart M. Asking the Right Questions. 224p. 1981. pap. text ed. 6.95 (ISBN 0-13-049395-3). P-H.

Dirkes, M. Ann. Learning to Think--to Learn. LC 80-65613. 145p. 1981. perfect bdg. 11.50 (ISBN 0-86548-032-X). Century Twenty One.

Unger, Carl. Trails of Thinking, Feeling & Willing. 1980. pap. 3.00 (ISBN 0-916786-47-1). St George Bk Serv.

Wydro, Kenneth. Think on Your Feet: The Art of Thinking & Speaking Under Pressure. 192p. 1981. text ed. 11.95 (ISBN 0-13-917815-5, Spec); pap. text ed. 4.95 (ISBN 0-13-917807-4, Spec). P-H.

THRIFT

see Saving and Thrift

THROMBOLYTIC AGENTS

see Fibrinolytic Agents

THROMBOSIS

Boeynaems, J. M. & Herman, A. G., eds. Prostaglandins, Prostacyclin, Thromboxanes Measurement. (Developments in Pharmacology Ser.: No. 1.). (Illus.). 209p. 1981. PLB 34.00 (ISBN 90-247-2417-1, Pub. by Martinus Nijhoff). Kluwer Boston.

Sharnoff, J. G. The Prevention of Venous Thrombosis & Pulmonary Thromboembolism. (Medical Publicatons Ser.). 1980. lib. bdg. 25.00 (ISBN 0-8161-2223-7). G K Hall.

THUCYDIDES

Cogan, Marc. The Human Thing: The Speeches & Principles of Thucydides' History. LC 80-24226. (Chicago Original Paperback Ser.). 248p. 1981. lib. bdg. 19.00x (ISBN 0-226-11194-6). U of Chicago Pr.

Rawlings, Hunter R. Structure of Thucydides' History. LC 80-8572. 312p. 1981. 21.00x (ISBN 0-691-03555-5). Princeton U Pr.

THUGS

Taylor, Phillip M. The Confessions of a Thug, 3vols.in 2. LC 80-2500. 1981. Repr. of 1839 ed. 104.00 (ISBN 0-404-19136-3). AMS Pr.

THYROID GLAND

Ashkar, F. S., ed. Thyroid & Endocrine System Investigations with Radionuclides & Radioassays. (Illus.). 544p. 1979. 40.50 (ISBN 0-89352-070-5). Masson Pub.

THYROID GLAND–DISEASES

see also Goiter; Graves' Disease

Livolsi, Virginia A. & Logerfo, Paul. Thyroiditis. 192p. 1981. 54.95 (ISBN 0-8493-5705-5). CRC Pr.

TIBET–CIVILIZATION

Salisbury, Charlotte. Tibetan Diary: Travels Along the Ancient Silk Route. LC 80-54816. 1981. 9.95 (ISBN 0-8027-0683-5). Walker & Co.

TIBET–HISTORY

Mehra, Parshotam. The North-East Frontier: A Documentary Study of the Internecine Rivalry Between India, Tibet & China, Vol. 1, 1906-14. 270p. 1979. text ed. 9.95x (ISBN 0-19-561158-6). Oxford U Pr.

TIBET–RELIGION

Snellgrove, David. Himalayan Pilgrimage: A Study of Tibetan Religion. (Illus.). 326p. (Orig.). 1981. pap. 12.50 (ISBN 0-87773-720-7). Great Eastern.

TIBETAN ART

see Art, Tibetan

TIGERS

Hunt, Patricia. Tigers. LC 80-2785. (A Skylight Bk.). (Illus.). 64p. (gr. 2-5). 1981. PLB 5.95 (ISBN 0-396-07932-6). Dodd.

TILES

Austwick, Jill & Austwick, Brian. The Decorative Tile: An Illustrated History of English Tile-Making & Design. (Illus.). 1981. 30.00 (ISBN 0-684-16761-1). Scribner.

Burch, Monte. Tile: Indoors & Out. Horowitz, Shirley M. & Kummings, Gail, eds. (Illus.). 144p. (Orig.). 1980. 14.95 (ISBN 0-932944-27-2); pap. 5.95 (ISBN 0-932944-28-0). Creative Homeowner.

Southwell, B. C. Making & Decorating Pottery Tiles. 1972. 9.95 (ISBN 0-571-09603-4, Pub. by Faber & Faber). Merrimack Bk Serv.

TILLICH, PAUL, 1886-1965

Bulman, Raymond F. A Blueprint for Humanity: Paul Tillich's Theology of Culture. LC 78-75208. 248p. 1981. 18.50 (ISBN 0-8387-5000-1). Bucknell U Pr.

TIMBER

see also Forests and Forestry; Pulpwood; Trees; Wood also names of timber-trees, e.g. Oak, Pine

Desch, H. E. Timber: Its Structure, Properties, & Utilization. 6th ed. 416p. (Orig.). 1980. pap. text ed. 24.95x (ISBN 0-917304-62-4, Pub. by Timber Press). Intl Schol Bk Serv.

Hyde, William F. Timber Supply, Land Allocation, & Economic Efficiency. LC 80-8021. (Illus.). 248p. 1980. text ed. 19.00x (ISBN 0-8018-2489-3). Johns Hopkins.

Thomas Telford Ltd. Editorial Staff. Non-Destructive Testing of Concrete & Timber. 126p. 1980. 80.00x (ISBN 0-901948-27-6, Pub. by Telford England). State Mutual Bk.

TIME–JUVENILE LITERATURE

Buck, Peggy J. Tommy Learns About Time & Eternity. (Illus.). 68p. (Orig.). (gr. 1-3). 1980. pap. 2.50 (ISBN 0-89323-006-5). BMA Pr.

Humphrey, Henry & Humphrey, Deirdre. When Is Now: Experiments with Time & Timekeeping Devices. (Illus.). 80p. (gr. 6-7). 1981. 7.95a (ISBN 0-385-13215-8); PLB (ISBN 0-385-13216-6). Doubleday.

Zokeisha. What Time Is It? (Puppet Story Board Bks.). (Illus.). 12p. (ps-k). Date not set. boards 2.95 (ISBN 0-671-42646-X, Little Simon). S&S.

TIME (THEOLOGY)

Herrmann, Siegfried. Time & History. Belvins, James L., tr. LC 80-25323. (Biblical Encounter Ser.). 208p. (Orig.). 1981. pap. 7.95 (ISBN 0-687-42100-4). Abingdon.

TIME ALLOCATION

Rutherford, Robert D. Just in Time: The Inner Game of Time Management. 186p. 1981. 13.95 (ISBN 0-471-08434-4, Pub. by Wiley-Interscience). Wiley.

TIME AND MOTION STUDY

Kolstee, Hans M. Motion & Power. (Illus.). 256p. 1981. text ed. 19.95 (ISBN 0-13-602953-1). P-H.

Lowry, S. M., et al. Time & Motion Study & Formulas for Wage Incentives. 3rd ed. LC 80-12407. 446p. 1981. Repr. of 1940 ed. write for info. (ISBN 0-89874-174-2, Pub. by McGraw). Krieger.

McDowall, David, et al. Interrupted Time Series Analysis. LC 80-52761. (Quantitative Applications in the Social Sciences Ser.: No. 21). (Illus.). 96p. 1980. pap. 3.50 (ISBN 0-8039-1493-8). Sage.

Plumb, J. H. Death of the Past. 152p. 1978. text ed. 12.50x (ISBN 0-333-06050-4). Humanities.

TIME AND SPACE

see Space and Time

TIME BUDGETS

see Time Allocation

TIME IN LITERATURE

Barthold, Bonnie J. Black Time: Fiction of Africa, the Caribbean, & the United States. LC 80-24336. (Illus.). 224p. 1981. 17.50x (ISBN 0-300-02573-4). Yale U Pr.

TIME MEASUREMENTS

see also Clocks and Watches; Sun-Dials

Humphrey, Henry & Humphrey, Deirdre. When Is Now: Experiments with Time & Timekeeping Devices. (Illus.). 80p. (gr. 6-7). 1981. 7.95a (ISBN 0-385-13215-8); PLB (ISBN 0-385-13216-6). Doubleday.

TIME PRODUCTION STANDARDS

see Production Standards

TIME-SERIES ANALYSIS

Brillinger, David R. Time Series: Data Analysis & Theory. enl. ed. (Illus.). 552p. 1980. Repr. of 1975 ed. text ed. 25.00 (ISBN 0-8162-1150-7); foreign ed. 29.95 (ISBN 0-686-69028-1). Holden-Day.

TIME STUDY

Engstrom, Ted W. & McKenzie, R. A., trs. Administracao Do Tempo. (Portugese Bks.). (Port.). 1979. 1.40 (ISBN 0-8297-0637-2). Life Pubs Intl.

--Como Aprovechar el Tiempo. (Spanish Bks.). (Span.). 1978. 1.50 (ISBN 0-8297-0518-X). Vida Pub.

Jay, Tony A. Time Study. (Illus.). 1981. 17.50 (ISBN 0-7137-1085-3, Pub. by Blandford Pr England); pap. 9.95 (ISBN 0-7137-1126-4). Sterling.

TINCTORIAL SUBSTANCES

see Dyes and Dyeing

TINY OBJECTS

see Miniature Objects

TISSUE COMPATIBILITY

see Histocompatibility

TISSUE TRANSPLANTATION

see Transplantation of Organs, Tissues, etc.

TISSUES

see also Elastic Tissue; Histology; Lymphoid Tissue; Transplantation of Organs, Tissues, etc. also names of particular tissues or organs, e.g. Bone, Kidneys

Fung, Y. C. Biomechanics: Mechanical Properties of Living Tissues. (Illus.). 400p. 1980. 29.80 (ISBN 0-387-90472-7). Springer-Verlag.

Kocsis, James J., et al, eds. The Effects of Taurine on Excitable Tissue. 1980. write for info. (ISBN 0-89335-125-3). Spectrum Pub.

TISSUES–TRANSPLANTATION

see Transplantation of Organs, Tissues, etc.

TISSUES, VEGETABLE

see Botany–Anatomy

TITANIC (STEAMSHIP)

Brown, Rustie. The Titanic, the Psychic & the Sea. LC 80-70551. (Illus.). 176p. 1981. 12.95 (ISBN 0-9605278-0-X). Blue Harbor.

TITHES

Ryves, Thomas. The Poore Vicars Plea. Declaring That a Competencie of Means Is Due to Them Out of the Tithes..Notwithstanding the Impropriations. LC 79-84135. (English Experience Ser.: No. 953). 164p. 1979. Repr. of 1620 ed. lib. bdg. 17.00 (ISBN 90-221-0953-4). Walter J Johnson.

TITIAN (TIZIANO, VECELLI), 1477-1576

Crowe, J. A. & Cavalcaselle, G. B. Titan, His Life & Times: With Some Account of His Family, 2 vols. Freedberg, Sydney J., ed. LC 77-19373. (Connoisseurship Criticism & Art History Ser.: Vol. 8). 1032p. 1979. lib. bdg. 80.00 (ISBN 0-8240-3265-9). Garland Pub.

TITLES (MOVING-PICTURES)

see Moving-Pictures–Editing

TITO, JOSIP BROZ, PRES. YUGOSLAVIA, 1892-1980

Djilas, Milovan. Tito: The Story from Inside. 1980. 9.95 (ISBN 0-686-68552-0). HarBraceJ.

TIUTCHEV, FEDOR IVANOVICH, 1803-1873

Conant, Roger. The Political Poetry & Idealogy of F. I. Tiutchev. (Ardis Essay Ser.: No. 6). 1981. 10.00. Ardis Pubs.

TIZIANO, VECELLI

see Titian (Tiziano, Vecelli), 1477-1576

TOADSTOOLS

see Mushrooms

TOBACCO–PHYSIOLOGICAL EFFECT

Fried & Oxern. Smoking for Two: Cigarettes & Pregnancy. 102p. Date not set. 8.95 (ISBN 0-02-910720-2). Macmillan.

TOBACCO HABIT

see Smoking; Tobacco–Physiological Effect

TOCCATAS AND FUGUES

see Canons, Fugues, etc.

TOE DANCING

see Ballet Dancing

TOES

see also Nails (Anatomy)

Gerbert, Joshua, ed. Textbook of Bunion Surgery. LC 80-68895. (Illus.). 300p. 1981. monograph 24.50 (ISBN 0-87993-153-1). Futura Pub.

TOILET (GROOMING)

see Beauty, Personal

TOKENS

Leighton, Philip. Coins & Tokens. (Junior Reference Ser.). (Illus.). 64p. (gr. 7 up). 1972. 7.95 (ISBN 0-7136-1238-X). Dufour.

TOLERANCE, IMMUNOLOGICAL

see Immunological Tolerance

TOLKIEN, JOHN RONALD RUEL, 1892-1973

Crabbe, Katharyn F. J. R. R. Tolkien. LC 80-53699. (Modern Literature Ser.). 200p. 1981. 9.95 (ISBN 0-8044-2134-X); pap. 4.95 (ISBN 0-8044-6091-4). Ungar.

Fonstad, Karen W. The Atlas of the Middle-Earth. 224p. 1981. 14.95 (ISBN 0-686-69045-1). HM.

TOLSTOI, LEV NIKOLAEVICH, GRAF, 1828-1910

Edwards, Anne. Sonya: The Life of Countess Tolstoy. 1981. 13.95 (ISBN 0-671-24040-4). S&S.

Eikhenbaum, Boris. Tolstoi in the Seventies. Kaspin, A., tr. 1981. 15.00 (ISBN 0-88233-472-7). Ardis Pubs.

TOMATOES

Mittleider, Jacob R. Let's Grow Tomatoes. LC 80-84563. (Illus.). 150p. 1981. pap. 4.95 (ISBN 0-88290-176-1, 4820). Horizon Utah.

Tomatoes in Peat. 76p. 1980. pap. 9.95x (ISBN 0-901361-32-1, Pub. by Grower Bks England). Intl Schol Bk Serv.

TOMBSTONE, ARIZONA

Hattich, William. Tombstone. LC 80-5947. (Illus.). 64p. 1981. 9.95 (ISBN 0-8061-1753-2). U of Okla Pr.

TOMBSTONES

see Sepulchral Monuments

TOMOGRAPHY

Berry, R. J., ed. Computerized Tomographic Scanners on Radiotheraopy in Europe. 1980. 20.00x (Pub. by Brit Inst Radiology England). State Mutual Bk.

Herman, G. T. & Natterer, F., eds. Mathematical Aspects of Computerized Tomography: Proceedings. (Lecture Notes in Medical Information Ser.: Vol. 8). 309p. 1981. pap. 28.10 (ISBN 0-387-10277-9). Springer-Verlag.

Pitcoff, Ramsey K. & Powell, Herb. Neuroradiology with Computed Tomography. 575p. 1981. text ed. price not set (ISBN 0-7216-7444-5). Saunders.

Valk, J. Computed Tomography & Cerebral Infarctions. 190p. 1980. 29.50 (ISBN 0-89004-646-8). Raven.

TONGA TRIBE

see Thonga Tribe

TONGUE TWISTERS

Brandreth, Gyles. Biggest Tongue Twister Book in the World. LC 78-7784. (Illus.). 123p. (gr. 3 up). 1980. pap. 2.95 (ISBN 0-8069-8972-6). Sterling.

TONGUES, GIFT OF

see Glossolalia

TONNAGE

see also Freight and Freightage

Tonnage Measurement: Treatment of Shelter-Deck & Other "Open" Spaces. 15p. 1964. 5.50 (IMCO). Unipub.

TOOL AND DIE INDUSTRY

International Labour Office, Geneva. Tool & Die. (Equipment Planning Guide for Vocational & Technical Training & Education Programmes Ser.: No. 2). x, 214p. (Orig.). 1980. pap. 22.80 spiral (ISBN 92-2-101891-1). Intl Labour Office.

TOOLS

see also Agricultural Implements; Agricultural Machinery; Home Workshops; Machine-Tools; Tool and Die Industry also specific tools

Advice About Tools & Home Repair. (Home Adviser Ser.). 80p. (Orig.). 1981. pap. 1.95 (ISBN 0-8326-2406-3, 7055). Delair.

Bartlett, J. V. Handy Farm & Home Devices. (Illus.). 320p. (Orig.). 1981. pap. price not set. MIT Pr.

Clark, Stephen & Lyman, Daniel, eds. Incredible Illustrated Tool Book. (Illus.). 415p. Date not set. price not set (ISBN 0-89196-082-1, Domus Bks). Quality Bks IL.

Fraser, T. M. Ergonomic Principles in the Design of Hand Tools. International Labour Office, ed. (Occupational Safety & Health Ser.: No. 44). (Illus.). vii, 93p. (Orig.). 1980. pap. 8.55 (ISBN 0-686-69012-5). Intl Labour Office.

Ritchie, James. Successful Homeowner's Tools. (Successful Ser.). 192p. 1980. 14.95 (ISBN 0-912336-85-4); pap. 7.95 (ISBN 0-912336-86-2). Structures Pub.

TOOLS–JUVENILE LITERATURE

Kesselman, Judi R. & Peterson, Franklynn. I Can Use Tools. (Illus.). 32p. (gr. 1-4). 1981. 5.95 (ISBN 0-525-66725-3). Elsevier-Nelson.

TOOLS, AGRICULTURAL

see Agricultural Implements

TOOTH

see Teeth

TOPECTOMY

see Brain–Surgery

TOPOGRAPHY, MEDICAL

see Medical Geography

TOPOLOGICAL VECTOR SPACES

see Linear Topological Spaces

TOPOLOGY

see also Algebraic Topology; Algebras, Linear; Banach Spaces; Geometry, Algebraic; Graph Theory; Homotopy Theory; Lattice Theory; Linear Topological Spaces

Murdeshwar, M. G. General Topology. LC 80-18434. 480p. 1981. 19.95 (ISBN 0-470-26916-2). Halsted Pr.

Wilansky, Albert. Topology for Analysis. 400p. 1981. Repr. of 1970 ed. lib. bdg. price not set (ISBN 0-89874-343-5). Krieger.

TORBUTS

see Flatfishes

TORT LIABILITY OF EMPLOYERS

see Employers' Liability

TORT LIABILITY OF PHYSICIANS

see Malpractice

TORT LIABILITY OF THE GOVERNMENT

see Government Liability

TORTURE

see also Inquisition

Sadist, Golem N. Cruel & Unusual Punishments: From the Here & the Hereafter. (Odd Books for Odd Moments Ser.). (Illus.). 72p. (Orig.). 1980. pap. 3.95 (ISBN 0-938338-03-X). Winds World Pr.

TOSCANINI, ARTURO, 1867-1957

Sachs, Harvey. Toscanini. (Da Capo Quality Paperbacks Ser.). (Illus.). 380p. 1981. pap. 8.95 (ISBN 0-306-80137-X). Da Capo.

TOTAL ABSTINENCE

see Temperance

TOUCH
McClain, Mary, illus. First Things to Touch. (Floppies Ser.). (Illus.). 6p. (ps-k). Date not set. 3.95 (ISBN 0-671-42533-1, Little Simon). S&S.
TOUR GUIDES (MANUALS)
see subdivisions Description and Travel as appropriate under names of countries, regions, cities, etc.
TOURISM
see Tourist Trade
TOURIST TRADE
see also Travel; Travel Agents
Dicke, Karen & Goeldner, C. R. Bibliography of Tourism & Travel Research Studies, Reports, & Articles, 9 vols. 1980. Set. 60.00 (ISBN 0-89478-052-2). U CO Busn Res Div.
Metelka, Charles J., ed. The Dictionary of Tourism. 1981. 14.95 (ISBN 0-916032-10-8). Merton Hse.
OECD. Tourism Policy & International Tourism in OECD Member Countries, 1980. (Illus.). 189p. (Orig.). 1980. pap. text ed. 19.50x (ISBN 92-64-12123-4). OECD.
Paraskevopoulos, George N. An Econometric Analysis of International Tourism. (Lecture Ser.: No. 31). (Illus.). 110p. (Orig.). 1977. pap. 8.50x (ISBN 0-8002-2743-3). Intl Pubns Serv.
Tourism's Top Twenty. 86p. 1980. 15.00 (ISBN 0-89478-053-0). U CO Busn Res Div.
Travel Trends, Nineteen Eighty-One. 1981. 25.00 (ISBN 0-686-69389-2). U CO Busn Res Div.
TOURISTS
see Tourist Trade
TOURS
see subdivisions Description and Travel as appropriate under names of countries, regions, cities, etc.
TOWBOATS
see Tugboats
TOWING
see also Tugboats
Cohen, Stuart. Proceedings of Towing Tank Conference, 2 vols. 1275p. 1981. Set. text ed. 88.00 (ISBN 0-250-40444-3). Ann Arbor Science.
TOWN MEETING
see Local Government
TOWN OFFICERS
see Municipal Officials and Employees
TOWN PLANNING
see City Planning
TOWN PLANNING LAW
see City Planning and Redevelopment Law
TOWNS
see Cities and Towns
TOWNSHIP GOVERNMENT
see Local Government
TOXIC SUBSTANCES
see Poisons
TOXICOLOGY
see also Industrial Toxicology
Ayres, John C. & Kirschman, John C., eds. Impact of Toxiology on Food Processing. (Institute of Food Technologists Basic Symposia Ser.). (Illus.). 1981. lib. bdg. price not set (ISBN 0-87055-388-7). AVI.
Bababunmi, E. A. & Smith, R. L. Toxicology in the Tropics. 280p. 1980. 37.50 (ISBN 0-85066-194-3, Pub. by Taylor & Francis England). J K Burgess.
Chambers, P. L. & Klinger, W., eds. Further Studies in the Assessment of Toxic Actions: Proceedings. (Archives of Toxicology Supplementum Ser.: No. 4). (Illus.). 507p. 1981. pap. 57.80 (ISBN 0-387-10191-8). Springer-Verlag.
Clayton, G. D. & Clayton, F. E. Pattys Industrial Hygiene & Toxicology, 4 vols. 3rd ed. 1981. 305.00 (ISBN 0-471-08431-X). Wiley.
Jakoby, William B. Enzymatic Basis of Detoxication, Vol. 2. LC 80-17350. (Biochemical Pharmacology & Toxicology Ser.). 1980. lib ed 38.50 (ISBN 0-12-380002-1). Acad Pr.
Lee, Si D. & Grant, Lester, eds. Toxicology & Toxicological Health Assessment for Polycyclic Agents. 1980. pap. text ed. 13.50 (ISBN 0-930376-20-X). Pathotox Pubs.
Oliver, John S., ed. Forensic Toxicology. 320p. 1980. 50.00x (Pub. by Croom Helm England). State Mutual Bk.
Prasad, Kedar N. & Vernadakis, Antonia, eds. Mechanisms of Neurotoxic Substances. 1981. text ed. price not set (ISBN 0-89004-638-7). Raven.
Toxicological Evaluation of Parathion & Azinphosmethyl in Freshwater Model Ecosystems. (Agricultural Research Reports: No. 898). 112p. 1980. pap. 20.75 (ISBN 90-220-0732-4, PDC210, Pudoc). Unipub.
Vander, Arthur J. Nutrition, Stress & Toxic Chemicals: An Approach to Environmental Health Controversies. 360p. 1981. text ed. 18.00 (ISBN 0-472-09329-0); pap. 9.95 (ISBN 0-472-06329-4). U of Mich Pr.
Vettorazzi, Gaston. Hand Book of International Food Regulatory Toxicology, 2 vols. Incl. Vol. 1. Evaluations. 176p. 1980 (ISBN 0-89335-086-9); Vol. 2. Profiles. 256p. 1981. text ed. 30.00 ea. Spectrum Pub.
TOXINS AND ANTITOXINS
see also Immunity; Mycotoxins; Serumtherapy
Instructions for the Selection & Presentation of Data for the International Register of Potentially Toxic Chemicals with Sixty Illustrative Chemical Data Profiles. (IRPTC Register Attribute Ser.: No. 2). 386p. 1979. pap. 40.00 (UNEP 41, UNEP). Unipub.
Kimmel, Carole A. & Buelke-Sam, Judith, eds. Developmental Toxicity. (Target Organ Toxicity Ser.). 1981. price not set. Raven.
O'Flaherty, Ellen. Toxicants & Drugs: Kinetics & Synamics. 320p. 1981. 27.50 (ISBN 0-471-06047-X, Pub. by Wiley-Interscience). Wiley.
TOY AUTOMOBILES
see Automobiles–Models
TOY-MAKING
Greenhouse, Jean. Making Miniature Toys & Dolls. 1980. 19.95 (ISBN 0-7134-3271-3). David & Charles.
Jaffke, Freya. Making Soft Toys. Gebert, Rosemary, tr. from Ger. LC 80-66665. Orig. Title: Spielzeug Von Eltern Selbstgemacht. (Illus.). 1981. pap. 6.95 (ISBN 0-89742-044-6). Dawne-Leigh.
Peppe, Rodney. Rodney Peppe's Moving Toys. (Illus.). 128p. 1981. 14.95 (ISBN 0-8069-5422-1); lib. bdg. 13.29 (ISBN 0-8069-5423-X); pap. 6.95 (ISBN 0-8069-5424-8). Sterling.
TOYNBEE, ARNOLD JOSEPH, 1889-
Morton, S. Fiona, ed. A Bibliography of Arnold J. Toynbee. 300p. 1980. 74.00 (ISBN 0-19-215261-0). Oxford U Pr.
TOYS
see also Dolls; Electronic Toys; Miniature Objects; Toy-Making
Ayres, William. The Warner Collectors' Guide to American Toys. (Orig.). 1981. pap. 9.95 (ISBN 0-446-97632-6). Warner Bks.
Sansweet, Stephen. Science Fiction Toys & Models, Vol. I. 1980. pap. 3.95 (ISBN 0-931064-27-9). O'Quinn Studio.
TOYS–JUVENILE LITERATURE
DiFiore. Toys. 121p. Date not set. 2.95 (ISBN 0-07-016921-7). McGraw.
TRACE ELEMENTS
see also names of specific elements, e.g. Boron
Reid, E. Trace-Organic Sample Handling. (Methodological Surveys Analysis). 400p. 1981. 110.00 (ISBN 0-470-27071-3). Halsted Pr.
TRACERS, RADIOACTIVE
see Radioactive Tracers
TRACK-ATHLETICS
see also Cycling; Running
Aaseng, Nathan. Track's Magnificent Milers. LC 80-27404. (The Sports Heroes Library). (Illus.). (gr. 4 up). 1981. PLB 5.95 (ISBN 0-8225-1066-9). Lerner Pubns.
Lovesey, Peter. Five Fings of Distance. (Illus.). 197p. 1981. 10.95 (ISBN 0-312-29484-0). St Martin.
TRACK-ATHLETICS FOR WOMEN
Sullivan, George. Better Track for Girls. LC 80-21399. (Better Sports Ser.). (Illus.). 64p. (gr. 5 up). 1981. PLB 6.95 (ISBN 0-396-07911-3). Dodd.
TRACKS OF ANIMALS
see Animal Tracks
TRADE
see Business; Commerce
TRADE, RESTRAINT OF
see Restraint of Trade
TRADE AGREEMENTS (COMMERCE)
see Commercial Treaties
TRADE AND PROFESSIONAL ASSOCIATIONS–DIRECTORIES
Wright, Rita & Anderson, Mildred, eds. Texas Trade & Professional Associations (1981 Edition) rev. ed. 75p. (Orig.). 1981. pap. 5.00 (ISBN 0-686-69074-5). U of Tex Busn Res.
Zils, Michael, ed. World Guide to Trade Associations. 2nd ed. (Handbook of International Documentation & Information Ser.: Vol. 12). 845p. 1980. 180.00 (ISBN 3-598-20513-9, Dist by Gale Research Co.). K G Saur.
TRADE BARRIERS
see Commercial Policy
TRADE FAIRS
see Fairs
TRADE-MARKS
Frankenstein, George & Frankenstein, Diane. Brand Names: Who Owns What. 384p. 1981. lib. bdg. 45.00 (ISBN 0-87196-420-1). Facts on File.
Matlack, Helena, ed. Brand Name & Trademark Guide: 1896, 1904, 1915, 1922, 1943, 1950, 1965, 1969. 10th ed. (Illus.). 300p. 1978. 19.95 (ISBN 0-931744-03-2). Jewelers Circular.
Oathout, John D. Trademarks in the Marketplace. (Illus.). 192p. 1981. 12.95 (ISBN 0-684-16844-8, ScribT). Scribner.
Silfen, Martin E. Counseling Clients in the Entertainment Industry 1980, 2 vols. LC 80-80021. (Patents, Copyrights, Trademarks, & Literary Property Course Handbook Ser.). 1433p. 1980. pap. text ed. 25.00 (ISBN 0-686-68822-8, G6-3666). PLI.
Stiling, Marjorie. Famous Brand Names, Emblems and Trademarks. LC 80-69353. (Illus.). 64p. 1981. 8.95 (ISBN 0-7153-8098-2). David & Charles.
Wolfenstine, Manfred R. The Manual of Brands & Marks. Adams, Ramon F., ed. LC 68-31379. (Illus.). 355p. 1981. 24.95 (ISBN 0-8061-0867-3). U of Okla Pr.
TRADE NAMES
see Trade-Marks
TRADE REGULATION
see also Advertising Laws; Antitrust Law; Competition, Unfair; Consumer Protection; Copyright; Law; Legislation; Licenses; Monopolies; Patent Laws and Legislation; Restraint of Trade; Trade-Marks
Calvert, Thomas H. Regulation of Commerce Under the Federal Constitution. (Studies in Constitutional Law). xiv, 380p. 1981. Repr. of 1907 ed. lib. bdg. 32.50x (ISBN 0-8377-0429-4). Rothman.
Weiss, Leonard. Trade Liberalization & the National Interest, Vol. II. LC 80-80932. (Significant Issues Ser.: No. 2). 60p. 1980. 5.95 (ISBN 0-89206-016-6). CSI Studies.
White, Lawrence J. Reforming Regulation: Processes & Problems. (Illus.). 240p. 1981. text ed. 13.95 (ISBN 0-13-770115-2); pap. text ed. 8.95 (ISBN 0-13-770107-1). P-H.
TRADE-UNIONS
Here are entered general works on Trade Unions. For works on trade unions of specific countries see appropriate subdivision, e.g. Trade-Unions–Africa.
see also Arbitration, Industrial; Collective Bargaining; Friendly Societies; Strikes and Lockouts; Teachers' Unions
also American Federation of Labor and Congress of Industrial Organizations; and other specific unions
Cooke, Frederick H. The Law of Trade & Labor Combinations As Applicable to Boycotts, Strikes, Trade Conspiracies, Monopolies, Pools, Trusts, & Kindred Topics. xxv, 214p. 1981. Repr. of 1898 ed. lib. bdg. 24.00x (ISBN 0-8377-0430-8). Rothman.
Denker, Joel S. Unions & Universities: The Rise of the New Labor Leader. LC 80-67093. 192p. 1981. text ed. 20.00 (ISBN 0-916672-58-1). Allanheld.
Howie, Will. Trade Unions & the Professional Engineer. 80p. 1980. 15.00x (ISBN 0-7277-0044-8, Pub. by Telford England). State Mutual Bk.
Korn, Richard. Union & Its Retired Workers: A Case Study of the UMW. (Key Issues Ser.: No. 21). 1976. pap. 3.00 (ISBN 0-87546-230-8). NY Sch Indus Rel.
Pitrone, Jean M. Myra: The Life & Times of Myra Wolfgang, Trade-Union Leader. LC 80-68386. (Illus.). 226p. 1980. 10.00 (ISBN 0-686-28855-6). Calibre Bks.
Poole, Michael. Theories of Trade Unionism. 280p. 1981. 35.00 (ISBN 0-7100-0695-0). Routledge & Kegan.
Seaton, Douglas P. Catholics & Radicals: The Association of Catholic Trade Unionists & the American Labor Movement, from Depression to Cold War. 300p. 1981. 18.50 (ISBN 0-8387-2193-1). Bucknell U Pr.
TRADE-UNIONS–OFFICIALS AND EMPLOYEES
Nash, Al. Union Steward: Duties, Rights, & Status. (Key Issues Ser.: No. 22). 1977. pap. 3.00 (ISBN 0-87546-235-9). NY Sch Indus Rel.
TRADE-WINDS
see Winds
TRADES
see Industrial Arts
TRADES UNION CONGRESS
Martin, Ross M. Tuc: The Growth of a Pressure Group Eighteen Sixty Eight to Nineteen Seventy Six. 408p. 1980. text ed. 42.00x (ISBN 0-19-822475-3). Oxford U Pr.
TRADES WASTE
see Factory and Trade Waste
TRADITION (THEOLOGY)
Tradition for Crisis: A Study in Hosea. LC 68-21008. 164p. 1981. pap. 6.95 (ISBN 0-8042-0181-1). John Knox.
TRADITION, ORAL
see Oral Tradition
TRADITIONS
see Folk-Lore; Legends; Superstition
TRAFFIC ACCIDENTS–PREVENTION
see Traffic Safety
TRAFFIC CONTROL
see Traffic Engineering
TRAFFIC ENGINEERING
see also Traffic Safety
also names of types of transportation, e.g. Automobiles; Aeronautics, Commercial, etc.
Institute of Civil Engineers, UK. Traffic Data Collection. 178p. 1980. 40.00x (ISBN 0-7277-0061-8, Pub. by Telford England). State Mutual Bk.
--Transport for Society. 180p. 1980. 75.00x (ISBN 0-7277-0015-4, Pub. by Telford England). State Mutual Bk.
--Transportation Engineering. 174p. 1980. 50.00x (Pub. by Telford England). State Mutual Bk.
Morse, Leon W. Practical Handbook of Industrial Traffic Management. 6th ed. LC 77-9240. 552p. 1980. text ed. write for info. (ISBN 0-87408-020-7). Traffic Serv.
Wells, G. R. Traffic Engineering: An Introduction. 190p. 1979. 34.50x (ISBN 0-85264-254-7, Pub. by Griffin England). State Mutual Bk.
TRAFFIC MANAGEMENT, INDUSTRIAL
see Shipment of Goods
TRAFFIC REGULATION
see Traffic Engineering
TRAFFIC SAFETY
Fleischer, G. A. Contingency Table Analysis for Road Safety Studies. (NAtO Advanced Study Institute Ser.: Applied Science, No. 42). 300p. 1980. 32.50x (ISBN 90-286-0960-1). Sijthoff & Noordhoff.
TRAGEDY
Corrigan, Robert W. Tragedy: Vision & Form. 2nd ed. 384p. 1980. pap. text ed. 10.95 scp (ISBN 0-06-041371-9, HarpC). Har-Row.
McLaughlin, Iona H. Triumph Over Tragedy. (Festival Ser.). 128p. 1981. pap. 1.50 (ISBN 0-687-42640-5). Abingdon.
TRAILS
see also Cattle Trade; Garden Walks
Newey, Bob. East Bay Trails. 4th, rev. ed. LC 80-69075. (Illus.). 144p. 1981. pap. 4.95 (ISBN 0-9605186-0-6). Footloose Pr.
TRAINED NURSES
see Nurses and Nursing
TRAINING, FOOTBALL
see Football–Training
TRAINING, OCCUPATIONAL
see Occupational Training
TRAINING, PHYSICAL
see Physical Education and Training
TRAINING, VOCATIONAL
see Occupational Training
TRAINING OF CHILDREN
see Children–Management
TRAINING OF EMPLOYEES
see Employees, Training of
TRAINING OF EXECUTIVES
see Executives, Training of
TRAINING OF THE MEMORY
see Mnemonics
TRAINING SCHOOLS FOR NURSES
see Nursing Schools
TRAINING WITHIN INDUSTRY
see Employees, Training of
TRAMPING
see Hiking
TRAMPS
see also Rogues and Vagabonds
Rosseau, Ann M. Shopping Bag Ladies. (Illus.). 244p. 1981. 16.95 (ISBN 0-8298-0413-7). Pilgrim NY.
TRAMWAYS
see Street-Railroads
TRANQUILIZING DRUGS
see also names of individual drugs, e.g. Rauwolfia
Hughes, Richard & Brewin, Robert. Tranquilizing of America. 1980. pap. 2.95 (ISBN 0-446-93638-3). Warner Bks.
TRANSACTIONAL ANALYSIS
Barker, Dave. TA & Training: The Theory & Use of Transactional Analysis. 226p. 1980. text ed. 29.50x (ISBN 0-566-02118-8, Pub. by Gower Pub Co England). Renouf.
Freed, Alvyn M. TA for Tots Coloring Book. (Transactional Analysis for Everybody Ser.). 1976. pap. 1.95 (ISBN 0-915190-33-8); spirit masters 3.95. Jalmar Pr.
Romano, Anne T. Transactional Analysis for Police Personnel. write for info. (ISBN 0-398-04175-X). C C Thomas.
Wagner, Abe. The Transactional Manager: How to Solve People Problems with Transactional Analysis. (Illus.). 208p. 1981. 11.95 (ISBN 0-13-928192-4, Spec); pap. 5.95 (ISBN 0-13-928184-3). P-H.
TRANSATLANTIC FLIGHTS
see Aeronautics–Flights
TRANSCENDENCE OF GOD
Daly, Gabriel. Transcendence & Immanence: A Study in Catholic Modernism & Integralism. 266p. 1980. 34.95x (ISBN 0-19-826652-9). Oxford U Pr.
TRANSCENDENTAL MEDITATION
What Everyone Should Know About Transcendential Meditation. (Orig.). pap. 1.50 (ISBN 0-89129-234-9). Jove Pubns.
TRANSCENDENTALISM
see also Idealism; Immanence of God
Orr, Robert P. The Meaning of Transcendence. Dietrich, Wendell, ed. LC 80-12872. (American Academy of Religion Dissertation Ser.). 1981. 13.50 (ISBN 0-89130-407-X); pap. 9.00. Scholars Pr CA.
TRANSCRIPTION (SHORTHAND)
see Shorthand
TRANSFER MACHINES
see Machine-Tools
TRANSFER OF EMPLOYEES
see Employees, Transfer of
TRANSFER OF TECHNOLOGY
see Technology Transfer
TRANSFER TAX
see Inheritance and Transfer Tax
TRANSFERENCE (PSYCHOLOGY)
Langs, Robert. Interactions: The Realm of Transference & Countertransference. LC 80-68042. 575p. 1980. 30.00 (ISBN 0-87668-425-8). Aronson.
TRANSFORMERS, ELECTRIC
see Electric Transformers
TRANSFUSION OF BLOOD
see Blood–Transfusion
TRANSIENT LABOR
see Migrant Labor
TRANSIT SYSTEMS
see Local Transit
TRANSITION METALS
see also Ligand Field Theory
also names of special metals, e.g. Iron, Molybdenum, Tungsten
Slocum, D. W. & Hughes, O. R., eds. Transition Metal Mediated Organic Syntheses. LC 79-24735. (N.Y. Academy of Sciences Annals: Vol. 333). 301p. 1980. 55.00x (ISBN 0-89766-039-0). NY Acad Sci.

TRANSITS
Lunsted, Betty. Transits: The Time of Your Life. 1980. pap. 7.95 (ISBN 0-87728-503-9). Weiser.
TRANSLATING AND INTERPRETING
Newmark, Peter. Approaches to Translation: Aspects of Translation. LC 80-41008. (MFLP Ser.). 160p. 1980. 23.95 (ISBN 0-08-024603-6); pap. 11.95 (ISBN 0-08-024602-8). Pergamon.
TRANSMISSION OF DATA
see Data Transmission Systems
TRANSMISSION OF HEAT
see Heat–Transmission
TRANSMISSIONS, AUTOMOBILE
see Automobiles–Transmission Devices
TRANSMITTING SETS, RADIO
see Radio–Transmitters and Transmission
TRANSMUTATION OF METALS
see Alchemy
TRANSPLANTATION OF ORGANS, TISSUES, ETC.
see also Biomedical Materials; Immunological Tolerance; Preservation of Organs, Tissues, etc.; Skin-Grafting; Surgery, Plastic; Vascular Grafts
also subdivision Transplantation under specific organs, etc. e.g. Cornea–Transplantation
Lalezari, Parviz & Krakauer, Henry, eds. Organ Specific Alloantigens. (Transplantations Proceedings Reprint Ser.). 1980. 24.50 (ISBN 0-8089-1324-7). Grune.
Madison, Arnold. Transplanted & Artificial Body Organs. (Illus.). 192p. (gr. 7 up). 1981. 8.95 (ISBN 0-8253-0050-9). Beaufort Bks NY.
Scott, Russell. The Body As Property. 1981. 14.95 (ISBN 0-670-17743-1). Viking Pr.
TRANSPORT AIRCRAFT
see Transport Planes
TRANSPORT PLANES
Keyes, Lucille S. Regulatory Reform in Air Cargo Transportation. 1980. pap. 4.25 (ISBN 0-8447-3371-7). Am Enterprise.
TRANSPORT WORKERS
Murphy, G. J. The Transport Operators Guide to Professional Competence. 314p. 1980. pap. 21.00x (ISBN 0-09-141591-8, Pub. by Busn Bks England). Renouf.
TRANSPORTATION
see also Aeronautics, Commercial; Air Travel; Automobiles; Bridges; Canals; Carriages and Carts; Coastwise Navigation; Commerce; Freight and Freightage; Harbors; Inland Water Transportation; Local Transit; Ocean Travel; Pipe Lines; Postal Service; Railroads; Roads; Shipping; Steam-Navigation; Steamboats and Steamboat Lines; Streets; Traffic Engineering; Vehicles
also subdivision Transportation under special subjects, e.g. Farm Produce–Transportation
The Arabian Transport Directory 1980-81. 1980. 95.00x (Pub. by Parrish-Rogers England). State Mutual Bk.
International Symposium on Theory & Practice in Transport Economics, 8th, Istanbul, 24-28 Sept. 1979. Transport & the Challenge of Structural Change: Proceedings. (Illus.). 539p. (Orig.). 1980. pap. 20.00x (ISBN 92-821-1061-3). OECD.
Stopher, Peter R., et al, eds. New Horizons in Travel-Behavior Research. LC 78-24830. 1981. price not set (ISBN 0-669-02850-9). Lexington Bks.
Vuchic, Vukan. Urban Public Transportation. (Illus.). 672p. 1981. text ed. 38.95 (ISBN 0-13-939496-6). P-H.
Wells, G. R. Comprehensive Transport Planning. 157p. 1975. 39.50x (ISBN 0-85264-233-4, Pub. by Griffin England). State Mutual Bk.
TRANSPORTATION–ACCOUNTING
Transfers Through the Transport Sector: Evaluation of Re-Distribution Effects. (ECMT Roundtable Ser.: No. 48). (Illus.). 93p. (Orig.). 1980. pap. text ed. 6.00x (ISBN 92-821-1064-8). OECD.
TRANSPORTATION–FINANCE
Transfers Through the Transport Sector: Evaluation of Re-Distribution Effects. (ECMT Roundtable Ser.: No. 48). (Illus.). 93p. (Orig.). 1980. pap. text ed. 6.00x (ISBN 92-821-1064-8). OECD.
TRANSPORTATION–FREIGHT
see Freight and Freightage
TRANSPORTATION–HISTORY
Antalffy, Gyula. A Thousand Years of Travel in Old Hungary. Hoch, Elisabeth, tr. Orig. Title: Igy Utaztunk Hajdanaban. (Illus.). 337p. (Orig.). 1980. pap. 8.50x (ISBN 963-13-0909-6). Intl Pubns Serv.
Young, Andrew D. & Provenzo, Eugene F., Jr. The History of the St. Louis Car Company. (Illus.). 304p. 1981. Repr. of 1978 ed. 27.50 (ISBN 0-8310-7114-1). A S Barnes.
--The History of the St. Louis Car Company. (Illus.). 304p. 1981. Repr. of 1978 ed. 27.50 (ISBN 0-8310-7114-1). Howell-North.
TRANSPORTATION, AUTOMOTIVE
see also Automobiles; Motor-Trucks; Motor Vehicles; School Children–Transportation; Traffic Safety
Guide for Motorist Aid System. 1974. 0.50. AASHTO.
Markets for Small Scale Electrical Generation Systems: E-043. 1981. 875.00 (ISBN 0-89336-284-0). BCC.
TRANSPORTATION AND STATE
Dunn, James A., Jr. Transportation Policy in Comparative Perspective. (Transportation Ser.). 288p. 1981. text ed. 25.00x (ISBN 0-262-04062-X). MIT Pr.
Guide on Citizen Participation in Transportation Planning. 1978. 7.00. AASHTO.
TRANSPORTATION INSURANCE
see Insurance, Marine
TRANSPORTATION OF SCHOOL CHILDREN
see School Children–Transportation
TRANSPORTATION POLICY
see Transportation and State
TRAPPISTS
Jones, W. P. The Province Beyond the River: A Protestant's Days in a Trappist Monastery. 144p. (Orig.). 1981. pap. 5.95 (ISBN 0-8091-2363-0). Paulist Pr.
Nouwen, Henri J. The Genesee Diary: Report from a Trappist Monastery. 192p. 1981. pap. 3.95 (ISBN 0-385-17446-2, Im). Doubleday.
TRASH
see Refuse and Refuse Disposal
TRAUMATISM
see also Shock; Wounds;
also subdivision Wounds and Injuries under names of organs, and regions of the body, e.g. Brain–Wounds and Injuries
Franklin, Jon & Doelp, Alan. Shocktrauma. 256p. 1981. pap. 2.95 (ISBN 0-449-24387-7, Crest). Fawcett.
Mills. Trauma, Vol. 1. 1981. pap. text ed. 25.00 (ISBN 0-443-02018-3). Churchill.
Stillman, Richard M. Surgery Review & Assessment: Tumor, Trauma, & Specialties. 1981. pap. 12.50 (ISBN 0-686-69608-5). ACC.
Valeri, C. Robert & Altschule, Mark D. Hypovalemic Anemia of Trauma: The Missing Blood Syndrome. 224p. 1981. 64.95 (ISBN 0-8493-5389-0). CRC Pr.
TRAVEL
Here are entered works on the art of travel, etc. Works on voyages and travels are entered under the heading Voyages and Travels.
see also Air Travel; Automobile Touring; Ocean Travel; Steamboats and Steamboat Lines; Tourist Trade; Voyages and Travels
also subdivision Description and Travel under names of countries, or Description under names of cities, e.g. France–Description and Travel; London–Description
Carlson, Kenneth N. Manual for Travel Counsellors. 12th, rev. ed. LC 73-92320. (Illus.). 260p. 1981. 11.75x (ISBN 0-938428-00-4). Res Pubns WA.
Dicke, Karen & Goeldner, C. R. Bibliography of Tourism & Travel Research Studies, Reports, & Articles, 9 vols. 1980. Set. 60.00 (ISBN 0-89478-052-2). U CO Busn Res Div.
Dickerman, Patricia. Adventure Travel. LC 79-57153. 256p. 1980. 7.95 (ISBN 0-913216-03-8). Berkshire Traveller.
Kaye, Dena. The Traveling Woman. 384p. 1981. pap. 2.95 (ISBN 0-553-14714-5). Bantam.
Mayo, Edward J. & Jarvis, Lance P. The Psychology of Leisure Travel: Effective Marketing & Selling of Travel Services. 448p. 1981. 9.95 (ISBN 0-8436-2204-0). CBI Pub.
Metelka, Charles J., ed. The Dictionary of Tourism. 1981. 14.95 (ISBN 0-916032-10-8). Merton Hse.
Robinson, H. A Geography of Tourism. (Illus.). 512p. 1976. pap. 17.50x (ISBN 0-7121-0721-5, Pub. by Macdonald & Evans England). Intl Ideas.
TRAVEL–COSTS
see Travel Costs
TRAVEL–GUIDEBOOKS
see Voyages and Travels–Guidebooks
TRAVEL AGENTS
Your Travel Agent: A Consumer's Guide. 1980. 1.95 (ISBN 0-916752-32-1). Green Hill.
TRAVEL BOOKS
see Voyages and Travels
also subdivision Description and Travel under names of countries, regions, etc.
TRAVEL COSTS
Berg, Rick. The Art & Adventure of Traveling Cheaply. 1981. pap. 2.95 (ISBN 0-451-09729-7, E9729, Sig). NAL.
TRAVEL IN LITERATURE
Santi, Paul & Hill, Richard, eds. The Europeans in the Sudan Eighteen Thirty Four to Eighteen Seventy Eight. (Illus.). 352p. 1980. 45.00 (ISBN 0-19-822718-3). Oxford U Pr.
TRAVEL PHOTOGRAPHY
Gilchrist, Peter S. My Amateur World. (Illus.). 200p. 1975. text ed. 10.00. Gilchem Corp.
TRAVELERS
Nashe, Thomas. The Unfortunate Traveler: Or the Life of Jack Wilton. 194p. 1980. Repr. of 1926 ed. 30.00 (ISBN 0-89760-605-1). Telegraph Bks.
TRAVELS
see Voyages and Travels
TRAWLS AND TRAWLING
see also Fisheries
Hjul, Peter, ed. The Stern Trawler. (Illus.). 228p. 22.50 (ISBN 0-85238-025-9, FN). Unipub.
Pair Trawling with Small Boats. (FAO Training Ser.: No. 1). 77p. 1981. pap. 6.75 (ISBN 92-5-100627-X, F2095, FAO). Unipub.
TREASON
West, Richard, et al. Discourse Concerning Treasons & Bills of Attainder. Berkowitz, David S. & Thorne, Samuel E., eds. LC 77-89246. (Classics of English Legal History in the Modern Era Ser.: Vol. 77). 273p. 1979. lib. bdg. 40.00 (ISBN 0-8240-3176-8). Garland Pub.
TREASURE-TROVE
Smith, Alan. Getting Started in Treasure Hunting. (Illus.). 192p. 1981. pap. 7.95 (ISBN 0-8117-2045-4). Stackpole.
TREATIES
see also Arbitration, International; Commercial Treaties; Congresses and Conventions; Indians of North America–Treaties
Dockrill, Michael & Gould, Douglas. Peace Without Promise: Britain & the Peace Conferences 1919-1923. 320p. 1981. 25.00 (ISBN 0-208-01909-X, Archon). Shoe String.
Ferraris, Luigi V., ed. Report on a Negotiation: Helsinki-Geneva-Helsinki Nineteen Seventy-Two to Nineteen Seventy-Five. Barber, Marie-Claire, tr. from Italian. (Collections De Relations Internationales Ser.). 439p. 1980. 46.00x (ISBN 9-0286-0779-X). Sijthoff & Noordhoff.
Multilateral Treaties in Respect of Which the Secretary General Performs Depository Functions. 677p. 1980. pap. 34.00 (ISBN 0-686-68960-7, UN80/5/10, UN). Unipub.
OAS General Secretariat Bureau of Legal Affairs, ed. Status of Inter-American Treaties & Conventions. rev. ed. (Treaty Ser.: No. 5). 53p. text ed. 5.00 (ISBN 0-8270-1147-4). OAS.
Slusser, Robert M. & Ginsburgs, George. A Calendar of Soviet Treaties: 1958-1973. LC 80-50453. 990p. 1980. 125.00x (ISBN 90-286-0609-2). Sijthoff & Noordhoff.
TREATIES–CATALOGS
Parry, C. Index Guide to Treaties, Vol. 1. 1979. 75.00 (ISBN 0-379-13002-5). Oceana.
TREE BREEDING
Rowland, Lorna. Growing Herbs. (Practical Gardening Ser.). (Illus.). 112p. (Orig.). 1979. pap. 10.50 (ISBN 0-589-01244-4, Pub. by Reed Bks Australia). C E Tuttle.
TREE SQUIRRELS
see Squirrels
TREES
see also Dwarf Fruit Trees; Forests and Forestry; Fruit-Culture; Landscape Gardening; Lumbering; Nurseries (Horticulture); Nuts; Plant Lore; Pruning; Shrubs; Timber; Wood
also classes, orders, species, etc. of trees, e.g. Elm, Pine, Spruce
Clouston, Brian & Stansfield, Kathy, eds. After the Elm. (Illus.). 186p. 1980. text ed. 24.50x (ISBN 0-8419-6107-7). Holmes & Meier.
Darlington, Arnold. World of a Tree. 1972. 6.95 (ISBN 0-571-09624-7, Pub. by Faber & Faber). Merrimack Bk Serv.
Hora, Bayard, ed. Oxford Encyclopedia of Trees of the World. (Illus.). 1981. write for info. Oxford U Pr.
Kramer, Jack. Indoor Trees. 1980. 25.00x (ISBN 0-232-51399-6, Pub. by Darton-Longman-Todd England). State Mutual Bk.
Little, Brown Editorial Staff, ed. Trees: West Coast Ed. (Explorer's Notebooks Ser.). (Illus.). 32p. (Orig.). (gr. 5 up). 1981. pap. 1.95 (ISBN 0-316-52769-6). Little.
The New Alchemy Tree Crop Book. 96p. 1981. pap. 4.95 (ISBN 0-931790-22-0). Brick Hse Pub.
Poplars & Willows. (Forestry Ser.: No. 10). 328p. 1958. pap. 36.75 (ISBN 92-5-100500-1, F2046, FAO). Unipub.
TREES–BREEDING
see Tree Breeding
TREES–JUVENILE LITERATURE
Little, Brown Editors, ed. Trees: East Coast Edition. (Explorer's Notebooks). (Illus.). 32p. (Orig.). (gr. 5 up). 1981. pap. 1.95 (ISBN 0-316-52769-6). Little.
TREES–GREAT BRITAIN
Bean, W. J., compiled by. Trees & Shrubs: Hardy in the British Isles, 4 vols. 8th ed. Clarke, D. L. & Taylor, George, eds. (Illus.). 850p. 1981. 280.00x set (ISBN 0-312-81742-8). St Martin.
Harz, Kurt. Trees & Shrubs. (Illus.). 144p. 1981. pap. 8.95 (ISBN 0-7011-2542-X, Pub. by Chatto-Bodley-Jonathan). Merrimack Bk Serv.
TREES–NEW ZEALAND
Adams, Nancy M. New Zealand Native Trees, Vol. 1. (Mobil New Zealand Nature Ser.). (Illus.). 84p. 1967. pap. 7.50 (ISBN 0-589-00052-7, Pub. by Reed Bks Australia). C E Tuttle.
TREES–UNITED STATES
Barnes, Burton V. & Wagner, Warren H., Jr. Michigan Trees: A Guide to the Trees of Michigan & the Great Lakes. (Biological Science). (Illus.). 360p. 1981. text ed. 10.95 (ISBN 0-472-08017-2); pap. text ed. 5.95 (ISBN 0-472-08018-0). U of Mich Pr.
McMinn, Howard E. & Maino, Evelyn. An Illustrated Manual of Pacific Coast Trees. 1981. pap. 6.95 (ISBN 0-520-04364-2). U of Cal Pr.
TREES IN THE BIBLE
see Bible–Natural History
TRIAL BY JURY
see Jury
TRIAL EVIDENCE
see Evidence (Law)
TRIAL PRACTICE
see also Appellate Procedure; Civil Procedure; Criminal Procedure; Cross-Examination; Defense (Criminal Procedure); Equity Pleading and Procedure; Evidence (Law); Instructions to Juries; Jury; Probate Law and Practice
Nolan, Joseph R. Cases & Materials on Trial Practice. (American Casebook Ser.). 514p. 1981. text ed. 17.95 (ISBN 0-686-69319-1). West Pub.
The Total Trial System. 175p. 1980. 14.95 (ISBN 0-9605222-0-4). Total Trial.
TRIAL REPORTING
see Crime and the Press; Newspaper Court Reporting
TRIALS–GREAT BRITAIN
Dunphy, Thomas & Cummins, Thomas J. Remarkable Trials of All Countries; Particularly of the United States, Great Britain, Ireland & France: With Notes & Speeches of Counsel. Containing Thrilling Narratives of Fact from the Court-Room, Also Historical Reminiscences of Wonderful Events. 464p. 1981. Repr. of 1867 ed. lib. bdg. 35.00x (ISBN 0-8377-0512-6). Rothman.
TRIALS–UNITED STATES
Dunphy, Thomas & Cummins, Thomas J. Remarkable Trials of All Countries; Particularly of the United States, Great Britain, Ireland & France: With Notes & Speeches of Counsel. Containing Thrilling Narratives of Fact from the Court-Room, Also Historical Reminiscences of Wonderful Events. 464p. 1981. Repr. of 1867 ed. lib. bdg. 35.00x (ISBN 0-8377-0512-6). Rothman.
TRIALS (MURDER)
Silverman, Milton J. & Winslow, Ron. Open & Shut. 1981. 15.95 (ISBN 0-393-01442-8). Norton.
TRIALS IN THE PRESS
see Crime and the Press; Newspaper Court Reporting
TRIAZINES
Temple, Carroll. Triazoles, One, Two, Four. (Monographs). 752p. 1980. 175.00 (ISBN 0-471-04656-6, Pub. by Wiley-Interscience). Wiley.
TRIBUNALS, ECCLESIASTICAL
see Ecclesiastical Courts
TRICK-TRACK
see Backgammon
TRICKS
see also Card Tricks; Conjuring; Magic
Fulves, Karl. Self-Working Table Magic: Ninety-Seven Foolproof Tricks with Everyday Objects. (Illus.). 128p. (Orig.). 1981. pap. price not set (ISBN 0-486-24116-5). Dover.
Kettelkamp, Larry. Magic Made Easy. rev. ed. LC 80-22947. (Illus.). 96p. (gr. 4-6). 1981. pap. 6.95 (ISBN 0-688-00377-X); PLB 6.67 (ISBN 0-688-00458-X). Morrow.
White, Laurence B., Jr. & Broekel, Ray. The Surprise Book: Seventy-Seven Stupendously Silly Practical Jokes You Can Play on Your Friends. (Illus.). 96p. 1981. 7.95a (ISBN 0-385-15832-7); PLB (ISBN 0-385-15833-5). Doubleday.
TRICYCLES
see Bicycles and Tricycles
TRIGONOMETRY
Hestenes, Marshall & Hill, Richard. Algebra & Trigonometry with Calculators. (Illus.). 512p. 1981. text ed. 17.95 (ISBN 0-13-021857-X). P-H.
Keedy, Mervin L. & Bittinger, Marvin L. Fundamental Algebra & Trigonometry. 2nd ed. (Mathematics-Remedial & Precalculus Ser.). (Illus.). 576p. 1981. text ed. 15.95 (ISBN 0-201-03839-0). A-W.
Lial, Margaret L. & Miller, Charles D. Trigonometry. 2nd ed. 1981. text ed. 16.95x (ISBN 0-673-15432-7). Scott F.
Steffensen, Arnold J. & Johnson, L. M. Algebra & Trigonometry. 1980. pap. text ed. 16.95 (ISBN 0-673-15371-1). Scott F.
Steinlage, Ralph. College Algebra & Trigonometry. 1981. text ed. write for info. (ISBN 0-8302-1640-5). Goodyear.
Zimmer, Rudolf A. Applications in Technology of Right Triangular Trigonometry: Unit 5. 64p. 1980. pap. text ed. 4.95 (ISBN 0-8403-2278-X). Kendall-Hunt.
Zimmer, Rudolph A. Basic Trigonometry with Applications in Technology. LC 80-82834. 256p. 1980. pap. text ed. 10.95 (ISBN 0-8403-2273-9). Kendall-Hunt.
--Primary Trigonometric Ratios: Unit 3. 49p. 1980. pap. text ed. 4.50 (ISBN 0-8403-2276-3). Kendall-Hunt.
--Secondary (Reciprocal) Trigonometric Ratios: Unit 4. 49p. 1980. pap. text ed. 4.50 (ISBN 0-8403-2277-1). Kendall-Hunt.
TRINIDAD
Lieber, Michael. Street Life: Afro-American Culture in Urban Trinidad. (University Book Ser.). 1981. lib. bdg. 15.95 (ISBN 0-8161-9033-X). G K Hall.
TRINITY
see also God; Holy Spirit; Jesus Christ; Socinianism; Unitarianism
Jungel, Eberhard. La Doctrina de la Trinidad. Canclini, Arnoldo, tr. from Eng. 152p. (Orig., Span.). 1980. pap. 3.95 (ISBN 0-89922-153-X). Edit Caribe.
Merrill, Dean, tr. Magnificos Tres. (Spanish Bks.). (Span.). 1979. 1.50 (ISBN 0-8297-0733-6). Life Pubs Intl.
--Tres Magnificos, Os. (Portugese Bks.). (Port.). 1979. 2.20 (ISBN 0-8297-0892-8). Life Pubs Intl.
Moltmann, Jurgen. The Trinity & the Kingdom. LC 80-8352. 320p. 1981. 15.00 (ISBN 0-06-065906-8, HarpR). Har-Row.

Stephens, Bruce M. God's Last Metaphor: The Doctrine of the Trinity in New England Theology. LC 80-11421. (American Academy of Religion Studies in Religion). 12.00x (ISBN 0-89130-385-5, 01 00 24); pap. 7.50x (ISBN 0-89130-386-3). Scholars Pr CA.

Tavard, George H. The Vision of the Trinity. LC 80-5845. 166p. (Orig.). 1981. lib. bdg. 17.75 (ISBN 0-8191-1412-X); pap. text ed. 8.75 (ISBN 0-8191-1413-8). U Pr of Amer.

TRITIUM

Muentzig, Arne. Triticale: Results & Problems. (Advances in Plant Breeding Ser.: Vol. 10). (Illus.). 103p. (Orig.). 1979. pap. text ed. 35.00 (ISBN 3-489-76210-X). Parey Sci Pubs.

TROLLOPE, ANTHONY, 1815-1882

Lansbury, Coral. The Reasonable Man: Trollope's Legal Fictions. LC 80-8560. 260p. 1981. 16.50x (ISBN 0-691-06457-1). Princeton U Pr.

Super, Robert H. Trollope in the Post Office. 1981. text ed. 10.00 (ISBN 0-472-10013-0). U of Mich Pr.

TROPICAL AGRICULTURE

see Tropical Crops

TROPICAL CROPS

see also special crops, e.g. Coffee

Courtenay, P. P. Plantation Agriculture. 2nd rev. ed. 250p. 1980. lib. bdg. 30.00x (ISBN 0-86531-090-4). Westview.

On-Farm Maize Drying & Storage in the Humid Tropics. (FAO Agricultural Services Bulletin: No. 40). 69p. 1981. pap. 6.00 (ISBN 92-5-100944-9, F2077, FAO). Unipub.

Priorities for Alleviating Soil-Related Constraints to Food Production in the Tropics. 468p. 1981. pap. 31.50 (R133, IRRI). Unipub.

Williams, C. N. & Chew, W. Y. Tree & Field Crops of the Wetter Regions of the Tropics. (Intermediate Tropical Agriculture Series). (Illus.). 262p. 1981. pap. text ed. 5.95x (ISBN 0-582-60319-6). Longman.

TROPICAL DISEASES

see Tropical Medicine

TROPICAL FISH

see also Aquariums

Axelrod, H., et al. Exotic Tropical Fishes. rev. ed. (Illus.). 1302p. 1980. 25.00 (ISBN 0-87666-543-1, H-1028); looseleaf 30.00. TFH Pubns.

May. Tropical Fish: Their Care & Breeding. (Illus.). 96p. 1981. 3.95 (ISBN 0-903264-23-4, 5216-3, Pub. by K & R Bks England). Arco.

Walker, Braz. Tropical Fish Identifier. LC 76-126851. (Illus.). 256p. 1981. pap. 6.95 (ISBN 0-8069-8968-8). Sterling.

TROPICAL MEDICINE

see also specific diseases, e.g. Malaria; Yellow Fever

Behrman, Jack N. Tropical Diseases: Responses of Pharmaceutical Companies. 1980. pap. 4.25 (ISBN 0-8447-3393-8). Am Enterprise.

Prance, Ghillean T. Biological Diversification in the Tropics. 752p. 1981. 40.00x (ISBN 0-231-04876-9). Columbia U Pr.

TROPICAL PLANTS

Buritica, P. & Hennen, J. F. Pucciniosireae: Uredinales, Pucciniaceae. LC 79-27151. (Flora Neotropica Monograph: No. 24). (Illus.). 50p. 1980. pap. 7.75 (ISBN 0-89327-219-1). NY Botanical.

Gentry, Alwyn H. Bignoniaceae: Crescentieae & Tourretieae, Pt. 1. LC 80-10846. (Flora Neotropica Monograph: No. 25). (Illus.). 132p. 1980. pap. 15.75 (ISBN 0-89327-222-1). NY Botanical.

TROPICS–DISEASES AND HYGIENE

see Tropical Medicine

TROPICS–SANITATION

see Tropical Medicine

TROTSKY, LEON, 1879-1940

Wistrich, Robert. Trotsky: Fate of a Revolutionary. LC 80-6163. 235p. 1981. 14.95 (ISBN 0-8128-2774-0). Stein & Day.

TROTTING-RACES

see Harness Racing

TROUBADOURS

see also Courtly Love; Trouveres

Appel, Carl L. Der Trobador Uc Brunec Oder Brunenc: Abhandlungen Herrn Prof. Adolf Tobler. LC 80-2177. 1981. Repr. of 1895 ed. 15.00 (ISBN 0-404-19003-0). AMS Pr.

Jordan, Raimon. Le Troubadour Raimon Jordan Vicomte De Saint-Antonin. LC 80-2189. Repr. of 1922 ed. 25.00 (ISBN 0-404-19017-0). AMS Pr.

Linskill, Joseph, ed. The Poems of the Troubadour Raimbaut De Vaqueiras. LC 80-2190. 1981. Repr. of 1964 ed. 45.00 (ISBN 0-404-19014-6). AMS Pr.

Pattison, W. T. Life & Works of the Troubadour Raimbaut D'Orange. LC 80-2182. 1981. Repr. of 1952 ed. 35.00 (ISBN 0-404-19015-4). AMS Pr.

TROUT

Roberts, Ronald J. & Shepherd, C. Jonathan. Handbook of Trout & Salmon Diseases. (Illus.). 172p. 21.25 (ISBN 0-85238-066-6, FN). Unipub.

TROUT FISHING

Eaton, Roy. Trout & Salmon Fishing. LC 80-68897. (Illus.). 192p. 1981. 22.50 (ISBN 0-7153-8117-2). David & Charles.

Gooch, Bob. Spinning for Trout. (Illus.). 192p. 1981. 12.50 (ISBN 0-684-16843-X, ScribT). Scribner.

Stevenson, John P. Trout Farming Manual. (Illus.). 1980. text ed. 26.50x (ISBN 0-85238-102-6). Scholium Intl.

TROUVERES

see also Chansons De Geste; Courtly Love; Troubadours

Linskill, Joseph, ed. The Poems of the Troubadour Raimbaut De Vaqueiras. LC 80-2190. 1981. Repr. of 1964 ed. 45.00 (ISBN 0-404-19014-6). AMS Pr.

Pattison, W. T. Life & Works of the Troubadour Raimbaut D'Orange. LC 80-2182. 1981. Repr. of 1952 ed. 35.00 (ISBN 0-404-19015-4). AMS Pr.

Petersen-Dyggve, Holgern. Trouveres et Protecteurs De Trouveres Dans les Cours Seigneuriales De France. LC 80-2168. 1981. Repr. of 1942 ed. 41.50 (ISBN 0-404-19032-4). AMS Pr.

TRUANCY (SCHOOLS)

see School Attendance

TRUCK CAMPERS AND COACHES

see Campers and Coaches, Truck

TRUCK FARMING

see also Vegetable Gardening

Watts, Leslie. Flower & Vegetable Plant Breeding. (Orig.). 1980. pap. 22.50 (ISBN 0-901361-35-6, Pub. by Grower Bks England). Intl Schol Bk Serv.

TRUCKS, AUTOMOBILE

see Motor-Trucks

TRUMAN, HARRY S., PRES. U. S. 1884-1972

Melton, David. Harry S. Truman: The Man Who Walked with Giants. (Illus.). 128p. (gr. 5 up). 1980. 20.00 (ISBN 0-8309-0293-7). Independence Pr.

Robbins, Jhan. Bess & Harry. large print ed. LC 80-27985. 1981. Repr. of 1980 ed. 9.95 (ISBN 0-89621-263-7). Thorndike Pr.

Stueck, William W., Jr. The Road to Confrontation: American Policy Toward China & Korea, 1947 - 1950. LC 80-11818. (Illus.). 337p. 1981. 22.00x (ISBN 0-8078-1445-8); pap. 10.00x (ISBN 0-8078-4080-7). U of NC Pr.

Truman, Margaret. Harry S. Truman in Family. LC 80-70224. 256p. 1981. 12.95 (ISBN 0-87795-313-9). Arbor Hse.

TRUMPET

Johnson, Keith. The Art of Trumpet Playing. 168p. 1981. 11.95. Iowa St U Pr.

TRUSSES

see also Bridges; Roofs

Midwest Plan Service Engineers. Designs for Glued Trusses. 4th ed. Midwest Plan Service Staff, ed. LC 80-39547. (Illus., 4#80). 1981. pap. 3.00 (ISBN 0-89373-051-3, MWPS-9). Midwest Plan Serv.

TRUSTEES

see Trusts and Trustees

TRUSTS, CHARITABLE

see Charitable Uses, Trusts and Foundations

TRUSTS, INDUSTRIAL–LAW AND LEGISLATION

see Antitrust Law

TRUSTS AND TRUSTEES

Here are entered general works, and those concerned with trusts and trustees in the United States For works dealing with other countries, or individual states in the United States see appropriate subdivision.

see also Charitable Uses, Trusts and Foundations; Equity; Executors and Administrators; Guardian and Ward

Kirsch, Charlotte. A Survivor's Manual to Wills, Trusts, Maintaining Emotional Stability. LC 80-977. 240p. 1981. 11.95 (ISBN 0-385-15879-3, Anchor Pr). Doubleday.

Spelling, Thomas C. A Treatise on Trusts & Monopolies, Containing an Exposition of the Rule of Public Policy Against Contracts & Combinations in Restraint of Trade, & a Review of Cases, Ancient & Modern. xxvii, 274p. 1981. Repr. of 1893 ed. lib. bdg. 27.50x (ISBN 0-8377-1116-9). Rothman.

TRUTH

see also Knowledge, Theory Of; Pragmatism; Reality

Jyoti, Amar. Retreat into Eternity. LC 80-54236. (Illus.). 128p. (Orig.). 1980. pap. 10.95 (ISBN 0-933572-03-4). Truth Consciousness.

Rawson, Natasha. Search for Truth. 100p. 1981. write for info. (Pub. by the Linolean Press). Larksdale.

TSCHAIKOVSKY, PETER, 1840-1893

see Tchaikovsky, Peter, 1840-1893

TSIMSHIAN INDIANS

see Indians of North America–Northwest, Pacific

TSONGA TRIBE

see Thonga Tribe

TUBE WELL

see Wells

TUBERCULOSIS

Gracey, Douglas R. Tuberculosis. Addington, Whitney W., ed. LC 79-88043. (Discussions in Patient Management Ser.). 1979. pap. 9.50 (ISBN 0-87488-875-1). Med Exam.

TUDOR, HOUSE OF

Plowden, Alison. The House of Tudor. LC 76-6936. 272p. 1981. pap. 8.95 (ISBN 0-8128-6123-X). Stein & Day.

TUGBOATS

see also Towing

Lang, Steven & Spectre, Peter. On the Hawser: A Tugboat Album. LC 79-67416. (Illus.). 506p. 1980. 30.00 (ISBN 0-89272-071-9). Down East.

TUITION

see College Costs; Education–Finance; Universities and Colleges–Finance

TULAROSA VALLEY

Sonnichsen, C. L. Tularosa--Last of the Frontier West. 356p. 1980. 14.95x (ISBN 0-8263-0563-6); pap. 7.95 (ISBN 0-8263-0561-X). U of NM Pr.

TULLE EMBROIDERY

see Lace and Lace Making

TUMORS

see also Antineoplastic Agents; Cancer; Lymphoma; Melanoma; Oncology

also subdivision Diseases under names of organs and regions of the body, e.g. Brain–Diseases

Aszalos, Adorjan, ed. Antitumor Compounds of Natural Origin. 1981. Vol. 1. 64.95 (ISBN 0-8493-5520-6); Vol. 2. 67.95 (ISBN 0-8493-5521-4). CRC Pr.

Blasecki. Mechanisms of Immunity to Virus-Induced Tumors. 376p. 1981. 49.50. Dekker.

Delellis. Diagnostic Immunohistochemistry of Tumor Markers. 1981. write for info. Masson Pub.

Jain, Rakesh K. & Gullino, Pietro M., eds. Thermal Characteristics of Tumors: Applications in Detection & Treatment. LC 80-13379. (N.Y. Academy of Sciences Annals: Vol. 335). 542p. 1980. 95.00x (ISBN 0-89766-046-3). NY Acad Sci.

M. D. Anderson Symposia on Fundamental Cancer Research, 33rd. Genes, Chromosomes, & Neoplasia. Arrighi, Frances E., et al, eds. 550p. 1981. 49.50 (ISBN 0-89004-532-1). Raven.

Morson, B. C. Histological Typing of Intestinal Tumours. LC 70-101520. (International Histological Classification of Tumours (World Health Organization) Ser.). (Illus.). 69p. 1976. text ed. 53.00 (ISBN 92-4-176015-X); text & slides 142.00. Am Soc Clinical.

Nicholson. Pediatric Ocular Tumors. 1981. price not set (ISBN 0-89352-125-6). Masson Pub.

Salman, Sydney E., ed. Cloning of Human Tumor Stem Cells. LC 80-19600. (Progress in Clinical & Biological Research: Vol. 48). 366p. 1980. 44.00 (ISBN 0-8451-0048-3). A R Liss.

Schajowicz, F. Tumors & Tumor Like Lesions of Bone & Joints. (Illus.). 650p. 65.00 (ISBN 0-387-90492-1). Springer-Verlag.

Sherbet, G. V., ed. Phenomenon of Control of Growth in Neoplastic & Differentiative Systems. (Illus.). xii, 184p. 1981. 58.75 (ISBN 3-8055-2305-X). S Karger.

Stillman, Richard M. Surgery Review & Assessment: Tumor, Trauma, & Specialties. 1981. pap. 12.50 (ISBN 0-686-69608-5). ACC.

Von Kleist, Sabine & Breuer, H., eds. Critical Evaluation of Tumor Markers. (Beitraege zur Onkologie (Contributions to Oncology): Vol. 7). (Illus.). x, 144p. 1981. pap. 28.75 (ISBN 3-8055-2353-X). S Karger.

Wolf, P., ed. Tumor Associated Markers: The Importance of Identification in Clinical Medicine. LC 79-87540. (Illus.). 208p. 1979. 25.50 (ISBN 0-89352-065-9). Masson Pub.

TUNA FISHERIES

Nakamura, Hiroshi. Tuna: Distribution & Migration. (Illus.). 84p. 8.25 (ISBN 0-85238-002-X, FN). Unipub.

TUNNELS AND TUNNELING

see also Boring; Excavation; Subways

also names of individual tunnels

Rapid Excavation & Tunneling Conference, 1979. R E T C Proceedings, 2 vols. Hustrulid, William A. & Maevis, Alfred C., eds. LC 79-52280. (Illus.). 1819p. 1979. 55.00x (ISBN 0-89520-266-2). Soc Mining Eng.

Thomas Telford Editorial Staff, Ltd, ed. Computer Methods in Tunnel Design. 284p. 1980. 70.00x (ISBN 0-7277-0061-8, Pub. by Telford England). State Mutual Bk.

TURBOJET PLANE ENGINES

see Airplanes–Turbojet Engines

TURBOMACHINES

see also Pumping Machinery

Sawyer, John W. & Hallberg, Kurt, eds. Sawyer's Turbomachinery Maintenance Handbook, 3 vols. LC 80-63559. (Illus.). 1060p. 1981. Set. 115.50 (ISBN 0-937506-03-6). Busn Journals.

--Sawyer's Turbomachinery Maintenance Handbook, Vol. III: Support Services & Equipment. LC 80-53539. (Illus.). 340p. 1981. 38.00 (ISBN 0-937506-02-8). Busn Journals.

TURBULENCE

Bradbury, J. S., et al, eds. Turbulent Shear Flows, Two. (Illus.). 480p. 1980. 68.00 (ISBN 0-387-10067-9). Springer-Verlag.

Libby, P. A. & Williams, F., eds. Turbulent Reacting Flows. (Topics in Applied Physics Ser.: Vol. 44). (Illus.). 260p. 1981. 49.50 (ISBN 0-387-10192-6). Springer Verlag.

Swinney, H. L. & Gollup, J. P., eds. Hydrodynamic Instabilities & the Transition to Turbulence. (Topics in Applied Physics Ser.: Vol. 45). (Illus.). 320p. 1981. 56.60 (ISBN 0-387-10390-2). Springer-Verlag.

TURCO-BALKAN WAR, 1912-1913

see Balkan Peninsula–History

TURF MANAGEMENT

Beard, James B. Turfgrass Management: The Golf Course. (Orig.). 1981. write for info. (ISBN 0-8087-2872-5). Burgess.

Madison, John H. Principles of Turfgrass Culture. 412p. 1981. Repr. of 1971 ed. lib. bdg. price not set (ISBN 0-89874-197-1). Krieger.

TURGOT, ANNE ROBERT JACQUES, BARON DE L'AULNE, 1727-1781

Rutledge, Kenneth R. The Thoughts of Robert Jacques Turgot As They Apply to the Economic Complexities of Our Present Age. (The Living Thoughts of the Great Economists Ser.). (Illus.). 93p. 1981. 17.55 (ISBN 0-918968-86-0). Inst Econ Finan.

TURK LANGUAGES

see Turko-Tataric Languages

TURKEY–FOREIGN RELATIONS

Zeine, Zeine N. Arab-Turkish Relations & the Emergence of Arab Nationalism. LC 80-25080. 156p. 1981. Repr. of 1958 ed. lib. bdg. 19.75x (ISBN 0-313-22705-5, ZEAT). Greenwood.

TURKEY–HISTORY

Deluca, Anthony R. Great Power Rivalry at the Turkish Straits: The Montreux Conference & Convention of 1936. (East European Monographs: No. 77). 224p. 1981. text ed. 16.00x (ISBN 0-914710-71-0). East Eur Quarterly.

Inalcik, Halil. The Ottoman Empire: Conquest, Organization & Economy. 362p. 1980. 60.00x (ISBN 0-86078-032-5, Pub. by Variorum England). State Mutual Bk.

Minorsky, Vladimir. The Turks, Iran & the Caucasus in the Middle Ages. 368p. 1980. 69.00x (ISBN 0-86078-028-7, Pub. by Variorum England). State Mutual Bk.

Weiker, Walter F. Modernization in Turkey Nineteen Twenty-Three to Nineteen Seventy-Nine. LC 80-24514. 250p. 1980. text ed. 24.00x (ISBN 0-8419-0503-7). Holmes & Meier.

TURKEY–POLITICS AND GOVERNMENT

Dodd, C. H. Democracy & Development in Turkey. 1980. text ed. 27.50 (ISBN 0-906719-01-1); pap. text ed. 13.75x (ISBN 0-906719-00-3). Humanities.

TURKISH ART

see Art, Turkish

TURKISH LANGUAGE

Goodenough, Ward H. & Sugita, Hiroshi. Trukese-English Dictionary. LC 79-54277. (Memoir Ser.: Vol. 141). 1980. 10.00 (ISBN 0-87169-141-8). Am Philos.

Gronbech, Vilhelm. Preliminary Studies in Turkic Historical Phonology. Krueger, John, tr. (Indiana University Uralic & Altaic Ser.: Vol. 135). 162p. 1979. 8.00. Ind U Res Inst.

TURKO-TATARIC LANGUAGES

see also Turkish Language

Gronbech, Vilhelm. Preliminary Studies in Turkic Historical Phonology. Krueger, John, tr. (Indiana University Uralic & Altaic Ser.: Vol. 135). 162p. 1979. 8.00. Ind U Res Inst.

TURNER, JOSEPH MALLORD WILLIAM, 1775-1851

Wilton, Andrew. Turner & the Sublime. (Illus.). 192p. 1981. 40.00 (ISBN 0-930606-24-8, 06188-4, Pub. by British Museum). U of Chicago Pr.

TUSCANY

Cipolla, Carlo M. Faith, Reason, & the Plague in Seventeenth-Century Tuscany. 128p. 1981. pap. 3.95 (ISBN 0-393-00045-1). Norton.

TUSCARORA INDIANS

see Indians of North America–Eastern States

TUTELAGE

see Guardian and Ward

TVA

see Tennessee Valley Authority

TWAIN, MARK

see Clemens, Samuel Langhorne, 1835-1910

TWANA INDIANS

see Indians of North America–Northwest, Pacific

TWENTY-ONE (GAME)

see Blackjack (Game)

TWINS

Gill, Frances M. & Abbe, Kathryn M. Twins on Twins. 1980. 17.95 (ISBN 0-517-54149-1, 541491). Potter.

TWO-PHASE FLOW

Azbel, David. Two Phase Flows in Chemical Engineering. LC 80-20936. (Illus.). 400p. Date not set. price not set (ISBN 0-521-23772-6). Cambridge U Pr.

Saha, P. & Farukhi, N. M., eds. Scaling in Two-Phase Flows. (HTD: Vol. 14). 53p. 1980. 12.00 (G00187). ASME.

TWO-PHASE MATERIALS

see Composite Materials

TYPE AND TYPE-FOUNDING

see also Advertising Layout and Typography; Newspaper Layout and Typography; Type-Setting

Rodmell, Ken. How to Use Type. 120p. 1981. pap. 7.95 (ISBN 0-442-29801-3). Van Nos Reinhold.

Sabin, Tracy. Getting the Type You Want. (Illus.). 1980. pap. 7.95 (ISBN 0-930904-01-X). Graphic Dimens.

TYPE-SETTING

see also Newspaper Layout and Typography; Printing–Layout and Typography; Type and Type-Founding

Rice, Stanley. CRT Typesetting Handbook. 415p. 1981. 35.00 (ISBN 0-442-23889-4). Van Nos Reinhold.

TYPEWRITERS–HISTORY

Behrman, Carol H. The Remarkable Writing Machine. (Illus.). 64p. (gr. 3-5). 1981. PLB 6.97 (ISBN 0-686-69297-7). Messner.

TYPEWRITING
Farmer, et al. Business Applications in Typewriting. 368p. 1976. text ed. 15.27 (ISBN 0-7715-0878-6); tchr's. manual 7.93 (ISBN 0-7715-0879-4); stationery & business forms 6.60 (ISBN 0-7715-0880-8); Set Of 26 Cassettes. 269.50 (ISBN 0-7715-0882-4). Forkner.
--Personal Applications in Typewriting. 272p. 1976. text ed. 13.27 (ISBN 0-7715-0875-1); Set Of 26 =cassettes. tchr's. manual 6.67 (ISBN 0-7715-0876-X); 269.50 (ISBN 0-7715-0882-4); book of resource materials 39.93 (ISBN 0-7715-0831-X); typing facts & tips 3.00 ea. (ISBN 0-7715-0889-1); typing facts & tips, package of 10 21.33 (ISBN 0-7715-0896-4); certificate of proficiency (personal, 1 per student) free (ISBN 0-7715-0865-4); roll of honor for production efficiency (1 per classroom) free (ISBN 0-7715-0864-6). Forkner.
--Professional Applications in Typewriting. 260p. 1977. text ed. 15.27 (ISBN 0-7715-0886-7); tchr's. manual 7.67 (ISBN 0-7715-0887-5); stationery & business forms 6.60 (ISBN 0-7715-0888-3); book of resource materials 44.60 (ISBN 0-7715-0833-6); typing facts & tips 3.00 ea. (ISBN 0-7715-0889-1); typing facts & tips, package of 10 21.33 (ISBN 0-7715-0896-4); certificate of proficiency (professional, 1 per student) free (ISBN 0-7715-0867-0); roll of honor for production efficiency (1 per classroom) free (ISBN 0-7715-0864-6). Forkner.
Hanson, Robert N. & Rigby, D. Sue. Keyboarding for Information Processing. (Illus.). 96p. 1981. pap. text ed. 6.95 (ISBN 0-07-026105-9, G). McGraw.
Heller, Jack. Typing for Individual Achievement. Rubin, Audrey, ed. LC 80-26244. (Illus.). 192p. 1981. text ed. 13.80 (ISBN 0-686-69551-8). McGraw.
Pate, Ellen & Spengler, Barbara. Handbook for Typists. 96p. 1980. 6.95 (ISBN 0-8403-2194-5). Kendall-Hunt.
Yacht. Clear & Simple Guide to Touch Typing. (Clear & Simple Guides Ser.). (Illus.). 96p. (Orig.). 1981. pap. 5.95 (ISBN 0-671-42223-5). Monarch Pr.

TYPEWRITING-PROGRAMMED INSTRUCTION
Pate, Ellen & Spengler, Barbara. Typewriting for the Modern Office: A Self-Paced Learning Activity Program. 288p. 1980. 10.95 (ISBN 0-8403-2196-1). Kendall-Hunt.

TYPISTS
see also Typewriting
Pate, Ellen & Spengler, Barbara. Handbook for Typists. 96p. 1980. 6.95 (ISBN 0-8403-2194-5). Kendall-Hunt.

TYPOGRAPHY
see Printing-Layout and Typography

TYPOGRAPHY, ADVERTISING
see Advertising Layout and Typography

TYRANTS
see Dictators

TYRELL, GEORGE
Wells, David. The Prophetic of George Tyrrell. LC 79-27097. (American Academy of Religion Monograph: No. 22). 12.00x (ISBN 0-89130-375-8, 01 00 22); pap. 7.50x (ISBN 0-89130-376-6). Scholars Pr CA.

TYRRELL, GEORGE, 1861-1909
Weaver, Mary J., ed. Letters from a "Modernist". The Letters from George Tyrrell to Wilfrid Ward, 1893-1908. LC 80-28372. 230p. 1981. 30.00 (ISBN 0-915762-12-9). Patmos Pr.

U

UFO
see Flying Saucers

UGANDA
Richardson, Michael L. After Amin: The Bloody Pearl. LC 80-23249. (Illus.). 224p. (Orig.). 1980. pap. 4.95 (ISBN 0-9604968-0-7, 737). Majestic Bks.

UGANDA-SOCIAL LIFE AND CUSTOMS
Potholm, Christian P. & Fredland, Richard A., eds. Integration & Disintegration in East Africa. LC 80-5914. 229p. 1980. lib. bdg. 17.75 (ISBN 0-8191-1298-4); pap. text ed. 9.75 (ISBN 0-8191-1299-2). U Pr of Amer.

UGRO-FINNISH LANGUAGES
see Finno-Ugrian Languages

UHF RADIO
see Radio, Short Wave

UKRAINE-HISTORY
Armstrong, John A. Ukranian Nationalism. 2nd ed. LC 79-25529. 361p. 1980. Repr. of 1963 ed. 30.00x (ISBN 0-87287-193-2). Libs Unl.
Kostruba, T., tr. from Ukrainian. Halyts'ko-Volyns'kyi Litopys, 2 vols. 258p. 1967. 17.50. Slavia Lib.

UKRAINE-POLITICS AND GOVERNMENT
Armstrong, John A. Ukranian Nationalism. 2nd ed. LC 79-25529. 361p. 1980. Repr. of 1963 ed. 30.00x (ISBN 0-87287-193-2). Libs Unl.
Farmer, Kenneth C. Ukrainian Nationalism in the Post-Stalin Era: Myth, Symbols & Ideology in Soviet Nationalities Policy. (Studies in Contemporary History: Vol. 4). 253p. 1980. lib. bdg. 36.50 (ISBN 90-247-2401-5, Pub. by Martinus Nijhoff). Kluwer Boston.

UKRAINIAN LITERATURE
Kotsiubynsky, Mykhailo. Shadows of Forgotten Ancestors. Carynnk, Marco, tr. from Ukrainian. (Ukrainian Classics in Translation Ser.: No. 4). 215p. 1981. lib. bdg. 9.50 (ISBN 0-87287-205-X, Ukrainian Acad Pr). Libs Unl.
Ukrainka, Lesia. Boiarynia. 56p. 1970. pap. 2.00. Slavia Lib.

UKRAINIANS IN THE UNITED STATES
Sokolyszyn, Aleksander & Wertsman, Vladimir, eds. Ukrainians in Canda & the United States: A Guide to Information Sources. (Ethnic Studies Information Guide Ser.: Vol. 7). 375p. 1981. 32.00 (ISBN 0-8103-1494-0). Gale.
Wynar, Christine G. The Ukrainian American Index: The Ukrainian Weekly, Nineteen Seventy-Nine. 119p. (Orig.). 1980. pap. 9.50 (ISBN 0-934760-02-0). Ukrainian Res.

ULTRAHIGH FREQUENCY RADIO
see Radio, Short Wave

ULTRAHIGH TEMPERATURES
see High Temperatures

ULTRASONIC DIAGNOSIS
see Diagnosis, Ultrasonic

ULTRASONICS
Leopold, I. H. Cases in Diagnostic Ultrasound. 224p. 1980. 22.00 (ISBN 0-471-08731-9, Pub. by Wiley Med). Wiley.
Rozenberg, L. D., ed. Physical Principles of Ultrasonic Technology, 2 vols. Incl. Vol. 1. 515p. 49.50 (ISBN 0-306-35041-6); Vol. 2. 544p. 47.50 (ISBN 0-306-35042-4). (Ultrasonic Technology Monographs Ser.). (Illus.). 1973 (Plenum Pr). Plenum Pub.

ULTRASONICS IN MEDICINE
Goldberg, Barry B. Ultrasound in Cancer. (Clinics in Diagnostic Ultrasound Ser.: Vol. 6). (Illus.). 224p. 1980. 20.50 (ISBN 0-443-08144-1). Churchill.
Leopold, I. H. Cases in Diagnostic Ultrasound. 224p. 1980. 22.00 (ISBN 0-471-08731-9, Pub. by Wiley Med). Wiley.
Nanda, Navin. Two Dimensional Echocardiography. 1981. write for info. (ISBN 0-87993-134-5). Futura Pub.
Repacholi, M. H. & Bewell, D. A., eds. Essentials of Medical Ultrasound. (Medical Methods Ser.). (Illus.). 1981. 24.50 (ISBN 0-89603-028-8). Humana.
Taylor, Kenneth J. & Viscomi, Gregory N. Ultrasound in Emergency Medicine. (Clinics in Diagnostic Ultrasound). (Illus.). 225p. 1981. lib. bdg. 20.50 (ISBN 0-443-08156-5). Churchill.
Thompson, H. E. & Bernstine, R. L. Diagnostic Ultrasound in Clinical Obstetrics & Gynecology. 192p. 1978. 34.95 (ISBN 0-471-86080-8, 1-322). Wiley.

ULTRASTRUCTURE (BIOLOGY)
Fawcett, Don. The Cell. 2nd ed. (Illus.). 928p. 1981. text ed. write for info. (ISBN 0-7216-3584-9). Saunders.
Tseng, C. Howard, ed. Atlas of Ultrastructure: Ultrastructural Features in Pathology. 224p. 1980. 32.50x (ISBN 0-8385-0462-0). ACC.

UNCERTAINTY (COMMUNICATION THEORY)
Fiddle, Seymour, ed. Uncertainty: Behavioral & Social Dimensions. LC 80-82073. 410p. 1980. 26.95 (ISBN 0-03-057022-0). Praeger.

UNCOOKED FOOD
see Food, Raw

UNDERDEVELOPED AREAS
see also Community Development; Technical Assistance
Class & Nation, Historically & in the Current Crisis. LC 79-3022. 292p. 1981. pap. 6.50 (ISBN 0-85345-523-6). Monthly Rev.
The Collective Self-Reliance of Developing Countries in the Fields of Science & Technology. 23p. 1981. pap. 6.75 (ISBN 92-808-0173-2, T*U*N*U 108, UNU). Unipub.
Morris, Morris D. Measuring the Condition of the World's Poor: The Physical Quality of Life Index. LC 79-16613. 190p. 1979. pap. 5.95 (ISBN 0-08-023889-0). Overseas Dev Council.
Olness, Karen. Practical Pediatrics in Less-Developed Countries. 1980. pap. 9.95 (ISBN 0-9602790-2-4). The Garden.
--Practical Pediatrics in Less-Developed Countries. 1980. pap. 7.95 (ISBN 0-9602790-2-4). The Garden.
Riddell, Robert. Ecodevelopment. 1980. 27.50 (ISBN 0-312-22585-7). St Martin.
Sauvant, K. P. The Third World Without Superpowers, Vols. 1-4. 1978. 42.50 ea. Oceana.
Sims, Michael. United States Doctoral Dissertations in Third World Studies, 1869-1978. 436p. 1980. 60.00. African Studies Assn.
Thompson, Carol L., et al, eds. The Current History Encyclopedia of Developing Nations. (Illus.). 384p. 1981. 34.95 (ISBN 0-07-064387-3, P&RB). McGraw.

UNDERDEVELOPED AREAS-AGRICULTURE
Agriculture: Toward Two Thousand Twentieth Session. 257p. 1981. pap. 18.50 (F2093, FAO). Unipub.

UNDERDEVELOPED AREAS-BIBLIOGRAPHY
Thompson, Carol L., et al, eds. The Current History Encyclopedia of Developing Nations. (Illus.). 384p. 1981. 34.95 (ISBN 0-07-064387-3, P&RB). McGraw.

UNDERDEVELOPED AREAS-COMMERCE
Erb, Guy F. Negotiations on Two Fronts: Manufactures & Commodities. LC 78-57199. (Development Papers: No. 25). 80p. 1978. pap. 1.50 (ISBN 0-686-28674-X). Overseas Dev Council.
Franko, Lawrence & Stephenson, Sherry. French Export Behavior in Third World Markets, Vol. II. LC 80-66695. (Significant Issues Ser.: No. 6). 96p. 1980. 4.00. CSI Studies.
Kumar, Krishna & McLeod, Maxwell G., eds. Multinationals from Developing Countries. LC 80-8531. 1981. write for info. (ISBN 0-669-04113-0). Lexington Bks.
The Nickel Industry & the Developing Countries. 100p. 1980. pap. 8.00 (UN80-2A2, UN). Unipub.
Sideri, S. & Johns, S., eds. Mining for Development in the Third World: Multinationals, State Enterprises & the International Economy. LC 80-20930. (Pergamon Policy Studies on International Development). 376p. 1980. 35.00 (ISBN 0-08-026308-9). Pergamon.

UNDERDEVELOPED AREAS-ECONOMIC CONDITIONS
Agh, Attila. Labyrinth in the Mode of Production Controversy. (Studies on Developing Countries: No. 105). 79p. (Orig.). 1980. pap. 8.50x (ISBN 963-301-062-4). Intl Pubns Serv.
Caldwell, Malcolm. Wealth of Some Nations. 192p. 1977. 10.00 (ISBN 0-905762-01-0); pap. 6.00. Lawrence Hill.
Cleveland, Harlan, ed. Energy Futures of Developing Countries: The Neglected Victims of the Energy Crisis. 1980. 19.95 (ISBN 0-03-058669-0). Praeger.
Cline, William R. & Weintraub, Sidney. Economic Stabilization in Developing Countries. LC 80-70079. 514p. 1981. 26.95 (ISBN 0-8157-1466-1); pap. 11.95 (ISBN 0-8157-1465-3). Brookings.
Coats, Warren L. & Khatkhate, Deena R., Jr., eds. Money & Monetary Policy in Less Developed Countries: A Survey of Issues & Evidence. LC 79-42703. (Illus.). 834p. 1980. 105.00 (ISBN 0-08-024041-0); pap. 25.00 (ISBN 0-08-024042-9). Pergamon.
Colclough, Christopher & McCarthy, Stephen. The Politocal Economy of Botswana: A Study of Growth & Distribution. (Illus.). 308p. 1980. 37.50 (ISBN 0-19-877136-3). Oxford U Pr.
Cole, J. P. The Development Gap: A Spatial Analysis of World Poverty & Inequality. 416p. 1981. write for info. (ISBN 0-471-27796-7, Pub. by Wiley-Interscience). Wiley.
Erb, Guy F. & Kallab, Valeriana, eds. Beyond Dependency: The Developing World Speaks Out. LC 75-23960. 268p. 1975. pap. 3.95 (ISBN 0-686-28707-X). Overseas Dev Council.
Frank, Charles R., Jr. Adjustment Assistance: American Jobs & Trade with the Developing Countries. LC 73-84869. (Development Papers: No. 13). 50p. 1973. pap. 1.00 (ISBN 0-686-28678-2). Overseas Dev Council.
Freeman, Howard E., et al. Evaluating Social Projects in Developing Countries. 239p. (Orig.). 1980. pap. text ed. 9.00x (ISBN 92-64-12040-8). OECD.
Hyden, Goran, et al. Development Administration: The Kenyon Experience. (Illus.). 384p. 1970. text ed. 12.95x. Oxford U Pr.
Mahbub ul Haq. The Third World & the International Economic Order. (Development Papers: No. 22). 54p. 1976. pap. 1.50 (ISBN 0-686-28676-6). Overseas Dev Council.
Mathieson, John A. The Advanced Developing Countries: Emerging Actors in the World Economy. LC 79-91996. (Development Papers: No. 28). 72p. 1979. pap. 3.00 (ISBN 0-686-28672-3). Overseas Dev Council.
Morris, Morris D. Measuring the Condition of the World's Poor: The Physical Quality of Life Index. LC 79-16613. 190p. 1979. pap. 5.95 (ISBN 0-08-023889-0). Overseas Dev Council.
Olaitan, Samson O. & Agusiobo, Obiora N. Introduction to the Teaching of Home Economics. 320p. 1981. write for info. (ISBN 0-471-27807-6, Pub. by Wiley-Interscience); pap. write for info. (ISBN 0-471-27806-8). Wiley.
Robinson, Richard D., et al. Foreign Investment in the Third World: A Comparative Study of Selected Developing Country Investment Promotion Programs. 1980. 10.00 (6005). Chamber Comm US.
Sideri, S. & Johns, S., eds. Mining for Development in the Third World: Multinationals, State Enterprises & the International Economy. LC 80-20930. (Pergamon Policy Studies on International Development). 376p. 1980. 35.00 (ISBN 0-08-026308-9). Pergamon.
Smith, Gordon W. The External Public Debt Prospects of the Non-Oil-Exporting Developing Countries. LC 77-90866. (Monographs: No. 10). 64p. 1977. 4.00 (ISBN 0-686-28685-5). Overseas Dev Council.
Sommer, John G. U. S. Voluntary Aid to the Third World: What Is Its Future? LC 75-43481. (Development Papers: No. 20). 68p. 1975. pap. 1.50 (ISBN 0-686-28677-4). Overseas Dev Council.
Stockwell, Edward G. & Laidlaw, Karen A. Third World Development: Problems & Prospects. LC 79-24088. 362p. 1981. text ed. 21.95 (ISBN 0-88229-532-2); pap. text ed. 10.95 (ISBN 0-88229-751-1). Nelson-Hall.
Tinker, Irene, et al, eds. Women & World Development with an Annotated Bibliography. 2 vols. 416p. 1976. pap. 6.95. Overseas Dev Council.
U Tun Wai. Economic Essays on Developing Countries. LC 80-83264. 512p. 1980. 70.00 (ISBN 90-286-0150-3). Sijthoff & Noordhoff.

UNDERDEVELOPED AREAS-EDUCATION
see Education-Underdeveloped Areas

UNDERDEVELOPED AREAS-FINANCE
Radetzki, Marian & Zorn, Stephen. Financing Mining Projects in Developing Countries. 1980. 35.00x (Pub. by Mining Journal England). State Mutual Bk.
Watson, Paul M. Debt & the Developing Countries: New Problems & New Actors. LC 78-57185. (Development Papers: No. 26). 88p. 1978. pap. 1.50 (ISBN 0-686-28673-1). Overseas Dev Council.

UNDERDEVELOPED AREAS-POLITICS AND GOVERNMENT
Hachey, Thomas & Weber, Ralph E. The Awakening of a Sleeping Giant: Third World Leaders & National Liberation. LC 80-12517. 160p. 1981. pap. text ed. 6.50 (ISBN 0-89874-081-9). Krieger.
Johnson, John J., ed. The Role of the Military in Underdeveloped Countries: Papers of a Conference Sponsored by the Rand Corp. at Santa Monica, Calif. in August 1959. LC 80-25808. viii, 423p. 1981. Repr. of 1962 ed. lib. bdg. 39.75x (ISBN 0-313-22784-5, JORM). Greenwood.

UNDERDEVELOPED AREAS-SOCIAL CONDITIONS
Conde, Julien, et al. Mortality in Developing Countries. OECD Deveopment Centre, ed. (Development Centre Studies). (Orig.). 1980. Tome 1 & 2, 1266p. pap. 85.00 (ISBN 9-2640-2097-7, 41-80-05-3); Tome 3, 550p. pap. 30.00 (ISBN 9-2640-2120-5, 41-80-06-1). OECD.
Freeman, Howard E., et al. Evaluating Social Projects in Developing Countries. 239p. (Orig.). 1980. pap. text ed. 9.00x (ISBN 92-64-12040-8). OECD.
Huston, Perdita. Third World Women Speak Out: Interviews in Six Countries on Change, Development, & Basic Needs. LC 78-32180. 172p. 1979. pap. 4.95 (ISBN 0-686-28701-0). Overseas Dev Council.
Johnson, John J., ed. The Role of the Military in Underdeveloped Countries: Papers of a Conference Sponsored by the Rand Corp. at Santa Monica, Calif. in August 1959. LC 80-25808. viii, 423p. 1981. Repr. of 1967 ed. lib. bdg. 39.75x (ISBN 0-313-22784-5, JORM). Greenwood.
McDowell & Lavitt. Third World Voices for Children. 1981. 7.95. Okpaku Communications.
Olaitan, Samson O. & Agusiobo, Obiora N. Introduction to the Teaching of Home Economics. 320p. 1981. write for info. (ISBN 0-471-27807-6, Pub. by Wiley-Interscience); pap. write for info. (ISBN 0-471-27806-8). Wiley.
On Social Indicators & Development. 36p. 1981. pap. 10.00 (ISBN 92-808-0147-3, TUNU 107, UNU). Unipub.
Rihani, May. Development As If Women Mattered: An Annotated Bibliography with a Third World Focus. LC 78-57205. (Occasional Papers: No. 10). 144p. 1978. pap. 3.00 (ISBN 0-686-28694-4). Overseas Dev Council.
Valdes, Alberto, ed. Food Security for Developing Countries. 350p. 1981. lib. bdg. 25.00x (ISBN 0-86531-071-8). Westview.

UNDERDEVELOPED AREAS-WOMEN
Huston, Perdita. Third World Women Speak Out: Interviews in Six Countries on Change, Development, & Basic Needs. LC 78-32180. 172p. 1979. pap. 4.95 (ISBN 0-686-28701-0). Overseas Dev Council.
Tinker, Irene, et al, eds. Women & World Development with an Annotated Bibliography, 2 vols. 416p. 1976. pap. 6.95. Overseas Dev Council.

UNDERDEVELOPED AREAS, AID TO
see Technical Assistance

UNDERGRADUATES
see College Students

UNDERGROUND CONSTRUCTION
see also Foundations; Subways; Tunnels and Tunneling
Let's Reach for the Sun: Thirty Original Solar & Earth Sheltered Home Designs. rev. ed. (Illus.). 144p. 1981. pap. 9.95 (ISBN 0-9603570-1-7). Space-Time.
Reynoldson, George. Let's Reach for the Sun: 30 Original Solar & Earth Sheltered Home Designs. rev. ed. Erdahl, Jeanne, ed. (Illus.). 144p. 1981. pap. 9.95 (ISBN 0-9603570-1-7). Space-Time.
Werning, David & Werning, Mary K. The Mistake Proof Earth Shelter Handbook. (Illus.). 160p. 1981. price not set (ISBN 0-89196-087-2, Domus Bks); pap. price not set. Quality Bks IL.

UNDERGROUND PRESS
Here are entered works about publications issued legally (and usually serially) and produced by radical, anti-establishment, counter-culture groups. Works about publications issued clandestinely and contrary to government regulations are entered under Underground literature.
Armstrong, David. A Trumpet to Arms: Alternative Media in America. 384p. 1981. 12.95 (ISBN 0-87477-158-7). J P Tarcher.
UNDERGROUND RAILROAD
see also Slavery in the United States–Fugitive Slaves
Blockson, Charles L. The Underground Railroad in Pennsylvania. LC 80-69847. (Illus.). 1981. 12.95 (ISBN 0-933184-21-2); pap. 6.95 (ISBN 0-933184-22-0). Flame Intl.
UNDERGROUND RAILROADS
see Subways
UNDERGROUND STRUCTURES
see Underground Construction
UNDERGROUND WATER
see Water, Underground
UNDERSEA RESEARCH STATIONS, MANNED
see Manned Undersea Research Stations
UNDERWATER EXPLORATION
see also Marine Biology; Treasure-Trove
Dillon, Lawrence S. Ultrastructure,Macromolecules, & Evolution. 750p. 1981. 69.50 (ISBN 0-306-40528-8, Plenum Pr). Plenum Pub.
Hackman, Donald J. & Caudy, Don W. Underwater Tools. (Illus.). 176p. 1981. 32.95 (ISBN 0-935470-08-5). Battelle.
UNDERWRITING
see Insurance; Securities
UNDULATED PARAKEET
see Budgerigars
UNDULATORY THEORY
see Wave-Motion, Theory Of
UNEMPLOYED
see also Food Relief; Full Employment Policies; Insurance, Unemployment; Job Vacancies; Migrant Labor; Public Welfare
Carrol, Frieda. Guide for the Unemployed: Keeping Busy Until... LC 80-70495. 103p. 1981. 16.95 (ISBN 0-9605246-5-7); pap. 12.95. Biblio Pr Ga.
Leventman, Paula G. Professionals Out of Work. LC 80-1645. (Illus.). 1981. 19.95 (ISBN 0-02-918800-8). Free Pr.
Malinvaud, Edmond & Fitouss, Jean-Paul, eds. Unemployment in Western Countries. LC 79-29710. 560p. 1980. 40.00 (ISBN 0-312-83268-0). St Martin.
Morley. Inflation & Unemployment. 2nd ed. 1979. pap. 6.95 (ISBN 0-03-041016-9). Dryden Pr.
Pierson, Frank C. The Minimum Level of Unemployment & Public Policy. 194p. 1980. text ed. 8.50 (ISBN 0-911558-76-4); pap. text ed. 5.50 (ISBN 0-911558-75-6). Upjohn Inst.
Showler, Brian & Sinfield, Adrian. The Workless State: A Study of Unemployment. 252p. 1981. 20.00x (ISBN 0-85520-327-7, Pub. by Martin Robertson England); pap. 9.95x (ISBN 0-85520-340-4). Biblio Dist.
UNEMPLOYED–GREAT BRITAIN
Garside, W. R. The Measurement of Unemployment: Methods & Sources in Great Britain. 300p. 1981. 37.50x (ISBN 0-631-12643-0). Biblio Dist.
UNEMPLOYMENT
see Labor Supply; Unemployed; Unemployment, Technological
UNEMPLOYMENT, TECHNOLOGICAL
Torrens, Robert. On Wages & Combination. (The Development of Industrial Society Ser.). 133p. 1980. Repr. of 1834 ed. 10.00x (ISBN 0-7165-1595-4, Pub. by Irish Academic Pr Ireland). Biblio Dist.
UNEMPLOYMENT BENEFITS, SUPPLEMENTAL
see Supplemental Unemployment Benefits
UNEMPLOYMENT INSURANCE
see Insurance, Unemployment
UNESCO
see United Nations Educational, Scientific and Cultural Organization
UNFAIR COMPETITION
see Competition, Unfair
UNICAMERAL LEGISLATURES
see Legislative Bodies
UNIDENTIFIED FLYING OBJECTS
see Flying Saucers
UNIFICATION CHURCH
Kemperman, Steve. Moonies. LC 80-54091. 192p. 1981. pap. 2.95 (ISBN 0-8307-0780-8). Regal.
UNIFIED SCIENCE
see Semantics (Philosophy)
UNIFORM COMMERCIAL CODE
Clark, Barkley, ed. Warranties in the Sale of Goods 1980: Course Handbook. 2 vols. LC 78-643376. (Nineteen Eighty to Nineteen Eighty-One Commercial Law & Practice Course Handbook Ser.). 1131p. 1980. pap. text ed. 25.00 (ISBN 0-686-69173-3, A6-3091). PLI.
LeVine, Robert. The Uniform Commercial Code: An Operational Translation. LC 80-68569. 1980. 16.50 (ISBN 0-933718-00-4). Browning Pubns.
UNIFORMS, MILITARY
see also subdivision Army or Navy under names of countries, with or without the additional subdivision Uniforms
Bannermans Catalogue of Military Goods 1927. facsimile ed. LC 80-68006. (Illus.). 384p. 1981. pap. 12.95 (ISBN 0-910676-20-8). DBI.
Haythornthwaite, Philip J. Uniforms of the French Revolutionary Wars 1789-1802. (Illus.). 160p. 1981. 19.95 (ISBN 0-7137-0936-7, Pub. by Blandford Pr England). Sterling.
L. Sachse & Co. Full-Color Uniforms of the Prussian Army: Seventy-Two Plates from the Year 1830. (Illus.). 80p. 1981. pap. price not set (ISBN 0-486-24085-1). Dover.
Mollo, Andrew, et al. World Army Uniforms: Nineteen Thirty-Nine to the Present. (Illus.). 360p. 1981. 24.95 (ISBN 0-7137-1189-2, Pub. by Blandford Pr England). Sterling.
Summers, Jack L. & Chartrand, Rene. Military Uniforms in Canada. (Illus.). 220p. 1981. 35.00 (ISBN 0-660-10346-X, 56434-7, Pub. by Natl Mus Canada). U of Chicago Pr.
Wilkinson. Uniforms & Weapons of the Crimean War. pap. 14.95 (ISBN 0-7134-0666-6). David & Charles.
Windrow, Martin. Uniforms of the French Foreign Legion 1831-1981. (Illus.). 160p. 1981. 19.95 (ISBN 0-7137-1010-1, Pub. by Blandford Pr England). Sterling.
UNIFORMS, NAVAL
see Uniforms, Military
UNION, MYSTICAL
see Mystical Union
UNION CATALOGS
see Catalogs, Union
UNION LISTS OF PERIODICALS
see Periodicals–Bibliography–Union Lists
UNION WITH CHRIST
see Mystical Union
UNIONS, TRADE
see Trade-Unions
UNIT CONSTRUCTION
Jones, Arthur J., et al. Principles of Unit Construction. 232p. 1980. Repr. of 1939 ed. lib. bdg. 20.00 (ISBN 0-89984-261-5). Century Bookbindery.
UNITARIANISM
see also Humanism, Religious; Jesus Christ–Divinity; Socinianism; Trinity
Eglash, Albert. Died on the Fourth of July: A Jewish Unitarian Psychologist Flees a Fascist Fellowship. LC 80-53581. (Illus.). 100p. (Orig.). 1981. pap. 20.00 (ISBN 0-935320-22-9). Quest Pr.
Wigmore-Beddoes, Dennis G. Yesterday's Radicals: A Study of the Affinity Between Unitarianism & Broad Church Anglicanism in the Nineteenth Century. 182p. Repr. of 1971 ed. 10.00 (ISBN 0-227-67751-X). Attic Pr.
UNITED ARAB REPUBLIC
Bedouins, Wealth, & Change: A Study of Rural Development in the United Arab Emirates & the Sultanate of Oman. 64p. 1980. pap. 11.75 (TUNU 086, UNU). Unipub.
UNITED MINE WORKERS OF AMERICA
Korn, Richard. Union & Its Retired Workers: A Case Study of the UMW. (Key Issues Ser.: No. 21). 1976. pap. 3.00 (ISBN 0-87546-230-8). NY Sch Indus Rel.
UNITED NATIONS
Here are entered works about the United Nations and about its relations with other countries, either as a group or individually.
Basic Facts About the United Nations. 133p. 1980. pap. 1.95 (ISBN 0-686-68944-5, UN80/1/5, UN). Unipub.
Broad Terms for United Nations Programmes & Activities, 1979. 186p. 1980. pap. 13.00 (ISBN 0-686-68945-3, UN79/0/1, UN). Unipub.
Eckhard, Frederic & Puchala, Donald J., eds. Issues Before the Thirty-Fifth General Assembly of the United Nations. 150p. 1980. text ed. 12.50x (ISBN 0-8147-2159-1). NYU Pr.
Espiell, Hector G., ed. The Right to Self-Determination: Implementation of United Nations Resolutions. 1980. 8.00 (E.79.XIV5). UN.
Everyone's United Nations. 477p. 1979. pap. 7.95 (ISBN 0-686-68955-0, UN79.1/5, UN). Unipub.
Moskowitz, Moses. The Roots & Reaches of United Nations Actions & Decisions. LC 80-51741. 220p. 1980. 28.50x (ISBN 90-286-0140-6). Sijthoff & Noordhoff.
Wilkins, Gregory L. African Influence in the United Nations, 1967-1975: The Politics & Techniques of Gaining Compliance to U. N. Principles & Resolutions. LC 80-5735. 263p. (Orig.). 1981. lib. bdg. 19.25 (ISBN 0-8191-1424-3); pap. text ed. 10.50 (ISBN 0-8191-1425-1). U Pr of Amer.
UNITED NATIONS–BIBLIOGRAPHY
Hufner, Klaus, ed. United Nations System: International Bibliography. Naumann, Jens. 286p. 1977. 58.00 (ISBN 3-7940-2251-3, Dist. by Gale Research Co). K G Saur.
--United Nations System; International Bibliography: Vol. 1, Learned Journals & Monographs Nineteen Forty-Five to Nineteen Sixty-Five. Naumann, Jens. 520p. 1976. 65.00 (ISBN 3-7940-2250-5, Dist. by Gale Research Co). K G Saur.
Hufner, Klaus & Naumann, Jens, eds. United Nations System; Internaional Bibliography: Vol. 2B, Learned Journals Nineteen Seventy-One to Nineteen Seventy-Five. 436p. 1977. 68.00 (ISBN 3-7940-2252-1, Dist. by Gale Research Co). K G Saur.
--United Nations System; International Bibliography: Vol. 3A, Monographs & Articles in Collective Volumes Nineteen Sixty-Five to Nineteen Seventy. 492p. 1978. 68.00 (ISBN 3-7940-2253-X, Dist. by Gale Research Co). K G Saur.
UNITED NATIONS–SECURITY COUNCIL
Davidson, Nicole & UNITAR, eds. Paths to Peace: The UN Security & Its Prsidency. LC 80-20166. (Pergamon Policy Studies on International Politics). 380p. 1981. 42.50 (ISBN 0-08-026322-4). Pergamon.
UNITED NATIONS–SPECIALIZED AGENCIES
see International Agencies
UNITED NATIONS–YEARBOOKS
UNESCO Statistical Yearbook 1978-1979. 1226p. 1980. pap. 88.75 (ISBN 92-3-001800-7, U1020, UNESCO). Unipub.
UNITED NATIONS EDUCATIONAL, SCIENTIFIC AND CULTURAL ORGANIZATION
Records of the General Conference Twentieth Session: Proceedings, Vol. 3. 1157p. 1980. pap. 37.50 (ISBN 9-2300-1776-0, U1038, UNESCO). Unipub.
Workshop of the Phenomenon Known As 'El Nino' Proceedings. 284p. 1980. pap. 22.50 (ISBN 92-3-101509-5, U1019, UNESCO). Unipub.
UNITED STATES–AIR FORCE
Aero Staff. Airman's Information Manual, 1981. LC 70-186849. 256p. 1981. pap. write for info. (ISBN 0-8168-1360-4). Aero.
Kinney, A. J. The Air Force Officer's Guide. 25th, rev. ed. (Illus.). 416p. 1981. pap. 10.95 (ISBN 0-8117-2055-1). Stackpole.
Miller, Thomas G., Jr. The Cactus Air Force. 256p. 1981. pap. 2.50 (ISBN 0-553-14766-8). Bantam.
Puryear, Edgar F., Jr. Stars in Flight: Studies in Air Force Leadership. 310p. 1981. 14.95 (ISBN 0-89141-127-5); pap. 8.95 (ISBN 0-89141-128-3). Presidio Pr.
Rust, Kenn C. Tenth Air Force Story. (Illus.). 1980. pap. 7.50 (Pub. by Hist. Avn. Album). Aviation.
Stiehm, Judith H. Bring Me Men & Women: Mandated Changes at the U. S. Air Force Academy. 1981. 19.95 (ISBN 0-520-04045-7). U of Cal Pr.
The U.S. Airforce: From Balloons to Spaceships. (Illus.). 64p. (gr. 3-7). 1981. write for info. (ISBN 0-671-34020-4). Messner.
UNITED STATES–AIR FORCE–JUVENILE LITERATURE
Doss, Helen. The Air Force: From Balloons to Space Ships. (Illus.). 64p. (gr. 4-6). 1981. PLB 6.97 (ISBN 0-686-69305-1). Messner.
UNITED STATES–ALIENS
see Aliens
UNITED STATES–ANTIQUITIES
see also Indians of North America–Antiquities
Gould, Richard A. & Schiffer, Michael, eds. The Archaeology of U. S. LC 80-2332. (Studies in Archaeology). 1981. price not set (ISBN 0-12-293580-2). Acad Pr.
Oppelt, Norman T. Guide to Prehistoric Ruins of the Southwest. 200p. (Orig.). 1981. pap. 6.95 (ISBN 0-87108-587-9). Pruett.
UNITED STATES–ARCHIVES
see Archives
UNITED STATES–ARMED FORCES
see also United States–Air Force
Binkin, Martin & Kyriakopoulos, Irene. Paying the Modern Military. LC 80-70080. (Studies in Defense Policy). 100p. 1981. pap. 3.95 (ISBN 0-8157-0971-4). Brookings.
UNITED STATES–ARMED FORCES–AFRO-AMERICANS
Carisella, P. J. & Ryan, James W. The Black Swallow of Death. LC 72-75762. (Illus.). 271p. 1972. 8.95 (ISBN 0-911721-87-8). Aviation.
UNITED STATES–ARMED FORCES–OFFICERS
Sarkesian, Sam C. American Military Professionalism. LC 80-27027. (Pergamon Policy Studies on International Politics). 1981. 25.00 (ISBN 0-08-027178-2). Pergamon.
UNITED STATES–ARMY–ENLISTMENT
see United States–Army–Recruiting, Enlistment, etc.
UNITED STATES–ARMY–FLAGS
see Flags–United States
UNITED STATES–ARMY–HANDBOOKS, MANUALS, ETC.
Crocker, Lawrence P. The Army Officer's Guide. 41st, rev. ed. (Illus.). 560p. (Orig.). 1981. pap. 12.95 (ISBN 0-8117-2040-3). Stackpole.
UNITED STATES–ARMY–HISTORY
see also United States–History, Military
Edmonds, David C. Yankee Autumn in Acadiana: A Narrative of the Great Texas Overland Expedition Through Southwestern Louisiana. 2nd ed. LC 79-67333. (Illus.). 512p. 1980. Repr. 15.95 (ISBN 0-937614-01-7). Acadiana Pr.
Sawicki, James A. Infantry Regiments of the US Army. LC 80-53362. (Illus.). 500p. 1981. 24.95 (ISBN 0-9602404-3-8); pap. 16.95 (ISBN 0-9602404-4-6). Wyvern.
Whiting, Charles. Death of a Division. LC 80-5717. (Illus.). 176p. 1981. 11.95 (ISBN 0-8128-2760-0). Stein & Day.
UNITED STATES–ARMY–RECRUITING, ENLISTMENT, ETC.
Davis, James W., Jr. & Dolbeare, Kenneth M. Little Groups of Neighbors: The Selective Service System. LC 80-25861. xv, 276p. 1981. Repr. of 1968 ed. lib. bdg. 35.00x (ISBN 0-313-22777-2, DALN). Greenwood.
UNITED STATES–BIOGRAPHY
Bigelow, Elfreda M. Hairdresser's Memoirs. 1981. 6.75 (ISBN 0-8062-1643-3). Carlton.
Collister, Peter. The Sulivans & the Slave Trade. (Illus.). 199p. 1981. 14.95x (ISBN 0-8476-3611-9). Rowman.
Cramer, C. H. Newton D. Baker: A Biography. Freidel, Frank, ed. LC 78-66521. (The History of the United States: Vol. 4). 316p. 1979. lib. bdg. 24.00 (ISBN 0-8240-9708-4). Garland Pub.
Cronkite, Kathy. On the Edge of the Spotlight: Celebrities' Children Speak Out About Their Lives. LC 80-21255. (Illus.). 320p. 1981. 12.95 (ISBN 0-688-00357-5). Morrow.
Elmer, June A. Scout of Santa Fe. (Illus.). 1981. 8.95 (ISBN 0-8062-1677-8). Carlton.
Helgesen, Sally. Wildeaters. LC 79-7867. 168p. 1981. 9.95 (ISBN 0-385-14637-X). Doubleday.
Henderson, Bill. His Son: A Child of the Fifties. 1981. 12.95 (ISBN 0-393-01439-8). Norton.
Jenkins, Ruth, et al. Four Great Southern Cooks. LC 80-68989. (Illus.). 200p. (Orig.). 1980. pap. 7.95 (ISBN 0-938072-00-5). DuBose Pub.
Matthews, Archibald M. Reminiscences of a Small County Lawyer. 1981. 5.75 (ISBN 0-8062-1689-1). Carlton.
Mebane, Mary E. Mary: An Autobiography. LC 80-51999. 256p. 1981. 12.95 (ISBN 0-670-45938-0). Viking Pr.
Olson, Nels. Time in Many Places. 218p. 1980. 9.00 (ISBN 0-87839-036-7). North Star.
Stokes, John W. The Man Who Lived Two Lives. LC 79-57548. 1981. 6.75 (ISBN 0-533-04561-4). Vantage.
Thomson, J. S. Personalities of the West & Midwest. 6th ed. 579p. 1980. 44.95x (ISBN 0-934544-07-7, Pub. by Intl Biog). Biblio Dist.
Winn, Lela P. The Marsh: A Century of Cranberries. 144p. 1981. 7.50 (ISBN 0-682-49697-9). Exposition.
UNITED STATES–BIOGRAPHY–BIBLIOGRAPHY
Fletcher, Colin. The Man from the Cave. LC 80-22548. (Illus.). 352p. 1981. 16.95 (ISBN 0-394-40695-8). Knopf.
UNITED STATES–BIOGRAPHY–DICTIONARIES
National Cyclopedia of American Biography, Vol. 59. 1980. 69.50 (ISBN 0-88371-031-5). J T White.
UNITED STATES–BIOGRAPHY–JUVENILE LITERATURE
Lowenherz, Robert J. & Lowenherz, Lila. Americans of Dream & Deed. (Orig.). (gr. 7-8). 1981. pap. text ed. 7.08 (ISBN 0-87720-397-0). AMSCO Sch.
UNITED STATES–CENTRAL INTELLIGENCE AGENCY
CIA & the Third World: A Study in Cryptodiplomacy. 22.50 (ISBN 0-7069-1292-6, Pub. by Vikas India). Advent Bk.
Goehlert, Robert & Hoffmeister, Elizabeth R. The CIA: A Bibliography. (Public Administration Ser.: Bibliography P-498). 79p. 1980. pap. 8.50. Vance Biblios.
Kumar, Satish. Cryptodiplomacy: CIA & the Third World. 210p. 1981. text ed. 22.50x (ISBN 0-7069-1292-6, Pub by Vikas India). Advent Bk.
Lefever, Ernest W. & Godson, Roy. The C. I. A. & the American Ethic: An Unfinished Debate. 176p. 1980. 9.50 (ISBN 0-89633-032-X); pap. 5.00 (ISBN 0-89633-031-1). Ethics & Public Policy.
UNITED STATES–CIVIL SERVICE
see Civil Service–United States
UNITED STATES–CIVILIZATION
Nicholas, H. G. The Nature of American Politics. 142p. 1980. 12.95 (ISBN 0-19-219121-7). Oxford U Pr.
Pole, J. R. American Individualism & the Promise of Progress: Inaugural Lecture. (Inaugural Lecture Ser.). 30p. pap. 5.95 (ISBN 0-19-951526-3). Oxford U Pr.
UNITED STATES–CIVILIZATION–FOREIGN INFLUENCES
Jones, George F. & Wilson, Renate, eds. Detailed Reports on the Salzburger Emigrants Who Settled in America, Vol. 6. LC 67-27137. (Wormsloe Foundation Publication Ser.: No. 15). 360p. 1981. 20.00 (ISBN 0-8203-0512-X). U of Ga Pr.
UNITED STATES–CIVILIZATION–JUVENILE LITERATURE
Boy Scouts, of America. American Cultures. LC 19-600. (Illus.). 32p. (gr. 6-12). 1980. pap. 0.70x (ISBN 0-8395-3388-8, 3388). BSA.
UNITED STATES–CIVILIZATION–1783-1865
Ziff, Larzer. Literary Democracy: The Declaration of Cultural Independence in America 1837-1861. 1981. 17.95 (ISBN 0-670-43026-9). Viking Pr.
UNITED STATES–CLIMATE
Rose, Martin R., et al. The Past Climate of Arroyo Hondo, New Mexico, Reconstructed from Tree Rings. (Arroyo Hondo Archaeological Ser.: Vol. 4). (Illus., Orig.). 1981. pap. 6.25 (ISBN 0-933452-05-5). Schol Am Res.

UNITED STATES–COMMERCE
see also Small Business
OAS General Secretariat International Trade & Export Development Program. The United States Generalized System of Preferences: Coverage & Administrative Procedures in Force in 1980. (International Trade Ser.). 58p. 1980. text ed. 5.00 (ISBN 0-8270-1101-6). OAS.
UNITED STATES–COMMERCE–HISTORY
Cochran, Thomas C. Frontiers of Change: Early Industrialism in America. 175p. 1981. 15.00 (ISBN 0-19-502875-9). Oxford U Pr.
UNITED STATES–COMMERCE–STATISTICS
see United States–Commerce
UNITED STATES–COMMERCE–AFRICA
Samuels, Michael A., et al. Implications of Soviet & Cuban Activities in Africa for U. S. Policy, Vol. 1. LC 79-90797. (Significant Issues Ser.: No. 5). 73p. 1979. write for info. (ISBN 0-89206-010-7). CSI Studies.
UNITED STATES–COMMERCE–EAST (FAR EAST)
Graham, Thomas. Impact of Tokyo Round Agreements on U. S. Export Competitiveness, Vol. II. LC 80-67709. (Significant Issues Ser.: No. 10). 30p. 1980. 5.95 (ISBN 0-89206-024-7). CSI Studies.
UNITED STATES–COMMERCIAL LAW
see Commercial Law
UNITED STATES–COMMERCIAL POLICY
Behrman, Jack & Mikesell, Raymond. The Impact of U. S. Foreign Direct Investment on U. S. Export Competitiveness in Third World Markets, Vol. II. LC 80-65189. (Significant Issues Ser.: No. 1). 34p. 1980. 5.95 (ISBN 0-89206-014-X). CSI Studies.
UNITED STATES–CONGRESS
Ashworth, William. Under the Infulence: Congress, Lobbies, & the American Park Barreling System. 1981. pap. 7.95 (ISBN 0-8015-5929-4, Hawthorn). Dutton.
Brownson, Charles B., ed. Advance Locator for Capital Hill, 1981: With Biographical Material. 19th ed. LC 59-13987. (Congressional Staff Directory Ser.). 1981. pap. 9.00. Congr Staff.
--Congressional Staff Directory. LC 59-13987. 1981. Repr. of 1978 ed. 25.00. Congr Staff.
--Congressional Staff Directory, 1981. 23rd ed. 1096p. 1981. pap. 25.00. Congr Staff.
Review - Nineteen Seventy Nine Session of the Congress: Nineteen Seventy-Nine Session of the Congress. 1980. pap. 3.75 (ISBN 0-8447-0228-5). Am Enterprise.
Review: Nineteen Seventy-Eight Session of the Congress. 1979. pap. 3.75 (ISBN 0-8447-0215-3). Am Enterprise.
Review: Nineteen Seventy-Six Session of the Congress. 1977. pap. 2.00 (ISBN 0-8447-0183-1). Am Enterprise.
UNITED STATES–CONGRESS–ELECTIONS
Brownson, Anna L., ed. Election Index: Nineteen Eighty. LC 59-13987. 1980. pap. 8.00 (87289). Congr Staff.
UNITED STATES–CONGRESS–HISTORY
Bibby, John F., et al. Vital Statistics on Congress Nineteen Eighty. 1980. 12.25 (ISBN 0-8447-3408-X); pap. 5.25 (ISBN 0-8447-3401-2). Am Enterprise.
Holt, Pat M. War Powers Resolution: The Role of Congress in U. S. Armed Intervention. 1978. pap. 4.25 (ISBN 0-8447-3299-0). Am Enterprise.
UNITED STATES–CONGRESS–HOUSE
Shannon, W. Wayne. Party, Constituency & Congressional Voting: A Study of Legislative Behavior in the United States House of Representatives. LC 80-25798. (Louisiana State University Studies, Social Science Ser.: No. 14). (Illus.). xii, 202p. 1981. Repr. of 1968 ed. lib. bdg. 23.50x (ISBN 0-313-22771-3, SHPV). Greenwood.
UNITED STATES–CONGRESS–POWERS AND DUTIES
Robinson, James A. Congress & Foreign Policy-Making: A Study in Legislative Influence & Initiative. LC 80-20372. x, 262p. 1980. Repr. of 1962 ed. lib. bdg. 27.50x (ISBN 0-313-22706-3, ROCF). Greenwood.
UNITED STATES–CONGRESS–SENATE
Sisk, B. F. A Congressional Record: The Memoir of Bernie Sisk. Dickman, A. I., ed. LC 80-84208. (Illus.). 280p. 1980. 20.00 (ISBN 0-914330-36-5). Panorama West.
UNITED STATES–CONSTITUTION
Constitution of the United States. 1978. 0.30. Lucas.
Goldwin, Robert A. & Schambra, William A., eds. How Democratic Is the Constitution? 1980. 12.25 (ISBN 0-8447-3400-4); pap. 5.25. Am Enterprise.
Lee, Rex E. A Lawyer Looks at the Constitution. (Illus.). 256p. 1981. 19.95 (ISBN 0-8425-1904-1). Brigham.
Lockhart, William B., et al. The American Constitution. Cases-Comments-Questions. 5th ed. LC 80-54210. 1181p. 1980. text ed. 20.95 (ISBN 0-8299-2132-X). West Pub.
Malbin, Michael J. Religion & Politics: The Intentions of the Athors of the First Amendment. 1978. pap. 3.25 (ISBN 0-8447-3302-4). Am Enterprise.
Miller, Samuel F. Lectures on the Constitution of the United States. xxi, 765p. 1981. Repr. of 1893 ed. lib. bdg. 45.00x (ISBN 0-8377-0836-2). Rothman.
Moore, W. S. & Penner, Rudolph G., eds. Constitution & the Budget. 1980. 13.25 (ISBN 0-8447-2179-4); pap. 7.25 (ISBN 0-8447-2180-8). Am Enterprise.
UNITED STATES–CONSTITUTION–BIBLIOGRAPHY
Sachs, B. F. United States Constitutions Subject Index, Release 1. 1980. 35.00 (ISBN 0-379-20413-4). Oceana.
UNITED STATES–CONSTITUTIONAL HISTORY
Constitutional Change: Amendment Politics & Supreme Court Litigation Since 1900. LC 72-1965. (A Twentieth Century Fund Study). 1972. pap. 30.00 (ISBN 0-527-02785-5). Kraus Repr.
Reid, John P. In Defiance of the Law: The Standing-Army Controversy, the Two Constitutions, & the Coming of the American Revolution. LC 80-14002. (Studies in Legal History). 295p. 1981. 20.00x (ISBN 0-8078-1449-0). U of NC Pr.
UNITED STATES–CONSTITUTIONAL LAW
Allen Bakke Vs. Regents of the University of California, 6 vols. 1978. 44.00 ea. Oceana.
Lockhart, William B., et al. Cases & Materials on Constitutional Rights & Liberties. 5th ed. LC 80-54541. (American Casebook Ser.). 1298p. 1980. text ed. 21.95 (ISBN 0-8299-2135-4). West Pub.
Supreme Court of the United States & Kurland, Philip B. Landmark Briefs & Arguments of the Supreme Court of the United States: Constitutional Law, 80 vols. 1977. Set. 4640.00 (ISBN 0-89093-000-7). U Pubns Amer.
UNITED STATES–CONSTITUTIONAL LAW–CASES
Constitutional Change: Amendment Politics & Supreme Court Litigation Since 1900. LC 72-1965. (A Twentieth Century Fund Study). 1972. pap. 30.00 (ISBN 0-527-02785-5). Kraus Repr.
Rotunda, Ronald D. Modern Constitutional Law: Cases & Notes. (American Casebook Ser.). 1058p. 1981. text ed. price not set (ISBN 0-8299-2136-2). West Pub.
UNITED STATES–COPYRIGHT
see Copyright–United States
UNITED STATES–COUNCIL OF ECONOMIC ADVISERS
White, Lawrence J. Reforming Regulation: Processes & Problems. (Illus.). 240p. 1981. text ed. 13.95 (ISBN 0-13-770115-2); pap. text ed. 8.95 (ISBN 0-13-770107-1). P-H.
UNITED STATES–COURTS
see Courts
UNITED STATES–DECLARATION OF INDEPENDENCE
Corn, Ira G., Jr. The Story of the Declaration of Independence. 1980. 8.95 (ISBN 0-89474-010-5). Green Hill.
UNITED STATES–DEPARTMENT OF DEFENSE
Ward, Harry M. The Department of War, Seventeen Eighty-One to Seventeen Ninety-Five. LC 80-28410. xi, 287p. 1981. Repr. of 1962 ed. lib. bdg. 29.75x (ISBN 0-313-22895-7, WADW). Greenwood.
UNITED STATES–DESCRIPTION AND TRAVEL
see also subdivision Description and Travel under names of states, geographic areas, etc.
Worldmark Press Ltd. The Worldmark Encyclopedia of the States. Sachs, Moshe, ed. LC 80-8218. (Illus.). 700p. 1981. pre-july 54.95 (ISBN 0-06-014733-4, HarpT); 54.95. Har-Row.
UNITED STATES–DESCRIPTION AND TRAVEL–GUIDEBOOKS
The Amoco Motor Club Guide to Mini-Vacations in the Southeast. (Illus.). 1981. 14.95 (ISBN 0-8092-7122-2); pap. 6.95 (ISBN 0-8092-7121-4). Contemp Bks.
Dickerman, Patricia. Farm, Ranch, Countryside Guide. LC 60-2113. 256p. 1981. 7.95 (ISBN 0-913214-03-5). Berkshire Traveller.
Frome, Michael, intro. by. Hosteling U. S. A. The Offical American Youth Hostels Handbook. rev. ed. (Illus.). 250p. (Orig.). 1981. pap. 6.95 (ISBN 0-914788-33-7). East Woods.
Patten, Marion & Sherwin, Mary. Know Your America, Vols. 1 & 2. 1981. 16.95 (ISBN 0-385-18503-0). Doubleday.
Reader's Digest. Drive America. (Illus.). 1981. 22.95 (ISBN 0-89577-085-7, Pub. by Reader's Digest). Norton.
Scheller, William G. Train Trips: Exploring America by Rail. (Illus.). 270p. (Orig.). 1981. pap. 6.95 (ISBN 0-914788-34-5). East Woods.
Vegetarian Times Magazine. The Vegetarian Times Guide to Dining in the U. S. A. 1980. pap. 8.95 (ISBN 0-689-10966-0). Atheneum.
UNITED STATES–DESCRIPTION AND TRAVEL–VIEWS
Morris, Wright. God's Country & My People. LC 80-23155. (Illus.). 176p. 1981. pap. 15.95 (ISBN 0-8032-3067-2, BB 752, Bison). U of Nebr Pr.
Sandler, Martin W. This Was America. 1980. 19.95 (ISBN 0-316-77022-1). Little.
UNITED STATES–DIRECTORIES
Moravisin, Sylvester. Why Our Universities Are Turning Out Ordinary Barbarians. (American Culture Library). (Illus.). 105p. 1981. 47.85 (ISBN 0-89266-299-9). Am Classical Coll Pr.
UNITED STATES–DISCOVERY AND EXPLORATION
see United States–Exploring Expeditions
UNITED STATES–ECONOMIC CONDITIONS
Castells, Manuel. The Economic Crisis & American Society. 285p. 20.00; pap. 7.50. Princeton U Pr.
Evans, James R. America's Choice. 150p. (Orig.). 1981. lib. bdg. 11.95 (ISBN 0-933028-17-2); pap. 6.95 (ISBN 0-933028-16-4). Fisher Inst.
Fourth Franklin Conference. Innovation & the American Economy. 140p. 1980. pap. text ed. 8.95 (ISBN 0-89168-033-0). Franklin Inst Pr.
Harrington, Michael. Decade of Decision: The Crisis of the American System. 354p. 11.95. S&S.
McNall, Scott. Political Economy: A Critique of American Society. 1981. pap. text ed. 7.95x (ISBN 0-673-15424-6). Scott F.
Moore, W. S. & Penner, Rudolph G., eds. Constitution & the Budget. 1980. 13.25 (ISBN 0-8447-2179-4); pap. 7.25 (ISBN 0-8447-2180-8). Am Enterprise.
Muller, Fred. America's Coming Nightmare Inflation, Economic Collapse & Crime Revolution. 120p. 1980. 10.00 (ISBN 0-686-68648-9). State Ptg.
O'Toole, James. Making America Work: Productivity & Responsibility. 244p. 1981. 14.95 (ISBN 0-8264-0045-0). Continuum.
UNITED STATES–ECONOMIC CONDITIONS–1918-1945
Day, Richard B. Crisis & the "Crash". Soviet Studies of the West'(1917-1939) 320p. 1981. 22.50 (Pub. by NLB England). Schocken.
UNITED STATES–ECONOMIC CONDITIONS–1945-
Darby, Michael R. Effects of Social Security on Income & the Capital Stock. 1979. pap. 4.25 (ISBN 0-8447-3329-6). Am Enterprise.
UNITED STATES–ECONOMIC CONDITIONS–1961-
Backman, Jules, ed. Economic Growth or Stagnation. LC 78-10874. (ITT Key Issue Lecture Ser.). 168p. text ed. 9.95 (ISBN 0-672-97323-5); pap. text ed. 4.95 (ISBN 0-672-97322-7). Bobbs.
Bell, Daniel & Kristol, Irving, eds. The Crisis in Economic Theory. LC 80-70392. 242p. 1981. 13.95 (ISBN 0-465-01476-3); pap. 4.95. Basic.
Harrington, Michael. Decade of Decision. 1981. pap. 6.95 (ISBN 0-671-42808-X, Touchstone). S&S.
McCune, James A. Why Deflation Is Coming in the Nineteen Eighties. (Illus.). 1981. 8.95 (ISBN 0-686-69292-6). Yorkshire Pub.
Macmillan, Duncan D. The Problem of the Economic & Political Survival of the United States. (The Major Currents in Contemporary World History Library). (Illus.). 117p. 1981. 37.85 (ISBN 0-930008-80-4). Inst Econ Pol.
Rose, Tom & Metcalf, Robert. The Coming Victory: Proposals on How to Overcome the Troubles That Plague Us. LC 80-68679. 192p. 1980. pap. 6.95. American Ent Texas.
Schwartz-Nobel, Loretta. Starving in the Shadow of Plenty. 256p. 1981. 12.95 (ISBN 0-399-12522-1). Putnam.
UNITED STATES–ECONOMIC POLICY
Douglas, J. Andrew. The Amazing Lost Money-Secret of the U. S. Government. 228p. 1981. 9.95 (ISBN 0-8119-0417-2, Pegasus Rex). Fell.
Hamberg, Daniel. The U. S. Monetary System: Money, Banking, & Financial Markets. 1981. text ed. 16.95 (ISBN 0-316-34096-0). Little.
Katz, Samuel I., ed. U. S.-European Monetary Relations. 1979. 13.25 (ISBN 0-8447-2150-6); pap. 7.25 (ISBN 0-8447-2149-2). Am Enterprise.
Novak, Michael. American Vision: Essay on the Future of Democratic Capitalism. 1978. pap. 4.25 (ISBN 0-8447-3324-5). Am Enterprise.
UNITED STATES–ECONOMIC POLICY–1971-
Hanson, Kermit & Roehl, Thomas, eds. The United States & the Pacific Economy in the 1980's. LC 80-16599. (ITT Key Issue Lecture Ser.). 160p. 1980. pap. text ed. 6.95. Bobbs.
Holroyd, Howard B. Quest for Valid Economics. 1981. 12.95 (ISBN 0-533-04830-3). Vantage.
Leveson, Irving. Economic Future of the United States. (Hudson Institute Studies on the Prospects for Mankind). 300p. 1981. lib. bdg. 27.50x (ISBN 0-86531-097-1). Westview.
Schwartz, Gail G. & Choate, Pat. Being Number One: Rebuilding the U. S. Economy. 1980. 14.95 (ISBN 0-669-04308-7). Lexington Bks.
UNITED STATES–ELECTIONS
see Elections–United States
UNITED STATES–EMIGRATION AND IMMIGRATION
see also Emigration and Immigration Law
Jones, George F. & Wilson, Renate, eds. Detailed Reports on the Salzburger Emigrants Who Settled in America, Vol. 6. LC 67-27137. (Wormsloe Foundation Publication Ser.: No. 15). 360p. 1981. 20.00 (ISBN 0-8203-0512-X). U of Ga Pr.
UNITED STATES–EXPLORING EXPEDITIONS
Hutchings, James M. Seeking the Elephant, Eighteen Forty-Nine: James Mason Hutchings' Journal of His Overland Trek to California. Sargent, Shirley, ed. LC 80-67777. (American Trail Ser.: No. XII). (Illus.). 210p. 1981. 30.00 (ISBN 0-87062-136-X). A H Clark.
UNITED STATES–FEDERAL BUREAU OF INVESTIGATION
Greene, Robert W. The Sting Man. (Illus.). 256p. 1981. 12.95 (ISBN 0-525-20985-9). Dutton.
UNITED STATES–FEDERAL RESERVE BOARD
Josephson, Emanuel. The Federal Reserve Conspiracy & the Rockefellers: Their Gold Corner. LC 68-29455. (Blacked-Out History Ser.). 374p. 1968. 12.50 (Pub. by Chedney); pap. 8.00. Alpine Ent.
Keyserling, Leon H. & Conference of Economic Staff. Money, Credit, & Interest Rates: Their Gross Mismanagement by the Federal Reserve System. (Illus.). 1980. 3.00. Conf Econ Prog.
UNITED STATES–FEDERAL TRADE COMMISSION
Clarkson, Kenneth, et al, eds. Economic Regulation & Consumer Welfare: The Federal Trade Commission Since 1970. (Illus.). 448p. Date not set. price not set (ISBN 0-521-23378-X). Cambridge U Pr.
UNITED STATES–FLAGS
see Flags–United States
UNITED STATES–FOREIGN ECONOMIC RELATIONS
see also Economic Assistance, American
Institute for Research on Public Policy, Canada & Brookings. Conferences on Canadian-U. S. Economic Relations. 94p. 1978. pap. text ed. 3.00x (ISBN 0-920380-09-3, Pub. by Inst Res Pub Canada). Renouf.
Sommer, John G. Beyond Charity: U. S. Voluntary Aid for a Changing Third World. LC 77-89276. 192p. 1977. pap. 3.95 (ISBN 0-686-28706-1). Overseas Dev Council.
U. S. Programs That Impede U. S. Export Competitiveness: The Regulatory Environment. (Significant Issues Ser.: Vol. II, No. 3). 45p. 1980. pap. 7.50 (ISBN 0-89206-017-4, CSIS011, CSIS). Unipub.
Yearbook of the United States, Vol. 31. 1303p. 1980. pap. 50.00 (ISBN 0-686-68982-8, UN79/1/1, UN). Unipub.
UNITED STATES–FOREIGN OPINION
see also subdivision Foreign Public Opinion under names of wars, e.g. United States–History–Civil War, 1861-1865–Foreign Public Opinion
Debating the Direction of U. S. Foreign Policy 1979-80: High School Debate Analysis. 1979. pap. 3.25 (ISBN 0-8447-1830-0). Am Enterprise.
UNITED STATES–FOREIGN RELATIONS
This heading is subdivided in three ways: First by subject, according to the nature of the materials, e.g. United States–Foreign Relations–Treaties; second chronologically, e.g. United States–Foreign Relations–1783-1865; Third geographically, e.g. United States–Foreign Relations–Great Britain.
America & the World 1980. (Pergamon Policy Studies on International Politics). 1981. 30.01 (ISBN 0-08-027515-X); pap. 6.95 (ISBN 0-08-027514-1). Pergamon.
Cline, Ray S. U. S. Power in a World of Conflict, Vol. II. (Significant Issues Ser.: No. 7). 45p. 1980. 5.95 (ISBN 0-89206-021-2). CSI Studies.
Dallek, Robert. Franklin D. Roosevelt & American Foreign Policy, 1932-1945. (A Galaxy Book: No. 628). 690p. 1981. pap. 9.95 (ISBN 0-19-502894-5). Oxford U Pr.
Finger, Seymour M. & Harbert, Joseph R., eds. U. S. Policy in International Institutions: Defining Reasonable Options in an Unreasonable World. rev. & updated ed. (Special Studies in International Relations). 200p. (Orig.). 1981. lib. bdg. 20.00x (ISBN 0-86531-105-6); pap. 8.50x (ISBN 0-86531-106-4). Westview.
Franck. U. S. Foreign Relations Law, Vol. 1. 1980. 40.00 (ISBN 0-379-20355-3). Oceana.
Franck, Thomas M., ed. The Tethered Presidency: A Study of New Congressional Restraints on Presidential Power & Their Effect on America's Ability to Conduct an Effective Foreign Policy. 272p. 1981. text ed. 17.50x (ISBN 0-8147-2567-8). NYU Pr.
Glennon, Michael J & Franck, Thomas M. United States Foreign Relations Law, Documents & Sources, 3 vols. Bowman, Ronald C., ed. Incl. Vol. 1. Executive Agreements. 1200p. (ISBN 0-379-20355-3); Vol. 2. Treaties. 1200p. (ISBN 0-379-20356-1); Vol. 3. The War Power. 1200p. (ISBN 0-379-20357-X). LC 80-18165. 40.00 set (ISBN 0-686-68787-6). Oceana.
Grant, Stan. Jimmy Carter's Odyssey to Black Africa: Part One. (Illus.). 9.50. Courier Pr FL.
Haines, Gerald K. & Walker, J. Samuel, eds. American Foreign Relations: A Historiographical Review. LC 80-545. (Contributions in American History: No. 90). (Illus.). xiii, 369p. 1981. lib. bdg. 35.00 (ISBN 0-313-21061-6, HAF/). Greenwood.
Herz, Martin F. How the Cold War Is Taught: Six American History Textbooks Examined. 82p. 1978. pap. 3.00 (ISBN 0-89633-009-5). Ethics & Public Policy.
Lefever, Ernest W. & Godson, Roy. The C. I. A. & the American Ethic: An Unfininished Debate. 176p. 1980. 9.50 (ISBN 0-89633-032-X); pap. 5.00 (ISBN 0-89633-031-1). Ethics & Public Policy.
Lefever, Ernest W., ed. Morality & Foreign Policy: A Symposium on President Carter's Stance. 82p. 1977. pap. 3.00 (ISBN 0-89633-005-2). Ethics & Public Policy.

Maghroori, Ray & Gorman, Stephen M. The Yom Kippur War: A Case Study in Crisis Decision Making in American Foreign Policy. LC 80-5811. 98p. 1981. lib. bdg. 14.75 (ISBN 0-8191-1373-5); pap. text ed. 6.75 (ISBN 0-8191-1374-3). U Pr of Amer.

Olson, Robert K. U. S. Foreign Policy & the New International Economic Order. (Special Studies in International Relations). 184p. 1981. lib. bdg. 20.00x (ISBN 0-86531-125-0). Westview.

Poole, Peter A. Profiles in American Foreign Policy: Stimson, Kennan, Acheson, Dulles, Rusk, Kissinger, & Vance. LC 80-5624. (Illus.). 54p. (Orig.). 1981. lib. bdg. 17.00 (ISBN 0-8191-1422-7); pap. text ed. 7.75 (ISBN 0-8191-1423-5). U Pr of Amer.

Robinson, James A. Congress & Foreign Policy-Making: A Study in Legislative Influence & Initiative. LC 80-20372. x, 262p. 1980. Repr. of 1962 ed. lib. bdg. 27.50x (ISBN 0-313-22706-3, ROCF). Greenwood.

Shaffer, Stephen M. & Shaffer, Lisa R. The Politics of International Cooperation: A Comparison of U. S. Experience in Space & in Security. (Monograph Series in World Affairs). 73p. Date not set. pap. 4.00 (ISBN 0-87940-063-3). U of Denver Intl.

U. S. Power in a World Conflict. (Significant Issues Ser.: Vol. II, No. 7). (Illus.). 45p. 1980. pap. 5.00 (ISBN 0-89206-021-2, CSIS015, CSIS). Unipub.

The United States, Western Europe, & the Third World: Allied & Adversaries. (Significant Issues Ser.: Vol. II, No. 4). 53p. 1980. pap. 7.50 (ISBN 0-89206-018-2, CSIS012, CSIS). Unipub.

Waldmann, Raymond J., ed. U S Foreign Trade Zones. (Orig.). 1981. pap. 45.00 (ISBN 0-933678-02-9). Transnatl Invest.

UNITED STATES–FOREIGN RELATIONS–1783-1865

Bemis, Samuel F. John Quincy Adams & the Foundations of American Foreign Policy. LC 80-23039. (Illus.). xix, 588p. 1981. Repr. of 1949 ed. lib. bdg. 49.75x (ISBN 0-313-22636-9, BEAD). Greenwood.

UNITED STATES–FOREIGN RELATIONS–1865-1898

Devine, Michael J. John W. Foster: Politics & Diplomacy in the Imperial Era-1873-1917. LC 80-17387. (Illus.). 200p. 1981. 14.95x (ISBN 0-8214-0437-7). Ohio U Pr.

UNITED STATES–FOREIGN RELATIONS–1898-1901

Devine, Michael J. John W. Foster: Politics & Diplomacy in the Imperial Era-1873-1917. LC 80-17387. (Illus.). 200p. 1981. 14.95x (ISBN 0-8214-0437-7). Ohio U Pr.

UNITED STATES–FOREIGN RELATIONS–20TH CENTURY

Berger, Jason. A New Deal for the World: Eleanor Roosevelt & American Foreign Policy, 1920-1962. 240p. 1981. 20.00x (ISBN 0-930888-07-3). Brooklyn Coll Pr.

Ninkovich, F. A. The Diplomacy of Ideas: U. S. Foreign Policy & Cultural Relations, 1938-1950. 256p. Date not set. 24.95 (ISBN 0-521-23241-4). Cambridge U Pr.

UNITED STATES–FOREIGN RELATIONS–1901-1913

Devine, Michael J. John W. Foster: Politics & Diplomacy in the Imperial Era-1873-1917. LC 80-17387. (Illus.). 200p. 1981. 14.95x (ISBN 0-8214-0437-7). Ohio U Pr.

UNITED STATES–FOREIGN RELATIONS–1913-1921

Devine, Michael J. John W. Foster: Politics & Diplomacy in the Imperial Era-1873-1917. LC 80-17387. (Illus.). 200p. 1981. 14.95x (ISBN 0-8214-0437-7). Ohio U Pr.

UNITED STATES–FOREIGN RELATIONS–1921-1933

Myers, William S. The Foreign Policies of Herbert Hoover, 1929-1933. Freidel, Frank, ed. LC 78-66558. (The History of the United States Ser.: Vol. 14). 272p. 1979. lib. bdg. 20.00 (ISBN 0-8240-9699-1). Garland Pub.

UNITED STATES–FOREIGN RELATIONS–1933-1945

Anderson, Terry H. The United States, Great Britain, & the Cold War: 1944-1947. LC 80-25838. 256p. 1981. text ed. 23.00x (ISBN 0-8262-0328-0). U of Mo Pr.

UNITED STATES–FOREIGN RELATIONS–1945-

Anderson, Terry H. The United States, Great Britain, & the Cold War: 1944-1947. LC 80-25838. 256p. 1981. text ed. 23.00x (ISBN 0-8262-0328-0). U of Mo Pr.

UNITED STATES–FOREIGN RELATIONS–1945-1961

Divine, Robert A. Eisenhower & the Cold War. (Illus.). 160p. 1981. 14.95 (ISBN 0-19-502823-6). Oxford U Pr.

--Eisenhower & the Cold War. 160p. 1981. pap. 3.95 (ISBN 0-19-502824-4, 621, GB). Oxford U Pr.

Stueck, William W., Jr. The Road to Confrontation: American Policy Toward China & Korea, 1947 - 1950. LC 80-11818. (Illus.). 337p. 1981. 22.00x (ISBN 0-8078-1445-8); pap. 10.00x (ISBN 0-8078-4080-7). U of NC Pr.

UNITED STATES–FOREIGN RELATIONS–1961-

Foreign Policy Association. Great Decisions Nineteen Eighty-One. (Illus.). 96p. (Orig.). 1981. pap. 5.00 (ISBN 0-87124-066-1). Foreign Policy.

Kearns, Graham. Arms for the Poor: President Carter's Poloicies on Arms Transfers to the Third World. 136p. (Orig.). 1980. pap. text ed. 10.95 (ISBN 0-908160-57-7). Bks Australia.

Kissinger, Henry. For the Record: Selected Statements, 1977 to 1980. 288p. 1981. 12.95 (ISBN 0-316-49663-4). Little.

Nathan & Oliver. U. S. Foreign Policy & World Order. 2nd ed. 475p. (Orig.). 1981. pap. text ed. 10.95 (ISBN 0-316-59851-8). Little.

UNITED STATES–FOREIGN RELATIONS–ARAB COUNTRIES

Bradley, C. Paul. The Camp David Peace Process: A Study of Carter Administration Policies (1977-1980) LC 81-50100. (Illus.). viii, 79p. 1981. pap. text ed. 4.50 (ISBN 0-936988-03-7). Tompson & Rutter.

Polk, William R. The Arab World: Fourth Edition of the United States & the Arab World. LC 80-16995. (American Foreign Policy Library). 1981. text ed. 22.50x (ISBN 0-674-04316-2); pap. text ed. 8.95x (ISBN 0-674-04317-0). Harvard U Pr.

UNITED STATES–FOREIGN RELATIONS–ASIA

Here are entered general works on Asia. For smaller areas see the name of the country or area, e.g.–Near East, or–China.

Shawcross, William. Sideshow. rev. ed. 1981. price not set (ISBN 0-671-25414-6, Touchstone). S&S.

UNITED STATES–FOREIGN RELATIONS–AUSTRALIA

Cuddy, Dennis L. Contemporary Australian-American Relations. LC 80-65615. 155p. 1981. perfect bdg. 12.95 (ISBN 0-86548-027-3). Century Twenty One.

Renwick, George W. InterAct: Australia-U.S. LC 80-83910. (Country Orientation Ser.). 80p. 1980. pap. text ed. 10.00 (ISBN 0-933662-16-5). Intercult Pr.

UNITED STATES–FOREIGN RELATIONS–CHINA

Stueck, William W., Jr. The Road to Confrontation: American Policy Toward China & Korea, 1947 - 1950. LC 80-11818. (Illus.). 337p. 1981. 22.00x (ISBN 0-8078-1445-8); pap. 10.00x (ISBN 0-8078-4080-7). U of NC Pr.

UNITED STATES–FOREIGN RELATIONS–CHINA–1949-

Schell, Orville. Watch Out for the Foreign Guests! China Encounters the West. 1981. 8.95 (ISBN 0-394-51331-2). Pantheon.

Stoessinger, John G. Nations in Darkness: China, Russia, & America. 3rd ed. 263p. 1981. pap. text ed. 6.95 (ISBN 0-394-32657-1). Random.

UNITED STATES–FOREIGN RELATIONS–EUROPE

Here are entered general works on Europe, as well as those on the separate countries of Europe except great britain and russia.

Katz, Samuel I., ed. U. S.-European Monetary Relations. 1979. 13.25 (ISBN 0-8447-2150-6); pap. 7.25 (ISBN 0-8447-2149-2). Am Enterprise.

UNITED STATES–FOREIGN RELATIONS–GERMANY

Catudal, Honore M. Kennedy & the Berlin Wall Crisis: A Case Study in U. S. Decision Making. (Illus.). 358p. (Orig.). 1980. pap. 20.00x (ISBN 3-87061-160-X). Intl Pubns Serv.

UNITED STATES–FOREIGN RELATIONS–IRAN

Alexander, Yonah & Nanes, Allan, eds. United States & Iran: A Documentary History. 450p. 1980. 24.00 (ISBN 0-89093-183-6); pap. 8.00 (ISBN 0-89093-184-4). U Pubns Amer.

Dreyfuss, Robert. Hostage to Khomeini. LC 80-24288. (Illus.). 260p. (Orig.). 1981. pap. 3.95 (ISBN 0-933488-11-4). New Benjamin.

Ledeen, Michael & Lewis, William. Debacle: The American Failure in Iran. LC 80-27149. 320p. 12.95 (ISBN 0-686-69414-7). Knopf.

UNITED STATES–FOREIGN RELATIONS–ISRAEL

Bradley, C. Paul. The Camp David Peace Process: A Study of Carter Administration Policies (1977-1980) LC 81-50100. (Illus.). viii, 79p. 1981. pap. text ed. 4.50 (ISBN 0-936988-03-7). Tompson & Rutter.

UNITED STATES–FOREIGN RELATIONS–JAPAN

Nishi, Toshio. The American Experiment: Japan 1945-1952, No. 244. 380p. 1981. 19.95 (ISBN 0-8179-7441-5). Hoover Inst Pr.

UNITED STATES–FOREIGN RELATIONS–KOREA

Stueck, William W., Jr. The Road to Confrontation: American Policy Toward China & Korea, 1947 - 1950. LC 80-11818. (Illus.). 337p. 1981. 22.00x (ISBN 0-8078-1445-8); pap. 10.00x (ISBN 0-8078-4080-7). U of NC Pr.

UNITED STATES–FOREIGN RELATIONS–MEXICO

Erb, Richard D. & Ross, Stanley R., eds. U. S. Policies Toward Mexico: Perceptions & Perspectives. 1979. pap. 4.25 (ISBN 0-8447-2166-2). Am Enterprise.

Ladman, Jerry R., et al, eds. U.S.-Mexican Energy Relationships: Realities & Prospects. LC 80-8878. 1981. price not set (ISBN 0-669-04398-2). Lexington Bks.

UNITED STATES–FOREIGN RELATIONS–NEAR EAST

Here are entered works on Eastern Asia and Turkey as a whole, as well as those on separate countries of the Near East.

The Impact of U. S. Foreign Direct Investment on U. S. Export Competitiveness in Third World Markets. (Significant Issues Ser.: Vol. II, No. 1). 25p. 1980. pap. 5.00 (ISBN 0-89206-014-X, CSIS009, CSIS). Unipub.

UNITED STATES–FOREIGN RELATIONS–PHILIPPINE ISLANDS

Cottrell, Alvin J. & Hanks, Robert J. The Military Utility of the U. S. Facilities in the Philippines, Vol. II. LC 80-83128. (Significant Issues Ser.: No.11). 34p. 1980. 5.95 (ISBN 0-89206-027-1). CSI Studies.

UNITED STATES–FOREIGN RELATIONS–RUSSIA

Balfour, Michael. The Adversaries: America, Russia and the Open World 1941-1962. 224p. 1981. price not set (ISBN 0-7100-0687-X). Routledge & Kegan.

Douglas, Roy. From War to Cold War: 1942-48. 1980. 19.95 (ISBN 0-312-30862-0). St Martin.

Eidelberg, Paul. Beyond Detente: Toward an American Foreign Policy. 12.95 (ISBN 0-89385-000-4). Green Hill.

Herz, Martin F., ed. Decline of the West? George Kennan & His Critics. 189p. 1978. 9.50 (ISBN 0-89633-036-2); pap. 5.00 (ISBN 0-89633-018-4). Ethics & Public Policy.

Stoessinger, John G. Nations in Darkness: China, Russia, & America. 3rd ed. 263p. 1981. pap. text ed. 6.95 (ISBN 0-394-32657-1). Random.

UNITED STATES–FOREIGN RELATIONS–SOUTH AFRICA

Lemarchand, Rene, ed. American Policy in Southern Africa: The Stakes & the Stance. 2nd ed. LC 80-6222. 513p. 1981. lib. bdg. 22.75 (ISBN 0-8191-1436-7); pap. text ed. 12.50 (ISBN 0-8191-1437-5). U Pr of Amer.

UNITED STATES–FOREIGN RELATIONS–THAILAND

Fieg, John. InterAct: Thailand-U.S. Renwick, George W., ed. LC 80-83909. (Country Orientation Ser.). 1980. pap. text ed. 10.00 (ISBN 0-933662-14-9). Intercult Pr.

UNITED STATES–FULL EMPLOYMENT POLICIES

see Full Employment Policies

UNITED STATES–GENEALOGY

see also subdivision Genealogy under names of individual states, e.g. Virginia–Genealogy

Algee, Isabelle R. Moorings - Past & Present. (Illus.). 557p. 1980. lib. bdg. 35.00 (ISBN 0-918518-18-0); pap. 20.00 (ISBN 0-918518-17-2). St Luke TN.

Boyer, Carl, 3rd. Ancestral Lines Revised. 1981. 40.00 (ISBN 0-936124-05-9). C Boyer.

Coldham, Peter W. American Loyalist Claims. LC 80-8609. 615p. 24.00 (ISBN 0-915156-45-8). Natl Genealogical.

Hershey, Virginia S. Those Southern Milners: A Collection of Record Abstracts for the Southern States Between 1606 & 1850 with Biographical & Historical Sketches, Family Records, & Genealogies up to 1900. (Illus.). 426p. 1980. 40.00x (ISBN 0-9605320-0-5, TX-578-128). Hershey.

Kent, David L. Foreign Origins. LC 80-85008. 100p. 1981. softcover 10.00 (ISBN 0-9604886-3-4). C M Kent.

Richards, Dennis L., ed. Montana's Genealogical Records. (The Gale Genealogy & Local History Ser.: Vol. 11). 330p. 1981. 30.00 (ISBN 0-8103-1487-8). Gale.

Rowland, Ralph S. & Rowland, Star W. Clary Genealogy: Four Early American Lines & Related Families. LC 80-54651. 1980. write for info. R & S Rowland.

--Clary Genealogy: Four Early American Lines & Related Families. 1980. 17.50. R & S Rowland.

Stryker, William N. The Stryker Family in America: A History of the Stryker & Striker Families, Vol 2. LC 78-75351. (Illus.). 500p. 1981. lib. bdg. 45.00 (ISBN 0-9602936-2-0). W N Stryker.

Underhill, Lonnie E. Genealogy Records of the First Arizona Volunteer Infantry Regiment. LC 80-24778. (Illus.). iv, 124p. 1980. pap. 18.50 (ISBN 0-933234-02-3). Roan Horse.

Versailles, Elizabeth S. Hathaways Twelve Hundred to Nineteen-Eighty. 621p. (YA) 1980. lib. bdg. write for info. Versailles.

Wright, Norman E. Building an American Pedigree: A Guide to Family & Local History Research. 2nd, rev. ed. (Illus.). 1981. pap. text ed. 12.95 (ISBN 0-8425-1863-0). Brigham.

UNITED STATES–GENEALOGY–BIBLIOGRAPHY

Parker, J. Carlyle, ed. Library Service for Genealogists. LC 80-26032. (The Gale Genealogy & Local History Ser.: Vol. 15). 285p. 1981. 30.00 (ISBN 0-8103-1489-4). Gale.

UNITED STATES–GOVERNMENT

see United States–Politics and Government

UNITED STATES–GOVERNMENT PUBLICATIONS

Johnson, Nancy P. Sources of Compiled Legislative Histories: Bibliography of Government Documents, Periodical Articles & Books, 1st Congress - 94th Congress. (AALL Publications Ser.: No. 14). 146p. 1979. loose-leaf in vinyl, 3-ring binder 22.50x (ISBN 0-8377-0112-0). Rothman.

UNITED STATES–GOVERNMENT PUBLICATIONS–BIBLIOGRAPHY

Newsome, Walter L. Government Reference Books 78-79: A Biennial Guide to U. S. Government Publications, 6th Biennial Volume. 450p. 1980. lib. bdg. 25.00x (ISBN 0-87287-192-4). Libs Unl.

Research Libraries of the New York Public Library & the Library of Congress. Bibliographic Guide to Government Publications - U. S. 1980. (Library Catalogs-Bib. Guides Ser.). 1981. lib. bdg. 195.00 (ISBN 0-8161-6887-3). G K Hall.

UNITED STATES–HISTORICAL GEOGRAPHY–MAPS

Wesley, Edgar B. Our United States...Its History in Maps. rev. ed. (Illus.). 96p. 1980. pap. text ed. 9.10x (ISBN 0-87453-001-6, 81001). Denoyer.

UNITED STATES–HISTORY

see also subdivision History under names of states, e.g. Pennsylvania–History; also under various geographic subdivisions of the United States e.g. New England States–History

Anthony, Irvin. Paddle Wheels & Pistols. 329p. 1980. Repr. of 1929 ed. lib. bdg. 30.00 (ISBN 0-8495-0075-3). Arden Lib.

Bernier, Olivier. Pleasure & Privilege: Life in France, Naples & America. LC 79-6174. (Illus.). 304p. 1981. 14.95 (ISBN 0-385-15780-0). Doubleday.

Brugger, Robert J., ed. Ourselves-Our Past: Psychological Approaches to American History. LC 80-81425. 448p. 1981. text ed. 26.50x (ISBN 0-8018-2312-9); pap. text ed. 8.95x (ISBN 0-8018-2382-X). Johns Hopkins.

Burner, David, et al. The American People, 2 vols. Incl. Vol. I. To Eighteen Seventy-Seven. 342p (ISBN 0-9603726-2-8); Vol. II. From Eighteen Sixty. 440p (ISBN 0-9603726-3-6). (Illus., Orig.). 1980. Combined Edition. pap. text ed. 14.95 (ISBN 0-9603726-0-1); pap. text ed. 9.75 ea. Revisionary.

Cordasco, Francesco & Pitkin, Thomas M. The White Slave Trade & the Immigrants: A Chapter in American Social History. LC 80-25556. 1981. write for info. (ISBN 0-87917-077-8); pap. write for info. (ISBN 0-87917-076-X). Blaine Ethridge.

Cornwall, Rebecca & Arrington, Leonard J. Rescue of the Eighteen Fifty-Six Handcraft Companies. (Charles Redd Monographs in Western History: No. 11). (Illus.). 64p. 1981. pap. text ed. 4.95 (ISBN 0-8425-1941-6). Brigham.

Dollar, C. M. America Changing Time: A Brief History. LC 80-10684. 729p. 1980. 12.95 (ISBN 0-471-06087-9). Wiley.

Friedman, Leon, ed. Episodes of Violence in U.S. History, 3 vols. Incl. Vol. 1. Dynamite. Adamic, Louis. LC 80-21964; Vol. 2. The Dorr War. Mowry, Arthur M. LC 80-21969; Vol. 3. The Molly Maguires. Broehl, Wayne G., Jr. LC 80-21794. (Illus.). 750p. 1981. Repr. of 1970 ed. Set. 50.00 (ISBN 0-87754-133-7). Chelsea Hse.

Gruver, Rebecca B. American History. 3rd ed. (Illus.). 1076p. 1981. One Vol. Ed. text ed. 17.95 (ISBN 0-201-05051-X); Vol. I. pap. 12.95 (ISBN 0-201-05052-8); Vol. II. pap. 12.95 (ISBN 0-201-05053-6). A-W.

--An American History. 3rd ed. LC 75-14794. 1981. text ed. write for info. (ISBN 0-201-05051-X); Vol. 1. pap. text ed. 12.95 (ISBN 0-201-05052-8); Vol. 2. pap. text ed. 12.95 (ISBN 0-201-05053-6); write for info. mstr's manual (ISBN 0-201-05054-4); Vol. 1. write for info. study guide (ISBN 0-201-05055-2); Vol. 2. write for info. study guide (ISBN 0-201-05056-0). A-W.

Heaston, Michael D., ed. From Mississippi to California. Date not set. 9.50 (ISBN 0-8363-0157-9). Jenkins.

Hindle, Brooke. Emulation & Invention. (The Anson G. Phelps Lectureship Ser. on Early American History). (Illus.). 224p. 1981. text ed. 19.50x (ISBN 0-8147-3409-X). NYU Pr.

Jones, Robert & Seligman, Gustav L. The Sweep of American History, Vol. 1. 400p. 1981. pap. text ed. 8.95 (ISBN 0-471-07898-0). Wiley.

--The Sweep of American History, Vol. 2. 400p. 1981. pap. text ed. 8.95 (ISBN 0-471-07897-2). Wiley.

McJimsey, George. Dividing & Reuniting of America. LC 80-68811. (Orig.). 1981. pap. text ed. 7.95x (ISBN 0-88273-108-4). Forum Pr MO.

McPhee, John. Basin & Range. 1981. 10.95 (ISBN 0-374-10914-1). FS&G.

Nevins, Allan & Commager, Henry S. A Pocket History of the United States. 2nd, rev. ed. 1981. pap. write for info. PB.

Poe, Susan. Americana Mazes. 32p. (Orig.). (gr. 3 up). 1980. pap. 1.50 (ISBN 0-937518-07-7). Hartley Hse.

Rosenberg, Emily. Spreading the American Dream. 1981. 12.95 (ISBN 0-8090-8798-7); pap. 4.95 (ISBN 0-8090-0146-2). FS&G.

Rossum, Ralph A. & McDowell, Gary L., eds. The American Founding: Politics, Statesmanship, & the Constitution. (National University Publications, Political Science Ser.). 1981. 17.50 (ISBN 0-8046-9283-1). Kennikat.

Schutz, John. Dawning of America. LC 80-68812. (Orig.). 1981. pap. text ed. 7.95x (ISBN 0-88273-109-2). Forum Pr MO.

Toepperwein, Fritz & Toepperwein, Emilia. Footnotes of the Buckhorn: Centennial Edition 1881-1981. pap. 3.50 (ISBN 0-910722-14-5). Highland Pr.

Traub, Hamilton P. The Call of Destiny: The Epic of the American Republic. LC 79-52732. (Illus.). 614p. 1980. 14.95x (ISBN 0-9605364-0-X); pap. 9.95x. Golden Hill.

Weinstein, Allen. Freedom & Crisis: An American History. 972p. 1981. text ed. 18.95 (ISBN 0-394-32415-3). Random.

--Freedom & Crisis: An American History, 2 vols. 3rd ed. 1981. Vol. 1, 498p. pap. text ed. 12.95 (ISBN 0-394-32611-3); Vol. 2, 539p. pap. text ed. 12.95 (ISBN 0-394-32612-1). Random.

Williams, T. Harry. A History of American Wars: From Colonial Times to World War I. LC 80-2717. 512p. 1981. 20.00 (ISBN 0-394-51167-0). Knopf.

UNITED STATES–HISTORY–ADDRESSES, ESSAYS, LECTURES

Dennis, Frank A., ed. Southern Miscellany: Essays in Honor of Glover Moore. LC 80-20373. 202p. 1981. 15.00 (ISBN 0-87805-129-5). U Pr of Miss.

UNITED STATES–HISTORY–ANECDOTES

Boochever, Florence & Jackson, Raymond, eds. Writings from the Beaver Trail. (Illus.). 312p. (Orig.). 1979. pap. 5.50 (ISBN 0-9605090-0-3). Albany Pub Lib.

Hope, Thelma P. Seven Daughters. (Americana Ser.). 150p. (Orig.). 1981. pap. 6.90 (ISBN 0-686-69154-7). Gusto Pr.

UNITED STATES–HISTORY–ATLASES

see United States–Historical Geography–Maps

UNITED STATES–HISTORY–BIBLIOGRAPHY

Tutorow, Norman E., compiled by. The Mexican-American War: An Annotated Bibliography. LC 80-1789. (Illus.). 456p. 1981. lib. bdg. 39.95 (ISBN 0-313-22181-2, TMA/). Greenwood.

UNITED STATES–HISTORY–HUMOR, CARICATURES, ETC.

Carol, Estelle & Simpson, Bob. The Incredible Shrinking Dream: An Illustrated People's History of the United States. (Illus.). 180p. (Orig.). 1981. pap. 6.95 (ISBN 0-932870-07-4). Alyson Pubns.

UNITED STATES–HISTORY–MAPS

see United States–Historical Geography–Maps

UNITED STATES–HISTORY–PERSONAL NARRATIVES

Heinrichs, Waldo H., Jr. American Ambassador: Joseph C. Grew & the Development of the United States Diplomatic Tradition. Freidel, Frank, ed. LC 78-66536. (The History of the United States Ser.: Vol. 7). 474p. 1979. lib. bdg. 35.00 (ISBN 0-8240-9705-X). Garland Pub.

UNITED STATES–HISTORY–COLONIAL PERIOD, ca. 1600-1775

Fowler, William & Coyle, E. Wallace. The American Revolution: Changing Perspectives. 2nd ed. LC 79-88424. (Illus.). 231p. 1981. pap. text ed. 9.95x (ISBN 0-930350-21-9). NE U Pr.

Jenkins, John. Early American Imprints, 2 vols. (Illus.). Date not set. Vol. 1. 15.00 (ISBN 0-8363-0158-7). Vol. 2 (ISBN 0-8363-0163-3). Jenkins.

Johnson, Richard R. Adjustment to Empire: The New England Colonies in the Era of the Glorious Revolution, 1675-1715. (Illus.). 448p. 1981. 29.50 (ISBN 0-8135-0907-6). Rutgers U Pr.

Wright, Louis B. The American Heritage History of the Thirteen Colonies. LC 67-23814. (Illus.). 384p. 1981. pap. 12.95 (ISBN 0-8281-0429-8, Dist. by Scribner). Am Heritage.

UNITED STATES–HISTORY–FRENCH AND INDIAN WAR, 1755-1763

Baxter, James P. The Pioneers of New France in New England. 450p. 1980. Repr. of 1894 ed. 20.00 (ISBN 0-917890-20-5). Heritage Bk.

UNITED STATES–HISTORY–REVOLUTION, 1775-1783

Bradford. A Better Guide Than Reason. 12.95 (ISBN 0-89385-006-3); pap. 4.95. Green Hill.

Jensen, Merrill. The New Nation: A History of the United States During the Confederation 1781-1789. 446p. 1981. text ed. 19.95 (ISBN 0-930350-15-4); pap. text ed. 9.95 (ISBN 0-930350-14-6). NE U Pr.

Scribner, Robert L. & Tarter, Brent, eds. The Time for Decision, 1776: A Documentary Record. LC 72-96023. (Revolutionary Virginia Ser.: The Road to Independence, Vol. VI). 1981. write for info. (ISBN 0-8139-0880-9). U Pr of Va.

Stone, Merlin. Ancient Mirrors of Womanhood: Our Goddess & Heroine Heritage, Vol. 2. (Illus.). 224p. Date not set. pap. 7.95 (ISBN 0-9603352-1-8). New Sibylline.

White, Morton. The Philosophy of the American Revolution. 321p. 1981. pap. 6.95 (ISBN 0-19-502891-0, GB 625, OPB). Oxford U Pr.

UNITED STATES–HISTORY–REVOLUTION, 1775-1783–BIBLIOGRAPHY

Adams, Thomas R. The American Controversy: A Bibliographical Study of the British Pamphlets About the American Disputes, 1764-1783, 2 vols. LC 77-76348. 1140p. 1981. Set. text ed. 60.00 (ISBN 0-87057-150-8). U Pr of New Eng.

UNITED STATES–HISTORY–REVOLUTION, 1775-1783–BIOGRAPHY

Johannes Schwalm the Hessian, No. 3. (Illus.). 53p. 1979. 5.75. Johannes Schwalm Hist.

Johannes Schwalm the Hessian, No. 4. (Illus.). 72p. 1980. 6.50. Johannes Schwalm Hist.

Ritchie, Arthur W. Heros of Seventy-Six! They Aren't What They Used to Be, but Then They Never Were. LC 80-50612. (Illus.). 255p. 1981. 9.95 (ISBN 0-9604516-0-9). Sigma Pr.

UNITED STATES–HISTORY–REVOLUTION, 1775-1783–FRENCH PARTICIPATION

Hoffman, Ronald & Albert, Peter J., eds. Diplomacy & Revolution: The Franco-American Alliance of 1778. LC 80-13931. 1981. write for info. (ISBN 0-8139-0864-7). U Pr of Va.

UNITED STATES–HISTORY–REVOLUTION, 1775-1783–GERMAN MERCENARIES

Johannes Schwalm the Hessian, No. 3. (Illus.). 53p. 1979. 5.75. Johannes Schwalm Hist.

Johannes Schwalm the Hessian, No. 4. (Illus.). 72p. 1980. 6.50. Johannes Schwalm Hist.

UNITED STATES–HISTORY–REVOLUTION, 1775-1783–JUVENILE LITERATURE

Bliven, Bruce, Jr. The American Revolution. LC 80-20813. (Landmark Bks.). (Illus.). 160p. (gr. 5-9). 1981. pap. 2.95 (ISBN 0-394-84696-6). Random.

Dorson, Richard M. America Rebels: Personal Narratives of the American Revoulution. 354p. Date not set. pap. 3.95 (ISBN 0-394-73277-4). Pantheon.

UNITED STATES–HISTORY–REVOLUTION, 1775-1783–PROPAGANDA

Schlesinger, Arthur M. Prelude to Independence: The Newspaper War on Britain 1764-1776. LC 80-22830. 340p. 1980. pap. text ed. 8.95x (ISBN 0-930350-13-8). NE U Pr.

UNITED STATES–HISTORY–1783-1809

Jensen, Merrill. The New Nation: A History of the United States During the Confederation 1781-1789. 446p. 1981. text ed. 19.95 (ISBN 0-930350-15-4); pap. text ed. 9.95 (ISBN 0-930350-14-6). NE U Pr.

UNITED STATES–HISTORY–1783-1865

Berlin, Ira. Slaves Without Masters: The Free Negro in the Antebellum South. 446p. 1981. pap. 6.95 (ISBN 0-19-502905-4, GB 629, OPB). Oxford U Pr.

Report About & from America: Given from First-Hand Observation in the Years 1848 &1849. (Mississippi Valley Collection Bulletin, No. 3). 84p. 1970. pap. 5.95 (ISBN 0-87870-080-3). Memphis St Univ.

UNITED STATES–HISTORY–19TH CENTURY

Foner, Eric. Politics & Ideology in the Age of the Civil War. 256p. 1981. pap. 5.95 (ISBN 0-19-502926-7, GB 646, GB). Oxford U Pr.

UNITED STATES–HISTORY–WAR WITH MEXICO, 1845-1848

Tutorow, Norman E., ed. The American-Mexican War: An Annotated Bibliography. LC 80-1789. (Illus.). 456p. 1981. lib. bdg. 39.95 (ISBN 0-313-22181-2, TMA/). Greenwood.

Tutorow, Norman E., compiled by. The Mexican-American War: An Annotated Bibliography. LC 80-1789. (Illus.). 456p. 1981. lib. bdg. 39.95 (ISBN 0-313-22181-2, TMA/). Greenwood.

UNITED STATES–HISTORY–CIVIL WAR, 1861-1865

Here are entered general works about the Civil War. Titles concerning the Civil War in specific states are listed under the names of individual states with the subdivision History.

Barney, William L. Flawed Victory: A New Perspective on the Civil War. LC 80-68972. 225p. 1980. lib. bdg. 19.00 (ISBN 0-8191-1273-9); pap. text ed. 8.75 (ISBN 0-8191-1274-7). U Pr of Amer.

Cromie, Alice H. Tour Guide to the Civil War. 1975. 12.95 (ISBN 0-87690-153-4). Dutton.

Cuttino, George P. Saddle Bag & Spinning Wheel. LC 80-83663. 330p. 1981. 18.95x (ISBN 0-86554-004-7). Mercer Univ Pr.

King, Spencer B., Jr. Darien: The Death & Rebirth of a Southern Town. LC 80-83662. (Illus.). 100p. 1981. 13.95x (ISBN 0-86554-003-9). Mercer Univ Pr.

Nesbitt, Mark. If the South Won Gettysburg. LC 80-52561. (Illus.). 200p. (Orig.). 1980. pap. 2.50 (ISBN 0-937740-01-2). Reliance Pub.

Ropes, John C. The Story of the Civil War, Vol. 4. 749p. 1980. Repr. of 1894 ed. lib. bdg. 375.00 (ISBN 0-8495-4634-6). Arden Lib.

Woodward, C. Vann, ed. Mary Chesnut's Civil War. LC 80-36661. (Illus.). 960p. 1981. 29.95x (ISBN 0-300-02459-2). Yale U Pr.

UNITED STATES–HISTORY–CIVIL WAR, 1861-1865–PERSONAL NARRATIVES

Baird, Samuel E. With Merrill's Cavalry. Annegan, Charles, ed. LC 80-69601. (Illus.). 64p. 1981. 15.95 (ISBN 0-9605200-0-7). Bk Habit.

Cummins, D. Duane & Hohweiler, Daryl, eds. An Enlisted Soldier's View of the Civil War: The Wartime Papers of Joseph R. Ward, Jr. (Illus., Orig.). 1981. pap. price not set (ISBN 0-9605732-0-8). Belle Pubns.

Forten, Charlotte L. The Journal of Charlotte L. Forten. Billington, Ray A., ed. 286p. 1981. pap. 4.95 (ISBN 0-393-00046-X). Norton.

UNITED STATES–HISTORY–CIVIL WAR, 1861-1865–REGIMENTAL HISTORIES

Dunkelman, Mark H. & Winey, Michael J. The Hardtack Regiment: An Illustrated History of the 154th Regiment, New York State Infantry Volunteers. LC 79-64502. (Illus.). 220p. 1981. 20.00 (ISBN 0-8386-3007-3). Fairleigh Dickinson.

UNITED STATES–HISTORY–CIVIL WAR, 1861-1865–REGISTERS, LISTS, ETC.

Krick. The Confederate Death Roster at Gettysburg. 10.00. Pr of Morningside.

UNITED STATES–HISTORY–1865-1898

see also Reconstruction

Savitt, Todd L. Medicine & Slavery: The Health Care of Blacks in Antebellum Virginia. LC 78-8520. (Blacks in the New World Ser.). (Illus.). 321p. 1981. pap. 7.50 (ISBN 0-252-00874-X). U of Ill Pr.

UNITED STATES–HISTORY–WAR OF 1898

Trask, David F. The War with the Spain in Eighteen Ninety-Eight. Morton, Louis, ed. LC 80-2314. (The Macmillan Wars of the United States Ser.). (Illus.). 775p. 1981. 29.95 (ISBN 0-02-932950-7). Macmillan.

UNITED STATES–HISTORY–20TH CENTURY

Roth, Russell. Muddy Glory: America's Indian Wars in the Phillipines, 1899 to 1935. 1981. 12.95 (ISBN 0-8158-0402-4). Chris Mass.

UNITED STATES–HISTORY–20TH CENTURY–SOURCES

Eckert, Thomas B. The Young Apostle: A Story of Torment & Revelation. LC 79-67515. 122p. 1980. 6.50 (ISBN 0-533-04471-5). Vantage.

UNITED STATES–HISTORY–1919-1933

Daniels, Jonathan. The Time Between the Wars: Armistice to Pearl Harbor. Freidel, Frank, ed. LC 78-66523. (The History of the United States Ser.: Vol. 5). 382p. 1979. lib. bdg. 24.00 (ISBN 0-8240-9707-6). Garland Pub.

Feinman, Ronald L. Twilight of Progressivism: The Western Republican Senators & the New Deal. LC 80-20124. (Johns Hopkins Studies in Historical & Political Science). (Illus.). 288p. 1981. text ed. 18.50x (ISBN 0-8018-2373-0). Johns Hopkins.

UNITED STATES–HISTORY–1933-1945

Daniels, Jonathan. The Time Between the Wars: Armistice to Pearl Harbor. Freidel, Frank, ed. LC 78-66523. (The History of the United States Ser.: Vol. 5). 382p. 1979. lib. bdg. 24.00 (ISBN 0-8240-9707-6). Garland Pub.

Robinson, John L. Living Hard: Southern Americans in the Great Depression. LC 80-5817. 272p. 1981. lib. bdg. 19.75 (ISBN 0-8191-1379-4); pap. text ed. 10.75 (ISBN 0-8191-1380-8). U Pr of Amer.

UNITED STATES–HISTORY–1945-

Days, G. D., ed. Threshold of the McCarthy Era & the McCarthy Era - Beginning of the End. 60p. 1980. pap. 19.95 includes cassettes (ISBN 0-918628-54-7, 54/7). Congeros Pubns.

UNITED STATES–HISTORY, COMIC, SATIRICAL, ETC.

see United States–History–Humor, Caricatures, Etc.

UNITED STATES–HISTORY, LOCAL

The Fifth Infantry Division in Thee ETO. (Divisional Ser.: No. 18). (Illus.). 254p. 1980. Repr. of 1945 ed. 27.50. Battery Pr.

Thunderbolt: The History of the Eleventh Armored Division. (Divisional Ser.: No. 17). (Illus.). 1980. Repr. of 1948 ed. 22.50 (ISBN 0-89839-041-9). Battery Pr.

UNITED STATES–HISTORY, LOCAL–BIBLIOGRAPHY

Parker, J. Carlyle, ed. Library Service for Genealogists. LC 80-26032. (The Gale Genealogy & Local History Ser.: Vol. 15). 285p. 1981. 30.00 (ISBN 0-8103-1489-4). Gale.

UNITED STATES–HISTORY, MILITARY

The History of the Joint Chiefs of Staff: The Joint Chiefs of Staff & National Policy, 4 vols. Incl. Vol. 1. 1945-1947. Schnabel, James P; Vol. 2. 1947-1949. Condit, Kenneth W; Vol. 3. The Korean War, 2 pts. Schnabel, James F. & Watson, Robert J. Vol. 4, 1950-1952. 49.00. Set. 179.00 (ISBN 0-89453-148-4). M Glazier.

Williams, T. Harry. The History of American Wars: From Colonial Times to World War I. LC 80-2717. 1981. 20.00 (ISBN 0-394-51167-0). Knopf.

UNITED STATES–HISTORY, POLITICAL

see United States–Politics and Government

UNITED STATES–IMMIGRATION

see United States–Emigration and Immigration

UNITED STATES–IMPRINTS

American Book Publishing Record Cumulative 1980. 1260p. 1981. 59.00 (ISBN 0-8352-1245-9). Bowker.

American Book Publishing Record Cumulative 1975-1979. 1981. 125.00 (ISBN 0-8352-1371-4). Bowker.

Books in Print Supplement 1980-1981. 2700p. 1981. 58.00 (ISBN 0-8352-1328-5). Bowker.

UNITED STATES–INDUSTRIES

see also Small Business

Bereny, et al. Baseline Study of U.S. Industry Solar Exports for Nineteen Seventy-Nine. 73p. 1981. Repr. of 1980 ed. 35.00 (ISBN 0-89934-080-6). Solar Energy Info.

State Industrial Directories Corp. Maine State Industrial Directory, 1981. 1980. pap. write for info. (ISBN 0-89910-045-7). State Indus Dir.

UNITED STATES–INDUSTRIES–HISTORY

Cochran, Thomas C. Frontiers of Change: Early Industrialism in America. 175p. 1981. 15.00 (ISBN 0-19-502875-9). Oxford U Pr.

William Marples & Sons Price List of American Tools & Hardware, Nineteen Hundred Nine. 1980. pap. 4.50 (ISBN 0-913602-41-8). K Roberts.

UNITED STATES–JUDICIARY

see Courts

UNITED STATES–LAW

see Law–United States

UNITED STATES–LEARNED INSTITUTIONS AND SOCIETIES

see Learned Institutions and Societies

UNITED STATES–LEGISLATIVE BODIES

see Legislative Bodies

UNITED STATES–MAIL

see Postal Service

UNITED STATES–MILITARY POLICY

Abrahamson, James L. America Arms for a New Century: The Making of a Great Military Power. LC 80-69716. (Illus.). 1981. 17.95 (ISBN 0-02-900190-0). Free Pr.

Bertram, Christoph, ed. Strategic Deterrence in a Changing Environment. LC 80-67841. (Adelphi Library: Vol. 6). 200p. 1981. text ed. 29.50 (ISBN 0-916672-75-1). Allanheld.

Cottrell, Alvin J. & Hanks, Robert J. The Military Utility of the U. S. Facilities in the Philippines, Vol. II. LC 80-83128. (Significant Issues Ser.: No.11). 34p. 1980. 5.95 (ISBN 0-89206-027-1). CSI Studies.

Higham, Robin, ed. Guide to the Sources of U. S. Military History: Supplement. 1981. 37.50 (ISBN 0-208-01750-X, Archon). Shoe String.

The History of the Joint Chiefs of Staff: The Joint Chiefs of Staff & National Policy, 4 vols. Incl. Vol. 1. 1945-1947. Schnabel, James P; Vol. 2. 1947-1949. Condit, Kenneth W; Vol. 3. The Korean War, 2 pts. Schnabel, James F. & Watson, Robert J. Vol. 4, 1950-1952. 49.00. Set. 179.00 (ISBN 0-89453-148-4). M Glazier.

Sarkesian, Sam C., ed. U. S. Policy & Low-Intensity Conflict: Potentials for Military Struggles in the 1980s. 224p. (Orig.). 1981. pap. 9.95 (ISBN 0-87855-851-9). Transaction Bks.

Sobel, Lester A., ed. U. S. Military Dilemma. 200p. 1981. 17.50x (ISBN 0-87196-202-0, Checkmark). Facts on File.

Whisker, James B. The Citizen Soldier & United States Military Policy. 7.50 (ISBN 0-88427-035-1); pap. 4.95 (ISBN 0-88427-036-X). Green Hill.

UNITED STATES–NATIONAL LABOR RELATIONS BOARD

Practice & Procedure Before the National Labor Relations Board. 3rd ed. 219p. 1980. pap. 15.00 (L027B). ALI-ABA.

UNITED STATES–NATIONAL PARK SERVICE

Maxwell, R. A. Geologic & Historic Guide to the State Parks of Texas. (Illus.). 197p. 1973. Repr. of 1970 ed. 3.00 (GB 10). Bur Econ Geology.

UNITED STATES–NATURALIZATION

see Naturalization

UNITED STATES–NAVY–HISTORY

Bauer, K. Jack, ed. The New American State Papers: Naval Affairs, 1949 to 1979, 10 vols. LC 80-53884. 3000p. 1981. Set. lib. bdg. 595.00 (ISBN 0-686-69283-7). Scholarly Res Inc.

Heine, Irwin M. The U. S. Maritime Industry in the National Interest: A Comprehensive History & Statistical Reference. 1981. pap. 11.95 (ISBN 0-87491-518-X). Acropolis.

Pearce, George F. The U S Navy in Pensacola: From Sailing Ships to Naval Aviation, Eighteen Twenty-Five to Nineteen Thirty. LC 80-12167. (Illus.). vii, 207p. 1980. 17.00 (ISBN 0-8130-0665-1). U Presses Fla.

UNITED STATES–NAVY–JUVENILE LITERATURE

Mohn, Peter B. Naval Special Warfare Teams. LC 80-26004. (Illus.). 48p. (gr. 4-8). 1981. PLB 9.25 (ISBN 0-686-69420-1). Childrens.

UNITED STATES–NAVY–OFFICERS

Sobel, Samuel. Intrepid Sailor. LC 80-13026. (Illus.). 1980. 12.95 (ISBN 0-936082-04-6). Cresset Pubs.

UNITED STATES–PATENTS

see Patents

UNITED STATES–POLITICS AND GOVERNMENT

Alexander, Josephine. America Through the Eye of My Needle: Common Sense for the 80's. 192p. 1981. 9.95 (ISBN 0-8037-0194-2). Dial.

American Government. (Wiley Self-Teaching Guides Ser.). 200p. 1981. write for info. (ISBN 0-471-01351-X). Wiley.

Aranson, Peter H. American Government: Strategy & Choice 1980. (Political Science Ser.). (Illus.). 600p. 1981. text ed. 18.95 (ISBN 0-87626-023-7). Winthrop.

Berman, David R. & Bollens, John C. American Government: Ideas & Issues. LC 80-83670. 1981. pap. 6.95 (ISBN 0-913530-22-0). Palisades Pubs.

Burns, James M., et al. Government by the People. 3 pts. 11th ed. Incl. National, State, Local. 800p. text ed. 19.95 (ISBN 0-13-361253-8); Basic. 480p. text ed. 16.95 (ISBN 0-13-361238-4); National. 640p. text ed. 17.95 (ISBN 0-13-361246-5). (Illus.). 1981. P-H.

Clubb, Jerome, et al. Partisan Realignment: Voters, Parties, & Government in American History. LC 80-16474. (Sage Library of Social Research: Vol. 108). 320p. 1980. 18.00 (ISBN 0-8039-1445-8); pap. 8.95 (ISBN 0-8039-1446-6). Sage.

De Tocqueville, Alexis C. Journey to America. rev. ed. Mayer, J. P., ed. Lawrence, George, tr. from Fr. LC 80-22556. xvi, 424p. 1981. Repr. of 1971 ed. lib. bdg. 35.00x (ISBN 0-313-22712-8, TOJA). Greenwood.

Diamond, Martin. The Founding of the Democratic Republic. LC 80-84210. 192p. 1981. pap. text ed. 5.50 (ISBN 0-87581-271-6). Peacock Pubs.

Dolbeare, Kenneth M. & Edelman, Murray J. American Politics: Policies, Power, & Change. 4th ed. 592p. 1981. pap. text ed. 12.95 (ISBN 0-669-03348-0); student guide 5.95 (ISBN 0-669-03957-8); instructor's guide (ISBN 0-669-03701-X). Heath.

Dorsey, John M. American Government: Conscious Self Sovereignty. 1969. 4.95x (ISBN 0-8143-1637-9). Wayne St U Pr.

Evans, James R. America's Choice. 150p. (Orig.). 1981. lib. bdg. 11.95 (ISBN 0-933028-17-2); pap. 6.95 (ISBN 0-933028-16-4). Fisher Inst.

Feldman, Daniel L. Reforming Government: Winning Strategies Against Waste, Corruption, & Mismanagement. LC 80-24963. 225p. 1981. 11.95 (ISBN 0-688-03729-1). Morrow.

Feldman, Elliot J. & Nevitte, Neil. The Future of North America: Canada, the United States, & Quebec Nationalism. 378p. 1979. pap. text ed. 9.50x (ISBN 0-87674-045-X, Pub. by Inst Res Pub Canada). Renouf.

Ford, Gerald R. A Vision for America. (YA) 1981. limited signed ed. 50.00 (ISBN 0-935716-08-4). Lord John.

Gordon, Milton M. & Lambert, Richard D., eds. America As a Multicultural Society. (Annals of the American Academy of Political & Social Science Ser.: No. 454). 250p. 1981. 7.50 (ISBN 0-87761-260-9); pap. 6.00 (ISBN 0-87761-261-7). Am Acad Pol Soc Sci.

Gray, Lee L. How We Chose A President. 5th ed. 1980. 8.95 (ISBN 0-312-39411-X). St Martin.

Halper. Power, Politics & American Democracy. 368p. (Orig.). 1981. pap. write for info. (ISBN 0-8302-7130-9). Goodyear.

Hinckley, Barbara. Outline of American Government: The Continuing Experiment. (Illus.). 288p. 1981. pap. 7.95 (ISBN 0-13-645200-0). P-H.

Kamath, P. M. Executive Privilege Vs. Democratic Accountability: The Special Assistant to the President for National Security Affairs, 1961-1969. 485p. 1980. text ed. 33.75x (ISBN 0-391-02173-7). Humanities.

Kharasch, Robert N. Institutional Imperative. LC 72-95169. 1979. pap. 7.95x (ISBN 0-582-28106-7). Longman.

Kiernan, Vernon. America: The New Imperialism. 306p. 1978. 19.00 (ISBN 0-905762-18-5, Pub. by Zed Pr). Lawrence Hill.

Maidens. Life, Death & the Government Regulating America's Health. 192p. 1981. lib. bdg. 19.95 (ISBN 0-87196-336-1). Facts on File.

Mason, Alpheus T. & Leach, Richard H. In Quest of Freedom: American Political Thought & Practice. LC 80-5749. 432p. 1981. pap. text ed. 12.00 (ISBN 0-8191-1473-1). U Pr of Amer.

Mercer, James L. & Philips, Ronald J., eds. Public Technology: Key to Improved Government Productivity. 451p. 1981. 24.95 (ISBN 0-8144-5546-8). Am Mgmt.

Nicholas, H. G. The Nature of American Politics. 142p. 1980. 12.95 (ISBN 0-19-219121-7). Oxford U Pr.

Nimmo, D. & Combs, J. Subliminal Politics: Myths & Mythmakers in America. 1980. 10.95 (ISBN 0-13-859116-4); pap. 4.95 (ISBN 0-13-859108-3). P-H.

Novak, Michael, et al. Values in an American Government Textbook: Three Appraisals. Lefever, Ernest W., ed. 57p. 1978. pap. 3.00. Ethics & Public Policy.

Pierpoint, Robert C. At the White House: Assignments to Six Presidents. (Illus.). 192p. 1981. 10.95 (ISBN 0-399-12281-8). Putnam.

Press, Charles. American Policy Studies. 200p. 1981. pap. text ed. 7.95 (ISBN 0-471-07866-2). Wiley.

Redenius, Charles. The American Ideal of Equality & Constitutional Change: From Jefferson's Declaration to the Burger Court. (National University Publications, Political Science Ser.). 1981. 17.50 (ISBN 0-8046-9282-3). Kennikat.

Rossum, Ralph A. & McDowell, Gary L., eds. The American Founding: Politics, Statesmanship, & the Constitution. (National University Publications, Political Science Ser.). 1981. 17.50 (ISBN 0-8046-9283-1). Kennikat.

Saffell, David C. The Politics of American National Government. 4th ed. (Illus.). 560p. 1981. pap. text ed. 12.95 (ISBN 0-87626-641-3). Winthrop.

Sharkansky, Ira. Wither the State? Politics & Public Enterprise in Three Countries. 9.95 (ISBN 0-934540-01-2); pap. 7.95 (ISBN 0-934540-00-4). Chatham Hse Pubs.

Strouse, James C., et al, eds. Making Government Work: Essays in Honor of Conley H. Dillon. LC 80-8308. 478p. 1981. lib. bdg. 23.75 (ISBN 0-8191-1306-9); pap. text ed. 15.75 (ISBN 0-8191-1307-7). U Pr of Amer.

Szanton, Peter, ed. Federal Reorganization. 1981. pap. 12.95x (ISBN 0-934540-11-X). Chatham Hse Pubs.

Thompson, James C. & Vidmer, Richard F. Political Administration in the Soviet Union & the United States. 240p. 1981. 22.95 (ISBN 0-89789-009-4). J F Bergin.

U. S. Power in a World Conflict. (Significant Issues Ser.: Vol. II, No. 7). (Illus.). 45p. 1980. pap. 5.00 (ISBN 0-89206-021-2, CSIS015, CSIS). Unipub.

Watson, Richard A. & Fitzgerald, Michael R. Promise & Performance of American Democracy: National Editon. 4th ed. 570p. 1981. text ed. 14.95 (ISBN 0-471-08380-1). Wiley.

--Promise & Performance of American Democracy: State Edition. 4th ed. 650p. 1981. text ed. 16.95 (ISBN 0-471-08381-X). Wiley.

Way, H. Frank. Liberty in the Balance. 5th, rev. ed. (Foundations of American Government & Political Science Ser.). 144p. 1981. pap. text ed. 6.95 (ISBN 0-07-068661-0, C). McGraw.

Woll. Behind the Scenes in American Government. 3rd ed. 1981. pap. text ed. 7.95 (ISBN 0-316-95137-4); tchrs'. manual free. Little.

Yearbook of the United States, Vol. 31. 1303p. 1980. pap. 50.00 (ISBN 0-686-68982-8, UN79/1/1, UN). Unipub.

UNITED STATES–POLITICS AND GOVERNMENT–ADDRESSES, ESSAYS, LECTURES

Berman, Ronald, ed. Solzhenitsyn at Harvard: The Address, Twelve Early Responses, & Six Later Reflections. 160p. 1980. 9.50 (ISBN 0-89633-034-6); pap. 5.00 (ISBN 0-89633-023-0). Ethics & Public Policy.

Bush, George & Crane, Philip. Great Issues 79-80: A Forum on Important Questions Facing the American Public, Vol. 11. 1980. 14.95 (ISBN 0-916624-32-3). TSU Pr.

Churchill, Winston S. & Glubb, John. Great Issues 71: A Forum on Important Questions Facing the American Public. 1972. 5.95. TSU Pr.

Faulk, Odie B. & Von Kuehneli, Erik M. Great Issues 75: A Forum on Important Questions Facing the American Public, Vol. 7. LC 76-26349. (Illus.). 1976. 10.95 (ISBN 0-916624-03-X). TSU Pr.

Kirk, Russell & Chamberlain, John. Great Issues 73: A Forum on Important Questions Facing the American Public, Vol. 5. 1974. 5.95. TSU Pr.

Leach, Douglas E. & Buchanan, Patrick J. Great Issues 78: A Forum on Important Questions Facing the American Public, Vol.10. LC 75-648855. 1979. 13.95 (ISBN 0-916624-28-5). TSU Pr.

McCracken, Paul W. & Izard, Ralph. Great Issues 77: A Forum on Important Questions Facing the American Public, Vol. 9. LC 78-65990. 1978. 12.95 (ISBN 0-916624-26-9). TSU Pr.

Parkinson, C. Northcote & Armstrong, O. K. Great Issues: A Forum on Important Questions Facing the American Public. 1971. 5.95. TSU Pr.

Tate, William & Moorer, Thomas H. Great Issues 74: A Forum on Important Questions Facing the American Public, Vol. 6. 5.95. TSU Pr.

Teller, Edward & Yoder, Paul V. Great Issues 72: Imortant Questions Facing the American Public. 1973. 5.95. TSU Pr.

Woll. American Government: Readings & Cases. 7th ed. 1981. pap. text ed. 8.95 (ISBN 0-316-95143-9); tchrs'. manual free (ISBN 0-316-95144-7). Little.

UNITED STATES–POLITICS AND GOVERNMENT–MISCELLANEA

Burch, Philip H. Elites in American History: The Civil War to the New Deal. 300p. text ed. 20.00x (ISBN 0-8419-0595-9). Holmes & Meier.

UNITED STATES–POLITICS AND GOVERNMENT–COLONIAL PERIOD, ca. 1600-1775

Lockridge, Kenneth A. Settlement & Unsettlement in Early America: The Crisis of Political Legitimacy Before the Revolution. LC 80-25658. (Illus.). 96p. Date not set. price not set (ISBN 0-521-23707-6). Cambridge U Pr.

Steinberg, Samuel. Seven Against Odds: Shapers of Our Democratic Heritage. Date not set. 7.95 (ISBN 0-533-04639-4). Vantage.

UNITED STATES–POLITICS AND GOVERNMENT–1815-1861

Burch, Philip H., Jr. Elites in American History: The Federalist Years to the Civil War, Vol. 1. 320p. 1981. text ed. 20.00x (ISBN 0-8419-0594-0). Holmes & Meier.

Cook, Charles M. The American Codification Movement: A Study of Antebellum Legal Reform. LC 80-662. (Contributions in Legal Studies: No. 14). 272p. 1981. lib. bdg. 35.00 (ISBN 0-313-21314-3, CAC/). Greenwood.

Gunderson, Robert G. Old Gentlemen's Convention: The Washington Peace Conference of 1861. LC 80-24747. (Illus.). xiii, 168p. 1981. Repr. of 1961 ed. lib. bdg. 17.50x (ISBN 0-313-22584-2, GUOG). Greenwood.

UNITED STATES–POLITICS AND GOVERNMENT–20TH CENTURY

Joyce, James E. The Federal Government Is Run by Idiots: Political Commentary. (Illus.). 1980. 3.50 (ISBN 0-932212-19-0). Avery Color.

Weinstein, James. The Corporate Ideal in the Liberal State: 1900-1918. LC 80-22211. xvii, 263p. 1981. Repr. of 1968 ed. lib. bdg. 25.00x (ISBN 0-313-22709-8, WECI). Greenwood.

UNITED STATES–POLITICS AND GOVERNMENT–1919-1933

Silva, Ruth C. Rum, Religion, & Votes: Nineteen Twenty-Eight Re-Examined. LC 80-24997. ix, 76p. 1981. Repr. of 1962 ed. lib. bdg. 22.50x (ISBN 0-313-22768-3, SIRR). Greenwood.

Warren, Harris G. Herbert Hoover & the Great Depression. LC 80-19603. x, 372p. 1980. Repr. of 1970 ed. lib. bdg. 28.75x (ISBN 0-313-22659-8, WAHO). Greenwood.

UNITED STATES–POLITICS AND GOVERNMENT–1933-1945–BIBLIOGRAPHY

Nicholas, H. G., ed. Dispatches from Washington, 1941 to 1945: Weekly Political Reports from the British Embassy. 748p. 1981. 40.00 (ISBN 0-226-58004-0). U of Chicago Pr.

UNITED STATES–POLITICS AND GOVERNMENT–1945-

Rovere, Richard H. The American Establishment & Other Reports, Opinions, & Speculations. LC 80-22247. x, 308p. 1981. Repr. of 1962 ed. lib. bdg. 27.50x (ISBN 0-313-22646-6, ROAE). Greenwood.

UNITED STATES–POLITICS AND GOVERNMENT–1945-1961

Cook, Blanche W. The Declassified Eisenhower: A Divided Legacy. LC 80-699. 360p. 1981. 15.95 (ISBN 0-385-05456-4). Doubleday.

Ewald, William B., Jr. Eisenhower the President: Crucial Days, 1951-1960. LC 80-22929. 420p. 1981. 12.95 (ISBN 0-13-246868-9). P-H.

UNITED STATES–POLITICS AND GOVERNMENT–1961-

Califano, Joseph. Crossfire. 15.95 (ISBN 0-671-25428-6). S&S.

Ferguson, John, et al. The American Federal Government. 14th ed. 592p. 1981. text ed. 17.95 (ISBN 0-07-020527-2, C); instr's manual 4.95 (ISBN 0-07-020529-9). McGraw.

Ferguson, John H. & McHenry, Dean E. The American System of Government. 14th ed. Munson, Eric M., ed. (Illus.). 688p. Date not set. text ed. price not set (ISBN 0-07-020528-0, C); instr's manual 4.95 (ISBN 0-07-020529-9). McGraw.

Hertzog, Ed. Slowly Strangle All Political Rapists: The Story of the Voters' Vendetta. LC 80-83137. 1981. 15.00 (ISBN 0-937894-00-1); pap. 10.00 (ISBN 0-937894-01-X). Life Arts.

Horne, A. D., ed. The Wounded Generation: America After Vietnam. (A Washington Post Bk.). 160p. 1981. 10.95 (ISBN 0-13-969154-5); pap. 5.95 (ISBN 0-13-969147-2). P-H.

Kearns, Graham. Arms for the Poor: President Carter's Polocies on Arms Transfers to the Third World. 136p. (Orig.). 1980. pap. text ed. 10.95 (ISBN 0-908160-57-7). Bks Australia.

McIntyre, Thomas J. & Obert, John C. The Fear Brokers: Peddling the Hate Politics of the New Right. LC 80-70413. 384p. 1981. pap. 7.95 (ISBN 0-8070-3247-6, BP 620). Beacon Pr.

Macmillan, Duncan D. The Problem of the Economic & Political Survival of the United States. (The Major Currents in Contemporary World History Library). (Illus.). 117p. 1981. 37.85 (ISBN 0-930008-80-4). Inst Econ Pol.

Ogden, Daniel M., Jr. & Bone, Hugh A. Washington Politics: Published Under the Auspices of the Citizenship Clearing House. LC 80-25647. (Illus.). vi, 77p. 1981. Repr. of 1960 ed. lib. bdg. 19.75x (ISBN 0-313-22803-5, OGWP). Greenwood.

Papp, Daniel S. Vietnam: The View from Moscow, Peking, Washington. LC 80-20117. (Illus.). 263p. 1981. lib. bdg. 17.95x (ISBN 0-89950-010-2). McFarland & Co.

Pomper, Gerald M. The Election of 1980: Reports & Interpretations. 224p. (Orig.). 1980. 12.95 (ISBN 0-934540-10-1); pap. text ed. 7.95 (ISBN 0-934540-09-8). Chatham Hse Pubs.

President's Commission for a National Agenda for the Eighties. A National Agenda for the Eighties. 1981. pap. 2.95 (ISBN 0-451-62011-9, ME2011, Ment). NAL.

Rice, Joseph B. A Positive Plan for a Revolutionary Change in the Political Structure of the United States. (American Culture Library Bk). (Illus.). 128p. 1981. 28.15 (ISBN 0-89266-290-5). Am Classical Coll Pr.

Szanton, Peter, ed. Federal Reorganization: What Have We Learned? (Chatham House Series on Change in American Politics). 184p. 1981. pap. text ed. 12.95x (ISBN 0-934540-11-X). Chatham Hse Pubs.

UNITED STATES–POPULAR CULTURE
see also United States–Civilization

Anson, Robert S. Gone Crazy & Back Again: The Rise & Fall of the Rolling Stone Generation. LC 80-5448. 384p. 1981. 14.95 (ISBN 0-385-13114-3). Doubleday.

UNITED STATES–POSTAL SERVICE
see Postal Service

UNITED STATES–PRESIDENTS
see Presidents–United States

UNITED STATES–PUBLIC DOCUMENTS
see United States–Government Publications

UNITED STATES–PUBLIC LANDS

Coggins, George C. & Wilkinson, Charles F. Federal Public Land & Resources Law. (University Casebook Ser.). 1018p. 1981. text ed. write for info. (ISBN 0-88277-022-5). Foundation Pr.

UNITED STATES–PUBLICATION BOARD–BIBLIOGRAPHY

Drazan, Joseph G. The Unknown Eric: A Selection of Documents for the General Library. LC 80-25975. 239p. 1981. lib. bdg. 12.50 (ISBN 0-8108-1402-1). Scarecrow.

UNITED STATES–RACE RELATIONS

Barrera, Mario. Race & Class in the Southwest: A Theory of Racial Inequality. LC 78-62970. 261p. 1980. pap. text ed. 5.95 (ISBN 0-268-01601-1). U of Notre Dame Pr.

Edelman, Marian W. Portrait of Inequality: Black & White Children in America. LC 80-68585. 144p. (Orig.). 1980. pap. 5.00 (ISBN 0-938008-00-5). Childrens Defense.

Higham, John. Strangers in the Land: Patterns of American Nativism, 1860 to 1925. LC 80-22204. (Illus.). xiv, 431p. 1981. Repr. of 1963 ed. lib. bdg. 35.50x (ISBN 0-313-22459-5, HISL). Greenwood.

Jenkins, Lee C. Faulkner & Black-White Relations: A Psychoanalytic Approach. LC 80-21937. 288p. 1981. 20.00x (ISBN 0-231-04744-4). Columbia U Pr.

Katz, Irwin. Stigma: A Social Psychological Analysis. LC 80-20765. 180p. 1981. ref. 16.50 (ISBN 0-89859-078-7). L Erlbaum Assocs.

Lawhorne, Clifton O. The Supreme Court & Libel. (New Horizons in Journalism Ser.). 1981. 19.95 (ISBN 0-8093-0998-X). S Ill U Pr.

Lumpkin, Katharine D. The Making of a Southerner. LC 80-24622. (Brown Thrasher Ser.). 264p. 1981. pap. 6.95 (ISBN 0-8203-0545-6). U of Ga Pr.

Ratcliffe, Peter. Racism & Reaction: A Profile of Handsworth. (International Library of Sociology). 280p. 1981. price not set (ISBN 0-7100-0696-9). Routledge & Kegan.

Rose, Peter I. They & We: Racial & Ethnic Relations in the United States. 252p. 1981. pap. text ed. 7.95 (ISBN 0-394-32402-1). Random.

Swan, L. Alex. Survival & Progress: The Afro-American Experience. LC 80-1197. (Contributions in Afro-American & African Studies: No. 58). (Illus.). 280p. 1981. lib. bdg. 25.00 (ISBN 0-313-22480-3, SSU). Greenwood.

Woods, Randall B. A Black Odyssey: John Lewis Waller & the Promise of American Life, 1878-1900. LC 80-18965. (Illus.). 272p. 1981. 20.00x (ISBN 0-7006-0207-0). Regents Pr KS.

UNITED STATES–RELATIONS (GENERAL) WITH FOREIGN COUNTRIES

Davis, Allan F., ed. For Better or Worse: The American Influence in the World. LC 80-1048. (Contributions in American Studies Ser.: No. 51). 240p. 1981. lib. bdg. 29.95 (ISBN 0-313-22342-4, DBO/). Greenwood.

Nixon, Richard. The Real War. 400p. 1981. pap. 3.50 (ISBN 0-446-96136-1). Warner Bks.

UNITED STATES–RELATIONS (GENERAL) WITH JAPAN

The Occupation of Japan: Economic Policy & Reform. 382p. pap. 6.00. MacArthur Memorial.

Redford, Lawrence H., ed. The Occupation of Japan: Impact of Legal Refor, 212p. pap. 5.00. MacArthur Memorial.

UNITED STATES–RELIGION

Jones, Peter D. & Holli, Melvin G., eds. Ethnic Chicago. 336p. (Orig.). 1981. pap. 12.95 (ISBN 0-8028-1821-8). Eerdmans.

Kelly, George A. The Battle for the American Church. LC 80-22348. 528p. 1981. pap. 8.95 (ISBN 0-385-17433-0, Im). Doubleday.

UNITED STATES–REVENUE
see Taxation

UNITED STATES–RURAL CONDITIONS

Bryan, Frank M. Politics in Rural America: People, Parties, & Policy. (Special Study Ser.). 320p. (Orig.). lib. bdg. 26.50x (ISBN 0-89158-561-3); pap. text ed. 10.00x (ISBN 0-89158-984-8). Westview.

Carlson & Lassey. Rural Society & Environment in America. (Agricultural Science Ser.). (Illus.). 448p. 1981. text ed. 15.95x (ISBN 0-07-009959-6, C). McGraw.

UNITED STATES–SECRET SERVICE
see Secret Service

UNITED STATES–SHIPPING
see Shipping–United States

UNITED STATES–SOCIAL CONDITIONS

Bernardo, Stephanie. The Ethnic Almanac. LC 78-14694. (Illus.). 576p. 1981. 19.95 (ISBN 0-385-14143-2). Doubleday.

--The Ethnic Almanac. LC 80-14694. (Illus.). 576p. 1981. pap. 10.95 (ISBN 0-385-14144-0, Dolp). Doubleday.

Bridenbaugh, Carl. Early Americans. (Illus.). 256p. 1981. 19.95 (ISBN 0-19-502788-4). Oxford U Pr.

Capp, Al & Wallace, George. Great Issues: A Forum on Important Questions Facing the American Public. 1970. 5.95. Troy State Univ.

Kneeter, Robert. America's Gauntlet: Manuscript 1 of the Humanist Papers. pap. 5.00 (ISBN 0-938722-01-8). Word Ent.
--The Humanist Papers, 4 vols, Vols. 1 & 2. pap. write for info. (ISBN 0-938722-00-X). Word Ent.
Kolko, Gabriel. Wealth & Power in America: An Analysis of Social Class & Income Distribution. LC 62-11584. 178p. 1962. pap. text ed. 4.95x (ISBN 0-03-037491-X). Praeger.
Montagu, Ashley & Rowe, David N. Great Issues 76: A Forum on Important Questions Facing the American Public, Vol. 8. LC 77-85525. 11.95 (ISBN 0-916624-11-0). Troy State Univ.
Muller, Fred. America's Coming Nightmare Inflation, Economic Collapse & Crime Revolution. 120p. 1980. 10.00 (ISBN 0-686-68648-9). State Ptg.
Ringer. Restoring the American Dream. 1981. pap. 2.95 (ISBN 0-449-24314-1). Fawcett.
Sweet, David G. & Nash, Gary B., eds. Struggle & Survival in Colonial America. 1981. 25.00 (ISBN 0-520-04110-0). U of Cal Pr.
Uncommon Sense: Manuscript 2 of the Humanist Papers. pap. 5.00 (ISBN 0-938722-02-6). Word Ent.

UNITED STATES–SOCIAL CONDITIONS–1960-

McNeil, Don. Moving Through Here. 252p. 10.95 (ISBN 0-934558-08-6); pap. 5.95 (ISBN 0-934558-09-4). Entwhistle Bks.
Mead, Margaret & Metraux, Rhoda. Aspects of the Present. 288p. 1981. pap. 6.95. Morrow.

UNITED STATES–SOCIAL LIFE AND CUSTOMS

American Dissent from Thomas Jefferson to Cesar Chavez: The Rhetoric of Reform & Revolution. LC 80-12577. 180p. 1980. pap. text ed. 6.50 (ISBN 0-89874-083-5). Krieger.
Bly, Carol. Letters from the Country. LC 80-8194. 192p. 1981. 9.95 (ISBN 0-06-010357-4, HarpT). Har-Row.
Campbell, Leslie K. Architects of Destruction. 282p. (Orig.). 1980. pap. 4.95 (ISBN 0-9605164-4-1). Self.
Gordon, Milton M. & Lambert, Richard D., eds. America As a Multicultural Society. (Annals of the American Academy of Political & Social Science Ser.: No. 454). 250p. 1981. 7.50 (ISBN 0-87761-260-9); pap. 6.00 (ISBN 0-87761-261-7). Am Acad Pol Soc Sci.
Harrison, Barbara G. Off Center. LC 81-80030. 320p. 1981. pap. 2.95 (ISBN 0-87216-870-0). Playboy Pbks.
Jacobs, Norman. Fab Fifties. 1980. pap. 2.25. O'Quinn Studio.
Kneeter, Robert. America's Gauntlet: Manuscript 1 of the Humanist Papers. pap. 5.00 (ISBN 0-938722-01-8). Word Ent.
--The Humanist Papers, 4 vols, Vols. 1 & 2. pap. write for info. (ISBN 0-938722-00-X). Word Ent.
McClymer, John. Thinking About the American People. 98p. 4.50 (ISBN 0-686-68744-2). Revisionary.
Martineau, Harriet. Society in America. Lipset, Seymour M., ed. (Socialscience Classics). 357p. 1981. 18.95 (ISBN 0-87855-420-3); pap. 7.95 (ISBN 0-87855-853-5). Transaction Bks.
Morris, Wright. God's Country & My People. LC 80-23155. (Illus.). 176p. 1981. pap. 15.95 (ISBN 0-8032-3067-2, BB 752, Bison). U of Nebr Pr.
Rothstein, Arthur. The American West in the Thirties: One Hundred Twenty-Two Photographs by Arthur Rothstein. (Illus.). 128p. (Orig.). 1981. pap. price not set (ISBN 0-486-24106-8). Dover.
Ryan, Mary P. Cradle of the Middle Class: The Family in Oneida County, New York, 1780-1865. LC 80-18460. (Interdisciplinary Perspectives on Modern History Ser.). (Illus.). 336p. Date not set. price not set (ISBN 0-521-23200-7). Cambridge U Pr.
Sandler, Martin W. This Was America. 1980. 19.95 (ISBN 0-316-77022-1). Little.
Uncommon Sense: Manuscript 2 of the Humanist Papers. pap. 5.00 (ISBN 0-938722-02-6). Word Ent.
Veroff, Joseph, et al. The Inner American: Life, Work, & Mental Health from 1957-1976. LC 80-68187. 492p. 1981. 30.00 (ISBN 0-465-03293-1). Basic.
Walker, Alice. You Can't Keep a Good Woman Down: Stories by Alice Walker. LC 80-8761. 180p. 1981. 10.95 (ISBN 0-15-199754-3). HarBraceJ.
Willis, Ellen. Beginning to See the Light: Pieces of a Decade. LC 80-22890. 320p. 1981. 12.95 (ISBN 0-394-51137-9). Knopf.
Wright, Norman E. Preserving Your American Heritage: A Guide to Family & Local History. rev. ed. (Illus.). 1981. pap. text ed. 12.95 (ISBN 0-8425-1863-0). Brigham.

UNITED STATES–SOCIAL LIFE AND CUSTOMS–BIBLIOGRAPHY

Jones, Peter D. & Holli, Melvin G., eds. Ethnic Chicago. 336p. (Orig.). 1981. pap. 12.95 (ISBN 0-8028-1821-8). Eerdmans.

UNITED STATES–SOCIAL LIFE AND CUSTOMS–COLONIAL PERIOD, ca. 1600-1775

Sweet, David G. & Nash, Gary B., eds. Struggle & Survival in Colonial America. 1981. 25.00 (ISBN 0-520-04110-0). U of Cal Pr.

UNITED STATES–SOCIAL POLICY

Schwartz-Nobel, Loretta. Starving in the Shadow of Plenty. 256p. 1981. 12.95 (ISBN 0-399-12522-1). Putnam.

UNITED STATES–SUPREME COURT

Danelski, David J. A Supreme Court Justice Is Appointed. LC 80-21229. (Studies in Political Science). x, 242p. 1980. Repr. of 1964 ed. lib. bdg. 23.50x (ISBN 0-313-22652-0, DASJ). Greenwood.
Dornan, Robert K. & Vedlik, Csaba. Judicial Supremacy: The Supreme Court on Trial. LC 80-82300. (The Nordland Series in Contemporary American Social Problems). 145p. (Orig.). 1980. pap. 5.95 (ISBN 0-913124-38-9). Nordland Pub.
Fein, Bruce E. Significant Decisions of the Supreme Court: 1978-1979 Term. 1980. pap. 6.25 (ISBN 0-8447-3387-3). Am Enterprise.
Lewis. Criminal Procedure: The Supreme Court's View - Cases. (Criminal Justice Ser.). 131p. 1980. pap. text ed. write for info. (ISBN 0-8299-0321-6); 1980 supplement avail. West Pub.
McGehee, Lucius P. Due Process of Law Under the Federal Constitution. (Studies in Constitutional Law). x, 452p. 1981. Repr. of 1906 ed. lib. bdg. 37.50x (ISBN 0-8377-0837-0). Rothman.
Supreme Court of the United States & Kurland, Philip B. Landmark Briefs & Arguments of the Supreme Court of the United States: Constitutional Law, 80 vols. 1977. Set. 4640.00 (ISBN 0-89093-000-7). U Pubns Amer.
Woodward, Bob & Armstrong, Scott. The Brethren. 1980. pap. 3.50 (ISBN 0-380-52183-0, 52183). Avon.

UNITED STATES–TAXATION

see Taxation

UNITED STATES–TRAVEL

see United States–Description and Travel

UNITED STATES–VICE-PRESIDENTS

see Vice-Presidents–United States

UNITY OF SCIENCE MOVEMENT

see Logical Positivism

UNIVERSAL HISTORY

see World History

UNIVERSAL MILITARY TRAINING

see Military Service, Compulsory

UNIVERSE

see Cosmogony; Cosmology

UNIVERSITIES AND COLLEGES

see also Degrees, Academic; Education, Higher; Junior Colleges; Libraries, University and College; Medical Colleges; Students
also headings beginning with the word College, and names of universities and colleges, e.g. Yale University; California, University of

Howie-Willis, Ian. A Thousand Graduates: Conflict in University Development in Papua New Guinea, 1961-1976. Fisk, E. K., ed. (Pacific Research Series Monograph: No. 3). 362p. 1980. pap. text ed. 12.95 (ISBN 0-909150-01-X, 0014). Bks Australia.
Nash, Al. Ruskin College: A Challenge to Adult & Labor Education. 1981. pap. price not set (ISBN 0-87546-084-4). NY Sch Indus Rel.
Peterson's Guides Editors, compiled by. The Competitive Colleges: Who Are They? 250p. 1981. pap. 6.95 (ISBN 0-87866-127-1). Petersons Guid.
Raichle, Donald R. From a Normal Beginning: The Origins of Kean College of New Jersey. (Illus.). 432p. 1980. 20.00 (ISBN 0-8386-4500-3). Fairleigh Dickinson.
Smith, Charles B. Troy State University: Nineteen Thirty-Seven to Nineteen Seventy, Troy Alabama. (Illus.). 1972. pap. 3.50 (ISBN 0-916624-34-X). TSU Pr.

UNIVERSITIES AND COLLEGES–ADMINISTRATION

see also Personnel Service in Education

Fordham, Adrian & Ainley, John. Evolution of Staff Development in Technical & Further Education: A Proposed Methodology. (Australian Council for Educational Research Monograph: No. 7). 266p. 1980. pap. text ed. 22.50 (ISBN 0-85563-207-0). Verry.
Hopkins, David S. & Massy, William F. Planning Models for Colleges & Universities. LC 78-66176. (Illus.). 576p. 1981. 28.50x (ISBN 0-8047-1023-6). Stanford U Pr.
Powell, John W. Campus Security & Law Enforcement. 250p. 1981. text ed. 19.95 (ISBN 0-409-95028-9). Butterworth.
Richardson, Richard C., Jr. & Leslie, Larry L. The Impossible Dream? Financing Community College's Evolving Mission. (Horizon Issues Monograph Ser.). 52p. (Orig.). 1980. pap. 5.00 (ISBN 0-87117-105-8). Am Assn Comm Jr Coll.

UNIVERSITIES AND COLLEGES–ADMISSION

Association of Commonwealth Universities. Compendium of University Entrance Requirements for First Degree Courses in the United Kingdom, 1981-82. 18th ed. LC 74-648109. 347p. (Orig.). 1980. pap. 12.50x (ISBN 0-85143-065-1). Intl Pubns Serv.
Blaker, Charles W. The College Matchmaker. LC 80-67604. (Illus.). 56p. (Orig.). (gr. 11-12). 1980. pap. text ed. 3.25 (ISBN 0-9604614-0-X). Rekalb Pr.
Corderman, Susan & McGarry, Jane, eds. College Admissions Data Service Handbook, 1980-81: 1980-81 Edition. rev. ed. Incl. Northeast Regional. 628p. pap. text ed. 30.00x (ISBN 0-933510-07-1); Southeast Regional. 602p. pap. text ed. 30.00x (ISBN 0-933510-08-X); Mid-West Regional. 520p. pap. text ed. 25.00x (ISBN 0-933510-09-8); West Regional. 502p. pap. text ed. 25.00x (ISBN 0-933510-10-1). 1980. Orchard Hse MA.
Flood, Robert. Graduation: A New Start. 128p. 1981. pap. 5.95. Moody.
Hayden, Thomas C. Handbook for College Admissions. LC 80-66009. 1981. 12.95 (ISBN 0-689-11095-2); pap. 6.95 (ISBN 0-686-69529-1). Atheneum.
Leana, Frank C. Getting into College. 1980. 11.95 (ISBN 0-8090-4921-X); pap. 5.95 (ISBN 0-8090-1393-2). Hill & Wang.
Proia, Nicholas C. Barron's Handbook of College Transfer Information. (Barron's Educational Ser.). 304p. 1980. pap. 5.95 (ISBN 0-8120-2166-5). Barron.
Undergraduate Admissions: The Realities of Institutional Policies, Practices, & Procedures. LC 80-70480. (Illus.). 72p. (Orig.). 1980. pap. 8.50 (ISBN 0-87447-136-2). College Bd.

UNIVERSITIES AND COLLEGES–ALUMNI

see also College Graduates

Alberger, Patricia L., ed. Building Your Alumni Program. 100p. (Orig.). 1980. pap. 14.50 (ISBN 0-89964-165-2). CASE.

UNIVERSITIES AND COLLEGES–ATHLETICS

see College Sports

UNIVERSITIES AND COLLEGES–CURRICULA

see also Independent Study

Peterson's Guides Editors, ed. Who Offers Part-Time Degree Programs? A National Survey of Postsecondary Institutions Offering Daytime, Evening, Weekend, Summer & External Degree Programs-1981 Edition. 250p. 1981. pap. 6.00 (ISBN 0-87866-121-2). Petersons Guid.
Tonkin, Humphrey. The World in the Curriculum: Curricular Strategies for the 21st Century. LC 80-69765. 200p. (Orig.). 1980. pap. 6.95 (ISBN 0-915390-28-0). Change Mag.

UNIVERSITIES AND COLLEGES–DIRECTORIES

American Association of College for Teacher Education. AACTE Directory 1980. 118p. (Orig.). 1980. pap. text ed. 6.00 (ISBN 0-89333-020-5). AACTE.
Barron's Guide to Graduate Schools. Incl. Vol. 2. Natural Sciences, Health Agriculture (ISBN 0-8120-0581-3); Vol. 3. English Communications, Foreign Languages (ISBN 0-8120-0580-5); Vol. 4. Math, Physical Sciences, Computer Science (ISBN 0-8120-0582-1); Vol. 5. Education (ISBN 0-8120-0583-X); Vol. 6. Engineering (ISBN 0-8120-0584-8). Date not set. pap. price not set. Barron.
Brawner, Julie R., et al. From the Kudzu to the Ivy: How to Find Your College: a Southerner's Guide to Northeastern Colleges. 256p. (Orig.). (YA) (gr. 11-12). 1980. pap. 5.95. Kudzu-Ivy.
College Division of Barron's Educational Ser., Inc. Barron's Compact Guide to Colleges. 2nd ed. LC 80-26124. (Illus.). 352p. (gr. 11-12). 1980. pap. 2.75 (ISBN 0-8120-2288-2). Barron.
Schwartz, Lester J. Choosing the Right College. 128p. Date not set. pap. 4.95 (ISBN 0-553-01276-2). Bantam.
The American College Testing Program. College Planning - Search Book. 6th ed. LC 75-28517. (Illus., Orig.). (gr. 9-12). pap. text ed. 6.00 (ISBN 0-937734-00-4). Am Coll Testing.
Welch, June R. The Colleges of Texas. (Illus.). 230p. 1981. 17.95 (ISBN 0-912854-11-1). GLA Pr.

UNIVERSITIES AND COLLEGES–ENTRANCE REQUIREMENTS

see Universities and Colleges–Admission

UNIVERSITIES AND COLLEGES–EXAMINATIONS

Boyajian, Lee G. The Comprehensive Verbal Graduate Record Exam Study Guide. 1981. 6.95 (ISBN 0-533-04508-8). Vantage.
Rich, Dale. How You Can Get Straight A's in College by Beating the System. 123p. (Orig.). 1981. 9.95 (ISBN 0-89896-099-1). Larksdale.

UNIVERSITIES AND COLLEGES–FACULTY

Bergquist, William H. & Phillips, Steven R. Handbook for Faculty Development, Vol. 3. Quehl, Gary H. & Bernard, Jean B., eds. LC 80-69254. 1981. pap. 15.00 (ISBN 0-937012-11-4). Coun Advance Small Colleges.
Hopkins, David S. & Massy, William F. Planning Models for Colleges & Universities. LC 78-66176. (Illus.). 576p. 1981. 28.50x (ISBN 0-8047-1023-6). Stanford U Pr.

UNIVERSITIES AND COLLEGES–FINANCE

see also College Costs; Federal Aid to Higher Education

Hopkins, David S. & Massy, William F. Planning Models for Colleges & Universities. LC 78-66176. (Illus.). 576p. 1981. 28.50x (ISBN 0-8047-1023-6). Stanford U Pr.
Peterson's Guides Editors, compiled by. After Scholarships, What: Sixteen Ways to Reduce Your College Costs. 400p. 1981. pap. 8.00 (ISBN 0-87866-129-8). Petersons Guid.
Richardson, Richard C., Jr. & Leslie, Larry L. The Impossible Dream? Financing Community College's Evolving Mission. (Horizon Issues Monograph Ser.). 52p. (Orig.). 1980. pap. 5.00 (ISBN 0-87117-105-8). Am Assn Comm Jr Coll.

UNIVERSITIES AND COLLEGES–GRADUATE WORK

Barron's Guide to Graduate Schools. Incl. Vol. 2. Natural Sciences, Health Agriculture (ISBN 0-8120-0581-3); Vol. 3. English Communications, Foreign Languages (ISBN 0-8120-0580-5); Vol. 4. Math, Physical Sciences, Computer Science (ISBN 0-8120-0582-1); Vol. 5. Education (ISBN 0-8120-0583-X); Vol. 6. Engineering (ISBN 0-8120-0584-8). Date not set. pap. price not set. Barron.
Careers Research & Advisory Centre, ed. Graduate Studies: The Guide to Postgraduate Study in the UK, 1980 to 1981. 7th ed. 1191p. 1980. 135.00x (ISBN 0-86021-342-0). Intl Pubns Serv.

UNIVERSITIES AND COLLEGES–HISTORY

Caraman, Philip. The University of the Nations: The Story of the Geogorian University. (Illus.). 160p. (Orig.). 1981. pap. 6.95 (ISBN 0-8091-2355-X). Paulist Pr.
Cohen, Stan B. & Miller, Don C. The University of Montana: A Pictorial History. LC 80-53616. (Illus.). 96p. 1980. pap. 5.95 (ISBN 0-933126-12-3). Pictorial Hist.
Cooper, Russell M. & Fisher, Margaret B. The Vision of a Contemporary University: A Case Study of Expansion & Development in American Higher Education, 1950-75. LC 80-29022. (Illus.). iv, 380p. 1981. 12.95 (ISBN 0-8130-0702-X). U Presses Fla.
Langill, Ellen. Carroll College, the First Century, 1846-1946. LC 79-54879. (Illus.). 1980. text ed. 20.95 (ISBN 0-916120-06-6). Carroll Coll.
Meritt, Lucy S. History of the American School of Classical Studies at Athens, Nineteen Thirty-Nine to Nineteen Eighty. 1981. price not set (ISBN 0-87661-942-1). Am Sch Athens.
Raichle, Donald R. From a Normal Beginning: The Origins of Kean College of New Jersey. (Illus.). 432p. 1980. 20.00 (ISBN 0-8386-4500-3). Fairleigh Dickinson.

UNIVERSITIES AND COLLEGES–LAW

see Educational Law and Legislation

UNIVERSITIES AND COLLEGES–SELECTION

see College, Choice Of

UNIVERSITIES AND COLLEGES–SPORTS

see College Sports

UNIVERSITIES AND COLLEGES–STUDENTS

see College Students

UNIVERSITIES AND COLLEGES–CANADA

Johnston, Charles M. McMaster University, Vol. 2: The Early Years in Hamilton, 1930-1957. 329p. 1981. 25.00x (ISBN 0-8020-3372-5). U of Toronto Pr.

UNIVERSITIES AND COLLEGES–GREAT BRITAIN

Brawner, Julie R., et al. From the Kudzu to the Ivy: How to Find Your College: a Southerner's Guide to Northeastern Colleges. 256p. (Orig.). (YA) (gr. 11-12). 1980. pap. 5.95. Kudzu-Ivy.
Chaloner, W. H. The Movement for the Extension of Owens College, Manchester, Eighteen Sixty-Three to Seventy-Three. 136p. 1973. 9.00x (ISBN 0-7190-0552-3, Pub by Manchester U Pr England). State Mutual Bk.

UNIVERSITIES AND COLLEGES–LATIN AMERICA

New Trends & New Responsibilities for Universities in Latin America. 96p. 1980. pap. 8.50 (ISBN 92-3-101830-2, U1040, UNESCO). Unipub.

UNIVERSITY DEGREES

see Degrees, Academic

UNIVERSITY GRADUATES

see College Graduates

UNIVERSITY LIBRARIES

see Libraries, University and College

UNIVERSITY OF IOWA

see Iowa, University Of

UNIVERSITY OF OKLAHOMA

see Oklahoma, University Of

UNIVERSITY OF UTAH

see Utah, University Of

UNIVERSITY PRESIDENTS

see Universities and Colleges–Administration

UNIVERSITY RADIO STATIONS

see Radio Stations

UNIVERSITY READERS

see College Readers

UNIVERSITY STUDENTS

see College Students

UNMARRIED MOTHERS

Roberts, Robert W., ed. The Unwed Mother. LC 80-20554. (Readers in Social Problems). viii, 270p. 1980. Repr. of 1966 ed. lib. bdg. 25.00x (ISBN 0-313-22677-6, ROUM). Greenwood.

UNMARRIED PEOPLE

see Single People

UNMARRIED WOMEN

see Single Women

UPANISHADS

Deussen, Paul. Sixty Upanishads, 2 vols. Bedekar, V. M. & Palsule, G. B., trs. 1030p. 1980. text ed. 45.00x (ISBN 0-8426-1645-4). Verry.

UPDIKE, JOHN

Detweiler, Robert, ed. John Updike. LC 74-187611. (Twayne's U. S. Authors Ser.). 183p. 1972. pap. text ed. 4.95 (ISBN 0-672-61506-1). Bobbs.

UPHOLSTERY

see also Furniture; Interior Decoration

Zimmernman, Fred W. Upholstering Methods. LC 80-25308. (Illus.). 196p. 1981. text ed. 12.00 (ISBN 0-87006-313-8). Goodheart.

URALIAN LANGUAGES
see Finno-Ugrian Languages

URANIUM
see also Nuclear Fuels

Annual Uranium Seminar, 3rd. Proceedings. LC 79-48044. (Illus.). 177p. 1980. pap. 15.00x (ISBN 0-89520-260-3). Soc Mining Eng.

Bickel, Lennard. The Deadly Element: The Story of Uranium. LC 78-66243. (Illus.). 320p. 1980. pap. 7.95 (ISBN 0-8128-6089-6). Stein & Day.

Brawner, Charles O., ed. First International Conference on Uranium Mine Waste Disposal. LC 80-69552. (Illus.). 626p. 1980. 22.00x (ISBN 0-89520-279-4). Soc Mining Eng.

Radetzki, Marian. Uranium: Economic & Political Instability in a Strategic Commodity Market. 1981. 30.00 (ISBN 0-312-83424-1). St Martin.

Schlitt, W. J. & Shock, D. A., eds. In Situ Uranium Mining & Ground Water Restoration. LC 79-52217. (Illus.). 137p. 1979. pap. 15.00x (ISBN 0-89520-267-0). Soc Mining Eng.

Uranium Evaluation & Mining Techniques. 550p. 1981. pap. 69.50 (ISBN 92-0-040280-1, ISP 524, IAEA). Unipub.

Uranium Guidebook for Wyoming. 1976. xerox copy 40.00. Minobras.

Uranium in the Pine Creek Geosyncline: Proceedings. (Illus.). 759p. 1980. pap. 93.75 (ISBN 92-0-140080-2, ISP-555, IAEA). Unipub.

Warnecke, Steven J. Uranium, Nonproliferation & Energy Security. (Atlantic Papers Ser.: No. 37). 121p. 1980. write for info. 0.00 (ISBN 0-916672-77-8). Allanheld.

URANIUM ORES

Uranium Deposits of Arizona, California & Nevada. 1978. 40.30. Minobras.

Uranium Deposits of the Northern U. S. Region. 1977. 37.10. Minobras.

Uranium Resources of the Central & Southern Rockies. 1979. 33.80. Minobras.

Uranium Seminar, Fourth. Proceedings. LC 80-70454. (Uranium Seminars Ser.). 1980. pap. 20.00x (ISBN 0-89520-280-8). Soc Mining Eng.

URBAN AREAS
see Cities and Towns; Metropolitan Areas

URBAN DESIGN
see City Planning

URBAN DEVELOPMENT
see City Planning

URBAN ECONOMICS

Bryce, Herrington J., ed. Cities & Firms. LC 80-8367. (The Urban Roundtable Ser.). 272p. 1980. 18.95x (ISBN 0-669-04042-8). Lexington Bks.

Neenan. Urban Public Economics. 1981. text ed. write for info. Duxbury Pr.

Phillips, E. Barbara & LeGates, Richard T. City Lights: An Introduction to Urban Studies. (Illus.). 608p. 1981. pap. text ed. 14.95x (ISBN 0-19-502797-3). Oxford U Pr.

Richardson. Urban Economics. 1978. 20.95 (ISBN 0-275-24430-X). Dryden Pr.

URBAN EDUCATION
see Education, Urban

URBAN PLANNING
see City Planning

URBAN POLICY
see City Planning

URBAN RENEWAL
see also City Planning; Community Organizations

Black, J. Thomas & Hoben, James E., eds. Urban Land Markets: Price Indices, Supply Measures, & Public Policy Effects. LC 80-53134. (ULI Research Report: No. 30). (Illus.). 238p. 1980. pap. 14.75 (ISBN 0-87420-593-X). Urban Land.

Butler, Stuart. Enterprise Zones. (Illus.). 192p. 1981. text ed. 12.50 (ISBN 0-87663-350-5). Universe.

Koenigsberger, O. H., et al, eds. Work of Charles Abrams: Housing & Urban Renewal in the U. S. A. & the Third World. (Illus.). 264p. 1980. 55.00 (ISBN 0-08-026111-6). Pergamon.

Muchnick, David M. Urban Renewal in Liverpool. 120p. 1970. pap. text ed. 6.25x (Pub. by Bedford England). Renouf.

Newman, Oscar. Community of Interest. (Illus.). 368p. 1981. pap. 8.95 (ISBN 0-385-11124-X, Anch). Doubleday.

Ramati, Racquel & Urban Design Group of the Department of City Planning, New York. How to Save Your Own Street. LC 78-14709. (Illus.). 176p. 1981. pap. 19.95 (ISBN 0-385-14814-3, Dolp). Doubleday.

White, Michael J. Urban Renewal & the Changing Residential Structure of the City. (Illus.). 225p. (Orig.). 1980. pap. text ed. write for info. (ISBN 0-89836-029-3). Comm & Family.

URBAN RENEWAL–LAW AND LEGISLATION
see City Planning and Redevelopment Law

URBAN SOCIOLOGY
see Sociology, Urban

Beshers, James M. Urban Social Structure. LC 80-27972. vii, 207p. 1981. Repr. of 1962 ed. lib. bdg. 19.75x (ISBN 0-313-22714-4, BEUR). Greenwood.

URBAN TRAFFIC
see Traffic Engineering

URBAN TRANSIT
see Local Transit

URBANISM
see Cities and Towns

URBANIZATION
see also Rural-Urban Migration

Golden, Hilda. Urbanization & Cities: A Historical & Comparitive Perspective on Our Urbanizing World. 384p. 1981. text ed. 18.95 (ISBN 0-669-03175-5). Heath.

O'Connor, A. M. Urbanization in Tropical Africa, Nineteen Sixty to Nineteen Seventy-Nine: An Annotated Bibliography. (Reference Bks.). 1981. lib. bdg. 48.00 (ISBN 0-8161-8262-0). G K Hall.

Palen, J. John. The Urban World. 2nd ed. Munson, Eric M., ed. 480p. 1981. text ed. 17.95 (ISBN 0-07-048107-5, C). McGraw.

Peil, Margaret. Cities & Suburbs: Urban Life in West Africa. LC 80-26440. (New Library of African Affairs). 330p. 1981. text ed. 24.00x (ISBN 0-8419-0685-8). Holmes & Meier.

Scott, A. J. The Urban Land Nexus & the State. 256p. 1980. 24.00 (ISBN 0-85086-079-2, 6390). Methuen Inc.

URDU LANGUAGE
see also Hindi Language

Becker, Donald. Reverse Dictionary of Urdu. 1980. 38.00x (ISBN 0-8364-0656-7, Pub. by Manohaar India). South Asia Bks.

UREDINALES
see Rusts (Fungi)

URETHANES

Polyurethanes: Looking Ahead to the Eighties. LC 80-65994. 133p. 1980. 25.00 (ISBN 0-87762-284-1). Technomic.

URINARY BLADDER
see Bladder

URINARY INCONTINENCE
see Urine–Incontinence

URINARY ORGANS–DISEASES
see also Urology;
also names of individual organs with or without the subdivision Diseases; names of particular diseases, e.g. Bright's Disease

Migone, L., ed. Urinary Proteins. (Contributions to Nephrology Ser.: Vol. 26). (Illus.). vi, 150p. 1981. pap. 54.00 (ISBN 3-8055-1848-X). S Karger.

Performing Urologic Procedures. (Nursing Photobook Ser.). (Illus.). 160p. 1981. text ed. 12.95 (ISBN 0-916730-32-8). Intermed Comm.

Stamey, Thomas A. Pathogenesis & Treatment of Urinary Tract Infections. (Illus.). 624p. 1980. 54.00 (ISBN 0-683-07909-3). Williams & Wilkins.

URINE

Armstrong, John W. The Water of Life. 136p. 1971. pap. 4.75x (ISBN 0-8464-1060-5). Beekman Pubs.

URINE–INCONTINENCE
see also Enuresis

Mandelstam, Dorothy, ed. Incontinence & Its Management. (Illus.). 233p. 1980. bds. 25.00x (ISBN 0-7099-0088-0, Pub. by Croom Helm Ltd England). Biblio Dist.

Meadow. Help for Bedwetting. Date not set. pap. text ed. 2.75 (ISBN 0-443-02236-4). Churchill.

Stanton, S. L. & Tanagho, E. A., eds. Surgery of Female Incontinence. (Illus.). 203p. 1980. 58.00 (ISBN 0-387-10155-1). Springer-Verlag.

UROGENITAL ORGANS
see Genito-Urinary Organs

UROLOGY
see also Genito-Urinary Organs; Pediatric Urology

Resnick, Martin I. Current Studies in Urology. (Illus.). 190p. 1981. write for info. (7216-1). Williams & Wilkins.

UROLOGY, OPERATIVE
see Genito-Urinary Organs–Surgery

USAGES
see Etiquette

USE OF LAND
see Land Use

USED AIRCRAFT

Aviation Consumer. The Aviation Consumer Used Aircraft Guide. Weeghman, Richard, ed. (McGraw-Hill Series in Aviation). (Illus.). 224p. 1981. 18.95 (ISBN 0-07-002543-6). McGraw.

USED CAR TRADE

Edmonston, Phil. The Used Car Guide. (Illus.). 254p. 1981. pap. 8.95 (ISBN 0-8253-0051-7). Beaufort Bks NY.

Green, Michael L., ed. Used Car Prices. rev. ed. (Buyer's Guide Ser.). 96p. (Orig.). Date not set. pap. 2.50 (ISBN 0-89552-065-6). DMR Pubns.

--Used Truck & Van Prices. rev. ed. (Buyer's Guide Ser.). 96p. (Orig.). Date not set. pap. 2.25 (ISBN 0-89552-066-4). DMR Pubns.

USEFUL ARTS
see Industrial Arts; Technology

USES, CHARITABLE
see Charitable Uses, Trusts and Foundations

USURY
see Interest and Usury

UTAH–DESCRIPTION AND TRAVEL

Welsh, Stan. Utah Two. (Illus.). 128p. 1981. 27.50 (ISBN 0-912856-65-3). Graphic Arts Ctr.

UTAH–HISTORY

Long, E. B. The Saints & the Union: Utah Territory During the Civil War. LC 80-16775. (Illus.). 292p. 1981. 17.95 (ISBN 0-252-00821-9). U of Ill Pr.

Vexler, R. I. Utah Chronology & Factbook, Vol. 44. 1978. 8.50 (ISBN 0-379-16169-9). Oceana.

UTAH, UNIVERSITY OF

Haglund, Elizabeth, ed. Remembering: The University of Utah. (Illus.). 250p. 1981. 25.00 (ISBN 0-87480-191-5). U of Utah Pr.

UTE INDIANS
see Indians of North America–Southwest, New

UTERUS–CANCER

Bates, T. D. & Berry, R. J., eds. High Dose-Rate Afterloading in the Treatment of Cancer of the Uterus. 1980. 90.00x (Pub. by Brit Inst Radiology). State Mutual Bk.

Simon & Silverstone. Cancer of the Uterus. 1981. price not set (ISBN 0-89352-016-0). Masson Pub.

UTERUS–HEMORRHAGE
see Hemorrhage, Uterine

UTILITARIANISM
see also Pragmatism; Secularism

Regan, Donald. Utilitarianism & Cooperation. 296p. 1980. text ed. 37.50x (ISBN 0-19-824609-9); pap. 15.95x. Oxford U Pr.

UTILITIES
see Public Utilities

UTILIZATION OF LAND
see Land Use

UTOPIAN LITERATURE
see Utopias

UTOPIAS

Andrea, Johann V. Johann Valentin Andreae's Christianopolis: An Ideal State of the Seventeenth Century. Held, Felix E., tr. from Lat. (Illus.). x, 287p. 1981. Repr. of 1916 ed. lib. bdg. 20.00x (ISBN 0-87991-958-2). Porcupine Pr.

Davis, C. J. Utopia & the Ideal Society. 410p. Date not set. price not set (ISBN 0-521-23396-8). Cambridge U Pr.

Morson, Gary S. The Boundaries of Genre: Dostoevsky's "Diary of a Writer" & the Traditions of Literary Utopia. 272p. 1981. text ed. 25.00x (ISBN 0-292-70732-0). U of Tex Pr.

V

VACCINES
see also Viruses

Hertmann, A. I., et al, eds. New Developments with Human & Veterinary Vaccines. Kohn, A. LC 80-19130. (Progress in Clinical & Biological Research: Vol. 47). 444p. 1980. 36.00 (ISBN 0-8451-0047-5). A R Liss.

VACUUM

McGregor, Donald R. The Inertia of the Vacuum: A New Foundation for Theoretical Physics. 96p. 1981. 6.00 (ISBN 0-682-49722-3). Exposition.

VACUUM-TUBES
see also Cathode Ray Tubes; Electronics; X-Rays

Howard W. Sams Engineering Staff. Tube Substitution Handbook. 21st ed. LC 80-13842. 1980. pap. 3.95 (ISBN 0-672-21746-5). Sams.

VADE-MECUMS
see Handbooks, Vade-Mecums, etc.

VAGABONDS
see Gipsies; Rogues and Vagabonds; Tramps

VAGINA

Copenhaver, Edward H. Surgery of the Vulva & Vagina: A Practical Guide. (Illus.). 100p. 1981. text ed. write for info. (ISBN 0-7216-2718-8). Saunders.

Stanton, S. L. & Tanagho, E. A., eds. Surgery of Female Incontinence. (Illus.). 203p. 1980. 58.00 (ISBN 0-387-10155-1). Springer-Verlag.

Vaginal Health. 1981. pap. 2.50 (ISBN 0-440-09368-6). Dell.

VAGRANTS
see Tramps

VAGUS NERVE

Holle, F. & Holle, G. E., eds. Vagotomy & Pyloroplasty: Latest Advances, 1975-1980. (Illus.). 160p. 1980. pap. 58.00 (ISBN 0-387-10083-0). Springer-Verlag.

VALENCE (THEORETICAL CHEMISTRY)
see also Chemical Bonds; Macromolecules

Brown, David B., ed. Mixed-Valence Compounds: Theory & Applications in Chemistry, Physics, Geology & Biology. (NATO Advanced Study Institute, C. Mathematical & Physical Sciences Ser.: No. 58). 525p. 1980. lib. bdg. 60.50 (ISBN 90-277-1152-6, Pub. by D. Reidel). Kluwer Boston.

VALENTINES

D'Immperio, Dan. Antique Valentines. LC 80-23002. (Illus.). 160p. 1981. write for info. (ISBN 0-498-02505-5). A S Barnes.

VALUATION
Here are entered only the most general works. Works on valuation for taxing purposes are entered under assessment. Materials dealing with valuation of special classes of property are entered under Mine valuation; Railroads–Valuation; Real Estate Business; Real Property–Valuation, etc.

Desmond, Glenn M. & Kelley, Richard E. Business Valuation Handbook. rev ed. LC 80-51554. 1980. 42.50 (ISBN 0-930458-02-8). Valuation.

VALUATION OF LAND
see Real Property–Valuation; Valuation

VALUE
Here are entered works on the theory of value in economics. Works on moral and aesthetic values, etc. are entered under values.
see also Money; Supply and Demand

Wood, E. G. Added Value: The Key to Prosperity. 148p. 1978. text ed. 22.00x (ISBN 0-220-66349-1, Pub. by Busn Bks England). Renouf.

VALUES
Here are entered works on moral and esthetic values, etc. Works on the economic theory of value are entered under value.
see also Social Values; Spirituality

The Big Rock Candy Mountain: A Paradigm of the Values of the Mass Consumption Society. 20p. 1981. pap. 10.00 (ISBN 92-808-0154-6, TUNU 106, UNU). Unipub.

Gow, K. M. Yes Virginia, There Is Right & Wrong! Values Education Survival Kit. 248p. 1980. 15.95 (ISBN 0-471-79954-8); pap. 9.95 (ISBN 0-471-79953-X). Wiley.

McFadden, Johnnie & Rotter, Joseph C. Values Orientation in School. LC 80-69238. 90p. 1981. perfect bdg. 4.50 (ISBN 0-86548-045-1). Century Twenty One.

Wittgenstein, Ludwig. Culture & Value. Von Wright, G. H., ed. Winch, Peter, tr. LC 80-15234. 1980. 20.00x (ISBN 0-226-90432-6). U of Chicago Pr.

VALVULAR DISEASES
see Heart–Diseases

VANCOUVER, BRITISH COLUMBIA

Murphy, Daniel. Queen Elizabeth Park & the Bloedel Conservatory. Campbell, M., ed. (Illus.). 50p. (Orig.). 1981. pap. 4.95 (ISBN 0-88839-088-2). Hancock Hse.

VANDALISM

Casserly, Michael D., et al. School Vandalism: Strategies for Prevention. LC 80-8118. 1980. 17.95 (ISBN 0-669-03956-X). Lexington Bks.

Williams, Robert B. & Venturini, Joseph L. School Vandalism: Cause & Cure. LC 80-69230. 130p. 1981. perfect bdg. 9.50 (ISBN 0-86548-060-5). Century Twenty One.

VANDERBILT, GLORIA

Goldsmith, Barbara. Little Gloria: Happy at Last. Date not set. pap. 3.50 (ISBN 0-440-15109-0). Dell.

VAN GOGH, VINCENT, 1853-1890

Roskill, Mark, ed. The Letters of Vincent Van Gogh. LC 63-13089. 1963. pap. 4.95 (ISBN 0-689-70167-5). Atheneum.

VANISHING ANIMALS
see Rare Animals

VANISHING BIRDS
see Rare Birds

VAN JOHN (GAME)
see Blackjack (Game)

VANS
see also Campers and Coaches, Truck

Rich, Mark. Custom Vans. LC 80-25792. (On the Move Ser.). (Illus.). 48p. (gr. 3-6). 1981. PLB 9.25 (ISBN 0-516-03885-0). Childrens.

VANZETTI, BARTOLOMEO
see Sacco-Vanzetti Case

VAPOR-PHASE CHROMATOGRAPHY
see Gas Chromatography

VAQUEROS
see Cowboys

VARIABLE PARAMETER AMPLIFIERS
see Parametric Amplifiers

VARIABLES (MATHEMATICS)

Nikol'ski, S. M., ed. Theory & Applications of Differentiable Functions of Several Variables, Vol. 4. LC 68-1677. (Proceedings of the Steklov Institute). 1974. 43.60 (ISBN 0-8218-3017-1, STEKLO-117). Am Math.

VARIATIONS, CALCULUS OF
see Calculus of Variations

VARNISH PAINTS
see Paint

VASCULAR DISEASES
see Blood-Vessels–Diseases; Cardiovascular System–Diseases

VASCULAR GRAFTS

Bergan, John J. & Yao, James S., eds. Operative Techniques in Vascular Surgery. 1980. write for info. (ISBN 0-8089-1334-4). Grune.

VASCULAR HYPERTENSION
see Hypertension

VASCULAR PLANTS
see Botany; Plants

VASCULAR SYSTEM
see Blood-Vessels; Cardiovascular System

VASCULAR SYSTEM OF PLANTS

Duncan, Wilbur H. & Kartesz, John T. Vascular Flora of Georgia: An Annotated Checklist. 149p. 1981. pap. 5.00 (ISBN 0-8203-0538-3). U of Ga Pr.

VASES–GREECE

Hambidge, Jay. The Greek Vase: Dynamic Symmetry. (Promotion of the Arts Library Bks.). (Illus.). 131p. Date not set. Repr. of 1917 ed. 77.45 (ISBN 0-89901-030-X). Found Class Reprints.

Hayes, John, ed. Corpus Vasorum Antiquorum Canada: Royal Ontario Museum, Ontario. (Corpus Vasorum Antiquorum Ser.). (Illus.). 64p. 1980. 89.00 (ISBN 0-19-726000-4). Oxford U Pr.

VASODILATORS

Vanhoutte, Paul M. & Leusen, Isadore, eds. Vasodilatation. 475p. 1981. 46.00 (ISBN 0-89004-602-6). Raven.

VAUGHAN, HENRY, 1622-1695

Calhoun, Thomas O. Henry Vaughan: The Achievement of Silex Scintillans. LC 79-51851. 272p. 1980. 22.50 (ISBN 0-87413-165-0). U Delaware Pr.

Rudrum, Alan, ed. Henry Vaughan: The Complete Poems. LC 80-53979. 718p. 1981. text ed. 30.00x (ISBN 0-300-02680-3); pap. 7.95x (ISBN 0-300-02687-0). Yale U Pr.

VAZQUEZ DE CORONADO, FRANCISCO, 1510-1549

Bolton, Herbert E. Coronado: Knight Pueblos & Plains. LC 64-17854. 491p. 1974. Repr. of 1964 ed. 12.95. U of NM Pr.

VECTOR ANALYSIS

see also Calculus of Tensors; Linear Programming; Spinor Analysis; Vector Spaces

Marsden, Jerrold E. & Tromba, Anthony J. Vector Calculus. 2nd ed. LC 80-24663. (Illus.). 1981. text ed. 22.95x (ISBN 0-7167-1244-X). W H Freeman.

VECTOR SPACES

see also Linear Topological Spaces

Graves, William H. Conference on Integration, Topology and Geometry in Linear Spaces: Proceedings, Vol. 2. LC 80-25417. (Contemporary Mathematics Ser.). 1980. 14.00 (ISBN 0-8218-5002-4). Am Math.

Weron, A., ed. Probability Theory an Vector Spaces II: Proceedings. (Lecture Notes in Mathematics Ser.: Vol. 828). 324p. 1981. pap. 19.50 (ISBN 0-387-10253-1). Springer-Verlag.

VECTOR TOPOLOGY

see Linear Topological Spaces

VEDANTA

In the Company of the Holy Mother. Orig. Title: At Holy Mother's Feet. 382p. 1980. pap. 5.95 (ISBN 0-87481-208-9). Vedanta Pr.

Mainkar, T. G. The Making of the Vedanta. 1980. 14.00x (ISBN 0-8364-0623-0, Pub. by Ajanta). South Asia Bks.

Sandal, M. L., tr. Mimansa Sutras of Jaimini, 2 vols. 1022p. 1980. text ed. 60.00 (ISBN 0-8426-1651-9). Verry.

Swami Vishwashrayananda. Swami Vijnanananda: His Life & Sayings. Devavrata Basu Ray, tr. from Bongali. 72p. 1981. pap. 1.95 (ISBN 0-87481-502-9). Vedanta Pr.

VEDIC MYTHOLOGY

see Mythology, Hindu

VEGA CARPIO, LOPE FELIX DE, 1562-1635

Portuondo, Augusto A. Diez Comedias Atribuidas a Lope De Vega: Estudio Do Su Autenticidad. 1980. pap. 17.00 (ISBN 84-499-3788-4). Biblio Siglo.

VEGETABLE GARDENING

see also Truck Farming; Vegetables

Grounds, Roger. Growing Vegetables & Herbs. (Orig.). 1980. pap. 6.95x (ISBN 0-8464-1016-8). Beekman Pubs.

Newcomb, Duane. Growing Vegetables the Big Yield-Small Space Way. (Illus.). 272p. 1981. pap. 7.95 (ISBN 0-87477-170-6). J P Tarcher.

Seabrook, Peter. The Complete Vegetable Gardener. (Illus.). 128p. 1981. 17.95 (ISBN 0-686-69382-5); pap. 7.95 (ISBN 0-686-69383-3). A & W Pubs.

Shewell-Cooper, W. E. Complete Vegetable Grower. 1973. pap. 5.50 (ISBN 0-571-04797-1, Pub. by Faber & Faber). Merrimack Bk Serv.

Toleman, Eric. Growing Vegetables. (Practical Gardening Ser.). (Illus.). 112p. (Orig.). 1979. pap. 10.50 (ISBN 0-589-01239-8, Pub. by Reed Bks Australia). C E Tuttle.

Vegetable Farming. (Country Home Ser.). 96p. 2.95 (ISBN 0-88453-008-6). Berkshire Traveller.

Vilmorin-Andrieux, M. M. The Vegetable Garden. 620p. 1981. pap. 11.95 (ISBN 0-89815-041-8). Ten Speed Pr.

Wilbur, Alan. Growing Unusual Vegetables. 1980. pap. 4.50 (ISBN 0-7153-7904-6). David & Charles.

VEGETABLE KINGDOM

see Botany

VEGETABLE MOLD

see Soils

VEGETABLE OILS

see Oils and Fats

VEGETABLE PATHOLOGY

see Plant Diseases

VEGETABLES

see also Cookery (Vegetables); Food, Raw; Vegetable Gardening; Vegetarianism;
also names of vegetables, e.g. Corn, Potatoes

Celery. 93p. 1980. pap. 9.95x (ISBN 0-901361-29-1, Pub. by Grower Bks England). Intl Schol Bk Serv.

Vegetable Farming. (Country Home Ser.). 96p. 2.95 (ISBN 0-88453-008-6). Berkshire Traveller.

VEGETARIAN COOKERY

Beasley, Sonia. The Spirulina Cookbook: Recipes for Rejuvenating the Body. (Illus.). 160p. (Orig.). 1981. pap. 6.95 (ISBN 0-916438-39-2). Univ of Trees.

Shandler, Michael & Shandler, Nina. The Complete Guide & Cookbook for Raising Your Child As a Vegetarian. 384p. 1981. 15.50x (ISBN 0-8052-3758-5); pap. 8.95. Schocken.

Szilard, Paula & Woo, Juliana J. Electric Vegetarian: Natural Cooking the Food Processor Way. 1980. pap. 10.95 (ISBN 0-933472-50-1). Johnson Colo.

VEGETARIANISM

see also Food, Raw; Vegetarian Cookery

Altman, Nathaniel. Nathaniel Altman's Vegetarian Book. LC 80-85343. 1981. pap. 2.95. Keats.

Annual Directory of Vegetarian Restaurants. 288p. 1980. 6.95 (ISBN 0-686-28725-8). Daystar Pub Co.

Better Homes & Gardens Books Editors, ed. Meatless Main Dishes. (Illus.). 96p. 1981. 4.95 (ISBN 0-696-00645-6). Meredith Corp.

Giehl, Dudley. Vegetarianism: A Way of Life. 272p. 1981. pap. 3.95 (ISBN 0-06-464045-0, BN). Har-Row.

International Vegetarian Health Food Handbook. 208p. 1979. pap. 3.95x (ISBN 0-8464-1026-5). Beekman Pubs.

New Vegetarian Restaurant Guide. 288p. pap. 6.95 (ISBN 0-686-28809-2). Daystar Pub Co.

Szilard, Paula & Woo, Juliana J. The Electric Vegetarian: Natural Cooking the Food Processor Way. 1981. 12.95. Johnson VA.

Van Dessel, Sabine. How to Survive Without Meat. 1981. 6.95 (ISBN 0-533-04833-8). Vantage.

Vegetarian Times Magazine. The Vegetarian Times Guide to Dining in the U. S. A. 1980. pap. 8.95 (ISBN 0-689-10966-0). Atheneum.

Wilson, Frank A. Food Fit for Humans. 1975. 7.25x (ISBN 0-8464-1011-7). Beekman Pubs.

VEGETATION MAPPING

Vegetation Map of Papua New Guinea. (Land Research Ser.: No. 35). 24p. 1975. 13.50 (ISBN 0-643-00138-7, CSIRO). Unipub.

VEGETATIVE NERVOUS SYSTEM

see Nervous System, Autonomic

VEHICLES

see also Automobiles; Bicycles and Tricycles; Carriages and Carts; Motor Vehicles; Motorcycles; Wagons; Wheels

Shacket, Sheldon R. The Complete Book of Electric Vehicles. rev. ed. (Illus.). 224p. 1981. price not set (ISBN 0-89196-085-6, Domus Bks); pap. price not set (ISBN 0-89196-086-4). Quality Bks IL.

VEHICLES, ARMORED (MILITARY SCIENCE)

see Armored Vehicles, Military

VEHICLES, MILITARY

see also Armored Vehicles, Military

Spence, Dennis R., ed. Army Vehicle Manuals. (Military Vehicle Reference Ser.: No. 1). 121p. 1980. pap. 15.00x (ISBN 0-938242-00-8). Portrayal.

VEINS

see also Arteries; Blood–Circulation; Blood-Vessels

Hobson, Robert W., II, ed. Venous Trauma & Its Management. Date not set. price not set (ISBN 0-87993-155-8). Futura Pub.

VELOCIPEDES

see Bicycles and Tricycles

VELOCITY OF CHEMICAL REACTION

see Chemical Reaction, Rate Of

VENDUES

see Auctions

VENEREAL DISEASES

Harris, ed. Recent Advances in Sexually Transmitted Diseases, No. 2. 1981. text ed. 45.00 (ISBN 0-443-01817-0). Churchill.

VENEZUELA–DESCRIPTION AND TRAVEL

Lanier, Alison R. Update -- Venezuela. (Country Orientation Ser.). 1980. pap. text ed. 25.00 (ISBN 0-686-28736-3). Intercult Network.

VENEZUELA–FOREIGN RELATIONS

Yepes, Jose A. The Challenge of Venezuelan Democracy. 175p. 1981. 19.95 (ISBN 0-87855-401-7); text ed. 19.95 (ISBN 0-686-68055-3). Transaction Bks.

VENEZUELA–HISTORY

Carl, George E. First Among Equals: Great Britain & Venezuela, 1810-1910. Robinson, David J., ed. LC 80-17481. (Dellplain Latin American Studies: No. 5). (Illus.). 188p. (Orig.). 1980. pap. 17.75 (ISBN 0-8357-0574-9, SS-00142, Pub. by Syracuse U Dept Geog). Univ Microfilms.

VENICE–DESCRIPTION–GUIDEBOOKS

Blue Guide - Venice. 1980. pap. 19.95 (ISBN 0-528-84609-4). Rand.

VENICE–HISTORY

Howard, Deborah. The Architectural History of Venice. LC 80-24856. (Illus.). 260p. 1981. pap. text ed. 32.50x (ISBN 0-8419-0681-5). Holmes & Meier.

Muir, Edward. Civic Ritual in Renaissance Venice. LC 80-8568. (Illus.). 368p. 1981. 17.50x (ISBN 0-691-05325-1). Princeton U Pr.

VENOMOUS SNAKES

see Poisonous Snakes

VENTILATION

see also Air Conditioning; Heating
also subdivision Heating and Ventilation or Ventilation under special subjects

Havrella, Raymond. Heating, Ventilating & Air Conditioning Fundamentals. LC 80-17155. (Contemporary Construction Ser.). (Illus.). 288p. (gr. 10-12). 1981. text ed. 16.95x (ISBN 0-07-027281-6, G); wkbk. avail. (ISBN 0-07-027283-2). McGraw.

VENUS (PLANET)

Asimov, Isaac. Venus, Near Neighbor of the Sun. (Illus.). 224p. (gr. 5 up). 1981. 8.95 (ISBN 0-688-41976-3); PLB 8.59 (ISBN 0-688-51976-8). Morrow.

VERDI, GIUSEPPE, 1813-1901

Budden, Julian. The Operas of Verdi, Vol. 3: From Don Carlos to Falstaff. 1981. 39.95 (ISBN 0-19-520254-6). Oxford U Pr.

Kimbell, R. B. Verdi in the Age of Italian Romanticism. (Illus.). 800p. Date not set. price not set (ISBN 0-521-23052-7). Cambridge U Pr.

Mann, William. Aida: Verdi. Mann, William & Parker, Roger, eds. Tracey, Edmund, tr. 1980. pap. 4.95 (ISBN 0-7145-3770-5). Riverrun NY.

Martin, George. Verdi, His Music, Life & Times. (Music Reprint Ser.). 1979. Repr. of 1963 ed. 35.00 (ISBN 0-306-79549-3). Da Capo.

Southwell-Sander, Peter. Verdi, His Life & Times. expanded ed. (Illus.). 192p. Repr. of 1978 ed. 19.95 (ISBN 0-87666-639-X). Paganiniana Pubns.

VERGIL (PUBLIUS VERGILIUS MARO)

Camps, W. A. An Introduction to Virgil's Aeneid. 174p. (Orig.). 1969. pap. 9.95x (ISBN 0-19-872024-6). Oxford U Pr.

VERMES

see Worms

VERMONT

see also names of cities, towns, etc. in Vermont

Archer, Ruth. Dayspring. 1981. pap. 2.95 (ISBN 0-935236-18-X). Nurseco.

Crosier, Barney. Vermont Blood. 128p. 1980. pap. 5.95 (ISBN 0-9603900-6-5). Lanser Pr.

VERMONT–DESCRIPTION AND TRAVEL

Aiken, George D., et al. Vermont for Every Season. (Illus.). 160p. 1980. 30.00 (ISBN 0-936896-00-0). VT Life Mag.

Hancock, William, et al, eds. The Vermont Atlas & Gazetteer. (Illus.). 96p. (Orig.). 1978. pap. 6.95 (ISBN 0-89933-005-3). DeLorme Pub.

VERMONT–GENEALOGY

Haviland, William & Power, Marjory W. The Original Vermonters: Native Inhabitants, Past & Present. (Illus.). 320p. 1981. 16.50 (ISBN 0-87451-196-8). U Pr of New Eng.

VERMONT–HISTORY

Hance, Dawn. Shrewsbury, Vermont: Our Town As It Was. LC 80-69447. 328p. 1980. 20.00 (ISBN 0-914960-28-8). Academy Bks.

Morrissey, Charles T. Vermont: The States & the Nation. (Illus.). 240p. 1981. 12.95 (ISBN 0-393-05625-2). Norton.

Vexler, R. I. Vermont Chronology & Factbook. 1978. 8.50 (ISBN 0-379-16170-2). Oceana.

VERMONT–SOCIAL LIFE AND CUSTOMS

Combes, Angela, ed. The Vermont Symphony Cookbook. (Illus.). 128p. 1981. pap. cancelled (ISBN 0-8397-8571-2). Eriksson.

VERNE, JULES, 1829-1905

Evans, I. O. Jules Verne & His Work. 188p. 1980. Repr. of 1965 ed. lib. bdg. 35.00 (ISBN 0-89760-224-2). Telegraph Bks.

VERSAILLES, TREATY OF, JUNE 28, 1919 (GERMANY)

Dockrill, Michael & Gould, Douglas. Peace Without Promise: Britain & the Peace Conferences 1919-1923. 320p. 1981. 25.00 (ISBN 0-208-01909-X, Archon). Shoe String.

VERSIFICATION

see also Alliteration; Poetry
also subdivison Versification under names of modern languages, e.g. English Languages–Versification; subdivision Metrics and Rhythmics under names of ancient languages, e.g. Greek Languages–Metrics and Rhythmics; and special forms of verse, e.g. Hexameter

Carruth, William H. Verse Writing. 123p. 1980. Repr. of 1925 ed. lib. bdg. 15.00 (ISBN 0-8482-3554-1). Norwood Edns.

VERTEBRAE

Wallace, H. Vertebrate Limb Regeneration. 320p. 1981. price not set (ISBN 0-471-27877-7, Pub. by Wiley-Interscience). Wiley.

VERTEBRAL COLUMN

see Spine

VERTEBRATES

see also Amphibians; Birds; Fishes; Mammals; Reptiles

Pearson, Ronald & Ball, John N. Lecture Notes on Vertebrate Zoology. 225p. 1981. pap. 19.95 (ISBN 0-470-27143-4). Halsted Pr.

Thurmond, John T. & Jones, Douglas E. Fossil Vertebrates of Alabama. LC 80-13075. (Illus.). 256p. 1981. 22.50x. U of Ala Pr.

VERTEBRATES–ANATOMY

see also Nervous System–Vertebrates

Lepori, N. G. Sex Differentiation, Hermaphroditism & Intersexuality in Vertebrates Including Man. (Illus.). 372p. 1980. text ed. 49.50x (ISBN 88-212-0747-1, Pub. by Piccin Italy). J K Burgess.

VERTEBRATES, FOSSIL

Zallinger, Peter. Prehistoric Animals. (Pictureback Ser.). (Illus.). 32p. (ps-3). 1981. PLB 4.99 (ISBN 0-394-93737-6); pap. 1.25 (ISBN 0-394-83737-1). Random.

VERTEBRATES, FOSSIL–BIBLIOGRAPHY

Gregory, Joseph L., et al. Bibliography of Fossil Vertebrates, 1978. 384p. (Orig.). 1981. 50.00 (ISBN 0-913312-52-5). Am Geol.

VERTIGO

Paparella, Michael M., et al. Sensorineural Hearing Loss, Vertigo & Tinnitus: International Symposium. 232p. 1981. write for info. (6750-8). Williams & Wilkins.

VESEY, DENMARK, 1767-1823

Killens, John O. Great Gittin up Morning: The Story of Denmark Vesey. Rivera, Louis R., ed. (Illus.). 128p. 1980. pap. 5.50 (ISBN 0-917886-06-2). Shamal Bks.

VESICO-URETERAL REFLUX

Hodson, C. J., et al. The Pathogenesis of Reflux Nephropathy. Maling, T. M. & McManamon, P. J., eds. 1980. 10.00x (Pub. by Brit Inst Radiology). State Mutual Bk.

Ransley, P. G. & Ridson, R. A. Reflux & Renal Scarring. 1980. 15.00x (Pub. by Brit Inst Radiology). State Mutual Bk.

VESPERTILIO

see Bats

VESSELS (SHIPS)

see Ships

VETERANS

Here are entered general works relating to ex-servicemen. Specific topic are entered under appropriate heading, e.g. Pensions, Military Veterans, Disabled–Rehabilitation.
see also Soldiers

Cleland, Max. Strong at the Broken Places. 1980. 6.95 (ISBN 0-912376-55-4). Word Bks.

Meade, James P., Jr. Making Reality: Coping with Limitations Successfully. 1981. 7.50 (ISBN 0-8062-1652-2). Carlton.

Russell, Harold & Ferullo, Dan. The Best Years of My Life. (Illus.). 224p. 1981. 12.95 (ISBN 0-8397-1026-7). Eriksson.

VETERINARIANS

see also Veterinary Medicine As a Profession

Taylor, David. Going Wild: Adventures of a Zoo Vet. LC 80-18432. (Illus.). 242p. 1981. 12.95 (ISBN 0-8128-2756-2). Stein & Day.

VETERINARY DIAGNOSIS

see Veterinary Medicine–Diagnosis

VETERINARY HISTOLOGY–LABORATORY MANUALS

Banks, William J. Applied Veterinary Histology. (Illus.). 540p. 1981. write for info. (0410-7). Williams & Wilkins.

VETERINARY MEDICINE

see also Domestic Animals; Parasitology
also subdivision Diseases under classes of animals, e.g. Cattle–Diseases; Horses–Diseases; names of particular diseases, e.g. Foot-and-Mouth disease; and headings beginning with the word veterinary

Davis, John W., et al, eds. Infectious Diseases of Wild Mammals. 2nd ed. 436p. 1981. text ed. 35.00 (ISBN 0-8138-0445-0). Iowa St U Pr.

Gelatt, Kirk N., ed. Textbook of Veterinary Opthalmology. LC 80-17291. (Illus.). 788p. 1981. text ed. write for info. (ISBN 0-8121-0686-5). Lea & Febiger.

Gillespie, James H. & Timoney, John F. Hagan & Bruner's Infectious Diseases of Domestic Animals. 7th rev. ed. LC 80-15937. (Illus.). 912p. 1981. 39.50x (ISBN 0-8014-1333-8). Cornell U Pr.

Marcus, Leonard C. Veterinary Biology & Medicine of Captive Amphibians & Reptiles. LC 80-24859. (Illus.). 236p. 1981. text ed. write for info. (ISBN 0-8121-0700-4). Lea & Febiger.

Ryan, Gerald D. Radiographic Positioning of Small Animals. LC 80-26069. (Illus.). 147p. 1981. text ed. write for info. (ISBN 0-8121-0774-8). Lea & Febiger.

Willinger, Herman & Weber, Albert, eds. Echerichia coli Infections in Domestic Animals. (Advances in Veterinary Medicine Ser.: Vol. 29). (Illus.). 86p. (Orig.). 1979. pap. text ed. 25.90 (ISBN 3-489-77916-9). Parey Sci Pubs.

VETERINARY MEDICINE–DIAGNOSIS

Davis, John W., et al, eds. Infectious Diseases of Wild Mammals. 2nd ed. 436p. 1981. text ed. 35.00 (ISBN 0-8138-0445-0). Iowa St U Pr.

Kahrs, Robert F. Viral Diseases of Cattle. (Illus.). 224p. 1981. text ed. 15.00 (ISBN 0-8138-0860-X). Iowa St U Pr.

Taylor, David. Going Wild: Adventures of a Zoo Vet. LC 80-18432. (Illus.). 242p. 1981. 12.95 (ISBN 0-8128-2756-2). Stein & Day.

VETERINARY MEDICINE AS A PROFESSION

see also Veterinarians

Younker, Lucas & Fried, John J. Animal Doctor: The Making of a Veterinarian. 256p. 1981. pap. 2.50. Jove Pubns.

VETERINARY MICROBIOLOGY

Cottral, George E., ed. Manual of Standardized Methods for Veterinary Microbiology. LC 77-90900. (Illus.). 720p. 1978. 40.00 (ISBN 0-8014-1119-X). Comstock.

VETERINARY SCIENCE

see Veterinary Medicine

VETERINARY SURGEONS

see Veterinarians

VETERINARY SURGERY

see also First Aid for Animals

Knecht, Charles D., et al. Fundamental Techniques Veterinary Surgery. (Illus.). 250p. 1981. text ed. price not set (ISBN 0-7216-5463-0). Saunders.

VIBRATION

see also Damping (Mechanics); Frequencies of Oscillating Systems; Light; Materials–Fatigue; Oscillations; Shock (Mechanics); Structural Dynamics; Time Measurements; Waves

Pain, H. J. The Physics of Vibrations & Waves. 2nd ed. 357p. 1976. 32.50 (ISBN 0-471-99407-3); pap. 16.50 (ISBN 0-471-99408-1). Wiley.

Wilson, W. Ker. Vibration Engineering. 292p. 1959. 65.00x (ISBN 0-85264-023-4, Pub. by Griffin England). State Mutual Bk.

VICE-PRESIDENTS–UNITED STATES

Alotta, Robert I. A Look at the Vice Presidency. 2ed ed. 1981. write for info. Messner.

--Number Two: A Look at the Vice Presidency. (Illus.). 256p. (gr. 8 up). 1981. PLB price not set. Messner.

Vexler, R. I. Vice Presidents & Cabinet Members: Biographies Arranged Chronologically by Administration, Vols. 1-2. 1975. 35.00 ea. Vol. 1 (ISBN 0-379-12089-5). Vol. 2 (ISBN 0-379-12090-9). Oceana.

Williams, Irving G. Rise of the Vice-Presidency. 5.00 (ISBN 0-8183-0204-6). Pub Aff Pr.

VICKSBURG, MISSISSIPPI–SIEGE, 1863

Foster, William L. & Urquhart, Kenneth T. Vicksburg: Southern City Under Siege. LC 80-84685. (Illus.). xxv, 82p. 1980. 15.00x (ISBN 0-917860-02-0). Historic New Orleans.

VICTORIA, QUEEN OF GREAT BRITAIN, 1819-1901

Plowden, Alison. The Young Victoria. LC 80-5908. (Illus.). 208p. 1981. 12.95 (ISBN 0-8128-2766-X). Stein & Day.

Young, Lesley. Queen Victoria. (Profiles Ser.). (Illus.). 64p. (gr. 3-6). 1981. 7.95 (ISBN 0-241-10480-7, Pub. by Hamish Hamilton England). David & Charles.

VICTORIA, AUSTRALIA–SOCIAL CONDITIONS

Serville, Paul De. Port Philip Gentlemen. (Illus.). 256p. 1980. 49.00x (ISBN 0-19-554212-6). Oxford U Pr.

VIDAL, GORE, 1925-

Stanton, Robert J. Gore Vidal: A Primary & Secondary Bibliography. (Reference Publications). 1980. lib. bdg. 25.00 (ISBN 0-8161-8109-8). G K Hall.

VIDEO TAPE RECORDERS AND RECORDING

The Video Tape/Disc Guide: Children's Programs. 160p. 9.95 (ISBN 0-686-68289-0). Natl Video.

Home Video Tape-Disc Guide: Children's Program. 1980. pap. 12.95 (ISBN 0-452-25256-3, Z5256, Plume). NAL.

Reed, Maxine K., ed. Le Video Source Book: France. (Illus.). 250p. (Orig.). 1981. pap. 30.00 (ISBN 0-935478-08-6). Natl Video.

--The Video Source Book: UK. (Illus.). 280p. (Orig.). 1981. pap. 24.00 (ISBN 0-935478-07-8). Natl Video.

--The Video Tape - Disc Guide: Religion. (Illus.). 200p. (Orig.). 1981. pap. 19.95 (ISBN 0-935478-06-X). Natl Video.

Robinson, J. F. & Lowe, Stephen. Videotape Recording. 3rd ed. LC 80-41244. 1981. 27.95 (ISBN 0-240-51083-6). Focal Pr.

Utz, Peter. Video User's Handbook. rev. ed. LC 79-379. (Video Bookshelf Ser.). (Illus.). 410p. 1980. Repr. of 1980 ed. text ed. 19.95x (ISBN 0-914236-78-4). Knowledge Indus.

VIDEO TAPES

Beardsley, Rick, ed. The Videolog: General Interest & Education. 1980-81 ed. (Videolog Ser.). 500p. 1981. pap. 34.50 (ISBN 0-88432-071-5). J Norton Pubs.

--The Videolog in Business. 1980-81 ed. (Videolog Ser.). 300p. 1981. pap. 39.50 (ISBN 0-88432-070-7). J Norton Pubs.

--The Videolog in the Health Sciences. 1980-81 ed. (Videolog Ser.). 1981. pap. 49.50 (ISBN 0-88432-069-3). J Norton Pubs.

Jevnikar, Jana M. Video Service Profiles. 60p. (Orig.). 1981. pap. price not set (ISBN 0-935654-02-X, Pub. by Ctr for Arts Info). Pub Ctr Cult Res.

Lebaron, John. Making Television: A Video Guide for Teachers. (Orig.). 1981. pap. 12.50 (ISBN 0-8077-2636-2). Tchrs Coll.

Reed, Maxine K. The Video Programs Update. (Illus.). 64p. (Orig.). 1981. (ISBN 0-935478-09-4). Natl Video.

Sigel, Efrem, et al. Video Discs: The Technology, the Applications & the Future. LC 80-23112. (Video Bookshelf Ser.). (Illus.). 183p. 1980. text ed. 29.95x (ISBN 0-914236-56-3). Knowledge Indus.

Video Resources in New York State. 64p. (Orig.). 1975. pap. 3.00 (ISBN 0-89062-015-6). Film & Video.

VIENNA–HISTORY

Boyer, John W. Political Radicalism in Late Imperial Vienna: Origins of the Christian Social Movement, 1848-1897. LC 80-17302. (Illus.). 1981. lib. bdg. price not set (ISBN 0-226-06957-5). U of Chicago Pr.

VIENNESE CIRCLE

see Logical Positivism

VIETNAM–HISTORY

Duiker, William J. Vietnam Since the Fall of Saigon. LC 80-21166. (Southeast Asia Ser., Ohio University Papers in International Studies). (Illus.). 78p. (Orig.). 1981. pap. 9.00 (ISBN 0-89680-106-3). Ohio U Ctr Intl.

Marr, David G. Vietnamese Tradition on Trial, Nineteen Twenty to Nineteen Forty-Five. (Illus.). 450p. 1981. 25.00 (ISBN 0-520-04180-1, CAMPUS 271); pap. 9.95 (ISBN 0-520-04277-8). U of Cal Pr.

Porter, Gareth. Vietnam: a History in Documents. pap. write for info. (F553, Meridian Bks). NAL.

VIETNAM–POLITICS AND GOVERNMENT

Smyser, W. R. The Independent Vietnamese: Vietnamese Communism Between Russia & China, 1959 to 1969. (Southeast Asia Ser., Ohio University Center for International Studies). 143p. (Orig.). 1980. pap. 12.75 (ISBN 0-89680-105-5, 80-18308). Ohio U Ctr Intl.

VIETNAMESE CONFLICT, 1961-1975

Chandler, Robert W. War of Ideas: The U. S. Propaganda Compaign in Vietnam. (Westview Special Studies in National Defense & Security Ser.). 301p. 1981. lib. bdg. 25.00x (ISBN 0-86531-082-3). Westview.

Cisneros, Louis. Good Mornin', Vietnam. 1981. 4.95 (ISBN 0-8062-1568-2). Carlton.

French, Robert. Vietnam: Both Sides. (Orig.). 1979. pap. 2.25 (ISBN 0-532-23177-5). Manor Bks.

Papp, Daniel S. Vietnam: The View from Moscow, Peking, Washington. LC 80-20117. (Illus.). 263p. 1981. lib. bdg. 17.95x (ISBN 0-89950-010-2). McFarland & Co.

VIETNAMESE CONFLICT, 1961-1975–PERSONAL NARRATIVES

Baker, Mark. Nam. 288p. 1981. 10.95 (ISBN 0-688-00086-X). Morrow.

Bleier, Rocky & O'Neil, Terry. Fighting Back. rev. ed. LC 75-12865. (Illus.). 240p. 1980. 12.95 (ISBN 0-8128-2767-8). Stein & Day.

VIETNAMESE IN FOREIGN COUNTRIES

Henkin, Alan B. & Liem Thanh Nguyen. Between Two Cultures: The Vietnamese in America. LC 80-69333. 125p. 1981. perfect bdg. 7.95 (ISBN 0-86548-039-7). Century Twenty One.

VIEWS

see also Geography–Pictorial Works;

also subdivision Description and Travel–Views under names of countries, regions, etc., e.g. Austria–Description and Travel–Views; subdivision Description–Views under names of cities and of universities and colleges, etc.

America: An Aerial View. Date not set. 5.95 (ISBN 0-517-25701-7). Aerial Photo.

VIKINGS

Here are entered works on the Norse seawarriors only. General works are entered under the heading Northmen.

Brogger, W. W. & Shetelig, Hakon. The Viking Ships. (Illus.). 196p. 1980. 27.50 (ISBN 0-906191-40-8, Pub. by Thule Pr England). Intl Schol Bk Serv.

Leirfall, Jon. West Over Sea. 160p. 1980. 14.95 (ISBN 0-906191-15-7, Pub. by Thule Pr England). Intl Schol Bk Serv.

VILLAGES

see also Community Development; Local Government; Rural Conditions; Sociology, Rural

Critchfield, Richard. Villages. LC 80-1721. (Illus.). 384p. 1981. 17.95 (ISBN 0-385-17212-5). Doubleday.

VILLIERS, BARBARA, LADY CASTLEMAINE AND DUTCHESS OF CLEVELAND, 1641-1709

Lafranche, Gaston M. The Intimate Memoirs of Barbara, the Duchess of Cleveland. (The Great Women of History Library). (Illus.). 93p. 1981. 19.85 (ISBN 0-89266-276-X). Am Classical Coll Pr.

VINES

see Climbing Plants

VINEYARDS

see Grapes

VINGT ET UN (GAME)

see Blackjack (Game)

VIOLENCE

Friedman, Leon, ed. Episodes of Violence in U.S. History, 3 vols. Incl. Vol. 1. Dynamite. Adamic, Louis. LC 80-21964; Vol. 2. The Dorr War. Mowry, Arthur M. LC 80-21969; Vol. 3. The Molly Maguires. Broehl, Wayne G., Jr. LC 80-21794. (Illus.). 750p. 1981. Repr. of 1970 ed. Set. 50.00 (ISBN 0-87754-133-7). Chelsea Hse.

Hirsch, Miriam F. Women & Violence. 416p. 1980. text ed. 17.95. Van Nos Reinhold.

Kaunda, Kenneth. The Riddle of Violence. LC 80-8348. 192p. 1981. 9.95 (ISBN 0-06-250450-9, HarpR, HarpR). Har-Row.

Warner, Carmen G. Conflict Intervention in Social-Domestic Violence. (Illus.). 256p. 1981. text ed. 14.95 (ISBN 0-87619-855-8); pap. text ed. 11.95 (ISBN 0-87619-854-X). R J Brady.

VIOLENCE–MORAL AND RELIGIOUS ASPECTS

see also War and Religion

Olson, Bruce, tr. Por Esta Cruz Te Matare. (Spanish Bks.). (Span.). 1979. 1.90 (ISBN 0-8297-0592-9). Life Pubs Intl.

--Por Esta Cruz Te Matarei. (Portuguese Bks.). 1979. 1.40 (ISBN 0-8297-0797-2). Life Pubs Intl.

Wilkerson, David, tr. La Cruz y el Punal. (Spanish Bks.). 1979. 1.90 (ISBN 0-8297-0522-8). Life Pubs Intl.

--Depois De a Cruz E O Punhal. (Portuguese Bks.). 1979. 1.40 (ISBN 0-8297-0731-X). Life Pubs Intl.

--Despues De la Cruz y el Punal. (Spanish Bks.). (Span.). 1978. 1.75 (ISBN 0-8297-0537-6). Life Pubs Intl.

VIOLINISTS, VIOLONCELLISTS, ETC.–CORRESPONDENCE, REMINISCENCES, ETC.

see Musicians–Correspondence, Reminiscences, etc.

VIOLONCELLO AND PIANO MUSIC

Piatagorsky, Gregor. Cellist Music. 1979. Repr. of 1965 ed. 27.50 (ISBN 0-306-70822-1). Da Capo.

VIPERS

see Snakes

VIRGIL

see Vergil (Publius Vergilius Maro)

VIRGIN BIRTH

see also Mary, Virgin

Gromacki, Robert. The Virgin Birth of Christ. 200p. 1981. pap. 5.95 (ISBN 0-8010-3765-4). Baker Bk.

VIRGIN ISLANDS

Radlauer, Ruth. Virgin Islands National Park. LC 80-22457. (Parks for People Ser.). (Illus.). 48p. (gr. 3 up). 1981. PLB 9.25 (ISBN 0-516-07741-4). Childrens.

VIRGIN MARY

see Mary, Virgin

VIRGINIA–DESCRIPTION AND TRAVEL

Higginbotham, Don. Guide to Virginia. LC 80-53941. 1981. pap. 7.95 (ISBN 0-528-84540-3). Rand.

Wamsley, James. Virginia. (Illus.). 128p. 1981. 27.50 (ISBN 0-912856-66-1). Graphic Arts Ctr.

VIRGINIA–DESCRIPTION AND TRAVEL–GUIDEBOOKS

Osler, Jack & Burgin, Tricia. Fifty Great Mini-Trips for Washington D. C. - Virginia. (Jack Osler's Mini-Trip Ser.). Date not set. pap. price not set (ISBN 0-89645-009-0). Media Ventures.

VIRGINIA–GENEALOGY

Hall, Virginius C., Jr. Portraits in the Collection of the Virginia Historical Society: A Catalogue. LC 80-14079. 1981. price not set (ISBN 0-8139-0813-2). U Pr of Va.

VIRGINIA–HISTORY

Dabney, Virginius. Virginia: The New Dominion, a History from 1607 to the Present. LC 78-157580. (Illus.). 629p. 14.95 (ISBN 0-385-07150-7). U Pr of Va.

Hall, Virginius C., Jr. Portraits in the Collection of the Virginia Historical Society: A Catalogue. LC 80-14079. 1981. price not set (ISBN 0-8139-0813-2). U Pr of Va.

Roeber, A. G. Faithful Magistrates & Republican Lawyers: Creators of Virginia Legal Culture, 1680-1810. LC 80-19524. (Studies in Legal History). 352p. 1981. 24.00x (ISBN 0-8078-1461-X). U of NC Pr.

VIRGINIA–HISTORY–SOURCES

Swindler, W. F. Chronology & Documentary Handbook of the State of Virginia. 1978. 8.50 (ISBN 0-379-16157-5). Oceana.

VIRGINIA–HISTORY–COLONIAL PERIOD, ca. 1600-1775

see also Raleigh's Roanoke Colonies, 1584-1590

Cope, Robert S. Carry Me Back: Slavery & Servitude in Seventeenth Century Virginia. (Illus.). xv, 179p. 1973. 2.00. Pikeville Coll.

VIRGINIA–HISTORY–COLONIAL PERIOD, ca. 1600-1775–SOURCES

Reese, George, ed. The Official Papers of Francis Fauquier, Lieutenant Governor of Virginia, 1758-1768: Vol. II, 1761-1763. LC 80-19866. (Virginia Historical Society Documents Ser.: Vol. 15). 1981. price not set (ISBN 0-8139-0895-7). U Pr of Va.

VIRGINIA–POLITICS AND GOVERNMENT

Roeber, A. G. Faithful Magistrates & Republican Lawyers: Creators of Virginia Legal Culture, 1680-1810. LC 80-19524. (Studies in Legal History). 352p. 1981. 24.00x (ISBN 0-8078-1461-X). U of NC Pr.

VIRGINIA AND TRUCKEE RAILROAD

Beebe, Lucius & Clegg, Charles. Virginia & Truckee. LC 63-14279. (Illus.). 64p. 1980. pap. 2.95 (ISBN 0-8310-6007-7). Howell-North.

VIRGINIA CITY, NEVADA

Lord, Eliot. Comstock Miners & Mining. (Illus.). 578p. Repr. of 1959 ed. 20.00 (ISBN 0-8310-7008-0). A S Barnes.

VIRGINIA DEER

see White-Tailed Deer

VIRIAL COEFFICIENTS

Dymond, J. H. & Smith, E. B. The Second Virial Coefficients of Pure Gases & Mixtures: A Critical Compilation. (Oxford Science Research Papers Ser.). (Illus.). 534p. 1980. pap. text ed. 69.00x (ISBN 0-19-855361-7). Oxford U Pr.

VIROLOGY

see also Virus Diseases; Viruses

Conrat, Heinz F. & Wagner, Robert, eds. Comprehensive Virology: Methods Used in the Study of Viruses, Vol. 17. 425p. 1981. 39.50 (ISBN 0-306-40418-4). Plenum Pub.

Dulbecco, Renato & Ginsberg, Harold. Virology. (Illus.). 408p. 1980. 20.00 (ISBN 0-06-140725-9, Harper Medical). Har-Row.

Eleventh Gustave Stern Symposium on Perspectives in Virology, New York, February 1980. Perspectives in Virology, Vol. 11: Proceedings. Pollard, Morris, ed. 324p. 1981. 40.00x (ISBN 0-8451-0800-X). A R Liss.

Fraenkel-Conrat, Heinz & Wagner, Robert, eds. Comprehensive Virology: Volume 16, Virus-Host Interactions. 385p. 1980. 39.50 (ISBN 0-306-40488-5, Plenum Pr). Plenum Pub.

Gardner, P. S. & McQuillan, J. Rapid Virus Diagnosis. 2nd ed. LC 80-40239. (Illus.). 336p. 1980. text ed 79.95 (ISBN 0-407-38441-3). Butterworths.

Hsiung, Gueh-Djen. Recent Advances in Clinical Virology. 128p. 1981. 19.95 (ISBN 0-03-059013-2); pap. 8.95 (ISBN 0-03-059014-0). Praeger.

Joklik, Wolfgang K. Principles of Animal Virology. 320p. 1980. text ed. 21.95x (ISBN 0-8385-7920-5). ACC.

Romberger, John A. Virology in Agriculture. LC 76-42139. (Beltsville Symposia in Agricultural Reasearch Ser.: No. 1). 320p. 1977. text ed. 23.50 (ISBN 0-916672-14-X). Allanheld.

Waterson, A. P., ed. Recent Advances in Clinical Virology, No. 2. (Illus.). 178p. 1980. text ed. 40.00 (ISBN 0-443-02094-9). Churchill.

VIRTUE AND VIRTUES

see also Character; Ethics

also specific virtues, e.g. Charity, Kindness

MacIntyre, Alasdair. After Virtue. LC 80-53073. 320p. 1981. text ed. 15.95 (ISBN 0-268-00662-8). U of Notre Dame Pr.

Thompson, Murray S. Grace & Forgiveness in Ministry. LC 80-23613. 176p. (Orig.). 1981. pap. 6.95 (ISBN 0-687-15680-7). Abingdon.

VIRUS DISEASES

Lauffer, Max A., et al, eds. Advances in Virus Research, Vol. 26. (Serial Publication). 1981. write for info. (ISBN 0-12-039826-5). Acad Pr.

VIRUSES

see also Interferons; Virus Diseases

Blasecki. Mechanisms of Immunity to Virus-Induced Tumors. 376p. 1981. 49.50. Dekker.

Eron, Carol. The Virus That Ate Cannibals: And Other True Stories. 256p. 1981. 12.95 (ISBN 0-02-536250-X). Macmillan.

Koch, Gebhard & Richter, Dietmar. Biosynthesis, Modification & Processing of Cellular & Viral Polyproteins. 1980. 29.00 (ISBN 0-12-417560-0). Acad Pr.

Palese, Peter & Roizman, Bernard, eds. The Genetic Variation of Viruses, Vol. 354. LC 80-25770. 501p. 1980. write for info. (ISBN 0-89766-097-8); pap. write for info. (ISBN 0-89766-098-6). NY Acad Sci.

VISCERAL LEARNING

see Biofeedback Training

VISIBLE SPEECH

see Deaf–Means of Communication

VISION

see also Eye; Visual Perception

Getz, Donald J. & McGraw, Lora. Vision Training for Better Learning. 1981. spiral bound 12.95 (ISBN 0-87804-430-2). Mafex.

Royal Society Discussion, March 7 & 8, 1979. The Psychology of Vision. Longuet-Higgins, H. C. & Sutherland, N. S., eds. (Illus.). 218p. 1980. text ed. 61.00x (ISBN 0-85403-141-3, Pub. by Royal Soc London). Scholium Intl.

VISIONS

see also Apparitions; Dreams; Fantasy

Wilkerson, David, tr. La Vision. (Spanish Bks.). (Span.). 1979. 1.65 (ISBN 0-8297-0608-9). Vida Pub.

--La Vision. (French Bks.). (Fr.). 1979. 1.95 (ISBN 0-686-28823-8). Vida Pub.

VISUAL AIDS

see also Visual Education;

also Moving Pictures in Education; Moving Pictures in Industry and similar headings; names of individual aids, e.g. Moving-Pictures; Posters

Lidstone, John & Lewis, Stanley. Reinhold Visuals Study Guide. 160p. 1980. pap. 8.95 (ISBN 0-442-25399-0). Van Nos Reinhold.

VISUAL ARTS

see Art

VISUAL DATA PROCESSING

see Optical Data Processing

VISUAL EDUCATION

see also Audio-Visual Education; Bulletin Boards; Moving-Pictures in Education; Visual Aids

Helmantoler, Michael C., ed. Mass Media College Catalog. rev. ed. 132p. 1980. pap. 15.00 (ISBN 0-87117-048-5). Am Assn Comm Jr Coll.

Thompson, Philip & Davenport, Peter, eds. Dictionary of Visual Language. (Illus.). 288p. 1981. 30.00x (ISBN 0-312-20108-7). St Martin.

VISUAL PERCEPTION

Feldman, E., ed. Varieties of Visual Experience. 3rd ed. 1981. pap. 15.95. P-H.

Fineman, Mark. The Inquisitive Eye. (Illus.). 224p. 1981. pap. text ed. 7.95x (ISBN 0-19-502773-6). Oxford U Pr.

Getty, David J. & Howard, James H., Jr. Auditory & Visual Pattern Recognition. 240p. 1981. professional ref. text 16.50 (ISBN 0-89859-087-6). L Erlbaum Assocs.

Rosner, Jerome. Visual Perceptual Skillsbook. (gr. k-3). 1981. 11.70 (ISBN 0-8027-9126-3). Walker & Co.

VISUALLY HANDICAPPED

Moravisin, Sylvester. Why Our Universities Are Turning Out Ordinary Barbarians. (American Culture Library). (Illus.). 105p. 1981. 47.85 (ISBN 0-89266-299-9). Am Classical Coll Pr.

National Accreditation Council. Section D-9, Low Vision Services. (Self-Study & Evaluation Guide). 1981. 1.50. NACASBVH.

Rhyne, Jane M. Curriculum for Teaching the Visually Impaired. 320p. 1981. text ed. 27.50 (ISBN 0-398-04161-X); pap. text ed. 27.50 spiral bdg. (ISBN 0-398-04161-X). C C Thomas.

VISUALLY HANDICAPPED CHILDREN

Gardiner, P. A. Development of Vision, Vol.4. 240p. 1981. 17.50 (ISBN 0-88416-379-2). PSG Pub.

Scholl, Geraldine T. Self Study & Evaluation Guide for Day School Programs for Visually Handicapped Pupils: A Guide for Program Improvement. LC 80-68282. 128p. 1980. pap. 14.50 (ISBN 0-86586-111-0). Coun Exc Child.

VISUALLY HANDICAPPED CHILDREN–EDUCATION

see Blind–Education

VITAMIN DEFICIENCY

see Avitaminosis

VITAMIN METABOLISM

Adams, Ruth & Murray, Frank. Body, Mind, & the B Vitamins. rev. ed. 317p. 1972. pap. 1.95x (ISBN 0-915962-02-0). Larchmont Bks.

--Improving Your Health with Vitamin A. (Larchmont Preventive Health Library). 125p. (Orig.). 1978. pap. 1.25 (ISBN 0-915962-24-1). Larchmont Bks.

VITAMIN THERAPY

Adams, Ruth. The Complete Home Guide to All the Vitamins. 432p. 1972. pap. 2.75 (ISBN 0-915962-05-5). Larchmont Bks.

Adams, Ruth & Murray, Frank. Body, Mind, & the B Vitamins. rev. ed. 317p. 1972. pap. 1.95x (ISBN 0-915962-02-0). Larchmont Bks.

--Improving Your Health with Vitamin A. (Larchmont Preventive Health Library). 125p. (Orig.). 1978. pap. 1.25 (ISBN 0-915962-24-1). Larchmont Bks.

--Megavitamin Therapy. 277p. (Orig.). 1973. pap. 1.95. Larchmont Bks.

Lesser, Michael. Nutrition & Vitamin Therapy. 224p. 1981. pap. 2.50 (ISBN 0-553-14437-5). Bantam.

Newbold, H. L. Vitamin C Against Cancer. LC 79-5301. (Illus.). 384p. 1981. pap. 7.95 (ISBN 0-8128-6098-5). Stein & Day.

Ross, Harvey. Fighting Depression. 221p. (Orig.). 1975. pap. 1.95. Larchmont Bks.

VITAMINS

see also Vitamin Metabolism; Vitamin Therapy

Adams, Ruth. The Complete Home Guide to All the Vitamins. 432p. 1972. pap. 2.75 (ISBN 0-915962-05-5). Larchmont Bks.

Adams, Ruth & Murray, Frank. The Vitamin B-Six Book. 176p. (Orig.). 1980. pap. 1.75 (ISBN 0-915962-30-6). Larchmont Bks.

Bauerfeind, Jack C., ed. Carotenoid As Colorants & Vitamin A Precursors: Technological & Nutritional Applications. LC 79-8850. (Food Science & Technology Ser.). 1981. write for info. (ISBN 0-12-082850-2). Acad Pr.

Borsook, Henry. Vitamins: What They Are. (Orig.). pap. 1.75 (ISBN 0-515-05132-2). Jove Pubns.

Briggs, M. H. Vitamins in Human Biology & Medicine. 304p. 1981. 69.95 (ISBN 0-8493-5673-3). CRC Pr.

Dolphin, David. Vitamin B-Twelve, Vols. 1 & 2. 1070p. 1981. Set. 95.00 (ISBN 0-471-03655-2, Pub. by Wiley-Interscience). Wiley.

Flodin, Nestor W. Vitamin-Trace Mineral-Protein Interactions, Vol. 3. Horribin, David F., ed. (Annual Research Reviews). 362p. 1980. 38.00 (ISBN 0-88831-085-4). Eden Med Res.

Munson, P. L., et al, eds. Vitamins & Hormones, Vol. 38. (Serial Publication Ser.). 1981. write for info. (ISBN 0-12-709838-0). Acad Pr.

Vitamin C, the Common Cold & the Flu. rev. ed. 224p. 1981. pap. 2.75 (ISBN 0-425-04853-5). Berkley Pub.

VITAMINS–THERAPEUTIC USE

see Vitamin Therapy

VOCABULARY

Here are entered general works and works on English vocabulary. Works dealing with the vocabularies of other languages are entered under names of specific languages, with subdivision Vocabulary, e.g. French Language–Vocabulary.

see also Children–Language

also subdivisions Dictionaries and Glossaries, Vocabularies, Etc. under names of languages.

Basic Skills Word List. 1980. pap. 14.95 (ISBN 0-932166-02-4). Instruct Object.

Brownstein & Weiner. Basic Word List. 1981. pap. 2.50 (ISBN 0-8120-0709-3). Barron.

Canney, John, et al. Working on Words. vi, 250p. (Orig.). 1981. pap. text ed. 6.95 (ISBN 0-913580-72-4). Gallaudet Coll.

Ehrlich, Ida L. Instant Vocabulary. pap. 2.95 (ISBN 0-671-42415-7). PB.

Fletcher, Paul F. & Elson, Milton. Words You Need. 288p. (Orig.). 1981. pap. 6.00 (ISBN 0-8215-9821-X). Sadlier.

Freundlich, Charles I. College Vacabulary Builder. 256p. (Orig.). 1981. pap. 5.95 (ISBN 0-671-41337-6). Monarch Pr.

Gregorich, Barbara. Expanding Your Vocabulary. LC 78-730053. (Illus.). 1978. pap. text ed. 99.00 (ISBN 0-89290-126-8, 327-SATC). Soc for Visual.

Levine, Harold & Levine, Robert T. Vocabulary Foundations for the College Student. (Orig.). 1980. pap. text ed. 7.50 (ISBN 0-87720-962-6). AMSCO Sch.

Lewick-Wallace, Mary. Vocabulary Building & Word Study. Raygor, Alton, ed. (Communication Skills Ser.). 240p. (Orig.). 1981. pap. text ed. 8.95 (ISBN 0-07-067902-9, C). McGraw.

Lewis, Norman. Word Power Made Easy. pap. 2.95 (ISBN 0-671-42416-5). PB.

Licklider, Patricia. Building a College Vocabulary. 256p. (Orig.). 1981. pap. text ed. 7.95 (ISBN 0-316-52424-7); tchrs'. manual free (ISBN 0-316-52425-5). Little.

Nurnberg, Maxwell. I Always Look up the Word "Egregious". 196p. 1981. 10.00 (ISBN 0-13-448720-6). P-H.

Oliver, Kenneth A. Words Every College Student Should Know. 465p. (Orig.). 1981. pap. 12.95 (ISBN 0-913244-50-3). Hapi Pr.

Sheeler, W. D. & Markley, R. W. Words, Words, Words, Bk 2. (Words, Words, Words). 128p. (gr. 9-12). 1981. pap. text ed. 6.95 (ISBN 0-88345-449-1). Regents Pub.

Shepherd, James F. RSVP: The Houghton Mifflin Reading, Study, & Vocabulary Program. (Illus.). 352p. 1981. pap. text ed. 8.50 (ISBN 0-395-29342-1); write for info. instr's manual (ISBN 0-395-29343-X). HM.

Sherk, Bill. More Brave New Words. LC 80-1729. (Illus.). 240p. 1981. pap. 6.95 (ISBN 0-385-17250-8). Doubleday.

Stanford, Gene. McGraw-Hill Vocabulary, Bk 1. 2nd ed. Weeden, Hester E., ed. (Illus.). 128p. (gr. 7-12). 1981. pap. text ed. 3.84 (ISBN 0-07-060771-0). McGraw.

--McGraw-Hill Vocabulary: Book 2. 2nd ed. (McGraw-Hill Vocabulary Ser.). Orig. Title: Vocab 2. (Illus.). 128p. 1981. pap. text ed. 4.24 (ISBN 0-07-060772-9). McGraw.

VOCABULARY–JUVENILE LITERATURE

Lewis, Norman. Instant Word Power. (Orig.). 1981. pap. text ed. price not set (ISBN 0-87720-963-4). AMSCO Sch.

Sarnoff, Jane. Words?! A Book About the Origins of Everyday Words & Phrases. (Illus.). 48p. (gr. 4-7). 1981. 8.95 (ISBN 0-686-69286-1). Scribner.

Scarry, Richard. Richard Scarry's Lowly Worm Word Book. LC 80-53103. (Chunky Bks.). (Illus.). 28p. (ps). 1981. pap. 2.50 board (ISBN 0-686-69031-1). Random.

VOCAL CULTURE

see Singing

VOCALISTS

see Singers

VOCATION

see also Professions; Vocational Guidance

McCarthy, Marianthy. Readings in English: Careers, Bk 3. 112p. (gr. 9-12). 1981. pap. text ed. price not set (ISBN 0-88345-425-4, 18884). Regents Pub.

VOCATION, CHOICE OF

see Vocational Guidance

VOCATIONAL EDUCATION

Here are entered works on vocational instruction within the standard educational system. Works on the vocationally oriented process of endowing people with a skill after either completion or termination of their formal education are entered under Occupational Training. Works on retraining persons with obsolete vocational skills are entered under Occupational Retraining. Works on the training of employees on the job are entered under Employees, Training Of.

see also Deaf–Education; Employees, Training Of; Forestry Schools and Education; Medical Colleges; Occupational Training

Careers Research & Advisory Centre, ed. Graduate Studies (United Kingdom), Nineteen Eighty to Eighty-One. 1191p. 1980. 135.00x (ISBN 0-86021-342-0). Intl Pubns Serv.

Dowding, Howard & Boyce, Sheila. Getting the Job You Want. (Orig.). 1980. pap. 5.95x (ISBN 0-8464-1012-5). Beekman Pubs.

Edelhart, Michael. Breaking in Book Two: Real Life Stories on the Career Trail. LC 80-2047. 240p. 1981. pap. 6.95 (ISBN 0-385-15581-6, Anch). Doubleday.

Hoyt, Kenneth. Career Education: Where It Is & Where It's Going. 280p. 1981. text ed. price not set (ISBN 0-913420-92-1). Olympus Pub Co.

Marten, Elizabeth. Work-a-Day: Your Classrookm Employment Agency. 59p. 1979. pap. 4.95 (ISBN 0-914634-73-9, 7919). DOK Pubs.

Powell, C Randall & Kirts, Donald K. Career Sevices Today: A Dynamic College Profession. LC 79-54801. 1980. pap. 11.95 (ISBN 0-913936-13-8). Coll Placement.

Wright, R. Thomas & Jensen, Thomas R. Manufacturing Laboratory Manual. 192p. 1980. 4.00 (ISBN 0-87006-292-1). Goodheart.

Zunker, Vernon G. Career Counseling. LC 80-23030. 357p. 1980. text ed. 16.95 (ISBN 0-8185-0428-5). Brooks-Cole.

VOCATIONAL GUIDANCE

see also Blind–Education; Counseling; Deaf–Education; Personnel Service in Education; Professions; Vocational Rehabilitation

Aldan, Daisy. Breakthrough. 6.95 (ISBN 0-913152-02-1). Green Hill.

Barrett, James & Williams, Geoffrey. Test Your Own Job Aptitude: Exploring Your Career Potential. 128p. 1981. pap. 2.95 (ISBN 0-14-005809-5). Penguin.

Bolles, R. N. What Color Is Your Parachute? 1981 Ed. (Illus.). 1981. 14.95 (ISBN 0-89815-047-7); pap. 6.95 (ISBN 0-89815-046-9). Ten Speed Pr.

Bolles, Richard N. The Quick Job-Hunting Map: Advanced Version Trade. pap. 1.50 (ISBN 0-89815-008-6). Ten Speed Pr.

--What Color Is Your Parachute? rev. ed. 352p. 1981. 14.95 (ISBN 0-89815-047-7); pap. 6.95 (ISBN 0-89815-046-9). Ten Speed Pr.

Borchard, David C., et al. Your Career: Choices, Chances, Changes. 368p. 1980. pap. text ed. 15.95 (ISBN 0-8403-2293-3). Kendall-Hunt.

Bostwick, Burdette. One Hundred One Proven Techniques for Getting the Job Interview. 256p. 1981. 12.95 (ISBN 0-471-07762-3, Pub. by Wiley-Interscience). Wiley.

Brooks, Patrice M. How to Get Any Job You Really Want. 1980. write for info. Unique Ent.

The Career Directory. 1981. pap. 9.95 (ISBN 0-686-69085-0). Dial.

Career Planning & Decision-Making for College Students. 5.95; instrs'. 7.50. McKnight.

Corwen, Leonard. Your Job: Where to Find It---How to Get It. LC 80-22251. 256p. 1981. lib. bdg. 11.95 (ISBN 0-668-05129-9); pap. 6.95 (ISBN 0-668-05131-0). Arco.

Doyle, Robert V. Careers for a Small World: Working & Living with Appropriate Technology. (Illus.). 190p. (gr. 9-12). 1981. PLB price not set. Messner.

DuPre, Flint O. Your Career in Federal Civil Service. 288p. 1981. pap. 4.95 (ISBN 0-06-463529-5, EH529, EH). Har-Row.

Erdlen, John A., ed. Job Hunting Guide. 2nd ed. LC 75-3824. (Career Guide Management Ser.). 160p. 1981. 12.95 (ISBN 0-89047-044-8); pap. 5.95 (ISBN 0-89047-043-X). Herman Pub.

Fregly, Bert. Help Wanted: Everything You Need to Get the Job You Deserve. pap. 9.95 (ISBN 0-88280-071-X). Chicago Review.

German, Donald R. & German, Joan W. How to Find a Job When Jobs Are Hard to Find. 387p. 1981. 14.95 (ISBN 0-8144-5677-4). Am Mgmt.

Greco, Ben. How to Get the Job That's Right for You: A Career Guide for the 80's. rev. ed. LC 79-56085. 210p. (Orig.). 1981. pap. 6.95 (ISBN 0-87094-194-1). Dow Jones-Irwin.

Hammell, Grandin K. The Sure Way to Get Job Interviews. Brown, Karen A., ed. (Educational Ser.). (Illus.). 78p. (Orig.). (gr. 11-12). 1980. tchrs. ed. 4.50 (ISBN 0-936510-00-5, 101); wkbk. 9.00. Diamond Pubs.

Herr, Edwin L. & Moore, Roberta. Your Working Life: A Guide to Getting & Holding a Job. LC 79-28360. Orig. Title: Career Education. (Illus.). 464p. 1980. 13.28 (ISBN 0-07-028342-7, G); tchrs. manual 3.00 (ISBN 0-07-028344-3); student wkbk. 5.00 (ISBN 0-07-028343-5). McGraw.

Johnson, Joanna. Working at Home for Profit. 243p. 1980. 25.00x (ISBN 0-631-12771-2, Pub. by Basil Blackwell); pap. 9.95x (ISBN 0-631-12583-3). Biblio Dist.

Jones, Marilyn. Exploring Careers in Special Education. (Careers in Depth Ser.). (Illus.). 128p. 1981. lib. bdg. 5.97 (ISBN 0-8239-0539-X). Rosen Pr.

Kingstone, Brett M. The Student Entrepreneur's Guide. 192p. (Orig.). 1981. pap. 4.95 (ISBN 0-89815-045-0). Ten Speed Pr.

Lathrop, Richard. Don't Use a Resume. 1980. pap. 1.95 (ISBN 0-89815-027-2). Ten Speed Pr.

Lewis, Florence. Help Wanted: A Guide to Career Counseling in the Bay Area. 4.95 (ISBN 0-931018-03-X). Green Hill.

Lombardi, Thomas P. Career Adaptive Behavior Inventory Activity Book. Preston, J. B., ed. 88p. (Orig.). 1980. pap. text ed. 10.00x (ISBN 0-87562-066-3). Spec Child.

Martin, Phyllis. Martin's Magic Formula for Getting the Right Job. 160p. 1981. 10.95 (ISBN 0-312-51702-5). St Martin.

Miller, Gordon. How to Choose a Career After College. 128p. 1981. 4.95 (ISBN 0-346-12443-3). Cornerstone.

Mitchell, Ian. Job Hunting Blueprint: How to Get the Job You Want. (Orig.). 1981. pap. 5.95 (ISBN 0-938306-00-6). Shoreline Pub.

Noer, David. How to Beat the Employment Game. Date not set. pap. 4.95 (ISBN 0-913668-96-6). Ten Speed Pr.

Pearson, Henry G. Your Hidden Skills: Clues to Careers & Future Pursuits. (Illus.). 150p. (Orig.). 1981. pap. price not set (ISBN 0-9605368-0-9). Mowry Pr.

Perry, William E. Orchestrating Your Career. 192p. 1981. pap. 13.95 (ISBN 0-8436-0799-8). CBI Pub.

Polking, Kirk, ed. Internships Nineteen Hundred Eighty-One. (Orig.). 1981. pap. 6.95 (ISBN 0-89879-036-0). Writers Digest.

R. B. Uleck Associates. Federal Career Guide. (Illus., Orig.). 1979. pap. 5.95 (ISBN 0-937562-03-3). Uleck Assoc.

R. B Uleck Associates. Life Sciences Jobs Handbook. (Illus., Orig.). 1979. pap. 9.95 (ISBN 0-937562-01-7). Uleck Assoc.

R. B. Uleck Associates. Social & Behavioral Sciences Jobs Handbook. (Illus.). 48p. (Orig.). 1979. pap. 9.95 (ISBN 0-937562-02-5). Uleck Assoc.

Raelin, Joseph A. Building a Career: The Effect of Initial Job Experiences & Related Work Attitudes on Later Employment. LC 80-24848. 178p. 1980. text ed. 7.00 (ISBN 0-911558-74-8); pap. text ed. 4.50 (ISBN 0-911558-73-X). Upjohn Inst.

Rinella, Richard J. & Robbins, Claire C. Career Power. 281p. 1981. 14.95 (ISBN 0-8144-5630-8); comb-bound 16.95 (ISBN 0-8144-7009-2). Am Mgmt.

Schmidt, Peggy J. Making It on Your First Job: When You're Young, Inexperienced & Ambitious. 288p. 1981. pap. 2.95 (ISBN 0-380-77354-6). Avon.

Shapiro, Stanley J. Exploring Careers in Science. (Careers in Depth Ser.). (Illus.). 140p. 1981. lib. bdg. 5.97 (ISBN 0-8239-0535-7). Rosen Pr.

Smith, Brenda H. & Shambaugh, Irvin C. AIMS Information About Aptitudes. rev. ed. 201p. 1980. pap. 10.00 (ISBN 0-9602710-1-5). Aptitude Inventory.

Tack, Alfred. Sell Your Way to Success. 6th ed. 256p. 1978. pap. 13.50x (ISBN 0-220-66366-1, Pub. by Busn Bks England). Renouf.

Taylor, F. J. The Right Way to a Good Job. 174p. 1979. pap. 9.75x (ISBN 0-220-66364-5, Pub. by Busn Bks England). Renouf.

Tomlinson, James & Dibden, Kenneth. Information Sources in Education & Work. LC 80-41801. (Butterworths Guides to Information Sources Ser.). 168p. 1980. text ed. 22.95 (ISBN 0-408-70923-5). Butterworths.

Ulrich, Heinz & Conner, Robert. National Job Finding Guide. LC 79-6182. 336p. 1981. pap. 10.95 (ISBN 0-385-15782-7, Dolp). Doubleday.

Van Roden, Albert. You're Hired! (Illus.). 64p. 1981. pap. 2.95 (ISBN 0-89709-025-X). Liberty Pub.

Wray, Monika J., et al. Unified Vocational Preparation: An Evaluation of the Pilot Programme. (Report of the National Foundation for Educational Research in England & Wales). 289p. 1980. pap. text ed. 19.25x (ISBN 0-85633-199-6). Humanities.

Zehring, John W. Careers in State & Local Government. LC 80-67448. (Illus.). 236p. 1980. pap. 10.95 (ISBN 0-912048-15-8). Garrett Pk.

VOCATIONAL GUIDANCE–RELIGIOUS ASPECTS

see Vocation

VOCATIONAL GUIDANCE FOR WOMEN

see also Women–Employment; Women in Business also subdivision Vocational Guidance under appropriate subjects

Catalyst Staff. Making the Most of Your First Job. 288p. 1981. 11.95 (ISBN 0-399-12609-0). Putnam.

Tobin, McLean. The Black Female Ph.D. Education & Career Development. LC 80-5578. 133p. 1980. lib. bdg. 15.25 (ISBN 0-8191-1312-3); pap. text ed. 7.25 (ISBN 0-8191-1313-1). U Pr of Amer.

Wider Opportunities for Women, Inc. Suit Yourself...Shopping for a Job. Kaplan, Roberta, ed. LC 80-53209. (Illus.). 52p. (Orig.). 1980. pap. text ed. 5.00 (ISBN 0-934966-02-8). WOW Inc.

VOCATIONAL NURSING

see Practical Nursing

VOCATIONAL OPPORTUNITIES

see Vocational Guidance

VOCATIONAL REHABILITATION

see also Handicapped–Employment; Vocational Guidance

Crawford, Fred L. Career Planning for the Blind: A Manual for Students & Teachers. 189p. 1966. 3.95 (ISBN 0-374-11905-8). FS&G.

Weisgerber, Robert A., et al. Training the Handicapped for Productive Employment. 450p. 1980. text ed. 29.50 (ISBN 0-89443-331-8). Aspen Systems.

VOCATIONAL TRAINING

see Occupational Training

VOICE

see also Automatic Speech Recognition; Larynx; Phonetics; Public Speaking; Respiration; Singing; Speech

Large, John, ed. Contributions of Voice Research to Singing. LC 79-57539. (Illus.). 432p. 1980. pap. text ed. 30.00 (ISBN 0-933014-53-8). College-Hill.

VOICE–CARE AND HYGIENE

Greene, Margaret. The Voice & Its Disorders. 4th ed. 446p. 1980. 47:50. Lippincott.

VOLCANOES

see also Rocks, Igneous;

also names of volcanoes, e.g. Hekla, Vesuvius

Asimov, Isaac. How Did We Find Out About Volcanoes? (History of Science Ser.). (Illus.). 64p. (gr. 4-7). 1981. 6.95 (ISBN 0-8027-6411-8); PLB 7.85 (ISBN 0-8027-6412-6). Walker & Co.

Kelso, Linda. Mount St. Helens & Other Volcanoes of the West. Shangle, Robert D., ed. (Illus.). 144p. 1980. 27.50 (ISBN 0-89802-202-9). Beautiful Am.

Radlauer, Ruth. Volcanoes. LC 80-25464. (Illus.). 48p. (gr. 3 up). 1981. PLB 9.25g (ISBN 0-516-07835-6, Elk Grove Bks). Childrens.

Ritchie, David. The Ring of Fire. LC 80-69391. (Illus.). 296p. 1981. 12.95 (ISBN 0-689-11150-9). Atheneum.

Secor, R. J. Mexico's Volcanoes: A Climbing Guide. (Illus.). 96p. (Orig.). 1981. pap. 6.95 (ISBN 0-89886-016-4). Mountaineers.

Williams, Chuck. Mount St. Helens: A Changing Landscape. (Illus.). 128p. 27.50 (ISBN 0-912856-63-7). Graphic Arts Ctr.

VOLITION

see Will

VOLKSWAGEN (AUTOMOBILE)

see Automobiles, Foreign–Types–Volkswagen

VOLLEYBALL

Fernandez, Linda & Evans, Walt. Volleyball. (Burns Sports Ser.). 156p. Date not set. pap. cancelled (ISBN 0-695-81570-9). Follett.

VOLT OHMMETER

see Voltohmmeter

VOLTAIRE, FRANCOIS MARIE AROUET DE, 1694-1778

Andrews, Wayne. Voltaire. LC 80-29565. (Illus.). 1981. 13.95 (ISBN 0-8112-0800-1); pap. 5.95 (ISBN 0-8112-0802-8, NDP519). New Directions.
--Voltaire. (Illus.). 13.95 (ISBN 0-8112-0800-1); pap. 5.95 (ISBN 0-8112-0802-8, NDP519). New Directions.
Chase, Cleveland B. The Young Voltaire. 253p. 1980. Repr. of 1926 ed. lib. bdg. 35.00 (ISBN 0-8495-0799-5). Arden Lib.
Voltaire. (Twayne's World Authors Ser.: No. 583). Date not set. cloth 10.95 (ISBN 0-8057-6425-9). Twayne.

VOLTOHMMETER

Middleton, Robert G. One Hundred & One Ways to Use Your VOM, TVM, DVM. 3rd ed. LC 80-52934. 1980. pap. 9.95 (ISBN 0-672-21756-2). Sams.

VOLUME FEEDING

see Food Service

VOLUNTARY ORGANIZATIONS

see Associations, Institutions, etc.

VOLUNTEER MILITARY SERVICE

see Military Service, Voluntary

VOLUNTEER WORKERS IN SOCIAL SERVICE

Kramer, Ralph M. Voluntary Agencies in the Welfare State. 400p. 1981. 24.95x (ISBN 0-520-04290-5). U of Cal Pr.

VOLVO (AUTOMOBILE)

see Automobiles, Foreign–Types–Volvo

VOM

see Voltohmmeter

VONNEGUT, KURT, JR., 1922-

Schatt, Stanley, ed. Kurt Vonnegut, Jr. LC 76-41754. (Twayne's U. S. Authors Ser.). 174p. 1976. pap. text ed. 4.95 (ISBN 0-672-61510-X). Bobbs.
Vonnegut, Kurt. Palm Sunday. 1981. 13.95 (ISBN 0-440-06593-3). Delacorte.

VOODOOISM

Haskins, Jim. Voodoo & Hoodoo. LC 77-17213. (Illus.). 226p. 1981. pap. 6.95 (ISBN 0-8128-6085-3). Stein & Day.

VORTEX-MOTION

see also Wakes (Fluid Dynamics)

Swift, Walter L., et al, eds. Vortex Flows. 171p. 1980. 28.00 (G00181). ASME.

VOTERS, REGISTRATION OF

NASSP. Voter Education Curriculum Guide. Bruce, Carol, ed. 78p. (Orig.). 1980. pap. text ed. 10.00 (ISBN 0-88210-114-5). Natl Assn Principals.

VOTING

see also Voters, Registration Of

Fiorina, Morris P. Retrospective Voting in American National Electiona. LC 80-24454. (Illus.). 288p. 1981. text ed. 35.00x (ISBN 0-300-02557-2); pap. 9.95 (ISBN 0-300-02703-6). Yale U Pr.
Keech, William R. The Impact of Negro Voting: The Role of the Vote in the Quest for Equality. LC 80-26518. (American Politics Research Ser.). ix, 113p. 1981. Repr. of 1968 ed. lib. bdg. 19.75x (ISBN 0-313-22774-8, KEIN). Greenwood.

VOYAGES AND TRAVELS

see also Adventure and Adventurers; Aeronautics–Flights; Air Travel; Buccaneers; Discoveries (In Geography); Mountaineering; Ocean Travel; Pirates; Seafaring Life; Shipwrecks; Travel; Travelers; Whaling; Yachts and Yachting

also subdivision Description and Travel (or Description, Geography) and Discovery and Exploration under names of countries, regions, etc., names of regions, e.g. Antarctic Regions; and names of ships

Barhydt, Hap. Voyage of a Lifetime: A Journal. (Illus.). 75p. (Orig.). 1980. pap. 4.95 (ISBN 0-9605346-0-1). Remarkable Pubns.
Boit, John. The Log of the Union: John Boit's Remarkable Voyage, 1794-1796. Hayes, Edmund, Sr., intro. by. LC 80-83181. (North Pacific Studies: No. 6). (Illus.). 250p. 1981. 14.95 (ISBN 0-87595-068-X); pap. 9.95 (ISBN 0-87595-089-2). Oreg Hist Soc.
Davidson, Robyn. Tracks. (Illus.). 1981. 11.95 (ISBN 0-394-51473-4). Pantheon.
Davison, Ann, et al. Great Voyages in Small Boats Solo Transatlantic. 1981. 15.00 (ISBN 0-8286-0085-6). De Graff.
Dutton, June. The Adventures of the S. S. Happiness Crew: Cap'n Joshua's Dangerous Dilemma. (Illus.). 1980. 4.95 (ISBN 0-915696-36-3). Determined Prods.
Gerbault, Alain. Firecrest Round the World. 1981. 12.50 (ISBN 0-679-51026-5). McKay.
Gilchrist, Peter S. My Amateur World. (Illus.). 200p. 1975. text ed. 10.00. Gilchem Corp.
Guggenheim, Hans G. Around the World in Eighty Ways. 64p. (Orig.). 1981. pap. 6.00 (ISBN 0-682-49683-9). Exposition.
Hamilton, Frederic. Here, There & Everywhere. 332p. 1980. Repr. of 1921 ed. lib. bdg. 20.00 (ISBN 0-8492-5273-3). R West.
James, Henry. Transatlantic Sketches. 448p. 1981. cancelled (ISBN 0-8180-1177-7). Horizon.
Jones, Tristan. Saga of a Wayward Sailor. 272p. (Orig.). 1980. pap. 2.75 (ISBN 0-380-52985-8, 52985). Avon.
Kennedy, James Y. South Seas Odyssey: An Escape. LC 79-904. (Illus.). 182p. (Orig.). 1979. pap. 5.95 (ISBN 0-9605088-0-5). Kennedy Pub.
Kiseli, Karl. Incompatible Destinies. 1980. 10.95 (ISBN 0-533-04518-5). Vantage.
McKelvy, John E., Jr. Translantic Summer. 1981. 10.00 (ISBN 0-533-04786-2). Vantage.
Miller, Christian. Daisy, Daisy: A Journey Across America on a Bicycle. LC 80-2946. 192p. 1981. 11.95 (ISBN 0-385-17475-6). Doubleday.
Rankin, Jake & Rankin, Marni. Getaway Guide II: More Short Vacations in the Pacific Northwest. 192p. 1981. pap. 8.95 (ISBN 0-914718-56-8). Pacific Search.
Smith, Herbert. Dreams of Natural Places: A New England Schooner Odyssey, LC 80-69529. (Illus.). 102p. 1981. 15.95 (ISBN 0-89272-107-3). Down East.
Stewart, Harris B., Jr. & Henderson, J. Welles, eds. Challenger Sketchbook: B. Shephard's Sketchbook of the H.M.S. Challenger Expedition 1872-1874. (Illus.). 34p. 1972. 25.00 (ISBN 0-913346-01-2). Phila Maritime Mus.
Zarian, Gostan. The Traveller & His Road. Baliozian, Ara, tr. from Armenian, LC 80-22809. 160p. (Orig.). 1981. pap. 5.95 (ISBN 0-935102-04-3). Ashod Pr.

VOYAGES AND TRAVELS–GUIDEBOOKS

Burckhardt, Jakob. The Cicerone: An Art Guide to Painting in Italy for the Use of Travellers & Students. Freedberg, Sydney J., ed. LC 77-18677. (Connoisseurship, Criticism & Art History Ser.: Vol. 3). 305p. 1979. lib. bdg. 30.00. Garland Pub.
Carroll, Frieda, compiled by. The People's Travel Book. LC 80-70869. 115p. 1981. 17.95; pap. 12.95. Biblio Pr Ga.
Clark, Merrian E. Ford's Freighter Travel Guide: Published Semi-Annually, March & September. 57th ed. D'Ascenzo, Juliann & Wilson, Bonnie, eds. LC 54-3845. (Illus.). 140p. pap. 4.95 (ISBN 0-916486-57-5). Fords Travel.
--Ford's International Cruise Guide. 28th ed. Wilson, Bonnie & D'Ascenzo, Juliann, eds. LC 75-29725. (Illus.). 160p. 1981. pap. 5.95 (ISBN 0-916486-56-7). M Clark.
--Ford's International Cruise Guide: Summer 1981. 29th ed. Wilson, Bonnie & D'Ascenzo, Juliann, eds. LC 75-29725. (Illus.). 160p. 1981. pap. 5.95 (ISBN 0-916486-59-1). M Clark.
Curtiss, Richard A. Taking off. Schriver, Peter, ed. 188p. (Orig.). 1981. pap. 4.95 (ISBN 0-517-53901-2, Harmony). Crown.
Discovery Magazine Editors. Traveler's Choice: A Treasury of America's Regional Restaurants & Their Favorite Recipes. LC 80-53813. (Illus.). 256p. (Orig.). 1981. pap. 4.95 (ISBN 0-528-88042-X). Rand.
Fielding's Worldwide Guide to Cruises. 320p. 1981. Fieldingflex 11.95 (ISBN 0-688-00422-9). Morrow.
Heise, Jon O., ed. The Travel Books: Guide to the Travel Guides. (Popular Bks.). 304p. 1981. pap. 24.95 (ISBN 0-8352-1337-4). Bowker.
London, Mel. Easy Going: A Guide to Good Health & Good Spirits on Your Journey Away from Home. (Illus.). 320p. (Orig.). 1981. 12.95 (ISBN 0-87857-331-3); pap. 9.95 (ISBN 0-87857-345-3). Rodale Pr Inc.
MacRobbie, Bill. Add Spice to Your Travels. (Illus.). 196p. 1980. pap. 4.95 (ISBN 0-9605244-0-1). B Sales.
Rand McNally. Pocket Vacation Guide. 1981. pap. 3.95 (ISBN 0-528-84547-0). Rand.
Road Notes. LC 80-53814. 1981. pap. 6.95 (ISBN 0-528-84546-2). Rand.
Sinor, John. Small Escapes Under the Sun. 1981. pap. 4.95 (ISBN 0-935572-10-4). Alive Pubns.
Weintz, Caroline & Weintz, Walter. The Discount Guide for Travelers Over Fifty-Five. 1981. pap. 5.95 (ISBN 0-525-93175-9). Dutton.

VOYAGES AND TRAVELS–VIEWS

see Geography–Pictorial Works; Views

VULCANITE

see Rubber

VULVA

Copenhaver, Edward H. Surgery of the Vulva & Vagina: A Practical Guide. (Illus.). 100p. 1981. text ed. write for info. (ISBN 0-7216-2718-8). Saunders.
Stening, Malcolm. Cancer & Related Lesions of the Vulva. (Illus.). 184p. 1980. text ed. 45.00 (ISBN 0-909337-22-5). ADIS Pr.

W

WAFFLES

see Pancakes, Waffles, etc.

WAGE-FUND

see Wages

WAGE-PRICE CONTROLS

see Wage-Price Policy

WAGE-PRICE GUIDELINES

see Wage-Price Policy

WAGE-PRICE POLICY

Gould, John & Bittlingmayer, George. Economics of the Davis-Bacon Act: An Analysis of Prevailing Wage Laws. 1980. pap. 4.25 (ISBN 0-8447-3381-4). Am Enterprise.

WAGES

Here are listed general works and those dealing primarily with the United states. Note other subdivisions below, e.g., Wages–Statistics, Wages–Great Britain, etc.

see also Cost and Standard of Living; Non-Wage Payments; Payrolls; Profit-Sharing; Wage-Price Policy

Adie, Douglas K. An Evaluation of Postal Service Wage Rates. 1977. pap. 3.75 (ISBN 0-8447-3265-6). Am Enterprise.
Chastain, Sherry. Winning the Salary Game: Salary Negotiation for Women. 192p. 1980. text ed. 9.95 (ISBN 0-471-08433-6); pap. text ed. 6.95 (ISBN 0-471-08023-3). Wiley.
International Labour Office. Wage Determination in Asia & the Pacific: The Views of Employers' Organisations-Reports & Documents Submitted to an ILO-DANIDA Regional Seminar (Singapore, October 8-12, 1979) (Labour-Management Relations Ser.: No. 58). ii, 169p. (Orig.). 1980. pap. 11.40 (ISBN 92-2-102492-X). Intl Labour Office.
Langer, Steven, ed. Compensation in Human Resource Development. 1981. pap. 75.00 (ISBN 0-916506-59-2). Abbott Langer Assocs.
--Compensation of Industrial Engineering. 6th ed. 1981. 60.00 (ISBN 0-916506-63-0). Abbott Langer Assocs.
--Inter-City Wage & Salary Differentials, 1981. 1981. pap. 75.00 (ISBN 0-916506-62-2). Abbott Langer Assocs.
--Salaries & Related Matters in the Service Department, 1981. 1981. pap. 85.00 (ISBN 0-686-69467-8). Abbott Langer Assocs.
Sgro, Pasquale M. Wage Differentials & Economic Growth. 147p. 1980. 28.50x (ISBN 0-389-20002-6). B&N.
Whitmore, D. A. & Ibbetson, J. The Management of Motivation & Renumeration. 230p. 1977. text ed. 29.50x (ISBN 0-220-66319-X, Pub. by Busn Bks England). Renouf.

WAGES–MINIMUM WAGE

Welch, Finis. Minimum Wages: Issues & Evidence. 1978. pap. 4.25 (ISBN 0-8447-3308-3). Am Enterprise.

WAGES–JAPAN

Wage Increases & Labour Productivity in Japanese Smaller Business. 34p. 1972. 2.75 (APO11, APO). Unipub.

WAGNER, COSIMA (LISZT), 1837-1930

Marek, George R. Cosima Wagner. LC 80-7591. (Illus.). 256p. 1981. 15.95 (ISBN 0-06-012704-X, HarpT). Har-Row.

WAGNER, RICHARD, 1813-1883

Adorno, Theodor. In Search of Wagner. 160p. 1981. 14.50 (ISBN 0-8052-7087-6, Pub. by NLB England). Schocken.
Barth, Herbert, ed. Internationale Wagner - Bibliographie: 1967-1978. LC 80-483676. 175p. (Orig.). 1979. pap. 12.50 (ISBN 3-921733-08-1). Intl Pubns Serv.
Beckett, Lucy. Richard Wagner: Parsifal. (Cambridge Opera Handbooks Ser.). (Illus.). 220p. Date not set. price not set (ISBN 0-521-22825-5); pap. price not set (ISBN 0-521-29662-5). Cambridge U Pr.
Josserand, Frank B. Richard Wagner: Patriot & Politician. LC 80-5638. 351p. (Orig.). 1981. lib. bdg. 20.50 (ISBN 0-8191-1418-9); pap. text ed. 11.75 (ISBN 0-8191-1419-7). U Pr of Amer.
Neumann, Angelo. Personal Recollections of Wagner. (Music Reprint Ser.). 329p. 1976. Repr. of 1906 ed. 25.00. Da Capo.

WAGNER, RICHARD, 1813-1883–JUVENILE LITERATURE

Marie Eugene. I Want to See God. M. Verda Clare, tr. 1981. pap. cancelled (ISBN 0-87061-051-1). Chr Classics.

WAGONS

see also Carriages and Carts

Smith, D. J. Collecting & Restoring Horse-Drawn Vehicles. (Illus.). 192p. 1981. 39.95 (ISBN 0-85059-429-4). Aztex.

WAGONS, ARMY

see Vehicles, Military

WAITING-LINE THEORY

see Queuing Theory

WAKEFULNESS

see Insomnia

WAKES (FLUID DYNAMICS)

French, Henri, ed. Heat Transfer & Fluid Flow in Nuclear Systems. 300p. 1981. 30.01 (ISBN 0-08-027181-2). Pergamon.

WALAPAI INDIANS

see Indians of North America–Southwest, New

WALDORF-ASTORIA HOTEL, NEW YORK

Morehouse, Ward, III. The Waldorf: The Story Behind America's Grandest Hotel. (Illus.). 320p. 1981. 11.95 (ISBN 0-399-12541-8). Putnam.

WALES–ANTIQUITIES

McBryde, Isabel. Coast & Estuary: Archaeological Coast of New South Wales at Wombah & Schnapper Point. (Australian Institute of Aboriginal Studies). 1981. pap. text ed. write for info. (ISBN 0-391-02194-X). Humanities.

WALES–DESCRIPTION AND TRAVEL

see also Great Britain–Description and Travel

Wales Tourist Board. Wales: Going Places. (Illus.). 72p. 1980. pap. write for info. (ISBN 0-900784-76-8, Pub. by Auto Assn-British Tourist Authority England). Merrimack Bk Serv.

WALES–DESCRIPTION AND TRAVEL–GUIDEBOOKS

Wales Tourist Board. Castles & Historic Places in Wales. rev. ed. (Illus.). 104p. 1981. pap. write for info. (ISBN 0-900784-77-6, Pub. by Auto Assn-British Tourist Authority England). Merrimack Bk Serv.
--Mid Wales: A Tourist Guide. (Illus.). 84p. Date not set. pap. price not set (ISBN 0-900784-72-5, Pub. by Auto Assn-British Tourist Authority England). Merrimack Bk Serv.
--North Wales: A Tourist Guide. rev. ed. (Illus.). 84p. Date not set. pap. price not set (ISBN 0-900784-71-7, Pub. by Auto Assn-British Tourist Authority England). Merrimack Bk Serv.
--South Wales: A Tourist Guide. rev. ed. (Illus.). 84p. 1981. pap. write for info. (ISBN 0-900784-73-3, Pub. by Auto Assn-British Tourist Authority England). Merrimack Bk Serv.
--Wales: Where to Stay. rev. ed. (Illus.). 380p. 1981. pap. price not set (ISBN 0-900784-79-2, Pub. by Auto Assn-British Tourist Authority England). Merrimack Bk Serv.

WALES–ECONOMIC CONDITIONS

Rees, Gareth & Rees, Teresa L., eds. Poverty & Social Inequality in Wales. 279p. 1980. 30.00x (ISBN 0-7099-2200-0, Pub. by Croom Helm Ltd England). Biblio Dist.

WALES–HISTORY

Morgan, Kenneth O. Rebirth of a Nation: Wales 1880-1980. (History of Wales Ser.: Vol. VI). 1981. 25.00 (ISBN 0-19-821736-6). Oxford U Pr.

WALHALLA, AUSTRALIA

Paull, Raymond. Old Walhalla: Portrait of a Gold Town. 148p. 1980. pap. 8.00x (ISBN 0-522-84212-7, Pub. by Melbourne U Pr Australia). Intl Schol Bk Serv.

WALKING

see also Hiking; Trails

Carothers, Merlin, tr. La Alabanza En Accion. (Spanish Bks.). (Span.). 1979. 1.60 (ISBN 0-8297-0490-6). Life Pubs Intl.
--Louvor Em Acao. (Portugese Bks.). (Port.). 1979. 1.25 (ISBN 0-8297-0638-0). Life Pubs Intl.
Consumer Guide, ed. The Complete Book of Walking. 1980. 5.95 (ISBN 0-671-41286-8, Fireside). S&S.
Dreyfack, Raymond. The Complete Book of Walking. LC 80-26185. (Illus.). 288p. 1981. pap. 5.95 (ISBN 0-668-05167-1, 5167). Arco.
Rowan, Lilian & Laiken, D. S. Speedwalking: The Exercise Alternative. 1980. 9.95 (ISBN 0-686-68357-9). Putnam.
Stutman, Fred A. & Africano, Lillian. The Doctor's Walking Book. (Orig.). 1980. pap. 6.95 (ISBN 0-345-28764-9). Ballantine.
Westacott, Hugh D. The Walker's Handbook. (Illus., Orig.). 1979. pap. 5.95 (ISBN 0-14-046267-8). Penguin.

WALKING PATIENT CARE

see Ambulatory Medical Care

WALKS, GARDEN

see Garden Walks

WALL-PAPER

see also Tapestry

Lynn, Catherine. Wallpaper in America: From the Seventeenth Century to World War I. (Illus.). 1980. 45.00 (ISBN 0-393-01448-7, A Barra Foundation - Cooper-Hewitt Bk). Norton.

WALL STREET

Little, Jeffrey B. & Rhodes, Lucien. Understanding Wall Street. LC 78-54787. (Illus.). 220p. 1980. pap. 7.95 (ISBN 0-89709-010-1). Liberty Pub.

WALLACE, EDGAR, 1875-1932

Lane, Margaret. Edgar Wallace. 423p. 1980. Repr. lib. bdg. 30.00 (ISBN 0-8495-3259-0). Arden Lib.

WALLACE, HENRY AGARD, 1888-1965

Macdonald, Dwight. Henry Wallace: The Man & the Myth. Freidel, Frank, ed. LC 78-66546. (The History of the United States Ser.: Vol. 11). 188p. 1979. lib. bdg. 15.00 (ISBN 0-8240-9701-7). Garland Pub.

WALLS

see also Foundations; Masonry

Banov, Abel & Lytle, Marie-Jeanne. Successful Wallcoverings & Decoration. 2nd ed. Case, Virginia A., ed. (Successful Ser.). (Illus.). 136p. 1981. 17.95 (ISBN 0-89999-021-5); pap. 7.95 (ISBN 0-89999-022-3). Structures Pub.
Greener. The Everything Book of Floors, Walls, & Ceilings. (Illus.). 250p. 1980. 14.95 (ISBN 0-8359-1803-3); pap. 7.95 (ISBN 0-8359-1802-5). Reston.
Institute of Civil Engineers. Diaphragm Walls & Anchorages. 234p. 1980. 79.00x (ISBN 0-7277-0005-7, Pub. by Telford England). State Mutual Bk.
--A Review of Diaphragm Walls. 158p. 1980. 35.00x (ISBN 0-7277-0045-6, Pub. by Telford England). State Mutual Bk.
Russell, James E. Walks, Walls & Fences. Horowitz, Shirley M. & Auer, Marilyn M., eds. (Illus., Orig.). 1981. pap. 6.95 (ISBN 0-932944-36-1). Creative Homeowner.

WALNUT

Thompson, Bruce. Black Walnut for Profit: A Guide to Risks & Rewards. (Illus.). 285p. Date not set. pap. 7.95 (ISBN 0-917304-40-3). Walnut AZ.

WALPOLE, HORACE, 4TH EARL OF OXFORD, 1717-1797
Riely, John C. The Age of Horace Walpole in Caricature: An Exhibition of Satirical Prints & Drawings from the Collection of W. S. Lewis. 48p. 1981. pap. text ed. 5.00x (ISBN 0-300-03509-8, 73-88450). Yale U Pr.
Stuart, Dorothy M. Horace Walpole. 229p. 1980. Repr. of 1927 ed. lib. bdg. 30.00 (ISBN 0-8492-8119-9). R West.
WALTER, BRUNO, 1877-1962
Walter, Bruno. Theme & Variations: An Autobiography. Galston, James A., tr. from Ger. LC 80-25558. (Illus.). xi, 344p. 1981. Repr. of 1946 ed. lib. bdg. 35.00x (ISBN 0-313-22635-0, WATV). Greenwood.
WAR
see also Air Warfare; Armies; Atomic Warfare; Battles; Chemical Warfare; Civil War; Disarmament; Martial Law; Militarism; Military Art and Science; Military Policy; Naval Art and Science; Peace; Psychological Warfare; Sociology, Military; Soldiers; Strategy; Tank Warfare; War and Society
also specific wars, battles, etc., Russo-Japanese War, 1904-1905; United States–History–Queen Anne's War, 1702-1713; Gettysburg, Battle of, 1863
Beer, Francis A. Peace Against War: The Ecology of International Violence. LC 80-27214. (International Relations Ser.). (Illus.). 1981. text ed. 18.95x (ISBN 0-7167-1250-4); pap. text ed. 9.95x (ISBN 0-7167-1251-2). W H Freeman.
Dennis, Lawrence & Martin, James J. The Dynamics of War & Revolution. 2nd ed. 259p. 1941. pap. 10.00 (ISBN 0-911038-91-4, Inst Hist Rev). Noontide.
Friedan, Leon, compiled by. The Law of War: A Documentary History, 2 vols. LC 72-765. 1972. Set. lib. bdg. 85.00 (ISBN 0-313-20133-1). Greenwood.
Moore, Roberta & Moore, Joseph. The Problem of War: A Global Issue. 144p. (gr. 10 up). 1980. pap. text ed. 6.19x (ISBN 0-8104-6073-4). Hayden.
Rollins, Leighton. Disasters of War. LC 80-69430. 1981. signed limited ed. 20.00 (ISBN 0-932274-16-1); pap. 4.00 (ISBN 0-932274-15-3). Cadmus Eds.
Rummel, Rudolph J. Understanding Conflict & War, 2 vols. Incl. Vol. 1. 342p. 18.95 (ISBN 0-470-74501-0); Vol. 2. The Conflict Helix. 17.50 (ISBN 0-470-15123-4). LC 74-78565. 1975-76. Halsted Pr.
Willmott, Ned & Pimlott, John. Strategy & Tactics of War. (Illus.). 240p. 1980. 16.95 (ISBN 0-85685-503-0). Quality Bks IL.
Ziegler. War, Peace & International Relations. 2nd ed. 1981. pap. text ed. 8.95 (ISBN 0-316-98493-0). Little.
WAR–LITERARY COLLECTIONS
see also War Poetry
Sayre, Joel & Faulkner, William. The Road to Glory: A Screenplay. Bruccoli, Matthew J., ed. (Illus.). 168p. 1981. price not set (ISBN 0-8093-0995-5); pap. price not set (ISBN 0-8093-0996-3). S Ill U Pr.
WAR–MORAL ASPECTS
see War and Morals; War and Religion
WAR–POETRY
see War Poetry
WAR–SOCIAL ASPECTS
see War and Society
WAR, MARITIME
see Naval Art and Science; Naval Battles
WAR, PRISONERS OF
see Prisoners of War
WAR AND CHRISTIANITY
see War and Religion
WAR AND MORALS
see also War and Religion
Eller, Vernard. War & Peace from Genesis to Revelation. 232p. 1981. pap. 8.95 (ISBN 0-8361-1947-9). Herald Pr.
WAR AND RELIGION
see also Conscientious Objectors; Nonviolence; Pacifism; War and Morals
also subdivision Religious Aspects under specific wars, e.g. World War, 1939-1945–Religious Aspects
Clouse, Robert G., ed. War: Four Christian Views. 220p. 1981. pap. 5.95 (ISBN 0-87784-801-7). Inter Varsity.
WAR AND SOCIETY
see also Sociology, Military
Mandelbaum, Michael. The Nuclear Revolution: International Politics Before & After Hiroshima. LC 80-24194. 256p. Date not set. price not set (ISBN 0-521-23819-6); pap. price not set (ISBN 0-521-28239-X). Cambridge U Pr.
Martin, Donald L. To the People: Prepare for War. 64p. 1981. 7.95 (ISBN 0-89962-043-4). Todd & Honeywell.
WAR CRIME TRIALS–NUREMBERG, 1945-1946
see Nuremberg Trial of Major German War Criminals, 1945-1946
WAR FILMS
Sayre, Joel & Faulkner, William. The Road to Glory: A Screenplay. Bruccoli, Matthew J., ed. (Illus.). 168p. 1981. price not set (ISBN 0-8093-0995-5); pap. price not set (ISBN 0-8093-0996-3). S Ill U Pr.
WAR GAMES
Sandars, John. Introduction to Wargaming. 11.95 (ISBN 0-7207-0861-3, Pub. by Michael Joseph). Merrimack Bk Serv.
WAR MAPS
see Geography, Historical–Maps; United States–Historical Geography–Maps
WAR OF NERVES
see Psychological Warfare
WAR OF 1914
see European War, 1914-1918
WAR OF SECESSION (U. S.)
see United States–History–Civil War, 1861-1865
WAR OF THE AMERICAN REVOLUTION
see United States–History–Revolution, 1775-1783
WAR POETRY
Winning Hearts & Minds: War Poems by Vietnam Veterans. LC 72-12486. 1972. pap. 3.50. Packrat Pr.
WAR PROFITS TAX
see Excess Profits Tax
WAR-SHIPS
see Warships
WARBLING PARAKEET
see Budgerigars
WARD, ARTEMUS
see Browne, Charles Farrar, 1834-1867
WARD, WILLIAM GEORGE, 1812-1882
Weaver, Mary J., ed. Letters from a "Modernist". The Letters from George Tyrrell to Wilfrid Ward, 1893-1908. LC 80-28372. 230p. 1981. 30.00 (ISBN 0-915762-12-9). Patmos Pr.
WARDS
see Guardian and Ward
WAREHOUSES
see also Pallets (Shipping, Storage, etc.)
Powell, Victor G. Warehousing: Analysis for Effective Operations. 240p. 1976. text ed. 29.50x (ISBN 0-220-66301-7, Pub. by Busn Bks England). Renouf.
WARING'S PROBLEM
see Partitions (Mathematics)
WARM-UP
see Exercise
WARPING
see Weaving
WARRANTS (LAW)
Berkowitz, David S. & Thorne, Samuel E., eds. An Enquiry into the Doctrine Concerning Libels, Warrants, & the Seizure of Papers. LC 77-86678. (Classics of English Legal History in the Modern Era Ser.: Vol. 52). 99p. 1979. lib. bdg. 40.00 (ISBN 0-8240-3151-2). Garland Pub.
Biddle, Arthur. A Treatise on the Law of Warranties in the Sale of Chattels. xx, 308p. 1981. Repr. of 1884 ed. lib. bdg. 30.00x (ISBN 0-8377-0316-6). Rothman.
WARREN, ROBERT PENN, 1905-
Graziano, Frank, ed. Homage to Robert Penn Warren. 80p. (Orig.). 1981. price not set (ISBN 0-937406-12-0); pap. price not set (ISBN 0-937406-11-2); price not set limited ed. (ISBN 0-937406-13-9). Logbridge-Rhodes.
WARS
see Military History; Naval History; War
WARSAW PACT, 1955
Dawisha, Karen & Hanson, Philip, eds. Soviet-East European Dilemmas. LC 80-28573. 226p. 1981. text ed. 31.00x (ISBN 0-8419-0697-1); pap. text ed. 15.00x (ISBN 0-8419-0698-X). Holmes & Meier.
WARSHIPS
see also Submarines
also navies of the various countries, e.g. Great Britain–Navy; also names of ships
Albrecht, G., ed. Weyer's Warships of the World: 1979-81 Flottentaschenbuch. 55th ed. LC 46-43961. (Illus.). 680p. (Eng. & Ger.). 1979. 48.95x (ISBN 0-933852-20-7). Nautical & Aviation.
Beaver, Paul. German Capital Ships: World War Two Photo Album. (Illus.). 96p. 1981. pap. 5.95 (ISBN 0-89404-038-3). Aztex.
--World War Two Photo Album: German Destroyers & Escorts. (Illus.). 96p. 1981. pap. 5.95 (ISBN 0-89404-060-X). Aztex.
Conway Maritime Press, ed. All the World's Fighting Ships, 1922-1946. (Illus.). 448p. 1980. 65.00 (ISBN 0-8317-0303-2). Mayflower Bks.
Overshiner, Elwyn E. Course Zero-Nine-Five to Eternity: The Saga of Destroyer Squadron Eleven. LC 80-82005. (Illus.). 224p. (Orig.). 1981. pap. 4.95 (ISBN 0-937480-00-2). Overshiner.
Polmar, Norman. The Ships & Aircraft of the U. S. Fleet. 12th ed. 416p. 1981. 24.95 (ISBN 0-87021-643-0). Naval Inst Pr.
WASHINGTON, BOOKER TALIAFERRO, 1859?-1915
Harlan, Louis R. & Smock, Raymond W., eds. Booker T. Washington Papers, Vol. 10: 1909-11. LC 75-186345. 525p. 1981. 20.00 (ISBN 0-252-00800-6). U of Ill Pr.
WASHINGTON, GEORGE, PRES. U. S., 1732-1799
Anderson, Patricia A. Promoted to Glory: The Apotheosis of George Washington. (Illus.). 68p. (Orig.). 1980. pap. 8.75 (ISBN 0-87391-017-6). Smith Coll Mus Art.
Morgan, Edmund S. The Genius of George Washington. 1981. 12.95 (ISBN 0-393-01440-1). Norton.
Muir, Dorothy T. General Washington's Headquarters: Seventeen Seventy-Five to Seventeen Eighty-Three. LC 76-45927. (Illus.). 1977. 19.95 (ISBN 0-916624-06-4). TSU Pr.
Twohig, Dorothy, ed. Journal of the Proceedings of the President: 1793 to 1797. LC 80-17174. (Papers of George Washington). 1981. price not set (ISBN 0-8139-0874-4). U Pr of Va.
Washington, George. Diaries of George Washington: January 1790 to December1799, Vol. 6. Jackson, Donald, ed. 1980. 30.00x (ISBN 0-8139-0807-8). U Pr of Va.
WASHINGTON (STATE)–DESCRIPTION AND TRAVEL
Darvill, Fred T., Jr. Stehekin: The Enchanted Valley. LC 80-16628. (Illus.). 96p. (Orig.). 1980. pap. 5.95 (ISBN 0-913140-42-2). Signpost Bk Pub.
Gill, Spencer. Washington Shores. (Illus.). 128p. 1981. 27.50 (ISBN 0-912856-68-8). Graphic Arts Ctr.
Hart, Herbert M. Tour Guide to Old Forts of Oregon, Idaho, Washington, California, Vol. 3. (Illus.). 65p. (Orig.). 1981. pap. 3.95 (ISBN 0-87108-582-8). Pruett.
Thollander, Earl. Back Roads of Washington. (Illus.). 208p. 1981. 15.95 (ISBN 0-517-54269-2); pap. 9.95 (ISBN 0-517-54270-6). Potter.
WASHINGTON (STATE)–HISTORY
Rosen, Shirley. Truman of St. Helens: The Man & His Mountain. (Illus.). 200p. 1981. 9.95 (ISBN 0-914842-57-9). Madrona Pubs.
Vexler, R. I. Washington Chronology & Factbook, Vol. 47. 1978. 8.50 (ISBN 0-379-16172-9). Oceana.
WASHINGTON, D. C.–DESCRIPTION
National Archives of the United States Office of Education. Washington: Design for the Federal City. 1981. pap. 9.95 (ISBN 0-87491-417-5). Acropolis.
WASHINGTON, D. C.–DESCRIPTION–GUIDEBOOKS
Geoghegan, Sheilah. Dining Out & Dining in: Memorable Menus & Recipes from Washington's Finest Restaurants. 128p. 1981. 10.00 (ISBN 0-914440-47-0). EPM Pubns.
Osler, Jack & Burgin, Tricia. Fifty Great Mini-Trips for Washington D. C. - Virginia. (Jack Osler's Mini-Trip Ser.). Date not set. pap. price not set (ISBN 0-89645-009-0). Media Ventures.
WASHINGTON, D. C.–DIRECTORIES
Brownson, Charles B., ed. Advance Locator for Capital Hill, 1981: With Biographical Material. 19th ed. LC 59-13987. (Congressional Staff Directory Ser.). 1981. pap. 9.00. Congr Staff.
--Congressional Staff Directory. LC 59-13987. 1981. Repr. of 1978 ed. 25.00. Congr Staff.
--Congressional Staff Directory, 1981. 23rd ed. 1096p. 1981. pap. 25.00. Congr Staff.
WASHINGTON, D. C.–HISTORY
Lee, Richard M. Civil War Washington: A Guide to Mr. Lincoln's City. 272p. 1981. pap. price not set (ISBN 0-914440-48-9). EPM Pubns.
WASHINGTON, D. C.–JUVENILE LITERATURE
Lumley, Kay. District of Columbia. (Young People's Stories of Our States Ser.). (Illus.). 48p. (gr. 2-5). 1981. PLB 8.65g (ISBN 0-516-03951-2, Time Line). Childrens.
WASHO INDIANS
see Indians of North America–Southwest, New
WASTE, DISPOSAL OF
see Factory and Trade Waste; Refuse and Refuse Disposal; Sewage Disposal
WASTE AS FUEL
see Refuse As Fuel
WASTE OIL
see Petroleum Waste
WASTE RECYCLING
see Recycling (Waste, etc.)
WASTE REUSE
see Recycling (Waste, etc.)
WASTE WATERS
see Sewage
WASTES, AGRICULTURAL
see Agricultural Wastes
WASTES, NUCLEAR
see Radioactive Wastes
WASTES, RADIOACTIVE
see Radioactive Wastes
WATCH MAKERS
see Clock and Watch Makers
WATCH MAKING
see Clock and Watch Making
WATCHES
see Clocks and Watches
WATER–COMPOSITION
see also Water Quality
Rockland, Louis B. & Stewart, George F., eds. Water Activity: Influences on Food Quality: Proceedings of Second International Symposium on Properties of Water Affecting Food Quality. LC 79-26632. 1980. 60.00 (ISBN 0-12-591350-8). Acad Pr.
WATER–CONSERVATION
see Water-Conservation
WATER–FLOW
see Hydraulics
WATER–LAWS AND LEGISLATION
see also Fishery Law and Legislation; Water–Pollution; Water-Rights
Bowden, Gerald. Coastal Aquaculture Law & Policy: A Case Study of California. (Special Studies in Agricultural Science & Policy). 300p. 1981. lib. bdg. 25.00x (ISBN 0-86531-108-0). Westview.
WATER–OIL POLLUTION
see Oil Pollution of Water
WATER–POLLUTION
see also Factory and Trade Waste; Oil Pollution of Water; Sewage Disposal; Water–Laws and Legislation; Water-Supply
Cousteau, Jacques-Yves. A Bill of Roghts for Future Generations. (Illus.). 33p. (Orig.). 1980. pap. 1.50 (ISBN 0-913098-31-0). Myrin Institute.
Eisenreich, Steven J. Atmospheric Pollutants in Natural Waters. 1981. text ed. 40.00 (ISBN 0-250-40369-2, Dist. by Butterworths). Ann Arbor Science.
Halasi-Kun, George J. Pollution & Water Resources: Pollution & Hydrology of Surface & Groundwater - - Selected Reports. LC 78-100896. (Columbia University Seminar Ser.: Vol. XIII, Pt. 3). (Illus.). 205p. 1981. 25.00 (ISBN 0-08-027511-7). Pergamon.
Halasi-Kun, George J., ed. Pollution & Water Resourses: Pollution & Hydrology of Surface & Ground Water - Selected Reports. (Columbia University Seminar Ser.: Vol. XIII-2, 1980). (Illus.). 187p. 1981. 20.00 (ISBN 0-08-027215-0). Pergamon.
Hudson, James F., et al. Pollution-Pricing: Industrial Response to Wastewater Charges. LC 80-8363. 1981. price not set (ISBN 0-669-04033-9). Lexington Bks.
International Convention for the Prevention of Pollution of the Sea by Oil, 1954. 25p. 1978. 7.00 (IMCO). Unipub.
Jenkins, S. H. Mediterranean Pollution: Proceedings of a Conference Held in Palma, Mallorca, Sept. 1979. (Progress in Water Technology Ser.: Vol. 12, Nos. 1 & 4). 850p. 1980. 100.00 (ISBN 0-08-026058-6). Pergamon.
Nuclear Techniques in Groundwater Pollution Research. 285p. 1981. pap. 36.25 (ISBN 92-0-141080-8, ISP 518, IAEA). Unipub.
Report of the Indo-Pacific Fishery Commission Working Party on Aquaculture & Environment. 16p. 1981. pap. 6.00 (ISBN 92-5-100962-7, F2074, FAO). Unipub.
Stiff, M. J., ed. River Pollution Control. 300p. 1980. 99.95x (ISBN 0-470-27004-7). Halsted Pr.
Suess, M. J. Examination of Water for Pollution Control: Handbook for Management & Analysts. (Illus.). 1700p. 1981. 300.00 (ISBN 0-08-025255-9). Pergamon.
WATER–PURIFICATION
see also Water-Supply Engineering
American Water Works Association. Water Disinfection with Ozone, Chloramines, or Chlorine Dioxide. (Handbooks-Proceedings Ser.). (Illus.). 224p. 1980. pap. text ed. 10.00 (ISBN 0-89867-244-9). Am Water Wks Assn.
Cooper, William J. Chemistry in Water Reuse, Vol. 2. 1981. text ed. 39.95 (ISBN 0-250-40391-9). Ann Arbor Science.
Lewis, W. M., ed. Developments in Water Treatment - One. (Illus.). xii, 195p. 1980. 42.50x (ISBN 0-85334-902-9). Burgess-Intl Ideas.
--Developments in Water Treatment-2. (Illus.). xii, 225p. 1981. 39.00x (ISBN 0-85334-903-7). Burgess-Intl Ideas.
WATER–QUALITY OF
see Water Quality
WATER–THERAPEUTIC USE
see Hydrotherapy
WATER–WASTE
see also Water-Conservation
Adams, Carl E., et al. Development of Design & Operational Criteria for Wastewater Treatment. LC 80-69077. (Illus.). 550p. 1980. text ed. 40.00 (ISBN 0-937976-00-8). Enviro Pr.
Stephens, H. S. & Priestley, G., eds. The Profitable Aeration of Waste Water. (Illus.). 98p. (Orig.). 1980. pap. 45.00x (ISBN 0-906085-44-6). BHRA Fluid.
WATER, UNDERGROUND
see also Hydrogeology; Divining-Rod; Wells
Everett, Lorne G. Groundwater Monitoring. LC 80-82885. (Illus.). 480p. 1980. 150.00x (ISBN 0-931690-14-5). GE Tech Market.
Institute of Civil Engineers, UK. Thames Groundwater Scheme. 242p. 1980. 60.00x (ISBN 0-7277-0060-X, Pub. by Telford England). State Mutual Bk.
Kovacs, G., et al. Subterranean Hydrology. 1981. 45.00 (ISBN 0-918334-35-7). WRP.
Nuclear Techniques in Groundwater Pollution Research. 285p. 1981. pap. 36.25 (ISBN 92-0-141080-8, ISP 518, IAEA). Unipub.
Plummer, F. B. & Sargent, E. C. Underground Waters & Subsurface Temperatures of the Woodbine Sand in Northeast Texas. (Illus.). 178p. 1931. 1.00 (BULL 3138). Bur Econ Geology.
Schlitt, W. J. & Shock, D. A., eds. In Situ Uranium Mining & Ground Water Restoration. LC 79-52217. (Illus.). 137p. 1979. pap. 15.00x (ISBN 0-89520-267-0). Soc Mining Eng.
WATER ANIMALS
see Aquatic Animals
WATER-BIRDS
see also Sea Birds; Shore Birds
also families and names of water-birds, e.g. Anatidae; Gulls, Murres, Terns
Thiede, Walter. Water & Shore Birds. (Illus.). 144p. 1981. pap. 5.95 (ISBN 0-7011-2527-6, Pub. by Chatto-Bodley-Jonathan). Merrimack Bk Serv.
WATER CHEMISTRY
see also Limnology

Maki, A. W., et al, eds. Biotransformation & Fate of Chemicals in the Aquatic Environment. (Illus.). 1980. write for info. (ISBN 0-914826-28-X). Am Soc Microbio.

WATER-COLOR PAINTING

Kautzky, Ted. Painting Trees & Landscapes in Watercolor. 1981. pap. 9.95 (ISBN 0-442-21918-0). Van Nos Reinhold.

WATER-COLOR PAINTING–TECHNIQUE

Blake, Vernon. The Way to Sketch: With Special Reference to Water Color. (Illus.). 144p. (Unabridged replication of 2nd ed.). 1981. pap. price not set (ISBN 0-486-24119-X). Dover.

Cohn, Marjorie B. Wash & Gouache: A Study of the Development of the Materials of Watercolor. LC 77-176. 120p. 1980. pap. 7.50 (ISBN 0-916724-06-9). Fogg Art.

Schink, Christopher. Mastering Color & Design in Watercolor. 144p. 1981. 22.50 (ISBN 0-8230-3015-6). Watson-Guptill.

Shook, Georg & Witt, Gary. Sharp Focus Watercolor Painting: Techniques for Hot-Pressed Surfaces. 144p. 1981. 21.95 (ISBN 0-8230-4794-6). Watson-Guptill.

WATER COLORS

Chi Chen. Chen Chi Watercolors, Drawings, Sketches: Deluxe Edition. (Illus.). 108p. 1980. leather bound 100.00 (ISBN 0-9604652-1-9). Chen Chi Studio.

Parramon, J. M. & Fresquet, G. Watercolors. (Art Ser.). (Orig.). 1980. pap. 4.95 (ISBN 0-89586-074-0). H P Bks.

WATER-CONSERVATION

see also Water-Supply

Halasi-Kun, George J., ed. Pollution & Water Resourses: Pollution & Hydrology of Surface & Ground Water - Selected Reports. (Columbia University Seminar Ser.: Vol. XIII-2, 1980). (Illus.). 187p. 1981. 20.00 (ISBN 0-08-027215-0). Pergamon.

Hickling, C. F. Water As a Productive Environment. 250p. 1980. 29.00x (ISBN 0-85664-062-X, Pub. by Croom Helm England). State Mutual Bk.

WATER CONTAMINATION

see Water–Pollution

WATER-CURE

see Hydrotherapy

WATER-FLIES

see Flies

WATER GARDENS

see also Aquatic Plants

Heritage, Bill. Ponds & Water Gardens. (Illus.). 176p. 1981. 12.95 (ISBN 0-7137-1015-2, Pub. by Blandford Pr England); pap. 6.95 (ISBN 0-7137-1141-8). Sterling.

WATER-MAINS

see Water-Pipes

WATER-PIPES

see also Pipe

Shuldener, Henry L. & Fullman, James B. Water & Piping Problems: A Troubleshooter's Guide for Large & Small Buildings. 275p. 1981. 19.95 (ISBN 0-471-08082-9, Pub. by Wiley-Interscience). Wiley.

WATER PLANTS

see Aquatic Plants

WATER POLLUTION

see Water–Pollution

WATER-POLO

Barr, David & Gordon, Andrew. Water Polo. (Illus.). 112p. (YA) 1981. 12.95 (Pub. by EP Publishing England). Sterling.

WATER-POWER

see also Dams; Hydraulic Engineering; Hydraulic Machinery

Brown, Ruben S. Hydro for the Eighties: Bringing Hydroelectric Power to Poor People. (Orig.). 1980. 15.00 (ISBN 0-936130-01-6). Intl Sci Tech.

WATER POWER–LAW AND LEGISLATION

see Water–Laws and Legislation

WATER-POWER ELECTRIC PLANTS

see also Electric Power Distribution

Nelson, Robert V. Hydro-Electric Energy: Past - or Future? Ide, Arthur F., ed. & illus. (E Equals MC Squared Ser.: Vol. 14). (Illus.). 60p. 1980. 10.00 (ISBN 0-86663-802-4); pap. 6.95 (ISBN 0-86663-803-2). Ide Hse.

Noyes, Robert, ed. Small & Micro Hydroelectric Power Plants: Technology & Feasibility. LC 80-19099. (Energy Tech. Rev. 60). (Illus.). 457p. 1981. 42.00 (ISBN 0-8155-0819-0). Noyes.

WATER PURIFICATION

see Water–Purification

WATER QUALITY

American Water Works Association. Upgrading Water Treatment Plants to Improve Water Quality. (Handbooks-Proceedings). (Illus.). 132p. 1980. pap. text ed. 10.50 (ISBN 0-89867-245-7). Am Water Wks Assn.

Biswas, Asit K. Models for Water Quality Management. (M-H Series in Water Resources & Environmental Engineering). (Illus.). 392p. 1980. text ed. 44.50 (ISBN 0-07-005481-9). McGraw.

Drinking Water & Health. Incl. Vol. I. 1977. 20.75 (ISBN 0-309-02619-9); Vol. II. 1980. 17.00 (ISBN 0-686-64937-0); Vol. III. 1980. 15.00 (ISBN 0-309-02932-5). Natl Acad Pr.

WATER RESOURCES DEVELOPMENT

see also Flood Control; Irrigation; Water-Power; Water-Supply

Barr, Charles W. Waterfront Development: A Bibliography. (Public Administration Ser.: Bibliography P-462). 51p. 1980. pap. 5.50. Vance Biblios.

Biswas, Asit K. Models for Water Quality Management. (M-H Series in Water Resources & Environmental Engineering). (Illus.). 392p. 1980. text ed. 44.50 (ISBN 0-07-005481-9). McGraw.

Colorado Energy Research Institute, Colorado School of Mines. Water & Energy in Colorado's Future. 330p. 1981. lib. bdg. 25.00x (ISBN 0-86531-118-8). Westview.

Haimes, Y. & Kindler, J., eds. Water & Related Land Resource Systems: Proceedings of the IFAC Symposium, Cleveland, Ohio, U. S. A., 28-31 May 1980. LC 80-41690. (IFAC Proceedings Ser.). (Illus.). 550p. 1981. 120.00 (ISBN 0-08-027307-6). Pergamon.

Henderson, G. E. Planning for an Individual Water System. 7.95 (ISBN 0-914452-45-2). Green Hill.

Hickling, C. F. Water As a Productive Environment. 250p. 1980. 29.00x (ISBN 0-85664-062-X, Pub. by Croom Helm England). State Mutual Bk.

Institute of Civil Engineers, UK. Management of National & Regional Water Resources. 98p. 1980. 60.00x (ISBN 0-901948-65-9, Pub. by Telford England). State Mutual Bk.

Kundell, James E., ed. Georgia Water Resources: Issues & Options. 114p. 1980. pap. 10.00x. U of GA Inst Govt.

Parker, Dennis J. & Penning-Rowsell, Edmund C. Water Planning in Britain. (Resource Management Ser.: No. 1). (Illus.). 288p. (Orig.). 1980. text ed. 34.00x (ISBN 0-04-711006-6); pap. text ed. 17.95x (ISBN 0-04-711007-4). Allen Unwin.

WATER-RIGHTS

see also Water–Laws and Legislation

Foreman, Richard L. Indian Water Rights. 1980. pap. text ed. 8.95x (ISBN 0-8134-2160-8, 2160). Interstate.

WATER-SUPPLY

see also Arid Regions; Dams; Droughts; Forests and Forestry; Irrigation; Reservoirs; Water–Pollution; Water–Purification; Water-Conservation; Water Quality; Wells

American Water Works Association. Distribution Systems: Actions & Innovations. (General Handbooks). (Illus.). 256p. 1980. pap. text ed. 20.00 (ISBN 0-89867-246-5). Am Water Wks Assn.

Farm Level Water Management in Selected Asian Countries. 159p. 1980. pap. 13.25 (ISBN 92-833-1461-1, APO 88, APO). Unipub.

Halasi-Kun, George J. Pollution & Water Resources: Pollution & Hydrology of Surface & Groundwater - Selected Reports. LC 78-100896. (Columbia University Seminar Ser.: Vol. XIII, Pt. 3). (Illus.). 205p. 1981. 25.00 (ISBN 0-08-027511-7). Pergamon.

WATER SUPPLY–LAWS AND LEGISLATION

see Water–Laws and Legislation

WATER-SUPPLY–UNITED STATES

Kundell, James E., ed. Georgia Water Resources: Issues & Options. 114p. 1980. pap. 10.00x. U of GA Inst Govt.

WATER-SUPPLY ENGINEERING

see also Boring; Hydraulic Engineering

Cooper, William J. Chemistry in Water Reuse, Vol. 2. 1981. text ed. 39.95 (ISBN 0-250-40391-9). Ann Arbor Science.

Faust, Aly. Chemistry of Natural Waters. 450p. 1981. text ed. 40.00 (ISBN 0-250-40387-0). Ann Arbor Science.

Garb, Forrest A. Waterflood Calculations for Hand-Held Computers. (Illus.). 200p. 1981. 19.95 (ISBN 0-87201-895-4). Gulf Pub.

WATER TRANSPORTATION

see Inland Water Transportation; Shipping

WATER WITCHING

see Divining-Rod

WATERFOWL SHOOTING

Taylor, Zack. Successful Waterfowling. 288p. (Orig.). 1981. pap. 13.95 (ISBN 0-8117-2147-7). Stackpole.

WATERGATE AFFAIR, 1972-

Garza, Hedda, compiled by. The Watergate Hearings: Index to the Senate Select Committee Reports. LC 80-53886. 625p. 1981. lib. bdg. price not set (ISBN 0-8420-2175-2). Scholarly Res Inc.

Liddy, G. Gordon. Will. 1981. pap. 3.50 (ISBN 0-440-09666-9). Dell.

WATERLOO, BATTLE OF, 1815

Chandler, David. Waterloo: The Hundred Days. LC 80-36696. 224p. 1981. 18.95. Macmillan.

WATERSHEDS

Casebook of Methods of Computation of Quantitative Changes in the Hydrological Regime of River Basins Due to Human Activities. (Studies & Reports in Hydrology: No. 28). 330p. 1980. pap. 24.25 (ISBN 92-3-101798-5, U1037, UNESCO). Unipub.

Watershed Development. (FAO Soils Bulletin: No. 44). 266p. 1980. pap. 14.25 (ISBN 92-5-100859-0, F1966, FAO). Unipub.

WATERWORKS

see Water-Supply

WATSON, THOMAS EDWARD, 1856-1922

Watson, Thomas E. Life & Speeches of Thomas E. Watson. (Studies in Populism). 1980. lib. bdg. 75.00 (ISBN 0-686-68880-5). Revisionist Pr.

--Mr. Watson's Editorials on the War Issues. (Studies in Populism). 1980. lib. bdg. 69.95 (ISBN 0-686-68881-3). Revisionist Pr.

WAUGH, EVELYN, 1903-1966

Davis, Robert M. A Catalogue of the Evelyn Waugh Collection at the Humanities Research Center: The Universtiy of Texas at Austin. LC 80-50840. 375p. 1981. 25.00x (ISBN 0-87875-194-7). Whitston Pub.

--Evelyn Waugh, Writer: The Making of a Man of Letters. 270p. 1980. 21.95x (ISBN 0-937664-00-6). Pilgrim Bks OK.

Lane, Calvin W. Evelyn Waugh. (English Authors Ser.: No. 301). 1981. lib. bdg. 9.95 (ISBN 0-8057-6793-2). Twayne.

WAVE MECHANICS

see also Matrix Mechanics; Quantum Statistics; Spinor Analysis

Ross, D. Energy from the Waves. 2nd rev. ed. LC 80-41076. (Illus.). 160p. 1981. 21.00 (ISBN 0-08-026715-7); pap. 9.00 (ISBN 0-686-68875-9). Pergamon.

WAVE-MOTION, THEORY OF

see also Light, Wave Theory Of; Sound; Spectrum Analysis

Chapple, M. A Level Physics: Wave Motion-Sound & Light, Vol. 2. 2nd ed. (Illus.). 240p. (Orig.). 1979. pap. text ed. 10.95x (ISBN 0-7121-0155-1, Pub. by Macdonald & Evans England). Intl Ideas.

WAVEFRONT RECONSTRUCTION IMAGING

see Holography

WAVES

see also Damping (Mechanics); Light; Radiation; Turbulence; Wave Mechanics

Bolton, W. Waves, Rays & Oscillations, Bk. 6. LC 80-41396. (Study Topics in Physics). 96p. 1980. pap. text ed. write for info. (ISBN 0-408-10657-3). Butterworths.

Minikin, R. R. Winds, Waves & Maritime Structures. 295p. 1963. 29.75x (ISBN 0-85264-091-9, Pub. by Griffin England). State Mutual Bk.

Pain, H. J. The Physics of Vibrations & Waves. 2nd ed. 357p. 1976. 32.50 (ISBN 0-471-99407-3); pap. 16.50 (ISBN 0-471-99408-1). Wiley.

WAVES, ELECTROMAGNETIC

see Electromagnetic Waves

WAX MODELING

Kallenberg, Lawrence. Modeling in Wax for Jewelry & Sculpture. LC 80-70384. (Illus.). 288p. 1981. 18.50 (ISBN 0-686-69521-6); text ed. 18.50 (ISBN 0-686-69522-4). Chilton.

WAX PORTRAITS

see Wax Modeling

WAY OF LIFE, JEWISH

see Jewish Way of Life

WEALTH

see also Capital; Consumption (Economics); Cost and Standard of Living; Income; Income Tax; Money; Poverty; Profit; Property; Saving and Investment; Success; Value

Guidelines on Statistics of Tangible Assets. (Statistical Papers Ser. M: No. 68). 63p. 1980. pap. 6.00 (ISBN 0-686-68959-3, UN80/17/2, UN). Unipub.

Hill, Harold, tr. Como Vivir Como un Hijo Del Rey. (Spanish Bks.). (Span.). 1978. 1.90 (ISBN 0-8297-0517-1). Life Pubs Intl.

WEAPONS

see Arms and Armor; Atomic Weapons; Firearms

WEAPONS SYSTEMS

Kemp, Anthony. Weapons & Equipment of the Marlborough Wars. (Illus.). 192p. 1981. 24.95 (ISBN 0-7137-1013-6, Pub. by Blandford Pr England). Sterling.

WEATHER

see also Climatology; Meteorology; Rain and Rainfall; Weather Control; Weather Forecasting; Winds also names of countries, cities, etc., with or without the subdivision Climate

Persinger, Michael A. Weather Matrix & Human Behavior. LC 80-18422. 300p. 1980. 27.95 (ISBN 0-03-057731-4). Praeger.

WEATHER CONTROL

see also Meteorology in Aeronautics; Water-Supply

Ruffner, James & Bair, Frank, eds. Weather Almanac: A Reference Guide to Weather & Climate of the United States & Its Key Cities. (Illus.). 700p. 1981. 42.00 (ISBN 0-8103-1053-8). Gale.

Wegman & DePrist. Statistical Analysis of Weather Modification Experiments. 184p. 1980. write for info. (ISBN 0-8247-1177-7). Dekker.

WEATHER FORECASTING

see also Meteorology in Aeronautics

Dabberdt, Walter. Weather for Outdoormen. (Illus.). 224p. 1981. 12.95 (ISBN 0-684-16865-0, ScribT). Scribner.

First Planning Meeting for TOPEX. (Topex Report Ser.: No. 1). 83p. 1981. pap. 10.00 (ISBN 92-63-10565-0, W479, WMO). Unipub.

Sloane, Eric. Sloan's Almanac & Weather Forecaster. 1977. pap. 3.50 (ISBN 0-8015-6877-3, Hawthorn). Dutton.

WEATHER MODIFICATION

see Weather Control

WEAVING

see also Basket Making; Hand Weaving; Indians of North America–Textile Industry and Fabrics; Indians of South America–Textile Industry and Fabrics; Lace and Lace Making; Silk Manufacture and Trade; Textile Fabrics also woven articles, e.g. Blankets, Carpets, Rugs

Brostoff, Laya. Duble Weave: Theory & Practice. LC 79-91202. (Illus.). 54p. 1979. 4.95 (ISBN 0-934026-01-7). Interweave.

Hobden, Eileen. Fun with Weaving. (Learning with Fun Ser.). (Illus.). 64p. (gr. 5 up). text ed. 11.50x (ISBN 0-7182-1317-3, SpS). Soccer.

Mitchell, Lillias. Irish Spinning Dyeing & Weaving. (Illus.). 1978. 12.95 (ISBN 0-85221-101-5). Dufour.

Nass, Ulla. Weaves of the Incas. (Illus.). 108p. soft cover 16.95. Nass.

Scarlett, James D. How to Weave Fine Cloth. 208p. 1981. 14.95 (ISBN 0-8359-2987-6); pap. 7.95 (ISBN 0-8359-2986-8). Reston.

WEBER, KARL MARIA FRIEDRICH ERNST, FREIHERR VON, 1786-1826

Stebbins, Lucy & Stebbins, Richard P. Enchanted Wanderer: The Life of Carl Maria Von Weber. LC 80-2301. 1981. Repr. of 1940 ed. 39.50 (ISBN 0-404-18870-2). AMS Pr.

WEBSTER, JOHN, 1580?-1625?

Corballis, R. & Harding, J. M. John Webster Concordance, Vol. 2, Pt. 3. (Jacobean Drama Studies: No. 70). 1979. pap. text ed. 25.00x (ISBN 0-391-01761-6). Humanities.

Lutze. John Websters Tragodienstil Als Ausdruck der Leidenschaftlichkeit. (Jacobean Ser.). (Ger.). 1980. pap. text ed. 25.00x (ISBN 0-391-02196-6). Humanities.

WEEDS

Fischer, Bill, et al. Growers Weed Identification Handbook. (Illus.). 183p. 1978. 40.00x (ISBN 0-931876-43-5, 4030). Ag Sci Pubns.

Muenscher, Walter C. Weeds. 2nd ed. LC 79-48017. (Illus.). 560p. 1980. 29.50x (ISBN 0-8014-1266-8). Comstock.

Smith, William. Wonders in Weeds. 187p. 1977. 13.00x (ISBN 0-8464-1062-1). Beekman Pubs.

WEELKES, THOMAS, 1570-1623

Brown, David. Thomas Weelkes. 1979. Repr. of 1969 ed. lib. bdg. 22.50 (ISBN 0-306-79523-X). Da Capo.

WEIGHING MACHINES

see also Weights and Measures

Griffiths, E. H. Weighing Machines: Application of Electricity & Electronics to Weighting Machines, Vol. 3. 248p. 1970. 49.75x (ISBN 0-85264-160-5, Pub. by Griffin England). State Mutual Bk.

Metcalfe, T. J. Weighing Machines: Non-Self-Indicating Mechanisms, Vol. 1. 192p. 1969. 42.50x (ISBN 0-85264-095-1, Pub. by Griffin England). State Mutual Bk.

--Weighing Machines: Semi-Self-Indicating & Self-Indicating Mechanisms, Vol. 2. 178p. 1969. 44.95x (ISBN 0-686-68843-0, Pub. by Griffin England). State Mutual Bk.

WEIGHT LIFTING

Ashpaugh, Bill & Miller, Holly. Powerlift. LC 80-81758. 150p. 1981. pap. 4.95 (ISBN 0-914850-67-9). Impact Tenn.

Bentley, Stacy. Weight Training. (Burns Sports Ser.). 156p. Date not set. pap. 4.95 (ISBN 0-695-81572-5). Follett.

Hatfield, Frederick C. Powerlifting: A Scientific Approach. (Illus.). 1981. 12.95 (ISBN 0-8092-7002-1); pap. 6.95 (ISBN 0-8092-7001-3). Contemp Bks.

Zuver, Jean. Getting Your Shape in Shape: A New Weight Conditioning Program for Women. LC 80-26725. (Illus.). 128p. 1981. 7.95 (ISBN 0-498-02536-5). A S Barnes.

WEIGHT REDUCING PREPARATIONS

Benziger, Barbara. Controlling Your Weight. (Illus.). (YA) (gr. 7-9). 1975. pap. 1.25 (ISBN 0-671-29735-X). PB.

G-Jo Institute. Permanent Weight Loss Program. 1980. pap. 4.50 (ISBN 0-916878-11-2). Falkynor Bks.

Gandhi, Hans. A Novel Approach to Losing Weight. 1981. 10.00 (ISBN 0-533-04724-2). Vantage.

Stern, Frances M., et al. Mind Trips to Help You Lose Weight. LC 76-44202. 192p. 1981. pap. 2.25 (ISBN 0-87216-786-0). Playboy Pbks.

WEIGHTS AND MEASURES

see also Decimal System; Gravity; Mensuration; Metric System; Weighing Machines also units of weight or measure

Managing Metrication in Business & Industry. 203p. 1976. 37.00 (ISBN 0-8247-6469-2). Am Natl.

Metrication: The Australian Experience. 210p. 1975. 4.00. Am Natl.

WEIMAR

Bessel, Richard & Feuchtwanger, E. J., eds. Social Change & Political Development in Weimar Germany. 297p. 1981. 27.00x (ISBN 0-389-20176-6). B&N.

WELDING

see also Oxyacetylene Welding and Cutting also specific materials or objects, with or without the subdivision Welding

Flood, Charles R. Welding & Metal Fabrication. 1981. text ed. price not set (ISBN 0-408-00448-7). Butterworths.

Jackson, M. D. Welding: Methods & Metallurgy. 422p. 1967. 37.50x (ISBN 0-85264-003-X, Pub. by Griffin England). State Mutual Bk.

Jefferson, T. B. & Jefferson, D. T., eds. Welding Encyclopedia. 18th ed. (Monticello Bks). 1981. 20.00 (ISBN 0-686-28906-4). Jefferson Pubns.

Kielhorn, William. Welding Guidelines with Aircraft Supplement. (Aviation Maintenance Training Course Ser.). (Illus.). 187p. 1978. text ed. 10.95 (ISBN 0-89100-136-0, E*A-W*B-2). Aviation Maintenance.
Material Specifications: Welding Rods, Electrodes & Filler Metals, 3 pts, Pt. C. (Boiler & Pressure Vessel Code Ser.: Sec. II). 1980. loose leaf 70.00 (P0002C); pap. 70.00 l00se leaf (V0002C). ASME.
Stewart, John P. The Welder's Handbook. 1981. 25.95 (ISBN 0-8359-8605-5). Reston.
Thielsch, Helmut. Sense & Nonsense of Weld Defects. 2nd ed. (Monticello Bks). 56p. 1981. soft cover 5.00 (ISBN 0-686-28905-6). Jefferson Pubns.

WELFARE ECONOMICS
Kramer, Ralph M. Voluntary Agencies in the Welfare State. 400p. 1981. 24.95x (ISBN 0-520-04290-5). U of Cal Pr.

WELFARE WORK
see Public Welfare

WELL-BORING
see Boring

WELLESLEY, RICHARD COLLEY WELLESLEY, MARQUIS, 1760-1842
Severn, John K. A Wellesley Affair: Richard Marquess Wellesley & the Conduct of Anglo-Spanish Diplomacy, 1809-1812. LC 80-25416. x, 294p. 1980. 21.50 (ISBN 0-8130-0684-8). U Presses Fla.

WELLS, HERBERT GEORGE, 1866-1946
The Science Fiction of H. G. Wells: A Concise Guide. LC 80-65231. 60p. 1980. pap. 2.25 (ISBN 0-9602738-1-6). Auriga.

WELLS
see also Boring; Gas, Natural; Petroleum; Water, Underground; Water-Supply
Corrosion & Encrustation in Water Wells. (FAO Irrigation & Drainage Paper Ser.: No. 34). 108p. 1981. pap. 5.75 (ISBN 92-5-100933-3, F2080, FAO). Unipub.
Feray, D. E. & Starnes, J. L. Index to Well Samples. rev. ed. 148p. 1950. 1.65 (PUB 5015). Bur Econ Geology.
Institute of Civil Engineers, UK. Safety in Wells & Boreholes. 1980. pap. 12.00x (ISBN 0-901948-57-8, Pub. by Telford England). State Mutual Bk.

WELSH LANGUAGE
Williams, Stephen J. A Welsh Grammar. 184p. 1980. pap. text ed. 20.00 (ISBN 0-7083-0737-X). Verry.

WELSH TALES
see Tales, Welsh

WELTY, EUDORA, 1909-
Evans, Elizabeth. Eudora Welty. LC 80-53702. (Modern Literature Ser.). 180p. 1981. 9.95 (ISBN 0-8044-2187-0). Ungar.

WESLEY, CHARLES, 1707-1788
Flint, Charles. Charles Wesley & His Colleagues. 7.00 (ISBN 0-8183-0230-5). Pub Aff Pr.

WESLEY, JOHN, 1703-1791
Dobree, Bonamy. Three Eighteenth Century Figures: Sarah Churchill, John Wesley, Giacomo Casanova. LC 80-19398. xi, 248p. 1981. Repr. of 1962 ed. lib. bdg. 25.00x (ISBN 0-313-22682-2, DOTF). Greenwood.

WESLEYAN METHODIST CHURCH OF AMERICA
Stokes, Mack B. The Bible in the Wesleyan Heritage. LC 80-23636. 96p. (Orig.). 1981. pap. 3.95 (ISBN 0-687-03100-1). Abingdon.

WEST, MAE
West, Mae. Goodness Had Nothing to Do with It. (A Belvedere Bk.). 312p. 1981. pap. 6.95 (ISBN 0-87754-301-1). Chelsea Hse.

WEST-BIOGRAPHY
Rush, N. Orwin. Diversions of a Westerner: With Emphasis Upon Owen Wister's & Frederic Remington's Books & Libraries. LC 78-53134. (Illus.). 224p. 1979. 10.00 (ISBN 0-932068-05-7). South Pass Pr.

WEST-DESCRIPTION AND TRAVEL-GUIDEBOOKS
Sterling, E. M. Western Trips & Trails. (Illus.). 350p. (Orig.). 1981. pap. 6.95 (ISBN 0-87108-584-4). Pruett.
Whitman, John. The Best Free Attractions in the West. Grooms, Kathe, ed. (The Best Free Attractions Ser.). (Illus.). 200p. 1981. pap. 3.95 (ISBN 0-915658-36-4). Meadowbrook Pr.

WEST-HISTORY
Adams, Alexander B. The Disputed Lands. 480p. 1981. 17.95 (ISBN 0-399-12530-2). Putnam.
Heaston, Michael D., ed. From Mississippi to California. Date not set. 9.50 (ISBN 0-8363-0157-9). Jenkins.
Lewis, Betty. Watsonville: More Memories That Linger, Vol. 2. LC 76-41500. (Illus.). 168p. 1980. 11.95 (ISBN 0-934136-08-4, Valley Calif). Western Tanager.
Taylor, A. J. Politicians, Socialism & Historians. LC 80-6217. 252p. 1981. 15.95 (ISBN 0-8128-2796-1). Stein & Day.

WEST-HISTORY-PICTORIAL WORKS
Brown, Robert L. Saloons of the American West. (Illus.). 144p. 16.50 (ISBN 0-913582-24-7). Sundance.
Roberts, Jack. Lord Gore. (Illus.). 220p. 27.00 (ISBN 0-913582-07-7). Sundance.

WEST-JUVENILE LITERATURE
Hoare, Robert. When the West Was Wild. (Junior Reference Ser.). (Illus.). 64p. (gr. 7 up). 1976. 7.95 (ISBN 0-7136-1619-9). Dufour.

WEST-SOCIAL LIFE AND CUSTOMS
Taylor, A. J. Politicians, Socialism & Historians. LC 80-6217. 252p. 1981. 15.95 (ISBN 0-8128-2796-1). Stein & Day.

WEST AFRICA
see Africa, West

WEST ARMENIAN LANGUAGE
see Armenian Language

WEST INDIAN LITERATURE
Allis, Jeannette B. West Indian Literature: An Index to Criticism, 1930-1975. (Reference Bks.). 1981. lib. bdg. 30.00 (ISBN 0-8161-8266-3). G K Hall.

WEST VIRGINIA-HISTORY
Bice, David A. A Panorama of West Virginia. LC 79-89608. 319p. (gr. 8). 1979. text ed. 12.95 (ISBN 0-934750-00-9); tchr's guide 4.00 (ISBN 0-934750-01-7); wkbk. 3.50 (ISBN 0-934750-03-3). Jalamap.
Vexler, R. I. West Virginia Chronology & Factbook, Vol. 48. 1978. 8.50 (ISBN 0-379-16173-7). Oceana.

WESTERN AND COUNTRY MUSIC
see Country Music

WESTERN ART
see Art

WESTERN CIVILIZATION
see Civilization, Occidental

WESTERN FILMS
Noyes, Stanley. Western. 32p. (Orig.). 1980. pap. 3.00 (ISBN 0-88235-044-7). San Marcos.
Rothel, David. The Singing Cowboys. LC 77-89646. (Illus.). 272p. (Orig.). 1981. pap. 10.95 (ISBN 0-498-02523-3). A S Barnes.

WESTERN STORIES
Great Westerns from the Saturday Evening Post. LC 76-41559. 1976. 5.95 (ISBN 0-89387-004-8). Sat Eve Post.
Noyes, Stanley. Western. 32p. (Orig.). 1980. pap. 3.00 (ISBN 0-88235-044-7). San Marcos.

WHALES
Hoyt, Erich. The Whale Called Killer. (Illus.). 28p. 1981. 15.95 (ISBN 0-525-22970-1). Dutton.
Spears, John R. The Fighting Whales As Whalers Knew Them. (American Culture Library Bk). (Illus.). 137p. 1981. 27.45 (ISBN 0-89266-289-1). Am Classical Coll Pr.

WHALING
see also Scrimshaws
Trotter, Alexander. To the Greenland Whaling. 80p. 1980. pap. 9.95 (ISBN 0-906191-24-6, Pub. by Thule Pr England). Intl Schol Bk Serv.

WHARTON, EDITH NEWBOLD (JONES) 1862-1937
McDowell, Margaret B. Edith Wharton. LC 75-44094. (Twayne's U. S. Authors Ser.). 158p. 1976. pap. text ed. 4.95 (ISBN 0-672-61509-6). Bobbs.

WHEAT
Australian Wheat Varieties. 126p. 1975. pap. 15.50 (ISBN 0-643-00143-3, CO08, CSIRO). Unipub.
Australian Wheat Varieties, Suppl. 1. 30p. 1978. pap. 13.50 (ISBN 0-643-00325-8, CO01, CSIRO). Unipub.
Yamazaki, W. T. Soft Wheat: Production, Breeding, Milling, & Uses. LC 80-65826. (The AACC Monograph: Vol. VI). 352p. 1980. 36.00 (ISBN 0-913250-17-1). Am Assn Cereal Chem.

WHEATLEY, PHILLIS, AFTERWARD PHILLIS PETERS, 1753?-1784
Robinson, William H. Phillis Wheatley: A Bio-Bibliography. (Reference Books Ser.). 1981. 18.00 (ISBN 0-8161-8318-X). G K Hall.

WHEELS
Turner, Katy. The Legacy of the Great Wheel. LC 80-83331. (Illus.). 128p. 1980. pap. 8.95 (ISBN 0-910458-15-4). Select Bks.

WHISKEY
Cooper, Derek. Guide to the Whiskies of Scotland. 1979. 2.95 (ISBN 0-346-12425-5). Cornerstone.

WHISKY
see Whiskey

WHISTLER, JAMES ABBOTT MCNEILL, 1834-1903
Sickert, Bernhard. Whistler. 175p. 1980. Repr. lib. bdg. 25.00 (ISBN 0-8495-5039-4). Arden Lib.

WHITE, WILLIAM ALLEN, 1868-1944
Johnson, Walter. William Allen White's America. Freidel, Frank, ed. LC 78-66541. (The History of the United States Ser.: Vol. 10). 630p. 1979. lib. bdg. 50.00 (ISBN 0-8240-9702-5). Garland Pub.

WHITE BLOOD CELLS
see Leucocytes

WHITE COLLAR CRIMES
see also Embezzlement; Fraud; Tax Evasion
Clinard, Marshall B. & Yeager, Peter C. Corporate Crime. LC 80-2156. (Illus.). 352p. 1980. 16.95 (ISBN 0-02-905710-8). Free Pr.
White Collar Crimes. 389p. 1980. 50.00 (ISBN 0-686-28718-5, C168). ALI-ABA.

WHITE COLLAR WORKERS
see also classes of white collar workers, e.g. Clerks; Executives; Teachers; etc.
Juddery, Bruce. White Collar Power: A History of the ACOA. 320p. 1981. text ed. 27.50x (ISBN 0-86861-138-7, 2519); pap. text ed. 12.50x (ISBN 0-86861-146-8, 2520). Allen Unwin.

WHITE MOUNTAINS, NEW HAMPSHIRE
The White Mountains: Place & Perceptions. LC 80-68935. (Illus.). 200p. pap. 10.00 (ISBN 0-87451-190-9). U Pr of New Eng.

WHITE RUSSIAN LITERATURE
see Russian Literature (Collections)

WHITE-SLAVE TRAFFIC
see Prostitution

WHITE-TAILED DEER
Mattis, George. Whitetail: Fundamentals & Fine Points for the Hunter. rev. ed. 290p. 1980. 15.95 (ISBN 0-442-23355-8). Van Nos Reinhold.

WHITEFIELD, GEORGE, 1714-1770
Dallimore, Arnold. George Whitefield: The Life & Times of the Great Evangelist of the 18th Century Revival, Vol. 1. LC 79-67152. 598p. 1980. 19.95 (ISBN 0-89107-167-9, Cornerstone Bks). Good News.
Whitefield, George. George Whitefield's Journals. 1978. 14.95 (ISBN 0-85151-147-3). Banner of Truth.

WHITEHEAD, ALFRED NORTH, 1861-1947
Hartshorne, Charles & Peden, Creighton. Whitehead's View of Reality. 96p. (Orig.). Date not set. pap. 6.95 (ISBN 0-8298-0381-5). Pilgrim NY.

WHITMAN, WALT, 1819-1892
Bly, et al. Walt Whitman: The Measure of His Song. 1st ed. Perlman, Jim & Campion, Dan, eds. LC 80-85268. (Illus.). 288p. (Orig.). 1981. 13.95 (ISBN 0-930100-09-3); pap. 7.95 (ISBN 0-930100-08-5). Holy Cow.
Dello Buono, Carmen J. Rare Early Essays on Walt Whitman. 202p. 1980. lib. bdg. 17.50 (ISBN 0-8482-3699-8). Norwood Edns.
Eitner, Walter H. Walt Whitman's Western Jaunt. LC 80-29336. (Illus.). 144p. 1981. text ed. 18.00 (ISBN 0-7006-0212-7). Regents Pr KS.

WHITMAN, WALT, 1819-1892-BIBLIOGRAPHY
Boswell, Jeanetta. Walt Whitman & the Critics: A Checklist of Criticism, 1900-1978. LC 80-20528. (The Scarecrow Author Bibliographies Ser.: No. 51). 270p. 1980. 14.50 (ISBN 0-8108-1355-6). Scarecrow.

WHITSUNDAY
see Pentecost Festival

WHITTLING
see Wood-Carving

WHO'S WHO IN AMERICA
The International Who's Who 1980-1981. 1385p. 1980. 90.00 (ISBN 0-905118-48-0, EUR021, Europa). Unipub.
Matney, William C., ed. Who's Who Among Black Americans, 1980-1981. 3rd ed. LC 76-643293. 1981. 49.95 (ISBN 0-915130-33-5). Who's Who Black Am.
Who's Who in the East. 18th ed. 944p. 1981. 62.50 (ISBN 0-8379-0618-0). Marquis.
Who's Who of American Women. 12th ed. LC 58-12364. 920p. 1981. 62.50 (ISBN 0-8379-0412-9). Marquis.

WIDOWS
see also Remarriage; Single-Parent Family; Women; Women-Legal Status, Laws, etc.
Comings, Pamela. Widow's Walk. Baron, Carole, ed. 1981. 12.95 (ISBN 0-686-68920-8). Crown.
Fisher, Ida & Lane, Byron. The Widow's Guide to Life: How to Adjust-How to Grow. 224p. 1981. 13.95 (ISBN 0-13-959452-3, Spec); pap. 6.95 (ISBN 0-13-959445-0). P-H.
Lippi, Otty. The Second Time Around: An Honest Widow Reveals Her Intimate & Humorous Experiences in the Dating & Mating Game. LC 80-27189. 1981. 12.95 (ISBN 0-934878-03-X). Dembner Bks.
Mooney, Elizabeth. Alone: Surviving As a Widow. 320p. 1981. 10.95 (ISBN 0-399-12601-5). Putnam.
Start, Clarissa. Second Song. 232p. (Orig.). 1980. pap. 5.95 (ISBN 0-86629-013-3). Sunrise MO.
Taves, Isabella. The Widow's Guide. LC 80-6219. 256p. 1981. 9.95 (ISBN 0-8052-3769-0). Schocken.

WIENER KREIS
see Logical Positivism

WIFE ABUSE
Hirsch, Miriam F. Women & Violence. 416p. 1980. text ed. 17.95. Van Nos Reinhold.
Langley, Roger & Levy, Richard C. Wife Beating: The Silent Crisis. 1977. 9.95 (ISBN 0-87690-231-X). Dutton.
Miller, Nick. Battered Spouses. 69p. 1975. pap. text ed. 5.00x (ISBN 0-7135-1936-3, Pub. by Bedford England). Renouf.
Moore, Donna M. Battered Women. LC 79-982. (Focus Editions Ser.: Vol. 9). (Illus.). 232p. 1979. 18.95 (ISBN 0-8039-1162-9); pap. 9.95 (ISBN 0-8039-1163-7). Sage.
O'Connor, Mariell. Born to Be Hurt. Date not set. 6.95 (ISBN 0-8062-1685-9). Carlton.

WIFE AND HUSBAND
see Husband and Wife

WILD ANIMALS
see Animals; Mammals

WILD FLOWERS
Borland, Hal. A Countryman's Flowers. LC 80-2698. (Illus.). 208p. 1981. 22.50 (ISBN 0-394-51893-4). Knopf.
Phillips, Arthur M., 3rd. Grand Canyon Wildflowers. Priehs, T. J., ed. LC 79-54236. (Illus.). 145p. 1979. pap. 6.50 (ISBN 0-938216-01-5). GCNHA.
Scott, Thomas G. & Wasser, Clinton H. Checklist of North American Plants for Wildlife Biologists. LC 79-89208. 58p. (Orig.). 1979. pap. 4.50 (ISBN 0-933564-07-4). Wildlife Soc.

WILD FLOWERS-AUSTRALIA
Galbraith, Jean. Collinsfield Guide to the Wild Flowers of Southeast Australia. 450p. 1980. 13.95x (ISBN 0-00-219246-2, Pub. by W Collins Australia). Intl Schol Bk Serv.
Grieve, B. J. & Blackall, W. E., eds. How to Know Western Australian Wildflowers: A Key to the Flore of the Flora of the Extratropical Regions of Western Australia, Pt. IIIA. 350p. 1980. 39.50x (ISBN 0-85564-160-6, Pub. by U of West Australia Pr Australia). Intl Schol Bk Serv.

WILD FLOWERS-NEW ZEALAND
Adams, Nancy M. Mountain Flowers in New Zealand. (Mobil New Zealand Nature Ser.). (Illus.). 80p. (Orig.). 1980. pap. 6.95 (ISBN 0-589-01328-9, Pub. by Reed Bks Australia). C E Tuttle.

WILD FLOWERS-NORTH AMERICA
Kavasch, E. B. Introducing Eastern Wildflowers. (Northeast Color Ser.). (Illus.). 50p. 1981. pap. 3.95 (ISBN 0-88839-092-0). Hancock Hse.
Keator, Glenn. Sierra Flower Finder: A Guide to Sierra Nevada Wildflowers. (Illus.). 1980. pap. 3.00 (ISBN 0-912550-09-0). Nature Study.

WILD FLOWERS, PROTECTION OF
see Plants, Protection of

WILD-FOWL
see Water-Birds

WILD LIFE CONSERVATION
see Wildlife Conservation

WILD LIFE REFUGES
see Wildlife Refuges

WILDE, OSCAR, 1854-1900
Pearson, Hesketh. The Life of Oscar Wilde. 389p. 1980. Repr. of 1947 ed. lib. bdg. 35.00 (ISBN 0-89987-658-7). Century Bookbindery.

WILDERNESS AREAS
Rutstrum, Calvin. Backcountry. LC 80-22052. (Illus.). 200p. 1981. pap. 10.00 (ISBN 0-934802-07-6). Ind Camp Supply.

WILDERNESS SURVIVAL
Fredrickson, Olive A. & East, Ben. Silence of the North. 224p. 1981. pap. 2.50 (ISBN 0-446-81559-4). Warner Bks.
Lehman, Charles A. Emergency Survival. Fessler, Diane M., ed. (Illus.). 160p. 1979. pap. 6.95 (ISBN 0-935810-03-X). Primer Pubs.
Neimark, Paul. Survival. (Wilderness World Ser.). (Illus.). 64p. (gr. 3 up). 1981. PLB 9.25 (ISBN 0-516-02454-X). Childrens.

WILDFLOWERS
see Wild Flowers

WILDLIFE CONSERVATION
see also National Parks and Reserves; Wilderness Areas; Wildlife Management
Bailey, James A., et al, eds. Readings in Wildlife Conservation. LC 74-28405. (Illus.). 722p. (Orig.). 1974. pap. 9.00 (ISBN 0-933564-02-3). Wildlife Soc.
Hobusch, Erich. Fair Game: A History of Hunting, Shooting & Animal Conservation. Michaelis-Jena, Ruth & Murray, Patrick, trs. from Ger. LC 80-19008. (Illus.). 280p. 1981. 29.95 (ISBN 0-668-05101-9, 5101). Arco.
Teague, Richard D. & Decker, Eugene, eds. Wildlife Conservation Principles & Practices. rev. ed. LC 79-2960. (Illus.). 280p. 1979. pap. 7.50 (ISBN 0-933564-06-6). Wildlife Soc.
Wildlife & Protected Areas: An Overview. (UNEP Report Ser.: No. 6). 50p. 1981. pap. 7.00 (ISBN 0-686-69543-7, UNEP 38, UNEP). Unipub.
Wildlife Society, Inc. A Manual of Wildlife Conservation. Teague, Richard D., ed. LC 72-143895. (Illus.). 206p. (Orig.). 1971. pap. text ed. 4.25 (ISBN 0-933564-01-5). Wildlife Soc.

WILDLIFE CONSERVATION-LAW AND LEGISLATION
see also Fishery Law and Legislation
International Congress of Game Biologists, Thirteenth, Atlanta, Ga., March 11-15, 1977. Proceedings. Peterle, Tony J., ed. (Illus.). 538p. (Orig.). 1978. pap. 10.00 (ISBN 0-933564-04-X). Wildlife Soc.
Legislation on Wildlife, Hunting & Protected Areas in Some European Countries. (Legislative Study Ser.: No. 20). 49p. 1980. pap. 6.00 (ISBN 92-5-100878-7, F2042, FAO). Unipub.
Tober, James. Who Owns the Wildlife? The Political Economy of Conservation in Nineteenth Century America. LC 80-23482. (Contributions in Economics & Economic History Ser.: No. 37). (Illus.). 300p. 1981. lib. bdg. 29.95 (ISBN 0-313-22597-4, TOW/). Greenwood.

WILDLIFE CONSERVATION-AFRICA
Hayes, Harold T. The Last Place on Earth. LC 76-15562. (Illus.). 288p. 1980. pap. 8.95 (ISBN 0-8128-6087-X). Stein & Day.

WILDLIFE CONSERVATION-LATIN AMERICA
McClung, Robert M. Vanishing Wildlife of Latin America. LC 80-25639. (Illus.). 160p. (gr. 7-9). 1981. 8.95 (ISBN 0-688-00378-8); PLB 8.59 (ISBN 0-688-00379-6). Morrow.

WILDLIFE CONSERVATION-NORTH AMERICA
Bryant, Jeannette, ed. Conservation Directory. 301p. 1981. 6.00 (ISBN 0-912186-39-9). Natl Wildlife.

WILDLIFE MANAGEMENT
see also Animal Populations
Dasmann, Raymond F. Wildlife Biology. 256p. 1981. text ed. 17.95 (ISBN 0-471-08042-X). Wiley.

Hobusch, Erich. Fair Game: A History of Hunting, Shooting & Animal Conservation. Michaelis-Jena, Ruth & Murray, Patrick, trs. from Ger. LC 80-19008. (Illus.). 280p. 1981. 29.95 (ISBN 0-668-05101-9, 5101). Arco.

Wildlife Society. Wildlife Management Techniques Manual. 4th ed. Schemnitz, Sanford D., ed. LC 80-19970. (Illus.). 722p. 1980. 20.00 (ISBN 0-933564-08-2). Wildlife Soc.

WILDLIFE REFUGES

see also names of specific Wildlife refuges

Riley, Laura & Riley, William. Guide to the National Wildlife Refuges. (Illus.). 672p. 1981. pap. 9.95 (ISBN 0-385-14015-0, Anch). Doubleday.

WILL

see also Belief and Doubt; Free Will and Determinism; Self

Bain, Alexander. Emotions & the Will. (Contributions to the History of Psychology Ser.: No. 5, Pt. a: Orientations). 1978. Repr. of 1859 ed. 30.00 (ISBN 0-89093-154-2). U Pubns Amer.

Unger, Carl. Trails of Thinking, Feeling & Willing. 1980. pap. 3.00 (ISBN 0-916786-47-1). St George Bk Serv.

WILLIAM 1ST, THE CONQUEROR, KING OF ENGLAND, 1027-1087

Histoire De Guillaume le Conquerant: Le Duc De Normandie, Vol. 1. LC 80-2252. 1981. Repr. of 1936 ed. 39.00 (ISBN 0-404-18777-3). AMS Pr.

WILLIAM 3RD, KING OF GREAT BRITAIN, 1650-1702

Ryskamp, Charles & Vliegenthart, A. W. William & Mary & Their House. (Illus.). 266p. 1980. 59.00x (ISBN 0-19-520185-X). Oxford U Pr.

WILLIAMS, HANK, 1923-1953

Flippo, Chet. Your Cheatin' Heart: A Biography of Hank Williams. 1981. 12.95 (ISBN 0-671-24114-1). S&S.

WILLIAMS, TENNESSEE, 1914-

Williams, Edwina D. & Freeman, Lucy. Remember Me to Tom. 2nd ed. 336p. 1980. pap. 5.95 (ISBN 0-86629-006-0). Sunrise MO.

Williams, Tennessee. Tennessee Williams' Letters to Donald Windham. 1976. 110.00x (ISBN 0-917366-01-8). S Campbell.

WILLS

see also Executors and Administrators; Probate Law and Practice

Harris, Virgil M. Ancient Curious & Famous Wills. xiii, 472p. 1981. Repr. of 1911 ed. lib. bdg. 39.50x (ISBN 0-8377-0633-5). Rothman.

Kirsch, Charlotte. A Survivor's Manual to Wills, Trusts, Maintaining Emotional Stability. LC 80-977. 240p. 1981. 11.95 (ISBN 0-385-15879-3, Anchor Pr). Doubleday.

Warner, Gerald. Being of Sound Mind: A Book of Eccentric Wills. (Illus.). 112p. 1981. 14.50 (ISBN 0-241-10471-8, Pub. by Hamish Hamilton England). David & Charles.

WILLS–GREAT BRITAIN

Swinburne, Henry. A Brief Treatise of Testaments & Last Wills. Berkowitz, David S. & Thorne, Samuel E., eds. LC 77-89255. (Classics of English Legal History in the Modern Era Ser.: Vol. 80). 342p. 1979. lib. bdg. 40.00 (ISBN 0-8240-3179-2). Garland Pub.

--A Briefe Treatise of Testaments & Last Wils, Newly Corrected & Augmented. LC 79-84140. (English Experience Ser.: No. 957). 620p. 1979. Repr. of 1635 ed. lib. bdg. 58.00 (ISBN 90-221-0957-7). Walter J Johnson.

WILMINGTON, DELAWARE

Hoffecker, Carol E. Wilmington: A Pictorial History. Friedman, Donna R., ed. (Illus.). 208p. 1981. pap. write for info. (ISBN 0-89865-057-7). Donning Co.

WILSON, EDITH (BOLLING) GALT, 1872-1962

Shachtman, Tom. Edith & Woodrow. 288p. 1981. 12.95 (ISBN 0-399-12446-2). Putnam.

WILSON, WOODROW, PRES. U. S., 1856-1924

Link, Arthur S., et al, eds. The Papers of Woodrow Wilson, Vol. 36: January-May, 1916. LC 66-10880. (Illus.). 648p. 1981. 30.00x (ISBN 0-691-04682-4). Princeton U Pr.

Shachtman, Tom. Edith & Woodrow. 288p. 1981. 12.95 (ISBN 0-399-12446-2). Putnam.

Tribble, Edwin, ed. A President in Love: The Courtship Letters of Woodrow Wilson & Edith Bolling Galt. (Illus.). 1981. 12.95 (ISBN 0-395-29482-7). HM.

Wilson, Woodrow. The Papers of Woodrow Wilson, Vol. 18-33. Link, Arthur S., ed. Incl. Vol. 18. 1908-1909. 1974. 30.00x (ISBN 0-691-04631-X); Vol. 19. Jan.-July 1910. 1975. 30.00x (ISBN 0-691-04633-6); Vol. 20. Jauary 12 - July 15, 1910. 1975. 30.00 (ISBN 0-691-04635-2); Vol. 21. July-Nov. 1910. 1976. 30.00 (ISBN 0-691-04636-0); Vol. 22. 1911. 1976-1977. 30.00 (ISBN 0-691-04638-7); Vol. 23. 1911-1912. 1976-1977. 30.00 (ISBN 0-691-04643-3); Vol. 24. January-August, 1912. (Illus.). 1977. text ed. 30.00 (ISBN 0-691-04645-X); Vol. 25. August - November, 1912. (Illus.). 1978. text ed. 30.00 (ISBN 0-691-04650-6); Vol. 26. Contents & Index, Vols. 14-25. 1980. 25.00 (ISBN 0-691-04664-6); Vol. 27. January - June 1913. (Illus.). 1978. 30.00 (ISBN 0-691-04652-2); Vol. 28. 1913. (Illus.). 1978. text ed. 30.00 (ISBN 0-691-04653-0); Vol. 29. 1913-1914. 1979. 30.00x (ISBN 0-691-04659-X); Vol. 30. May - December 1914. 30.00x (ISBN 0-691-04663-8); Vol. 31. September - December 1914. 1979. 30.00x (ISBN 0-691-04666-2); Vol. 32. 1979. 30.00x (ISBN 0-691-04667-0); Vol. 33. April - July 1915. (Illus.). 30.00x (ISBN 0-691-04668-9). LC 66-10880. Princeton U Pr.

WIND

see Winds

WIND INSTRUMENTS

see also Bands (Music);

also names of wind instruments, e.g. Flute, Horn (Musical Instrument), Trumpet

Robinson, Trevor. The Amateur Wind Instrument Maker, Revised Edition. LC 80-5381. (Illus.). 136p. 1981. pap. 8.95 (ISBN 0-87023-312-2). U of Mass Pr.

WIND POWER

see also Windmills

Hunt, V. Daniel. Windpower: Handbook of Wind Energy Conversion. 640p. 1981. text ed. 39.50 (ISBN 0-442-27389-4). Van Nos Reinhold.

Jarass, L., et al. Wind Energy. (Illus.). 230p. 1981. 43.70 (ISBN 0-387-10362-7). Springer-Verlag.

Pacific Northwest Laboratory. Sitting Handbook for Small Wind Energy Conversion Systems. 85p. Date not set. 21.95 (ISBN 0-89934-121-7); pap. 10.95 (ISBN 0-89934-122-5). Solar Energy Info.

Raytheon Service Co. Wind Energy Systems Program Summary Nineteen Eighty. 230p. 1981. pap. 19.50 (ISBN 0-89934-108-X). Solar Energy Info.

Stephens, H. S. & Stapleton, C. A., eds. Papers Presented at the Third International Symposium on Wind Energy Systems. (Illus.). 579p. 1980. pap. 99.00 (ISBN 0-906085-47-0). BHRA Fluid.

Symposium on Wind Energy, 1st. Proceedings. 1977. 65.00. BHRA Fluid.

Symposium on Wind Energy, 3rd. Proceedings. 1980. pap. 99.00 (ISBN 0-906085-47-0). BHRA Fluid.

Torrey, Volta. Wind-Catchers: American Windmills of Yesterday & Tomorrow. (Illus.). 240p. (Orig.). 1981. pap. 9.95 (ISBN 0-8289-0438-3). Greene.

WINDMILLS

see also Wind Power

Moison, Lawrence G. Home Windmills. (Illus.). 60p. (Orig.). 1980. pap. text ed. 2.95. Mod Handcraft.

The New Alchemy Water Pumping Windmill. 96p. 4.95 (ISBN 0-931790-23-9). Brick Hse Pub.

WINDOWS, STAINED GLASS

see Glass Painting and Staining

WINDS

see also Monsoons

Lawson, T. V. Wind Effects on Buildings: Vol. 1, Design Applicatons. (Illus.). xii, 344p. 1980. 55.00x (ISBN 0-85334-887-1). Burgess-Intl Ideas.

--Wind Effects on Buildings: Volume 2--Statistics & Meteorology. (Illus.). xii, 160p. 1980. 30.00x (ISBN 0-85334-893-6). Burgess-Intl Ideas.

Marko, Katherine D. How the Wind Blows. LC 80-22754. 32p. (gr. 2-4). 1981. 5.95g (ISBN 0-687-17680-?). Abingdon.

Minikin, R. R. Winds, Waves & Maritime Structures. 295p. 1963. 29.75x (ISBN 0-85264-091-9, Pub. by Griffin England). State Mutual Bk.

WINDSOR, H. R. H., THE DUKE OF

see Edward 8th, King of Great Britain, 1894-1972

WINDSOR, WALLIS WARFIELD, DUCHESS OF, 1896-

Bryan, James & Murphy, Charles. The Windsor Story. 1981. pap. 3.95 (ISBN 0-440-19346-X). Dell.

Mosley, Diana. The Duchess of Windsor. LC 80-20793. (Illus.). 224p. 1980. 14.95 (ISBN 0-8128-2759-7). Stein & Day.

WINE AND WINE MAKING

see also Brandy

Abel, Doninick. Guide to the Wines of the United States. 1979. 2.95 (ISBN 0-346-12427-1). Cornerstone.

Amerine, Maynard A., ed. Wine Production Technology in the United States. LC 80-28041. (Symposium Ser.: No. 145). 1981. price not set (ISBN 0-8412-0596-5); pap. price not set (ISBN 0-8412-0602-3). Am Chemical.

Emmery, Lena & Taylor, Sally. Grape Expeditions: Bicycle Tours of the California Wine Country, Vol. 2. (Illus.). 48p. 1980. pap. text ed. 2.40 (ISBN 0-9604904-0-X). Taylor & Friends.

Haynes, Irene W. Ghost Wineries of Napa Valley. (Illus.). 80p. (Orig.). 1980. pap. 2.40 (ISBN 0-9604904-1-8). Taylor & Friends.

Heckmann, Manfred. Corkscrews: An Introduction to Their Appreciation. Sullivan, Maurice, ed. (Illus.). 124p. 1981. 12.95 (ISBN 0-686-69566-6). Wine Appreciation.

Kleinsinger, Irene J. Wine Log. (Illus.). 96p. 1980. 9.95 (ISBN 0-9605146-1-9); pap. 4.95 (ISBN 0-9605146-0-0). Kleinsinger.

Meredith, Ted. Northwest Wine. LC 80-80917. (Illus.). 180p. 1980. pap. 6.95 (ISBN 0-936666-00-5). Nexus Pr.

Michaels, Marjorie. Stay Healthy with Wine: Natural Cures & Beauty Secrets from the Vineyards. 256p. 1981. 11.95 (ISBN 0-686-69092-3). Dial.

Morris, Roger. The Genie in the Bottle: Unravelling the Myths About Wine. (Illus.). 204p. 1981. 12.95 (ISBN 0-89104-213-X); pap. 5.95 (ISBN 0-89104-198-2). A & W Pubs.

Pratt, James N. The Wine Bibber's Bible. rev. ed. (Illus.). 192p. 1981. pap. 6.95 (ISBN 0-89286-182-7). One Hurd One Prods.

Shanken, Marvin R. The Impact American Wine Market Review & Forecast: Nineteen-Eighty-One Edition. 7th ed. (Illus.). 60p. 1981. pap. price not set (ISBN 0-918076-13-7). Tasco.

Vine, Richard P. Commercial Winemaking: Processing & Controls. (Illus.). 1981. text ed. 19.50 (ISBN 0-87055-376-3). AVI.

Yoxall, H. W. The Wines of Burgundy: The International Wire & Food Society's Guide. LC 78-57582. (Illus.). 192p. 1980. pap. 5.95 (ISBN 0-8128-6091-8). Stein & Day.

WINE AND WINE-MAKING–DICTIONARIES

Hamlyn Pocket Dictionary of Wines. 1980. pap. 3.95. Larousse.

Lichine, Alexis. Alexis Lichine's New Encyclopedia of Wines & Spirits. 3rd ed. LC 80-22385. (Illus.). 736p. 1981. 29.95 (ISBN 0-394-51781-4). Knopf.

WINE AND WINE-MAKING–AUSTRALIA

Halliday, James. Wines & Wineries of New South Wales. 165p. 1981. text ed. 10.95x (ISBN 0-7022-1570-8). U of Queensland Pr.

Major Wine Grape Varieties of Australia. 61p. 1979. pap. 6.50 (ISBN 0-643-02517-0, CO12, CSIRO). Unipub.

Some Wine Grape Varieties for Australia. 50p. 1976. pap. 5.00 (ISBN 0-643-00180-8, CO09, CSIRO). Unipub.

WINE AND WINE-MAKING–EUROPE

Read, Jan. Wines of Spain & Portugal. (Illus.). 1980. 13.95 (ISBN 0-571-10266-2, Pub. by Faber & Faber). Merrimack Bk Serv.

WINE AND WINE-MAKING–FRANCE

Brown, Michael. Food & Wine of Southwest France. (Illus.). 216p. 1981. 35.00 (ISBN 0-7134-1847-8, Pub. by Batsford England). David & Charles.

WINE AND WINE MAKING–GERMANY

Siegel, Hans. Guide to the Wines of Germany. 1979. pap. 2.95 (ISBN 0-346-12426-3). Cornerstone.

WINNEBAGO INDIANS

see Indians of North America–Northwest, Old

WINTER–JUVENILE LITERATURE

Allington, Richard L. & Krull, Kathleen. Winter. LC 80-25115. (Beginning to Learn About Ser.). (Illus.). 32p. (ps-2). 1981. PLB 9.65 (ISBN 0-8172-1340-6). Raintree Child.

Freedman, Russell. When Winter Comes. LC 80-22831. (Illus.). (gr. 1-3). 1981. PLB 7.95 (ISBN 0-525-42583-7). Dutton.

WINTER WAR, 1939-1940

see Russo-Finnish War, 1939-1940

WINTERTHUR MUSEUMS

see Henry Francis Dupont Winterthur Museum

WIRE EXPLOSIONS, ELECTRIC

see Exploding Wire Phenomena

WIRE-TAPPING

Fishman, Clifford. Wiretapping & Eavesdropping, Vol. 1. LC 78-18629. 1978. 47.50. Lawyers Co-Op.

WIRETAPPING

see Wire-Tapping

WIRING, ELECTRIC

see Electric Wiring

WISCONSIN–DESCRIPTION AND TRAVEL

Canoe Trails of Northern Wisconsin. (Illus.). 64p. (Orig.). 1981. pap. 6.95 (ISBN 0-915024-25-X). Tamarack Edns.

Daniel, Glenda & Sullivan, Jerry. A Sierra Club Naturlist's Guide to the North Woods of Michigan, Wisconsin, & Minnesota. (Naturalist's Guide Ser.). (Illus.). 384p. 1981. 24.95 (ISBN 0-87156-248-0); pap. 9.95 (ISBN 0-87156-277-4). Sierra.

Isherwood, Justin. Wisconsin. (Illus.). 128p. 1981. 27.50 (ISBN 0-912856-67-X). Graphic Arts Ctr.

Umhoefer, Jim. Guide to Wisconsin's State Parks, Forests, & Trails. (Illus.). 160p. (Orig.). 1981. pap. 7.95 (ISBN 0-915024-26-8). Tamarack Edns.

WISCONSIN–HISTORY

Anderson-Sannes, Barbara. Alma on the Mississippi, 1848-1932. Doyle, Michael, et al, eds. LC 80-68241. (Illus.). 198p. (Orig.). 1980. pap. 11.95 (ISBN 0-9604684-0-4). Alma Hist Soc.

Vexler, R. I. Wisconsin Chronology & Factbook, Vol. 49. 1978. 8.50 (ISBN 0-379-16174-5). Oceana.

WISCONSIN–SOCIAL LIFE AND CUSTOMS

Blei, Norbert. The Door Way. 240p. 1980. 16.95 (ISBN 0-933180-22-5). Ellis Pr.

Hachten, Harva. The Flavor of Wisconsin: An Informal History of Food & Eating in the Badger State. LC 80-26172. (Illus.). 300p. 1981. 12.95 (ISBN 0-87020-204-9). State Hist Soc Wis.

WISDOM

see also Judgment

Bennett, J. G. The Masters of Wisdom. 1980. pap. 5.95 (ISBN 0-87728-466-0). Weiser.

Wei Wu-Wei. Unwordly Wise. 88p. 1981. 6.50 (ISBN 0-85656-103-7). Great Eastern.

WISDOM LITERATURE

Gittner, Louis. Listen Listen Listen. Farish, Starr, ed. 320p. (Orig.). 1980. pap. 7.95 (ISBN 0-9605492-0-X). Louis Found.

Murphy, Roland E. Wisdom Literature: Ruth, Esther, Job, Proverbs, Ecclesiastes, Canticles. (The Forms of the Old Testament Literature Ser.). (Orig.). 1981. pap. write for info. (ISBN 0-8028-1877-3). Eerdmans.

Rutstrum, Calvin. Chips from a Wilderness Log. LC 77-20847. 256p. 1981. pap. 6.95 (ISBN 0-8128-6124-8). Stein & Day.

WISTER, OWEN, 1860-1938

Rush, N. Orwin. Diversions of a Westerner: With Emphasis Upon Owen Wister's & Frederic Remington's Books & Libraries. LC 78-53134. (Illus.). 224p. 1979. 10.00 (ISBN 0-932068-05-7). South Pass Pr.

Stokes, Frances K. My Father Owen Wister. 54p. (Orig.). 1952. pap. 5.00. South Pass Pr.

WIT AND HUMOR

see also Comedy; Epigrams; Humorists; Limericks; Political Satire; Puns and Punning

also American Wit and Humor; English Wit and Humor; and similar headings

Adams, Joey. Strictly for Laughs. 224p. 1981. 8.95 (ISBN 0-89479-079-X). A & W Pubs.

Beetle Bailey Shape up or Ship Out. (Beetle Bailey Cartoon Ser.). 128p. 1981. pap. 1.50 (ISBN 0-448-12659-1, Tempo). G&D.

Bombeck, Erma. Aunt Erma's Cope Book. 1980. pap. 2.75 (ISBN 0-449-24334-6, Crest). Fawcett.

Bonham, Tal D. The Treasury of Clean Jokes. LC 80-67639. (Orig.). 1981. pap. 2.95 (ISBN 0-8054-5703-8). Broadman.

Coren, Alan. The Best of Alan Coren. 424p. 1981. 15.95 (ISBN 0-312-07711-4). St Martin.

Crowquill, Alfred, ed. The Laughing Philosopher. 329p. 1980. Repr. of 1899 ed. lib. bdg. 40.00 (ISBN 0-89760-123-8). Telegraph Bks.

Curtis, Richard. How to Prosper in the Coming Apocalypse. (Illus.). 96p. 1981. pap. 3.95 (ISBN 0-312-39611-2); prepack 39.50 (ISBN 0-312-39612-0). St Martin.

De Bartolo, Dick & North, Henry. Mad Guide to Fraud & Deception. 192p. (Orig.). 1981. pap. 1.75 (ISBN 0-446-94154-9). Warner Bks.

Dekay, Ormonde. N'heures Souris Rames: The Coucy Castle Manuscript. (Clarkson N. Potter Bks.). 1980. 7.95 (ISBN 0-517-54081-9). Crown.

Diller, Phyllis. The Joys of Aging & How to Avoid Them. LC 79-7863. (Illus.). 192p. 1981. 8.95 (ISBN 0-385-14555-1). Doubleday.

Fagan, Kevin. Drabble. 132p. (Orig.). 1981. pap. 3.95 (ISBN 0-449-90052-5, Columbine). Fawcett.

Gately, George. Heathcliff Rides Again. 128p. 1981. pap. 1.50 (ISBN 0-448-12629-X, Tempo). G&D.

Guisewite, Cathy. What's a Nice Girl Like You Doing with a Double Bed. 160p. 1981. pap. 4.95 (ISBN 0-553-01316-5). Bantam.

Harvey Comics. Casper Far Out Fables. 1981. pap. 1.25 (ISBN 0-448-17251-8, Tempo). G&D.

Hayduke, George. Get Even Two. (Get Even Ser.: Vol. 2). (Illus.). 170p. 1981. 9.95 (ISBN 0-87364-213-9). Paladin Ent.

Kaeppel, Al. The Cat Testrophy. LC 79-91599. (Illus., Orig.). 1981. 3.95 (ISBN 0-89896-000-2). Larksdale.

Ketchum, Hank. Dennis the Menace: Good Intenshuns. 128p. 1981. pap. 1.50 (ISBN 0-449-14395-3, GM). Fawcett.

Kilthau, Gus. How to Write Dumb Poems. LC 79-88250. (Orig.). 1981. price not set (ISBN 0-89896-013-4). Larksdale.

Kivley, Melvin. Hadlock Hill. LC 79-56885. 178p. 1981. 7.95 (ISBN 0-533-04545-2). Vantage.

Lazarus, Mell. Momma. 128p. (Orig.). 1981. pap. 1.75 (ISBN 0-553-14788-9). Bantam.

Locks, Renee & McHugh, Joseph. Abandon Yourself to Love. LC 80-67343. (Illus.). 112p. 1981. 4.95 (ISBN 0-89087-304-6). Celestial Arts.

Mackintosh, Prudence. Thundering Sneakers. LC 80-1124. 192p. 1981. 9.95 (ISBN 0-385-12879-7). Doubleday.

McPhee, Nancy. Book of Insults II. 144p. 1981. 7.95 (ISBN 0-312-08930-9). St Martin.

Mad Magazine Editors. Pumping Mad. (Mad Ser.: No. 56). (Illus.). 192p. (Orig.). 1981. pap. 1.75 (ISBN 0-446-94820-9). Warner Bks.

Myers, Russell. Life Begins at One Thousand Five Hundred. 128p. 1981. pap. 1.50 (ISBN 0-449-14378-3, GM). Fawcett.

Paley, Frederick A. Greek Wit: A Collection of Smart Sayings & Anecdotes. 128p. 1980. Repr. of 1881 ed. lib. bdg. 20.00 (ISBN 0-8492-2190-0). R West.

Palin, Michael & Jones, Terry. More Ripping Yarns. (Illus.). 1981. pap. 5.95 (ISBN 0-394-74810-7). Pantheon.

Parham, William. The Book of Melvin. LC 80-53663. (Illus.). 64p. (Orig.). 1981. pap. 3.95 (ISBN 0-938264-00-1). Veritas Pubns.

Parker, et al. Are Those Your Good Pants? 128p. (Orig.). 1981. pap. 1.75 (ISBN 0-449-14390-2, GM). Fawcett.

Peake, Mervyn. Peake's Progress: Selected Writings & Drawings of Mervyn Peake. Gilmore, Maeve, ed. LC 80-83054. (Illus.). 576p. 1981. 25.00 (ISBN 0-87951-121-4). Overlook Pr.

Phillips, Bob. The Fun Joke Book. pap. 1.95 (ISBN 0-89081-235-7). Harvest Hse.

Pierce, Guy, compiled by. Cuttings: The Pick of "Country Life" from Punch. (Illus.). 64p. 1981. pap. 4.50 (ISBN 0-241-10496-3, Pub. by Hamish Hamilton England). David & Charles.

Porter, Mike. Funny Mouth: Comedy Material for All Occasions. 1981. spiral bdg. 12.95 (ISBN 0-914598-70-8); pap. 9.95 (ISBN 0-914598-71-6). Padre Prods.

Rees, Nigel. Love, Death & the Universe. (Illus.). 128p. 1981. pap. 6.95 (ISBN 0-02-029340-2). Macmillan.

Reiser, Judy. And I Thought I Was Crazy! Quirks, Idiosyncrasies & Meshugass That People Are into. LC 80-15360. (Illus.). 138p. (Orig.). 1980. pap. 4.95 (ISBN 0-671-25399-9, 91707-2, Fireside). S&S.

Rivers, Caryl & Lupo, Alan. For Better! for Worse! 256p. 1981. 12.95 (ISBN 0-671-25446-4). Summit Bks.

Ryan, Tom K. Tumbleweed Express. 128p. (Orig.). 1981. pap. 1.75 (ISBN 0-449-14407-0, GM). Fawcett.

Schulz, Charles. The Beagle Has Landed, Vol. II. 128p. 1981. pap. 1.75 (ISBN 0-449-24373-7, Crest). Fawcett.

Schwartz, Toby D. Mercy, Lord! My Husband's in the Kitchen & Other Equal Opportunity Conversations with God. LC 80-715. (Illus.). 96p. 1981. 6.95 (ISBN 0-385-17058-0). Doubleday.

Trudeau, G. B. A Tad Overweight but Violet Eyes to Die for. 1981. pap. 1.75 (ISBN 0-553-14337-9). Bantam.

Twain, Mark, pseud. Mark Twain in Hawaii. Jones, William R., ed. (Illus.). 96p. 1981. pap. 4.95 (ISBN 0-89646-070-3). Outbooks.

Unger, Jim. Herman Hang-Ups. 20p. (gr. 4 up). 1980. pap. 4.95 (ISBN 0-8362-1954-6). Andrews & McMeel.

Walton, Sally & Wilkinson, Faye. We're Number One: State--Ole Miss Jokes. rev. ed. (Illus.). 72p. 1980. pap. 3.95 (ISBN 0-937552-04-6). Quail Ridge.

Wilde, Larry. The Complete Doctor's Joke Book. 208p. (Orig.). 1981. pap. 1.95 (ISBN 0-553-14751-X). Bantam.

--More: The Official Sex Maniac's Joke Book. 176p. (Orig.). 1981. pap. 1.95 (ISBN 0-553-14623-8). Bantam.

--The Official Italian Joke Book. rev. ed. 160p. 1981. pap. 1.75 (ISBN 0-523-41196-0). Pinnacle Bks.

--The Official Polish Joke Book. rev. ed. 160p. 1981. pap. 1.75 (ISBN 0-523-41195-2). Pinnacle Bks.

Wilson, Tom. Ziggy's Door Openers. 20p. (gr. 4 up). 1980. pap. 4.95 (ISBN 0-8362-1914-7). Andrews & McMeel.

Wood, Debby. Oh, God, Not Another Beautiful Day! LC 80-69857. (Illus.). 128p. 1980. pap. 3.95 (ISBN 0-89305-032-6). Anna Pub.

Youngman, Henny. Henny Youngman's Five Hundred All-Time Greatest One-Liners. 160p. (Orig.). 1981. pap. 1.95 (ISBN 0-523-41142-1). Pinnacle Bks.

WIT AND HUMOR–HISTORY AND CRITICISM

Billington, Ray A. Limericks Historical & Hysterical: Plagiarized, Arranged, Annotated & Some Written by Ray Allen Billington. 1981. 9.95 (ISBN 0-393-01453-3). Norton.

Fine, George. Sex Jokes & Male Chauvinism. (Illus.). 192p. 1981. 9.95 (ISBN 0-8065-0753-5). Citadel Pr.

Leacock, Stephen. Humor & Humanity. 232p. 1980. Repr. of 1938 ed. lib. bdg. 35.00 (ISBN 0-89984-322-0). Century Bookbindery.

Schulz, Max F. Black Humor Fiction of the Sixties: A Pluralistic Definition of Man & His World. LC 72-85538. 156p. 1980. pap. 5.95x (ISBN 0-8214-0574-8). Ohio U Pr.

WIT AND HUMOR–JUVENILE LITERATURE

see Wit and Humor, Juvenile

WIT AND HUMOR–PSYCHOLOGY

Fisher, Seymour & Fisher, Rhoda L. Pretend the World Is Funny & Forever: A Psychological Analysis of Comedians, Clowns, & Actors. LC 80-7777. 288p. 1981. profess. & reference 19.95 (ISBN 0-89859-073-6). L Erlbaum Assocs.

WIT AND HUMOR, JUVENILE

The Bananas Yearbook 1980. (gr. 7-12). 1980. pap. 2.25 (ISBN 0-590-31471-8, Schol Pap). Schol Bk Serv.

Dachs. TV Jokes. (gr. 7-12). pap. 1.25 (ISBN 0-590-05402-3, Schol Pap). Schol Bk Serv.

De Reginiers. Abraham Lincoln Joke Book. (gr. 3-5). 1980. pap. 1.25 (ISBN 0-590-30968-4, Schol Pap). Schol Bk Serv.

Johnson, William. Famous Monster Funbooks. (Illus.). 48p. (Orig.). 1981. pap. 2.50 (ISBN 0-89844-030-0). Troubador Pr.

Kirk, Tim, illus. Fozzie's Big Book of Sidesplitting Jokes (Please Laugh) LC 80-23776. (Muppet Show Bks.). (Illus.). 32p. (gr. 1-5). 1981. pap. 1.95 (ISBN 0-394-84675-3). Random.

Myers, Bernice Myers' Book of Giggles. (ps-3). 1980. pap. 1.25 (ISBN 0-590-30067-9, Schol Pap). Schol Bk Serv.

Poole, Gary. Gag Galaxy Outer Space Jokes & Riddles. (Illus.). 128p. (Orig.). 1981. pap. 1.25 (ISBN 0-448-17165-1, Tempo). G&D.

Simon, Seymour. Silly Animal Jokes & Riddles. 64p. (gr. 1-3). 7.95 (ISBN 0-07-057397-2). McGraw.

Weigle, Oscar, ed. Great Big Joke & Riddle Book. LC 79-129734. (Illus.). 224p. (gr. 1-5). 1981. 6.95 (ISBN 0-448-02584-1); PLB 10.15 (ISBN 0-448-03167-1). G&D.

WIT AND HUMOR, PICTORIAL

see also Caricatures and Cartoons; Cartoonists; Comic Books, Strips, Etc.;
also American Wit and Humor, Pictorial; English Wit and Humor, Pictorial, and similar headings

Brooks, Charles, ed. Best Editorial Cartoons of the Year: Nineteen Eighty-One Edition. (Best Editorial Cartoons of the Year Ser.: Vol. 9). (Illus.). 160p. 1981. pap. 7.95 (ISBN 0-88289-280-0); pap. 5.95 (ISBN 0-88289-281-9). Pelican.

Hawkins, Hale. Your Old Balls. (Illus.). 80p. (Orig.). 1980. pap. 4.95 (ISBN 0-938194-00-3). Lively Hills.

WITCHCRAFT

see also Demonology; Medicine-Man; Occult Sciences; Science; Voodooism

Byars, Emma L. Witchcraft. 1981. 4.50 (ISBN 0-8062-1580-1). Carlton.

Elwood, Roger. Historias Extranas de Brujeria. Lockward, George, tr. from Eng. Orig. Title: Strange Things Are Happening. 112p. (Orig., Span.). 1974. pap. 1.50 (ISBN 0-89922-028-2). Edit Caribe.

Holzer, Hans. Inside Witchcraft. (Orig.). 1980. pap. 2.25 (ISBN 0-532-23220-8). Manor Bks.

Hoyt, Charles A. Witchcraft. 1981. price not set (ISBN 0-8093-0964-5); pap. price not set (ISBN 0-8093-1015-5). S Ill U Pr.

WITNESS BEARING (CHRISTIANITY)

see also Evangelistic Work; Martyrdom; Prophecy (Christianity)

Petersen, Jim. Evangelism As a Lifestyle. LC 80-83874. 1980. pap. 3.95 (ISBN 0-89109-475-X). NavPress.

WITTGENSTEIN, LUDWIG, 1889-1951

Bindeman, Steven L. Heidegger & Wittgenstein: The Poetics of Silence. LC 80-6066. 159p. 1980. lib. bdg. 15.75 (ISBN 0-8191-1350-6); pap. text ed. 7.50 (ISBN 0-8191-1351-4). U Pr of Amer.

Canfield, John V. Wittgenstein: Language & World. 256p. 1981. lib. bdg. 17.50x (ISBN 0-87023-318-1); pap. text ed. 7.50x (ISBN 0-87023-319-X). U of Mass Pr.

Peterson, Thomas D. Wittgenstein for Preaching: A Model for Communication. LC 80-5802. 192p. 1980. lib. bdg. 17.00 (ISBN 0-8191-1342-5); pap. text ed. 8.75 (ISBN 0-8191-1343-3). U Pr of Amer.

Rubenstein, David. Marx & Wittgenstein. 240p. 1981. write for info. (ISBN 0-7100-0688-8). Routledge & Kegan.

WIVES

see also Air Force Wives; Clergymen's Wives; Presidents–United States–Wives and Children

Funt, Marilyn. Are You Anybody? 352p. 1981. pap. 2.75 (ISBN 0-523-41413-7). Pinnacle Bks.

Griffith, Wickham. Young Wives Encyclopedia. 7.95 (ISBN 0-392-08135-0, SpS). Soccer.

WODEHOUSE, PELHAM GRENVILLE, 1881-1975

Jasen, David A. P. G. Wodehouse: Portrait of a Master. (Illus.). 352p. 1981. 17.50 (ISBN 0-8264-0046-9); pap. 8.95 (ISBN 0-8264-0033-7). Continuum.

WOLVES

Frame, George & Frame, Lory. Swift & Enduring: Cheetahs & Wild Dogs of the Serengeti. 1981. 15.95 (ISBN 0-525-93060-4). Dutton.

Mech, L. David. The Wolf: The Ecology & Behavior of an Endangered Species. LC 80-27364. (Illus.). 385p. 1981. pap. 8.95 (ISBN 0-8166-1026-6). U of Minn Pr.

WOMAN

see Women

WOMEN

see also Female Offenders; Feminism; Mothers; Single Women; Widows; Wives
also subdivision Women under names of ethnic groups, e.g. Indians of North America–Women; and headings beginning with the word Women

Boslooper, Thomas. Image of Women. LC 79-57637. (Illus.). 228p. 1980. 19.95 (ISBN 0-932894-04-6). Unif Theol Seminary.

Dahlberg, Francis, ed. Woman the Gatherer. LC 80-25262. (Illus.). 288p. 1981. text ed. 15.00x (ISBN 0-300-02572-6). Yale U Pr.

Hall, Nor. The Moon & the Virgin: Reflections on the Archetypal Feminine. LC 78-2138. (Illus.). 1981. pap. 5.95 (ISBN 0-06-090793-2, CN 793, CN). Har-Row.

Lee, Linda. Today I Am a Woman. 2.95 (ISBN 0-912216-17-4). Green Hill.

Nicol, Davidson & D'Onofrio-Flores, Pamela, eds. Scientific-Technological Change & the Role of Women in Development. (Special Studies in Social, Political, & Economic Development). 200p. 1981. lib. bdg. 25.00x (ISBN 0-86531-145-5). Westview.

Rein, Natalie. Daughters of Rachel: Women in Israel. 1980. pap. 4.95 (ISBN 0-14-005731-5). Penguin.

Schaef, Anne W. Woman's I View. Orig. Title: Another Reality: the Female System & White Male System. 180p. (Orig.). 1981. 12.95 (ISBN 0-03-059061-2); pap. 6.95 (ISBN 0-03-059061-2). Winston Pr.

Tinker, Irene, et al, eds. Women & World Development with an Annotated Bibliography. 2 vols. 416p. 1976. pap. 6.95. Overseas Dev Council.

WOMEN–ANATOMY AND PHYSIOLOGY

Federation of Feminist Women's Health Centers. A New View of a Woman's Body: A Totally Illustrated Guide. 1981. 14.95 (ISBN 0-671-41214-0); pap. 6.95 (ISBN 0-671-41215-9). S&S.

WOMEN–BIBLIOGRAPHY

Farr, Sidney S. Appalachian Women: An Annotated Bibliography. LC 80-5174. 224p. 1981. price not set (ISBN 0-8131-1431-4). U Pr of Ky.

Faunce, Patricia S. Women & Ambition: A Bibliography. LC 79-18347. 724p. 1980. lib. bdg. 32.50 (ISBN 0-8108-1242-8). Scarecrow.

WOMEN–BIOGRAPHY

Bergert, Fritz. Die Von Den Trobadors Genannten Oder Gefeierten Damen. LC 80-2164. 1981. Repr. of 1913 ed. 26.50 (ISBN 0-404-19028-6). AMS Pr.

Brough, James. The Vixens. 1981. 12.95 (ISBN 0-671-22688-6). S&S.

Clark, Eleanor D. When Mama Was a Little Girl: Memories of a Georgia Childhood. (Illus.). 64p. 1980. 6.00 (ISBN 0-682-49663-4). Exposition.

Cooke, Hope. Time Change: An Autobiography. 1981. 12.95 (ISBN 0-671-41225-6). S&S.

Fredrickson, Olive A. & East, Ben. Silence of the North. 224p. 1981. pap. 2.50 (ISBN 0-446-81559-4). Warner Bks.

Hawley, Gloria H. Frankly Feminine: God's Idea of Womanhood. 160p. (Orig.). 1981. pap. 3.50 (ISBN 0-87239-455-7, 2969). Standard Pub.

Holder, Maryse. Give Sorrow Words: Maryse Holder's Letters from Mexico. 336p. (Orig.). 1980. pap. 2.50 (ISBN 0-380-51466-4, 51466). Avon.

Irwin, Inez. The Story of Alice Paul. 6.95 (ISBN 0-87714-058-8). Green Hill.

Kirkman, Francis. The Counterfeit Lady Unveiled: Being a Full Account of the Birth, Life, Most Remarkable Actions, & Untimely Death of Mary Carleton, Known by the Name of the German Princess. Bd. with The Memoirs of Mary Carleton, Commonly Stiled, the German Princess: Being a Narrative of Her Life & Death. LC 80-2486. 1981. 74.50 (ISBN 0-404-19120-7). AMS Pr.

Le Lievre, Audrey. Miss Willmott of Warley Place. (Illus.). 240p. 1981. 28.00 (ISBN 0-571-11622-1, Pub. by Faber & Faber). Merrimack Bk Serv.

Leva, Laudia. Hard to Kill. 1981. 6.95 (ISBN 0-533-04672-6). Vantage.

Madden, Virginia M. Across America on the Yellow Brick Road. (Illus.). 1980. pap. 8.95 (ISBN 0-937760-00-5). Crow Canyon.

Manning, Anne, et al. Mary Powell & Deborah's Diary. Rhys, Ernest, ed. 228p. 1980. Repr. lib. bdg. 20.00 (ISBN 0-8495-3796-7). Arden Lib.

Martin, Sadie E. The Life & Professional Career of Emma Abbott. LC 80-2290. 1981. Repr. of 1891 ed. 28.50 (ISBN 0-404-18858-3). AMS Pr.

Nathan, Isaac. Memoirs of Madame Malibran De Beriot. LC 80-2291. 1981. Repr. of 1836 ed. 18.50 (ISBN 0-404-18860-5). AMS Pr.

O'Neil, Kitty & Libby, Bill. Kitty: A Story of Triumph in a Soundless World. (Illus.). 224p. 1981. 9.95 (ISBN 0-688-00355-9). Morrow.

Panther, Ida S. Doctor & Annie. 1981. 5.75 (ISBN 0-8062-1628-X). Carlton.

Raven, Susan & Weir, Alison. Women in History. (Illus.). 288p. 1981. 19.95 (ISBN 0-517-53982-9, Harmony). Crown.

Reid, Ruby D. My Life. 1981. 4.95 (ISBN 0-8062-1694-8). Carlton.

Ross, Macye. The Will-God's Way: The True Autobiography of an Orphan. 1981. 8.95 (ISBN 0-533-04846-X). Vantage.

Safran, Rose. Woman Ahead of Her Time. 1981. pap. 5.95 (ISBN 0-9602786-2-1). Tide Bk Pub Co.

Tardiff, Olive. They Paved the Way: A History of N. H. Women. vi, 98p. (gr. 9-12). 1980. pap. text ed. 3.95 (ISBN 0-917890-22-1). Heritage Bk.

Toth, Susan A. Blooming: A Small-Town Girlhood. 244p. 1981. 10.95 (ISBN 0-316-85076-4). Little.

Walkington, Ethlyn. Gently Down the Stream. 1981. 5.95 (ISBN 0-8062-1606-9). Carlton.

Walters, Dottie, ed. The Pearl of Potentiality. LC 79-91548. 296p. 1980. 11.95 (ISBN 0-8119-0338-9, Pub. by Royal CBC). Fell.

--Success Secrets of Successful Women. LC 78-68596. (Illus.). 276p. 1978. 11.95 (ISBN 0-8119-0339-7, Pub. by Royal CBC). Fell.

Watson, Alice S. Troubled Waters. 6.95 (ISBN 0-8062-1587-9). Carlton.

Williams, Masha. White Among the Reds. 224p. 1980. 25.00x (ISBN 0-85683-044-5, Pub. by Shepheard-Walwyn England). State Mutual Bk.

WOMEN–BIOGRAPHY–JUVENILE LITERATURE

Davis, Blanche W. As I Remember. 1981. 7.95 (ISBN 0-8062-1660-3). Carlton.

Johnston. They Led the Way: Fourteen American Women. (gr. 3-5). pap. 1.50 (ISBN 0-590-11908-7, Schol Pap). Schol Bk Serv.

Land, Barbara. The New Explorers: Women in Antarctica. LC 80-2778. (Illus.). 224p. (gr. 7 up). 1981. PLB 8.95 (ISBN 0-396-07924-5). Dodd.

WOMEN–CLOTHING

see Clothing and Dress; Costume

WOMEN–CLUBS

see Women–Societies and Clubs

WOMEN–COSTUME

see Costume

WOMEN–CRIME

see Female Offenders

WOMEN–DEFENSE

see Self-Defense for Women

WOMEN–DRESS

see Clothing and Dress; Costume

WOMEN–ECONOMIC CONDITIONS

Briles, Judith. The Woman's Guide to Financial Savvy. 192p. 1981. 10.95 (ISBN 0-312-88649-7). St Martin.

Dublin, Thomas. Farm & Factory: The Mill Experience & Women's Lives in New England, Eighteen Thirty to Eighteen Sixty. LC 80-28084. 220p. 1981. 15.00x (ISBN 0-231-05118-2). Columbia U Pr.

International Labour Office, Geneva. Women in Rural Development: Critical Issues. (a WEP Study) x, 214p. (Orig.). 1980. pap. 7.15 (ISBN 92-2-102388-5). Intl Labour Office.

Loutfi, Martha F. Rural Women: Unequal Partners in Development, a WEP Study. Intl Labour Office, ed. (Illus.). iii, 81p. 1980. pap. 7.15 (ISBN 92-2-102389-3). Intl Labour Office.

Minkow, Rosalie. Money Management for Women. LC 80-84373. 256p. (Orig.). 1981. pap. 2.50 (ISBN 0-87216-816-6). Playboy Pbks.

Wiesen-Cooke, Blanche. Women & Support Networks. (Out & Out Pamphlet Ser.). pap. 2.00 (ISBN 0-918314-10-0). Out & Out.

Zeidenstein, Sondra, ed. Learning About Rural Women. (Studies in Family Planning Ser.: Vol. 10, Nos. 11-12). 118p. (Orig.). 1979. pap. 2.50. Population Coun.

WOMEN–EDUCATION

see Education of Women

WOMEN–EMANCIPATION

see Women's Rights

WOMEN–EMPLOYMENT

see also Vocational Guidance for Women

Abarbanel, Karin & Siegel, Gonnie M. Woman's Work Book. 1977. pap. 2.50 (ISBN 0-446-81353-2). Warner Bks.

Abarbanol, Karin & Siegel, Gonnie M. The Woman's Work Book. 352p. 1981. pap. 3.50 (ISBN 0-446-91658-7). Warner Bks.

Braybon, Gail. Women Workers in the First World War: The British Experience. 224p. 1981. 24.50x (ISBN 0-389-20100-6). B&N.

Catalyst Staff. Making the Most of Your First Job. 288p. 1981. 11.95 (ISBN 0-399-12609-0). Putnam.

Chastain, Sherry. Winning the Salary Game: Salary Negotiation for Women. 192p. 1980. text ed. 9.95 (ISBN 0-471-08433-6); pap. text ed. 6.95 (ISBN 0-471-08023-3). Wiley.

Dublin, Thomas. Farm & Factory: The Mill Experience & Women's Lives in New England, Eighteen Thirty to Eighteen Sixty. LC 80-28084. 220p. 1981. 15.00x (ISBN 0-231-05118-2). Columbia U Pr.

--Women at Work: The Transformation of Work & Community in Lowell, Massachusetts, 1826-1860. 360p. 1981. pap. 7.50x (ISBN 0-231-04167-5). Columbia U Pr.

Edelstein, Barbara. The Woman Doctor's Diet for Teenage Girls. 288p. 1981. pap. 2.50 (ISBN 0-345-28879-3). Ballantine.

Epstein, Vivian S. The ABC's of What a Girl Can Be. (Illus.). 32p. (ps-3). 1980. pap. 3.95 (ISBN 0-9601002-2-9). V S Epstein.

Goldfein, Donna. Every Woman's Guide to Getting Ready for the Career You Want. LC 80-83692. 128p. (Orig.). 1981. pap. 5.95 (ISBN 0-89087-935-4). Celestial Arts.

Harris, Sarah. Women at Work. (History in Focus Ser.). (Illus.). 72p. (gr. 6-9). 1981. 14.95 (ISBN 0-7134-3551-8, Pub. by Batsford England). David & Charles.

Hine, Lewis. Women at Work: One Hundred Fifty Photographs by Lewis Hine. (Illus.). 128p. (Orig.). 1981. pap. price not set (ISBN 0-486-24154-8). Dover.

Howe, Florence & Rothermich, John A., eds. With These Hands: Women Working on the Land. (Women's Lives - Women's Work). (Orig.). pap. text ed. 6.45 (ISBN 0-07-020441-1). Webster-McGraw.

--Women Have Always Worked: An Historical Overview. (Women's Lives - Women's Work Ser.). 208p. (Orig.). 1980. pap. text ed. 4.71 (ISBN 0-07-020435-7). Webster-McGraw.

International Labour Office, Geneva. Standards & Policy Statements of Special Interest to Workers Adopted Under the Auspices of the International Labour Office. 132p. (Orig.). 1980. pap. 7.15 (ISBN 92-2-102441-5). Intl Labour Office.

--Work & Family Life: The Role of the Social Infrastructure in Eastern European Countries. (Illus.). vi, 77p. (Orig.). 1980. pap. 8.55 (ISBN 92-2-102167-X). Intl Labour Office.

King, David & Levine, Karen. Best Way in the World for a Woman to Make Money. 1980. pap. 4.95 (ISBN 0-446-97515-X). Warner Bks.

Kleinman, Carol. Women's Networks. 1981. pap. 2.95 (ISBN 0-345-29355-X). Ballantine.

Selected Standards & Policy Statements of Special Interest to Women Workers Adopted Under the Auspices of the ILO. 132p. 1980. pap. 8.00 (ISBN 92-2-102441-5, ILO150, ILO). Unipub.

Skurzynski, Gloria. Safeguarding the Land. LC 80-8805. (Illus.). 192p. (gr. 7 up). 1981. 9.95 (ISBN 0-15-269956-2, HJ). HarBraceJ.

Wider Opportunities for Women, Inc. Suit Yourself...Shopping for a Job. Kaplan, Roberta, ed. LC 80-53209. (Illus.). 52p. (Orig.). 1980. pap. text ed. 5.00 (ISBN 0-934966-02-8). WOW Inc.

WOMEN–EMPLOYMENT–GREAT BRITAIN

Black, Clementina. Married Women's Work: Being the Report of an Inquiry Undertaken by the Women's Industrial Council, London Nineteen Fifteen. LC 79-56947. (The Englishworking Class Ser.). 1980. lib. bdg. 25.00 (ISBN 0-8240-0102-8). Garland Pub.

Cadbury, Edward, et al. Women's Work & Wages: London. Nineteen Nine. LC 79-56954. (The English Working Class). 1980. lib. bdg. 30.00 (ISBN 0-8240-0108-7). Garland Pub.

Hutchins, B. L. Women in Modern Industry: London Nineteen Fifteen. LC 79-56959. (The English Working Class Ser.). 1980. lib. bdg. 28.00 (ISBN 0-8240-0112-5). Garland Pub.

Macdonald, J. Ransay, ed. Women in the Printing Trades: A Sociological Study, London Nineteen Four. LC 79-56961. (The English Working Class Ser.). 1980. lib. bdg. 18.00 (ISBN 0-8240-0114-1). Garland Pub.

WOMEN–ENFRANCHISEMENT

see Women–Suffrage

WOMEN–HEALTH AND HYGIENE

see also Beauty, Personal; Clothing and Dress; Cosmetics; Sports for Women

Airola, Paavo. Everywoman's Book. (Illus.). 640p. 1981. pap. 12.95 (ISBN 0-932090-10-9). Health Plus.

Better Homes & Gardens Books Editors, ed. Woman's Health & Medical Guide. (Illus.). 96p. 1981. 24.95 (ISBN 0-696-00275-2). Meredith Corp.

Cooke, Cynthia W. & Dworkin, Susan. The Ms. Guide to a Woman's Health. 1981. pap. 3.95 (ISBN 0-425-04796-2). Berkley Pub.

Dean, Patricia G. Self-Assessment of Current Knowledge in Gynecologic Nursing & Women's Health Care. LC 79-92917. 1980. pap. 9.50 (ISBN 0-87488-268-0). Med Exam.

Edelstein, Barbara. The Woman Doctor's Diet for Women. 199p. 1981. pap. 2.50 (ISBN 0-345-29488-2). Ballantine.

Farmer, Kathleen. Woman in the Woods. LC 80-22021. (Illus.). 1980. pap. 5.95 (ISBN 0-934802-08-4). Ind Camp Supply.

Federation of Feminist Women's Health Centers. A New View of a Woman's Body: A Totally Illustrated Guide. 1981. 14.95 (ISBN 0-671-41214-0); pap. 6.95 (ISBN 0-671-41215-9). S&S.

Gold, Sharon. The Woman's Day Book of Beauty, Health & Fitness Hints. LC 80-12022. (Illus.). 166p. 1980. pap. 5.95 (ISBN 0-688-08611-X, Quill). Morrow.

Marshall, John L. & Barbash, Heather. The Sports Doctor's Fitness Book for Women. 1981. 12.95 (ISBN 0-440-08201-3). Delacorte.

Mendelson, Robert S. Male Practice: How Doctors Manipulate Women. 1981. 10.95 (ISBN 0-8092-5974-5). Contemp Bks.

Milan, Albert R. Breast Self-Examination. LC 79-56529. (Illus.). 128p. 1980. pap. 3.50 (ISBN 0-89480-124-4). Liberty Pub.

Research on Service Delivery to Battered Women & Crime Victims. 1980. 3.00. Comm Coun Great NY.

Roberts, Helen. Women, Health & Reproduction. 208p. (Orig.). 1981. pap. 11.95 (ISBN 0-7100-0703-5). Routledge & Kegan.

Stewart, Felicia & Hatcher, Robert. My Body, My Health. 592p. 1981. pap. 9.95 (ISBN 0-553-01299-1). Bantam.

Tiegs, Cheryl. The Way to Natural Beauty. (Illus.). 1980. 12.95 (ISBN 0-686-68753-1, 24894). S&S.

Utian, Wulf H. Your Middle Years: A Doctor's Guide for Today's Woman. (Appleton Consumer Health Guides). 109p. 1980. 12.95 (ISBN 0-8385-9938-9); pap. 5.95 (ISBN 0-8385-9937-0). ACC.

Utlan. Your Middle Years: A Doctor's Guide for Today's Woman. 12.95 (ISBN 0-8385-9938-9). P-H.

WOMEN–HISTORY

Here are entered comprehensive works on the history of women, including works which deal collectively with their socio-economic, political and legal position, participation in historical events, contribution to society, etc. Works which deal specifically with their social condition and status, including historical discussions of the same, are entered under Women–Social conditions.

see also Women–Legal Status, Laws, etc.

Anderson, Karen. Wartime Women: Sex Roles, Family Relations, & the Status of Women During World War II. LC 80-1703. (Contributions in Women's Studies Ser.: No. 20). 224p. 1981. lib. bdg. 22.95 (ISBN 0-313-20884-0, AWW/). Greenwood.

Baker, Derek. Medieval Women. (Illus.). 412p. 1981. pap. 16.95x (ISBN 0-631-12539-6, Pub. by Basil Blackwell England). Biblio Dist.

Blade, Melinda K. The Education of Women in the Italian Renaissance. Ide, Arthur F., ed. LC 79-19011. (Woman in History Ser.: Vol. 21). (Illus.). 90p. (Orig.). 1981. 20.00 (ISBN 0-86663-024-4); pap. 14.95 (ISBN 0-86663-050-3). Ide Hse.

Blashfield, Jean. Hellraisers, Heroines, & Holy Women. 256p. 1981. 14.95 (ISBN 0-312-36736-8); pap. 7.95. St Martin.

Bott, Alan, ed. Our Mothers. 220p. 1980. Repr. of 1932 ed. lib. bdg. 30.00 (ISBN 0-8495-0461-9). Arden Lib.

Brady, Mary L., et al. Woman Power! (Illus.). 156p. 1981. pap. 4.95. J P Tarcher.

Claviere, Maude la & Rene de, Marie Alphonse. The Women of the Renaissance. 510p. 1980. Repr. of 1905 ed. lib. bdg. 50.00 (ISBN 0-8482-5077-X). Norwood Edns.

Heale, William & Swinburne, Henry. An Apologie for Women. Berkowitz, David S. & Thorne, Samuel E., eds. LC 77-86658. (Classics of English Legal History in the Modern Era Ser.: Vol. 42). 322p. 1979. lib. bdg. 40.00 (ISBN 0-8240-3091-5). Garland Pub.

Ide, Arthur F. Woman in Ancient Greece. LC 79-19011. (Woman in History Ser.: Vol. 7). (Illus.). 51p. 1980. 9.00 (ISBN 0-86663-012-0); pap. 6.00 (ISBN 0-86663-013-9). Ide Hse.

--Woman in Biblical Israel. LC 79-19011. (Woman in History Ser.: Vol. 5). (Illus.). 50p. 1980. 9.00 (ISBN 0-86663-008-2); pap. 6.00 (ISBN 0-86663-009-0). Ide Hse.

--Woman in the American Colonial South. LC 79-19011. (Woman in History Ser.: Vol. 30). 88p. (Orig.). 1980. 12.00 (ISBN 0-86663-018-X); pap. 8.00 (ISBN 0-86663-019-8). Ide Hse.

--Woman in the Civilization of the Ancient Near East. LC 79-19011. (Woman in History Ser.: Vol. 2). (Illus.). 82p. (Orig.). 1981. 8.00 (ISBN 0-86663-006-6); pap. 6.00 (ISBN 0-86663-007-4). Ide Hse.

Ide, Frederick. Woman in Ancient Rome. LC 79-19011. (Woman in History Ser.: Vol. 6). (Illus.). 54p. 1980. 9.00 (ISBN 0-86663-010-4); pap. 7.00 (ISBN 0-86663-011-2). Ide Hse.

Lerner, Gerda. The Majority Finds Its Past: Placing Women in History. (A Galaxy Book: No. 624). 250p. 1981. pap. 5.95 (ISBN 0-19-502899-6). Oxford U Pr.

Levine, Suzanne, et al. The Decade of Women: A Ms. History of the Seventies in Words & Pictures. 17.95 (ISBN 0-399-12490-X). Putnam.

Perica, Esther. The American Woman: Her Role in the Revolutionary War. LC 80-28294. (Cameo Series of Notable Women). 1981. pap. price not set (ISBN 0-912526-28-9). Lib Res.

SorBello, Marisa. Woman in Reformation Europe. Ide, Arthur F., ed. LC 79-19011. (Woman in History Ser.: Vol. 19). (Illus.). 80p. (Orig.). 1981. 16.95 (ISBN 0-86663-053-8); pap. 10.95 (ISBN 0-86663-054-6). Ide Hse.

Sweeeney, Francis, ed. The Knowledge Explosion: Liberation & Limitations. 249p. 1969. 4.95 (ISBN 0-374-18204-3). FS&G.

Tempelton, Darlene. Woman in Yorkist England. Ide, Arthur F., ed. LC 79-19011. (Woman in History Ser.: Vol. 16). (Illus.). 80p. 12.95 (ISBN 0-86663-051-1); pap. 9.95. Ide Hse.

Templeton, Darlene, et al. Woman & Medieval England. LC 79-19011. (Woman in History Ser.: Vol. 13). (Illus.). 80p. 1980. 15.95 (ISBN 0-86663-057-0); pap. 9.00 (ISBN 0-86663-058-9). Ide Hse.

Weiser, Marjorie P. & Arbeiter, Jean S. Womanlist. LC 80-65983. (Illus.). 512p. 1981. 19.95 (ISBN 0-689-11083-9); pap. 10.95 (ISBN 0-689-11113-4). Atheneum.

WOMEN–LEGAL STATUS, LAWS, ETC.

see also Divorcees; Husband and Wife; Women–Suffrage; Women's Rights

Jenkins, D. & Owen, M. E., eds. The Welsh Law of Women: Studies Presented to Professor Daniel A. Binchy-1980. 1980. write for info. (ISBN 0-7083-0771-X). Verry.

Junod, Mae A. The W-O-T Position or Self-Actualization for Women. 280p. 12.95 (ISBN 0-938968-00-9). Impact MI.

Laws Respecting Women. 1973. 27.50 (ISBN 0-379-20200-X). Oceana.

Lee, Rex E. A Lawyer Looks at the Equal Rights Amendment. LC 80-22202. (Illus.). 150p. 1980. pap. 7.95 (ISBN 0-8425-1883-5). Brigham.

The Legal Status of Rural Women: Limitations on the Economic Participation of Women in Rural Development. (FAO Economic & Social Development Paper Ser.: No. 9). 73p. 1980. pap. 7.50 (ISBN 92-5-100858-2, F1956, FAO). Unipub.

Pomroy, Martha. What Every Woman Needs to Know About the Law. LC 80-85109. 432p. 1981. pap. 3.95 (ISBN 0-87216-835-2). Playboy Pbks.

Research on Service Delivery to Battered Women & Crime Victims. 1980. 3.00. Comm Coun Great NY.

WOMEN–OCCUPATIONS

see Women–Employment

WOMEN–POLITICAL ACTIVITY

see Women in Politics

WOMEN–PORTRAITS

see also Women in Art

Gowland, Peter. The Secrets of Photographing Women. Michelman, Herbert, ed. (Illus.). 224p. 1981. 12.95 (ISBN 0-517-54180-7, Michelman Books). Crown.

WOMEN–PSYCHOLOGY

see also Femininity (Psychology)

Bardwick, Judith M., et al. Feminine Personality & Conflict. LC 80-24191. (Contemporary Psychology Ser.). vii, 102p. 1981. Repr. of 1970 ed. lib. bdg. 19.75 (ISBN 0-313-22504-4, BAFP). Greenwood.

Dowling, Colette. The Cinderella Complex: Women's Hidden Fear of Independence. 288p. 1981. 13.95 (ISBN 0-671-40052-5). Summit Bks.

Lichtenstein, Grace. Machisma: Women & Daring. LC 79-7114. 360p. 1981. 14.95 (ISBN 0-385-15109-8). Doubleday.

Mariechild, Diane. Mother Wit: A Feminist Guide to Psychic Development. (Illus.). 200p. 1981. 12.95 (ISBN 0-89594-050-7); pap. 5.95 (ISBN 0-89594-051-5). Crossing Pr.

Rubin, Lillian. Women of a Certain Age: The Midlife Search for Self. LC 79-1681. 320p. 1981. pap. 4.95 (ISBN 0-06-090833-5, CN 833, CN). Har-Row.

WOMEN–RELIGIOUS LIFE

Clark, Linda, et al. Image Breaking - Image Building. 148p. (Orig.). 1981. pap. 7.95 (ISBN 0-8298-0407-2). Pilgrim NY.

Jicks, John M. & Morton, Bruce L. Woman's Role in the Church. pap. 2.95 (ISBN 0-89315-362-1). Lambert Bk.

Schlafly, Phyllis. The Power of the Christian Woman. (Orig.). 1981. pap. 3.50 (ISBN 0-87239-457-3, 2972). Standard Pub.

WOMEN–RIGHTS OF WOMEN

see Women'S Rights

WOMEN–SELF-DEFENSE

see Self-Defense for Women

WOMEN–SOCIAL CONDITIONS

Here are entered works which deal specifically with the social conditions and status of women, including historical discussions of the same. Comprehensive works on the history of women, including works which deal collectively with their socio-economic, political and legal position, participation in historical events, contribution to society, etc. are entered under Women–History.

see also Women–Legal Status, Laws, Etc.

Bernard, Jessie. The Female World. LC 80-69880. (Illus.). 1981. 17.95 (ISBN 0-02-903000-5). Free Pr.

Claviere, Maude la & Rene de, Marie Alphonse. The Women of the Renaissance. 510p. 1980. Repr. of 1905 ed. lib. bdg. 50.00 (ISBN 0-8482-5077-X). Norwood Edns.

Epstein, Vivian S. The ABC's of What a Girl Can Be. (Illus.). 32p. (ps-3). 1980. pap. 3.95 (ISBN 0-9601002-2-9). V S Epstein.

Gundry, Patricia. The Complete Woman. LC 79-8928. 240p. 1981. 10.95 (ISBN 0-385-15521-2, Galilee). Doubleday.

Hunt, Gladys. Esa Soy Yo. Roberts, Grace S., tr. from Eng. LC 77-83671. 172p. (Orig., Span.). 1977. pap. 2.25 (ISBN 0-89922-094-0). Edit Caribe.

Lee, Dorothy E. & Clifton, A. Kay. Minority Status: The Position of Women. LC 79-65259. 155p. 1981. perfect bdg. 13.50 (ISBN 0-86548-044-3). Century Twenty One.

Lincoln, Bruce. Emerging from the Chrysalis: Studies in Rituals of Women's Initiation. LC 80-24189. (Illus.). 208p. 1981. text ed. 18.50 (ISBN 0-674-24840-6). Harvard U Pr.

Minai, Naila. Women in Islam. LC 80-52405. 320p. 1981. 11.95 (ISBN 0-87223-666-8). Seaview Bks.

Nebeker, Helen. Jean Rhys: Woman in Passage. 250p. 1981. price not set (ISBN 0-920792-04-9). Eden Women.

Nickles, Elizabeth & Ashcraft, Laura. The Coming Matriarchy: How Women Will Gain the Balance of Power. (Illus.). 352p. 1981. 13.95 (ISBN 0-87223-686-2). Seaview Bks.

Wiesen-Cooke, Blanche. Women & Support Networks. (Out & Out Pamphlet Ser.). pap. 2.00 (ISBN 0-918314-10-0). Out & Out.

Zeidenstein, Sondra, ed. Learning About Rural Women. (Studies in Family Planning Ser.: Vol. 10, Nos. 11-12). 118p. (Orig.). 1979. pap. 2.50. Population Coun.

WOMEN–SOCIETIES AND CLUBS

see also names of individual societies and clubs

Carrol, Frieda, compiled by. The Woman's Index. LC 80-70675. 200p. 1981. 12.95 (ISBN 0-9605246-6-5); pap. 9.95. Biblio Pr Ga.

WOMEN–SPORTS

see Sports for Women

WOMEN–STERILIZATION

see Sterilization of Women

WOMEN–SUFFRAGE

Grimes, Alan P. The Puritan Ethic & Woman Suffrage. LC 80-21799. xiii, 159p. 1980. Repr. of 1967 ed. lib. bdg. 19.50x (ISBN 0-313-22689-X, GRPE). Greenwood.

Ware, Susan. Beyond Suffrage: Women in the New Deal. (Illus.). 224p. 1981. text ed. 18.50 (ISBN 0-674-06921-8). Harvard U Pr.

WOMEN–SUFFRAGE–GREAT BRITAIN

Anstey, Thomas, et al. The Lawes Resolutions of Women's Rights. Thorne, Samuel E., ed. LC 77-89253. (Classics of English Legal History in the Modern Era Ser.: Vol. 82). 529p. 1979. lib. bdg. 40.00 (ISBN 0-8240-3181-4). Garland Pub.

WOMEN–UNDERDEVELOPED AREAS

see Underdeveloped Areas–Women

WOMEN–AFRICA

Njoku, John E. The World of the African Woman. LC 80-23832. 132p. 1980. 10.00 (ISBN 0-8108-1350-5). Scarecrow.

WOMEN–ASIA

Jahan, Rounaq & Papanek, H., eds. Women & Development: Perspectives from South & Southeast Asia. 439p. 1979. text ed. 27.00 (ISBN 0-8426-1657-8). Verry.

Manderson, Lenore. Women, Politics, & Change: The Kaum Ibu UMNO Malaysia, 1945-1972. (East Asian Social Science Monographs). (Illus.). 260p. 1981. 34.50 (ISBN 0-19-580437-6). Oxford U Pr.

WOMEN–AUSTRALIA

Bell, Diane & Ditton, Pam. Law. (Illus.). 147p. 1980. pap. text ed. 9.95 (ISBN 0-908160-77-1). Bks Australia.

Huffer, Virginia, et al. The Sweetness of the Pig: Aboriginal Women in Transition. LC 80-21658. (Illus.). 244p. 1981. 15.00 (ISBN 0-295-95790-5). U of Wash Pr.

Rischbrith, Bessie S. March of Australian Women. 15.00x (ISBN 0-392-08104-0, SpS). Soccer.

WOMEN–ENGLAND

see Women–Great Britain

WOMEN–GERMANY

Meissner, Hans-Oho. Magda Goebbels: The First Lady of the Third Reich. (Illus.). 288p. 1981. 14.95 (ISBN 0-686-69087-7). Dial.

Shaffer, Harry G. Women in the Two Germanies: A Comparative Study of a Socialist & a Non-Socialist Society. (Pergamon Policy Studies on Social Policy). (Illus.). 256p. 1981. 26.00 (ISBN 0-08-023862-9). Pergamon.

Woolf, Charlotte. Hindsight. Campbell, Dennis, ed. 312p. 1981. 20.00 (ISBN 0-89182-035-3). Charles River Bks.

WOMEN–GREAT BRITAIN

Braybon, Gail. Women Workers in the First World War: The British Experience. 224p. 1981. 24.50x (ISBN 0-389-20100-6). B&N.

The Lawes Resolutions of Womens Rights: Or, the Lawes Provision for Women. LC 79-84103. (English Experience Ser.: No. 922). 424p. 1979. Repr. of 1632 ed. lib. bdg. 40.00 (ISBN 90-221-0922-4). Walter J Johnson.

Tempelton, Darlene. Woman in Yorkist England. Ide, Arthur F., ed. LC 79-19011. (Woman in History Ser.: Vol. 16). (Illus.). 80p. 12.95 (ISBN 0-86663-051-1); pap. 9.95. Ide Hse.

Templeton, Darlene, et al. Woman & Medieval England. LC 79-19011. (Woman in History Ser.: Vol. 13). (Illus.). 80p. 1980. 15.95 (ISBN 0-86663-057-0); pap. 9.00 (ISBN 0-86663-058-9). Ide Hse.

WOMEN–GREECE

Ide, Arthur F. Woman in Ancient Greece. LC 79-19011. (Woman in History Ser.: Vol. 7). (Illus.). 51p. 1980. 9.00 (ISBN 0-86663-012-0); pap. 6.00 (ISBN 0-86663-013-9). Ide Hse.

WOMEN–INDIA

Vreede-de Stuers, Cora. Parda: A Study of Muslim Women's Life in Northern India. LC 70-1402. (Samenlevingen Buiten Europa--Non-European Societies Ser.: No. 8). (Illus.). xii, 128p. 1981. Repr. of 1968 ed. lib. bdg. 19.75x (ISBN 0-313-22915-5, VRPA). Greenwood.

WOMEN–ISRAEL

Datan, Nancy, et al. A Time to Reap: The Middle Age of Women in Five Israeli Subcultures. LC 80-26776. 176p. 1981. text ed. 14.00x (ISBN 0-8018-2516-4). Johns Hopkins.

Ide, Arthur F. Woman in Biblical Israel. LC 79-19011. (Woman in History Ser.: Vol. 5). (Illus.). 50p. 1980. 9.00 (ISBN 0-86663-008-2); pap. 6.00 (ISBN 0-86663-009-0). Ide Hse.

WOMEN–JAPAN

Pharr, Susan J. Political Women in Japan: The Search for a Place in Political Life. 275p. 1981. 17.50x (ISBN 0-520-04071-6). U of Cal Pr.

WOMEN–LATIN AMERICA

Hahner, June E., ed. Women in Latin American History: Their Lives & Views. rev. ed. LC 80-620044. (Latin American Studies: Vol. 51). 1981. pap. text ed. price not set (ISBN 0-87903-051-8). UCLA Lat Am Ctr.

Randall, Margaret. Women in Cuba--Twenty Years Later. (Illus.). 182p. 1981. 15.95 (ISBN 0-918266-15-7); pap. 6.95 (ISBN 0-918266-14-9). Smyrna.

WOMEN–NEW ZEALAND

Hughes, Beryl & Bunkle, Phillida, eds. Women in New Zealand Society. 304p. 1980. text ed. 21.00x (ISBN 0-86861-026-7, 2521); pap. text ed. 11.50x (ISBN 0-86861-034-8, 2522). Allen Unwin.

WOMEN–ROME

Ide, Frederick. Woman in Ancient Rome. LC 79-19011. (Woman in History Ser.: Vol. 6). (Illus.). 54p. 1980. 9.00 (ISBN 0-86663-010-4); pap. 7.00 (ISBN 0-86663-011-2). Ide Hse.

WOMEN–RUSSIA

McAulay, Alastair. Women's Work & Wages in the Soviet Union. 248p. 1981. text ed. 28.50x (ISBN 0-04-339020-X, 2605). Allen Unwin.

WOMEN–UNITED STATES

see also Presidents–United States–Wives and Children

Chinoy, Helen K. & Jenkins, Linda W. Women in American Theatre. Michelman, Herber, ed. (Illus.). 384p. 1981. 15.95 (ISBN 0-517-53729-X, Michaelman Books). Crown.

Degler, Carl N. At Odds: Women & the Family in America from the Revolution to the Present. 544p. 1981. pap. 8.95 (ISBN 0-19-502934-8, GB 645, GB). Oxford U Pr.

Ide, Arthur F. Woman in the American Colonial South. LC 79-19011. (Woman in History Ser.: Vol. 30). 88p. (Orig.). 1980. 12.00 (ISBN 0-86663-018-X); pap. 8.00 (ISBN 0-86663-019-8). Ide Hse.

Norton, Mary B. Liberty's Daughters: The Revolutionary Experience of American Women. 1980. 15.00 (ISBN 0-316-61251-0); pap. 7.95 (ISBN 0-316-61252-9). Little.

Rasmussen, Linda, et al, eds. A Harvest Yet to Reap: A History of Prairie Women. (Illus.). 240p. 1976. pap. 12.50 (ISBN 0-88961-050-9). U of Nebr Pr.

WOMEN–UNITED STATES–BIBLIOGRAPHY

Haber, Barbara. Women in America: A Guide to Books, 1963-1975, with an Appendix on Books Published 1976-1979. 360p. 1981. pap. 6.95 (ISBN 0-252-00826-X). U of Ill Pr.

Manning, Beverley. Index to American Women Speakers, Eighteen Twenty-Eight to Nineteen Seventy-Eight. LC 79-26928. viii, 672p. 1980. lib. bdg. 30.00 (ISBN 0-8108-1282-7). Scarecrow.

WOMEN–UNITED STATES–BIOGRAPHY

Elsasser, Nan, et al. Las Mujeres: Conversations from an Hispanic Community. (Women's Lives - Women's Work Ser.). (Illus.). 192p. (gr. 11-12). 1981. 14.95 (ISBN 0-912670-84-3); pap. 4.95 (ISBN 0-912670-70-3). Feminist Pr.

Goodfriend. The Ages of Woman: Female Lives in American History. (Orig.). 1981. pap. text ed. 7.95 (ISBN 0-316-32005-6). Little.

Hanft, Ethel W. & Manley, Paula J. Outstanding Iowa Women: Past & Present. LC 80-53730. (Illus.). 135p. 1980. pap. 4.95 (ISBN 0-9605162-0-4). River Bend.

Thomas, Sherry. We Didn't Have Much but We Sure Had Plenty: Stories of Rural Women. LC 80-956. (Illus.). 208p. 1981. pap. 7.95 (ISBN 0-385-14951-4, Anch). Doubleday.

WOMEN, AFRO-AMERICAN

see Afro-American Women

WOMEN, ARAB

Meghdessian, Samira R. The Status of the Arab Woman: A Select Bibliography. LC 80-1028. 176p. 1980. lib. bdg. 32.50 (ISBN 0-313-22548-6, MEA/). Greenwood.

WOMEN, DISCRIMINATION AGAINST

see Sex Discrimination

WOMEN, ISLAMIC

see Women, Muslim

WOMEN, MUSLIM

Lemu, B. Aisha & Heeren, Gatima. Woman in Islam. 51p. 1980. pap. 2.95x (ISBN 0-86037-004-6, Pub. by Islamic Council of Europe England). Intl Schol Bk Serv.

WOMEN (IN RELIGION, FOLKLORE, ETC.)

Luke, Helen. Spirit Woman: The Spirirtuality of the Feminine in Symbol & Myth. 144p. 1981. 9.95 (ISBN 0-8245-0018-0). Crossroad NY.

Stone, Merlin. Ancient Mirrors of Womanhood: Our Goddess & Heroine Heritage, Vol. 2. (Illus.). 224p. Date not set. pap. 7.95 (ISBN 0-9603352-1-8). New Sibylline.

WOMEN ACTORS

see Actors and Actresses

WOMEN AND RELIGION

see also Women–Religious Life; Women Clergy

Foh, Susan T. Women & the Word of God: A Response to Biblical Feminism. 280p. 1981. pap. 6.95. Baker Bk.

O'Hair, Madalyn M. Women & Atheism: The Ultimate Liberation. 1979. pap. 3.00. Am Atheist.

Ruether, Rosemary & Keller, Rosemary. Women & Religion in America: Vol 1, the Nineteenth Century. LC 80-8346. (Illus.). 352p. 1981. 15.00 (ISBN 0-06-066829-6, HarpR). Har-Row.

WOMEN AND SOCIALISM

see also Communism; Socialism

Barrett, Michele. Women's Oppression Today: Problems in Marxist Feminst Analysis. 280p. 1981. 19.50x (ISBN 0-8052-7091-4, Pub. by NLB England); pap. 8.50 (ISBN 0-8052-7090-6). Schocken.

Miller, Sally M., ed. Flawed Liberation: Socialism & Feminism. LC 80-1050. (Contributions to Women's Studies Ser.: No. 19). 240p. 1981. lib. bdg. 27.50 (ISBN 0-313-21401-8, MFL/). Greenwood.

WOMEN ARTISTS

Here are entered works on the attainments of women as artists. Works dealing with women as represented in art are entered under Women in Art.

Collins, J. L. & Opitz, Glenn. Women Artists in America: Eighteenth Century to Present. rev. ed. (Illus.). 1981. 60.00 (ISBN 0-938290-00-2). Apollo.

Harmon, Lily. Freehand. 1981. 13.95 (ISBN 0-671-41452-6). S&S.

Mochon, Anne. Gabriele Muunter: Between Munich & Murnau. Walsh, Peter & Matthews, Paula, eds. LC 80-21810. (Illus.). 65p. 1980. pap. 9.95 (ISBN 0-916724-19-0). Fogg Art.

Nelson-Rees, Walter A. Lillie May Nicholson: 1884-1964 an Artist Rediscovered. LC 80-53867. (Illus.). 88p. 1981. 38.50 (ISBN 0-938842-00-5). WIM Oakland.

Sherman, Claire R. & Holcomb, Adele M., eds. Women As Interpreters of the Visual Arts, 1820-1979. LC 80-785. (Contributions in Women's Studies: No. 18). (Illus.). 512p. 1981. lib. bdg. 35.00 (ISBN 0-313-22056-5, SWS/). Greenwood.

WOMEN AS MUSICIANS

see Women Musicians

Zaimont, Judith L. & Famera, Karen, eds. Contemporary Concert Music by Women: A Directory of the Composers & Their Works. LC 80-39572. (Illus.). 320p. 1981. lib. bdg. 25.00 (ISBN 0-313-22921-X, ZCM/). Greenwood.

WOMEN AS TEACHERS

see Women Teachers

WOMEN AUTHORS

Here are entered works on the attainments of women as authors. Collections of works written by women are entered under Women's Writings. Collections of works in two or more literary forms written about women are entered under Women–Literary Collections. Works which discuss the representation of women in literature are entered under Women in Literature.

Bree, Germaine. Women Writers in France: Variations on a Theme. 104p. 1973. 7.00 (ISBN 0-8135-0771-5). Rutgers U Pr.

Bucknall, Barbara. Ursula le Guin. LC 80-53696. (Recognitions Ser.). 160p. 9.95 (ISBN 0-8044-2085-8). Ungar.

Mrs. Ewing, Mrs. Molesworth, & Mrs. Hodgson Burnett. 121p. 1980. Repr. of 1950 ed. lib. bdg. 20.00 (ISBN 0-8492-1634-6). R West.

Olauson, Judith. The American Woman Playwright: A View of Criticism & Characterization. LC 80-51605. 190p. 1981. 12.50x (ISBN 0-87875-198-X). Whitston Pub.

Savage, Thomas. Her Side of It. Date not set. price not set. Little.

Todd, Janet, ed. Be Good, Sweet Maid: An Anthology of Women & Literature. 175p. 1981. text ed. 22.00x (ISBN 0-8419-0692-0). Holmes & Meier.

--Bibliography of Women & Literature. 150p. 1981. text ed. 22.00x (ISBN 0-8419-0693-9). Holmes & Meier.

Travitsky, Betty, ed. The Paradise of Women: Writings by Englishwomen of the Rennaissance. LC 80-1705. (Contributions in Women's Studies: No. 22). 312p. 1981. lib. bdg. 29.95 (ISBN 0-313-22177-4, TPW/). Greenwood.

Waelti-Walters, Jennifer. Fairy Tales & the Female Imagination. 225p. 1981. price not set (ISBN 0-920792-07-3). Eden Women.

Waldman, Bess. The Book of Tziril: A Family Chronicle. 270p. 1981. pap. 6.00x (ISBN 0-916288-09-9). Micah Pubns.

Yates, Elizabeth. My Diary - My World. LC 80-24977. (Illus.). (gr. 5-9). 1981. 8.95 (ISBN 0-664-32675-7). Westminster.

WOMEN CLERGY

Weidman, Judith L., ed. Women Ministers: How Women Are Redifining Traditional Roles. LC 80-8345. 192p. (Orig.). 1981. pap. 5.95 (ISBN 0-06-069291-X, RD 345, HarpR). Har-Row.

WOMEN CRIMINALS

see Female Offenders

WOMEN EXECUTIVES

Thompson, Ann M. & Wood, Marcia D. Management Strategies for Women: Or, Now That I'm Boss, How Do I Run This Place? 1981. 10.95 (ISBN 0-671-25476-6). S&S.

WOMEN IN ART

Here are entered works dealing with women as represented in art. Works on the attainments of women artists are entered under the heading Women Artists.

Bachtold, Louise M. Gifted Women in Politics & the Arts & Sciences. LC 80-69361. 135p. 1981. perfect bdg. 10.95 (ISBN 0-86548-022-2). Century Twenty One.

WOMEN IN BUSINESS

Douglass, Leslie S. Women in Business: How to Make Yourself Marketable. (Illus.). 192p. 1980. 9.95 (Spec); pap. 4.95. P-H.

Forisha, Barbara L. & Goldman, Barbara. Outsiders on the Inside: Women & Organizations. (Illus.). 352p. 1981. 14.95 (ISBN 0-13-645382-1, Spectrum); pap. 6.95 (ISBN 0-13-645374-0). P-H.

Hennig, Margaret & Jardim, Anne. The Managerial Woman. 221p. 1981. pap. 5.95 (ISBN 0-385-02291-3, Anch). Doubleday.

Jarvis, N. L. Woman's Guide to Wall Street. 195p. 1981. 28.50 (ISBN 0-686-68312-9). Porter.

Landau, Susanne & Bailey, Geoffrey. The Landau Strategy: How Working Women Win Top Jobs. LC 80-83564. 224p. 1981. pap. 2.50 (ISBN 0-87216-806-9). Playboy Pbks.

Landau, Suzanne & Bailey, Geoffrey. The Landau Strategy: How Working Women Win Top Jobs. 1981. pap. 4.95 (ISBN 0-686-68906-2). Bantam.

Lester, Mary. A Woman's Guide to Starting a Small Business. LC 80-24298. pap. 2.50 (ISBN 0-87576-093-7). Pilot Bks.

McVicar, Marjorie & Craig, Julia F. Minding My Own Business: Entrepreneurial Women Share Their Secrets for Success. 425p. 1981. 12.95 (ISBN 0-399-90116-7). Marek.

Murphy, Patricia & Taylor-Gordon, Elaine. The Business-Woman's Guide to Thirty American Cities. 400p. 1981. 19.95 (ISBN 0-312-92072-5); pap. 9.95 (ISBN 0-312-92073-3). St Martin.

Struggs, Callie F. Woman in Business. Ide, Arthur F., ed. LC 79-19011. (Woman in History Ser.: Vol. 56). (Illus.). 80p. (Orig.). 1981. 8.95 (ISBN 0-86663-020-1); pap. 6.95 (ISBN -086663-021-X). Ide Hse.

Wisely, Rae & Sanders, Gladys. The Independent Woman. 192p. 1981. 9.95 (ISBN 0-87477-176-5). J P Tarcher.

WOMEN IN CHRISTIANITY

see also Women Clergy; Women in the Bible

Ide, Arthur F. Woman in Early Christianity & Christian Society. LC 79-19011. (Woman in History Ser.: Vol. 9). (Illus.). 53p. 1980. 9.00 (ISBN 0-86663-016-3); pap. 6.95 (ISBN 0-86663-017-1). Ide Hse.

Ide, Arthur F. & Ide, Charles A. Woman in the Age of Christian Martyrs. LC 79-19011. (Woman in History Ser.: Vol. 10). (Illus.). ix, 98p. 1980. 9.00 (ISBN 0-86663-000-7); pap. 8.00 (ISBN 0-86663-001-5). Ide Hse.

Popson, Martha. That We Might Have Life. LC 80-2080. 128p. (gr. 6 up). 1981. pap. 2.75 (ISBN 0-385-17438-1, Im). Doubleday.

WOMEN IN CHURCH WORK

see also Clergymen's Wives; Women–Religious Life

Capetti, Giselda, ed. Cronistoria, 5 vols. 400p. (Orig.). 1980. Set. pap. write for info. (ISBN 0-89944-043-6); Vol. 1. pap. (ISBN 0-89944-044-4); Vol. 2. pap. (ISBN 0-89944-045-2); Vol. 3. pap. (ISBN 0-89944-046-0); Vol. 4. pap. (ISBN 0-89944-047-9); Vol. 5. pap. (ISBN 0-89944-048-7). D Bosco Pubns.

Eldred, O. John. Women Pastors. 128p. 1981. pap. 4.95 (ISBN 0-8170-0901-9). Judson.

Feucht, Oscar E. Guidelines for Women's Groups in the Congregation. 1981. pap. 3.95 (ISBN 0-570-03828-6, 12-2793). Concordia.

Jicks, John M. & Morton, Bruce L. Woman's Role in the Church. pap. 2.95 (ISBN 0-89315-362-1). Lambert Bk.

WOMEN IN DRAMA

see Women in Literature

WOMEN IN HINDUISM

Alfassa, Mira. Glimpses of the Mother's Life, Vol. 2. Das, Nilima, ed. 335p. 1980. 11.00 (ISBN 0-89071-291-3). Matagiri.

Nebeker, Helen. Jean Rhys: Woman in Passage. 250p. 1981. price not set (ISBN 0-920792-04-9). Eden Women.

Waelti-Walters, Jennifer. Fairy Tales & the Female Imagination. 225p. 1981. price not set (ISBN 0-920792-07-3). Eden Women.

WOMEN IN LITERATURE

Here are entered works which discuss the representation of women in literature. Collections of works in two or more literary forms written about women are entered under Women–Literary Collections. Collections of works written by women are entered under Women's Writings. Works on the attainments of women as authors are entered under Women Authors.

Ferguson, Mary Anne. Images of Women in Literature. 3rd ed. LC 80-82761. (Illus.). 528p. 1981. pap. text ed. 10.50 (ISBN 0-395-29113-5). HM.

McCadden, Joseph F. The Flight from Women in the Fiction of Saul Bellow. LC 80-5641. 299p. 1980. lib. bdg. 18.75 (ISBN 0-8191-1308-5); pap. text ed. 10.50 (ISBN 0-8191-1309-3). U Pr of Amer.

Monaghan, Patricia. The Book of Goddesses & Heroines. 1981. pap. 9.95 (ISBN 0-525-47664-4). Dutton.

Navaretta, Cynthia, ed. Voices of Women: Three Critics on Three Poets on Three Heroines. LC 80-80281. (Illus.). 1980. pap. 4.50. Midmarch Assocs.

O'Brien, Aline & Rasmussen, Chrys, eds. Womanblood: Portraits of Women in Poetry & Prose. LC 80-69814. 200p. (Orig.). 1981. pap. 5.95 (ISBN 0-939140-00-4). Continuing SAGA.

Taylor, Anne R. Male Novelists & Their Female Voices: Literary Masquerades. LC 80-50841. 238p. 1981. 15.00x (ISBN 0-87875-195-5). Whitston Pub.

WOMEN IN MEDICINE

see also Women Physicians

Stage, Sarah. Female Complaints: Lydia Pinkham & the Business of Women's Medicine. (Illus.). 304p. 1981. pap. 4.95 (ISBN 0-393-00033-8). Norton.

WOMEN IN POLITICS

Bachtold, Louise M. Gifted Women in Politics & the Arts & Sciences. LC 80-69361. 135p. 1981. perfect bdg. 10.95 (ISBN 0-86548-022-2). Century Twenty One.

Castle, Barbara. Castle Diaries Nineteen Seventy-Four to Seventy-Six. 788p. 1981. text ed. 40.00 (ISBN 0-8419-0689-0). Holmes & Meier.

FitzGerald, Kathleen W. Brass: Jane Byrne & the Pursuit of Power. 1981. 11.95 (ISBN 0-8092-7006-4). Contemp Bks.

Mandel, Ruth B. In the Running: The New Woman Candidate. LC 80-24190. 304p. 1981. 12.95 (ISBN 0-89919-027-8). Ticknor & Fields.

Pharr, Susan J. Political Women in Japan: The Search for a Place in Political Life. 275p. 1981. 17.50x (ISBN 0-520-04071-6). U of Cal Pr.

Rischbrith, Bessie S. March of Australian Women. 15.00x (ISBN 0-392-08104-0, SpS). Soccer.

Stineman, Esther. American Political Women: Comtemporary & Historical Profiles. LC 80-24478. 225p. 1980. lib. bdg. 19.50x (ISBN 0-87287-238-6). Libs Unl.

Tinker, Irene & Bramsen, Michelle B., eds. Women & World Developmemt, 2 vols, Vol.1. Incl. Vol. 2. An Annotated Bibliography. Buvinic, Mayra. 416p. Set. pap. 6.95. Overseas Dev Council.

Ware, Susan. Beyond Suffrage: Women in the New Deal. (Illus.). 224p. 1981. text ed. 18.50 (ISBN 0-674-06921-8). Harvard U Pr.

WOMEN IN RELIGION

see also Women in Christianity; Women in Church Work; Women in Hinduism

Ulanov, Ann B. Receiving Woman: Studies Inthe; Psychology & Theology Jof the Feminine0. LC 80-26813. 1981. pap. 9.95 (ISBN 0-664-24360-6). Westminster.

WOMEN IN THE BIBLE

Blanton, Alma E. Our Gospel's Women. (Illus.). 114p. (Orig.). 1979. pap. 3.00 (ISBN 0-938134-01-9). Loving Pubs.

Chavez, Moises. La Ishah, la Mujer en la Biblia. LC 76-43123. 180p. (Orig., Span.). 1976. pap. 3.25 (ISBN 0-89922-078-9). Edit Caribe.

Foh, Susan T. Women & the Word of God: A Response to Biblical Feminism. 280p. 1981. pap. 6.95. Baker Bk.

WOMEN IN THE MASS MEDIA INDUSTRY

Baeher, Helen, ed. Women & Media. LC 80-41424. (Illus.). 150p. 1980. 14.25 (ISBN 0-08-026061-6). Pergamon.

Smith, Betsy. Breakthrough: Women in Television. LC 80-54704. (Illus.). 192p. 1981. 9.95 (ISBN 0-8027-6420-7). Walker & Co.

Women in the Media. 119p. 1980. pap. 7.00 (ISBN 92-3-101687-3, U1027, UNESCO). Unipub.

WOMEN IN TRADE-UNIONS

see also Trade-Unions

Boyd, Marilyn S. Women's Liberation Ideology & Union Participation: A Study. LC 79-65257. 135p. 1981. perfect bdg. 10.95 (ISBN 0-86548-024-9). Century Twenty One.

WOMEN MINISTERS

see Women Clergy

WOMEN MOVING-PICTURE ACTRESSES

see Moving-Picture Actors and Actresses

WOMEN MUSICIANS

Eldred, Patricia M. Debby Boone. (gr. 4-12). 1979. PLB 5.95 (ISBN 0-87191-696-7); pap. 2.95 (ISBN 0-89812-096-9). Creative Ed.

Handy, D. Antoinette. Black Women in American Bands & Orchestras. LC 80-19380. 394p. 1981. 17.50 (ISBN 0-8108-1346-7). Scarecrow.

Nilsson, Birgit. My Memoirs in Pictures. Teal, Thomas, tr. from Swedish. LC 78-22343. (Illus.). 128p. 1981. 19.95 (ISBN 0-385-14835-6). Doubleday.

O'Day, Anita & Eells, George. High Times, Hard Times. 320p. 1981. 12.95 (ISBN 0-399-12505-1). Putnam.

WOMEN ORATORS

Manning, Beverley. Index to American Women Speakers, Eighteen Twenty-Eight to Nineteen Seventy-Eight. LC 79-26928. viii, 672p. 1980. lib. bdg. 30.00 (ISBN 0-8108-1282-7). Scarecrow.

WOMEN PHYSICIANS

Woolf, Charlotte. Hindsight. Campbell, Dennis, ed. 312p. 1981. 20.00 (ISBN 0-89182-035-3). Charles River Bks.

WOMEN POETS

Cowell, Pattie. Women Poets in Pre-Revolutionary America, 1650-1775. LC 80-50492. (Illus.). 400p. 1981. 25.00x (ISBN 0-87875-192-0). Whitston Pub.

Harter, Hugh A. Gertrudis Gomez De Avellaneda. (World Authors Ser.: No. 599). 1981. lib. bdg. 14.95 (ISBN 0-8057-6441-0). Twayne.

Mendoza, Ester F. Juana De Ibarbourou: Oficio De Poesia. LC 80-20020. (Mente y Palabra Ser.). (Illus.). xi, 370p. (Span.). 1980. 6.25 (ISBN 0-8477-0572-2); pap. 5.00 (ISBN 0-8477-0573-0). U of PR Pr.

Woman Poet - the Midwest. 1981. pap. 12.95 (ISBN 0-935634-05-3); pap. text ed. 6.00 (ISBN 0-935634-04-5). Women-in-Lit.

Woman Poet: The South. 1981. pap. 12.95 (ISBN 0-935634-07-X); pap. text ed. 6.00 (ISBN 0-935634-06-1). Women-in-Lit.

WOMEN SCIENTISTS

Bachtold, Louise M. Gifted Women in Politics & the Arts & Sciences. LC 80-69361. 135p. 1981. perfect bdg. 10.95 (ISBN 0-86548-022-2). Century Twenty One.

Committee on the Education & Employment of Women in Science & Engineering. Women Scientists in Industry & Government: How Much Progress in the 1970's. LC 80-80079. vii, 56p. 1980. pap. text ed. 5.00 (ISBN 0-309-03023-4). Natl Acad Pr.

Weiss, Iris R. & Place, Carol, eds. Women Scientists Roster. 143p. (Orig.). 1979. pap. 3.50 (ISBN 0-87355-015-3). Natl Sci Tchrs.

Williams, Barbara. Women in Archaeology. 174p. 1981. 9.95. Walker & Co.

WOMEN STUDIES

see Women'S Studies

WOMEN TEACHERS

Hoffman, Nancy. Woman's "True" Profession: Voices from the History of Teaching. (Women's Lives - Women's Work Ser.). (Illus.). 352p. (Orig.). (gr. 11-12). 1981. 17.95 (ISBN 0-912670-93-2); pap. 6.95 (ISBN 0-912670-72-X). Feminist Pr.

Sokolosky, Barbara A., ed. American Association of University Women Archives 1881-1976. 115p. 1980. pap. write for info. (ISBN 0-667-00651-6). Microfilming Corp.

Struggs, Callie F. Woman in Contemporary Education. Ide, Arthur F., ed. LC 79-19011. (Woman in History Ser.: Vol. 61). (Illus.). 82p. (Orig.). 1981. 12.95 (ISBN 0-86663-022-8); pap. 9.00 (ISBN 0-86663-023-6). Ide Hse.

WOMEN WORKERS

see Women–Employment

WOMEN'S CLOTHING

see Clothing and Dress; Costume

WOMEN'S CLUBS

see Women–Societies and Clubs

WOMEN'S COLLEGES

see Education of Women

WOMEN'S EDUCATION

see Education of Women

WOMEN'S LIB

see Feminism

WOMEN'S LIBERATION

see Women's Rights

WOMEN'S LIBERATION MOVEMENT

see Feminism

WOMEN'S RIGHTS

see also Sex Discrimination; Women–Legal Status, Laws, etc.; Women–Suffrage

Harris, James K., ed. The Complete Text of the Equal Rights Amendment. 132p. 1981. 3.95 (ISBN 0-9605188-0-0). Ganis & Harris.

The Lawes Resolutions of Womens Rights: Or, the Lawes Provision for Women. LC 79-84103. (English Experience Ser.: No. 922). 424p. 1979. Repr. of 1632 ed. lib. bdg. 40.00 (ISBN 90-221-0922-4). Walter J Johnson.

Lederer, Laura, ed. Take Back the Night: Women on Pornography. LC 80-17084. 352p. 1980. 14.95 (ISBN 0-688-03728-3). Morrow.

Lee, Rex E. A Lawyer Looks at the Equal Rights Amendment. LC 80-22202. (Illus.). 150p. 1980. pap. 7.95 (ISBN 0-8425-1883-5). Brigham.

WOMEN'S STUDIES

Halas, Celia. Why Can't a Woman Be More Like a Man? 288p. 1981. 10.95 (ISBN 0-02-547430-8). Macmillan.

Hayden, Dolores. A Grand Domestic Revolution: Feminism, Socialism & the American Home, 1870-1930. (Illus.). 425p. 1981. text ed. 19.95x (ISBN 0-262-08108-3). MIT Pr.

Lerner, Gerda. The Majority Finds Its Past: Placing Women in History. 250p. 1981. pap. 5.95 (ISBN 0-19-502899-6, GB 624, OPB). Oxford U Pr.

Mayhall, Carole. Del Corazon de una Mujer. Rojas, Juan, tr. from Eng. 111p. (Orig., Span.). 1978. pap. 2.25 (ISBN 0-89922-130-0). Edit Caribe.

Roberts, Helen, ed. Doing Feminist Research. 224p. (Orig.). 1981. pap. price not set (ISBN 0-7100-0772-8). Routledge & Kegam.

Stimpson, Catherine, et al, eds. Women & the American City. LC 80-53136. 280p. 1981. lib. bdg. 16.00x (ISBN 0-226-77478-3); pap. 5.95 (ISBN 0-226-77479-1). U of Chicago Pr.

Trip, Maggie, ed. Woman in the Year Two Thousand. LC 74-80707. 1981. pap. 6.00 (ISBN 0-686-68893-7). Arbor Hse.

Wyckoff, Hogie. Solving Women's Problems: Through Awareness, Action, & Contact. pap. 4.95 (ISBN 0-394-17003-2, E668, Ever). Grove.

WOMEN'S WRITINGS

Here are entered collections of works written by women. Works on the attainments of women as authors are entered under Women Authors. Collections of works in two or more literary forms written about women are entered under Women–literary Collections. Works which discuss the representation of women in literature are entered under Women in Literature.

Cooper, Jilly & Hartman, Tom, eds. Violets & Vinegar. LC 80-9059. 231p. 1981. 15.95 (ISBN 0-8128-2813-5). Stein & Day.

Dubois, Ellen, ed. Elizabeth Cady Stanton-Susan B. Anthony: Correspondence, Writings, Speeches. LC 80-6190. (Studies in the Life of Women Ser.). 1981. 17.95x (ISBN 0-8052-3759-3); pap. 6.95 (ISBN 0-8052-0672-8). Schocken.

Lederer, Laura, ed. Take Back the Night: Women on Pornography. LC 80-17084. 352p. 1980. 14.95 (ISBN 0-688-03728-3). Morrow.

Travitsky, Betty, compiled by. The Paradise of Women: Writings by Englishwomen of the Renaissance. LC 80-1705. (Contributions in Women's Studies: No. 22). 312p. 1981. lib. bdg. 29.95 (ISBN 0-313-22177-4, TPW/). Greenwood.

WONDER, STEVIE

Edwards, A. & Wohl, G. The Picture Life of Stevie Wonder. 1977. pap. 1.75 (ISBN 0-380-01907-8, 51656, Camelot). Avon.

WONDERS

see Curiosities and Wonders

WOOD

see also Forests and Forestry; Pulpwood; Woodwork; Woody Plants

also kinds of woods, e.g. Mahogany, Walnut

Smith, Nigel. Wood: An Ancient Fuel with a New Future. LC 80-54881. (Worlwatch Papers). 1981. pap. 2.00 (ISBN 0-916468-41-0). Worldwatch Inst.

WOOD AS FUEL

Cohen, Maurice. Woodcutter's Companion: A Guide to Locating, Cutting, Transporting & Storing Your Own Firewood. Rowland, Amy, ed. (Illus.). 160p. (Orig.). 1981. 11.95 (ISBN 0-87857-328-3); pap. 7.95 (ISBN 0-87857-329-1). Rodale Pr Inc.

WOOD-CARVING

Carstenson, Cecil C. The Craft & Creation of Wood Sculpture. (Illus.). 192p. 1981. pap. price not set (ISBN 0-486-24094-0). Dover.

Gottshall, Franklin H. Wood Carving & Whittling for Everyone. LC 77-23224. (Illus.). 1980. pap. 9.95 (SL 921, ScribT). Scribner.

Shourds, Harry V. & Hillman, Anthony. Carving Duck Decoys, with Full-Size Patterns for Hollow Contruction. (Illus.). 64p. (Orig.). 1981. pap. price not set (ISBN 0-486-24083-5). Dover.

WOOD-CARVING–TECHNIQUE

Bridgewater, Alan & Bridgewater, Gill. The Craft of Wood Carving. LC 80-18562. (Illus.). 160p. 1981. 15.95 (ISBN 0-668-04985-5, 4985). Arco.

Skinner, Robert. How to Design & Make Wood Assemblages & Reliefs. (Illus.). 64p. (Orig.). Date not set. pap. price not set (ISBN 0-486-24057-6). Dover.

Tangerman, E. J. Carving Flora & Fables in Wood. LC 80-54336. (Illus.). 128p. 1981. pap. 5.95 (ISBN 0-8069-8982-3). Sterling.

WOOD-ENGRAVING–HISTORY

Ottley, William Y. An Inquiry into the Origin & Early History of Engraving Upon Copper & Wood, 2 vols. Freedberg, Sydney J., ed. LC 77-25757. (Connosseurship Criticism & Art History Ser.: Vol. 14). 835p. 1979. Set. lib. bdg. 80.00 (ISBN 0-8240-3272-1). Garland Pub.

WOOD-ENGRAVINGS

McLean, Ruari. The Wood Engravings of Joan Hassall. LC 80-6193. (Illus.). 120p. 1981. pap. 7.95 (ISBN 0-8052-0675-2). Schocken.

WOOD FINISHING

see also Furniture Finishing

Frank, George. Eighty-Eight Rue de Charonne: Adventures in Wood Finishing. LC 80-54431. (Illus.). 128p. 1981. 9.95 (ISBN 0-918804-06-X, Dist. by Van Nostrand Reinhold). Taunton.

WOOD-WIND INSTRUMENTS

see Wind Instruments

WOODCUTS

see Wood-Engravings

WOODWORK

see also Cabinet-Work; Carpentry; Furniture Making; Home Workshops; Wood-Carving; Wood Finishing

Douglass, J. H. Woodworking Basics. 320p. 1980. 14.95 (ISBN 0-442-23152-0). Van Nos Reinhold.

Jones, Bernard E. The Complete Woodworker. LC 80-634. (Illus.). 1980. pap. 7.95 (ISBN 0-89815-022-1). Ten Speed Pr.

Karp, Ben. Ornamental Carpentry of Nineteenth-Century American Houses: One Hundred Sixty Five Photographs. rev. ed. Orig. Title: Wood Motifs in American Domestic Architecture. (Illus.). 96p. 1981. pap. price not set (ISBN 0-486-24144-0). Dover.

Krenov, James. James Krenov Worker in Wood. (Illus.). 128p. 1981. 24.95 (ISBN 0-442-26336-8). Van Nos Reinhold.

Leggatt, Alex. Carpentry for the Home. (Illus.). 144p. 1981. 22.50 (ISBN 0-7134-1886-9, Pub. by Batsford England). David & Charles.

Marshall, Mel. How to Choose & Use Lumber, Plywood, Panelboards, & Laminates. LC 79-4710. 1980. pap. 4.95 (ISBN 0-06-090724-X, CN 724, CN). Har-Row.

Oumet, Ronald P. Eighty Woodcraft Projects. 320p. 1980. 17.95 (ISBN 0-8246-0260-9). Jonathan David.

Punter, Ian. Woodwork Projects & Design. (Illus.). 96p. 1981. 14.95 (ISBN 0-7134-3549-6, Pub. by Batsford England). David & Charles.

Sainsbury, John. Sainsbury's Woodturning Projects for Dining. LC 80-54347. (Illus.). 160p. 1981. 14.95 (ISBN 0-8069-5436-1). Sterling.

Scott, Ernest. Working in Wood. 1980. 25.00 (ISBN 0-686-68362-5). Putnam.

Spielman, Patrick. Making Wood Signs. LC 80-54342. (Illus.). 144p. 1981. 10.95 (ISBN 0-8069-5434-5); lib. bdg. 9.89 (ISBN 0-8069-5435-3); pap. 6.95. Sterling.

Thompson, David T. Easy Woodstuff for Kids. LC 80-84599. (Illus.). 130p. 1981. pap. 7.95 (ISBN 0-87659-101-2). Gryphon Hse.

Zechlin, Katharina. Making Games in Wood. LC 80-54353. (Illus.). 80p. 1981. pap. 6.95 (ISBN 0-8069-8996-3). Sterling.

WOODWORKING MACHINERY

Roberts, Kenneth D. Some Nineteenth Century English Woodworking Tools. (Illus.). 496p. 1980. text ed. 40.00x (ISBN 0-913602-40-X). K Roberts.

WOODY PLANTS

see also Climbing Plants; Forest Ecology; Shrubs; Trees

Kozlowski, T. T. Water Deficits & Plant Growth: Woody Plant Communities, Vol. 6. 1981. write for info. (ISBN 0-12-424156-5). Acad Pr.

Lynch, Daniel. Native & Naturalized Woody Plants of Austin & the Hill Country. Mosely, Jane, ed. LC 80-53737. (Illus.). 160p. (Orig.). 1980. pap. 6.95 (ISBN 0-938472-00-3). St Edwards Univ.

WOOLF, VIRGINIA (STEPHEN) 1882-1941

Cecil, David. Poets & Story-Tellers. 201p. 1980. Repr. of 1968 ed. lib. bdg. 30.00 (ISBN 0-8495-0852-5). Arden Lib.

Poresky, Louise A. The Elusive Self: Psyche & Spirit in Virginia Woolf's Novels. LC 79-64503. 288p. 1981. 22.50 (ISBN 0-87413-170-7, 170). U Delaware Pr.

Spilka, Mark. Virginia Woolf's Quarrel with Grieving. LC 80-11792. xii, 142p. 1980. 13.50x (ISBN 0-8032-4120-8). U of Nebr Pr.

Woolf, Virginia. The Diary of Virginia Woolf: Volume Four 1931-1935. Bell, Ann O. & McNeillie, Andrew, eds. 1981. price not set. HarBraceJ.

WOOLMAN, JOHN, 1720-1772

Reynolds, Reginald. The Wisdom of John Woolman: With a Selection from His Writings As a Guide to the Seekers of Today. LC 79-8724. xii, 178p. 1981. Repr. of 1948 ed. lib. bdg. 22.50x (ISBN 0-313-22190-1, REJW). Greenwood.

WORD (THEOLOGY)

see Communication (Theology)

WORD-BLINDNESS, PARTIAL

see Dyslexia

WORD GAMES

see also Crossword Puzzles

Arnold, Henri & Lee, Bob. Jumble: That Scrambled Word Game, No. 17. (Orig.). 1980. pap. 1.50 (ISBN 0-451-09492-1, W9492, Sig). NAL.

--Jumble: That Scrambled Word Game, No. 18. (Orig.). 1981. pap. 1.50 (ISBN 0-451-09740-8, W9240, Sig). NAL.

Brandreth, Cyles. Pears Book of Words. Oxford English Dict., ed. 204p. 1981. 13.95 (ISBN 0-7207-1186-X). Merrimack Bk Serv.

Espy, Willard R. Another Almanac of Words at Play. (Illus.). 1980. 14.95 (ISBN 0-517-53187-9); pap. 8.95 (ISBN 0-517-53188-7). Potter.

Gerger, Dawn. Tempo World Finds, No. 6. 128p. pap. 1.50 (ISBN 0-448-05777-8, Tempo). G&D.

Graves, Ian D. Enneagrams: A Game of Nine Letter-Words. (Oleander Games & Pastimes Ser.: Vol. 4). (Illus.). 64p. 1981. 9.95 (ISBN 0-900891-78-5); pap. 4.75 (ISBN 0-900891-79-3). Oleander Pr.

Griffiths, John. Complete Word Game Finisher. 1980. pap. 7.95 (ISBN 0-446-97582-6). Warner Bks.

Halcombe, Alvin. Find-a-Word Puzzles for Vo-Ag Students: Set 1. 1981. pap. 9.95 (ISBN 0-8134-2164-0, 2164). Interstate.

Haubrick, Judd. Scrabble Grams. Bell, Harriet, ed. 96p. 1981. pap. 2.95 (ISBN 0-517-54271-4, Harmony). Crown.

Lindley, Letty A. Leaping into Language with Sound-a-Roo. 1981. pap. 9.95 (ISBN 0-8134-2165-9). Interstate.

Manchester, Richard B. The Third Mammoth Book of Word Games. 512p. 1981. pap. 8.95 (ISBN 0-89104-202-4). A & W Pubs.

WORD GAMES–JUVENILE LITERATURE

Brown, Marcia. All Butterflies. (Illus.). 32p. (ps-2). pap. 2.95 (ISBN 0-689-70483-6, A-110, Aladdin). Atheneum.

Debnam, Betty & Avery, Lois. The Mini Page & Your Newspaper Activity Book. 128p. (gr. k-6). 1980. pap. 5.95 (ISBN 0-8362-4209-2). Andrews & McMeel.

Doherty, Linda. Tempo Word Finds, No. 4. 128p. (gr. 4 up). 1981. pap. 1.25 (ISBN 0-448-05572-4, Tempo). G&D.

Espeland, Pamela. How to Play Word Games. (Creative Activities, Games, Projects Ser.). (Illus.). 32p. (gr. 4-8). 1981. PLB 5.95 (ISBN 0-87191-797-1); pap. 2.75 (ISBN 0-89812-249-X). Creative Ed.

WORD PROCESSING (OFFICE PRACTICE)

Bergerud, Marly & Gonzalez, Jean. Word Information Processing Concepts: Careers Technology, & Applications. 512p. 1981. text ed. 16.95 (ISBN 0-471-08499-9). Wiley.

--Word Processing: Concepts & Careers. 2nd ed. (Wiley Word Processing Ser.). 256p. 1981. text ed. 14.95 (ISBN 0-471-06010-0); write for info. tchrs'. ed. (ISBN 0-471-09093-X); write for info. resource manual (ISBN 0-471-09093-X). Wiley.

Ellis, Bettie H. Word Processing. (Concepts & Applications). (Illus.). 48p. 1980. 7.48 (ISBN 0-07-019242-1, G). McGraw.

Hansen, Gladys O. Word Processing Systems Manual for Support Staff. (Illus.). 1980. pap. text ed. 22.50 (ISBN 0-936512-01-6). Telecom Lib.

--Word Processing Systems Manual (1) for Originators & Support Staff. & for Support Staff. (Illus., Orig.). 1980. pap. text ed. 40.00 set (ISBN 0-936512-02-4). Telecom Lib.

Layman, N. Kathryn & Renner, Adrienne G. Word Processors: A Programmed Training Guide with Practical Applications. (Illus.). 352p. 1981. text ed. 19.95 (ISBN 0-13-963520-3). P-H.

Papers & Proceedings of Syntopican VII. 299p. 1979. write for info. (ISBN 0-935220-00-3). Intl Word Process.

Papers & Proceedings of Syntopican VIII. 463p. 1980. write for info. (ISBN 0-935220-03-8). Intl Word Process.

Rosen, A. & Freiden, R. Word Processing. 2nd ed. 1981. 15.95 (ISBN 0-13-963488-6). P-H.

Skelcher, Derek. Word Processing Equipment Survey. 222p. (Orig.). 1980. pap. 125.00x (ISBN 0-903796-56-2, Pub. by Online Conferences England). Renouf.

Van Uchelen, Rod. Word Processing: A Guide to Typography, Taste & in-House Graphics. 128p. 1980. 14.95 (ISBN 0-442-28647-3); pap. 7.95 (ISBN 0-442-28646-5). Van Nos Reinhold.

Word Processing: Current Practices & Future Developments. 300p. (Orig.). 1980. pap. text ed. 80.00x (ISBN 0-903796-55-4, Pub. by Online Conferences England). Renouf.

WORDS–HISTORY

Davies, Peter. Roots: Family Histories of Familiar Words. (Illus.). 224p. Date not set. 15.95 (ISBN 0-07-015449-X, P&RB). McGraw.

Schafer, Jurgen. Documentation in the O. E. D. Shakespeare & Nashe As Test Cases. (Illus.). 186p. 1980. text ed. 29.50x (ISBN 0-19-811938-0). Oxford U Pr.

Sperling, Susan K. Tenderfeet & Ladyfingers: A Visceral Approach to Words & Their Origins. LC 80-51778. (Illus.). 160p. 1981. 9.95 (ISBN 0-670-69633-1). Viking Pr.

WORDS, STOCK OF

see Vocabulary

WORDSWORTH, WILLIAM, 1770-1850

Elton, Oliver. Wordsworth. 96p. 1980. Repr. of 1924 ed. 15.00 (ISBN 0-8492-0788-6). R West.

Jones, Henry J. The Egotistical Sublime: A History of Wordsworth's Imagination. LC 78-2460. ix, 212p. 1979. Repr. of 1954 ed. lib. bdg. 19.25x (ISBN 0-313-20307-5). Greenwood.

Knight, William A. Through the Wordsworth Country. 268p. 1980. Repr. of 1887 ed. lib. bdg. 35.00 (ISBN 0-8482-4196-7). Norwood Edns.

Roper, Derek. Wordsworth & Coleridge - Lyrical Ballads 1805. 2nd ed. 432p. 1976. pap. 12.95 (ISBN 0-7121-0140-3, Pub. by Macdonald & Evans England). Intl Ideas.

Stanley, Hiram M. Essays on Literary Art: Tennyson, Wordsworth, Jane Austen, Thoreau. 164p. 1980. Repr. of 1897 ed. lib. bdg. 25.00 (ISBN 0-8414-8035-4). Folcroft.

WORK

see also Industrial Sociology; Job Satisfaction; Labor and Laboring Classes; Performance; Vocation

Esland, Geoff & Salaman, Graeme, eds. The Politics of Work & Occupations. 416p. 1981. pap. 11.00x (ISBN 0-8020-6429-9). U of Toronto Pr.

Gardell, Bertil & Johansson, Bunn. Working Life: Social Science Contribution to Work Reform. 352p. 1981. write for info. (ISBN 0-471-27801-7, Pub. by Wiley-Interscience). Wiley.

Helldorfer, Martin. The Work Trap. LC 80-53205. (Illus.). 140p. 1981. pap. 4.95 (ISBN 0-88489-127-5). St Mary's.

Hoffman, W. Michael & Wyly, Thomas J., eds. The Work Ethic in Business: Proceedings of the Third National Conference on Business Ethics. LC 80-22708. (Ethics Resource Center Ser.). 320p. 1981. lib. bdg. 22.50 (ISBN 0-89946-068-2). Oelgeschlager.

Oxenbury, Helen. Working. (Baby Board Bks.). (Illus.). 12p. (ps-k). Date not set. boards 3.50 (ISBN 0-671-42112-3, Little Simon). S&S.

WORK–MEASUREMENT

see Work Measurement

WORK–PHYSIOLOGICAL ASPECTS

Esland, Geoff & Salaman, Graeme, eds. The Politics of Work & Occupations. 416p. 1981. pap. 11.00x (ISBN 0-8020-6429-9). U of Toronto Pr.

Hofstede, Geert. Culture's Consequences: International Differences in Work-Related Values. LC 80-16327. (Sage Ser. on Cross-Cultural Research & Methodology: Vol. 5). (Illus.). 475p. 1980. 29.95 (ISBN 0-8039-1444-X). Sage.

Mellerowicz, Harald. Ergometry: Basics of Medical Exercise Testing. Smodlaka, Vojin N., ed. Rice, Allan L., tr. from Ger. 1981. text ed. write for info. (ISBN 0-8067-1241-4). Urban & S.

WORK–PSYCHOLOGICAL ASPECTS

Macholoitz, Marilyn. Workaholics: Living with Them, Working with Them. 1981. pap. 2.95 (ISBN 0-451-61971-4, ME1971, Mentor Bks). NAL.

WORK, PSYCHOLOGY OF

see Work–Psychological Aspects

Hughes, Everett C. Men & Their Work. LC 80-29143. 184p. 1981. Repr. of 1958 ed. lib. bdg. 17.50x (ISBN 0-313-22791-8, HUMW). Greenwood.

WORK, THERAPEUTIC EFFECT OF

see Occupational Therapy

WORK EXPERIENCE

see Apprentices; Vocational Education

WORK FUNCTION, ELECTRONIC

see Electrons–Emission

WORK MEASUREMENT

see also Performance

Mellerowicz, Harald. Ergometry: Basics of Medical Exercise Testing. Smodlaka, Vojin N., ed. Rice, Allan L., tr. from Ger. 1981. text ed. write for info. (ISBN 0-8067-1241-4). Urban & S.

WORK PERFORMANCE STANDARDS

see Performance Standards

WORK STANDARDS

see Production Standards

WORK STOPPAGES

see Strikes and Lockouts

WORKERS

see Labor and Laboring Classes

WORKING-CLASSES

see Labor and Laboring Classes

WORKING MEN

see Labor and Laboring Classes

WORKING-MEN'S ASSOCIATIONS

see Trade-Unions

WORKING-MEN'S LUNCH ROOMS

see Restaurants, Lunchrooms, etc.

WORKINGMEN

see Labor and Laboring Classes

WORKMEN'S COMPENSATION

see also Employers' Liability

Hunt, H. Allan. Inflation Protection for Workers' Compensation Claimants in Michigan: A Simulation Study. LC 80-28834. 125p. (Orig.). 1981. pap. text ed. write for info. (ISBN 0-911558-77-2). Upjohn Inst.

WORKSHOP

see Agricultural Machinery; Home Workshops

WORKSHOPS, TEACHERS'

see Teachers' Workshops

WORKSHOPS FOR THE HANDICAPPED

see Vocational Rehabilitation

WORLD, END OF

see End of the World

WORLD AND THE CHURCH

see Church and the World

WORLD COUNCIL OF CHURCHES

Lefever, Ernest. Amsterdam to Nairobi: The World Council of Churches & the Third World. 126p. 1979. 10.00 (ISBN 0-89633-025-7); pap. 5.00 (ISBN 0-89633-024-9). Ethics & Public Policy.

WORLD ECONOMICS

see Commercial Policy; Competition, International; Economic Policy; Geography, Economic

Dicks, G. R., ed. Sources of World Financial & Banking Information. LC 80-28654. 720p. 1981. lib. bdg. 125.00 (ISBN 0-313-22966-X, DSW/). Greenwood.

WORLD FEDERATION

see International Organization

WORLD GOVERNMENT

see International Organization

WORLD HISTORY

see also Geography; History, Ancient; Middle Ages–History

Botsford, George W. A Brief History of the World. (Illus.). 518p. 1980. Repr. of 1917 ed. lib. bdg. 35.00 (ISBN 0-8492-3591-X). R West.

Caidin, Martin. Black Thursday. 272p. 1981. pap. 2.50 (ISBN 0-553-13582-1). Bantam.

Chambers Atlas of World History. 136p. 1980. 25.00x (ISBN 0-550-14001-8, Pub. by W & R Chambers Scotland). State Mutual Bk.

Dawson, Christopher. Dynamics of World History. 12.95 (ISBN 0-89385-009-8). Green Hill.

Dickens, Peter. Night Action. 256p. 1981. pap. 2.50 (ISBN 0-553-14764-1). Bantam.

Grenville, J. A. A World History of the Twentieth Century: Western Dominance 1900-45, Vol. 1. (Illus.). 605p. 1981. 32.50x (ISBN 0-389-20171-5). B&N.

Hansen, Ben. Winning of the World. 176p. (Orig.). 1980. pap. 4.95 (ISBN 0-931590-04-3). Antietam Pr.

Holmes, W. J. Double-Edged Secrets. 1981. pap. 2.95 (ISBN 0-425-04714-8). Berkley Pub.

Kazanjian, Nuber. East & West. 1981. 8.95 (ISBN 0-533-04669-6). Vantage.

Kitchen, Ruben P., Jr. Pacific Carrier. (Zebra World at War Ser.: No. 23). (Orig.). 1980. pap. 2.50 (ISBN 0-89083-683-3, Kable News Co). Zebra.

Leeds, C. A. Twentieth-Century History Nineteen Hundred to Nineteen Forty-Five. (Illus.). 224p. 1979. pap. text ed. 9.95x (ISBN 0-7121-2025-4, Pub. by Macdonald & Evans England). Intl Ideas.

Lorain, Pierre. Clandestine Armament, 1941-1944. (Illus.). 192p. 1981. 12.50 (ISBN 0-02-575200-6). Macmillan.

McNeill, William H., et al. The World...Its History in Maps. rev. ed. (Illus.). 96p. 1980. pap. text ed. 9.10x (ISBN 0-87453-011-3, 81011). Denoyer.

The New Cambridge Modern History. Incl. Vol. 1. The Renaissance, 1493-1520. Potter, G. R., ed. 1957. 49.95 (ISBN 0-521-04541-X); pap. 21.95 (ISBN 0-521-09974-9); Vol. 2. The Reformation, 1520-1559. Elton, G. R., ed. 1958. 53.00 (ISBN 0-521-04542-8); pap. 22.95 (ISBN 0-521-09960-9); Vol. 3. Counter-Reformation & Price Revolution, 1559-1610. Wernham, R. B., ed. 1968. 49.95 (ISBN 0-521-04543-6); Vol. 4. The Decline of Spain & the Thirty Years War, 1609-59. Cooper, J. P., ed. 1970. 59.95 (ISBN 0-521-07618-8); Vol. 5. The Ascendary of France, 1648-88. Carsten, F. L., ed. 1961. 49.95 (ISBN 0-521-04544-4); Vol. 6. The Rise of Great Britain & Russia, 1688-1725. Bromley, J. S., ed. 1970. 69.00 (ISBN 0-521-07524-6); pap. 24.95 (ISBN 0-521-29396-0); Vol. 7. The Old Regime 1713-1763. Lindsay, J. O., ed. 1957. 79.95 (ISBN 0-521-04545-2); Vol. 8. The American & French Revolutions, 1763-93. Goodwin, A. 1965. 59.50 (ISBN 0-521-04546-0); pap. 22.95 (ISBN 0-521-29108-9); Vol. 9. War & Peace in an Age of Upheaval, 1793-1830. Crawley, C. W., ed. 1965. 59.95 (ISBN 0-521-04547-9); Vol. 10. The Zenith of European Power 1830-1870. Bury, J. P., ed. 1960. 59.95 (ISBN 0-521-04548-7); Vol. 11. Material Progress & World-Wide Problems, 1870-98. Hinsley, F. H., ed. 1962. 59.95 (ISBN 0-521-04549-5); pap. 22.95 (ISBN 0-521-29109-7); The Shifting Balance of World Forces, 1898-1945. 2nd ed. Mowat, C. L., ed. 1960. 65.95 (ISBN 0-521-04551-7); Vol. 13. Companion Volume. Burke, Peter, ed. 1979. 34.95 (ISBN 0-521-22128-5); pap. 13.95 (ISBN 0-521-28017-6); Vol. 14. Atlas. Darby, H. C. & Fullard, Harold, eds. (Illus.). 1970. 65.00 (ISBN 0-521-07708-7); pap. 22.95 (ISBN 0-521-09908-0). Set. 600.00 (ISBN 0-521-08787-2). Cambridge U Pr.

O'Kane, Richard H. Clear the Bridge. 496p. 1981. pap. 2.95 (ISBN 0-553-14516-9). Bantam.

Pluto Press. State of the World Atlas. 1981. 14.95 (ISBN 0-671-42438-6, Touchstone); pap. 9.95 (ISBN 0-671-42439-4). S&S.

The Saturday Evening Post Reflections of a Decade, 1901-1910. LC 80-67053. (Illus.). 1980. 13.95 (ISBN 0-89387-044-7). Sat Eve Post.

Tucker, Frank H. The Frontier Spirit & Progress. LC 79-19372. 368p. 1981. text ed. 23.95 (ISBN 0-88229-376-1); pap. text ed. 11.95 (ISBN 0-88229-757-0). Nelson-Hall.

WORLD HISTORY–STUDY AND TEACHING

see History–Study and Teaching

WORLD LITERATURE

see Literature

WORLD MAPS

Smith, A. G., et al. Phanerozoic Paleocontinental World Maps. LC 79-42669. (Cambridge Earth Science Ser.). 96p. Date not set. 29.50 (ISBN 0-521-23257-0); pap. 13.95 (ISBN 0-521-23258-9). Cambridge U Pr.

WORLD NEWS

see Foreign News

WORLD ORGANIZATION

see International Organization

WORLD POLITICS

Here are entered historical accounts of international intercourse. Theoretical works are entered under International Relations.

see also Detente

Boyd, Gavin & Pentland, Charles, eds. Issues in Global Politics. LC 80-69282. 1981. pap. text ed. 9.95 (ISBN 0-02-904470-7). Free Pr.

Flynn, Gregory A., et al, eds. The Internal Fabric of the Atlantic Alliance. 350p. 1981. text ed. 32.50 (ISBN 0-86598-039-X). Allanheld.

Greene, John C. Science, Ideology, & World View: Essays in the History of Evolutionary Ideas. 1981. 14.00 (ISBN 0-520-04217-4); pap. 4.95 (ISBN 0-520-04218-2). U of Cal Pr.

Smith, Michael, et al, eds. Perspectives on World Politics. 224p. 1981. 32.50x (ISBN 0-7099-2302-3, Pub. by Croom Helm Ltd England). Biblio Dist.

Snow, Donald M. Introduction to World Politics: A Conceptual & Developmental Perspective. LC 80-5851. 230p. 1981. lib. bdg. 18.25 (ISBN 0-8191-1398-0); pap. text ed. 9.75 (ISBN 0-8191-1399-9). U Pr of Amer.

Spiegel, Steven L. Dominance & Diversity: The International Hierarchy. LC 80-8295. 317p. 1980. lib. bdg. 19.00 (ISBN 0-8191-1331-X); pap. text ed. 10.50 (ISBN 0-8191-1332-8). U Pr of Amer.

Thomas, Harold. The World Power Foundation: Its Goals & Platform. 1980. pap. 6.95. Loompanics.

WORLD POLITICS–YEARBOOKS

Countries of the World & Their Leaders Yearbook 1981. (Illus.). 1000p. 1981. 48.00 (ISBN 0-8103-1052-X). Gale.

WORLD POLITICS–1933-1945

Alexander, Robert J. The Right Opposition: The Lovestoneites & the International Communist Opposition of the 1930's. LC 80-1711. (Contributions in Political Science Ser.: No. 54). 320p. 1981. lib. bdg. 32.50 (AOP/). Greenwood.

WORLD POLITICS–1945-

see also Atomic Power–International Control

Sarkesian, Sam C., ed. Non-Nuclear Conflicts in the Nuclear Age. 360p. 1980. 29.95 (ISBN 0-03-056138-8). Praeger.

WORLD POLITICS–1975-

Kissinger, Henry. For the Record: Selected Statements, 1977 to 1980. 288p. 1981. 12.95 (ISBN 0-316-49663-1). Little.

WORLD SERIES (BASEBALL)

Devaney, John & Goldblatt, Burt. The World Series: A Complete Pictorial History. rev. ed. (Illus.). 416p. 1981. pap. 10.95 (ISBN 0-528-88044-6). Rand.

WORLD WAR, 1914-1918

see European War, 1914-1918

WORLD WAR, 1939-1945

Baydot. Historical Encyclopedia of World War II. Date not set. 25.00 (ISBN 0-87196-401-5). Facts on File.

Breitman, George. Fighting Racism in World War II. 1980. 20.00 (ISBN 0-913460-81-8); pap. 5.95 (ISBN 0-913460-82-6). Monad Pr.

Cross, George L. The University of Oklahoma & World War II: A Personal Account, 1941-1946. LC 80-16934. (Illus.). 320p. 1980. 15.95 (ISBN 0-8061-1662-5). U of Okla Pr.

Fish, Hamilton. F D R: The Other Side of the Coin. 255p. 1976. pap. 8.00 (ISBN 0-911038-64-7, Inst Hist Rev). Noontide.

Goralski, Robert. World War Two Almanac: Nineteen Thirty-One to Nineteen Forty-Five A Political & Military Record. new ed. (Illus.). 484p. 1981. 17.95 (ISBN 0-399-12548-5). Putnam.

Irving, David. The War Between the Generals: Inside the Allied High Command. (Illus.). 384p. 1981. 17.95 (ISBN 0-312-92920-X). Congdon & Lattes.

WORLD WAR, 1939-1945–AERIAL OPERATIONS

Campbell, Christopher. Aces & Aircraft of World War One. (Illus.). 128p. 1981. 24.95 (Pub. by Blandford Pr England). Sterling.

Overy, R. J. The Air War, Nineteen Thirty-Nine to Nineteen Forty-Five. LC 80-6200. 288p. 1981. 16.95 (ISBN 0-8128-2792-9). Stein & Day.

Rust, Kenn C. The Tenth Air Force Story. (World War II Forces History). (Illus.). 64p. 1980. pap. 7.50 (ISBN 0-911852-87-5). Hist Aviation.

WORLD WAR, 1939-1945–AERIAL OPERATIONS, AMERICAN

Bove, Arthur. First Over Germany: A Story of the 306th Bombardment Group. LC 80-69557. (Aviation Ser.: No. 4). (Illus.). 138p. Repr. 20.00 (ISBN 0-89839-038-9). Battery Pr.

Glines, Carroll V. Doolittle's Tokyo Raiders. 464p. 1981. pap. 7.95 (ISBN 0-442-21925-3). Van Nos Reinhold.

Pay, Don. Thunder from Heaven: The Story of the 17th Airborne Division in WW II. LC 80-69273. (Airborne Ser.: No. 4). (Illus.). 179p. 1980. Repr. 22.50 (ISBN 0-89839-037-0). Battery Pr.

Spight, Edwin & Spight, Jeanne. Eagles of the Pacific: Consairways Service During WW-II. (Illus.). 1980. 12.95 (ISBN 0-911852-88-3, Pub. by Hist Avn. Album). Aviation.

Thomas, Gordon & Witts, Max M. Enola Gay. 400p. pap. 2.75 (ISBN 0-671-42116-6). PB.

WORLD WAR, 1939-1945–AERIAL OPERATIONS, BRITISH

Johnson, David. The London Blitz: The City Ablaze, December 29, 1940. LC 80-6199. 224p. 1981. 13.95 (ISBN 0-8128-2799-6). Stein & Day.

WORLD WAR, 1939-1945–AFRO-AMERICANS

Buchanan, A. Russell. Black Americans in World War II. LC 76-53577. 149p. 1977. pap. 6.95 (ISBN 0-87436-277-6). ABC-Clio.

WORLD WAR, 1939-1945–BIOGRAPHY

Rosenfeld, Oscar. The Phony War. Date not set. 8.95 (ISBN 0-533-04782-X). Vantage.

Vis, Johan W. Scherzo. Date not set. 8.95 (ISBN 0-533-04811-7). Vantage.

WORLD WAR, 1939-1945–CAMPAIGNS

see also names of individual battles, campaigns, etc.

Hoyt, Edwin P. To the Marianas: War in the Central Pacific: 1944. 192p. 1980. deluxe ed. 12.95 (ISBN 0-442-26105-5). Van Nos Reinhold.

Piekalkiewicz, Janusz. The Cavalry of World War II. LC 80-5800. (Illus.). 256p. 1980. 25.00 (ISBN 0-8128-2749-X). Stein & Day.

Quarrie, Bruce. German Paratroops in the Mediterranean: World War Two Photo Album. (Illus.). 96p. 1981. pap. 5.95 (ISBN 0-89404-049-9). Aztex.

Rigge, Simon. War in the Outposts. Editors of Time-Life Books, ed. (World War II Ser.). (Illus.). 208p. 1981. 13.95 (ISBN 0-8094-3379-6). Time-Life.

Whiting, Charles. Death of a Division. LC 80-5717. (Illus.). 176p. 1981. 11.95 (ISBN 0-8128-2760-0). Stein & Day.

WORLD WAR, 1939-1945–CAMPAIGNS–AFRICA

Mitcham, Samual W., Jr. Rommel's Desert War: The Life & Death of the Afrika Korps. LC 80-6153. 228p. 1981. 13.95 (ISBN 0-8128-2784-8). Stein & Day.

WORLD WAR, 1939-1945–CAMPAIGNS–FRANCE

Kemp, Anthony. The Maginot Line: Myth & Reality. LC 80-6260. 128p. 1981. 11.95 (ISBN 0-8128-2811-9). Stein & Day.

Mockler, Anthony. Our Enemies the French: Being an Account of the War Fought Between the French & the British - Syria 1941. (Illus.). xix, 252p. 1976. 18.00 (ISBN 0-85052-194-7). Shoe String.

Wilt, Alan F. The French Riviera Campaign of August Nineteen Forty-Four. LC 80-23041. 1981. price not set (ISBN 0-8093-1000-7). S Ill U Pr.

WORLD WAR, 1939-1945–CAMPAIGNS–GERMANY

Baron, Richard, et al. Raid: The Untold Story of Patton's Secret Mission. 288p. 1981. 12.95 (ISBN 0-399-12597-3). Putnam.

Hewitt, Robert L. Workhorse of the Western Front: The Story of the 30th Infantry Division. LC 80-68981. (Divisional Ser.: No. 16). (Illus.). 404p. 1980. Repr. of 1946 ed. 25.00 (ISBN 0-89839-036-2). Battery Pr.

Hillgruber, Andreas. Germany & the Two World Wars. Kirby, William C., tr. LC 80-27036. 144p. 1981. text ed. 14.50 (ISBN 0-674-35321-8). Harvard U Pr.

Rostow, W. W. Pre-Invasion Bombing Strategy: General Eisenhower's Decision of March 25, 1944. 176p. 1981. text ed. 18.00 (ISBN 0-292-76470-7); pap. 8.95 (ISBN 0-686-69545-3). U of Tex Pr.

Time-Life Books Editors & Ziemke, Earl. The Soviet Juggernaut. (World War II Ser.). (Illus.). 208p. 1981. 13.95 (ISBN 0-8094-3387-7). Time-Life.

WORLD WAR, 1939-1945–CAMPAIGNS–GUADALCANAL ISLAND

Hoyt, Edwin P. Guadalcanal. LC 80-5433. 320p. 1981. 14.95 (ISBN 0-8128-2735-X). Stein & Day.

WORLD WAR, 1939-1945–CAMPAIGNS–RUSSIA

Panzers in Russia Nineteen Forty-Three to Forty-Five: World War Two Photo Album. (Illus.). 96p. 1981. pap. 5.95 (ISBN 0-89404-058-8). Aztex.

Quarrie, Bruce. Panzers in Russia, 1941-1943: World War II Photo Album. (Illus.). 96p. 1981. pap. 5.95 (ISBN 0-89404-055-3). Aztex.

WORLD WAR, 1939-1945–CAMPAIGNS–SICILY

Skipper, G. C. Sicily. (World at War Ser.). (Illus.). 48p. (gr. 3-8). PLB 7.95 (ISBN 0-516-04792-2). Childrens.

WORLD WAR, 1939-1945–FICTION

Follett, Ken. The Key to Rebecca. LC 80-16760. 1980. 12.95 (ISBN 0-688-03734-8). Morrow.

Klein, Ed. Parachutists. LC 77-82953. 406p. 1981. 10.95 (ISBN 0-385-12573-9). Doubleday.

Rybakov, Anatoli. Heavy Sand. Shukman, Harold, tr. from Rus. 384p. 1981. 13.95 (ISBN 0-670-36499-1). Viking Pr.

Tonner, Leslie. The Five Towns. LC 80-52418. 416p. 1981. 12.95 (ISBN 0-87223-652-8). Seaview Bks.

WORLD WAR, 1939-1945–HISTORIOGRAPHY

Goralski, Robert. World War Two Almanac: Nineteen Thirty-One to Nineteen Forty-Five A Political & Military Record. new ed. (Illus.). 484p. 1981. 17.95 (ISBN 0-399-12548-5). Putnam.

WORLD WAR, 1939-1945–JUVENILE LITERATURE

Allen, Eleanor. Wartime Children, 1939-1945. (Junior Reference Ser.). (Illus.). 64p. (gr. 7 up). 7.95 (ISBN 0-7136-1503-6). Dufour.

Battle of the Coral Sea. LC 80-25088. (World at War Ser.). (Illus.). 48p. (gr. 3-8). 1981. PLB 7.95 (ISBN 0-516-04787-6). Childrens.

Carter, Hodding. The Commandos of World War II. LC 80-21142. (Landmark Bks.). (Illus.). 160p. (gr. 5-9). 1981. 2.95 (ISBN 0-394-84735-0, BYR); PLB 5.99 (ISBN 0-394-90561-X). Random.

Fyson, Nance L. Growing up in the Second World War. (Growing up Ser.). (Illus.). 72p. (gr. 6 up). 1981. 14.95 (ISBN 0-7134-3574-7, Pub. by Batsford England). David & Charles.

Lawson, Ted. Thirty Seconds Over Tokyo. LC 53-6522. (Landmark Bks.). (Illus.). 208p. (gr. 5-9). 1981. pap. 2.95 (ISBN 0-394-84698-2). Random.

Skipper, G. C. Battle of Leyte Gulf. LC 80-27265. (World at War Ser.). (Illus.). 48p. (gr. 3-8). 1981. PLB 7.95 (ISBN 0-516-04788-4). Childrens.

WORLD WAR, 1939-1945–MILITARY OPERATIONS

see World War, 1939-1945–Aerial Operations; World War, 1939-1945–Campaigns; World War, 1939-1945–Naval Operations

WORLD WAR, 1939-1945–MISCELLANEA

McCarthy, Robert. World War Two German Military Collectibles. (Illus.). 1980. pap. 6.95 (ISBN 0-89145-135-8). Collector Bks.

WORLD WAR, 1939-1945–NAVAL OPERATIONS

Winton, John. Sink the Haguro! The Last Destroyer of the Second World War. (Illus.). x, 182p. 1978. 19.50 (ISBN 0-85422-152-2). Shoe String.

WORLD WAR, 1939-1945–NAVAL OPERATIONS–SUBMARINE

Schaeffer, Heinz. U-Boat Nine Hundred Seventy-Seven. (War Book). 208p. 1981. pap. 2.50 (ISBN 0-553-14591-6). Bantam.

WORLD WAR, 1939-1945–NAVAL OPERATIONS, GERMAN

Beaver, Paul. German Destroyers & Escorts: World War Two Photo Album. (Illus.). 96p. 1981. pap. 5.95 (ISBN 0-89404-060-X). Aztex.

WORLD WAR, 1939-1945–PERSONAL NARRATIVES

Boeman, John. Morotai: A Memoir of War. LC 80-697. 288p. 1981. 12.95 (ISBN 0-385-15586-7). Doubleday.

Cohen, Bernard C. Political Process & Foreign Policy: The Making of the Japanese Peace Settlement. LC 80-19832. x, 293p. 1980. Repr. of 1957 ed. lib. bdg. 37.50x (ISBN 0-313-22715-2, COPF). Greenwood.

Irving, David. The War Between the Generals. (Illus.). 480p. 1981. 17.95 (ISBN 0-312-92920-X). St Martin.

WORLD WAR, 1939-1945–PERSONAL NARRATIVES, AMERICAN
Brown, Walter L. Up Front with U. S. Day by Day in the Life of a Combat Infantryman in General Patton's Third Army. LC 79-54035. (Illus.). 744p. 1979. 12.95x (ISBN 0-9604822-0-2); lib. bdg. write for info. (ISBN 0-9604822-0-2). Brown's Studio.
WORLD WAR, 1939-1945–PERSONAL NARRATIVES, EUROPEAN
Grant, Ian. Cameraman at War. (Illus.). 200p. 1981. 31.95 (ISBN 0-85059-489-8). Aztex.
WORLD WAR, 1939-1945–PERSONAL NARRATIVES, FRENCH
Dubosq, Genevieve. My Longest Night. Woodward, Richard S., tr. from Fr. LC 80-23169. (Illus.). 288p. 1981. 12.95 (ISBN 0-394-51590-0). Seaver Bks.
WORLD WAR, 1939-1945–PERSONAL NARRATIVES, HUNGARIAN
Fisher, Marianne & Roper, Gayle. Time of Storm. LC 80-69310. 160p. 1981. pap. 5.95 (ISBN 0-915684-82-9). Christian Herald.
WORLD WAR, 1939-1945–PERSONAL NARRATIVES, JEWISH
Wenzel, Gertrude. Granny. (Illus.). 272p. 1981. 12.50 (ISBN 0-682-49694-4). Exposition.
WORLD WAR, 1939-1945–PHOTOGRAPHY
Grant, Ian. Cameraman at War. (Illus.). 200p. 1981. 31.95 (ISBN 0-85059-489-8). Aztex.
WORLD WAR, 1939-1945–PICTORIAL WORKS
Beaver, Paul. World War Two Photo Album: German Destroyers & Escorts. (Illus.). 96p. 1981. pap. 5.95 (ISBN 0-89404-060-X). Aztex.
Quarrie, Bruce. World War Two Photo Album: Panzers in the Balkans & Italy. (Illus.). 96p. 1981. pap. 5.95 (ISBN 0-89404-059-6). Aztex.
WORLD WAR, 1939-1945–PRISONERS AND PRISONS, AMERICAN
Parnell, Wilma T. & Taber, Robert. The Killing of Corporal Kunze. (Illus.). 224p. 1981. 10.00 (ISBN 0-8184-0313-6). Lyle Stuart.
WORLD WAR, 1939-1945–PRISONERS AND PRISONS, GERMAN
Parnell, Wilma T. & Taber, Robert. The Killing of Corporal Kunze. (Illus.). 224p. 1981. 10.00 (ISBN 0-8184-0313-6). Lyle Stuart.
WORLD WAR, 1939-1945–PRISONERS AND PRISONS, JAPANESE
Blair, Joan & Blair, Clay, Jr. Return from the River Kwai. 320p. 1981. pap. 2.75 (ISBN 0-345-29007-0). Ballantine.
WORLD WAR, 1939-1945–SUBMARINE OPERATIONS
see World War, 1939-1945–Naval Operations–Submarine
WORLD WAR, 1939-1945–GREAT BRITAIN
Halpenny, Bruce B. Action Stations Two: Military Airfields of Lincolnshire & the East Midlands. (Illus.). 232p. 1981. 37.95 (ISBN 0-85059-484-7). Aztex.
WORLD WAR, 1939-1945–JAPAN
Time-Life Books Editors & Halloran, Richard. The Home Front: Japan. (World War II Ser.). (Illus.). 208p. 1981. 13.95 (ISBN 0-8094-3415-6). Time-Life.
WORLD WAR, 1939-1945–MEDITERRANEAN SEA
Whipple, A. B. & Time-Life Books Editors. The Mediterranean. (World War II Ser). (Illus.). 208p. 1981. 13.95 (ISBN 0-8094-3383-4). Time-Life.
WORLD WAR, 1939-1945–PHILIPPINE ISLANDS
Firth, Robert H. A Matter of Time. rev. ed. LC 80-68365. 143p. 1981. pap. write for info. (ISBN 0-9605060-0-4). Firth.
WORLDLINESS (THEOLOGY)
see Church and the World
WORLD'S FAIRS
see Exhibitions
WORMS
see also Earthworms
also names of classes, orders, genera, etc.
Meteorological Factors Affecting the Epidemology of the Cotton Leaf Worm & the Pink Boolworm. (Technical Note Ser.: No. 167). 46p. 1980. pap. 10.00 (ISBN 92-63-10532-4, W473, WMO). Unipub.
WORRY
see also Anxiety
Henderson, Janice A. Don't Worry. 250p. 1981. 8.95 (ISBN 0-396-07901-6). Dodd.
Patterson, Katherine. Partners in Pluralism: A Study Guide. (Orig.). 1981. pap. 2.95 (ISBN 0-377-00111-2). Friend Pr.
WORSHIP
see also Church Attendance; Devotional Exercises; God–Worship and Love; Idols and Images; Liturgics; Meditation; Prayer; Public Worship; Ritual; Sun-Worship
Bailey, Robert W. New Ways in Christian Worship. 1981. pap. 5.95. Broadman.
Clark, Linda, et al. Image Breaking - Image Building. 148p. (Orig.). 1981. pap. 7.95 (ISBN 0-8298-0407-2). Pilgrim NY.
Hislop, D. H. Our Heritage in Public Worship. LC 36-2187. 350p. 7.50. Attic Pr.
Maldonado, Luis & Power, David, eds. Symbol & Art in Worship, Concilium 132. (New Concilium 1980). 128p. 1980. pap. 5.95 (ISBN 0-8164-4765-9). Crossroad NY.
Price, Carl E. Worship Without Walls. LC 80-51409. (Orig.). 1980. pap. 1.00x (ISBN 0-8358-0404-6). Upper Room.
Watkins, Keith. Faithful & Fair: Transcending Sexist Language in Worship. LC 80-39698. 128p. 1981. pap. 4.95 (ISBN 0-687-12707-6). Abingdon.
WORTH
see Values
WOUNDED, FIRST AID TO
see First Aid in Illness and Injury
WOUNDS
see also Surgery; Traumatism
also subdivision Wounds and Injuries under names of organs and regions of the body, e.g. Brain–Wounds and Injuries; Chest–Wounds and Injuries
Hunt, Thomas K., ed. Wound Healing & Wound Infection: Theory & Surgical Practice. 303p. 1980. 18.95x (ISBN 0-8385-9836-6). ACC.
WRECKS
see Shipwrecks
WRIGHT BROTHERS–JUVENILE LITERATURE
Reynolds, Quentin. The Wright Brothers. LC 50-11766. (Landmark Bks.). (Illus.). 160p. (gr. 5-9). 1981. pap. 2.95 (ISBN 0-394-84700-8). Random.
WRITERS
see Authors
WRITING
Here are entered works dealing with the art and history of writing in general. Works dealing with the writing of a particular language are entered under the name of that language with subdivisions Alphabet and Writing. For a system of writing used by several peoples, the heading Writing, followed by the name of the system, is preferred, e.g. Writing, Arabic. General and comparative works dealing with the Semitic alphabet and its ancient and modern derivatives or with similar series of characters employed to represent the sounds of a language are entered under the heading Alphabet. Works dealing with variations in the style of writing in the past, and especially with ancient and medieval handwriting, are entered under the heading Paleography.
see also Abbreviations; Alphabet; Calligraphers; Calligraphy; Ciphers; Cryptography; Graphology; Penmanship; Shorthand; Typewriting
Agee, Anne & Kline, Gary. The Basic Writer's Book. (Illus.). 384p. 1981. text ed. 11.95 (ISBN 0-13-069476-2). P-H.
Barnes, Gregory. Crisscross: Structured Writing in Context. (Illus.). 208p. 1981. pap. text ed. 8.95 (ISBN 0-13-193920-3). P-H.
Colles, William M. & Cresswell, Henry. Success in Literature. 360p. 1980. Repr. of 1911 ed. lib. bdg. 20.00 (ISBN 0-89760-116-5). Telegraph Bks.
Fredericksen, Carl H., et al, eds. Variation in Writing: Functional & Linguistic-Cultural Differences, Vol. 1. 240p. 1981. prof. - refer. 16.50 (ISBN 0-89859-099-X). L Erlbaum Assocs.
Plimpton, George, ed. Writers at Work. LC 80-18030. (The Paris Review Interviews Ser.: No. 5). (Illus.). 416p. 1981. 17.95 (ISBN 0-670-79098-2). Viking Pr.
Underwood, Virginia & Kett, Merriellyn. College Writing Skills. 2nd ed. 320p. 1981. pap. text ed. 10.95 (ISBN 0-675-08046-0); test bank 3.95 (ISBN 0-686-69487-2); instr's. manual 3.95 (ISBN 0-686-69488-0); write for info 9 audiocassettes (ISBN 0-675-08031-2). Merrill.
WRITING–STUDY AND TEACHING
see Penmanship
WRITING (AUTHORSHIP)
see Authorship
WRITING, ITALIC
Lehman, Charles. Italic Handwriting & Calligraphy for the Beginner: A Craft Manual. (Illus.). 160p. (Orig.). 1981. pap. 3.95 (ISBN 0-8008-4290-1, 80-53415, Pentalic). Taplinger.
WRITING AS A PROFESSION
see Authorship
WRITING OF LETTERS
see Letter-Writing
WYATT, THOMAS SIR, 1503-1542
Rebholz, R. A., ed. Sir Thomas Wyatt: The Complete Poems. LC 80-53980. 558p. 1981. text ed. 25.00x (ISBN 0-300-02681-1); pap. 5.95x (ISBN 0-300-02688-9). Yale U Pr.
WYOMING–DESCRIPTION AND TRAVEL
Federal Writers' Project of the Works Projects Administration. Wyoming: A Guide to Its History, Highways, & People. LC 80-23038. (Illus.). xxxviii, 490p. 1981. 24.50x (ISBN 0-8032-1958-X); pap. 9.75 (ISBN 0-8032-6854-8, BB 757, Bison). U of Nebr Pr.
Urbanek, Mae. Ghost Trails of Wyoming. (Illus.). 236p. 1978. 16.95; pap. 8.95. Urbanek.
WYOMING–HISTORY
Federal Writers' Project of the Works Projects Administration. Wyoming: A Guide to Its History, Highways, & People. LC 80-23038. (Illus.). xxxviii, 490p. 1981. 24.50x (ISBN 0-8032-1958-X); pap. 9.75 (ISBN 0-8032-6854-8, BB 757, Bison). U of Nebr Pr.
Vexler, R. I. Wyoming Chronology & Factbook, Vol. 50. 1978. 8.50 (ISBN 0-379-16189-3). Oceana.

X

X CHROMOSOME
see Sex Chromosomes
X-RAY DIAGNOSIS
see Diagnosis, Radioscopic
X-RAY MICROSCOPE
Parsons, Donald F., ed. Ultrasoft X-Ray Microscopy: Its Application to Biological & Physical Sciences. (N.Y. Academy of Sciences: Vol. 342). 402p. 1980. 70.00 (ISBN 0-89766-066-8); pap. write for info. (ISBN 0-89766-067-6). NY Acad Sci.
X-RAY SPECTROSCOPY
Bruce, W. R. & Johns, H. E. The Spectra of X Rays Scattered in Low Atomic Number Materials. 1980. 10.00x (Pub. by Brit Inst Radiology). State Mutual Bk.
Heinrich, Kurt F. Electron Beam X-Ray Microanalysis. 608p. 1980. text ed. 42.50 (ISBN 0-442-23286-1). Van Nos Reinhold.
X-RAYS
see also Diagnosis, Radioscopic; Electron Spectroscopy; Electron Spectroscopy; Radiotherapy; Vacuum-Tubes; X-Ray Microscope; X-Ray Spectroscopy
Beaman, Donald R., et al, eds. Eighth International Congress on X-Ray Optics & Microanalysis. LC 77-18656. 665p. 90.00 (ISBN 0-87812-180-3). Pendell Pub.
Bonnelle, C. & Mande, C., eds. Advances in X-Ray Spectroscopy: A Reference Text in Honour of Professor Y Cauchois. (Illus.). 400p. 1981. 60.00 (ISBN 0-08-025266-4). Pergamon.
Du Boulay, G. H. Principles of X-Ray Diagnosis of the Skull. 2nd ed. (Illus.). 384p. 1979. text ed. 115.00x. Butterworths.
Graham, Daniel & Thomson, John. Grenz Rays: An Illustrated Guide to the Theory & Practical Applications of Soft X-Rays. LC 79-42745. (Illus.). 164p. 1980. 24.00 (ISBN 0-08-025525-6). Pergamon.
Rhodes, John S., et al, eds. Advances in X-Ray Analysis, Vol. 23. 400p. 1980. 45.00 (ISBN 0-306-40435-4). Plenum Pub.
X-RAYS–THERAPEUTIC USE
see Radiotherapy
X-RAYS IN DENTISTRY
see Teeth–Radiography
XENOPHON
Chrimes, K. M. T. The Respublica Lacedaemoniorum Ascribed to Xenophon. 119p. 1948. 24.00x (ISBN 0-7190-1207-4, Pub. by Manchester U Pr England). State Mutual Bk.
XYLOGRAPHY
see Wood-Engravings

Y

Y CHROMOSOME
see Sex Chromosomes
YACHT RACING
Page, Frank. Alone Against the Atlantic: The Observer Single-Handed Transatlantic Race, 1960-1980. LC 80-69349. (Illus.). 128p. 1981. 27.00x (ISBN 0-7153-8116-4). David & Charles.
YACHTS AND YACHTING
see also Sailing; Yacht Racing
Fagan, Brian. Passagemakers Guide from San Francisco to Ensenada. (Illus.). 120p. (Orig.). 1981. pap. 12.95 (ISBN 0-88496-161-3). Capra Pr.
Jones, Charles. Glass Fibre Yachts: Improvement & Repair. 128p. 1980. 12.00x (Pub. by Nautical England). State Mutual Bk.
Odin, Paula & Odin, Dexter. Yachtsman's Legal Guide to Co-Ownership. 1981. 10.00 (ISBN 0-686-69463-5). De Graff.
Stephens, W. P. Traditions & Memories of American Yachting: Complete Edition. LC 80-83038. (Illus.). 384p. write for info. (ISBN 0-87742-132-3). Intl Marine.
Time-Life Books Editors & Whipple, A. B. The Racing Yachts. (The Seafarers Ser.). (Illus.). 176p. 1981. 14.95 (ISBN 0-8094-2693-5). Time-Life.
YACHTS AND YACHTING–HISTORY
Martin, Fred W. Nineteen Hundred & One Album of Designs for Boats, Launches & Yachts. rev. ed. LC 80-69290. (Illus.). 80p. 1980. pap. 5.00. Altair Pub Co.
YAKIMA INDIANS
see Indians of North America–Northwest, Pacific
YANA INDIANS
see Indians of North America–Southwest, New
YANOMAMO
Lizot, Jacques. Circle of Fires: Life Among the Yanomami. Simon, Ernest, tr. from Fr. 224p. 1981. 22.50x (ISBN 0-8476-6968-8). Rowman.
YEARBOOKS
see also Almanacs; Calendars
also subdivision Yearbooks under special subjects, e.g. Literature–Yearbooks; Medicine–Yearbooks
Pragnell, Mervyn O. & Keillor, Jean-Pierre, eds. International Yearbook & Statesman's Who's Who. 28th ed. LC 53-1425. 1454p. 1980. 105.00x (ISBN 0-610-00526-X). Intl Pubns Serv.
World Book-Childcraft International, Inc. Today, 1981: A Personal Record & Reference Book. LC 76-27228. (World Book Today Yearly Diaries Ser.). (Illus.). 192p. 1980. write for info. (ISBN 0-7166-2032-4). World Bk-Childcraft.
YEATS, WILLIAM BUTLER, 1865-1939
Dougan, R. O. W. B. Yeats, Manuscripts & Printed Books, Exhibited in the Library of Trinity College, Dublin. 50p. 1980. Repr. of 1956 ed. lib. bdg. 10.00 (ISBN 0-8492-4216-9). R West.
Harper. Critical Edition of Yeats' A Vision. 1980. text ed. 42.50x (ISBN 0-333-21299-1). Humanities.
Jeffares, A. Norman. Yeats, Sligo & Ireland. 1981. text ed. 23.50x (ISBN 0-86140-041-0). Humanities.
Jeffares, A. Norman, ed. Yeats, Sligo & Ireland: Essays to Mark the 21st Yeats International Summer School. (Irish Literary Studies: No. 6). 267p. 1980. 24.75x (ISBN 0-389-20095-6). B&N.
Krimm, Bernard G. W. B. Yeats & the Emergence of the Irish Free State, 1918-1939: Living in the Explosion. 324p. 1981. 20.00x (ISBN 0-87875-200-5). Whitston Pub.
O'Hara, Daniel T. Tragic Knowledge: Yeat's Autobiography & Hermeneutics. LC 80-26825. 224p. 1981. 20.00x (ISBN 0-231-05204-9). Columbia U Pr.
Thuente, Mary W. W. B. Yeats & Irish Folklore. 286p. 1981. 26.50x (ISBN 0-389-20161-8). B&N.
Wrenn, Charles L. W. B. Yeats: A Literary Study. 50p. 1980. Repr. of 1920 ed. lib. bdg. 10.00 (ISBN 0-8492-2998-7). R West.
YELLS
see Cheers and Cheerleading
YOGA
Alfassa, Mira. Glimpses of the Mother's Life, Vol. 2. Das, Nilima, ed. 335p. 1980. 11.00 (ISBN 0-89071-291-3). Matagiri.
Cooper, Joan. The Ancient Teaching of Yoga & the Spiritual Evolution of Man. 218p. 1980. 14.75x (ISBN 0-7050-0064-8, Pub. by Skilton & Shaw England). State Mutual Bk.
Dass, Baba Hari. A Child's Garden of Yoga. LC 80-80299. (Illus.). 108p. (Orig.). (gr. 3-12). 1980. pap. 5.95 (ISBN 0-918100-02-X). Starmont Hse.
Dasss, Baba Hari, et al. Silence Speaks--from the Chalkboard of Baba Hari Dass. LC 76-53902. (Illus.). 224p. (Orig.). 1977. pap. 4.95 (ISBN 0-918100-01-1). SRI Rama.
De Segonzac, Catherine. Jewish Yoga: A System of Visualization & Movement Rooted in Genesis. 208p. 1981. pap. 7.95 (ISBN 0-87728-529-2). Weiser.
Houston, Ralph. Talk Does Not Cook the Rice: The Teachings of Agni Yoga. Phillips, Amelia, ed. 416p. 1981. pap. 7.95 (ISBN 0-87728-530-6). Weiser.
Kriyananda, Swami. The Story of Search for Meaning: An Autobiography. abr. ed. 240p. 1980. pap. 3.95 (ISBN 0-916124-19-3). Ananda.
Michaelle. Yoga & Prayer. Cumming, Diane, tr. pap. 6.50 (ISBN 0-87061-059-7). Chr Classics.
Patanjali. Patanjali's Yoga Sutras. 2nd ed. Prasada, Rama, tr. from Sanskrit. 321p. 1981. Repr. of 1912 ed. 15.95 (ISBN 0-89744-996-7, Pub. by Orient Reprint India). Auromere.
Pearce, Joseph C. The Bond of Power. 1981. 10.95 (ISBN 0-525-06950-X). Dutton.
Rawls, Eugene. A Handbook of Yoga for Modern Living. (Orig.). pap. 1.50 (ISBN 0-515-00958-X). Jove Pubns.
Shekhawat, Virenda. Yoga: The Technique of Liberation. 90p. 1979. text ed. 7.50 (ISBN 0-89684-264-9, Pub. by Sterling India). Orient Bk Dist.
Sri Aurobindo. Bases of Yoga. 168p. 1979. pap. 1.75 (ISBN 0-89071-288-3, Pub. by Sri Aurobindo Ashram India). Matagiri.
Yogi Vithaldas. Yoga System of Health. 1981. pap. 3.95 (ISBN 0-686-69341-8). Cornerstone.
YOGA, HATHA
Iyengar, B. K. Light on Pranayama: The Yogic Art of Breathing. 320p. 1981. 12.95 (ISBN 0-8245-0048-2). Crossroad NY.
Klipper, Ilse. My Magic Garden. (Illus., Orig.). (gr. 2-6). 1980. pap. 4.95 (ISBN 0-9605022-0-3). Pathway Pr.
Swami Muktananda. Kundalini-the Secret of Life. (Illus., Orig.). 1979. pap. 3.25 (ISBN 0-914602-47-0). SYDA Found.
--Reflections of the Self. LC 80-50391. (Illus., Orig.). 1980. pap. 5.95 (ISBN 0-914602-50-0). SYDA Found.
YOGA EXERCISES
see Yoga, Hatha
YOM KIPPUR WAR, 1973
see Israel-Arab War, 1973
YORKSHIRE, ENGLAND
Herriot, James. James Herriot's Yorkshire. (Illus.). 224p. 1981. pap. 9.95 (ISBN 0-312-43971-7). St Martin.
YORUBAN FOLK-SONGS
see Folk-Songs, Yoruban
YOSEMITE NATIONAL PARK
Jores, William R. Ten Trail Trips in Yosemite National Park. (Illus.). 1980. pap. 3.95 (ISBN 0-89646-064-9). Outbooks.

YOUNG, BRIGHAM, 1801-1877
Brigham Young: The New York Years. (Charles Redd Monographs in Western History: No. 12). (Illus.). 1981. pap. text ed. 6.95 (ISBN 0-8425-1942-4). Brigham.
Cooley, Everett L., ed. Diary of Brigham Young, 1857. (Utah, the Mormons, & the West Ser). 132p. 1981. 17.50 (ISBN 0-87480-195-8, Tanner). U of Utah Pr.
Harrison, et al. Brigham Young. (Illus.). 35p. (gr. 1-9). 1981. 2.95 (ISBN 0-86575-188-9). Dormac.
YOUNG, EDWARD, 1683-1765
Vines, Sherard. Georgian Satirists: Edward Young, Christopher Smart, Charles Churchill. 217p. 1980. Repr. of 1934 ed. lib. bdg. 25.00 (ISBN 0-8495-5528-0). Arden Lib.
YOUNG PEOPLE'S MEETINGS (CHURCH WORK)
Robinson, James H. & Darline, R. One Hundred Bible Quiz Activities for Church School Classes. 1981. pap. 3.95 (ISBN 0-570-03829-4, 12-2794). Concordia.
YOUNG'S MODULUS
see Elasticity
YOUTH
see also Adolescence; Children; Conduct of Life; Etiquette for Children and Youth; Marriage Counseling; Recreation Centers; Social Work with Youth
The Activities of Some Centres Engaged in Research & Information Programmes in the Field of Youth. 212p. 1980. pap. 15.00 (UN80-4-2, UN). Unipub.
Eagan, Andrea B. Why Am I So Miserable If These Are the Best Years of My Life? 1979. pap. 2.25 (ISBN 0-380-46136-6, 46136). Avon.
Kelly & Landers. Today's Teen. rev. ed. (gr. 7-9). 1981. text ed. 14.60 (ISBN 0-87002-323-3). Bennett IL.
Milbauer, Barbara. Teenagers in Other Societies. 192p. (gr. 7 up). 1981. write for info. (ISBN 0-671-32891-3). Messner.
Rice, F. Phillip. The Adolescent: Development, Relationships, & Culture. 3rd ed. 700p. 1981. text ed. 17.95 (ISBN 0-205-07303-4, 2473038); free tchr's ed. (ISBN 0-205-07304-2). Allyn.
YOUTH-CONDUCT OF LIFE
Baker, Pat. Help! I've Just Given Birth to a Teenager. 128p. (Orig.). 1981. pap. 4.95 (ISBN 0-8010-0799-2). Baker Bk.
Hoff, Syd. Dinosaur Do's & Don't's. LC 80-13729. (Illus.). 48p. (ps-2). 1980. pap. 2.95 (ISBN 0-671-41200-0, Pub. by Windmill). S&S.
YOUTH-EMPLOYMENT
see also Vocational Guidance
Reubens, Beatrice G. The Youth Labor Force. LC 80-67390. (Conservation of Human Resources Ser.: No. 13). 1981. text ed. 32.50 (ISBN 0-86598-027-6). Allanheld.
YOUTH-HEALTH AND HYGIENE
Aten, Marilyn J. & McAnarney, Elizabeth R. A Behavioral Approach to the Care of Adolescents. 200p. 1981. pap. text ed. 10.50 (ISBN 0-8016-3201-3). Mosby.
Comerci, George D., et al. Adolescent Medicine Case Studies. LC 78-61736. 1979. pap. 18.00 (ISBN 0-87488-053-X). Med Exam.
Lauton, Barry & Freese, Arthur. You & Your Adolescent. 2244p. 1981. 9.95 (ISBN 0-684-16819-7, ScribT). Scribner.
Lauton, Barry & Freese, Arthur S. The Healthy Adolescent: A Parent's Manual. 224p. 1981. 10.95 (ISBN 0-684-16819-7). Scribner.
YOUTH-LAW AND LEGISLATION
see Children-Law
YOUTH-LITERARY COLLECTIONS
Lenz, Millicent & Mahood, Ramona, eds. Young Adult Literature: Background & Criticisms. LC 80-23489. 524p. 1980. 30.00 (ISBN 0-8389-0302-9). ALA.
YOUTH-POLITICAL ACTIVITY
Jennings, M. Kent & Niemi, Richard G. Generations & Politics: A Panel Study of Young Adults & Their Parents. LC 80-8555. (Illus.). 408p. 1981. 25.00x (ISBN 0-691-07626-X); pap. 6.95x (ISBN 0-691-02201-1). Princeton U Pr.
Sigel, Roberta S. & Hoskin, Marilyn. The Political Involvement of Adolescents. 320p. 1981. 22.00 (ISBN 0-8135-0897-5). Rutgers U Pr.
YOUTH-PSYCHOLOGY
see Adolescent Psychology
YOUTH-RELIGIOUS LIFE
see also Jesus People
Harris, Maria. Portrait of Youth Ministry: Young People & the Church. 224p. (Orig.). 1981. pap. 7.95 (ISBN 0-8091-2354-1). Paulist Pr.
YOUTH-LATIN AMERICA
Escobar, Samuel. Irrupcion Juvenil. LC 77-17648. 96p. (Orig., Span.). 1978. pap. 1.95 (ISBN 0-89922-106-8). Edit Caribe.
YOUTH AND ALCOHOL
see Alcohol and Youth
YOUTH CENTERS
see Recreation Centers
YOUTH EMPLOYMENT
see Youth-Employment
YOUTH IN POLITICS
see Youth-Political Activity
YOUTH MOVEMENT
McNeil, Don. Moving Through Here. 252p. 10.95 (ISBN 0-934558-08-6); pap. 5.95 (ISBN 0-934558-09-4). Entwhistle Bks.
YUAN, SHIH-K'AI, 1859-1916
MacKinnon, Stephen R. Power & Politics in Late Imperial China: Yuan Shi-kai in Beijing & Tianjin, 1901-1908. (Center for Chinese Studies Ser.). (Illus.). 400p. 1981. 18.50x (ISBN 0-520-04025-2). U of Cal Pr.
YUCHI INDIANS
see Indians of North America-Eastern States
YUGOSLAVIA-ECONOMIC CONDITIONS
Tyson, Laura D. The Yugoslav Economic System & Its Performance in the Nineteen Seventies. LC 80-24650. (Research Ser.: No. 44). x, 115p. 1980. pap. 4.50x (ISBN 0-87725-144-4). U Cal LA Indus Rel.
YUKON TERRITORY
Theberge, John. Kluane: Pinnacle of the Yukon. LC 80-1078. (Illus.). 224p. 1981. 35.00 (ISBN 0-385-17122-6). Doubleday.

Z

ZAHARIAS, BABE DIDRIKSON, 1911-1956
Hahn, James & Hahn, Lynn. Babe! Mildred Didrickson Zaharias. Schroeder, Howard, ed. (Sports Legends Ser.). (Illus.). 48p. (Orig.). (gr. 3-5). 1981. PLB 5.95 (ISBN 0-89686-122-8); pap. text ed. 2.95 (ISBN 0-89686-137-6). Crestwood Hse.
ZAIRE-HISTORY
Reefe, Thomas O. The Rainbow & the Kings: A History of the Luba Empire to 1891. 1981. 21.00x (ISBN 0-520-04140-2). U of Cal Pr.
ZAMBESIA-HISTORY
Vail, Leroy & White, Landeg. Capitalism & Colonialism in Mozambique: A Study of the Quelimane District. LC 80-22702. (Illus.). 424p. 1981. 45.00x (ISBN 0-8166-1039-8). U of Minn Pr.
ZAMBIA
Shaw, Timothy M. & Anglin, Douglas G. Alternative Sources of Event Data on Zambian Foreign Policy. (Foreign & Comparative Studies Program, African Ser.: No. XXXVI). 1981. pap. text ed. price not set (ISBN 0-915984-60-1). Syracuse U Foreign Comp.
Van Binsbergen, Wim M. J. Religious Change in Zambia: Exploratory Studies. (Monographs from the African Studies Centre, Leiden). (Illus.). 416p. 1981. price not set (ISBN 0-7103-0000-X). Routledge & Kegan.
ZANUCK, DARRYL FRANCIS, 1902-
Gussow, Mel. Don't Say Yes Until I Finish Talking. (Illus.). 318p. Date not set. pap. 7.95 (ISBN 0-306-80132-9). Da Capo.
ZANZIBAR
Baily, Martin. Union of Tanganyika & Zanzibar-a Study in Political Intergration. (Foreign & Comparative Studies-Eastern African Ser.: No.9). 114p. 1973. pap. 4.50x (ISBN 0-915984-05-9). Syracuse U Foreign Comp.
Cooper, Frederick. From Slaves to Squatters: Plantation Labor & Agriculture in Zanibar & Coastal Kenya, 1890-1925. LC 80-5391. (Illus.). 352p. 1981. text ed. 25.00 (ISBN 0-300-02454-1). Yale U Pr.
ZEBRA PARAKEET
see Budgerigars
ZEN BUDDHISM
Hammitzch, Horst. Zen in the Art of Tea Ceremony. 104p. 1981. 7.95 (ISBN 0-312-89859-2). St Martin.
Johnston, William. Christian Zen: A Way of Meditation. 2nd ed. LC 80-8430. (Illus.). 144p. 1981. pap. 4.95 (ISBN 0-06-064198-3, RD 343, HarpR). Har-Row.
Kasulis, T. P. Zen Action-Zen Person. LC 80-27858. 192p. 1980. 12.95 (ISBN 0-8248-0702-2). U Pr of Hawaii.
Mountain, Marian. The Zen Environment: The Impact of Zen Meditation. 288p. 1981. 10.95 (ISBN 0-688-00350-8). Morrow.
Owens, Claire M. Zen & the Lady. LC 79-50288. 311p. (Orig.). 1981. pap. 6.95 (ISBN 0-88238-996-3). Great Eastern.
Stryk, Lucien. Encounter with Zen: Writings on Poetry & Zen. 1981. 16.95 (ISBN 0-8040-0405-6); pap. 8.95 (ISBN 0-8040-0406-4). Swallow.
ZEN BUDDHIST LITERATURE
see Zen Literature
ZEN LITERATURE
Chase, Mildred P. Just Being at the Piano. LC 80-8999. 112p. (Orig.). 1981. 9.95 (ISBN 0-915238-44-6); pap. 5.95 (ISBN 0-915238-45-4). Peace Pr.
Yuasa, Nobuyuki, tr. from Jap. The Zen Poems of Ryokan. LC 80-8585. (Princeton lbrary of Asian Translations). (Illus.). 196p. 1981. 17.50x (ISBN 0-691-06466-0). Princeton U Pr.
ZEOLITES
Scott, Jeanette, ed. Zeolite Technology & Applications: Recent Advances. LC 80-19308. (Chemical Tech. Rev. 170). (Illus.). 381p. 1981. 64.00 (ISBN 0-8155-0817-4). Noyes.
ZEPHYR AUTOMOBILE
see Automobiles, Foreign-Types-Zephyr
ZHABOTINSKII, VLADIMIR EUGENEVICH
see Jabotinsky, Vladimir Eugenevich, 1880-1940
ZIMBABWE, MASHONALAND
Chanaiwa, David. Zimbabwe Controversy-a Case of Colonial Historiography. (Foreign & Comparative Studies-Eastern African Ser.: No. 8). 142p. 1973. pap. 4.50x (ISBN 0-915984-05-9). Syracuse U Foreign Comp.
Pollak, Oliver & Pollak, Karen. Rhodesia-Zimbabwe. (World Bibliographical Ser.: No. 4). 197p. 1979. 25.25 (ISBN 0-903450-14-3). ABC-Clio.
Zimbabwe Directory 1980-81: Including Botswana. 71st ed. LC 38-1460. Orig. Title: Rhodesia Directory. (Illus.). 996p. (Orig.). 1980. pap. 45.00x (ISBN 0-8002-2747-6). Intl Pubns Serv.
ZINC
Morgan, S. W. Zinc & Its Alloys. (Illus.). 224p. 1977. pap. 13.95x (ISBN 0-7121-0945-5, Pub. by Macdonald & Evans England). Intl Ideas.
ZION NATIONAL PARK
Rudig, Doug. Zion Adventure Guide. 32p. 1978. 1.95. Zion.
Yandell, M. D. National Parkways, Zion & Bryce Canyon National Parks. (Illus.). 64p. 1972. 2.95. Zion.
ZIONISM
Here are entered works dealing with the movement looking toward the creation and maintenance of a Jewish state or a national home in Palestine.
see also Jews-Political and Social Conditions
Alexander, Yona & Chertoff, Mordecai, eds. Bibliography on Israel & Zionism. 1980. write for info. Herzl Pr.
Cohen, Saul B. Jerusalem Undivided. 1980. pap. 3.00 (ISBN 0-930832-58-2). Herzl Pr.
Davis, Moshe, ed. Zionism in Transition. 1980. pap. 8.00 (ISBN 0-930832-61-2). Herzl Pr.
Glubb, Faris. Zionist Relations with Nazi Germany. 3.00. New World Press NY.
Kaganoff, Nathan M., ed. Solidarity & Kinship: Essays on American Zionism. (Illus.). 1980. 5.00. Am Jewish Hist Soc.
Karta, Neturei. Judaism & Zionism: Principles & Definitions. 1980. lib. bdg. 59.95 (ISBN 0-686-68745-0). Revisionist Pr.
Marmorstein, Emil. The Murder of Jacob De Haan by the Zionists: A Martyr's Message. 1980. lib. bdg. 59.95 (ISBN 0-686-68747-7). Revisionist Pr.
Meah Shaerim Centennial: A Study of the Neturei Karta. 1980. lib. bdg. 59.95 (ISBN 0-686-68746-9). Revisionist Pr.
Navon, Yitzhak. The Six Days & the Seven Gates. 1980. 6.00 (ISBN 0-930832-57-4); pap. 4.00. Herzl Pr.
Rose, Norman. Lewis Namier & Zionism. 192p. 1980. 29.50x (ISBN 0-19-822621-7). Oxford U Pr.
Rotenstreich, Nathan, ed. Essays on Zionism & the Contemporary Jewish Condition. 1981. price not set. Herzl Pr.
Ruoff, Norman D., ed. The Writings of President Frederick M. Smith, Vol. III: The Zionic Enterprise. 1981. pap. price not set (ISBN 0-8309-0300-3). Herald Hse.
Urofsky, Melvin, ed. Essays in American Zionism Nineteen-Seventeen to Nineteen Forty-Eight. 1979. 12.50 (ISBN 0-930832-56-6). Herzl Pr.
Weismandel, Michael B. Ten Questions to the Zionists or, Zionist Complicity in Nazi War Atrocities. 1980. lib. bdg. 59.95 (ISBN 0-686-68886-4). Revisionist Pr.
ZODIAC
Anrais, David. Man & the Zodiac. pap. 5.95 (ISBN 0-87728-014-2). Weiser.
Moore, Eric V. Rhythm of the Zodiac & the Wisdom Dinner. LC 80-51680. (Illus.). 80p. (Orig.). 1980. pap. 4.00 (ISBN 0-937236-00-4, 4W). Sonrise Prods.
ZONING LAW
see also Building Laws
Garon, Philip A. Zoning Law Anthology, Vol. Ii. LC 78-66283. 1980. 59.95. Intl Lib.
ZOO
see Zoological Gardens
ZOOGEOGRAPHY
see also Animal Migration
Berger, Gilda. All in the Family: Animal Species Around the World. (Science Is What & Why Bk.). (Illus.). 48p. (gr. 7-10). 1981. PLB 5.99 (ISBN 0-698-30730-5). Coward.
ZOOLOGICAL GARDENS
Bendiner, Robert. The Fall of the Wild, the Rise of the Zoo. (Illus.). 256p. 1981. 13.95 (ISBN 0-525-10270-1). Dutton.
Serventy, Vincent. Zoo Walkabout. 160p. 1980. 17.95x (ISBN 0-00-216420-5, Pub. by W Collins Australia). Intl Schol Bk Serv.
ZOOLOGICAL SPECIMENS-COLLECTION AND PRESERVATION
Ashworth, J. H. Catalogue of the Chaetopoda in the British Museum (Natural History) A. Polychaeta. (Illus.). xii, 175p. 1912. 15.00x (ISBN 0-565-00102-7, Pub. by British Mus Nat Hist England). Sabbot-Natural Hist Bks.
Clark, Hubert L. Catalogue of the Recent Sea-Urchins (Echinoidea) in the Collection of the British Museum (Natural History) (Illus.). xxviii, 250p. 1925. 21.00x (ISBN 0-565-00165-5, Pub. by British Mus Nat Hist England). Sabbot-Natural Hist Bks.
Gunther, Albert. Catalogue of Colubrine Snakes in the Collection of the British Museum. xvi, 281p. 1971. Repr. of 1858 ed. 4.50x (ISBN 0-565-00709-2, Pub. by British Mus Nat Hist England). Sabbot-Natural Hist Bks.
Theodor, Oskar. An Illustrated Catalogue of the Rothschild Collection of Nycteribiidae (Diptera) in the British Museum (Natural History) (Illus.). viii, 506p. 1967. 66.50x (ISBN 0-565-00655-X, Pub. by British Mus Nat Hist England). Sabbot-Natural Hist Bks.
ZOOLOGY
see also Anatomy, Comparative; Animals; Animals, Habits and Behavior of; Aquatic Animals; Domestic Animals; Embryology; Entomology; Evolution; Extinct Animals; Fresh-Water Biology; Fresh-Water Fauna; Laboratory Animals; Marine Fauna; Ornithology; Paleontology; Physiology, Comparative; Poisonous Animals; Psychology, Comparative; Zoogeography; Zoological Specimens-Collection and Preservation; Zoology, Experimental
also divisions, classes, orders, etc. of the animal kingdom, e.g. Invertebrates, Vertebrates; Birds, Insects, Mammals; Crustacea, and particular animals, e.g. Bears, Rabbits
Florkin, Marcel & Sheer, Bradley T., eds. Chemical Zoology. 11 vols. Incl. Vol. 1. 1967. 72.50 (ISBN 0-12-261031-8); Vol. 2. 1968. 62.50 (ISBN 0-12-261032-6); Vol. 3. 1968. 68.50 (ISBN 0-12-261033-4); Vol. 4. 1969. 58.50 (ISBN 0-12-261034-2); Vol. 5. 1970. 52.50 (ISBN 0-12-261035-0); Vol. 6. 1971. 58.50 (ISBN 0-12-261036-9); Vol. 7. 1972. 57.00 (ISBN 0-12-261037-7); Vol. 8. 1974. 75.00 (ISBN 0-12-261038-5); Vol. 9. 1974. 72.50 (ISBN 0-12-261039-3); Vol. 10. 1978. 56.50 (ISBN 0-12-261040-7); Vol. 11. Mammalia. 1979. 49.50 (ISBN 0-12-261041-5). LC 67-23158. Set. 588.75. Acad Pr.
Kolisko, Eugen. Zoology for Everybody, Vol. 4: Protozoa. 1980. pap. 4.25x (ISBN 0-906492-24-6, Pub. by Kolisko Archives). St George Bk Serv.
Lawrence, R. D. The Zoo That Never Was. LC 80-18956. (Illus.). 304p. 1981. 12.95 (ISBN 0-03-056811-0). HR&W.
ZOOLOGY-ECOLOGY
see Animal Ecology
ZOOLOGY-GEOGRAPHICAL DISTRIBUTION
see Zoogeography
ZOOLOGY-JUVENILE LITERATURE
see also Nature Study-Juvenile Literature
Berger, Gilda. All in the Family: Animal Species Around the World. (Science Is What & Why Bk.). (Illus.). 48p. (gr. 7-10). 1981. PLB 5.99 (ISBN 0-698-30730-5). Coward.
ZOOLOGY-LABORATORY MANUALS
see also Dissection
Hartman, Margaret & Russell, Mercer P. Laboratory Manual for Biology of Animals. 1980. coil binding 7.50 (ISBN 0-88252-108-X). Paladin Hse.
Wodsedalek, J. E., ed. General Zoology Laboratory Guide: Shortversion. 8th ed. Lytle, Charles F. 237p. 1981. write for info. wire coil. Wm C Brown.
ZOOLOGY-MORPHOLOGY
see Anatomy, Comparative
ZOOLOGY-AFRICA
Matthiessen, Peter. Sand Rivers. LC 80-36703. (Illus.). 240p. 1981. 19.95 (ISBN 0-670-61696-6, Studio). Viking Pr.
ZOOLOGY-AMERICA
Collins, Henry H., Jr., ed. Harper & Row's Complete Field Guide to North American Wildlife: Eastern Edition. LC 80-8198. (Illus.). 810p. 1981. 17.50 (ISBN 0-690-01977-7, HarpT); flexible vinyl cover 12.95 (ISBN 0-690-01969-6). Har-Row.
ZOOLOGY, EXPERIMENTAL
Sperlinger, David. Animals in Research: New Perspectives in Animal Experimentation. 384p. 1980. 49.50 (ISBN 0-471-27843-2, Pub. by Wiley-Interscience). Wiley.
ZOOLOGY OF THE BIBLE
see Bible-Natural History
ZOONOSES
Beran, George. Viral Zoonoses. (CRC Handbook in Zoonoses Sect B: Vol. 1). 480p. 1981. 64.95 (ISBN 0-8493-2911-6). CRC Pr.
Beran, George, ed. Viral Zoonoses. (Handbook Series in Zoonoses Sect. B: Vol. 2). 464p. 1981. 64.95 (ISBN 0-8493-2912-4). CRC Pr.
ZOOPHYTA
see Coelenterata
ZOOTOMY
see Anatomy, Comparative

KEY TO PUBLISHERS' AND DISTRIBUTORS' ABBREVIATIONS

The following is a list of abbreviations for publishers and distributors names used in the listing of *BOOKS IN PRINT SUPPLEMENT 1980-1981*. The entries in this list contain: Full name, ISBN prefix, editorial address, telephone number, ordering address (if different from the editorial address), and imprints following the abbreviation. For example:

Bowker, (Bowker, R. R., Co., 0-8352), A Xerox Publishing Co., 1180 Ave. of the Americas, New York, NY 10036 Tel 212-764-5100; Orders To: P.O. Box 1807, Ann Arbor, MI 48106.

Titles which include the words "Pub. by" should be ordered from the distributor, not the publisher. For example, the title listed below should be ordered from Merrimack Bk Serv.

Land Girl at Large Frances Wilding. 1972 5.95 (ISBN 0-236-17693-5, Pub. by Paul Eleck) Merrimack Bk Serv.

A A Spohler, *(Spohler, Albert A.),* P.O. Box 2322, Palos Verdes, CA 90274 Tel 213-375-7775; 5417 Littlebow Rd., Palos Verdes, CA 90274.

A & W Pubs, *(A & W Pubs., Inc.; 0-89479),* 95 Madison Ave., New York, NY 10016 Tel 212-725-4970; Do Not Confuse with A-W, Addison-Wesley Publishing Co., Inc.

A & W Visual Library
See A & W Pubs

A Cartwright
See N P Cartwright

A Frommer
See Frommer-Pasmantier

A G Peterson, *(Peterson, Arthur G.),* P.O. Box 252, DeBary, FL 32713 Tel 305-668-6587.

A G Sweetser, *(Sweetser, Albert G.; 0-9605500),* 17 Broadleaf Dr., Clifton Park, NY 12065 Tel 518-371-7674.

A Glaser, *(Glaser, Anton; 0-9600324),* 1237 Whitney Rd., Southampton, PA 18966 Tel 215-357-6306.

A Gonshorowski, *(Gonshorowski, Addie; 0-9600982),* (Addie's Recipe Box), Drawer 5426-B, Eugene, OR 97405 Tel 503-343-5868.

A H Clark, *(Clark, Arthur H., Co.; 0-87062),* P.O. Box 230, Glendale, CA 91209 Tel 213-245-9119.

A Hardy & Assocs, *(Hardy, Arthur, & Associates; 0-930892),* P.O. Box 8058, New Orleans, LA 70182 Tel 504-282-2326.

A Hyde, *(Hyde, Arnout; 0-9604590),* 418 Lehigh Terrace, Charleston, WV 25302.

A J Phillips, *(Phillips, A.J.; 0-9605268),* 245-38 W. Bobier Dr., Vista, CA 92083.

A J Pub, *(A. J. Publishing Co.; 0-914190),* P.O. Box 3012, Duluth, MN 55803 Tel 218-722-3253.

A James Bks
See Alicejamesbooks

A Jones, *(Jones, Anson, Press; 0-912432),* P.O. Box 65, Salado, TX 76571 Tel 817-947-5414.

A L Kerth, *(Kerth, A. L.; 0-9601188),* Jericho Run, Buckland Valley Farms, Washington Crossing, PA 18977.

A M Newman, *(Newman, Albert M., Enterprises),* P.O. Box 88196, Honolulu, HI 96815 Tel 808-923-4489.

A M Rymer
See Rymer Bks

A Meriwether, *(Meriwether, Arthur, Education Resources, Inc.; 0-916260),* Div. of Arthur Meriwether Educational Resources, Inc., P.O. Box 457, 1529 Brook Dr., Downers Grove, IL 60515 Tel 312-495-0300.

A N Palmer, *(Palmer, A. N., Co., The; 0-914268),* 1720 W. Irving Park Rd., Schaumburg, IL 60193 Tel 800-323-9563.

A P M Pr, *(A.P.M. Press; 0-937612),* 650 Ocean Ave., Brooklyn, NY 11226.

A R Koester Bks, *(Koester, Arthur R., Books; 0-9602558),* P.O. Box 344, Burbank, CA 91503.

A R Liss, *(Liss, Alan R., Inc.; 0-8451),* 150 Fifth Ave., New York, NY 10011 Tel 212-741-2515.

A R Pragare
See Pine Mntn

A S Barnes, *(Barnes, A. S., & Co., Inc.; 0-498),* 11175 Flintkote Ave., Suite C, San Diego, CA 92121 Tel 714-457-3200.

A T Weinberg, *(Weinberg, Alyce T.; 0-9604552),* Box 16, Braddock Heights, MD 21714.

A-W, *(Addison-Wesley Publishing Co., Inc.; 0-201),* Jacob Way, Reading, MA 01867 Tel 617-944-3700. *Imprints:* A-W Childrens (Addison-Wesley Children's Books); Adv Bk Prog (Advance Book Program).

A-W Childrens *Imprint of* **A-W**

A Whitman, *(Whitman, Albert, & Co.; 0-8075),* 560 W. Lake St., Chicago, IL 60606 Tel 312-782-7536.

A Yards, *(Yards, A.; 0-9603108),* P.O. Box 4428, Mountain View, CA 94040 Tel 415-961-0741.

AA *Imprint of* **U of Mich Pr**

AAASPD, *(American Assn. for the Advancement of Science, Pacific Division; 0-934394),* c/o California Academy of Sciences, San Francisco, CA 94118.

AACTE, *(American Assn. of Colleges for Teacher Education; 0-910052; 0-89333),* One Dupont Circle, Suite 610, Washington, DC 20036 Tel 202-293-2450.

AAES, *(American Assn. of Engineering Societies; 0-87615),* 345 E. 47th St., New York, NY 10017 Tel 212-644-7840.

AAFH, *(Academy of American Franciscan History; 0-88382),* P.O. Box 34440, Washington, DC 20034 Tel 301-365-1763.

AAI, *(African-American Institute; 0-87862),* 833 United Nations Plaza, New York, NY 10017 Tel 212-949-5727.

AAP, *(Assn. of American Pubs., Inc.; 0-933636),* 1 Park Ave., New York, NY 10016 Tel 212-689-8920.

Aardvark Pubs, *(Aardvark Pubs. Inc.; 0-917384),* Div. of Bookthrift, Inc., One West 39th St., New York, NY 10018 Tel 212-221-4610.

Aaron Pubs, *(Aaron Pubs., Inc.; 0-936076),* P.O. Box 2572, Sarasota, FL 33578.

AASHTO, *(American Assn. of State Highway & Transportation Officials),* 444 N. Capitol St., N.W., Suite 225, Washington, DC 20001 Tel 202-624-5800.

AASLH, *(American Assn. for State & Local History; 0-910050),* 1400 Eighth Ave., S., Nashville, TN 37203.

Aatec Pubns, *(Aatec Pubns.; 0-937948),* P.O. Box 7119, Ann Arbor, MI 48107.

AAU Pubns, *(Amateur Athletic Union of the United States; 0-89710),* 3400 W. 86th St., Indianapolis, IN 46268 Tel 317-872-2900.

AAWS, *(Alcoholics Anonymous World Services, Inc.; 0-916856),* 468 Park Ave. S., New York, NY 10016 Tel 212-686-1100; Orders to: Box 459, Grand Central Sta., New York, NY 10163.

Aazunna, *(Aazunna Publishing; 0-934444),* 801 S. Victoria Ave. Suite 106, Ventura, CA 93003.

Abacus
See Camelot Pub

Abaris Bks, *(Abaris Books, Inc.; 0-913870; 0-89835),* 24 W. 40th St., New York, NY 10018 Tel 212-354-1313.

Abbeville Pr, *(Abbeville Press Inc.; 0-89659),* 505 Park Ave., New York, NY 10022 Tel 212-888-1969.

Abbincott, *(Abbincott Publishing Co.; 0-938490),* 1501 Broadway, Rm. 1414, New York, NY 10036.

Abbott Langer Assocs, *(Abbott, Langer & Associates; 0-916506),* P.O. Box 275, Park Forest, IL 60466 Tel 312-756-3990.

Abby Cooks
See Cuisinart Cooking

ABC, *(American Book Co.; 0-278),* Div. of Litton Educational Publishing, Inc., 135 W. 50th St., New York, NY 10020 Tel 212-265-8700; Orders to: 7625 Empire Dr., Florence, KY 41042 Tel 800-354-9815.

ABC-Clio, *(American Bibliographical Center-Clio Press; 0-87436),* 2040 Alameda Padre Serra, P.O. Box 4397, Santa Barbara, CA 93103 Tel 805-963-4221.

Abingdon, *(Abingdon Press; 0-687),* 201 Eighth Ave. S., Nashville, TN 37202 Tel 615-749-6403; Orders to: Customer Service Dept., 201 Eighth Ave. S., Nashville, TN 37202 Tel 615-749-6347. *Imprints:* Apex (Apex Books).

Ablex Pub, *(Ablex Publishing Corp.; 0-89391),* 355 Chestnut St., Norwood, NJ 07648 Tel 201-767-8450.

Abrams, *(Abrams, Harry N., Inc.; 0-8109),* Subs. of Times Mirror Co., 110 E. 59th St., New York, NY 10022 Tel 212-758-8600.

Abraxas, *(Abraxas Press; 0-932868),* 2322 Rugby Row, Madison, WI 53705 Tel 608-231-1440.

Abt Assoc, *(Abt Associates, Inc.; 0-89011),* Orders to: 55 Wheeler St., Cambridge, MA 02138 Tel 617-492-7100.

AC Pubns, *(AC Pubns.; 0-935496),* P.O. Box 238, Homer, NY 13077 Tel 607-749-4040.

Acad Educ Dev, *(Academy for Educational Development, Inc.; 0-89492),* 680 5th Ave., New York, NY 10019 Tel 212-397-0040; 1414-22nd St., N.W., Washington, DC 20037.

Acad of Mgmt, *(Academy of Management; 0-915350),* Dept. of Administration, College of Business Administration, Wichita State Univ., Wichita, KS 67208; Orders to: Dennis F. Ray, The Academy of Management College of Business, Mississippi State University, Mississippi State, MS 39762.

Acad Pr, *(Academic Press, Inc.; 0-12),* 111 Fifth Ave., New York, NY 10003 Tel 212-741-6800.

Acad Therapy, *(Academic Therapy Pubns.; 0-87879),* 20 Commercial Blvd., Novato, CA 94947 Tel 415-883-3314.

Academic Intl, *(Academic International; 0-87569),* P.O. Box 1111, Gulf Breeze, FL 32561.

Academic World, *(Academic World, Inc.; 0-915582),* Div. of Acaworld Corp., Drawer 4037, Greenville, NC 27834 Tel 919-756-4169.

Academy Bks, *(Academy Books; 0-914960),* P.O. Box 757, Rutland, VT 05701 Tel 802-773-9194.

Academy Chi Ltd, *(Academy Chicago, Ltd.; 0-915864),* 360 N. Michigan Ave., Chicago, IL 60601 Tel 312-782-9826.

Acadiana Pr, *(Acadiana Press, The; 0-937614),* P.O. Box 42290, USL, Lafayette, LA 70504.

ACC, *(Appleton-Century-Crofts; 0-8385),* 292 Madison Ave., New York, NY 10017 Tel 212-532-1700; Orders to: Prentice-Hall, Order Dept., Englewood Cliffs, NJ 07632.

Accel Devel, *(Accelerated Development Inc.; 0-915202),* 2515 W. Jackson St., Muncie, IN 47303 Tel 317-284-7511.

Accelerated Index, *(Accelerated Indexing Systems, Inc.; 0-89593),* 19 W. South Temple, Suite 600 Union Pacific Annex, Salt Lake City, UT 84101 Tel 801-531-0098.

Accent Bks, *(Accent Books; 0-89636; 0-916406),* P.O. Box 15337, Lakewood Sta., Denver, CO 80215 Tel 303-988-5300; 12100 W. Sixth Ave., Denver, CO 80215.

Accent Liv
See Cheever Pub

Accura, *(Accura Music, Inc.; 0-918194),* Box 887, Athens, OH 45701 Tel 614-594-3547.

ACE, *(American Council on Education; 0-8268),* 1 Dupont Circle, Washington, DC 20036 Tel 202-833-4785.

Ace Bks, *(Ace Books; 0-441),* Div. of Charter Communications Inc., c/o Grosset & Dunlap, 51 Madison Ave., New York, NY 10010 Tel 212-689-9200.

ACEI, *(Assn. for Childhood Education International; 0-87173),* 3615 Wisconsin Ave., N.W., Washington, DC 20016 Tel 202-363-6963.

ACI, *(American Concrete Institute; 0-87031),* 22400 W. Seven Mile Rd., P.O. Box 19150, Detroit, MI 48219 Tel 313-532-2600.

Acoma Bks, *(Acoma Books; 0-916552),* P.O. Box 4, Ramona, CA 92065 Tel 714-789-1288.

Acropolis, *(Acropolis Books; 0-87491),* 2400 17th St. N.W., Washington, DC 20009 Tel 202-387-6805.

Action Link, *(Action Link Pubns.; 0-936148),* 53 Condon Court, San Mateo, CA 94403.

Activity Resources, *(Activity Resources Co., Inc.; 0-918932),* P.O. Box 4875, 20655 Hathaway Ave., Hayward, CA 94541 Tel 415-782-1300.

Adams County, *(Adams County Historical Society; 0-934858),* P.O. Box 102, Hastings, NE 68901 Tel 402-463-5838.

Adams Inc MA, *(Adams, Bob, Inc.),* 30 Kinross Rd., Brookline, MA 02146 Tel 617-277-1373.

Adams Minn, *(Adams Press; 0-914828),* 59 Seymour Ave., S.E., Minneapolis, MN 55414 Tel 612-378-9076; Orders to: Lerner Publications Co., 241 First Ave. N., Minneapolis, MN 55401.

Adastra Pr, *(Adastra Press; 0-938566),* 101 Strong St., Easthampton, MA 01027.

ADC NY, *(Art Directors Club of New York),* Dist. by: Robert Silver Associates, 95 Madison Ave., New York, NY 10016.

Addresso'set, *(Addresso'set; 0-916944),* P.O. Box 1530, Vallejo, CA 94590 Tel 707-644-6358.

Addressoset
See Addresso'set

Adelphi Univ, *(Adelphi Univ. Press; 0-88461),* South Ave., Garden City, NY 11530 Tel 516-248-2020.

ADIS Pr, *(ADIS Press USA, Inc.; 0-909337),* 515 Madison Ave., New York, NY 10022.

ADK Mtn Club, *(Adirondack Mountain Club, Inc.; 0-935272),* 172 Ridge St., Glens Falls, NY 12801 Tel 518-793-7737.

Adler, *(Adler's Foreign Books, Inc.; 0-8417),* 162 Fifth Ave., New York, NY 10010 Tel 212-691-5151.

ADM Co, *(A.D.M. Co., Inc.; 0-937974),* P.O. Box 10462, Phoenix, AZ 85016 Tel 602-279-2070.

Adm Nimitz Foun, *(Admiral Nimitz Foundation),* P.O. Box 777, Fredericksburg, TX 78624.

Adriatic Stamp, *(Adriatic Stamp Co.; 0-9603474),* P.O. Box 1651, Maitland, FL 32751.

Adult Ed, *(Adult Education Assn. of the U.S.A.; 0-88379),* 810 18th St., N.W., Suite 500, Washington, DC 20006 Tel 202-347-9574.

Adv Bk Prog *Imprint of* **A-W**

Adv Bk Prog *Imprint of* **Benjamin-Cummings**

Adv Prof Seminars, *(Advanced Professional Seminars, Inc.; 0-9604532),* 7033 Ramsgate Place, Suite "A", Los Angeles, CA 90045; Orders to: P.O. Box 45791, Los Angeles, CA 90045 Tel 213-776-0113.

Adv Psychiatry, *(Group for the Advancement of Psychiatry; 0-87318),* 30 E. 29th St., New York, NY 10016 Tel 212-889-5760.

Advance Planning, *(Advance Planning Pubns.; 0-9600524),* Rte. 3, St. Croix Cove, Hudson, WI 54016.

Advent, *(Advent Pubs., Inc.; 0-911682),* P.O. Box A3228, Chicago, IL 60690.

Advent Bk, *(Advent Books, Inc; 0-89891),* 141 E. 44th St., Suite 511, New York, NY 10017 Tel 212-697-0887.

Advocate, *(Advocate Press; 0-911866),* Franklin Springs, GA 30639 Tel 404-245-7272.

Advocate Pub Group, *(Advocate Publishing Group; 0-89894),* 6810 E. Main St., Reynoldsburg, OH 43068.

AE-J *Imprint of* **Apollo Eds**

Aegean Park Pr, *(Aegean Park Press; 0-89412),* P.O. Box 2837, Laguna Hills, CA 92653 Tel 714-586-8811.

Aeonian Pr
See Amereon Ltd

Aerial Photo, *(Aerial Photography Services, Inc.),* 2300 Dunavant St., Charlotte, NC 28203.

Aero, *(Aero Pubs., Inc.; 0-8168),* 329 W. Aviation Rd., Fallbrook, CA 92028 Tel 714-728-8456.

Aero-Medical, *(Aero-Medical Consultants, Inc.; 0-912522),* 10912 Hamlin Blvd., Largo, FL 33540 Tel 813-596-2551.

Aerodrome Pr, *(Aerodrome Press; 0-935092),* Box 44, Story City, IA 50248.

Aerofacts, *(Aerofacts; 0-934268),* P.O. Box 11347, Las Vegas, NV 89111 Tel 702-458-3754.

Affirmation, *(Affirmation Books; 0-89571),* 456 Hill St., Whitinsville, MA 01588 Tel 617-234-6266.

Afi Pubns, *(Afi Pubns; 0-912460),* P.O. Box 8, Fleetwood, Mount Vernon, NY 10552 Tel 914-667-6575.

AFIPS Pr, *(AFIPS Press; 0-88283),* P.O. Box 9657, 1815 N. Lynn St., Suite 800, Arlington, VA 22209 Tel 703-558-3680.

African Policy, *(African Policy Institute),* 120 Wall St., Suite 1044, New York, NY 10005.

African Studies Assn, *(African Studies Assn.; 0-918456),* Epstein Service Bldg., Brandeis Univ., Waltham, MA 02254 Tel 617-899-3079.

Africana *Imprint of* **Holmes & Meier**

Afro-Am, *(Afro-Am Publishing Co., Inc.; 0-910030),* 910 S. Michigan Ave., Rm. 556, Chicago, IL 60605 Tel 312-922-1147.

Ag Sci Pubns, *(Agricultural Sciences Pubns. Univ. of California; 0-931876),* 1422 Harbour Way S., Richmond, CA 94804 Tel 415-642-2431.

Agascha Prods
See Shabazz Pr

Agate Pr, *(Agate Press, Inc.; 0-937266),* 51 E. 42nd St., New York, NY 10017.

Agni Yoga Soc, *(Agni Yoga Society, Inc.; 0-933574),* 319 W. 107th St., New York, NY 10025 Tel 212-864-7752.

Agora Pr, *(Agora Press; 0-934622),* P.O. Box 1085, La Jolla, CA 92038.

Agrinde Bks
See Agrinde Pubns

Agrinde Pubns, *(Agrinde Pubns., Ltd.; 0-9601068),* c/o Barbara J. Hendra Associates, Inc., 350 Fifth Ave., Suite 1101, New York, NY 10118 Tel 212-947-9898.

AHM Pub, *(AHM Publishing Corp.; 0-88295),* 3110 N. Arlington Heights Rd., Arlington Heights, IL 60004 Tel 312-253-9720.

Ahsahta Pr, *(Ahsahta Press; 0-916272),* Dept. of English, Boise State Univ., Boise, ID 83725 Tel 208-385-1246; Orders to: Univ. Bookstore, Boise State Univ., Boise, ID 83725.

Ai, *(Ai; 0-938454),* 118 E. 25th St., New York, NY 10010.

Aim-High *Imprint of* **Fell**

AIR Systems, *(American Institutes for Research, Systems Division; 0-89785),* 41 North Rd., Bedford, MA 01730 Tel 617-275-0800.

Aircraft Chart & Rent, *(Aircraft Charter & Rental Tariff Information Service of North America; 0-9603908),* Box 3000, Oak Park, IL 60303 Tel 217-546-1491.

Airline Job, *(Airline Job Kit),* P.O. Box 66895 ABI, Seattle, WA 98166.

Airmont, *(Airmont Publishing Co., Inc.; 0-8049),* 22 E. 60th St., New York, NY 10022.

Akiba Pr, *(Akiba Press; 0-934764),* Box 13086, Oakland, CA 94611 Tel 415-339-1283.

Al-Anon, *(Al-Anon Family Group Headquarters, Inc.; 0-910034),* 1 Park Ave., Second Floor, New York, NY 10016 Tel 212-481-6565.
ALA, *(American Library Assn.; 0-8389),* 50 E. Huron St., Chicago, IL 60611 Tel 312-944-6780.
Aladdin *Imprint of* **Atheneum**
Alandale Pr, *(Alandale Press; 0-937748),* R.D. 5, Ballston Rd., Amsterdam, NY 12010.
Alaska Northwest, *(Alaska Northwest Publishing Co.; 0-88240),* 130 Second Ave. S., Edmonds, WA 98020 Tel 206-774-4111.
Alaska Pacific, *(Alaska Pacific Univ. Press; 0-935094),* Alaska Pacific University, Anchorage, AK 99504 Tel 907-276-8181.
Alba, *(Alba House; 0-8189),* Div. of the Society of St. Paul, 2187 Victory Blvd., Staten Island, NY 10314 Tel 212-761-0047.
Albany Hist & Art, *(Albany Institute of History & Art),* 125 Washington Ave., Albany, NY 12210 Tel 518-463-4478.
Albany Pub Lib, *(Albany Public Library; 0-9605090),* 161 Washington Ave., Albany, NY 12210.
Albion Am Bks, *(Albion-American Books),* P.O. Box 50011, Tucson, AZ 85703.
Alchemist-Light, *(Alchemist/Light Publishing; 0-9600650),* P.O. Box 5530, San Francisco, CA 94101 Tel 415-342-7804.
Alchemy Bks, *(Alchemy Books; 0-931290),* 681 Market, Suite 755, San Francisco, CA 94105 Tel 415-362-2708.
Alcott Pr, *(Alcott Press, Inc.; 0-936998),* P.O. Box 335, Edwardsville, IL 62025 Tel 618-656-7445.
Aldebaran Rev, *(Aldebaran Review; 0-917744),* 2209 California St., Berkeley, CA 94703 Tel 415-549-2456.
Aldine
See Beresford Bk Serv
Aldine Pub, *(Aldine Publishing Co., Inc.; 0-202),* Div. of Walter De Gruyter, Inc., 200 Saw Mill River Rd., Hawthorne, NY 10532 Tel 914-747-0115.
Alembic Pr, *(Alembic Press; 0-934184),* 1744 Slaterville Rd., Ithaca, NY 14850.
Alexander Graham, *(Alexander Graham Bell Assn. for the Deaf, The; 0-88200),* 3417 Volta Place N.W., Washington, DC 20007 Tel 202-337-5220.
Alexandria Hse, *(Alexandria House Books; 0-932496),* Div. of Kephart Communications, Inc., c/o Kephart Communications Inc., 901 N. Washington St., Rm. 605, Alexandria, VA 22314 Tel 703-836-3313; Orders to: 236 Foest Park Place, Ottawa, IL 61350.
Alfa Sierra, *(Alfa Sierra Pubns.; 0-9604728),* P.O. Box 9636, San Diego, CA 92109.
Alfred Pub, *(Alfred Publishing Co., Inc.; 0-88284),* 15335 Morrison St., Sherman Oaks, CA 91403 Tel 213-995-8811.
ALI-ABA, *(ALI-ABA),* 4025 Chestnut St., Philadelphia, PA 19104 Tel 215-243-1600.
Alicejamesbooks, *(Alicejamesbooks; 0-914086),* 138 Mt. Auburn St., Cambridge, MA 02138.
Alive Pubns, *(Alive Pubns. Ltd.; 0-935572),* 11 Park Place, New York, NY 10007 Tel 212-962-0316.
Allanheld, *(Allanheld, Osmun & Co., Inc.; 0-916672; 0-86598),* 6 S. Fullerton Ave., Montclair, NJ 07042 Tel 201-783-5555; Dist. by: Biblio Distr. Ctr., 81 Adams Dr., Totowa, NJ 07512 Tel 201-256-8600.
Allanheld & Schram, *(Allanheld & Schram; 0-8390),* 36 Park St., Montclair, NJ 07042.
Allegheny, *(Allegheny Press; 0-910042),* 522 East St., California, PA 15419 Tel 412-938-8548.
Allegro Pub, *(Allegro Publishing Co.; 0-9601042),* P.O. Box 39892, Los Angeles, CA 90039 Tel 213-665-6783.
Alleluia Pr, *(Alleluia Press; 0-911726),* P.O. Box 103, Allendale, NJ 07401 Tel 201-327-3513; 672 Franklin Turnpike, NJ 07401.
Allen Pr, *(Allen Press, Inc.; 0-935868),* P.O. Box 368, Lawrence, KS 66044.
Allen Unwin, *(Allen & Unwin, Inc.; 0-04; 0-86861),* 9 Winchester Terrace, Winchester, MA 01890 Tel 617-729-0830; Orders to: P.O. Box 978, Building 424 Raritan Center, Edison, NJ 08817 Tel 201-225-1900.
Allenson
See Allenson-Breckinridge
Allenson-Breckinridge, *(Allenson-Breckinridge Books; 0-8401),* P.O. Box 447, Geneva, AL 36340.
Alliance Coll, *(Alliance College),* Cambridge Springs, PA 16403.
Allison Pubs, *(Allison Pubs.),* 1 La Playa, Box 733, Cochise, AZ 85606.
Ally Pr, *(Ally Press; 0-915408),* P.O. Box 30340, St. Paul, MN 55175; Orders to: P.O. Box 30340, Dept. BP, St. Paul, MN 55175.
Allyn, *(Allyn & Bacon, Inc.; 0-205),* 470 Atlantic Ave., Boston, MA 02210 Tel 617-482-9220; Orders to: College Division, Rockleigh, NJ 07647.
Alma Hist Soc, *(Alma Historical Society; 0-9604684),* P.O. Box 87, Alma, WI 54610.
Almar, *(Almar Press; 0-930256),* 4105 Marietta Dr., Binghamton, NY 13903 Tel 607-722-6251.
Alperin
See Junius Inc
Alpha Omega, *(Alpha Omega Publishing Co.; 0-931608),* P.O. Box 4130, Medford, OR 97501 Tel 503-826-7302.
Alpha Printing, *(Alpha Printing Ltd.; 0-937268),* 6301-B Central Ave., N.W., Albuquerque, NM 87105.
Alpine Ent, *(Alpine Enterprises),* P. O. Box 766, Dearborn, MI 48121.
Alpine Fine Arts, *(Alpine Fine Arts Collection, Ltd.; 0-933516),* 527 Madison Ave., New York, NY 10022; Dist. by: Hippocrene Books Inc., 171 Madison Ave., New York, NY 10016.
Alpine Pubns, *(Alpine Pubns.; 0-931866),* 1901 S. Garfield, Loveland, CO 80537 Tel 303-667-2017.
Alpine-Tahoe, *(Alpine-Tahoe Press; 0-9604574),* Box 1484, Tahoe City, CA 95730 Tel 916-583-3273.
Altair Pub Co, *(Altair Publishing Co.; 0-9604976),* 217 S. Louis St., Mt. Prospect, IL 60056.
Alyson Pubns, *(Alyson Pubns., Inc.; 0-932870),* 75 Kneeland St., No. 309, Boston, MA 02111 Tel 617-542-5679.
Am Acad Inst Arts, *(American Academy & Institute of Arts & Letters; 0-915974),* 633 W. 155th St., New York, NY 10032 Tel 212-368-5900.
Am Acad Pol Soc Sci, *(American Academy of Political & Social Science; 0-87761),* 3937 Chestnut St., Philadelphia, PA 19104 Tel 215-386-4594.
Am Antiquarian, *(American Antiquarian Society; 0-912296),* 185 Salisbury St., Worcester, MA 01609 Tel 617-755-5221; Dist. by: Univ. Press of Virginia, P.O. Box 3608, University Sta., Charlottesville, VA 22903.
Am Assn Cereal Chem, *(American Assn. of Cereal Chemists; 0-913250),* 3340 Pilot Knob Rd., St. Paul, MN 55121 Tel 612-454-7250.
Am Assn Clinical Chem, *(American Assn. for Clinical Chemistry; 0-915274),* 1725 K St., N.W., Washington, DC 20006.
Am Assn Comm Jr Coll, *(American Assn. of Community & Junior Colleges; 0-87117),* 1 Dupont Circle, N.W., Washington, DC 20036 Tel 202-293-7050.
Am Assn Conn
See Am Assn Comm Jr Coll
Am Astronaut, *(American Astronautical Society; 0-87703),* Orders to: Univelt, Inc., P.O. Box 28130, San Diego, CA 92128 Tel 714-746-4005.
Am Atheist, *(American Atheist Press; 0-911826),* P.O. Box 2117, Austin, TX 78768 Tel 512-458-1244.
Am Bar Foun, *(American Bar Foundation; 0-910058; 0-910059),* 1155 E. 60th St., Chicago, IL 60637 Tel 312-667-4700.
Am Biog Ctr, *(American Biographical Center; 0-9601168),* P.O. Box 473, Williamsburg, VA 23185 Tel 804-725-2234.
Am Bk Prices, *(American Book Prices Current, Bancroft-Parkman, Inc.; 0-914022),* 121 E. 78th St., New York, NY 10021 Tel 212-737-2715.
AM Books CA, *(AM Books; 0-935190),* 13415 Ventura Blvd., Sherman Oaks, CA 91423 Tel 213-995-3329.
Am Bur Metal, *(American Bureau of Metal Statistics; 0-910064),* 420 Lexington Ave., Rm. 420, New York, NY 10017 Tel 212-867-9450.
Am Busn Comm Assn, *(American Business Communication Assn.; 0-931874),* 911 S. Sixth St., Univ. of Illinois, Champaign, IL 61820 Tel 217-333-0458.
Am Busn Consult, *(American Business Consultants, Inc.; 0-937152),* 1540 Nuthatch Lane, Sunnyvale, CA 94087 Tel 408-732-8931.
Am Canadian, *(American-Canadian Pubs., Inc.; 0-913844),* Drawer 2078, Portales, NM 88130 Tel 505-356-4082.
Am Canal & Transport, *(American Canal & Transportation Center; 0-933788),* 809 Rathton Rd., York, PA 17403 Tel 717-843-4035.
Am Cancer Minn, *(American Cancer Society, Minnesota Division, Inc.),* 2750 Park Ave., Minneapolis, MN 55407 Tel 612-871-2111.
Am Cath Philo, *(American Catholic Philosophical Assn.; 0-918090),* Catholic University of America, Washington, DC 20064 Tel 202-635-5518.
Am Chemical, *(American Chemical Society; 0-8412),* 1155 16th St., N.W., Washington, DC 20036 Tel 202-872-4600.
Am Chiro Acad, *(American Chiropractic Academic Press; 0-936948),* 6716 N.W. 16th, Suite 129, Oklahoma City, OK 73127.
Am Classical Coll Pr, *(American Classical College Press; 0-913314; 0-89266),* P.O. Box 4526, Albuquerque, NM 87106 Tel 505-843-7749.
Am Coll Heraldry, *(American College of Heraldry, Inc., The; 0-9605668),* P.O. Box CG, University, AL 35486.
Am Coll Testing, *(American College Testing Program; 0-937734),* 2201 N. Dodge St., P. O. Box 168, Iowa City, IA 52243 Tel 319-356-3701.
Am Consul Eng, *(American Consulting Engineers Council; 0-910090),* 1015 15th St., N.W., Washington, DC 20005.
Am Council Arts, *(American Council for the Arts; 0-915400),* 570 Seventh Ave., New York, NY 10018 Tel 212-354-6655.
Am Craft, *(American Craft Council; 0-88321),* 22 W. 55th St., New York, NY 10019 Tel 212-397-0600.
Am Crafts
See Am Craft
Am Dental, *(American Dental Assn.; 0-910074),* Order Section , 211 E. Chicago Ave., Chicago, IL 60611 Tel 312-440-2892.
Am Educ Res, *(American Educational Research Assn.; 0-935302),* 1230 17th St., N.W., Washington, DC 20036 Tel 202-223-9485.
Am Enterprise, *(American Enterprise Institute for Public Policy Research; 0-8447),* 1150 17th St., N.W., Washington, DC 20036 Tel 202-862-5800.
Am Entom Inst, *(American Entomological Institute),* 5950 Warren Rd., Ann Arbor, MI 48105 Tel 313-662-8476.
Am Fed Arts, *(American Federation of Arts; 0-917418),* 41 E. 65th St., New York, NY 10021 Tel 212-988-7700.
Am Forestry, *(American Forestry Assn., Book Edit Dept.; 0-935050),* 1319 18th St., N.W., Washington, DC 20036 Tel 202-467-5810.
Am Foun Blind, *(American Foundation for the Blind; 0-89128),* 15 W. 16th St., New York, NY 10011 Tel 212-620-2151.
Am Geol, *(American Geological Institute; 0-913312),* One Skyline Place, 5205 Leesburg Pike, Falls Church, VA 22041 Tel 703-379-2480.
Am Geophysical, *(American Geophysical Union; 0-87590),* 2000 Florida Ave. N.W., Washington, DC 20009 Tel 202-462-6903.
Am Guidance, *(American Guidance Service, Inc; 0-913476),* Publishers' Bldg., Circle Pines, MN 55014 Tel 612-786-4343.
Am Heart, *(American Heart Assn., Inc.; 0-87493),* 7320 Greenville Ave., Dallas, TX 75231 Tel 214-750-5465.
Am Heritage, *(American Heritage Publishing Co.; 0-8281),* 10 Rockefeller Plaza, New York, NY 10020 Tel 212-399-8900.
Am Hist Pubs, *(American Historical Pubs., Inc.; 0-937862),* 177 E. Riverside, Newport Beach, CA 92663.
Am Hospital, *(American Hospital Assn.; 0-87258),* 840 N. Lake Shore Dr., Chicago, IL 60611 Tel 312-280-6235; Orders to: P.O. Box 96003, Chicago, IL 60690
Am Ind Mus
See Mus Am Ind
Am Inst Arch, *(American Institute of Architects; 0-913962),* 1735 New York Ave., N.W., Washington, DC 20006 Tel 202-626-7474.
Am Inst Cons Eng
See Am Consul Eng

Am Inst Cooperation, *(American Institute of Cooperation; 0-938868),* 1800 Massachusetts Ave., N. W., Suite 508, Washington, DC 20036 Tel 202-296-6825.
Am Inst CPA, *(American Institute of Certified Public Accountants; 0-87051),* 1211 Avenue of the Americas, New York, NY 10036 Tel 212-575-6200.
Am Inst Indus Eng, *(American Institute of Industrial Engineers; 0-89806),* 25 Technology Park-Atlanta, Norcross, GA 30092 Tel 404-449-0460.
Am Inst Marxist, *(American Institute for Marxist Studies; 0-89977),* 20 E. 30th St., New York, NY 10016 Tel 212-689-4530.
Am Inst Pharmacy, *(American Institute of the History of Pharmacy; 0-931292),* Pharmacy Bldg., Univ. of Wisconsin, Madison, WI 53706 Tel 608-262-5378; c/o Ex. Sec. Roy Bowers, Rutgers College of Pharmacy, Box 789, Piscataway, NJ 08854.
Am Inst Physics, *(American Institute of Physics; 0-88318),* 335 E. 45th St., New York, NY 10017 Tel 212-661-9404.
Am Inst Psych, *(American Institute for Psychological Research, The; 0-89920),* 614 Indian School Rd. N.W., Albuquerque, NM 87102 Tel 505-843-7749.
Am Inst Real Estate Appraisers, *(American Institute of Real Estate Appraisers; 0-911780),* 430 N. Michigan Ave., Chicago, IL 60611 Tel 312-440-8171; Dist. by: Ballinger Pub. Co., 17 Dunster St., Cambridge, MA 02138 Tel 617-492-0670.
Am Inst Res, *(American Institutes for Research; 0-89785),* P.O. Box 1113, Palo Alto, CA 94302.
Am Inst Writing Res, *(American Institute for Writing Research, Corp.; 0-917944),* Box 2129, Grand Central Sta., New York, NY 10163 Tel 212-266-2897.
Am Jewish Comm, *(American Jewish Committee; 0-87495),* 165 E. 56th St., New York, NY 10022 Tel 212-751-4000.
Am Jewish Hist Soc, *(American Jewish Historical Society; 0-911934),* 2 Thornton Rd., Waltham, MA 02154 Tel 617-891-8110.
Am Journal Nurse, *(American Journal of Nursing Co.),* 10 Columbus Circle, New York, NY 10019 Tel 212-582-8820.
Am Judicature, *(American Judicature Society),* 200 W. Monroe, Suite 1606, Chicago, IL 60606 Tel 312-558-6900.
Am Lang Acad, *(American Language Academy; 0-934270),*C/O Catholic Univ. of America Marist Bldg., Washington, DC 20064.
Am Law Inst, *(American Law Institute; 0-8318),* 4025 Chestnut St., Philadelphia, PA 19104 Tel 215-243-1600.
Am Lawn Bowlers, *(American Lawn Bowlers' Guide; 0-9600068),* P.O. Box 824, Laguna Beach, CA 92652 Tel 714-494-2606.
Am Lib Pub Co, *(American Library Publishing Co., Inc.; 0-87729),* 275 Central Park, W., New York, NY 10024 Tel 212-787-0766.
Am Malacologists, *(American Malacologists, Inc.; 0-915826),* Box 2255, Melbourne, FL 32901 Tel 305-725-2260.
Am Map, *(American Map Co., Inc.; 0-8416),* 1926 Broadway, New York, NY 10023 Tel 212-595-6582.
Am Math, *(American Mathematical Society; 0-8218),* P.O. Box 6248, Providence, RI 02940 Tel 401-272-9500; Orders to: P.O. Box 1571, Annex Sta., Providence, RI 02901.
Am Metric, *(American Metric Journal),* P.O. Box 847, Tarzana, CA 91356 Tel 805-484-5787.
Am Mgmt, *(American Management Assn., Inc.; 0-8144),* 135 W. 50th St., New York, NY 10020 Tel 212-586-8100.
Am Mideast, *(American Mideast Research),* 55 Sutter, Suite 712, San Francisco, CA 94104 Tel 415-921-5002.
Am Mktg, *(American Marketing Assn.; 0-87757),* 222 S. Riverside Plaza, Chicago, IL 60606 Tel 312-648-0536.
Am Mutuality, *(American Mutuality Foundation; 0-938844),* 9428 S. Western Ave., Los Angeles, CA 90047.
Am Natl, *(American National Metric Council; 0-916148),* 1625 Massachusetts Ave., N. W., Washington, DC 20036 Tel 202-232-4545.
Am Nuclear Soc, *(American Nuclear Society; 0-89448),* 555 N. Kensington Ave., La Grange Park, IL 60525 Tel 312-352-6611.
Am Numismatic, *(American Numismatic Society; 0-89722),* Broadway at 155th St., New York, NY 10032 Tel 212-234-3130.
Am Orient Soc, *(American Oriental Society),* 329 Sterling Memorial Library, Yale Sta., New Haven, CT 06520 Tel 203-436-1040.
Am Personnel, *(American Personnel & Guidance Assn.),* 2 Skyline Place, Suite 400, 5203 Leeburg Pike, Falls Church, VA 22041 Tel 703-820-4700.
Am Petroleum, *(American Petroleum Institute Pubns.; 0-89364),* 2101 "L" St., N.W., Washington, DC 20037 Tel 202-833-5790.
Am Pharm Assn, *(American Pharmaceutical Assn.; 0-917330),* 2215 Constitution Ave., N.W., Washington, DC 20037 Tel 202-628-4410.
Am Philos, *(American Philosophical Society; 0-87169),* 104 S. Fifth St., Philadelphia, PA 19106 Tel 215-627-0706.
Am Phytopathol Soc, *(American Phytopathological Society; 0-89054),* 3340 Pilot Knob Rd., St. Paul, MN 55121 Tel 612-454-7250.
Am Pine Barrens, *(American Pine Barrens Pub. Co.; 0-937438),* P.O. Box 22820, 1400 Washington Ave., Albany, NY 12222.
Am Poetry Pr, *(American Poetry Press; 0-933486),* P. O. Box 634, Claymont, DE 19703 Tel 302-366-1423; 4210 Lankershim Blvd., North Hollywood, CA 91602 Tel 213-980-9891.
Am Powder Metal, *(American Powder Metallurgy Institute),* 105 College Road E., Princeton, NJ 08540.
Am Psychiatric, *(American Psychiatric Assn.; 0-89042),* Pubn. Sales, 1700 18th St., N.W., Washington, DC 20009 Tel 202-797-4911.
Am Psychol, *(American Psychological Assn.; 0-912704),* 1200 17th St., N.W., Washington, DC 20036 Tel 202-833-7600.
Am Pub Co WI, *(American Publishing Company),* 2909 Syene Rd., Madison, WI 53713 Tel 608-271-6544.
Am Pub Health, *(American Public Health Assn. Pubns.; 0-87553),* 1015 15th St. N.W., Washington, DC 20005 Tel 202-789-5600.
Am Pub Welfare, *(American Public Welfare Assn.; 0-910106),* 1125 15th St., N. W., Washington, DC 20005 Tel 202-293-7550.
Am Public Works, *(American Public Works Assn.; 0-917084),* 1313 E. 60th St., Chicago, IL 60637 Tel 312-947-2541.
Am Quality, *(American Quality Books; 0-936956),* 12415 E. DeSmet, No. 35, Spokane, WA 99216 Tel 509-928-0061.
Am Radio, *(American Radio Relay League, Inc.; 0-87259),* 225 Main St., Newington, CT 06111 Tel 203-666-1541.
Am Register
See Thomas Intl Pub
Am Repr-Rivercity Pr, *(American Reprint Co./Rivercity Press; 0-89190),* P.O. Box 1200, Mattituck, NY 11952 Tel 516-298-5100; Dist. by: Amereon Ltd., P.O. Box 1200, Mattituck, NY 11952 Tel 516-298-5100.
Am Reprints, *(American Reprints Co.; 0-915706),* 111 West Dent, Ironton, MO 63650.
Am Res Ctr Egypt, *(American Research Center in Egypt, The; 0-936770),* c/o Columbia University, 1117 International Affairs Bldg., New York, NY 10027.
Am Res Pr, *(American Research Press; 0-937616),* 5153 Elkmont, Rancho Palos Verdes, CA 90274.
Am Samizdat, *(American Samizdat; 0-935500),* 724 Tenth Ave., Apt. 4A, New York, NY 10019 Tel 212-586-5780.
Am Scandinavian, *(American-Scandinavian Foundation; 0-89067),* 127 E. 73rd St., New York, NY 10021 Tel 212-879-9779; Orders to: Heritage Resource Center, P.O. Box 26305, Minneapolis, MN 55426.
Am Sch Athens, *(American School of Classical Studies at Athens; 0-87661),* c/o Institute for Advanced Study, Princeton, NJ 08540 Tel 609-734-8387.
Am Sch Health, *(American School Health Assn.; 0-917160),* P.O. Box 708, Kent, OH 44240 Tel 216-678-1601.
Am Sciences Pr, *(American Sciences Press, Inc.; 0-935950),* P.O. Box 21161, Columbus, OH 43221.
Am Showcase, *(American Showcase, Inc.; 0-931144),* 724 Fifth Ave., New York, NY 10019 Tel 212-245-0981; Dist. by: Mayflower Books, 575 Lexington Ave., New York, NY 10022; Dist. by: Fleetbooks, S.A., 100 Park Ave, New York, NY 10017.
Am Soc Appraisers, *(American Society of Appraisers; 0-937828),* Dulles International Airport, P.O. Box 17265, Washington, DC 20041 Tel 703-620-3838.
Am Soc Civil Eng, *(American Society of Civil Engineers; 0-87262),* 345 E. 47th St., New York, NY 10017 Tel 212-752-6800.
Am Soc Clinical, *(American Society of Clinical Pathologists; 0-89189),* Educational Products Division, 2100 W. Harrison St., Chicago, IL 60612 Tel 312-738-1336.
Am Soc Hosp Pharm, *(American Society of Hospital Pharmacists; 0-930530),* 4630 Montgomery Ave., Washington, DC 20014 Tel 301-657-3000.
Am Soc Microbio, *(American Society for Microbiology; 0-914826),* 1913 "I" St., N.W., Washington, DC 20006 Tel 202-833-9680.
Am Spelling, *(American Spelling Headquarters; 0-935276),* 2120 Jimmy Durante Dr., Del Mar, CA 92014.
Am Sports Sales, *(American Sports Sales, Inc.; 0-912354),* P.O. Box 160, Orangeburg, NY 10962 Tel 914-359-5300.
Am Stud Pr, *(American Studies Press, Inc.; 0-934996),* 13511 Palmwood Lane, Tampa, FL 33624 Tel 813-961-7200.
Am Technical, *(American Technical Pubs., Inc.; 0-8269),* 5608 Stony Island Ave., Chicago, IL 60637 Tel 800-621-2404.
Am Theatre Assoc, *(American Theatre Assn.),* 1000 Vermont Ave., N.W., Washington, DC 20005 Tel 202-628-4634.
Am U Beirut *Imprint of* **Syracuse U Pr**
Am Univ Artforms, *(American Universal Artforms Corp.; 0-913632),* P.O. Box 4574, Austin, TX 78765 Tel 512-451-3588.
Am Voc Assn, *(American Vocational Assn., Inc.; 0-89514),* 2020 N. 14th St., Arlington, VA 22201.
Am Water Wks Assn, *(American Water Works Assn.; 0-89867),* 6666 W. Quincy Ave., Denver, CO 80235 Tel 303-794-7711.
Amazon Pr, *(Amazon Press; 0-931458),* 1101 Keeler Ave., Berkeley, CA 94708; Dist. by: Bookpeople, 2940 Seventh St., Berkeley, CA 94710 Tel 415-549-3033.
Amber Crest, *(Amber Crest Books, Inc.),* Div. of New World Communications, 7060 Hollywood Blvd., Suite 503, Los Angeles, CA 90028 Tel 213-461-8193.
AmCen *Imprint of* **Hill & Wang**
AMCO Intl, *(AMCO International, Inc.; 0-9602406),* P.O. Box 347, Staten Island, NY 10301 Tel 518-356-3967.
Ameco, *(Ameco Publishing Corp.; 0-912146),* 275 Hillside Ave., Williston Park, NY 11596 Tel 516-741-5030.
Amer Bar Assn, *(American Bar Assn.; 0-89707),* 1155 E. 60th St., Chicago, IL 60637 Tel 312-947-3607.
Amereon Ltd, *(Amereon Ltd.; 0-88411),* P.O. Box 1200, Mattituck, NY 11952 Tel 516-298-5100.
American Ent Pubns, *(American Enterprise Pubns.),* Box 6690 R.D.6, Mercer, PA 16137 Tel 412-748-3726.
American Music, *(American Music Conference; 0-918196),* Public Relations Board, Inc., 150 E. Huron St., Chicago, IL 60611 Tel 312-266-7200; c/o American Music Conference, 1000 Skokie Blvd., Wilmette, IL 60091 Tel 312-251-1600.
American Pr, *(American Press; 0-89641),* 520 Commonwealth Ave., No. 416, Boston, MA 02215 Tel 617-247-0022.
Americanist, *(Americanist Press; 0-910120),* 1525 Shenkel Rd., Pottstown, PA 19464 Tel 215-323-5289.
Americans Energy Ind, *(Americans for Energy Independence; 0-934458),* 1629 K St., N.W., Suite 1201, Washington, DC 20006 Tel 202-466-2105.
AMG Pubs, *(AMG Pubs.; 0-89957),* 6815 Shallowford Rd., Chattanooga, TN 37421.
Amherst Media, *(Amherst Media; 0-936262),* 418 Homecrest Dr., Amherst, NY 14226.
Amherst Pr, *(Amherst Press),* Amherst, WI 54406 Tel 715-824-3214.
AMI Pr, *(AMI International Press; 0-911988),* Mountain View Rd., Washington, NJ 07822 Tel 201-689-1700.

Amon Carter, *(Amon Carter Museum of Western Art; 0-88360),* P.O. Box 2365, Fort Worth, TX 76113 Tel 817-738-1933.
Amonics, *(Amonics; 0-918166),* P.O. Box 1045, Norman, OK 73069 Tel 405-321-8076.
Amphoto, *(American Photographic Book Publishing Co., Inc.; 0-8174),* Div. of Watson-Guptill Pubns., Inc., 1 Astor Plaza, 1515 Broadway, 39th Floor, New York, NY 10036 Tel 212-764-7510.
AMS Pr, *(AMS Press, Inc.; 0-404),* 56 E. 13th St., New York, NY 10003 Tel 212-777-4700.
AMSCO Sch, *(AMSCO School Pubns., Inc.; 0-87720),* Orders to: 315 Hudson St., New York, NY 10013 Tel 212-675-7000.
Anaheim Pub Co, *(Anaheim Publishing Co.; 0-88236),* 1120 E. Ash, Fullerton, CA 92631 Tel 714-879-7922.
Analog Devices, *(Analog Devices, Inc.; 0-916550),* P.O. Box 280, Norwood, MA 02062 Tel 617-329-4700; Orders to: P.O. Box 796, Norwood, MA 02062.
Ananda, *(Ananda Pubns.; 0-916124),* 14618 Tyler Foote Rd., Nevada City, CA 95959 Tel 916-265-5877.
Anch *Imprint of* **Doubleday**
Anchor Pr *Imprint of* **Doubleday**
Anchorage, *(Anchorage Press; 0-87602),* P. O. Box 8067, New Orleans, LA 70182 Tel 504-283-8868.
Ancient Age, *(Ancient Age Press; 0-9605224),* P.O. Box 84431, Veterans Administration Branch, Los Angeles, CA 90073.
And Bks, *(And Books; 0-89708),* 702 S. Michigan, Suite 836, South Bend, IN 46618 Tel 219-232-8500.
And-Or Pr, *(And-or Press, Inc.; 0-915904),* P.O. Box 2246, Berkeley, CA 94702 Tel 415-849-2665.
Anderson Kramer, *(Anderson Kramer Associates, Inc.; 0-910136),* 1722 "H" St., N.W., Washington, DC 20006 Tel 202-298-8010.
Anderson Pub Co, *(Anderson Publishing Co.; 0-87084),* 646 Main St., Cincinnati, OH 45201.
Anderson World, *(Anderson World, Inc.; 0-89037),* 1400 Stierlin Road, Mountain View, CA 94043 Tel 415-965-8777.
Andover MA
See Town of Andover MA
Andover Pr, *(Andover Press; 0-939014),* 516 W. 34th St., New York, NY 10001.
Andre Deutsch, *(Andre Deutsch; 0-233),* c/o Elsevier Dutton, 2 Park Ave., New York, NY 10016.
Andrew Mtn Pr, *(Andrew Mountain Press; 0-9603840),* P.O. Box 14353, Hartford, CT 06114.
Andrews & McMeel, *(Andrews & McMeel, Inc.; 0-8362),* 4400 Johnson Dr., Fairway, KS 66205 Tel 913-362-1523.
Anemone Edns, *(Anemone Editions, Ltd.; 0-9604818),* P.O. Box 6056, Carmel, CA 93921.
Angel City, *(Angel City Books; 0-9605416),* 8033 Sunset Blvd., No. 366, Hollywood, CA 90046.
Angel Pr, *(Angel Press Publishers; 0-912216),* 171 Webster St., Monterey, CA 93940 Tel 408-372-1658; Dist. by: Caroline House Distributors, 2 Ellis Place, Ossining, NY 10562.
Anhinga Pr, , *(Anhinga Press; 0-938078),* Zapalachee Poetry Ctr., 410 Williams Bldg., Florida State Univ., Tallahassee, FL 32306.
Anima Bks
See Anima Pubns
Anima Pubns, *(Anima Pubns.; 0-89012),* 1053 Wilson Ave., Chambersburg, PA 17201 Tel 717-263-8303.
Animal Owners, *(Animal Owners Motivation Programs; 0-9604576),* Center Rd., Frankfort, IL 60423.
Animal Welfare, *(Animal Welfare Institute),* P.O. Box 3650, Washington, DC 20007 Tel 202-337-2333.
Anma Libri, *(Anma Libri; 0-915838),* P.O. Box 876, Saratoga, CA 95070 Tel 415-851-3375.
Ann Arbor FL, *(Ann Arbor Pubs.; 0-89039),* P.O. Box 7249, Naples, FL 33940.
Ann Arbor Pubs, *(Ann Arbor Pubs.; 0-910138),* 2057 Charlton, Ann Arbor, MI 48103 Tel 313-665-9130; Orders to: P.O. Box 7249, Naples, FL 33940.
Ann Arbor Science, *(Ann Arbor Science Pubs.; 0-250),* c/o Butterworth Publishers, Inc., 10 Tower Office Park, Woburn, MA 01801 Tel 617-935-9361.
Anna Pub, *(Anna Publishing, Inc.; 0-89305),* 2469 Aloma Ave., Winter Park, FL 32792 Tel 305-671-5995.
Annual Reviews, *(Annual Reviews, Inc.; 0-8243),* 4139 El Camino Way, Palo Alto, CA 94306 Tel 415-493-4400.
ANSI, *(American National Standards Institute),* 1430 Broadway, New York, NY 10018 Tel 212-354-3311.
Anthony, *(Anthony, C. & R., Pubs., Inc.; 0-910140),* 300 Park Ave., S., New York, NY 10010 Tel 212-677-3170.
Anthony Pub Co, *(Anthony Publishing Co.; 0-9603832),* 218 Gleasondale Rd., Stow, MA 01775 Tel 617-897-7191.
Anthroposophic, *(Anthroposophic Press, Inc.; 0-910142),* 258 Hungry Hollow Rd., Spring Valley, NY 10977 Tel 914-352-2295.
Antietam Pr, *(Antietam Press; 0-931590),* P.O. Box 62, Boonsboro, MD 21713 Tel 301-432-8079.
Antiquarium, *(Antiquarium, The),* 66 Humiston Dr., Bethany, CT 06525 Tel 203-393-2723.
Antiquary Pr, *(Antiquary Press; 0-937864),* P.O. Box 9523, Baltimore, MD 21237 Tel 301-734-6366.
Antique Clocks, *(Antique Clocks Publishing; 0-933396),* P.O. Box 21387, Concord, CA 94521 Tel 415-682-6512.
Antique Radio, *(Antique Radio Services),* 646 Kenilworth Terrace, Kenilworth, IL 60043 Tel 312-251-0089.
Aperture, *(Aperture, Inc.; 0-89381; 0-912334),* Elm St., Millerton, NY 12546 Tel 518-789-4491.
Apex *Imprint of* **Abingdon**
APO *Imprint of* **Unipub**
Apollo, *(Apollo; 0-938290),* 391 South Rd., Poughkeepsie, NY 12601.
Apollo Eds, *(Apollo Editions; 0-8152),* C/O Harper & Row Pubs., 10 E. 53rd St., New York, NY 10022; Dist. by: Harper & Row Pubs., Keystone Industrial Park, Scranton, PA 18512. *Imprints:* AE-J (Apollo Editions Juvenile Books).
Apostolic Formation, *(Apostolic Formation Center for Christian Renew-All, Inc.; 0-935488),* Box 355, Somers, CT 06071.
Appalach Consortium, *(Appalachian Consortium, Inc.),* 202 Appalachian St., Boone, NC 28607 Tel 704-262-2064.
Appalach Mtn, *(Appalachian Mountain Club; 0-910146),* 5 Joy St., Boston, MA 02108 Tel 617-523-0636.
Appel, *(Appel, Paul P., Pub.; 0-911858),* 119 Library Lane, Mamaroneck, NY 10543 Tel 914-698-8115.
Appellate Pub, *(Appellate Publishing; 0-9603848),* P. O. Box 10687, Edgemont Branch, Golden, CO 80401.
Apple-Gems, *(Apple-Gems; 0-9602122),* P.O. Box 16292, San Francisco, CA 94116 Tel 415-587-9752.
Apple Pub Co, *(Apple Publishing Co.; 0-9604134),* Box 2498, Grand Central Sta., New York, NY 10163.
Apple Tree, *(Apple Tree Press, Inc.; 0-913082),* P.O. Box 1012, Flint, MI 48501 Tel 313-234-5451.
Apple Wood, *(Apple-Wood Books; 0-918222),* Box 2870, Cambridge, MA 02139 Tel 617-964-5150.
Applewhite, *(Applewhite, Karen Miller; 0-9603472),* 5702 N. Tenth Ave., Phoenix, AZ 85013 Tel 602-246-8243.
Applezaba, *(Applezaba Press; 0-930090),* 410 St. Louis, Long Beach, CA 90814 Tel 213-434-7761.
Applied Arts, *(Applied Arts Pubs.; 0-911410),* Div. of Sowers Printing Co., Box 479, Lebanon, PA 17042 Tel 717-272-6667.
April Hill, *(April Hill Pubs.),* 79 Elm St., Springfield, VT 05156.
Apt Bks, *(Apt Books, Inc.; 0-86590),* 141 E. 44th St., New York, NY 10017.
Aptitude Inventory, *(Aptitude Inventory Measurement Service; 0-9602710),* 2506 McKinney Ave., Suite B, Dallas, TX 75201.
Aqua-Sol Ent, *(Aqua-Sol Enterprises; 0-9604874),* P.O. Box 18646, Fort Worth, TX 76118 Tel 817-284-8003.
Aquarian Bk Pubs, *(Aquarian Book Pubs.; 0-9605126),* 7011 Hammond Ave., Dallas, TX 75223.
Aquarian Pr, *(Aquarian Press; 0-902146),* P.O. Box 625, Stockbridge, MA 01262 Tel 413-298-3066.
Aquin Pub, *(Aquin Publishing Co.; 0-915352),* 1608 Pacific Ave., Venice, CA 90291 Tel 213-396-9633.
Arbit, *(Arbit, B, Books; 0-930038),* 8050 N. Port Washington Rd., Milwaukee, WI 53217 Tel 414-352-4404.
Arbor Hse, *(Arbor House Publishing Co.; 0-87795),* 235 E. 45th St., New York, NY 10017 Tel 212-599-3131.
Arc Bks, *(Arc Books; 0-668),* Div. of Arco Publishing Inc./Prentice-Hall, Inc., Dist. by: Arco Publishing Inc., 219 Park Ave., S., New York, NY 10003 Tel 212-777-6300.
Arcadia Pr, *(Arcadia Press; 0-938186),* 80 Fifth Ave., New York, NY 10011 Tel 212-477-5331.
Arcane Bks
See Arcane Pubns
Arcane Pubns, *(Arcane Pubns.; 0-912240),* Box 36, York Harbor, ME 03911 Tel 207-363-3333.
Archer Edns, *(Archer Editions Press; 0-89097),* P.O. Box 562, Danbury, CT 06810 Tel 203-438-0282.
Architectural, *(Architectural Book Publishing Co.),* Dist. by: Hastings House Pubs., Inc., 10 E. 40th St., New York, NY 10016 Tel 212-689-5400.
Architectural Rec Bks *Imprint of* **McGraw**
Archival Pr, *(Archival Press, Inc.; 0-915882),* P.O. Box 93, MIT Branch Sta., Cambridge, MA 02139.
Archway, *(Archway Paperbacks; 0-671),* c/o Pocket Books, 1230 Avenue of the Americas, New York, NY 10020 Tel 212-246-2121.
Arco, *(Arco Publishing, Inc.; 0-668),* Div. of Prentice-Hall, Inc., 219 Park Ave., S., New York, NY 10003 Tel 212-777-6300.
Arden Lib, *(Arden Library; 0-8495),* Mill & Main Sts., Darby, PA 19023 Tel 215-726-5505.
Ardis Pubs, *(Ardis Pubs.; 0-88233),* 2901 Heatherway, Ann Arbor, MI 48104 Tel 313-971-2367.
ARE Pr, *(A.R.E. Press; 0-87604),* P.O. Box 595, Editorial Dept., Virginia Beach, VA 23451 Tel 804-428-3588.
Ares, *(Ares Pubs., Inc.; 0-89005),* 612 N. Michigan Ave., Suite 216, Chicago, IL 60611 Tel 312-642-7850.
Arete, *(Arete Publishing Co., Inc.; 0-933880),* Princeton Forrestal Ctr., 101 College Rd. E., Princeton, NJ 08540 Tel 609-452-8090.
Arete Pr, *(Arete Press; 0-934958),* Dept. of English, Case Western Reserve University, Cleveland, OH 44106 Tel 216-368-2340.
Argee Pub, *(Argee Publishing Co.; 0-931084),* 2663 Anchor Ave., W. Los Angeles, CA 90064 Tel 213-559-7603.
Argo *Imprint of* **Atheneum**
Argo Bks, *(Argo Books; 0-912148),* Main St., Norwich, VT 05055 Tel 802-649-1000.
Argosy, *(Argosy-Antiquarian, Ltd.; 0-87266),* 116 E. 59th St., New York, NY 10022.
Argus Comm, *(Argus Communications; 0-913592; 0-89505),* 7440 Natchez Ave., Niles, IL 60648 Tel 312-647-7800.
Ariadne Pr, *(Ariadne Press; 0-918056),* 4817 Tallahassee Ave., Rockville, MD 20853 Tel 301-949-2514.
Ariel Bks
See Ariel Pr
Ariel Pr, *(Ariel Press),* P.O. Box 9183, Berkeley, CA 94709; Tel 415-548-8204; Do Not Confuse with Ariel Pubns, WA.
Aries Pr, *(Aries Press; 0-933646),* P. O. Box 30081, Chicago, IL 60630.
Ark Books MN
See Landmark Bks
Ark Hse NY, *(Ark House Ltd.; 0-935764),* 100 E. 42nd St., New York, NY 10017 Tel 212-697-0205; Dist. by: Associated Booksellers, P.O. Box 6361, Bridgeport, CT 06606 Tel 203-366-5494.
Arkham, *(Arkham House Pubs.; 0-87054),* Sauk City, WI 53583 Tel 608-643-4500.
Arlington Hse, *(Arlington House Pubs.; 0-87000),* 333 Post Rd. W., Westport, CT 06880 Tel 203-226-6383.
Arma Pr, *(Arma Press; 0-9603662),* Rte. 139, North Branford, CT 06471.
Armado & Moth, *(Armado & Moth; 0-9603626),* 2131 Arapahoe, Boulder, CO 80302 Tel 303-442-1415.

Armory Pubns, *(Armory Pubns.; 0-9604982),* P.O. Box 44372, Tacoma, WA 98444.
Arno, *(Arno Press; 0-405),* 3 Park Ave., New York, NY 10016 Tel 212-725-2050.
Arnold-Porter Pub, *(Arnold-Porter Publishing Co.; 0-9605048),* P.O. Box 646, Keego Harbor, MI 48033 Tel 313-338-4478.
ARO Pub, *(ARO Publishing Co.; 0-89868),* Box 193, 398 S. 1100 West, Provo, UT 84601 Tel 801-377-8218.
Aro Pub Co
See ARO Pub
Aronson, *(Aronson, Jason, Inc.; 0-87668),* 111 Eighth Ave., New York, NY 10011 Tel 212-924-6663.
Arrowhead Bks, *(Arrowhead Books; 0-9604152),* 3005 Fulton, Berkeley, CA 94705 Tel 415-548-5110.
Art Alliance, *(Art Alliance Press; 0-87982),* Div. of Associated University Presses, 4 Cornwall Dr., Suite 30, East Brunswick, NJ 08816 Tel 201-254-0132.
Art Dir, *(Art Direction Book Co.; 0-910158),* Dist. by: Advertising Trade Pubns., Inc., 19 W. 44th St., New York, NY 10036 Tel 212-354-0450.
Art Educ, *(Art Education, Inc.; 0-912242),* 28 E. Erie St., Blauvelt, NY 10913 Tel 914-359-2233.
Art Fettig
See Growth Unltd
Art History, *(Art History Pubs.; 0-9600002),* Rte. 2, Red Wing, MN 55066 Tel 612-388-4046.
Art Inst Chi, *(Art Institute of Chicago; 0-86559),* Michigan Ave. & Adams St., Chicago, IL 60603 Tel 312-443-3539; Dist. by: Univ. of Chicago Press, 11030 S. Langley Ave., Chicago, IL 60628 Tel 312-568-1550.
Art Mus Gall, *(Art Museum & Galleries, CSULB, The; 0-936270),* 1250 Bellflower Blvd., Long Beach, CA 90840.
Arte Publico, *(Arte Publico Press; 0-934770),* Revista Chicano-Riquena, Univ. of Houston Central Campus, Houston, TX 77004.
Artech Hse, *(Artech House, Inc.; 0-89006),* 610 Washington St., Dedham, MA 02026 Tel 617-326-8220.
Artemis Pr, *(Artemis Press; 0-9604664),* P.O. Box 58572, Los Angeles, CA 90058 Tel 213-232-5203.
Arthur Pubns, *(Arthur Pubns., Inc.; 0-932782),* P.O. Box 23101, Jacksonville, FL 32217 Tel 904-389-6515.
Artichoke, *(Artichoke Press; 0-9603916),* 3274 Parkhurst Dr., Rancho Palos Verdes, CA 90274.
Article One, *(Article I),* Merrill Rd., McCammon, ID 83250.
Artisan Sales, *(Artisan Sales; 0-934666),* P.O. Box 1497, Thousand Oaks, CA 91360 Tel 805-482-8076.
Artist-Dealer
See Davenport
Artists USA
See Foun Adv Artists
Artmans Pr, *(Artman's Press),* 1511 McGee Ave., Berkeley, CA 94703.
Arts End, *(Arts End Books; 0-933292),* P.O. Box 162, Newton, MA 02168 Tel 617-965-2478.
As-Shabazz Pr
See Shabazz Pr
Ascension, *(Ascension Academy Chinese Project; 0-9600176),* 4401 W. Braddock Rd., Box 9210, Alexandria, VA 22304 Tel 703-379-6050.
Asclepiad, *(Asclepiad Pubns., Inc.; 0-935718),* 1590 E. Maple, Birmingham, MI 48008.
Ash-Kar Pr, *(Ash-Kar Press; 0-9605308),* 519 Castro St., San Francisco, CA 94114.
Ash Pub
See Am Sports Sales
Ashford, *(Ashford Pubns.),* Box 61648, Houston, TX 77208.
Ashlar Pr, *(Ashlar Press; 0-932534),* Box 120277, Nashville, TN 37212.
Ashley Bks, *(Ashley Books, Inc.; 0-87949),* 30 Main St., Port Washington, NY 11050 Tel 516-883-2221; Orders to: P.O. Box 768, Port Washington, NY 11050 Tel 516-883-2221.
Ashod Pr, *(Ashod Press; 0-935102),* 620 E. 20th St, 11F, New York, NY 10009; Orders to: 138-40 64th Ave., Flushing, NY 11367.
Ashrod
See Ashod Pr
ASI Pubs Inc, *(ASI Pubs., Inc.; 0-88231),* 127 Madison Ave., New York, NY 10016 Tel 212-679-5676.
Asia, *(Asia Publishing House; 0-210),* Dist. by: APT Books, Inc., 141 E. 44th St., Suite 511, New York, NY 10017 Tel 212-697-0887.
Asia Bk Corp, *(Asia Book Corp. of America),* 94-41 218th St., Queens Village, NY 11426.
Asia Soc, *(Asia Society, Inc.; 0-87848),* 725 Park Ave., New York, NY 10021 Tel 212-288-6400.
Asian Am Stud, *(Asian American Studies Center, UCLA),* 3232 Campbell Hall, Univ. of California, Los Angeles, CA 90024 Tel 213-825-2974.
Asian Humanities *Imprint of* **Lancaster-Miller**
Asian Music Pub, *(Asian Music Pubns.; 0-913360),* University of WA, School of Music, Seattle, WA 98195 Tel 206-543-0974.
ASIS *Imprint of* **Knowledge Indus**
ASM, *(American Society for Metals; 0-87170),* 9275 Kinsman Rd., Metals Park, OH 44073 Tel 216-338-5151.
ASME, *(American Society of Mechanical Engineers; 0-87053),* 345 E. 47th St., New York, NY 10017 Tel 212-644-7703.
ASP, *(American Society of Photogrammetry; 0-937294),* 105 N. Virginia Ave., Falls Church, VA 22046 Tel 703-534-6617.
Aspen Pr
See Rue Morgue
Aspen Systems, *(Aspen Systems Corp.; 0-912862; 0-89443),* 1600 Research Blvd., Rockville, MD 20850 Tel 301-251-5000.
ASSE, *(American Society of Safety Engineers),* 850 Busse Hwy., Park Ridge, IL 60068 Tel 312-692-4121.
Assembling Pr, *(Assembling Press; 0-915066),* P.O. Box 1967, Brooklyn, NY 11202.
Assn Am Geographers, *(Assn. of American Geographers; 0-89291),* 1710 16th St., N.W., Washington, DC 20009 Tel 202-234-1450.
Assn Baptist Profs, *(Assn. of Baptist Professors of Religion; 0-932180),* Box A, Mercer Univ., Macon, GA 31207.
Assn Consumer Res, *(Assn. for Consumer Research; 0-915552),* Grad. Sch. of Business Admin., Univ. of Michigan, Ann Arbor, MI 48109.
Assn Ed Comm Tech, *(Assn. for Educational Communications & Technology; 0-89240),* 1126 Sixteenth St., N.W., Washington, DC 20036 Tel 202-833-4180.
Assn Family Living, *(Assn. for the Study of Family Living, The; 0-9602670),* P.O. Box 130, Brooklyn, NY 11208 Tel 212-647-7406.
Assn Supervision, *(Assn. for Supervision & Curriculum Development; 0-87120),* 225 N. Washington St., Alexandria, VA 22314 Tel 703-549-9110.
Assn Univ Progs Hlth, *(Assn. of Univ. Programs in Health Administration),* One Dupont Circle, Washington, DC 20036 Tel 202-659-4354.
Assoc Coun Arts
See Am Council Arts
Assoc Creative Writers, *(Associated Creative Writers; 0-933362),* 9231 Molly Woods Ave., La Mesa, CA 92041.
Assoc Writing Progs, *(Associated Writing Programs; 0-936266),* c/o Old Dominion Univ., Norfolk, VA 23508.
Assocs James Bell, *(Associates of the James Ford Bell Library; 0-9601798),* 472 Wilson Library, Univ. of Minnesota, 309 19th Ave. S., Minneapolis, MN 55455 Tel 612-373-2888.
Astor-Honor, *(Astor-Honor, Inc.; 0-8392),* 48 E. 43rd St., New York, NY 10017.
Astro Artz, *(Astro Artz; 0-937122),* 240 S. Broadway, Los Angeles, CA 90012.
Astro Comp Serv, *(Astro Computing Services; 0-917086),* P.O. Box 16297, San Diego, CA 92116 Tel 714-297-5648; Dist. by: Para Research, Whistlestop Mall, Rockport, MA 01966 Tel 617-546-3413.
Astroart Ent, *(Astroart Enterprises; 0-917814),* P.O. Box 503, South Houston, TX 77587 Tel 713-649-6601.
Astron Cal, *(Astronomical Calendar; 0-934546),* Dept. of Physics, Furman Univ., Greenville, SC 29613.
ASU Lat Am St, *(Arizona State Univ., Center for Latin American Studies; 0-87918),* Tempe, AZ 85281 Tel 602-965-5127.
Ata Bks, *(Ata Books; 0-931688),* 1928 Stuart St., Berkeley, CA 94703 Tel 415-841-9613.
Atelier-AFI Films
See Afi Pubns
Atheneum, *(Atheneum Pubs.; 0-689),* 597 Fifth Ave., New York, NY 10017 Tel 212-486-2700; Dist. by: Scribner Dist. Center, Vreeland Ave., Boro of Totowa, Paterson, NJ 07512. *Imprints:* Aladdin (Aladdin Books); Argo (Argo Books); McElderry Bk (McElderry Book).
Athletic, *(Athletic Press; 0-87095),* P.O. Box 2314-D, Pasadena, CA 91105 Tel 213-283-3446.
Athlone Pr *Imprint of* **Humanities**
Atlantic Pub Co, *(Atlantic Publishing Co.; 0-937866),* P.O. Box 67, Tabor City, NC 28463.
Attic Bks, *(Attic Books Ltd.; 0-915018),* 41 E. 57th St., Suite 1210, New York, NY 10022 Tel 212-593-3970; Orders to: P.O. Box 38, South Salem, NY 10590.
Attic Pr, *(Attic Press; 0-87921),* Stony Point, Rte. 2, Greenwood, SC 29646 Tel 803-374-3013.
Auburn Hse, *(Auburn House Publishing Co., Inc.; 0-86569),* 131 Clarendon St., Boston, MA 02116 Tel 617-247-2650.
Audel, *(Audel, Theodore; 0-672),* Dist. by: Bobbs-Merrill, 4300 W. 62nd St., Indianapolis, IN 46206 Tel 317-298-5400.
Audit Investment, *(Audit Investment Research, Inc.; 0-912840),* 230 Park Ave., New York, NY 10017 Tel 212-661-1710.
Augsburg, *(Augsburg Publishing House; 0-8066),* 426 S. Fifth St., Minneapolis, MN 55415 Tel 612-330-3300.
August Corp, *(August Corp.; 0-933482),* P.O. Box 582, Scottsdale, AZ 85252 Tel 602-949-7366.
Aum Pubns, *(Aum Pubns.; 0-88497),* P.O. Box 32433, Jamaica, NY 11431 Tel 212-523-3471.
Aura Bks, *(Aura Books; 0-937736),* 7911 Willoughby Ave., Los Angeles, CA 90046.
Aurelian Pr, *(Aurelian Press; 0-918844),* P.O. Box 366, Wilmette, IL 60091 Tel 312-251-6718.
Auriga, *(Auriga; 0-9602738),* Box F, 8 Candlelight Court, Clifton Park, NY 12065 Tel 518-371-2015.
Auromere, *(Auromere; 0-89744),* 1291 Weber St., Pomona, CA 91768 Tel 714-629-8255.
Aurora Pubs, *(Aurora Pubs.; 0-87695),* P.O. Box 120616, Nashville, TN 37212 Tel 615-254-5842.
Austin Inst Pub Aff
See LBJ Sch Public Affairs
Australiana, *(Australiana Pubns.; 0-909162),* 6511 Riviera Dr., Coral Gables, FL 33146 Tel 305-666-9404; Name Formerly Dryden Press of Australia.
Authors Co-op, *(Authors' Co-op Publishing Co.; 0-931150),* Rte. 4, Box 137, Franklin, TN 37064 Tel 615-646-3757.
Autumn Pr, *(Autumn Press; 0-914398),* 1318 Beacon St., Brookline, MA 02146 Tel 617-738-5680; Dist. by: Random House, Inc., 400 Hahn Rd, Westminster, MD 21157.
Ave Maria, *(Ave Maria Press; 0-87793),* Notre Dame, IN 46556 Tel 219-287-2831.
Avery Color, *(Avery Color Studios; 0-932212),* Star Route Box 275, Au Train, MI 49806 Tel 906-892-8251.
Avery Pub, *(Avery Pub. Group, Inc.; 0-89529),* 142 Fulton Ave., Garden City Park, NY 11040 Tel 516-741-2155; Orders to: 89 Baldwin Terrace, Wayne, NJ 07470.
AVI, *(AVI Publishing Co., Inc.; 0-87055),* 250 Post Rd. E., P.O. Box 831, Westport, CT 06881 Tel 203-226-0738.
Avi
See AVI
Aviation, *(Aviation Book Co.; 0-911720; 0-911721),* 1640 Victory Blvd., Glendale, CA 91201 Tel 213-240-1771.
Aviation Maintenance, *(Aviation Maintenance Publishers; 0-89100),* P.O. Box 890, Basin, WY 82410 Tel 307-568-2413.
Avon, *(Avon Books; 0-380),* 959 Eighth Ave., New York, NY 10019 Tel 212-262-5700. *Imprints:* Bard (Avon Bard Books); Camelot (Avon Camelot Books); Discus (Avon Discus Books).
Avons Res, *(Avons Research Pubns.; 0-913772),* P.O. Box 40, La Canada, CA 91011.

Awakening Prods, *(Awakening Productions; 0-914706),* 4132 Tuller Ave., Culver City, CA 90230.
Awani Pr, *(Awani Press; 0-915266),* P.O. Box 881, Fredericksburg, TX 78624.
Ayer Pr, *(Ayer Press; 0-910190),* 1 Bala Ave., Bala Cynwyd, PA 19004 Tel 215-664-6203.
Aylmer Pr, *(Aylmer Press; 0-932314),* P.O. Box 2735, Madison, WI 53701 Tel 608-251-2506.
AZ Hist Foun, *(Arizona Historical Foundation; 0-910152),* Hayden Memorial Library, Arizona State University, Tempe, AZ 85281 Tel 602-966-8331.
Aztex, *(Aztex Corp.; 0-89404),* 1126 N. Sixth Ave., P.O. Box 50046, Tucson, AZ 85703 Tel 602-882-4656; Dist. by: Elsevier-Dutton, 2 Park Ave., New York, NY 10016 Tel 212-725-1818.
B & M Waite Pr, *(Waite, Benjamin & Martha, Press, Ltd.; 0-934528),* 1126 E. 59th St., Chicago, IL 60637.
B C Scribe, *(Scribe, B. C., Pubns.; 0-930548),* P.O. Box 4705, Berkeley, CA 94704 Tel 415-548-6787.
B Franklin, *(Franklin, Burt, Pub.; 0-89102),* Dist. by: Lenox Hill Publishing & Distributing Corp., 235 E. 44th St., New York, NY 10017.
B Greene, *(Greene, Bill; 0-934668),* Box 810, Mill Valley, CA 94942.
B Klein Pubns, *(Klein, B., Pubns.; 0-87340),* P.O. Box 8503, Coral Springs, FL 33065 Tel 305-752-1708.
B Loft, *(Loft, Barnell, Ltd.; 0-87965),* 958 Church St., Baldwin, NY 11510 Tel 516-868-6064.
B O'Hara, *(O'Hara, Betsy; 0-9604188),* P.O. Box 31510, San Francisco, CA 94131.
B Owens
See Working Pr CA
B P Reynolds, *(Reynolds, Bryan P.),* P.O. Box 186, Palos Park, IL 60464 Tel 312-425-8342.
B Sales, *(Sales, Billee; 0-9605244),* 2638 N.W. 59th Ave., Margate, FL 33063.
B W Brace, *(Brace, Beverly W.),* 455 Crescent Dr., No. 27, Sunnyvale, CA 94087 Tel 408-737-1304.
B Warrior, *(Warrior, Betsy; 0-9601544),* 46 Pleasant St., Cambridge, MA 02139.
B West, *(West, Bill; 0-911614),* 536 E. Ada Ave., Glendora, CA 91740 Tel 213-335-7060.
B Witt, *(Witt, Bud; 0-9604932),* P.O. Box 2527, 4212 W. Olive, Fullerton, CA 92633.
Back Bay, *(Back Bay Books, Inc.),* P.O. Box 1396, Newport Beach, CA 92663.
Backdraft, *(Backdraft Pubns.; 0-936174),* P.O. Box 152, Morristown, NJ 07960 Tel 201-766-7937.
Backdrift
See Backdraft
Backeddy Bks, *(Backeddy Books; 0-9603566),* Box 301, Cambridge, ID 83610.
Backpacker Inc
See Foot Trails
Baha'i, *(Baha'i Publishing Trust; 0-87743),* 415 Linden Ave., Wilmette, IL 60091 Tel 312-251-1854.
Baja Trail, *(Baja Trail Pubns., Inc.; 0-914622),* P.O. Box 6088, Huntington Beach, CA 92646 Tel 714-536-8081.
Baker Bk, *(Baker Book House; 0-8010),* P.O. Box 6287, 6030 E. Fulton, Grand Rapids, MI 49506 Tel 616-676-9186.
Baker Library *Imprint of* **Kelley**
Baker's Plays, *(Baker, Walter H., Co.; 0-87440),* 100 Chauncy St., Boston, MA 02111 Tel 617-482-1280.
Bala Bks, *(Bala Books; 0-89647),* 51 W. Allens Lane, Philadelphia, PA 19119 Tel 215-247-4600.
Bala Pub Div, *(Bala Publishing Division),* 1500 W. 3rd Ave., Suite 329, Columbus, OH 43212.
Balboa Pub, *(Balboa Publishing; 0-935902),* 583 Tenth Ave., San Francisco, CA 94118.
Bale Bks, *(Bale Books; 0-912070),* P.O. Box 2727, New Orleans, LA 70176 Tel 504-895-5306.
Ballantine, *(Ballantine Books, Inc.; 0-345),* Div. of Random House, Inc., 201 E. 50th St., New York, NY 10022 Tel 212-751-2600; Orders to: 400 Hahn Rd., Westminster, MD 21157.
Ballena Pr, *(Ballena Press; 0-87919),* P.O. Box 1366, Socorro, NM 87801 Tel 505-835-2934.
Ballinger Pub, *(Ballinger Publishing Co.; 0-88410),* Subs. of Harper & Row, Inc., 17 Dunster St., Harvard Square, Cambridge, MA 02138 Tel 617-492-0670.
Baltica Pr, *(Baltica Press, Pubs.; 0-910198),* P.O. Box 7847, St. Matthews Sta., Louisville, KY 40207 Tel 502-897-1241.
Baltimore Co Pub Lib, *(Baltimore County Public Library; 0-937076),* 320 York Rd., Towson, MD 21204.
Baltimore Mus, *(Baltimore Museum of Art; 0-912298),* Art Museum Dr., Baltimore, MD 21218 Tel 301-396-6316; Orders to: The Museum Shop, Art Museum Dr., Baltimore, MD 21218 Tel 301-396-6338.
Banbury *Imprint of* **Dell**
Bancroft Parkman, *(Bancroft Parkman Inc.; 0-914022),* 121 E. 78th St., New York, NY 10021 Tel 212-737-2715.
Bancroft Pr, *(Bancroft Press; 0-914888),* 27 McNear Dr., San Rafael, CA 94901 Tel 415-454-7094.
B&B Hochberg, *(Hochberg, Bette & Bernard; 0-9600990),* 333 Wilkes Circle, Santa Cruz, CA 95060 Tel 408-427-2127.
B&N, *(Barnes & Noble Books; 0-389),* Div. of Littlefield, Adams & Co., 81 Adams Dr., Totowa, NJ 07512 Tel 201-256-8600.
Bandon Hist, *(Bandon Historical Society; 0-932368),* P.O. Box 737, Bandon, OR 97411 Tel 503-347-2164.
Banjo Pr
See Tamarack Edns
Bankers, *(Bankers Publishing Co.; 0-87267),* 210 South St., Boston, MA 02111 Tel 617-426-4495.
Banner *Imprint of* **Exposition**
Banner of Truth, *(Banner of Truth, The; 0-85151),* P.O. Box 621, Carlisle, PA 17013 Tel 717-249-5747.
Banner Pr IL, *(Banner Press; 0-916650),* P.O. Box 6469, Chicago, IL 60680 Tel 312-663-1843.
Banning Pr, *(Banning, Arthur J., Press; 0-938060),* 305 Foshay Tower, Minneapolis, MN 55402 Tel 612-335-4259.
Bantam, *(Bantam Books, Inc.; 0-553),* 666 Fifth Ave., New York, NY 10019 Tel 212-765-6500; Orders to: 414 E. Golf Rd., Des Plaines, IL 60016. *Imprints:* Skylark (Skylark).
Banyan Bks, *(Banyan Books; 0-916224),* P.O. Box 431160, Miami, FL 33143 Tel 305-665-6011.
Banyan Tree, *(Banyan Tree Books; 0-9604320),* 1963 El Dorado Ave., Berkeley, CA 94707; Dist. by: Bookpeople, 2940 Seventh St., Berkeley, CA 94710 Tel 415-549-3033.
Baptist Pub Hse, *(Baptist Publishing House; 0-89114),* 1319 Magnolia, Texarkana, TX 75501.
Baptist Span
See Casa Bautista
Bar Guide, *(Bar Guide Enterprises; 0-918338),* P.O. Box 4044, Terminal Annex, Los Angeles, CA 90051 Tel 213-883-5369.
Bar-None, *(Bar-None Press; 0-9605672),* 6520 Selma Ave., No. 538, Los Angeles, CA 90028.
Baraka Bk, *(Baraka Books, Ltd.),* 453 Greenwich St., New York, NY 10013 Tel 212-966-6658.
Baraka Pr
See Baraka Bk
Barber Pr, *(Barber, Lilian, Press; 0-936508),* Box 4224, Grand Central Sta., New York, NY 10163.
Barclay Bridge, *(Barclay Bridge Supplies, Inc.; 0-87643),* 8 Bush Ave., Port Chester, NY 10573 Tel 914-937-4200.
Bard *Imprint of* **Avon**
Bardic, *(Bardic Echoes Brochures; 0-915020),* 125 Somerset Dr., N.E., Grand Rapids, MI 49503 Tel 616-454-2807.
Bark-Back, *(Bark-Back; 0-9603338),* P.O. Box 235, Glenshaw, PA 15116 Tel 412-364-3743.
Barleycorn, *(Barleycorn Books; 0-935566),* 290 S.W. Tualatin Loop, West Linn, OR 97068 Tel 503-225-0234.
Barnard Roberts, *(Barnard, Roberts & Co., Inc.; 0-934118),* 6655 Amberton Dr., Rte. 100 Business Park, Baltimore, MD 21227 Tel 301-796-5655.
Barnegat, *(Barnegat Light Press; 0-937996),* Box 305, Barnegat Light, NJ 08006.
Barnstable, *(Barnstable Books; 0-918230),* 799 Broadway, Rm. 506A, New York, NY 10003 Tel 212-473-8681.
Barre, *(Barre Publishing Co.),* Valley Rd., Barre, MA 01005 Tel 617-355-2914; Dist. by: Crown Publishers, Inc., 1 Park Ave., New York, NY 10016.
Barrie & Jenkins, *(Barrie & Jenkins; 0-214),* Dist. by: Arco, 219 Park Ave. S., New York, NY 10003 Tel 212-777-6300.
Barrington, *(Barrington Press, Inc.; 0-938814),* 200 James St., Barrington, IL 60010 Tel 312-381-9200.
Barron, *(Barron's Educational Series, Inc.; 0-8120),* 113 Crossways Park Dr., Woodbury, NY 11797 Tel 516-921-8750.
Basic, *(Basic Books, Inc.; 0-465),* 10 E. 53rd St., New York, NY 10022 Tel 212-593-7057.
Basic Eng Rev, *(Basic English Revisited),* 275 Robins Row, Burlington, WI 53105.
Basic Sci Pr, *(Basic Science Press; 0-917410),* 1608 Via Lazo, Palos Verdes Estates, CA 90274 Tel 213-375-6740; Formerly Named Lucknow Publishing Co.
Basic Science Prep Ctr, *(Basic Science Preparation Center; 0-9604722),* 55 Willow Tree Lane, Irvine, CA 92715; Orders to: 1601 Vivian Lane, Louisville, KY 40205.
Basil Blackwell
See Biblio Dist
Baskin Pubs, *(Baskin Pubs.; 0-935854),* P.O. Box 3127, San Diego, CA 92103.
Bath St Pr, *(Bath Street Press; 0-937618),* 1016 Bath, Ann Arbor, MI 48103 Tel 313-663-2071.
Battelle, *(Battelle Press; 0-935470),* Div. of Columbus Laboratories of Batelle Memorial Institute, 505 King Ave., Columbus, OH 43201 Tel 614-424-4448; Dist. by: Van Nostrand Reinhold, 135 W. 50th St., New York, NY 10020 Tel 212-265-8700.
Battery Pk, *(Battery Park Book Co.; 0-89782),* Box 710, Forest Hills, NY 11375.
Battery Pr, *(Battery Press; 0-89839),* P.O. Box 3107, Uptown Sta., Nashville, TN 37219 Tel 615-298-1401.
Bauhan, *(Bauhan, William L., Inc.; 0-87233),* Old County Rd., Dublin, NH 03444 Tel 603-563-8020.
Bawa Muhaiyad
See Fellowship Pr PA
Baylor Univ Pr, *(Baylor Univ. Press; 0-918954),* Orders to: Book Dept., Baylor Book Store, P.O. Box 6325, Waco, TX 76706 Tel 817-755-2161.
Baywood Pub, *(Baywood Publishing Co., Inc.; 0-89503),* 120 Marine St., P.O. Box D, Farmingdale, NY 11735 Tel 516-293-7130.
BBM Assocs
See Calif Street
BC *Imprint of* **Grove**
BCC, *(Business Communications Co. Inc. (BCC); 0-89336),* P.O. Box 2070C, 9 Viaduct Rd., Stamford, CT 06906 Tel 203-325-2208.
BCM Inc, *(Bible Club Movement, Inc.),* 237 Fairfield Ave., Upper Darby, PA 19082 Tel 215-352-7177.
BCM Pubns
See BCM Inc
Bd of Pubns CRC, *(Board of Publicatons of the Christian Reformed Church; 0-933140),* 2850 Kalamazoo Ave. S.E., Grand Rapids, MI 49560 Tel 616-241-1691.
Beachcomber Bks, *(Beachcomber Books; 0-913076),* 3829 N. Oracle Rd., Tucson, AZ 85705.
Beacon Pr, *(Beacon Press, Inc.; 0-8070),* 25 Beacon St., Boston, MA 02108 Tel 617-742-2110; Orders to: Harper & Row Pubs., Inc., Keystone Industrial Park, Scranton, PA 18512.
Bean Assoc
See Bean Pub
Bean Pub, *(Carolyn Bean Publishing, Ltd.; 0-916860),* 120 Second St., San Francisco, CA 94105 Tel 415-957-9574.
Beau Lac, *(Beau Lac Pubs.; 0-911980),* P.O. Box 248, Chuluota, FL 32766 Tel 305-365-3830.
Beaufort Bks NY, *(Beaufort Books; 0-8253),* 9 E. 40th St., New York, NY 10016.
Beautiful Am, *(Beautiful America Publishing Co.; 0-89802; 0-915796),* P.O. Box 608, Beaverton, OR 97075 Tel 503-641-2272.
Beckwith, *(Beckwith, Burnham Putnam; 0-9603262),* 656 Lytton Ave., (C430), Palo Alto, CA 94301 Tel 415-324-0342.

Beeberry Bks, *(Beeberry Books; 0-9601996),* Box 3888, Stanford, CA 94306.
Beech Hill, *(Beech Hill Publishing Co.; 0-933786),* Box 29, Mt. Desert, ME 04660 Tel 207-244-3931.
Beech Hill Ent
See Beech Hill
Beekman Pubs, *(Beekman Pubs., Inc.; 0-8464),* 38 Hicks St., Brooklyn Heights, NY 11201 Tel 212-624-4514.
Beer Adv
See D Bull
Behavioral Pubns
See Human Sci Pr
Behavioral Re
See Learning Line
Behrman, *(Behrman House, Inc.; 0-87441),* 1261 Broadway, New York, NY 10001 Tel 212-689-2020.
Beinfeld Pub, *(Beinfeld Publishing, Inc.; 0-917714),* 12767 Saticoy St., North Hollywood, CA 91605.
Being Bks, *(Being Books),* 19834 Gresham St., Northridge, CA 91324 Tel 213-341-0283.
Belier Pr, *(Belier Press, Inc.; 0-914646),* P.O. Box C, Gracie Sta., New York, NY 10028 Tel 212-989-5722.
Bell Assn Deaf, *(A. G. Bell Assn. for the Deaf; 0-88200),* 3417 Volta Place, N.W., Washington, DC 20007 Tel 202-337-5220.
Bell Springs Pub, *(Bell Springs Pub; 0-917510),* P.O. Box 640, Laytonville, CA 95454 Tel 707-984-6746.
Belle Pubns, *(Belle Pubns.; 0-9605732),* 172 Pathway Lane, W. Lafayette, IN 47906.
Bellefontaine Bks, *(Bellefontaine Books; 0-932786),* P.O. Box 501, Arroyo Grande, CA 93420 Tel 805-489-6242.
Belleridge, *(Belleridge Press; 0-938632),* P.O. Box 970, Rancho Santa Fe, CA 92067.
Bellman, *(Bellman Publishing Co.; 0-87442),* P.O. Box 164, Arlington, MA 02174 Tel 617-894-3000.
Belmont-Tower
See Tower Bks
Bender Pub CA, *(Bender, R. James, Publishing; 0-912138),* P.O. Box 23456, San Jose, CA 95123 Tel 408-225-5777.
Benedict Con Adoration, *(Benedictine Convent of Perpetual Adoration; 0-913180),* 3888 Paducah Dr., San Diego, CA 92117 Tel 714-274-1030.
Beninda, *(Beninda Books; 0-931868),* P.O. Box 9251, Canton, OH 44711.
Benjamin Co, *(Benjamin Co., Inc.; 0-87502),* 485 Madison Ave., New York, NY 10022 Tel 212-759-6920.
Benjamin-Cummings, *(Benjamin-Cummings Publishing Co.; 0-8053),* Subs. of Addison-Wesley Publishing Co., 2727 Sand Hill Rd., Menlo Park, CA 94025 Tel 415-854-6020; Orders to: South St., Reading, MA 01867. *Imprints:* Adv Bk Prog (Advance Book Program).
Bennett Co
See Bennett IL
Bennett IL, *(Bennett Publishing Co.; 0-87002),* 809 W. Detweiller Dr., Peoria, IL 61615 Tel 309-691-4454.
Bentley, *(Bentley, Robert, Inc.; 0-8376),* 872 Massachusetts Ave., Cambridge, MA 02139 Tel 617-547-4170.
Benziger
See Glencoe
Beresford Bk Serv, *(Beresford Book Service; 0-202),* 1525 E. 53rd St., Suite 431, Chicago, IL 60615.
Berkeley Poets, *(Berkeley Poets' Workshop & Press),* P.O. Box 459, Berkeley, CA 94701 Tel 415-848-9098.
Berkeley Sci, *(Berkeley Scientific Pubns.),* Div. of Scientific Newsletters, Inc., P.O. Box 4546, Anaheim, CA 92803.
Berkeley Slavic, *(Berkeley Slavic Specialities; 0-933884),* P.O. Box 4605, Berkeley, CA 94704 Tel 415-653-8048.
Berkley Pub, *(Berkley Publishing Corp.; 0-425),* Affiliate of G. P. Putnam's Sons, 200 Madison Ave., New York, NY 10016 Tel 212-686-9820. *Imprints:* Highland (Highland Books); Medallion (Medallion Books).
Berkshire Traveller, *(Berkshire Traveller Press; 0-912944),* Pine St., Stockbridge, MA 01262 Tel 413-298-3636.
Bermont Bks, *(Bermont Books; 0-930686),* 815 15th St., N.W., Suite 1108, Washington, DC 20005.
Best Bks, *(Best Books, Inc.; 0-910228),* 44 Madison St., Oak Park, IL 60302.
Bet Yoatz Lib Serv
See BYLS Pr
Beta Bk, *(Beta Book Co.; 0-89293),* 10857 Valiente Court, San Diego, CA 92124 Tel 714-293-3832.
Beta Phi Mu, *(Beta Phi Mu Chapbooks; 0-910230),* College of Library Science; Univ. of KY, Lexington, KY 40506.
Bethany Coll
See Bethany Coll KS
Bethany Coll KS, *(Bethany College Pubns. - Kansas; 0-916030),* P.O. Box 111, Lindsborg, KS 67456.
Bethany Fell, *(Bethany Fellowship, Inc.; 0-87123),* 6820 Auto Club Rd., Minneapolis, MN 55438 Tel 612-944-2121.
Bethany Pr, *(Bethany Press; 0-8272),* 2640 Pine Blvd., Box 179, St. Louis, MO 63166 Tel 314-371-6900.
BETOM Pubns, *(BETOM Pubns; 0-9605172),* P.O. Box 47, New London, WI 54961.
Better Am Corp, *(Better America Corp., A; 0-9605156),* P.O. Box 8746, Pembroke Pines, FL 33024.
Better Baby, *(Better Baby Press, The; 0-936676),* 8801 Stenton Ave., Philadelphia, PA 19118.
Better Bks, *(Better Books Pub.),* 3736 S. E. 33rd Ave., Portland, OR 97202 Tel 503-238-0442.
Betterway Pubns, *(Betterway Pubns; 0-932620),* White Hall, VA 22987 Tel 804-823-5661.
Beverage Media, *(Beverage Media, Ltd.; 0-9602566),* 251 Park Ave. S., New York, NY 10010.
Bewick Edns, *(Bewick Editions; 0-935590),* 1443 Bewick, Detroit, MI 48214.
BGSU Dept Phil, *(Bowling Green State Univ., Dept. of Philosophy; 0-935756),* Bowling Green State Univ., Bowling Green, OH 43403 Tel 419-372-2117.
BGTC
See B Greene
BH Ent, *(BH Enterprises; 0-9604896),* P.O. Box 216, Midwood Sta., Brooklyn, NY 11230 Tel 212-336-0521.
Bhaktivedanta, *(Bhaktivedanta Book Trust; 0-912776),* 3764 Watseka Ave., Los Angeles, CA 90034 Tel 213-559-4455.
BH&G, *(Better Homes & Gardens Books; 0-696),* Div. of Meredith Corp., 1716 Locust St., Des Moines, IA 50336 Tel 515-284-2844.
BHRA Fluid, *(BHRA Fluid Engineering; 0-900983),* Dist. by: Air Science Co., P.O. Box 143, Corning, NY 14830 Tel 607-962-5591.
Bi World Indus, *(Bi World Industries, Inc.; 0-89557),* P.O. Box 62, Provo, UT 84601 Tel 801-224-5803.
Bibl Based Develop, *(Biblically Based Developmental Training Books, Inc.; 0-937442),* P.O. Box 15124, Atlanta, GA 30333.
Bibl Evang Pr, *(Biblical Evangelism Press; 0-914012),* 11 Blvd. Motif, Brownsburg, IN 46112 Tel 317-852-3535; Orders to: P.O. Box 157, Brownsburg, IN 46112.
Bibl Res Pr, *(Biblical Research Press; 0-89112),* 1334 Ruswood, Abilene, TX 79601 Tel 915-672-6702.
Bible Light, *(Bible Light Pubns.; 0-937078),* P.O. Box 168, Jerome Ave. Sta., New York, NY 10468.
Biblio Dist, *(Biblio Distribution Centre),* 81 Adams Dr., P.O. Box 327, Totowa, NJ 07511 Tel 201-256-8600.
Biblio Pr GA, *(Bibliotheca Press; 0-9605246),* P.O. Box 98378, Atlanta, GA 30359 Tel 404-588-1328.
Biblio Siglo, *(Biblioteca Siglo de Oro),* 530 N. First St., Charlottesville, VA 22901 Tel 804-295-1021.
Bibliotheca, *(Bibliotheca Islamica, Inc.; 0-88297),* P.O. Box 1536, Chicago, IL 60690.
Biblo, *(Biblo & Tannen Booksellers & Pubs., Inc.; 0-8196),* P.O. Box 302, 321 Sandbank Rd., Cheshire, CT 06410.
Bieler, *(Bieler Press; 0-931460),* P.O. Box 3856, St. Paul, MN 55165 Tel 612-292-9936.
Big Moose, *(Big Moose Press; 0-914692),* P.O. Box 180, Big Moose, NY 13331 Tel 315-357-2821.
Binford, *(Binford & Mort Pubs.; 0-8323),* 2536 S.E. 11th Ave., Portland, OR 97202 Tel 503-238-9666.
Bio Pubs & Dists, *(Biobehavioral Pubs. & Distributors, Inc.; 0-938176),* 8467 Indian Hills Blvd., Shreveport, LA 71107 Tel 318-929-7133; Orders to: P. O. Box 1102, Houston, TX 77001.
Bio Res Inst
See World Natural Hist
Biobehavioral Pr, *(Biobehavioral Press; 0-938176),* Dist. by: Stress Management Research Associates, 5801 Lumberdale, Suite 213, Houston, TX 77092 Tel 713-681-6725.
Biofeed Pr, *(Biofeedback Press),* 3428 Sacramento St., San Francisco, CA 94118 Tel 415-621-5455.
Biomedical Pr *Imprint of* **Elsevier**
BioServ Corp, *(BioService Corp.; 0-938278),* 500 S. Racine Ave., Suite 302, Chicago, IL 60607.
Birkhauser, *(Birkhauser Boston Inc.; 3-7643),* 380 Green St., Cambridge, MA 02139 Tel 617-876-2333.
Birth Day, *(Birth Day Publishing Co.; 0-9600958),* P.O. Box 7722, San Diego, CA 92107 Tel 714-296-3194.
Bisbee Pr, *(Bisbee Press Collective; 0-938196),* Drawer HA, Bisbee, AZ 85603.
Bishop Mus, *(Bishop Museum Press; 0-910240),* P.O. Box 19000-A, Honolulu, HI 96819 Tel 808-847-3511.
Biviano, *(Biviano, Ronald; 0-9605476),* 505 N. Lakeshore Dr., Chicago, IL 60611.
Biworld
See Bi World Indus
BJ Pub Group, *(BJ Publishing Group),* 200 Madison Ave., New York, NY 10016 Tel 212-686-9820.
Bk Habit, *(Book Habit, The; 0-9605200),* P.O. Box 941, San Marcos, CA 92069.
Bklyn Botanic, *(Brooklyn Botanic Garden),* 1000 Washington Ave., Brooklyn, NY 11225 Tel 212-622-4433.
Bklyn Mus, *(Brooklyn Museum; 0-87273; 0-913696),* Pubns. & Marketing Services, Eastern Pkwy., Brooklyn, NY 11238 Tel 212-638-5000.
Bks Australia, *(Books Australia, Inc.),* 15601 S.W. 83rd Ave., Miami, FL 33157 Tel 305-251-3934.
Bks Business, *(Books for Business, Inc.; 0-89499),* 1100 Seventeenth St., N.W., Washington, DC 20036 Tel 202-466-2372.
Bks in Focus, *(Books in Focus, Inc.; 0-916728),* 160 E. 38th St., Suite 31B, New York, NY 10016 Tel 212-490-0334.
Black Buzzard, *(Black Buzzard Press; 0-938872),* 2217 Shorefield Rd., No. 532, Wheaton, MD 20902.
Black Light Fellow, *(Black Light Fellowship; 0-933176),* P.O. Box 5369, Chicago, IL 60680 Tel 312-277-1361.
Black Oak, *(Black Oak Press; 0-930674),* Box 4663, University Place Sta., Lincoln, NE 68504.
Black Sparrow, *(Black Sparrow Press; 0-87685),* P.O. Box 3993, Santa Barbara, CA 93105 Tel 805-687-5014.
Black Stone, *(Black Stone Press; 0-937002),* 865 Florida St., San Francisco, CA 94110 Tel 415-282-8806.
Black Swan CT, *(Black Swan Books Ltd.; 0-933806),* P.O. Box 327, Redding Ridge, CT 06876 Tel 203-938-9548.
Blackburn Coll, *(Blackburn College Press),* Lumpkin Library, Carlinville, IL 62626.
Blackjack Ent, *(Blackjack Enterprises; 0-935110),* P.O. Box 328, Scottsdale, AZ 85252; Dist. by: Golden Hind Publishing Co., 36 W. Del Rio Circle, Tempe, AZ 85282.
Blackwell Sci, *(Blackwell Scientific Pubns., Inc.),* 52 Beacon St., Boston, MA 02108; Dist. by: Blackwell/Mosby Book Distributors, 11830 Westline Industrial Dr., St. Louis, MO 63141.
Blagrove Pubns, *(Blagrove Pubns.; 0-9604466),* 80 Pitkin St., P.O. Box 584, Manchester, CT 06040 Tel 203-647-1785.
Blaine Ethridge, *(Blaine Ethridge Books; 0-87917),* 13977 Penrod St., Detroit, MI 48223 Tel 313-838-3363.
Blair, *(Blair, John F., Pub.; 0-910244; 0-89587),* 1406 Plaza Dr., Winston-Salem, NC 27103 Tel 919-768-1374.
Blitz Pub Co, *(Blitz Publishing Co.),* 1600 Verona St., Middleton, WI 53562 Tel 608-836-7550.

Bloch, *(Bloch Publishing Co.; 0-8197),* 915 Broadway, New York, NY 10010 Tel 212-673-7910.
Bloch & Co OH, *(Bloch & Co.),* P.O. Box 18058, Cleveland, OH 44118 Tel 216-371-0979.
Blood Horse
See Thoroughbred Own & Breed
Blue Harbor, *(Blue Harbor Press; 0-9605278),* P.O. Box 1028, Lomita, CA 90717.
Blue Heron, *(Blue Heron Press, Inc.),* 1728 Herrick N.E., Grand Rapids, MI 49505 Tel 616-363-7810.
Blue Lagoon, *(Blue Lagoon Pubs.; 0-9605338),* 3606 Coldwater Canyon, Studio City, CA 91604.
Blue Leaf, *(Blue Leaf Editions; 0-915206),* P.O. Box 857, New London, CT 06320 Tel 203-445-7391.
Blue Mtn Arts
See Blue Mtn Pr CO
Blue Mtn Pr CO, *(Blue Mountain Press, Inc.; 0-88396),* P.O. Box 1007, Boulder, CO 80306 Tel 303-449-0536; Orders to: P.O. Box 4549, Boulder, CO 80306.
Blue Oak, *(Blue Oak Press; 0-912950),* P.O. Box 27, Sattley, CA 96124.
Blue River, *(Blue River Publishing Co.; 0-936324),* P.O. Box 882, Sheboygan, WI 53081.
Blue Wind, *(Blue Wind Press; 0-912652),* P.O. Box 7175, Berkeley, CA 94707 Tel 415-526-1905.
Blustein-Geary, *(Blustein/Geary; 0-9605248),* 46 Glen Circle, Waltham, MA 02154.
Blyden Pr, *(Blyden, Edward W., Press, Inc.; 0-914110),* P.O. Box 621, Manhattanville Sta., New York, NY 10027 Tel 212-222-6000.
BM Surveying
See CARBEN Survey
BMA Pr, *(BMA Press; 0-89323),* P.O. Box 12000, St. Louis, MO 63112.
BMH Bks, *(BMH Books; 0-88469),* P.O. Box 544, Winona Lake, IN 46590 Tel 219-267-7158.
BNA, *(Bureau of National Affairs, Inc.; 0-87179),* 1231 25th St., N.W., Washington, DC 20037 Tel 202-452-4276.
Board of Pubn
See Bd of Pubns CRC
Boardman, *(Boardman, Clark, Co., Ltd.; 0-87632),* 435 Hudson St., New York, NY 10014 Tel 212-929-7500.
Boardroom, *(Boardroom Books, Inc.; 0-932648),* Div. of Boardroom Reports, 500 5th Ave., New York, NY 10036 Tel 212-354-0005.
Boardroom Repr
See Boardroom
Bobbs, *(Bobbs-Merrill Co., Inc.; 0-672),* A Thomas Audel Co., 4300 W. 62nd St., Indianapolis, IN 46468 Tel 317-298-5400.
Bodine, *(Bodine & Associates, Inc.; 0-910254),* 1101 St. Paul St., Baltimore, MD 21202 Tel 301-385-1103.
Boian Bks, *(Boian Books; 0-9604420),* 246 West End Ave., No. 10 B, New York, NY 10023.
Bold Strummer Ltd, *(Bold Strummer, Ltd; 0-933224),* 1 Webb Rd., Westport, CT 06880 Tel 203-226-8230.
Bolder Landry, *(Bolder Landry),* 8925 San Salvador Circle, Buena Park, CA 90620.
Bonanza, *(Bonanza, Inc.; 0-932952),* 1010-12th St., Sparks, NV 89431.
Bond Pub Co, *(Bond Publishing Co.),* 226 Massachusetts Ave. N.E., Washington, DC 20002.
Bonney, *(Bonney, Orrin H.; 0-931620),* 625 E. 14th St., Houston, TX 77008 Tel 713-864-8697.
Book & Tackle, *(Book & Tackle Shop; 0-910258),* 29 Old Colony Rd., Chestnut Hill, MA 02167 Tel 617-965-0459.
Book-Lab, *(Book-Lab, Inc.; 0-87594),* 1449 37th St., Brooklyn, NY 11218 Tel 212-853-4140.
Book Promo Unltd, *(Book Promotions Unlimited; 0-933586),* P.O. Box 122, Flushing, MI 48433 Tel 313-659-6683.
Book Pub Co, *(Book Publishing Co., The; 0-913990),* 156 Drakes Lane, Summertown, TN 38483 Tel 615-964-3571.
Book Searchers, *(Book Searchers; 0-932484),* 2622 15th Ave., Forest Grove, OR 97116 Tel 503-357-6948.
Bookcraft Inc, *(Bookcraft, Inc.; 0-88494),* 1848 W. 2300, S., Salt Lake City, UT 84119 Tel 801-972-6180.
Bookery, *(Bookery; 0-930822),* 8193 Riata Dr., Redding, CA 96002 Tel 916-365-8068; Dist. by: Caroline House, 2 Ellis Place, Ossining, NY 10562.
Bookfinger, *(Bookfinger; 0-913774),* P.O. Box 487, Peter Stuyvesant Sta., New York, NY 10009.
Booklegger Pr, *(Booklegger Press; 0-912932),* 555 29th St., San Francisco, CA 94131 Tel 415-647-9074.
Bookmaker, *(Bookmaker Publishing; 0-934778),* 1212 E. 131st St., Burnsville, MN 55337.
Bookman Dan, *(Bookman Dan!; 0-934780),* P.O. Box 13492, Baltimore, MD 21203 Tel 301-235-8818.
Bookpeople, *(Bookpeople),* 2940 Seventh St., Berkeley, CA 94710 Tel 415-549-3030.
Boosey & Hawkes, *(Boosey & Hawkes, Inc.; 0-913932),* P.O. Box 130, Oceanside, NY 11572 Tel 516-678-2500.
Borden, *(Borden Publishing Co.; 0-87505),* 1855 W. Main St., Alhambra, CA 91801 Tel 213-283-5031.
Borf Bks, *(Borf Books; 0-9604894),* Brownsville, KY 42210 Tel 502-597-2187.
Borgo Pr, *(Borgo Press; 0-89370),* P.O. Box 2845, San Bernardino, CA 92406 Tel 714-884-5813.
Boss Bks, *(Boss Books; 0-932430),* P.O. Box 370, Madison Square Sta., New York, NY 10159 Tel 212-683-3274.
Boston Public Lib, *(Boston Public Library; 0-89073),* P.O. Box 286, Boston, MA 02117 Tel 617-536-5400.
Bouregy, *(Bouregy, Thomas, & Co., Inc.; 0-8034),* 22 E. 60th St., New York, NY 10022 Tel 212-753-8410.
Bowker, *(Bowker, R. R., Co.; 0-8352),* A Xerox Publishing Co., 1180 Ave. of the Americas, New York, NY 10036 Tel 212-764-5100; Orders to: P.O. Box 1807, Ann Arbor, MI 48106.
Bowling Green Univ, *(Bowling Green Univ., Popular Press; 0-87972),* Bowling Green State Univ., Popular Culture Ctr., Bowling Green, OH 43403 Tel 419-372-2981.
Bowmar
See Bowmar-Noble
Bowmar-Noble, *(Bowmar/Noble Publishers, Inc.; 0-8372; 0-8107),* 4563 Colorado Blvd., Los Angeles, CA 90039 Tel 213-247-8995.
Boxwood, *(Boxwood Press; 0-910286),* 183 Ocean View Blvd., Pacific Grove, CA 93950 Tel 408-375-9110.
Boyd & Fraser, *(Boyd & Fraser Publishing Co.; 0-87835),* 3627 Sacramento St., San Francisco, CA 94118 Tel 415-346-0686.
Boykin, *(Boykin, James H.; 0-9603342),* 1260 N.W. 122nd St, Miami, FL 33167.
Boynton & Assoc, *(Boynton & Associates; 0-933168),* Clifton House, Clifton, VA 22024.
Boys Clubs, *(Boys' Clubs of America),* 771 First Ave., New York, NY 10017 Tel 212-557-7755.
Boys Town Ctr, *(Boys Town Center for the Study of Youth Development; 0-938510),* Boys Town, NE 68010.
Bradbury Pr, *(Bradbury Press; 0-87888),* 2 Overhill Rd., Scarsdale, NY 10583 Tel 914-472-5100; Dist. by: E. P. Dutton & Co., Inc., 2 Park Ave., New York, NY 10016.
Bradford Bks, *(Bradford Books Pubs., Inc.; 0-89706),* Box 28, Montgomery, VT 05470 Tel 802-933-4193.
Bradley CPA, *(Bradley CPA Study Aids, Inc.; 0-932788),* 21146 Ventura Blvd., Suite 203, Woodland Hills, CA 91364 Tel 213-340-3779.
Bradt Ent, *(Bradt Enterprises Pubns.; 0-933982; 0-9505797),* 54 Dudley St., Cambridge, MA 02140 Tel 617-492-8776.
Branch-Smith, *(Branch-Smith, Inc.; 0-87706),* P.O. Box 1868, Fort Worth, TX 76101 Tel 817-332-6377; 120 St. Louis Ave., Fort Worth, TX 76101.
Branden, *(Branden Press, Inc.; 0-8283),* P.O. Box 843, Brookline Village, 21 Station St., Boston, MA 02147 Tel 617-734-2045.
Brandywine Bks, *(Brandywine Books; 0-9604986),* 5020 73rd St., Suite B, San Diego, CA 92115.
Brandywine Conserv, *(Brandywine Conservancy),* P.O. Box 141, Chadds Ford, PA 19317 Tel 215-388-7601.
Branford, *(Branford, Charles T., Co.; 0-8231),* 19 Calvin Rd., P.O. Box 16, Watertown, MA 02172 Tel 617-924-1020.
Braziller, *(Braziller, George, Inc.; 0-8076),* One Park Ave., New York, NY 10016 Tel 212-889-0909.
Breaking Point, *(Breaking Point, Inc.; 0-917020),* P.O. Box 328, Wharton, NJ 07885 Tel 201-361-7238.
Brethren, *(Brethren Press; 0-87178),* 1451 Dundee Ave., Elgin, IL 60120 Tel 312-742-5100.
Breton Pubs *Imprint of* **Wadsworth Pub**
Brevet Pr, *(Brevet Press; 0-88498),* Box 1404, Sioux Falls, SD 57101 Tel 605-339-2330.
Brick Hse Pub, *(Brick House Publishing Co.; 0-931790),* 34 Essex St., Andover, MA 01810 Tel 617-475-9568.
Bricker Pubns
See Bricker's Intl
Bricker's Intl, *(Bricker's International Directory; 0-916404),* 425 Family Farm Rd., Woodside, CA 94062 Tel 415-851-3090.
Bridges Pr, *(Bridges Pr),* 2212 "D" St., Vancouver, WA 98663 Tel 206-694-6695; Orders to: Pragmatix Management Resources, 408 S.W. 2nd Ave., Suite 425, Portland, OR 97204 Tel 503-223-7524.
Bridges Sound, *(Bridges to the Sound Publishing Corp.; 0-938316),* P.O. Box 260607, Tampa, FL 33685.
Brigadoon, *(Brigadoon Pubns., Inc.; 0-938512),* 3911 Richmond Ave., Staten Island, NY 10312.
Brigham, *(Brigham Young Univ. Press; 0-8425),* 218 University Press Bldg., Provo, UT 84602 Tel 801-378-4707; Orders to: 205 University Press Bldg., Provo, UT 84602 Tel 801-378-2809.
Bright Spirit, *(Bright Spirit Press; 0-937346),* P.O. Box 4254, San Rafael, CA 94913 Tel 415-453-5412.
Brighton Pub Co, *(Brighton Publishing Co.; 0-89832),* P.O. Box 6235, Salt Lake City, UT 84106 Tel 801-466-4044.
Brighton Pubns, *(Brighton Pubns.; 0-918420),* P.O. Box 12706, New Brighton, MN 55112 Tel 612-636-2220.
British Bk Ctr, *(British Book Center; 0-8277),* Fairview Park, Elmsford, NY 10523 Tel 914-592-7700.
Britton Pub, *(Britton Publishing Co.; 0-938318),* Box 9628, North Hollywood, CA 91609 Tel 213-506-4682.
Bro Life Bks, *(Brotherhood of Life, Inc.; 0-914732),* 110 Dartmouth, S.E., Albuquerque, NM 87106 Tel 505-255-8980.
Broadman, *(Broadman Press; 0-8054),* 127 Ninth Ave., N., Nashville, TN 37234 Tel 615-251-2544.
Brodart, *(Bro-Dart Publishing Co.; 0-87272),* 1609 Memorial Ave., Williamsport, PA 17701 Tel 717-326-2461.
Broken Whisker, *(Broken Whisker Studio; 0-932220),* Printers Row, 711 S. Dearborn, Loft 505, Chicago, IL 60605 Tel 312-969-8311.
Brookings, *(Brookings Institution; 0-8157),* 1775 Massachusetts Ave., N.W., Washington, DC 20036 Tel 202-797-6254.
Brooklyn Coll Pr, *(Brooklyn College Press; 0-930888),* 562 W. 113th St., New York, NY 10025.
Brooks-Cole, *(Brooks/Cole Publishing Co.; 0-8185),* Div. of Wadsworth, Inc., 555 Abrego St., Monterey, CA 93940 Tel 408-373-0728; Orders to: Wadsworth, Inc., 10 Davis Dr., Belmont, CA 94002 Tel 415-595-2350.
Brooks Pub Co, *(Brooks Publishing Co.; 0-932370),* 1226 Chester Ave., Bakersfield, CA 93301 Tel 805-322-0687.
Brooks-Sterling, *(Brooks-Sterling Co.; 0-914418),* P.O. Box 265, Danville, CA 94526 Tel 415-837-1318.
Broude, *(Broude Brothers Ltd., Music; 0-8450),* 56 W. 45th St., New York, NY 10036 Tel 212-687-4735.
Broude Intl Edns, *(Broude International Editions, Inc.; 0-89371),* 56 W. 45th St., New York, NY 10036 Tel 212-687-4735.
Brown Bk, *(Brown Book Co.; 0-910294),* 120 Secatogue Ave., Farmingdale, NY 11735 Tel 516-293-6969.
Brown Hse Gall, *(Brown House Galleries Ltd.; 0-9604534),* 5717 Hammersley Rd., P.O. Box 4243, Madison, WI 53711.

Brown Rabbit, *(Brown Rabbit Press; 0-933988),* P.O. Box 19111, Houston, TX 77024 Tel 713-465-1168.
Browning Pubns, *(Browning Pubns.; 0-933718),* P.O. Box 81306, Atlanta, GA 30366 Tel 404-455-3430.
Brown's Studio, *(Brown's Studio; 0-9604822),* 53 Middle St., Oakland, ME 04963.
BRuach HaTorah, *(B'ruach HaTorah Pubns.; 0-89655),* P.O. Box 391221, Miami Beach, FL 33139 Tel 305-673-1654.
Bruce Pub Co
See Glencoe
Brun Pr, *(Brun Press; 0-932574),* 701 N.E. 67th St., Miami, FL 33138 Tel 305-756-6249.
Brunner-Mazel, *(Brunner/Mazel, Inc.; 0-87630),* 19 Union Square W., New York, NY 10003 Tel 212-924-3344.
Brunswick Pub, *(Brunswick Publishing Co.; 0-931494),* P.O. Box 555, Lawrenceville, VA 23868 Tel 804-848-3865.
BSA, *(Boy Scouts of America; 0-8395),* Orders to: Supply Division, P.O. Box 61030, Dallas/Fort Worth Airport, TX 75261 Tel 214-659-2000.
BUC Intl, *(BUC International Corp.; 0-911778),* 1881 N.E. 26th St., Suite 95, Fort Lauderdale, FL 33305 Tel 305-565-6715.
Buccaneer Bks, *(Buccaneer Books; 0-89966),* P.O. Box 168, Cutchogue, NY 11935.
Buck Hill, *(Buck Hill Associates; 0-917420),* Garnet Lake Rd., Johnsburg, NY 12843 Tel 518-251-2743.
Buckley Pubns, *(Buckley Pubns., Inc.; 0-915388),* 233 E. Erie St., Suite 402, Chicago, IL 60611 Tel 312-943-2066.
Bucknell U Pr, *(Bucknell Univ. Press; 0-8387),* Div. of Associated University Presses, 4 Cornwall Dr., Suite 30, E. Brunswick, NJ 08816 Tel 201-254-0132.
Bucks Co Hist, *(Bucks County Historical Society; 0-910302),* Pine & Ashland Sts., Doylestown, PA 18901 Tel 215-345-0210.
Bucyrus-Erie Co, *(Bucyrus-Erie Co.; 0-9604136),* P.O. Box 56, S. Milwaukee, WI 53172.
Buddhist Bks, *(Buddhist Books Intl; 0-914910),* Orders to: P.O. Box 665, Chatsworth, CA 91311 Tel 213-998-8485.
Buddhist Study, *(Buddhist Study Center, The; 0-938474),* Office of Buddhist Education, 1727 Pali Hwy., Honolulu, HI 96813.
Buddhist Text, *(Buddhist Text Translation Society; 0-917512),* City of Ten Thousand Buddhas, Talmage, CA 95481 Tel 707-462-0939.
Budlong, *(Budlong Press Co.; 0-910304),* 649 Hinmam, Evanston, IL 60202; Orders to: 5915 N. Northwest Hwy., Chicago, IL 60631.
Buffalo Acad, *(Buffalo Fine Arts Academy; 0-914782),* Albright-Knox Art Gallery, 1285 Elmwood Ave., Buffalo, NY 14222 Tel 716-882-8700.
Builders of Adytum, *(Builders of the Adytum, Ltd.),* 5105 N. Figueroa St., Los Angeles, CA 90042 Tel 213-255-7141; Orders to: P.O. Box 42278, Dept., O, Los Angeles, CA 90042.
Bull Pub, *(Bull Publishing Co.; 0-915950),* P.O. Box 208, Palo Alto, CA 94302 Tel 415-322-2855.
Bunting, *(Bunting & Lyon, Inc.; 0-913094),* 238 N. Main St., Wallingford, CT 06492 Tel 203-269-3333.
Bur Busn Res U Nebr, *(Bureau of Business Research, Univ. of Nebraska-Lincoln),* 200 CBA Bldg., Univ. of Nebr., Lincoln, NE 68588 Tel 402-472-2334.
Bur Econ Geology, *(Bureau of Economic Geology),* Div. of Univ. of Texas at Austin, University Sta., Box X, Austin, TX 78712 Tel 512-471-1534.
Burda Pubns, *(Burda Pubns.; 0-914926),* Rockefeller Ctr., Suite 3005, 1270 Ave. of the Americas, New York, NY 10020.
Bureau Busn Res U Wis, *(Bureau of Business Research, Univ. of Wisconsin, Graduate School of Business),* 1155 Observatory Dr., Rm 110, Commerce Bldg., Madison, WI 53706 Tel 608-262-1550.
Burgess, *(Burgess Publishing Co.; 0-8087),* 7108 Ohms Lane, Minneapolis, MN 55435 Tel 612-831-1344.
Burgess-Intl Ideas, *(Burgess, Jack K. Inc., -International Ideas Inc.),* Orders to: Jack K. Burgess, Inc., 44 Engle St., Englewood, NJ 07631 Tel 201-569-7477; Orders to: International Ideas Inc., 1627 Spruce St., Philadelphia, PA 19103 Tel 215-546-0392.
Burkehaven Pr, *(Burkehaven Press; 0-914062),* Penacook Rd., Contoocook, NH 03229 Tel 603-746-3625.
Burn-Hart, *(Burn, Hart & Co., Pubs.; 0-918060),* 632 Calle Yucca, Box 1772, Thousand Oaks, CA 91360 Tel 805-498-3985.
Burning Bush, *(Burning Bush Press, The; 0-937528),* P.O. Box 7708, Newark, DE 19711 Tel 302-737-3670.
Burning Deck, *(Burning Deck; 0-930900; 0-930901),* 71 Elmgrove Ave., Providence, RI 02906 Tel 401-351-0015.
Burrill-Ellsworth, *(Burrill-Ellsworth Assoc.; 0-935310),* 26 Birchwood Place, Tenafly, NJ 07670; Orders to: Box 295, Tenafly, NJ 07670.
Business Brokers, *(Business Brokers Assn.),* P.O. Box 23934, Fort Lauderdale, FL 33307 Tel 305-561-1392.
Business Pubns, *(Business Pubns., Inc.; 0-256),* Subs. of Richard D. Irwin, Inc., 200 Chisholm Place, Suite 240, Plano, TX 75075 Tel 214-422-4389.
Busn *Imprint of* **P-H**
Busn Journals, *(Business Journals, Inc.; 0-937506),* 22 S. Smith St., Norwalk, CT 06855 Tel 203-853-6015.
Busn News, *(Business News Publishing Co.; 0-912524),* P.O. Box 2600, Troy, MI 48084 Tel 313-362-3700.
Busn Proposals
See Courier Pr FL
Busn Psych, *(Business Psychology International; 0-931918),* 890-6 National Press Bldg., Washington, DC 20045 Tel 202-638-3951.
Busn Res Pubns, *(Business Research Publications, Inc.),* 817 Broadway, New York, NY 10003 Tel 212-673-4700; Orders to: 87 Terminal Dr., Plainview, NY 11803 Tel 516-349-1010.
Busn Systems Res, *(Business Systems Research Group; 0-9603584),* 10218 Chimney Hill, Dallas, TX 75243 Tel 214-644-0222.
Buten Mus, *(Buten Museum of Wedgwood; 0-912014),* 246 N. Bowman Ave., Merion, PA 19066 Tel 215-664-9069.
Buteo, *(Buteo Books; 0-931130),* P.O. Box 481, Vermillion, SD 57069 Tel 605-624-4343.
Butterfly Pr, *(Butterfly Press; 0-918766),* P.O. Box 19571, Houston, TX 77024 Tel 713-464-7570; Formerly Terzarima System.
Butterick Pub, *(Butterick Publishing; 0-88421),* Div. of American Can Co., 708 Third Ave., New York, NY 10017 Tel 212-599-6599; Orders to: P.O. Box 1914, Altoona, PA 16603.
Butterworth, *(Butterworth Pubs., Inc.),* 10 Tower Office Park, Woburn, MA 01801 Tel 617-933-8260. *Imprints:* Newnes-Butterworth (Newnes-Butterworth).
Butterworths
See Butterworth
Buyer's Directory, *(Buyer's Directory),* R.D. 3, Box 533, Olean, NY 14760 Tel 716-372-0514.
By By Prods, *(By By Productions; 0-938826),* P.O. Box 1743, Glendora, CA 91740.
By Hand & Foot, *(By Hand & Foot, Ltd.; 0-938670),* Green River Rd., P.O. Box 611, Brattleboro, VT 05301.
BYLS Pr, *(BYLS Press),* Div. of Bet Yoatz Library Services, 6247 N. Francisco Ave., Chicago, IL 60659 Tel 312-262-8959.
BYR *Imprint of* **Random**
BYTE Bks *Imprint of* **McGraw**
C B Pub & Dist
See Caratzas Bros
C B Slack, *(Slack, Charles B., Inc.; 0-913590),* 6900 Grove Rd., Thorofare, NJ 08086 Tel 609-848-1000.
C Berke, *(Berke, Carl),* 20 Simmons Dr., Milford, MA 01757.
C Boyer, *(Boyer, Carl; 0-936124),* P.O. Box 333, Newhall, CA 91322.
C C Brown Pub, *(Brown, C. C., Publishing Co.; 0-9600378),* Box 462, Airway Heights, WA 99001 Tel 509-244-5807.
C C Fisher, *(Fisher, Clay C.),* 702 Tenth St., N.E., Massillon, OH 44646.
C C Pierce, *(Pierce, Clayton C.; 0-9601564),* 325 Carol Dr., Ventura, CA 93003 Tel 805-653-1949.
C C Thomas, *(Thomas, Charles C., Pub.; 0-398),* 301-327 E. Lawrence Ave., Springfield, IL 62717 Tel 217-789-8980.
C Clements, *(Clements, Christine),* 1257 E, 81st St., Los Angeles, CA 90001.
C E M Comp, *(C. E. M. Co.; 0-930004),* 3154 Coventry Dr., Bay City, MI 48706 Tel 517-686-4208.
C E Tuttle, *(Tuttle, Charles E., Co., Inc.; 0-8048),* P.O. Drawer F, Rutland, VT 05701 Tel 802-773-8930.
C Franklin Pr, *(Franklin, Chas., Press, The; 0-9603516),* 18409 90th Ave. W., Edmonds, WA 98020 Tel 206-774-6979.
C G Jung Foun, *(Jung, C. G., Foundation Publications; 0-913430),* 28 E. 39th St., New York, NY 10016 Tel 212-697-6430.
C Gebhardt, *(Gebhardt, Chuck; 0-9601410),* P.O. Box 6821, San Jose, CA 95150.
C H Neuffer, *(Neuffer, Claude Henry),* U. S. C. English Dept., Columbia, SC 29208 Tel 803-787-3823.
C Hallberg, *(Hallberg, Charles, & Co., Inc.; 0-87319),* P.O. Box 547, Delavan, WI 53115 Tel 414-728-2331.
C Hungness, *(Hungness, Carl, Publishing; 0-915088),* P.O. Box 24308, Speedway, IN 46224 Tel 317-244-4792.
C I B A Pharm, *(C I B A Pharmaceutical Co.; 0-914168),* 556 Morris Ave., Summit, NJ 07901; Orders to: P. O. Box R-195, Summit, NJ 07901.
C J Frompovich, *(Frompovich, C. J., Pubns.; 0-935322),* R.D. 1, Chestnut Rd., Coopersburg, PA 18036 Tel 215-346-8461.
C Jordan, *(Jordan, Carol; 0-9605360),* 654 Jerome St., Davis, CA 95616.
C Kerr Ent, *(Kerr, Charles, Enterprises, Inc.; 0-936002),* 129 N. Main St., New Hope, PA 18938 Tel 215-862-9618; Orders to: P. O. Box 22, New Hope, PA 18938.
C L Cook, *(Cook, Chester L.; 0-9604670),* P. O. Box 1511, Slidell, LA 70458.
C L Pelton, *(Pelton, Charles L.; 0-931470),* 201 S. Lloyd, Suite 230 Physician's Plaza, Aberdeen, SD 57401.
C M Kent, *(Kent, Carol Miller; 0-9604886),* 831 So. Frederick, Arlington, VA 22204.
C Schneider, *(Schneider, Coleman),* P.O. Box 762, Tenafly, NJ 07670.
C Stark, *(Stark, Claude, & Co., Pubs.; 0-89007),* P.O. Box 843, Brookline Village, 21 Station St., Boston, MA 02147 Tel 617-734-2045.
Cadillac, *(Cadillac Publishing Co., Inc.; 0-87445),* 709 S. Skinker Blvd., St. Louis, MO 63105 Tel 314-862-7560; 6611 Clayton Rd., St. Louis, MO 63117.
Cadmus Eds, *(Cadmus Editions; 0-932274),* P.O. Box 4725, Santa Barbara, CA 93103.
Cagg, *(Cagg, Richard D.),* 423 W. Fourth, Cameron, MO 64429.
Cahners
See CBI Pub
Caislan Pr, *(Caislan Press; 0-937444),* Box 28371, San Jose, CA 95159 Tel 408-398-4979.
Cal Inst Intl, *(California Institute of International Studies; 0-912098),* 766 Santa Ynez, Stanford, CA 94305 Tel 415-322-2026.
Cal Inst Public, *(California Institute of Public Affairs; 0-912102),* Affiliate of the Claremont Colleges, P.O. Box 10, Claremont, CA 91711 Tel 714-624-5212.
Cal Journal, *(California Journal Press; 0-930302),* 1617 10th St., Sacramento, CA 95814 Tel 916-444-2840.
Cal Living Bks, *(California Living Books; 0-89395),* The Hearst Bldg., Suite 501, Third & Market Sts., San Francisco, CA 94103 Tel 415-543-5981.
Cal-Syl Pr, *(Cal-Syl Press; 0-930638),* 3960 E. 14th St., Oakland, CA 94601 Tel 415-534-5032.
Calamus Bks, *(Calamus Books; 0-930762),* Box 689, Cooper Sta., New York, NY 10276.
Caledonia Pr, *(Caledonia Press; 0-932282),* P.O. Box 245, Racine, WI 53401 Tel 414-637-6200.
Calibre Bks, *(Calibre Books),* 2953 Fort St., Wyandotte, MI 48192.
Calico Pr, *(Calico Press; 0-912714),* P.O. Box 758, Twenty-Nine Palms, CA 92277 Tel 714-367-7661.

Calif Health, *(California Health Pubns.; 0-930926),* 3900 Shenandoah Dr., Oceanside, CA 92054.
Calif Hist, *(California Historical Society; 0-910312),* P.O. Box 3370, San Diego, CA 92103; Orders to: 2090 Jackson St., San Francisco, CA 94109 Tel 415-567-1848.
Calif Street, *(California Street; 0-915090),* 723 Dwight Way, Berkeley, CA 94710 Tel 415-548-8273.
Callarman Hse, *(Callarman House; 0-930092),* 2564 N. Spinnaker Ave., Port Hueneme, CA 93041 Tel 805-985-6554.
Calligraphy Donna, *(Calligraphy by Donna; 0-9604308),* 565 SE Airpark Dr., Bend, OR 97701 Tel 503-382-8215.
Camaro Pub, *(Camaro Publishing Co.; 0-913290),* Worldway Postal Sta., P.O. Box 90430, Los Angeles, CA 90009 Tel 213-837-7500.
Camberleigh & Hall, *(Camberleigh & Hall, Pubs.; 0-935880),* P.O. Box 18914, N. Hills Sta., Raleigh, NC 27619.
Cambrian, *(Cambrian Pubns.; 0-912548),* P.O. Box 191, Little River Sta., Miami, FL 33138 Tel 305-751-1122.
Cambric, *(Cambric Press; 0-918342),* 912 Strowbridge Dr., Huron, OH 44839 Tel 419-433-4221.
Cambridge Bk, *(Cambridge Book Co., Inc.; 0-8428),* Div. of the N.Y. Times Co., 888 Seventh Ave., New York, NY 10106 Tel 212-957-5313.
Cambridge Corp, *(Cambridge Corp.; 0-939008),* P.O. Box 64, Cambridge, MA 01938.
Cambridge U Pr, *(Cambridge Univ. Press; 0-521),* 32 E. 57th St., New York, NY 10022 Tel 212-688-8885; Orders to: 510 North Ave., New Rochelle, NY 10801.
Camden Hse, *(Camden House, Inc.; 0-938100),* Drawer 2025, Columbia, SC 29202.
Camelot *Imprint of* **Avon**
Camelot Pub, *(Camelot Publishing Co.; 0-89218),* P.O. Box 1357, Ormond Beach, FL 32074 Tel 904-672-5672.
Cameo Pr, *(Cameo Press; 0-937868),* 373 Fifth Ave., Suite 1102, New York, NY 10016.
Cameron & Co, *(Cameron & Co.; 0-918684),* Russ Bldg., Suite 1470, 235 Montgomery St., San Francisco, CA 94104 Tel 415-981-1135.
Campus Crusade, *(Campus Crusade for Christ, International; 0-918956),* P.O. Box 1576, 2700 Little Mountain Dr., Bldg. "B", San Bernardino, CA 92402 Tel 714-886-7981.
Campus Scope, *(Campus Scope Press),* 2928 Dean Parkway, Apt. 4D, Minneapolis, MN 55416.
Can-Do Bks, *(Can-Do-Books; 0-9604192),* 2119 Lone Oak Ave., Napa, CA 94558.
Canaveral, *(Canaveral Press, Inc.),* Orders to: 309 Santa Monica Blvd., Suite 224, Santa Monica, CA 90401 Tel 213-394-4542.
Cancer Care, *(Cancer Care Inc.),* National Cancer Foundation, 1 Park Ave., New York, NY 10016 Tel 212-679-5700.
Canning Pubns, *(Canning Pubns., Inc.; 0-938516),* 925 Anza Ave., Vista, CA 92083.
Canterbury Pr, *(Canterbury Press; 0-933993),* 5540 Vista Del Amigo, Anaheim, CA 92807.
Capital Pub Corp, *(Capital Publishing Corp.; 0-914470),* P.O. Box 348, Two Laurel Ave., Wellesley Hills, MA 02181 Tel 617-235-5405.
Capital Tech, *(Capital Technology, Inc.; 0-9603460),* 2 Fairview Plaza, Suite 116, 5950 Fairview Rd., Charlotte, NC 28210.
Capitalist Pr OH, *(Capitalist Press),* P.O. Box 1911, Akron, OH 44309.
Capra Pr, *(Capra Press; 0-912264; 0-88496),* P.O. Box 2068, Santa Barbara, CA 93120 Tel 805-966-4590.
Caprock Pr, *(Caprock Press; 0-912570),* 4806 17th St., Lubbock, TX 79416 Tel 806-795-7599.
Carabelle, *(Carabelle Books; 0-938634),* Box 2711, Reston, VA 22091.
Caratzas Bros, *(Caratzas Brothers, Pubs.; 0-89241),* 481 Main St. (P.O. Box 210), New Rochelle, NY 10802 Tel 914-632-8487.
Caravan Bks, *(Caravan Books; 0-88206),* P.O. Box 344, Delmar, NY 12054 Tel 518-439-6146; Orders to: Publishers Marketing Group Intl., P.O. Box 350, Momence, IL 60954 Tel 815-472-2661.
CARBEN Survey, *(CARBEN Surveying Reprints),* 274 Winthrop Rd., Columbus, OH 43214; Formerly Named BM Surveying Book Reprints.
Career Pub, *(Career Publishing, Inc.; 0-89262),* 924 N. Main St., P.O. Box 5486, Orange, CA 92667 Tel 714-997-0130.
Carib Hse, *(Carib House (USA); 0-936378),* P. O. Box 38834, Hollywood, CA 90038; Orders to: 25562 Camino Vista, Hayward, CA 94541.
Carlton, *(Carlton Press; 0-8062),* 84 Fifth Ave., New York, NY 10011 Tel 212-243-8800.
Carlton Pubns CA, *(Carlton Pubns.,Inc.; 0-937348),* 10949 Fruitland Dr., Studio City, CA 91604.
Carnation, *(Carnation Press; 0-87601),* P.O. Box 101, State College, PA 16801 Tel 814-238-3577.
Carnegie Endow, *(Carnegie Endowment for International Peace; 0-87003),* 11 Dupont Circle, Washington, DC 20036 Tel 202-797-6425.
Carnegie Inst, *(Carnegie Institution of Washington; 0-87279),* 1530 "P" St., N.W., Washington, DC 20005 Tel 202-387-6411.
Carnegie-Mellon, *(Carnegie-Mellon Univ. Press; 0-915604),* Carnegie-Mellon Univ., Baker Hall 233, Pittsburgh, PA 15213; Dist. by: Univ. of Pittsburgh Press, 127 N. Bellefield Ave., Pittsburgh, PA 15260 Tel 412-624-4110.
Carnot Pr, *(Carnot Press; 0-917308),* P.O. Box 1544, Lake Oswego, OR 97034 Tel 503-636-6894.
Carolina Acad Pr, *(Carolina Academic Press; 0-89089),* P.O. Box 8795, Durham, NC 27707 Tel 919-688-5155.
Carolina Wren, *(Carolina Wren Press, The; 0-932112),* 300 Barclay Rd., Chapel Hill, NC 27514.
Caroline Hse, *(Caroline House Pubs.),* P.O. Box 738, Ottawa, IL 61350 Tel 815-434-7905; Orders to: 2 Ellis Place, Ossining, NY 10562 Tel 914-941-9271.
Carolrhoda Bks, *(Carolrhoda Books, Inc.; 0-87614),* 241 First Ave., N., Minneapolis, MN 55401 Tel 612-332-3344.
Carousel Pr, *(Carousel Press; 0-917120),* P.O. Box 6061, Albany, CA 94706 Tel 415-527-5849.
Carpatho-Rusyn Res Ctr, *(Carpatho-Rusyn Research Center; 0-917242),* 1583 Massachusetts Ave., Cambridge, MA 02138 Tel 617-495-3692; Orders to: 355 Delano Place, Fairview, NJ 07022.
Carpenter Pr, *(Carpenter Press; 0-914140),* Rte. 4, Pomeroy, OH 45769 Tel 614-992-7520.
Carrier Pigeon, *(Carrier Pigeon; 0-932870),* 75 Kneeland St. Rm. 309, Boston, MA 02111 Tel 617-542-5679.
Carroll Coll, *(Carroll College Press; 0-916120),* 100 North East Ave., Waukesha, WI 53186 Tel 414-547-1211.
Carroll Pr, *(Carroll Press; 0-910328),* P.O. Box 8113, 43 Squantum St., Cranston, RI 02920 Tel 401-942-1587.
Carrollton Pr, *(Carrollton Press, Inc., U.S. Historical Documents Institute; 0-8408),* 1911 Fort Meyer Dr., Arlington, VA 22209 Tel 703-525-5942.
Carstens Pubns, *(Carstens Pubns., Inc.; 0-911868),* P.O. Box 700, Newton, NJ 07860 Tel 201-383-3355.
Carter, *(Carter),* P.O. Box 138, Monmouth Junction, NJ 08852 Tel 215-348-2015.
Carver Pub, *(Carver Publishing, Inc.; 0-915044),* P.O. Box 6002, Hampton Institute, Hampton, VA 23668 Tel 804-727-5000.
Carves, *(Carves Cards),* 179 South St., Brookline, MA 02167 Tel 617-469-9175.
Cary Arboretum
See NY Botanical
CAS, *(Competence Assurance Systems; 0-89147),* Harvard Square, P. O. Box 81, Cambridge, MA 02138 Tel 617-661-9151.
Casa Bautista, *(Casa Bautista De Publicaciones; 0-311),* P.O. Box 4255, 7000 Alabama St., El Paso, TX 79914 Tel 915-566-9656. *Imprints:* Edit Mundo (Editorial Mundo Hispano).
CASE, *(Council for Advancement & Support of Education; 0-911966),* 11 Dupont Circle, Suite 400, Washington, DC 20036 Tel 202-328-5900; Orders to: CASE Publications Order Dept., P.O. Box 298, Alexandria, VA 22314.
Casino Gaming, *(Casino Gaming Specialists; 0-9605112),* 1 Britton Place, Suite 16, Voorhees, NJ 08043.
Castalia Pub, *(Castalia Publishing Co.; 0-916154),* P.O. Box 1587, Eugene, OR 97440.
Castelli-Artspace, *(Castelli Graphics/Artspace; 0-9604140),* 4 E. 77th St., New York, NY 10021.
Castle Pub Co, *(Castle Publishing Co.; 0-9603372),* P.O. Box 188, Portland, ME 04112 Tel 207-799-2254.
Castro, *(Castro, Mercedes; 0-9604748),* 78-10 147th St., Apt. 3D, Flushing, NY 11367.
Cataract Pr, *(Cataract Press; 0-914764),* P.O. Box 4875, Chicago, IL 60680 Tel 416-638-0659.
Cath Health, *(Catholic Health Assn.; 0-87125),* 1438 S. Grand Blvd., St. Louis, MO 63104 Tel 314-773-0646.
Cath Hospital
See Cath Health
Cath Lib Assn, *(Catholic Library Assn.; 0-87507),* 461 W. Lancaster Ave., Haverford, PA 19041 Tel 215-649-5251.
Cath U Pr, *(Catholic Univ. of America Press; 0-8132),* 620 Michigan Ave., N.E., Washington, DC 20064 Tel 202-635-5052; Dist. by: International Scholarly Book Services, Inc., P.O. Box 555, Forest Grove, OR 97116 Tel 503-357-7192; All Titles Dist. by Intl Schol Bk Serv.
Cathedral of Knowledge, *(Cathedral of Knowledge),* 235 N.E. 84th Ave., Portland, OR 97220 Tel 503-255-3859.
Cato Inst, *(Cato Institute; 0-932790),* 747 Front St., San Francisco, CA 94111 Tel 415-433-4316.
Caverne Pub, *(Caverne Publishing, Inc.; 0-937844),* P.O. Box 1327, Hollywood, CA 90028 Tel 213-876-1990.
Caxton, *(Caxton Printers, Ltd.; 0-87004),* P.O. Box 700, Caldwell, ID 83605 Tel 208-459-7421.
CAYC Learning Tree, *(CAYC Learning Tree),* 9998 Ferguson Rd., Dallas, TX 75228 Tel 214-235-4565.
Cayucos, *(Cayucos Books; 0-9600372),* P.O. Box 2113, Monterey, CA 93940 Tel 408-375-5289.
CBI Pub, *(CBI Publishing Co. Inc.; 0-8436),* Member of the Wadsworth Publishing Group, 51 Sleeper St., Boston, MA 02210 Tel 617-426-2224.
CCG *Imprint of* **Doubleday**
CCPr *Imprint of* **Macmillan**
Cedar Rock, *(Cedar Rock Press; 0-930024),* 1121 Madeline, New Braunfels, TX 78130 Tel 512-625-6002.
Celestial Arts, *(Celestial Arts Publishing Co.; 0-912310; 0-89087),* 231 Adrian Rd., Millbrae, CA 94030 Tel 415-692-4500.
Cellar, *(Cellar Book Shop),* 18090 Wyoming, Detroit, MI 48221 Tel 313-861-1776.
Celo Pr, *(Celo Press; 0-914064),* Rte. 5, Burnsville, NC 28714 Tel 704-675-4925.
Centaur, *(Centaur Books, Inc.; 0-87818),* 799 Broadway, New York, NY 10003 Tel 212-677-1720.
Centaur Dumfries, *(Centaur Pubns.; 0-9602404),* P.O. Box 188, Dumfries, VA 22026 Tel 703-670-3527.
Centaur Pubn VA, *(Centaur Publication Co.; 0-932700),* 7807 Stovall Court, Lorton, VA 22079.
Centennial, *(Centennial Press; 0-8220),* Div. of Cliff's Notes, Inc., P.O. Box 80728, Lincoln, NE 68501 Tel 402-477-6971.
Centennial Photo Serv, *(Centennial Photo Services; 0-931838),* P.O. Box 36, Grantsburg, WI 54840 Tel 715-689-2153.
Center Pubns, *(Center Pubns.; 0-916820),* 905 S. Normandie Ave., Los Angeles, CA 90006 Tel 213-387-2356; Dist. by: Great Eastern Book Co., P.O. Box 271, Boulder, CO 80302.
Central Conf, *(Central Conference of American Rabbis; 0-916694),* 790 Madison Ave., Suite 601, New York, NY 10021 Tel 212-734-7166.
Central Electric, *(Central Electric Railfans' Assn.; 0-915348),* P.O. Box 503, Chicago, IL 60690.
Centurion Pr, *(Centurion Press),* Drawer 62, Los Angeles, CA 90028.
Century Bookbindery, *(Century Bookbindery; 0-89984),* P.O. Box 6471, Philadelphia, PA 19145.

Century One, *(Century One Press; 0-937080),* 2325 E. Platte Ave., Colorado Springs, CO 80909 Tel 303-471-1322.
Century Three, *(Century Three Press; 0-933400),* 411 S. 13th St. Suite 315, Lincoln, NE 68508.
Century Twenty One, *(Century Twenty One Publishing; 0-86548),* P.O. Box 8, Saratoga, CA 95070.
CEP, *(Council on Economic Priorities, Inc.; 0-87871),* 84 Fifth Ave., New York, NY 10011 Tel 212-691-8550.
CERA, *(CERA; 0-936706),* P.O. Box 18103, San Francisco, CA 94118.
Cerridwen & Co, *(Cerridwen & Co., Pubs.; 0-919345),* P.O. Box 10, Custer, WA 98240.
CES, *(Continuing Education Systems, Inc.; 0-916780),* 112 S. Grant St., Hinsdale, IL 60521 Tel 312-654-2596.
Chain Store Pub
See Lebhar Friedman
Chalfant Pr, *(Chalfant Press, Inc.; 0-912494),* P.O. Box 787, Bishop, CA 93514 Tel 714-873-3535.
Chamber Comm US, *(Chamber of Commerce of the U. S., Special Publications Dept.; 0-89834),* 1615 "H" St., N.W., Washington, DC 20062 Tel 202-659-5602.
CHAMH, *(CHAMH; 0-938666),* 15 Park Row, New York, NY 10038.
Champion Athlete, *(Champion Athlete Publishing Co.; 0-938074),* Box 2936, Richmond, VA 23235 Tel 804-794-6034.
Chan Shal Imi, *(Chan Shal Imi Society Press; 0-936380),* P.O. Box 1365, Stone Mountain, GA 30086.
Chandler & Sharp, *(Chandler & Sharp Pubs., Inc.; 0-88316),* 11A Commercial Blvd., Novato, CA 94947 Tel 415-883-2353.
Change Mag, *(Change Magazine Press; 0-915390),* 271 North Ave., Suite 1200, New Rochelle, NY 10801 Tel 914-235-8700.
Channing Bks, *(Channing Books & Whaleship Plans; 0-9600496),* P.O. Box 552, 35 Main St., Marion, MA 02738 Tel 617-748-0087.
Channings
See Channing Bks
Character Res, *(Character Research Press; 0-915744),* 207 State St., Schenectady, NY 12305 Tel 518-370-6012.
Charioteer, *(Charioteer Press; 0-910350),* P.O. Box 28055 Central, Washington, DC 20005 Tel 202-965-5046.
Charisma Pr, *(Charisma Press; 0-933402),* P.O. Box 263, St. Francis Seminary, Andover, MA 01810 Tel 617-851-7910.
Charisma Pubns, *(Charisma Pubns., Inc.; 0-937008),* P.O. Box 40321, Indianapolis, IN 46240 Tel 317-844-0719.
Chariton Review, *(Chariton Review Press; 0-933428),* Northeast Missouri State Univ., Kirksville, MO 63501 Tel 816-665-5121.
Charles, *(Charles Press Pubs.; 0-913486; 0-89303),* Div. of Robert J. Brady, Co., Rtes. 197 & 450, Bowie, MD 20715 Tel 301-262-6300.
Charles River Bks, *(Charles River Books; 0-89182),* 1 Thompson Square, Boston, MA 02129 Tel 617-742-9493.
Charter Bks, *(Charter Books; 0-441),* Div. of Ace Books, 51 Madison Ave., New York, NY 10010 Tel 212-689-9200.
ChartGuide, *(ChartGuide; 0-938206),* 300 N. Wilshire Ave., Suite 5, Anaheim, CA 92801.
Chartmasters, *(Chartmasters; 0-917190),* P.O. Box 1264, Covington, LA 70434 Tel 504-892-9135.
Chartrand, *(Chartrand, Robert Lee),* 5406 Dorset Ave., Chevy Chase, MD 20015.
Chatham Hse Pubs, *(Chatham House Pubs., Inc.; 0-934540),* P.O. Box 1, Chatham, NJ 07928 Tel 201-635-2059.
Chatham Pr, *(Chatham Press; 0-85699),* 143 Sound Beach, Old Greenwich, CT 06870 Tel 203-637-4531; Dist. by: The Devin-Adair Co., Old Greenwich, CT 06870.
Chatham Pub CA, *(Chatham Pub. Co.; 0-89685),* P.O. Box 283, 1012 Oak Grove Ave., Burlingame, CA 94010 Tel 415-348-0331.
Chatto-Bodley-Jonathan
See Merrimack Bk Serv
CHCUS Inc, *(CHCUS, Inc.; 0-937256),* P.O. Box 444, Oak Park, IL 60303 Tel 312-848-2210.
Cheever Pub, *(Cheever Publishing, Inc.; 0-915708),* P.O. Box 700, Bloomington, IL 61701 Tel 309-378-2961.
Chelsea Hse, *(Chelsea House Pubs.; 0-87754),* 133 Christopher St., New York, NY 10014 Tel 212-924-6414.
Chelsea Pub, *(Chelsea Publishing Co.; 0-8284),* 432 Park Ave. S., Rm. 503, New York, NY 10016 Tel 212-889-8095.
Chem Econ, *(Chemical Economic Services; 0-912060),* P.O. Box 468, Palmer Square, Princeton, NJ 08540 Tel 609-921-8468.
Chem Educ, *(Journal of Chemical Education; 0-910362),* 238 Kent Rd., Springfield, PA 19064.
Chem Eng *Imprint of* **McGraw**
Chem Pub, *(Chemical Publishing Co., Inc.; 0-8206),* 155 W. 19th St., New York, NY 10011 Tel 212-255-1950.
Chen Chi Studio, *(Chen Chi Studio; 0-9604652),* 15 Gramercy Park, New York, NY 10003.
Cherokee, *(Cherokee Publishing Co.; 0-87797),* P.O. Box 1081, Covington, GA 30209 Tel 404-786-0565.
Cherry Valley, *(Cherry Valley Editions; 0-916156),* 14200 Pear Tree Lane, No. 11, Wheaton, MD 20906 Tel 301-460-7682; Dist. by: Book Bus, 892 S. Clinton Ave., Rochester, NY 14620 Tel 716-473-2590.
Cherubim, *(Cherubim; 0-938574),* 434 Beach 47th St., Edgemere, NY 11691.
Chesbro, *(Chesbro Press; 0-938006),* 17370 Hawkins Lane, P.O. Box 1326, Morgan Hill, CA 95037 Tel 408-779-5930.
Cheshire, *(Cheshire Books; 0-917352),* 514 Bryant St., Palo Alto, CA 94301 Tel 415-321-2449; Dist. by: Van Nostrand Reinhold Co., 7625 Empire Dr., Florence, KY 41042.
Chicago Contemp Photo, *(Chicago Center for Contemporary Photography; 0-932026),* Columbia College, 600 S. Michigan Ave., Chicago, IL 60605 Tel 312-663-1600.
Chicago Hist, *(Chicago Historical Society; 0-913820),* Clark St. at North Ave., Chicago, IL 60614 Tel 312-642-4600.
Chicago Psych, *(Chicago Institute for Psychoanalysis; 0-918568),* 180 N. Michigan Ave., Chicago, IL 60601 Tel 312-726-6300.
Chicago Review, *(Chicago Review Press, Inc.; 0-914090),* 820 N. Franklin St., Chicago, IL 60610 Tel 312-644-5457.
Chicago Theology & Culture, *(Chicago Institute of Theology & Culture, The; 0-936978),* 5401 S. Cornell Ave., Chicago, IL 60645.
Chicago Visual Lib *Imprint of* **U of Chicago Pr**
Chicorel Lib
See Am Lib Pub Co
Child & Family Ent, *(Child & Family Enterprises, Inc.; 0-935202),* 7 Leonard Place, Albany, NY 12202.
Child Focus Co, *(Child Focus Co.; 0-933892),* 1230 Keats St., Manhattan Beach, CA 90266 Tel 213-379-4144.
Child Welfare, *(Child Welfare League of America, Inc.; 0-87868),* 67 Irving Place, New York, NY 10003 Tel 212-254-7410.
Children First, *(Children First Press; 0-9603696),* Box 8008, Ann Arbor, MI 48107 Tel 313-668-8056.
Children Learn Ctr, *(Children's Learning Center, Inc.; 0-917206),* 4660 E. 62nd St., Indianapolis, IN 46220 Tel 317-251-6241.
Childrens, *(Childrens Press; 0-516),* 1224 W. Van Buren St., Chicago, IL 60607 Tel 312-666-4200. *Imprints:* Elk Grove Bks (Elk Grove Books).
Children's Defense, *(Children's Defense Fund; 0-938008),* 1520 New Hampshire Ave., NW, Washington, DC 20036.
Childs World, *(Child's World, Inc., The; 0-89565; 0-913778),* 980 N. McLean, Elgin, IL 60120 Tel 312-741-7591; Orders to: P.O. Box 681, Elgin, IL 60120.
Chilmark Hse, *(Chilmark House; 0-937532),* 4224 38th St. N.E., Washington, DC 20016.
Chilton, *(Chilton Book Co.; 0-8019),* Orders to: School, Library Services, Chilton Way, Radnor, PA 19089 Tel 215-687-8200.
China Bks, *(China Books & Periodicals, Inc.; 0-8351),* 2929 24th St., San Francisco, CA 94110 Tel 415-282-2994.
Chinese Materials, *(Chinese Materials Center, Inc.; 0-89644),* 809 Taraval St., San Francisco, CA 94116.
Chips, *(Chip's Bookshop, Inc.; 0-912378),* Box 639, Cooper Sta., New York, NY 10276 Tel 212-362-9336.
Chiron Pr, *(Chiron Press, Inc.; 0-913462),* 24 W. 96th St., New York, NY 10025 Tel 212-662-5486; Orders to: Publishers' Storage & Shipping Corp., 2352 Main St., Concord, MA 01742 Tel 617-897-9332.
Chiropractic, *(Who's Who in Chiropractic, International Pub. Co.; 0-918336),* P.O. Box 2615, Littleton, CO 80161 Tel 303-333-1581.
Chong-Donnie, *(Chong-Donnie; 0-938918),* 246 E. 62nd St., New York, NY 10021.
Chosen Bks Pub, *(Chosen Books Publishing Co., Ltd.; 0-912376),* Lincoln, VA 22078 Tel 703-338-4131; Dist. by: Spring Arbor, P.O. Box 985, Ann Arbor, MI 48106 Tel 800-521-3690.
Chr Classics, *(Christian Classics, Inc.; 0-87061),* P.O. Box 30, Westminster, MD 21157 Tel 301-848-3065.
Chr Light
See Christian Light
Chr Lit, *(Christian Literature Crusade, Inc.; 0-87508),* Pennsylvania Ave., Fort Washington, PA 19034.
Chr Marriage, *(Christian Marriage Enrichment; 0-938786),* 8000 E. Girard, No. 301, Denver, CO 80231.
Chr Pubns, *(Christian Pubns., Inc.; 0-87509),* 25 S. Tenth St., Harrisburg, PA 17101 Tel 717-233-6728.
Chr Sch Intl, *(Christian Schools International; 0-87463),* 3350 E. Paris Ave. S.E., P.O. Box 8709, Grand Rapids, MI 49508 Tel 616-957-1070.
Chr Stud Ctr, *(Christian Studies Center),* P.O. Box 11110, Memphis, TN 38111.
Chris Mass, *(Christopher Publishing House (Mass); 0-8158),* 1405 Hanover St., West Hanover, MA 02339 Tel 617-878-4656.
Christ Nations, *(Christ for the Nations, Inc.; 0-89985),* 3404 Conway St., Box 24910, Dallas, TX 75224.
Christendom Educ
See Christendom Pubns
Christendom Pubns, *(Christendom Pubns.; 0-931888),* Rt. 3 Box 87, Front Royal, VA 22630 Tel 703-636-2908.
Christian Fellow Pubs, *(Christian Fellowship Pubs., Inc.; 0-935008),* 11515 Allecingie Pkwy., Richmond, VA 23235 Tel 804-794-5333.
Christian Herald, *(Christian Herald Books; 0-915684),* 40 Overlook Dr., Chappaqua, NY 10514 Tel 914-769-9000.
Christian Light, *(Christian Light Pubns., Inc.; 0-87813),* P.O. Box 1126, Harrisonburg, VA 22801 Tel 703-434-0768.
Christian Success, *(Christian Success Publishing House; 0-934178),* P.O. Box 521, Irrigon, OR 97844.
Christianica, *(Christianica Center; 0-911346),* 6 N. Michigan Ave., Chicago, IL 60602 Tel 312-782-4230.
Christs Mission, *(Christ's Mission; 0-935120),* Box 176, Hackensack, NJ 07602 Tel 201-342-6202.
Christward, *(Christward Ministry; 0-910378),* Rte. 5, Box 206, Escondido, CA 92025 Tel 714-744-1500.
Chrome Yellow, *(Chrome Yellow Private Press; 0-935656),* P.O. Box 14082, Gainesville, FL 32604 Tel 904-373-6798.
Chron Guide, *(Chronicle Guidance Pubns.; 0-912578),* Moravia, NY 13118 Tel 315-497-0330.
Chronicle Bks, *(Chronicle Books; 0-87701),* Div. of Chronicle Publishing Co., 870 Market St., Suite 915, San Francisco, CA 94102 Tel 415-777-7240.
Chulainn Press, *(Chulainn Press, Inc.; 0-917600),* 1040 Butterfield Rd., P.O. Box 770, San Anselmo, CA 94960.
Church History, *(Church History Research & Archives; 0-935122),* Rte. 4, Box 38, Lafayette, TN 37083 Tel 615-666-4834.
Churches Alive, *(Churches Alive; 0-934396),* P.O. Box 3800, San Bernardino, CA 92413 Tel 714-886-5361.

Churchill, *(Churchill Livingstone Inc.),* 19 W. 44th St., Suite 301, New York, NY 10036 Tel 212-921-0430; Dist. by: J.A. Majors Co., 3770 Zip Industrial Blvd., Atlanta, GA 30354; Dist. by: Brown & Connolly, Inc., 1399 Boylston St., Boston, MA 02215; Dist. by: Login Brothers Books Co, Inc., 1450 W. Randolph St., Chicago, IL 60607; Dist. by: J.A. Majors Co., 2221 Walnut Hill Lane, Irving, TX 75061; Dist. by: J.A. Majors Co., 1806 Southgate Blvd., Houston, TX 77025; Dist. by: Eliot Books, Inc., 35-53 24th St., Long Island City, NY 11106; Dist. by: J.A. Majors Co., 3909 Bienville St., New Orleans, LA 70119; Dist. by: Rittenhouse Book Distributors, Inc., 251 S. 24th St., Philadelphia, PA 19103; Dist. by: Medical & Technical Books, Inc., 11511 Tennessee Ave., Los Angeles, CA 90064; Dist. by: Longman, Inc., 19 W. 44th St., 10th Floor, New York, NY 10036 Tel 212-764-3955.
CIBC, *(Council on Interracial Books for Children, Inc.; 0-930040),* 1841 Broadway, New York, NY 10023 Tel 212-757-5339.
Circle Fine Art, *(Circle Fine Art Corp.; 0-932240),* 232 E. Ohio St., Chicago, IL 60611.
CIRS *Imprint of* **Unipub**
Cistercian Pubns, *(Cistercian Pubns., Inc.; 0-87907),* WMU Sta., Kalamazoo, MI 49008 Tel 616-383-4985.
Citadel Pr, *(Citadel Press; 0-8065),* Subs. of Lyle Stuart, Inc., 120 Enterprise Ave., Secaucus, NJ 07094 Tel 201-866-0490.
Citation *Imprint of* **Schol Bk Serv**
Citizens Energy, *(Citizens' Energy Project; 0-89988),* 1110 Sixth St. N.W., No. 300, Washington, DC 20001.
Citizens Law, *(Citizens Law Library; 0-89648),* 6 W. Loudoun St., P.O. Box 1745, Leesburg, VA 22075.
City Lights, *(City Lights Books; 0-87286),* 261 Columbus Ave., San Francisco, CA 94133 Tel 415-362-8193; Dist. by: Subterranean Co., P.O. Box 10233, Eugene, OR 97440.
Claremont House, *(Claremont House; 0-913860),* 231 E. San Fernando St., No. 1, San Jose, CA 95112 Tel 408-293-8650.
Claretian Pubns, *(Claretian Pubns.; 0-89570),* 221 W. Madison St., Chicago, IL 60606 Tel 312-236-7782.
Clarion *Imprint of* **HM**
Clark County Hist Soc, *(Clark County Historical Society),* 300 W. Main St., Springfield, OH 45504 Tel 513-324-0657.
Clark Pub, *(Clark Publishing Co.; 0-931054),* Dist. by: The Caxton Printers, Ltd., P.O. Box 700, Caldwell, ID 83605 Tel 208-459-7421.
Classic Furn Kits, *(Classic Furniture Kits),* 343 Lantana St., Camarillo, CA 93010.
Classic Pub, *(Classic Publishing; 0-937222),* Prospect, KY 40059.
Classical Folia, *(Classical Folia),* c/o College of the Holy Cross, Worcester, MA 01610.
Classics Unltd, *(Classics Unlimited, Inc.; 0-936660),* 2121 Arlington Ave., Caldwell, ID 83605.
Clawson, *(Clawson Printing Co.),* 107 W. 2nd, Frankfort, KS 66427.
Clayton Pub Hse, *(Clayton Publishing House, Inc.; 0-915644),* 6901 Manchester Ave., St. Louis, MO 63143 Tel 314-781-1070.
Clearwater OR, *(Clearwater Press; 0-9605512),* 1115 W Ave., La Grande, OR 97855.
Clearwater Pub, *(Clearwater Publishing Co.; 0-8287),* 1995 Broadway, New York, NY 10023 Tel 212-873-2100.
Cleveland St Univ Poetry Ctr, *(Cleveland State Univ. Poetry Center; 0-914946),* Cleveland State Univ., Cleveland, OH 44115 Tel 216-687-3986; Dist. by: Nacscorp, Inc. (Poetry Ser. Only), Oberlin, OH 44074 Tel 216-775-1561; Dist. by: Field (Poetry Ser. only), Oberlin College, Oberlin, OH 44074 Tel 216-775-8408.
Cleveland St Univ Poetry Ser
See Cleveland St Univ Poetry Ctr
Cliffs, *(Cliff's Notes, Inc.; 0-8220),* 1701 "P" St., Lincoln, NE 68501 Tel 402-477-6971.
Climate Bks, *(Climate Books),* 204 Greens Grove, Washington, GA 30673 Tel 404-678-1823; Formerly Named Garland Press, Point Blanc Press.
Cline-Sigmon, *(Cline-Sigmon Pubs.; 0-914760),* P.O. Box 367-T, Hickory, NC 28601 Tel 704-322-5090.
Clinical Psych, *(Clinical Psychology Publishing Co., Inc.; 0-88422),* 4 Conant Square, Brandon, VT 05733 Tel 802-247-6871.
Clodele, *(Clodele Enterprises, Inc.; 0-930416),* 2004 Vaugine Ave., Pine Bluff, AR 71601 Tel 501-534-8804.
Cloudburst
See Madrona Pubs
Clyde Pr, *(Clyde Press, The; 0-933190),* 373 Lincoln Pkwy, Buffalo, NY 14216 Tel 716-875-4713.
Clymer Pubns, *(Clymer Pubns.; 0-89287),* 12860 Muscatine St., Arleta, CA 91331 Tel 213-767-7660.
CMG Prods, *(C. M. G. Productions, Inc.; 0-933724),* P.O. Box 3838, Grand Junction, CO 81502.
CN *Imprint of* **Har-Row**
CO RR Mus, *(Colorado Railroad Museum; 0-918654),* P.O. Box 10, Golden, CO 80401 Tel 303-279-4591.
Cobb Ent, *(Cobb Enterprizes; 0-9602968),* P.O. Box 295, Rolla, MO 65401 Tel 314-364-5458; Dist. by: Paperback Supply, 4121 Forest Park, St. Louis, MO 63108.
Cobbers, *(Cobbers; 0-934680),* Div. of Martensen Co., Inc., P.O. Box 261, Williamsburg, VA 23185 Tel 804-220-2828.
Coda Pr, *(Coda Press, Inc.; 0-930956),* 700 W. Badger Rd., Suite 101, Madison, WI 53713.
Coffeetable, *(Coffeetable Pubns.; 0-938252),* P.O. Box 8236, 101 N. Haardt Dr., Montgomery, AL 36110.
Coin & Curr, *(Coin & Currency Institute, Inc.; 0-87184),* 1359 Broadway, New York, NY 10018 Tel 212-947-0370.
Colby, *(Colby College Press; 0-910394),* Library, Waterville, ME 04901 Tel 207-873-0311.
Cold Spring Harbor, *(Cold Spring Harbor Laboratory; 0-87969),* P.O. Box 100, Cold Spring Harbor, NY 11724 Tel 516-367-8351.
Cole-Outreach, *(Cole, David M./Outreach Books),* P.O. Box 425, Corona, CA 91720 Tel 213-926-9381.
Coll & U Pr, *(College & Univ. Press; 0-8084),* 267 Chapel St., New Haven, CT 06513 Tel 203-562-3101.
Coll Ent Exam
See College Bd
Coll Placement, *(College Placement Council, Inc.; 0-913936),* P.O. Box 2263, Bethlehem, PA 18001 Tel 215-868-1421.
Coll Wooster, *(College of Wooster, Office of Pubns.; 0-9604658),* Wooster, OH 44691 Tel 216-264-1234.
Colleasius Pr, *(Colleasius Press),* P.O. Box 15545, Colorado Springs, CO 80935 Tel 303-599-0041.
Collector Bks, *(Collector Books; 0-89145),* P.O. Box 3009, Paducah, KY 42001 Tel 502-898-6211.
Collectors Choice, *(Collector's Choice; 0-9602742),* c/o French-Bray Inc., P.O. Box 698, Glen Burnie, MD 21061 Tel 301-768-6000.
College Bd, *(College Board, The; 0-87447),* 888 Seventh Ave., New York, NY 10019 Tel 212-582-6210; Orders to: College Board Pubns, P.O. Box 2815, Princeton, NJ 08541 Tel 609-921-9000.
College-Hill, *(College-Hill Press, Inc.; 0-933014),* P.O. Box 35728, Houston, TX 77035.
College Pr Pub, *(College Press Publishing Co.; 0-89900),* Box 1132, 205 N. Main, Joplin, MO 64801 Tel 417-623-6280.
Collegium Bk Pubs, *(Collegium Book Pubs., Inc.; 0-89669),* 525 Executive Blvd., Elmsford, NY 10523.
Collier *Imprint of* **Macmillan**
Collins Pubs, *(Collins, William, Pubs., Inc.),* 2080 W. 117th St., Cleveland, OH 44111 Tel 216-941-6930; 200 Madison Ave., Suite 1405, New York, NY 10016.
Collins-World
See Collins Pubs
Colman Pubs, *(Colman Pubs.; 0-9602456),* 1147 Elmwood, Stockton, CA 95204 Tel 209-946-2148.
Colo Assoc, *(Colorado Associated Univ. Press, Univ. of Colorado; 0-87081),* Box 480, Univ. of Colorado, Boulder, CO 80309 Tel 303-492-7191.
Colo Fiber, *(Colorado Fiber Center, Inc.; 0-937452),* P.O. Box 2049, Boulder, CO 80306.
Colo Sch Mines, *(Colorado School of Mines; 0-918062),* Publications Dept./Sales, Golden, CO 80401 Tel 303-279-0300.
Colo Sch Mining
See Colo Sch Mines
Cologne Pr, *(Cologne Press; 0-9602310),* P.O. Box 682, Cologne, NJ 08213 Tel 609-965-5163.
Colonial Soc MA *Imprint of* **U Pr of Va**
Colophon, *(Colophon Book Shop, The),* 700 S. Sixth Ave., La Grange, IL 60525 Tel 312-354-0022.
Colton Bk, *(Colton Book Imports),* P.O. Box 526, San Francisco, CA 94101.
Coltsfoot, *(Coltsfoot Press, Inc.; 0-917372),* 507 Fifth Ave., Suite 307, New York, NY 10017.
Columbia Bks, *(Columbia Books Inc., Pubs.; 0-910416),* 777 14th St., N.W., Suite 1336, Washington, DC 20005 Tel 202-737-3777.
Columbia Bookkeeping, *(Columbia Bookkeeping Systems, Inc.; 0-9604828),* 24 Gould St., Reading, MA 01867.
Columbia Graphs, *(Columbia Graphs),* P.O. Box 445, Danielson, CT 06239.
Columbia Pub, *(Columbia Publishing Co., Inc.; 0-914366),* Frenchtown, NJ 08825 Tel 201-996-2141; Dist. by: Vanguard Press, Inc., 424 Madison Ave., New York, NY 10017 Tel 212-753-3906.
Columbia U Ctr Soc Sci, *(Columbia Univ., Center for the Social Sciences; 0-938436),* 420 W. 118th St., 814 I.A.B., New York, NY 10027.
Columbia U Pr, *(Columbia Univ. Press; 0-231),* 562 W. 113th St., New York, NY 10025 Tel 212-678-6777; Orders to: 136 S. Broadway, Irvington-on-Hudson, NY 10533 Tel 914-591-9111.
Colwyn-Tango, *(Colwyn-Tango),* 96 Old River Rd., Wilkes Barre, PA 18702.
Comm & Family, *(Community & Family Study Center; 0-89836),* 1411 E. 60th St., Chicago, IL 60637 Tel 312-753-2518.
Comm Chi Hist & Arch, *(Commission on Chicago Historical & Architectural Landmarks; 0-934076),* 320 N. Clark, Chicago, IL 60610; Dist. by: Chicago Review Press, 215 W. Ohio St., Chicago, IL 60610 Tel 312-644-5457.
Comm Consultants, *(Communication Consultants International; 0-938320),* P.O. Box 1212, San Diego, CA 92112.
Comm Coun Great NY, *(Community Council of Greater New York),* 225 Park Ave., S., New York, NY 10003 Tel 212-777-5000.
Comm Creat, *(Communication Creativity; 0-918880),* P.O. Box 213, Saguache, CO 81149 Tel 303-655-2502.
Comm Econ Dev, *(Committee for Economic Development; 0-87186),* 477 Madison Ave., New York, NY 10022 Tel 212-688-2063.
Comm Pr Inc, *(Communications Press, Inc.; 0-89461),* 1346 Connecticut Ave., N.W., Washington, DC 20036 Tel 202-785-0865.
Comm Serv, *(Community Service, Inc.; 0-910420),* P.O. Box 243, Yellow Springs, OH 45387 Tel 513-767-2161.
Comm Unltd, *(Communicatons Unlimited),* 7057 Wright Court, Arvada, CO 80004.
Commerce, *(Commerce Clearing House, Inc.; 0-8080),* 4025 W. Peterson Ave., Chicago, IL 60646 Tel 312-583-8500.
Commerce Pr
See Pennwell Pub
Commonweal Bks, *(Commonwealth Books, Inc.; 0-918596),* P.O. Box 4433, Lexington, KY 40504; Moved, Left No Forwarding Address.
Commonwealth Pr, *(Commonwealth Press, Inc.; 0-89227),* 415 First St., Radford, VA 24141 Tel 703-639-2475.
Communication Skill, *(Communication Skill Builders, Inc.; 0-88450),* 3130 N. Dodge Blvd., P.O. Box 42050, Tucson, AZ 85733 Tel 602-327-6021.
Commuter Airlines, *(Commuter Airlines Press; 0-9602554),* P.O. Box 15064, San Diego, CA 92115 Tel 714-287-5080; Dist. by: Aviation Book Co., 1640 Victory Blvd., Glendale, CA 91201 Tel 213-240-1771.
Compact Pubns, *(Compact Pubns., Inc.; 0-936320),* 3014 Willow Lane, Hollywood, FL 33021.
CompCare, *(CompCare Pubns.; 0-89638),* 2415 Annapolis Lane, Minneapolis, MN 55441.
Compton, *(Compton, F. E., Co.),* Div. of Encyclopaedia Britannica, Inc., 425 N. Michigan Ave., Chicago, IL 60611.

CompuSoft, *(CompuSoft Publishing; 0-932760),* Div. of CompuSoft, Inc., 1050 Pioneer Way, Suite E, El Cajon, CA 92020 Tel 714-588-0996.
Computer Sci, *(Computer Science Press, Inc.; 0-914894),* 11 Taft Court, Rockville, MD 20850 Tel 301-251-9050; Orders to: P.O. Box 34913, Washington, DC 20034.
Computerist, *(Computerist, Inc., The; 0-938222),* P.O. Box 3, Chelmsford, MA 01824; Dist. by: Micro Ink, Inc., P.O. Box 6502, Chelmsford, MA 01824.
Computing Trends, *(Computing Trends),* 6925 56th Ave. S., Seattle, WA 98118.
Comstock, *(Comstock Publishing Associates),* Dist. by: Cornell Univ. Press, Sales Manager, 124 Roberts Place, Ithaca, NY 14850.
Concept Design, *(Conceptual Design; 0-9604902),* 9 Glenmore Rd., Troy, NY 12180 Tel 518-283-6467.
Concerned Pubns, *(Concerned Pubns., Inc.; 0-939286),* P.O. Box 1024, Clermont, FL 32711.
Conch Mag, *(Conch Magazine Ltd. (Pubs.); 0-914970),* 102 Normal Ave., Buffalo, NY 14213 Tel 716-885-3686.
Concordant, *(Concordant Publishing Concern; 0-910424),* 15570 W. Knochaven Rd., Canyon Country, CA 91351 Tel 805-252-2112.
Concordia, *(Concordia Publishing House; 0-570),* 3558 S. Jefferson Ave., St. Louis, MO 63118 Tel 314-664-7000.
Conduit, *(Conduit; 0-9631781),* P.O. Box 388, Iowa City, IA 52244.
Cone-Heiden, *(Cone-Heiden),* 417 E. Pine St., Seattle, WA 98122.
Conf Econ Prog, *(Conference on Economic Progress; 0-910428),* 2610 Upton St., N.W., Washington, DC 20008 Tel 202-363-6222.
Conf Faith & Hist, *(Conference on Faith & History; 0-913446),* Indiana State Univ., Dept. of History, Terre Haute, IN 47809 Tel 812-232-6311.
Confed Arms, *(Confederate Arms Pubs.; 0-87833),* P.O. Box 220802, Charlotte, NC 28222.
Conference Bd, *(Conference Board, Inc., The; 0-8237),* 845 Third Ave., New York, NY 10022 Tel 212-759-0900.
Confluence Pr, *(Confluence Press, Inc.; 0-917652),* Spalding Hall, Lewis-Clark Campus, Lewiston, ID 83501 Tel 208-746-2341.
Cong Info, *(Congressional Information Service; 0-912380),* 7101 Wisconsin Ave., Washington, DC 20014 Tel 301-654-1550.
Cong Shaarai, *(Congregation Shaarai Shomayim),* 508 N. Duke St., Lancaster, PA 17602 Tel 717-397-5575.
Congdon & Lattes, *(Congdon & Lattes),* Empire State Bldg., New York, NY 10001 Tel 212-736-4883; Dist. by: St. Martin's Press, 175 Fifth Ave., New York, NY 10010 Tel 212-674-5151.
Congeros Pubns, *(Congeros Pubns.; 0-918628),* 123 N. Sultand Ave., P.O. Box 1387, Ontario, CA 91762.
Congr Quarterly, *(Congressional Quarterly, Inc.; 0-87187),* 1414 22nd St., N.W., Washington, DC 20037 Tel 202-296-6800.
Congr Staff, *(Congressional Staff Directory, Ltd.; 0-87289),* P.O. Box 62, Mount Vernon, VA 22121 Tel 703-765-3400.
Conn Hist Soc, *(Connecticut Historical Society),* 1 Elizabeth St., Hartford, CT 06105 Tel 203-236-5621.
Conocheague
See Anima Pubns
Conquest, *(Conquest Pubns.; 0-930220),* P.O. Box 11965, Winston-Salem, NC 27106 Tel 919-945-9686.
Conservation Foun, *(Conservation Foundation; 0-89164),* 1717 Massachusetts Ave. N.W, Washington, DC 20036 Tel 202-797-4300.
Consolidated Bk
See Delair
Consortium
See McGrath
Consortium *Imprint of* **McGrath**
Construct Educ, *(Constructive Educational Concepts, Inc.; 0-934734),* 213 Duncaster Rd., Box 667, Bloomfield, CT 06002.
Consultants *Imprint of* **Plenum Pub**
Consulting Psychol, *(Consulting Psychologists Press, Inc.; 0-89106),* 577 College Ave., Palo Alto, CA 94306 Tel 415-857-1444.
Consumertronics, *(Consumertronics Co.; 0-934274),* 2011 Crescent Dr., P.O. Box 475, Almagordo, NM 88310.
Contact Two, *(Contact/II Pubns.; 0-936556),* P.O. Box 451, Bowling Green, New York, NY 10004; Dist. by: Bookslinger, 2163 Ford Pkwy., St. Paul, MN 55116.
Contemp Bks, *(Contemporary Books, Inc.; 0-8092),* 180 N. Michigan Ave., Chicago, IL 60601 Tel 312-782-9181; Formerly Named Henry Regnery .o.
Contemp Pub
See Nursing Res
Contemp Pub Co of Raleigh, *(Contemporary Publishing Co. of Raleigh; 0-89892),* 1501 S. Blount St., Raleigh, NC 27603 Tel 919-821-0167.
Contemp Pub O
See Contemp Pub Co of Raleigh
Context Pubns, *(Context Pubns.; 0-932654),* 20 Lomita Ave., San Francisco, CA 94122.
Continent Divide, *(Continental Divide Trail Society; 0-934326),* P.O. Box 30002, Washington, DC 20014.
Continent Edns, *(Continental Editions; 0-916868),* 2300 Indian Hills Dr., 3-231, Sioux City, IA 51104 Tel 712-239-5954.
Continent Herit, *(Continental Heritage Press; 0-932986),* P.O. Box 1620, Tulsa, OK 74101 Tel 918-582-6000.
Continuing SAGA, *(Continuing SAGA Press),* 1822 Mason St., San Francisco, CA 94133.
Continuum, *(Continuum Publishing Corp.; 0-8264),* 18 E. 41st St., 7th Fl., New York, NY 10017; Dist. by: The Seabury Press, 815 Second Ave., New York, NY 10017 Tel 212-557-0500.
Control Data, *(Control Data Education Co.; 0-918852),* P.O. Box O, (HQA03Y), Minneapolis, MN 55440 Tel 612-853-7340.
Conway Pubns, *(Conway Pubns., Inc.; 0-910436),* 1954 Airport Rd. NE., Atlanta, GA 30341 Tel 404-458-6026.
Cook, *(Cook, David C., Publishing Co.; 0-89191; 0-912692),* 850 N. Grove Ave., Elgin, IL 60120 Tel 312-741-2400.
Cookbook Pubs, *(Cookbook Pubs.; 0-934474),* Lenexa, KS 66215 Tel 501-741-7340; Dist. by: Southern Star, Inc., P.O. Box 968, Harrison, AR 72601.
Cookie Pr, *(Cookie Press; 0-938236),* 4225 University, Des Moines, IA 50311 Tel 515-255-3552.
Cooper Sq, *(Cooper Square Pubs., Inc.; 0-8154),* 81 Adams Dr., Totowa, NJ 07512 Tel 201-256-8600.
Copley Bks, *(Copley Books; 0-913938),* P.O. Box 957, 7776 Ivanhoe Ave., La Jolla, CA 92038 Tel 714-454-1842.
Copper Beech, *(Copper Beech Press),* Box 1852, Brown University, Providence, RI 02912.
Coraco, *(Coraco; 0-917628),* 1017 S. Arlington Ave., Los Angeles, CA 90019 Tel 213-737-1066.
Core Collection, *(Core Collection Books, Inc.; 0-8486),* 11 Middle Neck Rd., Great Neck, NY 11021 Tel 516-466-3676.
CORE Collection
See Core Collection
Corinth Bks, *(Corinth Books; 0-87091),* 7308 Maple Ave., Chevy Chase, MD 20015 Tel 301-652-1016; Orders to: Bookslinger, 2163 Ford Pkwy., St. Paul, MN 55116.
Corinth Hse, *(Corinth House Pubs.; 0-938280),* 2238 E. Vermont Ave., Anaheim, CA 92806 Tel 714-635-6930.
Corinthian, *(Corinthian Press, The; 0-86551),* 3592 Lee Rd., Shaker Heights, OH 44120 Tel 216-751-7300.
Cornell Maritime, *(Cornell Maritime Press, Inc.; 0-87033),* P.O. Box 456, Centreville, MD 21617 Tel 301-758-1075.
Cornell Mod Indo, *(Cornell Modern Indonesia Project; 0-87763),* 102 West Ave., Ithaca, NY 14850 Tel 607-256-4359.
Cornell SE Asia, *(Cornell Univ., Southeast Asia Program; 0-87727),* 120 Uris Hall, Ithaca, NY 14853 Tel 607-256-2378.
Cornell U Pr, *(Cornell Univ. Press; 0-8014),* 124 Roberts Place, P.O. Box 250, Ithaca, NY 14850 Tel 607-257-7000.
Cornell U Sch Hotel, *(Cornell Univ., School of Hotel Administration; 0-937056),* 327 Statler Hall, Ithaca, NY 14853 Tel 607-256-5093.
Corner, *(Corner Book Shop; 0-910442),* 102 Fourth Ave., New York, NY 10003 Tel 212-254-7714.
Cornerstone, *(Cornerstone Library, Inc.; 0-346),* Div. of Simon & Schuster, Inc., Orders to: Simon & Schuster, Inc., 1230 Avenue of the Americas, New York, NY 10020 Tel 212-245-6400.
Cornerstone Pr, *(Cornerstone Press; 0-918476),* P.O. Box 28048, St. Louis, MO 63119 Tel 314-843-5195.
Corning, *(Corning Museum of Glass; 0-87290),* Corning Glass Ctr., Corning, NY 14830 Tel 607-937-5371.
Corona Pub, *(Corona Publishing Co.; 0-931722),* 1037 S. Alamo, San Antonio, TX 78210 Tel 512-227-1771.
COS *Imprint of* **Har-Row**
Cottage Indus, *(Cottage Industries; 0-938348),* Box 244, Cobalt, CT 06414.
Cotton Lane, *(Cotton Lane Press; 0-9604810),* 2 Cotton Lane, Augusta, GA 30902 Tel 404-722-0232.
Coun Advance Small Colleges, *(Council for the Advancement of Small Colleges; 0-937012),* 1 Dupont Circle, Suite 320, Washington, DC 20036 Tel 202-659-3795.
Coun Am Affairs, *(Council on American Affairs; 0-930690),* 1629 K St., N.W., Suite 520, Washington, DC 20006 Tel 202-232-1040.
Coun Exc Child, *(Council for Exceptional Children; 0-86586),* 1920 Association Dr., Reston, VA 22091 Tel 703-620-3660.
Coun on Municipal, *(Council on Municipal Performance; 0-916450),* 84 Fifth Ave., New York, NY 10011 Tel 212-243-6603.
Coun Plan Lib
See CPL Biblios
Coun Rel & Intl, *(Council on Religion & International Affairs; 0-87641),* 170 E. 64th St., New York, NY 10021 Tel 212-838-4120.
Coun Soc Studies, *(National Council for the Social Studies; 0-87986),* Social Education, 3615 Wisconsin Ave. N.W.,, Washington, DC 20016 Tel 202-966-7840.
Coun State Plan, *(Council of State Planning Agencies, The; 0-934842),* 444 N. Capital St., Washington, DC 20001 Tel 202-624-5386.
Counting Hse, *(Counting House Publishing Co.; 0-915026),* 182 S. Main St., Thiensville, WI 53092 Tel 414-242-2460.
Country Bazaar, *(Country Bazaar Publishing; 0-936744),* Honey Inc. Bldg. Rt.2 Box 190, Berryville, AR 72616 Tel 501-423-3131.
Country Music Found, *(Country Music Foundation Press; 0-915608),* 4 Music Square E., Nashville, TN 37203 Tel 615-256-1639.
Countryman, *(Countryman Press, Inc.; 0-914378),* Woodstock, VT 05091 Tel 802-457-1049.
Countryside Bks, *(Countryside Books; 0-88453),* 1845 N. Farwell Ave., Suite 201, Milwaukee, WI 53202 Tel 414-272-6700.
Countryside Studio, *(Countryside Studio, Inc.; 0-9605428),* P.O. Box 88, Hwy. 25 W., Cottontown, TN 37048.
Courier Pr FL, *(Courier Press; 0-934602),* 428 N.E. 82nd St. Suite 1, Miami, FL 33138.
Cove View, *(Cove View Press; 0-931896),* Box 637, Garberville, CA 95440 Tel 707-923-3476.
Coward, *(Coward, McCann & Geoghegan, Inc.; 0-698),* A Member of the Putnam Publishing Group, 200 Madison Ave., New York, NY 10016 Tel 212-576-8900; Orders to: 1050 W. Wall St., Lyndhurst, NJ 07071 Tel 201-933-9292.
Cowley Pubns, *(Cowley Pubns.),* 980 Memorial Dr., Cambridge, MA 02138.
Cox, *(Cox, Harold E.; 0-911940),* 80 Virginia Terrace, Forty Fort, PA 18704 Tel 717-287-7647.
Cozzolino Assocs, *(Cozzolino Associates; 0-9601408),* 12 Chippenham Dr., West Berlin, NJ 08091.
CPA Study
See Bradley CPA
CPL Biblios, *(CPL Bibliographies),* 1313 E. 60th St., Merriam Ctr., Chicago, IL 60637 Tel 312-947-2007.
Crabtree, *(Crabtree Publishing; 0-937070),* P.O. Box 3451, Federal Way, WA 98003.
Craftsman, *(Craftsman Book Co.; 0-910460),* 542 Stevens Ave., Solana Beach, CA 92075 Tel 714-755-0161.
Cragmont Pubns, *(Cragmont Pubns.; 0-89666),* China Basin Bldg., 161 Berry St., Suite 6410, San Francisco, CA 94107 Tel 415-546-0646.

Crain Bks, *(Crain Books; 0-87251)*, Div. of Crain Communications, Inc., 740 Rush St., Chicago, IL 60611 Tel 312-649-5250.
Crambruck, *(Crambruck Press; 0-87699)*, 381 Park Ave. S., New York, NY 10016 Tel 212-532-0871.
Cranbrook Pub, *(Cranbrook Publishing; 0-9604690)*, 2815 Cranbrook, Ann Arbor, MI 48104.
Crane Pub Co, *(Crane Publishing Co.; 0-89075)*, Div. of MLP, 1301 Hamilton Ave., Box 3713, Trenton, NJ 08629 Tel 609-393-1111.
Crane-Russak Co, *(Crane, Russak & Co., Inc.; 0-8448)*, 3 E. 44th St, New York, NY 10017 Tel 212-867-1490.
CRC Pr, *(CRC Press; 0-87819; 0-8493)*, 2000 N.W. 24th St., Boca Raton, FL 33431 Tel 305-994-0555.
CRCS Pubns NV, *(CRCS Pubns.; 0-916360)*, P.O. Box 20850, Reno, NV 89515 Tel 702-358-2850.
CRCS Pubns WA
See CRCS Pubns NV
Creation Hse, *(Creation House; 0-88419)*, 396 E. St. Charles Rd., Carol Stream, IL 60187 Tel 312-653-1472.
Creations Unltd, *(Creations Unlimited; 0-938900)*, P.O. Box 2591, Farmington Hills, MI 48018.
Creative Arts Bk, *(Creative Arts Book Co.; 0-916870)*, 833 Bancroft Way, Berkeley, CA 94710 Tel 415-848-4777.
Creative Bks, *(Creative Books; 0-914606)*, P.O. Box 5162, Carmel, CA 93921 Tel 408-624-7573.
Creative Ed, *(Creative Education, Inc.; 0-87191)*, 1422 W. Lake St., Suite 301, Minneapolis, MN 55408 Tel 612-825-9154; Orders to: 123 S. Broad St., Mankato, MN 56001 Tel 507-388-6273.
Creative Eye, *(Creative Eye Press; 0-916480)*, P.O. Box 4191, Modesto, CA 95352 Tel 209-524-8603.
Creative Homeowner, *(Creative Homeowner Press; 0-932944)*, Div. of Federal Marketing Corp., 2266 N. Prospect, No. 410, Milwaukee, WI 53202 Tel 414-276-4755.
Creative Infomatics, *(Creative Infomatics, Inc.; 0-917634)*, P.O. Box 11300, Aspen, CO 81611 Tel 303-925-8515.
Creative Learning, *(Creative Learning Press, Inc.; 0-936386)*, P.O. Box 320, Mansfield Center, CT 06250 Tel 203-281-4036.
Creative Pubns, *(Creative Pubns.; 0-88488)*, 1101 San Antonio Rd., Mountain View, CA 94043 Tel 415-968-1101; Orders to: P.O. Box 10328, Palo Alto, CA 94303 Tel 415-968-3977.
Creative Pubs
See Creative Pubns
Creative Storytime, *(Creative Storytime Press; 0-934876)*, P.O. Box 572, Minneapolis, MN 55440 Tel 612-926-5986.
Creative Texas, *(Creative Publishing Co.; 0-932702)*, P.O. Box 9292, College Sta., TX 77840 Tel 713-846-7907.
Creative Therapeutics, *(Creative Therapeutics; 0-933812)*, 155 County Rd., Cresskill, NJ 07626.
Crescent Pubns, *(Crescent Pubns., Inc.; 0-914184)*, 5410 Wilshire Blvd., Suite 400, Los Angeles, CA 90036.
Cresset Pubs, *(Cresset Pubs.; 0-936082)*, 519 E. Tabor Rd., Philadelphia, PA 19120.
Crest *Imprint of* **Fawcett**
Crestwood Hse, *(Crestwood House, Inc.; 0-89686; 0-913940)*, P.O. Box 3427, Hwy. 66 South, Mankato, MN 56001 Tel 507-388-1616.
Crime & Justice Hist, *(Crime & Justice History Group, The)*, Dist. by: John Jay Press, 444 W. 56th St., New York, NY 10019.
Crime & Soc Justice, *(Crime & Social Justice; 0-935206)*, P.O. Box 4373, Berkeley, CA 94704.
Croissant & Co, *(Croissant & Co.; 0-912348)*, P.O. Box 282, Athens, OH 45701 Tel 614-593-8339.
Crome & Soc Justice
See Crime & Soc Justice
Croner, *(Croner Pubns.; 0-87514)*, 211-03 Jamaica Ave., Queens Village, NY 11428 Tel 212-464-0866.
Crosby County, *(Crosby County Pioneer Memorial)*, P. O. Box 386, Crosbyton, TX 79322 Tel 806-675-2331.
Cross Country, *(Cross Country Press; 0-916696)*, P.O. Box 21081, Woodhaven, NY 11421 Tel 212-896-7648.
Cross Cult, *(Cross-Cultural Communications; 0-89304)*, 239 Wynsum Ave., Merrick, NY 11566 Tel 516-868-5635.
Crossbar Ent, *(Crossbar Enterprises; 0-9604994)*, 9522 Stevebrook Rd., Fairfax, VA 22032.
Crosscut Saw, *(Crosscut Saw Press; 0-931020)*, Orders to: Bookpeople, 2940 7th St., Berkeley, CA 94710.
Crossing Pr, *(Crossing Press, The; 0-89594; 0-912278)*, Box 640, Trumansburg, NY 14886 Tel 607-387-6217.
Crossroad NY, *(Crossroad Publishing Co.; 0-8245)*, 18 E 41st St., New York, NY 10017.
Crow Canyon, *(Crow Canyon Press; 0-937760)*, 1900 Las Trampas Rd., Alamo, CA 94507.
Crown, *(Crown Pubs., Inc.; 0-517)*, 1 Park Ave., New York, NY 10016 Tel 212-532-9200.
Cruikshank, *(Cruikshank, Eleanor P.)*, 194 San Carlos Ave., Sausalito, CA 94965.
CSA Pr, *(CSA Press; 0-87707)*, Lakemont, GA 30552 Tel 404-782-3931.
CSG Pr, *(CSG Press)*, 11301 Rockville Pike, Kensington, MD 20795.
CSI Studies, *(Center for Strategic & International Studies; 0-89206)*, 1800 "K" St. N.W., Washington, DC 20006 Tel 202-877-0200.
CSLA, *(Church & Synagogue Library Assn.; 0-915324)*, P.O. Box 1130, Bryn Mawr, PA 19010 Tel 215-853-2870.
CSS Pub, *(C.S.S. Publishing Co.; 0-89536)*, 628 S. Main St., Lima, OH 45804 Tel 419-227-1818.
CSU Ctr Busn Econ, *(California State Univ., Center for Business & Economic Research; 0-9602894)*, Chico, CA 95929.
CSU Oral Hist
See CSUF Oral Hist
CSUF Oral Hist, *(California State Univ. Fullerton, Oral History Program; 0-930046)*, Fullerton, CA 92634 Tel 714-773-3580.
CSUN, *(California State Univ., Northridge Library)*, 18111 Nordhoff St., Northridge, CA 91330 Tel 213-885-2271.
Ctr Afro-Am Stud, *(Center for Afro-American Studies (UCLA); 0-934934)*, 3111 Campbell Hall, 405 Hilgard Ave., Los Angeles, CA 90024 Tel 213-825-3528.
Ctr Appl Ling, *(Center for Applied Linguistics; 0-87281)*, 3520 Prospect St. Nw., Washington, DC 20007 Tel 202-298-9292.
Ctr Appl Res, *(Center for Applied Research in Education, Inc., The; 0-87628)*, Subs. of Prentice-Hall, C/o Prentice-Hall, Englewood Cliffs, NJ 07632 Tel 201-592-2483; Orders to: P.O. Box 130, W. Nyack, NY 10994 Tel 201-767-5195.
Ctr Applications Psych, *(Center for Applications of Psychological Type, Inc.; 0-935652)*, 1441 N.W. Sixth St., Suite B400, Gainesville, FL 32601 Tel 904-375-0160.
Ctr Art Living, *(Center for the Art of Living; 0-9602552)*, 2203 N. Sheffield, Chicago, IL 60614 Tel 312-871-5681.
Ctr Bus Devel, *(Center for Business Development & Research, College of Business & Economics)*, Univ. of Idaho, Moscow, ID 83843 Tel 208-885-6611.
Ctr Byzantine *Imprint of* **Dumbarton Oaks**
Ctr Calif Public
See Cal Inst Public
Ctr Cont Poetry, *(Center for Contemporary Poetry)*, Murphy Library, Univ. of Wisconsin at La Crosse, La Crosse, WI 54601.
Ctr Criminal
See Ctr Res Criminal
Ctr Econ Analysis, *(Center for Economic Analysis, George Mason Univ.; 0-933588)*, Box 1329, Cullowhee, NC 28723 Tel 704-293-5433.
Ctr Educ Policy Mgmt, *(Center for Educational Policy & Management)*, College of Education, Univ. of Oregon, Eugene, OR 97403 Tel 503-686-5072.
Ctr for NE & North African Stud, *(Univ. of Michigan Center for Near Eastern & North African Studies; 0-932098)*, 144 Lane Hall, Univ. of Michigan, Ann Arbor, MI 48109 Tel 313-764-0350.
Ctr Intl Stud Duke, *(Center for International Studies, Duke Univ.)*, Durham, NC 27706.
Ctr Korean U HI at Manoa, *(Center for Korean Studies, Univ. of Hawaii at Manoa; 0-917536)*, 1881 East-West Rd., Honolulu, HI 96822 Tel 808-949-1833.
Ctr Landscape Arch *Imprint of* **Dumbarton Oaks**
Ctr Migration, *(Center for Migration Studies; 0-913256)*, Dist. by: Jerome S. Ozer Pub., Inc., 340 Tenafly Rd., Englewood, NJ 07631 Tel 201-567-7040.
Ctr Natl Security, *(Center for National Security Studies; 0-86566)*, 122 Maryland Ave. NE, Washington, DC 20002.
Ctr Pre-Columbian *Imprint of* **Dumbarton Oaks**
Ctr Prof Adv, *(Center for Professional Advancement; 0-86553)*, 197 Rt. 18, P.O. Box H, E. Brunswick, NJ 08816 Tel 201-249-1400.
Ctr Renewable, *(Center for Renewable Resources; 0-937446)*, 1001 Connecticut Ave., N.W., No. 510, Washington, DC 20036.
Ctr Res Criminal, *(Center for Research on Criminal Justice; 0-917404)*, P.O. Box 4373, Berkeley, CA 94704; Orders to: Synthesis Publications, P. O. Box 40099, San Francisco, CA 94140 Tel 415-282-5272.
Ctr Res Soc Chg, *(Center for Research in Social Change; 0-89937)*, Emory University, Atlanta, GA 30322 Tel 404-329-7525.
Ctr Responsive Law, *(Center for Study of Responsive Law)*, P.O. Box 19367, Washington, DC 20036; Dist. by: Education Exploration Center, P.O. Box 7339, Minneapolis, MN 55407.
Ctr S&SE Asian, *(Univ. of Michigan, Center for South & Southeast Asian Studies; 0-89148)*, Univ. of Michigan, Center for S. & Se. Asian Studies, 130 Lane Hall, Ann Arbor, MI 48109 Tel 313-764-0352.
Ctr Sci Public, *(Center for Science in the Public Interest; 0-89329)*, 1755 "S" St., N.W., Washington, DC 20009 Tel 202-332-9110.
Ctr Sci Study, *(Center for the Scientific Study of Religion; 0-913348)*, 5757 University Ave., Chicago, IL 60637 Tel 312-752-5757.
Ctr South Folklore, *(Center for Southern Folklore; 0-89267)*, 1216 Peabody Ave., P.O. Box 40105, Memphis, TN 38104 Tel 901-726-4205.
Ctr Study Crime
See Ctr Res Criminal
Ctr Western Studies, *(Center for Western Studies; 0-931170)*, Augustana College, Sioux Falls, SD 57197 Tel 605-336-4007.
Cuisinart Cooking, *(Cuisinart Cooking Club; 0-936662)*, 411 W. Putnam Ave., Greenwich, CT 06830.
Cummings
See Benjamin-Cummings
Cummington Pub, *(Cummington Publishing, Inc.; 0-938350)*, 17 Old Orchard Rd., New Rochelle, NY 10804.
Cunningham Pr, *(Cunningham Press)*, 3063 W. Main, Alhambra, CA 91801 Tel 213-283-8838; Dist. by: Theosophy Co., 245 W. 33rd St., Los Angeles, CA 90007.
Curbstone, *(Curbstone Press; 0-915306)*, 321 Jackson St., Willimantic, CT 06226 Tel 203-423-9190.
Curbstone Pub NY TX, *(Curbstone Publishing; 0-931604)*, P.O. Box 1613, New York, NY 10116 Tel 212-360-1542; Orders to: P.O. Box 7445, Austin, TX 78712 Tel 512-444-9463.
Curriculum Info Ctr, *(Curriculum Information Center, Inc.; 0-914608; 0-89770)*, Ketchum Place, P.O. Box 510, Westport, CT 06881 Tel 203-226-8941.
Curry County, *(Curry County Historical Society; 0-932368)*, P.O. Box 1856, Wedderburn, OR 97491.
Curtin & London, *(Curtin & London, Inc.; 0-930764)*, 6 Vernon St., Somerville, MA 02145 Tel 617-625-1200.
Custer, *(Custer, Marquis, Pubns.; 0-9600274)*, 1021 S. Lee Ave., Lodi, CA 95240 Tel 209-368-0502.
CWS Group Pr, *(CWS Group Press; 0-9604324)*, P.O. Box 543, 807 W. 15th St., Vinton, IA 52349 Tel 313-472-3552.
D A Duke, *(Duke, David A.; 0-9605056)*, P.O. Box 725, Whitehouse, TX 75791 Tel 214-839-4837.
D Armstrong, *(Armstrong, D., Co., Inc.; 0-918464)*, 2000-B Governor's Circle, Houston, TX 77092 Tel 713-688-1441.

D Bosco Pubns, *(Don Bosco Pubns.; 0-89944),* Div. of Salsian Society, Inc., Box T, 148 Main St., New Rochelle, NY 10802 Tel 914-632-6562.
D Brown Bks, *(Brown, D., Books),* 511 Capp St., San Francisco, CA 94110.
D Bull, *(Bull, Donald; 0-9601190),* P.O. Box 106, Trumbull, CT 06611 Tel 203-261-2398.
D C Parker, *(Parker, D. Coffey),* 28 Abbot Rd., Springfield, IL 62704 Tel 217-787-7620.
D C Raemsch
See Raemsch Pubns
D D Murphy, *(Murphy, Dennis D.; 0-918788),* 4573 S. 23rd St., Apt. 1, Milwaukee, WI 53221.
D D Shepard, *(Shepard, Dennis D.; 0-9601234),* 1414 S. Miller St., Santa Maria, CA 93454 Tel 805-922-3527.
D Hannon, *(Hannon, Douglas; 0-937866),* Rte. 2, Box 991, Odessa, FL 33556; Dist. by: Great Outdoors Publishing Co., St. Petersburg, FL 33714.
D J Fortunato, *(Fortunato, Donald J.),* 7 Halko Dr., Cedar Knolls, NJ 07927 Tel 201-540-8852.
D J Gingery, *(Gingery, David J.; 0-9604330);* 2045 Boonville, Springfield, MO 65803.
D J Perkins, *(Perkins, Dorothy J.; 0-9604742),* Box 194, Moylan, PA 19065.
D Lem Assocs, *(Lem, Dean, Associates, Inc.; 0-914218),* 9229 Sunset Blvd, Suite 301, Los Angeles, CA 90069 Tel 213-275-3129; Orders to: P.O. Box 46086, Los Angeles, CA 90046.
D M Battle Pubns, *(Battle, Dennis M., Pubns.; 0-933464),* P.O. Box 67, Elyria, OH 44036 Tel 216-323-1729.
D M Chase, *(Chase, Don M.; 0-918634),* 8569 Lawrence Lane, Sebastopol, CA 95472.
D Polk, *(Polk, Donice; 0-9605430),* 1973 Reedy, Highland, CA 92346.
D Ponicsan, *(Ponicsan, Darryl),* P.O. Box 5094, Ojai, CA 93023 Tel 805-646-4215.
D R Bell, *(Bell, D. Rayford; 0-9604820),* 1225 McDaniel Ave., Evanston, IL 60202.
D Van Nostrand, *(Van Nostrand, D., Co.; 0-442),* 135 W. 50th St., New York, NY 10020 Tel 212-265-8700; Orders to: LEPI Order Processing, 7625 Empire Dr., Florence, KY 41042.
D Varden Pubns, *(Dolly Varden Pubns.),* P.O. Box 2017, Oceanside, CA 92054 Tel 714-729-1736.
Da Capo, *(Da Capo Press, Inc.; 0-306),* 227 W. 17th St., New York, NY 10011 Tel 212-255-0713.
Dabbs, *(Dabbs, Jack A.; 0-911494),* 2806 Cherry Lane, Austin, TX 78703 Tel 512-472-7463.
Dada Ctr, *(Dada Center Pubns.; 0-930608),* 2319 W. Dry Creek Rd., Healdsburg, CA 95448 Tel 707-433-2161.
Dadant & Sons, *(Dadant & Sons, Inc.; 0-915698),* 51 S. Second St., Hamilton, IL 62341 Tel 217-847-3324.
Dairy Goat, *(Dairy Goat Journal),* P.O. Box 1808, Scottsdale, AZ 85252 Tel 602-991-4628.
Daisy, *(Daisy Press; 0-935424),* P.O. Box 884, La Mesa, CA 92041.
Dalton, *(Dalton, Pat),* 410 Lancaster Ave., Haverford, PA 19041.
Dame Pubns, *(Dame Pubns., Inc.; 0-931920),* P.O. Box 35556, Houston, TX 77035 Tel 713-995-1000.
Dan River Pr, *(Dan River Press; 0-89754),* P.O. Box 249, Stafford, VA 22554 Tel 703-659-6771.
Dance Films, *(Dance Films Assn., Inc.; 0-914438),* 250 W. 57th St., Rm. 2201, New York, NY 10019 Tel 212-586-2142.
Dance Horiz, *(Dance Horizons; 0-87127),* 1801 E. 26th St., Brooklyn, NY 11229 Tel 212-645-9607.
Dance Notation, *(Dance Notation Bureau Press; 0-932582),* 505 Eighth Ave., New York, NY 10018 Tel 212-736-4350.
Dancin Bee, *(Dancin' Bee Co.; 0-933192),* 107 Maple Ave., P.O. Box 237, Ridgely, MD 21660.
Dandelion Pr, *(Dandelion Press; 0-89799),* RFD No. 2, Box 118, Bedford, NY 10506 Tel 914-764-8172; Orders to: 184 Fifth Ave., New York, NY 10010 Tel 212-929-0090.
Dandy Lion, *(Dandy Lion Pubns.; 0-931724),* P.O. Box 190, San Luis Obispo, CA 93406 Tel 805-544-3598.
Dangary Pub, *(Dangary Publishing Co.; 0-910484),* 606 N. Eutaw St., Baltimore, MD 21201 Tel 301-728-3322.
Dante U Am, *(Dante Univ. of America Press, Inc.),* Box 843, 21 Station St., Brookline Village, MA 02147.
Dante Univ Bkshlf, *(Dante Univ. Bookshelf),* Dist. by: Branden Press, Inc., P.O. Box 843, 21 Station St., Brookline Village, MA 02147 Tel 617-734-2045.
Daratech, *(Daratech Associates; 0-938484),* P.O. Box 410, Cambridge, MA 02238.
Darby Bks, *(Darby Books; 0-89987),* P.O. Box 148, Darby, PA 19023.
Daring Pr, *(Daring Press; 0-938936),* 5060 Navarre Rd., S.W., Canton, OH 44706.
Dark Sun, *(Dark Sun Press; 0-937968),* c/o MFA Photography, Rochester Institute of Technology, 1 Lomb Mem. Dr., Rochester, NY 14623 Tel 716-475-2616.
Dartnell Corp, *(Dartnell Corp.; 0-85013),* 4660 Ravenswood Ave., Chicago, IL 60640 Tel 312-561-4000.
Darwin Pr, *(Darwin Press, Inc.; 0-87850),* P.O. Box 2202, Princeton, NJ 08540 Tel 609-924-3938.
Datar Pub, *(Datar Publishing Co.; 0-931572),* 6410 Cates Ave., Suite 2W, University City, MO 63130.
Datarule, *(Datarule Publishing Co., Inc.; 0-911740),* P.O. Box 448, New Canaan, CT 06840 Tel 914-533-2263.
Davenport, *(Davenport, May, Publisher; 0-9603118),* 26313 Purissima Rd., Los Altos Hills, CA 94022 Tel 415-948-6499.
David & Charles, *(David & Charles, Inc.; 0-7153),* P.O. Box 57, North Pomfret, VT 05053 Tel 802-457-1911.
Davida Pubns, *(Davida Pubns.; 0-9603022),* P.O. Box 1925, West Covina, CA 91790 Tel 213-968-4148; Dist. by: Devorss & Co., Marina Del Rey, CA 90291.
Davis Co, *(Davis, F. A., Co.; 0-8036),* 1915 Arch St., Philadelphia, PA 19103 Tel 215-568-2270.
Davis Mass, *(Davis Pubns., Inc.; 0-87192),* 50 Portland St., Worcester, MA 01608.
Davis Pubns, *(Davis Pubns., Inc.; 0-89559),* 380 Lexington Ave., New York, NY 10017 Tel 212-557-9100.
Davison, *(Davison Publishing Co.; 0-87515),* P.O. Box 477, Ridgewood, NJ 07451 Tel 201-445-3135.
DAW Bks, *(DAW Books; 0-87997),* Dist. by: New American Library, 1633 Broadway, New York, NY 10019 Tel 212-397-8000.
Dawn Horse Pr, *(Dawn Horse Press; 0-913922),* P.O. Box 3680, Clearlake Highlands, CA 95422 Tel 707-994-8281; Dist. by: Publisher's Services, Box 3914, San Rafael, CA 94902 Tel 415-549-3033.
Dawn Valley, *(Dawn Valley Press; 0-936014),* P.O. Box 58, New Wilmington, PA 16142 Tel 412-946-2948.
Dawne-Leigh, *(Dawne-Leigh Pubns.; 0-89742),* 231 Adrian Rd., Millbrae, CA 94030 Tel 415-692-4500; Dist. by: Atheneum Publishers, 597 Fifth Ave., New York, NY 10017 Tel 212-486-2655.
Dawson & Co, *(Dawson & Co.; 0-918010),* P.O. Box 40157, Tucson, AZ 85717 Tel 602-323-8128.
Dawson Pub, *(Dawson Publishing; 0-7129),* Dist. by: Shoe String Press, Inc., P.O. Box 4327, 995 Sherman Ave., Hamden, CT 06514 Tel 203-248-6307.
Dawsons, *(Dawson's Book Shop; 0-87093),* 535 N. Larchmont Blvd., Los Angeles, CA 90004 Tel 213-469-2186.
Daystar Pub Co, *(Daystar Publishing Co.),* P.O. Box 707, Angwin, CA 94508.
Dayton Labs, *(Dayton Laboratories; 0-916750),* 3235 Dayton Ave., Lorain, OH 44055 Tel 216-246-1397.
DBA Bks, *(DBA Books; 0-9605276),* 130 Marlborough St., Boston, MA 02116.
DBI, *(DBI Books, Inc.; 0-910676),* 1 Northfield Plaza, Northfield, IL 60093 Tel 312-441-7010; Dist. by: Follett Publishing Co., P.O. Box 5705, Chicago, IL 60680.
DCT Ent, *(DCT Enterprises; 0-9604998),* 2888 Bluff St., Suite 218, Boulder, CO 80301.
De Graff, *(De Graff, John, Inc.; 0-8286),* Clinton Corners, NY 12514; Dist. by: International Marine Publishing Co., 21 Elm St., Camden, ME 04843 Tel 207-236-4342.
De Gruyter, *(De Gruyter, Walter, Inc.; 3-11; 0-89925),* 200 Saw Mill River Rd., Hawthorne, NY 10532 Tel 914-747-0110.
De La Ree, *(De La Ree, Gerry, Publisher; 0-938192),* 7 Cedarwood Lane, Saddle River, NJ 07458 Tel 201-327-6621.
De Vorss, *(De Vorss & Co.; 0-87516),* P.O. Box 550, Marina Del Rey, CA 90291 Tel 213-870-7478.
Decatur Hse, *(Decatur House Press, Ltd; 0-916276),* 2122 Decatur Place, N.W., Washington, DC 20008 Tel 202-387-3913.
Deem Corp, *(Deem Corp., The; 0-918822),* 5860 W. Sioux Dr,, Sedalia, CO 80135 Tel 303-688-9249.
Deep River Pr, *(Deep River Press; 0-935232),* 7319 Dinwiddie St., Downey, CA 90241 Tel 213-928-6815.
Definition, *(Definition Press; 0-910492),* 141 Greene St., New York, NY 10012 Tel 212-777-4490.
Dekker, *(Dekker, Marcel, Inc.; 0-8247),* 270 Madison Ave., New York, NY 10016 Tel 212-889-9595.
Del Oeste, *(Del Oeste Press; 0-89632),* P.O. Box 397, Tarzana, CA 91356.
Del Valley, *(Delaware Valley Poets; 0-937158),* P.O. Box 6203, Lawrenceville, NJ 08648.
Delacorte, *(Delacorte Press),* c/o Dell Publishing Co., 1 Dag Hammarskjold Plaza, 245 E. 47th St., New York, NY 10017 Tel 212-832-7300. *Imprints:* E Friede (Eleanor Friede); Sey Lawr (Seymour Lawrence).
Delafield Pr, *(Delafield Press; 0-916872),* P.O. Box 335, Suttons Bay, MI 49682 Tel 616-271-3826; P.O. Box 09118, Detroit, MI 48209 Tel 313-849-5123.
Delair, *(Delair/Consolidated; 0-8326),* Div. of Delair Publishing Co., 420 Lexington Ave., Rm. 1621, New York, NY 10170 Tel 212-867-2255.
Delamar Duverus
See Duverus Pub
Delanie Way, *(Delanie Way Pub.; 0-9602290),* 685 Delanie Way, Stone Mountain, GA 30083 Tel 404-292-9121.
Delbridge Pub Co, *(Delbridge Publishing Co.; 0-88232),* P.O. Box 2989, Stanford, CA 94305 Tel 408-446-3131.
Delford Pr, *(Delford Press; 0-931726),* P.O. Box 27, Oradell, NJ 07649 Tel 201-262-0647.
Dell, *(Dell Publishing Co., Inc.; 0-440),* 1 Dag Hammarskjold Plaza, 245 E. 47th St., New York, NY 10017 Tel 212-832-7300. *Imprints:* Banbury (Banbury); Dell Trade Pbks (Dell Trade Paperbacks); Delta (Delta Books); LE (Laurel Editions); LFL (Laurel Leaf Library); YB (Yearling Books).
Dell Trade Pbks *Imprint of* **Dell**
Delmar, *(Delmar Pubs.; 0-8273),* Div. of Litton Educ. Pub., Inc., 50 Wolf Rd., Albany, NY 12205; Orders to: 7625 Empire Dr., Florence, KY 41042.
DeLong & Assocs, *(DeLong & Associates; 0-9603414),* P.O. Box 1732, Annapolis, MD 21404 Tel 301-923-2308.
DeLorme Pub, *(DeLorme Publishing Co.; 0-89933),* P.O. Box 81, Yarmouth, ME 04096 Tel 207-846-9764.
Delphi Info, *(Delphi Information Sciences, Inc.; 0-930306),* 1414 Sixth St., Santa Monica, CA 90401.
Delta *Imprint of* **Dell**
Delta Systems, *(Delta Systems Co., Inc.; 0-937354),* 215 N. Arlington Hts. Rd., Arlington Hts, IL 60004 Tel 312-394-5760.
Deluxe Co, *(Deluxe Co., The; 0-938012),* P.O. Box 4246, Shreveport, LA 71104.
Dembner Bks, *(Dembner Books; 0-934878),* Div. of Red Dembner Enterprises Corp., 1841 Broadway, New York, NY 10023 Tel 212-265-1250; Dist. by: W.W. Norton & Co., Inc., 500 Fifth Ave., New York, NY 10036 Tel 212-354-5500.
Demetrius-Victor
See Caratzas Bros
Denison, *(Denison, T. S., & Co., Inc.; 0-513),* 9601 Newton Ave. S., Minneapolis, MN 55431 Tel 612-888-1460.
Denlingers, *(Denlingers Pubs., Ltd.; 0-87714),* P.O. Box 76, Fairfax, VA 22030 Tel 703-631-1501.
Denoyer, *(Denoyer-Geppert Co.; 0-87453),* Subs. of Times Mirror Co., 5235 Ravenswood Ave., Chicago, IL 60640 Tel 312-561-9200.

Denver Art Mus, *(Denver Art Museum; 0-914738),* 100 W. 14th Ave. Pkwy., Denver, CO 80204 Tel 303-575-5582.
Denver Mus Natl Hist, *(Denver Museum of Natural History; 0-916278),* City Park, Denver, CO 80205 Tel 303-575-3931.
Der Angriff, *(Der Angriff Pubns.; 0-9604770),* 1024 Sixth St., Huntington, WV 25701.
Derek Prince, *(Prince, Derek, Pubns.; 0-934920),* P.O. Box 14306, Fort Lauderdale, FL 33302 Tel 305-763-5202.
Deseret Bk, *(Deseret Book Co.; 0-87747),* 40 E. South Temple, P.O. Box 30178, Salt Lake City, UT 84130 Tel 801-534-1515.
Desert Botanical, *(Desert Botanical Garden),* P.O. Box 5415, Phoenix, AZ 85010 Tel 602-941-1217.
Desert Pr, *(Desert Press, The; 0-937764),* Box K, Bouse, AZ 85325.
Design Ent SF, *(Design Enterprises of San Francisco; 0-932538),* P.O. Box 14695, San Francisco, CA 94114 Tel 415-282-8813.
Determined Prods, *(Determined Productions, Inc.; 0-915696),* 315 Pacific Ave. at Battery, P.O. Box 2150, San Francisco, CA 94126 Tel 415-433-0660.
Developmental Arts, *(Developmental Arts),* P.O. Box 389, Arlington, MA 02174.
Devin, *(Devin-Adair Co., Inc.; 0-8159),* 143 Sound Beach Ave., Old Greenwich, CT 06870 Tel 203-637-4531.
Dghtrs St Paul, *(Daughters of St. Paul; 0-8198),* 50 St. Paul's Ave., Boston, MA 02130 Tel 617-522-8911.
Dharma Pub, *(Dharma Publishing; 0-913546; 0-89800),* 2425 Hillside Ave., Berkeley, CA 94704 Tel 415-548-5407.
Di-Tri Bks, *(Di-Tri Books; 0-9603374),* 261 Waubesa St., Madison, WI 53704 Tel 608-244-3466.
Dial, *(Dial Press; 0-8037),* 1 Dag Hammarskjold Plaza, 245 E. 47th St., New York, NY 10017 Tel 212-832-7300.
Dialogue Hse, *(Dialogue House Library; 0-87941),* 80 E. 11th St., New York, NY 10003 Tel 212-673-5880.
Diamond Heights, *(Diamond Heights Publishing Co., Inc.; 0-936182),* 25 Grand View Ave., San Francisco, CA 94114.
Diamond Pubs, *(Diamond Pubs; 0-936510),* 23818 Twin Pines Lane, Diamond Bar, CA 91765.
Diana Pr, *(Diana Press, Inc.; 0-88447),* 4400 Market St., Oakland, CA 94608 Tel 415-658-5558.
Diane Bks, *(Diane Books Publishing, Inc.; 0-88264),* 1111 E. Chevy Chase, Glendale, CA 91205 Tel 213-244-5600.
Dickenson, *(Dickenson Publishing Co.; 0-8221),* c/o Wadsworth, Inc., 10 Davis Dr., Belmont, CA 94002 Tel 415-595-2350.
Dicul Pub, *(Dicul Publishing; 0-938784),* P.O. Box 368, Nashville, IN 47448.
Didactic Syst, *(Didactic Systems Inc.; 0-89401),* P.O. Box 457, Cranford, NJ 07016 Tel 212-789-2194.
Digital Pr, *(Digital Press/Digital Equipment Corp.; 0-932376),* 12 Crosby Dr., Bldg. D-2, Bedford, MA 01730; Orders to: 12-A Esquire Rd., North Billerica, MA 01862.
Dilithium Pr, *(Dilithium Press; 0-918398),* 30 N.W. 23rd Place, Portland, OR 97210 Tel 503-243-1158; Orders to: P.O. Box 606, Beaverton, OR 97075.
Dillon, *(Dillon Press, Inc.; 0-87518),* 500 S. Third St., Minneapolis, MN 55415 Tel 612-336-2691.
Dimond Pubs, *(Dimond Pubs.),* 3431 Fruitvale Ave., Oakland, CA 94602.
Dinograph SW, *(Dinograph Southwest, Inc.; 0-932680),* P.O. Box 1600, Alamogordo, NM 88310.
Dinosaur, *(Dinosaur Press, The),* P.O. Box 372, Amherst, MA 01004 Tel 413-549-0404.
Diotima Bks, *(Diotima Books; 0-935772),* Box H, Glen Carbon, IL 62034.
DiPaul, *(DiPaul, H. Bert; 0-9605418),* 1066 Brennan Dr., Warminster, PA 18974.
Directions
See Easi-Bild
Directions Pr, *(Directions Press),* P.O. Box 1811, Thousand Oaks, CA 91360.
Directories Intl, *(Directories International, Inc.; 0-912794),* 1718 Sherman Ave., Evanston, IL 60201 Tel 312-491-0019.
Directories Pub, *(Directories Publishing Co., Inc.),* P.O. Box 1372, Ormond Beach, FL 32074 Tel 904-673-1241.
Discus *Imprint of* **Avon**
Displays Sch, *(Displays for Schools, Inc.; 0-9600962),* P.O. Box 163, Gainesville, FL 32602 Tel 904-373-2030.
Divry, *(Divry, D.C., Inc.; 0-910516),* 293 Seventh Ave., New York, NY 10001 Tel 212-255-2153.
DJD Prods, *(DJD Productions; 0-9603964),* 1712 S. Highland, Arlington Heights, IL 60005 Tel 312-640-7778.
DMR Pubns, *(D. M. R. Pubns., Inc.; 0-89552),* 1410 E. Capitol Dr., Milwaukee, WI 53211 Tel 414-961-0120.
Do It Yourself Pubs, *(Do-It-Yourself Pubs., Inc.; 0-932704),* 150 Fifth Ave., New York, NY 10011 Tel 212-242-2840.
Doane Agricultural, *(Doane Agricultural Service, Inc.; 0-932250),* 8900 Manchester Rd., St. Louis, MO 63144 Tel 314-968-1000.
Doctor Jazz, *(Doctor Jazz Press; 0-934002),* P.O. Box 1043, Auburn, AL 36830.
Documentary Pubns, *(Documentary Pubns.; 0-89712),* Rte. 12, Box 480, Salisbury, NC 28144.
DODC, *(Directory of Directors Co., Inc.; 0-936612),* P.O. Box 462, Southport, CT 06490 Tel 203-255-8525.
Dodd, *(Dodd, Mead & Co.; 0-396),* 79 Madison Ave., New York, NY 10016 Tel 212-685-6464.
DOK Pubs, *(DOK Pubs., Inc.; 0-914634),* 71 Radcliffe Rd., Buffalo, NY 14214 Tel 716-837-3391.
Doll Collect Am, *(Doll Collectors of America, Inc.; 0-9603210),* Dist. by: Hazel Toon, 167 Round Cove Rd., Chatham, MA 02633.
Dolp *Imprint of* **Doubleday**
Domjan Studio, *(Domjan Studio; 0-933652),* West Lake Rd., Tuxedo Park, NY 10987 Tel 914-351-4596; Dist. by: Wind, Sun & Stars, Pheasant Ridge Rd., W. Redding, CT 06896 Tel 203-938-9476.
Domus Bks
See Quality Bks IL
Domus Bks *Imprint of* **Quality Bks IL**
Donnelly, *(Donnelly, Sister Mary Louise),* P.O. Box 306, Burke, VA 22015.
Donning Co, *(Donning Co. Pubs.; 0-915442; 0-89865),* 5041 Admiral Wright Rd., Virginia Beach, VA 23462 Tel 804-499-0589. *Imprints:* Starblaze (Starblaze); Unilaw (Unilaw).
Dooryard, *(Dooryard Press; 0-937160),* P.O. Box 221, Story, WY 82842.
Dorison Hse, *(Dorison House Pubs., Inc.; 0-916752),* 824 Park Square Bldg., Boston, MA 02116 Tel 617-426-1715.
Dormac, *(Dormac, Inc; 0-86575),* P.O. Box 752, Beaverton, OR 97075 Tel 503-641-3128.
Dorrance, *(Dorrance & Co.; 0-8059),* Cricket Terrace Ctr., Ardmore, PA 19003 Tel 215-642-8303.
Dorsey, *(Dorsey Press; 0-256),* Div. of Richard D. Irwin, Inc., 1818 Ridge Rd., Homewood, IL 60430 Tel 312-798-6000.
Dots Pubns, *(Dots Pubns.),* P.O. Box 563, Ventura, CA 93002.
Double M Pr, *(Double M Press; 0-916634),* 16455 Tuba St., Sepulveda, CA 91343 Tel 213-366-1056.
Doubleday, *(Doubleday & Co., Inc.; 0-385),* 501 Franklin Ave., Garden City, NY 11530 Tel 516-294-4561. *Imprints:* Anch (Anchor Books); Anchor Pr (Anchor Press); CCG (College Course Guides); Dolp (Dolphin Books); Echo (Echo Books); Galilee (Galilee); Im (Image Books); Made (Made Simple Books); Zenith (Zenith Books); Zephyr (Zephyr).
Doubleshoe, *(Doubleshoe Pubs.; 0-9603270),* 5131 E. Shea Blvd., Scottsdale, AZ 85253 Tel 602-948-0355.
Douglas-McKay, *(Douglas-McKay, Inc.; 0-915712),* P.O. Box 15565, Milwaukee, WI 53215 Tel 414-481-7207.
Douglas-West, *(Douglas-West Pubs., Inc.; 0-913264),* 7060 Hollywood Blvd., Suite 503, Los Angeles, CA 90028 Tel 213-461-8195.
Douglass Pubs, *(Douglass Publishers, Inc.; 0-935392),* P.O. Box 3270, Alexandria, VA 22302 Tel 703-522-4000; Dist. by: National Council on Alcoholism, 733 Third Ave., New York, NY 10017.
Dover, *(Dover Pubns., Inc.; 0-486),* 180 Varick St., New York, NY 10014 Tel 212-255-3755.
Dow Jones-Irwin, *(Dow Jones-Irwin; 0-87094),* 1818 Ridge Rd., Homewood, IL 60430 Tel 312-798-6000.
Down East, *(Down East Books; 0-89272),* Div. of Down East Enterprise Inc., P.O. Box 679, Camden, ME 04843 Tel 207-594-9544.
Downtown Poets, *(Downtown Poets Co-Op; 0-917402),* GPO Box 1720, Brooklyn, NY 11202 Tel 212-625-4245.
Dragon Co, *(Dragon Co.; 0-937456),* P.O. Box 14682, Houston, TX 77021.
Dragon Ent, *(Dragon Enterprises),* P.O. Box 200, Genoa, NV 89411 Tel 702-782-2486.
Drake's Ptg & Pub, *(Drake's Printing & Pub.),* 225 N. Magnolia Ave., Orlando, FL 32801 Tel 305-841-3491.
Drama *Imprint of* **Hill & Wang**
Drama Bk, *(Drama Book Specialists (Pubs.); 0-910482; 0-89676),* 150 W. 52nd St., New York, NY 10019 Tel 212-582-1475.
Dramatists Play, *(Dramatists Play Service, Inc.; 0-8222),* 440 Park Ave. S., New York, NY 10016.
Dream Place, *(Dream Place Pubns.; 0-930486),* P.O. Box 9416, Stanford, CA 94305 Tel 415-494-6083.
Dreams Unltd, *(Dreams Unlimited),* P.O. Box 247, Middleton, WI 53562 Tel 608-238-6575.
Drelwood Pubns, *(Drelwood Pubns.; 0-937766),* P.O. Box 10605, Portland, OR 97210; Dist. by: Communication Creativity, 5644 La Jolla Blvd., La Jolla, CA 92037 Tel 714-459-4489.
Drivers License, *(Drivers License Guide Co.),* 1492 Oddstad Dr., Redwood City, CA 94063.
Drug Intl Pubns, *(Drug Intelligence Pubns.; 0-914768),* 7752 Woodmont Ave., Washington, DC 20014 Tel 301-654-8736; Orders to: 1241 Broadway, Hamilton, IL 62341.
Dryden Pr, *(Dryden Press; 0-8498),* Div. of Holt, Rinehart & Winston, Inc., 901 N. Elm, Hinsdale, IL 60521 Tel 312-325-2985.
Duane Shinn, *(Duane Shinn Pubns.; 0-912732),* 5090 Dobrot, Central Point, OR 97501 Tel 503-664-2317.
DuBose Pub, *(DuBose Publishing; 0-938072),* P.O. Box 924, Atlanta, GA 30301.
Duck Down, *(Duck Down Press; 0-916918),* P.O. Box 1047, Fallon, NV 89406 Tel 702-423-6643.
Ducky Ent, *(Duck, B.K., Enterprises),* 8836 S. Vermont Ave., No. 2, Los Angeles, CA 90044 Tel 213-377-0216.
Dufour, *(Dufour Editions, Inc.; 0-8023),* Chester Springs, PA 19425 Tel 215-458-5005.
Duke, *(Duke Univ. Press; 0-8223),* 6697 College Sta., Durham, NC 27708 Tel 919-684-2173.
Dumbarton Oaks, *(Dumbarton Oaks; 0-88402),* 1703 32nd St., N.W., Washington, DC 20007 Tel 202-342-3200; Orders to: Ctr Byzantine Only: J.J. Augustin, Inc., Locust Valley, NY 11560. *Imprints:* Ctr Byzantine (Center for Byzantine Studies); Ctr Landscape Arch (Center for Landscape Architecture); Ctr Pre-Columbian (Center for Pre-Columbian Studies).
Duquesne, *(Duquesne Univ. Press; 0-8207),* Dist. by: Humanities Press, Inc., Atlantic Highlands, NJ 07716.
Durbin Assoc, *(Durbin Associates; 0-936786),* 3711 Southwood Dr., Easton, PA 18042.
Durrell, *(Durrell Pubns., Inc.; 0-911764),* P.O. Box 743, Mast Cove Lane, Kennebunkport, ME 04046 Tel 207-985-3904.
Dustbooks, *(Dustbooks; 0-913218),* Box 100, Paradise, CA 95969 Tel 916-877-6110.
Dutton, *(Dutton, E. P.; 0-525),* 2 Park Ave., New York, NY 10016 Tel 212-725-1818. *Imprints:* Elsevier-Phaidon (Elsevier-Phaidon); Evman (Everyman); Gingerbread (Gingerbread House); Hawthorn (Hawthorn Books).
Duverus Pub, *(Duverus Publishing Corp.; 0-918700),* Duverus Bldg., Seligman, MO 65745.
Duxbury Pr, *(Duxbury Press; 0-87872),* Div. of Wadsworth Inc., 20 Providence St., Statler Bldg., Boston, MA 02116 Tel 617-482-2344; c/o Wadsworth, Inc., 10 Davis Dr., Belmont, CA 94002.
Dyco Inc, *(Dyco, Inc.; 0-937224),* 6702 E. Cactus Rd., Scottsdale, AZ 85254.
Dynamic Learn Corp, *(Dynamic Learning Corp.; 0-915890),* 59 Commercial Wharf, Boston, MA 02110 Tel 617-742-9493.

E C Schirmer, *(Schirmer, E. C., Music Co.; 0-911318),* 112 South St., Boston, MA 02111 Tel 617-426-3137.
E C Temple, *(Temple, Ellen C.; 0-936650),* 32 Sundown Pkwy., Austin, TX 78746
E Friede *Imprint of* **Delacorte**
E Keys, *(Keys, Elsie),* 1239 E. Marshall Ave., Phoenix, AZ 85014.
E Kinkead, *(Kinkead, Eugene; 0-9600476),* Colebrook, CT 06021 Tel 203-379-6843.
E Langstaff, *(Langstaff, E., Books; 0-89986),* 919 Fremont Ave., South Pasadena, CA 91030 Tel 213-441-3233.
E M Coleman Ent, *(Coleman, Earl M., Enterprises, Inc.; 0-930576),* P.O. Box 143, Pine Plains, NY 12567 Tel 518-398-7193.
E Mellen, *(Mellen, Edwin Press; 0-88946),* P.O. Box 450, Lewiston, NY 14092 Tel 716-754-8566.
E P Edwards, *(Edwards, Ernest P.; 0-911882),* P.O. Box AQ, Sweet Briar, VA 24595 Tel 804-381-5442.
E P Klein, *(Klein, Elizabeth Pfahning; 0-9604250),* 11041 S.W. 46th St., Miami, FL 33165.
E S Cunningham, *(Cunningham, Eileen S.),* R.R. 2, Carrollton, IL 62016.
E S Davis, *(Davis, Elsie Spry; 0-9605618),* 710 Second St., Coronado, CA 92118.
E Torres & Sons, *(Torres, Eliseo, & Sons; 0-88303),* Box 2, Eastchester, NY 10709.
E-W Pub Co, *(East/West Publishing Co.; 0-934788),* 838 Grant Ave., Suite 307, San Francisco, CA 94108.
E Whittle & F A Dockery, *(Whittle, E., & F. A. Dockery; 0-9604046),* 795-B Beech Circle N. W., Cleveland, TN 37311.
Eagle Comm, *(Eagle Communications; 0-9605462),* 340 W. Main St., Missoula, MT 59806.
Eakin Pubns, *(Eakin Pubns.; 0-89015),* P.O. Drawer A G, Burnet, TX 78611 Tel 512-756-6911.
Eakins, *(Eakins Press Foundation; 0-87130),* 155 E. 42nd St., New York, NY 10017 Tel 212-986-4077.
Eardley Pubns, *(Eardley Pubns.; 0-937630),* P.O. Box 281, Rochelle Park, NJ 07662.
Earth-Song, *(Earth-Song Press),* 202 Hartnell Place, Sacramento, CA 95825 Tel 916-927-6863.
Easi-Bild, *(Easi-Bild Directions Simplified, Inc.; 0-87733),* 529 N. State Rd., P.O. Box 215, Briarcliff Manor, NY 10510 Tel 914-941-6600.
East Eur Quarterly, *(East European Quarterly; 0-914710),* Dist. by: Columbia Univ. Press, 562 W. 113th St., New York, NY 10025 Tel 212-678-6777.
East Ridge Pr, *(East Ridge Press; 0-914896),* Hankins, NY 12741 Tel 914-887-5499; Dist. by: Twenty-Four Book Service, 161 E. Ridge Rd., Hankins, NY 12741.
East River Anthol, *(East River Anthology; 0-917238),* 75 Gates Ave., Montclair, NJ 07042 Tel 201-746-5941.
East Woods, *(East Woods Press, Inc.; 0-914788),* Subs. of Fast & McMillan, Pubs., 820 E. Blvd., Charlotte, NC 28203 Tel 704-334-0897.
Eastern Acorn, *(Eastern Acorn Press),* 339 Walnut St., Philadelphia, PA 19106 Tel 215-597-7129.
Eastern CT St Coll Fdn, *(Eastern Connecticut State College Foundation; 0-915884),* P.O. Box 431, Willimantic, CT 06226 Tel 203-456-2231.
Eastern Natl Park
See Eastern Acorn
Eastham Edns, *(Eastham Editions; 0-915102),* P.O. Box 10, Prospect, NY 13435 Tel 315-896-6388.
Eastman Kodak, *(Eastman Kodak Co.; 0-87985),* 343 State St., Bldg. 16, 2nd Floor, Dept. 373, Rochester, NY 14650; Orders to: 343 State St., Dept. 454, Rochester, NY 14650 Tel 716-722-2599.
Eastview, *(Eastview Editions, Inc.; 0-89860),* P.O. Box 783, Westfield, NJ 07091 Tel 201-233-0474.
Eberly Pr, *(Eberly Press; 0-932296),* 430 N. Harrison, East Lansing, MI 48823 Tel 517-351-7299.
Ebony Pub
See Carver Pub
ECA Assoc, *(ECA Associates; 0-938818),* P.O. Box 15004, Great Bridge Sta., Chesapeake, VA 23320 Tel 804-547-5542; P.O. Box 57, Lefferts Sta., Brooklyn, NY 11225.
ECA Pub, *(ECA Publishing Co.),* P.O. Box 1057, Menlo Park, CA 94025 Tel 415-325-7569; Formerly Educational Consortium of America.
Ecclesia *Imprint of* **William Carey Lib**
Ecco Pr, *(Ecco Press; 0-912946),* 1 W. 30th St., New York, NY 10001 Tel 212-736-2599; Dist. by: W.W. Norton & Co., Inc., Keystone Industrial Park, Scranton, PA 18512.
Echo *Imprint of* **Doubleday**
Economy Co, *(Economy Co.; 0-87892; 0-8332),* 1901 N. Walnut, P.O. Box 25308, Oklahoma City, OK 73125 Tel 405-528-8444.
Ed & Training, *(Education & Training Consultants Co.; 0-87657),* Box 2085, Sedona, AZ 86336 Tel 602-282-3009.
Ed Assocs, *(Education Assocs.; 0-918772),* P.O. Box 8021, Athens, GA 30603 Tel 404-542-4244.
Ed Bk Pubs OK, *(Educational Book Pubs.; 0-932188),* P.O. Box 1219, Guthrie, OK 73044.
Ed Consortium
See ECA Pub
Ed Dev Assn, *(Educational Development Assn.),* P.O. Box 181, Hazel Crest, IL 60429.
Ed Direct, *(Educational Directories Inc.; 0-910536),* P.O. Box 199, Mt. Prospect, IL 60056 Tel 312-392-1811.
Ed Prog, *(Educators Progress Service, Inc.; 0-87708),* 214 Center St., Randolph, WI 53956 Tel 414-326-3126.
Ed Solutions, *(Educational Solutions, Inc.; 0-87825),* 80 Fifth Ave., New York, NY 10011 Tel 212-924-1744.
Ed Tecnicos
See French & Eur
Edelson, *(Edelson, Mary Beth; 0-9604650),* 110 Mercer St., New York, NY 10012 Tel 212-226-0832.
Eden Med Res, *(Eden Medical Research, Inc.; 0-88831),* P.O. Box 51, St. Albans, VT 05478 Tel 514-931-3910.
Eden Women
See EPWP
Edgepress, *(Edgepress; 0-918528),* P.O. Box 69, Point Reyes, CA 94956 Tel 415-663-8430.
Edgewood, *(Edgewood Press; 0-9602472),* 2865 East Rock Rd., Clare, MI 48617.
Ediciones, *(Ediciones Universal; 0-89729),* 3090 S.W. 8th St., Miami, FL 33135 Tel 305-642-3234.
Edins Hispamerica, *(Ediciones Hispamerica; 0-935318),* 5 Pueblo Court, Gaithersburg, MD 20760 Tel 301-948-3494.
Edit Caribe, *(Editorial Caribe; 0-89922),* 3934 S. W. 8th St., Suite 303, Miami, FL 33134 Tel 305-445-0564.
Edit Consult, *(Editorial Consultants, Inc.; 0-917636),* 655 Sutter, San Francisco, CA 94102 Tel 415-474-7656.
Edit Mundo *Imprint of* **Casa Bautista**
Edit Res Serv, *(Editorial Research Service; 0-933592),* P.O. Box 1832, Kansas City, MO 64141.
Editorial Justa, *(Editorial Justa Pubns. Inc.; 0-915808),* 2831 Seventh St., Berkeley, CA 94710 Tel 415-848-3628; Orders to: P.O. Box 2131-C, Berkeley, CA 94702.
Editors, *(Editors & Engineers, Ltd.; 0-672),* Dist. by: Bobbs-Merrill Co., Inc., 4300 W. 62nd St., Indianapolis, IN 46206 Tel 317-298-5400.
EDITS Pubs, *(EDITS Pubs.),* P.O. Box 7234, San Diego, CA 92107 Tel 714-488-1666.
Edmund Miller, *(Miller, Edmund; 0-9600486),* 61-07 Woodside Ave., Apt. 5J, Woodside, NY 11377 Tel 212-424-0480.
Educ Comm, *(Educational Communications, Inc.; 0-915130),* 3105 Macarthur Blvd., Northbrook, IL 60062 Tel 312-564-2020.
Educ Guide, *(Education Guide, Inc.; 0-914880),* P.O. Box 421, Randolph, MA 02368 Tel 617-961-2217.
Educ Indus, *(Education Industries, Inc.; 0-86652),* P.O. Box 52, Madison, WI 53701.
Educ Inst Am Hotel, *(Educational Institute of the American Hotel & Motel Assn.; 0-86612),* 1407 S. Harrison Rd., East Lansing, MI 48823.
Educ Res MA, *(Education Research Associates; 0-913636),* P.O. Box 767, Amherst, MA 01004.
Educ Serv, *(Educational Service, Inc.; 0-89273),* P.O. Box 219, Stevensville, MI 49127 Tel 616-429-1451.
Educ Tech Pubns, *(Educational Technology Pubns, Inc.; 0-87778),* 140 Sylvan Ave., Englewood Cliffs, NJ 07632 Tel 201-871-4007.
Educ Today
See Pitman Learning
Educalc Pubns, *(EduCALC Pubns; 0-936356),* P.O. Box 974, Laguna Beach, CA 92652 Tel 714-497-3600.
Eerdmans, *(Eerdmans, Wm. B., Publishing Co.; 0-8028),* 255 Jefferson Ave., S.E., Grand Rapids, MI 49503 Tel 616-459-4591.
Effect Learning GA, *(Effective Learning Pubns.; 0-933594),* 111 Holly Dr., Statesboro, GA 30458.
Eggplant Pr, *(Eggplant Press; 0-935060),* P.O. Box 18641, Denver, CO 80218.
EH *Imprint of* **Har-Row**
EHUD, *(EHUD International Language Foundation),* 1755 Trinity Ave., No. 79, Walnut Creek, CA 94596 Tel 415-937-4841; Orders to: Box 2082, Dollar Ranch Sta., Walnut Creek, CA 94595 Tel 415-937-4841.
Eighties Pr, *(Eighties Press; 0-87390),* 308 First St., Moose Lake, MN 55767; Dist. by: Bookpeople, 2940 Seventh St., Berkeley, CA 94710.
Eisenbrauns, *(Eisenbrauns; 0-931464),* P.O. Box 275, Winona Lake, IN 46590 Tel 219-269-2011.
EKS Pub Co, *(EKS Publishing Co.; 0-939144),* 484 Lake Park Ave., No. 118, Oakland, CA 94610.
El-Shabazz Pr
See Shabazz Pr
Elar Pub Co, *(Elar Publishing Co.,Inc.),* 1120 Old Country Rd., Plainview, NY 11803 Tel 516-433-6530.
Elgen Pub Co, *(Elgen Publishing Co.; 0-935774),* 1004 Taurus Dr., Colorado Springs, CO 80906.
Eliopoulos, *(Eliopoulos),* P.O. Box 65, Oak Park, IL 60303.
Elk Grove Bks *Imprint of* **Childrens**
Ell Ell Diversified, *(Ell Ell Diversified, Inc.; 0-937428),* 1100 Butler Ave., P.O. Box 1702, Santa Rosa, CA 95402 Tel 707-542-8663.
Elliots Bks, *(Elliot's Books; 0-911830),* P.O. Box 6, Northford, CT 06472 Tel 203-484-2184.
Ellis Pr, *(Ellis Press, The; 0-933180),* P.O. Box 1443, Peoria, IL 61655.
Elmer, *(Elmer, William B.; 0-9601028),* 2 Chestnut St., Andover, MA 01810 Tel 617-475-1020.
Elmer Edwards, *(Edwards, Elmer Eugene),* P.O. Box 584, Miami, FL 33161.
ELS Intl, *(ELS International Inc.; 0-89318),* 5761 Buckingham Pkwy., Culver City, CA 90230 Tel 213-642-0994.
Elsevier, *(Elsevier-North Holland Pub. Co.; 0-444; 0-7204),* 52 Vanderbilt Ave., New York, NY 10017 Tel 212-867-9040. *Imprints:* Biomedical Pr (Elsevier North-Holland Biomedical Press); Excerpta Medica (Excerpta-Medica); North Holland (North-Holland); Thomond Pr (Thomond Press).
Elsevier-Nelson, *(Elsevier/Nelson Books; 0-525),* 2 Park Ave., New York, NY 10016 Tel 212-725-1818.
Elsevier-Phaidon *Imprint of* **Dutton**
Elsevier Sci
See Elsevier
Elysium, *(Elysium Growth Press; 0-910550),* 5436 Fernwood Ave., Los Angeles, CA 90027 Tel 213-465-7121.
Embee Pr, *(Embee Press; 0-89816),* 82 Pine Grove, Kingston, NY 12401.
Embroidy Bk
See C Schneider
EMC, *(EMC Corp.; 0-88436; 0-912022),* 180 E. Sixth St., St. Paul, MN 55101 Tel 612-227-7366.
Emerald Hse, *(Emerald House; 0-936958),* P.O. Box 388, Santa Rosa, CA 95402.
Emerson, *(Emerson Books, Inc.; 0-87523),* Reynolds Lane, Buchanan, NY 10511 Tel 914-739-3506.
En Passant Poet, *(En Passant Poetry Press; 0-9605098),* 4612 Sylvanus Dr., Wilmington, DE 19803 Tel 302-774-4571.
Encino Pr, *(Encino Press; 0-88426),* 510 Baylor St., Austin, TX 78703 Tel 512-476-6821.

Ency Brit Ed, *(Encyclopaedia Britannica Educational Corp.; 0-87827),* Affiliate of Encyclopaedia Britannica, Inc., 425 N. Michigan Ave., Chicago, IL 60611 Tel 312-321-6800.

Energy Educ, *(Energy Education Pubs.),* P.O. Box 6488, Grand Rapids, MI 49506 Tel 616-454-8264.

Eng Joint Coun
See AAES

Eng Language, *(English Language Services; 0-87789),* Div. of Washington Educational Research Associates, Inc., 5761 Buckingham Pkwy., Culver City, CA 90230 Tel 213-642-0994.

Eng Pr, *(Engineering Press, Inc.; 0-910554),* P.O. Box 1, San Jose, CA 95103 Tel 408-258-4503.

Eng Pubns, *(Engineering Pubns.; 0-9605004),* P.O. Box 302, Blacksburg, VA 24060.

Engelmeier, *(Engelmeier, Philip A.; 0-9605002),* 909 Geary-517, San Francisco, CA 94109.

Engineers Pr, *(Engineer's Press; 0-930644),* P.O. Box 1651, Coral Gables, FL 33134 Tel 305-856-0031.

English Lang, *(English Language Services, Inc.; 0-89285),* 5761 Buckingham Pkwy., Culver City, CA 90230 Tel 213-642-0994.

Enoch Pratt, *(Enoch Pratt Free Library; 0-910556),* 400 Cathedral St., Baltimore, MD 21201 Tel 301-396-5494.

Enrich, *(Enrich; 0-933358; 0-86582),* Div. of Ohaus, 760 Kifer Rd., Sunnyvale, CA 94086 Tel 408-733-5850.

Enslow Pubs, *(Enslow Pubs. Inc.; 0-89490),* Bloy St. & Ramsey Ave., Box 777, Hillside, NJ 07205 Tel 201-964-4116.

Entelek, *(Entelek, Inc.; 0-87567),* Ward-Whidden House, The Hill, P. O. Box 1303, Portsmouth, NH 03801 Tel 603-436-0439.

Enterprise Del, *(Enterprise Publishing Co.; 0-913864),* 725 Market St., Wilmington, DE 19801 Tel 302-654-0110.

Entity Pub Co, *(Entity Publishing Co.; 0-89913),* 1314 Larmor Ave., Rowland Heights, CA 91748 Tel 714-598-1755.

Entomol Soc, *(Entomological Society of America),* 4603 Calvert Rd., College Park, MD 20740 Tel 301-864-1334.

Entomological Repr, *(Entomological Reprint Specialists; 0-911836),* P.O. Box 77224, Dockweiler Sta., Los Angeles, CA 90007 Tel 213-227-1285.

Entropy Ltd, *(Entropy Ltd.),* South Great Rd., Lincoln, MA 01773.

Entwhistle Bks, *(Entwhistle Books; 0-9601428; 0-934558),* P.O. Box 611, Glen Ellen, CA 95442 Tel 707-996-3901.

Enviro Pr, *(Enviro Press; 0-937976),* P.O. Box 40284, Nashville, TN 37204 Tel 615-794-0110; Dist. by: CBI Publishers, 51 Sleeper St., Boston, MA 02210.

Environ Des VA, *(Environmental Design Press; 0-918436),* Div. of Educational & Research Management, Inc., P.O. Box 2187, Reston, VA 22090 Tel 703-471-1267.

Environ Design, *(Environmental Design & Research Ctr.; 0-915250),* 142 Lowell Ave., Newtonville, MA 02160 Tel 617-965-5910.

Environ Info, *(Environment Information Center, Inc., (EIC); 0-89947),* 292 Madison Ave., New York, NY 10017 Tel 212-949-9471.

Environ Pr, *(Environmental Press; 0-936960),* P.O. Box 701, Buffalo, NY 14205 Tel 301-942-0119.

Environ Res Inst, *(Environmental Research Institute of Michigan; 0-9603590),* P.O. Box 8618, Ann Arbor, MI 48107.

Ephemera, *(Ephemera & Books; 0-934792),* 7159 Crowley Ct., P.O. Box 19681, San Diego, CA 92119.

Epic Pubns, *(Epic Pubns., Inc.; 0-914244),* 4420 Westover Dr., Orchard Lake, MI 48033 Tel 313-626-6217.

Epiphany Pr, *(Epiphany Press; 0-916700),* P.O. Box 14606, San Francisco, CA 94114 Tel 415-431-1917.

EPM Pubns, *(EPM Pubns.; 0-914440),* 1003 Turkey Run Rd., McLean, VA 22101 Tel 703-356-5111; Orders to: P.O. Box 490, McLean, VA 22101.

EPWP, *(Eden Press Women's Pubns.; 0-920792),* P.O. Box 51, St. Albans, VT 05478 Tel 514-931-3910.

Equal Employ, *(Equal Employment Advisory Council; 0-937856),* 1015 Fifteenth St., N.W., Suite 1220, Washington, DC 20005.

Equipment Guide, *(Equipment Guide Book),* Div. of Dataquest, 2800 W. Bayshore Rd., Palo Alto, CA 94303 Tel 415-327-5100.

Era Davidson, *(Era Press; 0-9605270),* Box 548, Davidson, NC 28036.

Era Pr NC, *(E R A Press; 0-918234),* Subs. of The New East Magazine, Box 1673, Greenville, NC 27834 Tel 919-752-7829.

Erbonia Bks, *(Erbonia Books, Inc.),* P. O. Box 396, New Paltz, NY 12561 Tel 914-895-3614.

Eriksson, *(Eriksson, Paul S., Pubs.; 0-8397),* Battell Bldg., Middlebury, VT 05753 Tel 802-388-7303; Dist. by: Independent Publishers Group, 14 Vanderventer Ave., Port Washington, NY 11050 Tel 516-944-9325.

Erskine, *(Erskine, Kathryn A.; 0-9605058),* Box 398, Hurricane, WV 25526.

ESE Calif, *(ESE California; 0-912076),* 509 N. Harbor Blvd., La Habra, CA 90631 Tel 213-691-0737.

Esoteric Pubns, *(Esoteric Pubns.; 0-89861),* P.O. Box 325, Cottonwood, AZ 86326 Tel 602-634-7424.

ESPress, *(ESPress; 0-917200),* P.O. Box 8606, Washington, DC 20011 Tel 202-723-4578.

Esselte Video
See Nord Media

Esselte Video
See Nord Media

Essence Pubns, *(Essence Pubns.),* 168 Woodbridge Ave., Highland Park, NJ 08904 Tel 201-572-3120.

Essex Inst, *(Essex Institute; 0-88389),* 132 Essex St., Salem, MA 01970 Tel 617-744-3390.

Estacado Bks, *(Estacado Books),* P.O. Box 4516, Lubbock, TX 79409 Tel 806-742-3115.

ETC Pubns, *(ETC Pubns.; 0-88280),* 700 E. Vereda del Sur, Palm Springs, CA 92262 Tel 714-325-5352; Orders to: Pubns. Dept., P.O. Drawer 1627-A, Palm Springs, CA 92263.

Eternal Ent, *(Eternal Enterprises; 0-917578),* P.O. Box 60913, Sacramento, CA 95860; Name Formerly L P Price.

Ethics & Public Policy, *(Ethics & Public Policy Center, Inc.; 0-89633),* 1211 Connecticut Ave., NW, Washington, DC 20036 Tel 202-857-0595.

Euclid Pub, *(Euclid Publishing Co., The; 0-935490),* Dist. by: Bond & Bacon Assocs., P.O. Box 121, Cathedral Sta., New York, NY 10025.

Eur-Am Music, *(European American Music; 0-913574),* 195 Allwood Road, Clifton, NJ 07012 Tel 201-777-2680.

Eurail Guide, *(Eurail Guide Annual; 0-912442),* 27540 Pacific Coast Hwy, Malibu, CA 90265 Tel 213-457-7286.

Europa *Imprint of* **Unipub**

Evanel, *(Evanel Associates; 0-918948),* Box 42, Northfield, OH 44067 Tel 216-467-1750.

Evang & Ref, *(Evangelical & Reformed Historical Society; 0-910564),* 555 W. James St., Lancaster, PA 17603.

Evang Sisterhood Mary, *(Evangelical Sisterhood of Mary),* 9849 N. 40th St., Phoenix, AZ 85028 Tel 602-996-4040.

Evang Tchr, *(Evangelical Teacher Training Assn.; 0-910566),* 110 Bridge St., P.O. Box 327, Wheaton, IL 60187 Tel 312-668-6400.

Evangel Indiana, *(Evangel Press),* 301 N. Elm, Nappanee, IN 46550.

Evans
See M Evans

Ever *Imprint of* **Grove**

Everest Hse, *(Everest House Pubs.; 0-89696),* 1133 Ave. of the Americas, New York, NY 10036 Tel 212-764-3400; Orders to: Box 978, Edison, NJ 08817.

Everest Pub, *(Everest Publishing Co.; 0-931034),* Box 2686 Century Sta., Raleigh, NC 27602 Tel 919-787-8009.

Everett-Edwards, *(Everett/Edwards, Inc.; 0-912112),* P.O. Box 1060, DeLand, FL 32720 Tel 904-734-7458.

Evergreen, *(Evergreen Press, Inc.; 0-914510),* P.O. Box 4971, Walnut Creek, CA 94596 Tel 415-825-7850.

Evergreen Christmas
See Evergreen

Evergreen Pr, *(Evergreen Press; 0-913056),* P.O. Box 1711, Oceanside, CA 92054 Tel 714-757-5976.

Evman *Imprint of* **Dutton**

Ex Libris Sun, *(Ex Libris Sun Valley; 0-9605212),* Sun Valley, ID 83353.

Examiner Spec Proj
See Cal Living Bks

Exanimo Pr, *(Exanimo Press; 0-89316),* P.O. Box 18, 23520 Hwy. 12, Segundo, CO 81070.

Excerpta Medica *Imprint of* **Elsevier**

Exec Ent, *(Executive Enterprises Pubns. Co., Inc.; 0-917386),* Div. of Executive Enterprises, Inc., 33 W. 60th St., Ninth Floor, New York, NY 10023 Tel 212-489-2671.

Exec West, *(Executives West Publishing Co.),* P.O. Box 15966, Phoenix, AZ 85060.

Executive Comm, *(Executive Communications; 0-917168),* 400 E. 54th St., New York, NY 10022 Tel 212-421-3713.

Exelrod Pr, *(Exelrod Press; 0-917388),* P. O. Box 2303, Pleasant Hill, CA 94523 Tel 415-934-3357.

Existential Bks, *(Existential Books; 0-89231),* 1816 Stevens Ave.,S., Suite 25, Minneapolis, MN 55403 Tel 612-871-7275.

Exploration Pr, *(Exploration Press; 0-913552),* Chicago Theological Seminary, 5757 S. Univ. Ave., Chicago, IL 60637 Tel 312-752-5757.

Explorer Pub Co, *(Explorer Publishing Co.),* P.O. Box 385, Boston, MA 02117 Tel 617-536-3583.

Exposition, *(Exposition Press, Inc.; 0-682),* 325 Kings Highway, Smithtown, NY 11787 Tel 516-582-6655. *Imprints:* Banner (Banner); Lochinvar (Lochinvar); University (University).

Express, *(Express),* P.O. Box 1373, Richmond, CA 94802 Tel 415-233-0167.

ExPressAll, *(ExPressAll; 0-936190),* 260 Dean Rd., Brookline, MA 02146 Tel 617-734-1297.

Expressions TX, *(Expressions, Inc.; 0-937768),* P.O. Box 1091, Arlington, TX 76010 Tel 817-461-5255.

Eyecontact, *(Eyecontact; 0-938112),* 465 Lexington Ave., New York, NY 10017.

F Allen
See F Sypher

F Amato Pubns, *(Amato, Frank, Pubns.; 0-936608),* P.O. Box 02112, Portland, OR 97202 Tel 503-236-2305.

F Asbury Pub Co, *(Asbury, Francis, Publishing Co.),* P.O. Box 7, Wilmore, KY 40390.

F Cass Co
See Biblio Dist

F F Fournies
See F Fournies

F Fournies, *(Fournies, F., & Associates, Inc.; 0-917472),* 129 Edgewood Dr., Bridgewater, NJ 08807 Tel 201-526-2442.

F H Breise, *(Breise, Frederic H.; 0-938576),* 5750 Severin Dr., La Mesa, CA 92041.

F I Comm, *(F. I. Communications; 0-89533),* 45 Alhambra, Portola Valley, CA 94025 Tel 415-851-0254; Orders to: P.O. Box 3121, Stanford, CA 94305.

F M Roberts, *(Robert, F. M., Enterprises; 0-912746),* P.O. Box 608, Dana Point, CA 92629 Tel 714-493-1977.

F Sypher, *(Sypher, Francis),* 220 E. 50th St., New York, NY 10022.

Faber & Faber
See Merrimack Bk Serv

Fablewaves, *(Fablewaves Press),* P.O. Box 7874, Van Nuys, CA 91409 Tel 213-785-9042.

Fabmath, *(Fabmath; 0-937138),* P.O. Box 568, Warrington, PA 18976.

Facts on File, *(Facts on File, Inc.; 0-87196),* 119 W. 57th St., New York, NY 10019 Tel 212-265-2011.

Fade In, *(Fade in Pubs.; 0-936748),* 312 S. 6th, Bozeman, MT 59715.

Fairchild, *(Fairchild Books & Visuals; 0-87005),* 7 E. 12th St., New York, NY 10003 Tel 212-675-1242.

Fairfield, *(Fairfield Press, Inc.; 0-913158),* 128 E. 62nd St., New York, NY 10021 Tel 212-838-7424.

Fairleigh Dickinson, *(Fairleigh Dickinson Univ. Press; 0-8386),* Div. of Associated University Presses, 4 Cornwall Dr., East Brunswick, NJ 08816 Tel 201-254-0132.

Faith & Life, *(Faith & Life Press; 0-87303),* 718B Main St., Box 347, Newton, KS 67114 Tel 316-283-5100.

Faith Messenger, *(Faith Messenger Pubns.; 0-938544),* 1677 Cliffbranch Dr., Diamond Bar, CA 91765.

Faith Pub Hse, *(Faith Publishing House),* P. O. Box 518, 920 W. Mansur, Guthrie, OK 73044 Tel 405-282-1479.
Falcon Pr MT, *(Falcon Press Publishing; 0-934318),* P.O. Box 279, Billings, MT 59103.
Falkynor Bks, *(Falkynor Books; 0-916878),* Div. of G-Jo Institute, 4950 S.W. 70th Ave., Davie, FL 33314 Tel 305-581-4950.
Fallen Angel, *(Fallen Angel Press; 0-931598),* 1981 W. McNichols Cl, Highland Park, MI 48203 Tel 313-864-0982.
Family Pub CA, *(Family Publishing Co., The; 0-937770),* Star Mountain Ranch, P.O. Box 462, Bodega, CA 94923 Tel 707-875-9925.
Family Therapy
See Mehetabel & Co
Family YMCA Stanislaus, *(Family Young Men's Christian Assn. of Stanislaus County; 0-9604096),* 2700 McHenry Ave., Modesto, CA 95350 Tel 209-578-9622.
F&S Pr, *(F&S Press; 0-86621),* Div. of Frost & Sullivan, 106 Fulton St., New York, NY 10038.
FAO *Imprint of* **Unipub**
Far West Pr, *(Far West Press; 0-914480),* 3231 Pierce St., San Francisco, CA 94123.
Farm & Ranch, *(Farm & Ranch Vacations, Inc.; 0-913214),* 36 E. 57th St., New York, NY 10022 Tel 212-355-6334.
Farm Journal, *(Farm Journal, Inc.; 0-89795),* 230 W. Washington Square, Philadelphia, PA 19105.
Farmer Ent, *(Farmer, Wesley M., Enterprises,Inc.; 0-937772),* P.O. Box 26653, Tempe, AZ 85282.
Farnswth Pub, *(Farnsworth Publishing Co., Inc.; 0-910580; 0-87863),* 78 Randall Ave., Rockville Ctr., NY 11570 Tel 516-536-8400.
Farrar Pub, *(Farrar Publishing; 0-9605588),* 25 Library Ave., Warrensburg, NY 12885.
Faubus, *(Faubus, Orval E.),* c/o Pioneer Press, P.O. Box 191, Little Rock, AR 72201 Tel 501-374-0271; Orders to: 114 E. 2nd St., Little Rock, AR 72203.
Fawcett, *(Fawcett Book Group; 0-449),* 1515 Broadway, New York, NY 10036 Tel 212-975-7660. *Imprints:* Crest (Crest Books); GM (Gold Medal Books); Juniper (Juniper); Prem (Premier Books).
Fawcett World
See Fawcett
Fax Collect, *(Fax Collector's Editions, Inc.; 0-913960),* P.O. Box 851, Mercer Island, WA 98040 Tel 206-232-8484.
Faxon, *(Faxon, F. W., Co., Inc.; 0-87305),* 15 Southwest Park, Westwood, MA 02090 Tel 617-329-3350.
Fearon-Pitman
See Pitman Learning
FEB, *(First Edition Books/FEB Co.; 0-89502),* FEB Bldg., 120 Clairton Blvd., Pittsburgh, PA 15236 Tel 412-655-9733.
Fed Aviation, *(Federal Aviation Exams Co.; 0-938706),* 1669 Maple, Suite 6, Solvang, CA 93463.
Fed Employees, *(Federal Employees News Digest, Inc.; 0-910582),* P.O. Box 457, Merrifield, VA 22116 Tel 703-533-3031.
Fed Res Bank MN, *(Federal Reserve Bank of Minneapolis; 0-915484),* 250 Marquette Ave, Minneapolis, MN 55480 Tel 612-340-2345.
Federlin, *(Federlin, Tom; 0-9603136),* 106 Macdougal St., New York, NY 10012.
Fell, *(Fell, Frederick, Publishers, Inc.; 0-8119),* 386 Park Ave., S., New York, NY 10016 Tel 212-685-9017. *Imprints:* Aim-High (Aim-High); Pegasus Rex (Pegasus Rex).
Fellowship Pr PA, *(Fellowship Press; 0-914390),* 5820 Overbrook Ave., Philadelphia, PA 19131 Tel 215-879-8604.
Fels & Firn, *(Fels & Firn Press; 0-918704),* 1843 Vassar Ave., Mountain View, CA 94043 Tel 415-965-4291.
Feminist Pr, *(Feminist Press; 0-912670; 0-935312),* SUNY/College at Old Westbury, Box 334, Old Westbury, NY 11568 Tel 516-997-7660.
Fenimore Bk, *(Fenimore Book Store),* Lake Rd., Cooperstown, NY 13326 Tel 607-547-2533.
Fenn Gall Pub, *(Fenn Galleries Publishing; 0-937634),* 1075 Paseo De Peralta, Santa Fe, NM 87501.
Ferry Pr
See SBD
Fertig, *(Fertig, Howard, Inc.; 0-86527),* 80 E. 11th St., New York, NY 10003 Tel 212-982-7922.
Festival Pubns, *(Festival Pubns.; 0-930828),* P.O. Box 10180, Glendale, CA 91209 Tel 213-766-1798.
Fibonacci Corp, *(Fibonacci Corp.; 0-915494),* Golden Bridge, NY 10526 Tel 914-232-4293.
FICOA, *(Film Instruction Co. of America; 0-931974),* 2901 S. Wentworth Ave., Milwaukee, WI 53207.
Fiction Coll, *(Fiction Collective, Inc.; 0-914590),* c/o George Braziller, Inc., One Park Ave., New York, NY 10016.
Fictioneer Bks, *(Fictioneer Books, Ltd; 0-934882),* Box B.I.P, Screamer Mountain, Clayton, GA 30525 Tel 404-782-3318.
Fideler, *(Fideler Co.; 0-88296),* 31 Ottawa Ave., N. W., Grand Rapids, MI 49503 Tel 616-456-8577.
Fides Claretian, *(Fides/Claretian; 0-8190),* 333 N. Lafayette, South Bend, IN 46601 Tel 219-288-3050.
Field Ent
See World Bk-Childcraft
Field Mus, *(Field Museum of Natural History; 0-914868),* Roosevelt Rd., at Lake Shore Dr., Chicago, IL 60605 Tel 312-922-9410.
Field Oberlin, *(Field Translations Series/Oberlin College; 0-932440),* Rice Hall, Oberlin College, Oberlin, OH 44074 Tel 216-775-8407.
Fielding, *(Fielding Pubns.),* 105 Madison Ave., New York, NY 10016 Tel 212-889-3050; Dist. by: William Morrow & Co., 6 Henderson Dr., West Caldwell, NJ 07006.
Fiesta Pub, *(Fiesta Publishing Corp.; 0-88473),* 6360 N.E. 4th Court, Miami, FL 33138 Tel 305-751-1181.
Film & Video
See **Pub Ctr Cult Res**
Filmrow Pubns, *(Filmrow Pubns.),* 8272 Sunset Blvd., W. Hollywood, CA 90046 Tel 213-654-8310.
Filter, *(Filter Press; 0-910584; 0-86541),* P.O. Box 5, Palmer Lake, CO 80133 Tel 303-481-2523.
Finan Exec, *(Financial Executives Research Foundation; 0-910586),* 633 Third Ave., New York, NY 10017 Tel 212-953-0500.
Finan Pub, *(Financial Publishing Co.; 0-87600),* 82 Brookline Ave., Boston, MA 02215 Tel 617-262-4040.
Fine Arts Mus, *(Fine Arts Museums of San Francisco; 0-88401),* M.H. De Young Museum, Golden Gate Park, San Francisco, CA 94118 Tel 415-558-2887.
Fine Arts Soc, *(Fine Arts Society; 0-932192),* 50459 N. Portage Rd., South Bend, IN 46628 Tel 219-272-9290; Orders to: 2314 W. Sixth St., Mishawaka, IN 46544 Tel 219-255-8606.
Fineline, *(Fineline Co.; 0-917520),* 303 Fifth Ave., New York, NY 10016 Tel 212-684-3369.
Finney Co, *(Finney Co.; 0-912486),* 3350 Gorham Ave., Minneapolis, MN 55426 Tel 612-929-6165.
FireBuilders, *(FireBuilders, The; 0-9601794),* RR1, Box 620, Stetson Rd., Brooklyn, CT 06234 Tel 203-774-4824.
Fireside *Imprint of* **S&S**
Fireside Bks, *(Fireside Books; 0-87527),* Div. of Warren H. Green, Inc., 8356 Olive Blvd., St. Louis, MO 63132 Tel 314-991-1335.
First Amend, *(First Amendment Press),* P.O. Box 7334, Stanford, CA 94305 Tel 415-851-3391.
First Church, *(First Church of Christ Scientist),* 1 Norway St., Boston, MA 02115 Tel 617-262-2300.
First Impressions, *(First Impressions Publishing Co.; 0-934794),* P.O. Box 9073, Madison, WI 53715 Tel 608-238-6254.
First Person, *(First Person; 0-916452),* Washington Spring Rd., Palisades, NY 10964 Tel 914-359-2995.
Firth, *(Firth, Robert H.; 0-9605060),* P.O. Box 155, Walnut, CA 91789.
Fischer Inc NY, *(Fischer, Carl, Inc.; 0-8258),* 62 Cooper Square, New York, NY 10003.
Fisher Inst, *(Fisher Institute, The; 0-933028),* 6350 LBJ Fwy., Suite 183E, Dallas, TX 75240.
FitzGerald & Assocs, *(FitzGerald, Jerry, & Associates; 0-932410),* 506 Barkentine Lane, Redwood City, CA 94065 Tel 415-591-5676.
Five Arms Corp, *(Five Arms Corp.; 0-9604892),* 3813 Briar Place, Office 9, Dayton, OH 45405.
Five Assocs
See Mus Graphics
Flame Intl, *(Flame International Inc.; 0-933184),* 2622 Wavell St., Jacksonville, NC 28542 Tel 919-353-7575.
Fleet, *(Fleet Press Corp.; 0-8303),* 160 Fifth Ave., New York, NY 10010 Tel 212-243-6100.
Fleschner, *(Fleschner Publishing Co.; 0-937878),* 41 Village Lane, Bethany, CT 06525.
Flint Hills, *(Flint Hills Book Co.),* 1735 Fairview, Manhattan, KS 66502.
Florham, *(Florham Park Press, Inc.; 0-912598),* P.O. Box 303, Florham Park, NJ 07932 Tel 201-377-3670.
Flourtown Pub, *(Flourtown Publishing Co.; 0-9603376),* P.O. Box 148, Flourtown, PA 19031.
Flying Buttress, *(Flying Buttress Pubns.; 0-918348),* P.O. Box 254, Endicott, NY 13760 Tel 607-785-5423.
Flying Diamond Bks, *(Flying Diamond Books; 0-918532),* Box D301, Hettinger, ND 58639 Tel 701-567-2646.
Focal Pr, *(Focal Press, Inc.),* 10 E. 40th St., Suite 3600, New York, NY 10016 Tel 212-679-1777.
Fogg Art, *(Fogg Art Museum; 0-916724),* Div. of Harvard University, 32 Quincy St., Cambridge, MA 02138 Tel 617-495-2387.
Folcroft, *(Folcroft Library Editions; 0-8414),* P.O. Box 182, Folcroft, PA 19032.
Folder Edns, *(Folder Editions; 0-913152),* 103-26 68th Rd., Apt A63, Forest Hills, NY 11375; Dist. by: Caroline House Books, 2 Ellis Place, Ossining, NY 10562.
Folger Bks, *(Folger Books; 0-918016),* Folger Shakespeare Library, 201 E. Capitol St., S.E., Washington, DC 20003 Tel 202-546-3176.
Folio, *(Folio Magazine Pub. Corp.; 0-918110),* P.O. Box 697, 125 Elm St., New Canaan, CT 06840 Tel 203-972-0761.
Folk-Legacy, *(Folk-Legacy Records, Inc.),* Sharon Rd., Sharon, CT 06069.
Follett, *(Follett Publishing Co.; 0-695),* Div. of Follett Corp., 1010 W. Washington Blvd., Chicago, IL 60607 Tel 312-666-5858.
Fontana Pap *Imprint of* **Watts**
Food Processors, *(Food Processors Institute, The; 0-937774),* 1133 20th St. NW, Washington, DC 20036.
Food Res Action, *(Food Research & Action Center Inc.; 0-934220),* 2011 Eye St. N.W., Washington, DC 20006.
Foot Trails, *(Foot Trails Pubns., Inc.; 0-933710),* The Pottingshed, Bedford Rd., Greenwich, CT 06830; Dist. by: Simon & Schuster, Inc., 1230 Ave. of the Americas, New York, NY 10020 Tel 212-245-6400.
Football Hobbies, *(Football Hobbies, Pubs.; 0-912122),* 4216 McConnell, El Paso, TX 79904 Tel 915-565-7354.
Foothills Art
See Riverstone Foothills
Footloose Pr, *(Footloose Press),* P.O. Box 3353, Hayward, CA 94540 Tel 415-538-1197.
Ford Found, *(Ford Foundation; 0-916584),* 320 E. 43rd St., New York, NY 10017 Tel 212-573-4812; Orders to: P.O. Box 559, Naugatuck, CT 06770.
Fordham, *(Fordham Univ. Press; 0-8232),* University Box L, Bronx, NY 10458 Tel 212-933-2233.
Fordham Pub, *(Fordham Equipment & Publishing Co.; 0-913308),* 3308 Edson Ave., Bronx, NY 10469 Tel 212-379-7300.
Fords Travel, *(Fords Travel Guides; 0-916486),* Box 505, 22151 Clarendon St., Woodland Hills, CA 91365 Tel 213-347-1677.
Foreign Policy, *(Foreign Policy Assn.; 0-87124),* 205 Lexington Ave., New York, NY 10016 Tel 212-481-8450.
Forest Hill, *(Forest Hill Press; 0-9605472),* 3974 Forest Hill Ave., Oakland, CA 94602.
Forest Hist Soc, *(Forest History Society, Inc.; 0-89030),* 109 Coral St., Santa Cruz, CA 95060 Tel 408-426-3770.
Forest Pr, *(Forest Press Division Lake Placid Education Foundation; 0-910608),* 85 Watervliet Ave., Albany, NY 12206 Tel 518-489-8549.

Forest Pub, *(Forest Publishing; 0-9605118),* 222 Wisconsin, Lake Forest, IL 60045.
Foris Pubns, *(Foris Pubns.),* Box 1132, Delran, NJ 08075 Tel 609-829-6830; Orders to: Box C-50, Cinnaminson, NJ 08077.
Forkner, *(Forkner Publishing Corp.; 0-912036),* P.O. Box 652, Ridgewood, NJ 07451 Tel 201-447-0661.
Fortress, *(Fortress Press; 0-8006),* 2900 Queen Lane, Philadelphia, PA 19129 Tel 800-523-3824.
Forty Whacks, *(40 Whacks Press),* P.O. Box 591, Shelton, CT 06484.
Forum Pr MO, *(Forum Press, Inc.; 0-88273),* 2640 Pine, St. Louis, MO 63103 Tel 314-371-6907; Orders to: P.O. Box 179, St. Louis, MO 63166.
Forward Movement, *(Forward Movement Pubns.),* 412 Sycamore St., Cincinnati, OH 45202 Tel 513-721-6659.
FOSG
See FOSG Pubns
FOSG Pubns, *(Factory Outlet Shopping Guide; 0-913464),* Box 239, Oradell, NJ 07649 Tel 201-384-2500.
Foto Res, *(Foto Research Co.),* 234 Main St., Millbury, MA 01527 Tel 617-754-4612.
Foun Adv Artists, *(Foundation for the Advancement of Artists; 0-912916),* 1315 Walnut St. Bldg., Philadelphia, PA 19107 Tel 215-546-3336.
Foun Econ Ed, *(Foundation for Economic Education, Inc.; 0-910614),* 30 S. Broadway, Irvington-on-Hudson, NY 10533 Tel 914-591-7230.
Foun Human Under, *(Foundation of Human Understanding; 0-933900),* P.O. Box 34036, Los Angeles, CA 90034 Tel 213-559-3711.
Foun Natl Prog, *(Foundation for National Progress; 0-938806),* Housing Information Ctr., P.O. Box 3396, Santa Barbara, CA 93105.
Foun Pr
See Foun Pubns
Foun Pubns, *(Foundation Pubns., Inc.; 0-910618),* P.O. Box 6439, Anaheim, CA 92806 Tel 714-630-6450.
Found Class Reprints, *(Foundation for Classical Reprints, The; 0-89901),* 607 McKnight St. N.W., Albuquerque, NM 87102.
Found Class Rep
See Found Class Reprints
Foundation Ctr, *(Foundation Center, The; 0-87954),* 888 Seventh Ave., New York, NY 10106 Tel 212-975-1120.
Foundation Pr, *(Foundation Press, Inc.; 0-88277),* P.O. Box 3056, Textbook Dept., 8F, St. Paul, MN 55165.
Fountain Hse East, *(Fountain House East; 0-914736),* Box 99298, Jeffersontown, KY 40299 Tel 502-267-5414.
Fountainhead, *(Fountainhead Pubs., Inc.; 0-87310),* 475 Fifth Ave., New York, NY 10017.
Four Seas Bk, *(Four Seasons Book Pubs.; 0-9605400),* Box 222, West Chester, PA 19380.
Four Seasons Foun, *(Four Seasons Foundation; 0-87704),* P.O. Box 31411, San Francisco, CA 94131 Tel 415-824-5774; Dist. by: Subterranean Co., P.O. Box 10233, Eugene, OR 97440 Tel 503-343-6324.
Four Winds *Imprint of* **Schol Bk Serv**
Four Zoas Pr, *(Four Zoas Press),* RFD, Ware, MA 01082.
Foxmoor, *(Foxmoor Press; 0-938604),* Box 47, Rte. 2, Tahlequah, OK 74464.
Framo Pub, *(Framo Publishing; 0-936398),* 530 W. Surf St., Chicago, IL 60657.
Franklin Inst Pr, *(Franklin Institute Press, The; 0-89168),* Box 2266, Philadelphia, PA 19103 Tel 215-448-1551.
Fraser Pub Co, *(Fraser Publishing Co.; 0-87034),* Div. of Fraser Management Assocs., Inc., 309 S. Willard St., Burlington, VT 05401 Tel 802-658-0322; Orders to: Box 494, Burlington, VT 05402.
Free Church Pubns, *(Free Church Pubns.; 0-911802),* 1515 E. 66th St., Minneapolis, MN 55423 Tel 612-866-3343.
Free Life, *(Free Life Editions; 0-914156),* 41 Union Square, W., New York, NY 10003 Tel 212-989-3750.
Free Pr, *(Free Press; 0-02),* Div. of Macmillan Publishing Co., Inc., 866 Third Ave., New York, NY 10022 Tel 212-935-2000; Dist. by: Macmillan Co., Riverside, NJ 08370.
Freedom Bks, *(Freedom Books; 0-930374),* P.O. Box 5303, Hamden, CT 06518 Tel 203-281-6791.
Freedom Hse, *(Freedom House; 0-932088),* 20 W. 40th St., New York, NY 10018 Tel 212-730-7744.
Freedom Unltd, *(Freedom Unlimited; 0-938014),* P.O. Box 599, Garden Grove, CA 92642.
Freelance Pubns, *(Freelance Pubns.; 0-9602050),* P.O. Box 8, Bayport, NY 11705 Tel 516-472-1799.
Freeland Pubns, *(Freeland Pubns.; 0-936868),* P.O. Box 18941, Philadelphia, PA 19119.
Freeman C, *(Freeman, Cooper & Co.; 0-87735),* 1736 Stockton St., San Francisco, CA 94133 Tel 415-362-6171.
Freer, *(Freer Gallery of Art, Smithsonian Institution; 0-934686),* 12th & Jefferson Dr., S.W., Washington, DC 20560 Tel 201-381-5342.
French & Eur, *(French & European Pubns., Inc.; 0-8288),* 115 Fifth Ave., New York, NY 10003 Tel 212-673-7400.
French Forum, *(French Forum Pubs., Inc.; 0-917058),* P.O. Box 5108, Lexington, KY 40505 Tel 606-299-9530.
French Inst, *(French Institute-Alliance Francaise; 0-933444),* 22 E. 60th St., New York, NY 10022 Tel 212-355-6100.
Fresh Pr, *(Fresh Press; 0-9601398),* 774 Allen Court, Palo Alto, CA 94303 Tel 415-493-3596.
FreshCut, *(FreshCut Press),* 133 Clara Ave., Ukiah, CA 95482; 45 N. Prospect, Oberlin, OH 44074.
Freshwater, *(Freshwater Press, Inc.; 0-912514),* 334 the Arcade, Cleveland, OH 44114 Tel 216-241-0373.
Friedman, *(Friedman, Ira J., Inc.; 0-87198),* Div. of Kennikat Press, Inc., 90 S. Bayles Ave., Port Washington, NY 11050 Tel 516-883-0570.
Friend Freedom, *(Friends of Freedom Foundation Pubs. & Investors),* P.O. Box 6124, Waco, TX 76706 Tel 817-662-2695.
Friend Pr, *(Friendship Press; 0-377),* 475 Riverside Dr., Rm. 772, New York, NY 10027 Tel 212-870-2497; Orders to: Friendship Press Distribution, P.O. Box 37844, Cincinnati, OH 45237 Tel 513-761-2100.
Friendly City, *(Friendly City Publishing Co.; 0-938212),* P.O. Box 1946, Athens, TN 37303; Dist. by: Harlo Press, 50 Victor Ave., Detroit, MI 48203.
Friendly Fairways, *(Friendly Fairways of America),* P.O. Box 237-A, Royal Oak, MI 48068 Tel 313-652-8099.
Friendly Pr, *(Friendly Press; 0-938070),* 2744 Friendly St., Eugene, OR 97405.
Friends Aberdeen, *(Friends of the Aberdeen Public Library; 0-9605152),* 121 E. Market St., Aberdeen, WA 98520.
Friends Earth, *(Friends of the Earth, Inc.; 0-913890),* 124 Spear, San Francisco, CA 94105 Tel 415-495-4770.
Friends Israel-Spearhead Pr, *(Friends of Israel-Spearhead Press, The),* P.O. Box 123, West Collingswood, NJ 08107 Tel 215-922-3030.
Friends Peace Comm, *(Friends Peace Committee, Nonviolence & Children Program; 0-9605062),* 1515 Cherry St., Philadelphia, PA 19102.
Friends Photography, *(Friends of Photography, The; 0-933286),* P.O. Box 500, Sunset Ctr., Carmel, CA 93921 Tel 408-624-6330.
Friends Refugees, *(Friends of Refugees of Eastern Europe; 0-86639),* 1383 President St., Brooklyn, NY 11213.
Friends United, *(Friends United Press; 0-913408),* 101 Quaker Hill Dr., Richmond, IN 47374 Tel 317-962-7573.
Frog in Well, *(Frog in the Well; 0-9603628),* 430 Oakdale Rd., East Palo Alto, CA 94303.
From Here, *(From Here Press; 0-89120),* P. O. Box 219, Fanwood, NJ 07023 Tel 201-322-5928.
Frommer-Pasmantier, *(Frommer-Pasmantier Pubs.; 0-671),* 1230 Ave. of the Americas, New York, NY 10020 Tel 212-245-6400.
Front Row, *(Front Row Experience; 0-915256),* 540 Discovery Bay Blvd., Byron, CA 94514 Tel 415-634-5710.
Frontier Pr Co, *(Frontier Press Co.; 0-912168),* P.O. Box 1098, Columbus, OH 43216 Tel 614-864-3737.
Frost & Sullivan, *(Frost & Sullivan, Inc.),* 106 Fulton St., New York, NY 10038 Tel 212-233-1080.
Frost Art, *(Frost Art Distributors; 0-9604802),* 781 S. Kohler St., Los Angeles, CA 90021 Tel 213-626-3830.
FS&G, *(Farrar, Straus & Giroux, Inc.; 0-374),* 19 Union Square, W., New York, NY 10003 Tel 212-741-6900.
Full Court NY, *(Full Court Press, Inc.; 0-916190),* 15 Laight St., New York, NY 10013 Tel 212-966-6196.
Fulness Hse, *(Fulness House, Inc.; 0-937778),* P.O. Box 79350, Fort Worth, TX 76179.
Fun Pub, *(Fun Pub. Co; 0-918858),* P.O. Box 2049, Scottsdale, AZ 85252 Tel 602-946-2093.
Fur Line Pr, *(Fur Line Press; 0-912662),* Dist. by: ManRoot Press, Box 982, South San Francisco, CA 94080.
Futura Pub, *(Futura Publishing Co., Inc.; 0-87993),* P.O. Box 330, 295 Main St., Mount Kisco, NY 10549 Tel 914-666-3505.
Future Pr, *(Future Press; 0-918406),* P. O. Box 73, Canal St., New York, NY 10013.
Future Shop, *(Future Shop; 0-930490),* P.O. Box 903, Ventura, CA 93001 Tel 805-653-5419.
Futures Group, *(Futures Group, The; 0-9605196),* 76 Eastern Blvd., Glastonbury, CT 06033.
G A Eversaul, *(Eversaul, George A.; 0-9601978),* Box 19476, Las Vegas, NV 89119.
G & BJ's Serv, *(G & BJ's Services; 0-9604838),* 1350 Grandridge Blvd., Kennewick, WA 99336.
G Brune, *(Brune, Gunnar),* 2014 Royal Club Court, Arlington, TX 76017 Tel 817-465-3171.
G D L Inc, *(G.D.L., Inc.; 0-937358),* P.O. Box 1248, Birmingham, MI 48011.
G Davis, *(Davis, Grant, Co., Inc.; 0-934786),* P.O. Box 692, Lewisville, TX 75067.
G F Ritchie, *(Ritchie, George F.; 0-9604392),* 665 Pine St., No. 503, San Francisco, CA 94108 Tel 415-433-6115.
G F Stickley Co, *(Stickley, George F., Co.; 0-89313),* 210 W. Washington Square, Philadelphia, PA 19106 Tel 215-922-7126.
G Gannett, *(Gannett, Guy, Publishing Co.; 0-930096),* 390 Congress St., Portland, ME 04104.
G K Hall, *(Hall, G. K., & Co.; 0-8161),* 70 Lincoln St., Boston, MA 02111 Tel 617-423-3990. *Imprints:* Large Print Bks (Large Print Books Series).
G Ohsawa, *(Ohsawa, George, Macrobiotic Foundation; 0-918860),* 902 14th St., Oroville, CA 95965 Tel 916-533-7702.
G R Schoepfer, *(Schoepfer, G. R.; 0-931436),* 338 Concord Ave., West Hempstead, NY 11552.
G W May, *(May, George W.; 0-9605566),* Rte. 1 Box 221, Metropolis, IL 62960.
G Witzstrock Pub Hse, *(Witzstrock, Gerhard, Publishing House, Inc.; 0-933682),* 30 E. 40th St., Suite 703, New York, NY 10016.
Ga St U Busn Pub, *(Georgia State Univ., College of Business Administration; 0-88406),* Business Publishing Div., Univ. Plaza, Atlanta, GA 30303 Tel 404-658-4253.
Gabriel Bks
See Minn Scholarly
Gabriel Hse, *(Gabriel House, Inc.; 0-936192),* 9329 Crawford Ave., Evanston, IL 60203 Tel 312-674-6476.
Gala Bks, *(Gala Books & Gifts; 0-912448),* P. O. Box 659, Laguna Beach, CA 92652 Tel 714-494-6655.
Gale, *(Gale Research Co.; 0-8103),* Book Tower, Detroit, MI 48226 Tel 313-961-2242.
Galilee *Imprint of* **Doubleday**
Gallaudet Coll, *(Gallaudet College Press; 0-913580),* Kendall Green, Washington, DC 20002 Tel 202-651-5595.
Gallery Pr, *(Gallery Press; 0-913622),* 98 N. Main St., Essex, CT 06426 Tel 203-767-0313.
Galley OR, *(Galley Press),* P.O. Box 892, Portland, OR 97207 Tel 206-693-1397.
Galliard Pr, *(Galliard Press; 0-936616),* P.O. Box 296, Claremont, CA 91711.
Gallimaufry, *(Gallimaufry; 0-916300),* Dist. by: Apple-Wood Press, P.O. Box 2870, Cambridge, MA 02139 Tel 617-964-5150.
Gallopade Pub Group, *(Gallopade Publishing Group; 0-935326),* P.O. Box 469, Rocky Mount, NC 27801; P.O. Box 1537, Tryon, NC 28782 Tel 704-859-9253.

Galloway, *(Galloway Pubns. Inc.; 0-87874),* 2940 N.W. Circle Blvd., Corvallis, OR 97330.
Gambit, *(Gambit Inc. Pubs.; 0-87645),* 27 N. Main St., Ipswich, MA 01938 Tel 617-356-2956.
Gamblers, *(Gambler's Book Club/GBC Press; 0-911996; 0-89650),* 630 S. 11th St., P.O. Box 4115, Las Vegas, NV 89106 Tel 702-382-7555.
Gamesmasters, *(Gamesmasters Pubs. Assn.; 0-935426),* 20 Almont St., Nashua, NH 03060.
Gamma Bks, *(Gamma Books; 0-933124),* 307 Willow Ave., Ithaca, NY 14850.
G&D, *(Grosset & Dunlap, Inc.; 0-448),* 51 Madison Ave., New York, NY 10010 Tel 212-689-9200. *Imprints:* Tempo (Tempo Books).
G&G Pubs, *(G & G Pubs.; 0-937534),* Route 7, No.65, Hopewell Junction, NY 12533.
Ganis & Harris, *(Ganis & Harris, Inc.; 0-9605188),* 119 W. 57th St., New York, NY 10019.
Gannon, *(Gannon, William; 0-88307),* P.O. Box 2610, Santa Fe, NM 87501 Tel 505-983-1579.
Garabed, *(Garabed Books),* 23 Leroy St., New York, NY 10014.
Garden Way Pub, *(Garden Way Publishing Co.; 0-88266),* Charlotte, VT 05445 Tel 802-425-2171.
Gardner Pr, *(Gardner Press, Inc.; 0-89876),* 19 Union Square W., New York, NY 10003.
Garland Pub, *(Garland Publishing, Inc.; 0-8240),* 136 Madison Ave., 2nd Floor, New York, NY 10016 Tel 212-686-7492.
Garrard, *(Garrard Publishing Co.; 0-8116),* 107 Cherry St., New Canaan, CT 06840 Tel 203-966-4581; Orders to: 1607 N. Market St., Champaign, IL 61820 Tel 217-352-7685.
Garrett-Helix, *(Garrett Pubns.-Helix Press; 0-912326),* Orders to: Taplinger Publishing Co., 200 Park Ave, S., New York, NY 10003.
Garrett Pk, *(Garrett Park Press; 0-912048),* Garrett Park, MD 20766 Tel 301-946-2553.
Gaslight, *(Gaslight Pubns.; 0-934468),* 112 E. Second, Bloomington, IN 47401 Tel 812-332-5169.
Gateway Ed Ltd
See Regnery-Gateway
GATT *Imprint of* **Unipub**
Gay Pr NY, *(Gay Presses of New York; 0-9604724),* P.O. Box 294, New York, NY 10014.
Gay Sunshine, *(Gay Sunshine Press; 0-917342),* Box 40397, San Francisco, CA 94140 Tel 415-824-3184; Dist. by: Bookpeople, 2940 Seventh St., Berkeley, CA 94710 Tel 800-227-1516.
Gaylord Prof Pubns, *(Gaylord Professional Pubns.; 0-915794),* Div. of Gaylord Bros., Inc., P.O. Box 4264, Hamden, CT 06514 Tel 203-288-8707; Orders to: P.O. Box 4901, Syracuse, NY 13221.
Gazelle Pubns, *(Gazelle Pubns.; 0-930192),* 20601 W. Paoli Lane, Colfax, CA 95713.
GB *Imprint of* **Oxford U Pr**
GCNHA, *(Grand Canyon Natural History Assn.; 0-938216),* P.O. Box 399, Grand Canyon, AZ 86023.
GE-PS Cancer, *(GE-PS Cancer Memorial; 0-9601644),* 519 Austin Ave., Park Ridge, IL 60068 Tel 312-823-5425.
GE Tech Marketing, *(General Electric Co., Technology Marketing Operation; 0-931690),* 120 Erie Blvd., Schenectady, NY 12305.
GE Tech Prom & Train, *(General Electric Co., Technical Promotion & Training Services; 0-932078),* 1 River Rd., Bldg. 22, Rm. 232, Box MK, Schenectady, NY 12345.
GE Train & Ed
See GE Tech Prom & Train
Gearhart-Edwards, *(Gearhart-Edwards Press),* 2266 N. Prospect Ave., Suite 502, Milwaukee, WI 53202.
Gemini Pub Co, *(Gemini Publishing Co.; 0-937164),* 2801 W. Bay Area Blvd., Suite 811, Webster, TX 77598 Tel 713-482-9520.
Gen Welfare, *(General Welfare Pubns.; 0-87312),* P.O. Box 19098, Sacramento, CA 95819 Tel 916-677-1610.
Genealog Inst, *(Genealogical Institute),* Dist. by: Family History World, 19 W. South Temple, Suite 761, Salt Lake City, UT 84101 Tel 801-532-3327.
Genealogy Res, *(Genealogy Research; 0-9603214),* P.O. Box 1763, Sacramento, CA 95808.
General Educ, *(General Education Pubns.; 0-914504),* 99 S. Van Ness Ave., San Francisco, CA 94103 Tel 415-621-5410.
Geneva Pr, *(Geneva Press, The; 0-664),* 925 Chestnut St., Philadelphia, PA 19107.
Geographics, *(Geographics; 0-930722),* Box 133, Easton, CT 06425.
Geol Soc, *(Geological Society of America, Inc.; 0-8137),* 3300 Penrose Place, Boulder, CO 80301 Tel 303-447-2020.
Georgetown U Pr, *(Georgetown Univ. Press; 0-87840),* Georgetown University Press, School of Language & Linguistics, Georgetown University, Washington, DC 20057 Tel 202-625-4824.
Geothermal, *(Geothermal Resources Council; 0-934412),* P.O. Box 98, Davis, CA 95616.
Germainbooks, *(Germainbooks; 0-914142),* 91 St. Germain Ave., San Francisco, CA 94114 Tel 415-731-8155.
Ghost Dance, *(Ghost Dance Press),* ATL EBH MSU, East Lansing, MI 48824 Tel 517-351-5977.
Ghost Town, *(Ghost Town Pubns.; 0-933818),* P.O. Drawer 5998, Carmel, CA 93921 Tel 408-373-2885.
Gibson Pubs, *(Gibson, Tyler, Pubs.; 0-9605520),* 404 Riverside Dr., New York, NY 10025.
Gilchem Corp, *(Gilchem Corp.; 0-917122),* Woodlawn Rd., Suite 112, Bldg. 3, Woodlawn Green, Box 11291, Charlotte, NC 28209 Tel 704-523-2889.
Gingerbread *Imprint of* **Dutton**
Ginkgo Hut, *(Ginkgo Hut; 0-936620),* 13 Augusta Dr., Lincroft, NJ 07738.
Ginn Custom, *(Ginn Custom Publishing; 0-536),* Div. of Ginn & Co., 191 Spring St., Lexington, MA 02173 Tel 617-861-1670.
GLA Pr, *(G. L. A. Press; 0-912854),* P. O. Box 5312, Irving, TX 75062 Tel 214-579-5340.
Glanville, *(Glanville Pubs., Inc.; 0-87802),* 75 Main St., Dobbs Ferry, NY 10522 Tel 914-693-1320.
Glass Works, *(Glass Works Press; 0-934280),* P.O. Box 81782, San Diego, CA 92138 Tel 714-282-8000.
Glen-L Marine, *(Glen-L Marine Design),* 9152 Rosecrans, Bellflower, CA 90706.
Glen Pr, *(Glen Press; 0-9603518),* 2247 Glen Ave., Berkeley, CA 94709.
Glencoe, *(Glencoe Publishing Co., Inc.; 0-02),* c/o Macmillan Publishing Co., Inc., 866 Third Ave., New York, NY 10022 Tel 212-935-2000.
Glendale Advent Med, *(Glendale Adventist Medical Center; 0-87313),* P.O. Box 871, Glendale, CA 91209 Tel 213-240-2819.
Glenmary Res Ctr, *(Glenmary Research Center; 0-914422),* 4606 East-West Hwy., Washington, DC 20014 Tel 301-654-7501.
Glenn Vargas, *(Vargas, Glenn; 0-917646),* 85-159 Ave. 66, Thermal, CA 92274 Tel 714-397-4264.
Glide
See New Glide
Global Eng, *(Global Engineering Documents; 0-912702),* Div. of Information Handling Services, 2625 S. Hickory St., Santa Ana, CA 92707 Tel 714-540-9870.
Global Pubns WI, *(Global Pubns.; 0-9604752),* 731 N. 16th St., Milwaukee, WI 53233 Tel 414-344-2664.
Globe Pequot, *(Globe Pequot Press; 0-87106),* Old Chester Rd., Box Q, Chester, CT 06412 Tel 203-526-9572; CT History Ser., Dist. Only by the Center for CT Studies of Eastern CT State College, Willimantic, CT 06226.
Gloucester Art, *(Gloucester Art Press; 0-930582),* P.O. Box 4526, Albuquerque, NM 87196 Tel 505-843-7749.
GM *Imprint of* **Fawcett**
Gnomon Pr, *(Gnomon Press; 0-917788),* P.O. Box 106, Frankfort, KY 40602 Tel 502-223-1858.
God Unltd-U of Healing, *(God Unlimited-Univ. of Healing),* Rte. 1, Box 745, 32134 Hwy. 94, Campo, CA 92006 Tel 714-766-4643.
Godine, *(Godine, David R., Pub., Inc.; 0-87923),* 306 Dartmouth St., Boston, MA 02116 Tel 617-536-0761. *Imprints:* Nonpareil Bks (Nonpareil Books).
Godiva Pub, *(Godiva Publishing; 0-938018),* P.O. Box 42305, Portland, OR 97242 Tel 503-233-1228.
Gold-Kane Ent, *(Gold/Kane Enterprises; 0-9604430),* 1580 Garfield St., Denver, CO 80206 Tel 303-333-9659.
Gold Penny, *(Gold Penny Press, The; 0-87786),* Box 2177, Canoga Park, CA 91306 Tel 213-368-1417.
Gold Quill Pubs CA, *(Golden Quill Publishers, Inc.; 0-933904),* P.O. Box 1278-R, Colton, CA 92324 Tel 714-783-0119.
Golden Bell, *(Golden Bell Press; 0-87315),* 2403 Champa St., Denver, CO 80205 Tel 303-572-1777.
Golden Hill, *(Golden Hill Books; 0-9605364),* 2456 Broadway, San Diego, CA 92102.
Golden Owl Pub, *(Golden Owl Pubs.; 0-9601258),* 117 Essex South Dr., Lexington Park, MD 20653 Tel 301-863-9253.
Golden Pr *Imprint of* **Western Pub**
Golden Quill, *(Golden Quill Press; 0-8233),* Francestown, NH 03043 Tel 603-547-6622.
Golden West, *(Golden West Books; 0-87095),* P. O. Box 8136, San Marino, CA 91108 Tel 213-283-3446.
Golden West Hist, *(Golden West Historical Pubns.; 0-930960),* P.O. Box 1906, Ventura, CA 93002.
Golden West Pub, *(Golden West Pubs.; 0-914846),* 4113 N. Longview, Phoenix, AZ 85014 Tel 602-265-4392.
Golf Digest, *(Golf Digest/Tennis, Inc.; 0-914178),* 445 Westport Ave., Norwalk, CT 06856 Tel 203-847-5811.
Golf Digest Bks
See Golf Digest
Gondolier, *(Gondolier Press; 0-935824),* P.O. Box 467, Woodstock, NY 12498 Tel 914-679-9235.
Good Apple, *(Good Apple, Inc.; 0-916456; 0-86653),* P.O. Box 299, Carthage, IL 62321 Tel 217-357-3981.
Good Food Bks, *(Good Food Books; 0-932398),* 17 Colonial Terrace, Maplewood, NJ 07040.
Good Life VA, *(Good Life Publishers; 0-917374),* 14200 Nash Rd., Chesterfield, VA 23832 Tel 804-794-4954.
Good News, *(Good News Pubs.; 0-89107),* 9825 W. Roosevelt Rd., Westchester, IL 60153 Tel 312-345-7474.
Good Sign, *(Good Sign Pubns.; 0-937730),* 457 Ruthven Ave., Palo Alto, CA 94301.
Goodheart, *(Goodheart-Willcox Co., Inc.; 0-87006),* 123 W. Taft Dr., South Holland, IL 60473 Tel 312-333-7200.
Goodyear, *(Goodyear Publishing Co.; 0-87620; 0-8302),* 1640 Fifth St., Santa Monica, CA 90401 Tel 213-393-6731; Orders to: 4700 S. 5400 West, Box 18486, Salt Lake City, UT 84118 Tel 801-966-1411.
Gordian, *(Gordian Press, Inc.; 0-87752),* 85 Tompkins St., Staten Island, NY 10304 Tel 212-273-4700.
Gordon, *(Gordon & Breach Science Pubs., Inc.; 0-677),* 1 Park Ave., New York, NY 10016 Tel 212-689-0360.
Gordon-Cremonesi, *(Gordon-Cremonesi Book),* Dist. by: Atheneum Pubs., 597 Fifth Ave., New York, NY 10017 Tel 212-486-2700.
Gordon Pr, *(Gordon Press Pubs.; 0-87968),* P.O. Box 459, Bowling Green Sta., New York, NY 10004.
Gordons & Weinberg, *(Gordons & T. Weinberg; 0-9603484),* Berthoud Falls, P.O. Box 666, Empire, CO 80438.
Gordonstown, *(Gordonstown Press; 0-9603942),* Box U, Dillon, CO 80435.
Gordy Pr, *(Gordy Press; 0-936472),* 330 Pine Ridge Rd., Jackson, MS 39206 Tel 601-362-6518.
Gospel Advocate, *(Gospel Advocate Co., Inc.; 0-89225),* P.O. Box 150, Nashville, TN 37202 Tel 615-254-8781.
Gospel Pub, *(Gospel Publishing House; 0-88243),* 1445 Boonville Ave., Springfield, MO 65802 Tel 417-862-2781.
Gospel Pubns FL, *(Gospel Pubns. Inc. of Jax, Florida; 0-937408),* P.O. Box 16824, Jax, FL 32216.
Gotuit Ent, *(Gotuit Enterprises; 0-931490),* P.O. Box 2568, Seal Beach, CA 90740; Dist. by: Pelican Publishing Co., 630 Burmaster St., Gretna, LA 70053 Tel 504-368-1175.
Gould, *(Gould Pubns.; 0-87526),* 199 State St., Binghamton, NY 13901 Tel 607-724-3000.
Gourmet Guides, *(Gourmet Guides; 0-937024),* 1767 Stockton St., San Francisco, CA 94133.
Gov Insts, *(Government Institutes, Inc.; 0-86587),* 966 Hungerford Dr., No. 24, Rockville, MD 20850.

Gov Printing Office, *(Government Printing Office),* 710 N. Capitol St. NW., Washington, DC 20402 Tel 202-783-3238.
Gowan, *(Gowan, J.C.),* 1426 Southwind, Westlake Village, CA 91361 Tel 213-991-0342.
Gower *Imprint of* **Unipub**
Graceway, *(Graceway Publishing Co.; 0-932126),* P.O. Box 159, Station "C", Flushing, NY 11367 Tel 212-261-0759.
Grad School, *(Graduate School Press),* U. S. Dept. Agriculture, Rm. 6847, S. Bldg., Washington, DC 20250 Tel 202-447-7123.
Grand Canyon, *(Grand Canyon Pubns., Inc.; 0-9604276),* 443 S. 600 East St., Salt Lake City, UT 84102 Tel 801-272-2824.
Granger Bk, *(Granger Book Co., Inc.; 0-89609),* P.O. Box 406, Great Neck, NY 11021 Tel 516-466-3676.
Graph Arts Res RIT, *(Graphic Arts Research Center, Rochester Institute of Technology; 0-89938),* 1 Lomb Memorial Dr., Rochester, NY 14623 Tel 716-475-2761.
Graph Arts Trade, *(Graphic Arts Trade Journals; 0-910762),* P.O. Box 81, Farmingdale, NY 11735 Tel 516-694-4842.
Graphic Arts Ctr, *(Graphic Arts Center Publishing Co.; 0-912856),* P.O. Box 10306, Portland, OR 97210 Tel 503-224-7777.
Graphic Crafts, *(Graphic Crafts, Inc.),* P.O. Box 248, 300 Beaver Valley Pike, Willow Street, PA 17584 Tel 717-464-2733.
Graphic Dimensions, *(Graphic Dimensions; 0-930904),* 8 Frederick Rd., Pittsford, NY 14534 Tel 716-381-3428.
Graphic Pr, *(Graphic Press; 0-89284),* Div. of Carl Nelson Associates, Inc., P.O. Box 13056, Washington, DC 20009 Tel 202-232-2927.
Graphics Calif, *(Graphics Press; 0-937536),* 3010 Santa Monica Blvd. Suite 406, Santa Monica, CA 90404 Tel 213-395-2676.
Graywolf, *(Graywolf Press; 0-915308),* P.O. Box 142, Port Townsend, WA 98368 Tel 206-385-1160.
Great Basin, *(Great Basin Press; 0-930830),* Box 11162, Reno, NV 89510 Tel 702-826-7729.
Great Comm Pubns, *(Great Commission Pubns.; 0-934688),* 7401 Old York Rd., Philadelphia, PA 19126 Tel 215-635-6510.
Great Eastern, *(Great Eastern Book Co.; 0-87773),* P.O. Box 271, Boulder, CO 80306 Tel 303-449-6113. *Imprints:* Prajna (Prajna Press).
Great Northwest, *(Great Northwest Publishing & Distributing Co.; 0-937708),* 1207 E. Lyons, No.198, Spokane, WA 99208.
Great Ocean, *(Great Ocean Pubs.; 0-915556),* 738 S. 22nd St., Arlington, VA 22202 Tel 703-920-8978.
Great Western, *(Great Western Pubns.; 0-9604572),* 1842 W. 169th St., Gardena, CA 90247 Tel 213-323-7606.
Greater Phila, *(Greater Philadelphia Chamber of Commerce; 0-918964),* 1617 John F. Kennedy Blvd., Suite 1960, Philadelphia, PA 19103 Tel 215-568-4040.
Greater Portland, *(Greater Portland Landmarks, Inc.; 0-9600612),* 165 State St., Portland, ME 04101 Tel 207-744-5561.
Green, *(Green, Warren H., Inc.; 0-87527),* 8356 Olive Blvd., St. Louis, MO 63132 Tel 314-991-1335.
Green Hill, *(Green Hill Pubs.; 0-916054; 0-89803),* 236 Forest Park Place, Ottawa, IL 61350 Tel 815-434-7905; Dist. by: Caroline House Pubs., Inc., 2 Ellis Place, Ossining, NY 10562 Tel 914-941-9271.
Green Hut, *(Green Hut Press; 0-916678),* 24051 Rotunda Rd., Valencia Hills, CA 91355 Tel 805-259-5290.
Green Note Music, *(Green Note Music Pubns.; 0-912910),* P.O. Box 519, Pt. Reyes Sta., CA 94956 Tel 415-663-1453; Dist. by: Warner Bros. Pubns., Inc., 75 Rockefeller Plaza, New York, NY 10019.
Green River, *(Green River Press, Inc.),* Box 56, University Center, MI 48710 Tel 517-790-4376.
Green Tiger, *(Green Tiger Press; 0-914676),* P.O. Box 868, La Jolla, CA 92038 Tel 714-238-1001.
Greenberg Pub Co, *(Greenberg Publishing Co.; 0-89778),* 729 Oklahoma Rd., Sykesville, MD 21784 Tel 301-795-7447.
Greene, *(Greene, Stephen, Press; 0-8289),* Fessenden Rd. at Indian Flat, P.O. Box 1000, Brattleboro, VT 05301 Tel 802-257-7757.
Greenhaven, *(Greenhaven Press; 0-912616; 0-89908),* 577 Shoreview Park Rd., St. Paul, MN 55112 Tel 612-482-1582.
Greenlf Bks, *(Greenleaf Books; 0-934676),* Weare, NH 03281.
Greenvale, *(Greenvale Press; 0-911876),* P.O. Box 242, Kopperl, TX 76652 Tel 817-772-8576.
Greenwillow, *(Greenwillow Books; 0-688),* Div. of William Morrow & Co., Inc., 105 Madison Ave., New York, NY 10016 Tel 212-889-3050; Orders to: William Morrow & Co., Inc., Wilmor Warehouse, 6 Henderson Dr., West Caldwell, NJ 07006.
Greenwood, *(Greenwood Press; 0-8371; 0-313),* 88 Post Rd. W., Westport, CT 06881 Tel 203-226-3571. *Imprints:* Quorum Bks (Quorum Books).
Greenwood Hse, *(Greenwood House; 0-9601982),* 1655 Flatbush Ave., Brooklyn, NY 11210.
Gregg, *(Gregg Press, Inc.; 0-8398),* Div. of G. K. Hall & Co., 70 Lincoln St., Boston, MA 02111 Tel 617-423-3990.
Gregory Pubns, *(Gregory Pubns.; 0-917224),* Gateway Station, Box T, Aurora, CO 80014.
Grey Fox, *(Grey Fox Press; 0-912516),* P.O. Box 31411, San Francisco, CA 94131; Dist. by: Subterranean Co., P.O. Box 10233, Eugene, OR 97440 Tel 503-343-6324.
Greylock Pubs, *(Greylock Pubs.; 0-89223),* 13 Spring St., Stamford, CT 06901.
Grid Pub, *(Grid Publishing, Inc.; 0-88244),* 4666 Indianola Ave., Columbus, OH 43214 Tel 614-261-6565.
Grilled Flowers Pr, *(Grilled Flowers Press; 0-931238),* P.O. Box 3254, Durango, CO 81301.
Grolier Club, *(Grolier Club),* Dist. by: Univ. Press of Virginia, Univ. Sta., P.O. Box 3608, Charlottesville, VA 22903 Tel 804-924-3131.
Grolier Ed Corp, *(Grolier Educational Corp.; 0-7172),* Subs. of Grolier, Inc., Sherman Turnpike, Danbury, CT 06816 Tel 203-797-3500.
Grolier Inc
See Grolier Ed Corp
Grossman Stamp, *(Grossman Stamp Co., Inc.; 0-912618),* 860 Broadway, New York, NY 10003 Tel 212-254-6100.
Groupwork Today, *(Groupwork Today Inc.; 0-916068),* P.O. Box 258, South Plainfield, NJ 07080 Tel 201-755-4803.
Grove, *(Grove Press, Inc.; 0-8021; 0-394),* 196 W. Houston St., New York, NY 10014 Tel 212-242-4900; Orders to: Grove Press Order Dept., 196 W. Houston St., New York, NY 10014. *Imprints:* BC (Black Cat Books); Ever (Evergreen Books).
Groves Dict Music, *(Grove's Dictionaries of Music, Inc.),* 1283 National Press Bldg., Washington, DC 20045.
Growing Together, *(Growing Together Press; 0-9604118),* P.O. Box 2983, Stanford, CA 94305.
Growth Assoc, *(Growth Associates; 0-918834),* P.O. Box 8429, Rochester, NY 14618 Tel 716-244-1225.
Growth Unltd, *(Growth Unlimited; 0-9601334),* 31 East Ave., S., Battle Creek, MI 49017 Tel 616-964-4821.
Grune, *(Grune & Stratton; 0-8089),* c/o Academic Press, 111 Fifth Ave., 12th Fl., New York, NY 10003 Tel 212-741-4888.
Gryphon Hse, *(Gryphon House, Inc.; 0-87659),* 3706 Otis St., P.O. Box 217, Mt. Rainier, MD 20822 Tel 301-779-6200.
GS, *(Girl Scouts of the USA; 0-88441),* National Equipment Service, 830 Third Ave., New York, NY 10022 Tel 212-940-7500.
Guarionex Pr, *(Guarionex Press Ltd.; 0-935966),* 201 W. 77th St., New York, NY 10024.
Guide Pr, *(Guide Press; 0-915472),* 7101 Glenbrook Rd., Bethesda, MD 20014 Tel 301-654-3572.
Guild Bks, *(Guild Books; 0-912080),* 86 Riverside Dr., New York, NY 10024 Tel 212-799-2600.
Guild of Tutors, *(Guild of Tutors, International College; 0-89615),* 1019 Gavley Ave., Los Angeles, CA 90024.
Guild Prof Trans
See Translation Research
Guilford Pr, *(Guilford Press, The; 0-89862),* 200 Park Ave. S., New York, NY 10003.
Guitar Player, *(Guitar Player Productions; 0-89122),* Div. of Guitar Player Magazine, Dist. by: Music Sales Corp., 33 W. 60th St., New York, NY 10023 Tel 212-246-0325.
Gulf Pub, *(Gulf Publishing Co.; 0-87201),* P.O. Box 2608, Houston, TX 77001 Tel 713-529-4301.
Gun Hill, *(Gun Hill Publishing Co.; 0-9600228),* P.O. Box 187B, Yazoo City, MS 39194 Tel 601-746-3196.
Gun Room, *(Gun Room Press; 0-88227),* 127 Raritan Ave., Highland Park, NJ 08904 Tel 201-545-4344.
Gusto Pr, *(Gusto Press; 0-933906),* P.O. Box 1009, 2960 Philip Ave., Bronx, NY 10465 Tel 212-931-8964.
Gutenberg, *(Gutenberg Press, The; 0-9603872),* P.O. Box 26345, San Francisco, CA 94126 Tel 415-548-3776.
Gwenthie Pub
See Gwethine Pub Co
Gwethine Pub Co, *(Gwethine Publishing Co.),* 201 N. Wells St., Chicago, IL 60606 Tel 312-372-8105.
H Allen Enterprises
See Howard Allen
H & H Ent, *(H & H Enterprises, Inc.; 0-89079),* P.O. Box 1070, 946 Tennessee, Lawrence, KS 66044 Tel 913-843-4793.
H D Seyer, *(Seyer, Herman D.; 0-9600784),* 3848 Country Center Dr., Visalia, CA 93277 Tel 209-734-7537.
H Estes, *(Estes, Hiawatha, & Associates; 0-911008),* P.O. Box 404-RR, Northridge, CA 91328 Tel 213-885-6588.
H. H. Wait
See N S Wait
H J Cichy, *(Cichy, Helen J., Mrs.; 0-9601852),* Brandon, MN 56315.
H L Markow, *(Markow, Herbert L.; 0-934108),* P.O. Box 011451, Miami, FL 33101 Tel 305-448-0873.
H M Gousha, *(Gousha, H. M.; 0-913040),* 2001 The Alameda, P.O. Box 6227, San Jose, CA 95150 Tel 408-296-1060.
H M Rogers, *(Rogers, Helga M.; 0-9602294),* 1270 Fifth Ave., New York, NY 10029 Tel 212-348-0204.
H M Shelton, *(Shelton, Herbert M.),* P.O. Box 6636 - AH Sta, San Antonio, TX 78209 Tel 512-822-5263.
H P Bks, *(H. P. Books; 0-912656; 0-89586),* 341 Ponce de Leon Ave., N.E., Rm. 416, Tucson, AZ 85703 Tel 602-888-2150.
H S Marks, *(Marks, Henry S.),* 301 Terry-Hutchins Bldg. 102 Clinton Ave. W., Huntsville, AL 35801.
H Spriggle, *(Spriggle, Howard),* 1010 Chestnut St., Collingdale, PA 19023.
H Vogt, *(Vogt, Helen; 0-9602542),* 121 Blaine Ave., Brownsville, PA 15417 Tel 412-785-3804.
H W Hall, *(Hall, H. W.; 0-935064),* 3608 Meadow Oaks Lane, Bryan, TX 77801 Tel 713-846-0798.
Haas Ent NH, *(Haas Enterprises; 0-9605552),* 7 N. Main, Box 218, Ashland, NH 03217 Tel 603-968-7177.
Habel, *(Habel, Robert E.; 0-9600444),* 1529 Ellis Hollow Rd., Ithaca, NY 14850 Tel 607-272-3199.
Hacker, *(Hacker Art Books; 0-87817),* 54 W. 57th St., New York, NY 10019 Tel 212-757-1450.
Hackett Pub, *(Hackett Publishing Co.; 0-915144),* P. O. Box 55573, 4047 N. Pennsylvania St., Indianapolis, IN 46205 Tel 317-283-8187.
Hafner, *(Hafner Press; 0-02),* Div. of Macmillan Publishing Co., Inc., 866 Third Ave., New York, NY 10022 Tel 212-935-2000; Dist. by: Collier-Macmillan Distribution Ctr., Riverside, NJ 08075.
Hagin Evangelistic
See Hagin Ministries
Hagin Ministries, *(Hagin, Kenneth, Ministries, Inc.; 0-89276),* P.O. Box 50126, Tulsa, OK 74150 Tel 918-258-1588.
Haimo, *(Haimo, Oscar),* 252 E. 61st St., New York, NY 10021 Tel 212-838-6627.
Hake, *(Hake's Americana & Collectibles; 0-918708),* P.O. Box 1444, York, PA 17405 Tel 717-843-3731.
Halcyon Ithaca, *(Halcyon Press of Ithaca; 0-9604006),* 111 Halcyon Hill Rd., Ithaca, NY 14850.

Haldon Pubns, *(Haldon Pubns., Inc.),* 1204 N. 20th Ave., Hollywood, FL 33020 Tel 305-929-1956; Orders to: P.O. Box 2226, Hollywood, FL 33022; Moved, Left No Forwarding Address.
Halfrubber, *(Halfrubber Press; 0-9604808),* P.O. Box 312, Lithonia, GA 30058.
Hall Pr, *(Hall Press; 0-932218),* P.O. Box 5375, San Bernardino, CA 92412 Tel 714-887-3466.
Halldin Pub, *(Halldin, A. G., Publishing Co.; 0-935648),* P.O. Box 667, Indiana, PA 15701 Tel 412-463-8450.
Halsted Pr, *(Halsted Press),* Div. of John Wiley & Sons, Inc., 605 Third Ave., New York, NY 10158 Tel 212-850-6418.
Hamber
See BH Ent
Hamilton Hse, *(Hamilton House; 0-917908),* 936 N. 5th, Philadelphia, PA 19123 Tel 215-923-9161.
Hamilton Inst, *(Hamilton, Alexander, Institute, Inc.),* 1633 Broadway, New York, NY 10019 Tel 212-397-3580.
Hamilton Pr
See Citizens Law
Hammond Inc, *(Hammond, Inc.; 0-8437),* 515 Valley St., Maplewood, NJ 07040 Tel 201-763-6000.
Hamoroh Pr, *(Hamoroh Press; 0-9604754),* P.O. Box 48862, Los Angeles, CA 90048.
Hancock Hse, *(Hancock House Pubs., Ltd.; 0-88839),* Dist. by: Universe Books, 183 Munroe St., Passaic, NJ 07055.
Handel & Sons, *(Handel & Sons Publishing, Inc.; 0-917080),* 4227 Herschel, Suite 400, Dallas, TX 75219 Tel 214-234-3365.
Hang Gliding, *(Hang Gliding Press; 0-938282),* Box 22552, San Diego, CA 92122.
Hanging Loose, *(Hanging Loose Press; 0-914610),* 231 Wyckoff St., Brooklyn, NY 11217 Tel 212-643-9559.
Hansen Pub MI, *(Hansen Publishing Co.; 0-930098),* P.O. Box 1723, East Lansing, MI 48823 Tel 517-332-5946; Dist. by: Holley International Co., 63 Kercheval, Suite 204A, Grosse Pointe Farms, MI 48236 Tel 313-882-0405.
Hapi Pr, *(Hapi Press; 0-913244),* 512 S.W. Maplecrest Dr., Portland, OR 97219 Tel 503-246-9632.
Happiness Pr, *(Happiness Press; 0-916508),* 160 Wycliff Way, Drawer ADD, Magalia, CA 95954 Tel 916-873-0294; Orders to: P.O. Box Add, Magalia, CA 95954.
Happy History, *(Happy History, Inc.; 0-918430),* P.O. Box 2160, Boca Raton, FL 33432 Tel 305-391-8030; Box 726, New Canaan, CT 06840.
Har-Row, *(Harper & Row Pubs., Inc.; 0-06),* 10 E. 53rd St., New York, NY 10022 Tel 212-593-7000; 1700 Montgomery St., San Francisco, CA 94111 Tel 415-989-9000; Orders to: Keystone Industrial Park, Scranton, PA 18512. *Imprints:* CN (Colophon Books); COS (College Outline Series); EH (Everyday Handbooks); HarpC (Harper's College Division); Harper Medical (J.B. Lippincott/Harper & Row Medical Division); HarpJ (Juvenile Books); HarpR (Harper Religious Books); HarpT (Harper Trade Books); HW (Harrow Books Paperback Department); IntlDept (International Department); PL (Perennial Library); SchDept (School Department); Torch (Torchbooks); Trophy (Trophy).
Harbinger Pr, *(Harbinger Press Library; 0-936092),* 347 Willow Ave., Corte Madera, CA 94925 Tel 415-924-6490.
Harbor Pub CA, *(Harbor Publishing Inc.; 0-936602),* Ferry Building Suite 321, San Francisco, CA 94111; Dist. by: G.P. Putnam's Sons, 200 Madison Ave., New York, NY 10016.
HarBraceJ, *(Harcourt Brace Jovanovich, Inc.; 0-15),* 757 Third Ave., New York, NY 10017 Tel 212-888-4433. *Imprints:* Harv (Harvest Books); Hbgr (Harbinger Books); HC (Harcourt Brace Jovanovich, Inc., College Dept.); HPL (Harbrace Paperback Library); Psych Corp (Psychological Corp.); VoyB (Voyager Books).
Harian Creative, *(Harian Creative Press; 0-911906),* 47 Hyde Blvd., Ballston Spa, NY 12020 Tel 518-885-7397.
Harlo Pr, *(Harlo Press; 0-8187),* 50 Victor Ave., Detroit, MI 48203 Tel 313-883-3600.
Harmony & Co, *(Harmony & Co.; 0-89967),* Box 133, Greenport, NY 11944.
Harmony Soc, *(Harmony Society Press; 0-937640),* Box A 57, Clark University, Worcester, MA 01610.
Harold Hse, *(Harold House, Pubs.; 0-930138),* P.O. Box 59, 203 Walnut St., Marshall, AR 72650 Tel 501-448-5170.
HarpC *Imprint of* **Har-Row**
Harper Medical *Imprint of* **Har-Row**
HarpJ *Imprint of* **Har-Row**
HarpR *Imprint of* **Har-Row**
HarpT *Imprint of* **Har-Row**
Harris & Co, *(Harris, H. E., & Co., Inc.; 0-937458),* Div. of General Mills, Inc., 645 Summer St., Boston, MA 02210 Tel 617-269-5200; Orders to: Box A, Boston, MA 02117.
Harris Pub, *(Harris Publishing Co.; 0-916512),* 2057-2 East Aurora Rd., Twinsburg, OH 44087 Tel 216-425-9143.
Hartley Hse, *(Hartley House; 0-937518),* P.O. Box 1352, Hartford, CT 06143 Tel 203-525-2376.
Harv *Imprint of* **HarBraceJ**
Harvard Law Intl Tax, *(Harvard Law School, International Tax Program; 0-915506),* Harvard Law School, Cambridge, MA 02138 Tel 617-495-4407.
Harvard U Pr, *(Harvard Univ. Press; 0-674),* 79 Garden St., Cambridge, MA 02138 Tel 617-495-2600; Orders to: Customer Service, Harvard Univ. Press, 79 Garden St., Cambridge, MA 02138.
Harvest Hse, *(Harvest House Pubs., Inc.; 0-89081),* 2861 McGaw, Irvine, CA 92714 Tel 714-549-8112.
Harvest Pubns, *(Harvest Pubns.; 0-939074),* 907 Santa Barbara St., Santa Barbara, CA 93101 Tel 805-685-1358.
Harvey, *(Harvey House, Pubs.; 0-8178),* 20 Waterside Plaza, New York, NY 10010 Tel 212-889-9520; Orders to: 128 W. River St., Chippewa Falls, WI 54729 Tel 715-723-2814.
Harwood Academic, *(Harwood Academic Pubs.; 3-7186),* P.O. Box 786, Cooper Sta., New York, NY 10276 Tel 212-242-4464.
Haskell, *(Haskell Booksellers, Inc.; 0-8383),* P.O. Box FF, Blythebourne Sta., Brooklyn, NY 11219 Tel 212-435-0500.
Hastings, *(Hastings House Pubs., Inc.; 0-8038),* 10 E. 40th St., New York, NY 10016 Tel 212-689-5400.
Hastings Ctr Inst Soc, *(Hastings Center, Institute of Society, Ethics & Life Sciences; 0-916558),* 360 Broadway, Hastings-on-Hudson, NY 10706 Tel 914-478-0500.
Hatfield, *(Hatfield, Glen; 0-9600216),* P.O. Box 329, Kankakee, IL 60901 Tel 815-939-1818.
Hawkes Pub Inc, *(Hawkes Publishing Inc.; 0-89036),* 3775 S. 500 West, Box 15711, Salt Lake City, UT 84115 Tel 801-262-5555.
Hawley, *(Hawley, W. M.; 0-910704),* 8200 Gould Ave., Hollywood, CA 90046 Tel 213-654-1573.
Hawley Cooke Orr, *(Hawley, Cooke, & Orr Pubs.; 0-937246),* P.O. Box 6052, Louisville, KY 40207 Tel 502-893-0133.
Haworth Pr, *(Haworth Press Inc., The; 0-917724),* 149 Fifth Ave., New York, NY 10010 Tel 212-228-2800.
Hawthorn *Imprint of* **Dutton**
Hayden, *(Hayden Book Co., Inc.; 0-8104),* 50 Essex St., Rochelle Park, NJ 07662 Tel 201-843-0550. *Imprints:* Spartan (Spartan Books, Inc.).
Hayes Bk Co, *(Hayes Book Co.),* Hueysville, KY 41640.
Haymark, *(Haymark Pubns.; 0-933910),* P.O. Box 243, Fredericksburg, VA 22401 Tel 703-373-1144.
Hays Rolfes, *(Hays, Rolfes & Assocs.; 0-9602448),* P.O. Box 11465, Memphis, TN 38111 Tel 901-682-8128.
Hazelden, *(Hazelden Foundation; 0-89486),* P.O. Box 176, Center City, MN 55012 Tel 800-328-9288.
Hbgr *Imprint of* **HarBraceJ**
HC *Imprint of* **HarBraceJ**
Headway Pubns, *(Headway Pubns.; 0-89537),* 1700 Port Manleigh Circle, Newport Beach, CA 92660 Tel 714-640-0736.
Health Admin Pr, *(Health Administration Press; 0-914904),* 1021 E. Huron St., Univ. of Michigan, Ann Arbor, MI 48109 Tel 313-764-1380.
Health Plus, *(Health Plus, Pubs.; 0-932090),* P.O. Box 22001, Phoenix, AZ 85028 Tel 602-992-0589.
Health Sci Consort, *(Health Sciences Consortium, Inc.; 0-938938),* 200 Eastowne Dr., Suite 213, Chapel Hill, NC 27514 Tel 919-942-8731.
Healthworks, *(Healthworks, Inc.; 0-938480),* 31582 S. Coast Hwy., S. Laguna, CA 92677.
Hearst Bks, *(Hearst Books; 0-910992; 0-87851; 0-910990),* Div. of the Hearst Corp., 224 W. 57th St., Rm. 307, New York, NY 10019 Tel 212-262-8605; Orders to: P.O. Box 1406, Radio City Sta., New York, NY 10019.
Heart Am Pr, *(Heart of America Press; 0-913902),* P.O. Box 9808, 10101 Blue Ridge Blvd., Kansas City, MO 64134 Tel 816-761-0080.
Heart of the Lakes, *(Heart of the Lakes Publishing; 0-932334),* Interlaken, NY 14847 Tel 607-532-4204.
Hearthside, *(Hearthside Press, Inc.; 0-8208),* Orders to: Ingram Book Co., 347 Redwood Dr., Nashville, TN 37217.
Hearthstone, *(Hearthstone Press; 0-937308),* 708 Inglewood Dr., Broderick, CA 95605 Tel 916-372-0250.
Heartwork Pr, *(Heartwork Press; 0-935598),* 881 Lovell Ave., Mill Valley, CA 94941.
Heath, *(Heath, D.C., & Co., Elhi Dept.; 0-669),* Div. of Raytheon Co., 125 Spring St., Lexington, MA 02173 Tel 617-862-6650; Orders to: D. C. Heath & Co., Distribution Center, 2700 N. Richardt Ave., Indianapolis, IN 46219 Tel 317-359-5585.
Heathcote, *(Heathcote Publishers; 0-9602350),* P.O. Box 135, Monmouth Jct., NJ 08852 Tel 201-297-4891.
Heather Foun, *(Heather Foundation; 0-9600300),* P.O. Box 48, San Pedro, CA 90733 Tel 213-831-6269.
Hebrew Pub, *(Hebrew Publishing Co.; 0-88482),* 80 Fifth Ave., New York, NY 10011 Tel 212-675-3878.
Heffron Ent, *(Heffron, Dan, Enterprises; 0-9605104),* P.O. Box 9019, Cleveland, OH 44137.
Heian Intl, *(Heian International Publishing, Inc.; 0-89346),* Div. of Heian International, Inc., P.O. Box 2042, South San Francisco, CA 94080 Tel 415-467-0222.
Heidelberg Graph, *(Heidelberg Graphics; 0-918606),* P.O. Box 3606, Chico, CA 95927.
Heinemann Ed, *(Heinemann Educational Books Inc.; 0-435),* 4 Front St., Exeter, NH 03833 Tel 603-778-0534.
Heinle & Heinle, *(Heinle & Heinle Pubs.),* Div. of Science Books International, Inc., 51 Sleeper St., Boston, MA 02210 Tel 617-475-4582.
Heinman, *(Heinman, William S.; 0-88431),* 1966 Broadway, New York, NY 10023 Tel 212-787-3154.
Helios, *(Helios Book Publishing Co., Inc.; 0-87037),* 150 W. 28th St., New York, NY 10001 Tel 212-255-6112.
Hellenic Coll Pr, *(Hellenic College Press; 0-916586),* Div. of Holy Cross Orthodox Press, 50 Goddard Ave., Brookline, MA 02146.
Helm Pub, *(Helm Publishing),* Box 10512, Costa Mesa, CA 92627 Tel 714-645-3107.
Hemisphere Hse, *(Hemisphere House Books; 0-930770),* 530 S. Tancahua St.-Numero 4, Corpus Christi, TX 78401.
Hemisphere Pub, *(Hemisphere Publishing Corp.; 0-89116),* 1025 Vermont Ave., N.W., Washington, DC 20005 Tel 202-783-3958; Orders to: 19 W. 44th St., New York, NY 10036 Tel 212-921-0606.
Hemmings, *(Hemmings Motor News; 0-917808),* Box 256, Bennington, VT 05201 Tel 802-442-3101.
Hemphill, *(Hemphill Publishing Co.; 0-914696),* 1400 Wathen Ave., Austin, TX 78703 Tel 512-476-9422.
Hendershot, *(Hendershot Bibliography; 0-911832),* 4114 Ridgewood Dr., Bay City, MI 48706 Tel 517-684-3148.
Hendricks House, *(Hendricks House, Inc.; 0-87532),* 488 Greenwich St., New York, NY 10013 Tel 212-966-1765.

Hennessey, *(Hennessey & Ingalls, Inc.; 0-912158),* 10814 W. Pico Blvd., Los Angeles, CA 90064 Tel 213-474-2541.
Herald Bks, *(Herald Books; 0-910714),* P.O. Box 17, Pelham, NY 10803 Tel 914-576-1121.
Herald Hse, *(Herald House; 0-8309),* Drawer HH, 3225 S. Noland Rd., Independence, MO 64055 Tel 816-252-5010.
Herald Pr, *(Herald Press; 0-8361),* 616 Walnut Ave., Scottdale, PA 15683 Tel 412-887-8500.
Herbal Med, *(Herbal Medicine Research Foundation; 0-930074),* P.O. Box 29187, San Antonio, TX 78229 Tel 512-699-0783.
Herbert Pubs, *(Herbert Pubs.; 0-935780),* P.O. Box 162, Mount Laurel, NJ 08054.
Heres Life, *(Here's Life Pubs., Inc.; 0-89840),* Box 1576, 2700 Little Mountain Dr., Bldg. "B", San Bernardino, CA 92402 Tel 714-886-7981.
Heresy Pr, *(Heresy Press; 0-9603276),* 713 Paul St., Newport News, VA 23605.
Heritage Bk, *(Heritage Books, Inc.; 0-917890),* 3602 Maureen Lane, Bowie, MD 20715 Tel 301-464-1159.
Heritage Found, *(Heritage Foundation; 0-89195),* 513 "C" St., N.E., Washington, DC 20002 Tel 202-546-4400.
Heritage Kansas, *(Heritage Books),* Rte. 6 Box 25, Salina, KS 67401 Tel 913-827-7861.
Heritage Rec, *(Heritage Recording; 0-9602888),* Box 8132, St Paul, MN 55113 Tel 612-484-7481.
Herman Pub, *(Herman Publishing; 0-89046; 0-89047),* 45 Newbury St., Boston, MA 02116 Tel 617-536-5810.
Hermes Hse, *(Hermes House Press; 0-9605008),* 1615c Harmon St., Berkeley, CA 94703 Tel 415-655-9675.
Hermon, *(Sepher-Hermon Press, Inc.; 0-87203),* 53 Park Place, New York, NY 10007 Tel 212-349-1860.
Hershey, *(Hershey, Virginia Sharpe; 0-9605320),* 5325 Wikiup Bridgeway, Santa Rosa, CA 95404.
Herzl Pr, *(Herzl Press; 0-930832),* 515 Park Ave., New York, NY 10022 Tel 212-752-0600.
Heyday Bks, *(Heyday Books; 0-930588),* P.O. Box 9145, Berkeley, CA 94709 Tel 415-849-1438.
Heyden, *(Heyden & Son, Inc.),* 247 S. 41st St., Philadelphia, PA 19104 Tel 215-382-6673.
Heydent
See Heyden
Hi Country Pubs, *(Hi-Country Pubs.; 0-938354),* P.O. Box 2362, Littleton, CO 80161.
Hi Willow, *(Hi Willow Research & Publishing; 0-931510),* Box 1801, Fayetteville, AR 72701 Tel 501-575-5444.
Hiawatha Pub Iowa
See Pyramid Iowa
Hidden Hse *Imprint of* **Music Sales**
Hidden Valley, *(Hidden Valley Press; 0-935710),* 7051 Poole Jones Rd., Frederick, MD 21701 Tel 301-662-6745.
Highland *Imprint of* **Berkley Pub**
Highland Maya
See Indigenous Pubns
Highland Pr, *(Highland Press; 0-910722),* Rte. 3, Box 3125, Boerne, TX 78006.
Highlights, *(Highlights for Children, Inc.; 0-87534),* 803 Church St., Honesdale, PA 18431 Tel 717-253-1080; 2300 W. 5th Ave., P.O. Box 269, Columbus, OH 43216 Tel 614-486-0631.
Highly Specialized, *(Highly Specialized Promotions; 0-930194),* 391 Atlantic Ave., Brooklyn, NY 11217 Tel 212-858-3026; Orders to: P.O. Box 989, Brooklyn, NY 11202.
Hilary Hse Pubs, *(Hilary House Pubs., Inc.; 0-934464),* 1033 Channel Dr., Hewlett, NY 11557.
Hill & Wang, *(Hill & Wang, Inc.; 0-8090),* Div. of Farrar, Straus & Giroux, Inc., 19 Union Square, New York, NY 10003 Tel 212-741-6900. *Imprints:* AmCen (American Century Series); Drama (Dramabooks); Mermaid (Mermaid Dramabooks); New Mermaid (New Mermaid Dramabooks); Terra Magica (Terra Magica Books).
Hill Jr Coll, *(Hill Junior College Press; 0-912172),* P.O. Box 619, Hillsboro, TX 76645 Tel 817-582-2555.
Hillsdale Educ, *(Hillsdale Educational Pubs., Inc.; 0-910726),* 39 North St., Box 245, Hillsdale, MI 49242 Tel 517-437-3179.
Hilltop Pubns, *(Hilltop Pubns., Inc.; 0-937782),* 111 E. 61st St., New York, NY 10021.
Himalaya Hse, *(Himalaya House; 0-89654),* P.O. Box 792, Wheat Ridge, CO 80033 Tel 303-423-3170.
Himalayan Inst
See Himalayan Intl Inst
Himalayan Intl Inst, *(Himalayan International Institute; 0-89389),* RD 1, Box 88, Honesdale, PA 18431 Tel 717-253-5551.
Hippocrates, *(Hippocrates Books),* 25 Exeter St., Boston, MA 02116.
Hippocrene Bks, *(Hippocrene Books, Inc.; 0-88254),* 171 Madison Ave., New York, NY 10016 Tel 212-685-4372.
Hispanic Seminary, *(Hispanic Seminary of Medieval Studies),* 3734 Ross St., Madison, WI 53705.
Hispanic Soc, *(Hispanic Society of America; 0-87535),* 613 W. 155th St., New York, NY 10032 Tel 212-926-2234.
Hist Aviation, *(Historical Aviation Album; 0-911852),* P.O. Box 33, Temple City, CA 91780 Tel 213-286-7655.
Hist Tales, *(Historical Tales Ink; 0-938404),* 7344 Rich St., Reynoldsburg, OH 43068.
Historic New Orleans, *(Historic New Orleans Collection, The; 0-917860),* 533 Royal St., New Orleans, LA 70130.
Historic Photos, *(Historic Photos; 0-933206),* 3460 St. Helena Hwy. N., St. Helena, CA 94574 Tel 707-963-2855.
Hit Ent, *(Hit Enterprises; 0-935938),* 2945 Leticia Dr., Hacienda Heights, CA 91745.
HM, *(Houghton Mifflin Co.; 0-395),* 2 Park St., Boston, MA 02107 Tel 617-725-5000; Orders to: Wayside Road, Burlington, MA 01803 Tel 617-272-1500. *Imprints:* Clarion (Clarion Books).
HM Prof Med Div, *(Houghton Mifflin Professional Pubs., Medical Div.; 0-89289),* 2 Park St., Boston, MA 02107 Tel 617-725-5019.
HM Prof Pubs
See HM Prof Med Div
HMB Pubns, *(HMB Pubns.; 0-937086),* 7406 Monroe Ave., Hammond, IN 46324 Tel 219-932-1798.
HMS Pubns, *(HMS Pubns.; 0-9604812),* P.O. Box 5809, Santa Barbara, CA 93108 Tel 805-969-3421.
Hobby Hse, *(Hobby House Press; 0-87588),* 900 Frederick St., Cumberland, MD 21502 Tel 301-759-3770.
Hobby Pub Serv, *(Hobby Publishing Service; 0-917922),* 1318 Seventh St., N.W., Albuquerque, NM 87102 Tel 505-242-9465.
Hoffman Pubns, *(Hoffman Pubns., Inc.; 0-934890),* P.O. Box 11299, Fort Lauderdale, FL 33339 Tel 305-566-8401.
Holbrook Res, *(Holbrook Research Institute; 0-931248),* 57 Locust St., Oxford, MA 01540 Tel 617-987-0881.
Holden-Day, *(Holden-Day, Inc.; 0-8162),* 500 Sansome St., San Francisco, CA 94111 Tel 415-433-0220.
Holiday, *(Holiday House, Inc.; 0-8234),* 18 E. 53rd St., New York, NY 10022 Tel 212-688-0085.
Holland Hse Pr, *(Holland House Press; 0-913042),* 6215 Six Mile Rd., Northville, MI 48167 Tel 313-836-0286.
Hollow Spring Pr, *(Hollow Spring Press),* R.D. 1, Chester, MA 01011.
Holly Pr, *(Holly Press, The; 0-935968),* P.O. Box 306, Hockessin, DE 19707 Tel 302-239-2416.
Hollym Intl, *(Hollym International Corp.; 0-930878),* 18 Donald Place, Elizabeth, NJ 07208 Tel 201-353-1655.
Holman, *(Holman, A.J., Co.; 0-87981),* 127 Ninth Ave., N., Nashville, TN 37234 Tel 615-251-2611.
Holmes, *(Holmes Book Co.; 0-910740),* 274 14th St., Oakland, CA 94612 Tel 415-893-6860.
Holmes & Meier, *(Holmes & Meier Pubs., Inc.; 0-8419),* IUB Bldg., 30 Irving Place, New York, NY 10003 Tel 212-254-4100. *Imprints:* Africana (Africana Pub.).
Holmgangers, *(Holmgangers Press; 0-914974),* 22 Ardith Lane, Alamo, CA 94507 Tel 415-837-3831.
HoltC *Imprint of* **HR&W**
Holy Cow, *(Holy Cow! Press; 0-930100),* P.O. Box 618, Minneapolis, MN 55440.
Holy Cross Orthodox, *(Holy Cross Orthodox Press; 0-916586),* 50 Goddard Ave., Brookline, MA 02146 Tel 617-232-4544.
Holy Order Mans
See Epiphany Pr
Home Econ Educ, *(Home Economics Education Assn.),* 1201 Sixteenth St., N.W., Rm. 232, Washington, DC 20036 Tel 202-833-4138.
Home Equity, *(Home Equity Co.),* 802 Cascade Bldg., Portland, OR 97204 Tel 503-224-4522.
Home Frosted, *(Home of Frosted Sunshine, The; 0-937118),* R.R. 1, Box 612, Shermans Dale, PA 17090.
Home Mission, *(Home Mission of the Southern Baptist Convention; 0-937170),* 1350 Spring St., N.W., Atlanta, GA 30309 Tel 404-873-4041.
Homestead Bk, *(Homestead Book Co.; 0-930180),* 4009 Stone Way N., Seattle, WA 98103 Tel 206-634-2212.
Honey Hill, *(Honey Hill Publishing Co.; 0-937642),* 1022 Bonham Terrace, Austin, TX 78704 Tel 512-442-4177.
Hoover Inst Pr, *(Hoover Institution Press; 0-8179),* Stanford University, Stanford, CA 94305 Tel 415-497-3373.
Hopkinson, *(Hopkinson & Blake, Pubs.; 0-911974),* 50 W. 34th St., New York, NY 10001 Tel 212-947-8282; Not Publishing at This Time.
Horizon, *(Horizon Press Pubs.; 0-8180),* 156 Fifth Ave., New York, NY 10010 Tel 212-924-9225.
Horizon Bks CA, *(Horizon Books; 0-938840),* P.O. Box 3083, Fremont, CA 94538.
Horizon Utah, *(Horizon Pubs. & Distributors, Inc.; 0-88290),* P.O. Box 490, 50 S. 500 West, Bountiful, UT 84010 Tel 801-295-9451.
Horizons, *(Horizons; 0-932960),* P.O. Box 35008, Phoenix, AZ 85069.
Horn Bk, *(Horn Book, Inc.; 0-87675),* Park Square Bldg., 31 St. James Ave., Boston, MA 02116 Tel 617-482-5198.
Hornbeam Pr, *(Hornbeam Press, Inc.; 0-917496),* 6520 Courtwood Dr., Columbia, SC 29206 Tel 803-782-7667.
Horse & Bird, *(Horse & Bird Press, The; 0-9602214),* P.O. Box 67C89, Los Angeles, CA 90067.
Horticult Pubns, *(Horticultural Pubns.; 0-938378),* Box 231, Nichol Ave., Cook College, New Brunswick, NJ 08903.
Horticult Research, *(Horticultural Research Institute, Inc.; 0-935336),* 230 Southern Bldg., Washington, DC 20005 Tel 202-737-4060.
Horticultural, *(Horticultural Books, Inc.; 0-9600046),* P.O. Box 107, Stuart, FL 33495 Tel 305-287-1091.
Hosp Res & Educ, *(Hospital Research & Educational Trust; 0-87914),* 840 N. Lake Shore Dr., Chicago, IL 60611 Tel 312-280-6381.
Hospital Finan, *(Hospital Financial Management Assn.; 0-930228),* 1900 Spring Rd., Suite 500, Oak Brook, IL 60521 Tel 312-655-4600.
Host Assoc, *(Host, Jim, & Associates, Inc.; 0-934554),* 120 Kentucky Ave., Suite A-1, Lexington, KY 40502.
Hove Camera, *(Hove Camera Foto Books; 0-85242),* Dist. by: Morgan & Morgan, 145 Palisades St., Dobbs Ferry, NY 10522 Tel 914-693-9303.
How-to Pr, *(How-to Press; 0-938356),* P.O. Box 483, Arlington, TX 76010.
Howard Allen, *(Howard, Allen, Enterprises, Inc.; 0-914576),* P.O. Box 76, Cape Canaveral, FL 32920.
Howard U Pr, *(Howard Univ. Press; 0-88258),* 2900 Van Ness St., N.W., Washington, DC 20008 Tel 202-686-6696.
Howell Bk, *(Howell Book House Inc.; 0-87605),* Helmsley Bldg., 230 Park Ave., New York, NY 10169 Tel 212-986-4488.
Howell North, *(Howell-North Pubs., Inc.; 0-8310),* Subs. of Leisure Dynamics, Inc., 11175 Flintkote Ave., Suite C, San Diego, CA 92121 Tel 714-457-3200.
Howell-North
See Howell North
HPL *Imprint of* **HarBraceJ**

HRAFP, *(Human Relations Area File Press; 0-87536),* 4695 Main St., Snyder, NY 14226; Orders to: P.O. Box 2015 Y.S., New Haven, CT 06520 Tel 203-777-2334.
HR&W, *(Holt, Rinehart & Winston, Inc.; 0-03),* 383 Madison Ave., New York, NY 10017 Tel 212-688-9100. *Imprints:* HoltC (Holt College Department).
Hse of Affirmation
See Affirmation
Hse of Charles, *(House of Charles; 0-9605344),* 4833 NE 238th Ave., Vancouver, WA 98662.
Hse of Collectibles, *(House of Collectibles, Inc.; 0-87637),* 773 Kirkman Rd., Suite 120, Orlando, FL 32811 Tel 305-299-9343.
Hudson Hills, *(Hudson Hills Press, Inc.; 0-933920),* 30 Rockefeller Plaza, Suite 4323, New York, NY 10112 Tel 212-247-3400.
Huebner Foun Insur, *(Huebner, S. S., Foundation for Insurance Education),* 3641 Locust Walk CE, Philadelphia, PA 19104 Tel 215-243-5644; Dist. by: Richard D. Irwin, Inc., 1818 Ridge Rd., Homewood, IL 60430.
Huenefeld Co, *(Huenefeld Co., Inc.; 0-931932),* 119 The Great Rd., Bedford, MA 01730.
Hughes Pr, *(Hughes Press; 0-912560),* 500 23rd St., N.W., Box B203, Washington, DC 20037 Tel 202-293-2686.
Huguley Co, *(Huguley, John, Co., Inc.; 0-9605064),* 269 King St., Charleston, SC 29401.
Human Dev Pr, *(Human Development Press; 0-938024),* 10701 Lomas NE, 210, Albuquerque, NM 87112.
Human Dev Train, *(Human Development Training Institute; 0-86584),* 1727 Fifth Ave., San Diego, CA 92101 Tel 714-233-7023.
Human Kinetics, *(Human Kinetics Pubs.; 0-931250),* P.O. Box 5076, Champaign, IL 61820 Tel 217-351-5076.
Human Policy Pr, *(Human Policy Press; 0-937540),* P.O. Box 127, Syracuse, NY 13210.
Human Res Dev Pr, *(Human Resource Development Press; 0-914234),* 22 Amherst Rd., Amherst, MA 01002 Tel 413-253-3488.
Human Sci Pr, *(Human Sciences Press, Inc.; 0-87705; 0-89885),* 72 Fifth Ave., New York, NY 10011 Tel 212-243-6000; Dist. by: Independent Publishers Group, 14 Vanderventer Ave., Port Washington, NY 11050; Formerly Named Behavioral Pubns. Inc.
Humana, *(Humana Press, The; 0-89603),* Crescent Manor, P.O. Box 2148, Clifton, NJ 07015 Tel 201-773-4389.
Humanics Ltd, *(Humanics Ltd.; 0-89334),* P.O. Box 7447, Atlanta, GA 30309.
Humanities, *(Humanities Press, Inc.; 0-391),* Atlantic Highlands, NJ 07716 Tel 201-872-1441. *Imprints:* Athlone Pr (Athlone Press); NFER (National Foundation for Educational Research).
Humbird Hopkins, *(Humbird Hopkins Inc., Pubs.; 0-931854),* 625 Broadway, Seventh Floor, San Diego, CA 92101 Tel 714-234-4141.
Hummingbird, *(Hummingbird Press; 0-912998),* 2400 Hannett, N.E., Albuquerque, NM 87106 Tel 505-268-6277.
Humphrey
See Graph Arts Trade
Hungarian Cultural, *(Hungarian Cultural Foundation; 0-914648),* P.O. Box 364, Stone Mountain, GA 30086 Tel 404-377-2600.
Hunt Inst Botanical, *(Hunt Institute for Botanical Documentation; 0-913196),* Carnegie-Mellon Univ., Pittsburgh, PA 15213 Tel 412-578-2434.
Hunter Bks, *(Hunter Books; 0-917726),* 201 McClellar Rd., Kingwood, TX 77339 Tel 713-358-7575.
Hunter Hse, *(Hunter House, Inc.; 0-89793),* 824 W. Harrison, Suite 204, Claremont, CA 91711 Tel 714-624-2277.
Hunter Ministries
See Hunter Bks
Hunter NC, *(Hunter Publishing Co.; 0-89459),* P.O. Box 5867, Winston-Salem, NC 27103 Tel 919-765-0070.
Hunterdon Hse, *(Hunterdon House; 0-912606),* 38 Swan St., Lambertville, NJ 08530 Tel 609-397-2523.
Huntington Lib, *(Huntington Library Pubns.; 0-87328),* 1151 Oxford Rd., San Marino, CA 91108 Tel 213-792-6141.
Husher & Welch, *(Husher & Welch; 0-9603944),* 50 Nahant Rd., Nahant, MA 01908.
Hutchinson
See Merrimack Bk Serv
HW *Imprint of* **Har-Row**
Hwong Pub, *(Hwong Publishing Co.; 0-89260),* 10353 Los Alamitos Blvd., Los Alamitos, CA 90720 Tel 213-598-2428.
Hyperion Conn, *(Hyperion Press, Inc.; 0-88355; 0-8305),* 45 Riverside Ave., Westport, CT 06880 Tel 203-226-1091.
I & O Pub, *(I & O Publishing Co.; 0-911752),* P.O. Box 906, Boulder City, NV 89005.
I J Hoffman, *(Hoffman, Irwin J., Inc.; 0-9604082),* 5734 S. Ivanhoe St., Denver, CO 80111.
I S Gardner Mus, *(Isabella Stewart Gardner Museum; 0-914660),* 2 Palace Rd., Boston, MA 02115 Tel 617-566-1401.
IAEA *Imprint of* **Unipub**
IAFWA, *(International Assn. of Fish & Wildlife Agencies (IAFWA); 0-932108),* 1412 16th St., N.W., Washington, DC 20036 Tel 202-232-1652.
IAUS, *(Institute for Architecture & Urban Studies, The; 0-932628),* 8 W. 40th St., New York, NY 10018 Tel 212-398-9474.
IBM Armonk, *(IBM Corp.; 0-933186),* Armonk, NY 10504.
IBMA Pubns, *(Independent Battery Manufacturers Assn.; 0-912254),* 100 Larchwood Dr., Largo, FL 33540 Tel 813-586-1409.
IC&P, *(Issues in Cooperation & Power),* Subs. of Cooperation Corporation, P.O. Box 5039, Berkeley, CA 94705.
Icarus, *(Icarus Press, Inc.; 0-89651),* P.O. Box 1225, South Bend, IN 46624 Tel 219-291-3200.
ICPSR, *(Inter-university Consortium for Political & Social Research; 0-89138),* P.O. Box 1248, Ann Arbor, MI 48106 Tel 313-763-5010.
ICS Bks, *(I C S Books, Inc.; 0-934802),* P.O. Box 8002, Merrillville, IN 46410 Tel 219-769-0585.
ICS Pubns, *(I.C.S. Pubns., Institute of Carmelite Studies; 0-9600876; 0-935316),* 2131 Lincoln Rd., N.E., Washington, DC 20002 Tel 202-832-6622.
Idaho Mus Nat Hist, *(Idaho Museum of Natural History),* Campus Box 8096, Idaho State Univ., Pocatello, ID 83209 Tel 208-236-3168.
Ide Hse, *(Ide House, Inc.; 0-86663),* 4631 Harvey Dr., Mesquite, TX 75149.
Ideals, *(Ideals Publishing Corp.; 0-89542),* 11315 Watertown Plank Rd., Milwaukee, WI 53226 Tel 414-771-2700.
IDHHB, *(Institute for the Development of the Harmonious Human Being Inc.; 0-89556),* P.O. Box 370, Nevada City, CA 95959 Tel 916-878-8505.
IDRC *Imprint of* **Unipub**
IEAS Ctr Chinese Stud, *(Univ. of California, Institute of East Asian Studies, Center for Chinese Studies; 0-912966),* Institute of East Asian Studies, Pubns. Office, Berkeley, CA 94720 Tel 415-642-2816.
IFI Plenum, *(I F I/Plenum Data Corp.; 0-306),* Dist. by: Plenum Publishing Corp., 227 W. 17th St., New York, NY 10011.
Igaku-Shoin, *(Igaku-Shoin Medical Pubs.; 0-89640),* 50 Rockefeller Plaza, New York, NY 10020 Tel 212-765-9581.
Ignatius Pr, *(Ignatius Press; 0-89870),* P.O. Box 18990, San Francisco, CA 94118 Tel 415-387-2324.
IHS-Library & Educ Div
See IHS-PDS
IHS-PDS, *(Information Handling Services/PDS Hard Copy Publishing; 0-910972; 0-89847),* 15 Inverness Way E., P.O. Box 1154, Englewood, CO 80150 Tel 303-779-0600.
IIR *Imprint of* **Unipub**
IISJ, *(Institute for Independent Social Journalism; 0-917654),* 33 W. 17th St., New York, NY 10011 Tel 212-691-0404.
IIWPA, *(International Information/Word Processing Assn.; 0-935220),* 1015 North York Rd., Willow Grove, PA 19090 Tel 215-657-6300.
IJG Inc, *(IJG, Inc.; 0-936200),* 569 N. Mountain Ave., Suite A & B, Upland, CA 91786.
Ill Regional Lib Coun, *(Illinois Regional Library Council; 0-917060),* 425 N. Michigan, Suite 1303, Chicago, IL 60611 Tel 312-828-0928.
Ill St Hist Lib, *(Illinois State Historical Library; 0-912154),* Old State Capitol, Springfield, IL 62706 Tel 217-782-4836.
Ill St Hist Soc, *(Illinois State Historical Society; 0-912226),* Old State Capitol, Springfield, IL 62706 Tel 217-782-4836.
Illum Eng, *(Illuminating Engineering Society; 0-87995),* 345 E. 47th St., New York, NY 10017 Tel 212-644-7923.
Illuminations Pr, *(Illuminations Press),* 1321-L Dwight Way, Berkeley, CA 94710 Tel 415-849-2102.
Illusive Unicorn, *(Illusive Unicorn Pubns.),* P.O. Box 6841, San Jose, CA 95150 Tel 408-279-1520.
Im *Imprint of* **Doubleday**
IMA Ed, *(IMA Education & Research Foundation; 0-918486),* P.O. Box 526, Newtonville, NY 12128 Tel 518-434-3859.
Image Gallery, *(Image Gallery; 0-918362),* 1017 S. W. Morrison St., Rm. 307, Portland, OR 97205 Tel 503-224-9629.
Image West, *(Image West Press; 0-918966),* P.O. Box 5511, Eugene, OR 97405 Tel 503-342-3797.
Images Pr, *(Images Press; 0-9600374),* P.O. Box 9444, Berkeley, CA 94709 Tel 415-843-8834.
Imagesmith, *(Imagesmith; 0-938700),* P.O. Box 1524, Bellevue, WA 98009.
Immediate Pr, *(Immediate Press),* 13 Spring St., Stamford, CT 06901 Tel 203-327-5770.
Imp Pr, *(Imp Press; 0-9603008),* P.O. Box 93, Buffalo, NY 14213 Tel 716-881-5391.
Impact MI, *(Impact Press; 0-938968),* P.O. Box 475, Roseville, MI 48066.
Impact Pub, *(Impact Publishing Co.; 0-9601530),* 1601 Oak Park Blvd., Pleasant Hill, CA 94523.
Impact Pubs Cal, *(Impact Pubs., Inc.; 0-915166),* P.O. Box 1094, San Luis Obispo, CA 93406 Tel 805-543-5911.
Impact Tenn, *(Impact Books; 0-914850; 0-86608),* Div. of the Benson Co., 365 Great Circle Rd., Nashville, TN 37228 Tel 615-259-9111.
Imported Pubns, *(Imported Pubns.; 0-8285),* 320 W. Ohio St., Chicago, IL 60610 Tel 312-787-9017.
Impressions, *(Impressions),* P.O. Box 6191, Harrisburg, PA 17112.
Imprimis, *(Imprimis Press, Ltd),* Manassas, VA 22110.
Incentive Pubns, *(Incentive Pubns., Inc.; 0-913916),* P.O. Box 120189, Nashville, TN 37212 Tel 615-385-2934.
Ind Camp Supply
See ICS Bks
Ind Mus Art, *(Indianapolis Museum of Art; 0-936260),* 1200 W. 38th St., Indianapolis, IN 46208.
Ind Sch Pr, *(Independent School Press; 0-88334),* 51 River St., Wellesley Hills, MA 02181 Tel 617-237-2591.
Ind St Univ, *(Indiana State Univ),* Terre Haute, IN 47809 Tel 812-232-6311.
Ind U Pr, *(Indiana Univ. Press; 0-253),* Tenth & Morton Sts., Bloomington, IN 47405 Tel 812-337-6804.
Ind U Res Inst, *(Indiana Univ. Research Institute for Inner Asian Studies; 0-933070),* Goodbody Hall 101, Bloomington, IN 47405.
Ind-US Inc, *(Ind-US, Inc.),* Box 56, East Glastonbury, CT 06025 Tel 203-633-0045.
Independence Pr, *(Independence Press; 0-8309),* Div. of Herald House, Drawer HH, Independence, MO 64055 Tel 816-252-5010.
Index Co, *(Index Co.; 0-914054),* 319 Elm St., Kalamazoo, MI 49007; Moved, Left No Forwarding Address.
Indian Feather, *(Indian Feather Publishing; 0-937962),* 7218 SW Oak, Portland, OR 97223.
Indigenous Pubns, *(Indigenous Pubns.; 0-930740),* 160 Ribier, Modesto, CA 95350 Tel 209-529-5087.
Indisota Pubs, *(Indisota Publishers; 0-9603420),* 3166 Ridge Court, Placerville, CA 95667.
Individual Learn, *(Individual Learning Systems, Inc.; 0-86589),* P.O. Box 225447, Dallas, TX 75265 Tel 214-630-0313.
Indus Pr, *(Industrial Press Inc.; 0-8311),* 200 Madison Ave., New York, NY 10157 Tel 212-889-6330.

Indus Rel, *(Industrial Relations Counselors, Inc. (IRC); 0-87330),* P.O. Box 1530, New York, NY 10101 Tel 212-541-6086.
Indus Res Serv, *(Industrial Research Service, Inc.),* 90 Washington St., Dover, NH 03820 Tel 603-742-1919.
Indus Res Unit-Wharton, *(Industrial Research Unit-The Wharton School; 0-89546),* Univ. of Pennsylvania, Vance Hall/CS, 3733 Spruce St., Philadelphia, PA 19104 Tel 215-243-5606.
Info Alternative, *(Information Alternative; 0-936288),* Box 657, Woodstock, NY 12498.
Info Clearing House, *(Information Clearing House, Inc.; 0-931634),* 500 Fifth Ave., New York, NY 10110.
Info Coord, *(Information Coordinators, Inc.; 0-911772; 0-89990),* 1435-37 Randolph St., Detroit, MI 48226.
Info Prods, *(Information Products; 0-937978),* 2604 Artesia Blvd., Suite 4, Redondo Beach, CA 90278.
Info Resources, *(Information Resources Press; 0-87815),* Div. of Herner & Co., 1700 N. Moore St., Suite 700, Arlington, VA 22209 Tel 703-558-8270.
Info Retrieval, *(Information Retrieval Inc.; 0-917000),* Subs. of Information Retrieval Ltd., 250 W. 57th St., New York, NY 10022 Tel 703-548-0868.
INFORM, *(INFORM; 0-918780),* 25 Broad St., New York, NY 10004 Tel 212-425-3550.
Inform
See INFORM
Inglewood CA, *(Inglewood Public Library; 0-913578),* 101 W. Manchester Blvd., Inglewood, CA 90301 Tel 213-649-7397; Orders to: Inglewood Finance Dept., P.O. Box 6500, Inglewood, CA 90301.
Inkululeko, *(Inkululeko Pubns.),* Dist. by: Imported Publications, 320 W. Ohio St., Chicago, IL 60610 Tel 312-787-9017.
Inner Circle, *(Inner Circle Publishing Co.; 0-938284),* P.O. Box 1617, Detroit, MI 48231.
Inner Tradit, *(Inner Traditions International, Ltd.; 0-89281),* 377 Park Ave. S., New York, NY 10016 Tel 212-889-8350.
Innova Assoc, *(Innova Associates),* 2006 Franklin St., Suite 205, Huntsville, AL 35801.
Insiders Pub, *(Insiders' Publishing Group; 0-932338),* 349 W. Bute St., Room C-5, Norfolk, VA 23510 Tel 804-627-9925.
Insight Pr CA, *(Insight Press; 0-935218),* 614 Vermont St., San Francisco, CA 94107.
Inst Adv Philo, *(Institute for the Advancement of Philosophy for Children, Division 107; 0-916834),* Montclair State College, Upper Montclair, NJ 07043 Tel 201-893-4277.
Inst Am Music, *(Institute for Studies in American Music; 0-914678),* Dept. of Music, Brooklyn College, Brooklyn, NY 11210 Tel 212-780-5655.
Inst Analysis, *(Institute for the Analysis, Evaluation & Design of Human Action; 0-938526),* 44 Clifford Ave., Pelham, NY 10803.
Inst Contemporary, *(Institute for Contemporary Studies; 0-917616),* 260 California St., Suite 811, San Francisco, CA 94111 Tel 415-398-3010.
Inst Dev Harmonious
See IDHHB
Inst Ecological, *(Institute for Ecological Policies; 0-937786),* 9208 Christopher St., Fairfax, VA 22031.
Inst Econ Finan, *(Institute for Economic & Financial Research; 0-918968),* Dist. by: American Classical College Press, P.O. Box 4526, Albuquerque, NM 87196 Tel 505-843-7749.
Inst Econ Pol, *(Institute for Economic & Political World Strategic Studies; 0-930008),* P.O. Box 4526, Sta. A, Albuquerque, NM 87196 Tel 505-843-7749.
Inst Ed Management, *(Institute for Educational Management; 0-934222),* Harvard University, 337 Gutman Library, Appian Way, Cambridge, MA 02138 Tel 617-495-2655.
Inst Elect Eng, *(Institution of Electrical Engineers; 0-85296),* 445 Hoes Lane, Piscataway, NJ 08854 Tel 201-981-0060.
Inst Electrical, *(Institute of Electrical & Electronics Engineers; 0-87942),* 345 E. 47th St., New York, NY 10017 Tel 212-644-7558; Orders to: IEEE Ctr., 445 Hoes Lane, Piscataway, NJ 08854 Tel 201-981-0060.
Inst Evolutionary, *(Institute for Evolutionary Research; 0-938710),* 200 Park Ave., New York, NY 10166.
Inst Food & Develop, *(Institute for Food & Development Policy; 0-935028),* 2588 Mission St., San Francisco, CA 94110 Tel 415-648-6090.
Inst for Environ Action, *(Institute for Environmental Action; 0-936020),* 81 Leonard St., New York, NY 10013.
Inst for the Arts, *(Institute for the Arts, Rice Univ.; 0-914412),* P.O. Box 1892, Houston, TX 77001 Tel 713-527-4858.
Inst Foreign Policy Anal, *(Institute for Foreign Policy Analysis, Inc.; 0-89549),* 675 Massachusetts Ave., Central Plaza Bldg. 10th Fl., Cambridge, MA 02139 Tel 617-492-2116.
Inst Found Employ
See Intl Found Employ
Inst Gen Semantics, *(Institute of General Semantics; 0-910780),* R.R. 1, P.O. Box 215, Lakeville, CT 06039 Tel 203-435-9174.
Inst Gov Stud Berk, *(Univ. of California Institute of Governmental Studies; 0-87772),* 109 Moses Hall, Berkeley, CA 94720 Tel 415-642-6722.
Inst Hist Rev, *(Institute for Historical Review; 0-911038),* P. O. Box 1306, Torrance, CA 90505.
Inst Humane, *(Institute for Humane Studies, Inc.; 0-89617),* 1177 University Dr., Menlo Park, CA 94025 Tel 415-323-2464; Orders to: P.O. Box 2256, Wichita, KS 67201 Tel 316-832-5604.
Inst Info Stud, *(Institute for Information Studies; 0-935294),* 200 Little Falls St., Suite 104, Falls Church, VA 22046.
Inst Inter Aud, *(Institute of Internal Auditors, Inc.; 0-89413),* 249 Maitland Ave., Altamonte Springs, FL 32701 Tel 305-830-7600.
Inst Intl Educ, *(Institute of International Education; 0-87206),* 809 United Nations Plaza, New York, NY 10017 Tel 212-883-8258.
Inst Jesuit, *(Institute of Jesuit Sources, The; 0-912422),* Fusz Memorial, St. Louis Univ., 3700 W. Pine Blvd., St. Louis, MO 63108 Tel 314-652-5737.
Inst Liv Skills
See Bridges Pr
Inst Mediaeval Mus, *(Institute of Mediaeval Music; 0-912024; 0-931902),* c/o L.A. Dittmer, Paradise Falls, Cresco, PA 18326 Tel 717-629-1278.
Inst Mgmt & Labor, *(Institute of Management & Labor Relations),* Public Education Dept., Ryders Lane, Cook Campus, New Brunswick, NJ 08903.
Inst Mid East & North Africa, *(Institute of Middle Eastern & North African Affairs; 0-934484),* P.O. Box 1764, Hyattsville, MD 20788.
Inst Mod Lang, *(Institute of Modern Languages, Inc.; 0-88499),* 2622 Pittman Dr., Silver Spring, MD 20910 Tel 301-565-2580.
Inst Paper Chem, *(Institute of Paper Chemistry; 0-87010),* P.O. Box 1039, Appleton, WI 54912 Tel 414-734-9251.
Inst Personality & Ability, *(Institute for Personality & Ability Testing, Inc.; 0-918296),* P. O. Box 188, Champaign, IL 61820 Tel 217-352-4739.
Inst Policy Stud, *(Institute for Policy Studies; 0-89758),* 1901 "Q" St., N.W., Washington, DC 20009 Tel 202-234-9382.
Inst Product, *(Institute for Product Safety; 0-938830),* 1410 Duke University Rd., Durham, NC 27701.
Inst Pubs, *(Institute Pubs.; 0-86664),* 7422 Mountioy, Huntington Beach, CA 92648.
Inst Rational-Emotive, *(Institute for Rational-Emotive Therapy; 0-917476),* 45 E. 65th St., New York, NY 10021 Tel 212-535-0822.
Inst Real Estate, *(Institute of Real Estate Management; 0-912104),* 430 N. Michigan Ave., Chicago, IL 60611 Tel 312-440-8683.
Inst Responsive, *(Institute for Responsive Education; 0-917754),* 704 Commonwealth Ave., Boston, MA 02215.
Inst Self Dev, *(Institute for Self Development),* 50 Maple Place, Manhasset, NY 11030 Tel 516-627-0048.
Inst Study Human, *(Institute for the Study of Human Issues (ISHI); 0-89727; 0-915980),* 3401 Market St., Suite 252, Philadelphia, PA 19104 Tel 215-387-9002.
Inst Study Psych
See Inst Rational-Emotive
Instru Soc, *(Instrument Society of America; 0-87664),* P.O. Box 12277, 67 Alexander Dr., Research Triangle Park, NC 27709 Tel 919-549-8411.
Instruct Object, *(Instructional Objectives Exchange; 0-932166),* 11411 W. Jefferson Blvd., Culver City, CA 90230 Tel 213-391-6295.
Instrumental Co, *(Instrumentalist Co.),* 1418 Lake St., Evanston, IL 60204 Tel 312-328-6000.
Integrated Ed Assoc, *(Integrated Education Associates; 0-912008),* Univ. of Massachusetts School of Education, Amherst, MA 01003 Tel 413-545-0327.
Integrity, *(Integrity Press; 0-918048),* 3888 Morse Rd., Columbus, OH 43219 Tel 614-471-2759.
Inter-Am Tropical, *(Inter-American Tropical Tuna Commission; 0-9603078),* P.O. Box 1529, La Jolla, CA 92093.
Inter Am U Pr, *(Inter American Univ. Press; 0-913480),* G.P.O. Box 3255, San Juan, PR 00936 Tel 809-763-9622.
Inter-Crescent, *(Inter-Crescent Publishing Co., Inc.; 0-916400),* P.O. Box 8481, Dallas, TX 75205 Tel 214-341-4792.
Inter-Varsity, *(Inter-Varsity Press; 0-87784; 0-8308),* P.O. Box F, Downers Grove, IL 60515 Tel 312-964-5700.
Interbk Inc, *(Interbook, Inc.; 0-913456; 0-89192),* 13 E. 16th St., New York, NY 10003 Tel 212-924-4263.
Intercont Press, *(Intercontinental Press; 0-933142),* P.O. Box 565, Auburn, AL 36830 Tel 205-887-5297.
Intercontinental Pubns, *(Intercontinental Pubns.; 0-917408),* 25 Sylvan Rd. S., P.O. Box 5017, Westport, CT 06881 Tel 203-226-7463.
Intercult Network
See Intercult Pr
Intercult Pr, *(Intercultural Press, Inc.; 0-933622),* 70 W. Hubbard St., Chicago, IL 60610 Tel 312-321-0075.
InterCulture, *(InterCulture Associates; 0-88253; 0-89253),* Quaddick Rd., P.O. Box 277, Thompson, CT 06277 Tel 203-923-9494.
Intergalactic Pub, *(Intergalactic Publishing Co.; 0-914632),* 2301 Stuart St., Berkeley, CA 94705; Orders to: P.O. Box 5171, Berkeley, CA 94705.
InterMed Comm, *(InterMed Communications, Inc.; 0-916730),* 132 Welsh Rd., Horsham, PA 19044 Tel 215-657-4600.
Intermtn Air, *(Intermountain Air Press; 0-914680),* 171 S. Second E., Preston, ID 83263.
Interpersonal Comm, *(Interpersonal Communication Programs, Inc.; 0-917340),* 1925 Nicollet Ave., Minneapolis, MN 55403 Tel 612-871-7388.
Interstate, *(Interstate; 0-8134),* 19-27 N. Jackson St., Danville, IL 61832 Tel 217-446-0500.
Interurban, *(Interurban Press; 0-916374),* P.O. Box 6444, Glendale, CA 91205 Tel 213-240-9130.
Interurbans
See Interurban
Interweave, *(Interweave Press, Inc.; 0-934026),* 306 N. Washington Ave., Loveland, CO 80537 Tel 303-669-7672.
Intl Arts & Sci
See M E Sharpe
Intl Bk Ctr, *(International Book Centre; 0-917062),* P.O. Box 295, Troy, MI 48099 Tel 313-879-8436.
Intl City Mgr
See Intl City Mgt
Intl City Mgt, *(International City Management Assn.; 0-87326),* 1140 Connecticut Ave., N.W., Washington, DC 20036 Tel 202-828-3600.
Intl Comm Christ, *(International Community of Christ; 0-936202),* Pub. Dept. Chancellery, 643 Ralston St., Reno, NV 89503.

Intl Comm Rad Meas, *(International Commission on Radiation Units & Measurements; 0-913394),* 7910 Woodmont Ave., Suite 1016, Bethesda, DC 20014 Tel 301-657-2652; Orders to: P.O. Box 30165, Washington, DC 20014.
Intl Comm Serv, *(International Commercial Service; 0-935402),* P.O. Box 4082, Irvine, CA 92716 Tel 714-552-8494.
Intl Coun Shop, *(International Council of Shopping Centers; 0-913598),* 665 Fifth Ave., New York, NY 10022 Tel 212-421-8181.
Intl Ctr Environment, *(International Center for Environmental Research; 0-914704),* 141 Emerald Bay, Laguna Beach, CA 92651; P.O. Box 4664, Anaheim, CA 92803.
Intl Develop Res
See Intl Development
Intl Development, *(International Development Institute; 0-89249),* 400 E. 7 St., Bloomington, IN 47401 Tel 812-337-8596.
Intl Dialogue Pr, *(International Dialogue Press; 0-89881; 0-931364),* P.O. Box 924, Davis, CA 95616 Tel 916-758-6500.
Intl Educ Systems, *(International Educational Systems, Inc.),* 5521 W. 110th St., Oak Lawn, IL 60653 Tel 312-423-1717.
Intl Electrical
See Inst Electrical
Intl Exhibit Foun, *(International Exhibitions Foundation; 0-88397),* 1729 "H" St., N.W., Suite 310, Washington, DC 20006 Tel 202-298-7010.
Intl Fire Prot
See Intl Fire Serv
Intl Fire Serv, *(International Fire Service Training Assn.; 0-87939),* Oklahoma State Univ., Stillwater, OK 74078 Tel 405-624-5723.
Intl Found Biosocial Dev, *(International Foundation for Biosocial Development & Human Health; 0-934314),* c/o Lifshutz & Polland, 400 Park Ave., New York, NY 10022.
Intl Found Employ, *(International Foundation of Employee Benefit Plans; 0-89154),* P.O. Box 69, 18700 W. Bluemound Rd., Brookfield, WI 53005 Tel 414-786-6700.
Intl Friend, *(International Friendship; 0-935340),* Waxhaw, NC 28173 Tel 704-843-3168.
Intl Gen Semantics, *(International Society for General Semantics; 0-918970),* P.O. Box 2469, San Francisco, CA 94126 Tel 415-543-1747.
Intl General, *(International General; 0-88477),* P.O. Box 350, New York, NY 10013.
Intl Ideas, *(International Ideas Inc.; 0-89563),* 1627 Spruce St., Philadelphia, PA 19103 Tel 215-546-0392.
Intl Intertrade, *(International Intertrade Index Printing Consultants, Pubs.; 0-910794),* P.O. Box 636, Federal Square, Newark, NJ 07101 Tel 201-623-2864.
Intl Labour Office, *(International Labour Office; 92-2),* Washington Branch, 1750 New York Ave., N.W., Suite 311, Washington, DC 20006.
Intl Learn Syst, *(International Learning Systems, Inc.),* 1715 Connecticut Ave., N.W., Washington, DC 20009 Tel 202-232-4111.
Intl Lib, *(International Library-Book Pubs.; 0-914250),* 2425 Wilson Blvd., Arlington, VA 22201 Tel 703-538-4211.
Intl Marine, *(International Marine Publishing Co.; 0-87742),* 21 Elm St., Camden, ME 04843 Tel 207-236-4342.
Intl Ozone, *(International Ozone Assn.; 0-918650),* c/o Executives Consultants, Inc., 301 Maple Ave., W., Suite 500, Vienna, VA 22180 Tel 703-938-7433.
Intl Program Labs, *(International Program of Laboratories for Population Statistics; 0-89383),* NCNB Plaza, Suite 400, 136 E. Rosemary St., Chapel Hill, NC 27514 Tel 919-966-1131.
Intl Psych Pr, *(International Psychological Press, Inc.; 0-915662),* 1850 Hanover Dr., No. 69, Davis, CA 95616 Tel 916-758-0685.
Intl Pub Co, *(International Pubs. Co.; 0-7178),* 381 Park Ave., S., Suite 1301, New York, NY 10016 Tel 212-685-2864.
Intl Pubns Serv, *(International Pubns. Service; 0-8002),* 114 E. 32nd St., New York, NY 10016 Tel 212-685-9351.
Intl Reading, *(International Reading Assn.; 0-87207),* 800 Barksdale Rd., Box 8139, Newark, DE 19711 Tel 302-731-1600.
Intl Res Eval, *(International Research & Evaluation; 0-930318),* Research Pubns. Div., 21098 IRE Control Ctr., Eagan, MN 55121 Tel 612-888-9635.
Intl Research Serv, *(International Research Service, Inc.; 0-934366),* P.O. Box 225, Blue Bell, PA 19422.
Intl Review, *(International Review Service; 0-87138),* 15 Washington Place, New York, NY 10003 Tel 212-751-0833; UN Bureau: Rm. 301, United Nations, New York, NY 10017.
Intl Schl Psych, *(International School of Psychology; 0-917668),* 92 S. Dawson Ave., Columbus, OH 43209.
Intl Schol Bk Serv, *(International Scholarly Book Services, Inc. (ISBS, Inc.); 0-89955),* P.O. Box 555, Forest Grove, OR 97116 Tel 503-357-7192.
Intl Sci Tech, *(International Science & Technology Institute, Inc.; 0-936130),* 2033 M St. N.W., Suite 300, Washington, DC 20036 Tel 202-466-7290.
Intl Univs Pr, *(International Universities Press, Inc.; 0-8236),* 315 Fifth Ave., New York, NY 10016 Tel 212-684-7900.
Intl Wealth, *(International Wealth Success, Inc.; 0-914306),* 24 Canterbury Rd., Rockville Center, NY 11570 Tel 516-766-5850.
Intl Word Process
See IIWPA
IntlDept *Imprint of* **Har-Row**
Intraworld Trade, *(Intraworld Trade News; 0-9605190),* 1500 N.W. 103rd Lane, Coral Springs, FL 33065.
Invest Eval, *(Investment Evaluations Corp.; 0-9603282),* 2000 Goldenvue Dr., Golden, CO 80401 Tel 303-278-3464.
Investor Pubns, *(Investor Pubns., Inc.; 0-914230),* 219 Parkade, Cedar Falls, IA 50613 Tel 319-277-6341; 2930 Huntington Dr., Arlington Heights, IL 60004 Tel 312-577-2525.
Investrek, *(Investrek Publishing; 0-9604914),* 1025 Sea Breeze Dr., Costa Mesa, CA 92627.
IO Pubns
See North Atlantic
Iota Pr, *(Iota Press; 0-936412),* 2749 Mt. Hope Rd., Okemos, MI 48864.
Iowa St U Pr, *(Iowa State Univ. Press; 0-8138),* 2121 S. State Ave., Ames, IA 50010 Tel 515-294-5280.
IPIC
See Inter-Crescent
Iqra, *(Iqra, Inc.; 0-935290),* P.O. Box 12511, San Antonio, TX 78212 Tel 512-734-7552.
Irego, *(Irego; 0-911732),* P.O. Box 286, Lenox Hill Sta., 221 E. 70th St., New York, NY 10021.
Irish Bk Ctr, *(Irish Book Center),* 245 W. 104th St., New York, NY 10025 Tel 212-866-0309.
Irish Bks Media, *(Irish Books & Media; 0-937702),* 683 Osceola Ave., St. Paul, MN 55105.
Irvington, *(Irvington Pubs.; 0-89197; 0-8290),* 551 Fifth Ave., New York, NY 10176 Tel 212-697-8100.
Irwin, *(Irwin, Richard D., Inc.; 0-256),* 1818 Ridge Rd., Homewood, IL 60430 Tel 312-798-6000.
ISI Pr, *(ISI Press; 0-89495),* Div. of Institute for Scientific Information, 3501 Market St., University City Science Ctr., Philadelphia, PA 19104 Tel 215-386-0100.
Island CA, *(Island Press; 0-933280),* Div. of Round Valley Agrarian Institute, Star Route 1, Box 38, Covelo, CA 95428.
Island Her, *(Island Heritage Ltd.; 0-89610),* 104 Ward Plaza at 210 Ward Ave., Honolulu, HI 96814 Tel 808-526-1126.
Island Pr, *(Island Press; 0-87208),* 175 Bahia Via, Fort Myers Beach, FL 33931 Tel 813-463-9482.
Island Writers, *(Island Writers Publishing Co.; 0-9604798),* Box 25382, Honolulu, HI 96825 Tel 808-395-2615.
ITA
See Pitman Learning
IUCN *Imprint of* **Unipub**
Ivy Hill, *(Ivy Hill Press; 0-9601542),* 8817 Greenview Place, Spring Valley, CA 92077.
Ivystone, *(Ivystone Pubns.; 0-935604),* Box 23, Ada, MI 49301.
J A Allen, *(Allen, J. A., & Co. Ltd.; 0-85131),* Dist. by: Sporting Book Center, Inc., Canaan, NY 12029 Tel 518-794-8998.
J A Lohmann, *(Lohmann, Jeanne A.),* 722 Tenth Ave., San Francisco, CA 94118 Tel 415-387-7644.
J Alden, *(Alden, Jay, Pubs.; 0-914844),* P.O. Box 1295, 546 S. Hofgaarden St., La Puente, CA 91749 Tel 213-968-6424.
J & J Dist, *(J. & J. Distributors),* P.O. Box 247, Raymondville, TX 78580 Tel 512-689-2523.
J & L Lee, *(Lee, J. & L., Co.; 0-934904),* P.O. Box 5575, Lincoln, NE 68505.
J Arvidson, *(Arvidson, J., Press; 0-9602098),* P.O. Box 4022, Helena, MT 59601 Tel 406-442-0354.
J-B Pubs, *(J-B Publishing Co.; 0-916170),* 430 Ivy Ave., Crete, NE 68333 Tel 402-826-3356.
J Barton
See J&M Barton
J Calvin Keene, *(Keene, J. Calvin; 0-9603084),* 134 Verna Rd., Lewisburg, PA 17837.
J Custis
See D Brown Bks
J De Graff
See De Graff
J Domjan
See Domjan Studio
J Donaghey, *(Donaghey, John, Pubns.; 0-9604298),* P.O. Box 402021, Garland, TX 75040.
J F Bergin, *(Bergin, J. F., Pubs., Inc.; 0-89789),* One Hansen Place, Brooklyn, NY 11243 Tel 212-638-0729; 65 S. Oxford St., Brooklyn, NY 11217 Tel 212-237-9221.
J F Wine, *(Wine, J. F.),* 924 Woodland Ave., Winchester, VA 22601 Tel 703-662-5735.
J Freedman Liturgy, *(Freedman, Jacob, Liturgy Research Foundation),* P.O. Box 317 Forest Park Sta., Springfield, MA 01108.
J H Roush, *(Roush, John H., Jr.; 0-9600830),* 27 Terrace Ave., Kentfield, CA 94904 Tel 415-453-7130.
J J Johnson
See Carver Pub
J K Burgess, *(Burgess, Jack K., Inc.),* 44 Engle St., Englewood, NJ 07631 Tel 201-569-7477.
J L Barbour, *(Barbour, James L.),* P.O. Box 326, Port Tobacco, MD 20677.
J Larsen, *(Larsen, J., Publishing; 0-9602474),* P.O. Box 586, Deer Lodge, MT 59722 Tel 406-846-2610.
J M Bryant, *(Bryant, James M.),* P.O. Box 412, Normangee, TX 77871 Tel 713-828-4265.
J M Friedman, *(Friedman, James Michael; 0-9604232),* 2545 Pomeroy Court, S. San Francisco, CA 94080.
J N Summers, *(Summers, June Nay),* P.O. Box 334, Tecate, CA 92080.
J Norton Pubs, *(Norton, Jeffrey, Pubs., Inc.; 0-88432),* 145 E. 49th St., New York, NY 10017 Tel 212-753-1783.
J P Getty Mus, *(Getty, J. Paul, Museum; 0-89236),* 17985 Pacific Coast Hwy., Malibu, CA 90265 Tel 213-459-2306.
J P Tarcher, *(Tarcher, J. P., Inc.; 0-87477),* 9110 Sunset Blvd., Suite 250, Los Angeles, CA 90069 Tel 213-273-3274; Dist. by: Houghton Mifflin Co., Wayside Rd., Burlington, MA 01803 Tel 800-225-3362.
J Palmer, *(Palmer, J., Pub.),* P.O. Box 498, 86 Friend St., Amesbury, MA 01913 Tel 617-388-1337.
J R Weckstein, *(Weckstein, Joyce R.; 0-9600980),* 28290 Tavistock Trail, Southfield, MI 48034 Tel 313-353-6221.
J Simon, *(Simon, Joseph; 0-934710),* Box 4071, Malibu, CA 90265 Tel 213-457-3293.
J T White, *(White, James T., & Co.; 0-88371),* 1700 State Hwy. 3, Clifton, NJ 07013 Tel 201-773-9300.
J V Willis, *(Willis, J. V., Pubs.; 0-913732),* 825 May St., Hammond, IN 46320 Tel 219-931-2672.
J W Bell, *(Bell, James W., Publisher; 0-939130),* 7611 Briarwood Dr., Little Rock, AR 72205; Dist. by: Publishers Distribution Service, 7509 Cantrell Rd., Little Rock, AR 72207.
J W Linn, *(Linn, Jo White; 0-918470),* Box 1948, Salisbury, NC 28144 Tel 704-633-3575.
J W Van De Water
See Jonsalvania
J Wampler, *(Wampler, Joseph Carson; 0-935080),* Box 45, Berkeley, CA 94701.
J Willert, *(Willert, James; 0-930798),* 12804 S. Graff Dr., La Mirada, CA 90638.
J Young, *(Young, Joy),* 78 Peterboro, Detroit, MI 48201.

Jacada Pubns, *(Jacada Pubns.; 0-915700),* Northway Square Bldg. 2150 N. 10th St., Suite 350, Seattle, WA 98133 Tel 206-362-3001.
Jackpine Pr, *(Jackpine Press; 0-917492),* 1878 Meadowbrook Dr., Winston-Salem, NC 27104 Tel 919-725-8828.
Jackson St Hse
See Rainy Day Oreg
Jacobs, *(Jacobs Publishing Co.; 0-918272),* 4747 N. 16th St., Suite B-132, Phoenix, AZ 85016 Tel 602-277-3203.
Jacobs Enter
See J & J Dist
Jai Pr, *(Jai Press, Inc.; 0-89232),* Div. of Johnson Associates, Inc., 165 W. Putnam Ave., Greenwich, CT 06830 Tel 203-661-7602.
Jaks Pub Co, *(Jaks Publishing Co.; 0-935674),* 1106 N. Washington St., P.O. Box 5625, Helena, MT 59601.
Jalamap, *(Jalamap Pubns., Inc.; 0-934750),* 833 Scenic Dr., Charleston, WV 25311.
Jalapeno Pr, *(Jalapeno Press; 0-935342),* Rte. 2, Box 600, Bandon, OR 97411.
Jalmar Pr, *(Jalmar Press, Inc.; 0-915190),* 6501 Elvas Ave., Sacramento, CA 95819 Tel 916-451-2897.
Jama Bks, *(Jama Books; 0-934130),* P.O. Box 30751, Santa Barbara, CA 93105; Dist. by: LaMere Distributors, 1120 Beach St., Flint, MI 48502.
Jamestown Pubs, *(Jamestown Pubs., Inc.; 0-89061),* P.O. Box 6743, Providence, RI 02940 Tel 401-351-1915.
J&M Barton, *(Barton, John & Margaret; 0-937216),* 6157 Coleman Creek Rd., Medford, OR 97501 Tel 503-535-1244.
J&W Tex-Mex, *(J&W Tex-Mex; 0-9604842),* P.O. Box 983, Arlington, VA 22216.
Janevar Pub, *(Janevar Publishing Co.; 0-937174),* R. R. 11, Box 129, Muncie, IN 47302 Tel 317-289-3137.
Janus Bks, *(Janus Book Pubs.; 0-915510),* 2501 Industrial Pkwy. W., Hayward, CA 94545 Tel 415-887-7070.
Janus Pr, *(Janus Press; 0-916172),* P.O. Box 578, Rogue River, OR 97537 Tel 503-582-1520.
Japan Pubns, *(Japan Pubns. Inc.; 0-87040),* C/O Kodansha International, Inc., 10 E. 53rd St., New York, NY 10022 Tel 212-593-7050; Dist. by: Harper & Row Pubs., Inc., Keystone Industrial Park, Scranton, PA 18512.
Jargon Soc, *(Jargon Society, Inc., The; 0-912330),* Dist. by: Gnomon Distribution, P.O. Box 106, Frankfort, KY 40602 Tel 502-223-1858.
Jawbone Pr, *(Jawbone Press; 0-918116),* 17023 5th Ave., N.E., Seattle, WA 98155 Tel 206-363-1547.
Jazz Pr, *(Jazz Press; 0-937310),* 3650 W. Pico, Los Angeles, CA 90019.
JCP Corp VA, *(J.C.P. Corp. of Virginia; 0-938694),* P.O. Box 814, Virginia Beach, VA 23451.
JD-J *Imprint of* **John Day**
Jeannes Dreams, *(Jeanne's Dreams),* P.O. Box 211, La Farge, WI 54639 Tel 608-625-2425.
Jedick Ent, *(Jedick, Peter, Enterprises; 0-9605568),* 3637 W. 47th St., Cleveland, OH 44102.
Jefferson Pubns, *(Jefferson Pubns., Inc.),* Monticello Books Div., 44 S. Old Rand Rd., Box 19, Lake Zurich, IL 60047 Tel 312-438-4114.
Jelm Mtn, *(Jelm Mountain Pubns.),* 209 Grand Ave., Suite 205, Laramie, WY 82070.
Jemta Pr, *(Jemta Press),* 11313 Beech Daly, Redford Township, MI 48239 Tel 313-937-1986.
Jenfred Pr, *(Jenfred Press),* P.O. Box 767, Trinidad, CA 95570.
Jenkins, *(Jenkins Publishing Co.; 0-8363),* P.O. Box 2085, Austin, TX 78767 Tel 512-444-6616.
Jeppesen Sanderson, *(Jeppesen Sanderson; 0-88487),* Affiliate of Times Mirror Co., 55 Inverness Drive E., Englewood, CO 80112 Tel 303-779-5757.
Jepson Herbarium, *(Jepson Herbarium; 0-935628),* Botany Dept., Univ. of California, Berkeley, Berkeley, CA 94720 Tel 415-642-2465; Dist. by: Lubrecht & Cramer, RFD 1, Box 227, Monticello, NY 12701 Tel 914-794-8539.
Jesuit Bks, *(Jesuit Books; 0-913452),* Seattle University, Seattle, WA 98122 Tel 206-775-7545.
Jesuit Hist, *(Jesuit Historical Institute),* c/o Loyola Univ. Press, 3441 N. Ashland Ave., Chicago, IL 60657.
Jesus-First, *(Jesus-First Pubs., Inc.; 0-9602440),* 1116-4th St., N.W, Ruskin, FL 33570 Tel 813-645-5726.
Jet'iquette, *(Jet'iquette; 0-9600786),* 510 Michigan Ave., Charlevoix, MI 49720 Tel 616-547-6443.
Jewelers Circular, *(Jewelers' Circular-Keystone; 0-931744),* Chilton Way, Radnor, PA 19089 Tel 215-687-8200.
Jewish Bd Family, *(Jewish Board of Family & Children's Services, Inc.),* 120 W. 57th St., New York, NY 10019 Tel 212-582-9100.
Jewish Pubn, *(Jewish Publication Society of America; 0-8276),* 117 S. 17th St., Philadelphia, PA 19103 Tel 215-564-5925.
JH Pr, *(JH Press; 0-935672),* P.O. Box 294, Village Sta., New York, NY 10014.
Jifunza Educ, *(Jifunza Educational Pubns.; 0-931310),* 641 Dory Lane, Redwood City, CA 94065.
JJ Pub FL, *(JJ Publishing; 0-9604610),* 1312 Arthur St., Hollywood, FL 33019 Tel 305-929-3559.
JLJ Pubs, *(JLJ Pubs.; 0-937172),* 824 Shrine Rd., Springfield, OH 45504.
Joby Bks, *(Joby Books),* Box 2603, San Rafael, CA 94901; Dist. by: Bookpeople, 2940 Seventh St., Berkeley, CA 94710 Tel 415-549-3033.
Jochum, *(Jochum, Helen Parker),* 79 Huntington Rd., Garden City, NY 11530; Dist. by: Skills, 24 S. Prospect St., Amherst, MA 01002 Tel 413-253-9500.
Johannes, *(Johannes Press; 0-910810),* c/o Galerie St. Etienne, 24 W. 57th St., New York, NY 10019 Tel 212-245-6734.
Johannes Schwalm Hist, *(Johannes Schwalm Historical Assn., Inc.),* 4983 S. Sedgewick Rd., Lyndhurst, OH 44124.
John Day, *(John Day Co., Inc.; 0-381),* C/O Harper & Row Pubs., 10 E. 53rd St., New York, NY 10022; Dist. by: Harper & Row Pubs., Keystone Industrial Park, Scranton, PA 18512. *Imprints:* JD-J (John Day Juvenile Books).
John Jay Pr, *(John Jay Press; 0-89444),* 444 W. 56th St., New York, NY 10019 Tel 212-489-3515.
John Knox, *(John Knox Press; 0-8042),* 341 Ponce De Leon Ave., N.E., Rm. 416, Atlanta, GA 30365 Tel 404-873-1531.
John Muir, *(Muir, John, Pubns.; 0-912528),* P.O. Box 613, Santa Fe, NM 87501 Tel 505-982-4078; Dist. by: Bookpeople, 2940 Seventh St., Berkeley, CA 94710.
Johnny Inc
See K Diehl
Johnny Reads, *(Johnny Reads, Inc.; 0-910812),* P.O. Box 12834, St. Petersburg, FL 33733 Tel 813-867-7647.
Johns Hopkins, *(Johns Hopkins Univ. Press; 0-8018),* Baltimore, MD 21218 Tel 301-338-7861.
Johnson Colo, *(Johnson Publishing Co.; 0-933472),* P.O. Box 990, 1880 S. 57th Court, Boulder, CO 80301 Tel 303-443-1576.
Johnson NC, *(Johnson Publishing Co.; 0-930230),* P. O. Box 217, Murfreesboro, NC 27855.
Johnson Repr, *(Johnson Reprint Corp.; 0-384),* Subs. of Harcourt, Brace & Jovanovich, Inc., 111 Fifth Ave., New York, NY 10003 Tel 212-741-6800.
Johnson VA, *(Johnson Publishing Co., Inc.; 0-934572),* P.O. Box 192, Forest, VA 24551 Tel 804-525-4129.
Joint Comm Hosp, *(Joint Commission on Accreditation of Hospitals),* Dept. of Pubns., 875 N. Michigan Ave., Chicago, IL 60611 Tel 312-642-6061.
Jonathan David, *(Jonathan David Pubs., Inc.; 0-8246),* 68-22 Eliot Ave., Middle Village, NY 11379 Tel 212-456-8611.
Jonathan Pubns, *(Jonathan Pubns.; 0-9603348),* 660 Prospect Ave., Hartford, CT 06105.
Jones Med, *(Jones Medical Pubns.; 0-930010),* 355 Los Cerros Dr., Greenbrae, CA 94904 Tel 415-461-3749.
Jonsalvania, *(Jonsalvania Publishing Co.),* Russell Rd., Canton, NY 13617 Tel 315-386-4007.
Jordan & Co, *(Jordan & Co., Pubs., Inc.; 0-918908),* 1213 Laskin Rd. Suite 205, Virginia Beach, VA 23451 Tel 804-422-5426.
Joseph Nichols, *(Joseph Nichols Publisher; 0-912484),* P.O. Box 2394, Tulsa, OK 74101 Tel 918-583-3390.
Joseph Pub Co, *(Joseph Publishing Co.; 0-915878),* P.O. Box 770, San Mateo, CA 94401 Tel 415-345-4100.
Jossey-Bass, *(Jossey-Bass Inc., Pubs.; 0-87589),* 433 California St., San Francisco, CA 94104 Tel 415-433-1740.
Journal Herald, *(Journal Herald, The; 0-938492),* 37 S. Ludlow St., Dayton, OH 45342.
Journey Pr, *(Journey Press; 0-918572),* 1828 Virginia St., Berkeley, CA 94703 Tel 415-848-0311.
Journey Pubns, *(Journey Pubns.; 0-918038),* P.O. Box 423, Woodstock, NY 12498 Tel 914-679-2250.
Jove Pubns, *(Jove Pubns., Inc.; 0-515),* Div. of Berkley/Jove Publishing Group, 200 Madison Ave., New York, NY 10016 Tel 212-686-9820.
Joybug, *(Joybug Teaching Aids, Inc.; 0-931218),* P.O. Box 733, Parsons, KS 67357 Tel 316-421-0634.
Joyce Media, *(Joyce Media Inc.; 0-917002),* 8753 Shirley Ave., P.O. Box 458, Northridge, CA 91328 Tel 213-885-7181; Orders to: Sign Language Store, 8753 Shirley Ave., P.O. Box 458, Northridge, CA 91328 Tel 800-423-5413.
Joyce Motion Pict
See Joyce Media
Joyful Noise, *(Joyful Noise Productions, International; 0-936874),* 109 Minna St., Suite 153, San Francisco, CA 94105.
JP Pubns WI, *(JP Pubns.; 0-9602978),* P.O. Box 41731, Madison, WI 53711 Tel 608-231-2373.
Jr League Columbus, *(Junior League of Columbus. GA., Inc.),* 1440 Second Ave., Columbus, GA 31901.
Jr League Montclair-Newark, *(Junior League of Montclair-Newark, Inc.; 0-9605328),* Church St. & Trinity Place, Montclair, NJ 07042.
Jr League New Orleans, *(Junior League of New Orleans, Inc.; 0-9604774),* 4319 Carondelet, New Orleans, LA 70115.
Jr League Rochester, *(Junior League of Rochester, Inc.; 0-9605612),* 33 S. Washington St., Rochester, NY 14608.
Jr League Shreveport, *(Junior League of Shreveport, Inc.; 0-9602246),* P.O. Box 4648, Shreveport, LA 71104 Tel 318-868-7866.
Jr League Tulsa, *(Junior League of Tulsa Pubns.),* 167 London Square, Tulsa, OK 74105 Tel 918-743-9767.
Judaica Pr, *(Judaica Press, Inc.; 0-910818),* 521 Fifth Ave., New York, NY 10017 Tel 212-260-0520.
Judson, *(Judson Press; 0-8170),* Valley Forge, PA 19481 Tel 215-768-2111.
Jungle Garden, *(Jungle Garden Press),* 47 Oak Rd., Fairfax, CA 94930 Tel 415-456-4884.
Juniper *Imprint of* **Fawcett**
Juniper Pr WI, *(Juniper Press; 0-910822),* 1310 Shorewood Dr., La Crosse, WI 54601 Tel 608-788-0096.
Junius Inc, *(Junius, Inc.; 0-9603932),* 842 Lombard St., Philadelphia, PA 19147 Tel 215-627-8298.
Jupiter Pr, *(Jupiter Press; 0-933104),* P.O. Box 101, Lake Bluff, IL 60044 Tel 312-234-3997.
Justice Pr, *(Justice Press, Inc.; 0-936802),* P.O. Box 16204, Tampa, FL 33617.
Juvenescent, *(Juvenescent Research Corp.; 0-9600148),* 807 Riverside Dr., New York, NY 10032 Tel 212-795-8765.
K & K Pubs, *(K & K Pubs; 0-9604218),* 216 N. Batavia Ave., Batavia, IL 60510 Tel 312-879-6214.
K C Pubns
See KC Pubns
K Diehl, *(Diehl, Kathryn; 0-9603552),* 554 N. McDonel, Lima, OH 45801 Tel 419-223-7207.
K G Saur, *(Saur, K. G., Publishing, Inc.; 0-89664),* 45 N. Broad St., Ridgewood, NJ 07450 Tel 201-652-6360.
K Roberts, *(Roberts, Ken, Publishing Co.; 0-913602),* P.O. Box 151, Fitzwilliam, NH 03447 Tel 603-585-6612.

KaChunk Pr, *(KaChunk Press; 0-9604292),* Box 1043, Iowa City, IA 52244.

Kagg Pr, *(Kagg Press; 0-912200),* 9910 Columbus Circle, Nw, Albuquerque, NM 87114 Tel 505-898-4541.

Kalimat, *(Kalimat Press; 0-933770),* 10889 Wilshire Blvd., Suite 270, Los Angeles, CA 90024 Tel 213-478-0559.

Kalmbach, *(Kalmbach Publishing Co.; 0-89024),* 1027 N. Seventh St., Milwaukee, WI 53233 Tel 414-272-2060.

Kalum Pr, *(Kalum Press; 0-937788),* 596 Joey Ave., El Cajon, CA 92020.

Kanchenjunga Pr, *(Kanchenjunga Press; 0-913600),* 22 Rio Vista Lane, Red Bluff, CA 96080.

Kansas St Hist, *(Kansas State Historical Society; 0-87726),* Memorial Bldg., 120 W. 10th St., Topeka, KS 66612 Tel 913-296-3251.

Kar Ben, *(Kar-Ben Copies, Inc.; 0-930494),* 11216 Empire Lane, Rockville, MD 20852 Tel 301-984-8733.

Karoma, *(Karoma Pubs., Inc.; 0-89720),* 3400 Daleview Dr., Ann Arbor, MI 48103 Tel 313-665-3331.

Karz Howard
See Karz Pub

Karz Pub, *(Karz Pubs.; 0-918294),* 320 W. 105th St., New York, NY 10025 Tel 212-663-9059.

Kavanagh, *(Kavanagh, Peter, Hand Press; 0-914612),* 250 E. 30th St., New York, NY 10016 Tel 212-686-5099.

Kayak, *(Kayak; 0-87711),* 325 Ocean View Ave., Santa Cruz, CA 95062.

Kazi Pubns, *(Kazi Pubns.; 0-935782),* 1520 N. Wells St., Chicago, IL 60610 Tel 312-642-1291.

KC Pubns, *(KC Pubns.; 0-916122),* P.O. Box 14883, 2901 Industrial Rd., Las Vegas, NV 89114 Tel 702-731-3123.

Keats, *(Keats Publishing, Inc.; 0-87983),* 36 Grove St., P.O. Box 876, New Canaan, CT 06840 Tel 203-966-8721.

Keeble Pr, *(Keeble Press, The; 0-933144),* 3634 Winchell Rd., Shaker Heights, OH 44122.

Keithwood, *(Keithwood Publishing Co.),* 6835 Greenway Ave., Philadelphia, PA 19142 Tel 215-727-0883.

KEL Pubns, *(KEL Pubns.; 0-9605710),* 443 Schley Rd., Annapolis, MD 21401.

Kelley, *(Kelley, Augustus M., Pubs.; 0-678),* 1140 Broadway, Room 901, New York, NY 10001 Tel 212-685-7202; Orders to: 300 Fairfield Rd., P.O. Box 1308, Fairfield, NJ 07006 Tel 201-575-7338. *Imprints:* Baker Library (Baker Library).

Kelly, *(Kelly, Thomas; 0-910832),* 227 Midland Ave., East Orange, NJ 07017 Tel 201-672-9238.

Kelsey St Pr, *(Kelsey St. Press; 0-932716),* P.O. Box 9235, Berkeley, CA 94709 Tel 415-841-2044.

Kelso, *(Kelso Manufacturing Co.),* 651 N. Broadway, Greenville, MS 38701.

Kemsley Pub
See Foot Trails

Kenan Pr *Imprint of* **S&S**

Kendall-Hunt, *(Kendall/Hunt Publishing Co.; 0-8403),* 2460 Kerper Blvd., Dubuque, IA 52001 Tel 319-588-1451.

Kenilworth, *(Kenilworth Press; 0-9603876),* 421 W. Grant Ave., Eau Claire, WI 54701 Tel 715-832-2161.

Kennedy Pub, *(Kennedy Publishing; 0-9605088),* P.O. Box 2, Chatsworth, CA 91311 Tel 213-883-7939.

Kennikat, *(Kennikat Press, Corp.; 0-8046),* 90 S. Bayles Ave., Port Washington, NY 11050 Tel 516-883-0570.

Kent Popular, *(Kent Popular Press; 0-933522),* P.O. Box 715, Kent, OH 44240.

Kent Pub Co, *(Kent Publishing Co.; 0-534),* Div. of Wadsworth, Inc., 20 Providence St., Boston, MA 02116 Tel 617-542-1629; Orders to: 10 Davis Dr., Belmont, CA 94002 Tel 415-595-2350.

Kent Pubns, *(Kent Pubns.; 0-917458),* 18301 Halstead St., Northridge, CA 91325 Tel 213-349-5088.

Kent St U Pr, *(Kent State Univ. Press; 0-87338),* Kent, OH 44242 Tel 216-672-7913.

Kentucky Hist, *(Kentucky Historical Society; 0-916968),* Old-State-House, Box H, Frankfort, KY 40602 Tel 502-564-3016.

Kenyon, *(Kenyon Pubns.; 0-934286),* 361 Pin Oak Lane, Westbury, NY 11590 Tel 516-333-3236; Dist. by: G. Schirmer, Inc., 866 Third Ave., New York, NY 10022 Tel 212-935-5636.

Kephart Comm Inc
See Alexandria Hse

Kepley, *(Kepley, Ray R.; 0-9604248),* Rt. 2 Box 128A, Ulysses, KS 67880.

Keramos Bks, *(Keramos Books; 0-935066),* Subs. of Westwood Ceramic Supply Co., P.O. Box 2305, Bassett, CA 91746 Tel 213-330-0631; 14400 Lomitas Ave., City of Industry, CA 91746.

Kerr Assoc, *(Kerr Associates, Inc.; 0-937890),* 1942 Irving Ave., S., Minneapolis, MN 55403 Tel 612-374-5438.

Kesend Pub Co
See Kesend Pub Ltd

Kesend Pub Ltd, *(Kesend, Michael, Publishing, Ltd.; 0-935576),* 1025 Fifth Ave., New York, NY 10028 Tel 212-249-5150.

Kesher, *(Kesher Press; 0-9602394),* 1817 21 Ave. S., Nashville, TN 37212.

Key Curr Proj, *(Key Curriculum Project; 0-913684),* P.O. Box 2304, Berkeley, CA 94702 Tel 415-548-2304.

Keystone Pubns, *(Keystone Pubns., Inc.; 0-912126),* 1657 Broadway, 2nd Fl., New York, NY 10019 Tel 212-582-2254.

Khaniqahi-Nimatullahi, *(Khaniqahi Nimatullahi Pubns.; 0-933546),* 306 W. 11th St., New York, NY 10014 Tel 212-924-7739.

Kickapoo, *(Kickapoo Press; 0-933180),* P.O. Box 1443, Peoria, IL 61655.

Kindinger, *(Kindinger, Michael),* 931 W. 3rd Ave., Columbus, OH 43216 Tel 614-294-3227.

Kings Farspan, *(King's Farspan, Inc.; 0-932814),* 1473 S. La Luna Ave., Ojai, CA 93023 Tel 805-646-2928.

Kings Pr
See Kings Farspan

Kingsfield, *(Kingsfield Publishing Co.; 0-938494),* 10405 Town & Country Way, Suite 100, Houston, TX 77024.

Kirk Pr, *(Kirk Press),* 1811 Hammond Ave., Superior, WI 54880.

Kitchen Harvest, *(Kitchen Harvest Press; 0-917234),* 3N 681 Bittersweet Dr., St. Charles, IL 60174 Tel 312-584-4084.

Kjos, *(Kjos, Neil A., Music Co.; 0-910842; 0-8497),* 4382 Jutland Dr., San Diego, CA 92117 Tel 714-270-9800.

Klassen, *(Klassen, Beatrice C. Harris),* P.O. Box 794, La Conner, WA 98257.

Kleinsinger, *(Kleinsinger, Irene J.; 0-9605146),* 16 Holbrooke Rd., White Plains, NY 10605.

Kline, *(Kline, Charles H., & Co., Inc.; 0-917148),* 330 Passaic Ave., Dept. 39, Fairfield, NJ 07006 Tel 201-227-6262.

Klock & Klock, *(Klock & Klock Christian Pubs.; 0-86524),* 2527 Girard Ave. N., Minneapolis, MN 55411 Tel 612-522-2244.

Klutz Enterprises
See Klutz Pr

Klutz Pr, *(Klutz Press; 0-932592),* P.O. Box 2992, Stanford, CA 94305 Tel 415-857-0888.

Kluwer Boston, *(Kluwer Boston, Inc.),* 160 Old Derby St., Hingham, MA 02043 Tel 617-749-5262.

KMG Pubns OR, *(KMG Pubns.; 0-938928),* 195 Cambridge St., Ashland, OR 97520.

KMS Pr CO, *(KMS Press),* P.O. Box 6516, Denver, CO 80206.

Knapp
See EDITS Pubs

Knapp Pr, *(Knapp Press, The; 0-89535),* Div. of Knapp Communications Corp., 5900 Wilshire Blvd., Los Angeles, CA 90036 Tel 213-937-3454.

Knauff, *(Knauff, Thomas),* Julian, PA 16844.

Knollwood Pub, *(Knollwood Publishing Co.; 0-915614),* P.O. Box 735, 513 Benson Ave. E., Willmar, MN 56201 Tel 612-235-4950.

Knopf, *(Knopf, Alfred A., Inc.; 0-394),* Subs. of Random House, Inc., 201 E. 50th St., New York, NY 10022 Tel 212-757-2600; Orders to: 400 Hahn Rd., Westminster, MD 21157.

Know Inc, *(Know, Inc.; 0-912786),* P.O. Box 86031, Pittsburgh, PA 15221 Tel 412-241-2844.

Knowledge Bank, *(Knowledge Bank Pubs., Inc.),* P.O. Box 2364, Falls Church, VA 22042.

Knowledge Indus, *(Knowledge Industry Pubns.; 0-914236),* 2 Corporate Park Dr., White Plains, NY 10604 Tel 914-694-8686. *Imprints:* ASIS (American Society for Information Science).

Knowles, *(Knowles, Alison; 0-914162),* 122 Spring St., New York, NY 10012.

Kobro Pubns, *(Kobro Pubns., Inc.; 0-9604676),* 192 Lexington Ave., New York, NY 10016.

Kodansha, *(Kodansha International, Ltd.; 0-87011),* 10 E. 53rd St., New York, NY 10022; Dist. by: Harper & Row Pubs., Inc., Keystone Industrial Park, Scranton, PA 18512.

Konglomerati, *(Konglomerati Florida Foundation for Literature & the Book Arts, Inc.; 0-916906),* P.O. Box 5001, Gulfport, FL 33737 Tel 813-323-0386.

Korakas-Roberts-Kirby, *(Korakas, Roberts & Kirby),* 600 N.W. 46th St., Oklahoma City, OK 73118.

Korea Devel Inst *Imprint of* **U Pr of Hawaii**

Kosciuszko, *(Kosciuszko Foundation, Inc.; 0-917004),* 15 E. 65th St., New York, NY 10021 Tel 212-734-2130.

KOSMOS, *(KOSMOS; 0-916426),* 2580 Polk St., San Francisco, CA 94109 Tel 415-928-4332.

Kosmos
See KOSMOS

Kraus Intl, *(Kraus International; 0-527),* Div. of Kraus-Thomson Organization Ltd., Rte. 100, Millwood, NY 10546 Tel 914-762-2200.

Kraus Repr, *(Kraus Reprint; 0-527),* U.S. Div. of Kraus-Thomson Organization, Ltd., Rte. 100, Millwood, NY 10546 Tel 914-762-2200.

Krause Pubns, *(Krause Pubns., Inc.; 0-87341),* 700 E. State St., Iola, WI 54945 Tel 715-445-2214.

Kregel, *(Kregel Pubns.; 0-8254),* P.O. Box 2607, Grand Rapids, MI 49501 Tel 616-459-9444. *Imprints:* RBDH (Religious Book Discount House Pubns.).

Krieger, *(Krieger, Robert E., Pub. Co., Inc.; 0-88275; 0-89874),* P.O. Box 542, Huntington, NY 11743 Tel 516-271-5252.

Kronos Pr, *(Kronos Press; 0-917994),* Glassboro State College, Glassboro, NJ 08028 Tel 609-445-6048.

Kruzas Assoc, *(Kruzas, Anthony T., Associates),* 1810 Longshore Dr., Ann Arbor, MI 48103 Tel 313-665-7189; Dist. by: Gale Research Co., Book Tower, Detroit, MI 48226 Tel 313-961-2242.

Ktav, *(Ktav Publishing House, Inc.; 0-87068),* 75 Varick St., New York, NY 10013 Tel 212-966-6980.

KTO Pr
See Kraus Intl

Kudzu-Ivy, *(Kudzu-Ivy; 0-9605142),* P.O. Box 52743, Atlanta, GA 30355.

Kumarian Pr, *(Kumarian Press; 0-931816),* 29 Bishop Rd., West Hartford, CT 06119.

Kurios Pr, *(Kurios Press; 0-916588),* P.O. Box 946, Bryn Mawr, PA 19010 Tel 215-527-4635.

Kusel, *(Kusel, George; 0-9604476),* 600 Lakevue Dr., Willow Grove, PA 19090.

Kwik Sew, *(Kwik Sew Pattern Co., Inc.; 0-913212),* 300 Sixth Ave. N., Minneapolis, MN 55401 Tel 612-339-9348.

Kylix Pr, *(Kylix Press; 0-914408),* 1485 Maywood, Ann Arbor, MI 48103 Tel 313-761-5399.

L E Edwards, *(Edwards, Lowell E.; 0-936024),* P.O. Box 255714, Sacramento, CA 95825.

L Erlbaum Assocs, *(Erlbaum, Lawrence, Assocs., Inc.; 0-89859),* 365 Broadway, Hillsdale, NJ 07642 Tel 201-666-4110.

L J Fry, *(Fry, L. John; 0-9600984),* 1223 N. Nopal St., Santa Barbara, CA 93103 Tel 805-965-6891.

L J Martin, *(Martin, Louis J., & Associates, Inc.; 0-916800),* 95 Madison Ave., New York, NY 10016 Tel 212-725-2157.

L Lawler, *(Lawler, Louise; 0-931706),* 407 Greenwich St., New York, NY 10013.

L McMaster, *(McMaster, Linda, Ms),* War Cycles Institute, P.O. Box 1673, Kalispell, MT 59901.

L Orr, *(Orr, Leonard),* Orders to: Rebirth America, 301 Lyon St., San Francisco, CA 94117 Tel 415-929-1743.

L P Pubns, *(L P Pubns.; 0-916192),* P.O. Box 7601, San Diego, CA 92107 Tel 714-225-0133.

L R Frank, *(Frank, Leonard Roy; 0-9601376),* 2300 Webster St., San Francisco, CA 94115 Tel 415-922-3029.
L Shogren Quilt
See Pieceful Pleasures
L Ziman, *(Ziman, Larry; 0-933456),* P.O. Box 67485, Los Angeles, CA 90067.
LA Co Art Mus, *(Los Angeles County Museum of Art; 0-87587),* 5905 Wilshire Blvd., Los Angeles, CA 90036 Tel 213-937-4250.
La Siesta, *(La Siesta Press; 0-910856),* P.O. Box 406, Glendale, CA 91209 Tel 213-244-9305.
La State U Pr, *(Louisiana State Univ. Press; 0-8071),* Baton Rouge, LA 70803 Tel 504-388-2071.
Lacis Pubns, *(Lacis Pubns; 0-916896),* 2990 Adeline St., Berkeley, CA 94703 Tel 415-843-7178.
Lake County, *(Lake County Press),* Box 669, Ronan, MT 59864; Dist. by: Montana Writers, Inc., Box 21133, Billings, MT 59104.
Lakstun Pr, *(Lakstun Press; 0-9603706),* P.O. Box 429, Bensalem, PA 19020.
Lambert Bk, *(Lambert Book House, Inc.; 0-89315),* 133 Kings Hwy., Box 4007, Shreveport, LA 71104 Tel 318-861-3140.
Lame Johnny, *(Lame Johnny Press; 0-917624),* P.O. Box 66, Hermosa, SD 57744 Tel 605-255-4466.
Lamm-Morada, *(Lamm-Morada Publishing Co., Inc.; 0-932128),* Box 7607, Stockton, CA 95207 Tel 209-931-1056.
Lampkin Pub, *(Lampkin, J. G., Publishing; 0-9604918),* 15346 Stone Ave. N., Seattle, WA 98133.
Lamplight Pub, *(Lamplight Publishing Inc.; 0-88308),* 559 W. 26th St., New York, NY 10001 Tel 212-695-8222.
Lancaster-Miller, *(Lancaster-Miller Pubs.; 0-89581),* 3165 Adeline St., Berkeley, CA 94703 Tel 415-845-3782. *Imprints:* Asian Humanities (Asian Humanities Press).
Landmark Bks, *(Landmark Books, Inc.; 0-934400),* 7847 12th Ave. S., Bloomington, MN 55420 Tel 612-854-3345.
Lands End Bks, *(Lands End Books; 0-9603558),* Rte. 3, Box 370, Gloucester, VA 23061 Tel 804-693-4262.
Lane
See Sunset-Lane
Lang Svcs CA, *(Language Services),* 2725 Via Casa Loma, San Clemente, CA 92672 Tel 714-492-6528.
Lange, *(Lange Medical Pubns.; 0-87041),* Drawer L, Los Altos, CA 94022 Tel 415-948-4526.
Lankey, *(Lankey Pub. Co.; 0-918300),* Subs. of Huber Enterprises, Inc., R.D. 1, Box 205, West Newton, PA 15089 Tel 412-722-3507
Lanser Pr, *(Lanser Press; 0-9603900),* P.O. Box 38, Plainfield, VT 05667.
Lantern, *(Lantern Press, Inc. Pubs.; 0-8313),* 354 Hussey Rd., Mount Vernon, NY 10552 Tel 914-668-9736.
Larchmont Bks, *(Larchmont Books; 0-915962),* 6 E. 43rd St., New York, NY 10017 Tel 212-581-8840.
Large Print Bks *Imprint of* **G K Hall**
Larimi Comm, *(Larimi Communications; 0-935224),* 151 E. 50th St., New York, NY 10022 Tel 212-935-9262.
Larksdale, *(Larksdale Press, The; 0-89896),* 133 S. Heights Blvd., Houston, TX 77007 Tel 713-869-9092.
Larousse, *(Larousse & Co., Inc.; 0-88332),* 572 Fifth Ave., New York, NY 10036 Tel 212-575-9515.
Larren Pubs, *(Larren Pubs.; 0-9604370),* 707 W. Burton, Nevada, MO 64772 Tel 417-667-3706.
Lathrop, *(Lathrop, Norman, Enterprises; 0-910868),* P.O. Box 198, Wooster, OH 44691 Tel 216-262-5587.
Latin Am Ctr
See UCLA Lat Am Ctr
Latitudes Pr, *(Latitudes Press),* 3215 Lafayette Ave., Austin, TX 78722 Tel 512-478-1454; Dist. by: SBD: Small Press Distribution, 1636 Oceanview, Kensington, CA 94707.
Laurel Inst, *(Laurel Institute, The; 0-87012),* RD 1, Box 10, Farmington, PA 15437.
Laurida, *(Laurida Book Publishing Co.; 0-934810),* P.O. Box 2061, Hollywood, CA 90028 Tel 213-466-1707.
Law & Psych, *(Law & Psychology Press; 0-9603630),* 4344 Promenade Way, Suite 106P, Marina Del Rey, CA 90291 Tel 213-823-4460; Orders to: P. O. Box 9489, Venice, CA 90291.
Lawrence Hill, *(Hill, Lawrence, & Co., Inc.; 0-88208),* 520 Riverside Ave., Westport, CT 06880 Tel 203-226-9392.
Lawyers & Judges, *(Lawyers & Judges Publishing Co.; 0-88450),* Div. of Communication Skill Builders, Inc., 3130 N. Dodge Blvd., P.O. Box 42050, Tucson, AZ 85733 Tel 602-327-6021.
Lawyers Co-Op, *(Lawyers Co-Operative Publishing Co.),* Aqueduct Bldg., Rochester, NY 14694 Tel 716-546-5530.
LBJ Sch Public Affairs, *(L B J School of Public Affairs, Univ. of Texas Austin),* Drawer Y, Univ. Sta., Austin, TX 78712 Tel 512-471-4962.
LE *Imprint of* **Dell**
Lea & Febiger, *(Lea & Febiger; 0-8121),* 600 S. Washington Square, Philadelphia, PA 19106 Tel 215-922-1330.
Leadership Pr, *(Leadership Press; 0-936626),* 2870 N. Towne Ave., Suite 108, Pomona, CA 91767.
Learn Concepts OH, *(Learning Concepts, Inc.; 0-934902),* 7601 Mentor Ave., Mentor, OH 44060 Tel 216-946-6437.
Learn Mich, *(Learn; 0-9604634),* 827 CNB Bldg., Detroit, MI 48226.
Learn Pathways, *(Learning Pathways, Inc.; 0-89146),* Evergreen, CO 80439; Dist. by: J & J Distributors, P.O. Box 247, Raymondville, TX 78580.
Learn Res Intl Stud, *(Learning Resources in International Studies; 0-936876),* 60 E. 42nd St., Suite 1231, New York, NY 10165.
Learned Info, *(Learned Information, Inc.; 0-938734),* P.O. Box 550, Marlton, NJ 08053.
Learning Concepts, *(Learning Concepts, Inc.; 0-89384),* 400 E. Anderson Lane, Suite 318, Austin, TX 78753 Tel 512-837-9953; Orders to: Learning Concepts/Univ. Associates, 8517 Production Ave., San Diego, CA 92126 Tel 800-854-2143.
Learning Hse, *(Learning House; 0-9602730),* 38 South St., Roslyn Heights, NY 11577 Tel 516-621-5755; Dist. by: Liberty Publishing Co., 550 Scott Adam Rd., Cockeysville, MD 21030.
Learning Inc., *(Learning Inc.; 0-913692),* Learning Place, Manset, ME 04656 Tel 207-244-5015.
Learning Line, *(Learning Line, The; 0-8449),* P.O. Box 577, Palo Alto, CA 94302 Tel 415-854-4400.
Learning Syst, *(Learning Systems Co.; 0-256),* Div. of Richard D. Irwin, Inc., 1818 Ridge Rd., Homewood, IL 60430 Tel 312-798-6000.
Lebhar Friedman, *(Lebhar-Friedman Books; 0-912016),* Subs. of Lebhar-Friedman, Inc., 425 Park Ave, New York, NY 10022 Tel 212-371-9400.
Leetes Isl, *(Leete's Island Books; 0-918172),* P.O. Box 1131, New Haven, CT 06505 Tel 203-481-2536; Dist. by: Independent Publishers Group, 14 Vanderventer Ave., Port Washington, NY 11050.
Legacy Bks, *(Legacy Books; 0-913714),* Box 494, 12 Meetinghouse Rd., Hatboro, PA 19040 Tel 215-675-6762.
Legacy Pub Co, *(Legacy Pub. Co.; 0-918784),* 2008 Perkins Rd., Baton Rouge, LA 70808 Tel 504-343-0366.
Legal Bk Corp, *(Legal Book Corp.; 0-910874),* 316 W. Second St., Los Angeles, CA 90012 Tel 213-626-3494.
Legal Mgmt Serv, *(Legal Management Services, Inc.; 0-937542),* 250 W. 94th St., New York, NY 10025 Tel 212-864-6169; Dist. by: LMS Distribution Center, P.O. Box 2614, LaCrosse, WI 54601.
Leisure Pr, *(Leisure Press; 0-918438),* P.O. Box 3, West Point, NY 10996 Tel 914-446-7110.
LenChamps Pubs, *(LenChamps Publishers; 0-917230),* P.O. Box 23432, Washington, DC 20024 Tel 202-488-8787.
Lerner Bks
See Lerner Pubns
Lerner Pubns, *(Lerner Publications Co.; 0-8225),* 241 First Ave., N., Minneapolis, MN 55401 Tel 612-332-3344.
Les Femmes Pub, *(Les Femmes Publishing; 0-89087),* 231 Adrian Rd., Millbrae, CA 94030 Tel 415-692-4500.
Levada, *(Levada Services; 0-9605014),* P.O. Box 686, 11300 Eastside Rd., Fort Jones, CA 96032.
Levenson Pr, *(Levenson Press; 0-914442),* P.O. Box 19606, Los Angeles, CA 90019.
Levi Pub, *(Levi Publishing Co., Inc.; 0-910876),* P.O. Box 730, Sumter, SC 29150.
Leviathan Hse, *(Leviathan House),* Dist. by: Hippocrene Books, P.O. Box 978, Edison, NJ 08817.
Lewis, *(Lewis, A. F., & Co., Inc.; 0-910880),* 79 Madison Ave., New York, NY 10016 Tel 212-679-0770.
Lewis Carroll Soc, *(Lewis Carroll Society of North America; 0-930326),* 617 Rockford Rd., Silver Spring, MD 20902.
Lewis Pub Co, *(Lewis Publishing Co., The; 0-86616),* 15 Muzzey St., Lexington, MA 02173; Dist. by: Stephen Greene Press, Fessenden Rd. at Indian Flat, P.O. Box 1000, Brattleboro, VT 05301 Tel 802-257-7757.
Lex Bk Co CA, *(Lexington Book Co.; 0-9604372),* 4872 Old Cliffs Rd., San Diego, CA 92120 Tel 714-583-8348.
Lexik Hse, *(Lexik House Pubs.; 0-936368),* 75 Main St., P.O. Box 247, Cold Spring, NY 10516 Tel 914-256-2822.
Lexington Bks, *(Lexington Books; 0-669),* Div. of D. C. Heath & Co., Dist. by: D. C. Heath & Co., 125 Spring St., Lexington, MA 02173 Tel 617-862-6650.
Lexington Data, *(Lexington Data, Inc.; 0-914428),* Box 371, Ashland, MA 01721 Tel 617-881-2576.
LFL *Imprint of* **Dell**
Lib Res, *(Library Research Associates; 0-912526),* Dunderberg Rd., R.D. 5, Box 41, Monroe, NY 10950 Tel 914-783-1144.
Lib Soc Sci, *(Library of Social Science; 0-915042),* 475 Amsterdam Ave., New York, NY 10024 Tel 212-874-6718.
Liberator Pr, *(Liberator Press; 0-930720),* Box 7128, Chicago, IL 60680 Tel 312-663-4329.
Libertarian, *(Libertarian Press; 0-910884),* P.O. Box 218, 366 E. 166th St., South Holland, IL 60473 Tel 312-333-0031.
Liberty Fund, *(Liberty Fund, Inc.; 0-913966),* 7440 N. Shadeland Ave., Indianapolis, IN 46250 Tel 317-842-0880.
Liberty Lobby, *(Liberty Lobby; 0-935036),* 300 Independence Ave., S.E., Washington, DC 20003 Tel 202-546-5611.
Liberty Pub, *(Liberty Publishing Co., Inc.; 0-89709),* 50 Scott Adam Rd., Cockeysville, MD 21030 Tel 301-667-6680.
Libra, *(Libra Pubs., Inc.; 0-87212),* 391 Willets Rd., Roslyn Heights, L. I., NY 11577 Tel 516-484-4950.
Library Pr *Imprint of* **Open Court**
Libs Unl, *(Libraries Unlimited, Inc.; 0-87287),* P.O. Box 263, Littleton, CO 80160 Tel 303-770-1220.
Libty Pr MI, *(Liberty Press; 0-9604958),* 2115 Mark Ave., Lansing, MI 48912.
Lidiraven Bks, *(Lidiraven Books; 0-936162),* Box 5567, Sherman Oaks, CA 91413 Tel 213-892-0059.
Life Arts, *(Life Arts Publishing; 0-937894),* 116 Curryer South, Santa Maria, CA 93454 Tel 505-762-5063.
Life Enrich, *(Life Enrichment Pubs.; 0-938736),* Box 526, Canton, OH 44701.
Life Office
See LOMA
Life Pubs Intl, *(Life Pubs. International; 0-8297),* 3360 N.W. 110th St., Miami, FL 33167 Tel 305-685-6334.
Life Skills, *(Life Skills Training Associates; 0-9604510),* P.O. Box 48133, Chicago, IL 60648 Tel 312-823-0650.
Lifetime Learn, *(Lifetime Learning Pubns.; 0-534),* Div. of Wadsworth Inc., 10 Davis Dr., Belmont, CA 94002 Tel 415-595-2350.
Light & Life, *(Light & Life Press; 0-89367),* 999 College Ave., Winona Lake, IN 46590.
Light Impressions, *(Light Impressions Corp.; 0-87992),* P.O. Box 3012, Rochester, NY 14614 Tel 716-271-8960.
Light&Life Pub Co MN, *(Light & Life Publishing Co.; 0-937032),* 3450 Irving Ave. S., Minneapolis, MN 55408 Tel 612-925-3888.
Lighthouse Pr NY
See Lightyear

Lightning Tree, *(Lightning Tree; 0-89016),* P.O. Box 1837, Santa Fe, NM 87501 Tel 505-983-7434.
Lighton Pubns, *(Lighton Pubns.; 0-910892),* 73223 Sunnyvale Dr., Twentynine Palms, CA 92277 Tel 714-367-7386.
Lightyear, *(Lightyear Press, Inc.; 0-89968),* P.O. Box 507, Laurel, NY 11948.
Liguori Pubns, *(Liguori Pubns.; 0-89243),* 1 Liguori Dr., Liguori, MO 63057 Tel 800-325-9521.
Lime Rock Pr, *(Lime Rock Press, Inc.; 0-915998),* Mount Riga Rd., Box 363, Salisbury, CT 06068 Tel 203-435-2236.
Limestone Pr, *(Limestone Press; 0-919642),* P.O. Box 1604, Kingston, Ontario, Canada K7l 5c8,; Dist. by: A. S. Donnelly, 125 Southwood Dr., Vestal, NY 13850.
Lincoln Inst Land, *(Lincoln Institute of Land Policy),* 26 Trowbridge St., Cambridge, MA 02138 Tel 617-661-3016.
Lincoln Pub, *(Lincoln Publishing; 0-918898),* P.O. Box 50173, Palo Alto, CA 94303 Tel 415-494-7448.
Lincoln's Leadership, *(Lincoln's Leadership Library; 0-89764),* 5516 E. 35th, Tulsa, OK 74135.
Lindahl, *(Lindahl, Judy; 0-9603032),* 3211 N.E. Siskiyou, Portland, OR 97212 Tel 503-288-0772.
Lindell Pubs, *(Lindell Pubs.; 0-9604940),* P.O. Box 28, Bucks County, Springtown, PA 18081.
Linden *Imprint of* **S&S**
Linden Bks, *(Linden Books; 0-9603288),* Interlaken, NY 14847 Tel 607-387-9398.
Linden Pubs, *(Linden Pubs.; 0-89642),* 1750 N. Sycamore, Hollywood, CA 90028.
Lineal Cleworth, *(Lineal/Cleworth Books, Inc.; 0-916628),* 23 Leroy Ave., Darien, CT 06820 Tel 203-655-7676.
Lingua Pr, *(Lingua Press),* Box 481, Ramona, CA 92065 Tel 714-789-8389.
Linstok Pr, *(Linstok Press, Inc.; 0-932130),* 9306 Mintwood St., Silver Spring, MD 20901 Tel 301-585-1939.
Lion, *(Lion Press; 0-87460),* Dist. by: Sayre Publishing, Inc., 111 E. 39th St., New York, NY 10016.
Lion Ent, *(Lion Enterprises; 0-930962),* RR3 Box 127, Walkerton, IN 46574 Tel 219-369-9394.
Lionhead Pub, *(Lionhead Publishing; 0-89018),* 2521 East Stratford Court, Shorewood, Milwaukee, WI 53211 Tel 414-332-7474.
Liplop, *(Liplop Press; 0-936016),* P.O. Box 4520, Berkeley, CA 94704.
Lippincott, *(Lippincott, J. B., Co.; 0-397),* 10 E. 53rd St., New York, NY 10022 Tel 212-593-7213; E. Washington Sq., Philadelphia, PA 19105 Tel 215-574-4200; Orders to: Harper & Row, Publishers, Inc., Keystone Industrial Park, Scranton, PA 18512 Tel 717-343-4761.
Lippincott & Crowell, *(Lippincott & Crowell Pubs.; 0-690),* 521 Fifth Ave., New York, NY 10017 Tel 212-687-3980.
Little, *(Little, Brown & Co.; 0-316),* 34 Beacon St., Boston, MA 02106 Tel 617-227-0730; Orders to: 200 West St., Waltham, MA 02154 Tel 617-890-0250.
Little Brick Hse, *(Little Brick House, The; 0-9601648),* 621 Saint Clair St., Vandalia, IL 62471 Tel 618-283-0024.
Little Cajun, *(Little Cajun Books; 0-931108),* 4182 Blecker Dr., Baton Rouge, LA 70809 Tel 504-925-0355.
Little London, *(Little London Press; 0-936564),* 716 E. Washington, Colorado Springs, CO 80907 Tel 303-471-1322.
Little Red Hen, *(Little Red Hen, Inc.; 0-933046),* P.O. Box 4260, Pocatello, ID 83201.
Little Simon *Imprint of* **S&S**
Littlebird, *(Littlebird Pubns.; 0-937896),* 126 Fifth Ave., New York, NY 10011.
Littlefield, *(Littlefield, Adams & Co.; 0-8226),* 81 Adams Dr., Box 327, Totowa, NJ 07511 Tel 201-256-8600.
Litton Educ Pub, *(Litton Educational Publishing, International; 0-442),* 135 W. 50th St., New York, NY 10020 Tel 212-265-8700.
Liturgical Pr, *(Liturgical Press; 0-8146),* 74 Engle Blvd., Collegeville, MN 56321 Tel 612-363-2213.
Liv Bibles Int'l, *(Living Bibles International),* 1809C Mill St., Naperville, IL 60540 Tel 312-369-0100.
Lively Hills, *(Lively Hills Publishing Corp.; 0-938194),* P.O. Box 1186, St. Charles, MO 63301.
Liveright, *(Liveright Publishing Corp.; 0-87140),* Subs. of W. W. Norton Co., Inc., 500 Fifth Ave., New York, NY 10036 Tel 212-354-5500.
Living Flame Pr, *(Living Flame Press; 0-914544),* P.O. Box 74, Locust Valley, NY 11560 Tel 516-676-4265.
Living Love, *(Living Love Pubns.; 0-9600688; 0-915972),* 232 Monterey St., Santa Cruz, CA 95060 Tel 502-691-6006; Dist. by: DeVorss & Company, P.O. Box 550, Marina Del Rey, CA 90291 Tel 213-870-7478.
LJR Inc, *(LJR, Inc.; 0-936624),* 224 Joseph Square, Columbia, MD 21044 Tel 301-730-5365.
LL Co, *(LL Co.; 0-937892),* 1647 Manning Ave., Los Angeles, CA 90024 Tel 213-278-6803.
Llewellyn
See Llewellyn Pubns
Llewellyn Pubns, *(Llewellyn Pubns.; 0-87542),* Div. of Chester-Kent, Inc., P.O. Box 43383, St. Paul, MN 55164 Tel 612-291-1970.
Lloyd & Lipow, *(Lloyd, D. K., & M. Lipow; 0-9601504),* 201 Calle Miramar, Redondo Beach, CA 90277 Tel 213-535-3204.
Locare, *(Locare Research Group; 0-913986),* 910 N. Fairfax Ave., Los Angeles, CA 90046 Tel 213-656-4420.
Lochinvar *Imprint of* **Exposition**
Lodima, *(Lodima Press; 0-9605646),* Revere, PA 18953.
Loeffler
See Prod Hse
Loftin Pubs, *(Loftin, Tee, Pubs.,Inc.; 0-934812),* 3100 R St., N.W., Washington, DC 20007.
Log Boom, *(Log Boom Brewing; 0-9604130),* Box 1825, Boulder, CO 80306.
Logan Design, *(Logan Design Group; 0-9603856),* P. O. Box 997, N. Hollywood, CA 91603.
Logbridge-Rhodes, *(Logbridge-Rhodes, Inc.; 0-937406),* P.O. Box 3254, Durango, CO 81301.
Logos, *(Logos International; 0-912106; 0-88270),* 201 Church St., Plainfield, NJ 07060.
Loizeaux, *(Loizeaux Brothers, Inc.; 0-87213),* 1238 Corlies Ave., Box 277, Neptune, NJ 07753 Tel 201-774-8144.
Lollipop Power, *(Lollipop Power, Inc.; 0-914996),* P.O. Box 1171, Chapel Hill, NC 27514 Tel 919-929-4857.
LOMA, *(Life Office Management Assn.; 0-915322),* 100 Colony Square, Atlanta, GA 30361 Tel 404-892-7272; Orders to: Professional Book Distributors, P.O. Box 02055, 555 E. Hudson St., Columbus, OH 43202 Tel 800-848-0773.
Lomond, *(Lomond Pubns.; 0-912338),* P.O. Box 88, Mt. Airy, MD 21771 Tel 301-829-1496.
Lone Oak, *(Lone Oak Books; 0-936550),* 10,000 Old Georgetown Rd., Bethesda, MD 20014.
Longhorn Pr, *(Longhorn Press; 0-914208),* c/o J. W. Sitton, Box 150, Cisco, TX 76437 Tel 817-442-2530.
Longman, *(Longman Inc.),* 19 W. 44th St., Suite 1012, New York, NY 10036 Tel 212-764-3950.
Longwood Pr, *(Longwood Press, Ltd.; 0-89341),* Shady Nook Rd., West Newfield, ME 04095 Tel 207-793-2288.
Longyear Res, *(Longyear, J. M., Research Library),* c/o Marquette County Historical Society, 213 N. Front St., Marquette, MI 49855 Tel 906-226-6821.
Lonstein Pubns, *(Lonstein Pubns.),* 1 Terrace Hill, Box 351, Ellenville, NY 12428.
Loompanics, *(Loompanics Unlimited),* P.O. Box 264, Mason, MI 48854 Tel 517-694-2240.
Lord John, *(Lord John Press; 0-935716),* 19073 Los Alimos St., Northridge, CA 91326.
Lord Pub, *(Lord Publishing; 0-930204),* 46 Glen St., Dover, MA 02030 Tel 617-785-1575.
Lorian Pr, *(Lorian Press; 0-936878),* P.O. Box 1095, Elgin, IL 60120.
Lorien Hse, *(Lorien House; 0-934852),* P.O. Box 1112, Black Mountain, NC 28711 Tel 704-669-6211.
Lost Data, *(Lost Data Press; 0-937468),* 4410c Burnet Rd., Austin, TX 78756; Dist. by: Bookpeople, Inc., P.O. Box 40397, San Francisco, CA 94140 Tel 415-824-3184.
Lost Roads, *(Lost Roads Pubs.; 0-918786),* P.O. Box 11143, San Francisco, CA 94101.
Lothrop, *(Lothrop, Lee & Shepard Books; 0-688),* Div. of William Morrow & Co., Inc., 105 Madison Ave., New York, NY 10016 Tel 212-889-3050; Orders to: William Morrow & Co., Inc., Wilmor Warehouse, 6 Henderson Dr., West Caldwell, NJ 07006.
Lotus, *(Lotus Press, Inc.; 0-916418),* P.O. Box 21607, Detroit, MI 48221 Tel 313-861-1280.
Louis Found, *(Louis Foundation; 0-9605492),* Box 210, Eastsound, WA 98245 Tel 206-376-2581.
Love Street, *(Love Street Books; 0-915216),* P.O. Box 58163, Louisville, KY 40258 Tel 502-458-0604.
Loving Pubs, *(Loving Pubs.; 0-938134),* 4576 Alla Rd., Los Angeles, CA 90066.
Low-Tech, *(Low-Tech Press; 0-9605626),* 30-73 47th St., Long Island City, NY 11103.
Lowell & Lynwood, *(Lowell & Lynwood, Ltd.; 0-8484),* 965 Church St., Baldwin, NY 11510.
Lowell Pr, *(Lowell Press; 0-913504),* 115 E. 31st St., Box 1877, Kansas City, MO 64141 Tel 816-753-4545.
Loyola, *(Loyola Univ. Press; 0-8294),* 3441 N. Ashland Ave., Chicago, IL 60657 Tel 312-281-1818.
Lubrecht & Cramer, *(Lubrecht & Cramer),* RFD 1, Box 227, Monticello, NY 12701 Tel 914-794-8539.
Lucas, *(Lucas Brothers Pubs.; 0-87543),* 909 Lowry St., Missouri Store Bldg., Columbia, MO 65201 Tel 314-442-6161.
Lucas Pubs CA, *(Lucas Pubs.; 0-9604806),* 58 Arden Way, P.O. Box 15224, Sacramento, CA 95813.
Lucis, *(Lucis Publishing Co.; 0-85330),* 866 United Nations Plaza, Suite 566, New York, NY 10017 Tel 212-421-1577.
Lumeli Pr, *(Lumeli Press; 0-930592),* P.O. Box 909, San Carlos, CA 94070 Tel 415-593-7181.
Luna Bisonte, *(Luna Bisonte Prods.; 0-935350),* 137 Leland Ave., Columbus, OH 43214 Tel 614-846-4126.
Lunchroom Pr, *(Lunchroom Press, The; 0-938136),* Box 36027, Grosse Pointe Farms, MI 48236.
Lust, *(Lust, Benedict, Pubns.; 0-87904),* 25 Dewart Rd., Greenwich, CT 06830 Tel 203-661-0980; Orders to: P.O. Box 404, New York, NY 10156.
Lustrum Pr, *(Lustrum Press; 0-912810),* Dist. by: Amphoto, 1515 Broadway, New York, NY 10036 Tel 212-764-7300.
Luth Acad, *(Lutheran Academy for Scholarship; 0-913160),* 1901 McCord Rd., Valparaiso, IN 46383 Tel 219-464-5459.
LWV NYS, *(League of Women Voters of NYS; 0-938588),* 817 Broadway, New York, NY 10003.
LWV US, *(League of Women Voters of the U.S.; 0-89959),* 1730 M. St. N.W., Washington, DC 20036 Tel 202-296-1770.
Lyle Stuart, *(Stuart, Lyle, Inc.; 0-8184),* 120 Enterprise Ave., Secaucus, NJ 07094 Tel 201-866-0490.
M-A Pr, *(M/A Press; 0-930206),* 30 NW 23rd Place, Portland, OR 97210; Orders to: P.O. Box 606, Beaverton, OR 97075.
M & A Products, *(Machinery & Allied Products Institute),* 1200 18th St., N.W., Washington, DC 20036.
M Brinser, *(Brinser, Marlin; 0-9602298),* 643 Stuyvesant Ave., Irvington, NJ 07111.
M Burk, *(Burk, Margaret),* P.O. Box 22, Ambassador Sta, Los Angeles, CA 90070.
M C Clausen, *(Clausen, Muriel C.; 0-9603664),* 780 W. Grand Ave., Oakland, CA 94612.
M Clark, *(Clark, Merrian E.; 0-910384),* 22151 Clarendon St., P.O. Box 505, Woodland Hills, CA 91365 Tel 213-347-1677.
M Demou & Assocs, *(Demou, Morris, & Associates; 0-9604794),* 2013 Big Oak Dr., Burnsville, MN 55337 Tel 612-890-3579.
M E Gant, *(Gant, Margaret Elizabeth; 0-9603138),* 7500 Deer Track Dr., Raleigh, NC 27612 Tel 919-781-6062.
M E Sharpe, *(Sharpe, M. E., Inc.; 0-87332),* 80 Business Park Dr., Armonk, NY 10504 Tel 914-273-1800.
M Evans, *(Evans, M., & Co., Inc.; 0-87131),* 216 E. 49th St., New York, NY 10017 Tel 212-688-2810; Dist. by: E. P. Dutton, 2 Park Ave., New York, NY 10016.

M G L S Pub, *(M G L S Publishing; 0-9601682),* 700 S. First St., Marshall, MN 56258 Tel 507-532-3553.

M Glazier, *(Glazier, Michael, Inc.; 0-89453),* 1210A King St., Wilmington, DE 19801 Tel 302-654-1635.

M Hutson, *(Hutson, Martha),* P.O. Box 185, Orefield, PA 18069.

M Jones, *(Jones,, Marshall,, Co.; 0-8338),* Div. of Golden Quill Press, Francestown, NH 03043.

M K Heller, *(Heller, Marjorie K.; 0-915362),* Box 78, Bayside, NY 11361 Tel 212-229-7715.

M La Pice, *(La Pice, Margaret; 0-9604508),* 210 Montcalm, San Francisco, CA 94110.

M Loke, *(Mele Loke Publishing Co.; 0-930932),* P.O. Box 7142, Honolulu, HI 96821 Tel 808-734-8611.

M Lukman, *(Lukman, Mphahlele; 0-9602660),* 9110 Avenue "A", Brooklyn, NY 11236.

M M Bruce, *(Bruce, Martin M., Pubs.; 0-935198),* Box 228, New Rochelle, NY 10804 Tel 914-235-4450.

M M Chamberlain, *(Chamberlain, Mildred Mosher; 0-9604142),* 128 Potters Ave., Warwick, RI 02886.

M Molek Inc, *(Molek, M., Inc.; 0-9603142),* P.O. Box 453, Dover, DE 19901 Tel 302-678-1260.

M Robertson
See Biblio Dist

M S Wright, *(Wright, Mildred S., G.R.S.; 0-917016),* 140 Briggs, Beaumont, TX 77707 Tel 713-832-2308.

M Sturgeon
See Newport Beach

M W Riley, *(Riley, Maurice W.; 0-9603150),* 512 Roosevelt Blvd., Ypsilanti, MI 48197.

M West Pubs, *(West, Mark, Pubs.),* P.O. Box 413, Fulton, CA 95439.

M Wiener, *(Wiener, Moshe; 0-9605406),* 854 Newburg Ave., North Woodmere, NY 11581.

Macalester, *(Macalester Park Publishing Co.; 0-910924),* 1571 Grand Ave., St. Paul, MN 55105 Tel 612-698-8877.

MacArthur Memorial, *(MacArthur Memorial),* MacArthur Square, Norfolk, VA 23510 Tel 804-441-2256.

McBooks Pr, *(McBooks Press; 0-935526),* 106 N. Aurora, Ithaca, NY 14850 Tel 607-272-6602; Dist. by: Crossing Press, 17 W. Main St., Trumansburg, NY 14886 Tel 607-387-6217.

McCahan Found, *(McCahan Foundation; 0-937094),* 270 Bryn Mawr Ave., Bryn Mawr, PA 19010 Tel 215-896-4542.

McCartan & Root, *(McCartan & Root, Pubs.; 0-935786),* 325 E. 57th St., New York, NY 10022 Tel 212-421-2641.

McCormick-Mathers, *(McCormick-Mathers Publishing Co.; 0-8009),* Div. of Litton Educational Publishing, 135 W. 50th St, New York, NY 10020 Tel 212-265-8700; Orders to: 7625 Empire Dr., Florence, KY 41042.

McCutchan, *(McCutchan Publishing Corp.; 0-8211),* P.O. Box 774A, 2526 Grove St., Berkeley, CA 94701 Tel 415-841-8616.

McDougal-Littell, *(McDougal, Littell & Co.; 0-88343),* P.O. Box 1667, Evanston, IL 60204 Tel 312-256-5240.

McElderry Bk *Imprint of* **Atheneum**

McFarland & Co, *(McFarland & Co., Inc.; 0-89950),* Box 611, Jefferson, NC 28640 Tel 919-246-4460.

McGill-Queens U Pr, *(McGill-Queens Univ. Press; 0-7735),* 1020 Pine Ave., W., Montreal, Canada H3A 1A2, Tel 514-392-4421; Orders to: University of Toronto Press, 33 E. Tupper St., Buffalo, NY 14203.

McGlynn, *(McGlynn, June A.; 0-9601350),* 1529 Meadowlark Dr., Great Falls, MT 59404 Tel 406-452-3486.

McGrath, *(McGrath Publishing Co.; 0-8434),* P.O. Box 9001, Wilmington, NC 28402 Tel 919-763-3757. *Imprints:* Consortium (Consortium Books).

McGraw, *(McGraw-Hill Book Co.; 0-07),* 1221 Ave. of the Americas, New York, NY 10020 Tel 212-997-1221. *Imprints:* Architectural Rec Bks (Architectural Record Books); BYTE Bks (BYTE Books); Chem Eng (Chemical Engineering).

McGraw-Pretest, *(McGraw-Hill Book Co., Health Professions Division, PreTest Series),* P.O. Box 330, 71 S. Turnpike, Wallingford, CT 06492 Tel 203-265-5604; Orders to: McGraw-Hill Book Co., PreTest Series, P.O. Box 400, Hightstown, NJ 08520.

Mack Pub, *(Mack Publishing Co.; 0-912734),* 20th & Northampton Sts., Easton, PA 18042 Tel 215-258-9111.

McKay, *(McKay, David, Co., Inc.; 0-679),* 2 Park Ave., New York, NY 10016 Tel 212-340-9800.

Mackinac Island, *(Mackinac Island State Park Commission; 0-911872),* Box 370, Mackinac Island, MI 49757 Tel 906-847-3328.

McKnight, *(McKnight Publishing Co.),* 808 I.A.A. Dr., P.O. Box 2854, Bloomington, IL 61701 Tel 309-663-1341; Dist. by: Taplinger Publishing Co., 200 Park Ave., S., New York, NY 10003.

Macmillan, *(Macmillan Publishing Co., Inc.; 0-02),* 866 Third Ave., New York, NY 10022 Tel 212-935-2000; Orders to: Front & Brown Sts., Riverside, NJ 08370. *Imprints:* CCPr (Crowell-Collier Press); Collier (Collier Books).

Macmillan Info, *(Macmillan Information; 0-02),* Div. of Macmillan Publishing Co., Inc., 866 Third Ave., New York, NY 10022 Tel 212-935-2000.

McMillan Pubns, *(McMillan Pubns.; 0-934228),* 3208 Halsey Dr., Woodridge, IL 60517 Tel 312-968-3933.

McNally, *(McNally & Loftin, Pubs.; 0-87461),* P.O. Box 1316, Santa Barbara, CA 93102 Tel 805-964-5117.

Macoy Pub, *(Macoy Publishing & Masonic Supply Co., Inc.; 0-910928),* P.O. Box 9759, Richmond, VA 23228 Tel 804-262-6551.

Macro Bks, *(Macro Books; 0-913080),* P.O. Box 26661, Tempe, AZ 85282 Tel 602-949-5559.

Macromedia Inc, *(Macromedia Inc.; 0-9601170),* P.O. Box 1025, Lake Placid, NY 12946 Tel 518-523-2713.

Mad River, *(Mad River Press; 0-916422),* Rte. 2, Box 151-B, Eureka, CA 95501 Tel 707-443-2947.

Made *Imprint of* **Doubleday**

Madison Pub, *(Madison Co.; 0-913808),* P.O. Box 206, Berea, KY 40403 Tel 606-986-9744.

Madrona Pr, *(Madrona Press, Inc.; 0-89052),* P.O. Box 3750, Austin, TX 78764 Tel 512-327-2683.

Madrona Pubs, *(Madrona Pubs., Inc.; 0-914842),* 2116 Western Ave., Seattle, WA 98121 Tel 206-624-6840.

Maelstrom, *(Maelstrom Press; 0-917554),* P. O. Box 4261, Long Beach, CA 90804 Tel 213-439-7033.

Mafex, *(Mafex Associates, Inc.; 0-87804),* 90 Cherry St., Johnstown, PA 15902 Tel 814-535-3597.

Mag Indus, *(Magazines for Industry, Inc.; 0-89451),* 747 Third Ave., New York, NY 10017 Tel 212-838-7778.

Magi Bks, *(Magi Books, Inc.; 0-87343),* 33 Buckingham Dr., Albany, NY 12208 Tel 518-482-7781.

Magic Circle Pr, *(Magic Circle Press; 0-913660),* 10 Hyde Ridge Rd., Weston, CT 06883 Tel 203-226-1903; Dist. by: Walker & Co., 720 Fifth Ave, New York, NY 10019.

Magic Ltd, *(Magic Limited-Lloyd E. Jones; 0-915926),* P.O. Box 3186, San Leandro, CA 94578 Tel 415-352-1854; 4064 39th Ave., Oakland, CA 94619 Tel 415-531-5490.

Magnamusic, *(Magnamusic-Baton, Inc.; 0-918812),* 10370 Page Industrial Blvd, St. Louis, MO 63132 Tel 314-427-5660.

Magnolia Lab, *(Magnolia Laboratory),* 701 Beach Blvd., Pascagoula, MS 39567 Tel 601-762-1643.

Maguey Pr, *(Maguey Press, The; 0-930778),* Box 3395, Tucson, AZ 85722.

Maher Ventril Studio, *(Maher Ventriloquist Studios),* P.O. Box 420, Littleton, CO 80160 Tel 303-798-6830.

Mail Order, *(Mail Order U.S.A.; 0-914694),* 3100 Wisconsin Ave. N.W., Washington, DC 20016 Tel 202-686-9521; Orders to: P.O. Box 19083, Washington, DC 20036.

Maine St Mus, *(Maine State Museum Pubns.; 0-913764),* State House, Sta. 83, Augusta, ME 04333 Tel 207-289-2301.

Majestic Bks, *(Majestic Books; 0-9604968),* 2338 Henderson Mill Court, Atlanta, GA 30345.

Majors
See S Karger

Maledicta, *(Maledicta Press; 0-916500),* 331 S. Greenfield Ave., Waukesha, WI 53186 Tel 414-542-5853.

Malki Mus Pr, *(Malki Museum Press),* Dept. of Linguistics, Univ. of California, Los Angeles, CA 90024 Tel 213-474-0169; Orders to: 11-795 Fields Rd., Morongo Indian Reservation, Banning, CA 92220 Tel 714-849-7289.

Man-Root, *(Man-Root),* P. O. Box 982, South San Francisco, CA 94080.

Management Advisory Pubns, *(Management Advisory Pubns.),* Box 151, 44 Washington St., Wellesley Hills, MA 02181 Tel 617-235-2895.

Manas, *(Manas Pubns.; 0-911804),* 1868 Shore Dr. S., No. 205, St. Petersburg, FL 33707 Tel 813-343-1428.

Mandala
See Irvington

Manet Guild, *(Manet Guild; 0-9602418),* 310 Franklin St., Dept. 535, Boston, MA 02110 Tel 617-449-3792.

Mangan Bks, *(Mangan Books; 0-930208),* 6245 Snowheights Ct., El Paso, TX 79912 Tel 915-584-1662.

Mann Pubs, *(Mann Pubs.; 0-936632),* P.O. Box 7 AK, Jersey City, NJ 07307 Tel 201-659-8324.

Manoa Pr, *(Manoa Press, Inc.; 0-9605502),* Box 25355, Honolulu, HI 96825.

Manor Bks, *(Manor Books, Inc.; 0-532),* 45 E. 30th St., New York, NY 10016 Tel 212-686-9100.

Manufacturing Confectioner, *(Manufacturing Confectioner),* 175 Rock Rd., Glen Rock, NJ 07452 Tel 201-652-2655.

Manuscript Pr, *(Manuscript Press; 0-936414),* Box 307, Kingston, NJ 08528 Tel 609-921-0151; Dist. by: PDA Enterprises, Box 8010, New Orleans, LA 70182.

Maple Mont, *(Maplegrove & Montgrove Press),* 4055 N. Keystone Ave., Chicago, IL 60641 Tel 312-286-2655.

Mar Vista, *(Mar Vista Publishing Co.; 0-9604064),* 11917 Westminster Place, Los Angeles, CA 90066.

Mara Pr MA, *(Mara Press),* Box 790, Marblehead, MA 01945 Tel 617-631-0624.

Maran Pub, *(Maran Publishing Co.; 0-916526),* 320 N. Eutaw St., Baltimore, MD 21201.

Maranatha Evangelical
See Maranatha Hse Pubs

Maranatha Hse Pubs, *(Maranatha House Pubs.; 0-89337),* 705 S. Hwy. 101, Solana Beach, CA 92075 Tel 714-755-0962.

Marburger, *(Marburger Pubns.; 0-915730),* P.O. Box 422, Manhasset, NY 11030.

MARC, *(MARC, Missions Advanced Research & Communication Center; 0-912552),* 919 W. Huntington Dr., Monrovia, CA 91016 Tel 213-357-7979.

MARCC
See MARC

Marcella, *(Marcella Press; 0-938468),* P.O. Box 1105, Palm Desert, CA 92261.

March of Dimes, *(National Foundation-March of Dimes),* 1275 Mamaroneck Ave., White Plains, NY 10605 Tel 914-428-7100.

Marconi
See Tele Cable

Marek, *(Marek, Richard, Pubs., Inc.; 0-399),* Subs. of G.P. Putnam's Sons, 200 Madison Ave., New York, NY 10016 Tel 212-576-8900.

Margoe Jane, *(Margoe Jane Pubns.; 0-9602330),* Matthew 778, North Bangor, NY 12966 Tel 518-483-0842; Dist. by: National Ataxia Foundation, 6681 Country Club Dr., Minneapolis, MN 55427 Tel 612-546-6220.

Marine Bio, *(Marine Biological Laboratory; 0-912544),* Woods Hole, MA 02543.

Marine Educ, *(Marine Education Textbooks; 0-934114),* 124 N. Van Ave., Houma, LA 70360.

Mariner, *(Mariner Books; 0-910954),* 1949 Haywood Rd., Apt. 15, Hendersonville, NC 28739 Tel 704-693-8045.

Mariners Boston, *(Mariners Press, Inc., The; 0-913352),* P.O. Box 540, Boston, MA 02117 Tel 617-749-5759.

Mark Foster Mus, *(Mark Foster Music Co.; 0-916656),* P.O. Box 4012, Champaign, IL 61820 Tel 217-367-9932.
Market Ed, *(Market Ed Inc.; 0-937470),* P.O. Box 45181, Westlake, OH 44145 Tel 216-779-4689.
Marketing Econs, *(Marketing Economics Institute, Ltd.; 0-914078),* 108 W. 39th St., New York, NY 10018 Tel 212-869-8260.
Marlborough Pubns, *(Marlborough Pubns; 0-9604594),* P.O. Box 16406, San Diego, CA 92116 Tel 714-280-8310.
Marlin, *(Marlin Pubns., International, Inc.; 0-930624),* 485 Fifth Ave., New York, NY 10017 Tel 212-986-7752.
Marquest Colorguide, *(Marquest Colorguide Books; 0-916240),* P.O. Box 132, Palos Verdes Estates, CA 90274 Tel 213-373-4301.
Marquette, *(Marquette Univ. Press; 0-87462),* 1324 W. Wisconsin Ave., Rm. 409, Milwaukee, WI 53233 Tel 414-224-1564.
Marquette Cnty, *(Marquette County Historical Society, Inc.),* 213 N. Front St., Marquette, MI 49855 Tel 906-226-3571.
Marquis, *(Marquis Who's Who, Inc.; 0-8379),* 200 E. Ohio St., Chicago, IL 60611 Tel 312-787-2008; Orders to: 4300 W. 62nd St., Indianapolis, IN 46206 Tel 317-298-5400.
Marr Pubns, *(Marr Pubns.; 0-938712),* P.O. Box 1421, New York, NY 10101 Tel 516-822-7744.
Martin Motorsports, *(Martin Motorsports; 0-9605068),* P.O. Box 12654, Fort Wayne, IN 46864.
Martin Res
See Qwint Systems
Marvanco, *(Marvanco Enterprises; 0-9604336),* 25 Floral Rd., Peekskill, NY 10566.
Marxist Educ, *(Marxist Educational Press; 0-930656),* c/o Dept. of Anthropology, Univ. of Minnesota, 215 Ford Hall, 224 Church St., S.E., Minneapolis, MN 55455 Tel 612-373-5803.
Maryben Bks, *(Maryben Books; 0-913184),* 619 Warfield Dr., Rockville, MD 20850 Tel 301-762-5291.
Maryland Hist Pr, *(Maryland Historical Press; 0-917882),* 9205 Tuckerman St., Lanham, MD 20801 Tel 301-577-2436.
MAS De Reinis, *(M.A.S. De Reinis; 0-937370),* Div. of Polymath, Inc., Box 2820, Grand Central Sta., New York, NY 10017 Tel 212-625-4336.
Mason Charter
See Van Nos Reinhold
Mason Clinic, *(Mason Clinic, The; 0-9601944),* 1100 Ninth Ave., P.O. Box 900, Seattle, WA 98111 Tel 206-223-6985.
Mason Pub, *(Mason Publishing Co.; 0-917126),* 366 Wacouta St., St. Paul, MN 55101 Tel 612-224-5367.
Mass Hist Soc, *(Massachusetts Historical Society),* 1154 Boylston St., Boston, MA 02215 Tel 617-536-1608.
Masson Pub, *(Masson Publishing U.S.A., Inc.; 0-89352),* 14 E. 60th St., New York, NY 10022 Tel 212-838-8510.
Master Pr, *(Master Press; 0-9600818),* P. O. Box 432, Dayton, OR 97114 Tel 503-864-2987.
Masterco Pr, *(Masterco Press, Inc.; 0-912164),* P.O. Box 7382, Ann Arbor, MI 48107 Tel 313-428-8300.
Matagiri, *(Matagiri Sri Aurobindo Center, Inc.; 0-89071),* Mt. Tremper, NY 12457 Tel 914-679-8322.
Math Assn, *(Mathematical Assn. of America; 0-88385),* 1529 Eighteenth St., N.W., Washington, DC 20036 Tel 202-387-5200.
Math Counsel Inst, *(Math Counseling Institute Press; 0-9605756),* 4518 Corliss Ave. N., Seattle, WA 98103.
Math Hse, *(Math House; 0-917792),* Div. of Mosaic Media, Inc., P.O. Box 711, Glen Ellyn, IL 60137 Tel 312-790-1117.
Math Sci Pr, *(Math-Sci Press; 0-915692),* 53 Jordan Rd., Brookline, MA 02146 Tel 617-738-0307.
Mathco, *(Mathco; 0-912938),* P.O. Box 240, Rockport, MA 01966 Tel 617-546-6368.
Mathom, *(Mathom Pub. Co.; 0-930000),* 68 E. Mohawk St., Oswego, NY 13126 Tel 315-343-3035.
Matrix Pubns, *(Matrix Pubns., Inc.; 0-936554),* 27 Benefit St., Providence, RI 02904.
Mawa Pub, *(Mawa Publishing Co.; 0-935053),* Box 22525, Makiki, HI 96822.
Maxims Bks, *(Maxim's Books),* P.O. Box 480451, Los Angeles, CA 90048.
Maxwell Schl Citizen, *(Maxwell School of Citizenship & Public Affairs; 0-915984),* 119 College Place, Syracuse, NY 13210 Tel 315-423-2552.
Maxwell Sci Intl, *(Maxwell Scientific International, Inc.; 0-8277),* Fairview Park, Elmsford, NY 10523 Tel 914-592-9141.
May Murdock, *(May-Murdock; 0-932916),* Box 343, 90 Glenwood Ave., Ross, CA 94957 Tel 415-454-1771.
Mayapple Pr, *(Mayapple Press; 0-932412),* P.O. Box 7508, Liberty Sta., Ann Arbor, MI 48107 Tel 313-971-2223.
Mayfield Pub, *(Mayfield Publishing Co.; 0-87484),* 285 Hamilton Ave., Palo Alto, CA 94301 Tel 415-326-1640.
Mayflower Bks, *(Mayflower Books, Inc.; 0-8317),* 575 Lexington Ave., New York, NY 10022 Tel 212-888-9200.
Maznaim, *(Maznaim Publishing Corp.),* 413 E. 3rd St., Brooklyn, NY 11218.
MCL Assocs, *(MCL Associates; 0-930696),* P.O. Box 26, McLean, VA 22101 Tel 703-356-5979.
MD Hall Records, *(Maryland Hall of Records Commission),* P.O. Box 828, Annapolis, MD 21404 Tel 301-269-3915.
Md Hist, *(Maryland Historical Society),* 201 W. Monument St., Baltimore, MD 21201.
MD Pubns, *(MD Pubns.; 0-910922),* 30 E. 60th St., New York, NY 10022.
Me Pubns, *(Me Pubns.; 0-937706),* P.O. Box 14005, Minneapolis, MN 55414.
Mead Co, *(Mead Co., The; 0-934422),* 21176 S. Alameda St., Long Beach, CA 90810.
Meadow Lane, *(Meadow Lane Pubns.; 0-934826),* 2716 Edgewood, P.O. Box 640, Provo, UT 84601; Moved, Left No Forwarding Address.
Meadowbrook Pr, *(Meadowbrook Press; 0-915658),* 18318 Minnetonka Blvd., Deephaven, MN 55391 Tel 612-473-5400.
Means, *(Means, Robert Snow, Co., Inc.; 0-911950),* 100 Construction Plaza, Kingston, MA 02364 Tel 617-747-1270.
Meckler Bks, *(Meckler Books; 0-930466),* 520 Riverside Ave., P.O. Box 405, Saugatuck Sta., Westport, CT 06880 Tel 203-226-6967.
Med Economics, *(Medical Economics Books; 0-87489),* 680 Kinderkamack Rd., Oradell, NJ 07649 Tel 201-262-3030; Orders to: Box 157, Florence, KY 41042.
Med Educ, *(Medical Education Consultants; 0-937142),* Box 67101, Century City, Los Angeles, CA 90067 Tel 213-475-5141.
Med Exam, *(Medical Examination Publishing Co., Inc.; 0-87488),* 969 Stewart Ave., Garden City, NY 11530 Tel 516-222-2277.
Med Lib Assn, *(Medical Library Assn., Inc.; 0-912176),* 919 N. Michigan Ave., Suite 3208, Chicago, IL 60611 Tel 312-266-2456.
Medallion *Imprint of* **Berkley Pub**
Medi-Pub, *(Medi-Publishing Group),* 1975 E. Sunrise Blvd., Box 327, Fort Lauderdale, FL 33302 Tel 305-467-0189.
Media Awards, *(Media Awards Handbook; 0-910744),* 621 Sheri Lane, Danville, CA 94526 Tel 415-837-7562.
Media Concepts, *(Media Concepts Press; 0-935608),* 331 N. Broad St., Philadelphia, PA 19107 Tel 215-923-2545.
Media Inst, *(Media Institute, The; 0-937790),* 3017 M St., N.W., Washington, DC 20007.
Media Materials, *(Media Materials Inc.; 0-912974; 0-89539; 0-86601),* 2936 Remington Ave., Baltimore, MD 21211 Tel 301-235-1700.
Media Ventures, *(Media Ventures, Inc.; 0-89645),* 5055 N. Main St., Suite 240, Dayton, OH 45415 Tel 513-275-5142.
Medical Busn, *(Medical Business Service; 0-933916),* Butler & Maple Aves., Ambler, PA 19002 Tel 215-643-0400.
Medieval, *(Medieval & Renaissance Society; 0-913904),* P.O. Box 13348, N. Texas State Univ., Denton, TX 76203 Tel 817-788-2101.
Medieval Acad, *(Medieval Academy of America; 0-910956),* 1430 Massachusetts Ave., Cambridge, MA 02138 Tel 617-491-1622.
Medieval Inst, *(Medieval Institute Pubns.; 0-918720),* Western Michigan Univ., Kalamazoo, MI 49008 Tel 616-383-1685.
Medieval Latin, *(Medieval Latin Press; 0-916760),* P.O. Box 7847, St. Matthews Sta., Louisville, KY 40207 Tel 502-897-1241.
Medusa, *(Medusa; 0-9601714),* 4112 Emery Place, N.W., Washington, DC 20016.
Meeker Pub, *(Meeker Publishing Co.; 0-935068),* 2605 Virginia St., N.E., Albuquerque, NM 87110 Tel 505-299-6406.
Meher Baba Info, *(Meher Baba Information),* Box 1101, Berkeley, CA 94701; Dist. by: Book People, 2940 Seventh St., Berkeley, CA 94710 Tel 415-549-3033.
Mehetabel & Co, *(Mehetabel & Co.; 0-936094),* 4340 Redwood Hwy., Suite 307, San Rafael, CA 94903 Tel 415-472-2850.
Meiklejohn Civ Lib, *(Meiklejohn Civil Liberties Institute; 0-913876),* 1715 Francisco St., Berkeley, CA 94703 Tel 415-848-0599; Orders to: Box 673, Berkeley, CA 94701.
Melrose Pub Co, *(Melrose Publishing Co.; 0-934972),* 384 N. San Vicente Blvd., Los Angeles, CA 90048 Tel 213-655-5177.
Membrane Pr, *(Membrane Press; 0-87924),* P.O. Box 11601, Shorewood, Milwaukee, WI 53211.
Memphis St Univ, *(Memphis State Univ. Press; 0-87870),* Memphis State Univ., Memphis TN 38152 Tel 901-454-2752.
Menaid, *(Menaid Press; 0-918424),* Div. of Fichter Enterprises, P.O. Box 7664, Colorado Springs, CO 80933 Tel 303-598-8058.
Ment *Imprint of* **NAL**
Mer *Imprint of* **NAL**
Mercer Univ Pr, *(Mercer Univ. Press; 0-86554),* Macon, GA 31207 Tel 912-745-6811.
Merchants Pub Co, *(Merchants Pub. Co.; 0-89484),* 20 Mills St., Kalamazoo, MI 49001 Tel 616-345-1175.
Merck, *(Merck & Co., Inc.; 0-911910),* P.O. Box 2000, Rahway, NJ 07065 Tel 201-574-5403.
Meredith
See BH&G
Meredith Corp, *(Meredith Corp.; 0-696),* Orders to: Better Homes & Gardens Books, 1716 Locust, Des Moines, IA 50336.
Merganzer Pr, *(Merganzer Press; 0-9602648),* 659 Northmoor Rd., Lake Forest, IL 60045.
Merging Media, *(Merging Media; 0-934536),* 59 Sandra Circle A3, Westfield, NJ 07090 Tel 201-232-7224.
Merit Pubns, *(Merit Pubns., Inc.; 0-87803),* 610 NE 124th St., N. Miami, FL 33161.
Merk, *(Merk),* 377 Merk Rd., Watsonville, CA 95076.
Merlin Pr, *(Merlin Press; 0-930142),* P.O. Box 5602, San Jose, CA 95150.
Mermaid *Imprint of* **Hill & Wang**
Merriam, *(Merriam, G. & C., Co.; 0-87779),* Subs. of Encyclopaedia Britannica, Inc., 47 Federal St., Springfield, MA 01101 Tel 413-734-3134.
Merriam-Eddy, *(Merriam-Eddy Co., Inc.; 0-914562),* P.O. Box 25, South Waterford, ME 04081 Tel 207-583-4645.
Merrill, *(Merrill, Charles E., Publishing Co.; 0-675),* Div. of Bell & Howell Co., 1300 Alum Creek Dr., Columbus, OH 43216 Tel 614-258-8441.
Merrimack Bk Serv, *(Merrimack Book Service, Inc.),* 5 S. Union St, Lawrence, MA 01843 Tel 617-686-6409; Orders to: 99 Main St., Salem, NH 03079 Tel 617-685-4636.
Merritt Co, *(Merritt Co.; 0-930868),* 1661 Ninth St., Santa Monica, CA 90406.
Merton Hse, *(Merton House Publishing Co.; 0-916032),* 937 W. Liberty Dr., Wheaton, IL 60187 Tel 312-668-7410.
Mesa Pr IL, *(Mesa Press),* 5835 Kimbark Ave, Chicago, IL 60637 Tel 312-753-4013.
Mesorah Pubns, *(Mesorah Pubns., Ltd.; 0-89906),* 1969 Coney Island Ave., Brooklyn, NY 11223.
Messner, *(Messner, Julian; 0-671),* A Simon & Schuster Div. of Gulf & Western Corp., 1230 Ave. of the Americas, New York, NY 10020 Tel 212-245-6400.
Met Mus Art
See Metro Mus Art
Meta Pubns, *(META Pubns.; 0-916990),* P.O. Box 565, Cupertino, CA 95015 Tel 415-326-6465.
Metal Powder, *(Metal Powder Industries Federation; 0-918404),* 105 College Rd. E., Princeton, NJ 08540 Tel 609-452-7700.
Metaphysical, *(Metaphysical & Christian Science; 0-910964),* P.O. Box 6454, Metropolitan Sta., Los Angeles, CA 90055.

Metcut Res Assocs, *(Metcut Research Associates, Inc.; 0-936974),* 3980 Rosslyn Dr., Cincinnati, OH 45209.

Meth U Pr
See SMU Press

Methuen Inc, *(Methuen Inc.; 0-416),* 733 Third Ave, New York, NY 10017
Tel 212-922-3550; Dist. by: Transworld Distribution Services, Inc., 80 Northfield Ave., Raritan Center, Edison, NJ 08817.

Methuselah Bks, *(Methuselah Books; 0-937092),* Rt. 1 Spindle Rd., Ellsworth, ME 04605.

Metis Pr Inc, *(Metis Press, Inc.; 0-934816),* P.O. Box 25187, Chicago, IL 60625.

Metro Mus Art, *(Metropolitan Museum of Art; 0-87099),* 5th Ave. and 82nd St., New York, NY 10028 Tel 212-879-5500.

Mettler Studios, *(Mettler Studios, Inc.; 0-912536),* Tucson Creative Dance Ctr., 3131 N. Cherry Ave., Tucson, AZ 85719
Tel 602-327-7453.

Meyerbooks, *(Meyerbooks; 0-916638),* P.O. Box 427, 235 W. Main St., Glenwood, IL 60425
Tel 312-757-4950.

Mgmt Advisory, *(Management Advisory Associates, Inc.),* P.O. Box 703, Bowling Green, OH 43402 Tel 419-352-7782.

Mgmt & Indus Res Pubns, *(Management & Industrial Research Pubns.; 0-933684),* P.O. Box 7133, Kansas City, MO 64113
Tel 816-444-6622.

Micah Pubns, *(Micah Pubns.; 2-916288),* 255 Humphrey St., Marblehead, MA 01945
Tel 617-631-7601.

Mich St U Busn, *(Michigan State Univ., Div. of Research, Grad. School of Business Administration; 0-87744),* 5J Berkey Hall, East Lansing, MI 48824 Tel 517-355-7560.

Mich St U Pr, *(Michigan State Univ. Press; 0-87013),* 1405 S. Harrison Rd., 25 Manly Miles Bldg., East Lansing, MI 48824
Tel 517-355-9543.

Mich United Conserv, *(Michigan United Conservation Clubs; 0-933112),* P.O. Box 30235, Lansing, MI 48909
Tel 517-371-1041.

Michael Joseph
See Merrimack Bk Serv

Michelin, *(Michelin Guides & Maps),* Dept. of Michelin Tire Corp., P.O. Box 5022, New Hyde Park, NY 11042 Tel 212-895-2342.

Michelin Tire
See Michelin

Michie, *(Michie Co.; 0-87215),* P.O. Box 7587, Charlottesville, VA 22906
Tel 804-295-6171.

Mickler Hse, *(Mickler House Pubs., The; 0-913122),* P.O. Box 38, Chuluota, FL 32766 Tel 305-365-3636.

Microcomputer Appns, *(Microcomputer Applications; 0-935230),* P.O. Box E, Suisun City, CA 94585 Tel 707-422-1465.

Microfilming Corp, *(Microfilming Corp. of America; 0-88455; 0-667),* 1620 Hawkins Ave., P.O. Box 10, Sanford, NC 27330
Tel 919-775-3451.

Microform Rev, *(Microform Review; 0-913672),* 520 Riverside Ave., P.O. Box 405, Saugatuck Sta., Westport, CT 06880 Tel 203-226-6967.

Microwave Helps, *(Microwave Helps; 0-9602930),* P.O. Box 32223, Minneapolis, MN 55432 Tel 612-571-6091.

Mid-Am Coll, *(Mid-America College Art Assn.; 0-938852),* Art Dept., Univ. of Missouri-Kansas City, Kansas City, MO 64110.

Mid Am Pr, *(Mid-America Press; 0-9604672),* P.O. Box 21241, Columbia Heights, MN 55421 Tel 612-566-1968.

Mid Atlantic, *(Middle Atlantic Press; 0-912608),* P.O. Box 263, Wallingford, PA 19086
Tel 215-565-2445.

Mid South Sci Pubs, *(Mid-South Scientific Pubs.; 0-935974),* Box FM, Hwy. 82 E., Mississippi State Univ., Mississippi State, MS 39762.

Middle East Edit, *(Middle East Editorial Associates; 0-918992),* 1717 Massachusetts Ave., NW, Suite 100, Washington, DC 20036 Tel 202-797-7900.

Middleburg Pr, *(Middleburg Press, The; 0-931940),* Box 166, Orange City, IA 51401.

Midland Pub Co, *(Midland Publishing Co.),* Box 7, Sister Bay, WI 54234.

Midmarch Assocs, *(Midmarch Assocs.; 0-9602476),* Box 3204, Grand Central Sta., New York, NY 10017.

Midwest Heritage, *(Midwest Heritage Publishing Co.; 0-934582),* 108 Pearl St., Iowa City, IA 52240.

Midwest Plan Serv, *(Midwest Plan Service; 0-89373),* 122 Davidson Hall, Iowa State Univ., Ames, IA 50011 Tel 515-294-4337.

Midwest Pubns, *(Midwest Pubns. Co., Inc.; 0-910974; 0-89455),* P.O. Box 448, Pacific Grove, CA 93950 Tel 408-375-2455.

Milady, *(Milady Publishing Corp.; 0-87350),* 3839 White Plains Rd., Bronx, NY 10467
Tel 212-881-3000.

Military Aff Aero, *(Military Affairs/Aerospace Historian; 0-89126),* Eisenhower Hall, Kansas State University, Manhattan, KS 66506 Tel 913-532-6733.

Military Coll, *(Military Collectors News Press; 0-912958),* P.O. Box 7582, Tulsa, OK 74105.

Milky Way-Kosmos
See KOSMOS

Millenium Hse, *(Millenium House Pubs.; 0-916538),* P.O. Box 85, Agoura, CA 91301
Tel 213-889-3711.

Miller Bks, *(Miller Books; 0-912472),* 2908 W. Valley Blvd., Alhambra, CA 91803
Tel 213-284-7607.

Miller Freeman, *(Miller Freeman Pubns., Inc.; 0-87930),* 500 Howard St., San Francisco, CA 94105 Tel 415-397-1881.

Mills Pub Co, *(Mills Publishing Co.; 0-935356),* Box 6158, King Sta., Santa Ana, CA 92706
Tel 714-636-3830.

Milwaukee County, *(Milwaukee County Historical Society; 0-938076),* 910 N. Third St., Milwaukee, WI 53203
Tel 414-273-8288.

Milwaukee Journal, *(Milwaukee Journal, Public Service Bureau),* 333 W. State St., Milwaukee, WI 53201 Tel 414-224-2120; Orders to: P.O. Box 661, Milwaukee, WI 53201.

Milwaukee Pub Mus, *(Milwaukee Public Museum; 0-89326),* 800 W. Wells St., Milwaukee, WI 53233 Tel 414-278-2771.

Ministry Pubns, *(Ministry Pubns.; 0-938234),* P.O. Box 276, Redlands, CA 92373.

Minn Geol Surv, *(Minnesota Geological Survey; 0-934938),* University of Minnesota, 1633 Eustis St., St. Paul, MN 55108
Tel 612-373-3372.

Minn Hist, *(Minnesota Historical Society; 0-87351),* 690 Cedar St., St. Paul, MN 55101 Tel 612-296-2264; Orders to: 1500 Mississippi St., St. Paul, MN 55101.

Minn Rev Pr, *(Minnesota Review Press; 0-936484),* P.O. Box 211, Bloomington, IN 47402.

Minn Scholarly, *(Minnesota Scholarly Press, Inc.; 0-933474),* P.O. Box 224, Mankato, MN 56001 Tel 507-387-4964; Dist. by: Independent Pubs. Group, 14 Vanderventer Ave., Port Washington, NY 11050.

Minneapolis Inst Arts, *(Minneapolis Institute of Arts; 0-912964),* 2400 Third Ave., S., Minneapolis, MN 55404 Tel 612-870-3029.

Minobras, *(Minobras-Mining Services & Research),* P.O. Box 262, Dana Point, CA 92629 Tel 714-493-6066.

MIR PA, *(MIR; 0-935352),* 845 Suismon Dr., Pittsburgh, PA 15212 Tel 412-322-1319; Orders to: P.O. Box 962, Pittsburgh, PA 15230.

Mission Adv Res Com Ctr
See MARC

Mission Dolores, *(Mission Dolores Pubs.; 0-912748),* 193 Los Robles Dr., Burlingame, CA 94010.

Mission Pubs CA
See Mission Dolores

MIT Outing, *(MIT Outing Club; 0-9601698),* W20-461, MIT, Cambridge, MA 02139
Tel 617-253-2988.

MIT Pr, *(MIT Press; 0-262),* 28 Carleton St., Cambridge, MA 02142 Tel 617-253-2884.

Mitchell Pub, *(Mitchell Publishing, Inc.; 0-938188),* 116 Royal Oak, Santa Cruz, CA 95066.

MJ Pubns, *(MJ Pubns.; 0-9605144),* 6363 Lynwood Hill Rd., McLean, VA 22101.

MJG Co, *(MJG Co.; 0-932632),* P.O. Box 7743, Midland, TX 79703 Tel 915-682-3184.

MLM Pubs, *(MLM Pubs.; 0-939102),* 515 S. We-Go Trail, Mt. Prospect, IL 60056.

MLP
See Crane Pub Co

MLP Ent, *(MLP Enterprises),* P.O. Box 31-516, San Francisco, CA 94131 Tel 415-626-3131.

MN Pubs, *(M. N. Pubs.; 0-932964),* R
55, Bonnerdale, AR 71933
Tel 501-991-3815.

MNP Star, *(MNP Star Enterprises; 0-938*
P.O. Box 8267, S.F. International Airpo
San Francisco, CA 94128.

Mockingbird Bks, *(Mockingbird Books; 0-89176),* Box 624, St. Simons Island, G
31522 Tel 912-638-7212.

Mod Handcraft, *(Modern Handcraft, Inc.; 0-86675),* 4251 Pennsylvania Ave., Kansas City, MO 64111.

Mod Media Inst, *(Modern Media Institute; 0-935742),* 556 Central Ave., St. Petersburg, FL 33701 Tel 813-821-9494.

Modern Curr, *(Modern Curriculum Press; 0-87895),* Div. of Esquire, Inc., 13900 Prospect Rd., Cleveland, OH 44136
Tel 216-238-2222.

Modern Lang, *(Modern Language Assn. of America; 0-87352),* 62 Fifth Ave., New York, NY 10011 Tel 212-741-5588.

Modern Signs, *(Modern Signs Press; 0-916708),* 3131 Walker Lee Dr., Rossmoor, CA 90720; Orders to: P.O. Box 1181, Los Alamitos, CA 90720 Tel 213-596-8548.

Moffett, *(Moffett Publishing Co.),* Rt. 3, Box 175A, Cushing, OK 74023.

Mojave Bks, *(Mojave Books; 0-87881),* 7040 Darby Ave., Reseda, CA 91335
Tel 213-342-3403.

Mole Pub Co, *(Mole Pub. Co.; 0-9604464),* Route 1, Box 618, Bonners Ferry, ID 83805
Tel 208-267-7349.

Momos, *(Momo's Press; 0-917672),* P.O. Box 14061, San Francisco, CA 94114.

Mona Pub, *(Mona Publishing Co., Ltd.; 0-938952),* 79 Wall St., Suite 501, New York, NY 10005.

Monad Pr, *(Monad Press; 0-913460),* Dist. by: Pathfinder Press, 410 West St., New York, NY 10014 Tel 212-741-0690.

Monarch Pr, *(Monarch Press; 0-671),* Div. of Simon & Schuster, Inc., 1230 Ave. of the Americas, 12th Fl., New York, NY 10020
Tel 212-245-6400.

Money Digest
See Zimmerman

Monitor, *(Monitor Book Co., Inc.; 0-9600252),* 195 S. Beverly Dr., Beverly Hills, CA 90212
Tel 213-271-5558.

Monkey Man, *(Monkey Man Press; 0-9605594),* 8710 Wonderland Pk. Ave., Los Angeles, CA 90046 Tel 213-654-9154.

Monkey Sisters, *(Monkey Sisters, The; 0-933606),* 22971 Via Cruz, Laguna Niguel, CA 92677 Tel 714-496-1445.

Monroe County Lib, *(Monroe County Library System),* 3700 S. Custer Rd., Monroe, MI 48161.

Montaigne, *(Montaigne Publishing, Inc.; 0-917430),* 99 El Toyonal, Orinda, CA 94563 Tel 415-254-8082.

Montessori Learn
See Parent-Child Pr

Montessori Wkshps, *(Montessori Workshop; 0-915676),* 501 Salem Dr., Ithaca, NY 14850.

Montfort Pubns, *(Montfort Pubns.; 0-910984),* 26 S. Saxon Ave., Bay Shore, NY 11706
Tel 516-665-0726.

Montgomery Co Govt, *(Montgomery County Govt.; 0-9601094),* 99 Maryland Ave., Rockville, MD 20850 Tel 301-279-1401.

Montgomery Mus, *(Montgomery Museum of Fine Arts; 0-89280),* 440 S. McDonough St., Montgomery, AL 36104 Tel 205-834-3490.

Monthly Rev, *(Monthly Review Press; 0-85345),* 62 W. 14th St., New York, NY 10011
Tel 212-691-2555.

Moody, *(Moody Press; 0-8024),* 2101 Howard St., Evanston, IL 60645 Tel 312-973-7800; Orders to: 1777 Shermer Rd., Northbrook, IL 60062.

Moon Over Mntn, *(Moon Over the Mountain Publishing Co.; 0-9602970),* 6700 W. 44th Ave., Wheatridge, CO 80033
Tel 303-420-4272.

Moonlight Pubns, *(Moonlight Pubns.; 0-931350),* Box 671, La Jolla, CA 92038.

Moore Pub Co, *(Moore Publishing Co.; 0-87716),* P.O. Box 3036, W. Durham Sta., Durham, NC 27705 Tel 919-286-2250.

Moore-Taylor-Moore
See MTM Pub Co

Mor-Mac, *(Mor-Mac Publishing Co., Inc.; 0-912178),* P.O. Box 984, Fairborn, OH 45324 Tel 513-876-1535.

...*hing Corp.;* ...vd., P.O. Box ... 70896 ... by: Aviation Book ...vd., Glendale, CA 91201

...*ouse-Barlow Co.; 0-8192),* ..., Wilton, CT 06897 ...0721.

...*Moretus Press, Inc. The; 0-89679),* ...ison Ave., New York, NY 10016 ...2-685-2250; Orders to: P.O. Box 530, ...sburg, PA 17108 Tel 717-545-2097.

...**,** *(Morgan & Morgan, Inc.; 0-87100),* 145 Palisades St., Dobbs Ferry, NY 10522 Tel 914-693-9303.

Morgan-Pacific, *(Morgan-Pacific Corp.; 0-89430),* P. O. Box 456, Lomita, CA 90717 Tel 213-833-2194; Orders to: P. O. Box 4627, Mountain View, CA 94042.

Morgan Pr CA
See Morgan-Pacific

Morgan Pr-Farag
See Morgan-Pacific

Morning Glory, *(Morning Glory Press; 0-930934),* 6595 San Haroldo Way, Buena Park, CA 90620 Tel 714-828-1998.

Morningstar, *(Morningstar, Jim; 0-9604856),* 2728 N. Prospect Ave., Milwaukee, WI 53211.

Morrow, *(Morrow, William, & Co., Inc.; 0-688),* 105 Madison Ave., New York, NY 10016 Tel 212-889-3050; Orders to: Wilmor Warehouse, 6 Henderson Dr., West Caldwell, NJ 07006.

Morse Pr, *(Morse Press, Inc.; 0-933350),* 417 E. Pine, Seattle, WA 98122 Tel 206-323-1820.

Morton Pub, *(Morton Publishing Co.; 0-89582),* 2700 E. Bates Ave., Box 10128, Denver, CO 80210 Tel 303-759-2112.

Mosaic Pr, *(Mosaic Press, The; 0-934696),* P.O. Box 41502, Tucson, AZ 85717.

Mosby, *(Mosby, C. V., Co.; 0-8016),* 11830 Westline Industrial Dr., St. Louis, MO 63141 Tel 314-872-8370.

Moss Pubns, *(Moss Pubns.; 0-930870),* P.O. Box 644, Berkeley, CA 94701 Tel 415-653-6458.

Mother Earth, *(Mother Earth News, The; 0-938432),* P.O. Box 70, Hendersonville, NC 28791.

Motorbooks Intl, *(Motorbooks International, Pubs. & Wholesalers, Inc.; 0-87938),* P.O. Box 2, 729 Prospect Ave, Osceola, WI 54020 Tel 800-826-6600.

Motormatics, *(Motormatics Pubns.; 0-930968),* c/o Beach Cities Enterprises, 3640 E. Tenth St., Long Beach, CA 90804 Tel 213-434-6701.

Mott Media, *(Mott Media; 0-915134),* 1000 E. Huron, Milford, MI 48042 Tel 313-685-8773.

Mountain Pr, *(Mountain Press Publishing Co., Inc.; 0-87842),* P.O. Box 2399, Missoula, MT 59806 Tel 406-728-1900.

Mountain St Tel, *(Mountain States Telephone & Telegraph Co., Regulatory Matters Division; 0-9602580),* 931-14th St., Rm. 1010, Denver, CO 80202.

Mountaineers, *(Mountaineers-Books; 0-916890; 0-89886),* 719-B Pike St., Seattle, WA 98101 Tel 206-682-4636.

Mouton, *(Mouton Pubs.),* Div. of Walter De Gruyter, Inc., 200 Saw Mill River Rd., Hawthorne, NY 10532 Tel 914-747-0111.

Mouvement Pubns, *(Mouvement Pubns.; 0-932392),* 102 Irving Place, Ithaca, NY 14850 Tel 607-273-1745.

Move Short Soc, *(Movement Shorthand Society, Inc.; 0-914336),* P.O. Box 7344, Newport Beach, CA 92660 Tel 714-644-8342.

Movement New Soc, *(Movement for A New Society Press),* 4722 Baltimore Ave., Philadelphia, PA 19143 Tel 215-724-1464.

Mowry Pr, *(Mowry Press; 0-9605368),* Box 405, Wayland, MA 01778.

MSC Inc, *(Management & Systems Consultants, Inc.; 0-918356),* Univ. Stn., Box 40457, Tucson, AZ 85717 Tel 602-299-9615.

MT Coun Indian, *(Montana Council for Indian Education; 0-89992),* 3311-R 4th Ave. N., Billings, MT 59101 Tel 406-252-2071.

MT Mag, *(Montana Magazine, Inc.; 0-938314),* Box 5630, Helena, MT 59601 Tel 406-443-2842.

MTI Tele, *(MTI Teleprograms Inc.; 0-916070),* 3710 Commercial Ave., Northbrook, IL 60062 Tel 312-291-9400.

MTM Pub Co, *(M/T/M Publishing Co.),* P.O. Box 245, Washougal, WA 98671.

Mudborn, *(Mudborn Press; 0-930012),* 209 W. De La Guerra, Santa Barbara, CA 93101 Tel 805-962-9996.

Multimedia, *(Multimedia Publishing Corp.; 0-8334),* 7 Garber Hill Rd., Blauvelt, NY 10913 Tel 914-359-9292.

Multnomah, *(Multnomah Press; 0-930014),* 10209 S.E. Division St., Portland, OR 97266 Tel 503-257-0526.

Munger Africana Lib, *(Munger Africana Library; 0-934912),* Tel 213-795-6811; c/o California Institute of Technology, Pasadena, CA 91125.

Munger Oil, *(Munger Oil Information Service),* 9800 S. Sepulveda Blvd., Los Angeles, CA 90045 Tel 213-776-3990.

Muns, *(Muns, George F.; 0-9604924),* 721 E. Blanco Blvd., P.O. Box 878, Bloomfield, NM 87413 Tel 505-632-3987.

Murrison Co, *(Murrison Co., The; 0-9602110),* 3879 Northstrand Dr., Decatur, GA 30035.

Mus Am China Trade, *(Museum of the American China Trade; 0-937650),* 215 Adams St., Milton, MA 02186 Tel 617-696-1815.

Mus Am Ind, *(Museum of the American Indian; 0-934490),* Broadway at 155th St., New York, NY 10032 Tel 212-283-2420.

Mus Anthro MO, *(Univ. of Missouri, Museum of Anthropology; 0-913134),* 104 Swallow Hall, Columbia, MO 65211 Tel 314-882-3764.

Mus Fine Arts Boston, *(Museum of Fine Arts, Boston; 0-87846),* 465 Huntington Ave., Boston, MA 02115 Tel 617-267-9300.

Mus Graphics, *(Museum Graphics; 0-913832),* 2643-B Fair Oaks Ave., Redwood City, CA 94063 Tel 415-368-5531; Orders to: Little, Brown & Co., 200 West St., Waltham, MA 02154.

Mus Sci & Hist, *(Museum of Science & History, The; 0-9604642),* MacArthur Park, Little Rock, AR 72202.

Mus Sys, *(Museum Systems),* 817 N. La Cienaga Blvd., Los Angeles, CA 90069 Tel 213-657-5811.

Museum Mobile, *(Museum of the City of Mobile; 0-914334),* 355 Government St., Mobile, AL 36602 Tel 205-438-7569.

Museum Mod Art, *(Museum of Modern Art; 0-87070),* 11 W. 53rd St., New York, NY 10019 Tel 212-956-7216; Orders to: Customer Sales Service, 11 W. 53rd St., New York, NY 10019 Tel 212-956-7264.

Museum NM Pr, *(Museum of New Mexico Press; 0-89013),* P.O. Box 2087, Santa Fe, NM 87503 Tel 505-827-2352.

Museum of NM Pr
See Museum NM Pr

Mushroom Cave, *(Mushroom Cave, Inc., The; 0-9601516),* P.O. Box 894, Battle Creek, MI 49016 Tel 616-962-3497.

Music Sales, *(Music Sales Corp.; 0-8256),* Dist. by: Quick Fox, Inc., 33 W. 60th St., New York, NY 10023 Tel 212-246-0325. *Imprints:* Hidden Hse (Hidden House); Quick Fox (Quick Fox).

Musical Box Soc, *(Musical Box Society International, The; 0-915000),* 495 Springfield Ave., Summit, NJ 07901.

Musicdata, *(Musicdata, Inc.; 0-88478),* 18 W. Chelten Ave., Philadelphia, PA 19144 Tel 215-842-0555.

Myriade, *(Myriade Press, Inc., The; 0-918142),* Seven Stony Run, New Rochelle, NY 10804 Tel 914-235-8470.

Myrin Institute, *(Myrin Institute, Inc.; 0-913098),* 521 Park Ave., New York, NY 10021 Tel 212-758-6475.

Mysterious Pr, *(Mysterious Press; 0-89296),* 129 W. 56th St., New York, NY 10019.

Mystic Seaport, *(Mystic Seaport Museum, Inc.; 0-913372),* Mystic, CT 06355 Tel 203-536-2631.

N Dak Inst, *(North Dakota Institute for Regional Studies; 0-911042),* State College Sta., Fargo, ND 58105 Tel 701-237-8338.

N H Ludlow, *(Ludlow, Norman H.; 0-916706),* 516 Arnett Blvd., Rochester, NY 14619 Tel 716-235-0951.

N Hays, *(Hays, Nicolas, Ltd.),* P.O. Box 612, York Beach, ME 03910 Tel 207-363-4393; Dist. by: Samuel Weiser Inc., 625 Broadway, New York, NY 10012.

N Ill U Pr, *(Northern Illinois Univ. Press; 0-87580),* DeKalb, IL 60115 Tel 815-753-1826.

N Miller, *(Miller, Neil; 0-9601444),* 747 Bruce Dr., East Meadow, NY 11554 Tel 516-292-9569.

N P Cartwright, *(Cartwright, Nellie Parodi, Mrs.; 0-9601482),* 4348 Via Frascati, Rancho Palos Verdes, CA 90274 Tel 213-833-7586.

N P Evans, *(Evans, Norma P.; 0-937418),* 2211 Liberty, Beaumont, TX 77701 Tel 713-835-7175.

N Point Pr, *(North Point Press),* 850 Talbot Ave., Berkeley, CA 94706 Tel 415-527-6260.

N S Wait, *(N. S. Wait; 0-911588),* Box 407, Valparaiso, IN 46383; Formerly H. H. Wait Pub.

N Stonington, *(North Stonington Press; 0-938538),* 14 Zaccheus Mead Lane, Greenwich, CT 06830.

N T Smith, *(Smith, Nicholas T.; 0-935164),* P.O. Box 66, Bronxville, NY 10708 Tel 914-337-2794.

N Watson, *(Neale Watson Academic Pubns. Inc.; 0-88202),* 156 Fifth Ave., Suite 1100, New York, NY 10010 Tel 212-675-7480.

NACASBVH, *(National Accreditation Council for Agencies Serving the Blind & Visually Handicapped; 0-912948),* 79 Madison Ave., Suite 1406, New York, NY 10016 Tel 212-683-8581.

NACM, *(National Assn. of Credit Management; 0-934914),* Book Edit Dept., 475 Park Ave., S., New York, NY 10016 Tel 212-578-4431.

NAEB, *(National Assn. of Educational Broadcasters; 0-8105),* 1346 Connecticut Ave., N.W., Washington, DC 20036 Tel 202-785-1100.

NAIA Pubns, *(National Assn. of Intercollegiate Athletics),* 1221 Baltimore St., Kansas City, MO 64105 Tel 816-842-5050.

Naiad Pr, *(Naiad Press; 0-930044),* P. O. Box 10543, Tallahassee, FL 32302 Tel 904-539-9322.

NAIS, *(National Assn. of Independent Schools; 0-934388),* 18 Tremont St., Boston, MA 02108 Tel 617-723-6900.

NAL, *(New American Library; 0-451; 0-452; 0-453),* 1633 Broadway, New York, NY 10019 Tel 212-397-8000; Orders to: 120 Woodbine St., Bergenfield, NJ 07621 Tel 201-387-0600. *Imprints:* Ment (Mentor Books); Mer (Meridian Books); Plume (Plume Books); Sig (Signet Books); Sig Classics (Signet Classics).

Nantucket Nautical, *(Nantucket Nautical Pubs.),* 5 New Mill St., Nantucket, MA 02554.

Nash Pub, *(Nash Publishing Corp.; 0-8402),* 1290 Ave. of Americas, Suite 4150, New York, NY 10019 Tel 212-977-9500.

Nass, *(Nass, Sylvan & Ulla),* 220 Sunnybrook Rd., Flourtown, PA 19031.

Nat Learn Res, *(Natural Learning Resources; 0-936214),* 5151 Monroe, P.O. Box 8443, Toledo, OH 43623.

Nat Therapy, *(Natural Therapy Foundation Press, The; 0-937792),* 5 Greenleaf, Irvine, CA 92714.

Natl Acad Pr, *(National Academy Press; 0-309),* 2101 Constitution Ave., Washington, DC 20418 Tel 202-389-6942; Orders to: Publications Sales Office, 2101 Constitution Ave., Washington, DC 20418 Tel 202-389-6731.

Natl Acad Sci
See Natl Acad Pr

Natl Alliance, *(National Alliance; 0-937944),* Box 3535, Washington, DC 20007 Tel 703-525-3223.

Natl Art Ed, *(National Art Education Assn.; 0-937652),* 1916 Association Dr., Reston, VA 22091 Tel 703-860-8000.

Natl Assn Child Ed, *(National Assn. for the Education of Young Children; 0-912674),* 1834 Connecticut Ave., N.W., Washington, DC 20009 Tel 202-232-8777.

Natl Assn Coll, *(National Assn. of College & University Business Officers; 0-915164),* 1 Dupont Circle, Suite 510, Washington, DC 20036 Tel 202-296-2344.

Natl Assn Deaf, *(National Assn. of the Deaf; 0-913072),* 814 Thayer Ave., Silver Spring, MD 20910 Tel 301-587-1788.

Natl Assn Principals, *(National Assn. of Secondary School Principals; 0-88210),* 1904 Association Dr., Reston, VA 22091 Tel 703-860-0200.

Natl Assn Soc Wkrs, *(National Assn. of Social Workers; 0-87101),* 2 Park Ave., New York, NY 10016 Tel 212-689-9771; Orders to: Publications Sales, NASW,, 1425 "H" St., N.W., Washington, DC 20005.
Natl Assn Women, *(National Assn. for Women Deans, Administrators & Counselors),* 1625 Eye St., N.W., Washington, DC 20006 Tel 202-659-9330.
Natl Audubon, *(National Audubon Society; 0-930698),* 950 Third Ave., New York, NY 10022 Tel 212-546-9139; Orders to: Service Dept., 950 Third Ave., New York, NY 10022 Tel 212-546-9112.
Natl Behavior, *(National Behavior Systems; 0-937654),* 11601 Balboa Blvd., Granada Hills, CA 91344 Tel 213-363-7160.
Natl Book, *(National Book Co.; 0-89420),* Div. of Educational Research Associates, 333 S.W. Park Ave., Portland, OR 97205 Tel 503-228-6345.
Natl Cable, *(National Cable Television Assn.),* 918 Sixteenth St., N.W., Washington, DC 20006.
Natl Cath Educ, *(National Catholic Educational Assn.),* 1 Dupont Circle, Suite 350, Washington, DC 20036 Tel 202-293-5954.
Natl Cath Reporter, *(National Catholic Reporter Publishing Co., Inc.; 0-934134),* 115 E. Armour, Box 281, Kansas City, MO 64141 Tel 816-531-0538.
Natl Christian Pr, *(National Christian Press, Inc.; 0-934916),* P. O. Box 49118, Algood, TN 38501 Tel 615-537-9434.
Natl Clearinghse Bilingual Ed, *(National Clearinghouse for Bilingual Education; 0-89763),* 1300 Wilson Blvd., Suite B2-11, Rosslyn, VA 22209 Tel 800-336-4560.
Natl Ctr Educ Broker, *(National Center for Educational Brokering; 0-935612),* 405 Oak St., Syracuse, NY 13203.
Natl Ctr Health Stats, *(National Center for Health Statistics; 0-8406),* Federal Center Bldg., Rm. 1-57, 3700 East-West Hwy., Hyattsville, MD 20782 Tel 301-436-8586.
Natl Ctr St Courts, *(National Center for State Courts; 0-89656),* 300 Newport Ave., Williamsburg, VA 23185 Tel 804-253-2000.
Natl Ed Res, *(National Educational Resources, Inc.; 0-89498),* 1525 E. 53rd St., Suite 824, Chicago, IL 60615 Tel 312-684-4920.
Natl Ed Stand, *(National Education Standards; 0-918192),* 617 W. 7th St., Suite 300, Los Angeles, CA 90017 Tel 213-623-9135.
Natl Finan
See Lincoln Pub
Natl Fire Prot, *(National Fire Protection Assn.; 0-87765),* 470 Atlantic Ave., Boston, MA 02110 Tel 617-482-8755.
Natl Genealogical, *(National Genealogical Society; 0-915156),* 1921 Sunderland Place, N.W., Washington, DC 20036 Tel 202-785-2123.
Natl Geog, *(National Geographic Society; 0-87044),* 17th & "M" Sts., N.W., Washington, DC 20036 Tel 202-857-7000.
Natl Inst Burn, *(National Institute for Burn Medicine; 0-917478),* 909 E. Ann St., Ann Arbor, MI 48104 Tel 313-769-9000.
Natl Journal, *(National Journal; 0-89234),* 1730 "M" St., N.W., Washington, DC 20036 Tel 212-833-8000.
Natl Judicial Coll, *(National Judicial College),* Judicial College Bldg., Univ. of Nevada, Reno, NV 89557 Tel 702-784-6747.
Natl Learning, *(National Learning Corp.; 0-8373; 0-8293),* 212 Michael Dr., Syosset, NY 11791 Tel 516-921-8888.
Natl Marriage, *(National Marriage Encounter; 0-936098),* 955 Lake Dr., St. Paul, MN 55120.
Natl Micrograph, *(National Micrographics Assn.; 0-89258),* 8719 Colesville Rd., Silver Spring, MD 20910 Tel 301-587-8202.
Natl Notary, *(National Notary Assn.; 0-9600158; 0-933134),* 23012 Ventura Blvd., Woodland Hills, CA 91364 Tel 213-347-2035.
Natl Planning, *(National Planning Assn.),* 1606 New Hampshire Ave N.W., Washington, DC 20009 Tel 202-265-7685.
Natl Pub IL, *(National Publishing Corp., Pubs.),* 2720 Des Plaines Ave., Des Plaines, IL 60018 Tel 312-297-5115.
Natl Rail Hist Soc DC Chap, *(National Railway Historical Society, Washington D.C. Chapter; 0-933954),* P.O. Box 3512, Central Sta., Arlington, VA 22203.
Natl Rail Hist Soc DC
See Natl Rail Hist Soc DC Chap
Natl Rail Rochester, *(National Railway Historical Society, Rochester Chapter; 0-9605296),* P.O. Box 664, Rochester, NY 14602 Tel 716-726-3903.
Natl Recycling, *(National Assn. of Recycling Industries),* 330 Madison Ave., New York, NY 10017 Tel 212-867-7330.
Natl Register, *(National Register Publishing Co. Inc.; 0-87217),* Subs. of Standard Rate & Data Inc., 5201 Old Orchard Rd., Skokie, IL 60077 Tel 312-470-3100.
Natl Ret Merch, *(National Retail Merchants Assn.; 0-87102),* 100 W. 31st St., New York, NY 10001 Tel 212-244-8780.
Natl Rifle Assn, *(National Rifle Assn.; 0-935998),* 1600 Rhode Island Ave. N.W., Washington, DC 20036 Tel 202-828-6000; Dist. by: John Olson Co., 294 W. Oakland Ave., Oakland, NJ 07436 Tel 201-337-3355.
Natl Rural, *(National Rural Electric Cooperative Assn.),* 1800 Massachusetts Ave., N.W., Washington, DC 20036 Tel 202-857-9500.
Natl Sch PR, *(National School of Public Relations Assn.; 0-87545),* 1801 N. Moore St., Arlington, VA 22209 Tel 703-528-5840.
Natl Sci Tchrs, *(National Science Teachers Assn.; 0-87355),* Affiliate of American Association for the Advancement of Science, 1742 Connecticut Ave., N.W., Washington, DC 20009 Tel 202-328-5872.
Natl Sq Dance, *(National Square Dance Directory; 0-9605494),* P.O. Box 54055, Jackson, MS 39208 Tel 601-825-6831.
Natl Tech Info, *(National Technical Information Service, U.S. Dept. of Commerce),* U.S. Dept. of Commerce, 425 13th St., N.W., Suite 620, Washington, DC 20004 Tel 202-724-3383; Orders to: U.S. Dept of Commerce, 5285 Port Royal Rd., Springfield, VA 22161 Tel 703-487-4650.
Natl Textbk, *(National Textbook Co.; 0-8442),* 8260 N. Elmwood, Skokie, IL 60077 Tel 312-679-4210; Orders to: 8259 Niles Ctr. Rd., Skokie, IL 60077.
Natl Underwriter, *(National Underwriter Co.; 0-87218),* 420 E. Fourth St., Cincinnati, OH 45202 Tel 513-721-2140.
Natl Video, *(National Video Clearinghouse, Inc., The; 0-935478),* 100 Lafayette Dr., Syosset, NY 11791 Tel 516-364-3686.
Natl Wildlife, *(National Wildlife Federation; 0-912186),* 8925 Leesburg Pike, Vienna, VA 22180 Tel 703-790-4431.
Natural History Bks
See Sabbot-Natural Hist Bks
Nature Bks Pubs, *(Nature Books Pubs.; 0-912542),* P.O. Box 12157, Jackson, MS 39211 Tel 601-956-5686.
Nature Study, *(Nature Study Guild; 0-912550),* P.O. Box 972, Berkeley, CA 94701.
Naturegraph, *(Naturegraph Pubs., Inc.; 0-911010; 0-87961),* P.O. Box 1075, Happy Camp, CA 96039 Tel 916-493-5353.
NAUI, *(National Assn. of Underwater Instructors; 0-916974),* P.O. Box 630, Colton, CA 92324 Tel 714-824-5440.
Nautical & Aviation, *(Nautical & Aviation Publishing Co. of America, The; 0-933852),* 8 Randall St., Annapolis, MD 21401 Tel 301-267-8522.
Nautical Avia
See Nautical & Aviation
Navajo Curr, *(Navajo Curriculum Center Press; 0-936008),* Rough Rock Demonstration School, Star Rte. 1, Rough Rock, AZ 86503.
Naval Inst Pr, *(Naval Institute Press; 0-87021),* Annapolis, MD 21402 Tel 301-268-6110.
NavPress, *(NavPress Publishing Co.; 0-89109),* Div. of The Navigators, P. O. Box 6000, Colorado Springs, CO 80934 Tel 303-598-1212.
Nazarene, *(Nazarene Publishing House; 0-8341),* P.O. Box 527, Kansas City, MO 64141 Tel 816-931-1900.
NC Archives, *(North Carolina Division of Archives & History; 0-86526),* 109 E. Jones St., Raleigh, NC 27611 Tel 919-733-7442.
NC Natl Hist, *(North Carolina State Museum of Natural History; 0-917134),* 102 N. Salisbury St., P.O. Box 27647, Raleigh, NC 27611 Tel 919-733-7450.
NCCB, *(National Citizens Committee for Broadcasting; 0-9603466),* P.O. Box 12038, N.W., Washington, DC 20005.
NCCE, *(National Committee for Citiz Education; 0-934460),* Wilde Lake Green, Suite 410, Columbia, MD 21 Tel 301-997-9300.
NCTE, *(National Council of Teachers of 0-8141),* 1111 Kenyon Rd., Urbana, IL 61801 Tel 217-328-3870.
NCTM, *(National Council of Teachers of Mathematics; 0-87353),* 1906 Association Dr., Reston, VA 22091 Tel 703-620-9840.
NE Bks, *(Northeast Books; 0-937374),* 431 Wyoming Ave., I.B.E.W. Bldg., Scranton, PA 18503.
NE Conf Teach Foreign, *(Northeast Conference on the Teaching of Foreign Languages; 0-915432),* P.O. Box 623, Middlebury, VT 05753 Tel 802-388-2598.
NE U Pr, *(Northeastern Univ. Press; 0-930350),* 360 Huntington Ave., Rm. 17w, Northeastern Univ., Boston, MA 02115 Tel 617-437-2783; Orders to: P.O. Box 116, Boston, MA 02117.
NEA, *(National Education Assn.; 0-8106),* 1201 16th St., N.W., Washington, DC 20036 Tel 202-833-4062; Orders to: The Academic Bldg., Saw Mill Rd., West Haven, CT 06516 Tel 203-934-2669.
Neal Assoc, *(Neal, Richard, Associates),* 370 S. George Mason Dr., 1715-N, Falls Church, VA 22041.
Neal-Schuman, *(Neal-Schuman Pubs., Inc.; 0-918212),* 64 University Place, New York, NY 10003 Tel 212-473-5170; Orders to: P.O. Box 1687, FDR Sta., New York, NY 10150.
Nebraska Hist, *(Nebraska State Historical Society),* 1500 R St, Lincoln, NE 68503 Tel 402-471-3270.
Neechee Assoc, *(Neechee Associates, Inc.; 0-9602582),* 6664 Paseo Dorado, Tucson, AZ 85715.
Negro U Pr, *(Negro Universities Press; 0-8371),* Affiliate of Greenwood Press, 88 Post Rd. West, Westport, CT 06881 Tel 203-226-3571.
Neihardt Found, *(Neihardt, John G., Foundation, Inc.),* Bancroft, NE 68004 Tel 402-648-3388.
Nelson, *(Nelson, Thomas, Inc.; 0-8407),* P.O. Box 946, 407 Seventh Ave. S., Nashville, TN 37203 Tel 800-251-1236.
Nelson B Robinson, *(Robinson, Nelson B. Bookseller; 0-930352),* P.O. Box 153, Rockport, MA 01966 Tel 617-546-3828.
Nelson-Hall, *(Nelson-Hall Inc.; 0-911012; 0-88229; 0-8304),* 111 N. Canal St., Chicago, IL 60606 Tel 312-930-9446.
Nembutsu Pr, *(Nembutsu Press; 0-912624),* 6257 Golden West Ave., Temple City, CA 91780.
Nesbit, *(Nesbit, Norman L.; 0-911746),* 2104 Goddard Place, Boulder, CO 80303 Tel 303-494-6206.
Nettleton Hse, *(Nettleton House),* 737 Fifth Ave., San Francisco, CA 94118.
Nevada Pubns, *(Nevada Pubns.; 0-913814),* P.O. Box 15444, Las Vegas, NV 89114 Tel 702-871-1800.
New Age, *(New Age Press, Inc.; 0-87613),* 3912 Wilshire Blvd., Los Angeles, CA 90010 Tel 213-387-7103.
New-Age Foods
See Soyfoods-New Age
New Age Pr NM, *(New Age Press Inc.),* 320 Artist Rd., Santa Fe, NM 87501 Tel 505-982-1500.
New Benjamin, *(New Benjamin Franklin House, The; 0-933488),* 304 W. 58th St., 5th Fl., New York, NY 10019 Tel 212-247-7484.
New Capernaum, *(New Capernaum Works),* 4615 N.E. Emerson St., Portland, OR 97218.
New City, *(New City Press; 0-911782),* 206 Skillman Ave., Brooklyn, NY 11211 Tel 212-782-2844.
New Comm Pr, *(New Community Press; 0-934698),* P.O. Box 428, Columbia, MD 21045 Tel 301-596-3755.
New Day Pr, *(New Day Press; 0-913678),* c/o Karamu House, 2355 E. 89th St., Cleveland, OH 44106.
New Dimen Studio, *(New Dimension Studio; 0-916928),* 3872 Augusta Dr., Rm. 1, Nashville, TN 37209 Tel 615-227-6648; Orders to: P.O. Box 90492, Nashville, TN 37209.

Publishing
...ve., New York,
...30; Dist. by: W.
... Ave., New York,

Books; 0-918258), 58
...ew York, NY 10003
...2.

...NC
..., *(New England Press Inc., The;*
...*),* P.O. Box 525, Shelburne, VT
...Tel 802-985-2569.
...**and Marine**
...*e* URI MAS
...**Era,** *(New Era Press; 0-937590),* P.O. Box 124, Weaverville, CA 96093.
...**ew Era** *Imprint of* **World Merch Import**
...**New Glide,** *(New Glide Pubns., Inc.; 0-912078),* 330 Ellis St., Rm. 404, San Francisco, CA 94102 Tel 415-775-0918.
New Hope, *(New Hope Publishing Co.; 0-915460),* Dist. by: Midway Copy Services, P.O. Box 378, Lahaska, PA 18931 Tel 212-794-5757.
New Horizons, *(New Horizons Press; 0-914914),* P.O. Box 1758, Chico, CA 95927 Tel 916-345-0225.
New Issues MI, *(New Issues Press; 0-932826),* Institute of Public Affairs, Western Michigan Univ., Kalamazoo, MI 49008 Tel 616-383-3983.
New Leaf, *(New Leaf Press; 0-89221),* P.O. Box 1045, Harrison, AR 72601 Tel 501-741-2514.
New Letters, *(New Letters Books; 0-938652),* 5346 Charlotte, Kansas City, MO 64110 Tel 816-276-1168.
New London County, *(New London County Historical Society),* 11 Blinman St., New London, CT 06320 Tel 203-443-1209.
New Mermaid *Imprint of* **Hill & Wang**
New Orleans Mus Art, *(New Orleans Museum of Art; 0-89494),* P. O. Box 19123, New Orleans, LA 70179 Tel 504-488-2631.
New Orleans Poetry, *(New Orleans Poetry Journal Press, The; 0-938498),* 2131 General Pershing St., New Orleans, LA 70115.
New Outlook, *(New Outlook Pubs. & Distributors; 0-87898),* 239 W. 23rd St., New York, NY 10011.
New Poets, *(New Poets Series; 0-932616),* 541 Piccadilly Rd., Baltimore, MD 21204 Tel 301-321-2868.
New Republic, *(New Republic Books; 0-915220),* 1220 19th St. N.W., Suite 205, Washington, DC 20036 Tel 202-331-1250.
New Seed, *(New Seed Press),* P.O. Box 3016, Stanford, CA 94305.
New Sibylline, *(New Sibylline Books, Inc.; 0-9603352),* Box 266, Village Sta., New York, NY 10014.
New South Co, *(New South Co., The; 0-917990),* Suite 935, 924 Westwood Blvd., Los Angeles, CA 90024 Tel 213-879-0927.
New Victoria Pubs, *(New Victoria Pubs. Inc.; 0-934678),* 7 Bank St., Lebanon, NH 03766 Tel 603-448-2264.
New World
See New World Press NY
New World Bks, *(New World Books; 0-917480),* 4515 Saul Rd, Kensington, MD 20795.
New World Press NY, *(New World Press; 0-911026),* P.O. Box 416, New York, NY 10017 Tel 212-682-1154.
Newberry, *(Newberry Library; 0-911028),* 60 W. Walton St., Chicago, IL 60610 Tel 312-943-9090.
Newbury Bks Inc, *(Newbury Books, Inc.; 0-912728; 0-912729),* Box 29, Topsfield, MA 01983 Tel 617-887-5082.
Newbury Hse, *(Newbury House Pubs.; 0-88377; 0-912066),* 54 Warehouse Lane, Rowley, MA 01969 Tel 617-948-2704.
Newcastle Pub, *(Newcastle Publishing Co., Inc.; 0-87877),* 13419 Saticoy St., North Hollywood, CA 91605 Tel 213-873-3191; Orders to: P.O. Box 7589, Van Nuys, CA 91409.
Newhouse Pr, *(Newhouse Press; 0-918050),* 146 N. Rampart Blvd., Los Angeles, CA 90026 Tel 213-383-1089; Orders to: P.O. Box 76145, Los Angeles, CA 90076.
Newnes-Butterworth *Imprint of* **Butterworth**
Newport Beach, *(Newport Beach Pubs; 0-9602980),* 3901 MacArthur Blvd., Suite 211, Newport Beach, CA 92660 Tel 714-752-2268.
News Circle, *(News Circle; 0-915652),* P.O. Box 74637, Los Angeles, CA 90057 Tel 213-483-5111; 2007 Wilshire Blvd., Suite 900, Los Angeles, CA 90057.
Newspaper Bk, *(Newspaper Book Service; 0-936294),* P.O. Box 50342, Columbia, SC 29250.
Newspaper Ent, *(Newspaper Enterprise Assn., Inc.; 0-915106),* 200 Park Ave., New York, NY 10017 Tel 212-557-9651.
Newspaper Serv, *(Newspaper Services; 0-918488),* P.O. Box 62, Hutchinson, MN 55350 Tel 612-587-2375.
Newsweek, *(Newsweek; 0-88225),* 444 Madison Ave., New York, NY 10022 Tel 212-350-2528.
Nexus Pr, *(Nexus Press; 0-932526),* 608 Forrest Rd., N.E., Atlanta, GA 30312 Tel 404-577-3579.
NFAIS, *(National Federation of Abstracting & Indexing Services),* 112 S. 16th St., Philadelphia, PA 19102 Tel 215-563-2406.
NFER *Imprint of* **Humanities**
NFSAIS
See NFAIS
NH Pub Co, *(New Hampshire Publishing Co.; 0-912274; 0-89725),* P.O. Box 70, Somersworth, NH 03878 Tel 603-692-3727.
Nichols Pub, *(Nichols Publishing Co.; 0-89397),* P.O. Box 96, New York, NY 10024 Tel 212-580-8079.
Nighthawk Pr, *(Nighthawk Press; 0-936518),* Box 813, Forest Grove, OR 97116.
Nilgiri Pr, *(Nilgiri Press; 0-915132),* P.O. Box 477, Petaluma, CA 94953 Tel 707-878-2369; Name Formerly Sadhana Pr.
Nin-Ra Ent, *(Nin-Ra Enterprises; 0-933276),* 1721 La Barranca Rd., La Canada, CA 91011.
Ninth Sign, *(Ninth Sign Pubns.; 0-930840),* M-525, Hoboken, NJ 07030.
NIRH, *(National Institute of Reboundology & Health Inc.; 0-938302),* 7907 212th S.W., Edmonds, WA 98020 Tel 206-774-6403.
Nitty Gritty, *(Nitty Gritty Productions; 0-911954),* P.O. Box 5457, Concord, CA 94524 Tel 415-682-3144.
NM Philatelist
See Hobby Pub Serv
No Dead Lines, *(No Dead Lines; 0-931832),* 241 Bonita, Portola Valley, CA 94025 Tel 415-851-1847.
Noble
See Bowmar-Noble
Nodin Pr, *(Nodin Press; 0-931714),* c/o The Bookmen, Inc., 519 N. Third St., Minneapolis, MN 55401.
Noit Amrofer, *(Noit Amrofer Publ Co.; 0-932998),* Box 15176, Seattle, WA 98115; 5706 30th Ave. N.E., Seattle, WA 98105.
Nolo Pr, *(Nolo Press; 0-917316),* P.O. Box 544, Occidental, CA 95465 Tel 707-874-3105.
Non-Stop Bks, *(Non-Stop Books; 0-936816),* P.O. Box 1047, Berkeley, CA 94701.
Nonpareil Bks *Imprint of* **Godine**
Noon Rock, *(Noon Rock; 0-9602934),* Station Hill Rd., Barrytown, NY 12507 Tel 914-758-6682.
Noontide, *(Noontide Press/Institute for Historical Review, The; 0-911038),* P.O. Box 1248, Torrance, CA 90505.
NORC, *(NORC, National Opinion Research Center; 0-932132),* 6030 S. Ellis Ave., Chicago, IL 60637 Tel 312-753-1487.
Nord Media, *(Nord Media Inc.; 0-917226),* 127 W. 56th St., New York, NY 10019 Tel 212-245-1090.
Nordland Pub, *(Nordland Publishing International, Inc.; 0-913124),* P.O. Box 454, Woodside, NY 11377 Tel 212-335-1412; 3009 Plumb St., P.O. Box 25388, Houston, TX 77005 Tel 713-661-6126.
Nordon Pubns, *(Nordon Pubns, Inc; 0-8439),* 2 Park Ave., Suite 910, New York, NY 10016 Tel 212-679-7707; Orders to: Increased Sales Co., Inc., 327 Main Ave., Norwalk, CT 06852 Tel 203-846-2027; Dist. by: Wholesale: Kable, P.O. Box 270, Norwalk, CT 06852.
Norman & Sandra, *(Norman & Sandra; 0-936520),* P.O. Box 218, Orient, NY 11957 Tel 516-323-3602.
Nortex Pr
See Eakin Pubns
North Am Consumer, *(North American Consumer's Group Press),* 3747 S.E. Washington, Portland, OR 97124.
North Am Fal Hunt, *(North American Falconry & Hunting Hawks; 0-912510),* P.O. Box 1484, Denver, CO 80201 Tel 303-651-1472.
North Am Pub Co, *(North American Publishing Co.; 0-912920),* 401 N. Broad St., Philadelphia, PA 19108 Tel 215-574-9600.
North Atlantic, *(North Atlantic Books; 0-938190; 0-913028),* 635 Amador St., Richmond, CA 94805.
North Castle, *(North Castle Books, Inc.; 0-911040),* 212 Bedford Rd., Greenwich, CT 06830 Tel 203-869-7766.
North Country, *(North Country Books, Inc.; 0-932052),* P.O. Box 506, Sylvan Beach, NY 13157 Tel 315-762-5140.
North Holland *Imprint of* **Elsevier**
North Plains, *(North Plains Press; 0-87970),* P.O. Box 1830, Aberdeen, SD 57401 Tel 605-225-5360.
North River, *(North River Press, Inc.; 0-88427),* P.O. Box 241, Croton-on-Hudson, NY 10520 Tel 914-941-7175.
North Star, *(North Star Press; 0-87839),* P.O. Box 451, St. Cloud, MN 56301 Tel 612-253-1636.
Northern Mich, *(Northern Michigan Univ. Press; 0-918616),* 607 Cohodas Administrative Center, Marquette, MI 49855 Tel 906-227-2720; Orders to: NMU Bookstore, Don H. Bottum University Center, Marquette, MI 49855 Tel 906-227-2480.
Northland, *(Northland Press; 0-87358),* P.O. Box N, Flagstaff, AZ 86002 Tel 602-774-5251.
Northland Pubns WA, *(Northland Pubns.),* P.O. Box 12157, Seattle, WA 98102.
Northland Pubns
See Northland Pubns WA
Northwest Pub, *(Northwestern Publishing House; 0-8100),* 3624 W. North Ave., Milwaukee, WI 53208 Tel 414-442-1810.
Northwest Regional, *(Northwest Regional Educational Laboratory; 0-89354),* P. O. Box 414, Portland, OR 97207 Tel 503-248-6950.
Northwestern U Pr, *(Northwestern Univ. Press; 0-8101),* 1735 Benson Ave., Evanston, IL 60201 Tel 312-492-5313.
Northwood Inst, *(Northwood Institute Press; 0-87359),* 3225 Cook St., Midland, MI 48640 Tel 517-631-1600.
Northwoods-Bassett
See Northwoods Pr
Northwoods Pr, *(Northwoods Press, Inc.; 0-89002),* P.O. Box 249, Stafford, VA 22554 Tel 703-659-6771.
Norton, *(Norton, W. W., & Co., Inc.; 0-393),* 500 Fifth Ave., New York, NY 10110 Tel 212-354-5500. *Imprints:* NortonC (Norton College Division).
NortonC *Imprint of* **Norton**
Norwood
See Norwood Edns
Norwood Edns, *(Norwood Editions; 0-88305; 0-8482),* P.O. Box 38, Norwood, PA 19074 Tel 215-583-4550.
Nostalgia Pr, *(Nostalgia Press, Inc.; 0-87897),* 72 Franklin Ave., Franklin Square, NY 11010 Tel 516-488-4748; Orders to: P.O. Box 293, Franklin Square, NY 11010.
Nova Venturion, *(Nova Venturion; 0-915254),* P.O. Box 5182, Walnut Creek, CA 94596.
Noyes, *(Noyes Data Corp.; 0-8155),* Mill Rd. at Grand Ave., Park Ridge, NJ 07656 Tel 201-391-8484. *Imprints:* NP (Noyes Press).
NP *Imprint of* **Noyes**
NPD Corp, *(N.P.D. Corp; 0-937230),* P.O. Box 10161, Austin, TX 78766; 7701 N. Lamar Blvd., Austin, TX 78752 Tel 512-453-6154.
NPP Bks, *(NPP Books; 0-916182),* P.O. Box 1491, Ann Arbor, MI 48106.
Nuance Pr, *(Nuance Press Inc.; 0-917924),* 542 N. High St., Columbus, OH 43215.
NUCS
See Chr Sch Intl
Numarc Bk Corp, *(Numarc Book Corp.; 0-88471),* 1280 Main St., Buffalo, NY 14209 Tel 716-882-1155.
Nurseco, *(Nurseco, Inc.; 0-935236),* P.O. Box 145, Pacific Palisades, CA 90272.
Nursing Res, *(Nursing Resources, Inc.; 0-913654),* 12 Lakeside Office Park, Wakefield, MA 01880 Tel 617-245-9530.
NY Acad Sci, *(New York Academy of Sciences; 0-89072; 0-89766),* Pubns. Dept., 2 E. 63rd St., New York, NY 10021 Tel 212-838-0230.

NY Botanical, *(New York Botanical Garden, Pubns. Office; 0-89327),* Bronx, NY 10458 Tel 212-220-8721.
NY Chiro Coll, *(New York Chiropractic College; 0-938470),* P.O. Box 167, Glen Head, NY 11545.
NY Hunting, *(New York Hunting & Fishing Guide, Inc.; 0-937328),* 45 Gibbs St., Rochester, NY 14604.
NY Lit Forum, *(New York Literary Forum; 0-931196),* 21 E. 79th St., New York, NY 10021.
NY Prod Manual, *(New York Production Manual, Inc.; 0-935744),* Washington Square Village, Suite 8p, New York, NY 10012 Tel 212-777-4002.
NY Pub Lib, *(New York Public Library; 0-87104),* Fifth Ave. & 42nd St., New York, NY 10018 Tel 212-790-6285; Orders to: Readex Books, 101 Fifth Ave., New York, NY 10003; Ordering Address for NYPL Branch Libraries Imprint Only: Eight E. 40th St., N.Y., N.Y. 10016.
NY Sch Indus Rel, *(New York State School of Industrial & Labor Relations; 0-87546),* ILR Publications Division, Cornell University, Box 1000, Ithaca, NY 14853 Tel 607-256-3061.
NY St Coll Ag, *(New York State College of Agriculture & Life Sciences; 0-9605314),* Distribution Ctr., 7 Research Park, Cornell Univ., Ithaca, NY 14850.
NY St Eng Coun, *(New York State English Council; 0-930348),* 131 West Broad St., Rochester, NY 14608 Tel 716-325-4560.
NY Zoetrope, *(New York Zoetrope; 0-918432),* 31 E. 12th St., New York, NY 10003 Tel 212-473-2729.
Nyerges, *(Nyerges, Anton N.; 0-9600954),* 201 Langford Ct., Richmond, KY 40475 Tel 606-623-7153.
NYGS, *(New York Graphic Society, Ltd.; 0-8212),* 34 Beacon St., Boston, MA 02106 Tel 617-227-0730; Dist. by: Little, Brown & Co., 200 West St., Waltham, MA 02154.
NYGS CT, *(New York Graphic Society in Greenwich),* 140 Greenwich Ave., Greenwich, CT 06830 Tel 617-227-0730.
NYSCA, *(New York State Council on the Arts),* 80 Center St., New York, NY 10013.
NYU Pr, *(New York Univ. Press; 0-8147),* Dist. by: Columbia University Press, 562 W. 113th St., New York, NY 10025 Tel 212-678-6777.
O & B Bks, *(O & B Books, Inc.; 0-9601586),* 1215 N.W. Kline Place, Corvallis, OR 97330 Tel 503-752-2178.
O N Holmes, *(Holmes, Oakley N.),* c/o Black Artists in America, Macgowan Enterprises, 39 Wilshire Dr., Spring Valley, NY 10977.
Oak Tree Pubns, *(Oak Tree Pubns. Inc.; 0-916392),* 11175 Flintkote Ave., Suite C, San Diego, CA 92121 Tel 714-457-3200.
OAS, *(Organization of American States; 0-8270; 0-87549),* Dept. of Pubns., Washington, DC 20006 Tel 703-941-1578.
Oasis Pr
See PSI Res
Obol Intl, *(Obol International; 0-916710),* Div. of Unigraphics Inc., 8 S. Michigan Ave., Chicago, IL 60603 Tel 312-267-3662.
Oceana, *(Oceana Pubns.; 0-379),* 75 Main St., Dobbs Ferry, NY 10522 Tel 914-693-5944.
Ocelot Pr, *(Ocelot Press; 0-912434),* P.O. Box 504, Claremont, CA 91711 Tel 714-624-2439.
Octagon, *(Octagon Books; 0-374),* 19 Union Square W., New York, NY 10003 Tel 212-741-6961.
Octameron Assocs, *(Octameron Associates; 0-917760),* 820 Fontaine St., Alexandria, VA 22302 Tel 703-836-1019; Orders to: P.O. Box 3437, Alexandria, VA 22302.
October, *(October House; 0-8079),* P.O. Box 454, Stonington, CT 06378 Tel 203-535-3725.
October Pr, *(October Press, Inc., The; 0-935440),* 708 Stemmons Tower South, Dallas, TX 75207.
Oddo, *(Oddo Publishing, Inc.; 0-87783),* Storybook Acres-Box 68, Fayetteville, GA 30214 Tel 404-461-7627.
Odyssey Pr, *(Odyssey Press; 0-8399),* Dist. by: Bobbs-Merrill Co., Inc., 4300 W. 62nd St., Indianapolis, IN 46206 Tel 317-291-3100.
OECD, *(Organization for Economic Cooperation & Development),* 1750 Pennsylvania Ave., Suite 12072, N.W., Washington, DC 20006 Tel 202-724-1857.
Oelgeschlager, *(Oelgeschlager, Gunn & Hain, Pubs., Inc.; 0-89946),* 1278 Massachusetts Ave., Cambridge, MA 02138 Tel 617-876-5100.
OES Pubns, *(OES Pubns.; 0-89779),* College of Engineering, Univ. of KY, Lexington, KY 40506 Tel 606-257-2843.
Off off Broadway, *(Off off Broadway Alliance; 0-933750),* 162 W. 56th St., Room 206, New York, NY 10019 Tel 212-757-4473.
Ohara Pubns, *(O'Hara Pubns., Inc.; 0-89750),* 1847 W. Empire Ave., Burbank, CA 91504 Tel 213-843-4444.
Ohio Acad Sci, *(Ohio Academy of Science, The; 0-933128),* 445 King Ave., Columbus, OH 43201 Tel 614-424-6045.
Ohio Lib Foun, *(Ohio Library Foundation; 0-911060),* 40 S. 3rd St., Suite 409, Columbus, OH 43215.
Ohio Mag, *(Ohio Magazine; 0-938040),* 40 S. Third St., Columbus, OH 43215.
Ohio St U Pr, *(Ohio State Univ. Press; 0-8142),* Hitchcock Hall, Rm. 316, 2070 Neil Ave., Columbus, OH 43210 Tel 614-422-6930.
Ohio U Ctr Intl, *(Ohio Univ. Center for International Studies; 0-89680),* Athens, OH 45701.
Ohio U Pr, *(Ohio Univ. Press; 0-8214),* Scott Quadrangle, Athens, OH 45701 Tel 614-594-5852.
OK Street, *(OK Street Inc.; 0-917278),* 12800 Hillcrest Rd., Suite 215, Dallas, TX 75230 Tel 214-387-0953.
Okpaku Communications, *(Okpaku Communications; 0-89388),* 444 Central Park W., New York, NY 10025 Tel 212-866-9140.
Old Army, *(Old Army Press; 0-88342),* P.O. Box 2243, Fort Collins, CO 80521 Tel 303-484-5535.
Old Mill, *(Old Mill Press; 0-934700),* P.O. Box 388, Old Chelsea Sta., New York, NY 10113 Tel 212-929-4958.
Old NY Bk Shop, *(Old New York Book Shop Press; 0-937036),* 1069 Juniper St., NE, Atlanta, GA 30309.
Old Oaktree, *(Old Oaktree Motor Co.; 0-9603194),* 2012 Hyperion Ave., Los Angeles, CA 90027.
Old Ursuline, *(Old Ursuline Convent Cookbook; 0-9604718),* P.O. Box 7491, Metairie, LA 70010.
Old Violin, *(Old Violin-Art Publishing; 0-918554),* Box 500, 225 S. Cooke, Helena, MT 59601 Tel 406-442-8963.
Oleander Pr, *(Oleander Press; 0-902675; 0-900891; 0-906672),* 210 Fifth Ave., New York, NY 10010.
Olivia & Hill, *(Olivia & Hill Press Inc., The; 0-934034),* P.O. Box 7396, Ann Arbor, MI 48107 Tel 313-663-0235.
Olken Pubns, *(Olken Pubns.; 0-934818),* 2830 Kennedy St., Livermore, CA 94550 Tel 415-447-5177.
Oll Korrect, *(Oll Korrect Press),* 119 W. Ocotillo Vista, Tucson, AZ 85704 Tel 602-742-2070.
Olympic Media, *(Olympic Media Information; 0-88367),* 71 W. 23rd St., New York, NY 10010 Tel 212-675-4500.
Olympus Pub Co, *(Olympus Publishing Co.; 0-913420),* 1670 E. 13th St., Salt Lake City, UT 84105 Tel 801-583-3666.
OMango, *(OMango D'Press; 0-933278),* P.O. Box 64, Rte. 171, Woodstock Valley, CT 06282 Tel 203-974-2511.
Omega Pub Co, *(Omega Publishing Co., Inc.),* P.O. Box 323, Snohomish, WA 98290.
Omega Pubns OR, *(Omega Pubns.),* P.O. Box 4130, Medford, OR 97501 Tel 503-826-7302.
OMF Bks, *(OMF Books),* 404 S. Church St., Robesonia, PA 19551.
Omkara Pr, *(Omkara Press; 0-934094),* 51 Scott St., San Francisco, CA 94117 Tel 414-626-9407.
Omni Pubs, *(Omni Pubs.; 0-89127),* 218 E. Grand Ave., No. 201, Escondido, CA 92025 Tel 714-746-5833.
One Hund First Air, *(101st Airborne Division Assn.),* P.O. Box 101 Ab, Court Sta., Kalamazoo, MI 49005 Tel 616-388-5801.
One Hund One Prods, *(101 Productions; 0-912238; 0-89286),* 834 Mission St., San Francisco, CA 94103 Tel 415-495-6040; Dist. by: Charles Scribner's Sons, Book Warehouse, Vreeland Ave., Totowa, NJ 07512.
One Percent, *(One Percent Publishing; 0-935442),* 2888 Bluff St., Suite 143, Boulder, CO 80301.
Onset Pubns, *(Onset Pubns.; 0-89411),* 692 Elkader St., Ashland, OR 97520 Tel 503-482-0088.
Ontario Rev NJ, *(Ontario Review Press, The; 0-86538),* 9 Honey Brook Dr., Princeton, NJ 08540; Dist. by: Persea Books, Inc., 225 Lafayette St., New York, NY 10012 Tel 212-431-5270.
Oolp Pr, *(OOLP (Out of London Press) Inc.; 0-915570),* 12 W. 17th St, New York, NY 10011 Tel 212-691-8310.
Open Court, *(Open Court Publishing Co.; 0-87548; 0-89688),* Div. of Carus Corp., P.O. Box 599, LaSalle, IL 61301 Tel 815-223-2520. *Imprints:* Library Pr (Library Press).
Open Path, *(Open Path, The; 0-9602722),* 703 N. 18th St., Boise, ID 83702.
Open Roads, *(Open Roads Press; 0-937838),* P.O. Box 8061, San Diego, CA 92102 Tel 714-232-0714.
Ophthalmic, *(Ophthalmic Publishing Co.),* 435 N. Michigan Ave., Suite 1415, Chicago, IL 60611 Tel 312-787-3853.
Optical Soc, *(Optical Society of America; 0-9600380),* 1816 Jefferson Place, Washington, DC 20036 Tel 202-223-8130.
O'Quinn Studio
See Starlog
Orange County Genealog, *(Orange County Genealogical Society; 0-9604116),* 101 Main St., Goshen, NY 10924.
Orbis Bks, *(Orbis Books; 0-88344),* Maryknoll, NY 10545 Tel 914-941-7590.
Orchard Hse MA, *(Orchard House, Inc.; 0-933510),* Balls Hill Rd., Concord, MA 01742 Tel 617-369-0467.
Oreg Hist Soc, *(Oregon Historical Society; 0-87595),* 1230 S.W. Park Ave., Portland, OR 97205 Tel 503-222-1741.
Oreg St U Pr, *(Oregon State Univ. Press; 0-87071),* 101 Waldo Hall, Oregon State University, Corvallis, OR 97331 Tel 503-754-3166.
ORES Pubns
See OES Pubns
Organ Lit, *(Organ Literature Foundation, The; 0-913746),* 45 Norfolk Rd, Braintree, MA 02184 Tel 617-848-1388.
Oriel *Imprint of* **Routledge & Kegan**
Orient Bk Dist, *(Orient Book Distributors; 0-89684),* P.O. Box 100, Livingston, NJ 07039 Tel 201-992-6992.
Orient Longman *Imprint of* **South Asia Bks**
Orient Res Partners, *(Oriental Research Partners; 0-89250),* P.O. Box 158, Newtonville, MA 02160 Tel 617-965-4399.
Oriental Inst, *(Oriental Institute of the Univ. of Chicago; 0-918986),* 1155 E. 58th St., Chicago, IL 60637 Tel 312-753-2478; Orders to: 1155 E. 58th St., Chicago, IL 60637 Tel 312-753-3875.
Ortho, *(Ortho Books; 0-917102),* Div. of Chevron Chemical Co., Subs. of Standard Oil Co. of Calif., c/o Chevron Chemical Co., P.O. Box 3744, San Francisco, CA 94119 Tel 415-894-2593.
Orthodox Chr, *(Orthodox Christian Education Society; 0-938366),* 1916 W. Warner Ave., Chicago, IL 60613 Tel 312-549-0584.
Oryx Pr, *(Oryx Press; 0-912700; 0-89774),* 2214 N. Central Ave., Phoenix, AZ 85004 Tel 602-254-6156.
Osborne & Assocs
See Osborne-McGraw
Osborne-McGraw, *(Osborne/McGraw-Hill, Inc.; 0-931988),* P.O. Box 2036, Berkeley, CA 94702; 630 Bancroft Way, Berkeley, CA 94710 Tel 415-548-2805.
O'Sullivan Woodside, *(O'Sullivan, Woodside & Co.; 0-89019),* 2218 E. Magnolia, Phoenix, AZ 85034 Tel 602-244-0304; Dist. by: Follett Publishing Co., 1010 W. Washington Blvd., Chicago, IL 60607 Tel 312-666-5858.
Otafra, *(Otafra Press; 0-9605220),* 209 Capri Arc, Las Cruces, NM 88001.
Otterden, *(Otterden Press; 0-918868),* 111 Plymouth Rd., Hillsdale, NJ 07642 Tel 201-664-2583.

Our Sunday Visitor, *(Our Sunday Visitor, Inc.; 0-87973),* 200 Noll Plaza, Huntington, IN 46750 Tel 219-356-8400.
Ourobourus
See **New Age Pr NM**
Out & Out, *(Out & Out Books; 0-918314),* 476 Second St., Brooklyn, NY 11215
Outbooks, *(Outbooks; 0-89646),* 217 Kimball Ave., Golden, CO 80401.
Outdoor Assocs, *(Outdoor Associates),* 1279 Dean St., Schenectady, NY 12309
Overlook Pr, *(Overlook Press; 0-87951),* 667 Madison Ave., Suite 401A, New York, NY 10021; c/o Viking Press, 625 Madison Ave, New York, NY 10022 Tel 212-755-4330.
Overseas Dev Council, *(Overseas Development Council),* 1717 Massachusetts Ave., N.W., Washington, DC 20036 Tel 202-234-8701.
Overshiner, *(Overshiner Press; 0-937480),* 92 Buckwood Place, Santa Rosa, CA 95405 Tel 707-538-0181.
Owlswick Pr, *(Owlswick Press; 0-913896),* P.O. Box 8243, Philadelphia, PA 19101 Tel 215-382-5415.
Owlswood Prods, *(Owlswood Productions; 0-915942),* 1355 Market St., San Francisco, CA 94103 Tel 415-626-2480.
Ox Bow, *(Ox Bow Press; 0-918024),* P.O. Box 4045, Woodbridge, CT 06525 Tel 203-387-5900.
Oxford U Pr, *(Oxford Univ. Press, Inc.; 0-19),* 200 Madison Ave., New York, NY 10016 Tel 212-679-7300; Orders to: 16-00 Pollitt Dr., Fair Lawn, NJ 07410 Tel 201-796-8000; New York Accounts Use 212-564-6680. *Imprints:* GB (Galaxy Books).
Oxmoor Hse, *(Oxmoor House, Inc.; 0-8487),* P.O. Box 2262, Birmingham, AL 35201 Tel 205-870-4440; Dist. by: Harper & Row, Pubs., Inc., Keystone Industrial Park, Scranton, PA 18512 Tel 800-233-4175.
Ozer, *(Ozer, Jerome S., Pub., Inc.; 0-89198),* 340 Tenafly Rd., Englewood, NJ 07631 Tel 201-567-7040.
P A Abbott, *(Abbott, P.A., Pubns.; 0-938564),* P.O. Box 2085, Kalamazoo, MI 49003.
P A Janzen, *(Janzen, P. A.; 0-9604458),* 1405 Redwood Lane, Libertyville, IL 60048.
P Andersen, *(Andersen, Paul; 0-9604720),* P.O. Box 2184, Laguna Hills, CA 92653.
P Elek
See Merrimack Bk Serv
P G Partington, *(Partington, Paul G.; 0-9602538),* 7320 S. Gretna Ave., Whittier, CA 90606.
P Gaines Co, *(Gaines, P., Co., The; 0-936284),* P.O. Box 705, Oak Park, IL 60303 Tel 312-996-7829.
P-H, *(Prentice-Hall, Inc.; 0-13),* Englewood Cliffs, NJ 07632 Tel 201-592-2000; Orders to: Box 500, Englewood Cliffs, NJ 07632. *Imprints:* Busn (Business & Professional Div.); Parker (Parker Publishing Co.); Reward (Reward Books); Spec (Spectrum Books).
P H Brookes, *(Brookes, Paul H., Pubs.; 0-933716),* P.O. Box 10624, Baltimore, MD 21204 Tel 301-433-8100.
P H Perkins, *(Perkins, Percy H.; 0-9603090),* 5450 Peachtree-Dunwoody Rd., Atlanta, GA 30342 Tel 404-261-1740.
P J Thompson, *(Thompson, Paul J.; 0-9601288),* c/o Y.M.C.A., 2200 Prospect Ave., Rm. 437, Cleveland, OH 44115 Tel 216-344-7724.
P Juul Pr, *(Juul, Peter, Press, Inc.; 0-915456),* P.O. Box 40605, Tucson, AZ 85717 Tel 602-622-3409.
P Krejcarek, *(Krejcarek, Philip),* 1735 N. 57th, Milwaukee, WI 53208.
P L Johnstone
See Mission Dolores
P Odegard
See Advance Planning
P R Feltus, *(Feltus, Peter R.),* 5709 Keith Ave., Oakland, CA 94618.
P R Pub Co, *(PR Publishing Co., Inc.),* P.O. Box 600, 14 Front St., Exeter, NH 03833 Tel 603-778-0514.
P Robinson, *(Robinson, Peggy),* 1326 Fell St., San Francisco, CA 94117 Tel 415-387-9339; Dist. by: Far West Book Service, 3515 N.E. Hassalo, Portland, OR 97232.
P S & M Inc, *(Phelon, Sheldon & Marsar, Inc.),* 32 Union Square, New York, NY 10003 Tel 212-473-2590.
P Sawyer, *(Sawyer, Philip L.; 0-911308),* 108 South St., Auburn, NY 13021.
Pa Hist & Mus, *(Pennsylvania Historical & Museum Commission; 0-911124; 0-89271),* Division of History, Box 1026, Harrisburg, PA 17120 Tel 717-783-9868.
Pa St U Pr, *(Pennsylvania State Univ. Press; 0-271),* 215 Wagner Bldg., University Park, PA 16802 Tel 814-865-1320.
Pacesetter Pr, *(Pacesetter Press; 0-88415),* Div. of Gulf Publishing Co., P.O. Box 2608, Houston, TX 77001 Tel 713-529-4301.
Pachart Pub Hse, *(Pachart Publishing House; 0-912918),* P.O. Box 35549, Tucson, AZ 85740 Tel 602-297-4797.
Pacific-Asian, *(Pacific/Asian American Mental Health Research Center; 0-934584),* 1640 W. Roosevelt Rd., Chicago, IL 60608 Tel 312-226-0117.
Pacific Bks, *(Pacific Books, Pubs.; 0-87015),* P.O. Box 558, Palo Alto, CA 94302 Tel 415-856-0550.
Pacific Edns, *(Pacific Editions; 0-938226),* P.O. Box 27366, San Francisco, CA 94127 Tel 415-334-5716.
Pacific Mer, *(Pacific Meridian Publishing Co.; 0-911092),* 13540 Lake City Way, N. E., Seattle, WA 98125 Tel 206-362-0900.
Pacific NW Labor, *(Pacific Northwest Labor History Assn.; 0-932942),* P.O. Box 25048, Northgate Sta., Seattle, WA 98125.
Pacific Pipeline, *(Pacific Pipeline, Inc.),* P.O. Box 3711, Seattle, WA 98124 Tel 206-682-8820.
Pacific Pr MO
See Pacific Santa Barbara
Pacific Pr Pub Assn, *(Pacific Press Publishing Assn.; 0-8163),* 1350 Villa St., Mountain View, CA 94042 Tel 415-961-2323.
Pacific Santa Barbara, *(Pacific Press Santa Barbara; 0-911094),* P.O. Box 219, Pierce City, MO 65723 Tel 417-476-2034.
Pacific Search, *(Pacific Search Press; 0-914718),* 222 Dexter Ave. N., Seattle, WA 98109 Tel 206-682-5044.
Packard Pub, *(Packard Publishing Co.; 0-937798),* 321 S. Hobart, Los Angeles, CA 90020.
Packrat Pr, *(Packrat Press Books),* P.O. Box 74, Cambridge, ID 83610.
Paddington, *(Paddington Press, Ltd.),* 95 Madison Ave, New York, NY 10016 Tel 212-689-4801; Orders to: Grosset & Dunlap, 51 Madison Ave., New York, NY 10010.
Paddlewheel, *(Paddlewheel Press; 0-938274),* 15100 SW 109th, Tigard, OR 97223.
Padre Prods, *(Padre Productions; 0-914598),* P.O. Box 1275, San Luis Obispo, CA 93406 Tel 805-543-5404.
Paganiniana Pubns, *(Paganiniana Pubns., Inc.; 0-87666),* Div. of T.F.H Pubns., Inc., P.O. Box 427, Neptune, NJ 07753 Tel 201-988-8400.
Pajarito Pubns, *(Pajarito Pubns; 0-918358),* 2633 Granite N. W., Albuquerque, NM 87104 Tel 505-242-8075.
PAL Pr, *(P.A.L. Press; 0-938034),* P.O. Box 487, San Anselmo, CA 94960 Tel 805-453-8547.
Pal Pub, *(Pal Pub.; 0-918104),* Witter Springs, CA 95493 Tel 707-275-2766; P. O. Box 807, Northridge, CA 91328 Tel 213-360-0600.
Paladin Ent, *(Paladin Enterprises; 0-87364),* P.O. Box 1307, Boulder, CO 80306 Tel 303-443-7250.
Paladin Hse, *(Paladin House Pubs.; 0-88252),* 530 Lark St., Geneva, IL 60134 Tel 312-232-2711.
Paladin Pr
See Paladin Ent
Paladium Pr, *(Paladium Press; 0-9694090),* P.O. Box 42, Beltsville, MD 20705.
Palatine Pubns, *(Palatine Pubns., Inc.),* P.O. Drawer 1265, Ruston, LA 71270.
Paleo Res, *(Paleontological Research Institution; 0-87710),* 1259 Trumansburg Rd., Ithaca, NY 14850 Tel 607-273-6623.
Palisades Pub, *(Palisades Pubs.; 0-913530),* P.O. Box 744, Pacific Palisades, CA 90272 Tel 213-454-0826.
Palmer-Pletsch, *(Palmer-Pletsch Associates; 0-935278),* P.O. Box 8422, Portland, OR 97207 Tel 503-231-4908.
Palmer Pub CA, *(Palmer Publishing),* P.O. Box 966, Orangevale, CA 95662 Tel 916-445-5525.
Palmetto Pub, *(Palmetto Publishing Co.; 0-915096),* 4747 28th St., N., St. Petersburg, FL 33714.
Palomar Bks, *(Palomar Books; 0-932882),* P.O. Box 445, Palmdale, CA 93550 Tel 805-947-5093.
Pan Am Nav, *(Pan American Navigation Service, Inc.; 0-87219),* P.O. Box 9046, Van Nuys, CA 91409 Tel 213-345-2744.
Pan-Am Publishing Co, *(Pan-American Publishing Co.; 0-932906),* P.O. Box 1505, Las Vegas, NM 87701.
Pan Am Pubns, *(Pan Am Pubns.; 0-87582),* Pan Am Bldg., New York, NY 10017.
Panjandrum, *(Panjandrum Books; 0-915572),* 11321 Iowa Ave., Suite 1, Los Angeles, CA 90025 Tel 213-477-8771; Dist. by: Publisher's Group West, 5855 Beaudry, Emeryville, CA 94608 Tel 415-549-3033; Dist. by: Robert Rainer Assocs, 318 Happ Rd., Northfield, IL 60093; Dist. by: Crissales, Crissie Lossing, 3236 Clubhouse Rd., Merrick, NY 11566; Dist. by: Doug Paton, North East Book Sales, 802 Oak Ridge Ave., North Attleboro, MA 02760; Dist. by: Bookpeople, 2940 Seventh St., Berkeley, CA 94710; Dist. by: Wisdom Garden Books, 238 N. Juanita, Los Angeles, CA 90004; Dist. by: Ingram Book Co., 347 Reedwood Dr., Nashville, TN 37217; Dist. by: Henry Walck, Jr., 731 E. Shore Dr., Ithaca, NY 14850; Dist. by: Henry Walck, Jr., 702 S. Michigan, South Bend, IN 46618.
Panjandrum Pr
See Panjandrum
Panorama West, *(Panorama West Books; 0-914330),* 8 E. Olive Ave., Fresno, CA 93728.
Pantheon, *(Pantheon Books),* Div. of Random House, Inc., 201 E. 50th St., New York, NY 10022 Tel 212-751-2600; Orders to: Random House, Inc., 400 Hahn Rd., Westminster, MD 21157.
Paper Tiger Pap, *(Paper Tiger Paperbacks, Inc.; 0-933334),* 1512 N.W. Seventh Place, Gainesville, FL 32603 Tel 904-373-2383; Orders to: P.O. Box 14015, Gainesville, FL 32604.
Paper Vision
See Western Tanager
Paper Vision *Imprint of* **Western Tanager**
Paperweight Pr, *(Paperweight Press; 0-933756),* 761 Chestnut St., Santa Cruz, CA 95060.
PAR Inc, *(Programs for Achievement in Reading - P.A.R., Inc.; 0-913310; 0-89702),* 274 Weybosset St., Abbot Park Place, Providence, RI 02903 Tel 401-331-0130.
Para Pub, *(Para Publishing; 0-915516),* P.O. Box 4232-R, Santa Barbara, CA 93103.
Para Res, *(Para Research, Inc.; 0-914918),* Whistlestop Mall, Rockport, MA 01966 Tel 617-546-3413.
Paraclete Bks, *(Paraclete Books; 0-936100),* GPO 2058, New York, NY 10001 Tel 212-849-5849.
Paradigm Pr, *(Paradigm Press; 0-937572),* 127 Greenbrae Boardwalk, Greenbrae, CA 94904 Tel 415-461-5457; Dist. by: Bookpeople, 2940 Seventh St., Berkeley, CA 94710; Dist. by: Publishers Group West, 5855 Beaudry St., Emeryville, CA 94608.
Paragon, *(Paragon Book Reprint Corp.; 0-8188),* 14 E. 38th St., New York, NY 10016 Tel 212-532-4920.
Parapsych Foun, *(Parapsychology Foundation, Inc.; 0-912328),* 228 E. 71st St., New York, NY 10021 Tel 212-628-1550.
Parchment Pr, *(Parchment Press; 0-88428),* P.O. Box 8534, Chattanooga, TN 37411 Tel 615-624-9063.
Parent-Child Pr, *(Parent-Child Press; 0-9601016),* P.O. Box 767, 4201 Second Ave., Altoona, PA 16603 Tel 814-946-5213.
Parenthesis Pr, *(Parenthesis Press; 0-9601580),* P.O. Box 114, Bridgewater College, Bridgewater, VA 22812 Tel 703-828-6656.
Parenting Pr, *(Parenting Press; 0-9602862),* 7750 31st Ave. N.E., Seattle, WA 98115.
Parents, *(Parents Magazine Press; 0-8193),* 685 Third Ave., New York, NY 10017 Tel 212-878-8611; Dist. by: Elsevier-Dutton Publishing Co., 2 Park Ave., Dept. JH, New York, NY 10016 Tel 212-725-1818.
Parey Sci Pubs, *(Parey, Paul, Scientific Pubs.),* 461 Park Ave. S., No. 903, New York, NY 10016 Tel 212-686-3605.

Park Pub, *(Park Publishing, Inc.; 0-9603294),* 1999 Shepard Rd., St. Paul, MN 55116 Tel 612-698-1667.
Park View, *(Park View Press, Inc.; 0-87813),* 1066 Mt. Clinton Pike, Harrisonburg, VA 22801 Tel 703-434-0765.
Parker *Imprint of* **P-H**
Parker & Son, *(Parker & Son Pubns., Inc.; 0-911110),* Box 60001, Los Angeles, CA 90060 Tel 213-724-6622.
Parkway Pr, *(Parkway Press, Inc.; 0-930408),* 3347 E. Calhoun Pkwy., Minneapolis, MN 55408 Tel 612-827-3347.
Parnassus, *(Parnassus Press; 0-87466),* 6421 Regent St., Oakland, CA 94618 Tel 415-654-1368; Orders to: Houghton Mifflin Co., Wayside Rd., Burlington, MA 01803.
Partisan Pr, *(Partisan Press, Inc.; 0-935150),* P.O. Box 2193, Seattle, WA 98111.
Partner Pr, *(Partner Press; 0-933212),* Box 124, Livonia, MI 48152.
Pasadena Art, *(Pasadena Art Alliance; 0-937042),* 314 S. Mentor Ave., Pasadena, CA 91106 Tel 213-795-9276.
Pascal Pubs, *(Pascal Pubs),* 21 Sunnyside Ave., Wellesley, MA 02181.
Pass, *(Pass Press; 0-9601870),* 170 2nd Ave., 2A, New York, NY 10003.
Passive Solar, *(Passive Solar Institute; 0-933490),* P.O. Box 722, Davis, CA 95616 Tel 415-526-1549.
Passport Pr, *(Passport Press; 0-930016),* Box 596, Moscow, VT 05662 Tel 802-253-9387.
Path Pr NY, *(Pathfinder Press; 0-87348),* 410 West St., New York, NY 10014 Tel 212-741-0690.
Pathotox Pubs, *(Pathotox Pubs., Inc.; 0-930376),* 2405 Bond St., Park Forest South, IL 60466 Tel 312-534-1770.
Pathway Bks, *(Pathway Books; 0-935538),* 700 Parkview Terrace, Golden Valley, MN 55416 Tel 612-377-2997.
Pathway Pr, *(Pathway Press; 0-87148),* 922-1080 Montgomery Ave., Cleveland, TN 37311 Tel 615-476-4512.
Patmos Pr, *(Patmos Press, The; 0-915762),* P.O. Box V, Shepherdstown, WV 25443 Tel 304-876-2086.
Patrice Pr, *(Patrice Press; 0-935284),* Box 42, Gerald, MO 63037 Tel 314-764-2801.
Patriotic Educ, *(Patriotic Education, Inc.; 0-912530),* P.O. Box 2121, Daytona Beach, FL 32015 Tel 904-252-3414.
Pattecky Music, *(Pattecky Music Pubs.; 0-9602178),* Box T, College Park, MD 20740.
Patterson Smith, *(Smith, Patterson, Publishing Corp.; 0-87585),* 23 Prospect Terrace, Montclair, NJ 07042 Tel 201-744-3291.
Paulist-Newman
See Paulist Pr
Paulist Pr, *(Paulist Press; 0-8091),* 545 Island Rd., Ramsey, NJ 07446 Tel 201-825-7300; Orders to: 301 Island Rd., Mahwah, NJ 07430.
Paunch, *(Paunch; 0-9602478),* 123 Woodward Ave., Buffalo, NY 14214.
Pawnee Pub, *(Pawnee Publishing Co., Inc.; 0-913688),* P.O. Box 630, Higginsville, MO 64037 Tel 816-394-2424.
Pawson, *(Pawson, John R.; 0-9602080),* Box 411, Willow Grove, PA 19090.
PB, *(Pocket Books, Inc.; 0-671),* Div. of Simon & Schuster, Inc., 1230 Ave. of the Americas, New York, NY 10020 Tel 212-246-2121.
PBBC Pr, *(PBBC Press),* 315 S. Grove St., Owatonna, MN 55060 Tel 507-451-2710.
PBI Petrocelli
See Petrocelli
PDA Pubs, *(PDA Publishers Corp.; 0-914886),* 1200 S. Sharon Chapel Rd., P.O. Box 3075, W. Lafayette, IN 47906 Tel 317-743-1101.
Peabody Found, *(Peabody, Robert S., Foundation for Archaeology),* P. O. Box 71, Andover, MA 01810 Tel 617-475-0248.
Peabody Harvard, *(Peabody Museum of Archaeology & Ethnology, Harvard Univ.; 0-87365),* 11 Divinity Ave., Cambridge, MA 02138 Tel 617-495-3938.
Peabody Mus Salem, *(Peabody Museum of Salem; 0-87577),* East India Square, Salem, MA 01970 Tel 617-745-1876.
Peace & Pieces
See SF Arts & Letters
Peace Pr, *(Peace Press, Inc.; 0-915238),* 3828 Willat Ave., Culver City, CA 90230 Tel 213-838-7387.
Peachtree Pubs, *(Peachtree Pubs., Ltd.; 0-931948),* 494 Armour Circle, N.E., Atlanta, GA 30324 Tel 404-876-8761.
Peacock Pubs, *(Peacock, F. E., Pubs., Inc.; 0-87581),* 401 W. Irving Park Rd., Itasca, IL 60143 Tel 312-773-1155.
Peanut Butter, *(Peanut Butter Publishing; 0-89716),* 2733 4th Ave. S., Seattle, WA 98134 Tel 206-682-9320.
Pecalhen, *(Pecalhen Co.; 0-938910),* 14401 S.W. 85th Ave., Miami, FL 33158.
Peebles Pr, *(Peebles Press International Inc.; 0-85690),* 1865 Broadway, New York, NY 10023 Tel 212-586-2800; Dist. by: Farrar, Straus & Giroux, Inc., 19 Union Square, New York, NY 10003 Tel 212-741-6900.
Peek Pubns, *(Peek Pubns.; 0-917962),* 164 E. Dana St., Mountain View, CA 94041 Tel 415-964-2334; Orders to: P.O. Box 50123, Palo Alto, CA 94303.
Peerless, *(Peerless Pub. Co.; 0-930234),* 2745 Lafitte Ave., New Orleans, LA 70119 Tel 504-486-6225.
Pegasus, *(Pegasus),* Affiliated with Bobbs-Merrill Co., Inc., 4300 W. 62nd St., Indianapolis, IN 46206 Tel 317-291-3100.
Pegasus Rex *Imprint of* **Fell**
Pegasus Rex NJ, *(Pegasus Rex Press,Inc.,The; 0-937484),* 695 Bloomfield Ave., Montclair, NJ 07042 Tel 201-744-3774.
Pelican, *(Pelican Publishing Co., Inc.; 0-911116; 0-88289),* 1101 Monroe St., Gretna, LA 70053 Tel 504-368-1175. *Imprints:* Pelican (*Imprint of* Pengui).
Pella Pub, *(Pella Publishing Co., Inc.; 0-918618),* 461 Eighth Ave., New York, NY 10001 Tel 212-279-9586.
Peloquin Pubns, *(Peloquin Pubns.; 0-936448),* P.O. Box 121, Richland, WA 99352.
PEM Pr, *(PEM Press),* Div. of Pathescope Educational Media, Inc., 71 Weyman Ave., P.O. Box 719, New Rochelle, NY 10802 Tel 914-235-0800.
Pen & Podium, *(Pen & Podium Pubns.; 0-9603982),* 40 Central Park S., New York, NY 10019.
Pen-Art, *(Pen-Art Pubs.),* 402 Fairview Ave., Westwood, NJ 07675 Tel 201-664-8412.
Pendel Hill
See Pendle Hill
Pendell Pub, *(Pendell Publishing Co.; 0-87812),* 1700 James Savage Rd., P.O. Box 1666 Bip, Midland, MI 48640 Tel 517-496-3337.
Pendle Hill, *(Pendle Hill Pubns.; 0-87574),* Pendle Hill, 338 Plush Mill Rd, Wallingford, PA 19086 Tel 215-566-4507.
Pendragon NY, *(Pendragon Press; 0-918728),* 162 W. 13th St., New York, NY 10011.
Pendulum Pr, *(Pendulum Press, Inc.; 0-88301),* Academic Bldg., Saw Mill Rd., West Haven, CT 06516 Tel 203-933-2551.
Penguin, *(Penguin Books, Inc.; 0-14),* 625 Madison Ave., New York, NY 10022 Tel 212-755-4330. *Imprints:* Pelican (Pelican Books); Puffin (Puffin Books).
Peninsula, *(Peninsula Publishing; 0-932146),* P.O. Box 867, Los Altos, CA 94022 Tel 415-948-2511.
Peninsula Pub WA
See Peninsula WA
Peninsula Pubns, *(Peninsula Pubns.; 0-914372),* 26030 New Bridge Dr., Los Altos Hills, CA 94022 Tel 415-857-0381.
Peninsula WA, *(Peninsula Publishing, Inc.; 0-918146),* P.O. Box 412, Port Angeles, WA 98362 Tel 206-457-7550.
Penmaen Pr, *(Penmaen Press, Ltd.; 0-915778),* Old Sudbury Rd., Lincoln, MA 01773 Tel 617-259-0842.
Penmaen Pr & Design
See Penmaen Pr
Penns Valley, *(Penns Valley Pubs.; 0-931992),* 1298 S. 28th St., Harrisburg, PA 17111 Tel 717-232-5844.
Pennwell Pub, *(Pennwell Publishing Co.; 0-87814),* P.O. Box 1260, Tulsa, OK 74101 Tel 918-835-3161.
Pennypress, *(Pennypress, The; 0-937604),* 1100 23rd Ave., E., Seattle, WA 98112 Tel 206-325-5098.
Penrith, *(Penrith Publishing Co.; 0-936522),* P.O. Box 18070, Cleveland Heights, OH 44118.
Pentagram, *(Pentagram Press; 0-915316; 0-937596),* Box 379, Markesan, WI 53946 Tel 414-398-2161.
Penthouse Pr, *(Penthouse Press, Ltd.; 0-89110),* 909 Third Ave., New York, NY 10022.
Penumbra Press, *(Penumbra Press, The),* Box 12, Lisbon, IA 52253 Tel 319-455-2182.
People Places, *(People Places, Inc.; 0-9604068),* P.O. Box 110, Verona, VA 24482.
Peoples Computer, *(People's Computer Co.; 0-918790),* P.O. Box E, 1263 El Camino, Menlo Park, CA 94025 Tel 415-323-3111.
Pepper Pub, *(Pepper Publishing; 0-914468),* 2901 E. Mabel, Tucson, AZ 85716 Tel 602-881-0783.
Peppercorn *Imprint of* **Putnam**
Peppertree, *(Peppertree Publishing; 0-936822),* Box 1712, Newport Beach, CA 92663 Tel 714-642-3669.
Pequot
See Globe Pequot
Peregrine Pr, *(Peregrine Press; 0-933614),* Box 751, Old Saybrook, CT 06475 Tel 203-388-0285.
Peregrine Smith, *(Peregrine Smith, Inc.; 0-87905),* P.O. Box 667, 1877 E. Gentile St., Layton, UT 84041 Tel 801-376-9800.
Performance Pub, *(Performance Publishing Corp.),* 1660 N. LaSalle, Suite 4211, Chicago, IL 60614.
Pergamon, *(Pergamon Press, Inc.; 0-08),* Maxwell House, Fairview Park, Elmsford, NY 10523 Tel 914-592-7700.
Periday, *(Periday Co.),* Box 583, Woodland Hills, CA 91365.
Perigee *Imprint of* **Putnam**
Peripatetic, *(Peripatetic Press, The; 0-9602870),* P.O. Box 68, Grinnell, IA 50112.
Perivale Pr, *(Perivale Press; 0-912288),* 13830 Erwin St., Van Nuys, CA 91401 Tel 213-785-4671.
Periwinkle Pr, *(Periwinkle Press; 0-9602584),* P.O. Box 1305, Woodland Hills, CA 91365 Tel 213-346-3415.
Permanent Pr, *(Permanent Press, The; 0-932966),* Sagaponack, NY 11962 Tel 516-324-5993.
Perry Omega, *(Perry-Omega Publishing, Inc; 0-9602586),* P.O. Box 27097, Escondido, CA 92027 Tel 714-741-6235.
Persea Bks, *(Persea Books, Inc.; 0-89255),* 225 Lafayette St., New York, NY 10012 Tel 212-431-5270.
Persephone, *(Persephone Press, Inc.; 0-930436),* P.O. Box 7222, Watertown, MA 02172 Tel 617-924-0336.
Personal Christianity, *(Personal Christianity; 0-938148),* Box 549, Baldwin Park, CA 91706 Tel 213-338-7333.
Personnel Dev, *(Personnel Development Associates; 0-911128),* P.O. Box 3005 Roosevelt Field Sta., Garden City, NY 11530 Tel 516-746-7868.
Peter Glenn, *(Glenn, Peter, Pubns., Inc.; 0-87314),* 17 E. 48th St., New York, NY 10017 Tel 212-688-7940.
Peter Pauper, *(Peter Pauper Press; 0-8342),* 135 W. 50th St., New York, NY 10020 Tel 212-247-3507.
Peter Smith, *(Smith, Peter, Publisher Inc.; 0-8446),* 6 Lexington Ave., Magnolia, MA 01930 Tel 617-525-3562.
Petereins Pr, *(Petereins Press, The),* P.O. Box 10446, Glendale, CA 91209.
Petersen Pub, *(Petersen Publishing Co., Book Division; 0-8227),* 6725 Sunset Blvd., Los Angeles, CA 90028 Tel 213-657-5100.
Petersons Guides, *(Peterson's Guides Inc.; 0-87866),* 228 Alexander St., Princeton, NJ 08540 Tel 609-924-5338; Orders to: P.O. Box 978, Edison, NJ 08817.
Petrocelli, *(Petrocelli Books; 0-89433),* 1101 State Rd., Princeton, NJ 08540 Tel 609-924-5851.
Petrocelli-Charter
See Van Nos Reinhold
Petroglyph, *(Petroglyph Press Ltd.; 0-912180),* 201 Kinoole St., Hilo, HI 96720.
Petroleum Pub
See Pennwell Pub
PFC, *(P. F. C. Publishing Co.; 0-9603830),* 525 W. 26th St., New York, NY 10001 Tel 212-242-0179.
Pflaum Pr, *(Pflaum Press),* 2451 E. River Rd., Dayton, OH 45439.
Pflaum-Standard, *(Pflaum/Standard; 0-8278),* c/o CEBCO Standard Publishing, 9 Kulick Rd, Fairfield, NJ 07006; Name Changed to CEBCO-Standard.
PFOS, *(People for Open Space; 0-9605262),* 46 Kearny St., San Francisco, CA 94108.

Phaeton, *(Phaeton Press, Inc.; 0-87753),* Orders to: Gordian Press, 85 Tompkins St., Staten Island, NY 10304 Tel 212-273-4700.
Phaidon
See Dutton
Phantasia Pr, *(Phantasia Press; 0-932096),* 13101 Lincoln, Huntington Woods, MI 48070; Dist. by: F & SF Book Co., P.O. Box 415, Staten Island, NY 10302.
Pheasant Run, *(Pheasant Run Pubns.; 0-936978),* Box 14043, St. Louis, MO 63178 Tel 314-291-3439.
Phi Delta Kappa, *(Phi Delta Kappa, Inc.; 0-87367),* 8th & Union, P.O. Box 789, Bloomington, IN 47402 Tel 812-339-1156.
Phiebig
See S Karger
Phila Maritime Mus, *(Philadelphia Maritime Museum; 0-913346),* 321 Chestnut St., Philadelphia, PA 19106 Tel 215-925-5439.
Phila Mus Art, *(Philadelphia Museum of Art; 0-87633),* P.O. Box 7646, Philadelphia, PA 19101 Tel 215-763-8100.
Philbrook, *(Philbrook Art Center),* P.O. Box 52510, Tulsa, OK 74152.
Philomel, *(Philomel Books),* 200 Madison Ave., Suite 1405, New York, NY 10016.
Philos Document, *(Philosophy Documentation Center; 0-912632),* Bowling Green State University, Bowling Green, OH 43403 Tel 419-372-2419.
Philos Lib, *(Philosophical Library, Inc.; 0-8022),* 200 W. 57th St., New York, NY 10019 Tel 212-265-6050.
Philos Res, *(Philosophical Research Society, Inc.; 0-89314),* 3910 Los Feliz Blvd., Los Angeles, CA 90027 Tel 213-663-2167.
Philos Sci Assn, *(Philosophy of Science Assn.; 0-917586),* 18 Morrill Hall, Philosophy Dept., Michigan State Univ., East Lansing, MI 48824 Tel 517-353-9392.
Phipps Pub, *(Phipps Pub. Co.; 0-918442),* Subs. of New England Mfgr. Co., 66 Bridge St., Norwell, MA 02061 Tel 617-659-7003.
Phistiklakis & Eliopoulos
See Eliopoulos
Phoenix Bk Shop, *(Phoenix Book Shop; 0-916228),* 22 Jones St., New York, NY 10014 Tel 212-675-2795.
Phoenix Bks, *(Phoenix Books Pubs.; 0-914778),* 6505 N. 43rd Place, Paradise Valley, AZ 85253 Tel 602-952-0163; P.O. Box 32008, Phoenix, AZ 85064.
Phoenix Laguna, *(Phoenix),* P.O. Box 2225, Laguna Hills, CA 92653.
Phoenix Pub, *(Phoenix Publishing; 0-914016),* Canaan, NH 03741 Tel 603-523-9902.
Photo Memorabila, *(Photographic Memorabila; 0-9604352),* P. O. Box 351, Lexington, MA 02173 Tel 617-862-1222.
Photo Res, *(Photographic Research Pubns.; 0-934918),* P.O. Box 333, Seven Oaks, Detroit, MI 48235 Tel 313-493-3503.
Photographit, *(Photographit; 0-9605168),* 12 S. Gallatin Ave., Uniontown, PA 15401.
Physsardt, *(Physsardt Pubs.; 0-916062),* Dist. by: Bloomington Distribution Group, P.O. Box 841, Bloomington, IN 47402.
Pi Pr, *(Pi Press, Inc.; 0-931420),* Box 23371, Honolulu, HI 96822.
Pi Yee Pr, *(Pi Yee Press; 0-935926),* P.O. Box 1144, La Jolla, CA 92038.
Pica Pr *Imprint of* **Universe**
Pick Pub, *(Pick Publishing Corp.; 0-87551),* 21 West St., New York, NY 10006 Tel 212-425-0591.
Pickwick, *(Pickwick Press; 0-915138),* 5001 Baum Blvd., Pittsburgh, PA 15213 Tel 412-362-5610.
Pictorial Hist, *(Pictorial Histories Publishing Co.; 0-933126),* 713 South 3rd W., Missoula, MT 59801.
Pieceful Pleasures, *(Pieceful Pleasures; 0-933758),* 566 30th Ave., San Mateo, CA 94403 Tel 415-573-9243.
Pierce Pubs, *(Pierce Pubs.; 0-9603980),* 309 High St., Chestertown, MD 21620 Tel 301-778-1121.
Pierian, *(Pierian Press; 0-87650),* P.O. Box 1808, Ann Arbor, MI 48106 Tel 313-434-5530.
Pierpont Morgan, *(Pierpont Morgan Library; 0-87598),* 29 E. 36th St., New York, NY 10016 Tel 212-685-0008.
Pierson Pubs, *(Romaine Pierson Pubs., Inc.; 0-935466),* 80 Shore Rd., Port Washington, NY 11050 Tel 516-883-6350.
Pig Iron Pr, *(Pig Iron Press; 0-917530),* P.O. Box 237, Youngstown, OH 44501 Tel 216-744-2258.
Pigiron Pr
See Pig Iron Pr
Pika Pr, *(Pika Press; 0-935160),* P.O. Box C-9, Mammoth Lakes, CA 93546.
Pikes Peak, *(Pikes Peak Poets, Inc.),* P.O. Box 6411, Colorado Springs, CO 80934.
Pikestaff Pr, *(Pikestaff Press, The; 0-936044),* Div. of Pikestaff Publications, Inc., P.O. Box 127, Normal, IL 61761 Tel 309-452-4831.
Pikeville Coll, *(Pikeville College Press; 0-933302),* Pikeville, KY 41501 Tel 606-432-9227.
Pilgrim Bks OK, *(Pilgrim Books; 0-937664),* P.O. Box 2399, Norman, OK 73070.
Pilgrim NY, *(Pilgrim Press, The; 0-8298),* 132 W. 31st St., New York, NY 10001 Tel 212-594-8555; Orders to: Seabury Service Center, Somers, CT 06071.
Pilgrim Pr, *(Pilgrim Press, The; 0-933476),* 39 University Place, Princeton, NJ 08540 Tel 609-924-9095.
Pilgrim Pubns, *(Pilgrim Pubns.),* P.O. Box 66, Pasadena, TX 77501 Tel 713-477-2329.
Pillsbury Pr
See PBBC Pr
Pilot Bks, *(Pilot Books; 0-87576),* 347 Fifth Ave., New York, NY 10016 Tel 212-685-0736.
Pilot Pubns, *(Pilot Pubns.),* P.O. Box 9307, Mobile, AL 36691 Tel 205-666-0577; Dist. by: Aviation Book Co., 1640 Victory Blvd., Glendale, CA 91201 Tel 213-240-1771.
Pin Prick, *(Pin Prick Press, The; 0-936424),* 3877 Meadowbrook Blvd., University Heights, OH 44118 Tel 216-932-2173.
Pine Mntn, *(Pine Mountain Press, Inc.; 0-89769),* P.O. Box 19746, West Allis, WI 53219 Tel 414-546-2310.
Pine Pr, *(Pine Press; 0-930502),* Box 263c, R.D. 1, Landisburg, PA 17040.
Pinecliff
See HM Prof Med Div
Pinewood, *(Pinewood Press; 0-9604498),* P.O. Box 79104, Houston, TX 77024.
Pink Hse Pub, *(Pink House Publishing Co.; 0-915946),* 410 Magellan Ave., Penthouse 1002, Honolulu, HI 96813 Tel 808-537-1875.
Pinnacle Bks, *(Pinnacle Books; 0-523),* 1 Century Plaza, 2029 Century Park E., Los Angeles, CA 90067 Tel 213-552-9111.
Pintores Pr, *(Pintores Press; 0-934116),* Box 1597, Roswell, NM 88201.
Pioneer Bk TX, *(Pioneer Book Pubs.; 0-933512),* Box 426, Seagraves, TX 79359 Tel 806-546-2498.
Pioneer Pr, *(Pioneer Press, Inc.; 0-913150),* P.O. Box 684, Union City, TN 38261 Tel 901-885-0374.
Pioneer Pub Co, *(Pioneer Publishing Co.; 0-914330),* 8 E. Olive Ave., Fresno, CA 93728 Tel 209-485-2631.
Pioneer VT, *(Pioneer Press, The; 0-9603426),* Newfane, VT 05345; Orders to: The Pioneer Press, Box 43, Schooley's Mt., NJ 07870 Tel 201-852-5407.
PIP, *(Partners in Publishing; 0-937660),* P.O. Box 50347, Tulsa, OK 74150 Tel 918-587-4275.
Pisces Pr TX, *(Pisces Press; 0-938326),* P.O. Box 4075, Lubbock, TX 79409.
Pitman
See Pitman Learning
Pitman Learning, *(Pitman Learning, Inc.; 0-8224),* 6 Davis Dr., Belmont, CA 94002 Tel 415-592-7810.
Pittore Euforico, *(Pittore Euforico; 0-934376),* P.O. Box 1132, Peter Stuyvesant Sta., New York, NY 10009.
PJD Pubns, *(PJD Pubns., Ltd.; 0-9600290; 0-915340),* P.O. Box 966, Westbury, NY 11590 Tel 516-626-0650.
PL *Imprint of* **Har-Row**
Plan Parent, *(Planned Parenthood Federation of America, Inc.; 0-934586),* 810 Seventh Ave, New York, NY 10019 Tel 212-541-7800.
Planetary Pr, *(Planetary Press; 0-938330),* P.O. Box 4641, Baltimore, MD 21212.
Planners Pr, *(Planners Press; 0-918286),* 1313 E. 60th St., Chicago, IL 60637 Tel 312-947-2560.
Platt, *(Platt & Munk Pubs.; 0-448),* Div. of Grosset & Dunlap, 51 Madison Ave., New York, NY 10010 Tel 212-689-9200.
Playboy, *(Playboy Press; 0-87223),* Div. of P.E.I. Books, Inc., 747 Third Ave., New York, NY 10017 Tel 212-245-9160; Dist. by: Harper & Row Pubs., Inc., Keystone Industrial Park, Scranton, PA 18512.
Playboy Pbks, *(Playboy Paperbacks; 0-87216),* Div. of P.E.I. Books, Inc., 747 Third Ave., New York, NY 10017 Tel 212-688-3030.
Playboy Pr Pbks
See Playboy Pbks
Plays, *(Plays, Inc.; 0-8238),* 8 Arlington St., Boston, MA 02116 Tel 617-536-7420.
Please Pr, *(Please Press Ltd.),* Box 3036, Flint, MI 48502.
Plenum Pr *Imprint of* **Plenum Pub**
Plenum Pub, *(Plenum Publishing Corp.; 0-306),* 227 W. 17th St., New York, NY 10011 Tel 212-255-0713. *Imprints:* Consultants (Consultants Bureau); Plenum Pr (Plenum Press); Rosetta (Plenum Rosetta).
Plexus Pub, *(Plexus Publishing, Inc.; 0-937548),* P.O. Box 550, Marlton, NJ 08053 Tel 609-654-6500.
PLI, *(Practising Law Institute; 0-87224),* Orders to: 810 Seventh Ave., New York, NY 10019 Tel 212-765-5700.
Plough, *(Plough Publishing House of the Hutterian Society of Brothers; 0-87486),* Rifton, NY 12471 Tel 914-658-3141.
Plum Nelly, *(Plum Nelly Shop, Inc., The),* 1201 Hixson Pike, Chattanooga, TN 37405 Tel 615-266-0585.
Plumbers Ink, *(Plumbers Ink Press; 0-935684),* P.O. Box 2565, Taos, NM 87571.
Plume *Imprint of* **NAL**
Plycon Pr, *(Plycon Press; 0-916434),* P.O. Box 220, Redondo Beach, CA 90277 Tel 213-530-1033; Dist. by: Burgess Publishing Co., 7108 Ohms Lane, Minneapolis, MN 55435.
Plymouth
See Plymouth Pr
Plymouth Pr, *(Plymouth Press; 0-935540),* P. O. Box 390205, Miami, FL 33119 Tel 305-949-5599.
PMI Inc, *(Photography Media Institute, Inc.; 0-936524),* P.O. Box 78, Staten Island, NY 10304 Tel 212-447-3280.
Poet Gal Pr, *(Poet Gallery Press; 0-913054),* 224 W. 29th St., New York, NY 10001.
Poetasumanos, *(Poetasumanos Press; 0-938254),* 949 Capp St., No. 10, San Francisco, CA 94110.
Poets & Writers, *(Poets & Writers; 0-913734),* 201 W. 54th St., New York, NY 10019 Tel 212-757-1766.
Point Blanc Pr
See Climate Bks
Point Loma Pub, *(Point Loma Pubns., Inc.; 0-913004),* P.O. Box 6507, 3727 Charles St., San Diego, CA 92106 Tel 714-222-3291.
Point Pr, *(Point Press; 0-9601474),* Box 14, Point Pleasant, NJ 08742 Tel 201-892-9480.
Pol Stud Assocs, *(Policy Studies Associates; 0-936826),* P.O. Box 337, Croton-on-Hudson, NY 10520 Tel 914-271-8802.
Polaris Pr, *(Polaris Press; 0-930504),* 16540 Camellia Terrace, Los Gatos, CA 95030.
Policy Studies, *(Policy Studies Organization; 0-918592),* 361 Lincoln Hall, Univ. of Illinois at Urbana-Champaign, Urbana, IL 61801 Tel 217-359-8541.
Poly Tone, *(Poly Tone Press; 0-933830),* 16027 Sunburst St., Sepulveda, CA 91343 Tel 213-892-0044.
Polycrystal Bk Serv, *(Polycrystal Book Service; 0-9601304),* P.O. Box 11567, Pittsburgh, PA 15238 Tel 412-963-7878.
PolyScience, *(PolyScience Corp.; 0-913106),* 6366 Gross Point Rd., Niles, IL 60648 Tel 312-647-0611.
Pomegranate Calif, *(Pomegranate Pubns.; 0-917556),* Box 748, Corte Madera, CA 94925 Tel 415-924-8141.
Pong, *(Pong, Ted),* P.O. Box 321, Freeland, WA 98249.
Popcorn Pubs, *(Popcorn Pubs; 0-930506),* P.O. Box 1308, Pittsfield, MA 01202 Tel 413-443-5601.
Pope John Ctr, *(Pope John Center; 0-935372),* 1438 S. Grand Blvd., St. Louis, MO 63104.
Popular Lib, *(Popular Library, Inc.; 0-445),* Unit of CBS Pubns., 1515 Broadway, New York, NY 10036 Tel 212-975-7663.
Population Coun, *(Population Council, Inc.; 0-87834),* One Dag Hammarskjold Plaza, New York, NY 10017 Tel 212-644-1300.

Population Ref, *(Population Reference Bureau; 0-917136),* 1337 Connecticut Ave., N.W, Washington, DC 20036 Tel 202-785-4664.
Porcupine Pr, *(Porcupine Press, Inc.; 0-87991),* 1317 Filbert St., Philadelphia, PA 19107 Tel 215-563-2288.
Portals Pr, *(Portals Press; 0-916620),* P.O. Box 1048, Tuscaloosa, AL 35403 Tel 205-758-1874.
Porter, *(Porter, Bern; 0-911156),* 22 Salmond Rd., Belfast, ME 04915.
Porter Sargent, *(Porter Sargent Pubs., Inc.; 0-87558),* 11 Beacon St., Boston, MA 02108 Tel 617-523-1670.
Portland Symphony, *(Portland Symphony Orchestra Women's Committee; 0-9601266),* Box 332, Downtown Sta., Portland, ME 04112 Tel 207-854-4630.
Portolan, *(Portolan Press; 0-916762),* 825 Rathjen Rd., Brielle, NJ 08730 Tel 201-528-8264.
Portrayal, *(Portrayal Press; 0-938242),* P.O. Box 1913, Bloomfield, NJ 07003.
Portriga Pubns, *(Portriga Pubns.; 0-9602274),* 823 N. Edinburg Ave., Los Angeles, CA 90046.
Positive Pub, *(Positive Publishing),* 2402 N. Wishon, Fresno, CA 93704 Tel 209-225-1813.
Postscript, *(Postscript Productions; 0-9604850),* P.O. Box 307, Suisun, CA 94585.
Pot of Gold, *(Pot of Gold Pubns.),* 1152 11th St., Manhattan Beach, CA 90266.
Potomac, *(Potomac Books, Inc., Pubs.; 0-87107),* 4418 MacArthur Blvd., N.W., Washington, DC 20007 Tel 202-338-5774; Orders to: P.O. Box 40604, Palisades Sta., Washington, DC 20016 Tel 202-333-6779.
Potomac Appalach, *(Potomac Appalachian Trail Club; 0-915746),* 1718 N. St., N.W, Washington, DC 20036 Tel 202-638-5307.
Potter, *(Potter, Clarkson N., Inc.; 0-8257),* Dist. by: Crown Pubs., 1 Park Ave., New York, NY 10016 Tel 212-532-9200.
Pottle, *(Pottle, Ralph R.; 0-911162),* 407 N. Magnolia St., Hammond, LA 70401 Tel 504-345-2105.
Poudre Pub Co, *(Poudre Publishing Co.; 0-935240),* P.O. Box 181, La Porte, CO 80535 Tel 303-484-2267.
Pr Arden Park, *(Press of Arden Park),* 861 Los Molinos Way, Sacramento, CA 95825 Tel 916-481-7881.
Pr of Morningside, *(Press of Morningside Bookshop; 0-89029),* P.O. Box 1087, Dayton, OH 45401 Tel 513-461-6736.
Pr Vision Studios, *(Press at Vision Studios, The; 0-936888),* P.O. Box 241, La Grange, IL 60525.
Practical Pubns, *(Practical Pubns.; 0-912914),* 6272 W. North Ave., Chicago, IL 60639 Tel 312-237-2986.
Praeger, *(Praeger Pubs.; 0-275),* Div. of Holt, Rinehart & Winston/CBS, 521 Fifth Ave., New York, NY 10175 Tel 212-599-8400.
Praestant, *(Praestant Press; 0-930112),* P.O. Box 43, Delaware, OH 43015 Tel 614-363-1458.
Prajna *Imprint of* **Great Eastern**
Prakken, *(Prakken Pubns., Inc.; 0-911168),* P.O. Box 8623, 416 Longshore Dr., Ann Arbor, MI 48107 Tel 313-769-1211.
Precious Res, *(Precious Resources; 0-937836),* Box 259A, Rt. 1, Union, KY 41091 Tel 606-586-9943.
Precision Pub Co, *(Precision Publishing Co.),* P.O. Box 172, Fort Myers, FL 33902.
Prem *Imprint of* **Fawcett**
Prem Press, *(Premier Press; 0-912722),* P.O. Box 4428, Berkeley, CA 94704.
Presby & Reformed, *(Presbyterian & Reformed Publishing Co.; 0-87552),* Order Dept., Box 817, Phillipsburg, NJ 08865.
PRESCOB, *(PRESCOB Publishing Co.),* 5110 S. 67th E. Place, Tulsa, OK 74145 Tel 918-664-6717.
Preservation Pr, *(Preservation Press, National Trust for Historic Preservation; 0-89133),* 1785 Massachusetts Ave., N.W., Washington, DC 20036 Tel 202-673-4000.
Presidio Pr, *(Presidio Press; 0-89141),* 31 Pamaron Way, Novato, CA 94947 Tel 415-883-1373; Orders to: Presidio Press Distribution Center, P.O. Box 978, Edison, NJ 08817 Tel 201-225-1900.
Press West, *(Press West; 0-914592),* Box 4107, Chico, CA 95927 Tel 916-343-0642.
Pressure, *(Pressure Vessel Handbook Publishing, Inc.; 0-914458),* P.O. Box 35365, Tulsa, OK 74135 Tel 918-742-9637.
Preston-Hill, *(Preston-Hill, Inc.; 0-914616),* P.O. Box 572, Chapel Hill, NC 27514 Tel 919-967-7904.
Preston St Pr, *(Preston Street Press),* 6 Preston St., Rye, NY 10580.
Prestressed Concrete, *(Prestressed Concrete Institute),* 201 N. Wells St., Chicago, IL 60606 Tel 312-346-4071.
Pretest
See McGraw-Pretest
Priam Pr, *(Priam Press Inc; 0-911180),* 134 S. La Salle St., Chicago, IL 60603 Tel 312-726-0569.
Price Stern, *(Price, Stern, Sloan, Pubs., Inc.; 0-8431),* 410 N. La Cienega Blvd., Los Angeles, CA 90048 Tel 213-657-6100.
Primary Pr, *(Primary Press),* Box 105a, Parker Ford, PA 19457 Tel 215-495-7529.
Primavera, *(Primavera; 0-916980),* Ida Noyes Hall, Univ. of Chicago, 1212 E. 59th St., Chicago, IL 60637 Tel 312-752-5655.
Prime Natl Pub, *(Prime National Publishing Co.; 0-932834),* 470 Boston Post Rd., Weston, MA 02193 Tel 617-899-2702.
Primer Pubs, *(Primer Pubs.; 0-935810),* 5738 N. Central, Phoenix, AZ 85012 Tel 602-266-1043; Dist. by: Med Tech Books, Inc., 11511 Tennessee Ave., Los Angeles, CA 90064.
Prince Scientific, *(Prince Scientific Press; 0-933340),* P.O. Box 2355, Univ. of GA Sta., Athens, GA 30602.
Princeton Bk Co, *(Princeton Book Co.),* P. O. Box 109, Princeton, NJ 08540.
Princeton Lib, *(Princeton Univ. Library; 0-87811),* Princeton, NJ 08544 Tel 609-452-3215.
Princeton Pub, *(Princeton Publishing Inc.; 0-915038),* 221 Nassau St., Princeton, NJ 08540 Tel 609-924-7555; Orders to: Automobile Quarterly Publications, 245 W. Main St., Kutztown, PA 19530 Tel 215-683-8352.
Princeton U Pr, *(Princeton Univ. Press; 0-691),* 41 William St., Princeton, NJ 08540 Tel 609-452-4900.
Prindle, *(Prindle, Weber & Schmidt; 0-87150),* Statler Office Bldg., 20 Providence St., Boston, MA 02116 Tel 617-482-2344.
Prinit Pr, *(Prinit Press; 0-932970),* Box 65, Dublin, IN 47335.
Print Mail Serv, *(Printing, Mailing Services, Inc.),* 126 N. Ontario St., Toledo, OH 43624 Tel 419-241-4266.
Printed Edns, *(Printed Editions; 0-914162),* 122 Spring St., New York, NY 10012 Tel 212-966-5232; Dist. by: New York Small Press Assn., P.O. Box 1264, Radio City Sta., New York, NY 10019.
Printed Matter, *(Printed Matter, Inc.; 0-89439),* 7 Lispenard St., New York, NY 10013 Tel 212-925-0325.
Printek, *(Printek; 0-938042),* 6989 Oxford St., Minneapolis, MN 55426.
Pro Lingua, *(Pro Lingua Associates; 0-86647),* 15 Elm St., Brattleboro, VT 05301.
Pro West, *(Pro West),* 5745 Via los Ranchos, Paradise Valley, AZ 85253.
ProActive Pr, *(ProActive Press; 0-914158),* P.O. Box 296, Berkeley, CA 94701 Tel 415-841-7802.
Probe
See Veritas
Process Pr, *(Process Press; 0-9605378),* 2322 Haste, No. 31, Berkeley, CA 94704.
Prod Hse, *(Production House Corp.; 0-932638),* 4307 Euclid Ave., San Diego, CA 92115 Tel 714-287-2560.
Prof Bks, *(Professional Books; 0-933478),* P.O. Box 3494, Jackson, TN 38301 Tel 901-424-4665.
Prof Educ IL, *(Professional Education Pubns.; 0-89707),* 1155 E. 60th St., Chicago, IL 60637.
Prof Engine, *(Professional Engineering Registration Program; 0-932276),* P.O. Box 911, San Carlos, CA 94070 Tel 415-593-9731.
Prof Press, *(Professional Press, Inc.; 0-87873),* 101 E. Ontario St., Chicago, IL 60611.
Prof Pubns NY, *(Professional Pubns.; 0-932836),* Div of MetaData, Inc., 441 Lexington Ave., New York, NY 10017; Orders to: P.O. Box 319, Huntington, NY 11743.
Prof Pubns Ohio, *(Professional Pubns., Inc.; 0-934706),* 1609 Northwest Blvd., Columbus, OH 43212 Tel 614-488-8236.
Prog Grocer, *(Progressive Grocer; 0-911790),* 708 Third Ave., New York, NY 10017 Tel 212-490-1000.
Prog Studies, *(Programmed Studies, Inc.; 0-917194),* P.O. Box 113, Stow, MA 01775 Tel 617-897-2130.
Progresiv Pub, *(Progresiv Publishr; 0-89670),* 401 E. 32nd St., No. 1002, Chicago, IL 60616.
Progress Pubs, *(Progress Pubs.),* Orders to: Imported Pubns., 320 W. Ohio St., Chicago, IL 60610.
Prologue, *(Prologue Pubns; 0-930048),* P.O. Box 640, Menlo Park, CA 94025 Tel 415-322-1663.
Prometheus Bks, *(Prometheus Books; 0-87975),* 1203 Kensington Ave., Buffalo, NY 14215 Tel 716-837-2475.
Prometheus Nemesis, *(Prometheus Nemesis Books),* P.O. Box 2082, Del Mar, CA 92014.
Promise Corp, *(Promise Corp.; 0-936982),* P.O. Box 1534, Pawtucket, RI 02862.
Proscenium, *(Proscenium Press; 0-912262),* P.O. Box 361, Newark, DE 19711 Tel 215-255-4083.
Proteus Pub NY, *(Proteus Publishing Co., Inc.; 0-906071),* 733 Third Ave., Suite 901, New York, NY 10017; Dist. by: Charles Scribner's Sons, 597 Fifth Ave., New York, NY 10017.
Province Pub, *(Province Publishing Co.; 0-932348),* 11307 Vela Dr., San Diego, CA 92126 Tel 714-566-6355.
Provision, *(Provision House; 0-935446),* P.O. Box 5487, Austin, TX 78763 Tel 512-452-1417.
Prudent Pub Co, *(Prudential Publishing Company; 0-934432),* 311 California St., Suite 711, San Francisco, CA 94104 Tel 916-541-8360.
Pruett, *(Pruett Publishing Co.; 0-87108),* 3235 Prairie Ave., Boulder, CO 80301 Tel 303-449-4919.
Prytaneum Pr, *(Prytaneum Press; 0-907152),* 16 Fair Way, Poughkeepsie, NY 12603.
PSG Pub, *(PSG Pub. Co., Inc.; 0-88416),* 545 Great Rd., Littleton, MA 01460 Tel 617-486-8971.
PSI Res, *(PSI Research; 0-916378),* Subs. of Publishing Services, Inc., P.O. Box 6836, Oakland, CA 94603 Tel 415-523-7969.
PSI Rhythms, *(P.S.I. Rhythms, Inc.; 0-918882),* P. O. Box 1838, Ormond Beach, FL 32074 Tel 904-255-6444; 2085 South Halofax, Daytona Beach, FL 32018.
Psych & Consul Assocs, *(Psychology & Consulting Associates Press; 0-930626),* P.O. Box 1837, La Jolla, CA 92038 Tel 714-459-1135.
Psych Corp *Imprint of* **HarBraceJ**
Psych Graphic, *(Psych Graphic Pubs.; 0-932382),* 470 Nautilus St., Suite 303, La Jolla, CA 92037 Tel 714-459-0531.
Psych Pr WA, *(Psychological Press; 0-937668),* Box 5435, Seattle, WA 98105 Tel 206-524-0194.
Psych Res Assoc, *(Psychology Research Associates),* 9000 W. Sunset Blvd., Suite 305, Los Angeles, CA 90069.
Psychohistory Pr, *(Psychohistory Press),* Div. of Atcom, Inc., Pubs., 2315 Broadway, New York, NY 10024 Tel 212-873-3760.
PT Marketing, *(P. T. Marketing; 0-9605106),* 13836 Bora Bora Way, Marina Del Rey, CA 90291; Moved, Left No Forwarding Address.
Ptolemy Pr, *(Ptolemy Press Ltd.; 0-933550),* P.O. Box 243, Grove City, PA 16127 Tel 412-794-7309.
Pub Aff Pr, *(Public Affairs Press; 0-8183),* 419 New Jersey Ave., Washington, DC 20003 Tel 202-544-3024.
Pub Ctr Cult Res, *(Publishing Center for Cultural Resources, Inc.; 0-89062),* 625 Broadway, New York, NY 10012 Tel 212-260-2010.
Pub Serv Ctr, *(Publishing Services Center),* Dist. by: William Kaufmann, Inc., 1 First St., Los Altos, CA 94022 Tel 415-948-5810.
Pub Vaidava, *(Publisher Vaidava; 0-936302),* 1621 S. 21st St., Lincoln, NE 68502.
Public Info Pr, *(Public Information Press, Inc.; 0-934954),* P.O. Box 402611, Miami Beach, FL 33140 Tel 305-538-5308.

Public Relations, *(Public Relations Publishing Co.; 0-913046),* 888 Seventh Ave., New York, NY 10106 Tel 212-582-7373.
Public Serv Materials, *(Public Service Materials Center),* 415 Lexington Ave., New York, NY 10017.
Publish or Perish, *(Publish or Perish, Inc.; 0-914098),* 2000 Center St., Box 1404, Berkeley, CA 94704 Tel 404-329-0372.
Pubns Living, *(Pubns. for Living; 0-912128),* 11224 Big Bend Blvd., St. Louis, MO 63122 Tel 314-821-6177.
Puckerbrush, *(Puckerbrush Press; 0-913006),* 76 Main St., Orono, ME 04473 Tel 207-866-4868.
Pueblo Pub Co, *(Pueblo Publishing Co., Inc.; 0-916134),* 1860 Broadway, New York, NY 10023 Tel 212-541-7665.
Puerto Rico Almanacs, *(Puerto Rico Almanacs, Inc.; 0-934642),* P.O. Box 9582, Santurce, PR 00908 Tel 809-724-2402.
Puffin *Imprint of* **Penguin**
Pundarika, *(Pundarika Pubns.),* P.O. Box 444, Mountain Home, NC 28758.
Purchase Pr, *(Purchase Press, The; 0-938266),* P.O. Box 5, Harrison, NY 10528.
Purdue, *(Purdue Univ. Press; 0-911198),* S. Campus Courts-D, West Lafayette, IN 47907 Tel 317-749-6083.
Purdue Univ Bks, *(Purdue Univ. Books; 0-931682),* Bldg. D, South Campus Courts, West Lafayette, IN 47907.
PURRC, *(Princeton Urban & Regional Research Center; 0-938882),* Woodrow Wilson School, Princeton University, Princeton, NJ 08544.
Pushcart Bk Pr
See Pushcart Pr
Pushcart Pr, *(Pushcart Press, The; 0-916366),* P.O. Box 845, Yonkers, NY 10701 Tel 212-228-2269.
Putnam, *(Putnam's, G. P., Sons; 0-399),* 200 Madison Ave., New York, NY 10016 Tel 212-576-8900; Orders to: 1050 Wall St. W., Lyndhurst, NJ 07071 Tel 201-933-9292. *Imprints:* Peppercorn (Peppercorn); Perigee (Perigee Books).
Pyquag, *(Pyquag Books, Pubs.; 0-912492),* P.O. Box 328, Wethersfield, CT 06109.
Pyramid Iowa, *(Pyramid Pubs. of Iowa),* P.O. Box 400, Perry, IA 50220 Tel 515-465-5500; Dist. by: Hiawatha Book Co., 7567 N.E. 102nd Ave., Bondurant, IA 50035 Tel 515-967-4025.
Pyxidium Pr, *(Pyxidium Press; 0-936568),* Box 462, Old Chelsea Sta., New York, NY 10011 Tel 212-242-5224.
QED Info Sci, *(Q.E.D. Information Sciences, Inc.; 0-89435),* P.O. Box 181, 180 Linden St., Wellesley, MA 02181 Tel 617-237-5656.
Quadrangle
See Times Bks
Quail Ridge, *(Quail Ridge Press, Inc.; 0-937552),* P.O. Box 123, Brandon, MS 39042.
Quail Run, *(Quail Run Pubns., Inc.; 0-930380),* 3336 N.32nd St., Suite 104, Phoenix, AZ 85018 Tel 602-955-5953.
Quaker, *(Quaker Press; 0-911200),* 3218 O St. N.W., Washington, DC 20007 Tel 202-338-3391.
Quality Bks IL, *(Quality Books Inc.; 0-89196),* 400 Anthony Trail, Northbrook, IL 60062 Tel 312-498-4000. *Imprints:* Domus Bks (Domus Books).
Quality Circle, *(Quality Circle Institute; 0-937670),* 1425 Vista Way, Airport Industrial Park, P. O. Box Q, Red Bluff, CA 96080.
Quality Educ, *(Quality Educators, Ltd.),* 1236 S.E. Fourth Ave., Ft. Lauderdale, FL 33316 Tel 305-522-2249.
Quality Hill, *(Quality Hill Books; 0-9605044),* 674 Church St., San Luis Obispo, CA 93401.
Quality Pubns, *(Quality Pubns.; 0-89137),* Div. of Quality Printing Co., Inc., P.O. Box 1060, Abilene, TX 79604 Tel 915-677-6262.
Quam Pr, *(Quam, Martin, Press),* 1515 Columbia Dr., Cedar Falls, IA 50613 Tel 319-273-2648; Orders to: 201 Rio St., Rio, WI 53960.
Quantal, *(Quantal Publishing Co.; 0-936596),* P.O. Box 1598, Goleta, CA 93117 Tel 805-964-7293; Dist. by: Ross-Erikson, Inc., 629 State St., Suite 222, Santa Barbara, CA 93101 Tel 805-962-1175.
Quarterman, *(Quarterman Pubns., Inc.; 0-88000),* 5 S. Union St., Lawrence, MA 01843 Tel 617-259-8047.
Queens Hse, *(Queens House; 0-89244),* 105 Grovers Ave., Bridgeport, CT 06605 Tel 203-367-1578.
Quest *Imprint of* **Theos Pub Hse**
Quest Pr, *(Quest Press; 0-935320),* Box 998, San Luis Obispo, CA 93406 Tel 805-543-8500.
Quest Utah, *(Quest Publishing Inc.; 0-938662),* P.O. Box 27317, Salt Lake City, UT 84127.
Quick Fox *Imprint of* **Music Sales**
Quicksilver Prod, *(Quicksilver Productions; 0-930356),* P.O. Box 340, Ashland, OR 97520 Tel 503-482-5343.
Quigley Pub Co, *(Quigley Publishing Co. Inc.; 0-900610),* 159 W. 53rd. St., New York, NY 10019 Tel 212-247-3100.
Quinn-Gallagher, *(Quinn-Gallagher Press; 0-935282),* 6372 Forward Ave., Pittsburgh, PA 15217 Tel 412-521-1863.
Quint Pub Co, *(Quintessence Publishing Co., Inc.; 0-931386),* 10 S. LaSalle St., Chicago, IL 60603 Tel 312-782-3221.
Quintessence, *(Quintessence Pubns.; 0-918466),* 356 Bunker Hill Mine Rd., Amador City, CA 95601 Tel 209-267-5470.
Quist, *(Quist, Harlin, Books; 0-8252),* Dist. by: Dial/Delacorte Sales, 1 Dag Hammarskjold Plaza, 245 E. 47th St., New York, NY 10017 Tel 212-832-7300.
Quixote, *(Quixote Press; 0-9600306),* P.O. Box 70013, Allen Sta., Houston, TX 77007 Tel 713-227-2638.
Quorum Bks *Imprint of* **Greenwood**
Qwint Systems, *(Qwint Systems, Inc.),* 3693 Commercial Ave., Northbrook, IL 60062 Tel 312-498-5060.
R A Green, *(Green, Robert Alan; 0-9600266),* 214 Key Haven Rd., Key West, FL 33040 Tel 518-624-5591.
R & D Pubns, *(R & D Pubns., Inc.; 0-938152),* Box 1032, New York, NY 10028.
R & H Pubs, *(R & H Publishers; 0-935246),* Box 3587, Georgetown Sta., Washington, DC 20007 Tel 703-524-4226.
R & S Rowland, *(Rowland, Ralph & Star),* 4209 San Juan Dr., Fairfax, VA 22030 Tel 703-273-4891.
R B Forster, *(Forster, Reginald Bishop, Associates Inc.; 0-931398),* 2344 Nicollet Ave, Suite 100, Minneapolis, MN 55404 Tel 612-871-1395.
R C Rapier, *(Rapier, Regina C.; 0-9600584),* Rte. 1, Box 292, Social Circle, GA 30279 Tel 404-464-2582.
R Collier, *(Collier, Robert, Pub., Inc.; 0-912576),* P.O. Box 3684, Indialantic, FL 32903.
R Curtis Bks, *(Curtis, Ralph, Books; 0-88359),* 2633 Adams St., Hollywood, FL 33020 Tel 305-925-4639; Orders to: 520 N. Dixie Hwy., Hollywood, FL 33020 Tel 305-925-4639.
R E Todd, *(Todd, Richard E.; 0-9605324),* 3601 Linden Ave., Long Beach, CA 90807.
R Enslow
See Enslow Pubs
R H Sang & Son, *(Sang, R. H., & Son Pubs. Inc.; 0-932844),* 211 E. Delaware Place, Chicago, IL 60611 Tel 312-787-9565.
R J Brady, *(Brady, Robert J., Co.; 0-87618; 0-87619),* Subs. of Prentice Hall, Inc., Rtes. 197 & 450, Bowie, MD 20715 Tel 301-262-6300.
R J Liederbach, *(Liederbach, Robert J.; 0-934906),* 2720 East Boulevard, Cleveland, OH 44104 Tel 216-231-8896.
R J Pub, *(Jay, Robert, Publishing),* P.O. Box 1171, Madison, WI 53701.
R Kuppinger, *(Kuppinger, Roger),* 77 Woodland Lane, Arcadia, CA 91006 Tel 213-489-3900.
R L Bell, *(Bell, Robert L.; 0-9602450),* 48-50 Melrose St., Boston, MA 02116.
R L Shep, *(Shep, R. L.; 0-914046),* Box C-20, Lopez, WA 98261.
R L Thomas, *(Thomas, Ralph L.),* 5023 Frew Ave., Pittsburgh, PA 15213 Tel 412-683-4420.
R Marek
See Marek
R Morris Assocs, *(Morris, Robert, Associates; 0-936742),* 1616 Philadelphia National Bank Bldg., Philadelphia, PA 19107 Tel 215-665-2850.
R Nader, *(Nader, Ralph; 0-936486),* P.O. Box 19312, Washington, DC 20036.
R Nicholson
See Barrie & Jenkins
R Oman Pubns, *(Oman, Robert, Pubns.; 0-931660),* 204 Fair Oaks Park, Needham, MA 02192.
R Pagliotti, *(Pagliotti, Rick; 0-9602694),* 342 Pebble Hill Place, Santa Barbara, CA 93111 Tel 805-967-4630.
R S Hart, *(Hart, R. S.),* 6636 Wash. Blvd., Box 53, Elkridge, MD 21227.
R Seaver Bks
See Seaver Bks
R Shoemaker, *(Shoemaker, Rhoda; 0-9600474),* 1141 Orange Ave., Menlo Park, CA 94025 Tel 415-854-5768.
R T Matthews, *(Matthews, Robert T.; 0-9601150),* 2400 Pfefferkorn Rd., West Friendship, MD 21794.
R Thrift, *(Thrift, Richard),* 108 Clarke Court, Charlottesville, VA 22903.
R Tirtha, *(Tirtha, Ranjit),* Eastern Michigan University, Dept. of Geography, Ypsilanti, MI 48197 Tel 313-487-0218.
R West, *(West, Richard; 0-8492; 0-8274),* Box 6404, Philadelphia, PA 19145.
R Woodrow, *(Woodrow, Ralph, Evangelistic Assn., Inc.; 0-916938),* Box 124, Riverside, CA 92502 Tel 714-686-5467.
RA Corp, *(RA Corp.; 0-934434),* P.O. Box 483, Stanhope, NJ 07874 Tel 201-347-2715.
Racz Pub, *(Racz Publishing Co.; 0-916546),* P.O. Box 287, Oxnard, CA 93032 Tel 805-642-1186.
Rada Pr, *(Rada Press; 0-9604212),* 2297 Folwell, St. Paul, MN 55108.
Radio City, *(Radio City Book Store; 0-911202),* 324 W. 47th St., New York, NY 10036 Tel 212-245-5754.
Radio Pubns, *(Radio Pubns., Inc.; 0-933616),* Box 149, Wilton, CT 06897 Tel 914-967-5774.
Radix Bks, *(Radix Books Inc.),* P.O. Box 171, Beaver Falls, PA 15010 Tel 412-843-2806.
Raemsch Pubns, *(Raemsch Pubns.; 0-9605398),* Box 149, West Oneonta, NY 13861 Tel 607-432-4836.
Ragan Comm, *(Ragan, Lawrence, Communications, Inc.; 0-931368),* 407 S. Dearborn St., Chicago, IL 60605 Tel 312-922-8245.
Ragnarok
See Merging Media
Ragusan Pr, *(Ragusan Press; 0-918660),* 936 Industrial Ave., Palo Alto, CA 94303 Tel 415-494-1112.
Rail-Europe
See Rail-Europe-Baxter
Rail-Europe-Baxter, *(Rail-Europe/Baxter Guides; 0-913384),* P.O. Box 3255, Alexandria, VA 22302.
Railsearch, *(Railsearch Publishing, Inc.; 0-937060),* P.O. Box 84, Chalfont, PA 18914.
Rainbow-Betty, *(Rainbow Books/Betty Wright),* Dept. 1-H, P.O. Box 1069, Moore Haven, FL 33471 Tel 813-946-0293.
Rainbow Pub Co, *(Rainbow Publishing Co.; 0-936218),* P.O. Box 397, Chesterland, OH 44026.
Rainey Day Or
See Rainy Day Oreg
Raintree Child, *(Raintree Childrens Books; 0-8172; 0-8393),* Div. of Raintree Publishers Group, 205 W. Highland Ave., Milwaukee, WI 53203 Tel 414-273-0873.
Raintree Pubs, *(Raintree Pubs., Inc.; 0-8172),* 205 W. Highland Ave., Milwaukee, WI 53203 Tel 414-273-0873.
Raintree Pubs Ltd
See Raintree Pubs
Rainy Day Oreg, *(Rainy Day Press; 0-931742),* P.O. Box 3035, Eugene, OR 97403 Tel 503-484-4626.
Ramakrishna, *(Ramakrishna-Vivekananda Center; 0-911206),* 17 E. 94th St., New York, NY 10028 Tel 212-534-9445.
RaMar, *(RaMar Press; 0-935798),* Seven Lakes Box 548, West End, NC 27376 Tel 919-673-0571.
Ramfre, *(Ramfre Press; 0-911208),* 1206 N. Henderson, Cape Girardeau, MO 63701 Tel 314-335-6582.
Ramparts, *(Ramparts Press; 0-87867),* P.O. Box 50128, Palo Alto, CA 94303 Tel 415-325-7861.
Rana Hse, *(Rana House; 0-930172),* Box 2997, St. Louis, MO 63130.
RanC *Imprint of* **Random**
Rand, *(Rand McNally & Co.; 0-528),* P.O. Box 7600, Chicago, IL 60680 Tel 312-673-9100.

Rand-Tofua, *(Rand Editions/Tofua Press; 0-914488),* 10457-F Roselle St., San Diego, CA 92121 Tel 714-453-4774.
Randall Hse, *(Randall House Pubns.; 0-89265),* 114 Bush Rd., P.O. Box 17306, Nashville, TN 37217 Tel 615-361-1221.
R&M Pub Co, *(R&M Publishing Co.; 0-936026),* P.O. Box 210, Marion, SC 29571 Tel 803-423-6711.
Random, *(Random House, Inc.; 0-394),* Random House Publicity (11-6), 201 E. 50th St., New York, NY 10022 Tel 212-751-2600; Orders to: 400 Hahn Rd., Westminster, MD 21157. *Imprints:* BYR (Books for Young Readers); RanC (Random House College Division); Vin (Vintage Trade Books).
Ranger Assocs, *(Ranger Assocs., Inc.; 0-934588),* P.O. Box 1357, Manassas, VA 22110 Tel 703-369-5336.
Ransom Hill, *(Ransom Hill Press; 0-9604342),* P.O. Box 325, Ramona, CA 92065.
Rateavers, *(Rateavers; 0-9600698; 0-915966),* Pauma Valley, CA 92061 Tel 714-566-8994.
Rather Pr, *(Rather Press),* 3200 Guido St., Oakland, CA 94602 Tel 415-531-2938.
Rational Isl, *(Rational Island Pubs.; 0-911214),* 719 Second Ave. N., Seattle, WA 98109 Tel 206-284-0311; Orders to: P.O. Box 2081, Main Office Sta., Seattle, WA 98111.
Rational Living, *(Institute for Rational Living, Inc.; 0-917476),* 45 E. 65th St., New York, NY 10021 Tel 212-535-0822.
Raven, *(Raven Press, Pubs.; 0-89004),* 1140 Ave. of the Americas, New York, NY 10036 Tel 212-575-0335.
Raven Pub Co, *(Raven Publishing Co.),* 911 E. Mahanoy Ave., Mahanoy City, PA 17948 Tel 717-773-1586.
Rawson Assocs
See Rawson Wade
Rawson Wade, *(Rawson, Wade Pubs., Inc.; 0-89256),* 630 Third Ave., New York, NY 10017 Tel 212-867-6610; Dist. by: Atheneum Pubs., 122 E. 42nd St., New York, NY 10017.
Ray Riling, *(Riling, Ray, Arms Books; 0-9603096),* P.O. Box 18925, 6844 Gorsten St., Philadelphia, PA 19119 Tel 215-438-2456.
Raycol Prods, *(Raycol Products; 0-9605176),* 5346 E. 9th St., Tucson, AZ 85711.
RBDH *Imprint of* **Kregel**
RC&J
See Reed & Cannon
RCP Pubns, *(RCP Pubns.; 0-89851),* P.O. Box 3486, Merchandise Mart, Chicago, IL 60654 Tel 312-663-5920.
RDIC Pubns, *(Rudolf Dreikurs Institute of Colorado Pubns.; 0-933450),* P.O. Box 3118, Boulder, CO 80307 Tel 303-499-4500.
RE *Imprint of* **WSP**
Readers Digest Pr, *(Reader's Digest Press; 0-88349),* 200 Park Ave., New York, NY 10017; Dist. by: McGraw-Hill Book Co., 1221 Ave. of the Americas, New York, NY 10020.
Readex Bks, *(Readex Books; 0-918414),* Div. of Readex Microprint Corp., 101 Fifth Ave., New York, NY 10003 Tel 212-243-3822.
Readex Microprint
See Readex Bks
Reading Gems, *(Reading Gems; 0-915988),* P.O. Box 806, Madison, WI 53701.
Real Comp & Int, *(Real Computers & Intelligence; 0-934190),* P.O. Box 74, Santa Clara, CA 95050 Tel 408-688-0676.
Real Estate Ed Co, *(Real Estate Education Co.; 0-88462),* 500 N. Dearborn St., Chicago, IL 60610 Tel 312-836-4400; Dist. by: Follett Publishing Co., 1010 W. Washington, Chicago, IL 60610.
Real Estate Pub, *(Real Estate Publishing Co.; 0-914256),* P.O. Box 41177, Sacramento, CA 95841 Tel 916-677-3864.
Realtors Natl, *(Realtors National Marketing Institute; 0-913652),* 430 Michigan Ave., Chicago, IL 60611 Tel 312-440-8514.
Realvest Pub Co, *(Realvest Publishing Co.; 0-933928),* Div. of Charter Management Associates, Inc., 79 S. Pleasant St., Amherst, MA 01002 Tel 413-253-2554.
Rechs Pubns, *(Rechs Pubns.; 0-937568),* 8157 Madison Ave., South Gate, CA 90280.
Recipes Unltd, *(Recipes Unlimited, Inc.; 0-918620),* P.O. Box 1202, Burnsville, MN 55337 Tel 612-890-6655.
Record Research, *(Record Research Inc.; 0-89820),* P.O. Box 200, Menomonee Falls, WI 53051; Dist. by: Gale Research Co., Book Tower, Detroit, MI 48226 Tel 313-961-2242.
Red Dust, *(Red Dust Inc.; 0-87376),* P.O. Box 630, Gracie Sta., New York, NY 10028 Tel 212-348-4388.
Red Earth, *(Red Earth Press; 0-918434),* P.O. Box 26641, Albuquerque, NM 87125 Tel 505-268-3077; Formerly Named Yarbrough Mountain Press.
Red Feather, *(Red Feather Pubs.; 0-936430),* P.O. Box 906, Lubbock, TX 79408 Tel 806-741-7075.
Red Herring, *(Red Herring Press; 0-932884),* 1209 W. Oregon, Urbana, IL 61801 Tel 217-344-1176.
Red River, *(Red River Press; 0-938898),* 4806 Danberry, Wichita Falls, TX 76308.
Red Sun Pr, *(Red Sun Press; 0-932728),* 51 Bristol St., Boston, MA 02118 Tel 617-542-4821.
Redgrave Pub Co, *(Redgrave Publishing Co.; 0-913178),* Div. of Docent Corp., 430 Manville Rd., Pleasantville, NY 10570 Tel 914-769-3629.
Redwood Pub Co, *(Redwood Publishing Co.; 0-937316),* 3860 S. Niguera, Space 105, San Luis Obispo, CA 93401; Do Not Confuse with Redwood Publishers in Menlo Park, CA.
Reebie Assoc, *(Reebie Associates, Inc.; 0-9604776),* P.O. Box 1278, Greenwich, CT 06830 Tel 203-661-8661.
Reed, *(Reed, A. H. & A. W., Books; 0-589),* Dist. by: Charles E. Tuttle, Inc., 28 S. Main St., Rutland, VT 05701 Tel 802-773-8930.
Reed & Cannon, *(Reed & Cannon Co.; 0-918408),* 2140 Shattuck Ave., Rm. 311, Berkeley, CA 94704 Tel 415-527-1586.
Reel Res, *(Reel Research),* P.O. Box 6037, Albany, CA 94706 Tel 415-549-0923.
Ref Guides, *(Reference Guides),* Rte. 2, Box 162, Detroit, TX 75436.
Ref Pubns, *(Reference Pubns., Inc.; 0-917256),* Box 344, 218 St. Clair River Dr., Algonac, MI 48001 Tel 313-794-5722.
Ref Serv Pr, *(Reference Service Press; 0-918276),* 9023 Alcott, Suite 201, Los Angeles, CA 90035 Tel 213-271-1955.
Reg Baptist, *(Regular Baptist Press; 0-87227),* 1300 N. Meacham Rd., P.O. Box 95500, Schaumburg, IL 60195 Tel 312-843-1600.
Regal, *(Regal Books),* Div. of G/L Pubns., P.O. Box 3875, Ventura, CA 93006 Tel 805-644-6869.
Regenbogen-Verlag, *(Regenbogen-Verlag),* Box 6214, Silver Spring, MD 20906 Tel 301-933-8521.
Regent Graphic Serv, *(Regent Graphic Services; 0-912710),* P.O. Box 8372, Swissvale, PA 15218 Tel 412-371-7128.
Regents Pr KS, *(Regents Press of Kansas; 0-7006),* 303 Carruth-O'leary, Lawrence, KS 66045 Tel 913-864-4154.
Regents Pub, *(Regents Publishing Co., Inc.; 0-88345),* Div. of Hachette, 2 Park Ave., New York, NY 10016 Tel 212-889-2780.
Regional Ctr Educ, *(Regional Center for Educational Training; 0-915892),* 45 Lyme Rd., Hanover, NH 03755 Tel 603-643-5666.
Regnery
See Contemp Bks
Regnery-Gateway, *(Regnery/Gateway, Inc.; 0-89526),* 116 S. Michigan, Suite 300, Chicago, IL 60603 Tel 312-346-6646.
Rehab Intl, *(Rehabilitation International; 0-9605554),* 432 Park Ave. S., New York, NY 10016.
Reidel Pub
See Kluwer Boston
Reiff Pr, *(Reiff Press; 0-911246),* 160 Mt. Holly Rd., Amelia, OH 45102 Tel 513-753-5278.
Reilly & Lee
See Contemp Bks
Reiman Assocs, *(Reiman Associates; 0-89821),* 733 N. Van Buren, Milwaukee, WI 53202 Tel 414-272-5410; Orders to: 611 E. Wells St., Milwaukee, WI 53202.
Reiner, *(Reiner Pubns.; 0-87377),* Swengel, PA 17880 Tel 717-922-3213.
Rekalb Pr, *(Rekalb Press; 0-9604614),* 6203 Jane Lane, Columbus, GA 31904 Tel 404-324-1392.
Reliance Pub, *(Reliance Publishing Co.; 0-937740),* 380 Steinwehr Ave., Gettysburg, PA 17325 Tel 717-334-1103.
Religious Educ, *(Religious Education Press, Inc.; 0-89135),* 1531 Wellington Rd., Birmingham, AL 35209 Tel 205-879-4040.
Remarkable Pubns, *(Remarkable Pubns.; 0-9605346),* 8005 Bleriot Ave., Westchester, CA 90045.
Renfro Studios, *(Renfro, Nancy, Studios; 0-931044),* 1117 W. 9th St., Austin, TX 78703 Tel 512-472-2140.
Renouf, *(Renouf USA, Inc.; 0-604),* Brookfield, VT 05036 Tel 802-276-3355.
Reprint, *(Reprint Co.; 0-87152),* P.O. Box 5401, 601 Hillcrest Offices, Spartanburg, SC 29304 Tel 803-582-0732.
Res & Educ, *(Research & Education Assn.; 0-87891),* 505 Eighth Ave., New York, NY 10018 Tel 212-695-9487.
Res Media
See CAS
Res Press, *(Research Press Co.; 0-87822),* Box 3177, Champaign, IL 61820 Tel 217-352-3273.
Res Pubns Conn, *(Research Pubns., Inc.; 0-89235),* 12 Lunar Dr., Woodbridge, CT 06525 Tel 203-397-2600.
Res Pubns WA, *(Researcher Pubns., Inc.; 0-938428),* 18806-40th Ave., W., Lynnwood, WA 98036.
Res Stud Pr, *(Research Studies Press, Inc.; 0-89355),* Box 10766, Portland, OR 97210 Tel 503-243-1158.
Research Servs Corp, *(Research Services Corp.; 0-915074),* P.O. Box 16549, Fort Worth, TX 76133 Tel 817-292-4272.
Resolute Pr, *(Resolute Press; 0-9604382),* 13 Regent Court, Edison, NJ 08817.
Resource Pubns, *(Resource Pubns.; 0-89390),* P.O. Box 444, Saratoga, CA 95070 Tel 408-252-4195.
Responsible Action
See Intl Dialogue Pr
Reston, *(Reston Publishing Co., Inc.; 0-87909; 0-8359),* 11480 Sunset Hills Rd., Reston, VA 22090 Tel 703-437-8900; Dist. by: Prentice-Hall, Inc., Englewood Cliffs, NJ 07632.
Retail Report, *(Retail Reporting Bureau; 0-934590),* 101 Fifth Ave., New York, NY 10003 Tel 212-255-9595.
Retriever, *(Retriever Books; 0-9604628),* 250 W. 87th St., New York, NY 10024 Tel 212-874-5579.
Revell, *(Revell, Fleming H., Co.; 0-8007),* 184 Central Ave., Old Tappan, NJ 07675 Tel 201-768-8060.
Review & Herald, *(Review & Herald Publishing Assn.; 0-8280),* P.O. Box 59, Nashville, TN 37202 Tel 615-883-4463.
Revisionary, *(Revisionary Press; 0-9603726),* Box 158A, St. James, NY 11780 Tel 516-862-9296.
Revisionist Pr, *(Revisionist Press; 0-87700),* P.O. Box 2009, Brooklyn, NY 11202.
Reward *Imprint of* **P-H**
Reymont, *(Reymont Associates; 0-918734),* 29 Reymont Ave., Rye, NY 10580 Tel 914-967-8185.
Reynal, *(Reynal & Co.; 0-688),* 105 Madison Ave., New York, NY 10016 Tel 212-889-3050; Dist. by: William Morrow & Co., Order Dept., 6 Henderson Dr., West Caldwell, NJ 07006.
Reynolds Morse, *(Reynolds Morse Foundation; 0-934236),* 21709 Chagrin Blvd., Cleveland, OH 44122; Dist. by: L.D.S. Books, P.O. Box 67, MCS, Dayton, OH 45402.
Rhineburgh Pr, *(Rhineburgh Press Inc.; 0-9604746),* 595 Madison Ave., New York, NY 10022 Tel 212-355-0162.
Rhinos Pr, *(Rhino's Press, The; 0-937382),* 157 Streamwood, Irvine, CA 92714 Tel 714-730-0342.
Rho-Delta Pr, *(Rho-Delta Press; 0-913770),* 8831 Sunset Blvd., Suite 203, P.O. Box 69540, Los Angeles, CA 90069 Tel 213-657-1925.
RI Bicentennial
See RI Pubns Soc
RI Mayflower, *(Rhode Island Mayflower Society; 0-930272),* 128 Massasoit Dr., Warwick, RI 02888 Tel 401-781-6759.
RI Pubns Soc, *(Rhode Island Pubns. Society; 0-917012),* Old State House, 150 Benefit St., Providence, RI 02903 Tel 401-272-1776.
Rice Univ, *(Rice University Studies; 0-89263),* History Dept., Houston, TX 77001 Tel 713-527-8101; Orders to: Rice Campus Store, P.O. Box 1892, Houston, TX 77001.

Richards Pub, *(Richards, Frank E., Publishing Co., Inc.; 0-88323),* P.O. Box 66, Phoenix, NY 13135 Tel 315-695-7261.
Ridgefield Pub, *(Ridgefield Publishing Co.),* 18411 Hatteras St., No. 228, Tarzana, CA 91356.
Ridgeview, *(Ridgeview Publishing Co.; 0-917930),* Box 686, Atascadero, CA 93422 Tel 805-466-7252.
Ridgeview Jr High Pr, *(Ridgeview Junior High Press; 0-936920),* 9424 Highlander Court, Walkersville, MD 21793.
RIFD, *(Registry of Interpreters for the Deaf, Inc.; 0-9602220),* 814 Thayer Ave., Silver Spring, MD 20910.
Rigel, *(Rigel, Inc.; 0-937234),* 2644 Capitol Trail, Newark, DE 19711.
Ringling Mus Art, *(John & Mable Ringling Museum of Art Foundation; 0-916758),* 5401 Bayshore Rd., Sarasota, FL 33578 Tel 813-355-5101.
Rio Grande, *(Rio Grande Press, Inc.; 0-87380),* P.O. Box 33, Glorieta, NM 87535 Tel 505-757-6275.
Rip off, *(Rip off Press; 0-89620),* P.O. Box 14158, San Francisco, CA 94114 Tel 415-863-5359.
Rising Wolf, *(Rising Wolf Inc.; 0-936710),* 240 N. Higgins, No. 4, Missoula, MT 59801.
Risk & Ins, *(Risk & Insurance Mgt. Society, Inc.; 0-937802),* 205 E. 42nd St., New York, NY 10017.
RIT Graph Arts Res
See Graph Arts Res RIT
Ritger Sports, *(Ritger Sports Co.; 0-933554),* P.O. Box 1321, Tempe, AZ 85281 Tel 602-838-3974.
Rittenhouse, *(Rittenhouse Book Distributors; 0-87381),* 511 Feheley Dr., King of Prussia, PA 19406 Tel 215-277-1414.
River Basin, *(River Basin Publishing Co.; 0-936106),* P.O. Box 30573, St. Paul, MN 55175 Tel 612-291-7470.
River Bend, *(River Bend Publishing; 0-9605162),* 905 Leroy St., Muscatine, IA 52761.
Riverhouse Pubns, *(Riverhouse Pubns.; 0-933258),* 20 Waterside Plaza, New York, NY 10010 Tel 212-685-2376; c/o Harvey House, 128 W. River St., Chippewa Fall, WI 54792 Tel 715-723-2814.
Riverrun NY, *(Riverrun Press Inc.; 0-7145),* 175 Fifth Ave., Suite 814, New York, NY 10010 Tel 212-228-0390.
Riverrun Texas
See Riverrun NY
Riverstone Foothills, *(Riverstone Press of the Foothills Art Center; 0-936600),* 809 15th St., Golden, CO 80401.
Rizzoli Intl, *(Rizzoli International Pubns., Inc.; 0-8478),* 712 Fifth Ave., New York, NY 10019 Tel 212-397-3740.
RK Edns, *(RK Editions; 0-932360),* P.O. Box 73, Canal St., New York, NY 10013.
Roadrunner Tech, *(Roadrunner-Technical Pubns., Inc.; 0-89741),* Div. of Desert Laboratories, Inc., 3136 E. Columbia St., Tucson, AZ 85714 Tel 602-294-3431.
Roan Horse, *(Roan Horse Press; 0-933234),* 11 Silverweed Court, Pueblo, CO 81001.
Roberts Ent, *(Roberts Enterprises; 0-9604184),* 6322 N. Barcelona Lane, No. 516, Tucson, AZ 85704.
Robertson, *(Robertson, Donald W.),* Star Rte. 2, Box 216, Canyon Lake, TX 78130 Tel 512-935-2172.
Robin & Russ, *(Robin & Russ Handweavers),* 533 N. Adams St., McMinnville, OR 97128 Tel 503-472-5760.
Robotics Pr, *(Robotics Press; 0-89661),* 30 NW 23rd Place, Portland, OR 97210 Tel 503-243-1158; Orders to: P.O. Box 606, Beaverton, OR 97075.
Rock Harbor, *(Rock Harbor Press; 0-932260),* P.O. Box 1206, Hyannis, MA 02601.
Rockefeller, *(Rockefeller Univ. Press; 0-87470),* 1230 York Ave., Box 291, New York, NY 10021 Tel 212-360-1217; Orders to: Box 269, 1230 York Ave., New York, NY 10021 Tel 212-360-1367.
Rockets, *(Rockets; 0-912468),* P.O. Box 591, Corona, CA 91720 Tel 714-735-0169.
Rockland County Hist, *(Historical Society of Rockland County),* 20 Zukor Rd., New York, NY 10956.
Rocky Mtn Bks, *(Rocky Mountain Books),* P.O. Box 10663, Denver, CO 80210.
Rocky Mtn Pr, *(Rocky Mountain Press; 0-9603386),* 2754 Mariquita St., Long Beach, CA 90803.
Rod & Staff, *(Rod & Staff Pubs., Inc.),* Crockett, KY 41413 Tel 606-522-4348.
Rodale Pr Inc, *(Rodale Press, Inc.; 0-87857),* 33 E. Minor St., Emmaus, PA 18049 Tel 215-967-5171.
Roehrs, *(Roehrs Co.; 0-911266),* P.O. Box 125, 227A Paterson Ave., East Rutherford, NJ 07073 Tel 201-939-0090.
Rogers Bk, *(Rogers Book Service; 0-911268),* 217 W. 18th St, Box V, New York, NY 10011.
Rogers Hse Mus, *(Rogers House Museum Gallery; 0-9600686),* 102 E. Main South, Ellsworth, KS 67439 Tel 914-472-3255.
Romance, *(Romance Monographs, Inc.),* P.O. Box 7553, University, MS 38677 Tel 601-234-0001.
Romney Pr, *(Romney Press; 0-9604640),* 308 Fourth Ave., Iowa City, IA 52240; Dist. by: Eble Music Co., P.O. Box 2570, Iowa City, IA 52244.
Ronald Pr, *(Ronald Press),* 605 Third Ave., New York, NY 10158 Tel 212-850-6418.
Rooney Pubns, *(Rooney Pubns.; 0-9604600),* P.O. Box 44146, Panorama City, CA 91412 Tel 213-894-2585.
Rose Hill, *(Rose Hill Press; 0-917264),* 12368 Old Pen Mar Rd., Waynesboro, PA 17268 Tel 717-762-7072.
Rosen Pr, *(Rosen, Richards, Press, Inc.; 0-8239),* 29 E. 21st St., New York, NY 10010 Tel 212-777-3017.
Rosenbach Found
See Rosenbach Mus & Lib
Rosenbach Mus & Lib, *(Rosenbach Museum & Library, The),* 2010 De Lancey Place, Philadelphia, PA 19103 Tel 215-732-1600.
Rosetta *Imprint of* **Plenum Pub**
Rosetta Pub Co, *(Rosetta Publishing Co., The; 0-935850),* P.O. Box 17942, Raleigh, NC 27619; Moved, Left No Forwarding Address.
Ross, *(Ross & Haines Old Books Co.; 0-87018),* 639 E. Lake St., Wayzata, MN 55391 Tel 612-473-7551.
Ross-Erikson, *(Ross-Erikson, Inc.; 0-915520),* 629 State St., Suite 222, Santa Barbara, CA 75343 Tel 805-962-1175.
Rothman, *(Rothman, Fred B., & Co.; 0-8377),* 10368 W. Centennial Rd., Littleton, CO 80127 Tel 303-979-5657.
Rothman Repr
See Rothman
Rotz, *(Rotz, Anna Overcash; 0-9605108),* Box 266, 12182 Main St., Fort Loudon, PA 17224.
Routledge & Kegan, *(Routledge & Kegan Paul, Ltd.; 0-7100),* 9 Park St., Boston, MA 02108 Tel 617-742-5863. *Imprints:* Oriel (Oriel Press).
Rowan Tree, *(Rowan Tree Press, Ltd.; 0-937672),* 124 Chestnut St., Boston, MA 02108.
Rowman, *(Rowman & Littlefield, Inc.; 0-87471; 0-8476),* Div. of Littlefield, Adams, & Co., 81 Adams Dr., Box 327, Totowa, NJ 07511 Tel 201-256-8600.
Royal Calif, *(Royal Publishing; 0-930440),* P.O. Box 5027, Beverly Hills, CA 90210.
Rue Morgue, *(Rue Morgue Press; 0-915230),* P.O. Box 4119, Boulder, CO 80306 Tel 303-443-8346.
Rumbleseat, *(Rumbleseat Press, Inc.; 0-913444),* 3835 Scott St., San Francisco, CA 94123 Tel 415-929-1191.
Running Pr, *(Running Press; 0-89471),* 125 S. 22nd St., Philadelphia, PA 19103 Tel 215-567-5080.
Russell Sage, *(Russell Sage Foundation; 0-87154),* 633 Third Ave., New York, NY 10017 Tel 212-949-8990; Orders to: Basic Books, Inc., 10 E. 53rd St., New York, NY 10022.
Russica Bk Art
See Russica Pubs
Russica Pubs, *(Russica Publishers; 0-89830),* C/O Russica Book & Art Co., 799 Broadway, New York, NY 10003.
Rutan Pub, *(Rutan Publishing; 0-936222),* 2717 Lyndale Ave. S., Minneapolis, MN 55408.
Rutgers Ctr Alcohol, *(Rutgers Center of Alcohol Studies Pubns.; 0-911290),* Smithers Hall, Rutgers Univ., New Brunswick, NJ 08903 Tel 201-932-3510; Orders to: P.O. Box 969, Piscataway, NJ 08854 Tel 201-932-2011.
Rutgers U Pr, *(Rutgers Univ. Press; 0-8135),* 30 College Ave., New Brunswick, NJ 08903 Tel 201-932-7764.
RWS Bks, *(RWS Books),* 4296 Mulholland St., Salt Lake City, UT 84117.
RWU Parachuting Pubns, *(RWU Parachuting Pubns.),* 1656 Beechwood Ave., Fullerton, CA 92635 Tel 714-990-0369.
RWunderground
See RWU Parachuting Pubns
Ryerse, *(Ryerse Publishing Co.; 0-9603388),* 40 Bernice Dr., Freehold, NJ 07728 Tel 201-462-5068.
Rymer Bks, *(Rymer Books; 0-9600792),* P.O. Box 104, Tollhouse, CA 93667 Tel 209-855-8540.
S Appalachian Res, *(Southern Appalachian Resource Catalog),* Rt. 1, Box 71A, Warne, NC 28909 Tel 704-389-8323.
S Aronson, *(Aronson, Sam; 0-9604554),* 8650 Gulana Ave., Suite C-3064, Playa Del Rey, CA 90291 Tel 213-822-9940.
S Campbell, *(Campbell, Sandy M.; 0-917366),* 230 Central Park S., New York, NY 10019 Tel 212-582-6286.
S Carver
See Carves
S F Vanni, *(Vanni, S.F.; 0-913298),* 30 W. 12th St., New York, NY 10011 Tel 212-675-6336.
S G Phillips, *(Phillip's, S. G., Inc.; 0-87599),* 305 W. 86th St., New York, NY 10024 Tel 212-787-4405.
S Green, *(Green, Stanford J.; 0-9604656),* 5892 E. Jefferson Ave., Denver, CO 80237.
S H Park, *(Park, S.H.; 0-9604440),* 34 Lawnside Dr., Trenton, NJ 08648 Tel 609-883-3551.
S Ill U Pr, *(Southern Illinois Univ. Press; 0-8093),* P.O. Box 3697, Carbondale, IL 62901 Tel 618-453-2281.
S J Durst, *(Durst, Sanford J.; 0-915262),* 170 E. 61st St., New York, NY 10021 Tel 212-593-3514.
S Karger, *(Karger, S., AG; 3-8055),* 150 Fifth Ave., Suite 1103, New York, NY 10011 Tel 212-924-9222; Dist. by: Albert J. Phiebig, P.O. Box 352, White Plains, NY 10602.
S Meth U Pr
See SMU Press
S R Guggenheim, *(Guggenheim, Solomon R., Foundation; 0-89207),* 1071 Fifth Ave., New York, NY 10028 Tel 212-860-1300.
S Regional Ed, *(Southern Regional Education Board),* 130 Sixth St., N.W., Atlanta, GA 30313 Tel 404-875-9211.
S Res Inst, *(Southern Research Institute),* 2000 Ninth Ave., S., Birmingham, AL 35255 Tel 205-323-6592.
Sabbot-Natural Hist Bks, *(Sabbot, Rudolph Wm., - Natural History Books),* 5239 Tendilla Ave., Woodland Hills, CA 91364 Tel 213-346-7164.
Sachem Pr, *(Sachem Press; 0-937584),* P.O. Box 9, Old Chatham, NY 12136.
Sadlier, *(Sadlier, William H., Inc.; 0-8215),* 11 Park Place, New York, NY 10007 Tel 212-227-2120.
Sag Scriptory, *(Sagittarian Scriptory Enterprises; 0-931908),* P.O. Box 2786, Napa, CA 94558 Tel 707-224-4814.
Sagamore Bks, *(Sagamore Books; 0-87905),* Juvenile Div. of Peregrine Smith, Inc., P.O. Box 667, Layton, UT 84041 Tel 801-376-9800.
Sagamore Pr, *(Sagamore Press; 0-936640),* P.O. Box 3315, Terre Haute, IN 47803.
Sagarin Pr, *(Sagarin Press; 0-915298),* Box 251, Sand Lake, NY 12153 Tel 518-674-2998.
Sage, *(Sage Pubns., Inc.; 0-8039),* 275 S. Beverly Dr., Beverly Hills, CA 90212 Tel 213-274-8003.
Sagebrush Pr, *(Sagebrush Press; 0-930704),* P.O. Box 87, Morongo Valley, CA 92256.
Saifer, *(Saifer, Albert, Pub.; 0-87556),* P.O. Box 239 W.O.B., West Orange, NJ 07052.
Sail Bks, *(Sail Books, Inc.; 0-914814),* 38 Commercial Wharf, Boston, MA 02110; Dist. by: W. W. Norton & Co., Inc., 500 Fifth Ave., New York, NY 10036.
Salem Pr, *(Salem Press, Inc.; 0-89356),* Box 1097, Englewood Cliffs, NJ 07632 Tel 201-871-3700.
Sales & Mktg, *(Sales & Marketing Management; 0-89846),* 633 Third Ave., New York, NY 10017 Tel 212-986-4800.
Saltzman Co
See Eurail Guide

Salvation Army, *(Salvation Army: Supplies & Purchasing Dept.),* 1424 N.E. Expressway, Atlanta, GA 30329 Tel 404-321-7870.
SamHar Pr, *(SamHar Press),* Div. of Story House Corp., Charlotteville, NY 12036 Tel 607-397-8725.
Samisdat, *(Samisdat),* Box 129, Richford, VT 05476.
Sams, *(Sams, Howard W., & Co., Inc.; 0-672),* Subs. of ITT, 4300 W. 62nd St., Indianapolis, IN 46206 Tel 317-298-5400.
San Bernardino, *(San Bernardino County Museum Assn.; 0-915158),* 2024 Orange Tree Lane, Redlands, CA 92373 Tel 714-792-1334.
San Francisco Opera, *(San Francisco Opera Guild Auxiliary; 0-9600758),* War Memorial Opera House, San Francisco, CA 94102 Tel 415-863-2524.
San Jacinto, *(San Jacinto Publishing Co.; 0-911982),* c/o Texas A&M University Press, Drawer C, College Station, Houston, TX 77843 Tel 713-845-1436.
San Marcos, *(San Marcos Press; 0-88235),* P.O. Box 53, Cerrillos, NM 87010.
Sandlapper Pr
See Sandlapper Store
Sandlapper Store, *(Sandlapper Store, Inc.; 0-87844),* Box 841, 101 W. Main, Lexington, SC 29072 Tel 803-359-6571; Formerly Sandlapper Press, Inc.
Sandollar Pr, *(Sandollar Press),* P.O. Box 4157, Santa Barbara, CA 93103 Tel 805-569-0337.
Sandpiper OR, *(Sandpiper Press; 0-9603748),* P.O. Box 286, Brookings, OR 97415 Tel 503-468-5588.
Sandrock & Foster, *(Sandrock & Foster),* Memorial Foundation, Box 841, Winona, MN 55987 Tel 507-452-1859.
S&S, *(Simon & Schuster, Inc.; 0-671),* 1230 Ave. of the Americas, New York, NY 10020 Tel 212-245-6400. *Imprints:* Fireside (Fireside Paperbacks); Kenan Pr (Kenan Press); Linden (Linden); Little Simon (Little Simon); Touchstone Bks (Touchstone Books).
S&S Co OR, *(S&S Co., The),* 11047 Antiock Rd, Central Point, OR 97502 Tel 503-826-7870; Do Not Confuse with S&S, Simon & Schuster, Inc.
Sandstone, *(Sandstone Press, The; 0-913720),* 321 E. 43rd St., New York, NY 10017 Tel 212-682-5519.
Sanguinaria, *(Sanguinaria Publishing),* 85 Ferris St., Bridgeport, CT 06605.
Sant Bani Ash, *(Sant Bani Ashram, Inc.),* Franklin, NH 03235 Tel 603-934-4209.
Santa Barb Botanic, *(Santa Barbara Botanic Garden; 0-916436),* 1212 Mission Canyon Rd., Santa Barbara, CA 93105 Tel 805-682-4726.
Santa Barbara Mus Nat Hist, *(Santa Barbara Museum of Natural History; 0-936494),* 2559 Puesta del Sol Rd., Santa Barbara, CA 93105 Tel 805-682-4711.
Santa Monica Pub, *(Santa Monica Publishing Co.; 0-917640),* 605 E. Garcia, Santa Fe, NM 87501.
Santam, *(Santam Two, Ltd.),* Box 11642, Phoenix, AZ 85017.
Santarasa Pubns, *(Santarasa Pubns.; 0-935548),* 937 Broadway, Boulder, CO 80302.
Saphrograph, *(Saphrograph Co.; 0-87557),* 4910 Fort Hamilton Parkway, Brooklyn, NY 11219 Tel 212-925-7840.
Sargent
See Porter Sargent
SAS Inst, *(SAS Institute Inc.; 0-917382),* SAS Circle, Cary, NC 27511 Tel 919-467-8000.
Sassafras Pr, *(Sassafras Press; 0-930528),* P.O. Box 1366, Evanston, IL 60204 Tel 312-649-0888.
Sat Eve Post, *(Saturday Evening Post Co., The; 0-89387),* 1100 Waterway Blvd., Indianapolis, IN 46202 Tel 317-634-1100.
Sat Rev Pr
See Dutton
Saucerian, *(Saucerian Press; 0-911306),* P.O. Box 2228, Clarksburg, WV 26301 Tel 304-269-2719.
Saunders, *(Saunders, W. B., Co.; 0-7216),* Subs. of Columbia Broadcasting System, W. Washington Square, Philadelphia, PA 19105 Tel 215-574-4700.
Saurian Pr, *(Saurian Press; 0-936830),* New Mexico Tech, Socorro, NM 87801 Tel 505-835-5445.
Savage, *(Savage, Ella H.; 0-9605150),* P.O. Box 353, Lefferts Sta., Brooklyn, NY 11225.
Sawan Kirpal Pubns, *(Sawan Kirpal Pubns.; 0-918224),* 115 S. "O" St., Lake Worth, FL 33460 Tel 305-588-1287; Orders to: Rt. 1, Box 24, Bowling Green, VA 22427 Tel 804-633-5789.
Saxon, *(Saxon House),* Dist. by: Atheneum Pubs., 597 Fifth Ave., New York, NY 10017.
SBD, *(SBD: Small Press Distribution; 0-914068),* 1784 Shattuck Ave., Berkeley, CA 94709 Tel 415-529-3336.
SBS Pub, *(SBS Publishing, Inc.; 0-89961),* 14 W. Forest Ave., Englewood, NJ 07631 Tel 201-569-8700.
Scandia Pubs, *(Scandia Pubs.; 0-937242),* P.O. Box 1044, Lyons, CO 80540 Tel 303-823-5072.
Scanning Electron, *(Scanning Electron Microscopy, Inc.; 0-931288),* P.O. Box 66507, AMF O'Hare, Chicago, IL 60666 Tel 312-529-6677.
Scarab Pr, *(Scarab Press; 0-912962),* 63 Bates Blvd., Orinda, CA 94563.
Scarecrow, *(Scarecrow Press, Inc.; 0-8108),* Subs. of Grolier Educational Corp., 52 Liberty St., Box 656, Metuchen, NJ 08840 Tel 201-548-8600.
Scepter Pubs, *(Scepter Pubs.; 0-933932),* The Publishers Bldg., 481 Main St., New Rochelle, NY 10801 Tel 914-636-3377.
Sch Lib Sci, *(School of Library Science, Emporia State University),* 1200 Commercial, Emporia, KS 66801 Tel 316-343-1200.
Sch Living Pr
See Wisconsin Bks
Schalkenbach, *(Schalkenbach, Robert, Foundation; 0-911312),* 50 E. 69th St., New York, NY 10021 Tel 212-734-2468.
SchDept *Imprint of* **Har-Row**
Schenkman, *(Schenkman Publishing Co., Inc.; 0-87073),* 3 Mt. Auburn Place, Cambridge, MA 02138 Tel 617-492-4952.
Schiffer, *(Schiffer Publishing Ltd.; 0-916838),* P.O. Box E, Exton, PA 19341 Tel 215-363-6889.
Schirmer Bks, *(Schirmer Books; 0-02),* Div. of Macmillan Publishing Co., 866 Third Ave., New York, NY 10022 Tel 212-935-7642; Orders to: 100 Brown St., Riverside, NJ 08370.
Schmul Pub Co, *(Schmul Publishing Co. Inc.),* P.O. Box 4068, Salem, OH 44460.
Schocken, *(Schocken Books, Inc.; 0-8052),* 200 Madison Ave., New York, NY 10016 Tel 212-685-6500.
Schoenhof, *(Schoenhof's Foreign Books, Inc.; 0-87774),* 1280 Massachusetts Ave., Cambridge, MA 02138 Tel 617-547-8855.
Schol Am Res, *(School of American Research Press; 0-933452),* P.O. Box 2188, Santa Fe, NM 87501.
Schol Bk Serv, *(Scholastic Book Services; 0-590),* Div. of Scholastic Inc., 50 W. 44th St., New York, NY 10036 Tel 212-944-7700; Orders to: 906 Sylvan Ave., Englewood Cliffs, NJ 07632. *Imprints:* Citation (Citation Press); Four Winds (Four Winds Press); Schol Pap (Scholastic Paperbacks).
Schol Facsimiles, *(Scholars' Facsimiles & Reprints; 0-8201),* P.O. Box 344, Delmar, NY 12054 Tel 518-439-6146.
Schol Pap *Imprint of* **Schol Bk Serv**
Schol Test, *(Scholastic Testing Service, Inc.; 0-936224),* 480 Meyer Rd., Bensenville, IL 60106 Tel 312-766-7150.
Scholarly, *(Scholarly Press Inc.; 0-403),* 19722 E. Nine Mile Rd., Saint Clair Shores, MI 48080 Tel 313-773-4250.
Scholarly Res Inc, *(Scholarly Resources Inc.; 0-8420),* 104 Greenhill Ave.; Wilmington, DE 19805 Tel 302-654-7713.
Scholars Bk, *(Scholars Book Co.; 0-914348),* 4431 Mt. Vernon, Houston, TX 77006 Tel 713-528-4395.
Scholars Pr
See Scholars Pr CA
Scholars Pr CA, *(Scholars Press; 0-89130),* 101 Salem St., Chico, CA 95926 Tel 916-343-1651.
Scholars Pr MI
See Scholars Pr CA
Scholium Intl, *(Scholium International, Inc; 0-87936),* 265 Great Neck Rd., Great Neck, NY 11021 Tel 516-466-5181.
Schroeppel, *(Schroeppel, Tom; 0-9603718),* P.O. Box 521110, Miami, FL 33152.
Schulte, *(Schulte, Terry T.),* Box 1672, St. Cloud, MN 56301.
Schumacher Pubns, *(Schumacher Publications; 0-917378),* 9229 Lawn St., Proctor, MN 55810 Tel 218-624-7728.
Sci & Behavior, *(Science & Behavior Books, Inc.; 0-8314),* P.O. Box 11457, Palo Alto, CA 94306 Tel 415-326-6465.
Sci & Tech Pr, *(Science & Technology Press),* P.O. Box 614, Latham, NY 12110 Tel 518-783-0313.
Sci Newsletters, *(Scientific Newsletters, Inc.; 0-930914),* P.O. Box 4546, Anaheim, CA 92803 Tel 714-828-1371.
Sci of Mind, *(Science of Mind Pubns.; 0-911336),* P.O. Box 75127, Los Angeles, CA 90075 Tel 213-388-2181; Dist. by: Devorss & Co., P.O. Box 550, Marina Del Rey, CA 90291.
Sci Res Assoc Coll, *(Science Research Associates, Inc., College Division),* 1540 Page Mill Rd., P.O. Box 10021, Palo Alto, CA 94303 Tel 415-493-4700.
Scienspot, *(Scienspot Pubns.; 0-937926),* 39 Brunswick Ave., Troy, NY 12180.
Scientific Pr, *(Scientific Press, The; 0-89426),* 670 Gilman St., Palo Alto, CA 94301 Tel 415-322-5221.
Scott F, *(Scott, Foresman & Co.; 0-673),* 1900 E. Lake Ave., Glenview, IL 60025 Tel 312-729-3000.
Scott Pubns CA, *(Scott Pubns.; 0-935930),* P.O. Box 3277, Chico, CA 95926.
Scribner, *(Scribner's, Charles, Sons; 0-684),* 597 Fifth Ave., New York, NY 10017 Tel 212-486-2703; Orders to: Shipping & Service Ctr., Vreeland Ave., Totowa, NJ 07512.
Scrip Pr
See Victor Bks
Sea Chall, *(Sea Challengers; 0-930118),* 1851 Don Ave., Los Osos, CA 93402 Tel 805-528-0529.
Sea Harvest, *(Sea Harvest Press; 0-937496),* 421 Arileen, Grand Blanc, MI 48439.
Sea Horse, *(Sea Horse Press, Ltd., The; 0-933322),* 307 W. 11th St., New York, NY 10014 Tel 212-691-9066.
Sea Urchin, *(Sea Urchin Press; 0-9605208),* P.O. Box 10503, Oakland, CA 94610.
Seabury, *(Seabury Press, Inc.; 0-8164),* 815 Second Ave., New York, NY 10017 Tel 212-557-0500; Orders to: Seabury Service Center, Somers, CT 06071.
Seahawk Pr, *(Seahawk Press; 0-913008),* 6840 S.W. 92nd St., Miami, FL 33156 Tel 305-667-4051.
SeaHorse Pr
See Sea Horse
Seal Pr WA, *(Seal Press),* 533 11th, Seattle, WA 98188 Tel 206-322-2322; Moved, Left No Forwarding Address.
Seattle Art, *(Seattle Art Museum; 0-932216),* 14th E. & E. Prospect, Seattle, WA 98112 Tel 206-447-4710.
Seaver Bks, *(Seaver Books; 0-394),* 333 Central Park West, New York, NY 10025 Tel 212-866-9278; Orders to: Grove Press, Inc., 196 W. Houston St., New York, NY 10014.
Seaview Bks, *(Seaview Books; 0-87223),* Div. of P.E.I. Books, Inc., 1633 Broadway, New York, NY 10019 Tel 212-245-9160; Dist. by: Harper & Row Pubs., Inc., Keystone Industrial Park, Scranton, PA 18512.
Second Chance, *(Second Chance Press; 0-933256),* Sagaponack, NY 11962 Tel 516-324-5993.
Second Coming, *(Second Coming Press; 0-915016),* P.O. Box 31249, San Francisco, CA 94131 Tel 415-647-3679.
Second Soc Foun, *(Second Society Foundation),* 333 N. Michigan Ave., Suite 707, Chicago, IL 60601.
Secure Futures, *(Secure Futures Pubns.; 0-938064),* P.O. Box 3362, San Diego, CA 92103 Tel 714-692-0588.
Security World
See Butterworth
Seed Center, *(Seed Center; 0-916108),* P.O. Box 658, Garberville, CA 95440.
Select Bks, *(Select Books; 0-910458),* Rte. 1 Box 129C, Mountain View, MO 65548 Tel 417-934-6775.
Selective, *(Selective Pubs, Inc.; 0-912584),* P.O. Box 1140, Clearwater, FL 33517 Tel 813-442-5440.
Self, *(Self),* Box 1498, Quincy, CA 95917; Moved, Left No Forwarding Address.

Self-Prog Control, *(Self-Programmed Control Press; 0-9601926),* P.O. Box 49939, Los Angeles, CA 90049 Tel 213-826-1959.
Self Therapy
See Wingbow Pr
Sellens, *(Sellens),* 134 Clark St., Augusta, KS 67010.
Seluzicki Poetry, *(Seluzicki, Charles, Poetry Bookseller; 0-931356),* Box 12367, Salem, OR 97309.
Seminary Pr, *(Seminary Press; 0-912832),* P.O. Box 2218, Univ. Sta., Enid, OK 73701 Tel 405-237-4433.
Senterfitt, *(Senterfitt, Arnold, Pubns.; 0-937260),* Drawer 27310, Escondido, CA 92027 Tel 714-489-0590.
Septima, *(Septima, Inc.),* P.O. Box 2096, Sarasota, FL 33578 Tel 813-349-4634.
Serendipity Pr, *(Serendipity Press; 0-915396),* Div. of Price/Stern/Sloan, 410 N. LaCienega Blvd., Los Angeles, CA 90048 Tel 213-657-6100.
Serina, *(Serina Press; 0-911952),* 70 Kennedy St., Alexandria, VA 22305 Tel 703-548-4080.
Servant, *(Servant Publications; 0-89283),* P.O. Box 8617, 840 Airport Blvd., Ann Arbor, MI 48107 Tel 313-761-8505; Orders to: Customer Service Dept., Box 8617, Ann Arbor, MI 48107 Tel 313-761-8983; Formerly Named Word of Life.
Seven Locks Pr, *(Seven Locks Press; 0-932020),* P.O. Box 72, Cabin John, MD 20731 Tel 202-638-1598.
Seven Oaks, *(Seven Oaks Press; 0-932508),* 405 S. 7th St., St. Charles, IL 60174 Tel 312-584-0187.
Seven Seven Search, *(Seven Seven Search Pubns.; 0-934726),* P.O. Box 252, Solana Beach, CA 92075 Tel 714-436-4843.
Seventies Pr
See Eighties Pr
Sew-Fit, *(Sew/Fit Publishing Co.),* 960 N. Ridge, Lombard, IL 60148.
Sey Lawr *Imprint of* **Delacorte**
Seybold, *(Seybold Pubns., Inc.; 0-918514),* Box 644, Media, PA 19063 Tel 215-565-2480.
SF Arts & Letters, *(San Francisco Arts & Letters Foundation; 0-914024),* P.O. Box 99394, San Francisco, CA 94109 Tel 415-771-3431.
SF Bay Area, *(San Francisco Bay Area People's Yellow Pages),* P.O. Box 31291, San Francisco, CA 94131 Tel 415-641-4011.
Shaarai Shomayim, *(Shaarai Shomayim; 0-9605482),* 508 N. Duke St., Lancaster, PA 17602.
Shabazz Pr, *(El-Hajj Malik Shabazz Press; 0-913358),* 445 Park Rd. N. W., Washington, DC 20010; Orders to: Liberation Information Distributing Co., 4206 Edson Place N.E., Washington, DC 20019.
Shade Tree, *(Shade Tree Books; 0-930742),* P.O. Box 2268, Huntington Beach, CA 92647 Tel 714-846-3869.
Shaker Mus, *(Shaker Museum Foundation Inc.; 0-937942),* Shaker Museum Rd., Old Chatham, NY 12136 Tel 518-794-9100.
Shamal Bks, *(Shamal Books, Inc.; 0-917886),* G.P.O. Box 16, New York, NY 10001 Tel 212-622-4426.
Shambhala Pubns, *(Shambhala Pubns., Inc.; 0-87773),* 1920 13th St., P.O. Box 271, Boulder, CO 80306 Tel 303-449-6111; Dist. by: Random House, Inc., 400 Hahn Rd., Westminster, MD 21157.
Shameless Hussy, *(Shameless Hussy Press; 0-915288),* Box 3092, Berkeley, CA 94703 Tel 415-548-7800.
Sharing Co, *(Sharing Co., The),* P.O. Box 2224, Austin, TX 78767 Tel 512-452-4366.
Shaw Inc, *(Shaw, Mara Lynn, Inc.; 0-9605602),* 165 E. 72nd St., Suite 12n, New York, NY 10021.
Shaw Pubs, *(Shaw, Harold, Pubs.; 0-87788),* Box 567, 388 Gundersen Dr., Wheaton, IL 60187 Tel 312-665-6700.
Shawnee County Hist, *(Shawnee County Historical Society; 0-916934),* 1205 W. 29th St., Rm. 329, Topeka, KS 66611 Tel 913-267-0309; P.O. Box 56, Topeka, KS 66601.
Shayna Ltd, *(Shayna Ltd.; 0-9604208),* 100 Andrew St., Newton, MA 02161 Tel 617-244-1870.
Sheep Meadow, *(Sheep Meadow Press, The; 0-935296),* 145 Central Park W., New York, NY 10023; Dist. by: Persea Books, Inc., 225 Lafayette St., New York, NY 10012 Tel 212-431-5270.
Sheephead Bks, *(Sheephead Books; 0-9604644),* P.O. Box 1103, Vidalia, GA 30474.
Sheffield Pr, *(Sheffield Press; 0-917044),* P.O. Box 723, Manhattan Beach, CA 90266 Tel 213-545-7974.
Shelter Pubns
See Random
Shelter Pubns, *(Shelter Pubns.; 0-936070),* P.O. Box 279, Bolinas, CA 94924 Tel 415-868-0280; Dist. by: Random House, 400 Hahn Rd., Westminster, MD 21157.
Shengold, *(Shengold Pubs., Inc.; 0-88400),* 45 W. 45th St., New York, NY 10036 Tel 212-246-6911.
Sheriar Pr, *(Sheriar Press, Inc.; 0-913078),* 801 13th Ave. S., N. Myrtle Beach, SC 29582 Tel 803-272-5311.
Sheridan, *(Sheridan House, Inc.; 0-911378),* 175 Orawaupum St., White Plains, NY 10606 Tel 914-948-1806.
Sherwood Co, *(Sherwood Co., The; 0-933056),* P.O. Box 21645, Denver, CO 80221 Tel 303-423-6481.
Shetal Ent, *(Shetal Enterprises; 0-932888),* 1787 "B" W. Touhy, Chicago, IL 60626 Tel 312-262-1133.
Shields Illinois
See Shields WI
Shields WI, *(Shields Pubns.; 0-9600102; 0-914116),* P.O. Box 669, Eagle River, WI 54521 Tel 715-479-4810.
Shinn Music
See Duane Shinn
Shirjieh Pubs, *(Shirjieh Pubs.; 0-912496),* P.O. Box 259, Menlo Park, CA 94025 Tel 415-323-9954.
Shoal Creek Pub, *(Shoal Creek Pubs.; 0-88319),* P.O. Box 9737, Austin, TX 78766 Tel 512-451-7545.
Shoe String, *(Shoe String Press, Inc.; 0-208),* P.O. Box 4327, 995 Sherman Ave., Hamden, CT 06514 Tel 203-248-6307.
Shoreline Pub, *(Shoreline Publishing; 0-938306),* 212-08 75th Ave., Bayside, NY 11364.
Shorey, *(Shorey Pubns.; 0-8466),* 110 Union St., Seattle, WA 98111 Tel 206-624-0221.
Showcase Fairfield, *(Showcase Publishing Co.; 0-88205),* Div. of Entrepreneur Press, 3422 Astoria Circle, Fairfield, CA 94533 Tel 707-422-6822; Dist. by: Elsevier-Dutton, Inc., 2 Park Ave., New York, NY 10016 Tel 212-725-1818.
Shreveport Pub, *(Shreveport Publishing Corp.; 0-939042),* P.O. Box 31110, Shreveport, LA 71130.
Shulsinger Bros
See Shulsinger Sales
Shulsinger Sales, *(Shulsinger Sales, Inc.; 0-914080),* 50 Washington St., Brooklyn, NY 11201 Tel 212-852-0042.
Shumway, *(George Shumway Publisher; 0-87387),* R.D. 7, Box 388B, York, PA 17402 Tel 717-755-1196.
Sierra, *(Sierra Club Books; 0-87156),* 530 Bush St., San Francisco, CA 94108 Tel 415-981-8634; Dist. by: Charles Scribner's Sons, Scribner Distribution Center, Vreeland Ave., Totowa, NJ 07512.
Sig *Imprint of* **NAL**
Sig Classics *Imprint of* **NAL**
Sightseer, *(Sightseer Pubns.; 0-937928),* 5990 Moss Ranch Rd., Miami, FL 33156.
Sigma Pr, *(Sigma Press Inc.; 0-9604516),* P.O. Box 379, South Bound Brook, NJ 08880.
Signpost Bk Pub, *(Signpost Book Publishing Co.; 0-913140),* 8912 192nd St. S.W., Edmonds, WA 98020 Tel 206-776-0370.
Signpost Pubns
See Signpost Bk Pub
Signs of Times, *(Signs of the Times Publishing Co.; 0-911380),* 407 Gilbert Ave., Cincinnati, OH 45202 Tel 513-421-2050.
Sijthoff & Noordhoff, *(Sijthoff & Noordhoff International Publishing Co.),* 1600 Research Blvd., Rockville, MD 20850 Tel 301-251-0950.
Silbert Bress, *(Silbert & Bress Pubns.; 0-89544),* P.O. Box 68, Mahopac, NY 10541 Tel 914-628-7910.
Silver, *(Silver Burdett Co.; 0-382),* Div. of General Learning Co., 250 James St., Morristown, NJ 07960 Tel 201-285-8100.
Silverado, *(Silverado Publishing Co.; 0-87938),* St. Helena, CA 94574; Dist. by: Motorbooks International, Pubs. & Wholesalers, P.O. Box 2, 729 Prospect Ave., Osceola, WI 54020 Tel 715-294-3345.
Simplex Comm, *(Simplex Communications, Inc.; 0-935248),* P.O. Box 9133, Fort Wayne, IN 46783 Tel 219-672-3702.
Simplicity, *(Simplicity Pattern Co., Inc.; 0-918178),* 200 Madison Ave., New York, NY 10016 Tel 212-481-1777; Orders to: Simplicity Educational Div., 901 Wayne St., Niles, MI 49121.
Simply Elegant, *(Simply Elegant; 0-9600492),* 3801 N. Mission Hills Rd., Northbrook, IL 60062 Tel 312-564-2221; Orders to: P.O. Box 74, Winnetka, IL 60093.
Simpson-Hirshman, *(Simpson-Hirshman Publishing; 0-938406),* 1008 Western Ave., Seattle, WA 98104.
Simtek, *(Simtek; 0-933836),* P.O. Box 109, Cambridge, MA 02139 Tel 617-232-5020.
Simul Pubns, *(Simulations Pubns, Inc.; 0-917852),* 257 Park Ave. S., New York, NY 10010 Tel 212-673-4103.
Sinauer Assoc, *(Sinauer Associates, Inc.; 0-87893),* N. Main St, Sunderland, MA 01375 Tel 413-665-3722.
Single Impressions, *(Single Impressions; 0-938562),* 642 W. Zia Dr., Tucson, AZ 85704.
Singles World, *(Singles World Publishing Co.; 0-936890),* 1094 Cudahy, No. 102, San Diego, CA 92110; Dist. by: Communication Creativity, P.O. Box 213, Saguache, CO 81149 Tel 303-655-2502.
Singletary, *(Singletary, Milly; 0-9601256),* 1655 Makaloa St., Suite 906, Honolulu, HI 96814 Tel 808-949-1968; Dist. by: Press Pacifica, Box 47, Kailua, HI 96734.
Sirius Bks, *(Sirius Books; 0-917108),* P.O. Box 6294, Eureka, CA 95501 Tel 707-442-8481.
Sitnalta Pr, *(Sitnalta Press; 0-931826),* 1881 Sutter St., No. 103, San Francisco, CA 94115 Tel 415-922-8223.
Skipworth Pr, *(Skipworth Press, Inc.; 0-931804),* P.O. Box 9367, Richmond, VA 23227 Tel 804-746-3551.
Sky Pub, *(Sky Publishing Corp.; 0-933346),* 49 Bay State Rd., Cambridge, MA 02238 Tel 617-864-7360.
Skye Terrier, *(Skye Terrier Club of America; 0-9600722),* 2222 S. 12th St., St. Louis, MO 63104 Tel 314-367-4444.
Skylark *Imprint of* **Bantam**
Skyview Pub, *(Skyview Publishing; 0-934618),* Box L, Bellmore, NY 11710.
SLA, *(Special Libraries Assn.; 0-87111),* 235 Park Ave., S., New York, NY 10003 Tel 212-477-9250.
Slavia Lib, *(Slavia Library; 0-918884),* 418 W. Nittany Ave., State College, PA 16801.
Slavica, *(Slavica Publishers Inc.; 0-89357),* P.O. Box 14388, Columbus, OH 43214.
Sleepy Hollow, *(Sleepy Hollow Press, The; 0-912882),* 150 White Plains Rd., Tarrytown, NY 10591 Tel 914-631-8200; Dist. by: Independent Publishers Group, 14 Vanderventer Ave., Port Washington, NY 11050 Tel 516-944-9325.
Slohm Assoc, *(Slohm, Natalie, Associates, Inc.; 0-916840),* 49 W. Main St., Cambridge, NY 12816 Tel 518-677-3040.
Slurry Transport, *(Slurry Transport Assn.; 0-932066),* 490 L'Enfant Plaza East., S.W. Suite 3210, Washington, DC 20024.
SLUSA, *(SLUSA),* 88 Eastern Ave., Somerville, NJ 08876.
Small Busn Pubns, *(Small Business Pubns.; 0-9605436),* Drawer 330, Osterville, MA 02655.
SME, *(Society of Manufacturing Engineers; 0-87263),* P.O. Box 930, One SME Dr., Dearborn, MI 48128 Tel 313-271-1500.
Smith & Assoc, *(Smith & Associates; 0-938260),* Box 61648, Houston, TX 77208.
Smith Coll, *(Smith College, Pubns.; 0-87391),* College Hall 26, Northampton, MA 01063 Tel 413-584-2700; Dist. by: Neilson Library, Office of the Director of Technical Services, Northampton, MA 01063.
Smith Coll Mus Art, *(Smith College Museum of Art),* Elm at Bedford Terrace, Northampton, MA 01063 Tel 413-584-2700.

Smithsonian, *(Smithsonian Institution Press; 0-87474),* Rm. 2280, Arts & Industries Bldg., Washington, DC 20560 Tel 202-357-1912; Orders to: P.O. Box 1579, Washington, DC 20013 Tel 202-357-1793; Booksellers Order from: Publications Sales, 1111 North Capitol St., Washington, DC 20560 Tel 202-357-1793.
Smithsonian Expo Bks, *(Smithsonian Exposition Books; 0-89599),* 475 L'enfant Plaza, Rm. 2800, Washington, DC 20560 Tel 202-287-3388.
SMU Press, *(Southern Methodist Univ. Press; 0-87074),* Dallas, TX 75275 Tel 214-692-2263.
Smyrna, *(Smyrna Press; 0-918266),* P.O. Box 1803, GPO, Brooklyn, NY 11202 Tel 212-638-8939.
SNAG, *(Society of North American Goldsmiths; 0-9604446),* 8589 Wonderland NW, Clinton, OH 44216.
Snowstorm, *(Snowstorm Pubns.; 0-9605366),* Box 2310, Breckenridge, CO 80424.
Snug Harbor NY, *(Snug Harbor Cultural Center; 0-9604254),* 914 Richmond Terrace, Staten Island, NY 10301.
Snyder Inst Res, *(Snyder Institute of Research),* 508 N. Pacific Coast Hwy., Redondo Beach, CA 90277 Tel 213-372-4469.
Soc Adv Material, *(Society for the Advancement of Materials & Process Engineering (S.A.M.P.E.)),* Box 613, Azusa, CA 91702 Tel 213-334-1810.
Soc Am Archivists, *(Society of American Archivists; 0-931828),* 330 S. Wells St., Suite 810, Chicago, IL 60606 Tel 312-922-0140.
Soc Animal Rights, *(Society for Animal Rights, Inc.; 0-9602632),* 421 S. State St., Clarks Summit, PA 18411 Tel 717-586-2200.
Soc Auto Engineers, *(Society of Automotive Engineers, Inc.; 0-89883),* 400 Commonwealth Dr., Warrendale, PA 15096 Tel 412-776-4841.
Soc Exploration, *(Society of Exploration Geophysicists; 0-931830),* P.O. Box 3098, Tulsa, OK 74135 Tel 918-743-1365.
Soc for Visual, *(Society for Visual Education, Inc.; 0-89290),* 1345 W. Diversey Pkwy., Chicago, IL 60614 Tel 312-525-1500.
Soc Mining Eng, *(Society of Mining Engineers of A. I. M. E.; 0-89520),* Caller No. D, Littleton, CO 80127 Tel 303-973-9550.
Soc Naval Arch, *(Society of Naval Architects & Marine Engineers; 0-9603048),* One World Trade Center, 1369, New York, NY 10048 Tel 212-432-0310.
Soc Nuclear Med, *(Society of Nuclear Medicine, Inc.; 0-932004),* 475 Park Ave. So., New York, NY 10016 Tel 212-889-0717.
Soc Photo Sci & Eng, *(Society of Photographic Scientists & Engineers; 0-89208),* 1411 "K" St., N.W., Suite 930, Washington, DC 20005 Tel 202-347-1140.
Soc Sci & Soc Res, *(Social Science & Sociological Resources; 0-915574),* P.O. Box 241, Aurora, IL 60507.
Soc Sci Ed, *(Social Science Education Consortium, Inc; 0-89994),* 855 Broadway, Boulder, CO 80302 Tel 303-492-8154.
Soc Tech Comm, *(Society for Technical Communication; 0-914548),* 815 15th St. N.W., Suite 506, Washington, DC 20005 Tel 202-737-0035; Dist. by: Univelt, Inc., P.O. Box 28130, San Diego, CA 92128 Tel 714-746-4005.
Soccer, *(Sportshelf & Soccer Associates; 0-392),* P.O. Box 634, New Rochelle, NY 10802 Tel 914-235-2347.
Soccer for Am, *(Soccer for Americans; 0-916802),* P.O. Box 836, Manhattan Beach, CA 90266 Tel 213-372-9000.
Society Sp & Sp-Am, *(Society of Spanish & Spanish-American Studies; 0-89295),* Society of Spanish and Spanish-American Studies, Dept. of Modern Languages & Literatures, Univ. of Nebraska-Lincoln, Lincoln, NE 68588 Tel 402-472-3745.
Soho Bodhi, *(Soho Bodhi; 0-9605096),* 242 Lafayette St., New York, NY 10012.
Soil Conservation, *(Soil Conservation Society of America; 0-935734),* 7515 N.E. Ankeny Rd., Ankeny, IA 50021.
Solar Energy Info, *(Solar Energy Information Services (SEIS); 0-930978; 0-89934),* 18 Second Ave., P.O. Box 204, San Mateo, CA 94401 Tel 415-347-2640.
SolarVision, *(SolarVision, Inc.; 0-918984),* Church Hill, Harrisville, NH 03450 Tel 603-827-3347.
Soldier Creek, *(Soldier Creek Press; 0-936996),* Box 863, Lake Crystal, MN 56055.
Solo Pr, *(Solo Press),* 7670 Valle, Atascadero, CA 93422 Tel 805-466-0947.
Some Place
See Lacis Pubns
Somerset Hse, *(Somerset House; 0-914146; 0-89887),* 206 N. Alfred St., Alexandria, VA 22314 Tel 703-549-7369; Orders to: 417 Maitland Ave., Teaneck, NJ 07666 Tel 201-833-1795.
Somerset Pub, *(Somerset Pubs.),* Div. of Scholarly Press, Inc., 19722 E. Nine Mile Rd, St. Clair Shores, MI 48080.
Sonica Pr, *(Sonica Press),* 6255 Sunset Blvd., Suite 609, Los Angeles, CA 90028 Tel 213-393-1590.
Sonoma County, *(Sonoma County Bike Trails),* 50 Crest Way, Penngrove, CA 94951.
Sonrise Prods, *(SONrise Productions),* 746 E. 79th St., Box 186, Chicago, IL 60619.
Sooty-Face, *(Sooty-Face Publishing Co.; 0-9602366),* P.O. Box 26, Clairton, PA 15025 Tel 412-233-6141.
Sorger Assocs, *(Sorger Associates Inc.; 0-9604072),* 229 Humphrey St., Marblehead, MA 01945.
Soundview Bks, *(Soundview Books; 0-934924),* 100 Heights Rd., Darien, CT 06820 Tel 203-655-1436; Dist. by: Caroline House, 2 Ellis Place, Ossining, NY 10562 Tel 914-941-9271.
Soup to Nuts, *(Soup to Nuts Press; 0-9604780),* 582 Fernando Dr., Novato, CA 94947.
Sourcebook, *(Sourcebook Project, The; 0-9600712; 0-915554),* P.O. Box 107, Glen Arm, MD 21057 Tel 301-668-6047.
Sources, *(Sources; 0-9603232),* 26 Hart Ave., Hopewell, NJ 08525 Tel 609-466-0051.
South Asia Bks, *(South Asia Books; 0-88386; 0-8364),* P.O. Box 502, Columbia, MO 65205 Tel 314-449-1359. *Imprints:* Orient Longman (Orient Longman).
South End Pr, *(South End Press; 0-89608),* Box 68, Astor Sta., Boston, MA 02123 Tel 617-266-0629.
South Pass Pr, *(South Pass Press; 0-932068),* 2220 S. Bonham St., Amarillo, TX 79109 Tel 806-354-4068.
Southern Hist Pr, *(Southern Historical Press; 0-89308),* P.O. Box 738, Easley, SC 29640 Tel 803-859-2336.
Southern Pub, *(Southern Publishing Assn.; 0-8127),* Box 59, 1900 Elm Hill Pike, Nashville, TN 37202 Tel 615-889-8000.
Southwest Screen Print, *(Southwest Screen Print Ind., Inc.; 0-9603530),* P.O. Box 423, Scottsdale, AZ 85252.
Sovereign Bks, *(Sovereign Books),* Div. of Simon & Schuster, c/o Cornerstone Library, 1230 Ave. of the Americas, New York, NY 10020 Tel 212-245-6400.
Sovereign Pr, *(Sovereign Press; 0-914752),* 326 Harris Rd., Rochester, WA 98579 Tel 206-273-5109.
Soyfoods-New Age, *(Soyfoods Center/New-Age Foods; 0-933332),* P.O. Box 234, Lafayette, CA 94549 Tel 415-283-2991.
Space-Time, *(Space/Time Designs, Inc.; 0-9603570),* P.O. Box 1989, Sedona, AZ 86336 Tel 602-282-3639.
Spaceman Pr, *(Spaceman Press; 0-9603546),* 139 Carmel Ave., Pacific Grove, CA 93950 Tel 408-372-5915.
Sparks Pr, *(Sparks Press; 0-916822),* 900 W. Morgan St., P.O. Box 26747, Raleigh, NC 27611 Tel 919-834-8283.
Sparrow Pr, *(Sparrow Press; 0-935552),* 103 Waldron St., West Lafayette, IN 47906 Tel 317-743-1991.
Spartan *Imprint of* **Hayden**
Spec *Imprint of* **P-H**
Spec Child, *(Special Child Pubns.; 0-87562),* 4535 Union Bay Place N.E., Seattle, WA 98105 Tel 206-522-2036.
Spec Learn Corp, *(Special Learning Corp.; 0-89568),* 42 Boston Post Rd., Guilford, CT 06437 Tel 203-453-6525.
Spec Lit Pr, *(Special Literature Press),* P.O. Box 4397, Benson Sta., Omaha, NE 68104.
Spec Pr NJ, *(Specialty Press, Inc.; 0-913556),* P.O. Box 2187, Ocean, NJ 07712 Tel 201-774-8447.
Specialist, *(Specialist Publishing Co.; 0-911416),* 109 La Mesa Dr., Burlingame, CA 94010
Specialty Pr, *(Specialty Press Pubs. & Wholesalers, Inc.; 0-933424),* Box 426, 729 Prospect Ave., Osceola, WI 54020 Tel 715-294-2090.
Spectrum Pub, *(Spectrum Pubns., Inc.; 0-89335),* 175-20 Wexford Terrace, Jamaica, NY 11432 Tel 212-658-0888; Do Not Confuse with Spectrum CA or Spectrum Prods.
Speech & Hearing
See Press West
Speer Bks, *(Speer Books; 0-917832),* 234 S. Main St., Red Bluff, CA 96080.
Speleo Pr, *(Speleo Press; 0-914092),* P.O. Box 7037, Austin, TX 78712 Tel 512-847-2709.
Spevack, *(Spevack, Jerome M., Inc.; 0-9604480),* 224 E. Hickory St., No.2, Arcadia, FL 33821.
Spice West, *(Spice West Co.; 0-9602812),* Box 2044, Pocatello, ID 83201.
Spin-A-Test Pub, *(Spin-A-Test Publishing Co.; 0-915048),* 404 Old Orchard Court, Danville, CA 94526 Tel 415-837-4532; P.O. Box 881, Alamo, CA 94507.
Spindrift, *(Spindrift Press; 0-914864),* P.O. Box 3252, Catonsville, MD 21228 Tel 301-944-3317.
Spinsters Ink, *(Spinsters, Ink; 0-933216),* R.D. 1, Argyle, NY 12809 Tel 518-854-3109.
Spirit That Moves, *(Spirit That Moves Us, The; 0-930370),* P.O. Box 1585, Iowa City, IA 52244 Tel 319-338-5569.
Spiritual Comm, *(Spiritual Community Pubns.; 0-913852),* P.O. Box 1080, San Rafael, CA 94902 Tel 415-457-2990.
Spiritual Renaissance, *(Spiritual Renaissance Press; 0-938380),* P.O. Box 347, Berkeley, CA 94701.
Spoken Lang Serv, *(Spoken Language Services, Inc.; 0-87950),* P.O. Box 783, Ithaca, NY 14850 Tel 607-257-0500.
Spoon Riv Poetry, *(Spoon River Poetry Press; 0-933180),* P.O. Box 1443, Peoria, IL 61655 Tel 309-676-7611; Do Not Confuse with the Spoon River Press.
Spoon River, *(Spoon River Press, The; 0-930358),* P.O. Box 3635, Peoria, IL 61614 Tel 309-682-2286; Do Not Confuse with Spoon River Poetry Press.
Sport Fishing, *(Sports Fishing Institute; 0-9602382),* 608 13th St. N.W., Suite 801, Washington, DC 20005 Tel 202-737-0668.
Spring Pubns, *(Spring Pubns.; 0-88214),* P. O. Box 222069, Dallas, TX 75222.
Springer Pub, *(Springer Publishing Co., Inc.; 0-8261),* 200 Park Ave., S., New York, NY 10003 Tel 212-475-2494.
Springer-Verlag, *(Springer-Verlag New York, Inc.; 0-387),* 175 Fifth Ave., New York, NY 10010 Tel 212-477-8200.
Springfield, *(Springfield Art Museum; 0-934306),* 1111 E. Brookside Dr., Springfield, MO 65807 Tel 417-866-2716.
Springfield Pub Co, *(Springfield Publishing Co.; 0-937500),* P.O. Box 96, Northridge, CA 91328 Tel 213-886-2317.
Sproing, *(Sproing Books; 0-916176),* 1150 St. Paul St., Denver, CO 80206 Tel 303-321-4248.
Spyglass, *(Spyglass Co.; 0-914922),* 2415 Mariner Square Dr., Alameda, CA 94501 Tel 415-769-8410.
Spyglass Catalog
See Spyglass
Squad Sig Pubns, *(Squadron Signal Pubns.; 0-89747),* 1115 Crowley Dr., Carrolton, TX 75005 Tel 214-242-4485.
Squarebooks, *(Squarebooks; 0-916290),* P.O. Box 144, Mill Valley, CA 94942 Tel 415-383-0202.
SRA, *(Science Research Associates, Inc.; 0-574),* Subs. of IBM, College Div., 1540 Page Mill Rd., Palo Alto, CA 94304 Tel 415-493-4700; Orders to: 155 N. Wacker Dr., Chicago, IL 60606.
Sri Rama, *(Sri Rama Publishing; 0-918100),* 161 Robles Dr., Santa Cruz, CA 95060 Tel 408-429-1176; Orders to: P.O. Box 2550, Santa Cruz, CA 95063 Tel 408-429-1176.
SRL Pub Co, *(SRL Publishing Co.; 0-918152),* P.O. Box 2277, Sta. A, Champaign, IL 61820 Tel 217-356-1523.
SSC *Imprint of* **Unipub**
SSSR
See Soc Sci & Soc Res

St Alban Pr, *(St. Alban Press; 0-918980),* Rev. Alfred Strauss, 10525 Downey Ave., Apt. F, Downey, CA 90241 Tel 213-861-7569; Orders to: St. Albans Press, P.O. Box 598, Ojai, CA 93023 Tel 805-646-6790.
St Andrews NC, *(St. Andrews Press; 0-932662),* St. Andrews College, Laurinburg, NC 28352 Tel 919-276-3652.
St Anthony Mess Pr, *(St. Anthony Messenger Press; 0-912228),* 1615 Republic St., Cincinnati, OH 45210 Tel 513-241-5616.
St Clair Pr
See Wiley
St Edns, *(Street Editions),* 20 Desbrosses St., New York, NY 10013; Orders to: SBD: Small Press Distribution, 1636 Ocean View Ave., Kensington, CA 94707 Tel 415-524-2107.
St Edwards Univ, *(Saint Edward's Univ.; 0-938472),* 3001 S. Congress Ave., Austin, TX 78704.
St George Bk Serv, *(St. George Book Service; 0-916786),* P.O. Box 225, Spring Valley, NY 10977 Tel 914-623-7852.
St George Pr, *(St. George Press; 0-932104),* 3500 N. Coltrane Rd., Oklahoma City, OK 73121 Tel 405-427-5005.
St Luke TN, *(St. Luke's Press; 0-918518),* Mid-Memphis Tower, Suite 401, 1407 Union Ave., Memphis, TN 38104 Tel 901-357-5441.
St Martin, *(St. Martin's Press, Inc.; 0-312),* 175 Fifth Ave., New York, NY 10010 Tel 212-674-5151.
St Mary's, *(St. Mary's Press; 0-88489),* Winona, MN 55987 Tel 507-452-9090.
St Nectarios, *(St. Nectarios Press; 0-913026),* 10300 Ashworth Ave. N., Seattle, WA 98133 Tel 206-522-4471.
St Petersburg Times, *(St. Petersburg Times Publishing Co.; 0-9605382),* P.O. Box 1121, St. Petersburg, FL 33731.
ST Pubns
See Signs of Times
St Thomas, *(St. Thomas Press),* P.O. Box 35096, Houston, TX 77035 Tel 713-666-3111.
St Vartan, *(St. Vartan Press; 0-934728),* 630 Second Ave., New York, NY 10016.
St Vladimirs, *(St. Vladimir's Seminary Press; 0-913836),* 575 Scarsdale Rd., Crestwood, NY 10707 Tel 914-961-8313.
Stack the Deck, *(Stack the Deck, Inc.; 0-933282),* 10628 S. Prospect Ave., Chicago, IL 60643.
Stackpole, *(Stackpole Books, Inc.; 0-8117),* Cameron & Kelker Sts., Harrisburg, PA 17105 Tel 717-234-5091.
Standard Arts, *(Standard Arts Press; 0-911426),* 2324 Butler Rd., Butler, MD 21023 Tel 301-472-4698.
Standard Ed, *(Standard Educational Corp.; 0-87392),* 200 W. Monroe, Chicago, IL 60606 Tel 312-346-7440.
Standard Edns, *(Standard Editions; 0-918746),* P.O. Box 1297, Stuyvesant Sta., New York, NY 10009.
Standard Pub, *(Standard Publishing Co.; 0-87239),* 8121 Hamilton Ave., Cincinnati, OH 45231 Tel 513-931-4050.
Standing Orders, *(Standing Orders, Inc.; 0-8491),* 156 5th Ave., Suite 1122, New York, NY 10010 Tel 212-243-0370; Orders to: P.O. Box 183, Patterson, NY 12563.
Stanford U Pr, *(Stanford Univ. Press; 0-8047),* Stanford, CA 94305 Tel 415-497-9434.
StanGib Ltd, *(StanGib Ltd.; 0-85259),* 601 Franklin Ave., Garden City, NY 11530 Tel 516-746-4666.
Stanton & Lee, *(Stanton & Lee Pubs., Inc.; 0-88361),* 44 E. Mifflin St., Madison, WI 53703 Tel 608-255-3254; Orders to: Sauk City, WI 53583.
Star Pub CA, *(Star Publishing Co.; 0-89863),* 701 Welch Rd., Suite 1119, Palo Alto, CA 94304 Tel 415-591-3505.
Star Pubns MO, *(Star Pubns.; 0-932356),* 1211 W. 60th Terrace, Kansas City, MO 64113 Tel 816-523-8228.
Star Rover, *(Star Rover House; 0-932458),* 306-12th St., Suite 26, Oakland, CA 94607 Tel 415-839-6822.
Starblaze *Imprint of* **Donning Co**
Starform, *(Starform, Inc.; 0-9604946),* 620 Taylor Way, No. 14, Belmont, CA 94002.
Starkey Labs, *(Starkey Laboratories, Inc.; 0-9601970),* 6700 Washington Ave. S., Eden Prairie, MN 55344 Tel 800-328-8602.
Starlight Pr, *(Starlight Press; 0-9605438),* Box 3102, Long Island City, NY 11103.
Starlog, *(Starlog Press; 0-931064),* 475 Park Ave. So., New York, NY 10016 Tel 212-689-2830.
Starlog Pr, *(Starlog Press; 0-931064),* 475 Park Ave. S., New York, NY 10016 Tel 212-689-2830.
Starmont Hse, *(Starmont House; 0-916732),* Box 851, Mercer Island, WA 98040 Tel 206-232-8484.
State Hist Iowa, *(State Historical Society of Iowa; 0-89033),* 402 Iowa Ave., Iowa City, IA 52240 Tel 319-353-6689.
State Hist Soc Wis, *(State Historical Society of Wisconsin; 0-87020),* 816 State St., Madison, WI 53706 Tel 608-262-9604.
State Indus Dir, *(State Industrial Directories Corp.; 0-916112),* 2 Penn Plaza, New York, NY 10001 Tel 212-564-0340.
State Mutual Bk, *(State Mutual Book & Periodical Service, Ltd.; 0-89771),* 521 Fifth Ave., New York, NY 10017 Tel 212-682-5844.
State Ptg, *(State Printing Co.; 0-911432),* 1305 Sumter St., Columbia, SC 29201.
State U NY Pr, *(State Univ. of New York Press; 0-87395),* State University Plaza, Albany, NY 12246 Tel 518-474-6050; Orders to: P.O. Box 4830, Hampden Sta., Baltimore, MD 21211.
Steelstone, *(Steelstone Press; 0-9605678),* 4607 Claussen Lane, Valparaiso, IN 46383.
Steffanides, *(Steffanides, George F.; 0-9600114),* 66 Lourdes Dr., W.D., Fitchburg, MA 01420 Tel 617-342-1997.
Stein & Day, *(Stein & Day; 0-8128),* Scarborough House, Briarcliff Manor, NY 10510 Tel 914-762-2151.
Steinerbks, *(Steinerbooks),* 7 Garber Hill Rd., Blauvelt, NY 10913 Tel 914-359-9292.
Stelle, *(Stelle Group; 0-9600308),* Administration Bldg., Stelle, IL 60919 Tel 815-949-1111.
Stemmer Hse, *(Stemmer House Pubs., Inc.; 0-916144),* 2627 Caves Rd., Owings Mills, MD 21117 Tel 301-363-3690.
Stenospeed
See Intl Educ Systems
Sterling, *(Sterling Publishing Co., Inc.; 0-8069),* 2 Park Ave., New York, NY 10016 Tel 212-532-7160.
Sterling Swift, *(Sterling Swift Pub., Co.; 0-88408),* P.O. Box 188, Manchaca, TX 78652 Tel 512-444-7570.
Stern, *(Stern, Clarence Ames; 0-9600116),* P.O. Box 2294, Oshkosh, WI 54903 Tel 414-231-6786.
Stevenson Pr, *(Stevenson Press; 0-89482),* Div. of Callcott, Inc., P.O. Box 10021, Austin, TX 78766 Tel 512-255-8623.
Steves Wide World, *(Steves Wide World Studios),* 111 4th Ave. N., Edmonds, WA 98020.
Stillgate, *(Stillgate Pubs.; 0-938286),* Box 67, Alstead, NH 03602.
Stillwater Canyon Pr, *(Stillwater Canyon Press; 0-933762),* P.O. Box 1557, Flagstaff, AZ 86002 Tel 602-774-3778.
Stipes, *(Stipes Publishing Co.; 0-87563),* 10-12 Chester St., Champaign, IL 61820 Tel 217-356-8391.
Stirrup Assoc, *(Stirrup Associates, Inc.; 0-937420),* 115 Church St., Decatur, GA 30030.
Stoeger Pub Co, *(Stoeger Publishing Co.; 0-88317),* 55 Ruta Court, South Hackensack, NJ 07606 Tel 201-440-2700; Dist. by: Follett Publishing Co., 1010 W. Washington Blvd., Chicago, IL 60607 Tel 312-666-5858.
Stokes, *(Stokes Publishing Co.; 0-914534),* 1125 Robin Way, Sunnyvale, CA 94087 Tel 408-736-4637.
Stone Country, *(Stone Country Press; 0-930020),* 20 Lorraine Rd., Madison, NJ 07940 Tel 201-377-3727.
Stone Pr MI, *(Stone Pr.),* 1790 Grand River, Okemos, MI 48864.
Stone Wall Pr, *(Stone Wall Press, Inc.; 0-913276),* 1241 30th St. N.W., Washington, DC 20007 Tel 202-333-1860; Dist. by: The Stephen Greene Press, Box 1000, Brattleboro, VT 05301.
Stonehill Pub Co, *(Stonehill Publishing Co., Inc.; 0-88373),* 1140 Ave. of Americas, 19th Fl., New York, NY 10036 Tel 212-658-5980; Dist. by: Farrar, Straus & Giroux, Inc., 19 Union Square, New York, NY 10003 Tel 212-741-6900.
Stonehouse, *(Stonehouse Pubns.; 0-9603236),* Sweet, ID 83670.
Story Pr, *(Story Press; 0-931704),* P.O. Box 10040, Chicago, IL 60610 Tel 312-442-7295.
Stratford Hse, *(Stratford House Publishing Co.; 0-938614),* P.O. Box 7077, Burbank, CA 91510.
Strathcona, *(Strathcona Publishing Co.; 0-931554),* Box 350, Royal Oak, MI 48068 Tel 313-368-8945.
Stratton Intercon
See Thieme-Stratton
Stravon, *(Stravon Educational Press; 0-87396),* 845 Third Ave., New York, NY 10022 Tel 212-371-2880.
Strawberry Hill, *(Strawberry Hill Press; 0-89407),* 2594 15th Ave., San Francisco, CA 94127 Tel 415-228-6888.
Strawberry Pr NY, *(Strawberry Press; 0-936574),* P.O. Box 451, Bowling Green Sta., New York, NY 10004.
Street Fiction, *(Street Fiction Press, Inc.; 0-914908),* 130 Touro St., P.O. Box 625, Newport, RI 02840 Tel 401-847-1067.
Street Pr, *(Street Press; 0-935252),* P.O. Box 555, Port Jefferson, NY 11777 Tel 516-979-7392.
Strode, *(Strode Pubs.; 0-87397),* 720 Church St., NW., Huntsville, AL 35801 Tel 205-539-2187.
Structures Pub, *(Structures Publishing Co.; 0-912336; 0-89999),* 24277 Indoplex Circle, P.O. Box 1002, Farmington, MI 48024 Tel 313-477-2600.
Studia Hispanica, *(Studia Hispanica Editors; 0-934840),* Univ. of Texas at Austin, Batts Hall 112, Austin, TX 78712 Tel 512-471-4936; Orders to: P. O. Box 7304, Univ. Sta., Austin, TX 78712 Tel 512-458-5413.
Studia Slovenica, *(Studia Slovenica, Inc.),* P.O. Box 232, New York, NY 10032.
Stuttman, *(Stuttman, H. S., Inc.; 0-87475),* 333 Post Rd. W., Westport, CT 06889.
Success Unltd, *(Success Unlimited, Inc.; 0-918448),* 401 N. Wabash, Chicago, IL 60611 Tel 312-828-9500.
Sue Ann, *(Sue Ann; 0-9604172),* Box 2, North Haven, CT 06473 Tel 203-288-1913.
Sufi Order Pubns, *(Sufi Order Pubns.; 0-930872),* P.O. Box 568, Lebanon Springs, NY 12114.
Suhrkamp, *(Suhrkamp/Insel Pubs. Boston Inc.; 3-458),* 380 Green St., Cambridge, MA 02139 Tel 617-876-2333.
Sullivan Prod, *(Sullivan, Dorothy, Production; 0-9604928),* P.O. Box 7045, St. Petersburg, FL 33734.
Sumac Mich, *(Sumac Press; 0-912090),* P.O. Box 39, Fremont, MI 49412 Tel 616-924-3464.
Summer Inst Ling, *(Summer Institute of Linguistics; 0-88312),* Academic Pubns., 7500 W. Camp Wisdom Rd., Dallas, TX 75236 Tel 214-298-3331.
Summit Bks, *(Summit Books),* Subs. of Simon & Schuster, 1230 Ave. of the Americas, New York, NY 10020 Tel 212-246-2471.
Summit Pub Co
See Gold Penny
Summit Univ, *(Summit Univ. Press; 0-916766),* Box A, Malibu, CA 90265 Tel 213-991-4751.
SUN, *(SUN; 0-915342),* 347 W. 39th St., New York, NY 10018 Tel 212-594-8428.
Sun Pub, *(Sun Publishing Co.; 0-914172; 0-89540),* P.O. Box 4383, Albuquerque, NM 87196 Tel 505-255-6550.
Sun-Scape Pubns, *(Sun-Scape Pubns.; 0-919842),* P.O. Box 42725, Tucson, AZ 85733 Tel 602-743-0209.
Sunbury Pr, *(Sunbury Press; 0-915548),* P. O. Box 1778, Raleigh, NC 27602 Tel 919-832-6417.
Sundance, *(Sundance Pubns., Ltd.; 0-913582),* P.O. Box 597, Silverton, CO 81433 Tel 303-387-5784.
Sundial Bks *Imprint of* **Sunstone Pr**
Sundowner Serv, *(Sundowner Services; 0-932241),* 2559-47th Ave., San Francisco, CA 94116 Tel 415-564-0068.

Sunflower Ink, *(Sunflower Ink; 0-931104),* Palo Colorado Canyon, Carmel, CA 93923.
Sunrise MO, *(Sunrise Publishing Co.; 0-86629),* 10617 Liberty Ave., St. Louis, MO 63132.
Sunrise PA, *(Sunrise Publishing Co.),* P.O. Box 215, Hatfield, PA 19440.
Sunrise Pub OR, *(Sunrise Publishing; 0-9604344),* 3441 Stark St., Eugene, OR 97404.
Sunset-Lane, *(Sunset Books/Lane Publishing Co.; 0-376),* Willow & Middlefield Rds., Menlo Park, CA 94025 Tel 415-321-3600.
SunShine, *(SunShine; 0-937710),* Box 4351, Austin, TX 78765 Tel 512-459-6717.
Sunshine
See SunShine
Sunshine Arts WA, *(Sunshine Arts),* W. 1018 Shannon, Spokane, WA 99205.
Sunstone Pr, *(Sunstone Press, The; 0-913270; 0-86534),* P.O. Box 2321, Santa Fe, NM 87501 Tel 505-988-4418. *Imprints:* Sundial Bks (Sundial Books).
SUNY Environ, *(State Univ. of New York, College of Environmental Science & Forestry),* Syracuse, NY 13210 Tel 315-473-8711.
Superior Pub, *(Superior Publishing Co.; 0-87564),* 708 Sixth Ave., N., Box 1710, Seattle, WA 98111 Tel 206-282-4310.
Superlove, *(Superlove),* 4245 Ladoga Ave., Lakewood, CA 90713.
Survival Ed Assoc, *(Survival Education Assn.; 0-913724),* 9035 Golden Givens Rd., Tacoma, WA 98445 Tel 206-531-3156.
Sutter House, *(Sutter House; 0-915010),* 77 Main St., P.O. Box 212, Lititz, PA 17543 Tel 717-626-0800.
SW Mission, *(Southwestern Mission Research Center; 0-915076),* Arizona State Museum, Tucson, AZ 85721.
SW Pks Mnmts, *(Southwest Parks & Monuments Assn.; 0-911408),* P.O. Box 1562, Globe, AZ 85501 Tel 602-425-4392.
Swallow, *(Swallow Press; 0-8040),* Scott Quadrangle, Athens, OH 45701 Tel 614-594-5852; Orders to: Publishers Marketing Group, P.O. Box 350, Momence, IL 60954 Tel 815-472-2661.
Swanson, *(Swanson Publishing Co.; 0-911466),* P.O. Box 334, Moline, IL 61265.
Swedenborg, *(Swedenborg Foundation, Inc.; 0-87785),* 139 E. 23rd St., New York, NY 10010 Tel 212-673-7310.
Sweet, *(Sweet Publishing Co.; 0-8344),* Box 4055, Austin, TX 78765 Tel 512-255-4171.
Sweetbrier, *(Sweetbrier Press; 0-936736),* 536 Emerson St., Palo Alto, CA 94301.
Swets North Am, *(Swets North America),* P. O. Box 517, Berwyn, PA 19312.
Swets Pub Nor
See Swets North Am
Sword of Lord, *(Sword of the Lord Pubs.; 0-87398),* P.O. Box 1099, 224 Bridge Ave., Murfreesboro, TN 37130 Tel 615-893-6700.
Sybex, *(Sybex, Inc.; 0-89588),* 2020 Milbia St., Berkeley, CA 94704 Tel 415-848-8233.
Sycamore Pr, *(Sycamore Press, Inc.; 0-916768),* P.O. Box 552, Terre Haute, IN 47808 Tel 812-299-2458.
SYDA Found, *(SYDA Foundation; 0-914602),* P.O. Box 605, South Fallsburg, NY 12779 Tel 914-434-4850.
Syentek Bks, *(Syentek Books Co., Inc.; 0-914082),* 555 Battery St., P.O. Box 26588, San Francisco, CA 94126 Tel 415-441-7521.
Sylvan Inst, *(Sylvan Institute; 0-918428),* 7104 N. E. Hazel Dell Ave., Vancouver, WA 98665 Tel 206-694-0911.
Symposium Pr, *(Symposium Press, The),* 1620 Greenfield, Los Angeles, CA 90025.
Synapse Pubns, *(Synapse Pubns.; 0-935170),* 1310 Benedum Trees Bldg., Pittsburgh, PA 15222.
Synergistic Pr, *(Synergistic Press, Inc.; 0-912184),* 3965 Sacramento St., San Francisco, CA 94118 Tel 415-387-8180.
Synthesis Pubns, *(Synthesis Pubns.; 0-89935),* P.O. Box 40099, San Francisco, CA 94140 Tel 415-282-5272.
Syracuse U Foreign Comp, *(Syracuse Univ., Foreign & Comparative Studies Program; 0-915984),* 119 College Place, Syracuse, NY 13210 Tel 315-423-2552.
Syracuse U Pr, *(Syracuse Univ. Press; 0-8156),* 1011 E. Water St., Syracuse, NY 13210 Tel 315-423-2596. *Imprints:* Am U Beirut (American Univ. of Beirut Pubns.).
T Beckman & Assoc, *(Beckman, Tom, & Assoc.; 0-937204),* P.O. Box 20081, Cincinnati, OH 45219.
T D Anthony, *(Anthony, Travis D.; 0-9604686),* P.O. Box 646, Rush Springs, OK 73082 Tel 405-476-2211.
T K Sanderson, *(Sanderson, T. K., Organization),* 200 E. 25th St., Baltimore, MD 21218 Tel 301-235-3383.
T L Jaynes, *(Jaynes, Thomas L.; 0-935514),* P.O. Box 651038, Miami, FL 33165.
T M Johnson, *(Johnson, LTC Thomas M.; 0-9600906),* P.O. Box 7152, Alexandria, VA 22307 Tel 703-360-6241.
T Weinberg
See Gordons & Weinberg
T Y Crowell, *(Crowell, Thomas Y., Co.; 0-690),* 10 E. 53rd St., New York, NY 10022 Tel 212-593-3900; Dist. by: Harper & Row Pubs., Keystone Industrial Park, Scranton, PA 18512. *Imprints:* TYC-J (Crowell, T Y, Juvenile Books).
TAB Bks, *(Tab Books, Inc.; 0-8306),* Blue Ridge Summit, PA 17214 Tel 717-794-2191.
Tafnews, *(Tafnews Press; 0-911520; 0-911521),* Div. of Track & Field News, Inc., P.O. Box 296, Los Altos, CA 94022 Tel 415-948-8188.
Taft Corp, *(Taft Corporation; 0-914756),* 1000 Vermont Ave., N.W., Washington, DC 20005 Tel 202-347-0788.
Tales Mojave Rd, *(Tales of the Mojave Road Pub., Co.; 0-914224),* P.O. Box 307, Norco, CA 91760 Tel 714-737-3150.
Talisman, *(Talisman Press; 0-934612),* P.O. Box 455, Georgetown, CA 95634 Tel 916-333-4486.
Tamal Land, *(Tamal Land Press; 0-912908),* 39 Merwin Ave., Fairfax, CA 94930 Tel 415-456-4705.
Tamarack Edns, *(Tamarack Editions; 0-918092),* 909 Westcott St., Syracuse, NY 13210 Tel 315-478-6495.
Tamarack Pr, *(Tamarack Press; 0-915024),* P.O. Box 5650, Madison, WI 53705 Tel 608-831-3363.
Tamburitza, *(Tamburitza Press; 0-936922),* 1801 Blvd. of the Allies, Pittsburgh, PA 15219.
Tam's Bks, *(Tam's Books, Inc.; 0-89179),* 3333 S. Hoover St., Los Angeles, CA 90007 Tel 213-746-1141.
TAN Bks Pubs, *(TAN Books & Pubs., Inc.; 0-89555),* 2135 N. Central Ave., Rockford, IL 61105 Tel 815-962-2662; Orders to: P.O. Box 424, Rockford, IL 61105.
Tanam Pr, *(Tanam Press; 0-934378),* 40 White St., New York, NY 10013.
Tandem Pr, *(Tandem Press Pubs.; 0-913024),* P.O. Box 237, Tannersville, PA 18372 Tel 717-629-2250.
Tao of Wing, *(Tao of Wing Chun Do; 0-918642),* 2912-C S. Skagit Hwy., Sedro Woolley, WA 98284 Tel 206-826-3848.
Taplinger, *(Taplinger Publishing Co., Inc.; 0-8008),* 132 W. 22nd St., New York, NY 10011 Tel 212-741-0801.
TAPPI, *(Technical Assn. of the Pulp & Paper Industry; 0-89852),* 1 Dunwoody Park, Atlanta, GA 30338 Tel 404-394-6130.
Taraxacum, *(Taraxacum; 0-9602822),* 1227 30th St. N.W., Washington, DC 20007.
Tasa Pub Co, *(Tasa Publishing Co.; 0-935698),* 5230 W. 73rd St., Minneapolis, MN 55435.
Tasco, *(Tasco Pub. Corp.; 0-918076),* 305 E. 53rd St., Suite 3, New York, NY 10022 Tel 212-751-6500.
Tashmoo, *(Tashmoo Press, The; 0-932384),* RFD, Vineyard Haven, MA 02568.
Tatsch, *(Tatsch Associates; 0-912890),* 120 Thunder Rd., Sudbury, MA 01776 Tel 617-443-6343.
Taugus Hse, *(Taugus House Pubs., Inc.; 0-938556),* 1890 San Pablo Dr., San Marcos, CA 92069.
Taunton, *(Taunton Press, Inc.; 0-918804),* Box 355, Newtown, CT 06470 Tel 203-426-8171.
Taxlogs, *(Taxlogs Unlimited; 0-935802),* 20 Galli Dr., Ignacio, CA 94947 Tel 415-883-7768.
Taylor & Friends, *(Taylor, Sally, & Friends; 0-9604904),* 756 Kansas St., San Francisco, CA 94107.
Taylor & Ng, *(Taylor & Ng),* Box 200, Brisbane, CA 94005 Tel 415-467-2600.
Taylor-Carlisle, *(Taylor-Carlisle),* 245 Seventh Ave., New York, NY 10001 Tel 212-674-7788.
Taylor Museum, *(Taylor Museum),* Dist. by: Colorado Springs Fine Arts Ctr., 30 W. Dale St., Colorado Springs, CO 80903 Tel 303-634-5581.
TBW Bks, *(TBW Books; 0-931474),* Box 58, Day's Ferry Rd., Woolwich, ME 04579 Tel 207-442-7632.
Tchrs & Writers Coll, *(Teachers & Writers Collaborative; 0-915924),* 84 Fifth Ave., New York, NY 10011 Tel 212-691-6590.
Tchrs Coll, *(Teachers College Press, Columbia Univ.; 0-8077),* 1234 Amsterdam Ave., New York, NY 10027 Tel 212-678-3919; Orders to: 81 Adams Dr., Totowa, NJ 07512 Tel 201-265-8600.
Te Cum Tom, *(Te-Cum-Tom Pubns.; 0-913508),* 570 Sunset Way, Grants Pass, OR 97526 Tel 503-479-9091.
Teach'em, *(Teach'em, Inc.; 0-931028),* 160 E. Illinois St., Chicago, IL 60611.
Tech Ed Serv, *(Technical Education Services; 0-930552),* Univ. of Missouri, Columbia, MO 65201.
Tech Info Proj, *(Technical Information Project, Inc.),* 1346 Connecticut Ave. N.W., Suite 217, Washington, DC 20036 Tel 202-466-2954.
Tech Marketing, *(Technology Marketing Corp.),* 17 Park St., Norwalk, CT 06851 Tel 203-846-2029.
Techkits, *(Techkits, Inc.; 0-918662),* P.O. Box 105, Demarest, NJ 07627 Tel 201-684-7500.
Technocracy, *(Technocracy, Inc.),* P.O. Box 238, Savannah, OH 44874 Tel 419-962-4712.
Technomic, *(Technomic Publishing Co.; 0-87762),* 265 Post Road West, Westport, CT 06880 Tel 203-226-7203.
Tecolote Pr, *(Tecolote Press, Inc.; 0-915030),* P.O. Box 188, Glenwood, NM 88039 Tel 505-539-2183.
Tele Cable, *(Telegraphic Cable & Radio Registrations, Inc.; 0-916446),* 1600 Harrison Ave., Mamaroneck, NY 10543.
Telecom Lib, *(Telecom Library, The),* 205 W. 19th St., New York, NY 10011 Tel 212-691-8215.
Telegraph Bks, *(Telegraph Books; 0-89760),* Box 38, Norwood, PA 19074 Tel 215-583-4550.
Teleometrics, *(Teleometrics International, Inc.; 0-937932),* 2203 Timberloch Place, Suite 104, The Woodlands, TX 77380 Tel 713-367-0060.
Telephone Bks, *(Telephone Books Press; 0-916382),* P.O. Box 672, Old Chelsea Sta., New York, NY 10011 Tel 203-453-4415.
Telos Pr, *(Telos Press Ltd.; 0-914386),* Box 3111, St. Louis, MO 63130 Tel 314-361-8472.
Temple Bar, *(Temple Bar Bookshop),* 9 Boylston St., Cambridge, MA 02138 Tel 617-876-6025.
Temple U Pr, *(Temple Univ. Press; 0-87722),* Philadelphia, PA 19122 Tel 215-787-8787.
Templegate, *(Templegate Pubs.; 0-87243),* P.O. Box 5152, Springfield, IL 62705 Tel 217-522-3361.
Templeman, *(Templeman, Eleanor Lee; 0-911044),* 3001 N. Pollard St., Arlington, VA 22207 Tel 703-528-1112.
Tempo *Imprint of* **G&D**
Ten Penny, *(Ten Penny Players, Inc.; 0-934830),* 799 Greenwich St., New York, NY 10014 Tel 212-929-3169.
Ten Speed Pr, *(Ten Speed Press; 0-913668; 0-89815),* P.O. Box 7123, Berkeley, CA 94707 Tel 415-845-8414.
Ten Talents, *(Ten Talents; 0-9603532),* P.O. Box 86A, Rte. 1, Chisholm, MN 55719 Tel 218-254-5357.
Tendril, *(Tendril; 0-937504),* P.O. Box 512, Green Harbor, MA 02041.
Tern Pr, *(Tern, Eddie, Press; 0-9605388),* 430 SW 206th St., Seattle, WA 98166.
Terra Magica *Imprint of* **Hill & Wang**
Terraspace, *(Terraspace Inc.; 0-918990),* 304 N. Stonestreet Ave., Rockville, MD 20850 Tel 301-424-0090.
Teton Bkshop, *(Teton Bookshop Publishing Co.; 0-933160),* Box 1903, Jackson, WY 83001.
Tetra Tech, *(Tetra Tech, Inc.; 0-916646),* 1911 Ft. Myer Dr., Suite 601, Arlington, VA 22209.
Tex A & M Lang
See Dabbs
Tex A&M Univ Pr, *(Texas A & M Univ. Press; 0-89096),* Drawer "C", College Station, TX 77843 Tel 713-845-1436.

Tex Consumer, *(Texas Consumer Assn.; 0-937606),* 302 W. 15th St., Suite 202, Austin, TX 78701.
Tex Instr Inc, *(Texas Instruments Inc.; 0-89512),* P.O. Box 225012 MS54, Dallas, TX 75265 Tel 214-995-5516.
Tex Portfolio
See Cedar Rock
Tex St Hist Assn, *(Texas State Historical Assn.; 0-87611),* 2-306 Richardson Hall, Univ. Sta., Austin, TX 78712 Tel 512-471-1525.
Tex Tech Pr, *(Texas Tech Press; 0-89672),* P.O. Box 4460, Lubbock, TX 79409 Tel 806-742-2781; Orders to: Texas Tech University Library, Texas Tech University, Lubbock, TX 79409.
Tex Western, *(Texas Western Press, Univ. of Texas at El Paso; 0-87404),* El Paso, TX 79968 Tel 915-747-5688.
Texan-Am Pub, *(Texan-American Publisher's Co.; 0-935622),* 1101 Natchez Dr., Texas City, TX 77590 Tel 713-935-9576.
Texas Month Pr, *(Texas Monthly Press; 0-932012),* P.O. Box 1569, Austin, TX 78767 Tel 512-476-7085.
Texian, *(Texian Press; 0-87244),* P.O. Box 1684, Waco, TX 76703 Tel 817-754-5636.
Text-Fiche, *(Text-Fiche Press, The; 0-89969),* 540 Drexel Ave., Glencoe, IL 60022 Tel 312-835-4420; Orders to: Box 382, Glencoe, IL 60022.
Textile Bk, *(Textile Book Service, Inc.; 0-87245),* P.O. Box 25, Broadway, NJ 08808 Tel 201-689-2230.
TFH Pubns, *(T. F. H. Pubns.; 0-87666),* 211 W. Sylvania Ave., Neptune, NJ 07753 Tel 201-988-8400.
Thames Hudson, *(Thames & Hudson; 0-500),* Dist. by: W.W. Norton, & Co., Inc., 500 Fifth Ave., New York, NY 10036 Tel 212-354-3763.
That New Pub, *(That New Pub. Co.; 0-918270),* 1525 Eielson St., Fairbanks, AK 99701 Tel 907-452-3007.
The Garden, *(The Garden; 0-9602790),* 6605 Rowland Rd., Eden Prairie, MN 55344 Tel 612-944-2404.
The Harian
See Harian Creative
The Smith, *(Smith, The; 0-912292),* 5 Beekman St., New York, NY 10038 Tel 212-732-4821; Dist. by: Horizon Press, 156 Fifth Ave, New York, NY 10010.
Theatre Arts, *(Theatre Arts Books; 0-87830),* 153 Waverly Place, New York, NY 10014 Tel 212-675-1815.
Thelema Pub TN
See Troll Pub
Thelema Pubns, *(Thelema Pubns.; 0-913576),* P.O. Box 1093, Kings Beach, CA 95719.
Theos Pub Hse, *(Theosophical Publishing House; 0-8356),* 306 W. Geneva Rd., Wheaton, IL 60187 Tel 312-665-0123. *Imprints:* Quest (Quest Books).
Theos U Pr, *(Theosophical Univ. Press; 0-911500),* P.O. Bin "C", Pasadena, CA 91109 Tel 213-798-8020.
Theoscience Found, *(Theoscience Foundation Pub.; 0-917802),* 193 Los Robles Dr., Burlingame, CA 94010.
Theosophy, *(Theosophy Co.),* 245 W. 33rd St., Los Angeles, CA 90007 Tel 213-748-7244.
Theotes, *(Theotes-Logos Research, Inc.; 0-911806),* 4318 York Ave. S., Minneapolis, MN 55410 Tel 612-922-3202.
Thieme-Stratton, *(Thieme-Stratton, Inc.; 0-913258; 0-86577),* 381 Park Ave., S., New York, NY 10016 Tel 212-683-5088.
Third Pr
See Okpaku Communications
Third World, *(Third World Press; 0-88378),* 7524 S. Cottage Grove, Chicago, IL 60019 Tel 312-651-0700.
Thomas Intl Pub, *(Thomas International Publishing Co., Inc.; 0-937200),* Subs. of Thomas Publishing Co., 1 Penn Plaza, New York, NY 10001 Tel 212-695-0500.
Thomas More, *(More, Thomas, Press; 0-88347),* 225 W. Huron St., Chicago, IL 60610 Tel 312-951-2100.
Thomas Paine Pr, *(Thomas Paine Press; 0-934162),* 6674 Danville Ave., San Diego, CA 92120 Tel 714-462-8120.
Thomas Pr, *(Thomas Press; 0-89732),* 2030 Ferdon Rd., Ann Arbor, MI 48104 Tel 313-662-1275.
Thomond Pr *Imprint of* **Elsevier**
Thomson Pub CA, *(Thomson Pubns.; 0-913702),* P.O. Box 9335, Fresno, CA 93791 Tel 209-435-2163.
Thor, *(Thor Publishing Co.; 0-87407),* P.O. Box 1782, Ventura, CA 93002 Tel 805-648-4560.
Thorndike Pr, *(Thorndike Press; 0-89621),* Thorndike, ME 04986 Tel 207-948-2962.
Thoroughbred Own & Breed, *(Thoroughbred Owners & Breeders Assn.),* P.O. Box 4038, Lexington, KY 40544 Tel 606-278-2361.
Three Continents, *(Three Continents Press; 0-89410; 0-914478),* 1346 Connecticut Ave., Suite 1131, Washington, DC 20036 Tel 202-457-0288.
Thut Ctr World Ed
See World Educ Proj
Ticknor & Fields, *(Ticknor & Fields; 0-89919),* 383 Orange St., New Haven, CT 06511 Tel 203-776-1878; 52 Vanderbilt Ave., New York, NY 10017 Tel 212-687-8996; Dist. by: Houghton Mifflin Co., 2 Park St., Boston, MA 02107 Tel 617-725-5000.
Tidal Pr, *(Tidal Press, The),* Cranberry Isles, ME 04625 Tel 207-244-3090.
Tide Bk Pub Co, *(Tide Book Publishing Co.; 0-9602786),* P.O. Box 268, Manchester, MA 01944 Tel 617-526-4887; Orders to: Academy Chicago Ltd., 360 N. Michigan Ave., Chicago, IL 60601 Tel 312-782-9826.
Timberline Bks, *(Timberline Books; 0-913488),* 25890 Weld Rd. 53, Kersey, CO 80644 Tel 303-353-3785.
Time Bks
See Times Bks
Time-Lee Pubns, *(Time-Lee Pubns.; 0-937210),* P.O. Box 116, Melbourne, FL 32901 Tel 305-727-3010.
Time-Life, *(Time-Life Books; 0-8094),* Div. of Time, Inc., 777 Duke St., Alexandria, VA 22314 Tel 703-960-5000; Dist. by: Little, Brown & Co., 34 Beacon St., Boston, MA 02106; Dist. by: Morgan & Morgan Co., 400 Warburton Ave., Hastings on Hudson, NY 10706; Lib. & School Orders to: Silver Burdett Co., Morristown, NJ 13664.
Timeless Bks, *(Timeless Books; 0-931454),* Orders to: P.O. Box 60, Porthill, ID 83853 Tel 604-227-9220.
Timely Bks, *(Timely Books; 0-931328),* P.O. Box 267, New Milford, CT 06776 Tel 203-354-1110.
Times Bks, *(Times Books; 0-8129),* Div. of The New York Times Co., 3 Park Ave., New York, NY 10016 Tel 212-725-2050; Dist. by: Harper & Row, Keystone Industrial Park, Scranton, PA 18512.
Times-M Pr, *(Times-Mirror Press; 0-911510),* 1115 S. Boyle Ave, Los Angeles, CA 90023 Tel 213-265-6767.
Tioga Pub Co, *(Tioga Publishing Co.; 0-935382),* P.O. Box 98, Palo Alto, CA 94302 Tel 415-854-2445.
Tipton Woman, *(Tipton Woman's Club-Cookbook),* P.O. Box 25, Tipton, IA 52772 Tel 319-886-2730.
Tiresias Pr, *(Tiresias Press, Inc.; 0-913292),* 116 Pinehurst Ave., New York, NY 10033 Tel 212-568-9570.
TIS Inc, *(T.I.S., Inc.; 0-89917),* P.O. Box 1998, 1928 Arlington Rd., Bloomington, IN 47401 Tel 812-332-3307.
TL Enterprises, *(TL Enterprises, Inc.; 0-934798),* 29901 Agoura Rd., Agoura, CA 91301 Tel 213-991-4980.
TM Prods, *(TM Productions; 0-937522),* Box 189, Wilmette, IL 60091.
Todd & Honeywell, *(Todd & Honeywell Inc.; 0-89962),* 10 Cuttermill Rd., Great Neck, NY 11021 Tel 516-487-9777.
Tofua Pr
See Rand-Tofua
Toggitt, *(Toggitt, Joan, Ltd.; 0-911514),* 246 Fifth Ave., New York, NY 10001.
Toledo Mus Art, *(Toledo Museum of Art, The; 0-935172),* Box 1013, Toledo, OH 43697 Tel 419-255-8000; Dist. by: Pennsylvania State Univ. Press, 215 Wagner Bldg., University Park, PA 16802.
Tolvan Co, *(Tolvan Co.; 0-916774),* P.O. Box 1933, Appleton, WI 54911 Tel 414-766-1828.
Tombouctou, *(Tombouctou Books),* P.O. Box 265, Bolinas, CA 94924; Dist. by: Bookpeople, 2940 Seventh St., Berkeley, CA 94710 Tel 415-549-3030; Dist. by: Bookslinger, P.O. Box 1651, 2163 Ford Pkwy,, St. Paul, MN 55116 Tel 612-690-0293; Dist. by: Dark Horse, 2636 Etna, No 4, Berkeley, CA 94704 Tel 415-843-5796; Dist. by: Barbary Coast Distribution, 635 Amador, Richmond, CA 94805 Tel 415-236-1197; Dist. by: Serendipity Books Distribution, 1970 Shattuck Ave., Berkeley, CA 94704 Tel 415-549-3336; Dist. by: Word Works, 1421 Second Ave., N. Seattle, WA 98109 Tel 206-284-8127; Dist. by: New York State Small Press Assn., P.O. Box 1264, Radio City Sta., New York, NY 10019.
Tompson & Rutter, *(Tompson & Rutter, Inc.; 0-936988),* P.O. Box 297, Grantham, NH 03753.
Toothpaste, *(Toothpaste Press; 0-915124),* P.O. Box 546, West Branch, IA 52358 Tel 319-643-2604.
Topgallant, *(Topgallant Publishing Co., Ltd.; 0-914916),* Elizabeth Bldg. 845 Mission Lane, Honolulu, HI 96813 Tel 808-524-0884.
Torch *Imprint of* **Har-Row**
Total Trial, *(Total Trial System, The; 0-9605222),* P.O. Box 3663, St. Paul, MN 55165.
Touchstone Bks *Imprint of* **S&S**
Touchstone Pr OR, *(Touchstone Press; 0-911518),* P.O. Box 81, Beaverton, OR 97075 Tel 503-646-8081.
Tourism Ctr
See Travel & Tourism
Toward the Light, *(Toward the Light Publishing House; 0-937054),* 16645 Bosque Dr., Encino, CA 91436.
Tower
See Tower Bks
Tower Bks, *(Tower Books, Inc.; 0-505),* 2 Park Ave., Suite 910, New York, NY 10016 Tel 212-679-7707; Orders to: Increased Sales Co., Inc., 327 Main Ave., Norwalk, CT 06852 Tel 203-846-2027.
Tower Pub Co, *(Tower Publishing Co.; 0-89442),* 163 Middle St., P. O. Box 7220, Portland, ME 04112 Tel 207-774-9813.
Town of Andover MA, *(Town of Andover, MA; 0-9603160),* Town Hall, 20 Main St., Andover, MA 01810 Tel 617-475-5560.
Townsend Pr, *(Townsend Press; 0-935990),* 330 Charlotte Ave., Nashville, TN 37201 Tel 615-256-6589.
Toys 'N Things, *(Toys 'N Things; 0-934140),* Training & Resource Center, 906 North Dale, St. Paul, MN 55103 Tel 612-488-7284.
Tradd St Pr, *(Tradd Street Press; 0-937684),* 38 Tradd St., Charleston, SC 29401 Tel 803-722-4293.
Trade Ship Pub Co, *(Trade Ship Publishing Co.; 0-934592),* 60 State St., 34th Fl. Tower, Boston, MA 02109.
Trademark Reg, *(Trademark Register; 0-911522),* 454 Washington Bldg., Washington, DC 20005.
Traders Pr, *(Traders Press, Inc.; 0-934380),* P.O. Box 10344, Greenville, SC 29603 Tel 803-288-3900.
Trado-Medic, *(Trado-Medic Books; 0-932426),* Div. of Conch Magazine, Ltd., Pubs., 102 Normal Ave., Buffalo, NY 14213.
Traffic Serv, *(Traffic Service Corp.; 0-87408),* 1435 "G" St. N.W., Suite 815, Washington, DC 20005 Tel 202-783-7325.
Trail-R, *(Trail-R Club of America; 0-87593),* 610 W. Ninth Ave., Suite 14, Escondido, CA 92025 Tel 714-743-8648; Orders to: P.O. Box 1376, Beverly Hills, CA 90213.
Trailer Life
See TL Enterprises
Train Res Assoc, *(Training Resource Associates; 0-933794),* 5 S. Miller Rd., Harrisburg, PA 17109.
Trans-Anglo, *(Trans-Anglo Books; 0-87046),* P.O. Box 38, Corona Del Mar, CA 92625 Tel 714-645-7393.
Trans-Media Pub, *(Trans-Media Publishing, Co.; 0-913338),* Affiliated with Oceana Pubns., 75 Main St., Dobbs Ferry, NY 10522 Tel 914-693-5956.
Trans Tech, *(Trans Tech Pubns.; 0-87849),* 16 Bear Skin Neck, Rockport, MA 01966 Tel 617-546-6426.

Trans Tech Mgmt, *(Trans Tech Management Press; 0-938398),* P.O. Box 23032, Sacramento, CA 95823.
Transaction Bks, *(Transaction Books; 0-87855),* Bldg. 4051, Rutgers-State Univ., New Brunswick, NJ 08903 Tel 201-932-2280; Orders to: P.O. Box 978, Edison, NJ 08817.
Transatlantic, *(Transatlantic Arts, Inc.; 0-693),* 88 Bridge Rd., Central Islip, NY 11722 Tel 516-234-0055.
Transculture Inc, *(Transculture, Inc.; 0-935862),* Village Box 104, New York, NY 10014.
Transform Berkeley, *(Transformations Press; 0-930162),* 1625 Jaynes St., Berkeley, CA 94703 Tel 415-524-8391.
Transitour, *(Transitour Inc.; 0-939108),* 111 St. Charles Ave., New Orleans, LA 70130.
Translation Pr, *(Translation Press; 0-931556),* 2901 Heatherway, Ann Arbor, MI 48104.
Translation Research, *(Translation Research Institute; 0-917564),* 5914 Pulaski Ave., Philadelphia, PA 19144 Tel 215-848-7084.
Transmedia, *(Transmedia; 0-912750),* P.O. Box 2847, La Mesa, CA 92041 Tel 714-466-2138.
Transnatl Invest, *(Transnational Investments, Ltd.; 0-933678),* 1101 Connecticut Ave., N.W., Suite 600, Washington, DC 20036 Tel 202-857-0600.
Transrep, *(Transrep/Bibliographics; 0-918370),* P.O. Box 22678, Denver, CO 80222 Tel 303-756-4861.
Transworld
See Carpatho-Rusyn Res Ctr
Trask Hse Bks, *(Trask House Books, Inc.; 0-932264),* 2754 S.E. 27th Ave., Portland, OR 97202 Tel 503-235-1898.
Travel & Tourism, *(Travel & Tourism Press; 0-935638),* 313 Barson St., No. 5, Santa Cruz, CA 95060 Tel 408-426-1576.
Travis, *(Travis Piano Service; 0-9600394),* P.O. Box 4359, 8012 Carroll Ave., Takoma Park, MD 20012 Tel 301-439-4111.
Treasure Chest, *(Treasure Chest Pubns.; 0-918080),* 1842 W. Grant Rd., Suite 107, Tucson, AZ 85705 Tel 602-623-9558; Orders to: P.O. Box 5250, Tucson, AZ 85903.
Tree Bks, *(Tree Books),* Box 9005, Berkeley, CA 94709; Dist. by: Book People, 2940 Seventh St., Berkeley, CA 94710.
Tree Roots
See Treeroots
Treeroots, *(Treeroots Press; 0-9604450),* P. O. Box 684, Berkeley, CA 94704.
Trempealeau, *(Trempealeau Press; 0-912540),* 800 Hillcrest Dr., Santa Fe, NM 87501 Tel 505-983-1947.
Trend House, *(Trend House; 0-88251),* Div. of Florida Trend, Inc., P.O. Box 611, St. Petersburg, FL 33731 Tel 813-893-8511.
Trends Pub, *(Trends Publishing Co.; 0-9602426),* 23100 Providence Dr., Suite 270, Southfield, MI 48075 Tel 313-552-1175.
Tri-B Pubns, *(Tri-B Pubns.; 0-938054),* P.O. Box 26203, Tempe, AZ 85283; Dist. by: Multi-Marketing International, 6963 Washington Ave. S., Minneapolis, MN 55435.
Tri-Med, *(Tri-Med Press),* 65 Christopher St., Montclair, NJ 07042.
Triad Pr TX, *(Triad Press),* P.O. Box 42006-K, Houston, TX 77042 Tel 713-789-0424.
Triangle Pr, *(Triangle Press; 0-937144),* Rte. 6 Box 327, Kemp, TX 75143.
Triangle Pubns, *(Triangle Pubns., Inc.; 0-9603684),* 4 Radnor Corporate Ctr., Radnor, PA 19088 Tel 215-293-8500.
Trinity Pub Hse, *(Trinity Publishing House, Inc.; 0-933656),* 2171 Bayard Ave., St. Paul, MN 55116.
Trinity U Pr, *(Trinity Univ. Press; 0-911536),* 715 Stadium Dr., San Antonio, TX 78284 Tel 512-736-7619.
Troll Assocs, *(Troll Associates; 0-89375),* 320 Rte. 17, Mahwah, NJ 07430 Tel 201-529-4000.
Troll Pub, *(Troll Publishing Co.; 0-933454),* Box 90213, Nashville, TN 37209 Tel 615-297-4436.
Trolley Talk, *(Trolley Talk; 0-914196),* 59 Euclid Ave., Wyoming, OH 45215.
Trophy *Imprint of* **Har-Row**
Troubador Pr, *(Troubador Press; 0-912300; 0-89844),* 385 Fremont St., San Francisco, CA 94105 Tel 415-397-3716.
Troy State Univ
See TSU Pr
Truedog, *(Truedog Press; 0-937212),* 216 W. Academy St., Lonoke, AR 72086.
Truth Consciousness, *(Truth Consciousness; 0-933572),* Gold Hill, Salina Star Rte., Boulder, CO 80302.
TSU Pr, *(Troy State University Press; 0-916624),* Wallace Hall, Troy, AL 36081 Tel 205-566-3000.
Tuffy Bks, *(Tuffy Books, Inc.; 0-89828),* 949 Broadway, New York, NY 10010 Tel 212-228-8080.
Tulane Romance Lang, *(Tulane Studies in Romance Languages & Literature; 0-912788),* Newcomb Coll., Tulane Univ., New Orleans, LA 70118 Tel 504-865-4572.
Tulane Stud Pol, *(Tulane Studies in Political Science; 0-930598),* Tulane Univ., College of Arts & Sciences, Dept. of Political Science, New Orleans, LA 70118 Tel 504-865-6191.
Tulane U Ctr Busn
See Tulane Univ
Tulane Univ, *(Tulane Univ.),* Tulane University, New Orleans, LA 70118; Dist. by: Center for Business History Studies, History Bldg., Tulane Univ., New Orleans, LA 70118.
Tuppence, *(Tuppence, Inc.),* 2701 S. 35th, Lincoln, NE 68506.
Turkey Pr, *(Turkey Press; 0-918824),* 6746 Sueno Rd., Isla Vista, CA 93017 Tel 805-685-3603.
Turtle Isl Foun, *(Turtle Island Foundation, Netzahaulcoyotl Historical Society; 0-913666),* 2845 Buena Vista Way, Berkeley, CA 94708 Tel 415-845-0984.
TUVOTI, *(Unspeakable Visions of the Individual, The; 0-934660),* P. O. Box 439, California, PA 15419 Tel 412-938-8956.
TV Factbk, *(Television Factbook; 0-911486),* 1836 Jefferson Place, N.W., Washington, DC 20036 Tel 202-872-9200.
Twayne, *(Twayne Pubs.; 0-8057),* Div. of G. K. Hall, Dist. by: G. K. Hall & Co., 70 Lincoln St., Boston, MA 02111.
Two Eighteen, *(Two-Eighteen Press),* P.O. Box 218, Village Sta., New York, NY 10014 Tel 212-966-5877.
Two Rivers, *(Two Rivers Press; 0-89756),* Box 626, Aurora, OR 97002 Tel 503-266-2922.
TYC-J *Imprint of* **T Y Crowell**
Tyndale, *(Tyndale House Pubs.; 0-8423),* 336 Gundersen Dr., Wheaton, IL 60187 Tel 312-668-8300.
U Cal AISC, *(Univ. of California, American Indian Studies Center),* 3220 Campbell Hall, Los Angeles, CA 90024 Tel 213-825-7315.
U Cal Hist Sci Tech, *(Univ. of California., Berkeley, Office of History of Science & Technology; 0-918102),* 470 Stephens Hall, Univ. of California, Berkeley, CA 94720 Tel 415-642-4581.
U Cal LA Indus Rel, *(Univ. of California, Institute of Industrial Relations; 0-89215),* 405 Hilgard Ave., Los Angeles, CA 90024 Tel 213-825-9191.
U Chi Ctr Policy, *(Univ. of Chicago, Center for Policy Study),* 5801 S. Ellis Ave., Rm. 200, Chicago, IL 60637.
U Chicago Dept Geog, *(Univ. of Chicago, Department of Geography, Research Papers; 0-89065),* 5828 S. University Ave., Chicago, IL 60637 Tel 312-753-3930.
U CO Busn Res Div, *(Univ. of Colorado, Business Research Division; 0-89478),* Campus Box 420, Univ of Colorado, Boulder, CO 80309 Tel 303-492-8227.
U Delaware Pr, *(Univ. of Delaware Press; 0-87413),* c/o Associated Univ. Presses, Inc., 4 Cornwall Dr., East Brunswick, NJ 08816 Tel 201-254-0132.
U HI at Manoa Korean
See Ctr Korean U HI at Manoa
U Mich Busn Div Res, *(Univ. of Michigan, Division of Research, Grad. School of Business Administration; 0-87712),* Ann Arbor, MI 48109 Tel 313-764-1366.
U Mich Div Res
See U Mich Busn Div Res
U Mich Mus Anthro, *(Univ. of Michigan, Museum of Anthropology, Pubns. Dept.; 0-932206),* 4009 Museums Bldg., 1109 Geddes, Ann Arbor, MI 48109 Tel 313-764-6867.
U MO-St Louis, *(Univ. of Missouri-Saint Louis; 0-9601616),* 8001 Natural Bridge Rd., St. Louis, MO 63121 Tel 314-553-5168.
U MS Bus Econ, *(Univ. of Mississippi, Bureau of Business & Economic Research),* University, MS 38677 Tel 601-232-7481.
U NC Inst Res Soc Sci, *(Univ. of North Carolina, Institute for Research in Social Science; 0-89143),* IRSS Publications, Manning Hall 026A, Chapel Hill, NC 27514 Tel 919-966-3204.
U of AK Inst Marine, *(Univ. of Alaska, Inst of Marine Science; 0-914500),* Fairbanks, AK 99701 Tel 907-479-7843.
U of Ala Pr, *(Univ. of Alabama Press; 0-8173),* Box 2877, University, AL 35486 Tel 205-348-5180.
U of Ariz Pr, *(Univ. of Arizona Press; 0-8165),* P.O. Box 3398, Tucson, AZ 85722 Tel 602-626-1441.
U of Cal Intl St, *(Univ. of California, Institute of International Studies; 0-87725),* 215 Moses Hall, Berkeley, CA 94720 Tel 415-642-4065.
U of Cal Pr, *(Univ. of California Press; 0-520),* 2223 Fulton St., Berkeley, CA 94720
U of Chicago Pr, *(Univ. of Chicago Press; 0-226),* 5801 Ellis Ave., Chicago, IL 60637 Tel 312-753-3344; Orders to: 11030 S. Langley Ave., Chicago, IL 60628 Tel 312-568-1550. *Imprints:* Chicago Visual Lib (Chicago Visual Library).
U of Denver Intl, *(Univ. of Denver, Colorado Seminary, Grad. School of International Studies; 0-87940),* Graduate School of International Studies, Univ. of Denver, Denver, CO 80208 Tel 303-753-2324.
U of GA Inst Govt, *(Univ. of Georgia, Institute of Government; 0-89854),* Terrell Hall, Athens, GA 30602.
U of Ga Pr, *(Univ. of Georgia Press; 0-8203),* Terrell Hall, Athens, GA 30602 Tel 404-542-2830.
U of Guelph, *(Univ. of Guelph; 0-88955),* c/o John Erickson, 1545 University Dr., Lawrence, KS 66044.
U of Ill Lib Sci, *(Univ. of Illinois Graduate School of Library Science; 0-87845),* Pubns. Office, 249 Armory Bldg., Champaign, IL 61820 Tel 217-333-1359.
U of Ill Pr, *(Univ. of Illinois Press; 0-252),* 54 E. Gregory Dr., P.O. Box 5081, Sta. A, Champaign, IL 61820 Tel 217-333-0957.
U of Iowa Pr, *(Univ. of Iowa Press; 0-87745),* 214 Graphic Services Bldg., Iowa City, IA 52242 Tel 319-353-3181.
U of Iowa Sch Soc Wk, *(Univ. of Iowa, School of Social Work; 0-934936),* Iowa City, IA 52242.
U of KS Ind Stud Div, *(Univ. of Kansas, Independent Study, Div. of Continuing Education; 0-936352),* Lawrence, KS 66045.
U of KS Mus Nat Hist, *(Univ. of Kansas, Museum of Natural History; 0-89338),* Lawrence, KS 66044 Tel 913-864-4540.
U of KS Pubns, *(Univ. of Kansas Pubns.),* Watson Library, Univ. of Kansas, Lawrence, KS 66045.
U of Ky OES Pubns, *(Office of Engineering Services(O E S Pubns.); 0-89779),* College of Engineering, Univ. of Kentucky, Lexington, KY 40506 Tel 606-257-2843.
U of Mass Pr, *(Univ. of Massachusetts Press; 0-87023),* P.O. Box 429, Amherst, MA 01004 Tel 413-545-2217.
U of Miami Pr, *(Univ. of Miami Press; 0-87024),* Orders to: P.O. Box 4836, Hampden Sta., Baltimore, MD 21211 Tel 301-338-7886.
U of Mich Busn Res
See U Mich Busn Div Res
U of Mich Ctr Chinese, *(Univ. of Michigan, Center for Chinese Studies; 0-89264),* 104 Lane Hall, Ann Arbor, MI 48109 Tel 313-763-5888.
U of Mich Inst Labor, *(Univ. of Michigan, Wayne State, Institute of Labor & Industrial Relations; 0-87736),* 401 Fourth St., Ann Arbor, MI 48103 Tel 313-763-1187.
U of Mich Pr, *(Univ. of Michigan Press; 0-472),* P.O. Box 1104, Ann Arbor, MI 48106 Tel 313-764-4330. *Imprints:* AA (Ann Arbor Books).
U of Mich Soc Res, *(Univ. of Michigan, Institute for Social Research; 0-87944),* Publishing Div., P.O. Box 1248, Ann Arbor, MI 48106.
U of Minn Bell Mus, *(Univ. of Minnesota, Bell Museum of Pathology; 0-912922),* P.O. Box 302, Mayo Memorial Bldg., Minneapolis, MN 55455.
U of Minn Comp Ctr, *(Univ. of Minnesota Computer Center; 0-936992),* University of Minnesota, Duluth, MN 55812.

U of Minn Pr, *(Univ. of Minnesota Press; 0-8166),* 2037 University Ave. S.E., Minneapolis, MN 55414 Tel 612-373-3266.
U of Mo Pr, *(Univ. of Missouri Press; 0-8262),* 200 Lewis, Columbia, MO 65211 Tel 314-882-7641.
U of MT Pubns Hist, *(Univ. of Montana Pubns. in History),* Missoula, MT 59812 Tel 406-243-2231.
U of NC Pr, *(Univ. of North Carolina Press; 0-8078),* P.O Box 2288, Chapel Hill, NC 27514 Tel 919-966-3561.
U of Nebr Pr, *(Univ. of Nebraska Press; 0-8032),* 901 N. 17th St., Lincoln, NE 68588 Tel 402-472-3581.
U of Nev Pr, *(Univ. of Nevada Press; 0-87417),* Reno, NV 89557 Tel 702-784-6573.
U of NM Nat Am Std, *(Univ. of New Mexico, Native American Studies; 0-934090),* 1812 Las Lomas N.E., Albuquerque, NM 87131.
U of NM Pr, *(Univ. of New Mexico Press; 0-8263),* Albuquerque, NM 87131 Tel 505-277-2346.
U of Notre Dame Pr, *(Univ. of Notre Dame Press; 0-268),* P.O. Box L, Notre Dame, IN 46556 Tel 219-283-6346; Dist. by: Harper & Row Pubs., Keystone Industrial Park, Scranton, PA 18512.
U of Okla Pr, *(Univ. of Oklahoma Press; 0-8061),* 1005 Asp Ave., Norman, OK 73019 Tel 405-325-5111.
U of Pa Contemp Art, *(Univ. of Pennsylvania, Institute of Contemporary Art; 0-88454),* 34th & Walnut Sts., Philadelphia, PA 19104 Tel 215-243-7108.
U of Pa Pr, *(Univ. of Pennsylvania Press; 0-8122),* 3933 Walnut St., Philadelphia, PA 19104 Tel 215-243-6261.
U of Pittsburgh Pr, *(Univ. of Pittsburgh Press; 0-8229),* 127 N. Bellefield Ave., Pittsburgh, PA 15260 Tel 412-624-4110.
U of PR Pr, *(Univ. of Puerto Rico Press; 0-8477),* P.O. Box X, U.P.R. Sta., Rio Piedras, PR 00931 Tel 809-763-0812.
U of Queensland Pr, *(Univ. of Queensland Press),* Orders to: 5 S. Union St., Lawrence, MA 01843 Tel 617-685-3306.
U of SC Pr, *(Univ. of South Carolina Press; 0-87249),* Columbia, SC 29208 Tel 803-777-5243.
U of Tenn Pr, *(Univ. of Tennessee Press; 0-87049),* 293 Communications Bldg., Knoxville, TN 37916 Tel 615-974-3321.
U of Tex Arlington Pr, *(Univ. of Texas at Arlington Press, The; 0-87706),* Box 19075, Arlington, TX 76019; Orders to: 501 Monroe, Arlington, TX 76019.
U of Tex Busn Res, *(Univ. of Texas, Bureau of Business Research; 0-87755),* Univ. of Texas at Austin, P.O. Box 7459, Univ. Sta., Austin, TX 78712 Tel 512-471-1616.
U of Tex Hum Res, *(Univ. of Texas, Humanities Research Ctr.; 0-87959),* P.O. Box 7219, Austin, TX 78712 Tel 512-471-1833.
U of Tex Inst Tex Culture, *(Univ. of Texas, Institute of Texan Cultures; 0-933164),* P.O. Box 1226, San Antonio, TX 78294.
U of Tex Pr, *(Univ. of Texas Press; 0-292),* P.O. Box 7819, University Sta., Austin, TX 78712 Tel 512-471-4032.
U of Toronto Pr, *(Univ. of Toronto Press; 0-8020),* Orders to: 33 E. Tupper St., Buffalo, NY 14203 Tel 416-978-2052.
U of Utah Pr, *(Univ. of Utah Press; 0-87480),* Salt Lake City, UT 84112 Tel 801-581-6771.
U of Wash Pr, *(Univ. of Washington Press; 0-295),* Seattle, WA 98105 Tel 206-543-4050.
U of Wis Arch-Urban Pl
See U of Wis Ctr Arch-Urban
U of Wis Ctr Arch-Urban, *(Univ. of Wisconsin-Milwaukee, Center for Architecture & Urban Planning Research),* P.O. Box 413, Milwaukee, WI 53201 Tel 414-963-4014.
U of Wis Pr, *(Univ. of Wisconsin Press; 0-299),* 114 North Murray St., Madison, WI 53715 Tel 608-262-4922.
U of Wis-Stevens Point, *(Univ. of Wisconsin-Stevens Point; 0-932310),* Stevens Point, WI 54481.
U OK Ctr Econ, *(Univ. of Oklahoma, Center for Economic & Management Research; 0-931880),* College of Business Administration, 307 West Brooks St., Rm. 4, Norman, OK 73019 Tel 405-325-2931.
U Pr of Amer, *(University Press of America; 0-8191),* 4720 Boston Way, Lanham, MD 20801 Tel 301-459-3366.
U Pr of Hawaii, *(Univ. Press of Hawaii; 0-8248),* 2840 Kolowalu St., Honolulu, HI 96822 Tel 808-948-8255. *Imprints:* Korea Devel Inst (Korea Development Institute).
U Pr of Idaho, *(Univ. Press of Idaho; 0-89301),* Div. of the Idaho Research Foundation, Inc., University Sta., Box 3368, Moscow, ID 83843 Tel 208-885-7925.
U Pr of Ky, *(Univ. Press of Kentucky; 0-8131),* Lexington, KY 40506 Tel 606-258-2951.
U Pr of Miss, *(Univ. Press of Mississippi; 0-87805),* 3825 Ridgewood Rd., Jackson, MS 39211 Tel 601-982-6205.
U Pr of New Eng, *(Univ. Press of New England; 0-87451),* P. O. Box 979, Hanover, NH 03755 Tel 603-646-3348.
U Pr of Va, *(Univ. Press of Virginia; 0-8139),* P.O. Box 3608, University Sta., Charlottesville, VA 22903 Tel 804-924-3131. *Imprints:* Colonial Soc MA (Colonial Society of Massachusetts).
U Presses Fla, *(Univ. Presses of Fla.; 0-8130),* 15 N.W. 15th St., Gainesville, FL 32603 Tel 904-392-1351.
U Pubns Amer, *(University Pubns. of America, Inc.; 0-89093),* 5630 Connecticut Ave., Washington, DC 20015.
U S Cal Andrus Geron
See USC Andrus Geron
U Tex Austin Film Lib, *(Univ. of Texas at Austin Film Library; 0-913648),* Drawer W, University Sta., Austin, TX 78712 Tel 512-471-3573.
U Tex Studia
See Studia Hispanica
U TX Austin Gen Libs, *(Univ. of Texas at Austin, General Libraries; 0-930214),* Univ. of Texas at Austin, P.O. Box P, Austin, TX 78712 Tel 512-471-3811.
U Wis Grad Sch Busn, *(Univ. of Wisconsin-Madison, Graduate School of Business),* 1155 Observatory Dr., Madison, WI 53706.
UAHC, *(Union of American Hebrew Congregations; 0-8074),* 838 Fifth Ave., New York, NY 10021 Tel 212-249-0100.
UC Ctr S&SE Asian, *(University of California, Berkeley, Center for SE Asian Studies),* Dist. by: Cellar Book Shop, 18090 Wyoming, Detroit, MI 46221.
UCDLA, *(Univ. of California, Div. of Library Automation; 0-913248),* 2150 Shattuck Ave., Berkeley, CA 94720 Tel 415-642-9485.
Uchill, *(Uchill, Ida Libert; 0-9604468),* P.O. Box 22608, Wellshire Sta., Denver, CO 80222 Tel 303-355-9829.
UCLA Arch, *(Univ. of California, Los Angeles, Institute of Archaeology; 0-917956),* 405 Hilgard Ave., Los Angeles, CA 90024 Tel 213-825-1720.
UCLA Busn Forecasting, *(Univ. of California, Los Angeles, Business Forecasting Project; 0-913404),* Graduate School of Management, Rm. 6249 C, Los Angeles, CA 90024 Tel 213-825-1623.
UCLA Chicano Stud, *(Univ. of California, Los Angeles Chicano Studies Research Center, Pubns. Unit; 0-89551),* 3122 Campbell Hall, 405 Hilgard Ave., Los Angeles, CA 90024 Tel 213-825-2642.
UCLA Dept Biomath, *(Univ. of California, Los Angeles, Dept. of Biomathematics; 0-935386),* Los Angeles, CA 90024 Tel 213-825-2164.
UCLA Lat Am Ctr, *(Univ. of California, Latin American Center; 0-87903),* 405 Hilgard Ave., Los Angeles, CA 90024 Tel 213-825-6634.
UCLA Tissue, *(UCLA Tissue Typing Laboratory; 0-9604606),* UCLA School of Medicine, Los Angeles, CA 90024.
Ukrainian Acad, *(Ukrainian Academic Press; 0-87287),* Div. of Libraries Unlimited, Inc., P.O. Box 263, Littleton, CO 80160 Tel 303-770-1220.
Ukrainian Res, *(Ukrainian Research Foundation; 0-934760),* 6931 S. Yosemite St., Englewood, CO 80112.
Uleck Assoc, *(Uleck, R. B., Associates; 0-937562),* 34 Goodport Court, Gaithersburg, MD 20760.
Ulrich, *(Ulrich's Books, Inc.; 0-914004),* 549 E. University Ave., Ann Arbor, MI 48104 Tel 313-662-3201.
UN, *(United Nations; 0-680),* Sales Section, Publishing Division, New York, NY 10017.
UNABASHED Lib, *(UNABASHED Librarian; 0-916444),* G.P.O. Box 2631, New York, NY 10001.
Unarius, *(Unarius Educational Foundation; 0-932642),* 145 S Magnolia Ave., El Cajon, CA 92021 Tel 714-447-4170; Orders to: P.O. Box 1042, El Cajon, CA 92022.
Undena Pubns, *(Undena Pubns.; 0-89003),* P.O. Box 97, Malibu, CA 90265.
Undersea Res, *(Undersea Resources, Ltd.; 0-916630),* P.O. Box 15844, Honolulu, HI 96815 Tel 808-941-5471.
Underwood-Miller, *(Underwood/Miller; 0-934438),* 239 N. 4th St., Columbia, PA 17512; P.O. Box 5402, San Francisco, CA 94101 Tel 415-754-7920; Dist. by: F&SF Book Co., Inc., P.O. Box 415, Staten Island, NY 10302.
UNESCO *Imprint of* **Unipub**
Ungar, *(Ungar, Frederick, Publishing Co., Inc.; 0-8044),* 250 Park Ave. S., New York, NY 10003 Tel 212-473-7885.
Unicorn Pr, *(Unicorn Press; 0-87775),* P.O. Box 3307, Greensboro, NC 27402 Tel 919-273-2688.
Unicorn VA, *(Unicorn; 0-9604564),* P.O. Box 1153, Fredericksburg, VA 22401.
Unif Theol Seminary, *(Unification Theological Seminary; 0-932894),* 10 Dock Rd., Barrytown, NY 12507 Tel 914-758-8838; Dist. by: Rose of Sharon Press, Inc., G.P.O. Box 2432, New York, NY 10116.
Unilaw *Imprint of* **Donning Co**
Union League PA, *(Union League of Philadelphia; 0-915810),* 140 S. Broad St., Philadelphia, PA 19102 Tel 215-563-6500.
Unipub, *(Unipub; 0-89059),* A Xerox Publishing Co., 345 Park Ave. S., New York, NY 10010 Tel 212-686-4707. *Imprints:* APO (Asian Productivity Organization); CIRS (Cambridge Information & Research Services, Ltd.); Europa (Europa); FAO (Food & Agriculture Organization); GATT (General Agreement on Tariffs & Trade); Gower (Gower Press Pubns.); IAEA (International Atomic Energy Agency); IDRC (International Development Research Centre); IIR (International Institute of Refrigeration); IUCN (International Union for Conservation of Nature & Natural Resources); SSC (Supplies & Services, Government of Canada); UNESCO (United Nations Educational, Scientific & Cultural Organization); WIPO (World Intellectual Property Organization); WMO (World Meterological Organization); WW (World Watch).
Unique Ent, *(Unique Enterprises),* 1225 N. Edgemont, No. 34, Los Angeles, CA 90029.
Unique Pubns, *(Unique Pubns.; 0-86568),* 7011 Sunset Blvd., Hollywood, CA 90028.
Unitarian, *(Unitarian Universalist Church, The),* E. Main St., Canton, NY 13617.
United Bible, *(United Bible Societies),* 1865 Broadway, New York, NY 10023.
United Church Pr
See Pilgrim NY
United Front
See Banner Pr IL
United Pub NY, *(United Publishing Co., The; 0-938584),* P.O. Box 719, East Worcester, NY 12064.
United Syn Bk, *(United Synagogue Book Service; 0-8381),* 155 Fifth Ave., New York, NY 10010 Tel 212-533-7800.
Unity Bks, *(Unity Books; 0-87159),* Unity School of Christianity, Unity Village, MO 64065, Tel 816-524-3550.
Unity Pr, *(Unity Press; 0-913300),* 235 Hoover Rd., Santa Cruz, CA 95065 Tel 408-462-3344.
Univ Assocs, *(University Associates; 0-88390),* 8517 Production Ave., P. O. Box 26240, San Diego, CA 92126 Tel 714-578-5900.
Univ Bks, *(University Books, Inc.; 0-8216),* Div. of Lyle Stuart, Inc., 120 Enterprise Ave., Secaucus, NJ 07094 Tel 201-866-0490.
Univ Goddess, *(Universal Goddess Center Inc.; 0-937946),* P.O. Box 671, Malibu, CA 90265 Tel 213-457-7119; Dist. by: The Distributors, 702 S. Michigan, South Bend, IN 46618.
Univ Marketing, *(Universal Marketing Service, Inc.),* 4090 Jason St., Denver, CO 80211.

Univ Microfilms, *(University Microfilms International; 0-8357),* A Xerox Publishing Co., 300 N. Zeeb Rd., Ann Arbor, MI 48106 Tel 313-761-4700; Any Book with Standard-Size Type Can Be Reproduced in Large Type Format with Permission from Author or Publisher.
Univ Mus of U PA, *(University Museum, Univ. of Pennsylvania),* 33rd & Spruce Sts., Philadelphia, PA 19104 Tel 215-243-4119.
Univ of Trees, *(Univ. of the Trees Press; 0-916438),* P.O. Box 644, 13165 Pine St., Boulder Creek, CA 95006 Tel 408-338-2161.
Univ of Wis Latin Am, *(Univ. of Wisconsin-Milwaukee, Center for Latin America; 0-930450),* Univ. of Wisconsin-Milwaukee, Box 413, Milwaukee, WI 53201 Tel 414-963-5987.
Univ Park, *(University Park Press; 0-8391),* 300 N. Charles St., Baltimore, MD 21201 Tel 301-547-0700.
Univ Place, *(University Place Book Shop; 0-911556),* 821 Broadway, New York, NY 10003 Tel 212-254-5998.
Univ Pr OH, *(Univ. Press, Inc.; 0-9603614),* P.O. Box 24268, Cleveland, OH 44124 Tel 216-442-0800.
Univ SC Natl Info, *(University of Southern California National Information Center for Educational Media; 0-89320),* NICEM/USC, University Park, Los Angeles, CA 90007 Tel 213-743-6681.
Univ Sci Bks, *(University Science Books; 0-935702),* 20 Edgehill Rd., Mill Valley, CA 94941.
Univ-Wide Lib
See UCDLA
Univelt Inc, *(Univelt, Inc.),* P.O. Box 28130, San Diego, CA 92128 Tel 714-746-4005.
Universe, *(Universe Books, Inc.; 0-87663),* 381 Park Ave., S., New York, NY 10016 Tel 212-685-7400. *Imprints:* Pica Pr (Pica Press).
Universe Pub Co, *(Universe Publishing Co.; 0-935484),* 185 W. Demarest Ave., Englewood, NJ 07631 Tel 201-567-4296.
Universitet, *(Universitetsforlaget; 82-00),* C/O Columbia Univ. Press, 562 W. 113th St., New York, NY 10025; Dist. by: Columbia Univ. Press, 136 S. Broadway, Irvington-on-Hudson, NY 10533.
University *Imprint of* **Exposition**
Unmuzzled Ox, *(Unmuzzled Ox Press),* 105 Hudson St., New York, NY 10013 Tel 212-431-8829.
Unpublished Edns
See Printed Edns
UPB, *(Univ. Press Books; 0-8295),* 302 Fifth Ave., New York, NY 10001 Tel 212-564-2049.
UPBS
See UPB
Upjohn Inst, *(Upjohn, W.E., Institute for Employment Research; 0-911558),* 300 S. Westnedge Ave., Kalamazoo, MI 49007 Tel 616-343-5541.
Upland Pr, *(Upland Press; 0-932554),* P.O. Box 7390, Chicago, IL 60680 Tel 312-266-2087.
Upper Room, *(Upper Room; 0-8358),* 1908 Grand Ave., Nashville, TN 37202 Tel 615-327-2700.
Uranus Pub, *(Uranus Publishing Co.; 0-9601080),* 5050 Calatrana Dr., Woodland Hills, CA 91364.
Urban & S, *(Urban & Schwarzenberg; 0-8067),* 7 E. Redwood St., Baltimore, MD 21202 Tel 301-539-2550.
Urban Bks, *(Urban Books),* 295 Grizzly Peak Blvd., Berkeley, CA 94708 Tel 415-524-3315.
Urban Inst, *(Urban Institute Press; 0-87766),* 2100 "M" St., N.W., Washington, DC 20037 Tel 202-223-1950.
Urban Land, *(Urban Land Institute; 0-87420),* 1090 Vermont Ave. N. W., Washington, DC 20005 Tel 202-289-8500.
Urbanek, *(Urbanek, Mae),* Lusk, WY 82225 Tel 307-334-2473.
URI MAS, *(Univ. of Rhode Island, Marine Advisory Service),* Univ. of Rhode Island, Narragansett Bay Campus, Narragansett, RI 02882 Tel 401-792-6211.
Urizen Bks, *(Urizen Books, Inc.; 0-89396; 0-916354),* 66 W. Broadway, New York, NY 10007 Tel 212-962-3413.
US Capitol Hist Soc, *(U.S. Capitol Historical Society; 0-916200),* 200 Maryland Ave. N.E., Washington, DC 20002 Tel 202-543-8919.
US Coast Guard, *(United States Coast Guard Auxiliary National Board Inc.; 0-930028),* 306 Wilson Rd., Newark, DE 19711 Tel 302-731-4650.
US Comm Refugees, *(U. S. Committee for Refugees; 0-936548),* 20 W. 40th St., 7th Floor, New York, NY 10018.
US Comm Unicef, *(U. S. Committee for UNICEF; 0-935738),* 331 E. 38th St., New York, NY 10016 Tel 212-686-5522.
US Games Syst, *(U. S. Games Systems, Inc.; 0-913866),* 38 E. 32nd St., New York, NY 10016 Tel 212-685-4300.
US Pubs, *(U. S. Pubs. Assn., Inc.; 0-911548),* 46 Lafayette Ave., New Rochelle, NY 10801 Tel 914-576-1121.
US Ski, *(U.S. Ski Assn.; 0-9604162),* Box 777, Brattleboro, VT 05301.
US Trademark, *(U. S. Trademark Assn.),* 6 E. 45th St., New York, NY 10017 Tel 212-986-5880.
USC Andrus Geron, *(Univ. of Southern California, Andrus Gerontology Center),* Publications Office, University Park, CA 90007 Tel 213-743-5160.
USTA, *(U. S. Tennis Assn.),* USTA Pubns., 729 Alexander Rd., Princeton, NJ 08540 Tel 609-452-2580.
UTA Pr, *(UTA Press; 0-932408),* Box 929, Univ. of Texas at Arlington, Arlington, TX 76019 Tel 817-273-3391.
Utah St Hist Soc, *(Utah State Historical Society; 0-913738),* 300 Rio Grande, Salt Lake City, UT 84101 Tel 801-533-6024.
Utah St U Pr, *(Utah State Univ. Press; 0-87421),* UMC 95, Logan, UT 84322 Tel 801-750-1362.
UWSP Found Pr, *(UWSP Foundation Press; 0-932310),* Univ. of Wisconsin-Stevens Point, Stevens Point, WI 54481.
Uzzano Pr, *(Uzzano Press; 0-930600),* c/o Robert Schuler, 511 Sunset Dr., Menomonie, WI 54751; Orders to: Bookslinger, 2163 Ford Pkwy., Saint Paul, MN 55116.
V E Wysinger, *(Wysinger, Vossa E.),* P.O. Box 158, Berkeley, CA 94701 Tel 415-655-1742.
V H Ho, *(Ho, Van H., Assocs.; 0-9602904),* P.O. Box 130, Harbor City, CA 90710.
V S Epstein, *(Epstein, Vivian Sheldon; 0-9601002),* 212 S. Dexter St., Denver, CO 80222 Tel 303-322-7450.
V S Morris, *(Morris, Victoria S., Books; 0-914318),* 39 Gleneden Ave., Oakland, CA 94611 Tel 415-652-2013.
VA Bk, *(Virginia Book Co.; 0-911578),* Box 431, Berryville, VA 22611 Tel 703-955-1428.
VA City Rest, *(Virginia City Restoration Corp.),* P.O. Box 334, Los Altos, CA 94022.
VA Mus Fine Arts, *(Virginia Museum of Fine Arts; 0-917046),* Boulevard & Grove Ave., Richmond, VA 23221 Tel 804-257-0818.
VA State Lib, *(Virginia State Library; 0-88490),* 12th & Capitol Sts., Richmond, VA 23219 Tel 804-786-2312.
Vagabond Pr, *(Vagabond Press; 0-912824),* 1610 N. Water St., Ellensburg, WA 98926 Tel 509-925-5634.
Val-Hse Pub, *(Val-House Publishing; 0-939354),* 2903 Carriage Lane, P.O. Box 490443, College Park, GA 30349.
Valencia, *(Valencia, Jerry; 0-9604784),* 7525 Raytheon Rd., San Diego, CA 92111; Orders to: P.O. Box 758, La Jolla, CA 92038 Tel 714-226-1181.
Valkyrie Pr, *(Valkyrie Press, Inc.; 0-912760; 0-934616),* 2135 First Ave., S., St. Petersburg, FL 33712 Tel 813-822-6069.
Vallentine Mitchell
See Biblio Dist
Valley Calif
See Western Tanager
Valley Calif *Imprint of* **Western Tanager**
Valley Sun, *(Valley of the Sun Publishing Co.; 0-911842),* Box 4276, Scottsdale, AZ 85258 Tel 602-945-2644.
Valuation, *(Valuation Press Inc.; 0-930458),* 661 Washington St., Marina Del Rey, CA 90291; Orders to: P.O. Box 1080, Marina Del Ray, CA 90291 Tel 213-822-3691.
Value Comm, *(Value Communications, Inc.; 0-916392),* Subs. of Oak Tree Pubns., Inc., 11175 Flintkote Ave., Suite C, San Diego, CA 92121 Tel 714-457-3200.
Van Nos Reinhold, *(Van Nostrand Reinhold Co.; 0-442),* Div. of Litton Educational Publishing, Inc., 135 W. 50th St., New York, NY 10020 Tel 212-265-8700; Orders to: Lepi Order Processing, 7625 Empire Dr., Florence, KY 41042.
Van Nostrand
See D Van Nostrand
Vance Biblios, *(Vance Bibliographies),* 112 N. Charter St., Monticello, IL 61856 Tel 217-762-3831.
Vanderbilt U Pr, *(Vanderbilt Univ. Press; 0-8265),* 2505(Rear) West End Ave., Nashville, TN 37203 Tel 615-322-3585.
Vanguard, *(Vanguard Press, Inc.; 0-8149),* 424 Madison Ave., New York, NY 10017 Tel 212-753-3906.
VanMeer Pubns, *(VanMeer Pubns., Inc.; 0-937826),* P.O. Box 1289, Clearwater, FL 33517 Tel 813-725-3503.
Vanous, *(Vanous, Arthur, Co.; 0-89918),* 616 Kinderkamack Rd., River Edge, NJ 07661 Tel 201-265-7555; Orders to: P.O. Box A, River Edge, NJ 07661.
Vantage, *(Vantage Press, Inc.; 0-533),* 516 W. 34th St., New York, NY 10001 Tel 212-736-1767.
Variety Pr, *(Variety Press),* 5214 Starkridge, Houston, TX 77035 Tel 713-721-5919.
Vector Assocs, *(Vector Associates; 0-930808),* P.O. Box 6215, Bellevue, WA 98007 Tel 415-794-0462.
Vedanta Pr, *(Vedanta Press; 0-87481),* 1946 Vedanta Place, Hollywood, CA 90068 Tel 213-465-7114; Orders to: P.O. Box 290, Hollywood, CA 90028.
Vedanta Soc
See Vedanta Soc St Louis
Vedanta Soc St Louis, *(Vedanta Society of St. Louis; 0-916356),* 205 S. Skinker Blvd., St. Louis, MO 63105 Tel 314-721-5118.
Vendome, *(Vendome Press, The; 0-86565),* 515 Madison Ave., New York, NY 10022; Dist. by: Viking Press, 625 Madison Ave., New York, NY 10022.
Ventnor, *(Ventnor Pubs.; 0-911566),* P.O. Box 2078, Ventnor, NJ 08406.
Ventura
See Ventura Pr
Ventura Pr, *(Ventura Press; 0-917438),* P.O. Box 1076, Guerneville, CA 95446.
Verbatim, *(Verbatim; 0-930454),* Box 668, Essex, CT 06426 Tel 203-767-8248.
Veritas, *(Veritas Foundation; 0-911568),* P.O. Box 111, West Sayville, NY 11796; Formerly Named Probe.
Veritas Pubns, *(Veritas Pubns.; 0-938264),* P.O. Box 4418, Arlington, VA 22204.
Verlag Chemie, *(Verlag Chemie International; 0-89573),* 1020 N.W. 6th St., Plaza Centre, Suite E, Deerfield Beach, FL 33441 Tel 305-428-5566.
Vermeer Arts, *(Vermeer Arts, Ltd.; 0-934744),* 1676 W. 3rd Ave., Durango, CO 81301 Tel 303-247-3960.
Vermont Bks, *(Vermont Books, Inc.; 0-911570),* 38 Main St., Middlebury, VT 05753 Tel 802-388-2061.
Vermont Crossroads, *(Vermont Crossroads Press; 0-915248),* P.O. Box 30, Waitsfield, VT 05667 Tel 802-496-2469; Orders to: Rd 1, Box 147, Plainfield, VT 05667 Tel 802-454-7715.
Verry, *(Verry, Lawrence, Inc.; 0-8426),* Mystic, CT 06355 Tel 203-536-7373.
Versailles, *(Versailles, Elizabeth Starr),* 42 Nash Hill Rd., Williamsburg, MA 01096 Tel 413-268-7576.
Verta Pr, *(Verta Press; 0-930876),* 15 Randolph Place, N.W., Washington, DC 20001 Tel 202-387-0414.
Vestal, *(Vestal Press Ltd.; 0-911572),* P.O. Box 97, 320 N. Jensen Rd., Vestal, NY 13850 Tel 607-797-4872.
Vicky Bird Bks
See V S Morris
Victor Bks, *(Victor Books; 0-88207; 0-89693),* P.O. Box 1825, Wheaton, IL 60187 Tel 312-668-6000; Orders to: 1825 College Ave., Wheaton, IL 60187.
Victoria Hse, *(Victoria House, Pubs.; 0-918480),* 2218 N.E. 8th Ave., Portland, OR 97212 Tel 503-284-4801.
Victorious Ministry, *(Victorious Ministry Through Christ, Inc.; 0-9605178),* P.O. Box 1804, Winter Park, FL 32790; Dist. by: Impact Books, Kirkwood, MO 63122.

Vida Pubs *See* Life Pubs Intl
Video-Info, *(Video-Info Pubns.; 0-931294),* P.O. Box 1507, Santa Barbara, CA 93102 Tel 805-682-1198.
Viking Pr, *(Viking Press, Inc.; 0-670),* 625 Madison Ave., New York, NY 10022 Tel 212-755-4330; Orders to: Viking/Penguin, Inc., 299 Murray Hill Pkwy., East Rutherford, NJ 07073.
Vin *Imprint of* **Random**
Vintage Bk Co, *(Vintage Book Co.; 0-938164),* Box 16182, Elway Sta., St. Paul, MN 55116 Tel 612-690-2363.
Virtuoso, *(Virtuoso Pubns., Inc.; 0-918624),* 206 S.E. 46th Lane, Cape Coral, FL 33904 Tel 813-549-1802; Orders to: 206 S. E. 46th Lane, Cape Coral, FL 33904.
Visage Pr, *(Visage Press, Inc.; 0-916818),* 200 N. Glebe Rd., Suite 906, Arlington, VA 22203 Tel 703-528-8872.
Visibility Ent, *(Visibility Enterprises; 0-9603740),* 11 W. 81st St., New York, NY 10024.
Vision Hse, *(Vision House Pubs.; 0-88449),* 1651 E. Edinger, Suite 104, Santa Ana, CA 92705 Tel 714-558-0511.
Visual Evangels, *(Visual Evangels Publishing Co.; 0-915398),* 1401 Ohio St., Michigan City, IN 46360.
Vitality Assocs, *(Vitality Associates; 0-930918),* P.O. Box 154, Saratoga, CA 95070 Tel 408-867-1241.
Volkwein Bros, *(Volkwein Brothers, Inc.; 0-913650),* 117 Sandusky St., Pittsburgh, PA 15212 Tel 412-322-5100.
Volunteer Pubns, *(Volunteer Pubns.; 0-938310),* P.O. Box 171156, Memphis, TN 38117.
VoyB *Imprint of* **HarBraceJ**
VSBE, *(Very Serious Business Enterprises; 0-9605304),* P.O. Box 356, Newark, NJ 07101.
VT Hist Soc, *(Vermont Historical Society; 0-934720),* 109 State St., Montpelier, VT 05602 Tel 802-828-2291.
VT Life Mag, *(Vermont Life Magazine; 0-936896),* 61 Elm St., Montpelier, VT 05602.
W A Benjamin
See A-W
W A Benjamin
See Benjamin-Cummings
W A Jewell, *(Jewell, Willis A.),* 502 Benton St., Port Townsend, WA 98368 Tel 206-385-4342.
W A Linder, *(Linder, William A., Co., Pubs.; 0-934844),* P.O. Box 443, Lindsborg, KS 67456 Tel 913-227-2514.
W A Reilly, *(Reilly, William A.; 0-934258),* P.O. Box 63, 6 Crest Dr., Dover, MA 02030 Tel 617-785-0401.
W A Tieck, *(Tieck, W. A.; 0-9600398),* 3930 Bailey Ave., Bronx, NY 10463 Tel 212-549-5566.
W Bailey Pub, *(Bailey, William, Pub.; 0-9604196),* P.O. Box 985, Santa Barbara, CA 93102 Tel 805-965-3686.
W D Farmer, *(Farmer, W. D., Residence Designer, Inc.; 0-931518),* P.O. Box 49463, Atlanta, GA 30359 Tel 404-934-7380.
W D Leyerle, *(Leyerle, William D.; 0-9602296),* 28 Stanley St., Mt. Morris, NY 14510 Tel 716-658-2193; Orders to: Vocal Development Through Organic Imagery, or Leyerle Pubns., Box 384, Geneseo, NY 14454.
W D Linscott, *(Linscott, William D.; 0-9604920),* 40 Glen Dr., Mill Valley, CA 94941 Tel 415-383-1014.
W Fox, *(Fox, Wesley; 0-9604122),* P.O. Box 492, Brisbane, CA 94005.
W Fraser Pubs, *(Fraser, Worden, Pubs.; 0-936582),* 605 Cowper St., Palo Alto, CA 94301; Dist. by: Semiconductor Industry Assn., 20380 Town Center Lane, No. 155, Cupertino, CA 95014.
W H Anderson
See Anderson Pub Co
W H Freeman, *(Freeman, W. H., & Co.; 0-7167),* 660 Market St., San Francisco, CA 94104 Tel 415-391-5870.
W H Lord, *(Lord, William H.),* 9210 N. College Ave., Indianapolis, IN 46240 Tel 317-846-3907.
W H Wise, *(Wise, Wm. H., & Co., Inc; 0-8349),* 336 Mountain Rd., Union City, NJ 07087 Tel 201-864-5200.
W J Johnson
See Walter J Johnson
W Kaufmann, *(Kaufmann, William, Inc.; 0-913232; 0-86576),* 1 First St., Los Altos, CA 94022 Tel 415-948-5810.
W L Sheppard *(W. L. Sheppard)* 923 Old Manoa Rd., Havertown, PA 19083
W M Taylor, *(Taylor, William M.),* Essex Professional Ctr., 412 Red Hill Ave., San Anselmo, CA 94960 Tel 415-457-2214.
W N Stryker, *(Stryker, William Norman),* 7935 San Leandro Place, Alexandria, VA 22309.
W R Corliss
See Sourcebook
W R Palmer
See Heathcote
W S Hein, *(Hein, William S., & Co., Inc.; 0-89941; 0-930342),* Hein Bldg. 1285 Main St., Buffalo, NY 14209 Tel 716-882-2600.
W S Sullwold, *(Sullwold, William S., Publishing, Inc.; 0-88492),* 18 Pearl St., Taunton, MA 02780 Tel 617-823-0924.
W Thomas Taylor, *(Taylor, W. Thomas, Bookseller; 0-935072),* P.O. Box 5343, Austin, TX 78763 Tel 512-451-5406.
W Torda, *(Torda, W.),* 101 W. 12th St., New York, NY 10011.
W W Gaunt, *(Gaunt, Wm. W., & Sons, Inc.; 0-912004),* 3011 Gulf Dr., Holmes Beach, FL 33510 Tel 813-778-5211.
Wadsworth
See Wadsworth Pub
Wadsworth Pub, *(Wadsworth Publishing Co.; 0-534),* 10 Davis Dr., Belmont, CA 94002 Tel 415-595-2350. *Imprints:* Breton Pubs (Breton Pubs.).
Wake-Brook, *(Wake-Brook House; 0-87482),* 960 N.W. 53rd St., Fort Lauderdale, FL 33309 Tel 305-776-5884; June 1st Through October 15th, Contact at: P.O. Box 153, Hyannis, MA 02601, Tel: 617-775-5860.
Wake Forest, *(Wake Forest Univ. Press; 0-916390),* P.O. Box 7333, Reynolda Sta., Winston Salem, NC 27109 Tel 919-761-5448.
Walck, *(Walck, Henry Z., Inc.; 0-8098),* Div. of David McKay Co. Inc., c/o David McKay Co., Inc., 2 Park Ave., New York, NY 10016 Tel 212-340-9800.
Walden Pr, *(Walden Press; 0-911938),* 423 S. Franklin Ave., Flint, MI 48503.
Waldrop Pubns, *(Waldrop Pubns.; 0-9603364),* Box 396, Mt. Baldy, CA 91759 Tel 714-985-6128.
Walker & Co, *(Walker & Co.; 0-8027),* 720 Fifth Ave., New York, NY 10019 Tel 212-265-3632.
Walker Educ, *(Walker Educational Book Corp.; 0-8027),* Affiliate of Walker & Co., 720 Fifth Ave., New York, NY 10019 Tel 212-265-3632.
Walkers Manual, *(Walkers Manual Inc.; 0-916234),* 5855 Naples Plaza, Suite 101, Long Beach, CA 90803 Tel 213-434-3468.
Wallace-Homestead, *(Wallace-Homestead Book Co.; 0-87069),* 1912 Grand Ave., Des Moines, IA 50305 Tel 515-243-6181.
Wallcur Inc, *(Wallcur, Inc.; 0-918082),* 700 Island View Dr., Seal Beach, CA 90740 Tel 213-598-2385.
Walnut AZ, *(Walnut Press; 0-931318),* P.O. Box 17210, Fountain Hills, AZ 85268 Tel 602-837-9118.
Walter J Johnson, *(Johnson, Walter J., Inc.; 0-8472),* 355 Chestnut St., Norwood, NJ 07648 Tel 201-767-1303.
Walterick Pubs, *(Walterick Pubs.; 0-937396),* Box 2216, Kansas City, KS 66110 Tel 913-371-3273.
Walters, *(Walters),* 3100 N. Lake Shore Dr., Suite 2103, Chicago, IL 60657 Tel 212-989-1784.
Wampeter Pr, *(Wampeter Press; 0-931694),* P.O. Box 512, Green Harbor, MA 02041.
Wanderer Bks, *(Wanderer Books; 0-671),* Div. of Simon & Schuster, 1230 Ave. of the Americas, New York, NY 10020 Tel 212-245-6400.
Wards Comm, *(Wards Communications, Inc.),* 28 W. Adams, Detroit, MI 48226 Tel 313-962-4433.
Warman, *(Warman, E. G., Publishing,Inc.; 0-911594),* 540 Morgantown Rd., Uniontown, PA 15401 Tel 412-437-9717.
Warne, *(Warne, Frederick, & Co., Inc.; 0-7232),* 2 Park Ave., New York, NY 10016 Tel 212-686-9630.
Warner Bks, *(Warner Books, Inc.; 0-446),* Orders to: Independent News Co., 75 Rockefeller Plaza, New York, NY 10019 Tel 212-484-8000; Name Formerly Paperback Lib.
Wasatch Pubs, *(Wasatch Pubs., Inc.; 0-915272),* 4647 Idlewild Rd., Salt Lake City, UT 84117 Tel 801-278-3174.
Wash Busn Info, *(Washington Business Information, Inc.; 0-914176),* 235 National Press Bldg., Washington, DC 20045 Tel 202-737-2232.
Wash Intl Arts, *(Washington International Arts Letter; 0-912072),* 325 Pennsylvania Ave., S.E., Washington, DC 20003 Tel 202-488-0800; Orders to: P.O. Box 9005, Washington, DC 20003.
Wash Launderan, *(Wash Launderan Press; 0-9605326),* 5804 Ingersoll Ave., Des Moines, IA 50312.
Wash Park, *(Washington Park Press; 0-9605460),* 7 Englewood Place, Albany, NY 12203.
Wash Res, *(Washington Researchers; 0-934940),* 918 Sixteenth St. N.W., Washington, DC 20006 Tel 202-833-2230.
Wash U Gallery, *(Washington Univ., Gallery of Art; 0-936316),* Campus Box 1189, St. Louis, MO 63130.
Wash Writers Pub, *(Washington Writers Publishing House; 0-931846),* P.O. Box 50068, Washington, DC 20004.
Washingtonian, *(Washingtonian Books; 0-915168),* 1828 L St., N.W. Suite 200, Washington, DC 20036 Tel 202-296-3600.
Water Info, *(Water Information Center, Inc.; 0-912394),* The North Shore Atrium, 6800 Jericho Turnpike, Syosset, NY 11791 Tel 516-921-7690.
Water Mark, *(Water Mark Press; 0-931956),* 175 East Shore Rd., Huntington Bay, NY 11743 Tel 516-549-1150.
Waterfall Pr, *(Waterfall Press; 0-932278),* 1357 Hopkins St., Berkeley, CA 94702 Tel 415-527-7790.
Waterside, *(Waterside Press; 0-936628),* Box 1298, Stuyvesant Sta., New York, NY 10009.
Watson-Guptill, *(Watson-Guptill Pubns., Inc.; 0-8230),* 1 Astor Plaza, 1515 Broadway, New York, NY 10036 Tel 212-764-7300; Orders to: 2160 Patterson St., Cincinnati, OH 45214 Tel 513-381-6450. *Imprints:* Whitney Lib (Whitney Library).
Watts, *(Watts, Franklin, Inc.; 0-531),* Subs. of Grolier Inc., 730 Fifth Ave., New York, NY 10019 Tel 212-757-4050. *Imprints:* Fontana Pap (Fontana Paperbacks).
Waumbek, *(Waumbek Books; 0-9603106),* P.O. Box 573, Ashland, NH 03217 Tel 603-968-7959.
Waveland Pr, *(Waveland Press Inc.; 0-917974),* P.O. Box 400, Prospect Heights, IL 60070 Tel 312-634-0081.
Way of Seeing *(A Way of Seeing Inc.),* 2869 Grant Dr., Ann Arbor, MI 48104
Wayne St U Pr, *(Wayne State Univ. Press; 0-8143),* The Leonard N. Simons Bldg., 5959 Woodward Ave., Detroit, MI 48202 Tel 313-577-4603.
Weatherford, *(Weatherford, R.M., Press; 0-9604078),* 10902 Woods Creek Rd., Monroe, WA 98272 Tel 206-794-4318.
Weatherhill, *(Weatherhill, John, Inc.; 0-8348),* Asia House, Derby Square, Salem, MA 01970 Tel 617-745-8257; Dist. by: Charles E. Tuttle, Co., Inc., 28 S. Main St., Rutland, VT 05701.
Weatherman, *(Weatherman, Hazel Marie; 0-913074),* Rte. 1, Box 357A, Ozark, MO 65721 Tel 417-485-7812; c/o Glassbooks, Inc., Rte. 1, Box 357A, Ozark, MO 65721.
Web Pub Hse, *(Web Publishing House, Inc., The),* P.O. Box 374, Olney, MD 20832.
Webb-Newcomb, *(Webb-Newcomb Company, Inc.; 0-935054),* 308 N.E. Vance St., Wilson, NC 27893 Tel 919-291-7231.
Webster-McGraw, *(Webster),* Div. of McGraw-Hill Book Co., 1221 Ave. of Americas, New York, NY 10020.
Wedge Pub, *(Wedge Publishing),* c/o Radix Books, Inc., P.O. Box 171, Beaver Falls, PA 15010.
Wee Smile, *(Wee Smile Books; 0-9605444),* P.O. Box 1329, Sparks, NV 89431.
Weills
See Berkley Pub
Weinberg, *(Weinberg, Michael Aron; 0-9601014),* P.O. Box 27957, Los Angeles, CA 90027 Tel 213-661-9844.

Weiner
See Public Relations
Weiser, *(Weiser, Samuel, Inc.; 0-87728),* P.O. Box 612, York Beach, ME 03910 Tel 207-363-4393.
Weiss Pub, *(Weiss Publishing Co., Inc.; 0-916720),* 5309 W. Grace St., Richmond, VA 23226 Tel 804-282-4641.
Weist Pub OH, *(Weist Publishing Co., The; 0-938166),* P.O. Box 164, Englewood, OH 45322.
Wellington, *(Wellington Books),* Dist. by: Charles T. Branford Co., 19 Calvin Rd., Box 16, Watertown, MA 02172.
Wendover
See Bio Pubs & Dists
Wescott Cove, *(Wescott Cove Pub. Co.; 0-918752),* Box 130, Stamford, CT 06904 Tel 203-322-0998.
Wesleyan U Pr, *(Wesleyan Univ. Press; 0-8195),* Dist. by: Columbia University Press, 562 W. 113th St., New York, NY 10025 Tel 212-678-6764.
West Coast, *(West Coast Poetry Review; 0-915596),* 1335 Dartmouth Dr., Reno, NV 89509 Tel 702-322-4467.
West Coast Plays, *(West Coast Plays; 0-934782),* P.O. Box 7206, Berkeley, CA 94707.
West End, *(West End Press; 0-931122),* Box 697, Cambridge, MA 02139 Tel 816-753-4587.
West Pub, *(West Publishing Co.; 0-8299),* 50 W. Kellogg Blvd., P.O. Box 3526, St. Paul, MN 55165 Tel 612-228-2721; Orders to: 170 Old Country Rd., Mineola, NY 11501 Tel 516-248-1900.
West SW Pub Co, *(West Southwest Publishing Co.),* P.O. Box 4064, Redding, CA 96099.
West Va U Lib
See West Va U Pr
West Va U Pr, *(West Virginia Univ. Press; 0-937058),* Morgantown, WV 26506 Tel 304-293-4040.
West Village, *(West Village Publishing Co.; 0-933308),* 2904 E. Vanowen Ave., Orange, CA 92667 Tel 714-633-1420.
West Wash St Coll
See West Wash Univ
West Wash Univ, *(Western Washington Univ., Center for East Asian Studies; 0-914584),* Bellingham, WA 98225 Tel 206-676-3041.
Westburg, *(Westburg Associates, Pubs.; 0-87423),* 1745 Madison St., Fennimore, WI 53809 Tel 608-822-6237.
Western Heritage
See Pintores Pr
Western Ill Univ, *(Western Illinois Univ.; 0-934312),* Macomb, IL 61455.
Western Islands, *(Western Islands; 0-88279),* 395 Concord Ave., Belmont, MA 02178 Tel 617-489-0600.
Western Marine Ent, *(Western Marine Enterprises Inc.; 0-930030),* Box Q, Ventura, CA 93002 Tel 805-644-6043.
Western NC Pr, *(Western North Carolina Press, Inc.; 0-915948),* P.O. Box 29, Dillsboro, NC 28725 Tel 704-586-6253.
Western Psych, *(Western Psychological Services; 0-87424),* Div. of Manson Western Corp., 12031 Wilshire Blvd., Los Angeles, CA 90025 Tel 213-478-2061.
Western Pub, *(Western Publishing Co., Inc.; 0-307),* 850 Third Ave., New York, NY 10022 Tel 212-753-8500; Orders to: Dept. M, 1220 Mound Ave., Racine, WI 53404. *Imprints:* Golden Pr (Golden Press).
Western Pubs
See Western Pubs OH
Western Pubs OH, *(Western Pubs.; 0-9602218),* P.O. Box 848, Jamestown, OH 45335.
Western Tanager, *(Western Tanager Press; 0-934136),* 1111 Pacific Ave., Santa Cruz, CA 95060 Tel 408-425-5758. *Imprints:* Paper Vision (Paper Vision Press); Valley Calif (Valley Pubs.).
Westernlore, *(Westernlore Pubns.; 0-87026),* 126 La Porte, Unit F, Arcadia, CA 91006 Tel 213-445-7119; Orders to: P.O. Box 4304, Pasadena, CA 91106.
Westinghouse Learn, *(Westinghouse Learning Corp.; 0-88250),* 5005 W. 110th St., Oak Lawn, IL 60453 Tel 312-425-0804.
Westlake, *(Westlake, Kevin L.; 0-9604862),* RR 2, Montpelier, ID 83254.
Westminster, *(Westminster Press; 0-664),* 925 Chestnut St., Philadelphia, PA 19107 Tel 215-928-2700; Orders to: Order Dept., P.O. Box 718 Wm. Penn Annex, Philadelphia, PA 19105.
Westminster Comm & Pubns, *(Westminster Communication & Pubns., Inc.; 0-934506),* 601 13th St. N.W., Suite 203, Washington, DC 20005 Tel 202-737-1716.
Westrom, *(Westrom Co., The; 0-938230),* P.O. Box 85527, Los Angeles, CA 90072.
Westsea Pub, *(Westsea Publishing Co., Inc.; 0-937820),* P.O. Box 122, Old Bethpage, NY 11804.
Westview, *(Westview Press; 0-89158; 0-86531),* 5500 Central Ave., Boulder, CO 80301 Tel 303-444-3541.
Westwind Pr, *(Westwind Press),* Rte.1, Box 208, Farmington, WV 26571.
Weybright
See McKay
Whatever Pub, *(Whatever Publishing, Rising Sun Records; 0-931432),* 158 E. Blithedale, Suite 4, Mill Valley, CA 94941 Tel 415-383-2434.
Wheelchair Bowlers, *(Wheelchair Bowlers of Southern California; 0-9605306),* 6512 Cadiz Circle, Huntington Beach, CA 92647.
Wheelwright, *(Bond Wheelwright Co.; 0-87027),* Box 296, Freeport, ME 04032 Tel 207-865-4951.
Whirlpool, *(Whirlpool Corp.; 0-938336),* Consumer Affairs Training Center, Benton Harbor, MI 49022.
Whitaker Hse, *(Whitaker House; 0-88368),* Pittsburgh & Colfax Sts., Springdale, PA 15144 Tel 412-274-4444.
White Ewe, *(White Ewe Press; 0-917976),* P.O. Box 996, Adelphi, MD 20783.
White Pine, *(White Pine Press; 0-934834),* P.O. Box 236, Niagara Square Sta., Buffalo, NY 14201 Tel 716-825-8671.
Whitehall Co, *(Whitehall Co.; 0-87655),* 1200 S. Willis Ave., Wheeling, IL 60090 Tel 312-541-9290.
Whitenwife Pubns, *(Whitenwife Pubns.; 0-9603656),* 149 Magellan St., Capitola, CA 95010 Tel 408-476-2730.
Whitfield, *(Whitfield; 0-930920),* 1841 Pleasant Hill Rd., Pleasant Hill, CA 94523 Tel 415-934-8054.
Whitney Lib *Imprint of* **Watson-Guptill**
Whitston Pub, *(Whitston Publishing Co., Inc.; 0-87875),* P.O. Box 958, Troy, NY 12181 Tel 518-283-4363.
Whole Person, *(Whole Person Associates, Inc.; 0-938586),* P.O. Box 3151, Duluth, MN 55803.
Who's Who Black Am, *(Who's Who Among Black Americans, Inc.),* 3105 MacArthur Blvd., Northbrook, IL 60062 Tel 312-564-2020.
Wide World, *(Wide World Publishing; 0-933174),* P.O. Box 476, San Carlos, CA 94070 Tel 415-593-2839.
Wideview Bks, *(Wideview Books; 0-87223),* Div. of P.E.I. Books, Inc., 1633 Broadway, New York, NY 10019 Tel 212-688-3030; Dist. by: Harper & Row Pubs., Inc., Keystone Industrial Park, Scranton, PA 18512 Tel 212-593-7000.
Wild Horses Potted Plant, *(Wild Horses Potted Plant Pubs.; 0-9601088; 0-937148),* 226 Hamilton Ave., Palo Alto, CA 94301 Tel 415-326-6513.
Wilderness, *(Wilderness Press; 0-89997; 0-911824),* 2440 Bancroft Way, Berkeley, CA 94704 Tel 415-843-8080.
Wilderness Poetry
See Wilderness Pr
Wilderness Pr, *(Wilderness Press, The; 0-933326),* P.O. Box H, Albion, CA 95410 Tel 707-937-5560.
Wildfire Pub, *(Wildfire Publishing Co.; 0-938444),* 326 Toro Canyon Rd., Carpinteria, CA 93013.
Wildflower, *(Wildflower Press; 0-938370),* P.O. Box 255, Topanga, CA 90290.
Wildlife Educ, *(Wildlife Education, Ltd.; 0-937934),* 930 W. Washington, Suite 14, San Diego, CA 92103.
Wildlife Soc, *(Wildlife Society, Inc.; 0-933564),* 7101 Wisconsin Ave., No. 611, Washington, DC 20014 Tel 301-986-8700.
Wildwood Pubns MI, *(Wildwood Pubns.; 0-914104),* P.O. Box 629, Traverse City, MI 49684 Tel 616-941-7160.
Wiley, *(Wiley, John, & Sons, Inc.; 0-471),* 605 Third Ave., New York, NY 10158 Tel 212-850-6418.
Wilk Pub, *(Wilk Publishing Co.),* P.O. Box 320, Park Ridge, IL 60068 Tel 312-725-4878.
Willard-Bower, *(Willard/Bower),* 100 Marilyn Ave., Roseville, CA 95678.
William & Rich, *(William & Richards, Pubs.; 0-9600202),* P.O. Box 2546, San Francisco, CA 94126.
William Carey Lib, *(William Carey Library Pubs.; 0-87808),* 1705 N. Sierra Bonita Ave., P.O. Box 128-C, Pasadena, CA 91104 Tel 213-798-0819. *Imprints:* Ecclesia (Ecclesia Pubns.).
Williams & Wilkins, *(Williams & Wilkins Co.; 0-683),* 428 E. Preston St., Baltimore, MD 21202 Tel 301-528-4221.
Williams Ent, *(Williams, Bill, Enterprises; 0-934488),* 188 Merchant St., Honolulu, HI 96809; Moved, Left No Forwarding Address.
Williamsburg, *(Colonial Williamsburg Foundation; 0-910412; 0-87935),* Publications Dept., P.O. Box C, Williamsburg, VA 23185 Tel 804-229-1000; Orders to: Merchandising Office, P.O. Box Ch, Williamsburg, VA 23185.
Willow Creek, *(Willow Creek Press; 0-932558),* Div. of Wisconsin Sportsman, P.O. Box 2266, Oshkosh, WI 54903 Tel 414-233-4143.
Willowood Pr, *(Willowood Press; 0-938376),* P.O. Box 22321, Lexington, KY 40522.
Willows Pr, *(Willows Press; 0-9602924),* P.O. Box 2779, Long Beach, CA 90801 Tel 213-433-6276.
Willyshe Pub, *(Willyshe Publishing Co., Inc.; 0-936112),* 112 Mountain Rd., Linthicum Heights, MD 21090.
Wilmington Pr, *(Wilmington Press),* 13315 Wilmington Dr., Dallas, TX 75234.
Wilshire, *(Wilshire Book Co.; 0-87980),* 12015 Sherman Rd., North Hollywood, CA 91605 Tel 213-875-1711.
Wilson, *(Wilson, H. W.; 0-8242),* 950 University Ave., Bronx, NY 10452 Tel 212-588-8400.
Wilson Bks
See Anima Pubns
Wilson Bros, *(Wilson Brothers Pubns.; 0-934944),* P.O. Box 712, Yakima, WA 98907 Tel 509-457-8275.
Wilton, *(Wilton Enterprises, Inc., Book Div.; 0-912696),* 1603 S. Michigan Ave., Chicago, IL 60616 Tel 312-663-5096.
WIM Oakland, *(WIM; 0-938842),* 6000 Contra Costa Rd., Oakland, CA 94618.
WIM Pubns, *(WIM Pubns.; 0-934172),* P.O. Box 5037, Inglewood, CA 90310 Tel 213-774-5230.
Winchester Pr, *(Winchester Press; 0-87691),* P.O. Box 1260, Tulsa, OK 74101 Tel 918-835-3161.
Windflower Pr, *(Windflower Press; 0-931534),* P.O. Box 82213, Lincoln, NE 68501 Tel 402-475-0904.
Windham Bay, *(Windham Bay Press),* Box 1332, Juneau, AK 99802.
Windless Orchard, *(Windless Orchard Series; 0-87883),* Indiana Univ., English Dept., Fort Wayne, IN 46805 Tel 219-482-5386.
Windmill Bks, *(Windmill Books, Inc.; 0-87807),* an Intext Publisher, 1230 Ave of the Americas, New York, NY 10020 Tel 212-245-6400.
Winds World Pr, *(Winds of the World Press; 0-938338),* 35 Whittemore Rd., Framingham, MA 01701.
Windsinger, *(Windsinger Enterprises, Inc.),* P.O. Box 128, Wellsville, UT 84339 Tel 801-245-4030.
Windsor, *(Windsor Books Division),* P.O. Box 280, Brightwaters, NY 11718.
Windyridge, *(Windyridge Press; 0-913366),* P. O. Box 591, Rogue River, OR 97537; Orders to: Northwest Textbook Depository, P.O. Box 3708, Portland, OR 97208 Tel 503-639-3193.
Wine Appreciation, *(Wine Appreciation Guide, The; 0-932664),* 1377 Ninth Ave., San Francisco, CA 94122; 60 Federal St., San Francisco, CA 94107.
Wine Bks, *(Wine Books; 0-9604488),* P.O. Box 1015, San Marcos, CA 92069.
Wine Consul Calif, *(Wine Consultants of California; 0-916040),* P.O. Box 27187, San Francisco, CA 94127 Tel 415-681-8989.
Wine Pubns, *(Wine Pubns.; 0-913840),* 96 Parnassus Rd., Berkeley, CA 94708 Tel 415-843-4209.

Winfoto, *(Winfoto; 0-9605522),* 1790 Kearney St., Denver, CO 80220.
Wingbow Pr, *(Wingbow Press; 0-914728),* Dist. by: Bookpeople, 2940 Seventh St., Berkeley, CA 94710 Tel 415-549-3033.
Wings Pr, *(Wings Press; 0-930324),* P.O. Box 25296, Houston, TX 77005 Tel 713-668-7953.
Winston Pr, *(Winston Press, Inc.; 0-03),* Subs. of CBS Educational Publishing, 430 Oak Grove, Suite 203, Minneapolis, MN 55403 Tel 612-871-7000.
Winter Pub Co, *(Winter Publishing Co.),* P.O. Box 36536, Tucson, AZ 85740; 5613 N. Calle De la Reina, Tucson, AZ 85718 Tel 602-299-1528.
Winterthur, *(Winterthur Museum; 0-912724),* Winterthur, DE 19735 Tel 302-656-8591.
Winthrop, *(Winthrop Publishing Co.; 0-87626),* Subs. of Prentice-Hall, Inc., Dist. by: Prentice-Hall, Englewood Cliffs, NJ 07632 Tel 201-592-2154.
WIPO *Imprint of* **Unipub**
Wis Ev Luth, *(Wisconsin Ev. Lutheran Synod Board for Parish Education; 0-938272),* 3614 W. North Ave., Milwaukee, WI 53208 Tel 414-445-4030.
Wisc T & T
See Tamarack Pr
Wisconsin Bks, *(Wisconsin Books),* c/o R. B. Allison, 2025 Dunn Place, Madison, WI 53713 Tel 608-257-4126; Formerly Named School of Living Press.
Wisconsin Sptmn, *(Wisconsin Sportsman; 0-932558),* P.O. Box 2266, Oshkosh, WI 54903 Tel 414-233-1327.
Wisdom Garden, *(Wisdom Garden Books; 0-914794),* Box 29448, Los Angeles, CA 90029 Tel 213-380-1968.
Wise Pub, *(Wise Publishing Co.; 0-915766),* 5625 Wilhelmina Ave., Woodland Hills, CA 91364.
Wish Bklets, *(Wish Booklets; 0-913786),* 11909 Blue Spruce Rd, Reston, VA 22091 Tel 703-620-4966.
Wittenborn, *(Wittenborn, George, Inc.; 0-8150),* 1018 Madison Ave., New York, NY 10021 Tel 212-288-1558.
Wizards, *(Wizards Bookshelf; 0-913510),* Box 6600, San Diego, CA 92106 Tel 714-223-4005.
Wm C Brown, *(Brown, William C., Co., Pubs.; 0-697),* 2460 Kerper Blvd., Dubuque, IA 52001 Tel 319-588-1451.
WMO *Imprint of* **Unipub**
Woburn Pr
See Biblio Dist
Wolf Hse, *(Wolf House Books; 0-915046),* P.O. Box 209K, Cedar Springs, MI 49319 Tel 616-696-2772.
Womack Assoc, *(Womack Associates; 0-9605530),* 1616 Idylwild, Prescott, AZ 86301.
Women-in-Lit, *(Women-in-Literature, Inc.; 0-935634),* P.O. Box 12668, Reno, NV 89510 Tel 702-825-8104.
Women on Words, *(Women on Words & Images; 0-9600724),* 30 Valley Rd., Princeton, NJ 08540 Tel 609-921-8653; Orders to: P. O. Box 2163, Princeton, NJ 08540.
Women's Aglow, *(Women's Aglow Fellowship),* P.O. Box I, Lynnwood, WA 98036 Tel 206-775-7282.
Womens Research Act, *(Women's Research Action Project; 0-930522),* 72 Cornell St., Roslindale, MA 02131 Tel 617-327-5016.
Woodall, *(Woodall Publishing Co.; 0-912082),* 500 Hyacinth Place, Highland Park, IL 60035.
Woodbridge Pr, *(Woodbridge Press Publishing Co.; 0-912800),* P.O. Box 6189, Santa Barbara, CA 93111 Tel 805-965-7039.
Woodcraft Supply, *(Woodcraft Supply Corp.; 0-918036),* 313 Montvale Ave., Woburn, MA 01888 Tel 617-935-5860.
Wooden Shoe, *(Wooden Shoe),* P.O. Box 174, Pleasantville, NY 10570 Tel 914-769-5580; Orders to: Music Sales Corp., 33 W. 60th St., New York, NY 10023.
Woodland, *(Woodland Publishing Co., Inc.; 0-934104),* 230 Manitoba Ave., Wayzata, MN 55391 Tel 612-473-2725.
Word Bks, *(Word, Inc.; 0-87680; 0-8499),* P.O. Box 1790, Waco, TX 76796 Tel 817-772-7650.
Word Ent, *(Word Enterprise; 0-938722),* P.O. Box 535, Fairview, NJ 07022.
Word Factory, *(Word Factory; 0-936854),* 3345 Clairemont Dr., San Diego, CA 92117.
Word for Today, *(Word for Today, The; 0-936728),* P.O. Box 8000, Costa Mesa, CA 92626 Tel 714-979-0706.
Word-Fraction, *(Word-Fraction Math Aid Co.; 0-911642),* P.O. Box 475, Woodland Hills, CA 91366.
Word of Life
See Servant
Word Shop, *(Word Shop Publications, The; 0-932238),* 3737 Fifth Ave., Suite 203, San Diego, CA 92103 Tel 714-291-9126.
Word Works, *(Word Works, Inc.; 0-915380),* P.O. Box 4054, Washington, DC 20015 Tel 703-524-0999.
Wordtree, *(Wordtree, The; 0-936312),* 7306 Brittany, Merriam, KS 66203 Tel 913-236-7733.
Work in Amer, *(Work in America Institute Inc.; 0-89361),* 700 White Plains Rd., Scarsdale, NY 10583 Tel 914-472-9600.
Working Pr CA, *(Working Press; 0-9602462),* P.O. Box 687, Livermore, CA 94550 Tel 415-449-6995.
Workman Pub, *(Workman Publishing Co., Inc.; 0-911104; 0-89480),* 1 W. 39th St., New York, NY 10018 Tel 212-398-9160.
Workmen's Circle, *(Workmen's Circle Education Department),* 45 E. 33rd St., New York, NY 10016.
World Action, *(World Action Pubs.; 0-932742),* 135 Ridge Rd., Wethersfield, CT 06109.
World Almanac, *(World Almanac; 0-911818),* 200 Park Ave., New York, NY 10017 Tel 212-557-9651.
World Authors, *(World Authors, Ltd.; 0-89975),* 191/2 E. 62nd St., New York, NY 10021 Tel 212-759-7305; Dist. by: Hippocrene Books, Inc., 171 Madison Ave., New York, NY 10016 Tel 212-685-4371.
World Bible, *(World Bible Pubs., Inc.),* P. O. Box 2008, Iowa Falls, IA 50126 Tel 800-247-5195; Orders to: P. O. Box 1058, Iowa Falls, IA 50126 Tel 800-247-5111.
World Bk-Childcraft, *(World Book-Childcraft International, Inc.; 0-7166),* Merchandise Mart Plaza, Rm 510, Chicago, IL 60654 Tel 312-245-2801.
World Book
See World Bk-Childcraft
World Digest
See World Natural Hist
World Educ Proj, *(World Education Project; 0-918158),* Box U-32, School of Education, Univ. of Conn., Storrs, CT 06268 Tel 203-486-3321.
World Evang Fellow, *(World Evangelical Fellowship; 0-936444),* P.O. Box 670, Colorado Springs, CO 80901 Tel 303-635-1612.
World Food, *(World Food Press; 0-930922),* 10 Myrtle St., Jamaica Plain, MA 02130; Dist. by: Bookland, Inc., 56 Suffolk St., Holyoke, MA 01040 Tel 413-533-8475.
World Free Flight, *(World Free Flight Press; 0-933066),* 7513 Sausalito Ave., Canoga Park, CA 91307 Tel 213-340-1704.
World Future, *(World Future Society; 0-930242),* 4916 St. Elmo Ave., Washington, DC 20014 Tel 301-656-8274.
World Issues, *(World Issues Information Bureau; 0-9605110),* 1234 W. Loyola Ave., Chicago, IL 60626.
World Merch Import, *(World Merchandise-Import Center; 0-937514),* 609-613 Chetco Ave., P.O. Box 1389, Brookings, OR 97415 Tel 503-469-3218. *Imprints:* New Era (New Era Pubns.).
World Natural Hist, *(World Natural History Pubns.; 0-916846),* P.O. Box 550, Marlton, NJ 08053 Tel 609-654-6500.
World Pubns
See Anderson World
World Trade, *(World Trade Academy Press; 0-8360),* 50 E. 42nd St., New York, NY 10017 Tel 212-697-4999.
World Univ Pr, *(World Univ. Press; 0-938340),* 31 High St., New Haven, CT 06511.
World Wide Pubs, *(World Wide Pubns.; 0-89066),* 1303 Hennepin Ave., Minneapolis, MN 55403 Tel 612-336-0940.
Worldwatch Inst, *(Worldwatch Institute; 0-916468),* 1776 Massachusetts Ave., N.W., Washington, DC 20036 Tel 202-452-1999.
Wormhoudt, *(Wormhoudt, Arthur, Dr.; 0-916358),* Dept. of Language & Literature, William Penn College, Oskaloosa, IA 52577 Tel 515-673-3091.
Wormwood Rev, *(Wormwood Review Press; 0-935390),* P.O. Box 8840, Stockton, CA 95204 Tel 209-466-8231.
Worth, *(Worth Pubs., Inc.; 0-87901),* 444 Park Ave. S., New York, NY 10016 Tel 212-689-9630.
Worth Co, *(Worth, H. S., Co.),* P.O. Box 601, Oakridge, OR 97463.
WOW Inc, *(Wider Opportunities for Women; 0-934966),* 1511 "K" St., N.W., Suite 345, Washington, DC 20005 Tel 202-638-3143.
Wrightwill Pub, *(Wrightwill Publishing Co.),* 256 S. Robertson Blvd., Beverly Hills, CA 90211 Tel 213-926-6994.
Write to Sell, *(Write to Sell; 0-9605078),* P.O. Box 706-A, Carpinteria, CA 93013 Tel 805-684-2469.
Writer, *(Writer, Inc.; 0-87116),* 8 Arlington St., Boston, MA 02116 Tel 617-536-7420.
Writers Digest, *(Writers Digest Books; 0-89879; 0-911654),* 9933 Alliance Rd., Cincinnati, OH 45242 Tel 513-984-0717.
Writing, *(Writing Works Inc.; 0-916076),* 7438 S.E. 40th St., Mercer Island, WA 98040 Tel 206-232-2171.
WRP, *(Water Resources Pubns.; 0-918334),* 309 Yoakum Pkwy, No. 1401, Alexandria, VA 22304 Tel 703-370-5588; Orders to: P.O. Box 2841, Littleton, CO 80161 Tel 303-779-6685.
WSP, *(Washington Square Press, Inc.),* Div. of Simon & Schuster, Inc., 1230 Ave. of the Americas, New York, NY 10020. *Imprints:* RE (Readers Enrichment Series).
WW *Imprint of* **Unipub**
Wyden, *(Wyden Books; 0-87223),* Div. of P.E.I. Books, Inc., P.O. Box 151, Ridgefield, CT 06877 Tel 203-438-9631; Dist. by: Harper & Row Pubs., Inc., Keystone Industrial Park, Scranton, PA 18512.
Wyvern, *(Wyvern Pubns.; 0-9602404),* P.O. Box 188, Dumfries, VA 22026.
X Press Pr
See Downtown Poets
Xenos Bks, *(Xenos Books; 0-934724),* 13524 Crenshaw Blvd., Gardena, CA 90249 Tel 213-538-5000.
Xerox Ed Pubns, *(Xerox Education Publications; 0-8374),* Div. of Xerox Corp., 245 Long Hill Rd., Middletown, CT 06457 Tel 203-347-7251; Orders to: P.O. Box 16629, Columbus, OH 43216 Tel 614-253-0892.
Xerox Learning, *(Xerox Learning Systems; 0-935268),* A Xerox Publishing Co., One Pickwick Plaza, Greenwich, CT 06830 Tel 203-622-5300.
Yale Art Gallery, *(Yale University Art Gallery; 0-89467),* 2006 Yale Sta., 1111 Chapel St., New Haven, CT 06520 Tel 203-436-0574.
Yale U Anthro, *(Yale Univ. Pubns. in Anthropology),* P.O. Box 2114, Yale Sta., New Haven, CT 06520 Tel 203-432-3847.
Yale U Pr, *(Yale Univ. Press; 0-300),* 302 Temple St., New Haven, CT 06520 Tel 203-432-4975; Orders to: 92A Yale Sta., New Haven, CT 06520 Tel 203-432-4969.
Yama Pub, *(Yama Publishing Co; 0-937290),* 2266 Fifth Ave., No. 136, New York, NY 10037.
Yankee Bks, *(Yankee Books; 0-911658; 0-89909),* Dublin, NH 03444 Tel 603-563-8111.
Yankee Bookmen
See Heritage Bk
Yankee Inc
See Yankee Bks
Yankee Peddler, *(Yankee Peddler Book Co.; 0-911660),* 38 Hampton Rd., Drawer O, Southampton, NY 11968.
YB *Imprint of* **Dell**
Y'bird, *(Y'bird; 0-931676),* 2140 Shattuck Ave., Rm. 311, Berkeley, CA 94704 Tel 415-527-1586.
Ye Galleon, *(Ye Galleon Press; 0-87770),* P.O. Box 25, Fairfield, WA 99012 Tel 509-283-2422.
Ye Olde Print, *(Ye Olde Printery; 0-932606),* 5815 Cherokee Dr., Cincinnati, OH 45243 Tel 513-561-4338.
Year Bk Med, *(Year Book Medical Pubs., Inc.; 0-8151),* 35 E. Wacker Dr., Chicago, IL 60601 Tel 312-726-9733.

Yellow Bk PA, *(Yellow Book of Pa. Inc.; 0-9604612),* 715 Twining Rd., P.O. Box 7, Dresher, PA 19025.

Yellowstone Lib, *(Yellowstone Library & Museum Assn., The; 0-934948),* Yellowstone Park, WY 82190.

Yerba Buena
See Taylor & Ng

Yoknapatawpha, *(Yoknapatawpha Press; 0-916242),* Box 248, Oxford, MS 38655 Tel 601-234-0909.

Yorke Med, *(Yorke Medical Books; 0-914316),* 666 Fifth Ave., New York, NY 10103 Tel 212-489-4679.

Yorkshire Pub, *(Yorkshire Publishing Co.; 0-9604732),* P.O. Box 358, Fairfield, OH 45014.

Yourdon, *(Yourdon Press; 0-917072),* 1133 Ave. of the Americas, New York, NY 10036 Tel 212-730-2670.

Youth Sports, *(Youth Sports Press; 0-936446),* 6801 S. LaGrange Rd., LaGrange, IL 60525.

Zanel Pubns, *(Zanel Pubns.),* P.O. Box 11316, Tahoe Paradise, CA 95708 Tel 916-922-8320.

Zaner-Bloser, *(Zaner-Bloser, Inc.; 0-88309),* 823 Church St., Honesdale, PA 43215 Tel 717-253-5192; Orders to: 612 N. Park St., Columbus, OH 43215 Tel 614-221-5851.

Zartscorp, *(Zartscorp, Inc. Books),* 267 W. 89th St., New York, NY 10024 Tel 212-724-5071.

Zebra, *(Zebra Books; 0-89083),* 21 E. 40th St., New York, NY 10016 Tel 212-889-2299; Dist. by: Kable News Co., 777 3rd Ave., New York, NY 10017.

Zenith *Imprint of* **Doubleday**

Zentner Pubns, *(Zentner Pubns.; 0-934950),* 7735 Ophelia Court, Citrus Heights, CA 95610 Tel 916-722-5024.

Zephyr, *(Zephyr Pubs.; 0-931782),* P.O. Box 43-1275, South Miami, FL 33143 Tel 305-279-7817.

Zephyr *Imprint of* **Doubleday**

Zephyrus Pr, *(Zephyrus Press, Inc.; 0-914264),* 417 Maitland Ave., Teaneck, NJ 07666 Tel 201-833-0717; Orders to: Caroline House Pubs., 2 Ellis Place, Ossining, NY 10662.

Ziesing Bros, *(Ziesing Bros. Book Emporium),* 768 Main St., Willimantic, CT 06226.

Ziff-Davis Pub, *(Ziff-Davis Publishing Co.; 0-87165),* 1 Park Ave., Rm. 1011, New York, NY 10016 Tel 212-725-3639; Dist. by: McGraw-Hill Book Co., Order Services, Princeton Rd., Hightstown, NJ 08520.

Zimmerman, *(Zimmerman, Gary; 0-916202),* G.P.O. Box 114, Brooklyn, NY 11202 Tel 212-854-4494.

Zion, *(Zion Natural History Assn.; 0-915630),* Zion National Park, Springdale, UT 84767 Tel 801-772-3256.

Zoe Pubns, *(Zoe Pubns.; 0-89841),* Box 133, Geneva, IL 60134 Tel 312-653-7300.

Zomeworks Corp, *(Zomeworks Corp.),* P.O. Box 712, Albuquerque, NM 87103 Tel 505-242-5354.

Zondervan, *(Zondervan Publishing House; 0-310),* 1415 Lake Dr., S.E., Grand Rapids, MI 49506 Tel 616-459-6900.

Zybert, *(Zybert, Richard),* 1169 Folsom St., San Francisco, CA 94103 Tel 415-863-7229.